DIZIONARIO
ITALIANO-INGLESE
INGLESE-ITALIANO
ITALIAN-ENGLISH
ENGLISH-ITALIAN
DICTIONARY

GIUNTI MARZOCCO COLLINS

DIZIONARIO ITALIANO-INGLESE INGLESE-ITALIANO

a cura di

Catherine E. Love

Giunti
Firenze

Collins
London · Glasgow · Toronto

COLLINS
GIUNTI MARZOCCO
CONCISE
ITALIAN-ENGLISH
ENGLISH-ITALIAN
DICTIONARY

by

Catherine E. Love

SIMON AND SCHUSTER

GENERAL EDITOR/A CURA DI
Catherine E. Love

COORDINATING EDITORS/REDAZIONE
Michela Clari   R. M. Kochanowska   Roberta Martignon

CONTRIBUTING EDITORS/HANNO COLLABORATO

Carla Zipoli	John M. Dodds
Mariolina Meliadò Freeth	Anthony Baldry
Giuliana Colantoni Checketts	Anne Rocchiccioli
Carla Muschio	Wendy V. A. Morris
Giovanna Mattea	Peter Terrell
Claudia Poglayen	Ada Strong
Gabriella Mugellesi	Carolyn Turner
Mariarosaria Cardines	Julia Marshall
Giovanna Ferraguti	Barbara J. Thomason

EDITORIAL STAFF/SEGRETERIA DI REDAZIONE

Daphne Trotter	Elizabeth Cunningham
Anne Marie McLure	Lorna Cardosi

CONSULTANTS/GRUPPO DI CONSULENZA
GIUNTI MARZOCCO

Wanda d'Addio	Stefania Nuccorini
Lunella Mereu	Angelo Carriere

prepared for Collins by/opera realizzata da

LEXUS

© Copyright 1985 William Collins Sons & Co Ltd

All rights reserved including the right
of reproduction in whole or in part in any form

Published by New World Dictionaries/Simon & Schuster
A division of Simon & Schuster, Inc.
Simon & Schuster Building
Rockefeller Center
1230 Avenue of the Americas
New York, New York 10020

Dictionary Editorial Offices: New World Dictionaries
850 Euclid Avenue, Cleveland, Ohio 44114

Originally published in Great Britain
Published by arrangement with William Collins Sons & Co Ltd

Simon & Schuster, Tree of Knowledge, Webster's New World and
colophons are trademarks of Simon & Schuster, Inc.

Manufactured in the United States of America

1 2 3 4 5 6 7 8 9 10
Library of Congress Cataloging in Publication Data

ISBN 0-671-44505-7

INTRODUZIONE

Compilato da un gruppo di esperti linguisti e lessicografi italiani e inglesi, questo dizionario di nuovissima concezione si rivolge con un lemmario ampio e articolato ad un vasto pubblico di lettori che vogliano imparare, leggere e capire l'inglese. Oltre ai termini di uso comune nella loro accezione più moderna, compaiono anche vocaboli di uso colloquiale e gergale, senza peraltro trascurare le espressioni di carattere più formale e dedicando inoltre ampio spazio alle terminologie specifiche in campo scientifico, tecnologico e commerciale.

Per facilitare la comunicazione nella lingua straniera e fornire al lettore la possibilità di esprimersi correttamente e modernamente sia nel parlare che nello scrivere, i lemmi di base e con maggior frequenza d'uso sono stati trattati in modo particolarmente esteso.

L'ampiezza del lemmario unitamente alla chiarezza, sinteticità e modernità delle traduzioni ne fanno uno strumento di lavoro adatto alle esigenze della vita scolastica, privata e professionale.

INTRODUCTION

This entirely new dictionary provides the user whose aim is to learn, read and understand Italian with wide-ranging and up-to-date coverage of current usage – from the colloquial to the more formal – as well as extensive treatment of all areas relevant to modern life.

To facilitate communication in the foreign language the basic, most frequently used words in the language are treated in depth, so that the user may express himself correctly and idiomatically – both orally and in writing.

Compiled by a team of experienced Italian and English linguists and lexicographers this reference book combines comprehensive coverage with outstanding clarity, simplicity and economy, making it an ideal working tool for school, self-study and professional life.

PREFAZIONE

A quali scopi si usa un dizionario bilingue, ed in particolare un dizionario dal taglio pedagogico come il Collins-Giunti Marzocco? La risposta immediatamente al suo scopo è ovvia è che lo si usa per apprendere, cioè per colmare un nostro 'deficit lessicale' nella lingua straniera. Questo scopo generale va però ulteriormente definito al suo interno prendendo in considerazione le varie esigenze che ci spingono ad una consultazione del dizionario, esigenze che possono rispecchiare usi della lingua diversi.

Secondo una prima generale distinzione, un dizionario bilingue può essere usato *a scopi di comprensione* e *a scopi di produzione.* Nel primo caso, che si verifica quando ascoltiamo o leggiamo nella lingua straniera, ricorriamo al dizionario per trovare il significato di parole o di espressioni che non conosciamo o di cui non siamo certi. Nel secondo caso, lo consultiamo quando, dovendo dire qualcosa nella nuova lingua, ci 'mancano le parole'. Entrambi gli usi non sono privi di difficoltà se non vi si è stati specificamente addestrati poiché, per 'trovare i significati', come per 'trovare le parole', sarà necessario compiere delle mediazioni tra le informazioni necessariamente generalizzate dei dizionari e le nostre esigenze specifiche di appropriatezza contestuale. Se il dizionario deve essere, come sembra giusto, uno strumento pedagogico, è necessario quindi che chi apprende una lingua straniera sia messo in grado di usare le varie strategie di consultazione che portino a corrette interpretazioni di quanto il dizionario offre. Egli deve acquisire una vera e propria 'abilità di consultazione', un'abilità specifica, cioè, che fa parte delle più generali *abilità di studio* (study skills), trasversali alle varie discipline, sulle quali la glottodidattica odierna pone particolarmente l'accento. L'uso del dizionario bilingue nello studio di una lingua straniera, quindi, lungi dall'essere ritenuto marginale o da evitare, come accadeva ai tempi dei metodi diretti e meccanicistici, può rivelarsi – naturalmente se usato nel modo giusto e nelle occasioni giuste – uno strumento assai utile per sviluppare le generali capacità di 'problem-solving' che stanno alla base di ogni tipo di apprendimento. Il problema, di carattere nettamente pedagogico, sta nel predisporre l'allievo ad un suo uso corretto e non ad un 'abuso', facendo sì che egli vi ricorra soltanto quando sia veramente necessario. Tanto per fare degli esempi, dovrebbe ricorrervi soltanto quando, leggendo, gli sia impossibile inferire dal contesto il significato di date parole non note o quando, intuitone il significato, voglia verificare se le sue ipotesi erano giuste. Non c'è nulla di più demotivante e dannoso per l'apprendimento dell'interrompere continuamente la lettura per consultare il dizionario. Nella produzione, poi, occorre essere ancora più cauti e non ritenere che il dizionario possa risolvere tutti i nostri problemi di espressione nella lingua straniera.

Innanzitutto bisogna avere abbastanza chiaro quel che si vuole dire per essere pronti ad usare sinonimi, opposti, parafrasi o addirittura riformulare tutta l'espressione. Del resto, è quanto molto spesso facciamo nella lingua materna se stentiamo lì per lì a 'trovare le parole'. Ma un uso corretto del dizionario pedagogico richiede soprattutto una certa consapevolezza di alcuni fondamentali aspetti della lingua. In una voce del dizionario si rispecchiano, infatti, fortemente condensati, fenomeni linguistici di primaria importanza quali, ad esempio, quello della polisemia delle parole, generalmente dissimmetrica tra L1 e L2, quello dei rapporti di significato tra gli elementi lessicali (sinonimia, antonimia, iperonimia, etc), quello dei vari *usi* delle parole nelle diverse varietà linguistiche e nei diversi registri e linguaggi specialistici, degli usi *figurati*, anch'essi diversi da lingua a lingua, e così via. Sono tutti concetti indispensabili per acquisire una vera competenza lessicale sia nella lingua materna che nella lingua straniera. Se queste conoscenze sono indispensabili per un uso corretto del dizionario, se esse stanno alla base di quella che è considerata una delle fondamentali abilità di studio, si potrebbe bene a ragione affermare che esse debbano necessariamente essere oggetto di insegnamento specifico, specialmente nel quadro dell'educazione linguistica. L'uso del dizionario così verrebbe a collocarsi in maniera organica nell'iter didattico e ad affiancarsi allo studio del lessico 'in contesto', vale a dire all'esperienza diretta della lingua.

Wanda d'Addio Colosimo

STRUTTURA DEL DIZIONARIO

Chi si serve di un dizionario bilingue lo fa per controllare il significato di una parola straniera che non conosce – in questo caso una parola inglese – o trovare l'equivalente di un vocabolo italiano nella lingua straniera. Le due operazioni sono alquanto differenti e così pure i problemi che si incontrano nel consultare l'una o l'altra sezione del dizionario. Qui di seguito abbiamo illustrato le principali caratteristiche del dizionario nella speranza che vi possano essere di aiuto.

I lemmi principali, tutti in nero, compaiono in ordine alfabetico. Ogni voce comincia con il lemma in nero e può contenere altri elementi in neretto, quali esempi illustrativi e parole composte.

La sezione 1. qui di seguito illustra il modo in cui vengono elencati questi elementi all'interno di ogni voce; la sezione 2. chiarifica la struttura interna delle voci più complesse; e la sezione 3. spiega come meglio servirsi delle varianti di traduzione.

I diversi caratteri di stampa usati servono ad individuare le tre principali categorie di elementi all'interno del dizionario. Tutti i vocaboli o frasi in nero o neretto costituiscono riferimenti legati alla lingua di partenza, di cui viene fornito un'equivalente nell'altra lingua. Tutti i vocaboli o frasi in tondo sono traduzioni. Mentre le parti in corsivo forniscono informazioni sulle parole che vengono tradotte, cioè indicatori atti ad identificare la traduzione più appropriata, o spiegazioni che riguardano la lingua di origine.

1. Dove cercare

1.1 Derivati

Per maggiore facilità d'uso, in questo dizionario, derivati quali 'happiness', 'caller', 'calling' e in italiano 'borsista', 'giornalista' compaiono tutti come lemmi principali.

1.2 Lemmi omografi

I lemmi omografi, cioè vocaboli aventi la medesima grafia, ma con significato ed etimologia diversi, come ad esempio in italiano **fine** (sottile etc) e **fine** (parte terminale), o in inglese **fine** (bello etc) e **fine** (multa), compaiono come lemmi distinti, in ordine alfabetico e sono contrassegnati da un numero esponenziale.

1.3 Fraseologia

Abbiamo cercato di fornire la più ampia fraseologia possibile, che va da esempi a carattere illustrativo che aiuteranno il lettore a capire come un vocabolo viene usato nei diversi contesti, ad espressioni e costruzioni idiomatiche. Particolare rilievo è stato dato a locuzioni verbali quali: 'mettersi al lavoro', 'mettere via', 'prendere fuoco', 'andare via', 'farsi avanti' etc, e anche alle costruzioni di base (vedi ad esempio le voci **apply**, **agree**).

Le locuzioni verbali con i verbi più importanti (come **fare**, **mettere**, **prendere**, o in inglese **set**, **do**, **get** etc) compaiono generalmente sotto il sostantivo o altra importante parte del discorso. Per

HOW TO USE THE DICTIONARY

In using a bilingual dictionary, you will either want to check the meaning of a foreign word you don't know – here, an Italian word – or find the correct word in the foreign language for an English word. These two operations are quite different, and so are the problems you may face when using one side of the dictionary or the other. In order to help you, we have tried to explain below the main features of this dictionary.

The 'wordlist' is the alphabetical list of all the items in large bold type, i.e. all the 'headwords'. Each 'entry', or article, is introduced by a headword, and may contain additional 'references' in smaller bold type, such as phrases and compound words.

Section 1. below deals with the way references are listed; section 2. explains the internal structure of complex entries; and section 3. advises on how best to use the translations provided.

The typography distinguishes between three broad categories of text within the dictionary. All items in bold type, large or smaller, are 'source language' references, for which an equivalent in the other language is provided. All items in standard type (roman typeface) are translations. Items in italics are information about the words being translated, i.e. either labels or 'signposts' pinpointing the appropriate translation, or explanations about the source language.

1. Where to look

1.1 Derivatives

Derivatives such as 'happiness', 'caller', 'calling', in Italian 'borsista', 'giornalista' all appear as headwords in this dictionary, for greater ease of reference.

1.2 Homographs

Homographs are words which are spelt in exactly the same way, like Italian **fine** (thin, fine) and **fine** (end), or English **fine** (nice etc) and **fine** (penalty). As a rule these are listed as separate headwords, distinguished by superior numbers.

1.3 Phrases

We have endeavoured to provide extensive phraseology, ranging from illustrative phrases meant to help the user understand how words are used in context, to idiomatic constructions and expressions. Particular emphasis is given to verbal phrases like 'mettersi al lavoro', 'mettere via', 'prendere fuoco', 'andare via', 'farsi avanti', etc, and also to basic constructions (see for instance the entries for **apply**, **agree**).

Verbal phrases with the ten or so basic verbs (like **fare**, **mettere**, **prendere**, or English **set**, **do**, **get** etc) are generally listed under the noun, or other important part of speech. For instance, **to give the** esempio **to give the lie to** compare alla voce **lie**[1], e **to do somebody proud** compare alla voce **proud**.

Altre locuzioni e frasi idiomatiche compaiono sotto il primo elemento fondamentale della locuzione (e cioè non sotto la preposizione o articolo con cui la locuzione comincia). Per esempio **filare dritto** si troverà alla voce **filare** e **to burn one's boats** si troverà alla voce **burn**.

1.4 Abbreviazioni e nomi propri

Per maggior facilità di consultazione le abbreviazioni, le sigle e i nomi propri sono stati inseriti in ordine alfabetico nel testo e non elencati in tavole a parte. Ad esempio **M.O.T.** e in italiano **I.V.A.** che al giorno d'oggi hanno assunto valore nominale sono stati inseriti nel lemmario come voci a se stanti.

1.5 Composti

Housewife, smoke screen, terremoto e dopobarba sono composti. I composti che formano un'unica parola non costituiscono un problema in quanto compaiono sotto i lemmi principali. Tuttavia in entrambe le lingue insorgono delle difficoltà quando i composti sono formati da due parole distinte o da due parole unite con un trattino.

1.5.1 Composti italiani

La maggior parte dei composti in italiano è in forma di un'unica parola (es. doposcuola, portacenere). Tuttavia esistono composti costituiti da due vocaboli come 'vagone ristorante', 'verde bottiglia', 'asilo nido'. Questo tipo di composti compare sotto il primo dei due elementi che costituiscono l'espressione, es. 'vagone ristorante' sarà sotto 'vagone', 'verde bottiglia' sarà sotto 'verde', 'asilo nido' sotto 'asilo'.

1.5.2 Composti inglesi

In inglese la collocazione dei composti è più problematica in quanto il composto può essere costituito sia da una sola parola che da due parole o ancora da due parole unite per mezzo di un trattino, es: 'airbed', 'air-bed' o 'air bed'. Se la forma più comunemente usata è quella costituita da una sola parola o da due parole unite da un trattino, il vocabolo verrà inserito come lemma principale in ordine alfabetico. Se invece la forma più comune è costituita da due parole separate l'espressione verrà inserita sotto il primo dei due elementi. Questo ultimo tipo di composti verrà elencato all'interno della voce principale ma sarà contraddistinto da un numerino indicante una diversa categoria grammaticale – e sarà comunque sempre collocato in fondo alla voce e contrassegnato dall'indicatore grammaticale 'cpd'. Vedi ad esempio le voci 'bicycle' e 'bird'.

Poiché la maggior parte dei composti inglesi può avere sia una forma che l'altra è buona norma per il lettore controllare in entrambe le possibili collocazioni.

1.6 Verbi pronominali italiani

Verbi come 'svegliarsi', 'sbagliarsi', 'ricordarsi' etc. vengono definiti 'pronominali' perché vengono usati in combinazione con un pronome personale: 'mi sono svegliato alle sette' etc.

lie to is entered under **lie**[1], and **to do somebody proud** is entered under **proud**.

Other phrases and idioms are listed under the first set key word (i.e. not a preposition or article). For instance, **filare diritto** is to be found under **filare**, in English **to burn one's boats** is under **burn**.

1.4 Abbreviations and proper names

For easier reference, abbreviations, acronyms and proper names have been listed alphabetically in the wordlist, as opposed to being relegated to the appendices. **M.O.T.** is used in every way like 'certificate' or 'permit', **I.V.A.** like 'imposta', and consequently these words are treated like any other noun.

1.5 Compounds

Housewife, smoke screen, terremoto and **dopobarba** are all compounds. One-word – or 'solid' – compounds like 'housewife' are not a problem when consulting the dictionary, since they will appear in only one place. When it comes to other compounds however – hyphenated compounds or compounds made up of separate words – each language presents its own peculiar problems.

1.5.1 Italian compounds

Most compounds in Italian are of the solid variety (e.g. doposcuola, portacenere). There are also compounds made up of two juxtaposed words, e.g. 'vagone ristorante', 'verde bottiglia', 'asilo nido'. Compounds made up of two separate words are listed under the first word, i.e. 'vagone ristorante' under 'vagone', 'verde bottiglia' under 'verde', 'asilo nido' under 'asilo'.

1.5.2 English compounds

Listing here is less straightforward than with Italian, because of less predictable spelling: is it 'airbed', 'air-bed' or 'air bed'? If the preferred form is solid or hyphenated, the word will appear as a headword in strict alphabetical order. If on the other hand the usual form is made up of two or more separate words, the compound will appear within the entry for the first element. The latter are given as a rule in a separate numbered category – always the last in the entry and labelled 'cpd'. See for instance the entries for 'bicycle' and 'bird'.

As many English compounds have alternative forms, the user is advised to check according to both systems as explained above.

1.6 Italian pronominal verbs

Verbs like 'svegliarsi', 'sbagliarsi', 'ricordarsi' etc. are called 'pronominal' because they are used with a personal pronoun: 'mi sono svegliato alle sette' etc. They must be distinguished from truly

Queste forme verbali devono essere distinte dalle forme riflessive o riflessive reciproche come ad es: 'lui si guarda allo specchio' (he is looking at himself in the mirror) e 'si parlano ogni giorno' (they talk to each other every day). Nel caso della forma pronominale del verbo si tratta infatti di verbi transitivi o intransitivi usati in connessione con un pronome o una particella pronominale. La forma pronominale quindi è stata differenziata (per mezzo di indicatori) dalle forme riflessive e riflessive reciproche all'interno della voce principale. Vedi ad esempio voci come 'svegliare' e 'sbagliare'.

Forme pronominali come 'lavarsi le mani', 'soffiarsi il naso' sono transitive in quanto prendono un oggetto diretto, pertanto sono state inserite come esempi sotto la categoria grammaticale del transitivo.

In inglese non esiste la forma pronominale del verbo, e quando un verbo viene usato in connessione con 'oneself' si tratta in generale di una forma riflessiva vera e propria. Confrontate ad esempio le traduzioni di 'ammazzarsi' (nel senso di 'suicidarsi' e quindi realmente riflessivo: to kill o.s.) e 'ammazzarsi' (nel senso di 'trovare la morte': to die, be killed).

reflexive or reciprocal uses like 'lui si guarda nello specchio' (he is looking at himself in the mirror) and 'si parlano ogni giorno' (they talk to each other every day). They are intransitive or transitive verbs in their own right.

Pronominal forms such as 'lavarsi le mani', 'soffiarsi il naso' are transitive in that they take a direct object, and have thus been shown under the transitive category of the verb.

There are no pronominal verbs as such in English, where a verb used with 'oneself' is, as a rule, truly reflexive. Compare for instance the translations for 'ammazzarsi' (in the sense of commit suicide, i.e. truly reflexive: kill o.s.) and 'ammazzarsi' (in the sense of to die, be killed). These verbs have been listed as separate senses (differentiated by means of indicators) under the verb concerned. See for instance the entries for 'svegliare', 'sbagliare'.

1.7 'Phrasal verbs' inglesi

Si definiscono 'phrasal verbs' verbi come **go off, blow up, cut down** etc. Queste forme spesso costituiscono un problema per gli studenti stranieri che incontrano delle difficoltà nel distinguerli dalle normali costruzioni con avverbi o preposizioni (ad es. 'he came into the room' normale costruzione con preposizione diversa dal 'phrasal verb' 'he came into money'). Queste forme compaiono in forma di sottolemmi in neretto alla fine del lemma principale, in ordine alfabetico, e sono state evidenziate per mezzo di una losanga in neretto.

1.7 English phrasal verbs

'Phrasal verbs' are verbs like **go off, blow up, cut down** etc. They often present problems for foreign learners, who are often unable to distinguish them from straightforward adverbial or prepositional constructions (i.e. 'he came into the room' vs. 'he came into money'). They have been listed in this dictionary at the end of the entry for the basic verb, in their own alphabetical sequence and highlighted by a solid lozenge.

I 'phrasal verbs' si dividono nelle seguenti categorie:

Phrasal verbs are divided into the following categories:

vt + avverbio	cioè 'phrasal verb' con la costruzione: 'the doctors managed to **pull** him **through**'	
vi + avverbio	cioè 'phrasal verb' con la costruzione: 'he's been very ill but I think he'll **pull through**'	
vt + preposizione	cioè 'phrasal verb' con la costruzione: 'the doctors **pulled** him **through** the illness'	
vi + preposizione	cioè 'phrasal verb' con la costruzione: 'he should **pull through** this bout of fever'	

vt + adverb	phrasal verb with the pattern: 'the doctors managed to **pull** him **through**'	
vi + adverb	phrasal verb with the pattern: 'he's been very ill but I think he'll **pull through**'	
vt + preposition	phrasal verb with the pattern: 'the doctors **pulled** him **through** the illness'	
vi + preposition	phrasal verb with the pattern: 'he should **pull through** this bout of fever'	

1.8 Forme irregolari

Per rendere più agevole la ricerca di un vocabolo per il lettore straniero abbiamo inserito in ordine alfabetico le principali forme irregolari di verbi e sostantivi con un rimando alla voce in cui il lemma viene trattato per esteso. Ad esempio participi passati quali 'blown' o 'got' o, in italiano 'composto', 'fatto' e plurali irregolari quali 'feet' o 'mila' compaiono in ordine alfabetico con un rimando alla voce principale.

1.8 Irregular forms

In order to help the foreign user, we have listed irregular forms of nouns or verbs in their alphabetical order, with a cross-reference to the basic form where the word is fully treated. For instance, past participles such as 'blown' or 'got' or in Italian 'composto', 'fatto', and irregular plurals such as 'feet' or 'mila' can be found alphabetically.

Nel caso di participi passati si può talvolta avere oltre allo stretto uso participiale anche un uso aggettivale o nominale, vedi ad es. 'conosciuto'. Questi usi particolari vengono trattati come lemmi autonomi ma dove lo si è ritenuto necessario è stato anche inserito un rimando alla voce da cui derivano direttamente (vedi ad es. la voce 'coperto').

In the case of past participles, it sometimes happens that in addition to the purely verbal form there is an adjectival or noun use, for instance 'conosciuto'. These usages are translated as autonomous words, but they are also cross-referred to the verb whenever appropriate (see for instance the entry for 'coperto').

2. Struttura delle voci

Tutte le voci, per quanto lunghe o complesse, sono state strutturate in modo sistematico ed improntate a criteri di particolare chiarezza e semplicità. In particolare in questo dizionario è stato introdotto un sistema di indicatori che serve a guidare il lettore nella scelta della traduzione più adatta in ogni caso specifico.

2. Entry layout

All entries, however long or complex, are arranged in a systematic manner, with the emphasis on clarity and simplicity. In particular this dictionary provides the user with a sophisticated system of semantic 'signposting' which leads to the appropriate translation in each context.

2.1 Indicatori di campo semantico

Se il lettore cerca sul dizionario un vocabolo inglese e si trova di fronte ad una serie di traduzioni italiane, di sicuro non avrà molti problemi a 'riconoscere' la traduzione più appropriata nel contesto dato, poiché ovviamente conoscerà il significato del vocabolo italiano e il contesto in cui avrà trovato la parola da tradurre servirà ad escludere automaticamente le traduzioni incorrette. E' ben diverso il caso in cui si tratta di trovare la traduzione inglese della parola capo nel particolare contesto 'un capo di biancheria' o 'abbiamo doppiato il capo la scorsa notte', e il lettore si trova di fronte ad una voce di questo tipo: 'head; boss; item; article; head, top; end; ply; cape. Si potrebbe ovviamente ricorrere al lato inglese/ italiano del dizionario e controllare il significato di ogni singola parola. Ma si tratterebbe di un'operazione molto lunga e non di sicura riuscita. Per questo motivo abbiamo inserito nel dizionario un sistema di indicatori che servono ad individuare ogni singola traduzione. Ad esempio la voce capo è stata sviluppata come segue:

2.1 Signposting of meanings

If you look up an Italian word and find a string of quite different English translations, you are unlikely to have much trouble finding out which is the relevant one in a given context, because you know what the English words mean, and the context will almost automatically rule out unsuitable translations. It is quite a different matter when you want to find the Italian for, say, lock in the context 'we got to the lock around lunchtime', and are faced with an entry that reads 'lock: serratura; chiusa; sterzo'. You can of course go to the other side and check what each translation means. But this is time-consuming, and it doesn't always work. This is why we have provided the user with a system of indicators – signposts – which pinpoint the relevant translation. For instance with lock, the entry reads:

capo ['kapo] **1** *sm* **(a)** *(Anat)* head; **a ~ chino/alto** with one's head bowed/held high; **da ~ a piedi** from head to foot; **mal di ~** headache; **rompersi il ~** *(fig)* to rack one's brains; **fra ~ e collo** *(all'improvviso)* out of the blue.

(b) *(persona: di fabbrica, ufficio)* head, boss *(fam)*; *(: di partito, movimento)* leader; **essere a ~ di qc** to head sth, be at the head of sth.

(c) *(oggetto)* item, article; **un ~ di biancheria/ vestiario** an item of underwear/clothing.

(d) *(estremità: di tavolo, scale)* head, top; *(: di filo)* end; **da un ~ all'altro** from one end to the other; **in ~ a** *(tempo)* within; *(luogo)* at the top of; **andare in ~ al mondo per qn** *(fig)* to go to the ends of the earth for sb; **ricominciare da ~** to start all over again; **andare a ~** to start a new paragraph; **'punto a ~'** 'full stop — new paragraph'; **un discorso senza né ~ né coda** a senseless *o* meaningless speech.

(e) *(di corda, lana)* ply; **lana a 3 ~i** 3-ply wool.

(f) *(Geog)* cape.

2: **~ d'accusa** *(Dir)* charge; **C~ d'Anno** = Capodanno; **~ di bestiame** head *inv* of cattle; **~ del personale** personnel manager; **~ di stato** head of state.

3 *ag inv (giardiniere, sorvegliante etc)* head *attr*; **redattore ~** chief editor.

Nei due esempi suggeriti più sopra è ora chiaro che nel primo caso la traduzione corretta sarà 'item', mentre nel secondo caso sarà 'cape'.

lock[1] [lɒk] *n (of hair)* ciocca; **~s** *(poet)* chioma.

lock[2] [lɒk] **1** *n* **(a)** *(on door, box etc)* serratura; *(Aut)*: **steering ~** bloccasterzo; **under ~ and key** sotto chiave; **~ stock and barrel** *(fig)* in blocco; **he moved out, ~ stock and barrel** se n'è andato con armi e bagagli. **(b)** *(of canal)* chiusa. **(c)** *(Aut: turning)* a tutto sterzo. **2** *vt (door etc)* chiudere a chiave; *(Tech)* bloccare; **she ~ed the steering mechanism** ha messo il bloccasterzo; **to ~ sb/sth in a place** chiudere qn/qc in un posto; **they were ~ed in each other's arms** erano abbracciati stretti; **to be ~ed in combat** lottare corpo a corpo. **3** *vi (door etc)* chiudersi; *(wheel etc)* bloccarsi.

♦ **lock away** *vt + adv (valuables)* tenere (rinchiuso(a)) al sicuro; *(criminal)* mettere dentro; *(mental patient)* rinchiudere.

♦ **lock in** *vt + adv* chiudere dentro (a chiave).

♦ **lock out** *vt + adv* chiudere fuori; *(Industry)*: **to ~ workers out** fare una serrata.

♦ **lock up 1** *vt + adv (object)* mettere al sicuro, chiudere (a chiave); *(criminal)* mettere dentro; *(mental patient)* rinchiudere; *(funds)* vincolare, immobilizzare; **she checked that the house was properly ~ed up** ha controllato che tutto fosse ben chiuso. **2** *vi + adv* chiudere tutto (a chiave).

For the context suggested above, it is now clear that 'chiusa' is the correct word.

2.2 Categorie grammaticali e semantiche

Le voci più complesse sono suddivise in categorie grammaticali contrassegnate da un numero a seconda delle diverse parti del discorso in cui il vocabolo si suddivide, ad es. **capo 1** *sm*, **2** *categoria composti*, **3** *ag inv*. Ogni categoria grammaticale si suddivide poi a sua volta in varie categorie di significato o semantiche, per cui le varie accezioni di un vocabolo saranno precedute da una letterina in neretto, vedi sopra **capo** categoria 1.

2.3 Vari tipi di indicatori

Gli indicatori sono di vario tipo: indicatori contestuali, sinonimi atti a sostituire il lemma, e indicatori di campo semantico.

2.3.1 Indicatori contestuali

Gli indicatori contestuali costituiscono una guida studiata per fornire al lettore il tipico contesto di uso della traduzione fornita. Si può trattare di soggetti tipici nel caso di un verbo intransitivo, di oggetti tipici nel caso di un verbo transitivo, o di sostantivi tipicamente usati in associazione con un determinato sostantivo o con un aggettivo. Ad esempio:

bloccare: 2: ~**rsi** *vr (motore)* to stall; *(freni, porta)* to jam, stick; *(ascensore)* to get stuck, stop...

analizzare [analid'dzare] *vt (gen)* to analyse; *(sangue, orina)* to test, analyse; *(Gram: frase)* to parse; *(poesia, testo)* to give a commentary on.

blando, a ['blando] *ag (medicina, rimedio)* mild; *(liquore)* weak; *(sapore, cibo)* bland; *(punizione)* light, mild.

leaf [li:f] *n, pl* **leaves (a)** *(of plant)* foglia. **(b)** *(of book)* foglio, pagina; **to turn over a new ~** *(fig)* cambiar vita; **to take a ~ out of sb's book** *(fig)* prendere esempio da qn. **(c)** *(of table: fold-down)* ribalta; *(: extending)* asse *f* estraibile.

2.3.2 Sinonimi

I sinonimi o parziali definizioni del lemma servono a distinguere le sfumature di significato che la traduzione può assumere, ad esempio:

ar·ti·choke ['a:tɪtʃəʊk] *n (globe ~)* carciofo; *(Jerusalem ~)* topinambur *m inv*.

affascinare [affaʃʃi'nare] *vt (ammaliare)* to bewitch; *(sedurre)* to charm, fascinate.

2.3.3 Indicatori di campo semantico e di stile

2.3.3.1 Indicatori di campo semantico

Gli indicatori di campo semantico (cioè: *Sport, Mil, Naut* etc) vengono usati per differenziare i vari significati del lemma secondo una specifica suddivisione in campi semantici, ad esempio:

bobina [bo'bina] *sf* **(a)** *(Elettr)* coil; ~ **d'accensione** *(Aut)* ignition coil. **(b)** *(Cine, Fot etc)* reel. **(c)** ...

Questi indicatori vengono anche usati quando il significato nella lingua di origine è chiaro, ma possono insorgere delle ambiguità nella lingua di arrivo, per esempio:

boccale¹ [bok'kale] *ag (Anat)* oral.

2.2 Grammatical categories and semantic categories

Complex entries are first broken down into grammatical categories according to the part of speech and numbered, e.g. **lock²** **1** *n*, **2** *vt*, **3** *vi*. Each grammatical category is then split where appropriate into the various meanings and preceded by a letter, as in **lock²** category 1 (above).

2.3 Types of semantic indicators

Indicators fall into three basic groups: contextual indicators, substitutes for the headword, and labels.

2.3.1 Contextual indicators

Contextual indicators provide the user with typical contexts in which he may find or wish to use a translation. These may be typical noun subjects of an intransitive verb, typical noun objects of a transitive verb, or typical noun complements of an adjective or another noun. For instance:

lock² ... **3** *vi (door etc)* chiudersi; *(wheel etc)* bloccarsi.

analizzare [analid'dzare] *vt (gen)* to analyse; *(sangue, orina)* to test, analyse; *(Gram: frase)* to parse; *(poesia, testo)* to give a commentary on.

blando, a ['blando] *ag (medicina, rimedio)* mild; *(liquore)* weak; *(sapore, cibo)* bland; *(punizione)* light, mild.

leaf [li:f] *n, pl* **leaves (a)** *(of plant)* foglia. **(b)** *(of book)* foglio, pagina; **to turn over a new ~** *(fig)* cambiar vita; **to take a ~ out of sb's book** *(fig)* prendere esempio da qn. **(c)** *(of table: fold-down)* ribalta; *(: extending)* asse *f* estraibile.

2.3.2 Substitutes for the headword

Substitutes take the form of synonyms or partial definitions, for instance:

ar·ti·choke ['a:tɪtʃəʊk] *n (globe ~)* carciofo; *(Jerusalem ~)* topinambur *m inv*.

affascinare [affaʃʃi'nare] *vt (ammaliare)* to bewitch; *(sedurre)* to charm, fascinate.

2.3.3 Labels

2.3.3.1 Field labels

Field labels (i.e. *Sport, Mil, Naut* etc) are used to differentiate various meanings of the headword according to specific semantic fields, for instance:

bobina [bo'bina] *sf* **(a)** *(Elettr)* coil; ~ **d'accensione** *(Aut)* ignition coil. **(b)** *(Cine, Fot etc)* reel. **(c)** ...

They are also used when the meaning in the source language is clear but may be ambiguous in the target language, for instance:

boccale¹ [bok'kale] *ag (Anat)* oral.

2.3.3.2 Indicatori di stile

Tutti i vocaboli che esulano dal linguaggio 'standard' sono stati contrassegnati in base a due registri:
(i) uso formale *(frm)* e informale o colloquiale *(fam)*
(ii) uso antiquato *(ant)* e letterario o poetico *(poet)*
Questo tipo di indicatori viene fornito sia per la lingua di origine che per la lingua di arrivo e serve innanzitutto a mettere in guardia il lettore straniero rispetto all'uso di un particolare vocabolo, ad esempio:

hereby [,hɪə'baɪ] *adv (frm)* con questo.
finocchio [fi'nɔkkjo] *sm* **(a)** *(Bot)* fennel. **(b)** *(fam: omosessuale)* queer, poof.
whither ['wɪðəʳ] *adv (poet)* dove.

Per ulteriori informazioni sui colloquialismi e sul linguaggio volgare vedi al paragrafo 3.5 qui di seguito.

3. Come usare le traduzioni

3.1 Genere

Dal lato inglese-italiano del dizionario sono state indicate tutte le desinenze femminili degli aggettivi. Si potrebbe pensare che questa non sia altro che una ripetizione di quanto già illustrato nell'altra sezione del dizionario, ma siamo sicuri che tale aggiunta risulterà utile in molti casi. Abbiamo anche indicato la traduzione femminile di vocaboli come **driver, teacher, researcher** quando si tratta di un vocabolo di uso corrente in italiano.

3.2 Plurali

I plurali irregolari sono stati indicati subito dopo il lemma in entrambe le sezioni del dizionario.

3.3 Verbi irregolari

Quando compaiono come traduzione i verbi irregolari non sono stati indicati come tali, in caso di dubbio il lettore dovrebbe consultare le tavole dei verbi irregolari riportate in appendice al volume. Dalla parte inglese-italiano tutte le forme dei verbi forti sono state indicate sia subito dopo il lemma che in ordine alfabetico con un rimando al lemma principale. Dalla parte italiano-inglese invece sono stati indicati in ordine alfabetico tutti i participi passati irregolari con un rimando al lemma principale.

3.4 Verbi ausiliari

E' stato indicato l'ausiliare 'essere' per quei verbi italiani che ne richiedono l'uso nella formazione dei tempi composti. Vedi ad esempio 'andare', 'mancare'.

3.5 Colloquialismi e linguaggio volgare

Come regola il lettore dovrebbe usare molta cautela nel servirsi di espressioni informali o volgari in una lingua straniera. Quando un vocabolo è stato identificato con un indicatore *(fam)*, e cioè familiare, anche la traduzione avrà il medesimo livello di informalità. Quando invece un vocabolo è stato identificato con un indicatore *(fam!)* o una traduzione è stata fatta seguire da (!) si tratta di un'espressione volgare e il lettore dovrebbe usare estrema cautela nel servirsene a meno che non si trovi tra amici.

2.3.3.2 Style labels

All words which are not standard language have been labelled according to two separate registers:
(i) formal *(frm)* and informal or colloquial usage *(fam)*
(ii) old-fashioned *(old)* and literary or poetic usage *(poet)*
This labelling is given for both source and target languages and serves primarily to provide a warning to the non-native speaker, for instance:

hereby [,hɪə'baɪ] *adv (frm)* con questo.
finocchio [fi'nɔkkjo] *sm* **(a)** *(Bot)* fennel. **(b)** *(fam: omosessuale)* queer, poof.
whither ['wɪðəʳ] *adv (poet)* dove.

For further advice on colloquial usage see 3.5 below.

3. Using the translations

3.1 Gender

All feminine endings for Italian adjectives have been given on the English-Italian side of the dictionary. This may appear to duplicate information given on the other side, but we feel it is a useful reminder where and when it matters. The feminine version is given as a translation of words like **driver, teacher, researcher** etc where appropriate.

3.2 Plurals

Irregular plural forms are shown on both sides of the dictionary for headwords.

3.3 Irregular verbs

Irregular verbs appearing as translations have not been marked as such, and the user should refer to the verb tables at the end of the dictionary when in doubt. On the English-Italian side, all English strong verbs have their irregular forms shown both at the main entry and at their alphabetical position, while on the Italian-English side all irregular past participles appear at their alphabetical position.

3.4 Auxiliary verbs

Those Italian verbs which require 'essere' as their auxiliary in compound tenses have been marked appropriately. See, for instance, 'andare', 'mancare'.

3.5 Colloquial language

You should as a rule proceed with great caution when handling foreign language which has a degree of informality. When a word or phrase has been labelled *(fam)*, i.e. familiar or colloquial, you must assume that the translation belongs to a similar level of informality. If the item has been labelled *(fam!)*, or if a translation is followed by (!) you should exercise extreme caution, or better still avoid it unless with close friends!

3.6 Formule di cortesia

Nel fornire e nel tradurre esempi si è privilegiato in questo dizionario l'uso del pronome **tu**, oggi entrato a far parte del lessico quotidiano. Il pronome **lei** è tuttavia stato mantenuto nel caso di formule di cortesia, in cui l'uso del pronome **tu** sarebbe scortese.

3.7 Traduzioni con un certo livello di approssimazione ed equivalenti culturali

Non sempre è possibile fornire una traduzione assolutamente corrispondente all'originale. Ne può essere un esempio il caso di oggetti o istituzioni che esistono in italiano e non trovano un equivalente in inglese. In questo caso si può solo fornire una traduzione che di necessità ha un certo livello di approssimazione oppure una spiegazione. Gli equivalenti culturali sono preceduti da un segno ≈, mentre le spiegazioni vengono riportate in corsivo. Vedi ad esempio le voci **speaker** *(Brit Parliament)*, **comprehensive school**, e dalla parte italiano-inglese **A.C.I., ginnasio.**

3.8 Varianti di traduzione

Tutte le traduzioni separate da una virgola si possono considerare intercambiabili con riferimento al significato indicato in parentesi. Ogniqualvolta un contesto diverso richiede una diversa traduzione questo è stato segnalato per mezzo di indicatori che si riferiscono alla lingua di origine.

In alcuni casi all'interno di una voce compare un rimando che si riferisce al sistema di indicatori di un'altra voce. Ciò succede ad esempio con alcuni derivati. In questo caso le varianti di traduzione anche se separate semplicemente da un punto e virgola (non seguito da un indicatore) non devono essere considerate intercambiabili. Vedi ad esempio alla voce **sensitivity** e dalla parte italiano-inglese **abbandono, acclamazione.**

3.6 'tu' versus 'lei'

Throughout the dictionary, in phrases and in the translation of phrases, 'you' singular has been rendered by **tu**, which is the familiar form. **Lei** has only been used when the context clearly demands the polite form.

3.7 'Approximate' translations and cultural equivalents

It is not always possible to give a genuine translation, when for instance an English word denotes a thing or institution which either doesn't exist in Italy, or is quite different. Therefore only an approximate equivalent can be given, or else an explanation. Such equivalents are preceded by a ≈, and explanations are shown in italics. See for instance the entries for **speaker** *(Brit Parliament)*, **comprehensive school**, and on the Italian-English side **A.C.I., ginnasio.**

3.8 Alternative translations

As a rule, translations separated by commas can be regarded as interchangeable for the meaning indicated. Whenever a different context warrants a different translation, it has been shown by means of indicating words – signposts – in the source language.

There is occasionally a reference from an entry to the signposting structure of another, in the case for instance of nominalizations. In this case only, alternative translations may be separated by semi-colons, and should not be regarded as interchangeable. See for instance the entry for **sensitivity** and on the Italian-English side **abbandono, acclamazione.**

Trademarks
Words which we have reason to believe constitute registered trademarks are designated as such. However, neither the presence nor the absence of such designation should be regarded as affecting the legal status of any trademark.

TRASCRIZIONE FONETICA

PHONETIC TRANSCRIPTION

CONSONANTS / CONSONANTI

NB. The pairing of some vowel sounds only indicates approximate equivalence/La messa in equivalenza di certi suoni indica solo una rassomiglianza approssimativa.

puppy	p	*padre*
baby	b	*bambino*
tent	t	*tutto*
daddy	d	*dado*
cork kiss chord	k	*cane che*
gag guess	g	*gola ghiro*
so rice kiss	s	*sano*
cousin buzz	z	*svago esame*
sheep sugar	ʃ	*scena*
pleasure beige	ʒ	
church	tʃ	*pece lanciare*
judge general	dʒ	*giro gioco*
farm raffle	f	*afa faro*
very rev	v	*vero bravo*
thin maths	θ	
that other	ð	
little ball	l	*letto ala*
	ʎ	*gli*
rat brat	r	*rete arco*
mummy comb	m	*ramo madre*
no ran	n	*no fumante*
	ɲ	*gnomo*
singing bank	ŋ	
hat reheat	h	
yet	j	*buio piacere*
wall bewail	w	*uomo guaio*
loch	x	

VOWELS / VOCALI

NB. **p, b, t, d, k, g** are not aspirated in Italian/sono seguiti da un'aspirazione in inglese.

heel bead	iː i	*vino idea*
hit pity	ɪ	
	e	*stella edera*
set tent	ɛ	*epoca eccetto*
apple bat	æ a	*mamma amore*
after car calm	ɑː	
fun cousin	ʌ	
over above	ə	
urn fern work	ɜː	
wash pot	ɒ ɔ	*rosa occhio*
born cork	ɔː	
	o	*ponte ognuno*
full soot	ʊ u	*utile zucca*
boon lewd	uː	

DIPHTHONGS / DITTONGHI

ɪə	*beer tier*
ɛə	*tear fair there*
eɪ	*date plaice day*
aɪ	*life buy cry*
aʊ	*owl foul now*
əʊ	*low no*
ɔɪ	*boil boy oily*
ʊə	*poor tour*

MISCELLANEOUS / VARIE

ʳ per l'inglese: la 'r' finale viene pronunciata se seguita da una vocale.

ˈ precedes the stressed syllable/precede la sillaba accentata.

abbreviation	**abbr**	abbreviazione
adjective	**adj**	aggettivo
administration	**Admin**	amministrazione
adverb	**adv**	avverbio
aviation, aeronautics	**Aer**	aeronautica, trasporti aerei
adjective	**ag**	aggettivo
agriculture	**Agr**	agricoltura
American	**Am**	americano
administration	**Amm**	amministrazione
anatomy	**Anat**	anatomia
old	**ant**	antico
archaeology	**Archeol**	archeologia
architecture	**Archit**	architettura
article	**art**	articolo
astronomy	**Astron**	astronomia
attributive	**attr**	attributivo
auxiliary	**aus**	ausiliare
cars and motoring	**Aut**	automobile, automobilismo
auxiliary	**aux**	ausiliare
adverb	**av**	avverbio
biology	**Bio**	biologia
botany	**Bot**	botanica
British, Great Britain	**Brit**	britannico, Gran Bretagna
chemistry	**Chem, Chim**	chimica
cinema	**Cine**	cinema
commerce	**Comm**	commercio
comparative	**comp**	comparativo
conditional	**cond**	condizionale
conjunction	**cong**	congiunzione
subjunctive	**congiunt**	congiuntivo
conjunction	**conj**	congiunzione
building trade	**Constr**	edilizia
compound element: noun used as adjective and which cannot follow the noun it qualifies	**cpd**	sostantivo usato come aggettivo, non può essere usato dopo il sostantivo qualificato
cooking	**Culin**	culinaria, cucina
before	**dav a**	davanti a
definite	**def**	definito
demonstrative	**dem**	dimostrativo
determining	**det**	determinativo
dialect	**dial**	dialetto
demonstrative	**dimostr**	dimostrativo
law	**Dir**	diritto
direct	**dir**	diretto
economics	**Econ**	economia
building trade	**Edil**	edilizia
electricity, electronics	**Elec, Elettr**	elettricità, elettronica
exclamation	**escl**	esclamazione
especially	**esp**	specialmente
et cetera	**etc**	eccetera
euphemistic	**euph, euf**	eufemismo
exclamation	**excl**	esclamazione
feminine	**f**	femminile
informal, colloquial, familiar	**fam**	familiare, colloquiale
vulgar, offensive, taboo	**fam!**	volgare, tabù
railways	**Ferr**	ferrovia
figurative	**fig**	figurato
finance	**Fin**	finanza
physics	**Fis**	fisica
photography	**Fot**	fotografia
formal	**frm**	formale
football	**Ftbl**	calcio
generally, in most senses	**gen**	generale, nella maggior parte dei casi
geography	**Geog**	geografia
geology	**Geol**	geologia
geometry	**Geom**	geometria
grammar	**Gram**	grammatica
humorous	**hum**	scherzoso
impersonal	**impers**	impersonale
indefinite	**indef**	indefinito
indefinite	**indet**	indeterminativo
indicative	**indic**	indicativo

indirect	**indir**	indiretto
infinitive	**infin**	infinito
computers	**Inform**	informatica, computers
interrogative	**interrog**	interrogativo
invariable	**inv**	invariabile
Irish	**Ir**	irlandese
ironical	**iro**	ironico
irregular	**irreg**	irregolare
masculine	**m**	maschile
mathematics	**Math, Mat**	matematica
medicine	**Med**	medicina
meteorology, weather	**Met, Meteor**	meteorologia
either masculine or feminine	**m/f**	maschile o femminile,
depending on sex		secondo il sesso
military	**Mil**	militare
music	**Mus**	musica
noun	**n**	sostantivo
nautical, naval	**Naut**	nautica
negative	**neg**	negativo
no plural	**no pl**	niente plurale
object	**obj, ogg**	oggetto
oneself	**o.s.**	
passive	**pass**	passivo
past historic	**pass rem**	passato remoto
pejorative	**pej, peg**	peggiorativo
personal	**pers**	personale
photography	**Phot**	fotografia
physics	**Phys**	fisica
plural	**pl**	plurale
poetic, literary	**poet**	poetico, letterario
politics	**Pol**	politica
possessive	**poss**	possessivo
past participle	**pp**	participio passato
predicative	**pred**	predicativo
prefix	**pref**	prefisso
preposition	**prep**	preposizione
present	**pres**	presente
pronoun	**pron**	pronome
present participle	**prp**	participio presente
psychology	**Psych, Psic**	psicologia
past tense	**pt**	passato
	qc	qualcosa
	qn	qualcuno
religion	**Rel**	religione
relative	**rel**	relativo
noun	**s**	sostantivo
somebody	**sb**	
humorous	**scherz**	scherzoso
school	**Scol**	sistema scolastico
Scottish	**Scot**	scozzese
singular	**sg**	singolare
sociology	**Sociol**	sociologia
subject	**sog**	soggetto
especially	**spec**	specialmente
something	**sth**	
subjunctive	**sub**	congiuntivo
subject	**subj**	soggetto
suffix	**suf**	suffisso
superlative	**superl**	superlativo
specialist's term	**T**	termine da specialista
technology, technical	**Tech, Tecn**	tecnica, tecnologia
telecommunications	**Telec**	telecomunicazioni
typography, printing	**Tip**	tipografia
television	**TV**	televisione
typography, printing	**Typ**	tipografia
university	**Univ**	università
usually	**usu**	di solito
verb	**vb**	verbo
intransitive verb	**vi**	verbo intransitivo
transitive verb	**vt**	verbo transitivo
zoology	**Zool**	zoologia
registered trade mark	®	marchio registrato
vulgar, offensive, taboo	!	volgare, tabù

A

A, a[1] [a] *sf o m inv* (*lettera*) A, a; **dall'a alla zeta** from A to Z.

a[2] [a] *prep* (*a+il* = **al**, *a+lo* = **allo**, *a+l'* = **all'**, *a+la* = **alla**, *a+i* = **ai**, *a+gli* = **agli**, *a+le* = **alle**) **(a)** (*complemento di termine*) to (*spesso omesso*); **dare qc a qn** to give sth to sb, give sb sth; **ho dato un giocattolo ~ Sandro** I gave Sandro a toy, I gave a toy to Sandro; **gli ho dato un giocattolo** I gave him a toy, I gave a toy to him.

(b) (*stato in luogo: posizione*) at; (*: in*) in; (*: su*) on; **abitare ~ Milano/al terzo piano** to live in Milan/on the third floor; **essere ~ scuola/~ casa/al cinema** to be at school/at home/at the cinema; **è ~ 10 km da qui** it's 10 km from here; **alla televisione/radio** on television/the radio; **lavora alle poste/alle ferrovie** he works at the Post Office/on the railways.

(c) (*moto a luogo*) to; **andare ~ casa/~Roma/ al mare** to go home/to Rome/to the seaside.

(d) (*tempo*) at; (*epoca, stagione*) in; (*fino a*) to, till, until; **~ mezzanotte/Natale** at midnight/ Christmas; **alle 3** at 3 o'clock; **~ domani/lunedì!** see you tomorrow/on Monday!; **all'alba** at dawn; **~ primavera/maggio** in spring/May; **dalle 3 alle 5** from 3 to o till 5 (o'clock); **tornerà ~ minuti/~ giorni** he'll be back in a few minutes/a few days; **~ 18 anni si diventa maggiorenni** at 18 you come of age.

(e) (*mezzo, modo*) on, by, with; **andare ~ piedi/cavallo** to go on foot/horseback; **fatto ~ mano** made by hand, handmade; **scrivere qc ~ matita** to write sth in pencil *o* with a pencil; **entrare ~ uno ~ uno** to come in one by one; **una barca ~ motore** a motorboat; **bistecca alla fiorentina/ai ferri** T-bone/grilled steak; **pasta al pomodoro** pasta in tomato sauce; **gonna ~ pieghe/strisce** pleated/striped skirt; **alla milanese** the Milanese way, in the Milanese fashion.

(f) (*rapporto*) by, per; (*con prezzi*) at; **viaggiare ~ 100 km all'ora** to travel at 100 km an *o* per hour; **essere pagato ~ ore/giornata** to be paid by the hour/day; **prendo 500.000 lire al mese** I get 500,000 lire a *o* per month; **vendere qc ~ 500 lire il chilo** to sell sth at 500 lire a *o* per kilo.

(g) (*scopo, fine*) for, to; **restare ~ cena** to stay for dinner.

A. [a] *abbr* (= *autostrada*): **sull'~ 1** ≃ on the M1.
abate [a'bate] *sm* abbot.
abbacchiato, a [abbak'kjato] *ag* down, depressed; **ha un'aria ~a** he's looking a bit down.
abbacinare [abbatʃi'nare] *vt* to dazzle.
abbagliante [abbaʎ'ʎante] **1** *ag* dazzling; **fare uso dei fari ~i** to use one's headlights on full beam. **2** *sm* (*Aut*): **accendere gli ~i** to put one's headlights on full beam.
abbagliare [abbaʎ'ʎare] *vt* (*anche fig*) to dazzle; (*illudere*) to delude; **non lasciarti ~** don't be taken in.
abbaglio [ab'baʎʎo] *sm* blunder; **prendere un ~** to make a blunder.
abbaiare [abba'jare] *vi*: **~ (a)** to bark (at); (*fig: parlare rabbiosamente*) to bawl (at).
abbaino [abba'ino] *sm* (*Archit*) dormer window; (*soffitta*) attic.

abbandonare [abbando'nare] **1** *vt* **(a)** (*gen*) to abandon; (*famiglia, paese*) to abandon, desert; **~ qn a se stesso** to leave sb to his (*o* her) own devices; **il coraggio lo abbandonò** his courage deserted him; **~ la nave** to abandon ship; **~ il campo** (*Mil*) to retreat. **(b)** (*lasciare indietro*) to leave behind, abandon. **(c)** (*trascurare: casa, lavoro*) to neglect. **(d)** (*rinunciare a*) to give up; (*: studi, progetto*) to abandon, give up; **~ la speranza** to give up hope. **(e)** (*lasciare andare: redini*) to loosen; **~ la presa** to let go; **abbandonò la testa sul cuscino** he let his head fall back on the cushion.

2: **~rsi** *vr* to let o.s. go; **~rsi a** (*cedere*) to give o.s. up to; **~rsi a qn** (*sessualmente*) to give o.s. to sb; **~rsi al bere** to take to drink; **si abbandonò sul divano** he collapsed onto the couch.
abbandonato, a [abbando'nato] *ag* **(a)** (*casa*) deserted; (*miniera*) disused. **(b)** (*trascurato: terreno, podere*) neglected. **(c)** (*bambino*) abandoned.
abbandono [abban'dono] *sm* **(a)** (*vedi vt*) desertion; abandonment; neglecting; giving up. **(b)** (*trascuratezza*) neglect; **lasciare qc in stato di ~** to neglect sth. **(c)** (*Sport*) withdrawal. **(d)** (*rilassamento, cedimento*) abandon; **momenti di ~** moments of abandon.
abbarbicarsi [abbarbi'karsi] *vr*: **~ (a)** (*anche fig*) to cling (to).
abbassamento [abbassa'mento] *sm* lowering; (*di pressione, livello dell'acqua*) fall; (*di prezzi*) reduction; **~ di temperatura** drop in temperature.
abbassare [abbas'sare] **1** *vt* **(a)** to lower; (*pedale*) to press down; (*finestrino della macchina*) to roll down; (*finestrino del treno, tapparella*) to pull down; **~ le armi** (*Mil*) to lay down one's arms; **abbassò la testa per la vergogna** he hung his head in shame. **(b)** (*volume: Radio, TV*) to turn down; (*voce*) to lower. **(c)** (*diminuire: prezzi*) to reduce, bring down. **(d)** (*luce*) to dim; (*fari*) to dip. **(e)** (*Mat: perpendicolare*) to drop. **2:** **~rsi** *vr* **(a)** (*chinarsi*) to bend down, stoop; (*: per evitare*) to duck; (*fig: umiliarsi*): **~rsi a fare qc** to lower o.s. to do sth. **(b)** (*temperatura, prezzi*) to drop, fall; (*marea*) to go out; (*sole*) to go down; (*sipario*) to fall. **(c)** (*peggiorare: vista*) to get worse.
abbasso [ab'basso] **1** *escl*: **~ il re!** down with the king! **2** *av* down.
abbastanza [abbas'tantsa] *av* **(a)** (*a sufficienza*) enough; **non mangia ~** he doesn't eat enough; **non ho ~ tempo/denaro** I don't have enough *o* sufficient time/money; **hai trovato una casa ~ grande?** have you found a big enough house?; **non ho ~ denaro per comprarlo** I don't have enough money to buy it; **averne ~ di qn/qc** to have had enough of sb/sth, be fed up with sb/sth. **(b)** (*alquanto*) quite, rather, fairly; **un vino ~ dolce** quite a sweet wine, a fairly sweet wine; **ti piace il film? — sì, ~** are you enjoying the film? — yes, fairly.
abbattere [ab'battere] **1** *vt* **(a)** (*edificio*) to knock down; (*albero*) to fell, cut down; (*aereo*) to shoot down; (*porta*) to break down; (*fig: governo*) to overthrow. **(b)** (*uccidere: persona, selvaggina*) to shoot; (*: bestie da macello*) to slaughter; (*: cane, cavallo*) to destroy. **(c)** (*prostrare*) to lay low; **non lasciarti ~** don't be disheartened. **2:** **~rsi** *vr* **(a)**

(cadere): ~**rsi a terra** *o* **al suolo** to fall to the ground. **(b)** *(piombare)*: ~**rsi su** *(sog: maltempo)* to beat down on; *(: disgrazia)* to hit, strike. **(c)** *(avvilirsi)* to lose heart.

abbattimento [abbatti'mento] *sm* **(a)** *(di albero)* felling; *(di muro)* knocking down; *(di casa)* demolition. **(b)** *(prostrazione: fisica)* exhaustion; *(: morale)* despondency.

abbattuto, a [abbat'tuto] *ag* despondent, depressed.

abbazia [abbat'tsia] *sf* abbey.

abbecedario [abbetʃe'darjo] *sm* spelling book.

abbellimento [abbelli'mento] *sm* **(a)** *(ornamento)* embellishment. **(b)** *(Mus)* grace note.

abbellire [abbel'lire] **1** *vt* to make (more) attractive; *(racconto)* to embellish. **2**: ~**rsi** *vr* to become more attractive.

abbeverare [abbeve'rare] **1** *vt* to water. **2**: ~**rsi** *vr (animale)* to drink.

abbeveratoio [abbevera'tojo] *sm* drinking trough.

abbiccì [abbit'tʃi] *sm inv (alfabeto)* alphabet; *(abbecedario)* spelling book; **l'~ del fai da te** the abc of do-it-yourself.

abbiente [ab'bjɛnte] **1** *ag* well-to-do, prosperous. **2**: **gli ~i** *smpl* the well-to-do; **gli ~i e i non ~i** the haves and the have-nots.

abbietto [ab'bjɛtto] *etc* = **abietto** *etc.*

abbigliamento [abbiʎʎa'mento] *sm (indumenti, modo di vestire)* clothes *pl*; *(vestiario)* clothing; **capo** *o* **articolo di** ~ article of clothing; ~ **maschile/femminile** men's/women's fashions; **industria dell'** ~ clothing industry.

abbigliare [abbiʎ'ʎare] **1** *vt (aiutare a vestire)* to dress; *(agghindare)* to dress up. **2**: ~**rsi** *vr* to dress up.

abbinamento [abbina'mento] *sm (vedi vb)* combination; linking.

abbinare [abbi'nare] *vt*: ~ **(con** *o* **a) (gen)** to combine (with); *(nomi)* to link (with).

abbindolare [abbindo'lare] *vt (fig)* to trick, take in.

abbisognare [abbizoɲ'ɲare] *vi* **(a)** *(aus essere) (essere necessario)*: ~ **a: chiedi ciò che ti abbisogna** ask for what you need; **mi abbisogna il tuo aiuto** I need your help. **(b)** *(aver bisogno)*: ~ **di** to need; **non abbisognano dei tuoi consigli** they don't need your advice.

abboccamento [abbokka'mento] *sm* **(a)** *(colloquio)* preliminary meeting. **(b)** *(Tecn: di tubi)* connection.

abboccare [abbok'kare] **1** *vi (pesce)* to bite; *(fig: farsi raggirare)* to swallow the bait; ~ **all'amo** *(anche fig)* to rise to the bait. **2** *vt (Tecn: tubi, conduttore)* to connect, join. **3**: ~**rsi** *vr* to meet.

abboccato, a [abbok'kato] *ag (vino)* sweetish.

abboffarsi [abbof'farsi] *etc* = **abbuffarsi** *etc.*

abbonamento [abbona'mento] *sm* **(a)**: ~ **(a)** *(rivista)* subscription (to); *(teatro, trasporti)* season ticket (for); ~ **settimanale/mensile** *(a teatro, trasporti)* weekly/monthly ticket; **fare l'**~ **a qc** to take out a subscription to sth; to buy a season ticket for sth; **in** ~ for subscribers only; for season ticket holders only. **(b)** *(al telefono)* rental; ~ **alla radio/alla televisione** radio/television licence.

abbonare[1] [abbo'nare] *vt (cifra)* to deduct; *(fig: perdonare)* to forgive.

abbonare[2] [abbo'nare] **1** *vt*: ~ **qn (a qc)** *(rivista)* to take out a subscription (to sth) for sb; *(teatro, trasporti)* to buy sb a season ticket (for sth); *(televisione etc)* to take out a licence (for sth) for sb. **2**: ~**rsi** *vr*: ~**rsi a** *(rivista)* to subscribe (to); *(teatro, trasporti)* to buy a season ticket (for); ~**rsi al telefono** to have the telephone installed;

~**rsi alla radio/alla televisione** to take out a radio/television licence.

abbonato, a [abbo'nato] **1** *ag (fig: abituato)*: **viene a cena da noi ogni settimana: ormai c'è** ~! he comes to our house for dinner every week: it has become a habit with him now! **2** *sm/f (vedi abbonare*[2]*)* subscriber; season ticket holder; licence holder; ~ **al telefono** telephone subscriber; **elenco degli** ~**i** telephone directory.

abbondante [abbon'dante] *ag* **(a)** *(gen)* abundant; *(misure)* generous; *(nevicata)* heavy. **(b)** *(abito: troppo grande)* too big; *(: ampio)* loose-fitting.

abbondanza [abbon'dantsa] *sf (gran quantità)* abundance; **ci sono pere in** ~ there are plenty of pears, there is an abundance of pears. **(b)** *(ricchezza)*: **vivere nell'**~ to live in plenty.

abbondare [abbon'dare] *vi* **(a)** *(aus essere)* to abound, be plentiful. **(b)**: ~ **di** to be full of, abound in; ~ **in** *o* **di cortesie** to be extremely polite.

abbordabile [abbor'dabile] *ag (persona)* approachable; *(prezzo)* reasonable.

abbordare [abbor'dare] *vt* **(a)** *(Naut)* to go alongside. **(b)** *(curva, salita)* to take. **(c)** *(persona)* to accost; *(questione, argomento)* to tackle.

abbottonare [abbotto'nare] **1** *vt* to button (up); ~**rsi il cappotto** to button (up) one's coat. **2**: ~**rsi** *vr* to button (up).

abbottonato, a [abbotto'nato] *ag (fig)* reserved.

abbottonatura [abbottona'tura] *sf* buttons *pl*; **questo cappotto ha l'**~ **da uomo/da donna** this coat buttons on the man's/woman's side.

abbozzare [abbot'tsare] *vt* **(a)** *(scultura)* to rough-hew; *(disegno)* to sketch; *(romanzo)* to sketch out. **(b)** *(fig: idea, progetto)* to outline; *(: contratto)* to draft; ~ **un sorriso** to give a faint smile; ~ **un saluto** *(con la mano)* to half wave; *(con un cenno del capo)* to half nod.

abbozzo [ab'bɔttso] *sm* **(a)** *(di scultura, disegno)* sketch; *(di libro)* rough outline. **(b)** *(fig: di progetto)* outline; *(: di contratto)* draft; *(: accenno)* hint; **un** ~ **di sorriso** the ghost of a smile.

abbracciare [abbrat'tʃare] **1** *vt* **(a)** to embrace, hug; **ti abbraccio** *(in una lettera)* lots of love. **(b)** *(professione)* to take up; *(fede)* to embrace. **(c)** *(includere)* to take in; ~ **qc con lo sguardo** to take sth in at a glance; **la sua opera abbraccia due secoli di storia** his work covers two hundred years of history. **2**: ~**rsi** *vr* to embrace (one another), hug (one another).

abbraccio [ab'brattʃo] *sm* embrace, hug.

abbrancare [abbran'kare] **1** *vt* to grasp, seize; ~ **per il colletto qn** to seize hold of sb by the collar. **2**: ~**rsi** *vr*: ~**rsi a qc** to grab hold of sth.

abbreviare [abbre'vjare] *vt (gen)* to shorten; *(parola)* to abbreviate.

abbreviazione [abbrevjat'tsjone] *sf (vedi vb)* shortening; abbreviation.

abbronzante [abbron'dzante] **1** *ag (prodotto)* suntan *attr*. **2** *sm (crema)* suntan cream; *(olio)* suntan oil.

abbronzare [abbron'dzare] **1** *vt* to tan. **2**: ~**rsi** *vr* to tan, get a tan; **stare ad** ~**rsi** to sunbathe.

abbronzato, a [abbron'dzato] *ag (sun)*tanned.

abbronzatura [abbrondza'tura] *sf (sun)*tan.

abbrustolire [abbrusto'lire] **1** *vt (pane)* to toast; *(semi, caffè)* to roast. **2**: ~**rsi** *vr*: ~**rsi al sole** *(fig)* to soak up the sun.

abbrutimento [abbruti'mento] *sm (vedi vb)* exhaustion; degradation.

abbrutire [abbru'tire] *vt* **(a)** *(snervare, stancare)* to exhaust. **(b)** *(degradare)* to degrade; **essere abbrutito dall'alcool** to be ruined by drink.

abbuffarsi [abbuf'farsi] *vr (fam):* ~ **(di qc)** to stuff o.s. (with sth).

abbuffata [abbuf'fata] *sf (fam)* nosh-up; **farsi un'**~ to stuff o.s.

abbuiare [abbu'jare] **1** *vb impers* to get dark. **2:** ~**rsi** *vr (farsi buio)* to grow dark; *(fig: espressione, volto)* to darken.

abbuonare [abbwo'nare] *vt* = **abbonare**¹.

abbuono [ab'bwono] *sm* **(a)** *(Comm)* discount. **(b)** *(Ippica)* handicap.

abdicare [abdi'kare] *vi* **(a)** *(al trono):* ~ **(a)** to abdicate (from). **(b)** *(rinunciare):* ~ **a** to renounce, give up.

abdicazione [abdikat'tsjone] *sf* abdication.

aberrante [aber'rante] *ag* aberrant.

aberrazione [aberrat'tsjone] *sf* aberration.

abetaia [abe'taja] *sf* fir wood.

abete [a'bɛte] *sm (albero)* fir (tree); *(legno)* fir; ~ **bianco** silver fir; ~ **rosso** spruce.

abietto, a [a'bjɛtto] *ag (spregevole: persona, azione)* despicable, vile; *(squallido: condizioni)* abject.

abiezione [abjet'tsjone] *sf (vedi ag)* vileness; abjection.

abile ['abile] *ag* **(a)** *(capace)* skilful; **essere ~ in qc** to be good at sth; ~ **chirurgo/artigiano** skilful surgeon/craftsman. **(b)** *(accorto)* clever; *(astuto)* shrewd; **un ~ uomo d'affari** a shrewd businessman. **(c)** *(idoneo, Mil):* ~ **a qc/a fare qc** fit for sth/to do sth; **fare qn** ~ to pass sb as fit for military service.

abilità [abili'ta] *sf* **(a)** *(capacità)* ability; *(destrezza)* skill; ~ **nel fare qc** ability to do sth; skill in doing sth. **(b)** *(accortezza)* cleverness; *(astuzia)* shrewdness.

abilitante [abili'tante] *ag* qualifying; **corsi ~i** *(Scol)* ≈ teacher training.

abilitare [abili'tare] *vt:* ~ **qn a qc/a fare qc** to qualify sb for sth/to do sth; **è stato abilitato all'insegnamento** he has qualified as a teacher.

abilitato, a [abili'tato] **1** *ag* qualified. **2** *sm/f* qualified person; **solo gli ~i possono partecipare** only those with the required qualifications may take part.

abilitazione [abilitat'tsjone] *sf* qualification; **esame di** ~ qualifying exam; **conseguire l'**~ to qualify.

abissale [abis'sale] *ag* abysmal; *(fig: senza limiti)* profound.

abissino, a [abis'sino] *ag, sm/f* Abyssinian.

abisso [a'bisso] *sm (anche fig)* abyss, gulf; **c'è un** ~ **tra noi** we are poles apart; **essere sull'orlo dell'**~ to be on the brink of ruin; **è un** ~ **di ignoranza** he is utterly ignorant.

abitacolo [abi'takolo] *sm (Aer: cabina di guida)* cockpit; *(di macchina)* inside; *(di camion)* driver's cabin.

abitante [abi'tante] *sm/f (di città, paese)* inhabitant; *(di casa)* occupant.

abitare [abi'tare] **1** *vi:* ~ **(in, a)** to live (in). **2** *vt (casa)* to live in; *(luogo)* to inhabit.

abitato, a [abi'tato] **1** *ag (casa, appartamento)* occupied. **2** *sm (anche:* **centro** ~*)* built-up area.

abitazione [abitat'tsjone] *sf (casa)* house; **sai dov'è la sua** ~? do you know where he lives?

abito ['abito] *sm* **(a)** *(da donna)* dress; *(da uomo)* suit; ~**i** clothes; ~ **civile** civilian clothes *pl*, civvies *pl (fam)*; **in** ~ **da cerimonia** in formal dress; **'è gradito l'**~ **scuro'** 'dress formal'; ~ **da sera** *(da donna)* evening dress; **in** ~ **da sera** in evening dress; ~ **militare** military attire. **(b)** *(sistema di valori):* ~ **mentale** way of thinking. **(c)** *(Rel)* habit; **l'**~ **non fa il monaco** *(Proverbio)* you can't judge by appearances.

abituale [abitu'ale] *ag* usual; *(cliente, frequentatore)* regular.

abitualmente [abitual'mente] *av* usually, normally.

abituare [abitu'are] **1** *vt:* ~ **qn a qc/a fare qc** to accustom sb to sth/to doing sth, get sb used to sth/to doing sth. **2:** ~**rsi** *vr:* ~**rsi a qc/a fare qc** to get used to o accustomed to sth/to doing sth; **adesso mi sono abituato** I've become used to it now.

abitudinario, a [abitudi'narjo] **1** *ag* of fixed habits. **2** *sm/f* creature of habit.

abitudine [abi'tudine] *sf* habit; **aver l'**~ **di fare qc** to be in the habit of doing sth, to be used to doing sth; **per** ~ out of habit; **come d'**~ as usual; **d'**~ usually; **buona** o **bella/cattiva** o **brutta** ~ good/bad habit; **ci ho fatto l'**~ I've got used to it.

abiurare [abju'rare] *vt (Rel)* to abjure; *(principi)* to renounce.

ablativo [abla'tivo] *sm* ablative.

abnegazione [abnegat'tsjone] *sf* (self-)abnegation, self-denial; **con** ~ selflessly.

abnorme [ab'nɔrme] *ag (enorme)* extraordinary; *(anormale)* abnormal.

abolire [abo'lire] *vt* to abolish; **abbiamo abolito lo zucchero dalla nostra dieta** we have eliminated sugar from our diet.

abolizione [abolit'tsjone] *sf* abolition.

abominevole [abomi'nevole] *ag* abominable.

aborigeno, a [abo'ridʒeno] **1** *ag* aboriginal. **2** *sm* aboriginal, aborigine; ~ **australiano** Aborigine.

aborrire [abor'rire] *vt* to abhor, loathe.

abortire [abor'tire] *vi* **(a)** *(Med)* to abort; *(: spontaneamente)* to have a miscarriage; *(: artificialmente)* to have an abortion. **(b)** *(aus essere)* *(fig: progetto etc)* to fail, come to nothing.

aborto [a'bɔrto] *sm* **(a)** *(provocato)* abortion; *(spontaneo)* miscarriage; ~ **clandestino** backstreet abortion. **(b)** *(feto)* aborted foetus; **è un** ~ **di quadro** *(fig)* it's a terrible painting.

abrasione [abra'zjone] *sf* abrasion.

abrasivo, a [abra'zivo] *ag, sm* abrasive.

abrogare [abro'gare] *vt* to abrogate.

abrogazione [abrogat'tsjone] *sf* abrogation.

abruzzese [abrut'tsese] *ag* of (o from) the Abruzzi.

abside ['abside] *sf* apse.

abusare [abu'zare] *vi:* ~ **di** *(gen)* to abuse; *(persona)* to take advantage of; ~ **dell'altrui cortesia** to impose on sb's kindness; ~ **dell'alcool/dei cibi** to drink/eat to excess; ~ **di una donna** *(violentarla)* to rape a woman.

abusivo, a [abu'zivo] *ag* unauthorized, unlawful; *(occupante)* ~ *(di una casa)* squatter.

abuso [a'buzo] *sm (uso eccessivo)* excessive use; *(uso improprio)* abuse, misuse; ~ **di potere** abuse of power; ~ **di medicinali** drug abuse; **fare** ~ **di** *(stupefacenti, medicine)* to abuse.

a. C. *(abbr di avanti Cristo)* B.C.

acacia, cie [a'katʃa] *sf* acacia.

acaro ['akaro] *sm (Zool)* mite, tick.

acca ['akka] *sf* letter H; **non capire un'**~ not to understand a thing; **non sai un'**~ **di latino** you don't know a thing about Latin; **non m'importa un'**~ I couldn't care less.

accademia [akka'dɛmja] *sf* academy; ~ **di Belle Arti** art school.

accademico, a, ci, che [akka'dɛmiko] **1** *ag* academic; *(fig: pedante)* pedantic; **anno** ~ academic year. **2** *sm* academician.

accadere [akka'dere] *(aus essere)* **1** *vb impers* to happen; **mi è accaduto di incontrarlo** I happened to meet him. **2** *vi* to happen.

accaduto [akka'duto] *sm* event; **in seguito all'**~

following what happened.

accalappiacani [akkalappja'kani] *sm inv* dog-catcher.

accalappiare [akkalap'pjare] *vt (animali, fig: persona)* to catch.

accalcare [akkal'kare] *vt*, ~**rsi** *vr* to crowd, throng; **i tifosi accalcavano lo stadio, i tifosi si accalcavano nello stadio** the fans crowded *o* thronged the stadium.

accaldarsi [akkal'darsi] *vr* to get hot; **era tutto accaldato dopo la corsa** he was very hot after the race.

accalorarsi [akkalo'rarsi] *vr (infervorarsi)* to become worked up.

accampamento [akkampa'mento] *sm* **(a)** *(Mil, di zingari etc)* camp, encampment; **togliere/porre l'**~ to strike/pitch camp. **(b)** *(campeggio)* camp site.

accampare [akkam'pare] **1** *vt* **(a)** *(Mil)* to encamp. **(b)** *(fig: diritti)* to assert; *(: pretese)* to advance; ~ **scuse** to make excuses. **2**: ~**rsi** *vr (Mil)* to pitch camp; *(fare campeggio)* to camp; *(sistemarsi alla meglio)* to bed down.

accanimento [akkani'mento] *sm (odio, furia)* fury; *(tenacia)* tenacity, perseverance; **con** ~ *(furiosamente)* furiously; *(tenacemente)* assiduously, very hard.

accanirsi [akka'nirsi] *vr* **(a)** *(infierire)*: ~ **(contro)** to rage (against). **(b)** *(persistere)*: ~ **(a** *o* **nel fare qc)** to persist (in doing sth).

accanitamente [akkanita'mente] *av (vedi ag)* fiercely; assiduously, doggedly.

accanito, a [akka'nito] *ag (odio, gelosia)* fierce; *(lavoratore)* assiduous, dogged; *(giocatore)* inveterate; *(tifoso, sostenitore)* keen; **fumatore** ~ chain smoker.

accanto [ak'kanto] **1** *av* nearby; **la casa** ~ the house next door; **abito qui** ~ *(di fianco)* I live next door; *(vicino)* I live near here. **2**: ~ **a** *prep* next to, beside; ~ **ai suoi meriti non vanno dimenticate le sue colpe** her bad points must be remembered along with her good points.

accantonare [akkanto'nare] *vt (denaro, viveri)* to put aside; *(progetto, idea)* to shelve; *(argomento)* to leave aside.

accaparrare [akkapar'rare] *vt* **(a)** *(assicurare con caparra)* to secure (by deposit). **(b)** *(fare incetta di beni)* to buy up. **(c)**: ~**rsi qc** to secure sth (for o.s.); ~**rsi il mercato** to corner the market; ~**rsi il posto migliore** to grab the best seat.

accapigliarsi [akkapiʎ'ʎarsi] *vr* to come to blows; *(fig)* to squabble.

accappatoio [akkappa'tojo] *sm (da bagno)* bathrobe; *(da spiaggia)* beach robe.

accapponare [akkappo'nare] *vt*: **fare** ~ **la pelle a qn** to give sb goosepimples *o* gooseflesh; **mi si è accapponata la pelle** I came out in goosepimples *o* gooseflesh.

accarezzare [akkaret'tsare] *vt* **(a)** to caress *(animali, capelli)* to stroke; ~**rsi il mento** to stroke one's chin. **(b)** *(fig: progetto, idea)* to toy with.

accartocciare [akkartot'tʃare] **1** *vt (carta)* to roll up, screw up. **2**: ~**rsi** *vr (foglie)* to curl up.

accasarsi [akka'sarsi] *vr (sposarsi)* to get married.

accasciarsi [akkaʃ'ʃarsi] *vr* to collapse; *(fig: deprimersi)* to lose heart; ~**rsi su una sedia** to collapse into a chair.

accatastare [akkatas'tare] *vt* to stack, pile.

accattonaggio [akkatto'naddʒo] *sm* begging.

accattone, a [akkat'tone] *sm/f* beggar.

accavallare [akkaval'lare] **1** *vt (gambe)* to cross. **2**: ~**rsi** *vr (sovrapporsi: muscolo, nervo)* to come out of place; *(fig: avvenimenti)* to overlap.

accecare [attʃe'kare] **1** *vt* to blind; *(abbagliare)* to dazzle. **2**: ~**rsi** *vr* to become blind.

accedere [at'tʃedere] *vi*: ~ **a (a)** *(aus essere)* *(luogo)* to enter; *(scuola: essere ammesso)* to enter, be admitted to. **(b)** *(aus essere)* *(poter raggiungere: notizia, fonte)* to gain access to. **(c)** *(acconsentire: richiesta)* to accede to.

accelerare [attʃele'rare] **1** *vt* to speed up; ~ **il passo** to quicken one's pace. **2** *vi* to accelerate, speed up.

accelerato, a [attʃele'rato] **1** *ag (rapido)* quick, rapid; **tempo/ritmo** ~ fast tempo/rhythm. **2** *sm (treno)* local train, stopping train.

acceleratore [attʃelera'tore] *sm* accelerator.

accelerazione [attʃelerat'tsjone] *sf* acceleration.

accendere [at'tʃendere] **1** *vt* **(a)** *(fiammifero, candela, sigaretta)* to light; ~ **il camino** to light the fire; **mi fa** ~? do you have a light? **(b)** *(radio, luce, lampada)* to turn on, switch on; *(gas)* to light; *(motore)* to switch on. **(c)** *(fig: speranza, desiderio)* to arouse. **(d)** *(Fin)*: ~ **un debito** to contract a loan; ~ **un'ipoteca** to raise a mortgage; ~ **un conto** to open an account. **2**: ~**rsi** *vr* **(a)** *(fuoco)* to start; *(riscaldamento)* to come on. **(b)** *(fig: di sentimenti)*: ~**rsi di gioia** *(occhi, volto)* to light up with joy; **l'entusiasmo si accese in lei** she was fired with enthusiasm. **(c)** *(fig: lotta, conflitto)* to break out.

accendino [attʃen'dino] *sm* lighter; ~ **a gas/elettronico** gas/electronic lighter.

accendisigaro [attʃendi'sigaro] *sm* lighter.

accennare [attʃen'nare] **1** *vt* **(a)** *(indicare)* to indicate, point out; **le accennai la porta** I showed her the door. **(b)** *(abbozzare)*: ~ **un saluto** *(con la mano)* to make as if to wave; *(col capo)* to half nod; ~ **un sorriso** to half smile. **(c)** *(citare)* to mention; **mi ha accennato qualcosa a proposito del suo progetto** he mentioned something to me about his project. **(d)** *(Mus)* to pick out the notes of. **2** *vi* **(a)** *(far cenno)*: **mi accennò di star zitto** he signalled to me to keep quiet. **(b)** *(dare segno di)*: ~ **a fare qc** to show signs of doing sth; **accenna a piovere** it looks as if it's going to rain. **(c)**: ~ **a** *(menzionare)* to mention; *(alludere a)* to hint at; **ha accennato al fatto che vuole partire** he mentioned that he wants to leave.

accenno [at'tʃenno] *sm (fig)* hint; **con un** ~ **di sorriso** with a hint of a smile; **non ha fatto** ~ **all'accaduto** he made no mention of what had happened.

accensione [attʃen'sjone] *sf* **(a)** *(vedi* **accendere***)* lighting; switching on; *(Fin)* contracting; raising; opening. **(b)** *(Aut)* ignition.

accentare [attʃen'tare] *vt (scrivendo)* to accent; *(parlando)* to stress.

accentazione [attʃentat'tsjone] *sf (vedi vb)* accentuation; stressing.

accento [at'tʃento] *sm* **(a)** *(pronuncia)* accent; **parla con un** ~ **straniero** he speaks with a foreign accent. **(b)** *(Fonetica)* accent, stress; *(fig)* stress, emphasis; **mettere l'**~ **su qc** to stress sth. **(c)** *(segno grafico)* accent; ~ **grave/acuto/circonflesso** grave/acute/circumflex accent. **(d)** *(inflessione)* tone (of voice); **un breve** ~ **di tristezza** a slight note of sadness.

accentramento [attʃentra'mento] *sm (Amm)* centralization.

accentrare [attʃen'trare] *vt (potere etc)* to centralize; *(fig: interesse, sguardi)* to attract, draw.

accentratore, trice [attʃentra'tore] *ag (persona)* unwilling to delegate; **politica** ~**trice** policy of centralization.

accentuare [attʃentu'are] **1** *vt* **(a)** *(sillaba, parola)* to stress. **(b)** *(mettere in rilievo)* to emphasize, accentuate. **2:** ~**rsi** *vr (tendenza)* to become more marked *o* pronounced; *(crisi)* to become worse.

accerchiare [attʃer'kjare] *vt* to encircle, surround.

accertamento [attʃerta'mento] *sm (verifica)* check; *(: Fisco)* assessment; *(Dir)* investigation; **essere in corso di** ~ to be under investigation.

accertare [attʃer'tare] **1** *vt* **(a)** *(verificare)* to verify, check. **(b)** *(Fisco)* to assess. **2:** ~**rsi** *vr:* ~**rsi di qc/che** to make sure of sth/that, ascertain sth/that.

acceso, a [at'tʃeso] **1** *pp di* **accendere**. **2** *ag* **(a)** *(fuoco, lampada)* lit; *(luce elettrica, televisore, gas)* on. **(b)** *(intenso: colore)* bright, vivid; *(: infervorato: discussione, parole)* heated; ~ **di** *(ira, entusiasmo etc)* burning with.

accessibile [attʃes'sibile] *ag (luogo):* ~ **(a)** accessible (to); *(persona)* approachable; ~ **a tutti** *(prezzo, articolo)* within everyone's means; *(concetto, materia)* within the reach of everyone.

accesso [at'tʃɛsso] *sm* **(a)** access; **vietato l'**~ no entry, no admittance; **di facile** ~ *(luogo)* (easily) accessible; **avere** ~ **a** to have access to; ~ **casuale** *(Inform)* random access. **(b)** *(di stizza, gelosia, tosse)* fit; *(di febbre)* attack, bout. **(c)** *(TV):* **programmi dell'**~ educational programmes.

accessorio, a [attʃes'sɔrjo] **1** *ag* secondary; **parti** ~**e** *(Aut etc)* accessories. **2** *sm (Aut, Moda etc)* accessory.

accetta [at'tʃetta] *sf* hatchet; **fatto con l'**~ *(fig: lavoro etc)* clumsily done.

accettabile [attʃet'tabile] *ag* acceptable.

accettare [attʃet'tare] *vt (gen, Comm)* to accept; *(proposta)* to agree to, accept; ~ **di fare qc** to agree to do sth; ~ **qn per** *o* **come amico** to accept sb as a friend.

accettazione [attʃettat'tsjone] *sf* **(a)** *(gen)* acceptance. **(b)** *(di albergo, ospedale etc)* reception; ~ **bagagli** *(Aer)* check-in.

accetto, a [at'tʃetto] *ag* welcome; **(ben)** ~ **a tutti** *(persona)* well-liked by everybody.

accezione [attʃet'tsjone] *sf* meaning, sense.

acchiappare [akkjap'pare] *vt (prendere, catturare)* to catch; *(afferrare)* to seize.

acciaccato, a [attʃak'kato] *ag* **(a)** *(persona)* full of aches and pains. **(b)** *(abito)* crushed.

acciacco, chi [at'tʃakko] *sm* ailment; ~**chi** aches and pains.

acciaieria [attʃaje'ria] *sf* steelworks *sg*.

acciaio [at'tʃajo] *sm* steel; **d'**~ *(trave)* steel *attr*, of steel; *(fig: uomo, nervi)* of steel; ~ **inossidabile** stainless steel.

accidentale [attʃiden'tale] *ag* accidental; **in circostanze** ~**i** accidentally.

accidentalmente [attʃidental'mente] *av (per caso)* by chance; *(non deliberatamente)* accidentally, by accident.

accidentato, a [attʃiden'tato] *ag (terreno)* uneven, rough; *(strada)* bumpy, uneven.

accidente [attʃi'dɛnte] *sm* **(a)** *(gen, Filosofia)* accident; *(disgrazia)* mishap; **quando ho visto il conto mi è venuto un** ~! I had a fit when I saw the bill! **(b)** *(fig: niente):* **non vale un** ~ it's not worth a damn; **non capisco un** ~ it's as clear as mud to me. **(c):** ~**i!** *(fam: per rabbia)* damn (it)!; *(: per meraviglia)* good heavens!; ~**i a lui!** damn him!; **mandare un** ~ **a qn** to curse sb; **ma che** ~**i vuole?** what on earth does he want?

accidia [at'tʃidja] *sf* sloth.

accigliato, a [attʃiʎ'ʎato] *ag* frowning.

acciottolato [attʃotto'lato] *sm* cobbles *pl*.

acciuffare [attʃuf'fare] *vt* to seize, catch.

acciuga, ghe [at'tʃuga] *sf* anchovy; **magro come un'**~ as thin as a rake; **stretti come** ~**ghe** packed like sardines.

acclamare [akkla'mare] **1** *vt* **(a)** *(salutare)* to cheer, applaud. **(b)** *(eleggere)* to acclaim. **2** *vi:* ~ **a** to cheer, applaud.

acclamazione [akklamat'tsjone] *sf (vedi vb)* applause; acclamation.

acclimatare [akklima'tare] **1** *vt* to acclimatize. **2:** ~**rsi** *vr* to become acclimatized.

acclimatazione [akklimat'tsjone] *sf* acclimatization.

accludere [ak'kludere] *vt:* ~ **(a)** to enclose (with).

accluso, a [ak'kluzo] **1** *pp di* **accludere**. **2** *ag* enclosed; **qui** ~ **è...** please find enclosed....

accoccolarsi [akkokko'larsi] *vr* to crouch (down).

accodarsi [akko'darsi] *vr* to follow, tag on (behind).

accogliente [akkoʎ'ʎɛnte] *ag (atmosfera)* welcoming, friendly; *(stanza)* pleasant, cosy.

accoglienza [akkoʎ'ʎɛntsa] *sf* welcome, reception; **fare una buona** ~ **a qn** to welcome sb; **fare una cattiva** ~ **a qn** to give sb a cool reception.

accogliere [ak'kɔʎʎere] *vt* **(a)** *(persona: ricevere)* to receive; *(: calorosamente)* to welcome; *(: ospitare)* to accommodate; **questa sala può** ~ **600 persone** this hall can hold *o* accommodate 600 people. **(b)** *(notizia)* to receive. **(c)** *(richieste)* to agree to, accept.

accollare [akkol'lare] **1** *vt (fig):* ~ **qc a qn** to force sth on sb. **2:** ~**rsi** *vr:* ~**rsi qc** to take sth upon o.s., shoulder sth.

accollato, a [akkol'lato] *ag (vestito)* high-necked.

accoltellare [akkoltel'lare] *vt* to knife, stab.

accolto, a [ak'kolto] *pp di* **accogliere**.

accomandita [akko'mandita] *sf (Comm):* **(società in)** ~ limited partnership.

accomiatare [akkomja'tare] **1** *vt* to dismiss. **2:** ~**rsi** *vr:* ~**rsi (da)** to take one's leave (of), say goodbye (to).

accomodamento [akkomoda'mento] *sm (accordo)* arrangement, agreement; *(Dir)* settlement out of court.

accomodante [akkomo'dante] *ag* accommodating.

accomodare [akkomo'dare] **1** *vt* **(a)** *(riparare)* to fix, repair. **(b)** *(sistemare)* to arrange; *(: fig: questione, lite)* to settle; ~**rsi i capelli** *(: fig)* to tidy one's hair. **2:** ~**rsi** *vr* **(a)** *(sedersi)* to sit down; **si accomodi!** *(venga avanti)* come in!; *(mi segua)* this way please!; *(si sieda)* take a seat! **(b)** *(accordarsi):* ~**rsi (con qn su qc)** to come to an agreement (with sb on sth). **(c)** *(fig: risolversi: situazione)* to work out.

accompagnamento [akkompaɲɲa'mento] *sm* **(a)** *(Mus)* accompaniment; **senza** ~ unaccompanied. **(b)** *(Comm):* **lettera di** ~ accompanying letter. **(c)** *(Mil)* supporting fire.

accompagnare [akkompaɲ'ɲare] **1** *vt* **(a)** *(gen, Mus)* to accompany; ~ **qn a casa** to see sb home; **ti accompagno** I'll come with you; ~ **qn alla porta** to show sb out; ~ **qn al piano** to accompany sb on the piano; ~ **un regalo con un biglietto** to put in *o* send a card with a present. **(b)** *(fig: seguire)* to follow; ~ **qn con lo sguardo** to follow sb with one's eyes; ~ **la porta** to close the door gently. **2:** ~**rsi** *vr* **(a)** *(armonizzarsi)* to go well together; ~**rsi a** *(colori)* to go with, match; *(cibi)* to go with. **(b)** *(frequentare):* ~**rsi a** to frequent.

accompagnatore, trice [akkompaɲɲa'tore] *sm/f* **(a)** companion, escort; *(guida turistica)* courier.

(b) *(Mus)* accompanist. **(c)** *(Sport)* team manager.

accomunare [akkomu'nare] *vt* **(a)** *(ricchezze etc)* to pool, share. **(b)** *(persone)* to unite, join; **molti interessi ci accomunano** we have many interests in common; **non voglio che mi si accomuni a lui** I don't want to be associated with him.

acconciatura [akkontʃa'tura] *sf (pettinatura)* hairstyle; *(ornamento)* headdress.

accondiscendente [akkondiʃʃen'dɛnte] *ag* affable.

accondiscendere [akkondiʃ'ʃendere] *vi:* ~ **a** to agree to, consent to.

accondisceso, a [akkondiʃ'ʃeso] *pp di* **accondiscendere**.

acconsentire [akkonsen'tire] *vi:* ~ **(a)** to agree (to), consent (to); **chi tace acconsente** silence means consent.

accontentare [akkonten'tare] **1** *vt* to satisfy. **2:** ~**rsi** *vr:* ~**rsi (di)** to be content (with), be satisfied (with); **chi si accontenta gode** there's no point in complaining.

acconto [ak'konto] *sm (sullo stipendio)* advance; *(caparra)* deposit.

accoppiamento [akkoppja'mento] *sm (vedi vb)* mating; coupling, connecting (up).

accoppiare [akkop'pjare] **1** *vt* **(a)** *(persone, cose):* **essere ben accoppiati** to be well matched, go well together. **(b)** *(animali)* to mate. **(c)** *(Tecn)* to couple, connect (up). **2:** ~**rsi** *vr (animali)* to mate.

accorato, a [akko'rato] *ag* heartfelt.

accorciare [akkor'tʃare] **1** *vt* to shorten. **2:** ~**rsi** *vr (giorni)* to grow shorter; *(vestiti: nel lavaggio)* to shrink.

accordare [akkor'dare] **1** *vt* **(a)** *(concedere):* ~ **qc a qn** to grant sb sth *o* sth to sb. **(b)** *(Mus)* to tune. **(c)** *(Gram):* ~ **un verbo/un aggettivo (con qc)** to make a verb/an adjective agree (with sth). **2:** ~**rsi** *vr (mettersi d'accordo):* ~**rsi (con qn su qc)** to come to an agreement (with sb on sth), agree (with sb on sth).

accordo [ak'kɔrdo] *sm* **(a)** *(gen, Gram)* agreement; *(armonia)* harmony; ~ **sulla parola** gentlemen's agreement; **decidere di buon** ~ **di fare qc** to be in complete agreement about doing sth; **andare d'**~ **(con qn)** to get on well (with sb); **essere d'**~ to agree, be in agreement; **mettersi d'**~ **(con qn)** to agree *o* come to an agreement with sb; **d'**~**!** agreed!, all right!, O.K.! *(fam)*; **sono d'accordissimo** I quite agree. **(b)** *(Mus)* chord; **conosci gli** ~**i di quella canzone?** can you play that song?

accorgersi [ak'kɔrdʒersi] *vr:* ~**rsi di** *(notare)* to notice; *(capire)* to realize; ~**rsi che** to notice *(o* realize*)* that.

accorgimento [akkordʒi'mento] *sm* **(a)** *(espediente)* trick, device. **(b)** *(astuzia)* shrewdness.

accorrere [ak'korrere] *vi (aus essere):* ~ **(a)** to rush up (to), hurry (to); **gente accorreva da tutte le parti** people rushed up from all directions; ~ **in aiuto di qn** to rush to sb's aid.

accorso, a [ak'korso] *pp di* **accorrere**.

accortezza [akkor'tettsa] *sf (avvedutezza)* good sense; *(astuzia)* shrewdness.

accorto, a [ak'kɔrto] **1** *pp di* **accorgersi**. **2** *ag* shrewd, alert; **stare** ~ to be on one's guard.

accostare [akkos'tare] **1** *vt* **(a):** ~ **qc a qc** *(mettere vicino: oggetto)* to move sth near sth; *(: colori, stili)* to match sth with sth; *(appoggiare: scala etc)* to lean sth against sth; **accosta la sedia al tavolo** move your chair near the table; **ha accostato la tazza alle labbra** he put the cup to his lips. **(b)** *(avvicinare: persona)* to approach, come up to. **(c)** *(socchiudere: persiane)* to half-close; *(: porta)* to

push *(o* pull*)* to; **lasciare la porta accostata** to leave the door ajar.

2 *vi* **(a):** ~ **(a)** *(Aut)* to draw up (at); *(Naut)* to come alongside. **(b)** *(Naut: modificare la rotta)* to alter course.

3: ~**rsi** *vr* **(a)** *(andare o venire vicino):* ~**rsi (a)** to approach, go *(o* come*)* nearer; *(Aut):* ~**rsi a qc/qn** to draw up at sth/next to sb; *(Naut)* to come alongside; **questi colori si accostano male** these colours don't go well together. **(b)** *(fig: abbracciare):* ~**rsi a** *(fede, religione)* to turn to; *(idee politiche)* to come to agree with. **(c)** *(somigliare):* ~**rsi a** to be like, resemble.

accovacciarsi [akkovat'tʃarsi] *vr* to crouch down.

accozzaglia [akkot'tsaʎʎa] *sf (peg: di persone)* odd assortment; *(: di cose, idee)* jumble, hotchpotch.

accreditare [akkredi'tare] **1** *vt* **(a)** *(convalidare)* to confirm; *(: voce)* to substantiate. **(b)** *(Comm, Fin):* ~ **qc a** *o* **a favore di qn** to credit sb with sth; ~ **su un conto** to credit to an account; **si sono accreditati il merito della scoperta** they took all the credit for the discovery. **(c)** *(diplomatico)* to accredit. **2:** ~**rsi** *vr (teoria etc)* to gain ground.

accredito [ak'kredito] *sm (Comm, Fin: atto)* crediting; *(: effetto)* credit.

accrescere [ak'kreʃʃere] **1** *vt* to increase. **2:** ~**rsi** *vr* to grow, increase.

accrescimento [akkreʃʃi'mento] *sm* increase, growth.

accrescitivo, a [akkreʃʃi'tivo] *ag, sm (Gram)* augmentative.

accucciarsi [akkut'tʃarsi] *vr (cane)* to lie down; *(persona)* to crouch down.

accudire [akku'dire] **1** *vi:* ~ **a** to attend to. **2** *vt* to look after.

acculturazione [akkulturat'tsjone] *sf (Sociol)* integration.

accumulare [akkumu'lare] **1** *vt (gen)* to accumulate; *(energia)* to store; **il treno ha accumulato un ritardo di 3 ore** the train is running 3 hours late. **2:** ~**rsi** *vr* to accumulate; *(Fin)* to accrue.

accumulatore [akkumula'tore] *sm* accumulator, *(storage)* battery.

accumulazione [akkumulat'tsjone] *sf (vedi vb)* accumulation; storage.

accumulo [ak'kumulo] *sm* accumulation.

accuratezza [akkura'tettsa] *sf* care, thoroughness.

accurato, a [akku'rato] *ag* careful, thorough.

accusa [ak'kuza] *sf (gen)* accusation; *(Dir)* charge; **l'**~ *(Dir)* the prosecution; **fare** *o* **muovere un'**~ **a qn** to make an accusation against sb; **mettere qn sotto** ~ *(Dir)* to indict sb; **in stato di** ~ *(Dir)* committed for trial.

accusabile [akku'zabile] *ag (Dir)* chargeable.

accusare [akku'zare] *vt* **(a)** *(incolpare):* ~ **qn di (fare) qc** to accuse sb of (doing) sth; *(biasimare):* ~ **qn/qc di qc** to blame sb/sth for sth; *(Dir):* ~ **qn di qc** to charge sb with sth. **(b)** *(sentire: dolore)* to feel; *(mostrare):* ~ **la fatica** to show signs of exhaustion; **ha accusato il colpo** *(anche fig)* you could see that he had felt the blow. **(c)** *(Comm):* ~ **ricevuta (di)** to acknowledge receipt (of).

accusativo, a [akkuza'tivo] *ag (Gram)* accusative.

accusato, a [akku'zato] *sm/f* accused.

accusatore, trice [akkuza'tore] **1** *ag* accusing. **2** *sm/f* accuser; *(Dir)* prosecutor.

acerbo, a [a'tʃerbo] *ag* **(a)** *(aspro)* sour. **(b)** *(non maturo: frutto)* unripe; *(: persona)* immature; **è una ragazza** ~**a** she's very young. **(c)** *(destino, rimprovero)* bitter, harsh.

acero [ˈatʃero] *sm* maple.

acerrimo, a [a'tʃerrimo] *ag* very fierce.

acetato [atʃe'tato] *sm* acetate.

acetilene [atʃeti'lɛne] *sm* acetylene.
aceto [a'tʃeto] *sm* vinegar; **sotto ~** pickled; **mettere sotto ~** to pickle.
acetone [atʃe'tone] *sm* acetone.
A.C.I. ['atʃi] *abbr m* (= *Automobile Club d'Italia*) ≃ A.A.
acidità [atʃidi'ta] *sf* (*vedi ag*) acidity; sourness, tartness; **~ (di stomaco)** heartburn.
acido, a ['atʃido] **1** *ag* (*anche fig*) acid, sour, tart; (*Chim*) acid. **2** *sm* acid; **sapere di ~** to taste sour.
acidulo, a [a'tʃidulo] *ag* slightly sour, slightly acid.
acino ['atʃino] *sm*: **~ (d'uva)** grape.
acme ['akme] *sf* **(a)** (*fig*) acme, peak. **(b)** (*Med*) crisis.
acne ['akne] *sf* (*anche*: **~ giovanile**) acne.
acqua ['akkwa] *sf* **1 (a)** (*gen*) water; (*pioggia*) rain; **~e** *sfpl* (*Med, di fiume, lago, mare*) waters; **prendere l'~** to get caught in the rain, get wet; **far la cura delle ~e** to take the waters.
   (b) (*fraseologia*): **~, ~!** (*in giochi*) you're cold!; **~ in bocca!** mum's the word!; **buttare ~ sul fuoco** (*fig*) to pour oil on troubled waters; **è sempre stata un'~ cheta** she has always seemed a quiet one; **fare ~ (da tutte le parti)** (*barca*) to leak, let in water; (*fig: situazione, posizione*) to be shaky; **la sua versione dei fatti fa ~ da tutte le parti** his version of what happened won't hold water; **essere con** *o* **avere l'~ alla gola** to be in great difficulty; **tirare ~ al proprio mulino** to feather one's own nest; **è passata molta ~ sotto i ponti** (*fig*) a lot of water has flowed under the bridge; **è stata una faccenda all'~ di rose** it was all plain sailing; **trovarsi** *o* **navigare in cattive ~e** (*fig*) to be in deep water.
   2: ~ di colonia eau de Cologne, cologne; **~ corrente** running water; **~ dolce** fresh water; **~ di mare** sea water; **~ minerale** mineral water; **~ ossigenata** hydrogen peroxide; **~ piovana** rain water; **~ potabile** drinking water; **~ ragia** = **acquaragia; ~ salata** *o* **salmastra** salt water; **~ santa** = **acquasanta; ~ sorgiva** *o* **di sorgente** spring water.
acquaforte [akkwa'fɔrte] *sf, pl* **acqueforti** etching.
acquaio [ak'kwajo] *sm* (kitchen) sink.
acquamarina [akkwama'rina] *sf* (*pietra, colore*) aquamarine.
acquaragia [akkwa'radʒa] *sf* turpentine.
acquarello [akkwa'rello] *sm* = **acquerello.**
acquario [ak'kwarjo] *sm* **(a)** (*vasca per pesci, edificio*) aquarium. **(b)** (*Astrologia*): **A~** Aquarius; **essere dell'A~** to be Aquarius.
acquartierare [akkwartje'rare] *vt* (*Mil*) to quarter.
acquasanta [akkwa'santa] *sf* holy water.
acquasantiera [akkwasan'tjera] *sf* holy water font.
acquatico, a, ci, che [ak'kwatiko] *ag* aquatic.
acquattarsi [akkwat'tarsi] *vr* to crouch (down).
acquavite [akkwa'vite] *sf, pl* **~i** *o* **acqueviti** brandy.
acquazzone [akkwat'tsone] *sm* heavy shower, downpour.
acquedotto [akkwe'dotto] *sm* (*conduttura*) aqueduct; (*intero sistema*) water system.
acqueo, a [ak'kweo] *ag*: **vapore ~** water vapour; **umore ~** aqueous humour.
acquerello [akkwe'rɛllo] *sm* (*tecnica*) watercolours; (*opera*) watercolour.
acquerugiola [akkwe'rudʒola] *sf* drizzle.
acquiescente [akkwjeʃ'ʃɛnte] *ag* acquiescent.
acquiescenza [akkwjeʃ'ʃɛntsa] *sf* acquiescence.
acquietare [akkwje'tare] **1** *vt* (*dolore*) to ease; (*desiderio, fame*) to appease. **2: ~rsi** *vr* to calm down.

acquirente [akkwi'rɛnte] *sm/f* buyer, purchaser.
acquisire [akkwi'zire] *vt* (*diritto, proprietà*) to acquire; (*qualità, cognizione*) to acquire, gain.
acquisizione [akkwizit'tsjone] *sf* acquisition.
acquistare [akkwis'tare] **1** *vt* **(a)** (*casa, mobili*) to buy, purchase; (*beni, diritti*) to acquire; **~ a rate** to buy on hire purchase; **~ in contanti** to buy for cash. **(b)** (*fig: esperienza, pratica etc*) to gain; **~ terreno** to gain ground. **2** *vi* to improve; **~ in bellezza** to become more beautiful; **ha acquistato in salute** his health has improved.
acquisto [ak'kwisto] *sm* purchase; **andare a fare ~i** to go shopping; **fare molti ~i** to buy a lot of things; **fare un buon/cattivo ~** to get a good/bad buy; **ecco il nostro ultimo ~** (*persona*) here is the latest addition to the staff.
acquitrino [akkwi'trino] *sm* bog, marsh.
acquitrinoso, a [akkwitri'noso] *ag* boggy, marshy.
acquolina [akkwo'lina] *sf*: **far venire l'~ in bocca a qn** to make sb's mouth water; **ho l'~ in bocca, mi viene l'~ in bocca** my mouth is watering.
acquoso, a [ak'kwoso] *ag* watery.
acre ['akre] *ag* (*sapore, odore*) acrid; (*fig: polemica, critica*) bitter.
acredine [a'krɛdine] *sf* (*fig*) bitterness.
acrilico, a, ci, che [a'kriliko] *ag* acrylic.
acrimonia [akri'mɔnja] *sf* acrimony.
acrobata, i, e [a'krɔbata] *sm/f* acrobat.
acrobatico, a, ci, che [akro'batiko] *ag* (*ginnastica*) acrobatic; (*Aer*) aerobatic.
acrobazia [akrobat'tsia] *sf* **(a)** (*ginnica: movimento*) acrobatic feat; **fare ~e** (*anche fig*) to perform acrobatics. **(b)** (*aerea: esercizio*) aerobatic feat; **~e aeree** aerobatics.
acropoli [a'krɔpoli] *sf inv* acropolis.
acuire [aku'ire] **1** *vt* to sharpen; (*appetito*) to whet. **2: ~rsi** *vr* (*gen*) to increase; (: *crisi*) to worsen.
aculeo [a'kuleo] *sm* (*di riccio, istrice, pianta*) prickle; (*di vespa, ape*) sting.
acume [a'kume] *sm* acumen, perspicacity.
acuminato, a [akumi'nato] *ag* sharp.
acustica [a'kustika] *sf* (*scienza*) acoustics *sg*; (*di ambiente*) acoustics *pl*.
acustico, a, ci, che [a'kustiko] *ag* acoustic; **apparecchio ~** hearing aid; **cornetto ~** ear trumpet.
acutezza [aku'tettsa] *sf* (*vedi ag*) acuteness; keenness; intensity; sharpness; shrillness; (*Mus*) high pitch.
acutizzare [akutid'dzare] **1** *vt* (*fig*) to intensify. **2: ~rsi** *vr* (*fig: crisi, malattia*) to become worse, worsen.
acuto, a [a'kuto] *ag* **1 (a)** (*Mat, Med, Gram*) acute; (*vista, udito, senso dell'umorismo*) keen; (*desiderio, fastidio*) intense; (*mente, osservazione, dolore*) sharp, acute. **(b)** (*voce, suono*) shrill, high-pitched; (*Mus*) high. **2** *sm* (*Mus*) high note.
adagiare [ada'dʒare] **1** *vt* to lay down (carefully). **2: ~rsi** *vr* (*mettersi comodo*) to make o.s. comfortable; (*sdraiarsi*) to lie down; **si è adagiato nella situazione** (*fig*) he sat back.
adagio[1] [a'dadʒo] *av* (*lentamente*) slowly; (*con cura*) with care, gently; **vacci ~ con la birra!** go easy on the beer!; **~!** easy does it!; **~ ~** gradually.
adagio[2] [a'dadʒo] *sm* **(a)** (*Mus*) adagio. **(b)** (*proverbio*) adage, saying.
adamitico, a, ci, che [ada'mitiko] *ag*: **in costume ~** in one's birthday suit.
adattabile [adat'tabile] *ag* (*oggetto, persona*) adaptable; **questa poltrona è ~ a letto** this armchair can be converted into a bed.
adattabilità [adattabili'ta] *sf* adaptability.
adattamento [adatta'mento] *sm* (*Bio, Med, di romanzo*) adaptation; (*di stanza*) conversion;

avere spirito di ~ to be adaptable.

adattare [adat'tare] **1** vt (gen): ~ qc (a) to adapt sth (to); (camera) to convert sth (into); **mi sono fatta ~ il cappotto di mia madre** I've had my mother's coat altered to fit me. **2**: ~rsi vr (a) (all'ambiente, ai tempi): ~rsi (a) to adapt (to); **si adatta facilmente** she adapts easily, she's very adaptable. (b) (accontentarsi): ~rsi a qc/a fare qc to make the best of sth/of doing sth; **dobbiamo ~rci** we'll have to make the best of it.

adatto, a [a'datto] ag: ~ (a) (giusto) right (for); (appropriato) suitable (for); **è la persona più ~a a fare questo lavoro** he is the most suitable person for this job o to do this job.

addebitare [addebi'tare] vt (Comm): ~ qc (in conto) a qn to debit sb with sth, debit sb's account with sth.

addebito [ad'debito] sm (Comm) debit.

addendo [ad'dɛndo] sm (Mat) addend.

addensamento [addensa'mento] sm (vedi vb) thickening; gathering.

addensare [adden'sare] **1** vt to thicken. **2**: ~rsi vr (nebbia) to get thicker; (nuvole, folla) to gather.

addentare [adden'tare] vt (panino) to bite into.

addentrarsi [adden'trarsi] vr: ~ in (posto) to penetrate, go into; (fig: problema) to go (deeply) into.

addentro [ad'dentro] av (fig): **essere ~ a** o **in qc** to be well up on sth.

addestramento [addestra'mento] sm training.

addestrare [addes'trare] **1** vt: ~ qn/qc a o per qc to train sb/sth for sth; **quel cane è stato addestrato alla guardia** that dog has been trained as a watchdog. **2**: ~rsi vr: ~rsi (a o in qc) to train (in sth).

addetto, a [ad'detto] **1** pp di **addirsi**. **2** ag: ~ a (persona) assigned to; (oggetto) intended for. **3** sm (a): ~ **al telex** telex operator; ~i **alle pulizie** cleaning staff; '**vietato l'ingresso ai non ~i ai lavori**' 'authorized personnel only'; **gli ~i ai lavori** (fig) those in the know. (b) (Diplomazia) attaché; ~ **commerciale/stampa** commercial/press attaché.

addì [ad'di] av (Amm): ~ **28 aprile 1985** on the 28th of April 1985.

addiaccio [ad'djattʃo] sm (Mil) bivouac; **dormire all'**~ to sleep in the open.

addietro [ad'djɛtro] av (nel passato, prima) before, ago; **è venuto tempo** ~ he came some time ago.

addio [ad'dio] **1** escl goodbye, farewell (old); **se arrivano i bambini,** ~ **pace!** if the children turn up, it's goodbye to peace and quiet! **2** sm goodbye, farewell; **dire** ~ **a qn/qc** (anche fig) to say goodbye to sb/sth.

addirittura [addirit'tura] av (a) (perfino) even; ~! really!; **il suo comportamento è** ~ **ridicolo** his behaviour is downright ridiculous. (b) (direttamente) directly, right away.

addirsi [ad'dirsi] vr: ~ a to suit, be suitable for; **questo comportamento non si addice a un padre di famiglia** such behaviour ill befits a married man.

additare [addi'tare] vt to point out.

additivo, a [addi'tivo] ag, sm additive.

addizionale [addittsjo'nale] **1** ag additional. **2** sf (anche: **imposta** ~) surtax.

addizionare [addittsjo'nare] vt to add (up); ~ **qc a qc** to add sth to sth.

addizione [addit'tsjone] sf addition; **fare un'**~ to add (up).

addobbare [addob'bare] **1** vt (a) (edificio etc) to decorate; ~ **a festa** to deck out. (b) (fig: persona) to dress up. **2**: ~rsi vr to dress up.

addobbo [ad'dɔbbo] sm decoration; ~i **natalizi** Christmas decorations.

addolcire [addol'tʃire] **1** vt (a) (caffè etc) to sweeten; ~ **la pillola** (fig) to sugar the pill. (b) (fig: mitigare: brutta notizia, carattere) to soften; (: calmare) to soothe, calm. (c) (Tecn: acqua) to soften: (: acciaio) to temper. **2**: ~rsi vr (fig: carattere, persona) to mellow, soften.

addolorare [addolo'rare] **1** vt to grieve. **2**: ~rsi vr: ~rsi (per) to be distressed (by).

addolorato, a [addolo'rato] ag distressed, upset; **l'A~a** (Rel) Our Lady of Sorrows.

addome [ad'dɔme] sm abdomen.

addomesticabile [addomesti'kabile] ag which can be tamed; **poco** ~ difficult to tame.

addomesticare [addomesti'kare] vt (anche fig) to tame; **è riuscita ad** ~ **il marito** she's managed to domesticate her husband.

addomesticato, a [addomesti'kato] ag tame.

addominale [addomi'nale] ag abdominal; (**muscoli** mpl) ~i **stomach muscles**.

addormentare [addormen'tare] **1** vt (anche fig: persona): (**far**) ~ to send to sleep. **2**: ~rsi vr to go to sleep, fall asleep; **mi si è addormentato un piede** my foot has gone to sleep.

addormentato, a [addormen'tato] ag sleeping, asleep; (fig: tardo) stupid, dopey.

addossare [addos'sare] **1** vt (a) (appoggiare): ~ qc a qc to lean sth against sth. (b) (imputare): ~ **la colpa/la responsabilità di qc a qn** to lay the blame/the responsibility for sth on sb; **si addossò la colpa** he took the blame. **2**: ~rsi vr: ~rsi a (appoggiarsi) to stand against; **stava addossato al muro** he was standing with his back to the wall; **si sono addossati gli uni agli altri** they crowded together.

addosso [ad'dɔsso] **1** av (sulla persona) on; **mettersi** ~ **il cappotto** to put one's coat on; **non ho soldi** ~ I don't have any money on me; **avere la febbre** ~ to have a temperature; **ho una tale sfortuna** ~ **in questo periodo** I've had such a run of bad luck recently. **2**: ~ a prep (sopra) on; (molto vicino) right next to; **gli ombrelloni sono uno** ~ **all'altro sulla spiaggia** the umbrellas are practically one on top of the other on the beach; **andare** (o **venire**) ~ a (Aut: altra macchina) to run into; (: pedone) to run over; **dare** ~ **a qn** (fig) to attack sb; **mettere gli occhi** ~ **a qn/qc** to take quite a fancy to sb/sth; **mettere le mani** ~ **a qn** (picchiare, catturare, molestare) to lay hands on sb; **la polizia ci sta** ~ the police are breathing down our necks.

addotto, a [ad'dotto] pp di **addurre**.

addurre [ad'durre] vt (a) (prove, esempi) to produce. (b) (citare: scuse, argomenti) to advance, put forward.

adeguamento [adegwa'mento] sm adjustment.

adeguare [ade'gware] **1** vt: ~ (a) (stipendio) to adjust (to); (produzione, struttura) to bring into line (with). **2**: ~rsi vr (conformarsi): ~rsi (a) to adapt (to).

adeguato, a [ade'gwato] ag (proporzionato): ~ (a) adequate (to); (adatto): ~ (a) suitable (for); (equo) fair.

adempiere [a'dɛmpjere] **1** vi: ~ a, vt (gen) to carry out, fulfil; (ordine) to carry out. **2**: ~rsi vr (avverarsi) to be fulfilled.

adempimento [adempi'mento] sm (vedi vb) fulfilment; carrying out; **nell'**~ **del proprio dovere** in the performance of one's duty.

adempire [adem'pire] = **adempiere**.

adenoidi [ade'nɔidi] sfpl adenoids.

adepto [a'dɛpto] sm disciple, follower.

aderente [ade'rɛnte] **1** ag (sostanza) adhesive;

(abiti) close-fitting. **2** *sm/f:* ~ **(a)** follower (of), supporter (of).

aderenza [ade'rɛntsa] *sf* **(a)** *(gen, Med)* adhesion; *(Aut: di ruota)* grip. **(b)**: ~**e** *sfpl (fig: conoscenze)* connections, contacts.

aderire [ade'rire] *vi:* ~ **(a) (a)** to adhere (to), stick (to); ~ **alla strada** *(Aut)* to grip the road. **(b)** *(partito)* to join; *(idea)* to support. **(c)** *(richiesta)* to agree to.

adescare [ades'kare] *vt* **(a)** *(attirare)* to lure, entice. **(b)** *(Tecn: pompa)* to prime.

adesione [ade'zjone] *sf* **(a)** adhesion. **(b)** *(assenso)* agreement, acceptance; *(appoggio)* support.

adesivo, a [ade'zivo] *ag, sm* adhesive.

adesso [a'dɛsso] *av (ora)* now; *(poco fa)* just now; *(fra poco)* any moment now; **da** ~ **in poi** from now on; **per** ~ for the moment, for now.

adiacente [adja'tʃɛnte] *ag* adjacent, adjoining; ~ **a** adjacent to.

adiacenze [adja'tʃɛntse] *sfpl* vicinity *sg*, environs.

adibire [adi'bire] *vt:* ~ **qc a** to use sth as; **questo edificio è adibito a deposito merci** this building is used as a goods depot.

adiposo, a [adi'poso] *ag (Anat)* adipose.

adirarsi [adi'rarsi] *vr:* ~ **(con** o **contro qn per qc)** to get angry (with sb over sth).

adirato, a [adi'rato] *ag* angry.

adire [a'dire] *vt (Dir):* ~ **le vie legali** to resort to o institute legal proceedings; ~ **un'eredità** to take legal possession of an inheritance.

adito ['adito] *sm:* **dare** ~ **a** *(sospetti)* to give rise to.

adocchiare [adok'kjare] *vt (scorgere)* to catch sight of; *(desiderare)* to have one's eye on.

adolescente [adoleʃ'ʃɛnte] **1** *ag* adolescent. **2** *sm/f* adolescent, teenager.

adolescenza [adoleʃ'ʃɛntsa] *sf* adolescence.

adombrare [adom'brare] **1** *vt (fig: celare)* to veil, conceal. **2:** ~**rsi** *vr (cavallo)* to shy; *(persona: aversene a male)* to be offended.

adoperare [adope'rare] **1** *vt* to use. **2:** ~**rsi** *vr:* ~**rsi (per fare)** to make every effort (to do); ~**rsi in favore di qn** to do one's best for sb.

adorabile [ado'rabile] *ag* adorable.

adorare [ado'rare] *vt (gen)* to adore; *(Rel)* to adore, worship.

adorazione [adorat'tsjone] *sf (vedi vb)* adoration; worship.

adornare [ador'nare] **1** *vt (anche fig):* ~ **(di** o **con)** to adorn (with). **2:** ~**rsi** *vr:* ~**rsi (di** o **con)** to adorn o.s. (with).

adorno, a [a'dorno] *ag:* ~ **(di)** adorned (with).

adottare [adot'tare] *vt (gen)* to adopt; *(libro di testo)* to choose, select.

adottivo, a [adot'tivo] *ag (genitori)* adoptive; *(figlio, patria)* adopted.

adozione [adot'tsjone] *sf (vedi vb)* adoption; selection; **si rende necessaria l'**~ **di misure di sicurezza** security measures will have to be adopted.

adriatico, a, ci, che [adri'atiko] **1** *ag* Adriatic. **2** *sm:* **l'A**~ the Adriatic.

adulare [adu'lare] *vt* to flatter.

adulatore, trice [adula'tore] *sm/f* flatterer.

adulatorio, a [adula'tɔrjo] *ag* flattering.

adulazione [adulat'tsjone] *sf* flattery.

adulterare [adulte'rare] *vt* to adulterate; *(fig: informazione)* to distort.

adulterio [adul'tɛrjo] *sm* adultery.

adultero, a [a'dultero] **1** *ag* adulterous. **2** *sm/f* adulterer.

adulto, a [a'dulto] **1** *ag* adult. **2** *sm/f* adult, grown-up.

adunanza [adu'nantsa] *sf* meeting, assembly.

adunare [adu'nare] **1** *vt* to assemble, gather; ~ **le forze** *(fig)* to gather one's strength. **2:** ~**rsi** *vr* to assemble, gather.

adunata [adu'nata] *sf (Mil)* muster.

adunco, a, chi, che [a'dunko] *ag* hooked.

aerazione [aerat'tsjone] *sf* **(a)** ventilation. **(b)** *(Tecn)* aeration.

aereo, a [a'ɛreo] **1** *ag* **(a)** *(gen, Aer, Posta)* air *attr;* *(navigazione, fotografia)* aerial; *(linea elettrica)* overhead *attr.* **(b)** *(Bot: radice)* aerial. **2** *sm (abbr di* **aeroplano***)* plane; ~ **da caccia** fighter (plane); ~ **di linea** airliner; ~ **a reazione** jet (plane).

aerobica [ae'rɔbika] *sf* aerobics *sg.*

aerodinamica [aerodi'namika] *sf* aerodynamics *sg.*

aerodinamico, a, ci, che [aerodi'namiko] *ag (Fis)* aerodynamic; *(affusolato)* streamlined.

aeromodellismo [aeromodel'lizmo] *sm* model aircraft building.

aeromodello [aeromo'dɛllo] *sm* model aircraft.

aeronauta, i [aero'nauta] *sm* pilot.

aeronautica [aero'nautika] *sf* aeronautics *sg;* ~ **civile** civil aviation; ~ **militare** air force.

aeronautico, a, ci, che [aero'nautiko] *ag* aeronautical.

aeronavale [aerona'vale] *ag (forze, manovre)* air and sea *attr.*

aeroplano [aero'plano] *sm* aeroplane, airplane *(Am).*

aeroporto [aero'pɔrto] *sm* airport.

aeroportuale [aeroportu'ale] *ag* airport *attr.*

aeroscalo [aeros'kalo] *sm* airstrip.

aerosol [aero'sɔl] *sm inv* aerosol.

aerospaziale [aerospat'tsjale] *ag* aerospace.

aerostatico, a, ci, che [aeros'tatiko] *ag* aerostatic; **pallone** ~ air balloon.

aerostato [ae'rɔstato] *sm* aerostat.

afa ['afa] *sf* sultriness, closeness; **c'è un'**~ **terribile** it's terribly sultry o close.

affabile [af'fabile] *ag* affable.

affabilità [affabili'ta] *sf* affability.

affaccendarsi [affattʃen'darsi] *vr:* ~ **a fare qc** to be busy doing sth, bustle about doing sth; **si affaccendava intorno ai fornelli** she was busy at the cooker.

affaccendato, a [affattʃen'dato] *ag* busy.

affacciare [affat'tʃare] **1** *vt (dubbio)* to raise, put forward. **2:** ~**rsi** *vr (sporgersi):* ~**rsi (a)** to appear (at); **il balcone si affaccia sulla piazza** the balcony looks onto the square; ~**rsi alla vita** *(bambino, fiore)* to come into the world; **un dubbio gli si affacciò alla mente** a sudden doubt came into his mind.

affamato, a [affa'mato] *ag* starving, hungry; ~ **di potere** greedy for power; ~ **d'affetto** starved of affection.

affannare [affan'nare] **1** *vt* to leave breathless; *(fig)* to trouble, worry. **2:** ~**rsi** *vr (fig):* ~**rsi (per)** to worry (about), get worked up (about); ~**rsi a fare qc** to worry about doing sth; **è inutile che ti affanni a trovar scuse** don't waste your breath looking for excuses.

affanno [af'fanno] *sm* **(a)** breathlessness. **(b)** *(fig)* anxiety, worry; **mettersi in** ~ **per qc** to get worked up over sth, become anxious about sth.

affannosamente [affannosa'mente] *av (respirare)* with difficulty; *(fig)* anxiously.

affannoso, a [affan'noso] *ag (respiro)* laboured; *(fig: attesa, ricerca)* anxious.

affare [af'fare] *sm* **(a)** *(faccenda)* matter, affair; *(Dir)* case; **è stato un brutto** ~ it was a nasty business o affair; **questo non è affar tuo** this is none of your business; **sono** ~**i miei** that's my business; **bada agli ~i tuoi!** mind your own business!; ~ **di cuore** love affair; ~ **di Stato** *(Pol)* affair of state.

(b) *(transazione)* piece of business, (business) deal; *(occasione)* bargain; ~ **fatto!** done!, it's a deal!; **concludere un** ~ to conclude a (business) deal; **hai fatto un (buon)** ~ you got a bargain.

(c) *(fam: coso)* thing; **come funziona quest'**~? how does this thing *o* contraption work?

(d): ~**i** *pl* *(gen, Pol)* affairs; *(commercio)* business *sg*; **è qua per** ~**i** he's here on business; **uomo d'**~**i** businessman; **Ministro degli A**~**i Esteri** Foreign Secretary *(Brit)*, Secretary of State *(Am)*.

affarista, i, e [affa'rista] *sm/f* shrewd businessman/woman; *(peg)* profiteer.

affascinante [affaʃʃi'nante] *ag* fascinating.

affascinare [affaʃʃi'nare] *vt* *(ammaliare)* to bewitch; *(sedurre)* to charm, fascinate.

affastellare [affastel'lare] *vt* *(rami)* to tie up in bundles.

affaticamento [affatika'mento] *sm* tiredness.

affaticare [affati'kare] **1** *vt* to tire. **2**: ~**rsi** *vr (stancarsi)* to get tired; ~**rsi a fare qc** to tire o.s. out doing sth.

affatto [af'fatto] *av (interamente)* completely; **non ... ~** not ... at all; **non mi piace** ~ I don't like it at all; **non sei** ~ **divertente** you're not at all funny; **niente** ~! not at all!

affermare [affer'mare] **1** *vt (sostenere)* to maintain; *(: diritti)* to assert; **afferma di essere innocente** he maintains that he is innocent. **2** *vi (dir di si)* to say yes; **affermò col capo** he nodded. **3**: ~**rsi** *vr (imporsi)* to make o.s. known.

affermativamente [affermativa'mente] *av* in the affirmative, affirmatively.

affermativo, a [afferma'tivo] *ag* affirmative; **dare una risposta** ~**a** to say yes.

affermazione [affermat'tsjone] *sf* **(a)** assertion, affirmation. **(b)** *(successo)* achievement.

afferrare [affer'rare] **1** *vt* *(prendere)* to seize, grasp; *(fig: idea)* to grasp; ~ **un'occasione** to seize an opportunity. **2**: ~**rsi** *vr*: ~**rsi a** to grasp at.

affettare[1] [affet'tare] *vt (carne etc)* to slice.

affettare[2] [affet'tare] *vt (ostentare)* to affect.

affettato[1]**, a** [affet'tato] **1** *ag* sliced. **2** *sm* (sliced) cold meat.

affettato[2]**, a** [affet'tato] *ag (lezioso)* affected.

affettatrice [affetta'tritʃe] *sf* meat slicer.

affettazione [affettat'tsjone] *sf* affectation.

affettivo, a [affet'tivo] *ag* affective; *(vita)* emotional.

affetto[1] [af'fetto] *sm* **(a)** *(sentimento)* affection; *(nelle lettere)*: **con (molto)** ~ with love, affectionately yours. **(b)** *(persona, cosa)* object of affection; **gli** ~**i familiari** one's nearest and dearest.

affetto[2]**, a** [af'fetto] *ag*: **essere** ~ **da** to suffer from.

affettuosamente [affettuosa'mente] *av* affectionately; *(nelle lettere)* **(ti saluto)** ~**, Roberta** love, Roberta.

affettuosità [affettuosi'ta] *sf inv* **(a)** affection. **(b)** ~ *pl (manifestazioni)* demonstrations of affection.

affettuoso, a [affettu'oso] *ag* affectionate; *(nelle lettere)*: **un saluto** *o* **un abbraccio** ~**, Roberta** love, Roberta.

affezionarsi [affettsjo'narsi] *vr*: ~ **a qn/qc** to grow fond of sb/sth.

affezionato, a [affettsjo'nato] *ag* **(a)**: ~ **a qn/qc** fond of sb/sth; *(attaccato)* attached to sb/sth. **(b)** *(abituale: cliente)* regular.

affezione [affet'tsjone] *sf* **(a)** *(sentimento)* affection. **(b)** *(Med)* ailment.

affiancare [affjan'kare] *vt* **(a)** *(mettere a fianco)*: ~ **a** to put beside; *(accompagnare)* to accompany. **(b)** *(Mil)* to flank. **(c)** *(fig: sostenere)* to support.

affiatamento [affjata'mento] *sm* understanding; **c'è molto** ~ **fra di loro** they get on well together.

affiatarsi [affja'tarsi] *vr* to get to know one another; **sono molto affiatati** they get on very well.

affibbiare [affib'bjare] *vt* **(a)** *(allacciare)* to buckle. **(b)** *(fig: appioppare)*: ~ **qc a qn** *(soprannome, colpa)* to pin sth on sb; *(compito sgradevole)* to saddle sb with sth; ~ **uno schiaffo a qn** to slap sb in the face.

affidabilità [affidabili'ta] *sf* reliability.

affidamento [affida'mento] *sm* **(a)** *(fiducia)* trust, confidence; *(garanzia)* assurance; **dare** ~ to seem reliable; **fare** ~ **su qn/qc** to rely *o* count on sb/sth; **quel tipo lì non mi dà nessun** ~ I don't trust that chap at all. **(b)** *(Dir: di bambino)* custody.

affidare [affi'dare] **1** *vt*: ~ **qn/qc a qn** to entrust sb/sth to sb; ~ **un incarico a qn** to entrust sb with a task. **2**: ~**rsi** *vr*: ~**rsi a qn/qc** to place one's trust in sb/sth; **mi affido alla tua discrezione** I rely on your discretion.

affievolire [affjevo'lire] **1** *vt (forze)* to weaken; *(suoni)* to make faint. **2**: ~**rsi** *vr (suoni)* to grow faint; *(passione, affetto)* to fade.

affiggere [af'fiddʒere] *vt* to stick up.

affilare [affi'lare] **1** *vt* to sharpen. **2**: ~**rsi** *vr (persona)* to slim down.

affilato, a [affi'lato] *ag (gen)* sharp; *(volto, naso)* thin.

affiliare [affi'ljare] **1** *vt* **(a)** *(Dir: bambino)* to foster. **(b)** *(aggregare)* to affiliate. **2**: ~**rsi** *vr*: ~**rsi (a qc)** to join (sth), become a member (of sth).

affiliato, a [affi'ljato] *sm/f* **(a)** *(Dir)* fostered child. **(b)** *(membro)* affiliated member.

affiliazione [affiljat'tsjone] *sf (vedi vt)* fostering; affiliation.

affinare [affi'nare] *vt (Tecn, fig: gusto)* to refine; *(: ingegno)* to sharpen.

affinché [affin'ke] *cong* in order that, so that.

affine [af'fine] **1** *ag* similar. **2** *sm/f* **(a)** *(di coniuge)* in-law. **(b)** *(prodotto dello stesso tipo)* similar product; **sapone e** ~**i** soap and allied products.

affinità [affini'ta] *sf inv* affinity.

affiorare [affjo'rare] *vi* **(a)** *(venire in superficie)*: ~ **(su)** to appear on the surface (of); ~ **da** to emerge from. **(b)** *(fig: indizi)* to come to light.

affissione [affis'sjone] *sf* billposting; **'divieto di ~'** 'post no bills'.

affisso, a [af'fisso] **1** *pp di* **affiggere**. **2** *sm* **(a)** *(avviso)* notice; *(manifesto)* poster, bill. **(b)** *(Edil)* fixture. **(c)** *(Gram)* affix.

affittacamere [affitta'kamere] *sm/f inv* landlord/lady; **fare l'**~ to take in lodgers.

affittare [affit'tare] *vt* **(a)** *(dare in affitto: casa)* to rent (out), let; *(: macchina)* to hire (out). **(b)** *(prendere in affitto: casa)* to rent; *(noleggiare)* to hire.

affitto [af'fitto] *sm* **(a)** *(vedi vb)* renting; hiring; **dare in** ~ to rent (out), let; to hire (out); **prendere in** ~ to rent; to hire. **(b)** *(prezzo)* rent.

affliggere [af'fliddʒere] **1** *vt* **(a)** *(malattia, lamentela)* to trouble; **i dolori reumatici la affliggono da tempo** she has been troubled with rheumatics for years. **(b)** *(notizia)* to grieve, distress. **2**: ~**rsi** *vr*: ~**rsi (per)** *(rattristarsi)* to grieve (over); *(preoccuparsi)* to worry (over).

afflitto, a [af'flitto] **1** *pp di* **affliggere**. **2** *ag*: **aver**

l'aria ~**a** to look miserable. **3** *sm/f:* **gli** ~**i** the afflicted.

afflosciarsi [afflo∫'∫arsi] *vr* **(a)** *(perdere tensione: tenda, vela)* to become limp; *(: pelle)* to become flabby, sag. **(b)** *(sgonfiarsi: palloncino)* to go down. **(c)** *(accasciarsi: persona)* to collapse.

affluente [afflu'ente] *sm (Geog)* tributary.

affluenza [afflu'entsa] *sf (di persone, merci)* influx; *(di liquidi)* flow.

affluire [afflu'ire] *vi (aus* **essere) (a)** *(liquidi)* to flow. **(b)** *(persone, merci)* to pour in; ~ **in** to pour into.

afflusso [af'flusso] *sm (di gente, prodotti)* influx; *(di liquidi)* flow.

affogare [affo'gare] **1** *vt (gen, fig)* to drown; ~ **i dispiaceri nell'alcool** to drown one's sorrows in drink. **2** *vi (aus* **essere)** to drown.

affogato, a [affo'gato] *ag* **(a)** drowned; **è morta** ~**a** she drowned. **(b)** *(Culin: uova)* poached.

affollamento [affolla'mento] *sm* **(a)** crowding. **(b)** *(folla)* crowd.

affollare [affol'lare] **1** *vt (gen, fig)* to crowd. **2:** ~**rsi** *vr (gen, fig)* to crowd; ~**rsi intorno a qn/qc** to crowd round sb/sth.

affollato, a [affol'lato] *ag:* ~ **(di)** crowded (with).

affondamento [affonda'mento] *sm (di nave)* sinking; *(di ancora)* dropping.

affondare [affon'dare] **1** *vt* **(a)** *(mandare a fondo: nave)* to sink; *(: ancora)* to drop. **(b)** *(immergere):* ~ **in** to sink into; ~ **le mani in tasca** to dig one's hands into one's pockets. **2** *vi (aus* **essere) (a)** *(andare a fondo)* to sink. **(b)** *(penetrare):* ~ **in qc** to sink into sth.

affondo [af'fondo] *sm (Scherma)* lunge.

affossamento [affossa'mento] *sm (avvallamento)* hollow.

affrancare [affran'kare] *vt* **(a)** *(con francobolli)* to stamp; ~ **(a macchina)** to frank. **(b)** *(liberare: schiavo, popolo)* to liberate, free; *(beni, proprietà)* to redeem.

affrancatrice [affranka'trit∫e] *sf* franking machine.

affrancatura [affranka'tura] *sf (valore)* postage; *(operazione)* stamping; franking.

affranto, a [af'franto] *ag (dallo sconforto, dal dolore):* ~ **(da)** overcome (with).

affresco, schi [af'fresko] *sm* fresco.

affrettare [affret'tare] **1** *vt (lavoro, operazione)* to speed up; *(partenza)* to bring forward; ~ **il passo** to quicken one's pace. **2:** ~**rsi** *vr (sbrigarsi)* to hurry up; ~**rsi a rispondere/a scusarsi/a aggiungere** to hasten to answer/to apologize/to add.

affrettato, a [affret'tato] *ag (veloce: passo, ritmo)* quick, fast. **(b)** *(frettoloso: decisione)* hurried, hasty; *(: lavoro)* rushed.

affrontare [affron'tare] **1** *vt (nemico, pericolo)* to face, confront; *(situazione)* to face up to; *(questione)* to deal with, tackle; ~ **una spesa** to meet an expense. **2:** ~**rsi** *vr (venire a confronto)* to confront each other.

affronto [af'fronto] *sm* affront; **fare un** ~ **a qn** to insult sb.

affumicare [affumi'kare] *vt* **(a)** *(riempire di fumo)* to fill with smoke. **(b)** *(annerire)* to blacken with smoke. **(c)** *(alimenti)* to smoke.

affumicato, a [affumi'kato] *ag (salmone etc)* smoked; *(occhiali)* tinted.

affusolato, a [affuso'lato] *ag* tapering.

aforisma, i [afo'rizma] *sm* aphorism.

afoso, a [a'foso] *ag* close, sultry.

Africa ['afrika] *sf* Africa.

africano, a [afri'kano] *ag, sm/f* African.

afrodisiaco, a, ci, che [afrodi'ziako] *ag, sm* aphrodisiac.

agata ['agata] *sf* agate.

agave ['agave] *sf (Bot)* agave.

agenda [a'dʒɛnda] *sf* **(a)** *(taccuino)* diary; ~ **tascabile/da tavolo** pocket/desk diary. **(b)** *(in una riunione)* agenda.

agente [a'dʒɛnte] *sm* **(a)** *(incaricato)* agent, representative; ~ **di cambio** stockbroker; ~ **delle tasse** tax inspector; ~ **teatrale** theatrical agent; ~ **di vendita** sales agent. **(b)** *(Polizia):* ~ **di polizia** o **di Pubblica Sicurezza** policeman; ~ **di custodia** prison officer. **(c)** *(Chim, Med, Meteor)* agent.

agenzia [adʒen'tsia] *sf* **(a)** *(succursale)* branch office. **(b)** *(impresa)* agency; ~ **di collocamento** employment agency; ~ **immobiliare** estate agent's (office); ~ **d'informazione** information office; ~ **matrimoniale** marriage bureau; ~ **pubblicitaria** advertising agency; ~ **di viaggi** travel agency.

agevolare [adʒevo'lare] *vt* **(a)** *(facilitare: compito, operazione):* ~ **qc (a qn)** to make sth easy (for sb), facilitate sth (for sb). **(b)** *(aiutare):* ~ **qn (in qc)** to help sb (with sth).

agevolazione [adʒevolat'tsjone] *sf (facilitazione economica)* facility; ~ **di pagamento** payment on easy terms; ~**i creditizie** credit facilities; ~**i fiscali** tax concessions.

agevole [a'dʒevole] *ag (salita, compito)* easy; *(strada)* smooth.

agganciare [aggan't∫are] *vt (unire con un gancio)* to hook; *(ricevitore del telefono)* to hang up; *(Ferr: vagone, vettura)* to couple; *(fig: persona)* to catch.

aggancio [ag'gant∫o] *sm* **(a)** *(Tecn)* coupling. **(b)** *(fig: conoscenza)* contact.

aggeggio [ad'dʒeddʒo] *sm* gadget, contraption.

aggettivo [addʒet'tivo] *sm* adjective.

agghiacciare [aggjat't∫are] **1** *vt:* ~ **qn**, ~ **il sangue a qn** to make sb's blood run cold. **2:** ~**rsi** *vr:* **mi si è agghiacciato il sangue** my blood ran cold.

aggiogare [addʒo'gare] *vt (buoi)* to yoke; *(popolo)* to subjugate.

aggiornamento [addʒorna'mento] *sm (vedi vb)* updating; revision; postponement; adjournment; **corso di** ~ refresher course.

aggiornare [addʒor'nare] **1** *vt* **(a)** *(testo)* to update; *(: rivedere)* to revise; *(persona)* to bring up to date; **tienimi aggiornato!** keep me up to date on what's happening! **(b)** *(rimandare):* ~ **(a)** to postpone (till), put off (till); *(: Dir)* to adjourn (till). **2:** ~**rsi** *vr:* ~**rsi (su qc)** to bring *(o* keep) o.s. up to date (about sth); **mi piace tenermi aggiornato su ciò che succede** I like to keep up to date with what's happening.

aggiotaggio [addʒo'taddʒo] *sm (Econ)* rigging the market.

aggirare [addʒi'rare] **1** *vt (andare intorno a)* to go round. **2:** ~**rsi** *vr* **(a)** *(girare qua e là):* ~**rsi in** *o* **per** to hang about, go about. **(b)** *(approssimarsi):* **la spesa si aggira sui 2 milioni** the cost is about *o* in the region of 2 million.

aggiudicare [addʒudi'kare] *vt (premio, merito):* ~ **qc a qn** to award sb with sth, award sth to sb; *(all'asta)* to knock sth down to sb; **aggiudicato!** *(all'asta)* gone!; **si è aggiudicato il primo posto** he won first place.

aggiungere [ad'dʒundʒere] **1** *vt* to add. **2:** ~**rsi** *vr:* ~**rsi a** to add to.

aggiunta [ad'dʒunta] *sf* addition; **in** ~... what's more... .

aggiunto, a [ad'dʒunto] **1** *pp di* **aggiungere. 2** *ag (Amm: aiuto)* assistant; *(: sostituto)* stand-in; **sin-**

daco ~ deputy mayor. **3** *sm (Amm)* assistant.

aggiustare [addʒus'tare] **1** *vt* **(a)** *(riparare)* to repair, mend. **(b)** *(adattare: vestito)* to alter; *(correggere: tiro, mira)* to correct; ~**rsi la cravatta/gli occhiali** to adjust one's tie/glasses. **(c)** *(fig: sistemare: lite, conto)* to settle; **ti aggiusto io!** I'll fix you! **2:** ~**rsi** *vr* **(a)** *(reciproco: accordarsi)* to come to an agreement; *(per soldi)* to settle (up). **(b)** *(mettersi in ordine)* to tidy o.s. up.

agglomerato [agglome'rato] *sm* **(a)** *(di rocce)* conglomerate. **(b)** *(Tecn)* agglomeration; ~ **di legno** chipboard. **(c):** ~ **urbano** built-up area.

aggomitolare [aggomito'lare] **1** *vt* to wind. **2:** ~**rsi** *vr* to curl up.

aggrapparsi [aggrap'parsi] *vr (anche fig):* ~ **(a)** to cling (to).

aggravamento [aggrava'mento] *sm* worsening; **c'è stato un** ~ there has been a turn for the worse.

aggravante [aggra'vante] *(Dir)* **1** *ag* aggravating. **2** *sf* aggravation.

aggravare [aggra'vare] **1** *vt (situazione)* to worsen; *(: pena)* to increase. **2:** ~**rsi** *vr (situazione etc)* to get worse, worsen.

aggraziato, a [aggrat'tsjato] *ag (movimenti)* graceful; *(lineamenti)* pretty; *(modi)* gracious.

aggredire [aggre'dire] *vt* to attack.

aggregare [aggre'gare] **1** *vt:* ~ **qn a qc** to include sb in sth; *(a un club)* to admit sb to sth. **2:** ~**rsi** *vr:* ~**rsi (a)** to tag on (to).

aggregato, a [aggre'gato] **1** *ag (associato)* associated; **socio** ~ associate member; ~ **a un reparto** attached to a section. **2** *sm (gen, Bot, Geol)* aggregate.

aggregazione [aggregat'tsjone] *sf (gen, Fis, Chim)* aggregation.

aggressione [aggres'sjone] *sf* **(a)** *(contro una persona)* attack, assault; ~ **a mano armata** armed assault. **(b)** *(Mil, Pol: contro un paese)* aggression; **patto di non** ~ non-aggression pact.

aggressività [aggressivi'ta] *sf* aggressiveness.

aggressivo, a [aggres'sivo] *ag* aggressive.

aggressore [aggres'sore] *sm* attacker; *(Pol)* aggressor.

aggrottare [aggrot'tare] *vt:* ~ **le sopracciglia**, ~ **la fronte** to frown.

aggrovigliare [aggroviʎ'ʎare] **1** *vt (fili, matassa)* to (en)tangle; ~ **la matassa** *(fig)* to complicate things. **2:** ~**rsi** *vr* to become tangled; *(fig)* to become complicated.

agguantare [aggwan'tare] *vt* to catch hold of.

agguato [ag'gwato] *sm* **(a)** *(insidia)* trap; **tendere un** ~ **a qn** to set a trap for sb; **cadere in un** ~ to fall into a trap. **(b)** *(appostamento)* ambush; **stare** *o* **essere in** ~ to lie in ambush.

agguerrito, a [aggwer'rito] *ag (sostenitore, nemico)* fierce.

aghiforme [agi'forme] *ag* needle-shaped.

agiatezza [adʒa'tettsa] *sf* prosperity; **vivere nell'**~ to live in comfort.

agiato, a [a'dʒato] *ag (vita, condizione)* comfortable; *(persona)* well-off, well-to-do.

agile ['adʒile] *ag* agile, nimble.

agilità [adʒili'ta] *sf* agility, nimbleness.

agio ['adʒo] *sm* **(a)** ease; **sentirsi/trovarsi a proprio** ~ to feel/be at one's ease; **mettiti a tuo** ~ make yourself at home. **(b)** *(opportunità):* **dare** ~ **a qn di fare qc** to give sb the chance of doing sth. **(c):** ~**i** *smpl:* **vivere negli** ~**i** to live in comfort.

agire [a'dʒire] *vi* **(a)** *(gen)* to act; *(comportarsi)* to behave; **bisogna** ~ **immediatamente** we must act *o* take action at once; **ha agito male verso i colleghi** he behaved badly towards his col-

leagues; **non mi piace il suo modo di** ~ I don't like the way he does things; ~ **su qn/qc** to act on sb/sth; **una medicina che agisce rapidamente** a medicine which acts *o* takes effect quickly; **la leva agisce sul cambio** the lever operates the gear. **(b)** *(Dir):* ~ **contro qn** to take legal action against sb, to start proceedings against sb.

agitare [adʒi'tare] **1** *vt* **(a)** *(liquido, bottiglia)* to shake; *(mano, fazzoletto)* to wave; '~ **prima dell'uso'** 'shake well before use'; **il vento agitava le foglie** the wind was blowing the leaves about. **(b)** *(fig: incitare)* to incite; *(: turbare)* to trouble. **2:** ~**rsi** *vr* **(a)** *(rami etc)* to sway; *(bambino)* to fidget; *(mare)* to get rough; *(dubbio, pensiero, folla)* to stir; ~**rsi nel sonno** to toss and turn in one's sleep. **(b)** *(turbarsi)* to get worked up; *(eccitarsi)* to get excited. **(c)** *(Pol)* to agitate.

agitato, a [adʒi'tato] **1** *ag* **(a)** *(persona malata)* restless; *(bambino)* fidgety; *(mare)* rough. **(b)** *(persona: turbato)* worried; *(: eccitato)* excited. **2** *sm/f (in ospedale psichiatrico)* manic patient.

agitatore, trice [adʒita'tore] *sm/f (Pol)* agitator.

agitazione [adʒitat'tsjone] *sf* **(a)** *(inquietudine)* agitation; **essere in uno stato di** ~ to be worked up; **mettersi in** ~ to get worked up. **(b)** *(Pol)* agitation, unrest.

agli ['aʎʎi] *prep + art vedi* **a**[2].

aglio ['aʎʎo] *sm* garlic.

agnello [aɲ'ɲɛllo] *sm* lamb.

agnosticismo [aɲɲosti'tʃismo] *sm* agnosticism.

agnostico, a, ci, che [aɲ'ɲɔstiko] *ag* agnostic.

ago, ghi ['ago] *sm (gen)* needle; *(della bilancia)* pointer; **lavoro ad** ~ needlework; ~ **da calza** knitting needle; **è come cercare un** ~ **in un pagliaio** it's like looking for a needle in a haystack.

agonia [ago'nia] *sf* **(a)** *(Med)* death throes *pl*; **entrare in** ~ to be at death's door; **è stata una lunga** ~ it was a slow death. **(b)** *(fig)* agony.

agonistico, a, ci, che [ago'nistiko] *ag (Sport, fig)* competitive.

agonizzante [agonid'dzante] *ag* dying.

agonizzare [agonid'dzare] *vi (malato)* to be dying; *(fig: civiltà etc)* to decline.

agopuntura [agopun'tura] *sf* acupuncture.

agosto [a'gosto] *sm* August; *per uso vedi* **luglio**.

agraria [a'grarja] *sf* agriculture.

agrario, a [a'grarjo] **1** *ag (scuola, scienza)* agricultural; *(leggi)* agrarian; **riforma** ~**a** land reform. **2** *sm* landowner.

agricolo, a [a'grikolo] *ag (gen)* agricultural; *(lavoratori, prodotti, macchine)* farm *attr*; *(popolazione)* farming.

agricoltore [agrikol'tore] *sm* farmer.

agricoltura [agrikol'tura] *sf* agriculture.

agrifoglio [agri'fɔʎʎo] *sm* holly.

agro, a ['agro] *ag* sour, bitter.

agrodolce [agro'doltʃe] **1** *ag (sapore, fig)* bittersweet; *(salsa)* sweet and sour. **2** *sm (Culin)* sweet and sour sauce.

agronomia [agrono'mia] *sf* agronomy.

agronomo [a'grɔnomo] *sm* agronomist.

agrume [a'grume] *sm (pianta)* citrus; *(frutto)* citrus fruit.

agrumeto [agru'meto] *sm* citrus grove.

aguzzare [agut'tsare] *vt* to sharpen; ~ **gli occhi** *o* **la vista** to strain to see; ~ **le orecchie** to prick up one's ears; ~ **l'ingegno** to use one's wits.

aguzzino, a [agud'dzino] *sm/f* jailer; *(fig)* tyrant.

aguzzo, a [a'guttso] *ag* sharp.

ah [a] *escl* ah!, oh!; ~ **si?** really?

ahi ['ai] *escl (dolore)* ouch!

ahimè [ai'mɛ] *escl* alas!

ai ['ai] *prep* + *art vedi* **a**².

Aia ['aja] *sf*: **l'~** the Hague.

aia ['aja] *sf* (*per battere il grano*) threshing floor; (*cortile*) farmyard.

aiola [a'jɔla] *sf* = **aiuola**.

airone [ai'rone] *sm* heron.

air-terminal ['ɛə,təːminl] *sm inv* air terminal.

aitante [ai'tante] *ag* robust.

aiuola [a'jwɔla] *sf* flower bed; '**non calpestare le ~e**' 'keep off the flower beds'.

aiutante [aju'tante] *sm/f* (**a**) (*nel lavoro*) assistant; **fare da ~ a qn** to be sb's assistant. (**b**) (*Mil*) adjutant; **~ di campo** aide-de-camp. (**c**) (*Naut*) master-at-arms; **~ di bandiera** flag lieutenant.

aiutare [aju'tare] **1** *vt* to help; (*assistere*) to assist; **~ qn (a fare qc)** to help sb (to do sth); **~ la digestione** to aid (the) digestion. **2**: **~rsi** *vr* (**a**) to help o.s.; **aiutati, che Dio ti aiuta** God helps those who help themselves. (**b**) (*uso reciproco*) to help one another.

aiuto [a'juto] **1** *sm* (**a**) (*soccorso*) help, assistance, aid; **prestare o dare ~ a qn** to help sb; **venire in ~ di qn** to help sb, come to sb's assistance; **essere di ~** to be a help; **mi è stata di grande ~** she has been a great help to me; **chiedere ~ a qn** to ask sb for help; **correre in ~ di qn** to rush to sb's assistance. (**b**) (*aiutante, assistente*) assistant; **~ contabile/regista** assistant accountant/director. **2** *escl* help!

aizzare [ait'tsare] *vt* (**a**) (*cani*): **~ contro qn** to set on sb. (**b**) (*folla*) to incite; (*contendenti*) to urge on.

al [al] *prep* + *art vedi* **a**².

ala ['ala] *sf*, *pl* **ali** (*gen*) wing; (*di cappello*) brim; (*di mulino*) sail; **fare ~** to make way; **avere le ~i ai piedi** (*fig*) to have wings; **mettere le ~i** (*fig*) to spread one's wings; **prendere qn sotto le proprie ~i** (*fig*) to take sb under one's wing.

alabastro [ala'bastro] *sm* alabaster.

alacre ['alakre] *ag* (*persona*) eager; (*mente, fantasia*) lively.

alacrità [alakri'ta] *sf* promptness, speed.

alambicco, chi [alam'bikko] *sm* still (*Chim*).

alano [a'lano] *sm* Great Dane.

alare¹ [a'lare] *ag* wing *attr*.

alare² [a'lare] *sm* (*di camino*) firedog.

alato, a [a'lato] *ag* winged.

alba ['alba] *sf* dawn; **all'~** at dawn, at daybreak; **spunta l'~** dawn is breaking; **alzarsi all'~** to get up at dawn.

albanese [alba'nese] *ag, sm/f, sm* Albanian.

Albania [alba'nia] *sf* Albania.

albatro ['albatro] *sm*, **albatros** ['albatros] *sm inv* albatross.

albeggiare [albed'dʒare] (*aus essere*) *vi, vb impers* to dawn; **comincia ad ~** day is dawning; **albeggiava quando arrivò a casa** day was breaking when he arrived home.

alberato, a [albe'rato] *ag* (*viale, piazza*) lined with trees, tree-lined.

alberatura [albera'tura] *sf* (*Naut*) masts *pl*.

albergare [alber'gare] **1** *vt* (**a**) (*dare albergo*) to accommodate. (**b**) (*poet: sentimenti*) to harbour. **2** *vi* (*poet*) to dwell.

albergatore, trice [alberga'tore] *sm/f* (*proprietario*) hotel owner; (*gestore*) hotel manager/manageress.

alberghiero, a [alber'gjero] *ag* hotel *attr*.

albergo, ghi [al'bergo] *sm* hotel; **~ della gioventù** youth hostel; **~ diurno** *public toilets with washing and shaving facilities etc*.

albero ['albero] *sm* (**a**) (*pianta*) tree; **~ da frutto** fruit tree; **~ genealogico** family tree; **~ di**

Natale Christmas tree. (**b**) (*Naut*) mast. (**c**) (*Tecn*) shaft; **~ a camme** camshaft; **~ a gomiti** crankshaft.

albicocca, che [albi'kɔkka] *sf* apricot.

albicocco, chi [albi'kɔkko] *sm* apricot tree.

albino, a [al'bino] *ag, sm/f* (*Bio*) albino.

albo ['albo] *sm* (*registro professionale*) register, roll; (*Amm: bacheca*) notice board; (*fascicolo illustrato*) album.

album ['album] *sm inv* (*libro, disco*) album; **~ da disegno** sketch book; **~ per francobolli/fotografie** stamp/photo album.

albume [al'bume] *sm* (**a**) (*Bio*) albumen. (**b**) (*bianco d'uovo*) egg white.

albumina [albu'mina] *sf* albumin.

alcalino, a [alka'lino] *ag* alkaline.

alce ['altʃe] *sm* elk.

alchimia [alki'mia] *sf* alchemy.

alchimista, i, e [alki'mista] *sm/f* alchemist.

alcol ['alkol] *sm inv* = **alcool**.

alcolicità [alkolitʃi'ta] *sf* alcohol(ic) content.

alcolico, a, ci, che [al'kɔliko] **1** *ag* alcoholic. **2** *sm* alcohol; **non faccio uso di ~ci** I don't drink.

alcolismo [alko'lizmo] *sm* alcoholism.

alcolizzato, a [alkolid'dzato] *ag, sm/f* alcoholic.

alcool ['alkool] *sm inv* (*gen, Chim*) alcohol; **~ etilico** ethyl alcohol; **~ denaturato** methylated spirits *pl*.

alcova [al'kɔva] *sf* alcove.

alcuno, a [al'kuno] **1** *ag* (*dav sm:* **alcun**+*consonante, vocale,* **alcuno**+*s impura, gn, pn, ps, x, z; dav sf:* **alcuna**+*consonante,* **alcun'**+*vocale*) (**a**) (*nessuno*): **non ... ~** no, not any; **non c'è ~a fretta** there's no hurry, there isn't any hurry; **senza alcun riguardo** without any consideration. (**b**): **~i(e)** some, a few. **2**: **~i(e)** *pron pl* some, a few.

aldilà [aldi'la] *sm inv*: **l'~** the next life, the afterlife.

aleatorio, a [alea'tɔrjo] *ag* (*incerto*) uncertain.

aletta [a'letta] *sf* (*Tecn*) fin.

alfa ['alfa] *ag inv, sm o f inv* alpha.

alfabetico, a, ci, che [alfa'bɛtiko] *ag* alphabetical.

alfabeto [alfa'beto] *sm* alphabet.

alfiere [al'fjere] *sm* (*Mil*) standard-bearer; (*Scacchi*) bishop.

alga, ghe ['alga] *sf* strand of seaweed; **~ghe** seaweed *sg*, algae.

algebra ['aldʒebra] *sf* algebra; **questo per me è ~** (*fig*) this is Greek to me.

Algeria [aldʒe'ria] *sf* Algeria.

algerino, a [aldʒe'rino] *ag, sm/f* Algerian.

aliante [ali'ante] *sm* glider.

alibi ['alibi] *sm inv* alibi.

alienare [alje'nare] **1** *vt* (*gen*) to alienate; (*Dir: trasferire*) to transfer; **~rsi un amico** to alienate a friend. **2**: **~rsi** *vr*: **~rsi (da)** to cut o.s. off (from).

alienato, a [alje'nato] **1** *ag* (*pazzo*) insane. **2** *sm/f* lunatic.

alienazione [aljenat'tsjone] *sf* (*gen*) alienation; (*Dir*) transfer; (*Psic*): **~ mentale** insanity.

alieno, a [a'ljɛno] **1** *ag*: **~ (da)** opposed (to), averse (to). **2** *sm/f* alien.

alimentare¹ [alimen'tare] **1** *ag* food *attr*; **generi ~i** foodstuffs; **regime ~** diet. **2**: **~i** *smpl* (*anche:* **negozio di ~i**) grocer's shop.

alimentare² [alimen'tare] *vt* (**a**) (*Tecn*) to feed, supply; (*: stufa*) to add fuel to; (*: caldaia*) to stoke; (*: fuoco*) to stoke up. (**b**) (*fig: tener vivo*) to sustain, keep going. (**c**) (*nutrire*) to nourish, feed.

alimentazione [alimentat'tsjone] *sf* (**a**) (*nutrizione*) nutrition; (*cibi*) diet; **~ equilibrata/priva di grassi** balanced/low fat diet. (**b**) (*Tecn*) feeding; (*: di caldaia*) stoking.

alimento [ali'mento] *sm* (**a**): ~, ~i *(cibo)* food; **contenitore per** ~i food container. (**b**): ~i *pl (Dir)* alimony.

aliquota [a'likwota] *sf* (**a**) *(Mat)* aliquot. (**b**) *(Fin)* rate.

aliscafo [alis'kafo] *sm* hydrofoil.

alito ['alito] *sm (anche fig)* breath; **avere l'**~ **cattivo** to have bad breath; **non c'è un** ~ **di vento** there isn't a breath of wind.

all. *abbr* (= *allegato*) encl.

alla ['alla] *prep* + *art vedi* **a**[2].

allacciamento [allattʃa'mento] *sm (Tecn)* connection; **far fare l'**~ **dell'acqua/del gas** to have the water/gas connected.

allacciare [allat'tʃare] **1** *vt* (**a**) *(cintura, mantello, cerniera etc)* to fasten; *(scarpe con lacci)* to lace (up); ~**rsi il cappotto** to fasten one's coat; ~ **due funi** to tie two ropes together. (**b**) *(Tecn)* to connect. (**c**) *(fig: rapporti)* to form, establish. **2**: ~**rsi** *vr (vestito)* to fasten.

allacciatura [allattʃa'tura] *sf* fastening.

allagamento [allaga'mento] *sm (atto)* flooding; *(effetto)* flood.

allagare [alla'gare] *vt,* ~**rsi** *vr* to flood.

allampanato, a [allampa'nato] *ag* lanky.

allargare [allar'gare] **1** *vt* (**a**) *(passaggio, buco)* to widen; *(vestito)* to let out; *(scarpe)* to stretch; *(fig: orizzonti etc)* to widen, broaden. (**b**) *(aprire: braccia)* to open; **si sentì** ~ **il cuore** his heart gladdened. **2** *vi:* ~ **in curva** *(Aut)* to take a bend wide. **3**: ~**rsi** *vr (gen)* to widen; *(scarpe, pantaloni)* to stretch; *(espandersi: problema, fenomeno)* to spread.

allarmare [allar'mare] **1** *vt* to alarm. **2**: ~**rsi** *vr* to become alarmed.

allarme [al'larme] *sm (gen)* alarm; **dare l'**~ to give *o* sound the alarm; ~ **aereo** air-raid warning; **essere in** ~ **per qc** to be alarmed about sth; **mettere qn in** ~ to alarm sb.

allarmismo [allar'mizmo] *sm* scaremongering.

allarmista, i, e [allar'mista] *sm/f* alarmist, scaremonger.

allarmistico, a, ci, che [allar'mistiko] *ag* alarmist.

allattamento [allatta'mento] *sm (vedi vb)* (breast-)feeding; suckling; ~ **naturale** breast-feeding; ~ **artificiale** bottle-feeding.

allattare [allat'tare] *vt (sog: donna)* to (breast-)feed; *(: animale)* to suckle; ~ **artificialmente** to bottle-feed.

alle ['alle] *prep* + *art vedi* **a**[2].

alleanza [alle'antsa] *sf* alliance.

alleare [alle'are] **1** *vt* to unite. **2**: ~**rsi** *vr* to form an alliance; ~**rsi a qn** to become allied with sb; **l'Italia e la Germania si allearono contro la Francia** Italy and Germany joined forces against France.

alleato, a [alle'ato] **1** *ag* allied. **2** *sm/f* ally.

allegare [alle'gare] *vt* (**a**) *(in una lettera):* ~ **(a)** to enclose (with); **alleghiamo alla presente una fotocopia** we enclose herewith a photocopy. (**b**) *(gen, Dir: addurre)* to adduce, put forward. (**c**) *(denti)* to set on edge.

allegato, a [alle'gato] **1** *ag* enclosed. **2** *sm* enclosure; **in** ~ enclosed.

alleggerimento [alleddʒeri'mento] *sm (gen)* lightening; *(di sofferenza, coscienza)* easing; *(di tasse)* reduction.

alleggerire [alleddʒe'rire] *vt (rendere più leggero)* to lighten, make lighter; *(fig: responsabilità)* to lighten; *(: sofferenza)* to relieve, lessen; *(: tasse)* to reduce; *(: coscienza)* to ease; **lo hanno al-**

leggerito del portafoglio *(scherz)* he's had his wallet pinched.

allegoria [allego'ria] *sf* allegory.

allegorico, a, ci, che [alle'gɔriko] *ag* allegorical.

allegria [alle'gria] *sf* cheerfulness, gaiety; **mettere** ~ **a qn** to cheer sb up; **su, un po' di** ~! come on, cheer up!; **tutte queste luci colorate fanno** ~ all these coloured lights make things more cheerful.

allegro, a [al'legro] **1** *ag* (**a**) *(persona)* cheerful, merry; *(colore)* bright; *(musica)* lively; **c'è poco da stare** ~**i** things are pretty grim. (**b**) *(un po' brillo)* merry, tipsy. **2** *sm (Mus)* allegro.

alleluia [alle'luja] *sm inv, escl* hallelujah.

allenamento [allena'mento] *sm* training; **essere fuori** ~ to be out of training.

allenare [alle'nare] *vt,* ~**rsi** *vr* to train.

allenatore, trice [allena'tore] *sm/f* trainer, coach.

allentare [allen'tare] **1** *vt* (**a**) *(nodo, cintura)* to loosen; ~ **le redini** *(anche fig)* to slacken the reins; ~ **il passo** to slacken one's pace. (**b**) *(diminuire: disciplina)* to relax. **2**: ~**rsi** *vr (nodo, stringhe)* to loosen, become loose; *(ingranaggio, vite)* to loosen, work loose.

allergia, gie [aller'dʒia] *sf* allergy.

allergico, a, ci, che [al'lɛrdʒiko] *ag:* ~ **(a)** allergic (to).

allestimento [allesti'mento] *sm* preparation, setting up; **in** ~ in preparation.

allestire [alles'tire] *vt* (**a**) *(spettacolo, mostra, fiera)* to organize; *(vetrina)* to prepare. (**b**) *(Naut)* to rig out, fit out.

allettante [allet'tante] *ag* attractive, alluring.

allettare [allet'tare] *vt* to attract, entice; **l'idea non mi alletta** the idea doesn't appeal to me.

allevamento [alleva'mento] *sm* (**a**) *(di animali)* breeding, rearing; **pollo d'allevamento** battery hen. (**b**) *(luogo)* farm; *(: per cavalli)* stud farm; *(: per cani)* kennels *pl*.

allevare [alle'vare] *vt (animali)* to breed, rear; *(bambini)* to bring up; **allevato male** *(bambino)* badly brought up.

allevatore [alleva'tore] *sm* breeder.

alleviare [alle'vjare] *vt* to alleviate, relieve.

allibire [alli'bire] *vi (aus essere) (impallidire)* to go white, turn pale; *(essere turbato)* to be disconcerted.

allibito, a [alli'bito] *ag (vedi vb)* pale; disconcerted.

allibratore [allibra'tore] *sm* bookmaker.

allietare [allje'tare] **1** *vt* to make happy, cheer (up). **2**: ~**rsi** *vr* to become happy, rejoice.

allievo [al'ljɛvo] *sm* pupil, student.

alligatore [alliga'tore] *sm* alligator.

allineamento [allinea'mento] *sm* alignment.

allineare [alline'are] **1** *vt* to align, line up; *(Mil)* to draw up in lines. **2**: ~**rsi** *vr (anche Mil)* to line up; *(Pol):* ~**rsi a o con** to align o.s. with.

allineato, a [alline'ato] *ag* aligned, in line; **paesi non** ~**i** *(Pol)* non-aligned countries.

allo ['allo] *prep* + *art vedi* **a**[2].

allocco, a, chi, che [al'lɔkko] **1** *sm (Zool)* tawny owl. **2** *sm/f* fool, dolt.

allocuzione [allokut'tsjone] *sf* address.

allodola [al'lɔdola] *sf* lark.

alloggiare [allod'dʒare] **1** *vt* to accommodate, put up. **2** *vi:* ~ **(in)** to stay (at); **sono alloggiato al Ritz** I'm staying at the Ritz.

alloggio [al'lɔddʒo] *sm* (**a**) *(abitazione provvisoria)* lodging, accommodation; **vitto e** ~ board and lodging. (**b**) *(appartamento)* flat; **la crisi degli** ~**i** the housing problem; **cercare** ~ to look for somewhere to live.

allontanamento [allontana'mento] *sm (gen)* separation; *(affettivo)* estrangement; *(di funzionario, studente)* removal; **c'è stato un graduale ~ fra i 2 paesi** relations between the 2 countries have grown cooler.

allontanare [allonta'nare] **1** *vt* **(a)** *(persona)* to take away; *(oggetto)* to move away, take away; *(fig: affetti, amici)* to alienate; **~ una poltrona dal fuoco** to move an armchair away from the fire; **la maestra ha allontanato Maria da Roberto** the teacher has separated Maria and Roberto. **(b)** *(mandare via)* to send away; *(licenziare)* to dismiss. **(c)** *(fig: pericolo, sospetti)* to avert; **~ qn dall'idea di fare qc** to deter sb from doing sth. **(d)** *(dilazionare)* to space out. **2:** **~rsi** *vr* to go away; *(fig: possibilità)* to grow more remote; **~rsi da qn** to wander away from sb; *(fig)* to grow away from sb; **c'eravamo allontanati troppo** we had wandered too far.

allora [al'lora] *av* **(a)** *(in quel momento)* then, at that moment; *(a quel tempo)* then, in those days, at that time; **la gente di ~** people then *o* in those days; **da ~ in poi** since then. **(b)** *(in questo caso)* then, in that case, so; *(dunque)* well then, so; **hai paura? — ~ dillo!** are you frightened? — (well) then, say so!; **~ vieni?** well (then), are you coming?; **e ~?** *(che fare?)* what now?; *(e con ciò?)* so what?

alloro [al'lɔro] *sm* laurel; **riposare** *o* **dormire sugli ~i** to rest on one's laurels.

alluce ['allutʃe] *sm* big toe.

allucinante [allutʃi'nante] *ag* *(scena, spettacolo)* awful, terrifying; *(fam: incredibile)* amazing.

allucinato, a [allutʃi'nato] *ag* terrified; *(fuori di sé)* bewildered, confused.

allucinazione [allutʃinat'tsjone] *sf* hallucination; **avere le ~i** *(anche fig)* to hallucinate.

allucinogeno, a [allutʃi'nɔdʒeno] **1** *ag* hallucinogenic. **2** *sm* hallucinogen.

alludere [al'ludere] *vi:* **~ a** to allude to, hint at.

alluminio [allu'minjo] *sm* aluminium.

allunaggio [allu'naddʒo] *sm* moon landing.

allunare [allu'nare] *vi* to land on the moon.

allungabile [allun'gabile] *ag* extendable.

allungare [allun'gare] **1** *vt* **(a)** *(rendere più lungo)* to lengthen; **~ il passo** to quicken one's step; **~ la strada** to take the long way round. **(b)** *(tendere)* to stretch out; **~ le gambe** to stretch one's legs; **~ le orecchie/il collo** to strain one's ears/crane one's neck; **~ le mani** *(rubare)* to pick pockets; **non ~ le mani sulla mia ragazza** keep your hands off my girlfriend. **(c)** *(fam: porgere)* to pass, hand; **mi allunghi il sale per favore?** could you pass me the salt please?; **gli allungò uno schiaffo** he took a swipe at him. **(d)** *(diluire)* to dilute, water down. **2:** **~rsi** *vr* **(a)** *(diventare più lungo)* to grow longer; *(: ombre)* to lengthen; *(: bambino, pianta)* to grow taller; *(: vestito, maglione)* to stretch. **(b)** *(stendersi)* to stretch out.

allusione [allu'zjone] *sf:* **~ (a)** allusion (to), hint (at).

allusivo, a [allu'zivo] *ag* allusive.

alluso, a [al'luzo] *pp di* alludere.

alluvionato, a [alluvjo'nato] **1** *ag* *(regione, città)* flooded. **2** *sm/f* flood victim.

alluvione [allu'vjone] *sf* flood.

almanacco, chi [alma'nakko] *sm* almanac.

almeno [al'meno] **1** *av* at least. **2** *cong* if only; **(se) ~ piovesse!** if only it would rain!

alone [a'lone] *sm* *(di sole, luna)* halo; *(di fiamma, lampada)* glow; *(di macchia)* ring; **un ~ di mistero** an aura of mystery.

alpe ['alpe] *sf* *(montagna)* alp; *(pascolo)* mountain pasture.

alpeggio [al'peddʒo] *sm* mountain pasture.

alpestre [al'pestre] *ag* *(delle alpi)* alpine; *(montuoso)* mountainous.

Alpi ['alpi] *sfpl:* **le ~** the Alps.

alpinismo [alpi'nizmo] *sm* mountaineering.

alpinista, i, e [alpi'nista] *sm/f* mountaineer.

alpino, a [al'pino] **1** *ag* alpine. **2:** **~i** *smpl* *(Mil)* Italian Alpine troops.

alquanto, a [al'kwanto] **1** *ag* a certain amount of, some; **~i(e)** quite a few, several. **2** *pron* a certain amount, some; **~i(e)** quite a few, several. **3** *av* rather, somewhat.

alt [alt] **1** *escl* halt!, stop! **2** *sm* order to halt, order to stop; **dare l'~** to call a halt.

altalena [alta'lena] *sf* *(a funi)* swing; *(in bilico)* seesaw; **la mia vita è un'~ di fortuna e disgrazie** my life is a series of ups and downs.

altare [al'tare] *sm* altar; **~ maggiore** high altar.

alterare [alte'rare] **1** *vt* **(a)** *(fatti, verità)* to distort; *(qualità)* to affect, impair; *(alimenti)* to adulterate. **(b)** *(piani etc)* to alter, change. **2** *vi* *(aus essere)* *(cambiare)* to alter, change; **alterò in viso per lo sgomento** his face became distorted with fear. **3:** **~rsi** *vr* **(a)** *(fatti etc)* to become distorted; *(salute etc)* to be affected, be impaired; *(alimenti)* to go bad; *(vino)* to spoil. **(b)** *(cambiare)* to change, alter. **(c)** *(sdegnarsi)* to get angry.

alterazione [alterat'tsjone] *sf* *(vedi vb)* distortion; impairment; adulteration; alteration, change.

altercare [alter'kare] *vi* to argue, quarrel.

alterco, chi [al'terko] *sm* row, altercation.

alternanza [alter'nantsa] *sf* alternation; *(Agr)* rotation.

alternare [alter'nare] **1** *vt* *(avvicendare):* **~ qc a o con** to alternate sth with; *(Agr)* to rotate. **2:** **~rsi** *vr:* **~rsi (a o con)** to alternate (with).

alternativa [alterna'tiva] *sf* alternative; **non abbiamo ~e** we have no alternative; **in ~** as an alternative.

alternativo, a [alterna'tivo] *ag* *(anche fig: società etc)* alternative.

alternato, a [alter'nato] *ag* alternate; *(Elettr)* alternating.

alternatore [alterna'tore] *sm* alternator.

alterno, a [al'terno] *ag* *(gen)* alternate; *(mutevole: fortuna, vicenda)* changing; **a giorni ~i** every other day, on alternate days.

altero, a [al'tero] *ag* proud.

altezza [al'tettsa] *sf* **(a)** *(di edificio, persona)* height; *(quota)* height, altitude; *(di suono)* pitch; *(di acqua, pozzo etc)* depth; *(di tessuto)* width; **~ sul mare** height above sea level; **da un'~ di 2000 metri** from a height of 2000 metres; **essere all'~ di una situazione** *(fig)* to be equal to a situation; **non sono all'~** *(fig)* I'm not up to it. **(b)** *(Geom)* perpendicular height; *(: linea)* perpendicular; *(Astron)* elevation, altitude. **(c)** *(prossimità):* **all'~ della farmacia** near the chemist's; **all'~ di Capo Horn** off Cape Horn. **(d)** *(titolo):* **Vostra A~** Your Highness.

altezzoso, a [altet'tsoso] *ag* haughty, arrogant.

altisonante [altiso'nante] *ag* *(fig)* high-sounding, pompous.

altitudine [alti'tudine] *sf* altitude.

alto, a ['alto] **1** *ag* **(a)** *(gen)* high, tall; **un muro ~ 10 metri** a wall 10 metres high; **un uomo ~ 1 metro 80** a man 6 feet tall; **andare a testa ~a** *(fig)* to carry one's head high. **(b)** *(suono: elevato)* high; *(: forte)* loud; **ad ~a voce** out loud, aloud. **(c)** *(fig: elevato: carica, dignitario)* high; *(: sentimenti, pensieri)* lofty, noble; **avere un'~a opinione di sé** to have a high opinion of o.s. **(d)** *(profondo: acqua, sonno, silenzio)* deep; **essere in ~ mare** *(fig)* to be far from a solution. **(e)** *(Geog)*: **l'~ Italia** Northern Italy; **l'A~ Volta** Upper Volta; **l'~ Po** the upper reaches of the Po. **(f)** *(largo: tessuto)* wide.

2 *sm (parte superiore)* top; **mani in ~!** hands up!; **guardare in ~** to look up; **là in ~** up there; **dall'~** from on high; **dall'~ di** from the top of; **guardare dall'~ in basso qn** *(fig)* to look down on sb; **~i e bassi** ups and downs.

3 *av* high; *(parlare, gridare)* aloud, out loud; **'~'** *(su casse di imballaggio)* 'this side up'.

4: ~ comando *(Mil)* high command; **~ commissario** high commissioner; **~a fedeltà** high fidelity, hi-fi; **~a moda** haute couture; **l'A~ Medioevo** the Early Middle Ages; **~a società** high society; **~a stagione** high season.

altoatesino, a [altoate'zino] *ag* of *(o* from*)* the Alto Adige.

altoforno [alto'forno] *sm* blast furnace.

altolocato, a [altolo'kato] *ag* of high rank, highly placed; **amicizie ~e** friends in high places.

altoparlante [altopar'lante] *sm* loudspeaker.

altopiano [alto'pjano] *sm, pl* **altipiani** upland plain, plateau.

altrettanto, a [altret'tanto] **1** *ag* as much; **~i(e)** as many; **ho ~a fiducia in te** I have as much *o* the same confidence in you. **2** *pron* as much; **~i(e)** as many; **domani dovrò comprarne ~** I'll have to buy as much *o* the same tomorrow; **sono 2 mesi che cerco lavoro, e temo che ne passeranno ~i prima di trovarlo** I have been looking for work for 2 months now, and I'm afraid it'll be as long again before I find any; **se n'è andato ed io ho fatto ~** he left and so did I *o* and I followed suit; **tanti auguri! — grazie, ~** all the best! — thank you, the same to you. **3** *av* equally; **lui è ~ bravo** he is equally clever, he is just as clever.

altri ['altri] *pron pers (qualcuno)* somebody; *(: in espressioni negative)* anybody; *(un'altra persona)* another (person).

altrimenti [altri'menti] *av* **(a)** *(in caso contrario)* otherwise, or else. **(b)** *(in modo diverso)* differently.

altro, a ['altro] **1** *ag indef* **(a)** *(diverso)* other, different; **questa è un'~a cosa** that's another *o* a different thing; **erano ~i tempi** things were different then.

(b) *(supplementare)* other; **prendi un ~ cioccolatino** have another chocolate; **gli ~i allievi usciranno più tardi** the other pupils *o* the rest of the pupils will come out later.

(c) *(opposto)* other; **dall'~a parte della strada** on the other *o* opposite side of the street.

(d) *(nel tempo)*: **l'~ giorno** the other day; **l'~ ieri** the day before yesterday, the day before last; **domani l'~** the day after tomorrow; **quest'~ mese** next month.

(e): **d'~a parte** on the other hand; **chi/dove/chiunque ~** who/where/anybody else; **noi ~i, voi ~i = noialtri, voialtri**.

2 *pron indef* **(a)** *(persona, cosa diversa o supplementare)*: **un(a) ~(a)** another (one); **~i(e)** others; **se non lo fai tu lo farà un ~** if you don't do it someone else will; **prendine un ~** take another one; **da un giorno all'~** from day to day; *(qualsiasi giorno)* any day now.

(b) *(opposizione)*: **l'~(a)** the other (one); **gli(le) altri(e)** the others; **non questo, l'~** not this one, the other one.

(c) *(sostantivato: solo maschile)* something else; *(in espressioni interrogative)* anything else; **non ho ~ da dire** I have nothing else to say, I don't have anything else to say; **ci vuole ~ per**

spaventarmi! it takes a lot more (than this) to frighten me!; **gli dirò questo ed ~!** I'll tell him this and more besides!; **tra l'~** among other things; **ci mancherebbe ~!** that's all we need!; **non faccio ~ che studiare** I do nothing but study; **sei contento? — tutt'~!** are you pleased? — on the contrary!; **se non ~** at least; **più che ~** above all.

altroché [altro'ke] *escl* certainly!, and how!

altronde [al'tronde] *av*: **d'~** on the other hand.

altrove [al'trove] *av* elsewhere, somewhere else.

altrui [al'trui] *ag inv* other people's, others'; **la roba ~** other people's belongings *pl*.

altruismo [altru'izmo] *sm* altruism.

altruista, i, e [altru'ista] **1** *ag* altruistic. **2** *sm/f* altruist.

altruistico, a, ci, che [altru'istiko] *ag* altruistic.

altura [al'tura] *sf* **(a)** *(luogo alto)* height, high ground. **(b)** *(Naut)*: **pesca d'~** deep-sea fishing.

alunno, a [a'lunno] *sm/f* pupil.

alveare [alve'are] *sm* beehive.

alveo ['alveo] *sm* riverbed.

alzabandiera [altsaban'djɛra] *sm (Mil)*: **l'~** the raising of the flag.

alzare [al'tsare] **1** *vt* **(a)** *(gen)* to raise; *(pacco etc)* to lift; **~ gli occhi** *o* **lo sguardo** to raise one's eyes. **(b)** *(issare: bandiera, vela)* to hoist. **(c)** *(costruire, erigere)* to build, erect. **(d)** *(fraseologia)*: **~ le carte** to cut the cards; **non ha alzato nemmeno un dito per aiutarmi** he didn't lift a finger to help me; **~ il gomito** to drink too much; **~ le mani su qn** to raise one's hand to sb; **~ le spalle** to shrug one's shoulders; **~ i tacchi** to take to one's heels. **2**: **~rsi** *vr* **(a)** *(persona)* to rise, get up; **~rsi (in piedi)** to stand up; **~rsi da tavola** to get up from the table; **~rsi col piede sbagliato** to get out of bed on the wrong side. **(b)** *(aumentare: prezzi, temperatura)* to rise. **(c)** *(sorgere: sole, luna)* to rise; *(: vento)* to rise, get up. **(d)** *(crescere di statura)* to grow (tall).

alzata [al'tsata] *sf* **(a)** *(vedi vb)* lifting; raising. **(b)** *(di mobile)* upper part, top. **(c)** *(per dolci)* cake-stand.

alzato, a [al'tsato] **1** *sm (Archit)* elevation. **2** *ag (braccio)* raised; *(persona: in piedi)* up, out of bed.

A.M. *abbr (= Aeronautica Militare)* ≃ RAF.

amabile [a'mabile] *ag* **(a)** *(persona, conversazione)* pleasant, amiable. **(b)** *(vino)* sweet.

amabilità [amabili'ta] *sf* pleasantness, amiability.

amaca, che [a'maka] *sf* hammock.

amalgama, i [a'malgama] *sm (Chim)* amalgam; *(fig)* amalgam, mixture; *(peg)* (strange) combination.

amalgamare [amalga'mare] **1** *vt* to amalgamate, combine; *(impastare)* to mix. **2**: **~rsi** *vr (sostanze)* to combine; *(Culin, fig: persone)* to mix.

amante [a'mante] **1** *ag (appassionato)*: **~ di** fond of, keen on. **2** *sm/f* lover; *(extraconiugale)* lover/mistress.

amaranto [ama'ranto] **1** *sm (Bot)* love-lies-bleeding. **2** *ag inv*: **color ~** reddish purple.

amare [a'mare] **1** *vt (provare affetto)* to love; *(: amante, marito)* to love, be in love with; *(amico, musica, sport etc)* to like, be fond of; **noi amiamo la musica classica** we like *o* enjoy *o* are fond of classical music; **~ fare qc** to like doing *o* to do sth; **farsi ~ da qn** to win sb's love. **2**: **~rsi** *vr (uso reciproco)* to be in love, love each other.

amareggiare [amared'dʒare] **1** *vt* to sadden, upset. **2**: **~rsi** *vr* to get upset; **~rsi la vita** to make one's life a misery.

amarena [ama'rɛna] *sf* black cherry.

amaretto [ama'retto] *sm (dolce)* macaroon; *(li-*

quore) bitter liqueur made with almonds.

amarezza [ama'rettsa] *sf* bitterness; **le ~e della vita** life's disappointments.

amaro, a [a'maro] **1** *ag (sapore, fig)* bitter; *(senza zucchero)* unsweetened; *(triste)* unhappy, painful; **avere la bocca ~a** to have a bitter taste in one's mouth. **2** *sm* **(a)** *(liquore)* bitters *pl*. **(b)** *(gusto)* bitter taste; *(fig: tristezza, dolore)* bitterness; **mi ha lasciato l'~ in bocca** it left a bitter taste in my mouth.

amarognolo, a [ama'roɲɲolo] *ag* slightly bitter.

amato, a [a'mato] **1** *ag* beloved, loved, dear. **2** *sm/f* loved one.

amatore, trice [ama'tore] *sm/f* **(a)** *(amante)* lover. **(b)** *(appassionato)* lover; *(intenditore: di vini etc)* connoisseur. **(c)** *(dilettante)* amateur.

amazzone [a'maddzone] *sf* **(a)** Amazon. **(b)** *(cavallerizza)* horsewoman; *(abito)* riding habit; **cavalcare all'~** to ride sidesaddle.

ambasceria [ambaʃʃe'ria] *sf* embassy.

ambasciata [ambaʃ'ʃata] *sf* embassy.

ambasciatore, trice [ambaʃʃa'tore] *sm/f* ambassador.

ambedue [ambe'due] **1** *ag inv* both; **~ i ragazzi** both boys. **2** *pron inv* both.

ambidestro, a [ambi'dɛstro] *ag* ambidextrous.

ambientale [ambjen'tale] *ag* environmental; *(temperatura)* ambient.

ambientare [ambjen'tare] **1** *vt (film, racconto)* to set. **2**: **~rsi** *vr* to get used to one's surroundings, settle down.

ambientazione [ambjentat'tsjone] *sf* setting.

ambiente [am'bjente] *sm* **(a)** environment; *(classe, gruppo)* sphere, circle. **(b)** *(stanza)* room.

ambiguità [ambigui'ta] *sf inv* ambiguity.

ambiguo, a [am'biguo] *ag* ambiguous, equivocal; *(persona)* doubtful, shady.

ambire [am'bire] *vt (anche: vi: ~ a)* to aspire to; **un premio molto ambito** a much sought-after prize.

ambito ['ambito] *sm* environment; *(fig: cerchia)* sphere, circle.

ambivalente [ambiva'lɛnte] *ag* ambivalent; **questo apparecchio è ~** this is a dual-purpose device.

ambivalenza [ambiva'lɛntsa] *sf* ambivalence.

ambizione [ambit'tsjone] *sf* ambition.

ambizioso, a [ambit'tsjoso] *ag* ambitious.

ambo ['ambo] **1** *ag inv* both. **2** *sm (al gioco)* double.

ambra ['ambra] *sf* amber; **~ grigia** ambergris.

ambrosia [am'brɔzja] *sf* ambrosia.

ambulante [ambu'lante] **1** *ag* travelling, itinerant; *(suonatore)* strolling, travelling; *(biblioteca)* mobile; **sei un vocabolario ~!** you're a walking encyclopaedia! **2** *sm* pedlar.

ambulanza [ambu'lantsa] *sf (veicolo)* ambulance; *(Mil)* field hospital.

ambulatoriale [ambulato'rjale] *ag (Med)* outpatient⌀ *attr;* **operazione ~** operation as an outpatient; **visita ~** visit to the doctor's surgery.

ambulatorio, a [ambula'tɔrjo] *sm (di medico)* surgery, consulting rooms *pl; (di ospedale)* outpatients' department.

ameba [a'mɛba] *sf* amoeba.

amen ['amen] *av* amen; **in un ~** *(fig)* in the twinkling of an eye.

amenità [ameni'ta] *sf inv* **(a)** *(di luogo, pensieri)* pleasantness. **(b)** *(facezia)* pleasantry.

ameno, a [a'mɛno] *ag* **(a)** *(luogo, lettura, pensieri)* pleasant, agreeable. **(b)** *(faceto: tipo, discorso)* droll, amusing.

America [a'mɛrika] *sf* America; **~ latina** Latin America.

americanata [amerika'nata] *sf (peg):* **le Olimpiadi sono stati una vera ~** the Olympics were a

typical American extravaganza; **gli piacciono le ~e** he likes everything that comes from America.

americanismo [amerika'nizmo] *sm (espressione)* Americanism; *(ammirazione)* love of America.

americanizzare [amerikanid'dzare] **1** *vt* to americanize. **2**: **~rsi** *vr* to become americanized.

americano, a [ameri'kano] *ag, sm/f* American.

ametista [ame'tista] *sf* amethyst.

amianto [a'mjanto] *sm* asbestos.

amichevole [ami'kevole] *ag (anche Sport)* friendly.

amichevolmente [amikevol'mente] *av* in a friendly fashion.

amicizia [ami'tʃittsja] *sf* **(a)** *(rapporto)* friendship; **fare ~ con qn** to make friends with sb. **(b)**: **~e** *(amici)* friends.

amico, a, ci, che [a'miko] **1** *ag* friendly. **2** *sm/f* **(a)** friend; **~ del cuore** best friend; **~ d'infanzia** childhood friend; **Michela e le sue ~che** Michela and her (girl)friends; **farsi qn ~** to make friends with sb; **senza ~ci** friendless; **un mio ~ avvocato** a lawyer friend of mine. **(b)** *(amante)* lover. **(c)** *(appassionato)* lover, enthusiast; **~ degli animali** animal lover; **club degli ~ci della musica** music club.

amido ['amido] *sm* starch.

ammaccare [ammak'kare] **1** *vt (auto, pentola, cappello)* to dent; *(frutta, braccio)* to bruise. **2**: **~rsi** *vr (vedi vt)* to get dented; to bruise.

ammaccatura [ammakka'tura] *sf (segno: su auto etc)* dent; *(: su braccio etc)* bruise.

ammaestrare [ammaes'trare] *vt (insegnare)* to teach; *(: animali)* to train; **leone/cavallo ammaestrato** performing lion/horse.

ammainabandiera [ammainaban'djɛra] *sm (Mil):* **l'~** the lowering of the flag.

ammainare [ammai'nare] *vt (vela, bandiera)* to lower, strike.

ammalare [amma'lare] *vi (aus essere),* **~rsi** *vr* to fall ill, become ill.

ammalato, a [amma'lato] **1** *ag* ill, unwell, sick. **2** *sm/f* sick person; *(paziente)* patient.

ammaliare [amma'ljare] *vt (con sortilegio)* to bewitch; *(fig)* to bewitch, enchant, charm.

ammaliatore, trice [ammalja'tore] **1** *sm/f* enchanter/enchantress; *(fig)* charmer, enchantress *(female only).* **2** *ag* bewitching, charming.

ammanco, chi [am'manko] *sm (Amm)* deficit; **c'è stato un ~ di cassa di 30 sterline** the till was £30 short.

ammanettare [ammanet'tare] *vt* to handcuff.

ammansire [amman'sire] *vt (animale)* to tame; *(fig: persona)* to calm down, placate.

ammaraggio [amma'raddʒo] *sm (vedi vb)* (sea) landing; splashdown.

ammarare [amma'rare] *vi (aus essere) (Aer)* to make a sea landing; *(astronave)* to splash down.

ammassare [ammas'sare] **1** *vt (cose)* to pile up, accumulate, amass; *(fig: ricchezze)* to amass, accumulate; *(persone)* to pack. **2**: **~rsi** *vr (cose)* to pile up, accumulate; *(persone)* to crowd.

ammasso [am'masso] *sm (cumulo)* pile, heap; *(Econ)* stockpile.

ammattire [ammat'tire] *vi (aus essere) (anche fig)* to go mad, be driven mad.

ammazzare [ammat'tsare] **1** *vt (uccidere)* to kill; *(fig: affaticare)* to exhaust, wear out; **~ il tempo** to kill time. **2**: **~rsi** *vr (suicidarsi)* to kill o.s.; *(trovare la morte)* to die, be killed; **~rsi di lavoro** to kill o.s. with work, work o.s. to death.

ammenda [am'mɛnda] *sf* **(a)** *(Dir)* fine. **(b)** *(riparazione):* **fare ~** to make amends.

ammesso, a [am'messo] *pp di* **ammettere**.

ammettere [am'mettere] vt (a) *(far entrare: visitatore)* to admit, let in, allow in; *(accettare: nuovo socio, studente)* to admit; ~ qn in un club to admit sb to a club; **alla prova orale saranno ammessi solo quelli che superano la prova scritta** only those who pass the written exam will be eligible for *o* will be allowed to sit the oral exam. (b) *(riconoscere: colpa, errore)* to admit, acknowledge. (c) *(supporre)* to suppose, assume; **ammettiamo che sia vero** let us suppose *o* assume that it's true; **ammesso (e non concesso) che** assuming that. (d) *(tollerare: scuse, comportamento)* to accept; *(permettere)* to allow; **non ammetto che si bestemmi** I will not tolerate swearing.

ammezzato [ammed'dzato] *sm* entresol, mezzanine.

ammiccare [ammik'kare] *vi:* ~ (a) to wink (at).

amministrare [amminis'trare] vt (a) *(ditta)* to manage, direct, run; *(patrimonio)* to administer; *(stato)* to run, govern. (b) *(Rel, Dir)* to administer.

amministrativo, a [amministra'tivo] *ag* administrative.

amministratore [amministra'tore] *sm (Amm)* administrator; *(di stabile)* flats manager; ~ **delegato** managing director, chief executive *(Am)*.

amministrazione [amministrat'tsjone] *sf* (a) *(vedi vb)* management, running; administration; government. (b) *(complesso di amministratori)* administration, management; **consiglio d'**~ board of directors; **la pubblica** ~ public administration; **l'**~ **comunale** local government.

ammiraglia [ammi'raʎʎa] *sf* flagship.

ammiraglio [ammi'raʎʎo] *sm* admiral.

ammirare [ammi'rare] vt to admire.

ammiratore [ammira'tore] *sm* admirer.

ammirazione [ammirat'tsjone] *sf* admiration.

ammirevole [ammi'revole] *ag* admirable.

ammissibile [ammis'sibile] *ag (Dir: testimonianza)* admissible; *(comportamento)* acceptable.

ammissione [ammis'sjone] *sf* (a) *(a club)* admission, entry; *(a scuola)* entrance, acceptance; **esame d'**~ entrance exam. (b) *(di colpa etc)* admission.

ammobiliare [ammobi'ljare] vt to furnish.

ammodo [am'mɔdo] **1** *av (per bene)* well, properly. **2** *ag inv* well-behaved, respectable.

ammogliare [ammoʎ'ʎare] **1** vt to find a wife for. **2:** ~rsi vr to marry, take a wife.

ammoniaca [ammo'niaka] *sf* ammonia.

ammonimento [ammoni'mento] *sm (rimprovero)* reprimand; *(lezione)* lesson, warning.

ammonire [ammo'nire] vt (a) *(rimproverare)* to admonish, reprimand; *(avvertire: anche Sport)* to warn. (b) *(Dir)* to caution.

ammonizione [ammonit'tsjone] *sf* (a) *(monito: anche Sport)* warning; *(rimprovero)* reprimand. (b) *(Dir)* caution.

ammontare [ammon'tare] **1** vi *(aus essere)*: ~ a *(assommare)* to amount to, add up to. **2** *sm (somma)* amount.

ammonticchiare [ammontik'kjare] vt to pile up.

ammorbare [ammor'bare] vt (a) *(diffondere malattia)* to infect. (b) *(sog: odore)* to taint, foul.

ammorbidire [ammorbi'dire] **1** vt to soften. **2:** ~rsi vr to soften; ~rsi con l'età *(fig)* to mellow with age.

ammortamento [ammorta'mento] *sm* redemption.

ammortare [ammor'tare] vt *(Fin: debito)* to pay off, redeem; *(: spese d'impianto)* to write off.

ammortizzamento [ammortiddza'mento] *sm* (a)

(Fin) = **ammortamento**. (b) *(Aut)* cushioning.

ammortizzare [ammortid'dzare] vt (a) *(Fin: debito)* to pay off, redeem; *(: spese d'impianto)* to write off. (b) *(Aut: attutire)* to cushion.

ammortizzatore [ammortiddza'tore] *sm (Aut)* shock absorber.

ammucchiare [ammuk'kjare] **1** vt *(disporre in mucchio)* to heap, pile up; *(: denaro etc)* to pile up, accumulate. **2:** ~rsi vr *(cose)* to pile up, accumulate; *(persone)* to crowd.

ammuffire [ammuf'fire] vi *(aus essere)* to grow mouldy; *(fig: persona)* to moulder, languish.

ammuffito, a [ammuf'fito] *ag* mouldy; *(fig)* fossilized; **è una vecchia** ~a she's an old fossil.

ammutinamento [ammutina'mento] *sm* mutiny.

ammutinarsi [ammuti'narsi] vr to mutiny.

ammutinato, a [ammuti'nato] **1** *ag* mutinous. **2** *sm* mutineer.

ammutolire [ammuto'lire] vi *(aus essere)* to be struck dumb.

amnesia [amne'zia] *sf* amnesia.

amnistia [amnis'tia] *sf* amnesty.

amo ['amo] *sm (Pesca)* (fish) hook; *(fig)* bait; **l'abbiamo preso all'**~ *(fig)* he's swallowed the bait.

amorale [amo'rale] *ag* amoral.

amore [a'more] *sm* (a) *(affetto)* love, affection; *(sessuale)* love; **il suo** ~ **per lui/per le piante** her love for him/of plants; **fare qc con** ~ to do sth with loving care; **fare l'**~ *o* **all'**~ **(con)** to make love (to); **mi ha raccontato tutto dei suoi** ~i he told me all about his love affairs. (b) *(persona)* love; **vieni,** ~ come here, darling; **che** ~ **di vestito!** what a lovely dress!; **il tuo bambino è un** ~ your baby is a darling. (c) *(fraseologia):* **per l'amor di Dio!** for God's sake!; **per** ~ **di** for love of; **per** ~ **o per forza** willy-nilly; **andare d'**~ **e d'accordo con qn** to get on like a house on fire with sb; ~ **libero** free love; **amor proprio** self-esteem; ~ **di sé** egoism, selfishness.

amoreggiare [amored'dʒare] vi to flirt.

amorevole [amo'revole] *ag* loving.

amorfo, a [a'mɔrfo] *ag* amorphous; *(fig)* colourless; **ma come sei** ~! how apathetic you are!

amorino [amo'rino] *sm* cupid.

amoroso, a [amo'roso] **1** *ag (affettuoso)* loving, affectionate; *(d'amore: sguardo)* amorous; *(: poesia, lettera, relazione)* love attr. **2** *sm/f* lover.

ampère [ã'pɛr] *sm inv (Elettr)* ampère, amp.

ampiezza [am'pjettsa] *sf* (a) *(vedi ag a)* spaciousness; breadth, width. (b) *(Fis, Mus)* range; *(fig)* breadth, range; ~ **di vedute** broad-mindedness.

ampio, a ['ampjo] *ag* (a) *(vasto: spazio, sala)* spacious; *(: strada, corridoio)* wide, broad; **di** ~ **respiro** *(fig: ricerca, articolo)* far-reaching. (b) *(largo: vestito)* loose; *(: gonna)* full. (c) *(abbondante: garanzie, dettagli)* ample.

amplesso [am'plɛsso] *sm (sessuale)* intercourse.

ampliamento [amplia'mento] *sm (di strada)* widening; *(di aeroporto)* expansion; *(fig)* broadening.

ampliare [ampli'are] **1** vt *(allargare)* to widen; *(fig: discorso)* to enlarge on; *(: raggio di azione)* to widen; ~ **la propria cultura** to broaden one's mind. **2:** ~rsi vr to grow, increase.

amplificare [amplifi'kare] vt *(suono)* to amplify; *(fig: sensazione)* to increase.

amplificatore [amplifika'tore] *sm* amplifier.

ampolla [am'polla] *sf* (a) *(per olio, aceto)* cruet. (b) *(Chim)* round-bottom flask.

ampolloso, a [ampol'loso] *ag* bombastic.

amputare [ampu'tare] vt *(Med)* to amputate; *(fig: testo, scritto)* to cut.

amputazione [amputat'tsjone] *sf* amputation.

amuleto [amu'lɛto] *sm* amulet.

anabbagliante [anabbaʎˈʎante] *(Aut)* **1** *ag* dipped. **2** *sm* dipped headlight.

anacronismo [anakroˈnizmo] *sm* anachronism.

anacronistico, a, ci, che [anakroˈnistiko] *ag* anachronistic.

anagrafe [aˈnagrafe] *sm (Amm: registro)* register of births, marriages and deaths; *(: ufficio)* registry office.

anagrafico, a, ci, che [anaˈgrafiko] *ag (Amm)*: **dati ~ci** personal data; **comune di residenza** ~a district where resident.

anagramma, i [anaˈgramma] *sm* anagram.

analcolico, a, ci, che [analˈkɔliko] **1** *ag* non-alcoholic; **bevanda** ~a soft drink. **2** *sm* soft drink.

anale [aˈnale] *ag* anal.

analfabeta, i, e [analfaˈbɛta] *ag, sm/f* illiterate.

analfabetismo [analfabeˈtizmo] *sm* illiteracy.

analgesico, a, ci, che [analˈdʒɛziko] *ag, sm* analgesic.

analisi [aˈnalizi] *sf inv* **(a)** *(gen)* analysis; *(di orina, sangue)* test; **all'~ dei fatti** on examining the facts; **in ultima ~** in conclusion, in the final analysis; **sono in ~ da 5 anni** *(Psic)* I've been seeing a psychoanalyst for the past 5 years; **~ del sangue** blood test; **~ di mercato** market analysis. **(b)** *(Gram)*: **~ grammaticale** parsing; **~ logica** sentence analysis; **fare l'~ di un brano** to do a commentary on a passage.

analista, i, e [anaˈlista] *sm/f (Chim, Med, Inform)* analyst; *(Psic)* (psycho)analyst.

analitico, a, ci, che [anaˈlitiko] *ag* analytical; **indice ~** index.

analizzare [analidˈdzare] *vt (gen)* to analyse; *(sangue, orina)* to test, analyse; *(Gram: frase)* to parse; *(poesia, testo)* to give a commentary on.

anallergico, a, ci, che [analˈlɛrdʒiko] *ag, sm (Med)* hypoallergenic.

analogia, gie [analoˈdʒia] *sf* analogy; **per ~ (con)** by analogy (with).

analogico, a, ci, che [anaˈlɔdʒiko] *ag* analogical.

analogo, a, ghi, ghe [aˈnalogo] *ag*: **~ (a)** analogous (to), similar (to).

ananas [ˈananas] *sm inv* pineapple.

anarchia [anarˈkia] *sf* anarchy.

anarchico, a, ci, che [aˈnarkiko] **1** *ag* anarchistic. **2** *sm/f* anarchist.

A.N.A.S. *abbr di Azienda Nazionale Autonoma delle Strade.*

anatema, i [anaˈtɛma] *sm (Rel)* anathema; **scagliare** *o* **gettare l'~ contro** to anathematize.

anatomia [anatoˈmia] *sf (gen)* anatomy; *(analisi)* analysis.

anatomico, a, ci, che [anaˈtɔmiko] *ag* anatomical; **sedile ~** contoured seat.

anatomizzare [anatomidˈdzare] *vt* to anatomize.

anatra [ˈanatra] *sf* duck; **~ selvatica** mallard.

anatroccolo [anaˈtrɔkkolo] *sm* duckling.

anca, che [ˈanka] *sf (Anat)* hip.

ancestrale [antʃesˈtrale] *ag* ancestral.

anche [ˈanke] *cong* **(a)** *(pure)* also, too; **e va ~ a Roma** and he's going to Rome too, and he's also going to Rome; **parla inglese e ~ italiano** he speaks English and Italian too *o* as well; **vengo anch'io!** I'm coming too!; **gli ho parlato ieri — anch'io** I spoke to him yesterday — so did I; **~ oggi non potrò venire** I won't be able to come today either; **potrebbe ~ cambiare idea, ma...** he may well change his mind, but.... . **(b)** *(perfino)* even; **~ se** even if; **~ volendo, non finiremmo in tempo** even if we wanted to, we wouldn't finish in time.

ancheggiare [ankedˈdʒare] *vi* to wiggle (one's hips).

anchilosato, a [ankiloˈzato] *ag* stiff.

ancora¹ [ˈankora] *sf (Naut, fig)* anchor; **gettare/levare l'~** to cast/weigh anchor; **~ di salvezza** *(fig)* last hope.

ancora² [anˈkora] **1** *av* **(a)** *(tuttora)* still; **è ~ innamorato di lei** he's still in love with her. **(b)** *(di nuovo)* again; **~ tu!** (not) you again!; **sei andato ~ a Parigi da allora?** have you been back to Paris since then? **(c)**: **non ~** not yet; **il direttore non è ~ qui** the manager isn't here yet. **(d)** *(più)* more; **~ un po'** a little more; **vuoi ~ zucchero?** would you like some more sugar?; **ne vorrei ~** I'd like some more; **prendi ~ un biscotto** have another biscuit; **ci sono ~ caramelle?** are there any sweets left?; **cosa vuoi ~?** what else do you want?; **~ per una settimana** for another week, for one week more; **~ un po' e finivamo in acqua** we almost ended up in the water.

2 *cong (nei comparativi)* even, still; **~ di più/meno** even more/less; **~ meglio/peggio** even *o* still better/worse; **~ altrettanto** as much again; **oggi fa ~ più freddo** it's even colder today.

ancoraggio [ankoˈraddʒo] *sm* anchorage; **tassa d'~** anchorage dues *pl*.

ancorare [ankoˈrare] *vt*, **~rsi** *vr* to anchor.

andamento [andaˈmento] *sm (di strada, malattia)* course; *(della Borsa)* trend; *(del mercato)* state.

andare [anˈdare] **1** *vi (aus essere)* **(a)** *(gen)* to go; **~ e venire** to come and go; **vado e vengo** I'll be back in a minute; **~ a Roma/a letto** to go to Rome/to bed; **~ in città a piedi/in bicicletta/in macchina** to go to town on foot/by bike/by car, walk/cycle/drive to town; **~ lontano** *(anche fig)* to go far; **dove va (messa) questa vite?** where does this screw go?; **andrò all'università l'anno prossimo** I'm going to university next year; **~ per i 50** *(età)* to be getting on for 50.

(b) *(essere)*: **~ fiero di qc/qn** to be proud of sth/sb; **~ perduto** to be lost; **va sempre vestita di rosso** she always wears red; **vado pazzo per la pizza** I'm crazy about pizza, I adore pizza; **se non vado errato** if I'm not mistaken; **non va trascurato il fatto che...** we shouldn't forget *o* overlook the fact that...; **la situazione va peggiorando** the situation is getting worse.

(c) *(salute, situazione)*: **come va? — bene grazie** how are you? — fine thanks; **come va (la salute)? — va bene** how are you? — I'm well; **va bene** all right, O.K. *(fam)*; **come va la scuola?** how's school?; **come vai a scuola?** how are you getting on at school?; **com'è andata?** how did it go?; **ti è andata bene** you have got away with it; **~ di bene in meglio** to get better and better.

(d) *(funzionare)* to work; **la macchina va a benzina** the car runs on petrol.

(e): **~ a qn** *(calzare: scarpe, vestito)* to fit sb; *(essere gradito)*: **quest'idea non mi va** I don't like this idea; **ti va il cioccolato?** do you like chocolate?; **ti va di andare al cinema?** do you feel like going to the cinema?; **ti va (bene) se ci vediamo alle 5?** does it suit you if we meet at 5?; **non mi vanno più questi jeans** these jeans don't fit me any more.

(f) *(essere venduto)* to sell; *(essere di moda)* to be fashionable; **le mele vanno molto** apples are selling well.

(g) *(+infin)*: **~ a pescare/sciare** *etc* to go fishing/skiing *etc*; **~ a prendere qc/qn** to go and fetch sth/sb; **~ a vestirsi** to go and get dressed.

(h): **andiamo!** let's go!; *(coraggio!)* come on!; **va da sé** *(è naturale)* it goes without saying; **va là che ti conosco bene** come off it, I know you too well; **per questa volta vada** let's say no more

about it this time; **vada per una birra** all right, beer it is; **chi va piano va sano e va lontano** *(Proverbio)* slow and steady wins the race; **vai a quel paese!** *(fam)* get lost!
 (i): **andarsene** to go away; **me ne vado** I'm off, I'm going.
 (j) *(+av, prep)* *vedi* **fuori, via** *etc.*
 2 *sm*: **con l'andar del tempo** with the passing of time; **a lungo** ~ in time; ~ **e venire** coming and going; **racconta storie a tutto** ~ she's forever talking rubbish.

andata [an'data] *sf*: **(viaggio di)** ~ outward journey; **all'**~ **c'era brutto tempo** on the outward journey there was bad weather; **biglietto di sola** ~/**di** ~ **e ritorno** single/return ticket.

andatura [anda'tura] *sf* **(a)** *(modo di camminare)* gait, walk. **(b)** *(Sport)* pace; **imporre l'**~ to set the pace.

andazzo [an'dattso] *sm (peg)*: **con o di questo** ~, **finiremo male** the way things are going, we'll finish up in a mess; **le cose stanno prendendo un brutto** ~ things are taking a turn for the worse.

andirivieni [andiri'vjeni] *sm inv* coming and going.

andito ['andito] *sm* hall.

androgino, a [an'drɔdʒino] **1** *ag* androgynous. **2** *sm* hermaphrodite.

androne [an'drone] *sm* entrance hall.

aneddoto [a'neddoto] *sm* anecdote.

anelare [ane'lare] *vi*: ~ **a qc/a fare qc** to long *o* yearn for sth/to do sth.

anelito [a'nelito] *sm (respiro affannoso)* panting; *(fig)*: ~ **(di)** longing (for), yearning (for).

anello [a'nello] *sm (gen, fig)* ring; *(di catena)* link; **ad** ~ ring-shaped; ~ **di fidanzamento/nuziale** engagement/wedding ring.

anemia [ane'mia] *sf* anaemia.

anemico, a, ci, che [a'nɛmiko] **1** *ag* anaemic. **2** *sm/f* anaemic person.

anemone [a'nɛmone] *sm* anemone.

anestesia [aneste'zia] *sf* anaesthesia; **fare a qn un'**~ **locale/totale** to give sb a local/general anaesthetic; **sotto** ~ under anaesthetic, under anaesthesia.

Ande ['ande] *sfpl*: **le** ~ the Andes.

anestesista, i, e [aneste'zista] *sm/f* anaesthetist.

anestetico, a, ci, che [anes'tɛtiko] *ag, sm* anaesthetic.

anestetizzare [anestetid'dzare] *vt* to anaesthetize.

anfibio, a [an'fibjo] **1** *ag* amphibious. **2** *sm* **(a)** *(Zool, veicolo)* amphibian. **(b)**: ~**i** *pl (scarpe)* heavy-duty boots.

anfiteatro [anfite'atro] *sm* amphitheatre.

anfitrione [anfitri'one] *sm* host.

anfora ['anfora] *sf* amphora.

anfratto [an'fratto] *sm* cleft.

angariare [anga'rjare] *vt* to vex.

angelico, a, ci, che [an'dʒeliko] *ag* angelic.

angelo ['andʒelo] *sm* angel; ~ **custode** guardian angel.

angheria [ange'ria] *sf* vexation.

angina [an'dʒina] *sf (tonsillite)* tonsillitis; ~ **pectoris** angina.

anglicanesimo [anglika'nezimo] *sm* anglicanism.

anglicano, a [angli'kano] *ag, sm/f* Anglican.

anglicismo [angli'tʃizmo] *sm* anglicism.

anglicizzare [anglitʃid'dzare] **1** *vt* to anglicize. **2**: ~**rsi** *vr* to become anglicized.

anglista, i, e [an'glista] *sm/f* anglicist.

anglofilo, a [an'glɔfilo] **1** *ag* anglophilic. **2** *sm/f* anglophile.

anglosassone [anglo'sassone] *ag, sm/f* Anglo-Saxon.

angolare [ango'lare] *ag (gen, Geom)* angular;

mobile ~ corner unit; **pietra** ~ *(Archit, fig)* cornerstone.

angolazione [angolat'tsjone] *sf* **(a)** *(di angolo)* angulation. **(b)** *(Fot, Cine, TV, fig)* angle; **visto da questa** ~ seen from this angle.

angolo ['angolo] *sm* **(a)** *(di stanza, tavolo, strada, bocca)* corner; **fare** ~ **con** *(strada)* to run into; **all'**~ **della strada** on *o* at the corner of the street; **scendo al negozio all'**~ I'm just going down to the shop round the corner; **dietro l'**~ *(anche fig)* round the corner; **abito in Via Cairoli** ~ **Via Bersaglio** I live on the corner of Via Cairoli and Via Bersaglio; **ho scoperto degli** ~**i di Londra che non conoscevo** I've discovered some hidden parts of London I never knew before. **(b)** *(Geom)* angle; ~ **retto/acuto/ottuso** right/acute/obtuse angle.

angoloso, a [ango'loso] *ag (oggetto)* angular; *(volto, corpo)* angular, bony.

angora ['angora] *sf*: **d'**~ *(Zool, lana)* angora *attr*.

angoscia [an'gɔʃʃa] *sf (gen, Psic)* anguish.

angosciare [angoʃ'ʃare] **1** *vt* to cause anguish to; **la scena mi ha angosciato** I was very upset by what I saw; **il pensiero della morte mi angoscia** the thought of dying terrifies me. **2**: ~**rsi** *vr*: ~**rsi (per)** *(preoccuparsi)* to become anxious (about); *(provare angoscia)* to get upset (about *o* over).

angoscioso, a [angoʃ'ʃoso] *ag (scena, situazione)* distressing, harrowing; *(attesa)* agonizing.

anguilla [an'gwilla] *sf* eel.

anguria [an'gurja] *sf* watermelon.

angustia [an'gustja] *sf* **(a)** *(di spazio)* lack of space. **(b)** *(povertà)* poverty, want; **vive in** ~ he lives in straitened circumstances. **(c)** *(tristezza)* anguish, distress.

angustiare [angus'tjare] **1** *vt* to torment. **2**: ~**rsi** *vr*: ~**rsi (per)** to become distressed (about).

angusto, a [an'gusto] *ag (locale, letto)* narrow; *(fig: pensiero)* mean, petty; (: *mente)* narrow.

anice ['anitʃe] *sm* **(a)** *(Bot: pianta)* anise; (: *frutto)* aniseed. **(b)** *(liquore)* anisette.

anidride [ani'dride] *sf (Chim)*: ~ **carbonica/solforosa** carbon/sulphur dioxide.

anima ['anima] *sf* **(a)** *(gen)* soul; ~ **gemella** soul mate; **l'**~ **della festa** the life and soul of the party; **volere un bene dell'**~ **a qn** to be extremely fond of sb; **con tutta l'**~ with all one's heart; **mettere l'**~ **in qc/nel fare qc** to put one's heart into sth/into doing sth; **vendere l'**~ **(al diavolo)** to sell one's soul (to the devil); **scommettere l'**~ **(su/che)** *(fig)* to bet one's life (on/that); ~ **e corpo** body and soul, wholeheartedly; **rompere l'**~ **a qn** to drive sb mad; **mi hai rotto l'**~ I've had enough of you; **il nonno buon'**~... Grandfather, God rest his soul...; **la buon'**~ **di Mario** *(defunto)* the dear departed Mario.
 (b) *(persona)* soul; *(abitante)* inhabitant; **un'**~ **in pena** *(anche fig)* a tormented soul; **non c'era neanche un'**~ there wasn't a soul; **non c'era viva** there wasn't a living soul; **il paese conta 1000** ~**e** the town has 1000 inhabitants.

animale [ani'male] **1** *sm (gen, fig)* animal. **2** *ag* animal.

animalesco, a, schi, sche [anima'lesko] *ag (gesto, atteggiamento)* animal-like.

animare [ani'mare] **1** *vt* **(a)** *(dare vita a)* to animate; *(serata, conversazione)* to liven up, enliven; **la gioia le animava il volto** her face shone with joy. **(b)** *(sog: sentimento)* to drive, impel; **era animato dal desiderio di libertà** he was driven by a desire for freedom. **(c)** *(incoraggiare: persona, commercio)* to encourage. **2**: ~**rsi**

vr (persona, oggetto, strada) to come to life; *(festa)* to liven up, become animated; *(scaldarsi: conversazione, persona)* to become animated.

animato, a [ani'mato] ag **(a)** *(vivace)* lively; *(: conversazione)* lively, animated. **(b)** *(vivo)* animate.

animatore, trice [anima'tore] **1** *ag (principio)* guiding; *(forza)* driving. **2** *sm/f (turistico, di festa, gruppo)* organizer; *(di spettacolo)* compère; è sempre lui l'~ della festa he's always the life and soul of the party.

animazione [animat'tsjone] *sf (eccitazione)* excitement; *(vivacità)* liveliness; *(di città, strada)* bustle; *(Cine)* animation; ~ teatrale amateur dramatics.

animo ['animo] *sm* **(a)** *(mente)* mind; stato d'~ state of mind; avere in ~ di fare qc to have a mind to do sth, intend to do sth; mettersi l'~ in pace to set one's mind at rest; ho l'~ turbato I'm upset. **(b)** *(coraggio)* courage; perdersi d'~ to lose heart; fare qc di buon ~ to do sth willingly; fare ~ a qn to cheer sb up; farsi ~ to pluck up courage; fatti ~!, ~! cheer up!, take heart!

animosità [animosi'ta] *sf* animosity.

anisetta [ani'zetta] *sf* anisette.

anitra ['anitra] *sf* = **anatra.**

annacquare [annak'kware] *vt* to dilute; *(vino)* to water down.

annaffiare [annaf'fjare] *vt (fiori, piante)* to water.

annaffiatoio [annaffja'tojo] *sm* watering can.

annali [an'nali] *smpl* annals.

annaspare [annas'pare] *vi (nell'acqua)* to flounder; *(fig: nel buio, nell'incertezza)* to grope.

annata [an'nata] *sf (gen)* year; *(di vino)* vintage, year; vino di ~ vintage wine.

annebbiare [anneb'bjare] **1** *vt (gen, fig)* to cloud. **2:** ~rsi *vr* to become foggy; *(vista)* to become blurred.

annegamento [annega'mento] *sm* drowning; è morto per ~ he drowned.

annegare [anne'gare] **1** *vi (aus essere)* to drown. **2** *vt* to drown; ~ le preoccupazioni nel vino to drown one's sorrows. **3:** ~rsi *vr* to drown o.s.

annegato, a [anne'gato] *sm/f* drowned man/woman.

annerire [anne'rire] **1** *vi (aus essere)* to get black. **2** *vt* to blacken. **3:** ~rsi *vr* to go o become black.

annessione [annes'sjone] *sf (Pol)* annexation.

annesso, a [an'nesso] **1** *pp di* **annettere. 2** *ag (attaccato: gen)* attached; *(: Pol)* annexed; fra ~i e connessi... what with one thing and another...; mi occupo del nuovo progetto con tutti gli ~i e connessi I'm working on the new project and everything relating to it.

annettere [an'nettere] *vt (Pol)* to annexe.

annichilire [anniki'lire] *vt* to annihilate; *(fig)* to devastate.

annidarsi [anni'darsi] *vr (uccello)* to nest; *(fig: persona)* to hide; *(paura, dubbio)* to take root.

annientamento [annjenta'mento] *sm* annihilation, destruction.

annientare [annjen'tare] *vt* to annihilate, destroy.

anniversario [anniver'sarjo] *sm* anniversary.

anno ['anno] *sm* **(a)** year; ~ per ~, ~ dopo ~ year after year; è aperto tutto l'~ it's open all year round; uno studente del primo ~ a first year student; gli ~i 20 the 20s; un ~ di affitto a year's rent; sono ~i che non ti vedo it's been ages since I last saw you, I haven't seen you for ages; correva l'~ di grazia... it was in the year of grace...; ~ luce *(Astron)* light year; ~ santo holy year; Buon A~! Happy New Year! **(b)** *(età):* quanti ~i hai? — ho 40 ~i how old are you? — I'm 40 (years old); quando compi gli ~i? when is

your birthday?; un bambino di 6 ~i a 6-year-old child; porta bene gli ~i she doesn't look her age; porta male gli ~i she looks older than she is.

annodare [anno'dare] *vt (lacci)* to tie; *(cravatta, fune, corda)* to knot; *(: due corde)* to knot o tie together; ~rsi la cravatta to tie one's tie.

annoiare [anno'jare] **1** *vt (recare noia)* to bore; *(seccare)* to annoy; *(disturbare)* to bother. **2:** ~rsi *vr* to get bored.

annoso [an'noso] *ag (albero)* old; *(fig: problema etc)* age-old.

annotare [anno'tare] *vt* **(a)** *(scrivere)* to note down, take down. **(b)** *(Letteratura: testo)* to annotate.

annotazione [annotat'tsjone] *sf* **(a)** *(appunto)* note. **(b)** *(di testo)* annotation.

annottare [annot'tare] *vb impers (aus essere):* annotta night is falling.

annoverare [annove'rare] *vt* to number.

annuale [annu'ale] *ag* annual, yearly.

annualmente [annual'mente] *av* annually, yearly.

annuario [annu'arjo] *sm (gen)* annual publication; *(di scuola etc)* yearbook.

annuire [annu'ire] *vi (assentire: anche:* ~ col capo*)* to nod; *(acconsentire)* to agree.

annullamento [annulla'mento] *sm (vedi vb)* annihilation; cancellation; annulment; quashing.

annullare [annul'lare] **1** *vt* **(a)** *(distruggere)* to annihilate. **(b)** *(francobollo, ordine, contratto)* to cancel; *(Dir: testamento, matrimonio)* to annul; *(: sentenza)* to quash. **2:** ~rsi *vr:* ~rsi a vicenda to cancel each other out; si è completamente annullato nel suo lavoro *(fig)* he has become absorbed in his work to the exclusion of all else.

annullo [an'nullo] *sm (Amm)* cancelling.

annunciare [annun'tʃare] *vt (gen)* to announce; *(predire)* to foretell; *(essere segno di)* to be a sign of; ~ una brutta notizia a qn to break a piece of bad news to sb; il barometro annuncia pioggia the barometer is indicating rain; entrò senza farsi ~ he came in without being announced.

annunciatore, trice [annuntʃa'tore] *sm/f (Radio, TV)* announcer.

annunciazione [annuntʃat'tsjone] *sf (Rel)* annunciation.

annuncio [an'nuntʃo] *sm (gen)* announcement; *(presagio)* sign; mettere un ~ sul giornale to place o put an advertisement in the newspaper; ~ (pubblicitario) advertisement; ~i mortuari *(colonna)* obituary column; ~i economici classified advertisements, small ads.

annuo, a ['annuo] *ag* annual, yearly.

annusare [annu'sare] *vt (anche fig)* to smell; *(cane)* to smell, sniff; ~ tabacco to take snuff.

annuvolamento [annuvola'mento] *sm* clouding (over).

annuvolare [annuvo'lare] **1** *vt* to cloud. **2:** ~rsi *vr* to become cloudy, cloud over.

ano ['ano] *sm* anus.

anodo ['anodo] *sm* anode.

anomalia [anoma'lia] *sf (gen)* anomaly; *(Med)* abnormality; ~ di funzionamento *(Tecn)* technical fault.

anomalo, a [a'nɔmalo] *ag* anomalous.

anonimato [anoni'mato] *sm* anonymity; conservare l'~ to remain anonymous.

anonimo, a [a'nɔnimo] **1** *ag* anonymous; un tipo ~ *(peg)* a colourless character; società ~a *(Comm)* joint stock company. **2** *sm/f (persona)* unknown person; *(pittore etc)* anonymous painter *(o* writer *etc)*.

anormale [anor'male] **1** *ag* abnormal. **2** *sm/f* abnormal person.

anormalità [anormali'ta] *sf inv* abnormality.

ansa ['ansa] *sf (Anat, Geog: curva)* loop.

ansante [an'sante] *ag* out of breath, panting.

ansia ['ansja] *sf* anxiety; **stare in** ~ **(per qn/qc)** to be anxious (about sb/sth); **con** ~ anxiously.

ansietà [ansje'ta] *sf* anxiety.

ansimare [ansi'mare] *vi* to pant, gasp for breath; *(respirare pesantemente)* to breathe heavily.

ansioso, a [an'sjoso] *ag* anxious; *(desideroso):* ~ **di fare qc** anxious *o* eager to do sth.

anta ['anta] *sf (di armadio)* door; *(di finestra)* shutter.

antagonismo [antago'nizmo] *sm* antagonism.

antartico, a, ci, che [an'tartiko] **1** *ag* Antarctic. **2** *sm:* **l'A**~ the Antarctic.

Antartide [an'tartide] *sf* Antarctica.

ante... ['ante] *pref* pre..., ante... .

antebellico, a, ci, che [ante'belliko] *ag* prewar *attr.*

antecedente [antetʃe'dɛnte] **1** *ag* previous, preceding. **2** *sm (Gram, Filosofia)* antecedent; **gli** ~**i** previous history *sg.*

antefatto [ante'fatto] *sm* prior event; **gli** ~**i dell'incidente** the events prior to the accident, what happened before the accident.

anteguerra [ante'gwɛrra] *sf* prewar period; **dell'**~ prewar.

ante litteram ['ante 'litteram] *ag inv* ahead of one's time.

antenato [ante'nato] *sm* ancestor, forefather.

antenna [an'tenna] *sf (Zool)* antenna, feeler; *(Radio, TV)* aerial; **rizzare le** ~**e** *(fig)* to prick up one's ears.

anteporre [ante'porre] *vt:* ~ **qc a qc** to place *o* put sth before sth.

anteposto, a [ante'posto] *pp di* **anteporre**.

anteprima [ante'prima] *sf (Teatro, Cine)* preview; **presentare qc in** ~ to preview sth; **comunichiamo in** ~ **la notizia di...** we are bringing you advance news of... .

anteriore [ante'rjore] *ag* **(a)** *(tempo)* previous, preceding. **(b)** *(parte, sedile)* front *attr.*

antesignano [antesiɲ'ɲano] *sm (fig)* forerunner; *(Storia)* standard-bearer.

anti... ['anti] *pref* **(a)** *(contro)* anti... . **(b)** *(prima)* ante... .

antiaereo, a [antia'ɛreo] *ag* anti-aircraft *attr.*

antiatomico, a, ci, che [antia'tɔmiko] *ag* antinuclear; **rifugio** ~ fallout shelter.

antibiotico, a, ci, che [antibi'ɔtiko] *ag, sm* antibiotic.

anticaglia [anti'kaʎʎa] *sf* junk *no pl.*

anticamera [anti'kamera] *sf (ingresso)* hall; *(Archit)* antechamber; hall; **fare** ~ to be kept waiting; **non mi passerebbe neanche per l'**~ **del cervello** it wouldn't even cross my mind.

antichità [antiki'ta] *sf inv* **(a)** antiquity. **(b):** ~ *pl* antiques; **negozio di** ~ antique shop.

anticiclone [antitʃi'klone] *sm* anticyclone.

anticipare [antitʃi'pare] **1** *vi* to come early, arrive early; ~ **di un giorno** to come *o* arrive a day early. **2** *vt* **(a)** *(spostare prima nel tempo)* to bring forward; ~ **un incontro di 3 giorni** to bring a meeting forward 3 days; ~ **i tempi** *(accelerare)* to speed things up; *(precorrere)* to be ahead of one's time. **(b)** *(precedere: reazione, risposta etc)* to anticipate; ~ **qn nel fare qc** to do sth before sb; **mi ha anticipato** he did it before me. **(c)** *(sorpresa, notizia)* to reveal. **(d)** *(pagare)* to pay in advance; *(prestare)* to lend.

anticipato, a [antitʃi'pato] *ag (prima del previsto)* early; **pagamento** ~ payment in advance.

anticipazione [antitʃipat'tsjone] *sf* **(a)** *(spostamento)* bringing forward; *(pagamento)* payment in advance. **(b)** *(percezione futura)* anticipation; **vi diamo delle** ~**i sui risultati** we have advance news for you on the results.

anticipo [an'titʃipo] *sm (gen, Fin)* advance; **con due giorni di** ~ two days in advance; **arrivare in** ~ to arrive early *o* ahead of time; **avvertire qn in** ~ to warn sb in advance *o* beforehand; **gli ho dato un** ~ **sullo stipendio** I gave him an advance on his salary.

anticlericale [antikleri'kale] *ag, sm/f* anticlerical.

antico, a, chi, che [an'tiko] **1** *ag* **(a)** *(vecchio: mobile, quadro)* antique; *(: manoscritto)* ancient; **all'**~**a** old-fashioned. **(b)** *(di antichità)* ancient. **2:** **gli** ~**chi** *smpl* the ancients.

anticoncezionale [antikontʃettsjo'nale] *ag, sm* contraceptive.

anticonformista, i, e [antikonfor'mista] *ag, sm/f* nonconformist.

anticongelante [antikondʒe'lante] *ag, sm* antifreeze.

anticongiunturale [antikondʒuntu'rale] *ag (Fin):* **misure** ~**i** measures to remedy the economic situation; **soluzione** ~ solution to the (unfavourable) economic situation.

anticorpo [anti'kɔrpo] *sm* antibody.

anticostituzionale [antikostituttsjo'nale] *ag* unconstitutional.

anticrittogamico, a, ci, che [antikritto'gamiko] **1** *ag* fungicidal. **2** *sm* fungicide.

antidiluviano, a [antidilu'vjano] *ag (anche fig)* antediluvian.

antidoping ['anti'doupiŋ] *sm inv (Sport)* dope test.

antidoto [an'tidoto] *sm* antidote.

antieconomico, a, ci, che [antieko'nɔmiko] *ag* uneconomic(al).

antiestetico, a, ci, che [anties'tɛtiko] *ag* unsightly.

antifascismo [antifaʃ'ʃizmo] *sm* antifascism.

antifona [an'tifona] *sf (Mus, Rel)* antiphon; *(fig)* hint; **capire l'**~ to take the hint.

antifurto [anti'furto] *sm* anti-theft device.

antigelo [anti'dʒelo] **1** *ag inv* antifreeze *attr.* **2** *sm (per motore)* antifreeze; *(per cristalli)* de-icer.

antigienico, a, ci, che [anti'dʒeniko] *ag* unhygienic.

Antille [an'tille] *sfpl:* **le** ~ the West Indies.

antilope [an'tilope] *sf* antelope.

antimonio [anti'mɔnjo] *sm* antimony.

antincendio [antin'tʃendjo] *ag inv* fire *attr;* **bombola** ~ fire extinguisher.

antinebbia [anti'nebbja] *sm inv (anche:* **faro** ~**:** *Aut)* fog lamp.

antinevralgico, a, ci, che [antine'vraldʒiko] **1** *ag* painkilling. **2** *sm* painkiller.

antiorario [antio'rarjo] *ag:* **in senso** ~ in an anti-clockwise direction, anticlockwise.

antipastiera [antipas'tjera] *sf* hors d'œuvre tray.

antipasto [anti'pasto] *sm* hors d'œuvre.

antipatia [antipa'tia] *sf* antipathy, dislike; **prendere in** ~ to take an aversion *o* a dislike to.

antipatico, a, ci, che [anti'patiko] **1** *ag* unpleasant, disagreeable. **2** *sm/f* unpleasant person; *(rompiscatole)* nuisance.

antipodi [an'tipodi] *smpl:* **gli** ~ the antipodes; **essere agli** ~ *(fig)* to be poles apart.

antiquariato [antikwa'rjato] *sm (cose antiche)* antiques *pl;* *(Comm)* antique trade; **negozio di** ~ antique shop; **un pezzo d'**~ an antique.

antiquario [anti'kwarjo] *sm* antique dealer; **negozio di** ~ antique shop.

antiquato, a [anti'kwato] *ag* antiquated, old-fashioned.

antiruggine |anti'ruddʒinc| 1 *ag* anti-rust *attr*. 2 *sf* rust preventer.
antisemita, i, e |antisc'mita| 1 *ag* anti-semitic. 2 *sm* anti-semite.
antisemitismo |antiscmi'tizmo| *sm* anti-semitism.
antisettico, a, ci, che |anti'sɛttiko| *ag, sm* antiseptic.
antistante |antis'tantc| *ag* opposite.
antitesi |an'titczi| *sf inv* antithesis.
antitetanico, a, ci, che |antitc'taniko| *ag (siero, iniezione etc)* tetanus *attr*.
antitetico, a, ci, che |anti'tctiko| *ag* antithetical.
antivigilia |antivi'dʒilja| *sf*: **l'~ di Natale/Capodanno** the day before Christmas Eve/New Year's Eve.
antologia, gie |antolo'dʒia| *sf* anthology.
antonomasia |antono'mazja| *sf* antonomasia; **per ~ par** excellence.
antracite |antra'tʃitc| *sf* anthracite.
antro |'antro| *sm* cave, cavern.
antropofago, a, gi, ghe |antro'pɔfago| 1 *ag* cannibal *attr*, man-eating. 2 *sm* cannibal, man-eater.
antropologia |antropolo'dʒia| *sf* anthropology.
antropologico, a, ci, che |antropo'lɔdʒiko| *ag* anthropological.
antropologo, a, gi, ghe |antro'pɔlogo| *sm/f* anthropologist.
anulare |anu'larc| 1 *ag* ring *attr*; **raccordo ~** *(Aut)* ring road. 2 *sm (Anat)* ring finger.
anzi |'antsi| *cong* **(a)** *(avversativo)* on the contrary. **(b)** *(rafforzativo)* or rather, or better still.
anzianità |antsjani'ta| *sf (età avanzata)* old age; *(nel lavoro)* seniority.
anziano, a |an'tsjano| 1 *ag (vecchio)* elderly, old; *(socio)* senior. 2 *sm/f* senior citizen, old person.
anziché |antsi'kc| *cong* rather than.
anzitempo |antsi'tcmpo| *av (in anticipo)* early; **morire ~** to die before one's time.
anzitutto |antsi'tutto| *av* first of all.
aorta |a'ɔrta| *sf* aorta.
apartheid |a'parthcit| *sm (Pol)* apartheid.
apartitico, a, ci, che |apar'titiko| *ag (Pol)* nonparty *attr*.
apatia |apa'tia| *sf* apathy.
apatico, a, ci, che |a'patiko| *ag* apathetic.
ape |'apc| *sf* bee; **~ regina** queen bee.
aperitivo |apcri'tivo| *sm* aperitif.
apertamente |apcrta'mcntc| *av* openly.
aperto, a |a'pcrto| 1 *pp di* **aprire**. 2 *ag (gen, fig)* open; *(rubinetto)* on, running; *(gas)* on; *(mentalità)* open-minded; **lasciare la macchina ~a** to leave the car unlocked; **a cuore ~** *(fig)* frankly, sincerely; **a bocca ~a** open-mouthed; **rimanere a bocca ~a** *(fig)* to be taken aback; **all'aria ~a** in the open air; **all'~** *av* outdoors; *ag (cinema, piscina etc)* open-air *attr*; *(giochi, vacanze)* outdoor *attr*.
apertura |apcr'tura| *sf (gen, Carte)* opening; *(Fot)* aperture; **in ~ di** at the beginning of; **~ alare** wing span; **~ mentale** open-mindedness.
apice |'apitʃc| *sm (di montagna)* peak, summit; *(fig)* height, peak; **essere all'~ del successo** to be at the height *o* peak of one's success.
apicoltore |apikol'torc| *sm* beekeeper.
apicoltura |apikol'tura| *sf* beekeeping.
apnea |ap'nɛa| *sf*: **immergersi in ~** to dive without breathing apparatus.
apocalisse |apoka'lissc| *sf (Rel)*: **l'A~** (the book of) Revelation, the Apocalypse; *(fig)* apocalypse.
apocalittico, a, ci, che |apoka'littiko| *ag* apocalyptic.
apocrifo, a |a'pɔkrifo| *ag* apocryphal.
apogeo |apo'dʒɛo| *sm (Astron, fig)* apogee.

apolide |a'pɔlidc| *(Pol)* 1 *ag* stateless. 2 *sm/f* stateless person.
apolitico, a, ci, che |apo'litiko| *ag (neutrale)* nonpolitical; *(indifferente)* apolitical.
apologia, gie |apolo'dʒia| *sf* apology, apologia; **fare l'~ di qn** to praise sb; **accusare qn di ~ di reato** *(Dir)* to accuse sb of criminal sympathies.
apoplettico, a, ci, che |apo'plɛttiko| *ag* apoplectic; **colpo ~** apoplectic fit.
a posteriori |a poste'rjɔri| 1 *ag inv* after the event *(dopo sostantivo)*. 2 *av* looking back.
apostolato |aposto'lato| *sm (Rel)* apostolate; **fare opera di ~** *(anche fig)* to spread the word.
apostolico, a, ci, che |apos'tɔliko| *ag* apostolic.
apostolo |a'pɔstolo| *sm* apostle.
apostrofare |apostro'farc| *vt* **(a)** *(parola)* to write with an apostrophe. **(b)** *(persona)* to address.
apostrofo |a'pɔstrofo| *sm (segno)* apostrophe.
apoteosi |apotc'ɔzi| *sf inv* apotheosis.
appagamento |appaga'mcnto| *sm (vedi vb)* satisfaction; fulfilment.
appagare |appa'garc| 1 *vt (gen)* to satisfy; *(desiderio)* to fulfil; *(sete, fame)* to appease, satisfy. 2: **~rsi** *vr*: **~rsi (di)** to be satisfied (with).
appaiare |appa'jarc| *vt (oggetti)* to pair; *(animali)* to match.
appallottolare |appallotto'larc| 1 *vt (carta, foglio)* to screw into a ball. 2: **~rsi** *vr (gatto)* to roll up into a ball.
appaltare |appal'tarc| *vt (dare in appalto)* to let out on contract; *(assumere in appalto)* to undertake on contract.
appaltatore |appalta'torc| *sm* contractor.
appalto |ap'palto| *sm* contract; **dare in ~** to let out on contract; **prendere in ~** to take on a contract for; **gara di ~** invitation to tender.
appannare |appan'narc| 1 *vt* to steam up. 2: **~rsi** *vr (vetro, superficie)* to steam up; *(vista)* to blur.
apparato |appa'rato| *sm* **(a)** equipment, machinery; **~ scenico** *(Teatro)* set; **~ burocratico** bureaucratic machinery. **(b)** *(Anat, Bio)* apparatus. **(c)** *(sfoggio)* display, pomp.
apparecchiare |apparck'kjarc| *vt* to prepare, get ready; **~ (la tavola)** to set *o* lay the table.
apparecchiatura |apparckkja'tura| *sf* **(a)** *(Tecn: impianto)* equipment *no pl*; *(: macchina)* machine, device. **(b)** *(Tessitura)* finishing.
apparecchio |appa'rckkjo| *sm* **(a)** *(gen)* instrument, device; *(per denti)* brace; **~ acustico** hearing aid. **(b)** *(Radio, TV)* set. **(c)** *(Aer)* aircraft *inv*.
apparente |appa'rcntc| *ag* apparent.
apparenza |appa'rcntsa| *sf* **(a)** *(aspetto)* appearance; **l'~ inganna** appearances can be deceptive; **in o all'~** to all appearances; **questo lavoro è facile all'~** this job looks easy. **(b)**: **~e** *pl (convenienze sociali)* appearances; **badare alle ~e** to care about appearances.
apparire |appa'rirc| 1 *vi (aus* **essere)** **(a)** *(mostrarsi)* to appear; **la verità gli apparve all'improvviso** the truth suddenly dawned on him. **(b)** *(sembrare)* to seem, appear; **appare che...** it appears *o* turns out that.... 2 *vt (sembrare)* to appear to be.
appariscente |apparif'fcntc| *ag (vestito)* showy; *(colore)* gaudy, garish; *(bellezza)* striking.
apparizione |appari'tsjonc| *sf (comparsa)* appearance; *(fantasma)* apparition.
apparso, a |ap'parso| *pp di* **apparire**.
appartamento |apparta'mcnto| *sm* flat, apartment *(Am)*.
appartarsi |appar'tarsi| *vr* to withdraw.
appartato, a |appar'tato| *ag (luogo)* secluded.
appartenente |apparte'ncntc| 1 *ag*: **~ a** belonging to. 2 *sm/f*: **~ (a)** member (of).

appartenenza [apparte'nɛntsa] *sf:* ~ **(a)** *(gen)* belonging (to); *(a un partito, club)* membership (of).

appartenere [apparte'nere] *vi:* ~ **a (a)** *(chiesa, fede)* to belong to; *(club, partito)* to be a member of. **(b)** *(essere di proprietà)* to belong to; **mi appartiene di diritto** it belongs to me by right.

appassionante [appassjo'nante] *ag* thrilling, exciting.

appassionare [appassjo'nare] **1** *vt* to grip, fascinate. **2:** ~**rsi** *vr:* ~**rsi a** to develop a passion for.

appassionato, a [appassjo'nato] **1** *ag* **(a)** *(entusiasta):* ~ **(di)** keen (on). **(b)** *(passionale)* passionate. **2** *sm/f* enthusiast.

appassire [appas'sire] *vi (aus essere) (pianta)* to wither; *(fig: speranze)* to fade.

appellare [appel'lare] **1** *vt (chiamare)* to call. **2:** ~**rsi** *vr:* ~**rsi a** to appeal to; **mi appello alla vostra generosità** I appeal to your generosity; **si è appellato contro la sentenza** *(Dir)* he appealed against the sentence.

appellativo [appella'tivo] *sm* name.

appello [ap'pɛllo] *sm* **(a)** *(chiamata per nome)* roll-call; **fare l'**~ *(Scol)* to call the register; *(Mil)* to call the roll. **(b)** *(Univ: sessione d'esame)* exam session. **(c)** *(Dir)* appeal; **corte d'**~ court of appeal. **(d)** *(invocazione)* appeal; **fare** ~ **a** *(anche fig)* to call upon.

appena [ap'pena] **1** *av (a stento)* hardly, scarcely; *(solamente, da poco)* just; **sono** ~ **le 9** it's only just 9 o'clock; **sarà alto** ~ ~ **un metro e 80** he is certainly no more than 6 feet tall. **2** *cong* as soon as; ~ **possibile** as soon as possible; ~ **(furono) arrivati...** as soon as they had arrived...; ~ **...che** *o* **quando no sooner** ... than; **era appena tornato quando è dovuto ripartire** no sooner *o* scarcely had he returned than he had to leave again; **non** ~ **ho finito, vado** I'll leave the moment I've finished.

appendere [ap'pendere] **1** *vt:* ~ **(a** *o* **su)** to hang (on). **2:** ~**rsi** *vr:* ~**rsi a qc/qn** to hang on to sth/sb.

appendiabiti [appendi'abiti] *sm inv* hook, peg; *(mobile)* hall stand.

appendice [appen'ditʃe] *sf (Anat, di libro)* appendix; **romanzo d'**~ popular serial; **letteratura d'**~ popular literature.

appendicite [appendi'tʃite] *sf* appendicitis.

Appennini [appen'nini] *smpl:* **gli** ~ the Apennines.

appenninico, a, ci, che [appen'niniko] *ag* Apennine.

appesantire [appesan'tire] **1** *vt (anche fig)* to weigh down; *((atmosfera)* to make strained; **tutti questi dolci mi hanno appesantito lo stomaco** all these sweet things are lying on my stomach. **2:** ~**rsi** *vr (gen)* to grow heavier; *(ingrassare)* to put on weight; *(fig: atmosfera)* to become strained.

appeso, a [ap'peso] *pp di* **appendere**.

appestare [appes'tare] *vt (Med)* to infect with plague; *(: contagiare)* to infect; **il fumo delle sigarette ha appestato la stanza** the cigarette smoke made the room stink.

appestato, a [appes'tato] *ag (Med)* infected with plague; *(: contagioso)* infected; *(aria)* stinking.

appetibile [appe'tibile] *ag (cibo)* appetizing; *(lavoro, ragazza)* attractive.

appetito [appe'tito] *sm (gen, fig)* appetite; **avere** ~ to have an appetite; **non ho** ~ I'm not hungry; **buon** ~! enjoy your meal!; **stuzzicare l'**~ to whet one's appetite.

appetitoso, a [appeti'toso] *ag (cibo)* appetizing; *(fig)* attractive.

appezzamento [appettsa'mento] *sm (anche:* ~ **di terreno)** plot, piece of ground.

appianamento [appjana'mento] *sm (vedi vt)* levelling; ironing out, settlement.

appianare [appja'nare] **1** *vt (terreno)* to level; *(fig: contesa, lite)* to iron out, settle. **2:** ~**rsi** *vr (divergenze)* to be ironed out.

appiattire [appjat'tire] **1** *vt* to flatten; *(fig: rendere monotono)* to make dull, make boring. **2:** ~**rsi** *vr (oggetto)* to become flatter; *(persona)* to flatten o.s.; *(fig)* to become dull; **si appiatti al o contro il muro** he flattened himself against the wall.

appiccare [appik'kare] *vt:* ~ **il fuoco a qc** to set fire to sth, set sth on fire.

appiccicare [appittʃi'kare] **1** *vi* to be sticky. **2** *vt:* ~ **(a, su)** to stick (on); ~ **un soprannome a qn** to pin a nickname on sb. **3:** ~**rsi** *vr:* ~**rsi (a)** to stick (to); *(fig: persona)* to cling (to).

appiccicoso, a [appittʃi'koso] *ag*, **appiccicaticcio, a, ci, ce** [appittʃika'tittʃo] *ag* sticky; *(fig: persona):* **essere** ~ to cling like a leech.

appiedato, a [appje'dato] *ag:* **rimanere** ~ to be left without means of transport.

appigliarsi [appiʎ'ʎarsi] *vr:* ~ **a** *(gen)* to grasp, seize (hold of); **non appigliarti a quella scusa** don't try that as an excuse.

appiglio [ap'piʎʎo] *sm* handhold; *(fig: pretesto)* pretext, excuse.

appiombo [ap'pjombo] **1** *sm* perpendicularity; *(di muro)* plumb. **2** *av* perpendicularly.

appioppare [appjop'pare] *vt:* ~ **qc a qn** *(nomignolo)* to pin sth on sb; *(compito difficile)* to saddle sb with sth; **gli ha appioppato un pugno sul muso** he punched him in the face.

appisolarsi [appizo'larsi] *vr* to doze off.

applaudire [applau'dire] **1** *vi* to applaud, clap. **2** *vt (anche fig)* to applaud.

applaudito, a [applau'dito] *ag* famous, celebrated.

applauso [ap'plauzo] *sm* applause *no pl;* **un** ~ **a** round of applause.

applicabile [appli'kabile] *ag:* ~ **(a)** applicable (to).

applicare [appli'kare] **1** *vt (gen)* to apply; *(cucire)* to sew on; ~ **la mente a qc** to apply one's mind to sth; **(fare)** ~ **una legge** to enforce a law; ~ **una tassa** to impose a tax. **2:** ~**rsi** *vr:* ~**rsi (a, in)** to apply o.s. (to).

applicato, a [appli'kato] **1** *ag (arte, scienze)* applied. **2** *sm (Amm)* clerk.

applicazione [applikat'tsjone] *sf* **(a)** *(gen)* application; *(di legge, norma)* enforcement; ~**i tecniche** *(a scuola)* practical subjects. **(b)** *(su stoffa)* appliqué.

applique [a'plik] *sf inv* wall light.

appoggiare [appod'dʒare] **1** *vt* **(a)** *(posare):* ~ **qc su qc** to put sth (down) on sth, lay sth (down) on sth. **(b)** *(mettere contro):* ~ **qc a qc** to lean *o* rest sth against sth. **(c)** *(sostenere: idea, candidato)* to support, back. **2** *vi:* ~ **su** to rest on. **3:** ~**rsi** *vr (reggersi):* ~**rsi a** to lean against; *(fig)* to rely on.

appoggiatesta [appoddʒa'testa] *sm inv* headrest.

appoggio [ap'poddʒo] *sm (gen, fig)* support; **ho un** ~ **importante al ministero** I have an important contact in the ministry.

appollaiarsi [appolla'jarsi] *vr (anche fig)* to perch.

apporre [ap'porre] *vt (sigillo, nome)* to affix; *(firma)* to append.

apportare [appor'tare] *vt (novità, cambiamento)* to bring (about); ~ **modifiche a** to modify.

apporto [ap'porto] *sm (gen, Fin)* contribution.

appositamente [appozita'mente] *av (apposta)* on purpose; *(specialmente)* specially.

apposito, a [ap'pozito] *ag (adatto)* appropriate, proper; *(fatto appositamente)* special.

apposizione [appozit'tsjone] *sf (Gram)* apposition.

apposta [ap'posta] *av (intenzionalmente)* on purpose, intentionally; (*proprio*) specially; **neanche a farlo ~,** ... by sheer coincidence, ...

appostamento [apposta'mento] *sm* (*agguato*) ambush; (*Mil*) post.

appostare [appos'tare] **1** *vt* (*Mil*) to post, station. **2:** **~rsi** *vr* to lie in wait.

apposto, a [ap'posto] *pp di* **apporre.**

apprendere [ap'prɛndere] **1** *vi* to learn. **2** *vt* (*imparare*) to learn; (*venire a sapere*) to learn, find out; **hai appreso la notizia?** have you heard the news?

apprendimento [apprendi'mento] *sm* learning.

apprendista, i, e [appren'dista] *sm/f* apprentice.

apprendistato [apprendis'tato] *sm* apprenticeship; **fare l'~** to serve one's apprenticeship.

apprensione [appren'sjone] *sf* apprehension; **essere in uno stato di ~** to be anxious; **non stare in ~ don't** worry.

apprensivo, a [appren'sivo] *ag* apprehensive, anxious.

appreso, a [ap'preso] *pp di* **apprendere.**

appresso [ap'presso] **1** *av* (*vicino*) nearby, close by. **2: ~ a** *prep* near, close to; **me lo porto sempre ~ I** always carry it with me. **3** *ag inv*: **il giorno ~** the next day, the day after.

apprestare [appres'tare] **1** *vt* to prepare, get ready. **2: ~rsi** *vr*: **~rsi a fare qc** to get ready to do sth.

appretto [ap'pretto] *sm* starch.

apprezzabile [appret'tsabile] *ag* (*notevole*) noteworthy, significant; (*percepibile*) appreciable; **è un'opera ~ da tutti** it is a work which everybody can enjoy.

apprezzamento [apprettsa'mento] *sm* **(a)** appreciation. **(b)** (*commento*) comment; **fare ~i su** to make comments about, pass comment on.

apprezzare [appret'tsare] *vt* to appreciate.

approccio [ap'prɔttʃo] *sm* approach.

approdare [appro'dare] *vi* (*Naut*) to land; (*fig*): **~ a** to arrive at; **non approderà a nulla** (*piano, progetto*) it won't come to anything; (*persona*) he won't achieve anything.

approdo [ap'prɔdo] *sm* (*Naut: l'approdare*) landing; ((*luogo*) landing place.

approfittare [approfit'tare] *vi*: **~ di** (*persona, situazione etc*) to take advantage of; **dovresti ~ dell'occasione** you should make the most of the opportunity.

approfondimento [approfondi'mento] *sm* deepening; **per l'~ di questo argomento si consulti...** for a thorough examination of this subject consult... .

approfondire [approfon'dire] **1** *vt* (*fossa*) to deepen, make deeper; (*fig: conoscenza*) to deepen, increase; (*argomento*) to go into; **~ un problema** to go into a problem in more depth. **2: ~rsi** *vr* (*gen, fig*) to deepen; (*peggiorare*) to get worse.

approntare [appron'tare] *vt* to prepare, get ready.

appropriarsi [appro'prjarsi] *vr*: **~ di qc** to appropriate sth, take possession of sth.

appropriato, a [appro'prjato] *ag* appropriate, suitable.

appropriazione [approprjat'tsjone] *sf* appropriation; **~ indebita** (*Dir*) embezzlement.

approssimare [approssi'mare] **1** *vt* (*cifra*): **~ per eccesso/per difetto** to round up/down. **2: ~rsi** *vr*: **~rsi a** to approach, draw near.

approssimativo, a [approssima'tivo] *ag* (*calcolo*) rough; (*numero*) approximate; **è stato molto ~ nel darmi informazioni** the information he gave me was very vague.

approssimazione [approssimat'tsjone] *sf* approximation; **per ~** approximately, roughly.

approvare [appro'vare] *vt* **(a)** (*comportamento,*

decisione) to approve of. **(b)** (*candidato, legge*) to pass; (*mozione*) to approve.

approvazione [approvat'tsjone] *sf* (*vedi vb*) approval; passing.

approvvigionamento [approvvidʒona'mento] *sm* **(a)** (*di cibo*) supplying. **(b): ~i** *pl* provisions, supplies.

approvvigionare [approvvidʒo'nare] **1** *vt*: **~ (di)** to supply (with). **2: ~rsi** *vr* (*fare provviste*): **~rsi (di)** to stock up (with).

appuntamento [appunta'mento] *sm* (*d'affari, dal medico*) appointment; (: *con amici, amoroso*) date.

appuntare[1] [appun'tare] **1** *vt* **(a)** (*matita*) to sharpen. **(b)** (*puntare: dito, spada*) to point. **(c)** (*fissare con spillo*) to pin (on). **2: ~rsi** *vr* (*interesse, attenzione*): **~rsi su** to be focussed on.

appuntare[2] [appun'tare] *vt* (*prendere appunti*) to note down, take note of.

appuntato [appun'tato] *sm* (*Carabinieri*) corporal.

appuntino [appun'tino] *av* perfectly.

appuntire [appun'tire] *vt* to sharpen.

appunto[1] [ap'punto] *sm* **(a)** (*nota*) note; **prendere ~i** to take notes. **(b)** (*rimprovero*) reproach; **fare un ~ a qn** to find fault with sb.

appunto[2] [ap'punto] *av* (*precisamente*) exactly; **dicevo ~ ieri** I was just saying yesterday; **si parlava (per l')~ di questo** we were talking about that very thing.

appurare [appu'rare] **1** *vt* (*verificare*) to check, verify; (: *verità*) to ascertain. **2: ~rsi** *vr*: **~rsi di qc/che** to make sure of sth/that, check sth/that.

apribottiglie [apribot'tiʎʎe] *sm inv* bottle-opener.

aprile [a'prile] *sm* April; **pesce d'~!** April Fool!; *per uso vedi* **luglio.**

a priori [a pri'ɔri] *av* a priori.

aprioristico, a, ci, che [aprio'ristiko] *ag* a priori.

apripista [apri'pista] *sm inv* (*Sci*) forerunner.

aprire [a'prire] **1** *vt* **(a)** (*gen*) to open; (*porta chiusa a chiave*) to unlock; (*vestito, camicia*) to undo, unfasten; (*ali: anche fig*) to spread; **va' ad aprire (la porta)** go and answer the door; **non ha aperto bocca** (*fig*) he didn't say a word, he didn't open his mouth; **tutto ciò mi ha aperto gli occhi** (*fig*) all that was an eye-opener to me; **questo dolce mi ha appena aperto lo stomaco** this cake has only just whetted my appetite; **apri bene gli orecchi** listen carefully; **~rsi un passaggio nella folla** to cut one's way through the crowd; **il corteo ha aperto un varco tra la folla** the procession made its way through the crowd.

(b) (*gas, radio*) to turn on, switch on, put on; (*acqua, rubinetto*) to turn on.

(c) (*istituire: negozio, club, conto*) to open (up); (*inchiesta*) to open, set up; (*strada*) to build; **~ bottega** to open shop.

(d) (*cominciare: anno, stagione*) to start, open; (*lista*) to head; (*processione*) to lead; **~ (il gioco)** (*Carte*) to open play; **~ le ostilità** (*Mil*) to start up *o* begin hostilities.

(e) (*Dir: testamento*) to read.

2: ~rsi *vr* **(a)** (*gen*) to open; (*fiore*) to open (up); **la finestra si apre sulla piazza** the window looks onto the square; **la porta dev'essersi aperta** the door must have come open; **quest'abito si apre sul davanti** this dress undoes *o* unfastens at the front; **la vita che le si apre davanti** the life which is opening in front of *o* before her; **mi si aprì davanti la vista del mare** the sea appeared before me; **mi si è aperto lo stomaco** I feel rather peckish; **davanti a quella scena si è aperto il cuore** (*commuoversi*) she was moved by the scene before her; (*rallegrarsi*) the scene gladdened her heart; **apriti cielo!** heaven forbid!

(b): ~**rsi a** *(amore, esperienza)* to become aware of; *(persona: confidarsi)* to open one's heart to.

(c) *(cominciare)* to start, open.

apriscatole [apris'katole] *sm inv* tin-opener.

aquila ['akwila] *sf* eagle; ~ **reale** golden eagle; **sei un'~!** *(anche iro)* you're a genius!

aquilino, a [akwi'lino] *ag* aquiline.

aquilone [akwi'lone] *sm* **(a)** *(vento)* north wind. **(b)** *(giocattolo)* kite.

ara ['ara] *sf* altar.

arabesco, schi [ara'besko] *sm* arabesque.

Arabia Saudita [a'rabja sau'dita] *sf* Saudi Arabia.

arabico, a, ci, che [a'rabiko] *ag* Arabic; **deserto ~** Arabian desert; **penisola ~a** Arabian peninsula.

arabile [a'rabile] *ag* arable.

arabo, a ['arabo] **1** *ag (popolo, paesi)* Arab; *(lingua, arte)* Arabic, Arab; **numeri ~i** Arabic numerals. **2** *sm/f* Arab. **3** *sm (lingua)* Arabic; **questo per me è ~** *(fig)* it's all Greek to me; **parlare ~** *(fig)* to speak double-dutch.

arachide [a'rakide] *sf* peanut, groundnut.

aragosta [ara'gosta] **1** *sf* spiny lobster. **2** *ag inv: color ~* bright orange.

araldica [a'raldika] *sf* heraldry.

araldo [a'raldo] *sm* herald.

aranceto [aran'tʃeto] *sm* orange grove.

arancia, ce [a'rantʃa] *sf* orange.

aranciata [aran'tʃata] *sf* orangeade.

arancio [a'rantʃo] **1** *sm* orange tree; *(colore)* orange; **fiori di ~** orange blossom *sg.* **2** *ag inv* orange.

arancione [aran'tʃone] *ag inv:* **(color)** ~ bright orange.

arare [a'rare] *vt* to plough.

aratore [ara'tore] *sm* ploughman.

aratro [a'ratro] *sm* plough.

aratura [ara'tura] *sf* ploughing.

arazzo [a'rattso] *sm* tapestry.

arbitraggio [arbi'traddʒo] *sm* **(a)** *(Sport)* refereeing; *(: Tennis, Cricket)* umpiring. **(b)** *(Dir)* arbitration.

arbitrare [arbi'trare] *vt (Sport)* to referee; *(: Tennis, Cricket)* to umpire.

arbitrario, a [arbi'trarjo] *ag* arbitrary.

arbitrio [ar'bitrjo] *sm (capacità, potere)* will; **libero ~** free will; **prendersi l'~ di fare qc** to take the liberty of doing sth.

arbitro ['arbitro] *sm* **(a)** *(Sport)* referee; *(: Cricket, Tennis)* umpire. **(b)** *(di contese)* arbitrator; *(fig: di moda etc)* arbiter.

arboscello [arboʃ'ʃɛllo] *sm* sapling.

arbusto [ar'busto] *sm* shrub.

arca ['arka] *sf* ark; ~ **di Noè** Noah's Ark.

arcaico, a, ci, che [ar'kaiko] *ag* archaic.

arcaismo [arka'izmo] *sm* archaism.

arcangelo [ar'kandʒelo] *sm* archangel.

arcano, a [ar'kano] **1** *ag* arcane. **2** *sm* mystery.

arcata [ar'kata] *sf (Archit, Anat)* arch.

archeologia [arkeolo'dʒia] *sf* archaeology.

archeologico, a, ci, che [arkeo'lɔdʒiko] *ag* archaeological.

archeologo, a, gi, ghe [arke'ɔlogo] *sm/f* archaeologist.

archetipo [ar'kɛtipo] *sm* archetype.

archetto [ar'ketto] *sm (Mus)* bow.

architettare [arkitet'tare] *vt (fig: ideare)* to devise; *(: macchinare)* to plan, concoct.

architetto [arki'tetto] *sm* architect.

architettonico, a, ci, che [arkitet'tɔniko] *ag* architectural.

architettura [arkitet'tura] *sf* architecture.

architrave [arki'trave] *sm* architrave.

archiviare [arki'vjare] *vt (documenti)* to file; *(Dir)* to dismiss; **per questa volta archiviamo la faccenda** *(passiamoci sopra)* let's forget about it this time.

archivio [ar'kivjo] *sm (insieme di documenti, luogo)* archives *pl*; *(in ufficio: mobile)* filing cabinet.

archivista, i, e [arki'vista] *sm/f (Amm)* archivist; *(in ufficio)* filing clerk.

arciere [ar'tʃere] *sm* archer.

arcigno, a [ar'tʃiɲɲo] *ag (espressione)* frowning; *(persona)* severe.

arcione [ar'tʃone] *sm* saddlebow; **montare in ~** to get into the saddle.

arcipelago, ghi [artʃi'pelago] *sm* archipelago.

arcivescovile [artʃivesko'vile] *ag* of an archbishop *(o archbishops)*; **palazzo ~** archbishop's palace.

arcivescovo [artʃi'veskovo] *sm* archbishop.

arco, chi ['arko] *sm* **(a)** *(arma, Mus)* bow; ~**chi** *(strumenti ad ~)* string(ed) instruments, strings. **(b)** *(Geom)* arc; *(Archit, forma)* arch; **ad ~** arched; ~ **trionfale** triumphal arch. **(c)** *(lasso di tempo)* space; **nell'~ di 3 settimane** within the space of 3 weeks; **la somma verrà pagata in un ~ di 6 mesi** the sum will be paid over a period of 6 months.

arcobaleno [arkoba'leno] *sm* rainbow.

arcuare [arku'are] *vt (schiena)* to arch; *(bastone)* to bend.

arcuato, a [arku'ato] *ag (gen)* curved, bent; *(sopracciglia)* arched.

ardente [ar'dɛnte] *ag (sole, fuoco)* blazing, burning; *(sguardo)* passionate; *(ammiratore)* ardent; *(passione)* ardent, burning; *(preghiera, desiderio)* fervent.

ardere ['ardere] **1** *vt (anche fig)* to burn; **legna da ~** firewood. **2** *vi (aus essere)* to burn; ~ **di passione/dalla curiosità** to burn with passion/curiosity; ~ **d'amore** to burn with love.

ardesia [ar'dɛzja] *sf (minerale)* slate; *(colore)* slate-grey.

ardimento [ardi'mento] *sm* daring.

ardimentoso, a [ardimen'toso] *ag* daring, bold.

ardire [ar'dire] **1** *vi:* ~ **(di) fare qc** to dare (to) do sth. **2** *sm (audacia)* daring, boldness; *(impudenza)* impudence.

ardito, a [ar'dito] *ag (coraggioso)* brave; *(temerario)* daring; *(impertinente)* forward; **impresa ~a** risky undertaking; **scollatura ~a** daring neckline.

ardore [ar'dore] *sm (calore intenso)* heat; *(fig: passione)* ardour; *(: fervore)* fervour, eagerness.

arduo, a ['arduo] *ag (impresa)* arduous; *(problema)* difficult; *(salita)* steep.

area ['area] *sf* **(a)** *(gen, Geom)* area; ~ **di rigore** *(Sport)* penalty area; ~ **di servizio** *(Aut)* service area; **nell'~ dei partiti di sinistra** among the parties of the left. **(b)** *(Edil)* land, ground; ~ **fabbricabile** building land.

arena [a'rena] *sf (gen, fig)* arena; *(sabbia)* sand.

arenarsi [are'narsi] *vr (Naut)* to run aground; *(fig: trattative)* to come to a standstill; **la mia pratica si è arenata** my file is lying forgotten on somebody's desk.

arenaria [are'narja] *sf* sandstone.

arenile [are'nile] *sm* strand.

argano ['argano] *sm* winch; *(Naut)* capstan.

argentare [ardʒen'tare] *vt* to silver-plate.

argentato, a [ardʒen'tato] *ag* silver-plated; *(colore)* silver, silvery; *(capelli)* silver(-grey).

argenteo, a [ar'dʒɛnteo] *ag* silver, silvery.

argenteria [ardʒente'ria] *sf (oggetti)* silverware, silver; *(fabbrica)* silverware factory.

argentiere [ardʒen'tjɛre] *sm* silversmith.

Argentina [ardʒen'tina] sf Argentina.

argentino¹, a [ardʒen'tino] ag silvery.

argentino², a [ardʒen'tino] ag, sm/f (dell'Argentina) Argentinian.

argento [ar'dʒento] sm **(a)** silver; **piatto d'**~ silver dish; **capelli d'**~ silver(-grey) hair; ~ **vivo** (Chim) quicksilver; **avere l'**~ **(vivo) addosso** (fig) to be fidgety. **(b):** ~**i** pl (argenteria) silverware sg, silver sg.

argilla [ar'dʒilla] sf clay.

argilloso, a [ardʒil'loso] ag clayey.

arginare [ardʒi'nare] vt (fiume, acque) to embank; (: con diga) to dyke up; (fig: inflazione, corruzione) to check; (: spese) to limit; ~ **la piena** to stem the flow of water; ~ **l'avanzata nemica** to hold the enemy advance.

argine ['ardʒine] sm (di fiume) embankment, bank; **far** ~ **a, porre un** ~ **a** (fig) to check, hold back.

argomentare [argomen'tare] **1** vt to deduce, infer. **2** vi: ~ (**su** o **di qc**) to argue (about sth).

argomentazione [argomentat'tsjone] sf argument.

argomento [argo'mento] sm **(a)** (tema) subject; ~ **di conversazione** topic of conversation; **qual'è l'**~ **del film/del libro?** what is the film/book about?; **cambiare** ~ to change the subject; **visto che siamo entrati in** ~**...** since we're on the subject.... **(b)** (argomentazione) argument.

arguire [argu'ire] vt to deduce, infer.

arguto, a [ar'guto] ag (battuta, conversazione) witty; (persona) quick-witted; (sguardo) sharp, keen.

arguzia [ar'guttsja] sf (spirito) wit; (battuta) witty remark.

aria¹ ['arja] sf **(a)** (gen) air; ~ **di mare/montagna** sea/mountain air; **all'**~ **(aperta)** in the open (air); **vivere all'**~ **aperta** to live an outdoor life; **mettere le lenzuola all'**~ to air the sheets; **cambiare l'**~ **in una stanza** to air a room; **esco a prendere una boccata d'**~ I'm going out for a breath of fresh air; **manca l'**~ it's stuffy; **che** ~ **tira?** (fig: atmosfera) what's the atmosphere like?; **c'è** ~ **di burrasca** (anche fig) there's a storm brewing; ~ **condizionata** air conditioning; ~ **compressa** compressed air.

(b): **andare all'**~ (piano, progetto) to come to nothing; **buttare** o **mandare all'**~ (progetto, piano) to ruin, upset; **discorsi a mezz'**~ vague remarks; **ha la testa per** ~ his head is in the clouds; **lasciare tutto per** ~ (in disordine) to leave everything in a mess; **sta sempre con la pancia all'**~ he's always lazing about.

aria² ['arja] sf **(a)** (aspetto) look, air; (modi) manner, air; **hai l'**~ **così stanco oggi** you look so tired today; **quel ragazzo ha l'**~ **intelligente** that boy looks o seems intelligent; **ha l'**~ **della persona onesta** he looks (like) o seems (to be) an honest person; **ha l'**~ **di voler piovere** it looks like rain; **ha un'**~ **di famiglia** there is a family likeness; **cos'è quell'**~ **da funerale?** what are you looking so gloomy about? **(b):** ~**e** pl airs (and graces); **darsi delle** ~**e, mettere su** ~**e** to put on airs and graces.

aria³ ['arja] sf (Mus: di opera) aria; (: di canzonetta) tune.

aridità [aridi'ta] sf aridity, dryness; (fig) lack of feeling.

arido, a ['arido] ag (suolo, regione) arid; (clima) dry; (fig: persona) insensitive; **cuore** ~ heart of stone.

arieggiare [arjed'dʒare] vt **(a)** (stanza, casa) to air. **(b)** (somigliare) to resemble; (imitare) to imitate.

ariete [a'rjete] sm (Zool) ram; (Astrologia): **A**~ Aries; **essere dell'A**~ to be Aries.

arietta [a'rjetta] sf (brezza) breeze; (Mus) arietta.

aringa, ghe [a'ringa] sf herring; ~ **affumicata** smoked herring, kipper; ~ **marinata** pickled herring.

arioso, a [a'rjoso] ag airy.

arista ['arista] sf (Culin) chine of pork.

aristocratico, a, ci, che [aristo'kratiko] **1** ag (gen, fig) aristocratic. **2** sm/f aristocrat.

aristocrazia [aristokrat'tsia] sf aristocracy.

aritmetica [arit'mɛtika] sf arithmetic.

aritmetico, a, ci, che [arit'mɛtiko] ag arithmetical.

arlecchino [arlek'kino] sm (Teatro) harlequin; **fare l'**~ (fig) to act the fool o clown.

arma, i ['arma] sf **(a)** (anche fig) weapon; ~**i atomiche** atomic weapons; ~ **da fuoco** firearm; **battersi all'**~ **bianca** to fight with blades; **all'**~**i!** to arms!; **passare qn per le** ~**i** to execute sb; ~ **a doppio taglio** (anche fig) double-edged weapon; **combattere ad** ~**i pari** (anche fig) to fight on equal terms; **deporre le** ~**i** (anche fig) to lay down one's arms; **essere alle prime** ~**i** (fig) to be a novice; **prendere** ~**i e bagagli e partire** (fig) to pack up and go. **(b)** (corpo dell'esercito) arm, force; (dei carabinieri) force. **(c)** (servizio militare): **essere sotto le** ~**i** to be in the army o in the forces; **andare sotto le** ~**i** to join the army o forces; **chiamare alle** ~**i** to call up.

armadio [ar'madjo] sm (gen) cupboard, closet (Am); (per abiti) wardrobe; ~ **a muro** built-in cupboard.

armaiolo [arma'jɔlo] sm **(a)** (fabbricante) armourer; (: di armi da fuoco) gunsmith. **(b)** (venditore) arms dealer.

armamentario [armamen'tarjo] sm (attrezzatura) equipment; (chirurgico) instruments pl; (scherz) paraphernalia.

armamento [arma'mento] sm **(a)** (azione: di paese) armament; (Naut) fitting out, equipping; (: provvedere di uomini) manning. **(b)** (armi: di soldato) arms pl, weapons pl; (: di paese): ~**i arms, armaments; **la corsa agli** ~**i** the arms race; **società di** ~ shipowning company.

armare [ar'mare] **1** vt **(a)** (persona, paese, fortezza) to arm. **(b)** (Naut) to equip, fit out; (: di uomini) to man. **(c)** (Edil) to prop up, shore up. **2:** ~**rsi** vr: ~**rsi (di)** (anche fig) to arm o.s. (with).

armata [ar'mata] sf (esercito) army; (flotta) fleet; **corpo d'**~ army corps sg.

armato, a [ar'mato] **1** ag **(a):** ~ **(di)** (anche fig) armed (with); ~ **fino ai denti** armed to the teeth; **sono partiti** ~**i di tutto punto** they set off equipped for anything; **rapina a mano** ~**a** armed robbery. **(b)** (Tecn: cemento, volta) reinforced. **2** sm (soldato) soldier.

armatore, trice [arma'tore] **1** ag shipping attr. **2** sm shipowner.

armatura [arma'tura] sf **(a)** (corazza) (suit of) armour. **(b)** (Edil) framework. **(c)** (Elettr: di cavo) sheath; (: di condensatore) plate.

armeggiare [armed'dʒare] vi (affaccendarsi): ~ (intorno a qc) to mess about (with sth).

armento [ar'mento] sm herd.

armeria [arme'ria] sf (deposito) armoury; (collezione) collection of arms.

armistizio [armis'tittsjo] sm armistice.

armonia [armo'nia] sf (concordia, Mus) harmony; (conformità) agreement; **vivere in** ~ **con qn** to live in harmony with sb, get on very well with sb.

armonica, che [ar'mɔnika] sf (Mus) harmonica; ~ **a bocca** mouth organ.

armonico, a, ci, che [ar'mɔniko] ag **(a)** (Mus) harmonic; **cassa** ~**a** sound box. **(b)** (ben proporzionato) harmonious.

armonioso, a [armo'njoso] ag (voce) melodious;

(suono) harmonious; *(lingua)* musical; *(colori)* well matched; *(corpo)* well-proportioned.

armonizzare [armonid'dzare] **1** *vt (Mus)* to harmonize; *(fig: colori)* to match. **2** *vi:* ~ **(con)** to harmonize (with); to match.

arnese [ar'nese] *sm* **(a)** *(strumento, utensile)* tool, implement; ~**i da giardino/falegname** gardening/joiner's tools. **(b)** *(oggetto qualsiasi)* gadget, thing. **(c): essere male in** ~ *(vestito male)* to be poorly dressed; *(di salute malferma)* to be in poor health; *(di condizioni economiche)* to be hard up.

arnia ['arnja] *sf* (bee)hive.

aroma, i [a'rɔma] *sm (odore)* aroma; ~**i** *pl* seasoning *sg; (erbe)* herbs; ~**i naturali/artificiali** natural/artificial flavouring *sg*.

aromatico, a, ci, che [aro'matiko] *ag* aromatic.

aromatizzare [aromatid'dzare] *vt* to season, flavour.

arpa ['arpa] *sf* harp.

arpeggiare [arped'dʒare] *vi (suonare l'arpa)* to play the harp; *(fare arpeggi)* to play arpeggios.

arpia [ar'pia] *sf (Mitologia, fig)* harpy.

arpionare [arpjo'nare] *vt* to harpoon.

arpione [ar'pjone] *sm (Pesca)* harpoon; *(uncino: anche Alpinismo)* hook; *(cardine)* hinge.

arrabattarsi [arrabat'tarsi] *vr:* ~ **per fare qc** to do all one can to do sth, strive to do sth.

arrabbiare [arrab'bjare] **1** *vi (aus essere)* **(a)** *(cane)* to be affected with rabies. **(b)** *(persona):* **far** ~ **qn** to make sb angry. **2:** ~**rsi** *vr* to get angry, fly into a rage.

arrabbiato, a [arrab'bjato] *ag* **(a)** *(cane)* rabid. **(b)** *(persona)* angry; **un giocatore** ~ *(fig: entusiasta)* a keen player.

arrabbiatura [arrabbja'tura] *sf:* **prendersi un'**~ **(per qc)** to become furious (over sth).

arraffare [arraf'fare] *vt* to snatch, seize; *(rubare)* to pinch.

arrampicarsi [arrampi'karsi] *vr* to climb (up); ~**rsi sul tetto** to climb (up) onto the roof; ~**rsi sui vetri** *o* **sugli specchi** *(fig)* to clutch at straws.

arrampicata [arrampi'kata] *sf* climb.

arrampicatore, trice [arrampika'tore] *sm/f (gen, Sport)* climber; ~ **sociale** *(fig)* social climber.

arrancare [arran'kare] *vi* to limp, hobble; *(fig)* to struggle along.

arrangiamento [arrandʒa'mento] *sm* **(a)** *(gen, Mus)* arrangement. **(b)** *(accordo)* agreement.

arrangiare [arran'dʒare] **1** *vt (gen, Mus)* to arrange; **abbiamo arrangiato un pranzo alla bell'e meglio** we've rustled up some lunch; **ti arrangio io!** *(fig)* I'll fix you! **2:** ~**rsi** *vr (cavarsela)* to get by, manage; **con l'arte di** ~**rsi si risolve tutto** with a bit of improvisation you can cope with anything; **arrangiati un po' tu!** *(fam)* sort it out for yourself!

arrecare [arre'kare] *vt* to cause.

arredamento [arreda'mento] *sm* **(a)** *(azione)* furnishing; *(mobilia)* furniture. **(b)** *(arte)* interior design.

arredare [arre'dare] *vt* to furnish.

arredatore, trice [arreda'tore] *sm/f* interior designer.

arredo [ar'rɛdo] *sm* furnishings *pl;* **per l'**~ **della vostra casa...** to furnish your home...; ~**i sacri** religious ornaments.

arrembaggio [arrem'baddʒo] *sm (Naut)* boarding; **buttarsi all'**~ **in qc** *(fig)* to throw o.s. enthusiastically into sth.

arrendersi [ar'rɛndersi] *vr (persona):* ~ **(a)** *(polizia, nemico)* to give o.s. up (to), surrender (to); ~ **all'evidenza (dei fatti)** to face (the) facts.

arrendevole [arren'devole] *ag (persona)* yielding, compliant.

arrendevolezza [arrendevo'lettsa] *sf* compliancy.

arreso, a [ar'reso] *pp di* **arrendere.**

arrestare [arres'tare] **1** *vt (fermare)* to stop; *(Dir)* to arrest. **2:** ~**rsi** *vr* to stop.

arrestato [arres'tato] *sm* person under arrest.

arresto [ar'resto] *sm* **(a)** *(azione)* stopping; *(sosta, pausa)* interruption; **aspettate l'**~ **del treno** wait until the train stops; **segnale d'**~ stop sign; ~ **cardiaco** *(Med)* cardiac arrest; **il gioco ebbe una battuta d'**~ the game was interrupted; **le discussioni fra i due partiti subirono un** ~ discussions between the two parties came to a standstill. **(b)** *(Dir)* arrest; **mandato d'**~ warrant of arrest; **essere in stato di** ~ to be under arrest; **la dichiaro in** ~ I'm putting you under arrest; **essere/mettere agli** ~**i** *(Mil)* to be/place under arrest.

arretrare [arre'trare] **1** *vt* to move back. **2** *vi (aus essere)* to move back; ~ **davanti** *o* **di fronte a qc** *(fig)* to shrink from sth.

arretratezza [arretra'tettsa] *sf* backwardness.

arretrato, a [arre'trato] **1** *ag* **(a)** *(paese, zona)* backward. **(b)** *(numero di giornale, pagamento, interesse)* back *attr;* **ho un sacco di lavoro** ~ **da finire** I've got a huge backlog of work to finish. **2** *sm* **(a): essere in** ~ **con qc** to be behind with sth. **(b):** ~**i** *pl* arrears; **gli** ~**i dello stipendio** back pay *sg*.

arricchimento [arrikki'mento] *sm* enrichment.

arricchire [arrik'kire] **1** *vt* to make rich; ~ **qc di** *o* **con qc** *(fig)* to enrich sth with sth. **2:** ~**rsi** *vr (persona)* to grow rich; *(collezione):* ~**rsi di** to be enriched with.

arricchito [arrik'kito] *sm* nouveau riche.

arricciare [arrit'tʃare] **1** *vt* **(a)** *(capelli, baffi)* to curl; ~ **il naso** *(fig)* to turn up one's nose. **(b)** *(Edil: muri)* to render. **2:** ~**rsi** *vr* to become curly.

arridere [ar'ridere] *vi:* ~ **a qn** *(fortuna, successo)* to smile on sb.

arringa [ar'ringa] *sf (gen)* harangue; *(Dir)* address.

arringare [arrin'gare] *vt* to harangue.

arrischiare [arris'kjare] **1** *vt (vita, denaro)* to risk; *(parola, giudizio)* to venture, hazard. **2:** ~**rsi** *vr:* ~**rsi (a fare qc)** to venture (to do sth), dare (to do sth).

arrischiato, a [arris'kjato] *ag* foolhardy, rash.

arriso, a [ar'riso] *pp di* **arridere.**

arrivare [arri'vare] *vi (aus* **essere)** **(a)** *(essere a destinazione)* to arrive; *(avvicinarsi)* to come; *(raggiungere):* ~ **a** to reach, arrive at, get to; ~ **a casa** to arrive *o* get *o* reach home; ~ **a Roma/in Italia** to arrive in Rome/in Italy; **mi è arrivato un pacco dall'Italia** a parcel has arrived for me from Italy, I've had a parcel from Italy; ~ **a destinazione** to arrive at *o* reach one's destination; ~ **allo scopo** to reach one's goal; ~ **al potere** to come to power; ~ **primo** *(in un luogo)* to be the first to arrive; *(in classifica)* to come in first; ~ **al punto di fare qc** to reach the stage of doing sth; **arrivo!** (I'm) coming!; **siamo arrivati** we're here; **per fare** ~ **la corrente alla macchina** in order to connect the machine up to the electricity supply; **l'acqua mi arrivava alle ginocchia** the water came up to my knees; **la notizia è arrivata fino a lui** the news reached him; **non ci arrivo** *(a prendere qc)* I can't reach it; *(a capire qc)* I can't understand it; **a questo siamo arrivati!** so this is what we've come to!; **il mio stipendio non arriva al milione di lire** my salary doesn't reach the million lire mark; **dove ti arriva la gonna?** how long is the skirt on you?; **chi tardi arriva**

male alloggia (*Proverbio*) the early bird catches the worm.

(**b**) (*riuscire*): ~ **a fare qc** to manage to do sth, succeed in doing sth; **non arriverò mai a capirlo** I'll never understand him; **non arriverà a niente** he'll never get anywhere, he'll never achieve anything; **non ci arrivo da solo** I can't do it on my own.

arrivato, a [arri'vato] **1** *ag* (**a**) (*persona: di successo*) successful. (**b**): **ben** ~! welcome! **2** *sm/f* (**a**) (*persona: di successo*): **essere un** ~ to have made it. (**b**): **nuovo** ~ newcomer; **l'ultimo** ~ the last to arrive; **non sono l'ultimo** ~! (*fig*) I'm no fool!

arrivederci [arrive'dertʃi] *escl* goodbye!; ~ **a domani!** see you tomorrow!

arrivederla [arrive'derla] *escl* goodbye!

arrivismo [arri'vizmo] *sm* (*gen*) ambitiousness; (*sociale*) social climbing.

arrivista, i, e [arri'vista] *sm/f* go-getter; (*sociale*) social climber.

arrivo [ar'rivo] *sm* (**a**) arrival; **al mio** ~ on my arrival; **telefonami al tuo** ~ **in Italia** phone me when you arrive in *o* get to Italy; **il treno è in** ~ **al binario 7** the train is arriving *o* coming in at platform 7; ~**i e partenze** arrivals and departures. (**b**) (*Sport*) finish, finishing line. (**c**) (*Comm*): **ultimi** ~**i** latest arrivals; **ci sono nuovi** ~**i?** has anything new come in?

arroccare [arrok'kare] **1** *vt* (*Scacchi*) to castle. **2**: ~**rsi** *vr*: ~**rsi dietro qc** (*fig*) to shelter behind sth.

arrogante [arro'gante] *ag* arrogant.

arroganza [arro'gantsa] *sf* arrogance.

arrogarsi [arro'garsi] *vr*: ~**rsi il diritto di fare qc** to assume the right to do sth; ~**rsi il merito di qc** to claim credit for sth.

arrossamento [arrossa'mento] *sm* reddening.

arrossare [arros'sare] *vi* (*aus* **essere**), ~**rsi** *vr* to go *o* become red.

arrossire [arros'sire] *vi* (*aus* **essere**): ~ (**di, per**) (*vergogna, imbarazzo*) to blush (with); (*piacere*) to flush (with), blush (with); **arrossì di vergogna** *o* **per la vergogna** he blushed with shame; ~ **fino alle orecchie** to go bright red, blush to the roots of one's hair.

arrostire [arros'tire] **1** *vt* (*al forno*) to roast; (*: ai ferri, alla griglia*) to grill; **sotto un sole che arrostiva** under a blazing sun. **2**: ~**rsi** *vr* (*Culin*) to roast; ~**rsi al sole** to soak up the sun.

arrosto [ar'rɔsto] **1** *ag inv* (*vedi vb*) roast; grilled. **2** *sm* roast; ~ **di manzo** roast beef.

arrotare [arro'tare] *vt* (**a**) (*lame, coltelli*) to sharpen; (*vetro*) to grind. (**b**) (*investire con un veicolo*) to run over.

arrotino [arro'tino] *sm* knife-grinder.

arrotolare [arroto'lare] *vt* (*stoffa, sigaretta*) to roll; (*carta*) to roll up.

arrotondare [arroton'dare] *vt* (*cifra*) to round up; (*fig: stipendio*) to supplement.

arrovellarsi [arrovel'larsi] *vr* (*anche*: ~ **il cervello**) to rack one's brains.

arroventare [arroven'tare] **1** *vt* to make red hot. **2**: ~**rsi** *vr* to become red hot.

arroventato, a [arroven'tato] *ag* red-hot.

arruffare [arruf'fare] **1** *vt* to ruffle. **2**: ~**rsi** *vr* to become tousled.

arruffato, a [arruf'fato] *ag* (*capelli, pelo*) tousled, ruffled; (*piume*) ruffled.

arrugginire [arruddʒi'nire] **1** *vi* (*aus* **essere**) to rust, get rusty. **2** *vt* to rust. **3**: ~**rsi** *vr* (*metallo*) to rust, get rusty; (*atleta, memoria*) to become rusty; (*muscoli*) to get stiff.

arruolamento [arrwola'mento] *sm* enlistment.

arruolare [arrwo'lare] **1** *vt* to enlist. **2**: ~**rsi** *vr* to enlist; ~**rsi volontario** to join up, enlist.

arsenale [arse'nale] *sm* (*cantiere*) dockyard; (*fabbrica e deposito di armi*) arsenal; **il suo studio è un vero** ~ (*fig*) his study is full of all sorts of things; **si è portato dietro un** ~ he had everything but the kitchen sink with him, he brought everything but the kitchen sink.

arsenico [ar'sɛniko] *sm* arsenic.

arso, a [ˈarso] **1** *pp di* **ardere. 2** *ag* (*bruciato*) burnt; (*arido*) dry.

arsura [ar'sura] *sf* (**a**) (*calore: del sole*) burning heat; (*: di febbre*) burning. (**b**) (*siccità*) drought; (*sete*) thirst.

arte [ˈarte] *sf* (**a**) (*gen*) art; (*abilità*) skill; (*mestiere, attività*) craft; **opera d'**~ work of art; **con** ~ skilfully; **a regola d'**~ (*fig*) perfectly; **avere l'**~ **di fare qc** to have the knack of doing sth; **senz'**~ **né parte** penniless and out of a job. (**b**) (*Storia*) guild; **l'**~ **della lana** the woollen guild.

artefatto, a [arte'fatto] *ag* (*stile, modi*) artificial; (*cibo*) adulterated.

artefice [ar'tefitʃe] *sm* (*fig: autore*) author.

arteria [ar'tɛrja] *sf* (*Anat, fig*) artery.

arteriosclerosi [arterjoskle'rɔzi] *sf* arteriosclerosis, hardening of the arteries.

arteriosclerotico, a, ci, che [arterjoskle'rɔtiko] *ag* (*Med*) suffering from hardening of the arteries; (*fig scherz*) senile.

arterioso, a [arte'rjoso] *ag* (*Anat*) arterial.

artesiano, a [arte'zjano] *ag*: **pozzo** ~ artesian well.

artico, a, ci, che [ˈartiko] **1** *ag* Arctic. **2** *sm*: **l'A**~ the Arctic.

articolare[1] [artiko'lare] *ag* articular.

articolare[2] [artiko'lare] **1** *vt* (**a**) (*muovere: giunture*) to move. (**b**) (*parole*) to articulate. (**c**) (*discorso, idee: suddividere*) to split (up); **ha articolato bene il suo discorso** he presented his speech very clearly. **2**: ~**rsi** *vr*: ~**rsi in** (*discorso, progetto*) to be divided into.

articolato, a [artiko'lato] *ag* (**a**) (*Aut*) articulated. (**b**) (*linguaggio*) articulate; **preposizione** ~**a** preposition combined with the definite article; **un ragionamento ben** ~ a clear and well developed argument.

articolazione [artikolat'tsjone] *sf* (**a**) (*Anat, Tecn*) joint. (**b**) (*di voce, concetto*) articulation.

articolo [ar'tikolo] *sm* (**a**) (*Gram*) article. (**b**) (*di giornale, legge, regolamento*) article; ~ **di fondo** editorial; ~ **di fede** (*Rel*) article of faith. (**c**) (*Comm*) item, article; ~**i per la casa/d'importazione** household/imported products; ~**i di lusso** luxury goods; ~ **da regalo** gift; **quel suo amico è un bell'**~ (*fig*) that friend of his is a real character.

Artide [ˈartide] *sm*: **l'**~ the Arctic.

artificiale [artifi'tʃale] *ag* (*gen*) artificial; (*allegria*) forced, unnatural.

artificiere [artifi'tʃere] *sm* (*Mil*) artificer; (*: per disinnescare bombe*) bomb disposal expert.

artificio [arti'fitʃo] *sm* artifice; **fuochi d'**~ fireworks.

artificioso, a [artifi'tʃoso] *ag* (*non spontaneo*) unnatural, forced.

artigianale [artidʒa'nale] *ag* craft *attr*; **produzione** ~ production by craftsmen; **lavoro** ~ craftsmanship; **è un pezzo** ~ it's made by craftsmen.

artigianato [artidʒa'nato] *sm* (**a**) (*arte*) craft; **corso di** ~ arts and crafts course. (**b**) (*prodotti*) arts and crafts *pl*. (**c**) (*ceto*) artisans *pl*, craftsmen *pl*.

artigiano, a [arti'dʒano] **1** *ag* craft *attr*. **2** *sm/f* craftsman, artisan; (*fig*) craftsman.

artigliere [artiʎ'ʎere] *sm* artilleryman.

artiglieria [artiʎʎe'ria] sf artillery; **tiro di** ~ artillery fire.

artiglio [ar'tiʎʎo] sm (di felini) claw; (di uccelli) talon; **sfoderare gli** ~**i** (fig) to show one's claws; **cadere negli** ~**i di qn** (fig) to fall into sb's clutches.

artista, i, e [ar'tista] sm/f (pittore, scultore etc) artist; (di spettacolo) artiste; ~ **del cinema** film actor/actress; ~ **di varietà** variety artist; **un lavoro da** ~ (fig) a professional piece of work.

artistico, a, ci, che [ar'tistiko] ag artistic.

arto ['arto] sm limb.

artrite [ar'trite] sf arthritis.

artritico, a, ci, che [ar'tritiko] ag, sm/f arthritic.

artrosi [ar'trɔzi] sf osteoarthritis.

arzigogolare [ardzigogo'lare] vi (fantasticare) to daydream; (cavillare) to quibble.

arzigogolato, a [ardzigogo'lato] ag tortuous.

arzillo, a [ar'dzillo] ag lively, sprightly.

ascella [aʃ'ʃɛlla] sf (Anat) armpit.

ascellare [aʃʃel'lare] ag underarm attr.

ascendente [aʃʃen'dɛnte] **1** ag (moto, piano) ascending, upward; (Mus: scala) ascending. **2** sm **(a)** (antenato) ancestor. **(b)** (autorità, influenza): ~ **(su)** ascendancy (over). **(c)** (Astrologia) ascendant.

ascendenza [aʃʃen'dɛntsa] sf ancestry.

ascendere [aʃ'ʃɛndere] vi (aus essere) (frm): ~ **al trono** to ascend the throne; ~ **a grandi onori** to rise to great honours.

ascensionale [aʃʃensjo'nale] ag (forza, moto) upward; **velocità** ~ (Aer) rate of climb.

ascensione [aʃʃen'sjone] sf **(a)** (Alpinismo) ascent, climb; (Aer) ascent. **(b)** (Rel): **l'A**~ the Ascension.

ascensore [aʃʃen'sore] sm lift, elevator (Am).

ascesa [aʃ'ʃesa] sf (gen) ascent, climb; (fig: al trono) accession; (: al potere) rise.

ascesi [aʃ'ʃezi] sf asceticism.

asceso, a [aʃ'ʃeso] pp di **ascendere**.

ascesso [aʃ'ʃesso] sm abscess.

asceta, i [aʃ'ʃeta] sm ascetic.

ascetico, a, ci, che [aʃ'ʃetiko] ag ascetic(al).

ascia, sce ['aʃʃa] sf axe; (più piccola) hatchet.

ascissa [aʃ'ʃissa] sf (Mat) x-axis.

asciugacapelli [aʃʃugaka'pelli] sm inv hairdryer.

asciugamano [aʃʃuga'mano] sm towel; ~ **da bagno** bath towel.

asciugare [aʃʃu'gare] **1** vt (gen) to dry; (sudore) to wipe; ~ **i piatti** to wipe o dry the dishes; ~**rsi le mani/le lacrime** to dry one's hands/one's eyes. **2** vi (aus essere) to dry; **stendere i panni ad** ~ to hang the clothes out to dry. **3**: ~**rsi** vr to dry; ~**rsi al sole** (panni) to dry in the sun; (persona) to dry o.s. in the sun.

asciugatrice [aʃʃuga'tritʃe] sf spin-dryer.

asciuttezza [aʃʃut'tettsa] sf (anche fig) dryness; (di risposta) curtness.

asciutto, a [aʃ'ʃutto] **1** ag (gen, fig) dry; (scarno: viso, corpo etc) lean; (brusco: risposta) curt; **rimanere** o **restare a bocca** ~**a** (fig) to be disappointed. **2** sm: **tenere all'**~ to keep in a dry place; **rimanere** o **restare all'**~ (fig) to be broke, be hard up.

ascoltare [askol'tare] vt (persona, musica, radio, discorso etc) to listen to; ~ **qn parlare/cantare** to listen to sb talking/singing; ~ **qn con un orecchio solo** to half listen to sb; ~ **il consiglio di qn** to heed sb's advice; ~ **la messa/una lezione** to attend Mass/a lesson; ~ **un testimonio** (Dir) to hear a witness.

ascoltatore, trice [askolta'tore] sm/f listener.

ascolto [as'kolto] sm **(a)** (Radio) reception; (gen,

anche Radio): **essere** o **stare in** ~ **(di qc)** to be listening (to sth); **mettersi in** ~ **(di qc)** to listen (to sth); **indice di** ~ (TV, Radio) audience rating. **(b)** (attenzione): **dare** o **prestare** ~ **a qn/ai consigli di qn** to listen to o heed sb/sb's advice.

ascritto, a [as'kritto] pp di **ascrivere**.

ascrivere [as'krivere] vt **(a)** (attribuire): ~ **qc a qn** to attribute sth to sb; ~ **qc a merito di qn** to give sb credit for sth. **(b)** (annoverare): ~ **(tra)** to number (among).

asessuale [asessu'ale] ag asexual.

asessuato, a [asessu'ato] ag = **asessuale**.

asettico, a, ci, che [a'settiko] ag aseptic.

asfaltare [asfal'tare] vt to asphalt.

asfalto [as'falto] sm asphalt.

asfissia [asfis'sia] sf asphyxia.

asfissiante [asfis'sjante] ag (gas) asphyxiant; (fig: calore, ambiente) stifling, suffocating; (: persona) tiresome.

asfissiare [asfis'sjare] **1** vt to asphyxiate, suffocate; (fig: opprimere) to stifle; (: infastidire) to get on sb's nerves; ~ **(con il gas)** to gas; **è morto asfissiato** he died of suffocation; **la sta asfissiando con la sua gelosia** he's stifling her with his jealousy. **2** vi (aus essere) to suffocate, asphyxiate. **3**: ~**rsi** vr to suffocate o.s.; ~**rsi col gas** to gas o.s.

Asia ['azja] sf Asia.

asiatica [a'zjatika] sf (Med) Asian flu.

asiatico, a, ci, che [a'zjatiko] ag, sm/f Asian, Asiatic.

asilo [a'zilo] sm **(a)**: ~ **(infantile)** nursery (school); ~ **nido** crèche. **(b)** (rifugio) shelter, refuge; (Pol) asylum; **diritto di** ~ right of asylum.

asimmetria [asimme'tria] sf asymmetry.

asimmetrico, a, ci, che [asim'metriko] ag asymmetric(al).

asina ['asina] sf she-ass.

asinello [asi'nɛllo] sm (little) donkey.

asinino, a [asi'nino] ag: **tosse** ~**a** whooping cough.

asino ['asino] sm (Zool) donkey, ass; (fig) fool, ass; (: scolaro) dunce; **la bellezza dell'**~ (fig: di ragazza) the beauty of youth; **qui casca l'**~! there's the rub!

asma ['azma] sf asthma.

asmatico, a, ci, che [az'matiko] ag, sm/f asthmatic.

asociale [aso'tʃale] ag antisocial.

asocialità [asotʃali'ta] sf antisocial behaviour.

asola ['azola] sf buttonhole.

asparago, gi [as'parago] sm (Bot) asparagus; (Culin): ~**i** asparagus sg.

aspergere [as'perdʒere] vt: ~ **(di** o **con)** to sprinkle (with).

asperità [asperi'ta] sf inv (di terreno, roccia) roughness, ruggedness; (fig) harshness; **le** ~ **della vita** the trials of life.

asperrimo, a [as'perrimo] ag superl di **aspro**.

asperso, a [as'perso] pp di **aspergere**.

aspettare [aspet'tare] vt **(a)** (attendere) to wait for; **aspettiamo che arrivi** let's wait for him to come; **aspetta un po'** wait a second, hold on; **aspetta a giudicare!** wait and see!; ~ **la fine** (di film etc) to wait until the end; ~ **conferma** (Comm) to await confirmation; ~ **un bambino** (essere incinta) to be expecting (a baby); **è mezz'ora che ti aspetto** I've been waiting for you for half an hour; **fare** ~ **qn** to keep sb waiting; **farsi** ~ to keep people waiting; **chi la fa, l'aspetti!** it'll all come home to roost. **(b)** (essere in serbo: notizia, evento etc) to be in store for, lie ahead of; **non sapeva che cosa lo aspettasse** he didn't know what was in store for him o lay ahead of him. **(c)**: ~**rsi qc** to expect sth; **non mi aspettavo che partisse** I didn't expect him to leave; **quando meno te l'aspetti** when you least expect it; **me l'aspettavo!** I thought as much!

aspettativa [aspetta'tiva] *sf* **(a)** *(previsione, speranza)* expectation; **contro le mie ~e...** contrary to my expectations...; **corrispondere alle/deludere le ~e di qn** to come up to/fall short of sb's expectations. **(b)**: **essere/mettersi in ~** *(Amm)* to be on/take leave of absence.

aspetto [as'pɛtto] *sm* **(a)** *(apparenza)* appearance, look; **un uomo di bell'~** a good-looking man; **all'~** *o* **a giudicare dall'~**, **pare una persona onesta** to look at him, he seems an honest person; **avere l'~ di** to look like. **(b)** *(di questione etc)* aspect, side; **sotto un certo ~** in some ways.

aspide ['aspide] *sm* asp.

aspirante [aspi'rante] **1** *ag* **(a)** *(Tecn)* suction *attr*. **(b)** *(fig: attore, artista etc)* aspiring. **2** *sm/f (a un titolo)* aspirant; *(candidato)* candidate.

aspirapolvere [aspira'polvere] *sm inv* vacuum cleaner, hoover®; **passare l'~** to vacuum, hoover.

aspirare [aspi'rare] **1** *vt* **(a)** *(aria, profumo)* to breathe in; *(fumo)* to inhale. **(b)** *(Tecn)* to suck up. **(c)** *(Fonetica)* to aspirate. **2** *vi (anelare)*: **~ a qc/a fare qc** to aspire to sth/to do sth.

aspiratore [aspira'tore] *sm (di aria, gas)* extractor fan; *(di liquidi)* aspirator, extractor.

aspirazione [aspirat'tsjone] *sf* **(a)** *(Tecn)* suction. **(b)** *(anelito)* aspiration; *(ambizione)* ambition. **(c)** *(Fonetica)* aspiration.

aspirina [aspi'rina] *sf* aspirin.

asportare [aspor'tare] *vt (anche Med)* to remove.

asportazione [asportat'tsjone] *sf (anche Med)* removal.

asprezza [as'prettsa] *sf inv (vedi ag)* sharpness; sourness; pungency; rugged nature; severity; harshness; strictness.

asprigno, a [as'priɲɲo] *ag* rather sour.

aspro, a ['aspro] *ag (vino)* sharp; *(agrumi)* sour; *(odore)* pungent; *(paesaggio)* rugged; *(clima)* severe, harsh. **(b)** *(fig: voce, giudizio)* harsh; *(: disciplina, regime)* strict; *(: cammino, salita)* difficult, hard. **(c)** *(Fonetica)*: **'s' ~a** unvoiced 's'.

assaggiare [assad'dʒare] *vt (pietanza, bevanda)* to taste, try; **fammi ~** let me have a taste; **gli hanno fatto ~ la frusta** *(fig)* they gave him a taste of the whip.

assaggiatore, trice [assaddʒa'tore] *sm/f* taster.

assaggio [as'saddʒo] *sm (prova, degustazione)* tasting, sampling; *(piccola quantità)* taste; *(campione)* sample.

assai [as'sai] *av (abbastanza)* enough; *(molto)* a lot, much; *(: con ag)* very; **è ~ più giovane di me** she is very much younger than me; **ha fatto ~ per quel suo amico** he's done a lot for that friend of his; **sono ~ contento** I'm very pleased; **c'era ~ gente** there were a lot of people; **m'importa ~ di lui!** what do I care about him!

assalire [assa'lire] *vt* to attack, assail; *(fig)* to assail; **~ a parole** to attack verbally.

assalitore, trice [assali'tore] *sm/f* attacker, assailant.

assaltare [assal'tare] *vt (Mil)* to storm; *(banca)* to raid; *(treno, diligenza)* to hold up.

assalto [as'salto] *sm* **(a)** *(Mil)* attack, assault; **truppe d'~** assault troops. **(b)** *(rapina)* raid; **prendere d'~** *(fig: negozio, treno)* to storm; *(: personalità)* to besiege.

assaporare [assapo'rare] *vt* to savour.

assassinare [assassi'nare] *vt (gen)* to murder; *(Pol)* to assassinate.

assassinio [assas'sinjo] *sm* murder; **~ (politico)** assassination.

assassino, a [assas'sino] **1** *ag (sguardo, occhiata)* seductive. **2** *sm/f* murderer; *(Pol)* assassin.

asse¹ ['asse] *sf (di legno)* board; **~ di equilibrio** *(Ginnastica)* beam; **~ da stiro** ironing board.

asse² ['asse] *sm (Geom)* axis; *(Tecn)* axle; **l'~ terrestre** the earth's axis; **l'~ Roma-Berlino** *(Pol)* the Rome-Berlin axis.

assecondare [assekon'dare] *vt*: **~ qn (in qc)** to go along with sb (in sth); **~ i desideri di qn** to go along with sb's wishes; **~ i capricci di qn** to give in to sb's whims.

assediare [asse'djare] *vt (anche fig)* to besiege.

assediato, a [asse'djato] **1** *ag* besieged. **2**: **~i** *smpl* people under siege.

assedio [as'sɛdjo] *sm* siege; **porre in stato di ~** to lay siege to.

assegnamento [asseɲɲa'mento] *sm* **(a)** *(vedi vb)* assignment; allocation; allotment. **(b)**: **fare ~ su qn/qc** *(fig)* to rely on sb/sth.

assegnare [asseɲ'ɲare] *vt*: **~ (a)** *(gen)* to assign (to); *(premio, borsa di studio)* to award (to); *(somma)* to allocate (to), allot (to).

assegnatario [asseɲɲa'tarjo] *sm (Dir)* assignee; **l'~ del premio** the person awarded the prize.

assegnazione [asseɲɲat'tsjone] *sf (di casa, somma)* allocation; *(di carica)* assignment; *(di premio, borsa di studio)* awarding.

assegno [as'seɲɲo] *sm* **(a)** *(somma destinata)* allowance; **~i familiari** family allowance *sg*. **(b)** *(Fin, Comm)*: **~ (bancario)** cheque, check *(Am)*; **un ~ per** *o* **di 100.000 lire** a cheque for 100,000 lire; **contro ~** cash on delivery; **~ in bianco** blank cheque; **~ circolare** bank draft; **~ turistico** traveller's cheque; **~ a vuoto** dud cheque.

assemblaggio [assem'bladdʒo] *sm (Industria)* assembly.

assemblea [assem'blɛa] *sf (gen)* assembly; *(raduno, adunanza)* meeting; **~ generale** general meeting; *(di scioperanti etc)* mass meeting.

assembramento [assembra'mento] *sm* (public) gathering; **divieto di ~** ban on public meetings.

assennatezza [assenna'tettsa] *sf (vedi ag)* good sense; wisdom.

assennato, a [assen'nato] *ag* sensible, wise.

assenso [as'sɛnso] *sm* approval, assent.

assentarsi [assen'tarsi] *vr (gen)* to go out; **il capoufficio dovrà ~ per un paio di giorni** the head clerk will be away for a couple of days; **si assenta spesso dal lavoro** he is frequently absent from work.

assente [as'sɛnte] **1** *ag* **(a)**: **~ (da)** *(gen)* away (from); *(malato, scolaro)* absent (from); **il direttore è momentaneamente ~** the manager is out at the moment. **(b)** *(aspetto, aria)* vacant; **avere lo sguardo ~** to look miles away. **2** *sm/f* absentee; **quanti ~i ci sono oggi?** how many people are absent today?; **non sparlare degli assenti** don't speak ill of people behind their backs; **il grande ~ alla riunione** the most notable absentee at the meeting.

assenteismo [assente'izmo] *sm* absenteeism.

assenteista, i, e [assente'ista] *sm/f (dal lavoro)* absentee; **è un ~** he *(o* she) is often absent.

assentire [assen'tire] *vi*: **~ (a)** to agree (to), assent (to); **~ (con un cenno del capo)** to nod in agreement.

assenza [as'sɛntsa] *sf* absence; **in ~ di** in the absence of; **non ho fatto nessuna ~ a scuola/in ufficio** I haven't missed a day at school/at the office; **quanto durerà la sua assenza?** how long will he be away for?

asserire [asse'rire] *vt* to maintain, assert; **ha asserito di avere ragione** *o* **che aveva ragione** he maintained (that) he was right.

asserragliarsi [asserraʎ'ʎarsi] *vr*: ~ **(in)** to barricade o.s. (in).

assertore, trice [asser'tore] *sm/f* supporter, upholder.

asservimento [asservi'mento] *sm* *(azione)* enslavement; *(stato: anche fig)*: ~ **(a)** slavery (to), subservience (to).

asservire [asser'vire] **1** *vt* to enslave; *(fig: animo, passioni)* to subdue. **2**: ~**rsi** *vr*: ~**rsi (a)** to submit (to).

asserzione [asser'tsjone] *sf* assertion.

assessorato [assesso'rato] *sm* councillorship.

assessore [asses'sore] *sm* councillor.

assestamento [assesta'mento] *sm* *(gen, Geol)* settlement; **essere in via di** ~ *(terreno)* to be settling; **la situazione è in via di** ~ things are settling down.

assestare [asses'tare] **1** *vt (gen, Geol)* to settle; ~ **il bilancio** *(Comm)* to balance the books; ~ **un colpo a qn** to deal sb a blow; ~ **la mira** to adjust one's aim. **2**: ~**rsi** *vr (situazione etc)* to settle down; *(terreno)* to settle.

assestato, a [asses'tato] *ag*: **un colpo ben** ~ a well-aimed blow.

assetato, a [asse'tato] *ag* thirsty; *(campi, terra)* arid; ~ **di** *(fig)* thirsting for.

assetto [as'setto] *sm* **(a)** *(ordine)* order, arrangement; **dare un** ~ **nuovo a qc** to (re)arrange sth; **in** ~ **di guerra** ready for war. **(b)** *(Aer, Naut)* trim; *(Aut)* position.

assicurare [assiku'rare] **1** *vt* **(a)**: ~ **a qn che** to assure sb that; **te l'assicuro!** I assure you! **(b)** *(fissare)* to secure; ~**rsi qc** to secure *o* ensure sth for o.s.; ~**rsi un lavoro** to make sure of a job for o.s. **(c)** *(Fin: vita, casa)* to insure. **2**: ~**rsi** *vr* **(a)**: ~**rsi di/che** to make sure of/that. **(b)** *(legarsi)*: ~**rsi (a)** to fasten o.s. (to), tie o.s. (to). **(c)** *(Fin)*: ~**rsi (contro qc)** to insure o.s. (against sth).

assicurativo, a [assikura'tivo] *ag* insurance *attr*.

assicurata [assiku'rata] *sf* registered letter.

assicurato, a [assiku'rato] **1** *ag* insured. **2** *sm/f* policy holder.

assicuratore, trice [assikura'tore] **1** *ag* insurance *attr*; **società** ~**trice** insurance company. **2** *sm/f* insurance agent.

assicurazione [assikurat'tsjone] *sf* **(a)** *(conferma, garanzia)* assurance. **(b)** *(contratto)* insurance (policy); ~ **contro incendi/furti/terzi** fire/theft/third party insurance; ~ **sulla vita** life insurance.

assideramento [assidera'mento] *sm (Med)* exposure.

assiderare [asside'rare] **1** *vt* to freeze; **questo freddo mi sta assiderando** *(fig)* I'm chilled to the bone. **2**: ~**rsi** *vr* to freeze; **morire assiderato** to die of exposure.

assiduità [assidui'ta] *sf (vedi ag)* assiduity; regularity; ~ **alle lezioni** *(Scol)* regular attendance at classes; **viene a trovarmi con** ~ he comes to see me frequently.

assiduo, a [as'siduo] *ag (cure, studio, applicazione)* assiduous; *(visitatore, lettore)* regular.

assieme [as'sjeme] *av (insieme)* together; ~ **a** *prep* (together) with.

assillante [assil'lante] *ag (dubbio, pensiero)* nagging; *(creditore)* pestering.

assillare [assil'lare] *vt (sog: dubbio, pensiero, persona)* to nag at; *(: creditore)* to harass.

assillo [as'sillo] *sm (Zool)* horsefly, gadfly; *(fig: pensiero tormentoso)* nagging worry; **aver l'**~ **di**

qc to be constantly worrying about sth.

assimilabile [assimi'labile] *ag (sostanza)* easily assimilated; *(: cibo)* digestible.

assimilare [assimi'lare] *vt (anche fig)* to assimilate.

assimilazione [assimilat'tsjone] *sf* assimilation.

assiolo [assi'ɔlo] *sm* horned owl.

assioma [as'sjɔma] *sm* axiom.

assiomatico, a, ci, che [assjo'matiko] *ag* axiomatic.

assise [as'size] *sfpl (Dir)*: **(corte** *f* **d')a**~ ≈ crown court.

assistente [assis'tente] *sm/f (gen)* assistant; ~ **ai lavori** supervisor; ~ **universitario** (assistant) lecturer; ~ **sociale/sanitario** social/health worker; ~ **di volo** steward/stewardess.

assistenza [assis'tɛntsa] *sf (aiuto)* assistance; **dare** *o* **prestare** ~ **a qn** to assist sb, give assistance to sb; **fare opera di** ~ to help out; ~ **legale** legal aid; ~ **ospedaliera** free hospital treatment; ~ **sanitaria** health service; ~ **sociale** social security; ~ **tecnica** after-sales service.

assistenziale [assisten'tsjale] *ag (ente, organizzazione)* welfare *attr*; *(opera)* charitable.

assistere [as'sistere] **1** *vt* to assist; *(malato)* to look after. **2** *vi*: ~ **a** *(essere presente)* to be present at, attend; *(incidente)* to witness; *(fare sorveglianza: ai lavori, agli esami)* to supervise.

assistito, a [assis'tito] *pp di* **assistere**.

asso ['asso] *sm* **(a)** *(carta, dado)* ace; ~ **di picche/cuori** *etc* ace of spades/hearts *etc*; **avere l'**~ **nella manica** *(fig)* to have an ace up one's sleeve; **piantare qn in** ~ *(fig)* to leave sb in the lurch. **(b)** *(campione)* ace; ~ **del volante** ace driver.

associare [asso'tʃare] **1** *vt* **(a)**: ~ **(a)** *(idee, parole, fatti)* to associate (with); **il suo nome è stato associato alla Mafia** his name has been linked with the Mafia. **(b)**: ~ **qn a** *(ad una ditta)* to take sb into partnership in; *(ad un circolo)* to make sb a member of; ~ **qn alle carceri** to take sb to prison. **2**: ~**rsi** *vr*: ~**rsi a** *(ditta)* to enter into partnership in; *(circolo)* to join, become a member of; *(dolori, gioie)* to share in.

associativo, a [assotʃa'tivo] *ag* associative.

associazione [assotʃat'tsjone] *sf* **(a)** *(gen, Pol, Sport etc)* association; ~ **a delinquere** *(Dir)* criminal association. **(b)** *(di idee)* association; **per** ~ **di idee** by association of ideas.

assodare [asso'dare] **1** *vt (muro, posizione)* to strengthen; *(fatti, verità)* to ascertain. **2**: ~**rsi** *vr (sostanza)* to harden.

assoggettamento [assoddʒetta'mento] *sm* subjection.

assoggettare [assoddʒet'tare] **1** *vt (persone)* to subjugate; *(fig: passioni, istinti)* to curb. **2**: ~**rsi a** to submit to; *(adattarsi)* to adapt to.

assolato, a [asso'lato] *ag* sunny.

assoldare [assol'dare] *vt* to hire.

assolo [as'solo] *sm (Mus)* solo.

assolto, a [as'sɔlto] *pp di* **assolvere**.

assolutamente [assoluta'mente] *av* absolutely; **devo** ~ **andare** I simply *o* positively have to go; ~ **no** certainly not.

assolutismo [assolu'tizmo] *sm* absolutism.

assoluto, a [asso'luto] **1** *ag (gen, Pol, Gram)* absolute; **in caso di** ~ **a necessità** if absolutely essential. **2** *sm*: **l'**~ the absolute.

assoluzione [assolut'tsjone] *sf (Rel)* absolution; *(Dir)* acquittal; **dare l'**~ **a qn** to give sb absolution; to acquit sb.

assolvere [as'sɔlvere] *vt* **(a)**: ~ **qn (da)** *(Rel)* to absolve sb (from); *(Dir)* to acquit sb (of). **(b)** *(mansioni, compiti)* to carry out, perform.

assomigliare [assomiʎ'ʎare] **1** *vi*: ~ **a** to resemble, look like; **assomiglia a suo padre** he looks like *o* resembles his father. **2:** ~**rsi** *vr (uso reciproco)* to be alike, resemble each other; **si assomigliano come due gocce d'acqua** they are as like as two peas (in a pod).

assommare [assom'mare] **1** *vt (fig)* to combine. **2** *vi (aus essere) (ammontare):* ~ **a** to amount to, come to.

assonanza [asso'nantsa] *sf* assonance.

assonnato, a [asson'nato] *ag* sleepy; **hai l'aria** ~**a** you look sleepy.

assopimento [assopi'mento] *sm* doziness, sleepiness.

assopire [asso'pire] **1** *vt* **(a):** **far** ~ to make drowsy. **(b)** *(dolore)* to soothe. **2:** ~**rsi** *vr* to doze off.

assorbente [assor'bɛnte] **1** *ag* absorbent; **carta** ~ blotting paper. **2** *sm* absorbent; ~ **(igienico)** sanitary towel; ~ **interno** tampon.

assorbimento [assorbi'mento] *sm (Chim, Fis)* absorption.

assorbire [assor'bire] *vt (liquidi)* to absorb, soak up; *(suono)* to absorb; *(tempo, attenzione)* to take up, occupy; *(cultura, influenza)* to assimilate, absorb; **era assorbito nello studio** he was absorbed in his studies.

assordare [assor'dare] *vt* to deafen.

assortimento [assorti'mento] *sm* assortment, variety.

assortire [assor'tire] *vt (combinare)* to combine; *(: colori)* to match.

assortito, a [assor'tito] *ag* **(a)** *(combinato: persone, cose, colori):* **bene/male** ~ well/badly matched. **(b)** *(cioccolatini)* assorted.

assorto, a [as'sɔrto] *ag:* **essere** ~ **in qc** to be engrossed in sth.

assottigliare [assottiʎ'ʎare] **1** *vt* **(a)** *(affilare)* to sharpen. **(b)** *(ridurre: provviste)* to reduce; *(: caviglie)* to slim (down); *(girovita)* to reduce, slim down. **2:** ~**rsi** *vr (provviste)* to diminish; *(caviglie, girovita)* to slim down.

A.S.S.T. *abbr (= Azienda di Stato per i Servizi Telefonici)* ≃ British Telecom.

assuefare [assue'fare] **1** *vt:* ~ **a** to get used to, accustom to. **2:** ~**rsi** *vr:* ~**rsi a** to become accustomed *o* used to; *(droga)* to become addicted to.

assuefazione [assuefat'tsjone] *sf (Med)* addiction; **questo medicinale non dà** ~ this drug is not habit-forming.

assumere [as'sumere] *vt* **(a)** *(atteggiamento, espressione)* to assume; *(comando, potere)* to assume, take over; *(incarico)* to take up; ~**rsi il compito di fare qc** to take on the job of doing sth; ~ **informazioni su qn/qc** to make enquiries about sb/sth. **(b)** *(impiegato)* to take on, engage, employ. **(c)** *(supporre)* to assume; **assumendo (come ipotesi) che...** assuming that.... **(d)** *(innalzare a dignità)* to raise; ~ **al trono** to raise to the throne.

assunto, a [as'sunto] **1** *pp di* **assumere. 2** *sm (Filosofia)* proposition.

assunzione [assun'tsjone] *sf* **(a)** *(di impiegati)* employment, engagement; **ci sono state poche** ~**i** few people have been taken on *o* employed; **il problema delle** ~**i** the employment problem. **(b)** *(Rel):* **l'A**~ the Assumption.

assurdità [assurdi'ta] *sf inv* absurdity; **che** ~**!** how absurd!; **dire delle** ~ to talk nonsense; **fare delle** ~ to behave very strangely.

assurdo, a [as'surdo] *ag* absurd; **l'**~ **di tutto questo è...** the absurd thing about all this is... .

asta ['asta] *sf* **(a)** *(palo)* pole; **bandiera a mezz'**~ flag at half-mast. **(b)** *(di occhiali)* leg; *(di compasso, bilancia)* arm. **(c)** *(Comm)* auction; **met-**

tere all'~ to put up for auction; **vendere all'**~ to auction off; **vendita all'**~ auction sale; ~ **fallimentare** bankruptcy sale. **(d)** *(nella scrittura)* stroke.

astante [as'tante] *sm* bystander.

astemio, a [as'tɛmjo] **1** *ag* teetotal. **2** *sm/f* teetotaller.

astenersi [aste'nersi] *vr:* ~**rsi dal fare qc** to abstain *o* refrain from doing sth; ~**rsi dal dire** to refrain from saying; ~**rsi dal bere/dal fumo** to keep off drink/cigarettes.

astensione [asten'sjone] *sf* abstention.

astensionismo [astensjo'nizmo] *sm (Pol)* abstentionism.

asterisco, schi [aste'risko] *sm* asterisk.

asteroide [aste'rɔide] *sm* asteroid.

astice ['astitʃe] *sm* lobster.

astigmatismo [astigma'tizmo] *sm* astigmatism.

astinenza [asti'nɛntsa] *sf* abstinence; **fare** ~ **(da)** *(Rel)* to abstain (from).

astio ['astjo] *sm:* ~ **(contro)** rancour (against), resentment (towards); **portare** ~ **a qn** to bear sb a grudge.

astiosità [astjosi'ta] *sf* rancour, resentment.

astioso, a [as'tjoso] *ag* rancorous, resentful.

astrakan ['astrakan] *sm inv* astrakhan.

astrale [as'trale] *ag* astral; **influsso** ~ *(Astrologia)* influence of the planets.

astrarre [as'trarre] **1** *vt* to abstract. **2: astrarsi** *vr:* **astrarsi da** to cut o.s. off from.

astrattezza [astrat'tettsa] *sf* abstract nature; **con** ~ abstractly.

astrattismo [astrat'tizmo] *sm (Arte)* abstract art.

astratto, a [as'tratto] **1** *pp di* **astrarre. 2** *ag, sm* abstract; **in** ~ in the abstract.

astrazione [astrat'tsjone] *sf* abstraction.

astringente [astrin'dʒɛnte] *ag, sm* astringent.

astro ['astro] *sm (Astron, fig)* star; *(Bot)* aster.

astrofisica [astro'fizika] *sf* astrophysics *sg.*

astrologia [astrolo'dʒia] *sf* astrology.

astrologico, a, ci, che [astro'lɔdʒiko] *ag* astrological.

astrologo, a, gi, ghe [as'trɔlogo] *sm/f* astrologer.

astronauta, i, e [astro'nauta] *sm/f* astronaut.

astronautica [astro'nautika] *sf* astronautics *sg.*

astronautico, a, ci, che [astro'nautiko] *ag* astronautical.

astronave [astro'nave] *sf* spaceship.

astronomia [astrono'mia] *sf* astronomy.

astronomico, a, ci, che [astro'nɔmiko] *ag (anche fig)* astronomic(al).

astronomo, a [as'trɔnomo] *sm/f* astronomer.

astruso, a [as'truzo] *ag* abstruse.

astuccio [as'tuttʃo] *sm* case.

astuto, a [as'tuto] *ag* astute, shrewd; ~ **come una volpe** cunning as a fox.

astuzia [as'tuttsja] *sf (qualità)* astuteness, shrewdness; *(azione)* trick.

atavico, a, ci, che [a'taviko] *ag* atavistic.

atavismo [ata'vizmo] *sm* atavism.

ateismo [ate'izmo] *sm* atheism.

ateistico, a, ci, che [ate'istiko] *ag* atheistic.

atelier [atə'lje] *sm inv (laboratorio)* workshop; *(studio)* studio; *(sartoria)* fashion house.

Atene [a'tene] *sf* Athens.

ateneo [ate'nɛo] *sm* university.

ateo, a, i, e ['ateo] **1** *ag* atheistic. **2** *sm/f* atheist.

A.T.I. *abbr di Aereo Trasporti Italiani.*

atipico, a, ci, che [a'tipiko] *ag* atypical.

atlante [a'tlante] *sm (libro, Anat)* atlas.

atlantico, a, ci, che [a'tlantiko] **1** *ag* Atlantic. **2** *sm:* **l'A**~ the Atlantic.

atleta, i, e [a'tlɛta] *sm/f* athlete.

atletica [a'tletika] *sf* athletics *sg;* ~ **leggera** track and field events *pl.*

atletico, a, ci, che [a'tletiko] *ag* athletic.

atmosfera [atmos'fera] *sf (anche fig)* atmosphere.

atmosferico, a, ci, che [atmos'feriko] *ag* atmospheric.

atollo [a'tɔllo] *sm* atoll.

atomico, a, ci, che [a'tɔmiko] *ag* atomic; **bomba** ~a atom bomb; **guerra** ~a nuclear war.

atomistica [ato'mistika] *sf (Chim)* atomic theory.

atomizzatore [atomiddza'tore] *sm (di acqua, lacca)* spray; *(di profumo)* atomizer.

atomo ['atomo] *sm* atom.

atono, a ['atono] *ag (Fonetica)* unstressed.

atrio ['atrjo] *sm (di albergo)* entrance hall, lobby; *(di stazione)* concourse; *(Storia, Anat)* atrium.

atroce [a'trotʃe] *ag (delitto)* atrocious; *(sofferenza, destino)* terrible, dreadful; *(dolore)* excruciating; *(tempo)* ghastly, dreadful; **fa un freddo** ~ it's dreadfully cold; **in modo** ~ dreadfully; **ho l'~ dubbio che...** I have the horrible feeling that... .

atrocità [atrotʃi'ta] *sf inv (caratteristica)* atrocity, atrociousness; *(azione)* atrocity.

atrofia [atro'fia] *sf* atrophy.

attaccabrighe [attakka'brige] *sm/f inv* quarrelsome person.

attaccamento [attakka'mento] *sm* attachment.

attaccapanni [attakka'panni] *sm inv (su parete)* hook, peg; *(mobile)* hall stand.

attaccare [attak'kare] **1** *vt* **(a)** *(far aderire)* to attach; *(incollare: manifesto)* to stick up; *(: francobollo)* to stick on; *(cucire)* to sew on; *(legare)* to tie; *(appendere: quadro)* to hang up. **(b)** *(Mil, Sport, fig)* to attack. **(c)** *(cominciare: discorso, lite)* to start, begin; ~ **a suonare** to strike up; **mi ha attaccato discorso** he started up a conversation with me. **(d)** *(Med: colpire)* to affect; **ha attaccato il morbillo a sua cugina** he's given his cousin the measles.

2 *vi* **(a)** *(aver successo):* **la nuova moda non attacca** the new fashion isn't catching on; **con me non attacca!** it doesn't work with me! **(b)** *(cominciare)* to start, begin; **ha attaccato con una delle sue lamentele** *o* **a lamentarsi** he started complaining.

3: ~**rsi** *vr* **(a):** ~**rsi (a)** *(appiccicarsi)* to stick (to); *(aggrapparsi: anche fig)* to cling (to); **le pagine si sono attaccate** the pages have stuck together; **attaccati alla corda!** hold on tight to the rope!; **è inutile che ti attacchi a dei pretesti** there's no point in making excuses; ~**rsi alla bottiglia** *(fig)* to take to the bottle. **(b)** *(affezionarsi):* ~**rsi a** to become attached to.

attaccaticcio, a, ci, ce [attakka'tittʃo] *ag* sticky; **è una persona** ~**a** *(fig)* he (*o* she) clings like a leech.

attaccatura [attakka'tura] *sf (di manica)* join; ~ **(dei capelli)** hairline.

attacco, chi [at'takko] *sm* **(a)** *(Mil, Sport)* attack; *(giocatori)* forward line, forwards *pl;* **giocare in** ~ to play an attacking game; ~ **aereo** air raid. **(b)** *(Med)* attack; **un** ~ **di cuore/di tosse** a heart attack/coughing fit. **(c)** *(Sci)* binding. **(d)** *(Tecn)* connection.

attanagliare [attanaʎ'ʎare] *vt (anche fig)* to grip; **attanagliato dalla paura** gripped by fear.

attardarsi [attar'darsi] *vr:* ~**rsi a fare qc** *(fermarsi)* to stop to do sth; *(stare più a lungo)* to stay behind to do sth; **dev'essersi attardato in ufficio** he must have stayed on *o* behind at the office; ~**rsi da amici** to stay on at friends.

attecchire [attek'kire] *vi (pianta)* to take root; *(fig)* to catch on.

atteggiamento [atteddʒa'mento] *sm (disposizione mentale)* attitude; *(aria)* air; *(del corpo)* pose; **perché hai avuto quell'~ strano quando l'abbiamo incontrato?** why did you act so strangely when we met him?; **è tutto un** ~ **il suo** it's all an act with him.

atteggiare [atted'dʒare] **1** *vt:* ~ **il viso a compassione** to assume a sympathetic expression. **2:** ~**rsi** *vr:* ~**rsi ad artista** to play *o* act the artist, pretend to be an artist.

attempato, a [attem'pato] *ag* elderly.

attendarsi [atten'darsi] *vr* to camp, pitch one's tent.

attendente [atten'dɛnte] *sm (Mil)* orderly, batman.

attendere [at'tɛndere] **1** *vt (aspettare)* to wait for; **attendo l'arrivo di mio fratello** I'm waiting for my brother to arrive *o* arriving; **attenda qui, il Sig. Rossi sarà qui tra un attimo** if you wait here, Mr Rossi will be here in a moment. **2** *vi:* ~ **a to** attend to.

attendibile [atten'dibile] *ag (scusa, storia)* credible; *(fonte, testimone, notizia)* reliable; *(persona)* trustworthy.

attendibilità [attendibili'ta] *sf (vedi ag)* credibility; reliability; trustworthiness.

attenersi [atte'nersi] *vr:* ~**rsi a** to keep to, stick to.

attentare [atten'tare] *vi:* ~ **a** *(libertà, diritti)* to attack; ~ **alla vita di qn** to make an attempt on sb's life.

attentato [atten'tato] *sm (contro libertà, onore)* attack; *(contro persona)* assassination attempt; **commettere un** ~ **contro qn** to make an attempt on sb's life.

attentatore, trice [attenta'tore] *sm/f* attacker.

attenti [at'tenti] **1** *escl (Mil)* attention! **2** *sm:* **mettersi/stare sull'~** to come to/stand at attention.

attento, a [at'tento] *ag* **(a)** *(che presta attenzione)* attentive; **avere lo sguardo** ~ to watch attentively. **(b)** *(fatto con cura)* careful, thorough. **(c)** *(avviso di pericolo):* ~**!** (be) careful!, look out!; ~**i al cane** beware of the dog; **stai** ~**!** *(non distrarsi)* pay attention!; *(stare in guardia)* be careful!

attenuante [attenu'ante] *ag:* **(circostanze** *fpl)* ~**i** *(Dir)* extenuating circumstances.

attenuare [attenu'are] *vt (dolore)* to ease; *(fig: colpo)* to soften; *(Dir: colpa)* to mitigate.

attenuazione [attenuat'tsjone] *sf (vedi vb)* easing; softening; mitigation.

attenzione [atten'tsjone] *sf* **(a)** *(gen)* attention; *(cura)* care; **con** ~ *(ascoltare)* carefully, attentively; *(esaminare)* carefully, closely; ~**!** watch out!, careful!; ~ **al gradino** mind the step; **fare** *o* **prestare** ~ *(stare in guardia)* to be careful; *(ascoltare, guardare)* to pay attention. **(b):** ~**i** *pl (gentilezze)* attentions; **avere mille** ~**i per qn,** **coprire qn di** ~**i** to lavish attention on sb.

atterraggio [atter'raddʒo] *sm* landing; **all'~** on landing; ~ **di fortuna** emergency landing; **essere in fase di** ~ to be coming in to land.

atterrare [atter'rare] **1** *vi (Aer)* to land. **2** *vt (avversario)* to floor.

atterrire [atter'rire] **1** *vt* to terrify. **2:** ~**rsi** *vr* to become terrified.

attesa [at'tesa] *sf* wait; **l'~ durò a lungo** it was a long wait; **essere in** ~ **di qc** to be waiting for sth; **in** ~ **di una vostra risposta** *(Comm)* awaiting your reply; **è in** ~ **del terzo figlio** she is expecting her third baby.

atteso, a [at'teso] **1** *pp di* attendere. **2** *ag* long-awaited.

attestare [attes'tare] *vt:* ~ **qc/che** to testify to sth/(to the fact) that.

attestato [attes'tato] *sm (certificato)* certificate;

quest'~ **certifica che** this document testifies to the fact that.

attestazione [attestat'tsjone] *sf (certificato)* certificate; *(dichiarazione)* statement.

attico, ci ['attiko] *sm* attic; *(di lusso)* penthouse.

attiguo, a [at'tiguo] *ag (contiguo)* adjoining; *(adiacente)* adjacent; **il suo appartamento è ~ al nostro** his flat is next to ours.

attillato, a [attil'lato] *ag (vestito)* tight, close-fitting.

attimo ['attimo] *sm* moment; **fra un ~** in a minute *o* moment; **un ~ fa** a moment ago; **ci metto un ~** I'll just be a minute.

attinente [atti'nɛnte] *ag:* **~ (a)** relevant (to).

attinenza [atti'nɛntsa] *sf* connection.

attingere [at'tindʒere] *vt:* **~ da** *(acqua)* to draw from; **~ a** *(denaro, risorse)* to draw on; **~ informazioni a una fonte sicura** to obtain information from a reliable source.

attinto, a [at'tinto] *pp di* **attingere.**

attirare [atti'rare] *vt (attenzione, persona)* to attract; **l'idea mi attira** the idea appeals to me; **~rsi delle critiche** to incur criticism; **~rsi la simpatia di qn** to attract sb's sympathy.

attitudinale [attitudi'nale] *ag:* **esame ~** aptitude test.

attitudine [atti'tudine] *sf* aptitude; **avere ~ per qc** to have a flair for sth.

attivare [atti'vare] *vt (motore, azienda)* to start; *(dispositivo, mina)* to activate; **~ la circolazione** *(Med)* to stimulate the circulation.

attivismo [atti'vizmo] *sm* activism.

attivista, i, e [atti'vista] *sm/f* activist.

attivistico, a, ci, che [atti'vistiko] *ag* activist.

attività [attivi'ta] *sf inv* **(a)** *(gen)* activity; **essere/entrare in ~** to be/become active. **(b)** *(Comm: azienda)* business; **le ~ e passività di un'azienda** the assets and liabilities of a business.

attivo, a [at'tivo] **1** *ag (gen, Gram)* active; *(Comm)* profit-making; **bilancio ~** credit balance; **un'azienda ~a** a going concern. **2** *sm (Comm)* assets *pl;* **chiudere in ~** to show a profit; **avere qc al proprio ~** *(fig)* to have sth to one's credit.

attizzare [attit'tsare] *vt (fuoco)* to poke (up); *(fig: passioni, odi)* to stir up.

attizzatoio [attittsa'tojo] *sm* poker.

atto¹ ['atto] *sm* **(a)** *(azione)* action, deed; **~ eroico** heroic feat; **essere in ~** to be under way; **cogliere** *o* **sorprendere qn nell'~ di fare qc** to catch sb in the act of doing sth; **all'~ pratico** in practice; **mettere in ~** to put into action; **fare l'~ di fare qc** to make as if to do sth; **~i osceni (in luogo pubblico)** *(Dir)* indecent exposure. **(b)** *(dimostrazione):* **~ di fede/amicizia** *etc* act of faith/friendship *etc;* **dare ~ a qn di qc** to give sb credit for sth. **(c)** *(Dir: documento)* document; *(del parlamento)* act; *(notarile)* deed; *(di congressi etc):* **~i** proceedings; **~ di nascita/morte** birth/death certificate. **(d)** *(Teatro)* act; **una commedia in 3 ~i** a three-act play.

atto² ['atto] *ag:* **~ alle armi** fit for military service; **~ a proseguire gli studi** capable of going on with one's studies.

attonito, a [at'tonito] *ag* astonished, amazed.

attorcigliare [attortʃiʎ'ʎare] **1** *vt* to twist. **2: ~rsi** *vr* to twist; **le funi si sono attorcigliate** the cords have become twisted.

attore, trice [at'tore] *sm/f* actor/actress; *(Dir)* plaintiff.

attorniare [attor'njare] **1** *vt (circondare)* to surround. **2: ~rsi** *vr:* **~rsi di** to surround o.s. with.

attorno [at'torno] **1** *av* around; **è entrato e si è guardato ~** he came in and looked around *o*

about him; **tutt'~** all around; **d'~ = di torno. 2:** **~ a** *prep* around, round; **stare ~ a qn** to hang round sb; **~ al fuoco** around *o* round the fire.

attraccare [attrak'kare] *vt, vi (Naut)* to dock, berth.

attracco, chi [at'trakko] *sm (Naut: manovra)* docking, berthing; *(luogo)* berth.

attraente [attra'ente] *ag (gen)* attractive; *(idea)* appealing, attractive; **dai modi ~i** charming.

attrarre [at'trarre] *vt (anche fig)* to attract; **l'attrasse a sé** he drew her into his arms.

attrattiva [attrat'tiva] *sf* attraction; **esercitare un'~ su qn** to hold a great attraction for sb; **dotato di grande ~** charming.

attrattivo, a [attrat'tivo] *ag (Fis)* attractive.

attratto, a [at'tratto] *pp di* **attrarre.**

attraversamento [attraversa'mento] *sm* crossing; **~ pedonale** pedestrian crossing.

attraversare [attraver'sare] *vt (strada, fiume, ponte)* to cross; *(bosco, città)* to go through; **~ la strada di corsa** to rush across the road; **~ il fiume a nuoto** to swim across the river; **~ il ponte correndo** to run across the bridge; **il fiume attraversa la città** the river passes through the town; **~ un brutto periodo** *(fig)* to go through a bad patch; **la pallottola gli ha attraversato il braccio** the bullet went straight through his arm.

attraverso [attra'verso] *prep* **(a)** *(gen)* through; **abbiamo camminato ~ i campi** we walked through the fields; **ha ottenuto il lavoro ~ suo zio** he got the job through his uncle. **(b)** *(da una parte all'altra)* across; **ha nuotato ~ il fiume** he swam across the river. **(c)** *(di tempo)* over, through; **~ i secoli** over *o* through the centuries.

attrazione [attrat'tsjone] *sf (gen, Fis)* attraction; **uno spettacolo di grande ~** a very entertaining show.

attrezzare [attret'tsare] *vt (gen)* to equip; *(nave)* to rig.

attrezzatura [attrettsa'tura] *sf* equipment *no pl;* **~e turistiche/sportive** tourist/sports facilities.

attrezzista, i [attret'tsista] *sm (Atletica)* gymnast; *(Teatro)* property-man.

attrezzistica [attret'tsistika] *sf* gymnastics *sg.*

attrezzo [at'trettso] *sm* tool, implement; **gli ~i** *(Atletica)* the apparatus *sg.*

attribuire [attribu'ire] *vt (gen)* to attribute; *(premio)* to award; **non attribuirmi colpe che non ho** don't blame me for things I didn't do; **va attribuito a lui il merito di tale successo** he should be given the credit for this success; **~rsi il merito di qc** to take the credit for sth.

attributo [attri'buto] *sm (gen, Gram)* attribute.

attribuzione [attribut'tsjone] *sf (vedi vb)* attribution; awarding.

attrito [at'trito] *sm (anche fig)* friction.

attuabile [attu'abile] *ag* feasible.

attuabilità [attuabili'ta] *sf* feasibility.

attuale [attu'ale] *ag (presente)* present; *(di attualità)* topical; *(che è in atto)* current; **al momento ~** at the present moment; **lo stato ~ dell'economia** the present state of the economy; **le leggi ~i** the current legislation; **un problema ~** a current problem; **il suo ~ ragazzo** her current boyfriend.

attualità [attuali'ta] *sf inv* **(a)** *(di argomento)* topicality; **un problema di grande ~** a very topical question; **film d'~** topical film. **(b):** **~ pl** *(avvenimenti)* current affairs *pl;* **notizie d'~** *(TV)* the news *sg.*

attualmente [attual'mente] *av* at the moment, at present.

attuare [attu'are] **1** *vt* to carry out. **2: ~rsi** *vr* to be realized; **un piano difficile ad** *o* **da ~rsi** a difficult plan to carry out.

attuazione |attuat'tsjone| *sf* carrying out; **di facile/ difficile ~** easy/difficult to carry out; **l'~ del progetto sembra impossibile** it seems an impossible plan to carry out.

attutire |attu'tire| **1** *vt* (*suono*) to deaden; (*colpo, caduta*) to cushion; (*dolore*) to ease. **2: ~rsi** *vr* (*suono*) to die down; (*dolore*) to ease.

audace |au'datʃe| *ag* **(a)** (*coraggioso: persona*) daring, audacious; (: *impresa*) daring, bold. **(b)** (*provocatorio*) provocative; (: *vestito*) daring.

audacia |au'datʃa| *sf* (*vedi ag*) daring, audacity; boldness; provocativeness; (*sfrontatezza*) audacity; **tutti hanno notato l'~ del suo vestito** everyone noticed her daring dress.

audio |'audjo| *sm* (*TV, Radio, Cine*) sound.

audiovisivo, a |audjovi'zivo| *ag* audiovisual; **sussidi ~i** audiovisual aids.

auditorio |audi'tɔrjo| *sm* auditorium.

auge |'audʒe| *sf* (*della gloria, carriera*) height, peak; **essere in ~** to be at the top.

augurale |augu'rale| *ag*: **messaggio ~** greeting; **biglietto ~** greetings card.

augurare |augu'rare| *vt* (*buon viaggio, buonanotte etc*) to wish; **gli augurò di guarire presto** he wished him a speedy recovery; **~rsi qc/che succeda qc** to hope for sth/that sth may happen; **me lo auguro** I hope so; **mi auguro di no/sì** I hope not/so.

augurio |au'gurjo| *sm* **(a)** greeting; **~i di Natale/ Pasqua** Christmas/Easter greetings; **biglietto di ~i** greetings card; **fare gli ~i a qn** to give sb one's best wishes, wish sb all the best; **tanti ~i!** best wishes; (*di compleanno*) happy birthday!; (*buona fortuna*) good luck!; **~i di pronta guarigione!** get well soon! **(b)** (*presagio*): **essere di cattivo/di buon ~** to be ominous/a good omen.

augusto, a |au'gusto| *ag* august.

aula |'aula| *sf* (*di scuola*) classroom; (*di università*) lecture room; **~ del tribunale** courtroom; **silenzio in ~!** (*Dir*) silence in court!; **~ magna** main hall.

aulico, a, ci, che |'auliko| *ag* (*tono*) dignified; (*stile*) refined.

aumentare |aumen'tare| **1** *vt* (*prezzo*) to increase, put up; (*stipendi*) to increase, raise. **2** *vi* (*aus* **essere**) (*gen*) to increase; (*prezzi*) to go up, rise, increase; (*livello*) to rise; (*qualità*) to improve; **~ di peso** (*persona*) to put on weight.

aumento |au'mento| *sm*: **~ (di)** increase (in), rise (in); **un imprevisto ~ delle nascite** an unexpected rise in the birth rate; **ottenere un ~ (di stipendio)** to get a rise; **essere in ~** (*gen*) to be rising, be going up; (*qualità*) to be improving.

aura |'aura| *sf* (*poet: venticello*) light breeze; (*Med, fig*) aura.

aureo, a |'aureo| *ag* (*di oro*) gold *attr*; (*fig: colore, periodo*) golden.

aureola |au'rɛola| *sf* (*Rel, Astron*) halo.

auricolare |auriko'lare| **1** *ag* auricular, ear *attr*; **padiglione ~** external ear. **2** *sm* (*Radio*) earphone.

aurifero, a |au'rifero| *ag* gold *attr*.

aurora |au'rɔra| *sf* (*anche fig*) dawn.

auscultare |auskul'tare| *vt* (*Med*) to auscultate.

ausiliare |auzi'ljare| *ag* (*gen, Gram*) auxiliary.

ausiliaria |auzi'ljarja| *sf* (*Mil*) member of Women's Army Auxiliary Corps.

ausiliario, a |auzi'ljarjo| *ag, sm* auxiliary.

auspicabile |auspi'kabile| *ag* desirable; **è ~ che** it is to be hoped that.

auspicare |auspi'kare| *vt* to hope for; **ci si auspica che** it is hoped that.

auspicio |aus'pitʃo| *sm* **(a)** (*presagio*) omen; **essere di buon ~** to be a good omen. **(b)** (*incoraggiamento, aiuto*) auspices *pl*; **sotto gli ~i di** under the auspices of.

austerità |austeri'ta| *sf* (*gen, Econ*) austerity.

austerity |ɔs'teriti| *sf* (*Econ*) austerity.

austero, a |aus'tero| *ag* (*persona, vita*) austere; (*disciplina*) strict.

australe |aus'trale| *ag* southern.

Australia |aus'tralja| *sf* Australia.

australiano, a |austra'ljano| *ag, sm/f* Australian.

Austria |'austria| *sf* Austria.

austriaco, a, ci, che |aus'triako| *ag, sm/f* Austrian.

autarchia |autar'kia| *sf* (*Econ*) autarky; (*Pol*) autarchy.

autarchico, a, ci, che |au'tarkiko| *ag* (*sistema*) self-sufficient, autarkic; (*prodotto*) home *attr*, home-produced.

aut aut |'aut 'aut| *sm inv* ultimatum.

autenticare |autenti'kare| *vt* to authenticate.

autenticità |autentitʃi'ta| *sf* authenticity.

autentico, a, ci, che |au'tentiko| *ag* (*quadro, firma*) authentic, genuine; (*fatto*) true; **quel ragazzo è un ~ cretino** that boy is an out-and-out fool.

autista, i, e |au'tista| *sm/f* driver; (*personale*) chauffeur; **auto con ~** chauffeur-driven car.

auto |'auto| *sf inv* (*motor*) car, automobile (*Am*).

auto... |'auto| *pref* **(a)** self-, auto.... **(b)** (*Aut*) car *attr*.

autoadesivo, a |autoade'zivo| **1** *ag* self-adhesive. **2** *sm* sticker.

autoambulanza |autoambu'lantsa| *sf* ambulance.

autoarticolato |autoartiko'lato| *sm* articulated lorry.

autobiografia |autobiogra'fia| *sf* autobiography.

autobiografico, a, ci, che |autobio'grafiko| *ag* autobiographical.

autoblinda |auto'blinda| *sf* armoured car.

autobotte |auto'botte| *sf* tanker.

autobus |'autobus| *sm inv* bus; **~ a due piani** double-decker bus.

autocarro |auto'karro| *sm* lorry.

autocisterna |autotʃis'tɛrna| *sf* tanker.

autocolonna |autoko'lonna| *sf* convoy.

autocombustione |autokombus'tjone| *sf* spontaneous combustion.

autocontrollo |autokon'trollo| *sm* self-control.

autocrate |au'tɔkrate| *sm* autocrat.

autocratico, a, ci, che |auto'kratiko| *ag* autocratic.

autocrazia |autokrat'tsia| *sf* autocracy.

autocritica, che |auto'kritika| *sf* self-criticism.

autocritico, a, ci, che |auto'kritiko| *ag* self-critical.

autoctono, a |au'tɔktono| *ag, sm/f* native.

autodidatta, i, e |autodi'datta| *sm/f* autodidact, self-taught person; **è un ~** he is self-taught.

autodidattico, a, ci, che |autodi'dattiko| *ag* teach-yourself *attr*.

autodifesa |autodi'fesa| *sf* self-defence.

autodromo |au'tɔdromo| *sm* motor racing track.

autoferrotranviario, a |autoferrotran'vjarjo| *ag* public transport *attr*.

autofilotranviario, a |autofilotran'vjarjo| *ag* bus, trolley and tram *attr*.

autofurgone |autofur'gone| *sm* van.

autogeno, a |au'tɔdʒeno| *ag*: **saldatura ~a** welding.

autogoverno |autogo'vɛrno| *sm* self-government.

autografo, a |au'tɔgrafo| *ag, sm* autograph.

autogrill |auto'gril| *sm inv* motorway café.

autolesionismo |autolezjo'nizmo| *sm (fig)* self-destruction.

autolesionista, i, e |autolezjo'nista| *ag* self-destructive.

autolinea |auto'linea| *sf* bus company.

automa, i |au'tɔma| *sm (anche fig)* automaton.

automatico, a, ci, che |auto'matiko| **1** *ag* automatic; **selezione** ~**a** *(Telec)* direct dialling, subscriber trunk dialling. **2** *sm (bottone)* press stud.

automatismo |automa'tizmo| *sm (Psic)* automatism.

automatizzare |automatid'dzare| *vt* to automate.

automazione |automat'tsjone| *sf* automation.

automezzo |auto'mɛddzo| *sm* motor vehicle.

automobile |auto'mɔbile| *sf* (motor) car, automobile *(Am)*; **correre in** ~ *(Sport)* to race, be a racing driver; **viaggiare in** ~ to travel by car; ~ **da corsa** racing car.

automobilina |automobi'lina| *sf* (toy) car.

automobilismo |automobi'lizmo| *sm (gen)* motoring; *(Sport)* motor racing.

automobilista, i, e |automobi'lista| *sm/f* motorist.

automobilistico, a, ci, che |automobi'listiko| *ag (industria, assicurazione, incidente)* car *attr*, automobile *attr (Am)*; *(sport)* motor *attr*.

automotrice |automo'tritʃe| *sf* railcar.

autonoleggio |autono'leddʒo| *sm* car hire, car rental.

autonomia |autono'mia| *sf (Pol)* autonomy; *(fig: di idee, comportamento)* independence; *(Tecn: di macchine, motori)* range; ~ **di volo** *(Aer)* flight range.

autonomista, i, e |autono'mista| *ag, sm/f (Pol)* autonomist.

autonomo, a |au'tɔnomo| **1** *ag (Pol)* autonomous; *(sindacato, pensiero)* independent. **2:** ~**i** *smpl* independent trade union members.

autoparcheggio |autopar'keddʒo| *sm* car park.

autoparco, chi |auto'parko| *sm (parcheggio)* car park; *(insieme di automezzi)* transport fleet.

autopista |auto'pista| *sf* fairground race track.

autopompa |auto'pompa| *sf* fire engine.

autopsia |autop'sia| *sf* autopsy, post-mortem (examination).

autopubblica, che |auto'pubblika| *sf* taxi.

autopullman |auto'pulman| *sm inv (di linea)* bus; *(per gite turistiche)* coach.

autoradio |auto'radjo| *sf inv (apparecchio)* car radio; *(autoveicolo)* radio car.

autoraduno |autora'duno| *sm (Sport)* motor racing meeting.

autore, trice |au'tore| *sm/f (gen, scrittore)* author; *(di pittura)* painter; *(di scultura)* sculptor; *(di musica)* composer; **l'~ del delitto** the person who committed the crime; **quadro d'~** painting by a famous artist; **diritti d'~** copyright *sg*; *(compenso)* royalties.

autorevole |auto'revole| *ag (giudizio)* authoritative; *(influente: persona)* influential.

autorevolezza |autorevo'lettsa| *sf* authority.

autorimessa |autori'messa| *sf* garage.

autorità |autori'ta| *sf inv* **(a)** *(potere)* authority; **esercitare la propria** ~ **su qn** to exercise one's authority over sb. **(b)** *(esperto)* authority, expert. **(c)** *(prestigio)* repute. **(d)** *(Amm: di governo, ente)*: **l'~, le** ~ the authorities.

autoritario, a |autori'tarjo| *ag* authoritarian.

autoritarismo |autorita'rizmo| *sm* authoritarianism.

autoritratto |autori'tratto| *sm* self-portrait.

autorizzare |autorid'dzare| *vt* to give permission for, authorize; ~ **qn a fare qc** to give sb permission to do sth.

autorizzazione |autoriddzat'tsjone| *sf (permesso)* authorization, permission; *(documento)* permit.

autosalone |autosa'lone| *sm* car showroom.

autoscatto |autos'katto| *sm (Fot)* timer.

autoscontro |autos'kontro| *sm* dodgem car.

autoscuola |autos'kwɔla| *sf* driving school.

autosnodato |autozno'dato| *sm* articulated vehicle.

autostop |autos'tɔp| *sm* hitchhiking; **fare l'~** to hitchhike; **è andato a Parigi in** *o* **con l'~** he hitchhiked to Paris.

autostoppista, i, e |autostop'pista| *sm/f* hitchhiker.

autostrada |autos'trada| *sf* motorway.

autostradale |autostra'dale| *ag* motorway *attr*.

autosufficiente |autosuffi'tʃɛnte| *ag* self-sufficient.

autosufficienza |autosuffi'tʃɛntsa| *sf* self-sufficiency.

autosuggestionarsi |autosuddʒestjo'narsi| *vr* to get carried away.

autosuggestione |autosuddʒes'tjone| *sf (Psic)* autosuggestion.

autotrasporto |autotras'pɔrto| *sm (di persone)* road transport; *(di merci)* road haulage.

autotreno |auto'treno| *sm* trailer truck.

autoveicolo |autove'ikolo| *sm* motor vehicle.

autovettura |autovet'tura| *sf* (motor) car.

autunnale |autun'nale| *ag (di autunno)* autumn *attr*; *(da autunno)* autumnal.

autunno |au'tunno| *sm* autumn, fall *(Am)*.

avallare |aval'lare| *vt (Fin)* to guarantee; *(fig: sostenere)* to back; *(: confermare)* to confirm.

avallo |a'vallo| *sm (Fin)* guarantee.

avambraccio |avam'brattʃo| *sm* forearm.

avamposto |avam'posto| *sm (Mil)* outpost.

avana |a'vana| *sm inv (sigaro)* Havana (cigar); *(colore)* Havana brown.

avance, s |a'väs| *sf:* **fare delle** ~**s a qn** to make advances to sb.

avanguardia |avan'gwardja| *sf* **(a)** *(Mil, fig)* vanguard; **essere all'~** to be in the vanguard. **(b)** *(Arte)* avant-garde; **d'~** avant-garde *attr*.

avanguardismo |avangwar'dizmo| *sm* avant-garde trend.

avanguardista, i, e |avangwar'dista| *sm/f* avant-garde artist.

avanscoperta |avansko'pɛrta| *sf (Mil)* reconnaissance; **andare in** ~ to reconnoitre.

avanspettacolo |avanspet'takolo| *sm (Teatro)* curtain raiser.

avanti |a'vanti| **1** *av* **(a)** *(moto: andare, venire)* forward; **fare un passo** ~ to take a step forward; **farsi** ~ to come forward; **piegarsi in** ~ to bend forward; ~ **e indietro** backwards and forwards, to and fro; **sono un anno** ~ I'm a year ahead; **essere** ~ **negli studi** to be well ahead in one's studies; **essere** ~ **di 5 punti** *(Sport etc)* to be ahead *o* be leading by 5 points; **mettere le mani** ~ *(fig)* to safeguard o.s.; **tirare** ~ *(fig)* to get by. **(b)** *(tempo: prima)* before; **l'anno** ~ the year before. **(c)** *(tempo: posteriore a)*: **d'ora in** ~ from now on; **essere** ~ **con gli** *o* **negli anni** to be well on in years; **il mio orologio è** *o* **va** ~ my watch is fast; **mettere** ~ **l'orologio** to put the clock forward; **guardare** ~ to look ahead. **(d)**: **andare** ~ to go forward; *(continuare)* to go on, carry on; *(fig: fare progressi)* to get on; *(: tirare* ~*)* to get by; **non aspettatemi, andate** ~! don't wait for me, go on (ahead)!; **non possiamo andare** ~ **così** we can't carry on like this. **(e)**: **mandare** ~ **la famiglia** to provide for one's family; **mandare ~ un'azienda** to run a business.

(f): ~! *(entra)* come in!; *(non fare così)* come on!; ~! **si accomodi!** come *(o* go) in and sit down!; ~ **il prossimo!** next please!; ~, **march!** forward, march!; ~ **tutta!** *(Naut)* full speed ahead!

2 *prep (luogo)* before, in front of; *(tempo)* before; ~ **Cristo** before Christ.

3 *sm inv (Sport)* forward.

avantreno [avan'treno] *sm (Aut)* front chassis.

avanzamento [avantsa'mento] *sm (gen)* advance; *(fig: progresso)* progress; *(: promozione di grado)* promotion.

avanzare[1] [avan'tsare] **1** *vi (aus essere) (procedere)* to advance, move forward; *(stagioni)* to approach; *(fig)* to make progress; ~ **negli anni** to grow old; ~ **di grado** to be promoted; **con l'~ degli anni** with the passing of time. **2** *vt (spostare in avanti: oggetto)* to move forward; *(fig: proposta etc)* to put forward; ~ **qn di grado** to promote sb.

avanzare[2] [avan'tsare] **1** *vt (essere creditore)* to be owed; **avanzo mille lire da te** you owe me a thousand lire. **2** *vi (aus essere)* **(a)** *(essere d'avanzo)* to be left over, remain; **è avanzato del pane da ieri** there is some bread left over from yesterday; **non m'avanza molto tempo** I haven't much time left; **c'è da mangiare per tutti e ne avanza** there is more than enough food for everyone; **basta e avanza** that's more than enough. **(b)** *(Mat):* **sette diviso tre fa due e avanza uno** seven divided by three is two remainder one.

avanzata [avan'tsata] *sf (Mil)* advance.

avanzato, a [avan'tsato] *ag (teoria, tecnica)* advanced; **in età ~a** advanced in years, up in years; **a primavera ~a** late on in spring; **a un'ora ~a della notte** late at night.

avanzo [a'vantso] *sm* **(a)** *(gen, Mat)* remainder; *(di stoffa)* remnant; *(di carta)* scrap; ~ **di galera** *(fig)* jailbird; ~**i** *pl (di cibo)* leftovers. **(b)** *(sovrappiù):* **averne d'~** to have more than enough; **ce n'è d'~** there is more than enough. **(c)** *(Comm)* surplus; *(eccedenza di bilancio)* profit carried forward; ~ **di cassa** cash in hand.

avaria [ava'ria] *sf (danno)* damage; *(guasto meccanico)* breakdown, failure; **motore in ~** engine out of action.

avariare [ava'rjare] **1** *vt* to damage. **2:** ~**rsi** *vr (cibo)* to go off, go bad.

avariato, a [ava'rjato] *ag (merce)* damaged; *(cibo)* off.

avarizia [ava'rittsja] *sf (peccato)* avarice; *(tirchieria)* meanness, stinginess; **crepi l'~!** to hang with the expense!

avaro, a [a'varo] **1** *ag:* ~ **(di)** stingy (with), mean (with); *(fig: di complimenti)* sparing (with). **2** *sm/f* miser.

avem(m)aria ['avemma'ria] *sf inv (preghiera)* Hail Mary, Ave Maria; *(suono delle campane)* Angelus.

avena [a'vena] *sf* oats *pl*.

avere [a'vere] **1** *vt* **(a)** *(gen)* to have; *(ricevere, ottenere)* to get; *(indossare)* to wear, have on; **non ha soldi** he has no money, he doesn't have any money, he hasn't got any money; **ho le mani sporche** my hands are dirty; **aveva le mani che gli tremavano** his hands were shaking.

(b) *(età, forma, colore)* to be; **quanti anni hai?** how old are you?; **ho vent'anni** I am twenty (years old); **aveva la mia stessa età** he was the same age as me; **ha 2 anni più di me** he's two years older than me; **la mia gonna ha un colore rosa pallido** my skirt is pale pink; ~ **fame/paura**

etc to be hungry/afraid *etc*.

(c) *(tempo):* **quanti ne abbiamo oggi?** what's the date today?; **ne hai ancora per molto?** have you got much longer to go?; **ne avremo ancora per due giorni prima di arrivare a Londra** we've got another two days to go before we get to London.

(d) *(fraseologia):* **averne fin sopra i capelli** *o* **piene le tasche** *(fam)* to be fed up to the teeth; **cos'hai?** what's wrong *o* what's the matter (with you)?; **ma cos'hai da lamentarti?** what have you got to complain about?; **ce l'hai con me?** are you angry with me?; **questo non ha niente a che vedere con me** that's got nothing to do with me.

2 *vb aus* **(a)** *(con pp):* **lo hai/avevi sentito?** have/had you heard from him?; **l'ho incontrata ieri** I met her yesterday; **quando l'avrò visto, ti dirò** when I've seen him, I'll let you know.

(b) *(+da+infin: dovere):* ~ **qc da fare** to have sth to do; **ho ancora due lettere da scrivere** I have to *o* must write another two letters, I've still got 2 letters to write; **non hai che da dirglielo** you only have to tell him; **non hai da preoccuparti per me** you don't have to *o* needn't worry about me.

3 *vb impers:* **si è avuto un risultato imprevisto** there was a surprising result; **ieri si è avuto un abbassamento di temperatura** there was a drop in temperature yesterday.

4 *sm:* **il dare e l'~** *(Fin)* debits and credits; **gli ~i** *(ricchezze)* wealth *sg*.

aviatore, trice [avja'tore] *sm/f* aviator, pilot.

aviatorio, a [avja'torjo] *ag* air *attr*, aviation *attr*.

aviazione [avjat'tsjone] *sf* aviation; ~ **(militare)** air force.

avicoltura [avikol'tura] *sf (di pollame)* poultry farming; *(di uccelli)* bird breeding.

avidità [avidi'ta] *sf:* ~ **(di)** *(denaro etc)* greed (for); *(gloria)* thirst (for); ~ **di imparare** eagerness to learn.

avido, a ['avido] *ag:* ~ **(di)** greedy (for); *(fig: di conoscenza)* eager (for); ~ **di imparare** eager to learn.

aviere [a'vjɛre] *sm (Mil)* airman.

aviogetto [avjo'dʒɛtto] *sm* jet.

aviorimessa [avjori'messa] *sf* hangar.

avitaminosi [avitami'nɔzi] *sf* vitamin deficiency.

avo ['avo] *sm (antenato)* ancestor; *(letterario: nonno)* grandfather.

avocado [avo'kado] *sm (albero)* avocado; *(frutto)* avocado (pear).

avorio [a'vɔrjo] *sm* ivory.

avulso, a [a'vulso] *ag:* **parole ~e dal contesto** words out of context; ~ **dalla società** *(fig)* cut off from society.

Avv. *abbr di* **avvocato.**

avvalersi [avva'lersi] *vr:* ~ **di** to avail o.s. of.

avvallamento [avvalla'mento] *sm* depression.

avvalorare [avvalo'rare] *vt (comprovare)* to confirm.

avvampare [avvam'pare] *vi (aus essere) (fuoco)* to flare up; *(fig: cielo, nuvole)* to become red; *(: arrossire)* to blush; ~ **per la collera** to flare up with anger.

avvantaggiare [avvantad'dʒare] **1** *vt (favorire)* to favour, further. **2:** ~**rsi** *vr* **(a):** ~**rsi di qc** to take advantage of sth, profit by sth. **(b):** ~**rsi su qn** to get ahead of sb; ~**rsi negli affari** to get ahead in business.

avvedersi [avve'dersi] *vr:* ~**rsi di qn/qc** to notice sb/sth.

avvedutezza [avvedu'tettsa] *sf (vedi ag)* prudence; astuteness.

avveduto, a [avve'duto] *ag (accorto)* prudent; *(scaltro)* astute.

avvelenamento [avvelena'mento] *sm* poisoning; ~ **da cibo** food poisoning.

avvelenare [avvele'nare] **1** *vt* to poison; ~ **l'esistenza a qn** to make sb's life a misery. **2**: ~**rsi** *vr* to poison o.s.; **si è avvelenato mangiando dei funghi** he got food poisoning from eating mushrooms; **è inutile** ~**rsi il sangue per così poco** there's no point in making yourself miserable over nothing.

avvenente [avve'nɛnte] *ag* attractive.

avvenenza [avve'nɛntsa] *sf* attractiveness.

avvenimento [avveni'mento] *sm* event.

avvenire [avve'nire] **1** *vb impers, vi (aus* **essere)** to happen, occur. **2** *ag inv* future *attr.* **3** *sm (gen)* future; *(carriera)* future, prospects *pl;* **in** ~ **in the** future.

avveniristico, a, ci, che [avveni'ristiko] *ag* innovating.

avventare [avven'tare] **1** *vt (scagliare):* **gli avventò contro il cane** he set the dog on him. **2**: ~**rsi** *vr (scagliarsi):* ~**rsi su** *o* **contro qn/qc** to hurl o.s. at sb/sth.

avventatezza [avventa'tettsa] *sf* rashness.

avventato, a [avven'tato] *ag* rash.

avventizio, a [avven'tittsjo] **1** *ag (impiegato)* temporary; *(guadagno)* casual. **2** *sm* temporary clerk.

avvento [av'vɛnto] *sm* **(a)** *(venuta)* coming, advent; ~ **al trono** accession to the throne. **(b)** *(Rel):* **l'A** ~ Advent.

avventore [avven'tore] *sm* customer.

avventura [avven'tura] *sf (gen)* adventure; *(vicenda amorosa)* (love) affair; **avere spirito d'** ~ to be adventurous.

avventurare [avventu'rare] **1** *vt (proposta)* to venture. **2**: ~**rsi** *vr:* ~**rsi (in qc)** to venture (into sth).

avventuriero, a [avventu'rjɛro] *sm/f* adventurer/ adventuress.

avventuroso, a [avventu'roso] *ag* adventurous.

avvenuto, a [avve'nuto] *pp di* **avvenire.**

avverarsi [avve'rarsi] *vr* to come true.

avverbiale [avver'bjale] *ag* adverbial.

avverbio [av'vɛrbjo] *sm* adverb.

avversare [avver'sare] *vt* to oppose.

avversario, a [avver'sarjo] **1** *ag* opposing. **2** *sm/f (Sport)* opponent; *(Pol)* adversary, opponent.

avversione [avver'sjone] *sf:* ~ **(per)** loathing (for), aversion (to); **nutrire un'** ~ **per** to harbour a dislike for.

avversità [avversi'ta] *sf* adversity.

avverso, a [av'vɛrso] *ag (forze, sorte)* adverse, hostile; *(tempo)* unfavourable, adverse.

avvertenza [avver'tentsa] *sf* **(a)** *(avviso)* warning; ~ **ai lettori** *(prefazione)* foreword. **(b)** *(cautela)* care; **abbiate l'** ~ **di pulirvi le scarpe prima di entrare** make sure you wipe your feet before going in. **(c):** ~**e** *pl (per l'uso)* instructions.

avvertibile [avver'tibile] *ag (suono, movimento)* perceptible.

avvertimento [avverti'mento] *sm* warning.

avvertire [avver'tire] *vt* **(a)** *(informare):* ~ **(di)** to inform (of), let know (of); **avvertimi prima di partire** let me know when you're leaving. **(b)** *(ammonire)* to warn. **(c)** *(percepire: suono)* to perceive, hear; *(sentire: dolore)* to feel.

avvezzo, a [av'vettso] *ag:* ~ **a** accustomed to.

avviamento [avvia'mento] *sm* **(a)** *(gen: atto)* starting; *(: effetto)* start. **(b)** *(insegnamento preparatorio: ad una carriera)* training; *(: ad uno studio)* introduction. **(c)** *(Meccanica: messa in moto)* starting; **motorino d'** ~ starter (motor). **(d)** *(Econ, Comm)* goodwill.

avviare [avvi'are] **1** *vt* **(a)** *(indirizzare)* to lead, direct. **(b)** *(mettere in moto)* to start (up). **(c)** *(iniziare: attività)* to start up, set up; *(: discorso)* to start up; *(: lavoro a maglia)* to cast on. **2**: ~**rsi** *vr (incamminarsi):* ~**rsi (a** *o* **verso qc)** to set out (for sth); *(fig: essere sul punto di):* ~**rsi a fare qc** to be about to do sth, be on the point of doing sth; **avviati, poi ti raggiungo** you go on ahead and I'll catch up; **l'estate si avvia alla fine** summer is drawing to an end.

avvicendamento [avvitʃenda'mento] *sm (gen)* alternation; *(Agr: delle colture)* rotation; **c'è molto** ~ **di personale** there is a high turnover of staff.

avvicendare [avvitʃen'dare] **1** *vt* to alternate. **2**: ~**rsi** *vr* to alternate; **si avvicendano in cucina** they take it in turns in the kitchen.

avvicinabile [avvitʃi'nabile] *ag (fig: persona)* approachable.

avvicinamento [avvitʃina'mento] *sm (Mil)* approach; **ha ottenuto un** ~ *(soldato)* he has been posted nearer home; *(in un lavoro)* he has been given a transfer nearer home; **l'** ~ **dei due paesi** the rapprochement between the two countries.

avvicinare [avvitʃi'nare] **1** *vt* **(a)** *(mettere vicino):* ~ **(a)** to bring near (to); **avvicina la sedia al tavolo** bring the chair near(er) to the fire; **il dolore li ha avvicinati** *(fig)* their sorrow has brought them closer together. **(b)** *(farsi vicino a: persona)* to approach. **2**: ~**rsi** *vr (a) (andare vicino):* ~**rsi a** to approach, go (*o* come) up to; **il treno si avvicinava alla stazione** the train was approaching the station; **avvicinati! avvicinati!** come here!, come closer!; **mi si avvicinò un mendicante** a beggar came up to me. **(b)** *(essere imminente: stagione, periodo)* to draw near. **(c)** *(somigliare)* to be similar, to be close.

avvilente [avvi'lɛnte] *ag (umiliante)* humiliating; *(scoraggiante)* discouraging, disheartening.

avvilimento [avvili'mento] *sm (vedi vb)* discouragement; humiliation.

avvilire [avvi'lire] **1** *vt (scoraggiare)* to dishearten, discourage; *(mortificare)* to humiliate. **2**: ~**rsi** *vr* to lose heart, become discouraged.

avviluppare [avvilup'pare] *vt* **(a)** *(avvolgere):* ~ **(in)** to wrap up (in); *(sog: nebbia)* to envelop. **(b)** *(ingarbugliare)* to entangle.

avvinazzato, a [avvinat'tsato] **1** *ag* drunken. **2** *sm* drunkard.

avvincente [avvin'tʃɛnte] *ag (persona)* charming, fascinating; *(spettacolo etc)* gripping, fascinating.

avvincere [av'vintʃere] *vt (fig: sog: persona)* to charm; *(: spettacolo etc)* to enthral, fascinate.

avvinghiare [avvin'gjare] **1** *vt* to clutch, clasp. **2**: ~**rsi** *vr:* ~**rsi a** to cling to; **gli si avvinghiò al collo** she threw her arms round his neck.

avvinto, a [av'vinto] *pp di* **avvincere.**

avvio [av'vio] *sm* start, beginning; **dare l'** ~ **a qc** to start sth off; **prendere l'** ~ to get going, get under way.

avvisaglia [avvi'zaʎʎa] *sf* **(a)** *(sintomo: di temporale etc)* sign; *(di malattia)* manifestation, sign, symptom. **(b)** *(scaramuccia)* skirmish.

avvisare [avvi'zare] *vt* **(a)** *(informare)* to inform, notify. **(b)** *(mettere in guardia)* to warn.

avvisatore [avviza'tore] *sm (apparecchio d'allarme)* alarm; ~ **acustico** horn; ~ **d'incendio** fire alarm.

avviso [av'vizo] *sm* **(a)** *(avvertenza: al pubblico)* notice; **dare** ~ **a qn di qc** to give sb notice of sth.

(b) *(documento di notificazione)* notice; ~ **di sfratto** eviction order. **(c)** *(Comm)*: ~ **di consegna/spedizione** delivery/consignment note; ~ **di pagamento** payment advice. **(d)** *(consiglio, avvertimento)* warning; **dare un** ~ **a qn** to warn sb; **mettere qn sull'**~ to put sb on their guard. **(e)** *(opinione)* opinion; **a mio** ~ in my opinion. **(f)** *(annuncio)* announcement; *(inserzione pubblicitaria)* advertisement; ~ **economico** classified advertisement.

avvistamento [avvista'mento] *sm* sighting.

avvistare [avvis'tare] *vt* to sight.

avvitare [avvi'tare] **1** *vt (vite)* to screw in (*o* down); *(lampadina)* to screw in. **2**: ~**rsi** *vr (Aer)* to spin, go into a spin.

avvizzimento [avvittsi'mento] *sm* withering.

avvizzire [avvit'tsire] *vi (aus essere)*, ~**rsi** *vr* to wither.

avvocatessa [avvoka'tessa] *sf* (female) lawyer.

avvocato [avvo'kato] *sm* **(a)** *(gen)* lawyer; *(in corti inferiori)* solicitor; *(in corti superiori)* barrister, attorney(-at-law) *(Am)*; **consultare il proprio** ~ to consult one's lawyer; ~ **di parte civile/difensore** counsel for the plaintiff/the defence. **(b)** *(fig)* advocate, defender; ~ **del diavolo** devil's advocate; ~ **delle cause perse** defender of lost causes.

avvocatura [avvoka'tura] *sf* **(a)** *(professione)* legal profession; **esercitare l'**~ to practise law. **(b)** *(insieme degli avvocati)*: l'~ the Bar.

avvolgere [av'vɔldʒere] **1** *vt* **(a)** *(bambino, oggetto)* to wrap (up); *(arrotolare: tappeto)* to roll up; **avvolto dalla nebbia** enveloped in fog; **avvolto dal mistero/silenzio** shrouded in mystery/silence. **(b)**: ~ **qc intorno a qc** to wind sth round sth. **2**: ~**rsi** *vr*: **si avvolse nel mantello** he wrapped himself in his cloak.

avvolgibile [avvol'dʒibile] **1** *ag* roll-up *attr*. **2** *sm* roller blind.

avvolgimento [avvoldʒi'mento] *sm (Elettr)* winding.

avvolto, a [av'vɔlto] *pp di* **avvolgere**.

avvoltoio [avvol'tojo] *sm (gen, fig)* vulture.

avvoltolare [avvolto'lare] **1** *vt* to roll up. **2**: ~**rsi** *vr (rotolarsi: nel fango)* to roll (around).

azalea [adʒa'lɛa] *sf* azalea.

azienda [ad'dzjɛnda] *sf (gen)* business, firm, concern; ~ **agricola** (large-scale) farm; ~ **di soggiorno** tourist board.

aziendale [addzjen'dale] *ag* company *attr*; **mensa** ~ firm canteen; **organizzazione** ~ business administration.

azimut ['addzimut] *sm inv (Astron)* azimuth.

azionare [attsjo'nare] *vt* to activate.

azionario, a [attsjo'narjo] *ag* share *attr*; **mercato** ~ stock market; **capitale** ~ share capital.

azione[1] [at'tsjone] *sf* **(a)** *(l'agire)* action; **entrare in** ~ *(piano)* to come into operation; **passare all'**~ to take action; *(Mil)* to go into action. **(b)** *(atto)* action, act; **buona/cattiva** ~ good/bad deed. **(c)** *(effetto)* action; **l'**~ **dei gas tossici** the action of toxic gases. **(d)** *(Teatro, Sport)* action; *(trama)* plot; **romanzo/film d'**~ action novel/film. **(e)** *(Dir: processo)* (law)suit, action.

azione[2] [at'tsjone] *sf (Fin: titolo)* share; ~**i shares**, stocks; ~**i preferenziali** preference shares.

azionista, i, e [attsjo'nista] *sm/f* shareholder.

azoto [ad'dzɔto] *sm* nitrogen.

azzannare [attsan'nare] *vt* to maul, bite.

azzardare [addzar'dare] **1** *vt (soldi, vita)* to risk, hazard; *(domanda, ipotesi)* to hazard, venture. **2**: ~**rsi** *vr*: ~**rsi a fare qc** to dare (to) do sth.

azzardato, a [addzar'dato] *ag (ipotesi, dichiarazione)* rash; *(impresa)* risky; **non voglio dare un parere** ~, **ma...** I don't want to be hasty *o* rash, but... .

azzardo [ad'dzardo] *sm* risk; **gioco d'**~ game of chance; **gli piace giocare d'**~ *(anche fig)* he likes gambling.

azzeccare [attsek'kare] *vt (bersaglio)* to hit, strike; *(risposta, pronostico)* to get right; *(fig: indovinare)* to guess; **ha azzeccato il pronostico al totocalcio** he had a win on the pools; **non ne azzecca mai una** he never gets anything right.

azzerare [addze'rare] *vt* **(a)** *(Mat, Fis)* to make equal to zero, reduce to zero. **(b)** *(Tecn: di uno strumento)* to (re)set to zero.

azzimato, a [addzi'mato] *ag* dressed up, spruced up.

azzimo, a ['addzimo] **1** *ag (non lievitato: pane)* unleavened. **2** *sm* unleavened bread.

azzittire [attsit'tire] *vt*: ~ **qn** to silence sb, shut sb up.

azzoppare [attsop'pare] **1** *vt* to lame, make lame. **2**: ~**rsi** *vr* to become lame.

azzuffarsi [attsuf'farsi] *vr (gen)* to come to blows; *(bambini)* to squabble.

azzurrino, a [addzur'rino] *ag* light blue, pale blue.

azzurro, a [ad'dzurro] **1** *ag* **(a)** *(colore)* blue, azure; **il principe** ~ Prince Charming. **(b)** *(Sport: della nazionale italiana)* of the Italian (national) team. **2** *sm* **(a)** *(colore)* blue, azure. **(b)** *(Sport: atleta)* member of the Italian national team; **gli** ~**i** the Italian (national) team.

azzurrognolo, a [addzur'roɲɲolo] *ag* bluish.

B

B, b [bi] *sf o m inv (lettera)* B, b.
babau [ba'bau] *sm inv* ogre, bogey man.
babbeo [bab'bɛo] *sm* fool, idiot.
babbo ['babbo] *sm (fam)* dad, daddy; **B~ Natale** Father Christmas, Santa Claus.
babbuccia, ce [bab'buttʃa] *sf* (Turkish) slipper; *(per neonati)* bootee.
babbuino [babbu'ino] *sm* baboon.
babele [ba'bɛle] *sf* chaos, confusion.
babordo [ba'bordo] *sm (Naut)* port side; **a ~ to** port.
baby ['beibi] *smf inv (neonato)* (newborn) baby, infant.
bacato, a [ba'kato] *ag (frutto)* worm-eaten, maggoty; *(fig: mente)* diseased; *(: persona)* corrupt.
bacca, che ['bakka] *sf* berry.
baccalà [bakka'la] *sm inv (pesce)* dried salted cod; *(fig: persona sciocca)* dummy; **magro come un ~** as thin as a rake.
baccano [bak'kano] *sm* row, din; **fare ~ to make a** row *o* din.
baccello [bat'tʃɛllo] *sm* pod.
bacchetta [bak'ketta] *sf (bastoncino)* rod, stick; *(di tamburo)* drumstick; *(di direttore d'orchestra)* baton; **~ magica** magic wand; **comandare a ~ to** rule with a rod of iron.
bacchiare [bak'kjare] *vt* to knock down *(fruit, nuts etc)*.
bacheca, che [ba'kɛka] *sf* **(a)** *(mobile)* showcase, display case. **(b)** *(Univ, in ufficio)* notice board.
bachicoltura [bakikol'tura] *sf* breeding of silkworms.
baciamano [batʃa'mano] *sm*: **fare il ~ a qn** to kiss sb's hand.
baciare [ba'tʃare] **1** *vt* to kiss; **lo baciò sulla guancia** she kissed him on the cheek, she kissed his cheek; **le sponde baciate dal sole** the sun-kissed shores. **2**: **~rsi** *vr* to kiss (each other).
bacillare [batʃil'lare] *ag* bacterial.
bacillo [ba'tʃillo] *sm* bacillus, germ.
bacinella [batʃi'nɛlla] *sf (gen: recipiente)* bowl, basin; *(per lavarsi)* basin.
bacino [ba'tʃino] *sm* **(a)** *(Anat)* pelvis. **(b)** *(Geog)* basin. **(c)** *(Geol)* field; **~ carbonifero** coalfield; **~ petrolifero** oilfield. **(d)** *(Naut)* dock; **~ di carenaggio** dry dock; **~ galleggiante** floating dock.
bacio ['batʃo] *sm* kiss; **dare un ~ a qn** to give sb a kiss; **coprire qn di ~i** to smother sb with kisses; **dare il ~ della buonanotte a qn** to kiss sb goodnight; **tanti ~i** *(fine di lettera)* love and kisses.
baco, chi ['bako] *sm (gen: verme)* worm, maggot; *(larva)* grub; **~ da seta** silkworm.
bacucco, a, chi, che [ba'kukko] *ag* senile; **è un vecchio ~** he's an old fool.
bada ['bada] *sf*: **tenere qn a ~** *(tener d'occhio)* to keep an eye on sb; *(tenere a distanza)* to hold sb at bay.
badare [ba'dare] *vi*: **~ a (a)** *(occuparsi di: negozio, casa)* to look after, mind; *(: bambino, malato)* to take care of, look after; *(: cliente)* to attend to;

bada agli affari tuoi! mind your own business! **(b)** *(fare attenzione)* to pay attention to, mind; **nessuno gli ha badato** nobody paid any attention to him; **bada (a te)!** watch out!; **bada a non cadere** mind *o* be careful you don't fall. **(c)** *(preoccuparsi)* to care about; **non bada a ciò che dice la gente** he doesn't care what people say; **è un tipo che non bada a spese** money is no object with him.
badile [ba'dile] *sm* shovel.
baffo ['baffo] *sm* **(a)**: **~i** *pl (di persona)* moustache *sg*; *(di animale)* whiskers; **un pranzo da leccarsi i ~i** a mouth-watering meal; **ridere sotto i ~i** to laugh up one's sleeve; **di quello che mi ha detto me ne faccio un ~** *(fam)* I don't give *o* care a damn about what he said. **(b)** *(sgorbio, sbavatura)* smear, smudge.
baffuto, a [baf'futo] *ag (persona)* with a moustache.
bagagliaio [bagaʎ'ʎajo] *sm* **(a)** *(di auto)* boot, trunk *(Am)*; *(di treno)* luggage van, baggage car *(Am)*. **(b)** *(deposito bagagli)* left-luggage office.
bagaglio [ba'gaʎʎo] *sm* luggage, baggage; **fare/disfare i ~i** to pack/unpack; **~ appresso** accompanied luggage; **~ a mano** hand luggage; **ho preso armi e ~i e me ne sono andato** *(fig)* I packed up and left; **un ~ intellettuale** a store of knowledge.
bagattella [bagat'tɛlla] *sf* **(a)** *(inezia)* trifle. **(b)** *(Mus)* bagatelle.
baggianata [baddʒa'nata] *sf* foolish action; **dire ~e** to talk nonsense.
bagliore [baʎ'ʎore] *sm (di fuoco)* glow; *(di fari)* glare; *(di lampi)* flash; **un ~ di speranza** a gleam *o* ray of hope.
bagnante [baɲ'ɲante] *smf* swimmer, bather.
bagnare [baɲ'ɲare] **1** *vt* **(a)** *(gen)* to wet; *(inzuppare)* to soak; *(labbra)* to moisten; *(piante, fiori)* to water; **bagna la camicia prima di stirarla** damp the shirt before you iron it; **~rsi le labbra** to moisten one's lips; **le lacrime bagnavano il suo viso** her face was bathed in tears. **(b)** *(sog: fiume)* to flow through; *(: mare)* to wash, bathe; **il Mediterraneo bagna Genova** Genoa stands on the Mediterranean. **(c)** *(brindare)* to drink to, toast; **abbiamo bagnato la nuova macchina** we've celebrated the purchase of the new car. **2**: **~rsi** *vr* **(a)** *(fare il bagno)* to bathe. **(b)** *(prendere acqua)* to get wet; *(inzupparsi)* to get soaked, get drenched; **il bambino si è bagnato** the baby has wet himself.
bagnato, a [baɲ'ɲato] *ag* wet; **~ di lacrime** bathed in tears; **~ di sudore** *(viso, fronte)* bathed in sweat; *(camicia)* soaked with sweat; **~ fino alle ossa** soaked to the skin; **~ fradicio** wet through, drenched; **era come un pulcino ~** he looked like a drowned rat.
bagnino, a [baɲ'ɲino] *smf* lifeguard; *(in piscina)* bathing attendant.
bagno ['baɲɲo] *sm* **(a)** *(gen, Chim, Fot)* bath; *(in piscina)* swim; *(al mare)* swim, bathe; **fare il ~** *(nella vasca)* to have a bath; *(in piscina)* to go

swimming; *(al mare)* to go swimming *o* bathing; **(stanza da)** ~ bathroom; **(vasca da)** ~ bath, bathtub; ~ **di fango/sabbia** mud/sand bath; ~ **(di) schiuma** bubble bath; ~**i di mare** sea bathing *sg*; **mettere qc a** ~ to leave sth to soak. **(b)** *(stabilimento balneare)* bathing establishment; ~**i pubblici** public baths.

bagnomaria [baɲɲoma'ria] *sm:* **cuocere a** ~ to cook in a double saucepan.

baia ['baja] *sf (Geog)* bay.

baio, a ['bajo] *ag (cavallo)* bay.

baionetta [bajo'netta] *sf* bayonet.

baita ['baita] *sf* mountain hut.

balalaica, che [bala'laika] *sf* balalaika.

balaustra [bala'ustra] *sf*, **balaustrata** [balaus-'trata] *sf* balustrade.

balbettare [balbet'tare] **1** *vt (gen)* to stammer (out); *(sog: bambino)* to babble (out); ~ **delle scuse** to mumble an excuse. **2** *vi (vedi vt)* to stammer; to babble.

balbettio, ii [balbet'tio] *sm (vedi vb)* stammering; babbling.

balbuzie [bal'buttsje] *sf* stammer; **essere affetto da** ~ to have a stammer.

balbuziente [balbut'tsjɛnte] **1** *ag* stammering, mumbling; **essere** ~ to stammer. **2** *sm/f* stammerer.

balcone [bal'kone] *sm* balcony.

baldacchino [baldak'kino] *sm* canopy; **letto a** ~ four-poster (bed).

baldanza [bal'dantsa] *sf (sicurezza)* self-confidence; *(spavalderia)* audacity, boldness.

baldanzoso, a [baldan'tsoso] *ag (vedi sf)* self-confident; audacious, bold.

baldo, a ['baldo] *ag* bold.

baldoria [bal'dɔrja] *sf* merrymaking, revelry; **fare** ~ to have a riotous time.

balena [ba'lena] *sf (Zool)* whale; *(fig peg)* barrel of lard.

balenare [bale'nare] *vi (aus essere) (gen)* to flash; **mi è balenata un'idea** an idea flashed in *o* through my mind; **l'ira balenò nel suo sguardo** his eyes flashed angrily.

baleniera [bale'njɛra] *sf (per la caccia)* whaler, whaling ship.

baleno [ba'leno] *sm* flash; **in un** ~ in a flash.

balestra [ba'lɛstra] *sf (arma)* crossbow.

balia[1] ['balja] *sf (anche fig)* wet-nurse; ~ **asciutta** nanny.

balia[2] [ba'lia] *sf (potere assoluto):* **essere in** ~ **di** to be at the mercy of; **la nave era in** ~ **delle onde** the ship was at the mercy of the waves; **essere lasciato in** ~ **di se stesso** to be left to one's own devices.

balilla [ba'lilla] *sm inv (Storia)* member of Fascist youth group.

balistica [ba'listika] *sf* ballistics *sg*.

balistico, a, ci, che [ba'listiko] *ag* ballistic; **perito** ~ ballistics expert.

balla ['balla] *sf* **(a)** *(quantità)* bale. **(b)** *(fam: fandonia)* rubbish *no pl*; **raccontare una** ~ **a qn** to tell sb a tall story; **un sacco di** ~**e** a pack of lies, a load of rubbish.

ballabile [bal'labile] *sm (Mus)* dance number, dance tune.

ballare [bal'lare] **1** *vi* **(a)** to dance; **andare a** ~ to go dancing; ~ **come un orso** to dance like an elephant. **(b)** *(traballare: mobile)* to wobble; **le onde facevano** ~ **la nave** the waves tossed the ship about; **quella giacca gli balla addosso** he's lost in that jacket. **2** *vt* to dance; ~ **il valzer** to (dance the) waltz.

ballata [bal'lata] *sf* ballad.

ballatoio [balla'tojo] *sm* **(a)** *(terrazzina)* gallery. **(b)** *(per uccelli)* perch, swing.

ballerina [balle'rina] *sf* **(a)** (female) dancer; ~ **classica** ballerina, ballet dancer; **prima** ~ prima ballerina; ~ **di rivista** chorus girl. **(b)** *(scarpa)* ballet shoe. **(c)** *(uccello)* wagtail.

ballerino [balle'rino] *sm* dancer; *(classico)* ballet dancer.

balletto [bal'letto] *sm* **(a)** *(spettacolo)* ballet; *(Mus)* ballet music. **(b)** *(corpo di ballo)* dance troupe; *(:classico)* corps de ballet.

ballo ['ballo] *sm (danza, festa)* dance, ball; *(giro di danza)* dance; **fare un** ~ to have a dance; ~ **in maschera** *o* **mascherato** (fancy-dress) ball; **essere in** ~ *(fig)* to be at stake; **tirare in** ~ **qn** *(fig)* to involve sb; **tirare in** ~ **qc** to bring sth up, raise sth; **entrare in** ~ *(fig: persona)* to become involved; *(: cosa)* to be raised, be brought up.

ballottaggio [ballot'taddʒo] *sm* second ballot.

balneare [balne'are] *ag* bathing *attr*.

baloccare [balok'kare] **1** *vt (trastullare)* to distract, amuse. **2:** ~**rsi** *vr (perder tempo)* to fritter (one's) time away.

balocco, chi [ba'lɔkko] *sm* toy, plaything.

balordo [ba'lordo] *ag (sciocco)* silly, foolish; *(poco affidamento)* unreliable.

balsamico, a, ci, che [bal'samiko] *ag (aria, brezza)* balmy; **pomata** ~**a** balsam.

balsamo ['balsamo] *sm* balsam, balm; *(fig)* balm.

baluardo [balu'ardo] *sm (bastione)* bulwark, rampart; *(fig)* bulwark.

baluginare [baludʒi'nare] *vi (aus essere)* to flicker; *(fig):* **gli baluginò il sospetto che...** suddenly the suspicion came into his mind that... .

balza ['baltsa] *sf* **(a)** *(rupe)* crag. **(b)** *(di stoffa)* frill. **(c)** *(di cavallo)* white sock.

balzano, a [bal'tsano] *ag (persona, idea)* queer, odd; **è un cervello** ~ he's a queer fish.

balzare [bal'tsare] *vi (aus essere)* to leap, jump; ~ **in piedi** to leap *o* jump to one's feet; ~ **giù dal letto/dalla sedia** to leap *o* jump out of bed/up from one's chair; ~ **in macchina/a cavallo** to leap *o* jump into a car/onto a horse; **il cuore le balzò per la gioia/per la paura** her heart leapt with joy/with fear; **la verità balza agli occhi** the truth of the matter is obvious; **gli balzò alla mente che...** it came to him that... .

balzo[1] ['baltso] *sm (salto)* leap, jump; *(di palla)* bounce; **fare un** ~ to leap, jump; to bounce; **un** ~ **in avanti** *(fig)* a great leap forward; **prendere la palla al** ~ *(fig)* to seize one's opportunity.

balzo[2] ['baltso] *sm (di rupe)* crag, cliff.

bambagia [bam'badʒa] *sf (ovatta)* cottonwool; *(cascame)* cotton waste; **tenere qn nella** ~ *(fig)* to mollycoddle sb.

bambinaia [bambi'naja] *sf* nursemaid, nanny.

bambino, a [bam'bino] **1** *sm/f (gen)* child, (little) boy/girl; *(neonato)* baby; **quando ero** ~ when I was a child; **fare il** ~ to behave childishly; **è un** ~! he's really childish! **2** *ag:* **una scienza ancora** ~**a** a science still in its infancy.

bamboccio [bam'bɔtʃo] *sm (bambino)* chubby child; *(pupazzo)* rag doll; *(fig)* simpleton.

bambola ['bambola] *sf (giocattolo)* doll, dolly; *(fig: donna)* doll.

bambolotto [bambo'lɔtto] *sm* male doll.

bambù [bam'bu] *sm inv* bamboo.

banale [ba'nale] *ag (gen)* banal; *(idea, scusa)* trite; *(incidente)* trivial; *(persona)* ordinary; *(vita)* humdrum, dull; **è solo un** ~ **raffreddore** it's just a common or garden cold, it's just an ordinary cold.

banalità [banali'ta] *sf inv* **(a)** *(vedi ag)* banality;

triteness; triviality; ordinariness; dullness. **(b)** *(parole)* truism, trite remark; **dire una** ~ to make a trite remark.

banana [ba'nana] *sf* banana.

banano [ba'nano] *sm* banana tree.

banca, che ['banka] *sf (istituto, edificio)* bank; **in** ~ in the bank; **andare in** ~ to go to the bank; ~ **del sangue** blood bank.

bancarella [banka'rɛlla] *sf* stall.

bancario, a [ban'karjo] **1** *ag* bank *attr*; **assegno** ~ (bank) cheque. **2** *sm/f* bank employee.

bancarotta [banka'rɔtta] *sf (Fin)* bankruptcy; *(fig)* failure; **fare** ~, **andare in** ~ to go bankrupt.

banchettare [banket'tare] *vi* to banquet, feast.

banchetto [ban'ketto] *sm* banquet; **fare un** ~ **(a base di qc)** to feast (on sth).

banchiere [ban'kjɛre] *sm (Fin, nei giochi)* banker.

banchina [ban'kina] *sf* **(a)** *(di porto)* quay, wharf. **(b)** *(marciapiede)* platform. **(c)** *(per pedoni)* footpath; *(per ciclisti)* cycle path; ~ **spartitraffico** *(Aut)* traffic island.

banchisa [ban'kiza] *sf* ice pack.

banco, chi ['banko] *sm* **(a)** *(sedile)* seat, bench; *(: Parlamento)* bench; ~ **di chiesa** pew; ~ **degli imputati** *(Dir)* dock; ~ **di scuola** desk. **(b)** *(di negozio)* counter; *(di mercato)* stall; **sotto** ~ *(fig)* under the counter. **(c)** *(di officina)* (work)bench; ~ **di prova** test bed; *(fig)* testing ground. **(d)** *(Fin)* bank; ~ **del Lotto** lottery-ticket office; **tenere il** ~ *(nei giochi)* to be (the) banker; **tener** ~ *(fig)* to monopolize the conversation. **(e)** *(Meteor)* bank, patch; ~ **di nebbia** fog bank. **(f)** *(Geol: strato)* layer; *(: di coralli)* reef; ~ **di ghiaccio** ice floe; ~ **di sabbia** sandbank. **(g)** *(di pesci)* shoal.

bancogiro [banko'dʒiro] *sm* credit transfer.

banconota [banko'nɔta] *sf* banknote.

banda[1] ['banda] *sf (di suonatori)* band; *(di ladri, guerriglieri)* band, gang; *(di amici)* gang, group.

banda[2] ['banda] *sf* **(a)** *(di stoffa, metallo)* band, strip; *(di carta)* strip; *(di calcolatore)* tape; ~ **perforata** punch tape. **(b)** *(Fis, Radio)* band.

banderuola [bande'rwɔla] *sf* *(Meteor)* weathercock, weathervane; **essere una** ~ *(fig)* to be fickle.

bandiera [ban'djɛra] *sf* flag; **alzare** ~ **bianca** to wave the white flag; **battere** ~ **italiana** *(nave etc)* to fly the Italian flag; **cambiare** ~ *(fig)* to change sides; ~ **di comodo** flag of convenience.

bandire [ban'dire] *vt* **(a)** *(annunciare)* to announce. **(b)** *(porre al bando: prodotto, persona)* to ban; *(: Storia, fig: sentimenti)* to banish; *(: complimenti, ciance)* to dispense with; **l'hanno bandito dall'ordine degli avvocati** he has been struck off.

bandita [ban'dita] *sf* reserve.

banditismo [bandi'tizmo] *sm* banditry.

bandito [ban'dito] *sm* bandit, outlaw.

banditore [bandi'tore] *sm* **(a)** *(Storia)* town crier. **(b)** *(di aste)* auctioneer.

bando ['bando] *sm* **(a)** *(annuncio)* (public) announcement, (public) notice. **(b)** *(esilio)*: **mettere al** ~ **qn** to exile sb; *(fig)* to freeze sb out; ~ **alle ciance!** that's enough talk!

bandolo ['bandolo] *sm (di matassa)* end; **trovare il** ~ **della matassa** *(fig)* to find the key to the problem.

banjo ['bændʒou] *sm inv* banjo.

bar [bar] *sm inv (locale)* bar *(serving coffee, spirits, snacks etc)*; *(mobile)* cocktail cabinet.

bara ['bara] *sf* coffin; **avere un piede nella** ~ *(fig)* to have one foot in the grave.

baracca, che [ba'rakka] *sf* hut; *(fam peg: oggetto)* piece of junk; **mandare avanti la** ~ to keep

things going; **come va la** ~? how are you managing?; **piantare** ~ **e burattini** to throw everything up.

baraccato, a [barak'kato] *sm/f person living in temporary camp.*

baracchino [barak'kino] *sm* **(a)** *(chiosco)* stall. **(b)** *(apparecchio)* CB radio.

baraccone [barak'kone] *sm* booth, stall; ~**i** *(parco dei divertimenti)* funfair *sg*; **fenomeno da** ~ circus freak.

baraonda [bara'onda] *sf* chaos.

barare [ba'rare] *vi* to cheat.

baratro ['baratro] *sm (anche fig)* abyss.

barattare [barat'tare] *vt*: ~ **qc con qc** *(merce)* to barter sth for sth; *(francobolli, dischi etc)* to swap sth for sth.

baratto [ba'ratto] *sm (Comm)* barter; *(scambio)* exchange; **fare un** ~ **con qn** to swap with sb.

barattolo [ba'rattolo] *sm (di vetro, coccio)* jar, pot; *(di latta)* tin, can.

barba ['barba] *sf* **(a)** beard; **farsi la** ~ to shave; **una** ~ **di 3 giorni** 3 days' growth; **farla in** ~ **a qn** to fool sb; **servire qn di** ~ **e capelli** *(fig)* to teach sb a lesson; **che** ~! *(persona, libro etc)* what a bore! **(b)** *(Bot)* (fine) root.

barbabietola [barba'bjɛtola] *sf* beetroot; ~ **da zucchero** sugar beet.

barbarico, a, ci, che [bar'bariko] *ag (invasione)* barbarian; *(usanze, metodi)* barbaric.

barbarie [bar'barje] *sf inv (condizione)* barbarism; *(crudeltà)* barbarity.

barbaro, a ['barbaro] **1** *ag (popolo)* barbarian; *(comportamento, crimine)* barbaric, barbarous; *(stile, gusto)* appalling. **2** *sm* barbarian.

barbecue ['ba:bikju:] *sm inv* barbecue.

barbiere [bar'bjɛre] *sm* barber.

barbiturico, a, ci, che [barbi'turiko] **1** *ag* barbituric. **2** *sm* barbiturate.

barbone [bar'bone] *sm* **(a)** *(straccione)* vagrant. **(b)** *(anche: cane* ~) poodle.

barboso, a [bar'boso] *ag* boring.

barbuto, a [bar'buto] *ag* bearded.

barca[1]**, che** ['barka] *sf* boat; ~ **a vela/a remi** sailing/rowing boat; ~ **a motore** motorboat; **andare in** ~ *(a vela)* to go sailing; *(a remi etc)* to go boating; **mandare avanti la** ~ *(fig)* to keep things going.

barca[2]**, che** ['barka] *sf (fig: quantità)*: **una** ~ **di** heaps of, tons of.

barcaiolo [barka'jɔlo] *sm* boatman.

barcamenarsi [barkame'narsi] *vr (nel lavoro)* to get by; *(a parole)* to beat about the bush.

barcollare [barkol'lare] *vi* to stagger.

barcone [bar'kone] *sm (quadrangolare)* scow; *(per costruzione di ponti)* pontoon.

bardare [bar'dare] **1** *vt (cavallo)* to harness; *(fig: persona)* to dress up. **2**: ~**rsi** *vr* to dress up, deck o.s. out.

bardatura [barda'tura] *sf (di cavallo)* harness; *(fig)* finery.

bardo ['bardo] *sm* bard.

barella [ba'rɛlla] *sf (per malati)* stretcher.

barese [ba'rese] *ag* of *(o* from) Bari.

baricentro [bari'tʃɛntro] *sm* centre of gravity.

barile [ba'rile] *sm (gen)* barrel; *(di vino)* cask, barrel.

bario ['barjo] *sm* barium.

barista, i, e [ba'rista] *sm/f* barman/maid.

baritonale [barito'nale] *ag* baritone *attr*.

baritono [ba'ritono] *sm* baritone.

barlume [bar'lume] *sm* (faint) light; *(fig: di speranza, idea)* glimmer.

baro ['baro] *sm (Carte)* cardsharp.

barocco, a, chi, che [ba'rɔkko] *ag, sm* baroque.
barometro [ba'rɔmetro] *sm* barometer.
baronale [baro'nale] *ag* baronial.
barone [ba'rone] *sm* baron; **i ~i della medicina** *(fig peg)* the top brass in the medical faculty.
baronessa [baro'nessa] *sf* baroness.
baronetto [baro'netto] *sm* baronet.
barra ['barra] *sf* **(a)** *(gen)* bar; *(di legno, metallo)* rod, bar. **(b)** *(Naut)* helm; *(: piccola)* tiller. **(c)** *(segno grafico)* stroke.
barricare [barri'kare] **1** *vt* to barricade. **2**: ~**rsi** *vr*: ~**rsi in/dietro** to barricade o.s. in/behind; ~**rsi in camera** to shut o.s. up in one's room.
barricata [barri'kata] *sf* barricade; **essere dall'altra parte della ~** *(fig)* to be on the other side of the fence.
barriera [bar'rjɛra] *sf (gen,fig, Fis)* barrier; *(corallina)* reef; *(Calcio)* wall; ~ **doganale** trade *o* tariff barrier; ~ **del suono** sound barrier.
barrire [bar'rire] *vi* to trumpet.
barrito [bar'rito] *sm* trumpeting.
barroccio [bar'rɔttʃo] *sm* cart.
baruffa [ba'ruffa] *sf* squabble; **fare ~** to squabble.
barzelletta [barzel'letta] *sf* joke; **raccontare una ~** to tell *o* crack a joke.
basalto [ba'zalto] *sm* basalt.
basamento [baza'mento] *sm (parte inferiore, piedestallo)* base; *(Tecn)* bed, base plate.
basare [ba'zare] **1** *vt*: ~ **(su)** to base (on), found (on). **2**: ~**rsi** *vr*: ~**rsi su** *(sog: edificio, argomento)* to be based on, be founded on; *(: persona)* to base o.s. on.
basco, a, schi, sche ['basko] **1** *ag* Basque. **2** *sm/f* Basque. **3** *sm* **(a)** *(lingua)* Basque. **(b)** *(berretto)* beret.
bascula ['baskula] *sf* weighing machine, weighbridge.
base ['baze] **1** *sf* **(a)** *(gen, Mil, Chim, Mat)* base; *(Pol)*: **la ~ del partito** the rank and file of the party. **(b)** *(fig: fondamento)* basis; *(: di problema, idea)* origin, root; ~ **di partenza** starting point. **(c)**: ~**i** *pl (fondamento)* basis *sg*, foundation *sg*; **gettare le ~i per qc** to lay the basis *o* foundations for sth; **avere buone ~i** *(Scol)* to have a sound educational background. **(d)**: **prodotto a ~ di carne** meat-based product; **essere alla ~ di qc** to be at the root of sth; **servire da** *o* **come ~ a** *(punto di partenza)* to act as the basis for; **in ~ a** *(notizie, informazioni etc)* according to; **in ~ a ciò...** on that basis...; **sulla ~ di** on the basis of; **regole di ~** basic rules. **2** *ag inv (prezzo, problema, stipendio)* basic.
baseball ['beisbɔːl] *sm* baseball.
basetta [ba'zetta] *sf* side whisker.
basico, a, ci, che ['baziko] *ag (Chim)* basic.
basilare [bazi'lare] *ag* basic, fundamental.
basilica, che [ba'zilika] *sf* basilica.
basilico [ba'ziliko] *sm (Bot)* (sweet) basil.
basket ['baːskit] *sm (sport)* basketball.
bassa ['bassa] *sf* lowlands *pl*.
bassezza [bas'settsa] *sf (d'animo, di sentimenti)* baseness; *(azione)* base action.
basso, a ['basso] **1** *ag* **(a)** *(gen)* low; *(persona)* short; *(suono)* soft, low; *(: profondo)* deep; **i rami** ~**i** the lower *o* bottom branches; **a occhi** ~**i** with eyes lowered; **l'ho avuto a ~ prezzo** I got it cheap; **c'è** ~**a marea** it's low tide, the tide is out. **(b)** *(inferiore: qualità)* poor, inferior; *(abietto: azione, istinto)* base, mean. **(c)** *(Geog)*: **la B~a Italia** Southern Italy; **il ~ Po** the lower Po; **i Paesi B~i** the Netherlands. **(d)** *(Storia: tardo)* late; **il ~ Medioevo** the late Middle Ages; ~ **latino** low Latin.

2 *av (volare, mirare)* low; *(parlare)* softly, in a low voice.

3 *sm* **(a)** *(parte inferiore)* bottom; *(: di pagina)* foot, bottom; **in ~** at the bottom; **devo spostare quel bottone più in ~** I'll have to move that button lower down; **scendere da ~** to go downstairs; **cadere in ~** *(fig)* to come down in the world. **(b)** *(Mus)* bass.
bassofondo [basso'fondo] *sm, pl* **bassifondi** shallow, shoal; **i bassifondi (della città)** the seediest parts of the town.
bassopiano [basso'pjano] *sm* low-lying plain.
bassorilievo [bassori'ljevo] *sm* bas relief.
bassotto, a [bas'sɔtto] **1** *ag* squat. **2** *sm (cane)* dachshund.
bastante [bas'tante] *ag* sufficient.
bastardo, a [bas'tardo] **1** *ag (figlio)* illegitimate, *(anche peg)* bastard *attr*; *(animale)* crossbred; **cane ~** mongrel. **2** *sm/f (figlio)* illegitimate child, *(anche peg)* bastard; ~**!** *(fam)* (you) bastard! **3** *sm (cane)* mongrel.
bastare [bas'tare] **1** *vi (aus essere)* **(a)** to be enough, be sufficient; ~ **a qn** to be enough for sb; **mi bastano 5000 lire per oggi** 5000 lire will do me *o* will be sufficient (for me) for today; **50.000 lire ti bastano per 2 giorni** 50,000 lire will last you 2 days; ~ **a se stesso** to be self-sufficient. **(b)** *(fraseologia)*: **basta!** *(per interrompere un'azione)* that's enough!, stop it!; **punto e basta!** and that's that!; **basta con queste scuse** enough of these excuses; **basta così, grazie** that's enough, thank you; *(nei negozi)* that's all, thank you; **basta così?** is that enough?; *(nei negozi)* will that be all?; **basta e avanza** that's more than enough.

2 *vb impers* **(a)**: **basta rivolgersi all'ufficio competente** you just *o* only have to contact the relevant department; **non basta volere, bisogna sapere** it's not enough to want to, you have to know how to; **e come se non bastasse...** and as if that wasn't enough...; **basti dire che...** suffice it to say that...; **basta un niente per farla arrabbiare** the slightest thing is enough to get her annoyed, it only takes the slightest thing to annoy her; **quanto basta** as much as is necessary. **(b)**: **basta che** provided (that); **basta che tu lo chieda** you only have to ask.
bastian [bas'tjan] *sm*: ~ **contrario** awkward customer.
bastimento [basti'mento] *sm* ship, vessel.
bastione [bas'tjone] *sm* bastion.
basto ['basto] *sm* pack saddle.
bastonare [basto'nare] *vt* to beat, thrash; **avere l'aria di un cane bastonato** to look crestfallen.
bastonata [basto'nata] *sf* blow *(with a stick)*; **prendere qn a ~e** to give sb a good beating; **l'hanno ucciso a ~e** they beat him to death.
bastoncino [baston'tʃino] *sm (piccolo bastone)* small stick; *(Tecn)* rod; ~**i di pesce** *(Culin)* fish fingers.
bastone [bas'tone] *sm* **(a)** *(gen)* stick; *(Rel)* staff; ~ **da passeggio** walking stick; **mettere i ~i fra le ruote a qn** to put a spoke in sb's wheel. **(b)**: ~**i** *pl* *(Carte)* suit in Neapolitan pack of cards.
batacchio [ba'takkjo] *sm (di campana)* clapper; *(di porta)* (door-)knocker.
batista [ba'tista] *sf (tessuto)* batiste.
battaglia [bat'taʎʎa] *sf (Mil)* battle; *(fig)* fight.
battagliero, a [battaʎ'ʎɛro] *ag (esercito, popolo)* warlike; *(fig: spirito, persona)* aggressive.
battaglio [bat'taʎʎo] *sm (di campana)* clapper; *(di porta)* (door-)knocker.
battaglione [battaʎ'ʎone] *sm* battalion.
battelliere [battel'ljɛre] *sm* boatman.

battello [bat'tɛllo] *sm* *(gen)* boat; *(canotto)* dinghy; ~ **pneumatico** rubber dinghy; ~ **di salvataggio** lifeboat.

battente [bat'tɛnte] *sm* **(a)** *(di finestra)* shutter; *(di porta)* leaf, door; **porta a due** ~**i** double door; **chiudere i** ~**i** *(fig)* to shut up shop. **(b)** *(per bussare)* (door-)knocker.

battere ['battere] **1** *vt* **(a)** *(percuotere: persona)* to beat, strike, hit; *(: panni, tappeti, ferro)* to beat; *(: grano)* to thresh; ~ **qn a sangue** to beat sb up; ~ **il ferro quando è caldo** *(fig)* to strike while the iron is hot; **battè un pugno sul tavolo** he beat his fist on the table; ~**i il petto** to beat one's breast; ~ **(a macchina)** to type; ~ **il tempo**, ~ **il ritmo** *(Mus)* to beat time.

(b) *(avversario)* to beat, defeat; *(concorrenza, record)* to beat; **in matematica nessuno lo batte** there's no one to beat him at maths.

(c) *(urtare: parte del corpo)* to hit; **ha battuto il mento sul gradino** he hit his chin on the step; **batteva i denti per il freddo** his teeth were chattering with the cold; ~ **i piedi** to stamp one's feet; ~ **i tacchi** to click one's heels; ~ **le mani** to clap one's hands.

(d) *(sbattere: ali)* to beat; **senza** ~ **ciglio** without batting an eyelid; **in un batter d'occhio** in the twinkling of an eye.

(e) *(rintoccare: le ore)* to strike; **il pendolo batteva le 8** the grandfather clock was striking 8 o'clock.

(f) *(Culin)* to beat.

(g) *(Sport: palla)* to hit; ~ **un rigore** *(Calcio)* to take a penalty.

(h) *(percorrere: campagna, paese)* to scour, comb; *(Caccia)* to beat; ~ **il marciapiede** *(peg)* to walk the streets, be on the game.

(i): **battersela** to run off.

2 *vi* **(a)** *(cuore, polso)* to beat; *(pioggia, sole)*: ~ **(su)** to beat down (on); **la pioggia batteva contro i vetri** the rain beat *o* lashed against the window panes; ~ **in testa** *(Aut)* to knock.

(b) *(insistere)*: ~ **su** to insist on; ~ **su un argomento** to hammer home an argument.

(c) *(bussare)*: ~ **(a)** to knock (at).

(d): ~ **in ritirata** to beat a retreat, fall back.

3: ~**rsi** *vr* *(lottare)* to fight; *(: fig)* to fight, battle; ~**rsi all'ultimo sangue** to fight to the last.

batteria [batte'ria] *sf* **(a)** *(Mil, Elettr, Agr etc)* battery; ~ **da cucina** pots and pans *pl*. **(b)** *(Sport)* heat. **(c)** *(Mus)*: **la** ~ **the drums** *pl*.

battericida, i [batteri'tʃida] *sm* germicide.

batterico, a, ci, che [bat'tɛriko] *ag* bacterial.

batterio [bat'tɛrjo] *sm* bacterium.

batteriologia [batterjolo'dʒia] *sf* bacteriology.

batteriologico, a, ci, che [batterjo'lɔdʒiko] *ag* bacteriological; **guerra** ~**a** germ warfare.

batterista, i [batte'rista] *sm* drummer.

battesimale [battezi'male] *ag* baptismal.

battesimo [bat'tezimo] *sm* **(a)** *(sacramento)* baptism; *(rito)* christening, baptism; **tenere qn a** ~ to be godfather (*o* godmother) to sb. **(b)** *(di nave)* christening. **(c)**: ~ **dell'aria** first flight; ~ **del fuoco** baptism of fire.

battezzare [batted'dzare] *vt* **(a)** *(Rel)* to baptize, christen; *(fig: nave)* to christen. **(b)** *(chiamare)* to call, name, christen; *(fig: dare il soprannome)* to nickname.

battibaleno [battiba'leno] *sm*: **in un** ~ in a flash.

battibecco, chi [batti'bekko] *sm* squabble.

batticuore [batti'kwɔre] *sm (Med)* palpitations *pl*; **avevo il** ~ *(fig)* my heart was thumping.

battigia [bat'tidʒa] *sf* water's edge.

battimano [batti'mano] *sm* applause *no pl*, clapping *no pl*.

battipanni [batti'panni] *sm inv* carpet beater.

battiscopa [battis'kopa] *sm inv* skirting (board).

battista, i, e [bat'tista] *ag, sm/f* Baptist; **San Giovanni B**~ Saint John the Baptist.

battistero [battis'tɛro] *sm* baptistry.

battistrada [battis'trada] *sm inv* **(a)** *(Aut: di pneumatico)* tread. **(b)** *(Sport)* pacemaker; **fare da** ~ **a qn** *(fig)* to prepare the way for sb.

battito ['battito] *sm* *(pulsazione)* beat, throb; ~ **cardiaco** heartbeat.

battitore [batti'tore] *sm* **(a)** *(Cricket)* batsman; *(Baseball)* batter. **(b)** *(Caccia)* beater.

battitura [batti'tura] *sf* **(a)** *(anche:* ~ **a macchina)** typing. **(b)** *(del grano)* threshing.

battuta [bat'tuta] *sf* **(a)** *(Caccia)* beat; *(fig: di polizia)*: **fare una** ~ **in una zona** to scour *o* comb an area. **(b)** *(Mus)* bar; ~ **d'arresto** *o* **d'aspetto** bar rest; **gli affari hanno avuto una** ~ **d'arresto** business is at a standstill. **(c)** *(Teatro)* cue; *(fig: osservazione)* remark; *(: spiritosaggine)* witty remark; **fare una** ~ to crack a joke, make a witty remark; **aver la** ~ **pronta** *(fig)* to have a ready answer; **non perde mai una** ~ he never misses a thing; **è ancora alle prime** ~**e** it's just started. **(d)** *(Tennis)* service; **alla** ~ **Borg** Borg is now serving. **(e)** *(di macchina da scrivere)* stroke.

batuffolo [ba'tuffolo] *sm* wad.

bau bau ['bau 'bau] *escl* woof woof!, bow wow!

baule [ba'ule] *sm* *(valigia)* trunk; *(Aut)* boot, trunk *(Am)*.

bauxite [bauk'site] *sf* bauxite.

bava ['bava] *sf* *(di persona)* dribble; *(di cane idrofobo)* foam; *(di lumaca)* slime; *(di baco da seta)* silk filament; **aver la** ~ **alla bocca** *(anche fig)* to be foaming at the mouth; **non c'era nemmeno una** ~ **di vento** there wasn't even a puff of wind.

bavaglino [bavaʎ'ʎino] *sm* bib.

bavaglio [ba'vaʎʎo] *sm* gag; **mettere il** ~ **a qn** *(anche fig)* to gag sb.

bavero ['bavero] *sm* collar.

bavoso, a [ba'voso] *ag* dribbling.

bazar [bad'dzar] *sm inv* bazaar.

bazooka [ba'zu:kə] *sm inv* bazooka.

bazzecola [bad'dzɛkola] *sf* *(mere)* trifle.

bazzicare [battsi'kare] **1** *vt* *(persona)* to hang about with; *(posto)* to hang about. **2** *vi*: ~ **con qn** to hang about with sb; ~ **in un posto** to hang about a place.

bearsi [be'arsi] *vr*: ~ **di qc/a fare qc** to delight in sth/in doing sth; ~ **alla vista di** to enjoy looking at.

beatificare [beatifi'kare] *vt (Rel)* to beatify.

beatitudine [beati'tudine] *sf (Rel)* beatitude; *(felicità)* bliss.

beato, a [be'ato] *ag (Rel)* blessed; *(felice)* blissfully happy; **una vita** ~**a** a life of bliss; ~ **lui!** lucky him!, how lucky he is!

bebè [be'bɛ] *sm inv* baby.

beccaccia, ce [bek'kattʃa] *sf* woodcock.

beccaccino [bekkat'tʃino] *sm* snipe.

beccare [bek'kare] **1** *vt* **(a)** *(sog: uccello)* to peck (at). **(b)** *(fam: cogliere sul fatto)* to nab; **non mi becchi più un'altra volta!** you won't catch me out like that again! **(c)** *(fam: anche:* ~**rsi)** to get; ~ **un raffreddore** to catch a cold. **2**: ~**rsi** *vr* *(uso reciproco: uccelli)* to peck (at) one another; *(: fig)* to squabble.

beccata [bek'kata] *sf* peck.

beccheggiare [bekked'dʒare] *vi (Aer, Naut)* to pitch.

beccheggio [bek'keddʒo] *sm (Aer, Naut)* pitching.

becchime [bek'kime] *sm* birdseed.

becchino [bek'kino] *sm* gravedigger.

becco[1], **chi** ['bekko] *sm* **(a)** *(di uccello)* beak, bill; **non ho il ~ di un quattrino** I'm broke. **(b)** *(fam: bocca)* mouth; **chiudi il ~!** shut your mouth!, shut your trap!; **mettere il ~ in qc** to poke one's nose into sth; **mettere ~** to butt in. **(c)** *(bruciatore)* burner; **~ Bunsen** Bunsen burner.

becco[2], **chi** ['bekko] *sm* *(Zool)* billy-goat; *(fig fam)* cuckold.

beccuccio [bek'kuttʃo] *sm* *(di ampolla, bricco)* lip; *(di teiera)* spout.

beduino, a [bedu'ino] *ag, sm/f* Bedouin.

Befana [be'fana] *sf* **(a)** *(Epifania)* Epiphany. **(b)** *(personaggio)* kind old woman who, according to legend, brings children their presents at the Epiphany. **(c)**: **b~** *(donna brutta)* old hag, old witch.

beffa ['beffa] *sf*: **farsi ~ o ~e di qn** to make a fool of sb; **farsi ~ o ~e di qc** to make fun of sth; **ma questa è una ~!** but this must be some sort of a joke!

beffardo, a [bef'fardo] *ag* mocking.

beffare [bef'fare] **1** *vt* to make a fool of, mock. **2**: **~rsi** *vr*: **~rsi di** to scoff at.

beffeggiare [beffed'dʒare] *vt* to laugh at, mock.

bega, ghe ['bega] *sf* *(litigio)* quarrel, dispute; *(problema)*: **non voglio ~ghe** I don't want any trouble.

begli ['beʎʎi] *ag vedi* **bello.**

begonia [be'gɔnja] *sf* begonia.

beh [bɛ] *escl* well!

bei ['bei] *ag vedi* **bello.**

beige [bɛʒ] *ag inv* beige.

bel [bɛl] *ag vedi* **bello.**

belare [be'lare] *vi* *(Zool, fig)* to bleat.

belato [be'lato] *sm* bleating.

belga, gi, ghe ['bɛlga] *ag, sm/f* Belgian.

Belgio ['bɛldʒo] *sm* Belgium.

bella ['bɛlla] *sf* **(a)** beauty, belle; *(innamorata)* sweetheart; **la B~ addormentata nel bosco** the Sleeping Beauty. **(b)** *(anche: ~ copia)* fair copy. **(c)** *(Sport, Carte)* deciding match.

bellezza [bel'lettsa] *sf* **(a)** *(qualità)* beauty; *(: di donna)* beauty, loveliness; *(: di uomo)* handsomeness; **una donna di eccezionale ~** an exceptionally beautiful woman; **chiudere o finire qc in ~** to finish sth with a flourish; **e per finire in ~...** *(iro)* and to round it all off perfectly...; **che ~!** fantastic! **(b)** *(persona, cosa)* beauty; **ciao ~!** hello gorgeous!; **le ~e di Roma** the beauties o sights of Rome; **questo vestito è una ~** this dress is really lovely. **(c)** *(quantità)*: **ho pagato la ~ di 60.000 lire** I paid 60,000 lire, no less; **ha impiegato la ~ di 2 anni a finirlo** he took a good 2 years to finish it.

bellico, a, ci, che ['bɛlliko] *ag* war *attr.*

bellicoso, a [belli'koso] *ag* *(popolo, nazione)* warlike; *(fig: persona)* quarrelsome.

belligerante [bellidʒe'rante] *ag* belligerent.

belligeranza [bellidʒe'rantsa] *sf* belligerence.

bellimbusto [bellim'busto] *sm* dandy.

bello, a ['bɛllo] **1** *ag (dav sm* **bel** + *consonante,* **bell'** + *vocale,* **bello** + *s impura, gn, pn, ps, x, z, pl* **bei** + *consonante,* **begli** + *s impura etc o vocale)* **(a)** *(oggetto, donna, paesaggio)* beautiful, lovely; *(uomo)* handsome, good-looking; **che ~!** how lovely!; **una ~a pettinatura** a nice hairstyle; **è una gran ~a donna** she's a very beautiful woman; **~e maniere** elegant manners; **le B~ Arti** fine arts; **il bel mondo** high society. **(b)** *(tempo)* fine, beautiful, lovely; **è una ~a giornata** it's a lovely o beautiful day; **fa bel tempo, fa ~** it's lovely weather, the weather's lovely o beautiful. **(c)** *(quantità)* considerable; **non mi ha dato un bel niente** he gave me absolutely nothing; **ha avuto un bel coraggio** he was very brave; *(iro)* he had a nerve; **ce n'è rimasto un bel pezzo** there's still a good bit left. **(d)** *(buono)* good, fine; **una ~a azione** a good deed; **una ~a idea** a good o nice idea; **un bel posto** o **lavoro** a good job; **un bel pensiero** a kind thought; **una ~a tazza di tè** a nice cup of tea; **fare una ~a dormita** to have a nice long sleep; **avere una ~a riuscita** to be a big success. **(e)** *(rafforzativo)*: **sei un bel matto** you're a fine fool; **è bell'e fatto** it's done now; **è una truffa ~a e buona** it's a real fraud; **nel bel mezzo di** right in the middle of. **(f)** *(fraseologia)*: **farsi ~ (più) ~** to become more attractive; **è andata a farsi ~a** she's gone to make herself beautiful; **farsi ~ di qc** *(vantarsi)* to show off about sth; **fare la ~a vita** to lead an easy life; **alla bell'e meglio** somehow or other; **oh ~a!, anche questa è ~a!** that's nice!; **dirne delle ~e** to tell some fine tales; **farne delle ~e** to get up to mischief.

2 *sm* **(a)**: **il ~** the beautiful, beauty; **amare il ~** to love beauty o beautiful things; **il ~ è che...** the best bit about it is that...; **proprio sul più ~** at that very moment; **che fai di ~ stasera?** are you doing anything interesting this evening? **(b)** *(fidanzato)* sweetheart. **(c)** *(tempo)*: **si sta mettendo al ~** the weather is clearing up.

belva ['bɛlva] *sf* wild beast; **essere una ~** *(fig)* to be an animal.

belvedere [belve'dere] *sm inv* panoramic viewpoint.

benché [ben'ke] *cong* although, though.

benda ['bɛnda] *sf* *(Med)* bandage; *(per occhi)* blindfold; **avere gli occhi coperti da una ~** to be blindfolded; **avere la ~ agli occhi** *(fig)* to be blind.

bendaggio [ben'daddʒo] *sm* *(atto)* bandaging; *(effetto)* bandage.

bendare [ben'dare] *vt* *(ferita)* to bandage; *(occhi)* to blindfold.

bendisposto, a [bendis'posto] *ag*: **essere ~ a qn/qc** to be well-disposed towards sb/sth.

bene ['bɛne] **1** *av* **(a)** *(gen)* well; *(funzionare)* properly, well; **guida ~** he drives well, he's a good driver; **parla ~ l'italiano** he speaks Italian well, he speaks good Italian; **parlare ~ di qn** to speak well of sb; **ha preso ~ la notizia** he has taken the news well; **se ben ricordo, se ricordo ~** if I remember correctly; **hai fatto ~** you did the right thing; **faresti ~ a studiare** you'd do well o you'd be well advised to study; **ben fatto!** well done!; **va ~** all right, okay; **gente per ~** *(ben educata)* respectable people; **la gente ~** *(ricca, snob)* the upper classes. **(b)** *(completamente)*: **chiudi ~ la porta** close the door properly; **hai capito ~?** have you quite understood?; **ascoltami ~** listen to me carefully; **per ~, ben ~** thoroughly; **ho legato il pacco ben ~** I've tied the parcel securely; **ho sistemato le cose per ~** I've sorted things out properly. **(c)** *(molto)* *(+ag)* (very) much; *(: + comp, av)* (very) much; **ben meglio** (very) much better; **ben meglio così!** so much the better!; **ben contento** very pleased; **ben più lungo/caro** much longer/more expensive. **(d)** *(rafforzativo: appunto)*: **te l'avevo ben detto io che...** I DID tell you that..., I certainly did tell you that...; **sai** ~ **che non dovresti uscire** you know perfectly well you shouldn't go out; **lo so ben io, lo so fin troppo** ~ I know only too well; **come tu ben sai** as you well know; **lo credo** ~ I can well believe it, I can quite believe it; **lo spero** ~ I certainly hope so.

(e) *(addirittura, non meno di)* at least; **hai fatto ben 7 errori** you've made at least 7 mistakes; **sono ben 3 giorni che non la vedo** I haven't seen her for at least 3 days.

(f) *(in esclamazioni)*: **ho finito — ~!** I've finished — good!; **~, allora possiamo partire** well then, we can go; **~, puoi continuare da solo se vuoi** all right, you can continue on your own if you like; **~ ~!** good (good)!

(g): **di** ~ **in meglio** better and better; **né** ~ **né male** so-so *(fam)*; **tutto è** ~ **quel che finisce** ~ all's well that ends well.

2 *sm* **(a)** good; **far del** ~ to do good; **quella vacanza ti ha fatto** ~ that holiday has done you good; **a fin di** ~ for a good reason; **è stato un** ~ it was a good thing; **l'ho fatto per il suo** ~ I did it for his own good.

(b): **~i** *pl (proprietà: anche Dir)* possessions, property *sg*; *(Econ)* goods; **sul tavolo c'era ogni ben di Dio** there were all sorts of good things on the table; **~i di consumo** consumer goods; **~i di consumo durevole** consumer durables; **~i immobili** real estate *sg*; **~i mobili** personal *o* movable property *sg*; **~i spirituali** spiritual riches.

benedettino, a [benedet'tino] *ag, sm/f* Benedictine.

benedetto, a [bene'detto] **1** *pp di* **benedire**. **2** *ag* blessed; *(santo)* holy; **acqua** ~**a** holy water; **Dio** ~**!** Good Lord!

benedire [bene'dire] *vt* to bless; **che Dio ti benedica!** God bless you!; **l'ho mandato a farsi** ~ *(fig)* I told him to go to hell.

benedizione [benedit'tsjone] *sf (atto)* blessing; *(funzione)* benediction.

beneducato, a [benedu'kato] *ag* well-mannered.

benefattore, trice [benefat'tore] *sm/f* benefactor/ benefactress.

beneficenza [benefi'tʃɛntsa] *sf* charity; **fare opere di** ~ to do charity work; **istituto di** ~ charitable organization; **festa di** ~ function in aid of charity; **concerto di** ~ charity concert.

beneficiare [benefi'tʃare] *vi*: ~ **di** to benefit by, benefit from; ~ **di una borsa di studio** to be awarded a scholarship.

beneficiario, a [benefi'tʃarjo] *ag, sm/f* beneficiary.

beneficio [bene'fitʃo] *sm* benefit; **trarre** ~ **da** to benefit from *o* by; **con** ~ **d'inventario** *(fig)* with reservations; **il** ~ **del dubbio** the benefit of the doubt.

benefico, a, ci, che [be'nefiko] *ag (gen)* beneficial; *(persona)* charitable; **opera** ~**a** *(di carità)* work of charity.

Benelux ['beneluks] *sm*: **il** ~ the Benelux countries.

benemerenza [beneme'rentsa] *sf* merit; **attestato di** ~ certificate of merit.

benemerito, a [bene'merito] *ag* meritorious.

beneplacito [bene'platʃito] *sm (approvazione)* approval; *(permesso)* permission.

benessere [be'nessere] *sm (salute)* well-being; *(agiatezza)* comfort.

benestante [benes'tante] **1** *ag* well-to-do. **2** *sm*: **essere un** ~ to be well-off; **i** ~**i** the well-off; **una famiglia di** ~**i** a well-to-do family.

benestare [benes'tare] *sm inv* approval; **ha dato il suo** ~ **per il matrimonio della figlia** he gave his consent to his daughter's marriage.

benevolenza [benevo'lentsa] *sf* benevolence; **trattare qn con** ~ to treat sb kindly.

benevolo, a [be'nevolo] *ag* benevolent.

benfatto, a [ben'fatto] *ag (lavoro)* good; *(mobile)* well made; *(pietanza)* well cooked; **una ragazza** ~**a** a girl with a good figure.

bengodi [ben'godi] *sm* land of plenty.

beniamino, a [benja'mino] *sm/f* favourite; **è il** ~ **della maestra** he's the teacher's pet.

benignità [beniɲɲi'ta] *sf (cortesia)* kindness; **trattare con** ~ to treat kindly.

benigno, a [be'niɲɲo] *ag (gen, Med)* benign; *(sguardo, sorriso)* kindly.

benintenzionato, a [benintentsjo'nato] *ag* well-meaning; **in fondo era** ~ after all he meant well.

beninteso [benin'teso] **1** *av (certamente)* of course, certainly. **2**: ~ **che** *cong* provided that.

benpensante [benpen'sante] *sm/f* conformist.

benservito [benser'vito] *sm* reference; **dare il** ~ **a qn** *(sul lavoro)* to give sb the sack, fire sb; *(fig)* to send sb packing.

bensì [ben'si] *cong (ma)* but (rather); *(anzi)* on the contrary.

benvenuto, a [benve'nuto] **1** *ag* welcome. **2** *sm/f*: **essere il(la)** ~**(a)** to be welcome. **3** *sm* welcome; **dare il** ~ **a qn** to welcome sb.

benvisto, a [ben'visto] *ag*: **essere** ~ **(da)** to be well thought of (by).

benvolere [benvo'lere] *vt*: **farsi** ~ **da tutti** to win everybody's affection; **prendere a** ~ **qn/qc** to take a liking to sb/sth.

benvoluto, a [benvo'luto] *ag* loved, well liked.

benzina [ben'dzina] *sf* petrol, gasoline *(Am)*; **rimanere senza** ~ to run out of petrol; **fare** ~ to get petrol.

benzinaio, a [bendzi'najo] **1** *sm/f (persona)* petrol-pump attendant. **2** *sm (posto)* petrol station.

beone [be'one] *sm* heavy drinker.

bere ['bere] **1** *vt (gen)* to drink; *(fig: assorbire)* to soak up; ~ **un bicchiere di vino/un caffè** to have a glass of wine/a (cup of) coffee; **ti offro** *o* **ti pago da** ~ I'll buy you a drink; ~ **qc tutto d'un fiato** to down sth in one gulp; ~ **come una spugna** to drink like a fish; ~ **per dimenticare** to drown one's sorrows (in drink); ~ **alla salute di qn** to drink to sb's health; **il motore beve la benzina** the engine is heavy on petrol; ~ **le parole di qn** to drink in sb's words; **questa volta non me la dai a** ~! I won't be taken in this time! **2** *sm* drink; **si è lasciato andare al vizio del** ~ he has turned to drink.

bergamotto [berga'motto] *sm* bergamot.

berillio [be'riljo] *sm* beryllium.

berlina¹ [ber'lina] *sf*: **mettere alla** ~ *(fig)* to hold up to ridicule.

berlina² [ber'lina] *sf (Aut)* saloon car.

bermuda [ber'muda] *smpl (calzoni)* bermuda shorts.

bernoccolo [ber'nɔkkolo] *sm* bump; **avere il** ~ **per qc** *(fig: disposizione)* to have a bent *o* flair for sth.

berretta [ber'retta] *sf* cap; ~ **da prete** biretta.

berretto [ber'retto] *sm* cap; ~ **con visiera** peaked cap; ~ **da montagna** woolly hat.

bersagliare [bersaʎ'ʎare] *vt (colpire ripetutamente)* to bombard; ~ **di colpi** to bombard with gunfire; ~ **di domande** to bombard with questions; **è bersagliato dalla sfortuna** he's dogged by ill fortune.

bersagliere [bersaʎ'ʎere] *sm* member of rifle regiment in Italian army.

bersaglio [ber'saʎʎo] *sm (anche fig)* target; **colpire il** ~ to hit the target; *(fig)* to reach one's target;

era il ~ di tutti i loro scherzi he was the butt of all their jokes.

bertuccia, ce [ber'tuttʃa] *sf* Barbary ape.

besciamella [beʃʃa'mella] *sf* béchamel sauce.

bestemmia [bes'temmja] *sf (gen)* curse; *(Rel)* blasphemy; **dire una** ~ to swear; to blaspheme.

bestemmiare [bestem'mjare] *vt (gen)* to curse; *(Rel)* to blaspheme; ~ **come un turco** to swear like a trooper.

bestemmiatore, trice [bestemmja'tore] *sm/f (gen)* swearer; *(Rel)* blasphemer.

bestia ['bestja] *sf (anche fig)* beast, animal; ~ **feroce** *o* **selvaggia** wild beast *o* animal; ~ **da macello** animal for slaughter; ~ **da soma** beast of burden; ~ **da tiro** draught animal; **una** ~ **rara** *(fig: persona)* an oddball; **andare in** ~ *(fig)* to fly into a rage; **lavorare come una** ~ to work like a dog; ~! *(sciocco)* you stupid fool!

bestiale [bes'tjale] *ag (gen)* beastly; *(passione, istinto)* animal *attr*; *(fig: terribile)* beastly, terrible; **ha fatto un freddo** ~ it's been beastly cold; **ho una fame** ~ I could eat a horse; **fa un caldo** ~ it's terribly hot.

bestialità [bestjali'ta] *sf inv* **(a)** *(qualità)* bestiality. **(b)**: **dire/fare una** ~ **dopo l'altra** to say/do one idiotic thing after another.

betoniera [beto'njera] *sf* cement mixer.

bettola ['bettola] *sf* tavern; *(peg)* dive; **contegno da** ~ coarse behaviour.

betulla [be'tulla] *sf* birch.

bevanda [be'vanda] *sf* drink; ~ **alcolica/non alcolica** alcoholic/soft drink.

beveraggio [beve'raddʒo] *sm (per animali)* bran mash; *(pozione)* potion.

bevibile [be'vibile] *ag* drinkable.

bevitore, trice [bevi'tore] *sm/f* drinker; **un forte** ~ a heavy drinker.

bevuta [be'vuta] *sf* drink; **fare una (bella)** ~ to have a booze-up *(fam)*.

bevuto, a [be'vuto] *pp di* **bere**.

biada ['bjada] *sf* fodder.

biancheggiare [bjanked'dʒare] *vi* to look white.

biancheria [bjanke'ria] *sf (per casa)* linen; ~ **intima** underwear; ~ **da donna** ladies' underwear, lingerie.

bianchezza [bjan'kettsa] *sf* whiteness.

bianchiccio, a, ci, ce [bjan'kittʃo] *ag* whitish, off-white; *(persona)* pale.

bianco, a, chi, che ['bjanko] **1** *ag* **(a)** *(gen)* white; **essere** ~ **come uno straccio** to be as white as a sheet; **avere i capelli** ~**chi** to have white hair, be white-haired; **far venire i capelli** ~**chi a qn** *(fig)* to make sb's hair turn white; **notte** ~**a** sleepless night. **(b)** *(pagina)* blank; **votare scheda** ~**a** to return a blank voting slip. **(c)** *(Mus)*: **voce** ~**a** treble (voice).

2 *sm* **(a)** *(colore)* white; *(vino)* white wine; **vestire di** ~ to dress in white; **fotografie in** ~ **e nero** black and white photographs; **passare una notte in** ~ to have a sleepless night. **(b)** *(spazio)*: **un assegno in** ~ a blank cheque; **lasciare in** ~ to leave blank. **(c)** *(Culin)*: ~ **d'uovo** egg-white; **pesce/carne in** ~ boiled fish/meat; **mangiare in** ~ to follow a light diet.

3 *sm/f (persona)* white man/woman.

biancospino [bjankos'pino] *sm* hawthorn.

biascicare [bjaʃʃi'kare] *vt* to mumble.

biasimare [bjazi'mare] *vt* to blame.

biasimevole [bjazi'mevole] *ag* blameworthy.

biasimo ['bjazimo] *sm* blame; **degno di** ~ blameworthy.

bibbia ['bibbja] *sf* Bible.

biberon [bibe'rɔn] *sm inv* baby's bottle.

bibita ['bibita] *sf* drink; *(non alcolica)* soft drink.

biblico, a, ci, che ['bibliko] *ag* biblical.

bibliografia [bibljogra'fia] *sf* bibliography.

bibliografico, a, ci, che [bibljo'grafiko] *ag* bibliographical.

bibliografo, a [bibli'ɔgrafo] *sm/f* bibliographer.

biblioteca, che [bibljo'tɛka] *sf (edificio)* library; *(mobile)* bookcase.

bibliotecario, a [bibljote'karjo] *sm/f* librarian.

bicamerale [bikame'rale] *ag (Pol)* two-chamber *attr*.

bicarbonato [bikarbo'nato] *sm*: ~ **(di sodio)** bicarbonate (of soda).

bicchierata [bikkje'rata] *sf (contenuto di un bicchiere)* glass(ful); *(bevuta)* drink.

bicchiere [bik'kjere] *sm* glass; ~ **da vino** wine glass; ~ **di vino** glass of wine; ~ **di carta** paper cup; ~ **a calice** goblet; **bere un** ~ to have a drink; **è (facile) come bere un bicchier d'acqua** it's as easy as pie.

bicefalo, a [bi'tʃefalo] *ag* two-headed.

bicicletta [bitʃi'kletta] *sf* bicycle, bike; **andare in** ~ to cycle; **sai andare a** ~? can you ride a bicycle?; ~ **da corsa** racing cycle.

bicilindrico, a, ci, che [bitʃi'lindriko] *ag (Tecn)* two-cylinder *attr*.

bicipite [bi'tʃipite] *ag (che ha due teste)* two-headed; *(Anat)*: **(muscolo)** ~ biceps *pl inv*.

bicocca, che [bi'kɔkka] *sf* hovel.

bicolore [biko'lore] *ag* two-tone; **governo** ~ two-party government.

bicromia [bikro'mia] *sf (procedimento)* two-colour printing; *(illustrazione)* two-colour print.

bidè [bi'dɛ] *sm inv* bidet.

bidello, a [bi'dɛllo] *sm/f (di scuola)* janitor; *(di università)* porter.

bidimensionale [bidimensjo'nale] *ag* two-dimensional.

bidonare [bido'nare] *vt (fam: piantare in asso)* to let down; *(: imbrogliare)* to cheat, swindle.

bidonata [bido'nata] *sf (fam)* swindle; **fare** *o* **tirare una** ~ **a qn** *(piantare in asso)* to let sb down; *(imbrogliare)* to cheat *o* do sb.

bidone [bi'done] *sm* **(a)** *(recipiente)* drum; ~ **per la spazzatura** *o* **dei rifiuti** dustbin; ~ **da latte** churn. **(b)** = **bidonata**.

bidonville [bidɔ'vil] *sf inv* shanty town.

bieco, a, chi, che ['bjɛko] *ag* sinister.

biella [bi'jɛlla] *sf (Tecn)* connecting rod.

biennale [bien'nale] **1** *ag (che dura 2 anni)* two-year *attr*; *(che avviene ogni 2 anni)* two-yearly; **la mostra è** ~ the exhibition is held every two years. **2** *sf*: **la B**~ **di Venezia** the Venice Arts Festival.

biennio [bi'ɛnnjo] *sm* period of two years; **nel prossimo** ~ over the next two years.

bietola ['bjɛtola] *sf (Bot)* chard; *(: per estensione)* beet.

bifase [bi'faze] *ag (Elettr)* two-phase *attr*.

bifocale [bifo'kale] *ag* bifocal.

bifolco, a, chi, che [bi'folko] *sm/f (peg)* bumpkin, yokel.

bifora ['bifora] *sf (Archit)* mullioned window.

biforcarsi [bifor'karsi] *vr (fiume, strada)* to divide, fork; *(Ferr)* to branch.

biforcazione [biforkat'tsjone] *sf (di fiume, strada etc)* fork; *(Ferr)* junction.

biforcuto, a [bifor'kuto] *ag (anche fig)* forked; **lingua** ~**a** forked tongue.

bifronte [bi'fronte] *ag (anche fig)* two-faced.

big [big] *sm inv (dello spettacolo)* star; *(dell'industria)* big noise, big shot.

bigamia [biga'mia] *sf* bigamy.

bigamo, a ['bigamo] **1** *ag* bigamous. **2** *sm/f* bigamist.

bighellonare [bigello'nare] *vi* to loaf about.

bighellone, a [bigel'lone] *sm/f* loafer.

bigio, a, gi, ge *o* **gie** ['bidʒo] *ag* dull grey.

bigiotteria [bidʒotte'ria] *sf (gioielli)* costume jewellery; *(negozio)* jeweller's *(selling only costume jewellery)*.

biglia ['biʎʎa] *sf* = **bilia.**

bigliardo [biʎ'ʎardo] *sm* = **biliardo.**

bigliettaio, a [biʎʎet'tajo] *sm/f (nei treni)* ticket inspector; *(in autobus etc)* conductor/conductress; *(Cine, Teatro)* box-office attendant.

biglietteria [biʎʎette'ria] *sf (gen)* ticket office; *(per prenotazioni)* booking office; *(Cine, Teatro)* box office.

biglietto [biʎ'ʎetto] *sm* **(a)** *(per viaggio, entrata)* ticket; ~ **di andata** *o* **di corsa semplice/di andata e ritorno** single/return (ticket), one-way/round-trip ticket *(Am)*; **fare/comprare il** ~ to get/buy one's ticket; ~ **omaggio** complimentary ticket. **(b)** *(banconota)*: ~ **(di banca)** banknote, note, bill *(Am)*; **un** ~ **da 1000 (lire)** a 1000 lire note. **(c)** *(nota)* note; *(cartoncino)* card; ~ **di auguri** greetings card; ~ **di presentazione** letter of introduction; ~ **da visita** visiting card.

bignè [biɲ'nɛ] *sm inv* cream puff.

bigodino [bigo'dino] *sm* (hair-)curler, roller.

bigoncia, ce [bi'gontʃa] *sf* wooden tub.

bigotteria [bigotte'ria] *sf* overdevoutness.

bigotto, a [bi'gotto] **1** *ag* over-devout. **2** *sm/f* (religious) bigot.

bikini [bi'kini] *sm inv* bikini.

bilancia, ce [bi'lantʃa] *sf* **(a)** *(gen)* scales *pl*; *(a due piatti)* pair of scales; *(Chim, Fis)* balance; *(basculla)* weighing machine; **porre qc sulla** ~ *(anche fig)* to weigh sth up; **pesare con giusta** ~ to judge fairly. **(b)** *(Astrologia)*: **B~** Libra; **essere della B~** to be Libra. **(c)** *(Comm)*: ~ **commerciale/dei pagamenti** balance of trade/payments. **(d)** *(Pesca)* drop-net.

bilanciare [bilan'tʃare] **1** *vt* **(a)** *(tenere in equilibrio)* to balance; ~ **il carico** to spread the load evenly. **(b)** *(Comm)* to balance; ~ **le uscite e le entrate** to balance expenditure and revenue; **le uscite bilanciano le entrate** expenditure and revenue balance out. **2:** ~**rsi** *vr* **(a)** *(stare in equilibrio)* to balance (o.s.). **(b)** *(equipararsi)* to be equal.

bilanciere [bilan'tʃɛre] *sm (di orologio)* balance wheel; *(di motore)* compensator.

bilancio [bi'lantʃo] *sm (Comm: cifre)* balance; *(: documento)* balance sheet; **fare il** ~, **chiudere il** ~ to draw up the balance sheet; **far quadrare il** ~ to balance the books; **chiudere il** ~ **in attivo/passivo** to make a profit/loss; **fare il** ~ **della situazione** *(fig)* to assess the situation; ~ **preventivo** budget; ~ **consuntivo** final balance; ~ **settimanale/mensile** weekly/monthly balance.

bilaterale [bilate'rale] *ag* bilateral.

bile ['bile] *sf (Med)* bile; *(fig: rabbia)* anger, rage; **era verde dalla** ~ he was white with rage.

bilia ['bilja] *sf* **(a)** *(da biliardo: pallina)* billiard ball; *(: buca)* (billiard) pocket. **(b)** *(di vetro)* marble; **giocare a** ~**e** to play marbles.

biliardino [biljar'dino] *sm* (small) billiard table; *(~ elettrico)* pinball.

biliardo [bi'ljardo] *sm* billiards *pl*; **giocare a** ~ to play billiards.

biliare [bi'ljare] *ag (Med)* biliary; **calcolo** ~ gallstone.

bilico ['biliko] *sm*: **essere** *o* **stare in** ~ to be balanced; *(fig)* to be undecided; **essere in** ~ **tra la** vita e la morte to be suspended between life and death.

bilingue [bi'lingwe] *ag* bilingual.

bilinguismo [bilin'gwizmo] *sm* bilingualism.

bilione [bi'ljone] *sm* billion.

bilioso, a [bi'ljoso] *ag* bad-tempered.

bimbo, a ['bimbo] *sm/f (bambino)* child; *(bebè)* baby.

bimensile [bimen'sile] *ag* twice-monthly, fortnightly.

bimestrale [bimes'trale] *ag (che dura 2 mesi)* two-month *attr*; *(che avviene ogni 2 mesi)* two-monthly; **pagamento** ~ payment every 2 months; **rivista** ~ two-monthly magazine.

bimestre [bi'mɛstre] *sm* two-month period; **ogni** ~ every two months.

bimotore [bimo'tore] **1** *ag* twin-engined. **2** *sm (aereo)* twin-engined plane.

binario, a [bi'narjo] **1** *ag* binary. **2** *sm (rotaie)* (railway) track, (railway) line; *(piattaforma)* platform; ~ **unico/doppio** single/double track; **uscire dai** ~**i** *(anche fig)* to go off the rails.

binocolo [bi'nɔkolo] *sm (gen)* binoculars *pl*; *(Teatro)* opera glasses *pl*.

binomio [bi'nɔmjo] *sm* **(a)** *(Mat)* binomial. **(b)** *(fig: due persone)*: **il** ~ **Laurel e Hardy** the Laurel and Hardy duo.

biochimica [bio'kimika] *sf* biochemistry.

biochimico, a, ci, che [bio'kimiko] **1** *ag* biochemical. **2** *sm/f* biochemist.

biodegradabile [biodegra'dabile] *ag* biodegradable.

biofisica [bio'fizika] *sf* biophysics *sg*.

biofisico, a, ci, che [bio'fiziko] **1** *ag* biophysical. **2** *sm/f* biophysicist.

biografia [biogra'fia] *sf* biography.

biografico, a, ci, che [bio'grafiko] *ag* biographical.

biografo, a [bi'ɔgrafo] *sm/f* biographer.

biologia [biolo'dʒia] *sf* biology.

biologico, a, ci, che [bio'lɔdʒiko] *ag* biological.

biologo, a, ghi, ghe [bi'ɔlogo] *sm/f* biologist.

biondeggiare [bjonded'dʒare] *vi (messi etc)* to be golden.

biondo, a ['bjondo] **1** *ag (capelli)* fair, blond; *(persona)* fair, fair-haired; ~ **cenere/platino** ash/platinum blond. **2** *sm (colore)* blond; *(uomo)* fair-haired man. **3** *sf (donna)* blonde.

biopsia [bio'psia] *sf* biopsy.

bipartire [bipar'tire] *vt* to divide.

bipartitico, a, ci, che [bipar'titiko] *ag (Pol)* two-party *attr*.

bipartitismo [biparti'tizmo] *sm (Pol)* two-party system.

bipartito, a [bipar'tito] *(Pol)* **1** *ag* two-party *attr*. **2** *sm* two-party alliance.

bipartizione [bipartit'tsjone] *sf (Pol)* split.

bipede ['bipede] *ag, sm* biped.

biplano [bi'plano] *sm* biplane.

bipolare [bipo'lare] *ag* bipolar.

biposto [bi'posto] *ag inv* two-seater *attr*.

birba ['birba] *sf* rascal, rogue.

birbante [bir'bante] *sm* rascal, rogue.

birbonata [birbo'nata] *sf* naughty trick.

birbone, a [bir'bone] **1** *ag (bambino)* naughty; **fare un tiro** ~ **a qn** to play a naughty trick on sb. **2** *sm/f (bambino)* little rascal.

bireattore [bireat'tore] *sm* twin-engined jet.

birichinata [biriki'nata] *sf* prank, practical joke.

birichino, a [biri'kino] **1** *ag (bambino)* mischievous, impish; *(adulto)* sly; **sguardo** ~ sly look. **2** *sm/f (bambino)* little rascal.

birillo [bi'rillo] *sm* skittle; ~**i** *pl (gioco)* skittles *sg*.

Birmania [bir'manja] *sf* Burma.

birmano, a [bir'mano] *ag, smf* Burmese *(pl inv)*.

biro ['biro] *sf inv* biro.

birra ['birra] *sf (gen)* beer, ale; ~ **in bottiglia** bottled beer; ~ **alla spina** draught beer; ~ **chiara** lager; ~ **scura** stout; **fabbrica di** ~ brewery; **a tutta** ~ *(fig: veloce)* at top speed, flat out.

birraio [bir'rajo] *sm (fabbricante)* brewer.

birreria [birre'ria] *sf (locale)* ≈ bierkeller; *(fabbrica)* brewery.

bis [bis] **1** *escl* encore! **2** *sm inv* encore; **chiedere il** ~ *(Teatro)* to call for an encore; *(fig: a tavola)* to ask for a second helping. **3** *ag inv (treno, autobus)* relief; *(numero):* **12** ~ 12a.

bisaccia, ce [bi'zattʃa] *sf* knapsack.

bisavo, a [bi'zavo] *smf* great-grandfather/grandmother; ~**i** *pl (antenati)* forefathers.

bisavolo, a [bi'zavolo] *smf* = **bisavo, a.**

bisbetico, a, ci, che [biz'bɛtiko] *ag* ill-tempered, crabby.

bisbigliare [bizbiʎ'ʎare] *vt, vi (anche fig)* to whisper.

bisbiglio[1] [biz'biʎʎo] *sm (anche fig)* whisper.

bisbiglio[2] [bizbiʎ'ʎio] *sm (anche fig)* whispering.

bisboccia, ce [biz'bottʃa] *sf* binge, spree; **fare** ~ to have a binge.

bisca, sche ['biska] *sf* gambling den.

bischero ['biskero] *sm (a) (Mus)* peg. **(b)** *(fam: toscano)* fool, idiot.

biscia, sce ['biʃʃa] *sf* non-poisonous snake; ~ **d'acqua** water snake.

biscottato, a [biskot'tato] *ag* crisp; **fette** ~e rusks.

biscottiera [biskot'tjera] *sf* biscuit barrel; *(di latta)* biscuit tin.

biscottificio [biskotti'fitʃo] *sm* biscuit factory.

biscotto [bis'kɔtto] *sm* biscuit.

bisdrucciolo, a [biz'druttʃolo] *ag (Gram)* with the stress on the fourth-last syllable.

bisecare [bise'kare] *vt (Mat)* to bisect.

bisessuale [bisessu'ale] *ag* bisexual.

bisestile [bizes'tile] *ag:* **anno** ~ leap year.

bisettimanale [bisettima'nale] *ag* twice-weekly.

bisettrice [biset'tritʃe] *sf* bisector.

bisezione [biset'tsjone] *sf* bisection.

bisillabo, a [bi'sillabo] **1** *ag* disyllabic. **2** *sm* disyllable.

bislacco, a, chi, che [biz'lakko] *ag* odd, weird; **è una testa** ~a he's an odd fellow.

bislungo, a, ghi, ghe [biz'lungo] *ag* oblong.

bismuto [biz'muto] *sm* bismuth.

bisnipote [bizni'pote] *smf (di nonni)* great-grandchild, great-grandson/granddaughter; *(di zii)* great-nephew/niece.

bisnonno, a [biz'nɔnno] *smf* great-grandfather/grandmother.

bisognare [bizoɲ'ɲare] **1** *vb impers:* **bisogna partire** we must leave, we'll have to leave; **bisogna che arriviate in tempo** you must *o* you'll have to arrive on time; **bisognerebbe che si decidesse** he should make up his mind; **non bisogna lamentarsi sempre** one *o* you shouldn't complain all the time; **bisogna vedere!** *(dipende)* I'll *(o* you'll *etc)* have to see how things go!; **bisogna proprio dire che…** it has to be said that… . **2** *vi (aus essere) (aver bisogno)* to need, want; **cosa le bisogna?** *(in negozio)* can I help you?

bisognevole [bizoɲ'ɲevole] *ag:* ~ **di** in need of.

bisogno [bi'zoɲɲo] *sm* **(a)** *(necessità)* need, necessity; **aver** ~ **di** to need, be in need of; **aver** ~ **di fare qc** to need to do sth; **sentire il** ~ **di qc/di fare qc** to feel the need for sth/to do sth; **c'è** ~ **di te qui** we need you here; **non c'è** ~ **che venga anche tu** there's no need for you to come too; **in caso di** ~

if need be, if necessary; **non c'è** ~ **di gridare** there's no need to shout; **nel momento del** ~ in one's hour of need. **(b)** *(povertà)* poverty, need; **trovarsi nel** ~ to be in need. **(c)** *(necessità corporali):* **fare i** ~**i** *(persona)* to relieve o.s.; *(animale)* to do its business.

bisognoso, a [bizoɲ'ɲoso] *ag* **(a)** *(che ha bisogno):* ~ **di** in need of. **(b)** *(povero)* poor, needy.

bisonte [bi'zonte] *sm (Zool)* bison.

bisso ['bisso] *sm (tessuto)* fine linen.

bistecca, che [bis'tekka] *sf* steak; ~ **al sangue/ai ferri** rare/grilled steak.

bisticciare [bistit'tʃare] *vi,* ~**rsi** *vr* to bicker, quarrel.

bisticcio [bis'tittʃo] *sm* **(a)** *(litigio)* quarrel, squabble. **(b)** *(gioco di parole)* pun, play on words.

bistrattare [bistrat'tare] *vt* to maltreat.

bisturi ['bisturi] *sm inv (Med)* scalpel.

bisunto, a [bi'zunto] *ag (unto)* very greasy; **un cappotto unto e** ~ a filthy, greasy coat.

bitorzolo [bi'tortsolo] *sm (sulla testa)* bump; *(sul corpo)* lump.

bitorzoluto, a [bitortso'luto] *ag (albero)* gnarled, knotted; *(faccia)* warty.

bitter ['bitter] *sm inv* bitters *pl.*

bitumare [bitu'mare] *vt* to bituminize.

bitume [bi'tume] *sm* bitumen.

bituminoso, a [bitumi'noso] *ag* bituminous.

bivaccare [bivak'kare] *vi (Mil)* to bivouac; *(fig)* to bed down.

bivacco, chi [bi'vakko] *sm* bivouac.

bivio ['bivjo] *sm (di una strada)* fork, junction; **trovarsi davanti a un** ~ *(fig)* to be at a crossroads.

bizantino, a [biddzan'tino] *ag* Byzantine; *(fig: pedante)* pedantic.

bizza ['biddza] *sf* tantrum; **fare le** ~**e** to throw a tantrum; **la macchina fa le** ~**e oggi** the car is playing up today.

bizzarria [biddzar'ria] *sf* **(a)** *(qualità)* eccentricity, weirdness. **(b)** *(azione)* whim, caprice; *(cosa)* oddity.

bizzarro, a [bid'dzarro] *ag* **(a)** *(strano, eccentrico)* odd, queer, eccentric. **(b)** *(focoso: cavallo)* frisky.

bizzeffe [bid'dzeffe]: **a** ~ *av* in abundance; **avere soldi a** ~ to be rolling in money.

bizzoso, a [bid'dzoso] *ag (irascibile)* irritable, quick-tempered; *(capriccioso)* capricious, self-willed.

blandizie [blan'dittsje] *sfpl* blandishments.

blando, a ['blando] *ag (medicina, rimedio)* mild; *(liquore)* weak; *(sapore, cibo)* bland; *(punizione)* light, mild.

blasfemo, a [blas'femo] **1** *ag* blasphemous. **2** *smf* blasphemer.

blasone [bla'zone] *sm* coat of arms, escutcheon.

blaterare [blate'rare] **1** *vi* to blether. **2** *vt* to blether about; **ma cosa vai blaterando?** what are you blethering about?

blatta ['blatta] *sf* cockroach.

blazer ['bleiza] *sm inv* blazer.

blindare [blin'dare] *vt (veicolo)* to armour; *(porta)* to reinforce.

blindato, a [blin'dato] *ag* armoured; **vetro** ~ bulletproof glass; **camera** ~a strongroom.

bloccare [blok'kare] **1** *vt (a) (ostruire: strada)* to block (up); *(fermare: assegno, pallone, persona etc)* to stop; *(: comandi, meccanismo)* to block; *(: merci)* to stop, hold up; *(: negoziati)* to block, hold up; *(: prezzi, affitti)* to freeze; **il villaggio è stato bloccato da una frana** the village has been cut off by a landslide; **la polizia ha bloccato le vie**

d'accesso alla città the police have blocked off the access roads to the city; **sono rimasto bloccato in un ingorgo/nell'ascensore** I was stuck in a traffic jam/in the lift; **ha bloccato la macchina** he braked suddenly; **blocca la sicura** put on the safety catch. **(b)** *(Mil)* to blockade.

  2: ~**rsi** *vr (motore)* to stall; *(freni, porta)* to jam, stick; *(ascensore)* to get stuck, stop; **si è bloccato nel bel mezzo del discorso** he suddenly stopped in the middle of what he was saying.

bloccasterzo [blokkas'tɛrtso] *sm (Aut)* steering lock; *(: antifurto)* crook lock.

blocchetto [blok'ketto] *sm* notebook.

blocco¹, chi ['blɔkko] *sm* **(a)** *(gen)* block; ~**chi di partenza** *(Sport)* starting blocks; **considerare/condannare qc in** ~ *(fig)* to take/condemn sth as a whole. **(b)** *(per appunti)* notebook; *(di carta da lettere)* writing pad. **(c)** *(Pol)* bloc, coalition; **il** ~ **orientale** the Eastern bloc.

blocco², chi ['blɔkko] *sm* **(a)** *(Mil)* blockade; **posto di** ~ *(sul confine)* frontier post; *(di polizia: anche:* ~ **stradale)** road block. **(b)** *(Comm)* freeze; ~ **dei fitti** rent restrictions; ~ **dei salari** wage freeze. **(c)** *(Med):* ~ **cardiaco** cardiac arrest; ~ **renale** kidney failure.

bloc-notes [blɔk'nɔt] *sm inv* notebook, notepad.

blu [blu] *ag inv, sm* blue.

bluastro, a [blu'astro] *ag* bluish.

blue-jeans ['blu:dʒeinz] *smpl* (blue) jeans.

blues [blu:z] *sm inv* blues *pl.*

bluff [bluf] *sm inv (anche fig)* bluff; **un** ~ **pubblicitario** a publicity stunt.

bluffare [bluf'fare] *vi (anche fig)* to bluff.

blusa ['bluza] *sf (camicetta)* blouse; *(per pittore)* smock; *(per operaio)* overall.

blusante [blu'zante] *ag* loose-fitting.

blusotto [blu'zɔtto] *sm* jerkin.

boa¹ ['bɔa] *sm inv (serpente)* boa; *(sciarpa)* feather boa.

boa² ['bɔa] *sf (Naut)* buoy.

boato [bo'ato] *sm* roar; ~ **sonico** sonic boom.

bob [bɔb] *sm inv* bobsleigh.

bobina [bo'bina] *sf (Elettr)* coil; ~ **d'accensione** *(Aut)* ignition coil. **(b)** *(Cine, Fot etc)* reel. **(c)** *(di cotone etc)* reel, bobbin, spool.

bocca, che ['bokka] *sf* **(a)** *(gen)* mouth; **per** ~ orally; **rimanere a** ~ **asciutta** to have nothing to eat; *(fig)* to be disappointed; **rimanere a** ~ **aperta** *(fig)* to be taken aback; **non ha aperto** ~ *(parlare)* he didn't open his mouth; **vuoi chiudere la** ~? *(star zitto)* will you shut up?; **essere sulla** ~ **di tutti** *(persona, notizia)* to be the talk of the town; **essere di buona** ~ to be a hearty eater; *(fig)* to be easily satisfied; **farsi la** ~ **a qc** to acquire a taste for sth; **non voglio metter** ~ **in questa storia** I don't want to interfere; **mi hai tolto la parola di** ~ you took the words out of my mouth; **in** ~ **al lupo!** good luck!

  (b) *(di fiume, di recipiente etc)* mouth; ~ **d'acqua** hydrant.

  (c) *(Bot):* ~ **di leone** snapdragon.

boccaccia, ce [bok'kattʃa] *sf* **(a)** *(smorfia):* **fare le** ~**ce** to pull faces. **(b)** *(persona maldicente)* foul-mouthed person.

boccaglio [bok'kaʎʎo] *sm (Tecn)* nozzle; *(di respiratore)* mouthpiece.

boccale¹ [bok'kale] *ag (Anat)* oral.

boccale² [bok'kale] *sm (recipiente)* jug; *(per bere)* mug; ~ **da birra** beer mug, tankard.

boccascena [bokkaʃ'ʃɛna] *sm inv* proscenium.

boccata [bok'kata] *sf* mouthful; *(di fumo)* puff; **prendere una** ~ **d'aria** to go out for a breath of (fresh) air.

boccetta [bot'tʃetta] *sf* phial, small bottle.

boccheggiante [bokked'dʒante] *ag* **(a)** *(che boccheggia)* gasping (for breath). **(b)** *(morente)* at one's last breath.

boccheggiare [bokked'dʒare] *vi* to gasp.

bocchetta [bok'ketta] *sf* **(a)** *(di strumento musicale)* mouthpiece. **(b)** *(di serratura)* plate. **(c):** ~ **stradale** drain cover.

bocchino [bok'kino] *sm (di pipa, strumento musicale)* mouthpiece; *(per sigarette)* cigarette holder.

boccia, ce ['bɔttʃa] *sf (palla di legno, metallo)* bowl; **il gioco delle** ~**ce** bowls; **giocare alle** ~**ce** to play bowls.

bocciare [bot'tʃare] *vt* **(a)** *(respingere)* to reject; *(: agli esami)* to fail. **(b)** *(alle bocce)* to hit.

bocciatura [bottʃa'tura] *sf (agli esami)* failure.

boccino [bot'tʃino] *sm* jack.

boccio ['bɔttʃo] *sm* bud.

bocciodromo [bot'tʃɔdromo] *sm* bowling ground.

bocciolo [bot'tʃɔlo] *sm* bud; ~ **di rosa** rosebud.

boccola ['bokkola] *sf (fibbia)* buckle.

boccolo ['bokkolo] *sm* curl.

boccone [bok'kone] *sm (quantità di cibo)* mouthful; **mangiare un** ~ to have a bite to eat; **inghiottire un** ~ **amaro** *(fig)* to swallow a bitter pill; **finire tutto in un** ~ to down everything at one gulp.

bocconi [bok'koni] *av* face downwards; **cadere** ~ to fall flat on one's face.

bofonchiare [bofon'kjare] *vi* to grumble.

bohemien [boe'mjɛ̃] *ag, sm/f* Bohemian.

boia ['bɔja] *sm inv* **(a)** *(carnefice)* executioner; *(: in impiccagione)* hangman; *(fig: mascalzone)* rogue, scoundrel; *(: assassino)* murderer. **(b)** *(in escl: fam):* **mondo** ~!, ~ **d'un mondo ladro!** damn!, blast!; **fa un freddo** ~ it's cold as hell.

boiata [bo'jata] *sf (fam: azione)* dirty trick; *(: robaccia)* rubbish; **quel film era una** ~ that film was (a load of) rubbish.

boicottaggio [boikot'taddʒo] *sm* boycott; *(fig)* sabotage.

boicottare [boikot'tare] *vt (Econ, fig: persona)* to boycott; *(: piani)* to sabotage.

boiler ['bɔiler] *sm inv* water heater.

bolero [bo'lero] *sm* bolero.

bolgia, ge ['bɔldʒa] *sf (fig):* **c'era una tale** ~ **al cinema** the cinema was absolutely mobbed.

bolide ['bɔlide] *sm* **(a)** *(Astron)* meteor; **come un** ~ like a flash, at top speed; **entrare/uscire come un** ~ to charge in/out. **(b)** *(macchina: da corsa)* racing car; *(: elaborata)* performance car.

Bolivia [bo'livja] *sf* Bolivia.

bolla¹ ['bolla] *sf* bubble; *(Med)* blister; **fare ~e di sapone** to blow bubbles; **finire in una** ~ **di sapone** *(fig)* to come to nothing.

bolla² ['bolla] *sf* **(a)** *(Rel)* bull. **(b)** *(Comm)* bill, receipt.

bollare [bol'lare] *vt (timbrare)* to stamp; *(sigillare)* to seal; *(fig)* to brand; **bollato a vita** *(fig)* branded for life.

bollente [bol'lɛnte] *ag (che bolle)* boiling; *(caldissimo)* boiling (hot); **calmare i** ~**i spiriti** to sober up, calm down.

bolletta [bol'letta] *sf* **(a)** *(ricevuta)* receipt; ~ **di consegna** delivery note; **essere in** ~ *(fam)* to be broke. **(b)** *(conto: del gas etc)* bill; ~ **della luce** electricity bill.

bollettino [bollet'tino] *sm* **(a)** *(comunicato, periodico)* bulletin; ~ **meteorologico** weather forecast. **(b)** *(Comm: dei prezzi, dei cambi)* list; *(: modulo)* form; ~ **di ordinazione** order form; ~ **di spedizione** consignment note.

bollire [bol'lire] **1** *vt* to boil. **2** *vi* to boil, be boiling;

fare ~ *(acqua)* to boil, bring to the boil; *(biberon)* to sterilize; *(panni)* to boil; **sto bollendo (dal caldo)** I'm boiling (hot); **qualcosa bolle in pentola** *(fig)* there's something brewing.

bollito, a [bol'lito] **1** *ag* boiled. **2** *sm (Culin)* boiled meat.

bollitore [bolli'tore] *sm* **(a)** *(Tecn)* boiler. **(b)** *(Culin: per acqua)* kettle; *(: per latte)* milk pan.

bollitura [bolli'tura] *sf* **(a)** *(azione)* boiling. **(b)** *(acqua)* cooking liquid.

bollo ['bollo] *sm (timbro)* stamp; *(sigillo)* seal; *(su bestiame)* brand; ~ **di circolazione** *(Aut)* road fund licence; ~ **postale** postmark.

bollore [bol'lore] *sm*: **dare un** ~ **a qc** to bring sth to the boil; **i** ~**i della gioventù** *(fig)* youthful enthusiasm; **ti sono passati i** ~**i?** have you calmed down?

bolo ['bɔlo] *sm (alimentare)* bolus; *(di ruminante)* cud.

bolognese [boloɲ'ɲese] *ag* Bolognese, of *(o* from*)* Bologna; **spaghetti alla** ~ spaghetti bolognese.

bolscevico, a, chi, che [bolʃe'viko] *ag, sm/f* Bolshevik.

Bolscevismo [bolʃe'vizmo] *sm* Bolshevism.

bomba ['bomba] *sf* bomb; ~ **a mano** hand grenade; ~ **ad orologeria** time bomb; ~ **N** Neutron bomb; **la notizia fu una** ~ the news came as a bombshell; **sei stato una** ~**!** you were tremendous!; **guarda che** ~**!** *(donna, macchina etc)* what a beauty!; **tornare a** ~ *(al punto)* to get back to the point.

bombardamento [bombarda'mento] *sm (vedi vb)* bombardment; bombing; shelling; **un** ~ **aereo** an air raid; **morto sotto un** ~ killed during a bomb attack.

bombardare [bombar'dare] *vt (gen, Fis)* to bombard; *(con bombe)* to bomb; *(con cannone)* to shell; ~ **di domande/lettere** to bombard with questions/letters.

bombardiere [bombar'djɛre] *sm (aereo)* bomber; *(persona)* bombardier.

bombé [bɔ̃'be] *ag inv* rounded.

bombetta [bom'betta] *sf* bowler hat.

bombola ['bombola] *sf* cylinder; ~ **di ossigeṇo/del gas** oxygen/gas cylinder; ~ **d'insetticida** fly spray.

bomboniera [bombo'njɛra] *sf* box of sweets *(as souvenir at weddings, first communions etc)*.

bonaccia [bo'nattʃa] *sf (Naut)* dead calm; *(fig)* lull; **il mare è in** ~ the sea is dead calm.

bonaccione, a [bonat'tʃone] **1** *ag* good-natured, easy-going. **2** *sm/f* good-natured sort.

bonarietà [bonarje'ta] *sf (vedi ag)* good nature, affability; kindliness.

bonario, a [bo'narjo] *ag (persona)* good-natured, affable; *(modi, aspetto)* kindly.

bonifica, che [bo'nifika] *sf (operazione)* reclamation; **opere di** ~ land reclamation works.

bonificabile [bonifi'kabile] *ag* reclaimable.

bonificare [bonifi'kare] *vt* **(a)** *(terreno)* to reclaim; *(Mil)* to clear of mines *etc*. **(b)** *(Comm)* to give a discount to.

bonificazione [bonifikat'tsjone] *sf* = **bonifica**.

bonifico, ci [bo'nifiko] *sm (Comm: abbuono)* discount; *(Banca)* credit transfer.

bontà [bon'ta] *sf (gen)* goodness, kindness; *(di prodotti etc)* quality; ~ **d'animo** *o* **di cuore** goodness of heart; ~ **sua!** how kind of him!; **abbia la** ~ **di ascoltarmi!** will you please listen to me?

bonzo ['bondzo] *sm* Buddhist monk, bonze.

borace [bo'ratʃe] *sm* borax.

borbonico, a, ci, che [bor'bɔniko] *ag* Bourbon; *(fig)* backward, out of date.

borbottamento [borbotta'mento] *sm (vedi vb)* mut-

tering; grousing, grumbling; rumbling.

borbottare [borbot'tare] **1** *vt (pronunciare confusamente)* to mutter. **2** *vi* to mutter; *(lamentarsi)* to grouse, grumble; *(tuono, stomaco)* to rumble.

borbottio, ii [borbot'tio] *sm (vedi vb)* muttering; grousing, grumbling; rumbling.

borchia ['bɔrkja] *sf (di abiti, cinture, borse)* stud; *(Tecn)* boss; *(da tappezziere)* upholsterer's nail.

bordare [bor'dare] *vt* **(a)** *(fare il bordo a)* to hem, edge; **un vestito bordato di rosso** a dress with a red border. **(b)** *(Naut: vele)* to spread.

bordata [bor'data] *sf (Naut)* tack; *(di cannoni)* broadside.

bordatura [borda'tura] *sf (di abiti, tende)* border, edge.

bordeaux [bɔr'do] *sm (colore)* burgundy, maroon; *(vino)* Bordeaux.

bordeggiare [borded'dʒare] *vi (Naut)* to tack.

bordello [bor'dɛllo] *sm* brothel; **fare** ~ *(fam!)* to kick up a hell of a row; **questa stanza è un** ~ *(fam!)* this room's a shambles.

bordo ['bɔrdo] *sm* **(a)** *(orlo)* edge; *(guarnizione)* border; *(di cratere, ruota)* rim; **il** ~ **del tavolo** the edge of the table; **sul** ~ **della strada** at the roadside. **(b)** *(Naut, Aer)*: **a** ~ **(di)** aboard, on board; **fuori** ~ overboard; **era a** ~ **di una macchina rossa** he was in a red car; **salire a** ~ **(di qc)** *(aereo, nave)* to go on board (sth), board (sth); *(macchina)* to get in(to sth); **persona d'alto** ~ *(fig)* VIP.

bordura [bor'dura] *sf (di abiti, aiuole etc)* border; *(di pietanze)* garnish.

boreale [bore'ale] *ag* northern; **aurora** ~ northern lights *pl*, aurora borealis.

borgata [bor'gata] *sf (in campagna)* hamlet; *(a Roma)* working-class suburb.

borghese [bor'gese] **1** *ag* **(a)** *(gen)* middle-class; *(Pol, peg)* bourgeois. **(b)**: **essere in (abito)** ~ to be in civilian clothes *o* in civvies; **poliziotto in** ~ plainclothes policeman. **2** *sm/f (vedi ag)* middle-class person; bourgeois; **piccolo** ~ *(peg)* petty bourgeois.

borghesia [borge'zia] *sf* bourgeoisie, middle classes *pl*; **alta/piccola** ~ upper/lower middle classes *pl*.

borgo, ghi ['borgo] *sm (paese)* village; *(quartiere cittadino)* district; *(sobborgo)* suburb.

borgomastro [borgo'mastro] *sm* burgomaster.

boria ['bɔrja] *sf* conceit, arrogance.

borioso, a [bo'rjoso] *ag* conceited, arrogant.

borlotto [bor'lotto] *sm* kidney bean.

borotalco [boro'talko] *sm* talcum powder.

borraccia, ce [bor'rattʃa] *sf (per soldati, ciclisti etc)* water bottle; *(fiaschetta)* flask.

borraccina [borrat'tʃina] *sf (Bot)* moss.

borsa¹ ['borsa] **1** *sf (gen)* bag; *(~ da signora)* handbag; **aver le** ~**e sotto gli occhi** to have bags under one's eyes. **2**: ~ **dell'acqua calda** hot water bottle; ~ **da avvocato** briefcase; ~ **del ghiaccio** ice bag; ~ **di scuola** schoolbag; ~ **della spesa** shopping bag; ~ **di studio** (student's) grant; ~ **del tabacco** tobacco pouch; ~ **degli utensili** toolbag; ~ **da viaggio** travelling bag.

borsa² ['borsa] *sf (Fin)*: **B**~ Stock Exchange; **speculare in** ~ to speculate on the Stock Exchange.

borsaiolo, a [borsa'jɔlo] *sm/f* pickpocket.

borsanera [borsa'nera] *sf* black market.

borseggiatore, trice [borseddʒa'tore] *sm/f* pickpocket.

borseggio [bor'seddʒo] *sm* pickpocketing.

borsellino [borsel'lino] *sm* purse.

borsello [bor'sɛllo] *sm* gent's handbag.

borsetta [bor'setta] *sf* handbag; ~ **da sera** evening bag.

borsetto [bor'setto] *sm* = **borsello**.

borsista, i, e [bor'sista] *sm/f* **(a)** *(di borsa di studio)* grant holder. **(b)** *(Borsa)* speculator.

boscaglia [bos'kaʎʎa] *sf* brush.

boscaiolo [boska'jɔlo] *sm (legnaiuolo)* woodcutter; *(guardiano)* forester.

boschereccio, a, ci, ce [boske'rettʃo] *ag* woodland *attr*.

boschetto [bos'ketto] *sm* copse, grove.

boschivo, a [bos'kivo] *ag (terreno)* wooded, woody; *(piante, vegetazione)* woodland *attr*.

bosco, schi ['bɔsko] *sm* wood.

boscosità [boskosi'ta] *sf* density of woodland.

boscoso, a [bos'koso] *ag* wooded.

bosso ['bɔsso] *sm (pianta)* box; *(legno)* boxwood.

bossolo ['bɔssolo] *sm* cartridge case.

botanica [bo'tanika] *sf* botany.

botanico, a, ci, che [bo'taniko] **1** *ag* botanic(al). **2** *sm/f* botanist.

botola ['bɔtola] *sf* trapdoor.

botta ['bɔtta] *sf* **(a)** *(percossa)* blow; *(fig: colpo, danno)* blow, shock; **gli menò una ~ in testa** he struck him a blow on the head; **dare (un sacco di) ~e a qn** to give sb a good thrashing. **(b)** *(rumore)* bang. **(c)** *(Scherma)* thrust; **~ e risposta** *(fig)* cut and thrust.

bottaio [bot'tajo] *sm* cooper.

botte ['botte] *sf* barrel, cask; **volta a ~** *(Archit)* barrel vault; **volere la ~ piena e la moglie ubriaca** to want to have one's cake and eat it; **essere in una ~ di ferro** *(fig)* to be as safe as houses.

bottega, ghe [bot'tega] *sf (negozio)* shop; *(laboratorio)* workshop; **aprire/mettere su ~** to open/set up shop; **chiudere ~** *(fig)* to shut up shop; *(fig)* to give up; **stare a ~ (da qn)** to serve one's apprenticeship (with sb); **avere la ~ aperta** *(fam)* to have one's flies undone.

bottegaio, a [botte'gajo] *sm/f* shopkeeper.

botteghino [botte'gino] *sm (Teatro, Cine)* box office; *(del lotto)* lottery office.

bottiglia [bot'tiʎʎa] *sf* bottle; **~ di vino** bottle of wine; **~ da vino** wine bottle; **una ~ da 1 litro** a litre bottle; **birra in ~** bottled beer; **~ Molotov** Molotov cocktail.

bottiglieria [bottiʎʎe'ria] *sf (negozio)* wine shop; *(deposito)* wine cellar.

bottiglione [bottiʎ'ʎone] *sm* large bottle.

bottino¹ [bot'tino] *sm (di guerra)* booty; *(di rapina)* loot; **fare ~ di qc** *(anche fig)* to make off with sth.

bottino² [bot'tino] *sm (pozzonero)* cesspool, cesspit.

botto ['bɔtto] *sm (di mortaretti, spari)* crack; **di ~** *(fam)* suddenly; **d'un ~** *(fam)* in a flash.

bottone [bot'tone] *sm* **(a)** *(di giacca, TV, radio)* button; **~ automatico** press stud; **premere o spingere un ~** to press a button; **la stanza dei ~i** control room; *(fig)* nerve centre; **attaccare (un) ~ o con qn** to strike up a conversation with sb; *(trattenere)* to buttonhole sb. **(b)** *(Bot)* bud; **botton d'oro** buttercup.

bottoniera [botto'njera] *sf (Tecn)* control panel.

bouquet [bu'ke] *sm inv (di fiori, del vino)* bouquet.

bovaro [bo'varo] *sm* herdsman.

bove ['bɔve] *sm* = **bue**.

bovino, a [bo'vino] **1** *ag* bovine; *(allevamento)* cattle *attr*; **occhi ~i** *(fig)* protruding eyes. **2:** **~i** *smpl* cattle.

bowling ['bouliŋ] *sm inv (gioco)* (tenpin) bowling; *(luogo)* bowling alley.

box [bɔks] *sm inv (per cavalli)* horsebox; *(per macchina)* lock-up; *(per macchina da corsa)* pit; *(per bambini)* playpen.

boxare [bok'sare] *vi* to box.

boxe [bɔks] *sf* boxing.

boxeur [bɔk'sœr] *sm inv (pugile)* boxer.

boy ['bɔi] *sm inv (ballerino di rivista)* dancer; *(in albergo)* bellboy.

bozza¹ ['bɔttsa] *sf (fam: bernoccolo)* bump.

bozza² ['bɔttsa] *sf (di lettera, contratto, romanzo)* draft; *(Tip)* proof; **prima/seconda ~** first/revised proof; **~ in colonna** galley proof; **rivedere o correggere le ~e** to proofread.

bozzettista, i, e [bottset'tista] *sm/f (scrittore)* sketch writer; *(di pubblicità)* commercial artist.

bozzetto [bot'tsetto] *sm (disegno)* sketch; *(modello)* scale model.

bozzo ['bɔttso] *sm* bump.

bozzolo ['bɔttsolo] *sm* cocoon; **uscire dal ~** *(fig)* to come out of one's shell; **chiudersi nel proprio ~** *(fig)* to withdraw into one's shell.

BR *abbr fpl di* **Brigate Rosse**.

braca ['braka] *sf* **(a)** *(gamba di pantalone)* trouser leg; **~che** *(fam)* trousers; *(mutandoni)* drawers; **calare le ~che** *(fig fam)* to chicken out. **(b)** *(allacciatura: per operai)* (safety) harness; *(: per bambini)* harness.

braccare [brak'kare] *vt (anche fig)* to hunt.

braccetto [brat'tʃetto] *: a ~ av* arm in arm; **prendere qn a ~** to take sb by the arm; **tenersi a ~** to be arm in arm.

bracciale [brat'tʃale] *sm*, **braccialetto** [brattʃa'letto] *sm* bracelet.

bracciante [brat'tʃante] *sm* day labourer.

bracciata [brat'tʃata] *sf* **(a)** *(quantità)* armful; **a ~e** in armfuls. **(b)** *(nel nuoto)* stroke.

braccio ['brattʃo] *sm*, *pl(f)* **~a (a)** *(Anat)* arm; **tenere/prendere in ~** to hold/take in one's arms; **dare o offrire il ~ a qn** to give sb one's arm; **camminare sotto ~** to walk arm in arm; **è il suo ~ destro** he's his right-hand man; **~ di ferro** *(anche fig)* trial of strength; **alzare le ~a al cielo** to throw up one's arms; **a ~a** *(sollevare, portare)* with one's own hands; **a ~a aperte** with open arms; **incrociare le ~a** to fold one's arms; *(fig)* to down tools; **gettare le ~a al collo a qn** to throw one's arms round sb's neck; **mi sono cascate le ~a** *(fig)* I could have wept; **avere buone ~a** to be big and strong.

(b) *(Naut: unità di misura)* fathom.

(c) *(pl(m) ~i: di croce, gru, fiume, grammofono)* arm; *(: di edificio)* wing; **~ di mare** sound.

bracciolo [brat'tʃɔlo] *sm* arm.

bracco, chi ['brakko] *sm* hound.

bracconiere [brakko'njere] *sm* poacher.

brace ['bratʃe] *sf* embers *pl*.

braciere [bra'tʃɛre] *sm* brazier.

braciola [bra'tʃɔla] *sf (con osso)* chop; *(senza osso)* steak.

bradipo ['bradipo] *sm (Zool)* sloth.

brado, a ['brado] *ag (animale)* wild; **allo stato ~** in the wild *o* natural state.

braille [braj] *sf* braille.

brama ['brama] *sf:* **~ (di/di fare)** longing (for/to do), yearning (for/to do).

bramare [bra'mare] *vt:* **~ (qc/di fare qc)** to long (for sth/to do sth), yearn (for sth/to do sth).

bramire [bra'mire] *vi (cervo)* to bell; *(orso)* to roar.

bramito [bra'mito] *sm (di cervo)* bell; *(di orso)* roar.

bramosia [bramo'sia] *sf:* **~ (di)** longing (for), yearning (for).

bramoso, a [bra'moso] *ag (sguardo etc)* longing; **essere ~ di qc** to long *o* yearn for sth.

branca, che ['branka] *sf* **(a)** *(artiglio: di gatto)* claw; *(: di falco)* talon. **(b)** *(settore, ramo)* branch; **una ~ dello scibile** a branch of knowledge.

branchia ['brankja] *sf* gill.

branchiale [bran'kjale] *ag* branchial.

branco, chi ['branko] *sm (di pecore)* flock; *(di lupi)* pack; *(fig peg: di persone)* gang; **mettersi** *o* **entrare nel** ~ *(fig)* to go with the crowd.

brancolare [branko'lare] *vi* to grope; ~ **nel buio** *(fig)* to grope in the dark.

branda ['branda] *sf (da campo, per militari)* camp bed, folding bed; *(per marinai)* hammock; **giù dalle** ~**e!** everybody up!

brandello [bran'dɛllo] *sm* scrap, shred; **a** ~**i** in tatters, in rags; **fare a** ~**i** to tear to shreds.

brandire [bran'dire] *vt* to brandish.

brano ['brano] *sm (gen)* piece; *(di letteratura)* passage; **fare qc a** ~**i** *(fig)* to tear sth to pieces.

brasare [bra'zare] *vt (Culin)* to braise; *(Tecn)* to braze.

brasato, a [bra'zato] **1** *ag (Culin)* braised. **2** *sm* braised beef.

Brasile [bra'zile] *sm* Brazil.

brasiliano, a [brazi'ljano] *ag, sm/f* Brazilian.

bravata [bra'vata] *sf (azione spavalda)* act of bravado; ~**e** *(millanterie)* bravado *sg*.

bravo ['bravo] *ag (a) (abile)* good, clever, skilful; **essere** ~ **in qc/a fare qc** to be good at sth/at doing sth; **un** ~ **insegnante/medico** a good teacher/doctor; **essere** ~ **a scuola** to do well at school; ~**!** well done!; *(in chiusura di spettacolo)* bravo! **(b)** *(buono)* good; *(onesto)* honest; **è un brav'uomo** he's a decent chap; **sono** ~**e persone** they're good people; **fai il** ~ be good; **su da** ~**!** *(fam)* there's a good boy! **(c)** *(coraggioso)* brave. **(d)** *(rafforzativo)*: **mi sono fatto le mie** ~**e 8 ore di lavoro** I put in a full 8 hours' work; **se non si beve il suo** ~ **mezzo litro non è contento** he isn't happy unless he has had his usual pint.

bravura [bra'vura] *sf* cleverness, skill; **pezzo di** ~ *(Mus)* bravura piece.

breccia¹, ce ['brettʃa] *sf* breach; **essere sulla** ~ *(fig)* to be going strong; **fare** ~ **nell'animo** *o* **nel cuore di qn** to find the way to sb's heart.

breccia² ['brettʃa] *sf*, **brecciame** [bret'tʃame] *sm* road metal.

brefotrofio [brefo'trɔfjo] *sm* orphanage *(for abandoned children)*.

bresaola [bre'zaola] *sf (Culin)* kind of dried salted beef.

bretella [bre'tɛlla] *sf (a) (di sottoveste, reggiseno)* strap; *(di calzoni)*: ~**e** braces. **(b)** *(raccordo stradale)* motorway link road.

breve ['brɛve] **1** *ag (gen)* brief, short; *(vita, strada)* short; **tra** ~ shortly; **a** ~ **distanza** near, not far; **sarò** ~ I'll be brief; **per farla** ~ to cut a long story short; **in** ~ in short. **2** *sf (a) (Mus)* breve. **(b)** *(vocale)* short vowel; *(sillaba)* short syllable.

brevettare [brevet'tare] *vt* to patent.

brevetto [bre'vetto] *sm (a) (d'invenzione)* patent; **Ufficio B**~**i** Patent Office. **(b)** *(patente)*: ~ **di pilota** pilot's licence.

breviario [brevi'arjo] *sm (Rel)* breviary; *(compendio)* compendium.

brevità [brevi'ta] *sf* brevity.

brezza ['breddza] *sf* breeze.

bric-à-brac ['brika'brak] *sm* bric-à-brac.

bricco, chi ['brikko] *sm* jug.

bricconata [brikko'nata] *sf* mischievous trick.

briccone [brik'kone] *sm* rascal.

briciola ['britʃola] *sf (di pane etc)* crumb; *(frammento)* scrap; **non ha lasciato che le** ~**e** *(anche fig)* he only left the scraps; **ridurre in** ~**e** *(biscotto)* to crumble up; *(fig: persona)* to take to pieces.

briciolo ['britʃolo] *sm* bit; *(fig: di buon senso, verità)* grain.

bridge [bridʒ] *sm* bridge.

briga, ghe ['briga] *sf (a) (cura, fastidio)* bother, trouble; **darsi** *o* **prendersi la** ~ **di fare qc** to take the trouble to do sth. **(b)** *(lite)*: **attaccar** ~ to start a quarrel.

brigadiere [briga'djɛre] *sm (a) (dei carabinieri, Polizia etc)* ≈ sergeant. **(b)** *(comandante di brigata)* brigadier.

brigantaggio [brigan'taddʒo] *sm* brigandage; *(organizzazione)* brigands *pl*.

brigante [bri'gante] *sm* brigand, bandit; *(fig: bambino)* rascal.

brigantino [brigan'tino] *sm (Naut)* brig, brigantine.

brigata [bri'gata] *sf (a) (gruppo)* group; *(comitiva)* · party; **un'allegra** ~ **di amici** a lively bunch of friends. **(b)** *(Mil)* brigade; **generale di** ~ brigadier *(Brit)*, brigadier general *(Am)*; **le B**~**e Rosse** the Red Brigades.

brigatista, i, e [briga'tista] *sm/f (Pol) member of the Red Brigades*.

briglia ['briʎʎa] *sf (di cavallo, per bambino)* rein; **a** ~ **sciolta** at full gallop; *(fig)* at full speed; **allentare/tirare la** ~ *(anche fig)* to slacken/tighten the reins.

brillante [bril'lante] **1** *ag (a) (luce, raggi, colori)* bright; *(: più intenso)* brilliant; *(che luccica)* shining; *(: occhi)* sparkling. **(b)** *(successo, carriera, studioso)* brilliant; *(conversazione)* brilliant, sparkling; **è una persona** ~ he has a sparkling wit. **2** *sm (diamante)* diamond; *(anello)* diamond ring.

brillantina [brillan'tina] *sf* brilliantine.

brillare¹ [bril'lare] *vt (riso)* to husk.

brillare² [bril'lare] **1** *vi (a) (sole)* to shine; *(stelle)* to shine, twinkle; *(occhi)* to shine, sparkle; *(brillante)* to sparkle; **gli occhi le brillavano di gioia** her eyes sparkled *o* shone with joy; **brilla per la sua bellezza/intelligenza** she is outstandingly beautiful/intelligent. **(b)** *(mina)* to go off, explode. **2** *vt (mina)* to set off.

brillo, a ['brillo] *ag (fam)* tipsy.

brina ['brina] *sf (hoar)*frost.

brinare [bri'nare] *vb impers (aus essere)*: **stanotte è brinato** there was a frost last night.

brinata [bri'nata] *sf (hoar)*frost.

brindare [brin'dare] *vi* to make a toast; ~ **a qn/qc** to drink to *o* toast sb/sth; ~ **alla salute di qn** to drink to sb's health.

brindello [brin'dello] *sm* = **brandello.**

brindisi ['brindizi] *sm inv* toast; **fare un** ~ **(a qn/qc)** to drink a toast (to sb/sth).

brio ['brio] *sm* liveliness; **essere pieno di** ~ to be very lively *o* full of life.

brioche [bri'ɔʃ] *sf inv* brioche.

brioso, a [bri'oso] *ag* lively.

briscola ['briskola] *sf (a)* type of card game. **(b)** *(seme vincente)* trump(s); *(carta)* trump card.

britannico, a, ci, che [bri'tanniko] **1** *ag* British. **2** *sm/f* British person; **i B**~**ci** the British.

brivido ['brivido] *sm* shiver, shudder; **avere i** ~**i** *(anche fig)* to have the shivers; **far venire i** ~**i a qn** *(fig)* to give sb the shivers; **racconti del** ~ suspense stories.

brizzolato, a [brittso'lato] *ag (barba, capelli)* greyspeckled, grizzled; *(persona)* grey-haired, greying.

brocca, che ['brɔkka] *sf* jug.

broccato [brok'kato] *sm* brocade.

broccolo ['brɔkkolo] *sm (Bot, Culin)* broccoli *no pl*; *(fig)* clot, idiot.

broda ['brɔda] *sf (peg)* dishwater.

brodaglia [bro'daʎʎa] *sf (peg)* dishwater.

brodetto [bro'detto] *sm (brodo leggero)* light broth;

~ **alla marinara** sort of bouillabaisse.

brodo ['brɔdo] sm broth; ~ **di manzo** beef tea; **riso/pasta in** ~ rice/noodle soup; **tutto fa** ~ every little bit helps; **lasciare (cuocere) qn nel suo** ~ to let sb stew (in his own juice).

brogliaccio [broʎ'ʎattʃo] sm (Amm) daybook.

broglio ['brɔʎʎo] sm: ~ **elettorale** gerrymandering.

bromo ['brɔmo] sm bromine.

bromuro [bro'muro] sm bromide.

bronchiale [bron'kjale] ag bronchial.

bronchite [bron'kite] sf bronchitis.

broncio ['brontʃo] sm sulky expression; (malumore) sulkiness; **avere o tenere il** ~ to sulk; **gli tiene il** ~ he's not speaking to him.

bronco, chi ['bronko] sm bronchial tube.

broncopolmonite [bronkopolmo'nite] sf bronchial pneumonia.

brontolare [bronto'lare] 1 vt to mutter, mumble. 2 vi (mormorare) to mutter, mumble; (protestare) to grumble; **mi brontola lo stomaco** my stomach is rumbling.

brontolio, ii [bronto'lio] sm (vedi vb) mumbling; muttering; grumbling; rumbling.

brontolone, a [bronto'lone] 1 ag grumbling. 2 sm/f grumbler.

brontosauro [bronto'sauro] sm brontosaurus.

bronzeo, a ['brondzeo] ag (di bronzo) bronze; (color bronzo) bronze(-coloured).

bronzetto [bron'dzetto] sm bronze statuette.

bronzina [bron'dzina] sf (Tecn) bush.

bronzo ['brondzo] sm (metallo, oggetto) bronze; **che faccia di** ~! what a brass neck!

brossura [bros'sura] sf: **in** ~ (libro) limpback.

brucare [bru'kare] vt to browse on, nibble at.

bruciacchiare [brutʃak'kjare] 1 vt to singe, scorch. 2: ~**rsi** vr to become singed, become scorched.

bruciapelo [brutʃa'pelo]: **a** ~ av point-blank; **sparare a** ~ to fire at point-blank range.

bruciare [bru'tʃare] 1 vt (a) (gen) to burn; (edificio) to burn down; (stoffa: stirando) to scorch; (Med: verruca) to cauterize; **bruciato dal sole** (terreno) sun-scorched; (volto) sunburnt; (: ustionato) burnt by the sun. (b) (fraseologia): ~ **gli avversari** (Sport, fig) to leave the rest of the field behind; ~ **le cervella a qn** to blow sb's brains out; ~ **le tappe o i tempi** (Sport, fig) to shoot ahead; ~**rsi le ali** (fig) to burn one's fingers; ~**rsi la carriera** to put an end to one's career.

2 vi (aus essere) (a) (gen) to burn; (edificio, bosco etc) to be on fire. (b) (essere molto caldo) to be burning (hot); (: sole) to be scorching, be burning; ~ **di febbre** to run a high temperature. (c) (produrre bruciore): **gli occhi mi bruciano** my eyes are smarting o stinging; **il viso mi brucia** my face is burning; **mi brucia molto questa offesa** that insult really rankles.

3: ~**rsi** vr (persona) to burn o.s.; **si è bruciato l'arrosto** the joint is burnt.

bruciato, a [bru'tʃato] 1 ag burnt; **Gioventù** ~**a** Beat Generation. 2 sm: **odore di** ~ (smell of) burning; **questa zuppa sa di** ~ this soup tastes burnt.

bruciatore [brutʃa'tore] sm (Tecn) burner.

bruciatura [brutʃa'tura] sf (a) (atto) burning. (b) (parte bruciata) burn.

bruciore [bru'tʃore] sm burning (sensation); **provocare** ~ to sting.

bruco, chi ['bruko] sm (Zool) grub; (: di farfalla) caterpillar.

brufolo ['brufolo] sm pimple, spot.

brughiera [bru'gjera] sf moor, heath.

brûlé [bry'le] ag inv: **vin** ~ mulled wine.

brulicante [bruli'kante] ag: ~ **di** (anche fig) swarming with, teeming with.

brulicare [bruli'kare] vi to swarm; **il mercato brulicava di gente** the market was teeming with people.

brulichio, ii [bruli'kio] sm swarming.

brullo, a ['brullo] ag barren.

bruma ['bruma] sf mist, haze.

brunire [bru'nire] vt (metallo: levigare) to burnish, polish.

brunitura [bruni'tura] sf burnishing, polishing.

bruno, a ['bruno] 1 ag (capelli) brown, dark; (carnagione) dark. 2 sm/f dark-haired person.

brusca, sche ['bruska] sf scrubbing brush; (per cavalli) horse brush.

bruscamente [bruska'mente] av (in modo brusco) sharply, abruptly; (improvvisamente) suddenly.

bruschezza [brus'kettsa] sf brusqueness, abruptness.

brusco, a, schi, sche ['brusko] ag (movimento) abrupt, sudden; (modi, persona) abrupt, brusque.

bruscolo ['bruskolo] sm speck.

brusio, ii [bru'zio] sm hubbub, buzz; **i** ~**ii degli insetti** the buzzing of the insects.

brutale [bru'tale] ag rough, brutal; **per dirla in modo** ~ to put it bluntly.

brutalità [brutali'ta] sf inv brutality.

brutalizzare [brutalid'dzare] vt to brutalize.

bruto, a ['bruto] 1 ag: **forza** ~**a** brute force o strength. 2 sm (uomo violento) brute.

brutta ['brutta] sf rough copy, first draft.

bruttezza [brut'tettsa] sf ugliness.

brutto, a ['brutto] 1 ag (a) (persona, vestito, casa etc) ugly; ~ **come la fame** as ugly as sin. (b) (cattivo: gen) bad; (: ferita, malattia) nasty; (: carattere) unpleasant, nasty; ~ **cattivo!** you naughty boy!; ~ **stupido!** you stupid clown!; **ha fatto** ~ (tempo) ieri yesterday the weather was bad; **avere un** ~ **male** (euf) to have cancer; **passare un** ~ **momento** to go through a difficult period; **passare un** ~ **quarto d'ora** to have a nasty time of it; **vedersela** ~**a** (per un attimo) to have a nasty moment; (per un periodo) to have a bad time of it.

2 sm (a): **il** ~ (Arte etc) the ugly; **è il** ~ **della famiglia** he's the ugly member of the family; **il** ~ **è che...** the problem o unfortunate thing is that...; **stiamo andando verso il** ~ (Meteor) the weather is getting worse. (b): **di** ~: **guardare qn di** ~ to give sb a nasty look; **picchiare qn di** ~ to give sb a bad o nasty beating; **sta lavorando di** ~ he's working furiously.

bruttura [brut'tura] sf (azione, oggetto) horrible thing.

bubbone [bub'bone] sm (Med) swelling.

bubbonico, a, ci, che [bub'boniko] ag: **peste** ~**a** bubonic plague.

buca, che ['buka] sf (gen, Golf) hole; (più profondo) pit; (di biliardo) pocket; ~ **delle lettere** letterbox; **la** ~ **del suggeritore** (Teatro) prompter's box.

bucaneve [buka'neve] sm snowdrop.

bucaniere [buka'njere] sm buccaneer.

bucare [bu'kare] 1 vt (forare) to make a hole (o holes) in, pierce; (: biglietto) to punch; (: gomma) to puncture; **ho bucato una gomma** I've got a puncture; **avere le mani bucate** (fig) to be a spendthrift. 2: ~**rsi** vr to prick o.s.; (fam: drogarsi) to mainline; **mi si è bucata una gomma** I've got a puncture.

bucato [bu'kato] sm washing; **fare il** ~ to do the washing; **stirare il** ~ to do the ironing.

buccia, ce ['buttʃa] sf (di verdura, frutta: gen) skin;

(: *di agrumi, patate*) skin, peel; (: *di piselli*) pod; (*di salumi*) skin; (*di formaggio*) rind.

bucherellare [bukerel'lare] *vt* to riddle (with holes).

buco, chi ['buko] *sm* (*gen*) hole; (*omissione*) gap; (*orifizio, apertura*) aperture; **il ~ della serratura** keyhole; **fare un ~ nell'acqua** to fail, draw a blank; **farsi un ~** (*fam: drogarsi*) to have a fix.

bucolico, a, ci, che [bu'kɔliko] *ag* bucolic, pastoral.

buddismo [bud'dizmo] *sm* (*Rel*) Buddhism.

buddista, i, e [bud'dista] *ag, sm/f* Buddhist.

buddistico, a, ci, che [bud'distiko] *ag* Buddhist.

budello [bu'dɛllo] *sm* (*intestino: pl(f) ~a*) bowel, intestine, gut; (*tubo: di ruota*) tube. (**b**) (*materiale*) gut. (**c**) (*strada*) alley.

budgetario, a [buddʒe'tarjo] *ag* budgetary.

budino [bu'dino] *sm* pudding.

bue ['bue], *pl* **buoi** *sm* (**a**) (*Zool*) ox; **~ marino** dugong; **~ muschiato** musk ox; **~ selvatico** bison. (**b**) (*Culin*) beef; **uovo all'occhio di ~** fried egg.

bufalo ['bufalo] *sm* buffalo.

bufera [bu'fera] *sf* (*anche fig*) storm.

buffet [by'fe] *sm inv* (**a**) (*mobile*) sideboard. (**b**) (*bar*) buffet, refreshment bar.

buffetto [buf'fetto] *sm* flick.

buffo, a ['buffo] *ag* (*ridicolo*) funny, comical; (*divertente*) funny, amusing; (*strano*) funny, odd.

buffonata [buffo'nata] *sf* (*azione*) prank, jest; (*parola*) jest; **fare ~e** (*anche fig*) to clown about; **dire ~e** to joke; (*fig*) to talk rubbish.

buffone [buf'fone] *sm* (*anche fig*) clown, buffoon; (*peg*) joker; **fare il ~** (*fig*) to play the fool, clown about; **~ di corte** court jester.

buffoneria [buffone'ria] *sf* buffoonery.

buffonesco, a, schi, sche [buffo'nesko] *ag* clownish, comical.

buggerare [buddʒe'rare] *vt* to swindle, cheat.

bugia[1], gie [bu'dʒia] *sf* (*menzogna*) lie; **dire o raccontare ~e** to tell lies; **~ pietosa** white lie; **le ~e hanno le gambe corte** (*Proverbio*) truth will out.

bugia[2], gie [bu'dʒia] *sf* (*candelabro*) candleholder.

bugiardo, a [bu'dʒardo] **1** *ag* lying, deceitful. **2** *sm/f* liar.

bugigattolo [budʒi'gattolo] *sm* (*ripostiglio*) boxroom; (*peg*) poky little room.

bugliolo [buʎ'ʎɔlo] *sm* (*Naut*) (ship's) bucket.

bugna ['buɲɲa] *sf* (*Archit*) boss.

buio, a, i o ii, e ['bujo] **1** *ag* (*oscuro*) dark; (*tetro, triste*) gloomy, dismal. **2** *sm* dark, darkness; **al ~** in the dark; **si sta facendo ~** (*imbrunisce*) it is growing *o* getting dark.

bulbo ['bulbo] *sm* (*gen*) bulb; **~ oculare** eyeball.

Bulgaria [bulga'ria] *sf* Bulgaria.

bulgaro, a ['bulgaro] *ag, sm/f, sm* Bulgarian.

bulino [bu'lino] *sm* (*Tecn*) burin, graver; **lavorare a ~** to engrave.

bulldozer ['buldouzə] *sm inv* bulldozer.

bulletta [bul'letta] *sf* tack, stud.

bullo ['bullo] *sm* (*persona*) tough; **fare il ~** to act tough.

bullonare [bullo'nare] *vt* (*Tecn*) to bolt.

bullone [bul'lone] *sm* bolt.

bum [bum] **1** *escl* (*scoppio*) boom!, bang! **2** *sm inv* bang; **fare ~** to bang.

bungalow ['bʌngəlou] *sm inv* (*casa*) bungalow; (*per vacanze*) holiday chalet.

bunker ['bunker] *sm inv* (*Mil*) bunker.

buoi ['bwɔji] *smpl di* **bue.**

buonafede [bwona'fede] *sf* good faith; **in ~** in good faith.

buonanima [bwo'nanima] *sf*: **mio nonno ~..., la ~**

di mio nonno... my grandfather, God rest his soul... .

buonanotte [bwona'nɔtte] **1** *escl* = **buona notte. 2** *sf*: **dare la ~ a qn** to say good night to sb.

buonasera [bwona'sera] **1** *escl* = **buona sera. 2** *sf*: **dare la ~ a qn** to wish sb good evening; **signorina ~** (*TV*) female TV announcer.

buoncostume [bwonkos'tume] *sm* public morality; **la (squadra del) ~** (*Polizia*) the vice squad.

buondì [bwon'di] *escl* hello!

buongiorno [bwon'dʒorno] **1** *escl* = **buon giorno. 2** *sm*: **dare il ~ a qn** to wish sb good morning.

buongrado [bwon'grado]: **di ~** *av* willingly.

buongustaio, a [bwongus'tajo] *sm/f* gourmet.

buongusto [bwon'gusto] *sm* (good) taste; **abbi il ~ di non farti più vedere** I hope you'll have the good manners not to show your face again.

buono, a[1] [a] ['bwɔno] **1** *ag* (*dav sm:* **buon** + *consonante, vocale,* **buono** + *s impura, gn, pn, ps, x, z; dav sf:* **buona** + *consonante,* **buon'** + *vocale*) (**a**) (*gen*) good; (*prodotto*) good (quality); (*odore, ambiente, atmosfera*) good, nice, pleasant; (*posizione, ditta, impresa*) sound; **~a società** polite society; **buon senso** common sense; **essere in ~a compagnia** to be in good company; **avere un buon sapore/odore** to taste/smell good *o* nice; **più ~** better; **il più buon libro** the best book; **essere di ~a famiglia** to come from a good family; **tenere ~ qn** (*bambino*) to keep sb quiet; (*fig: persona influente*) to keep sb sweet; **(stai) ~!** behave!

(**b**) (*generoso: persona, azione*) good, kind, kindly; **è una ~a ragazza** she's a good-hearted girl; **una persona di buon cuore** a good-hearted person; **essere ~ come il pane** to have a heart of gold.

(**c**) (*abile, idoneo*): **essere ~ a nulla** to be no good *o* use at anything; **quest'acqua non è ~a da bersi** this water isn't safe to drink; **~ da buttar via** fit for the dustbin; **mi sembra ~ per questo lavoro** he seems suitable for the job.

(**d**) (*utile, vantaggioso*): **a buon mercato** cheap; **~ a sapersi** that's nice to know; **è stata una ~a scelta** it was a good choice.

(**e**) (*giusto, valido*) correct, right; (: *motivo*) valid; **al momento ~** at the right moment; **a buon diritto** rightfully; **ad ogni buon conto** in any case.

(**f**) (*utilizzabile*) usable; (: *biglietto, passaporto*) valid; **è ancora ~a questa vernice?** is this paint still okay *o* usable?; **non è più ~** (*latte*) it's off; (*pane*) it's stale.

(**g**) (*con valore intensivo*) good; **un buon numero** a good *o* large number; **di buon mattino** early in the morning; **deciditi una ~a volta** make up your mind once and for all; **ci vuole un buon mese** it takes a good month *o* a month at least; **peserà 10 kg ~i** it must weigh a good 10 kg.

(**h**) (*auguri*): **buon giorno!** good day!; (*in mattinata*) good morning!; **~a sera!** good evening!; **~a notte!** good night!; **buon appetito/viaggio/divertimento!** have a nice meal/journey/time!; **~a permanenza!** enjoy your stay!; **buon compleanno/Natale!** happy birthday/Christmas!; **buon riposo** sleep well; **tante ~e cose** all the best.

(**i**) (*fraseologia*): **fare qc alla ~a** to do sth simply *o* in a simple way; **stasera mi vesto alla ~a** I'm not getting dressed up this evening; **è un tipo alla ~a** he's an easy-going sort; **questa sì che è ~a!** that's a good one!; **con le ~e** (*maniere*) in a kind *o* friendly way; **accetterà con le ~e o con le cattive** he'll have to accept whether he wants to or not; **essere in ~e mani** to be in good hands; **mettere una ~a parola per qn** to put in a good word for sb; **essere a buon punto** to be well advanced; **siamo a buon punto con il pranzo** dinner's nearly ready; **mi dica, buon uomo…** tell me, my good man…; **fare buon viso a cattivo gioco** to put a good face on things; **l'ho fatto di ~a voglia** I did it willingly; **che Dio ce la mandi ~a!** here's hoping!

2 *sm/f (persona)* good *o* upright person; **i ~i e i cattivi** *(in film etc)* the goodies and the baddies.

3 *sm (bontà)* goodness, good; **di ~ c'è che…** the good thing about it is that…; **essere un poco di ~** to be a nasty piece of work; **è una poco di ~** she's a slut.

buono² ['bwɔno] *sm* **(a)** *(Comm)* coupon, voucher; **~ (d') acquisto** credit note, credit slip; **~ di consegna** delivery note; **~ per benzina** petrol coupon; **~ mensa** canteen voucher. **(b)** *(Fin)* bill, bond; **~ del Tesoro** Treasury bill; **~ fruttifero** interest-bearing bond.

buonora [bwo'nora] *sf (anche:* **buon'ora***)*: **di ~** early; **alla ~** finally, at last.

buonsenso [bwon'sɛnso] *sm* = **buon senso.**

buontempone, a [bwontem'pone] *sm/f* jovial person.

buonumore [bwonu'more] *sm* = **buon umore.**

buonuomo [bwo'nwɔmo] *sm* = **buon uomo.**

buonuscita [bwonuʃ'ʃita] *sf* **(a)** *(Industria)* golden handshake. **(b)** *(di affitti)* sum paid for the relinquishing of tenancy rights.

burattinaio [buratti'najo] *sm* puppeteer.

burattino [burat'tino] *sm (anche fig)* puppet; **fare la figura del ~** to cut a sorry figure.

burbero, a ['burbero] **1** *ag* surly, gruff. **2** *sm/f* surly person, gruff person; **~ benefico** rough diamond.

bureau [by'ro] *sm inv (mobile)* writing desk, bureau.

burla ['burla] *sf* prank, trick; **per ~** for fun, for a joke.

burlare [bur'lare] **1** *vt* to make fun of. **2**: **~rsi di ~** = *vt*.

burlesco, a, schi, sche [bur'lesko] *ag (tono, voce)* jesting; *(stile etc)* burlesque.

burlone, a [bur'lone] *sm/f* joker.

burocrate [bu'rɔkrate] *sm (anche fig)* bureaucrat; **cervello da ~** bureaucratic mind.

burocratico, a, ci, che [buro'kratiko] *ag (anche fig)* bureaucratic.

burocratismo [burokra'tizmo] *sm* bureaucratic attitude.

burocratizzare [burokratid'dzare] *vt* to bureaucratize.

burocrazia [burokrat'tsia] bureaucracy.

burrasca, sche [bur'raska] *sf (anche fig)* storm; **far ~** to be stormy; **mare in ~** stormy sea; **c'è ~ in famiglia** there's trouble at home.

burrascoso, a [burras'koso] *ag (anche fig)* stormy.

burrificio [burri'fitʃo] *sm* creamery.

burro ['burro] *sm* butter; **pasta/riso al ~** buttered noodles/rice; **uovo al ~** egg fried in butter; **~ di arachidi** peanut butter; **~ di cacao** *(Culin)* cocoa butter; *(per labbra)* lip salve; **questa bistecca è come ~** *(fig)* this steak melts in your mouth; **avere le mani di ~** *(fig)* to be butter-fingered.

burrone [bur'rone] *sm* ravine.

burroso, a [bur'roso] *ag* buttery.

buscare [bus'kare] *vt (anche:* **~rsi***: raffreddore, schiaffo etc)* to get; **buscarle** to catch it, get a good hiding.

busillis [bu'zillis] *sm inv*: **qui sta il ~** there's the rub.

bussare [bus'sare] *vi* **(a)** to knock; **~ alla porta** to knock at the door; **stanno bussando** there's somebody at the door; **~ a quattrini** *(fig)* to ask for money. **(b)** *(Carte)* to knock on the table to induce partner to play his highest card.

bussola ['bussola] *sf* **(a)** *(strumento nautico)* compass; **~ giroscopica/magnetica** gyro/magnetic compass; **perdere la ~** *(fig)* to lose one's head. **(b)** *(porta)* revolving door. **(c)** *(cassetta sigillata)* collection box.

bussolotto [busso'lɔtto] *sm (per dadi)* diceshaker.

busta ['busta] *sf* **(a)** envelope; **in ~ aperta** in an unsealed envelope; **~ a finestrella** window envelope; **~ paga** pay packet; *(listino)* pay slip. **(b)** *(astuccio: di occhiali etc)* case.

bustaia [bus'taja] *sf* corsetière.

bustarella [busta'rella] *sf* bribe.

bustina [bus'tina] *sf* **(a)** *(piccola busta)* envelope. **(b)** *(di cibi, farmaci)* sachet; **~ di tè** tea bag. **(c)** *(Mil)* forage cap.

bustino [bus'tino] *sm* corselet(te).

busto ['busto] *sm* **(a)** *(Anat, Scultura)* bust; **a mezzo ~** *(fotografia, ritratto)* half-length; **stare a ~ eretto** to stand up straight. **(b)** *(indumento)* corset.

butano [bu'tano] *sm* butane.

buttare [but'tare] **1** *vt* **(a)** *(gettare)* to throw; **~ fuori qn** to throw sb out; **~ qc addosso a qn** to throw sth at sb; **~ qc a qn** to throw sth to sb; **~ qc per terra** to throw sth on the ground; **~ la pasta/ verdura** *(Culin)* to put pasta/vegetables into boiling water; **~rsi addosso il cappotto** to throw one's coat on; **~rsi qc dietro alle spalle** to throw sth over one's shoulder; *(fig: passato etc)* to put sth behind one.

(b) *(anche:* **~ via***: nella spazzatura)* to throw away, discard; *(sprecare: soldi, tempo)* to waste; **non è un tipo da buttar via** he's not bad looking.

(c): **~ giù** *(scritto)* to jot down; *(cibo, boccone)* to gulp down; *(edificio)* to pull down, knock down; *(governo)* to bring down; **~ giù qn** *(deprimere)* to get sb down.

(d) *(fraseologia)*: **~ la colpa addosso a qn** to lay the blame on sb; **~ a mare** *(fig: soldi, occasione)* to throw away; **~ i soldi dalla finestra** to throw money down the drain; **ho buttato là una frase** I mentioned it in passing; **gli ha buttato in faccia tutto il suo disprezzo** she told him to his face how much she despised him; **mi ha buttato in faccia tutta la verità** he flung the truth at me.

2 *vi (germogliare)* to sprout.

3: **~rsi** *vr (saltare)* to jump; **buttiamoci!** *(saltiamo)* let's jump!; *(rischiamo)* let's have a go!; **~rsi in acqua** to jump into the water; **~rsi dalla finestra** to jump out of the window; **~rsi su** *o* **addosso a qn** to launch o.s. at sb; **~rsi nelle braccia di qn** to throw o.s. into sb's arms; **~rsi in ginocchio** to throw o.s. down on one's knees; **~rsi (anima e corpo) in qc** to throw o.s. (wholeheartedly) into sth; **~rsi giù** *(stendersi)* to lie down; *(stimarsi poco)* to have a low opinion of o.s.; *(scoraggiarsi)* to get depressed *o* miserable; **~rsi nella mischia** *(anche fig)* to throw o.s. into the fray; **~rsi sulla preda** *(anche fig)* to pounce on one's prey.

buttata [but'tata] *sf (Bot)* sprouting.

butterato, a [butte'rato] *ag* pock-marked, pitted.

buzzo ['buddzo] *sm (fam: pancia)* belly, paunch; **di ~ buono** *(con impegno)* with a will.

buzzurro, a [bud'dzurro] *sm/f (peg)* boor.

C

C, c [tʃi] *sf o m inv (lettera)* C, c.
cabala ['kabala] *sf (intrigo)* cabal.
cabaret [kaba'rɛ] *sm inv* cabaret.
cabina [ka'bina] **1** *sf (Naut, Aer)* cabin; *(di treno, autocarro etc) cab; (di ascensore)* cage; *(di funivia)* car; *(alla spiaggia)* beach hut; *(in piscina)* cubicle. **2:** ~ **di blocco** *o* **di manovra** *(Ferr)* signal box; ~ **elettorale** polling booth; ~ **elettrica** substation; ~ **di guida** driver's cab; ~ **passeggeri** *(Aer)* passenger cabin *o* compartment; ~ **piloti,** ~ **di pilotaggio** *(Aer)* flight deck; ~ **di proiezione** *(Cine)* projection booth; ~ **di registrazione** recording booth; ~ **telefonica** telephone booth *o* box.
cabinato, a [kabi'nato] **1** *ag (Naut)* with a cabin. **2** *sm* cabin cruiser.
cabinovia [kabino'via] *sf* two-seater cablecar.
cablaggio [ka'bladdʒo] *sm* wiring.
cablogramma [kablo'gramma] *sm* cable, cablegram.
cabotaggio [kabo'taddʒo] *sm* coastal navigation; **nave da** ~ tramp, coaster.
cabotare [kabo'tare] *vi* to ply along the coast.
cabrare [ka'brare] *vi (Aer)* to nose up.
cabrata [ka'brata] *sf (Aer)* nose-up.
cabriolet [kabriɔ'lɛ] *sm (Aut)* convertible; *(carrozza)* cabriolet.
cacao [ka'kao] *sm inv (albero)* cacao; *(polvere)* cocoa.
cacare [ka'kare] *vi (fam)* to shit.
cacatoa [kaka'toa] *sm inv,* **cacatua** [kaka'tua] *sm inv* cockatoo.
cacca ['kakka] *sf (fam: anche fig)* shit; **dover fare la** ~ *(linguaggio infantile)* to have to do a job.
caccia¹ ['kattʃa] **1** *sf* **(a)** hunting; *(col fucile)* shooting, hunting; **andare a** ~ to go hunting; **andare a** ~ **di leoni** to go lion-hunting; **battuta di** ~ hunting party. **(b)** *(anche:* **stagione della** ~*)* hunting *(o* shooting) season; *(selvaggina)* game. **(c)** *(fig: inseguimento, ricerca)* chase; **dare la** ~ **a qn** to give chase to sb; **essere a** ~ **di notizie/libri** to be on the lookout for news/books; **essere a** ~ **di uomini/soldi** to be after men/money; **andare a** ~ **di guai** to be asking for trouble. **2:** ~ **al cervo** deerstalking; ~ **grossa** big game hunting; ~ **alle streghe** witch-hunt; ~ **subacquea** harpoon fishing; ~ **al tesoro** treasure hunt; ~ **all'uomo** manhunt.
caccia² ['kattʃa] *sm inv (Aer)* fighter.
cacciagione [kattʃa'dʒone] *sf* game.
cacciare [kat'tʃare] **1** *vt* **(a)** *(Sport)* to hunt; *(col fucile)* to shoot, hunt.
  (b) *(mandar via: persona):* ~ **qn di casa/dal paese/dalla scuola** to throw sb out of the house/ the country/school; *(: nemico)* to drive away; *(: tristezza, malinconia, dubbio)* to chase away.
  (c) *(mettere):* ~ **qn in prigione** to throw sb into prison; ~**rsi qc in testa** *(cappello etc)* to pull sth on; *(idea)* to get sth into one's head; ~ **un pugnale nel petto a** *o* **di qn** to stab sb in the chest; ~ **qn in un mare di guai** to get sb into a fine mess;

dove hai cacciato quel libro? where have you put that book?
  (d) *(emettere):* ~ **un grido** to let out a cry.
  (e) *(estrarre):* ~ **fuori** to pull out; ~ **fuori un coltello** to pull out a knife; ~ **fuori la lingua** to put out one's tongue; ~ **fuori i soldi** to show the colour of one's money, pay up.
  2: ~**rsi** *vr* **(a)** *(nascondersi)* to hide o.s.; **ma dove si sarà cacciato?** where on earth can he (*o* it) have got to?
  (b) *(mettersi):* ~**rsi nei guai** *o* **in un bel pasticcio** to get o.s. into a nice mess; **è uno che si caccia sempre in avanti** he is a very pushy person.
cacciata [kat'tʃata] *sf (espulsione)* expulsion.
cacciatora [kattʃa'tora] *sf* **(a)** *(giacca)* hunting jacket. **(b)** *(Culin):* **pollo** *etc* **alla** ~ chicken *etc* chasseur.
cacciatore [kattʃa'tore] *sm (Sport, Mil)* hunter; *(a cavallo)* huntsman; ~ **di frodo** poacher; ~ **di scalpi** *o* **di teste** headhunter; ~ **di dote** fortunehunter.
cacciatorpediniere [kattʃatorpedi'njere] *sm* destroyer.
cacciavite [kattʃa'vite] *sm inv* screwdriver.
cacciucco [kat'tʃukko] *sm spiced fish soup.*
cachemire [kaʃ'mir] *sm inv* cashmere.
cachet [ka'ʃɛ] *sm* **(a)** *(Med)* capsule; *(: compressa)* tablet. **(b)** *(compenso)* fee. **(c)** *(colorante per capelli)* rinse.
cachi¹ ['kaki] *ag inv, sm* khaki.
cachi² ['kaki] *sm inv (albero, frutto)* persimmon.
cacio ['katʃo] *sm* cheese; **essere come il** ~ **sui maccheroni** to turn up at the right moment.
cacofonia [kakofo'nia] *sf* cacophony.
cactus ['kaktus] *sm inv* cactus.
cadauno, a [kada'uno] *ag, pron indef* each.
cadavere [ka'davere] *sm* corpse, (dead) body.
cadaverico, a, ci, che [kada'veriko] *ag (fig)* deathly pale; **rigidità** ~**a** rigor mortis.
cadente [ka'dɛnte] *ag* falling; *(fig: edificio)* tumbledown; *(: persona)* decrepit; **stella** ~ falling *o* shooting star.
cadenza [ka'dɛntsa] *sf (gen)* cadence; *(ritmo)* rhythm; *(inflessione)* intonation; *(Mus)* cadenza.
cadenzare [kaden'tsare] *vt* to mark the rhythm of.
cadere [ka'dere] *vi (aus essere)* **(a)** *(persona, oggetto)* to fall; ~ **dalla bicicletta/da un albero/dalle scale** to fall off one's bicycle/from a tree/down the stairs; ~ **bocconi** to fall flat on one's face; ~ **in ginocchio** to fall on(to) one's knees; ~ **lungo disteso** to go sprawling, fall headlong; ~ **in piedi** *(anche fig)* to land on one's feet; ~ **ai piedi di qn** to fall at sb's feet; ~ **dal sonno** to be falling asleep on one's feet; ~ **a terra** to fall down, fall to the ground; **far** ~ to knock over *o* down; **fa sempre** ~ **tutto dall'alto** he does everything as if it was a great favour; ~ **dalle nuvole** to be taken aback; **la conversazione cadde** the conversation died; **la conversazione cadde su Garibaldi** the conversation came round to Garibaldi; **questi pantaloni cadono bene** these trousers hang well.

(b) *(staccarsi: denti, capelli)* to fall out; *(: foglie)* to fall.

(c) *(pioggia, neve)* to fall, come down; *(vento)* to drop; *(notte, stelle)* to fall; *(aereo)* to crash.

(d) *(data)* to fall; **quest'anno il mio compleanno cade di martedì** my birthday falls on a Tuesday this year.

(e) *(venire a trovarsi)*: ~ **ammalato** to fall ill; ~ **in disgrazia** to fall into disgrace; ~ **in errore** to make a mistake; ~ **in miseria/oblio** to sink into poverty/oblivion.

(f) *(soldato, fortezza, governo)* to fall; **far** ~ **il governo** to bring down the government.

(g): **lasciar** ~ *(oggetto, fig: discorso, proposta)* to drop; *(frase, parola)* to slip in; **si lasciò** ~ **sulla poltrona** he dropped *o* fell into the armchair.

cadetto, a [ka'detto] **1** *ag* **(a)** younger; **ramo** ~ cadet branch. **(b)** *(Sport)* junior *attr.* **2** *sm (gen, Mil)* cadet; *(Sport)* junior.

cadmio ['kadmjo] *sm* cadmium.

caducità [kadutʃi'ta] *sf* transience.

caduco, a, chi, che [ka'duko] *ag* transient, fleeting; *(Bot)* deciduous.

caduta [ka'duta] *sf (gen, Rel)* fall; *(di pressione, febbre, temperatura)* drop; **ha fatto una brutta** ~ he had a nasty fall.

caduto, a [ka'duto] **1** *ag (morto)* dead. **2** *sm* dead soldier; **monumento ai** ~**i** war memorial.

caffè [kaf'fɛ] *sm inv* coffee; *(bar)* café; ~ **corretto** coffee with liqueur; ~ **decaffeinato/solubile** decaffeinated/instant coffee; ~ **in grani** coffee beans; ~ **lungo/ristretto** weak/strong black coffee; ~ **macchiato** coffee with a dash of milk; ~ **macinato/tostato** ground/roasted coffee; ~ **d'orzo** barley coffee; ~ **con panna** coffee with cream.

caffeario, a [kaffe'arjo] *ag* coffee *attr.*

caffeina [kaffe'ina] *sf* caffeine.

caffel(l)atte [kaffe'l(l)atte] *sm inv* white coffee.

caffettano [kaffet'tano] *sm* kaftan.

caffetteria [kaffette'ria] *sf* coffee bar.

caffettiera [kaffet'tjɛra] *sf (per fare il caffè)* coffeemaker; *(per servire il caffè)* coffeepot.

cafonaggine [kafo'naddʒine] *sf* boorishness.

cafone [ka'fone] *sm (contadino)* peasant; *(peg)* boor.

cagionare [kadʒo'nare] *vt* to cause.

cagione [ka'dʒone] *sf* cause.

cagionevole [kadʒo'nevole] *ag (salute etc)* delicate.

cagliare [kaʎ'ʎare] *vt, vi (aus essere)* to curdle.

caglio ['kaʎʎo] *sm* rennet.

cagna ['kaɲɲa] *sf (Zool)* bitch.

cagnara [kaɲ'ɲara] *sf (di cani)* loud barking; *(fig)* uproar.

cagnesco, a, schi, sche [kaɲ'ɲesko] *ag*: **guardare qn in** ~ to scowl at sb.

Cairo ['kairo] *sm*: **il** ~ Cairo.

cala ['kala] *sf* **(a)** *(baia)* bay. **(b)** *(Naut)* hold.

calabrese [kala'brese] *ag, sm/f* Calabrian.

calabrone [kala'brone] *sm* hornet.

calafatare [kalafa'tare] *vt (Naut)* to caulk.

calamaio [kala'majo] *sm* inkpot.

calamaro [kala'maro] *sm* squid.

calamita [kala'mita] *sf (anche fig)* magnet.

calamità [kalami'ta] *sf inv* disaster, calamity; **è una** ~ **naturale** *(fig)* he's a walking disaster.

calamitare [kalami'tare] *vt (anche fig)* to magnetize.

calamo ['kalamo] *sm (Zool, penna)* quill.

calante [ka'lante] *ag* falling; **sole** ~ setting sun; **luna** ~ waning moon.

calare [ka'lare] **1** *vt (gen)* to lower; *(Maglia)* to

decrease; *(ancora)* to drop, lower; *(perpendicolare)* to drop.

2 *vi (aus essere)* **(a)** *(gen)* to come down, fall; *(sole)* to set; *(notte, silenzio)* to fall. **(b)** *(diminuire: vento, febbre)* to drop; *(: temperatura, prezzo)* to drop, fall; *(: suono)* to drop, die away; ~ **di peso** to lose weight; **sono calato (di) 3 chili** I've lost 3 kilos; **cala!** *(non esagerare)* come off it! **(c)** *(invadere)*: ~ **(su)** to descend (on).

3: ~**rsi** *vr* **(a)** to lower o.s. **(b)**: ~**rsi nella parte** *(Teatro)*: **si è calato bene nella parte** he has really got into the part; **si è calato un po' troppo nella parte del giovane dirigente** *(fig)* he goes a bit too far in playing the young executive.

4 *sm*: **al calar del sole** at sunset; **al calar della luna** when the moon goes down.

calata [ka'lata] *sf (invasione)* invasion.

calca ['kalka] *sf* throng, press.

calcagno [kal'kaɲɲo] *sm (pl(f)* ~**a** *in alcuni usi figurati)* *(Anat, di scarpa)* heel; **aveva la polizia alle calcagna** the police were hot on his heels; **il mio capo mi sta sempre alle** ~**a** my boss is never off my back.

calcare[1] [kal'kare] **1** *vt* **(a)** *(premere)* to press down; *(: coi piedi)* to tread, press down; ~**rsi il cappello sugli occhi** to pull one's hat down over one's eyes; ~ **le scene** *(fig)* to be on the stage; ~ **le orme di qn** *(fig)* to follow in sb's footsteps; ~ **la mano** *(fig)* to overdo it, exaggerate. **(b)** *(mettere in rilievo)* to stress; ~ **le parole** to accentuate each syllable. **2** *vi (spingere)* to push; *(premere)* to press down, lean heavily.

calcare[2] [kal'kare] *sm* limestone.

calcareo, a [kal'kareo] *ag* limestone *attr.*

calce[1] ['kaltʃe] *sf* lime; ~ **viva** quicklime; ~ **spenta** slaked lime.

calce[2] ['kaltʃe] *sf (Amm)*: **in** ~ **a** at the foot of; **'firma in** ~**'** 'please sign below'.

calcestruzzo [kaltʃes'truttso] *sm* concrete.

calciare [kal'tʃare] *vt* to kick.

calciatore [kaltʃa'tore] *sm* (football) player.

calcificarsi [kaltʃifi'karsi] *vr* to calcify.

calcina [kal'tʃina] *sf* (lime) mortar.

calcinaccio [kaltʃi'nattʃo] *sm* flake of plaster; **un mucchio di** ~**ci** a pile of rubble.

calcio[1] ['kaltʃo] *sm* **(a)** *(pedata: anche Sport)* kick; **dare un** ~ **a qn** to give sb a kick, kick sb; ~ **d'angolo/di rigore** corner/penalty kick. **(b)** *(Sport)* football, soccer; **squadra di** ~ football team. **(c)** *(di fucile)* butt.

calcio[2] ['kaltʃo] *sm (Chim)* calcium.

calcistico, a, ci, che [kal'tʃistiko] *ag* football *attr.*

calco, chi ['kalko] *sm (Scultura)* cast; *(di disegno)* tracing; *(Linguistica)* loan translation.

calcografia [kalkogra'fia] *sf (incisione, arte)* copper engraving.

calcolare [kalko'lare] *vt (fare il conto di)* to calculate, work out; *(considerare)* to reckon on, take into account; **calcolo che sarò di ritorno fra 5 giorni** I reckon I'll be back in 5 days' time; ~ **i pro e i contro** to weigh up the pros and cons.

calcolatore, trice [kalkola'tore] **1** *ag (fig)* calculating; **macchina** ~**trice** calculator. **2** *sm* computer. **3** *sf* calculator; *(erroneamente)* computer. **4** *sm/f (persona)* calculating person.

calcolo ['kalkolo] *sm* **(a)** calculation; **fare il** ~ **di qc** to work sth out; **fare i propri** ~**i** *(fig)* to weigh up the pros and cons; ~ **differenziale/infinitesimale** differential/infinitesimal calculus; **a un** ~ **approssimativo** at a rough estimate. **(b)** *(Med)* stone; ~ **renale** stone in the kidneys.

caldaia [kal'daja] *sf* boiler.

caldarrosta [kaldar'rɔsta] *sf* roast chestnut.

caldeggiare [kalded'dʒare] *vt* to support.

calderone [kalde'rone] *sm* cauldron; *(fig)* hotchpotch; **mettere tutto nello stesso** ~ *(fig)* to treat everything in the same way.

caldo, a ['kaldo] **1** *ag (gen,fig)* warm; *(molto* ~*)* hot; *(cordiale: persona, accoglienza)* warm, friendly, cordial; **batti il ferro finché è** ~ strike while the iron is hot; **piangere a** ~**e lacrime** to weep bitterly; **essere una testa** ~**a** to be hot-headed. **2** *sm* heat; **fa** ~ it's warm; *(molto* ~*)* it's hot; **col** ~ **che fa...** in this heat...; **ho** ~ I'm warm; I'm hot; **ti tengo in** ~ **la minestra** I'm keeping your soup hot for you; **non mi fa né** ~ **né freddo** I couldn't care less; **quel ragazzo non fa né** ~ **né freddo** I'm indifferent to that boy; **a** ~ *(fig)* in the heat of the moment.

caleidoscopio [kaleidos'kɔpjo] *sm* kaleidoscope.

calendario [kalen'darjo] *sm* calendar.

calende [ka'lɛnde] *sfpl* calends; **rimandare qc alle** ~ **greche** to put sth off indefinitely.

calesse [ka'lesse] *sm* gig.

calibrare [kali'brare] *vt (Tecn)* to calibrate.

calibro ['kalibro] *sm (di arma)* calibre, bore; *(Tecn)* callipers *pl; (fig)* calibre; **di grosso** ~ *(fig)* prominent.

calice¹ ['kalitʃe] *sm (Bot)* calyx.

calice² ['kalitʃe] *sm (coppa)* goblet; *(bicchiere)* stem glass; *(Rel)* chalice.

caligine [ka'lidʒine] *sf (nebbia)* fog; *(: mista con fumo)* smog.

caliginoso, a [kalidʒi'noso] *ag (vedi sf)* foggy; murky.

calle ['kalle] *sf* narrow street *(in Venice)*.

callifugo, ghi [kal'lifugo] *sm* corn plaster.

calligrafia [kalligra'fia] *sf* handwriting; *(arte)* calligraphy.

calligrafico, a, ci, che [kalli'grafiko] *ag (vedi sf)* handwriting *attr;* calligraphic.

callista, i, e [kal'lista] *sm/f* chiropodist.

callo ['kallo] *sm* callus; *(ai piedi)* corn; **pestare i** ~**i a qn** *(fig)* to tread on sb's toes; **fare il** ~ **a qc** to get used to sth; ~ **osseo** callus.

calloso, a [kal'loso] *ag* callous.

calma ['kalma] *sf (vedi ag)* quietness, peacefulness; stillness; calm; *(tranquillità)* peace (and quiet), quietness; **con** ~ *(senza fretta)* slowly; **fai con** ~ take your time; **mare in** ~ calm sea; **è un giorno di** ~ **nel negozio** it's a quiet day in the shop; ~ **e sangue freddo!** keep cool *o* calm!

calmante [kal'mante] **1** *ag* relaxing. **2** *sm (Med)* painkiller; *(: sedativo)* tranquillizer.

calmare [kal'mare] **1** *vt (gen)* to calm; *(persona)* to calm (down); *(dolore)* to soothe. **2:** ~**rsi** *vr (mare, persona)* to calm down; *(dolore)* to ease; *(febbre, rabbia)* to subside.

calmierare [kalmje'rare] *vt (Comm: prezzi)* to control.

calmiere [kal'mjɛre] *sm (Comm):* ~ **dei prezzi** price control(s).

calmo, a ['kalmo] *ag (atmosfera)* quiet, peaceful; *(aria, cielo)* still; *(persona, mare)* calm.

calo ['kalo] *sm:* ~ **(di)** *(gen)* fall (in), drop (in); *(di prezzi)* fall (in); *(di peso)* loss (in); **la sua reputazione ha subito un grosso** ~ his reputation has suffered greatly.

calore [ka'lore] *sm (gen)* warmth; *(intenso, Fis)* heat; *(fig: impegno)* fervour; **accogliere qn con** ~ to welcome sb warmly; **essere in** ~ *(Zool)* to be on heat.

caloria [kalo'ria] *sf* calorie.

calorico, a, ci, che [ka'lɔriko] *ag* calorific.

calorifero [kalo'rifero] *sm* radiator.

calorifico, a, ci, che [kalo'rifiko] *ag* calorific,

heat producing.

calorosamente [kalorosa'mente] *av (fig: con cordialità)* warmly; *(: con fervore)* fervently.

caloroso, a [kalo'roso] *ag (persona):* **essere** ~ not to feel the cold; *(fig: accoglienza etc)* warm.

caloscia, sce [ka'lɔʃʃa] *sf* galosh.

calotta [ka'lɔtta] *sf* **(a)** *(Mat):* ~ **sferica** segment of a sphere. **(b)** *(Geog):* ~ **polare** icecap. **(c)** *(Anat):* ~ **cranica** skullcap. **(d)** *(di cappello)* crown.

calpestare [kalpes'tare] *vt* to tread on, trample on; **'vietato** ~ **le aiuole'** 'keep off the grass'; ~ **i diritti di qn** to encroach on sb's rights; **non farti** ~ *(fig)* don't let people walk all over you.

calpestio [kalpes'tio] *sm (di piedi)* tread, treading; *(: rumore)* stamping.

calunnia [ka'lunnja] *sf* slander; **spargere** ~**e sul conto di qn** to spread slander *o* slanderous remarks about sb.

calunniare [kalun'njare] *vt* to slander.

calunniatore, trice [kalunnja'tore] **1** *ag* slanderous. **2** *sm/f* slanderer.

calunnioso, a [kalun'njoso] *ag* slanderous.

Calvario [kal'varjo] *sm (Rel)* Calvary; **da allora la sua vita è stata un c**~ her life since then has been one of suffering.

calvinismo [kalvi'nizmo] *sm* Calvinism.

calvinista, i, e [kalvi'nista] *ag, sm/f* Calvinist.

calvizie [kal'vittsje] *sf* baldness.

calvo, a ['kalvo] **1** *ag* bald. **2** *sm* bald man.

calza ['kaltsa] *sf (da uomo)* sock; *(da donna)* stocking; ~**e di nailon** nylons, (nylon) stockings; ~**e elastiche** support stockings; ~**e con la cucitura/senza** seamed/seamless stockings; **fare la** ~ to knit; **le donne dovrebbero stare a casa a fare la** ~ *(fig)* a woman's place is in the home.

calzamaglia [kaltsa'maʎʎa] *sf* tights *pl; (per danza, ginnastica)* leotard.

calzante [kal'tsante] *ag* **1** *ag (fig)* appropriate, fitting. **2** *sm* shoehorn.

calzare [kal'tsare] **1** *vt (scarpe)* to wear; *(mettersi)* to put on. **2** *vi* to fit; ~ **a pennello** to fit like a glove; **questa descrizione gli calza a pennello** that describes him to a T.

calzatura [kaltsa'tura] *sf* footwear; **negozio di** ~**e** shoeshop.

calzaturiero, a [kaltsatu'rjɛro] *ag* shoe *attr.*

calzaturificio [kaltsaturi'fitʃo] *sm* shoe *o* footwear factory.

calzetta [kal'tsetta] *sf* ankle sock; **una mezza** ~ *(fig)* a nobody.

calzettone [kaltset'tone] *sm* knee-length sock.

calzificio [kaltsi'fitʃo] *sm* hosiery factory.

calzino [kal'tsino] *sm* (short) sock.

calzolaio [kaltso'lajo] *sm* shoemaker; *(che ripara)* cobbler.

calzoleria [kaltsole'ria] *sf (negozio)* shoeshop; *(arte)* shoemaking.

calzoncini [kaltson'tʃini] *smpl* shorts; ~ **da bagno** (swimming) trunks.

calzone [kal'tsone] *sm* **(a):** ~**i** *pl* trousers; ~**i corti** shorts; ~**i alla zuava** knickerbockers; **portare i** ~**i** *(anche fig)* to wear the trousers. **(b)** *(Culin)* savoury turnover made with pizza dough.

camaleonte [kamale'onte] *sm (Zool, fig)* chameleon.

cambiale [kam'bjale] *sf (Comm)* bill (of exchange); *(: pagherò cambiario)* promissory note; **firmare** ~**i per qc** to sign sth up in instalments.

cambiamento [kambja'mento] *sm* change.

cambiare [kam'bjare] **1** *vt* **(a)** *(gen)* to change; ~ **(l')aria in una stanza** to air a room; **vado in montagna per** ~ **aria** I'm going to the mountains for a change of air; **è ora di ~ aria** *(andarsene)* it's time to move on; **~ casa** to move house; **~ indirizzo** to change address; **~ marcia** *(Aut)* to change gear; **~ idea** to change one's mind; **~ le carte in tavola** *(fig)* to change one's tune. **(b)** *(scambiare)* to exchange; **ho cambiato la mia macchina con quella del mio amico** I exchanged cars with my friend. **(c)** *(valuta)* to change; **mi puoi ~ mille lire?** can you give me change of one thousand lire?

2 *vi (aus* **essere)** *(variare)* to change.

3: **~rsi** *vr* **(a)** *(modificarsi)* to change; **~rsi (d'abito)** to get changed, change (one's clothes). **(b)** *(scambiarsi)*: **~rsi (con)** to swap *o* change places (with).

cambiario, a [kam'bjarjo] *ag* (Fin) exchange *attr*.

cambiavalute [kambjava'lute] *sm inv* exchange office.

cambio ['kambjo] *sm* **(a)** *(gen)* change; *(modifica)* alteration, change; **dare il ~ a qn** to take over from sb, relieve sb; **fare il** *o* **un ~** to change (over); **facciamo a ~** let's change over *o* swap. **(b)** *(Fin)* exchange; *(tasso di cambio)* rate of exchange. **(c)** *(Aut)* gears *pl*; **~ di marcia** gear change; **macchina con il ~ automatico** automatic (car).

Cambogia [kam'bɔdʒa] *sf* Cambodia.

cambusa [kam'buza] *sf* (Naut) galley, storeroom.

camelia [ka'mɛlja] *sf* camellia.

camera ['kamera] **1** *sf* **(a)** *(gen)* room; *(~ da letto)* bedroom; *(mobili)* bedroom suite; **~ da pranzo** dining room; **~ singola** *o* **a un letto/a due letti/matrimoniale** single/twin-bedded/double room. **(b)** *(Pol)* Chamber, House; **C~ dei Deputati** Chamber of Deputies, ≈ House of Commons *(Brit)*, House of Representatives *(Am)*; **le C~e** ≈ (the Houses of) Parliament. **2:** **~ ardente** mortuary chapel; **~ d'aria** *(di pneumatico)* inner tube; *(di pallone)* bladder; **~ blindata** strongroom; **~ di combustione/di decompressione** combustion/decompression chamber; **~ di commercio** Chamber of Commerce; **~ a gas** gas chamber; **~ del lavoro** trades union centre; **~ oscura** *(Fot)* darkroom.

camerata[1] [kame'rata] *sf (dormitorio)* dormitory.

camerata[2] [kame'rata] *sm/f* comrade.

cameratesco, a, schi, sche [kamera'tesko] *ag*: **spirito ~** sense of comradeship.

cameratismo [kamera'tizmo] *sm* comradeship.

cameriera [kame'rjɛra] *sf (domestica)* maid; *(che serve a tavola)* waitress; *(che fa le camere)* chambermaid.

cameriere [kame'rjɛre] *sm (domestico)* (man)servant; *(di ristorante)* waiter.

camerino [kame'rino] *sm (Teatro)* dressing room.

camice ['kamitʃe] *sm (di medico, tecnico)* white coat; *(di chirurgo)* gown; *(di sacerdote)* alb.

camiceria [kamitʃe'ria] *sf (fabbrica)* shirt factory; *(negozio)* shirt shop.

camicetta [kami'tʃetta] *sf* blouse.

camicia, cie [ka'mitʃa] *sf* **(a)** *(da uomo)* shirt; *(da donna)* blouse; **sei ancora in ~?** aren't you dressed yet?; **nascere con la ~** to be born lucky; **sudare sette ~cie** *(fig)* to have a hell of a time; **~ da notte** *(da donna)* nightdress; *(da uomo)* nightshirt; **~ di forza** straitjacket; **C~ nera** *(fascista)* Blackshirt. **(b)** *(Tecn: involucro)* jacket.

camiciaio, a [kami'tʃajo] *sm/f* shirtmaker; *(che vende camicie)* shirtseller.

camiciola [kami'tʃɔla] *sf* vest.

camiciotto [kami'tʃɔtto] *sm (camicia sportiva)* casual shirt; *(per operai)* smock.

caminetto [kami'netto] *sm* hearth, fireplace.

camino [ka'mino] *sm* **(a)** *(focolare)* fireplace; **accendere il ~** to light the fire. **(b)** *(comignolo, ciminiera, di vulcano)* chimney.

camion ['kamjon] *sm inv* lorry, truck *(Am)*.

camionabile [kamjo'nabile] **1** *ag* for heavy vehicles. **2** *sf* road for heavy vehicles.

camioncino [kamjon'tʃino] *sm* van.

camionetta [kamjo'netta] *sf* jeep.

camionista, i [kamjo'nista] *sm* lorry driver, truck driver *(Am)*.

camma ['kamma] *sf* cam; **albero a ~** camshaft.

cammello [kam'mello] *sm (Zool, colore)* camel; *(stoffa)* camelhair.

cammeo [kam'mɛo] *sm* cameo.

camminare [kammi'nare] *vi* **(a)** *(gen)* to walk; **~ a carponi** *o* **a quattro zampe** to go on all fours; **~ a grandi passi** to stride (along); **~ a testa alta** *(fig)* to walk with one's head held high; **con questo traffico non si cammina** you can't move with all this traffic; **cammina cammina, siamo arrivati** after a long walk, we arrived; **cammina!** come on! **(b)** *(funzionare)* to work, go; **il mio orologio non cammina più** my watch has stopped; **gli autobus non camminano oggi** the buses aren't running today.

camminata [kammi'nata] *sf* walk; **fare una ~** to go for a walk.

camminatore, trice [kammina'tore] *sm/f* walker.

cammino [kam'mino] *sm*: **un'ora di ~** an hour's walk; **mettersi in ~** to set *o* start off; **riprendere il ~** to continue on one's way; **mentre era in ~**, **cammin facendo** on the way; **il ~ della virtù** the path of virtue.

camomilla [kamo'milla] *sf* camomile.

camorra [ka'mɔrra] *sf* Camorra; *(fig)* racket.

camorrista, i, e [kamor'rista] *sm/f* member of the Camorra; *(fig)* racketeer.

camoscio [ka'mɔʃʃo] *sm (Zool, pelle)* chamois; **scarpe di ~** suede shoes.

campagna [kam'paɲɲa] *sf* **(a)** *(gen)* country; *(paesaggio)* countryside; **vivere in ~** to live in the country; **andare in ~** to go to the country. **(b)** *(terra coltivata)* land. **(c)** *(Pol, Comm, Mil)* campaign; **fare una ~** to campaign.

campagnolo, a [kampaɲ'ɲɔlo] **1** *ag* country *attr*. **2** *sm/f* countryman/woman.

campale [kam'pale] *ag (Mil)* field *attr*; **una giornata ~** *(fig)* a hectic day.

campana [kam'pana] *sf* **(a)** bell; **suonare le ~e a martello/a morte** to sound the alarm bell/death knell; **sordo come una ~** as deaf as a doorpost; **sentire l'altra ~** *(fig)* to hear the other side of the story. **(b)** *(calotta)* ~ **pneumatica** diving bell; **~ (di vetro)** bell jar; **tenere qn sotto una ~ di vetro** *(fig)* to wrap sb up in cotton wool.

campanaccio [kampa'nattʃo] *sm (di mucca)* cowbell; *(di capra)* goatbell.

campanaro [kampa'naro] *sm* bell-ringer.

campanella [kampa'nɛlla] *sf* **(a)** (school) bell. **(b)** *(Bot)* campanula.

campanello [kampa'nello] *sm (di porta, scuola etc)* bell; **~ elettrico/della bicicletta** electric/bicycle bell; **~ d'allarme** *(anche fig)* alarm bell.

campanile [kampa'nile] *sm* bell tower, belfry.

campanilismo [kampani'lizmo] *sm* parochialism.

campanilista, i, e [kampani'lista] *ag* parochial.

campano, a [kam'pano] *ag* of *(o* from) Campania.

campanula [kam'panula] *sf (Bot)* bellflower; *(: genere)* campanula.

campare [kam'pare] *vi (aus* essere) to live; **~ di** *(soldi)* to get by on; **~ alla giornata, tirare a ~** to live from day to day; **~ d'aria** *(fig)* to live on air;

~ **alla bell'e meglio** to get by o manage somehow or other.

campata [kam'pata] *sf (Archit, Elettr)* span.

campato, a [kam'pato] *ag*: ~ **in aria** *(ragionamento etc)* unsound, unfounded.

campeggiare [kamped'dʒare] *vi* **(a)** *(gen, Mil)* to camp. **(b)** *(Pittura)* to stand out.

campeggiatore, trice [kampeddʒa'tore] *sm/f* camper.

campeggio [kam'peddʒo] *sm (luogo)* camp site; *(attività)* camping; **nel** ~ on the camp site; **vacanze in** ~ camping holidays; **fare (del)** ~, **andare in** ~ to go camping.

campestre [kam'pestre] *ag* country *attr*, rural; **corsa** ~ cross-country race.

camping [kæmpiŋ] *sm inv* camp site.

campionare [kampjo'nare] *vt (Comm)* to sample.

campionario, a [kampjo'narjo] **1** *sm (Comm)* collection of samples. **2** *ag*: **fiera** ~a trade fair.

campionato [kampjo'nato] *sm* championship.

campione [kam'pjone] *sm* **(a)** *(Sport, fig: sostenitore)* champion; ~ **di tennis/del mondo** tennis/world champion; **sei un** ~ **in** o **della matematica** *(fig)* you're brilliant at mathematics. **(b)** *(Comm)* sample; **comprare su** ~ to buy on sample. **(c)** *(Fis):* ~ **di misura** standard measure.

campo ['kampo] **1** *sm* **(a)** *(gen, Agr, Fis etc)* field; ~ **di grano** cornfield; **la vita dei** ~ life in the country, country life; **fiori di** ~ wild flowers. **(b)** *(di calcio)* field, pitch; *(da golf)* course; *(da tennis)* court; *(da cricket)* pitch. **(c)** *(Mil)* field, battlefield; *(: accampamento)* camp; **padrone del** ~ *(fig)* victor. **(d)** *(pittura)* background; *(Araldica)* field. **(e)** *(Cine, TV, Fot):* ~ **lungo** long shot; ~ **d'immagine** viewfield. **2:** ~ **d'aviazione** airfield; ~ **di concentramento** concentration camp; ~ **giochi** play area; ~ **petrolifero** oilfield; ~ **profughi** refugee camp; ~ **sportivo** sports ground; ~ **di visibilità** range of visibility; ~ **visivo** field of vision.

camposanto [kampo'santo] *sm* cemetery.

camuffare [kamuf'fare] **1** *vt*: ~ **(da)** to disguise (as); *(Mil)* to camouflage (as). **2:** ~**rsi** *vr*: ~**rsi (da)** to disguise o.s. (as); *(per ballo in maschera)* to dress up (as).

camuso, a [ka'muzo] *ag (naso)* snub; *(persona)* snub-nosed.

Canada [kana'da] *sm* Canada.

canadese [kana'dese] *ag, sm/f* Canadian.

canaglia [ka'naʎʎa] *sf (persona)* scoundrel, rogue.

canale [ka'nale] *sm (gen, Elettr, TV, fig)* channel; *(artificiale)* canal; *(condotto)* conduit; *(Anat)* duct, canal; ~ **di bonifica** o **di drenaggio** drainage canal; ~ **di Panama** Panama Canal; **Canal Grande** Grand Canal; **il** ~ **della Manica** English Channel.

canalizzare [kanalid'dzare] *vt* to canalize.

canalone [kana'lone] *sm (Geol)* gorge.

canapa ['kanapa] *sf (Bot, tessuto)* hemp; ~ **indiana** Indian hemp.

canapè [kana'pe] *sm inv (mobile)* settee, couch; *(Culin)* canapé.

canapo [ka'napo] *sm (Naut)* hawser.

canarino [kana'rino] *sm* canary.

cancan [kan'kan] *sm inv (ballo)* cancan; *(fig: confusione)* din, row; *(: scandalo)* fuss.

cancellare [kantʃel'lare] **1** *vt* **(a)** *(con gomma)* to erase, rub out; *(con penna)* to score out, cross out. **(b)** *(fig: eliminare)* to take off, remove; *(: annullare)* to annul, cancel; *(disdire)* to cancel; ~ **la lavagna** to clean the blackboard; ~ **qn dalla faccia della terra** to wipe sb off the face of the

earth. **2:** ~**rsi** *vr (scritto)* to be erased; *(ricordo)* to fade.

cancellata [kantʃel'lata] *sf* railings *pl*.

cancellatura [kantʃella'tura] *sf* **(a)** *(azione) (vedi vb)* erasing; crossing out; taking off; annulment; cancellation. **(b)** *(segno)* erasure; crossing out.

cancellazione [kantʃellat'tsjone] *sf (Dir, Comm)* cancellation.

cancelleria [kantʃelle'ria] *sf* **(a)** *(Dir, Amm)* chancery. **(b)** *(materiale per scrivere):* **(articoli di)** ~ stationery.

cancellierato [kantʃellje'rato] *sm (Amm)* chancellery.

cancelliere [kantʃel'ljere] *sm* **(a)** *(Dir)* clerk of the court. **(b)** *(Pol)* chancellor; **C~ dello Scacchiere** Chancellor of the Exchequer.

cancello [kan'tʃello] *sm* gate.

cancerizzarsi [kantʃerid'dzarsi] *vr* to become cancerous.

cancerogeno, a [kantʃe'rɔdʒeno] **1** *ag* carcinogenic. **2** *sm* carcinogen.

cancerologia [kantʃerolo'dʒia] *sf* study of cancer.

cancerologo, gi [kantʃe'rɔlogo] *sm* cancer specialist.

canceroso, a [kantʃe'roso] **1** *ag (Med)* cancerous. **2** *sm/f* cancer patient.

cancrena [kan'krena] *sf (Med)* gangrene; *(fig: corruzione)* corruption; **andare in** ~ to become gangrenous.

cancro ['kankro] *sm* **(a)** *(Med, fig)* cancer; *(Bot)* canker. **(b)** *(Astron, Astrologia):* **C~** Cancer; **essere del C~** to be Cancer.

candeggiante [kanded'dʒante] **1** *sm* bleach. **2** *ag* bleaching.

candeggiare [kanded'dʒare] *vt* to bleach.

candeggina [kanded'dʒina] *sf* bleach.

candeggio [kan'deddʒo] *sm* bleaching; **fare il** ~ **(di qc)** to bleach (sth).

candela [kan'dela] *sf* **(a)** *(gen)* candle; **a lume di** ~ by candlelight; **tenere la** ~ *(fig)* to play gooseberry. **(b)** *(Aut)* spark(ing) plug; **una lampadina da 100** ~**e** *(Elettr)* a 100 watt bulb.

candelabro [kande'labro] *sm* candelabra *inv*.

candeliere [kande'ljere] *sm* **(a)** candlestick. **(b)** *(Naut)* stanchion.

candelotto [kande'lɔtto] *sm* candle; ~ **lacrimogeno** tear gas grenade; ~ **di dinamite** stick of dynamite.

candidarsi [kandi'darsi] *vr*: ~ **(per)** *(Pol)* to present o.s. as candidate (for).

candidato, a [kandi'dato] *sm/f*: ~ **(a)** *(gen)* candidate (for); *(a un lavoro)* applicant (for).

candidatura [kandida'tura] *sf (gen)* candidature; *(a un lavoro)* application; **presentare la propria** ~ **alle elezioni** to stand for election.

candido, a ['kandido] *ag* **(a)** *(bianco)* (pure) white; ~ **come la neve** (as) white as snow. **(b)** *(fig: ingenuo)* ingenuous, naïve; *(: sincero)* candid, frank; *(: innocente)* pure, innocent.

candito, a [kan'dito] **1** *ag* candied. **2:** ~**i** *smpl* candied fruit *sg*.

candore [kan'dore] *sm (vedi ag)* brilliant white; ingenuousness, naïvety; candour, frankness; purity, innocence.

cane ['kane] **1** *sm (Zool)* dog; *(di fucile)* hammer; **comportarsi da** ~**i** to behave very badly; **qui si mangia da** ~**i** the food is rotten here; **è una vita da** ~**i** it's a dog's life; **questo lavoro è fatto da** ~**i** this job is a real botch; **quell'attore è un** ~ he's a rotten actor; **fa un freddo** ~ it's bitterly cold; **non c'era un** ~ there wasn't a soul; **essere solo come un** ~ to be all on one's own; **essere come** ~ **e gatto** to fight like cat and dog. **2:** ~ **barbone**

poodle; ~ **da caccia** hunting dog; ~ **per ciechi** guide dog; ~ **da guardia** watchdog; ~ **lupo** alsatian; ~ **da punta** pointer; ~ **di razza** pedigree (dog); ~ **da salotto** lap dog; ~ **da slitta** husky.

canestro [ka'nɛstro] *sm (gen, Sport)* basket; **centrare il** *o* **fare un** ~ *(Sport)* to shoot a basket.

canfora ['kanfora] *sf* camphor.

canforato, a [kanfo'rato] *ag* camphorated.

cangiante [kan'dʒante] *ag* iridescent; **seta** ~ shot silk.

canguro [kan'guro] *sm* kangaroo.

canicola [ka'nikola] *sf* scorching heat; **oggi c'è una** ~ today's a scorcher.

canile [ka'nile] *sm* kennel; *(di allevamento)* kennels *pl*; ~ **municipale** dog pound.

canino, a [ka'nino] **1** *ag (razza)* canine; *(mostra)* dog *cpd*; **tosse** ~**a** whooping cough; **rosa** ~**a** dog rose. **2** *sm (dente)* canine.

canizie [ka'nittsje] *sf (chioma bianca)* white hair; *(fig: vecchiaia)* old age.

canna ['kanna] *sf* **(a)** *(Bot)* reed; ~ **da zucchero** sugar cane. **(b)** *(bastone)* stick, cane; ~ **da pesca** fishing rod. **(c)** *(di fucile)* barrel; *(di organo)* pipe; *(di bicicletta)* crossbar; ~ **fumaria** chimney flue.

cannella¹ [kan'nɛlla] *sf (di conduttura, botte)* tap.

cannella² [kan'nɛlla] *sf (Bot, Culin)* cinnamon.

cannello [kan'nɛllo] *sm (forato)* tube; *(Chim)* pipette; *(non forato)* stick; *(Tecn)* blowpipe.

cannellone [kannel'lone] *sm (Culin)* pasta *stuffed with sauce and baked.*

canneto [kan'neto] *sm* bed of reeds.

cannibale [kan'nibale] *sm/f* cannibal.

cannibalismo [kanniba'lizmo] *sm* cannibalism.

cannocchiale [kannok'kjale] *sm* telescope.

cannolo [kan'nɔlo] *sm (Culin)* cream horn.

cannonata [kanno'nata] *sf* cannon shot; ~ **a salve** gun salute; **è una vera** ~**!** *(fig)* it's *(o he's etc)* fantastic!

cannoncino [kannon'tʃino] *sm* **(a)** *(Mil)* light gun. **(b)** *(di abito)* box pleat. **(c)** *(Culin)* cream horn.

cannone [kan'none] *sm* **(a)** *(arma)* gun; *(Storia)* cannon; *(fig: chi eccelle)* ace; **donna** ~ fat lady. **(b)** *(tubo)* pipe, tube. **(c)** *(di abito)* box pleat.

cannoneggiare [kannoned'dʒare] *vt* to shell.

cannoniera [kanno'njɛra] *sf (Naut)* gunboat; *(di fortificazione)* embrasure.

cannoniere [kanno'njɛre] *sm* **(a)** *(Naut)* gunner. **(b)** *(Calcio)* goal scorer.

cannuccia, ce [kan'nuttʃa] *sf* straw.

canoa [ka'nɔa] *sf* canoe; **andare in** ~ to go canoeing.

canoismo [kano'izmo] *sm* canoeing.

canoista, i, e [kano'ista] *sm/f* canoeist.

cañon [ka'ɲon] *sm inv* canyon.

canone ['kanone] *sm* **(a):** ~**i** *pl (criteri)* canons, rules; *(di comportamento)* norm. **(b)** *(pagamento periodico)* rent, fee; ~ **d'affitto** rent; ~ **agricolo** land rent; ~ **d'abbonamento alla TV** TV licence fee; **legge dell'equo** ~ fair rent act. **(c)** *(Rel, Mus)* canon.

canonica [ka'nɔnika] *sf* presbytery.

canonico, a, ci, che [ka'nɔniko] *(Rel)* **1** *ag* canonical; **diritto** ~ canon law. **2** *sm* canon.

canonizzare [kanonid'dzare] *vt* to canonize.

canonizzazione [kanoniddzat'tsjone] *sf* canonization.

canorità [kanori'ta] *sf* melodiousness.

canoro, a [ka'nɔro] *ag:* **uccello** ~ songbird.

canottaggio [kanot'taddʒo] *sm* rowing; **gara di** ~ boat race.

canottiera [kanot'tjɛra] *sf* vest.

canotto [ka'nɔtto] *sm* dinghy; ~ **pneumatico** rubber dinghy; ~ **di salvataggio** lifeboat.

canovaccio [kano'vattʃo] *sm* **(a)** *(tela)* canvas; *(per i piatti)* dish cloth; *(per pulire)* cloth. **(b)** *(Teatro)* plot.

cantante [kan'tante] *sm/f* singer; **fare il** ~ to be a singer; ~ **lirico** *o* **d'opera** opera singer.

cantare [kan'tare] **1** *vi (gen)* to sing; *(uccelli)* to sing, warble; *(gallo)* to crow; *(ruscello)* to babble; ~ **da tenore/da soprano** to be a tenor/soprano; **fare** ~ **qn** *(fig)* to make sb talk; **i complici hanno cantato** *(fam)* his accomplices grassed. **2** *vt (Mus)* to sing; *(Poesia: anche:* ~ **in versi)** to sing of; ~ **messa** to sing mass; ~ **vittoria** to crow.

cantastorie [kantas'tɔrje] *sm/f* story-teller.

cantata [kan'tata] *sf* singsong; *(Mus)* cantata.

cantautore, trice [kantau'tore] *sm/f inv* singer-songwriter.

canterellare [kanterel'lare] *vt, vi* to sing to o.s.; *(a bocca chiusa)* to hum.

canticchiare [kantik'kjare] *vt, vi* to sing to o.s., hum.

cantico, ci ['kantiko] *sm* canticle.

cantiere [kan'tjɛre] *sm (Naut)* shipyard; *(Edil)* (building) site.

cantieristico, a, ci, che [kantje'ristiko] *ag:* **industria** ~**a** shipbuilding industry.

cantilena [kanti'lɛna] *sf (filastrocca)* lullaby; *(intonazione)* singsong intonation; *(fig: lamentela)* whining.

cantina [kan'tina] *sf (locale)* cellar; *(bottega)* wine shop.

cantiniere [kanti'njɛre] *sm* cellarman.

canto¹ ['kanto] *sm (il cantare, arte)* singing; *(canzone)* song; *(Poesia)* lyric poem; *(: capitolo)* canto; **lezioni di** ~ singing lessons; **il** ~ **dell'usignolo** *(il cantare)* the singing *o* warbling of the nightingale; *(melodia)* the song of the nightingale; **al** ~ **del gallo** at cockcrow; ~ **di Natale** (Christmas) carol; ~ **gregoriano** Gregorian chant.

canto² ['kanto] *sm:* **da un** ~ **... d'altro** ~ on the one hand ... on the other hand; **da un** ~ **ti capisco** in a way I understand you.

cantonata [kanto'nata] *sf (di edificio)* corner; **prendere una** ~ *(fig)* to blunder.

cantone¹ [kan'tone] *sm (angolo)* corner; **in un** ~ *(fig: in disparte)* in a corner.

cantone² [kan'tone] *sm (Pol, Amm)* canton.

cantoniera [kanto'njɛra] *ag:* **(casa)** ~ road inspector's house.

cantore, a [kan'tore] *sm/f (Rel)* singer; *(fig: poeta)* poet.

cantoria [kanto'ria] *sf (luogo, persone)* choir.

cantuccio [kan'tuttʃo] *sm* corner, nook.

canuto, a [ka'nuto] *ag* white-haired.

canzonare [kantso'nare] *vt* to tease, make fun of.

canzonatore, trice [kantsona'tore] **1** *ag* teasing. **2** *sm/f* teaser, tease.

canzonatorio, a [kantsona'tɔrjo] *ag* teasing.

canzonatura [kantsona'tura] *sf* teasing; *(beffa)* joke.

canzone [kan'tsone] *sf (Mus)* song; *(poesia)* canzone; **è sempre la stessa** ~ *(fig)* it's always the same old story; ~ **di gesta** chanson de geste.

canzonetta [kantso'netta] *sf* popular song.

canzonettista, i, e [kantsonet'tista] *sm/f (cabaret)* singer.

canzoniere [kantso'njɛre] *sm (Mus)* song book; *(Letteratura)* collection of poems.

caolino [kao'lino] *sm* kaolin.

caos ['kaos] *sm (anche fig)* chaos.

caotico, a, ci, che [ka'ɔtiko] *ag* chaotic.

capace [ka'patʃe] *ag* **(a)** *(capiente)* large, capacious; **questa borsa è poco** ~ this bag doesn't hold much. **(b)** *(in grado, dotato)* able, capable; ~ **di fare qc** able to do sth, capable of doing sth; **è** ~ **di tutto** he's capable of anything; ~ **d'intendere e di volere** *(Dir)* in full possession of one's faculties; **è** ~ **di venire nonostante tutto** he's quite likely to come in spite of everything.

capacità [kapatʃi'ta] *sf inv* **(a)** *(capienza)* capacity. **(b)** *(abilità)* ability, capability; **è superiore alle sue** ~ it's beyond his capabilities. **(c)** *(Dir, Fis)* capacity; ~ **giuridica** legal capacity.

capacitarsi [kapatʃi'tarsi] *vr:* ~ **(di qc)** to realize (sth); **non riesce a** ~ **di ciò che è successo** he can't seem to take in what has happened.

capanna [ka'panna] *sf* hut.

capannello [kapan'nello] *sm* knot (of people).

capanno [ka'panno] *sm (di cacciatori)* hide; *(da spiaggia)* bathing hut.

capannone [kapan'none] *sm (gen)* shed; *(di stabilimento)* (factory) shed; *(Agr)* barn; *(Aer)* hangar.

caparbietà [kaparbje'ta] *sf* stubbornness, obstinacy.

caparbio, a [ka'parbjo] *ag* stubborn, obstinate.

caparra [ka'parra] *sf* deposit.

capeggiare [kaped'dʒare] *vt (rivolta etc)* to head, lead.

capello [ka'pello] *sm (uno)* hair; *(capigliatura):* ~**i** hair *sg*; **dai** ~**i scuri** dark-haired; **avere i** ~**i bianchi** to have white hair; ~**i d'angelo** *(Culin)* long thin pasta; **avere un diavolo per** ~ to be in a foul temper; **averne fin sopra i** ~**i di qc/qn** to be fed up to the teeth with sth/sb; **mettersi** *o* **cacciarsi le mani nei** ~**i** *(fig)* to be in despair; **prendersi per i** ~**i** *(fig)* to come to blows; **strapparsi i** ~**i** *(fig)* to tear one's hair out; **mi ci hanno tirato per i** ~**i** *(fig)* they dragged me into it; **tirato per i** ~**i** *(spiegazione)* far-fetched.

capellone, a [kapel'lone] *sm/f* hippie.

capelluto, a [kapel'luto] *ag:* **cuoio** ~ scalp.

capelvenere [kapel'venere] *sm (Bot)* maidenhair.

capestro [ka'pestro] *sm (di forca)* noose; *(per animali)* halter.

capezzale [kapet'tsale] *sm* bolster; *(fig)* bedside; **accorrere al** ~ **di qn** to rush to sb's bedside.

capezzolo [ka'pettsolo] *sm* nipple.

capidoglio [kapi'dɔʎʎo] *sm* = **capodoglio.**

capiente [ka'pjɛnte] *ag* capacious.

capienza [ka'pjɛntsa] *sf* capacity.

capigliatura [kapiʎʎa'tura] *sf* head of hair.

capillare [kapil'lare] **1** *ag (Anat, Fis)* capillary; *(fig: analisi, ricerca)* detailed. **2** *sm (Anat)* capillary.

capinera [kapi'nera] *sf (Zool)* blackcap.

capire [ka'pire] *vt* to understand; **si capisce che...** it is clear that...; **si capisce!** *(certamente!)* of course, certainly!; **capisco** I see, I understand; **capisci, è un problema di soldi** you see, it's a problem of money; **bisogna capirla, poverina** you've got to try and understand her, poor thing; ~ **al volo** to catch on straight away; **farsi** ~ to make o.s. understood; **ci siamo capiti** we understand one another.

capitale [kapi'tale] **1** *ag* **(a)** *(mortale):* **pena** ~ capital punishment; **sentenza** ~ death sentence; **i sette peccati** ~**i** the seven deadly sins. **(b):** **d'importanza** ~ of capital *o* the utmost importance. **2** *sf (Amm)* capital (city); *(fig: centro)* centre. **3** *sm (Fin)* capital; ~ **immobile** real estate; ~ **liquido** cash assets *pl*; ~ **mobile** movables *pl*; ~ **sociale** *(di società)* authorized capital; *(di club)* funds *pl*; **ho speso un** ~ **per quella macchina** *(fig)* I've spent a fortune on that car.

capitalismo [kapita'lizmo] *sm* capitalism.

capitalista, i, e [kapita'lista] *ag, sm/f* capitalist.

capitalistico, a, ci, che [kapita'listiko] *ag* capitalist.

capitalizzare [kapitalid'dzare] *vt* to capitalize.

capitanare [kapita'nare] *vt* to lead; *(Calcio)* to captain.

capitaneria [kapitane'ria] *sf:* ~ **(di porto)** port authorities.

capitano [kapi'tano] *sm (Mil, Naut, Sport)* captain; *(Aer: di squadriglia)* flight lieutenant; ~ **di industria** captain of industry; ~ **di lungo corso** master mariner; ~ **di ventura** *(Storia)* mercenary leader.

capitare [kapi'tare] **1** *vi (aus essere)* **(a)** *(giungere)* to arrive, turn up; ~ **a proposito/bene/male** to turn up at the right moment/at a good time/at a bad time. **(b)** *(accadere)* to happen; **se ti capita di vederlo** if you happen to see him; **mi è capitato un guaio** I had a spot of trouble; **sono cose che capitano** these things happen. **2** *vb impers* to happen; **capita spesso di incontrarci** *o* **che ci incontriamo** we often bump into one another.

capitello [kapi'tɛllo] *sm (Archit)* capital.

capitolare [kapito'lare] *vi (Mil)* to capitulate, surrender; *(fig)* to give in.

capitolato [kapito'lato] *sm (Dir)* terms *pl*, specifications *pl.*

capitolazione [kapitolat'tsjone] *sf (Mil, fig)* capitulation.

capitolino, a [kapito'lino] *ag* Capitoline.

capitolo [ka'pitolo] *sm* **(a)** *(di testo, Rel)* chapter; **non ho voce in** ~ *(fig)* I have no say in the matter. **(b):** ~**i pl** *(Comm)* items.

capitombolare [kapitombo'lare] *vi (aus essere)* to tumble, fall headlong.

capitombolo [kapi'tombolo] *sm* tumble, headlong fall; **fare un** ~ to take a tumble.

capitone [kapi'tone] *sm (Zool)* large (female) eel.

capo ['kapo] **1** *sm* **(a)** *(Anat)* head; **a** ~ **chino/alto** with one's head bowed/held high; **da** ~ **a piedi** from head to foot; **mal di** ~ headache; **rompersi il** ~ *(fig)* to rack one's brains; **fra** ~ **e collo** *(all'improvviso)* out of the blue.

(b) *(persona: di fabbrica, ufficio)* head, boss *(fam);* *(: di partito, movimento)* leader; **essere a** ~ **di qc** to head sth, be at the head of sth.

(c) *(oggetto)* item, article; **un** ~ **di biancheria/vestiario** an item of underwear/clothing.

(d) *(estremità: di tavolo, scale)* head, top; *(: di filo)* end; **da un** ~ **all'altro** from one end to the other; **in** ~ **a** *(tempo)* within; *(luogo)* at the top of; **andare in** ~ **al mondo per qn** *(fig)* to go to the ends of the earth for sb; **ricominciare da** ~ to start all over again; **andare a** ~ to start a new paragraph; **'punto a** ~**'** 'full stop — new paragraph'; **un discorso senza né** ~ **né coda** a senseless *o* meaningless speech.

(e) *(di corda, lana)* ply; **lana a 3** ~**i** 3-ply wool.

(f) *(Geog)* cape.

2: ~ **d'accusa** *(Dir)* charge; **C**~ **d'Anno** = **Capodanno;** ~ **di bestiame** head *inv* of cattle; ~ **del personale** personnel manager; ~ **di stato** head of state.

3 *ag inv (giardiniere, sorvegliante etc)* head *attr;* **redattore** ~ chief editor.

capobanda [kapo'banda] *sm, pl* **capibanda** *(Mus)* bandmaster; *(di malviventi, fig)* gang leader.

capocannoniere [kapokanno'njɛre] *sm, pl* **capicannonieri** *(Calcio)* leading goal scorer; *(Naut)* head gunner.

capocchia [ka'pɔkkja] *sf* head; ~ **di spillo** pin head.

capoccia [ka'pɔttʃa] *sm inv (di lavoranti)* overseer; *(peg: capobanda)* boss.

capoccione [kapot'tʃone] *sm (persona intelligente)* brainbox; *(fig peg: persona importante)* bigwig.

capocellula [kapo'tʃellula] *sm/f, pl(m)* **capicellula,** *pl(f) inv (Pol)* leader of a cell.

capoclasse [kapo'klasse] *sm/f, pl(m)* **capiclasse,** *pl(f) inv (Scol)* ≃ form captain.

capocomico, a, ci, che [kapo'kɔmiko] *sm/f* leader of a theatre company.

capocordata [kapokor'data] *sm, pl* **capicordata** *(Alpinismo)* leader (of roped party).

capocronista [kapokro'nista] *sm/f, pl(m)* **capicronista,** *pl(f)* **capocroniste** news editor.

capocuoco [kapo'kwɔko] *sm, pl* **capocuochi** *o* **capicuochi** head cook.

Capodanno [kapo'danno] *sm* New Year.

capodivisione [kapodivi'zjone] *sm, pl* **capidivisione** *(Amm)* head of department.

capodoglio [kapo'dɔʎʎo] *sm* sperm whale.

capofabbrica [kapo'fabbrika] *sm, pl* **capifabbrica** (factory) supervisor.

capofamiglia [kapofa'miʎʎa] *sm/f, pl(m)* **capifamiglia,** *pl(f) inv* head of the family.

capofila [kapo'fila] *sm/f, pl(m)* **capifila,** *pl(f) inv* leader; **in** ~ at the head of the line.

capofitto [kapo'fitto]: **a** ~ *av* headlong, headfirst; **gettarsi a** ~ **in qc** *(fig)* to rush headlong into sth.

capogiro [kapo'dʒiro] *sm* dizziness; **aver un** ~ to have a dizzy spell; **far venire il** ~ **a qn** to make sb dizzy; **da** ~ *(fig)* astonishing, staggering.

capogruppo [kapo'gruppo] *sm/f, pl(m)* **capigruppo,** *pl(f) inv* group leader.

capolavoro [kapola'voro] *sm (anche fig)* masterpiece.

capolinea [kapo'linea] *sm, pl* **capilinea** terminus.

capolino [kapo'lino] *sm*: **far** ~ to peep out *(o in etc)*.

capolista [kapo'lista] *sm/f, pl(m)* **capilista,** *pl(f) inv* (Pol) top candidate on electoral list.

capoluogo, ghi [kapo'lwɔgo] *sm*: ~ **(di provincia)** ≃ county town.

capomastro [kapo'mastro] *sm, pl* **capomastri** *o* **capimastri** master builder.

capopartito [kapopar'tito] *sm* party leader.

caporale [kapo'rale] *sm* lance corporal.

caporalesco, a, schi, sche [kapora'lesko] *ag (peg)* bossy.

caporalmaggiore [kaporalmad'dʒore] *sm (Mil)* corporal.

caporedattore, trice [kaporedat'tore] *sm/f, pl(m)* **capiredattore,** *pl(f)* **caporedattrici** editor in chief.

caporeparto [kapore'parto] *sm/f, pl(m)* **capireparto,** *pl(f) inv (di operai)* foreman; *(di ufficio, negozio)* head of department.

caporione [kapo'rjone] *sm* gang leader, ringleader.

caposala [kapo'sala] *sf inv (Med)* ward sister.

caposaldo [kapo'saldo] *sm, pl* **capisaldi** *(Mil)* stronghold; *(Topografia)* datum point; *(fig)* cornerstone.

caposcuola [kapo'skwɔla] *sm/f, pl(m)* **capiscuola,** *pl(f) inv (Arte, Mus etc)* founder.

caposervizio [kaposer'vittsjo] *sm/f, pl(m)* **capiservizio,** *pl(f) inv* departmental *o* section head; ~ **alla redazione sportiva** Sports editor.

caposezione [kaposet'tsjone] *sm, pl* **capisezione** section *o* departmental head.

caposquadra [kapos'kwadra] *sm, pl* **capisquadra** *(di operai)* foreman, ganger; *(Mil)* squad leader; *(Sport)* team captain.

caposquadriglia [kaposkwa'driʎʎa] *sm, pl* **capisquadriglia** *(Aer, Naut)* squadron leader.

capostazione [kapostat'tsjone] *sm, pl* **capistazione** *(Ferr)* station master.

capostipite [kapos'tipite] *sm* progenitor; *(fig)* earliest example.

capotavola [kapo'tavola] *sm/f, pl(m)* **capitavola,** *pl(f) inv (persona)* head of the table; **sedere a** ~ to sit at the head of the table.

capote [ka'pɔt] *sf inv (Aut)* hood, soft top.

capotreno [kapo'treno] *sm, pl* **capitreno** *o* **capotreni** *(Ferr)* guard.

capotribù [kapotri'bu] *sm, pl* **capitribù** chief.

capottare [kapot'tare] *vi* = **cappottare.**

capoturno [kapo'turno] *sm/f, pl(m)* **capiturno,** *pl(f) inv* shift supervisor.

capoufficio [kapouf'fitʃo] *sm/f, pl(m)* **capiufficio,** *pl(f) inv* head clerk.

capoverso [kapo'verso] *sm* **(a)** *(di verso, periodo)* first line; *(Tip)* indent; *(paragrafo)* paragraph. **(b)** *(Dir: comma)* section.

capovolgere [kapo'vɔldʒere] **1** *vt (gen)* to turn upside down; *(barca)* to capsize, overturn; *(macchina)* to overturn; *(fig: situazione, posizione)* to reverse, change completely. **2:** ~**rsi** *vr (gen)* to overturn; *(barca)* to capsize; *(fig)* to be reversed.

capovolgimento [kapovoldʒi'mento] *sm (fig)* reversal, complete change.

capovolto, a [kapo'vɔlto] **1** *pp di* **capovolgere. 2** *ag* upside down; *(barca)* capsized.

cappa[1] ['kappa] *sf* **(a)** *(mantello)* cloak; **film/romanzo di** ~ **e spada** romantic adventure film/novel; **sentirsi sotto una** ~ **di piombo** to feel oppressed. **(b)** *(del camino)* hood; *(Industria)* chimney. **(c)** *(Naut)*: **mettersi in** ~ to heave to.

cappa[2] ['kappa] *sm o f inv (lettera)* K, k.

cappella [kap'pɛlla] *sf (Rel)* chapel; *(: cantori)* choir.

cappellaio, a [kappel'lajo] *sm/f* hatter.

cappellano [kappel'lano] *sm* chaplain; ~ **militare** army chaplain.

cappelleria [kappelle'ria] *sf* hat shop.

cappelliera [kappel'ljera] *sf* hat box.

cappello [kap'pɛllo] *sm* hat; *(di chiodo)* head; *(di fungo)* cap; ~ **di paglia** straw hat; ~ **a cilindro** top hat; ~ **a bombetta** bowler hat; **levarsi/togliersi il** ~ to raise/take off one's hat; **ti faccio tanto di** ~! *(fig)* I take my hat off to you!

cappero ['kappero] *sm (Bot, Culin)* caper; ~**i!** *(fam)* gosh!

cappio ['kappjo] *sm* slip-knot; *(nodo scorsoio)* noose.

cappone [kap'pone] *sm* capon.

cappottare [kappot'tare] *vi (Aut)* to overturn.

cappotto[1] [kap'pɔtto] *sm* (over)coat.

cappotto[2] [kap'pɔtto] *sm*: **dare** *o* **fare** ~ *(nei giochi)* to win the grand slam.

cappuccino[1], a [kapput'tʃino] *ag, sm (Rel)* Capuchin.

cappuccino[2] [kapput'tʃino] *sm* frothy white coffee, cappuccino.

cappuccio [kap'puttʃo] *sm* **(a)** hood; *(di frate)* cowl; *(di penna)* top. **(b)** *fam abbr di* **cappuccino.**

capra ['kapra] *sf* **(a)** *(Zool)* (she-)goat, *(fam)* nannygoat. **(b)** *(Tecn)* trestle.

capraio [ka'prajo] *sm* goatherd.

caprese [ka'prese] *ag* from *(o* of) Capri.

capretto [ka'pretto] *sm* kid.

capriata [kapri'ata] *sf (Edil)* truss.

capriccio [ka'prittʃo] *sm* **(a)** *(gen)* whim, caprice; *(di bambino)* tantrum; **levarsi** *o* **togliersi il** ~ to indulge one's whim; **fare i** ~**i** to be awkward, be naughty; **fare un** ~ to throw a tantrum; ~**i della moda** whims of fashion; ~ **della natura** freak of nature; ~ **della sorte** quirk of fate. **(b)** *(Mus)* capriccio.

capriccioso, a [kaprit'tʃoso] *ag* capricious,

whimsical; *(bambino)* naughty; **insalata** ~**a** *(Culin)* mixed salad with mayonnaise.

Capricorno [kapri'kɔrno] *sm* Capricorn; **essere del** ~ *(Astrologia)* to be Capricorn.

caprifoglio [kapri'fɔʎʎo] *sm* honeysuckle.

caprino, a [ka'prino] **1** *ag* goat *attr.* **2** *sm (formaggio)* goat's (milk) cheese.

capriola [kapri'ɔla] *sf (salto)* somersault; *(Danza)* cabriole; *(Equitazione)* capriole; **fare una** ~ to turn a somersault; **fare le** ~**e per la gioia** to be head over heels with joy.

capriolo [kapri'ɔlo] *sm* roe deer; *(maschio)* roe-buck.

capro ['kapro] *sm* (he-)goat, *(fam)* billy-goat; ~ **espiatorio** scapegoat.

caprone [ka'prone] *sm* = **capro.**

capsula ['kapsula] *sf (di medicinali, Anat, Spazio)* capsule; *(di dente)* crown; *(di arma, per bottiglie)* cap.

captare [kap'tare] *vt (trasmissione)* to pick up; *(pensiero)* to read; ~ **lo sguardo di qn** to catch sb's eye.

capzioso, a [kap'tsjoso] *ag* specious.

carabattole [kara'battole] *sfpl* odds and ends.

carabina [kara'bina] *sf* rifle.

carabiniere [karabi'njɛre] *sm* carabiniere *(member of Italian military police force).*

caracollare [karakol'lare] *vi* to caracole.

caraffa [ka'raffa] *sf* carafe; *(per vino, liquori)* decanter.

carambola [ka'rambola] *sf (Biliardo)* cannon.

caramella [kara'mɛlla] *sf (dolciume)* sweet; *(monocolo)* monocle.

caramellare [karamel'lare] *vt (zucchero)* to caramelize; *(stampo, arance)* to coat with caramel.

caramello [kara'mɛllo] *sm* caramel.

carato [ka'rato] *sm* **(a)** *(di oro, diamante etc)* carat. **(b)** *(Naut)* twenty-fourth part of the ownership of a ship. **(c)** *(Comm)* share.

carattere [ka'rattere] *sm* **(a)** *(gen)* character, nature; **avere un buon/brutto** ~ to be good-/ill-natured, be good-/bad-tempered; **aver** ~ to have character; **mancare di** ~ to lack character, have no backbone; **informazione di** ~ **tecnico/ confidenziale** information of a technical/ confidential nature; **essere in** ~ **con qc** *(intonarsi)* to be in harmony with sth. **(b)** *(spesso pl: caratteristica)* characteristic, feature. **(c)** *(Tip)* character, letter; **scrivere a** *o* **con** ~**i chiari/ illeggibili** to write clearly/illegibly; **in** ~ **corsivo/neretto** *o* **grassetto** in italic/bold type.

caratteriale [karatte'rjale] *ag (studio, indagine)* character *attr*; *(disturbi)* emotional.

caratterino [karatte'rino] *sm* difficult nature *o* character.

caratterista, i, e [karatte'rista] *sm/f* character actor/actress.

caratteristica, che [karatte'ristika] *sf* characteristic, feature.

caratteristico, a, ci, che [karatte'ristiko] *ag (tipico)* typical, characteristic; *(distintivo)* distinctive; **segni** ~**ci** *(su passaporto etc)* distinguishing marks.

caratterizzare [karatterid'dzare] *vt* to characterize, be typical *o* characteristic of.

caratterizzazione [karatteriddzat'tsjone] *sf* characterization.

caravella [kara'vɛlla] *sf* caravel.

carboidrato [karboi'drato] *sm* carbohydrate.

carbonaia [karbo'naja] *sf (catasta di legna)* charcoal pit; *(locale)* coal cellar.

carbonaio [karbo'najo] *sm (chi fa carbone)* char-

coal-burner; *(commerciante)* coalman, coal merchant.

carbonaro [karbo'naro] *sm (Storia)* member of the Carbonari society.

carbonato [karbo'nato] *sm* carbonate.

carbonchio [kar'bonkjo] *sm (Med, Veterinaria)* anthrax; *(Bot)* smut.

carboncino [karbon'tʃino] *sm (bastoncino)* charcoal crayon; *(disegno)* charcoal drawing.

carbone [kar'bone] *sm* coal; *(anche:* ~ **di legna)** charcoal; *(di lampada ad arco)* carbon; ~ **bianco** hydroelectric power; ~ **fossile** (pit) coal; **essere** *o* **stare sui** ~**i ardenti** to be like a cat on hot bricks.

carbonella [karbo'nɛlla] *sf* charcoal slack.

carboneria [karbone'ria] *sf (Storia)* secret society of the Carbonari.

carbonico, a, ci, che [kar'boniko] *ag* carbonic.

carbonifero, a [karbo'nifero] *ag* carboniferous, coal *attr.*

carbonio [kar'bɔnjo] *sm (Chim)* carbon.

carbonizzare [karbonid'dzare] *vt (legna)* to carbonize; *(: parzialmente)* to char; **morire carbonizzato** to be burned to death; **hanno trovato i resti carbonizzati della vittima** they found the charred remains of the victim.

carburante [karbu'rante] **1** *ag* combustible. **2** *sm* fuel.

carburare [karbu'rare] *vi:* ~ **bene/male** *(Aut)* to be well/badly tuned.

carburatore [karbura'tore] *sm* carburettor.

carburazione [karburat'tsjone] *sf* carburation.

carburo [kar'buro] *sm* carbide.

carcassa [kar'kassa] *sf* **(a)** *(di animale)* carcass; *(fig peg: macchina etc)* (old) wreck. **(b)** *(struttura portante)* framework, frame; *(: di nave)* hulk.

carcerario, a [kartʃe'rarjo] *ag* prison *attr.*

carcerato, a [kartʃe'rato] *sm/f* prisoner.

carcerazione [kartʃerat'tsjone] *sf* imprisonment.

carcere ['kartʃere] *sm, pl(f)* ~**i** *(edificio)* prison, jail; *(pena)* imprisonment; **condannato a due anni di** ~ sentenced to two years' imprisonment; **essere/mettere in** ~ to be in/send to prison *o* jail.

carceriere, a [kartʃe'rjɛre] *sm/f (anche fig)* jailer.

carciofo [kar'tʃɔfo] *sm* artichoke.

cardamomo [karda'mɔmo] *sm* cardamom.

cardanico, a, ci, che [kar'daniko] *ag:* **giunto** ~ universal joint.

cardare [kar'dare] *vt* to card.

cardellino [kardel'lino] *sm* goldfinch.

cardiaco, a, ci, che [kar'diako] *ag* cardiac; **attacco** ~ heart attack.

cardigan ['kardigan] *sm inv* cardigan.

cardinale [kardi'nale] **1** *ag* cardinal. **2** *sm (Rel)* cardinal.

cardine ['kardine] *sm (di porta, finestra)* hinge.

cardiologia [kardjolo'dʒia] *sf* cardiology.

cardiologo, gi [kar'djɔlogo] *sm* heart specialist, cardiologist.

cardo ['kardo] *sm* **(a)** *(Bot)* thistle; *(commestibile)* cardoon. **(b)** *(per cardare)* teasel.

carena [ka'rɛna] *sf (Naut)* keel.

carenare [kare'nare] *vt (Naut)* to careen; *(veicolo)* to streamline.

carente [ka'rɛnte] *ag:* ~ **di** lacking in.

carenza [ka'rɛntsa] *sf* shortage; *(Med)* deficiency; ~ **vitaminica** vitamin deficiency.

carestia [kares'tia] *sf* famine; *(fig)* scarcity, lack.

carezza [ka'rettsa] *sf* caress; **dare** *o* **fare una** ~ **a** *(persona)* to caress; *(animale)* to stroke, pat.

carezzare [karet'tsare] *vt* = **accarezzare.**

carezzevole [karet'tsevole] *ag* sweet, endearing.

cargo, ghi ['kargo] *sm (nave)* cargo boat, freighter; *(aereo)* freighter.

cariarsi [ka'rjarsi] *vr (denti)* to decay.

cariatide [ka'rjatide] *sf* caryatid.

carica, che ['karika] *sf* **(a)** *(ufficio, funzione)* position, office; ~ **onorifica** honorary appointment; **ricoprire** *o* **rivestire una** ~ to hold a position; **entrare/essere in** ~ to come into/be in office; **uscire di** ~ to leave office. **(b)** *(di orologio)* winding; **è finita la** ~ it's wound down; **dare la** ~ **a** to wind up; *(fig: persona)* to back up. **(c)** *(di arma, missile)* charge. **(d)** *(attacco: Mil, di animali)* charge; **tornare alla** ~ *(fig)* to insist, persist; **entrare a passo di** ~ to charge in.

caricare [kari'kare] **1** *vt* **(a)** *(gen)* to load; *(fig: esagerare)* to exaggerate; *(tinta)* to deepen. **(b)**: ~ **su/in** *(merci etc)* to load on/into; ~ **in macchina** *(dare un passaggio)* to give a lift to; *(mettere)* to put into the car. **(c)** *(sovraccaricare)*: ~ **(di)** *(merci etc)* to overload (with); *(fig: di lavoro, responsabilità)* to burden (with). **(d)** *(orologio, molla)* to wind up; *(batteria, accumulatore)* to charge; *(fucile, macchina fotografica)* to load; *(pipa, stufa)* to fill; *(caldaia, altoforno)* to stoke. **(e)** *(attaccare: Mil)* to charge; *(: Sport)* to tackle.
2: ~**rsi** *vr*: ~**rsi di** to burden *o* load o.s. with; *(fig: di responsabilità, impegni)* to burden o.s. with.

caricatore [karika'tore] **1** *sm* **(a)** *(di armi)* magazine; *(Fot)* cartridge. **(b)** *(operaio)* loader. **2** *ag*: **piano** ~ loading platform.

caricatura [karika'tura] *sf* caricature; **fare la** ~ **di** *o* **a qn** to do a caricature of sb.

caricaturale [karikatu'rale] *ag* ridiculous, grotesque.

caricaturista, i, e [karikatu'rista] *sm/f* caricaturist.

carico, a, chi, che ['kariko] **1** *ag* **(a)** *(veicolo)*: ~ **(di)** loaded *o* laden (with), full (of); *(persona)*: ~ **di** laden with; ~ **di debiti** up to one's ears in debt; ~ **di lavoro** weighed down with work. **(b)** *(forte: colore)* strong. **(c)** *(caricato: molla, orologio)* wound up; *(: fucile, macchina fotografica)* loaded; *(: pipa, penna)* full; *(: batteria)* charged; *(bomba)* live.
2 *sm* **(a)** *(azione di caricare)* loading; **fare il** ~ to load. **(b)** *(materiale caricato)* load; *(: su nave)* freight, cargo; **a pieno** ~ with a full load. **(c)** *(Elettr)* charge. **(d)** *(Econ)*: **essere a** ~ **di qn** *(onere)* to be charged to sb, be payable by sb; *(persona)* to be dependent on sb, be supported by sb; **hai dei familiari a** ~? do you have any dependants? **(e)** *(Dir)* charge; **essere a** ~ **di qn** *(accusa, prova)* to be against sb; **testimone a** ~ witness for the prosecution.

carie ['karje] *sf (Med)* decay; *(Bot)* rot.

carillon [kari'jõ] *sm inv* musical box.

carino, a [ka'rino] *ag (gen)* nice; *(ragazza, bambino)* pretty, lovely; *(ragazzo)* good-looking; **è stato molto** ~ **da parte tua** that was really nice *o* kind of you.

carisma [ka'rizma] *sm* charisma.

carismatico, a, ci, che [kariz'matiko] *ag* charismatic.

carità [kari'ta] *sf (gen, Rel)* charity; **chiedere la** ~ **(a qn)** to beg for charity (from sb); *(fig)* to come begging (to sb); **fare la** ~ **a** to give (something) to; **per** ~! *(figurarsi)* you've got to be joking!; *(per favore)* please!; *(non ti disturbare!)* please don't bother!; *(non è un disturbo)* not at all!, it's no trouble at all!; **fammi la** ~ **di star zitto** please be so kind as to keep quiet.

caritatevole [karita'tevole] *ag* charitable.

carlinga, ghe [kar'linga] *sf* fuselage.

carlona [kar'lona] *sf*: **alla** ~ carelessly, roughly.

carme ['karme] *sm* solemn poem.

carnagione [karna'dʒone] *sf* complexion.

carnaio [kar'najo] *sm (ammasso di cadaveri)* charnel house; *(fig: strage)* carnage, slaughter; *(: luogo affollato)*: **è un** ~ it's swarming with people.

carnale [kar'nale] *ag* **(a)** *(sessuale: desiderio, istinto)* carnal. **(b)** *(consanguineo: fratello, sorella)* full.

carne ['karne] *sf* **(a)** *(gen, fig)* flesh; **in** ~ **e ossa** in the flesh, in person; ~ **da macello** cannon fodder; **color** ~ flesh coloured; ~ **viva** raw flesh; **essere (bene) in** ~ to be well padded, be plump; **è** ~ **della mia** ~ he's my own flesh and blood. **(b)** *(Culin)* meat; **non essere né** ~ **né pesce** *(fig)* to be neither fish nor fowl; **mettere troppa** ~ **al fuoco** *(fig)* to have too many irons in the fire; ~ **ai ferri/bollita/arrosto** grilled/boiled/roast meat; ~ **di maiale** pork; ~ **di manzo** beef; ~ **in scatola** tinned meat; ~ **di vitello** veal.

carnefice [kar'nefitʃe] *sm (boia)* executioner; *(nell'impiccagione)* hangman; *(fig)* torturer.

carneficina [karnefi'tʃina] *sf* carnage; *(fig)* disaster; **fare una** ~ to carry out a massacre.

carnevale [karne'vale] *sm* carnival.

carnevalesco, a, schi, sche [karneva'lesko] *ag* carnival *attr*.

carniere [kar'njɛre] *sm* game bag.

carnivoro, a [kar'nivoro] **1** *ag* carnivorous. **2** *sm* carnivore.

carnosità [karnosi'ta] *sf* fleshiness; *(di labbra)* fullness.

carnoso, a [kar'noso] *ag (gen)* fleshy; *(pianta, frutto, radice)* pulpy; *(labbra)* full.

caro, a ['karo] **1** *ag (a)* *(amato)*: ~ **(a)** dear (to); *(: ricordo)* fond; **mi è tanto** ~ it *(o* he) is very dear to me; **C**~ **Paolo** *(nelle lettere)* Dear Paul; **tanti** ~**i saluti** best wishes; ~**a signora!** my dear lady!; **se ti è** ~**a la vita** if you value your life; **tener** ~ **il ricordo di qn/qc** to cherish the memory of sb/sth; **tientelo** ~, **un uomo così non lo trovi più** make sure you look after him, you won't find another man like him. **(b)** *(costoso)* dear, expensive; **a** ~ **prezzo** at a high price; **vendere** ~**a la pelle** *(fig)* to sell one's life dear. **2** *sm/f*: **mio** ~, **mia** ~**a** my dear; **i miei** ~**i** my dear ones. **3** *av (costare, pagare)* a lot, a great deal; **questo insulto ti costerà** ~ you'll pay dearly for that insult.

carogna [ka'roɲɲa] *sf* carrion *inv*; *(fam: persona vile)* swine *inv*.

carognata [karoɲ'ɲata] *sf (fam)* rotten trick; **fare una** ~ **a qn** to play a rotten trick on sb.

carosello [karo'zello] *sm (giostra)* merry-go-round, *(Am)* carousel.

carota [ka'rɔta] *sf* carrot.

carotide [ka'rɔtide] *sf* carotid.

carovana [karo'vana] *sf (gen)* caravan; *(convoglio)* convoy.

carovaniero, a [karova'njɛro] *ag* caravan *attr*; **strada** ~**a** caravan route.

carovita [karo'vita] *sm inv* cost of living; *(indennità)* cost of living allowance.

carpa ['karpa] *sf* carp.

carpenteria [karpente'ria] *sf* carpentry.

carpentiere [karpen'tjɛre] *sm* carpenter.

carpire [kar'pire] *vt (attenzione)* to catch; *(bacio)* to steal; ~ **un segreto/un'informazione a qn** to worm a secret/information out of sb.

carpo ['karpo] *sm (Anat)* wrist joint, carpus *(T)*.

carponi [kar'poni] *av* on all fours, on one's hands and knees; **mettersi/stare a** ~ to get down/be on all fours.

carrabile [kar'rabile] *ag* suitable for vehicles; **'passo ~'** 'keep clear'.

carraio, a [kar'rajo] *ag* carriage *attr;* **passo ~** driveway.

carré [ka're] **1** *sm inv (Culin: lombata)* loin. **2** *ag inv:* **pan ~** toasting loaf.

carreggiabile [karred'dʒabile] *ag:* **(strada) ~** road open to light traffic.

carreggiata [karred'dʒata] *sf (Aut)* carriageway; **strada a due ~e** dual carriageway; **tenersi in ~** *(fig)* to keep to the right path; **rimettersi in ~** *(fig: recuperare)* to catch up.

carrellare [karrel'lare] *vi (Cine, TV)* to track.

carrellata [karrel'lata] *sf (Cine, TV: tecnica)* tracking; *(: scena)* running shot; **~ di successi** medley of hit tunes.

carrello [kar'rɛllo] *sm (gen, Ferr)* trolley; *(della teleferica)* hopper; *(Aer)* undercarriage; *(della macchina da scrivere)* carriage; *(Cine, TV)* dolly; **~ elevatore** fork-lift truck.

carretta [kar'retta] *sf (piccolo carro)* cart; *(peg: veicolo)* old wreck; **tirare la ~** *(fig)* to plod along.

carrettiere [karret'tjɛre] *sm* carter; **usa un linguaggio da ~!** he talks like a navvy!

carretto [kar'retto] *sm* hand cart; **~ a mano** wheelbarrow.

carriera [kar'rjɛra] *sf* career; **fare ~** to get on in one's job, to have a successful career; **prospettive di ~** promotion prospects; **ufficiale di ~** *(Mil)* regular officer; **di** *o* **a gran ~** *(fig)* at full speed.

carriola [karri'ɔla] *sf* wheelbarrow.

carrista, i [kar'rista] *sm (Mil: guidatore)* tank driver; *(: soldato)* tank soldier.

carro ['karro] **1** *sm* **(a)** cart, wagon; *(per carnevale)* float; **mettere il ~ avanti ai buoi** *(fig)* to put the cart before the horse. **(b)** *(Astron):* **il Gran/Piccolo C~** the Great/Little Bear. **2: ~ armato** *(Mil)* tank; **~ attrezzi** *(Aut)* breakdown van; **~ funebre** hearse; **~ merci/bestiame** *(Ferr)* goods/animal wagon.

carrozza [kar'rɔtsa] **1** *sf (gen, Ferr)* carriage, coach; **(signori) in ~!** all aboard! **2: ~ letto** sleeper; **~ ristorante** dining car.

carrozzabile [karrot'tsabile] *ag:* **(strada) ~** road open to vehicles.

carrozzella [karrot'tsɛlla] *sf (per bambini)* pram; *(per invalidi)* wheelchair.

carrozzeria [karrottse'ria] *sf* **(a)** *(Aut: rivestimento)* bodywork, body; **~ portante** chassis. **(b)** *(Aut: officina)* body repairer's.

carrozziere [karrot'tsjɛre] *sm (Aut: progettista)* car designer; *(: meccanico)* coachbuilder.

carrozzina [karrot'tsina] *sf* pram.

carrozzino [karrot'tsino] *sm (di motocicletta)* side-car.

carrozzone [karrot'tsone] *sm (da circo, di zingari)* caravan.

carrucola [kar'rukola] *sf* pulley.

carta ['karta] **1** *sf* **(a)** *(gen)* paper; *(statuto)* charter; *(anche:* **~ geografica)** map; **sulla ~** *(in teoria)* on paper; **in ~ libera** *(Amm)* on plain paper.

(b) *(gioco)* card; **dare le ~e** to deal the cards; **giocare una carta** to play a card; **giocare l'ultima carta** *(anche fig)* to play one's last card; **a ~e scoperte** *(anche fig)* cards on the table; **mettere le ~e in tavola** to lay one's cards on the table; **cambiare le ~e in tavola** *(fig)* to shift one's ground; **fare le ~e a qn** *(Cartomanzia)* to tell sb's fortune *(using cards)*.

(c) *(documento)* paper; **devo fare tutte le ~e per il concorso** I've got to sort out all the documents and forms for that examination; **fare ~e**

false *(fig)* to go to great lengths; **avrebbe fatto ~e false pur di ottenere quel posto** he would have gone to any lengths to get that job.

(d) *(Ristorante):* **alla ~** à la carte; **~ dei vini** wine list.

2: ~ assorbente blotting paper; **~ automobilistica** road map; **~ bianca: dare ~ bianca a qn** to give sb carte blanche; **~ bollata** *(Amm)* official stamped paper; **~ di credito** credit card; **~ da disegno** drawing paper; **~ di giornale** newspaper; **~ d'identità** identity card; **~ igienica** toilet paper; **~ d'imbarco** embarkation card; **~ da lettere** writing paper; **~ millimetrata** graph paper; **~ oleata** waxed paper; **~ da pacchi, ~ da imballo** wrapping paper, brown paper; **~ da parati** wallpaper; **~ da regalo** *(gift)* wrapping paper; **~ da ricalco** tracing paper; **~ stagnola** tinfoil; **~ vetrata** sandpaper; **(color) ~ da zucchero** mid blue.

cartacarbone [kartakar'bone] *sf* carbon paper.

cartaccia, ce [kar'tattʃa] *sf* waste paper.

cartaceo, a, cei, cee [kar'tatʃeo] *ag* paper *attr.*

cartamodello [kartamo'dɛllo] *sm* paper pattern.

cartamoneta [kartamo'neta] *sf* paper money.

cartapecora [karta'pɛkora] *sf* parchment, vellum.

cartapesta [karta'pesta] *sf* papier mâché; **di ~** papier mâché *attr; (fig)* weak; **eroe di ~** tin god.

cartario, a [kar'tarjo] *ag* paper *attr.*

cartastraccia, ce [kartas'trattʃa] *sf* waste paper.

carteggio [kar'teddʒo] *sm* correspondence.

cartella [kar'tɛlla] *sf* **(a)** *(di cartoncino)* folder; *(borsa: di professionista)* briefcase; *(: di scolaro)* schoolbag; *(pratica, incartamento)* file; **~ clinica** *(Med)* case sheet. **(b)** *(Tip)* page. **(c)** *(Lotteria)* lottery ticket; *(Tombola)* tombola card.

cartellino [kartel'lino] *sm (etichetta)* label; *(su porta)* notice; *(scheda)* card; **~ delle ore di lavoro** time card; **timbrare il ~** *(all'entrata)* to clock in; *(all'uscita)* to clock out.

cartello¹ [kar'tɛllo] *sm (avviso)* notice, sign; *(segnale stradale)* road sign; *(di dimostranti, pubblicitario)* placard; *(di negozio)* shop sign.

cartello² [kar'tɛllo] *sm (Econ, Pol)* cartel.

cartellone [kartel'lone] *sm (pubblicitario)* poster, placard; *(Teatro)* bill, playbill; *(Cine)* poster; *(di tombola)* board; **tenere il ~** *(Teatro)* to have a long run.

cartellonista, i, e [kartello'nista] *sm/f* poster designer.

carter ['karter] *sm inv (di bicicletta, moto)* chain guard; *(Aut)* oil sump.

cartiera [kar'tjɛra] *sf* paper mill.

cartiglio [kar'tiʎʎo] *sm* scroll.

cartilagine [karti'ladʒine] *sf* cartilage.

cartina [kar'tina] *sf* **(a)** *(Geog)* map. **(b)** *(di sigarette)* cigarette paper; *(piccolo involto)* packet.

cartoccio [kar'tɔttʃo] *sm* **(a)** *(involucro)* paper bag; *(: a forma di cono)* cornet; **cuocere al ~** *(Culin)* to bake in tinfoil; **patate al ~ ≃** jacket potatoes. **(b)** *(Mil)* powder charge.

cartografia [kartogra'fia] *sf* cartography.

cartografo [kar'tɔgrafo] *sm* cartographer.

cartolaio, a [karto'lajo] *sm/f* stationer.

cartoleria [kartole'ria] *sf* stationer's (shop).

cartolina [karto'lina] *sf (anche:* **~ postale)** postcard; **~ di auguri** greetings card; **~ illustrata** picture postcard; **~ precetto** *o* **rosa** *(Mil)* call-up card.

cartomante [karto'mante] *sm/f* fortune-teller *(using cards).*

cartomanzia [kartoman'tsia] *sf* fortune-telling *(using cards).*

cartoncino [karton'tʃino] *sm (materiale)* thin cardboard; *(biglietto)* card.

cartone [kar'tone] *sm* **(a)** cardboard. **(b)** *(Arte)* cartoon; ~ **animato** *(Cine)* cartoon. **(c)** *(scatola)* large cardboard box; *(: del latte, dell'aranciata)* carton.

cartuccia, ce [kar'tuttʃa] *sf (di armi, penna)* cartridge; ~ **a salve** blank cartridge; **mezza** ~ *(fig: persona)* good-for-nothing.

cartucciera [kartut'tʃɛra] *sf* cartridge belt.

casa ['kasa] **1** *sf* **(a)** *(edificio)* house; ~ **a quattro piani** four-storey house; ~ **di campagna** *(grande)* house in the country; *(piccola)* country cottage; ~ **di mattoni** brick house; ~ **popolare** council house *(o* flat); **la C~ Bianca** *(Pol)* the White House.

(b) *(abitazione)* home; **essere/stare a** *o* **in** ~ to be/stay at home; **tornare a** ~ to come *(o* go) back home; **c'è nessuno in** ~? is anybody in?; **vieni a** ~ **nostra?** are you coming to our house *o* place?; **uscire di** ~ to leave home; **dove sta di** ~? where does he live?; **non sa dove sta di** ~ **la cortesia** he doesn't know the meaning of courtesy; **essere di** ~ to be like one of the family; **è una ragazza tutta** ~ **e chiesa** she is a home-loving, church-going girl; **fatto in** ~ home-made; **fai come se fossi a** ~ **tua** make yourself at home; **abitare a** ~ **del diavolo** to live in the back of beyond.

(c) *(casato, stirpe)* house, family; ~ **d'Asburgo** House of Hapsburg.

(d) *(ditta)* firm, company.

2: ~ **di correzione** approved school; ~ **di cura** nursing home; ~ **editrice** publishing house; ~ **di moda** fashion house; ~ **dello studente** hall of residence; ~ **di tolleranza,** ~ **d'appuntamenti** brothel.

casacca, che [ka'zakka] *sf (Mil)* coat; *(giacca)* jacket.

casaccio [ka'zattʃo] *sm:* **a** ~ *(per caso)* at random; *(senza cura)* any old how.

casale [ka'sale] *sm* hamlet; *(casolare)* farmhouse.

casalinga, ghe [kasa'linga] *sf* housewife.

casalingo, a, ghi, ghe [kasa'lingo] **1** *ag* **(a)** *(occupazione, lavoro)* domestic, household *attr.* **(b)** *(fatto in casa)* home-made; **cucina** ~**a** home cooking. **2:** ~**ghi** *smpl* household articles.

casamento [kasa'mento] *sm* block (of flats).

casata [ka'sata] *sf* **(a)** family, lineage. **(b)** = **casato.**

casato [ka'sato] *sm* family name; **è di** ~ **nobile** he's of noble birth.

cascame [kas'kame] *sm (Tessile)* waste.

cascamorto [kaska'mɔrto] *sm* woman chaser; **fare il** ~ to chase women; **non fare il** ~ **con me** there's no point in chasing after me.

cascante [kas'kante] *ag* drooping, droopy; **avere le guance/le spalle** ~**i** to be heavy-jowled/round-shouldered.

cascare [kas'kare] *vi (aus* **essere**) to fall; **far** ~ **qc** to drop sth; ~ **per terra** to fall to the ground, fall down; ~ **dalla fame** to be faint with hunger; ~ **dal sonno** to be falling asleep on one's feet; ~ **dalle nuvole** *(fig)* to be taken aback; ~ **bene/male** *(fig)* to land lucky/unlucky; **gli ho detto che tu eri partito e lui c'è cascato** I told him you had left and he fell for it; **caschi il mondo** no matter what; **non cascherà il mondo se...** it won't be the end of the world if... .

cascata [kas'kata] *sf (di acqua)* waterfall, cascade; *(fig: di capelli etc)* cascade; **le** ~**e Vittoria** the Victoria Falls.

cascina [kaʃ'ʃina] *sf* farmstead.

cascinale [kaʃʃi'nale] *sm (casolare)* farmhouse;

(cascina) farmstead.

casco, schi ['kasko] *sm* **(a)** *(Mil, Sport)* helmet; *(da motociclista)* crash helmet; *(da parucchiera)* (hair-)dryer; **i** ~**schi blu** the UN peace-keeping troops. **(b)** *(di banane)* bunch.

caseario, a [kaze'arjo] *ag* dairy *attr.*

caseggiato [kased'dʒato] *sm (edificio)* large block of flats; *(gruppo di case)* group of houses.

caseificio [kazei'fitʃo] *sm* creamery.

casella [ka'sɛlla] *sf (quadretto)* box; *(di scacchiera)* square; *(di mobile, schedario)* pigeonhole; ~ **postale** *(abbr* **C.P.**) Post Office Box *(abbr* P.O. box).

casellante [kasel'lante] *sm (Ferr)* signalman; *(: al passaggio livello)* level-crossing keeper; *(su autostrada)* toll collector.

casellario [kasel'larjo] *sm (mobile)* filing cabinet; *(raccolta di pratiche)* files *pl;* ~ **penale** police files *pl;* ~ **giudiziale** court records *pl.*

casello [ka'sɛllo] *sm (Ferr)* signal box; *(di autostrada)* tollgate.

casereccio, a, ci, ce [kase'rettʃo] *ag* home-made.

caserma [ka'sɛrma] *sf* barracks *pl.*

casermone [kaser'mone] *sm (peg)* barracks *pl.*

casino [ka'sino] *sm* **(a)** *(fam: bordello)* brothel; *(fig fam: rumore)* row; *(: disordine)* mess; **ha fatto un** ~ he made an awful row; he messed everything up; **c'era un** ~ **di macchine** there was a hell of a lot of traffic. **(b):** ~ **di caccia** hunting lodge.

casinò [kazi'nɔ] *sm inv* casino.

casistica [ka'zistika] *sf (Med)* record of cases; **secondo la** ~ **degli incidenti stradali** according to road accident data.

caso ['kazo] *sm* **(a)** *(fatalità, destino)* chance; **è un puro** ~ it's sheer chance; **il** ~ **ha voluto che...** by chance...; **non è un** ~ it's no coincidence; **si dà il** ~ **che** it so happens that; **guarda** ~ strangely enough; **a** ~ at random.

(b) *(fatto, Gram, Med, Dir)* case; **per lui è un** ~ **di coscienza** he is in a moral dilemma; **questi sono i** ~**i della vita!** that's life!; ~ **limite** extreme case.

(c) *(bisogno):* **fare al** ~ **di qn** to be just what sb needs; **non è il** ~ **che tu te la prenda** there's no need for you to be upset; **non mi sembra il** ~ **di insistere** I wouldn't insist on that; **è il** ~ **che ce ne andiamo** we'd better go.

(d) *(possibilità, evenienza):* **i** ~**i sono due** there are two possibilities; **in ogni** ~, **in tutti i** ~**i** in any case, at any rate; **in** ~ **contrario** otherwise; **in tal** ~, **in questo** ~, **in quel** ~ in that case; **in** ~ **di necessità** *o* **bisogno** in case of need; **al** ~ if need be; **per** ~ by chance; ~ **mai** if by chance; ~ **mai non possiate venire...** if (by chance) you can't come...; **dovrei essere lì alle 5,** ~ **mai aspetta** I should be there for 5, if (by any chance) I'm not, wait; **fare** *o* **porre** *o* **mettere il** ~ **che** to suppose that; **a seconda dei** ~**i, secondo il** ~ depending on the circumstances.

(e) *(attenzione):* **far** ~ **a qc/qn** to pay attention to sth/sb; **hai fatto** ~ **al suo cappello?** did you notice his hat?; **non farci** ~ don't pay any attention.

casolare [kaso'lare] *sm* cottage.

casomai [kazo'mai] *cong* = **caso mai.**

casotto [ka'sɔtto] *sm* **(a)** *(di sentinella)* sentry box; *(di guardiano)* shelter; *(in spiaggia)* bathing hut, bathing cabin. **(b)** *(fam)* = **casino (a).**

caspita ['kaspita] *escl (di sorpresa)* good heavens!; *(di impazienza)* for goodness' sake!

cassa ['kassa] **1** *sf* **(a)** *(gen, Tip, di orologio, mobile)* case; *(gabbia)* crate. **(b)** *(Comm: macchina)* cash register; *(: sportello)* cash desk; **'si prega di pagare alla** ~**'** 'please pay at the desk'; **'**~**'** 'pay here'; **battere** ~ *(fig)* to come looking for money. **(c)** *(ente finanziario)* fund. **2:** ~ **acustica** *(Mus)* speaker; ~ **d'aria** *(Naut)* airlock; ~ **armonica** *(Mus)* sound chest; ~ **del fucile** rifle stock; ~ **integrazione: mettere in** ~ **integrazione** ≃ to lay off; ~ **malattia** sickness fund; **C**~ **del Mezzogiorno** *development fund for the South of Italy;* ~ **da morto** coffin; ~ **di risonanza** *(Fis)* resonance chamber; ~ **di risparmio** savings bank; ~ **toracica** *(Anat)* chest.

cassaforte [kassa'fɔrte] *sf, pl* **casseforti** safe.

cassapanca, che [kassa'panka] *sf* settle.

cassare [kas'sare] *vt (Dir: annullare)* to annul, repeal.

cassata [kas'sata] *sf (gelato)* tutti-frutti.

cassazione [kassat'tsjone] *sf (Dir)* cassation.

cassero ['kassero] *sm* quarter-deck.

casseruola [kasse'rwɔla] *sf* saucepan; **pollo in** ~ chicken casserole.

cassetta [kas'setta] *sf* box; *(per preziosi)* jewel box; *(di magnetofono)* cassette; *(sedile del cocchiere)* coachman's seat; ~ **delle lettere** letterbox; ~ **degli arnesi** toolbox; **pane a** *o* in ~ toasting loaf; **film di** ~ *(commerciale)* box-office draw.

cassettiera [kasset'tjɛra] *sf* chest of drawers.

cassetto [kas'setto] *sm* drawer.

cassettone [kasset'tone] *sm (mobile)* chest of drawers; **soffitto a** ~**i** *(Archit)* panelled ceiling.

cassiere, a [kas'sjɛre] *sm/f* cashier; *(in supermercato)* check-out assistant; ~ **di banca** bank teller.

cassone [kas'sone] *sm (cassa)* large case, large chest.

casta ['kasta] *sf* caste.

castagna [kas'taɲɲa] *sf* chestnut; **prendere qn in** ~ *(fig)* to catch sb in the act.

castagnaccio [kastaɲ'nattʃo] *sm* chestnut cake.

castagno [kas'taɲɲo] *sm (albero)* chestnut (tree); *(legno)* chestnut.

castagnola [kastaɲ'nɔla] *sf (petardo)* cracker.

castano, a [kas'tano] *ag (capelli)* chestnut (brown); *(persona)* brown-haired.

castellano, a [kastel'lano] *sm/f* lord/lady of the manor.

castello [kas'tello] *sm* **(a)** castle; **fare** ~**i in aria** to build castles in the air; **letti a** ~ bunk-beds. **(b)** *(Naut)*: ~ **di poppa** quarter-deck; ~ **di prua** fo'c'sle.

castigare [kasti'gare] *vt* to punish, chastise.

castigatezza [kastiga'tettsa] *sf (irreprensibilità)* faultlessness, sobriety.

castigato, a [kasti'gato] *ag (casto, modesto)* pure, chaste; *(emendato: prosa, versione)* expurgated, amended.

castigo, ghi [kas'tigo] *sm* punishment; **mettere/ essere in** ~ to punish/be punished; ~ **di Dio** *(fig)* scourge.

castità [kasti'ta] *sf* chastity.

casto, a ['kasto] *ag* chaste.

castorino [kasto'rino] *sm* coypu; **pelliccia di** ~ nutria fur.

castoro [kas'tɔro] *sm* beaver.

castrare [kas'trare] *vt (gen)* to castrate; *(cavallo)* to geld; *(gatto)* to neuter; *(fig: iniziativa)* to frustrate.

castrato, a [kas'trato] **1** *ag (vedi vb)* castrated; gelded; neutered. **2** *sm (agnello)* wether; *(Culin)* mutton.

castrazione [kastrat'tsjone] *sf* castration.

castroneria [kastrone'ria] *sf (fam)*: **dire** ~**e** to talk rubbish.

casuale [kazu'ale] *ag* chance *attr*, fortuitous; **incontro** ~ chance meeting.

casualità [kazuali'ta] *sf* chance nature.

casupola [ka'supola] *sf* simple little cottage.

cataclisma, i [kata'klizma] *sm* cataclysm; **sembra che ci sia stato un** ~ **qui** this place looks as though a bomb has hit it.

catacomba [kata'komba] *sf* catacomb.

catafalco, chi [kata'falko] *sm* catafalque.

catafascio [kata'faʃʃo] *sm*: **mandare a** ~ to wreck; **andare a** ~ to collapse.

catalessi [kata'lessi] *sf*, **catalessia** [katales'sia] *sf (Med)* catalepsy; **entrare** *o* **cadere in** ~ to have a cataleptic fit; *(fig)* to go into a trance.

catalizzatore [kataliddza'tore] *sm (anche fig)* catalyst.

catalogare [katalo'gare] *vt* to catalogue, list.

catalogo [ka'talogo] *sm* catalogue; ~ **dei prezzi** price list.

catapecchia [kata'pekkja] *sf* hovel.

cataplasma, i [kata'plazma] *sm (Med)* poultice.

catapulta [kata'pulta] *sf* catapult.

catapultare [katapul'tare] *vt*, ~**rsi** *vr* to catapult.

cataratta [kata'ratta] *sf* = **cateratta**.

catarifrangente [katarifran'dʒɛnte] **1** *ag* reflecting. **2** *sm* reflector.

catarro [ka'tarro] *sm* catarrh.

catarsi [ka'tarsi] *sf* catharsis.

catasta [ka'tasta] *sf* pile, stack.

catastale [katas'tale] *ag (Amm)*: **ufficio** ~ land office; **rilievo** ~ cadastral survey.

catasto [ka'tasto] *sm (Amm: inventario)* land register, cadaster; *(anche:* **ufficio del** ~*)* land office.

catastrofe [ka'tastrofe] *sf* catastrophe, disaster.

catastrofico, a, ci, che [katas'trɔfiko] *ag (evento)* catastrophic, disastrous; *(persona, previsione)* pessimistic.

catechismo [kate'kizmo] *sm* catechism.

catechista, i, e [kate'kista] *sm/f* catechist.

categoria [katego'ria] *sf (gen)* category; *(di albergo)* class; **fare un salto di** ~ *(fig)* to move up in the world; **di terza** ~ *(albergo, locale: anche peg)* third-class.

categorico, a, ci, che [kate'gɔriko] *ag (gen)* categorical; *(rifiuto)* flat.

catena [ka'tena] *sf (gen)* chain; *(di montagne)* range, chain; *(di negozi)* string, chain; *(fig: legame)* bond, chain; **reazione a** ~ chain reaction; **susseguirsi a** ~ to happen in quick succession; **tenere un cane alla** ~ to keep a dog on a chain; ~ **di montaggio** *(Tecn)* assembly line; ~**e da neve** *(Aut)* snow chains.

catenaccio [kate'nattʃo] *sm* bolt; **chiudere con il** ~ to bolt; **fare** ~ *(Calcio)* to play defensively.

catenella [kate'nɛlla] *sf (ornamento)* chain; *(di orologio)* watch chain; *(di porta)* door chain; **punto a** ~ *(in ricamo, maglia)* chain stitch.

cateratta [kate'ratta] *sf* **(a)** *(Geog)* cataract; *(saracinesca)* sluice, sluice gate. **(b)** *(Med)* cataract.

caterva [ka'tɛrva] *sf (di cose)* loads *pl*, heaps *pl*; *(di persone)* horde.

catetere [kate'tere] *sm (Med)* catheter.

catinella [kati'nɛlla] *sf* basin; **piovere a** ~**e** to rain cats and dogs.

catino [ka'tino] *sm* basin.

catodico, a, ci, che [ka'tɔdiko] *ag* cathode *attr*.

catodo ['katodo] *sm* cathode.

catorcio [ka'tɔrtʃo] *sm (peg)* old wreck.

catramare [katra'mare] *vt* to tar.

catrame [ka'trame] *sm* tar.

cattedra ['kattedra] *sf* **(a)** *(mobile)* (teacher's) desk; **salire** *o* **montare in** ~ *(fig)* to pontificate. **(b)** *(incarico: Scol)* teaching post; *(: Univ)* chair, professorship.

cattedrale [katte'drale] *sf* cathedral.

cattedratico, a, ci, che [katte'dratiko] **1** *ag*

(insegnamento) university *attr; (iro)* pedantic. **2** *sm/f* professor.

cattiveria [katti'vɛrja] *sf* **(a)** *(qualità)* wickedness, nastiness; *(: di bambino)* naughtiness; **lo ha fatto per pura** ~ he did it out of spite. **(b)** *(azione)* nasty *o* wicked action; **fare una** ~ to do something nasty; *(bambino)* to be naughty.

cattività [kattivi'ta] *sf (di animali)* captivity.

cattivo, a [kat'tivo] **1** *ag* **(a)** *(persona, azione)* bad, wicked; *(bambino: birichino)* naughty; **brutto** ~! you naughty boy!; **quel ragazzo è un** ~ **soggetto** that boy's a bit of a rascal; **farsi** ~ **sangue** to worry, get in a state; **farsi un** ~ **nome** to earn a bad reputation for o.s. **(b)** *(di qualità: gen)* bad; *(odore, sapore)* bad, nasty; *(cibo: guasto)* off; *(insegnante, salute)* bad. **2** *sm/f* bad *o* wicked person; **fare il** *(o* **la)** ~**(a)** *(bambino)* to be naughty; **i** ~**i** *(nei film)* the baddies, *(Am)* the bad guys. **3** *sm:* **accettare il buono e il** ~ *(fig)* to take the good with the bad.

cattolicesimo [kattoli'tʃezimo] *sm* Catholicism.

cattolico, a, ci, che [kat'tɔliko] *ag, sm/f* (Roman) Catholic.

cattura [kat'tura] *sf* capture.

catturare [kattu'rare] *vt (gen, fig: attenzione)* to capture, catch; **riuscì a** ~ **il suo sguardo** she managed to catch his eye.

Caucaso ['kaukazo] *sm:* **il** ~ the Caucasus.

caucciù [kaut'tʃu] *sm* India rubber.

causa ['kauza] *sf* **(a)** *(motivo, ragione)* cause, reason; *(ideale)* cause; **essere** ~ **di qc** to be the cause of sth, be the reason for sth; **a** ~ **di** because of; **per** ~ **sua** because of him; ~ **persa** *(anche fig)* lost cause; **far** ~ **comune** to make common cause. **(b)** *(Dir)* case; **intentare** ~ **a qn** to take legal action against sb; **perorare una** ~ to plead a case; **parte in** ~ litigant; **tu non sei parte in** ~ **in tutto ciò** this doesn't concern you at all; **rimettere qc in** ~ *(fig)* to bring sth up again.

causalità [kauzali'ta] *sf* causality.

causare [kau'zare] *vt* to cause.

caustico, a, ci, che ['kaustiko] *ag (Chim, fig)* caustic.

cautela [kau'tɛla] *sf* **(a)** *(prudenza)* caution; '**maneggiare con** ~' 'handle with care'. **(b)** *(precauzione)* precaution.

cautelare¹ [kaute'lare] *ag* precautionary.

cautelare² [kaute'lare] **1** *vt* to protect. **2:** ~**rsi** *vr:* ~**rsi (da** *o* **contro)** to take precautions (against).

cauterizzare [kauterid'dzare] *vt* to cauterize.

cauto, a ['kauto] *ag* prudent, cautious; **andare** ~ *(fig)* to tread carefully.

cauzione [kaut'tsjone] *sf* **(a)** *(Dir: deposito)* security, guarantee; *(: per libertà provvisoria)* bail; **rilasciare dietro** ~ to release on bail. **(b)** *(somma)* caution money.

cav. *abbr di* **cavaliere.**

cava ['kava] *sf* quarry.

cavalcare [kaval'kare] *vt, vi* to ride.

cavalcata [kaval'kata] *sf* ride; **fare una** ~ to go for a ride.

cavalcatore, trice [kavalka'tore] *sm/f* rider.

cavalcatura [kavalka'tura] *sf* mount.

cavalcavia [kavalka'via] *sm inv* flyover; *(sopra ferrovia)* railway bridge.

cavalcioni [kaval'tʃoni]: **a** ~ **di** *prep* astride.

cavaliere [kava'ljɛre] *sm* **(a)** rider, horseman; *(Mil)* cavalryman, trooper. **(b)** *(fig: accompagnatore)* escort; *(: nel ballo)* partner; *(: gentiluomo)* gentleman. **(c)** *(titolo, Storia)* knight; **l'hanno fatto** ~ **del lavoro** he has been knighted for services to industry.

cavalla [ka'valla] *sf* mare.

cavalleggero [kavalled'dʒɛro] *sm* light cavalryman.

cavalleresco, a, schi, sche [kavalle'resko] *ag* knightly; *(fig: comportamento)* chivalrous, noble; **poema** ~ poem of chivalry.

cavalleria [kavalle'ria] *sf* **(a)** *(Mil)* cavalry. **(b)** *(Storia, fig: lealtà, cortesia)* chivalry.

cavallerizza [kavalle'rittsa] *sf (maneggio)* riding school; **alla** ~ *(abbigliamento, stivali)* riding *attr.*

cavallerizzo [kavalle'rittso] *sm (nel circo)* circus rider; *(maestro di equitazione)* riding instructor.

cavalletta [kaval'letta] *sf (Zool)* grasshopper; *(: dannosa)* locust.

cavalletto [kaval'letto] *sm (supporto)* trestle; *(di pittore)* easel; *(Fot)* tripod.

cavallina [kaval'lina] *sf* **(a)** *(Zool)* filly. **(b)** *(gioco)* leapfrog. **(c)** *(attrezzo ginnico)* (vaulting) horse.

cavallino, a [kaval'lino] *ag (fig: volto, risata)* horsy.

cavallo [ka'vallo] **1** *sm* horse; *(Scacchi)* knight; *(attrezzo ginnico)* (vaulting) horse; *(anche:* ~ **vapore)** horsepower; **a** ~ on horseback; **a** ~ **di** *(sedia, moto, bici)* astride; **andare a** ~ to go on horseback, ride; **essere a** ~ to ride; **siamo a** ~ *(fig)* we've made it; **montare a/scendere da** ~ to mount/dismount; **denti da** ~ horsy teeth; **da** ~ *(fig: dose)* drastic; *(: febbre)* raging; **vivere a** ~ **tra due periodi** to straddle two periods. **2:** ~ **di battaglia** *(Teatro)* tour de force; *(fig)* hobby-horse; ~ **a dondolo** rocking horse; ~ **purosangue** *o* **di razza** thoroughbred; ~ **di sella** saddle horse; ~ **da soma** packhorse.

cavallone [kaval'lone] *sm (onda)* breaker; *(fig: persona sgraziata)* clodhopper.

cavalluccio [kaval'luttʃo] *sm:* ~ **marino** sea horse.

cavare [ka'vare] **1** *vt* **a** *(gen)* to take out; *(marmo)* to extract; *(dente)* to pull, extract; *(informazioni, soldi)* to obtain, get; ~ **gli occhi a qn** *(anche fig)* to scratch sb's eyes out; **me l'hai cavato di bocca** you took the words out of my mouth; **non gli ho cavato una parola (di bocca)** I couldn't get a word out of him; **non ci caverai un bel nulla** you'll get nothing out of him. **(b):** ~**rsi** *(desiderio, capriccio)* to satisfy; ~**rsi il pane di bocca** *(fig)* to make sacrifices. **2:** ~**rsi** *vr (liberarsi):* ~**rsi da** *(guai, problemi)* to get out of. **3: cavarsela** *(farcela)* to manage; *(da impiccio)* to find a way out; **come te la cavi?** how are things?; **cavarsela (a buon mercato)** to come off lightly; **se l'è cavata bene** *(in un processo)* he got off lightly; *(in un esame etc)* he did quite well; **se l'è cavata con qualche graffio** she came out of it with only a few scratches.

cavatappi [kava'tappi] *sm inv,* **cavaturaccioli** [kavatu'rattʃoli] *sm inv* corkscrew.

caverna [ka'verna] *sf* cave, cavern; **uomo delle** ~**e** caveman.

cavernoso, a [kaver'noso] *ag (luogo)* cavernous; *(fig: voce)* deep; *(: tosse)* raucous.

cavezza [ka'vettsa] *sf* halter.

cavia ['kavja] *sf (anche fig)* guinea pig.

caviale [ka'vjale] *sm* caviar.

cavicchio [ka'vikkjo] *sm (Tecn)* wooden pin; *(Agr)* dibble.

caviglia [ka'viλλa] *sf (Anat)* ankle; *(cavicchio)* pin, peg.

cavigliera [kaviλ'λera] *sf (fascia elastica)* ankle bandage.

cavillare [kavil'lare] *vi* to quibble, split hairs.

cavillo [ka'villo] *sm* quibble.

cavilloso, a [kavil'loso] *ag* quibbling, hair-splitting.

cavità [kavi'ta] *sf inv* hollow; *(Anat)* cavity.

cavo¹, a ['kavo] *ag, sm* hollow.

cavo² ['kavo] *sm (gen, Tecn, Telec)* cable; *(Naut)* rope.

cavolata [kavo'lata] *sf (fam)* stupid thing, foolish thing; **dire ~e** to talk rubbish *o* nonsense; **fare ~e** to do stupid things.

cavolfiore [kavol'fjore] *sm* cauliflower.

cavolo ['kavolo] *sm* **(a)** *(Bot)* cabbage; **~ cappuccio** spring cabbage; **questo ci entra come il ~ a merenda** that's completely beside the point. **(b)** *(fam: euf per cazzo)*: **non fa un ~ dalla mattina alla sera** he doesn't do a damn thing from morning till night; **non m'importa un ~** I don't give two hoots; **che ~ vuoi?** what the heck do you want?; **~!** damn!

cazzata [kat'tsata] *sf (fam!: stupidaggine)* stupid thing, something stupid; **dire ~e** to talk rubbish; **ha fatto un'altra delle sue ~e!** he's boobed again!

cazzo ['kattso] *sm* **(a)** *(fam!: pene)* prick. **(b)** *(fig fam!)*: **non gliene importa un ~** he doesn't give a damn about it; **che ~ vuoi?** what the hell do you want?; **fatti i ~i tuoi** mind your own bloody business; **~!** bloody hell!

cazzotto [kat'tsɔtto] *sf* punch; **tirare un ~** to throw a punch; **fare a ~i** to have a punch-up.

cazzuola [kat'tswɔla] *sf* trowel.

c/c *abbr di* **conto corrente.**

ce [tʃe] *pron, av vedi* **ci.**

cece ['tʃetʃe] *sm* chick pea.

cecità [tʃetʃi'ta] *sf* blindness.

ceco, a, chi, che ['tʃɛko] *ag, sm/f* Czech.

Cecoslovacchia [tʃekozlo'vakkja] *sf* Czechoslovakia.

cecoslovacco, a, chi, che [tʃekozlo'vakko] *ag, sm, sm/f* Czechoslovakian.

cedere ['tʃedere] **1** *vt* **(a)** *(concedere)*: **~ qc (a qn)** to give up sth (to sb); *(eredità, diritto)* to transfer sth (to sb); **~ il posto a qn** *(in autobus etc)* to give sb one's seat; **~ il passo (a qn)** to let (sb) pass in front; **~ il passo a qc** *(fig)* to give way to sth; **~ la parola (a qn)** to hand over (to sb). **(b)** *(Comm: vendere)* to sell; **'cedo', 'cedesi'** 'for sale'. **2** *vi* **(a)** *(crollare: persona)* to give in; *(: muro, terreno)* to give way; **il suo cuore ha ceduto** his heart couldn't take the strain. **(b)** *(soccombere)*: **~ a qn/qc** to give way to *o* yield to sb/sth. **(c)** *(deformarsi: terreno, tessuto, scarpe)* to give.

cedevole [tʃe'devole] *ag (materiale)* supple, pliable, yielding; *(terreno, rami)* soft.

cedibilità [tʃedibili'ta] *sf (Comm)* transferability.

cediglia [tʃe'diʎʎa] *sf* cedilla.

cedimento [tʃedi'mento] *sm (di terreno)* sinking, subsiding; **ha avuto un ~** *(terreno)* it has collapsed; *(fig: persona)* he broke down.

cedola ['tʃɛdola] *sf (Comm, Fin)* coupon; *(di assegno)* counterfoil.

cedrata [tʃe'drata] *sf* citron juice.

cedro¹ ['tʃedro] *sm (frutto, albero)* citron.

cedro² ['tʃedro] *sm (legno, albero)* cedar.

ceduo, a ['tʃeduo] *ag*: **bosco ~** copse, coppice.

C.E.E. *abbr f vedi* **comunità.**

cefalea [tʃefa'lɛa] *sf (Med)* headache.

ceffo ['tʃeffo] *sm (peg)* ugly mug.

ceffone [tʃef'fone] *sm* slap, smack; **dare un ~ a qn** to slap sb.

celare [tʃe'lare] **1** *vt* to conceal; **~ qc alla vista di qn** to conceal sth from sb. **2**: **~rsi** *vr (nascondersi)* to hide, conceal o.s.; *(stare nascosto)* to be hidden, be concealed.

celeberrimo, a [tʃele'bɛrrimo] *ag superl di* **celebre.**

celebrante [tʃele'brante] *sm (Rel)* celebrant.

celebrare [tʃele'brare] *vt (messa, matrimonio, festa)* to celebrate; *(cerimonia)* to hold; **~ le lodi di qc/qn** to sing the praises of sth/sb.

celebrazione [tʃelebrat'tsjone] *sf* celebration.

celebre ['tʃɛlebre] *ag* famous.

celebrità [tʃelebri'ta] *sf (fama, notorietà)* fame; *(persona)* celebrity; **arrivare alla ~** to become famous; **raggiungere la ~** to rise to fame.

celere ['tʃelere] **1** *ag* quick, fast. **2** *sf (Polizia)* riot police.

celerità [tʃeleri'ta] *sf* quickness, speed.

celeste [tʃe'lɛste] **1** *ag* **(a)** *(di cielo)* celestial; *(divino)* heavenly, celestial; **volta ~** sky. **(b)** *(colore)* pale blue, sky blue. **2** *sm (colore)* pale blue, sky blue.

celestiale [tʃeles'tjale] *ag* heavenly, celestial.

celia ['tʃɛlja] *sf* joke; **per ~** for a joke.

celibato [tʃeli'bato] *sm* celibacy.

celibe ['tʃɛlibe] **1** *ag* single, unmarried; *(prete)* celibate. **2** *sm* single *o* unmarried man.

cella ['tʃɛlla] *sf* cell; **essere in ~ di rigore** to be in solitary confinement; **~ frigorifera** cold store.

cellophane [sɛlɔ'fan] *sm* cellophane.

cellula ['tʃɛllula] *sf (in ogni senso)* cell.

cellulare [tʃellu'lare] **1** *ag* cellular; **segregazione ~** *(Dir)* solitary confinement. **2** *sm (furgone)* police van.

cellulite [tʃellu'lite] *sf* cellulitis.

celluloide [tʃellu'lɔide] *sf* celluloid.

cellulosa [tʃellu'losa] *sf* cellulose.

celtico, a, ci, che ['tʃɛltiko] *ag, sm* Celtic.

cembalo [tʃembalo] *sm (Mus)* harpsichord.

cementare [tʃemen'tare] *vt (anche fig)* to cement.

cemento [tʃe'mento] *sm* cement; **~ armato** reinforced concrete.

cena ['tʃena] *sf* dinner; **invitare qn a ~** to invite sb to dinner; **andare fuori a ~** to go out for dinner; **l'Ultima C~** *(Rel)* the Last Supper.

cenacolo [tʃe'nakolo] *sm (circolo)* coterie, circle; *(Rel, dipinto)* (the) Last Supper.

cenare [tʃe'nare] *vi* to have dinner.

cenciaiolo [tʃentʃa'jɔlo] *sm* ragman.

cencio ['tʃentʃo] *sm (straccio)* rag; *(: per pulire)* cloth; **vestito di ~i** dressed in rags; **essere ridotto a un ~** to feel washed out; **essere bianco come un ~** to be as white as a sheet.

cencioso, a [tʃen'tʃoso] *ag (persona)* (dressed) in rags; *(indumento)* tattered.

cenere [tʃenere] *sf* **(a)** ash, ashes *pl*; *(di carbone, di legno)* cinders *pl*; **color ~** ash grey. **(b)** *(Rel, di defunto)*: **~i** *pl* ashes.

Cenerentola [tʃene'rɛntola] *sf (anche fig)* Cinderella.

cenno [tʃenno] *sm* **(a)** *(segno)* sign, signal; *(: con la testa)* nod; *(: con gli occhi)* wink; *(: con la mano)* gesture; *(: di saluto)* wave; **capirsi/parlare a ~i** to understand each other/speak with gestures; **~ d'intesa** sign of agreement; **fare ~ di sì/no** to nod/shake one's head; **mi fece un ~ di saluto con la mano/con la testa** he waved/nodded to me; **mi ha fatto ~ di avvicinarmi** he beckoned to me to come forward. **(b)** *(breve esposizione)* mention; **fare ~ a qc/qn** to mention sth/sb; **~i di storia dell'arte** an outline of the history of art. **(c)** *(indizio)* sign; **al primo ~ di pioggia** at the first sign of rain.

cenone [tʃe'none] *sm*: **~ di Capodanno** New Year's Eve dinner.

cenotafio [tʃeno'tafjo] *sm* cenotaph.

censimento [tʃensi'mento] *sm* census; **fare il ~** to take a census.

censire [tʃen'sire] *vt*: **~ qc** to take a census of sth.

censo ['tʃɛnso] *sm (Storia)* census; *(ricchezza)* wealth.

censore [tʃen'sore] *sm (anche Storia)* censor; *(fig: critico)* critic.

censura [tʃen'sura] *sf (Cine, Stampa: controllo)* censorship; *(: ufficio)* board of censors; *(fig, Pol, Rel)* censure; *(Psic)* censor.

censurare [tʃensu'rare] *vt (Cine, Stampa)* to censor; *(fig, Pol, Rel)* to censure.

centauro [tʃen'tauro] *sm* centaur; *(fig)* motorcycle rider.

centellinare [tʃentelli'nare] *vt* to sip; *(fig)* to savour.

centenario, a [tʃente'narjo] **1** *ag* **(a)** *(che ha cento anni)* one hundred years old; **un albero** ~ a one hundred-year-old tree. **(b)** *(che avviene ogni cento anni)* centennial. **2** *sm/f (persona)* centenarian. **3** *sm (anniversario)* centenary.

centennale [tʃenten'nale] *ag* centennial; **tradizione** ~ age-old tradition.

centesimale [tʃentezi'male] *ag* hundredth.

centesimo, a [tʃen'tezimo] **1** *ag* hundredth. **2** *sm (moneta: di dollaro)* cent; *(: di franco)* centime; **non vale un** ~ it's not worth a penny; **essere senza un** ~ to be penniless.

centigrado [tʃen'tigrado] *ag m* centigrade; **gradi** ~**i** degrees centigrade.

centilitro [tʃen'tilitro] *sm* centilitre.

centimetro [tʃen'timetro] *sm* **(a)** *(misura)* centimetre. **(b)** *(nastro)* measuring tape *(in centimetres)*.

centinaio [tʃenti'najo] *sm, pl(f)* **centinaia** hundred; **un** ~ **di persone** about a hundred people, a hundred or so people; **a** ~**a** *(merce: vendere)* by the hundred; *(persone: ve..ire)* in (their) hundreds.

cento ['tʃento] **1** *ag inv* a hundred, one hundred; ~**uno** one o a hundred and one; **sei**~ six hundred; ~ **di questi giorni!** many happy returns (of the day)! **2** *sm inv* a hundred, one hundred; **per** ~ per cent; **al** ~ **per** ~ a hundred per cent; *per fraseologia vedi* **cinque**.

centodieci [tʃento'djetʃi] *ag inv, sm inv* one hundred and ten; *(Univ):* **laurearsi con** ~ **e lode** ≃ to graduate with first-class honours.

centometrista, i, e [tʃentome'trista] *sm/f* one hundred metres runner *(o swimmer)*.

centomila [tʃento'mila] *ag inv* a o one hundred thousand; **te l'ho detto** ~ **volte** *(fig)* I've told you a thousand times.

centrale [tʃen'trale] **1** *ag (gen)* central; *(stazione, ufficio)* main; **sede** ~ head office. **2** *sf (sede principale)* head office; ~ **elettrica** power station, power plant; ~ **del latte** dairy; ~ **nucleare** nuclear power plant *o* station; ~ **di polizia** police headquarters *pl*; ~ **telefonica** telephone exchange.

centralinista, i, e [tʃentrali'nista] *sm/f (Telec)* operator; *(in ditta, albergo)* switchboard operator.

centralino [tʃentra'lino] *sm (Telec)* telephone exchange; *(di ditta, albergo)* switchboard.

centralizzare [tʃentralid'dzare] *vt* to centralize.

centralizzazione [tʃentraliddzat'tsjone] *sf* centralization.

centrare [tʃen'trare] *vt (gen, Sport)* to centre; *(bersaglio)* to hit the centre; ~ **(in pieno)** *(freccette etc)* to score a bull's eye; ~ **una risposta** to get the right answer; **hai centrato il problema** you've hit the nail on the head.

centrattacco, chi [tʃentrat'takko] *sm*, **centravanti** [tʃentra'vanti] *sm inv* centre forward.

centrifuga, ghe [tʃen'trifuga] *sf (Tecn)* centrifuge; *(per biancheria)* spin-dryer.

centrifugare [tʃentrifu'gare] *vt (Tecn)* to centrifuge; *(biancheria)* to spin-dry.

centrifugo, a, ghi, ghe [tʃen'trifugo] *ag:* **forza** ~**a** centrifugal force.

centrino [tʃen'trino] *sm* doily.

centripeto, a [tʃen'tripeto] *ag:* **forza** ~**a** centripetal force.

centrista, i, e [tʃen'trista] *ag (Pol)* centre *attr*.

centro ['tʃentro] *sm (gen)* centre; *(di città)* (town *o* city) centre; *(di bersaglio)* bull's eye; **fare** ~ to hit the bull's eye; *(Calcio)* to score; *(fig)* to hit the nail on the head; **si crede il** ~ **del mondo** he thinks the universe revolves around him; ~ **balneare** seaside resort; ~ **commerciale** shopping centre; *(città)* commercial centre; ~ **nervoso** *(Anat)* nerve centre; ~ **ospedaliero** hospital complex; ~ **sportivo/di ricerche** sports/research centre; ~**i vitali** *(anche fig)* vital organs.

centrocampo [tʃentro'kampo] *sm (Sport)* midfield.

centrodestra [tʃentro'dɛstra] *sm (Pol)* centre right.

centrodestro [tʃentro'dɛstro] *sm (Calcio)* inside right.

centromediano [tʃentrome'djano] *sm (Calcio)* centre half.

centrosinistra [tʃentrosi'nistra] *sm (Pol)* centre left.

centrosinistro [tʃentrosi'nistro] *sm (Calcio)* inside left.

centrosostegno [tʃentrosos'teɲɲo] *sm* = **centromediano**.

centrotavola [tʃentro'tavola] *sm, pl* **centritavola** centrepiece.

centroterzino [tʃentroter'tsino] *sm (Calcio)* central defender.

centuplo, a ['tʃɛntuplo] **1** *ag* a hundred times as much. **2** *sm:* **il** ~ **di 2** a hundred times 2.

centurione [tʃentu'rjone] *sm* centurion.

ceppo ['tʃeppo] *sm* **(a)** *(di albero)* (tree) stump; *(fig: genealogico)* stock. **(b)** *(ciocco)* log; *(per decapitazione)* (chopping) block. **(c)** *(di aratro, ancora)* stock; *(Tecn)* brake shoe. **(d):** ~**i** *pl (di prigioniero)* shackles, fetters.

cera ['tʃera] *sf* **(a)** *(sostanza)* wax; ~ **d'api** beeswax; ~ **per pavimenti** floor polish; **dare la** ~ **(a qc)** to polish (sth); **museo delle** ~**e** waxworks *sg*. **(b)** *(fig: aspetto):* **avere una bella/brutta** ~ to look well/ill.

ceralacca [tʃera'lakka] *sf* sealing wax.

ceramica [tʃe'ramika] *sf* **(a)** *(materiale)* baked clay; *(Arte)* ceramics *sg*. **(b):** ~**che** *pl* pottery.

cerato, a [tʃe'rato] **1** *ag* waxed, wax *attr*; **tela** ~**a** oilskin. **2** *sm* oilcloth.

cerbiatto [tʃer'bjatto] *sm* fawn.

cerbottana [tʃerbot'tana] *sf (arma)* blowpipe; *(giocattolo)* peashooter.

cerca ['tʃerka] *sf:* **andare/essere in** ~ **di qc** to go/be looking for sth.

cercare [tʃer'kare] *vt (gen)* to look for; *(fama, gloria)* to seek; ~ **di fare qc** to try to do sth; **l'hai cercato sul dizionario?** have you looked it up in the dictionary?; ~ **lavoro/casa** to look for work/a house; ~ **moglie/marito** to be looking for a wife/husband; ~ **qn con gli occhi** to look round for sb; ~ **le parole** to search for words; ~ **guai** to be looking for trouble; ~ **fortuna** to seek one's fortune.

cercatore [tʃerka'tore] *sm* searcher, seeker; ~ **d'oro** gold digger.

cerchia ['tʃerkja] *sf (anche fig)* circle; ~ **di mura** city walls.

cerchiare [tʃer'kjare] *vt (botte)* to hoop.

cerchiato, a [tʃer'kjato] *ag*: **occhiali ~i d'osso** horn-rimmed spectacles; **hai gli occhi ~i** you've got dark rings under your eyes.

cerchio ['tʃerkjo] *sm* (*gen, Geom, di persone*) circle; (*di ruota*) rim; (*di botte*) hoop; **mettersi in ~** to stand in a circle; **dare un colpo al ~ e uno alla botte** (*fig*) to keep two things going at the same time.

cerchione [tʃer'kjone] *sm* (wheel)rim.

cereale [tʃere'ale] *ag, sm* cereal.

cerebrale [tʃere'brale] *ag* cerebral.

cereo, a ['tʃereo] *ag* wan, waxen.

ceretta [tʃe'retta] *sf* (*per depilazione*) depilatory wax.

cerimonia [tʃeri'mɔnja] *sf* (**a**) ceremony; (*Rel*) service. (**b**): **~e** *pl* ceremony *sg*; **fare ~e** to stand on ceremony; **senza tante ~e** (*senza formalità*) informally; (*bruscamente*) unceremoniously, without so much as a by your leave.

cerimoniale [tʃerimo'njale] *sm* (*regole*) ritual, custom; (*libro*) book of etiquette; **~ di corte** court ritual.

cerimoniere [tʃerimo'njere] *sm* master of ceremonies.

cerimonioso, a [tʃerimo'njoso] *ag* ceremonious, formal.

cerino [tʃe'rino] *sm* (*fiammifero*) (wax) match; (*stoppino*) taper.

cernia ['tʃɛrnja] *sf* (*anche: ~ gigante*) grouper; (*anche: ~ di fondo*) stone bass.

cerniera [tʃer'njɛra] *sf* (*di porte, finestre*) hinge; (*di abito: anche: ~ lampo*) zip; (*di bracciale*) clasp.

cernita ['tʃɛrnita] *sf* selection; **fare una ~ di** to select.

cero ['tʃero] *sm* (church) candle.

cerone [tʃe'rone] *sm* (*trucco*) greasepaint.

cerotto [tʃe'rɔtto] *sm* (*Med*) plaster; **attaccarsi a qn come un ~** to cling to sb like a limpet.

certamente [tʃerta'mente] *av* certainly, surely.

certezza [tʃer'tettsa] *sf* certainty, assurance; **avere la ~ che** to be certain *o* sure that; **sapere con ~ che** to know for sure that.

certificare [tʃertifi'kare] *vt* to certify.

certificato [tʃertifi'kato] *sm* certificate; **~ di matrimonio/nascita** marriage/birth certificate; **~ medico** doctor's certificate.

certo, a ['tʃɛrto] **1** *ag* (**a**) (*dopo sostantivo: indubbio: gen*) certain; (*: prova*) sure, positive, definite; **è cosa ~a** it's quite certain, there's no doubt about it;` **un sintomo ~ di malattia** it's a sure sign of illness, it's undoubtedly a sign of illness. (**b**) (*sicuro*) certain, sure; **essere ~ di qc/di fare qc** to be sure *o* certain of sth/of doing sth.

2 *ag indef* (*prima del sostantivo*) (**a**) certain; **devo sbrigare una ~a faccenda** there is a certain matter I must attend to; **un ~ signor Bonanno** a (certain) Mr Bonanno; **c'è un ~ Stefano che ti cerca** someone called Stefano is looking for you; **in un ~ senso** in a way, in a certain sense; **in ~i casi** in some *o* certain cases. (**b**) (*con valore intensivo*) some; **un fatto di una ~a importanza** a fact of some importance; **avere una ~a età** to be getting on; **in quel locale c'erano ~e facce!** there were some really unpleasant faces in that place!; **ho visto ~e borse oggi — le avrei comprate tutte** I saw some terrific bags today — I could have bought the lot.

3 *pron indef*: **~i(e)** *pl* (*persone*) some (people); (*cose*) some.

4 *av* certainly, (*senz'altro*) of course; **~ che sì/no** certainly/certainly not; **~ che puoi!** of course you can!

certosino [tʃerto'zino] *sm* Carthusian monk; (*li-*

quore) chartreuse; **è un lavoro da ~** it's a pernickety job.

certuni [tʃer'tuni] *pron pl indef* some (people).

cerume [tʃe'rume] *sm* (ear) wax.

cervello [tʃer'vello] *sm* (**a**) (*Anat: pl(f) ~a*) brain, brains; **far saltare il ~** *o* **le ~a a qn** to blow sb's brains out. (**b**) (*fig: intelligenza*): **avere molto ~** to be very brainy; **ha poco ~** he's not very bright; **avere il** *o* **essere un ~ fino** to be sharpwitted; **avere il ~ di una gallina** to be brainless *o* peabrained; **dovevi avere abbastanza ~ da evitarlo** you should have had enough sense to avoid it; **è uscito di ~, gli è dato di volta il ~** he's gone off his head; **è lui il ~ della banda?** is he the brains behind the operation?; **~ elettronico** computer.

cervellotico, a, ci, che [tʃervel'lɔtiko] *ag* bizarre, unreasonable.

cervicale [tʃervi'kale] *ag* cervical.

cervo ['tʃɛrvo] *sm* (**a**) (*mammifero*) deer; (*: maschio*) stag; (*: femmina*) doe; **carne di ~** venison. (**b**) (*insetto*): **~ volante** stag beetle.

cesareo, a [tʃe'zareo] *ag* (*anche Med*) Caesarian; **parto ~** Caesarian (section).

cesellare [tʃezel'lare] *vt* to chisel; (*incidere*) to engrave.

cesellatore [tʃezella'tore] *sm* engraver.

cesellatura [tʃezella'tura] *sf* (*lavoro*) chiselling; (*Arte*) engraving.

cesello [tʃe'zɛllo] *sm* (*strumento*) chisel; (*Arte*) engraving.

cesoie [tʃe'zoje] *sfpl* shears.

cespo ['tʃespo] *sm* tuft.

cespuglio [tʃes'puʎʎo] *sm* bush.

cespuglioso, a [tʃespuʎ'ʎoso] *ag* (*anche fig*) bushy.

cessare [tʃes'sare] **1** *vi* (*finire: aus essere*) to cease, stop; (*ditta*) to stop *o* cease trading. **2** *vt* to stop, put an end to; (*produzione*) to discontinue; (*~ di fare qc* to stop doing sth; **~ il fuoco** (*Mil*) to cease fire; **il medico ha fatto ~ il sangue** the doctor staunched the flow of blood; **'cessato allarme'** 'all clear'.

cessate il fuoco [tʃes'sate il 'fwɔko] *sm inv* ceasefire.

cessazione [tʃessat'tsjone] *sf* cessation; (*interruzione*) suspension.

cessione [tʃes'sjone] *sf* transfer.

cesso ['tʃɛsso] *sm* (*fam: gabinetto*) bog; (*: peg: luogo*) dive; **quel film era proprio un ~** that film was a load of shit.

cesta ['tʃesta] *sf* basket.

cestello [tʃes'tello] *sm* (*per bottiglie*) crate; (*di lavatrice*) drum.

cestinare [tʃesti'nare] *vt* to throw away; (*fig: proposta*) to turn down; (*: romanzo*) to reject.

cestino [tʃes'tino] *sm* basket; **~ (dei rifiuti)** wastepaper basket; **~ da viaggio** packed lunch (*for train travellers*); **~ da lavoro** (*Cucito*) work basket, sewing basket.

cesto ['tʃesto] *sm* (**a**) (*gen, Sport*) basket. (**b**) (*Bot*) head.

cetaceo [tʃe'tatʃeo] *sm* sea mammal.

ceto ['tʃeto] *sm* (*social*) class.

cetra ['tʃetra] *sf* zither; (*fig: di poeta*) lyre.

cetriolino [tʃetrio'lino] *sm* gherkin.

cetriolo [tʃetri'ɔlo] *sm* cucumber.

cfr. *abbr* (= *confronta*) cf.

C.G.I.L. *abbr f* (= *Confederazione Generale Italiana del Lavoro*) Italian Trades Union Organization.

chalet [ʃa'le] *sm* chalet.

champagne [ʃã'paɲ] *sm inv* champagne.

chance [ʃãs] *sf inv* chance.

charme [ʃarm] *sm* charm.

charter ['tʃaːtə] **1** *ag inv (volo)* charter; *(aereo)* chartered. **2** *sm inv (aereo)* chartered plane.

chassis [ʃa'si] *sm inv* chassis.

che [ke] **1** *pron* **(a)** *(relativo: persona: soggetto)* who; *(: oggetto)* that, whom; *(: cosa, animale)* which, that *(spesso omesso)*; **l'uomo ~ sta parlando** the man who is speaking; **la ragazza ~ hai visto** the girl whom you saw; **i bambini ~ vedi nel cortile** the children that *o* whom you see in the yard; **l'anno ~ scoppiò la guerra** the year (that) war broke out.
(b) *(la qual cosa)* which; **dovrei ottenere il massimo dei voti, il ~ è improbabile** I ought to get top marks, which is unlikely.
(c) *(indefinito)*: **quell'uomo ha un ~ di losco** there's something suspicious about that man; **un certo non so ~** an indefinable something; **quella ragazza ha un non so ~ di affascinante** there's something fascinating about that girl; **quel film non era un gran ~** that film was nothing special.
(d) *(interrog)* what; **~ (cosa) fai?** what are you doing?; **di ~ (cosa) hai bisogno?** what do you need?; **non so ~ dire** I don't know what to say; **ma ~ dite!** what are you saying!
2 *ag* **(a)** *(interrog)* what; *(: di numero limitato)* which; **~ giorno è oggi?** what day is it today?; **~ lenzuola metti sul letto?** what *(o* which) sheets are you putting on the bed?; **di ~ attore stai parlando?** which actor are you talking about?
(b) *(escl)* what; **~ bel ragazzo!** what a good-looking boy!; **guarda in ~ stato sei ridotto!** look at the mess you're in!
3 *(cong)* **(a)** *(con proposizioni subordinate)* that *(talvolta omesso)*; **so ~ tu c'eri** I know (that) you were there; **voglio ~ tu venga** I want you to come; **nasconditi qui ~ non ti veda nessuno** hide here, so nobody can see you; **ero così felice ~ corsi a dirlo a tutti** I was so happy (that) I ran off to tell everyone.
(b) *(temporale)*: **era appena uscita di casa ~ suonò il telefono** she had no sooner gone out than *o* she had hardly gone out when the telephone rang; **mi sono svegliato ~ era ancora buio** I woke up while it was still dark; **sono anni ~ non lo vedo** I haven't seen him for years, it's years since I saw him.
(c) *(in frasi imperative, concessive)*: **~ venga pure!** let him come by all means!; **~ sia benedetto!** may God bless him!
(d): **non è ~ non mi interessi la commedia, è ~ sono stanco e vorrei andare a letto** it's not that the play doesn't interest me, it's just that I'm tired and I'd like to go to bed; **non ~ sia stupido** not that he's stupid; **~ tu venga o no, noi partiamo lo stesso** we're leaving whether you come or not.
(e) *(comparativo: con più, meno)* than; **è più furbo ~ intelligente** he's more cunning than intelligent; *vedi* **più, meno, così** *etc.*

checca, che ['kekka] *sf (fam: omosessuale)* fairy.

chef [ʃef] *sm inv* chef.

chela ['kela] *sf* nipper.

chemisier [ʃəmi'zje] *sm inv* shirtwaister.

chepì [ke'pi] *sm inv* kepi.

chèque [ʃɛk] *sm inv* cheque.

cherosene [kero'zɛne] *sm* kerosene.

cherubino [keru'bino] *sm (anche fig)* cherub.

chetare [ke'tare] **1** *vt* to hush, silence. **2: ~rsi** *vr* to quieten down, fall silent.

chetichella [keti'kella] *sf*: **alla ~** unobtrusively, stealthily; **andarsene alla ~** to slip away.

cheto, a ['keto] *ag* quiet.

chi [ki] *pron* **(a)** *(interrog: sog)* who; *(: ogg)* who, whom; **~ l'hai visto?** who saw him?; **~ viene di voi?** which of you is coming?; **~ hai visto?** who *o* whom did you see?; **con ~ desidera parlare?** who do you wish to speak to?; **di ~ è questo libro?** whose book is this?, whose is this book?; **di ~ stai parlando?** who are you talking about?; **non sapevo a ~ rivolgermi** I didn't know who to ask; **ha telefonato non so ~ per te** somebody or other was on the phone for you; **dimmi ~ ti piace di più tra loro** tell me which of them you like best.
(b) *(rel)* whoever, anyone who; **invita ~ vuoi** invite whoever *o* anyone you like; **~ arriva prima vince** whoever gets there first wins; **lo racconterò a ~ so io** I know who I'll tell about it; **lo riferirò a ~ di dovere** I'll pass it on to the relevant person; **so io di ~ parlo** I'm naming no names; **esco con ~ mi pare** I'll go out with whoever I like.
(c): **~ ... ~ : i bambini hanno avuto i regali: ~ dolci, ~ giocattoli e così via** the children have had their presents: some got sweets, others toys and so on; **~ dice una cosa, ~ l'altra** some say one thing, others another.
(d): **~ si somiglia si piglia** birds of a feather flock together; **~ si salvi ~ può** every man for himself; **ride bene ~ ride ultimo** he who laughs last laughs best; **~ va piano va sano e va lontano** more haste less speed.

chiacchiera ['kjakkjera] *sf* **(a)**: **~e** *pl*: **fare due** *o* **quattro ~e** to have a chat; **perdersi in ~e** to waste time talking. **(b)** *(pettegolezzo)*: **~e** *pl* gossip *sg*, talk *sg*.

chiacchierare [kjakkje'rare] *vi* to chat; *(parlottare)* to chatter; *(spettegolare)* to gossip; **la molto chiacchierata relazione tra...** the much talked about relationship between... .

chiacchierata [kjakkje'rata] *sf* chat; **farsi una ~** to have a chat.

chiacchierio [kjakkje'rio] *sm* chattering.

chiacchierone, a [kjakkje'rone] **1** *sm/f* chatterbox *(fam)*; *(peg)* gossip. **2** *ag* talkative; *(peg)* gossipy.

chiamare [kja'mare] **1** *vt* **(a)** *(persona)* to call; *(nome)* to call out; *(per telefono)* to call, phone; **~ qn per nome** to call *o* address sb by his *(o* her) name; **~ qn a gran voce** to call out loudly to sb; **~ qn da parte** to take sb aside; **~ (qn in) aiuto** to call (sb) for help; **mandare a ~ qn** to send for sb, call sb in; **mi sono fatto ~ presto stamattina** *(svegliare)* I asked to be called early this morning. **(b)** *(dare un nome)* to call, name; *(soprannominare)* to (nick)name, call; **e chiamala sfortuna!** and you call that bad luck! **(c)** *(Mil)*: **~ alle armi** to call up. **(d)** *(Dir)*: **~ qn in giudizio** *o* **in causa** to summons sb; **non mi ~ in causa!** *(fig)* don't bring me into it!
2: ~rsi *vr*: **come ti chiami? — mi chiamo Michela** what's your name? — my name is Michela *o* what are you called? — my name is Michela *o* I'm called Michela; **questo è quello che si chiama un buon affare** that's what you call a bargain.

chiamata [kja'mata] *sf (gen)* call; *(Dir)* summons; **fare una ~** *(Telec)* to make a (phone) call; **~ telefonica** phone call; **~ urbana/interurbana** local/long-distance call; **~ alle armi** *(Mil)* call-up; **~ alle urne** *(Pol)* election.

chiappa ['kjappa] *sf (Anat fam)* cheek; **~e** *pl* bottom *sg*; **alza le ~e!** get up off your backside!

chiara ['kjara] *sf* egg white.

chiarezza [kja'rettsa] *sf (anche fig)* clearness, clarity.

chiarificare [kjarifi'kare] *vt (anche fig)* to clarify, make clear.

chiarificatore, trice [kjarifika'tore] *ag*

clarifying, explanatory; **avere un incontro** ~ **to have a meeting to clarify matters.**

chiarificazione [kjarifikat'tsjone] *sf* clarification *no pl*, explanation.

chiarimento [kjari'mento] *sm* clarification *no pl*, explanation.

chiarire [kja'rire] **1** *vt (gen)* to clarify, explain; *(mistero, dubbio)* to clear up; ~ **le idee a qn** to clarify things for sb; **ti chiarisco io le idee!** I'll sort you out! **2:** ~**rsi** *vr* **(a)** to become clear(er). **(b)** *(uso reciproco)*: **si sono chiariti** they've sorted things out.

chiaro, a ['kjaro] **1** *ag* **(a)** *(di colore: mobili, vestiti)* light-coloured; *(colore)* light, pale; *(capelli, carnagione)* fair; **pantaloni verde** ~ **light green trousers. (b)** *(limpido: anche fig)* clear; *(luminoso)* bright; **si sta facendo** ~ **the day is dawning; un no** ~ **e tondo a very definite no; sarò** ~ **I'll come to the point; sia** ~ **a una cosa let's get one thing straight. (c)** *(evidente, ovvio)* obvious, clear; **è** ~ **e lampante it's blatantly obvious.**
2 *sm* **(a)** *(colore)*: **vestirsi di** ~ **to wear light colours** *o* **light-coloured clothes. (b)** *(luce, luminosità)* day, daylight; **fa** ~ **alle 7 it gets light at 7 o'clock;** ~ **di luna moonlight; partiamo col** ~ **let's leave during daylight; mettere in** ~ **qc** *(fig)* **to clear sth up.**
3 *av (parlare, vedere)* clearly; **parliamoci** ~ **let's be frank.**

chiarore [kja'rore] *sm* (diffuse) light; **col** ~ **della luna in the moonlight.**

chiaroscuro [kjaros'kuro] *sm* (Pittura) chiaroscuro.

chiaroveggente [kjaroved'dʒente] *ag, sm/f* clairvoyant.

chiaroveggenza [kjaroved'dʒentsa] *sf* clairvoyance.

chiasso ['kjasso] *sm* din, uproar; **far** ~ **to make a din;** *(fig)* **to make a fuss;** *(: scalpore)* **to cause a stir.**

chiassoso, a [kjas'soso] *ag (rumoroso)* noisy, rowdy; *(vistoso: colori etc)* showy, gaudy.

chiatta ['kjatta] *sf* barge.

chiave ['kjave] **1** *sf* **(a)** *(gen, fig)* key; **chiudere a** ~ **to lock; tenere sotto** ~ *(anche fig)* **to keep under lock and key; prezzo** ~**i in mano** *(di macchina)* **on the road price;** *(di casa)* **price with immediate entry** *o* **possession; in** ~ **politica in political terms; rifare qc in** ~ **moderna to produce a modern version of sth; la** ~ **di lettura di questo brano... the key to an understanding of this passage...;** ~ **di basso/di violino** *(Mus)* **bass/treble clef. (b)** *(Tecn)* spanner; *(: più grande)* wrench; ~ **inglese** (monkey) wrench; ~ **a forcella fork spanner. (c)** *(Archit)*: ~ **di volta** *(anche fig)* **keystone. 2** *ag inv* **key** *attr.*

chiavetta [kja'vetta] *sf* (Tecn) key; *(di orologio etc)* winder.

chiavistello [kjavis'tɛllo] *sm* bolt.

chiazza ['kjattsa] *sf* stain, splash.

chiazzare [kjat'tsare] *vt* to stain, splash.

chichessia [kikkes'sia] *pron indef* anyone, anybody.

chicco, chi ['kikko] *sm (di cereale, riso)* grain; *(di caffè)* bean; *(di rosario)* bead; ~ **d'uva grape;** ~ **di grandine hailstone.**

chiedere ['kjɛdere] **1** *vt* **(a)** *(per sapere)* to ask; *(per avere)* to ask for; *(: intervista)* to ask for, request; *(: riunione, intervento, volontari)* to call for; ~ **qc a qn** to ask sb for sth; ~ **scusa a qn** to apologise to sb; **chiedo scusa!** I'm sorry!; ~ **a qn di fare qc** *o* **che faccia qc** to ask sb to do sth; ~ **il permesso di** to ask permission to; ~ **notizie di qn** to inquire *o*

ask after sb; **mi ha chiesto del mio viaggio** he asked me about my journey; **ci chiede di partire** he wants us *o* is asking us to go.
(b) *(fraseologia)*: ~ **il divorzio** to ask for a divorce; ~ **l'elemosina** to beg; ~ **giustizia** to demand justice; ~ **l'impossibile** to ask (for) the impossible; ~ **qn in matrimonio,** ~ **la mano di qn** to ask for sb's hand in marriage; ~ **la pace** to sue for peace; **non chiedo altro** that's all I want; **non chiedo altro che partire con te** all I want is to leave with you.
2 *vi:* ~ **di qn** *(salute)* to ask about sb; *(per vederlo)* to ask for sb; **il padrone chiede di te** the boss wants to see you.
3: ~**rsi** *vr:* ~**rsi (se)** to wonder (whether).

chierica ['kjerika] *sf (Rel)* tonsure; *(fig)* bald patch.

chierichetto [kjeri'ketto] *sm* altar boy.

chierico, ci ['kjeriko] *sm (Rel)* cleric; *(: seminarista)* seminarist.

chiesa ['kjɛza] *sf* church; **C~ anglicana** Church of England; **C~ cattolica** (Roman) Catholic Church; **essere di** ~ to be a churchgoer.

chiesto, a ['kjɛsto] *pp di* **chiedere.**

chiglia ['kiʎʎa] *sf* keel.

chilo¹ ['kilo] **1** *sm* kilo. **2** *pref* kilo... .

chilo² ['kilo] *sm:* **fare il** ~ to have a nap after lunch *(o* dinner).

chilogrammo [kilo'grammo] *sm* kilogram(me).

chilometraggio [kilome'traddʒo] *sm (Aut)* ≈ mileage.

chilometrico, a, ci, che [kilo'mɛtriko] *ag* kilometric; *(fig)* endless.

chilometro [ki'lɔmetro] *sm* kilometre.

chilowatt ['kilovat] *sm inv* kilowatt.

chilowattora [kilovat'tora] *sm inv* kilowatt hour.

chimera [ki'mɛra] *sf* chimera.

chimica ['kimika] *sf* chemistry.

chimico, a, ci, che ['kimiko] **1** *ag* chemical; **sostanza** ~**a** a chemical. **2** *sm/f* chemist.

chimono [ki'mɔno] *sm inv* kimono.

china¹ ['kina] *sf (pendenza)* slope; *(salita)* incline; **risalire la** ~ *(fig)* to be on the road to recovery.

china² ['kina] *sf (albero)* cinchona; *(liquore)* drink made with alcohol and cinchona bark.

china³ ['kina] *sf (inchiostro)* Indian ink.

chinare [ki'nare] **1** *vt* to lower, bend; ~ **il capo** *(anche fig)* to bow one's head. **2:** ~**rsi** *vr* to stoop, bend over; *(fig)* to give way, submit.

chincaglieria [kinkaʎʎe'ria] *sf* **(a)** *(negozio)* fancy-goods shop. **(b):** ~**e** *sfpl (cianfrusaglie)* fancy goods, knick-knacks.

chinino [ki'nino] *sm* quinine.

chino, a ['kino] *ag:* **a capo** ~, **a testa** ~ a head bent *o* bowed.

chinotto [ki'nɔtto] *sm (bevanda)* type of bitter orange drink.

chioccia, ce ['kjɔttʃa] *sf* broody hen.

chioccio, a, ci, ce ['kjɔttʃo] *ag (voce)* clucking.

chiocciola ['kjɔttʃola] *sf (Zool)* snail; **scala a** ~ spiral staircase.

chiodo ['kjɔdo] *sm* **(a)** *(Tecn)* nail; *(: per lamiere)* rivet; *(da scarpone)* hobnail; *(Alpinismo)* piton; *(di scarpe da calcio)* stud; *(di scarpe da atleta, pneumatico)* spike; **per lui è diventato un** ~ **fisso** it's become a fixation with him; **roba da** ~**i!** it's unbelievable!; ~ **scaccia** ~ *(Proverbio)* one problem drives away another. **(b)** *(Culin)*: ~ **di garofano** clove.

chioma ['kjɔma] *sf (capelli)* head of hair; *(di cavallo)* mane; *(di albero)* foliage; *(di cometa)* tail.

chiosa ['kjɔza] *sf* gloss, note.

chiosare [kjo'zare] *vt* to gloss, annotate.

chiosco, schi ['kjɔsko] *sm* kiosk, stall.

chiostro [ˈkjɔstro] *sm* cloister.

chiromante [kiroˈmante] *sm/f* palmist; *(indovino)* fortune-teller.

chiromanzia [kiromanˈtsia] *sf (vedi* **chiromante***)* palmistry; fortune-telling.

chirurgia [kirurˈdʒia] *sf* surgery.

chirurgico, a, ci, che [kiˈrurdʒiko] *ag* surgical.

chirurgo, ghi *o* **gi** [kiˈrurgo] *sm* surgeon.

chissà [kisˈsa] *av*: ~! who knows!; I wonder!; ~ **chi/come** goodness knows who/how; ~ **che non riesca** you never know, he might succeed.

chitarra [kiˈtarra] *sf* guitar.

chitarrista, i, e [kitarˈrista] *sm/f* guitarist, guitar player.

chiudere [ˈkjudere] **1** *vt* **(a)** to close, shut; *(pugno, lista, caso)* to close; *(busta, lettera)* to seal; *(giacca, camicia)* to do up, fasten; *(gas, rubinetto)* to switch off, turn off; ~ **a chiave** to lock; ~ **al catenaccio** to bolt; ~ **sotto chiave** to lock up; **sta sempre chiusa in casa** she never goes out; ~ **la porta in faccia a qn** *(anche fig)* to slam the door in sb's face; ~ **un occhio su** *(fig)* to turn a blind eye to; ~ **gli occhi davanti a** *(fig)* to close one's eyes to; **non ho chiuso occhio tutta la notte** I didn't sleep a wink all night; **chiudi la bocca!** *o* **il becco!** shut up! **(b)** *(strada)* to block off; *(frontiera)* to close; *(aeroporto, negozio, scuola)* to close (down), shut (down).

2 *vi (porta, ombrello)* to close, shut; *(scuola, negozio)* to close; *(periodo lungo, vacanze)* to finish.

3: ~**rsi** *vr* to close, shut; *(fiore, ferita)* to close up; ~**rsi le dita nella porta** to catch one's fingers in the door; ~**rsi in casa** to shut o.s. up in the house; ~**rsi in se stesso** to withdraw into o.s.

chiunque [kiˈunkwe] **1** *pron rel* whoever, anyone who; ~ **mi chiami, di' che non ci sono** if anyone phones, tell them I'm not in; ~ **sia, fallo entrare** whoever that is, let them in; **di** ~ **sia la colpa, nessuno la passerà liscia** I don't care who is to blame, nobody's going to get away with it; ~ **lo abbia fatto...** whoever did it.... **2** *pron indef* anyone, anybody; ~ **ti direbbe che hai torto** ask anybody and they'd tell you you're wrong; **potrebbe farlo** ~ anyone could do that; **puoi chiederlo a** ~ you can ask anybody; ~ **altro** anyone else, anybody else; **posso farlo meglio di** ~ **altro** I can do it better than anyone else.

chiusa [ˈkjusa] *sf* **(a)** *(terreno circondato)* enclosure. **(b)** *(sbarramento fluviale)* sluice; *(: per navigazione)* lock. **(c)** *(di discorso)* conclusion.

chiuso, a [ˈkjuso] **1** *pp di* **chiudere. 2** *ag* **(a)** *(porta)* shut, closed; *(: a chiave)* locked; *(senza uscita: strada, corridoio)* blocked off; *(rubinetto)* off; '~' *(negozio etc)* 'closed'; '~ **al pubblico'** 'no admittance to the public'. **(b)** *(persona)* uncommunicative; *(mente)* narrow; *(ambiente, club)* exclusive. **(c)** *(concluso: discussione, seduta)* finished; *(iscrizione, lista)* closed. **3** *sm*: **stare al** ~ *(fig)* to be shut up.

chiusura [kjuˈsura] *sf* **(a)** *(fine)* end; *(Comm: definitiva)* closing down; ~ **annuale** annual closure; **orario di** ~ closing time; **termine di** ~ closing date; **discorso di** ~ closing speech. **(b)** *(di porta)* lock; *(di cassaforte)* catch; *(di vestito)* fastening; ~ **lampo®** zip; ~ **ermetica** hermetic seal. **(c)** *(Pol)*: ~ **verso la destra/sinistra** refusal to collaborate with the right/left.

choc [ʃɔk] *sm inv* shock.

ci [tʃi] *(dav lo, la, li, le, ne diventa* **ce***)* **1** *pron pers* **(a)** *(ogg diretto)* us; ~ **hanno visto** they saw us; **ascolta**~ listen to us. **(b)** *(complemento di termine)* (to) us; ~ **dai da mangiare?** will you give us some-

thing to eat?; **ce l'hanno dato** they gave it to us; ~ **dissero di tornare più tardi** they told us to come back later. **(c)** *(con verbi riflessivi, pronominali, reciproci)*: ~ **siamo divertiti** we enjoyed ourselves; ~ **siamo annoiati** we got bored; ~ **vediamo più tardi!** see you later!; ~ **amiamo** we love one another.

2 *pron dimostr*: **non so che far**~ I don't know what to do about it; **che c'entro io?** what have I got to do with it?; ~ **puoi giurare,** ~ **puoi scommettere** you can bet on it; ~ **puoi contare** you can depend on it; ~ **penserò** I'll think about it.

3 *av* **(a)** *(qui)* here; *(lì)* there; **qui non** ~ **ritorno più** I'm not coming back here again; **son qui e** ~ **resto** here I am and here I stay; ~ **andiamo?** shall we go there?; ~ **sei mai stato?** have you ever been there?; ~ **sei?** *(sei pronto)* are you ready?; *(hai capito)* do you follow?; **non** ~ **si sta tutti, non** ~ **stiamo tutti** we won't all fit in. **(b)**: **c'è** there is; ~ **sono** there are; **non c'era nessuno** there was nobody there; **c'è nessuno in casa?** is (there) anybody in?; **c'era una volta...** once upon a time.... **(c)** *(con verbi di moto)*: ~ **passa sopra un ponte** a bridge passes over it; **non** ~ **passa più nessuno per di qua** nobody comes this way anymore; *vedi* **mancare, stare, volere** *etc.*

ciabatta [tʃaˈbatta] *sf* slipper; **trattare qn come una** ~ to treat sb like dirt.

ciabattare [tʃabatˈtare] *vi* to shuffle about (in one's slippers).

ciabattino [tʃabatˈtino] *sm* cobbler.

ciac [tʃak] **1** *escl (camminando sul fango etc)* squelch!; ~, **si gira!** action! **2** *sm (Cine)* clapper board.

cialda [ˈtʃalda] *sf* wafer.

cialtrone [tʃalˈtrone] *sm* good-for-nothing.

ciambella [tʃamˈbella] *sf* **(a)** *(Culin)* ring-shaped cake; **non tutte le** ~ **riescono col buco** *(Proverbio)* things can't be expected to turn out right every time. **(b)** *(oggetto: gen)* ring-shaped object; *(: cuscino)* round cushion; *(: salvagente per bambini)* rubber ring; *(: per dentizione)* teething ring; **a** ~ ring-shaped.

ciambellano [tʃambelˈlano] *sm* chamberlain.

ciancia, ce [ˈtʃantʃa] *sf* gossip, tittle-tattle.

cianciare [tʃanˈtʃare] *vi* to gossip, tittle-tattle.

ciancicare [tʃantʃiˈkare] *vt (parole)* to mumble; *(cibo)* to chew slowly; *(vestito)* to crush.

cianfrusaglia [tʃanfruˈzaʎʎa] *sf* knick-knack; ~**e** bits and pieces.

cianuro [tʃaˈnuro] *sm* cyanide.

ciao [ˈtʃao] *escl (buongiorno)* hello!, hi!; *(arrivederci)* bye-(bye)!, cheerio!

ciarlare [tʃarˈlare] *vi* to chatter; *(peg)* to gossip.

ciarlatano [tʃarlaˈtano] *sm (peg: gen)* charlatan; *(: medico)* quack.

ciarliero, a [tʃarˈljero] *ag* chatty, talkative.

ciarpame [tʃarˈpame] *sm* rubbish, junk.

ciascuno, a [tʃasˈkuno] **1** *ag (dav sm:* **ciascun**+*consonante, vocale,* **ciascuno**+*s impura, gn, pn, ps, x, z; dav sf:* **ciascuna**+*consonante,* **ciascun'**+*vocale) (con valore distributivo)* every, each; *(ogni)* every; **ciascun ragazzo** every *o* each boy; **ciascun uomo nasce libero** every man is born free. **2** *pron indef* **(a)** *(con valore distributivo)* each (one); ~ **di** each (one) *o* every one of; ~ **di noi avrà la sua parte** each of us will have his share; **ci ha dato 10.000 lire (per)** ~ he gave each of us 10,000 lire; **costano 50.000 lire** ~ they cost 50,000 lire each. **(b)** *(tutti)* everyone, everybody; **a** ~ **il suo** to each his own.

cibaria [tʃiˈbarja] *sf* foodstuffs *pl*, provisions *pl*.

cibarsi [tʃi'barsi] *vr*: ~ **di** *(anche fig)* to live on.
cibernetica [tʃiber'nɛtika] *sf* cybernetics *sg*.
cibo ['tʃibo] *sm* food; **~i precotti** ready-cooked food; **son 2 giorni che non tocca** ~ he hasn't eaten for 2 days.
cicala [tʃi'kala] *sf (Zool)* cicada; **~ di mare** squilla.
cicalare [tʃika'lare] *vi* to chatter (away), jabber (away).
cicaleccio [tʃika'lettʃo] *sm (di persone)* chatter, chattering; *(di uccelli)* chirping.
cicalio [tʃika'lio] *sm* chatter, chattering.
cicatrice [tʃika'tritʃe] *sf (anche fig)* scar.
cicatrizzare [tʃikatrid'dzare] *vt, vi,* **~rsi** *vr* to heal.
cicca, che ['tʃikka] *sf* **(a)** *(mozzicone: di sigaretta)* cigarette end, stub; *(: di sigaro)* cigar butt; **non vale una** ~ *(fig)* it's not worth tuppence. **(b)** *(fam: sigaretta)* fag.
cicchetto [tʃik'ketto] *sm* **(a)** *(bicchierino)* drop, nip; **andiamo a farci un** ~ let's go for a jar. **(b)** *(rimprovero)* telling-off, ticking-off.
ciccia ['tʃittʃa] *sf* fat, flab; **avere troppa** ~ to be on the plump side.
ciccione, a [tʃit'tʃone] *sm/f (fam)* fatty.
cicerone [tʃitʃe'rone] *sm (guida turistica)* guide; **fare da** ~ **a qn** to show sb around.
cicisbeo [tʃitʃiz'bɛo] *sm (Storia)* gallant; *(damerino)* dandy.
ciclabile [tʃi'klabile] *ag* suitable for cycling, cycle *attr*.
ciclamino [tʃikla'mino] *sm* cyclamen.
ciclico, a, ci, che ['tʃikliko] *ag* cyclical.
ciclismo [tʃi'klizmo] *sm* cycling.
ciclista, i, e [tʃi'klista] *sm/f* cyclist.
ciclistico, a, ci, che [tʃi'klistiko] *ag* cycle *attr*.
ciclo ['tʃiklo] *sm (gen, Chim, Fis)* cycle; *(di lezioni, conferenze)* series, course; **la malattia deve fare il suo** ~ the illness must run its course.
ciclomotore [tʃiklomo'tore] *sm* moped.
ciclone [tʃi'klone] *sm* cyclone; *(fig)* whirlwind.
ciclonico, a, ci, che [tʃi'kloniko] *ag* cyclonic.
Ciclope [tʃi'klɔpe] *sm (Mitologia)* Cyclops.
ciclopico, a, ci, che [tʃi'klɔpiko] *ag (fig)* gigantic, huge.
ciclopista [tʃiklo'pista] *sf* cycle path, cycle track.
ciclostilare [tʃiklosti'lare] *vt* to cyclostyle.
ciclostile [tʃiklos'tile] *sm* **(a)** *(macchina)* cyclostyle. **(b)** *(foglio)* duplicate copy.
cicogna [tʃi'koɲɲa] *sf* **(a)** *(Zool)* stork. **(b)** *(autotreno)* trailer lorry o truck.
cicoria [tʃi'kɔrja] *sf* chicory.
cicuta [tʃi'kuta] *sf* hemlock.
ciecamente [tʃeka'mente] *av (anche fig)* blindly.
cieco, a, chi, che ['tʃɛko] **1** *ag (anche fig)* blind; **essere** ~ **da un occhio** to be blind in one eye; **alla ~a** *(anche fig)* blindly; **andare alla ~a** to grope along; ~ **come una talpa** as blind as a bat; **essere** ~ **d'amore** to be blind with love; **vicolo** ~ *(anche fig)* blind alley. **2** *sm/f* blind man/woman; **i ~chi** the blind.
cielo ['tʃɛlo] *sm* **(a)** sky; *(letterario)* heavens *pl*; **miniera a** ~ **aperto** opencast mine; **toccare il** ~ **con un dito** *(fig)* to walk on air; **essere al settimo** ~ to be in seventh heaven; **volare nel** ~ **italiano** *(Aer)* to fly in Italian airspace. **(b)** *(Rel)* heaven; **il regno dei** ~**i** the kingdom of heaven; **santo** ~! good heavens!; **per amor del** ~! for heaven's sake!; **voglia il** ~ **che torni presto** I hope to heaven (that) he comes back soon.
cifra ['tʃifra] *sf* **(a)** *(numero)* figure, numeral; **un numero di 5 ~e** a five-figure number; **scrivere un numero in ~e** to write a number in figures. **(b)** *(somma)* figure, sum; **è una** ~ **astronomica** it's an astronomical figure. **(c)**: ~**e** *pl (monogramma)* initials, monogram *sg*. **(d)** *(codice)* code, cipher.
cifrare [tʃi'frare] *vt* **(a)** *(messaggio)* to (put into) code, cipher. **(b)** *(lenzuola, camicie etc)* to embroider initials o a monogram on.
cifrario [tʃi'frarjo] *sm* code book, cipher book.
cifrato, a [tʃi'frato] *ag* **(a)** *(codice)* coded, ciphered. **(b)** *(lenzuola, camicie)* monogrammed, initialled.
ciglio ['tʃiʎʎo] *sm* **(a)** *(pl(f) ~a)* (eye)lash; ~**a finte** false eyelashes; **non ha battuto** ~ *(fig)* he didn't bat an eyelid. **(b)** *(di strada, fossato)* edge, side.
cigno ['tʃiɲɲo] *sm* swan.
cigolare [tʃigo'lare] *vi (porta, ruota)* to squeak; *(parquet)* to creak.
cigolio [tʃigo'lio] *sm (vedi vb)* squeaking; creaking.
Cile ['tʃile] *sm* Chile.
cilecca [tʃi'lekka] *sf*: **far** ~ *(Mil, fig)* to misfire; **le ginocchia mi hanno fatto** ~ my knees gave way.
cileno, a [tʃi'leno] *ag, sm/f* Chilean.
cilicio [tʃi'litʃo] *sm* hair shirt.
ciliegia, gie o ge [tʃi'ljɛdʒa] *sf* cherry.
ciliegio [tʃi'ljɛdʒo] *sm (albero)* cherry (tree); *(legno)* cherry (wood).
cilindrata [tʃilin'drata] *sf (Tecn)* cubic capacity; **macchina di grossa/piccola** ~ a big-engined/small-engined car.
cilindrico, a, ci, che [tʃi'lindriko] *ag* cylindrical.
cilindro [tʃi'lindro] *sm (gen, Tecn, Geom)* cylinder; *(di macchina da scrivere)* roller; *(cappello)* top hat.
cima ['tʃima] *sf* **(a)** *(gen)* top; *(estremità)* end; *(di montagna)* top, summit, peak; *(fig: persona)* genius; **conquistare una** ~ *(Alpinismo)* to conquer a peak; **è una** ~ **in matematica** he's a genius at maths; **in** ~ **a** *(lista, classifica)* at the top of; *(montagna)* at the top of, on the summit of; **da** ~ **a fondo** from top to bottom; **leggere qc da** ~ **a fondo** to read sth from beginning to end. **(b)** *(Naut)* rope, cable. **(c)** *(Bot)* top, head.
cimasa [tʃi'maza] *sf* moulding.
cimelio [tʃi'mɛljo] *sm* relic.
cimentare [tʃimen'tare] **1** *vt (pazienza, persona)* to try, put to the test. **2**: ~**rsi** *vr* **(a)**: ~**rsi in qc** to undertake sth. **(b)**: ~**rsi con qn** to compete with sb.
cimento [tʃi'mento] *sm (prova rischiosa)* trial.
cimice ['tʃimitʃe] *sf* (bed)bug.
cimiero [tʃi'mjɛro] *sm* crest; *(fig: elmo)* helmet.
ciminiera [tʃimi'njɛra] *sf (di fabbrica)* chimney (stack); *(di nave)* funnel.
cimitero [tʃimi'tero] *sm* cemetery, graveyard; ~ **di automobili** scrapyard; **questo posto è un** ~! *(fig)* this place is like a morgue!
cimosa [tʃi'mosa] *sf (Tessitura)* selvage.
cimurro [tʃi'murro] *sm* distemper.
Cina ['tʃina] *sf* China.
cinabro [tʃi'nabro] *sm* cinnabar.
cinciallegra [tʃintʃal'legra] *sf* great tit.
cincillà [tʃintʃil'la] *sm inv* chinchilla.
cincin, cin cin [tʃin'tʃin] *escl* cheers!
cincischiare [tʃintʃis'kjare] *vt (perder tempo)* to mess about, fiddle about.
cine ['tʃine] *sm inv (fam)* cinema; **andare al** ~ to go to the pictures, *(Am)* to go to the movies.
cineamatore [tʃineama'tore] *sm* amateur filmmaker.
cineasta, i, e [tʃine'asta] *sm/f* **(a)** person in the film industry; **è un** ~ he's in films. **(b)** film-maker.
cinecamera [tʃine'kamera] *sf* cine camera.
cineclub [tʃine'klub] *sm inv* film club.
cineforum [tʃine'forum] *sm inv* cinema discussion.
cinegiornale [tʃinedʒor'nale] *sm* newsreel.

cinema ['tʃinema] *sm inv* cinema; **andare al** ~ **to go to the pictures** *o (Am)* movies; **cosa danno al** ~ **stasera?** what's on at the pictures *o (Am)* movies tonight?; **fare del** ~ to be in the film business; **industria/divo del** ~ film industry/star; ~ **muto** silent films; **è stato un vero** ~! *(fig)* it was a real performance!

cinema d'essai [sine'ma dɛ'sɛ] *sm inv (locale)* avant-garde cinema, experimental cinema.

cinematica [tʃine'matika] *sf (Fis)* kinematics *sg.*

cinematografia [tʃinematograˈfia] *sf (arte, tecnica)* cinematography; *(industria)* film-making industry, cinema.

cinematografico, a, ci, che [tʃinemato'grafiko] *ag* **(a)** film *attr*, cinema *attr*; **casa** ~ a film studio, film company; **regista** ~ film director. **(b)** *(fig: stile)* cinematographic.

cinematografo [tʃinema'tɔgrafo] *sm (locale)* cinema, *(Am)* movie theatre; *(arte)* cinema, films.

cineparco, chi [tʃine'parko] *sm* drive-in.

cinepresa [tʃine'presa] *sf* cine camera.

cinerario, a [tʃine'rarjo] *ag:* **urna** ~a funeral urn.

cinereo, a [tʃi'nɛreo] *ag (colore)* ash-grey; *(pallido)* pale, ashen.

cinescopio [tʃines'kɔpjo] *sm (TV)* cathode-ray tube.

cinese [tʃi'nese] **1** *ag* Chinese. **2** *sm/f* Chinese man/woman; **i C~ i** the Chinese. **3** *sm (lingua)* Chinese.

cineseria [tʃinese'ria] *sf* chinoiserie.

cineteca, che [tʃine'tɛka] *sf (collezione)* film collection, film library; *(locale)* film library.

cinetica [tʃi'nɛtika] *sf* kinetics *sg.*

cinetico, a, ci, che [tʃi'netiko] *ag* kinetic.

cingere ['tʃindʒere] *vt* **(a)** *(circondare)* to surround, encircle; ~ **una città di mura** to surround a city with walls; ~ **d'assedio** to besiege, lay siege to. **(b)** *(avvolgere)*: **le cinse la vita con le braccia** he put his arms round her waist; ~**rsi la vita con una corda** to tie a rope round one's waist; ~**rsi la testa con fiori** to wreath one's head with flowers.

cinghia ['tʃingja] *sf (cintura)* belt, strap; *(di portabagagli, zaino etc)* strap; *(Tecn)* belt; ~ **di trasmissione** drive belt; ~ **del ventilatore** fan belt; **tirare la** ~ *(fig)* to tighten one's belt.

cinghiale [tʃin'gjale] *sm (animale)* wild boar; *(pelle)* pigskin.

cingolato, a [tʃingo'lato] *ag (veicolo)* caterpillar *attr.*

cingolo ['tʃingolo] *sm (di veicoli)* caterpillar.

cinguettare [tʃingwet'tare] *vi (uccelli)* to twitter; *(bambini)* to chatter.

cinguettio [tʃingwet'tio] *sm (vedi vb)* twittering; chattering.

cinico, a, ci, che ['tʃiniko] **1** *ag* cynical. **2** *sm/f* cynic.

ciniglia [tʃi'niʎʎa] *sf* chenille.

cinismo [tʃi'nizmo] *sm* cynicism.

cinofilo, a [tʃi'nɔfilo] *sm/f* dog lover.

cinquanta [tʃin'kwanta] *ag inv* fifty; **gli anni** ~ the fifties, the 50s; **cinquantuno** fifty-one.

cinquantenario [tʃinkwante'narjo] *sm* fiftieth anniversary.

cinquantenne [tʃinkwan'tɛnne] **1** *ag* fifty-year-old; **un signore** ~ a man of fifty, a fifty-year-old man. **2** *sm/f* fifty-year-old man/woman; *(sulla cinquantina)* man/woman in his/her fifties.

cinquantennio [tʃinkwan'tɛnnjo] *sm (period of)* fifty years.

cinquantesimo, a [tʃinkwan'tɛzimo] *ag, sm/f, sm* fiftieth.

cinquantina [tʃinkwan'tina] *sf* **(a)**: **una** ~ **(di)** about fifty, fifty-odd, fifty or so; **eravamo una** ~ there were about fifty of us. **(b)** *(età)*: **avere una** ~ **d'anni, essere sulla** ~ *(persona)* to be about fifty, to be in one's fifties; **avere una** ~ **d'anni** *(mobile, casa etc)* to be about fifty years old.

cinque ['tʃinkwe] **1** *ag inv* five; **paragrafo/pagina/capitolo** ~ paragraph/page/chapter five; **i** ~ **settimi della cifra** five-sevenths of the amount; **abito in Via Cavour, numero** ~ I live at number five Via Cavour; **un bambino di** ~ **anni** a child of five; **ha** ~ **anni** he is five; **un biglietto da** ~ **sterline** a five-pound note; **siamo in** ~ there are five of us; **sono Je due meno** ~ it's five to two; **sono arrivati alle** ~ they arrived at five o'clock; **le** ~ **di sera** five o'clock in the evening; ~ **volte su dieci** five times out of ten; **mettersi in fila per** ~ to form rows of five.

2 *sm inv* five; **due più tre fa** ~ two plus three make five; **il** ~ **nel dieci ci sta due volte** five goes into ten twice; **uno sconto del** ~ **per cento** a five percent discount; **abito in Via Cavour** ~ I live at 5 Via Cavour; **arrivare il** ~ **ottobre** to arrive on October 5th; **oggi è il** ~ it's the fifth today; **prendere un** ~ *(Scol)* to get five out of ten; **il** ~ **di fiori** *(Carte)* the five of clubs.

cinquecentesco, a, schi, sche [tʃinkwetʃen-'tesko] *ag* sixteenth century.

cinquecento [tʃinkwe'tʃɛnto] **1** *ag inv* five hundred. **2** *sm inv* five hundred; *(secolo)*: **il C~** the sixteenth century. **3** *sf inv (Aut)* Fiat 500.

cinquemila [tʃinkwe'mila] *ag inv, sm inv* five thousand.

cinquina [tʃin'kwina] *sf (Lotto, Tombola)* set of five winning numbers.

cinta ['tʃinta] *sf (anche:* ~ **muraria)** city walls *pl*; **muro di** ~ *(di giardino etc)* surrounding wall.

cintare [tʃin'tare] *vt* to enclose.

cinto, a ['tʃinto] **1** *pp di* cingere. **2** *sm:* ~ **erniario** truss.

cintola ['tʃintola] *sf (cintura)* belt; *(vita)* waist.

cintura [tʃin'tura] *sf* **(a)** belt; ~ **di sicurezza** *(Aut, Aer)* seat belt; **allacciare la** ~ **(di sicurezza)** to fasten one's seat belt; ~ **industriale** *(Urbanistica)* industrial belt. **(b)** *(vita)* waist.

cinturino [tʃintu'rino] *sm* strap; ~ **dell'orologio** watch strap.

cinturone [tʃintu'rone] *sm* gun belt.

ciò [tʃɔ] *pron dimostr* **(a)** *(questa cosa)* this; *(quella cosa)* that; ~ **è vero** this *(o* that) is true; **di** ~ **parleremo più tardi** we'll talk about this *(o* that) later; **con tutto** ~ for all that, in spite of everything; **e con** ~ **ne me ne vado!** and now I'm off!; **e con** ~ **ha concluso il suo discorso** and with that he finished his speech; **e con** ~? so what?; **oltre a** ~ besides that, furthermore; **nonostante** ~, **e con** ~ **nonostante** nevertheless, in spite of that; **detto** ~... having said that.... **(b)**: ~ **che** what; ~ **che voglio dirti è importante** what I want to tell you is important; **gli sarò sempre grato per** ~ **che ha fatto** I'll always be grateful for what he's done; **questo è tutto** ~ **che hai fatto** this is all (that) you've done.

ciocca, che ['tʃɔkka] *sf* lock; **perde i capelli a** ~che her hair is coming out in handfuls.

ciocco, chi ['tʃɔkko] *sm* log.

cioccolata [tʃokko'lata] *sm* chocolate; **una tavoletta di** ~ a bar of chocolate; ~ **al latte/fondente** milk/plain chocolate; **una (tazza di)** ~ **calda** a (cup of) hot chocolate.

cioccolatino [tʃokkola'tino] *sm* chocolate; **una scatola di** ~**i** a box of chocolates.

cioccolato [tʃokko'lato] *sm* chocolate.

cioè [tʃo'ɛ] *av* that is (to say); **vengo tra poco —** ~**?** I'll come soon — what do you mean by soon?;

questo è il mio — ~ no — il tuo! this is mine — or rather, I mean yours!

ciondolare [tʃondo'lare] **1** *vi* to dangle; *(fig: bighellonare)* to hang around, loaf about; **l'ubriaco camminava ciondolando** the drunk swayed from side to side as he walked. **2** *vt (far dondolare)* to dangle, swing.

ciondolo ['tʃondolo] *sm* pendant; **~ portafortuna** charm.

ciondoloni [tʃondo'loni] *av*: **con le braccia/gambe ~** with arms/legs dangling.

ciononostante [tʃononos'tante] *av* nonetheless, nevertheless.

ciotola ['tʃotola] *sf* bowl.

ciottolo ['tʃottolo] *sm* pebble.

cipiglio [tʃi'piʎʎo] *sm* frown.

cipolla [tʃi'polla] *sf* **(a)** onion; **mangiare pane e ~** *(fig)* to live on bread and dripping. **(b)** *(Med)* bunion. **(c)** *(scherz: orologio)* turnip.

cippo ['tʃippo] *sm (celebrativo)* memorial stone; *(di confine)* boundary stone.

cipresso [tʃi'presso] *sm* cypress.

cipria ['tʃiprja] *sf* face powder; **~ compatta/in polvere** solid/loose powder.

cipriota, i, e [tʃipri'ɔta] **1** *ag* Cypriot; **la questione ~** the Cyprus question. **2** *sm/f* Cypriot.

Cipro ['tʃipro] *sm* Cyprus.

circa ['tʃirka] **1** *prep*: **~ (a)** regarding, concerning; **~ agli accordi presi in precedenza** with reference to previous agreements. **2** *av (quasi)* about, approximately; **erano ~ le 3 quando è partita, è partita alle 3 ~** she left at about 3; **mancano 20 minuti ~ all'arrivo del treno** the train is due in about 20 minutes.

circo, chi ['tʃirko] *sm* **(a)** *(Storia romana)* circus; **~ (equestre)** *(spettacolo)* circus. **(b)** *(Geog)* cirque, corrie.

circolante [tʃirko'lante] *ag* circulating.

circolare[1] [tʃirko'lare] *vi (gen, Anat, Econ)* to circulate; *(persone)* to go about; *(notizie, idee)* to circulate, go about; **~!** move along!; **~ in città diventa sempre più difficile** *(Aut)* driving in town is getting more and more difficult; **i camion non possono ~ di domenica** lorries are not allowed on the roads on Sundays; **circola voce che...** there is a rumour going about that... .

circolare[2] [tʃirko'lare] **1** *ag* circular; **assegno ~** banker's draft. **2** *sf* **(a)** *(lettera)* circular (letter). **(b)** *(linea di autobus)* circle line.

circolatorio, a [tʃirkola'tɔrjo] *ag* circulatory.

circolazione [tʃirkolat'tsjone] *sf (di sangue, aria, moneta)* circulation; *(di merci, veicoli)* movement; **mettere in ~** *(moneta etc)* to put into circulation; *(fig: voce, notizie)* to spread, put about; **togliere dalla ~** *(moneta etc)* to withdraw from circulation; *(fig: persona)* to remove; **~ monetaria** money in circulation; **~ stradale** *(Aut)* traffic; **tassa di ~** *(Aut)* road tax; **libretto di ~** *(Aut)* log book, registration book.

circolo ['tʃirkolo] *sm* **(a)** *(gen, Geog, Mat)* circle; **entrare in ~** *(Anat)* to enter the bloodstream; **~ vizioso** vicious circle. **(b)** *(club)* club; **~ ufficiali** officers' club; **~ letterario** literary circle *o* society.

circoncidere [tʃirkon'tʃidere] *vt* to circumcize.

circoncisione [tʃirkontʃi'zjone] *sf* circumcision.

circonciso, a [tʃirkon'tʃizo] *pp di* circoncidere.

circondare [tʃirkon'dare] **1** *vt (gen)* to surround; *(racchiudere)* to encircle; *(: con uno steccato)* to enclose; **~ qn di cure** to give sb the best of attention; **~ qn di attenzioni** to be very attentive towards sb; **è sempre stato circondato d'affetto** he has always been surrounded by affection. **2:**

~rsi *vr*: **~rsi di** to surround o.s. with.

circondariale [tʃirkonda'rjale] *ag*: **casa di pena ~** district prison.

circondario [tʃirkon'darjo] *sm* **(a)** *(Dir)* administrative district. **(b)** *(zona circostante)* neighbourhood.

circonferenza [tʃirkonfe'rentsa] *sf* circumference; **~ fianchi/vita** hip/waist measurement.

circonflesso, a [tʃirkon'flesso] *ag*: **accento ~** circumflex accent.

circonlocuzione [tʃirkonlokut'tsjone] *sf* circumlocution.

circonvallazione [tʃirkonvallat'tsjone] *sf* ring road.

circoscritto, a [tʃirkos'kritto] **1** *pp di* circoscrivere. **2** *ag (zona)* limited; *(fenomeno, contagio)* localized.

circoscrivere [tʃirkos'krivere] *vt (Geom)* to circumscribe; *(zona)* to mark out; *(incendio, contagio)* to contain, confine.

circoscrizionale [tʃirkoskrittsjo'nale] *ag* area *attr*, district *attr*.

circoscrizione [tʃirkoskrit'tsjone] *sf (Amm)* district, area; **~ elettorale** constituency.

circospetto, a [tʃirkos'petto] *ag* circumspect, cautious; **con fare ~** with a suspicious air.

circospezione [tʃirkospet'tsjone] *sf* circumspection, prudence, caution.

circostante [tʃirkos'tante] *ag (territorio)* surrounding; *(persone)* in the vicinity.

circostanza [tʃirkos'tantsa] *sf (occasione)* occasion; *(situazione)*: **~e** *pl* circumstances; **in questa ~** on this occasion; **date le ~e** in view of *o* under the circumstances; **~e aggravanti/attenuanti** *(Dir)* aggravating/mitigating circumstances; **parole di ~** words suited to the occasion.

circostanziato, a [tʃirkoskan'tsjato] *ag* detailed.

circuire [tʃirku'ire] *vt (fig)* to fool, take in.

circuito [tʃir'kuito] *sm* **(a)** *(Elettr)* circuit; **andare in** *o* **fare corto ~** to short-circuit; **~ chiuso/integrato** closed/integrated circuit. **(b)** *(Aut)* track, circuit; **~ di gara** racing track; **~ di prova** test circuit. **(c)** *(sale cinematografiche)* circuit.

circumnavigare [tʃirkumnavi'gare] *vt* to circumnavigate.

circumnavigazione [tʃirkumnavigat'tsjone] *sf* circumnavigation.

cirillico, a, ci, che [tʃi'rilliko] *ag* Cyrillic.

cirro ['tʃirro] *sm (Meteor)* cirrus.

cirrosi [tʃir'rozi] *sf (Med)* cirrhosis.

cisalpino, a [tʃizal'pino] *ag* cisalpine.

C.I.S.L. *abbr f* (= Confederazione Italiana Sindacati Lavoratori) Italian Trades Union Organization.

cisposo, a [tʃis'pozo] *ag*: **avere gli occhi ~i** to be bleary-eyed.

ciste ['tʃiste] *sf* = cisti.

cisterna [tʃis'terna] **1** *sf* tank. **2** *ag inv*: **nave ~** tanker; **camion ~** tanker (lorry).

cisti ['tʃisti] *sf inv* cyst.

cistifellea [tʃisti'fellea] *sf (Anat)* gall bladder.

cistite [tʃis'tite] *sf* cystitis.

C.I.T. [tʃit] *abbr f di* Compagnia Italiana del Turismo.

citare [tʃi'tare] *vt* **(a)** *(Dir)* to summon; *(: testimone)* to subpoena; **~ qn per danni** to sue sb. **(b)** *(passo, testo)* to quote, cite; **~ qn/qc a modello** *o* **ad esempio** to quote sb/sth as an example.

citazione [tʃitat'tsjone] *sf* **(a)** *(Dir: vedi vb)* summons *sg*; subpoena. **(b)** *(di testo)* quotation, citation. **(c)** *(menzione)* citation; **~ all'ordine del giorno** *(Mil)* mention in dispatches.

citofonare [tʃitofo'nare] *vi* to call on the entry phone.

citofono [tʃi'tɔfono] *sm (di appartamento)* entry phone; *(in uffici)* intercom.

citologico, a, ci, che [tʃito'lɔdʒiko] *ag:* **esame ~** test for detection of cancerous cells.

citrato [tʃi'trato] *sm* citrate; *(anche:* **~ di magnesia effervescente)** ≃ milk of magnesia.

citrico, a, ci, che ['tʃitriko] *ag* citric.

citrullo, a [tʃi'trullo] *sm/f (fam)* half-wit.

città [tʃit'ta] *sf inv (gen)* town; *(grande)* city; **abitare in ~** to live in town *(o* in the city); **andare in ~** to go to *o* into town; **vita di ~** town *(o* city) life; **la ~ vecchia/nuova** the old/new (part of) town; **~ giardino** garden city; **~ di mare/di provincia** seaside/provincial town; **~ universitaria** university town; **~ satellite** satellite town.

cittadella [tʃitta'dɛlla] *sf* citadel, stronghold.

cittadinanza [tʃittadi'nantsa] *sf* **(a)** *(città, popolazione)* town, citizens *pl;* **tutta la ~** the whole town. **(b)** *(Dir)* citizenship; **avere/prendere la ~ britannica** to have/take British citizenship.

cittadino, a [tʃitta'dino] **1** *ag (vie, popolazione, vita)* town *attr,* city *attr.* **2** *sm/f (non campagnolo)* townsman, city dweller; *privato* ~ private citizen; **~ britannico** British subject *o* citizen.

ciuccio ['tʃuttʃo] *sm (fam)* comforter, dummy, *(Am)* pacifier.

ciuco, a, chi, che ['tʃuko] *sm/f* ass; *(fig: persona)* ass, fool.

ciuffo ['tʃuffo] *sm (gen)* tuft; *(di prezzemolo etc)* bunch; *(di capelli):* **porta il ~ di lato** she wears her fringe to the side.

ciurma ['tʃurma] *sf (di nave)* crew.

ciurmaglia [tʃur'maʎʎa] *sf* mob, rabble.

civetta [tʃi'vetta] **1** *sf* owl; *(fig: donna)* flirt, coquette; **fare la ~ con qn** to flirt with sb. **2** *ag inv:* **auto/nave ~** decoy car/ship.

civettare [tʃivet'tare] *vt* to flirt.

civetteria [tʃivette'ria] *sf* coquetry, coquettishness.

civettuolo, a [tʃivet'twɔlo] *ag* flirtatious; **un cappellino ~** a pert little hat.

civico, a, ci, che ['tʃiviko] *ag* **(a)** *(museo)* town *attr,* municipal; **centro ~** civic centre; **guardia ~a** (town) policeman. **(b)** *(dovere)* civic; **senso ~** public spirit; **educazione ~a** civics *sg.*

civile [tʃi'vile] **1** *ag* **(a)** civil; **Diritto ~** Civil Law; **diritti ~i** civil rights; **convivenza ~** life in society; **stato ~** marital status. **(b)** *(non militare)* civilian; **abiti ~i** civvies. **(c)** *(civilizzato)* civilized; *(educato)* polite, civil. **2** *sm* private citizen, civilian.

civilista, i, e [tʃivi'lista] *sm/f (avvocato)* civil lawyer; *(studioso)* expert in civil law.

civilizzare [tʃivilid'dzare] **1** *vt (paese, popolo)* to civilize. **2: ~rsi** *vr (fig)* to become civilized, become more refined.

civilizzatore, trice [tʃiviliddza'tore] **1** *ag* civilizing. **2** *sm/f* civilizer.

civilizzazione [tʃiviliddzat'tsjone] *sf* civilization.

civiltà [tʃivil'ta] *sf inv* **(a)** civilization; **una società con un alto grado di ~** a highly civilized society. **(b)** *(gentilezza, educazione)* courtesy, civility; **con ~** in a civilized manner.

civismo [tʃi'vizmo] *sm* public-spiritedness.

clacson ['klakson] *sm inv (Aut)* horn, hooter; **suonare il ~** to sound the horn.

clamore [kla'more] *sm* din, clamour; *(fig: scalpore):* **suscitare** *o* **destare ~** to cause a sensation.

clamoroso, a [klamo'roso] *ag (gen: applausi, sconfitta)* resounding; *(notizia, processo)* sensational.

clan [klan] *sm inv* clan; *(fig: gruppo)* team; *(: di malviventi)* gang.

clandestinità [klandesti'ta] *sf (di attività)* secret nature; **vivere nella ~** to live in hiding; *(ricercato politico)* to live underground.

clandestino, a [klandes'tino] **1** *ag (illecito)* illicit; *(segreto: matrimonio, incontro)* clandestine, secret; *(: movimento, radio etc)* underground *attr.* **2** *sm/f (anche:* **passeggero ~)** stowaway.

claque [klak] *sf inv* claque.

clarinetto [klari'netto] *sm* clarinet.

clarinista, i, e [klari'nista] *sm/f* clarinet player, clarinettist.

clarino [kla'rino] *sm* clarinet.

classe ['klasse] *sf* **(a)** *(gen, fig)* class; **lotta di ~** class struggle; **~ di leva 1958** *(Mil)* class of 1958; **viaggiare in prima/seconda ~** to travel first/second class; **~ turistica** *(Aer)* economy class; **un albergo di prima ~** a first-class hotel; **una donna di (gran) ~** a woman with class. **(b)** *(Scol)* class; *(: aula)* classroom; **compagno di ~** schoolmate; **che ~ fai quest'anno?** what class are you in this year?

classicheggiante [klassiked'dʒante] *ag* in the classical style.

classicismo [klassi'tʃizmo] *sm* classicism.

classicista, i, e [klassi'tʃista] *sm/f* classicist.

classicità [klassitʃi'ta] *sf* **(a)** *(di opera artistica, letteraria)* classical nature. **(b)** *(mondo greco, latino)* classical antiquity.

classico, a, ci, che ['klassiko] **1** *ag* **(a)** *(arte, letteratura, civiltà)* classical; **studi ~ci** classical studies; **danza ~a** ballet dancing; **musica ~a** classical music. **(b)** *(moda, risposta, esempio)* classic; **un film ~** a classic film; **~!** that's typical! **2** *sm* **(a)** *(autore antico)* classical author; *(opera famosa)* classic. **(b)** *(anche:* **liceo ~)** secondary school with emphasis on the humanities.

classifica, che [klas'sifika] *sf (di gara sportiva)* placings *pl;* *(di concorso, esame)* list; *(di dischi)* charts *pl,* hit parade; **essere primo in ~** to be placed first, come first; *(disco)* to be number one (in the charts); **~ finale** final results *pl.*

classificare [klassifi'kare] **1** *vt* to classify. **2: ~rsi** *vr (Sport)* to be placed; **~rsi primo/secondo** to be placed first/second.

classificatore [klassifika'tore] *sm (cartella)* loose-leaf file; *(mobile)* filing cabinet.

classificazione [klassifikat'tsjone] *sf* classification.

classismo [klas'sizmo] *sm* class consciousness.

classista, i, e [klas'sista] **1** *ag* class-conscious. **2** *sm/f* class-conscious person.

classistico, a, ci, che [klas'sistiko] *ag (politica)* class *attr.*

claudicante [klaudi'kante] *ag (zoppo)* lame; *(fig: prosa)* halting.

claunesco, a, schi, sche [klau'nesko] *ag (aspetto, espressione)* clownish.

clausola ['klauzola] *sf* clause.

claustrofobia [klaustrofo'bia] *sf* claustrophobia.

clausura [klau'zura] *sf (Rel):* **monaca di ~** nun belonging to an enclosed order; **fare una vita di ~** *(fig)* to lead a cloistered life.

clava ['klava] *sf (arma primitiva)* club; *(attrezzo da ginnastica)* Indian club.

clavicembalo [klavi'tʃembalo] *sm* harpsichord.

clavicola [kla'vikola] *sf* collarbone.

clavicordo [klavi'kɔrdo] *sm* clavichord.

clemente [kle'mente] *ag (persona)* lenient; *(tempo, stagione)* mild.

clemenza [kle'mentsa] *sf (vedi ag)* leniency; mildness.

cleptomane [klep'tɔmane] *sm/f* kleptomaniac.

cleptomania [kleptoma'nia] *sf* kleptomania.

clergyman ['klɔ:dʒimən] *sm inv* clergyman's suit.

clericale [kleri'kale] **1** *ag* clerical; **potere** ~ power of the clergy. **2** *sm/f* clericalist, church supporter.

clero ['klɛro] *sm* clergy.

clessidra [kles'sidra] *sf (a sabbia)* hourglass; *(ad acqua)* water clock.

cliché [kli'ʃe] *sm inv (Tip)* plate; *(fig)* cliché.

cliente [kli'ɛnte] *sm/f (gen)* customer; *(di albergo)* guest; *(di professionista)* client; ~ **abituale/occasionale** regular/occasional customer; **sono un ~ fisso di quel bar** I'm a regular at that bar.

clientela [klien'tela] *sf (di negozio)* customers *pl*; *(di professionista)* clients *pl*; *(di sartoria etc)* clientele.

clientelismo [kliente'lizmo] *sm*: ~ **politico** political nepotism.

clima, i ['klima] *sm (anche fig)* climate; **c'è un ~ piuttosto teso** there's a rather tense atmosphere.

climaterio [klima'tɛrjo] *sm* climacteric.

climatico, a, ci, che [kli'matiko] *ag* climatic; **stazione** ~a health resort.

clinica, che ['klinika] *sf (a) (Med: disciplina):* ~ **medica/chirurgica** clinical medicine/surgery. **(b)** *(settore dell'ospedale)* clinic; *(ospedale privato)* clinic, nursing home.

clinico, a, ci, che ['kliniko] **1** *ag (medico, esame)* clinical; **quadro** ~ anamnesis; **avere l'occhio** ~ *(fig)* to have an expert eye. **2** *sm (medico)* clinician; *(docente)* professor of clinical medicine.

clip [klip] *sf inv (per foglio)* paper clip; *(di orecchino, abito)* clip; **orecchini a** ~ clip-on earrings.

clistere [klis'tɛre] *sm (Med)* enema; *(: apparecchio)* device used to give an enema.

clitoride [kli'tɔride] *sm o f (Anat)* clitoris.

cloaca, che [klo'aka] *sf (fogna)* sewer; *(pozzo nero)* cesspool, cesspit.

cloche [klɔʃ] *sf inv (Aer)* control stick, joystick; **cambio a** ~ *(Aut)* floor-mounted gear shift; **cappello a** ~ cloche hat.

cloridrico, a, ci, che [klo'ridriko] *ag* hydrochloric.

cloro ['klɔro] *sm* chlorine.

clorofilla [kloro'filla] *sf* chlorophyl.

cloroformio [kloro'fɔrmjo] *sm* chloroform.

cloruro [klo'ruro] *sm* chloride; ~ **di sodio** sodium chloride.

clou [klu] *sm inv*: **il ~ della serata** the highlight of the evening.

cm *abbr (= centimetro)* cm.

c.m. *abbr di* **corrente mese.**

coabitare [koabi'tare] *vi* to share a flat *(o* house).

coabitazione [koabitat'tsjone] *sf* sharing a flat *(o* house).

coadiutore [koadju'tore] *sm* assistant.

coadiuvare [koadju'vare] *vt*: ~ **(con) qn in qc** to cooperate with sb on sth.

coagulante [koagu'lante] **1** *ag* coagulative. **2** *sm* coagulant.

coagulare [koagu'lare] *vt*, ~**rsi** *vr (sangue)* to coagulate, clot; *(latte)* to curdle.

coagulazione [koagulat'tsjone] *sf (vedi vb)* coagulation, clotting; curdling.

coagulo [ko'agulo] *sm (di sangue)* clot; *(di latte)* curd.

coalizione [koalit'tsjone] *sf* coalition; **governo di** ~ coalition government.

coalizzare [koalid'dzare] **1** *vt* to unite in a coalition. **2** ~**rsi** *vr* to form a coalition.

coartare [koar'tare] *vt*: ~ **qn a fare qc** to coerce sb into doing sth.

coatto, a [ko'atto] *ag*: **condannare al domicilio** ~ to place under house arrest.

coautore, trice [koau'tore] *sm/f* co-author.

cobalto [ko'balto] *sm* cobalt.

cobaltoterapia [kobaltotera'pia] *sf (Med)* cobalt treatment, cobalt therapy.

cobra ['kɔbra] *sm inv* cobra.

coca[1] ['kɔka] *sf (Bot)* coca.

coca[2] ['kɔka] *sf abbr di* **Coca cola.**

Coca cola ['kɔka 'kɔla] *sf* ® Coca Cola ®, Coke ®.

cocaina [koka'ina] *sf* cocaine, coke *(fam)*.

cocainomane [kokai'nɔmane] *sm/f* cocaine addict.

cocca, che ['kɔkka] *sf (di freccia)* (arrow) notch.

coccarda [kok'karda] *sf* cockade.

cocchiere [kok'kjɛre] *sm* coachman.

cocchio ['kɔkkjo] *sm (carrozza)* coach; *(biga)* chariot.

coccige [kot'tʃidʒe] *sm* coccyx.

coccinella [kottʃi'nɛlla] *sf* ladybird.

cocciniglia [kottʃi'niʎʎa] *sf (Zool)* cochineal; **rosso di** ~ cochineal.

coccio ['kɔttʃo] *sm* **(a)** earthenware; **un vaso di** ~ an earthenware pot. **(b)** *(frammento)* fragment (of pottery), (broken) piece; **chi rompe paga e i cocci sono suoi** *(Proverbio)* any damage must be paid for.

cocciutaggine [kottʃu'taddʒine] *sf* stubbornness, pig-headedness.

cocciuto, a [kot'tʃuto] *ag* stubborn, pig-headed.

cocco[1]**, chi** ['kɔkko] *sm* coconut palm; **noce di** ~ coconut; **latte di** ~ coconut milk.

cocco[2]**, chi** ['kɔkko] *sm (batterio)* coccus.

cocco[3]**, a, chi, che** ['kɔkko] *sm/f (fam)* love; **è il ~ della mamma** he's mummy's darling.

coccodrillo [kokko'drillo] *sm* crocodile; **lacrime di** ~ *(fig)* crocodile tears.

coccolare [kokko'lare] **1** *vt* to cuddle. **2**: ~**rsi** *vr (uso reciproco)* to cuddle one another.

cocente [ko'tʃɛnte] *ag (sole)* burning, scorching; *(fig: dolore, rimorso)* deep, burning.

cocker ['kɔkə] *sm inv* cocker (spaniel).

cocktail ['kɔkteil] *sm inv* cocktail; *(festa)* cocktail party.

cocomero [ko'komero] *sm* watermelon.

cocuzzolo [ko'kuttsolo] *sm* summit, top; *(della testa)* crown, top (of the head).

coda ['koda] *sf* **(a)** tail; ~ **di cavallo** *(di capelli)* ponytail; **vettura/fanale di** ~ rear coach/light; **in** ~ **a** *(veicolo, treno)* at the rear of; *(processione)* at the tail end of; **con la** ~ **fra le gambe** *(fig)* with one's tail between one's legs; **avere la** ~ **di paglia** *(fig)* to have a guilty conscience; **guardare con la** ~ **dell'occhio** to look out of the corner of one's eye; **incastro a** ~ **di rondine** dovetail joint. **(b)** *(fila)* queue; **fare la** ~, **mettersi in** ~ to queue (up). **(c)** *(Zool):* ~ **di rospo** angler fish.

codardia [kodar'dia] *sf* cowardice.

codardo, a [ko'dardo] *ag, sm/f* coward.

codazzo [ko'dattso] *sm* throng.

codesto, a [ko'desto] *ag, pron dimostr (poet, Tosc)* this; that.

codice ['kɔditʃe] *sm* **(a)** code; **messaggio in** ~ message in code, coded message; ~ **civile/penale** civil/penal code; ~ **stradale** highway code; ~ **d'avviamento postale** *(abbr* **C.A.P.)** postal code, *(Am)* zip code. **(b)** *(manoscritto antico)* codex.

codicillo [kodi'tʃillo] *sm* codicil.

codifica [ko'difika] *sf* codification.

codificare [kodifi'kare] *vt (Dir)* to codify; *(informazioni, segreti, dati)* to encode.

codificazione [kodifikat'tsjone] *sf (vedi vb)* codification; encoding.

codino[1] [ko'dino] *sm (treccia)* pigtail.

codino², **a** [ko'dino] **1** *ag* reactionary. **2** *sm/f* (*fig: persona*) reactionary.

coeditore [koedi'tore] *sm* co-publisher.

coedizione [koedit'tsjone] *sf* co-edition.

coefficiente [koeffi'tʃɛnte] *sm* coefficient.

coercibile [koer'tʃibile] *ag* coercible; (*Fis*) compressible.

coercitivo, **a** [koertʃi'tivo] *ag* coercive.

coercizione [koertʃit'tsjone] *sf* coercion.

coerente [koe'rɛnte] *ag* (*Geol*) coherent; (*fig: pensiero, azione*) consistent, coherent.

coerenza [koe'rɛntsa] *sf* (*vedi ag*) coherence; consistency.

coesione [koe'zjone] *sf* cohesion.

coesistente [koezis'tɛnte] *ag* coexistent.

coesistenza [koezis'tɛntsa] *sf* coexistence.

coesistere [koe'zistere] *vi* (*aus essere*) to coexist.

coesistito, **a** [koezis'tito] *pp di* **coesistere**.

coesivo, **a** [koe'sivo] *ag* cohesive.

coetaneo, **a** [koe'taneo] **1** *ag* (of) the same age; **essere ~ di qn** to be the same age as sb. **2** *sm/f* contemporary; **preferisco la compagnia dei miei ~i** I prefer the company of people my own age.

coevo, **a** [ko'ɛvo] *ag* contemporary.

cofanetto [kofa'netto] *sm* casket; **~ dei gioielli** jewel case.

cofano ['kɔfano] *sm* (**a**) coffer. (**b**) (*Aut*) bonnet, (*Am*) hood.

coffa ['kɔffa] *sf* (*Naut*) top.

cogitabondo, **a** [kodʒita'bondo] *ag* thoughtful, deep in thought.

cogli ['koʎʎi] *prep + art vedi* **con**.

cogliere ['kɔʎʎere] *vt* (**a**) (*fiori, frutta*) to pick. (**b**) (*fig: afferrare*) to grasp, seize, take; **~ il significato di qc** to grasp the meaning of sth; **~ l'occasione (per fare)** to take the opportunity (to do); **ha colto l'occasione buona** he chose the right moment; **~ nel segno** (*fig*) to hit the nail on the head. (**c**) (*sorprendere*) to catch; **~ sul fatto/alla sprovvista** to catch red-handed/unprepared; **~ qn in fallo** to catch sb out.

coglione [koʎ'ʎone] *sm* (*fam!: testicolo*): **~i** balls(!); (: *fig: persona sciocca*) burk, twit; **rompere i coglioni a qn** to get on sb's tits(!).

cognac [kɔ'ɲak] *sm inv* cognac.

cognato, **a** [koɲ'ɲato] *sm/f* brother-/sister-in-law.

cognizione [koɲɲit'tsjone] *sf* (*conoscenza*) knowledge; (*Dir*) cognizance; (*Filosofia*) cognition; **con ~ di causa** with full knowledge of the facts.

cognome [koɲ'ɲome] *sm* surname.

coi ['koi] *prep + art vedi* **con**.

coincidenza [kointʃi'dɛntsa] *sf* (**a**) coincidence. (**b**) (*Ferr*) connection.

coincidere [koin'tʃidere] *vi* to coincide.

coinciso, **a** [koin'tʃizo] *pp di* **coincidere**.

coinquilino [koinkwi'lino] *sm* fellow tenant.

cointeressenza [kointeres'sɛntsa] *sf* (*Comm*): **avere una ~ in qc** to own shares in sth; **~ dei lavoratori** profit-sharing.

coinvolgere [koin'vɔldʒere] *vt* to involve, implicate; **~ qn in qc** to involve sb in sth.

coinvolto, **a** [koin'volto] *pp di* **coinvolgere**.

coito ['kɔito] *sm* coitus.

coke ['kouk] *sm inv*: (**carbone**) **~** coke.

col [kol] *prep + art vedi* **con**.

colà [ko'la] *av* there.

colabrodo [kola'brɔdo] *sm inv* colander, strainer.

colapasta [kola'pasta] *sm inv* colander.

colare [ko'lare] **1** *vt* (**a**) (*pasta*) to strain. (**b**) (*metalli*) to cast. **2** *vi* (*aus essere*) (**a**) (*cadere a gocce*) to drip; (*cera, formaggio*) to run; **il sudore gli colava dalla fronte** sweat dripped from his

brow; **mi cola il naso** my nose is running; **mi cola il sangue dal naso** my nose is bleeding. (**b**) (*nave*): **~ a picco** to sink straight to the bottom.

colata [ko'lata] *sf* (*di metallo fuso*) casting; (*di lava*) flow.

colazione [kolat'tsjone] *sf* (*anche*: **prima ~**) breakfast; (*anche*: **seconda ~**) lunch; **fare ~** to have breakfast (*o* lunch); **~ all'inglese** English *o* full breakfast.

colbacco, chi [kol'bakko] *sm* (*Mil*) busby; (*da donna, uomo*) fur hat.

colei [ko'lɛi] *pron dimostr* (*sog*) she; (*complemento*) her; **~ che** the woman who, the one who.

coleotteri [kole'ɔtteri] *smpl* coleoptera *pl*.

colera [ko'lɛra] *sm inv* cholera.

colesterolo [koleste'rɔlo] *sm* cholesterol.

colf [kɔlf] *sf abbr di* **collaboratrice familiare**.

colibrì [koli'bri] *sm* hummingbird.

colica ['kɔlika] *sf* colic.

colino [ko'lino] *sm* strainer; **~ per il tè** tea strainer.

colite [ko'lite] *sf* (*Med*) colitis.

colla¹ ['kɔlla] *sf* glue; **~ di farina** paste; **~ di pesce** fish glue, isinglass.

colla² ['kɔlla] *prep + art vedi* **con**.

collaborare [kollabo'rare] *vi*: **~ (a)** to contribute (to), collaborate (on); (*Pol*) to collaborate.

collaboratore, trice [kollabora'tore] *sm/f* (*vedi vb*) contributor; collaborator; **~ di un giornale** contributor to a newspaper; **~ esterno** freelance; **collaboratrice familiare** home help.

collaborazione [kollaborat'tsjone] *sf* (*vedi vb*) contribution; collaboration; **in ~ con** in collaboration with.

collana [kol'lana] *sf* (**a**) necklace; **~ di fiori** garland of flowers. (**b**) (*raccolta di libri, scritti*) collection, series *sg*.

collant [kɔ'lã] *sm inv* tights *pl*.

collare [kol'lare] *sm* collar.

collarino [kolla'rino] *sm* (*Rel*) clerical collar.

collasso [kol'lasso] *sm* collapse; **un ~ cardiaco** heart failure.

collaterale [kollate'rale] *ag* collateral.

collaudare [kollau'dare] *vt* to test.

collaudatore, trice [kollauda'tore] *sm/f* tester; **~ di aeroplani/automobili** test pilot/driver.

collaudo [kol'laudo] *sm* (*azione*) testing; (*prova*) test; **fare il ~ di qc** to test sth; **volo/giro di ~** test flight/run.

collazionare [kollattsjo'nare] *vt* to collate.

collazione [kollat'tsjone] *sf* collation.

colle¹ ['kɔlle] *sm* (*collina*) hill; (*valico*) pass.

colle² ['kolle] *prep + art vedi* **con**.

collega, ghi, ghe [kol'lɛga] *sm/f* colleague.

collegamento [kollega'mento] *sm* (**a**) (*gen, fig: legame*) connection. (**b**) (*Mil*) liaison; **ufficiale di ~** liaison officer. (**c**) (*Radio*) link(-up); **siamo ora in ~ con...** we are now linked to....

collegare [kolle'gare] **1** *vt* to connect, join; (*città, zone*) to join, link; (*Elettr*) to connect (up). **2**: **~rsi** *vr* to join, meet.

collegiale [kolle'dʒale] **1** (*riunione, decisione*) collective; (*Scol*) boarding school *attr*. **2** *sm/f* boarder; (*fig: persona timida e inesperta*) schoolboy/girl.

collegio [kol'lɛdʒo] *sm* (**a**) (*ordine di professionisti, Rel*) college. (**b**) (*convitto*) boarding school; **~ militare** military college. (**c**) (*Amm*): **~ elettorale** constituency.

collera ['kɔllera] *sf* anger; **andare in ~** to get angry; **essere in ~ con qn** to be angry with sb.

collerico, a, ci, che [kol'lɛriko] *ag* (*persona*)

hot-tempered; *(parole)* angry; *(temperamento)* choleric.

colletta [kol'lɛtta] *sf* collection.

collettivismo [kolletti'vizmo] *sm* collectivism.

collettività [kollettivi'ta] *sf* community.

collettivizzare [kollettivid'dzare] *vt* to collectivize.

collettivo, a [kollet'tivo] **1** *ag (benessere, bisogno, interesse)* common; *(responsabilità)* collective; *(impresa)* group *cpd;* **fenomeno ~** popular phenomenon; **società in nome ~** *(Comm)* partnership. **2** *sm (Pol)* collective.

colletto [kol'letto] *sm (di vestito, Bot: di albero)* collar; *(di dente)* neck; **~i bianchi** *(fig)* white-collar workers.

collettore [kollet'tore] *sm (Aut)* manifold; **~ di scarico** exhaust manifold.

collezionare [kollettsjo'nare] *vt* to collect.

collezione [kollet'tsjone] *sf* collection.

collezionista, i, e [kollettsjo'nista] *sm/f* collector.

collier [kɔ'lje] *sm inv* necklace.

collimare [kolli'mare] *vi:* **~ (con)** *(idee)* to coincide (with), agree (with).

collina [kol'lina] *sf* hill; *(zona)* hills; **una città di ~ a** town in the hills, a hill town.

collinare [kolli'nare] *ag* hill *attr.*

collinoso, a [kolli'noso] *ag* hilly.

collirio [kol'lirjo] *sm* eyedrops *pl,* eye lotion.

collisione [kolli'zjone] *sf (di veicoli)* collision; *(fig)* clash, conflict; **entrare in ~ con qc** to collide with sth.

collo¹ [ˈkɔllo] *sm* neck; **~ del piede** instep; **portare qc al ~** to wear sth round one's neck; **buttare le braccia al ~ di qn** to throw one's arms round sb; **fino al ~** *(anche fig)* up to one's neck; **è nei guai fino al ~** he's up to his neck in it.

collo² [ˈkɔllo] *sm (pacco)* parcel, package; *(bagaglio)* piece of luggage.

collo³ [ˈkollo] *prep + art vedi* **con.**

collocamento [kolloka'mento] *sm:* **agenzia di ~** employment agency; **ufficio di ~** job centre.

collocare [kollo'kare] *vt* **(a)** *(porre)* to place, position; *(: cavi)* to lay; **questo libro va collocato fra le sue opere migliori** this book ranks among his best works. **(b)** *(trovare un impiego a qn)* to place, to find a job for; **~ qn a riposo** to pension sb off. **(c)** *(Comm: merce)* to place, find a market for.

collocazione [kollokat'tsjone] *sf* **(a)** *(gen)* placing, positioning; **l'opera va considerata nella sua ~ storica** the work has to be considered within its historical setting. **(b)** *(in una biblioteca)* classification.

colloquiale [kollo'kwjale] *ag (gen)* colloquial; *(tono)* informal.

colloquiare [kollo'kwjare] *vi* to talk, converse.

colloquio [kol'lɔkwjo] *sm* **(a)** *(conversazione)* talk; *(udienza etc)* interview; **concedere un ~ a** to grant sb an interview; **avviare un ~ con qn** *(Pol etc)* to start talks with sb. **(b)** *(Univ)* preliminary oral exam.

colloso, a [kol'loso] *ag* sticky.

collottola [kol'lɔttola] *sf* nape *o* scruff of the neck; **afferrare qn per la ~** to grab sb by the scruff of the neck.

collusione [kollu'zjone] *sf (Dir)* collusion.

colluttazione [kolluttat'tsjone] *sf* scuffle.

colmare [kol'mare] *vt:* **~ (di)** *(riempire)* to fill (to the brim) (with); *(fig)* to fill (with); **~ una lacuna** *(fig)* to fill a gap; **~ un divario** *(fig)* to bridge a gap; **~ qn di gentilezze** to overwhelm sb with kindness.

colmo¹, a [ˈkolmo] *ag:* **~ (di)** full (of).

colmo² [ˈkolmo] *sm (punto più alto)* summit; *(fig):* **il**

~ della maleducazione the height of bad manners; **essere al ~ della disperazione** to be in the depths of despair; **essere al ~ dell'ira** to be in a towering rage; **e per ~ di sfortuna...** and to cap it all...; **è il ~!** that beats everything!

colomba [ko'lomba] *sf* dove; **~ pasquale** *dove-shaped Easter cake.*

colombaia [kolom'baja] *sf* dovecote; *(piccionaia)* pigeon coop.

colombo [ko'lombo] *sm (Zool)* pigeon; *(fig fam):* **~i** lovebirds.

colon ['kɔlon] *sm (Anat)* colon.

colonia¹ [ko'lɔnja] *sf (gen)* colony; *(per bambini)* holiday camp; **~ marina** seaside holiday camp.

colonia² [ko'lɔnja] *sf:* **(acqua di) ~** (eau de) cologne.

coloniale [kolo'njale] *ag, sm* colonial.

colonialismo [kolonja'lizmo] *sm* colonialism.

colonialista, i, e [kolonja'lista] *ag, sm/f* colonialist.

colonialistico, a, ci, che [kolonja'listiko] *ag* colonialist.

colonico, a, ci, che [ko'lɔniko] *ag:* **casa ~a** farmhouse.

colonizzare [kolonid'dzare] *vt* to colonize.

colonizzatore, trice [koloniddza'tore] **1** *ag* colonizing. **2** *sm/f* colonizer.

colonizzazione [koloniddzat'tsjone] *sf* colonization.

colonna [ko'lonna] *sf (gen)* column; **in ~** in a column; **stare in ~** *(Aut)* to be caught in a tailback; **una ~ di 10 chilometri** *(Aut)* a 10-kilometre tailback; **~ sonora** *(Cine)* sound track; **~ vertebrale** spine, spinal column.

colonnato [kolon'nato] *sm* colonnade.

colonnello [kolon'nɛllo] *sm* colonel.

colono [ko'lɔno] *sm* **(a)** *(contadino)* farmer. **(b)** *(abitante di una colonia)* colonist, settler.

colorante [kolo'rante] **1** *ag* colouring. **2** *sm* colorant.

colorare [kolo'rare] **1** *vt* to colour. **2:** **~rsi** *vr:* **il cielo si colorava di rosso** the sky was turning red.

colorazione [kolorat'tsjone] *sf (atto)* colouring; *(colore)* colour, colouring; **~ politica** political sympathies *pl.*

colore [ko'lore] *sm* **(a)** *(gen, fig)* colour; *(pittura)* paint; *(Carte)* suit; **di che ~ è?** what colour is it?; **di un ~ chiaro/scuro** light-/dark-coloured; **color fragola** strawberry-coloured; **senza** *o* **privo di ~** *(fig)* colourless; **la gente di ~** coloured people; **cambiare ~** *(anche fig)* to change colour; **a ~i** *(film, TV, foto)* colour *attr;* **~i a olio/a tempera** oil/tempera paints. **(b)** *(fraseologia)* **riprendere ~** *(fig)* to get one's colour back; **diventare di tutti i ~i** to turn scarlet; **dirne di tutti i ~i a qn** to hurl insults at sb; **farne di tutti i ~i** to get up to all sorts of tricks; **passarne di tutti i ~i** to go through all sorts of problems.

colorificio [kolori'fitʃo] *sm* dye factory.

colorire [kolo'rire] *vt (colorare)* to colour; *(fig)* to enliven, embellish.

colorito, a, [kolo'rito] **1** *ag (guance)* rosy; *(racconto, linguaggio)* colourful; **sei più ~ oggi** you've got more colour in your cheeks today. **2** *sm (carnagione)* complexion.

coloro [ko'loro] *pron dimostr pl (sog)* they; *(complemento)* them; **~ che** those who. **(b)** *(peg)* those people.

colossale [kolos'sale] *ag* colossal, huge.

colosso [ko'lɔsso] *sm (statua)* colossus; *(fig)* giant, colossus; **è un ~!** *(fisicamente)* he's enormous!

colpa [ˈkolpa] *sf (responsabilità)* fault; *(colpevolezza)* guilt; *(morale)* sin; **di chi è la ~?** whose fault is it?; **è ~ mia** it's my fault; **per ~ di** because of, thanks to; **per ~ sua** because of him, thanks to him; **essere in ~** to be at fault; **sentirsi in ~** to feel guilty; **senso di ~** sense of guilt; **confessare le proprie ~e** to admit one's faults; **dare la ~ a qn** *a qc* to blame sb for sth; **addossarsi la ~ di qc** to take the blame for sth.

colpevole [kol'pevole] **1** *ag* guilty; **dichiarare qn ~ (di qc)** to find sb guilty (of sth); **dichiararsi ~** to plead guilty. **2** *sm/f* culprit.

colpevolezza [kolpevo'lettsa] *sf* guilt.

colpire [kol'pire] *vt (anche fig)* to hit, strike; *(toccare)* to affect; **è stata colpita alla testa** she was hit *o* struck on the head; **lo ha colpito con un pugno** he punched him; **~ qn a morte** to strike sb dead; **il nuovo provvedimento colpirà gli spacciatori** the new measure will hit drug pushers; **~ nel segno** *(fig)* to hit the nail on the head, be spot on; **~ l'immaginazione** to catch the imagination; **la sua bellezza mi ha colpito** I was struck by her beauty; **un'epidemia che colpisce le persone anziane** an epidemic which affects old people; **colpito dalla paralisi/dalla sfortuna** stricken with paralysis/by misfortune; **è stato colpito da ordine di cattura** there is a warrant out for his arrest.

colpo ['kolpo] **1** *sm* **(a)** *(ostile)* blow, strike; *(urto)* knock; *(fig: affettivo)* blow, shock; **~ mortale** mortal blow; **~ di spada** sword-blow; **~ di remo** oar stroke; **dare un ~ in testa a qn** to hit sb over the head; **prendere un ~ in** *o* **alla testa** to bump one's head; **prendere qn a ~i di bastone** to set about sb with a stick; **darsi un ~ di pettine** to run a comb through one's hair; **è stato un brutto ~ per lui** *(fig)* it came as a hard blow to him; **un ~ di coda** *(di cavallo etc)* a flick of the tail; **con un ~ d'ala l'uccello si è librato in volo** with a flap of its wings the bird took flight.

(b) *(di arma da fuoco)* shot; **hanno sparato 10 ~i di cannone** they fired 10 cannon shots; **mi restano solo 2 ~i** I've only got 2 rounds left.

(c) *(Med)* stroke; **~ (apoplettico)** (apopleptic) fit; **~ d'aria** chill; **~ di calore** heat stroke; **~ di sole** sunstroke; **~ di tosse** fit of coughing; **ti venisse un ~!** *(fam)* drop dead!; **mi hai fatto venire un ~!** what a fright you gave me!

(d) *(Pugilato)* punch; *(Scherma)* hit; **~ basso** *(Pugilato, fig)* punch below the belt.

(e) *(furto)* raid; **fare un ~** to carry out a raid; **hanno preso gli autori di quel ~ in banca** they caught those responsible for the bank job *o* raid; **tentare il ~** *(fig)* to have a go; **ho fatto un buon ~** I pulled it off.

(f) *(fraseologia)*: **al primo ~** at the first attempt; **di ~, tutto d'un ~** suddenly; **far ~** to cause a sensation; **è morto sul ~** he died instantly; **sono andato in quel negozio a ~ sicuro** I went into that shop knowing I would find what I wanted; **il motore perde ~i** *(Aut)* the engine is misfiring.

2: **~ di fortuna** stroke of (good) luck; **~ di fulmine** love at first sight; **~ giornalistico** newspaper coup; **~ gobbo** smart move; *(al gioco)* lucky strike; **~ di grazia** *(fig)* finishing blow; **~ di mano** *(Mil)* surprise attack; *(fig)* surprise action; **a ~ d'occhio** at a glance; **avere ~ d'occhio** to have a good eye; **~ di scena** *(Teatro)* coup de théâtre; *(fig)* dramatic turn of events; **~i di sole** *(nei capelli)* highlights; **~ di Stato** coup (d'état); **dare un ~ di telefono a qn** to give sb a ring; **~ di testa** sudden impulse; **~ di vento** gust of wind; **~ di vita** *(fig)* high spot; **facciamo un ~ di vita!** let's live it up!

colposo, a [kol'poso] *ag*: **omicidio ~** manslaughter.

coltellata [koltel'lata] *sf (colpo)* stab; *(ferita)* knife wound.

coltelleria [koltelle'ria] *sf (fabbrica)* cutlery works *sg*; *(negozio)* cutler's (shop).

coltello [kol'tɛllo] *sm* knife; **~ a serramanico** flick knife; **avere il ~ dalla parte del manico** *(fig)* to have the whip hand; **c'era una nebbia che si tagliava con il ~** the fog was so thick you could have cut it with a knife.

coltivabile [kolti'vabile] *ag* fit for cultivation.

coltivare [kolti'vare] *vt (terreno, fig: amicizia)* to cultivate; *(piante)* to grow, cultivate; **~ un campo a grano** to plant a field with corn; **~ la mente** to cultivate one's mind.

coltivatore [koltiva'tore] *sm* grower, farmer; **~ diretto** small independent farmer.

coltivazione [koltivat'tsjone] *sf* growing, cultivation; **~ intensiva** intensive farming.

coltivo, a [kol'tivo] *ag (terreno)* cultivated, under cultivation.

colto¹, a ['kolto] *ag* cultured, well-educated.

colto², a ['kɔlto] *pp di* **cogliere.**

coltre ['kɔltre] *sf (anche fig)* blanket.

coltura [kol'tura] *sf* cultivation; **~ alternata** crop rotation. **(b)** *(Bio)* culture; **~ batterica** bacterial culture.

colui [ko'lui] *pron dimostr (sog)* he; *(complemento)* him; **~ che** the man who, the one who.

coma ['kɔma] *sm inv* coma.

comandamento [komanda'mento] *sm* commandment.

comandante [koman'dante] *sm (Mil)* commander, commanding officer; *(Aer, Naut)* captain; **~ del porto** harbour master; **~ in seconda** second-in-command.

comandare [koman'dare] **1** *vt* **(a)** *(ordinare)* to order, command; *(essere al comando)* to command, be in charge of; **~ a bacchetta** *(fig)* to rule with a rod of iron. **(b)** *(macchina: azionare)* to operate, control; **~ a distanza** to operate by remote control. **2** *vi* to be in charge, be in command; **qui comando io!** I'm in charge here!

comando [ko'mando] *sm* **(a)** *(ordine)* command, order; **ubbidire a un ~** to obey an order. **(b)** *(autorità, sede)* command; **essere al ~ (di)** to be in command *o* in charge (of); *(Sport: di classifica)* to be at the top (of); *(: di gara)* to be in the lead (in); **assumere il ~ di** to assume command of; *(Sport)* to take the lead in; **~ generale** general headquarters *pl.* **(c)** *(Tecn)* control; **doppi ~i** dual controls.

comare [ko'mare] *sf (madrina)* godmother; *(donna pettegola)* gossip; **le allegre ~i di Windsor** the Merry Wives of Windsor.

comatoso, a [koma'toso] *ag* comatose.

combaciare [komba'tʃare] *vi* to fit together; *(fig: idee)* to agree, coincide.

combattente [kombat'tɛnte] **1** *ag* fighting, combatant. **2** *sm* fighter, combatant.

combattere [kom'battere] **1** *vt* to fight; *(fig: teoria, malattia)* to combat, fight (against). **2** *vi* to fight.

combattimento [kombatti'mento] *sm (Mil)* battle, fight; *(Pugilato etc)* match; **mettere fuori ~** to knock out; **~ di galli** cockfighting.

combattività [kombattivi'ta] *sf* fighting spirit.

combattivo, a [kombat'tivo] *ag* pugnacious.

combattuto, a [kombat'tuto] *ag* **(a)** *(incerto: persona)* uncertain, undecided; **~ tra due possibilità** torn between two possibilities. **(b)** *(gara, partita)* hard fought.

combinare [kombi'nare] **1** *vt* **(a)** *(mettere insieme)* to combine. **(b)** *(organizzare: incontro)* to arrange; *(concludere: affare)* to conclude; **che cosa stai combinando?** what are you getting up to?; **ci hai combinato un bel guaio!** you've got us into a nice mess! **2** *vi (corrispondere)*: ~ **(con)** to correspond (with). **3:** ~**rsi** *vr* **(a)** *(Chim)* to combine. **(b)** *(fam: conciarsi)*: **ma come ti sei combinato?** what on earth have you got on?, what on earth have you done to yourself?

combinata [kombi'nata] *sf (Sci)* combination.

combinazione [kombinat'tsjone] *sf* **(a)** *(accostamento, unione)* combination. **(b)** *(caso)* chance; **per** ~ by chance; **(guarda) che** ~! what a coincidence!

combriccola [kom'brikkola] *sf (gruppo)* party; *(banda)* gang.

comburente [kombu'rɛnte] *sm (Chim)* combustive agent.

combustibile [kombus'tibile] **1** *ag* combustible. **2** *sm* fuel.

combustibilità [kombustibili'ta] *sf* combustibility.

combustione [kombus'tjone] *sf* combustion; **a lenta** ~ slow-burning.

combutta [kom'butta] *sf*: **essere in** ~ to be in league o in cahoots; **fare** ~ **con qn** to be in league o in cahoots with sb.

come ['kome] **1** *av* **(a)** *(alla maniera di, nel modo che)* as, like *(dav a sostantivo, pronome)*; **bianco** ~ **la neve** (as) white as snow; **veste** ~ **suo padre he** dresses like his father; **a scuola** ~ **a casa** both at school and at home, at school as well as at home; **ci vuole uno** ~ **lui** we need somebody like o such as him; **è** ~ **parlare al muro** it's like talking to the wall; **non hanno accettato il progetto:** ~ **dire che siamo fregati** they didn't accept the plan: which means we've had it; **com'è vero Dio** as God is my witness.

(b) *(in quale modo)* how; ~ **stai?** how are you?; ~ **glielo dico?** how will I tell him?; **non so** ~ **dirglielo** I don't know how to tell him; ~?, ~ **dici?** sorry?, what did you say?; **com'è il tuo amico?** what's your friend like?; **com'è che non hai telefonato?** how come you didn't phone?; **vieni?** — ~ **no!** are you coming? — of course! o and how!; ~ **mai?** how come?; ~ **mai non sei partito?** whyever didn't you leave?; **non hanno accettato il mio assegno** — ~ **mai?**; they didn't accept my cheque — whyever not?

(c) *(il modo in cui)*: **mi piace** ~ **scrive** I like the way he writes, I like his style of writing; **ecco** ~ **è successo** this is how it happened; **attento a** ~ **parli!** mind your tongue!

(d) *(in qualità di)* as; ~ **presidente, dirò che...** speaking as your president I must say that...; **ti parlo** ~ **amico** I'm speaking to you as a friend; **lo hanno scelto** ~ **rappresentante** they've chosen him as their representative.

(e) *(quanto)*: ~ **è brutto!** how ugly he (o it) is!; ~ **mi dispiace!** I'm terribly sorry!

(f): **A** ~ **Ancona** ≃ A for Andrew; **ora** ~ **ora** right now; **oggi** ~ **oggi** at the present time; ~ **non detto** let's forget it; *vedi* **così, tanto.**

2 *cong* **(a)** *(che, in quale modo)*: **mi scrisse** ~ **si era rotto un braccio** he wrote to tell me about how he had broken an arm; **mi ha spiegato** ~ **l'ha conosciuto** he told me how he met him; **dovevi vedere** ~ **lo picchiava** you should have seen the way he was hitting him.

(b) *(quanto)* how; **sai** ~ **ci tiene/sia permaloso** you know how much it matters to him/how touchy he is.

(c) *(correlativo)* as; *(con comparitivi di maggioranza)* than; **si comporta** ~ **ha sempre fatto** he

behaves as he has always done; **è meglio/peggio di** ~ **mi aspettavo** it is better/worse than I expected.

(d) *(appena che, quando)*: ~ **arrivò si mise a lavorare** as soon as he arrived he set to work, no sooner had he arrived than he set to work; ~ **se n'è andato, tutti sono scoppiati a ridere** no sooner had he left than everyone burst out laughing.

(e): ~ **(se)** as if, as though; **la trattano** ~ **(se) fosse la loro schiava** they treat her like a slave o as if she were their slave.

(f) *(in proposizioni incidentali)* as; ~ **sai** as you know; ~ **puoi constatare** as you can see.

3 *sm inv*: **il** ~ **e il perché** the whys and the wherefores; **non so dirti il** ~ **e il quando** di tutta **questa faccenda** I couldn't tell you how and when all this happened.

comedone [kome'done] *sm* blackhead.

cometa [ko'meta] *sf* comet.

comica, che ['kɔmika] *sf short slapstick silent film.*

comicità [komitʃi'ta] *sf (di libro, film, attore)* comic quality; *(di situazione)* funny side.

comico, a, ci, che ['kɔmiko] **1** *ag (gen: buffo)* comic(al); *(Teatro)* comic. **2** *sm* **(a)** *(comicità)*: **il** ~ **è che...** the funny thing is that.... **(b)** *(attore)* comedian.

comignolo [ko'miɲɲolo] *sm* chimney.

cominciare [komin'tʃare] **1** *vt* to start, begin; ~ **a fare qc** to begin o start to do o doing sth. **2** *vi (aus essere se usato assolutamente)* to start, begin; **una parola che comincia per J** a word beginning with J; ~ **col dire** to start off by saying; **tanto per** ~ to start with; **a** ~ **da domani** starting (from) tomorrow; **cominciamo bene!** *(iro)* we're off to a fine start!

comitato [komi'tato] *sm* committee, board; ~ **direttivo** steering committee; **far parte di un** ~ to be on a committee.

comitiva [komi'tiva] *sf* group, party; **viaggiare in** ~ to travel in o as a group.

comizio [ko'mittsjo] *sm* rally; ~ **elettorale** election rally.

comma, i ['kɔmma] *sm (Dir)* subsection.

commando [kom'mando] *sm* commando *(group)*.

commedia [kom'mɛdja] *sf* **(a)** *(Teatro)* play; *(: comica)* comedy; ~ **musicale** musical; **la Divina C**~ the Divine Comedy. **(b)** *(finzione)* sham, play-acting; **è tutta una** ~ it's just play-acting; **fare la** ~ to play-act.

commediante [komme'djante] *sm/f* comedian/ comedienne; *(fig: ipocrita)* sham.

commediografo, a [komme'djɔgrafo] *sm/f (autore)* comedy writer.

commemorare [kommemo'rare] *vt* to commemorate.

commemorativo, a [kommemora'tivo] *ag* commemorative, memorial.

commemorazione [kommemorat'tsjone] *sf* commemoration.

commendatore [kommenda'tore] *sm official title awarded for services to one's country.*

commensale [kommen'sale] *sm/f* table companion.

commensurabile [kommensu'rabile] *ag (Mat)* commensurable.

commentare [kommen'tare] *vt (annotare)* to annotate; *(dare un giudizio su: fatto, avvenimento)* to comment on.

commentatore, trice [kommenta'tore] *sm/f (di testo)* annotator; *(TV, Radio)* commentator.

commento [kom'mento] *sm (osservazione)* comment; *(letterario, TV, Radio)* commentary; **fare**

un ~ su qn/qc to comment on sb/sth; **fare il ~ di una partita** to give the commentary on a match; **senza fare ~i** without passing comment; **è meglio che io non faccia ~i** it is better if I don't say anything; ~ **musicale** *(Cine)* background music.

commerciabile [kommer'tʃabile] *ag* marketable, saleable.

commerciale [kommer'tʃale] *ag (gen)* commercial; *(corrispondenza)* business *attr*, commercial; *(fiera, bilancio)* trade *attr*; **interrompere i rapporti ~i con** to interrupt trade with.

commercialista, i, e [kommertʃa'lista] *sm/f (laureato)* graduate in economics and commerce; *(consulente)* business consultant.

commercializzare [kommertʃalid'dzare] *vt (prodotto)* to market; *(peg: arte)* to commercialize.

commerciante [kommer'tʃante] *sm* trader; *(negoziante)* shopkeeper, tradesman; ~ **all'ingrosso** wholesaler; ~ **di legname** timber merchant.

commerciare [kommer'tʃare] **1** *vi* to trade, deal; ~ **con qn** to do business with sb. **2** *vt* to trade in, deal in.

commercio [kom'mɛrtʃo] *sm (vendita, affari)* trade, commerce; ~ **all'ingrosso/al minuto** wholesale/retail trade; **il ~ della lana** the wool trade; **essere in ~** *(prodotto)* to be in the shops, be for sale; **mettere in ~** to put on the market.

commessa [kom'messa] *sf (a) (addetta alla vendita)* shop assistant, salesgirl. **(b)** *(ordinazione)* order.

commesso, a [kom'messo] **1** *pp di* **commettere. 2** *sm (a) (addetto alla vendita)* shop assistant; ~ **viaggiatore** travelling salesman. **(b)** *(impiegato)* clerk; ~ **di banca** bank clerk.

commestibile [kommes'tibile] **1** *ag* edible. **2** *smpl:* ~**i** foodstuffs.

commettere [kom'mettere] *vt (a) (sbaglio)* to make; *(delitto, peccato)* to commit. **(b)** *(ordinare)* to commission, order.

commiato [kom'mjato] *sm* leave-taking; **prendere ~ da qn** to take one's leave of sb.

commilitone [kommili'tone] *sm* fellow soldier, comrade-in-arms.

comminare [kommi'nare] *vt (Dir)* to make provision for.

commiserare [kommize'rare] *vt* to commiserate with.

commiserazione [kommizerat'tsjone] *sf* commiseration; **sorriso di ~** *(anche peg)* pitying smile.

commissariato [kommissa'rjato] *sm (a)* police station. **(b)** *(carica)* commissionership.

commissario [kommis'sarjo] *sm (a) (funzionario):* ~ **(di Pubblica Sicurezza)** (police) superintendent; ~ **di bordo** *(Naut)* purser; ~ **d'esame** member of an examining board. **(b)** *(Sport)* steward; ~ **di gara** race official; **il ~ tecnico della Nazionale** the national team manager.

commissionare [kommissjo'nare] *vt* to order, place an order for.

commissionario [kommissjo'narjo] *sm (Comm, Fin)* agent, broker.

commissione [kommis'sjone] *sf (a)* errand; **fare una ~** to go on an errand; **devo fare delle ~i** I have some shopping to do. **(b)** *(Comm: ordinazione)* order; *(: percentuale)* commission; **fatto su ~** made to order; **vendere su ~** to sell on commission. **(c)** *(comitato)* committee, board; ~ **d'esame** examining board; ~ **d'inchiesta** committee of enquiry; ~ **parlamentare** parliamentary commission.

commisurato, a [kommizu'rato] *ag:* ~ **a** in proportion to.

committente [kommit'tɛnte] *sm/f (Comm)* purchaser, customer.

commosso, a [kom'mɔsso] **1** *pp di* **commuovere. 2** *ag* moved, touched; **essere ~ fino alle lacrime** to be moved to tears.

commovente [kommo'vɛnte] *ag* moving, touching.

commozione [kommot'tsjone] *sf (a) (emozione)* emotion. **(b)** *(Med):* ~ **cerebrale** concussion.

commuovere [kom'mwɔvere] **1** *vt* to move, touch. **2:** ~**rsi** *vr* to be moved.

commutare [kommu'tare] *vt (a) (Dir)* to commute. **(b)** *(Elettr)* to switch, commutate.

commutatore [kommuta'tore] *sm (Elettr)* commutator.

commutazione [kommutat'tsjone] *sf (Dir, Elettr)* commutation.

comò [ko'mɔ] *sm* chest of drawers.

comodino [komo'dino] *sm* bedside table.

comodità [komodi'ta] *sf inv (a) (vedi ag)* convenience; handiness; comfort. **(b):** **le ~ della vita moderna** modern conveniences.

comodo, a ['kɔmodo] **1** *ag (opportuno)* convenient; *(pratico)* handy; *(confortevole)* comfortable; **gli piace la vita ~a** he likes an easy life; **stia ~!** don't bother to get up! **2** *sm:* **con ~** at one's convenience; **fai con ~** take your time; **fare il proprio ~** to please o.s.; **amare il proprio ~** to like one's comforts; **quei soldi mi hanno fatto ~** that money came in handy; **una macchina mi farebbe ~** a car would do me nicely, a car would be very handy; **una soluzione di ~** a convenient arrangement.

compaesano, a [kompae'zano] *sm/f* fellow townsman/woman; **è un mio ~** he comes from the same town (o district) as I do.

compagine [kom'padʒine] *sf (Pol):* **la ~ del partito** the party en bloc; **la ~ dello Stato** the government as a whole.

compagnia [kompaɲ'ɲia] *sf (a)* company; **fare ~ a qn** to keep sb company; **essere di ~** to be sociable; **dama di ~** lady-in-waiting. **(b)** *(gruppo di persone)* group, party; *(Mil, Comm, Teatro)* company.

compagno, a [kom'paɲɲo] *sm/f (gen)* companion; *(nel gioco)* partner; *(della vita)* mate; *(Pol)* comrade; ~ **di giochi** playmate; ~ **di lavoro** workmate; ~ **di scuola** schoolfriend; ~ **di sventura** companion in misfortune; ~ **di viaggio** fellow traveller.

companatico [kompa'natiko] *sm:* **pane e ~** ≈ bread and dripping.

comparativo, a [kompara'tivo] *ag, sm* comparative.

comparato, a [kompa'rato] *ag* comparative.

comparazione [komparat'tsjone] *sf* comparison.

compare [kom'pare] *sm (padrino)* godfather; *(complice)* accomplice; *(fam: amico)* old pal, old mate.

comparire [kompa'rire] *vi (aus essere) (presentarsi)* to appear; *(uscire: libro, giornale)* to come out; ~ **in giudizio** *(Dir)* to appear before the court.

comparizione [komparit'tsjone] *sf (Dir)* appearance; **mandato di ~** summons *sg*.

comparsa [kom'parsa] *sf (a) (apparizione)* appearance; **fare la propria ~** to put in an appearance; **nessuno si aspettava la sua ~** no one expected him to turn up. **(b)** *(Cine: persona)* extra.

comparso, a [kom'parso] *pp di* **comparire.**

compartecipare [kompartetʃi'pare] *vi (Comm):* ~ **a** to have a share in; ~ **agli utili** to share in the profits.

compartecipazione [kompartetʃipat'tsjone] *sf (divisione con altri)* sharing; *(quota)* share; ~ **agli**

utili profit-sharing; **in** ~ jointly.

compartecipe [kompar'tetʃipe] *ag*: **essere** ~ **agli utili** to share in the profits.

compartimentale [kompartimen'tale] *ag* district *attr*.

compartimento [komparti'mento] *sm* **(a)** *(circoscrizione)* district. **(b)** *(Naut)*: ~ **stagno** watertight compartment.

compassato, a [kompas'sato] *ag (persona)* composed; **freddo e** ~ cool and collected.

compassione [kompas'sjone] *sf* compassion, pity; **provare** *o* **sentire** ~ **per qn** to pity sb, feel sorry for sb; **fare** ~ to arouse pity; **mi ha fatto** ~ **vederli ridotti così** I was sorry to see them in such a state.

compassionevole [kompassjo'nevole] *ag (che sente compassione)* compassionate; *(che suscita compassione)* pitiful, pathetic.

compasso [kom'passo] *sm* (pair of) compasses *pl*; ~ **per spessori** callipers *pl*.

compatibile [kompa'tibile] *ag* **(a)** *(conciliabile)* compatible. **(b)** *(scusabile)* understandable, excusable.

compatibilità [kompatibili'ta] *sf* compatibility.

compatimento [kompati'mento] *sm*: **con aria di** ~ with a condescending air.

compatire [kompa'tire] *vt* to feel sorry for; **bisogna compatirlo, poveretto** *(iro)* you've got to make allowances for him, poor thing.

compatriota, i, e [kompatri'ɔta] *sm/f* fellow countryman/woman.

compattezza [kompat'tettsa] *sf (solidità)* compactness; *(fig: unità)* solidarity.

compatto, a [kom'patto] *ag (solido)* compact, solid; *(folla)* dense; *(partito)* united.

compendio [kom'pɛndjo] *sm* compendium, outline.

compenetrarsi [kompene'trarsi] *vr* to interpenetrate.

compensare [kompen'sare] **1** *vt* **(a)** *(lavoro)* to pay for; *(danno)* to give compensation for; **è stato compensato per il danno ricevuto** he has received compensation for the damage. **(b)** *(bilanciare)* to compensate for, make up for; **le perdite dell'anno scorso saranno compensate dagli utili di quest'anno** this year's profits will compensate for last year's losses. **2:** ~**rsi** *vr* to balance each other out.

compensato [kompen'sato] *sm (anche: **legno** ~)* plywood.

compensazione [kompensat'tsjone] *sf* compensation.

compenso [kom'pɛnso] *sm (retribuzione)* remuneration; *(onorario)* fee; *(ricompensa)* reward; **in** ~ *(d'altra parte)* on the other hand.

compera ['kompera] *sf*: **fare le** ~**e** to do the shopping.

comperare [kompe'rare] *vt* = **comprare**.

competente [kompe'tɛnte] *ag (gen, Dir)* competent; *(capace)* qualified; **è lui il** ~ **in materia** he's the expert.

competenza [kompe'tɛntsa] *sf* **(a)** *(capacità)* competence; *(Dir: autorità)* jurisdiction; **non ho** ~ **in materia** I'm not an expert on that; **è di** ~ **del tribunale di Milano** it comes under the jurisdiction of the Milan courts; **l'argomento non è di mia** ~ I am not qualified to speak on that subject; **questo lavoro non è di mia** ~ that's not my job. **(b)** *(onorario)*: ~**e** *pl* fees.

competere [kom'pɛtere] *vi* **(a)** *(gareggiare)* to compete. **(b)** *(Dir)*: ~ **a** to lie with, come under the jurisdiction of; *(spettare: compito etc)* to lie with; *(: denaro)* to be due to; **avrai ciò che ti**

compete you'll have what is due to you.

competitività [kompetitivi'ta] *sf* competitiveness.

competitivo, a [kompeti'tivo] *ag* competitive.

competitore, trice [kompeti'tore] *sm/f* competitor.

competizione [kompetit'tsjone] *sf* competition, contest; **spirito di** ~ competitive spirit; **auto da** ~ racing car.

compiacente [kompja'tʃɛnte] *ag* obliging; *(peg)* accommodating.

compiacenza [kompja'tʃɛntsa] *sf* courtesy; **abbia la** ~ **di aspettarmi** please be so good as to wait for me.

compiacere [kompja'tʃere] **1** *vt* to please, make happy. **2:** ~**rsi** *vr*: ~**rsi di** to be pleased with; ~**rsi con qn per qc** to congratulate sb for *o* on sth.

compiacimento [kompjatʃi'mento] *sm* satisfaction.

compiaciuto, a [kompja'tʃuto] *pp di* **compiacere**.

compiangere [kom'pjandʒere] *vt* to feel sorry for.

compianto, a [kom'pjanto] **1** *pp di* **compiangere**. **2** *ag*: **il** ~ **presidente** the late lamented president. **3** *sm* mourning, grief.

compiere ['kompjere] **1** *vt (adempiere)* to carry out, fulfil; *(finire)* to finish, complete; ~ **gli anni: ha compiuto 18 anni il mese scorso** he turned 18 last month; **quando compi gli anni?** when is your birthday?; **quanti anni compi?** how old will you be?; ~ **il proprio dovere** to carry out one's duty; ~ **una buona azione** to do a good deed. **2:** ~**rsi** *vr* **(a)** *(giungere a termine)* to end. **(b)** *(avverarsi: speranze)* to be fulfilled; *(: profezie)* to come true.

compilare [kompi'lare] *vt (gen)* to compile; *(modulo)* to complete, fill in.

compilatore, trice [kompila'tore] *sm/f* compiler.

compilazione [kompilat'tsjone] *sf (vedi vb)* compilation; completion.

compimento [kompi'mento] *sm (termine, conclusione)* completion, fulfilment; **portare a** ~ **qc** to conclude sth, bring sth to a conclusion.

compitare [kompi'tare] *vt* to spell out.

compitezza [kompi'tettsa] *sf* poise.

compito¹, a [kom'pito] *ag* poised.

compito² ['kompito] *sm* **(a)** *(lavoro)* job, task. **(b)** *(Scol: a casa)* piece of homework; *(: in classe)* class test; **fare i** ~**i** to do one's homework.

compiutezza [kompju'tettsa] *sf (completezza)* completeness; *(perfezione)* perfection.

compiuto, a [kom'pjuto] *ag*: **a 20 anni** ~**i** at 20 years of age; **un fatto** ~ a fait accompli.

compleanno [komple'anno] *sm* birthday.

complementare [komplemen'tare] *ag (gen, Geom)* complementary; *(materia di studio, esame)* subsidiary; **imposta** ~ supplementary tax.

complemento [komple'mento] *sm* **(a)** *(Gram)* complement; ~ **oggetto** *o* **diretto/indiretto** direct/indirect object. **(b)** *(Mil)* reserve; **di** ~ reserve *attr*.

complessato, a [komples'sato] *ag, sm/f*: **essere (un)** ~ to be full of complexes *o* hang-ups *(fam)*.

complessità [komplessi'ta] *sf* complexity.

complessivo, a [komples'sivo] *ag (giudizio)* comprehensive; *(ammontare, prezzo)* total; **visione** ~**a** overview.

complesso, a [kom'plɛsso] **1** *ag* complex, complicated; **numeri** ~**i** complex numbers; **proposizione** ~**a** a compound sentence. **2** *sm* **(a)** *(insieme)* whole; *(di leggi)* body; *(organizzazione, posto)* complex; **nel** *o* **in** ~ by and large, generally speaking; **il** ~ **delle manifestazioni culturali avverrà in luglio** the vast majority of cultural events will take place in July; ~ **industriale/**

turistico industrial/tourist complex. **(b)** *(Psic)* complex; ~ **d'inferiorità** inferiority complex. **(c)** *(Mus)* band, ensemble; *(: di musica leggera)* group.

completare [komple'tare] *vt* to complete, finish.

completezza [komple'tettsa] *sf* completeness.

completo, a [kom'plɛto] **1** *ag (gen)* complete; *(reso-conto, elenco)* full, complete; *(fiasco, fallimento)* complete, utter; **computer** ~ **di stampatrice** computer complete with printer. **2** *sm (abito)* suit; ~ **da sci** ski suit; **essere al** ~ *(albergo)* to be full; *(teatro)* to be sold out.

complicare [kompli'kare] **1** *vt* to complicate; **non per complicarti la vita, ma...** not that I want to make life difficult for you, but .... **2**: ~**rsi** *vr* to become complicated.

complicazione [komplikat'tsjone] *sf* complication; **salvo** ~**i** unless any difficulties arise.

complice ['kɔmplitʃe] *sm/f* accomplice.

complicità [komplitʃi'ta] *sf* complicity.

complimentarsi [komplimen'tarsi] *vr*: ~ **con qn per qc** to congratulate sb on sth.

complimento [kompli'mento] *sm* **(a)** *(lode)* compliment; **fare un** ~ **a qn** to compliment sb, pay sb a compliment. **(b)**: ~**i** *pl (congratulazioni)* congratulations; **le faccio i miei** ~**i per...** may I congratulate you on.... **(c)**: ~**i** *pl (cerimonie)*: **fa sempre tanti** ~**i** he always stands on ceremony; **non fare** ~**i,** *o* **senza** ~**i, se ti fa piacere resta con noi** feel free to stay with us if you'd like to; **senza tanti** ~**i ha preso la mia macchina e se n'è andato** without so much as a by your leave he took my car and off he went.

complimentoso, a [komplimen'toso] *ag (persona)* proper.

complottare [komplot'tare] *vi* to plot.

complotto [kom'plɔtto] *sm* plot, conspiracy.

componente [kompo'nɛnte] **1** *ag* component. **2** *sm/f (persona)* member. **3** *sm (Elettr)* component, part; *(Chim)* component. **4** *sf (fig: elemento)* element; **c'era in lui una** ~ **di sadismo** there was an element of sadism in his character.

componibile [kompo'nibile] *ag (mobili, cucina)* fitted.

componimento [komponi'mento] *sm* **(a)** *(gen, Mus)* composition; *(Letteratura)* work, writing. **(b)** *(Dir)* settlement.

comporre [kom'porre] **1** *vt* **(a)** *(creare: concerto, poesia)* to compose; **essere composto da** *o* to be composed of, consist of. **(b)** *(Telec)* to dial. **(c)** *(Tip)* to set. **(d)** *(Dir)* to settle. **2: comporsi** *vr*: **comporsi di** to consist of, be composed of.

comportamentismo [komportamen'tizmo] *sm (Psic)* behaviourism.

comportamento [komporta'mento] *sm* behaviour.

comportare [kompor'tare] **1** *vt (richiedere)* to call for, require; *(implicare)* to imply, involve; **ciò comporta una spesa ingente** it involves a huge financial outlay. **2:** ~**rsi** *vr* to behave; **comportati bene!** behave!; **non ci si comporta così** that's no way to behave.

composito, a [kom'pozito] *ag* composite.

compositore, trice [kompozi'tore] **1** *sm/f (Mus)* composer. **2** *sm (Tip)* typesetter. **3** *sf (Tip)* typesetting machine.

composizione [kompozit'tsjone] *sf* **(a)** *(gen, Chim, Mus)* composition. **(b)** *(Tip)* typesetting, composition. **(c)** *(Dir)* settlement.

compossesso [kompos'sɛsso] *sm (Dir)* joint possession.

composta [kom'posta] *sf (Culin)* stewed fruit, compote.

compostezza [kompos'tettsa] *sf* composure.

composto, a [kom'posto] **1** *pp di* **comporre. 2** *ag* **(a)** *(Gram)* compound; *(Mat)* composite. **(b)** *(atteggiamento)* composed; **stai seduto** ~ sit properly. **3** *sm (Chim)* compound; *(Culin)* mixture.

comprare [kom'prare] *vt* **(a)** to buy; ~ **qc a qn** to buy sth for sb, to buy sb sth; ~ **qc a occhi chiusi** *o* **a scatola chiusa** to buy sth with complete confidence. **(b)** *(giudice)* to bribe; *(voti)* to buy; ~ **il silenzio di qn** to bribe sb to keep quiet.

compratore, trice [kompra'tore] *sm/f* buyer.

compravendita [kompra'vendita] *sf (Comm)* (contract of) sale; **un atto di** ~ a deed of sale.

comprendere [kom'prendere] *vt* **(a)** *(includere)* to include. **(b)** *(capire)* to understand.

comprendonio [kompren'dɔnjo] *sm*: **essere duro di** ~ to be slow on the uptake.

comprensibile [kompren'sibile] *ag* understandable.

comprensione [kompren'sjone] *sf* understanding.

comprensivo, a [kompren'sivo] *ag* **(a)** *(Comm)*: ~ **(di)** inclusive (of). **(b)** *(tollerante)* understanding.

comprensorio [kompren'sɔrjo] *sm* area, territory; *(Amm)* district.

compreso, a [kom'preso] **1** *pp di* **comprendere. 2** *ag (incluso)* inclusive; **tutto** ~ all inclusive, all in; **dall'8 al 22** ~ from the 8th to the 22nd inclusive; **aperto tutta la settimana domenica** ~**a** open all week including Sunday.

compressa [kom'pressa] *sf (Med: garza)* compress; *(: pastiglia)* tablet.

compressione [kompres'sjone] *sf* compression.

compresso, a [kom'presso] **1** *pp di* **comprimere. 2** *ag* compressed.

compressore [kompres'sore] *sm* **(a)** compressor. **(b)** *(anche: rullo* ~**)** steamroller.

comprimere [kom'primere] *vt* to compress.

compromesso, a [kompro'messo] **1** *pp di* **compromettere. 2** *sm (accordo)* compromise; *(Dir)* arbitration agreement; **arrivare a un** ~ to reach a compromise; **soluzione di** ~ compromise solution; **vive di** ~ his life is a series of compromises.

compromettente [kompromet'tente] *ag* compromising.

compromettere [kompro'mettere] **1** *vt (reputazione)* to compromise, jeopardize; *(libertà, avvenire, risultato)* to jeopardize; ~**rsi la reputazione** to compromise *o* jeopardize one's reputation. **2:** ~**rsi** *vr* to compromise o.s.

comproprietà [komproprje'ta] *sf (Dir)* joint ownership.

comproprietario, a [komproprje'tarjo] *sm/f (Dir)* joint owner.

comprova [kom'prova] *sf*: **a** ~ **di** as proof of.

comprovabile [kompro'vabile] *ag* which can be proved, demonstrable.

comprovare [kompro'vare] *vt* to prove, confirm.

compunto, a [kom'punto] *ag (contrito)* contrite; **con fare** ~ *(iro)* with a solemn air.

compunzione [kompun'tsjone] *sf (vedi ag)* contrition; solemnity.

computabile [kompu'tabile] *ag* calculable.

computare [kompu'tare] *vt* to calculate, estimate.

computer [kam'pjutər] *sm inv* computer.

computerizzato, a [komputerid'dzato] *ag* computerized.

computisteria [komputiste'ria] *sf (Comm)* bookkeeping, accounting.

computo ['kɔmputo] *sm (calcolo)* counting; **fare il** ~ **di** to count.

comunale [komu'nale] *ag (del comune)* town *attr*, municipal; **è un impiegato** ~ he works for the local council; **consiglio/palazzo** ~ town council/hall.

comunanza [komu'nantsa] *sf:* ~ **di interessi** community of interests.

comune[1] [ko'mune] **1** *ag* **(a)** *(gen, Gram)* common; *(diffuso)* common, widespread; **è un problema molto** ~ it's a very common *o* widespread problem; **di intelligenza non** ~ of exceptional intelligence; **un nostro** ~ **amico** a mutual friend of ours; **il bene** ~ the common good; **di** ~ **accordo** by common consent; **di uso** ~ in common use; **un luogo** ~ a commonplace; **cassa** ~ kitty; **fare cassa** ~ to pool one's money; **mal** ~, **mezzo gaudio** a trouble shared is a trouble halved. **(b)** *(ordinario)* ordinary; **la gente** ~ ordinary folk. **2** *sm* **(a)** *(di più persone)*: **avere qc in** ~ to have sth in common; **avere il bagno in** ~ to share a bathroom, to have a communal bathroom; **mettere le provviste in** ~ to pool *o* share one's provisions. **(b)**: **fuori del** ~ out of the ordinary.

comune[2] [ko'mune] *sm* town council; **l'età dei C~i** *(Storia)* the age of the city states; **la Camera dei ~i, i C~i** *(Brit Pol)* the House of Commons, the Commons.

comune[3] [ko'mune] *sf (anche Storia)* commune.

comunella [komu'nɛlla] *sf:* **fare** ~ to band together.

comunicabile [komuni'kabile] *ag* communicable.

comunicando, a [komuni'kando] *sm/f (Rel)* communicant.

comunicante [komuni'kante] *ag* communicating.

comunicare [komuni'kare] **1** *vt* **(a)** *(trasmettere)* to communicate; ~ **una notizia a qn** to give sb a piece of news; ~ **qc a qn** to inform sb of sth. **(b)** *(Rel)* to administer communion to. **2** *vi (stanze, persone)* to communicate; **questa porta comunica con l'esterno** this door leads outside. **3**: ~**rsi** *vr* **(a)** *(propagarsi)* to spread. **(b)** *(Rel)* to receive communion.

comunicativa [komunika'tiva] *sf* communicativeness; **ha molta** ~ she is very communicative.

comunicativo, a [komunika'tivo] *ag* communicative.

comunicato [komuni'kato] *sm* communiqué; ~ **stampa** press release.

comunicazione [komunikat'tsjone] *sf* **(a)** *(collegamento)* communication; **porta di** ~ communicating door; **essere in** ~ **(con)** *(Anat, Tecn)* to be connected (with); **mettersi in** ~ **con qn** to contact sb; **vie di** ~ means of communication; **le ~i ferroviarie/stradali/telefoniche sono interrotte** rail/road/telephone communications have been interrupted. **(b)** *(Telec)* call; **le passo la** ~ I'll put the call through to you; **non riesco ad avere la** ~ I can't get through; **si è interrotta la** ~ we've been cut off. **(c)** *(messaggio)* message, communication; *(annuncio)* announcement; **ho una** ~ **urgente per lei** I have an urgent message for you.

comunione [komu'njone] *sf (Rel, fig)* communion; **fare la** ~ to receive communion; **fare la prima** ~ to make one's first communion; ~ **dei beni** *(Dir: tra coniugi)* joint ownership of property.

comunismo [komu'nizmo] *sm* communism.

comunista, i, e [komu'nista] *ag, sm/f* communist.

comunità [komuni'ta] *sf* community; **C~ Economica Europea** *(abbr* **C.E.E.***)* European Economic Community *(abbr* EEC*)*.

comunitario, a [komuni'tarjo] *ag* community *attr.*

comunque [ko'munkwe] **1** *av (in ogni modo)* anyhow, anyway; **devi farlo** ~ you'll have to do it anyway; **accetterà** ~ he'll accept in any case; **e** ~ **al biglietto ci penso io** and as for the ticket I'll

see to that. **2** *cong* **(a)** *(in qualunque modo)* however, no matter how; ~ **vada** whatever happens; ~ **sia** however that may be. **(b)** *(tuttavia)* however, nevertheless; ~ **potevi avvertirmi** however *o* nevertheless you could have let me know, you could have let me know though.

con [kon] *prep (può fondersi con l'articolo determinativo:* con+il = **col**, con+lo = **collo**, con+l' = **coll'**, con+la = **colla**, con+i = **coi**, con+gli = **cogli**, con+le = **colle**) **(a)** *(gen)* with; **ci andrò** ~ **lei** I'll go with her; ~ **chi sei stato?** who were you with?; ~ **chi era il film?** who was in the film?; **riso col burro** rice with butter; **un ragazzo** ~ **gli occhi azzurri** a boy with blue eyes, a blue-eyed boy; **è a letto** ~ **la febbre** he's in bed with a temperature.

(b) *(complemento di relazione)* with; *(nei confronti di)* with, towards; **sono in contatto** ~ **loro** I am in touch with them; **è sposata** ~ **uno scozzese** she's married to a Scot; **si è sposata** ~ **uno scozzese** she married a Scot, she got married to a Scot; **hai parlato** ~ **lui?** have you spoken to him?; **essere gentile** ~ **qn** to be kind to sb; **è brava** ~ **i bambini** she's good with children; **confrontare qc** ~ **qc** to compare sth with *o* to sth; **sono tutti** ~ **lui** *(dalla sua parte)* they are all on his side, they are all behind him.

(c) *(per mezzo di)* with; *(: aereo, macchina etc)* by; **scrivere** ~ **la penna** to write with a pen; **prendilo** ~ **le mani** pick it up with your hands; **condisci l'insalata** ~ **l'olio** dress the salad with oil; **la birra è fatta col luppolo** beer is made from hops; **arrivare col treno/l'aereo/** ~ **la macchina** to arrive by train/by plane/by car; **lo hanno fatto venire** ~ **una scusa** they used a pretext to get him to come, they got him to come by means of a pretext.

(d) *(complemento di modo o maniera)* with; ~ **pazienza** with patience, patiently; ~ **la forza** by force; ~ **molta attenzione** with great attention, very attentively; ~ **mia grande sorpresa** to my great surprise; **lo accolse** ~ **un sorriso** she greeted him with a smile.

(e) *(complemento di causa)*: ~ **questo freddo non potremo partire** we can't leave in this cold weather; ~ **tutti i debiti che ha...** with all his debts..., given all his debts...; ~ **il 1° di ottobre** as of October 1st; ~ **l'autunno cadono le foglie** with the coming of autumn the leaves fall from the trees.

(f) *(nonostante)*: ~ **tutti i suoi difetti...** in spite of all his faults...; ~ **tutto ciò** in spite of that, for all that; ~ **tutto che era arrabbiato** even though he was angry, in spite of the fact that he was angry.

(g) *(con l'infinito)*: **se vuoi dimagrire, comincia col mangiare meno** if you want to lose weight, start by eating less; **finì col dirgli che aveva ragione lei** he ended up saying she was right; ~ **l'insistere tanto l'hai fatto arrabbiare** you've annoyed him with your pestering; **col (passar del) tempo** with the passing of time, in the course of time; **col sorgere del sole** with the dawn.

(h): **e** ~ **ciò se n'è andato** and with that he left; **e** ~ **questo?** so what?; **come va** ~ **la tua gamba?** how's your leg?; **come va** ~ **Alberto?** how are you getting on with Alberto?

conato [ko'nato] *sm:* **avere un** ~ *o* ~**i di vomito** to retch.

conca, che ['konka] *sf (Geog)* valley, basin.

concatenare [konkate'nare] **1** *vt* to link up, connect. **2:** ~**rsi** *vr* to be connected.

concatenazione [konkatenat'tsjone] *sf* connection, link.

concavo, a ['kɔnkavo] *ag* concave.

concedere [kon'tʃedere] **1** *vt* **(a)** *(permettere)*: ~ a **qn di fare qc** to allow sb to do sth; *(dare)*: ~ **qc a qn** to grant sb sth; **gli concesse di uscire** he gave him permission to go out; ~ **un prestito** to grant a loan; **mi concedi un minuto d'attenzione** may I have your attention. **(b)** *(ammettere)*: ~ **(che)** to concede (that). **2**: ~**rsi** *vr* *(permettersi)* to allow o.s., treat o.s. to.

concentramento [kontʃentra'mento] *sm* concentration.

concentrare [kontʃen'trare] **1** *vt* to concentrate; ~ **l'attenzione su qc** to focus one's attention on sth. **2**: ~**rsi** *vr*: ~**rsi (in)** *(raccogliere l'attenzione)* to concentrate (on); *(adunarsi)* to assemble (in).

concentrato, a [kontʃen'trato] *sm* concentrate; ~ **di pomodoro** tomato purée.

concentrazione [kontʃentrat'tsjone] *sf* (gen) concentration; ~ **orizzontale/verticale** *(Econ)* horizontal/vertical integration.

concentrico, a, ci, che [kon'tʃɛntriko] *ag (Geom)* concentric.

concepibile [kontʃe'pibile] *ag* conceivable.

concepimento [kontʃepi'mento] *sm* conception.

concepire [kontʃe'pire] *vt* **(a)** *(bambino)* to conceive. **(b)** *(idea)* to conceive; *(progetto)* to devise, conceive; **un elettrodomestico concepito per vari usi** an electrical appliance devised for various purposes. **(c)** *(immaginare)* to imagine, understand; **non riesco a ~ una cosa simile** I just can't imagine such a thing.

conceria [kontʃe'ria] *sf* tannery.

concernere [kon'tʃɛrnere] *vt* to concern, regard; **per quanto mi concerne** as far as I'm concerned.

concertare [kontʃer'tare] *vt* *(combinare: piano)* to devise; *(Mus: spartito)* to harmonize; *(: sinfonia)* to rehearse.

concertista, i, e [kontʃer'tista] *sm/f (Mus)* concert performer.

concerto [kon'tʃɛrto] *sm (Mus)* concert; *(: composizione)* concerto; **sala per ~i** concert hall.

concessionario, a [kontʃessjo'narjo] **1** *ag* concessionary. **2** *sm* agent, dealer; ~ **esclusivo (di)** sole agent (for).

concessione [kontʃes'sjone] *sf* concession.

concessivo, a [kontʃes'sivo] *ag* concessive.

concesso, a [kon'tʃesso] *pp di* **concedere**.

concetto [kon'tʃɛtto] *sm (nozione)* concept; *(opinione)* opinion; **farsi un ~ di** to form an opinion of; **è un impiegato di ~** ≈ he's a white-collar worker; **lascialo in pace, sta facendo un lavoro di ~** *(iro)* leave him alone, he's concentrating.

concettoso, a [kontʃet'toso] *ag* full of conceits.

concettuale [kontʃettu'ale] *ag* conceptual.

concezione [kontʃet'tsjone] *sf* **(a)** *(ideazione)* conception. **(b)** *(idea)* view, idea; **che ~ hai della vita!** how do you see life?, what is your view of life?

conchiglia [kon'kiʎʎa] *sf (Zool)* shell; *(Culin)* pasta shell.

concia ['kontʃa] *sf (vedi vt a)* tanning; curing.

conciare [kon'tʃare] **1** *vt* **(a)** *(pelli)* to tan; *(tabacco)* to cure. **(b)** *(maltrattare: scarpe, libri)* to treat badly; *(: persona)* to ill-treat; **guarda come hai conciato quei libri** look at the mess you've made of those books; **ti hanno conciato una** ≈ per le feste! they've really beaten you up! **2**: ~**rsi** *vr* *(ridursi male)* to get into a mess; *(vestirsi male)*: **ma guarda come si è conciata!** look at the state she's in!; **è sempre conciato da far paura** he always looks a terrible fright.

conciatore [kontʃa'tore] *sm (vedi vt* **a)** tanner; curer.

conciatura [kontʃa'tura] *sf (vedi vt* **a)** tanning; curing.

conciliabile [kontʃi'ljabile] *ag* compatible.

conciliabilità [kontʃiljabili'ta] *sf* compatibility.

conciliabolo [kontʃi'ljabolo] *sm* secret meeting.

conciliante [kontʃi'ljante] *ag* conciliatory.

conciliare[1] [kontʃi'ljare] **1** *vt* **(a)** *(mettere d'accordo)* to reconcile; ~ **una contravvenzione** to settle a fine on the spot. **(b)** *(favorire)* to be conducive to. **(c)**: ~**rsi qc** *(stima, simpatia)* to win, gain. **2**: ~**rsi** *vr* *(trovare un accordo)* to be reconciled; **lo studio non si concilia con il mio lavoro** I can't combine studying with my job.

conciliare[2] [kontʃi'ljare] *ag* council *attr.*

conciliazione [kontʃiljat'tsjone] *sf (accordo)* reconciliation; *(Dir)* settlement; **la C~** *(Storia)* the Lateran Pact.

concilio [kon'tʃiljo] *sm* **(a)** *(Rel)* council. **(b)** *(riunione)* conference, meeting.

concimare [kontʃi'mare] *vt* to fertilize; *(con letame)* to manure.

concime [kon'tʃime] *sm* fertilizer; *(letame)* manure.

concione [kon'tʃone] *sf*: **tenere una ~** *(iro)* to speechify.

concisione [kontʃi'zjone] *sf* concision, conciseness.

conciso, a [kon'tʃizo] *ag* concise.

concistoro [kontʃis'tɔro] *sm (Rel)* consistory.

concitato, a [kontʃi'tato] *ag* excited, agitated.

concitazione [kontʃitat'tsjone] *sf* excitement, agitation.

concittadino [kontʃitta'dino] *sm* fellow citizen.

conclave [kon'klave] *sm (Rel)* conclave.

concludente [konklu'dɛnte] *ag (argomentazione)* conclusive, convincing; *(persona)*: **poco ~** inefficient.

concludere [kon'kludere] **1** *vt* **(a)** *(affare, trattato)* to conclude; *(discorso)* to finish, end; **non ho concluso nulla oggi** I haven't achieved anything today; **per ~...** and to conclude...; **cerchiamo di ~** let's try to come to a conclusion. **(b)** *(dedurre)*: ~ **che** to conclude that, come to the conclusion that. **2**: ~**rsi** *vr* *(finire)* to end, conclude.

conclusione [konklu'zjone] *sf (gen)* conclusion; *(di discorso)* close, end; **in ~** in conclusion.

conclusivo, a [konklu'zivo] *ag* final, closing.

concluso, a [kon'kluzo] *pp di* **concludere**.

concomitante [konkomi'tante] *ag* concomitant.

concomitanza [konkomi'tantsa] *sf (di circostanze, fatti)* combination.

concordanza [konkor'dantsa] *sf (anche Gram)* agreement; *(letteratura)* concordance.

concordare [konkor'dare] **1** *vt (fissare)* to agree on; *(Gram)* to make agree; ~ **una tregua** to agree to a truce. **2** *vi (essere d'accordo)* to agree, coincide; *(: testimonianze)* to agree, tally.

concordato [konkor'dato] *sm (patto)* agreement; *(Rel)* concordat.

concorde [kon'kɔrde] *ag* in agreement; ~**i nel condannarlo** unanimous in their condemnation of him.

concordia [kon'kɔrdia] *sf* concord.

concorrente [konkor'rɛnte] **1** *ag* **(a)** *(Geom)* concurrent. **(b)** *(Comm)* competing. **2** *sm/f (Comm, Sport)* competitor; *(a un concorso di bellezza)* contestant.

concorrenza [konkor'rɛntsa] *sf* competition; **le due ditte si fanno una ~ spietata** the two firms are in fierce competition with one another, there is fierce competition between the two firms; **non**

temono la ~ they are unbeatable.

concorrenziale [konkorren'tsjale] *ag* competitive.

concorrere [kon'korrere] *vi* (**a**): ~ (**a**) *(contribuire: a guarigione, spesa)* to contribute (to); *(partecipare: a un'impresa)* to take part (in). (**b**) *(competere)*: ~ (**a**) to compete (for).

concorso, a [kon'korso] **1** *pp di* **concorrere. 2** *sm* (**a**) *(gen)* competition; *(esame)* competitive examination; **partecipanti fuori** ~ non-competitors; ~ **di bellezza** beauty contest; **un** ~ **ippico** a showjumping event; ~ **per titoli** competitive examination for qualified candidates. (**b**) *(partecipazione)*: ~ (**a**) contribution (to); ~ **di colpa** *(Dir)* contributory negligence; ~ **in reato** *(Dir)* complicity in a crime. (**c**) *(affluenza)* gathering; ~ **di circostanze** combination of circumstances.

concretare [konkre'tare] **1** *vt (attuare)* to put into practice. **2:** ~**rsi** *vr (attuarsi)* to materialize, be realized.

concretezza [konkre'tettsa] *sf* concreteness.

concretizzare [konkretid'dzare] *vt* = **concretare.**

concreto, a [kon'krɛto] **1** *ag (gen)* concrete; *(vantaggi)* positive. **2** *sm:* **in** ~ in reality; **fare qualcosa di** ~ to get something concrete done.

concubina [konku'bina] *sf* concubine.

concubinato [konkubi'nato] *sm* cohabitation.

concubino [konku'bino] *sm:* **sono** ~**i** they are living together.

concupire [konku'pire] *vt* to lust after.

concupiscenza [konkupiʃ'ʃɛntsa] *sf* lust, concupiscence.

concussione [konkus'sjone] *sf (Dir)* extortion.

condanna [kon'danna] *sf* (**a**) *(Dir: sentenza)* sentence; ~ **a morte** death sentence; **scontare una** ~ to serve a sentence; **ha già avuto due** ~**e per furto** he has two previous convictions for theft. (**b**) *(disapprovazione)* condemnation.

condannabile [kondan'nabile] *ag (biasimevole)* open to censure.

condannare [kondan'nare] *vt* (**a**) *(Dir)* to sentence; ~ **qn a 5 anni di prigione** to sentence sb to 5 years' imprisonment; ~ **qn per rapina a mano armata** to convict sb *o* find sb guilty of armed robbery; **è condannato al letto** he is confined to bed. (**b**) *(disapprovare)* to condemn, censure.

condannato, a [kondan'nato] *sm/f* prisoner, convict.

condensa [kon'dɛnsa] *sf* condensation.

condensare [konden'sare] *vt*, ~**rsi** *vr* to condense.

condensato, a [konden'sato] **1** *ag (denso)* condensed; *(riassunto)* summarized; **latte** ~ condensed milk. **2** *sm (di bugie, errori etc)* heap.

condensatore [kondensa'tore] *sm* condenser.

condensazione [kondensat'tsjone] *sf* condensation.

condimento [kondi'mento] *sm (di insalata)* dressing; *(di carne)* seasoning; *(salsa)* sauce.

condire [kon'dire] *vt (cibo)* to season, flavour; *(insalata)* to dress; *(fig)* to spice, season; **hai condito la pasta?** have you mixed the sauce with the pasta?

condirettore, trice [kondiret'tore] *sm/f (gen)* joint manager/manageress; *(di giornale)* co-editor.

condiscendente [kondiʃʃen'dɛnte] *ag (indulgente)* obliging; *(arrendevole)* compliant.

condiscendenza [kondiʃʃen'dentsa] *sf (disponibilità)* obligingness; *(arrendevolezza)* compliance.

condiscendere [kondiʃ'ʃendere] *vi* = **accondiscendere.**

condiscepolo, a [kondiʃ'ʃepolo] *sm/f* fellow disciple.

condisceso, a [kondiʃ'ʃeso] *pp di* **condiscendere.**

condividere [kondi'videre] *vt* to share.

condiviso, a [kondi'vizo] *pp di* **condividere.**

condizionale [kondittsjo'nale] **1** *ag (Gram)* conditional. **2** *sm (Gram)* conditional (mood). **3** *sf* (**a**) *(Gram)* conditional clause. (**b**) *(Dir)* suspended sentence.

condizionamento [kondittsjona'mento] *sm* conditioning; ~ **d'aria** air conditioning.

condizionare [kondittsjo'nare] *vt (gen, Psic)* to condition.

condizionato, a [kondittsjo'nato] *ag* conditioned; **ad aria** ~**a** air conditioned.

condizionatore [kondittsjona'tore] *sm:* ~ (**d'aria**) air conditioner.

condizione [kondit'tsjone] *sf* (**a**) *(stato)* condition; **in buone** ~**i** in good condition; **in** ~**i pessime** in a very bad state, in poor condition; ~**i di salute** state of health; **migliorare le proprie** ~**i finanziarie** to improve one's financial position; ~**i di lavoro** working conditions.
(**b**) *(situazione)* situation; **essere** *o* **trovarsi in** ~ **di fare qc** to be in a position to do sth; **mettere qn in** ~ **di fare qc** to make it possible for sb to do sth; **mi trovo in una** ~ **assurda** I'm in an absurd situation.
(**c**) *(di patto)* condition; *(di contratto etc)* condition, term; **porre una** ~ to lay down *o* make a condition; **ad un'unica** ~ on one condition; **non lo farò a nessuna** ~ on no account will I do it; **a** ~ **che** on condition that, provided that; ~**i a convenirsi** terms to be arranged.

condoglianze [kondoʎ'ʎantse] *sfpl* condolences; **fare le proprie** ~ **e a qn** to offer one's sympathy *o* condolences to sb.

condominiale [kondomi'njale] *ag:* **riunione** ~ residents' meeting; **spese** ~**i** common charges.

condominio [kondo'minjo] *sm (Dir)* condominium; *(edificio)* block of flats, condominium *(Am).*

condomino [kon'domino] *sm* joint owner.

condonare [kondo'nare] *vt (Dir)* to remit.

condono [kon'dono] *sm (Dir)* remission.

condor ['kɔndor] *sm inv* condor.

condotta [kon'dotta] *sf* (**a**) *(comportamento)* behaviour, conduct; **tenere una buona/cattiva** ~ to behave well/badly. (**b**) *(Amm: di medico)* country medical practice controlled by a local authority. (**c**) *(Tecn: tubature)* piping.

condottiero [kondot'tjero] *sm (mercenary)* leader; *(Storia)* condottiere.

condotto¹, a [kon'dotto] *pp di* **condurre.**

condotto², a [kon'dotto] **1** *ag:* **medico** ~ local authority doctor *(in a country district).* **2** *sm* (**a**) *(Anat)* duct. (**b**) *(Tecn: di liquido)* pipe, conduit; *(: di aria)* duct.

conducente [kondu'tʃente] *sm* driver.

conducibilità [kondutʃibili'ta] *sf* = **conduttività.**

condurre [kon'durre] *vt* (**a**) *(persona: portare)* to take; *(: guidare)* to lead; ~ **qn a casa** *(a piedi)* to walk sb home; *(in macchina)* to drive *o* take sb home; ~ **qn per mano** to take sb by the hand; ~ **alla vittoria** to lead to victory; ~ **in salvo qn** to lead sb to safety; ~ **qn alla follia** to drive sb mad; **questo ci conduce a pensare che...** this leads us to think that.... (**b**) *(azienda, affari)* to run; *(trattative)* to hold, conduct; *(orchestra)* to conduct; ~ *(il gioco) (Sport)* to lead, be in the lead; ~ **a termine** to conclude. (**c**) *(macchina)* to drive; *(aereo)* to pilot; *(barca)* to steer. (**d**) *(Fis)* to conduct.

conduttività [konduttivi'ta] *sf (Fis)* conductivity.

conduttivo, a [kondut'tivo] *ag (Fis)* conductive.

conduttore, trice [kondut'tore] **1** *ag:* **filo** ~ *(fig)* thread; **motivo** ~ leitmotiv. **2** *sm* (**a**) *(Fis)*

conductor. **(b)** *(di mezzi pubblici)* driver.
conduttura [kondut'tura] *sf (gen)* pipe; *(di acqua, gas)* main.
conduzione [kondut'tsjone] *sf* **(a)** *(di affari, ditta)* management. **(b)** *(Dir: locazione)* lease. **(c)** *(Fis)* conduction.
confabulare [konfabu'lare] *vi* to confab.
confabulazione [konfabulat'tsjone] *sf* confab.
confacente [konfa'tʃɛnte] *ag*: ~ **a qn/qc** suitable for sb/sth; **clima** ~ **alla salute** healthy climate.
confarsi [kon'farsi] *vr (essere adatto)*: ~ **a qn/qc** to be suitable for sb/sth; **questo modo di parlare non ti si confà** it doesn't become you to speak like that; **questo clima non mi si confà** this climate isn't good for me.
confatto, a [kon'fatto] *pp di* **confarsi.**
confederale [konfede'rale] *ag* confederal.
confederarsi [konfede'rarsi] *vr* to form a confederation.
confederato, a [konfede'rato] *ag, sm/f* confederate.
confederazione [konfederat'tsjone] *sf* confederacy, confederation.
conferenza [konfe'rentsa] *sf* **(a)** *(discorso)* lecture; **fare** *o* **tenere una** ~ **su qc** to give a lecture on sth, lecture on sth; **sala** ~**e** lecture theatre. **(b)** *(Pol, Amm: riunione)* conference; ~ **al vertice** summit conference; ~ **stampa** press conference.
conferenziere, a [konferen'tsjere] *sm/f* lecturer, speaker.
conferimento [konferi'mento] *sm* conferring, awarding.
conferire [konfe'rire] **1** *vt*: ~ **(a)** *(premio, titolo, incarico)* to confer (on); *(tono, aria)* to give (to). **2** *vi* **(a)** *(avere un colloquio)* to confer. **(b)** *(contribuire, giovare)*: ~ **a qn/qc** to be good for sb/sth.
conferma [kon'ferma] *sf* confirmation; **dare** ~ to confirm; **a** ~ **di** in confirmation of.
confermare [konfer'mare] *vt* to confirm; **l'eccezione conferma la regola** the exception proves the rule; **si è confermato campione** he has confirmed his position as champion.
confessare [konfes'sare] **1** *vt (gen)* to confess, admit; *(Rel)* to confess; **confesso di essere stupito** I must admit I'm amazed; **l'omicida ha confessato** the murderer confessed. **2:** ~**rsi** *vr* **(a)** *(Rel)*: **(andare a)** ~**rsi** to go to confession. **(b):** ~**rsi colpevole** to admit one's guilt.
confessionale [konfessjo'nale] **1** *ag* confessional. **2** *sm (Rel)* confessional (box).
confessione [konfes'sjone] *sf* **(a)** *(gen, Rel)* confession. **(b)** *(fede)* denomination.
confesso, a [kon'fesso] *ag*: **esser reo** ~ to have pleaded guilty.
confessore [konfes'sore] *sm (Rel)* confessor.
confetto [kon'fetto] *sm* **(a)** *(dolciume)* sugared almond; **a quando i** ~**i?** have you *(o* has he *etc)* named the day? **(b)** *(pillola)* sugar-coated pill.
confettura [konfet'tura] *sf (gen)* jam; *(di arance)* marmalade.
confezionare [konfettsjo'nare] *vt* **(a)** *(pacco)* to wrap up. **(b)** *(cibo, piatto)* to prepare; *(articoli di abbigliamento)* to make; **confezionato su misura** made to measure.
confezione [konfet'tsjone] *sf* **(a)** *(gen)* making, preparation; *(di abiti: da uomo)* tailoring; *(: da donna)* dressmaking; ~**i da uomo** menswear; ~**i per signora** ladies' wear. **(b)** *(imballaggio)* packaging; ~ **natalizia/regalo** Christmas/gift pack; **mi può fare una** ~ **regalo?** could you giftwrap it for me?; ~ **risparmio** economy size.
conficcare [konfik'kare] **1** *vt*: ~ **in** *(chiodo, punta)* drive into, stick into; *(unghie)* to stick into, dig

into. **2:** ~**rsi** *vr* to be stuck.
confidare [konfi'dare] **1** *vt*: ~ **qc a qn** to confide sth to sb. **2** *vi*: ~ **in** *(persona, capacità etc)* to have confidence in; **confido nella tua discrezione** I am relying on your discretion; **confido in una buona riuscita** I am confident of a successful outcome. **3:** ~**rsi** *vr*: ~**rsi con qn** to confide in sb.
confidente [konfi'dɛnte] **1** *ag* confiding, trusting. **2** *sm/f (chi riceve confidenze)* confidant/confidante; **è un** ~ **della polizia** he is a police informer.
confidenza [konfi'dɛntsa] *sf* **(a)** *(familiarità)* intimacy, familiarity; **essere in** ~ *o* **avere** ~ **con qn** to be on friendly terms with sb; **prendersi (troppe)** ~**e** to take liberties. **(b)** *(rivelazione)* confidence; **fare una** ~ **a qn** to confide something to sb; **dire qc in** ~ **a qn** to tell sb sth in confidence. **(c)** *(dimestichezza)*: **prendere** ~ **col proprio lavoro** to become more confident about one's work.
confidenziale [konfiden'tsjale] *ag (lettera, informazione)* confidential; *(maniere, parole)* familiar; **in via** ~ confidentially.
configurarsi [konfigu'rarsi] *vr (fig)* to take shape.
configurazione [konfigurat'tsjone] *sf (gen)* shape, configuration; *(Astron, Geog)* configuration.
confinante [konfi'nante] *ag* neighbouring.
confinare [konfi'nare] **1** *vt* **(a)** *(relegare)*: ~ **qn in** to confine sb to; **la malattia l'ha confinata a casa** her illness confined her to the house. **(b)** *(Pol)* to intern. **2** *vi*: ~ **con** *(anche fig)* to border on. **3:** ~**rsi**: ~**rsi (in)** to shut o.s. up (in).
confinato, a [konfi'nato] **1** *ag* interned. **2** *sm/f* internee.
Confindustria [konfin'dustrja] *sf* ≈ Confederation of British Industry.
confine [kon'fine] *sm (di territorio, nazione)* border, frontier; *(di proprietà)* boundary; **territorio di** ~ border zone; **senza** ~ *(fig)* boundless; **i** ~**i della scienza** the frontiers of science.
confino [kon'fino] *sm (Pol)* internment; **mandare al** ~ **qn** to send sb into internal exile.
confisca [kon'fiska] *sf* confiscation.
confiscare [konfis'kare] *vt* to confiscate.
conflagrazione [konflagrat'tsjone] *sf (incendio)* conflagration; *(fig: guerra)* sudden outbreak of hostilities.
conflitto [kon'flitto] *sm (gen, Mil)* conflict; *(fig: contrasto)* clash, conflict; **essere in** ~ **con qc** to clash with sth; **essere in** ~ **con qn** to be at loggerheads with sb.
conflittuale [konflittu'ale] *ag*: **rapporto** ~ relationship based on conflict.
confluenza [konflu'entsa] *sf (di fiumi, fig)* confluence; *(di strade)* junction.
confluire [konflu'ire] *vi (acque)* to meet, flow into each other; *(vie)* to meet; *(fig: idee, persone)* to meet, come together.
confondere [kon'fondere] **1** *vt* **(a)** *(mischiare)* to mix up; ~ **le idee a qn** to mix sb up, confuse sb; ~ **le carte in tavola** *(fig)* to confuse the issue. **(b)** *(scambiare)*: ~ **qc con qc** to confuse sth with sth; **confondo sempre i due fratelli** I always get the two brothers mixed up. **(c)** *(turbare)* to confuse; *(imbarazzare)* to embarrass; *(disorientare: nemico, avversario)* to trick. **2:** ~**rsi** *vr* **(a)** *(colori, sagoma)* to merge; *(ricordi)* to become confused; *(persona)* ~**rsi tra la folla** to mingle with the crowd. **(b)** *(sbagliarsi)* to be mistaken, get mixed up. **(c)** *(turbarsi)* to become confused.
conformare [konfor'mare] **1** *vt*: ~ **(a)** to adapt (to). **2:** ~**rsi** *vr*: ~**rsi (a)** to conform (to).

conformazione [konformat'tsjone] *sf* conformation.

conforme [kon'forme] *ag*: ~ **a** *(simile)* similar to; *(corrispondente)* in keeping with sth.

conformismo [konfor'mizmo] *sm* conformity.

conformista [konfor'mista] *sm/f (gen)* conformist.

conformità [konformi'ta] *sf* conformity; **in** ~ **a** in conformity with.

confortante [konfor'tante] *ag* comforting.

confortare [konfor'tare] *vt* **(a)** *(consolare)* to comfort. **(b)** *(tesi, accusa)* to strengthen, support.

confortevole [konfor'tevole] *ag (comodo)* comfortable; *(confortante)* comforting.

conforto [kon'tɔrto] *sm* **(a)** *(consolazione, sollievo)* comfort, consolation; **i** ~**i** *(religiosi)* the last sacraments. **(b)** *(conferma)* support; **a** ~ **di qc** in support of sth.

confratello [konfra'tɛllo] *sm (Rel)* brother.

confraternita [konfra'tɛrnita] *sf* brotherhood.

confrontabile [konfron'tabile] *ag* comparable.

confrontare [konfron'tare] **1** *vt (paragonare)* to compare. **2**: ~**rsi** *vr (scontrarsi)* to have a confrontation.

confronto [kon'fronto] *sm* **(a)** *(paragone)* comparison; *(Dir, Mil, Pol)* confrontation; **a** ~ **di** *o* **in** ~ **a** compared with, in comparison to; **reggere al** ~ **con** to stand comparison with. **(b)** *(di testi)* collation. **(c)**: **nei miei** *(o* **tuoi** *etc)* ~**i** towards me *(o* you *etc).*

confusionale [konfuzjo'nale] *ag*: **stato** ~ *(Med)* confused state.

confusionario, a [konfuzjo'narjo] **1** *ag* muddle-headed. **2** *sm/f* muddle-headed person.

confusione [konfu'zjone] *sf (disordine, errore)* confusion; *(chiasso)* racket, noise; *(imbarazzo)* embarrassment; **c'è stata** ~ **tra i due nomi** there's been a mix-up over the two names, the two names have been confused; **far** ~ *(disordine)* to make a mess; *(chiasso)* to cause a racket; *(confondere)* to confuse things; **essere in uno stato di** ~ **mentale** to be confused in one's mind.

confuso, a [kon'fuzo] **1** *pp di* **confondere. 2** *ag (gen)* confused; *(discorso, stile)* muddled; *(persona: turbato)* embarrassed; *(immagine, ricordo)* hazy.

confutare [konfu'tare] *vt* to confute.

confutazione [konfutat'tsjone] *sf* confutation.

congedare [kondʒe'dare] **1** *vt (gen)* to dismiss; *(Mil: soldati)* to demob; *(licenziare)* to sack. **2**: ~**rsi** *vr*: ~**rsi (da)** to take one's leave (of); *(soldato)* to be demobbed (from).

congedo [kon'dʒɛdo] *sm* **(a)** *(commiato)*: **prendere** ~ **da qn** to take one's leave of sb. **(b)** *(permesso, Mil)* leave; **andare in** ~ *(Mil)* to go on leave; **chiedere un** ~ **per motivi di salute** to apply for sick leave; ~ **illimitato** *(Mil)* discharge. **(c)** *(Teatro: finale)* finale; *(Poesia: coda)* envoi.

congegnare [kondʒeɲ'nare] *vt (motore)* to construct, put together; *(fig: trama, scherzo)* to devise.

congegno [kon'dʒeɲɲo] *sm (dispositivo)* device; *(meccanismo)* mechanism; *(fig peg)* contraption.

congelamento [kondʒela'mento] *sm (gen)* freezing; *(Med)* frostbite.

congelare [kondʒe'lare] **1** *vt (gen, Econ)* to freeze. **2**: ~**rsi** *vr* to freeze.

congelatore [kondʒela'tore] **1** *ag* freezer *attr.* **2** *sm (macchina)* deep-freeze.

congelato, a [kondʒe'lato] *ag (gen, Econ)* frozen.

congelazione [kondʒelat'tsjone] *sf* = **congelamento.**

congeniale [kondʒe'njale] *ag* congenial.

congenialità [kondʒenjali'ta] *sf* congeniality.

congenito, a [kon'dʒenito] *ag* congenital.

congerie [kon'dʒerje] *sf inv (di oggetti)* heap; *(di idee)* muddle, jumble.

congestionare [kondʒestjo'nare] *vt (Med, strada)* to congest; **essere congestionato** *(persona, viso)* to be flushed.

congestione [kondʒes'tjone] *sf* congestion.

congettura [kondʒet'tura] *sf* conjecture; **fare mille** ~ to let one's imagination run riot.

congetturare [kondʒettu'rare] *vt* to conjecture.

congiungere [kon'dʒundʒere] **1** *vt (gen)* to join; *(punti)* to join, connect; *(luoghi)* to link, connect. **2**: ~**rsi** *vr (gen)* to join; *(Mil)* to join forces; ~**rsi in matrimonio** to be joined in matrimony.

congiungimento [kondʒundʒi'mento] *sm (vedi vb)* joining; connecting; linking; **mettere in atto un** ~ *(Mil)* to join forces.

congiuntivite [kondʒunti'vite] *sf (Med)* conjunctivitis.

congiuntivo, a [kondʒun'tivo] *ag, sm (Gram)* subjunctive.

congiunto, a [kon'dʒunto] **1** *pp di* **congiungere. 2** *ag (mani)* clasped, joined; *(azione, sforzo)* joint. **3** *sm/f (parente)* relative.

congiuntura [kondʒun'tura] *sf* **(a)** *(punto di contatto)* join. **(b)** *(circostanza)* juncture, circumstance; *(opportunità)* occasion; **in questa** ~ at this juncture. **(c)** *(Econ)* economic situation; **superare la (bassa)** ~ to overcome the economic crisis.

congiunturale [kondʒuntu'rale] *ag* of the economic situation; **crisi** ~ economic crisis.

congiunzione [kondʒun'tsjone] *sf (gen)* join; *(Anat)* joint; *(di due linee ferroviarie)* junction; *(Astron, Gram)* conjunction.

congiura [kon'dʒura] *sf (anche fig)* conspiracy, plot.

congiurare [kondʒu'rare] *vi*: ~ **(ai danni di** *o* **contro qn)** to conspire (against sb), plot (against sb); **tutto sembra** ~ **contro di me** everything seems to be conspiring against me.

congiurato, a [kondʒu'rato] *sm/f* conspirator.

conglomerare [konglome'rare] *vt (gen)* to amass; *(Econ: somme)* to lump together.

conglomerato [konglome'rato] *sm (gen)* conglomeration; *(Geol)* conglomerate; *(Edil)* concrete.

congratularsi [kongratu'larsi] *vr*: ~**rsi con qn (per qc)** to congratulate sb (on sth).

congratulazioni [kongratulat'tsjoni] *sfpl* congratulations; **fare le (proprie)** ~ **a qn per qc** to congratulate sb on sth.

congrega, ghe [kon'grega] *sf* gang.

congregazione [kongregat'tsjone] *sf* congregation.

congressista, i, e [kongres'sista] *sm/f* participant at a congress.

congresso [kon'grɛsso] *sm* congress; **sala (dei)** ~**i** conference hall.

congressuale [kongressu'ale] *ag* congressional.

congruo, a ['kɔngruo] *ag (prezzo, compenso)* adequate, fair; *(ragionamento)* coherent, consistent.

conguagliare [kongwaʎ'ʎare] *vt (Comm)* to balance; *(stipendio)* to adjust.

conguaglio [kon'gwaʎʎo] *sm* **(a)** *(vedi vb)* balancing; adjusting; **fare il** ~ **di** to balance; to adjust. **(b)** *(somma)* balance.

coniare [ko'njare] *vt (monete)* to mint; *(medaglie)* to strike; *(fig: parole nuove)* to coin.

conico, a, ci, che ['kɔniko] *ag* conic(al), cone-shaped.

conifera [ko'nifera] *sf* conifer.

conigliera [koniʎ'ʎɛra] *sf (gabbia)* rabbit hutch; *(più grande)* rabbit run.

coniglia [ko'niʎʎa] *sf* (doe) rabbit.

coniglietto [koniʎ'ʎetto] *sm* bunny.

coniglio [ko'niʎʎo] *sm (Zool)* rabbit; *(maschio)* buck; **pelliccia di ~** rabbit fur; **sei un ~!** *(fig)* you're chicken!

conio ['kɔnjo] *sm* **(a)** *(punzone)* minting die. **(b)** *(impronta)* stamp; **moneta di nuovo ~** newly-minted coin. **(c)** *(invenzione)* coining; **parole di nuovo ~** newly-coined words.

coniugale [konju'gale] *ag (amore, diritti)* conjugal; *(vita)* married, conjugal.

coniugare [konju'gare] *vt (Gram)* to conjugate.

coniugato, a [konju'gato] *ag (Amm)* married.

coniugazione [konjugat'tsjone] *sf (Gram)* conjugation.

coniuge ['kɔnjudʒe] *sm* spouse; **i ~i** the couple, the husband and wife; **i ~i Bianchi** Mr and Mrs Bianchi.

connaturale [konnatu'rale] *ag:* **~ a qn/qc** natural to sb/sth.

connaturarsi [konnatu'rarsi] *vr:* **~rsi in qn** *(abitudine, vizio)* to become second nature to sb.

connaturato, a [konnatu'rato] *ag* inborn.

connazionale [konnattsjo'nale] **1** *ag* of the same country. **2** *sm/f* compatriot, fellow countryman/woman.

connessione [konnes'sjone] *sf* connection; **~ di idee** association of ideas.

connesso, a [kon'nɛsso] **1** *pp di* **connettere. 2** *ag* connected.

connettere [kon'nɛttere] **1** *vt:* **~ (a)** *(gen, fig)* to connect (with), link (to); *(Elettr)* to connect (with). **2** *vi (ragionare)* to think straight.

connettivo, a [konnet'tivo] *ag:* **tessuto ~** connective tissue.

connivente [konni'vɛnte] *ag:* **essere ~ (in qc con qn)** to connive (at sth with sb).

connivenza [konni'vɛntsa] *sf (Dir)* connivance.

connotati [konno'tati] *smpl* distinguishing marks; **dare i ~i di qn** to give a description of sb; **rispondere ai ~i** to fit the description; **cambiare i ~i a qn** *(fam)* to beat sb up.

connubio [kon'nubjo] *sm (matrimonio)* marriage; *(fig)* union.

cono ['kɔno] *sm* cone.

conoscente [konoʃ'ʃɛnte] *sm/f* acquaintance.

conoscenza [konoʃ'ʃɛntsa] *sf* **(a)** *(sapere, nozione)* knowledge; *(Filosofia)* cognition; **essere a ~ di qc** to know sth; **venire a ~ di qc** to get to know sth, learn of sth; **portare qn a ~ di qc** to inform sb of sth; **la polizia è venuta a ~ (del fatto) che...** it has come to the knowledge of the police that...; **le mie ~e in questo campo** my knowledge in this field; **per vostra ~** for your information; **prendere ~ di qc** *(Dir, Amm)* to take cognizance of sth.

(b) *(amicizia, persona)* acquaintance; **fare la ~ di qn** to make sb's acquaintance; **lieto di fare la sua ~** pleased to meet you; **ti voglio far fare la ~ di mio marito** I'd like to introduce you to my husband; **ha ottenuto il lavoro grazie alle sue ~e** she got the job because of her contacts.

(c) *(sensi, coscienza)* consciousness; **perdere/riprendere ~** to lose/regain consciousness.

conoscere [ko'noʃʃere] **1** *vt* **(a)** *(gen)* to know; *(persona, avvenimento)* to be acquainted with, know; *(testo, abitudine)* to be familiar with, know; *(posto, ristorante)* to know of; **~ qn di vista** to know sb by sight; **l'ha conosciuto all'università** she met him at university; **conosci i motori?** do you know anything about engines?; **conosco**

la canzone *(fig)* I've heard it all before; **conosce il fatto suo** he knows what he's talking about; **non conosce il mondo** he isn't very worldly-wise.

(b) *(successo)* to enjoy, have; *(privazioni)* to know, experience; **~ tempi difficili** to go through hard times.

(c): **far ~ qn/qc** to make sb/sth known; **ti farò ~ mio marito** I'll introduce you to my husband; **mi ha fatto ~ la musica classica** he introduced me to classical music; **farsi ~** *(fig)* to make a name for o.s.

(d) *(riconoscere)*: **~ qn dalla voce** to recognize sb by his voice.

2: **~rsi** *vr* **(a)** *(se stessi)* to know o.s.

(b) *(uso reciproco)* to meet, know each other; **si sono conosciuti un anno fa** they met a year ago; **da quanto vi conoscete?** how long have you known one another?

conoscitivo, a [konoʃʃi'tivo] *ag* cognitive.

conoscitore, trice [konoʃʃi'tore] *sm/f* connoisseur.

conosciuto, a [konoʃ'ʃuto] **1** *pp di* **conoscere. 2** *ag (universo)* known; *(attore, autore, artista)* well-known; **~ in tutto il mondo** well-known throughout the world, world-famous.

conquista [kon'kwista] *sf (anche fig)* conquest; **partire alla ~ di qc** to set out to conquer sth; **le ~e della scienza** the achievements of science.

conquistare [konkwis'tare] *vt (territorio, fortezza)* to conquer; *(felicità, successo, ricchezza)* to gain; *(simpatia)* to win, gain; *(cuore)* to win over; **si è conquistato la simpatia di tutti** he's made himself popular with everybody.

conquistatore, trice [konkwista'tore] **1** *ag (esercito, truppe)* conquering. **2** *sm (in guerra)* conqueror; *(seduttore)* lady-killer.

consacrare [konsa'krare] **1** *vt* **(a)** *(Rel)* to consecrate; *(: sacerdote)* to ordain; *(: re)* to anoint; *(abitudine, tradizione)* to establish. **(b)** *(vita, tempo, sforzi)*: **~ (a)** to dedicate (to), devote (to). **2:** **~rsi** *vr (dedicarsi)*: **~rsi a qc/qn** to dedicate o.s. to sth/sb.

consacrazione [konsakrat'tsjone] *sf (Rel: vedi vb)* consecration; ordination; anointing.

consanguineità [konsangwinei'ta] *sf* consanguinity, blood relationship.

consanguineo, a [konsan'gwineo] **1** *ag* related by blood. **2** *sm/f* blood relation.

consapevole [konsa'pevole] *ag:* **~ di qc** aware *o* conscious of sth; **rendere qn ~ di qc** to make sb aware of sth.

consapevolezza [konsapevo'lettsa] *sf* awareness, consciousness; **acquistare ~ di qc** to become aware *o* conscious of sth.

conscio, a, sci, sce *o* **scie** ['kɔnʃo] *ag:* **~ (di)** aware (of), conscious (of); **è ~ dei suoi limiti** he is aware of *o* knows his limitations.

consecutivo, a [konseku'tivo] *ag* consecutive; **~ a** following upon.

consegna [kon'seɲɲa] *sf (a)* *(Comm: il consegnare)* delivery; *(: merce consegnata)* consignment; **~ a domicilio** home delivery; **~ in contrassegno, pagamento alla ~** cash on delivery. **(b)** *(custodia)*: **prendere in ~ qn** *(bambino)* to take sb into one's care; *(prigioniero)* to take custody of sb; **prendere qc in ~** to take sth into safekeeping; **dare qc in ~ a qn** to give sth to sb for safekeeping. **(c)** *(Mil: ordini)* orders *pl*; *(punizione)* confinement to barracks; **un soldato fedele alla ~** a soldier who obeys orders; **passare le ~e a qn** to hand over to sb.

consegnare [konseɲ'ɲare] *vt* **(a)**: **~ qc (a qn)** *(lettera, pacco, merce)* to deliver sth (to sb);

(lavoro finito) to hand sth in (to sb), submit sth (to sb); **il meccanico non mi ha ancora consegnato la macchina** I haven't had the car back from the mechanic yet; ~ **qn alla polizia** to hand sb over to the police. **(b)** *(Mil: soldato)* to confine to barracks.

consegnatario, a [konseɲɲa'tarjo] *sm/f* consignee.

consegnato [konseɲ'ɲato] *sm (Mil)* soldier confined to barracks.

conseguente [konse'gwɛnte] *ag* consequent.

conseguenza [konse'gwɛntsa] *sf* consequence; **di o per** ~ consequently; **senza lasciare** ~**e** without having any effect; **pagare le** ~**e** to pay the consequences.

conseguibile [konse'gwibile] *ag* achievable, attainable.

conseguimento [konsegwi'mento] *sm (di scopo, risultato etc)* achievement, attainment; **al** ~ **della laurea** on graduation.

conseguire [konse'gwire] **1** *vt (scopo)* to achieve, attain; *(vittoria)* to gain; ~ **la laurea** to graduate, obtain one's degree. **2** *vi (aus essere) (derivare)*: **ne consegue che...** it follows that... .

consenso [kon'sɛnso] *sm* approval, consent; **dare/ negare il proprio** ~ **a qc** to give/refuse one's consent to sth; **per comune** ~ unanimously.

consensuale [konsensu'ale] *ag (Dir)* by mutual consent.

consentire [konsen'tire] **1** *vi*: ~ **a qc/a fare qc** to agree *o* consent to sth/to do sth. **2** *vt*: ~ **a qn qc/di fare qc** to allow *o* permit sb sth/to do sth; **è un lavoro che non consente distrazioni** you can't afford to be distracted in this kind of job; **mi si consenta di ringraziare...** I would like to thank... .

consenziente [konsen'tsjɛnte] *ag (gen, Dir)* consenting.

consequenziale [konsekwen'tsjale] *ag* consequential.

conserto, a [kon'sɛrto] *ag*: **a braccia** ~**e** with one's arms folded.

conserva [kon'sɛrva] **1** *sf*: ~**e alimentari** tinned *(o* canned *o* bottled) foods; **mettere cibi in** ~ to preserve food. **2**: ~ **di frutta** preserve; ~ **di pomodoro** tomato purée.

conservare [konser'vare] **1** *vt* **(a)** *(gen)* to keep; *(andatura, velocità)* to maintain; ~ **la calma** to keep calm; ~ **il proprio sangue freddo** *(fig)* to keep one's head; **conservo sempre un buon ricordo di lui** I still have fond memories of him. **(b)** *(monumenti)* to preserve. **(c)** *(Culin)* to preserve; *(: in frigo)* to keep; ~ **le cipolline sotto aceto** to pickle onions; ~ **i pomodori in bottiglia** to bottle tomatoes. **2**: ~**rsi** *vr (cibo)* to keep; ~**rsi in buona salute** to keep healthy; **si conserva bene** *(persona)* he *(o* she) is well-preserved.

conservatore, trice [konserva'tore] **1** *ag (gen, Pol)* conservative; **il partito C**~ the Conservative Party. **2** *sm/f* **(a)** *(di museo)* curator; *(di biblioteca)* librarian; *(di archivio)* keeper. **(b)** *(Pol)* Conservative.

conservatorio [konserva'tɔrjo] *sm (di musica)* conservatory.

conservatorismo [konservato'rizmo] *sm (Pol)* conservatism.

conservazione [konservat'tsjone] *sf* **(a)** *(di cibi, monumenti)* preservation; **in buono stato di** ~ well-preserved; **istinto di** ~ instinct of self-preservation. **(b)** *(di energia, dell'ambiente naturale)* conservation.

conserviero, a [konser'vjero] *ag*: **industria** ~**a** canning industry.

consesso [kon'sɛsso] *sm (assemblea)* assembly; *(riunione)* meeting.

considerabile [konside'rabile] *ag* worthy of consideration.

considerare [konside'rare] **1** *vt* **(a)** *(gen)* to consider; **considerato che...** considering that...; **tutto considerato** all things considered; **ti considero un amico** I think of you *o* consider you as a friend; ~ **un onore fare qc** to consider it an honour to do sth. **(b)** *(stimare)*: ~ **molto qn** to think highly of sb. **(c)** *(Dir: contemplare)*: **la legge non considera questo caso** the law does not provide for this case. **2**: ~**rsi** *vr*: ~**rsi un genio** to consider o.s. a genius; **si considerano amici** they consider themselves friends.

considerato, a [konside'rato] *ag* **(a)** *(prudente)* cautious, careful. **(b)** *(stimato)* highly thought of, esteemed.

considerazione [konsiderat'tsjone] *sf* **(a)** *(esame, riflessione)* consideration; **agire senza** ~ to act rashly; **voglio che tu agisca con** ~ I'd like you to think carefully about what you're doing; **meritare** ~ to be worthy of consideration; **prendere qn/qc in** ~ to take sb/sth into consideration. **(b)** *(stima)* esteem; **godere di molta** ~ to be very highly thought of; **avere (una grande)** ~ **per qn** to think highly of sb. **(c)** *(pensiero, osservazione)* observation.

considerevole [konside'revole] *ag* considerable.

consigliabile [konsiʎ'ʎabile] *ag* advisable.

consigliare [konsiʎ'ʎare] **1** *vt* **(a)** *(raccomandare: ristorante, film, prudenza)*: ~ **(a qn)** to recommend (to sb); **che cosa mi consigli?** what do you recommend? **(b)** *(suggerire)*: ~ **a qn di fare qc** to advise sb to do sth; **si consiglia ai passeggeri di...** passengers are advised to... . **2**: ~**rsi** *vr*: ~**rsi con qn** to ask sb's advice; ~**rsi col proprio avvocato** to consult one's lawyer.

consigliere, a [konsiʎ'ʎere] *sm/f (gen)* adviser; *(Pol, Amm)* councillor, council member; ~ **comunale** town councillor; ~ **delegato** *(Comm)* managing director; ~ **d'amministrazione** *(Comm)* board member.

consiglio [kon'siʎʎo] *sm* **(a)** advice; **un** ~ some advice, a piece of advice; **un** ~ **da amico** a friendly piece of advice; **seguire il** ~ *o* **i** ~**i di qn** to take sb's advice. **(b)** *(assemblea)* council; ~ **d'amministrazione** board of directors; ~ **comunale** town council; ~ **di fabbrica** works council; **il C**~ **dei Ministri** *(Parlamento)* the Cabinet; **hanno fatto un** ~ **di famiglia** they held a family conference.

consiliare [konsi'ljare] *ag (decisione, assemblea)* council *attr*; *(: direzionale)* board *attr*.

consistente [konsis'tɛnte] *ag (tessuto)* solid; *(fig: prova, testimonianza)* sound.

consistenza [konsis'tɛntsa] *sf* **(a)** *(di impasto)* consistency; *(di stoffa)* texture. **(b)** *(di sospetti, voci, ragionamenti)*: **senza** ~ ill-founded, groundless; **acquistare** ~ to gain substance. **(c)** *(Comm, Dir)*: ~ **di cassa/di magazzino** cash/stock in hand; ~ **patrimoniale** financial solidity.

consistere [kon'sistere] *vi (aus essere) (essere composto di)*: ~ **di qc** to consist of sth, be made up of sth; *(fondarsi, risiedere in)*: ~ **in qc/nel fare qc** to consist in sth/in doing sth; **in che consiste il tuo lavoro?** what does your job entail?

consistito, a [konsis'tito] *pp di* **consistere**.

consociarsi [konso'tʃarsi] *vr* to go into partnership.

consociato, a [konso'tʃato] **1** *ag* associated. **2** *sm/f* associate.

consocio, a, ci, cie [kon'sɔtʃo] *sm/f* associate, partner.

consolante [konso'lante] *ag* consoling, comforting.

consolare[1] [konso'lare] **1** *vt* to console; **se ti può ~...** if it is of any consolation *o* comfort to you... . **2: ~rsi** *vr* to console o.s.; **la vedova si è consolata presto** the widow got over her loss quickly; **il bambino si è consolato vedendo le caramelle** the child cheered up when he saw the sweets.

consolare[2] [konso'lare] *ag* consular.

consolato [konso'lato] *sm (officio)* consulate; *(carica)* consulship.

consolatore, trice [konsola'tore] *ag* consoling, comforting.

consolazione [konsolat'tsjone] *sf* **(a)** comfort, consolation; **sei la mia unica ~** you're my one consolation; **premio di ~** consolation prize. **(b)** *(piacere)*: **è una ~ vederlo di nuovo in salute** it's a pleasure *o* joy to see him well again.

console ['konsole] *sm* consul.

consolidamento [konsolida'mento] *sm* consolidation.

consolidare [konsoli'dare] **1** *vt (anche fig)* to consolidate; **~ le proprie posizioni** *(Mil)* to consolidate one's position. **2: ~rsi** *vr (Geol)* to consolidate; *(fig: patrimonio, posizione)* to become more stable; **la società si è consolidata** the company has consolidated its position.

consolidato, a [konsoli'dato] *ag* consolidated; **è un'amicizia ormai ~a** it's a firm friendship; **debito ~** funded debt.

consolidazione [konsolidat'tsjone] *sf* consolidation.

consolle [kon'solle] *sf* console; **~ di comando** *o* **controllo** control panel.

consommé [kõsɔ'me] *sm inv* consommé.

consonante [konso'nante] *sf* consonant.

consonantico, a, ci, che [konso'nantiko] *ag* consonantal.

consonanza [konso'nantsa] *sf* consonance.

consono, a ['kɔnsono] *ag*: **~ a** consistent with, consonant with.

consorella [konso'rella] *ag f* sister *attr*.

consorte [kon'sɔrte] **1** *sm/f (coniuge)* consort. **2** *ag*: **principe ~** prince consort.

consorteria [konsorte'ria] *sf* clique.

consorziale [konsor'tsjale] *ag* consortium *attr*.

consorziarsi [konsor'tsjarsi] *vr* to form a consortium.

consorzio [kon'sɔrtsjo] *sm* consortium.

constare [kon'stare] **1** *vi (aus* **essere)** *(essere composto)*: **~ di** to consist of, be composed of, be made up of. **2** *vb impers (essere noto)*: **mi consta che...** I know that...; **a quanto mi consta** as far as I know.

constatare [konsta'tare] *vt* **(a)** *(notare, verificare)* to notice, note; **come può ~** as you can see; **non faccio che ~** I'm merely making an observation. **(b)** *(decesso)* to certify.

constatazione [konstatat'tsjone] *sf* observation; **fare una ~** to make an observation.

consueto, a [konsu'ɛto] **1** *ag* usual. **2** *sm*: **come di ~** as usual; **più/meno del ~** more/less than usual.

consuetudinario, a [konsuetudi'narjo] *ag (abituale)* usual, habitual; **diritto ~** *(Dir)* common law.

consuetudine [konsue'tudine] *sf* **(a)** *(abitudine)* habit; *(tradizione)* custom; **è sua ~ alzarsi prestissimo** he usually gets up very early, he is in the habit of getting up very early; **secondo la ~** according to custom. **(b)** *(Dir)* common law.

consulente [konsu'lɛnte] **1** *ag* consulting. **2** *sm (tecnico, amministrativo)* consultant; **~ legale** legal adviser.

consulenza [konsu'lɛntsa] *sf (prestazione professionale)* consultancy; *(consigli)* advice; **~ medica/legale** medical/legal advice; **chiedere una ~** to ask for professional advice; **ufficio di ~ fiscale** tax consultancy office.

consultare [konsul'tare] **1** *vt (medico, esperto)* to consult, seek the advice of; *(dizionario)* to look up, consult. **2: ~rsi** *vr* **(a)** *(uso reciproco)* to confer, consult each other. **(b): ~rsi con qn** to consult (with) sb.

consultazione [konsultat'tsjone] *sf* consultation; **~i** *(Pol)* talks, consultations; **dopo lunga ~** after much consultation; **libro di ~** reference book; **~ popolare** referendum.

consultivo, a [konsul'tivo] *ag* consultative.

consulto [kon'sulto] *sm (Med)* consultation.

consultorio [konsul'tɔrjo] *sm*: **~ familiare** *o* **matrimoniale** marriage guidance centre; **~ pediatrico** children's clinic.

consumare [konsu'mare] **1** *vt* **(a)** *(logorare: scarpe, vestiti, libri)* to wear out. **(b)** *(cibo)* to consume; *(sog: malattia, passione)* to consume, devour; **desidera ~ i pasti in camera?** *(in albergo)* would you like to have your meals brought up to your room? **(c)** *(usare: acqua, luce, benzina)* to use; *(finire)* to use up; **quanto consuma questa macchina?** what sort of mileage does your car do?; **la mia moto consuma molto** my motorbike uses a lot of petrol *o* is heavy on petrol. **(d)** *(Dir: matrimonio)* to consummate. **2: ~rsi** *vr (vestiario)* to wear (out); *(candela)* to burn down; *(penna, pennarello)* to run dry; *(persona: per malattia)* to waste away; **~rsi (di)** to be consumed (with).

consumato, a [konsu'mato] *ag* **(a)** *(vestiti, scarpe, tappeto)* worn. **(b)** *(persona: esperto)* accomplished.

consumatore, trice [konsuma'tore] *sm/f (Comm)* consumer.

consumazione [konsumat'tsjone] *sf* **(a)** *(al bar)* drink. **(b)** *(Dir: del matrimonio)* consummation.

consumismo [konsu'mizmo] *sm* consumerism.

consumistico, a, ci, che [konsu'mistiko] *ag* consumer *attr*.

consumo [kon'sumo] *sm* **(a)** *(gen)* consumption; **~ di benzina** petrol consumption; **fare largo ~ di qc** to use sth heavily; **per mio uso e ~** for my personal use. **(b)** *(Econ)*: **generi** *o* **beni di ~** consumer goods; **beni di largo ~** basic commodities; **imposta di ~** tax on consumer goods; **la società dei ~i** consumer society.

consuntivo, a [konsun'tivo] **1** *ag (Comm: bilancio)* final. **2** *sm (Comm)* final balance; **fare un ~ (della situazione)** *(fig)* to take stock (of the situation).

consunto, a [kon'sunto] *ag (abiti)* worn out, shabby; *(volto)* wasted.

consunzione [konsun'tsjone] *sf (Med)* consumption.

conta ['konta] *sf (nei giochi)*: **fare la ~** to see who is going to be 'it'.

contabile [kon'tabile] **1** *ag (Comm)* book-keeping *attr*. **2** *sm/f* book-keeper, accountant.

contabilità [kontabili'ta] *sf (Comm: di banca, ditta)* accounting, accountancy; *(insieme dei libri)* books *pl*, accounts *pl*; **tenere la ~** to keep the accounts; **ufficio ~** accounts department.

contachilometri [kontaki'lɔmetri] *sm inv* mileometer.

contadinesco, a, schi, sche [kontadi'nesko] *ag (campagnolo)* country *attr*; *(peg)* coarse, oafish.

contadino, a [konta'dino] **1** *ag (di campagna)* country *attr*; *(rurale)* peasant *attr*; **la rivolta ~a** the peasant revolt. **2** *sm/f* **(a)** *(bracciante)* countryman/woman; *(bracciante)* farm worker. **(b)** *(Storia,*

peg) peasant. **3** *sm (fattore)* tenant farmer.
contagiare [konta'dʒare] *vt (anche fig)* to infect.
contagio [kon'tadʒo] *sm* **(a)** *(contatto)* contagion; **il vaiolo si prende per** ~ smallpox is contracted by touch. **(b)** *(malattia)* disease; *(epidemia)* epidemic.
contagioso, a [konta'dʒoso] *ag (gen)* infectious; *(per contatto)* contagious; *(fig: riso, allegria)* infectious, contagious.
contagiri [konta'dʒiri] *sm inv (Aut)* rev counter.
contagocce [konta'gottʃe] *sm inv* dropper; **mi dà i soldi con il** ~ he counts every penny he gives me.
contaminare [kontami'nare] *vt (gen)* to contaminate; *(buon nome)* to tarnish; *(testo)* to corrupt.
contaminazione [kontaminat'tsjone] *sf* contamination.
contante [kon'tante] **1** *ag*: **denaro** ~ cash. **2**: ~**i** *smpl* cash *sg*; **pagare in** ~**i** to pay cash *o* cash down.
contare [kon'tare] **1** *vt* **(a)** *(calcolare, enumerare)* to count; **le telefonate non si contavano più** I *(o he etc)* couldn't keep count of the telephone calls; **ha sempre i minuti contati** he never has a spare moment; **ha i giorni contati, ha le ore contate** his days are numbered; **ho i soldi contati** I haven't a penny to spare. **(b)** *(mettere in conto)* to include, count (in); **senza** ~ *(senza includere)* not counting; *(senza parlare di)* not to mention; ~ **di fare qc** to intend to do sth. **(c)** *(fam: raccontare)* to tell; **contarle grosse** to tell tall stories. **2** *vi* **(a)** *(calcolare)* to count; ~ **fino a 100** to count to 100. **(b)** *(fare assegnamento)*: ~ **su qn/qc** to count on sb/sth; **puoi contarci** you can count on it. **(c)** *(avere importanza)* to count, matter; **la gente che conta** people who matter.
contatore [konta'tore] *sm* meter; ~ **del gas** gas meter.
contattare [kontat'tare] *vt* to contact.
contatto [kon'tatto] *sm* **(a)** *(gen)* contact; **essere o venire a** ~ **con qc** to be in/come into contact with sth; **a** ~ **con l'aria** in contact with (the) air; **non sopporto la lana a** ~ **con la pelle** I can't wear wool against my skin; **mettere qc a** ~ **con qc** to put sth against sth; **essere in** ~ **con qn** to be in touch with sb; **prendere** ~ **con** to get in touch *o* contact with; **mantenere i** ~**i (con qn)** to maintain contact (with sb). **(b)** *(Elettr, Radio)* contact; **aprire/chiudere il** ~ *(Elettr)* to make/break contact; **fare** ~ *(Elettr: fili)* to touch; **stabilire il** ~ *(Radio)* to make contact.
conte ['konte] *sm* count; *(Brit)* earl.
contea [kon'tɛa] *sf* **(a)** *(Storia)* earldom. **(b)** *(Amm)* county.
conteggiare [konted'dʒare] *vt (fare il conto di)* to work out; *(addebitare)* to charge for.
conteggio [kon'teddʒo] *sm* **(a)** *(gen)* reckoning, calculation; **fare il** ~ **di** to calculate. **(b)** *(Spazio)*: ~ **alla rovescia** countdown. **(c)** *(Pugilato)* count.
contegno [kon'teɲɲo] *sm* behaviour; **avere** *o* **tenere un** ~ **esemplare** to behave perfectly; **ha assunto un** ~ **poco simpatico nei nostri confronti** he assumed a rather unpleasant attitude towards us; **darsi un** ~ *(ostentare disinvoltura)* to act nonchalant; *(ricomporsi)* to pull o.s. together.
contegnoso, a [konteɲ'ɲoso] *ag (dignitoso)* dignified; *(riservato)* reserved.
contemplare [kontem'plare] *vt (paesaggio)* to gaze at; *(possibilità)* to contemplate; *(Dir: considerare)* to provide for.
contemplativo, a [kontempla'tivo] *ag* contemplative.

contemplazione [kontemplat'tsjone] *sf* contemplation.
contempo [kon'tɛmpo] *sm*: **nel** ~ meanwhile, in the meantime.
contemporaneo, a [kontempo'raneo] **1** *ag*: ~ **(di** *o* **a)** contemporary (with); **la sua partenza fu** ~**a al mio arrivo** his departure coincided with my arrival; **l'arte** ~**a** contemporary *o* modern art. **2** *sm/f* contemporary.
contendente [konten'dɛnte] **1** *ag* contending. **2** *sm/f (avversario)* opponent, adversary; *(per un titolo)* contestant.
contendere [kon'tɛndere] **1** *vt (contestare)*: ~ **qc a qn** to contend with sb for sth, be in competition with sb for sth; **si contendono il titolo** they are competing for the title; **si contendevano l'affetto della madre** they were vying with one another for their mother's affection. **2** *vi (disputare, litigare)*: ~ **(per qc)** to quarrel (over *o* about sth).
contenere [konte'nere] **1** *vt* **(a)** *(racchiudere)* to contain; *(: sog: recipienti, locali pubblici)* to hold; *(: cinema, veicoli)* to hold, seat. **(b)** *(frenare: entusiasmo, sentimenti, epidemia)* to contain; *(: truppe, avanzata nemica)* to hold in check. **2**: ~**rsi** *vr* to contain o.s.
contenitore [konteni'tore] *sm* container.
contentabile [konten'tabile] *ag*: **essere difficilmente** ~ to be difficult to please.
contentare [konten'tare] **1** *vt* to please; *(soddisfare)* to satisfy. **2**: ~**rsi** *vr*: ~**rsi (di)** to content o.s. (with); **si contenta di poco** he is easily satisfied.
contentezza [konten'tettsa] *sf (soddisfazione)* contentment; *(felicità)* happiness.
contentino [konten'tino] *sm* sop; **gli abbiamo dato un** ~ **per farlo smettere di piangere** we gave him a little something to stop him crying.
contento, a [kon'tento] *ag (lieto)* happy; *(soddisfatto)* satisfied, pleased; ~ **di** *(auto, persona)* pleased with; *(promozione, cambiamento)* happy *o* pleased about; **sono** ~ **di averti ritrovato** I'm happy to have met up with you again; **e non** ~ **di ciò...** and not content with that...; **sono** ~ **così** *(mi basta)* I've got enough; ~ **come una Pasqua** as happy as Larry.
contenuto, a [konte'nuto] **1** *ag (ira, entusiasmo)* restrained, suppressed; *(forza)* contained. **2** *sm (di cassa, valigia etc)* contents *pl*; *(di libro, film, discorso)* content.
contenzioso, a [konten'tsjoso] **1** *ag (Dir)* contentious. **2** *sm (Amm: ufficio)* legal department.
conterraneo, a [konter'raneo] *sm/f* fellow countryman/woman.
contesa [kon'tesa] *sf (litigio, contrasto)* quarrel, argument; *(Dir)* dispute.
conteso, a [kon'teso] **1** *pp di* **contendere**. **2** *ag (premio, carica)* sought after.
contessa [kon'tessa] *sf* countess.
contestabile [kontes'tabile] *ag* questionable, disputable.
contestare [kontes'tare] *vt (disputare)* to dispute, contest; ~ **a qn il diritto di fare qc** to contest sb's right to do sth; ~ **un reato a qn** *(Dir)* to charge sb with a crime; ~ **una contravvenzione a qn** to issue sb with a fine; ~ **il sistema** to protest against the system.
contestatario, a [kontesta'tarjo] *ag, sm/f* = **contestatore**.
contestatore, trice [kontesta'tore] **1** *ag* antiestablishment. **2** *sm/f* protester.
contestazione [kontestat'tsjone] *sf* **(a)** *(Dir: disputa)* dispute; **in caso di** ~ if there are any objections. **(b)** *(Dir: notifica)* notification; **si**

proceda alla ~ **delle accuse** please read out the charges. **(c)** *(Pol)* anti-establishment activity; **la ~ studentesca del '68** the student protests of '68.

contesto [kon'tɛsto] *sm* context; **visto nel ~** seen in context.

contestuale [kontestu'ale] *ag (gen)* contextual; *(Dir)* contemporary.

contiguità [kontigui'ta] *sf* proximity.

contiguo, a [kon'tiguo] *ag (camere, case)* adjoining, adjacent; **essere ~ a** to be adjacent *o* next to.

continentale [kontinen'tale] *ag* continental; **l'Europa ~** *(Geog)* continental Europe; *(per gli inglesi)* the Continent.

continente¹ [konti'nɛnte] *sm (gen)* continent; *(terraferma)* mainland.

continente² [konti'nɛnte] *ag* moderate; **essere ~ nel bere/mangiare** to drink/eat in moderation.

continenza [konti'nɛntsa] *sf* continence.

contingentare [kontindʒen'tare] *vt (Comm)* to place a quota on, fix a quota on.

contingente [kontin'dʒente] **1** *ag* contingent. **2** *sm* **(a)** *(gen, Mil, Filosofia)* contingent; **~ di leva** group of soldiers called up for military service. **(b)** *(Comm)* quota.

contingenza [kontin'dʒentsa] *sf* **(a)** *(gen)* contingency; *(circostanza)* circumstance. **(b): (indennità di) ~** cost-of-living allowance.

continuamente [kontinua'mente] *av (senza interruzione)* continuously, nonstop; *(ripetutamente)* continually; **perché vieni ~ a disturbarmi?** why do you keep coming and bothering me?

continuare [kontinu'are] **1** *vt (studi, progetto)* to continue (with), carry on with; *(viaggio)* to continue; *(tradizione)* to continue, carry on; **~ a fare qc** to go on *o* keep on *o* continue doing sth; **continuò la lettura** he went on reading. **2** *vi* to continue, go on; **continuò per la sua strada** he continued on his way; **la strada continua fino al bosco** the road carries on *o* continues as far as the wood; **se continua così...** if it *o* he goes on like this...; **se i dolori continuano...** if the pain persists...; **'continua'** *(di romanzi a puntate)* 'to be continued'; **'continua a pagina 9'** 'continued on page 9'. **3** *vb impers*: **continua a nevicare/a fare freddo** it's still snowing/cold.

continuativo, a [kontinua'tivo] *ag (occupazione)* permanent; *(periodo)* consecutive; **per 5 giorni ~i** for 5 consecutive days.

continuatore, trice [kontinua'tore] *sm/f*: **essere ~ di** *(tradizione etc)* to continue, carry on.

continuazione [kontinuat'tsjone] *sf* continuation; **la ~ di un romanzo** the sequel to a novel; **in ~** continuously.

continuità [kontinui'ta] *sf* continuity.

continuo, a [kon'tinuo] *ag (ininterrotto)* continuous; *(che si ripete)* continual; **di ~** continually.

contitolare [kontito'lare] *sm/f* co-owner.

conto ['konto] **1** *sm* **(a)** *(calcolo)* calculation; **fare di ~** to count.

(b) *(Banca, Comm)* account; *(fattura: di ristorante, albergo)* bill; *(: di prestazione)* account, bill; **pagare** *o* **saldare il ~** to pay the bill; **fare i ~i** to do the accounts; **dobbiamo fare il ~ delle spese** we must work out the expenses; **far bene/male i propri ~i** *(anche fig)* to get one's sums right/wrong; **non aveva fatto i ~i con possibili imprevisti** he hadn't allowed for anything unexpected happening; **fare i ~i senza l'oste** to forget the most important thing; **farò i ~i con te più tardi!** I'll sort you out later!; **avere un ~ in sospeso (con qn)** to have an outstanding account (with sb); *(fig)* to have a score to settle (with sb).

(c) *(stima, considerazione)*: **di poco/nessun ~** of little/no importance; **tener ~ di qn/qc** to take sb/sth into consideration *o* account; **tenere qc da ~** to take great care of sth.

(d) *(fraseologia)*: **a ~i fatti, in fin dei ~i** all things considered, when all is said and done; **ad ogni buon ~** in any case; **per ~ mio** *(a mio avviso)* in my opinion; *(a nome mio)* on my behalf; **voglio starmene per ~ mio** I went to be on my own; **mi hanno detto strane cose sul suo ~** I've heard some strange things about him; **fare ~ che** *(supporre)* to suppose that; **fare ~ su qn/qc** to rely *o* depend on sb/sth; **chiedere ~ di qc a qn** to ask sb to give an account *o* explanation of sth; **rendere ~ di qc a qn** to be accountable to sb for sth; **rendersi ~ di qc/che** to realize sth/that.

2: ~ in banca bank account; **~ corrente** current account; **~ corrente postale** ≈ National Girobank payment; **~ alla rovescia** countdown; **~ scoperto** overdrawn account; **avere il ~ scoperto** to be overdrawn.

contorcere [kon'tortʃere] **1** *vt* to twist; *(viso)* to contort. **2: ~rsi** *vr*: **~rsi dal dolore** to writhe with pain; **~rsi dalle risa** to be doubled up with laughter.

contorcimento [kontortʃi'mento] *sm* = **contorsione.**

contornare [kontor'nare] **1** *vt (gen, fig)* to surround; *(ornare)* to decorate, trim. **2: ~rsi** *vr*: **~rsi di** to surround o.s. with.

contorno [kon'torno] *sm* **(a)** *(linea esterna)* outline, contour; **fare da ~ a** to surround. **(b)** *(Culin)* vegetables *pl*; **arrosto con ~ di piselli** roast meat served with peas.

contorsione [kontor'sjone] *sf* contortion.

contorsionista, i, e [kontorsjo'nista] *sm/f* contortionist.

contorto, a [kon'tɔrto] **1** *pp di* **contorcere. 2** *ag* twisted; *(fig: ragionamento, stile)* tortuous.

contrabbandare [kontrabban'dare] *vt* to smuggle.

contrabbandiere [kontrabban'djere] *sm* smuggler.

contrabbando [kontrab'bando] *sm* smuggling, contraband; **fare il ~** to smuggle; **di ~** contraband, smuggled.

contrabbasso [kontrab'basso] *sm (Mus)* (double) bass.

contraccambiare [kontrakkam'bjare] *vt (favore, auguri)* to return; *(gentilezza)* to repay; **vorrei ~** I'd like to show my appreciation.

contraccettivo, a [kontrattʃet'tivo] *ag, sm* contraceptive.

contraccolpo [kontrak'kolpo] *sm (gen)* rebound; *(di arma da fuoco)* recoil.

contraccusa [kontrak'kuza] *sf (Dir)* counter-charge.

contrada [kon'trada] *sf (poet)* land.

contraddetto, a [kontrad'detto] *pp di* **contraddire.**

contraddire [kontrad'dire] **1** *vt* to contradict. **2: ~rsi** *vr* to contradict o.s.; *(uso reciproco: persone)* to contradict each other *o* one another; *(: testimonianze etc)* to be contradictory.

contraddistinguere [kontraddis'tingwere] *vt (merce)* to mark; *(fig: atteggiamento, persona)* to distinguish.

contraddistinto, a [kontraddis'tinto] *pp di* **contraddistinguere.**

contraddittorio, a [kontraddit'tɔrjo] **1** *ag (affermazione, testimonianza, personaggio)* contradictory; *(comportamento)* inconsistent; *(sentimenti)* conflicting. **2** *sm (Dir: di testimoni)* cross-examination; *(Pol: dibattito)* debate.

contraddizione [kontraddit'tsjone] *sf*

contradiction; **cadere in** ~ to contradict o.s.; **essere in** ~ *(tesi, affermazioni)* to contradict one another; **essere in** ~ **con** to contradict; **spirito di** ~ argumentativeness.

contraente [kontra'ɛnte] **1** *ag (Dir: parte)* contracting. **2** *sm/f* contracting party.

contraerea [kontra'ɛrea] *sf (Mil)* anti-aircraft artillery.

contraereo, a [kontra'ɛreo] *ag (Mil)* anti-aircraft *attr.*

contraffare [kontraf'fare] *vt (firma)* to forge; *(banconota)* to forge, counterfeit; *(voce)* to disguise; *(cibo, vino)* to adulterate.

contraffatto, a [kontraf'fatto] **1** *pp di* **contraffare**. **2** *ag (firma)* forged; *(banconota)* forged, counterfeit; *(voce)* disguised.

contraffattore, trice [kontraffat'tore] *sm/f (di firme)* forger; *(di monete)* forger, counterfeiter.

contraffazione [kontraffat'tsjone] *sf* **(a)** *(vedi vb)* forging, forgery; counterfeiting; *(di cibi etc)* adulteration. **(b)** *(esemplare contraffatto)* forgery.

contrafforte [kontraf'fɔrte] *sm* **(a)** *(Archit)* buttress. **(b)** *(Geog)* spur.

contralto [kon'tralto] *sm* alto, contralto.

contrappello [kontrap'pɛllo] *sm (Mil)* second roll call.

contrappesare [kontrappe'sare] **1** *vt* to counterbalance; *(fig: decisione)* to weigh up. **2:** ~**rsi** *vr* to counterbalance each other.

contrappeso [kontrap'peso] *sm* counterbalance.

contrapporre [kontrap'porre] **1** *vt* **(a)** *(opporre):* ~ **un rifiuto ad una richiesta** to counter a request with a refusal; ~ **un ostacolo a qc** to set an obstacle in the way of sth. **(b)** *(paragonare):* ~ **a** to compare with. **2:** ~**contrapporsi** *vr:* **contrapporsi a qc** to contrast with sth, be opposed to sth; **i loro punti di vista si contrappongono** they hold opposing points of view.

contrapposizione [kontrappozit'tsjone] *sf (opposizione)* juxtaposition; *(confronto)* comparison.

contrapposto, a [kontrap'posto] **1** *pp di* **contrapporre**. **2** *ag (argomenti, concetti)* contrasting; *(posizioni)* opposing.

contrappunto [kontrap'punto] *sm* counterpoint.

contrariamente [kontrarja'mente] *av:* ~ **a** contrary to; ~ **al solito** just for once; ~ **al solito non ha ottenuto un buon risultato** unusually for him he wasn't successful.

contrariare [kontra'rjare] *vt (ostacolare: persona)* to oppose; *(: piani)* to thwart; *(irritare)* to annoy.

contrariato, a [kontra'rjato] *ag* annoyed.

contrarietà [kontrarje'ta] *sf inv (avversità)* adversity, misfortune; *(fastidio)* trouble.

contrario, a [kon'trarjo] **1** *ag (gen)* opposite; *(avverso: sorte)* adverse; *(: venti)* contrary; **è** ~ **ai miei principi** it's against my principles; **sono** ~ **a questo tuo modo di comportarti** I disapprove of the way you behave; **in caso** ~ otherwise; **in direzione** ~**a** in the opposite direction. **2** *sm* opposite; **al** ~ on the contrary; **avere qc in** ~ to have some objection; **non ho niente in** ~ I've no objection; **è esattamente il** ~ it's quite the opposite *o* reverse.

contrarre [kon'trarre] **1** *vt* **(a)** *(muscoli, volto)* to tense. **(b)** *(malattia, debito, prestito)* to contract; *(abitudine, vizio)* to pick up; *(accordo, patto)* to enter into; ~ **matrimonio** to marry. **2: contrarsi** *vr (gen, Gram)* to contract.

contrassegnare [kontrasseɲ'ɲare] *vt* to mark.

contrassegno [kontras'seɲɲo] **1** *sm* *(distinguishing)* mark. **2** *av* = **contro assegno**.

contrastante [kontras'tante] *ag* contrasting.

contrastare [kontras'tare] **1** *vt (avanzata, piano etc)* to hinder; *(desiderio, diritto)* to dispute; **una vittoria contrastata** a hard-fought victory. **2** *vi:* ~ **(con)** to clash (with); **questi colori contrastano fra di loro** these colours clash.

contrasto [kon'trasto] *sm* **(a)** *(gen, TV, Fot)* contrast; **per** ~ in contrast; **un** ~ **di opinioni** a difference of opinion. **(b)** *(conflitto)* conflict; *(disputa, litigio)* quarrel, dispute; **essere in/ venire a** ~ **con qn** to be in/come into disagreement with sb.

contrattaccare [kontrattak'kare] *vi* to counter-attack.

contrattacco [kontrat'takko] *sm* counter-attack; **passare al** ~ *(fig)* to fight back.

contrattare [kontrat'tare] *vt (uso assoluto: trattare)* to negotiate; *(mercanteggiare)* to bargain; *(terreno, merce)* to bargain over, to negotiate the price of; ~ **il prezzo** to negotiate the price.

contrattazione [kontrattat'tsjone] *sf (trattativa)* negotiation; **dopo lunghe** ~**i ho spuntato un buon prezzo** after much bargaining I managed to get a good price.

contrattempo [kontrat'tempo] *sm* hitch; **per una serie di** ~**i** due to a series of difficulties.

contratto, a [kon'tratto] **1** *pp di* **contrarre**. **2** *ag (volto, muscoli)* tense; *(muscoli)* tense, contracted; *(Gram)* contracted. **3** *sm* contract; ~ **di lavoro** contract of employment; ~ **collettivo di lavoro** collective agreement.

contrattuale [kontrattu'ale] *ag* contractual; **forza** ~ *(di sindacato)* bargaining power.

contravvenire [kontravve'nire] *vi:* ~ **a** *(legge, regolamento)* to contravene; ~ **a un obbligo** to fail to meet an obligation.

contravventore, trice [kontravven'tore] *sm/f* offender.

contravvenuto, a [kontravve'nuto] *pp di* **contravvenire**.

contravvenzione [kontravven'tsjone] *sf* **(a)** *(trasgressione):* ~ **(a)** contravention (of). **(b)** *(Aut: multa)* fine; **fare una** ~ **a qn** to fine sb.

contrazione [kontrat'tsjone] *sf (gen, Med, Gram)* contraction; *(di prezzi, vendite):* ~ **(di)** decrease (in).

contribuente [kontribu'ente] *sm/f (Fisco)* taxpayer.

contribuire [kontribu'ire] *vi:* ~ **a qc** to contribute to sth; ~ **a fare qc** to help do sth; **tutto ciò ha contribuito a peggiorare la situazione** all this made things worse.

contributivo, a [kontribu'tivo] *ag* contributory.

contributo [kontri'buto] *sm* **(a)** *(gen)* contribution; **dare il proprio** ~ **a qc** to make one's contribution to sth. **(b):** ~**i** *pl* charges; ~**i prevedenziali** = national insurance contributions.

contribuzione [kontribut'tsjone] *sf* contribution.

contristare [kontris'tare] **1** *vt* to sadden, make sad. **2:** ~**rsi** *vr* to become sad.

contrito, a [kon'trito] *ag* contrite, penitent; **con aria** ~**a** penitently.

contrizione [kontrit'tsjone] *sf* contrition.

contro ['kontro] **1** *prep* **(a)** *(gen)* against; **sono tutti** ~ **di me** they are all against me; **lottare** ~ **qn/qc** to fight against sb/sth; **è** ~ **il divorzio** he's against *o* opposed to divorce; **il Milan** ~ **la Juventus** Milan versus *o* against Juventus; **pastiglie** ~ **l'emicrania** tablets for migraines, migraine tablets; **una medicina ottima** ~ **l'influenza** an excellent treatment for flu. **(b)** *(contatto, direzione)* against; **si appoggiò** ~ **la porta** he leaned against the door; **ho sbattuto** ~ **la porta** I bumped into the door; **puntò la**

pistola ~ **di me** he pointed his gun at me; **spararono** ~ **la polizia** they shot at the police.

(c) *(Comm: in cambio di)*: **pagamento** ~ **assegno** cash on delivery; ~ **pagamento/ricevuta** on payment/receipt.

(d) *(contrariamente a)*: ~ **ogni mia aspettiva** contrary to my expectations.

(e): ~ **corrente,** ~ **luce,** ~ **voglia** *etc vedi* **controcorrente, controluce, controvoglia** *etc.*

2 *av* against; **votare** ~ to vote against; **dar** ~ **a qn** to contradict sb; **per** ~ on the other hand.

3 *sm inv* con; **il pro e il** ~ the pros and cons.

4 *pref* counter...; **contraereo, a** *ag* anti-aircraft *attr*; **contrattacco** *sm* counter-attack; **controindicazione** *sf* contraindication.

controbattere [kontro'battere] *vt (ribattere)* to answer back; *(confutare)* to refute.

controbilanciare [kontrobilan'tʃare] *vt (gen, fig)* to counterbalance.

controcorrente [kontrokor'rɛnte] *av*: **nuotare** ~ *(in un fiume)* to swim upstream; *(nel mare)* to swim against the tide; **andare** ~ *(fig)* to swim against the tide.

controfagotto [kontrofa'gɔtto] *sm (Mus)* double bassoon.

controffensiva [kontroffen'siva] *sf (Mil, fig)* counter-offensive.

controfigura [kontrofi'gura] *sf* stuntman/woman; **fare la** ~ **di qn** to play sb's double.

controfinestra [kontrofi'nɛstra] *sf*: **mettere le** ~**e** to have double glazing installed.

controfirma [kontro'firma] *sf* countersignature.

controfirmare [kontrofir'mare] *vt* to countersign.

controindicazione [kontroindikat'tsjone] *sf* contraindication.

controllare [kontrol'lare] *vt* **(a)** *(verificare: gen)* to check; *(: biglietto)* to inspect, check. **(b)** *(sorvegliare)* to watch, keep a close watch on; *(: ufficio, impiegato)* to supervise. **(c)** *(tenere a freno, dominare: anche Mil)* to control. **2:** ~**rsi** *vr* to control o.s.

controllo [kon'trɔllo] *sm* **(a)** *(verifica: gen)* check; *(: dei biglietti)* inspection; **fare un** ~ **di** to check sth; to inspect sth; ~ **doganale** customs inspection; ~ **passaporti** passport control; ~ **qualità** quality control; **visita di** ~ *(Med)* checkup. **(b)** *(sorveglianza)* supervision; **telefono sotto** ~ tapped telephone; **base di** ~ *(Aer)* ground control. **(c)** *(padronanza, regolamentazione)* control; **esercitare il** ~ **su qc** to have control over sth; **perdere il** ~ **(di qc)** *(di macchina, situazione etc)* to lose control (of sth); **ha perso il** ~ **(di sé)** he lost control (of himself), he lost his self-control; ~ **dei prezzi/delle nascite** price/birth control.

controllore [kontrol'lore] *sm (di autobus, treno)* inspector; *(doganale)* customs officer.

controluce [kontro'lutʃe] **1** *sf inv (Fot)* backlit shot. **2** *av*: **(in)** ~ against the light; *(fotografare)* into the light.

contromano [kontro'mano] *av*: **guidare** ~ to drive on the wrong side of the road; *(in un senso unico)* to drive the wrong way up a one-way street.

contromarca, che [kontro'marka] *sf* pass-out (ticket).

contromarcia [kontro'martʃa] *sf (Mil)* counter-march; *(Aut)* reverse.

controparte [kontro'parte] *sf (Dir)* opposing party.

contropartita [kontropar'tita] *sf (fig: compenso)*: **come** ~ in return.

contropelo [kontro'pelo] **1** *av (di stoffa etc)* against the nap; **radersi** ~ to shave against the growth; **accarezzare un gatto** ~ to stroke a cat the wrong way. **2** *sm*: **fare il** ~ to shave against the growth.

contropiede [kontro'pjɛde] *sm (Sport)*: **azione di** ~ sudden counter-attack; **prendere qn in** ~ *(fig)* to catch sb off his *(o* her*)* guard.

controproducente [kontroprodu'tʃɛnte] *ag*: **essere** ~ to produce the opposite effect.

contrordine [kon'trordine] *sm* counter-order; **salvo** ~ unless I *(o* you *etc)* hear to the contrary.

controriforma [kontrori'forma] *sf (Storia)* Counter-Reformation.

controrivoluzione [kontrorivolut'tsjone] *sf* counter-revolution.

controsenso [kontro'sɛnso] *sm (di affermazione etc)* contradiction in terms; *(assurdità)* nonsense.

controspionaggio [kontrospio'naddʒo] *sm* counter-espionage.

controvento [kontro'vɛnto] *av* against the wind; **navigare** ~ *(Naut)* to sail to windward.

controversia [kontro'vɛrsja] *sf (gen)* controversy; *(Dir)* dispute; **ha suscitato molte** ~**e** it provoked a great deal of controversy.

controverso, a [kontro'vɛrso] *ag* controversial.

controvoglia [kontro'vɔʎʎa] *av*: **(di)** ~ reluctantly.

contumace [kontu'matʃe] **1** *ag (Dir)*: **rendersi** ~ to default, fail to appear in court. **2** *sm/f (Dir)* defaulter.

contumacia [kontu'matʃa] *sf (Dir)* default; **processare qn in** ~ to try sb in his *(o* her*)* absence; **giudizio in** ~ judgment by default.

contundente [kontun'dɛnte] *ag*: **corpo** ~ blunt instrument.

conturbante [kontur'bante] *ag (sguardo, bellezza)* disturbing.

conturbare [kontur'bare] *vt* to disturb.

contusione [kontu'zjone] *sf* bruise.

contuso, a [kon'tuzo] **1** *ag* bruised. **2:** ~**i** *smpl (in incidente etc)* those suffering from cuts and bruises.

conurbazione [konurbat'tsjone] *sf* conurbation.

convalescente [konvaleʃ'ʃɛnte] *ag, sm/f* convalescent.

convalescenza [konvaleʃ'ʃɛntsa] *sf* convalescence; **essere in** ~ to be convalescing; **ha fatto una** ~ **di 3 mesi** he spent 3 months convalescing.

convalida [kon'valida] *sf (vedi vb)* validation; confirmation.

convalidare [konvali'dare] *vt (Amm)* to validate; *(fig: dubbi, sospetti)* to confirm.

convegno [kon'veɲɲo] *sm (incontro)* meeting; *(riunione ufficiale)* convention, conference.

convenevoli [konve'nevoli] *smpl* courtesies; **scambiarsi i** ~ to exchange the usual courtesies.

conveniente [konve'njɛnte] *ag* **(a)** *(adatto, opportuno)*: ~ **(a)** suitable (for), fitting (for). **(b)** *(vantaggioso: prezzo)* cheap; *(: affare)* profitable.

convenienza [konve'njɛntsa] *sf* **(a)** *(l'essere vantaggioso: di prezzo)* cheapness; *(: di affare)* advantage, profit; **non vedo la** ~ **di trovarci a Milano** I feel our meeting in Milan would be to little purpose; **fare qc per** ~ to do sth out of self-interest; **non c'è** ~ **a vendere adesso** there's no advantage in selling at the moment; **la** ~ **di abitare in centro** the advantage of living in the centre; **matrimonio di** ~ marriage of convenience. **(b)** *(decoro)* propriety; **andare oltre i limiti della** ~ to go beyond the pale. **(c)**: **le** ~**e** *(norme sociali)* good manners, the proprieties.

convenire [konve'nire] **1** *vt* to agree upon; **come convenuto** as agreed; **resta convenuto che...** it is agreed that...; **in data da** ~ on a date to be agreed.

2 *vi* **(a)** *(essere d'accordo)*: ~ **(su qc/che)** to agree (upon sth/that); **devi** ~ **che hai torto** you must admit you are in the wrong. **(b)** *(aus essere: riunirsi)* to gather, assemble. **(c)** *(aus essere: essere vantaggioso)*: ~ **a qn** to be worthwhile for sb; **questo affare non mi conviene** this transaction isn't worth my while.

3 *vb impers (aus essere)*: ~ **(a qn)** *(essere vantaggioso)* to be worthwhile (for sb); *(essere consigliabile)* to be advisable (for sb); **ti conviene accettare** you would be well advised to accept; **non gli conviene fare il furbo** he'd better not try to get clever; **conviene andarsene** we'd better go.

4: ~**rsi** *vr*: ~**rsi a** to suit, befit; **come si conviene ad una signorina** as befits a young lady.

conventicola [konven'tikola] *sf (cricca)* clique; *(riunione segreta)* secret meeting.

convento [kon'vɛnto] *sm (di suore)* convent; *(di monaci)* monastery; **entrare in** ~ *(suora)* to enter a convent; **accontentiamoci di quel che passa il** ~ let's make the best of things.

conventuale [konventu'ale] *ag* of a convent.

convenuto, a [konve'nuto] **1** *pp di* **convenire. 2** *ag (ora, luogo, prezzo)* agreed. **3** *sm* **(a)** *(cosa pattuita)* agreement; **secondo il** ~ as agreed. **(b)** *(Dir)* defendant. **(c)**: **i** ~**i** *(i presenti)* those present.

convenzionale [konventsjo'nale] *ag (gen)* conventional.

convenzionato, a [konventsjo'nato] *ag (ospedale, clinica)* ≈ National Health Service *attr.*

convenzione [konven'tsjone] *sf* **(a)** *(Dir, Pol)* agreement. **(b)** *(assunto generale, tradizione)* convention; *(tacito accordo)* understanding; **le** ~**i (sociali)** social conventions; **la** ~ **vuole che tutti bacino la sposa** it's the custom for everyone to kiss the bride. **(c)** *(Pol, Dir: convegno)* convention.

convergente [konver'dʒɛnte] *ag* convergent.

convergenza [konver'dʒɛntsa] *sf* convergence.

convergere [kon'vɛrdʒere] *vi (aus essere)*: ~ **(su)** *(gen, Mat)* to converge (on); *(interesse)* to centre (on).

conversa [kon'vɛrsa] *sf (Rel)* lay sister.

conversare [konver'sare] *vi* to talk, have a conversation, converse *(frm)*.

conversazione [konversat'tsjone] *sf* conversation; **fare una** ~ to have a conversation *o* a talk; **fare** ~ *(chiacchierare)* to chat, have a chat.

conversione [konver'sjone] *sf (gen)*: ~ **(a/in)** conversion (to/into); ~ **a U** *(Aut)* U-turn.

converso, a [kon'vɛrso] **1** *pp di* **convergere. 2**: **per** ~ *av* conversely.

convertibile [konver'tibile] *ag*: ~ **(in)** convertible (into).

convertire [konver'tire] **1** *vt*: ~ **qn (a qc)** to convert sb (to sth); ~ **qc in qc** to convert sth into sth. **2**: ~**rsi** *vr*: ~**rsi (a qc)** *(persona)* to be converted (to sth).

convertito, a [konver'tito] **1** *ag* converted. **2** *sm/f* convert.

convertitore [konverti'tore] *sm (Elettr)* converter.

convessità [konvessi'ta] *sf* convexity.

convesso, a [kon'vɛsso] *ag* convex.

convettore [konvet'tore] *sm* convector.

convezione [konvet'tsjone] *sf* convection.

convincente [konvin'tʃɛnte] *ag* convincing.

convincere [kon'vintʃere] **1** *vt* **(a)** to convince; ~ **qn di qc** to convince sb of sth; ~ **qn a fare qc** to persuade sb to do sth, talk sb into doing sth. **(b)** *(Dir)*: ~ **qn di qc** to prove sb guilty of sth. **2**: ~**rsi** *vr*: ~**rsi di qc/che** to convince o.s. of sth/that.

convincimento [konvintʃi'mento] *sm* conviction, belief.

convinto, a [kon'vinto] **1** *pp di* **convincere. 2** *ag* convinced; **in tono** ~ with conviction; **reo** ~ *(Dir)* convicted criminal.

convinzione [konvin'tsjone] *sf* conviction; **ho la** ~ **di aver lasciato l'orologio a scuola** I'm positive I left my watch at school.

convissuto, a [konvis'suto] *pp di* **convivere.**

convitato, a [konvi'tato] *sm/f* guest.

convitto [kon'vitto] *sm* boarding school.

convivenza [konvi'vɛntsa] *sf* living together; *(Dir)* cohabitation; **la** ~ **con quell'uomo non dev'esser facile** it can't be easy living with that man.

convivere [kon'vivere] *vi* to live together; *(Dir)* to cohabit; ~ **con qn** to live with sb.

conviviale [konvi'vjale] *ag* convivial.

convocare [konvo'kare] *vt (riunione, parlamento)* to convene; *(persona subordinata)* to summon, send for; **tutti i genitori sono stati convocati** all parents have been asked to attend.

convocazione [konvokat'tsjone] *sf* **(a)** *(atto: vedi vb)* convening; summoning; **lettera di** ~ (letter of) notification to appear *o* attend. **(b)** *(riunione)* meeting.

convogliare [konvoʎ'ʎare] *vt* **(a)** *(dirigere)* to direct; *(: acque)* to channel; *(: fig: energie etc)*: ~ **su** to channel into. **(b)** *(trasportare)* to carry, transport.

convoglio [kon'vɔʎʎo] *sm* **(a)** *(Naut, Mil)* convoy; ~ **(ferroviario)** train. **(b)** *(corteo funebre)* funeral procession.

convolare [konvo'lare] *vi (aus essere)*: ~ **a (giuste) nozze** *(scherz)* to tie the knot.

convulsione [konvul'sjone] *sf (Med)* convulsion; *(di riso)* fit.

convulsivo, a [konvul'sivo] *ag* convulsive.

convulso, a [kon'vulso] *ag (gen)* convulsive; *(pianto)* uncontrollable; *(fig: stile, parlare)* jerky; *(: attività, ritmo)* feverish.

cooperare [koope'rare] *vi*: ~ **a qc/a fare qc** to cooperate in sth/to do sth.

cooperativa [koopera'tiva] *sf* cooperative.

cooperativo, a [koopera'tivo] *ag* cooperative.

cooperatore, trice [koopera'tore] *sm/f (collaboratore)* collaborator; *(socio di cooperativa)* cooperative member.

cooperazione [kooperat'tsjone] *sf* cooperation.

coordinamento [koordina'mento] *sm* coordination.

coordinare [koordi'nare] *vt* to coordinate.

coordinata [koordi'nata] *sf (Mat, Geog)* coordinate.

coordinato, a [koordi'nato] **1** *ag (gen, Mat)* coordinate. **2**: ~**i** *smpl (abbigliamento, arredamento)* coordinates.

coordinatore, trice [koordina'tore] *sm/f* coordinator.

coordinazione [koordinat'tsjone] *sf* coordination.

Copenhagen [koupn'heigən] *sf* Copenhagen.

coperchio [ko'pɛrkjo] *sm* lid.

coperta [ko'pɛrta] *sf* **(a)** blanket; *(da viaggio)* rug; ~ **elettrica** electric blanket. **(b)** *(Naut)* deck; **tutti in** ~**!** all hands on deck!

copertamente [koperta'mente] *av* covertly, secretly.

copertina [koper'tina] *sf (di libro, rivista etc)* cover; *(: sovraccoperta)* jacket; **in** ~ on the cover; **ragazza di** ~ cover girl.

coperto, a [ko'pɛrto] **1** *pp di* **coprire. 2** *ag (gen, Assicurazione)* covered; *(luogo: riparato)* sheltered; *(piscina, campo da tennis)* indoor *attr*; *(cielo)* overcast; ~ **di** covered with; **tieni il bambino ben** ~ keep the child well wrapped up. **3** *sm* **(a)**: **al** ~ under cover; **mettersi al** ~ to take shelter; **essere al** ~ *(fig)* to be safe. **(b)** *(posto a tavola)* place; **ho messo 12 ~i** I've set the table for 12; **(prezzo del) ~** *(al ristorante)* cover charge.

copertone [koper'tone] *sm* **(a)** *(Aut)* tyre. **(b)** *(telone impermeabile)* tarpaulin.

copertura [koper'tura] *sf* **(a)** *(gen: atto)* covering; *(Edil)* roofing; **materiali da ~** roofing (materials). **(b)** *(Econ, Comm, Assicurazione)* cover. **(c)** *(Sport)*: **fare un gioco di ~** to play a defensive game. **(d)** *(Mil)* cover.

copia ['kɔpja] *sf* *(gen)* copy; *(Fot)* print; **brutta/bella ~** rough/final copy; **~ carbone** carbon copy; **~ conforme** *(Dir)* certified copy; **~ omaggio** presentation copy; **essere l'esatta ~ di qn/qc** to be the spitting image of sb/sth.

copiare [ko'pjare] *vt* to copy; *(in compito a scuola)*: **~ (qc da qn)** to crib *o* (sth from sb).

copiativo, a [kopja'tivo] *ag*: **carta ~a** carbon paper; **inchiostro ~** indelible ink.

copiatrice [kopja'tritʃe] *sf* copier, copying machine.

copiatura [kopja'tura] *sf* copying; *(a scuola)* cribbing, copying.

copione [ko'pjone] *sm* *(Cine, Teatro etc)* script.

copioso, a [ko'pjoso] *ag* copious.

copisteria [kopiste'ria] *sf* copy bureau.

coppa[1] ['kɔppa] *sf* **(a)** *(gen, Sport)* cup; *(per gelato, frutta)* dish; *(per vino, spumante)* goblet; *(Rel)* chalice; **~ di gelato** *(in confezione)* tub of ice cream; **~ dell'olio** oil sump; **~ della ruota** hub cap. **(b)**: **~e** *pl* *(Carte)* suit in Neapolitan pack of cards.

coppa[2] ['kɔppa] *sf* **(a)** *(nuca)* nape. **(b)** *(Culin)* large pork sausage.

coppia ['kɔppja] *sf* *(di persone)* couple; *(di animali, Sport)* pair; **una ~ di sposi** a married couple; **a ~e, in ~** in pairs; **fare una bella ~** to make a nice couple; **gara a ~e** competition for pairs; **~ di forze** *(Fis)* torque.

copricapo [kopri'kapo] *sm* headgear; *(cappello)* hat.

copricostume [koprikos'tume] *sm* beach robe.

coprifuoco, chi [kopri'fwɔko] *sm* curfew.

copriletto [kopri'letto] *sm* bedspread.

coprire [ko'prire] **1** *vt* *(gen)* to cover; *(persona: proteggere: anche fig)* to cover, shield; *(fig: suono)* to drown; *(: segreto, sentimenti)* to conceal; **copri bene il bambino** wrap the child up well; **~ di, ~ con** *(gen)* to cover with; **era coperto di lividi** he was bruised all over *o* covered in bruises; **~ qn di insulti/di doni** to shower insults/gifts on sb; **~ qn di ridicolo** to cover sb with ridicule; **~ qn di baci** to smother sb with kisses; **~ qn alle spalle** *(in una sparatoria)* to cover sb from behind. **2**: **~rsi** *vr* *(gen)*: **~rsi (di)** to cover o.s. (with); *(vestirsi)* to wrap o.s. up (in); *(proteggersi)*: **~rsi (da)** to shield o.s. (from); *(Assicurazione)*: **~rsi contro** to insure o.s. against; **~rsi di gloria/di ridicolo** to cover o.s. with glory/with ridicule; **~rsi di macchie** to become covered in spots; **il cielo si è coperto di nuvole** the sky has clouded over.

copula ['kɔpula] *sf* *(Gram)* copula; *(congiunzione)* conjunction.

copulativo, a [kopula'tivo] *ag* copulative.

copyright ['kɔpirait] *sm inv* copyright.

coque [kɔk] *sf*: **uovo à la ~** boiled egg.

coraggio [ko'raddʒo] *sm* **(a)** courage; **aver ~** to be courageous, be brave; **dimostrare ~ in battaglia** to show courage *o* bravery in battle; **aver un ~ da leone** to be as brave as a lion; **non ho avuto il ~ di chiederglielo** I hadn't the nerve to ask him; **avere il ~ delle proprie azioni** to have the courage of one's convictions; **farsi ~** to pluck up

courage; **fare ~ a qn** to cheer sb up; **~!** *(forza!)* come on!; *(animo!)* cheer up! **(b)** *(sfacciataggine)* nerve, cheek; **hai un bel ~!** you've got a nerve *o* a cheek!

coraggioso, a [korad'dʒoso] *ag* brave, courageous.

corale [ko'rale] *ag* *(Mus)* choral; *(approvazione: unanime)* unanimous.

corallino, a [koral'lino] *ag* coral *attr*.

corallo [ko'rallo] *sm* coral.

corano [ko'rano] *sm* Koran.

corazza [ko'rattsa] *sf* *(Storia)* cuirass; *(Sport)* protective clothing; *(di animali)* carapace; **~ di indifferenza** *(fig)* hard shell of indifference.

corazzare [korat'tsare] *vt* to armour.

corazzata [korat'tsata] *sf* battleship.

corazzato, a [korat'tsato] *ag* *(Mil)* armoured.

corazziere [korat'tsjere] *sm* *(Storia)* cuirassier; *(guardia presidenziale)* carabiniere of the President's guard.

corbelleria [korbelle'ria] *sf* stupid remark; **non dire ~e!** don't talk nonsense!, don't be so silly!

corda ['kɔrda] *sf* **(a)** *(fune)* rope; **~e** *(Pugilato)* ropes; **di ~** *(suole)* rope *attr*; **scarpe di ~** espadrilles; **saltare la ~** to skip. **(b)** *(di violino, arco, racchetta)* string; **strumenti a ~** stringed instruments. **(c)** *(Anat)*: **~e vocali** vocal cords; **~ dorsale** spinal chord. **(d)** *(Geom)* chord. **(e)** *(fraseologia)*: **dare ~ a qn** *(fig)* to let sb have his (*o* her) way; **dare la ~ a un orologio** to wind a clock; **mettersi la ~ al collo** *(fig)* to put one's head in the noose; **essere giù di ~** to feel down; **tagliare la ~** *(fig)* to sneak off; **essere/tenere sulla ~** to be/keep on tenterhooks.

cordame [kor'dame] *sm* ropes *pl*; *(Naut)* rigging.

cordata [kor'data] *sf* *(Alpinismo)* roped party; **in ~** roped together.

cordiale [kor'djale] **1** *ag* *(accoglienza)* warm, cordial; *(persona)* warm; **~i saluti** *(in lettere)* best regards; **c'è una ~ antipatia tra noi** we cordially dislike one another. **2** *sm* *(bevanda)* cordial.

cordialità [kordjali'ta] *sf inv* **(a)** warmth, cordiality. **(b)** *(saluti)*: **~** *pl* best wishes.

cordialmente [kordjal'mente] *av* warmly, cordially.

cordigliera [kordiʎ'ʎera] *sf* cordillera.

cordoglio [kor'dɔʎʎo] *sm* grief, sorrow; *(lutto)* mourning; **esprimere il proprio ~ a qn** to offer sb one's sympathy *o* condolences.

cordone [kor'done] *sm* *(gen)* cord; *(di telefono)* cord, flex; *(di borsa)* string; *(fig: di poliziotti, soldati)* cordon; **~ litoraneo** *(Geog)* offshore bar; **~ ombelicale** *(Anat)* umbilical cord; **~ sanitario** quarantine line.

Corea [ko'rɛa] *sf* Korea.

coreano, a [kore'ano] *ag, sm, sm/f* Korean.

coreografia [koreogra'fia] *sf* choreography.

coreografico, a, ci, che [koreo'grafiko] *ag* choreographic.

coreografo, a [kore'ɔgrafo] *sm/f* choreographer.

coriaceo, a [ko'rjatʃeo] *ag* *(Bot, Zool)* coriaceous; *(fig)* tough.

coriandolo [ko'rjandolo] **(a)** *(Bot)* coriander. **(b)** *(per carnevale, matrimoni)* piece of confetti; **~i** confetti *sg*.

coricare [kori'kare] **1** *vt* *(persona: a letto)* to put to bed; *(: a terra, su divano)* to put down, lay down; *(bottiglia)* to rest, lay. **2**: **~rsi** *vr* *(andare a letto)* to go to bed; *(riposarsi)* to lie down.

corista, i, e [ko'rista] **1** *sm/f* *(Rel)* choir member, chorister; *(Teatro)* member of the chorus; **i ~i** *(Teatro)* the chorus. **2** *sm* tuning fork.

cormorano [kormo'rano] *sm* cormorant.

corna ['kɔrna] *sfpl vedi* **corno.**

cornacchia [kor'nakkja] *sf* crow.

cornamusa [korna'muza] *sf* bagpipes *pl.*

cornata [kor'nata] *sf* butt; **dare una ~ a qn** to butt sb; *(infilzare)* to gore sb.

cornea ['kɔrnea] *sf (Anat)* cornea.

corneo, a ['kɔrneo] *ag* horny.

corner ['kɔrner] *sm inv (Calcio)* corner (kick); **salvarsi in ~** *(fig: in gara, esame etc)* to get through by the skin of one's teeth; **mi son salvato in ~** *(in situazione imbarazzante)* I just managed to wriggle out of it.

cornetta [kor'netta] *sf (Mus)* cornet; *(di telefono)* receiver; **riattaccare la ~** to hang up.

cornetto [kor'netto] *sm* **(a)** *(Culin: brioche)* croissant; *(: fagiolino)* string bean. **(b)** *(amuleto)* horn-shaped talisman. **(c): ~ acustico** ear trumpet.

cornice [kor'nitʃe] *sf (gen)* frame; *(Archit)* cornice; *(Geog)* ledge; *(fig)* background, setting; **fare da ~ a** *(fig)* to frame.

corniciaio [korni'tʃajo] *sm* picture framer.

cornicione [korni'tʃone] *sm (di edificio)* ledge; *(: Archit)* cornice.

cornificare [kornifi'kare] *vt (fam: marito, moglie etc)* to cheat on.

corno ['kɔrno] *sm* **(a)** *(gen, Mus)* horn; **di ~** *(bottoni, manico etc)* horn *attr;* **~ da caccia** hunting horn; **~ inglese** *(Mus)* English horn, cor anglais; **~ delle scarpe** shoehorn. **(b)** *(Geog):* **C~ d'Africa** Horn of Africa. **(c)** *(pl: ~a: Zool: di toro, lumaca)* horn; *(: di cervo)* antler. **(d)** *(fam):* **fare le ~a** *(per scaramanzia)* to keep one's fingers crossed; **fare le ~a a qn** *(a marito, moglie etc)* to cheat on sb; **dire peste e ~a di qn** to call sb every name under the sun; **rompersi le ~a** to burn one's fingers; **un ~!** not on your life!; **felice? — un ~! happy? —** anything but!; **non me ne importa un ~!** I don't give a damn!; **non è vero, un ~!** that's rubbish!

cornuto, a [kor'nuto] **1** *ag* **(a)** *(con corna)* horned. **(b)** *(fam: tradito)* cheated; **arbitro ~!** bloody ref! **2** *sm/f (fam)* cheated husband/wife; **~!** *(insulto)* bastard!

coro ['kɔro] *sm (gen, fig)* chorus; *(Rel: cantori, luogo)* choir; **in ~** in chorus.

corolla [ko'rɔlla] *sf (Bot)* corolla.

corollario [korol'larjo] *sm* corollary.

corona [ko'rona] *sf* **(a)** *(di re, papa)* crown; *(di nobile)* coronet; **cingere la ~** to assume the crown; **fare ~ intorno a qn** *(fig)* to form a circle round sb. **(b)** *(di fiori)* wreath; **~ d'alloro/mortuaria** laurel/funeral wreath; **~ di spine** crown of thorns. **(c)** *(di dente)* crown. **(d)** *(Geom):* **~ circolare** outer circle.

coronamento [korona'mento] *sm* **(a)** *(di impresa)* completion; *(di carriera)* crowning achievement; **il ~ dei propri sogni** the fulfilment of one's dreams. **(b)** *(Edil)* crown; *(Naut)* taffrail.

coronare [koro'nare] *vt:* **~ (di)** *(anche fig)* to crown (with); **~ i propri sogni** to fulfil one's dreams; **coronato dal successo** crowned with success.

coronaria [koro'narja] *sf* coronary artery.

coronario, a [koro'narjo] *ag* coronary.

corpetto [kor'petto] *sm (da donna)* bodice; *(da uomo)* waistcoat.

corpo ['kɔrpo] **1** *sm (gen, Chim, fig)* body; *(cadavere)* corpse, (dead) body; *(di opere)* corpus; **non ho niente in ~** I haven't eaten anything; **darsi anima e ~ a** to give o.s. heart and soul to; **~ a ~** *(ag)* hand-to-hand; *(sm: lotta)* hand-to-hand fight; **andare di ~** to empty one's bowels; **dare ~ a qc** to give substance to sth; **prendere ~** *(idea, progetto)* to take shape; **ma che hai in ~?** what's got into

you?; **l'incendio ha divorato l'intero ~ dell'edificio** the fire destroyed the entire building; **l'intero ~ delle opere di Leopardi** the entire works of Leopardi.

2: ~ d'armata army corps *sg;* **~ di ballo** corps de ballet; **~ dei carabinieri** ≃ police force; **~ diplomatico** diplomatic corps *sg;* **~ elettorale** electorate; **~ estraneo** foreign body; **~ insegnante** teachers *pl,* teaching staff; **~ liquido/gassoso** liquid/gaseous substance; **~ dei pompieri** fire brigade; **~ del reato** material evidence; **~ di spedizione** *(Mil)* task force.

corporale [korpo'rale] *ag (bisogni)* bodily; *(punizione)* corporal.

corporativo, a [korpora'tivo] *ag* corporate.

corporatura [korpora'tura] *sf* build, physique.

corporazione [korporat'tsjone] *sf* professional body; *(Storia)* guild.

corposo, a [kor'poso] *ag (vino)* full-bodied.

corpulento, a [korpu'lento] *ag* stout, corpulent.

corpulenza [korpu'lentsa] *sf* stoutness, corpulence.

corpuscolo [kor'puskolo] *sm* corpuscle.

corredare [korre'dare] **1** *vt:* **~ di** *(apparecchio, laboratorio)* to equip with; **un elettrodomestico corredato di vari accessori** an electrical appliance complete with various accessories; **domanda corredata dai seguenti documenti** application accompanied by the following documents. **2: ~rsi** *vr:* **~rsi di** to equip o.s. with.

corredo [kor'redo] *sm (di attrezzi)* kit; *(da sposa)* trousseau.

correggere [kor'reddʒere] **1** *vt (gen)* to correct; *(esame)* to mark; *(Tip)* to proofread; *(fig: abuso)* to remedy. **2: ~rsi** *vr* to correct o.s.

corregionale [korredʒo'nale] **1** *ag:* **sono ~i** they come from the same area. **2** *sm/f:* **è un mio ~** he comes from the same area as me.

correlativo, a [korrela'tivo] *ag* correlative.

correlatore, trice [korrela'tore] *sm/f (Univ: di tesi)* assistant supervisor.

correlazione [korrelat'tsjone] *sf (gen)* correlation; **~ dei tempi** *(Gram)* sequence of tenses.

corrente [kor'rente] **1** *ag* **(a)** *(che scorre: acqua)* running. **(b)** *(uso, anno)* current; *(valuta)* valid; **è opinione ~ che...** it is commonly believed that...; **la vostra lettera del 5 ~ mese** *(in lettere commerciali)* in your letter of the 5th of this month. **(c)** *(ordinario: merce)* ordinary.

2 *sm:* **essere al ~ di** *(notizia)* to know about; *(scoperte scientifiche etc)* to be well-informed about; **tenere qn al ~** to keep sb informed; **mettere qn al ~ (di)** to inform sb (of).

3 *sf (Elettr, di acque)* current; *(di aria)* airstream, current of air; *(: spiffero)* draught; *(di opinioni etc)* trend; **c'è ~ qui dentro** there's a draught in here; **tagliare la ~** *(Elettr)* to cut off the power; **~ continua/alternata** *(Elettr)* direct/alternating current; **una ~ di simpatia** a wave of sympathy; **andare contro ~** *(anche fig)* to swim against the stream; **seguire la ~** *(fig)* to follow the trend; **la C~ del Golfo** the Gulf Stream.

correntemente [korrente'mente] *av (comunemente)* commonly; **parlare una lingua ~** to speak a language fluently.

correntista, i, e [korren'tista] *sm/f (Fin)* (current) account holder.

correo, a ['kɔrreo] *sm/f (Dir)* accomplice.

correre ['korrere] **1** *vi (aus* **essere** *quando si esprime o sottointende una meta) (gen)* to run; *(affrettarsi)* to hurry; *(precipitarsi)* to rush; *(Sport)* to race; **non ~!** *(anche fig)* not so fast!; **~ dietro a qn** *(anche fig)* to run after sb; **corre voce**

che it is rumoured that; **il tempo corre** time is getting on. **2** *vt (gen, Sport)* to run; **~ i 100 metri** to run in the 100 metres; **~ i 100 metri a tempo di record** to run the 100 metres in record time; **~ un rischio** to run a risk.

corresponsabile [korrespon'sabile] **1** *ag* jointly responsible; *(Dir)* jointly liable. **2** *sm* person jointly responsible; *(Dir: civile)* person jointly liable; *(: penale)* accomplice; *(: di divorzio)* co-respondent.

corresponsabilità [korresponsabili'ta] *sf (vedi ag)* joint responsibility; joint liability.

corresponsione [korrespon'sjone] *sf* payment.

correttezza [korret'tettsa] *sf (di comportamento)* correctness; *(Sport)* fair play; **è questione di ~** it's a question of propriety o good manners.

correttivo, a [korret'tivo] *ag* corrective.

corretto, a [kor'retto] **1** *pp di* **correggere. 2** *ag (gen)* correct; *(comportamento)* proper; **caffè ~ al cognac** coffee laced with cognac.

correttore, trice [korret'tore] *sm/f:* **~ di bozze** proofreader.

correzione [korret'tsjone] *sf* **(a)** *(gen)* correction; *(di esame)* marking; *(miglioramento)* improvement; **~ di bozze** proofreading. **(b)** *(castigo):* **casa di ~** borstal.

corrida [kor'rida] *sf* bullfight.

corridoio [korri'dojo] *sm (gen)* corridor, passage; *(laterale: di aereo, treno)* corridor; *(centrale: di aereo, pullman)* aisle; **manovre di ~** *(Pol)* lobbying; **~ aereo** air corridor.

corridore [korri'dore] *sm (Sport)* runner; *(: su veicolo)* racer.

corriera [kor'rjɛra] *sf* coach, bus.

corriere [kor'rjɛre] *sm (gen)* messenger; *(Mil, diplomatico etc)* courier; *(spedizioniere)* carrier.

corrimano [korri'mano] *sm* handrail.

corrispettivo [korrispet'tivo] *sm* amount due; **versare a qn il ~ di una prestazione** to pay the amount due for his (o her) services.

corrispondente [korrispon'dɛnte] **1** *ag* corresponding. **2** *sm/f (gen, Stampa, TV)* correspondent.

corrispondenza [korrispon'dɛntsa] *sf* **(a)** *(conformità)* correspondence; *(fig)* connection, relation; **non c'è ~ tra le due versioni** the two versions do not correspond. **(b)** *(posta: atto di scrivere)* correspondence; *(insieme di lettere)* mail; **corso per ~** correspondence course; **~ in arrivo/partenza** incoming/outgoing mail. **(c)** *(Mat)* relation.

corrispondere [korris'pondere] **1** *vt (pagare)* to pay. **2** *vi* **(a):** **~ (a)** *(equivalersi)* to correspond (to); **quello che ha detto non corrisponde a verità** what he said doesn't fit the facts. **(b)** *(per lettera):* **~ con** to correspond with.

corrisposto, a [korris'posto] **1** *pp di* **corrispondere. 2** *ag (affetto, sentimento)* reciprocated.

corroborante [korrobo'rante] **1** *ag* fortifying, stimulating; **clima ~** bracing climate. **2** *sm (liquore)* pick-me-up.

corroborare [korrobo'rare] *vt (rinvigorire)* to invigorate; *(fig: ipotesi)* to corroborate, bear out.

corrodere [kor'rodere] **1** *vt (metalli, fig)* to corrode; *(legno)* to eat into; **la carie corrode i denti** teeth are eaten away by decay. **2** *vi,* **~rsi** *vr (metalli)* to corrode; *(roccia)* to erode, wear away.

corrompere [kor'rompere] **1** *vt (gen, fig)* to corrupt; *(testimone, giudice etc)* to bribe, corrupt; *(linguaggio)* to debase. **2:** **~rsi** *vr (costumi)* to become corrupt; *(lingua)* to become debased.

corrosione [korro'zjone] *sf* corrosion.

corrosivo, a [korro'sivo] *ag, sm* corrosive.

corroso, a [kor'roso] *pp di* **corrodere.**

corrotto, a [kor'rotto] **1** *pp di* **corrompere. 2** *ag* corrupt.

corrucciarsi [korrut'tʃarsi] *vr* to become upset; **si corrucciò in viso** his face took on a worried expression.

corrugare [korru'gare] *vt:* **~ la fronte, ~ le sopracciglia** to frown, knit one's brows.

corruttela [korrut'tɛla] *sf* corruption, depravity.

corruttibile [korrut'tibile] *ag* corruptible.

corruttore, trice [korrut'tore] *sm/f* corrupter; *(con denaro)* briber.

corruzione [korrut'tsjone] *sf* corruption; **~ di minorenne** *(Dir)* corruption of a minor.

corsa [korsa] *sf* **(a)** *(azione)* running; **andare** *o* **essere di ~** to be in a hurry; **andarsene/arrivare di ~** to rush off/in; **ho dovuto fare una ~** I had to dash; **'vietato scendere dal treno in ~'** 'do not alight from the train while it is in motion'; **abbiamo preso i cappotti e via di ~** we grabbed our coats and off we went; **faccio una ~ e torno!** I'll be straight back!

(b) *(Sport: gara)* race; *(: disciplina)* racing; *(: atletica)* running; **da ~** *(auto, moto etc)* racing; **cavallo da ~** racehorse; **fare una ~** to run a race; **va spesso alle ~e** he often goes to the races; **è una ~ contro il tempo** it's a race against time; **~ automobilistica/ciclistica** motor/cycle racing; **~ campestre** cross-country race; **~ all'oro** gold rush; **~ ad ostacoli** *(Ippica)* steeplechase; *(Atletica)* hurdles race; **~ con i sacchi** sack race.

(c) *(di autobus, treno etc)* trip, journey; **a che ora c'è l'ultima ~?** when is the last bus *(o* train *etc)*?; **quanto costa la ~?** what's the fare?

(d) *(Fis: di pendolo)* movement; *(: di pistone)* stroke.

(e) *(Naut, Mil):* **guerra di ~** privateering.

corsaro, a [kor'saro] **1** *ag:* **nave ~a** privateer. **2** *sm* privateer.

corsetteria [korsette'ria] *sf* corsetry.

corsetto [kor'setto] *sm* corset.

corsia [kor'sia] *sf* **(a)** *(gen)* gangway, passage; *(Aut, Sport)* lane; **~ di accelerazione/decelerazione** *(Aut)* acceleration/deceleration lane; **~ di emergenza** *(Aut)* hard shoulder; **~ di sorpasso** *(Aut)* overtaking lane; **autostrada a 4 ~e** 4-lane motorway. **(b)** *(in ospedale)* ward; **è ricoverato in ~** he's a patient in the ward.

Corsica ['korsika] *sf* Corsica.

corsivo, a [kor'sivo] **1** *ag (scrittura)* cursive; *(Tip)* italic. **2** *sm* **(a)** cursive writing; *(Tip)* italics *pl.* **(b)** *(Stampa)* brief article of comment *(in italics).*

corso¹, a ['korso] *pp di* **correre.**

corso², a ['korso] *ag, sm/f* Corsican.

corso³ ['korso] *sm* **(a)** *(fluire: di acqua, tempo etc)* course; **~ d'acqua** *(naturale)* river, stream; *(artificiale)* waterway; **discendere il ~ del Nilo** to go down the Nile; **dare ~ a** to start; **in ~** *(lavori)* in progress, under way; *(anno, mese)* current; **in ~ di riparazione** in the process of being repaired; **nel ~ di** during; **nel ~ del tempo** in the course of time; **il nuovo ~ del partito Laburista** the new direction of the Labour Party.

(b) *(Scol, Univ)* course; **seguire un ~ serale** to go to an evening class; **tenere un ~ su** to give a course on; **primo anno di ~** first year; **studente fuori ~** undergraduate who has not completed course in due time.

(c) *(strada cittadina)* main street; *(nei nomi di strada)* avenue.

(d) *(Fin: di moneta)* circulation; *(: di titoli)* rate, price; **aver ~ legale** to be legal tender.

corte ['korte] *sf* **(a)** *(cortile)* courtyard. **(b)**

(seguito: del re) court; **fare la ~ a qn** *(per amore)* to court sb; *(per interesse)* to butter sb up. **(c)** *(Dir)* court; **~ d'appello** court of appeal; **C~ di Cassazione** Court of Cassation; **C~ dei Conti** *State audit court;* **C~ Costituzionale** *special court dealing with constitutional and ministerial matters;* **~ marziale** court-martial.

corteccia, ce [kor'tettʃa] *sf (di albero)* bark; *(Anat)* cortex.

corteggiamento [korteddʒa'mento] *sm* courtship.

corteggiare [korted'dʒare] *vt* to court, woo.

corteggiatore [korteddʒa'tore] *sm* suitor.

corteo [kor'teo] *sm* procession; **~ funebre** funeral cortège; **i dimostranti hanno sfilato in ~** the demonstrators marched past.

cortese [kor'teze] *ag* courteous; *(Letteratura)* courtly.

cortesia [korte'zia] *sf (qualità)* courtesy; *(atto)* favour; **fare una ~ a qn** to do sb a favour; **per ~, dov'è...?** excuse me, please, where is...?; **mi fai una ~, spegni quella radio** could you please turn off that radio.

cortigiano, a [korti'dʒano] **1** *sm/f* courtier. **2** *sf (prostituta)* courtesan.

cortile [kor'tile] *sm (di edificio: all'interno)* courtyard; *(: davanti)* forecourt; *(: all'esterno, dietro)* yard; *(di cascina)* farmyard.

cortina [kor'tina] *sf* curtain; **~ di fumo/nebbia** a wall of smoke/mist; **la ~ di ferro** the Iron Curtain.

cortisone [korti'zone] *sm* cortisone.

corto, a ['korto] **1** *ag (tutti i sensi)* short; **la settimana ~a** the 5-day week; **la strada più ~a** *(anche fig)* the quickest way; **avere la vista ~a** *(anche fig)* to be short-sighted; **essere o rimanere a ~ di qc** to be short of sth; **essere a ~ di parole** to be at a loss for words. **2** *av:* **tagliare ~** to come straight to the point.

cortocircuito [kortotʃir'kuito] *sm* short-circuit.

cortometraggio, gi [kortome'traddʒo] *sm (Cine)* short (feature film).

corvé [kor've] *sf inv (Mil)* fatigue duty; **sabato siamo di ~** *(scherz)* we are on chores on Saturday.

corvetta [kor'vetta] *sf* corvette, sloop.

corvino, a [kor'vino] *ag:* **capelli ~i** jet-black hair.

corvo ['korvo] *sm (anche:* **~ imperiale)** raven; **~ nero** rook.

cosa ['kɔsa] **1** *sf* **(a)** *(gen)* thing; **ogni ~, tutte le ~e** everything; **qualche ~** something; **nessuna ~** nothing; **è una ~ da poco** it's nothing; **devo dirti una ~** I've got something to tell you; **come prima ~** first of all; **facciamo le ~e per bene** let's do things properly; **tante belle ~e!** all the best! **(b)** *(situazione, fatto)* it, things; **la ~ non è chiara** it isn't clear, things aren't clear; **ti voglio spiegare la ~** let me explain things to you; **è successa una ~ strana** something strange has happened; **sono ~e da ragazzi** that's kids for you; **ormai è ~ fatta!** *(positivo)* it's in the bag!; *(negativo)* it's done now!; **a ~e fatte** when all is said and done; **le ~e stanno così** this is how things stand. **(c)** *(preoccupazione, problema)* matter; **brutta ~!** it's a nasty business *o* matter!; **la ~ non mi riguarda** the matter doesn't concern me; **è tutt'altra ~** that's quite another matter. **2** *pron interrog:* **(che) ~?** what?; *vedi anche* **che.**

cosacco, chi [ko'zakko] *sm* Cossack.

cosca, sche ['kɔska] *sf (di mafiosi)* clan.

coscia, sce ['kɔʃʃa] *sf (Anat)* thigh; *(Culin: di pollo etc)* leg.

cosciente [koʃ'ʃɛnte] *ag (gen, Med)* conscious; *(consapevole):* **~ di** aware *o* conscious of.

coscienza [koʃ'ʃɛntsa] *sf* **(a)** *(morale)* conscience; **aver qc sulla ~** to have sth on one's conscience; **avere la ~ a posto/sporca** to have a good *o* clear/ bad *o* guilty conscience; **in (tutta) ~** in all conscience *o* honesty. **(b)** *(sensi)* consciousness; **perdere/riacquistare ~** to lose/regain consciousness. **(c)** *(psicologica)* awareness; **~ politica** political awareness; **avere ~ di/che** to be aware *o* conscious of/that; **prendere ~ di qc** to become aware of sth, realize sth. **(d):** **~ professionale** conscientiousness; **persona di ~** honest *o* conscientious person.

coscienziosità [koʃʃentsjosi'ta] *sf* conscientiousness.

coscienzioso, a [koʃʃen'tsjoso] *ag* conscientious.

cosciotto [koʃ'ʃɔtto] *sm (Culin)* leg.

coscritto [kos'kritto] *sm (Mil)* conscript.

coscrizione [koskrit'tsjone] *sf (Mil)* conscription.

cosecante [kose'kante] *sf (Mat)* cosecant.

coseno [ko'seno] *sm (Mat)* cosine.

così [ko'si] **1** *av* **(a)** *(in tal modo)* so; *(in questo modo)* (in) this way, like this; **ho detto ~** that's what I said; **ha detto ~: 'sei bugiardo'** this is what he said: 'you're a liar'; **se fosse ~** if this were the case; **le cose stanno ~** this is how things stand; **vorrei una scatola larga ~ e lunga ~** *(accompagnato da gesti)* I'd like a box so wide and so long; **non scriverlo ~, ma ~!** don't write it like that, write it like this!; **e ~ feci anch'io** and I did likewise.

(b) *(talmente)* so; **fa ~ bello oggi** it's such a lovely day, the weather's so lovely today; **una persona ~ gentile** such a kind person; **è ~ lontano** it's so far away; **non sono mica ~ stupido!** I'm not that stupid!

(c): **~ ... come as ...** as; **non è ~ onesto come credi** he's not as *o* so honest as you think; **se si comporta ~ come ha sempre fatto...** if he goes on behaving like this...; **me lo dia ~ com'è** give it to me as it is.

(d): **per ~ dire** so to speak, so to say; **e ~ via** and so on; **è ~ o non è ~?** isn't that so?; **~ ~** so so; **e ~?** well?

2 *ag inv:* **non ho mai conosciuto una persona ~** I've never met such a person, I've never met a person like that.

3 *cong (perciò)* so, therefore; **pioveva, ~ sono rimasto a casa** it was raining so I stayed at home.

cosicché [kosik'ke] *cong* so (that).

cosiddetto, a [kosid'detto] *ag* so-called.

cosmesi [koz'mezi] *sf (scienza)* cosmetics *sg;* *(prodotti)* cosmetics *pl;* *(trattamento)* beauty treatment.

cosmetico, a, ci, che [koz'mɛtiko] *ag, sm* cosmetic.

cosmico, a, ci, che ['kɔzmiko] *ag* cosmic.

cosmo ['kɔzmo] *sm (universo)* cosmos; *(spazio)* outer space.

cosmologia [kozmolo'dʒia] *sf* cosmology.

cosmonauta, i, e [kozmo'nauta] *sm/f* cosmonaut.

cosmonave [kozmo'nave] *sf* spaceship.

cosmopolita, i, e [kozmopo'lita] *ag, sm/f (anche fig)* cosmopolitan.

coso ['kɔso] *sm (fam: oggetto)* thing, thingumabob; *(: aggeggio)* contraption; *(: persona)* what's his name, thingumabob.

cospargere [kos'pardʒere] *vt:* **~ di** to sprinkle with.

cosparso, a [kos'parzo] *pp di* **cospargere.**

cospetto [kos'petto] *sm (presenza):* **in o al ~ di** in the presence of; **giurare al ~ di Dio** to swear before God.

cospicuità [kospiku'ta] *sf* vast quantity; **la ~ delle sue risorse** his considerable resources.

cospicuo, a [kos'pikuo] *ag* considerable, large.

cospirare [kospi'rare] *vi (gen)* to conspire, plot; *(fig: circostanze etc)* to conspire.

cospiratore, trice [kospira'tore] *sm/f* plotter, conspirator; **con fare da ~** with a conspiratorial air.

cospirazione [kospirat'tsjone] *sf (anche fig)* plot, conspiracy.

costa ['kɔsta] *sf* **(a)** *(litorale)* coast; *(spiaggia)* shore; **navigare sotto ~** to hug the coast; **la C~ Azzurra** the French Riviera. **(b)** *(di montagna)* slope; **a mezza ~** halfway up (*o* down) the slope. **(c)** *(nervatura: di nave, Bot)* rib; *(: di tessuto)* ribbing; *(dorso: di libro)* spine; **punto a ~e** *(Maglia)* rib (stitch); **velluto a ~e** corduroy.

costà [kos'ta] *av (poet)* there.

costante [kos'tante] **1** *ag (gen, Mat)* constant; *(persona)* steadfast. **2** *sf (Mat)* constant; **è una ~ della letteratura del '900** it is a standard feature of 20th century literature.

costanza [kos'tantsa] *sf (gen)* constancy; *(fig)* constancy, steadfastness.

costare [kos'tare] **1** *vi (aus essere)* to cost; **~ caro** to be expensive, cost a lot; **~ poco** to be cheap; **cosa vuoi che ti costi** I am not asking much of you. **2** *vt (fig)* to cost; **~ un occhio della testa** to cost a fortune; **costi quel che costi** no matter what; **gli è costato la vita** it cost him his life.

costaricano, a [kostari'kano] *ag, sm/f* Costa Rican.

costata [kos'tata] *sf (Culin: di manzo)* large chop.

costato [kos'tato] *sm (Anat)* ribs *pl*.

costeggiare [kosted'dʒare] *vt (Naut)* to hug, skirt; *(sog: persona)* to walk (*o* drive *etc*) alongside; *(: strada)* to run alongside.

costei [kos'tei] *pron dimostr (sog)* she; *(complemento)* her; *(peg)* this woman.

costellare [kostel'lare] *vt:* **~ (di)** to stud (with); **il cielo era costellato di stelle** the sky was studded with stars.

costellazione [kostellat'tsjone] *sf* constellation.

costernare [koster'nare] *vt* to dismay, fill with consternation.

costernato, a [koster'nato] *ag* dismayed.

costernazione [kosternat'tsjone] *sf* dismay, consternation.

costì [kos'ti] *av (poet)* here.

costiera [kos'tjera] *sf (costa)* coast; *(strada)* coast road.

costiero, a [kos'tjero] *ag* coastal; **nave ~a** coaster.

costipato, a [kosti'pato] *ag (stitico)* constipated; *(raffreddato):* **essere ~** to have a bad cold.

costipazione [kostipat'tsjone] *sf (vedi ag)* constipation; bad cold.

costituente [kostitu'ente] **1** *ag (gen, Chim, Pol)* constituent *attr*. **2** *sm (Chim)* constituent. **3** *sf:* **la C~, l'Assemblea C~** the Constituent Assembly.

costituire [kostitu'ire] **1** *vt* **a)** *(fondare: società, governo)* to set up, form; *(accumulare: patrimonio, raccolta)* to build up, put together. **(b)** *(formare)* to constitute, make up. **(c)** *(essere, rappresentare)* to be; **costituisce un vero problema!** it's a real problem!; **il fatto non costituisce reato** *(Dir)* this is not a crime. **(d)** *(Dir: nominare):* **~ qn erede/presidente** to appoint sb heir/chairman. **2:** **~rsi** *vr* **(a)** *(organizzarsi):* **~rsi in società** to form a company; **~rsi in regione autonoma** to become an independent region. **(b)** *(ricercato)* to give o.s. up. **(c)** *(Dir):* **~rsi parte civile** *to associate in an action with the public prosecutor for damages.*

costitutivo, a [kostitu'tivo] *ag* constituent, com-

ponent; **atto ~** *(Dir: di società)* memorandum of association.

costituzionale [kostituttsjo'nale] *ag* constitutional.

costituzionalismo [kostituttsjona'lizmo] *sm* constitutionalism.

costituzione [kostitut'tsjone] *sf* **(a)** *(formazione)* setting-up, establishment; *(struttura)* composition, make-up; *(: Med)* constitution; **certificato di sana e robusta ~** certificate of good health. **(b)** *(Dir)* constitution.

costo ['kɔsto] *sm (anche fig)* cost; **~ della vita** cost of living; **determinazione dei ~i** costing; **sotto ~** for less than cost price; **a ogni** *o* **qualunque ~, a tutti i ~i** *(fig)* at all costs; **non vuol cedere a nessun ~** there's no way he'll give in, he won't give in no matter what.

costola ['kɔstola] *sf (Anat, Bot, Archit)* rib; **è magrissimo, gli si contano le ~e** he's so thin you can see his ribs; **se lo prendo gli rompo le ~e!** if I catch him I'll break every bone in his body!; **ha la polizia alle ~e** the police are hard on his heels.

costoletta [kosto'letta] *sf (Culin)* cutlet.

costoro [kos'toro] *pron dimostr pl (sog)* they; *(complemento)* them; *(peg)* these people.

costoso, a [kos'toso] *ag* costly, expensive.

costretto, a [kos'tretto] *pp di* **costringere**.

costringere [kos'trindʒere] *vt:* **~ qn (a fare qc)** to force *o* compel sb (to do sth); **mi ci hanno costretto con la forza** they forced me to do it; **la paralisi lo costringe a una sedia a rotelle** the paralysis confines him to a wheelchair; **vedersi costretto a fare qc** to find o.s. forced *o* compelled to do sth.

costrittivo, a [kostrit'tivo] *ag* coercive.

costrittore [kostrit'tore] *ag:* **muscolo ~** constrictor.

costrizione [kostrit'tsjone] *sf* **(a)** *(obbligo)* compulsion; **è legato da ~ morale** he is morally obliged. **(b)** *(violenza)* coercion, duress.

costruire [kostru'ire] *vt (gen)* to build, construct; *(fig: teoria, frasi, fortuna)* to construct, build up; **questo verbo si costruisce con il congiuntivo** this verb takes the subjunctive; **in questa città non si costruisce più da anni** there's been no building work done in this town for years.

costruttivo, a [kostrut'tivo] *ag (Edil)* building *attr*; *(fig)* constructive; **schema ~** *(Tecn)* design, plan; **tecnica ~a** *(Edil)* building techniques *pl*; *(Ingegneria)* assembly techniques *pl*.

costrutto [kos'trutto] *sm (Gram)* construction.

costruttore, trice [kostrut'tore] **1** *ag* building *attr*. **2** *sm (fabbricante)* manufacturer; *(Edil)* builder.

costruzione [kostrut'tsjone] *sf* **(a)** *(fabbricazione)* building, construction; *(struttura: anche Tecn, Gram)* construction; **di recente ~** of recent construction, recently built; **in (via di) ~** under construction; **materiali/legno da ~** building materials/timber; **scienza delle ~i** construction theory; **le ~i** *(gioco)* building blocks. **(b)** *(edificio)* building.

costui [kos'tui] *pron dimostr (sog)* he; *(complemento)* him; *(peg)* this fellow, this man.

costume [kos'tume] *sm* **(a)** *(gen)* custom; *(abitudine)* habit; **usi e ~i di una popolazione** habits and customs of a people; **donna di facili ~i** woman of easy morals. **(b)** *(indumento)* costume; **~ nazionale** national costume *o* dress; **~ da bagno** *(da donna)* bathing *o* swimming costume, swimsuit; *(da uomo)* bathing *o* swimming trunks *pl*.

costumista, i, e [kostu'mista] *sm/f* costume maker, costume designer.

cotangente [kotan'dʒente] *sf (Mat)* cotangent.

cotechino [kote'kino] *sm (Culin)* pork sausage.

cotenna [ko'tenna] *sf* bacon rind.

cotillon [kɔti'jɔ̃] *sm inv (piccolo omaggio)* favour.

cotogna [ko'toɲɲa] *sf (anche: mela ~)* quince.

cotognata [kotoɲ'ɲata] *sf* quince jelly.

cotogno [ko'toɲɲo] *sm* quince (tree).

cotoletta [koto'letta] *sf (di maiale, montone)* chop; *(di vitello, agnello)* cutlet.

cotonare [koto'nare] *vt (capelli)* to backcomb.

cotone [ko'tone] *sm* **(a)** *(gen)* cotton; ~ **da rammendo** darning thread; **di** ~ cotton *attr.* **(b)** *(anche:* ~ **idrofilo**) cotton wool; **batuffolo di** ~ wad of cotton wool.

cotoniero, a [koto'njɛro] *ag* cotton *attr.*

cotonificio, ci [kotoni'fitʃo] *sm* cotton mill.

cotta[1] ['kɔtta] *sf* **(a)** *(Rel)* surplice. **(b)** *(Storia):* ~ **d'arme** surcoat; ~ **di maglia** chain mail.

cotta[2] ['kɔtta] *sf:* **prendersi una** ~ **(per qn)** to have a crush (on sb).

cottimista, i, e [kotti'mista] *sm/f* pieceworker.

cottimo ['kɔttimo] *sm (anche:* **lavoro a** ~) piecework; **lavorare a** ~ to do piecework.

cotto, a ['kɔtto] **1** *pp di* **cuocere**. **2** *ag (Culin)* cooked; **ben** ~ well cooked; *(carne)* well done; **poco** ~ underdone; **troppo** ~ overdone; ~ **a puntino** cooked to perfection; **essere** ~ **(di qn)** *(fig fam)* to have a crush (on sb); **è proprio** ~! he's smitten!; **essere** ~ **(di sonno/stanchezza)** *(fam)* to be done in; **dirne di** ~**e e di crude a qn** to call sb every name under the sun; **farne di** ~**e e di crude** to get up to all kinds of mischief. **3** *sm* brickwork; **mattone di** ~ fired brick; **pavimento in** ~ tile floor.

cottura [kot'tura] *sf (Culin: gen)* cooking; *(: in forno)* baking; *(: di arrosto)* roasting; *(: in umido)* stewing; ~ **a fuoco lento** simmering; **angolo di** ~ cooking area.

coupé [ku'pe] *sm inv (Aut)* coupé.

coupon [ku'pɔ̃] *sm inv* coupon.

cova ['kova] *sf (di uccello: atto, periodo)* brooding; **fare la** ~ to brood, sit.

covare [ko'vare] **1** *vi (odio, rancore)* to smoulder; **qui gatta ci cova** there's something fishy about this. **(b)** *(uccello)* to sit on its eggs. **2** *vt (sog: uccello: uova)* to sit on. **(b)** *(fig):* **sta covando un raffreddore** he is sickening for a cold; ~ **odio verso qn** to nurse hatred for sb.

covata [ko'vata] *sf (anche fig)* brood.

covo ['kovo] *sm* den, lair; ~ **di terroristi** a terrorist base; **quel bar è un** ~ **di spacciatori** that bar is a haunt for drug pushers.

covone [ko'vone] *sm* sheaf.

coyote [ko'jɔte] *sm inv* coyote.

cozza ['kɔttsa] *sf* mussel.

cozzare [kot'tsare] **1** *vi (animali: con le corna)* to butt; *(veicoli)* to collide; *(fig: caratteri, idee)* to clash; ~ **contro un muro** to crash into a wall. **2** *vt (fig):* ~ **il capo contro il muro** to bang one's head against a brick wall.

cozzo ['kɔttso] *sm (di corna)* butt; *(di veicoli)* crash; *(fig: di idee)* clash.

C.P. *abbr vedi* **casella**.

crac [krak] *sm inv* **(a)** *(rumore)* crack. **(b)** *(rovina: economica)* crash; *(: fisica, psichica)* breakdown.

crampo ['krampo] *sm* cramp; **avere un** ~ **alla gamba** to have cramp in one's leg; **avere i** ~**i allo stomaco** to have stomach cramp; **ho i** ~**i allo stomaco dalla fame** I've got hunger pangs.

cranico, a, ci, che ['kraniko] *ag* cranial.

cranio ['kranjo] *sm* skull, cranium *(T)*; **avere il** ~ **duro** *(fig)* to be pig-headed.

cratere [kra'tɛre] *sm* crater.

crauti ['krauti] *smpl* sauerkraut *sg*.

cravatta [kra'vatta] *sf* tie; ~ **a farfalla** bow tie; **fare il nodo alla** ~ to tie one's tie.

cravattino [kravat'tino] *sm* bow tie.

crawl [krɔːl] *sm inv* crawl; **nuotare a** ~ to do the crawl.

creanza [kre'antsa] *sf* good manners *pl*; **per buona** ~ out of politeness.

creare [kre'are] *vt (gen)* to create; *(eleggere)* to make, appoint; *(fondare)* to set up; ~ **un precedente** to create a precedent; ~ **un problema a qn** to create a problem for sb; ~**rsi una clientela** to build up a clientele.

creativo, a [krea'tivo] *ag* creative.

creato [kre'ato] *sm:* **il** ~ the creation.

creatore, trice [krea'tore] **1** *ag* creative. **2** *sm/f* creator; *(fondatore)* founder; **un** ~ **di alta moda** fashion designer; **il C**~ *(Dio)* the Creator; **andare al C**~ to go to meet one's maker.

creatura [krea'tura] *sf* creature; **povera** ~! poor thing!; **le mie** ~**e** my babies.

creazione [kreat'tsjone] *sf (gen)* creation.

credente [kre'dɛnte] *sm/f (Rel)* believer.

credenza[1] [kre'dɛntsa] *sf (fede, opinione)* belief.

credenza[2] [kre'dɛntsa] *sf (mobile)* sideboard.

credenziale [kreden'tsjale] **1** *ag:* **lettere** *sfpl* ~**i** credentials. **2:** ~**i** *sfpl (anche fig)* credentials.

credere ['kredere] **1** *vt* **(a)** to believe; **lo o ci credo** I believe it; **voglio proprio crederci!** I should think so too!; **come puoi** ~ **una cosa simile?** how can you believe such a thing?; **lo credo bene!** I can well believe it!

(b) *(pensare)* to believe, think; **lo credo onesto** I believe him to be honest; **ti credevo morto** I thought you were dead; **credo che sia stato lui (a farlo)** I think it was him, I think he did it; **credeva di aver perso le chiavi** she thought she had lost her keys; **credo di sì/no** I think/don't think so; **voleva farmi** ~ **che...** he wanted me to think that...; **voleva darmi a** ~ **che non la conosceva** he tried to convince me that he didn't know her.

(c) *(ritenere opportuno):* **fai quello che credi o come credi** do as you please; **ha creduto bene di mollare tutto** he thought it best to let everything go.

2 *vi* to believe; ~ **a qn/qc** to believe sb/sth; ~ **in qn/qc** to believe in sb/sth; ~ **in Dio** to believe in God; **ti credo sulla parola** I'll take your word for it; **gli credo poco** I have little faith in him; **non credeva ai suoi occhi/alle sue orecchie** he could not believe his eyes/ears; **credevo a uno scherzo** I thought it was a joke; **si credeva a una truffa** it looked like a swindle.

3: ~**rsi** *vr:* **si crede furbo** he thinks he's smart; **chi ti credi di essere!** who do you think you are!

credibile [kre'dibile] *ag* credible, believable.

credibilità [kredibili'ta] *sf* credibility.

creditizio, a [kredi'tittsjo] *ag* credit.

credito ['kredito] *sm* **(a)** *(Fin)* credit; **comprare/ vendere a** ~ to buy/sell on credit *o* easy terms; **'non facciamo** ~**'** 'no credit', 'cash terms only'.

(b) *(fig: prestigio)* credit; **acquistare** ~ *(fig: teoria, partito)* to gain acceptance; **dare** ~ **a qc** *(fig)* to give credit to sth; **non puoi dar** ~ **alla sua parola** you can't trust him; **trovare** ~ **presso qn** *(fig)* to win sb's trust; **non è degno di** ~ he's not to be trusted.

creditore, trice [kredi'tore] *ag, sm/f* creditor.

credo ['krɛdo] *sm inv (Rel, fig)* creed; ~ **politico** political credo.

credulità [kreduli'ta] *sf* credulity, gullibility.

credulone, a [kredu'lone] *sm/f* simpleton, sucker *(fam)*.

crema ['krɛma] **1** *sf (gen, fig)* cream; **un gelato alla ~ vanilla ice. 2: ~ di bellezza** beauty cream; **~ di cacao** *(liquore)* crème de cacao; **~ al cioccolato** chocolate custard; **~ pasticciera** confectioner's custard; **~ di riso** rice custard.

cremagliera [kremaʎ'ʎɛra] *sf* rack; **ferrovia a ~** rack railway.

cremare [kre'mare] *vt* to cremate.

crematorio [krema'tɔrjo] **1** *ag* crematory. **2** *sm* crematorium.

cremazione [kremat'tsjone] *sf* cremation.

cremisi ['krɛmizi] *ag inv, sm inv* crimson.

cremoso, a [kre'moso] *ag* creamy.

cren [krɛn] *sm (Bot)* horseradish; *(salsa)* horseradish sauce.

crepa ['krɛpa] *sf* crack.

crepaccio [kre'pattʃo] *sm (nella roccia)* large crack, fissure; *(nel ghiaccio)* crevasse.

crepacuore [krepa'kwore] *sm:* **morire di ~** to die of a broken heart.

crepapelle [krepa'pɛlle] *av:* **ridere a ~** to split one's sides laughing; **mangiare a ~** to eat till one bursts.

crepare [kre'pare] **1** *vi (aus essere) (fam: morire)* to snuff it, kick the bucket; **~ dal ridere** *o* **dalle risa** to kill o.s. laughing; **~ dall'invidia** to be green with envy. **2: ~rsi** *vr (spaccarsi)* to crack.

crepitare [krepi'tare] *vi (fuoco)* to crackle; *(pioggia)* to patter; *(foglie)* to rustle.

crepitio, ii [krepi'tio] *sm (vedi vb)* crackling; pattering; rustling.

crepuscolare [krepusko'lare] *ag* twilight *attr;* **luce ~** twilight.

crepuscolo [kre'puskolo] *sm (anche fig)* twilight; **al ~** at twilight.

crescendo [kreʃ'ʃɛndo] *sm (anche fig)* crescendo; **suonare in ~** to play a crescendo; **la sua carriera è stata un ~ di successi** his career has gone from strength to strength.

crescente [kreʃ'ʃɛnte] *ag (gen)* growing, increasing; *(luna)* waxing.

crescere ['kreʃʃere] **1** *vi (aus essere)* **(a)** *(gen)* to grow; *(persona: diventare adulto)* to grow up; *(: diventare più alto)* to grow taller; **il bambino/l'albero è cresciuto** the child/tree has grown; **i suoi capelli non crescono molto** her hair doesn't grow very fast; **sono cresciuto in Sardegna** I grew up in Sardinia; **farsi ~ la barba/i capelli** to grow a beard/one's hair.

(b) *(aumentare: rumore, prezzo, numero)* to increase; *(: città, quartiere)* to expand; *(: luna)* to wax; **la popolazione mondiale cresce velocemente** the world's population is increasing rapidly; **i prezzi crescono ogni giorno** prices are going up daily; **la città è cresciuta a vista d'occhio** the city has grown before one's eyes.

(c) *(fam: avanzare):* **questo mese mi crescono i soldi** I've got some spare cash this month.

2 *vt (fam: coltivare)* to grow; *(: aumentare: prezzi etc)* to increase; *(: allevare: figli)* to raise.

crescione [kreʃ'ʃone] *sm* watercress; **~ inglese** *o* **degli orti** garden cress.

crescita ['kreʃʃita] *sf:* **~ (di)** growth (in); **~ zero** zero growth.

cresciuto, a [kreʃ'ʃuto] *pp di* **crescere.**

cresima ['krɛzima] *sf (Rel)* confirmation.

cresimare [krezi'mare] *(Rel)* **1** *vt* to confirm. **2: ~rsi** *vr* to be confirmed.

crespo, a ['krɛspo] **1** *ag (capelli)* frizzy. **2** *sm* crêpe.

cresta ['krɛsta] *sf (gen)* crest; *(di polli, uccelli)* crest, comb; *(di montagna)* ridge; **alzare la ~** *(fig)* to become cocky; **abbassare la ~** *(fig)* to climb down; **far abbassare la ~ a qn** to take sb down a

peg or two; **far la ~ sulla spesa** to keep some of the shopping money for o.s.; **essere sulla ~ dell'onda** to be riding high.

Creta ['kreta] *sf* Crete.

creta ['kreta] *sf (gesso)* chalk; *(argilla)* clay.

cretinata [kreti'nata] *sf (fam):* **dire/fare una ~** to say/do a stupid thing; **non dire ~e!** don't talk rubbish!

cretineria [kretine'ria] *sf* stupidity.

cretinismo [kreti'nizmo] *sm (Med)* cretinism.

cretino, a [kre'tino] **1** *ag (Med)* cretinous; *(peg)* cretinous *(fam).* **2** *sm/f (vedi ag)* cretin.

cric[1] [krik] *sm inv (rumore)* creak.

cric[2] [krik] *sm inv (Tecn)* jack.

cricca, che ['krikka] *sf* clique.

cricco, chi ['krikko] *sm (Tecn)* = **cric[2].**

criceto [kri'tʃeto] *sm* hamster.

criminale [krimi'nale] **1** *ag* criminal. **2** *sm/f* criminal; **~ della strada** road hog.

criminalità [kriminali'ta] *sf* **(a)** criminal nature. **(b)** *(delinquenza)* crime; **la ~ organizzata** organized crime.

crimine ['krimine] *sm (anche fig)* crime; **~i di guerra** war crimes.

criminologia [kriminolo'dʒia] *sf* criminology.

criminosità [kriminosi'ta] *sf* criminality.

criminoso, a [krimi'noso] *ag* criminal.

crinale [kri'nale] *sm* ridge.

crine ['krine] *sm* horsehair; **di ~** horsehair *attr;* **~ vegetale** vegetable fibre.

criniera [kri'njɛra] *sf (di animale)* mane.

cripta ['kripta] *sf* crypt.

crisalide [kri'zalide] *sf* chrysalis.

crisantemo [krizan'tɛmo] *sm* chrysanthemum.

crisi ['krizi] *sf inv (gen, Pol, Econ)* crisis; *(Med)* attack; *(di epilessia)* fit; **~ di nervi/di pianto** fit of hysterics/of tears; **essere in ~** *(partito, impresa etc)* to be in a state of crisis; *(persona)* to be upset; **mettere qn in ~** to put sb in a difficult position.

crisma ['krizma] *sf (Rel)* chrism.

cristalleria [kristalle'ria] *sf (fabbrica)* crystal glassworks *sg;* *(oggetti)* crystalware.

cristallino, a [kristal'lino] **1** *ag (Mineralogia)* crystalline; *(fig: suono, acque)* crystal clear. **2** *sm (Anat)* crystalline lens.

cristallizzare [kristallid'dzare] **1** *vi (aus essere),* **~rsi** *vr* to crystallize; *(fig)* to become fossilized. **2** *vt (gen)* to crystallize, turn into crystals; **zucchero cristallizzato** granulated sugar.

cristallizzazione [kristalliddzat'tsjone] *sf* crystallization.

cristallo [kris'tallo] *sm* crystal; *(di finestra)* pane (of glass); **~ di rocca** rock crystal.

cristianesimo [kristja'nezimo] *sm* Christianity.

cristiania [kris'tjania] *sm inv (Sci)* christie.

cristianità [kristjani'ta] *sf (condizione)* Christianity; *(popoli, territorio)* Christendom.

cristianizzare [kristjanid'dzare] *vt* to convert to Christianity.

cristiano, a [kris'tjano] **1** *ag* Christian. **2** *sm/f (anche fig)* Christian; **un povero ~** *(fig)* a poor soul *o* beggar; **non c'era un ~ per le strade** there wasn't a soul on the streets; **comportarsi da ~** *(fig)* to behave in a civilized manner.

cristo ['kristo] *sm* **(a)** C**~** Christ; **nell'anno 54 avanti/dopo C~** in 54 B.C./A.D.; **(un) povero ~** (a) poor beggar. **(b)** *(immagine, oggetto)* figure of Christ.

criterio [kri'tɛrjo] *sm* **(a)** *(norma)* criterion, rule; **con ~ approssimativo** approximately. **(b)** *(buon senso)* (common) sense; **dovresti avere più ~** you should have more sense; **è una persona di**

poco ~ he doesn't have much common sense.

critica ['kritika] *sf* **(a)** *(biasimo)* criticism. **(b)**: la ~ *(attività)* criticism; *(i critici)* critics *pl*; *(opera, studio)* appreciation, critique; *(recensione)* review; **fare la ~ di** *(libro, film etc)* to review.

criticabile [kriti'kabile] *ag* open to criticism.

criticare [kriti'kare] *vt* *(biasimare)* to criticize, find fault with; *(giudicare: opera)* to give a critique of.

critico, a, ci, che ['kritiko] **1** *ag* critical; **aver spirito ~** to have a critical mind; **al momento ~** at the vital *o* critical moment; **età ~a** *(gen)* difficult age; *(menopausa)* change of life. **2** *sm* *(gen)* critic; *(recensore)* reviewer.

criticone, a [kriti'kone] *sm/f* faultfinder; **sei il solito ~!** you're always finding fault!

crivellare [krivel'lare] *vt*: ~ **(di)** to riddle (with).

croccante [krok'kante] **1** *ag* crisp, crunchy. **2** *sm* *(Culin)* almond crunch.

crocchetta [krok'ketta] *sf* *(Culin)* croquette.

crocchia ['krɔkkja] *sf* chignon, bun.

crocchio ['krɔkkjo] *sm* *(di persone)* small group, cluster.

croce ['krotʃe] *sf* *(gen)* cross; **farsi il segno della ~** to make the sign of the cross, cross o.s.; **Cristo in ~** *o* **sulla ~** Christ on the cross; **mettere in ~** *(anche fig: criticare)* to crucify; *(tormentare)* to nag to death; **mettiamoci una ~ sopra** let's forget about it; **quella malattia è la sua ~** that illness is her cross in life; **ognuno ha la sua ~ da portare** we each have our cross to bear; **la C~ Rossa** the Red Cross; **chiama la C~ Rossa** *(uso improprio)* call an ambulance; ~ **uncinata** swastika.

crocefiggere [krotʃe'fiddʒere] *etc* = **crocifiggere** *etc*.

crocerossina [krotʃeros'sina] *sf* Red Cross nurse.

crocevia [krotʃe'via] *sm inv* crossroads *sg*.

crochet [krɔ'ʃe] *sm inv* **(a)** *(arnese)* crochet hook. **(b)** *(lavoro)* crochet.

crociata [kro'tʃata] *sf* *(anche fig)* crusade.

crociato, a [kro'tʃato] **1** *ag* cross-shaped; **parole ~e** crossword puzzle *sg*. **2** *sm* *(anche fig)* crusader.

crocicchio [kro'tʃikkjo] *sm* crossroads *sg*.

crociera [kro'tʃera] *sf* **(a)** *(viaggio)* cruise; **velocità di ~** *(Aer, Naut)* cruising speed; **altezza di ~** *(Aer)* cruising height; **andare in *o* fare una ~** to go on a cruise. **(b)** *(Archit)*: **volta a ~** cross vault.

crocifiggere [krotʃi'fiddʒere] *vt* *(anche fig)* to crucify.

crocifissione [krotʃifis'sjone] *sf* *(anche fig)* crucifixion.

crocifisso, a [krotʃi'fisso] **1** *pp di* **crocifiggere**. **2** *sm* crucifix.

crogiolarsi [krodʒo'larsi] *vr*: ~ **al sole** to bask in the sun.

crogiolo [krɔ'dʒɔlo] *sm* *(Chim, Metallurgia)* crucible; *(Vetreria)* pot; *(fig: di popoli)* melting pot.

crollare [krol'lare] **1** *vi* *(aus essere)* *(gen, fig)* to collapse; *(tetto)* to cave in; *(prezzi, titoli)* to slump; **far ~** *(anche fig: governo)* to bring down; **si lasciò ~ sul letto** he slumped down on the bed; **dopo 2 giorni di interrogatorio è crollato** he broke down after 2 days of interrogation. **2** *vt*: ~ **il capo** to hang one's head.

crollo ['krɔllo] *sm* *(anche fig)* collapse; *(Fin)* slump, sudden fall; **avere un ~** *(fisico)* to collapse; *(psichico)* to break down; ~ **in Borsa** slump in prices on the Stock Exchange; **il ~ del '29** the Wall Street Crash.

croma ['krɔma] *sf* *(Mus)* quaver.

cromare [kro'mare] *vt* to chromium-plate.

cromatico, a, ci, che [kro'matiko] *ag* chromatic;

sfumature ~che shades of colour.

cromatura [kroma'tura] *sf* chromium plating.

cromo ['krɔmo] **1** *sm* *(Chim)* chromium. **2** *ag inv*: **giallo ~** chrome yellow.

cromosoma, i [kromo'sɔma] *sm* chromosome.

cronaca, che ['krɔnaka] *sf* **(a)** *(Storia)* chronicle. **(b)** *(di giornale)* news *sg*; *(resoconto: sportivo)* commentary; *(: di viaggio etc)* coverage; **fatti di ~** news items; ~ **nera** crime news.

cronico, a, ci, che ['krɔniko] **1** *ag* *(anche fig)* chronic. **2** *sm* *(Med)* chronic invalid.

cronista, i, e [kro'nista] *sm/f* *(storico)* chronicler; *(Stampa)* reporter; *(Radio, TV)* commentator.

cronistoria [kronis'tɔrja] *sf* chronicle; *(fig iro)* blow-by-blow account.

cronologia [kronolo'dʒia] *sf* chronology.

cronologico, a, ci, che [krono'lɔdʒiko] *ag* chronological.

cronometraggio [kronome'traddʒo] *sm* *(precision)* timing.

cronometrare [kronome'trare] *vt* to time.

cronometrico, a, ci, che [krono'mɛtriko] *ag* chronometric(al); *(fig: puntualità)* perfect.

cronometrista, i, e [kronome'trista] *sm/f* timekeeper.

cronometro [kro'nɔmetro] *sm* chronometer; *(a scatto)* stopwatch.

cross [krɔs] *sm inv* *(Sport: motocross)* motocross; *(in Pugilato, Calcio)* cross; **moto da ~** rally bike.

crosta ['krɔsta] *sf* *(di formaggio, pane etc)* crust; *(Med)* scab; *(Zool)* shell; *(di ghiaccio)* layer; *(fig peg: quadro)* daub; ~ **terrestre** earth's crust; ~ **lattea** *(Anat)* cradle cap.

crostaceo [kros'tatʃeo] *sm* *(Zool)* shellfish *(no pl)*.

crostata [kros'tata] *sf* tart.

crostino [kros'tino] *sm* *(da brodo)* croûton; *(da antipasto)* canapé.

crucciare [krut'tʃare] **1** *vt* to torment, worry. **2**: ~**rsi** *vr*: ~**rsi per** to torment o.s. over.

crucciato, a [krut'tʃato] *ag* worried.

cruccio, ci ['kruttʃo] *sm* torment.

cruciale [kru'tʃale] *ag* crucial.

cruciverba [krutʃi'vɛrba] *sm inv* crossword (puzzle).

crudele [kru'dele] *ag* *(anche fig)* cruel.

crudeltà [krudel'ta] *sf* *(anche fig)* cruelty.

crudezza [kru'dettsa] *sf* *(vedi ag* **b)** severity, harshness; bluntness, forthrightness.

crudo, a ['krudo] *ag* **(a)** *(Culin, Tecn)* raw; *(acqua)* hard; **la bistecca è un po' ~a** the steak is underdone. **(b)** *(fig: clima)* severe, harsh; *(: descrizione, linguaggio)* blunt, forthright; ~**a realtà** harsh reality.

cruento, a [kru'ɛnto] *ag* bloody.

crumiro, a [kru'miro] *sm/f* *(peg)* blackleg, scab.

cruna ['kruna] *sf* eye (of a needle).

crusca ['kruska] *sf* bran.

cruscotto [krus'kɔtto] *sm* *(Aut)* dashboard.

Cuba ['kuba] *sf* Cuba.

cubano, a [ku'bano] *ag*, *sm/f* Cuban.

cubatura [kuba'tura] *sf* cubic capacity.

cubetto [ku'betto] *sm* (small) cube; ~ **di ghiaccio** ice cube.

cubico, a, ci, che ['kubiko] *ag* *(gen)* cubic; **radice ~a** cube root.

cubismo [ku'bizmo] *sm* cubism.

cubo, a ['kubo] **1** *ag* cubic. **2** *sm* *(gen)* cube; **elevare al ~** *(Mat)* to cube.

cuccagna [kuk'kaɲɲa] *sf* abundance, plenty; **paese della ~** land of plenty; **è finita la ~!** the party's over!; **albero della ~** greasy pole.

cuccetta [kut'tʃetta] *sf* *(di treno)* couchette; *(di nave)* berth.

cucchiaiata [kukkja'jata] *sf* spoonful.

cucchiaino [kukkja'ino] *sm* teaspoon; *(contenuto)* teaspoonful; *(Pesca)* spinner.

cucchiaio [kuk'kjajo] *sm (gen)* spoon; *(da tavola)* tablespoon; *(cucchiaiata)* spoonful; tablespoonful; ~ **da portata** serving spoon.

cuccia, ce ['kuttʃa] *sf (di cane: letto)* dog's basket; *(: canile)* kennel; **a ~!, fai la ~!** down (boy)!

cucciolata [kuttʃo'lata] *sf* litter.

cucciolo ['kuttʃolo] *sm (gen)* cub; *(di cane)* pup, puppy; *(fig: persona):* **vieni qua, ~!** come here, pet!

cucina [ku'tʃina] *sf (locale)* kitchen; *(arte)* cooking, cookery; *(cibo)* cooking, food; *(fornelli)* cooker; **mi piace la ~ greca** I like Greek cooking; **è molta brava in ~** she's very good at cooking; **da ~** *(utensile)* kitchen *attr*; **di ~** *(libro, lezione)* cookery *attr*; ~ **da campo** primus stove; ~ **componibile** fitted kitchen; ~ **economica** kitchen range.

cucinare [kutʃi'nare] *vt* to cook; **chi ha cucinato?** who did the cooking?

cuciniere, a [kutʃi'njɛre] *sm/f* cook.

cucinino [kutʃi'nino] *sm* kitchenette.

cucire [ku'tʃire] *vt (gen)* to sew; *(vestito, Med: ferita)* to sew up; *(libro, cuoio)* to stitch; ~ **a macchina** to machine-sew; **macchina da ~** sewing machine; ~ **la bocca a qn** *(fig)* to shut sb up.

cucito, a [ku'tʃito] **1** *ag (vedi vb)* sewn; stitched; ~ **a mano** hand-sewn; **stare ~ addosso a qn** *(fig: persona)* to cling to sb. **2** *sm* sewing; *(Scol)* sewing, needlework.

cucitrice [kutʃi'tritʃe] *sf (Tip: per libri)* stitching machine; *(per fogli)* stapler.

cucitura [kutʃi'tura] *sf (di stoffa, cuoio, libro)* stitching; *(costura)* seam.

cucù [ku'ku] *sm inv (Zool: anche: cuculo)* cuckoo; **orologio a ~** cuckoo clock; **far ~** to go boo; **~, eccomi qua!** peek-a-boo!

cuculo [ku'kulo] *sm vedi* **cucù.**

cuffia ['kuffja] *sf* bonnet, cap; *(da infermiera)* cap; *(per ascoltare)* headphones *pl*, headset; *(Tecn)* casing; ~ **da bagno** *(da piscina etc)* bathing cap; *(da doccia etc)* shower cap, bath cap.

cugino, a [ku'dʒino] *sm/f* cousin.

cui ['kui] *pron rel* **(a)** *(nei complementi indiretti: riferito a persona)* whom; *(: riferito a oggetto, animale)* which; **la persona (a) ~ si riferiva** the person he referred to is the person to whom he referred; **le ragazze di ~ ti ho parlato** the girls I spoke to you about *o* about whom I spoke to you; **il libro di ~ parlavo** the book I was talking about *o* about which I was talking; **il motivo per ~ non insisto** the reason I'm not insisting; **il quartiere in ~ abito** the area where I live; **l'anno in ~ prese la laurea** the year he took his degree, the year when *o* in which he took his degree.

(b) *(come genitivo possessivo: riferito a persona)* whose; *(: riferito a oggetto, animale)* of which, whose; **il signore la ~ figlia** ho incontrato ieri the gentleman whose daughter I met yesterday; **la persona di ~ ti ho dato il numero di telefono ieri** the person whose telephone number I gave you yesterday.

(c): **per ~** *(perciò)* therefore, so.

culinaria [kuli'narja] *sf* cuisine.

culinario, a [kuli'narjo] *ag* culinary.

culla ['kulla] *sf (anche fig)* cradle; **fin dalla ~** from the cradle, since (you were *etc*) a baby.

cullare [kul'lare] **1** *vt (bambino)* to rock; *(fig: idea, speranza)* to cherish. **2: ~rsi** *vr (gen)* to sway; **~rsi in vane speranze** *(fig)* to cherish fond hopes; **~rsi nel dolce far niente** *(fig)* to sit back and relax.

culminante [kulmi'nante] *ag:* **posizione ~** *(Astron)* highest point; **punto** *o* **momento ~** *(fig)* climax.

culminare [kulmi'nare] *vi (aus essere):* ~ **(in)** *(Astron)* to reach its highest point (at); ~ **in** *o* **con** *(fig)* to culminate in.

culmine ['kulmine] *sm (di torre, monte)* summit, top; *(fig):* **ero al ~ della felicità** my happiness knew no bounds; **era al ~ del successo** he was at the peak of his success.

culo ['kulo] *sm (fam!)* **(a)** *(sedere)* arse(!), backside; **alza il ~!** get up off your backside!; **prendere qn per il ~** to take the piss out of sb. **(b)** *(fortuna):* **aver ~** to have the luck of the devil; **che ~!** lucky sod!

culto ['kulto] *sm (religione)* religion; *(adorazione)* worship, adoration; *(venerazione: anche fig)* cult; ~ **della personalità** *(fig)* personality cult; ~ **degli eroi** hero worship; **avere un ~ per qn/di** *o* **per qc** to worship sb/sth; **avere il ~ della propria persona** to be vain about one's personal appearance.

cultore, trice [kul'tore] *sm/f:* **essere un ~ di** to have a keen interest in.

cultura [kul'tura] *sf (gen)* culture; *(conoscenza)* learning, knowledge; **ai ~** *(persona)* cultured; *(istituto)* cultural, of culture; ~ **generale** general knowledge.

culturale [kultu'rale] *ag* cultural.

culturismo [kultu'rizmo] *sm* body-building.

cumulare [kumu'lare] *vt (gen)* to accumulate; *(Amm: impieghi)* to hold concurrently.

cumulativo, a [kumula'tivo] *ag (gen)* cumulative; *(prezzo)* (all-)inclusive; *(biglietto)* group *attr*.

cumulo ['kumulo] *sm* **(a)** *(mucchio)* heap, pile; ~ **dei redditi** *(Fisco)* combined incomes; ~ **delle pene** *(Dir)* consecutive sentences. **(b)** *(Meteor)* cumulus.

cuneo ['kuneo] *sm* wedge.

cunetta [ku'netta] *sf* **(a)** *(di strada etc)* bump; **a ~e, pieno di ~e** bumpy. **(b)** *(scolo: nelle strade di città)* gutter; *(: di campagna)* ditch.

cunicolo [ku'nikolo] *sm (galleria)* tunnel; *(di miniera)* pit, shaft; *(di talpa)* hole.

cuocere ['kwɔtʃere] **1** *vt* **(a)** *(gen):* **(far) ~** to cook; ~ **al forno** *(pane)* to bake; *(arrosto)* to roast; ~ **in umido/a vapore/in padella** to stew/steam/fry; **da ~** *(frutta)* cooking *attr*. **(b)** *(mattoni)* to fire. **2** *vi (aus essere)* to cook. **3: ~rsi** *vr (cibo)* to cook; *(fig: al sole)* to get burnt.

cuoco, a, chi, che ['kwɔko] *sm/f* cook; *(di ristorante)* chef.

cuoiame [kwo'jame] *sm* leather goods *pl*.

cuoio ['kwɔjo] **1** *sm* leather; *(prima della concia)* hide; **in** *o* **di ~** leather *attr*; ~ **capelluto** *(Anat)* scalp. **2** *sfpl:* **~a: tirare le ~a** *(fam)* to kick the bucket.

cuore ['kwɔre] *sm* **(a)** *(Anat, fig: cosa centrale)* heart; **a ~** heart-shaped; **nel ~ della città/della notte/della mischia** in the heart of the city/middle of the night/midst of the fight; **operazione a ~ aperto** open-heart operation.

(b) *(fig: animo):* **aver buon ~** to be kind-hearted; **una persona di buon ~** a kind-hearted soul; **ho a ~ il successo del progetto** the success of the project matters to me; **col ~ in mano** open-handed, generous; **col ~ in gola** with one's heart in one's mouth; **senza ~** heartless; **aprire il proprio ~ a qn** to open one's heart to sb; **non ho il ~ di dirglielo** I haven't the heart to tell him; **il ~ mi dice che...** I feel in my heart that...; **un grazie di ~** heartfelt thanks; **avere un ~ da leone** to be brave-hearted; **mettiti il ~ in pace, non tornerà mai più** you'll have to accept that he'll never

come back; **avere la morte nel** ~ to be sick at heart; **nel profondo del** ~ in one's heart of hearts; **ringraziare di** ~ to thank sincerely; **mi sta molto a** ~ it's very important to me; **mi si stringeva il** ~, **mi piangeva il** ~ my heart ached; **mi piange il** ~ **a vedere questo spreco** I hate to see such waste; **toccare il** ~ **a qn** to move sb.
(**c**): ~**i** *pl* (*Carte*) hearts.

cupidigia [kupi'didʒa] *sf* greed, covetousness.

cupo, a ['kupo] *ag* (*caverna, notte*) pitch-black; (*voce, abisso*) deep; (*colore, cielo*) dark; (*suono*) dull; (*fig: carattere*) sullen, morose.

cupola ['kupola] *sf* (*di chiesa, osservatorio*) dome; (*più piccolo*) cupola; **a** ~ dome-shaped.

cura ['kura] *sf* (**a**) care; **avere** *o* **prendersi** ~ **di qn/qc** to look after sb/sth; **abbi** ~ **di fare come ti ho detto** be sure to do exactly as I've told you, take care to do exactly as I've told you; **abbi** ~ **di te** take care of yourself, look after yourself; **si dedica completamente alla** ~ **dell'azienda** he devotes all his time to running the company; **questa pianta ha bisogno di molte** ~**e** this plant needs a lot of attention; **a** ~ **di** (*Stampa*) edited by; **trasmissione a** ~ **di** (*TV, Radio*) programme produced by.
(**b**) (*accuratezza*) care, accuracy; **con** ~ carefully; **senza** ~ carelessly; **se lo facessi con un po' più di** ~... if you took a bit more care over it... .
(**c**) (*Med: trattamento*) (course of) treatment; **fare una** ~ to follow a course of treatment; **è in** ~ **presso il dott. Bianchi** she's one of Dr Bianchi's patients; **è stato in** ~ **presso i migliori medici** he has received treatment from the best doctors; **le hanno dato una** ~ **a base di ormoni** they prescribed a course of hormone treatment for her; ~ **dimagrante** diet; ~ **del sonno** sleep therapy.

curabile [ku'rabile] *ag* curable.

curante [ku'rante] *ag*: **medico** ~ doctor (in charge of a patient).

curare [ku'rare] **1** *vt* (**a**) (*Med*) to treat; (*: guarire*) to cure; **gli curarono la pertosse** they treated him for whooping cough; **farsi** ~ **da qn per qc** to be treated by sb for sth; **devi** ~ *o* **curarti questo raffreddore** you must see about that cold. (**b**) (*occuparsi di*) to look after; (*: azienda*) to run, look after; (*: libro*) to edit; ~ **l'edizione di un'antologia** to be the editor of an anthology.
2: ~**rsi** *vr* (**a**) (*Med*) to take care of o.s., look after o.s.; **si sta curando con delle vitamine** he's taking vitamins. (**b**) (*esteticamente*) to take trouble over one's appearance. (**c**): ~**rsi di** (*occuparsi di*) to look after; (*preoccuparsi di*) to bother about.

curaro [ku'raro] *sm* curare.

curatela [kura'tela] *sf* (*Dir*) guardianship.

curativo, a [kura'tivo] *ag* curative.

curato [ku'rato] *sm* (*Rel*) parish priest; (*: protestante*) vicar.

curatore, trice [kura'tore] *sm/f* (**a**) (*Dir*) guardian; ~ **fallimentare** receiver. (**b**) (*di antologia etc*) editor.

curia ['kurja] *sf* (**a**) (*Rel*): **la C**~ (**Romana**) the (Roman) Curia; ~ **vescovile** diocesan administration. (**b**) (*Dir*) local lawyers' association; ~ **notarile** notaries' association *o* guild.

curiosaggine [kurjo'saddʒine] *sf* nosiness.

curiosare [kurjo'sare] *vi* (*aggirarsi*) to look round, wander round; ~ **nei negozi** to look round *o* wander around the shops; ~ **tra le cose** to poke about among things; ~ **tra vecchi giornali** to browse amongst old newspapers; ~ **nelle faccende altrui** to poke one's nose into other people's affairs.

curiosità [kurjosi'ta] *sf inv* (**a**) (*gen*) curiosity; (*peg*) curiosity, inquisitiveness; **provare** ~ **per** to be curious about. (**b**) (*cosa rara*) curio, curiosity.

curioso, a [ku'rjoso] **1** *ag* (*gen*) curious; (*peg*) curious, inquisitive; (*strano*) odd; **un fatto/tipo** ~ an odd thing/person; **essere** ~ **di qc/di sapere qc** to be curious about sth/to know sth. **2** *sm/f* busybody, nosy parker; **una folla di** ~ a crowd of onlookers. **3** *sm*: **il** ~ **è che...** the funny *o* curious thing is that... .

curriculum [kur'rikulum] *sm inv*: ~ (**vitae**) curriculum vitae.

curva ['kurva] *sf* (**a**) (*gen, Mat, Tecn*) curve; (*traiettoria*) trajectory; ~ **della produzione** production curve; **una bionda tutta** ~**e** (*fam*) a curvaceous blonde. (**b**) (*di strada, fiume*) bend; ~ **a forcella** hairpin bend; ~ **stretta** sharp bend; **prendere una** ~ (*Aut*) to take a bend; **sorpassare in** ~ to overtake on a bend. (**c**) (*Geog*) contour; ~ **di livello** contour line.

curvare [kur'vare] **1** *vt* to bend. **2** *vi* (**a**) (*strada*) to bend, curve; ~ **a sinistra/destra** to bend to the left/right. (**b**) (*Aut*) to take a bend; ~ **a sinistra/destra** to follow the road to the left/right. **3**: ~**rsi** *vr* (*chinarsi*) to bend down; (*diventare curvo*) to become bent; (*legno*) to warp; ~**rsi cogli anni** (*persona*) to become stooped with old age.

curvatura [kurva'tura] *sf* (*gen, Mat*) curvature; (*di strada*) camber; ~ **alla spina dorsale** (*Med*) curvature of the spine.

curvilineo, a [kurvi'lineo] **1** *ag* (*gen, Mat*) curvilinear. **2** *sm* (*strumento*) drawing stencil.

curvo, a ['kurvo] *ag* (*gen*) curved; (*piegato*) bent; **camminare** ~ to walk with a stoop.

cuscinetto [kuʃʃi'netto] **1** *sm* (*per timbri*) pad; (*puntaspilli*) pincushion; (*Tecn*) bearing; ~ **a sfere** ball bearing. **2** *ag inv*: **stato** ~ (*fig*) buffer state.

cuscino [kuʃ'ʃino] *sm* (*gen*) cushion; (*guanciale*) pillow; ~ **di aria** cushion of air.

cuspide ['kuspide] *sf* (*Mat, Astron, Astrologia*) cusp; (*Archit*) spire.

custode [kus'tɔde] *sm/f* (*di museo*) keeper, custodian; (*di parco*) warden; (*di casa*) concierge; (*di fabbrica, carcere*) guard.

custodia [kus'tɔdja] *sf* (**a**) care; **avere qc in** ~ to look after sth; **dare qc in** ~ **a qn** to entrust sth to sb's care. (**b**) (*Dir*) custody; **affidare a qn la** ~ **di** to give sb custody of; **agente di** ~ prison warder; ~ **delle carceri** prison security. (**c**) (*astuccio*) case.

custodire [kusto'dire] *vt* (*conservare*) to keep; (*fare la guardia: casa, carcere*) to guard; **i gioielli sono custoditi in cassaforte** the jewels are kept in a strongbox.

cutaneo, a [ku'taneo] *ag* skin *attr*.

cute ['kute] *sf* (*Anat, Med*) skin.

cuticola [ku'tikola] *sf* cuticle.

C.V. *abbr* (= cavallo vapore) h.p.

D

D, d [di] *sf o m inv (lettera)* D, d.

da [da] *prep (da + il = **dal**, da + lo = **dallo**, da + l' = **dall'**, da + la = **dalla**, da + i = **dai**, da + gli = **dagli**, da + le = **dalle**) (a)* *(agente, mezzo)* by; **dipinto ~ un grande artista** painted by a great artist; **l'ho appreso dalla radio** I heard it on the radio; **fare qc ~ sé** to do sth (for) o.s.; **riconoscere qn dal passo** to recognize sb by his step.

(b) *(provenienza, distanza, separazione)* from; *(: fuori di)* out of; *(: giù ~)* off; **~ dove vieni?** where do you come from?; **arrivare ~ Milano** to arrive from Milan; **l'aereo parte ~ Gatwick** the plane departs from Gatwick; **a 3 km ~ Roma** 3 kms from Rome; **uscire dalla scuola** to come out of school; **scendere dal treno** to get off the train; **toglitelo dalla testa** get it out of your head; **staccarsi ~ qn** to leave *o* part from sb.

(c) *(stato in luogo)* at; *(: presso)* at, with; **sono ~ Pietro** I'm at Pietro's (house); **vive ~ un amico** he's living at a friend's *o* with a friend; **ti aspetto dal macellaio** I'll wait for you at the butcher's; **abita ~ quelle parti** he lives round there.

(d) *(moto a luogo)* to; *(moto per luogo)* through; **vado ~ Pietro/dal giornalaio** I'm going to Pietro's (house)/to the newsagent's; **è uscito dalla finestra** he went out through *o* by (way of) the window; **questo treno passa ~ Genova** this train goes through Genoa.

(e) *(tempo: durata)* for; *(: a partire da: nel passato)* since; *(: nel futuro)* from; **vivo qui ~ un anno** I've been living here for a year; **sono qui dalle 6/~ martedì** I've been here since 6 o'clock/since Tuesday; **~ quando sei qui** since you have been here; **~ allora** since then; **~ oggi in poi** from today onwards; **d'ora in poi** *o* **in avanti** from now on.

(f) *(qualità, caratteristica)*: **una ragazza dai capelli biondi/dagli occhi azzurri** a fair-haired/blue-eyed girl, a girl with fair hair/blue eyes; **un vestito ~ 100.000 lire** a 100,000 lire dress; **sordo ~ un orecchio** deaf in one ear; **è una cosa ~ poco** it's nothing special.

(g) *(modo)* like; **comportarsi ~ uomo** to behave like a man; **trattare qn ~ amico** to treat sb like *o* as a friend; **non è ~ lui** it's not like him; **è ~ vigliacco fare così** that's a cowardly way to behave.

(h) *(in qualità di)* as; **~ giovane/studente** as a youth/student; **fare ~ guida/maestro** to act as a guide/teacher; **fare ~ padre a** to be a father to.

(i) *(fine, scopo)*: **cavallo ~ corsa** racehorse; **vino ~ pasto** table wine; **abito ~ sera** evening dress.

(j) *(seguito da infinito: consecutivo)* that *(spesso omesso)*; *(: finale)* to; **ero così stanco ~ non stare più in piedi** I was so tired (that) I couldn't stand; **casa ~ affittare/vendere** house to let/for sale; **qualcosa ~ bere/mangiare** something to drink/eat.

(k): **~... a...** from... to...; **contare ~ 1 a 10** to count from 1 to 10; **dalle 3 alle 5** from 3 to *o* till 5 (o'clock); **c'erano dalle 30 alle 40 persone** there were between 30 and 40 people there; **è cambiato dall'oggi al domani** he changed overnight.

dabbasso [dab'basso] *av* = **da basso.**

dabbenaggine [dabbe'naddʒine] *sf (peg)* simplemindedness, credulity.

dabbene [dab'bene] *ag inv* honest, decent.

daccapo [dak'kapo] *av* = **da capo.**

dacché [dak'ke] *cong* since.

dado ['dado] *sm (Gioco)* dice, die; *(Culin)* stock cube; *(Tecn)* (screw)nut; *(Archit)* dado; **giocare a ~i** to play dice; **tagliare a ~i** *(Culin)* to dice; **il ~ è tratto** *(fig)* the die is cast.

daffare [daf'fare] *sm inv* work, toil; **avere un gran ~** to be very busy; **darsi ~ perché si faccia qc** to work hard to get sth done.

dagli ['daλλi], **dai** ['dai] *prep + art vedi* **da.**

daino ['daino] *sm* (fallow) deer; **pelle di ~** buckskin.

dal [dal] *prep + art vedi* **da.**

dalia ['dalja] *sf* dahlia.

dalla ['dalla], **dalle** ['dalle], **dallo** ['dallo] *prep + art vedi* **da.**

dalmata, i ['dalmata] *sm (cane)* Dalmatian.

daltonico, a, ci, che [dal'tɔniko] **1** *ag* colourblind. **2** *sm/f* colour-blind person.

daltonismo [dalto'nizmo] *sm* colour blindness.

dama ['dama] *sf* **(a)** lady; *(nei balli)* partner; **~ di corte** lady-in-waiting; **~ di compagnia** lady's companion. **(b)** *(gioco)* draughts *sg*; **far ~** to make a crown.

damasco, schi [da'masko] *sm* damask.

damigella [dami'dʒɛlla] *sf (Storia)* damsel; *(: titolo)* mistress; **~ di onore** *(di sposa)* bridesmaid.

damigiana [dami'dʒana] *sf* demijohn.

dammeno [dam'meno] *ag inv*: **per non essere ~ di qn** so as not to be outdone by sb; **è un grande imbroglione e sua moglie non è ~** he's an out-and-out trickster and so is his wife.

danaro [da'naro] *sm* = **denaro.**

danaroso, a [dana'roso] *ag* wealthy.

dancing ['da:nsiŋ] *sm inv* dance hall.

danese [da'nese] **1** *ag* Danish. **2** *sm/f* Dane. **3** *sm (lingua)* Danish; *(cane)* Great Dane.

Danimarca [dani'marka] *sf* Denmark.

dannare [dan'nare] **1** *vt (Rel)* to damn; **far ~ qn** *(fig)* to drive sb mad; **~rsi l'anima per qc** *(affannarsi)* to work o.s. to death for sth; *(tormentarsi)* to worry o.s. to death over sth. **2**: **~rsi** *vr*: **~rsi (per)** *(fig: tormentarsi)* to be worried to death (by).

dannato, a [dan'nato] **1** *ag* damned; **quella ~a macchina!** *(fam)* that damned car! **2**: **i ~i** *smpl* the damned.

dannazione [dannat'tsjone] *sf* damnation.

danneggiare [danned'dʒare] *vt (gen)* to damage; *(fig: persona)* to harm; **la parte danneggiata** *(Dir)* the injured party.

danno ['danno] *sm (gen)* damage; *(a persona)* harm, injury; **arrecare ~ a qc** to damage sth; **arrecare ~ a qn** to harm sb, do sb harm; **il maltempo ha**

provocato ingenti ~**i** the bad weather caused serious damage; **a** ~ **di qn** to sb's detriment; **non c'è stato nessun** ~ **alle persone** nobody was hurt; **in caso di perdita o** ~ in case of loss or damage; **chiedere/risarcire i** ~**i** to sue for/pay damages.

dannoso, a [dan'noso] *ag*: ~ **a** harmful to; **il fumo è** ~ **alla salute** cigarettes damage your health.

dantesco, a, schi, sche [dan'tesko] *ag* Dantesque; **l'opera** ~**a** Dante's work.

Danubio [da'nubjo] *sm* Danube.

danza ['dantsa] *sf*: **la** ~ dancing; **una** ~ a dance; **fare** ~ to study dancing; ~ **classica** ballet dancing; **scuola/maestro di** ~ school/dancing master; ~ **di guerra** war dance.

danzante [dan'tsante] *ag* dancing; **serata** ~ dance.

danzare [dan'tsare] *vi, vt* to dance.

danzatore, trice [dantsa'tore] *sm/f* dancer.

dappertutto [dapper'tutto] *av* everywhere.

dappocaggine [dappo'kaddʒine] *sf* ineptitude.

dappoco [dap'pɔko] *ag inv (anche: da poco: inetto)* inept; *(: insignificante)* insignificant.

dapprima [dap'prima] *av* at first.

dardo ['dardo] *sm* dart, arrow.

dare ['dare] **1** *vt* **(a)** *(gen)* to give; *(premio, borsa di studio)* to give, award; ~ **qc a qn** to give sb sth, give sth to sb; ~ **qc da fare a qn** to give sb sth to do; ~ **uno schiaffo/un calcio a qn** to give sb a slap/kick, slap/kick sb; **mi dai la macchina?** can I have the car?; ~ **a qn il permesso di fare qc** to give sb permission to do sth; **gli hanno dato ordine di sparare** they gave him the order to fire; **questo trucco ti dà un'aria volgare** that make-up makes you look cheap; **ha dato 6 milioni per la macchina** he paid 6 million (lire) for the car; **gli hanno dato 5 anni** *(di prigione)* they gave him 5 years; **quanti anni mi dai?** how old do you think I am?; **queste scene mi danno il vomito** these scenes make me feel sick; ~ **del cretino a qn** to call sb an idiot; ~ **la vita per qc** to give (up) one's life for sth; ~ **tutto se stesso a qn/qc** to give one's all to sb/sth; ~**rsi una pettinata** to give one's hair a comb.

(b) *(organizzare: festa, banchetto)* to hold, give; *(: spettacolo)* to perform, put on; *(: film)* to show; **danno ancora quel film?** is that film still showing?

(c) *(produrre: frutti, soldi)* to give, yield; *(: suono, calore)* to give off; **gli investimenti hanno dato il 10% di interesse** the investments yielded 10% interest; **gli ha dato un figlio** she bore him a son.

(d): ~ **qc per certo** to be sure of sth; ~ **qn per morto** to give sb up for dead; ~ **qc/qn per perso** to give sth/sb up for lost; ~ **qc per scontato** to take sth for granted; ~ **ad intendere a qn che...** to lead sb to believe that...; ~ **da mangiare/bere a qn** to give sb sth to eat/drink; **ciò mi dà da pensare** *((insospettire)* that gives me food for thought; *(preoccupare)* that worries me; **si dà il caso che...** it so happens that...; **non è dato a tutti di essere intelligenti** not everyone is blessed with intelligence; **dar via** to give away.

2 *vi* **(a)** *(finestra, casa: guardare)*: ~ **su** to overlook, give onto; **il giardino dà sulla strada** the garden faces onto the road.

(b) *(colore: tendere)*: ~ **su** to tend towards; **un colore che dà sul verde** a greenish colour.

3: ~**rsi** *vr* **(a)**: ~**rsi a** *(musica, politica etc)* to dedicate o.s. to; ~**rsi al bere/al gioco** to take to drink/to gambling; ~**rsi alla bella vita** to have a good time; ~**rsi ammalato** to report sick; ~**rsi prigioniero** to surrender; ~**rsi per vinto** to give in; ~**rsi da fare per fare qc** to go to a lot of bother

to do sth; **coraggio, diamoci da fare!** come on, let's go to it!

(b): **può** ~**rsi** maybe, perhaps; **può** ~**rsi che venga** he may come, perhaps he will come.

(c): **darsela a gambe** to take to one's heels.

4 *sm (Fin)*: **il** ~ **e l'avere** debits and credits *pl*.

darsena ['darsena] *sf (Naut)* dock.

data ['data] *sf* date; **che** ~ **è oggi?** what's today's date?; **in** ~ **da destinarsi** on a date still to be announced; **lettera in** ~ **4 febbraio** letter dated the 4th February; **in** ~ **odierna** as of today; **senza** ~ undated; ~ **di emissione** date of issue; ~ **di nascita** date of birth; ~ **di scadenza** expiry date; **amicizia di lunga** *o* **vecchia** ~ long-standing friendship.

datare [da'tare] **1** *vt* to date; **non datato** undated. **2** *vi*: ~ **da** to date back to.

datario [da'tarjo] *sm (timbro)* date stamp; *(di orologio)* (universal) calendar.

datazione [datat'tsjone] *sf* dating.

dativo, a [da'tivo] *ag, sm* dative.

dato, a ['dato] **1** *ag* **(a)** *(certo)*: **in quel** ~ **giorno** on that particular day; **in** ~**i casi** in certain cases. **(b)** *(stabilito)*: **entro quel** ~ **giorno** by that particular day. **(c)** *(considerato)*: ~**a la situazione** given *o* considering *o* in view of the situation; ~ **che...** given that...; ~ **a me** *(Mat, Scienza)* datum; ~**i data**; **è un** ~ **di fatto** it's a fact.

datore, trice [da'tore] *sm/f*: ~ **di lavoro** employer.

dattero ['dattero] *sm* **(a)** *(Bot: albero)* date palm; *(: frutto)* date. **(b)** *(Zool)* date mussel.

dattilografare [dattilogra'fare] *vt* to type.

dattilografia [dattilogra'fia] *sf* typing.

dattilografo, a [datti'lɔgrafo] *sm/f* typist.

dattiloscritto, a [dattilos'kritto] **1** *pp di* **dattiloscrivere**. **2** *sm* typescript.

dattorno, d'attorno [dat'torno] *av* = **di torno**.

davanti [da'vanti] **1** *av* in front; *(all'inizio: di gruppo, stanza)* at the front; *(dirimpetto)* opposite; **posso andare** ~? *(in macchina)* can I go *o* sit in front? ~ **c'era un bel giardino** at the front there was a nice garden.

2: ~ **a** *prep* **(a)** *(posizione: gen)* in front of; *(: dirimpetto a)* opposite; *(distanza)* ahead; **ogni mattina passo** ~ **alla tua casa** every morning I go past your house; **camminava** ~ **a me** he was walking ahead of *o* in front of me; **era seduto** ~ **a me** *(più in là)* he was sitting in front of me; *(faccia a faccia)* he was sitting opposite *o* facing me; **la mia casa è** ~ **al municipio** my house is opposite *o* faces the town hall. **(b)** *(al cospetto di)* before, in front of; **comparire** ~ **al giudice** to appear before the judge; ~ **a Dio** before God; ~ **al pericolo** in the face of danger.

3 *ag inv* front *attr*; **le file** ~ **sono occupate** the front rows are occupied; **zampe** ~ front *o* fore paws.

4 *sm inv* front.

davanzale [davan'tsale] *sm* (window)sill.

davanzo [da'vantso] *av* = **d'avanzo**.

davvero [dav'vero] *av* really; **è successo** ~ it really happened; **dico** ~ I mean it.

davvicino [davvi't∫ino] *av* = **da vicino**.

daziario, a [dat'tsjarjo] *ag* excise *attr*.

dazio ['dattsjo] *sm (tassa)* duty, tax; *(luogo)* customs *pl*; ~ **doganale** customs duty.

D.C. *abbr f di* **Democrazia Cristiana**.

d.C. *abbr (= dopo Cristo)* A.D.

DD *abbr di* **direttissimo**.

D.D.T. *abbr m* D.D.T.

dea ['dɛa] *sf (anche fig)* goddess.

debellare [debel'lare] *vt* to overcome, conquer.

debilitare [debili'tare] **1** vt to debilitate. **2**: ~**rsi** vr to become debilitated.

debilitazione [debilitat'tsjone] sf debilitation.

debitamente [debita'mente] av (vedi ag) duly; properly.

debito¹, a ['debito] ag (dovuto) due; (appropriato) proper; **a tempo** ~ in due course; **ogni cosa a tempo** ~ I'll (o we'll) think about it when the time comes.

debito² ['debito] sm (anche fig) debt; ~ **pubblico** national debt; **far** ~**i** to get into debt; **essere/ sentirsi in** ~ **verso qn** to be/feel indebted to sb.

debitore, trice [debi'tore] sm/f debtor; **ti sono** ~ (anche fig) I'm in your debt; **ti sono** ~ **di un favore** I owe you a favour.

debole ['debole] **1** ag (gen) weak; (luce) dim, faint; (speranza, lamento, suono) faint; (polso) faint, weak; (argomentazioni) weak, poor; **essere** ~ **di vista** to have weak o poor eyesight; **essere** ~ **di stomaco** to have a delicate stomach; **essere** ~ **di polmoni** to have weak lungs; **essere** ~ **in matematica** to be poor at mathematics; **è troppo** ~ **con lei** he's too soft with her. **2** sm/f (persona) weakling. **3** sm weakness; **ha un** ~ **per le bionde** blondes are his weakness, he's got a weakness for blondes.

debolezza [debo'lettsa] sf (anche fig) weakness.

debosciato, a [deboʃ'ʃato] **1** ag debauched. **2** sm/f debauchee.

debuttante [debut'tante] sm/f (gen) beginner, novice; (Teatro) actor/actress at the beginning of his (o her) career; **ballo delle** ~**i** debutantes' ball.

debuttare [debut'tare] vi to make one's debut.

debutto [de'butto] sm (anche fig) debut; **fare il proprio** ~ (anche fig) to make one's debut.

decade ['dekade] sf period of ten days.

decadente [deka'dɛnte] ag, sm/f (gen, Letteratura) decadent.

Decadentismo [dekaden'tizmo] sm Decadence.

decadenza [deka'dɛntsa] sf (processo) decline; (stato) decadence; **una città in** ~ a city in decline.

decadere [deka'dere] vi (aus essere) **(a)** (costumi) to fall into decline. **(b)** (scadere) to lapse.

decaduto, a [deka'duto] ag (persona) impoverished; (norma) lapsed.

decaedro [deka'edro] sm (Mat) decahedron.

decaffeinato, a [dekaffei'nato] ag decaffeinated.

decalcificare [dekaltʃifi'kare] vt (Med) to decalcify.

decalcificazione [dekaltʃifikat'tsjone] sf (Med, Geol) decalcification.

decalcomania [dekalkoma'nia] sf transfer.

decalitro [de'kalitro] sm decalitre, ten litres.

decametro [de'kametro] sm decametre, ten metres.

decano [de'kano] sm (Rel) dean; (fig) doyen.

decantare [dekan'tare] vt (virtù, bravura etc) to praise; (persona) to sing the praises of.

decapitare [dekapi'tare] vt (gen) to decapitate; (per pena capitale) to behead.

decapitazione [dekapitat'tsjone] sf (vedi vb) decapitation; beheading.

decappottabile [dekappot'tabile] ag (Aut) convertible.

decat(h)lon ['dɛkatlon] sm (Sport) decathlon.

decelerare [detʃele'rare] vt, vi to decelerate, slow down.

decelerazione [detʃelerat'tsjone] sf deceleration.

decennale [detʃen'nale] **1** ag (che dura 10 anni) ten-year attr; (che ricorre ogni 10 anni) ten-yearly,

every ten years. **2** sm (ricorrenza) tenth anniversary.

decenne [de'tʃenne] ag: **un bambino** ~ a ten-year-old child, a child of ten.

decennio [de'tʃɛnnjo] sm decade.

decente [de'tʃɛnte] ag (anche fig) decent.

decentralizzare [detʃentralid'dzare] vt (Amm) to decentralize.

decentramento [detʃentra'mento] sm decentralization.

decentrare [detʃen'trare] vt to decentralize, move out of o away from the centre.

decenza [de'tʃɛntsa] sf decency, propriety.

decesso [de'tʃɛsso] sm death.

decidere [de'tʃidere] **1** vt **(a)** (stabilire): ~ **qc** to decide on sth; ~ **che** to decide that; ~ **di fare qc/di non fare qc** to decide to do sth/against doing sth; **sta a lui** ~ it's up to him to decide; **ha deciso il nostro futuro** it determined our future. **(b)** (risolvere: disputa) to settle, resolve; ~ **una lite** (Dir) to settle a dispute.

2 vi (persona) to decide, make up one's mind; **è venuto il momento di** ~ it's time to decide o make a decision; **non so** ~ **tra questi modelli** I can't decide which of these models to choose; **fu quel fatto a** ~ **del mio futuro** that was what decided o determined my future.

3: ~**rsi** vr (persona) to come to o make a decision, make up one's mind; **finalmente si è deciso a parlare** he finally made up his mind to talk.

decifrare [detʃi'frare] vt (codice) to decode, decipher; (calligrafia) to decipher; (enigma) to find the key to; (fig: intenzioni, atteggiamento) to work out.

decilitro [de'tʃilitro] sm decilitre.

decima ['dɛtʃima] sf (Storia) tithe.

decimale [detʃi'male] ag, sm decimal.

decimare [detʃi'mare] vt (anche fig) to decimate.

decimazione [detʃimat'tsjone] sf (anche fig) decimation.

decimetro [de'tʃimetro] sm decimetre.

decimo, a ['dɛtʃimo] ag, sm/f, sm tenth; per uso vedi **quinto**.

decina [de'tʃina] sf **(a)** (Mat): **la colonna delle** ~**e** the tens column. **(b)** (circa 10) ten or so, about ten; ~**e di lettere** dozens of letters, letters by the dozen; vedi anche **cinquantina**.

decisionale [detʃizjo'nale] ag decision-making attr.

decisione [detʃi'zjone] sf **(a)** (scelta, Dir) decision; **prendere una** ~ to take a decision. **(b)** (risolutezza) decisiveness; **con** ~ decisively, resolutely.

decisivo, a [detʃi'zivo] ag (gen) decisive; (fattore, colpo) deciding.

deciso, a [de'tʃizo] **1** pp di **decidere**. **2** ag **(a)** (persona, carattere) determined; (tono) firm, resolute; **essere** ~ **a fare qc** to be determined to do sth; **essere** ~ **a tutto** to be ready to do anything; **sei proprio** ~? are you quite sure?; **entrò con passo** ~ he marched in resolutely. **(b)** (netto: colpo) clean; (: accento) pronounced. **(c)** (definitivo): **non c'è ancora niente di** ~ nothing has been decided yet.

declamare [dekla'mare] vt, vi to declaim.

declamatorio, a [deklama'tɔrjo] ag declamatory.

declassare [deklas'sare] vt to downgrade; **1ª declassata** (Ferr) first-class carriage which may be used by second-class passengers.

declinabile [dekli'nabile] ag declinable.

declinare [dekli'nare] **1** vi (pendio) to slope down; (fig: popolarità) to decline. **2** vt **(a)** (Gram) to decline; ~ **le proprie generalità** (fig) to give one's particulars. (b) *(rifiutare: invito, offerta)* to decline, turn down; ~ **ogni responsabilità** to disclaim all responsibility.

declinazione [deklinat'tsjone] *sf* (a) *(Gram)* declension. (b) *(Fis, Astron)* declination.

declino [de'klino] *sm* decline; **in** ~ declining, on the decline.

declivio [de'klivjo] *sm* downward slope.

decodificare [dekodifi'kare] *vt* to decode.

decodificazione [dekodifikat'tsjone] *sf* decoding.

decollare [dekol'lare] *vi (anche fig)* to take off.

décolleté [dekolo'te] **1** *ag inv (abito)* low-necked, low-cut. **2** *sm (di abito)* low neckline; *(di donna)* cleavage.

decollo [de'kollo] *sm (Aer, fig)* take-off; **al** ~ on take-off; **in fase di** ~ during take-off.

decolorante [dekolo'rante] **1** *ag* decolorizing; *(per capelli)* bleaching. **2** *sm (vedi ag)* decolorizing agent; bleach.

decolorare [dekolo'rare] *vt* to decolorize; *(capelli)* to bleach.

decomporre [dekom'porre] *vt*, **decomporsi** *vr* to decompose.

decomposizione [dekompozit'tsjone] *sf* decomposition; **un cadavere in** ~ a decomposing corpse.

decomposto, a [dekom'posto] *pp di* **decomporre**.

decompressione [dekompres'sjone] *sf* decompression.

decongelare [dekondʒe'lare] *vt* to defrost.

decongestionare [dekondʒestjo'nare] *vt (Med, traffico)* to relieve congestion in.

decorare [deko'rare] *vt* (a) *(ornare)* to decorate; *(: abito)* to trim. (b) *(Mil etc)* to decorate; ~ **qn al valor militare** to decorate sb for bravery.

decorativo, a [dekora'tivo] *ag* decorative.

decoratore, trice [dekora'tore] *sm/f* (a) (interior) decorator. (b) *(Teatro)* set designer.

decorazione [dekorat'tsjone] *sf (vedi vb)* decoration; trimming.

decoro [de'koro] *sm (decenza)* decorum; *(dignità)* dignity; **vestirsi con** ~ to dress properly.

decoroso, a [deko'roso] *ag (contegno, abito)* dignified, decorous; *(fig: stipendio etc)* decent.

decorrenza [dekor'rɛntsa] *sf*: **con** ~ **da** (as) from.

decorrere [de'korrere] *vt*: ~ **da** to have effect from; **a** ~ **da** (as) from, starting from.

decorso, a [de'korso] **1** *pp di* **decorrere**. **2** *sm (di malattia)* course.

decotto [de'kotto] *sm* decoction.

decrepito, a [de'krɛpito] *ag (anche fig)* decrepit.

decrescere [de'kreʃʃere] *vi (aus essere) (gen)* to decrease; *(prezzi, febbre)* to go down; *(luna)* to wane; *(marea)* to ebb.

decresciuto, a [dekreʃ'ʃuto] *pp di* **decrescere**.

decretare [dekre'tare] *vt (norma)* to decree; *(mobilitazione)* to order; ~ **lo stato d'emergenza** to declare a state of emergency; ~ **la nomina di qn** to decide on the appointment of sb.

decreto [de'kreto] **1** *sm* decree. **2**: ~ **legge** *decree with the force of law*.

decubito [de'kubito] *sm (Med)*: **piaghe** *fpl* **da** ~ bedsores.

decuplicare [dekupli'kare] *vt*, ~**rsi** *vr* to increase tenfold.

decuplo, a ['dɛkuplo] **1** *ag* tenfold. **2** *sm*: **guadagno il** ~ **di quanto guadagnassi** I earn ten times as much as I used to.

decurtare [dekur'tare] *vt* to reduce.

dedica, che ['dɛdika] *sf* dedication.

dedicare [dedi'kare] **1** *vt (gen, Rel)* to dedicate; *(energie, sforzi)* to devote. **2**: ~**rsi** *vr*: ~**rsi a** *(votarsi)* to devote o.s. to; ~**rsi alla casa** *(occupar-*

sene) to look after the house; ~**rsi anima e corpo a** to give o.s. up body and soul to.

dedicatorio, a [dedika'torjo] *ag* dedicatory.

dedito, a ['dedito] *ag*: ~ **a** devoted to; **essere** ~ **al bere** to be a heavy drinker.

dedizione [dedit'tsjone] *sf* dedication, devotion.

dedotto, a [de'dotto] *pp di* **dedurre**.

dedurre [de'durre] *vt* (a) *(capire, concludere)* to deduce, infer; **dal suo comportamento ho dedotto che era stanco** I gathered from the way he was behaving that he was tired. (b) *(togliere)*: ~ **(da)** to deduct (from).

deduttivo, a [dedut'tivo] *ag* deductive.

deduzione [dedut'tsjone] *sf (in tutti i sensi)* deduction.

défaillance [defa'jɑ̃s] *sf (Sport: crisi)* collapse; **avere un attimo di** ~ to have a momentary lapse.

defalcare [defal'kare] *vt* to deduct.

defecare [defe'kare] **1** *vt (Chim)* to refine. **2** *vi (Med)* to defecate.

defenestrare [defenes'trare] *vt* to throw out of the window; *(fig)* to remove from office.

defenestrazione [defenestrat'tsjone] *sf (fig: azione)* removal from office, dismissal.

deferente [defe'rente] *ag (persona)* deferential.

deferenza [defe'rɛntsa] *sf* deference.

deferire [defe'rire] *vt*: ~ **qc a** *(Dir)* to refer sth to.

defezionare [defettsjo'nare] *vi* to defect; *(Mil)* to desert.

defezione [defet'tsjone] *sf (vedi vb)* defection; desertion.

deficiente [defi'tʃɛnte] **1** *ag* (a) *(mancante)*: ~ **di** deficient in. (b) *(fig fam: sciocco)* half-witted. **2** *sm/f (Med)* mental defective; *(fig fam: sciocco)* half-wit.

deficienza [defi'tʃɛntsa] *sf (gen)* deficiency; *(carenza)* shortage; *(fig: lacuna)* weakness.

deficit ['defitʃit] *sm inv* deficit.

deficitario, a [defitʃi'tarjo] *ag (Fin)* in deficit.

defilarsi [defi'larsi] *vr (svignarsela)* to slip away, slip off.

défilé [defi'le] *sm inv* fashion parade.

definire [defi'nire] *vt* (a) *(precisare)* to define; **il suo comportamento si può** ~ **irresponsabile** his behaviour can be described as irresponsible. (b) *(risolvere: vertenza)* to settle.

definitiva [defini'tiva] *sf*: **in** ~ *(dopotutto)* when all is said and done; *(dunque)* well then.

definitivo, a [defini'tivo] *ag (gen)* final; *(chiusura, vittoria, edizione)* definitive.

definito, a [defi'nito] *ag (gen)* definite; **ben** ~ clear, clearcut.

definizione [definit'tsjone] *sf (gen)* definition; *(soluzione)* settlement.

deflagrare [defla'grare] *vi (anche fig)* to explode.

deflagrazione [deflagrat'tsjone] *sf* explosion.

deflazionare [deflattsjo'nare] *vt (Econ)* to deflate.

deflazione [deflat'tsjone] *sf (Econ)* deflation.

deflettore [deflet'tore] *sm (Aut)* quarter-light.

deflorazione [deflorat'tsjone] *sf* deflowering; defloration.

defluire [deflu'ire] *vi (aus essere)*: ~ **da** *(liquido)* to flow away from; *(fig: capitali)* to flow out of.

deflusso [de'flusso] *sm (anche fig)* flow; *(di marea)* ebb.

deformante [defor'mante] *ag (Med)* deforming; *(specchio)* distorting.

deformare [defor'mare] **1** *vt (oggetto)* to put out of shape; *(legno)* to warp; *(corpo)* to deform; *(fig: immagine, visione, verità)* to distort. **2**: ~**rsi** *vr (vedi vt)* to lose its shape; to warp; to become deformed; *(fig: immagine)* to become distorted.

deformazione [deformat'tsjone] *sf (Med)*

deformation; **questa è ~ professionale!** that's force of habit because of your (o his etc) job!

deforme [de'forme] ag (Med) deformed; (vestito) misshapen; (peg: bruttissimo) hideous.

deformità [deformi'ta] sf inv (Med) deformity.

defraudare [defrau'dare] vt: **~ qn di qc** to cheat o swindle sb out of sth, defraud sb of sth.

defunto, a [de'funto] **1** ag dead; **il ~ presidente** the late president. **2** sm/f deceased.

degenerare [dedʒene'rare] vi: **~ (in)** to degenerate (into).

degenerato, a [dedʒene'rato] ag, sm/f degenerate.

degenerazione [dedʒenerat'tsjone] sf degeneration, degeneracy.

degenere [de'dʒenere] ag degenerate.

degente [de'dʒɛnte] sm/f (di ospedale) in-patient.

degenza [de'dʒɛntsa] sf confinement in bed; **~ ospedaliera** period in hospital.

degli ['deʎʎi] prep + art vedi **di.**

deglutire [deglu'tire] vt to swallow.

deglutizione [deglutit'tsjone] sf swallowing.

degnare [deɲ'ɲare] **1** vt: **non mi ha degnato di uno sguardo** he didn't so much as look at me; **non mi ha degnato di una risposta** he didn't even deign to answer me. **2**: **~rsi** vr: **~rsi di fare qc** to deign o condescend to do sth; **vedo che ti sei degnato!** (iro) how gracious of you!

degno, a ['deɲɲo] ag (gen) worthy; (dignitoso) dignified; **~ di** worthy of; **~ di fiducia** trustworthy; **~ di fede** (persona, testimonianza) reliable; **~ di invidia** enviable; **~ di lode** praiseworthy; **non è ~ di te** (persona) he is not worthy of you; **fare una cosa del genere non è ~ di te** it's most unworthy of you to do a thing like that; **non è ~ di essere chiamato padre** he is not fit to be called a father; **il suo ~ figlio** (anche iro) his good o worthy son.

degradante [degra'dante] ag degrading.

degradare [degra'dare] **1** vt (Mil) to downgrade; (fig: persona) to degrade. **2**: **~rsi** vr to degrade o.s.

degradazione [degradat'tsjone] sf (vedi vb) downgrading; degradation.

degustare [degus'tare] vt to sample, taste.

degustazione [degustat'tsjone] sf **(a)** (azione) tasting, sampling. **(b)** (negozio): **~ di vini** specialist wine bar; **~ di caffè** specialist coffee shop.

dei ['dei] prep + art vedi **di.**

deificare [deifi'kare] vt to deify.

del [del] prep + art vedi **di.**

delatore, trice [dela'tore] sm/f informer.

delazione [delat'tsjone] sf secret accusation.

delega, ghe ['delega] sf **(a)** (di autorità, poteri) delegation. **(b)** (Dir) proxy; **per ~** by proxy; **per ~ notarile** through a solicitor.

delegare [dele'gare] vt to delegate; **~ qn a fare qc** to delegate sb to do sth; (Dir) to empower o authorise sb to do sth.

delegato, a [dele'gato] **1** ag: **amministratore ~, consigliere ~** managing director. **2** sm delegate.

delegazione [delegat'tsjone] sf delegation.

deleterio, a [dele'tɛrjo] ag deleterious, noxious.

Delfino [del'fino] sm (Storia) Dauphin.

delfino [del'fino] sm (Zool) dolphin; **nuotare a ~** (Sport) to do the butterfly (stroke).

delibera [de'libera] sf decision.

deliberare [delibe'rare] **1** vt: **~ qc** to come to a decision on sth; **~ di fare qc** to decide to do sth. **2** vi (Dir): **~ su qc** to rule on sth.

deliberato, a [delibe'rato] ag (intenzionale) deliberate.

deliberazione [deliberat'tsjone] sf decision.

delicatamente [delikata'mente] av (toccare) deli-

cately; (accarezzare, appoggiare) gently.

delicatezza [delika'tettsa] sf (vedi ag) delicacy; softness, paleness; lightness; gentleness; frailty; fragility; thoughtfulness, considerateness.

delicato, a [deli'kato] ag **(a)** (gen) delicate; (tessuto) delicate, fine; (colore) delicate, soft, pale; (profumo) delicate, light; (carezza) gentle; (salute) delicate, frail; (meccanismo) delicate, fragile; **è ~ di polmoni** he has weak lungs. **(b)** (che richiede tatto) delicate; (che dimostra tatto) thoughtful, considerate.

delimitare [delimi'tare] vt (anche fig) to delimit.

delimitazione [delimitat'tsjone] sf delimitation.

delineare [deline'are] **1** vt (anche fig) to outline. **2**: **~rsi** vr to be outlined; (fig: periodo) to emerge; (situazione) to take shape.

delinquente [delin'kwɛnte] sm/f delinquent, criminal; (fig: mascalzone) scoundrel, wretch; **~ abituale** (Dir) persistent offender.

delinquenza [delin'kwɛntsa] sf delinquency; **~ minorile** juvenile delinquency; **~ organizzata** organized crime.

deliquio [de'likwjo] sm (Med) swoon; **cadere in ~** to swoon.

delirante [deli'rante] ag (Med) delirious; (fig: folla) frenzied; (: discorso, mente) insane.

delirare [deli'rare] vi (Med) to be delirious; (fig) to rave.

delirio [de'lirjo] sm (Med) delirium; **in ~** (Med) delirious; **andare in ~ per qc** to go wild about sth; **mandare in ~** to send into a frenzy; **la folla in ~** the frenzied crowd.

delitto [de'litto] sm (misfatto, anche fig) crime; (Dir) crime, offence; **~ d'onore** crime committed to avenge one's honour.

delittuoso, a [delittu'oso] ag criminal.

delizia [de'littsja] sf delight; **con mia grande ~** to my delight; **che ~!** how delightful!

deliziare [delit'tsjare] **1** vt to delight. **2**: **~rsi** vr: **~rsi di qc/a fare qc** to take delight in sth/in doing sth.

delizioso, a [delit'tsjoso] ag (gen) delightful; (sapore, odore) delicious.

della ['della], **delle** ['delle], **dello** ['dello] prep + art vedi **di.**

delta ['dɛlta] **1** sm inv (Geog: anche: **foce a ~**) delta. **2** sm o f inv **(a)** (alfabeto greco) delta. **(b)** (Aer): **ala a ~** delta wing.

deltaplano [delta'plano] sm hang-glider; **volo col ~** hang-gliding.

delucidazione [delutʃidat'tsjone] sf clarification no pl; **vorrei delle ~i in merito** I would like to have some more details on that.

deludere [de'ludere] vt to disappoint.

delusione [delu'zjone] sf disappointment; **dare una ~ a qn** to disappoint sb.

deluso, a [de'luzo] **1** pp di **deludere. 2** ag disappointed.

demagogia [demago'dʒia] sf demagogy.

demagogico, a, ci, che [dema'gɔdʒiko] ag demagogic.

demagogo, ghi [dema'gɔgo] sm demagogue.

demaniale [dema'njale] ag state attr.

demanio [de'manjo] sm (Amm) state property; (: ufficio) state property office.

demarcare [demar'kare] vt to demarcate.

demarcazione [demarkat'tsjone] sf demarcation; **linea di ~** demarcation line.

demente [de'mɛnte] sm/f (anche fig) lunatic.

demenza [de'mɛntsa] sf (anche fig) madness, insanity; **~ senile** senile dementia.

demenziale [demen'tsjale] ag insane.

demerito [de'mɛrito] *sm* demerit; **ciò torna a tuo** ~ that reflects badly on you.

demistificare [demistifi'kare] *vt (mito etc)* to debunk.

democraticità [demokratitʃi'ta] *sf* democratic nature.

democratico, a, ci, che [demo'kratiko] **1** *ag* democratic. **2** *sm/f* democrat.

democratizzare [demokratid'dzare] *vt* to democratize.

democrazia [demokrat'tsia] *sf* democracy; ~ **popolare** people's democracy; **la D**~ **Cristiana** the Christian Democrat Party.

democristiano, a [demokris'tjano] *ag, sm/f* Christian Democrat.

démodé [demɔ'de] *ag inv* old-fashioned, out-of-date.

demografia [demogra'fia] *sf* demography.

demografico, a, ci, che [demo'grafiko] *ag* demographic; **incremento** ~ increase in population.

demolire [demo'lire] *vt (casa, oggetto, teoria)* to demolish; *(persona: criticare)* to tear to pieces.

demolitore, trice [demoli'tore] **1** *ag (anche fig)* destructive. **2** *sm (operaio)* demolition worker.

demolizione [demolit'tsjone] *sf (anche fig)* demolition.

demone ['dɛmone] *sm* demon.

demoniaco, a, ci, che [demo'niako] *ag* demoniacal; *(fig: diabolico)* fiendish.

demonico, a, ci, che [de'mɔniko] *ag* demonic.

demonio [de'mɔnjo] *sm* demon, devil; *(fig: genio)* genius; **il D**~ the Devil; **quel ragazzino è un** ~ that child is a little devil.

demoralizzare [demoralid'dzare] **1** *vt* to demoralize. **2**: ~**rsi** *vr* to become demoralized.

demoralizzazione [demoraliddzat'tsjone] *sf* demoralization.

demoscopia [demosko'pia] *sf* analysis of public opinion.

demoscopico, a, ci, che [demos'kɔpiko] *ag*: **indagine** ~**a** opinion poll.

denaro [de'naro] *sm* **(a)** money; ~ **contante** *o* **liquido** cash. **(b)** *(misura di seta)* denier. **(c)**: ~**i** *pl (Carte)* suit in Neapolitan pack of cards.

denaturato, a [denatu'rato] *ag*: **alcool** ~ methylated spirits, denatured alcohol *(Am)*.

denigrare [deni'grare] *vt* to denigrate, run down.

denigratorio, a [denigra'tɔrjo] *ag* disparaging, denigrating.

denigrazione [denigrat'tsjone] *sf* denigration.

denominare [denomi'nare] *vt* to name.

denominatore [denomina'tore] *sm* denominator; ~ **comune** *(Mat)* common denominator.

denominazione [denominat'tsjone] *sf* name, designation; ~ **di origine controllata** *(abbr* **D.O.C.***) mark guaranteeing the quality of a wine.*

denotare [deno'tare] *vt* to indicate, denote.

densità [densi'ta] *sf inv (gen, Fis)* density; *(di nebbia)* thickness, denseness; *(di vernice)* thickness; *(di folla)* denseness; **ad alta/bassa** ~ **di popolazione** densely/sparsely populated.

denso, a ['dɛnso] *ag (gen)* dense, thick; *(vernice, fumo, minestra)* thick; **una frase** ~**a di significativo** a phrase charged with meaning.

dentale [den'tale] *ag* dental.

dentario, a [den'tarjo] *ag* dental.

dentata [den'tata] *sf (morso)* bite; *(segno)* toothmark.

dentato, a [den'tato] *ag (Tecn)* toothed; *(Bot)* dentate.

dentatura [denta'tura] *sf* **(a)** set of teeth, teeth *pl*. **(b)** *(Tecn: di ruota)* serration.

dente ['dɛnte] *sm* **(a)** *(Anat)* tooth; ~ **da latte/del**

giudizio milk/wisdom tooth; ~**i sporgenti** buck teeth; **mettere i** ~**i** to teethe.

(b) *(di sega, pettine)* tooth; *(di ingranaggio)* cog; *(di forchetta, tridente)* prong.

(c) *(Geog)* jagged peak.

(d) *(Bot)*: ~ **di leone** dandelion.

(e) *(fraseologia)*: **al** ~ *(Culin)* al dente *(cooked so as to be firm when eaten)*; **avere il** ~ **avvelenato contro** *o* **con qn** to bear sb a grudge; **fuori il** ~ **fuori il dolore** once it's over I'll *(o you'll etc)* feel better; **mettere qc sotto i** ~**i** to have a bite to eat; **mostrare i** ~**i** *(anche fig)* to show one's teeth; **parlare a** ~**i stretti** to talk through one's teeth; **stringere i** ~**i** *(fig)* to grit one's teeth.

dentellare [dentel'lare] *vt (gen)* to indent, notch; *(francobollo)* to perforate; *(lama)* to serrate; *(stoffa)* to scallop, pink.

dentellato, a [dentel'lato] *ag (gen)* indented, notched; *(foglia)* serrated; *(Geog: cresta)* jagged; *(pizzo)* scalloped.

dentellatura [dentella'tura] *sf (gen)* indentation; *(di francobollo)* perforation; *(di cresta)* jagged outline; *(di pizzo)* scalloping.

dentice ['dɛntitʃe] *sm (Zool)* sea bream.

dentiera [den'tjera] *sf* **(a)** *(Med)* dentures *pl*. **(b)** *(Tecn)* rack.

dentifricio, a [denti'fritʃo] **1** *ag*: **pasta** ~**a** toothpaste. **2** *sm* toothpaste.

dentista, i, e [den'tista] *sm/f* dentist.

dentistico, a, ci, che [den'tistiko] *ag (gabinetto, studio)* dentist's; **studi** ~**ci** dentistry *sg*.

dentizione [dentit'tsjone] *sf* dentition.

dentro ['dentro] **1** *av* **(a)** *(all'interno)* inside; *(in casa)* indoors; **qui/là** ~ in here/there; **andare** ~ to go inside *(o indoors)*; **non ci va qui** ~ it won't go in here; **vieni** ~ come inside *o* in; **col freddo che c'era,** ~ **si stava bene** with the cold weather we were better off indoors; **hai visto** ~? have you seen inside?; **cioccolatini con** ~ **le nocciole** chocolates with hazelnut centres; **piegato in** ~ folded over; **o** ~ **o fuori!** either come in or go out!; **darci** ~ *(fig fam)* to slog away, work hard.

(b) *(fam: in carcere)* inside; **l'hanno messo** ~ they've put him away *o* inside; **è** ~ **da un anno** he's been inside for a year.

(c) *(fig: nell'intimo)* inwardly; **sentire qc** ~ to feel sth deep down inside o.s.; **tenere tutto** ~ to keep everything bottled up (inside o.s.).

2 *prep* in; ~ **l'armadio** in the cupboard; ~ **le mura/i confini** within the walls/frontiers; ~ **a: è** ~ **a quel cassetto** it's in that drawer; **è** ~ **alla politica/agli affari** he's involved in politics/business; ~ **di me pensai...** I thought to myself...; **ci sono** ~ **fino al collo** *(fig)* I'm in it up to my neck.

3 *sm* inside.

denudare [denu'dare] **1** *vt (persona)* to strip; *(parte del corpo)* to bare. **2**: ~**rsi** *vr* to strip.

denuncia, ce *o* **cie** [de'nuntʃa] *sf*, **denunzia** [de'nuntsja] *sf* **(a)** *(Dir)*: **fare una** ~ *o* **sporgere** ~ **contro qn** to report sb to the police. **(b)** *(Amm)*: ~ **dei redditi** income tax return; ~ **delle nascite** registration of births.

denunciare [denun'tʃare] *vt*, **denunziare** [denun'tsjare] *vt* **(a)** *(notificare: nascite, redditi etc)* to declare; *(accusare pubblicamente)* to denounce; *(rivelare)* to expose. **(b)** *(Dir)*: ~ **qn/qc (alla polizia)** to report sb/sth to the police.

denutrito, a [denu'trito] *ag* undernourished.

denutrizione [denutrit'tsjone] *sf* malnutrition.

deodorante [deodo'rante] *ag, sm* deodorant.

deodorare [deodo'rare] *vt* to deodorize.

depauperare [depaupe'rare] *vt* to impoverish.

dépendance [depā'dās] *sf inv* outbuilding.

deperibile [depe'ribile] *ag* perishable; **merce ~** perishables *pl*, perishable goods *pl*.

deperimento [deperi'mento] *sm (di persona)* wasting away; *(di merci)* deterioration; **il suo ~ è dovuto ad una cattiva alimentazione** he is run down due to poor eating habits.

deperire [depe'rire] *vi (aus essere) (persona)* to waste away; *(pianta)* to wilt; **ti trovo un po' deperito** you look rather run-down to me.

depilare [depi'lare] *vt* to depilate; **~rsi le sopracciglia** to pluck one's eyebrows; **~rsi le gambe** to shave one's legs.

depilatorio, a [depila'tɔrjo] **1** *ag* hair-removing *attr*, depilatory. **2** *sm (sostanza)* hair-remover, depilatory.

depilazione [depilat'tsjone] *sf* depilation, hair-removal.

dépliant [depli'ā] *sm inv* leaflet; *(opuscolo)* brochure.

deplorabile [deplo'rabile] *ag* deplorable.

deplorare [deplo'rare] *vt (biasimare)* to deplore; *(perdita)* to lament.

deplorazione [deplorat'tsjone] *sf* censure, disapproval.

deplorevole [deplo'revole] *ag* deplorable.

deponente [depo'nɛnte] *sm (Gram)* deponent.

deporre [de'porre] **1** *vt* **(a)** *(gen: valigia etc)* to put down; *(abbandonare: progetto, incarico)* to abandon, give up; *(: vecchio odio)* to put aside. **(b)** *(rimuovere: persona)* to remove; *(: re)* to depose; **lo deposero dalla carica** they removed him from office; **~ le armi** *(Mil)* to lay down arms. **(c)** *(sog: uccello)*: **~ le uova** to lay eggs. **(d)** *(Dir)*: **~ il vero** to tell the truth; **~ il falso** to give false evidence. **2** *vi (Dir)* to testify.

deportare [depor'tare] *vt* to deport.

deportato, a [depor'tato] **1** *ag* deported. **2** *sm/f* deportee.

deportazione [deportat'tsjone] *sf* deportation.

depositare [depozi'tare] **1** *vt* **(a)** *(gen: oggetto)* to put down, lay down; *(merci)* to store; **~ qc per terra** to put sth down; **ha depositato qui tutti i libri e se n'è andato** he dumped all his books here and then left. **(b)** *(Banca)* to deposit; **~ una somma in banca** to deposit a sum in the bank. **(c)** *(sog: fiume, vino etc)* to deposit. **2** *vi (liquido)* to leave some sediment. **3**: **~rsi** *vr (sabbia, polvere)* to settle.

depositario, a [depozi'tarjo] *sm/f (gen)* depository; *(fig: confidente)* repository.

deposito [de'pɔzito] *sm* **(a)** *(atto)*: **il ~ della merce ci è costato molto** we had to pay a lot for storing the goods; **il ~ dei bagagli è gratuito** there is no charge for left luggage. **(b)** *(di liquidi)* sediment, deposit; *(di acqua calcarea)* fur; **~ alluvionale** drift. **(c)** *(Fin)* deposit; **versare un ~** to put down *o* pay a deposit; **denaro in ~** money on deposit. **(d)** *(magazzino)* warehouse; *(Mil, di autobus)* depot; **lasciare in ~** *(merce)* to store; **~ bagagli** left-luggage office; **~ di legna** timber yard; **~ di munizioni** ammunition dump.

deposizione [depozit'tsjone] *sf (gen, Dir)* deposition; **rendere una falsa ~** to perjure o.s.

deposto, a [de'posto] *pp di* **deporre**.

depravare [depra'vare] *vt* to corrupt, pervert.

depravato, a [depra'vato] **1** *ag* depraved. **2** *sm/f* degenerate.

depravazione [depravat'tsjone] *sf* depravity.

deprecabile [depre'kabile] *ag* deplorable.

deprecare [depre'kare] *vt* to deplore, deprecate.

deprecativo, a [depreka'tivo] *ag* deprecating.

depredare [depre'dare] *vt* to plunder, loot; **~ qn di qc** to rob sb of sth.

depressione [depres'sjone] *sf (in tutti i sensi)* depression; **area** *o* **zona di ~** *(Meteor)* area of low pressure; *(Econ)* depressed area; **essere in uno stato di ~** *(Med)* to be depressed, be in a state of depression.

depressivo, a [depres'sivo] *ag* depressive; **in uno stato ~** in a depressed state, in a state of depression.

depresso, a [de'prɛsso] **1** *pp di* **deprimere**. **2** *ag* depressed.

deprezzamento [deprettsa'mento] *sm*: **~ (di)** depreciation (in).

deprezzare [depret'tsare] *vt* to bring down the value of.

deprimente [depri'mɛnte] *ag* depressing.

deprimere [de'primere] **1** *vt* to depress. **2**: **~rsi** *vr* to become depressed.

depurare [depu'rare] **1** *vt (liquido)* to purify; *(intestino etc)* to cleanse. **2**: **~rsi** *vr (liquido)* to be purified; *(corpo, anima)* to be cleansed.

depurativo, a [depura'tivo] *ag, sm* depurative.

depuratore, trice [depura'tore] **1** *ag* purifying. **2** *sm*: **~ d'acqua** water purifier; **~ di gas** scrubber.

depurazione [depurat'tsjone] *sf* purification; **impianto di ~** purification plant.

deputare [depu'tare] *vt (incaricare)*: **~ qn a fare qc** to delegate sb to do sth.

deputatessa [deputa'tessa] *sf* = **deputata**.

deputato, a [depu'tato] *sm/f* **(a)** *(Pol)* deputy, ≃ member of Parliament *(Brit)*, ≃ representative *(Am)*. **(b)** *(Amm)* delegate, representative.

deputazione [deputat'tsjone] *sf (gruppo)* deputation, delegation.

deragliamento [deraλλa'mento] *sm* derailment.

deragliare [deraλ'λare] *vi* to go off the rails; **far ~ un treno** to derail a train.

dérapage [dera'paʒ] *sm inv (di veicolo)* skid; *(Sci)* sideslipping.

derapare [dera'pare] *vi (veicolo)* to skid; *(Sci)* to sideslip.

derattizzazione [derattiddzat'tsjone] *sf* rodent control.

derelitto, a [dere'litto] **1** *ag* abandoned; *(casa)* derelict, abandoned. **2** *sm/f* destitute person; **i ~i** the destitute.

deretano [dere'tano] *sm (fam)* backside.

deridere [de'ridere] *vt* to mock, deride.

derisione [deri'zjone] *sf* mockery, derision; *(del pubblico)* jeers *pl*.

deriso, a [de'rizo] *pp di* **deridere**.

derisorio, a [deri'zɔrjo] *ag (gesto, tono)* mocking; *(situazione)* ludicrous, ridiculous.

deriva [de'riva] *sf* **(a)** *(Aer, Naut)* drift; **andare alla ~** *(anche fig)* to drift; **~ dei continenti** *(Geol)* continental drift. **(b)** *(dispositivo: Aer)* fin; *(: Naut)* centre-board.

derivare [deri'vare] **1** *vi (aus essere)*: **~ da** to derive from; **da ciò deriva che...** it follows that.... **2** *vt (Chim, Gram, Mat)* to derive; **da ciò ha derivato che...** hence he concluded that... .

derivata [deri'vata] *sf (Mat)* derivative.

derivato, a [deri'vato] **1** *ag* derived. **2** *sm (Chim, Gram)* derivative; *(prodotto)* by-product.

derivazione [derivat'tsjone] *sf* derivation; *(Elettr)* shunt.

dermatite [derma'tite] *sf* dermatitis.

dermatologia [dermatolo'dʒia] *sf* dermatology.

dermatologico, a, ci, che [dermato'lɔdʒiko] *ag* dermatological.

dermatosi [derma'tɔzi] *sf* dermatosis.

deroga, ghe ['dɛroga] *sf* (special) dispensation; **in ~ a** as a (special) dispensation to.

derogare [dero'gare] *vi (Dir)*: **~ a** to repeal in part.

derrate [der'rate] *sfpl*: **~ alimentari** foodstuffs.

derubare [deru'bare] *vt*: **~ qn di qc** to rob sb of sth, steal sth from sb.

descrittivo, a [deskrit'tivo] *ag* descriptive.

descritto, a [des'kritto] *pp di* **descrivere**.

descrivere [des'krivere] *vt (in tutti i sensi)* to describe.

descrivibile [deskri'vibile] *ag*: **facilmente ~** easy to describe; **non è ~** it's indescribable.

desertico, a, ci, che [de'zertiko] *ag* desert *attr*.

deserto, a [de'zɛrto] **1** *ag* deserted; **isola ~a** desert island. **2** *sm* desert.

desiderabile [deside'rabile] *ag* desirable.

desiderare [deside'rare] *vt* **(a)** *(volere)* to want; **~ (di) fare qc** to want *o* wish to do sth; **desidererei andarmene** I would like to leave; **desidero che lei venga domani** I'd like you to come tomorrow; **desideri fare una passeggiata?** would you like to go for a walk?; **desidera?** *(in bar)* what would you like?; *(in negozio, ufficio)* can I help you?; **sei desiderato al telefono** you're wanted on the phone; **farsi ~** *(fare il prezioso)* to play hard to get; *(farsi aspettare)* to take one's time; **lascia molto a ~** it leaves a lot to be desired; **la casa lascia un po' a ~** the house is not ideal. **(b)** *(sessualmente)* to desire.

desiderio [desi'dɛrjo] *sm (gen)* wish; *(più intenso, carnale)* desire; **sentì il ~ di andarsene** he felt a desire to leave; **esprimi un ~!** make a wish!

desideroso, a [deside'roso] *ag*: **~ di** eager for, longing for.

designare [desiɲ'ɲare] *vt (persona)* to designate, appoint; *(data, ora)* to fix; **la vittima designata** the intended victim.

designazione [desiɲɲat'tsjone] *sf* designation, appointment.

desinare [dezi'nare] **1** *vi* to dine, have dinner. **2** *sm* dinner.

desinenza [dezi'nɛntsa] *sf (Gram)* ending, inflexion.

desistere [de'sistere] *vi*: **~ (da qc/dal fare qc)** to give up (sth/doing sth).

desistito, a [desis'tito] *pp di* **desistere**.

desolante [dezo'lante] *ag* distressing.

desolato, a [dezo'lato] *ag (paesaggio)* desolate; *(persona: sconsolato)* distressed; **essere ~ (per qc)** *(spiacente)* to be terribly sorry (about sth).

desolazione [dezolat'tsjone] *sf* desolation.

despota, i ['dɛspota] *sm* despot.

dessert [de'sɛr] *sm inv* dessert; **da ~** dessert *attr*.

destare [des'tare] **1** *vt (svegliare)* to wake up; *(fig: dubbio, sospetti, pietà)* to arouse; *(: curiosità, invidia)* to arouse, awaken; **~ la preoccupazione/la sorpresa di qn** to cause sb concern/surprise; **non ~ il can che dorme** *(Proverbio)* let sleeping dogs lie. **2**: **~rsi** *vr* to wake up.

destinare [desti'nare] *vt* **(a)** *(designare)*: **~ qc a qn** to intend *o* mean sth for sb; **~ una somma all'acquisto di qc** to intend to use a sum *o* earmark a sum to buy sth; **i fondi saranno destinati alla ricerca** the money will be devoted to *o* used for research; **vi ha destinato questo posto** he intended *o* meant you to have this post; **era destinato a morir giovane** he was destined *o* fated to die young; **la sorte che gli è stata destinata** the fate that was in store for him; **libri destinati ai bambini** books (intended *o* meant) for children. **(b)** *(mandare)*: **sai dov'è destinata la lettera?** do you know where the letter is going?; **è desti-** nato alla nuova filiale he's been appointed to the new branch. **(c)** *(decidere)*: **~ un giorno a qc/a fare qc** to set aside a day for sth/to do sth; **in data da destinarsi** at some future date, at a date to be decided.

destinatario, a [destina'tarjo] *sm/f (di lettera)* addressee; *(di merce)* consignee; *(di mandato)* payee.

destinazione [destinat'tsjone] *sf* destination; *(scopo)* purpose; **giungere a ~** to reach one's destination.

destino [des'tino] *sm (sorte)* fate; *(futuro)* destiny; **era ~ che accadesse** it was fated to happen.

destituire [destitu'ire] *vt (gen)* to dismiss; *(re)* to depose.

destituzione [destitut'tsjone] *sf (vedi vb)* dismissal, deposition.

desto, a ['desto] *ag* awake; **tener ~ l'interesse del pubblico** to hold the public's attention.

destra ['dɛstra] *sf* **(a)** *(mano)* right hand. **(b)** *(parte)* right, right-hand side; **a ~** *(stato in luogo)* on the right; *(moto a luogo)* to the right; **a ~ di** to the right of; **corsia di ~** right-hand lane; **guida a ~** right-hand drive; **tenere la ~** to keep to the right. **(c)** *(Pol)*: **la ~** the right; **di ~** right-wing.

destreggiarsi [destred'dʒarsi] *vr* to manoeuvre.

destrezza [des'trettsa] *sf* skill, dexterity.

destriero [des'trjero] *sm* steed; *(da battaglia)* warhorse, charger.

destrismo [des'trizmo] *sm* **(a)** *(Med)* right-handedness. **(b)** *(Pol)* right-wing tendencies.

destro, a ['dɛstro] **1** *ag* **(a)** *(mano, braccio etc)* right; *(lato)* right(-hand). **(b)** *(persona: abile)* skilful, adroit. **2** *sm (Boxe)* right.

destrorso, a [des'trɔrso] **1** *ag (moto)* clockwise; *(Pol: scherz)* rightist. **2** *sm/f (Pol: scherz)* rightist.

destrosio [des'trɔzjo] *sm* dextrose.

desumere [de'sumere] *vt (dedurre)* to infer, deduce; *(trarre: informazioni)* to obtain; **desumo da ciò che te ne vuoi andare** I gather from that that you want to leave.

desunto, a [de'sunto] *pp di* **desumere**.

detenere [dete'nere] *vt (incarico, primato)* to hold; *(proprietà)* to have, possess; *(prigioniero)* to detain, hold.

detentivo, a [deten'tivo] *ag*: **mandato ~** imprisonment order; **pena ~a** prison sentence.

detentore, trice [deten'tore] *sm/f (di titolo, primato etc)* holder; *(di refurtiva)* possessor.

detenuto, a [dete'nuto] *sm/f* prisoner.

detenzione [deten'tsjone] *sf* **(a)** *(di titolo, primato)* holding; *(di armi, stupefacenti)* possession. **(b)** *(Dir)* detention.

detergente [deter'dʒɛnte] **1** *ag (gen)* detergent; *(crema, latte)* cleansing *attr*. **2** *sm* detergent.

detergere [de'tɛrdʒere] *vt (gen)* to clean; *(pelle, viso)* to cleanse; *(sudore)* to wipe (away).

deteriorabile [deterjo'rabile] *ag (gen)* liable to deteriorate; *(cibi)* perishable.

deterioramento [deterjora'mento] *sm*: **~ (di)** deterioration (in).

deteriore [dete'rjore] *ag (merce)* second-rate; *(significato)* pejorative; *(tradizione letteraria)* lesser, minor.

determinante [determi'nante] *ag* decisive, determining.

determinare [determi'nare] *vt (gen)* to determine; *(causare)* to bring about, cause.

determinativo, a [determina'tivo] *ag* determining; **articolo ~** *(Gram)* definite article.

determinato, a [determi'nato] *ag* **(a)** *(gen)*

certain; *(particolare)* specific. **(b)** *(risoluto)* determined, resolute.

determinazione |dcterminat'tsjonc| *sf (atto)* determining; *(decisione)* decision; *(risolutezza)* determination.

deterrente |detcr'rentc| *ag, sm* deterrent.

detersivo |detcr'sivo| *sm (gen)* detergent; *(per bucato)* washing powder; ~ **per lavatrice/per bucato a mano** washing machine/hand wash powder.

deterso, a |de'terso| *pp di* **detergere.**

detestabile |detes'tabile| *ag (carattere, abitudine)* detestable, odious; *(tempo, cibo)* dreadful, appalling.

detestare |detes'tare| *vt* to detest, hate.

detonante |deto'nante| **1** *ag* detonating, explosive. **2** *sm* explosive.

detonare |deto'nare| *vi* to detonate, explode.

detonatore |detona'tore| *sm* detonator.

detonazione |detonat'tsjonc| *sf (di esplosivo)* detonation, explosion; *(di arma)* bang; *(di motore)* pinking, knocking.

detrarre |de'trarre| *vt:* ~ **(da)** to deduct (from), take away (from).

detratto, a |de'tratto| *pp di* **detrarre.**

detrazione |detrat'tsjone| *sf* deduction.

detrimento |detri'mento| *sm:* **a** ~ **di** to the detriment of.

detrito |de'trito| *sm (Geol)* detritus; *(: fluviale)* silt, alluvium.

detronizzare |detronid'dzare| *vt (anche fig)* to dethrone.

detta |'detta| *sf:* **a** ~ **di** according to; **a** ~ **sua** according to him *(o* her).

dettagliante |detta/'/ante| *sm/f inv (Comm)* retailer, retail dealer.

dettagliare |detta/'/are| **1** *vt (racconto, descrizione)* to detail. **2** *vi* to give details.

dettagliatamente |detta//ata'mente| *av* in detail.

dettaglio |det'ta//o| *sm* **(a)** detail; **entrare** *o* **scendere nei** ~**i** to go into details *o* particulars. **(b)** *(Comm):* **al** ~ *(prezzo, vendita)* retail; **vendere al** ~ **to** (sell) retail.

dettame |det'tame| *sm* dictate, precept.

dettare |det'tare| *vt (lettera, condizioni etc)* to dictate; ~ **legge** *(fig)* to lay down the law; **fa come ti detta il cuore** follow your heart.

dettato |det'tato| *sm* dictation.

dettatura |detta'tura| *sf* dictation; **scrivere qc sotto** ~ to take sth down as a dictation; **l'ha scritto sotto** ~ it was dictated to him.

detto, a |'detto| **1** *pp di* **dire.** **2** *ag* **(a)** *(Amm, Comm: suddetto)* above-mentioned, aforementioned; ~**i prodotti vi saranno consegnati in settimana** the above-mentioned products will be delivered to you in the course of this week; **nel** ~ **giorno** on that day. **(b)** *(fraseologia):* ~ **fatto** no sooner said than done; **presto** ~**!** it's easier said than done!; **come non** ~ let's forget it. **3** *sm (motto)* saying.

deturpare |detur'pare| *vt (anche fig)* to disfigure.

deturpazione |deturpat'tsjonc| *sf* disfigurement.

devastare |devas'tare| *vt* to devastate; *(fig: sog: malattia)* to ravage.

devastatore, trice |devasta'tore| *ag* destructive.

devastazione |devastat'tsjone| *sf* devastation, destruction.

deviare |devi'are| **1** *vi (veicolo):* ~ **(da)** to turn off (from); *(pallone)* to deflect; **il viale devia dal corso principale** the avenue leads off the main road; **far** ~ **il traffico** to divert traffic; **far** ~ **il pallone** to deflect the ball; ~ **dalla retta via** *(fig)* to go astray. **2** *vt (traffico, fiume, conversazione)* to divert; *(proiettile, colpo, pallone)* to deflect; ~ **qn dalla retta via** to lead sb astray.

deviazione |deviat'tsjone| *sf (gen)* deviation; *(Aut)* diversion; **fare una** ~ to make a detour; ~ **della colonna vertebrale** curvature of the spine.

devitalizzare |devitalid'dzare| *vt (dente, nervo)* to devitalize, kill.

devoluto, a |devo'luto| *pp di* **devolvere.**

devoluzione |devolut'tsjone| *sf (Dir)* devolution, transfer; *(Fin)* endowment.

devolvere |de'volvere| *vt (somma)* to transfer; ~ **qc in beneficenza** to give sth to charity.

devoto, a |de'voto| **1** *ag (Rel)* devout, pious; *(affezionato)* devoted. **2** *sm/f* devout person; **i** ~**i** *(i fedeli)* the faithful.

devozione |devot'tsjone| *sf (Rel)* devoutness; *(affetto, dedizione)* devotion; ~**i** *(Rel: preghiere)* devotions; **avere una** ~ **per qn** to worship sb.

di |di| *(di + il = del, di + lo = dello, di + l' = dell', di + la = della, di + i = dei, di + gli = degli, di + le = delle)* **1** *prep* **(a)** *(possesso)* of; *(composto da, scritto da)* by; **la macchina del mio amico/dei miei amici** my friend's/friends' car, the car of my friend/friends; **la figlia dell'amica** ~ **mia madre** the daughter of my mother's friend, my mother's friend's daughter; **una commedia** ~ **Goldoni** a comedy by Goldoni; **l'ultimo libro** ~ **Moravia** Moravia's latest book, the latest book by Moravia.

(b) *(specificazione, denominazione)* of; **il sindaco** ~ **Milano** the mayor of Milan; **il mese** ~ **marzo** the month of March; **la vita** ~ **campagna** country life; **tavolo** ~ **cucina** kitchen table; **sala** ~ **lettura** reading-room; **il direttore dell'azienda** the manager of the company; **il professore d'inglese** the English teacher, the teacher of English; **è fatto** ~ **legno** it's made of wood; **una casa** ~ **mattoni** a brick house, a house made of brick; **il nome** ~ **Maria** the name Mary; **che razza d'imbecille!** what an idiot!

(c) *(provenienza)* from, out of; *(posizione)* in, on; **sono** ~ **Roma** I am *o* come from Rome; **uscire** ~ **casa** to come out of *o* leave the house; **i negozi** ~ **Milano** the Milan shops, the shops in Milan; **i vicini del piano** ~ **sopra** the neighbours on the floor above; **il migliore della città/classe** the best in the city/class.

(d) *(tempo)*: ~ **giorno** by day, during the day; ~ **mattina/sera** in the morning/evening; **d'estate** in (the) summer.

(e) *(misura)*: **un chilo** ~ **farina** a kilo of flour; **un bicchiere** ~ **vino** a glass of wine; **un viaggio** ~ **100 chilometri/2 giorni** a 100-kilometre/2-day journey; **una stanza** ~ **2 metri per 3** a room measuring 2 metres by 3; **un bimbo** ~ **2 anni** a 2-year-old child; **un milione** ~ **lire** a million lire; **un gioiello** ~ **valore** a valuable piece of jewellery.

(f) *(mezzo, modo, causa)*: **sporcare** ~ **sugo** to stain with sauce; **spalmare** ~ **burro** to spread with butter; **morire** ~ **cancro** to die of cancer; **è debole** ~ **cuore** he has a weak heart; **urlare** ~ **dolore** to scream with pain; **vestirsi** ~ **bianco** to dress in white; **ridere** ~ **gusto** to laugh heartily; **fermarsi** ~ **botto** to stop dead *o* suddenly; **rispondere** ~ **brutto** to answer brusquely.

(g) *(argomento)* about, of; **libro** ~ **storia** history book; **trattato** ~ **medicina** medical treatise; **parlare** ~ **qc** to talk about sth; **discutere del tempo** to discuss the weather.

(h) *(abbondanza, privazione)*: **ricco/povero** ~ **carbone** rich/poor in coal; **pieno** ~ full of; **privo** ~ lacking in.

(i) *(paragone: nei comparativi)* than; *(: nei superlativi)* of; **è meglio** ~ **me** he's better than me; **è il migliore** ~ **tutti** he is the best of all; **il migliore dei suoi libri** his best book, the best of his books.

(**j**) (*con l'infinito*): **tentò** ~ **scappare** he tried to escape; **credo** ~ **capire** I think (that) I understand; **sa** ~ **aver sbagliato** he knows (that) he has made a mistake; **è degno** ~ **esser ricordato** it's worth remembering; **ti chiedo** ~ **dirmi la verità** I beg you to tell me the truth.

2 *art partitivo* (*affermativo*) some; (*negativo*) any; (*interrogativo*) any, some; **vuoi dei biscotti/del vino?** would you like some biscuits/some wine?, do you want any biscuits/any wine?; **c'è del vero in quello che dici** there's some truth in what you say; **non c'è nulla** ~ **strano** there's nothing odd about it; **non vedo niente** ~ **meglio** I can't see anything better.

3 *art indef pl* some; (*negativo*) any, no; **c'erano delle persone che non conoscevo** there were some people I didn't know; **ho dei soldi** I've got some money; **non ho dei libri** I haven't any books, I have no books.

dì [di] *sm* day; **buon** ~! hallo!; **3 volte al** ~ 3 times a day; **a** ~ = **addì**.

diabete [dia'bɛte] *sm* diabetes *sg*.

diabetico, a, ci, che [dia'bɛtiko] *ag*, *sm/f* diabetic.

diabolico, a, ci, che [dja'bɔliko] *ag* (*anche fig*) diabolical.

diacono [di'akono] *sm* (*Rel*) deacon.

diadema, i [dia'dɛma] *sm* (*di sovrano, fig*) diadem; (*di donna*) tiara.

diafano, a [di'afano] *ag* diaphanous; (*fig: mani, volto*) transparent.

diaframma, i [dia'framma] *sm* (*Anat, Fot, contraccettivo*) diaphragm; (*schermo*) screen.

diagnosi [di'aɲɲozi] *sf inv* (*anche fig*) diagnosis *sg*.

diagnostica [diaɲ'nɔstika] *sf* diagnostics *sg*.

diagnosticare [diaɲnosti'kare] *vt* (*anche fig*) to diagnose.

diagnostico, a, ci, che [diaɲ'nɔstiko] **1** *ag* diagnostic. **2** *sm* diagnostician.

diagonale [diago'nale] **1** *ag* (*motivo, disegno*) diagonal; **in linea** ~ diagonally; **tessuto** ~ twill; **tiro** ~ (*Calcio*) cross. **2** *sf* diagonal; **in** ~ diagonally. **3** *sm* (**a**) (*tessuto*) twill. (**b**) (*Calcio*) cross.

diagramma, i [dia'gramma] *sm* (*gen, Mat*) diagram; (*grafico*) chart, graph.

dialettale [dialet'tale] *ag* dialectal; **poesia** ~ poetry in dialect.

dialettica [dia'lɛttika] *sf* dialectic.

dialettico, a, ci, che [dia'lɛttiko] *ag* dialectic.

dialetto [dia'letto] *sm* dialect.

dialisi [di'alizi] *sf* (*Chim, Med*) dialysis.

dialogare [dialo'gare] **1** *vi*: ~ (**con**) to have a dialogue (with); (*conversare*) to converse (with). **2** *vt* (*scena*) to write the dialogue for.

dialogico, a, ci, che [dia'lɔdʒiko] *ag* dialogue *attr*.

dialogo, ghi [di'alogo] *sm* (*anche fig*) dialogue; (*conversazione*) conversation.

diamante [dia'mante] *sm* (**a**) (*gen*) diamond; **di** ~, **di** ~**i** diamond *attr*. (**b**) (*Naut: di ancora*) crown.

diametralmente [diametral'mente] *av* diametrically.

diametro [di'ametro] *sm* diameter.

diamine ['djamine] *escl*: **che** ~? what on earth?

diapason [di'apazon] *sm* (*Mus: strumento*) tuning fork; (*: tono*) diapason.

diapositiva [diapozi'tiva] *sf* slide, transparency.

diaria [di'arja] *sf* daily (expense) allowance.

diario [di'arjo] *sm* (*gen*) diary, journal; ~ **di bordo** (*Naut*) logbook; ~ **di classe** (*Scol*) class register;

~ **degli esami** (*Scol*) exam timetable; ~ **scolastico** homework book.

diarrea [diar'rɛa] *sf* diarrhoea.

diatriba [di'atriba] *sf* diatribe.

diavoleria [djavole'ria] *sf* (**a**) (*azione*) act of mischief. (**b**) (*aggeggio*) weird contraption.

diavoletto, a [djavo'letto] *sm/f* (**a**) (*fig: bambino*) little devil, imp. (**b**) (*bigodino*) hair-curler.

diavolo ['djavolo] *sm* (**a**) devil; **povero** ~! poor devil!; **è un buon** ~ he's a good sort; **avere un** ~ **per capello** to be in a foul temper; **avere il** ~ **in corpo** (*bambino*) to have the devil in one; (*adulto*) to be fidgety; **avere una fame/un freddo del** ~ to be ravenously hungry/frozen stiff; **mandare qn al** ~ (*fam*) to tell sb to go to hell; **va al** ~! (*fam*) go to hell!; **fare il** ~ **a quattro** to kick up a fuss. (**b**): ~! for goodness' sake!; **che** ~ **vuoi?** what the devil do you want?; **dove** ~ **è finito?** where the devil has it (*o* he) got to?

dibattere [di'battere] **1** *vt* (**a**) (*argomento*) to debate, discuss. (**b**) (*agitare: ali*) to flap. **2**: ~**rsi** *vr* (*anche fig*) to struggle, wrestle; ~**rsi tra mille difficoltà** to struggle *o* wrestle with a host of difficulties; ~**rsi nel dubbio** to suffer agonies of doubt.

dibattimento [dibatti'mento] *sm* (*dibattito*) debate, discussion; (*Dir*) hearing.

dibattito [di'battito] *sm* (*gen*) debate, discussion; (*in parlamento*) debate.

dicastero [dikas'tero] *sm* ministry.

dicembre [di'tʃembre] *sm* December; *per uso vedi* **luglio**.

dicembrino [ditʃem'brino] *ag* December *attr*.

diceria [ditʃe'ria] *sf* rumour, piece of gossip; **sono solo** ~**e** it's just gossip.

dichiarare [dikja'rare] **1** *vt* (*gen*) to declare; (*annunciare*) to announce; ~ **guerra** (**a**) to declare war (on); ~ **qn colpevole** to declare sb guilty; **si dichiara che...** it is hereby declared that.... **2**: ~**rsi** *vr* (**a**) to declare o.s.; ~**rsi vinto** to acknowledge defeat; ~**rsi soddisfatto** to declare o.s. satisfied; ~**rsi a favore di/contro** to declare o.s. *o* come out in favour of/against. (**b**) (*innamorato*) to declare one's love.

dichiarato, a [dikja'rato] *ag* (*nemico, ateo*) avowed.

dichiarazione [dikjarat'tsjone] **1** *sf* (*proclamazione*) declaration; (*discorso, commento*) statement. **2**: ~ (**d'amore**) declaration of love; ~ **doganale** customs declaration; ~ **di guerra** declaration of war; ~ **dei redditi** statement of income; (*modulo*) tax return.

diciannove [ditʃan'nɔve] *ag inv*, *sm inv* nineteen; *per uso vedi* **cinque**.

diciannovenne [ditʃanno'venne] *ag*, *sm/f* nineteen-year-old; *per uso vedi* **cinquantenne**.

diciannovesimo, a [ditʃanno'vɛzimo] *ag*, *sm/f*, *sm* nineteenth; *per uso vedi* **quinto**.

diciassette [ditʃas'sette] *ag inv*, *sm inv* seventeen; *per uso vedi* **cinque**.

diciassettenne [ditʃasset'tenne] *ag*, *sm/f* seventeen-year-old; *per uso vedi* **cinquantenne**.

diciassettesimo, a [ditʃasset'tezimo] *ag*, *sm/f*, *sm* seventeenth; *per uso vedi* **quinto**.

diciottenne [ditʃot'tenne] *ag*, *sm/f* eighteen-year-old; *per uso vedi* **cinquantenne**.

diciottesimo, a [ditʃot'tɛzimo] *ag*, *sm/f*, *sm* eighteenth; *per uso vedi* **quinto**.

diciotto [di'tʃɔtto] **1** *ag inv* eighteen. **2** *sm inv* eighteen; (*Univ*) minimum satisfactory mark awarded in Italian universities; *per uso vedi* **cinque**.

dicitore, trice [ditʃi'tore] *sm/f* speaker.

dicitura [ditʃi'tura] *sf* wording, words *pl*.

dicotomia [dikoto'mia] *sf* dichotomy.

didascalia [didaska'lia] *sf (di illustrazione)* caption; *(Teatro)* stage directions *pl*; *(Cine)* subtitle.

didascalico, a, ci, che [didas'kaliko] *ag* didactic.

didattica [di'dattika] *sf (scienza)* didactics *sg*; *(metodologia)* teaching methodology.

didattico, a, ci, che [di'dattiko] *ag (gen)* didactic; *(programma, metodo)* teaching; *(centro, libro, direttore)* educational.

didentro [di'dentro] **1** *av* inside, indoors. **2** *sm inv (gen)* inside; *(di casa, auto)* interior; **dal** ~ from inside.

didietro [di'djetro] **1** *av* behind. **2** *ag inv (ruota, giardino)* back, rear *attr.* **3** *sm (di casa)* rear; *(fam: sedere)* backside.

dieci ['djetʃi] **1** *ag inv* ten. **2** *sm inv* ten; *(voto)*: **dare un** ~ **a qn** to give sb ten out of ten; *per uso vedi* **cinque.**

diecimila [djetʃi'mila] *ag inv, sm inv* ten thousand.

dieresi [di'erezi] *sf* dieresis *sg.*

diesel ['diːzəl] *ag inv, sm inv* diesel.

dieta ['djeta] *sf* **(a)** diet; **essere o stare a** ~ to be on a diet; **mettersi a** ~ to diet; **rompere la** ~ to interrupt one's diet. **(b)** *(Storia)* diet.

dietetica [die'tetika] *sf* dietetics *sg.*

dietetico, a, ci, che [die'tetiko] *ag* dietetic.

dietologo, gi [dje'tɔlogo] *sm* dietician.

dietro ['djetro] **1** *av* behind; *(in fondo: di gruppo, stanza)* at the back; **qua/là** ~ behind here/there; **2 file** ~ 2 rows (further) back; **vestito che si abbottona** ~ dress which buttons at the back; **non guardar** ~ don't look back; **guarda se arriva qualcuno (da)** ~ look and see if anyone is coming up behind you *(o him etc)*; **ti metti tu** ~? *(in macchina)* are you going in the back?; **la firma è** ~ the signature is on the back; **attacca il foglio** ~ attach the sheet to the back; **passa** ~! to go round the back!; **di** ~ *(entrare, stare)* at the back; **la porta di** ~ the back door; **zampe di** ~ hind legs; **da** ~ *(assalire)* from behind, from the rear; **da** ~ **non ti ho riconosciuto** I didn't recognize you from the back.

2 *prep* **(a)** *(anche:* ~ **a:** *posizione)* behind; ~ **la casa/il banco** behind the house/the counter; ~ **l'angolo** round the corner; ~ **di o a lui/lei** behind him/her; **guarda cosa c'è scritto** ~ **il foglio** look and see what is written on the back of the sheet; **camminare uno** ~ **l'altro** to walk one behind the other *o* in single file; **andare** ~ **a** *(anche fig)* to follow; **stare** ~ **a qn** *(sorvegliare)* to keep an eye on sb; *(corteggiare)* to hang around sb; **portarsi** ~ **qn/qc** to bring sb/sth with one, bring sb/sth along; **gli hanno riso/parlato** ~ they laughed at/talked about him behind his back.

(b) *(anche:* ~ **a:** *dopo)* after; **sono arrivati uno** ~ **l'altro** they arrived one after the other.

(c) *(Amm, Comm)*: ~ **pagamento/consegna** on payment/delivery; ~ **ricevuta** against receipt; ~ **richiesta** *(orale)* on demand, upon request; *(scritto)* on application.

3 *sm inv (di foglio, quadro, giacca)* back; *(di casa)* back, rear; *(di pantaloni)* seat.

4 *ag inv (vedi sm)*: **la parte** ~ the back; the rear; the seat.

dietro front ['djetro 'front] **1** *escl* about-turn! **2** *sm (Mil)* about-turn; *(fig)* volte-face, about-turn; **fare** ~ *(Mil, fig)* to about-turn; *(tornare indietro)* to turn around.

difatti [di'fatti] *cong* in fact, as a matter of fact.

difendere [di'fendere] **1** *vt (gen, Dir: proteggere)* to defend; *(: opinioni)* to defend, stand up for, uphold; *(: dal freddo)* to protect; ~ **gli interessi di qn** to look after sb's interests. **2**: ~**rsi** *vr* **(a)** *(proteggersi)*: ~**rsi (da/contro)** to defend o.s. (from/

against); ~**rsi dal freddo** to protect o.s. from the cold; **sapersi** ~ to know how to look after o.s. **(b)** *(cavarsela)* to get by; **a scuola mi difendo** I get by at school, I can hold my own at school.

difensiva [difen'siva] *sf*: **stare sulla** ~ to be on the defensive.

difensivo, a [difen'sivo] *ag* defensive.

difensore, a [difen'sore] **1** *sm/f (gen)* defender; *(di moralità etc)* upholder; *(Dir)* counsel for the defence. **2** *ag*: **avvocato** ~ defence counsel.

difesa [di'fesa] *sf (gen, Mil, Dir, Sport)* defence; **senza** ~**e** defenceless; **prendere le** ~**e di qn** to defend sb, take sb's part; **parola alla** ~! *(Dir)* the defence may speak!; **giocare in** ~ *(Sport)* to play in defence; **Ministro/Ministero della D**~ Minister/Ministry of Defence.

difeso, a [di'feso] *pp di* **difendere.**

difettare [difet'tare] *vi* **(a)** *(essere difettoso)* to be defective. **(b)** *(mancare)*: ~ **di** to be lacking in.

difettivo, a [difet'tivo] *ag (Gram)* defective.

difetto [di'fetto] *sm* **(a)** *(imperfezione: di fabbricazione)* fault, flaw, defect; *(: morale)* fault, failing, defect; *(: fisico)* defect; **è senza** ~**i** *(persona)* he's faultless; **l'arroganza è il suo** ~ pride is his failing; ~ **di pronuncia** speech defect. **(b)** *(mancanza)* lack; **se la memoria non mi fa** ~ if my memory serves me well.

difettoso, a [difet'toso] *ag* defective, faulty, imperfect.

diffamare [diffa'mare] *vt (a parole)* to slander; *(per iscritto)* to libel.

diffamatore, trice [diffama'tore] *sm/f (vedi vb)* slanderer; libeller.

diffamatorio, a [diffama'tɔrjo] *ag (vedi vb)* slanderous; libellous.

diffamazione [diffamat'tsjone] *sf (vedi vb)* slander; libel.

differente [diffe'rente] *ag*: ~ **(da)** different (from).

differenza [diffe'rentsa] *sf*: ~ **(di)** difference (in); ~ **di età** age difference, difference in age; **non fare** ~ **(tra)** to make no distinction (between); **a** ~ **di** unlike; **con la** ~ **che…** with the difference that…; **non fa** ~ **che venga o meno** it makes no difference whether he comes or not.

differenziale [differen'tsjale] **1** *ag* differential; **classi** ~**i** *(Scol)* special classes *(for backward children)*. **2** *sm (Aut, Mat)* differential.

differenziare [differen'tsjare] **1** *vt* to differentiate. **2**: ~**rsi** *vr (essere differente)* to be different, differ; *(diventare differente)* to become different.

differenziazione [differentsjat'tsjone] *sf* differentiation.

differimento [differi'mento] *sm* deferment, postponement.

differire [diffe'rire] **1** *vt* to defer, postpone; ~ **qc di un mese** to postpone *o* defer sth for a month. **2** *vi (essere differente)*: ~ **(da/in)** to differ (from/in), be different (from/in); ~ **per grandezza** to differ *o* be different in size.

difficile [dif'fitʃile] **1** *ag* **(a)** *(problema, lavoro, periodo etc)* difficult; *(situazione)* difficult, awkward; ~ **da fare** difficult *o* hard to do; **sta attraversando momenti** ~**i** he's going through a difficult *o* trying period; **non farla tanto** ~ don't make it more difficult than it is. **(b)** *(persona: intrattabile)* difficult, trying; *(: nei gusti)* fussy; **suo marito ha un carattere** ~ her husband is hard to get on with, her husband has a difficult nature; ~ **da accontentare** hard to please; **essere** ~ **nel mangiare** to be fussy about one's food. **(c)** *(improbabile)* unlikely; **è** ~ **che venga** he's unlikely to come.

2 *sm/f*: **fare il(la)** ~ to be difficult, be awkward.

3 *sm* difficulty; **il** ~ **è finire in tempo** the difficulty lies in finishing in time, what is difficult is to finish in time; **ora che il** ~ **è fatto...** now that the difficult part has been done... .

difficilmente [diffitʃil'mente] *av* **(a)** *(con difficoltà)* with difficulty. **(b)** *(improbabile)*: ~ **verrà** he's unlikely to come; **verrai?** — ~ will you come? — it's unlikely.

difficoltà [diffikol'ta] *sf inv* difficulty; ~ **finanziarie** financial difficulties; **trovare** ~ **a fare qc** to find it difficult to do sth; **fare delle** ~ to make difficulties, raise objections.

difficoltoso, a [diffikol'toso] *ag (compito)* difficult, hard; *(persona)* difficult, hard to please; **digestione** ~**a** poor digestion.

diffida [dif'fida] *sf (Dir)* notice, warning.

diffidare [diffi'dare] **1** *vi (sospettare)*: ~ **di** to distrust, be suspicious of. **2** *vt (Dir)*: ~ **qn dal fare qc** to warn sb not to do sth, caution sb against doing sth.

diffidente [diffi'dɛnte] *ag*: ~ **(nei confronti di)** distrustful (of).

diffidenza [diffi'dɛntsa] *sf* distrust.

diffondere [dif'fondere] **1** *vt (luce)* to give out, spread, diffuse; *(malattia, idea, notizie, scritto)* to spread; **la notizia è stata diffusa per radio** the news was broadcast on the radio. **2**: ~**rsi** *vr (anche fig)* to spread.

diffrazione [diffrat'tsjone] *sf (Fis)* diffraction.

diffusione [diffu'zjone] *sf (gen)* diffusion; *(di giornale)* circulation.

diffuso, a [dif'fuzo] **1** *pp di* **diffondere**. **2** *ag* **(a)** *(Fis)* diffuse. **(b)** *(notizia, malattia etc)* widespread; **è opinione** ~**a che...** it's widely held that... .

diffusore [diffu'zore] *sm (Tecn)* diffuser.

difilato [difi'lato] *av (subito)* straightaway; *(direttamente)* straight; **ho lavorato per 8 ore** ~ I worked 8 hours straight.

difterite [difte'rite] *sf (Med)* diphtheria.

diga, ghe ['diga] *sf (sbarramento)* dam; *(: portuale)* breakwater.

digerente [didʒe'rɛnte] *ag* digestive.

digeribile [didʒe'ribile] *ag* digestible.

digerire [didʒe'rire] *vt (cibo, fig: nozioni)* to digest; *(: insulto)* to stomach, put up with.

digestione [didʒes'tjone] *sf* digestion.

digestivo, a [didʒes'tivo] **1** *ag* digestive. **2** *sm (liquore)* liqueur taken to aid digestion.

digitale [didʒi'tale] **1** *ag (Anat, Tecn)* digital; **impronta** ~ fingerprint. **2** *sf (Bot)* foxglove.

digiunare [didʒu'nare] *vi* to fast.

digiuno, a [di'dʒuno] **1** *sm* fast, fasting; **a** ~ on an empty stomach; **sono a** ~ I haven't eaten; **stare a** ~ to fast; **è una medicina da prendersi a** ~ this medicine should be taken before meals. **2** *ag*: ~ **di** *(fig: di cognizioni)* ignorant of.

dignità [diɲɲi'ta] *sf inv* dignity.

dignitoso, a [diɲɲi'toso] *ag (contegno, abito)* dignified; *(fig: stipendio etc)* decent.

DIGOS *abbr f* (= *Divisione Investigazioni Generali e Operazioni Speciali)* ≃ Special Branch.

digradare [digra'dare] *vi (pendio)* to slope, decline.

digressione [digres'sjone] *sf* digression.

digrignare [digriɲ'ɲare] *vt*: ~ **i denti** *(animale)* to bare its teeth; *(persona)* to grind one's teeth.

digrossare [digros'sare] *vt (tronco etc)* to trim; *(pietra, marmo)* to rough-hew; *(fig: stile)* to polish, refine; *(: persona)* to smooth the rough edges off.

dilagare [dila'gare] *vi (aus essere)* to overflow; *(fig:* *corruzione)* to spread, be rampant; *(malattia)* to spread.

dilaniare [dila'njare] *vt* to tear to pieces; **era dilaniato dal rimorso** he was smitten by remorse.

dilapidare [dilapi'dare] *vt* to squander, waste, dissipate.

dilapidatore, trice [dilapida'tore] *sm/f* squanderer.

dilatare [dila'tare] **1** *vt (Anat)* to dilate; *(: stomaco)* to dilate, cause to expand; *(gas, metallo)* to cause to expand; *(tubo, buco)* to enlarge. **2**: ~**rsi** *vr (vedi vt)* to dilate; to expand; to become enlarged.

dilatazione [dilatat'tsjone] *sf (Anat)* dilation; *(di gas, metallo)* expansion.

dilazionare [dilattsjo'nare] *vt* to defer.

dilazione [dilat'tsjone] *sf* deferment.

dileggiare [diled'dʒare] *vt* to mock, scoff at, deride.

dileggio [di'leddʒo] *sm* mockery, scoffing, derision; **per** ~ in derision o mockery.

dileguare [dile'gware] **1** *vt* to dispel, disperse; **il vento ha dileguato le nubi** the wind has dispersed the clouds. **2**: ~**rsi** *vr (nebbia)* to disperse; *(fig: dubbio, persona)* to vanish, disappear.

dilemma, i [di'lemma] *sm* dilemma.

dilettante [dilet'tante] **1** *ag* amateur *attr*; *(peg)* amateur *attr*, dilettante *attr*. **2** *sm/f (vedi ag)* amateur; dilettante.

dilettantismo [dilettan'tizmo] *sm (peg)* amateurishness; *(Sport)* amateurism.

dilettantistico, a, ci, che [dilettan'tistiko] *ag (peg)* amateurish; *(Sport)* amateur *attr*.

dilettare [dilet'tare] **1** *vt* **(a)** *(dar piacere)* to delight, please; **mi dilettava l'idea di partire** I was delighted at the thought of leaving. **(b)** *(intrattenere)* to amuse, entertain. **2**: ~**rsi** *vr*: ~**rsi a fare qc** to delight in doing sth; ~**rsi di qc** to have sth as a hobby; **si diletta di pittura** painting is a hobby of his.

dilettevole [dilet'tevole] *ag* delightful.

diletto¹, a [di'letto] **1** *pp di* **diligere**. **2** *ag* beloved. **3** *sm/f* beloved, loved one.

diletto² [di'letto] *sm* delight, pleasure; **trarre** ~ **da** to take pleasure o delight in; **per** ~ for pleasure.

diligente [dili'dʒɛnte] *ag* diligent, hard-working.

diligenza¹ [dili'dʒɛntsa] *sf (qualità)* diligence.

diligenza² [dili'dʒɛntsa] *sf (carrozza)* stagecoach.

diluire [dilu'ire] *vt (gen: liquidi)* to dilute; *(vernice)* to thin (down); *(polverina, medicina)* to dissolve.

diluizione [diluit'tsjone] *sf (vedi vb)* dilution; thinning; dissolving.

dilungarsi [dilun'garsi] *vr* to talk at length; ~ **in una descrizione** to go into a detailed description.

diluviare [dilu'vjare] *vb impers* to pour, rain hard.

diluvio [di'luvjo] *sm (pioggia)* downpour, deluge; *(fig: di lettere)* flood; *(: di insulti)* torrent; **il** ~ **universale** the Flood.

dimagrante [dima'grante] *ag* slimming *attr*.

dimagrimento [dimagri'mento] *sm* loss of weight.

dimagrire [dima'grire] *vi (aus essere)* to become thin, lose weight; **è dimagrito di 5 kg** he has lost 5 kg.

dimenare [dime'nare] **1** *vt (braccia)* to wave (about); *(coda)* to wag. **2**: ~**rsi** *vr (agitarsi: nel letto)* to toss (about); *(: per liberarsi, ballando)* to fling o.s. about; *(: gesticolare)* to gesticulate wildly.

dimensionale [dimensjo'nale] *ag* dimensional.

dimensione [dimen'sjone] *sf* **(a)** *(Mat, Filosofia, Fis)* dimension; **a 3** ~**i** 3-dimensional. **(b)** *(misura)*: ~**i** *pl* dimensions, measurements; **di quali** ~**i è la stanza?** what are the dimensions o measurements of the room? **(c)** *(fig)*:

ricondurre qc alle giuste ~i to get sth back in perspective; considerare un discorso nella sua ~ politica to look at a speech in terms of its political significance; di ~i allarmanti of alarming proportions.

dimenticanza |dimcnti'kantsa| *sf (svista)* oversight; **per** ~ due to an oversight.

dimenticare |dimenti'karc| **1** *vt (gen)* to forget; *(preoccupazioni)* to forget (about); *(omettere)* to leave out; ~ **di fare qc** to forget to do sth; ~ *o* ~**rsi qc** to forget sth; **ho dimenticato l'ombrello in ufficio** I left my umbrella at the office. **2**: ~**rsi** *vr*: ~**rsi di qc/di fare qc** to forget (about) sth/to do sth; **non me ne dimenticherò** I won't forget.

dimenticatoio |dimɛntika'tojo| *sm (scherz)*: **cadere/mettere nel** ~ to sink into/consign to oblivion.

dimentico, a, chi, che |di'mentiko| *ag*: ~ **di** *(che non ricorda)* forgetful of; *(incurante)* oblivious of, unmindful of.

dimesso, a |di'mɛsso| **1** *pp di* **dimettere. 2** *ag* modest, unassuming; **in abiti** ~**i** simply dressed; **con voce** ~**a** humbly.

dimestichezza |dimɛsti'kettsa| *sf (familiarità)* familiarity; **avere** ~ **con qc** to be familiar with sth.

dimettere |di'mettɛrɛ| **1** *vt (da ospedale)* to discharge; *(da carcere)* to release; *(da carica)* to dismiss; **far** ~ **qn** to have sb dismissed. **2**: ~**rsi** *vr* to resign, hand *o* give in one's resignation.

dimezzare |dimed'dzarɛ| *vt* to cut in half, halve.

diminuire |diminu'irɛ| **1** *vt (gen)* to reduce, decrease; *(prezzi)* to bring down. **2** *vi (gen)* to diminish, decrease; *(vento, rumore)* to die down, die away; *(prezzo, valore, pressione)* to go down, fall, decrease; ~ **d'intensità** to decrease in intensity, subside; ~ **di volume** to be reduced in volume; ~ **di peso** *(persona)* to lose weight; *(Fis)* to be reduced in weight.

diminutivo, a |diminu'tivo| *ag, sm* diminutive.

diminuzione |diminut'tsjonɛ| *sf* reduction; *(calo)* decrease; *(: di temperatura, pressione)* fall; **in** ~ on the decrease; **nuvolosità in** ~ gradually dispersing cloud; ~ **della produttività** fall in productivity; ~ **di peso** loss of weight.

dimissionare |dimissjo'narɛ| *vt (Amm)* to dismiss.

dimissionario, a |dimissjo'narjo| *ag* outgoing, resigning.

dimissioni |dimis'sjoni| *sfpl* resignation *sg*; **dare** *o* **rassegnare le** ~ to give in *o* tender one's resignation.

dimora |di'mɔra| *sf (abitazione)* residence; **senza fissa** ~ of no fixed address *o* abode; **estrema** ~ *(euf)* last resting place.

dimorare |dimo'rarɛ| *vi (anche fig: sentimenti)* to dwell.

dimostrabile |dimos'trabilɛ| *ag* demonstrable.

dimostrante |dimos'trantɛ| *sm/f (Pol)* demonstrator.

dimostrare |dimos'trarɛ| **1** *vt (a)* *(verità, funzionamento)* to demonstrate; *(colpevolezza, teorema, tesi)* to prove; **ciò dimostra che hai ragione** this proves *o* shows you are right. **(b)** *(simpatia, affetto, interesse)* to show, display; **non dimostra la sua età** he doesn't look his age. **2** *vi (Pol etc)* to demonstrate. **3**: ~**rsi** *vr (a) (rivelarsi)* to prove to be; **si è dimostrato coraggioso** he proved to be brave. **(b)** *(apparire)*: ~**rsi entusiasta/interessato** to show one's enthusiasm/interest.

dimostrativo, a |dimostra'tivo| *ag (gen, Gram)* demonstrative; **azione** ~**a** *(Pol etc)* demonstration.

dimostratore, trice |dimostra'torɛ| *sm/f (Comm)* demonstrator.

dinamitardo, a |dinami'tardo| **1** *ag*: **attentato** ~ dynamite attack. **2** *sm/f* dynamiter.

dinamite |dina'mitɛ| *sf* dynamite.

dinamo |'dinamo| *sf inv* dynamo, generator.

dinanzi |di'nantsi| **1** *av* ahead; **levati** ~ get out of the way. **2**: ~ **a** *prep (di fronte)* in front of; *(al cospetto)* in the presence of, before; **si presentò** ~ **a me** he appeared before me; ~ **ad una tale situazione...** faced with such a situation... .

dinastia |dinas'tia| *sf* dynasty.

dinastico, a, ci, che |di'nastiko| *ag* dynastic(al).

diniego, ghi |di'njɛgo| *sm (rifiuto)* refusal; **ha opposto un netto** ~ he refused point-blank; **scuotere la testa in segno di** ~ to shake one's head.

dinoccolato, a |dinokko'lato| *ag* lanky; **camminare** ~ to walk with a slouch.

dinosauro |dino'sauro| *sm* dinosaur.

dintorno |din'torno| **1** *av* (a)round, (round)about. **2**: ~**i** *smpl* outskirts; **nei** ~**i di** in the vicinity *o* neighbourhood of; **Palermo e** ~**i** Palermo and the surrounding area.

dio |'dio| *sm (a) (Mitologia, fig)* god; **gli dei** the gods; **si crede un** ~ he thinks he's wonderful; **canta come un** ~ he sings divinely.

(b) *(Rel)*: **D**~ God; **D**~ **padre** God the Father; **un senza D**~ a godless person; **il buon D**~ the good Lord.

(c) *(fraseologia)*: **D**~ **mio!** my goodness, my God!; **D**~ **buono!, D**~ **santo!** for God's sake!; **per D**~**!** by God!; **grazie a D**~**!, D**~ **sia lodato** *o* **ringraziato!** thank God!; **com'è vero D**~ as God is my witness; **D**~ **sa quando finirà** God knows when it's going to be finished; **viene giù che D**~ **la manda** it's raining cats and dogs; **come D**~ **volle arrivammo** somehow or other we got there; **se D**~ **vuole...** God willing...; **D**~ **ce la mandi buona** let's hope for the best; **D**~ **ce ne scampi e liberi** God forbid.

diocesi |di'ɔtʃɛzi| *sf inv* diocese.

diodo |'diodo| *sm (Elettr)* diode.

dipanare |dipa'narɛ| *vt (matassa)* to wind (up *o* into a ball); *(fig: questione)* to sort out.

dipartimentale |dipartimen'talɛ| *ag (Amm, Scol)* departmental.

dipartimento |diparti'mento| *sm (gen)* department.

dipendente |dipen'dɛntɛ| **1** *ag (a) (Gram)* subordinate. **(b)**: **personale** ~ employees *pl.* **2** *sm/f* employee; ~**i** employees, staff *sg*, personnel *sg*. **3** *sf (Gram)* subordinate clause.

dipendenza |dipen'dɛntsa| *sf (a)* *(gen, di droga)* dependency, dependence; **un farmaco che provoca** ~ an addictive drug. **(b)**: **alle** ~**e di** employed by; **ha 10 persone alle sue** ~**e** *(datore di lavoro)* he employs 10 people; *(caporeparto)* he has 10 people under him.

dipendere |di'pɛndɛrɛ| *vi (aus essere)*: ~ **da (a)** *(gen)* to depend on; **dipende!** it depends!; **dipende solo da te** it depends entirely on you, it's entirely up to you; **la sua risposta è dipeso dal fatto che era nervosa** she answered that way because she was irritated. **(b)** *(impiegato, filiale)* to be answerable to; **la ditta dipendeva da una compagnia americana** the firm was controlled by an American company. **(c)** *(essere mantenuto, soggetto)* to depend (up)on, be dependent on.

dipeso, a |di'pɛso| *pp di* **dipendere.**

dipingere |di'pindʒɛrɛ| **1** *vt (gen, Arte)* to paint; *(fig)* to describe, depict. **2**: ~**rsi** *vr (tingersi)*: **gli si dipinse sul viso la delusione** disappointment showed *o* was written in his face; **il cielo si dipinse di rosso** the sky turned red.

dipinto, a [di'pinto] **1** *pp di* dipingere. **2** *sm (quadro)* painting.

diploma, i [di'plɔma] *sm* diploma, certificate; ~ **di maturità** school-leaving certificate; ~ **di laurea** degree (certificate).

diplomare [diplo'mare] **1** *vt* to award a diploma to, graduate *(Am)*. **2**: ~**rsi** *vr* to obtain a diploma, graduate *(Am)*.

diplomatico, a, ci, che [diplo'matiko] **1** *ag* diplomatic. **2** *sm (anche fig)* diplomat.

diplomato, a [diplo'mato] **1** *ag* qualified. **2** *sm/f* qualified person, holder of a diploma.

diplomazia [diplomat'tsia] *sf (anche fig)* diplomacy; *(corpo diplomatico)* diplomatic corps *sg*.

diporto [di'pɔrto] *sm*: **imbarcazione da** ~ pleasure craft *inv*.

diradare [dira'dare] **1** *vt (vegetazione)* to thin (out); *(nebbia, gas)* to clear, dissipate; ~ **le visite** to call less frequently. **2** *vi (aus* essere*)*, ~**rsi** *vr (vegetazione)* to thin out; *(folla, nebbia)* to disperse; *(visite)* to become less frequent.

diramare [dira'mare] **1** *vt (comunicato, ordine etc)* to issue; *(notizia)* to circulate. **2**: ~**rsi** *vr (fusti)* to branch; *(sentiero, strada)* to branch off; *(vene)* to spread; **la notizia si è diramata** the news spread.

diramazione [diramat'tsjone] *sf* **(a)** *(diffusione: di ordine)* issuing; *(: di notizia)* circulation. **(b)** *(biforcazione)* fork. **(c)** *(ramificazione)* branch.

dire ['dire] **1** *vt* **(a)** *(gen)* to say; ~ **qc a qn** to say sth to sb; **'non ci vado'** — **disse** 'I'm not going' — he said; ~ **di sì/no** to say yes/no; **disse che accettava** he said he would accept; **non disse una parola** he didn't say *o* utter a word; **dice sempre quello che pensa** he always says what he thinks; **sa quello che dice** he knows what he's talking about; **come dicono gli Inglesi** as the English would say; **di' liberamente ciò che pensi** feel free to say what you think; **lascialo** ~ *(esprimersi)* let him have his say; *(ignoralo)* just ignore him; **dicano pure quello che vogliono!** let them say what they like!; **dica?** *(in negozio)* what can I do for you?; **Roberta... — sì, dimmi** Roberta... — yes, what is it?; **si dice che...** they say that..., it is said that...; **si dice che siano ricchissimi** they are said to be very rich, people say they are very rich; **come si dice in inglese?** how do you say it in English?; **come si dice 'penna' in inglese?** what is the English for 'penna'?

(b) *(raccontare, riferire, indicare)* to tell; ~ **a qn qc/di fare qc** to tell sb sth/to do sth; **mi ha detto tutto** he told me everything; **può dirmi da che parte devo andare?** can you tell me which way I have to go?; **mi si dice che...** I am told that... .

(c) *(significare)* to mean; **come sarebbe a** ~? what do you mean?; **ti dice niente questo nome?** does this name mean anything to you?; **quel libro non mi ha detto niente** that book didn't appeal to me.

(d) *(recitare)* to say, recite; ~ **(la) Messa** to say Mass; ~ **a memoria** to recite by heart; ~ **le preghiere** to say one's prayers.

(e) *(pensare)* to think; **cosa** *o* **che ne dici di questa musica?** what do you think of this music?; **che ne diresti di andarcene?** how about leaving?; **si direbbe che non menta** you would think he was telling the truth; **chi l'avrebbe mai detto!** who would have thought it!

(f): *(ammettere)* to say, admit; **devi** ~ **che ha ragione** you must admit that he's right.

(g): **far** ~ **qc a qn** to make sb say sth; *(man-*

dare a ~, *riferire)* to let sb know sth; **gliel'ho fatto** ~ **dalla segretaria** I had my secretary tell him about it; **non me lo farò** ~ **due volte** I don't need to be told twice.

(h): ~**rsi** to say to o.s.; *(definirsi)* to call o.s., claim to be; *(uso reciproco)* to say to each other; **'coraggio'** — **si disse** 'come on' — he said to himself; **si dicono esperti** they say they are experts; **si dissero addio** they said goodbye (to each other); **si son detti qualcosa all'orecchio** they whispered something to one another.

(i) *(fraseologia)*: **per così** ~ so to speak; **lo conosco per sentito** ~ I've heard about him; **a dir poco** to say the least; **non c'è che** ~ there's no doubt about it; **e chi mi dice che è vero?** and who's to say that's true?; **l'idea è accattivante, non dico di no** the idea is tempting, I can't deny it; **a** ~ **il vero...** to tell the truth...; **il che è tutto** ~ need I say more?; **avere** *o* **trovare da** ~ **con qn** to have words with sb; **trovare da** ~ **su qc/qn** to find fault with sth/sb; **non ti dico la scena!** you can't imagine the scene!; **dico sul serio** I'm serious; **sono stanco** — **e a me lo dici!** I'm tired — if you're tired, how do you think I feel?; **dimmi con chi vai e ti dirò chi sei** *(Proverbio)* you can tell what sort of a person somebody is by the company he keeps.

2 *sm*: **tra il** ~ **e il fare c'è di mezzo il mare** it's easier said than done; **è un bel** ~ **il suo** what he says is all very well.

direttamente [diretta'mente] *av (immediatamente)* directly, straight; *(personalmente)* directly; *(senza intermediari)* direct, straight; **andiamo** ~ **a casa** let's go straight home; **non mi riguarda** ~ it doesn't directly concern me; **parla** ~ **col preside** speak to the headmaster direct.

direttissima [diret'tissima] *sf* **(a)** *(tragitto)* most direct route. **(b)** *(Dir)*: **processo per** ~ summary trial.

direttissimo [diret'tissimo] *sm (Ferr)* fast (through) train.

direttiva [diret'tiva] *sf* directive, instruction; **seguire le** ~**e del partito** to toe the party line.

direttivo, a [diret'tivo] **1** *ag (Pol, Amm)* executive; *(Comm)* managerial, executive. **2** *sm* leadership, leaders *pl*.

diretto, a [di'retto] **1** *pp di* dirigere. **2** *ag (gen, Gram)* direct; **è il suo** ~ **superiore** he's his immediate superior; **c'è una** ~**a dipendenza tra i due fatti** the two events are directly connected. **3** *sm* **(a)** *(Ferr: anche:* **treno** ~*)* through train. **(b)** *(pugno)* jab. **4** *sf*: **in (linea)** ~**a** *(Radio, TV)* live.

direttore [diret'tore] *sm (gen)* director; *(responsabile: di banca, fabbrica etc)* manager; ~ **artistico** *(Teatro, Mus)* artistic director; ~ **del carcere** prison governor; ~ **didattico** headmaster, principal *(Am)*; ~ **di macchina** *(Naut)* chief engineer; ~ **d'orchestra** conductor; ~ **del personale** personnel manager; ~ **di produzione** *(Cine)* producer; *(Industria)* production manager; ~ **responsabile** *(Stampa)* editor (in chief); ~ **sportivo** team manager; ~ **tecnico** *(Sport)* trainer.

direttrice[1] [diret'tritʃe] *sf (vedi* direttore*)* director; manageress; ~ **didattica** headmistress, principal *(Am)*.

direttrice[2] [diret'tritʃe] *sf* **(a)** *(Mat)* directrix. **(b)** *(fig: di partito etc)* policy, line.

direzionale [direttsjo'nale] *ag* directional.

direzione [diret'tsjone] *sf* **(a)** *(senso: anche fig)* direction; **in** ~ **di** towards, in the direction of; **in che** ~ **vai?** which way are you going?; **prendere la** ~ **giusta/sbagliata** to go the right/wrong way; **sbagliare** ~ to go the wrong way. **(b)**

dirigente *(conduzione: gen)* running; *(: di società)* management; *(: di giornale)* editorship; *(: di partito)* leadership; **assumere la ~ delle operazioni** to take on the directing of operations. **(c): la ~** *(direttori)* the management; *(ufficio)* director's *(o* manager's *o* editor's *o* headmaster's *etc)* office.

dirigente [diri'dʒɛnte] **1** *ag* managerial; **classe ~** ruling class. **2** *sm/f* executive.

dirigenza [diri'dʒɛntsa] *sf (di ditta etc)* management; *(di partito)* leadership.

dirigenziale [diridʒen'tsjale] *ag* managerial.

dirigere [di'ridʒere] **1** *vt* **(a)** *(pacco, lettera)* to address; *(arma):* **~ verso,** **~ contro** to point at; *(critiche):* **~ contro** to direct at, aim at; **~ l'attenzione su qc/qn** to turn one's attention to sth/sb; **~ i propri passi verso** to make one's way towards; **~ lo sguardo verso** to look towards; **a chi era diretta quell'osservazione?** who was that remark intended for?; **era diretto verso casa** he was heading home; **dove sei diretto?** where are you heading?; **il treno era diretto a Pavia** the train was heading for Pavia; **eravamo diretti a nord** we were heading north; **mi hanno diretto qui** they sent me here.

(b) *(condurre)* to run; *(ditta)* to manage; *(giornale)* to edit; *(partito, inchiesta)* to lead; *(operazioni, traffico)* to direct; *(orchestra)* to conduct.

2: ~rsi *vr (prendere una direzione):* **~rsi a** *o* **verso** *(luogo)* to make one's way towards; **~rsi verso** *(persona)* to make one's way towards, head for; **l'aereo si dirigeva a nord** the plane was heading *o* making its way north; **si diresse a** *o* **verso casa** he headed home, he made for home; **dove si è diretto?** which way did he go?

dirigibile [diri'dʒibile] *sm* airship.

dirimpetto [dirim'pɛtto] **1** *av* opposite. **2: ~ a** *prep* opposite; **era seduto ~ a me** he was sitting opposite me. **3** *ag inv* opposite; **la casa ~** the house opposite.

diritto¹, a [di'ritto] **1** *ag* **(a)** *(strada, palo, linea etc)* straight; *(persona: eretto)* erect, upright; *(fig: onesto)* upright, honest; **stare su ~** to stand up straight; **è andato ~ dal direttore** he went straight to the manager. **(b)** *(Maglia):* **punto ~** plain (stitch). **2** *av* straight; **verrò ~ al punto** I'll come straight to the point; **vai sempre ~ fino al semaforo** keep straight on as far as the traffic lights. **3** *sm* **(a)** *(di vestito etc)* right side. **(b)** *(Tennis)* forehand. **(c)** *(Maglia)* plain stitch.

diritto² [di'ritto] **1** *sm* **(a)** *(prerogativa)* right; **ti spetta di ~** it is yours by right; **a buon ~** quite rightly; **avere il ~ di fare qc** to have the right to do sth; **aver ~ a qc** to be entitled to sth; **ho il ~ di sapere** I have a right to know. **(b)** *(Dir):* **il ~** law. **2: ~ d'asilo** right of asylum; **~i (d'autore)** royalties; **~ al voto** right to vote.

dirittura [dirit'tura] *sf (Sport):* **~ (d'arrivo)** home straight.

diroccato, a [dirok'kato] *ag (semidistrutto)* in ruins; *(cadente)* dilapidated.

dirompente [dirom'pɛnte] *ag (anche fig)* explosive; **bomba ~** fragmentation bomb.

dirottamento [dirotta'mento] *sm:* **~ (aereo)** hijacking.

dirottare [dirot'tare] **1** *vt (traffico, aereo)* to divert; *(aereo: abusivamente)* to hijack. **2** *vi (Naut)* to change course.

dirotto, a [di'rotto] *ag:* **scoppiare in un pianto ~** to burst into tears; **piove a ~** it's pouring.

dirozzare [dirod'dzare] *vt (pietra, marmo)* to roughhew; *(fig: stile, maniere)* to polish, refine; *(: persona)* to smooth the rough edges off.

dirupo [di'rupo] *sm* precipice, crag.

disabitato, a [dizabi'tato] *ag* uninhabited.

disabituare [dizabitu'are] **1** *vt:* **~ qn a qc/a fare qc** to break sb of the habit of sth/of doing sth. **2: ~rsi** *vr:* **~rsi a qc/a fare qc** to get out of the habit of sth/of doing sth.

disaccordo [dizak'kordo] *sm* **(a)** disagreement; **essere in ~** to disagree. **(b)** *(Mus)* discord.

disadattamento [dizadatta'mento] *sm (Psic)* maladjustment.

disadattato, a [dizadat'tato] **1** *ag* maladjusted. **2** *sm/f* maladjusted person, misfit.

disadorno, a [diza'dorno] *ag* plain, unadorned.

disagevole [diza'dʒevole] *ag (scomodo)* uncomfortable; *(difficile)* difficult.

disagiato, a [diza'dʒato] *ag (povero)* poor, needy; **vivere in condizioni ~e** to live in poverty.

disagio [di'zadʒo] *sm* **(a)** *(scomodità)* discomfort; *(difficoltà)* difficulty. **(b)** *(imbarazzo)* uneasiness; **essere** *o* **trovarsi a ~** to be ill-at-ease *o* uncomfortable; **mettere qn a ~** to make sb feel ill-at-ease *o* uncomfortable.

disamina [di'zamina] *sf* close examination; **sottoporre a ~** to examine carefully.

disamorarsi [dizamo'rarsi] *vr:* **~ di qn** to fall out of love with sb, cease to love sb.

disappetenza [dizappe'tɛntsa] *sf* lack of appetite.

disapprovare [dizappro'vare] *vt:* **~ (qc)** to disapprove (of sth).

disapprovazione [dizapprovat'tsjone] *sf* disapproval.

disappunto [dizap'punto] *sm (delusione)* disappointment; *(fastidio)* annoyance; **con mio ~** to my disappointment *(o* annoyance).

disarcionare [dizartʃo'nare] *vt* to unhorse.

disarmare [dizar'mare] **1** *vt (Mil, fig)* to disarm; *(Naut)* to lay up. **2** *vi (Mil)* to disarm; *(fig)* to surrender, give in.

disarmo [di'zarmo] *sm (Mil)* disarmament; *(di nave)* laying up.

disarmonia [dizarmo'nia] *sf* disharmony.

disarticolare [dizartiko'lare] *vt* to dislocate.

disarticolato, a [dizartiko'lato] *ag (suoni, discorso)* inarticulate.

disastrato, a [dizas'trato] **1** *ag* devastated, badly hit; **zona ~a** disaster area. **2** *sm/f (di alluvione, terremoto etc)* victim.

disastro [di'zastro] *sm (anche fig)* disaster; **i ~i dovuti alla grandine** the damage caused by the hailstorm.

disastroso, a [dizas'troso] *ag (gen)* disastrous; **in condizioni ~e** in a terrible *o* appalling state.

disattento, a [dizat'tɛnto] *ag* careless, inattentive.

disattenzione [dizatten'tsjone] *sf* carelessness, lack of attention.

disattivare [dizatti'vare] *vt (bomba)* to de-activate, defuse.

disavanzo [diza'vantso] *sm (Econ)* deficit.

disbrigo [diz'brigo] *sm:* **~ (di)** dealing (with).

discapito [dis'kapito] *sm:* **a ~ di** to the detriment of; **lo fai a tuo ~** if you do it it will be to your detriment.

discendente [diʃʃen'dɛnte] **1** *ag* descending. **2** *sm/f* descendant.

discendenza [diʃʃen'dɛntsa] *sf* **(a)** descent, lineage; **di nobile/umile ~** of noble/humble descent. **(b)** *(discendenti)* descendants *pl.*

discendere [diʃ'ʃɛndere] **1** *vi (con essere)* **(a)** to come *(o* go) down, descend; **~ da** *(treno)* to get off; *(macchina)* to get out of; *(albero)* to get down from; **le tenebre discesero sulla città** darkness descended on the town. **(b)** *(essere discendente):* **~ da** to be descended from, come from. **2** *vt (scale)* to come *(o* go) down, descend.

discepolo, a [diʃˈʃepolo] *sm/f (Rel)* disciple; *(seguace)* follower, disciple; *(scolaro)* pupil.

discernere [diʃˈʃernere] *vt (distinguere: anche fig)* to discern; ~ **il bene dal male** to distinguish good from evil.

discernimento [diʃʃerniˈmento] *sm* discernment.

discesa [diʃˈʃesa] *sf* **(a)** *(atto)* descent; ~ **libera** *(Sci)* downhill (race); **la** ~ **dei barbari** the barbarian invasion. **(b)** *(pendio)* slope, downhill stretch; **in** ~ downhill *attr*, sloping.

discesista, i, e [diʃʃeˈsista] *sm/f (Sci)* downhill skier.

disceso, a [diʃˈʃeso] *pp di* **discendere.**

dischiudere [disˈkjudere] *vt (aprire)* to open; *(fig: rivelare)* to disclose, reveal.

dischiuso, a [disˈkjuso] *pp di* **dischiudere.**

discinto, a [diʃˈʃinto] *ag (anche:* **in abiti** ~**i)** half-undressed.

disciogliere [diʃˈʃɔʎʎere] **1** *vt* **(a)** *(nodo)* to untie, unfasten, loosen; *(fig: capelli)* to loosen, let down. **(b)** *(liquefare)* to melt; *(sciogliere: medicina, fig: partito)* to dissolve. **2:** ~**rsi** *vr (vedi vt* **b)** to melt; to dissolve.

disciolto, a [diʃˈʃɔlto] *pp di* **disciogliere.**

disciplina [diʃʃiˈplina] *sf (regola)* discipline; *(materia)* discipline, subject.

disciplinare[1] [diʃʃipliˈnare] *vt* to discipline.

disciplinare[2] [diʃʃipliˈnare] *ag* disciplinary.

disciplinato, a [diʃʃipliˈnato] *ag* disciplined.

disc-jockey [ˈdisk ˈdʒɔki] *sm inv* disc jockey.

disco, schi [ˈdisko] **1** *sm* **(a)** *(gen, Inform, Anat)* disc; *(Sport)* discus. **(b)** *(Mus)* record, disc; **cambia** ~! *(fam)* change the subject! **2:** ~ **magnetico** *(Inform)* magnetic disc; ~ **orario** *(Aut)* parking disc; ~ **volante** flying saucer.

discofilo, a [disˈkɔfilo] *sm/f* record collector.

discografia [diskograˈfia] *sf* **(a)** *(tecnica)* recording, record-making. **(b)** *(industria)* record industry.

discografico, a, ci, che [diskoˈgrafiko] **1** *ag* record *attr*, recording *attr*; **casa** ~**a** record(ing) company. **2** *sm* record producer.

discoide [disˈkɔide] *ag* disc-shaped.

discolo, a [ˈdiskolo] **1** *ag (bambino)* undisciplined, unruly. **2** *sm/f* rascal.

discolpa [disˈkolpa] *sf* defence, excuse; **a** ~ **di qn** in sb's defence.

discolpare [diskolˈpare] **1** *vt:* ~ **qn** to prove sb's innocence, clear sb. **2:** ~**rsi** *vr* to clear o.s., prove one's innocence; *(giustificarsi)* to excuse o.s.

disconoscere [diskoˈnoʃʃere] *vt (figlio)* to disown; *(meriti)* to ignore, disregard.

disconosciuto, a [diskonoʃˈʃuto] *pp di* **disconoscere.**

discontinuità [diskontinuiˈta] *sf (vedi ag)* discontinuity, irregularity.

discontinuo, a [diskonˈtinuo] *ag (linea)* discontinuous; *(rendimento, stile)* irregular; *(interesse)* sporadic.

discordante [diskorˈdante] *ag* discordant, conflicting, clashing.

discordanza [diskorˈdantsa] *sf (gen)* discordance, dissonance; *(Mus)* discord; ~ **di opinioni** difference of opinion; **ci sono** ~**e tra le due versioni** the two versions conflict *o* clash.

discordare [diskorˈdare] *vi:* ~ **(da)** *(suono, colore)* to clash (with); *(opinioni)* to conflict (with).

discorde [disˈkorde] *ag* conflicting; **essere di parere** ~ to be of a different opinion.

discordia [disˈkordja] *sf* discord, dissension; **essere in** ~ **con** to be at variance with.

discorrere [disˈkorrere] *vi:* ~ **(di)** to talk (about), chat (about).

discorsivo, a [diskorˈsivo] *ag (stile)* conversational, colloquial.

discorso, a [disˈkorso] **1** *pp di* **discorrere. 2** *sm (gen, Gram)* speech; **fare un** ~ *(in pubblico)* to make a speech; **gli ho fatto un bel** ~ **ieri** *(iro)* I gave him a piece of my mind yesterday; **cambiare** ~ to change the subject; **è un altro** ~ that's something different; **non son** ~**i da fare!** what sort of attitude is that?; **analisi del** ~ *(Gram)* sentence analysis; ~ **diretto/indiretto** *(Gram)* direct/indirect *o* reported speech.

discostare [diskosˈtare] **1** *vt* to move away; **ha discostato la sedia dal tavolo** he moved the chair away from the table. **2:** ~**rsi** *vr (anche fig):* ~**rsi da** to move away from.

discosto, a [disˈkosto] **1** *ag* distant, remote; **tenersi** ~ **da** to stay away from. **2** *av* at a distance, at some distance.

discoteca, che [diskoˈtɛka] *sf* **(a)** *(raccolta)* record library. **(b)** *(sala da ballo)* discotheque.

discredito [disˈkredito] *sm* discredit, disrepute; **cadere in** ~ to fall into disrepute; **gettare** ~ **su** to bring discredit on; **tornare a** ~ **di qn** to redound to sb's discredit.

discrepanza [diskreˈpantsa] *sf* discrepancy.

discreto, a [disˈkreto] *ag* **(a)** *(abbastanza buono)* reasonable. **(b)** *(non forte: tinta, trucco)* low-key, discreet. **(c)** *(persona: riservato)* discreet; **fu** ~ **da parte sua andarsene** he very discreetly left.

discrezionale [diskrettsjoˈnale] *ag* discretionary.

discrezione [diskretˈtsjone] *sf* **(a)** *(discernimento)* judgment, discretion; **a propria** ~ at one's own discretion. **(b)** *(riservatezza)* discretion; **ti prego la massima** ~ I'm relying on your absolute discretion.

discriminante [diskrimiˈnante] **1** *ag (fattore, elemento)* decisive. **2** *sf (Dir)* extenuating circumstance.

discriminare [diskrimiˈnare] *vt* to discriminate.

discriminazione [diskriminatˈtsjone] *sf* discrimination.

discussione [diskusˈsjone] *sf (gen)* discussion; *(lite)* argument; **fare una** ~ to have a discussion; to have an argument; **mettere in** ~ to bring into question; **fuori** ~ out of the question; **fila a letto, senza** ~**i!** go to bed and don't argue!; **ho avuto una** ~ **col capo** *(lite)* I had words with my boss.

discusso, a [disˈkusso] **1** *pp di* **discutere. 2** *ag* controversial.

discutere [disˈkutere] **1** *vt (dibattere)* to discuss, debate; *(contestare)* to question; **è da** ~ *(se ne parlerà ancora)* it's still up for discussion; *(è in dubbio)* it's questionable. **2** *vi* **(a)** *(conversare):* ~ **(di)** to talk (about), discuss. **(b)** *(litigare)* to argue.

discutibile [diskuˈtibile] *ag* questionable.

disdegnare [dizdeɲˈɲare] *vt* to disdain, scorn.

disdegno [dizˈdeɲɲo] *sm* disdain, contempt, scorn.

disdegnoso, a [dizdeɲˈɲoso] *ag* disdainful, scornful.

disdetta [dizˈdetta] *sf* **(a)** **dare la** ~ **di** *(contratto)* to cancel; **dare la** ~ **di un contratto d'affitto** to give notice (to quit). **(b)** *(sfortuna):* **per** ~ unfortunately; **che** ~! hard luck!

disdetto, a [disˈdetto] *pp di* **disdire.**

disdicevole [dizdiˈtʃevole] *ag* improper, unseemly.

disdire [dizˈdire] *vt (prenotazione, contratto)* to cancel; ~ **un contratto d'affitto** *(Dir)* to give notice (to quit).

diseducare [dizeduˈkare] *vt* to bring up badly.

disegnare [diseɲˈɲare] *vt* **(a)** *(gen)* to draw; *(a* *contorno)* to outline; *(fig: descrivere)* to describe, portray. **(b)** *(progettare: mobile etc)* to design; *(fig):* ~ **di fare qc** to plan to do sth.

disegnatore, trice [diseɲɲa'tore] *sm/f (tecnico)* draughtsman/woman; *(progettista)* designer.

disegno [di'seɲɲo] *sm* **(a)** drawing; *(schizzo)* sketch; ~ **a matita** pencil drawing; ~ **dal vero** real-life drawing. **(b)** *(su carta, stoffa etc)* design, pattern. **(c)** *(fig: schema)* outline, plan; *(: progetto)* plan, project; ~ **di legge** *(Dir)* bill.

diserbante [dizer'bante] **1** *ag* herbicidal. **2** *sm* herbicide, weed-killer.

diserbare [dizer'bare] *vt* to weed.

diseredare [dizere'dare] *vt* to disinherit.

diseredato, a [dizere'dato] **1** *ag* disinherited; *(fig)* deprived. **2** *sm/f* disinherited person; *(fig)* deprived person.

disertare [dizer'tare] **1** *vt* to desert, abandon, leave; **ieri ho disertato la riunione** yesterday I gave the meeting a miss. **2** *vi (Mil, fig):* ~ **(da qc)** to desert (sth).

disertore [dizer'tore] *sm (anche fig)* deserter.

diserzione [dizer'tsjone] *sf (Mil, fig)* desertion.

disfacimento [disfatʃi'mento] *sm (di cadavere)* decay; *(fig: di istituzione, impero, società)* decline, decay; **in** ~ in decay.

disfare [dis'fare] **1** *vt* **(a)** *(gen)* to undo; *(nodo)* to untie, undo; *(sciogliere)* to melt; *(meccanismo)* to take to pieces; *(impalcatura)* to take down; ~ **il letto** to strip the bed; ~ **le valigie** to unpack (one's cases). **(b)** *(distruggere: gen)* to destroy; *(: automobile)* to smash. **2:** ~**rsi** *vr* **(a)** *(nodo, pacco)* to come undone; *(neve etc)* to melt. **(b)** *(andare a pezzi)* to fall to pieces. **(c):** ~**rsi di** *(liberarsi)* to get rid of.

disfatta [dis'fatta] *sf (Mil)* (utter) defeat, rout.

disfattismo [disfat'tizmo] *sm* defeatism.

disfattista, i, e [disfat'tista] *sm/f* defeatist.

disfatto, a [dis'fatto] **1** *pp di* **disfare. 2** *ag (gen)* undone, untied; *(letto)* unmade; *(persona: sfinito)* exhausted, worn-out; *(: addolorato)* grief-stricken.

disfida [dis'fida] *sf (sfida)* challenge; *(duello)* duel.

disfunzione [disfun'tsjone] *sf (Med)* dysfunction; ~ **cardiaca** heart trouble.

disgelare [dizdʒe'lare] *vt, vi,* ~**rsi** *vr* to thaw.

disgelo [diz'dʒɛlo] *sm* thaw.

disgiungere [diz'dʒundʒere] *vt* to separate.

disgiuntivo, a [dizdʒun'tivo] *ag (Gram)* disjunctive.

disgiunto, a [dis'dʒunto] *pp di* **disgiungere.**

disgrazia [diz'grattsja] *sf* **(a)** *(sventura)* bad luck, misfortune; **per** ~ unfortunately. **(b)** *(incidente)* accident; *(terremoto etc)* disaster. **(c)** *(sfavore)* disgrace; **cadere in** ~ to fall into disgrace.

disgraziato, a [dizgrat'tsjato] **1** *ag (persona: povero)* poor, wretched; *(: sfortunato)* unfortunate, unlucky; *(: peg: sciagurato)* good-for-nothing; *(periodo, attività, impresa)* ill-fated, luckless. **2** *sm/f (povero)* poor wretch; *(sciagurato)* rascal, rogue, scoundrel.

disgregamento [dizgrega'mento] *sm* disintegration; *(fig)* break-up.

disgregare [dizgre'gare] **1** *vt* to cause to disintegrate, break up; *(fig: partito, famiglia)* to break up. **2:** ~**rsi** *vr* to disintegrate, break up; *(fig)* to break up.

disgregazione [dizgregat'tsjone] *sf* disintegration; *(fig)* break-up.

disguido [diz'gwido] *sm* hitch.

disgustare [dizgus'tare] **1** *vt* to disgust, sicken, make sick. **2:** ~**rsi** *vr* to be disgusted, be sickened.

disgusto [diz'gusto] *sm (anche fig)* disgust.

disgustoso, a [dizgus'toso] *ag* disgusting.

disidratare [dizidra'tare] *vt* to dehydrate.

disidratazione [dizidratat'tsjone] *sf* dehydration.

disilludere [dizil'ludere] **1** *vt* to disillusion, disenchant. **2:** ~**rsi** *vr* to be disillusioned, be disenchanted.

disillusione [dizillu'zjone] *sf* disillusion, disenchantment.

disilluso, a [dizil'luzo] **1** *pp di* **disilludere. 2** *ag* disillusioned, disenchanted. **3** *sm/f* disillusioned *o* disenchanted person.

disimparare [dizimpa'rare] *vt* to forget; **ho disimparato il francese** I've forgotten my French.

disimpegnare [dizimpeɲ'ɲare] **1** *vt* **(a)** *(persona: da obblighi)* to free; ~ **(da)** to release (from); *(ancora)* to clear. **(b)** *(oggetto in pegno)* to redeem, get out of pawn. **2:** ~**rsi** *vr:* ~**rsi da** *(obblighi etc)* to release o.s. from, free o.s. from.

disincagliare [dizinkaʎ'ʎare] **1** *vt (barca)* to refloat. **2:** ~**rsi** *vr* to get afloat again.

disincantare [dizinkan'tare] *vt* to disenchant.

disincantato, a [dizinkan'tato] *ag* disenchanted, disillusioned.

disincrostare [dizinkros'tare] *vt:* ~ **qc da qc** to scrape sth off sth.

disinfestante [dizinfes'tante] **1** *ag* disinfesting. **2** *sm* pesticide.

disinfestare [dizinfes'tare] *vt* to disinfest.

disinfestazione [dizinfestat'tsjone] *sf* disinfestation.

disinfettante [dizinfet'tante] *ag, sm* disinfectant.

disinfettare [dizinfet'tare] *vt* to disinfect.

disinfezione [dizinfet'tsjone] *sf* disinfection.

disingannare [dizingan'nare] *vt* to disillusion.

disinganno [dizin'ganno] *sm* disillusion.

disinnescare [dizinnes'kare] *vt* to defuse.

disinnestare [disinnes'tare] *vt (marcia)* to disengage.

disinserire [dizinse'rire] *vt (Elettr)* to disconnect.

disintasare [dizinta'sare] *vt (tubo)* to unblock, clear.

disintegrare [dizinte'grare] **1** *vt (gen)* to disintegrate; *(fig: edificio)* to shatter; *(: opposizione, avversari)* to annihilate. **2:** ~**rsi** *vr (anche fig)* to disintegrate.

disintegrazione [dizintegrat'tsjone] *sf* disintegration

disinteressare [dizinteres'sare] **1** *vt:* ~ **qn a qc** to cause sb to lose interest in sth. **2:** ~**rsi** *vr:* ~**rsi di** to take no interest in.

disinteressato, a [dizinteres'sato] *ag* disinterested.

disinteresse [dizinte'resse] *sm* **(a)** *(indifferenza)* disinterest, indifference. **(b)** *(generosità)* disinterestedness, unselfishness.

disintossicante [dizintossi'kante] *ag* purifying.

disintossicare [dizintossi'kare] **1** *vt* to detoxicate; *(alcolizzato, drogato)* to treat for alcoholism *(o* drug addiction); ~ **l'organismo** to clear out one's system. **2:** ~**rsi** *vr* to clear out one's system; *(alcolizzato, drogato)* to be treated for alcoholism *(o* drug addiction).

disintossicazione [dizintossikat'tsjone] *sf (vedi vb)* detoxication; treatment for alcoholism *(o* drug addiction).

disinvolto, a [dizin'vɔlto] *ag (sicuro)* confident; *(spigliato)* casual, nonchalant, free and easy; **con fare** ~ nonchalantly.

disinvoltura [dizinvol'tura] *sf (vedi ag)* confidence; casualness, nonchalance, ease; **con** ~ with ease, easily.

dislivello [dizli'vɛllo] *sm* difference in height; *(fig)* gap.

dislocare [dizlo'kare] *vt* **(a)** *(Mil)* to post, station; *(funzionario)* to post. **(b)** *(Naut)* to displace.

dismisura [dizmi'sura] *sf*: **a** ~ excessively.

disobbligare [dizobbli'gare] **1** *vt*: ~ **(da)** to free (from), release (from). **2**: ~**rsi** *vr* (*sdebitarsi*): ~**rsi con qn per qc** to pay sb back for sth.

disoccupato, a [dizokku'pato] **1** *ag* unemployed, out of work. **2** *sm/f* unemployed person; **i** ~**i the** unemployed, people out of work.

disoccupazione [dizokkupat'tsjone] *sf* unemployment.

disonestà [dizones'ta] *sf inv* dishonesty; **è una** ~ it's dishonest.

disonesto, a [dizo'nesto] **1** *ag* dishonest. **2** *sm/f* dishonest person.

disonorare [dizono'rare] **1** *vt* (*nome, famiglia*) to disgrace, dishonour; (*donna*) to dishonour. **2**: ~**rsi** *vr* to bring disgrace on o.s., bring dishonour on o.s.

disonore [dizo'nore] *sm* disgrace, dishonour; **essere il** ~ **della propria famiglia** to be a disgrace to one's family.

disonorevole [dizono'revole] *ag* dishonourable.

disopra [di'sopra] **1** *av* **= di sopra. 2** *sm inv* top, upper part.

disordinare [dizordi'nare] *vt* to mess up, disarrange; *(Mil)* to throw into disorder.

disordinato, a [dizordi'nato] *ag* (*persona*) untidy, disorderly; *(compito)* untidy; (*fuga, vita*) disorderly; ~ **nel lavoro** disorganized in one's work.

disordine [di'zordine] *sm* **(a)** (*confusione*) untidiness, disorderliness; **essere/mettere in** ~ to be/make untidy; **ho i capelli in** ~ my hair is untidy *o* in a mess; ~ **mentale** mental confusion; **che** ~! what a mess! **(b)**: ~**i** *pl* (*Pol etc*) disorder *sg*; (*tumulti*) riots.

disorganico, a, ci, che [dizor'ganiko] *ag* incoherent, disorganized.

disorganizzare [dizorganid'dzare] *vt* to disorganize.

disorganizzazione [dizorganiddzat'tsjone] *sf* disorganization.

disorientamento [dizorjenta'mento] *sm* (*fig*) confusion, bewilderment.

disorientare [dizorjen'tare] **1** *vt* (*anche fig*) to disorientate. **2**: ~**rsi** *vr* (*anche fig*) to lose one's bearings, become disorientated.

disorientato, a [dizorjen'tato] *ag* disorientated.

disossare [dizos'sare] *vt* (*Culin*) to bone.

disotto [di'sotto] **1** *adv* **= di sotto. 2** *sm inv* bottom, underside.

dispaccio [dis'pattʃo] *sm* dispatch.

disparato, a [dispa'rato] *ag* disparate; **le cose più** ~**e** all kinds of things.

dispari ['dispari] *ag inv* (*numero*) odd; *(Mil: forze)* unequal.

disparità [dispari'ta] *sf*: ~ **(di)** (*disuguaglianza*) disparity (in); *(divergenza*) difference (in).

disparte [dis'parte]: **in** ~ *av* (*da lato*) aside; **mettere qc in** ~ to put *o* set sth aside; **stare** *o* **tenersi in** ~ to stand apart; *(fig)* to keep to o.s., hold aloof.

dispendio [dis'pɛndjo] *sm* (*di denaro, energie*) expenditure; (: *spreco*) waste.

dispendioso, a [dispen'djoso] *ag* extravagant.

dispensa [dis'pɛnsa] *sf* **(a)** (*distribuzione*) distribution, handing out. **(b)** (*locale*) larder, pantry; (*mobile*) sideboard. **(c)** (*esenzione*): ~ **(da)** exemption (from); *(Rel)* dispensation (from).

(d) (*fascicolo*) instalment, number; *(Univ)* duplicated lecture notes *pl*.

dispensare [dispen'sare] **1** *vt* **(a)** (*elemosine, favori*) to distribute, hand out. **(b)** (*esonerare*): ~ **qn da/dal fare** to exempt sb from/from doing. **2**: ~**rsi** *vr*: ~**rsi da fare qc** to get out of *o* avoid doing sth.

disperare [dispe'rare] **1** *vi* to despair; ~ **di fare qc** to despair of doing sth. **2**: ~**rsi** *vr* to despair; **non disperarti in quel modo!** don't get so upset!

disperata [dispe'rata]: **alla** ~ *av* recklessly.

disperatamente [disperata'mente] *av* desperately.

disperato, a [dispe'rato] **1** *ag* (*persona*) in despair; *(caso)* hopeless; (*tentativo, gesto*) desperate; **grido** ~ cry of despair. **2** *sm/f* **(a)** (*squattrinato*) wretch. **(b)** (*agitato: bambino, ragazzo*): **è un** ~ he's wild; **lavorare come un** ~ to work furiously.

disperazione [disperat'tsjone] *sf* despair; **in preda alla** ~ overcome by despair; **quel bambino è la mia** ~ I despair of that child.

disperdere [dis'pɛrdere] **1** *vt* (*folla, nemico*) to scatter, disperse; (*energia, sostanze*) to waste, squander. **2**: ~**rsi** *vr* (*folla, nemico*) to scatter, disperse; (*energia, sostanze*) to be wasted; (*calore*) to be lost.

dispersione [disper'sjone] *sf* (*vedi vb*) scattering, dispersal; waste; *(Chim, Fis)* dispersion; ~ **di calore** heat loss.

dispersivo, a [disper'sivo] *ag* (*lavoro etc*) disorganized.

disperso, a [dis'pɛrso] **1** *pp di* **disperdere. 2** *ag* (*sparpagliato*) scattered, dispersed; (*smarrito: documenti*) lost; (: *persona*) missing. **3** *sm/f* missing person; *(Mil)* missing soldier.

dispetto [dis'pɛtto] *sm* **(a)** (*molestia*) spiteful trick; **fare un** ~ **a qn** to play a nasty *o* spiteful trick on sb; **a** ~ **di** in spite of, despite; **per** ~ out of spite. **(b)** (*stizza*) vexation; **con suo grande** ~ much to his annoyance.

dispettoso, a [dispet'toso] *ag* spiteful.

dispiacere [dispja'tʃere] **1** *sm* **(a)** (*rammarico*) regret, sorrow; (*dolore*) grief; **con mio grande** ~ much to my regret; **con grande** ~ **vi annuncio...** I regret to announce...; **impazzire dal** ~ to go mad with grief. **(b)** (*disappunto*) disappointment; **non puoi dare questo** ~ **a tua madre** you can't disappoint your mother in this way. **(c)**: ~**i** *pl* (*preoccupazioni*) worries; **il figlio le ha dato molti** ~**i** her son has been a disappointment to her.

2 *vi* (*aus* **essere**): ~ **a (a)** (*causare dolore*) to upset; (*causare disagio, noia*) to displease; **ciò che hai fatto è dispiaciuto ai tuoi** your parents are upset *o* displeased at your behaviour; **mi dispiace andarmene** I'm sorry to be leaving. **(b)** (*risultare sgradito*): **ti dispiace se fumo?** do you mind if I smoke?; **se non le dispiace...** if you don't mind...; **ti dispiace prestarmelo?** would you mind lending it to me?

3: ~**rsi** *vr*: ~**rsi (per** *o* **di qc)** to regret (sth).

dispiaciuto, a [dispja'tʃuto] *pp di* **dispiacere.**

displuvio [dis'pluvjo] *sm* **(a)** *(Geog)* watershed. **(b)** (*di tetto*) ridge.

disponibile [dispo'nibile] *ag* (*posto, merce, peg: donna*) available; **sei** ~ **stasera?** are you free this evening?; **è sempre molto** ~ he's always willing to help.

disponibilità [disponibili'ta] *sf* **(a)** (*gen*) availability; *(fig: di persona*) willingness to help. **(b)** *(Fin)*: ~ *pl* liquid assets.

disporre [dis'porre] **1** *vt* **(a)** (*mettere*) to place, put; (*sistemare*) to arrange; (*preparare*) to prepare, make ready; ~ **l'animo a fare qc** to put o.s. in the mood for doing sth. **(b)** *(ordinare)* to order; **la legge dispone che...** the law provides that...; **ha disposto che nessuno se ne andasse** he gave orders that no-one should leave.

2 *vi* **(a)** *(decidere)* to decide; **abbiamo disposto diversamente** we have decided otherwise, we have made other arrangements. **(b)**: ~ **di** to have, have at one's disposal; **lo stadio dispone di 50.000 posti** the stadium holds 50,000 people.

3: **disporsi** *vr* **(a)** *(posizione)* to put o.s., place o.s.; **disporsi in fila** to line up; **disporsi in cerchio** to form a circle. **(b)** *(prepararsi)*: **disporsi a fare qc** to prepare o.s. *o* get ready to do sth; **disporsi all'attacco** to prepare for an attack.

dispositivo [dispozi'tivo] *sm* **(a)** *(meccanismo)* device; ~ **di controllo** *o* **di comando** control device; ~ **di sicurezza** *(gen)* safety device; *(di arma da fuoco)* safety catch. **(b)** *(Mil: posizione)* order; ~ **di marcia** marching order. **(c)** *(Dir)* pronouncement.

disposizione [disposit'tsjone] *sf* **(a)** *(sistemazione: di mobili)* arrangement; *(: di locali)* layout; *(Sport: di squadra)* positioning; *(: di terreno)* situation.

(b) *(ordine)* order; *(: Dir)* provision; ~**i** *(preparativi, misure)* measures; **dare** ~ *o* ~**i a qn affinché faccia qc** to give orders to sb to do sth; **per** ~ **di legge** by law; ~**i di sicurezza** safety measures; ~ **testamentaria** provisions of a will; **le sue ultime** ~**i erano...** his last instructions were... .

(c): **a** ~: **avere a** ~ to have available *o* at one's disposal; **sono a tua** ~ I am at your disposal; **resti a** ~ **della polizia** be prepared to assist the police with their enquiries.

(d): ~ **d'animo** mood, frame of mind.

disposto, a [dis'posto] **1** *pp di* **disporre. 2** *ag (incline)*: ~ **a fare** disposed *o* prepared to do; **essere ben/mal** ~ **verso qn** to be well-/ill-disposed towards sb. **3** *sm (Dir)* provision.

dispotico, a, ci, che [dis'potiko] *ag* despotic; *(fig)* tyrannical, overbearing.

dispotismo [dispo'tizmo] *sm* despotism; *(fig)* tyranny.

dispregiativo, a [dispredʒa'tivo] *ag* disparaging; *(Gram)* pejorative.

dispregio [dis'predʒo] *sm* disparagement.

disprezzabile [dispret'tsabile] *ag* contemptible, despicable; **una somma non** ~ a not inconsiderable sum of money.

disprezzare [dispret'tsare] *vt (gen)* to scorn, despise; *(persona)* to look down on.

disprezzo [dis'prettso] *sm* scorn, contempt; **ha agito con** ~ **del pericolo** he acted with a total disregard for the danger involved.

disputa ['disputa] *sf* **(a)** *(dibattito)* dispute, argument. **(b)** *(lite)* argument.

disputare [dispu'tare] **1** *vi*: ~ **di** *(discutere)* to argue over. **2** *vt* **(a)** *(gara)* to take part in; *(partita)* to play; **quando si disputerà la gara?** when will the competition take place? **(b)** *(contrastare)* to contest, dispute; **gli hanno disputato il diritto di farlo** they contested *o* disputed his right to do it. **(c)**: ~**rsi qc** to compete for sth; ~**rsi il pallone** to fight for the ball.

disquisizione [diskwizit'tsjone] *sf* detailed analysis; **è inutile stare a fare** ~**i sul perché** there's no point discussing all the ins and outs of it.

dissacrare [dissa'krare] *vt* to desecrate.

dissalazione [dissalat'tsjone] *sf* desalination.

dissanguamento [dissangwa'mento] *sm (Med)* loss of blood.

dissanguare [dissan'gware] **1** *vt (fig: persona)* to bleed white; *(: patrimonio)* to suck dry. **2**: ~**rsi** *vr*

(Med) to lose blood; *(fig)* to ruin o.s.; **morire dissanguato** to bleed to death.

dissapore [dissa'pore] *sm* slight disagreement.

dissecare [disse'kare] *vt* to dissect.

disseccare [dissek'kare] *vt*, ~**rsi** *vr* to dry (up).

dissellare [dissel'lare] *vt* to unsaddle.

disseminare [dissemi'nare] *vt* to scatter, spread; *(fig: notizie)* to spread.

dissennato, a [dissen'nato] *ag (persona)* foolish; *(idea)* senseless.

dissenso [dis'senso] *sm* dissent; **scrittori del** ~ dissident writers.

dissenteria [dissente'ria] *sf* dysentery.

dissentire [dissen'tire] *vi* to dissent; ~ **da qn su qc** to disagree with sb on sth.

dissenziente [dissen'tsjɛnte] **1** *ag* dissenting. **2** *sm/f* dissenter.

disseppellire [disseppel'lire] *vt (esumare: cadavere)* to disinter, exhume; *(dissotterrare: anche fig)* to dig up, unearth; *(: rancori)* to resurrect.

dissertare [disser'tare] *vi*: ~ **di** *(parlare)* to speak on; *(scrivere)* to write on.

dissertazione [dissertat'tsjone] *sf* dissertation.

disservizio [disser'vittsjo] *sm* inefficiency.

dissestare [disses'tare] *vt (anche fig)* to upset, disturb; **queste spese hanno dissestato il bilancio familiare** these expenses have disrupted the household's finances.

dissestato, a [disses'tato] *ag (fondo stradale)* uneven; *(: per lavori in corso)*: **'strada** ~**a'** 'road up'; *(economia, finanze)* shaky.

dissesto [dis'sɛsto] *sm (Fin, Econ)* disorder; ~ **finanziario** serious financial difficulties; **in** ~ in disorder.

dissetante [disse'tante] *ag* refreshing, thirst-quenching.

dissetare [disse'tare] **1** *vt (persona)* to quench the thirst of; *(animale)* to water, give water to. **2**: ~**rsi** *vr* to quench one's thirst.

dissezione [disset'tsjone] *sf* dissection.

dissidente [dissi'dɛnte] *ag*, *sm/f* dissident.

dissidenza [dissi'dɛntsa] *sf* dissidence.

dissidio [dis'sidjo] *sm* quarrel, dispute; ~ **di opinioni** difference of opinion.

dissimile [dis'simile] *ag*: ~ **(da)** different (from), dissimilar (to).

dissimulare [dissimu'lare] **1** *vt* to hide, conceal. **2** *vi* to dissemble; **non sa** ~ he's not good at pretending.

dissimulatore, trice [dissimula'tore] *sm/f* dissembler.

dissimulazione [dissimulat'tsjone] *sf (vedi vb)* concealment; dissembling.

dissipare [dissi'pare] **1** *vt* **(a)** *(disperdere: nubi, nebbia)* to disperse; *(: odori, fig: dubbi, timori)* to dispel. **(b)** *(sprecare)* to waste, squander. **2**: ~**rsi** *vr (nubi)* to disperse; *(nebbia)* to clear, lift; *(odori, dubbi, timori)* to vanish, disappear.

dissipatezza [dissipa'tettsa] *sf* dissipation.

dissipato, a [dissi'pato] *ag* dissolute, dissipated.

dissipatore, trice [dissipa'tore] *sm/f* spendthrift.

dissipazione [dissipat'tsjone] *sf* **(a)** *(sperpero)* squandering, waste. **(b)** *(dissipatezza)* dissipation.

dissociare [disso't∫are] **1** *vt* to dissociate. **2**: ~**rsi** *vr (separarsi)* to split up; ~**rsi da** to dissociate o.s. from.

dissociativo, a [dissot∫a'tivo] *ag* dissociative.

dissociazione [dissot∫at'tsjone] *sf* dissociation.

dissodamento [dissoda'mento] *sm (Agr)* tillage.

dissodare [disso'dare] *vt (Agr)* to till, break up.

dissolto, a [dis'sɔlto] *pp di* **dissolvere.**

dissolutezza [dissolu'tettsa] *sf* dissoluteness;

vivere nella ~ to lead a dissolute life.

dissolutivo, a [dissolu'tivo] *ag (forza)* divisive; **processo** ~ *(anche fig)* process of dissolution.

dissoluto, a [disso'luto] 1 *ag* dissolute. 2 *sm/f* dissolute person.

dissoluzione [dissolut'tsjone] *sf* dissolution.

dissolvere [dis'sɔlvere] 1 *vt (sostanza)* to dissolve; *(nebbia)* to disperse, dispel, clear (away); *(fig: dubbio)* to dispel. 2: ~**rsi** *vr (vedi vt)* to dissolve; to disperse, dispel, clear (away); to be dispelled.

dissonante [disso'nante] *ag (suono)* dissonant, discordant.

dissonanza [disso'nantsa] *sf (di suoni)* dissonance, discord; *(fig: di opinioni)* clash.

dissotterrare [dissotter'rare] *vt (cadavere)* to disinter, exhume; *(tesori, rovine)* to dig up, unearth; *(fig: sentimenti, odio)* to bring up again, resurrect.

dissuadere [dissua'dere] *vt* to dissuade; ~ **qn da qc/da fare qc** to dissuade sb from sth/from doing sth.

dissuasione [dissua'zjone] *sf* dissuasion.

dissuasivo, a [dissua'zivo] *ag* dissuasive.

dissuaso, a [dissu'azo] *pp di* **dissuadere**.

distaccamento [distakka'mento] *sm (Mil)* detachment.

distaccare [distak'kare] 1 *vt* **(a):** ~ **(da)** *(persona)* to separate (from), take away (from); *(etichetta, francobollo)* to remove, take off; *(vagone, ricevuta)* to detach (from); ~ **lo sguardo da qn** to look away from sb. **(b)** *(Amm: dipendente)* to transfer; *(Mil: reparto)* to detach. **(c)** *(Sport)* to outdistance; **li distaccò di 20 metri** he outdistanced them by 20 metres. 2: ~**rsi** *vr (bottone, etichetta):* ~**rsi (da qc)** to come off (sth); *(persona):* ~**rsi (da qn)** to leave (sb).

distaccato, a [distak'kato] *ag* detached.

distacco, chi [dis'takko] *sm* **(a)** *(separazione)* detaching; *(: fig)* parting; **il** ~ **fu molto doloroso** it was very painful to part. **(b)** *(indifferenza)* detachment. **(c)** *(Sport):* **vincere con un** ~ **di...** to win by a distance of... .

distante [dis'tante] 1 *ag* **(a)** *(luogo):* **essere** ~ **(da)** to be a long way (from); **la casa è molto** ~ **dal centro** the house is a long way (away) from the centre; **è** ~ **da qui?** is it far from here?, is it a long way from here?; **non è** ~ it's not far. **(b)** *(tempo):* **essere** ~ **nel tempo** to be in the distant past; **sono** ~**i gli anni in cui...** it's a long time since... . **(c)** *(fig: persona, atteggiamento)* distant. 2 *av* far away, a long way away; **non si vede da così** ~ you can't see it from this distance *o* from so far away; **non abitano** ~ they don't live far away.

distanza [dis'tantsa] 1 *sf* **(a)** *(gen)* distance; **abito ad una certa** ~ **dal centro** I live a fair distance *o* quite a distance from the centre; **qual'è la** ~ **tra Glasgow ed Edimburgo?** how far is it from Glasgow to Edinburgh?, how far is Glasgow from Edinburgh?; **le 2 barche erano a 3 metri di** ~ the 2 boats were 3 metres apart; **comando a** ~ remote control. **(b)** *(tempo):* **a** ~ **di 2 giorni** 2 days later; **sono nati a qualche anno di** ~ they were born within a few years of one another. **(c)** *(Sport)* distance; **gara su media/lunga** ~ middle-/long-distance race. **(d)** *(fraseologia):* **prendere le** ~**e da qc/qn** to dissociate o.s. from sth/sb; **tenere** *o* **mantenere le** ~ to keep one's distance; **tener qn a** ~ to keep sb at arm's length.

2: ~ **di sicurezza** safe distance; *(Aut)* braking distance; ~ **focale** focal length; ~ **di tiro** range; ~ **di visibilità** visibility.

distanziare [distan'tsjare] *vt* **(a)** *(gen: oggetti)* to

space out. **(b)** *(Sport, fig):* ~ **qn** to leave sb behind, outdistance sb.

distare [dis'tare] *vi:* ~ **(da)** to be a long way (from); **la mia casa dista 2 ore da qui** my house is 2 hours (away) from here; **dista molto da qui?** is it far (away) from here?; **non dista molto** it's not far (away); **quanto dista?** how far is it?

distendere [dis'tɛndere] 1 *vt (braccia, gambe)* to stretch (out); *(muscoli)* to relax; *(cavo, corda)* to extend; *(tovaglia)* to spread; *(bucato)* to hang out; **fecero** ~ **il ferito sul letto** they laid the wounded man on the bed; **è ottimo per** ~ **i nervi** it's just the thing to help you relax. 2: ~**rsi** *vr* **(a)** *(persona)* to lie down, stretch out; *(fig: rilassarsi)* to relax. **(b)** *(estendersi):* **i prati si distendevano a perdita d'occhio** the fields stretched out as far as the eye could see.

distensione [disten'sjone] *sf* relaxation; *(Pol)* détente.

distensivo, a [disten'sivo] *ag (gen)* relaxing, restful; *(farmaco)* tranquillizing; *(Pol)* conciliatory.

distesa [dis'tesa] *sf* expanse, stretch; **la** ~ **del mare** the expanse of the sea; **le campane suonavano a** ~ the bells pealed out.

disteso, a [dis'teso] 1 *pp di* **distendere**. 2 *ag (allungato: persona, gamba)* stretched out; *(rilassato: persona, atmosfera)* relaxed; **cadere lungo** ~ to fall flat on one's face; **se ne stava** ~ **sul letto** he was stretched out on the bed; **avere un volto** ~ to look relaxed.

distillare [distil'lare] *vt* to distil; **acqua distillata** distilled water.

distillato [distil'lato] *sm* distillate.

distillazione [distillat'tsjone] *sf* distillation.

distilleria [distille'ria] *sf* distillery.

distinguere [dis'tingwere] 1 *vt* **(a)** *(differenziare)* to distinguish; ~ **il torto dalla ragione** to tell right from wrong; **la sua energia lo distingue dagli altri** his energy distinguishes him *o* sets him apart from the others. **(b)** *(percepire)* to distinguish, discern; **era troppo buio per** ~ **la faccia** it was too dark to see *o* make out his face. **(c)** *(contrassegnare: con etichetta ecc)* to mark, indicate.

2: ~**rsi** *vr* **(a)** *(essere riconoscibile)* to be distinguished. **(b)** *(emergere)* to stand out, be conspicuous, distinguish o.s.; **un whisky che si distingue per il suo aroma** a whisky with a distinctive bouquet; **si è sempre distinta per la sua eleganza** her elegance always makes her stand out from the crowd.

distinta [dis'tinta] *sf (Comm)* note; ~ **di pagamento** receipt; ~ **di versamento** pay-in slip.

distinto, a [dis'tinto] 1 *pp di* **distinguere**. 2 *ag* **(a)** *(differente)* different, distinct. **(b)** *(chiaro)* distinct, clear. **(c)** *(elegante, dignitoso)* distinguished, refined; ~**i saluti** *(in lettera)* yours faithfully *o* truly.

distinzione [distin'tsjone] *sf* **(a)** *(gen)* distinction; **non faccio** ~**i** *(tra persone)* I don't discriminate; *(tra cose)* it's all one to me; **senza** ~ **di razza/religione...** no matter what one's race/creed... . **(b)** *(signorilità)* distinction, refinement. **(c)** *(onore)* honour, distinction.

distogliere [dis'tɔʎʎere] *vt* **(a)** *(allontanare)* to remove, take away; ~ **lo sguardo** to look away. **(b)** *(fig: dissuadere)* to dissuade, deter; ~ **qn da qc** to deter sb from sth.

distolto, a [dis'tolto] *pp di* **distogliere**.

distorcere [dis'tɔrtʃere] 1 *vt* to twist; *(fig: verità, versione dei fatti)* to twist, distort. 2: ~**rsi** *vr (contorcersi)* to twist.

distorsione [distor'sjone] *sf* **(a)** *(Med)* sprain. **(b)** *(Fis, Ottica)* distortion.

distorto, a [dis'tɔrto] **1** *pp di* **distorcere. 2** *ag (Fis, Ottica, fig)* distorted.

distrarre [dis'trarre] **1** *vt (distogliere)* to distract, divert; *(divertire)* to amuse, distract; ~ **lo sguardo** to look away. **2: distrarsi** *vr* to be distracted, let one's mind wander; *(svagarsi)* to take one's mind off things; **non distrarti!** pay attention!

distrattamente [distratta'mente] *av* absent-mindedly, without thinking.

distratto, a [dis'tratto] **1** *pp di* **distrarre. 2** *ag (persona)* absent-minded; *(peg)* inattentive.

distrazione [distrat'tsjone] *sf* **(a)** *(caratteristica)* absent-mindedness, lack of attention; *(svista)* oversight; **errori di** ~ careless mistakes. **(b)** *(divertimento)* distraction, amusement.

distretto [dis'tretto] *sm* **(a)** *(circoscrizione)* district. **(b)** *(anche:* ~ **militare)** recruiting office.

distrettuale [distrettu'ale] *ag* district *attr*.

distribuire [distribu'ire] *vt* **(a)** *(dare: gen)* to distribute; *(posta)* to deliver; *(lavoro, mansioni: assegnare)* to allocate, assign; *(: ripartire)* to share out; *(carte)* to deal (out). **(b)** *(disporre)* to arrange; *(Mil)* to deploy.

distributivo, a [distribu'tivo] *ag* distributive.

distributore, trice [distribu'tore] **1** *sm/f* distributor. **2** *sm (apparecchio)* dispenser; *(Aut, Elettr)* distributor; ~ **automatico** slot machine; ~ **(di benzina)** petrol pump; *(stazione)* petrol station; ~ **di biglietti** ticket machine.

distribuzione [distribut'tsjone] *sf* **(a)** *(vedi vb)* distribution; delivery; allocation, assignment; sharing out; dealing; arrangement; deployment. **(b)** *(Comm, Aut, Tecn)* distribution.

districare [distri'kare] **1** *vt (sbrogliare)* to unravel, disentangle; *(fig: chiarire)* to unravel, sort out. **2:** ~**rsi** *vr* **(a):** ~**rsi da** to get out of, disentangle o.s. from. **(b)** *(fig: cavarsela)* to manage, get by.

distrofia [distro'fia] *sf* dystrophy.

distruggere [dis'truddʒere] *vt (gen)* to destroy; *(popolazione)* to wipe out; *(fig: speranze)* to ruin, destroy; *(: persona)* to shatter, destroy.

distruttivo, a [distrut'tivo] *ag* destructive.

distrutto, a [dis'trutto] *pp di* **distruggere.**

distruttore, trice [distrut'tore] **1** *ag* destructive. **2** *sm/f* destroyer.

distruzione [distrut'tsjone] *sf* destruction.

disturbare [distur'bare] **1** *vt (importunare)* to disturb, trouble, bother; *(portar scompiglio)* to disturb; **disturbo?** am I disturbing you?; **non vorrei** ~ I wouldn't like to be a nuisance; **non mi disturba affatto** it's no trouble at all. **2:** ~**rsi** *vr* to bother, put o.s. out; **non si disturbi** please don't bother; **non doveva** ~**rsi!** you shouldn't have gone to all that trouble!

disturbo [dis'turbo] *sm* **(a)** *(incomodo)* trouble, bother, inconvenience; **non è affatto un** ~ it's no trouble at all; **prendersi il** ~ **di fare qc** to take the trouble to do sth; **della quiete pubblica** *(Dir)* disturbance of the peace. **(b)** *(Med)* disorder; ~**i di stomaco** stomach trouble *sg*. **(c)** *(Radio, TV):* ~**i** *pl* noise *sg*, interference *sg*.

disubbidiente [dizubbi'djɛnte] *ag* disobedient.

disubbidienza [dizubbi'djɛntsa] *sf* disobedience.

disubbidire [dizubbi'dire] *vi* to disobey; ~ **alla legge** to break the law.

disuguaglianza [dizugwaʎ'ʎantsa] *sf* inequality.

disuguale [dizu'gwale] *ag* **(a)** *(gen: differente)* different. **(b)** *(non uniforme: superficie)* uneven, irregular.

disumanità [dizumani'ta] *sf* inhumanity.

disumano, a [dizu'mano] *ag* inhuman; **un grido** ~ a terrible cry.

disunione [dizu'njone] *sf (separazione)* disunity.

disunire [dizu'nire] **1** *vt (separare)* to take apart, separate; *(fig: disgregare)* to divide. **2:** ~**rsi** *vr* to come apart, separate.

disunito, a [dizu'nito] *ag* disunited, divided.

disuso [di'zuzo] *sm* disuse; **andare** *o* **cadere in** ~ to fall into disuse.

ditale [di'tale] *sm (per cucire)* thimble; *(per ferita)* fingerstall.

ditata [di'tata] *sf (colpo)* jab (with one's finger); *(segno)* fingermark.

dito ['dito] *sm*, *pl(f)* ~**a (a)** *(di mano, guanto)* finger; ~ **(del piede)** toe; **mettersi le** ~**a nel naso** to pick one's nose.

 (b) *(misura):* **per me solo un** ~ **di vino** just a drop of wine for me; **accorciare una gonna di un** ~ to shorten a skirt by an inch.

 (c) *(fraseologia):* **avere sulla punta delle** ~**a** *(materia)* to have at one's fingertips; **le volte che ha detto di no si possono contare sulle** ~**a di una mano** I can count the number of times he's said no on the fingers of one hand; **un pranzetto da leccarsi le** ~**a** a lip-smacking meal; **mettere il** ~ **sulla piaga** to touch a sore spot; **non ha mosso un** ~ **(per aiutarmi)** he didn't lift a finger (to help me); **ormai è segnato a** ~ everyone knows about him now.

ditta ['ditta] *sf* firm, company; **Spett. D**~ **F.lli Gobbi** *(su busta)* Messrs Gobbi; *(su lettera)* Dear Sirs; **usa la macchina della** ~ he uses the company car; **son due giorni che non viene in** ~ he hasn't been in to the office for the past two days.

dittafono [dit'tafono] *sm* dictaphone.

dittatore [ditta'tore] *sm* dictator; **fare il** ~ to be bossy.

dittatoriale [dittato'rjale] *ag* dictatorial.

dittatorio, a [ditta'tɔrjo] *ag* dictatorial.

dittatura [ditta'tura] *sf* dictatorship.

dittongo, ghi [dit'tɔngo] *sm* diphthong.

diuretico, a, ci, che [diu'rɛtiko] *ag* diuretic.

diurno, a [di'urno] *ag* day *attr*, daytime *attr*; **luce** ~**a** daylight; **lavoro** ~ day work; **spettacolo** ~ matinee; **turno** ~ day shift; **ore** ~**e** daytime *sg*.

diva ['diva] *sf* star; ~ **del cinema** film star; **come una** ~ like a prima donna.

divagare [diva'gare] *vi* to digress, wander; ~ **dal tema** to stray from the point.

divagazione [divagat'tsjone] *sf* digression; ~**i sul tema** variations on a theme.

divampare [divam'pare] *vi (aus essere) (incendio)* to flare up, break out; *(fig: rivolta)* to break out; *(: passione)* to blaze.

divano [di'vano] *sm* sofa, settee; *(senza schienale)* divan; ~ **letto** bed settee.

divaricare [divari'kare] *vt* to open (wide).

divario [di'varjo] *sm* difference.

divenire [dive'nire] **1** *vi (aus essere)* to become. **2** *sm (Filosofia)* becoming.

diventare [diven'tare] *vi (aus essere) (gen)* to become; ~ **famoso/medico** to become famous/a doctor; ~ **vecchio** to grow old; **le foglie sono diventate gialle** the leaves have turned yellow; **è diventato rosso in faccia** he turned *o* grew red in the face; **come sei diventato grande!** how tall you've grown!; **ora che sei diventato grande** now that you're grown up; **mangia la minestra, non farla** ~ **fredda** eat your soup, don't let it go cold; **c'è da** ~ **matti** it's enough to drive you mad.

divenuto, a [dive'nuto] *pp di* **divenire.**

diverbio [di'verbjo] *sm* dispute, quarrel.

divergente [diver'dʒɛnte] *ag* divergent.

divergenza [diver'dʒɛntsa] *sf* divergence; ~ **d'opinioni** difference of opinion.

divergere [di'vɛrdʒere] vi (Mat) to diverge, be divergent; (fig: opinioni) to differ, diverge.

diversamente [diversa'mente] av (a) (in modo differente) differently; ~ da quanto stabilito contrary to what had been decided. (b) (altrimenti) otherwise.

diversificare [diversifi'kare] 1 vt (gen) to vary; (Comm: prodotti) to diversify. 2: ~rsi vr: ~rsi (per) to differ (in).

diversificazione [diversifikat'tsjone] sf (a) (il diversificare) diversification. (b) (diversità) difference.

diversione [diver'sjone] sf (anche Mil) diversion.

diversità [diversi'ta] sf inv (differenza) difference; (varietà) variety, diversity.

diversivo, a [diver'sivo] 1 ag diversionary; **fare un'azione** ~a to create a diversion. 2 sm (divertimento) diversion, distraction.

diverso, a [di'vɛrso] 1 ag (differente): ~ (da) different (from); **secondo me è** ~ I don't see it like that. 2 ag indef: ~i(e) pl (alcuni, parecchi) several; ~i mesi fa some o several months ago; **gliel'ho detto** ~e volte I told him several times; **c'era** ~a **gente** there were quite a few people; ~e persone me l'hanno detto several o various people told me that. 3 pron: ~i(e) pl several; (persone) several (people); ~i dicono che... various people say that...; ne ho presi ~i (libri, bicchieri etc) I took several (of them). 4 sm (omosessuale) homosexual.

divertente [diver'tɛnte] ag (piacevole) amusing, entertaining; (comico) funny, amusing.

divertimento [diverti'mento] sm (a) (passatempo) amusement, entertainment, distraction; **fare qc per** ~ to do sth for fun; **buon** ~! enjoy yourself!, have a good time!; **bel** ~ (iro) that sounds like fun! (b) (Mus) divertimento, divertissement.

divertire [diver'tire] 1 vt to amuse, entertain. 2: ~rsi vr to enjoy o.s., amuse o.s.; **divertiti!** enjoy yourself!, have a good time!; ~rsi a fare qc to enjoy doing sth; ~rsi alle spalle di qn to have a laugh at sb's expense.

divertito, a [diver'tito] ag amused.

divezzare [divet'tsare] vt (anche fig): ~ (da) to wean (from).

dividendo [divi'dɛndo] sm (Fin, Mat) dividend.

dividere [di'videre] 1 vt (a) (gen, Mat) to divide; (compito, risorse) to share out; (dolce) to divide up; ~ **in 5 parti/per 5** to divide o split into 5 parts/in 5; ~ **100 per 2** to divide 100 by 2; **su questo argomento gli studiosi sono divisi** scholars are divided on this matter; **si stavano picchiando e hanno dovuto dividerli** they were fighting and had to be separated; **niente potrà dividerci** nothing can come between us; **è diviso dalla moglie** he's separated from his wife; **si sono divisi il bottino** they split o divided the loot between them. (b) (condividere) to share; **non ho niente da** ~ **con te** I have nothing in common with you.
2: ~**rsi** vr (a) (scindersi): ~**rsi (in)** to divide (into), split up (into); (ramificarsi) to fork; **il libro si divide in 5 capitoli** the book is divided into 5 chapters; **si divide tra casa e lavoro** he divides his time between home and work; **a questo punto le nostre strade si dividono** we must now go our separate ways. (b) (persone) to separate, part; (coppia) to divorce.

divieto [di'vjɛto] sm: '~ **di accesso**' 'no entry'; '~ **di caccia**' 'no hunting'; '~ **di parcheggio**' 'no parking'; '~ **di sosta**' 'no waiting'.

divinatorio, a [divina'tɔrjo] ag: **arte** ~a divination.

divincolarsi [divinko'larsi] vr to wriggle (free), struggle (free); **continuava a** ~ he was struggling to free himself.

divinità [divini'ta] sf inv divinity.

divinizzare [divinid'dzare] vt to deify.

divino, a [di'vino] ag (gen) divine; (fig fam) divine, heavenly.

divisa[1] [di'viza] sf (uniforme) uniform.

divisa[2] [di'viza] sf (Fin) currency.

divisibile [divi'zibile] ag divisible.

divisionale [divizjo'nale] ag (Mil: comandante) divisional; (: raggruppamento) in divisions.

divisione [divi'zjone] sf (gen) division; ~ **del lavoro** division of labour.

divismo [di'vizmo] sm (esibizionismo) playing to the crowd.

diviso, a [di'vizo] pp di **dividere**.

divisore [divi'zore] sm (Mat) divisor; **massimo comun** ~ highest common denominator.

divisorio, a [divi'zɔrjo] 1 ag (siepe, muro esterno) dividing; (muro interno) dividing, partition attr. 2 sm (in una stanza) partition.

divo, a ['divo] sm/f star.

divorare [divo'rare] 1 vt (cibo, fig: libro) to devour; (: patrimonio) to squander; (sog: passione, malattia, fuoco) to consume, devour; ~ **qn con gli occhi** to devour sb with one's eyes; ~ **qc con gli occhi** to eye sth greedily; **questa macchina divora i chilometri** this car eats up the miles. 2: ~**rsi** vr: ~**rsi da** to be consumed o eaten up with.

divoratore, trice [divora'tore] 1 ag (passione) devouring, consuming; (febbre) burning. 2 sm/f: **è un** ~ **di carne** he's a great meat eater; **una** ~**trice di uomini** (fig) a man-eater; **un** ~ **di libri** (fig) an avid reader.

divorziare [divor'tsjare] vi to get divorced; ~ **dalla moglie** to divorce one's wife.

divorziato, a [divor'tsjato] 1 ag divorced. 2 sm/f divorcee.

divorzio [di'vɔrtsjo] sm divorce.

divulgare [divul'gare] 1 vt (a) (segreto) to divulge, disclose. (b) (rendere accessibile: teoria) to popularize. 2: ~**rsi** vr (notizia, dottrina) to spread.

divulgazione [divulgat'tsjone] sf (vedi vb) disclosure; popularization; spread.

dizionario [dittsjo'narjo] sm dictionary.

dizione [dit'tsjone] sf (a) (modo di parlare) diction, delivery; (recitazione) recitation; (pronuncia) pronunciation. (b) (locuzione) idiom, expression.

do [dɔ] sm inv (Mus) C; (: solfeggiando la scala) do(h).

doccia, ce ['dottʃa] sf (a) (impianto) shower; **fare la** ~ to have a shower; ~ **fredda** (fig) slap in the face. (b) (grondaia) gutter.

docente [do'tʃɛnte] 1 ag teaching. 2 sm/f (Univ) lecturer.

docenza [do'tʃɛntsa] sf (Univ): **ottenere la libera** ~ to become a lecturer.

docile ['dɔtʃile] ag (persona) docile, meek; (animale) docile; (sostanza) malleable.

docilità [dotʃili'ta] sf (vedi ag) docility; meekness; (di sostanza) softness.

documentabile [dokumen'tabile] ag which can be proved (in writing).

documentare [dokumen'tare] 1 vt to document. 2: ~**rsi** vr: ~**rsi (su)** to gather information (about), gather material (about).

documentario, a [dokumen'tarjo] 1 ag documentary. 2 sm documentary (film).

documentazione [dokumentat'tsjone] sf documentation.

documento [doku'mento] sm (a) (gen) document; **ha un** ~ **d'identità?** do you have any identification?; ~i prego! may I see your papers, please? (b) (storico) historical document; i Nuraghi sono un importante ~ della preistoria the Nuraghi provide important evidence on the prehistoric period.

dodicenne [dodi'tʃɛnne] ag, sm/f twelve-year-old; per uso vedi **cinquantenne**.

dodicesimo, a [dodi'tʃezimo] ag, sm/f, sm twelfth; per uso vedi **quinto**.

dodici ['doditʃi] ag inv, sm inv twelve; per uso vedi **cinque**.

dogana [do'gana] sf customs; (tassa) (customs) duty; **passare la ~** to go through customs; **pagare la ~ su** qc to pay duty on sth.

doganale [doga'nale] ag customs attr.

doganiere [doga'njɛre] sm customs officer.

doge ['dɔdʒe] sm doge.

doglie ['dɔʎʎe] sfpl (Med) labour pains; **avere le ~** to be in labour.

dogma, i ['dɔgma] sm dogma.

dogmatico, a, ci, che [dog'matiko] 1 ag dogmatic. 2 sm/f dogmatic person.

dolce ['doltʃe] 1 ag (a) (zuccherato, piacevole) sweet; (formaggio, clima) mild; (modi, carattere) gentle, mild; (suono, voce) soft; (ricordo) pleasant; (pendio) gentle; (decollo) smooth; (legno, carbone) soft; **cerca di essere più ~ con tua madre** try to be kinder to your mother, try to be a little more pleasant with your mother; **mi piace ~ il caffè** I like my coffee sweet; **nutriva la ~ speranza di rivederlo** she cherished the hope of seeing him again; **il ~ far niente** sweet idleness; **la ~ vita** the good life. (b) (Fonetica) soft.

2 sm (a) sweetness; **preferire il ~ al salato** to prefer sweet things to savoury ones; **mi piacciono i ~i** I like sweet things. (b) (Culin: portata) sweet, dessert; (: torta) cake.

dolcezza [dol'tʃettsa] sf (vedi ag a) sweetness; mildness; gentleness; softness; pleasantness; smoothness; **parlare con ~** to speak gently.

dolciario, a [dol'tʃarjo] ag confectionery attr.

dolciastro, a [dol'tʃastro] ag (sapore) sweetish; (: stucchevole) sickly sweet; (fig: tono) ingratiating.

dolcificante [doltʃifi'kante] 1 ag sweetening. 2 sm sweetener.

dolcificare [doltʃifi'kare] vt to sweeten.

dolciumi [dol'tʃumi] smpl sweets, confectionery sg.

dolente [do'lɛnte] ag (a) (dolorante: braccio, gamba) sore, painful; (: dente, testa) aching. (b) (addolorato: espressione) sorrowful, doleful; **essere ~ per qc** to be very sorry about sth, regret sth profoundly.

dolere [do'lere] 1 vi (aus essere) (dente) to ache; (gamba, schiena) to hurt; **mi duole la testa** my head aches, I've got a headache. 2 : ~rsi vr: ~rsi di (errore, cattiva azione) to regret; (peccato) to repent of.

dollaro ['dɔllaro] sm dollar.

dolo ['dɔlo] sm (a) (Dir) malice. (b) (frode) fraud, deceit.

Dolomiti [dolo'miti] sfpl: **le ~** the Dolomites.

dolorante [dolo'rante] ag aching, sore; **sono ancora ~** I still ache.

dolore [do'lore] sm (fisico) pain; (morale) distress, sorrow; **avere un ~ a** (al braccio, dito etc) to have a pain in; **ha dei ~i di testa** he suffers from headaches; **se lo scoprono sono ~i!** if they find out there'll be trouble!

doloroso, a [dolo'roso] ag (operazione) painful; (situazione) distressing; (notizia) sad.

doloso, a [do'loso] ag (Dir) malicious; **incendio ~** arson.

domanda [do'manda] sf (interrogazione) question; (richiesta): ~ (di) request (for); (: d'impiego, d'iscrizione) application (for); (Econ): **la ~** demand; **fare una ~ a qn** to ask sb a question; **fare ~ d'impiego** to apply for a job; **fare ~ all'autorità giudiziaria** to apply to the courts; **far regolare ~ (di qc)** to apply through the proper channels (for sth); **presentare una ~** to send in an application; **~ di divorzio** divorce petition; **~ di matrimonio** proposal.

domandare [doman'dare] 1 vt (a) (per sapere: ora, nome, strada) to ask; **~ qc a qn** to ask sb sth. (b) (per ottenere: informazione, consiglio, aiuto) to ask for; **~ qc a qn** to ask sb for sth; **~ il permesso di o per fare qc** to ask permission to do sth; **~ scusa a qn** to beg sb's pardon, say sorry to sb; **~ un favore a qn** to ask sb a favour, ask a favour of sb; **~ la parola** to ask leave o permission to speak.

2 vi: **~ di qn** (chiedere come sta) to ask after sb; (voler vedere o parlare a) to ask for sb; **c'è un signore che domanda di te** (al telefono) there's a gentleman asking to speak to you; (voler vedere) there's a gentleman asking to see o speak to you.

3: **~rsi** vr to wonder, ask o.s.; **mi domando e dico perché devo rimanere qua?** why on earth have I got to stay here?

domani [do'mani] 1 av tomorrow; **~ mattina** tomorrow morning; **~ l'altro** the day after tomorrow; **~ a mezzogiorno** at midday tomorrow; **~ a otto** tomorrow week, a week tomorrow; **a ~!** see you tomorrow! 2 sm (a) (l'indomani) next day, following day. (b) (fig: il futuro) future; **un ~** some day; **chi sa cosa ci riserva il ~** who knows what the future holds.

domare [do'mare] vt (belva) to tame; (cavallo) to break in; (fig: popolo, rivolta) to subdue; (: incendio) to control; (: passione) to master, control.

domatore, trice [doma'tore] sm/f (gen) tamer; **~ di leoni** lion tamer; **~ di cavalli** horsebreaker.

domattina [domat'tina] av tomorrow morning.

domenica, che [do'menika] sf Sunday; **ha messo il vestito della ~** he is dressed in his Sunday best; **la ~ di Pasqua** Easter Sunday; per uso vedi **martedì**.

domenicale [domeni'kale] ag Sunday attr.

domenicano, a [domeni'kano] ag, sm/f Dominican.

domestico, a, ci, che [do'mestiko] 1 ag (lavori) domestic, household attr; (vita) domestic, family attr; (Zool) domestic, domesticated; **le pareti ~che** one's own four walls. 2 sm/f (domestic) servant; **una ~a a ore** a daily (woman).

domiciliare [domitʃi'ljare] 1 ag domiciliary; **arresto ~** house arrest; **fare una perquisizione ~** to carry out a search of sb's house. 2: ~rsi vr to take up residence.

domicilio [domi'tʃiljo] sm (gen) residence; (Dir) domicile; (indirizzo) address; **cambiare ~** to change one's address; **visita a ~** (Med) house call; **'recapito a ~'** 'deliveries'; **violazione di ~** (Dir) breaking and entering.

dominante [domi'nante] ag (colore, nota) dominant; (opinione) prevailing; (idea) main attr, chief attr; (posizione) dominating attr; (classe, partito) ruling attr. 2 sf (Mus) dominant.

dominare [domi'nare] 1 vt (gen) to dominate; (governare) to rule; (situazione, alunni) to control; (passioni) to master; **la fortezza domina la pianura** the fortress has a commanding position overlooking the plain; **~ i mari** to rule the seas o waves; **è dominato dal padre** he is dominated by his father; **da lassù si domina uno stupendo panorama** there is a wonderful view from up there. 2 vi (a) (regnare): **~ (su)** to reign (over). (b)

dominatore *(primeggiare)*: ~ **su tutti per intelligenza** to excel over everyone in intelligence.

dominatore, trice [domina'tore] 1 *ag* ruling *attr.* 2 *sm/f* ruler.

dominazione [dominat'tsjone] *sf* domination.

dominio [do'minjo] *sm* **(a)** *(Pol: supremazia)* rule; *(: potere)* power; **esercitare il ~ su** to exercise power over; **~i coloniali** colonies; **il ~ indiscusso di un artista** an artist's undisputed sway *o* influence; **essere di ~ pubblico** *(notizia etc)* to be common knowledge. **(b)** *(controllo: gen)* control; *(: delle passioni, di una materia)* mastery; **~ di sé** self-control.

domino ['domino] *sm inv* *(gioco)* dominoes *sg*.

don [don] *sm* *(sacerdote)* Father; *(titolo spagnolo o meridionale)* Don.

donare [do'nare] 1 *vt* *(gen)* to give; *(organo)* to donate; **~ sangue** to give blood; **~ qc a qn** to give sb sth; **~ tutto se stesso a qn** to dedicate o.s. to sb; **~ la vita per** to give one's life for. 2 *vi* *(abito, colore)*: **~ a** to suit, become.

donatore, trice [dona'tore] *sm/f* *(gen)* giver; *(Med)* donor; **~ di sangue** blood donor.

donazione [donat'tsjone] *sf* donation; **atto di ~** *(Dir)* deed of gift.

donde |'donde] *av* *(poet)* whence.

dondolare [dondo'lare] 1 *vt* *(sedia)* to rock; *(ciondolare: corda, gambe)* to dangle. 2 *vi* *(barca)* to rock, sway; *(altalena)* to sway; *(corda, lampadario)* to swing (to and fro). 3: **~rsi** *vr* *(su sedia)* to rock (backwards and forwards); *(su altalena)* to swing (backwards and forwards).

dondolio [dondo'lio] *sm* (gentle) rocking.

dondolo ['dondolo] *sm*: **cavallo/sedia a ~** rocking horse/chair.

dongiovanni [dondʒo'vanni] *sm* Don Juan, ladies' man.

donna ['donna] *sf* **(a)** woman; **da ~** *(abito)* woman's, lady's; **~ di casa** housewife; **~ (di servizio)** maid; **~ a ore** daily (help *o* woman); **~ delle pulizie** cleaning lady, cleaner; **~ di vita** *o* **di strada** prostitute, streetwalker; **figlio di buona ~!** *(fam)* son of a bitch! **(b)** *(titolo)* Donna. **(c)** *(Carte)* queen.

donnaiolo [donna'jolo] *sm* philanderer, lady-killer.

donnola ['donnola] *sf* weasel.

dono ['dono] *sm* **(a)** *(regalo)* gift, present; *(donazione)* donation; **fare un ~ a qn** to give sb a present; **portare qc in ~ a qn** to bring sth as a gift *o* present for sb. **(b)** *(dote)* gift, talent; **un ~ di natura** a natural gift *o* talent; **il ~ della parola** the gift of speech.

dopo ['dopo] 1 *av* **(a)** *(in seguito)* afterwards, after; *(poi)* then; *(più tardi)* later; **il giorno ~** the next *o* following day; **un anno ~** a year later; **parecchio/poco (tempo) ~** long/shortly after(wards); **prima studia, ~ usciremo** do your studying first then we'll go out, do your studying first and we'll go out afterwards; **prima pensa e ~ parla** think before you speak; **è accaduto 2 mesi ~** it happened 2 months later; **ci vediamo ~** see you later; **ho rimandato tutto a ~** I've postponed everything till later.

(b) *(oltre)* after, next; **ecco la chiesa — la mia casa è subito ~** there's the church — my house is just beyond *o* past it; **non questa strada, quella ~** not this street but the next one.

2 *prep* *(gen)* after; **~ un anno** after a year, a year later; **~ le vacanze** after the holidays; **rimandare qc a ~ Natale** to postpone sth till after Christmas; **è arrivato ~ cena/di me** he arrived after supper/me; **non l'ho più sentito ~ la sua partenza** I haven't heard from him again since he left; **uno ~ l'altro** one after the other; **è subito ~ la chiesa** it's just after *o* past the church; **come sarà il ~ Berlinguer?** what will things be like after Berlinguer?; **~ tutto** = **dopotutto**.

3 *cong* *(temporale)*: **~ mangiato va a dormire** after eating *o* after a meal he has a sleep; **~ aver mangiato è uscito** after having eaten *o* after eating he went out; **~ che è partito** after he left; **~ tutto ciò che gli ho detto** after all I have said to him; **~ che** = **dopoché**.

dopobarba [dopo'barba] *sm inv* after-shave.

dopoché [dopo'ke] *cong* after, when.

dopodiché [dopodi'ke] *av* after which.

dopodomani [dopodo'mani] *av, sm* the day after tomorrow.

dopoguerra [dopo'gwɛrra] *sm inv* post-war period.

dopolavoro [dopola'voro] *sm* recreational club.

dopopranzo [dopo'prandzo] *sm inv* afternoon.

doposci [dopoʃ'ʃi] *sm inv*: **i ~** *(stivali)* après-ski boots.

doposcuola [dopos'kwɔla] *sm inv* supervised study and recreation after school hours.

dopotutto [dopo'tutto] *av* after all.

doppiaggio [dop'pjaddʒo] *sm* *(Cine)* dubbing.

doppiare[1] [dop'pjare] *vt* **(a)** *(Sport)* to lap. **(b)** *(Naut)* to round.

doppiare[2] [dop'pjare] *vt* *(Cine)* to dub.

doppiatore, trice [doppja'tore] *sm/f* dubber.

doppietta [dop'pjetta] *sf* **(a)** *(fucile)* double-barrelled shotgun; *(sparo)* shot from both barrels. **(b)** *(Calcio)* double; *(Pugilato)* one-two. **(c)** *(Aut)* double-declutch.

doppiezza [dop'pjettsa] *sf* *(fig: di persona)* duplicity, double-dealing.

doppio, a ['doppjo] 1 *ag* *(gen)* double; *(vantaggio)* double, twofold; *(fig: persona)* deceitful; **battere una lettera in ~a copia** to type a letter with a carbon copy; **chiudere a ~a mandata** to double-lock; **un utensile a ~ uso** a dual-purpose utensil; **fare il ~ gioco** *(fig)* to play a double game; **~ senso** double entendre; **frase a ~ senso** sentence with a double meaning.

2 *sm* **(a)**: **pagare il ~** to pay twice as much *o* double the amount; **10 è il ~ di 5** 10 is twice *o* two times 5. **(b)** *(Sport: tennis)* doubles (match); **facciamo un ~** let's have a game of doubles. **(c)** *(attore)* understudy.

3 *av* *(anche fig)*: **vedere** *o* **vederci ~** to see double.

doppiofondo [doppjo'fondo] *sm* *(di valigia)* false bottom; *(Naut)* double hull.

doppione [dop'pjone] *sm* duplicate.

doppiopetto [doppjo'pɛtto] *sm inv* *(anche:* **giacca ~)** double-breasted jacket.

doppista, i, e [dop'pista] *sm/f* *(tennis)* doubles player.

dorare [do'rare] *vt* *(oggetto)* to gild; *(metallo)* to gold-plate; *(Culin: arrosto)* to brown; **~ la pillola** *(fig)* to sugar the pill.

dorato, a [do'rato] *ag* *(oggetto)* gilt, gilded; *(abbronzatura, giallo)* golden.

doratura [dora'tura] *sf* **(a)** *(vedi vb)* gilding; gold-plating; browning. **(b)** *(ornamento)* gilt.

dormicchiare [dormik'kjare] *vi* to doze.

dormiente [dor'mjɛnte] 1 *ag* sleeping. 2 *sm/f* sleeper.

dormiglione, a [dormiʎ'ʎone] *sm/f* sleepyhead.

dormire [dor'mire] 1 *vi* **(a)** to sleep; *(essere addormentato)* to be asleep, be sleeping; **vado a ~** I'm going to bed; **il caffè non mi fa ~** coffee keeps me awake; **sono pensieri che non mi fanno ~** I'm losing sleep thinking about all this; **i campi**

dormono sotto la neve the fields lie dormant under the snow. **(b)** *(fraseologia):* ~ **come un ghiro** to sleep like a log; ~ **della grossa** to sleep soundly, be dead to the world; ~ **con gli occhi aperti** *(fig)* to sleep with one eye open; ~ **in piedi** *(essere stanco)* to be asleep on one's feet; *(essere imbambolato):* **dormi in piedi!** you're half asleep!; ~ **tranquillo** *o* **tra due guanciali** *(senza preoccupazioni)* to rest easy; **è meglio dormirci sopra** it's best to sleep on it.

2 *vt* *(fig):* ~ **sonni tranquilli/agitati** to have a good/bad night's sleep, sleep well/badly; ~ **il sonno del giusto** to sleep the sleep of the just; ~ **il sonno eterno** to sleep the sleep of the dead.

dormita [dor'mita] *sf* sleep; **fare una bella** ~ to have a good sleep.

dormitorio [dormi'tɔrjo] **1** *sm (gen)* dormitory; ~ **pubblico** doss-house *(run by local authority).* **2** *ag inv:* **città** ~ dormitory town.

dormiveglia [dormi've ʎ ʎ a] *sm:* **essere in uno stato di** ~ to be half-asleep, be drowsy; **nel** ~ **ha sentito un rumore** he was half-asleep when he heard a noise.

dorsale [dor'sale] **1** *ag* dorsal; **spina** ~ backbone, spine. **2** *sm (di sedia)* back. **3** *sf (catena montuosa)* ridge.

dorsista, i, e [dor'sista] *sm/f (Nuoto)* backstroke swimmer.

dorso ['dɔrso] *sm* **(a)** *(gen)* back; *(di libro)* spine; *(di monte)* ridge; **a** ~ **di cavallo** on horseback; **a** ~ **d'asino** *(ponte)* humpback. **(b)** *(Nuoto)* backstroke.

dosaggio [do'zaddʒo] *sm (atto)* measuring out; **sbagliare il** ~ to get the proportions wrong.

dosare [do'zare] *vt (ingredienti)* to measure out; *(Med)* to dose; *(fig: forze, risorse)* to husband; **saper** ~ **le proprie forze** to know how much effort to expend.

dose ['dɔze] *sf (Med)* dose; *(di farina, zucchero)* amount, quantity; *(di whisky, vodka etc)* measure; **ha avuto la sua** ~ **di preoccupazioni** he's had his fair share of worries; **ci vuole una buona** ~ **di coraggio** it takes a lot of courage.

dossier [do'sje] *sm inv* dossier, file.

dosso ['dɔsso] *sm* **(a)** *(rilievo)* rise; *(: di strada)* bump. **(b):** **levarsi i vestiti di** ~ to take one's clothes off; **levarsi un peso di** ~ *(fig)* to take a weight off one's mind; **in** ~ = **indosso; a** ~ = **addosso.**

dotare [do'tare] *vt:* ~ **di** *(attrezzature)* to equip with; *(fig: qualità)* to endow with.

dotato, a [do'tato] *ag:* ~ **di** *(attrezzature)* equipped with; *(bellezza, intelligenza)* endowed with; **un uomo** ~ a gifted man.

dotazione [dotat'tsjone] *sf* **(a)** *(gen, Mil, Naut)* equipment; **dare qc in** ~ **a qn** to issue sth with sth, issue sth to sb; **avere in** ~ **una somma** to be supplied with a sum; **i macchinari in** ~ **alla fabbrica** the machinery in use in the factory. **(b)** *(rendita)* endowment.

dote ['dɔte] *sf (di sposa)* dowry; *(Fin)* endowment; *(fig)* gift, talent; **portare qc in** ~ to bring a dowry of sth; **avere** ~**i naturali per** to have a natural talent for.

Dott. *abbr (= dottore)* Dr.

dotto[1], a [a ['dotto] **1** *ag (persona)* erudite, learned; *(citazione)* learned; **lingue** ~**e** classical languages. **2** *sm/f* scholar.

dotto[2] ['dotto] *sm (Anat)* duct.

dottorale [dotto'rale] *ag* doctoral; *(iro: tono)* pedantic.

dottorato [dotto'rato] *sm* doctorate.

dottore, essa [dot'tore] *sm/f* **(a)** *(laureato)* graduate. **(b)** *(medico)* doctor; **andare dal** ~ to go to the doctor's. **(c)** *(studioso)* scholar.

dottrina [dot'trina] *sf (Filosofia, Rel)* doctrine; *(cultura)* learning, erudition.

dottrinale [dottri'nale] *ag* doctrinal.

dottrinario, a [dottri'narjo] **1** *ag* doctrinaire. **2** *sm/f* doctrinarian.

Dott.ssa *abbr (= dottoressa)* Dr.

double-face ['dublə'fas] *ag inv* reversible.

dove ['dove] **1** *av (gen)* where; *(in cui)* where, in which; *(dovunque)* wherever; ~ **vivi?** where do you live?; **di** ~ **sei?** where are you from?, where do you come from?; **non so da** ~ **iniziare** I don't know where to begin; **da** ~ **è entrato?** where did he get in?; **la città** ~ **abito** the city where I live *o* in which I live; **da** ~ **abito vedo...** from where I live I can see...; **per** *o* **da** ~ **sei passato?** which way did you go?; **siediti** ~ **vuoi** sit wherever you like; **ti do una mano fin** ~ **posso** I'll help you as much as I can; **(fin)** ~ **è arrivato con il programma?** how far has he got with the programme?

2 *cong* **(a)** *(mentre):* **mi sono beccato la colpa** ~ **invece era sua** I got the blame whereas it was really his fault. **(b)** *(allorquando):* **e** ~ **non vi piacesse fate come volete** and if you are not happy about it do as you wish.

3 *sm* where; **gente arrivava da ogni** ~ people were arriving from all over; **per ogni** ~ everywhere.

dovere [do'vere] **1** *vt (soldi, riconoscenza)* to owe; **gli devo il mio successo** I owe my success to him, I have him to thank for my success; **devo tutto ai miei genitori** I owe my parents everything, I am indebted to my parents for everything; **crede che tutto gli sia dovuto** he thinks he has a god-given right to everything.

2 *vb aus (nei tempi composti prende l'ausiliare del verbo che accompagna)* **(a)** *(obbligo)* to have to; **avrebbe dovuto farlo** he should have *o* ought to have done it; **devo farlo subito?** do I have to *o* have I got to do it immediately?; **non devi fare rumore** you mustn't *o* you're not to make a noise; **non devi zuccherarlo** *(non è necessario)* you needn't *o* don't have to add sugar; **come si deve** *(bene)* properly; *(meritatamente)* properly, as he *(o she etc)* deserves; **è una persona come si deve** he is a very proper person.

(b) *(fatalità):* **doveva accadere** it was bound to happen; **non doveva esserne informato che il giorno dopo** she was not to hear about it until the following day; **dovesse morire lo farebbe** he would do it even though he were to die in the attempt; **tutti dobbiamo morire** we all have to die.

(c) *(previsione):* **deve arrivare alle 10** he should *o* is due to arrive at 10; **sembra che le cose si debbano sistemare** things seem to be sorting themselves out.

(d) *(probabilità):* **deve essere difficile farlo** it must be difficult to do; **non deve essere uno stupido** he can't be stupid; **devono essere le 4** it must be 4 o'clock; **devo averlo fatto** I must have done it.

3 *sm (obbligo)* duty; **avere il senso del** ~ to have a sense of duty; **farsi un** ~ **di qc** to make sth one's duty; **fare il proprio** ~ **di elettore** to do one's duty as a voter; **rivolgersi a chi di** ~ to apply to the appropriate authority *o* person; **a** ~ *(bene)* properly; *(debitamente)* as he *(o she etc)* deserves.

doveroso, a [dove'roso] *ag (ubbidienza)* dutiful;

(rispetto) due; è ~ **avvertirlo** we *(o you etc)* have to warn him.

dovunque [do'vunkwe] *av* **(a)** *(in qualsiasi luogo)* wherever; ~ **vada** wherever I go; ~ **tu sia** wherever you are. **(b)** *(dappertutto)* everywhere; **si trovano** ~ they can be found everywhere; **c'erano libri un po'** ~ there were books all over the place.

dovutamente [dovuta'mente] *av* *(debitamente: redigere, compilare)* correctly; *(: rimproverare)* as he *(o she etc)* deserves.

dovuto, a [do'vuto] **1** *ag (denaro)* owing, owed; *(rispetto)* due; è ~ **al temporale** it's due to the storm, it's because of the storm; **nel modo** ~ in the proper way. **2** *sm* due; **mi hanno pagato più del** ~ they paid me more than my due; **ho lavorato più del** ~ I worked more than was necessary.

dozzina [dod'dzina] *sf* dozen; **c'erano persone/libri a** ~**e** there were dozens of people/books; **di** *o* **da** ~ *(scrittore, spettacolo)* second-rate.

dozzinale [doddzi'nale] *ag* cheap, shoddy.

draga, ghe ['draga] *sf* dredger.

dragaggio [dra'gaddʒo] *sm* dredging.

dragare [dra'gare] *vt* to dredge; ~ **il mare** *(per mine)* to sweep the sea.

drago, ghi ['drago] *sm* dragon; **in inglese è un** ~ *(fig fam)* he's a genius at English.

dramma, i ['dramma] *sm* **(a)** *(Teatro)* drama. **(b)** *(fig: vicenda tragica)* drama, tragedy; **fare un** ~ **di qc** to make a drama out of sth.

drammaticità [drammatitʃi'ta] *sf (Teatro)* dramatic force; *(fig: di situazione)* drama.

drammatico, a, ci, che [dram'matiko] *ag* dramatic.

drammatizzare [drammatid'dzare] *vt* to dramatize.

drammaturgia [drammatur'dʒia] *sf* drama.

drammaturgo, a, ghi, ghe [dramma'turgo] *sm/f* dramatist, playwright.

drappeggiare [drapped'dʒare] **1** *vt* to drape. **2**: ~**rsi** *vr* to drape o.s.

drappeggio [drap'peddʒo] *sm (tessuto)* drapery; *(di abito)* folds.

drappello [drap'pello] *sm (Mil)* squad, platoon.

drappo ['drappo] *sm* cloth.

drastico, a, ci, che ['drastiko] *ag* drastic.

drenaggio [dre'naddʒo] *sm* drainage.

drenare [dre'nare] *vt* to drain.

dribblare [drib'blare] *(Calcio)* **1** *vi* to dribble. **2** *vt (avversario)* to avoid, dodge.

dritta ['dritta] *sf (destra)* right, right hand; *(Naut)* starboard; **a** ~ **e a manca** *(fig)* on all sides, right, left and centre.

dritto, a ['dritto] **1** *ag* **(a)** = **diritto**[1]. **(b)** *(fam: scaltro: persona)* sharp, crafty. **2** *sm* = **diritto**[1]. **3** *sm/f (fam: furbo)*: **è un** ~ he's a crafty *o* sly one. **4** *av* = **diritto**[1].

drittofilo [dritto'filo] *sm inv (di tessuto)* grain; **tagliare in** ~ to cut on the grain.

drizzare [drit'tsare] **1** *vt (palo, quadro)* to straighten; *(innalzare: antenna, muro)* to erect; ~ **le orecchie** to prick up one's ears. **2**: ~**rsi** *vr*: ~**rsi in piedi** to rise to one's feet; ~**rsi a sedere** to sit up.

droga, ghe ['drɔga] *sf* **(a)** *(spezia)* spice. **(b)** *(stupefacente)* drug; **la** ~ drugs *pl*; **spacciare la** ~ to peddle drugs; **prendere la** ~ to take *o* be on drugs; ~**ghe pesanti** hard drugs.

drogare [dro'gare] **1** *vt* **(a)** *(Culin)* to season, spice. **(b)** *(persona, animale)* to drug, dope; **questa bevanda è drogata** this drink has been doped. **2**: ~**rsi** *vr* to take drugs, be on drugs.

drogato, a [dro'gato] *sm/f* drug addict.

drogheria [droge'ria] *sf* grocer's (shop).

droghiere, a [dro'gjɛre] *sm/f* grocer.

dromedario [drome'darjo] *sm* dromedary.

dualismo [dua'lizmo] *sm (Filosofia)* dualism; *(fig: contrasto)* conflict.

dubbio, a ['dubbjo] **1** *ag* **(a)** *(incerto: gen)* doubtful; *(: tempo, avvenire)* uncertain. **(b)** *(equivoco, discutibile: qualità, gusto)* dubious, questionable. **2** *sm* doubt; **mettere in** ~ to doubt, question; **avere il** ~ **che** to suspect (that); **essere in** ~ *(risultato)* to be doubtful *o* uncertain; **sono in** ~ **se partire o no** I don't know whether to go or not; **essere in** ~ **fra** to hesitate between; **nutrire seri** ~**i su qc** to have grave doubts about sth; **senza** ~ doubtless, no doubt; **senza alcun** ~ without a doubt; **esprimere un** ~ **su** to express (one's) doubts about.

dubbioso, a [dub'bjoso] *ag* **(a)** *(esitante)* hesitant, uncertain; *(perplesso: persona)* uncertain; *(: sguardo, aria)* puzzled; **essere** ~ **su qc** to be uncertain about sth, question the truth of sth. **(b)** *(incerto: esito, successo)* uncertain; *(: abilità)* questionable, dubious.

dubitare [dubi'tare] *vi*: ~ **di** *(onestà)* to doubt, have (one's) doubts as to; *(autenticità)* to question; *(riuscita)* to be doubtful of; ~ **di** sb to mistrust sb; **dubito che venga** I doubt if *o* whether he'll come; **non dubito che verrà** I have no doubt that he'll come, I'm sure he'll come; ~ **di sé** to be unsure of o.s.

duca, chi ['duka] *sm* duke.

ducale [du'kale] *ag* ducal.

ducato[1] [du'kato] *sm (titolo)* dukedom; *(territorio)* duchy, dukedom.

ducato[2] [du'kato] *sm (moneta)* ducat.

duce ['dutʃe] *sm (Storia)* captain; *(: del fascismo)* duce.

duchessa [du'kessa] *sf* duchess.

due ['due] **1** *ag inv* **(a)** two; ~ **volte** twice; **a** ~ **a** ~ two at a time, two by two. **(b)** *(fig: pochi)* a couple, a few; **dire** ~ **parole** to say a few words; **starò via** ~ **o tre giorni** I'll be away for two or three days; **ci metto** ~ **minuti** I'll have it done in a tick *o* jiffy. **2** *sm inv* two; *per uso vedi* **cinque**.

duecentesco, a, schi, sche [duetʃen'tesko] *ag* thirteenth century.

duecento [due'tʃɛnto] **1** *ag inv* two hundred. **2** *sm inv* two hundred; *(secolo)*: **il D**~ the thirteenth century.

duellante [duel'lante] *sm* duellist.

duellare [duel'lare] *vi* to fight a duel.

duello [du'ello] *sm duel;* **sfidare a** ~ to challenge to a duel; **disputare un** ~ to fight a duel.

duemila [due'mila] **1** *ag inv* two thousand. **2** *sm inv* two thousand; **il** ~ the year two thousand.

duepezzi, due pezzi [due'pettsi] *sm inv (da bagno)* bikini; *(abito)* two piece (suit).

duetto [du'etto] *sm (Mus)* duet.

duna ['duna] *sf* dune.

dunque ['dunkwe] **1** *cong (perciò)* therefore, so; *(allora)* well (now); **fallo** ~! do it then! **2** *sm inv*: **venire al** ~ to come to the point.

duo ['duo] *sm inv (Mus)* duet; *(Teatro, Cine, fig)* duo; **formano un** ~ **ben assortito** they're a well-matched pair *o* couple.

duodeno [duo'dɛno] *sm* duodenum.

duomo[1] ['dwɔmo] *sm* cathedral.

duomo[2] ['dwɔmo] *sm (Tecn)* dome.

duplex ['dupleks] *sm inv (Telec)* party line.

duplicare [dupli'kare] *vt* to duplicate.

duplicato [dupli'kato] *sm* duplicate.

duplicatore [duplika'tore] *sm* duplicator.

duplicazione [duplikat'tsjone] *sf* duplication.

duplice ['duplitʃe] *ag (gen)* double; *(incarico, scopo)* dual; **in ~ copia** in duplicate; **il problema ha un ~ aspetto** the problem is two-fold.

duplicità [dupliʃi'ta] *sf (fig)* duplicity.

durante [du'rante] *prep (nel corso di)* during, in the course of; *(per tutta la durata di)* throughout, for; **~ la notte** during the night; **~ l'intera giornata** throughout the day, for the entire day; **vita natural ~** for life.

durare [du'rare] **1** *vi (gen)* to last; **la festa durò tutta la notte** the party went on *o* lasted all night; **lo stipendio ti deve ~ tutto il mese** your salary will have to last you the month; **non può ~!** this can't go on any longer!; **questa storia dura da un pezzo** this business has been going on for a while; **~ in carica** to remain in office. **2** *vt:* **~ fatica a fare qc** to have a hard job doing sth, have difficulty in doing sth.

durata [du'rata] *sf (gen)* duration, length; *(di prodotto, pianta)* life; **per tutta la ~ di** throughout; **di breve ~** *(vacanza)* short; *(felicità)* short-lived; **di lunga ~** long-lasting; **~ media della vita** life expectancy.

duraturo, a [dura'turo] *ag* lasting.

durevole [du'revole] *ag (ricordo)* lasting; *(materiale)* durable.

durezza [du'rettsa] *sf (gen)* hardness; *(di spazzola)* stiffness; *(fig: di carattere)* severity; *(: di invasori)* harshness; *(: di clima)* rigidity, severity.

duro, a ['duro] **1** *ag* **(a)** *(resistente: gen)* hard; *(: serratura)* stiff; *(: carne)* tough; **~ d'orecchi** *(sordo)* hard of hearing; **~ di comprendonio** *o* **di testa** slow-witted; **avere la pelle ~a** *(fig: persona)* to be tough; **cappello ~** *(bombetta)* bowler (hat). **(b)** *(fig: severo: persona)* harsh, hard; *(: disciplina)* harsh, strict; *(: atteggiamento)* harsh, unbending; *(: clima)* severe, rigid; *(: inverno)* hard; **~ di cuore** hard-hearted. **(c)** *(ostinato)* stubborn, obstinate.

2 *sm* **(a)** *(di oggetto, pane)* hardness. **(b)** *(fig: difficoltà)* hard part; **il ~ deve ancora venire** the hard part is still to come.

3 *sm/f (persona)* tough one; **fare il ~** to act tough.

4 *av:* **tener ~** *(resistere)* to stand firm, hold out.

duttile ['duttile] *ag (sostanza)* malleable; *(fig: carattere)* docile, biddable; *(: stile)* adaptable.

E

E, e¹ [e] *sf o m inv (lettera)* E, e.

e² [e] *cong (spesso* **ed** *dav a vocale)* **(a)** and; **un metro** ~ **novanta** one metre ninety; **ho speso settemila** ~ **duecento lire** I spent seven thousand two hundred lire; **tutt'**~ **tre** all three of them; **tutt'**~ **due** both of them; **è bell'**~ **fatto** it's well and truly finished; **mi piace molto,** ~ **a te?** I like it a lot, what about you?
(b) *(avversativo)* but; *(eppure)* and yet; **lo credevo onesto** ~ **non lo è** I thought he was honest but he isn't; **sapeva di sbagliare,** ~ **l'ha fatto ugualmente** he knew he was in the wrong and yet he did it anyway.
(c) *(ebbene)* well, well then; ~ **deciditi dunque!** well make up your mind then!; ~ **smettila!** stop it!

E. *abbr (= est)* E.

ebanista, i [eba'nista] *sm* cabinet-maker.

ebanisteria [ebaniste'ria] *sf (arte)* cabinet-making; *(negozio)* cabinet-maker's shop.

ebano ['ɛbano] *sm* ebony.

ebbene [eb'bɛne] *cong* well (then).

ebbrezza [eb'brettsa] *sf* intoxication, inebriation; **in stato di** ~ drunk, inebriated; **l'**~ **del successo** *(fig)* the thrill o exhilaration of success.

ebbro, a ['ɛbbro] *ag* intoxicated, inebriated; ~ **di gioia** beside o.s. with joy.

ebdomadario, a [ebdoma'darjo] *ag, sm* weekly.

ebetaggine [ebe'taddʒine] *sf* stupidity.

ebete ['ɛbete] **1** *ag* idiotic. **2** *sm/f* idiot, half-wit.

ebetismo [ebe'tizmo] *sm* stupidity.

ebollizione [ebollit'tsjone] *sf:* **in** ~ boiling; **punto di** ~ boiling point; **portare ad** ~ to bring to the boil.

ebraico, a, ci, che [e'braiko] **1** *ag* Hebrew, Hebraic. **2** *sm (lingua)* Hebrew.

ebreo, a [e'brɛo] **1** *ag* Jewish. **2** *sm/f* Jew/Jewess.

eburneo, a [e'burneo] *ag* ivory *attr.*

ecatombe [eka'tombe] *sf (strage)* slaughter, massacre.

ecc. *abbr (= eccetera)* etc.

eccedente [ettʃe'dɛnte] *sm* surplus, excess.

eccedenza [ettʃe'dɛntsa] *sf* surplus, excess; **un'**~ **di peso** some excess weight.

eccedere [et'tʃɛdere] **1** *vt (competenza, limiti)* to overstep, exceed; *(aspettative)* to go beyond, exceed. **2** *vi* to go too far; ~ **nel mangiare** to overeat, eat too much; ~ **nel bere** to drink too much.

eccellente [ettʃel'lɛnte] *ag* excellent.

eccellenza [ettʃel'lɛntsa] *sf* **(a)** excellence; **per** ~ par excellence. **(b): Sua E**~ His Excellency.

eccellere [et'tʃɛllere] *vi* to excel; ~ **in tutto** to excel at everything; ~ **su tutti** to surpass everyone.

eccelso, a [et'tʃɛlso] **1** *ag (cima, montagna)* high; *(fig: ingegno)* great, exceptional. **2** *sm:* **l'E**~ *(Rel)* the Almighty.

eccentricità [ettʃentritʃi'ta] *sf inv* eccentricity.

eccentrico, a, ci, che [et'tʃentriko] **1** *ag (persona, Mat)* eccentric. **2** *sm (Tecn)* cam.

eccepibile [ettʃe'pibile] *ag (argomento, decisione)* questionable.

eccepire [ettʃe'pire] *vt:* ~ **che** to object that; **non avere niente da** ~ to have no objections.

eccessivo, a [ettʃes'sivo] *ag* excessive.

eccesso [et'tʃɛsso] *sm* **(a)** *(di denaro)* excess, surplus; *(di merce)* surplus, glut; **una cifra arrotondata per** ~ a figure which has been rounded up. **(b)** *(esagerazione)* excess; **gentile fino all'**~ excessively kind, kind to a fault; ~ **di velocità** *(Aut)* speeding; ~ **di zelo** overzealousness; **dare in** ~i to fly off the handle.

eccetera [et'tʃɛtera] *av* et cetera, and so on.

eccetto [et'tʃɛtto] **1** *prep* except, apart from. **2:** ~ **che** *cong:* ~ **che (non)** unless.

eccettuare [ettʃettu'are] *vt* to except; **se si eccettua questo** this apart, apart from o other than this; **eccettuati i presenti** present company excepted.

eccezionale [ettʃettsjo'nale] *ag* exceptional; **in via del tutto** ~ in this instance, exceptionally.

eccezione [ettʃet'tsjone] *sf* **(a)** exception; **d'**~ *(provvedimento)* exceptional, special; *(ospite)* special; **a** ~ o **con l'**~ **di** except for, with the exception of; **l'**~ **che conferma la regola** the exception which proves the rule; **fare un'**~ **alla regola** to make an exception to the rule. **(b)** *(Dir: obiezione)* objection.

ecchimosi [ek'kimozi] *sf inv* bruise, ecchymosis *(T).*

eccidio [et'tʃidjo] *sm* massacre.

eccipiente [ettʃi'pjɛnte] *sm (Med)* excipient.

eccitabile [ettʃi'tabile] *ag* excitable.

eccitante [ettʃi'tante] **1** *ag (gen)* exciting; *(sostanza)* stimulating. **2** *sm* stimulant.

eccitare [ettʃi'tare] *vt* **(a)** *(persona)* to arouse; *(sensi)* to arouse, excite; *(fantasia)* to stir; *(folla)* to incite. **(b)** *(innervosire)* to excite; **il caffè eccita** coffee acts as a stimulant. **2:** ~**rsi** *vr (sessualmente)* to become aroused; *(entusiasmarsi)* to get excited; *(innervosirsi)* to get worked up; *(irritarsi)* to get angry.

eccitazione [ettʃitat'tsjone] *sf (gen)* excitement; *(del sistema nervoso)* stimulation; *(Elettr)* excitation.

ecclesiastico, a, ci, che [ekkle'zjastiko] **1** *ag* ecclesiastical. **2** *sm* ecclesiastic.

ecco ['ɛkko] *av:* ~ **qui/là** here/there it is; ~ **i nostri amici** here are our friends; ~ **il treno** here is o here comes the train; ~**!** **(prendi)** here you are!; ~**mi** here I am; ~**ne due** here are two of them; ~ **perché** that's why; **ed** ~ **che sul più bello...** and just at that moment...; ~ **fatto** there, that's that done.

eccome [ek'kome] *av* rather; **ti piace?** —~**!** do you like it? — I'll say! o and how! o rather!; **lo so** ~**!** and don't I know it!

echeggiare [eked'dʒare] *vi* to echo; ~ **di** to echo o resound with.

eclettico, a, ci, che [e'klɛttiko] *ag, sm/f* eclectic.

eclettismo [eklet'tizmo] *sm* eclecticism.

eclissare [eklis'sare] **1** vt to eclipse; (fig) to eclipse, overshadow. **2**: ~**rsi** vr (persona: scherz) to slip away.

eclissi [e'klissi] sf inv eclipse.

eco ['ɛko] sm o f (pl(m) **echi**) echo; **fare** ~ **a qc/qn** to echo sth/sb; **suscitò** o **ebbe una profonda** ~ it caused quite a stir.

ecografia [ekogra'fia] sf (Med) ultrasound.

ecologia [ekolo'dʒia] sf ecology.

ecologico, a, ci, che [eko'lɔdʒiko] ag ecological.

ecologo, a, gi, ghe [e'kɔlogo] sm/f ecologist.

economato [ekono'mato] sm (Scol, Univ) bursar's office.

econometria [ekonome'tria] sf econometrics sg.

economia [ekono'mia] sf **(a)** (scienza) economics sg; (di paese, nazione) economy; ~ **politica** (Univ) political economy. **(b)** (risparmio) economy, thrift; **dobbiamo fare** ~ we must economize o make economies; **vivere in** ~ to live frugally; **costruito in** ~ built on the cheap.

economico, a, ci, che [eko'nɔmiko] ag (Econ) economic; (che costa poco) economical; **edizione** ~**a** economy edition.

economista, i, e [ekono'mista] sm/f economist.

economizzare [ekonomid'dzare] **1** vt (soldi, forze) to save. **2** vi: ~ (**su**) to economize (on), cut down (on).

economo, a [e'kɔnomo] **1** ag thrifty. **2** sm/f (Amm) bursar.

ecosistema, i [ekosis'tɛma] sm ecosystem.

ectoplasma [ekto'plazma] sm ectoplasm.

ecumenico, a, ci, che [eku'mɛniko] ag ecumenical.

ecumenismo [ekume'nizmo] sm ecumenicalism.

eczema [ek'dzɛma] sm eczema.

ed [ed] cong vedi **e**.

Eden ['eden] sm: **l'**~ Eden.

edera ['edera] sf ivy.

edicola [e'dikola] sf newspaper kiosk, newsstand; (che vende libri) bookstall.

edicolante [ediko'lante] sm/f news vendor (in kiosk).

edificante [edifi'kante] ag edifying; **è uno spettacolo poco** ~ it isn't a very edifying sight.

edificare [edifi'kare] vt (casa) to build, erect; (fig: moralmente) to edify.

edificazione [edifikat'tsjone] sf erection; (morale) edification.

edificio [edi'fitʃo] sm (costruzione) building; (struttura: sociale) structure, fabric; (: filosofico, critico) structure, framework.

edile [e'dile] **1** ag building attr, construction attr; **impresa** ~ building firm. **2** sm construction worker.

edilizia [edi'littsja] sf building (trade).

edilizio, a [edi'littsjo] ag building attr.

Edimburgo [edim'burgo] sf Edinburgh.

edito, a ['ɛdito] ag published.

editore[1], trice [edi'tore] **1** ag publishing attr. **2** sm/f publisher.

editore[2], trice [edi'tore] sm/f (chi cura la pubblicazione) editor.

editoria [edito'ria] sf publishing (trade).

editoriale [edito'rjale] **1** ag publishing attr. **2** sm (articolo di fondo) leader, editorial.

editorialista, i, e [editorja'lista] sm/f leader writer.

editto [e'ditto] sm edict.

edizione [edit'tsjone] sf **(a)** (di libro) edition; ~ **a tiratura limitata** limited edition. **(b)**: **la quarantesima** ~ **della Fiera di Milano** the fortieth Milan Trade Fair.

edonismo [edo'nizmo] sm hedonism.

edonista, i, e [edo'nista] sm/f hedonist.

edonistico, a, ci, che [edo'nistiko] ag hedonistic.

edotto, a [e'dɔtto] ag informed; **rendere qn** ~ **su qc** to inform sb about sth.

educanda [edu'kanda] sf boarder.

educare [edu'kare] vt (gen) to educate; (allevare) to bring up; (gusto, mente) to train; ~ **qn a rispettare qc** to bring sb up to respect sth.

educativo, a [eduka'tivo] ag educational.

educato, a [edu'kato] ag well-mannered, polite; **non è** ~ **fare così** it's not polite o good manners to do that.

educatore, trice [eduka'tore] sm/f educator; (pedagogista) educationalist.

educazione [edukat'tsjone] sf **(a)** (istruzione) education; (familiare) upbringing; ~ **fisica** physical education o training. **(b)** (comportamento) manners pl; **per** ~ out of politeness; **buona/cattiva** ~ good/bad manners; **questa è pura mancanza d'**~! this is sheer bad manners!

efelide [e'felide] sf freckle.

effeminatezza [effemina'tettsa] sf effeminacy.

effeminato, a [effemi'nato] ag effeminate.

efferatezza [effera'tettsa] sf brutality, ferocity.

efferato, a [effe'rato] ag brutal, savage.

effervescente [efferveʃ'ʃɛnte] ag (gen) effervescent; (fig: spirito, ingegno) sparkling; **bibita** ~ fizzy o effervescent drink.

effervescenza [efferveʃ'ʃɛntsa] sf effervescence.

effettivamente [effettiva'mente] av (in effetti) in fact; (a dire il vero) really, actually.

effettivo, a [effet'tivo] **1** ag **(a)** (reale) effective, real. **(b)** (impiegato, professore) permanent; (Mil) regular. **2** sm **(a)** (Amm): ~**i** pl permanent staff; (Mil) strength. **(b)** (di patrimonio etc) sum total.

effetto[1] [ef'fetto] sm **(a)** (risultato) effect; **avere** o **produrre un** ~ (**su**) to have an effect (on); **l'**~ **voluto** the desired effect; **far** ~ (medicina) to take effect, work; **sotto l'**~ **dell'alcool** under the influence of drink; **in** ~**i** in fact; **a questo** o **tale** ~ to this end o effect.
     (b) (fig: impressione) effect, impression; **ebbe l'**~ **di una bomba** it had a shattering effect; **fare** ~ **su qn** to make an impression on sb; **il sangue mi fa** ~ the sight of blood turns my stomach; **mi fa un** ~ **strano pensare che...** it gives me a strange feeling to think that...; **cercare l'**~ to seek attention; ~**i speciali** (Cine) special effects.
     (c) (Sport: di palla) spin; **colpire d'**~ to spin.
     (d) (Comm: cambiale) bill.

effetto[2] [ef'fetto] sm: ~**i personali** personal effects, personal belongings.

effettuare [effettu'are] vt (gen) to make; (controllo, volontà altrui) to carry out. **2**: ~**rsi** vr to take place.

efficace [effi'katʃe] ag (provvedimento) effective; (rimedio) efficacious.

efficacia [effi'katʃa] sf (vedi ag) effectiveness, efficacy.

efficiente [effi'tʃɛnte] ag (persona, macchina) efficient; (misura) effective.

efficienza [effi'tʃɛntsa] sf efficiency.

effigiare [effi'dʒare] vt to represent, portray.

effigie [ef'fidʒe] sf inv effigy; (ritratto) portrait.

effimero, a [ef'fimero] ag ephemeral, fleeting, short-lived.

effluvio [ef'fluvjo] sm (anche peg iro) scent, perfume.

effusione [effu'zjone] sf effusion; **con** ~ effusively.

egemonia [edʒemo'nia] sf hegemony.

Egeo [e'dʒɛo] sm: **l'**~, **il mare** ~ the Aegean (Sea).

egida [ˈɛdʒida] *sf*: **sotto l'~ di** under the aegis of.

Egitto [eˈdʒitto] *sm* Egypt.

egiziano, a [edʒitˈtsjano] *ag*, *sm/f* Egyptian.

egizio, a [eˈdʒittsjo] *ag*, *sm/f* (ancient) Egyptian.

egli [ˈeʎʎi] *pron pers* he; **~ stesso** he himself.

ego [ˈɛgo] *sm inv* (Psic) ego.

egocentrico, a, ci, che [egoˈtʃɛntriko] **1** *ag* egocentric(al). **2** *sm/f* self-centred person.

egocentrismo [egotʃenˈtrizmo] *sm* egocentricity.

egoismo [egoˈizmo] *sm* egoism, selfishness.

egoista, i, e [egoˈista] **1** *ag* egoistic, selfish. **2** *sm/f* egoist.

egoistico, a, ci, che [egoˈistiko] *ag* egoistic, selfish.

egotismo [egoˈtizmo] *sm* egotism.

egotista, i, e [egoˈtista] **1** *ag* egotistic. **2** *sm/f* egotist.

egr. *abbr di* **egregio.**

egregio, a, gi, gie [eˈgrɛdʒo] *ag* distinguished; **E~ Signore** (*nelle lettere*) Dear Sir.

egualitario, a [egwaliˈtarjo] *ag*, *sm/f* egalitarian.

egualitarismo [egwalitaˈrizmo] *sm* egalitarianism.

E.I. *abbr di esercito italiano.*

eiaculazione [ejakulatˈtsjone] *sf* ejaculation.

elaborare [elaboˈrare] *vt* (*gen*) to elaborate, work out; (*dati*) to process.

elaborato, a [elaboˈrato] *ag* elaborate; **motore ~** (*Aut*) souped-up engine.

elaboratore [elaboraˈtore] *sm*: **~ elettronico** computer.

elaborazione [elaboratˈtsjone] *sf* (*gen*) elaboration; (*Inform*): **~ dei dati** data processing.

elargire [elarˈdʒire] *vt* to hand out.

elargizione [elardʒitˈtsjone] *sf* donation.

elasticità [elastitʃiˈta] *sf* (*vedi* **elastico**) elasticity; spring; flexibility; accommodating nature.

elasticizzato, a [elastitʃidˈdzato] *ag* (*tessuto*) stretch *attr*.

elastico, a, ci, che [eˈlastiko] **1** *ag* (*materiale*) elastic; (*fig: andatura*) springy; (: *decisione, vedute*) flexible; (: *coscienza, misure*) accommodating. **2** *sm* (*per cucito: nastro*) elastic; (*di gomma*) elastic band, rubber band.

elefante [eleˈfante] *sm* elephant.

elefantesco, a, schi, sche [elefanˈtesko] *ag* elephantine.

elegante [eleˈgante] *ag* elegant.

eleganza [eleˈgantsa] *sf* elegance.

eleggere [eˈlɛddʒere] *vt*: **~ (a)** to elect (to).

elementare [elemenˈtare] **1** *ag* (*gen*) elementary; (*principi, nozioni*) rudimentary, elementary; (*Chim*) elemental; **scuola ~** primary school; **la prima ~** the first year of primary school. **2** *sfpl*: **le ~i** primary school *sg*.

elemento [eleˈmento] *sm* (*gen, Chim*) element; (*di meccanismo*) part, component; (*di pila*) cell; (*di cucina componibile etc*) unit; **~i di algebra** basic algebra; **la furia degli ~i** the fury of the elements; **non è stato scoperto nessun nuovo ~** there have been no new developments, no new facts have come to light; **è il migliore ~ della squadra** he's the best player in the team; **essere nel proprio ~** to be in one's element.

elemosina [eleˈmɔzina] *sf* charity, alms *pl*; **chiedere l'~** to beg; **dare qc in ~** to give sth to charity; **cassetta delle ~e** (*Rel*) alms box; **non ho bisogno della tua ~** (*fig*) I don't need your charity.

elemosinare [elemoziˈnare] **1** *vt* to beg for, ask for. **2** *vi* to beg.

elencare [elenˈkare] *vt* to list.

elenco, chi [eˈlɛnko] *sm* list; **~ telefonico** telephone directory; **fare un ~ di** (*scritto*) to make a list of, list; (*orale*) to list.

elettivo, a [eletˈtivo] *ag* (*carica*) assigned by vote.

eletto, a [eˈletto] **1** *pp di* **eleggere**. **2** *ag* (*Pol*) elected; (*Rel: popolo*) chosen; (*pubblico*) select. **3** *sm* (*Pol*) elected member; **gli ~i** (*Rel*) the chosen.

elettorale [eletoˈrale] *ag* electoral.

elettorato [eletoˈrato] *sm*: **~ (attivo)** electorate.

elettore, trice [eletˈtore] *sm/f* voter.

elettrauto [eletˈtrauto] *sm* (*officina*) workshop for car electrical repairs; (*tecnico*) car electrician.

elettricista, i [elettriˈtʃista] *sm* electrician.

elettricità [elettriʃiˈta] *sf* electricity; **c'è ~ nell'aria** (*fig*) the atmosphere is electric.

elettrico, a, ci, che [eˈlɛttriko] **1** *ag* (*gen*) electric; (*impianto, corrente*) electrical; **tariffe ~che** electricity charges. **2** *sm* (*operaio*) electricity worker, power worker.

elettrificare [elettrifiˈkare] *vt* (*linea ferroviaria*) to electrify.

elettrificazione [elettrifikatˈtsjone] *sf* electrification.

elettrizzante [elettridˈdzante] *ag* (*fig*) electrifying, thrilling.

elettrizzare [elettridˈdzare] **1** *vt* to charge (with electricity); (*fig: pubblico, atmosfera*) to electrify. **2**: **~rsi** *vr* to become charged with electricity; (*fig: persona*) to be thrilled.

elettrizzazione [elettriddzatˈtsjone] *sf* electrification; **stato di ~** (*fig*) state of excitement.

elettrocalamita [elettrokalaˈmita] *sf* electromagnet.

elettrocardiogramma, i [elettrokardjoˈgramma] *sm* electrocardiogram.

elettrodinamica [elettrodiˈnamika] *sf* electrodynamics *sg*.

elettrodo [eˈlettrodo] *sm* electrode.

elettrodomestico, a, ci, che [elettrodoˈmestiko] *ag*: **(apparecchio) ~** domestic (electrical) appliance.

elettroencefalogramma, i [elettroentʃefaloˈgramma] *sm* electroencephalogram.

elettrogeno, a [eletˈtrɔdʒeno] *ag*: **gruppo ~** generator.

elettrolisi [eletˈtrɔlizi] *sf* electrolysis.

elettromagnete [elettromaɲˈɲete] *sm* electromagnet.

elettromagnetico, a, ci, che [elettromaɲˈɲetiko] *ag* electromagnetic.

elettromagnetismo [elettromaɲɲeˈtizmo] *sm* electromagnetism.

elettromeccanico, a, ci, che [elettromekˈkaniko] *ag* electromechanical.

elettromotrice [elettromoˈtritʃe] *sf* electric train.

elettrone [eletˈtrone] *sm* electron.

elettronica [eletˈtrɔnika] *sf* electronics *sg*.

elettronico, a, ci, che [eletˈtrɔniko] *ag* (*gen*) electronic; (*carica, microscopio*) electron *attr*; **ingegneria ~a** electronics engineering.

elettroshock [elettroʃˈʃɔk] *sm inv* electroshock treatment.

elettrostatica [elettrosˈtatika] *sf* electrostatics *sg*.

elettrostatico, a, ci, che [elettrosˈtatiko] *ag* electrostatic.

elettrotecnica [elettroˈteknika] *sf* electrotechnology.

elettrotecnico, a, ci, che [elettroˈtekniko] **1** *ag* electrotechnical. **2** *sm* electrical engineer.

elevare [eleˈvare] **1** *vt* **(a)** (*alzare: muro*) to put up; (*fig: sguardo, occhi*) to raise, lift; (: *tenore di vita*) to raise; **~ un edificio di un piano** to add a floor to a building; **~ qn al rango di** to raise *o* elevate sb to the rank of; **~ al trono** to raise to the throne.

(b) *(Mat)* to raise; ~ **un numero al quadrato** to square a number. **(c)** *(Amm):* ~ **una contravvenzione** to impose a fine. **2**: ~**rsi** *vr (gen)* to rise; ~**rsi (con lo spirito)** *(fig)* to be uplifted.

elevatezza [eleva'tettsa] *sf (altezza)* elevation; *(di animo, pensiero)* loftiness.

elevato, a [ele'vato] *ag (gen)* high; *(cime)* high, lofty; *(fig: stile, sentimenti)* lofty; **poco** ~ low.

elevatore [eleva'tore] *sm* elevator, hoist.

elevazione [elevat'tsjone] *sf (gen, Mat)* raising; *(di terreno)* elevation; *(Sport)* lift; **l'E**~ *(Rel)* the Elevation.

elezione [elet'tsjone] *sf* **(a)** *(Pol, Amm)* election; **indire un'**~ to hold an election; **giorno delle** ~**i** election day. **(b)** *(scelta)* choice; **patria d'**~ chosen country.

elfo ['ɛlfo] *sm* elf.

elica, che ['ɛlika] *sf (Aer, Naut)* propeller, screw; *(Mat)* helix.

elicoidale [elikoi'dale] *ag* helicoidal.

elicottero [eli'kɔttero] *sm* helicopter.

elidere [e'lidere] **1** *vt (Fonetica)* to elide. **2**: ~**rsi** *vr (forze)* to cancel each other out, neutralize each other.

eliminare [elimi'nare] *vt (anche fig)* to eliminate.

eliminatorio, a [elimina'torjo] **1** *ag (prova, gara)* eliminatory. **2** *sf (Sport)* heat.

eliminazione [eliminat'tsjone] *sf* elimination.

elio ['ɛljo] *sm* helium.

eliocentrico, a, ci, che [eljo'tʃɛntriko] *ag* heliocentric.

eliporto [eli'pɔrto] *sm* heliport.

elisabettiano, a [elizabet'tjano] *ag* Elizabethan.

elisione [eli'zjone] *sf (Fonetica)* elision.

elisir [eli'zir] *sm inv* elixir.

eliso, a [e'lizo] *pp di* **elidere**.

elitario, a [eli'tarjo] *ag* elitist.

élite [e'lit] *sf inv* élite.

ella ['ella] *pron pers* she; ~ **stessa** she herself.

ellenico, a, ci, che [el'leniko] *ag* Hellenic.

ellisse [el'lisse] *sf (Geom)* ellipse.

ellissi [el'lissi] *sf inv (Gram)* ellipsis.

ellittico, a, ci, che [el'littiko] *ag (Geom, Gram)* elliptic(al).

elmetto [el'metto] *sm* helmet.

elmo ['elmo] *sm* helmet.

elogiare [elo'dʒare] *vt* to praise.

elogiativo, a [elodʒa'tivo] *ag* laudatory.

elogio [e'lɔdʒo] *sm* **(a)** praise; **fare l'**~ **di qn/qc** to praise sb/sth, sing sb's/sth's praises. **(b)** *(ufficiale)* eulogy; ~ **funebre** funeral oration.

eloquente [elo'kwɛnte] *ag* eloquent; **questi dati sono** ~**i** these facts speak for themselves.

eloquenza [elo'kwɛntsa] *sf* eloquence.

elsa ['elsa] *sf* hilt.

elucubrare [eluku'brare] *vt (piano)* to ponder about, ponder over; **che cosa stai elucubrando?** what are you thinking up now?

elucubrazioni [elukubrat'tsjoni] *sfpl (anche iro)* lucubrations.

eludere [e'ludere] *vt (gen)* to evade; *(sorveglianza, nemico)* to evade, elude.

elusivo, a [elu'zivo] *ag (sguardo)* elusive; *(risposta, parole)* evasive.

eluso, a [e'luzo] *pp di* **eludere**.

elvetico, a, ci, che [el'vetiko] *ag* Swiss.

emaciato, a [ema'tʃato] *ag* emaciated.

emanare [ema'nare] **1** *vt* **(a)** *(odore, calore)* to give off, send out; *(raggi)* to send out; *(fig: fascino)* to radiate. **(b)** *(emettere: legge)* to promulgate; *(: ordine, circolare)* to issue. **2** *vi*: ~ **da** to emanate from.

emanazione [emanat'tsjone] *sf* **(a)** *(di raggi, calore)*

emanation; *(di odori)* exhalation. **(b)** *(di legge)* promulgation; *(di ordine, circolare)* issuing.

emancipare [emantʃi'pare] **1** *vt* to emancipate. **2**: ~**rsi** *vr* to become liberated, become emancipated.

emancipato, a [emantʃi'pato] *ag* emancipated.

emancipazione [emantʃipat'tsjone] *sf* emancipation.

emarginare [emardʒi'nare] *vt (fig: socialmente)* to cast out.

emarginato, a [emardʒi'nato] *sm/f* outcast.

ematologia [ematolo'dʒia] *sf* haematology.

ematoma, i [ema'tɔma] *sm* bruise, haematoma *(T)*.

embargo, ghi [em'bargo] *sm* embargo.

emblema, i [em'blɛma] *sm* emblem.

emblematico, a, ci, che [emble'matiko] *ag* emblematic; *(fig: atteggiamento, parole)* symbolic.

embolia [embo'lia] *sf* embolism.

embrionale [embrio'nale] *ag* embryonic.

embrione [embri'one] *sm* embryo.

emendamento [emenda'mento] *sm (Dir)* amendment; *(di scritto)* emendation.

emendare [emen'dare] *vt (legge)* to amend; *(testo)* to emend.

emergente [emer'dʒɛnte] *ag* emerging.

emergenza [emer'dʒɛntsa] *sf (caso imprevisto)* emergency; **in caso di** ~ in an emergency; **stato di** ~ state of emergency.

emergere [e'mɛrdʒere] *vi (aus essere) (gen, anche fig: verità, fatti)* to emerge; *(fig: persona: distinguersi)* to stand out.

emerito, a [e'merito] *ag (insigne)* distinguished; **professore** ~ professor emeritus; **è un** ~ **cretino!** he's a right idiot!

emerso, a [e'mɛrso] **1** *pp di* **emergere**. **2** *ag (Geog)*: **Terra** ~**a** surface of the Earth.

emesso, a [e'messo] *pp di* **emettere**.

emetico, a, ci, che [e'metiko] *ag, sm* emetic.

emettere [e'mettere] *vt* **(a)** *(gen)* to emit; *(luce)* to give out; *(calore, odore)* to give off; *(suono, fischio)* to give, let out; *(Fis, Radio)* to transmit; ~ **un grido di dolore** to shout with pain, give a cry of pain; ~ **un gemito** to groan, utter a groan. **(b)** *(Fin: titoli, assegno etc)* to issue; *(: moneta)* to put into circulation, issue. **(c)** *(ordine, mandato di cattura)* to issue; ~ **la sentenza** to pass sentence.

emiciclo [emi'tʃiklo] *sm* semicircle, hemicycle; *(della Camera dei deputati)* floor.

emicrania [emi'kranja] *sf* migraine.

emigrante [emi'grante] *ag, sm/f* emigrant.

emigrare [emi'grare] *vi (aus essere)*: ~ **(in)** *(persona)* to emigrate (to); *(animale)* to migrate (to).

emigrato, a [emi'grato] **1** *ag* emigrant. **2** *sm/f* emigrant; *(Storia)* émigré.

emigrazione [emigrat'tsjone] *sf* **(a)** *(vedi vb)* emigration; migration. **(b)** *(di capitali)* flight.

emiliano, a [emi'ljano] *ag* of *o* from Emilia.

eminente [emi'nɛnte] *ag (cima, posizione)* high, lofty; *(fig: scienziato etc)* eminent, distinguished.

eminenza [emi'nɛntsa] *sf (qualità)* distinction, eminence. **(b)** *(titolo: di cardinale)*: **E**~ Eminence; ~ **grigia** *(fig)* éminence grise.

emirato [emi'rato] *sm* emirate.

emiro [e'miro] *sm* emir.

emisfero [emis'fɛro] *sm (gen)* hemisphere; ~ **australe/boreale** southern/northern hemisphere.

emissario [emis'sarjo] *sm* **(a)** *(Geog)* outlet, effluent. **(b)** *(inviato)* emissary.

emissione [emis'sjone] *sf (di suoni, onde, calore)* emission; *(di energia, Radio)* transmission; *(di francobolli, titoli, assegni, prestiti)* issue.

emittente [emit'tɛnte] **1** *ag (Radio, TV)* transmitting. **2** *sf (stazione)* transmitting station, broadcasting station.

emofilia [emofi'lia] *sf* haemophilia.

emoglobina [emoglo'bina] *sf* haemoglobin.

emolliente [emol'ljɛnte] *ag, sm* emollient.

emorragia, gie [emorra'dʒia] *sf* haemorrhage.

emorroide [emor'rɔide] *sf (gen pl)* haemorrhoid, pile.

emostatico, a, ci, che [emos'tatiko] *ag* haemostatic; **laccio** ~ tourniquet; **matita** ~a styptic pencil.

emotività [emotivi'ta] *sf* emotionalism.

emotivo, a [emo'tivo] *ag* emotional.

emozionale [emottsjo'nale] *ag* emotional.

emozionante [emottsjo'nante] *ag (che appassiona)* thrilling, exciting; *(che commuove)* moving.

emozionare [emottsjo'nare] **1** *vt (appassionare)* to thrill, excite; *(commuovere)* to move; **era tutto emozionato** he was very excited. **2:** ~**rsi** *vr (vedi vt)* to get excited; to be moved; ~**rsi facilmente** to be excitable; to be easily moved.

emozione [emot'tsjone] *sf* emotion; **a caccia di** ~ in search of excitement.

empatia [empa'tia] *sf* empathy.

empietà [empje'ta] *sf* impiety.

empio, a ['empjo] *ag (Rel)* impious; *(crudele)* wicked, cruel.

empirico, a, ci, che [em'piriko] *ag* empirical.

empirismo [empi'rizmo] *sm* empiricism.

emporio [em'pɔrjo] *sm* emporium.

emù [e'mu] *sm inv* emu.

emulare [emu'lare] *vt* to emulate.

emulazione [emulat'tsjone] *sf* emulation.

emulo, a ['emulo] *sm/f* imitator.

emulsionare [emulsjo'nare] *vt* to emulsify.

emulsione [emul'sjone] *sf* emulsion.

enciclica, che [en'tʃiklika] *sf* encyclical.

enciclopedia [entʃiklope'dia] *sf* encyclopaedia.

enciclopedico, a, ci, che [entʃiklo'pɛdiko] *ag* encyclopaedic.

enclave [ã'klav] *sm inv* enclave.

encomiabile [enko'mjabile] *ag* praiseworthy, commendable.

encomiare [enko'mjare] *vt* to commend, praise.

encomio [en'kɔmjo] *sm* commendation; ~ **solenne** *(Mil)* mention in dispatches.

endemico, a, ci, che [en'dɛmiko] *ag* endemic.

endovenosa [endove'nosa] *sf* intravenous injection.

endovenoso, a [endove'noso] *ag* intravenous.

E.N.E.L. ['enel] *abbr m (= Ente Nazionale per l'Energia Elettrica)* ≃ C.E.G.B.

energetico, a, ci, che [ener'dʒɛtiko] *ag (risorse, crisi)* energy *attr*; *(sostanza, alimento)* energy-giving.

energia, gie [ener'dʒia] *sf* **(a)** *(vigore)* energy; **avere molta** ~ to be very energetic; **avere poca** ~ to be unenergetic, have little energy; **dedicare tutte le proprie** ~**e a qc** to put all one's energy into sth. **(b)** *(Fis)* energy; *(Tecn)* power; **liberare** ~ to release energy; **consumo di** ~ power consumption.

energico, a, ci, che [e'nɛrdʒiko] *ag (uomo)* energetic; *(resistenza, rifiuto)* forceful, vigorous; *(cura)* powerful; *(provvedimenti)* drastic.

energumeno [ener'gumeno] *sm (scherz)* brute.

enfasi ['ɛnfazi] *sf* emphasis; **con** ~ emphatically; *(peg)* pompously; **porre l'**~ **su** to stress, place the emphasis on, emphasize.

enfatico, a, ci, che [en'fatiko] *ag (tono, discorso)* emphatic; *(: peg)* pompous.

enfatizzare [enfatid'dzare] *vt* to emphasize, stress.

enfisema, i [enfi'zɛma] *sm* emphysema.

enigma, i [e'nigma] *sm (mistero)* enigma, riddle; *(gioco)* puzzle, riddle.

enigmatico, a, ci, che [enig'matiko] *ag* enigmatic.

enigmistica [enig'mistika] *sf*: **essere un appassionato di** ~ to be very keen on puzzles; **giornale di** ~ puzzles magazine.

E.N.I.T. ['enit] *abbr di Ente Nazionale per il Turismo.*

ennesimo, a [en'nɛzimo] *ag (Mat, fam)* nth; **all'**~**a potenza** to the nth power *o* degree; **per l'**~**a volta** for the nth *o* umpteenth time.

enologo, gi [e'nɔlogo] *sm* oenologist.

enorme [e'norme] *ag (gen)* enormous, huge; *(distesa, riserva)* vast, enormous; *(pazienza, forza)* tremendous, enormous.

enormità [enormi'ta] *sf inv* **(a)** *(di peso, somma)* hugeness; *(di distesa)* vastness; *(di richiesta)* enormity; *(di prezzo)* unreasonableness. **(b)** *(stupidaggine)* blunder, howler; **non dire** ~**!** don't talk nonsense!; **l'ho pagato un'**~ I paid a fortune for it.

enoteca, che [eno'tɛka] *sf (negozio)* wine bar.

ensemble [ã'sãbl] *sm inv (Mus)* ensemble.

ente ['ɛnte] *sm* **(a)** *(Filosofia)* being. **(b)** *(Amm)* body, corporation.

enterite [ente'rite] *sf* enteritis.

entità [enti'ta] *sf* **(a)** *(Filosofia)* entity. **(b)** *(di perdita, danni, investimenti)* extent; *(di popolazione)* size; **di molta/poca** ~ *(avvenimento, incidente)* of great/slight importance.

entomologia [entomolo'dʒia] *sf* entomology.

entourage [ãtu'raʒ] *sm inv* entourage.

entrambi, e [en'trambi] *ag, pron* both; ~ **i ragazzi** both boys, both of the boys; ~**e le sorelle** both sisters, both of the sisters; **vennero** ~ they both came, both of them came.

entrante [en'trante] *ag (prossimo: mese, anno)* next, coming.

entrare [en'trare] *vi (aus essere)* **(a)** to go *(o* come) in, enter; *(con la macchina)* to drive in; ~ **in** to go *(o* come) into, enter; **entri pure!** do come in!; **'si prega di bussare prima di** ~**'** 'knock before entering'; ~ **dalla finestra** to get in by the window; **mi è entrato qualcosa nell'occhio** I've got something in my eye; **non** ~ **in acqua subito dopo aver mangiato!** don't go into the water just after you've eaten!

(b) *(soldi, prodotti)* to enter, come in; *(contenuto)* to go in; *(: adattarsi)* to fit in; **il regalo non entra nella scatola** the present won't go *o* fit into the box; **queste scarpe non mi entrano** I can't get into these shoes; **entra acqua dal tetto** there's water coming in through the roof; **la matematica non mi entra proprio in testa** I just can't get the hang of maths, I just can't get maths to sink in.

(c): far ~ *(visitatore, cliente)* to show in; *(animale)* to let in; *(oggetto)* to fit in; *(merce: d'importazione)* to bring in; *(: di contrabbando)* to smuggle in; **far** ~ **qn in un club** *(ammettere)* to get sb into a club; **far** ~ **qn in banca** *(come impiegato)* to get sb a job in a bank; **non riesco a fargli** ~ **in testa che ce la può fare** I can't get him to understand that he can do it; **gli hanno fatto** ~ **in testa la trigonometria** they've managed to teach him trigonometry.

(d): ~ **in** *(club, partito)* to join; *(mestiere, gruppo)* to go into; ~ **nella professione legale** to go into *o* enter law; ~ **in convento** to enter a convent; ~ **in affari** to go into business; ~ **in società/in commercio con qn** to go into partnership/business with sb; ~ **al servizio di qn** to enter sb's service; ~ **nella storia** to go down in history.

(**e**): ~ **in** (*cominciare*): ~ **in discussione con qn** to enter into discussions with sb; **entriamo in argomento** let's get down to the matter in hand; ~ **in ballo** o **in gioco** (*fig*) to come into play; ~ **in carica** to take up office; ~ **in guerra** (*all'inizio*) to go to war; (*durante*) to come into the war; ~ **in convalescenza** to begin one's convalescence; ~ **nei vent'anni di età** to turn twenty.

(**f**): **entrarci** to have to do with; **ciò che dici non c'entra** what you say has nothing to do with it; **tu non c'entri in questa faccenda** this is none of your business; **io non c'entro** it's got nothing to do with me.

entrata [en'trata] *sf* (**a**) (*l'entrare: di persona*) entry, entrance; (: *di merci, veicoli*) entry; **alla sua** ~ as he entered; **alla sua ~ in scena** (*Teatro*) on his entrance; **fare l'~ in società** to make one's debut (in society). (**b**) (*accesso*) admission; '**divieto di ~**' 'no admittance'; '**~ libera**' 'admission free'; **biglietto di** ~ (entrance) ticket. (**c**) (*porta*) entrance; (*vestibolo*) entrance (hall); ~ **degli artisti** (*Teatro*) stage door; ~ **di servizio** service o tradesmen's entrance. (**d**) (*inizio*): **all'~ in guerra degli Stati Uniti** when the United States came into the war; **dopo la sua ~ in carica** after he came to office; **con l'~ in vigore dei nuovi provvedimenti...** once the new measures come into effect.... (**e**): **~e** *pl* (*Econ*) income *sg*; (*Comm*) takings, receipts.

entrecôte [ātrǝ'kot] *sf inv* (*Culin*) entrecôte, rib steak.

entro ['entro] *prep* within; ~ **un mese** within a month; ~ **domani** by tomorrow; ~ **febbraio** by the end of February; **tornerò entro 5 minuti** I'll be back in 5 minutes.

entroterra [entro'terra] *sm inv* hinterland.

entusiasmante [entuzjaz'mante] *ag* exciting.

entusiasmare [entuzjaz'mare] **1** *vt* to fill with enthusiasm. **2**: **~rsi** *vr*: **~rsi per qc** to be enthusiastic about o over sth.

entusiasmo [entu'zjazmo] *sm* enthusiasm.

entusiasta, i, e [entu'zjasta] **1** *ag*: ~ (**di**) enthusiastic (about o over); **non sono** ~ **dei risultati** I'm not too happy about the results. **2** *sm/f* enthusiast.

entusiastico, a, ci, che [entu'zjastiko] *ag* enthusiastic.

enucleare [enukle'are] *vt* (*frm: chiarire*) to explain.

enumerare [enume'rare] *vt* to enumerate.

enumerazione [enumerat'tsjone] *sf* enumeration.

enunciare [enun'tʃare] *vt* (*pensiero*) to express; (*fatti*) to state; (*teorema*) to enunciate.

enzima, i [en'dzima] *sm* enzyme.

epatico, a, ci, che [e'patiko] *ag* hepatic; **cirrosi ~a** cirrhosis of the liver.

epatite [epa'tite] *sf* hepatitis.

epica ['ɛpika] *sf* epic (poetry).

epicentro [epi'tʃɛntro] *sm* epicentre.

epico, a, ci, che ['ɛpiko] *ag* (*anche fig*) epic.

epicureo, a [epiku'rɛo] *ag, sm/f* epicurean.

epidemia [epide'mia] *sf* epidemic.

epidemico, a, ci, che [epi'dɛmiko] *ag* epidemic.

epidermico, a, ci, che [epi'dɛrmiko] *ag* (*Anat*) skin *attr*; (*fig: interesse, impressioni*) superficial.

epidermide [epi'dɛrmide] *sf* (*Anat*) skin, epidermis (*T*).

Epifania [epifa'nia] *sf* Epiphany.

epigono [e'pigono] *sm* imitator.

epigrafe [e'pigrafe] *sf* epigraph; (*su libro*) dedication.

epigrafico, a, ci, che [epi'grafiko] *ag* epigraphic; (*fig: stile*) concise.

epigramma, i [epi'gramma] *sm* epigram.

epilessia [epiles'sia] *sf* epilepsy.

epilettico, a, ci, che [epi'lettiko] *ag, sm/f* epileptic.

epilogo, ghi [e'pilogo] *sm* (*letterario*) epilogue; (*fig*) conclusion.

episcopale [episko'pale] *ag* episcopal.

episcopato [episko'pato] *sm* episcopacy.

episodico, a, ci, che [epi'zɔdiko] *ag* (*romanzo, narrazione*) episodic; (*fig: occasionale*) occasional.

episodio [epi'zɔdjo] *sm* episode; **sceneggiato a ~i** serial.

epistola [e'pistola] *sf* epistle.

epistolare [episto'lare] *ag* epistolary; **essere in rapporto** o **relazione** ~ **con qn** to correspond o be in correspondence with sb.

epistolario [episto'larjo] *sm* letters *pl*.

epitaffio [epi'taffjo] *sm* epitaph.

epiteto [e'piteto] *sm* (*Gram*) attribute; (*fig*) epithet; **un** ~ **irripetibile** an unrepeatable insult.

epoca, che ['ɛpoka] *sf* (*gen*) time; (*Storia*) age, era, epoch; **mobili d'~** genuine antiques; **all'~ di** at the time of; **viviamo in un'~ difficile** we live in difficult times o in a difficult age; **fare** ~ (*scandalo*) to cause a stir; (*cantante, moda*) to mark a new era; **lo sbarco sulla luna ha fatto** ~ the moon landing was an epoch-making event.

epopea [epo'pɛa] *sf* (*anche fig*) epic.

eppure [ep'pure] *cong* and yet, nevertheless.

epurare [epu'rare] *vt* (*Pol*) to purge.

epurazione [epurat'tsjone] *sf* purge.

equanime [e'kwanime] *ag* (*imparziale*) fair, impartial.

equanimità [ekwanimi'ta] *sf* (*imparzialità*) fairness, impartiality.

equatore [ekwa'tore] *sm* equator.

equatoriale [ekwato'rjale] *ag* equatorial.

equazione [ekwat'tsjone] *sf* equation.

equestre [e'kwɛstre] *ag* equestrian; **circo** ~ circus.

equidistante [ekwidis'tante] *ag* equidistant.

equilatero [ekwi'latero] *ag* equilateral.

equilibrare [ekwili'brare] **1** *vt* (*gen*) to balance; (*controbilanciare*) to counterbalance; ~ **qc con qc** to balance sth against sth else. **2**: **~rsi** *vr* (*forze etc*) to counterbalance each other.

equilibrato, a [ekwili'brato] *ag* (*carico, fig: giudizio*) balanced; (*vita*) well-regulated; (*persona*) stable, well-balanced.

equilibratura [ekwilibra'tura] *sf* (*Aut*) balancing.

equilibrio [ekwi'librjo] *sm* (*gen*) balance, equilibrium; (*armonia*) harmony; **perdere l'~** to lose one's balance; **stare in** ~ **su** (*persona*) to balance on; (*oggetto*) to be balanced on; ~ **mentale** (mental) equilibrium o stability; ~ **economico** economic stability; ~ **politico** balance of power; **è una persona priva di** ~ he is not a very level-headed person.

equilibrismo [ekwili'brizmo] *sm* tightrope walking; (*fig, Pol*) juggling.

equilibrista, i, e [ekwili'brista] *sm/f* tightrope walker.

equino, a [e'kwino] *ag* horse *attr*; **carne ~a** horsemeat, horseflesh; **una razza ~a** a breed of horses.

equinozio [ekwi'nɔttsjo] *sm* equinox.

equipaggiamento [ekwipaddʒa'mento] *sm* (**a**) (*operazione: di nave*) equipping, fitting out; (: *di spedizione, esercito*) equipping, kitting out. (**b**) (*attrezzatura*) equipment; ~ **da sci/da sub** skiing/diving equipment.

equipaggiare [ekwipad'dʒare] **1** vt (nave, esercito, spedizione) to equip; (per uno sport) to kit out. **2:** ~rsi vr to equip o.s.

equipaggio [ekwi'paddʒo] sm (gen, Naut) crew; (Aer) (air)crew.

equiparare [ekwipa'rare] vt (Amm: stipendi, gradi) to make equal, level.

équipe [e'kip] sf (Sport, gen) team; **lavorare in** ~ to work as a team.

equipollente [ekwipol'lɛnte] ag equivalent.

equità [ekwi'ta] sf equity, fairness.

equitazione [ekwitat'tsjone] sf (horse-)riding.

equivalente [ekwiva'lɛnte] **1** ag: ~ **(a)** equivalent (to). **2** sm equivalent.

equivalenza [ekwiva'lɛntsa] sf equivalence.

equivalere [ekwiva'lere] **1** vi: ~ **a** to be equivalent to; **equivale a dire che...** that is the same as saying that... . **2:** ~rsi vr (forze etc) to counterbalance each other; (soluzioni) to amount to the same thing.

equivalso, a [ekwi'valso] pp di **equivalere**.

equivocare [ekwivo'kare] vi (capire male): ~ **(su qc)** to misunderstand (sth).

equivoco, a, ci, che [e'kwivoko] **1** ag (risposta, discorso) equivocal, ambiguous; (persona, ambiente) dubious. **2** sm (malinteso) misunderstanding; **dar luogo a un** ~ to cause a misunderstanding; **cadere in** ~ to misunderstand; **ci dev'essere stato un** ~ there must have been some misunderstanding.

equo, a ['ɛkwo] ag (gen) equitable, fair; **un** ~ **compenso** a fair o adequate reward.

era ['era] sf (gen) era; (Geol) period; **l'~ cristiana** the Christian era; **l'~ spaziale/della macchina** the space/mechanical age.

erariale [era'rjale] ag: **ufficio** ~ ≈ tax office; **spese** ~**i** public expenditure; **imposte** ~**i** revenue taxes.

erario [e'rarjo] sm: **l'~** ≈ the Treasury.

erba ['ɛrba] sf grass; (Culin, Med) herb; (fam: droga) grass, pot; **in** ~ (fig: pittore) budding; **fare di ogni** ~ **un fascio** (fig) to lump everything (o everybody) together.

erbaccia, ce [er'battʃa] sf weed.

erbaceo, a [er'batʃeo] ag herbaceous.

erbario [er'barjo] sm (raccolta) herbarium; (libro) herbal.

erbette [er'bette] sfpl beet tops.

erbicida, i, e [erbi'tʃida] **1** ag herbicidal. **2** sm weed-killer.

erbivendolo, a [erbi'vendolo] sm/f greengrocer.

erbivoro, a [er'bivoro] **1** ag herbivorous. **2** sm herbivore.

erborista, i, e [erbo'rista] sm/f herbalist.

erboristeria [erboriste'ria] sf (scienza) study of medicinal herbs; (negozio) herbalist's (shop).

erboso, a [er'boso] ag grassy; **tappeto** ~ lawn.

erculeo, a [er'kuleo] ag (anche fig) Herculean.

erede [e'rɛde] sm/f heir/heiress; ~ **di qc** heir to sth; ~ **al trono** heir to the throne; ~ **legittimo** heir-at-law; **nominare qn proprio** ~ to make sb one's heir.

eredità [eredi'ta] sf inv **(a)** (Dir) inheritance; (fig) heritage; **lasciare qc in** ~ **a qn** to leave o bequeath sth to sb; **ricevere qc in** ~ to inherit sth. **(b)** (Bio) heredity.

ereditare [eredi'tare] vt to inherit; ~ **qc da qn** to inherit sth from sb.

ereditarietà [ereditarje'ta] sf heredity.

ereditario, a [eredi'tarjo] ag hereditary.

ereditiera [eredi'tjera] sf heiress.

eremita, i [ere'mita] sm hermit.

eremitaggio [eremi'taddʒo] sm hermitage.

eremo ['eremo] sm hermitage; (fig) retreat.

eresia [ere'zia] sf (Rel, fig) heresy; **dire eresie** (fig) to talk nonsense.

eretico, a, ci, che [e'rɛtiko] **1** ag heretical. **2** sm/f heretic.

eretto, a [e'rɛtto] **1** pp di **erigere**. **2** ag (capo, busto) erect, upright.

erezione [eret'tsjone] sf erection.

ergastolano, a [ergasto'lano] sm/f prisoner serving a life sentence, lifer (fam).

ergastolo [er'gastolo] sm (pena) life imprisonment; (luogo di pena) prison (for those serving life sentence).

erica, che ['erika] sf heather.

erigere [e'ridʒere] **1** vt (monumento) to erect, raise. **2:** ~rsi vr (fig: costituirsi): ~rsi **a giudice/difensore (di)** to set o.s. up as a judge/a defender (of).

eritema [eri'tɛma] sm (Med) inflammation, erythema (T); ~ **solare** sunburn.

ermafrodito, a [ermafro'dito] ag, sm hermaphrodite.

ermellino [ermel'lino] sm (animale: d'inverno) ermine; (: d'estate) stoat; (pelliccia) ermine.

ermetico, a, ci, che [er'mɛtiko] ag **(a)** (chiusura, vaso) airtight, watertight, hermetic; (fig: sguardo, volto) impenetrable. **(b)** (Poesia) hermetic.

ernia ['ɛrnja] sf (Med) hernia; ~ **del disco** slipped disk.

erodere [e'rodere] vt to erode.

eroe [e'rɔe] sm hero.

erogare [ero'gare] vt (gas, luce) to supply; (somma) to distribute.

erogazione [erogat'tsjone] sf (vedi vb) supply; distribution.

eroico, a, ci, che [e'rɔiko] ag heroic.

eroicomico, a, ci, che [eroi'kɔmiko] ag mock-heroic.

eroina[1] [ero'ina] sf (donna) heroine.

eroina[2] [ero'ina] sf (droga) heroin.

eroismo [ero'izmo] sm heroism.

erompere [e'rompere] vi: ~ **(da)** (lava, folla) to erupt (from); ~ **in un pianto dirotto** to burst into tears.

erosione [ero'zjone] sf erosion.

erosivo, a [ero'zivo] ag erosive.

eroso, a [e'roso] pp di **erodere**.

erotico, a, ci, che [e'rɔtiko] ag erotic.

erotismo [ero'tizmo] sm eroticism.

erotomane [ero'tomane] sm erotomaniac.

erpete ['ɛrpete] sm herpes sg.

erpice [er'pitʃe] sm (Agr) harrow.

errabondo, a [erra'bondo] ag wandering.

errante [er'rante] ag wandering; **cavaliere** ~ knight errant.

errare [er'rare] vi **(a)** (vagare): ~ **(per)** to wander (about), roam (about); ~ **con la fantasia** to let one's imagination wander. **(b)** (sbagliare) to be mistaken, make a mistake; **se non erro...** if I'm not mistaken... .

errata corrige [er'rata 'kɔrridʒe] sm inv erratum, corrigendum.

errato, a [er'rato] ag (calcolo) wrong, incorrect; (idea, interpretazione) mistaken, erroneous; **se non vado** ~ if I am not mistaken.

erroneo, a [er'rɔneo] ag erroneous.

errore [er'rore] **1** sm mistake, error; **fare un** ~ to make a mistake; **per** ~ by mistake; **salvo** ~**i** (scritto) errors excepted; (nel parlare) if I am not mistaken. **2:** ~ **di calcolo** (anche fig) miscalculation; ~ **di gioventù** youthful error; ~**giudiziario** miscarriage of justice; ~ **di giudizio** o **di valutazione** error of judgment; ~ **di ortografia**

spelling mistake; ~ **di stampa** printing error, misprint.

erta ['erta] *sf* **(a)** *(salita)* steep slope. **(b): stare all'**~ *(vigilare)* to be on the alert.

erto, a ['erto] *ag* (very) steep.

erudire [eru'dire] *vt (frm, scherz)* to teach, educate.

erudito, a [eru'dito] **1** *ag (persona)* learned, erudite; *(opera)* scholarly. **2** *sm/f* scholar.

erudizione [erudit'tsjone] *sf* erudition, scholarship.

eruttare [erut'tare] *vt (lava)* to throw out, belch.

eruttivo, a [erut'tivo] *ag* eruptive.

eruzione [erut'tsjone] *sf (Geol)* eruption; *(Med)* rash.

esacerbare [ezatʃer'bare] *vt* to exacerbate.

esagerare [ezadʒe'rare] **1** *vi (gen)* to exaggerate; *(eccedere)* to go too far; ~ **con le pretese** to demand too much; ~ **con la prudenza** to be overcautious; **senza** ~ without exaggeration; ~ **nel bere** to drink too much; ~ **nel mangiare** to overeat. **2** *vt* to exaggerate.

esagerato, a [ezadʒe'rato] **1** *ag (notizia, proporzioni)* exaggerated; *(curiosità, pignoleria)* excessive; *(prezzo)* exorbitant; **sarebbe** ~ **dire che...** it would be an exaggeration to say that.... **2** *sm/f:* **sei il solito** ~ you are exaggerating as usual.

esagerazione [ezadʒerat'tsjone] *sf* exaggeration; **costare un'**~ to cost the earth; **che** ~! what nonsense!

esagitato, a [ezadʒi'tato] *ag (persona, animo)* restless.

esagonale [ezago'nale] *ag* hexagonal.

esagono [e'zagono] *sm* hexagon.

esalare [eza'lare] **1** *vt (odori)* to give off; ~ **l'ultimo respiro** *(fig)* to breathe one's last. **2** *vi:* ~ **(da)** to emanate (from).

esalazione [ezalat'tsjone] *sf (emissione)* exhalation; *(odore)* fumes *pl.*

esaltante [ezal'tante] *ag* exciting.

esaltare [ezal'tare] **1** *vt* **(a)** *(lodare: pregi, virtù)* to extol, exalt. **(b)** *(eccitare: immaginazione)* to fire; *(: folla)* to excite. **2:** ~**rsi** *vr:* ~**rsi (per qc)** to grow excited (about sth).

esaltato, a [ezal'tato] **1** *ag* excited; *(mente)* deranged. **2** *sm/f* fanatic.

esaltazione [ezaltat'tsjone] *sf* **(a)** *(elogio)* extolling, exalting. **(b)** *(nervosa)* intense excitement; *(mistica)* exaltation.

esame [e'zame] *sm* **(a)** *(gen)* examination; **essere all'**~ to be under study *o* examination; **prendere in** ~ to examine, consider; **fare un** ~ **di coscienza** to search one's conscience; **dopo un attento** ~ **della situazione** after careful study *o* consideration of the situation. **(b)** *(Med)* examination, test; ~ **del sangue** blood test; ~ **della vista** eye test; **farsi fare degli** ~**i** to have some tests done *o* carried out. **(c)** *(Scol)* exam, examination; **fare gli** ~**i** to sit *o* take one's exams; **dare un** ~ to sit *o* take an exam; ~ **di guida** driving test.

esaminando, a [ezami'nando] *sm/f* examinee.

esaminare [ezami'nare] *vt* **(a)** *(gen)* to examine; *(proposta, elementi)* to consider, examine. **(b)** *(oggetto)* to examine, study. **(c)** *(candidati)* to interview; *(Scol)* to examine.

esaminatore, trice [ezamina'tore] **1** *ag* examining *attr.* **2** *sm/f* examiner.

esangue [e'zangwe] *ag* bloodless; *(fig: pallido)* pale, wan; *(: privo di vigore)* lifeless.

esanime [e'zanime] *ag* lifeless.

esasperare [ezaspe'rare] **1** *vt (persona)* to exasperate; *(situazione)* to exacerbate. **2:** ~**rsi** *vr* to become exasperated.

esasperazione [ezasperat'tsjone] *sf* exasperation.

esattezza [ezat'tettsa] *sf (di calcolo, affermazione etc)* accuracy; **per l'**~ to be precise; **con** ~ exactly; **rispondere con** ~ *(in modo corretto)* to answer correctly; *(in modo preciso)* to answer accurately.

esatto, a [e'zatto] **1** *pp di* **esigere. 2** *ag (calcolo, risposta)* correct, right; *(ora)* exact, correct; *(dimensioni, quantità)* exact, precise; *(prezzo, peso)* exact; **è l'**~ **contrario** it's the exact opposite; **allora, hai deciso di partire?** — ~! so, you've decided to leave? — that's right!; **le scienze** ~**e** the exact sciences.

esattore, trice [ezat'tore] *sm/f:* ~ **delle tasse** tax collector; ~ **del gas/della luce** gas/electricity man.

esattoria [ezatto'ria] *sf:* ~ **comunale** district rates office.

esaudibile [ezau'dibile] *ag (desiderio, richiesta)* easily-granted.

esaudire [ezau'dire] *vt* to grant.

esauribile [ezau'ribile] *ag* exhaustible.

esauriente [ezau'rjente] *ag (gen)* exhaustive, thorough; *(risposta)* complete.

esaurimento [ezauri'mento] *sm (gen)* exhaustion; ~ **nervoso** nervous breakdown; **svendita ad** ~ *o* **fino ad** ~ **della merce** clearance sale.

esaurire [ezau'rire] **1** *vt* **(a)** *(consumare: scorte, risorse)* to exhaust, use up; *(: pozzo, miniera)* to exhaust; *(: carburante)* to consume, use up; *(: forze, energie)* to expend. **(b)** *(portare a termine: indagine)* to conclude; *(: argomento)* to exhaust. **(c)** *(persona)* to exhaust, wear out. **2:** ~**rsi** *vr* **(a)** *(persona)* to exhaust o.s., wear o.s. out. **(b)** *(provviste)* to run out; *(fondi)* to run out, dry up; *(ispirazione)* to dry up; **la prima edizione si è esaurita in breve tempo** the first edition sold out very quickly.

esaurito, a [ezau'rito] *ag (gen)* exhausted; *(merci)* sold out; *(libro: non più stampato)* out of print; **tutto** ~ sold out; **registrare il tutto** ~ *(Teatro)* to have a full house; **essere** ~ *(persona)* to be run down.

esausto, a [e'zausto] *ag (spossato)* exhausted, worn out.

esautorare [ezauto'rare] *vt (dirigente, funzionario)* to deprive of authority.

esazione [ezat'tsjone] *sf* collection (of taxes).

esca ['eska] *sf* **(a)** *(anche fig)* bait; **mettere l'**~ **all'amo** to bait the hook. **(b)** *(sostanza infiammabile)* tinder.

escandescenza [eskandeʃ'ʃentsa] *sf:* **dare in** ~**e** to lose one's temper, fly into a rage.

escavatore, trice [eskava'tore] **1** *ag* excavating. **2** *sm o f* excavator.

escavazione [eskavat'tsjone] *sf* excavation.

eschimese [eski'mese] **1** *ag* Eskimo; **cane** ~ husky. **2** *sm/f* Eskimo. **3** *sm (lingua)* Eskimo.

esclamare [eskla'mare] *vi* to exclaim.

esclamativo, a [eskla'mativo] *ag:* **punto** ~ exclamation mark.

esclamazione [esklamat'tsjone] *sf* exclamation.

escludere [es'kludere] *vt* **(a)** *(estromettere):* ~ **qn (da)** to exclude sb (from); **fu escluso dall'elenco** his name was left off the list. **(b)** *(ritenere o rendere impossibile)* to rule out, exclude; **escludo che si tratti di furto** robbery is out of the question; **la polizia ha escluso la tesi del suicidio** the police ruled out *o* excluded the suicide theory; **una teoria esclude l'altra** one theory excludes another; **vieni domani?** — **lo escludo!** *o* **è escluso!** are you coming tomorrow? — it's out of the question!

esclusione [esklu'zjone] *sf* exclusion; **a** ~ **di, fatta**

~ **per** except (for), apart from; **senza** ~ (**alcuna**) without exception; **senza** ~ **di colpi** (*fig*) with no holds barred; **procedere per** ~ to follow a process of elimination.

esclusiva [esklu'ziva] *sf* (**a**) (*Comm*): **avere l'**~ **di qc** to be the sole agent for sth; **avere l'**~ **di vendita** to have the exclusive *o* sole selling rights. (**b**) (*Stampa*) exclusive; **intervista in** ~ exclusive interview.

esclusivamente [eskluziva'mente] *av* exclusively, solely.

esclusivo, a [esklu'zivo] *ag* exclusive.

escluso, a [es'kluzo] **1** *pp di* **escludere**. **2** *ag*: **nessuno** ~ without exception; **è** ~ **che venga** there is no question of his coming; **non è** ~ **che lo si faccia** the possibility mustn't be ruled out; **IVA** ~**a** excluding VAT, exclusive of VAT.

escogitare [eskodʒi'tare] *vt* to devise, think up.

escoriare [esko'rjare] **1** *vt* to graze. **2**: ~**rsi** *vr* to graze o.s.

escoriazione [eskorjat'tsjone] *sf* abrasion, graze.

escrementi [eskre'menti] *smpl* excrement *sg*, faeces *pl*.

escrescenza [eskreʃ'ʃɛntsa] *sf* (*Bio*) outgrowth; (*Med*) growth.

escursione [eskur'sjone] *sf* (**a**) (*gita*) excursion, trip; (: *a piedi*) hike, walk. (**b**) (*Meteor*): ~ **termica** temperature range.

escursionista, i, e [eskursjo'nista] *sm/f* (*gitante*) (day) tripper; (: *a piedi*) hiker, walker.

esecrabile [eze'krabile] *ag* execrable, abominable.

esecrando, a [eze'krando] *ag* abhorrent, abominable.

esecrare [eze'krare] *vt* to abhor, loathe; (*persona*) to loathe.

esecutivo, a [ezeku'tivo] *ag, sm* executive.

esecutore, trice [ezeku'tore] *sm/f* (**a**) (*Dir*): ~ (**testamentario**) executor/executrix; **l'**~ **del progetto** the person who realized the project. (**b**) (*Mus*) performer.

esecuzione [ezekut'tsjone] *sf* (**a**) (*vedi vb*) execution; carrying out; performance; **mettere in** ~, **dare** ~ **a** (*progetto, ordine*) to carry out. (**b**) (*Dir*) execution.

eseguire [eze'gwire] *vt* (*lavoro, ordini, piano*) to carry out, execute; (*Mus: sinfonia, pezzo*) to perform, execute; **ha fatto** ~ **dei lavori** he had some work done; ~ **un pagamento** to effect a payment.

esempio [e'zɛmpjo] *sm* example; **ad** *o* **per** ~ for example *o* instance; **citare come** *o* **ad** ~ to quote as an example; **dare il buon/cattivo** ~ to set a good/bad example; **essere un** ~ **di virtù** to be a paragon of virtue; **fare un** ~ to give an example; **prendere** (**l'**)~ **da qn** to follow sb's example; **che ti serva d'**~! let that be a lesson to you!

esemplare [ezem'plare] **1** *ag* (*vita, punizione*) exemplary; (*allievo*) model *attr*; **dare una punizione** ~ **a qn** to make an example of sb. **2** *sm* (*Bot, Zool, Geol*) specimen; (*di francobollo, moneta*) example; (*di libro*) copy.

esemplificare [ezemplifi'kare] *vt* to illustrate, exemplify.

esemplificativo, a [ezemplifika'tivo] *ag* illustrative, exemplifying.

esentare [ezen'tare] *vt*: ~ **qn (da qc)** to exempt sb (from sth).

esentasse [ezen'tasse] *ag inv* tax-free.

esente [e'zɛnte] *ag*: ~ **da** (*dispensato da*) exempt from; **anche lui non è** ~ **da difetti** he isn't perfect either.

esenzione [ezen'tsjone] *sf*: ~ (**da**) exemption (from).

esequie [e'zɛkwje] *sfpl* funeral rites, obsequies.

esercente [ezer'tʃɛnte] *sm/f* (*gestore*) retailer; **unione** ~**i** retailers' association.

esercitare [ezertʃi'tare] **1** *vt* (**a**) (*professione*) to practise; (*diritto*) to exercise; ~ (**su**) (*controllo, influenza*) to exert (over); (*pressione*) to exert (on); (*autorità, potere*) to exercise (over); **quel medico non esercita più** that doctor is no longer in practice. (**b**) (*corpo, mente, voce*) to train, exercise. **2**: ~**rsi** *vr* (*sportivo, musicista*) to practise; ~**rsi nella guida** to practise one's driving; ~**rsi a fare qc** to practise doing sth; ~**rsi agli attrezzi** (*Sport*) to practise on the apparatus.

esercitazione [ezertʃitat'tsjone] *sf* (**a**) (*Univ: di materie scientifiche*) practical (class); (: *di lingue*) language class. (**b**) (*Mil*): ~ **navale/militare** naval/military exercise; ~**i di tiro** target practice *sg*.

esercito [e'zɛrtʃito] *sm* (*Mil*) army; (*fig: di persone*) host.

esercizio [ezer'tʃittsjo] *sm* (**a**) (*compito, movimento*) exercise; ~**i strutturali** (*Gram*) structural drills; **essere fuori** ~ to be out of practice; **fare** (**molto**) ~ to take a lot of exercise.

(**b**) (*di professione*) practice; (*di diritto*) exercising; (*di funzioni, culto*) exercise; **nell'**~ **delle proprie funzioni** in the execution of one's duties.

(**c**) (*Comm, Amm: gestione*) running, management; (: *azienda gestita*) business, concern; **costi d'**~ overheads; **quella ditta è in** ~ **da pochi mesi** that firm has only been in business for a few months; **aprire** *o* **avviare un** ~ to set up a business, open a shop (*o bar etc*); **pubblici** ~**i** commercial concerns; **licenza d'**~ licence to trade.

(**d**) (*Fin: anche*: ~ **finanziario**) financial year; **il bilancio dell'**~ **1984** the budget for the 1984 financial year.

esibire [ezi'bire] **1** *vt* (*bravura, capacità*) to exhibit, display; (*documenti*) to produce, present. **2**: ~**rsi** *vr* (*attore, artista*) to perform; (*fig*) to show off.

esibizione [ezibit'tsjone] *sf* (**a**) (*spettacolo*) performance. (**b**) (*sfoggio*) exhibition, showing off. (**c**) (*di documento*) presentation.

esibizionismo [ezibittsjo'nizmo] *sm* exhibitionism.

esibizionista, i, e [ezibittsjo'nista] *sm/f* exhibitionist.

esigente [ezi'dʒɛnte] *ag* (*gen*) demanding; **è** ~ **nel mangiare** he's particular about his food.

esigenza [ezi'dʒɛntsa] *sf* (*gen*) requirement, need; **aver troppe** ~**e** to be too demanding; **far fronte alle** ~**e del mercato** *o* **dei consumatori** to meet demand; **sentire l'**~ **di** to feel the need for.

esigere [e'zidʒere] *vt* (**a**) (*pretendere*) to demand; (*comportare, richiedere*) to require, call for; ~ **qc da qn** to demand sth from *o* of sb; ~ **che qn faccia qc** to expect sb to do sth; **esige il rispetto di tutti** he demands everybody's respect; ~ **troppo da se stesso** to expect too much from o.s. (**b**) (*riscuotere: debito*) to collect.

esiguo, a [e'ziguo] *ag* (*numero, quantità*) small, tiny; (*patrimonio, compenso*) meagre; (*risorse*) scanty.

esilarante [ezila'rante] *ag* hilarious; **gas** ~ laughing gas.

esile ['ɛzile] *ag* (*persona*) slender, slim; (*stelo*) thin; (*voce*) faint; **un** ~ **filo di speranza** a faint ray of hope, a glimmer of hope.

esiliare [ezi'ljare] **1** *vt* (*Pol*) to exile; (*fig*) to banish. **2**: ~**rsi** *vr* (*Pol*) to go into exile; ~**rsi dal mondo** (*fig*) to cut o.s. off from the world.

esiliato, a [ezi'ljato] **1** *ag* exiled. **2** *sm/f* exile.

esilio [e'ziljo] *sm* exile.

esilità [ezili'ta] *sf (vedi ag)* slenderness, slimness; thinnes; faintness.

esimere [e'zimere] **1** *vt:* ~ qn da qc to exempt sb from sth. **2:** ~rsi *vr:* ~rsi da qc/dal fare qc to get out of sth/doing sth.

esimio, a [e'zimjo] *ag* distinguished, eminent.

esistente [ezis'tɛnte] *ag (gen)* existing; **tuttora** ~ *(persona)* still alive *o* living; *(casa)* which still exists.

esistenza [ezis'tɛntsa] *sf (gen)* existence; *(vita)* life, existence.

esistenziale [ezisten'tsjale] *ag* existential.

esistere [e'zistere] *vi (aus essere) (gen)* to exist; **esistono ancora dubbi in merito** there are still some doubts about it; **questo modello esiste in due colori** this model comes *o* can be found in two colours.

esistito, a [ezis'tito] *pp di* **esistere.**

esitante [ezi'tante] *ag* hesitant; *(voce)* faltering.

esitare [ezi'tare] *vi* to hesitate; **esitava a prendere una decisione** he was reluctant to take a decision; **esitava tra il sì e il no** he wasn't sure whether to say yes or no; **esitò a rispondere** he hesitated before answering; **senza** ~ without (any) hesitation.

esitazione [ezitat'tsjone] *sf* hesitation; **dopo molte** ~i after much hesitation; **senza** ~ unhesitatingly, without (any) hesitation.

esito ['ɛzito] *sm* result, outcome; **avere buon** ~ to be successful; **quest'anno gli esami hanno avuto un** ~ **negativo** this year the exam results were poor; **le analisi hanno avuto un** ~ **negativo** the results of the tests were negative.

eskimo ['eskimo] *sm (giaccone)* parka.

esodo ['ɛzodo] *sm* exodus.

esofago, gi [e'zɔfago] *sm* oesophagus.

esonerare [ezone'rare] *vt:* ~ da *(servizio militare)* to exempt from; *(lezioni)* to excuse from.

esonero [e'zɔnero] *sm* exemption.

esorbitante [ezorbi'tante] *ag* exorbitant, excessive.

esorbitare [ezorbi'tare] *vi:* ~ da to go beyond.

esorcismo [ezor'tʃizmo] *sm* exorcism.

esorcista, i [ezor'tʃista] *sm* exorcist.

esorcizzare [ezortʃid'dzare] *vt* to exorcise.

esordiente [ezor'djɛnte] **1** *ag:* **un attore/calciatore** ~ an actor/ footballer who is making his professional debut. **2** *sm/f* beginner.

esordio [e'zɔrdjo] *sm* debut, first appearance; **la sua carriera è ancora agli** ~i his career is just beginning.

esordire [ezor'dire] *vi (nel teatro)* to make one's debut; *(fig)* to start out, begin (one's career); **esordì giovanissima** she made her debut when she was very young; **esordì dicendo che...** he began by saying (that).... .

esortare [ezor'tare] *vt* to exhort, urge; **lo esortai a partire al più presto** I urged him to leave as soon as possible.

esortazione [ezortat'tsjone] *sf* exhortation.

esoso, a [e'zozo] *ag* **(a)** *(prezzo)* exorbitant. **(b)** *(persona: avido)* grasping.

esoterico, a, ci, che [ezo'tɛriko] *ag* esoteric.

esotico, a, ci, che [e'zɔtiko] *ag* exotic.

esotismo [ezo'tizmo] *sm* exoticism.

espandere [es'pandere] **1** *vt (gen)* to expand; *(confini)* to extend; *(influenza)* to extend, spread. **2:** ~rsi *vr* to expand.

espansione [espan'sjone] *sf (estensione)* expansion; **in** ~ *(di economia)* booming; *(di universo)* expanding; **a** ~ *(Tecn: motori)* expansion *attr.*

espansionismo [espansjo'nizmo] *sm* expansionism.

espansionistico, a, ci, che [espansjo'nistiko] *ag* expansionist.

espansività [espansivi'ta] *sf* expansiveness.

espansivo, a [espan'sivo] *ag (persona)* expansive, communicative; **poco** ~ restrained, not very forthcoming.

espanso, a [es'panso] *pp di* **espandere.**

espatriare [espa'trjare] *vi (aus essere)* to leave the country.

espatrio [es'patrjo] *sm* expatriation; **permesso di** ~ authorization to leave the country.

espediente [espe'djɛnte] *sm* expedient; **cercare un** ~ **per trarsi d'impaccio** to try and find a way out of a difficult situation; **vivere di** ~i to live by one's wits.

espellere [es'pɛllere] *vt* **(a):** ~ *(da) (gen, da scuola)* to expel (from); *(da paese)* to deport (from); *(Sport):* ~ **(dal campo)** to send off (the field). **(b)** *(gas)* to discharge; *(cartucce usate)* to eject.

esperanto [espe'ranto] *sm* Esperanto.

esperienza [espe'rjɛntsa] *sf* **(a)** experience; **senza** ~ inexperienced; **avere molta** ~ **di/in** to have a lot of experience of/in; **parlare/sapere per** ~ to speak/know from experience; **fare** *o* **acquisire** ~ to gain experience; **ha dieci anni di** ~ **nell'insegnamento** he has ten years' teaching experience; ~e **di lavoro** work experience. **(b)** *(scientifico)* experiment.

esperimento [esperi'mento] *sm* experiment; **a titolo di** ~ experimentally; **sottoporre qc ad** ~ to carry out an experiment on sth.

esperto, a [es'pɛrto] **1** *ag* **(a)** *(competente)* expert; *(operaio)* skilled. **(b)** *(che ha esperienza)* experienced; **è abbastanza** ~ **nella guida** he is a fairly experienced driver. **2** *sm/f* expert; **è un** ~ **di botanica** he is a botany expert *o* an expert on botany.

espiare [espi'are] *vt* to expiate, atone for.

espiatorio, a [espia'tɔrjo] *ag* expiatory.

espiazione [espiat'tsjone] *sf:* ~ **(di)** expiation (of), atonement (for).

espirare [espi'rare] *vt, vi* to breathe out, exhale.

espirazione [espirat'tsjone] *sf* breathing out, exhalation.

espletamento [espleta'mento] *sm (Amm)* carrying out; **l'** ~ **delle pratiche richiede 2 mesi** the completion of all formalities will require 2 months.

espletare [esple'tare] *vt (Amm)* to carry out.

esplicare [espli'kare] *vt (incarico, attività)* to carry out, perform.

esplicativo, a [esplika'tivo] *ag* explanatory.

esplicito, a [es'plitʃito] *ag* explicit.

esplodere [es'plɔdere] **1** *vi (aus essere) (anche fig)* to explode; *(bomba)* to explode, blow up; **far** ~ **una bomba** to explode a bomb; ~ **per la rabbia** to explode with anger; ~ **in una risata** to burst out laughing; **è esplosa l'estate** summer has arrived with a bang. **2** *vt:* ~ **un colpo contro qn** to fire a shot at sb.

esplorare [esplo'rare] *vt* **(a)** *(gen, fig)* to explore. **(b)** *(Mil)* to reconnoitre.

esplorativo, a [esplora'tivo] *ag* exploratory.

esploratore [esplora'tore] *sm* explorer; *(militare)* scout; *(: nave)* scout (ship); **giovane** ~ (boy) scout.

esplorazione [esplorat'tsjone] *sf* exploration; *(Mil)* reconnaissance; **mandare qn in** ~ *(Mil)* to send sb to scout ahead.

esplosione [esplo'zjone] *sf (gen)* explosion; *(fig: di rabbia, gioia)* outburst.

esplosivo, a [esplo'zivo] *ag, sm* explosive.

esploso, a [es'plɔzo] *pp di* **esplodere.**

esponente [espo'nɛnte] **1** *sm/f (rappresentante)* exponent, representative. **2** *sm (Mat)* exponent.

esponenziale [esponen'tsjale] *ag (Mat)* exponential.

esporre [es'porre] **1** *vt* **(a)** *(esibire: merce)* to put on display, display; *(: quadri)* to exhibit, show; *(: avviso)* to put up, display; *(: bandiera)* to put up, raise; **esposto al pubblico** on display to the public. **(b)** *(spiegare)* to explain; *(argomento, teoria)* to put forward; *(fatti, ragionamenti)* to set out; *(dubbi, riserve)* to express; ~ **a voce/per iscritto** to explain verbally/in writing. **(c)** *(mettere in pericolo)*: ~ **qn al pericolo** to expose sb to danger; ~ **la propria vita a un rischio** to risk one's life; ~ **il fianco a critiche** to lay o.s. open to criticism. **(d)** *(alla luce, all'aria: anche Fot)* to expose.
    2: esporsi *vr*: **esporsi a** *(sole, pericolo)* to expose o.s. to; *(critiche)* to lay o.s. open to; **stai attento a non esporti troppo** be careful not to lay yourself open to criticism *(o punishment etc)*.

esportare [espor'tare] *vt* to export.

esportatore, trice [esporta'tore] **1** *ag* exporting *attr.* **2** *sm/f* exporter.

esportazione [esportat'tsjone] *sf (azione)* export, exportation; *(insieme di prodotti)* exports *pl*; **di** ~ *(agenzia, permesso)* export *attr.*

esposimetro [espo'zimetro] *sm (Fot)* exposure meter.

espositore, trice [espozi'tore] **1** *ag* exhibiting. **2** *sm/f* exhibitor.

esposizione [espozit'tsjone] *sf* **(a)** *(di merce)* display; *(di fatti, ragioni)* exposition. **(b)** *(fiera, mostra)* exhibition, show. **(c)** *(posizione di casa)* aspect; **casa con** ~ **a nord** house facing north. **(d)** *(Fot, al sole)* exposure.

esposto, a [es'posto] **1** *pp di* **esporre. 2** *ag* **(a)** *(edificio)*: ~ **a nord** facing north. **(b)** *(Med: frattura)* compound *attr.* **3** *sm (Amm)* statement, account; *(: petizione)* petition; **fare un** ~ **a qn** to send a report to sb, give sb a report.

espressamente [espressa'mente] *av (esplicitamente)* expressly, explicitly; *(appositamente)* especially.

espressione [espres'sjone] *sf (gen, Mat)* expression.

espressività [espressivi'ta] *sf* expressiveness.

espressivo, a [espres'sivo] *ag* expressive; **silenzio** ~ eloquent silence.

espresso[1], a [es'presso] *pp di* **esprimere.**

espresso[2], a [es'presso] **1** *ag (desiderio, treno)* express; *(caffè)* espresso. **2** *sm (lettera)* express letter; *(treno)* express; *(caffè)* espresso (coffee).

esprimere [es'primere] **1** *vt* to express; *(opinione)* to voice, express. **2:** ~**rsi** *vr* to express o.s.; ~**rsi a gesti** to use sign language.

esprimibile [espri'mibile] *ag* expressible.

espropriare [espro'prjare] *vt (terreni, edifici)* to place a compulsory purchase order on; **l'hanno espropriato dei suoi beni** they dispossessed him of his property, they expropriated his property.

espropriazione [esproprjat'tsjone] *sf*, **esproprio** [es'prɔprjo] *sm* expropriation; ~ **per pubblica utilità** compulsory purchase.

espugnare [espuɲ'ɲare] *vt* to take by force, storm.

espulsione [espul'sjone] *sf (vedi* **espellere** *a)* expulsion; deportation; sending off.

espulso, a [es'pulso] *pp di* **espellere.**

essa ['essa] *pron f*, **esse** ['esse] *pron fpl vedi* **esso.**

essenza [es'sɛntsa] *sf* **(a)** *(di argomento, libro)* gist, essence; *(Filosofia)* essence. **(b)** *(estratto: di piante)* (essential) oil, essence; *(alimentare)* essence.

essenziale [essen'tsjale] **1** *ag*: ~ **(a)** essential (to *o* for); **olio** ~ essential oil; **requisiti** ~ **i** prerequisites. **2** *sm*: **l'**~ *(oggetti necessari)* the (basic) essentials; *(punti principali)* the essentials; **riduciamo il discorso all'**~ let's restrict our discussion to the basic *o* essential points; **l'**~ **è che venga** the main *o* important thing is that he comes.

essere ['ɛssere] *(aus* **essere***)* **1** *vb copulativo* **(a)** *(gen)* to be; **è giovane/malato** he is young/ill; **è (un) professore** he is a teacher; **chi è quel tipo?** — **è Giovanni** who is that (guy)? — it's Giovanni; **non è vero** that's not true; **siamo in 10 a volerci andare** there are 10 of us wanting to go *o* who want to go.
    (b) *(data)*: **è il 12 giugno** it is June 12th; *(ora)*: **che ora è?** *o* **che ore sono?** — **sono le due** what's the time? *o* what time is it? — it's two o'clock.
    (c) *(appartenenza)*: **di chi è questo libro?** — **è mio** whose book is this? — it's mine *o* it belongs to me; **non potrò** ~ **uno dei vostri quest'estate** I shan't be able to join you this summer.
    2 *vb aus* **(a)** *(tempi composti: attivo)*: **è venuto?** has he come?; **è andato/stato in Inghilterra** he has gone/been to England; **sono cresciuto in Italia** I grew up in Italy.
    (b) *(tempi composti: passivo)*: **è stato fabbricato in India** it was made in India; **è stato investito da un'auto** he was run over by a car.
    (c) *(tempi composti: riflessivo)*: **si sono vestiti** they dressed, they got dressed.
    (d) *(+da+infin)*: **è da fare subito** it must be *o* is to be done immediately; **è da spedire stasera** it must be *o* is to be sent tonight.
    3 *vi* **(a)** *(esistere)* to be; ~ **o non** ~ to be or not to be; **sia la luce** — **e la luce fu** let there be light — and there was light; **è il miglior meccanico che ci sia** he is the best mechanic there is.
    (b) *(trovarsi)* to be; *(vivere)* to live; **sono qui da tre ore** I've been here for three hours; **è a tavola** he is eating; ~ **in piedi** to be standing; **è a Roma da due anni** he's been (living) in Rome for two years.
    (c) *(diventare)* to be; **quando sarai grande** when you grow up; **quando sarai calmo** when you calm down; **quando sarai medico** when you are a doctor.
    (d) *(provenire)*: **è di Genova** he comes from Genoa.
    4 *vb impers* **(a)**: **è tardi/Pasqua** it's late/Easter; **è da tre ore che ti aspetto** I've been waiting for you for three hours; **può** ~ perhaps; **sarà come dici tu** you may be right; **è che non mi piace** the fact is I don't like it; **è possibile che venga** he may come; **non è da te** it's not like you; **sia detto fra noi** between you and me; **come sarebbe a dire?** what do you mean?; **sarà quel che sarà** what will be will be; **che ne sarà della macchina?** what will happen to the car?; **come se niente fosse** as if nothing had happened; **sia quel che sia, io me ne vado** whatever happens I'm off.
    (b) *(costare)*: **quant'è?** how much is it?; **quant'è in tutto?** how much does that come to?; **sono mille lire** that's a thousand lire, that comes to a thousand lire.
    (c): **esserci: c'è** there is; **ci sono** there are; **quanti invitati ci saranno?** how many guests will there be?; **che (cosa)** *o* **cosa c'è?** what's wrong *o* the matter?; **che (cosa) di nuovo?** what's new?; **non c'è altro da dire** there's nothing else to be said; **ce n'è per tutti** there's enough for everybody; **c'è**

da strapparsi i capelli *(fig)* it's enough to drive you up the wall; **quanto c'è da qui a Edimburgo? how far is it from here to Edinburgh?; ci sono 60 km** it's 60 km; **c'era una volta...** once upon a time there was...; *vedi anche* **ci.**

5 *sm* being; ~ **umano** human being; **gli** ~**i viventi** the living *pl;* **è un** ~ **spregevole** he is despicable; **l'amava con tutto il suo** ~ he loved her with all his heart.

essi ['essi] *pron mpl vedi* **esso.**

essiccare [essik'kare] **1** *vt (gen)* to dry; *(legname)* to season; *(cibi)* to desiccate; *(bacino, palude)* to drain. **2:** ~**rsi** *vr (fiume, pozzo)* to dry up; *(vernice)* to dry (out).

essiccazione [essikkat'tsjone] *sf* drying (process); *(di cibi, Chim)* desiccation.

esso, a ['esso] *pron pers (neutro)* it; *(riferito a persona: sog)* he/she; *(: complemento)* him/her; ~**i, ~e** *(sog)* they; *(complemento)* them; **...o chi per** ~ ...or his delegate *o* representative.

est [est] **1** *sm* **(a)** east; **a** ~ **(di)** east (of); **verso** ~ eastward(s); **il vento dell'**~ the east wind. **(b)** *(Pol):* **l'E**~ the East; **i paesi dell'E**~ the Eastern bloc *sg.* **2** *ag inv (gen)* east; *(regione)* eastern; **è partito in direzione** ~ he set off eastwards *o* in an eastward direction.

estasi ['estazi] *sf inv (Rel, fig)* ecstasy; **andare in** ~ **(per)** *(fig)* to go into ecstasies *o* raptures (over); **mandare in** ~ to send into ecstasies *o* raptures.

estasiare [esta'zjare] **1** *vt* to send into raptures. **2:** ~**rsi** *vr:* ~**rsi (a, davanti a)** to go into ecstasies (over), go into raptures (over).

estate [es'tate] *sf* summer; **d'**~, **in** ~ in (the) summer; **un giorno d'**~ one summer's day, one day in summer.

estatico, a, ci, che [es'tatiko] *ag* ecstatic.

estemporaneo, a [estempo'raneo] *ag (discorso)* extempore, impromptu; *(brano musicale)* impromptu.

estendere [es'tendere] **1** *vt (gen)* to extend. **2:** ~**rsi** *vr* **(a)** *(diffondersi: epidemia, rivolta)* to spread; *(allargarsi: città)* to spread, expand; *(: attività commerciale)* to increase, expand. **(b)** *(foresta etc)* to stretch, extend; **la pianura si estendeva a perdita d'occhio** the plain stretched (away) as far as the eye could see.

estensibile [esten'sibile] *ag* **(a)** *(materiale)* extensible. **(b):** **una norma** ~ **a tutti i cittadini** a law which applies to all citizens.

estensione [esten'sjone] *sf* **(a)** *(ampliamento: di diritto, significato, contratto)* extension; *(di commercio, dominio)* expansion; **per** ~ by extension, in a wider sense; **in tutta l'**~ **del termine** in the widest sense of the word. **(b)** *(ampiezza: di fenomeno, territorio)* extent; *(superficie)* expanse. **(c)** *(Mus)* range.

estensivo, a [esten'sivo] *ag* extensive.

estensore [esten'sore] *sm* **(a)** *(Anat: anche:* **muscolo** ~*)* extensor (muscle). **(b)** *(attrezzo)* chest expander.

estenuante [estenu'ante] *ag* wearing, tiring.

estenuare [estenu'are] *vt (stancare)* to wear out, tire out.

esteriore [este'rjore] *ag (fig: esterno: aspetto, segni, manifestazioni)* outward *attr;* **il mondo** ~ the external world.

esteriorità [esterjori'ta] *sf inv* outward appearance.

esteriorizzare [esterjorid'dzare] *vt (gioia etc)* to show.

esternare [ester'nare] *vt* to express; ~ **un sospetto** to voice a suspicion.

esterno, a [es'terno] **1** *ag* **(a)** *(muro, superficie)*

outer, exterior; *(scala, gabinetto)* outside *attr;* *(rivestimento)* exterior; **l'aspetto** ~ **della casa** the outside of the house; **per uso** ~ *(Med)* for external use only. **(b)** *(fig: influenze, mondo)* external, outside *attr;* *(: interessi, minacce)* outside *attr;* *(: realtà)* external; **aspetto** ~ *(di persona)* outward appearance. **(c)** *(Geom):* **angolo** ~ exterior angle. **(d)** *(allievo)* day *attr;* *(candidato)* external; **commissione** ~**a** external examiners.

2 *sm (di edificio)* outside, exterior; *(di scatola)* outside; **all'**~ on the outside; **dall'**~ from outside; **gli** ~**i sono stati girati a Glasgow** *(Cine)* the location shots were taken in Glasgow.

3 *sm/f (Scol)* day pupil; *(: candidato)* external candidate.

estero, a ['estero] **1** *ag* foreign. **2** *sm:* **andare all'**~, **partire per l'**~ to go abroad; **vivere all'**~ to live abroad *o* in a foreign country; **commercio con l'**~ foreign trade; **Ministero degli E**~**i, gli E**~**i** Ministry for Foreign Affairs, ≈ Foreign Office *(Brit),* State Department *(Am).*

esterofilia [esterofi'lia] *sf* excessive love of foreign things.

esterrefatto, a [esterre'fatto] *ag (costernato)* horrified; *(sbalordito)* astounded.

esteso, a [es'teso] **1** *pp di* **estendere. 2** *ag (gen)* extensive; *(territorio)* vast; *(cultura, ricerca)* broad, wide-ranging; **(scrivere) per** ~ (to write) in full.

esteta, i, e [es'teta] *sm/f* aesthete.

estetica [es'tetika] *sf* aesthetics *sg;* **tiene molto all'**~ he's very concerned about his appearance; **gli manca completamente il senso dell'**~ he has no taste at all.

estetico, a, ci, che [es'tetiko] *ag* aesthetic; **chirurgia** ~**a** plastic surgery; **cura** ~**a** beauty treatment.

estetista [este'tista] *sf* beautician.

estimo ['estimo] *sm (stima)* valuation; *(disciplina)* surveying.

estinguere [es'tingwere] **1** *vt* **(a)** *(spegnere)* to put out, extinguish. **(b)** *(Comm: debito)* to pay off; *(: conto in banca)* to close. **2:** ~**rsi** *vr (fuoco)* to go out, die out; *(fig: fama)* to die out, fade away; *(: stirpe)* to die out.

estinto, a [es'tinto] **1** *pp di* **estinguere. 2** *ag* **(a)** *(incendio)* extinguished; *(specie, stirpe, vulcano)* extinct. **(b)** *(Comm: debito)* paid off; *(: conto)* closed. **3** *sm/f:* **i cari** ~**i** the dear departed *pl.*

estintore [estin'tore] *sm* (fire) extinguisher.

estinzione [estin'tsjone] *sf (gen)* extinction; *(di debito)* payment; *(di conto)* closing.

estirpare [estir'pare] *vt (pianta)* to uproot, pull up; *(dente)* to extract; *(tumore)* to remove; *(fig: vizio)* to eradicate.

estivo, a [es'tivo] *ag* summer *attr;* **nei mesi** ~**i** in summer(time).

estorcere [es'tortfere] *vt:* ~ **qc (a qn)** to extort sth (from sb).

estorsione [estor'sjone] *sf* extortion.

estorto, a [es'torto] *pp di* **estorcere.**

estradare [estra'dare] *vt (Dir)* to extradite.

estradizione [estradit'tsjone] *sf (Dir)* extradition.

estraneità [estranei'ta] *sf (non implicazione):* **ha tentato di dimostrare la propria** ~ **alla faccenda** he tried to prove that he had nothing to do with it.

estraneo, a [es'traneo] **1** *ag (gen)* extraneous; **corpo** ~ foreign body; *(a tema, argomento)* unrelated to; **sentirsi** ~ **a** *(famiglia, società)* to feel alienated from; **mantenersi** *o* **rimanere** ~ **a** *(litigio, complotto)* to take no part in. **2** *sm/f* stranger; **ingresso vietato agli** ~**i** no admittance to unauthorized personnel.

estraniarsi [estra'njarsi] vr: ~ **(da)** to cut o.s. off (from).

estrapolare [estrapo'lare] vt to extrapolate.

estrapolazione [estrapolat'tsjone] sf extrapolation.

estrarre [es'trarre] vt **(a)** (gen, Med, Mat) to extract; (carbone) to mine; (marmo) to quarry. **(b)** (sorteggiare) to draw; ~ **a sorte** to draw lots.

estratto, a [es'tratto] **1** pp di **estrarre**. **2** sm **(a)** (alimentare) extract; (per profumeria) essence. **(b)** (sommario: di discorso) abstract; (brano: di libro) extract, excerpt; ~ **di nascita** birth certificate; ~ **conto** (Banca) statement (of account).

estrazione [estrat'tsjone] sf **(a)** (vedi **estrarre**) extraction; mining; quarrying; drawing. **(b)** (sorteggio) draw; (fig: origine) extraction, birth.

estremismo [estre'mizmo] sm extremism.

estremista, i, e [estre'mista] sm/f extremist.

estremistico, a, ci, che [estre'mistiko] ag extremist.

estremità [estremi'ta] sf inv **(a)** (gen) end; (di ago, matita etc) point, tip; (di villaggio, lago, isola) extremity, limit; **da un'~ all'altra** from one end to the other. **(b):** ~ pl (Anat) extremities.

estremo, a [es'tremo] **1** ag (gen) extreme; (ultimo: ora, tentativo) final, last; (misure) drastic, extreme. **2** sm **(a)** (gen) extreme; (limite: di pazienza, forze) limit, end; **all'~ della disperazione** in the depths of despair; **passare da un ~ all'altro** to go from one extreme to the other; **è pignolo (fino) all'~** he is fussy in the extreme, he is extremely fussy; **spingere le cose agli ~i** to go too far; **ridursi agli ~i (della miseria)** to be reduced to abject poverty. **(b):** ~i pl (Amm: dati essenziali) details, particulars; (Dir) essential elements. **3:** ~**a destra/sinistra** (Pol) extreme right/left; **E~a Unzione** (Rel) Extreme Unction; **E~ Oriente** Far East.

estrinsecare [estrinse'kare] **1** vt to express, show. **2:** ~**rsi** vr to express o.s.; **le sue paure si sono estrinsecate** his fears became evident.

estrinseco, a, ci, che [es'trinseko] ag extrinsic.

estro ['estro] sm (ispirazione) inspiration; (dono) gift, bent; **gli è venuto l'~ di scrivere** he has taken it into his head to become a writer.

estrogeno, a [es'trɔdʒeno] ag, sm oestrogen.

estromesso, a [estro'messo] pp di **estromettere**.

estromettere [estro'mettere] vt: ~ **(da)** (partito, club etc) to expel (from); (discussione) to exclude (from).

estromissione [estromis'sjone] sf expulsion.

estroso, a [es'troso] ag (capriccioso) whimsical, fanciful; (creativo) inspired, talented.

estroverso, a [estro'verso] **1** ag extroverted. **2** sm/f extrovert.

estuario [estu'arjo] sm estuary.

esuberante [ezube'rante] ag (gen) exuberant.

esuberanza [ezube'rantsa] sf (di persona) exuberance.

esulare [ezu'lare] vi: ~ **da** (competenza) to be beyond; (compiti) not to be part of; **esula dalle mie possibilità aiutarti** it is not within my power to help you.

esule ['ezule] sm/f exile.

esultanza [ezul'tantsa] sf exultation.

esultare [ezul'tare] vi: ~ **(di)** to exult (with).

esumare [ezu'mare] vt (salma) to exhume, disinter; (fig) to unearth.

esumazione [ezumat'tsjone] sf exhumation, disinterment.

età [e'ta] sf inv (gen) age; **all'~ di 8 anni** at the age of 8, at 8 years of age; **avere l'~ per fare qc** to be old enough to do sth; **di mezza ~** middle-aged;

con l'~ è migliorato he has improved with age; **in ~ avanzata** advanced in years; **gente della nostra ~** people our age; **raggiungere la maggior ~** to come of age; **è giunto ad una bella ~** he has reached a good age; **limite di ~** age limit; **l'~ della ragione** the age of reason; **l'~ della pietra** the Stone Age.

etere ['etere] sm (Chim, poet) ether.

etereo, a [e'tɛreo] ag ethereal.

eternare [eter'nare] vt to immortalize.

eternità [eterni'ta] sf (anche fig) eternity; **impiegare o mettere un'~ a fare qc** to take ages to do sth; **ti aspetto da un'~** I've been waiting for you for ages.

eterno, a [e'tɛrno] **1** ag (Rel, Filosofia) eternal; (senza fine) eternal, everlasting; (duraturo) perpetual; (interminabile: lamenti, attesa) never-ending; **in ~** for ever, eternally. **2** sm eternity; **l'E~** (Dio) the Eternal.

eterogeneità [eterodʒenei'ta] sf heterogeneousness.

eterogeneo, a [etero'dʒɛneo] ag heterogeneous.

etica ['etika] sf ethics sg.

etichetta [eti'ketta] sf label; (cerimoniale): **l'~** etiquette.

etichettare [etiket'tare] vt to label.

etichettatrice [etiketta'tritʃe] sf (macchina) labelling machine, labeller.

etico, a, ci, che ['etiko] ag ethical.

etilico, a, ci, che [e'tiliko] ag: **alcool ~** ethyl alcohol.

etimologia [etimolo'dʒia] sf etymology.

etimologico, a, ci, che [etimo'lɔdʒiko] ag etymological.

etiope [e'tiope] ag, sm/f Ethiopian.

Etiopia [eti'ɔpja] sf Ethiopia.

etiopico, a, ci, che [eti'ɔpiko] **1** ag Ethiopian. **2** sm (lingua) Ethiopian.

etnico, a, ci, che ['etniko] ag ethnic.

etnografia [etnogra'fia] sf ethnography.

etnologia [etnolo'dʒia] sf ethnology.

etnologico, a, ci, che [etno'lɔdʒiko] ag ethnological.

etrusco, a, schi, sche [e'trusko] ag, sm/f Etruscan.

ettaro ['ettaro] sm hectare.

etto ['etto] **1** pref: ~... hecto.... **2** sm abbr di **ettogrammo**.

ettogrammo [etto'grammo] sm hectogram(me).

ettolitro [et'tɔlitro] sm hectolitre.

eucalipto [euka'lipto] sm eucalyptus.

eucaristia [eukaris'tia] sf: **l'~** the Eucharist.

eufemismo [eufe'mizmo] sm euphemism.

euforia [eufo'ria] sf euphoria.

euforico, a, ci, che [eu'fɔriko] ag euphoric.

eunuco, chi [eu'nuko] sm eunuch.

eurasiatico, a, ci, che [eura'zjatiko] ag, sm/f Eurasian.

eurodollaro [euro'dɔllaro] sm Eurodollar.

euromissile [euro'missile] sm Euromissile.

Europa [eu'rɔpa] sf Europe.

europeismo [europe'izmo] sm (Pol) Europeanism.

europeizzare [europeid'dzare] vt to europeanize.

europeo, a [euro'pɛo] ag, sm/f European.

Eurovisione [eurovi'zjone] sf Eurovision.

eutanasia [eutana'zia] sf euthanasia.

evacuamento [evakua'mento] sm evacuation.

evacuare [evaku'are] vt, vi (gen, Med) to evacuate.

evacuazione [evakuat'tsjone] sf evacuation.

evadere [e'vadere] **1** vt **(a)** (Amm: sbrigare: pratica) to deal with, dispatch; (Comm: rispondere a: corrispondenza) to deal with, clear; (: ordine) to deal with. **(b)** (Dir: tasse, imposte) to evade; ~ **il**

fisco to evade (income) tax. **2** *vi (aus essere)*: ~ **(da)** *(prigione)* to escape (from); *(situazione)* to escape (from), get out (of); **far** ~ **qn** to help sb to escape; **ho deciso di** ~ **un po'** I've decided to get away for a while.

evanescente [evaneʃ'ʃɛnte] *ag* evanescent.

evanescenza [evaneʃ'ʃɛntsa] *sf* evanescence.

evangelico, a, ci, che [evan'dʒɛliko] *ag, sm/f* evangelical.

evangelista, i [evandʒe'lista] *sm* Evangelist.

evangelizzare [evandʒelid'dzare] *vt* to evangelize.

evaporare [evapo'rare] *vt, vi (aus essere nel senso di 'diventare vapore'; avere nel senso di 'diminuire per evaporazione')* to evaporate.

evaporazione [evaporat'tsjone] *sf* evaporation.

evasione [eva'zjone] *sf* **(a)** *(anche fig)* escape; **letteratura d'**~ escapist literature. **(b)** *(Amm: disbrigo: di ordine)* carrying out, fulfilment; **qualcuno deve occuparsi dell'**~ **della corrispondenza** somebody must deal with the correspondence. **(c)** *(Fisco)* evasion; ~ **fiscale** tax evasion.

evasivo, a [eva'zivo] *ag* evasive.

evaso, a [e'vazo] **1** *pp di* **evadere. 2** *sm/f* escaped prisoner.

evasore [eva'zore] *sm*: ~ **(fiscale)** tax evader.

evenienza [eve'njɛntsa] *sf*: **nell'**~ **che ciò succeda** should that happen; **essere pronto ad ogni** ~ to be ready for anything *o* any eventuality; **in ogni** ~ **puoi metterti in contatto con me** you can get in touch with me should the need arise.

evento [e'vɛnto] *sm* event.

eventuale [eventu'ale] *ag (cliente, sostituto etc)* possible; **gli** ~**i guadagni saranno devoluti in beneficenza** any profit will be given to charity; **per** ~**i reclami rivolgersi a...** (any) claims should be addressed to... .

eventualità [eventuali'ta] *sf inv* eventuality, possibility; **tenersi pronto a ogni** ~ *o* **a tutte le** ~ to be prepared for any eventuality *o* for all eventualities; **nell'**~ **di** in the event of; **nell'**~ **che non dovesse tornare...** should he not return... .

eventualmente [eventual'mente] *av* if need be, if necessary; ~ **ci fossero difficoltà...** should there be any problems... .

eversione [ever'sjone] *sf* subversion.

eversivo, a [ever'sivo] *ag* subversive.

evidente [evi'dɛnte] *ag* obvious, evident; **è una prova** ~ **di...** it's clear proof of...; **è** ~ **che** it is obvious *o* evident that; **è** ~**!** obviously!

evidenza [evi'dɛntsa] *sf*: **l'**~ **dei fatti è schiacciante** the facts speak for themselves; **arrendersi di fronte all'**~ **dei fatti** to yield to the evidence; **negare l'**~ **(dei fatti)** to deny the facts *o* the

obvious; **mettere in** ~ *(problemi)* to highlight, bring to the fore.

evidenziatore [evidentsja'tore] *sm (penna)* highlighter.

evirare [evi'rare] *vt* to castrate.

evirazione [evirat'tsjone] *sf* castration.

evitabile [evi'tabile] *ag* avoidable.

evitare [evi'tare] *vt (gen)* to avoid; *(colpo)* to dodge; *(sguardo)* to evade; ~ **di fare qc** to avoid doing sth; ~ **che qc accada** to prevent sth (from) happening; ~ **qc a qn** to spare sb sth; **ciò gli ha evitato il fastidio di tornare indietro** that saved him the bother of going back; **evita di fare rumore** try not to make any noise.

evo ['ɛvo] *sm*: **l'**~ **moderno/antico** modern/ancient times.

evocare [evo'kare] *vt (gen)* to evoke; *(ricordo)* to recall, evoke.

evocativo, a [evoka'tivo] *ag* evocative.

evocazione [evokat'tsjone] *sf* evocation.

evolutivo, a [evolu'tivo] *ag (gen, Bio)* evolutionary; *(Med)* progressive.

evoluto, a [evo'luto] **1** *pp di* **evolversi. 2** *ag (popolo, civiltà)* (highly) developed, advanced; *(persona: emancipato)* independent; (: *senza pregiudizi)* broad-minded.

evoluzione [evolut'tsjone] *sf* **(a)** *(gen)* evolution; *(progresso)* progress, development; **teoria dell'**~ theory of evolution. **(b)** *(movimento)* movement; *(Mil)* manoeuvre.

evolversi [e'vɔlversi] **1** *vr* to evolve. **2** *sm*: **con l'**~ **della situazione** as the situation developed.

evviva [ev'viva] **1** *escl* hurrah; ~ **il re!** long live the King! **2** *sm inv* applause *no pl*.

ex [ɛks] **1** *pref* ex, former. **2** *sm/f inv* ex-boyfriend/girlfriend.

ex aequo [ɛg'zɛkwo] *av*: **classificarsi primo** ~ to come joint first, come equal first.

expertise [ɛksper'tiz] *sf inv (di opera d'arte)* authentication.

exploit [ɛks'plwa] *sm inv* exploit, feat.

extra ['ɛkstra] *ag inv, sm inv* extra.

extraconiugale [ɛkstrakonju'gale] *ag* extramarital.

extraeuropeo, a [ɛkstraeuro'pɛo] *ag* non-European.

extraparlamentare [ɛkstraparlamen'tare] *ag* extraparliamentary.

extrasensoriale [ɛkstrasenso'rjale] *ag* extrasensory.

extraterritoriale [ɛkstraterrito'rjale] *ag* extraterritorial.

extraurbano, a [ɛkstraur'bano] *ag* suburban.

ex voto [ɛks'vɔto] *sm inv* ex voto.

F

F, f [ˈeffe] *sf o m inv (lettera)* F, f.
F. *abbr di* **Fahrenheit**.
fa¹ [fa] **1** *3ᵃ pers sg del presente di* **fare. 2** *av:* **10 anni**
~ 10 years ago; quanto tempo ~? how long ago?
fa² [fa] *sm inv (Mus)* F; *(: solfeggiando)* fa.
fabbisogno [fabbiˈzoɲɲo] *sm* needs *pl*, requirements *pl;* **il ~ nazionale di petrolio** the country's oil requirements.
fabbrica, che [ˈfabbrika] *sf* factory; **~ di mattoni** brickyard; **~ di carta** paper mill.
fabbricante [fabbriˈkante] *sm/f* manufacturer.
fabbricare [fabbriˈkare] *vt (produrre: gen)* to make; *(: a livello industriale)* to manufacture; *(costruire: edificio)* to build, put up; *(fig: inventare: alibi, scuse)* to fabricate, make up.
fabbricato [fabbriˈkato] *sm* building.
fabbricazione [fabbrikatˈtsjone] *sf (vedi vb)* making; manufacture, manufacturing; building; fabrication; **di ~ italiana** made in Italy, of Italian make; **difetto di ~** manufacturing defect.
fabbro [ˈfabbro] *sm* smith; **~ ferraio** blacksmith.
faccenda [fatˈtʃenda] *sf (affare)* business, affair, matter; **una brutta ~** a nasty business; **devo sbrigare alcune ~e** I've got a few things *o* some business to see to; **le ~e domestiche** the housework.
faccetta [fatˈtʃetta] *sf (di pietra preziosa)* facet.
facchinaggio [fakkiˈnaddʒo] *sm* porterage.
facchino [fakˈkino] *sm (gen)* porter; **comportarsi come un ~** *(fig)* to behave like a navvy; **lavoro da ~** *(fig)* drudgery.
faccia, ce [ˈfattʃa] *sf* **(a)** *(viso, espressione)* face; **una ~ amica** a friendly face; **avere la ~ stanca** to look tired; **fare la ~ imbronciata** to sulk; **dovevi vedere la sua ~ quando...** you should have seen his face when...; **avere il sole in ~** to have the sun in one's eyes; **gliel'ho detto in ~** I told him to his face; **ridere in ~ a qn** to laugh in sb's face; **leggere qc in ~ a qn** to see sth written all over sb's face; **perdere/salvare la ~** to lose/save (one's) face; **avere la ~ (tosta) di dire/fare qc** to have the face *o* nerve to say/do sth.
(b) *(lato: gen)* side; *(: Geom)* face, side; *(: della terra)* face; *(: fig: di problema, questione)* side, aspect; **vorrei cancellarlo dalla ~ della terra** I'd like to wipe him off the face of the earth.
(c): (a) ~ a ~ face to face; **a ~ in su/giù** face up(wards)/down(wards); **fare qc alla ~ di qn** to do sth to spite sb; **di ~ a** opposite, facing; **visto di ~** seen from the front.
facciale [fatˈtʃale] *ag* facial.
facciata [fatˈtʃata] *sf* **(a)** *(Archit)* façade; *(fig: apparenza esterna)* appearances *pl;* **non giudicare dalla ~** don't judge by appearances. **(b)** *(di pagina)* side; **una lettera di 4 ~e** a 4-page letter.
faceto, a [faˈtʃeto] *ag* witty, humorous.
facezia [faˈtʃettsja] *sf* witticism, witty remark.
fachiro [faˈkiro] *sm* fakir.
facile [ˈfatʃile] *ag* **(a)** *(gen)* easy; **è più ~ a dirsi che a farsi** it's easier said than done; **è meno ~ di quanto sembri** it's harder than it looks; **far tutto**

~ to make light *o* little of everything; avere la pistola ~ to be ready with one's gun; **avere la lacrima ~** to be easily moved to tears; **è ~ all'ira/alla malinconia** he's easily angered/depressed; **avere un carattere ~** to be an easygoing person; **donna di ~i costumi** woman of easy virtue, loose woman. **(b)** *(probabile):* **è ~ che piova** it's likely to rain; **è ~ che venga** he's likely to come, he'll probably come.
facilità [fatʃiliˈta] *sf inv* **(a)** *(di lavoro, compito)* easiness; *(di vittoria)* ease; **studia con ~** he has no problem studying; **arrabbiarsi con ~** to be easily angered. **(b)** *(disposizione, dono)* ability, aptitude; **ha ~ a farsi amicizie** he makes friends easily.
facilitare [fatʃiliˈtare] *vt* to facilitate, make easier; **non faciliterà la situazione** it's not going to make matters any easier; **~ un cliente** *(Fin)* to assist a client financially.
facilitazione [fatʃilitatˈtsjone] *sf (gen)* facilities *pl;* **~i di pagamento** easy terms, credit facilities.
facilmente [fatʃilˈmente] *av (gen)* easily; *(probabilmente)* probably.
facilone, a [fatʃiˈlone] *sm/f (peg)* happy-go-lucky person.
faciloneria [fatʃiloneˈria] *sf* happy-go-lucky attitude, slapdash attitude.
facinoroso, a [fatʃinoˈroso] **1** *ag* violent. **2** *sm/f* thug.
facoltà [fakolˈta] *sf inv* **(a)** *(capacità mentale)* faculty; *(proprietà: Chim etc)* property; **nel pieno possesso delle proprie ~ mentali** in full possession of one's faculties. **(b)** *(autorità)* power; **dare ~ a qn di fare qc** to give sb the power *o* authority to do sth; **esula dalle mie ~** it's not within my power. **(c)** *(Univ:)* faculty.
facoltativo, a [fakoltaˈtivo] *ag* optional; **fermata ~a** request stop.
facoltoso, a [fakolˈtoso] *ag* wealthy, rich.
facsimile [fakˈsimile] *sm inv* facsimile; *(fig: cosa simile)* copy.
factotum [fakˈtɔtum] *sm/f inv:* **è il ~ della ditta** he does all the real work in the firm; **sarebbe una semplice segretaria ma in pratica è la ~** she's supposed to be a secretary but in reality she does a bit of everything.
faggio [ˈfaddʒo] *sm (albero, legno)* beech; **mobili di ~ in ~** beech(wood) furniture.
fagiano [faˈdʒano] *sm* pheasant.
fagiolino [fadʒoˈlino] *sm* French bean, string bean.
fagiolo [faˈdʒɔlo] *sm* bean; **capitare a ~** to come at the right time.
fagocitare [fagotʃiˈtare] *vt (Bio)* to phagocytize; *(fig: industria etc)* to absorb, swallow up; *(scherz: cibo)* to devour.
fagotto¹ [faˈgɔtto] *sm* bundle; **fare ~** to pack up and leave.
fagotto² [faˈgɔtto] *sm (Mus)* bassoon.
Fahrenheit [ˈfaːrənhait] *sm* Fahrenheit.
faida [ˈfaida] *sf* feud.

faina |fa'ina| *sf (Zool)* stone marten.

falange |fa'landʒe| *sf (Anat, Mil)* phalanx.

falcata |fal'kata| *sf* stride.

falce |'faltʃe| *sf* scythe; **una ~ di luna** a crescent moon; **~ e martello** *(Pol)* hammer and sickle.

falcetto |fal'tʃetto| *sm* sickle.

falciare |fal'tʃare| *vt (fieno)* to reap; *(erba)* to mow, cut; *(con la falce)* to scythe; **furono falciati da una raffica di mitra** they were mown down by machine-gun fire.

falciatrice |faltʃa'tritʃe| *sf (per fieno)* reaping machine; *(per erba)* mowing machine.

falciatura |faltʃa'tura| *sf (vedi vb)* reaping; mowing.

falco, chi |'falko| *sm (Zool, fig Pol)* hawk; **~ pescatore** osprey; **occhio di ~!** you're sharp-eyed!

falcone |fal'kone| *sm* falcon.

falconeria |falkone'ria| *sf* falconry.

falda |'falda| *sf (Geol)* layer, stratum; *(di cappello)* brim; *(di cappotto)* tails *pl*; *(di monte)* lower slope; *(di tetto)* pitch; *(di neve)* flake.

falegname |faleɲ'ɲame| *sm* carpenter.

falegnameria |faleɲɲame'ria| *sf (a) (mestiere)* carpentry. **(b)** *(locale)* carpenter's shop.

falena |fa'lena| *sf (Zool)* moth.

falla |'falla| *sf* leak.

fallace |fal'latʃe| *ag* misleading, deceptive.

fallacia, cie |fal'latʃa| *sf* fallacy.

fallico, a, ci, che |'falliko| *ag* phallic.

fallimentare |fallimen'tare| *ag (Comm)* bankruptcy *attr*; **bilancio ~** negative balance, deficit; **diritto ~** bankruptcy law; **'tutto a prezzo ~'** 'everything at drastically reduced prices'; **il bilancio della sua vita era ~** his life was simply a failure; **fu un'esperienza ~** it was simply a failure.

fallimento |falli'mento| *sm (a) (fiasco)* failure, flop. **(b)** *(Comm, Dir)* bankruptcy; **essere/andare in ~** to be/go bankrupt.

fallire |fal'lire| **1** *vt (colpo, bersaglio)* to miss. **2** *vi (aus essere)* **(a): ~ (in)** to fail (in), be unsuccessful (in). **(b)** *(Comm)* to go bankrupt.

fallito, a |fal'lito| **1** *ag (commerciante)* bankrupt; *(tentativo)* unsuccessful. **2** *sm/f (Comm)* bankrupt; *(fig)* failure.

fallo[1] |'fallo| *sm (a) (errore)* fault, error; **essere in ~** to be at fault *o* in error; **mettere il piede in ~** to slip; **cogliere qn in ~** to catch sb out (in a mistake); **senza ~** without fail. **(b)** *(difetto)* fault, defect. **(c)** *(Sport)* fault, foul.

fallo[2] |'fallo| *sm (Anat)* phallus.

fallocrate |fal'lɔkrate| *sm* male chauvinist.

falloso, a |fal'loso| *ag (Sport):* **gioco ~** foul play, incorrect play.

falò |fa'lɔ| *sm inv* bonfire.

falsare |fal'sare| *vt (notizia, realtà etc)* to distort.

falsariga, ghe |falsa'riga| *sf* lined page, ruled page; **sulla ~ di...** *(fig)* along the lines of... .

falsario |fal'sarjo| *sm* forger, counterfeiter.

falsetto |fal'setto| *sm (Mus)* falsetto; **cantare in ~** to sing falsetto.

falsificare |falsifi'kare| *vt (firma, documento, denaro)* to forge; *(conti)* to falsify.

falsificazione |falsifikat'tsjone| *sf* forging; **di difficile ~** difficult to forge.

falsità |falsi'ta| *sf inv* **(a)** *(di persona, notizia)* falseness. **(b)** *(bugia)* falsehood, lie.

falso, a |'falso| **1** *ag (denaro, documenti)* forged, fake; *(oro, gioielli)* imitation *attr*; *(pudore, promessa)* false; **fare un passo ~** to stumble; *(fig)* to slip up; **sotto ~a luce** in a false light; **~ allarme** false alarm; **~a partenza** *(anche fig)* false start; **essere un ~ magro** to be heavier than one looks.

2 *sm* **(a)** falsehood; **dire il ~** to lie, not to tell the truth; **giurare il ~** *(Dir)* to commit perjury. **(b)** *(Dir)* forgery; **~ in atto pubblico** forgery (of a legal document). **(c)** *(opera d'arte)* fake.

fama |'fama| *sf (a) (celebrità)* fame, renown; **raggiungere la ~** to become famous *o* well-known; **di ~ mondiale** world famous. **(b)** *(reputazione)* reputation, name; **conoscere qn di *o* per ~** to know sb by reputation; **ha (la) ~ di essere un dongiovanni** he has a reputation for being a Don Juan.

fame |'fame| *sf* hunger; **aver ~** to be hungry; **ho una ~ da lupo** I'm famished, I could eat a horse; **aver ~ di** *(fig: giustizia etc)* to hunger *o* long for; **fare la ~** *(fig)* to starve, exist at subsistence level.

famelico, a, ci, che |fa'mɛliko| *ag* ravenous.

famigerato, a |famidʒe'rato| *ag* notorious, ill-famed.

famiglia |fa'miʎʎa| *sf (gen, Zool, Bot)* family; **essere di buona ~** to come from a good family; **metter su ~** to start a family; **amico/festa di ~** family friend/celebration; **cerimonia in ~** quiet ceremony, family ceremony; **passare il Natale in ~** to spend Christmas with one's family; **è uno della ~** *(fig)* he's one of the family; **la Sacra F~** the Holy Family.

familiare |fami'ljare| **1** *ag (a) (di famiglia)* family *attr*; **vita ~** family life; **una FIAT ~** a FIAT estate car. **(b)** *(noto)* familiar; **questo nome mi è ~** I've heard this name before, I know the name. **(c)** *(intimo: rapporti, atmosfera)* friendly; *(: tono)* informal; *(lessico: colloquiale)* informal, colloquial. **2** *sm/f* relative, relation; **i miei ~i** my relations *o* family *sg*.

familiarità |familjari'ta| *sf* familiarity; **trattare qn con ~** to treat sb in a friendly way; **aver ~ con qc** to be familiar with sth.

familiarizzare |familjarid'dzare| *vi:* **~ (con)** to get to know; **abbiamo familiarizzato subito** we got on well together from the start; **~ *o* ~rsi con l'ambiente** to familiarize o.s. with one's environment.

famoso, a |fa'moso| *ag* famous, well-known.

fanale |fa'nale| *sm (Aut)* light; *(luce stradale)* lamp; *(di faro)* beacon; **~ di poppa** *(Naut)* stern light.

fanalino |fana'lino| *sm* light; **~ di coda** *(Aut, Aer)* tail light; *(fig)* tail end; **~ di posizione** *(Aut)* sidelight.

fanatico, a, ci, che |fa'natiko| **1** *ag* fanatical; **~ di *o* per** wild about. **2** *sm/f* fanatic; **è un ~ del golf/di Fellini** he is a golf/Fellini fanatic.

fanatismo |fana'tizmo| *sm* fanaticism.

fanciullesco, a, schi, sche |fantʃul'lesko| *ag* childlike; *(peg)* childish.

fanciullezza |fantʃul'lettsa| *sf* childhood.

fanciullo, a |fan'tʃullo| *sm/f* child.

fandonia |fan'dɔnja| *sf* fib, story; **~e!** nonsense!, rubbish!

fanfara |fan'fara| *sf (banda)* brass band; *(musica)* fanfare.

fanfarone |fanfa'rone| *sm* braggart.

fanghiglia |fan'giʎʎa| *sf* mire, mud.

fango, ghi |'fango| *sm* mud; **gettare ~ addosso a qn** *(fig)* to sling mud at sb; **fare i ~ghi** *(Med)* to take a course of mud baths.

fangoso, a |fan'goso| *ag* muddy.

fannullone, a |fannul'lone| *sm/f* idler, loafer.

fantapolitica |fantapo'litika| *sf* political fiction.

fantascientifico, a, ci, che |fantaʃʃen'tifiko| *ag* science fiction *attr*.

fantascienza |fantaʃ'ʃentsa| *sf* science fiction.

fantasia |fanta'zia| *sf (a) (facoltà)* imagination,

fancy; **avere** ~ to have imagination; **non ha** ~ he doesn't have any imagination; **lavori troppo di** ~ your imagination is running away with you; **sono** ~**e le tue!** it's just your imagination!; **nel mondo della** ~ in the realm of fantasy o fancy. **(b)** (*capriccio*) whim, caprice; ~ **passeggera** passing fancy. **(c)** (*decorazione*) pattern; **lo vuole tinta unita o** ~? would you like it plain or patterned? **(d)** (*Mus*) fantasia.

fantasioso, a [fanta'zjoso] *ag* (*dotato di fantasia*) imaginative; (*bizzarro*) fanciful, strange.

fantasista, i, e [fanta'zista] *sm/f* variety artist.

fantasma, i [fan'tazma] *sm* (*spettro*) ghost, spectre.

fantasmagoria [fantazmago'ria] *sf* phantasmagoria.

fantasmagorico, a, ci, che [fantazma'gɔriko] *ag* phantasmagorical.

fantasticare [fantasti'kare] *vi* to daydream.

fantasticheria [fantastike'ria] *sf* daydream.

fantastico, a, ci, che [fan'tastiko] *ag* (*gen*) fantastic; (*potenza, ingegno*) imaginative; **un mondo** ~ a world of fantasy; **il cinema** ~ the cinema of the fantastic; ~**!** fantastic!, terrific!

fante ['fante] *sm* **(a)** (*Mil*) infantryman. **(b)** (*Carte*) knave, jack.

fanteria [fante'ria] *sf* (*Mil*) infantry.

fantino [fan'tino] *sm* jockey.

fantoccio [fan'tottʃo] **1** *sm* (*manichino*) dummy; (*bambola*) doll; (*fig: persona*) puppet; ~ **di pezza** rag doll. **2** *ag inv*: **governo** ~ puppet government.

fantomatico, a, ci, che [fanto'matiko] *ag* (*nave, esercito*) phantom; (*personaggio*) mysterious.

farabutto [fara'butto] *sm* crook.

faraona [fara'ona] *sf* guinea fowl.

faraone [fara'one] *sm* **(a)** (*Storia*) Pharaoh. **(b)** (*Carte*) Faro.

faraonico, a, ci, che [fara'ɔniko] *ag* of the pharaohs; (*fig*) enormous, huge.

farcire [far'tʃire] *vt* (*carni, peperoni, pomodori*) to stuff; (*torte*) to fill; **farcito di errori** (*fig*) crammed o packed with mistakes.

fard [far] *sm inv* blusher.

fardello [far'dello] *sm* bundle; (*fig*) burden.

fare ['fare] **1** *vt* **(a)** (*fabbricare: gen*) to make; (*: casa*) to build; (*quadro*) to paint; (*disegno*) to draw; (*pasto*) to cook; (*pane, dolci*) to bake; (*assegno*) to make out; **hai fatto il letto/la stanza?** have you made the bed/cleaned the room?; **che cosa ne hai fatto di quei pantaloni?** what have you done with those trousers?; ~ **una promessa/un errore** to make a promise/a mistake; ~ **un corso** (*tenere*) to give a series of lessons, teach a course; (*seguire*) to do a course; **fanno la stessa classe** they are in the same year; ~ **una festa** to have o hold a party; **quest'albero non fa frutti** this tree doesn't bear fruit; **ha fatto un figlio** she's had a baby; **lo hanno fatto presidente** they made him president; **ha fatto la mia felicità** he made me so happy.

(b) (*attività: gen*) to do; (*vacanza, sogno*) to have; ~ **i compiti/la spesa** to do one's homework/the shopping; ~ **del tennis** to play tennis; **cosa fai?** (*adesso*) what are you doing?; (*nella vita*) what do you do?, what is your job?; **a scuola facciamo chimica** at school we do chemistry; **non posso farci nulla** I can't do anything about it.

(c) (*funzione*) to be; (*Teatro*) to play, be; ~ **il medico/l'avvocato** to be a doctor/a lawyer; ~ **il malato,** ~ **finta di essere malato** to pretend to be ill; ~ **l'innocente** to act the innocent; **nel film fa il padre** in the film he plays the father; **la cucina**

fa anche da sala da pranzo the kitchen also serves as o is also used as a dining room.

(d) (*percorrere*) to do; **abbiamo fatto 5 km** we've done 5 km; ~ **un viaggio** to go on a trip, make a journey; ~ **una passeggiata** to go for o take a walk; ~ **i 100 metri** (*competere*) to go in for o run in the 100 metres; **fa i 100 metri in 10,5** he does the 100 metres in 10.5.

(e) (*suscitare: sentimenti*) to arouse; ~ **paura a** to frighten; **mi fa rabbia** it makes me angry; **che differenza ti fa?** what difference does it make to you?; **fa niente se fumo?** is it O.K. if I smoke?; **fa niente** it doesn't matter.

(f) (*ammontare*): **2 più 2 fa 4** two plus two make(s) o equal(s) 4; **fa 5000 lire, signora** that'll be 5000 lire, madam; **Roma fa 2.000.000 di abitanti** Rome has 2,000,000 inhabitants; **che ora fa il tuo orologio?** what time is it by your watch?; **glielo faccio 100.000 lire** I'll give it to you o I'll let you have it for 100,000 lire.

(g) (*+ infin*): **fammi vedere** let me see; **l'hanno fatto entrare in macchina** (*costringere*) they forced him into the car, they made him get into the car; (*lasciare*) they let him get into the car; **le faremo avere la merce** we'll get the goods to you; **far scongelare** to defrost, thaw out; **far piangere/soffrire qn** to make sb cry/suffer; **far riparare la macchina** to have one's car repaired; **mi son fatto tagliare i capelli** I've had my hair cut; ~**rsi fregare** to let o.s. be cheated; **lo farò** ~ **a lei** I'll get her o I'll have her do it.

(h): ~**rsi:** ~**rsi una gonna** to make o.s. a skirt; ~**rsi un nome** to make a name for o.s.; ~**rsi la macchina/barca** to get a car/boat; **si fa da mangiare da solo** he does his own cooking; **si è fatto mia moglie** (*fam*) he's had it off with my wife.

(i) (*fraseologia*): **me l'hanno fatta!** (*imbrogliare*) I've been done!; (*derubare*) I've been robbed!; (*lasciare nei guai*) I've been lumbered!; **ne ha fatta una delle sue** he's done it again; **farcela** to succeed, manage; **non ce la faccio più** I can't go on; **ce la facciamo?** do you think we'll make it?; **ti facevo più intelligente** I thought you were more intelligent; **ti facevo al mare** I thought you were at the seaside; **ha fatto di sì con la testa** he nodded.

2 *vi* **(a)** (*agire*) to do; ~ **presto** to be quick; ~ **del proprio meglio** to do one's best; **fate come volete** do as you please; **non c'è niente da** ~ it's no use; **saperci** ~ **con** (*situazioni, persone*) to know how to deal with; **ci sa** ~ **con le donne/coi bambini/con le macchine** he's good with women/children/cars; **ci sa fare** he's very capable; **faccia pure!** go ahead!

(b) (*dire*) to say; **'davvero?'—fece** 'really?'— he said.

(c): ~**rsi: questo non si fa** it's not done; **si fa così** you do it like this, this is the way it's done; **non si fa così!** (*rimprovero*) that's no way to behave!; **questa festa non si farà!** this party won't take place!

(d) (*fraseologia*): ~ **per** (*essere adatto*) to be suitable for; (*essere sul punto di*) to be about to; **fece per uscire e poi si fermò** he made as if to go out and then stopped; **non fa per me** it isn't (suitable) for me; ~ **da padre a qn** to be like a father to sb; **fa proprio al caso nostro** it's just what we need; ~ **a pugni** to come to blows; (*fig*) to clash; ~ **in tempo a...** to be in time to...; **avere a che** ~ **con qn** to have sth to do with sb; **non so che farmene di lui** I don't know what to do with him; **il grigio fa vecchio** grey makes you look older.

3 vb impers: **fa freddo/caldo** it's cold/hot; **fa notte** it's getting dark.

4: ~**rsi** vr **(a)** (divenire) to become; ~**rsi bello/ grande** to become beautiful/tall; ~**rsi vecchio** to grow old; ~**rsi prete** to become a priest; **si fa notte** it's getting dark; **è andata a** ~**rsi bella** (iro) she's gone to make herself beautiful; ~**rsi amico di qn** to make friends with sb.

(b) (spostarsi): ~**rsi avanti/indietro** to move forward/back; **fatti più in là!** move along a bit!

(c) (gergo: drogarsi) to be a junkie.

5 sm: **con** ~ **distratto** absent-mindedly; **ha un** ~ **simpatico** he has a pleasant manner; **sul far del giorno/della notte** at daybreak/nightfall.

faretra [fa'retra] sf quiver.

farfalla [far'falla] sf **(a)** (Zool) butterfly. **(b)** (cravatta) bow tie. **(c)** (Nuoto) butterfly (stroke); **nuotare a** ~ to do the butterfly (stroke).

farfallone [farfal'lone] sm (fig) philanderer.

farfugliare [farfuʎ'ʎare] vt, vi to mumble, mutter.

farina [fa'rina] sf flour; ~ **gialla** maize flour; ~ **integrale** wholemeal flour; **questa non è** ~ **del tuo sacco** (fig) this isn't your own idea (o work).

farinaceo, a [fari'natʃeo] **1** ag farinaceous. **2:** ~**i** smpl starches.

faringe [fa'rindʒe] sf (Anat) pharynx.

faringeo, a [farin'dʒεo] ag (Anat) pharyngeal.

farinoso, a [fari'noso] ag (patate) floury; (neve, mela) powdery.

fariseo [fari'zεo] sm pharisee.

farmaceutica [farma'tʃeutika] sf pharmaceutics sg.

farmaceutico, a, ci, che [farma'tʃeutiko] ag pharmaceutical.

farmacia, cie [farma'tʃia] sf **(a)** (negozio) chemist's (shop), pharmacy. **(b)** (professione) pharmacy.

farmacista, i, e [farma'tʃista] sm/f (dispensing) chemist, pharmacist.

farmaco, ci ['farmako] sm drug, medicine.

farmacologia [farmakolo'dʒia] sf pharmacology.

farmacologico, a, ci, che [farmako'lɔdʒiko] ag pharmacological.

farmacopea [farmako'pεa] sf (catalogo) pharmacopoeia.

farneticare [farneti'kare] vi to rave, be delirious; **stai farneticando!** you're raving!, you're talking nonsense!

faro ['faro] sm **(a)** (Naut) lighthouse; (Aer) beacon; ~ **d'atterraggio** landing light. **(b)** (Aut) headlight; ~**i abbaglianti** headlights on full beam; ~**i anabbaglianti** dipped headlights.

farragine [far'radʒine] sf jumble.

farraginoso, a [farradʒi'noso] ag (stile) muddled, confused.

farsa ['farsa] sf (anche fig) farce.

farsesco, a, schi, sche [far'sesko] ag farcical.

fascetta [faʃ'ʃetta] sf (gen) narrow band, narrow strip; (di medaglia) ribbon; (Med) bandage; (di giornale) wrapper.

fascia, sce ['faʃʃa] sf **(a)** (di tessuto, carta, anche fig) strip, band; (Med) bandage; (di sindaco, ufficiale) sash; ~ **del cappello** hatband; ~ **di contribuenti** tax group o band; **ti conosco da quando eri ancora in** ~**sce** I've known you since you were a baby. **(b)** (Geog) strip, belt; ~ **equatoriale** equatorial belt. **(c)** (Tecn): ~ **elastica** piston ring.

fasciame [faʃ'ʃame] sm (Naut: di legno) planking; (: di metallo) plating.

fasciare [faʃ'ʃare] vt (gen) to bind; (Med) to bandage; ~ **un bambino** to put on a baby's nappy (Brit) o diaper (Am); **fasciati la mano** bandage

your hand; **quel vestito le fasciava i fianchi** the dress clung to her hips.

fasciato, a [faʃ'ʃato] ag bandaged.

fasciatura [faʃʃa'tura] sf (azione) bandaging; (fascia) bandage.

fascicolo [faʃ'ʃikolo] sm (gen) booklet, pamphlet; (Amm) file, dossier; (di pubblicazione) instalment.

fascina [faʃ'ʃina] sf faggot.

fascino ['faʃʃino] sm charm, fascination; **avere** ~ (persona) to be fascinating; **subire il** ~ **di qn** to succumb to sb's charm.

fascio ['faʃʃo] sm **(a)** (di legna) bundle; (di fieno, frecce) sheaf; (di fiori) bunch; (di luce) beam. **(b)** (Storia) fasces pl; (Pol: fascismo) fascism.

fascismo [faʃ'ʃizmo] sm fascism.

fascista, i, e [faʃ'ʃista] ag, sm/f fascist.

fase ['faze] sf **(a)** (gen, Chim) phase; **in** ~ **avanzata** at an advanced stage; **in** ~ **preliminare** in the preliminary stages. **(b)** (Tecn) stroke; **essere fuori** ~ (motore) to be rough; (fig) to feel rough; **mettere il motore in** ~ to tune the engine.

fastello [fas'tεllo] sm bundle.

fastidio [fas'tidjo] sm (disturbo) trouble, bother; **che** ~**!** what a nuisance!; **dare** ~ **a** to bother; **sento** ~ **al braccio** my arm is bothering me; **sento un po' di** ~ it just hurts a little; **il rumore mi dava** ~ the noise was annoying me; **mi dà** ~ **il suo modo di fare** his attitude annoys me; **le dà** ~ **se fumo?** do you mind if I smoke?; **ha avuto dei** ~**i con la polizia** he has had some trouble o bother with the police.

fastidioso, a [fasti'djoso] ag **(a)** (gen) annoying; (persona) tiresome, annoying; **un dolore** ~ a nagging pain. **(b)** (irritabile) irritable.

fasto ['fasto] sm pomp, splendour; **i** ~**i dell'antica Roma** the splendour(s) of ancient Rome.

fastosità [fastosi'ta] sf pomp, splendour.

fastoso, a [fas'toso] ag sumptuous, lavish.

fasullo, a [fa'zullo] ag (gen) fake; (dichiarazione, persona) false; (pretesto) bogus.

fata ['fata] sf fairy.

fatale [fa'tale] ag **(a)** (inevitabile) inevitable; **era** ~ **che succedesse** it was bound to happen. **(b)** (mortale: incidente, malattia) fatal; (: colpo) fatal, mortal; (fig: sguardo) irresistible; **errore** ~ fatal error; **essere** ~ **a qn** to be o prove fatal to sb; **donna** ~ femme fatale.

fatalismo [fata'lizmo] sm fatalism.

fatalista, i, e [fata'lista] sm/f fatalist.

fatalistico, a, ci, che [fata'listiko] ag fatalistic.

fatalità [fatali'ta] sf inv (fato) fate; (inevitabilità) inevitability; (disgrazia) misfortune, calamity.

fatato, a [fa'tato] ag (spada, chiave) magic; (castello) enchanted.

fatica, che [fa'tika] sf **(a)** (sforzo fisico) hard work, toil; **animale da** ~ beast of burden; **divisa da** ~ (Mil) fatigues pl; **uomo di** ~ odd-job man; **fare** ~ **a fare qc** to have a job doing sth; **faccio** ~ **a crederlo** I find that hard to believe; **il paziente deve evitare ogni** ~ the patient must avoid any heavy work; **risparmiarsi la** ~ **di fare qc** to save o.s. the bother o effort of doing sth; **accusare** o **sentire** ~ to feel tired; **non si è preso nemmeno la** ~ **di dirmelo** he didn't even take the trouble to tell me; **respirare a** ~ to have difficulty (in) breathing; **riusciva a** ~ **a tenere la testa dritta** he could hardly keep his head up; **l'ho convinto a** ~ I had a hard job convincing him; **le** ~**che di Ercole** the labours of Hercules. **(b)** (di metalli) fatigue.

faticaccia, ce [fati'kattʃa] sf: **fu una** ~ it was hard work, it was a hell of a job (fam).

faticare [fati'kare] *vi* to work hard, toil; ~ **per fare qc** to struggle to do sth; ~ **a fare qc** to have difficulty in doing sth.

faticata [fati'kata] *sf* hard work.

faticoso, a [fati'koso] *ag (viaggio, camminata)* tiring, exhausting; *(lavoro)* laborious.

fatidico, a, ci, che [fa'tidiko] *ag* fateful.

fato ['fato] *sm* fate, destiny.

fattaccio [fat'tattʃo] *sm* foul deed.

fatterello [fatte'rello] *sm* insignificant event.

fattezze [fat'tettse] *sfpl* features.

fattibile [fat'tibile] *ag* feasible, possible.

fattispecie [fattis'pɛtʃe] *sf*: **nella** *o* **in** ~ in this case *o* instance.

fatto[1], a ['fatto] **1** *pp di* **fare**. **2** *ag* **(a)** *(prodotto)* made; ~ **a macchina/a mano** machine/hand made; ~ **in casa** home-made; **abiti** ~**i** ready-made *o* off-the-peg clothes. **(b)** *(fraseologia)*: **sono** ~ **così** it's the way I'm made; **è ben** ~**a** she has a nice figure; **essere** ~ **per qc** to be made *o* meant for sth; **è** ~ **per l'archeologia** he's cut out to be an archeologist; **a giorno** ~ in broad daylight; **è** ~**a!** that's it!, I've (*o* we've *etc*) done it!

fatto[2] ['fatto] *sm* **(a)** *(accaduto)* fact; **i** ~**i parlano chiaro** the facts speak for themselves; **questo è un altro** ~ that's another matter; **di** ~ in fact; ~ **sta** *o* **è che** the fact remains *o* is that; **in** ~ **di macchine se ne intende** when it comes to cars he knows a lot about them.

(b) *(azione)* deed, act; **cogliere qn sul** ~ to catch sb red-handed *o* in the act; **porre qn di fronte al** ~ **compiuto** to present sb with a fait accompli; **c'è stato un nuovo** ~ **di sangue** there has been further bloodshed; ~ **d'arme** feat of arms; **è uno che sa il** ~ **suo** he knows what he's about; **gli ho detto il** ~ **suo** I told him what I thought of him; **fare i** ~**i propri** to mind one's own business; **immischiarsi nei** ~**i altrui** to stick one's nose into other people's business.

(c) *(avvenimento)* event, occurrence; *(di romanzo, film)* action, story; ~ **di cronaca** news item; ~ **nuovo** new development.

fattore [fat'tore] *sm* **(a)** *(elemento)* factor. **(b)** *(Agr)* farm manager.

fattoria [fatto'ria] *sf (gen)* farm; *(casa)* farmhouse.

fattorino [fatto'rino] *sm (gen)* errand boy; *(di ufficio)* office junior; *(d'albergo)* porter.

fattucchiera [fattuk'kjɛra] *sf* witch.

fattura [fat'tura] *sf* **(a)** *(Comm)* invoice. **(b)** *(confezione: di abito)* tailoring. **(c)** *(stregoneria)* spell; **fare una** ~ **a qn** to cast a spell on sb.

fatturare [fattu'rare] *vt* **(a)** *(Comm)* to invoice. **(b)** *(prodotto)*: ~ **prodotti di prima qualità** to turn out goods of the highest quality.

fatturato [fattu'rato] *sm (Comm)* turnover.

fatuità [fatui'ta] *sf* fatuousness.

fatuo, a ['fatuo] *ag* fatuous, vain; **fuoco** ~ *(anche fig)* will-o'-the-wisp.

fauci ['fautʃi] *sfpl (di leone etc)* jaws; *(di vulcano)* mouth *sg*.

fauna ['fauna] *sf (Zool)* fauna.

fauno ['fauno] *sm (Mitologia)* faun.

fausto, a ['fausto] *ag (frm)* happy; **un** ~ **evento** a happy event; **un** ~ **presagio** a good omen.

fautore, trice [fau'tore] *sm/f* advocate, supporter.

fava ['fava] *sf* broad bean.

favella [fa'vella] *sf* speech; **perdere il dono della** ~ to be struck dumb.

favilla [fa'villa] *sf* spark; *(fig: di speranza)* glimmer; **fare** ~**e** *(fig: cantante etc)* to give a sparkling performance.

favo ['favo] *sm (di api)* honeycomb.

favola ['favola] *sf (fiaba)* fairy tale; *(d'intento morale)* fable; *(fig: fandonia)* tall tale; **essere la** ~ **del paese** *(oggetto di critica)* to be the talk of the town; *(zimbello)* to be a laughing stock in the town; **la casa è una** ~ the house is a dream.

favoleggiare [favoled'dʒare] *vi* to tell stories.

favoloso, a [favo'loso] *ag (gen)* fabulous; **prezzi** ~**i** incredible prices.

favore [fa'vore] *sm* favour; **chiedere/fare un** ~ **a qn** to ask/do sb a favour; **per** ~ please; **godere del** ~ **del pubblico** to enjoy public favour; **prezzo/trattamento di** ~ preferential price/ treatment; **biglietto di** ~ complimentary ticket; **a** ~ **di** *(votare)* in favour of; *(testimoniare, raccogliere aiuti)* on behalf of; **col** ~ **delle tenebre** under cover of darkness.

favoreggiamento [favoreddʒa'mento] *sm (Dir)* aiding and abetting; ~ **bellico** collaboration (with the enemy).

favoreggiare [favored'dʒare] *vt* **(a)** to favour. **(b)** *(Dir)* to aid and abet.

favorevole [favo'revole] *ag*: ~ **a** *(situazione, vento etc)* favourable (to); *(persona)* in favour (of), favourable (to); **hanno avuto 70 voti** ~**i** they got 70 votes in favour; **aspettare il momento** ~ to wait for the right moment.

favorire [favo'rire] *vt* **(a)** *(gen)* to favour; *(commercio, industria, arti)* to promote, encourage; *(partito, opinione)* to support. **(b)** *(in espressioni di cortesia)*: **favorisca da questa parte** please come this way; **vuole** ~**?** won't you help yourself?; **favorite passarmi quel pacco** would you please pass me that package?; **mi favorisca i documenti** please may I see your papers?

favoritismo [favori'tizmo] *sm* favouritism.

favorito, a [favo'rito] *ag, sm/f* favourite.

fazione [fat'tsjone] *sf* faction.

faziosità [fattsjosi'ta] *sf* sectarianism.

fazioso, a [fat'tsjoso] *ag* sectarian, factious.

fazzoletto [fattso'letto] *sm (da naso)* handkerchief; *(da collo)* neckerchief; *(da testa)* headscarf, headsquare; **un** ~ **di terra** a patch of land.

febbraio [feb'brajo] *sm* February; *per uso vedi* **luglio**.

febbre ['febbre] *sf* **(a)** fever; **avere la** ~ to have a temperature; ~ **da fieno** hay fever; **la** ~ **dell'oro** gold fever. **(b)** *(erpes)* cold sore.

febbricitante [febbritʃi'tante] *ag* feverish.

febbrile [feb'brile] *ag* feverish.

febbrone [feb'brone] *sm* high temperature.

fecale [fe'kale] *ag* faecal.

feccia, ce ['fettʃa] *sf (anche fig)* dregs *pl*.

feci ['fetʃi] *sfpl* faeces, excrement *sg*.

fecola ['fɛkola] *sf* starch; ~ **di patate** ≃ cornflour.

fecondare [fekon'dare] *vt* to fertilize.

fecondativo, a [fekonda'tivo] *ag*: **un farmaco** ~ **a** fertility drug.

fecondazione [fekondat'tsjone] *sf* fertilization; ~ **artificiale** artificial insemination.

fecondità [fekondi'ta] *sf* fertility, fruitfulness; *(di scrittore)* prolificness.

fecondo, a [fe'kondo] *ag (terreno, donna, fig: ingegno)* fertile; *(albero, fig: penseiro, lavoro)* fruitful; (: *scrittore)* prolific.

fede ['fede] *sf* **(a)** *(credenza)* faith, belief; *(Rel)* faith. **(b)** *(fiducia)* faith, trust; *(fedeltà)* loyalty; **aver** ~ **in** to have faith in; **degno di** ~ trustworthy, reliable; **tener** ~ **a** *(ideale)* to remain loyal to; *(giuramento, promessa)* to keep; **essere in buona/cattiva** ~ to act in good/bad faith; **in** ~ **mia!** on my word! **(c)** *(anello nuziale)* wedding ring. **(d)** *(attestato)* certificate; **in** ~ **di** in proof of *o* as evidence of; **far** ~ **di** to be proof *o* evidence of; '**in** ~' (Dir) 'in witness whereof'.

fedele |feˈdele| **1** ag (a) (leale): ~ (a) faithful (to); **essere** ~ **alla parola data** to keep one's word; **suddito** ~ loyal subject. (b) (veritiero) true, accurate. **2** sm/f (Rel) believer; (seguace) follower; **i** ~**i** (Rel) the faithful pl.

fedeltà |fedelˈta| sf (a) (devozione) loyalty, faithfulness; (coniugale) fidelity; ~ **verso** o **a qn** loyalty to sb. (b) (esattezza: di copia, traduzione) accuracy. (c) (Radio): **alta** ~ high fidelity.

federa |ˈfedera| sf pillowslip, pillowcase.

federale |fedeˈrale| ag federal.

federalismo |federaˈlizmo| sm federalism.

federalista, i, e |federaˈlista| ag, sm/f federalist.

federarsi |fedeˈrarsi| vr to form a federation.

federativo, a |federaˈtivo| ag federative.

federazione |federatˈtsjone| sf federation.

fedifrago, a, ghi, ghe |feˈdifrago| ag faithless, perfidious.

fedina |feˈdina| sf (Dir): ~ (**penale**) record; **avere la** ~ **penale pulita** to have a clean record; **avere la** ~ **penale sporca** to have a police record.

fegatino |fegaˈtino| sm (di pollame) liver; ~ **di pollo** chicken liver.

fegato |ˈfegato| sm (a) (Anat, Culin) liver; ~ **ingrossato** (Med) swollen liver; ~ **di vitello** calf's liver; **mangiarsi** o **rodersi il** ~ to be consumed with rage. (b) (fig: coraggio) guts pl, nerve.

felce |ˈfeltʃe| sf fern.

feldmaresciallo |feldmareʃˈʃallo| sm (Mil) field marshal.

felice |feˈlitʃe| ag (a) (contento) happy; **sono** ~ **di fare la sua conoscenza** pleased to meet you; ~ **come una pasqua** as happy as a sandboy. (b) (fortunato) lucky; (: scelta) fortunate, happy; (: vento) favourable; **avere la mano** ~ to have nimble fingers; **non ho scelto il momento più** ~ **per venire** I don't seem to have chosen the best of times to come.

felicità |felitʃiˈta| sf happiness.

felicitarsi |felitʃiˈtarsi| vr: ~**rsi con qn (per qc)** to congratulate sb (on sth).

felicitazioni |felitʃitatˈtsjoni| sfpl congratulations.

felino, a |feˈlino| **1** ag (Zool) feline; (fig) feline, catlike. **2** sm feline.

felpato, a |felˈpato| **1** ag (tessuto) brushed; (passo) stealthy; **con passo** ~ stealthily. **2** sm brushed material.

feltro |ˈfeltro| sm felt; **cappello in** ~ felt hat.

feluca, che |feˈluka| sf (a) (Naut) felucca. (b) (cappello) cocked hat.

femmina |ˈfemmina| sf (Zool, Tecn) female; **ho due figli, un maschio e una** ~ I've got two children, a boy and a girl; **una** ~ **di panda, un panda** ~ a female panda.

femminile |femmiˈnile| ag (gen, Gram) feminine; (sesso) female; **moda** ~ women's fashion.

femminilità |femminiliˈta| sf femininity; **ha molta** ~ she is very feminine.

femminismo |femmiˈnizmo| sm feminism.

femminista, i, e |femmiˈnista| sm/f feminist.

femore |ˈfemore| sm thighbone, femur.

fendente |fenˈdente| sm (con sciabola) cut; (Calcio) powerful shot; **con un** ~ **mandò il pallone in rete** he slammed the ball into the back of the net.

fendere |ˈfendere| **1** vt (fig: aria, flutti, onde) to cut through, slice (through); **i fari fendevano la nebbia** the headlights cut through o pierced the fog. **2**: ~**rsi** vr (roccia) to crack.

fendinebbia |fendiˈnebbja| sm inv (Aut) fog lamp.

fenditura |fendiˈtura| sf (gen) crack; (di roccia) cleft, crack.

fenice |feˈnitʃe| sf (anche: **araba** ~) phoenix.

fenicottero |feniˈkɔttero| sm flamingo.

fenolo |feˈnɔlo| sm phenol.

fenomenale |fenomeˈnale| ag (gen) phenomenal.

fenomenico, a, ci, che |fenoˈmeniko| ag phenomenal; **mondo** ~ external world.

fenomeno |feˈnɔmeno| sm (gen) phenomenon; (persona: eccezionale) character; (: anormale) freak.

feretro |ˈferetro| sm coffin; **il** ~ **si avviava verso il cimitero** the funeral procession wound its way to the cemetery.

feriale |feˈrjale| ag: **giorno** ~ working day, weekday.

ferie |ˈferje| sfpl holidays, vacation sg (Am); ~ **retribuite** holiday with pay; **andare in** ~ to go on holiday; **ho fatto le** ~ **al mare** I spent my holidays at the seaside; **ho 2 settimane di** ~ I have 2 weeks' holiday(s).

ferimento |feriˈmento| sm wounding; **nella sparatoria si è avuto il** ~ **di 3 persone** 3 people were injured o wounded in the shooting.

ferire |feˈrire| **1** vt (a) (gen) to injure; (Mil) to wound; **fu ferito a morte** he was mortally wounded; **nell'incidente sono state ferite 4 persone** 4 people were injured in the accident. (b) (fig) to hurt, wound; ~ **qn nell'orgoglio** to hurt o wound o injure sb's pride; **le sue parole la ferirono** she was wounded o hurt by what he said. **2**: ~**rsi** vr to hurt o.s., injure o.s.; ~**rsi con un coltello** to cut o.s. with a knife; **mi sono ferito ad una mano** I've injured by hand.

ferita |feˈrita| sf (vedi vb) injury; wound; **riportò gravi** ~**e** he was seriously wounded.

ferito, a |feˈrito| sm/f wounded o injured man/woman; **un** ~ **grave** a seriously injured person.

feritoia |feriˈtoja| sf slit.

ferma |ˈferma| sf (Mil) (period of) service.

fermacarte |fermaˈkarte| sm inv paperweight.

fermacravatta |fermakraˈvatta| sm inv tiepin.

fermaglio |ferˈmaʎʎo| sm (gen) clasp; (per documenti) clip.

fermamente |fermaˈmente| av firmly.

fermare |ferˈmare| **1** vt (a) (gen) to stop; ~ **qn dal fare qc** to stop sb (from) doing sth; **fermò lo sguardo sul quadro** his eyes came to rest on the painting; **lo fermò con un gesto della mano** (far cenno) he gestured to him to stop; (bloccare) he put his hand out to stop him. (b) (fissare: bottone, cucitura) to fasten; (: porta) to stop. (c) (prenotare: stanza, albergo etc) to book. (d) (Polizia) to detain, hold. **2** vi to stop; **il treno ferma a...** the train calls at.... **3**: ~**rsi** vr (gen) to stop; ~**rsi a guardare/fare** to stop to look/do; **non posso fermarmi di più** I can't stop o stay any longer; **far segno di** ~**rsi a qn** to signal to sb to stop; (ad automobilista) to wave sb down; **la sua attenzione si fermò sul dipinto** his attention focused on the painting.

fermata |ferˈmata| sf stop; ~ **di autobus** bus stop; ~ **facoltativa** o **a richiesta** request stop; **scendo tra 2** ~**e** I get off 2 stops from here; **la corriera fa una** ~ **a Montelupo** the coach stops o makes a stop at Montelupo.

fermentare |fermenˈtare| **1** vi (anche fig) to ferment. **2** vt to ferment.

fermentazione |fermentatˈtsjone| sf fermentation.

fermento |ferˈmento| sm (a) (anche fig) ferment; **in** ~ in a ferment. (b) (Culin: lievito) yeast.

fermezza |ferˈmettsa| sf firmness; ~ **di mente/di animo** strength of mind/of character; ~ **di propositi** steadiness of purpose; **rispondere con** ~ to answer firmly, give a firm answer.

fermo, a |'fermo| **1** *ag* **(a)** *(immobile: persona)* still, motionless; *(: veicolo, traffico)* at a standstill; *(non in funzione)* not working; **era ~ in piedi** he was standing still; **stai ~!** keep still!; **stai ~ con le mani!** keep your hands still!; *(non toccarmi)* keep your hands to yourself!; **~!** don't move!, stay where you are!; **c'era una macchina ~a al bordo della strada** there was a car stationary at the side of the road; **il treno era ~ in stazione** the train was standing in the station; **gli affari sono ~i** business is at a standstill; **l'orologio è ~** the clock has stopped. **(b)** *(costante, risoluto)* firm; *(non tremante: voce, mano)* steady; **restare ~ sulle proprie posizioni** to stick to one's position; **resta ~ che...** it is settled that...; **~ restando che...** it being understood that... . **2** *sm* **(a)** *(Dir):* **~ di polizia** police detention. **(b)** *(di porta)* catch.

fermo posta |'fermo'posta| *av, sm* poste restante, general delivery *(Am)*.

feroce |fe'rotʃe| *ag (animale)* ferocious; *(persona)* fierce, cruel; *(critica)* savage; *(fame, dolore)* raging; **le bestie ~i** wild animals.

ferocia |fe'rɔtʃa| *sf* ferocity.

ferodo |fe'rɔdo| *sm* ® brake lining.

ferraglia |fer'raʎʎa| *sf* scrap iron; **rumore di ~** clanking noise.

ferragosto |ferra'gosto| *sm* ≃ August bank holiday *(15th August)*.

ferraio |fer'rajo| *ag:* **fabbro ~** blacksmith.

ferramenta |ferra'mɛnta| **1** *sfpl* hardware *sg,* ironmongery *sg.* **2** *sm (anche:* **negozio di ~)** ironmonger's.

ferrare |fer'rare| *vt (cavallo)* to shoe; *(botte)* to hoop.

ferrato, a |fer'rato| *ag* **(a)** *(Ferr):* **strada ~a** railway line, railroad line *(Am)*. **(b)** *(fig):* **essere ~ in** *(materia)* to be well up in.

ferravecchio |ferra'vɛkkjo| *sm* scrap merchant.

ferreo, a |'ferreo| *ag (anche fig)* iron *attr;* **volontà ~a** iron will; **salute ~a** iron constitution.

ferriera |fer'rjera| *sf* ironworks *sg o pl.*

ferro |'ferro| *sm* **(a)** *(metallo)* iron; **~ battuto** wrought iron; **l'età del ~** the Iron Age; **minerali di ~** iron ore; **ha una memoria di ~** he has an excellent memory; **ha una salute di ~** he has an iron constitution; **avere uno stomaco di ~** *(fig)* to have a cast-iron stomach; **avere un alibi di ~** to have a cast-iron alibi; **tocca ~!** touch wood!; **battere il ~ finché è caldo** to strike while the iron is hot.

(b) *(strumento: gen)* tool; **i ~i del mestiere** the tools of the trade; **~ da stiro** iron; **~i da calza** knitting needles; **~ di cavallo** horseshoe; **a ~ di cavallo** in the shape of a horseshoe; **i ~i del chirurgo** surgical instruments; **essere sotto i ~i** *(di chirurgo)* to be under the knife; **carne ai ~i** grilled meat; **cucinare** *o* **fare qc ai ~i** to grill sth.

(c) *(arma)* sword; **~i** *(ceppi)* irons, chains; **incrociare i ~i** to cross swords; **mettere a ~ e fuoco** to put to the sword; **essere ai ~i corti** *(fig)* to be at daggers drawn.

ferroso, a |fer'roso| *ag* ferrous.

ferrotranviario, a |ferrotran'vjarjo| *ag* public transport *attr.*

ferrotranviere |ferrotran'vjɛre| *sm* public transport employee.

ferrovia |ferro'via| *sf* railway, railroad *(Am)*.

ferroviario, a |ferro'vjarjo| *ag* railway *attr,* rail *attr,* railroad *attr (Am)*.

ferroviere |ferro'vjɛre| *sm* railwayman.

ferry-boat |'fɛri 'bout| *sm inv* ferry.

fertile |'fertile| *ag (anche fig)* fertile.

fertilità |fertili'ta| *sf* fertility.

fertilizzante |fertilid'dzante| **1** *ag* fertilizing. **2** *sm* fertilizer.

fertilizzare |fertilid'dzare| *vt* to fertilize.

fertilizzazione |fertiliddzat'tsjone| *sf* fertilization.

fervente |fer'vente| *ag* fervent, ardent.

fervere |'fervere| *vi:* **fervono i preparativi per l'arrivo del presidente** they are making feverish preparations for the president's arrival.

fervido, a |'fervido| *ag* fervent, fervid, ardent; **~e preghiere** impassioned pleas; **i miei più ~i auguri** my very best wishes.

fervore |fer'vore| *sm* fervour, ardour; **nel ~ di** *(discussione, lotta)* in the heat of.

fesa |'feza| *sf (Culin)* rump of veal.

fesseria |fesse'ria| *sf* stupidity; **quel film è una ~** that film is rubbish; **dire ~e** to talk nonsense; **fare una ~** to do something stupid.

fesso, a |'fesso| **1** *pp di* **fendere. 2** *ag* **(a)** *(spaccato)* cracked; **con voce ~a** in a cracked voice. **(b)** *(fam)* stupid, daft. **3** *sm/f* idiot, fool; **fare il ~** to play the fool; **dare del ~ a qn** to call sb a fool.

fessura |fes'sura| *sf (gen)* crack, split; *(per moneta, gettone)* slot.

festa |'festa| *sf* **(a)** *(religiosa)* feast; *(civile)* holiday; **giorno di ~** holiday; **il Natale è la ~ dei bambini** Christmas is a time for children.

(b) *(vacanza)* holidays *pl,* vacation *(Am);* **cosa fai per le ~e?** what are you doing over the holidays?; **la settimana scorsa ho avuto 3 giorni di ~** last week I was on holiday for 3 days.

(c) *(ricorrenza: compleanno)* birthday; *(: onomastico)* name day; **quand'è la tua ~?** when is your birthday?; **la ~ di San Giovanni** St John's Day, the feast of St John.

(d) *(sagra)* fair; **la ~ del paese** the town festival; **~ della birra** beer festival.

(e) *(ricevimento)* party; **dare** *o* **fare una ~** to give *o* have a party.

(f) *(fraseologia):* **un'aria di ~** a festive air; **fare ~** *(non lavorare)* to have a holiday; *(far baldoria)* to live it up; **fare le ~e a qn** to give sb a warm welcome; **tutta la città era in ~** the whole town was celebrating; **le campane suonavano a ~** the bells were pealing; **essere vestito a ~** to be dressed up to the nines.

2: ~ comandata *(Rel)* holiday of obligation; **la ~ della donna** International Women's Day; **la ~ della mamma/del papà** Mother's/Father's Day; **~ nazionale** national *o* public holiday.

festaiolo, a |festa'jɔlo| *ag (atmosfera)* festive; **è un tipo ~** he's a great one for parties.

festeggiamenti |festeddʒa'menti| *smpl* celebrations.

festeggiare |fested'dʒare| *vt (anniversario etc)* to celebrate; *(persona)* to have a celebration for, fête.

festeggiato, a |fested'dʒato| *sm/f* guest of honour; **sei tu il ~!** it's your party!

festino |fes'tino| *sm (festa)* party.

festival |'festival| *sm inv* festival.

festività |festivi'ta| *sf inv* festivity; **~ civile** public holiday.

festivo, a |fes'tivo| *ag (atmosfera)* festive; **giorno ~** holiday.

festone |fes'tone| *sm* festoon.

festoso, a |fes'toso| *ag* merry, joyful; **un'accoglienza ~a** a warm welcome.

fetale |fe'tale| *ag* foetal.

fetente |fe'tente| **1** *ag (puzzolente)* fetid; *(: comportamento)* disgusting. **2** *sm/f (fam)* stinker, rotter.

feticcio |fe'tittʃo| *sm* fetish.

feticismo |feti'tʃizmo| *sm* fetishism.

feticista, i, e [feti'tʃista] *ag, sm/f* fetishist.

fetido, a ['fetido] *ag* fetid, stinking.

feto ['feto] *sm* foetus.

fetore [fe'tore] *sm* stench, stink.

fetta ['fetta] *sf (gen)* slice; *(di terra)* strip; *(fig: porzione)* share; **fare a ~e** *(pane, prosciutto etc)* to slice; *(fig: persona)* to make mincemeat of; **una ~ di pane** a slice of bread; **una ~ del bottino** a share of the loot; **si vedeva solo una ~ di luna/cielo** you could just glimpse the moon/sky.

fettuccia, ce [fet'tuttʃa] *sf* tape, ribbon.

fettuccine [fettut'tʃine] *sfpl (Culin)* ribbon-shaped pasta.

feudale [feu'dale] *ag* feudal.

feudalesimo [feuda'lezimo] *sm* feudalism.

feudatario [feuda'tarjo] *sm* feudal lord.

feudo ['feudo] *sm (Storia)* fief; **un ~ democristiano** *(fig)* a Christian Democrat stronghold.

FF.SS. *abbr di Ferrovie dello Stato.*

fiaba ['fjaba] *sf* fairy tale; **paesaggio di ~** fairy-tale landscape.

fiabesco, a, schi, sche [fja'besko] *ag* fairy-tale *attr.*

fiacca ['fjakka] *sf (stanchezza)* weariness; *(svogliatezza)* listlessness; **avere la ~** to be listless; **battere la ~** to shirk.

fiaccare [fjak'kare] *vt* to exhaust, wear out; **l'artiglieria ha fiaccato le difese nemiche** the artillery wore down the enemy's defences.

fiacchezza [fjak'kettsa] *sf* weariness.

fiacco, a, chi, che ['fjakko] *ag (stanco)* tired, weary; *(svogliato)* listless; *(debole)* weak; *(: discorso)* weak, dull; *(fermo: mercato)* slack.

fiaccola ['fjakkola] *sf* torch.

fiaccolata [fjakko'lata] *sf* torchlight procession.

fiala ['fjala] *sf* phial.

fiamma ['fjamma] *sf* **(a)** flame; **andare in ~e** to go up in flames; **dare alle ~e** to set on fire, burn; **le ~e dell'inferno** hellfire. **(b)** *(fig: persona amata)* love, flame; **una vecchia ~** an old flame. **(c)** *(Mil, Naut)* pennant.

fiammante [fjam'mante] *ag (colore)* flaming; **rosso ~** flaming red, bright red; **nuovo ~** brand new.

fiammata [fjam'mata] *sf* blaze.

fiammeggiante [fjammed'dʒante] *ag* flaming, blazing; *(fig: occhi)* flashing.

fiammeggiare [fjammed'dʒare] *vi (anche fig: cielo)* to blaze; *(: occhi)* to flash; *(: spada)* to gleam.

fiammifero [fjam'mifero] *sm* match.

fiammingo, a, ghi, ghe [fjam'mingo] **1** *ag* Flemish. **2** *sm/f* Fleming; **i ~ghi** the Flemish. **3** *sm (lingua)* Flemish.

fiancata [fjan'kata] *sf (di nave etc)* side; *(Naut)* broadside.

fiancheggiare [fjanked'dʒare] *vt (gen)* to border; *(Mil)* to flank; *(fig: sostenere)* to support.

fiancheggiatore, trice [fjankeddʒa'tore] *sm/f* supporter.

fianco, chi ['fjanko] *sm (gen)* side; *(di persona)* hip; *(di animale, esercito)* flank; *(di montagna)* slope; **di ~** from the side; **di ~ a** *o* **a ~ di qn/qc** beside *o* next to sb/sth; **avere un dolore al ~** to have a pain in one's side; **stare al ~ di qn** *(anche fig)* to stand by sb; **ho sempre avuto qualcuno al mio ~** I have always had somebody by my side; **~ a ~** side by side; **stare con le mani sui ~chi** to stand with one's hands on one's hips; **avere ~chi larghi/ stretti** *(persona)* to have broad/narrow hips, be broad-/narrow-hipped; **una spina nel ~** *(fig)* a thorn in one's side; **mostrare il ~ al nemico** *(fig)* to reveal one's weak spot *o* Achilles' heel to one's enemy; **prestare il proprio ~ alle critiche** to

leave o.s. open to criticism; **~ destr/sinistr!** *(Mil)* right/left turn!

Fiandre ['fjandre] *sfpl*: **le ~** Flanders *sg.*

fiasca, sche ['fjaska] *sf* flask.

fiaschetteria [fjaskette'ria] *sf* wine shop.

fiasco, schi ['fjasko] *sm* flask; *(fig: fallimento)* fiasco; **fare ~** *(persona)* to come a cropper; *(spettacolo)* to be a flop.

fiatare [fja'tare] *vi (fig: parlare)*: **senza ~** without saying a word; **non osarono ~** they didn't dare breathe.

fiato ['fjato] *sm* **(a)** breath; **~ cattivo** bad breath; **avere il ~ grosso** to pant, be out of breath; **riprendere ~** *(anche fig)* to get one's breath back; **tirare il ~** to draw breath; *(fig)* to have a breather; **essere senza ~** to be out of breath; **restare senza ~** to be breathless; **sono rimasto senza ~** *(fig)* it took my breath away; **bere tutto d'un ~** to drink all in one go *o* gulp; **me l'ha raccontato tutto d'un ~** he told me the whole story without drawing breath; **è ~ sprecato** *(fig)* it's a waste of breath; **quella scena mi ha mozzato il ~** that scene took my breath away. **(b)** *(capacità di resistenza)* stamina, staying power. **(c)** *(Mus)*: **i ~i** *pl* wind instruments; **strumento a ~** wind instrument.

fibbia ['fibbja] *sf* buckle.

fibra ['fibra] *sf (gen)* fibre; *(fig: costituzione)* constitution; **persona di ~ forte** person with a strong constitution.

fibroso, a [fi'broso] *ag* fibrous; *(carne)* stringy.

ficcanaso [fikka'naso] *sm/f, pl(m)* **~i**, *pl(f) inv* busybody, nos(e)y parker.

ficcare [fik'kare] **1** *vt* **(a)** *(infilare: in borsa, cassetto)* to put; *(: con forza)* to thrust; *(palo, chiodo)* to drive; **mi ha ficcato un dito nell'occhio** he poked his finger in my eye; **ficcalo da qualche parte** stick it somewhere; **~ il naso negli affari altrui** *(fig)* to poke *o* stick one's nose into other people's business; **lo hanno ficcato dentro** *(fam: in prigione)* they put him away *o* inside. **(b)**: **~rsi le dita nel naso** to pick one's nose; **~rsi il cappello in testa** to put *o* thrust one's hat on one's head; **~rsi in testa qc** *(fig)* to get sth into one's head; **~rsi in testa di fare qc** *(fig)* to take it into one's head to do sth.

2: **~rsi** *vr (andare a finire)* to get to; **dove si sarà ficcato?** where can he (*o* it *etc*) have got to?; **~rsi nei pasticci** *o* **nei guai** to get into hot water *o* a fix; **perché ti devi sempre ~ in mezzo?** why do you always have to stick your oar in?

fiche [fiʃ] *sf inv (nei giochi d'azzardo)* chip.

fico¹, chi ['fiko] *sm (Bot)* fig; **~ secco** = ficosecco; **~ d'India** prickly pear.

fico², a, chi, che ['fiko] *(fam)* **1** *ag* great. **2** *sm/f* great guy/girl.

ficosecco [fiko'sekko] *pl* **fichisecchi** [fiki'sekki] *sm* dried fig; *(fig)*: **non vale un ~** it's not worth a fig *o* a straw; **non ci capisco un ~** I don't understand a thing.

fidanzamento [fidantsa'mento] *sm* engagement; **anello/festa di ~** engagement ring/party.

fidanzare [fidan'tsare] **1** *vt*: **~ a** to betroth to. **2**: **~rsi** *vr* to get engaged.

fidanzato, a [fidan'tsato] **1** *ag* engaged. **2** *sm/f* fiancé/fiancée; **i ~i** the engaged couple.

fidarsi [fi'darsi] *vr*: **~rsi di** to trust; *(fare affidamento)* to rely on; **non mi fido a uscire con questo tempo** I don't dare to go out in this weather; **~rsi è bene non ~rsi è meglio** *(Proverbio)* better safe than sorry.

fidatezza [fida'tettsa] *sf* trustworthiness, reliability.

fidato, a [fi'dato] *ag (degno di fiducia)* trustworthy, reliable; *(leale)* loyal, faithful.

fideiussione [fidejus'sjone] *sf (Dir)* guarantee.

fideiussore [fidejus'sore] *sm (Dir)* guarantor.

fido¹, a ['fido] *ag* faithful, loyal.

fido² ['fido] *sm (Comm)* credit; ~ **bancario** banker's credit.

fiducia [fi'dutʃa] *sf* (a) trust, confidence; **avere ~ in qn** to have trust *o* faith in sb, trust sb; **abbi ~ in Dio** have faith in the Lord; **riporre la propria ~ in qn/qc** to place one's trust in sb/sth; **devi avere più ~ in te stesso** you should have more confidence in yourself; **una persona di ~ a** trustworthy *o* reliable person; **un prodotto di ~ a** reliable product; **è il mio uomo di ~** he is my right-hand man; **ha un incarico di ~** he holds a responsible position. (b) *(Pol)*: **voto di ~** vote of confidence; ~ **del Parlamento al Governo** parliamentary vote of confidence; **porre la questione di ~** to ask for a vote of confidence.

fiduciario, a [fidu'tʃarjo] *ag, sm (Dir, Comm)* fiduciary.

fiducioso, a [fidu'tʃoso] *ag* trusting.

fiele ['fjɛle] *sm* gall; **parole piene di ~** bitter words.

fienagione [fjena'dʒone] *sf (operazione)* haymaking; *(stagione)* haymaking season.

fienile [fje'nile] *sm* hayloft.

fieno ['fjɛno] *sm* hay.

fiera¹ ['fjɛra] *sf (animale)* wild beast.

fiera² ['fjɛra] *sf* fair; ~ **campionaria** trade fair; ~ **di beneficenza** charity bazaar; ~ **del bianco** linen sale.

fierezza [fje'rettsa] *sf* pride.

fiero, a ['fjɛro] *ag* (a) *(orgoglioso)* proud; **essere** *o* **andare ~ di qn/qc** to be proud of sb/sth. (b) *(valente)* bold, intrepid.

fievole ['fjɛvole] *ag (luce)* dim; *(suono)* weak.

fifa ['fifa] *sf (fam)*: **che ~!** what a fright!; **avere ~** to have the jitters.

fifone [fi'fone] *sm/f (fam scherz)* coward.

figlia ['fiʎʎa] *sf* (a) daughter. (b) *(Comm)* counterfoil.

figliare [fiʎ'ʎare] *vi* to give birth.

figliastro, a [fiʎ'ʎastro] *sm/f* stepchild, stepson/daughter.

figlio ['fiʎʎo] **1** *sm* son; *(senza distinzione di sessi)* child; **hanno 2 figli** they have 2 children; **suo ~ è all'estero** his son is abroad. **2**: ~ **d'arte**: **essere ~ d'arte** to come from a theatrical *(o* musical *etc)* family; ~ **di papà** daddy's boy, spoilt and wealthy young man; ~ **di puttana** *(fam!)* son of a bitch*(!)*

figlioccio, a, ci, ce [fiʎ'ʎottʃo] *sm/f* godchild, godson/daughter.

figliola [fiʎ'ʎola] *sf* daughter; *(fig: ragazza)* girl.

figliolo [fiʎ'ʎolo] *sm (anche fig: ragazzo)* son.

figura [fi'gura] *sf (gen, Mat)* figure; *(illustrazione)* illustration; *(Carte)* face card; ~ **retorica** figure of speech; **ritratto a mezza ~** half-length portrait; **fare bella/brutta ~** to create a good/bad impression; **far fare una brutta ~ a qn** to give sb a showing-up, make sb look a fool; **fare la ~ dello scemo** to look a fool; **che ~!** how embarrassing!; **fare ~** to look good.

figuraccia, ce [figu'rattʃa] *sf*: **fare una ~** to create a bad impression.

figurante [figu'rante] *sm (Teatro, Cine)* extra.

figurare [figu'rare] **1** *vi* to appear, figure. **2** *vt*: **non riesco a figurarmelo** I can't picture it. **3**: ~**rsi** *vr* to imagine; **ti disturbo? — ma, figurati!** am I disturbing you? — no, not at all!; **figurati che...?** would you believe that...?; ~**rsi se non accetta-**

va! wouldn't you just know it — he accepted it!

figurativo, a [figura'tivo] *ag* figurative.

figurato, a [figu'rato] *ag* (a) *(allegorico)* figurative; **linguaggio ~** figurative language. (b) *(illustrato)* illustrated.

figurazione [figurat'tsjone] *sf (rappresentazione)* representation, depiction.

figurina [figu'rina] *sf* (a) *(statuetta)* figurine. (b) *(cartoncino)* picture card.

figurinista, i, e [figuri'nista] *sm/f* dress designer.

figurino [figu'rino] *sm* fashion sketch; **sembra un ~** she is like a fashion plate.

figuro [fi'guro] *sm*: **un losco ~** a suspicious character.

figurona [figu'rona] *sf*, **figurone** [figu'rone] *sm*: **fare una figurona** *o* **un figurone** *(persona, oggetto)* to look terrific; *(persona: con un discorso etc)* to make an excellent impression.

fila ['fila] *sf (gen)* line, row; *(coda)* queue; *(Mil)* rank; *(Teatro)* row; **in ~** in a row *o* line; **in ~ indiana** in single file; **mettetevi in ~ per due** line up in twos; **fare la ~** to queue; **serrare/rompere le ~e** *(Mil)* to close/break ranks; **di ~** in succession, one after the other; **è piovuto per due mesi di ~** it rained for two months on the trot *o* nonstop; **una ~ di avvenimenti** a series of events.

filamento [fila'mento] *sm* filament.

filamentoso, a [filamen'toso] *ag (verdura, carne)* stringy.

filanca [fi'lanka] *sf* ® stretch material.

filanda [fi'landa] *sf* spinning mill.

filante [fi'lante] *ag*: **stella ~** *(stella cadente)* shooting star; *(striscia di carta)* streamer.

filantropia [filantro'pia] *sf* philanthropy.

filantropico, a, ci, che [filan'trɔpiko] *ag* philanthropic(al).

filantropo [fi'lantropo] *sm* philanthropist.

filare¹ [fi'lare] **1** *vt* (a) *(lana)* to spin; *(metallo)* to draw; **quando Berta filava** in the good old days. (b) *(Naut: gomena)* to pay out; *(: remi)* to trail. **2** *vi* (a) *(liquido)* to trickle; *(candela)* to smoke; *(formaggio)* to go stringy. (b) *(aus essere) (persona)* to dash off, run; ~ **via, filarsela** to run away, make off; **fila (via)!** clear off!; **fila a letto subito** off to bed with you; **far ~ qn** to make sb behave; ~ **dritto** to behave; **la macchina fila che è una bellezza** the car goes like a dream. (c) *(discorso, ragionamento)* to be coherent. (d) *(amoreggiare)*: ~ **con** to go out with.

filare² [fi'lare] *sm (di alberi etc)* row, line.

filarmonica, che [filar'mɔnika] *sf* music society.

filarmonico, a, ci, che [filar'mɔniko] *ag* philharmonic.

filastrocca, che [filas'trɔkka] *sf* nursery rhyme.

filatelia [filate'lia] *sf* philately, stamp collecting.

filatelica [fila'tɛlika] *sf* philately, stamp collecting.

filatelico, a, ci, che [fila'tɛliko] **1** *ag* philatelic. **2** *sm/f* philatelist, stamp collector.

filato¹, a [fi'lato] **1** *ag* (a): **zucchero ~** candy floss. (b) *(di seguito)* on the trot, straight off; **ha parlato per 4 ore ~e** he spoke for 4 hours on the trot. **2** *av*: **vai dritto ~ a casa** go straight home.

filato² [fi'lato] *sm (di lana)* yarn; *(di altri tessuti)* thread.

filatoio [fila'tojo] *sm (macchina)* spinning wheel.

filatore, trice [fila'tore] *sm/f* spinner.

filatura [fila'tura] *sf* (a) *(operazione)* spinning. (b) *(fabbrica)* spinning mill.

filettare [filet'tare] *vt (Tecn: vite etc)* to thread.

filettatura [filetta'tura] *sf (di viti etc)* thread.

filetto¹ [fi'lɛtto] *sm* (a) *(ornamento)* braid. (b) *(Tecn)* thread.

filetto² [fi'letto] *sm (Culin)* fillet.

filiale¹ [fi'ljale] *ag* filial.

filiale² [fi'ljale] *sf (Comm)* branch; *(impresa dipendente)* subsidiary (company).

filibustiere [filibus'tjɛre] *sm* pirate; *(fig)* adventurer.

filiforme [fili'forme] *ag* threadlike; *(fig: magrissimo)* spindly.

filigrana [fili'grana] *sf (di oro)* filigree; *(di banconota)* watermark.

filippica [fi'lippika] *sf* invective.

filippino, a [filip'pino] *ag, sm/f* Filipino.

filisteo, a [filis'tɛo] *ag, sm/f* Philistine.

film [film] *sm inv (Fot)* film; *(Cine)* film, movie *(Am)*.

filmare [fil'mare] *vt (persona)* to film; *(scena)* to film, shoot.

filmato [fil'mato] *sm* short film.

filmina [fil'mina] *sf* film strip.

filo ['filo] *sm* **(a)** *(di cotone)* thread; *(di lana)* yarn; *(di perle, burattini)* string; *(di telefono, lampada etc)* cable, wire, flex; **i ~i della luce/del telefono** the electricity/telephone wires; **~ di ferro/spinato** wire/barbed wire; **~ elettrico** electric wire; **il ~ del traguardo** the finishing tape; **un ~ d'erba** a blade of grass; **~ a piombo** plumb line; **un ~ d'acqua** a trickle of water; **un ~ d'aria** *(fig)* a breath of air; **un ~ di luce** *(fig)* a ray of light; **un ~ di speranza** *(fig)* a ray o glimmer of hope; **con un ~ di voce** in a weak o feeble voice.

(b) *(di lama, rasoio)* edge; **essere o camminare o trovarsi sul ~ del rasoio** *(fig)* to be on the razor's edge.

(c) *(di legno)* grain.

(d) *(fraseologia)*: **perdere il ~** *(di un discorso)* to lose the thread; **ripetere qc per ~ e per segno** to repeat sth in detail o word for word; **dare del ~ da torcere a qn** to create difficulties for sb, make life difficult for sb; **è appeso a un ~** it's hanging by a thread; **fare il ~ a qn** *(corteggiare)* to be after sb, chase sb.

(e): **~a** *sfpl*: **le ~a di un complotto** the threads of a plot.

filoamericano, a [filoameri'kano] *ag* pro-American.

filobus ['filobus] *sm inv* trolley bus.

filocinese [filotʃi'nese] *ag* pro-Chinese.

filodiffusione [filodiffu'zjone] *sf* rediffusion.

filodrammatico, a, ci, che [filodram'matiko] **1** *ag*: **(compagnia) ~a** amateur dramatic society. **2** *sm/f* amateur actor/actress.

filologia [filolo'dʒia] *sf* philology.

filone [fi'lone] *sm* **(a)** *(di minerale)* seam; *(fig: culturale)* tradition; **un film che appartiene al ~ western** a film in the Western genre. **(b)** *(di pane)* Vienna loaf.

filosofale [filozo'fale] *ag*: **pietra ~** philosopher's stone.

filosofare [filozo'fare] *vi* to philosophize.

filosofeggiare [filozofed'dʒare] *vi (peg)* to philosophize.

filosofia [filozo'fia] *sf* philosophy; **con ~** *(fig)* philosophically.

filosoficamente [filozofika'mente] *av* philosophically.

filosofico, a, ci, che [filo'zɔfiko] *ag* philosophical.

filosofo, a [fi'lozofo] *sm/f* philosopher.

filosovietico, a, ci, che [filoso'vjetiko] *ag* pro-Soviet.

filovia [filo'via] *sf (linea)* trolley line; *(bus)* trolley bus.

filtrare [fil'trare] **1** *vt* to filter; *(fig: selezionare)* to screen. **2** *vi (aus essere)* to filter; **la luce filtrava**

dalla finestra the light filtered in through the window.

filtrazione [filtrat'tsjone] *sf (vedi vb)* filtration; screening.

filtro¹ ['filtro] *sm* filter; **sigaretta con ~** filter-tipped cigarette, filter tip; **~ dell'olio** *(Aut)* oil filter.

filtro² ['filtro] *sm (pozione)* potion.

filza ['filtsa] *sf (gen, anche fig)* string; **mi ha raccontato una ~ di bugie** he told me a string of lies.

finale [fi'nale] **1** *ag* final; **il giudizio ~** *(Rel)* the Last Judgment; **proposizione ~** *(Gram)* final clause. **2** *sm (di libro, film)* ending; *(Mus, di spettacolo)* finale; **~ a sorpresa** surprise ending. **3** *sf* **(a)** *(Sport)* final; **entrare in ~** to reach the final(s). **(b)** *(Gram)* last syllable *(o letter)*.

finalissima [fina'lissima] *sf (Sport)* final(s); *(di concorso di bellezza etc)* grand final.

finalista, i, e [fina'lista] *sm/f* finalist.

finalità [finali'ta] *sf inv (Filosofia)* finality; *(scopo)* aim, purpose; **gioco a ~ educativa** educational game.

finalizzare [finalid'dzare] *vt*: **~ a** to direct towards.

finalmente [final'mente] *av* at (long) last, finally; **~!** at (long) last!

finanza [fi'nantsa] *sf* **(a)** finance; **alta ~** high finance. **(b)**: **~e** *pl* finances; **Ministro delle ~e** Minister of Finance, ≃ Chancellor of the Exchequer *(Brit)*, Secretary of the Treasury *(Am)*. **(c)** *(Amm)*: **(Guardia di) ~** *(di frontiera)* ≃ Customs and Excise; **(Intendenza di) ~** ≃ Inland Revenue.

finanziamento [finantsja'mento] *sm (azione)* financing; *(denaro fornito)* funds *pl*; **la banca ha concesso un ~ alla ditta** the bank has agreed to finance o fund the company.

finanziare [finan'tsjare] *vt* to finance, fund.

finanziario, a [finan'tsjarjo] **1** *ag* financial. **2** *sf (anche: **società ~a**)* investment company.

finanziatore, trice [finantsja'tore] **1** *ag*: **ente ~, società ~trice** backer. **2** *sm/f* backer.

finanziere [finan'tsjɛre] *sm* **(a)** *(esperto di finanze)* financier. **(b)** *(guardia)* ≃ customs officer.

finché [fin'ke] *cong (fino a quando)* until; *(per tutto il tempo che)* as long as; **ti amerò ~ vivrò** I'll love you as long as I live; **non uscirai ~ non avrai finito il lavoro** you won't leave until you have finished your work.

fine¹ ['fine] *ag* **(a)** *(sottile: lamina, fetta)* thin; *(: capelli, lineamenti, pioggia)* fine; *(: voce)* thin, frail; **penna a punta ~** fine-point pen. **(b)** *(acuto: vista, udito)* sharp, keen; *(: odorato)* fine; *(fig: ingegno)* shrewd; *(: osservazione, ironia)* subtle. **(c)** *(raffinato: persona)* refined; **non è ~ mangiare con le mani** it's bad manners to eat with your fingers.

fine² ['fine] *sm (scopo)* aim, end, purpose; *(Filosofia)* end; **avere un secondo ~** to have an ulterior motive; **a fin di bene** with the best of intentions; **il ~ giustifica i mezzi** the end justifies the means; **al ~ di fare qc** (in order) to do sth. **(b)** *(conclusione)* end; **condurre qc a buon ~** to bring sth to a successful conclusion.

fine³ ['fine] *sf (gen)* end; *(di libro, film)* ending; **alla ~** in the end; **senza ~** *(av)* endlessly; *(ag)* endless; **porre ~ a** to put an end to; **a ~ anno/mese** at the end of the year/month; **alla ~ della giornata** at the end of the day; **verso la ~ di giugno** in late June; **alla fin ~** at the end of the day, in the end; **in fin dei conti** when all is said and done; *(tutto sommato)* after all; **volgere alla ~** to draw to an end; **fare una brutta ~** to come to a bad end; **che ~ ha fatto?** what became of him?; **essere in fin di**

vita to be at death's door; **è la ~ del mondo!** *(fig: stupendo)* it's out of this world!; *(peg)* what's the world coming to?; **buona ~ e buon principio!** *(augurio)* happy New Year!; **un quadro ~ Ottocento** a late nineteenth-century painting; **articoli di ~ serie** oddments; **svendita di ~ stagione** end-of-season sale.

fine settimana ['fine setti'mana] *sm o f inv* weekend.

finestra [fi'nεstra] *sf* window; **~ a saliscendi** sash window; **~ a battenti** casement window; **buttare il denaro dalla ~** *(fig)* to throw money down the drain.

finestrino [fines'trino] *sm (Aut, Ferr etc)* window.

finezza [fi'nettsa] *sf (vedi* **fine**[1]*)* thinness; fineness; sharpness; keenness; shrewdness; subtleness; refinement.

fingere ['findʒere] **1** *vt* to feign; **~ di fare qc** to pretend to do sth; **~ un grande dolore** to pretend to be in great pain. **2** *vi* to dissemble; **sa ~ molto bene** he's very good at dissembling. **3:** **~rsi** *vr* to pretend to be; **~rsi medico** to pretend to be a doctor.

finimenti [fini'menti] *smpl (di cavallo etc)* harness sg.

finimondo [fini'mondo] *sm* pandemonium; **successe un ~** all hell broke loose.

finire [fi'nire] **1** *vi (aus* essere) **(a)** *(gen)* to finish, end; *(pioggia, neve)* to stop, cease; **un altro giorno è finito** another day is over *o* has come to an end; **tra noi è tutto finito** it's all over between us; **ha finito di piovere/nevicare** it has stopped raining/snowing; **~ bene** *(film, libro etc)* to have a happy ending; **~ male** *(film, libro etc)* to have an unhappy ending; *(persona)* to come to a bad end; **per fortuna che tutto è finito bene** luckily everything turned out well in the end; **~ per** *o* **col fare qc** to end up (by) doing sth; **finì col fare il lavoro lui** he ended up doing the job himself; **com'è andata a ~?** what happened in the end?; **dov'è andato a ~ il libro?, dov'è finito il libro?** where has that book got to?; **dove vuoi andare a ~ con questo discorso?** what are you driving at?; **è finita!** *(non c'è rimedio)* it's all over!

(b) *(esaurirsi)* to be finished; **l'olio è finito** we have run out of oil, the oil is finished.

2 *vt* **(a)** *(gen)* to finish; *(lavoro, corso etc)* to finish, complete; *(discorso)* to end; **ha finito i propri giorni in prigione** he ended his days in prison; **finisci la minestra** finish *o* eat up your soup.

(b) *(smettere)* to stop; **~ di fare qc** to stop doing sth; **non ~ più di fare qc** to keep on doing sth; **non finisco di meravigliarmi della sua pazienza** her patience never ceases to amaze me.

(c) *(dare il colpo di grazia)* to finish off.

(d) *(rifinire)* to finish off, put the finishing touches to.

(e): **finirla: è ora di finirla con queste storie!** it's time you stopped this nonsense!; **finiscila!** stop it!; **devi farla finita con questi capricci** you'll have to stop these tantrums; **l'ho fatta finita con la droga** I've stopped taking drugs; **ho deciso di farla finita con Maria** I've decided to finish with Maria; **farla finita (con la vita)** to put an end to one's life.

3 *sm (fine)* end; **sul ~ della festa** towards the end of the party.

finissaggio [finis'saddʒo] *sm (Tecn: operazione)* finishing; *(: risultato)* finish.

finito, a [fi'nito] *ag* **(a)** *(Gram, Mat, Filosofia)* finite. **(b)** *(terminato, rifinito)* finished; **è un uomo ~** *(fig: rovinato)* he's finished. **(c)** *(esperto: cuoco)*

---

expert; *(: operaio, artigiano)* skilled.

finitura [fini'tura] *sf* finish; **le ultime ~e** the finishing touches.

finlandese [finlan'dese] **1** *ag* Finnish. **2** *sm/f* Finn. **3** *sm (lingua)* Finnish.

Finlandia [fin'landja] *sf* Finland.

fino[1]**, a** ['fino] *ag* **(a)** = **fine**[1]. **(b)** *(oro, argento)* pure; **cervello ~** quick brain.

fino[2] ['fino] **1** *av (pure, anche)* even; **hai detto fin troppo** you have said too much *o* more than enough.

2 *prep* **(a):** **~ a** *(tempo)* until, up to, till; *(luogo)* as far as; *(+ infin)* so that; **resto ~ a venerdì/al 15 gennaio** I'm staying until Friday/until the 15th of January; **vengo con te ~ al cinema** I'll come as far as the cinema with you; **ha lavorato ~ ad ammalarsi** he worked so hard that he became ill; **~ a quando?, fin quando?** until when?; **~ all'ultimo** until the end, to the end, till the end; **~ all'ultimo ha negato poi ha ceduto** he denied it up till the last minute, then gave in; **averne fin sopra i capelli** *(fig)* to be fed up to the back teeth; **andare ~ in fondo a qc** *(anche fig)* to get to the bottom of sth.

(b): **fin da** since, from; **fin dalla nascita/dall'infanzia** since birth/infancy; **fin da quando sei arrivato** since you arrived, from the time you arrived; **fin d'ora** as of now; **fin dall'alba** since daybreak.

finocchio [fi'nɔkkjo] *sm* **(a)** *(Bot)* fennel. **(b)** *(fam: omosessuale)* queer, poof.

finora [fi'nora] *av* up till now, so far; **~ Marco non si è visto** Marco hasn't turned up yet.

finta ['finta] *sf* **(a)** *(finzione)*: **fare ~ di fare qc** to pretend to do sth; **fa ~ di niente** he pretends not to notice; *(comportarsi normalmente)* he's behaving as if nothing had happened; **l'ho detto per ~** I was only pretending; *(per scherzo)* I was only kidding. **(b)** *(Pugilato)* feint. **(c)** *(Cucito)* flap.

fintantoché [fintanto'ke] *av (per tutto il tempo che)* as long as; *(fino al momento in cui)* until.

finto, a ['finto] **1** *pp di* **fingere. 2** *ag (capelli, dente)* false; *(fiori)* artificial; *(cuoio, pelle)* imitation *attr*; *(fig: simulato: pazzia etc)* feigned, sham.

finzione [fin'tsjone] *sf (simulazione)* pretence, sham; *(Teatro, Letteratura)* fiction, invention.

fio ['fio] *sm*: **pagare il ~ (di)** to pay the penalty (for).

fioccare [fjok'kare] *(aus* essere) **1** *vi (neve)* to fall; *(fig: insulti etc)* to fall thick and fast. **2** *vb impers* to snow.

fiocco[1]**, chi** ['fjɔkko] *sm* **(a)** *(di neve, cereali)* flake. **(b)** *(di lana)* flock. **(c)** *(nastro)* bow; **coi ~chi** *(fig)* first-rate; **un pranzo coi ~chi** a slap-up meal.

fiocco[2]**, chi** ['fjɔkko] *sm (Naut)* jib.

fiocina ['fjɔtʃina] *sf (Naut)* harpoon.

fioco, a, chi, che ['fjɔko] *ag (luce)* dim, weak; *(suono, voce)* faint, weak.

fionda ['fjonda] *sf (arma)* sling; *(giocattolo)* catapult.

fioraio, a [fjo'rajo] *sm/f (in negozio)* florist; *(ambulante)* flower seller.

fiorato, a [fjo'rato] *ag* floral.

fiordaliso [fjorda'lizo] *sm (Bot)* cornflower.

fiordo ['fjɔrdo] *sm* fjord.

fiore ['fjore] **1** *sm* **(a)** *(gen, anche fig)* flower; *(di albero)* blossom; **essere in ~** *(pianta, giardino)* to be in bloom *o* flower; *(albero)* to be in blossom; *(fig)* to be in full bloom; **~ d'arancio** orange blossom sg; **disegno a ~i** floral design; **nel ~ degli anni** in one's prime; **oggi sei un ~** you're looking lovely today; **'non ~i ma opere di bene'**

(negli annunci mortuari) 'no flowers please, but give to charity'.
(b) *(Carte)*: ~**i** pl clubs.
(c): **a fior di**: **a fior d'acqua** on (the surface of) the water; **a fior di labbra** in a whisper; **ho i nervi a fior di pelle** my nerves are all on edge.
(d): **un fior di ragazza** a really lovely girl; **è un fior di vestito** it's a very pretty dress; **è costato fior di soldi** it cost a pretty penny; **aver fior di quattrini** to be rolling in money; **il fior ~ della società** the cream of society.
2: **fior di farina** superfine flour; **fior di latte** cream.

fiorente [fjo'rɛnte] *ag (industria, paese)* flourishing; *(salute)* blooming; *(petto)* ample; **~ di** *(boschi, vigneti)* rich in.

fiorentina [fjoren'tina] *sf (Culin)* T-bone steak.

fiorentino, a [fjoren'tino] *ag, sm/f* Florentine.

fioretto[1] [fjo'retto] *sm (piccola rinuncia)* small sacrifice; *(buona azione)* good deed.

fioretto[2] [fjo'retto] *sm* **(a)** *(Scherma)* foil. **(b)** *(Tecn)* drilling bit.

fioriera [fjo'rjɛra] *sf (per piante)* flowerpot; *(per fiori recisi)* vase.

fiorino [fjo'rino] *sm* florin.

fiorire [fjo'rire] *vi (aus essere) (fiore)* to flower, bloom; *(albero)* to blossom, flower; *(fig: sentimento)* to blossom; *(: commercio, arte)* to flourish.

fiorista, i, e [fjo'rista] *sm/f* florist.

fiorito, a [fjo'rito] *ag (giardino)* in flower, in bloom; *(pianta)* in bloom; *(ramo)* in blossom; *(tessuto)* floral, flowered; *(stile)* flowery; **~ di errori** full of errors.

fioritura [fjori'tura] *sf* **(a)** *(di pianta)* flowering, blooming; *(di albero)* blossoming; *(fig: di commercio, arte)* flourishing. **(b)** *(insieme dei fiori)* flowers pl; **il ciliegio ha avuto una ~ abbondante quest'anno** the cherry tree produced a lot of flowers this year. **(c)** *(Mus)* fioritura.

fiotto ['fjɔtto] *sm (di lacrime)* flow, flood; *(di sangue)* gush, spurt; **scorrere a ~i** to gush out o forth.

Firenze [fi'rentse] *sf* Florence.

firma ['firma] *sf* signature; *(fig)* name; **apporre la propria ~ a** to put one's signature to; **le grandi ~e della moda** the big names in fashion.

firmamento [firma'mento] *sm* firmament.

firmare [fir'mare] *vt* to sign; **un maglione firmato da Missoni** a Missoni sweater, a sweater by Missoni.

firmatario, a [firma'tarjo] *sm/f* signatory.

fisarmonica, che [fizar'mɔnika] *sf* accordion.

fiscale [fis'kale] *ag* **(a)** fiscal, tax *attr*; **anno ~** tax year; **medico ~** doctor employed by Social Security to verify cases of sick leave. **(b)** *(meticoloso)* punctilious.

fiscalista, i, e [fiska'lista] *sm/f* tax consultant.

fiscalità [fiskali'ta] *sf inv (vedi ag)* tax system; punctiliousness.

fischiare [fis'kjare] **1** *vt* **(a)** *(canzone, motivo)* to whistle; **l'arbitro ha fischiato un rigore** the referee blew his whistle for a penalty. **(b)** *(in segno di disapprovazione)* to hiss, boo. **2** *vi (gen, fig)* to whistle; *(serpente)* to hiss; *(uccello)* to sing; **mi fischian le orecchie** my ears are singing; *(fig)* my ears are burning; **~ al cane** to whistle for one's dog.

fischiata [fis'kjata] *sf (azione)* whistling; *(fischio)* whistle; **le ~e del pubblico** the booing of the audience.

fischiettare [fiskjet'tare] *vi, vt* to whistle.

fischietto [fis'kjetto] *sm (strumento)* whistle.

fischio ['fiskjo] *sm (suono)* whistle; **prendere ~i**

per fiaschi to get hold of the wrong end of the stick.

fisco ['fisko] *sm (Amm)* ≃ Inland Revenue *(Brit)*, Internal Revenue *(Am)*.

fisica ['fizika] *sf* physics *sg*.

fisicamente [fizika'mente] *av* physically; **sono ~ impossibilitato a venire** it's physically impossible for me to come.

fisico, a, ci, che ['fiziko] **1** *ag (gen)* physical. **2** *sm (corpo)* physique; **avere un bel ~** to be good-looking; **hai il ~ dell'atleta** you have an athletic physique o the physique of an athlete. **3** *sm/f (studioso)* physicist.

fisima ['fizima] *sf* fixation.

fisiologia [fizjolo'dʒia] *sf* physiology.

fisiologico, a, ci, che [fizjo'lɔdʒiko] *ag* physiological.

fisionomia [fizjono'mia] *sf* physiognomy; **non ricordo bene la sua ~** I don't remember his face very well.

fisionomista, i, e [fizjono'mista] *sm/f*: **sei un buon ~** you have a good memory for faces.

fisioterapia [fizjotera'pia] *sf* physiotherapy.

fisioterapico, a, ci, che [fizjote'rapiko] *ag* physiotherapy *attr*.

fisioterapista, i, e [fizjotera'pista] *sm/f* physiotherapist.

fissaggio [fis'saddʒo] *sm (Fot)* fixing; **bisogna aspettare 2 ore per il ~ di questa vernice** you must wait 2 hours for this paint to dry.

fissare [fis'sare] **1** *vt* **(a)** *(attaccare)*: **~ (a o su)** to fix (to), fasten (to); *(sguardo)*: **~ (su)** to fix (on), fasten (on); **~ qn/qc** to stare at sb/sth; **~ qc nella memoria** to fix sth firmly in one's memory. **(b)** *(prezzo, data)* to fix, set; *(regola)* to lay down; *(appuntamento)* to arrange, fix; **all'ora fissata** at the agreed time; **è tutto fissato** it's all fixed o arranged. **(c)** *(prenotare)* to book, reserve. **(d)** *(Fot, Chim)* to fix.
2: **~rsi** *vr* **(a)**: **~rsi di fare qc** *(mettersi in testa di)* to set one's heart on doing sth; *(ostinarsi)* to insist on doing sth; **si è fissato di partire con noi** he has set his heart on coming with us; **si è fissato che vuole vederlo subito** he insists on seeing him at once. **(b)** *(concentrarsi)*: **l'attenzione del pubblico si è fissata su di lui** he was very much in the public eye. **(c)** *(uso reciproco)* to stare at each other.

fissativo, a [fissa'tivo] *ag, sm* fixative.

fissato, a [fis'sato] **1** *ag (gen)* fixed; *(ora)* set, agreed; *(prezzo)* agreed; **essere ~ con qc** to have a thing about sth. **2** *sm/f* person with an obsession; **ma quello è un ~!** he is obsessed!

fissatore [fissa'tore] *sm (Chim)* fixative; *(Fot)* fixer; *(per capelli)* setting lotion.

fissazione [fissat'tsjone] *sf (Psic)* obsession, fixation.

fissione [fis'sjone] *sf* fission.

fissità [fissi'ta] *sf (di sguardo)* steadiness; *(di principi)* fixedness.

fisso, a ['fisso] **1** *ag (gen)* fixed; *(lavoro, lavoratore)* permanent; *(stipendio)* regular; *(presenza)* constant; *(immagine, elemento)* recurring; **avere un ragazzo ~** to have a steady boyfriend; **senza ~a dimora** of no fixed abode. **2** *sm* fixed sum. **3** *av*: **guardar ~ qn/qc** to stare (at sb/sth).

fistola ['fistola] *sf (Med)* fistula.

fitta ['fitta] *sf* sharp pain; **una ~ di dolore** a sharp twinge of pain; **una ~ al cuore** *(fig)* a pang of grief.

fittavolo [fit'tavolo] *sm* tenant.

fittizio, a [fit'tittsjo] *ag (nome)* fictitious.

fitto[1]**, a** ['fitto] **1** *ag* **(a)** *(bosco, pelo)* thick; *(nebbia)* thick, dense; *(tessuto)* closely-woven; *(pettine)* fine; **è buio** ~ it's pitch dark. **(b)** *(intenso: interrogatorio)* close; *(: fuoco d'artiglieria)* heavy; **una giornata** ~**a di eventi** an eventful day. **2** *av (nevicare, piovere)* hard; **parlare** ~ ~ to be deep in conversation; **scritto** ~ ~ closely written. **3** *sm:* **nel** ~ **del bosco** in the heart *o* depths of the wood.

fitto[2] ['fitto] *sm (affitto)* rent; **blocco dei** ~**i** rents freeze.

fiumana [fju'mana] *sf (fiume in piena)* torrent; *(fig: di gente etc)* flood.

fiumara [fju'mara] *sf* torrent.

fiume ['fjume] **1** *sm* river; *(fig: di gente, parole)* stream; **scorrere a** ~**i** *(acqua, sangue)* to flow in torrents; **uscire a** ~**i (da)** *(acqua, sangue)* to pour out (from). **2** *ag inv:* **romanzo** ~ roman-fleuve; **processo** ~ long-drawn-out trial.

fiutare [fju'tare] *vt* to smell, sniff; *(cane da caccia)* to scent; ~ **tabacco** to take snuff; ~ **qc di losco** *(fig)* to smell a rat.

fiuto ['fjuto] *sm (odorato)* sense of smell; *(fig: intuito)* nose; **avere** ~ **nel fare qc** to have a good nose for doing sth.

flaccido, a ['flattʃido] *ag* flabby.

flacone [fla'kone] *sm* bottle.

flagellare [fladʒel'lare] **1** *vt* to flog, scourge; *(sog: onde)* to beat against. **2:** ~**rsi** *vr* to whip o.s.

flagellazione [fladʒellat'tsjone] *sf* flogging, scourging.

flagello [fla'dʒello] *sm (frusta, fig)* scourge.

flagrante [fla'grante] *ag:* **cogliere qn in** ~ to catch sb red-handed *o* in the act; **essere in** ~ **contraddizione** to be in blatant contradiction.

flan [flɑ̃] *sm (Culin)* flan.

flanella [fla'nɛlla] *sf* flannel.

flash [flæʃ] *sm inv* **(a)** *(Fot, Elettr)* flash. **(b)** *(Radio, TV)* newsflash.

flashback ['flæʃbæk] *sm inv (Cine):* ~ **(su** *o* **di)** flashback (to).

flautista, i, e [flau'tista] *sm/f* flautist.

flauto ['flauto] *sm:* ~ **(traverso)** flute; ~ **dolce** recorder.

flebile ['flɛbile] *ag* feeble, faint.

flebite [fle'bite] *sf* phlebitis.

fleboclisi [flebo'klisi] *sf inv (Med)* drip.

flemma ['flɛmma] *sf* phlegm, composure; **rispose con molta** ~ he answered very phlegmatically *o* coolly.

flemmatico, a, ci, che [flem'matiko] *ag* phlegmatic, cool.

flessibile [fles'sibile] *ag (materiale)* flexible, pliable; *(fig: carattere)* flexible, adaptable.

flessibilità [flessibili'ta] *sf* flexibility.

flessione [fles'sjone] *sf* **(a)** *(gen)* bending; *(Ginnastica: a terra)* sit-up; *(: in piedi)* forward bend; *(: sulle gambe)* knee-bend; **fare una** ~ to bend. **(b)** *(diminuzione)* slight drop, slight fall; ~ **economica** a downward trend in the economy. **(c)** *(Linguistica)* inflection.

flesso, a ['flɛsso] *pp di* **flettere**.

flessuosità [flessuosi'ta] *sf (vedi ag)* suppleness; grace(fulness).

flessuoso, a [flessu'oso] *ag (elastico)* supple; *(armonico: corpo femminile)* graceful; *(: movimenti)* flowing, graceful.

flettere ['flɛttere] **1** *vt* **(a)** *(gen)* to bend; ~ **il busto in avanti** to bend forward from the waist. **(b)** *(Linguistica)* to inflect. **2:** ~**rsi** *vr* to bend.

flipper ['flipper] *sm inv* pinball machine.

flirt [fləːt] *sm inv* brief romance, flirtation.

flirtare [flir'tare] *vi* to flirt.

F.lli *abbr (= fratelli)* Bros.

flora ['flɔra] *sf* flora.

floreale [flore'ale] *ag* floral; **una lampada in stile** ~ an Art Nouveau lamp.

floricoltore, trice [florikol'tore] *sm/f* flower grower.

floricoltura [florikol'tura] *sf* flower-growing, floriculture.

floridezza [flori'dettsa] *sf (di economia, industria)* flourishing state, prosperity; *(dei campi)* fertility; *(di persona)* glowing health.

florido, a ['flɔrido] *ag (industria)* flourishing, thriving, prosperous; *(campagna)* fertile; *(corpo)* healthy, glowing with health; **seno** *o* **petto** ~ ample bosom.

floruro [flo'ruro] *sm* fluoride.

floscio, a, sci, sce ['flɔʃʃo] *ag (cappello, tessuto)* soft, floppy; *(muscoli, carni)* flabby.

flotta ['flɔtta] *sf* fleet; ~ **aerea** fleet of aircraft.

flou [flu] *ag inv* **(a)** *(Fot, Cine: sfumato)* blurred. **(b)** *(abito)* flowing, loose(-fitting).

fluente [flu'ɛnte] *ag (fig: chioma, barba)* flowing; *(: discorso)* fluent.

fluidità [fluidi'ta] *sf (gen)* fluidity; *(fig: di stile)* fluency.

fluido, a ['fluido] **1** *ag (gen)* fluid. **2** *sm* fluid; *(forza magica)* mysterious power.

fluire [flu'ire] *vi (aus essere)* to flow.

fluorescente [fluoreʃ'ʃɛnte] *ag* fluorescent.

fluorescenza [fluoreʃ'ʃɛntsa] *sf* fluorescence.

fluoro [flu'ɔro] *sm* fluorine.

flusso ['flusso] *sm (gen, fig)* flow; *(Fis, Elettr)* flux.

fluttuante [fluttu'ante] *ag (Econ: moneta, prezzi)* fluctuating; **debito** ~ floating debt.

fluttuare [fluttu'are] *vi* **(a)** *(ondeggiare: mare)* to rise and fall; *(: barca)* to toss, rock; *(: bandiera)* to flutter. **(b)** *(Econ: moneta)* to fluctuate.

fluttuazione [fluttuat'tsjone] *sf (Econ, Fis, fig)* fluctuation.

fluviale [flu'vjale] *ag* river *attr*, fluvial; **pesca** ~ freshwater fishing; **navigazone** ~ river *o* inland navigation.

fobia [fo'bia] *sf* phobia; **ha la** ~ **dei ragni** he has a phobia about spiders.

foca, che ['fɔka] *sf (Zool)* seal.

focaccia, ce [fo'kattʃa] *sf (Culin)* kind of pizza; *(: dolce)* bun; **rendere pan per** ~ to get one's own back, give tit for tat.

focaia [fo'kaja] *ag f:* **pietra** ~ flint.

focale [fo'kale] *ag* focal.

focalizzare [fokalid'dzare] *vt (Fot: immagine)* to get into focus; ~ **la situazione** to get the situation into perspective; ~ **l'attenzione su** to focus one's attention on.

foce ['fotʃe] *sf (Geog)* mouth.

fochista, i [fo'kista] *sm* stoker; *(Ferr)* stoker, fireman.

focolaio [foko'lajo] *sm (Med)* centre (of infection), focus; *(fig)* hotbed, breeding ground; **il** ~ **della rivolta** the breeding ground of the rebellion.

focolare [foko'lare] *sm* hearth; **ritornare al** ~ **domestico** to return to home and hearth.

focoso, a [fo'koso] *ag* fiery; *(cavallo)* mettlesome, fiery.

fodera ['fɔdera] *sf (interna, di vestito)* lining; *(di libro)* dust jacket; *(di divano etc)* cover.

foderare [fode'rare] *vt (vestito)* to line; *(libro)* to cover.

fodero ['fɔdero] *sm (di spada)* scabbard; *(di pugnale)* sheath; *(di pistola)* holster.

foga ['fɔga] *sf* enthusiasm; **nella** ~ **della passione/ discussione** in the heat of passion/the discussion; **lavora con** ~ he throws himself into his work (with great enthusiasm); **si precipitò con** ~ **ad aprire** he rushed excitedly to the door.

foggia, ge ['fɔddʒa] *sf (forma)* shape; *(moda)* style; **un abito di ~ strana** a strange style of dress; **alla ~ degli anni venti** twenties style.

foggiare [fod'dʒare] *vt* to shape, mould.

foglia ['fɔʎʎa] *sf (Bot, di metallo)* leaf; **gli alberi stanno mettendo le ~e** the leaves are coming out (on the trees); **ha mangiato la ~** *(fig)* he's caught on; **tremare come una ~** *(fig)* to shake like a leaf; **~ d'argento** silver leaf; **~ di fico** fig leaf.

fogliame [foʎ'ʎame] *sm* foliage, leaves *pl*.

foglietto [foʎ'ʎetto] *sm* **(a)** *(piccolo foglio)* slip of paper, piece of paper; *(manifestino)* leaflet, handout. **(b)** *(Anat):* **~ pleurico** pleural layer.

foglio ['fɔʎʎo] *sm* **(a)** *(gen, di metallo)* sheet; *(di libro)* page, leaf; **~ rigato** *o* **a righe** sheet of lined *o* ruled paper; **~ a quadretti** sheet of squared paper; **~ protocollo** foolscap; **~ volante** leaflet, handout. **(b)** *(documento):* **~ rosa** *(Aut)* ≈ provisional driving licence; **~ di via** *(Dir)* expulsion order. **(c)** *(banconota)* (bank)note. **(d)** *(Tip):* **in ~** folio *attr*.

fogna ['foɲɲa] *sf* sewer; *(fig: luogo sporco)* pigsty; **topo di ~** sewer rat.

fognatura [foɲɲa'tura] *sf* sewerage.

föhn [fø:n] *sm inv* hair-dryer.

folaga, ghe ['fɔlaga] *sf* coot.

folata [fo'lata] *sf* gust; **il tuo arrivo ha portato una ~ di novità** your arrival was like a breath of fresh air.

folclore [fol'klore] *sm* folklore.

folcloristico, a, ci, che [folklo'ristiko] *ag (spettacolo, canzone)* folk *attr*; **costume ~** traditional dress.

folgorante [folgo'rante] *ag (fulmine)* dazzling; *(fig: sguardo)* withering; *(: passione)* violent; *(: dolore, male)* sudden.

folgorare [folgo'rare] **1** *vt (sog: fulmine)* to strike (down); **mi folgorò con uno sguardo** *(fig)* he gave me a withering look. **2** *vi (rilucere)* to flash.

folgorazione [folgorat'tsjone] *sf* electrocution; **ebbe una ~** *(fig: idea)* he had a brainwave.

folgore ['folgore] *sf* thunderbolt.

folk ['fouk] **1** *ag (cantante)* folk *attr*; *(abito)* peasant *attr*. **2** *sm (Mus)* folk; *(moda)* peasant look.

folla ['folla] *sf (di persone)* crowd; *(: peg)* mob; **una ~ di idee** a multitude *o* host of ideas.

folle ['fɔlle] **1** *ag* **(a)** *(anche fig: idee, trovata)* mad, insane; **a ritmo** *o* **velocità ~** at breakneck speed. **(b)** *(Tecn: ingranaggio)* idle. **2** *sm/f* madman/woman. **3** *sm (Aut):* **in ~** in neutral.

folleggiare [folled'dʒare] *vi (divertirsi)* to paint the town red.

folletto [fol'letto] *sm* elf.

follia [fol'lia] *sf* madness; *(atto)* act of madness, act of folly; **fare una ~** *(fig)* to do sth mad *o* crazy; **è stata una ~ fare ciò che ha fatto** it was madness *o* folly to do what he did; **costare una ~** to cost the earth; **amare qn alla ~** to love sb to distraction; **che ~!** what folly!, what madness!

follicolo [fol'likolo] *sm* follicle.

folto, a ['folto] **1** *ag (capelli, pelo, bosco)* thick; *(schiera)* dense. **2** *sm:* **nel ~ della mischia** in the thick of the fray.

fomentare [fomen'tare] *vt* to stir up, foment.

fomentatore, trice [fomenta'tore] *sm/f* agitator.

fomento [fo'mento] *sm* **(a)** *(Med)* poultice. **(b)** *(stimolo):* **dare ~ a** to stir up, foment.

fon [fɔn] *sm inv* = **föhn**.

fondale [fon'dale] *sm* **(a)** *(del mare)* bottom; **il ~ marino** the sea bed. **(b)** *(Teatro)* backdrop.

fondamentale [fondamen'tale] *ag* fundamental, basic; **è ~ che...** it's of prime importance that....

fondamento [fonda'mento] *sm* **(a)** foundation,

basis; **i ~i della matematica** the principles of mathematics. **(b):** **~a** *sfpl (Edil)* foundations; **gettare le ~a** *(anche fig)* to lay the foundations.

fondant [fɔ'dã] *sm* fondant.

fondare [fon'dare] **1** *vt (istituzione, città)* to found; *(teoria, sospetti)* to base. **2:** **~rsi** *vr (teorie):* **~rsi (su)** to be based (on).

fondatezza [fonda'tettsa] *sf* soundness.

fondatore, trice [fonda'tore] *sm/f* founder.

fondazione [fondat'tsjone] *sf* foundation.

fondere ['fondere] **1** *vt* **(a)** *(gen)* to melt; *(metallo)* to fuse, melt; *(fig: colori)* to blend, merge; *(: enti, classi)* to merge. **(b)** *(statua, campana)* to cast. **2** *vi* to melt; **mi fonde il cervello** *(fig)* I can't think straight any more, my brain has seized up. **3:** **~rsi** *vr (sciogliersi)* to melt; *(unirsi: correnti, enti)* to merge.

fonderia [fonde'ria] *sf* foundry.

fondiario, a [fon'djarjo] *ag* land *attr*; **possidente ~** landowner.

fondina [fon'dina] *sf* **(a)** *(piatto fondo)* soup plate. **(b)** *(portapistola)* holster.

fondista, i, e [fon'dista] *sm/f* (long-)distance runner; *(sciatore)* cross-country skier.

fondo[1], a ['fondo] **1** *ag* deep; **piatto ~** soup plate; **a notte ~a** at dead of night; **una buca ~a 3 metri** a hole 3 metres deep.

2 *sm* **(a)** *(di recipiente, vallata etc)* bottom; *(dei pantaloni)* seat; *(di mare, fiume)* bottom, bed; **~ stradale** road surface; **~ tinta** *(cosmetico)* foundation; **doppio ~** false bottom; **andare** *o* **colare a ~** *(Naut)* to go to the bottom, sink; **in ~ alla pagina** at the bottom of the page; **in ~ al vicolo** at the end of the alley; **laggiù in ~** *(lontano)* over there; *(in profondità)* down there; **nel ~ del bosco** in the depths *o* heart of the wood; **nel ~ del suo cuore** deep down, in his heart of hearts. **(b):** **~i** *pl (di vino, aceto)* dregs, lees; *(di caffè)* grounds; **~i di magazzino** old stock. **(c)** *(sfondo)* background; *(Araldica)* ground. **(d)** *(Sport):* **di ~** long-distance; **sci di ~** cross-country skiing.

(e) *(fraseologia):* **conoscere a ~** *(persona)* to know through and through; *(argomento, materia)* to have a thorough knowledge of; **studiare a ~** qc to study sth thoroughly *o* in depth; **andare a ~ in** *(affare losco)* to get to the bottom of; **dar ~ a** qc *(risorse etc)* to use up, consume; **senza ~** *(risorse)* infinite, never-ending; *(pozzo)* bottomless; **in ~** after all, all things considered; **in ~ in ~** when all's said and done; **toccare il ~** *(fig)* to plumb the depths.

fondo[2] ['fondo] *sm* **(a)** *(bene immobile)* land, property; **~ rustico** country estate; **~ urbano** town property. **(b)** *(riserva)* fund; **~ di previdenza** social insurance fund; **~ di riserva** reserve fund; **~ (di) cassa** cash in hand; *(per spese minute)* petty cash; **a ~ perduto** unsecured; **~ comune d'investimento** investment trust; **F~ Monetario (Internazionale)** International Monetary Fund. **(c):** **~i** *pl (capitale)* capital sg; **~i pubblici/segreti** public/secret funds; **~i d'esercizio** working capital; **~i liquidi** ready money, liquid assets.

fondovalle [fondo'valle] *sm* valley bottom.

fonduta [fon'duta] *sf (Culin)* fondue.

fonema [fo'nɛma] *sm* phoneme.

fonetica [fo'nɛtika] *sf* phonetics *sg*.

fonetico, a, ci, che [fo'nɛtiko] *ag* phonetic.

fonico, a, ci, che ['fɔniko] *ag* phonic; **apparecchio ~** hearing aid; **accento ~** stress.

fonoassorbente [fonoassor'bɛnte] *ag* sound-absorbent.

fonografo [fo'nɔgrafo] *sm* gramophone, phonograph (*Am*).

fontana [fon'tana] *sf* fountain; **piangere come una** ~ to weep great buckets of tears.

fontanella [fonta'nɛlla] *sf* **(a)** *(fontana)* drinking fountain. **(b)** *(Anat)* fontanelle.

fonte ['fonte] **1** *sf* *(sorgente)* spring; *(fig: di calore, informazioni)* source; **risalire alle** ~**i** to go back to the origins *o* roots. **2** *sm:* ~ **battesimale** *(Rel)* font.

footing ['futiŋ] *sm* jogging; **fare** ~ to jog.

foraggio [fo'raddʒo] *sm* fodder.

forare [fo'rare] **1** *vt (gen)* to make a hole in, pierce; *(biglietto)* to punch; *(pneumatico)* to puncture. **2** *vi (Aut)* to have a puncture. **3:** ~**rsi** *vr (gen)* to develop a hole; *(Aut, pallone, timpano)* to burst.

foratura [fora'tura] *sf* **(a)** *(vedi vb)* piercing; punching; puncturing. **(b)** *(di pneumatico)* puncture.

forbice ['fɔrbitʃe] *sf (spec pl)* scissors *pl*; **un paio di** ~**i** a pair of scissors; **dare un colpo di** ~ **a qc** to snip sth; ~ **da giardiniere** (gardening) shears *pl*; ~ **per potare** secateurs *pl*.

forbicina [forbi'tʃina] *sf* earwig.

forbito, a [for'bito] *ag (stile, modi)* polished; **parla una lingua** ~**a** he has an elegant turn of phrase.

forca, che ['fɔrka] *sf* **(a)** *(Agr)* pitchfork. **(b)** *(per impiccagione)* gallows *pl*.

forcella [for'tʃɛlla] *sf (gen, Tecn)* fork; *(per capelli)* hairpin; *(di volatile)* wishbone.

forchetta [for'ketta] *sf* fork; **essere una buona** ~ to enjoy one's food.

forcina [for'tʃina] *sf* hairpin.

forcipe ['fɔrtʃipe] *sm* forceps *pl*.

forcone [for'kone] *sm* pitchfork.

forcuto, a [for'kuto] *ag* forked.

forense [fo'rɛnse] *ag (linguaggio)* legal; **avvocato** ~ barrister.

foresta [fo'rɛsta] *sf* forest.

forestale [fores'tale] *ag* forest *attr*; **guardia** ~ forester.

foresteria [foreste'ria] *sf (di convento, palazzo etc)* guest rooms *pl*, guest quarters *pl*.

forestiero, a [fores'tjɛro] *sm/f* stranger; *(dall'estero)* foreigner.

forfait [for'fɛ] *sm inv* **(a): (prezzo a)** ~ fixed price, set price; **le diamo un** ~ **per il suo lavoro** we'll give you a lump sum for your work; **a** ~ on a lump-sum basis. **(b): dichiarare** ~ *(Sport)* to withdraw; *(fig)* to give up.

forfetario, a [forfe'tarjo] *ag:* **prezzo** ~ *(da pagare)* fixed *o* set price; *(da ricevere)* lump sum.

forfora ['forfora] *sf* dandruff.

forgiare [for'dʒare] *vt* to forge; *(fig: carattere)* to mould, form.

forma ['forma] *sf* **(a)** *(gen, Gram, Filosofia)* form; *(contorno)* form, shape; **di** ~ **quadrata** square; **a** ~ **di cuore** heart-shaped; **senza** ~ *(oggetto)* shapeless; *(pensiero)* formless; **prendere** ~ *(delinearsi)* to take shape; **prendere una medicina in** *o* **sotto** ~ **di compresse** to take a medicine in tablet form; **in** ~ **ufficiale/privata** officially/privately; ~ **mentale** *o* **mentis** way of thinking; **non c'è alcuna** ~ **di vita sulla luna** there is no form of life on the moon.

(b) *(stampo)* mould; *(per scarpe)* last; **una** ~ **di formaggio** a (whole) cheese.

(c) *(modo di esprimersi)* form; **errori di** ~ stylistic errors.

(d) *(~ fisica)* form; **essere/non essere in** ~ to be on/off form; **tenersi in** ~ to keep fit.

(e) *(apparenze)* appearances *pl*; **tenere alla** ~ to care about appearances.

formaggiera [formad'dʒɛra] *sf* cheese dish *(for grated Parmesan)*.

formaggino [formad'dʒino] *sm* processed cheese; **un** ~ a portion of processed cheese.

formaggio [for'maddʒo] *sm* cheese.

formale [for'male] *ag* formal.

formalismo [forma'lizmo] *sm (Arte, Filosofia)* formalism.

formalista, i, e [forma'lista] *ag, sm/f* formalist.

formalità [formali'ta] *sf inv* formality; **senza** ~ *(pasto etc)* informal.

formalizzare [formalid'dzare] **1** *vt* to formalize. **2:** ~**rsi** *vr (farsi scrupoli sulla forma)* to stand on ceremony; *(scandalizzarsi)* to be easily shocked.

formare [for'mare] **1** *vt* **(a)** *(gen)* to form; *(numero telefonico)* to dial; **questi pezzi formano una croce** these pieces make *o* form a cross; **l'appartamento è formato da 3 stanze** the flat is made up of 3 rooms; ~ **una famiglia** to get married and start a family. **(b)** *(educare: soldati, attori)* to train; *(intelligenza, carattere)* to form, develop. **2:** ~**rsi** *vr* **(a)** to form; **il treno si forma a Milano** the train starts from Milan. **(b)** *(educarsi)* to be educated; **Leopardi si formò sui classici greci** Leopardi had a classical Greek background.

formativo, a [forma'tivo] *ag* formative.

formato, a [for'mato] **1** *ag (maturo)* fully-developed, fully-grown. **2** *sm (dimensioni)* size, format; **foto** ~ **tessera** passport-size photo; ~ **famiglia** family size.

formazione [format'tsjone] *sf* **(a)** formation. **(b)** *(educazione)* education; *(addestramento)* training.

formella [for'mɛlla] *sf* tile.

formica¹, che [for'mika] *sf (Zool)* ant.

formica² ['fɔrmika] *sf* ® Formica ®.

formicaio [formi'kajo] *sm (sporgente)* anthill; *(sotterraneo)* ants' nest; **quella spiaggia è un** ~ *(fig)* that beach is always swarming with people.

formichiere [formi'kjɛre] *sm* anteater.

formicolare [formiko'lare] *vi* **(a)** *(brulicare):* ~ **di** to swarm with, be crawling with. **(b)** *(aus essere) (arto: essere intorpidito):* **mi formicola un braccio** I've got pins and needles in my arm.

formicolio [formiko'lio] *sm (brulichio)* swarming; *(prurito)* tingling; **sento un** ~ **al braccio** I've got pins and needles in my arm.

formidabile [formi'dabile] *ag (temibile)* formidable; *(meraviglioso)* amazing, tremendous, fantastic; **ho una fame** ~ I'm incredibly hungry.

formoso, a [for'moso] *ag* shapely.

formula ['formula] *sf (gen, Chim, Mat)* formula; ~ **di cortesia** *(nelle lettere)* letter ending; ~ **pubblicitaria** advertising slogan; ~ **1** *(Sport)* formula 1.

formulare [formu'lare] *vt (giudizio, pensiero)* to formulate.

formulario [formu'larjo] *sm (modulo)* form.

formulazione [formulat'tsjone] *sf* formulation; **è un pensiero di difficile** ~ **verbale** it's a difficult concept to put into words.

fornace [for'natʃe] *sf (Tecn)* kiln.

fornaio [for'najo] *sm* baker; **dal** ~ at the baker's.

fornello [for'nɛllo] *sm* **(a)** *(cuocivivande: a spirito, petrolio)* stove; *(: elettrico)* hotplate; *(: a gas)* ring. **(b)** *(di pipa)* bowl.

fornicare [forni'kare] *vi* to fornicate.

fornicazione [fornikat'tsjone] *sf* fornication.

fornire [for'nire] **1** *vt* **(a)** *(Comm):* ~ **qc a qn** to supply sth to sb, supply sb with sth. **(b)** *(procurare: abiti, viveri):* ~ **qc a qn**, ~ **qn di qc** to supply *o* provide sb with sth; ~ **qn di informazioni** to supply *o* provide sb with information, supply *o* provide information to sb. **2:** ~**rsi** *vr:* ~**rsi di**

(procurarsi) to provide o.s. with; **mi fornisco di pane da quel fornaio** I get my bread from that baker; **dobbiamo fornirci di legna per l'inverno** we'll have to stock up on wood for the winter.

fornito, a [for'nito] *ag:* **ben ~** *(negozio)* well-stocked.

fornitore, trice [forni'tore] *ag:* **ditta ~trice di...** company supplying... . **2** *sm/f* supplier.

fornitura [forni'tura] *sf* supply; **~e per ufficio** office supplies.

forno ['forno] *sm (gen)* oven; *(Industria)* furnace; **cuocere al ~** *(dolci, patate)* to bake; *(carne)* to roast; **pasta al ~** oven-baked pasta; **pollo al ~** roast chicken; **fare il ~i** to undergo heat treatment; **questa stanza è un ~!** this room's like an oven!; **~ crematorio** cremator.

foro¹ ['foro] *sm* hole.

foro² ['foro] *sm* **(a)** *(Storia)* forum. **(b)** *(Dir: tribunale)* (law) court; *(: autorità competente):* **del caso si occuperà il ~ di Milano** the case will be dealt with by the Milan judiciary; **gli avvocati del ~** ≃ the Bar.

forse ['forse] **1** *av* perhaps, maybe; *(circa)* about; **ti devo ~ 1000 lire** I must owe you about 1000 lire; **sei ~ tu il mio padrone?** so you think you own me, do you? **2** *sm:* **essere in ~** to be undecided *o* in doubt.

forsennato, a [forsen'nato] *sm/f* madman, lunatic.

forte¹ ['forte] **1** *ag* **(a)** *(gen, fig)* strong; *(luce, tinta)* strong, bright; *(nevicata, pioggia)* heavy; *(voce, musica)* loud; *(ceffone, colpo)* hard; *(somma, aumento)* large, big; **ho un ~ mal di testa/ raffreddore** I have a bad headache/heavy cold; **questo curry è un po' ~** this curry is rather hot; **taglie ~i** *(Abbigliamento)* outsize; **usare le maniere ~i** to use strong-arm methods; **piatto ~** *(Culin)* main dish; **pezzo ~** pièce de résistance; **dare man ~ a qn** to back sb up, support sb; **è ~ in matematica** he is good at maths; **essere ~ di qc** to be confident of sth; **farsi ~ di qc** to make use of *o* avail o.s. of sth; **non voglio piangere ma è più ~ di me** I don't want to cry but I can't help it.

(b) *(fam: bello, bravo)* amazing, great; **che ~!** amazing!, fantastic!

2 *av (velocemente)* fast; *(a volume alto)* loud(ly); *(violentemente)* hard; **tenersi ~** to hold tight; **giocare ~** to play for high stakes; **andare ~** *(fam: essere bravo)* to be amazing, be fantastic; *(: aver successo)* to be all the rage.

3 *sm (persona):* **il ~ e il debole** the strong and the weak; *(punto ~)* strong point, forte.

forte² ['forte] *sm (fortezza)* fort.

fortezza [for'tettsa] *sf* fortress.

fortificare [fortifi'kare] *vt* to strengthen, fortify.

fortificazione [fortifikat'tsjone] *sf* fortification.

fortino [for'tino] *sm* fort.

fortuito, a [for'tuito] *ag* chance, fortuitous; **per un caso ~** by pure chance.

fortuna [for'tuna] *sf* **(a)** *(destino)* fortune, destiny; *(: favorevole)* luck; **predire la ~ a qn** to tell sb's future; **la ruota della ~** the wheel of fortune; **tentare la ~** to try one's luck; **portare ~** to bring luck; **colpo di ~** stroke of luck; **cercare ~** to seek one's fortune; **per ~** luckily, fortunately; **(per) ~ che sei passato, a una ~ che tu sia passato** it's lucky that you were passing; **aver ~** to be lucky; **avere la ~ di fare qc** to be lucky enough to do sth; **è tutta ~ la sua!** it's his luck; **che ~!** what luck!; **buona ~!** good luck! **(b)** *(successo, ricchezza)* fortune; **costa una ~** it costs a fortune; **fare ~** to make one's fortune. **(c):** **di ~** *(installazione etc)* makeshift; *(atterraggio)* emergency *attr;* **albero di ~** *(Naut)* jury mast.

fortunale [fortu'nale] *sm* storm.

fortunatamente [fortunata'mente] *av* luckily, fortunately.

fortunato, a [fortu'nato] *ag* lucky, fortunate; *(felice)* happy; *(coronato da successo)* successful; **numero ~** lucky number.

foruncolo [fo'runkolo] *sm (Med)* boil.

forviare [forvi'are] **1** *vi* to go astray. **2** *vt (inseguitori, polizia)* to mislead; *(sospetti)* to allay; *(giovani: traviare)* to lead astray.

forza ['fortsa] *sf* **(a)** *(vigore)* strength; **perdere/ riacquistare le ~e** to lose/regain one's strength; **avere ~ nelle braccia** to be strong in the arm; **senza ~ o ~e** weak; **bella ~!** *(iro)* how clever of you!; **farsi ~** *(coraggio)* to pluck up one's courage; **fatti ~!** buck up!, come on!; **~! come on!; con la ~ della disperazione** with the strength born of desperation; **l'unione fa la ~** unity is strength; **~ d'animo** fortitude; **~ di volontà** willpower.

(b) *(di vento, tempesta)* force; **vento ~ 4** force 4 gale.

(c) *(violenza)* force; **ricorrere alla/adoperare la ~** to resort to/use violence; **a viva ~** by force; **~ bruta** brute force.

(d) *(Mil):* **le ~e armate** the armed forces; **la ~ pubblica** the police.

(e) *(Dir):* **in ~** in force; **avere ~ di legge** to have force of law.

(f) *(Fis, Tecn)* force; **~ di gravità** force of gravity; **~ motrice** motive force.

(g): **a ~, con la ~** by force; **a ~ di rimproveri/ di lavorare** by dint of scolding/working; **con ~** *(violentemente)* violently; *(fermamente)* firmly; **picchiare qn con ~** to hit sb hard; **lo devi fare per ~?** have you got to do it?; **l'ha fatto per ~** he had no choice but to do it, he was forced to do it; **per ~** *(ovviamente)* of course; **per causa di ~ maggiore** *(Dir)* by reason of an act of God; *(per estensione)* due to circumstances beyond one's control; **per ~ di cose** by force of circumstances.

forzare [for'tsare] *vt* **(a)** *(costringere):* **~ qn (a fare qc)** to force sb (to do sth), compel sb (to do sth); **hanno forzato la mia volontà** they forced me to do it. **(b)** *(cassaforte, porta)* to force open; *(serratura)* to force. **(c)** *(sforzare: voce)* to strain; **~ l'andatura** to force the pace; **~ il significato** *(di parola, testo)* to stretch the meaning; **non voglio ~ la situazione** I don't want to push things.

forzato, a [for'tsato] **1** *ag* forced; *(situazione)* artificial; **la mia è stata un'assenza ~a** my absence was due to circumstances beyond my control; **fare un sorriso ~** to force a smile. **2** *sm* convict.

forziere [for'tsjere] *sm* strongbox; *(di pirati)* treasure chest.

forzuto, a [for'tsuto] *ag (scherz)* big and strong.

foschia [fos'kia] *sf* haze; **oggi c'è molta ~** it's very hazy today.

fosco, a, schi, sche ['fosko] *ag (colore)* dark; *(cielo)* dull, overcast; *(fig: futuro, pensiero)* dark, gloomy; **dipingere qc a tinte ~sche** *(fig)* to paint a gloomy picture of sth.

fosfato [fos'fato] *sm* phosphate; **~ di sodio** sodium phosphate.

fosforescente [fosfore'fɛnte] *ag* phosphorescent; *(insegna, lancetta dell'orologio etc)* luminous.

fosforescenza [fosfore'fɛntsa] *sf* phosphorescence.

fosforo ['fosforo] *sm* phosphorus.

fossa ['fossa] *sf* **(a)** *(buca)* pit, hole; *(Oceanografia, Mil)* trench; **~ biologica** cesspool. **(b)** *(tomba)* grave; **~ comune** mass grave; **essere con un piede nella**

~ to have one foot in the grave. **(c)** *(Anat)* fossa.

fossato [fos'sato] *sm* ditch; *(di castello)* moat.

fossetta [fos'setta] *sf* dimple.

fossile ['fɔssile] *ag, sm (anche fig)* fossil.

fossilizzare [fossilid'dzare] *vt,* ~**rsi** *vr (anche fig)* to fossilize.

fosso ['fɔsso] *sm* ditch; *(di castello)* moat.

foto ['foto] *sf inv (abbr di* **fotografia)** photo, snap; ~ **ricordo** souvenir photo; ~ **tessera** passport (-type) photo; **fare una** ~ to take a photo *o* a snap.

fotocopia [foto'kɔpja] *sf* photocopy.

fotocopiare [fotoko'pjare] *vt* to photocopy.

fotocopiatrice [fotokopja'tritʃe] *sf* photocopier, photocopying machine.

fotoelettrico, a, ci, che [fotoe'lettriko] *ag* photoelectric.

fotogenico, a, ci, che [foto'dʒɛniko] *ag* photogenic.

fotografare [fotogra'fare] *vt* to photograph.

fotografia [fotogra'fia] *sf (arte)* photography; *(immagine)* photograph; ~ **a colori/in bianco e nero** colour/black and white photograph; **fare una** ~ to take a photograph; **farsi fare una** ~ to have one's photograph taken.

fotografico, a, ci, che [foto'grafiko] *ag* photographic; **macchina** ~**a** camera; **servizio** *o* **reportage** ~ photo feature; **studio** ~ photographer's studio.

fotografo, a [fo'tɔgrafo] *sm/f* photographer.

fotomodella [fotomo'dɛlla] *sf* photographic model.

fotomontaggio [fotomon'taddʒo] *sm* photomontage.

fotoreporter [fotore'pɔrter] *sm/f inv* newspaper *(o* magazine*)* photographer.

fotoromanzo [fotoro'mandzo] *sm* photo story.

fotosintesi [foto'sintezi] *sf* photosynthesis.

fottere ['fottere] *vt (fam!)* **(a)** *(avere rapporti sessuali)* to fuck(!), screw(!); **vai a farti** ~! fuck off! **(b)** *(rubare)* to pinch, swipe. **(c)** *(fregare):* **mi hanno fottuto** they did the dirty on me.

fottuto, a [fot'tuto] *ag (fam!)* bloody, fucking(!).

foulard [fu'lar] *sm inv* scarf.

foyer [fwa'je] *sm inv* foyer.

fra[1] [fra] *prep =* **tra.**

fra[2] [fra] *sm (dav a nomi propri) =* **frate.**

frac [frak] *sm inv* tails *pl.*

fracassare [frakas'sare] **1** *vt* to smash, shatter. **2:** ~**rsi** *vr* to smash, break; *(veicolo)* to crash; *(fare a piccoli pezzi)* to smash *o* break to smithereens, shatter.

fracasso [fra'kasso] *sm (baccano, confusione)* din; *(di piatti etc)* crash; **fare** ~ to make a din.

fradicio, a, ci, ce ['fraditʃo] *ag* soaked, soaking, drenched; **bagnato** ~ soaking wet; **ubriaco** ~ blind drunk.

fragile ['fradʒile] *ag (gen, fig)* fragile; *(salute)* delicate; *(vetro, nervi)* brittle; '~' *(sui pacchi)* 'fragile, with care'.

fragilità [fradʒili'ta] *sf (vedi ag)* fragility; delicacy; brittleness.

fragola ['fragola] *sf* strawberry.

fragore [fra'gore] *sm (di cascate, carro armato)* roar; *(di tuono)* rumble.

fragoroso, a [frago'roso] *ag* deafening; **un** ~ **ceffone** a resounding slap; **fare una risata** ~**a** to roar with laughter.

fragrante [fra'grante] *ag* fragrant.

fragranza [fra'grantsa] *sf* fragrance.

fraintendere [frain'tendere] *vt* to misunderstand.

frainteso, a [frain'teso] *pp di* **fraintendere.**

frammentario, a [frammen'tarjo] *ag* sketchy, fragmentary.

frammento [fram'mento] *sm (di roccia)* fragment, bit; *(di testo)* passage, extract.

frammesso, a [fram'messo] *pp di* **frammettere.**

frammettere [fram'mettere] **1** *vt* to interpose. **2:** ~**rsi** *vr* to intervene, interfere.

frammezzo [fram'meddzo] **1** *av* in between. **2:** ~ **a** *prep* among.

frammisto, a [fram'misto] *ag:* ~ **a** interspersed with, mixed with.

frana ['frana] *sf (Geol)* landslip, landslide; *(fig: persona):* **essere una** ~ to be useless, be a walking disaster area.

franare [fra'nare] *vi (aus* **essere)** *(Geol)* to slip; *(: roccia)* to fall; *(fig: resistenza)* to collapse.

francamente [franka'mente] *av* frankly.

francescano, a [franteʃes'kano] *ag, sm* Franciscan.

francese [fran'tʃeze] **1** *ag* French. **2** *sm/f* Frenchman/woman; **i F**~**i** the French. **3** *sm (lingua)* French.

franchezza [fran'kettsa] *sf* frankness.

franchigia, gie [fran'kidʒa] *sf* **(a)** *(Amm)* exemption; ~ **doganale** exemption from customs duty. **(b)** *(Dir)* franchise. **(c)** *(Naut)* shore leave.

Francia ['frantʃa] *sf* France.

franco[1]**, a, chi, che** ['franko] **1** *ag* **(a)** *(persona, sguardo: sincero)* frank, candid; **rispondere in modo** ~ to answer frankly. **(b)** *(Comm):* ~ **di porto** carriage free; ~ **di dazio** *o* **dogana** duty-free; **porto** ~ free port. **(c)** *(Mil):* ~ **tiratore** irregular (soldier); *(cecchino)* sniper. **(d):** **farla** ~**a** to get away with it. **2** *av (francamente)* frankly.

franco[2]**, a, chi, che** ['franko] **1** *ag (Storia)* Frankish. **2** *sm* Frank. **3** *pref:* ~... **Franco...** .

franco[3]**, chi** ['franko] *sm (moneta)* franc.

francobollo [franko'bollo] *sm* stamp.

francofilo, a [fran'kɔfilo] *ag, sm/f* francophile.

frangente [fran'dʒɛnte] *sm* **(a)** *(onda)* breaker. **(b)** *(scoglio affiorante)* reef. **(c)** *(circostanza)* situation, circumstance.

frangia, ge ['frandʒa] *sf (gen)* fringe; ~ **costiera** coastal strip; **le** ~**ge estremiste del partito** *(fig)* the extreme fringes of the party.

frangiflutti [frandʒi'flutti] *sm inv* breakwater.

frangivento [frandʒi'vento] *sm* windbreak.

franoso, a [fra'noso] *ag* unstable, subject to landslides.

frantoio [fran'tojo] *sm (Agr)* olive-press; *(Tecn)* crusher.

frantumare [frantu'mare] **1** *vt* to break (up). **2:** ~**rsi** *vr* to break, shatter.

frantumazione [frantumat'tsjone] *sf* breaking, crushing.

frantume [fran'tume] *sm:* **andare in** ~**i, mandare in** ~**i** to shatter, smash to pieces *o* smithereens.

frappé [frap'pe] *sm (Culin)* milk shake.

frapporre [frap'porre] **1** *vt:* ~ **ostacoli a qn** to place obstacles in the way of sb; **senza** ~ **indugi** without hesitating. **2: frapporsi** *vr:* **frapporsi a** *(interferire)* to interfere with.

frapposizione [frapposit'tsjone] *sf* interference.

frapposto, a [frap'posto] *pp di* **frapporre.**

frasario [fra'zarjo] *sm (gergo)* vocabulary, language.

frasca, sche ['fraska] *sf* bough, branch; **saltare di palo in** ~ to jump from one subject to another.

frase ['fraze] *sf* **(a)** *(proposizione)* sentence; ~ **fatta** stock phrase; ~ **d'amore** expression of love; **mi sussurrava** ~**i d'amore** he was whispering sweet nothings to me; **la** ~ **che ha detto non mi è piaciuta** I didn't like what he said. **(b)** *(Mus)* phrase.

fraseologia [frazeolo'dʒia] *sf* phraseology.

frassino ['frassino] *sm* ash (tree).

frastagliare [frasta λ'λare] *vt* to indent.

frastagliato, a [frasta λ'λato] *ag (costa)* indented, jagged.

frastornare [frastor'nare] *vt (intontire)* to daze; *(confondere)* to befuddle.

frastornato, a [frastor'nato] *ag* deafened; *(fig)* taken aback.

frastuono [fras'twɔno] *sm* noise, din.

frate ['frate] *sm (Rel)* brother, friar; **farsi** ~ to become a monk.

fratellanza [fratel'lantsa] *sf* brotherhood, fraternity.

fratellastro [fratel'lastro] *sm* stepbrother.

fratello [fra'tello] *sm* **(a)** *(gen)* brother; ~ **gemello** twin; ~ **siamese** Siamese twin; ~ **d'armi** brother in arms; **siamo** ~ **i, disse la donna** we are brother and sister, said the woman. **(b)** *(Rel)* brother; **i** ~**i cristiani** the Christian brethren.

fraternità [fraterni'ta] *sf* fraternity.

fraternizzare [fraternid'dzare] *vi* to fraternize.

fraterno, a [fra'tɛrno] *ag* fraternal, brotherly.

fratricida, i, e [fratri'tʃida] **1** *ag* fratricidal; **guerra** ~ civil war. **2** *sm/f* fratricide.

fratta ['fratta] *sf* thicket.

frattaglie [frat'taλλe] *sfpl (Culin: gen)* offal *sg;* (: *di pollo)* giblets.

frattanto [frat'tanto] *av* meanwhile, in the meantime.

frattempo [frat'tempo]: **nel** ~ *av* in the meantime, meanwhile.

frattura [frat'tura] *sf (Med, Geol)* fracture; *(fig: dissenso)* split, break.

fratturare [frattu'rare] **1** *vt (Med)* to fracture, break; ~**rsi un braccio/una gamba** to break one's arm/one's leg. **2** ~**rsi** *vr (Med)* to fracture, break; *(partito, gruppo)* to split.

fraudolento, a [fraudo'lɛnto] *ag* fraudulent.

fraudolenza [fraudo'lɛntsa] *sf* fraudulence.

frazionamento [frattsjona'mento] *sm* division, splitting up.

frazionare [frattsjo'nare] *vt* to divide, split up.

frazione [frat'tsjone] *sf* **(a)** *(gen, Mat)* fraction; **una** ~ **di secondo** a fraction of a second. **(b)** *(borgata)* village.

freatico, a, ci, che [fre'atiko] *ag (Geol)*: **falda** ~**a** phreatic layer.

freccia, ce ['frettʃa] *sf* **(a)** *(di arco)* arrow; **entrare/uscire come una** ~ to dash *o* shoot in/out. **(b)** *(Aut)* indicator; **mettere la** ~ **(a destra/sinistra)** to indicate that one is turning (right/left). **(c)** *(segnale stradale)* signpost.

frecciata [fret'tʃata] *sf*: **lanciare una** ~ to make a cutting remark.

freddare [fred'dare] **1** *vt (minestra etc)* to cool; *(fig: entusiasmo)* to put a damper on; *(fam: uccidere)* to do in, kill; **fai** ~ **la minestra** let the soup cool; ~ **qn con lo sguardo** to silence sb with an icy stare. **2** ~**rsi** *vr* to cool, become cold.

freddezza [fred'dettsa] *sf (fig)* coldness, coolness; **devi decidere cosa fare con** ~ you must decide what to do calmly *o* coolly; **accogliere qn con** ~ to give sb a cool welcome.

freddo, a ['freddo] **1** *ag (gen)* cold; *(accoglienza)* cool, cold; **a mente** ~**a capì di avere torto** when he had cooled down he realized that he was wrong; **la macchina è ancora** ~**a** the engine is still cold. **2** *sm* **(a)** *(gen)* cold; **avere** ~ to be cold; **prendere** ~ to catch cold; **soffrire il** ~ to feel the cold; **sudare** ~ to be in a cold sweat; **fa** ~ it's cold; **c'è stata un'ondata di** ~ there's been a cold spell. **(b)**: **a** ~ *(lavare)* in cold water; **a** ~ **ha poi**

negato di averlo detto when he had cooled down, he denied having said it.

freddoloso, a [freddo'loso] *ag*: **essere** ~ to feel the cold.

freddura [fred'dura] *sf* dry comment.

freezer ['friːzə] *sm inv* freezer.

fregare [fre'gare] *vt* **(a)** *(sfregare)* to rub; *(per pulire)* to polish; ~**rsi le mani/gli occhi** to rub one's hands/one's eyes. **(b)** *(fig fam)*: ~ **qn** *(imbrogliare)* to cheat sb, rip sb off; **questo indizio l'ha fregato** this piece of evidence gave him away; **mi frega sempre a carte** *(vincere)* he always beats me at cards; ~ **qc a qn** *(portar via)* to pinch sth from sb; **mi ha fregato il ragazzo** she pinched my boyfriend. **(c)** *(fig fam)*: **fregarsene (di qc/qn)** *(infischiarsene)* not to give a damn (about sth/sb); **non gliene frega niente** he doesn't give a damn; **me ne frego** I don't give a damn; **che ti frega?** none of your business!

fregata¹ [fre'gata] *sf* **(a)** *(vedi vb* **a)** rub; polish; **dare una** ~ **a qc** to rub sth; to polish sth. **(b)** *(fam)* = **fregatura**.

fregata² [fre'gata] *sf (Naut)* frigate.

fregatura [frega'tura] *sf (fam: imbroglio)* rip-off; **mi hanno tirato una** ~ they ripped me off; **è stata una** ~ *(delusione)* it's been a let-down.

fregiare [fre'dʒare] **1** *vt (Archit)* to adorn, embellish. **2** ~**rsi** *vr*: ~**rsi di** *(medaglia)* to be the bearer of.

fregio ['fredʒo] *sm (gen)* decoration, ornament; *(Archit)* frieze.

frego, ghi ['frego] *sm* line, mark.

fregola ['fregola] *sf* **(a)** *(Zool: calore)* heat. **(b)** *(fig: smania)*: **avere la** ~ **di fare qc** to have an itch to do sth.

fremere ['frɛmere] *vi* to shake, tremble; ~ **d'invidia** to be green with envy; ~ **d'impazienza** to be champing at the bit.

fremito ['frɛmito] *sm* shudder, shiver; **ebbe un** ~ **d'ira** he shook with anger.

frenare [fre'nare] **1** *vt (veicolo)* to pull up, slow down; *(progresso, avanzata)* to hold up; *(gioia, evoluzione)* to check; ~ **la lingua** to hold one's tongue; ~ **le lacrime** to hold back one's tears. **2** *vi (Aut)* to brake; *(Sci etc)* to slow down. **3**: ~**rsi** *vr* to restrain o.s., stop o.s.

frenata [fre'nata] *sf* braking; **fare una brusca** ~ to brake suddenly, hit the brakes.

frenesia [frene'zia] *sf* frenzy; **con** ~ frenziedly.

frenetico, a, ci, che [fre'netiko] *ag* frenetic.

freno ['freno] *sm* **(a)** *(Aut)* brake; *(di cavallo)* bit; *(fig)* restraint; **bloccare i** ~**i, azionare i** ~**i** to apply the brakes; ~ **a mano** handbrake, parking brake *(Am)*; ~ **a disco** disc brake. **(b)** *(fraseologia)*: **mettere o porre un** ~ **a** *(inflazione, tendenza etc)* to put a brake on, keep in check; **tenere a** ~ *(passioni etc)* to restrain; **tenere a** ~ **la lingua** to hold one's tongue; **agire da** ~ to act as a restraint.

frenulo ['frɛnulo] *sm (Anat)* fraenum.

frequentare [frekwen'tare] **1** *vt (scuola, corso)* to attend; *(persona)* to see (regularly); *(locale, casa)* to go to; ~ **cattive compagnie** to keep bad company; **il 'Lautrec's' è mal** ~ you get some shady types at 'Lautrec's'. **2** ~**rsi** *vr (uso reciproco)* to see each other (regularly); **si frequentano da anni** they have been seeing each other for years.

frequentato, a [frekwen'tato] *ag (locale)* busy.

frequentatore, trice [frekwenta'tore] *sm/f*: ~ **(di)** frequent visitor (to).

frequente [fre'kwɛnte] *ag* frequent; **di** ~ frequently.

frequentemente [frekwente'mente] *av* frequently, often.

frequenza [fre'kwɛntsa] *sf* (*gen, Fis, Radio, Elettr*) frequency; (*Scol*) attendance.

fresa ['frɛza] *sf* (*Tecn*) milling cutter.

fresare [fre'zare] *vt* (*Tecn*) to mill.

fresatrice [freza'tritʃe] *sf* (*Tecn*) milling machine.

freschezza [fres'kettsa] *sf* (*gen*) freshness; (*di serata*) coolness.

fresco, a, schi, sche ['fresko] **1** *ag* (*gen*) fresh; (*temperatura, clima*) fresh, cool; (*vernice*) wet; (*traccia, notizia, ferita*) recent, new; ~ **e riposato** (completely) refreshed; ~**a come una rosa** as fresh as a daisy; **bere qc di** ~ to drink sth cool and refreshing; ~ **di bucato** straight from the wash, newly washed; ~ **di università** (*fam*) fresh out of university; **se continui così stai** ~ (*fig*) if you go on like this you'll be in trouble. **2** *sm* (*temperatura*) cool; **è o fa** ~ it is cool; **mettere/tenere al** ~ (*oggetto*) to put/keep in a cool place; (*fig: persona: in prigione*) to put/keep inside *o* in the cooler; **fatto di** ~ newly done.

frescura [fres'kura] *sf* cool; **la** ~ **della sera** the cool of the evening.

fresia ['frɛzja] *sf* freesia.

fretta ['fretta] *sf* hurry; **in** ~ in a hurry; **in tutta** ~ hurriedly, quickly; **in** ~ **e furia** in a great *o* tearing hurry; **avere** ~ (**di fare qc**) to be in a hurry (to do sth); **fare qc in** ~ (*velocemente*) to d̄o sth quickly, hurry up with sth; (*troppo velocemente*) to do sth in a hurry; **l'ho fatto un po' troppo in** ~ I did it in too much of a hurry; **far** ~ **a qn** to hurry sb; **fai in** ~! hurry up!; **che** ~ **c'è?** what's the hurry?

frettolosamente [frettolosa'mente] *av* hurriedly, in a rush; **salutò** ~ **e se ne andò** he said a hurried goodbye and left.

frettoloso, a [fretto'loso] *ag* (*persona*) in a hurry; (*lavoro*) hurried; **diede una scorsa** ~**a al libro** he flicked through the book; **è un po' troppo** ~ **in quello che fa** he tends to rush things.

friabile [fri'abile] *ag* (*roccia*) friable; (*biscotto etc*) crumbly.

fricassea [frikas'sɛa] *sf* (*Culin*) fricassee; **pollo in** ~ chicken fricassee.

fricativo, a [frika'tivo] *ag, sf* fricative.

friggere ['friddʒere] **1** *vt* to fry; **vai a farti** ~! (*fam*) get lost! **2** *vi* (*grasso, olio*) to sizzle; (*fig*): ~ **dalla rabbia** to seethe with rage; ~ **d'impazienza** to fume with impatience.

friggitoria [friddʒito'ria] *sf* ≈ fish and chip shop.

friggitrice [friddʒi'tritʃe] *sf* deep fryer.

frigidità [fridʒidi'ta] *sf* frigidity.

frigido, a ['fridʒido] *ag* frigid.

frignare [friɲ'ɲare] *vi* to whine, snivel.

frignone, a [friɲ'ɲone] *sm/f* whiner, sniveller.

frigo, ghi ['frigo] *sm* fridge.

frigorifero, a [frigo'rifero] **1** *ag* refrigerating; **cella** ~**a** cold store. **2** *sm* refrigerator.

fringuello [frin'gwɛllo] *sm* chaffinch.

frinire [fri'nire] *vi* to chirp.

frittata [frit'tata] *sf* (*Culin*) omelette; **la** ~ **è fatta!** (*fig*) that's torn it!

frittella [frit'tɛlla] *sf* (*Culin*) fritter.

fritto, a ['fritto] **1** *pp di* **friggere**. **2** *ag* (*patatine, pesce etc*) fried; **ormai siamo** ~**i**! (*fig fam*) now we've had it!; **è un argomento** ~ **e rifritto** that's old hat. **3** *sm* fried food; ~ **misto** mixed fry; **odore di** ~ smell of frying.

frittura [frit'tura] *sf* (*cibo*) fried food; ~ **di pesce** mixed fried fish.

frivolezza [frivo'lettsa] *sf* frivolity.

frivolo, a ['frivolo] *ag* frivolous.

frizionare [frittsjo'nare] *vt* to rub, massage; ~**rsi il braccio** to rub *o* massage one's arm.

frizione [frit'tsjone] *sf* (a) (*massaggio*) rubbing, massage; **fare delle** ~**i con una pomata** to rub *o* massage in an ointment. (b) (*lozione*) lotion. (c) (*Fis*) friction. (d) (*Aut*) clutch.

frizzante [frid'dzante] *ag* (*gen*) fizzy, sparkling; (*vino*) sparkling; (*persona*) effervescent, bubbly (*fam*).

frizzare [frid'dzare] *vi* to sparkle, be fizzy.

frizzo ['friddzo] *sm* witticism.

frodare [fro'dare] *vt* to defraud, cheat; ~ **il fisco** to evade taxation.

frode ['frɔde] *sf* (*Dir*) fraud.

frodo ['frɔdo] *sm*: **di** ~ illegal, contraband; **pescatore di** ~, **cacciatore di** ~ poacher; **pescare di** ~, **cacciare di** ~ to poach.

frogia, gie ['frɔdʒa] *sf* (*di cavallo etc*) nostril.

frollare [frol'lare] *vi* (*aus essere*) (*carne*) to become high.

frollino [frol'lino] *sm* (*Culin*) pastry (with candied fruit).

frollo, a ['frɔllo] *ag* (*Culin: carne*) high; (: *pasta*) short(crust).

fronda¹ ['fronda] *sf* (*Bot*) leafy branch.

fronda² ['fronda] *sf* (*fig Pol*) rebellion.

frondista, i, e [fron'dista] *sm/f* (*fig Pol*) rebel.

frondoso, a [fron'doso] *ag* (*albero*) leafy; (*fig: stile*) ornate.

frontale [fron'tale] *ag* (*Anat, Mil*) frontal; **scontro** ~ (*Aut*) head-on collision.

fronte ['frɔnte] **1** *sf* (a) (*Anat*) brow, forehead; **a** ~ **alta** (*anche fig*) with one's head held high; **col sudore della** ~ by the sweat of one's brow; **testo a** ~ parallel text; **far** ~ **a** (*nemico, problema*) to confront; (*responsabilità*) to face up to; (*spese*) to cope with. (b) (*dirimpetto*) opposite; (*da davanti*) from the front; **di** ~ **a** opposite; (*a paragone di*) compared with; **vista di** ~ **la casa è più bella** seen from the front the house is much more attractive. **2** *sm* (*Mil, Pol, Meteor*) front.

fronteggiare [fronted'dʒare] *vt* (*affrontare: nemico, problema*) to face, confront; (*sostenere: spese*) to cope with.

frontespizio [frontes'pittsjo] *sm* (a) (*Archit*) frontispiece. (b) (*di libro*) title page.

frontiera [fron'tjɛra] *sf* frontier, border; (*fig*) frontier; **zona di** ~ frontier *o* border area; **guardia di** ~ frontier guard; **polizia di** ~ frontier police.

frontone [fron'tone] *sm* pediment.

fronzolo ['frondzolo] *sm* frill; **senza** ~**i** (*fig*) without (any) frills, plainly.

fronzuto, a [fron'dzuto] *ag* leafy.

frotta ['frɔtta] *sf* crowd; **in** ~, **a** ~**e** in their hundreds, in droves.

frottola ['frɔttola] *sf* (*bugia*) lie, fib; **raccontare un sacco di** ~**e** to tell a pack of lies.

frugale [fru'gale] *ag* frugal.

frugalità [frugali'ta] *sf* frugality.

frugare [fru'gare] **1** *vt* to search; ~**rsi le tasche** to search through one's pockets. **2** *vi*: ~ **in** to search, rummage around in.

frugoletto [frugo'letto] *sm* cutie-pie (*fam*).

fruibile [fru'ibile] *ag* enjoyable, usable; **è** ~ **da tutti** it's available to everybody.

fruire [fru'ire] *vi*: ~ **di qc** to enjoy sth, have the use of sth.

frullare [frul'lare] **1** *vt* (*gen*) to blend; (*frutta*) to blend, liquidize. **2** *vi* (*uccelli*) to flutter, whirr; **cosa ti frulla in mente?** what is going on in that mind of yours?

frullato [frul'lato] *sm* (*Culin*) milk shake; (: *con solo frutta*) fruit drink.

frullatore [frulla'tore] *sm* blender, liquidizer.

frullino [frul'lino] *sm* whisk.

frullio [frul'lio] *sm (di ali)* flutter.

frumentario, a [frumen'tarjo] *ag* grain *attr*, wheat *attr*.

frumento [fru'mento] *sm* grain, wheat.

frusciare [fruʃ'ʃare] *vi* to rustle.

fruscio, scii [fruʃ'ʃio] *sm* rustling.

frusta ['frusta] *sf* **(a)** *(per cavalli)* whip. **(b)** *(Culin)* whisk.

frustare [frus'tare] *vt* to whip.

frustata [frus'tata] *sf* lash.

frustino [frus'tino] *sm* riding crop.

frustrare [frus'trare] *vt* to frustrate.

frustrato, a [frus'trato] **1** *ag* frustrated. **2** *sm/f* frustrated person.

frustrazione [frustrat'tsjone] *sf* frustration.

frutta ['frutta] *sf* fruit; *(portata)* dessert; **torta alla ~** fruit cake; **gelato alla ~** fruit-flavoured ice cream; **~ candita/secca** candied/dried fruit.

fruttare [frut'tare] **1** *vt*: **il mio deposito in banca (mi) frutta il 10%** my bank deposits bring (me) in 10%; **quella gara gli fruttò la medaglia d'oro** he won the gold medal in that competition. **2** *vi (investimenti, deposito)* to bear dividends, give a return; **questo investimento ha fruttato poco** this investment did not give much of a return *o* gave a poor yield.

frutteto [frut'teto] *sm* orchard.

frutticolo, a [frut'tikolo] *ag* fruit *attr*.

frutticoltore [fruttikol'tore] *sm* fruit grower.

frutticoltura [fruttikol'tura] *sf* fruit growing.

fruttiera [frut'tjɛra] *sf* fruit dish.

fruttifero, a [frut'tifero] *ag* **(a)** *(albero etc)* fruit-bearing. **(b)** *(fig: che frutta)* fruitful, profitable; **deposito ~** interest-bearing deposit.

fruttificare [fruttifi'kare] *vi* to bear fruit.

fruttivendolo, a [frutti'vendolo] *sm/f* fruiterer, greengrocer; **dal ~** at the fruit shop, at the fruiterer's.

frutto ['frutto] *sm (anche fig)* fruit; **dare ~i** *(anche fig)* to bear fruit; **raccogliere i ~i di qc** *(fig)* to reap the rewards of sth; **essere ~ di** *(fig)* to be the fruit of; **è ~ della tua immaginazione** it's a figment of your imagination; **il ~ del mio lavoro** *(fig)* the fruits of my labour; **senza alcun ~** *(fig)* fruitlessly, in vain; **~i di mare** seafood *sg*.

fruttuoso, a [fruttu'oso] *ag* fruitful, profitable.

FS *abbr di* Ferrovie dello Stato.

fu [fu] **1** *3ª pers sg del passato remoto di* **essere. 2** *ag (defunto)*: **il ~ Mario Rossi** the late Mario Rossi.

fucilare [futʃi'lare] *vt* to shoot *o* execute (by firing squad).

fucilata [futʃi'lata] *sf* shot; **fu ucciso da una ~ alla schiena** it was a bullet in the back which killed him.

fucilazione [futʃilat'tsjone] *sf* execution (by firing squad).

fucile [fu'tʃile] *sm* rifle, gun; **~ da caccia** shotgun; **~ subacqueo** (underwater) spear gun; **~ a canne mozze** sawn-off shotgun.

fucina [fu'tʃina] *sf (Tecn)* forge; *(fig: di ingegni etc)* breeding ground.

fuco, chi ['fuko] *sm* drone.

fucsia ['fuksja] *sf* fuchsia.

fuga, ghe ['fuga] *sf* **(a)** escape, *(letterario)* flight; **mettere qn in ~** to put sb to flight; **nella ~ ha dimenticato le chiavi** he forgot his keys when he ran off *o* escaped. **(b)** *(perdita: di gas, notizie)* leak; **~ di capitali** flight of capital; **~ di cervelli** brain drain. **(c)** *(Mus)* fugue.

fugace [fu'gatʃe] *ag* fleeting.

fugare [fu'gare] *vt (dubbi, incertezze)* to dispel, drive out.

fuggevole [fud'dʒevole] *ag* fleeting.

fuggiasco, a, schi, sche [fud'dʒasko] **1** *ag* runaway *attr*. **2** *sm/f* fugitive; *(Mil)* deserter.

fuggifuggi [fuddʒi'fuddʒi] *sm* stampede.

fuggire [fud'dʒire] **1** *vt (anche fig)* to avoid, shun. **2** *vi (aus* **essere**) to run away, escape; *(fig: vita)* to fly by, slip by; **il tempo fugge** time flies.

fuggitivo, a [fuddʒi'tivo] **1** *ag* **(a)** *(in fuga)* fleeing, escaping. **(b)** *(fugace)* fleeting. **2** *sm/f* runaway; *(Mil)* deserter.

fulcro ['fulkro] *sm (Tecn)* fulcrum; *(fig: di discussione, teoria)* pivotal point, central point.

fulgido, a ['fuldʒido] *ag* bright, shining; *(fig: esempio)* shining.

fulgore [ful'gore] *sm* brightness, splendour.

fuliggine [fu'liddʒine] *sf* soot.

fuligginoso, a [fuliddʒi'noso] *ag* sooty.

fulminante [fulmi'nante] *ag* fulminating; *(sguardo)* blazing.

fulminare [fulmi'nare] **1** *vb impers*: **fulmina** there is lightning. **2** *vt (sog: fulmine)* to strike (by lightning); *(: elettricità)* to electrocute; *(fig: uccidere)* to shoot dead; **mi fulminò con uno sguardo** he looked daggers at me. **3**: **~rsi** *vr (lampadina)* to go, blow.

fulminato [fulmi'nato] *sm (Chim)* fulminate.

fulmine ['fulmine] *sm* bolt of lightning; **~i** lightning *sg*; **come un ~** like lightning; **~ a ciel sereno** bolt from the blue.

fulmineo, a [ful'mineo] *ag (fig: scatto)* rapid; *(minaccioso: sguardo)* threatening.

fulvo, a ['fulvo] *ag* tawny.

fumaiolo [fuma'jɔlo] *sm (gen)* chimney; *(Naut, Ferr)* funnel.

fumare [fu'mare] **1** *vt (sigaretta, pipa)* to smoke. **2** *vi (esalare: fumo)* to smoke; *(: vapore)* to steam; **smettere di ~** to give up smoking; **~ come un turco** to smoke like a chimney; **'vietato ~'** 'no smoking'.

fumario, a [fu'marjo] *ag*: **canna ~a** flue.

fumarola [fuma'rɔla] *sf* fumarole.

fumata [fu'mata] *sf* **(a)** *(il fumare)*: **farsi una ~** to have a smoke. **(b)** *(emissione di fumo)* cloud of smoke; **~ bianca/nera** *(in Vaticano)* signal that a new pope has/has not been elected.

fumatore, trice [fuma'tore] *sm/f* smoker.

fumé [fy'me] *ag inv* smoky grey.

fumettista, i, e [fumet'tista] *sm/f* cartoonist.

fumetto [fu'metto] *sm* **(a)** *(nuvoletta con parole)* bubble. **(b)** *(storia a vignette)* cartoon, comic strip; **giornale a ~i** comic.

fumo ['fumo] **1** *sm* **(a)** *(di fuoco, sigaretta etc)* smoke; *(vapore)* steam; **fare ~** to smoke; **i ~i industriali** industrial fumes; **i ~i dell'alcool** *(fig)* the after-effects of drink. **(b)** *(il fumare)* smoking; **il ~ fa male** smoking is bad for you. **(c)** *(fam: hascisc)* dope. **(d)** *(fraseologia)*: **andare in ~** to go up in smoke; **è solo ~** it's worthless; **è tutto ~ e niente arrosto** it has no substance to it; **gettare ~ negli occhi a qn** to pull the wool over sb's eyes; **lo vedo come il ~ negli occhi** I can't stand him. **2** *ag inv*: **grigio ~** smoky grey.

fumogeno, a [fu'mɔdʒeno] **1** *ag (candelotto)* smoke *attr*; **cortina ~a** smoke screen. **2** *sm* smoke bomb.

fumoso, a [fu'moso] *ag* **(a)** *(ambiente, stanza)* smoky. **(b)** *(idee)* woolly; *(progetto)* muddled.

funambolo, a [fu'nambolo] *sm/f* tightrope walker.

fune ['fune] *sf* rope.

funebre ['funebre] *ag (gen)* funeral *attr*; *(atmosfera)* gloomy; *(voce, sguardo)* funereal, mournful.

funerale [fune'rale] *sm* funeral.

funerario, a [fune'rarjo] *ag* funeral *attr*.

funereo, a [fu'nɛreo] *ag (gen)* funeral *attr*; *(sguardo, aspetto)* funereal, mournful.

funesto, a [fu'nɛsto] *ag (incidente)* fatal; *(errore, decisione)* fatal, disastrous; *(atmosfera)* gloomy, dismal.

fungaia [fun'gaja] *sf* mushroom bed.

fungere ['fundʒere] *vi*: ~ **da** to act as.

fungo, ghi ['fungo] *sm* **(a)** mushroom; **andare a** *o* **per** ~**ghi** to go mushrooming; **crescere come i** ~**ghi** *(fig)* to spring up overnight; ~**ghi secchi** dried mushrooms; ~ **atomico** atomic mushroom. **(b)** *(Med)* fungus. **(c)** *(di annaffiatoio)* rose.

funicolare [funiko'lare] *sf* funicular railway.

funivia [funi'via] *sf* cable railway.

funto, a ['funto] *pp di* **fungere**.

funzionale [funtsjo'nale] *ag* functional.

funzionalità [funtsjonali'ta] *sf* functionality.

funzionamento [funtsjona'mento] *sm (vedi vb* **a)** working; functioning.

funzionare [funtsjo'nare] *vi* **(a)** *(gen)* to work; *(sistema)* to function; *(macchina a benzina* it works *o* runs on petrol; **far** ~ to operate; **il telefono non funziona** the telephone is out of order. **(b)**: ~ **da** to act as.

funzionario [funtsjo'narjo] *sm (Amm: dirigente)* official; *(: impiegato)* employee; ~ **statale** civil servant; ~ **dell'amministrazione comunale** local authority employee.

funzione [fun'tsjone] *sf* **(a)** *(gen, Gram, Mat)* function; **in** ~ *(macchina)* in operation; **vive in** ~ **dei figli/della carriera** he lives for his children/his job; **participio usato in** ~ **di aggettivo** participle used as an adjective; **non il presidente ma il facente** ~ not the president but his substitute. **(b)** *(carica)* post, office; **cessare dalle** ~**i** to leave office; **far** ~ **di sindaco** to act as mayor; **nell'esercizio delle sue** ~**i** in the performance of his duties. **(c)** *(Rel)* service, religious ceremony.

fuoco, chi ['fwɔko] **1** *sm* **(a)** fire; **prendere** ~ to catch fire; **dar** ~ **a qc** to set fire to sth; **al** ~**!** fire!; **scherzare col** ~ *(fig)* to play with fire; **soffiare sul** ~ *(fig)* to add fuel to the flames. **(b)** *(Culin: fornello)* ring; **mettere qc sul** ~ to put sth on the stove; **cuocere a** ~ **lento/vivo** to cook over a low/brisk heat. **(c)** *(Mil: sparo)* fire; **far** ~ to fire; **cessare/aprire il** ~ to cease/open fire; ~ **incrociato** crossfire. **(d)** *(ardore, vivacità)* fire; **parole di** ~ heated words. **(e)** *(Mat, Ottica)* focus; **mettere a** ~ to focus; *(fig: problema)* to clarify. **(f)** *(fraseologia)*: **fare** ~ **e fiamme (per fare)** to do one's utmost (to do); **mettere la mano sul** ~ **per qc** to stake one's life on sth; **mettere a ferro e** ~ to put to fire and the sword. **2** *ag inv*: **rosso** ~ flame red. **3**: ~ **d'artificio** firework; ~ **di paglia** flash in the pan; ~ **fatuo** will-o'-the-wisp; ~ **sacro** *o* **di Sant'Antonio** *(Med fam)* shingles *pl*.

fuorché [fwor'ke] *cong, prep* except, apart from.

fuori ['fwɔri] **1** *av* **(a)** outside; *(all'aria aperta)* outdoors, outside; *(fuori casa)* out; *(all'estero)* abroad; **era lì** ~ **ad aspettarmi** he was outside waiting for me; **ceniamo** ~**?** *(all'aperto)* shall we eat outside?; *(al ristorante)* shall we go out for a meal?; **mandali a giocare** ~ send them out to play; **mio marito è** ~ my husband is out *o* is not at home; **ho vissuto in Italia e** ~ I've lived in Italy and abroad; **tiralo** ~ **dalla scatola** take it out of the box. **(b)** *(fraseologia)*: ~ **di qui!** get out (of here)!;

~ **i soldi!** hand over your money!; **essere di** ~ to be a stranger; **essere in** ~ *(sporgere)* to stick out; *(denti, occhi)* to be prominent; **finalmente ne sono** ~ I've seen the back of it at last; **far** ~ *(fam: soldi)* to spend; *(: cioccolatini)* to eat up; *(: rubare)* to nick; **far** ~ **qn** *(fam)* to do sb in; **lasciare/ mettere** ~ to leave/put out; **essere tagliato** ~ *(da un gruppo, ambiente)* to be excluded; **mi sento tagliato** ~ **qui** I feel cut off here; **uscire** ~ to come out; **andare/venire** ~ to go/come out; **giocare** ~ *(Sport)* to play away. **2** *prep* **(a)**: ~ **(di)** out of, outside; **è** ~ **città** he's out of town; **abita** ~ **Roma** he lives outside Rome. **(b)** *(fraseologia)*: **è** ~ **di sé (dalla gioia/rabbia)** he's beside himself (with joy/anger); **è** ~ **commercio** it's not for sale; ~ **fase** *(motore)* out of phase; ~ **mano** *(casa, paese)* out of the way; **abitare** ~ **mano** to live in an out-of-the-way place; ~ **luogo** *(osservazione)* out of place, uncalled for; ~ **orario** outside working hours; ~ **pasto** between meals; ~ **pericolo** out of danger; ~ **dai piedi!** get out of the way!; ~ **programma** unscheduled; **è** ~ **questione** *o* **discussione** it's out of the question; ~ **servizio** out of order; ~ **stagione** in the low season; **la macchina è andata** ~ **strada** the car left the road; **essere** ~ **tempo** *(Mus)* to be out of time; **è arrivato** ~ **tempo massimo** he arrived outside the time limit. **3** *sm* outside; **dal di** ~ from the outside.

fuoribordo [fwori'bordo] *sm (Naut: imbarcazione)* outboard; *(: motore)* outboard motor.

fuoricampo [fwori'kampo] *av (Cine)* out of the picture.

fuoriclasse [fwori'klasse] **1** *ag* unrivalled, unequalled. **2** *sm/f* undisputed champion.

fuoricorso [fwori'korso] *ag inv* **(a)** *(moneta)* no longer in circulation. **(b)** *(Univ)*: *(studente)* ~ *student who takes longer than normal to complete his university course.*

fuorigioco [fwori'dʒoko] *sm inv (Sport)*: **in** ~ offside; **fischiare un** ~ to blow the whistle for offside.

fuorilegge [fwori'leddʒe] *sm/f inv* outlaw.

fuoriprogramma, i [fworipro'gramma] *sm (TV)* unscheduled programme.

fuoriserie [fwori'sɛrje] **1** *ag inv (macchina etc)* specially built; *(fig: eccezionale)* outstanding. **2** *sf inv* custom-built car.

fuoristrada [fwori'strada] *sm (Aut)* cross-country vehicle; **fare del** ~ to drive cross-country.

fuor(i)uscita [fwor(i)uʃ'ʃita] *sf (di gas)* leakage, escape; *(di sangue, linfa)* seepage.

fuor(i)uscito, a [fwor(i)uʃ'ʃito] *sm/f* exile, refugee.

fuorviare [fworvi'are] = **forviare**.

furbacchione, a [furbak'kjone] *sm/f* cunning old devil.

furberia [furbe'ria] *sf (qualità)* cunning, slyness; *(azione)* cunning action, crafty action.

furbesco, a, schi, sche [fur'besko] *ag* cunning, sly, crafty; **lingua** ~**a** thieves' cant.

furbizia [fur'bittsja] *sf (vedi ag)* cleverness; cunning; sma ~ a cunning trick.

furbo, a ['furbo] **1** *ag* clever, smart; *(peg)* cunning. **2** *sm/f* clever person; cunning person; **fare il** ~ (try to) be clever *o* smart; **fatti** ~**!** show a bit of sense!

furente [fu'rɛnte] *ag* furious.

fureria [fure'ria] *sf (Mil)* orderly room.

furetto [fu'retto] *sm* ferret.

furfante [fur'fante] *sm* rascal, scoundrel.

furfanteria [furfante'ria] *sf* roguery.

furgoncino [furgon'tʃino] *sm* small van.

furgone [fur'gone] *sm* van.

furia ['furja] *sf* **(a)** *(ira, furore)* fury; *(velocità)* hurry, haste; **andare** *o* **montare su tutte le ~e** to get into a towering rage; **la ~ del vento** the violence of the wind; **a ~ di qc/fare qc** by means of sth/doing sth. **(b)** *(Mitologia):* **le F~e** the Furies.

furibondo, a [furi'bondo] *ag* furious.

furiere [fu'rjere] *sm* quartermaster.

furioso, a [fu'rjoso] *ag (gen)* furious; *(vento, assalto)* violent; **è un pazzo ~** he is a raving lunatic.

furore [fu'rore] *sm* fury; **nel ~ della battaglia** in the heat of the battle; **amare con ~** to love passionately; **a furor di popolo** by popular acclaim; **fare ~** to be all the rage.

furoreggiare [furored'dʒare] *vi* to be all the rage.

furtivo, a [fur'tivo] *ag (sguardo)* furtive; *(passo)* stealthy.

furto ['furto] *sm* theft; **~ con scasso** *(Dir)* burglary; **commettere un ~** to steal.

fusa ['fusa] *sfpl*: **fare le ~** to purr.

fuscello [fuʃ'ʃɛllo] *sm* twig; **magro come un ~** slender.

fusciacca, che [fuʃ'ʃakka] *sf* sash.

fusibile [fu'zibile] *sm (Elettr)* fuse.

fusillo [fu'sillo] *sm (Culin)* pasta spiral.

fusione [fu'zjone] *sf* **(a)** *(gen, Fis)* fusion; *(di metalli)* melting; *(fig: di idee)* merging, blending. **(b)** *(Comm)* merger, amalgamation.

fuso¹, a [fuzo] *pp di* **fondere.**

fuso² ['fuzo] *sm* **(a)** *(Tessile)* spindle; **diritto come un ~** as stiff as a ramrod. **(b):** **~ orario** time zone.

fusoliera [fuzo'ljera] *sf (Aer)* fusillage.

fustagno [fus'taɲɲo] *sm* fustian.

fustella [fus'tɛlla] *sf (su scatola di medicinali)* tear-off tab.

fustigare [fusti'gare] *vt (frustare)* to flog; *(fig: costumi)* to censure, denounce.

fustigatore, trice [fustiga'tore] *sm/f (fig)* critic.

fustigazione [fustigat'tsjone] *sf* flogging, beating.

fustino [fus'tino] *sm (di detersivo)* tub.

fusto ['fusto] *sm* **(a)** *(Anat, Bot: di albero)* trunk; *(: di pianta)* stem; *(colonna)* shaft. **(b)** *(recipiente: di metallo)* drum. **(c)** *(fam)* he-man.

futile ['futile] *ag* futile.

futilità [futili'ta] *sf* futility.

futurismo [futu'rizmo] *sm* futurism.

futuro, a [fu'turo] **1** *ag* future. **2** *sm* future; **~ anteriore** future perfect.

G

G, g [dʒi] *sf o m inv (lettera)* G, g.
g. *abbr (= grammo, grammi)* g.
gabardine [gabar'din] *sm (tessuto)* gabardine; *(soprabito)* gabardine raincoat.
gabbare [gab'bare] *vt* to deceive, trick.
gabbia ['gabbja] *sf (gen)* cage; **la ~ degli accusati** *(Dir)* the dock; **~ toracica** *(Anat)* rib cage; **~ di matti** *(fig)* madhouse.
gabbiano [gab'bjano] *sm* gull.
gabella [ga'bɛlla] *sf (Storia: tassa)* duty.
gabinetto [gabi'netto] *sm* **(a)** *(WC)* lavatory, toilet. **(b)** *(di medico)* surgery, consulting room. **(c)** *(Pol: ministero)* ≃ ministry; *(: di ministro)* advisers *pl.* **(d)** *(Scol)* laboratory, lab *(fam)*.
gaffe [gaf] *sf inv* blunder, boob *(fam)*.
gag [gæg] *sf inv (Cine, Teatro)* gag.
gagliardetto [gaʎʎar'detto] *sm* pennant.
gagliardo, a [gaʎ'ʎardo] *ag* strong, robust.
gaiezza [ga'jettsa] *sf (di persona, romanzo)* gaiety, cheerfulness; *(di colori)* brightness.
gaio, a ['gajo] *ag (persona)* cheerful, happy; *(colore, vestito)* bright, gay.
gala ['gala] **1** *sf* **(a)** *(ornamento)* bow. **(b)**: **mettersi in ~** to dress in all one's finery; **serata di ~ gala** evening; **uniforme di gran ~** full-dress uniform; **pranzo di ~** banquet. **2** *sm* gala, festivity.
galante [ga'lante] **1** *ag* **(a)** *(cortese)* gallant, chivalrous. **(b)** *(amoroso)* romantic; **avventura ~** love affair. **2** *sm* gallant.
galanteria [galante'ria] *sf* gallantry.
galantuomo [galan'twɔmo] *sm, pl* **-uomini** gentleman.
galassia [ga'lassja] *sf* galaxy.
galateo [gala'tɛo] *sm* etiquette.
galea [ga'lɛa] *sf* galley.
galeone [gale'one] *sm* galleon.
galeotto [gale'ɔtto] *sm (Storia)* galley slave; *(carcerato)* convict.
galera [ga'lɛra] *sf* **(a)** *(Naut)* galley. **(b)** *(fam)* prison, gaol; **avanzo di ~** jailbird; **vita da ~** *(fig)* dog's life.
galla¹ ['galla]: **a ~** *av* afloat; **stare a ~** to float; *(fig)* to keep one's head above water; **venire a ~** to surface, come to the surface; *(fig: verità)* to come out.
galla² ['galla] *sf (Bot)* gall.
galleggiabilità [galleddʒabili'ta] *sf* buoyancy.
galleggiamento [galleddʒa'mento] *sm* floating; **linea di ~** *(di nave)* water line.
galleggiante [galled'dʒante] **1** *ag* floating. **2** *sm (Tecn, Aer, Pesca)* float; *(natante)* barge; *(boa)* buoy.
galleggiare [galled'dʒare] *vi* to float.
galleria [galle'ria] *sf* **(a)** *(traforo)* tunnel; **~ del vento** *(Aer)* wind tunnel. **(b)** *(Archit, Arte)* gallery; *(strada coperta con negozi)* arcade; *(Cine)* balcony; *(Teatro)* circle.
Galles ['galles] *sm* Wales.
gallese [gal'lese] **1** *ag* Welsh. **2** *sm/f* Welshman/woman; **i G~i** the Welsh. **3** *sm (lingua)* Welsh.
galletta [gal'letta] *sf* cracker; *(Naut)* ship's biscuit.

galletto [gal'letto] *sm* young cock, cockerel; *(fig)* cocky young man; **fare il ~** to play the gallant.
gallicismo [galli'tʃizmo] *sm* gallicism.
gallico, a, ci, che ['gallico] *ag* Gallic.
gallina [gal'lina] *sf* hen; **~ lessa** boiled chicken; **andare a letto con le ~e** to go to bed early.
gallismo [gal'lizmo] *sm* machismo.
gallo ['gallo] **1** *sm* cock; **~ cedrone** capercaillie; **~ da combattimento** fighting cock; **al canto del ~** at daybreak, at cockcrow; **fare il ~** to play the gallant. **2** *ag inv (Pugilato)*: **peso ~** bantamweight.
gallone¹ [gal'lone] *sm* **(a)** *(Mil)* stripe; **guadagnarsi i ~i** to be promoted; **perdere i ~i** to lose one's stripes. **(b)** *(ornamento)* braid.
gallone² [gal'lone] *sm (unità di misura)* gallon.
galoppante [galop'pante] *ag (inflazione, tisi)* galloping.
galoppare [galop'pare] *vi (cavallo)* to gallop; *(fig: correre affannosamente)* to rush about; *(: fantasia, immaginazione)* to run wild, run riot; **sua madre lo fa ~!** his mother runs him off his feet!
galoppata [galop'pata] *sf (di cavallo)* gallop; **ho fatto una ~ per arrivare in tempo** *(fig)* I had to gallop to get here in time.
galoppino [galop'pino] *sm* **(a)** errand boy. **(b)** *(Pol)* canvasser.
galoppo [ga'lɔppo] *sm* gallop; **piccolo ~** canter; **al ~** *(anche fig)* at a gallop; **andare al ~** to gallop; **partire al ~** *(cavallo)* to set off at a gallop; *(persona)* to rush off *o* away.
galoscia, sce [ga'lɔʃʃa] *sf* = **caloscia**.
galvanizzare [galvanid'dzare] *vt (Tecn, anche fig)* to galvanize.
galvanizzazione [galvaniddzat'tsjone] *sf* galvanization.
gamba ['gamba] *sf (Anat, di mobile)* leg; *(di lettera)* stroke; **le ~e del tavolo** the table legs; **con le proprie ~e** on one's own two feet; **essere di buona ~ o di ~ lesta** to be a good walker; **scappare a ~e levate o in spalla** to take to one's heels; **darsela a ~e** to take to one's heels; **~e!** scatter!; **andare a ~e all'aria** to fall headlong; *(fig: progetto)* to fall through.
gambale [gam'bale] *sm* legging.
gamberetto [gambe'retto] *sm* shrimp.
gambero ['gambero] *sm* prawn; **~ di fiume** crayfish; **fare come i ~i** *(fig)* to go backwards.
gambetto [gam'betto] *sm (Scacchi)* gambit.
gambo ['gambo] *sm (di fiore, bicchiere)* stem; *(di frutta)* stalk.
gamella [ga'mɛlla] *sf* mess tin.
gamma¹ ['gamma] *ag inv*: **raggi** *mpl* **~** gamma rays.
gamma² ['gamma] *sf (Mus)* scale; *(fig)* range; **~ d'onda** *(Radio)* waveband.
ganascia, sce [ga'naʃʃa] *sf (Zool, Tecn)* jaw; **~sce dei freni** brake shoes; **mangiare a quattro ~sce** to eat like a horse.
gancio ['gantʃo] *sm (gen, Pugilato)* hook.
gang [gæŋ] *sf inv* gang.

ganghero ['gangero] sm hinge; **uscire dai ~i** (fig) to lose one's temper, go off the deep end; **essere fuori dai ~i** (fig) to be beside o.s. with rage.

ganglio ['ganglio] sm (Anat, Med) ganglion.

gangrena [gan'grɛna] sf = **cancrena**.

gangster ['gɛnstə] sm/f inv gangster; (fig) shark, crook.

gara ['gara] sf (a) (concorso) competition, contest; (: di velocità) race; ~ **di nuoto/tiro/canto** swimming/shooting/singing competition; ~e **automobilistiche/ciclistiche** car/cycle races; **entrare in** ~ to enter a competition (o race); **essere in** ~ to be competing; **hanno fatto a** ~ **a chi riusciva meglio** they competed o vied with each other to see who could do it best. (b) (Comm, Econ): ~ **d'appalto** tender.

garage [ga'raʒ] sm inv garage.

garagista, i, e [gara'dʒista] sm/f (proprietario) garage owner; (gestore) garage manager; (meccanico) mechanic.

garante [ga'rante] 1 ag: **farsi** ~ **di** o **per qc** to vouch for sth, guarantee sth; **farsi** ~ **di** o **per qn** to stand surety for sb. 2 sm/f guarantor.

garantire [garan'tire] 1 vt (gen) to guarantee; ~ **un debito** to stand surety for a debt; **ti garantisco che sarà pronto domani** I guarantee that it will be ready tomorrow. 2: ~**rsi** vr: ~**rsi da** o **contro** to insure o.s. against.

garantito, a [garan'tito] ag guaranteed; **il successo sembra ormai** ~ success now seems certain; **è** ~ **che pioverà** it's bound to rain; **se glielo chiedi dirà di no,** ~! if you ask him he'll certainly say no!

garanzia [garan'tsia] sf (gen, Comm) guarantee; (pegno) security, surety; **in** ~ under guarantee; **lasciare qc come** ~ to leave sth as security; **questa persona non dà alcuna** ~ this person is not to be trusted.

garbare [gar'bare] vi (aus essere): **non mi garba** I don't like it (o him etc).

garbatezza [garba'tettsa] sf (vedi ag) courtesy, politeness; kindness; **con** ~ politely; kindly.

garbato, a [gar'bato] ag (cortese) courteous, polite; (gentile) kind.

garbo ['garbo] sm (a) (grazia) grace; **muoversi con** ~/**senza** ~ to move gracefully/awkwardly; **non ha** ~ **nel vestire** she doesn't dress well. (b) (gentilezza) politeness, courtesy; **una persona di** ~ a well-mannered person.

garbuglio [gar'buʎʎo] sm tangle; (fig) muddle, mess.

gardenia [gar'dɛnja] sf gardenia.

gareggiare [gared'dʒare] vi: ~ **in qc** to compete in sth; ~ **con qn** to compete o vie with sb.

garganella [garga'nɛlla] sf: **a** ~ from the bottle.

gargarismo [garga'rizmo] sm gargle; **fare un** ~ o **dei** ~**i** to gargle.

garibaldino, a [garibal'dino] ag (Storia) of (o relating to) Garibaldi; **alla** ~**a** impetuously.

garitta [ga'ritta] sf (di caserma) sentry box.

garofano [ga'rɔfano] sm carnation.

garretto [gar'retto] sm hock.

garrire [gar'rire] vi to chirp.

garrulo, a ['garrulo] ag (a) (uccello) chirping. (b) (persona: loquace) garrulous, talkative.

garza ['gardza] sf (tessuto, Med) gauze; **una** ~ (Med) a gauze bandage.

garzone [gar'dzone] sm (di negozio etc) boy; **il** ~ **del macellaio** the butcher's boy.

gas [gas] 1 sm inv (a) gas; **l'uomo del** ~ the gasman; **scaldabagno/stufa a** ~ gas waterheater/ stove. (b) (Aut): **dare** ~ to step on the gas; **a tutto** ~ (anche fig) at full speed; **è partito a tutto** ~ he

roared off. 2: ~ **asfissiante** poison gas; ~ **esilarante** laughing gas; ~ **illuminante** town gas; ~ **lacrimogeno** tear gas.

gasare [ga'zare] 1 vt (a) (liquido) to aerate, make fizzy. (b) (uccidere col gas) to gas. 2: ~**rsi** vr (fam) to get excited.

gasato, a [ga'zato] 1 ag (bibita) aerated, fizzy. 2 sm/f (fam: persona molto eccitata) freak.

gasdotto [gaz'dotto] sm gas pipeline.

gasista, i [ga'zista] sm = **gassista**.

gasolina [gazo'lina] sf gasoline.

gasolio [ga'zɔljo] sm diesel oil.

gasometro [ga'zɔmetro] sm = **gassometro**.

gassare [gas'sare] vt = **gasare**.

gassato, a [gas'sato] ag = **gasato**.

gassificare [gassifi'kare] vt to gasify.

gassista, i [gas'sista] sm gasman.

gassometro [gas'sɔmetro] sm gasometer.

gassosa [gas'sosa] sf fizzy drink.

gassoso, a [gas'soso] ag gaseous.

gastrico, a, ci, che ['gastriko] ag gastric.

gastrite [gas'trite] sf gastritis.

gastroenterite [gastroente'rite] sf gastroenteritis.

gastronomia [gastrono'mia] sf gastronomy.

gastronomico, a, ci, che [gastro'nɔmiko] ag gastronomic.

gastronomo, a [gas'trɔnomo] sm/f gourmet, gastronome.

gatta ['gatta] sf (female) cat; **una** ~ **da pelare** (fam) a thankless task; **qui** ~ **ci cova!** I smell a rat!, there's something fishy going on here!

gattabuia [gatta'buja] sf (fam scherz: prigione) clink.

gatto ['gatto] 1 sm (gen) cat; (maschio) tomcat; **siamo rimasti in quattro** ~**i** there were only a few of us left; **quando il** ~ **non c'è i topi ballano** (Proverbio) when the cat's away the mice will play. 2: ~ **selvatico** wildcat; ~ **a nove code** cat-o'-nine-tails; ~ **delle nevi** (Sci) snowcat.

gattoni [gat'toni] av on all fours.

gattopardo [gatto'pardo] sm: ~ **africano** serval; ~ **americano** ocelot.

gattuccio [gat'tuttʃo] sm dogfish.

gaudente [gau'dɛnte] sm/f pleasure-seeker; **fare la vita del** ~ to live like a lord.

gaudio ['gaudjo] sm joy, happiness.

gavetta [ga'vetta] sf (Mil) mess tin; **venire dalla** ~ (fig) to rise from the ranks.

gazolina [gaddzo'lina] sf = **gasolina**.

gazza ['gaddza] sf magpie.

gazzarra [gad'dzarra] sf racket, din; **fare** ~ to make a din.

gazzella [gad'dzɛlla] sf (a) (Zool) gazelle. (b) (auto dei Carabinieri) (high-speed) police car.

gazzetta [gad'dzetta] sf gazette; **G~ Ufficiale** official gazette.

gazzettino [gaddzet'tino] sm (a) (di giornale: titolo) gazette; (: sezione) page; ~ **teatrale** theatre page; ~ **regionale** (alla radio) regional news sg. (b) (fig: persona pettegola) gossip.

gazzosa [gad'dzosa] sf = **gassosa**.

gelare [dʒe'lare] 1 vt to freeze; **mi ha gelato il sangue** (fig) it made my blood run cold. 2 vi (aus essere) to freeze; **il lago è gelato** the lake has frozen over; **chiudi la porta, si gela!** close the door, it's freezing! 3 vb impers to freeze; **gela** it's freezing.

gelata [dʒe'lata] sf frost.

gelataio, a [dʒela'tajo] sm/f (venditore) ice-cream man; (produttore) ice-cream maker.

gelateria [dʒela'teria] sf ice-cream shop, ice-cream parlour (Am).

gelatiera [dʒela'tjɛra] sf ice-cream machine.

gelatina [dʒela'tina] *sf (gen, Culin)* gelatine; ~ **di frutta** fruit jelly; ~ **esplosiva** gelignite.

gelatinoso, a [dʒelati'noso] *ag* gelatinous.

gelato, a [dʒe'lato] **1** *ag* frozen; **ho le mani** ~**e** my hands are frozen (stiff). **2** *sm* ice cream; ~ **di fragola/di crema** strawberry/dairy ice.

gelido, a ['dʒelido] *ag (aria, vento)* icy, freezing; *(mani, acqua)* freezing, ice-cold; *(fig: accoglienza, espressione, sguardo)* icy, frosty.

gelo ['dʒelo] *sm (temperatura)* intense cold; *(brina)* frost; *(fig: inverno)* cold weather; **il** ~ **invernale** the cold winter weather; **sentirsi il** ~ **nelle ossa** to feel a chill of fear; **il** ~ **della morte** the chill hand of death.

gelone [dʒe'lone] *sm* chilblain.

gelosia[1] [dʒelo'sia] *sf* jealousy; **conservare qc con gran** ~ to guard sth jealously.

gelosia[2] [dʒelo'sia] *sf (persiana)* shutter.

geloso, a [dʒe'loso] *ag* jealous.

gelso ['dʒelso] *sm* mulberry.

gelsomino [dʒelso'mino] *sm* jasmine.

gemellaggio [dʒemel'laddʒo] *sm* twinning.

gemellare [dʒemel'lare] **1** *ag* twin *attr.* **2** *vt (città)* to twin.

gemello, a [dʒe'mɛllo] **1** *ag (fratelli, letti)* twin *attr.* **2** *sm/f (persona, oggetto)* twin. **3:** ~**i** *smpl* **(a)** *(di camicia)* cuff links. **(b)** *(Astrologia):* **G**~**i** Gemini; **essere dei G**~**i** to be Gemini.

gemere ['dʒɛmere] *vi (ferito):* ~ **(di)** to groan (with), moan (with); *(cane)* to whine; *(ruote, molle)* to creak; *(piccione, tortora: tubare)* to coo.

gemito ['dʒɛmito] *sm* groan, moan.

gemma ['dʒɛmma] *sf* **(a)** *(Bot)* bud. **(b)** *(gioiello)* gem, jewel.

gendarme [dʒen'darme] *sm* policeman; **essere un** ~ *(fig)* to be a martinet.

gene ['dʒɛne] *sm* gene.

genealogia, gie [dʒenealo'dʒia] *sf* genealogy.

genealogico, a, ci, che [dʒenea'lɔdʒiko] *ag* genealogical; **albero** ~ family tree.

generale[1] [dʒene'rale] *ag* general; **nell'interesse** ~ in the general interest, for the common good; **un quadro** ~ **della situazione** a general *o* overall view of the situation; **l'opinione** ~ public opinion; **direttore** ~ managing director; **console** ~ consul general; **in** ~ generally, in general; **in** ~ **sto bene** on the whole I am quite well; **mantenersi** *o* **stare sulle** ~**i** to stick to generalities.

generale[2] [dʒene'rale] *sm* general; ~ **di brigata** brigadier.

generalesco, a, schi, sche [dʒenera'lesko] *ag (scherz)* military-like.

generalità [dʒenerali'ta] *sf inv* **(a)** *(qualità)* generality; ~ **d'assenso** general assent; **stare sulle** ~ *(in un discorso etc)* to stick to generalities. **(b)** *(maggioranza)* majority. **(c)** *(dati personali):* ~ *pl* particulars.

generalizzare [dʒeneralid'dzare] *vt* to generalize.

generalizzazione [dʒeneraliddzat'tsjone] *sf* generalization.

generalmente [dʒeneral'mente] *av* generally, usually.

generare [dʒene'rare] *vt* to generate.

generativo, a [dʒenera'tivo] *ag* generative.

generatore [dʒenera'tore] *sm (Elettr)* generator.

generazione [dʒenerat'tsjone] *sf* generation; **la nuova** ~ the new *o* younger generation.

genere ['dʒɛnere] *sm* **(a)** *(tipo)* kind, type, sort; **oggetti di ogni** ~ all kinds of things; **cose del** *o* **di questo** ~ such things; **non farmi più uno scherzo del** ~**!** don't ever play a similar trick on me again!; **è bravo nel suo** ~ in his own way he is quite good; **questo vaso è bello, nel suo** ~ this is a nice vase

of its kind; **in** ~ generally, usually; **i documentari non sono il mio** ~ documentaries aren't my scene. **(b)** *article;* ~**i di consumo** consumer goods; ~**i di prima necessità** basic essentials. **(c)** *(Bio, Zool, Bot)* genus; *(Gram)* gender; *(Letteratura, Arte)* genre; **il** ~ **umano** mankind, the human race.

genericità [dʒeneritʃi'ta] *sf* vagueness, generality; **l'argomento è stato trattato con troppa** ~ the subject was treated too vaguely.

generico, a, ci, che [dʒe'nɛriko] **1** *ag* generic; *(vago: descrizione etc)* vague, imprecise; **medico** ~ general practitioner. **2** *sm* generality; **i suoi discorsi non escono dal** ~ his speeches never get away from generalities.

genero ['dʒɛnero] *sm* son-in-law.

generosità [dʒenerosi'ta] *sf* generosity; **è un uomo di grande** ~ he's a very generous *o* liberal man.

generoso, a [dʒene'roso] *ag* generous; **non è** ~ **da parte tua** that's not very kind of you; **un vino** ~ a full-bodied wine.

genesi ['dʒɛnezi] *sf* genesis.

genetica [dʒe'nɛtika] *sf* genetics *sg.*

genetico, a, ci, che [dʒe'nɛtiko] *ag* genetic.

gengiva [dʒen'dʒiva] *sf* gum.

gengivale [dʒendʒi'vale] *ag* gum *attr.*

genia [dʒe'nia] *sf (peg)* mob, gang.

geniale [dʒe'njale] *ag (persona, artista)* of genius; *(idea, soluzione)* brilliant, inspired.

genialità [dʒenjali'ta] *sf (vedi ag)* genius; brilliance.

genialoide [dʒenja'lɔide] *sm/f* eccentric genius.

genio[1] ['dʒɛnjo] *sm* **(a)** *(persona, talento)* genius; **avere il** ~ **degli affari** to have a genius *o* flair for business; **essere un** ~ **in matematica** he is a mathematical genius *o* wizard; **non mi va a** ~ I am not very keen on it *(o him etc)*. **(b)** *(Mitologia: gen)* spirit; *(: arabo)* genie.

genio[2] ['dʒɛnjo] *sm* **(a)** *(Mil):* **il** ~ the Engineers. **(b):** ~ **civile** civil engineers *pl.*

genitale [dʒeni'tale] **1** *ag* genital. **2:** ~**i** *smpl* genitals.

genitivo, a [dʒeni'tivo] *ag, sm* genitive.

genitore, trice [dʒeni'tore] *sm/f* parent.

gennaio [dʒen'najo] *sm* January; *per uso vedi* **luglio.**

genocidio [dʒeno'tʃidjo] *sm* genocide.

Genova ['dʒɛnova] *sf* Genoa.

genovese [dʒeno'vese] *ag, sm/f* Genoese *(pl inv).*

gentaglia [dʒen'taʎʎa] *sf (peg)* rabble, scum.

gente ['dʒɛnte] *sf people pl;* **c'era tanta** ~ there were lots of people there; ~ **di campagna** countryfolk; ~ **di città** townspeople; ~ **di mare** seafaring folk; **è brava** ~ they are nice people *o* folk; **aspetto** ~ I'm waiting for somebody; **ho** ~ **a cena** I've got people to dinner; **le** ~**i anglosassoni** the Anglo-Saxon peoples; **diritto delle** ~**i** law of nations.

gentildonna [dʒentil'dɔnna] *sf* gentlewoman, lady.

gentile[1] [dʒen'tile] *ag* **(a)** kind, courteous; **è molto** ~ **da parte sua** it's very kind *o* nice of you; **vuoi essere tanto** ~ **da...?** would you be so kind as to...?; **i commessi sono sempre così** ~**i** the shop assistants are always so helpful. **(b)** *(delicato: lineamenti)* fine; *(: profumo)* delicate; **il gentil sesso** the gentle sex. **(c)** *(nelle lettere):* **G**~ **Signore** Dear Sir.

gentile[2] [dʒen'tile] *sm (Rel)* Gentile.

gentilezza [dʒenti'lettsa] *sf* **(a)** kindness, courtesy; ~**e** acts of kindness; **fare una** ~ **a qn** to do sb a favour; **fammi la** ~ **di chiudere la porta** please be so kind as to close the door; **per** ~ *(per* *favore*) please. **(b)** *(grazia: di lineamenti)* delicacy; *(: di movimento)* grace.

gentiluomo [dʒenti'lwɔmo] *sm, pl* **-uomini** gentleman.

genuflessione [dʒenufles'sjone] *sf* genuflexion.

genuflesso, a [dʒenu'flɛsso] *pp di* **genuflettersi.**

genuflettersi [dʒenu'flɛttersi] *vr* to genuflect, kneel.

genuinità [dʒenuini'ta] *sf (di prodotti)* naturalness; *(di sentimento)* sincerity, genuineness.

genuino, a [dʒenu'ino] *ag (prodotto)* natural; *(persona, sentimento)* genuine, sincere; *(risata)* natural, unaffected; **ha una ~a vocazione** he has a true *o* real vocation.

genziana [dʒen'tsjana] *sf* gentian.

geodesia [dʒeode'sia] *sf* geodesy.

geofisica [dʒeo'fizika] *sf* geophysics *sg.*

geografia [dʒeogra'fia] *sf* geography.

geografico, a, ci, che [dʒeo'grafiko] *ag* geographical; **atlante ~** atlas; **carta ~a** map.

geografo, a [dʒe'ɔgrafo] *sm/f* geographer.

geologia [dʒeolo'dʒia] *sf* geology.

geologico, a, ci, che [dʒeo'lɔdʒiko] *ag* geological.

geometra, i, e [dʒe'ɔmetra] *sm/f* surveyor.

geometrico, a, ci, che [dʒeo'mɛtriko] *ag* geometric(al).

geopolitica [dʒeopo'litika] *sf* geopolitics *sg.*

geotermico, a, ci, che [dʒeo'tɛrmiko] *ag* geothermal.

geranio [dʒe'ranjo] *sm* geranium.

gerarca, chi [dʒe'rarka] *sm (Storia: nel fascismo)* party official.

gerarchia [dʒerar'kia] *sf* hierarchy; **le più alte ~e** the upper echelons.

gerarchico, a, ci, che [dʒe'rarkiko] *ag* hierarchical.

gerente [dʒe'rɛnte] *sm/f* manager/manageress.

gerenza [dʒe'rɛntsa] *sf* management.

gergale [dʒer'gale] *ag (vedi sm)* slang *attr*; jargon *attr.*

gergo ['dʒergo] *sm (gen)* slang; *(professionale)* jargon; **~ della malavita** thieves' cant.

geriatria [dʒerja'tria] *sf* geriatrics *sg.*

geriatrico, a, ci, che [dʒe'rjatriko] *ag* geriatric.

gerla ['dʒerla] *sf* conical wicker basket.

Germania [dʒer'manja] *sf* Germany; **~ occidentale** West Germany; **~ dell'Est** *o* **orientale** East Germany.

germanico, a, ci, che [dʒer'maniko] *ag* Germanic.

germanismo [dʒerma'nizmo] *sm* Germanism.

germe ['dʒerme] *sm (gen)* germ; *(fig)* seed; **~i dell'influenza** flu germs; **i ~i della ribellione** the seeds of rebellion.

germinare [dʒermi'nare] *vi* to germinate.

germinazione [dʒerminat'tsjone] *sf* germination.

germogliare [dʒermoʎ'ʎare] *vi (germinare)* to germinate; *(emettere germogli)* to sprout.

germoglio [dʒer'moʎʎo] *sm (gen)* shoot; *(gemma)* bud.

geroglifico, ci [dʒero'glifiko] *sm* hieroglyphic.

gerontologia [dʒerontolo'dʒia] *sf* gerontology.

gerontologo, a, gi, ghe [dʒeron'tologo] *sm/f* specialist in geriatrics.

gerundio [dʒe'rundjo] *sm* gerund.

gessetto [dʒes'setto] *sm* piece of chalk.

gesso ['dʒesso] *sm (gen)* chalk; *(minerale)* gypsum; *(Scultura, Med, Edil)* plaster; *(statuetta)* plaster figure; **mi hanno tolto il ~** *(Med)* they've taken off my plaster cast.

gesta ['dʒesta] *sfpl (poet)* deeds, feats.

gestante [dʒes'tante] *sf* expectant mother.

gestazione [dʒestat'tsjone] *sf* gestation; **il progetto**

è ancora in ~ *(fig)* the project is still at the planning stage.

gesticolare [dʒestiko'lare] *vi* to gesticulate.

gestionale [dʒestjo'nale] *ag* administrative, management *attr.*

gestione [dʒes'tjone] *sf* management.

gestire [dʒes'tire] *vt* to manage, run.

gesto ['dʒesto] *sm* gesture; **ha fatto un ~ di rabbia** he made an angry gesture; **non ha fatto un ~ per aiutarmi** he didn't lift a finger to help me.

gestore [dʒes'tore] *sm* manager.

gestuale [dʒestu'ale] *ag*: **linguaggio ~** sign language.

Gesù [dʒe'zu] *sm* Jesus; **~ bambino** the Christ Child.

gesuita, i [dʒezu'ita] *sm* Jesuit.

gettare [dʒet'tare] **1** *vt* **(a)** *(lanciare)* to throw; *(: con forza)* to fling, hurl; *(: in aria)* to toss; **~ (via)** *(liberarsi di)* to throw away; **~ qc a qn** to throw sth to sb; **~ qc addosso a qn** *(sasso etc)* to throw sth at sb; *(acqua, sabbia)* to throw sth over sb; **si gettò un mantello sulle spalle** he threw a coat round his shoulders; **~ a terra qn** to throw sb to the ground; **~ le braccia al collo di qn** to throw *o* fling one's arms round sb's neck; **~ la colpa addosso a qn** to cast the blame on sb; **~ qc in faccia a qn** *(anche fig)* to throw sth in sb's face; **gettò un rapido sguardo intorno** he had a quick look round; **~ l'ancora** *(Naut)* to drop anchor; **~ a mare** *(fig: persona)* to abandon; **quella notizia l'ha gettato nella disperazione** he was plunged into despair at the news.

(b) *(metalli, cera)* to cast; *(fondamenta)* to lay; **~ un ponte su un fiume** to throw a bridge over a river.

(c) *(emettere: acqua)* to spout; *(: grido)* to utter, give.

(d) *(fraseologia)*: **~ le armi** *(anche fig)* to throw down one's weapons; **~ la spugna** *(Pugilato, fig)* to throw in the sponge; **~ la polvere negli occhi a qn** *(fig)* to throw dust in sb's eyes; **~ luce su qc** to shed light on sth.

2 *vi (pianta)* to sprout.

3: **~rsi** *vr* **(a)**: **~rsi ai piedi di qn** to throw o.s. at sb's feet; **~rsi in un'impresa** to throw o.s. into an enterprise; **~rsi nella mischia** to hurl o.s. into the fray; **~rsi contro** *o* **addosso a qn** to hurl o.s. at sb; **~rsi sulla preda** to pounce on one's prey.

(b) *(fiume)*: **~rsi in** to flow into.

gettata [dʒet'tata] *sf* **(a)** *(di cemento, bronzo, delle reti)* cast. **(b)** *(in balistica)* range. **(c)** *(diga)* jetty.

gettito ['dʒettito] *sm (rendita, introito)* yield.

getto¹ ['dʒetto] *sm* **(a)** *(azione)* throwing; *(risultato)* throw, cast. **(b)** *(di acqua)* jet; **a ~ continuo** in a continuous stream; **scrive novelle a ~ continuo** he writes one short story after another, he produces a constant stream of short stories; **di ~** *(scrivere)* in one go. **(c)** *(Bot)* shoot. **(d)** *(Metallurgia, Edil)* casting.

getto² ['dʒetto] *sm (Meteor)*: **corrente a ~** jet stream.

gettonare [dʒetto'nare] *vt (fam: telefonare)* to call, ring, phone; *(: juke-box)* to put money in, feed.

gettone [dʒet'tone] *sm (gen)* token; *(per giochi)* counter; *(: Roulette)* chip; **~ di presenza** attendance fee; **~ del telefono** telephone token.

geyser ['gaizə] *sm inv* geyser.

ghenga, ghe ['genga] *sf (fam)* gang, crowd.

ghepardo [ge'pardo] *sm* cheetah.

gheriglio [ge'riʎʎo] *sm* kernel.

ghermire [ger'mire] *vt* to grasp, clasp, clutch.

ghetta ['getta] *sf (gambale)* gaiter.

ghetto ['getto] *sm* ghetto.

ghiacciaia [gjat'tʃaja] sf (anche fig) icebox.

ghiacciaio [gjat'tʃajo] sm glacier.

ghiacciare [gjat'tʃare] 1 vi (aus essere) to freeze; (lago, fiume) to ice over, freeze (over); **mi si è ghiacciato il sangue** my blood ran cold; **questa notte è ghiacciato** there was a frost last night. 2 vt to freeze. 3 vt impers to freeze.

ghiacciato, a [gjat'tʃato] ag (gen) frozen; (bevanda) ice-cold; **avevo le mani ~e** my hands were frozen.

ghiaccio ['gjattʃo] sm ice; ~ **secco** dry ice; **hai le mani di ~** your hands are frozen; **restare di ~** to be dumbfounded; **quella donna è un pezzo di ~** that woman is as cold as ice.

ghiacciolo [gjat'tʃɔlo] sm (a) (formazione di ghiaccio) icicle. (b) (gelato) ice(d) lolly.

ghiaia ['gjaja] sf gravel.

ghiaioso, a [gja'joso] ag gravelly.

ghianda ['gjanda] sf (Bot) acorn.

ghiandaia [gjan'daja] sf jay.

ghiandola ['gjandola] sf gland.

ghiandolare [gjando'lare] ag glandular.

ghigliottina [giʎʎot'tina] sf guillotine.

ghigliottinare [giʎʎotti'nare] vt to guillotine.

ghignare [gin'nare] vi to sneer, laugh derisively.

ghignata [gin'nata] sf (fam) laugh; **fare una ~** to have a good laugh.

ghigno ['ginno] sm (espressione) sneer; (risata) mocking laugh.

ghingheri ['gingeri] smpl: **in ~** all dolled up; **mettersi in ~** to put on one's Sunday best.

ghiotto, a ['gjotto] ag (persona): ~ **(di)** greedy (for); (cibi) appetizing, delicious; (fig: notizia) juicy.

ghiottone, a [gjot'tone] sm/f (a) (persona) glutton. (b) (Zool) wolverine.

ghiottoneria [gjottone'ria] sf (a) greed, gluttony. (b) (cibo) delicacy, titbit.

ghiribizzo [giri'biddzo] sm whim; **gli è venuto il ~ della pittura** he's taken it into his head to paint.

ghirigoro [giri'gɔro] sm (scarabocchio) doodle, scribble; (arabesco) flourish.

ghirlanda [gir'landa] sf garland, wreath.

ghiro ['giro] sm dormouse.

ghisa ['giza] sf cast-iron.

già [dʒa] av (a) (gen) already; **te l'ho ~ detto** I have already told you; **ho finito — di ~?** I've finished — already?; ~ **che ci sei...** while you are at it...; **è successo ~ da molto tempo** it happened a long time ago; **fra qualche anno sarà ~ un pianista famoso** in just a few years he will be a famous pianist; ~ **da bambino amava la musica** even as a child he liked music; ~ **sua madre lo faceva** his mother used to do it too. (b) (ex) formerly; **lo Zimbabwe, ~ Rodesia** Zimbabwe, formerly Rhodesia. (c) (naturalmente) of course, naturally; ~, **avrei dovuto saperlo!** of course, I should have known!

giacca, che ['dʒakka] sf jacket; ~ **a vento** windcheater, anorak.

giacché [dʒak'ke] av as, since.

giacchetta [dʒak'ketta] sf jacket.

giaccone [dʒak'kone] sm heavy jacket.

giacente [dʒa'tʃɛnte] ag (merce) unsold; (posta) undelivered; (: non ritirata) unclaimed; (Fin: capitale) idle, uninvested.

giacenza [dʒa'tʃɛntsa] sf (Fin, Comm): ~ **di capitale** uninvested capital; **merce in ~** (non reclamata) unclaimed goods; (non recapitata) undelivered goods; ~**e di magazzino** unsold stock.

giacere [dʒa'tʃere] vi (aus essere) (gen) to lie; (Fin: capitale) to lie idle; **il paese giace ai piedi della montagna** the village lies o is situated at the foot of the mountain; ~ **nell'ozio** to live in idleness; **la mia domanda giace ancora negli uffici del consolato** my application is still buried somewhere in the consulate.

giaciglio [dʒa'tʃiʎʎo] sm bed, pallet.

giacimento [dʒatʃi'mento] sm (Mineralogia) deposit.

giacinto [dʒa'tʃinto] sm hyacinth.

giaculatoria [dʒakula'tɔrja] sf short prayer; (fig: discorso noioso) boring words pl.

giaciuto, a [dʒa'tʃuto] pp di giacere.

giada ['dʒada] sf jade.

giaggiolo [dʒad'dʒɔlo] sm iris.

giaguaro [dʒa'gwaro] sm jaguar.

giallastro, a [dʒal'lastro] ag yellowish; (carnagione) sallow.

giallo, a ['dʒallo] 1 ag (a) (colore) yellow; (carnagione) sallow. (b): **libro/film ~** detective novel/film. 2 sm (a) (colore) yellow; ~ **dell'uovo** egg yolk. (b) (romanzo) detective story; (film) thriller.

giallognolo, a [dʒal'lonnolo] ag yellowish, dirty yellow.

giammai [dʒam'mai] av never.

Giappone [dʒap'pone] sm Japan.

giapponese [dʒappo'nese] ag, sm/f, sm Japanese (inv).

giara ['dʒara] sf jar.

giardinaggio [dʒardi'naddʒo] sm gardening.

giardinetta [dʒardi'netta] sf estate car, station wagon (Am).

giardiniera [dʒardi'njɛra] sf (Culin: verdure sottaceto) mixed pickles pl.

giardiniere, a [dʒardi'njɛre] sm/f gardener.

giardino [dʒar'dino] sm garden; ~ **d'infanzia** nursery school, kindergarten; ~ **pubblico** public gardens pl, (public) park; ~ **zoologico** zoo.

giarrettiera [dʒarret'tjɛra] sf garter; **Ordine della G~** Order of the Garter.

giavellotto [dʒavel'lɔtto] sm javelin.

gibbone [dʒib'bone] sm gibbon.

gibbosità [dʒibbosi'ta] sf inv: **le ~ del terreno** the bumps in the ground.

gibboso, a [dʒib'boso] ag (superficie) bumpy; (naso) crooked.

giberna [dʒi'bɛrna] sf (Mil) cartridge case.

gigante [dʒi'gante] 1 ag gigantic. 2 sm giant; ~ **della letteratura** literary giant.

giganteggiare [dʒigantcd'dʒare] vi: ~ **su** to tower over.

gigantesco, a, schi, sche [dʒigan'tesko] ag gigantic, huge.

giglio ['dʒiʎʎo] sm lily.

gigolo [ʒigɔ'lo] sm inv gigolo.

gilè [dʒi'lɛ] sm inv (panciotto) waistcoat; (fatto a maglia) sleeveless cardigan.

gin [dʒin] sm inv gin.

gincana [dʒin'kana] sf gymkhana.

ginecologia [dʒinekolo'dʒia] sf gynaecology.

ginecologico, a, ci, che [dʒineko'lɔdʒiko] ag gynaecological.

ginecologo, a, gi, ghe [dʒine'kɔlogo] sm/f gynaecologist.

ginepro [dʒi'nepro] sm juniper.

ginestra [dʒi'nestra] sf broom.

Ginevra [dʒi'nevra] sf Geneva.

gingillarsi [dʒindʒil'larsi] vr (a) (perdere tempo) to fritter away one's time. (b) (trastullarsi): ~ **con** to fiddle with.

gingillo [dʒin'dʒillo] sm (ninnolo) knick-knack, trinket; (balocco) plaything.

ginnasio [dʒin'nazjo] sm 4th and 5th year of secondary school.

ginnasta, i, e [dʒin'nasta] *sm/f* gymnast.

ginnastica [dʒin'nastika] *sf (disciplina)* gymnastics *sg; (educazione fisica)* physical education; **fare ~** *(Scol)* to do gym; **dovresti fare un po' di ~** you should take some exercise.

ginnico, a, ci, che ['dʒinniko] *ag* gymnastic.

ginocchiata [dʒinok'kjata] *sf:* **mi ha dato una ~ nello stomaco** he kneed me in the stomach; **ho preso** *o* **battuto una ~ contro il letto** I bumped my knee on the bed.

ginocchiera [dʒinok'kjɛra] *sf (Sport)* kneepad; *(Med)* elasticated knee bandage.

ginocchio [dʒi'nɔkkjo] *sm, pl(f)* **~a** knee; **in ginocchio** on one's knees, kneeling; **siediti sulle mie ~a** come and sit on my lap.

ginocchioni [dʒinok'kjoni] *av* on one's knees; **cadere ~** to fall to one's knees.

giocare [dʒo'kare] **1** *vi* **(a)** *(gen, Sport)* to play; **~ a scacchi/ai soldatini/al pallone** to play (at) chess/soldiers/football; **giocava con l'accendino** *(trastullarsi)* he was toying *o* playing with the lighter; **~ in Nazionale** *(Calcio)* to play for Italy; **il Milan gioca in casa** Milan is playing at home; **~ con il fuoco** *(fig)* to play with fire.

(b) *(anche:* **~ d'azzardo)** to gamble; **~ in Borsa** to speculate *o* gamble on the Stock Exchange; **~ alla roulette** to play roulette; **~ ai cavalli** to bet on the horses.

(c) *(intervenire: fattore)* to matter, count; **ciò ha giocato a suo favore** that worked in his favour; **qui gioca l'elemento sorpresa** it is the surprise element which matters here.

(d) *(muoversi liberamente: vite etc)* to be loose, fit loosely.

(e) *(fraseologia):* **a che gioco giochiamo?** what are you playing at?; **~ a carte scoperte** to act openly; **~ sul sicuro** to play safe; **~ d'astuzia** to be crafty.

2 *vt* **(a)** *(partita, carta)* to play; **~ l'atout** to play trumps; **~ l'ultima carta** *(fig)* to play one's last card.

(b) *(scommettere):* **~ (su)** *(Casinò)* to stake (on), wager (on); *(Corse)* to bet (on), stake (on); **~ forte** to gamble heavily; **~rsi una cena** to play for a meal; **si è giocato anche la camicia** he has gambled away his last penny; **ci giocherei l'anima** I'd stake my life on it; **~rsi tutto** to risk everything; **si sta giocando la carriera** he's putting his career at risk; **ormai è troppo tardi, ti sei giocato la carriera** it's too late now, your career is ruined.

(c) *(imbrogliare)* to deceive, trick; **ci hanno giocato un brutto tiro** they played a dirty trick on us.

giocata [dʒo'kata] *sf* **(a)** *(partita)* game. **(b)** *(scommessa)* wager, bet.

giocatore, trice [dʒoka'tore] *sm/f* **(a)** *(gen, Sport)* player. **(b)** *(d'azzardo)* gambler.

giocattolo [dʒo'kattolo] *sm* toy.

giocherellare [dʒokerel'lare] *vi:* **~ con** *(giocattolo)* to play with; *(distrattamente)* to fiddle with.

giocherellone [dʒokerel'lone] *sm* joker.

giochetto [dʒo'ketto] *sm* **(a)** *(gioco)* game; **è un ~** *(cosa molto facile)* it's child's play. **(b)** *(tranello)* trick.

gioco, chi ['dʒɔko] *sm* **(a)** *(gen)* game; **~ d'azzardo/di abilità** game of chance/skill; **~ di pazienza** puzzle; **~ di società** parlour game; **il ~ degli scacchi/delle bocce** (the game of) chess/bowls *sg*.

(b) *(Sport: partita, modo di giocare)* game; **~ di squadra** team game; **due ~chi a uno** *(Tennis)* two

games to one; **i Giochi Olimpici** the Olympic Games.

(c) *(Carte: mano)* hand; **non avere ~** to have a bad hand.

(d): **il ~** *(Casinò)* gambling; *(Corse)* betting; **avere il vizio del ~** to be a gambler; **casa/tavolo da ~** gaming house/table; **fortunato al ~, sfortunato in amore** lucky at cards, unlucky in love.

(e) *(Tecn)* play; **lo sterzo ha troppo ~** there is too much play in the steering wheel.

(f): **~ chi di luce** play of light and shade; **~ chi d'acqua** play of water.

(g) *(fraseologia):* **~ di parole** play on words, pun; **è un ~ da ragazzi** it's child's play; **entrano in ~ diversi fattori** various factors come into play; **è in ~ la mia reputazione** my reputation is at stake; **ho deciso di fare il suo ~** I've decided to play his game; **stare al ~ di qn** to play along with sb; **scoprire il proprio ~** to show one's hand; **prendersi ~ di qn** to pull sb's leg; **per ~** in fun; **il ~ non vale la candela** the game's not worth the candle; **far buon viso a cattivo ~** to make the best of a bad job; **un bel ~ dura poco** never take a joke too far; **~ di mano, ~ di villano** never use your fists.

giocoforza [dʒoko'fɔrtsa] *sm:* **essere ~** to be inevitable.

giocoliere [dʒoko'ljɛre] *sm* juggler.

giocondità [dʒokondi'ta] *sf* cheerfulness.

giocondo, a [dʒo'kondo] *ag* cheerful, smiling.

giocoso, a [dʒo'koso] *ag* playful, jocular.

giogaia [dʒo'gaja] *sf* range of mountains.

giogo, ghi ['dʒogo] *sm (Agr, fig)* yoke; *(di montagna)* range; *(di bilancia)* beam; **sotto il ~ di** under the yoke of.

gioia¹ ['dʒɔja] *sf* **(a)** joy, delight; **essere pazzo di ~** to be beside o.s. with joy, be overjoyed; **darsi alla pazza ~** to live it up; **le ~e della vita** the joys of life. **(b):** **~ mia!** darling!; **è la nostra ~** he's the light of our life.

gioia² ['dʒɔja] *sf* jewel.

gioielleria [dʒojelle'ria] *sf* **(a)** *(arte)* jeweller's art. **(b)** *(negozio)* jeweller's shop.

gioielliere [dʒojel'ljɛre] *sm* jeweller.

gioiello [dʒo'jɛllo] *sm* jewel, piece of jewellery; *(fig)* jewel, treasure.

gioioso, a [dʒo'joso] *ag* joyful, cheerful.

gioire [dʒo'ire] *vt:* **~ di qc** to rejoice in sth, be delighted by sth.

Giordania [dʒor'danja] *sf* Jordan.

giornalaio, a [dʒorna'lajo] *sm/f* newsagent.

giornale [dʒor'nale] *sm* **(a)** newspaper, paper; *(periodico)* journal; **lo dicono i ~i, è sui ~i** it's in the papers; **~ a fumetti** comic; **~ murale** wall poster; **il ~ radio** the (radio) news. **(b)** *(diario)* diary, journal; **~ di bordo** *(Naut)* logbook, ship's log.

giornaletto [dʒorna'letto] *sm* children's comic.

giornaliero, a [dʒorna'ljɛro] **1** *ag* daily. **2** *sm* day labourer.

giornalino [dʒorna'lino] *sm* children's comic.

giornalismo [dʒorna'lizmo] *sm* journalism.

giornalista, i, e [dʒorna'lista] *sm/f* journalist.

giornalistico, a, ci, che [dʒorna'listiko] *ag* journalistic; **stile ~** journalese.

giornalmente [dʒornal'mente] *av* daily.

giornata [dʒor'nata] *sf* **(a)** day; **durante la ~** during the day; **durante la ~ di ieri** yesterday; **in ~** by the end of the day; **fresco di ~** *(uovo)* freshly laid; **lavorare/pagare a ~** to work/pay by the day; **è a una ~ di cammino/macchina** it's a day's walk/drive away; **come stai? — mah, va a ~e** how are you? — well, it varies from day to day; **vivere alla** ~ to live from day to day; **è proprio la mia** ~**!** *(iro)* it's not my day today! **(b)** *(paga)* day's wages, day's pay.

giorno ['dʒorno] *sm* **(a)** *(periodo di luce)* day(light), day(time); ~ **e notte** day and night; **si fa** ~ it's getting light; **è già** ~ it's daylight; **di** ~ by day, during the daytime; **in pieno** ~ in full daylight; **c'è differenza come dal** ~ **alla notte** there's absolutely no comparison.

(b) *(periodo di tempo)* day; ~ **feriale** week day; ~ **festivo** holiday; ~ **di paga** payday; **tutti i santi** ~**i** every blessed day; **tutto il santo** ~ all day long; **fra 2** ~**i** in 2 days' time; **è a 2** ~**i di cammino da qui** it's 2 days' walk from here; **uno di questi** ~**i** one of these days; **il** ~ **prima** the day before, the previous day; **il** ~ **dopo** the day after, the next day, the following day; **un** ~ **sì e uno no** on alternate days; **due** ~**i fa** two days ago; **fra quindici** ~**i** in a fortnight, in two weeks' time; **al** ~ **a day**; ~ **per** ~ day by day; **a** ~**i** *o* **da un** ~ **all'altro** any day now.

(c) *(periodo indeterminato)*: **al** ~ **d'oggi** nowadays; **ha i** ~**i contati** his days are numbered; **mettere fine ai propri** ~**i** to put an end to one's life; **passare i propri** ~**i a fare qc** to spend one's time doing sth.

giostra ['dʒostra] *sf* **(a)** *(nei luna park)* merry-go-round. **(b)** *(Storia)* joust.

giostrare [dʒos'trare] **1** *vi* **(a)** *(Storia)* to joust, tilt. **(b)** *(fig)*: ~ **fra la folla** to push one's way through the crowd. **2**: ~**rsi** *vr* to manage; ~**rsi fra i creditori** to manage one's creditors.

giovamento [dʒova'mento] *sm* benefit, help; **trarre** ~ **da qc** to benefit from sth; **non ho avuto nessun** ~ **dalla cura** the treatment hasn't done me any good.

giovane ['dʒovane] **1** *ag (gen)* young; *(aspetto)* youthful; **non è più tanto** ~ he is not as young as he was; **è più** ~ **di me** he is younger than me; **vestirsi da** ~ to wear young styles; **è morto in** ~ **età** he died young; ~ **di spirito** young at heart; **è** ~ **del mestiere** he's new to the job. **2** *sm* youth, young man; **i** ~**i** the young, young people; ~ **di bottega** apprentice. **3** *sf* girl, young woman.

giovanetto, a [dʒova'netto] *sm/f* young man/woman.

giovanile [dʒova'nile] *ag (aspetto)* youthful; *(scritti)* early; *(errore)* of youth.

giovanotto, a [dʒova'nɔtto] *sm/f* young man/woman.

giovare [dʒo'vare] **1** *vi*: ~ **a** *(essere utile)* to be useful to; *(far bene)* to be good for; **nascondere la verità non ti gioverà di sicuro** it certainly won't do you any good to conceal the truth; **lavorare fino a tardi non ti giova** working late isn't good for you. **2** *vb impers (essere bene, utile)* to be useful; **a che giova prendersela?** what's the point of getting upset?; **giova sapere che...** it's useful to know that.... **3**: ~**rsi** *vr*: ~**rsi di qn/qc** to make use of sb/sth.

Giove ['dʒove] *sm (Mitologia)* Jove; *(Astron)* Jupiter.

giovedì [dʒove'di] *sm inv* Thursday; *per uso vedi* **martedì**.

giovenca, che [dʒo'venka] *sf* heifer.

giovenco, chi [dʒo'venko] *sm* young ox.

gioventù [dʒoven'tu] *sf* **(a)** *(gen)* youth; **errori di** ~ errors of youth; **in** ~ in one's youth, in one's younger days. **(b)** *(persone)* young (people); **la** ~ **del giorno d'oggi** today's youth, young people today; **libri per la** ~ books for the young.

gioviale [dʒo'vjale] *ag* jolly, jovial.

giovialità [dʒovjali'ta] *sf* jollity, joviality.

giovinastro [dʒovi'nastro] *sm* young thug.

giovincello [dʒovin'tʃello] *sm* young lad.

giovinezza [dʒovi'nettsa] *sf (gen)* youth; *(di spirito)* youthfulness; **godersi la** ~ to enjoy one's youth.

girabile [dʒi'rabile] *ag (cambiale, assegno)* endorsable.

giradischi [dʒira'diski] *sm inv* record player.

giraffa [dʒi'raffa] *sf (Zool)* giraffe; *(TV, Cine, Radio)* boom.

giramento [dʒira'mento] *sm*: ~ **di testa** fit of dizziness; **mi è venuto un** ~ **di testa** I feel dizzy.

giramondo [dʒira'mondo] *sm/f inv* globetrotter.

girandola [dʒi'randola] *sf (fuochi artificiali)* Catherine wheel; *(giocattolo)* toy windmill; *(banderuola)* weathervane, weathercock.

girante [dʒi'rante] *sm/f (chi gira un assegno)* endorser.

girare [dʒi'rare] **1** *vt* **(a)** *(ruota, chiave, sguardo)* to turn; *(pagina)* to turn (over); **ha girato la testa dall'altra parte** he looked the other way; ~ **l'angolo** to turn the corner; **ha girato la domanda al presidente** he referred the question to the president; **non** ~ **il discorso** don't change the subject; **girala come ti pare** *(fig)* look at it whichever way you like.

(b) *(museo, città, negozio)* to go round; **ha girato il mondo** he has travelled the world; **ho girato tutta Londra per trovarlo** I searched all over London for it.

(c) *(cambiale, assegno)* to endorse.

(d) *(Cine, TV: scena)* to shoot, film; *(: film: fare le riprese)* to shoot; *(: esserne il regista)* to make.

2 *vi* **(a)** *(gen)* to turn; *(trottola)* to spin; *(ruota)* to revolve; *(tassametro)* to tick away; ~ **su se stesso** *(persona)* to turn around on o.s.; *(: rapidamente)* to spin round; **la terra gira intorno al proprio asse** the earth rotates around its axis; **continuavano a** ~ **intorno allo stesso argomento** they continued to talk round the matter; **gli gira intorno da mesi** she's been hanging round him for months; **la strada gira intorno al lago** the road runs round the lake.

(b) *(errare)* to go round, wander round; ~ **per i negozi** to go *o* wander round the shops.

(c) *(voltare)* to turn; **giri subito a destra** take the first turning on the right.

(d) *(denaro, notizie)* to circulate; **girano troppi drogati** there are too many drug addicts about.

(e) *(fraseologia)*: **mi gira la testa** I feel dizzy, my head's spinning; **quella ragazza fa** ~ **la testa a tutti** that girl is a real show stopper; **gira al** ~**!** keep your distance!; **gira e rigira...** after a lot of driving *(o walking)* about...; *(fig)* whichever way you look at it...; **cosa ti gira?** *(fam)* what's got into you?; **mi ha fatto** ~ **le scatole** *(fam)* he drove me round the bend.

3: ~**rsi** *vr (voltarsi)* to turn (round); *(: nel letto)* to turn over; **si girava e rigirava nel letto** he tossed and turned in bed; **non so più da che parte girarmi** *(fig)* I don't know which way to turn.

girarrosto [dʒirar'rosto] *sm (Culin)* spit.

girasole [dʒira'sole] *sm* sunflower.

girata [dʒi'rata] *sf (di cambiale, assegno)* endorsement.

giratario, a [dʒira'tarjo] *sm/f* endorsee.

giravolta [dʒira'volta] *sf* turn, twirl; *(di strada)* sharp bend; *(fig)* about-face, about-turn.

girellare [dʒirel'lare] *vi* to wander about, stroll about.

girello [dʒi'rello] *sm* **(a)** *(di bambino)* Babywalker®. **(b)** *(taglio di carne)* topside.

giretto [dʒi'retto] *sm (passeggiata)* walk, stroll; *(: in macchina)* drive, spin; *(: in bicicletta)* ride.

girevole [dʒi'revole] *ag (sedia)* swivel *attr; (porta, piattaforma)* revolving.

girino [dʒi'rino] *sm* tadpole.

giro ['dʒiro] *sm* **(a)** *(circuito, cerchio)* circle; *(di manovella, chiave)* turn; *(Tecn)* revolution; **compiere un intero ~** to go full circle; **un ~ di vite a** turn of the screw; **dare un ~ di vite** *(fig)* to put the screws on, put pressure on; **un ~ di parole** *(fig)* a circumlocution; **essere giù di ~i** *(fig)* to be depressed; **essere su di ~i** *(fig)* to be on top of the world; **~ d'affari** *(Comm)* turnover.

(b) *(passeggiata)* walk, stroll; *(: in macchina)* drive, spin; *(: in bicicletta, a cavallo)* ride; *(viaggio)* tour, trip; *(percorso intorno a)*: **fare il ~ di** *(parco, città)* to go round; **abbiamo dovuto fare un ~ intorno all'isolato** we had to go round the block; **abbiamo dovuto fare un lungo ~** we had to take the long way round; **abbiamo fatto un ~ in campagna** we went for a walk *(o* a drive *o* a ride) in the country; **~ turistico della città** sightseeing tour of the city; **fare il ~ del mondo** to go round the world; **~ d'ispezione** tour of inspection; **il medico sta facendo il ~ dei malati** the doctor is doing his rounds.

(c) *(Sport: di pista)* lap; *(Carte)* hand; **sono al primo ~** they are on the first lap; **~ d'onore** lap of honour; **~ di Francia** Tour de France.

(d) *(di parte del corpo)* measurement; **~ vita** waist measurement; **~ manica** sleeve seam.

(e) *(di tempo)*: **nel ~ di** in the course of; **a ~ di posta** by return of post.

(f) *(cerchia, ambiente)*: **non ti preoccupare, è del nostro ~** don't worry, he's one of us; **essere nel *o* del ~** to be one of a circle; **entrare in un ~** to become one of a set; **essere fuori dal ~** to be no longer part of a set.

(g): **in ~**: **guardarsi in ~** to look around; **andare in ~** to wander about; **sono stato in ~ tutto il giorno** I've been on the go all day; **non trovo la penna, ma dev'essere in ~** I can't find my pen, but it must be around somewhere; **prendere in ~ qn** to pull sb's leg, take sb for a ride; **lascia sempre tutto in ~** she always leaves everything lying about; **mettere in ~** *(voci, denaro)* to circulate; **c'è parecchio denaro falso in ~** there is a lot of counterfeit money in circulation; **c'è molta droga in ~** there are a lot of drugs around.

girocollo [dʒiro'kollo] *sm*: **a ~** crewneck.

giroconto [dʒiro'konto] *sm (Fin)* giro credit transfer.

girone [dʒi'rone] *sm* **(a)** *(dantesco)* circle. **(b)** *(Sport)* series of games; **~ di andata/ritorno** first/second half of the season.

gironzolare [dʒirondzo'lare] *vi* to wander about, stroll about; **~ intorno a qn** *(peg: importunare)* to hang around sb.

giroscopio [dʒiros'kɔpjo] *sm* gyroscope.

girotondo [dʒiro'tondo] *sm* ring-a-ring-o' roses; **in ~** in a circle.

girovagare [dʒirova'gare] *vi* to wander about.

girovago, a, ghi, ghe [dʒi'rovago] **1** *ag* wandering, strolling; **vita ~a** itinerant life. **2** *sm/f (vagabondo)* tramp; *(venditore)* pedlar; **una compagnia di ~i** a company of strolling actors.

gita ['dʒita] *sf* trip, outing; **fare una ~, andare in ~** to go for a trip, go on an outing; **~ in barca** boat trip.

gitano, a [dʒi'tano] *ag, sm/f* gypsy.

gitante [dʒi'tante] *sm/f* member of a tour.

giù [dʒu] *av* **(a)** *(gen)* down; *(dabbasso)* downstairs; **è sceso ~ in giardino** he's gone down to the garden; **scese ~ per le scale** he came down the stairs; **è ~ in cantina** he's down in the cellar; **scendi ~ dal tavolo!** get down off the table!; **mi tiri ~ quella scatola?** can you get that box down for me?; **vieni ~ un minuto** come down a minute; **è venuto ~ il tetto** the roof came down; **veniva ~ un'acqua!** it was pouring with rain!; **fagli mettere ~ quel libro** make him put that book down; **due isolati più in ~** two blocks further down; **la mia casa è un po' più in ~** my house is a bit further on; **cadere a testa in ~** to fall head first; **vai ~ di là** go down that way.

(b) *(al di sotto di)* below; **gli studenti dai vent'anni in ~** students under twenty, students below twenty years of age; **dal 10 in ~** up to 10; **ce n'erano 30 o ~ di lì** there were about 30, there were 30 or thereabouts.

(c) *(nelle esclamazioni)*: **~!** down!; **~ le mani!** hands off!; **~ di lì!** get down from there!; **e ~ botte!** and the fists flew!

(d) *(fraseologia)*: **essere ~** *(persona: di morale)* to be depressed; *(: di salute)* to be run down; **quel tipo non mi va ~** I can't stand that bloke; **non riesco a mandarla ~** *(fig)* it really sticks in my throat; **buttare ~** *vedi* buttare.

giubba ['dʒubba] *sf* jacket.

giubbetto [dʒub'betto] *sm* short jacket.

giubbone [dʒub'bone] *sm* heavy jacket.

giubbotto [dʒub'bɔtto] *sm* jerkin; **~ salvagente** life jacket.

giubilare [dʒubi'lare] *vi* to rejoice.

giubileo [dʒubi'lɛo] *sm* jubilee.

giubilo ['dʒubilo] *sm* rejoicing; **grida fpl di ~** shouts of joy.

giuda ['dʒuda] *sm inv* Judas, traitor.

giudaico, a, ci, che [dʒu'daiko] *ag* Jewish.

giudaismo [dʒuda'izmo] *sm* Judaism.

giudeo, a [dʒu'dɛo] **1** *ag* Jewish. **2** *sm/f* Jew.

giudicare [dʒudi'kare] **1** *vt* **(a)** *(Dir: causa)* to judge; *(: lite)* to arbitrate in; *(: accusato)*: **~ (per)** to try (for); **l'hanno giudicato e l'hanno trovato colpevole** they tried him and found him guilty; **l'hanno giudicato colpevole** they found him guilty; **il caso verrà giudicato il prossimo anno** the case will be heard next year. **(b)** *(valutare)* to judge; **non giudicarla con tanta severità** don't be so severe in your judgment of her; **~ qn abile alla leva/idoneo ad un lavoro** to judge sb fit for military service/suitable for a job; **fai presto a ~!** it's easy for you to judge!; **sta a voi ~** it's up to you to decide *o* judge. **(c)** *(stimare)*: **~ qn capace di fare qc** to consider sb able to do sth; **anche se mi giudicherai pazzo** even though you think I'm mad; **~ qn bene/male** to think well/badly of sb; **~ opportuno fare** to consider it advisable to do.

2 *vi (dare un giudizio)*: **~ di** to judge; **se devo ~ in base alla mia esperienza** judging by my experience; **a ~ da ciò che dice** judging by what he says; **~ dalle apparenze** to judge *o* go by appearances.

giudicato [dʒudi'kato] *sm (Dir)*: **passare in ~** to pass final judgment.

giudicatore, trice [dʒudika'tore] *ag* judging; **comitato ~** panel of judges; **commissione ~trice** examining board.

giudice ['dʒuditʃe] *sm (gen)* judge; **~ collegiale** member of the court; **~ conciliatore** magistrate, justice of the peace; **~ istruttore** examining magistrate; **~ popolare** member of a jury; **farsi ~ o erigersi a ~ di qc** to set o.s. up as a judge of sth.

giudiziale [dʒudit'tsjale] *ag* judicial.

giudiziario, a [dʒudit'tsjarjo] *ag* legal, judicial.

giudizio [dʒu'dittsjo] *sm* **(a)** *(opinione)* judgment, opinion; **dare** *o* **esprimere un** ~ **su qn/qc** to express an opinion on sb/sth; **non vorrei esprimere un** ~ **troppo affrettato** I wouldn't like to pass judgment, I wouldn't like to judge too hastily; **a** ~ **di qn** in sb's opinion; **chiedere il** ~ **di qn** to ask sb's opinion. **(b)** *(discernimento)* judgment; **essere privo di** ~ to lack judgment; **l'età del** ~ the age of reason; **denti del** ~ wisdom teeth; **fai** ~! be good! **(c)** *(Dir: processo)* trial; *(: verdetto)* sentence; *(: in processi civili)* decision; **essere in attesa di** ~ to be awaiting trial; **l'imputato è stato rinviato a** ~ the accused has been committed for trial; **citare in** ~ to summons. **(d)** *(Rel)* judgment.

giudizioso, a [dʒudit'tʃoso] *ag* judicious.

giuggiola ['dʒuddʒola] *sf*: **andare in brodo di** ~**e** *(fam)* to be over the moon.

giugno ['dʒuɲɲo] *sm* June; *per uso vedi* **luglio**.

giugulare [dʒugu'lare] *ag* jugular.

giulivo, a [dʒu'livo] *ag* merry.

giullare [dʒul'lare] *sm (Storia)* jester.

giumenta [dʒu'menta] *sf* mare.

giumento [dʒu'mento] *sm* pack animal.

giunco, chi ['dʒunko] *sm (Bot)* rush.

giungere ['dʒundʒere] **1** *vi (aus essere)*: ~ **a** to arrive at, reach; ~ **all'orecchio di qn** to come to sb's attention *o* notice; ~ **nuovo a qn** to come as news to sb; ~ **alla meta** to achieve one's aim; ~ **in porto** to reach harbour; *(fig)* to be brought to a successful outcome. **2** *vt (unire)* to join.

giungla ['dʒungla] *sf* jungle.

giunta¹ ['dʒunta] *sf* **(a)** *(Anat)* joint; *(punto in cui due cose si uniscono)* join. **(b)** addition; **questa gonna è troppo corta, dovrò fare una** ~ this skirt is too short, I'll have to add a piece of material; **per** ~ what's more.

giunta² ['dʒunta] *sf (Amm)* council, board; *(Mil)* junta.

giuntare [dʒun'tare] *vt* to join.

giunto, a ['dʒunto] **1** *pp di* **giungere**. **2** *sm (Tecn)* coupling, joint; ~ **cardanico** universal joint; ~ **elastico** flexible joint.

giuntura [dʒun'tura] *sf* **(a)** *(Cucitura)* seam. **(b)** *(Anat)* joint.

giunzione [dʒun'tsjone] *sf (Tecn)* joint; *(Elettr)* junction.

giuoco ['dʒwɔko] *etc* = **gioco** *etc*.

giuramento [dʒura'mento] *sm* oath; **fare** *o* **prestare un** ~ to take an oath; **venir meno a un** ~ to break an oath.

giurare [dʒu'rare] **1** *vt* to swear; ~ **su qc** to swear on sth; ~ **su qn** to swear by sb; ~ **di fare qc** to swear to do sth; ~ **fedeltà a qn** to swear *o* pledge loyalty to sb; ~ **il falso** to commit perjury; **ti giuro che non ne posso più** I swear I've had more than I can take; **giurerei di averlo visto prima** I would swear I had seen him somewhere before; **io non ci giurerei sopra** I wouldn't swear to it; **gliel'ho giurata** I swore I would get even with him. **2** *vi* to swear, take an oath.

giurato, a [dʒu'rato] **1** *ag* sworn; **nemico** ~ sworn enemy. **2** *sm/f* juror, juryman/woman.

giureconsulto [dʒurekon'sulto] *sm* jurist.

giuri [dʒu'ri] *sm inv (letterario)* jury.

giuria [dʒu'ria] *sf (Dir)* jury; *(di gara, concorso)* (panel of) judges.

giuridico, a, ci, che [dʒu'ridiko] *ag* legal.

giurisdizione [dʒurizdit'tsjone] *sf* jurisdiction.

giurisprudenza [dʒurispru'dentsa] *sf* jurisprudence.

giurista, i, e [dʒu'rista] *sm/f* jurist.

giustapporre [dʒustap'porre] *vt* to juxtapose.

giustapposizione [dʒustappozit'tsjone] *sf* juxtaposition.

giustapposto, a [dʒustap'posto] *pp di* **giustapporre**.

giustezza [dʒus'tettsa] *sf* **(a)** *(di calcoli)* accuracy; *(di ragionamento)* soundness; *(di osservazione)* aptness. **(b)** *(Tip)* justification.

giustificabile [dʒustifi'kabile] *ag* justifiable.

giustificare [dʒustifi'kare] **1** *vt (gen)* to justify; *(Amm: spese)* to account for; **il fine giustifica i mezzi** the end justifies the means; **posso giustificarlo** I can understand why he did it; ~ **il proprio ritardo** to justify one's lateness. **2**: ~**rsi** *vr*: ~**rsi di** *o* **per qc** to justify *o* excuse o.s. for (doing) sth.

giustificativo, a [dʒustifika'tivo] *ag (Amm)*: **nota** *o* **pezza** ~**a** receipt.

giustificazione [dʒustifikat'tsjone] *sf (spiegazione)* justification, explanation; *(prova)* proof; *(Scol)* excuse note.

giustizia [dʒus'tittsja] *sf* **(a)** *(gen)* justice; **render** ~ **a qn** to do sb justice; **farsi** ~ **(da sé)** *(vendicarsi)* to take the law into one's own hands; **con** ~ justly, with justice. **(b)** *(autorità)* law; **ricorrere alla** ~ to have recourse to the law; **affidarsi alla** ~ to give o.s. up.

giustiziare [dʒustit'tsjare] *vt* to execute.

giustiziere [dʒustit'tsjere] *sm* executioner.

giusto, a ['dʒusto] **1** *ag* **(a)** *(persona, sentenza)* just, fair; **per essere** ~ **verso di lui** *o* **nei suoi confronti** in fairness to him, to be fair to him; **non mi sembra** ~ it doesn't seem fair to me; **il** ~ **prezzo** the right price; **il** ~ **mezzo** the happy medium. **(b)** *(calcolo, risposta)* right, correct; *(ragionamento)* sound; *(osservazione)* apt; *(misura, peso, ora)* correct, exact; **tre ore** ~**e** exactly three hours; **queste scarpe mi sono un po'** ~**e** these shoes are a bit tight on me; ~ **di sale** with enough *o* the right amount of salt; ~ **di cottura** well-cooked.

2 *sm* righteous person; **i** ~**i** the just; *(Rel)* the righteous.

3 *av* **(a)** *(proprio)* just, exactly; **volevo** ~ **te** you're just *o* exactly the person I wanted; **saranno state** ~ **le quattro quando mi sono svegliato** it must have been exactly four o'clock when I woke up; **ho finito** ~ **adesso** I've only just finished; **è andato via** ~ **adesso** he's just left; ~**!** right!, of course!; *(a proposito)* that reminds me!; ~ **a me dovevi dare questo lavoro?** why did you have to give this work to me? **(b)** *(rispondere, capire)* correctly; *(indovinare)* rightly; **mirare** ~ to aim straight.

glabro, a ['glabro] *ag* hairless.

glaciale [gla'tʃale] *ag* icy, freezing; *(fig)* icy, frosty; **periodo** ~ *(Geol)* glacial period, Ice Age.

glaciazione [glatʃat'tsjone] *sf* glaciation.

gladiatore [gladja'tore] *sm* gladiator.

gladiolo [gla'diolo] *sm* gladiolus.

glande ['glande] *sm (Anat)* glans.

glandola ['glandola] *sf* = **ghiandola**.

glassa ['glassa] *sf (Culin)* icing.

glassare [glas'sare] *vt (Culin)* to ice.

gli¹ [ʎi] *art det mpl vedi* **il**.

gli² [ʎi] *pron pers* **(a)** *(a lui)* (to) him; *(a esso: riferito ad animale)* (to) it, (to) him; **dagli qualcosa da mangiare** *(persona)* give him something to eat; *(animale)* give it something to eat. **(b)** *(in coppia con lo, la, li, le, ne: a lui, a lei, a loro, a esso etc)*: **dagliela** give it to him *(o her o* them); **glieli hai promessi** you promised them to him *(o her o* them); **glielo ha detto** he told him *(o her o* them); **gliele ha spedite** he sent them to him *(o her o* them); **gliene ho parlato** I spoke to him (o her o them) about it.

glicerina [glitʃe'rina] sf glycerine.

glicine ['glitʃine] sm wistaria.

gliela ['ʎela] etc vedi **gli**[2].

globale [glo'bale] ag (gen) overall, inclusive; (spesa, reddito) total; (vista) global.

globo ['glɔbo] sm globe; ~ **oculare** eyeball; **il** ~ **terrestre** the globe.

globulare [globu'lare] ag (sferico) globular; (Anat) corpuscular.

globulo ['glɔbulo] sm globule; (Anat) corpuscle.

gloria ['glɔrja] sf (a) (fama) glory, fame; (Rel) glory; **coprirsi di** ~ to cover o.s. in glory; **lavorare per la** ~ to work for the glory of it. (b) (vanto) pride; **farsi** ~ **di qc** to pride o.s. on sth, take pride in sth.

gloriarsi [glo'rjarsi] vr: ~ **di qc** to pride o.s. on sth, glory o take pride in sth.

glorificare [glorifi'kare] vt to glorify.

glorificazione [glorifikat'tsjone] sf glorification.

glorioso, a [glo'rjoso] ag glorious.

glossa ['glɔssa] sf gloss.

glossario [glos'sarjo] sm glossary.

glottologia [glottolo'dʒia] sf linguistics sg.

glucosio [glu'kɔzjo] sm glucose.

glutammato [glutam'mato] sm: ~ **monosodico** monosodium glutamate.

gluteo ['gluteo] sm gluteus (T); ~**i** pl buttocks.

gnocco, chi ['ɲɔkko] sm (a) (Culin) small dumpling made of potato or semolina. (b) (fig fam) dolt, idiot.

gnomo ['ɲɔmo] sm gnome.

gnorri ['ɲɔrri] sm/f inv: **non fare lo** ~! stop acting as if you didn't know anything about it!

gnu [ɲu] sm, inv gnu.

goal ['goul] sm inv (Sport) goal.

gobba ['gɔbba] sf (Anat, Zool) hump; (di terreno, naso) bump.

gobbo, a ['gɔbbo] **1** ag (che ha una gobba) hunchbacked; (ricurvo) bent. **2** sm/f hunchback.

goccia, ce ['gottʃa] sf (gen) drop; (di sudore) bead; ~ **a** ~ drop by drop; ~ **di rugiada** dewdrop; **le prime** ~**ce di pioggia** the first drops o spots of rain; ~**ce per il naso/gli occhi** nose/eyedrops; **vuoi ancora una** ~ **di caffè?** would you like another drop o spot of coffee?; **orecchini a** ~ drop earrings; **somigliarsi come due** ~**ce d'acqua** to be as like as two peas in a pod; **avere la** ~ **al naso** to have a runny nose; **è la** ~ **che fa traboccare il vaso!** it's the last straw!

goccio ['gottʃo] sm drop, spot; **vuoi un** ~ **di vino?** would you like some wine?

gocciolare [gottʃo'lare] **1** vi to drip; **mi gocciola il naso** I have got a runny nose; **l'acqua gocciola dal rubinetto, il rubinetto gocciola** the tap's dripping; **l'acqua gocciola dal soffitto** there's water coming in through the ceiling. **2** vb impers to drizzle.

gocciolatoio [gottʃola'tojo] sm (Archit) dripstone.

gocciolio [gottʃo'lio] sm dripping.

godere [go'dere] **1** vt (gustare: pace, fresco) to enjoy; (: bene, rendita) to enjoy, benefit from; ~**rsi il sole** to soak up the sun; **godersela** to enjoy o.s.; **si è goduta sua suocera per due mesi** (iro) she put up with her mother-in-law for two months. **2** vi (a) (essere felice): ~ **di** to enjoy, rejoice at o in; ~ **nel fare qc** to enjoy o delight in doing sth; ~ **delle disgrazie altrui** to take pleasure in other people's misfortunes; ~ **della compagnia di qn** to enjoy sb's company; ~ **all'idea che...** to rejoice at the thought of.... (b) (possedere): ~ **di** (buona salute, reputazione) to enjoy;

~ **di riduzioni speciali** to benefit from special reductions.

godimento [godi'mento] sm (a) (piacere) pleasure, enjoyment. (b) (Dir) enjoyment, possession.

goffaggine [gof'faddʒine] sf clumsiness.

goffo, a ['gɔffo] ag (persona, gesto) clumsy, awkward; (vestito) inelegant.

gogna ['gɔɲɲa] sf pillory; **mettere qn alla** ~ (anche fig) to pillory sb.

go-kart ['gou kaːt] sm inv go-kart.

gol [gɔl] sm inv = **goal**.

gola ['gola] sf (a) (Anat) throat; **avere mal di** ~ to have a sore throat; **tagliare la** ~ **a qn** to cut sb's throat; **ricacciare il pianto** o **le lacrime in** ~ to swallow one's tears; **mettere il coltello alla** ~ **di qn** (fig) to hold a pistol to sb's head. (b) (golosità) gluttony, greed; **fare** ~ **a qn** to tempt sb. (c) (di montagna) gorge.

goletta [go'letta] sf (Naut) schooner.

golf[1] [gɔlf] sm (sport) golf.

golf[2] [gɔlf] sm inv jumper; (con bottoni) cardigan.

golfo ['golfo] sm gulf.

goliardico, a, ci, che [go'ljardiko] ag (canto, vita) student attr.

gollismo [gol'lizmo] sm Gaullism.

gollista, i, e [gol'lista] ag, sm/f Gaullist.

golosità [golosi'ta] sf inv greed, gluttony; **un tavolo pieno di** ~ a table laden with titbits.

goloso, a [go'loso] ag: ~ **(di)** greedy (for).

golpe ['golpe] sm inv (Pol) coup.

golpista, i, e [gol'pista] sm/f leader of a coup.

gomena ['gomena] sf (Naut) hawser.

gomitata [gomi'tata] sf: **dare una** ~ **a qn** to elbow sb; **farsi avanti a (forza o furia di)** ~**e** to elbow one's way through; **fare a** ~**e per qc** to fight to get sth.

gomito ['gomito] sm (Anat) elbow; (di tubatura, strada) bend; **a** ~ (tubo, giunto) L-shaped; ~ **a** ~ shoulder to shoulder; **alzare il** ~ (fig) to drink too much.

gomitolo [go'mitolo] sm (di lana, filo) ball.

gomma ['gomma] sf (a) (sostanza) gum; (: caucciù) rubber; (per cancellare) rubber, eraser; ~ **arabica** gum arabic; ~ **da masticare** chewing gum. (b) (pneumatico) tyre; **avere una** ~ **a terra** to have a flat tyre; ~ **rigenerata** (Aut) remould.

gommapiuma [gomma'pjuma] sf ® foam rubber.

gommare [gom'mare] vt to rubberize.

gommato, a [gom'mato] ag (tela) rubberized; (carta) gummed; **nastro** ~ adhesive tape.

gommino [gom'mino] sm (gen) rubber tip; (rondella) rubber washer.

gommista, i, e [gom'mista] sm/f tyre specialist.

gommone [gom'mone] sm rubber dinghy.

gommoso, a [gom'moso] ag rubbery.

gondola ['gondola] sf gondola.

gondoliere [gondo'ljɛre] sm gondolier.

gonfalone [gonfa'lone] sm (Storia) banner.

gonfiare [gon'fjare] **1** vt (a) (palloncino) to inflate, blow up; (: con una pompa) to inflate, pump up; (le guance) to puff out, blow out. (b) (fiume, vele) to swell; **la birra mi gonfia lo stomaco** beer makes me feel bloated. (c) (fig: notizia, fatto) to exaggerate. **2**: ~**rsi** vr (gen) to swell (up); (fiume) to rise.

gonfio, a ['gonfjo] ag (a) (occhi, piedi) swollen; (fiume) swollen, full; (stile) bombastic, wordy; ~ **di orgoglio** (persona) puffed up (with pride); **aveva il cuore** ~ (di dolore) her heart was heavy; **occhi** ~**i di pianto** eyes swollen with tears; **mi sento** ~ I feel bloated; **avere il portafoglio** ~ to have a bulging wallet. (b) (palloncino, gomme) inflated, blown up; (con pompa) pumped up.

gonfiore [gon'fjore] *sm* swelling.

gong [gɔŋg] *sm inv* gong.

gongolare [gongo'lare] *vi*: ~ **(per)** to look pleased with o.s. (about).

gonna ['gonna] *sf* skirt; ~ **pantalone** culottes *pl*; **stare attaccato alle** ~**e della madre** to cling to one's mother's apron strings.

gonzo ['gondzo] *sm* simpleton, dolt.

gorgheggiare [gorged'dʒare] *vi (uccello)* to warble.

gorgheggio [gor'geddʒo] *sm (Mus, di uccello)* trill.

gorgo, ghi ['gorgo] *sm* whirlpool; **essere preso nel** ~ **della passione** to be in the grip of passion.

gorgogliare [gorgoʎ'ʎare] *vi* to gurgle.

gorgoglio[1] [gor'goʎʎo] *sm* gurgle.

gorgoglio[2] [gorgoʎ'ʎio] *sm* gurgling.

gorgonzola [gorgon'dzɔla] *sm inv* gorgonzola.

gorilla [go'rilla] *sm inv* **(a)** *(Zool)* gorilla. **(b)** *(fig: guardia del corpo)* bodyguard.

gotico, a, ci, che ['gɔtiko] *ag, sm* Gothic.

gotta ['gotta] *sf* gout.

governante[1] [gover'nante] *sm* ruler.

governante[2] [gover'nante] *sf (donna di servizio)* housekeeper; *(di bambini)* governess.

governare [gover'nare] *vt* **(a)** *(stato, nazione)* to govern, rule. **(b)** *(barca, nave)* to steer; *(polli, mucche etc)* to look after, tend.

governativo, a [governa'tivo] *ag (politica, decreto)* government *attr*, governmental; *(stampa)* pro-government.

governatore, trice [governa'tore] *sm/f* governor.

governo [go'vɛrno] *sm (regime)* government; *(gabinetto)* Cabinet, Government; **crisi di** ~ Government crisis; ~ **ponte** caretaker government; **il partito al** ~ the party in power *o* in office.

gozzo ['gottso] *sm (Zool)* crop; *(Med)* goitre; *(fig fam)* throat; **restare sul** ~ *(fig)* to stick in one's throat; **se hai qualcosa sul** ~ **sarà meglio che parli** if something is bothering you, you'd better spit it out.

gozzovigliare [gottsoviʎ'ʎare] *vi* to make merry, carouse.

gracchiare [grak'kjare] *vi (cornacchia)* to caw, croak; *(telefono, radio)* to crackle; *(fig: persona)* to croak.

gracchio ['grakkjo] *sm* caw, croak.

gracidare [gratʃi'dare] *vi (rana)* to croak.

gracidio, ii [gratʃi'dio] *sm* croaking.

gracile ['gratʃile] *ag (persona, costituzione)* delicate; *(braccia, gambe)* slender, thin.

gracilità [gratʃili'ta] *sf (di persona)* delicateness.

gradasso [gra'dasso] *sm* braggart, boaster; **che** ~! what a loudmouth!

gradatamente [gradata'mente] *av* gradually, by degrees.

gradazione [gradat'tsjone] *sf* gradation; ~ **alcolica** alcoholic content *o* strength.

gradevole [gra'devole] *ag* agreeable, pleasant.

gradimento [gradi'mento] *sm* pleasure, satisfaction; **essere di mio** *(o* **tuo** *etc)* ~ to be to my *(o* your *etc)* taste.

gradinata [gradi'nata] *sf (scalinata)* (flight of) steps *pl*; *(di stadio)* terracing.

gradino [gra'dino] *sm (gen)* step; *(Alpinismo)* foothold; **'attenti al gradino'** 'mind the step'; **è salito di un** ~ **nella carriera** he has taken a step forward in his career; **è l'ultimo** ~ **della scala sociale** that's the bottom rung of the social ladder.

gradire [gra'dire] *vt* **(a)** *(accogliere, ricevere con piacere)* to accept (with pleasure); **ho gradito la sua visita** I enjoyed your visit; ~ **un dono/un**

invito to accept a gift/an invitation with pleasure; ... **tanto per** ~ ...I wouldn't like to refuse; **gradisca i miei omaggi** please accept my best wishes. **(b)** *(frm: desiderare)* to like, want; **gradisce un caffè?** would you like a coffee?; **gradirei avere un po' di pace** *(iro)* I should like some peace and quiet.

gradito, a [gra'dito] *ag* welcome.

grado[1] ['grado] *sm*: **di buon** ~ willingly.

grado[2] ['grado] *sm* **(a)** *(gen)* degree; *(livello)* degree, level; **per** ~**i** by degrees; **un cugino di primo/secondo** ~ a first/second cousin; **essere in** ~ **di** to be able to; **subire il terzo** ~ *(anche fig)* to be given the third degree. **(b)** *(Mil, sociale)* rank; **salire di** ~ to be promoted; **perdere i** ~**i** to lose one's stripes.

graduale [gradu'ale] *ag* gradual.

gradualità [graduali'ta] *sf* gradualness.

graduare [gradu'are] *vt (scala, termometro)* to graduate.

graduato, a [gradu'ato] **1** *ag (scala, termometro)* graduated. **2** *sm (Mil)* non-commissioned officer.

graduatoria [gradua'tɔrja] *sf (di concorso)* list; *(per la promozione)* order of seniority.

graduazione [graduat'tsjone] *sf* graduation.

graffa ['graffa] *sf (Tip: parentesi)* brace; *(punto metallico)* staple.

graffetta [graf'fetta] *sf* clip.

graffiare [graf'fjare] *vt* to scratch.

graffiatura [graffja'tura] *sf* scratch.

graffio ['graffjo] *sm* scratch.

graffiti [graf'fiti] *smpl* graffiti.

grafia [gra'fia] *sf (di parola)* spelling; *(scrittura)* handwriting.

grafica ['grafika] *sf* graphic arts *pl*.

grafico, a, ci, che ['grafiko] **1** *ag* graphic. **2** *sm* **(a)** *(diagramma)* graph. **(b)** *(disegnatore)* commercial artist; ~ **industriale** draughtsman.

grafite [gra'fite] *sf (minerale)* graphite.

gramaglie [gra'maʎʎe] *sfpl*: **in** ~ in mourning.

gramigna [gra'miɲɲa] *sf (Bot)* couch grass; *(erbaccia)* weed.

graminacee [grami'natʃee] *sfpl (Bot)* grasses.

grammatica, che [gram'matika] *sf* grammar; **un errore di** ~ a grammatical error; **libro di** ~ grammar book.

grammaticale [grammati'kale] *ag* grammatical.

grammo ['grammo] *sm* gram(me).

grammofono [gram'mɔfono] *sm* gramophone.

gramo, a ['gramo] *ag (vita)* wretched.

gran [gran] *ag vedi* **grande**.

grana[1] ['grana] *sf* grain; **di** ~ **grossa** coarse-grained.

grana[2] ['grana] *sf (fam: seccatura)* trouble; **avere delle** ~**e** to have problems; **piantare** ~**e** to stir up trouble.

grana[3] ['grana] *sm* cheese similar to Parmesan.

grana[4] ['grana] *sf (fam)* cash; **essere pieno di** ~ to be rolling in it, be stinking rich.

granaglie [gra'naʎʎe] *sfpl* corn *sg*, seed *sg*; **commerciante di** ~ corn *o* seed merchant.

granaio [gra'najo] *sm* barn, granary.

granata[1] [gra'nata] *sf (Mil)* grenade.

granata[2] [gra'nata] *sf (Bot)* pomegranate.

granatiere [grana'tjɛre] *sm (Mil)* grenadier; *(fig)* fine figure of a man.

granato [gra'nato] *sm (pietra preziosa)* garnet.

Gran Bretagna [granbre'taɲɲa] *sf* Great Britain.

grancassa [gran'kassa] *sf (Mus)* bass drum.

granchio ['grankjo] *sm (Zool)* crab; *(fig: errore)* blunder; **pigliare un** ~ *(fig)* to blunder.

grandangolo [gran'dangolo] *sm (Fot)* wide-angle lens.

grande ['grande] **1** *ag (qualche volta* **gran** + *consonante,* **grand'** + *vocale)* **(a)** *(gen)* big; *(quantità)* large; *(alto)* tall; *(: montagna)* high; *(largo)* wide, broad; *(lungo)* long; *(forte: rumore)* loud; *(: vento)* strong, high; *(: pioggia)* heavy; *(: caldo)* intense; *(: affetto, bisogno)* great; *(: sospiro)* deep; **un ragazzo ~ e grosso** a big strong boy; **una taglia più ~** a larger *o* bigger size; **è ~ per la sua età** he's big for his age; **la ~ maggioranza degli Italiani** the great *o* vast majority of Italians; **il gran pubblico** the general public; **un ~ invalido** a seriously disabled person.

(b) *(di età):* **mio fratello più ~** my big *o* older brother; **è più ~ di me** he's older than me; **sei abbastanza ~ per capire** you're big *o* old enough to understand; **farsi ~** to grow up; **hanno due figli ~i** they have two grown-up children.

(c) *(importante, rilevante)* great; *(illustre, nobile)* noble, great; **un ~ poeta/musicista** a great poet/musician; **le ~i potenze** *(Pol)* the major powers; **è arrivato il gran giorno** the great day dawned; **ha fatto ~i spese!** he's been spending his money!; **è un gran ~** he's a real gentleman.

(d) *(rafforzativo: lavoratore)* hard; *(: bevitore)* heavy; *(: amico, bugiardo)* great; **è un gran cretino** he's an utter fool; **ha fatto una gran risata** he laughed loudly; **è una gran bella donna** she's a very beautiful woman; **una gran bella vita** a great life; **di gran classe** *(prodotto)* high-class; **una donna di gran classe** a woman with class; **oggi fa un gran freddo/caldo** it's extremely cold/hot today; **con mia ~ sorpresa** to my great surprise; **per sua ~ fortuna non c'era la polizia** he was really lucky that the police weren't around; **la famiglia al gran completo** the entire family.

(e) *(fraseologia):* **non ne so (un) gran che** I don't know very much about it; **non è** *o* **non vale (un) gran che** it *(o* he *etc)* is nothing special, it *(o* he *etc)* is not up to much; **quel quadro non è poi (una) gran cosa** that painting's nothing special; **in gran parte** to a large extent, mainly; **ha una ~ opinione di sé** he has a high opinion of himself; **ti farà un gran bene** it'll do you good; **non ci ho fatto gran caso** I didn't really notice; **fare le cose in ~** to do things on a grand scale.

2 *sm/f* **(a)** *(persona adulta)* adult, grown-up; **cosa farai da ~?** what will you be *o* do when you grow up?

(b) *(persona importante)* great man/woman; **i quattro G~i** *(Pol)* the Big Four; **fare il ~** *(strafare)* to act big.

(c): **Pietro** *etc* **il G~** Peter *etc* the Great.

grandeggiare [granded'dʒare] *vi* **(a):** **~ (su)** to tower (over). **(b)** *(darsi arie)* to put on airs, give o.s. airs.

grandezza [gran'dettsa] *sf* **(a)** *(dimensione)* size; *(Astron)* magnitude; *(Mat, Fis)* quantity; **di media ~** of average size; **a** *o* **in ~ naturale** life-size(d). **(b)** *(fig: qualità)* greatness; **~ d'animo** nobility of soul. **(c)** *(fasto)* grandeur; **manie di ~** delusions of grandeur.

grandinare [grandi'nare] **1** *vb impers* to hail. **2** *vi (aus essere) (fig: bombe, proiettili)* to hail down.

grandine ['grandine] *sf* hail; **un chicco di ~** a hailstone.

grandiosità [grandjosi'ta] *sf* grandeur, magnificence.

grandioso, a [gran'djoso] *ag* grandiose, magnificent; **dalle idee ~e** with grandiose ideas; **avere un'idea ~a** to have a great idea.

granduca, chi [gran'duka] *sm* grand duke.

granducato [grandu'kato] *sm* grand duchy.

granduchessa [grandu'kessa] *sf* grand duchess.

granello [gra'nello] *sm (di sabbia, sale)* grain; *(di polvere)* speck; **un ~ di pepe** a peppercorn; **un ~ di fantasia/pazzia** *(fig)* a touch of fantasy/madness.

granita [gra'nita] *sf* kind of water ice.

granitico, a, ci, che [gra'nitiko] *ag (roccia)* granite *attr; (fig: fede)* rock-like.

granito [gra'nito] *sm* granite.

grano ['grano] *sm* **(a)** *(Bot)* grain. **(b)** *(chicco: gen)* grain; *(: di rosario)* bead; **un ~ di pepe** a peppercorn; **pepe in ~i** peppercorns.

granturco [gran'turko] *sm (Bot)* maize; **pannocchia di ~** corncob.

granulare [granu'lare] *ag* granular.

granulo ['granulo] *sm* granule.

granuloso, a [granu'loso] *ag* granular.

grappa ['grappa] *sf* grappa.

grappolo ['grappolo] *sm* bunch; **un ~ d'uva** a bunch of grapes.

grassetto [gras'setto] *sm (Tip)* bold (type).

grassezza [gras'settsa] *sf* fatness, stoutness.

grasso, a ['grasso] **1** *ag* **(a)** *(gen)* fat; *(cibo)* fatty; *(pelle, capelli)* greasy; *(terreno)* rich, fertile; **cucina ~a** oily cooking; **formaggio ~** full fat cheese; **un'annata ~a** *(Agr)* a good year; **pianta ~a** a succulent plant. **(b)** *(volgare)* lewd, coarse; **una ~a risata** a coarse laugh. **2** *sm (adipe, Culin)* fat; *(unto)* grease; **~ per cucinare** cooking fat; **~ (per lubrificare)** (lubricating) grease; **~ di balena** blubber.

grassoccio, a, ci, ce [gras'sɔttʃo] *ag* plump, podgy.

grassone, a [gras'sone] *sm/f (fam: persona)* dumpling.

grata ['grata] *sf* grating.

graticcio, ci [gra'tittʃo] *sm* trellis; *(stuoia)* mat.

graticola [gra'tikola] *sf (Culin)* grill.

gratifica, che [gra'tifika] *sf* bonus.

gratificare [gratifi'kare] *vt (fig):* **questo lavoro non mi gratifica, non mi sento gratificato in questo lavoro** I don't find this job rewarding; **~ qn di un sorriso** to give sb a smile.

gratificazione [gratifikat'tsjone] *sf (soddisfazione)* satisfaction, reward.

gratin [gra'tɛ̃] *sm inv (Culin):* **al ~** au gratin.

gratinare [grati'nare] *vt (Culin)* to cook au gratin.

gratis ['gratis] *av (viaggiare)* free; *(lavorare)* for nothing; **biglietto ~** free ticket; **ingresso ~** admission free.

gratitudine [grati'tudine] *sf* gratitude.

grato, a ['grato] *ag (riconoscente)* grateful; **ti sono molto ~** I am very grateful to you.

grattacapo [gratta'kapo] *sm* worry, headache.

grattacielo [gratta'tʃɛlo] *sm* skyscraper.

grattare [grat'tare] **1** *vt* **(a)** to scratch; **~ via** *(vernice etc)* to scrape off; **~rsi la testa** to scratch one's head; **~rsi la pancia** *(fig)* to twiddle one's thumbs; **~ il violino** *(fam)* to scrape on the violin. **(b)** *(grattugiare)* to grate. **(c)** *(fam: rubare)* to pinch, nick. **2** *vi (stridere)* to grate; *(Aut: marcia)* to grind. **3:** **~rsi** *vr* to scratch (o.s.).

grattata [grat'tata] *sf* **(a)** *(alla testa etc)* scratch; **darsi una ~ alla testa** to scratch one's head. **(b)** *(Aut fam):* **fare una ~** to grind the gears.

grattugia, gie [grat'tudʒa] *sf* grater.

grattugiare [grattu'dʒare] *vt* to grate; **pane grattugiato** breadcrumbs.

gratuità [gratui'ta] *sf (fig)* gratuitousness.

gratuito, a [gra'tuito] *ag* **(a)** *(gratis)* free. **(b)** *(fig: critiche, commenti)* gratuitous, uncalled-for.

gravame [gra'vame] *sm:* **~ fiscale** tax.

gravare [gra'vare] **1** *vt:* **~ di** *(responsabilità, impo-*

ste) to burden with. **2** *vi (aus* **essere**): ~ **su** to weigh on, lie heavy on.

grave ['grave] **1** *ag* **(a)** *(suono, voce)* deep, low-pitched; *(fig: pericolo, errore)* grave, serious; *(: responsabilità)* heavy, grave; *(: contegno)* grave, solemn; **un malato** ~ a seriously ill patient; **non è** ~ it's not serious. **(b)** *(Gram)*: **accento** ~ grave accent. **2** *sm (Fis)* (heavy) body.

gravidanza [gravi'dantsa] *sf* pregnancy.

gravido, a ['gravido] *ag* pregnant; ~ **di minaccia** *(fig)* fraught with *o* full of menace.

gravità [gravi'ta] *sf* **(a)** *(di errore, situazione, malattia)* seriousness, gravity; *(di comportamento, occasione)* solemnity, gravity; *(di punizione)* severity. **(b)** *(Fis)* gravity.

gravitare [gravi'tare] *vi (Fis):* ~ **intorno a** to gravitate round; *(fig):* ~ **verso** to gravitate towards.

gravitazionale [gravitattsjo'nale] *ag (Fis)* gravitational.

gravitazione [gravitat'tsjone] *sf (Fis)* gravitation.

gravoso, a [gra'voso] *ag (tasso, imposta)* heavy, onerous; **un compito** ~ a hard *o* onerous task.

grazia ['grattsja] *sf* **(a)** *(bellezza: di persona)* grace; **piena di** ~ graceful; **muoversi con** ~ to move gracefully; **di buona/mala** ~ with good/bad grace. **(b)** *(favore, benevolenza)* favour; **entrare nelle ~ e di qn** to win sb's favour; **essere nelle ~ e di qn** to be in sb's good graces *o* books; **mi ha fatto la** ~ **di accettare il mio invito** he did me the honour of accepting my invitation; **di** ~ *(iro)* if you please; **troppa** ~! *(iro)* you're too generous! **(c)** *(misericordia, Dir)* pardon; **concedere la** ~ to pardon; **ottenere la** ~ to be pardoned; **Ministero di G~ e Giustizia** Ministry of Justice, ≃ Lord Chancellor's Office *(Brit)*, Department of Justice *(Am)*. **(d)** *(Rel)* grace; **quanta** ~ **di Dio!** what abundance! **(e)** *(Mitologia):* **le tre G~e** the three Graces. **(f)** *(titolo):* **Sua G~** Your Grace.

graziare [grat'tsjare] *vt (Dir)* to pardon.

grazie ['grattsje] **1** *sm inv* thank you; **non ho avuto neanche un** ~ I did not get a word of thanks; **dille un** ~ **da parte mia** thank her for me. **2** *escl* thank you!, thanks!; **vuole un caffè?** — **(sì)** ~/**no** ~ would you like some coffee? — yes, please/ no, thank you; **hai trovato i libri?** — **sì** ~ did you find the books? — yes, thanks; **mille** *o* **tante** ~! many thanks!; **Marco non è mai stanco** — ~ **al cavolo** *o* ~ **tante, lui non fa mai niente!** Marco is never tired — and neither he should be, given that he never does a thing! **3:** ~ **a** *prep* thanks to.

grazioso, a [grat'tsjoso] *ag (piacevole)* delightful; *(gentile)* kind.

greca ['greka] *sf* (Greek) fret.

Grecia ['gretʃa] *sf* Greece.

greco, a, ci, che ['greko] *ag, sm/f, sm* Greek.

gregario, a [gre'garjo] **1** *ag (Bot, Zool)* gregarious. **2** *sm (ciclismo)* supporting rider; *(Pol)* follower, supporter.

gregge ['greddʒe] *sm, pl(f)* ~**i** *(gen, fig)* flock.

greggio, a, gi, ge ['greddʒo] **1** *ag (materia)* raw, unrefined; *(petrolio)* crude; *(diamante)* rough, uncut; *(cuoio)* untanned, untreated; *(tessuto)* unbleached. **2** *sm* crude oil.

gregoriano [grego'rjano] *ag* Gregorian.

grembiule [grem'bjule] *sm* apron; *(sopravveste)* overall.

grembo ['grembo] *sm* **(a)** *(ginocchia)* lap; **tenere qn in** ~ to have sb on one's knee *o* in one's arms. **(b)** *(ventre materno)* womb; **in** ~ **alla famiglia** in the bosom of one's family.

gremito, a [gre'mito] *ag:* ~ **di** crammed with, packed with.

greppia ['greppja] *sf* manger.

greto ['greto] *sm* (exposed) gravel bed of a river.

grettezza [gret'tettsa] *sf (vedi ag)* pettiness; meanness, stinginess; ~ **d'animo** narrow-mindedness.

gretto, a ['gretto] *ag* **(a)** *(meschino)* petty, narrow-minded. **(b)** *(avaro)* mean, stingy.

greve ['greve] *ag* heavy.

grezzo, a ['greddzo] *ag* = **greggio.**

gridare [gri'dare] **1** *vi (gen)* to shout, cry (out); *(strillare)* to scream, yell; *(animale)* to call; **smettila di** ~! stop shouting!; ~ **a squarciagola** to yell at the top of one's voice; ~ **di dolore** to cry out *o* scream out in pain. **2** *vt* to shout, yell; ~ **aiuto** to cry *o* shout for help; ~ **qc ai quattro venti** to shout *o* cry sth from the rooftops; ~ **vendetta** to cry out for vengeance.

grido ['grido] *sm, pl(f)* ~**a** *(gen)* shout, cry; *(strillo)* scream, yell; *(di animale: pl(m)* ~**i**) cry; **un** ~ **di dolore** a cry of pain; **un** ~ **di aiuto** a cry for help; **emettere** ~ **a di gioia** to shout for joy; **un cantante di** ~ *(fig)* a famous singer; **è l'ultimo** ~ **(della moda)** it's the latest fashion; **vestito all'ultimo** ~ dressed in the latest style.

grigiastro, a [gri'dʒastro] *ag* greyish.

grigio, a, gi, gie ['gridʒo] **1** *ag* grey; *(fig)* dull, boring; **materia** ~**a** grey matter. **2** *sm* grey.

grigioverde [gridʒo'verde] *ag* grey-green.

griglia ['griʎʎa] *sf* **(a)** *(di stufa, focolare)* grate; *(di apertura)* grating. **(b)** *(Culin)* grill; **alla** ~ grilled. **(c)** *(Aut)* grille.

grilletto [gril'letto] *sm* trigger; **premere il** ~ to pull the trigger.

grillo ['grillo] *sm (Zool)* cricket; **gli è saltato il** ~ **di...** he's taken it into his head to...; **ha dei** ~**i per la testa** his head is full of nonsense.

grimaldello [grimal'dello] *sm* picklock.

grinfia ['grinfja] *sf:* **cadere nelle** ~**e di qn** *(fig)* to fall into sb's clutches.

grinta ['grinta] *sf (di persona)* determination; **avere molta** ~ to be very determined; **una macchina che ha** ~ a car with aggressive acceleration.

grinza ['grintsa] *sf (di pelle)* wrinkle; *(di stoffa)* wrinkle, crease; **il tuo ragionamento non fa una** ~ your argument is faultless.

grinzoso, a [grin'tsoso] *ag (vedi sf)* wrinkled; creased.

grippare [grip'pare] *vi,* ~**rsi** *vr (Tecn)* to seize up, jam.

grisou [gri'zu] *sm* firedamp.

grissino [gris'sino] *sm* bread-stick.

Groenlandia [groen'landja] *sf* Greenland.

gronda ['gronda] *sf* eaves *pl.*

grondaia [gron'daja] *sf* gutter.

grondante [gron'dante] *ag* dripping; **un impermeabile** ~ **di pioggia** a soaking wet *o* dripping raincoat; ~ **di sudore** bathed in *o* dripping with sweat.

grondare [gron'dare] **1** *vi (aus* **essere**) to pour; **il sudore gli grondava dalla fronte** the sweat was pouring down his face. **2** *vt* to drip with.

groppa ['grɔppa] *sf (di quadrupede)* back, rump; *(fam: di persona)* back, shoulders *pl;* **salire in** ~ **a un cavallo** to mount a horse; **mi è rimasta tutta la merce sulla** ~ I've been left with all those goods on my hands; **ha un bel po' di anni sulla** ~ she's getting on a bit.

groppo ['groppo] *sm (groviglio)* tangle; **avere un** ~ **alla gola** *(fig)* to have a lump in one's throat.

groppone [grop'pone] *sm (scherz: di persona)* = **groppa.**

gros-grain [gro'grɛ̃] sm (nastro) petersham.

grossezza [gros'settsa] sf (dimensione) size; (spessore) thickness.

grossista, i, e [gros'sista] sm/f (Comm) wholesaler.

grosso, a ['grɔsso] **1** ag **(a)** (gen) big, large; (spesso) thick; (pesante) heavy. **(b)** (fig: errore, rischio) serious, great; (: patrimonio) large; (: tempo, mare) rough; **un pezzo** ~ **a** VIP, a bigwig; **un** ~ **industriale** a business magnate. **(c)** (non raffinato: sale etc, anche fig) coarse. **(d)** (fraseologia): **avere il fiato** ~ to be short of breath; **fare la voce** ~**a** to raise one's voice; **farla** ~**a** to do something very stupid; **questa volta l'hai fatta** ~**a!** now you've done it!; **dirla** o **spararla** ~**a** to tell tall stories o shoot a line; **sbagliarsi di** ~ to be completely wrong o mistaken; **questa è** ~**a!** that's a good one!; **dormire della** ~**a** to sleep like a log; ~ **modo** = **grossomodo**.

2 sm: **il** ~ **del lavoro è fatto** the bulk o the main part of the work is over; **il** ~ **dell'esercito** the main body of the army.

grossolanità [grossolani'ta] sf coarseness.

grossolano, a [grosso'lano] ag (gen) coarse; (lavoro) roughly done; (linguaggio) coarse, crude; (errore) stupid, gross.

grossomodo [grosso'mɔdo] av roughly.

grotta ['grɔtta] sf cave.

grottesco, a, schi, sche [grot'tesko] **1** ag grotesque. **2** sm: **il suo atteggiamento ha del** ~ his attitude is somewhat ridiculous.

groviera [gro'vjɛra] sf gruyère (cheese).

groviglio [gro'viʎʎo] sm (di fili, lana) tangle; (fig: di idee) muddle.

gru [gru] sf inv (Zool, Tecn) crane.

gruccia, ce ['gruttʃa] sf **(a)** (stampella) crutch. **(b)** (per abiti) coathanger.

grufolare [grufo'lare] vi to root about.

grugnire [gruɲ'ɲire] **1** vi (maiale) to grunt; (fig: persona) to grumble, growl. **2** vt to mutter, growl out.

grugnito [gruɲ'ɲito] sm grunt.

grugno ['gruɲɲo] sm (di maiale) snout; (fam: faccia) mug; **rompere il** ~ **a qn** to smash sb's face in.

grullaggine [grul'laddʒine] sf stupidity.

grullo, a ['grullo] **1** ag stupid, silly. **2** sm/f fool, idiot.

grumo ['grumo] sm (di sangue, latte etc) clot; (di farina, sale etc) lump.

grumoso, a [gru'moso] ag lumpy.

gruppetto [grup'petto] sm small group.

gruppo ['gruppo] sm **(a)** group; **suddividere in** ~**i di 10** to divide into groups of 10; **arrivare a** ~**i di 3** to arrive in groups of 3 o in threes; ~ **sanguigno** blood group; **un** ~ **di turisti** a group o party of tourists; **un** ~ **letterario** a literary circle o group; ~ **elettrogeno** generating set. **(b)** (Ciclismo) pack.

gruviera [gru'vjɛra] sf = **groviera**.

gruzzolo ['gruttsolo] sm (di denaro) hoard; **ha messo da parte un bel** ~ he has saved a fair bit.

guadagnare [gwadaɲ'ɲare] **1** vt **(a)** (stipendio, percentuale: anche fig) to earn; ~**rsi la vita/il pane** to earn one's living/one's bread and butter. **(b)** (fig: conquistare) to win; ~ **la fiducia/l'affetto di qn** to win sb's confidence/affection. **(c)** (ottenere) to gain; ~ **tempo** (temporeggiare) to gain time; (risparmiare) to save time; ~ **terreno** (Mil, fig) to gain ground; **che cosa ci guadagni a fare così?** what will you gain by doing that?; **tanto di guadagnato!** so much the better! **2** vi: **con quel vestito ci guadagna** that dress does a lot for her.

guadagno [gwa'daɲɲo] sm **(a)** earnings pl; (Comm) profit; ~ **lordo/netto** gross/net earnings;

fare grossi ~**i** to earn a packet; (Comm) to make a large profit. **(b)** (fig: vantaggio) advantage, gain.

guadare [gwa'dare] vt to ford.

guado ['gwado] sm ford; **passare a** ~ to ford.

guai [gwai] escl: ~ **a te** (o lui etc)! woe betide you (o him etc)!; **se non lo fai subito** ~! there will be trouble if you don't do it straight away!

guaina [gwa'ina] sf **(a)** (fodero) sheath. **(b)** (busto) girdle.

guaio ['gwajo] sm trouble, difficulty; (inconveniente) trouble, snag; **essere nei** ~**i** to be in trouble o in a mess; **mettersi** o **ficcarsi nei** ~**i** (fam) to get into trouble o into a spot of bother; **andare a caccia di** ~**i** (fam) to go looking for trouble; **il** ~ **è che...** the trouble o snag is that... .

guaire [gwa'ire] vi (cane) to yelp, whine; (persona) to whine.

guaito [gwa'ito] sm (di cane) yelp, whine; (il guaire) yelping, whining.

gualdrappa [gwal'drappa] sf (di cavallo) caparison.

guancia, ce ['gwantʃa] sf cheek; **porgere l'altra** ~ to turn the other cheek.

guanciale [gwan'tʃale] sm pillow; **dormire fra due** ~**i** (fig) to sleep easy, have no worries.

guanto ['gwanto] sm glove; **un paio di** ~**i** a pair of gloves; **trattare qn con i** ~**i** (fig) to handle sb with kid gloves; **gettare/raccogliere il** ~ to throw down/take up the gauntlet.

guantone [gwan'tone] sm boxing glove.

guardaboschi [gwarda'bɔski] sm inv forester.

guardacaccia [gwarda'kattʃa] sm inv gamekeeper.

guardacoste [gwarda'kɔste] sm inv (persona) coastguard; (nave) coastguard patrol vessel.

guardalinee [gwarda'linee] sm inv (Sport) linesman.

guardare [gwar'dare] **1** vt **(a)** (oggetto, paesaggio) to look at; (persona, cosa in movimento) to watch; ~ **la televisione** to watch television; ~ **dalla finestra** to look out of the window; **guarda un po' lì** (cerca) take a look over there; **ma guarda un po'**! good heavens!; **guarda chi c'è** o **chi si vede! look who's here!; **e guarda caso...** as if by coincidence... .

(b) (rapidamente) to glance at; (a lungo) to gaze at; ~ **di sfuggita** to steal a glance at; ~ **con diffidenza** to look warily at; ~ **di traverso** to scowl o frown at; ~ **fisso** to stare at; ~ **qc di buon/mal occhio** to look on o view sth favourably/unfavourably; ~ **qn dall'alto in basso** to look down on sb; ~ **qn in faccia** to look sb in the face; **non** ~ **in faccia a nessuno** (fig) to have no regard for anybody.

(c) (esaminare) to (have a) look at, check; ~ **una parola sul dizionario** to look up o check a word in the dictionary.

(d) (custodire) to look after; (proteggere) to guard; ~ **qn a vista** (prigioniero) to keep a close watch on sb; **chi guarda i bambini?** who is looking after the children?; **i soldati guardano il ponte** the soldiers are guarding the bridge; **Dio me ne guardi!** God forbid!

2 vi **(a)**: ~ **di** to try to; **guarda di non arrivare in ritardo** try not to be late.

(b) (badare): ~ **a** to mind, be careful about; **comprare qc senza** ~ **a spese** to buy sth without worrying about the expense; **per il matrimonio di sua figlia non ha guardato a spese** he spared no expense when his daughter got married.

(c) (essere rivolto): ~ **a** to face; ~ **su** to give o look onto.

3: ~**rsi** vr **(a)** (in vetrina, specchio) to look at

o.s.; **~rsi allo specchio** to look at o.s. in the mirror.
(b) *(uso reciproco)* to look at each other.
(c): **~rsi da** *(astenersi da)* to refrain from; *(stare in guardia)* to be wary of; **~rsi dal fare qc** to take care o be careful not to do sth.

guardaroba [gwarda'rɔba] *sm inv* **(a)** *(armadio)* wardrobe. **(b)** *(locale)* cloakroom.

guardarobiera [gwardaro'bjɛra] *sf* **(a)** *(in albergo, grande casa)* housekeeper. **(b)** *(in locale pubblico)* cloakroom attendant.

guardasigilli [gwardasi'dʒilli] *sm inv (Storia)* keeper of the seals.

guardia ['gwardja] **1** *sf* **(a)** *(individuo, corpo)* guard; **il cambio della ~** the changing of the guard; **essere della vecchia ~** to be one of the old guard; **giocare a ~e e ladri** to play cops and robbers.
(b) *(sorveglianza: gen, Naut)* watch; *(Mil: servizio)* guard duty, sentry duty; **lasciare qn a ~ di qc** to leave sb to look after o to keep an eye on sth, to leave sth in sb's care; **fare la ~ a qn/qc** to guard sb/sth; **essere di ~** to be on duty; **il medico di ~** the doctor on call; **il fiume ha raggiunto il livello di ~** the river has reached the high-water mark; **cane da ~** guard dog.
(c) *(Pugilato, Scherma)* guard; *(di spada)* hilt; **in ~!** on guard!; **mettersi in ~** to take one's guard; **mettere qn in ~ contro** *(fig)* to put sb on his guard against.
2: ~ del corpo bodyguard; **~ forestale** forest ranger; **~ giurata** security guard; **~ medica** emergency doctor service; **~ notturna** night security guard; **~ di pubblica sicurezza** policeman.

guardiano [gwar'djano] *sm (di carcere)* warder; *(di villa etc)* caretaker; *(di museo)* custodian; *(di faro)* keeper; **~ dei porci** swineherd; **un ~ notturno** a night watchman.

guardina [gwar'dina] *sf* cell.

guardingo, a, ghi, ghe [gwar'dingo] *ag* wary, cautious.

guardrail ['gaːdreil] *sm inv* guardrail.

guaribile [gwa'ribile] *ag* curable.

guarigione [gwari'dʒone] *sf* recovery; **essere in via di ~** to be on the way o road to recovery.

guarire [gwa'rire] **1** *vt (anche fig)* to cure; *(ferita)* to heal; **~ qn da qc** to cure sb of sth. **2** *vi (aus essere) (persona)* to recover; *(ferita)* to heal (up); **è guarito dal vizio del fumo** he is cured of smoking.

guaritore, trice [gwari'tore] *sm/f* healer.

guarnigione [gwarni'dʒone] *sf (Mil)* garrison.

guarnire [gwar'nire] *vt (ornare: abiti)* to trim; *(: Culin)* to garnish.

guarnizione [gwarnit'tsjone] *sf* **(a)** *(vedi vb)* trimming; garnish. **(b)** *(Aut)* gasket.

guastafeste [gwasta'fɛste] *sm/f inv* spoilsport.

guastare [gwas'tare] **1** *vt (danneggiare: gen)* to spoil, ruin; *(: meccanismo)* to break; *(: cibo)* to spoil. **2: ~rsi** *vr (meccanismo)* to break down; *(cibo)* to go bad, go off; *(tempo, persona)* to change for the worse.

guasto, a ['gwasto] **1** *ag* **(a)** *(non funzionante: gen)* broken; *(: telefono, distributore)* out of order. **(b)** *(andato a male)* bad, rotten; *(: dente)* decayed, bad; *(fig: corrotto)* depraved. **2** *sm (rottura completa)* breakdown; *(avaria)* failure; **~ al motore** engine failure.

guazza ['gwattsa] *sf* heavy dew.

guazzabuglio [gwattsa'buʎʎo] *sm* muddle, confusion.

guazzo ['gwattso] *sm (Pittura)* gouache.

guercio, a, ci, ce ['gwertʃo] **1** *ag* cross-eyed. **2** *sm/f* cross-eyed person.

guerra ['gwɛrra] *sf (conflitto)* war; *(tecnica bellica)* warfare; **corrispondente di ~** war correspondent; **~ fredda/mondiale** cold/world war; **in ~ con** at war with o against; **fare la ~ (a)** to wage war (against); **essere sul piede di ~** to be on a war footing; **ha fatto la Iª guerra mondiale** he fought in World War I; **sembra che abbia fatto la ~** *(fig)* it looks as if it has been through the wars; **tra di loro ormai c'è la ~ aperta** there is open war between them now.

guerrafondaio [gwerrafon'dajo] *sm* warmonger.

guerreggiare [gwerred'dʒare] *vi:* **~ (contro)** to wage war (on, against).

guerresco, a, schi, sche [gwer'resko] *ag (di guerra)* war *attr*; *(bellicoso)* warlike.

guerriero, a [gwer'rjɛro] **1** *ag* warlike. **2** *sm* warrior.

guerriglia [gwer'riʎʎa] *sf* guerrilla warfare.

guerrigliero, a [gwerriʎ'ʎɛro] *sm/f* guerrilla.

gufo ['gufo] *sm* owl.

guglia ['guʎʎa] *sf (Archit)* spire; *(di roccia)* needle.

gugliata [guʎ'ʎata] *sf* length of thread.

guida ['gwida] *sf* **(a)** *(manuale)* guide, manual; **~ telefonica** telephone directory. **(b)** *(capo)* guide; *(direzione)* guidance, direction; **sotto la ~ di qn** with sb's guidance; **essere alla ~ di** *(governo)* to head; *(spedizione, paese)* to lead; **far da ~ a qn** *(mostrare la strada)* to show sb the way; *(in una città)* to show sb round. **(c)** *(Aut)* driving; **~ a destra/sinistra** right-hand/left-hand drive; **lezioni/patente di ~** driving lessons/licence; **posto di ~** driving seat. **(d)** *(tappeto)* runner; *(Tecn)* runner, guide. **(e)** *(scout)* girl guide.

guidare [gwi'dare] *vt* **(a)** *(gen)* to guide; *(capeggiare)* to lead; **lasciarsi ~ dal proprio istinto** to let o.s. be guided by one's instincts; **~ qn sulla retta via** *(fig)* to steer sb in the right direction; **~ una spedizione** to lead an expedition; **~ la classifica** *(Sport)* to head the table. **(b)** *(Aut)* to drive; **~ bene/male** to drive well/badly.

guidatore, trice [gwida'tore] *sm/f* driver.

guinzaglio [gwin'tsaʎʎo] *sm* lead, leash; **tenere qn al ~** *(fig)* to keep sb on a tight rein.

guisa ['gwisa] *sf* manner, way; **a ~ di** like, in the manner of; **in tal ~** in such a way.

guizzante [gwit'tsante] *ag (luce, fiamma)* flickering; *(pesce)* darting, flashing.

guizzare [gwit'tsare] *vi* **(a)** *(pesce, serpente)* to dart; *(fiamma)* to flicker. **(b)** *(aus essere) (fuggire, balzare)*: **guizzò in piedi** he leapt to his feet; **mi guizzò via dalle mani** it leapt o slipped out of my hands; **il ladro riuscì a ~ via** the thief managed to slip away.

guizzo ['gwittso] *sm (di animale)* dart; *(di fulmine)* flash.

guru ['guru] *sm inv* guru.

guscio ['guʃʃo] *sm* shell; **uscire dal proprio ~** *(fig)* to come out of one's shell; **chiudersi nel proprio ~** *(fig)* to retreat into one's shell; **~ di noce** nut-shell; *(fig: barca)* cockleshell.

gustare [gus'tare] *vt* **(a)** *(assaggiare)* to taste. **(b)** *(assaporare)* to enjoy, savour; *(fig: apprezzare)* to enjoy, appreciate.

gustativo, a [gusta'tivo] *ag:* **papille fpl ~e** taste buds.

gusto ['gusto] *sm* **(a)** *(senso)* taste; *(sapore)* taste, flavour; **ha un ~ amaro/di lampone** it tastes bitter/of raspberries, it has a bitter/raspberry taste; **al ~ di fragola** strawberry-flavoured; **privo di ~** tasteless, flavourless. **(b)** *(senso estetico)* taste; **con ~** tastefully; **veste con buon ~** she has very good dress sense; **di buon/cattivo** ~ in good/bad taste; **abbiamo gli stessi** ~i we like the same things, we have the same tastes; **non è di mio** ~ it is not my taste. **(c)** *(piacere)*: **fare qc di** *o* **con** ~ to do sth with pleasure; **mangiare/ridere di** ~ to eat/laugh heartily; **prendere** ~ **a qc/a fare qc** to get a taste for sth/doing sth, get to like sth/doing sth; **non c'è** ~ **a...** there's no pleasure in...; **tutti i** ~**i sono** ~i there is no accounting for taste. **(d)** *(stile)* style; **di** ~ **barocco** in the baroque style.

gustoso, a [gus'toso] *ag (piatto)* tasty; *(romanzo, commedia)* enjoyable.

gutturale [guttu'rale] *ag* guttural.

H

H, h¹ ['akka] *sf o m inv (lettera)* H, h.
h² *abbr di* **ora; altezza.**
habitat ['abitat] *sm inv (Bot, Zool)* habitat.
habitué [abi'tɥe] *sm/f inv (di locale, ristorante)* regular customer.
hall [hɔːl] *sf inv (di albergo)* hall, foyer.
handicap ['hændikap] *sm inv (Sport, fig)* handicap.
handicappato, a [andikap'pato] **1** *ag* handicapped. **2** *sm/f* handicapped person, disabled person; **gli ~i** the handicapped.
hangar [ã'gar] *sm inv (Aer)* hangar.
happening ['hæpəniŋ] *sm inv* happening.
hardware ['haːdweə] *sm inv* hardware.
hascisc [aʃ'ʃiʃ] *sm inv* hashish.
haute-couture ['otku'tyr] *sf* haute couture.
henna ['ɛnna] *sf* henna.
herpes ['ɛrpes] *sm (Med)* herpes *sg*; **~ zoster** shingles *sg*.

hi-fi ['haifai] *sm inv, ag inv* hi-fi.
hinterland ['hintərlant] *sm* hinterland.
hippy ['hipi] *ag inv, sm/f inv* hippy.
hitleriano, a [itle'rjano] **1** *ag* Hitler. **2** *sm* Hitlerite.
hobby ['hɔbi] *sm inv* hobby.
hockey ['hɔki] *sm* hockey; **~ su ghiaccio** ice hockey.
holding ['houldiŋ] *sf inv* holding company.
hollywoodiano, a [ollivu'djano] *ag* Hollywood *attr; (fig)* spectacular.
hostess ['houstis] *sf inv* air hostess.
hot dog ['hɔtdɔg] *sm inv* **(a)** *(panino)* hot dog. **(b)** *(Sport: sci acrobatico)* hot-dogging.
hotel [o'tɛl] *sm inv* hotel.
hovercraft ['hɔvəkraːft] *sm inv* hovercraft.
humour ['hjuːmə] *sm* (sense of) humour.
humus ['umus] *sm* humus.

I

I, i¹ [i] *sf o m inv (lettera)* I, i.
i² [i] *art det mpl vedi* **il.**
iato [i'ato] *sm* hiatus.
iberico, a, ci, che [i'bɛriko] *ag* Iberian.
ibernare [iber'nare] **1** *vi* to hibernate. **2** *vt (Med)* to induce hypothermia in.
ibernazione [ibernat'tsjone] *sf* hibernation.
ibrido, a ['ibrido] *ag, sm* hybrid.
iceberg ['aisbɔːg] *sm inv* iceberg.
icona [i'kɔna] *sf* icon.
iddio [id'dio] *sm* God.
idea [i'dɛa] *sf* **(a)** *(gen)* idea; **non ho la minima** ~ I haven't the faintest *o* slightest idea; **farsi un'**~ **di qc** to get an idea of sth; **non hai** ~ **di quanto sia difficile** you have no idea how difficult it is; **un'**~ **geniale** a brilliant *o* clever idea; **chissà che** ~ **gli è saltato in mente adesso?** who knows what he may have taken it into his head to do now?; **tremo solo all'**~ **che possa venire** I tremble at the very thought *o* idea of his coming; **ho** ~ **che...** I have an idea *o* feeling that...; **nemmeno per** ~ not on your life; ~ **fissa** obsession.
  (b) *(opinione)* opinion, view; **avere le** ~**e chiare** to know one's mind; **cambiare** ~ to change one's mind; **essere dell'**~ **(che)** to be of the opinion (that), think (that).
  (c) *(intenzione)*: **avere una mezza** ~ **di fare qc** to have half a mind to do sth; **la mia** ~ **era di andare al cinema** I had thought of going to the pictures.
  (d) *(ideale)* ideal; **l'**~ **del bello/della pace** the ideal of beauty/of peace.
ideale [ide'ale] **1** *ag* ideal. **2** *sm* ideal; **l'**~ **sarebbe andarsene** the ideal thing would be to leave; **il mio** ~ **di casa** my ideal home.
idealismo [idea'lizmo] *sm* idealism.
idealista, i, e [idea'lista] *sm/f* idealist.
idealistico, a, ci, che [idea'listiko] *ag* idealistic.
idealizzare [idealid'dzare] *vt* to idealize.
idealizzazione [idealiddzat'tsjone] *sf* idealization.
idealmente [ideal'mente] *av* ideally.
ideare [ide'are] *vt (escogitare: scherzo, piano)* to think up; *(congegno)* to think up, invent.
ideatore, trice [idea'tore] *sm/f* author.
ideazione [ideat'tsjone] *sf* conception.
idem ['idem] *av* idem.
identico, a, ci, che [i'dɛntiko] *ag:* ~ **(a)** identical (to); **è la stessa** ~**a cosa** it's exactly the same thing.
identificabile [identifi'kabile] *ag* identifiable.
identificare [identifi'kare] **1** *vt* to identify. **2:** ~**rsi** *vr:* ~**rsi con** to identify o.s. with.
identificazione [identifikat'tsjone] *sf* identification.
identikit [identi'kit] *sm inv* identikit; **fare l'**~ **di** to produce an identikit of.
identità [identi'ta] *sf* identity; **carta d'**~ identity card.
ideologia, gie [ideolo'dʒia] *sf* ideology.
ideologico, a, ci, che [ideo'lɔdʒiko] *ag* ideological.

idilliaco, a, ci, che [idil'liako] *ag,* **idillico, a, ci, che** [i'dilliko] *ag* idyllic.
idillio [i'dilljo] *sm* idyll; **tra di loro è nato un** ~ they have fallen in love.
idioma, i [i'djɔma] *sm* idiom, language.
idiomatico, a, ci, che [idjo'matiko] *ag* idiomatic; **frase** ~**a** idiom.
idiosincrasia [idjosinkra'zia] *sf* **(a)** *(avversione)* dislike; **avere un'**~ **per qc** to dislike sth. **(b)** *(Med)* idiosyncrasy.
idiota, i, e [i'djɔta] **1** *ag (Med)* idiotic; *(fig)* idiotic, stupid. **2** *sm/f* idiot.
idiotismo [idjo'tizmo] *sm (Med)* idiocy.
idiozia [idjot'tsia] *sf (Med)* idiocy; *(fig)* idiocy, stupidity; **è una vera** ~ it's an idiotic thing to do *(o* say).
idolatra, i, e [ido'latra] **1** *ag* idolatrous. **2** *sm/f* idolater.
idolatrare [idola'trare] *vt (divinità)* to worship; *(fig: persona)* to idolize.
idolatria [idola'tria] *sf* idolatry.
idoleggiare [idoled'dʒare] *vt* to idolize.
idolo ['idolo] *sm (Rel, fig)* idol.
idoneità [idonei'ta] *sf* suitability, fitness; **esame** *m* **di** ~ qualifying examination; **certificato d'**~ certificate of eligibility.
idoneo, a [i'dɔneo] *ag:* ~ **(a)** fit (for), suitable (for); ~ **all'insegnamento** qualified to teach; **fare qn** ~ **(al servizio militare)** to pass sb as fit for military service.
idrante [i'drante] *sm* hydrant.
idratante [idra'tante] **1** *ag (crema)* moisturizing. **2** *sm* moisturizer.
idratare [idra'tare] *vt (pelle)* to moisturize.
idratazione [idratat'tsjone] *sf (della pelle)* moisturizing, hydration.
idraulica [i'draulika] *sf* hydraulics *sg.*
idraulico, a, ci, che [i'drauliko] **1** *ag* hydraulic. **2** *sm* plumber.
idrico, a, ci, che ['idriko] *ag* water *attr.*
idrocarburo [idrokar'buro] *sm* hydrocarbon.
idrofilo, a [i'drɔfilo] *ag:* **cotone** ~ cotton wool.
idrofobia [idrofo'bia] *sf (Med)* rabies *sg.*
idrofobo, a [i'drɔfobo] *ag (fig)* furious.
idrogeno [i'drɔdʒeno] *sm* hydrogen.
idrografia [idrogra'fia] *sf* hydrography.
idrografico, a, ci, che [idro'grafiko] *ag* hydrographic.
idrolisi [i'drɔlizi] *sf* hydrolysis.
idromele [idro'mɛle] *sm* mead.
idrometro [i'drɔmetro] *sm* hydrometer.
idropisia [idropi'zia] *sf (Med)* dropsy.
idroporto [idro'porto] *sm (Aer)* seaplane base.
idrorepellente [idrorepel'lɛnte] *ag* water-repellent.
idroscalo [idros'kalo] *sm* = **idroporto.**
idrovolante [idrovo'lante] *sm* seaplane.
idrovora [i'drɔvora] *sf* water pump.
iella ['jɛlla] *sf* bad luck.
iellato, a [jel'lato] *ag* plagued by bad luck.
iena ['jɛna] *sf* hyena.

ieratico, a, ci, che [je'ratiko] *ag (Rel: scrittura)* hieratic; *(fig: atteggiamento)* solemn.

ieri ['jɛri] **1** *av* yesterday; ~ **l'altro, l'altro** ~ the day before yesterday; ~ **sera** yesterday evening, last night; **non sono nato** ~ I wasn't born yesterday. **2** *sm* yesterday; **il giornale di** ~ yesterday's paper.

iettatore, trice [jetta'tore] *sm/f* jinx; **smettila di fare lo** ~! stop trying to put a jinx on things!

iettatura [jetta'tura] *sf* evil eye; **è una** ~! there must be a jinx on me *(o you etc)*!; **essere perseguitato dalla** ~ to be dogged by misfortune.

igiene [i'dʒɛne] *sf* hygiene; ~ **del corpo** personal hygiene; **norme d'**~ sanitary regulations; ~ **pubblica** public health; **ufficio d'**~ public health authority.

igienico, a, ci, che [i'dʒɛniko] *ag (gen)* hygienic; *(salubre: clima)* healthy; **carta** ~ a toilet paper.

igienista, i, e [idʒe'nista] *sm/f* hygienist.

igloo ['iglu] *sm inv* igloo.

ignaro, a [iɲ'ɲaro] *ag:* ~ **(di)** unaware (of), ignorant (of).

ignifugo, a [iɲ'ɲifugo] *ag* flame-resistant, fireproof.

ignobile [iɲ'ɲɔbile] *ag* vile, despicable.

ignominia [iɲɲo'minja] *sf* ignominy; **questo monumento è un'**~! *(scherz)* this monument is a disgrace!

ignominioso, a [iɲɲomi'njoso] *ag* ignominious.

ignorante [iɲɲo'rante] **1** *ag* ignorant. **2** *sm/f* ignoramus; *(villano)* boor.

ignoranza [iɲɲo'rantsa] *sf* ignorance; **è di un'**~ **spaventosa** his lack of knowledge is appalling.

ignorare [iɲɲo'rare] *vt* **(a)** *(non conoscere)* to be unaware of, be ignorant of; **ignoravo che...** I was unaware that..., I was ignorant of the fact that...; **ignoravo che tu fossi qui** I was unaware *o* I didn't know that you were here. **(b)** *(trascurare)* to ignore.

ignoto, a [iɲ'ɲɔto] **1** *ag* unknown; **il Milite I**~ the Unknown Soldier. **2** *sm/f* stranger, unknown person; **figlio di** ~ i child of unknown parentage. **3** *sm:* **l'**~ the unknown.

il [il] *art det m (pl(m) i; diventa* **lo** *(pl* **gli**) *dav s impura, gn, pn, ps, x, z; f* **la** *(pl* **le**)) **(a)** *(determinazione)* the; ~ **bambino ha la febbre** the baby has a temperature; **le ragazze non sono arrivate** the girls haven't arrived; **i figli dell'architetto** the architect's children; **lo zio di Roberta** Roberta's uncle; **gli studenti del primo anno** first-year students; **l'ora di cena** dinner time.

(b) *(generalizzazione, astrazione)* gen non tradotto; **l'uomo è un animale sociale** man is a social animal; **i cavalli dormono in piedi** horses sleep on their feet; **l'oro è un metallo prezioso** gold is a precious metal; **la leucemia** leukemia; **lo zucchero è caro** sugar is dear; **mi piace la musica classica** I like classical music; **non sopporto** ~ **rumore** I can't stand noise; **la gioventù** youth; ~ **bello** the beautiful; **i poveri** the poor.

(c) *(tempo)* the *(spesso omesso)*; **siamo arrivati** ~ **lunedì di Pasqua** we arrived on Easter Monday; **la settimana prossima** next week; **l'inverno scorso** last winter; **riceve** ~ **venerdì** he sees people on Fridays *o* on a Friday; **la sera in the evening**; **verso le 6** at about 6 o'clock; **è partito** ~ **20 luglio** he left on the 20th of July *o* on July the 20th *(lingua parlata)*; he left on July 20th *(scritto)*.

(d) *(distributivo)* a, an; **costano 2000 lire** ~ **paio/chilo** they cost 2000 lire a *o* per pair/kilo; **120 km l'ora** 120 km an *o* per hour; **ne abbiamo fatto la metà** we have done half of it.

(e) *(partitivo)* some, any; **hai messo lo zucchero?** have you added sugar?; **hai comprato** ~ **pane?** did you buy (some *o* any) bread?

(f) *(possesso)*: **ha aperto gli occhi** he opened his eyes; **mi fa male la gamba** my leg is sore; **mettiti le scarpe** put your shoes on; **la madre sorrise** her mother smiled at her; **prendo** ~ **caffè senza zucchero** I take my coffee without sugar; **aver le gambe corte** to have short legs.

(g) *(con nomi propri)*: **Plinio** ~ **giovane** Pliny the Younger; ~ **Petrarca** Petrarch; ~ **Presidente Mitterrand** President Mitterrand; **sono arrivati i Martignon** the Martignons have arrived; **le sorelle Clari** the Clari sisters; **dov'è la Giovanna?** where's Giovanna?; **ma dov'è finito** ~ **Cozzi?** whatever happened to the Cozzi boy?

(h) *(con nomi geografici)*: ~ **Tevere** the Tiber; **i Pirenei** the Pyrenees; **l'Everest** Everest; **l'Italia** Italy; ~ **Regno Unito** the United Kingdom.

ilare ['ilare] *ag* cheerful.

ilarità [ilari'ta] *sf* hilarity, mirth.

illanguidire [illangwi'dire] **1** *vt* to weaken. **2** *vi (aus* **essere**) to grow weak, grow feeble.

illazione [illat'tsjone] *sf* inference, deduction.

illecito, a [il'letʃito] *ag* illicit.

illegale [ille'gale] *ag* illegal, unlawful.

illegalità [illegali'ta] *sf* illegality, unlawfulness.

illeggibile [illed'dʒibile] *ag (scrittura)* illegible; *(romanzo)* unreadable.

illegittimità [illeddʒittimi'ta] *sf* illegitimacy.

illegittimo, a [ille'dʒittimo] *ag* illegitimate.

illeso, a [il'lezo] *ag* unharmed, unhurt.

illetterato, a [illette'rato] *ag, sm/f* illiterate.

illibatezza [illiba'tettsa] *sf (di donna)* virginity.

illibato, a [illi'bato] *ag:* **donna** ~ a virgin.

illimitato, a [illimi'tato] *ag (gen)* unlimited; *(fiducia)* absolute; *(congedo, visto)* indefinite.

illividire [illivi'dire] *vi (aus* **essere**) *(volto, mani)* to turn livid; *(cielo)* to grow leaden.

illogicità [illodʒitʃi'ta] *sf* illogicality.

illogico, a, ci, che [il'lɔdʒiko] *ag* illogical.

illudere [il'ludere] **1** *vt* to deceive, fool. **2**: ~ **rsi** *vr* to deceive o.s., delude o.s.; ~ **rsi sul conto di qn** to deceive *o* delude o.s. about sb; **si illuse di poter cambiare tutto** he deceived himself into thinking he could change everything.

illuminante [illumi'nante] *ag* illuminating, enlightening.

illuminare [illumi'nare] **1** *vt* **(a)** *(strada, stanza, volto)* to light (up), illuminate; *(con riflettori)* to floodlight. **(b)** *(fig: informare)* to enlighten. **2**: ~ **rsi** *vr (stanza, volto)* to light up.

illuminato, a [illumi'nato] *ag (fig: sovrano, spirito)* enlightened.

illuminazione [illuminat'tsjone] *sf* **(a)** *(vedi vb)* lighting, illumination; floodlighting; enlightenment. **(b)** *(lampo di genio)* flash of inspiration.

illuminismo [illumi'nizmo] *sm (Storia)* Enlightenment.

illusione [illu'zjone] *sf* illusion; ~ **ottica** optical illusion; **farsi** ~ i to deceive *o* delude o.s.; **non farti** ~ i don't delude yourself, don't kid yourself *(fam)*; **ha perso ogni** ~ he has become thoroughly disillusioned.

illusionismo [illuzjo'nizmo] *sm* conjuring.

illusionista, i, e [illuzjo'nista] *sm/f* conjurer.

illuso, a [il'luzo] **1** *pp di* **illudere**. **2** *ag* deluded. **3** *sm/f*: **sei un** ~ you are suffering from delusions.

illusorio, a [illu'zɔrjo] *ag* illusory.

illustrare [illus'trare] *vt* to illustrate.

illustrativo, a [illustra'tivo] *ag* illustrative.

illustrazione [illustrat'tsjone] *sf* illustration.

illustre [il'lustre] *ag* eminent, renowned, illustrious.

illustrissimo, a [illus'trissimo] *ag (negli indirizzi)* very revered.

imbacuccare [imbakuk'kare] **1** *vt* to wrap up. **2**: ~**rsi** *vr* to wrap (o.s.) up.

imbacuccato, a [imbakuk'kato] *ag* muffled up, wrapped up.

imbaldanzire [imbaldan'tsire] **1** *vt* to give confidence to. **2**: ~**rsi** *vr* to grow bold.

imballaggio [imbal'laddʒo] *sm* **(a)** *(gen)* packing; **cassa da** ~ packing case; **carta da** ~ wrapping *o* brown paper. **(b)** *(costo)* cost of packing.

imballare[1] [imbal'lare] *vt* to pack.

imballare[2] [imbal'lare] *vt (Aut: motore)* to race.

imballatore, trice [imballa'tore] *sm/f* packer.

imbalsamare [imbalsa'mare] *vt* to embalm.

imbalsamatore, trice [imbalsama'tore] *sm/f* embalmer.

imbalsamazione [imbalsamat'tsjone] *sf* embalming.

imbambolato, a [imbambo'lato] *ag (sguardo, espressione)* vacant, blank.

imbandierare [imbandje'rare] *vt* to deck with flags.

imbandire [imban'dire] *vt*: ~ **un banchetto** to prepare a lavish feast.

imbandito, a [imban'dito] *ag*: **tavola** ~**a** lavishly *o* sumptuously decked table.

imbarazzante [imbarat'tsante] *ag* embarrassing, awkward.

imbarazzare [imbarat'tsare] **1** *vt* **(a)** *(mettere a disagio)* to embarrass. **(b)** *(ostacolare: movimenti)* to hamper; *(: stanza)* to clutter up; *(: stomaco)* to lie heavily on. **2**: ~**rsi** *vr* to become embarrassed.

imbarazzato, a [imbarat'tsato] *ag (persona)* embarrassed; **avere lo stomaco** ~ to have an upset stomach.

imbarazzo [imba'rattso] *sm* **(a)** *(disagio)* embarrassment; **essere** *o* **trovarsi in** ~ to be in an awkward situation *o* predicament; **mettere in** ~ to embarrass. **(b)** *(perplessità)* bewilderment, puzzlement; **non hai che l'**~ **della scelta** your only problem will be that you have too great a choice. **(c)** *(pesantezza)*: ~ **di stomaco** indigestion.

imbarbarimento [imbarbari'mento] *sm* barbarization.

imbarbarire [imbarba'rire] **1** *vt (costumi)* to make less civilized; *(lingua)* to barbarize. **2**: ~**rsi** *vr (costumi)* to become less civilized; *(lingua)* to become barbarized.

imbarcadero [imbarka'dɛro] *sm* landing stage.

imbarcare [imbar'kare] **1** *vt (passeggeri)* to embark; *(merci)* to load; ~ **acqua** *(Naut)* to ship water. **2**: ~**rsi** *vr* **(a)**: ~**rsi su** *(nave)* to board, embark on; *(altro veicolo)* to board; ~**rsi per l'America** to sail for America. **(b)** *(fig)*: ~**rsi in** *(affare etc)* to embark on.

imbarcazione [imbarkat'tsjone] *sf* boat, craft *pl inv*; ~ **da pesca** fishing boat.

imbarco [im'barko] *sm* **(a)** *(di persone)* embarkation, boarding; *(di merci)* loading; **carta d'**~ boarding pass. **(b)** *(luogo)* embarkation point, departure point.

imbastardire [imbastar'dire] **1** *vt* to bastardize, debase. **2**: ~**rsi** *vr* to degenerate, become debased.

imbastire [imbas'tire] *vt (Cucito)* to baste, tack; *(fig: piano)* to sketch out, outline.

imbastitura [imbasti'tura] *sf (Cucito)* tacking.

imbattersi [im'battersi] *vr*: ~ **in** *qn* to bump

into *sb*, run into *sb*.

imbattibile [imbat'tibile] *ag* unbeatable.

imbattuto, a [imbat'tuto] *ag* unbeaten.

imbavagliare [imbavaʎ'ʎare] *vt (anche fig)* to gag.

imbeccare [imbek'kare] *vt (uccelli)* to feed; *(fig)* to prompt, put words into sb's mouth.

imbeccata [imbek'kata] *sf (di uccelli)* beakful of food; *(Teatro)* prompt; **dare l'**~ **a** *qn (Teatro)* to prompt sb; *(fig)* to give sb their cue.

imbecillaggine [imbetʃil'laddʒine] *sf* stupidity, foolishness; **questa è una vera** ~ this is a really idiotic thing to do (*o* say).

imbecille [imbe'tʃille] **1** *ag (Med)* imbecilic; *(fig)* idiotic, stupid. **2** *sm/f* idiot, imbecile; **fare l'**~ to play the fool.

imbecillità [imbetʃilli'ta] *sf inv (Med, fig)* imbecility, idiocy; **dire** ~ to talk nonsense.

imbellettare [imbellet'tare] **1** *vt (viso)* to make up, put make-up on. **2**: ~**rsi** *vr* to make o.s. up, put on one's make-up.

imbellire [imbel'lire] **1** *vt* to adorn, embellish. **2**: ~**rsi** *vr* to grow more beautiful.

imberbe [im'bɛrbe] *ag* beardless; **un giovanotto** ~ a callow youth.

imbestialire [imbestja'lire] **1** *vt* to infuriate. **2**: ~**rsi** *vr* to become infuriated, fly into a rage.

imbevere [im'bevere] **1** *vt*: ~ **qc di** to soak sth in. **2**: ~**rsi** *vr (anche fig)*: ~**rsi di** to soak up, absorb.

imbevuto, a [imbe'vuto] *ag (spugna)*: ~ **(di)** soaked (in); *(fig: nozione)*: ~ **di** imbued with.

imbiancare [imbjan'kare] **1** *vt (gen)* to whiten; *(muro: con il bianco di calce)* to whitewash; *(: con qualsiasi pittura)* to paint; **sepolcro** ~ *(fig)* whited sepulchre. **2**: ~**rsi** *vr* to turn white, go white.

imbiancatura [imbjanka'tura] *sf (di muro: con bianco di calce)* whitewashing; *(: con altre pitture)* painting.

imbianchino [imbjan'kino] *sm* painter, decorator.

imbiondire [imbjon'dire] **1** *vt (capelli)* to lighten; *(Culin: cipolla)* to brown. **2** *vi*, ~**rsi** *vr (capelli)* to lighten, go blonde, go fair; *(messi)* to turn golden, ripen.

imbizzarrirsi [imbiddzar'rirsi] *vr (cavallo)* to become frisky.

imboccare [imbok'kare] *vt* **(a)** *(bambino)* to feed. **(b)** *(tromba)* to put to one's mouth. **(c)** *(entrare in: strada)* to turn into, enter.

imboccatura [imbokka'tura] *sf* **(a)** *(di grotta, galleria, fiume)* mouth; *(di strada, porto)* entrance. **(b)** *(Mus, del morso)* mouthpiece.

imbocco, chi [im'bokko] *sm (di autostrada, galleria)* entrance.

imbonitore [imboni'tore] *sm (di spettacolo, circo)* barker.

imborghesimento [imborgezi'mento] *sm* trend towards a middle-class outlook.

imborghesirsi [imborge'zirsi] *vr* to become bourgeois.

imboscare [imbos'kare] **1** *vt (nascondere)* to hide. **2**: ~**rsi** *vr (Mil)* to evade military service; **quei due si sono imboscati di nuovo** *(fig)* those two have disappeared again.

imboscata [imbos'kata] *sf* ambush; **tendere un'**~ to lay an ambush.

imboscato [imbos'kato] *sm* draft dodger *(Am)*.

imboschimento [imboski'mento] *sm* afforestation.

imboschire [imbos'kire] **1** *vt* to afforest. **2**: ~**rsi** *vr* to become wooded.

imbottigliamento [imbottiʎʎa'mento] *sm (di vino)* bottling.

imbottigliare [imbottiʎ'ʎare] **1** *vt* **(a)** *(vino)* to bottle. **(b)** *(Mil: nemico)* to hem in, bottle up;

(: *porto*) to blockade; **siamo rimasti imbottigliati** we got stuck in a traffic jam. **2**: ~**rsi** *vr* to get stuck in a traffic jam.

imbottigliatrice [imbottiʎʎa'tritʃe] *sf* bottling machine.

imbottire [imbot'tire] **1** *vt* (*sedia, cuscino*) to stuff; (*giacca*) to pad; (*panino*) to fill; **gli hanno imbottito la testa di idee strane** they filled his head with silly notions. **2**: ~**rsi** *vr* (*coprirsi*) to wrap o.s. up; (*rimpinzarsi*): ~**rsi di** to stuff o.s. with.

imbottita [imbot'tita] *sf* quilt, eiderdown.

imbottito, a [imbot'tito] *ag* (*sedia*) upholstered; (*giacca*) padded; **panino** ~ filled roll.

imbottitura [imbotti'tura] *sf* (*vedi vb*) stuffing; padding; filling.

imbracciare [imbrat'tʃare] *vt* (*fucile*) to shoulder; (*scudo*) to grasp.

imbranato, a [imbra'nato] **1** *ag* clumsy, awkward. **2** *sm/f* clumsy person.

imbrattacarte [imbratta'karte] *sm/f* (*peg*) scribbler.

imbrattare [imbrat'tare] **1** *vt*: ~ (**di**) to dirty (with), smear (with), daub (with). **2**: ~**rsi** *vr*: ~**rsi (di)** to dirty o.s. (with).

imbrattatele [imbratta'tele] *sm/f* (*peg*) dauber.

imbrigliare [imbriʎ'ʎare] *vt* (*cavallo*) to bridle; (*acque*) to dam; (*passioni*) to curb.

imbroccare [imbrok'kare] *vt* (*bersaglio*) to hit; (*fig: risposta*) to guess correctly; **non riesco mai ad imbroccarne una!** I never manage to get anything right!

imbrogliare [imbroʎ'ʎare] **1** *vt* (**a**) (*ingannare*) to cheat, deceive. (**b**) (*confondere: faccenda, documenti*) to muddle up; (: *idee*) to confuse, muddle; (: *fili*) to tangle up; ~ **le carte** to confuse the issue. (**c**) (*Naut: vele*) to clew up. **2**: ~**rsi** *vr* (*vedi vt* **b**) to become muddled up; to become confused, become muddled; to become tangled up; **s'imbrogliò nel parlare** his speech became confused.

imbroglio [im'brɔʎʎo] *sm* (**a**) (*truffa*) swindle, cheat; **questo affare è un** ~ this business is a swindle; **niente** ~**i!** no cheating! (**b**) (*groviglio*) tangle; (*fig: situazione difficile*) mess; **cacciarsi in un** ~ to get into a mess.

imbroglione [imbroʎ'ʎone] *sm* cheat, swindler.

imbronciarsi [imbron'tʃarsi] *vr* (*persona*) to sulk; (*cielo*) to cloud over.

imbronciato, a [imbron'tʃato] *ag* (*persona*) sulky; (*cielo*) cloudy, threatening.

imbrunire [imbru'nire] **1** (*aus essere*) *vi, vb impers*, ~**rsi** *vr* to grow dark. **2** *sm*: **all'**~ at dusk.

imbruttire [imbrut'tire] **1** *vt* to make ugly. **2** *vi* (*aus essere*) to become ugly.

imbucare [imbu'kare] *vt* to post, mail (*Am*).

imburrare [imbur'rare] *vt* to butter.

imbutiforme [imbuti'forme] *ag* funnel-shaped.

imbuto [im'buto] *sm* funnel.

imene [i'mɛne] *sm* hymen.

imitare [imi'tare] *vt* (*gen*) to imitate; (*Teatro*) to impersonate; (*gesti*) to mimic; (*firma*) to forge.

imitativo, a [imita'tivo] *ag* imitative.

imitatore, trice [imita'tore] *sm/f* (*gen*) imitator; (*Teatro*) impersonator, impressionist.

imitazione [imitat'tsjone] *sf* (*vedi vb*) imitation; impersonation, impression; mimicry; forgery.

immacolato, a [immako'lato] *ag* immaculate, spotless; **l'I**~**a Concezione** (*Rel*) the Immaculate Conception.

immagazzinare [immagaddzi'nare] *vt* (*merce, energia*) to store; (*nozioni, idee*) to accumulate.

immaginabile [immadʒi'nabile] *ag* conceivable, imaginable.

immaginare [immadʒi'nare] *vt* (**a**) (*credere, supporre*) to imagine; ~ **che** to imagine *o* think that; **me lo immaginavo più giovane** I imagined him to be younger; **me lo immaginavo** I thought as much; **me lo sarei dovuto** ~ I should have expected it. (**b**) (*in espressioni di cortesia*): **s'immagini!** don't mention it!, not at all!

immaginario, a [immadʒi'narjo] *ag* imaginary; (*mondo*) make-believe.

immaginativa [immadʒina'tiva] *sf* imagination; **mancare d'**~ to lack imagination.

immaginativo, a [immadʒina'tivo] *ag* imaginative.

immaginazione [immadʒinat'tsjone] *sf* imagination; **è frutto della tua** ~ it's a figment of your imagination.

immagine [im'madʒine] *sf* (*gen, Fis*) image; (*rappresentazione, fotografia*) picture; **è l'**~ **della salute** (*fig*) he's the picture of health; **è l'**~ **di suo padre** he's the image of his father; **avere nella mente l'**~ **di qn/qc** to have a mental picture of sb/sth; **mi ero fatta di lui un'**~ **diversa** I had formed quite a different impression of him.

immaginoso, a [immadʒi'noso] *ag* (*linguaggio, stile*) fantastic.

immalinconire [immalinko'nire] **1** *vt* to sadden, depress. **2**: ~**rsi** *vr* to become depressed, become melancholy.

immancabile [imman'kabile] *ag* unfailing; **ecco l'**~ **Giovanna** here comes Giovanna as usual.

immancabilmente [immankabil'mente] *av* without fail, unfailingly.

immanente [imma'nɛnte] *ag* (*Filosofia*) inherent, immanent.

immanenza [imma'nɛntsa] *sf* (*Filosofia*) immanence.

immangiabile [imman'dʒabile] *ag* unpalatable, uneatable; **è** ~ I can't stomach it.

immateriale [immate'rjale] *ag* incorporeal, immaterial.

immatricolare [immatriko'lare] **1** *vt* (*veicolo etc*) to register. **2**: ~**rsi** *vr* (*Scol*) to matriculate, enrol.

immatricolazione [immatrikolat'tsjone] *sf* (*vedi vb*) registration; matriculation, enrolment.

immaturità [immaturi'ta] *sf* immaturity.

immaturo, a [imma'turo] *ag* (*frutto*) unripe; (*persona*) immature.

immedesimarsi [immedezi'marsi] *vr*: ~ **in** to identify with.

immedesimazione [immedezimat'tsjone] *sf*: ~ (**in**) identification (with).

immediatamente [immedjata'mente] *av* immediately, at once.

immediatezza [immedja'tettsa] *sf* immediacy.

immediato, a [imme'djato] *ag* (*gen*) immediate; (*intervento*) prompt.

immemorabile [immemo'rabile] *ag* immemorial; **da tempo** ~ from time immemorial.

immemore [im'mɛmore] *ag*: ~ **di** forgetful of.

immensità [immensi'ta] *sf* immensity.

immenso, a [im'mɛnso] *ag* (*gen*) immense, huge; (*spazio*) boundless; (*folla*) huge, enormous; (*fig: dolore, tristezza*) immense; **odio** ~ deep hatred.

immergere [im'mɛrdʒere] **1** *vt* (*gen*) to immerse; ~ **in acqua** (*mani*) to put in water; (*stoffa*) to steep in water; **immerso nello studio** immersed *o* absorbed in one's studies. **2**: ~**rsi** *vr* to immerse, plunge; (*sommergibile*) to dive, submerge; ~**rsi in** (*fig*) to immerse o.s. in, become absorbed in.

immeritato, a [immeri'tato] *ag* undeserved, unmerited.

immersione [immer'sjone] *sf* (*gen*) immersion; (*di sommergibile*) submersion, dive; (*di palombaro*) dive; **navigare in** ~ to sail underwater; **linea di** ~ *(Naut)* water line.

immerso, a [im'merso] *pp di* **immergere**.

immesso, a [im'messo] *pp di* **immettere**.

immettere [im'mettere] *vt (gen)* to introduce; ~ **aria nei polmoni** to take air into the lungs; ~ **dati in un computer** to feed information into a computer.

immigrante [immi'grante] *ag, sm/f* immigrant.

immigrare [immi'grare] *vi (aus* **essere***)* to immigrate.

immigrato, a [immi'grato] *ag, sm/f* immigrant.

immigrazione [immigrat'tsjone] *sf* immigration.

imminente [immi'nɛnte] *ag* imminent.

imminenza [immi'nɛntsa] *sf* imminence.

immischiare [immis'kjare] **1** *vt* to involve; ~ **qn in** to involve sb in; **trovarsi immischiato in uno scandalo** to find o.s. mixed up *o* involved in a scandal. **2**: ~**rsi** *vr*: ~**rsi in** to interfere *o* meddle in.

immiserimento [immizeri'mento] *sm* impoverishment.

immissario [immis'sarjo] *sm (Geog)* affluent, tributary.

immissione [immis'sjone] *sf (gen)* introduction; *(Tecn, Med)* intake.

immobile [im'mɔbile] **1** *ag* motionless, stationary. **2** *sm* item of real estate; **(beni)** ~**i** real estate *sg*.

immobiliare [immobi'ljare] **1** *ag* property *attr*; **patrimonio** ~ real estate; **agenzia** ~ estate agent's *(Brit)*, realtor *(Am)*; **società** ~ property company. **2** *sf* = **agenzia** ~.

immobilità [immobili'ta] *sf* immobility; ~ **politica** political inertia.

immobilizzare [immobilid'dzare] *vt (gen)* to immobilize; *(Fin)* to lock up.

immobilizzazione [immobiliddzat'tsjone] *sf (vedi vb)* immobilization; locking up.

immodestia [immo'dɛstja] *sf* immodesty.

immodesto, a͡ [immo'dɛsto] *ag* immodest, conceited.

immolare [immo'lare] **1** *vt*: ~ **(a)** to sacrifice (to). **2**: ~**rsi** *vr*: ~**rsi per** to sacrifice o.s. for.

immolazione [immolat'tsjone] *sf* sacrifice.

immondezza [immon'dettsa] *sf (spazzatura)* rubbish *(no pl)*, refuse *(no pl)*, trash *(no pl)* *(Am)*.

immondezzaio [immondet'tsajo] *sm* rubbish dump.

immondizia [immon'dittsja] *sf* = **immondezza**.

immondo, a [im'mondo] *ag (luogo)* filthy, foul; *(azione)* base, vile.

immorale [immo'rale] *ag* immoral.

immoralità [immorali'ta] *sf* immorality.

immortalare [immorta'lare] **1** *vt* to immortalize. **2**: ~**rsi** *vr* to win immortality for o.s.

immortale [immor'tale] *ag* immortal.

immortalità [immortali'ta] *sf* immortality.

immotivato, a [immoti'vato] *ag (azione)* unmotivated; *(critica)* groundless.

immune [im'mune] *ag*: ~ **da** *(esente)* exempt from; *(Med)* immune from.

immunità [immuni'ta] *sf (Med, Dir)* immunity; **l'**~ **parlamentare** = parliamentary privilege.

immunizzare [immunid'dzare] *vt*: ~ **contro** to immunize against.

immunizzazione [immuniddzat'tsjone] *sf* immunization.

immunologia [immunolo'dʒia] *sf* immunology.

immusonirsi [immuzo'nirsi] *vr (fam)* to sulk.

immusonito, a [immuzo'nito] *ag* sulky.

immutabile [immu'tabile] *ag (gen)* unchanging; *(decreto, decisione)* immutable.

immutato, a [immu'tato] *ag* unchanged.

impaccare [impak'kare] *vt* to pack.

impacchettare [impakket'tare] *vt* to wrap up, parcel up.

impacciare [impat'tʃare] *vt* to hamper, hinder; ~ **qn nei movimenti** to hamper sb's movements.

impacciato, a [impat'tʃato] *ag* **(a)** *(imbarazzato)* embarrassed. **(b)** *(goffo)* awkward, clumsy.

impaccio [im'pattʃo] *sm* **(a)** *(imbarazzo)* embarrassment; *(situazione imbarazzante)* awkward situation; **trarsi d'**~ *o* **da un** ~ to get out of an awkward situation. **(b)** *(ostacolo)* obstacle; **essere d'**~ **a qn** to be in sb's way.

impacco, chi [im'pakko] *sm (Med)* compress.

impadronirsi [impadro'nirsi] *vr*: ~ **di** *(città, ricchezze)* to seize, take possession of; *(fig: lingua)* to master.

impagabile [impa'gabile] *ag* priceless.

impaginare [impadʒi'nare] *vt (Tip)* to paginate, page (up).

impaginazione [impadʒinat'tsjone] *sf* pagination.

impagliare [impaʎ'ʎare] *vt* **(a)** *(animale: imbalsamare)* to stuff (with straw). **(b)**: ~ **una sedia** to put a raffia *o* cane seat on a chair.

impagliatore, trice [impaʎʎa'tore] *sm/f (di animali)* taxidermist; *(di sedie)* chair-mender.

impalare [impa'lare] **1** *vt* **(a)** *(persona)* to impale. **(b)** *(viti, piante)* to stake, prop up. **2**: ~**rsi** *vr (fig: bloccarsi)* to stand stock still; **non startene lì impalato, fai qualcosa!** don't just stand there, do something!

impalcatura [impalka'tura] *sf* scaffolding; *(fig)* framework, structure.

impallidire [impalli'dire] *vi (aus* **essere***)* to turn pale; *(colore, ricordo)* to fade.

impallinare [impalli'nare] *vt* to riddle with shot.

impalpabile [impal'pabile] *ag* impalpable.

impanare [impa'nare] *vt* **(a)** *(Culin)* to dip in breadcrumbs, roll in breadcrumbs. **(b)** *(Tecn: vite)* to thread.

impanatura [impana'tura] *sf* **(a)** *(vedi vb)* dipping in breadcrumbs; threading. **(b)** *(Culin)* breadcrumbs *pl*.

impantanarsi [impanta'narsi] *vr* to sink into mud; *(fig)* to get bogged down.

impaperarsi [impape'rarsi] *vr* to stumble over a word.

impappinarsi [impappi'narsi] *vr* to falter, stammer.

imparare [impa'rare] *vt* to learn; ~ **a fare qc** to learn to do sth; ~ **qc a memoria** to learn sth (off) by heart; ~ **qc a proprie spese** to learn sth to one's cost *o* the hard way; **così la prossima volta impari!** that'll teach you!

imparaticcio [impara'tittʃo] *sm* half-baked notions *pl*.

impareggiabile [impared'dʒabile] *ag* incomparable.

imparentare [imparen'tare] **1** *vt (famiglie)* to ally by marriage. **2**: ~**rsi** *vr*: ~**rsi con** to marry into, become related to.

impari ['impari] *ag (disuguale)* unequal.

impartire [impar'tire] *vt (ordine)* to give; *(benedizione)* to bestow.

imparziale [impar'tsjale] *ag* impartial, unbiased.

imparzialità [impartsjali'ta] *sf* impartiality.

impasse [ɛ̃'pas] *sf (fig)* impasse.

impassibile [impas'sibile] *ag* impassive.

impastare [impas'tare] *vt* **(a)** *(pane)* to knead. **(b)** *(cemento, malta)* to mix.

impastato, a [impas'tato] *ag (mani)* covered in dough; ~ **di fango** covered in mud; **avere la lingua** ~**a** *(fig)* to have a furry tongue; **avere gli occhi** ~**i di sonno** to feel drowsy.

impasto [im'pasto] *sm* (a) *(l'impastare: di pane)* kneading; *(: di cemento)* mixing. (b) *(pasta)* dough; *(mistura: anche fig)* mixture, blend.

impatto [im'patto] *sm (urto)* impact.

impaurire [impau'rire] 1 *vt* to frighten. 2 *vi*, ~**rsi** *vr* to become frightened.

impavido, a [im'pavido] *ag* intrepid, fearless.

impaziente [impat'tsjɛnte] *ag* impatient; ~ **di fare qc** eager to do sth.

impazienza [impat'tsjɛntsa] *sf (vedi ag)* impatience; eagerness.

impazzata [impat'tsata]: **all'**~ *av (fuggire, correre)* at breakneck speed; *(colpire)* wildly.

impazzire [impat'tsire] *vi (aus essere)* to go mad; ~ **per il dolore** to go mad with grief; ~ **per lo sport/il gelato** to be mad about sport/ice cream; **impazzisco d'amore per te** I'm mad *o* wild about you; **questo compito mi fa** ~ this homework's driving me mad; **sono impazzito a cercare un taxi** I went crazy trying to find a taxi.

impeccabile [impek'kabile] *ag* impeccable.

impedimento [impedi'mento] *sm* (a) *(ostacolo)* obstacle; **essere un** ~ *o* **d'**~ **a qc/qn** to be *o* stand in the way of sth/sb. (b) *(Dir)* impediment.

impedire [impe'dire] *vt* (a) *(proibire)*: ~ **a qn di fare qc** to prevent *o* stop sb (from) doing sth. (b) *(ostruire)* to obstruct. (c) *(impacciare)* to hamper, hinder; **era impedita dal vestito lungo** she was hampered by her long dress.

impegnare [impeɲ'ɲare] 1 *vt* (a) *(dare in pegno)* to pawn. (b) *(vincolare)* to bind. (c) *(sog: lavoro)* to keep busy; **quel compito di matematica ha impegnato tutta la classe** the maths exercise kept the whole class busy. (d) *(Mil)* to engage; *(Sport)* to put under pressure. 2 ~**rsi** *vr*: ~**rsi a fare qc** to undertake to do sth; ~**rsi con un contratto** to take on a contract; **mi sono già impegnato con qn** I have already come to an agreement with sb.

impegnativo, a [impeɲɲa'tivo] *ag (lavoro)* exacting, demanding; *(promessa)* binding.

impegnato, a [impeɲ'ɲato] *ag* (a) *(gioielli)* pawned. (b) *(persona: occupata)* busy; **sono già** ~ I have a prior engagement; **essere** ~ **con** *(lavoro)* to be busy with; *(ditta)* to be involved with. (c) *(fig: intellettuale, romanzo)* committed, engagé.

impegno [im'peɲɲo] *sm* (a) *(obbligo, promessa, di scrittore)* commitment; **assumere un** ~ to take on a commitment. (b) *(affare, incombenza)* engagement, appointment; **un** ~ **precedente** a previous engagement. (c) *(zelo)* enthusiasm, diligence; **studiare con** ~ to study hard.

impegolarsi [impego'larsi] *vr (fig)*: ~ **in** to get heavily involved in.

impelagarsi [impela'garsi] *vr* = **impegolarsi**.

impellente [impel'lɛnte] *ag* pressing, urgent.

impenetrabile [impene'trabile] *ag (bosco)* impenetrable; *(volto)* inscrutable; *(mistero, segreto)* complete.

impenitente [impeni'tɛnte] *ag* impenitent, unrepentant; **scapolo** ~ confirmed bachelor.

impennare [impen'nare] 1 *vt* (Aer): **far** ~ **l'aereo** to go into a climb. 2: ~**rsi** *vr* (a) *(aereo)* to go into a climb; *(cavallo)* to rear (up). (b) *(fig: arrabbiarsi)* to bridle, flare up.

impennata [impen'nata] *sf* (a) *(di cavallo)* rearing (up); *(di aereo)* climb, nose-up. (b) *(fig: scatto d'ira)* burst of anger.

impensabile [impen'sabile] *ag (inaccettabile)* unthinkable; *(difficile da concepire)* inconceivable.

impensato, a [impen'sato] *ag* unexpected.

impensierire [impensje'rire] 1 *vt* to worry. 2: ~**rsi** *vr*: ~**rsi (per)** to worry (about).

imperare [impe'rare] *vi (anche fig)* to rule, reign.

imperativo, a [impera'tivo] 1 *ag (tono, discorso)* commanding; *(Gram)* imperative. 2 *sm (Gram)* imperative.

imperatore, trice [impera'tore] *sm/f* emperor/empress.

impercettibile [impertʃet'tibile] *ag* imperceptible.

imperdonabile [imperdo'nabile] *ag* unforgivable, unpardonable.

imperfetto, a [imper'fɛtto] 1 *ag (gen, Gram)* imperfect; *(difettoso)* faulty, defective; *(incompleto)* unfinished. 2 *sm (Gram)*: **l'**~ the imperfect (tense).

imperfezione [imperfet'tsjone] *sf (gen)* imperfection; *(di gioiello)* flaw; *(della pelle)* blemish, imperfection.

imperiale [impe'rjale] *ag* imperial.

imperialismo [imperja'lizmo] *sm* imperialism.

imperialista, i, e [imperja'lista] *ag, sm/f* imperialist.

imperialistico, a, ci, che [imperja'listiko] *ag* imperialist(ic).

imperioso, a [impe'rjoso] *ag (autoritario)* imperious.

imperizia [impe'rittsja] *sf* inexperience, lack of experience.

imperlare [imper'lare] 1 *vt*: **il sudore gli imperlava la fronte** his brow was beaded with perspiration, beads of sweat stood out on his forehead. 2: ~**rsi** *vr*: ~**rsi di sudore** to be *(o* become) beaded with perspiration.

impermalire [imperma'lire] 1 *vt*: **far** ~ **qn** to offend sb. 2: ~**rsi** *vr*: ~**rsi (per)** to take offence *o* umbrage (at).

impermeabile [imperme'abile] 1 *ag (terreno)* impermeable; *(tessuto)* waterproof. 2 *sm (indumento)* raincoat.

impermeabilizzare [impermeabilid'dzare] *vt* to waterproof.

imperniare [imper'njare] 1 *vt*: ~ **qc su** to hinge sth on; *(fig: discorso, relazione etc)* to base sth on; **il mio discorso è imperniato su un unico concetto** my talk hinges on one basic concept. 2: ~**rsi** *vr (fig)*: ~**rsi su** to be based on.

impero [im'pero] 1 *sm* empire; **l'**~ **della ragione** *(fig)* the rule of reason. 2 *ag inv* empire *attr*.

imperscrutabile [imperskru'tabile] *ag* inscrutable.

impersonale [imperso'nale] *ag* impersonal.

impersonalità [impersonali'ta] *sf* impersonality.

impersonare [imperso'nare] 1 *vt* (a) *(qualità, concetto astratto)* to personify, symbolize. (b) *(Teatro)* to play (the part of). 2: ~**rsi** *vr* (a) *(incarnarsi)*: **in lei s'impersona la cupidigia** she is the personification of greed. (b) *(Teatro)*: ~**rsi in un ruolo** to get into a part, live a part.

imperterrito, a [imper'territo] *ag* unperturbed; **continuare** ~ **(a fare qc)** to carry on (doing sth) regardless *o* unperturbed.

impertinente [imperti'nɛnte] *ag* impertinent.

impertinenza [imperti'nɛntsa] *sf* impertinence.

imperturbabile [impertur'babile] *ag* imperturbable.

imperturbato, a [impertur'bato] *ag* unperturbed.

imperversare [imperver'sare] *vi (persona, tempesta, malattia)* to rage; *(scherz: moda, costumi)* to be all the rage.

impervio, a [im'pervjo] *ag (luogo)* inaccessible; *(strada)* impassable.

impeto ['impeto] *sm (moto, forza)* force, impetus; *(assalto)* onslaught; *(fig: d'odio, d'amore)* surge; **in un** ~ **d'ira lo uccise** he killed him in a fit of rage; **agire d'**~ to act on impulse; **con** ~ *(parlare)* forcefully, energetically.

impetrare [impe'trare] vt to beg for, beseech.

impettito, a [impet'tito] ag: **essere tutto ~** to be as stiff as a ramrod; **camminare ~** to strut.

impetuosità [impetuosi'ta] sf impetuosity.

impetuoso, a [impetu'oso] ag (gen) impetuous; (vento, corrente) raging.

impiallacciare [impjallat'tʃare] vt (mobile) to veneer.

impiallacciatura [impjallattʃa'tura] sf (tecnica) veneering; (materiale) veneer.

impiantare [impjan'tare] vt (installare) to set up, install; (avviare: azienda) to set up, establish.

impiantistica [impjan'tistika] sm plant design and installation.

impiantito [impjan'tito] sm flooring, floor.

impianto [im'pjanto] sm (a) (installazione) installation; **spese d'~** installation costs. (b) (complesso di attrezzature): **~ (industriale)** plant; **~ elettrico/di riscaldamento** electrical/heating system; **~ sportivo** sports complex.

impiastrare [impjas'trare] vt, **impiastricciare** [impjastrit'tʃare] vt: **~ di** (fango etc) to dirty with; (pittura, trucco) to smear with.

impiastro [im'pjastro] sm (a) (Med) poultice. (b) (fig fam: persona) nuisance.

impiccagione [impikka'dʒone] sf hanging.

impiccare [impik'kare] 1 vt to hang; **questo colletto m'impicca** (fig) this collar's choking me; **non lo farò nemmeno se m'impicchi!** there's no way I'll do that! 2: **~rsi** vr to hang o.s.; **impiccati!** (fam) go hang yourself!

impiccato [impik'kato] sm hanged man.

impicciare [impit'tʃare] 1 vt (sog: persona, tavolo) to be in the way of, get in the way of; (: abiti) to hinder. 2: **~rsi** vr: **~rsi di** o **in qc** to interfere o meddle in sth; **impicciati degli affari tuoi!** mind your own business!

impiccio [im'pittʃo] sm (a) (ostacolo) hindrance; **essere d'~** to be in the way. (b) (affare imbrogliato) mess (no pl); **cavare** o **togliere qn dagli ~i** to get sb out of trouble.

impiccione, a [impit'tʃone] sm/f busybody.

impiccolire [impikko'lire] 1 vt to make smaller, reduce. 2 vi (aus essere), **~rsi** vr to get smaller.

impiegare [impje'gare] 1 vt (a) (utilizzare) to use; (: tempo) to spend; (metterci: tempo) to take; (investire: denaro) to invest; **impiega il tempo libero a dipingere** he spends his free time painting; **impiego un quarto d'ora per andare a casa** it takes me o I take a quarter of an hour to get home. (b) (lavoratore) to employ. 2: **~rsi** vr to get a job, obtain employment.

impiegatizio, a [impjega'tittsjo] ag clerical, white-collar attr; **il ceto ~** clerical o white-collar workers pl.

impiegato, a [impje'gato] sm/f employee; **~ di banca** bank clerk; **~ statale** state employee.

impiego, ghi [im'pjɛgo] sm (a) (gen) use; (Econ) investment. (b) (occupazione) employment; (posto di lavoro) job, post; **un ~ fisso** a permanent job.

impietosire [impjeto'sire] 1 vt to move (to pity). 2: **~rsi** vr to be moved (to pity).

impietoso, a [impje'toso] ag pitiless, cruel.

impietrire [impje'trire] vt (anche fig) to petrify.

impigliare [impiʎ'ʎare] 1 vt to catch, entangle. 2: **~rsi** vr to get caught up, get entangled.

impigrire [impi'grire] 1 vt to make lazy. 2 vi (aus essere), **~rsi** vr to get lazy, grow lazy.

impilare [impi'lare] vt to stack, pile (up).

impinguare [impin'gware] vt (maiale etc) to fatten; (fig: tasche, casse dello Stato) to stuff with money.

impiombare [impjom'bare] vt (a) (saldare: tubo

etc) to seal (with lead); (sigillare: baule, cassa) to seal. (b) (dente) to fill.

implacabile [impla'kabile] ag implacable.

implicare [impli'kare] 1 vt (a) (sottintendere) to imply; (comportare) to entail. (b) (coinvolgere): **~ qn (in)** to involve sb (in), implicate sb (in). 2: **~rsi vr~rsi (in)** to get involved (in).

implicazione [implikat'tsjone] sf implication.

implicito, a [im'plitʃito] ag implicit.

implorante [implo'rante] ag beseeching, imploring.

implorare [implo'rare] vt to implore, beseech.

impluvio [im'pluvjo] sm (Geol): **linea di ~** watershed.

impollinare [impolli'nare] vt to pollinate.

impollinazione [impollinat'tsjone] sf pollination.

impolverare [impolve'rare] 1 vt to cover with dust. 2: **~rsi** vr to get covered with dust.

impomatare [impoma'tare] 1 vt (pelle) to put ointment on; (capelli) to pomade; (baffi) to wax. 2: **~rsi** vr (fam) to get spruced up.

imponderabile [imponde'rabile] 1 ag imponderable. 2 sm imponderable; **valutare l'~** to be prepared for the unexpected.

imponente [impo'nɛnte] ag (persona, monumento etc) imposing, impressive.

imponibile [impo'nibile] 1 ag taxable. 2 sm taxable income.

impopolare [impopo'lare] ag unpopular.

impopolarità [impopolari'ta] sf unpopularity.

imporporare [imporpo'rare] 1 vt (sog: tramonto) to redden, flush. 2: **~rsi** vr (cielo) to redden; (persona) to blush.

imporre [im'porre] 1 vt (gen) to impose; (compito) to set, impose; (condizioni) to impose, lay down; **~ a qn di impose sth on sb;** **~ a qn di fare qc** to oblige o force sb to do sth, make sb do sth; **~ la propria autorità** to assert one's authority, make one's authority felt; **~ la propria volontà** to have one's way; **imporsi qc** to impose sth on o.s.

2: **imporsi** vr (a) (farsi valere) to assert o.s., make o.s. respected; **si è imposto sugli altri con la sua competenza** he commanded the others' respect because of his ability. (b) (aver successo: moda) to become established; (: musicista, attore, sportivo) to come to the fore; **imporsi al pubblico** to come into the public eye. (c): **imporsi di fare qc** to make o.s. do sth, force o.s. to do sth. (d) (diventare necessario) to become necessary; **s'impone una scelta** a choice is called for.

importante [impor'tante] 1 ag (gen) important; (fatti) important, significant; (somma) sizeable; **poco ~** of little importance o significance; **è ~ che ci sia anche lui** it is important that he be there too. 2 sm: **l'~ è...** the important thing is....

importanza [impor'tantsa] sf (vedi ag) importance; significance; size; **di una certa ~** of considerable importance; **della massima ~** of the utmost importance; **avere ~** to be important; **assumere ~** to become more important; **dare troppa ~ a qc** to make too much of sth, attach too much importance to sth; **darsi ~** (darsi arie) to give o.s. airs.

importare¹ [impor'tare] vt to import.

importare² [impor'tare] vi, vb impers (aus **essere**) (essere importante) to matter, be important; **le tue ragioni non mi importano** your reasons aren't important to me, I don't care about your reasons; **ciò che importa di più è...** the most important thing is...; **non importa!** it doesn't matter!; **non m'importa niente** I couldn't care less, I don't care; **che importa?** what does that matter?; **non importa cosa/quando/dove** it doesn't matter what/when/where.

importatore, trice [importa'tore] **1** *ag* importing; **la ditta** ~**trice di questo prodotto** the firm which imports this product. **2** *sm/f* importer.

importazione [importat'tsjone] *sf (operazione)* importation; *(prodotto)* import; **merci/prodotti d'**~ imported goods/products.

importo [im'pɔrto] *sm* (total) amount.

importunare [importu'nare] *vt* **(a)** *(disturbare)* to bother, disturb; **non vorrei importunarti con le mie richieste** I don't wish to bother you with my requests. **(b)** *(molestare)* to pester, annoy.

importuno, a [impor'tuno] **1** *ag (visita)* inopportune; *(persona)* irksome, annoying. **2** *sm/f* irksome individual.

imposizione [impozit'tsjone] *sf* **(a)** *(atto)* imposition. **(b)** *(ordine)* order, command; **non accetto** ~**i da nessuno** I don't take orders from anyone.

impossessarsi [imposses'sarsi] *vr:* ~ **di** *(terreno, beni)* to seize, take possession of; *(segreto)* to get hold of; **sembra che il diavolo si sia impossessato di lui** *(fig)* he's like one possessed; **si è impossessato della mia stanza** *(fig)* he has taken over my room.

impossibile [impos'sibile] **1** *ag* impossible; **mi è** ~ **farlo** it's impossible for me to do it, I can't possibly do it. **2** *sm*: **fare l'**~ to do one's utmost, do all one can.

impossibilità [impossibili'ta] *sf* impossibility; **trovarsi nell'**~ **di fare qc** to find it impossible to *o* be unable to do sth.

impossibilitato, a [impossibili'tato] *ag*: **essere** ~ **a fare qc** to be unable to do sth.

imposta[1] [im'pɔsta] *sf (di finestra)* shutter.

imposta[2] [im'pɔsta] *sf (tassa)* tax; ~**e dirette/ indirette** direct/indirect taxation *sg*; **ufficio** ~**e** tax office; ~ **sul reddito** income tax; ~ **sul valore aggiunto** *(abbr* **I.V.A.***)* value added tax *(abbr* VAT).

impostare[1] [impos'tare] *vt* **(a)** *(servizio, organizzazione)* to set up; *(lavoro)* to organize, plan; *(resoconto, rapporto)* to plan; *(questione, problema)* to formulate, set out; *(Tip: pagina)* to lay out. **(b)** *(Mus)*: ~ **la voce** to pitch one's voice.

impostare[2] [impos'tare] *vt (lettera)* to post, mail *(Am)*.

impostazione[1] [impostat'tsjone] *sf (di problema, questione)* formulation, statement; *(di lavoro)* organization, planning; *(di attività)* setting up; *(Mus: di voce)* pitch.

impostazione[2] [impostat'tsjone] *sf (di lettera)* posting, mailing *(Am)*.

impostore, a [impos'tore] *sm/f* impostor.

impotente [impo'tente] **1** *ag* **(a)** *(persona, governo)* impotent, powerless; **essere** ~ **di fronte a qc** to be powerless in the face of sth; **sentirsi** ~ to feel helpless. **(b)** *(Med: incapace sessualmente)* impotent. **2** *sm (Med)* impotent man.

impotenza [impo'tentsa] *sf (vedi ag)* impotence; powerlessness.

impoverimento [impoveri'mento] *sm* impoverishment.

impoverire [impove'rire] **1** *vt* to impoverish. **2:** ~**rsi** *vr* to become poor(er).

impraticabile [imprati'kabile] *ag (strada)* impassable; *(Sport: campo)* unfit for play, unplayable.

impraticabilità [impratikabili'ta] *sf*: **l'**~ **delle strade** the fact that the roads are impassable; **partita sospesa per** ~ **del campo** *(Sport)* match abandoned due to the pitch being unplayable.

impratichirsi [imprati'kirsi] *vr (fare pratica)* to get practice, gain experience; ~ **in qc** to gain experience in (doing) sth.

imprecare [impre'kare] *vi* to curse, swear; ~

contro qn/qc to hurl abuse at sb/sth.

imprecazione [imprekat'tsjone] *sf* imprecation; **lanciare un'**~ **(contro qn/qc)** to curse (sb/sth).

imprecisabile [impretʃi'zabile] *ag* indeterminable.

imprecisato, a [impretʃi'zato] *ag* **(a)** *(non preciso: quantità, numero)* indeterminate. **(b)** *(non chiaro)*: **per motivi** ~**i** for reasons which are not clear.

imprecisione [impretʃi'zjone] *sf (vedi ag)* imprecision; inaccuracy.

impreciso, a [impre'tʃizo] *ag (definizione, descrizione)* imprecise, vague; *(calcolo)* inaccurate; **è** ~ **nel suo lavoro** he's a careless worker.

impregnare [impreɲ'ɲare] **1** *vt (stoffa)* to impregnate; *(aria, stanza)* to permeate, fill. **2:** ~**rsi** *vr:* ~**rsi di** *(vedi vt)* to become impregnated with; to become permeated *o* filled with.

imprenditore [imprendi'tore] *sm* entrepreneur; *(appaltatore)* contractor; **piccolo** ~ small businessman; ~ **edile** builder.

imprenditoriale [imprendito'rjale] *ag (ceto, classe)* entrepreneurial.

impreparato, a [imprepa'rato] *ag:* ~ **(a)** *(gen)* unprepared (for); *(lavoratore)* untrained (for); **quel professore di matematica è** ~ that maths teacher has a poor knowledge of his subject; **cogliere qn** ~ to catch sb unawares.

impreparazione [impreparat'tsjone] *sf* lack of preparation.

impresa [im'presa] *sf* **(a)** *(iniziativa)* enterprise, undertaking; **abbandonare un'**~ to abandon an enterprise *o* an undertaking; **è un'**~**!** that's quite an undertaking! **(b)** *(azione gloriosa)* feat, exploit. **(c)** *(ditta, azienda)* firm, concern; **mettere su un'**~ to set up a business.

impresario [impre'sarjo] *sm (Teatro)* theatre manager; *(: di teatri maggiori, o più teatri)* impresario; ~ **di pompe funebri** funeral director.

imprescindibile [impreʃʃin'dibile] *ag (necessità)* inescapable, unavoidable; *(condizione)* essential; *(obbligo)* binding.

impressionabile [impressjo'nabile] *ag (persona)* impressionable.

impressionante [impressjo'nante] *ag* **(a)** *(che suscita sgomento)* disturbing, upsetting. **(b)** *(che suscita sensazione)* impressive.

impressionare [impressjo'nare] **1** *vt* **(a)** *(sgomentare)* to upset; *(colpire)* to impress. **(b)** *(Fot)* to expose. **2:** ~**rsi** *vr (spaventarsi)* to get upset; **non impressionarti!** don't get upset!

impressione [impres'sjone] *sf* **(a)** *(sensazione)* impression; **far** ~ **a qn** *(colpire)* to impress sb; *(sgomentare)* to upset sb; **fare una buona/cattiva** *o* **brutta** ~ **a qn** to make a good/bad impression on sb; **che** ~ **ti ha fatto?** what was your impression of it *(o* him *etc)*?, what did you make of it *(o* him *etc)*?; **che** ~**!** how awful!, how ghastly! **(b)** *(Tip: stampa)* printing; *(: ristampa)* impression.

impressionismo [impressjo'nizmo] *sm* impressionism.

impresso, a [im'presso] *pp di* **imprimere**.

imprestare [impres'tare] *vt:* ~ **qc a qn** to lend sth to sb.

imprevedibile [impreve'dibile] *ag (destino, futuro)* unforeseeable; *(cambiamento)* unexpected; *(persona, risultato)* unpredictable.

imprevidente [imprevi'dente] *ag* lacking in foresight, improvident.

imprevidenza [imprevi'dentsa] *sf* improvidence, lack of foresight.

imprevisto, a [impre'visto] **1** *ag (arrivo, cambiamento)* unexpected; *(circostanza)* unforeseen, unexpected. **2** *sm*: **l'**~ the unexpected; **salvo** ~**i** unless anything unexpected happens.

impreziosire [imprettsjo'sire] *vt*: ~ **di** to embellish with.

imprigionamento [impridʒona'mento] *sm* imprisonment.

imprigionare [impridʒo'nare] *vt* (*chiudere in prigione*) to imprison; (*rinchiudere: in casa etc*) to shut up, confine; (*fig: intrappolare*) to trap; **la nave era imprigionata nel ghiaccio** the ship was icebound.

imprimatur [impri'matur] *sm inv* imprimatur.

imprimere [im'primere] **1** *vt* (**a**) (*marchio*) to impress, stamp; ~**rsi qc nella mente** to fix sth firmly in one's mind; **mi è rimasto impresso ciò che hai detto** I have never forgotten what you said. (**b**) (*trasmettere*): ~ (**un**) **movimento a** to impart *o* transmit movement to. **2**: ~**rsi** *vr* (*fig: ricordo*) to stamp itself, imprint itself.

improbabile [impro'babile] *ag* improbable, unlikely; **è ~ che venga** he's unlikely to come.

improbabilità [improbabili'ta] *sf* improbability, unlikelihood.

improbo, a ['improbo] *ag* (*fatica, lavoro*) hard, laborious.

improduttività [improduttivi'ta] *sf* unproductiveness.

improduttivo, a [improdut'tivo] *ag* (*gen*) unproductive; (*terreno*) unfruitful.

impronta [im'pronta] *sf* (**a**) (*di piedi, mani*) print; (*fig: di genio, maestro*) mark, stamp; ~ **del piede** footprint; ~**e digitali** fingerprints; **lasciare la propria ~ in qc** (*fig*) to leave one's mark on sth. (**b**) (*di moneta*) impression.

improntare [impron'tare] *vt* (**a**) (*imprimere*) to impress, imprint. (**b**) (*dare una certa espressione a*): **improntò il suo viso al dolore** his face took on a sad expression; **improntò il suo discorso alla massima semplicità** his speech was couched in terms of the utmost simplicity.

impronunciabile [impronun'tʃabile], **impronunziabile** [impronun'tsjabile] *ag* unpronounceable.

improperio [impro'perjo] *sm* (*insulto*) insult; **lanciare un ~** to swear; **coprire qn d'~i** to hurl abuse at sb.

improprietà [improprje'ta] *sf inv* impropriety; ~ **di linguaggio** linguistic impropriety.

improprio, a [im'prɔprjo] *ag* (*non corretto: uso*) incorrect, improper; (*sconveniente: tono, abbigliamento*) improper, inappropriate; **arma ~a** offensive weapon.

improrogabile [improro'gabile] *ag* (*termine*) that cannot be extended.

improvvisamente [improvviza'mente] *av* suddenly, unexpectedly.

improvvisare [improvvi'zare] **1** *vt* (*gen*) to improvise; (*cena, piatto*) to knock up, throw together, improvise; ~ **una festa** to hold an impromptu party. **2**: ~**rsi** *vr* to act as; **si è improvvisato cuoco per l'occasione** he acted as *o* took on the role of cook on that occasion.

improvvisata [improvvi'zata] *sf* surprise; **fare un'~ a qn** to give sb a surprise.

improvvisatore, trice [improvviza'tore] *sm/f* improviser; **è un abile ~** he's good at improvising.

improvvisazione [improvvizat'tsjone] *sf* improvisation; **spirito d'~** spirit of invention; **capacità d'~** ability to improvise.

improvviso [improv'vizo] *ag* (*inaspettato: arrivo etc*) unexpected; (*subitaneo: simpatia, cambiamento d'umore*) sudden; **all'~**, **d'~** (*inaspetta-*

tamente) unexpectedly; (*tutto d'un tratto*) suddenly.

imprudente [impru'dɛnte] **1** *ag* (*gen*) careless, foolish, imprudent; (*osservazione*) unwise. **2** *sm/f* imprudent person.

imprudenza [impru'dɛntsa] *sf* (*qualità*) carelessness, foolishness, imprudence; (*azione*): **è stata un'~** that was a foolish *o* imprudent thing to do.

impudente [impu'dɛnte] **1** *ag* impudent, cheeky. **2** *sm/f* impudent person.

impudenza [impu'dɛntsa] *sf* impudence, cheek; **avere l'~ di fare qc** to have the cheek to do sth.

impudicizia [impudi'tʃittsja] *sf* immodesty.

impudico, a, chi, che [impu'diko] *ag* immodest.

impugnabile [impuɲ'ɲabile] *ag* (*Dir*) subject to appeal.

impugnare [impuɲ'ɲare] *vt* (**a**) (*arma*) to grasp, seize. (**b**) (*Dir: sentenza*) to contest.

impugnatura [impuɲɲa'tura] *sf* (*di coltello, frusta*) handle; (*di spada*) hilt; (*di remo*) grip.

impulsività [impulsivi'ta] *sf* impulsiveness; **fare qc per ~** to do sth impulsively.

impulsivo, a [impul'sivo] *ag* impulsive.

impulso [im'pulso] *sm* (**a**) (*Fis, moto istintivo*) impulse; **agire d'~** to act on impulse; **sentì l'~ di picchiarlo** he was seized with an urge to hit him. (**b**) (*fig: spinta*) boost; **dare un ~ alle vendite** to boost sales.

impunemente [impune'mente] *av* with impunity; **fare qc ~** to get away with sth.

impunità [impuni'ta] *sf* impunity.

impunito, a [impu'nito] *ag* unpunished; **restare ~** to go unpunished.

impuntarsi [impun'tarsi] *vr* (*cavallo, asino*) to jib; (*fig: ostinarsi*) to dig one's heels in.

impuntura [impun'tura] *sf* stitching.

impurità [impuri'ta] *sf inv* impurity.

impuro, a [im'puro] *ag* impure; **esse ~a** (*Fonetica*) s impure.

imputabile [impu'tabile] *ag* (**a**) (*Dir*) chargeable. (**b**) (*attribuibile*): ~ **a** attributable to.

imputare [impu'tare] *vt* (**a**) (*Dir*): ~ **qn di** to charge sb with, accuse sb of. (**b**) (*attribuire*): ~ **qc a** to attribute *o* ascribe sth to.

imputato, a [impu'tato] *sm/f* (*Dir*) defendant, accused.

imputazione [imputat'tsjone] *sf* (*Dir*) charge.

imputridire [imputri'dire] **1** *vt* to putrefy. **2** *vi* (*aus essere*) to go bad, rot.

impuzzolentire [imputtsolen'tire] *vt* to stink out.

in [in] *prep* (*in + il = nel, in + lo = nello, in + l' = nell', in + la = nella, in + i = nei, in + gli = negli, in + le = nelle*) (**a**) (*stato in luogo*) in; (: *all'interno*) inside; **vivo ~ Scozia** I live in Scotland; **sono rimasto ~ casa** I stayed at home, I stayed indoors; **aveva le mani ~ tasca** he had his hands in his pockets; **è ~ fondo all'armadio** it is at the back of the wardrobe; **il pranzo è ~ tavola** dinner is on the table; **un giornale diffuso ~ tutta Italia** a newspaper found all over *o* throughout Italy; **è bravo ~ latino** he's good at Latin; **dottore ~ legge** doctor of law; **~ lui non c'era più speranza** there was no hope left in him; **nell'opera di Shakespeare** in Shakespeare's work; **~ lei ho trovato una sorella** I found a sister in her; **è nell'editoria/nell'esercito** he is in publishing/the army; **se fossi ~ te** if I were you.

(**b**) (*moto a luogo*) to; (: *dentro*) into; **andrò ~ Francia** I'll go to France; **andare ~ campagna/montagna** to go into the countryside/the mountains; **entrare ~ macchina/casa** to get into the car/go into the house; **gettare qc ~ acqua** to throw sth into the water; **l'ho messo là ~ alto/**

basso I put it up/down there; **spostarsi di città ~ città** to move from town to town; **inciampò ~ una radice** he tripped over a root.

(**c**) *(moto per luogo)*: **il corteo è passato ~ piazza** the procession passed through the square; **sta facendo un viaggio ~ Egitto** he's travelling in *o* around Egypt.

(**d**) *(tempo)* in; **nel 1960** in 1960; **~ luglio, nel mese di luglio** in July; **~ autunno** in autumn; **negli anni ottanta** in the eighties; **~ questo istante** at the moment; **~ passato/gioventù** in the past/one's youth; **lo farò ~ settimana** I'll do it within the week; **è cambiata molto ~ un anno** she has changed a lot in the course of a year; **di giorno ~ giorno** from day to day.

(**e**) *(mezzo)* by; **siamo andati ~ treno** we went by train; **mi piace viaggiare ~ aereo** I like travelling by plane; **ci andremo ~ macchina** we'll go there by car, we'll drive there; **pagare ~ contanti/dollari** to pay cash/in dollars.

(**f**) *(trasformazione: cambiare, tradurre etc)* into; **tagliare ~ due** to cut in two.

(**g**) *(modo, maniera)* in; **~ silenzio** in silence; **~ guerra** at war; **~ fiamme** on fire, in flames; **nell'oscurità** in the darkness; **scrivere ~ stampatello** to write in block letters; **~ versi/prosa** in verse/prose; **~ abito da sera** in evening dress; **~ gruppo** in a group; **~ piedi** standing, on one's feet.

(**h**) *(materia)* made of; **è ~ oro/legno** it's made of gold/wood; **braccialetto ~ oro** gold bracelet; **lo stesso modello ~ seta** the same model in silk.

(**i**) *(misura)* in; **~ lunghezza/altezza** in length/height; **sono ~ dieci** there are ten of them; **arrivarono ~ gran numero** they arrived in large numbers; **~ tutto** in all.

(**j**) *(fine, scopo)*: **me lo hanno dato ~ dono** they gave it to me as a gift; **spende tutto ~ divertimenti** he spends everything on entertainment; **~ onore di** in honour of; **~ favore di** in favour of.

(**k**) *(con infin)*: **si è fatto male nel salire sull'autobus** he hurt himself as he was getting onto the bus; **nell'udire la notizia** on hearing the news; **ha sbagliato nel rispondere male** he was wrong to be rude.

inabile [i'nabile] *ag (fisicamente, Mil)*: **~ (a)** unfit (for); *(per infortunio)* disabled; **~ al servizio militare** unfit for military service.

inabilità [inabili'ta] *sf (fisica, Mil)*: **~ (a)** unfitness (for); *(per infortunio)* disablement.

inabissare [inabis'sare] **1** *vt* to sink. **2**: **~rsi** *vr* to sink.

inabitabile [inabi'tabile] *ag* uninhabitable.

inabitato, a [inabi'tato] *ag* uninhabited.

inaccessibile [inattʃes'sibile] *ag (luogo)* inaccessible; *(spesa)* prohibitive; *(persona)* unapproachable; *(mistero)* unfathomable; *(teoria)* incomprehensible.

inaccettabile [inattʃet'tabile] *ag* unacceptable.

inaccostabile [inakkos'tabile] *ag (persona)* unapproachable.

inacerbire [inatʃer'bire] **1** *vt* to exacerbate. **2**: **~rsi** *vr (persona)* to become embittered.

inacidire [inatʃi'dire] **1** *vt (persona, carattere)* to embitter. **2** *vi (aus essere)*, **~rsi** *vr (latte)* to go sour; *(fig: persona, carattere)* to become sour, become embittered.

inadatto, a [ina'datto] *ag*: **~ (a)** *(persona)* unsuited (to), unfit (for); *(luogo, costruzione, lavoro)* unsuitable (for); *(parole, azione)* inappropriate (to).

inadeguato, a [inade'gwato] *ag*: **~ (a)** *(non sufficiente)* inadequate (for); *(inadatto)* not suitable (for).

inadempiente [inadem'pjɛnte] **1** *ag* defaulting. **2** *sm/f* defaulter.

inadempienza [inadem'pjɛntsa] *sf*: **~ a un contratto** non-fulfilment of a contract; **dovuto alle ~e dei funzionari** due to negligence on the part of the officials.

inadempimento [inadempi'mento] *sm* non-fulfilment.

inadempiuto, a [inadem'pjuto] *ag* unfulfilled, broken.

inafferrabile [inaffer'rabile] *ag (ladro, criminale)* elusive; *(fig: concetto, significato)* incomprehensible.

inalare [ina'lare] *vt* to inhale.

inalatore [inala'tore] *sm* inhaler.

inalazione [inalat'tsjone] *sf* inhalation.

inalberare [inalbe'rare] **1** *vt (bandiera, insegna)* to hoist, run up. **2**: **~rsi** *vr (fig: arrabbiarsi)* to flare up, fly off the handle.

inalienabile [inalje'nabile] *ag* inalienable.

inalterabile [inalte'rabile] *ag (colori)* permanent, fast; *(prezzo, qualità)* stable; *(amicizia)* steadfast; *(affetto)* unchanging; **i termini del contratto sono ~i** the terms of the contract are not subject to alteration.

inalterato, a [inalte'rato] *ag (prezzi)* stable; *(affetto, amicizia, termini di contratto)* unaltered, unchanged.

inamidare [inami'dare] *vt* to starch.

inamidato, a [inami'dato] *ag (colletto, camicia)* starched.

inammissibile [inammis'sibile] *ag (comportamento, reazione)* inadmissible, intolerable; *(Dir: prova)* inadmissible.

inamovibile [inamo'vibile] *ag (Amm: impiegato)* who cannot be dismissed.

inanimato, a [inani'mato] *ag (gen)* inanimate; *(svenuto)* unconscious; *(morto)* lifeless.

inappagabile [inappa'gabile] *ag (desiderio)* insatiable.

inappagato, a [inappa'gato] *ag* unfulfilled.

inappellabile [inappel'labile] *ag (decisione)* final, irrevocable; *(Dir)* not open to appeal, final.

inappetenza [inappe'tentsa] *sf (Med)* lack of appetite; **soffrire di ~** to have no appetite.

inappuntabile [inappun'tabile] *ag (persona)* irreproachable; *(contegno)* faultless, irreproachable; *(eleganza)* faultless, impeccable.

inarcare [inar'kare] **1** *vt (schiena)* to arch; *(sopracciglia)* to raise. **2**: **~rsi** *vr (legno)* to warp.

inaridimento [inaridi'mento] *sm (anche fig)* drying up.

inaridire [inari'dire] **1** *vt (terreno)* to parch, dry up; *(fig: vena poetica)* to dry up; *(: persona)* to sour. **2** *vi (aus essere)*, **~rsi** *vr (anche fig)* to dry up; *(persona)* to become soured.

inarrestabile [inarres'tabile] *ag* **(a)** *(processo)* irreversible; *(emorragia)* that cannot be stemmed. **(b)** *(corsa del tempo)* relentless.

inarticolato, a [inartiko'lato] *ag (suono)* inarticulate.

inascoltato, a [inaskol'tato] *ag* unheeded, unheard; **rimanere ~** to go unheeded *o* unheard.

inaspettatamente [inaspettata'mente] *av* unexpectedly.

inaspettato, a [inaspet'tato] *ag* unexpected.

inasprimento [inaspri'mento] *sm (vedi vt)* tightening up; embitterment; worsening.

inasprire [inas'prire] **1** *vt (disciplina)* to tighten up, make harsher; *(persona, carattere)* to embitter, sour; *(rapporti)* to make worse. **2**: **~rsi** *vr (vedi vt)* to become harsher; to become bitter; to become worse; **si sono inasprite le ostilità** hostilities have intensified.

inattaccabile [inattak'kabile] *ag (fortezza, castello)* unassailable, impregnable; *(fig: alibi)* cast-iron, unshakeable; *(: posizione)* unassailable; **~ dagli acidi** proof against acids.

inattendibile [inatten'dibile] *ag (versione dei fatti)* unreliable; *(testimone)* unreliable, untrustworthy.

inatteso, a [inat'teso] *ag* unexpected.

inattivo, a [inat'tivo] *ag (persona)* idle, inactive; *(Chim)* inactive.

inattuabile [inattu'abile] *ag* impracticable.

inaudito, a [inau'dito] *ag (crudeltà, ferocità)* unheard-of, unprecedented; *(somma, prezzo)* incredible.

inaugurale [inaugu'rale] *ag* inaugural; **la fase ~** the opening stages.

inaugurare [inaugu'rare] *vt (scuola, linea ferroviaria)* to open, inaugurate; *(mostra)* to open; *(monumento)* to unveil; *(fig: era, periodo)* to usher in, inaugurate; *(: sistema)* to inaugurate; *(: scherz: scarpe, vestito)* to christen.

inaugurazione [inaugurat'tsjone] *sf* inauguration, opening; **fare l'~ di** to inaugurate, open.

inavveduto, a [inavve'duto] *ag (gesto)* inadvertent, unintentional.

inavvertenza [inavver'tɛntsa] *sf* carelessness.

inavvertitamente [inavvertita'mente] *av* inadvertently, unintentionally.

inavvicinabile [inavvitʃi'nabile] *ag* unapproachable.

incagliarsi [inkaʎ'ʎarsi] *vr (nave, barca)* to run aground; *(fig: trattative)* to become bogged down, grind to a halt.

incalcolabile [inkalko'labile] *ag (gen)* incalculable; **il valore dei gioielli è ~** the jewels are priceless.

incallito, a [inkal'lito] *ag (a) (mani)* calloused. **(b)** *(fig: ladro, bugiardo)* hardened, inveterate; **è un ~ rubacuori** he's a regular ladies' man.

incalzare [inkal'tsare] **1** *vt (inseguire)* to pursue. **2** *vi:* **il tempo incalza** time is pressing.

incamerare [inkame'rare] *vt (Dir)* to expropriate, confiscate.

incamminarsi [inkammi'narsi] *vr* to set forth, set out; **~ verso** to set out for, head for; *(fig)* to head for.

incanalamento [inkanala'mento] *sm (di acque)* canalization.

incanalare [inkana'lare] **1** *vt (acque)* to canalize; *(traffico, folla)* to direct, channel. **2: ~rsi** *vr (folla);* **~rsi verso** to converge on.

incancrenire [inkankre'nire] *vi (aus essere),* **~rsi** *vr* to become gangrenous.

incandescente [inkandeʃ'ʃɛnte] *ag* incandescent, white-hot.

incantare [inkan'tare] **1** *vt (per magia, anche fig: persona)* to enchant, bewitch; *(serpente)* to charm; **non m'incanti con le tue chiacchiere!** you don't fool me with your fine words! **2: ~rsi** *vr (bloccarsi: meccanismo)* to stick, jam; *(: persona)* to be spellbound, be in a daze; **~rsi nel parlare** to hesitate in one's speech; **~rsi a guardare qc/qn** to stop and stare at sth/sb.

incantato, a [inkan'tato] *ag (anello, castello)* enchanted; *(fig: affascinato)* spellbound, entranced; **rimanere ~ davanti a qc** to stand entranced *o* spellbound before sth.

incantatore, trice [inkanta'tore] *sm/f* enchanter; **~ di serpenti** snake charmer.

incantesimo [inkan'tezimo] *sm* spell; **rompere l'~** *(anche fig)* to break the spell.

incantevole [inkan'tevole] *ag* enchanting, delightful.

incanto¹ [in'kanto] *sm (incantesimo)* spell; **quella ragazza/quel paese è un ~** that girl/village is enchanting; **sei un ~ stasera** you look enchanting this evening; **l'~ della montagna** the magic of the mountains; **come per ~** as if by magic; **ti sta d'~!** *(vestito etc)* it really suits you!

incanto² [in'kanto] *sm* auction; **vendita all'~** sale by auction.

incapace [inka'patʃe] **1** *ag* incapable; **essere ~ (di fare qc)** to be incapable (of doing sth). **2** *sm/f:* **essere un ~** to be incompetent, be a dead loss *(fam)*; **solo un ~ poteva...** only an idiot could.... .

incapacità [inkapatʃi'ta] *sf (a) (inabilità)* incapability, inability; **~ a fare qc** inability to do sth. **(b)** *(Dir)* incapacity; **~ d'intendere e di volere** diminished responsibility.

incappare [inkap'pare] *vi (aus essere):* **~ in** *(problema, guaio)* to run into, get into; *(persona)* to run into.

incappucciare [inkapput'tʃare] **1** *vt* to put a hood on. **2: ~rsi** *vr (persona)* to put on a hood; *(: coprirsi per bene)* to wrap up (well).

incapsulare [inkapsu'lare] *vt (Med: dente)* to crown.

incapricciarsi [inkaprit'tʃarsi] *vr:* **~ di qn/qc** to take a fancy to sb/sth.

incarcerare [inkartʃe'rare] *vt* to imprison, jail.

incaricare [inkari'kare] **1** *vt:* **~ qn di fare qc** to give sb the responsibility of doing sth, ask sb to do sth. **2: ~** *vr:* **~rsi di fare qc** to take it upon o.s. to do sth; **me ne incarico io** I'll see to it.

incaricato, a [inkari'kato] **1** *ag:* **~ (di)** in charge (of), responsible (for); **docente ~** *(Univ)* lecturer without tenure. **2** *sm/f* appointee, representative; **~ d'affari** chargé d'affaires.

incarico, chi [in'kariko] *sm (a) (gen: compito)* task, job; **dare un ~ a qn** to give sb a task *o* job to do; **ricevere un ~** to be given a task *o* job to do; **avere l'~ di fare qc** to have the job of doing sth; **per ~ di qn** on sb's behalf. **(b)** *(Scol, Univ)* temporary post.

incarnare [inkar'nare] **1** *vt (rappresentare)* to embody. **2: ~rsi** *vr (a) (Rel)* to become incarnate. **(b)** *(unghia)* to become ingrown.

incarnato, a [inkar'nato] *ag (unghia)* ingrown.

incarnazione [inkarnat'tsjone] *sf (Rel)* incarnation; *(fig)* embodiment; **è l'~ della virtù** he *(o* she) is the embodiment of virtue; **sembra l'~ di suo nonno** he *(o* she) is the image of his *(o* her) grandfather.

incarnire [inkar'nire] *vi,* **~rsi** *vr (unghia)* to become ingrown.

incartamento [inkarta'mento] *sm* dossier, file.

incartapecorire [inkartapeko'rire] *vi (aus essere),* **~rsi** *vr* to shrivel (up).

incartapecorito, a [inkartapeko'rito] *ag (pelle)* wizened, shrivelled.

incartare [inkar'tare] *vt* to wrap.

incasellare [inkasel'lare] *vt (posta)* to sort; *(fig: nozioni)* to pigeonhole.

incassare [inkas'sare] *vt (a) (Comm: denaro)* to take, receive; *(: assegno, cambiale)* to cash. **(b)** *(Pugilato: colpi)* to take, stand up to; *(: offese)* to take. **(c)** *(montare: pietra preziosa)* to set; *(: mobile)* to build in.

incassatore [inkassa'tore] *sm (pugile):* **è un buon ~** he can take a lot of punishment.

incasso [in'kasso] *sm (somma incassata)* takings *pl;* *(: per un incontro sportivo)* take; **~ giornaliero/mensile** daily/monthly takings; **fare un buon ~** to take in a lot of cash *o* money.

incastonare [inkasto'nare] *vt* to set.

incastonatura [inkastona'tura] *sf* setting.

incastrare [inkas'trare] **1** *vt* **(a)** *(gen: far combaciare)* to fit in, insert. **(b)** *(intrappolare)* to catch; **mi hanno incastrato di nuovo!** *(trattenuto)* I got caught again!; **la polizia lo ha incastrato** the police have nailed him. **2**: ~**rsi** *vr* **(a)** *(combaciare: pezzi meccanici)* to fit together; **questo pezzo s'incastra qui** this part fits *o* is fitted here. **(b)** *(rimanere bloccato)* to become stuck; **la chiave si è incastrata nella serratura** the key got stuck in the lock.

incastro [in'kastro] *sm (Falegnameria)* joint; *(scanalatura)* slot, groove; **gioco a** ~ interlocking puzzle; **sistema a** ~ interlocking system; ~ **a coda di rondine** dovetail joint.

incatenare [inkate'nare] *vt*: ~ **qc/qn a qc** to chain sth/sb to sth.

incatramare [inkatra'mare] *vt* to tar.

incattivire [inkatti'vire] **1** *vt* to make wicked. **2**: ~**rsi** *vr* to turn nasty.

incauto, a [in'kauto] *ag* imprudent, rash.

incavare [inka'vare] *vt* to hollow out.

incavato, a [inka'vato] *ag (gen)* hollow; *(occhi)* sunken, deep-set.

incavo [in'kavo] *sm* hollow.

incavolarsi [inkavo'larsi] *vr (fam)* to lose one's temper, get annoyed; ~ **per** *o* **a causa di qc** to get annoyed about sth, lose one's temper over sth; ~ **con qn** to get annoyed *o* lose one's temper with sb.

incazzarsi [inkat'tsarsi] *vr (fam!)* to get steamed up.

incedere [in'tʃedere] **1** *vi (poet)* to advance solemnly. **2** *sm* solemn gait.

incendiare [intʃen'djare] **1** *vt (gen)* to set fire to; *(fig: animi)* to fire. **2**: ~**rsi** *vr* to catch fire, burst into flames.

incendiario, a [intʃen'djarjo] **1** *ag* incendiary. **2** *sm/f* arsonist.

incendio [in'tʃendjo] *sm* fire; **provocare l'**~ **di** to set fire to; ~ **doloso** arson.

incenerimento [intʃeneri'mento] *sm (gen)* incineration; *(cremazione)* cremation.

incenerire [intʃene'rire] *vt (gen)* to incinerate; *(casa, albero)* to burn (down); *(cadavere)* to cremate; ~ **qn con uno sguardo** *(fig)* to give sb a withering look, crush sb with a glance.

inceneritore [intʃeneri'tore] *sm* incinerator.

incensiere [intʃen'sjere] *sm* censer, thurible.

incenso [in'tʃenso] *sm* incense.

incensurabile [intʃensu'rabile] *ag* irreproachable.

incensurato, a [intʃensu'rato] *ag (Dir)*: **essere** ~ to have a clean record.

incentivare [intʃenti'vare] *vt (produzione, vendite)* to boost; *(persona)* to motivate.

incentivazione [intʃentivat'tsjone] *sf (di produzione)* boosting; ~ **vendite** sales promotion.

incentivo [intʃen'tivo] *sm* incentive.

incentrarsi [intʃen'trarsi] *vr*: ~ **su** *(fig)* to centre on.

inceppare [intʃep'pare] **1** *vt (fig: operazione)* to obstruct, hamper. **2**: ~**rsi** *vr (fucile etc)* to jam.

incerare [intʃe'rare] *vt* to wax.

incerata [intʃe'rata] *sf (completo)* oilskins *pl; (tela)* oilcloth; *(: da letto)* waterproof sheet.

incertezza [intʃer'tettsa] *sf* **(a)** *(di notizie, fonti)* uncertainty, doubtful nature. **(b)** *(esitazione)* uncertainty, hesitation; **un momento d'**~ a moment's uncertainty *o* hesitation; **rispondere con** ~ to answer hesitantly. **(c)** *(insicurezza, instabilità)* uncertainty, doubt; **essere nell'**~ to be in a state of uncertainty; **tenere qn nell'**~ to

keep sb in suspense; **vivere nell'**~ to live in a state of uncertainty.

incerto, a [in'tʃerto] **1** *ag (esito, risultato)* uncertain, doubtful; *(tempo)* uncertain; **essere** ~ **su qc** to be uncertain *o* unsure about sth; **essere** ~ **sul da farsi** not to know what to do, be uncertain what to do; **camminare con passo** ~ to walk unsteadily. **2** *sm* uncertainty; **lasciare il certo per l'**~ to step out into the unknown, leave certainty behind one; **gli** ~**i del mestiere** the risks of the job.

incespicare [intʃespi'kare] *vi*: ~ **(in qc)** to trip (over sth).

incessante [intʃes'sante] *ag (gen)* unceasing, incessant; *(serie)* never-ending.

incesto [in'tʃesto] *sm* incest.

incestuoso, a [intʃestu'oso] *ag* incestuous.

incetta [in'tʃetta] *sf* buying up, hoarding; **fare** ~ **di** *(prodotti, merce)* to stockpile, buy up; **cercare di fare** ~ **di voti** to try to get as many votes as possible.

inchiesta [in'kjesta] *sf (gen, Dir)* inquiry, investigation; *(giornalistica)* report; **fare un'**~ **su qc** to investigate sth, carry out an investigation *o* inquiry into sth; to report on sth.

inchinare [inki'nare] **1** *vt (schiena)* to bend; *(testa, fronte)* to bow. **2**: ~**rsi** *vr* to bow; *(donna)* to curtsey; ~**rsi davanti a qn** to bow *(o* curtsey) to sb; **m'inchino davanti alla tua bravura** *(fig)* I take off my hat to you.

inchino [in'kino] *sm (gen)* bow; *(di donna)* curtsey; **fare un** ~ to bow; to curtsey.

inchiodare [inkjo'dare] *vt* to nail (down); ~ **qc a qc** to nail sth to sth; **il lavoro lo inchioda al tavolino** *(fig)* his work keeps him nailed to his desk; **con queste prove lo hanno inchiodato** *(fig)* they nailed him with this evidence; ~ **la macchina** to jam on the brakes.

inchiostro [in'kjostro] *sm* ink; ~ **di china** Indian ink; ~ **simpatico** invisible ink; **una macchia d'**~ an ink blot.

inciampare [intʃam'pare] *vi* to trip; ~ **in** *(gradino, pietra)* to trip over; *(fig: persona)* to run into; **far** ~ **qn** to trip sb (up).

inciampo [in'tʃampo] *sm* obstacle.

incidentale [intʃiden'tale] *ag* **(a)** *(casuale)* accidental. **(b)** *(secondario)* incidental; **questione** ~ *(Dir)* interlocutory matter; **proposizione** ~ *(Gram)* parenthetical clause.

incidentalmente [intʃidental'mente] *av (per caso)* by chance; *(per inciso)* incidentally, by the way.

incidente [intʃi'dente] *sm* **(a)** *(disgrazia)* accident; ~ **mortale** fatal accident; ~ **stradale** road accident; ~ **aereo/di macchina** plane/car crash. **(b)** *(episodio)* incident; **e con questo l'**~ **è chiuso** and that is the end of the matter; ~ **diplomatico** diplomatic incident.

incidenza [intʃi'dentsa] *sf* **(a)** *(Mat)*: **angolo di** ~ angle of incidence. **(b)** *(fig: effetto)*: **avere una forte** ~ **su qc** to affect sth greatly, have a considerable effect on sth.

incidere[1] [in'tʃidere] *vt* **(a)** *(tagliare: corteccia, legno)* to cut into, carve; *(scolpire: pietra, legno)* to engrave; ~ **un'iscrizione su** to engrave an inscription on; ~ **ad acquaforte** to etch; ~ **una ferita** *(Med)* to lance a wound. **(b)** *(canzone)* to record; ~ **un disco** to cut a record.

incidere[2] [in'tʃidere] *vi (influire)*: ~ **su** to influence, affect; **le spese di riscaldamento incidono molto sull'economia domestica** heating costs are an important item of household expenditure.

incinta [in'tʃinta] *ag f* pregnant; **restare** ~ to become *o* get pregnant; ~ **di 5 mesi** 5 months pregnant; **mettere** ~ **una ragazza** to get a girl pregnant.

incipiente [intʃi'pjɛnte] *ag* incipient.

incipriare [intʃi'prjare] **1** *vt* to powder. **2**: ~**rsi** *vr* to powder one's face.

incirca [in'tʃirka] *av*: **all'**~ more or less, approximately.

incisione [intʃi'zjone] *sf* **(a)** *(taglio)* cut; *(Med)* incision. **(b)** *(Arte)* engraving; ~ **ad acquaforte** etching; ~ **su legno** woodcut; ~ **su rame** copperplate engraving. **(c)** *(registrazione)* recording; ~ **su nastro** tape recording.

incisività [intʃizivi'ta] *sf* incisiveness.

incisivo, a [intʃi'zivo] *ag* **(a)** *(Anat)*: **(dente)** ~ incisor. **(b)** *(fig: parole, stile)* incisive.

inciso, a [in'tʃizo] **1** *pp di* **incidere. 2** *sm* *(Gram)* parenthesis; **per** ~ incidentally, by the way.

incisore [intʃi'zore] *sm* *(Arte)* engraver.

incitamento [intʃita'mento] *sm* incitement; **essere d'**~ **per** *o* **a** to be an incitement to.

incitare [intʃi'tare] *vt*: ~ **qn a (fare) qc** to incite sb to (do) sth.

incivile [intʃi'vile] **1** *ag* *(popolazione, costumi)* uncivilized; *(fig: persona, comportamento)* rude, impolite. **2** *sm/f* boor.

incivilire [intʃivi'lire] **1** *vt* to civilize. **2**: ~**rsi** *vr* to become civilized.

inciviltà [intʃivil'ta] *sf* **(a)** *(di popolazione)* barbarism. **(b)** *(fig: di trattamento)* barbarity; *(: maleducazione)* incivility, rudeness.

incl. *abbr (= incluso)* encl.

inclemente [inkle'mɛnte] *ag* *(giudice, sentenza)* severe, harsh; *(fig: clima)* harsh; *(: tempo)* inclement.

inclemenza [inkle'mɛntsa] *sf* *(vedi ag)* severity; harshness; inclemency.

inclinabile [inkli'nabile] *ag* *(schienale)* reclinable.

inclinare [inkli'nare] **1** *vt* **(a)** *(recipiente)* to tilt, tip; *(schienale)* to tilt (back), recline; ~ **il busto in avanti** to bend forward, lean forward. **2** *vi*: ~ **a** to be inclined to. **3**: ~**rsi** *vr* *(barca)* to list, heel; *(aereo)* to bank; *(ago magnetico)* to dip.

inclinato, a [inkli'nato] *ag* *(recipiente)* tilted; *(strada)* sloping; **piano** ~ *(Mat)* inclined plane.

inclinazione [inklinat'tsjone] *sf* **(a)** *(pendenza: di strada)* gradient; *(: di superficie)* slope; *(: di tetto)* slope, pitch; *(: di retta, piano)* inclination. **(b)** *(fig: tendenza)* inclination, bent; **seguire le proprie** ~**i** to follow one's inclinations.

incline [in'kline] *ag*: **essere** ~ **a pensare che...** to be inclined to think that...; **essere** ~ **alla collera** to be prone to anger, be irascible.

includere [in'kludere] *vt*: ~ **(in)** *(accludere)* to enclose (in); *(comprendere)* to include (in).

inclusione [inklu'zjone] *sf* inclusion.

incluso, a [in'kluzo] **1** *pp di* **includere. 2** *ag* **(a)** *(accluso)* attached. **(b)** *(compreso)* inclusive; **fino ad aprile** ~ until April inclusive; ~ **mio cugino** including my cousin, my cousin included; **spese** ~**e** inclusive of expenses.

incoerente [inkoe'rɛnte] *ag* **(a)** *(terreno, materiali)* loose. **(b)** *(fig: confuso)* incoherent; *(: illogico)* inconsistent.

incoerenza [inkoe'rɛntsa] *sf* *(vedi ag)* looseness; incoherence; inconsistency.

incognita [in'kɔɲɲita] *sf* *(Mat, fig: persona)* unknown quantity; *(: fatto, evento etc)* uncertainty.

incognito, a [in'kɔɲɲito] **1** *ag* unknown. **2** *sm*: **mantenere l'**~ to remain incognito; **viaggiare in** ~ to travel incognito.

incollare [inkol'lare] **1** *vt* *(gen)* to stick; *(legno, porcellana)* to glue, stick; ~ **un francobollo ad una lettera** to put *o* stick a stamp on a letter; ~

insieme dei cartoncini to stick *o* glue pieces of card together; ~ **gli occhi addosso a qn** *(fig)* to fix one's eyes on sb. **2**: ~**rsi** *vr (gen)*: ~**rsi (a)** to stick (to); ~**rsi a qn** *(fig)* to stick close to sb; **le pagine si sono incollate** the pages have stuck together.

incollatura [inkolla'tura] *sf* *(Ippica)*: **vincere/perdere di un'**~ to win/lose by a head.

incollerire [inkolle'rire] *vi* *(aus essere)*, ~**rsi** *vr* to lose one's temper.

incolmabile [inkol'mabile] *ag* *(vuoto)* unfillable; *(lacuna)* overwhelming; *(Sport: distacco)* irretrievable.

incolonnare [inkolon'nare] **1** *vt* *(cifre)* to put in columns; *(Mil: truppe)* to draw up in columns; *(Tip)* to set up in columns; *(con macchina da scrivere)* to tabulate. **2**: ~**rsi** *vr* *(truppe)* to draw up in columns.

incolore [inko'lore] *ag* colourless.

incolpare [inkol'pare] *vt* *(gen)*: ~ **(di)** to blame (for); ~ **qn di aver fatto qc** to accuse sb of having done sth; ~ **l'inesperienza** to blame one's inexperience.

incolto, a [in'kolto] *ag* *(terreno)* uncultivated; *(fig: barba)* neglected.

incolume [in'kɔlume] *ag* unhurt, safe and sound.

incolumità [inkolumi'ta] *sf* safety; **attentato all'**~ **di qn** attempt on sb's life.

incombente [inkom'bɛnte] *ag* *(pericolo)* imminent, impending.

incombenza [inkom'bɛntsa] *sf* duty, task.

incombere [in'kombere] *vi*: ~ **su** to hang over; threaten.

incombustibile [inkombus'tibile] *ag* incombustible.

incominciare [inkomin'tʃare] **1** *vt* to begin, start; ~ **a fare qc** to begin *o* start doing sth. **2** *vi* *(aus essere)* to begin, start.

incommensurabile [inkommensu'rabile] *ag* *(Mat)* incommensurable; *(fig: pregi, distanza)* immeasurable.

incomodare [inkomo'dare] **1** *vt* to trouble, inconvenience. **2**: ~**rsi** *vr* to put o.s. out.

incomodo [in'kɔmodo] *sm* trouble, inconvenience; **prendersi l'**~ **di fare qc** to take the trouble to do sth; **essere d'**~ **a qn** to be in sb's way; **togliere l'**~ *(andarsene)* to take o.s. off; **fare il terzo** ~ to play gooseberry.

incompatibile [inkompa'tibile] *ag* *(inconciliabile)* incompatible.

incompatibilità [inkompatibili'ta] *sf* incompatibility; ~ **di carattere** (mutual) incompatibility.

incompetente [inkompe'tɛnte] **1** *ag* *(gen, Dir)* incompetent; **essere** ~ **in qc** to be incompetent *o* useless *(fam)* at sth. **2** *sm/f* incompetent person; **è un** ~ he is incompetent.

incompetenza [inkompe'tɛntsa] *sf* incompetence.

incompiuto, a [inkom'pjuto] *ag* unfinished, incomplete; **rimanere** ~ to be left unfinished.

incompleto, a [inkom'plɛto] *ag* incomplete.

incomprensibile [inkompren'sibile] *ag* *(gen)* incomprehensible.

incomprensione [inkompren'sjone] *sf* **(a)** *(mancanza di comprensione)* lack of understanding. **(b)** *(malinteso)* misunderstanding.

incompreso, a [inkom'preso] **1** *ag* misunderstood. **2** *sm/f*: **è un** ~ he's misunderstood, people don't understand him.

incomunicabile [inkomuni'kabile] *ag* *(sentimento, sensazione)* incommunicable.

inconcepibile [inkontʃe'pibile] *ag* *(impensabile)* inconceivable, unthinkable; *(assurdo)* incredible.

inconciliabile [inkontʃi'ljabile] *ag* irreconcilable.

inconcludente [inkonklu'dɛnte] *ag (persona)* ineffectual; *(sforzi)* inconclusive; *(discorso: sconclusionato)* disconnected.

incondizionato, a [inkondittsjo'nato] *ag (approvazione etc)* unconditional; *(fiducia)* unquestioning, complete; **resa** ~**a** *(anche fig)* unconditional surrender.

inconfessabile [inkonfes'sabile] *ag (pensiero, peccato)* unmentionable.

inconfessato, a [inkonfes'sato] *ag (desiderio, voglia)* unconfessed, secret.

inconfondibile [inkonfon'dibile] *ag* unmistakeable.

inconfutabile [inkonfu'tabile] *ag* irrefutable.

incongruente [inkongru'ɛnte] *ag* inconsistent.

incongruenza [inkongru'ɛntsa] *sf* inconsistency.

incongruo, a [in'kɔngruo] *ag* insufficient, inadequate.

inconoscibile [inkonoʃ'ʃibile] *sm*: **l'**~ *(Filosofia)* the unknowable.

inconsapevole [inkonsa'pevole] *ag*: ~ **di** unaware of, ignorant of.

inconsapevolezza [inkonsapevo'lettsa] *sf* ignorance, lack of awareness.

inconscio, a, sci, sce [in'kɔnʃo] **1** *ag (desiderio, impulso)* unconscious. **2** *sm*: **l'**~ *(Psic)* the unconscious.

inconsistente [inkonsis'tɛnte] *ag (dubbio)* unfounded; *(ragionamento, prove)* tenuous, flimsy; *(patrimonio)* small, insubstantial.

inconsistenza [inkonsis'tɛntsa] *sf (di dubbio)* lack of foundation; *(di ragionamento, prove)* flimsiness; *(di patrimonio)* insubstantial nature.

inconsolabile [inkonso'labile] *ag* inconsolable.

inconsueto, a [inkonsu'eto] *ag* unusual.

inconsulto, a [inkon'sulto] *ag (gesto, azione)* rash, impetuous.

incontaminato, a [inkontami'nato] *ag* uncontaminated.

incontenibile [inkonte'nibile] *ag (sentimento, desiderio)* irrepressible, uncontrollable; *(assalto)* uncontainable.

incontentabile [inkonten'tabile] *ag (desiderio, avidità)* insatiable; *(persona: capriccioso)* hard to please, very demanding.

incontestabile [inkontes'tabile] *ag* incontrovertible, indisputable.

incontinenza [inkonti'nɛntsa] *sf (Med)* incontinence; *(fig: nelle passioni)* lack of restraint.

incontrare [inkon'trare] **1** *vt* **(a)** *(gen)* to meet; *(in riunione)* to have a meeting with; *(difficoltà, pericolo)* to meet with, run into, come up against; ~ **qn per caso** *o* **run** *o* **bump into sb**; ~ **il favore del pubblico** *(attore, prodotto etc)* to find favour with *o* be popular with the public; **questo prodotto non incontra** this product hasn't caught on. **(b)** *(Sport: squadra)* to meet, play (against); *(: pugile)* to meet, fight. **2**: ~**rsi** *vr* **(a)** *(trovarsi: su appuntamento)* to meet; *(: in riunione)* to have a meeting. **(b)** *(uso reciproco)* to meet (each other).

incontrario [inkon'trarjo]: **all'**~ *av*: **si è messo il maglione all'**~ he put his jumper on back to front; **leggeva all'**~ he was reading upside down; **camminare all'**~ to walk backwards; **fare qc all'**~ to do sth back to front; **dovresti farlo all'**~ you should do it the other way round.

incontrastato, a [inkontras'tato] *ag (successo, vittoria, verità)* uncontested, undisputed.

incontro[1] [in'kontro] *sm* **(a)** *(gen)* meeting; *(fortuito)* encounter; **un** ~ **al vertice** a summit (meeting); **a tarda notte si possono fare brutti** ~**i** you can have some nasty encounters late at night.

(b) *(Sport)* match; ~ **di calcio/pugilato** a football/boxing match.

incontro[2] [in'kontro]: ~ **a** *av* towards; **andare** ~ **a qn** to go to meet sb; *(fig: aiutare)* to meet sb halfway; **andare** ~ **a** *(brutte sorprese)* to come up against, meet; *(spese)* to incur; **andare** ~ **alla morte** to go to one's death; **stiamo ormai andando** ~ **alla primavera** we're moving towards spring now, it'll soon be spring.

incontrollabile [inkontrol'labile] *ag* uncontrollable.

inconveniente [inkonve'njɛnte] *sm* **(a)** *(difficoltà)* setback, mishap; **ho avuto degli** ~ **con la macchina** I had some problems with the car. **(b)** *(svantaggio)* drawback, disadvantage.

incoraggiamento [inkoraddʒa'mento] *sm* encouragement; **premio d'**~ consolation prize.

incoraggiare [inkorad'dʒare] *vt (esortare)* to encourage; ~ **qn a fare qc** to encourage sb to do sth; ~ **qn allo studio** to encourage sb to study.

incornare [inkor'nare] *vt* to gore.

incorniciare [inkorni'tʃare] *vt (quadro, ritratto)* to frame; *(fig)*: **i lunghi capelli le incorniciavano il volto** her long hair framed her face.

incoronare [inkoro'nare] *vt (anche fig)* to crown.

incoronazione [inkoronat'tsjone] *sf* coronation.

incorporare [inkorpo'rare] *vt*: ~ **(in)** *(gen, Comm)* to incorporate (into); *(sostanza)* to mix (with); '~ **gli albumi nell'impasto'** *(Culin)* 'fold the egg whites into the mixture'.

incorporeo, a [inkor'pɔreo] *ag* incorporeal; **esseri** ~**i** spirits.

incorreggibile [inkorred'dʒibile] *ag (gen)* incorrigible; *(giocatore)* inveterate.

incorrere [in'korrere] *vi (aus essere)*: ~ **in** *(pericolo, guaio)* to run into, come up against.

incorruttibile [inkorrut'tibile] *ag (funzionario)* incorruptible; *(fig: fede)* unshakeable; *(: bellezza)* unfading.

incorso, a [in'korso] *pp di* **incorrere**.

incosciente [inkoʃ'ʃɛnte] **1** *ag* **(a)** *(privo di sensi)* unconscious. **(b)** *(sventato)* reckless, thoughtless. **2** *sm/f* reckless person, thoughtless person.

incoscienza [inkoʃ'ʃɛntsa] *sf (vedi ag)* unconsciousness; recklessness, thoughtlessness.

incostante [inkos'tante] *ag (studente, impiegato)* inconsistent; *(carattere)* fickle, inconstant; *(rendimento)* sporadic.

incostanza [inkos'tantsa] *sf* inconstancy, fickleness.

incostituzionale [inkostituttsjo'nale] *ag* unconstitutional.

incostituzionalità [inkostituttsjonali'ta] *sf* unconstitutionality.

incredibile [inkre'dibile] *ag* incredible, unbelievable.

incredulità [inkreduli'ta] *sf* incredulity.

incredulo, a [in'kredulo] *ag* incredulous.

incrementare [inkremen'tare] *vt (vendite, produzione etc)* to increase.

incremento [inkre'mento] *sm*: ~ **(di)** increase (in); ~ **demografico** population rise *o* increase.

increscioso, a [inkreʃ'ʃoso] *ag (spiacevole)* unpleasant; **incidente** ~ regrettable incident.

increspare [inkres'pare] **1** *vt (capelli)* to curl; *(stoffa)* to gather; *(superficie del mare)* to ripple. **2**: ~**rsi** *vr (superficie: di mare, lago)* to ripple.

incriminabile [inkrimi'nabile] *ag (Dir)* chargeable.

incriminare [inkrimi'nare] *vt (Dir)*: ~ **qn di qc** to charge sb with sth.

incriminazione [inkriminat'tsjone] *sf (atto*

d'*accusa*) indictment, charge; **non c'erano prove sufficienti per la sua** ~ there wasn't sufficient evidence to charge him.

incrinare |inkri'nare] **1** *vt* (*vetro, specchio, vaso*) to crack; (*fig: rapporti, amicizia*) to cause to deteriorate. **2**: ~**rsi** *vr* (*vetro, ghiaccio, roccia*) to crack; (*rapporti, amicizia*) to deteriorate.

incrinatura [inkrina'tura] *sf* (*crepa*) crack; (*fig: di rapporti*) rift.

incrociare [inkro'tʃare] **1** *vt* (**a**) (*gen*) to cross; (*strada, linea*) to cut across; ~ **le gambe** to cross one's legs; ~ **le braccia** to fold one's arms; (*fig*) to down tools, refuse to work. (**b**) (*autoveicolo, persona*) to meet; **l'ho incrociato per strada** I met him in the street. (**c**) (*animali, piante*) to cross. **2** *vi* (*Naut, Aer*) to cruise. **3**: ~**rsi** *vr* (*strade, rette*) to cross, intersect; (*persone, veicoli*) to pass each other; (*fig: sguardi*) to meet; (*: battute*) to fly thick and fast.

incrociatore [inkrotʃa'tore] *sm* (*Naut*) cruiser.

incrocio [in'krotʃo] *sm* (**a**) (*di strade*) crossroads, junction. (**b**) (*Zool, Bot*) cross.

incrollabile [inkrol'labile] *ag* (*fede*) unshakeable, firm.

incrostare [inkros'tare] **1** *vt* to encrust. **2**: ~**rsi** *vr*: ~**rsi di** to become encrusted with.

incrostazione [inkrostat'tsjone] *sf* incrustation; (*di calcare*) scale; (*nelle tubature*) fur, scale.

incruento, a [inkru'ento] *ag* (*battaglia*) without bloodshed, bloodless.

incubatrice [inkuba'tritʃe] *sf* incubator.

incubazione [inkubat'tsjone] *sf* incubation.

incubo ['inkubo] *sm* (*anche fig*) nightmare; **ho l'**~ **degli esami** exams are a nightmare for me.

incudine [in'kudine] *sf* anvil; **trovarsi** *o* **essere tra l'**~ **e il martello** (*fig*) to be between the devil and the deep blue sea.

inculcare [inkul'kare] *vt*: ~ **qc a qn** to inculcate sth into sb, instil sth into sb.

incuneare [inkune'are] *vt* to wedge.

incurabile [inku'rabile] *ag, sm/f* incurable.

incurante [inku'rante] *ag*: ~ **di** heedless of, careless of.

incuria [in'kurja] *sf* negligence.

incuriosire [inkurjo'sire] **1** *vt* to arouse the curiosity of, make curious. **2**: ~**rsi** *vr* to become curious.

incursione [inkur'sjone] *sf* (*Mil, Aer*) incursion, foray, raid; (*di ladri etc*) raid.

incurvare [inkur'vare] **1** *vt* (*piegare*) to curve, bend; **non** ~ **la schiena!** don't stoop!; **il lavoro a tavolino gli ha incurvato la schiena** *o* **le spalle** working at a desk has made him round-shouldered *o* has given him a stoop. **2**: ~**rsi** *vr* (*gen*) to bend; (*legno*) to warp; (*persona*) to develop a stoop, become bent.

incusso, a [in'kusso] *pp di* **incutere**.

incustodito, a [inkusto'dito] *ag* (*bagaglio*) unattended; **passaggio a livello** ~ unmanned level crossing.

incutere [in'kutere] *vt*: ~ **rispetto a qn** to command sb's respect; ~ **spavento a qn** to strike fear into sb; ~ **soggezione a qn** to cow sb.

indaco ['indako] *ag inv, sm* indigo.

indaffarato, a [indaffa'rato] *ag*: ~ **(a fare qc)** busy (doing sth).

indagare [inda'gare] **1** *vi*: ~ **su** to investigate; ~ **sul conto di qn** to investigate sb, make enquiries about sb; **è meglio non** ~ it's better not to enquire too closely. **2** *vt* to investigate, look into.

indagatore, trice [indaga'tore] *ag* (*sguardo, domanda*) searching; (*mente*) inquiring; **rivolgere a qn uno sguardo** ~ to give sb a searching look.

indagine [in'dadʒine] *sf* (**a**) (*inchiesta*) investigation, enquiry; **fare** *o* **svolgere un'**~ **(su)** to carry out an investigation *o* enquiry (into). (**b**) (*ricerca*) research, study; **fare** *o* **svolgere un'**~ **su** to carry out research into, make a study of.

indebitamente [indebita'mente] *av* (*immeritatamente*) undeservedly; (*erroneamente*) wrongfully.

indebitarsi [indebi'tarsi] *vr* to get into debt, run into debt; **si è indebitato fino al collo** he is up to his eyes in debt.

indebito, a [in'debito] *ag* (*onori, accuse*) undeserved; **appropriazione** ~**a** embezzlement.

indebolimento [indeboli'mento] *sm* (**a**) weakening. (**b**) (*debolezza*) weakness.

indebolire [indebo'lire] **1** *vt* to weaken. **2**: ~**rsi** *vr* (*persona*) to grow weak, become feeble; (*vista*) to grow worse.

indecente [inde'tʃɛnte] *ag* indecent.

indecenza [inde'tʃɛntsa] *sf* indecency; **è un'**~! (*vergogna*) it's scandalous!, it's a disgrace!

indecifrabile [indetʃi'frabile] *ag* (*scrittura*) illegible, undecipherable; (*messaggio, testo*) incomprehensible.

indecisione [indetʃi'zjone] *sf* indecision, indecisiveness.

indeciso, a [inde'tʃizo] *ag* (*persona*) indecisive; (*questione, risultato*) undecided; (*tempo*) unsettled; (*colore, forma*) indistinct.

indeclinabile [indekli'nabile] *ag* (*Gram*) indeclinable.

indecoroso, a [indeko'roso] *ag* (*comportamento*) indecorous, unseemly.

indefesso, a [inde'fɛsso] *ag* indefatigable, untiring.

indefinibile [indefi'nibile] *ag* indefinable.

indefinito, a [indefi'nito] *ag* (*indeterminato: anche Gram*) indefinite; (*impreciso*) undefined; (*irrisolto: questione, controversia*) unresolved.

indeformabile [indefor'mabile] *ag* crushproof.

indegno, a [in'deɲɲo] *ag* (*atto*) shameful; (*persona*) unworthy; **è** ~ **di tanta ammirazione** he doesn't deserve so much admiration.

indelebile [inde'lɛbile] *ag* indelible.

indelicatezza [indelika'tettsa] *sf* tactlessness; **è stata un'**~ **da parte sua** that was tactless of him.

indelicato, a [indeli'kato] *ag* (*domanda*) indiscreet, tactless.

indemoniato, a [indemo'njato] **1** *ag* possessed (by the devil); **quel ragazzino è** ~ (*fig*) that boy is a little demon. **2** *sm/f* person possessed by the devil; **gridare come un** ~ to shout like one possessed.

indenne [in'dɛnne] *ag* (*illeso*) unscathed, unharmed.

indennità [indenni'ta] *sf inv* (**a**) (*rimborso*) allowance; ~ **di trasferta** travel allowance; ~ **parlamentare** member of parliament's salary. (**b**) (*compenso*) indemnity.

indennizzare [indennid'dzare] *vt* to indemnify, compensate.

indennizzo [inden'niddzo] *sm* (*somma*) indemnity, compensation.

inderogabile [indero'gabile] *ag* binding.

indescrivibile [indeskri'vibile] *ag* indescribable.

indesiderabile [indeside'rabile] *ag* undesirable.

indesiderato, a [indeside'rato] *ag* unwanted.

indeterminatezza [indetermina'tettsa] *sf* vagueness.

indeterminativo, a [indetermina'tivo] *ag* (*Gram*)

indeterminato, a [indetermi'nato] *ag* (*tempo*) unspecified, indefinite; (*quantità, spazio*) indeterminate; **rimandare qc a tempo** ~ to postpone sth indefinitely.

indetto, a [in'detto] *pp di* **indire**.

India ['indja] *sf* India.

indiano, a [in'djano] **1** *ag* Indian. **2** *sm/f (dell'India)* Indian; *(dell'America)* (Red *o* American) Indian; **fare l'~** *(fig)* to feign ignorance.

indiavolato, a [indjavo'lato] *ag (persona: arrabbiato)* furious; *(bambino)* high-spirited; *(chiasso)* terrible, awful; *(danza, ritmo)* frenzied.

indicare [indi'kare] *vt* **(a)** *(mostrare)* to show, indicate; **~ qc a qn** to show sb sth; **~ la strada a qn** to show sb the way; **~ qn col dito** to point to *o* at sb; **m'indicò l'uscita** he showed me where the exit was; **la lancetta grande indica i minuti** the big hand shows *o* indicates the minutes; **cosa indica questo segnale?** what does this signal mean?; **le varie tappe erano indicate sulla carta** the various stops were indicated *o* shown *o* marked on the map; **i risultati indicano che...** the results indicate *o* show that.... **(b)** *(consigliare)* to suggest, recommend; **mi indicò un medico** he suggested *o* recommended a doctor to me.

indicativo, a [indika'tivo] **1** *ag (gen, Gram)* indicative; *(prezzo)* approximate; **a titolo puramente ~** just as an indication. **2** *sm (Gram)* indicative.

indicato, a [indi'kato] *ag (consigliato)* advisable; *(adatto)*: **~ per** suitable for, appropriate for; **questa cura non è ~a in caso di gravidanza** this treatment is not advisable during pregnancy.

indicatore, trice [indika'tore] **1** *ag* indicating; **cartello ~** sign. **2** *sm (Tecn)* gauge, indicator; **~ di velocità** *(Aut)* speedometer; *(Aer)* airspeed indicator; **~ della benzina** petrol gauge.

indicazione [indikat'tsjone] *sf (gen)* indication; *(istruzione)* instruction, direction; *(informazione)* piece of information; **~i** *(Med)* directions; **non è stato in grado di fornirmi ~i utili** he was unable to give me any useful information; **mi ha dato le ~i giuste per arrivare lì** his directions for getting there were correct.

indice ['inditʃe] **1** *sm (Anat)* index finger, forefinger. **(b)** *(indicatore)* needle, pointer; **tale comportamento è ~ d'ignoranza/di pigrizia** such behaviour is a sign of ignorance/laziness. **(c)** *(di libro)* (table of) contents *pl*; **~ analitico** index. **(d)** *(Rel)*: **l'I~** the Index; **mettere all'I~** to put on the Index; *(fig)* to blacklist. **(e)** *(Mat, Statistica, rapporto)* index; **~ di produzione** production index; **~ di gradimento** popularity rating. **2** *ag*: **dito ~** index finger, forefinger.

indicibile [indi'tʃibile] *ag* inexpressible.

indicizzare [inditʃid'dzare] *vt*: **~ al costo della vita** to index-link.

indietreggiare [indjetred'dʒare] *vi (anche fig)* to draw back; *(Mil)* to retreat.

indietro [in'djetro] *av* **(a)** *(stato, tempo)* behind; **essere ~ col lavoro/negli studi** to be behind with one's work/in one's studies; **rimanere ~** *(persona: di proposito)* to stay back; *(: proprio malgrado)* to drop *o* lag behind; *(: orologio)* to be slow; **questo orologio rimane sempre ~** this watch keeps losing time; **mentre dettava sono rimasto ~** while he was dictating I got behind; **essere ~ con i pagamenti** to be behind *o* in arrears with one's payments.

(b) *(moto)* back, backwards; **tornare ~** to go back; **mandare ~** to send back; **andare avanti e ~** to walk up and down; **non vado né avanti né ~** *(fig)* I'm not getting anywhere, I'm getting nowhere; **voltarsi ~** to look back, look round; **farsi ~** to move back; **fare un passo ~** to take a step back *o* backwards; **facciamo un passo ~ agli**

anni venti let's go back *o* cast our minds back to the twenties; **mettere ~ l'orologio** to put one's watch back; **(state) ~!** get back!; **camminare all'~** to walk backwards; **cadere all'~** to fall over backwards.

(c): **dare qc ~ a qn** *(restituire)* to give sth back to sb.

indifeso, a [indi'feso] *ag (città, confine)* undefended; *(persona)* defenceless, helpless.

indifferente [indiffe'rente] **1** *ag* **(a)** indifferent (to); **mi è ~** I don't mind, it's all the same to me; **quell'uomo mi è ~** that man means nothing to me, I feel quite indifferent towards that man; **vorrei partire, ~ quale giorno** I'd like to leave, it doesn't really matter which day. **(b)**: **non ~** *(notevole: somma, spesa)* sizeable, not inconsiderable. **2** *sm*: **fare l'~** to pretend to be indifferent, be *o* act casual; *(fingere di non vedere o sentire)* to pretend not to notice.

indifferenza [indiffe'rentsa] *sf* indifference.

indifferibile [indiffe'ribile] *ag* not deferable.

indigeno, a [in'didʒeno] **1** *ag* indigenous, native. **2** *sm/f* native.

indigente [indi'dʒente] **1** *ag* destitute, poverty-stricken. **2** *sm/f* pauper; **gli ~i** the poor *o* needy.

indigenza [indi'dʒentsa] *sf* extreme poverty, destitution; **vivere nell'~** to live in extreme poverty.

indigestione [indidʒes'tjone] *sf* indigestion; **fare ~ di qc** to eat too much of sth; *(fig: di romanzi, film)* to have a surfeit of sth.

indigesto, a [indi'dʒesto] *ag* indigestible; **il latte mi è ~** I find milk indigestible; **quel tipo mi è ~** I can't stand that fellow.

indignare [indiɲ'ɲare] **1** *vt*: **~ qn** to make sb indignant, fill sb with indignation. **2**: **~rsi** *vr*: **~rsi per** to get indignant about.

indignato, a [indiɲ'ɲato] *ag*: **~ (per)** indignant (at).

indignazione [indiɲɲat'tsjone] *sf* indignation; **con sua grande ~** much to his indignation.

indimenticabile [indimenti'kabile] *ag* unforgettable.

indio, a ['indjo] *ag, sm/f* (South American) Indian.

indipendente [indipen'dente] **1** *ag (gen, Pol, Gram)*: **~ (da)** independent (of); **'affittasi camera con ingresso ~'** 'room to let with independent access'. **2** *sm/f (Pol)* independent.

indipendentemente [indipendente'mente] *av* **(a)** *(in modo libero)* independently. **(b)** *(a prescindere da)*: **verrò ~ dal fatto che lui venga o meno** I'll come irrespective of whether he comes or not; **~ dal fatto che gli piaccia o meno, verrà!** whether he likes it or not, he's coming!

indipendenza [indipen'dentsa] *sf* independence.

indire [in'dire] *vt (concorso)* to announce; *(elezioni)* to call.

indiretto, a [indi'retto] *ag (gen)* indirect; **per vie ~e** indirectly.

indirizzare [indirit'tsare] **1** *vt (lettera, osservazione, richiesta)* to address; **mi hanno indirizzato qui** they sent me here; **un libro indirizzato ai ragazzi** a book intended *o* written for young people; **~ i propri sforzi verso** to direct one's efforts towards; **l'hanno indirizzato alla segretaria del personale** he was referred to the personnel assistant. **2**: **~rsi** *vr (rivolgersi)*: **~rsi a qn** to speak to sb, go and see sb.

indirizzo [indi'rittso] *sm* **(a)** *(di domicilio)* address; **sbagliare ~** to have the wrong address; **se vieni da me in cerca di aiuto, hai sbagliato ~** if you're looking for help from me, you've come to the wrong person. **(b)** *(fig: direzione)* direction, course; *(: tendenza)* trend; **cambiare ~** to change course o direction; **stanno seguendo l'~ giusto** they're on the right lines, they're going in the right direction; **l'attuale ~ politico** the present political trend.

indisciplina [indiʃʃi'plina] *sf* indiscipline.

indisciplinato, a [indiʃʃipli'nato] *ag* undisciplined, unruly.

indiscreto, a [indis'kreto] *ag* indiscreet.

indiscrezione [indiskret'tsjone] *sf* **(a)** *(qualità)* indiscretion. **(b)** *(azione)* indiscretion; *(fuga di notizie)* unconfirmed report.

indiscriminato, a [indiskrimi'nato] *ag* indiscriminate.

indiscusso, a [indis'kusso] *ag* *(autorità, campione)* undisputed.

indiscutibile [indisku'tibile] *ag* indisputable, unquestionable.

indispensabile [indispen'sabile] **1** *ag* *(essenziale)* essential, indispensable; *(necessario)* necessary; **rendersi ~** to make o.s. indispensable. **2** *sm*: **porterò con me solo l'~** I'll take the absolute minimum with me; **ho l'~ per il picnic** I've got everything I need for the picnic.

indispettire [indispet'tire] **1** *vt* to irritate, annoy. **2**: **~rsi** *vr* to become irritated, become annoyed.

indisponente [indispo'nɛnte] *ag* irritating, annoying.

indisporre [indis'porre] *vt* to antagonize.

indisposizione [indispozit'tsjone] *sf* (slight) indisposition.

indisposto, a [indis'posto] **1** *pp di* **indisporre**. **2** *ag* indisposed, unwell.

indissolubile [indisso'lubile] *ag* indissoluble.

indistintamente [indistinta'mente] *av* **(a)** *(senza distinzioni)* indiscriminately, without exception. **(b)** *(in modo indefinito: vedere, sentire)* vaguely, faintly.

indistinto, a [indis'tinto] *ag* *(gen)* indistinct; *(colori)* vague.

indistruttibile [indistrut'tibile] *ag* indestructible.

indisturbato, a [indistur'bato] *ag* undisturbed.

indivia [in'divja] *sf* endive.

individuale [individu'ale] *ag* *(gen)* individual; *(libertà)* personal; *(qualità)* distinctive; **lezioni ~i** individual tuition.

individualismo [individua'lizmo] *sm* individualism.

individualista, i, e [individua'lista] *sm/f* individualist.

individualità [individuali'ta] *sf* *(unicità)* individuality; *(personalità)* personality.

individualizzare [individualid'dzare] *vt* to individualize.

individualizzazione [individualiddzat'tsjone] *sf* individualization.

individualmente [individual'mente] *av* individually.

individuare [individu'are] *vt* **(a)** *(determinare)* to identify; *(: posizione)* to locate. **(b)** *(riconoscere)* to pick out; **sono riuscito ad individuarlo tra la folla** I managed to pick him out in the crowd.

individuazione [individuat'tsjone] *sf* *(gen)* identification; *(di posizione, relitto etc)* location.

individuo [indi'viduo] *sm* *(gen)* individual; *(peg: uomo)* character, fellow.

indivisibile [indivi'zibile] *ag* *(Mat)* indivisible; **quei due sono ~i** *(fig)* those two are inseparable.

indivisibilità [indivizibili'ta] *sf (Mat)* indivisibility.

indiviso, a [indi'vizo] *ag* undivided.

indiziare [indit'tsjare] *vt*: **~ qn** to cast suspicion on sb; **essere indiziato di qc** to be suspected of sth.

indiziato, a [indit'tsjato] **1** *ag* suspected. **2** *sm/f* suspect.

indizio [in'dittsjo] *sm* *(segno)* indication, sign; *(traccia)* clue; *(Dir)* piece of evidence.

indoeuropeo, a [indoeuro'pɛo] *ag, sm/f* Indo-European.

indole ['indole] *sf* nature, character; **di ~ bonacciona** good-natured.

indolente [indo'lɛnte] *ag* indolent, lazy.

indolenza [indo'lɛntsa] *sf* indolence, laziness.

indolenzimento [indolentsi'mento] *sm* *(vedi vb)* stiffness, ache; numbness.

indolenzire [indolen'tsire] **1** *vt* *(gambe, braccia etc)* to make stiff, cause to ache; *(: intorpidire)* to numb. **2** *vi (aus essere)*, **~rsi** *vr* to become stiff; to go numb.

indolore [indo'lore] *ag* painless.

indomabile [indo'mabile] *ag* *(animale)* untameable; *(fig: volontà)* indomitable; *(: incendio)* uncontrollable.

indomani [indo'mani] *sm*: **l'~** the next day, the following day.

indonesiano, a [indone'zjano] *ag, sm/f, sm* Indonesian.

indorare [indo'rare] *vt* *(rivestire in oro)* to gild; *(Culin)* to dip in egg yolk; **~ la pillola** *(fig)* to sugar the pill.

indossare [indos'sare] *vt* *(mettere indosso)* to put on; *(avere indosso)* to wear, have on.

indossatore, trice [indossa'tore] *sm/f* model; **fare l'~** to be a model.

indotto, a [in'dotto] *pp di* **indurre**.

indottrinare [indottri'nare] *vt* to indoctrinate.

indovinare [indovi'nare] *vt* **(a)** *(gen)* to guess; *(il futuro)* to predict, foretell; **tirare a ~** to have a shot in the dark; **indovina chi viene a cena!** guess who's coming to dinner! **(b)** *(azzeccare: risposta)* to get right; **una festa indovinata** a successful party; **non ne indovini una** you never get anything right.

indovinello [indovi'nɛllo] *sm* riddle, enigma.

indovino, a [indo'vino] *sm/f* fortune-teller, soothsayer.

indù [in'du] *ag, sm/f* Hindu.

indubbiamente [indubbja'mente] *av* undoubtedly; **sarai a Parigi per la fine del mese? — ~** will you be in Paris by the end of the month? — definitely.

indubbio, a [in'dubbjo] *ag* undoubted, undeniable; **è ~ che...** there is no doubt that... .

indubitabile [indubi'tabile] *ag* indubitable.

indugiare [indu'dʒare] *vi (attardarsi)* to take one's time; **non ha indugiato ad accettare l'invito** he wasted no time in accepting the invitation.

indugio [in'dudʒo] *sm* delay; **senza ~** without delay, straight away.

induismo [indu'izmo] *sm* Hinduism.

indulgente [indul'dʒɛnte] *ag* *(gen)* indulgent; *(giudice)* lenient.

indulgenza [indul'dʒɛntsa] *sf* **(a)** *(vedi ag)* indulgence; leniency. **(b)** *(Rel)* indulgence; **~ plenaria** plenary indulgence.

indulgere [indul'dʒɛre] *vi*: **~ (in)** to indulge (in).

indulto, a [in'dulto] *pp di* **indulgere**.

indumento [indu'mento] *sm* garment; **un negozio di ~i usati** a secondhand clothes shop; **~i intimi** underwear *sg*.

indurimento [induri'mento] *sm* hardening.

indurire [indu'rire] **1** *vt (anche fig: cuore)* to harden. **2** *vi (aus essere)*, **~rsi** *vr* to harden, become hard.

indurre [in'durre] *vt*: **~ qn a fare qc** to induce o persuade sb to do sth; **~ in tentazione** to lead into temptation; **~ in errore** to mislead, lead astray.

industria [in'dustrja] *sf* **(a)** *(attività)* industry; **~ pesante/leggera** heavy/light industry; **la pic-**

cola/grande ~ small/big business. **(b)** *(impresa)* industry, industrial concern.

industriale [indus'trjale] **1** *ag* industrial. **2** *sm/f* industrialist.

industrializzare [industrjalid'dzare] *vt* to industrialize.

industrializzazione [industrjaliddzat'tsjone] *sf* industrialization.

industriarsi [indus'trjarsi] *vr* to do one's best, try hard.

industrioso, a [indus'trjoso] *ag* industrious.

induttivo, a [indut'tivo] *ag* inductive.

induttore, trice [indut'tore] **1** *ag* *(Elettr)* inductive. **2** *sm* *(Elettr)* inductor.

induzione [indut'tsjone] *sf* induction.

inebetire [inebe'tire] **1** *vt* to stupefy, daze. **2** *vi* *(aus* essere), ~rsi *vr* to become stupid.

inebetito, a [inebe'tito] *ag* dazed.

inebriante [inebri'ante] *ag* *(alcolico)* intoxicating; *(fig: eccitante)* heady, exciting, exhilarating.

inebriare [inebri'are] **1** *vt (anche fig)* to intoxicate. **2:** ~rsi *vr* to become intoxicated; ~rsi alla vista di qc to go into raptures on seeing sth.

ineccepibile [inettʃe'pibile] *ag* *(comportamento)* exemplary, unexceptionable.

inedia [i'nedja] *sf* starvation; **morire d'**~ to starve to death; *(fig)* to die of boredom.

inedito, a [i'nedito] **1** *ag (non pubblicato)* unpublished; **notizia** ~a fresh piece of news. **2** *sm* unpublished work.

ineffabile [inef'fabile] *ag* ineffable.

inefficace [ineffi'katʃe] *ag* ineffective.

inefficacia [ineffi'katʃa] *sf* inefficacy, ineffectiveness.

inefficiente [ineffi'tʃɛnte] *ag* inefficient.

inefficienza [ineffi'tʃɛntsa] *sf* inefficiency.

ineguagliabile [inegwaʎ'ʎabile] *ag* incomparable, matchless.

ineguaglianza [inegwaʎ'ʎantsa] *sf* *(sociale)* inequality; *(di superficie, livello)* unevenness.

ineguale [ine'gwale] *ag (non uguale)* unequal; *(irregolare)* uneven.

ineluttabile [inelut'tabile] *ag* inescapable.

ineluttabilità [ineluttabili'ta] *sf* inescapability.

inenarrabile [inenar'rabile] *ag* unutterable.

inequivocabile [inekwivo'kabile] *ag* unequivocal.

inerente [ine'rɛnte] *ag:* ~ **a** concerning, regarding.

inerme [i'nɛrme] *ag* defenceless, unarmed.

inerpicarsi [inerpi'karsi] *vr:* ~ **su per** *(persona)* to clamber up; **la strada si inerpicava fino in cima al colle** the road wound steeply up to the top of the hill.

inerte [i'nɛrte] *ag* **(a)** *(persona)* inactive, apathetic. **(b)** *(Chim)* inert.

inerzia [i'nɛrtsja] *sf (gen, Fis)* inertia; *(inoperosità)* inactivity, apathy; **per forza d'**~ *(anche fig)* through inertia.

inesattezza [inezat'tettsa] *sf* inaccuracy.

inesatto[1], a [ine'zatto] *ag (impreciso)* inaccurate, inexact; *(erroneo)* incorrect.

inesatto[2], a [ine'zatto] *ag (non riscosso)* uncollected.

inesauribile [inezau'ribile] *ag* inexhaustible.

inesistente [inezis'tɛnte] *ag* non-existent.

inesistenza [inezis'tɛntsa] *sf* non-existence.

inesorabile [inezo'rabile] *ag (destino, nemico, ostilità)* inexorable, relentless; *(giudice)* inflexible.

inesorabilità [inezorabili'ta] *sf (vedi ag)* inexorability, relentlessness; inflexibility.

inesorabilmente [inezorabil'mente] *av* inexorably, relentlessly.

inesperienza [inespe'rjɛntsa] *sf* inexperience.

inesperto, a [ines'pɛrto] *ag* inexperienced.

inesplicabile [inespli'kabile] *ag* inexplicable.

inesplorato, a [inesplo'rato] *ag* unexplored.

inesploso, a [ines'plɔzo] *ag* unexploded.

inespressivo, a [inespres'sivo] *ag (viso)* expressionless, inexpressive.

inespresso, a [ines'presso] *ag* unexpressed.

inesprimibile [inespri'mibile] *ag* inexpressible.

inespugnabile [inespuɲ'ɲabile] *ag (fortezza, torre etc)* impregnable.

inespugnato, a [inespuɲ'ɲato] *ag (fortezza etc)* unconquered.

inestimabile [inesti'mabile] *ag (bene, qualità)* inestimable; *(valore)* incalculable; **un quadro di valore** ~ a priceless painting.

inestinguibile [inestin'gwibile] *ag* inextinguishable.

inestirpabile [inestir'pabile] *ag* ineradicable.

inettitudine [inetti'tudine] *sf* ineptitude.

inetto, a [i'netto] **1** *ag* incompetent; *(sciocco)* inept. **2** *sm/f* incompetent.

inevaso, a [ine'vazo] *ag (pratica, corrispondenza)* outstanding.

inevitabile [inevi'tabile] **1** *ag (ostacolo)* unavoidable; *(risultato)* inevitable; **era** ~! it was inevitable!, it was bound to happen!; **era** ~ **che lo scoprisse** he was bound to discover it. **2** *sm:* **l'**~ the inevitable.

inevitabilmente [inevitabil'mente] *ag* inevitably.

inezia [i'nettsja] *sf* trifle, bagatelle.

infagottare [infagot'tare] **1** *vt* to bundle up, wrap up; **essere infagottato** to be well wrapped up. **2:** ~rsi *vr* to wrap o.s. up.

infallibile [infal'libile] *ag* infallible.

infallibilità [infallibili'ta] *sf* infallibility.

infamante [infa'mante] *ag (accusa)* defamatory, slanderous.

infame [in'fame] *ag (persona)* infamous; *(calunnia)* vile; *(fig: pessimo)* awful, dreadful.

infamia [in'famja] *sf* **(a)** *(disonore)* infamy. **(b)** *(azione)* infamous deed, vile deed.

infangare [infan'gare] **1** *vt* to cover with mud; *(fig: reputazione, nome)* to sully. **2:** ~rsi *vr* to get covered in mud; *(fig)* to be sullied.

infanticida, i, e [infanti'tʃida] *sm/f* infanticide *(person)*.

infanticidio [infanti'tʃidjo] *sm* infanticide.

infantile [infan'tile] *ag* **(a)** *(per bambini)* child *attr*; *(di bambino: grazia, ingenuità)* childlike; **asilo** ~ nursery school; **letteratura** ~ children's books. **(b)** *(immaturo)* childish, infantile.

infantilismo [infanti'lizmo] *sm* infantilism.

infanzia [in'fantsja] *sf* **(a)** *(periodo)* childhood; **prima** ~ infancy. **(b)** *(bambini)* children; **l'**~ **abbandonata** abandoned children.

infarcire [infar'tʃire] *vt (Culin, fig):* ~ **(di)** to fill (with), stuff (with).

infarinare [infari'nare] *vt* to dip in flour.

infarinatura [infarina'tura] *sf (fig: rudimenti)* smattering.

infarto [in'farto] *sm (Med)* coronary.

infastidire [infasti'dire] **1** *vt* to annoy, irritate. **2:** ~rsi *vr* to get annoyed, get irritated.

infaticabile [infati'kabile] *ag* indefatigable, tireless.

infatti [in'fatti] *cong* as a matter of fact, in fact, actually.

infatuarsi [infatu'arsi] *vr:* ~rsi **di** to become infatuated with.

infatuazione [infatuat'tsjone] *sf* infatuation.

infausto, a [in'fausto] *ag (infelice)* unhappy; **presagio** ~ ill omen.

infecondità [infekondi'ta] *sf* infertility.

infecondo, a [infe'kondo] *ag (anche fig)* infertile.
infedele [infe'dele] **1** *ag* unfaithful. **2** *sm/f (Storia)* infidel.
infedeltà [infedel'ta] *sf inv* infidelity.
infelice [infe'litʃe] **1** *ag* **(a)** *(persona, sguardo, vita)* unhappy; *(incontro, osservazione, posizione)* unfortunate; **una frase** ~ an unfortunate choice of words. **(b)** *(mal riuscito: traduzione)* bad, poor; **esito** ~ unsuccessful outcome. **2** *sm/f* poor wretch.
infelicità [infelitʃi'ta] *sf (gen)* unhappiness; *(inopportunità)* inopportuneness.
infeltrire [infel'trire] *vi (aus essere)*, ~**rsi** *vr (lana)* to become matted.
inferiore [infe'rjore] **1** *ag (parte, rango, velocità)* lower; *(quantità, numero)* smaller; *(qualità, intelligenza)* inferior; ~ **alla media** below average; **il piano** ~ the next floor down; ~ **a** *(numero, quantità)* less *o* smaller than, below; *(meno buono)* inferior to. **2** *sm/f* inferior.
inferiorità [inferjori'ta] *sf* inferiority; **complesso di** ~ inferiority complex.
inferire¹ [infe'rire] *vt*: ~ **un colpo a** to strike.
inferire² [infe'rire] *vt (dedurre)* to infer, deduce.
infermeria [inferme'ria] *sf (gen)* infirmary; *(di scuola, nave)* sick bay.
infermiera [infer'mjɛra] *sf* nurse.
infermiere [infer'mjɛre] *sm* male nurse.
infermità [infermi'ta] *sf inv (stato)* infirmity; *(malattia)* illness; ~ **di mente** mental illness.
infermo, a [in'fermo] **1** *ag (fisicamente debole)* infirm; *(malato)* ill; ~ **di mente** mentally ill. **2** *sm/f* invalid.
infernale [infer'nale] *ag (gen)* infernal; *(complotto, proposito)* diabolical; **fa un caldo** ~ *(fam)* it's roasting; **un tempo** ~ *(fam)* hellish weather.
inferno [in'ferno] *sm* hell; **la mia vita è un** ~ my life is hell; **fare una vita d'**~ to lead a dog's life; **mandare qn all'**~ to tell sb to go to hell; **soffrire le pene dell'**~ *(fig)* to go through hell.
inferocire [infero'tʃire] **1** *vt* to make fierce. **2** *vi (aus essere)*, ~**rsi** *vr* to become fierce.
inferriata [infer'rjata] *sf* grating.
inferto, a [in'ferto] *pp di* **inferire¹**.
infervorare [infervo'rare] **1** *vt* to arouse enthusiasm in. **2**: ~**rsi** *vr* to get excited, get carried away.
infestare [infes'tare] *vt* to infest; **infestato dai topi** infested with *o* overrun by mice.
infettare [infet'tare] **1** *vt (gen)* to infect; *(acqua, aria)* to pollute, contaminate. **2**: ~**rsi** *vr* to become infected.
infettivo, a [infet'tivo] *ag* infectious.
infetto, a [in'fetto] *ag (ferita)* infected; *(acque, aria)* polluted, contaminated.
infezione [infet'tsjone] *sf* infection.
infiacchire [infjak'kire] **1** *vt (anche fig)* to weaken, exhaust. **2**: ~**rsi** *vr* to grow weak.
infiammabile [infjam'mabile] *ag, sm* inflammable.
infiammare [infjam'mare] **1** *vt (gen)* to set fire to, set alight; *(Med: ferita, organo)* to inflame; **il suo discorso infiammò gli animi dei rivoltosi** his speech inflamed the rebels. **2**: ~**rsi** *vr (gen)* to catch fire; *(Med)* to become inflamed.
infiammatorio, a [infjamma'tɔrjo] *ag* inflammatory.
infiammazione [infjammat'tsjone] *sf* inflammation.
infiascare [infjas'kare] *vt (vino, olio)* to bottle.
inficiare [infi'tʃare] *vt (Dir: atto, dichiarazione)* to challenge.
infido, a [in'fido] *ag* unreliable, treacherous.

infierire [infje'rire] *vi*: ~ **su** *(fisicamente)* to attack furiously; *(verbalmente)* to rage at; *(epidemia, peste)* to rage over.
infiggere [in'fiddʒere] *vt*: ~ **qc in** to drive sth into, thrust sth into.
infilare [infi'lare] **1** *vt* **(a)** *(introdurre: moneta, chiave)* to insert; **infilò le mani in tasca** he put *o* slipped his hands into his pockets; **le infilò un anello al dito** he put *o* slipped a ring on her finger; **infilò la mano nel cassetto** he slid his hand into the drawer; **puoi** ~ **anche questo nella busta?** can you put this in the same envelope?; **riesci ad infilarci ancora qualcosa?** *(in borsa, valigia)* can you manage to squeeze anything else in?
(b) *(ago, perle)* to thread.
(c) *(indossare)* to put on; ~**rsi la giacca** to put on one's jacket.
(d) *(imboccare: strada)* to turn into, take; **infilò l'uscio e se ne andò** he slipped through the door and off he went.
2: ~**rsi** *vr (introdursi)*: ~**rsi in** to slip into; ~**rsi tra la folla** to merge into the crowd; **il gatto si è infilato lì sotto e non riesco a prenderlo** the cat slipped under there and I can't get it to come out; ~**rsi a letto** to slip into bed; ~**rsi in un taxi** to jump into a taxi.
infiltrarsi [infil'trarsi] *vr (gen)* to infiltrate; *(fumo, gas, luce)* to penetrate, filter through; *(umidità, liquido)* to penetrate, seep in; ~ **in** to infiltrate; to penetrate into; to filter (through) into; to seep into.
infiltrato, a [infil'trato] *sm/f* infiltrator.
infiltrazione [infiltrat'tsjone] *sf (vedi vb)* infiltration; penetration; seepage.
infilzare [infil'tsare] *vt (trafiggere)* to run through; *(sullo spiedo)* to skewer; ~ **un pollo sullo spiedo** to spit a chicken.
infimo, a ['infimo] *ag (qualità)* very poor; **un albergo di** ~ **ordine** a third-rate hotel.
infine [in'fine] *av (alla fine)* finally; *(per concludere)* in short.
infingardo, a [infin'gardo] **1** *ag* lazy. **2** *sm/f* slacker.
infinità [infini'ta] *sf* infinity; **un'**~ **di** an infinite number of; **ho un'**~ **di cose da fare** I have masses of things to do.
infinitamente [infinita'mente] *av (anche fig)* infinitely; **mi dispiace** ~ I'm extremely sorry; **amare qn** ~ to be madly in love with sb.
infinitesimale [infinitezi'male] *ag* infinitesimal.
infinitesimo, a [infini'tezimo] *ag, sm* infinitesimal.
infinito, a [infi'nito] **1** *ag (gen)* infinite; **con** ~ **rammarico** with deep regret; **con** ~ **a gioia** with great pleasure. **2** *sm* **(a)** *(Filosofia)*: **l'**~ the infinite; *(Mat, Fot)* infinity; **all'**~ *(senza fine)* endlessly; *(Mat)* to infinity; **te l'ho ripetuto all'**~! I've told you a thousand times! **(b)** *(Gram)* infinitive; **all'**~ in the infinitive.
infinocchiare [infinok'kjare] *vt (fam)* to hoodwink, bamboozle.
infiorare [infjo'rare] *vt* to deck with flowers.
infiorescenza [infjoreʃ'ʃentsa] *sf* inflorescence.
infirmare [infir'mare] *vt (Dir)* to invalidate.
infischiarsi [infis'kjarsi] *vr*: ~ **di** not to care about; **me ne infischio!** I couldn't care less!
infisso [in'fisso] **1** *pp di* **infiggere**. **2** *sm (di porta, finestra)* frame.
infittire [infit'tire] **1** *vt* to thicken. **2**: ~**rsi** *vr* to become thicker.
inflazionare [inflattsjo'nare] *vt (Econ)* to inflate.

inflazione [inflat'tsjone] *sf (Econ)* inflation; *(fig)* proliferation.

inflazionistico, a, ci, che [inflattsjo'nistiko] *ag (Econ)* inflationary.

inflessibile [infles'sibile] *ag (gen)* inflexible; *(carattere)* unyielding; *(volontà)* iron *attr*.

inflessibilità [inflessibili'ta] *sf* inflexibility.

inflessione [infles'sjone] *sf* inflexion.

infliggere [in'fliddʒere] *vt (pena, castigo)* to inflict; *(multa)* to impose.

inflitto, a [in'flitto] *pp di* **infliggere**.

influente [influ'ente] *ag* influential.

influenza [influ'entsa] *sf* **(a)** *(ascendente, peso)* influence; **è una persona che ha ~** he's an influential person; **avere ~ su qn/qc** to have an influence on sb/sth; **subire l'~ di qn/qc** to be influenced by sb/sth. **(b)** *(Med)* influenza, flu; **prendersi l'~** to catch (the) flu.

influenzabile [influen'tsabile] *ag* easily influenced.

influenzale [influen'tsale] *ag (Med)* influenza *attr*.

influenzare [influen'tsare] *vt* to influence, have an influence on.

influenzato, a [influen'tsato] *ag (ammalato)*: **essere ~** to have (the) flu; **è a letto ~** he's in bed with flu.

influire [influ'ire] *vi*: **~ su** to influence, affect.

influsso [in'flusso] *sm* influence.

infocare [info'kare] **1** *vt* to make red-hot. **2**: **~rsi** *(metallo)* to become red-hot; *(fig: persona)* to become excited.

infocato, a [info'kato] *ag (metallo etc)* red-hot; *(sabbia, guance)* burning; *(discorso)* heated, passionate.

infognarsi [infoɲ'narsi] *vr (fam)* to get into a mess; **~ in un mare di debiti** to be up to one's eyes in debt.

infoltire [infol'tire] **1** *vt* to thicken, make thicker. **2** *vi (aus essere)* to become thicker.

infondatezza [infonda'tettsa] *sf* groundlessness.

infondato, a [infon'dato] *ag* unfounded, groundless.

infondere [in'fondere] *vt*: **~ qc in qn** to instil sth in sb; **~ fiducia in qn** to inspire sb with confidence.

inforcare [infor'kare] *vt* **(a)** *(prendere con la forca)* to fork (up). **(b)** *(bicicletta, cavallo)* to mount, get on; *(occhiali)* to put on.

informale [infor'male] *ag* informal.

informare [infor'mare] **1** *vt*: **~ qn di qc** to inform sb of *o* about sth, tell sb of *o* about sth; **tenere informato qn** to keep sb informed. **2**: **~rsi** *vr* to make inquiries; **~rsi di** to inquire about, ask about, find out about; **un'altra volta informati!** next time make sure you're better informed!

informatica [infor'matika] *sf (scienza)* computer science; *(tecnica)* data processing.

informativo, a [informa'tivo] *ag* informative; **a titolo ~** for information only.

informatore, trice [informa'tore] **1** *ag* informative. **2** *sm/f* informer.

informazione [informat'tsjone] *sf* **(a)** *(ragguaglio)* piece of information; **può darmi un'~?** can you give me some information?; **chiedere/prendere ~i sul conto di qn** to ask for/get information about sb; **a titolo d'~** for information; **ufficio ~i** information *o* inquiry office. **(b)** *(Inform)* information; **teoria dell'~** information theory.

informe [in'forme] *ag* formless, shapeless.

informicolarsi [informiko'larsi] *vr*, **informicolirsi** [informiko'lirsi] *vr*: **mi si è informicolata una gamba** I've got pins and needles in my leg.

infornare [infor'nare] *vt* to put in the oven.

infornata [infor'nata] *sf (anche fig)* batch.

infortunarsi [infortu'narsi] *vr* to injure o.s., have an accident.

infortunato, a [infortu'nato] **1** *ag* injured, hurt. **2** *sm/f* injured person.

infortunio [infor'tunjo] *sm* accident; **~ sul lavoro** industrial accident, accident at work.

infortunistica [infortu'nistika] *sf* study of (industrial) accidents.

infossamento [infossa'mento] *sm (nel terreno)* hollow, depression.

infossarsi [infos'sarsi] *vr (terreno)* to sink; *(guance)* to become hollow.

infossato, a [infos'sato] *ag (guance)* hollow; *(occhi)* sunken.

infradiciare [infradi'tʃare] **1** *vt (inzuppare)* to soak, drench; *(marcire)* to rot. **2**: **~rsi** *vr (vedi vt)* to get soaked, get drenched; to rot.

infrangere [in'frandʒere] **1** *vt (legge, patto)* to violate, break. **2**: **~rsi** *vr (onde)* to break, smash; **le onde s'infrangevano sugli scogli** the waves were breaking on the rocks.

infrangibile [infran'dʒibile] *ag* unbreakable.

infranto, a [in'franto] **1** *pp di* **infrangere**. **2** *ag (anche fig: cuore)* broken.

infrarosso, a [infra'rosso] *ag, sm* infrared.

infrasettimanale [infrasettima'nale] *ag* midweek *attr*.

infrastruttura [infrastrut'tura] *sf* infrastructure.

infrazione [infrat'tsjone] *sf* infringement.

infreddolire [infreddo'lire] *vi (aus essere)*, **~rsi** *vr* to get cold.

infreddolito, a [infreddo'lito] *ag* cold, chilled; **sono tutto ~** I'm chilled through.

infrequente [infre'kwente] *ag* infrequent.

infrollire [infrol'lire] *vi (aus essere)*, **~rsi** *vr (selvaggina)* to become high.

infruttuoso, a [infruttu'oso] *ag (anche fig)* unfruitful, fruitless.

infuori [in'fwori] *av* **(a)**: **~, all'~** *(sporgere)* out, outwards; **avere i denti/gli occhi ~** to have prominent teeth/eyes. **(b)**: **all'~ di** *(eccetto)* except, apart from; **non so altro all'~ di questo** that's all I know.

infuriare [infu'rjare] **1** *vt* to enrage, make furious. **2**: **~rsi** *vr* to fly into a rage.

infusione [infu'zjone] *sf (operazione)* infusion; *(infuso)* infusion, herb tea; **lasciare in ~** to leave to infuse.

infuso, a [in'fuzo] **1** *pp di* **infondere**. **2** *ag*: **scienza ~a** *(anche iro)* innate knowledge. **3** *sm* infusion, herb tea.

Ing. *abbr di* **ingegnere**.

ingaggiare [ingad'dʒare] *vt (assumere: operai)* to take on, engage; *(: Sport: giocatore)* to sign; **~ battaglia** *(Mil)* to engage the enemy.

ingaggio [in'gaddʒo] *sm (di operaio)* taking on, engaging; *(Sport)* signing on; *(: somma)* signing-on fee.

ingagliardire [ingaʎʎar'dire] **1** *vt* to strengthen, invigorate. **2** *vi (aus essere)*, **~rsi** *vr* to grow stronger.

ingannare [ingan'nare] **1** *vt (imbrogliare)* to deceive; *(tradire: moglie, marito)* to cheat on; **le apparenze spesso ingannano** appearances can be deceptive; **~ il tempo** to while away the time; **abbiamo giocato a carte per ~ la noia** we had a game of cards to relieve the boredom. **2**: **~rsi** *vr* to be mistaken, be wrong; **~rsi sul conto di qn** to be mistaken about sb.

ingannatore, trice [inganna'tore] *ag (gen)* deceptive; *(persona, sguardo)* deceitful.

ingannevole [ingan'nevole] *ag (gen)* deceptive; *(consiglio)* misleading.

inganno [in'ganno] *sm (imbroglio)* deceit, deception; *(insidia)* trick; *(illusione)* illusion; **trarre in** ~ to deceive, mislead; **con l'**~ by a trick; ~ **dei sensi** sensory illusion.

ingarbugliare [ingarbuʎ'ʎare] **1** *vt (fili, corde)* to tangle; *(fig: situazione)* to muddle, confuse. **2**: ~**rsi** *vr (fili, corde, capelli)* to get tangled; *(fig: situazione)* to become muddled, become confused.

ingarbugliato, a [ingarbuʎ'ʎato] *ag (vedi vb)* tangled; muddled, confused.

ingegnarsi [indʒeɲ'ɲarsi] *vr* to use one's ingenuity; **non avevamo l'occorrente ma ci siamo ingegnati** we didn't have what we needed but we made do; ~ **per vivere** to live by one's wits; **basta** ~ **un po'** you just need a bit of ingenuity; **bisogna che ti ingegni** use *o* show a bit of ingenuity.

ingegnere [indʒeɲ'ɲere] *sm* engineer.

ingegneria [indʒeɲɲe'ria] *sf* engineering.

ingegno [in'dʒeɲɲo] *sm* **(a)** *(intelligenza)* intelligence, brains *pl*; *(attitudine, talento)* talent; *(ingegnosità)* ingenuity; **avere dell'**~ to have a creative mind; **aguzzare l'**~ to sharpen one's wits. **(b)** *(persona)* mind; **è un bell'**~ he has a good brain; **i più grandi** ~**i del secolo** the greatest minds of the century.

ingegnosità [indʒeɲɲosi'ta] *sf* ingenuity.

ingegnoso, a [indʒeɲ'ɲoso] *ag* ingenious, clever.

ingelosire [indʒelo'sire] **1** *vt* to make jealous. **2**: ~**rsi** *vr* to become jealous.

ingente [in'dʒɛnte] *ag* huge, enormous.

ingentilire [indʒenti'lire] **1** *vt* to refine, civilize. **2**: ~**rsi** *vr* to become more refined, become more civilized.

ingenuità [indʒenui'ta] *sf* naïvety, ingenuousness.

ingenuo, a [in'dʒɛnuo] **1** *ag* naïve, ingenuous. **2** *sm/f*: **è un** ~ he is naive; **fare l'**~ to act the innocent.

ingerenza [indʒe'rɛntsa] *sf* interference.

ingerire [indʒe'rire] *vt* to ingest.

ingessare [indʒes'sare] *vt* to put in plaster.

ingessatura [indʒessa'tura] *sf* plaster (cast).

ingestione [indʒes'tjone] *sf* ingestion.

Inghilterra [ingil'tɛrra] *sf* England.

inghiottire [ingjot'tire] *vt (anche fig)* to swallow; **la barca fu inghiottita dai flutti** the boat was swallowed up *o* engulfed by the waves; **essere inghiottito dal buio** to be swallowed up by the darkness; **ne ha inghiottite tante nella vita** *(fig: dispiaceri)* he's had so much to put up with in life.

inghippo [in'gippo] *sm* trick.

ingiallire [indʒal'lire] *vt, vi (aus essere)* to (turn) yellow.

ingiallito, a [indʒal'lito] *ag* yellowed.

ingigantire [indʒigan'tire] **1** *vt (immagine)* to enlarge, magnify; *(fig: problema)* to exaggerate. **2** *vi (aus essere)*, ~**rsi** *vr* to become gigantic, become enormous.

inginocchiarsi [indʒinok'kjarsi] *vr* to kneel (down); **essere inginocchiato** to be kneeling down, be on one's knees.

inginocchiatoio [indʒinokkja'tojo] *sm* prie-dieu.

ingioiellare [indʒojel'lare] *vt* to bejewel, adorn with jewels.

ingiù [in'dʒu] *av* down, downwards; **bambini dai dieci anni** ~ children of ten years old and under; **con la testa all'**~ head downwards.

ingiungere [in'dʒundʒere] *vt*: ~ **a qn di fare qc** to enjoin *o* order sb to do sth.

ingiunto, a [in'dʒunto] *pp di* **ingiungere**.

ingiunzione [indʒun'tsjone] *sf* injunction, command.

ingiuria [in'dʒurja] *sf (insulto)* insult; **coprire qn di** ~**e** to heap abuse on sb; **le** ~**e del tempo** the ravages of time.

ingiuriare [indʒu'rjare] *vt* to insult, abuse.

ingiurioso, a [indʒu'rjoso] *ag* insulting, abusive.

ingiustamente [indʒusta'mente] *av* unjustly.

ingiustificabile [indʒustifi'kabile] *ag* unjustifiable.

ingiustificato, a [indʒustifi'kato] *ag* unjustified.

ingiustizia [indʒus'tittsja] *sf* injustice; **ha commesso un'**~ he was unjust, he acted unjustly; **è un'**~! that's not fair!

ingiusto, a [in'dʒusto] *ag* unjust, unfair; **essere** ~ **con qn** to be unfair *o* unjust to sb.

inglese [in'glese] **1** *ag* English. **2** *sm/f* Englishman/woman; **gli I**~**i** the English, English people. **3** *sm (lingua)* English; **parlare (l')**~ to speak English.

inglorioso, a [inglo'rjoso] *ag* inglorious.

ingobbire [ingob'bire] *vi (aus essere)*, ~**rsi** *vr* to become stooped.

ingoiare [ingo'jare] *vt (anche fig)* to swallow; **se l'ingoiò in un boccone** he swallowed it in one (go); **furono ingoiati dai flutti** they were swallowed up *o* engulfed by the waves; **è stato un boccone amaro da** ~ *(fig)* it was a bitter pill to swallow; **ha dovuto** ~ **tante amarezze** he has had to endure so many disappointments; **ha dovuto** ~ **il rospo** *(fig)* he had to accept the situation, whether he liked it or not.

ingolfare [ingol'fare] **1** *vt (Aut)* to flood. **2**: ~**rsi** *vr (Aut)* to flood.

ingolosire [ingolo'sire] **1** *vt*: ~ **qn** to make sb's mouth water; *(fig)* to attract sb. **2** *vi (aus essere)*, ~**rsi** *vr*: ~ **o** ~**rsi (di)** *(anche fig)* to become greedy (for).

ingombrante [ingom'brante] *ag* cumbersome.

ingombrare [ingom'brare] *vt (strada)* to block, obstruct; *(stanza, tavolo)* to clutter up.

ingombro¹, a [in'gombro] *ag*: ~ **di** *(strada)* blocked by; *(stanza)* cluttered up with.

ingombro² [in'gombro] *sm* obstacle; **essere d'**~ to be in the way.

ingordigia [ingor'didʒa] *sf*: ~ **(di)** *(vedi ag)* greed (for); avidity (for).

ingordo, a [in'gordo] **1** *ag*: ~ **(di)** *(cibo)* greedy (for); *(fig: denaro)* greedy (for), avid (for). **2** *sm/f* glutton.

ingorgare [ingor'gare] **1** *vt* to block. **2**: ~**rsi** *vr* to get blocked.

ingorgo, ghi [in'gorgo] *sm* **(a)** *(di tubo etc)* blockage, obstruction. **(b)** *(anche:* ~ **stradale)** *(traffic)* jam.

ingozzare [ingot'tsare] **1** *vt (animali)* to fatten; *(fig: persona)*: ~ **(di cibo)** to stuff (with food). **2**: ~**rsi** *vr*: ~**rsi (di)** *(fig)* to stuff o.s. (with).

ingranaggio [ingra'naddʒo] *sm (Tecn)* gear; *(: di orologio)* mechanism; **gli** ~**i della burocrazia** the bureaucratic machinery; **essere preso nell'**~ *(fig)* to be caught in the system.

ingranare [ingra'nare] **1** *vi (Tecn)* to engage; **non riesco ad** ~ **nel nuovo lavoro** I can't seem to get into my stride in the new job. **2** *vt*: ~ **la marcia** *(Aut)* to engage gear, get into gear.

ingrandimento [ingrandi'mento] *sm (di città, azienda)* development, growth; *(di casa)* extension; *(di strada)* widening; *(Ottica)* magnification; *(Fot)* enlargement; **lente d'**~ magnifying glass.

ingrandire [ingran'dire] **1** *vt (azienda, città)* to develop, expand; *(locale)* to extend; *(strada)* to widen; *(Ottica)* to magnify; *(Fot)* to enlarge; *(fig: storia: esagerare)* to exaggerate. **2**: ~**rsi** *vr (gen)* to get bigger; *(azienda, città)* to grow, expand;

(strada) to get wider; *(potere)* to grow; *(problema)* to become exaggerated.

ingranditore [ingrandi'tore] *sm (Fot)* enlarger.

ingrassaggio [ingras'saddʒo] *sm* greasing.

ingrassare [ingras'sare] **1** *vt* **(a)** *(animali)* to fatten (up); *(persone)* to make fat; **questo vestito ti ingrassa** this dress makes you look fat; **i dolci ingrassano** sweets are fattening. **(b)** *(lubrificare)* to grease. **2** *vi (aus* essere*),* ~**rsi** *vr* to get fat, put on weight; ~**rsi alle spalle altrui** *(fig)* to thrive at the expense of others.

ingratitudine [ingrati'tudine] *sf* ingratitude, ungratefulness.

ingrato, a [in'grato] **1** *ag (persona)* ungrateful; *(lavoro)* thankless, unrewarding. **2** *sm/f* ungrateful person; **sei un** ~! you're an ungrateful wretch!

ingraziarsi [ingrat'tsjarsi] *vt:* ~ **qn** to ingratiate o.s. with sb.

ingrediente [ingre'djɛnte] *sm* ingredient.

ingresso [in'grɛsso] *sm* **(a)** *(porta)* entrance; *(atrio)* hall; ~ **principale** main entrance; ~ **di servizio** tradesmen's entrance. **(b)** *(accesso)* admission; **fare il proprio** ~ to make one's entrance; **vietato l'**~ no admittance; ~ **libero** admission free; **biglietto d'**~ admission ticket, entrance ticket; **prezzo d'**~ cost of admission.

ingrossamento [ingrossa'mento] *sm* swelling.

ingrossare [ingros'sare] **1** *vt (spessore, patrimonio)* to increase; *(fiume)* to swell; *(muscoli)* to develop; ~ **le file** *(Mil, fig)* to swell the ranks; **quest'abito ti ingrossa** this dress makes you (look) fat. **2** *vi (aus* essere*),* ~**rsi** *vr (vedi vt)* to increase; to swell; to develop; *(persona)* to put on weight.

ingrosso [in'grɔsso] *sm:* **all'**~ *(Comm)* wholesale; **prezzo all'**~ wholesale price; **vendere all'**~, **effettuare vendite all'**~ to sell wholesale.

ingrugnato, a [ingruɲ'ɲato] *ag* grumpy.

inguaiarsi [ingwa'jarsi] *vr* to get into trouble.

inguainare [ingwai'nare] *vt* to sheathe.

ingualcibile [ingwal'tʃibile] *ag* crease-resistant.

inguaribile [ingwa'ribile] *ag* incurable.

inguine ['ingwine] *sm (Anat)* groin.

ingurgitare [ingurdʒi'tare] *vt* to gulp down.

inibire [ini'bire] *vt* to inhibit.

inibito, a [ini'bito] **1** *ag* inhibited. **2** *sm/f* inhibited person.

inibitorio, a [inibi'tɔrjo] *ag (Psic)* inhibitory, inhibitive; *(provvedimento, misure)* restrictive.

inibizione [inibit'tsjone] *sf* inhibition.

iniettare [injet'tare] **1** *vt* to inject; ~**rsi una sostanza** to inject o.s. with a substance; **con gli occhi iniettati di sangue** with bloodshot eyes. **2:** ~**rsi** *vr:* **gli occhi gli si iniettarono di sangue** his eyes became bloodshot.

iniettore [injet'tore] *sm (Tecn)* injector.

iniezione [injet'tsjone] *sf* injection; **fare** *o* **farsi fare un'**~ to get an injection; **fare un'**~ **(a qn)** to give (sb) an injection.

inimicare [inimi'kare] **1** *vt* to alienate, make hostile; **si è inimicato gli amici di un tempo** he has alienated his old friends. **2:** ~**rsi** *vr:* ~**rsi con qn** to fall out with sb.

inimicizia [inimi'tʃittsja] *sf* enmity.

inimitabile [inimi'tabile] *ag* inimitable.

inimmaginabile [inimmadʒi'nabile] *ag* unimaginable.

ininfiammabile [ininfjam'mabile] *ag* nonflammable.

inintelligibile [inintelli'dʒibile] *ag* unintelligible.

ininterrottamente [ininterrotta'mente] *av* nonstop, continuously; **ha continuato a piovere** ~ **per 2 settimane** it rained non-stop *o* continuously

for 2 weeks.

ininterrotto, a [ininter'rotto] *ag (fila)* continuous, unbroken; *(viavai, rumore)* steady, uninterrupted.

iniquità [inikwi'ta] *sf* iniquity.

iniquo, a [i'nikwo] *ag* iniquitous.

iniziale [init'tsjale] *ag, sf* initial.

inizialmente [inittsjal'mente] *av* initially, at first.

iniziare [init'tsjare] *vt* **(a)** *(cominciare)* to begin, start; *(dibattito, ostilità)* to open; ~ **a fare qc** to start doing sth. **(b)** *(persona: a un culto)* to initiate into; *(: a un attività)* to introduce to.

iniziativa [inittsja'tiva] *sf (gen)* initiative; **di propria** ~ on one's own initiative; **l'**~ **privata** *(Comm)* private enterprise.

iniziato, a [init'tsjato] **1** *ag (a un culto)* initiated. **2** *sm/f* initiate; **gli** ~**i** the initiated.

iniziatore, trice [inittsja'tore] *sm/f* initiator.

iniziazione [inittsjat'tsjone] *sf* initiation.

inizio [i'nittsjo] *sm* beginning, start; **fin dall'**~ from the beginning; **all'**~ at the beginning, at the start; **essere agli** ~**i** *(progetto, lavoro etc)* to be in the initial stages.

innaffiare [innaf'fjare] *vt* to water.

innaffiatoio [innaffja'tojo] *sm* watering can.

innalzamento [innaltsa'mento] *sm (gen)* raising; *(fig: al trono)* elevation.

innalzare [innal'tsare] **1** *vt (gen: sollevare)* to raise; *(costruire: monumento)* to erect; ~ **gli occhi al cielo** to raise one's eyes to heaven; ~ **al trono** to raise to the throne. **2:** ~**rsi** *vr* to rise.

innamoramento [innamora'mento] *sm* falling in love.

innamorare [innamo'rare] **1** *vt* to enchant, charm; **un viso che innamora** an enchanting *o* a delightful face. **2:** ~**rsi** *vr* (**a**): ~**rsi (di qn)** to fall in love (with sb). **(b)** *(uso reciproco)* to fall in love with each other).

innamorato, a [innamo'rato] **1** *ag:* ~ **(di)** *(anche fig: di lavoro etc)* in love (with); **è** ~ **del suo bambino** he's very fond of his child. **2** *sm/f* lover; *(anche scherz)* sweetheart.

innanzi [in'nantsi] **1** *av* **(a)** *(stato in luogo)* in front, ahead; *(moto a luogo)* forward, on; **stare** *o* **essere** ~ to be in front *o* ahead; **farsi** ~ to step forward. **(b)** *(tempo)* before, earlier; **il giorno** ~ the day before; **d'ora** ~ from now on. **2** *prep (davanti):* ~ **a** before, in front of; ~ **tutto** above all; ~ **tempo** ahead of time; **morire** ~ **tempo** to die before one's time.

innato, a [in'nato] *ag* innate, inborn.

innaturale [innatu'rale] *ag* unnatural.

innegabile [inne'gabile] *ag* undeniable.

inneggiare [inned'dʒare] *vi:* ~ **a** to sing hymns to; *(fig)* to sing the praises of.

innervosire [innervo'sire] **1** *vt:* ~ **qn** *(rendere nervoso)* to make sb nervous; *(irritare)* to get on sb's nerves, annoy sb. **2:** ~**rsi** *vr (vedi vt)* to become nervous; to get annoyed.

innescare [innes'kare] *vt* **(a)** *(amo)* to bait. **(b)** *(ordigno esplosivo)* to prime; *(fig: serie di eventi etc)* to trigger off.

innesco, schi [in'nesko] *sm* primer, fuse.

innestare [innes'tare] *vt (Agr, Med)* to graft; *(Tecn)* to engage; *(Elettr: presa)* to insert.

innesto [in'nesto] *sm (Agr, Med)* graft; *(: azione)* grafting; *(Tecn)* clutch; *(Elettr)* connection.

inno ['inno] *sm (anche fig)* hymn; ~ **nazionale** national anthem.

innocente [inno'tʃɛnte] **1** *ag* **(a)** *(gen)* innocent; *(scherzo)* harmless. **(b)** *(Dir)* not guilty. **2** *sm/f* innocent person; *(bambino)* innocent.

innocenza [inno'tʃɛntsa] *sf* innocence.

innocuo, a [in'nɔkuo] *ag* innocuous, harmless.

innominabile [innomi'nabile] *ag* unmentionable.

innominato, a [innomi'nato] *ag* unnamed.

innovare [inno'vare] *vt* to make innovations in.

innovatore, trice [innova'tore] **1** *ag* innovatory. **2** *sm/f* innovator.

innovazione [innovat'tsjone] *sf* innovation.

innumerevole [innume'revole] *ag* innumerable, countless.

inoculare [inoku'lare] *vt (Med)* to inoculate.

inodoro, a [ino'doro] *ag (gen)* odourless; *(fiore)* scentless.

inoffensivo, a [inoffen'sivo] *ag* harmless.

inoltrare [inol'trare] **1** *vt (Amm: pratica)* to pass on, forward; *(lettera)* to send on, forward. **2**: ~rsi *vr* to advance, go forward.

inoltrato, a [inol'trato] *ag*: **a notte** ~**a** late at night; **a primavera** ~**a** late in the spring.

inoltre [i'noltre] *av* besides, moreover.

inoltro [i'noltro] *sm (Amm)* forwarding.

inondare [inon'dare] *vt (anche fig)* to flood; *(merca-to)*: ~ **(di)** to flood (with), inundate (with); **la folla inondava la piazza** the crowd flooded into the square; **il sole inondava la stanza** the sun flooded into the room; **le lacrime le inondavano il viso** her face was bathed in tears.

inondazione [inondat'tsjone] *sf* flood.

inoperosità [inoperosi'ta] *sf* idleness, inactivity.

inoperoso, a [inope'roso] *ag* idle, inactive.

inopinato, a [inopi'nato] *ag* unexpected.

inopportunità [inopportuni'ta] *sf (vedi ag)* inappropriateness; untimeliness.

inopportuno, a [inoppor'tuno] *ag (poco adatto)* inappropriate; *(intempestivo)* untimely, ill-timed; **è arrivato in un momento** ~ he arrived at an awkward *o* inopportune moment.

inoppugnabile [inoppuɲ'ɲabile] *ag* incontrovertible.

inorganico, a, ci, che [inor'ganiko] *ag* inorganic.

inorgoglire [inorgoʎ'ʎire] **1** *vt* to make proud. **2** *vi (aus* **essere**), ~rsi *vr* to become proud; ~rsi **di qc** to pride o.s. on sth.

inorridire [inorri'dire] **1** *vt* to horrify. **2** *vi (aus* **essere**) to be horrified.

inospitale [inospi'tale] *ag* inhospitable.

inosservante [inosser'vante] *ag*: **essere** ~ **di** to fail to comply with.

inosservanza [inosser'vantsa] *sf* non-observance.

inosservato, a [inosser'vato] *ag (non notato)* unobserved; **passare** ~ to go unobserved, escape notice.

inossidabile [inossi'dabile] *ag (acciaio)* stainless.

inquadramento [inkwadra'mento] *sm (Mil)* organization (into regiments).

inquadrare [inkwa'drare] *vt* **(a)** *(foto, immagine)* to frame; ~ **un autore nel suo periodo** to place an author in his historical context; **quando l'ho visto, l'ho inquadrato subito** I recognized his sort as soon as I saw him. **(b)** *(Mil)* to regiment; *(personale)* to organize.

inquadratura [inkwadra'tura] *sf (Cine, Fot: atto)* framing; *(: immagine)* shot; *(: sequenza)* sequence.

inqualificabile [inkwalifi'kabile] *ag* unspeakable.

inquietante [inkwje'tante] *ag* disturbing, worrying.

inquietare [inkwje'tare] **1** *vt (preoccupare)* to disturb, worry; *(irritare)* to upset. **2**: ~rsi *vr (vedi vt)* to worry, become anxious; to get upset.

inquieto, a [in'kwjɛto] *ag (agitato)* restless; *(preoccupato)* worried, anxious; *(arrabbiato)* upset.

inquietudine [inkwje'tudine] *sf* anxiety, worry.

inquilino, a [inkwi'lino] *sm/f* tenant.

inquinamento [inkwina'mento] *sm* pollution.

inquinare [inkwi'nare] *vt* to pollute.

inquinato, a [inkwi'nato] *ag* polluted.

inquirente [inkwi'rɛnte] *ag (Dir)*: **magistrato** ~ examining magistrate; **commissione** ~ commission of inquiry.

inquisire [inkwi'zire] *vt* to investigate.

inquisitore, trice [inkwizi'tore] **1** *ag (sguardo)* inquiring. **2** *sm* inquisitor.

inquisizione [inkwizit'tsjone] *sf* inquisition.

insabbiamento [insabbja'mento] *sm (fig: di pratica)* shelving.

insabbiare [insab'bjare] **1** *vt (fig: pratica)* to shelve. **2**: ~rsi *vr (barca)* to run aground; *(fig: pratica)* to be shelved.

insaccare [insak'kare] *vt (grano, farina etc)* to bag, put into sacks; *(carne)* to put into sausage skins.

insaccati [insak'kati] *smpl* sausages.

insalata [insa'lata] *sf (pianta)* lettuce; *(piatto)* salad; ~ **mista** mixed salad; ~ **russa** Russian salad.

insalatiera [insala'tjɛra] *sf* salad bowl.

insalubre [insa'lubre] *ag* insalubrious, unhealthy.

insalubrità [insalubri'ta] *sf* insalubrity, unhealthiness.

insanabile [insa'nabile] *ag (piaga)* which cannot be healed; *(fig: situazione)* irremediable; *(: odio)* implacable; **fra di loro si è creato una rottura** ~ a rift has developed between them which cannot be healed.

insanguinare [insangwi'nare] **1** *vt* to stain with blood; **arrivò tutto insanguinato** he arrived all covered in blood *o* bloodstained; **una feroce rivolta insanguinò la Francia** France was plunged into a bloody revolution. **2**: ~rsi *vr* to become covered in blood.

insania [in'sanja] *sf* insanity.

insaponare [insapo'nare] *vt* to soap; ~rsi **le mani** to soap one's hands.

insaponata [insapo'nata] *sf*: **dare un'**~ **a qc** to give sth a (quick) soaping.

insaponatura [insapona'tura] *sf* soaping.

insaporire [insapo'rire] **1** *vt* to flavour; *(con spezie)* to season. **2**: ~rsi *vr* to acquire flavour.

insaporo, a [insa'poro] *ag* tasteless, insipid.

insaputa [insa'puta] *sf*: **all'**~ **di qn** without sb's knowledge, unbeknown to sb.

insaziabile [insat'tsjabile] *ag* insatiable.

inscatolare [inskato'lare] *vt (frutta, carne)* to can.

inscenare [inʃe'nare] *vt (Teatro)* to stage, put on; ~ **una commedia** *(fig)* to put on an act.

inscindibile [inʃin'dibile] *ag (fattori)* inseparable; *(legame)* indissoluble.

inscritto, a [in'skritto] *pp di* **inscrivere**.

inscrivere [in'skrivere] *vt (Geom)* to inscribe.

insecchire [insek'kire] **1** *vt (seccare)* to dry up; *(: piante)* to wither. **2** *vi (aus* **essere**) *(vedi vt)* to dry up, become dry; to wither.

insediamento [insedja'mento] *sm* **(a)** *(Amm: in carica, ufficio)* installation. **(b)** *(villaggio, colonia)* settlement.

insediare [inse'djare] **1** *vt (Amm)* to install. **2**: ~rsi *vr* **(a)** *(Amm)* to take up office. **(b)** *(colonia, profughi etc)* to settle; *(Mil)* to take up positions.

insegna [in'seɲɲa] *sf* **(a)** *(stradale, di negozio)* sign; ~ **al neon** neon sign. **(b)** *(bandiera)* flag, banner; *(emblema)* emblem, sign.

insegnamento [inseɲɲa'mento] *sm* teaching; **che ti serva da** ~ let this be a lesson to you; **trarre** ~ **da un'esperienza** to learn from an experience, draw a lesson from an experience.

insegnante [inseɲ'ɲante] **1** *ag* teaching *attr*. **2** *sm/f* teacher; **fare l'**~ to be a teacher; ~ **di storia**

history teacher; ~ **di sostegno** remedial teacher.

insegnare [inseɲ'nare] **1** *vt* to teach; ~ **a qn qc/a fare qc** to teach sb sth/to do sth; **vi insegno io a comportarvi bene!** I'll teach you how to behave!; **come lei ben m'insegna...** *(iro)* as you will doubtless be aware...; **mi puoi ~ la strada?** can you tell me how to get there? **2** *vi* to teach.

inseguimento [insegwi'mento] *sm* pursuit; **darsi all'~ di qn** to give chase to sb; **(gara di) ~** *(Ciclismo)* pursuit (race).

inseguire [inse'gwire] *vt (anche fig)* to pursue.

inseguitore, trice [insegwi'tore] *sm/f* pursuer.

insellare [insel'lare] *vt* to saddle.

inselvatichire [inselvati'kire] **1** *vt (persona)* to make unsociable. **2** *vi (aus essere)*, **~rsi** *vr (giardino, animale domestico)* to grow wild; *(persona)* to become unsociable.

inseminazione [inseminat'tsjone] *sf* insemination.

insenatura [insena'tura] *sf* inlet, creek.

insensato, a [insen'sato] *ag* senseless, stupid.

insensibile [insen'sibile] *ag (anche fig)* insensitive; **è ~ al freddo** he doesn't feel the cold; **~ ai complimenti** indifferent to compliments.

insensibilità [insensibili'ta] *sf* insensitivity, insensibility.

inseparabile [insepa'rabile] *ag* inseparable.

insepolto, a [inse'polto] *ag* unburied.

inserimento [inseri'mento] *sm (gen)* insertion; **ha avuto problemi di ~ nella nuova scuola** he has had adjustment problems at his new school.

inserire [inse'rire] **1** *vt (introdurre)* to insert; *(Elettr: spina)* to insert, put in; *(allegare)* to enclose; **~ un annuncio sul giornale** to put *o* place an advert in the newspaper; **~ un apparecchio in un circuito elettrico** to connect a machine to an electrical circuit. **2**: **~rsi** *vr*: **~rsi in** *(ambiente)* to fit into, become part of.

inserto [in'serto] *sm* insert; **~ filmato** film clip.

inservibile [inser'vibile] *ag* useless.

inserviente [inser'vjɛnte] *sm/f* attendant.

inserzione [inser'tsjone] *sf (aggiunta)* insertion; *(avviso)* advertisement; **mettere un'~ sul giornale** to put an advert in the paper.

inserzionista, i, e [insertsjo'nista] *sm/f* advertiser.

insetticida, i, e [insetti'tʃida] *ag, sm* insecticide.

insetto [in'setto] *sm* insect; **è un ~** *(peg: persona)* he's scum.

insicurezza [insicu'rettsa] *sf* insecurity.

insicuro, a [insi'kuro] *ag* insecure.

insidia [in'sidja] *sf (pericolo)* hidden danger; *(inganno)* trap; **tendere un'~ a qn** to lay *o* set a trap for sb.

insidiare [insi'djare] *vt (a) (Mil)* to harass. **(b)**: **~ la vita di qn** to make an attempt on sb's life; **~ la virtù di una donna** to attempt to besmirch a woman's honour.

insidioso, a [insi'djoso] *ag* insidious.

insieme [in'sjɛme] **1** *av (a)* together; **tutti ~** all together; **stanno bene ~** *(persone)* they get on well together; **(colori)** they go well together; **quei due stanno proprio bene ~** *(coppia)* those two make a nice couple; **stanno ~ da due anni** they have been going out together for two years; **questo libro non sta più ~** this book is falling apart. **(b)** *(contemporaneamente)* at the same time; **vuol fare troppe cose ~** she wants to do too many things at the same time; **abbiamo finito ~** we finished together *o* at the same time.

2: **~ a** *prep* together with; **bevilo ~ al succo di frutta** take it with a drink of fruit juice; **mettilo ~ al mio** put it along with mine.

3 *sm (a) (totalità)* whole; **l'~ degli elettori** the

whole electorate; **l'~ dei cittadini/degli edifici** all the citizens/buildings; **nell'~** on the whole; **bisogna considerare la cosa nell'~** *o* **nel suo ~** we will have to look at the matter as a whole; **d'~** *(sguardo, veduta)* overall, general. **(b)** *(Mat)* set; *(Moda)* outfit, suit; **nella stanza c'era uno strano ~ di persone/oggetti** there was a strange collection of people/objects in the room.

insigne [in'siɲɲe] *ag (persona)* famous, distinguished, eminent; *(città, monumento)* notable.

insignificante [insiɲɲifi'kante] *ag (gen)* insignificant; *(somma)* trifling, insignificant.

insignire [insiɲ'ɲire] *vt* to honour, decorate; **~ qn del titolo di cavaliere** to dub sb knight.

insincero, a [insin'tʃɛro] *ag* insincere.

insindacabile [insinda'kabile] *ag* unquestionable, unchallengeable.

insinuante [insinu'ante] *ag (osservazione, sguardo)* insinuating; *(maniere)* ingratiating.

insinuare [insinu'are] **1** *vt (a) (introdurre)*: **~ qc in** to slip *o* slide sth into. **(b)** *(alludere)* to insinuate; **fu lei ad insinuargli il sospetto che...** she was the one who created the suspicion in his mind *o* made him suspect that...; **cosa vorresti ~?** what are you trying to insinuate? **2**: **~rsi** *vr (umidità, acqua)*: **~rsi (in qc)** to seep in(to sth), penetrate (sth); *(persona)*: **~rsi in** to worm one's way into, insinuate o.s. into; *(dubbio)*: **~rsi in** to creep into.

insinuazione [insinuat'tsjone] *sf* insinuation, innuendo; **fare ~i su qn** to make insinuations about sb.

insipido, a [in'sipido] *ag (anche fig)* insipid.

insistente [insis'tɛnte] *ag (che insiste)* insistent; *(: pioggia, mal di testa)* persistent.

insistenza [insis'tentsa] *sf (vedi ag)* insistence; persistence; **chiedere con ~** to ask insistently.

insistere [in'sistere] *vi*: **~ (su qc/a fare qc)** to insist (on sth/on doing sth); **~ (in qc/a fare qc)** *(perseverare)* to persist in sth/in doing sth.

insistito, a [insis'tito] *pp di* **insistere**.

insito, a ['insito] *ag*: **~ (in)** inherent (in).

insoddisfatto, a [insoddis'fatto] *ag (persona)* dissatisfied; *(desiderio)* unfulfilled, unsatisfied.

insofferente [insoffe'rɛnte] *ag (impaziente)* impatient; *(irrequieto)* edgy.

insofferenza [insoffe'rɛntsa] *sf* impatience.

insolazione [insolat'tsjone] *sf (Med)* sunstroke; **prendere un'~** to get sunstroke.

insolente [inso'lɛnte] **1** *ag* insolent. **2** *sm/f* insolent person.

insolenza [inso'lɛntsa] *sf (arroganza)* insolence; *(osservazione)* insolent remark; **è stata un'~ da parte sua** *(azione)* that was insolent of him.

insolito, a [in'sɔlito] *ag* unusual, out of the ordinary, strange.

insolubile [inso'lubile] *ag (a) (problema)* insoluble, insolvable. **(b)** *(sostanza)* insoluble.

insoluto, a [inso'luto] *ag (problema)* unsolved; *(debito)* unpaid, outstanding.

insolvente [insol'vɛnte] *ag (Dir)* insolvent.

insolvenza [insol'ventsa] *sf (Dir)* insolvency.

insomma [in'somma] **1** *av* in short, all in all. **2** *escl*: **~!** for Heaven's sake!

insondabile [inson'dabile] *ag* unfathomable.

insonne [in'sɔnne] *ag (notte)* sleepless.

insonnia [in'sɔnnja] *sf (Med)* insomnia, sleeplessness.

insonnolito, a [insonno'lito] *ag* sleepy, drowsy.

insopportabile [insoppor'tabile] *ag* unbearable.

insopprimibile [insoppri'mibile] *ag* unsuppressible.

insorgenza [insor'dʒentsa] *sf (di malattia)* onset.

insorgere [in'sordʒere] *vi (aus essere)* **(a)**

(ribellarsi) to rise up, rebel. **(b)** *(manifestarsi improvvisamente)* to arise.

insormontabile [insormon'tabile] *ag (ostacolo)* unsurmountable, insuperable.

insorto, a [in'sorto] **1** *pp di* **insorgere**. **2** *ag:* **il popolo** ~ the rebels, the insurgents. **3** *sm/f* rebel, insurgent.

insospettabile [insospet'tabile] *ag* **(a)** *(al di sopra di ogni sospetto)* above suspicion. **(b)** *(inatteso)* unsuspected.

insospettato, a [insospet'tato] *ag* unsuspected.

insospettire [insospet'tire] **1** *vt* to make suspicious, arouse suspicions in. **2:** ~**rsi** *vr:* ~**rsi (per/di qc)** to become suspicious (because of/about sth).

insostenibile [insoste'nibile] *ag* **(a)** *(posizione, teoria)* untenable. **(b)** *(dolore, situazione)* intolerable, unbearable; **le spese di manutenzione sono** ~**i** the maintenance costs are excessive.

insostituibile [insostitu'ibile] *ag (persona)* irreplaceable; *(aiuto, presenza)* invaluable.

insozzare [insot'tsare] **1** *vt* **(a)** *(pavimento)* to make dirty. **(b)** *(fig: reputazione, memoria di qn)* to tarnish, sully. **2:** ~**rsi** *vr* to get dirty.

insperabile [inspe'rabile] *ag:* **la guarigione/salvezza era** ~ there was no hope of a cure/of rescue; **abbiamo ottenuto risultati** ~**i** the results we achieved were far better than we had hoped.

insperato, a [inspe'rato] *ag* unhoped for.

inspiegabile [inspje'gabile] *ag* inexplicable.

inspirare [inspi'rare] *vt* to inhale, breathe in.

inspirazione [inspirat'tsjone] *sf* inhaling, breathing in.

instabile [in'stabile] *ag (carico, carattere, situazione)* unstable; *(tempo)* unsettled, changeable; *(umore)* uncertain, changeable.

instabilità [instabili'ta] *sf (gen)* instability; *(del tempo)* changeability; *(di umore)* inconstancy.

installare [instal'lare] **1** *vt (impianto, telefono)* to install, put in. **2:** ~**rsi** *vr (sistemarsi)* to settle, set up house; **si è installata a casa mia** she has moved in at my house.

installazione [installat'tsjone] *sf* **(a)** *(di telefono etc)* installation. **(b)** *(impianto)* installations *pl;* ~**i sanitarie** *o* **igieniche** sanitary fittings.

instancabile [instan'kabile] *ag* tireless, indefatigable.

instaurare [instau'rare] *vt (regola, sistema)* to establish, institute; *(moda etc)* to introduce.

instaurazione [instaurat'tsjone] *sf (vedi vb)* establishment, institution; introduction.

instillare [instil'lare] *vt* to instil.

instradare [instra'dare] *vt* = **istradare.**

insù [in'su] *av* up, upwards; **guardare all'**~ to look up *o* upwards; **naso all'**~ turned-up nose.

insubordinato, a [insubordi'nato] *ag* insubordinate.

insubordinazione [insubordinat'tsjone] *sf* insubordination.

insuccesso [insut'tʃɛsso] *sm* failure.

insudiciare [insudi'tʃare] **1** *vt* to dirty, soil; *(fig: reputazione, nome)* to sully, tarnish; ~**rsi i vestiti** to get one's clothes dirty, dirty one's clothes. **2:** ~**rsi** *vr* to get dirty.

insufficiente [insuffi'tʃɛnte] *ag* **(a):** ~ **a** *o* **per** *(quantità)* insufficient (for); *(qualità)* inadequate (for); **200 sterline sono** ~**i per vivere** £200 is not enough *o* sufficient to live on. **(b)** *(Scol: voto)* unsatisfactory; *(: compito)* below standard; **ho preso** ~ **in latino** I got a fail in Latin.

insufficienza [insuffi'tʃɛntsa] *sf* **(a)** *(di denaro, viveri)* shortage; *(di tempo, spazio)* lack; *(di preparazione)* inadequacy; *(Med)* insufficiency; ~ **di**

prove *(Dir)* lack of evidence. **(b)** *(Scol)* fail; **ho preso un'**~ **in chimica** I got a fail in chemistry.

insulare [insu'lare] *ag* island *attr*, insular; **l'Italia** ~ the Italian islands.

insulina [insu'lina] *sf (Chim)* insulin.

insulsaggine [insul'saddʒine] *sf (vedi ag)* dullness, insipidity; inanity.

insulso, a [in'sulso] *ag (persona)* dull, insipid; *(osservazione)* inane.

insultare [insul'tare] *vt* to insult.

insulto [in'sulto] *sm* insult; **coprire qn di** ~**i** to hurl abuse at sb, heap abuse on sb.

insuperabile [insupe'rabile] *ag* **(a)** *(ostacolo, difficoltà)* insuperable, unsurmountable. **(b)** *(eccellente: qualità, prodotto)* unbeatable; *(: persona, interpretazione)* unequalled.

insuperato, a [insupe'rato] *ag* unsurpassed, unequalled.

insuperbire [insuper'bire] **1** *vt* to make proud, make arrogant; **il successo lo ha insuperbito** success has gone to his head. **2** *vi (aus* **essere),** ~**rsi** *vr* to become arrogant.

insurrezionale [insurrettsjo'nale] *ag* insurrectionary.

insurrezione [insurret'tsjone] *sf* insurrection, revolt.

insussistente [insussis'tente] *ag (accusa, paura)* unfounded, groundless; *(pericolo)* non-existent.

intaccabile [intak'kabile] *ag (metallo)* corrodible; *(fig: teoria)* open to criticism.

intaccare [intak'kare] *vt* **(a)** *(sog: ruggine)* to corrode; *(: acido)* to eat into; **non vorrei** ~ **i miei risparmi** I wouldn't like to break into my savings. **(b)** *(fare tacche in)* to cut into, nick. **(c)** *(infettare, fig: reputazione)* to affect.

intacco, chi [in'takko] *sm* notch, nick.

intagliare [intaʎ'ʎare] *vt (legno, pietre)* to engrave.

intagliatore, trice [intaʎʎa'tore] *sm/f* engraver.

intaglio [in'taʎʎo] *sm* intaglio.

intangibile [intan'dʒibile] *ag* **(a)** *(bene, patrimonio)* untouchable. **(b)** *(fig: diritto)* inviolable; *(: differenza)* intangible.

intanto [in'tanto] *av (nel frattempo)* meanwhile, in the meantime; ~ **che** while; ~ **che aspetti leggiti questo** you can read this while you're waiting; **puoi scusarti quanto vuoi,** ~ **il male è già stato fatto** you can apologise as much as you like, but (the fact remains that) the damage has been done.

intarsiare [intar'sjare] *vt* to inlay.

intarsio [in'tarsjo] *sm (arte, tecnica)* marquetry; *(parte lavorata)* marquetry, inlaid work; **mobili lavorati a** ~ inlaid furniture.

intasamento [intasa'mento] *sm (ostruzione)* blockage, obstruction; *(Aut: ingorgo)* traffic jam.

intasare [inta'sare] **1** *vt (tubo etc)* to block; **ho il naso intasato** I've got a blocked *o* stuffed-up nose. **2:** ~**rsi** *vr* to become blocked, get blocked.

intascare [intas'kare] *vt (denaro, premio)* to pocket.

intatto, a [in'tatto] *ag (gen)* intact; *(facoltà mentali)* unimpaired; **la neve era** ~**a** there were no footprints in the snow.

intavolare [intavo'lare] *vt (discussione, trattative)* to open.

integerrimo, a [inte'dʒɛrrimo] *ag* honest, upright; **è un uomo** ~ he's a man of the utmost integrity.

integrale [inte'grale] **1** *ag* **(a)** *(gen)* complete; *(rimborso)* full; **edizione** ~ unabridged edition; **un film in versione** ~ uncut version of a film; **pane** ~ wholemeal bread. **(b)** *(Mat)* integral. **2** *sm (Mat)* integral.

integrante [inte'grante] *ag:* **essere parte** ~ **di** to be an integral part of.

integrare [inte'grare] 1 *vt* (a) *(completare)* to integrate; *(: personale)* to bring up to strength; *(: stipendio, dieta etc)* to supplement; **integra il proprio stipendio dando lezioni private** he supplements his income by giving private lessons. (b) *(Sociol, Mat)* to integrate. 2: ~**rsi** *vr (Sociol)* to become integrated.

integrativo, a [integra'tivo] *ag (assegno)* supplementary; *(Scol):* **esame** ~ *assessment test sat when changing schools.*

integrato, a [inte'grato] *ag (Elettr)* integrated.

integrazione [integrat'tsjone] *sf* integration.

integrità [integri'ta] *sf* (a) *(interezza: di patrimonio)* integrity. (b) *(onestà)* integrity, honesty, uprightness.

integro, a ['integro] *ag* (a) *(intero)* intact. (b) *(onesto)* honest, upright.

intelaiatura [intelaja'tura] *sf (Edil)* skeleton, framework; *(fig: economica, sociale)* framework.

intellegibile [intelle'dʒibile] *ag* = **intelligibile**.

intellettivo, a [intellet'tivo] *ag (facoltà)* intellectual.

intelletto [intel'lɛtto] *sm* intellect.

intellettuale [intellettu'ale] 1 *ag* intellectual; **sforzo** ~ mental effort. 2 *sm/f* intellectual.

intellettualizzare [intellettualid'dzare] *vt* to intellectualize.

intellettualoide [intellettua'lɔide] 1 *ag (peg: atteggiamento)* highbrow. 2 *sm/f (peg)* pseudo-intellectual, would-be intellectual.

intelligente [intelli'dʒɛnte] *ag (gen)* intelligent; *(brillante)* clever, bright; *(capace)* clever, able.

intelligenza [intelli'dʒɛntsa] *sf* intelligence; **ha un'~ viva** he's got a quick *o* sharp mind; **è una bella** ~ he has a fine mind *o* a good brain; **un lavoro fatto con** ~ a clever piece of work; **giocato con** ~ ably *o* cleverly played.

intellighenzia [intelli'gɛntsia] *sf* intelligentsia.

intelligibile [intelli'dʒibile] *ag* intelligible; **ripetilo in modo chiaro e** ~ repeat it loudly and clearly; **un messaggio poco** ~ an unclear message; **ha una scrittura chiara e** ~ he is clear, legible handwriting.

intemerato, a [inteme'rato] *ag (persona, vita)* blameless, irreproachable; *(coscienza)* clear; *(fama)* unblemished.

intemperante [intempe'rante] *ag* intemperate, immoderate.

intemperanza [intempe'rantsa] *sf* intemperance; ~**e** excesses.

intemperie [intem'pɛrje] *sfpl* bad weather *sg*; **esposto alle** ~ exposed to the elements; **resistente alle** ~ weatherproof.

intempestivo, a [intempes'tivo] *ag (intervento)* untimely, ill-timed.

intendente [inten'dɛnte] *sm:* ~ **di Finanza** inland revenue officer.

intendenza [inten'dɛntsa] *sf:* ~ **di Finanza** inland revenue office.

intendere [in'tɛndere] 1 *vt* (a) *(avere intenzione):* ~ **fare qc** to intend *o* mean to do sth, have the intention of doing sth; **non intendo farlo** I have no intention of doing it, I don't intend to do it; **cosa intendevi (dire)?** what did you mean? (b) *(capire)* to understand; **mi ha dato a ~ che...** he led me to believe that...; **mi ha lasciato ~ che...** he gave me to understand that...; **ma io non la intendo così** I don't see things that way; **puoi intenderla come vuoi** you can take it as you please; **non riesce a farsi** ~ he cannot make himself understood; **ho inteso dire che...** I've heard it said that...; **non vuole ~ ragione** he doesn't want to listen to reason; **s'intende**

naturally!, of course!; **s'intende che verrai anche tu!** you'll be coming too, of course!

2: ~**rsi** *vr* (a) *(conoscere bene):* ~**rsi di qc** to know about sth; *(: cibi, vini)* to be a connoisseur of sth; **me ne intendo poco** I know very little about it. (b) *(capirsi)* to understand each other; *(accordarsi):* ~**rsi con qn su qc** to come to an agreement with sb about sth; **intendiamoci** let's get it quite clear; **ci siamo intesi?** is that clear?, is that understood? (c): **intendersela (con qn)** to have an affair with sb.

intendimento [intendi'mento] *sm* intention.

intenditore, trice [intendi'tore] *sm/f* expert; *(di vini, cibi)* connoisseur; **a buon intenditor poche parole** *(Proverbio)* a word is enough to the wise.

intenerire [intene'rire] 1 *vt (commuovere)* to touch, move. 2: ~**rsi** *vr* to be touched, be moved.

intensificare [intensifi'kare] *vt,* ~**rsi** *vr* to intensify, increase.

intensificazione [intensifikat'tsjone] *sf* intensification.

intensità [intensi'ta] *sf inv (gen, Fis)* intensity; *(del vento)* force, strength.

intensivo, a [inten'sivo] *ag* intensive.

intenso, a [in'tɛnso] *ag (gen)* intense; *(luce, profumo)* strong; *(colore)* intense, deep.

intentare [inten'tare] *vt (Dir):* ~ **causa contro qn** to start *o* institute proceedings against sb.

intentato, a [inten'tato] *ag:* **non lasciare nulla d'**~ to leave no stone unturned, try everything.

intento¹, a [in'tɛnto] *ag* intent; **essere** ~ **a qc/a fare qc** to be intent on sth/absorbed in doing sth.

intento² [in'tɛnto] *sm* intention; **fare qc con l'**~ **di** to do sth with the intention of; **riuscire nell'**~ to achieve one's aim.

intenzionale [intentsjo'nale] *ag (gen)* intentional, deliberate; *(Dir: omicidio)* premeditated; **fallo** ~ *(Sport)* deliberate foul.

intenzionato, a [intentsjo'nato] *ag:* **essere** ~ **a fare qc** to intend to do sth, have the intention of doing sth; **ben** ~ well-meaning, well-intentioned; **mal** ~ ill-intentioned.

intenzione [inten'tsjone] *sf* intention; **avere (l')**~ **di fare qc** to intend to do sth, have the intention of doing sth; **è mia** ~ **farlo** I intend to do it; **è l'**~ **che conta** it's the thought that counts; **senza** ~ unintentionally; **secondo l'**~ *o* **le** ~**i di qn** in accordance with sb's wishes; **animato dalle migliori** ~**i** with the best of intentions.

intepidire [intepi'dire] *vt* = **intiepidire**.

interagire [intera'dʒire] *vi* to interact.

interamente [intera'mente] *av* entirely, completely.

interazione [interat'tsjone] *sf* interaction.

intercalare [interka'lare] 1 *vt:* ~ **a,** ~ **in** *(testo, discorso etc)* to insert into; **bisogna** ~ **un periodo di riposo ad uno di lavoro** a period of rest is necessary between periods of work. 2 *sm:* **il suo** ~ **preferito è 'cioè'** one of his favourite expressions is 'cioè'.

intercambiabile [interkam'bjabile] *ag* interchangeable.

intercapedine [interka'pɛdine] *sf* gap, cavity.

intercedere [inter'tʃɛdere] *vi:* **(presso/in favore di)** to intercede (with/on behalf of).

intercessione [intertʃes'sjone] *sf* intercession.

intercettamento [intertʃetta'mento] *sm* interception.

intercettare [intertʃet'tare] *vt (gen, Sport, Telec)* to intercept.

intercettatore [intertʃetta'tore] *sm* = **intercettore**.

intercettazione [intertʃettat'tsjone] *sf* interception.

intercettore [intertʃet'tore] *sm* interceptor.

intercomunicante [interkomuni'kante] *ag* (inter)communicating.

intercontinentale [interkontinen'tale] *ag* intercontinental.

intercorrere [inter'korrere] *vi (aus essere)* **(a)** *(passare: tempo)* to elapse. **(b)** *(esserci)* to exist; **fra loro intercorrono ottimi rapporti** they are on the very best of terms.

intercorso, a [inter'korso] *pp di* intercorrere.

interdetto, a [inter'detto] **1** *pp di* interdire. **2** *ag (sconcertato)*: **rimanere** ~ to be taken aback; **lasciare qn** ~ to disconcert sb. **3** *sm (Rel, Dir)* interdict.

interdipendente [interdipen'dɛnte] *ag* interdependent.

interdipendenza [interdipen'dɛntsa] *sf* interdependence.

interdire [inter'dire] *vt (gen: vietare)* to forbid, ban, prohibit; *(Rel)* to interdict; ~ **qn dai pubblici uffici** to ban *o* debar sb from public office.

interdizione [interdit'tsjone] *sf (divieto)*: ~ **(di)** ban (on); *(Rel)* interdict; *(Dir)* debarment.

interessamento [interessa'mento] *sm (interesse)* interest; *(intervento)* intervention, good offices *pl*; **grazie al suo** ~ **sono riuscito ad avere il lavoro** it was thanks to his good offices that I managed to get the job.

interessante [interes'sante] *ag (gen)* interesting; **essere in stato** ~ to be expecting (a baby).

interessare [interes'sare] **1** *vi (aus essere)*: ~ **(a qn)** to interest (sb); **forse ti interesserà sapere che...** perhaps you might be interested to know that...; **se ti interessa ti posso dare il suo indirizzo** if you are interested I can give you his address; **non m'interessa!** I'm not interested!; **a lui non interessano che i suoi libri** he's only interested in his books; **ci interessa che tutto vada bene** what matters to us is that everything should go well.

2 *vt* **(a)** *(suscitare interesse in)* to interest; ~ **qn a qc** to interest sb in sth. **(b)** *(riguardare)* to affect, concern; **precipitazioni che interessano le regioni settentrionali** rainfall affecting the north; **un provvedimento che interessa gli automobilisti** a regulation affecting *o* concerning motorists. **(c)** *(Comm)*: ~ **qn in** *(utili)* to give sb a share *o* an interest in.

3: ~**rsi** *vr* **(a)** *(mostrare curiosità)*: ~**rsi (a)** to show interest (in); **si è interessato molto a quel progetto** he showed a lot of interest in the project. **(b)** *(occuparsi)*: ~**rsi di** *o* **a** *(politica, pittura etc)* to be interested in, take an interest in; **si sono interessati al suo caso** they took up his case; **si è interessato alla mia promozione** he helped me get promotion; **si è interessato di farmi avere quei biglietti** he took the trouble to get me those tickets; **interessati degli affari tuoi!** mind your own business!

interessato, a [interes'sato] **1** *ag* **(a)** *(coinvolto)* interested, involved; **le parti** ~**e** the interested parties. **(b)** *(peg)*: **essere** ~ to act out of pure self-interest. **2** *sm/f (coinvolto)* person concerned; **a tutti gli** ~**i** to all those concerned, to all interested parties.

interesse [inte'resse] *sm* **(a)** *(gen)* interest; **ho sempre avuto un certo** ~ **per...** I've always had a certain interest in..., I've always been rather interested in... .

(b) *(Fin, Comm)* interest; **un** ~ **del 5%** 5% interest; ~ **semplice/composto** simple/compound interest; **ha degli** ~**i in quell'azienda** he has a financial interest in that company;

badare ai propri ~**i** to look after one's own interests *o* affairs.

(c) *(tornaconto)*: **fare qc per** ~ to do sth out of self-interest; **non pensa che a fare il proprio** ~ he only thinks of his own interests; **nell'**~ **dell'umanità** in the interests of mankind; **agire nell'**~ **comune** to act for the common good *o* in the common interest; **non ho alcun** ~ **a farlo, non è nel mio** ~ **farlo** it is not in my interest to do it; **lo ha sposato per** ~ she married him for gain; **quando c'è di mezzo l'**~**...** when personal interests are involved... .

interessenza [interes'sɛntsa] *sf (Econ)* profit-sharing.

interferenza [interfe'rɛntsa] *sf (gen, Tecn)* interference; **ci sono delle** ~**e nella linea** *(Telec)* there is interference on the line.

interferire [interfe'rire] *vi*: ~ **(in)** to interfere (in).

interfono [inter'fono] *sm* intercom *(fam)*; *(in una casa)* house phone.

intergalattico, a, ci, che [interga'lattiko] *ag* intergalactic.

interiezione [interjet'tsjone] *sf (Gram)* interjection.

interim ['interim] *sm inv* **(a)** *(periodo)* interim, interval; **ministro ad** ~ acting *o* interim minister. **(b)** *(incarico)* temporary appointment.

interiora [inte'rjora] *sfpl* entrails *pl*.

interiore [inte'rjore] *ag* **(a)** *(interno)* inner *attr*; **parte** ~ inside. **(b)** *(fig: vita, mondo)* inner *attr*.

interiorità [interjori'ta] *sf* inner being.

interiorizzare [interjorid'dzare] *vt* to internalize.

interlinea [inter'linea] *sf* **(a)** *(Dattilografia)* spacing; **doppia** ~ double spacing. **(b)** *(Tip)* leading.

interlineare [interline'are] **1** *ag* interlinear. **2** *vt* **(a)** *(spaziare le righe)* to space (out). **(b)** *(Tip)* to lead (out).

interlocutore, trice [interloku'tore] *sm/f* speaker; **il suo** ~ the person he was speaking to.

interlocutorio, a [interloku'tɔrjo] *ag* interlocutory.

interludio [inter'ludjo] *sm (Mus, fig)* interlude.

intermediario, a [interme'djarjo] **1** *ag* intermediary. **2** *sm/f* intermediary, go-between; *(Comm, Econ)* middleman.

intermedio, a [inter'mɛdjo] *ag* intermediate *attr*.

intermezzo [inter'mɛddzo] *sm (intervallo)* interval; *(breve spettacolo)* intermezzo.

interminabile [intermi'nabile] *ag* interminable, endless, never-ending.

interministeriale [interministe'rjale] *ag* interministerial.

intermittente [intermit'tente] *ag* intermittent.

intermittenza [intermit'tentsa] *sf*: **ad** ~ intermittent.

internamento [interna'mento] *sm (vedi vb)* internment; confinement (to a mental hospital).

internare [inter'nare] *vt (Pol)* to intern; *(Med)* to confine to a mental hospital.

internato[1], a [inter'nato] *(vedi vb)* **1** *ag* interned; confined (to a mental hospital). **2** *sm/f* internee; inmate (of a mental hospital).

internato[2] [inter'nato] *sm* **(a)** *(collegio)* boarding school. **(b)** *(Med)* period as a houseman *o* intern.

internazionale [internattsjo'nale] **1** *ag* international. **2** *sf (Pol: associazione)* International; *(: inno)* Internationale.

internista, i, e [inter'nista] *sm/f* specialist in internal medicine.

interno, a [in'tɛrno] **1** *ag (gen, Med)* internal; *(tasca)* inside *attr*; *(regione, navigazione, mare)* inland *attr*; *(politica, commercio, volo)* domestic; **alunno** ~ boarder; **commissione** ~**a** *(Scol)* internal examination board; **'per uso ~'** *(Med)* 'to be taken internally'.

2 *sm* **(a)** *(di edificio)* inside, interior; *(di scatola, cappotto)* inside; **dall'~** from the inside; **all'~ (della casa)** inside (the house); **girare gli ~i** *(Cine)* to film the indoor shots. **(b)** *(di paese)* interior; **regioni dell'~** inland areas, areas of the interior; **notizie dall'~** *(Stampa)* home news; **Ministero degli I~i** Ministry of the Interior, ≈ Home Office *(Brit)*, Department of the Interior *(Am)*. **(c)** *(di telefono)* extension; *(di appartamento)*: **abita in Via Mangili 6, 2° piano, ~ 5** he lives at number 6 Via Mangili, 2nd floor, flat 5.

intero, a [in'tero] **1** *ag* **(a)** *(gen)* whole, entire; *(quantità)* whole, full; *(Mat: numero)* whole; **latte ~** full-cream milk; **ti ho aspettato per un'ora ~a** I waited for you for a whole *o* full hour; **pagare il prezzo ~** to pay the full price; **ha ingoiato una prugna tutta ~a** he swallowed a plum whole; **ho trascorso l'~a settimana a studiare** I spent the whole *o* entire week studying; **ha girato il mondo ~** he's travelled all over the world, he's been all round the world. **(b)** *(intatto)* intact; **ho 50.000 lire ~e, me le cambi?** I have a 50,000 lire note, will you change it for me? **2** *sm (anche Mat)* whole; **scrivere per ~ qc** to write sth in full.

interparlamentare [interparlamen'tare] *ag* inter-parliamentary.

interpellanza [interpel'lantsa] *sf*: **presentare un'~** *(Pol)* to ask a question.

interpellare [interpel'lare] *vt (consultare)* to consult, ask; *(Pol)* to question.

interplanetario, a [interplane'tarjo] *ag* inter-planetary.

interpolare [interpo'lare] *vt* to interpolate.

interporre [inter'porre] **1** *vt* **(a)** *(ostacoli, difficoltà)*: **~ qc a qc** to put sth in the way of sth; *(influenza)* to use; **ha interposto i suoi buoni uffici per aiutarlo** he used his good offices to help him. **(b)**: **~ appello** *(Dir)* to appeal. **2**: **interporsi** *vr (intervenire)* to intervene; **interporsi fra** *(mettersi in mezzo)* to come between.

interposto, a [inter'posto] **1** *pp di* **interporre. 2** *ag*: **per ~a persona** through a third party.

interpretare [interpre'tare] *vt* **(a)** *(gen: spiegare, tradurre, capire)* to interpret; **~ male** to misinterpret. **(b)** *(Mus, Teatro)* to perform; *(personaggio, sonata)* to play; *(canzone)* to sing.

interpretariato [interpreta'rjato] *sm* interpreting.

interpretazione [interpretat'tsjone] *sf* interpretation; **~ simultanea** *(Lingue)* simultaneous interpreting.

interprete [in'terprete] *sm/f* **(a)** *(traduttore)* interpreter; *(portavoce)*: **farsi ~ di** to act as a spokesman for. **(b)** *(Teatro, Cine)* actor/actress, performer; *(Mus)* performer.

interpunzione [interpun'tsjone] *sf* punctuation; **segni di ~** punctuation marks.

interrare [inter'rare] *vt* **(a)** *(seme, pianta)* to plant; *(tubature etc)* to lay underground; *(Mil: pezzo d'artiglieria)* to dig in. **(b)** *(riempire di terra: canale)* to fill in.

interrato [inter'rato] *sm (anche: piano ~)* basement.

interregno [inter'reɲɲo] *sm* interregnum.

interrogare [interro'gare] *vt (gen)* to question; *(Scol, Dir)* to examine; **lo interrogarono in merito agli ultimi avvenimenti** they questioned him regarding recent events; **mi ha interrogato in matematica** he examined me in maths; **~ gli astri** *(Astrologia)* to consult the stars.

interrogativo, a [interroga'tivo] **1** *ag (sguardo, espressione)* questioning, inquiring; *(Gram)* in-terrogative; **punto ~** *(anche fig)* question mark. **2** *sm* question; *(fig: persona, futuro)* mystery; **porsi un ~** to ask o.s. a question.

interrogato, a [interro'gato] *sm/f* person examined *(o* questioned).

interrogatorio [interroga'tɔrjo] *sm* questioning; *(più severo)* interrogation; **subire un ~** to be questioned; *(anche fig)* to be interrogated.

interrogazione [interrogat'tsjone] *sf* **(a)** *(Scol)*: **~ (di)** *(oral)* examination (in). **(b)** *(Pol)*: **~ (parlamentare)** question.

interrompere [inter'rompere] **1** *vt (viaggio, studi, trattative etc)* to interrupt, break off; *(conversazione)* to interrupt; *(gravidanza)* to terminate; *(Elettr: circuito)* to break; **~ l'erogazione del gas/dell'acqua** to cut off the gas/water supply; **le comunicazioni con il nord sono interrotte** the north is cut off; **non ~!** don't interrupt!, don't butt in! **2**: **~rsi** *vr (gen)* to break off; *(corrente, linea telefonica)* to be cut off; *(circuito elettrico)* to be broken; *(trasmissione)* to be interrupted.

interrotto, a [inter'rotto] *pp di* **interrompere.**

interruttore [interrut'tore] *sm* switch.

interruzione [interrut'tsjone] *sf (azione)* interruption; *(stato)* break, interruption; **~ di gravidanza** termination of pregnancy; **senza ~** *(lavorare)* without a break; *(dormire, parlare)* non-stop.

intersecare [interse'kare] *vt*, **~rsi** *vr* to intersect.

intersezione [interset'tsjone] *sf* intersection.

interstizio [inter'stittsjo] *sm* interstice.

interurbano, a [interur'bano] **1** *ag* intercity *attr*; *(Telec: chiamata)* trunk *attr* (*Brit*), long-distance *attr*. **2** *sf (Telec)* trunk call *(Brit)*, long-distance call.

intervallare [interval'lare] *vt* to space out.

intervallo [inter'vallo] *sm* **(a)** *(di tempo, Teatro, Cine, Mus)* interval; *(a scuola)* break, interval; *(in ufficio)* (tea *o* coffee) break; *(Sport: fra due tempi)* half-time; **fare un ~ di 10 minuti** to have a 10-minute interval; to have a 10-minute break; **a ~i regolari** at regular intervals. **(b)** *(di spazio)* space, gap; **a ~i di 10 cm** at intervals of 10 cm, every 10 cm.

intervenire [interve'nire] *vi (aus essere)*: **(a)**: **~ (in)** *(in discussione)* to intervene (in); *(in programma)* to take part (in); **hanno dovuto far ~ l'esercito** the army had to be brought in. **(b)** *(insorgere: nuovi elementi)* to arise. **(c)** *(Med)*: **~ chirurgicamente** to operate.

intervento [inter'vento] *sm* **(a)** *(gen, Pol, Mil)* intervention; **politica del non ~** policy of non-intervention; **hanno chiesto l'~ della polizia** they asked for police assistance, they asked the police to intervene. **(b)** *(breve discorso)* speech; *(partecipazione)* participation; **fare un ~ nel corso di** *(dibattito, programma)* to take part in. **(c)** *(Med)* operation; **fare un ~** to carry out *o* perform an operation.

intervenuto, a [interve'nuto] **1** *pp di* **intervenire. 2**: **gli ~i** *smpl* those present.

intervista [inter'vista] *sf*: **~ (con)** interview (with); **fare un'~ a qn** to interview sb.

intervistare [intervis'tare] *vt* to interview.

intervistato, a [intervis'tato] *sm/f* person interviewed.

intervistatore, trice [intervista'tore] *sm/f* interviewer.

intesa [in'tesa] *sf (amicizia)* understanding; *(accordo)* agreement; **raggiungere un'~** *(comprendersi)* to understand each other; *(accordarsi)* to reach an agreement; **uno sguardo d'~** a knowing look.

inteso, a [in'teso] **1** *pp di* **intendere. 2** *ag* **(a)**

intessere [in'tɛssere] *vt* to interweave; *(fig)*: ~ **lodi a qn** to sing sb's praises.

intestardirsi [intestar'dirsi] *vr*: ~ **(su qc/a fare qc)** to insist (on sth/on doing sth); **si è intestardito che vuole andare a Parigi** he's taken it into his head that he wants to go to Paris.

intestare [intes'tare] *vt* **(a)** *(lettera, busta)* to address. **(b)**: ~ **a** *(casa, proprietà)* to register in the name of; **a chi è intestata la macchina?** in whose name is the car registered?; ~ **un assegno a qn** to make out a cheque to sb.

intestatario, a [intesta'tarjo] *sm/f* holder.

intestazione [intestat'tsjone] *sf (gen)* heading; *(su lettera)* letterhead; **qual'è l'~ dell'assegno?** who is the cheque made out to?

intestinale [intesti'nale] *ag* intestinal.

intestino, a [intes'tino] **1** *ag* internal; **guerra ~a** civil war. **2** *sm (Anat)* intestine; ~ **tenue/crasso** small/large intestine.

intiepidire [intjepi'dire] **1** *vt (riscaldare)* to warm (up); *(raffreddare)* to cool (down); *(fig: amicizia etc)* to cool. **2**: ~**rsi** *vr (vedi vt)* to warm (up); to cool (down); to cool.

intimamente [intima'mente] *av* intimately; **sono ~ convinto che...** I'm firmly *o* deeply convinced that...; **i due fatti sono ~ connessi** the two events are closely connected.

intimare [inti'mare] *vt*: ~ **a qn di fare qc** to order sb to do sth; ~ **la resa a qn** *(Mil)* to call upon sb to surrender.

intimazione [intimat'tsjone] *sf* order, command.

intimidatorio, a [intimida'torjo] *ag* threatening; **una telefonata a scopo** ~ **a** threatening phone call.

intimidazione [intimidat'tsjone] *sf* intimidation; **vittima di ~i** victim of intimidation *o* threats.

intimidire [intimi'dire] **1** *vt* to intimidate. **2**: ~**rsi** *vr* to become shy.

intimità [intimi'ta] *sf (vita privata)* privacy; *(di rapporto)* intimacy; **nell'~ della propria casa** in the privacy of one's own home.

intimo, a ['intimo] **1** *ag (igiene)* intimate; *(affetti, vita)* private; *(amico)* close, intimate; *(gioia, dolore)* deep; *(cerimonia)* quiet; *(atmosfera)* cosy, intimate; *(significato)* innermost, inmost; **biancheria ~a** underwear; **parti ~e** *(Anat)* private parts; **rapporti ~i** *(sessuali)* intimate relations. **2** *sm* **(a)** *(persona)* close friend. **(b)**: **nell'~ della sua coscienza** deep down in his conscience; **nell'~ del suo cuore** in his heart of hearts.

intimorire [intimo'rire] **1** *vt* to frighten, make afraid. **2**: ~**rsi** *vr* to become frightened.

intingere [in'tindʒere] *vt* to dip.

intingolo [in'tingolo] *sm (sugo)* sauce; *(pietanza)* tasty dish.

intinto, a [in'tinto] *pp di* **intingere**.

intirizzire [intirid'dzire] **1** *vt* to numb. **2**: ~**rsi** *vr* to grow numb (with cold).

intirizzito, a [intirid'dzito] *ag* numb (with cold).

intitolare [intito'lare] **1** *vt* **(a)** *(dare un titolo a)* to entitle; **come ha intitolato il suo ultimo romanzo?** what title has he given to his latest book? **(b)** *(dedicare: chiesa, monumento)* to dedicate. **2**: ~**rsi** *vr (libro, film)* to be called.

intoccabile [intok'kabile] *ag, sm/f* untouchable.

intollerabile [intolle'rabile] *ag* intolerable, unbearable.

intollerante [intolle'rante] *ag*: ~ **(nei confronti di)** intolerant (of).

intolleranza [intolle'rantsa] *sf* intolerance.

intonacare [intona'kare] *vt* to plaster.

intonaco, ci [in'tɔnako] *sm* plaster.

intonare [into'nare] **1** *vt (Mus: canzone)* to start to sing; *(fig: armonizzare)*: ~ **a** to tone in with, match with; ~ **due colori tra di loro** to match two colours. **2**: ~**rsi** *vr (colori)* to go together; ~**rsi a** *(armonizzarsi: alla circostanza, carnagione)* to suit; *(: al vestito)* to match, go with.

intonazione [intonat'tsjone] *sf (nel cantare)* tone; *(nel parlare)* intonation.

intontire [inton'tire] *vt (sog: botta)* to stun, daze; *(: gas, alcool)* to make dizzy, make woozy *(fam)*.

intontito, a [inton'tito] *ag (persona: da botta)* stunned, dazed; *(: da gas, alcool)* dizzy, woozy *(fam)*; *(sguardo)* glazed; ~ **dal sonno** stupid with sleep.

intopparsi [intop'parsi] *vr (congegno)* to stick; ~ **in** *(parola difficile, difficoltà)* to stumble over.

intoppo [in'tɔppo] *sm (ostacolo)* hitch; *(difficoltà)* difficulty.

intorbidare [intorbi'dare] *vt (liquido)* to make turbid; *(mente)* to cloud; ~ **le acque** *(fig)* to muddy the waters.

intorno [in'torno] **1** *av* around, round; **qui/lì** ~ round here/there; **c'è un castello e tutt'** ~ **un giardino** there is a castle with a garden all around it. **2**: ~ **a** *prep* **(a)** *(attorno a, circa)* around, (round) about; **smettila di girarmi** ~ stop hanging around me; **successe** ~ **al 1910** it happened around *o* (round) about 1910. **(b)** *(riguardo)* about.

intorpidimento [intorpidi'mento] *sm (delle membra)* numbness; *(della mente)* torpor, sluggishness.

intorpidire [intorpi'dire] **1** *vt (membra)* to numb; *(mente)* to slow down, make sluggish. **2**: ~**rsi** *vr (membra)* to grow numb; *(mente, persona)* to become sluggish.

intossicare [intossi'kare] **1** *vt* to poison. **2**: ~**rsi** *vr* to poison o.s.

intossicazione [intossikat'tsjone] *sf* poisoning.

intraducibile [intradu'tʃibile] *ag* untranslatable.

intralciare [intral'tʃare] *vt* to hamper, hinder.

intralcio [in'traltʃo] *sm* hitch.

intrallazzare [intrallat'tsare] *vi* to intrigue, scheme.

intrallazzatore, trice [intrallattsa'tore] *sm/f* wheeler dealer.

intrallazzo [intral'lattso] *sm (Pol)* intrigue, manoeuvre; *(traffico losco)* racket.

intramontabile [intramon'tabile] *ag* timeless.

intramuscolare [intramusko'lare] *ag* intramuscular.

intransigente [intransi'dʒente] *ag* uncompromising, intransigent; **è piuttosto** ~ **in fatto di amicizie** he's rather particular about the company he keeps.

intransigenza [intransi'dʒentsa] *sf* intransigence.

intransitivo, a [intransi'tivo] *ag (Gram)* intransitive.

intrappolare [intrappo'lare] *vt* to trap; **rimanere intrappolato** to be trapped; **farsi** ~ to get caught.

intraprendente [intrapren'dɛnte] *ag (che si dà da fare)* enterprising, go-ahead; *(: con le donne)* forward, bold.

intraprendenza [intrapren'dɛntsa] *sf* audacity, initiative; *(con le donne)* boldness.

intraprendere [intra'prɛndere] *vt (riforme)* to undertake; *(carriera)* to embark (up)on; ~ **una spedizione** to set out on an expedition.

intrapreso, a [intra'preso] *pp di* **intraprendere**.

intrattabile [intrat'tabile] *ag* intractable.

intrattenere [intratte'nere] **1** *vt* **(a)** *(divertire)* to entertain. **(b)** *(rapporti)* to have, maintain. **2:** ~**rsi** *vr (fermarsi: con ospiti)* to linger; ~**rsi su** *(argomento, questione)* to dwell on.

intravedere [intrave'dere] *vt* **(a)** *(vedere appena)* to make out, catch a glimpse of. **(b)** *(presagire: difficoltà, pericoli)* to foresee; *(: verità)* to have an inkling of.

intrecciare [intret'tʃare] **1** *vt (gen)* to plait, braid; *(intessere)* to weave; ~ **una relazione amorosa** *(fig)* to begin an affair; **s'intreccino le danze!** let the dance begin! **2:** ~**rsi** *vr (rami, corde)* to become interwoven, intertwine.

intreccio [in'trettʃo] *sm* **(a)** *(di tessuto)* weave; *(di paglia)* plaiting. **(b)** *(fig: di commedia)* plot.

intrepido, a [in'trɛpido] *ag* intrepid, dauntless.

intricare [intri'kare] **1** *vt (fili)* to tangle; *(fig: faccenda)* to complicate. **2:** ~**rsi** *vr (vedi vt)* to become tangled; to become complicated.

intrico, chi [in'triko] *sm (anche fig)* tangle.

intrigante [intri'gante] **1** *ag* scheming. **2** *sm/f* schemer, intriguer.

intrigare [intri'gare] *vi* to scheme, intrigue.

intrigo, ghi [in'trigo] *sm (complotto)* intrigue, scheme; *(situazione complicata)* tricky situation.

intrinseco, a, ci, che [in'trinseko] *ag* intrinsic.

intriso, a [in'trizo] *ag:* ~ **di** *(inzuppato)* soaked with; *(fig: testa, mente)* stuffed with.

intristire [intris'tire] *vi (aus essere) (persona: diventare triste)* to grow sad; *(pianta)* to wilt.

introdotto, a [intro'dotto] *pp di* **introdurre.**

introdurre [intro'durre] **1** *vt (gen)* to introduce; *(moneta, chiave)* to insert, introduce; *(descrizione, elemento)* to introduce, bring in; *(persona)* to show in; **gli ospiti venivano introdotti in sala** the guests were shown *o* ushered into the room; ~ **prodotti di contrabbando** to smuggle in goods. **2:** ~**rsi** *vr (penetrare):* ~**rsi in** to enter, get into; *(: furtivamente)* to sneak in, slip in.

introduttivo, a [introdut'tivo] *ag* introductory.

introduzione [introdut'tsjone] *sf* introduction; **lettera di** ~ letter of introduction.

introito [in'trɔito] *sm* **(a)** *(Comm: entrata: anche:* ~**i)** revenue, income. **(b)** *(Rel)* introit.

intromesso, a [intro'messo] *pp di* **intromettersi.**

intromettersi [intro'mettersi] *vr (immischiarsi)* to interfere, meddle; *(in conversazione)* to intervene.

intromissione [intromis'sjone] *sf (vedi vb)* interference, meddling; intervention.

introspettivo, a [introspet'tivo] *ag* introspective.

introspezione [introspet'tsjone] *sf* introspection.

introvabile [intro'vabile] *ag (persona, oggetto)* who *(o* which) cannot be found; *(libro etc)* unobtainable.

introversione [introver'sjone] *sf* introversion.

introverso, a [intro'verso], **introvertito, a** [introver'tito] **1** *ag* introverted. **2** *sm/f* introvert.

intrufolarsi [intrufo'larsi] *vr:* ~ **(in)** *(stanza)* to sneak in(to), slip in(to); *(conversazione)* to butt in(to).

intruglio [in'truʎʎo] *sm* concoction.

intrusione [intru'zjone] *sf* intrusion.

intrusivo, a [intru'zivo] *ag* intrusive.

intruso, a [in'truzo] *sm/f (estraneo)* intruder; *(: ad un ricevimento)* gatecrasher; **mi sento un** ~ I feel as if I don't belong; **mi trattano come un** ~ they treat me like an outsider.

intuibile [intu'ibile] *ag* deducible; **è facilmente** ~ **che...** one soon realizes that... .

intuire [intu'ire] *vt (presentire, accorgersi)* to realize; *(capire)* to grasp intuitively; *(indovinare)* to guess.

intuitivo, a [intui'tivo] *ag* intuitive.

intuito [in'tuito] *sm* intuition; **capire per** ~ to grasp intuitively.

intuizione [intuit'tsjone] *sf* intuition.

inturgidire [inturdʒi'dire] *vi (aus essere),* ~**rsi** *vr* to swell.

inumanità [inumani'ta] *sf inv* inhumanity.

inumano, a [inu'mano] *ag* inhuman.

inumare [inu'mare] *vt (seppellire)* to bury, inter.

inumazione [inumat'tsjone] *sf* burial, interment.

inumidire [inumi'dire] *vt (labbra)* to moisten; *(biancheria)* to dampen; ~**rsi le labbra** to moisten one's lips.

inurbamento [inurba'mento] *sm* urbanization.

inusitato, a [inuzi'tato] *ag* unusual.

inutile [i'nutile] *ag (che non serve)* useless; *(superfluo)* needless, unnecessary; **è** ~ **insistere** *o* **che tu insista** it's no use *o* no good insisting, there's no point in insisting; **è stato tutto** ~! it was all in vain!

inutilità [inutili'ta] *sf (vedi ag)* uselessness; needlessness.

inutilizzabile [inutilid'dzabile] *ag* unusable.

inutilizzato, a [inutilid'dzato] *ag* unused.

inutilmente [inutil'mente] *av (senza risultato)* fruitlessly; *(senza utilità, scopo)* unnecessarily, needlessly; **l'ho cercato** ~ I looked for him in vain; **ti preoccupi** ~ there's nothing for you to worry about, there's no need for you to worry.

invadente [inva'dɛnte] *ag* intrusive; **non vorrei essere** ~ I don't want to interfere.

invadenza [inva'dentsa] *sf* intrusiveness.

invadere [in'vadere] *vt (gen)* to invade; *(sog: dimostranti)* to overrun, swarm into; *(: acque)* to flood; **i tifosi hanno invaso il campo** the fans invaded the pitch; **le auto giapponesi hanno invaso il mercato** Japanese cars have flooded the market; ~ **la privacy di qn** to invade sb's privacy.

invaditrice [invadi'tritʃe] *ag f vedi* **invasore.**

invaghirsi [inva'girsi] *vr:* ~ **di** to take a fancy to.

invalicabile [invali'kabile] *ag (montagna)* impassable.

invalidare [invali'dare] *vt* to invalidate.

invalidità [invalidi'ta] *sf (vedi ag)* disablement, disability; infirmity; invalidity.

invalido, a [in'valido] **1** *ag* **(a)** *(Med)* disabled; *(: malato)* infirm. **(b)** *(Dir: nullo)* invalid. **2** *sm/f (Med)* disabled person; *(: malato)* invalid; ~ **di guerra** disabled ex-serviceman; ~ **del lavoro** industrially disabled person.

invalso, a [in'valso] *ag (diffuso)* established.

invano [in'vano] *av* in vain.

invariabile [inva'rjabile] *ag* invariable.

invariato, a [inva'rjato] *ag* unchanged.

invasare [inva'zare] *vt (pianta)* to pot.

invasato, a [inva'zato] **1** *ag* possessed (by the devil). **2** *sm/f* person possessed by the devil; **urlare come un** ~ to shout like a madman.

invasatura [invasa'tura] *sf (Naut)* slipway, slips *pl.*

invasione [inva'zjone] *sf* invasion.

invaso, a [in'vaso] *pp di* **invadere.**

invasore [inva'zore], **invaditrice** [invadi'tritʃe] **1** *ag* invading. **2** *sm* invader.

invecchiamento [invekkja'mento] *sm (di persona)* ageing; **questo whisky ha un** ~ **di 12 anni** this whisky has been matured for 12 years.

invecchiare [invek'kjare] **1** *vi (aus essere) (diventare vecchio)* to grow old; *(sembrare più vecchio)* to age; *(vino)* to age; **lo trovo invecchiato** I find he has aged. **2** *vt (persona)* to age, put years on; *(vino)* to age.

invece [in'vetʃe] *av (gen)* instead; *(ma)* but; **credevo di aver ragione** ~ **no** I thought I was right but

I wasn't; **io preferisco i romanzi; Peter ~ i gialli** I prefer novels whereas Peter prefers detective stories; **~ di qc/di o che fare qc** instead of sth/of doing sth; **potresti aiutarmi ~ di o che stare lì a guardare la TV** you could help me instead of sitting there watching TV; **preferisco lavorare in Italia ~ che all'estero** I prefer to work in Italy rather than abroad.

inveire [inve'ire] *vi*: **~ contro qn/qc** to rail against sb/sth.

invelenire [invele'nire] **1** *vt* to embitter. **2**: **~rsi** *vr* to become bitter.

invendibile [inven'dibile] *ag* unsaleable.

invenduto, a [inven'duto] *ag* unsold.

inventare [inven'tare] *vt* (*gen*) to invent; (*metodo*) to invent, devise; (*gioco, scusa*) to invent, make up, think up; **lui ne inventa di tutti i colori!** what will he think up next!; **se l'è inventata di sana pianta** he made the whole thing up.

inventariare [inventa'rjare] *vt* to make an inventory of, inventory.

inventario [inven'tarjo] *sm* (*gen*) inventory; (*Comm: registro*) stock list; (*: operazione*) stocktaking; **fare l'~ di** to make an inventory of; **mi ha fatto l'~ delle sue malattie** (*fig*) he regaled me with his medical history.

inventiva [inven'tiva] *sf* inventiveness.

inventore, trice [inven'tore] **1** *ag* inventive. **2** *sm/f* inventor.

invenzione [inven'tsjone] *sf* (*gen*) invention; **è tutta un'~** (*fig*) it's pure invention *o* fabrication; **una ricetta di mia ~** a recipe of my own creation.

inverecondia [invere'kondja] *sf* shamelessness, immodesty.

inverecondo, a [invere'kondo] *ag* shameless, immodest.

invernale [inver'nale] *ag* (*gen*) winter *attr*; (*simile all'inverno*) wintry.

inverno [in'verno] *sm* winter; **d'~** in (the) winter; **essere in pieno ~** to be in the depths of winter.

inverosimiglianza [inverosimiʎ'ʎantsa] *sf* improbability, unlikelihood.

inverosimile [invero'simile] **1** *ag* (*racconto, scusa*) unlikely, improbable; (*disordine, baccano*) incredible, unbelievable. **2** *sm*: **l'~** the improbable; **ha dell'~** it's hard to believe, it's incredible.

inversione [inver'sjone] *sf* inversion; **~ di tendenza** (*fig*) radical change of direction; (*peg: spec Pol*) U-turn; **'divieto d'~'** (*Aut*) 'no U-turns'.

inverso, a [in'verso] **1** *ag* (**a**) (*direzione*) opposite; **in ordine ~** in reverse order; **in ragione ~a** (*Mat*) in inverse ratio; **si è scontrato con una macchina che veniva in senso ~** he collided with a car coming in the opposite direction. (**b**) (*fig fam*) cross, bad-tempered. **2** *sm*: **l'~** the opposite, the reverse; **capisce tutto all'~** he always gets hold of the wrong end of the stick; **fa tutto all'~** he does everything the wrong way round.

invertebrato, a [inverte'brato] *ag, sm* invertebrate.

invertire [inver'tire] *vt* (*gen*) to invert; (*disposizione, posti*) to change; (*ruoli*) to exchange; **~ il senso di marcia** (*Aut*) to do a U-turn; **~ la rotta** (*Naut*) to go about; (*fig*) to do a U-turn.

invertito, a [inver'tito] **1** *ag* (*Chim*): **zucchero ~** invert sugar. **2** *sm* (*omosessuale*) homosexual.

investigare [investi'gare] **1** *vt* (*indagare*) to investigate; (*analizzare*) to examine. **2** *vi*: **~ su** to investigate.

investigativo, a [investiga'tivo] *ag*: **squadra ~a** detective squad; **agente ~** detective.

investigatore, trice [investiga'tore] *sm/f* investigator, detective.

investigazione [investigat'tsjone] *sf* investigation, inquiry.

investimento [investi'mento] *sm* (**a**) (*Econ*) investment. (**b**) (*di pedone*) running down, knocking down; (*di veicolo*) collision.

investire [inves'tire] **1** *vt* (**a**) (*Econ*) to invest. (**b**) (*sog: veicolo: pedone*) to run over, knock down; (*: altro veicolo*) to crash into, hit. (**c**) (*apostrofare*) to assail; **~ qn di o con qc** (*domande*) to besiege sb with sth, ply sb with sth; (*ingiurie, insulti*) to heap sth on sb. (**d**) (*Dir, Amm: incaricare*): **~ qn di** (*poteri*) to invest sb with; (*incarico*) to appoint sb to. **2**: **~rsi** *vr* (*fig*): **~rsi di una parte** to enter thoroughly into a role.

investitore, trice [investi'tore] *sm/f* driver responsible for an accident.

investitura [investi'tura] *sf* (*Amm, Pol*) appointment, nomination; (*Rel*) investiture.

inveterato, a [invete'rato] *ag* (*abitudine, vizio*) ingrained; (*fumatore, bugiardo etc*) inveterate.

invettiva [invet'tiva] *sf* invective; **lanciare ~e contro qn** to hurl abuse at sb.

inviare [invi'are] *vt* (*gen*) to send; (*merce*) to dispatch.

inviato, a [invi'ato] *sm/f* (*Pol*) envoy; (*Stampa*) correspondent.

invidia [in'vidja] *sf* envy; **fare ~ a qn** to make sb envious; **farebbe ~ ai migliori ristoranti** it would be the envy of the best restaurants; **avere o provare ~ per qn/qc** to be envious of sb/sth; **per ~** out of envy; **morire d'~** (*fig*) to be green with envy; **degno d'~** enviable; **che ~!** how I envy you!

invidiabile [invi'djabile] *ag* enviable.

invidiare [invi'djare] *vt*: **~ qc a qn** to envy sb sth; **~ qn per qc** to envy sb for sth; **non aver nulla da ~ a nessuno** to be as good as the next one.

invidioso, a [invi'djoso] *ag* envious.

invincibile [invin'tʃibile] *ag* (*esercito, nemico*) invincible; (*fig: antipatia, timidezza*) insurmountable.

invio, ii [in'vio] *sm* (**a**) (*vedi vb*) sending; dispatching; **chiedere l'~ di qc** to ask for sth to be sent (*o* dispatched). (**b**) (*insieme di merci*) consignment.

inviolabile [invio'labile] *ag* inviolable.

inviolato, a [invio'lato] *ag* (**a**) (*diritto, segreto*) inviolate. (**b**) (*foresta*) virgin *attr*; (*montagna, vetta*) unscaled.

inviperire [invipe'rire] *vi* (*aus essere*), **~rsi** *vr* to become furious, fly into a temper; **mi ha fatto ~** he made me furious.

inviperito, a [invipe'rito] *ag* furious.

invischiare [invis'kjare] **1** *vt* (*fig*): **~ qn in qc** to involve sb in sth, mix sb up in sth. **2**: **~rsi** *vr*: **~rsi con qn/in qc** to get mixed up *o* involved with sb/in sth.

invisibile [invi'zibile] *ag* (*gen, Econ*) invisible; **rendersi ~** (*scherz*) to make o.s. scarce.

inviso, a [in'vizo] *ag*: **~ a** unpopular with.

invitante [invi'tante] *ag* (*proposta, odorino*) inviting; (*sorriso*) appealing, attractive.

invitare [invi'tare] **1** *vt* (*gen*) to invite; **~ qn a fare qc** to invite sb to do sth; **~ a cena gli amici** to invite *o* ask one's friends to dinner; **furono invitati a entrare** they were invited *o* asked in; **è stato invitato a dimettersi** he was asked to resign; **è una giornata che invita a uscire** it's the sort of day that tempts one to go out. **2**: **~rsi** *vr*: **si invita sempre da solo** he always invites himself along.

invitato, a [invi'tato] *sm/f* guest.

invito [in'vito] *sm* invitation; **fare un ~ a qn** to extend an invitation to sb; **su ~ di qn** at sb's invitation.

invocare [invo'kare] *vt* (**a**) *(aiuto, pietà)* to beg for, cry out for; *(Dio)* to invoke, call upon. (**b**) *(Dir: legge, articolo)* to cite, refer to.

invocazione [invokat'tsjone] *sf* invocation.

invogliare [invoʎ'ʎare] *vt (stimolare)* to encourage; *(invitare)* to tempt, entice; **bisognerebbe invogliarlo a studiare** we should encourage him to study; **la giornata di sole invogliava ad uscire** the sunny day tempted one out of doors.

involgarire [involga'rire] **1** *vt (sog: abito, trucco)* to cause to appear vulgar. **2**: **~rsi** *vr* to become vulgar.

involontario, a [involon'tarjo] *ag (movimento)* involuntary; *(offesa, errore)* unintentional.

involtino [invol'tino] *sm (Culin)* roulade.

involto [in'volto] *sm (fagotto)* bundle.

involucro [in'volukro] *sm (rivestimento)* covering; *(confezione)* wrapping.

involutivo, a [involu'tivo] *ag*: **subire un processo ~** to regress.

involuto, a [invo'luto] *ag (stile)* convoluted.

involuzione [involut'tsjone] *sf* (**a**) *(di stile)* convolutedness. (**b**) *(regresso)*: **subire un'~** to regress.

invulnerabile [invulne'rabile] *ag* invulnerable.

invulnerabilità [invulnerabili'ta] *sf* invulnerability.

inzaccherare [intsakke'rare] **1** *vt* to spatter with mud. **2**: **~rsi** *vr* to get muddy.

inzuppare [intsup'pare] **1** *vt (gen)*: **~ qc (di)** to soak sth (in); **inzuppò i biscotti nel latte** he dipped the biscuits in the milk. **2**: **~rsi** *vr* to get soaked, get drenched.

io ['io] **1** *pron pers* I; **sono ~** it's me, *(più formale)* it is I; **~ e te** you and I; **il mio amico ed ~ ci andremo** my friend and I will go; **lo farò ~**, **io lo farò** i'LL do it; **~ stesso(a)** I myself. **2** *sm*: **l'~** the self, the ego.

iodio ['jɔdjo] *sm* iodine.

iogurt ['jɔgurt] *sm inv* = **yogurt**.

ione ['jone] *sm* ion.

ionico, a, ci, che ['jɔniko] *ag* (**a**) *(stile, periodo)* Ionic. (**b**) *(Geog)* Ionian.

Ionio ['jɔnjo] *sm*: **lo ~** the Ionian (Sea).

ionizzare [jonid'dzare] *vt* to ionize.

ionizzazione [joniddzat'tsjone] *sf* ionization.

iosa ['jɔsa]: **a ~** *av* in abundance, in great quantity; **ce ne sono a ~** there are thousands of them; **avere matite a ~** to have pencils galore.

iperbole [i'pɛrbole] *sf (Letteratura)* hyberbole; *(Mat)* hyperbola.

iperbolico, a, ci, che [iper'bɔliko] *ag (Letteratura, Mat)* hyperbolic(al); *(fig: esagerato)* exaggerated.

ipercritico, a, ci, che [iper'kritiko] *ag* hypercritical.

ipermercato [ipermer'kato] *sm* hypermarket.

ipersensibile [ipersen'sibile] *ag (persona)* hypersensitive; *(Fot: lastra, pellicola)* hypersensitized.

ipersensibilità [ipersensibili'ta] *sf* hypersensitivity.

ipertensione [iperten'sjone] *sf (Med)* high blood pressure, hypertension *(T)*.

iperteso, a [iper'teso] *ag, sm/f (Med)* suffering from high blood pressure.

ipnosi [ip'nɔzi] *sf* hypnosis.

ipnotico, a, ci, che [ip'nɔtiko] *ag, sm* hypnotic.

ipnotismo [ipno'tizmo] *sm* hypnotism.

ipnotizzare [ipnotid'dzare] *vt* to hypnotize.

ipocondria [ipokon'dria] *sf* hypochondria.

ipocondriaco, a, ci, che [ipokon'driako] *ag, sm/f* hypochondriac.

ipocrisia [ipokri'zia] *sf* hypocrisy; **è stata un'~ da parte sua** that was sheer hypocrisy on his part.

ipocrita, i, e [i'pɔkrita] **1** *ag* hypocritical. **2** *sm/f* hypocrite.

ipoteca, che [ipo'tɛka] *sf* mortgage; **fare o mettere un'~ su qc** to mortgage sth, raise a mortgage on sth.

ipotecabile [ipote'kabile] *ag* mortgageable.

ipotecare [ipote'kare] *vt (Dir, fig)* to mortgage.

ipotecario, a [ipote'karjo] *ag* mortgage *attr*.

ipotensione [ipoten'sjone] *sf (Med)* low blood pressure, hypotension *(T)*.

ipotenusa [ipote'nuza] *sf* hypotenuse.

ipotesi [i'pɔtezi] *sf inv* hypothesis; **facciamo l'~ che…, ammettiamo per ~ che…** let's suppose *o* assume that…; **nella peggiore/migliore delle ~i** at worst/best; **nell'~ che venga** should he come, if he comes; **se per ~ io partissi…** just supposing I were to leave… .

ipotetico, a, ci, che [ipo'tɛtiko] *ag (gen)* hypothetical; *(guadagni, profitti)* theoretical, hypothetical; *(mondo)* imaginary; **nel caso ~ che tu non arrivi a tempo** should you not arrive in time; **periodo ~** *(Gram)* conditional clause.

ipotizzare [ipotid'dzare] *vt*: **~ che** to form the hypothesis that.

ippica ['ippika] *sf* horseracing.

ippico, a, ci, che ['ippiko] *ag* horse *attr*.

ippocastano [ippokas'tano] *sm* horse chestnut (tree).

ippodromo [ip'pɔdromo] *sm* racecourse, racetrack.

ippopotamo [ippo'pɔtamo] *sm* hippopotamus.

ipsilon ['ipsilon] *sf o m inv (lettera)* Y, y; *(: dell'alfabeto greco)* upsilon.

ira ['ira] *sf* anger, fury, wrath; **l'~ di Dio** the wrath of God; **è successo un'~ di Dio** *(fig)* all hell broke loose; **con uno scatto d'~** in a fit of anger; **farsi prendere dall'~** to lose one's temper.

iracheno, a [ira'kɛno] *ag, sm/f* Iraqi.

iracondo, a [ira'kondo] *ag* irascible, quicktempered.

Iran ['iran] *sm* Iran.

iraniano, a [ira'njano] *ag, sm/f* Iranian.

Iraq ['irak] *sm* Iraq.

irascibile [iraʃ'ʃibile] *ag* irascible, quicktempered.

irato, a [i'rato] *ag (persona, sguardo)* irate, furious.

iride ['iride] *sf* (**a**) *(Anat, Bot)* iris. (**b**) *(arcobaleno)* rainbow.

iridescente [irideʃ'ʃɛnte] *ag* iridescent.

iridescenza [irideʃ'ʃɛntsa] *sf* iridescence.

Irlanda [ir'landa] *sf* Ireland; **~ del Nord** Northern Ireland, Ulster; **Repubblica d'~** Eire.

irlandese [irlan'dese] **1** *ag* Irish. **2** *sm/f* Irishman/woman; **gli I~i** the Irish.

ironia [iro'nia] *sf* irony; **fare dell'~ su qc** to be ironic(al) about sth.

ironico, a, ci, che [i'rɔniko] *ag* ironic(al).

ironizzare [ironid'dzare] *vt, vi*: **~ su** to be ironical about.

iroso, a [i'roso] *ag (sguardo, tono)* angry, wrathful; *(persona)* irascible.

irradiare [irra'djare] **1** *vt* (**a**) *(illuminare: anche fig)* to light up. (**b**) *(diffondere: calore, energia)* to radiate. **2** *vi (aus essere)* to radiate. **3**: **~rsi** *vr*: **~rsi (da)** *(strade, rette)* to radiate (from).

irradiazione [irradjat'tsjone] *sf (di calore, energia)* radiation.

irraggiamento [irraddʒa'mento] *sm (Fis)* radiation.

irraggiungibile [irraddʒun'dʒibile] *ag* unreachable; *(fig: meta)* unattainable.

irragionevole [irradʒo'nevole] *ag (privo di ragione)* irrational; *(fig: persona, pretese, prezzo)* unreasonable.

irrancidire [irrantʃi'dire] *vi (aus* **essere)** to turn rancid.

irrazionale [irrattsjo'nale] *ag (gen, Mat)* irrational.

irrazionalità [irrattsjonali'ta] *sf* irrationality.

irreale [irre'ale] *ag* unreal.

irrealizzabile [irrealid'dzabile] *ag (sogno, desiderio)* unattainable, unrealizable; *(progetto)* unworkable, impracticable.

irrealtà [irreal'ta] *sf* unreality.

irrecuperabile [irrekupe'rabile] *ag (gen)* irretrievable; *(fig: persona)* irredeemable.

irrecusabile [irreku'zabile] *ag* **(a)** *(prova)* indisputable, irrefutable. **(b)** *(offerta)* which cannot be refused.

irredentismo [irreden'tizmo] *sm (Storia)* irredentism.

irredimibile [irredi'mibile] *ag* irredeemable.

irrefrenabile [irrefre'nabile] *ag* uncontrollable.

irrefutabile [irrefu'tabile] *ag* irrefutable.

irregolare [irrego'lare] **1** *ag (gen)* irregular; *(terreno, passi)* uneven; *(sonno)* fitful; *(risultati, sviluppo)* erratic. **2** *sm (Mil)* irregular.

irregolarità [irregolari'ta] *sf inv* **(a)** *(vedi ag)* irregularity; unevenness; fitfulness; erratic nature. **(b)** *(azione irregolare)* irregularity; *(Sport)* foul.

irreligioso, a [irreli'dʒoso] *ag* irreligious.

irremovibile [irremo'vibile] *ag* unshakeable; **essere ~ in qc** to be adamant about sth.

irreparabile [irrepa'rabile] *ag* irreparable.

irreperibile [irrepe'ribile] *ag* who *(o* which) cannot be found.

irreprensibile [irrepren'sibile] *ag* irreproachable.

irrequietezza [irrekwje'tettsa] *sf* restlessness.

irrequieto, a [irre'kwjɛto] *ag (agitato)* restless; *(vivace)* lively.

irresistibile [irresis'tibile] *ag* irresistible.

irresolubile [irreso'lubile] *ag (mistero, problema)* unsolvable.

irresolutezza [irresolu'tettsa] *sf* irresoluteness, indecisiveness.

irresoluto, a [irreso'luto] *ag* irresolute, indecisive.

irresoluzione [irresolut'tsjone] *sf* irresolution, indecision.

irrespirabile [irrespi'rabile] *ag (aria)* unbreathable; *(: malsano)* unhealthy; *(fig: opprimente)* stifling, oppressive.

irresponsabile [irrespon'sabile] **1** *ag* irresponsible. **2** *sm/f* irresponsible person.

irresponsabilità [irresponsabili'ta] *sf* irresponsibility.

irrestringibile [irrestrin'dʒibile] *ag* unshrinkable.

irretire [irre'tire] *vt* to ensnare, catch.

irreversibile [irrever'sibile] *ag* irreversible.

irrevocabile [irrevo'kabile] *ag* irrevocable.

irriconoscibile [irrikonoʃ'ʃibile] *ag* unrecognizable.

irriducibile [irridu'tʃibile] *ag (frazione, cifra)* irreducible; *(fig: avversario)* indomitable; *(: ostinazione)* unyielding.

irriflessivo, a [irrifles'sivo] *ag* thoughtless.

irrigare [irri'gare] *vt (Agr, Med)* to irrigate.

irrigazione [irrigat'tsjone] *sf* irrigation.

irrigidimento [irridʒidi'mento] *sm (dei muscoli)* stiffening; *(fig: della disciplina)* tightening; *(: di posizione, atteggiamento)* hardening.

irrigidire [irridʒi'dire] **1** *vt (gen)* to stiffen; *(fig: disciplina)* to tighten. **2: ~rsi** *vr* to stiffen; **~rsi**

nella propria posizione *(fig)* to become entrenched in one's position.

irriguardoso, a [irrigwar'doso] *ag* disrespectful.

irriguo, a [ir'riguo] *ag (terreno)* irrigated; *(acque)* irrigation *attr.*

irrilevante [irrile'vante] *ag (trascurabile)* insignificant.

irrimediabile [irrime'djabile] *ag* irremediable; **danneggiato in modo ~** irremediably *o* irreparably damaged.

irripetibile [irripe'tibile] *ag* unrepeatable.

irrisorio, a [irri'zɔrjo] *ag* derisory.

irrispettoso, a [irrispet'toso] *ag* disrespectful.

irritabile [irri'tabile] *ag* irritable.

irritabilità [irritabili'ta] *sf* irritability.

irritante [irri'tante] *ag (atteggiamento)* irritating, annoying; *(Med)* irritant.

irritare [irri'tare] **1** *vt* **(a)** *(infastidire)* to irritate, annoy. **(b)** *(pelle, occhi)* to irritate. **2: ~rsi** *vr* **(a):** **~rsi per qc/con qn** to become irritated *o* annoyed at sth/with sb. **(b)** *(infiammarsi: pelle, occhi)* to become irritated.

irritato, a [irri'tato] *ag* irritated; **aver la gola ~a** to have a sore throat.

irritazione [irritat'tsjone] *sf (stizza)* irritation, annoyance; *(Med)* irritation; **mi da un senso d'~** he irritates me.

irriverente [irrive'rente] *ag* irreverent.

irriverenza [irrive'rentsa] *sf (qualità)* irreverence; *(azione)* irreverent action.

irrobustire [irrobus'tire] **1** *vt (persona)* to make stronger, make more robust; *(muscoli)* to strengthen. **2: ~rsi** *vr* to become stronger.

irrompere [ir'rompere] *vi:* **~ in** to burst into.

irrorare [irro'rare] *vt (bagnare)* to bathe.

irruente [irru'ɛnte] *ag (impetuoso)* impetuous; *(chiassoso)* boisterous.

irruenza [irru'entsa] *sf* impetuousness; **con ~** impetuously.

irruvidire [irruvi'dire] **1** *vt* to roughen. **2** *vi (aus* **essere)**, **~rsi** *vr* to become rough.

irruzione [irrut'tsjone] *sf:* **fare ~ in** *(sog: polizia)* to raid; **i tifosi hanno fatto ~ nel campo** the fans invaded the pitch.

irsuto, a [ir'suto] *ag (petto)* hairy; *(barba)* bristly.

irto, a ['irto] *ag (barba)* bristly; **~ di** *(anche fig)* bristling with.

iscritto[1], a [is'kritto] **1** *pp di* **iscrivere. 2** *sm/f* registered member *(o* student *o* candidate); **gli ~i alla gara** the competitors.

iscritto[2] [is'kritto]: **per ~** *av* in writing.

iscrivere [is'krivere] **1** *vt* **(a)** *(Scol):* **~ (a)** to register (in), enrol (in); *(all'anagrafe)* to register; **~ qn a un club** to enrol sb as a member of a club. **(b)** *(Comm)* to enter; **~ una spesa nel bilancio** to enter an item on the balance sheet. **2: ~rsi** *vr:* **~rsi a** *(partito, club)* to join; *(gara, concorso)* to enter; *(corso, università)* to enrol for.

iscrizione [iskrit'tsjone] *sf* **(a)** *(epigrafe)* inscription. **(b)** *(a scuola, università)* enrolment; *(all'anagrafe)* registration; **chiedere/fare l'~ a un club** to apply for membership of/join a club; **tassa di ~** *(a una gara)* entry fee; *(a un circolo)* membership fee. **(c)** *(Comm)* entering.

Islam [iz'lam] *sm* Islam.

islamico, a, ci, che [iz'lamiko] *ag* Islamic.

Islanda [iz'landa] *sf* Iceland.

islandese [izlan'dese] **1** *ag* Icelandic. **2** *sm/f* Icelander. **3** *sm (lingua)* Icelandic.

isobara [i'zɔbara] *sf* isobar.

isobata [i'zɔbata] *sf* isobath.

isola ['izola] *sf* island; **le I~e britanniche** the

British Isles; ~ **pedonale** pedestrian precinct; ~ spartitraffico traffic island.

isolamento [izola'mento] *sm* **(a)** *(gen)* isolation; *(solitudine)* loneliness, solitude; **mettere qn nella cella di** ~ to put sb in solitary confinement. **(b)** *(Tecn, Elettr)* insulation; ~ **acustico** soundproofing; ~ **termico** thermal insulation.

isolano, a [izo'lano] **1** *ag* island *attr.* **2** *sm/f* islander.

isolante [izo'lante] **1** *ag* insulating. **2** *sm* insulator.

isolare [izo'lare] **1** *vt* **(a)** *(gen)* to isolate; **la neve ha isolato il paese dal resto del mondo** snow has cut the village off from the rest of the world. **(b)** *(Tecn, Elettr)* to insulate; *(contro il rumore)* to soundproof. **2**: ~**rsi** *vr* to isolate o.s.

isolato¹, a [izo'lato] *ag* *(gen)* isolated; *(luogo)* lonely, remote.

isolato² [izo'lato] *sm* *(edifici)* block; **fare il giro dell'**~ to walk round the block.

isolatore [izola'tore] *sm* insulator.

isolazionismo [izolattsjo'nizmo] *sm* isolationism.

isolazionista, i, e [izolattsjo'nista] *sm/f* isolationist.

isolotto [izo'lɔtto] *sm* islet.

isometrico, a, ci, che [izo'metriko] *ag* isometric.

isoscele [i'zɔʃʃele] *ag* *(Geom)* isosceles *attr.*

isoterma [izo'tɛrma] *sf* isotherm.

isotopo, a [i'zɔtopo] **1** *ag* isotropic. **2** *sm* isotope.

ispanico, a, ci, che [is'paniko] *ag* Hispanic.

ispessimento [ispessi'mento] *sm* thickening.

ispessire [ispes'sire] **1** *vt* to thicken. **2**: ~**rsi** *vr* to get thicker, thicken.

ispettorato [ispetto'rato] *sm* inspectorate.

ispettore, trice [ispet'tore] *sm/f (Amm)* inspector; *(Comm)* supervisor; ~ **di zona** *(Comm)* area supervisor *o* manager.

ispezionare [ispettsjo'nare] *vt* to inspect.

ispezione [ispet'tsjone] *sf* inspection.

ispido, a [ˈispido] *ag (barba)* bristly; *(fig: carattere)* bristly, touchy.

ispirare [ispi'rare] **1** *vt (gen)* to inspire; ~ **fiducia a qn** to inspire sb with confidence; **è un tipo/ un'idea che non mi ispira** *o* **che mi ispira poco** I'm not all that keen on him/the idea; **l'idea m'ispira** the idea appeals to me. **2**: ~**rsi** *vr* **(a)** *(prendere ispirazione)*: ~**rsi a qn/qc** to be inspired by sb/sth, draw one's inspiration from sb/sth. **(b)** *(conformarsi)*: ~**rsi a qc** to be based on sth.

ispiratore, trice [ispira'tore] **1** *ag* inspiring. **2** *sm/f* inspirer; *(di ribellione)* instigator.

ispirazione [ispirat'tsjone] *sf* inspiration; **secondo l'**~ **del momento** according to the mood of the moment; **mi è venuto l'**~ **di telefonargli** I had the bright idea of phoning him.

Israele [izra'ele] *sm* Israel.

israeliano, a [izrae'ljano] *ag, sm/f* Israeli.

israelita, i, e [izrae'lita] *sm/f* Jew/Jewess; *(Storia)* Israelite.

israelitico, a, ci, che [izrae'litiko] *ag* Jewish.

issare [is'sare] *vt (bandiera, vela)* to hoist; *(oggetto)* to hoist, haul up; ~ **l'ancora** to weigh anchor; ~ **qn in spalla** to lift sb onto one's shoulders.

istantanea [istan'tanea] *sf (Fot)* snap.

istantaneità [istantanei'ta] *sf* instantaneousness, immediacy.

istantaneo, a [istan'taneo] *ag (gen)* instantaneous; *(che dura un istante)* momentary.

istante [is'tante] *sm* moment, instant; **all'**~, **sull'**~ at once, immediately; **in un** ~ in a flash; **fra un** ~, **tra qualche** ~ in a moment *o* minute; **abbiamo saputo proprio in questo** ~ **che...** we have just (this moment) heard that...; **l'aereo dovrebbe essere atterrato proprio in questo** ~ the plane should be landing at this very moment; **in**

quell'~ at that very *o* precise moment.

istanza [is'tantsa] *sf (richiesta: Amm, Dir)* request, petition; **fare** *o* **presentare un'**~ **a qn** to present a petition to sb; **su** ~ **di qn** at sb's request; **giudice di prima** ~ *(Dir)* judge of the court of first instance; **giudizio di seconda** ~ judgment on appeal; **in ultima** ~ *(fig)* finally; ~ **di divorzio** petition for divorce.

isteria [iste'ria] *sf* hysteria.

isterico, a, ci, che [is'teriko] **1** *ag* hysterical. **2** *sm/f (Med)* hysteric; *(peg)* hysterical type.

isterilire [isteri'lire] **1** *vt (terreno)* to render infertile; *(fig: fantasia)* to dry up. **2**: ~ **rsi** *vr (vedi vt)* to become infertile; to dry up.

isterismo [iste'rizmo] *sm* hysteria.

istigare [isti'gare] *vt*: ~ **qn a (fare) qc** to incite sb to (do) sth.

istigatore, trice [istiga'tore] *sm/f* instigator.

istigazione [istigat'tsjone] *sf* incitement; **su** ~ **di qn** (up)on sb's instigation; ~ **a delinquere** *(Dir)* incitement to crime.

istintivo, a [istin'tivo] **1** *ag* instinctive. **2** *sm/f*: **essere un** ~ to be guided by one's instincts.

istinto [is'tinto] *sm* instinct; ~ **di conservazione** instinct of self-preservation; **per** *o* **d'**~ instinctively.

istituire [istitu'ire] *vt (gen)* to institute; *(borsa di studio)* to found.

istituto [isti'tuto] *sm* **(a)** *(gen)* institute; *(Univ)* department; *(Scol)* college, school, institute; ~ **di bellezza** beauty salon; ~ **di credito** bank, banking institution; ~ **di francese/storia** *(Univ)* French/history department; ~ **tecnico** technical college. **(b)** *(istituzione)* institution.

istitutore, trice [istitu'tore] *sm/f* **(a)** *(fondatore)* founder. **(b)** *(precettore)* tutor/governess.

istituzionale [istituttsjo'nale] *ag* institutional.

istituzionalizzare [istituttsjonalid'dzare] *vt* to institutionalize.

istituzione [istitut'tsjone] *sf* **(a)** *(atto)* institution; founding. **(b)** *(ente, tradizione, norma)* institution; **lotta alle** ~**i** struggle against the Establishment; **essere un'**~ *(fig)* to be an institution. **(c)** *(Dir)*: ~**i** *pl* institutes.

istmo [ˈistmo] *sm* isthmus.

istologia [istolo'dʒia] *sf (Med)* histology.

istradare [istra'dare] *vt (fig: persona)*: ~ **(verso)** to direct (towards); ~ **qn sul giusto cammino** to put sb on the right path.

istriano, a [istri'ano] *ag, sm/f* Istrian.

istrice [ˈistritʃe] *sm (Zool)* porcupine; *(fig: persona)*: **essere un** ~ to be prickly.

istrione [istri'one] *sm (Teatro, fig)* ham; **fare l'**~ to ham.

istrionico, a, ci, che [istri'ɔniko] *ag* histrionic.

istruire [istru'ire] **1** *vt* **(a)** *(dare un'istruzione a)* to educate; *(dare istruzioni a)* to instruct; *(Mil)* to drill. **(b)** *(Dir)*: ~ **una causa** *o* **un processo** to prepare a case. **2**: ~ **rsi** *vr (informarsi)*: ~ **rsi su qc** to find out about sth.

istruito, a [istru'ito] *ag* educated.

istruttivo, a [istrut'tivo] *ag (esempio)* instructive; *(libro, film, discussione)* informative.

istruttore, trice [istrut'tore] **1** *ag*: **giudice** ~ *(Dir)* examining judge; **caporale** ~ *(Mil)* drill sergeant. **2** *sm/f* instructor; ~ **di scuola guida** driving instructor; ~ **di nuoto** swimming instructor.

istruttoria [istrut'tɔrja] *sf (Dir)* preliminary investigation; **formalizzare un'**~ to proceed to a formal hearing.

istruttorio, a [istrut'tɔrjo] *ag (Dir)* preliminary.

istruzione [istrut'tsjone] *sf* **(a)** *(gen)* training, instruction; *(Mil)* training; *(Scol, cultura)* education; **Ministero della Pubblica I**~ Ministry of Education. **(b)**: ~**i** pl *(direttive, avvertenze)* instructions, directions; ~**i per l'uso** instructions for use. **(c)** *(Dir)* investigation.

istupidire [istupi'dire] **1** vt *(sog: colpo)* to stun, daze; *(: droga, stanchezza)* to stupefy. **2**: ~**rsi** vr to become stupid.

Italia [i'talja] sf: **l'**~ Italy; **in** ~ in Italy.

italianità [italjani'ta] sf Italian character.

italianizzare [italjanid'dzare] vt to make Italian, italianize.

italiano, a [ita'ljano] **1** ag Italian; **all'**~**a** in the Italian style. **2** sm/f *(abitante)* Italian; **gli I**~**i** the Italians. **3** sm *(lingua)* Italian; **parlare (l')**~ speak Italian.

italico, a, ci, che [i'taliko] ag *(Storia)* Italic;

(Geog): **la penisola** ~**a** the Italian peninsula.

iter ['iter] sm passage, course; **l'**~ **burocratico** the bureaucratic process.

iterativo, a [litera'tivo] ag iterative.

itinerante [itine'rante] ag wandering, itinerant; **spettacolo** ~ travelling o touring show; **mostra** ~ touring exhibition.

itinerario [itine'rarjo] sm *(percorso)* route, itinerary; ~ **turistico** tourist route.

itterizia [litte'rittsja] sf *(Med)* jaundice.

ittico, a, ci, che ['ittiko] ag fish attr, fishing attr; **il mercato** ~ the fish market.

iugoslavo [jugoz'lavo] etc = **jugoslavo** etc.

iuta ['juta] sf jute.

I.V.A. ['iva] abbr di **imposta sul valore aggiunto**.

ivi ['ivi] av *(frm, poet)* therein; *(nelle citazioni)* ibid.

J

J, j |i'lunga| *sm o f inv (lettera)* J, j.
jazz |dʒaz| **1** *sm* jazz. **2** *ag inv* jazz attr.
jazzista, i |dʒad'dzista| *sm* jazz player.
jeans |dʒinz| *smpl* jeans.
jeep |dʒip| *sm inv* jeep.
jersey |'dʒɛrzi| *sm inv* jersey (cloth).
jockey |'dʒɔki| *sm inv* **(a)** *(Carte)* jack. **(b)** *(fantino)* jockey.
jodel |'jodel| *sm inv* yodel.
jogging |'dʒɔɡiŋ| *sm* jogging; **fare** ~ to go jogging.

jolly |'dʒɔli| *sm inv* joker.
jr. *abbr (= junior)* Jr., jr.
judo |dʒu'dɔ| *sm* judo.
Jugoslavia |jugoz'lavja| *sf* Yugoslavia.
jugoslavo, a |jugoz'lavo| *ag, sm/f* Yugoslav(ian).
juke-box |'dʒuk'bɔks| *sm inv* jukebox.
junior |'junjor| **1** *ag inv* junior. **2** *sm (Calcio):* **la Nazionale** ~**es** the under-21 team.
juta |'juta| *sf* = **iuta.**

K

K, k¹ |'kappa| *sf o m inv (lettera)* K, k.
k² *abbr (= kilo)* k.
kaki |'kaki| *ag inv, sm* = **cachi.**
kapoc |ka'pɔk| *sm* kapok.
kaputt |ka'put| *ag inv (fam)* kaput.
karakiri |kara'kiri| *sm* harakiri.
karatè |kara'tɛ| *sm* karate.
kasher |ka'ʃɛr| *ag inv* kosher.
kayak |ka'jak| *sm inv* kayak.
képi |ke'pi| *sm inv* kepi.
kerosene |kero'zɛne| *sm* = **cherosene.**
ketchup |'ketʃup| *sm inv* ketchup.
kg *abbr (= chilogrammo)* kg.
kibbutz |kib'buts| *sm inv* kibbutz.
kidnapping |'kidnapiŋ| *sm inv* kidnapping.

killer |'killer| *sm inv* gunman, hired gun.
kilo |'kilo| *etc* = **chilo** *etc.*
kilt |kilt| *sm inv* kilt.
kimono |ki'mɔno| *sm* = **chimono.**
kinesiterapia |kinezitera'pia| *sf* = **cinesiterapia.**
kitsch |kitʃ| *sm* kitsch.
km *abbr (= chilometro)* km.
km/h *abbr (= chilometri all'ora)* ≃ m.p.h.
knock out |nɔk'aut| **1** *ag inv* knocked out; **mettere qn** ~ to knock sb out. **2** *sm inv (colpo)* knockout punch.
K.O., k.o. *abbr di* **knock out.**
koala |ko'ala| *sm inv* koala (bear).
krapfen |'krapfən| *sm inv* doughnut.
KW *abbr (= kilowatt)* kw.

228

L

L¹, l¹ ['ɛlle] *sf o m inv (lettera)* L, l.
L², l² *abbr (= lira)* L., l.
l³ *abbr (= litro)* L., l.
l' *vedi* **il, la², lo².**
la¹ [la] *art det f vedi* **il.**
la² [la] *pron (dav vocale* **l')** **(a)** *(oggetto: riferito a persona)* her; (: *riferito a cosa)* it; *vedi anche* **lo. (b)** *(oggetto: forma di cortesia: anche:* **L~)** you; **in attesa di risentir~** I (*o* we) look forward to hearing from you; **molto lieto di conoscer~** pleased to meet you.
la³ [la] *sm inv (Mus)* A; (: *solfeggiando la scala)* la.
là [la] *av* **(a)** there; **mettilo ~** put it there; **eccolo ~!** there he (*o* it) is!; **resta ~ dove sei** stay where you are; **~ dentro/fuori/sopra/sotto** *etc* in/out/up/under *etc* there; **più in ~** *(spazio)* further on; *(tempo)* later on; **chi va ~?** who goes there?; **alto ~!** halt!
  (b): **di ~: di ~ dal fiume** beyond the river, on the other side of the river; **vieni via di ~** come away from there; **mia madre è di ~** my mother's in the other room; **per di ~** *(andare, passare etc)* that way; **se vai per di ~ allunghi** if you go that way it'll take you longer; **essere più di ~ che di qua** to be more dead than alive; **cerca di guardare al di ~ del fatto in sé** try to look beyond the event in itself.
  (c) *(fraseologia):* **~ per ~** *(sul momento)* there and then; **va' ~!** come off it!; **stavolta è andato troppo in ~** this time he's gone too far; **essere in ~ con gli anni** to be getting on (in years); *vedi* **quello.**
labbro ['labbro] *sm* **(a)** *(Anat: pl (f) ~a)* lip; **leccarsi le ~a** to lick one's lips; **mordersi le ~ a** *(fig)* to bite one's tongue; **parlare a fior di ~a** to murmur; **sorridere a fior di ~a** to smile faintly; **pendere dalle ~a di qn** *(fig)* to hang on sb's every word. **(b)** *(pl(m) ~i: di ferita, vaso etc)* lip.
labiale [la'bjale] *ag, sf* labial.
labile ['labile] *ag* fleeting, ephemeral; **avere una memoria ~** to have a poor memory.
labirinto [labi'rinto] *sm (anche fig)* labyrinth, maze.
laboratorio [labora'tɔrjo] *sm* **(a)** laboratory, lab *(fam)*; **esperimento di** *o* **da ~** laboratory experiment; **~ linguistico** language lab(oratory). **(b)** *(per lavori manuali)* workshop; *(stanza)* workroom; **~ fotografico** darkroom.
laboriosità [laborjosi'ta] *sf (industriosità)* industriousness.
laborioso, a [labo'rjoso] *ag (operoso)* industrious, hardworking; *(faticoso)* laborious, difficult.
laburismo [labu'rizmo] *sm (Pol)* Labour movement.
laburista, i, e [labu'rista] **1** *ag* Labour *attr.* **2** *sm/f* Labour Party member.
lacca, che ['lakka] *sf (per mobili)* varnish, lacquer; *(per capelli)* (hair) lacquer, hair spray; *(per unghie)* nail varnish, nail polish.
laccare [lak'kare] *vt (mobili)* to varnish, lacquer.
laccatura [lakka'tura] *sf* lacquering, varnishing.

lacchè [lak'kɛ] *sm inv* lackey.
laccio ['lattʃo] *sm* lace, string; **~i da scarpe** shoelaces; **~ emostatico** *(Med)* tourniquet.
lacerante [latʃe'rante] *ag (suono)* piercing, shrill.
lacerare [latʃe'rare] **1** *vt (vestiti, stoffa)* to rip, tear; *(Med, fig)* to lacerate; **un grido lacerò il silenzio** a piercing cry broke the silence. **2: ~rsi** *vr* to tear, rip.
lacerazione [latʃerat'tsjone] *sf (vedi vb)* tearing, ripping; laceration.
lacero, a ['latʃero] *ag* **(a)** *(abiti)* torn, ripped; *(persona)* ragged, in rags. **(b)** *(Med)* lacerated; **ferita lacero-contusa** cut with lacerations and bruising.
laconico, a, ci, che [la'kɔniko] *ag* laconic, concise.
lacrima ['lakrima] *sf* **(a)** tear; **con le ~e agli occhi** with tears in one's eyes; **essere/scoppiare in ~e** to be in/burst into tears; **~e di coccodrillo** crocodile tears. **(b)** *(goccia)* drop.
lacrimale [lakri'male] *ag (Anat)* tear *attr*, lachrymal.
lacrimare [lakri'mare] *vi (occhi)* to water; *(persona)* to cry, weep.
lacrimevole [lakri'mevole] *ag* heartrending, pitiful.
lacrimogeno, a [lakri'mɔdʒeno] **1** *ag:* **gas ~** tear gas. **2** *sm* tear-gas grenade; **hanno lanciato dei ~i** they fired tear gas.
lacrimoso, a [lakri'moso] *ag* tearful.
lacuna [la'kuna] *sf (vuoto)* gap; (: *in un testo)* blank (space); (: *di memoria)* lapse.
lacunoso, a [laku'noso] *ag* full of blanks *o* gaps.
lacustre [la'kustre] *ag* lake *attr.*
ladro, a ['ladro] **1** *ag* thieving; **governo ~!** *(fam)* damned government! **2** *sm/f* thief; *(di case)* burglar; **al ~!** stop thief!; **l'occasione fa l'uomo ~** *(fig)* opportunity makes the thief.
ladrocinio [ladro'tʃinjo] *sm* theft, robbery.
ladroneria [ladrone'ria] *sf* robbery.
ladruncolo, a [la'drunkolo] *sm/f* petty thief.
lager ['la:gər] *sm inv (Nazismo)* lager.
laggiù [lad'dʒu] *av (in basso)* down there; *(di là)* down *o* over there.
lagna ['laɲɲa] *sf (fam: persona, cosa)* drag, bore; **~e** whining *sg*, moaning *sg*; **fare la ~** to whine, moan.
lagnanza [laɲ'ɲantsa] *sf* complaint.
lagnarsi [laɲ'ɲarsi] *vr:* **~ (di, per)** to complain (about), grumble (about).
lago, ghi ['lago] *sm* lake; **il ~ di Garda** Lake Garda; **~ di sangue** *(fig)* pool of blood.
laguna [la'guna] *sf* lagoon.
laicismo [lai'tʃizmo] *sm* laicism.
laicizzare [laitʃid'dzare] *vt* to secularize.
laico, a, ci, che ['laiko] **1** *ag (Rel)* lay; *(stato, potere)* secular. **2** *sm/f* layman/woman. **3** *sm (frate converso)* lay brother.
laido, a ['laido] *ag* filthy, foul; *(fig: osceno)* obscene, filthy.
lama¹ ['lama] *sf (di rasoio, spada)* blade; *(spada)*

sword; **rasoio a doppia** ~ double-edged razor.
lama[2] ['lama] *sm inv (Rel)* lama.
lama[3] ['lama] *sm inv (Zool)* llama.
lambiccare [lambik'kare] *vt* to distil; **~rsi il cervello** *(fig)* to rack one's brains.
lambire [lam'bire] *vt (fig: acqua)* to lap; *(: fiamme)* to lick.
lambretta [lam'bretta] *sf* ® scooter.
lamé [la'me] *sm inv* lamé; **di** ~ lamé *attr.*
lamella [la'mɛlla] *sf* **(a)** *(di metallo etc)* thin sheet. **(b)** *(Bot, Bio)* lamella.
lamentare [lamen'tare] **1** *vt* to lament; **si lamentano gravi perdite** heavy losses are reported. **2:** ~**rsi** *vr* **(a)** *(gemere)* to moan. **(b)** *(lagnarsi):* ~**rsi (di)** to complain (about); **non mi lamento!** I can't complain!
lamentela [lamen'tela] *sf* complaint; ~**e** complaining *sg*, grumbling *sg*; **smettila con queste** ~**e!** stop grumbling!
lamentevole [lamen'tevole] *ag (voce)* plaintive, mournful; *(stato)* lamentable, pitiful.
lamento [la'mento] *sm (gemito)* groan, moan; *(: per la morte di qn)* lament.
lamentoso, a [lamen'toso] *ag* plaintive, mournful.
lametta [la'metta] *sf (da rasoio)* razor blade.
lamiera [la'mjɛra] *sf (Tecn)* sheet; ~ **di ferro/d'acciaio** sheet iron/steel; ~ **ondulata** corrugated iron.
lamina ['lamina] *sf (di metallo)* thin layer *o* sheet *o* plate; *(Bot)* lamina; ~ **d'oro** gold leaf.
laminare[1] [lami'nare] *ag* laminar.
laminare[2] [lami'nare] *vt* to laminate.
laminato [lami'nato] *sm* rolled section; ~ **plastico** laminated plastic.
lampada ['lampada] *sf* light, lamp; ~ **al neon** neon light; ~ **a petrolio/a gas** oil/gas lamp; ~ **di sicurezza** safety lamp; ~ **a spirito** blowlamp; ~ **a stelo** standard lamp; ~ **da tavolo** table lamp.
lampadario [lampa'darjo] *sm* chandelier.
lampadina [lampa'dina] *sf (Elettr)* bulb; **una** ~ **da 100 candele** a 100 watt bulb; ~ **tascabile** torch, flashlight.
lampante [lam'pante] *ag* **(a)** *(fig)* blatantly obvious, crystal clear. **(b):** **olio** ~ lamp oil.
lampara [lam'para] *sf* fishing lamp; *(barca)* boat for fishing by lamplight *(in Mediterranean)*.
lampeggiamento [lampeddʒa'mento] *sm* flashing.
lampeggiare [lamped'dʒare] **1** *vi (luce, occhi)* to flash; *(Aut)* to flash one's lights. **2** *vb impers:* **lampeggia** there is lightning.
lampeggiatore [lampeddʒa'tore] *sm (Aut)* indicator; *(Fot)* flash(gun).
lampione [lam'pjone] *sm* street lamp; *(palo)* lamppost.
lampo ['lampo] **1** *sm (gen)* flash; *(Meteor)* flash of lightning; ~**i** *(Meteor)* lightning *sg*; **in un** ~ in a flash; **passare come un** ~ to flash past *o* by; ~ **di speranza** glimmer of hope; ~ **di genio** flash of genius, sudden inspiration; ~ **al magnesio** *(Fot)* magnesium flash. **2** *ag inv (cerimonia, Mil: operazione)* lightning *attr*; **cerniera** ~ zip (fastener); **guerra** ~ blitzkrieg; **visita** ~ flying visit.
lampone [lam'pone] *sm (Bot)* raspberry.
lana ['lana] **1** *sf* wool; **di** ~ wool, woollen; **pura** ~ **vergine** pure new wool; **essere una buona** ~ *(fig)* to be a scoundrel *o* rogue. **2:** ~ **d'acciaio** steel wool; ~ **di cammello** camel hair; ~ **di vetro** fibreglass.
lancetta [lan'tʃetta] *sf (di orologio)* hand; *(di barometro etc)* needle.
lancia[1], **ce** ['lantʃa] *sf (arma)* lance, spear; *(Pesca)* harpoon; *(di pompa antincendio)* nozzle; **spezzare una** ~ **in favore di qn** *(fig)* to come to sb's de-

fence; **partire** ~ **in resta** *(fig)* to set off ready for battle.
lancia[2], **ce** ['lantʃa] *sf (Naut)* launch; ~ **di salvataggio** lifeboat.
lanciabombe [lantʃa'bombe] *sm inv (Mil)* mortar.
lanciafiamme [lantʃa'fjamme] *sm inv (Mil)* flamethrower.
lanciamissili [lantʃa'missili] **1** *ag inv* missile-launching. **2** *sm inv* missile launcher.
lanciarazzi [lantʃa'raddzi] **1** *ag inv* rocket-launching. **2** *sm inv* rocket launcher.
lanciare [lan'tʃare] **1** *vt* **(a)** *(gen)* to throw; *(bombe)* to drop; *(missili, siluri)* to launch; ~ **qc a qn** to throw sth to sb; *(per colpirlo)* to throw sth at sb; ~ **qc in aria** to throw sth into the air; ~ **una moneta in aria** to toss a coin; ~ **il peso** *(Sport)* to put the shot; ~ **il disco** *(Sport)* to throw the discus.
(b) *(emettere: grido)* to give out; *(: invettiva)* to hurl; *(: S.O.S.)* to send out; **mi ha lanciato un'occhiataccia** he flashed me a nasty look; **ha lanciato un urlo** he let out a yell.
(c) *(introdurre: idea, nave, prodotto)* to launch; **fu quel regista a lanciarla** it was that film producer who started her on her career.
(d) *(far andare veloce: macchina)* to get up to top speed; ~ **un cavallo** to give a horse his head. **2:** ~**rsi** *vr* **(a)** *(gen):* ~**rsi in qc** *(anche fig)* to throw o.s. into sth; ~**rsi contro qn** to hurl *o* fling o.s. at sb; ~**rsi nella mischia** to throw o.s. into the fray; ~**rsi all'inseguimento di qn** to set off in pursuit of sb; ~**rsi col paracadute** to parachute.
(b) *(fig: fare il primo passo):* ~**rsi in** to launch into, embark upon; **che aspetti? — lanciati!** what are you waiting for? — off you go!
lanciasiluri [lantʃasi'luri] *sm inv* torpedo tube.
lanciato, a [lan'tʃato] *ag* **(a)** *(affermato: attore, prodotto)* well-known, famous. **(b)** *(veicolo)* speeding along, racing along; ~ **a tutta velocità** racing along at top speed.
lancinante [lantʃi'nante] *ag (dolore)* stabbing, shooting; *(grido)* piercing; *(ricordo)* painful.
lancio ['lantʃo] *sm* **(a)** *(vedi vb* **1a, c)** throwing; dropping; launching. **(b)** *(Sport)* throw; ~ **del peso** putting the shot; ~ **del disco** throwing the discus.
landa ['landa] *sf* moor.
languido, a ['langwido] *ag (voce)* languid; *(sguardo, atteggiamento)* languishing.
languire [lan'gwire] *vi* **(a)** *(struggersi)* to pine, languish; ~ **d'amore** to be languishing with love. **(b)** *(perdere forza: persona)* to languish; *(: conversazione)* to flag; *(: affari, commercio)* to be slack; ~ **in carcere** to languish in prison.
languore [lan'gwore] *sm* **(a)** *(debolezza)* weakness, faintness; **sento un** ~ **allo stomaco** I'm feeling a bit peckish. **(b)** *(comportamento)* languor; **mi guardava con** ~ he gave me a languishing look.
laniero, a [la'njero] *ag* wool *attr.*
lanificio [lani'fitʃo] *sm* wool mill.
lanolina [lano'lina] *sf (Chim)* lanolin.
lanoso, a [la'noso] *ag* woolly.
lanterna [lan'tɛrna] *sf (lume, Archit)* lantern; *(faro)* lighthouse; ~ **magica** *(Cine)* magic lantern.
lanternino [lanter'nino] *sm:* **cercarsele col** ~ to be asking for trouble.
lanugine [la'nudʒine] *sf* down.
lapalissiano, a [lapalis'sjano] *ag* self-evident.
lapidare [lapi'dare] *vt* to stone (to death); *(fig)* to tear to pieces.
lapidario, a [lapi'darjo] *ag* lapidary; *(fig: stile)* succinct, terse.
lapide ['lapide] *sf* tombstone; *(lastra commemorativa)* memorial stone.

lapin |la'pɛ̃| *sm inv* rabbit skin.

lapis |'lapis| *sm inv* pencil.

Lapponia |lap'ponja| *sf* Lapland.

lapsus |'lapsus| *sm inv* slip (of the tongue); ~ **freudiano** Freudian slip.

lardellare |lardel'lare| *vt (Culin)* to lard.

lardo |'lardo| *sm* (bacon) fat, lard.

larga |'larga| *sf vedi* **largo 3**.

larghezza |lar'gettsa| *sf (Mat, misura)* width, breadth; **una stanza della** ~ **di 3 metri** a room 3 metres wide; ~ **di vedute** *(fig)* broad-mindedness.

largire |lar'dʒire| *vt* to give generously.

largo, a, ghi, ghe |'largo| **1** *ag* **(a)** *(dimensione, misura)* wide, broad; **un cappello a** ~**ghe falde** a wide-brimmed hat; **un uomo** ~ **di spalle** *o* **di spalle** ~**ghe** a broad-shouldered man; **a gambe** ~**ghe** with legs wide apart; **un corridoio** ~ **2 metri** a corridor 2 metres wide. **(b)** *(abiti)* loose; **questa gonna mi sta** ~**a** this skirt is loose on me; **questa giacca mi sta** ~**a di spalle** this jacket is wide in the shoulders on me. **(c)** *(ampio: parte, percentuale etc)* large, big; **in** ~**a misura** to a great *o* large extent; **su** ~**a scala** on a large scale; **di** ~**ghe vedute** *(fig: liberale)* broad-minded; **di manica** ~**a** generous, open-handed.

2 *sm* **(a)**: **fate** ~! make room!; **farsi** ~ **tra la folla** to make one's way through the crowd; **farsi** ~ **a gomitate** to elbow one's way. **(b)** *(piazzetta)* (small) square. **(c)** *(Naut)* open sea; **andare al** ~ to sail on the open sea; **non andare al** ~ *(nuotando)* don't go too far out; **al** ~ **di Genova** off the coast of Genoa. **(d)** *(Mus)* largo.

3 *sf*: **stare** *o* **tenersi alla** ~**a (da qn/qc)** to keep one's distance (from sb/sth), keep away (from sb/sth).

larice |'laritʃe| *sm (Bot)* larch.

laringe |la'rindʒe| *sf* larynx.

laringoiatra, i, e |laringo'jatra| *sm/f (medico)* throat specialist.

larva |'larva| *sf (Zool, Bio)* larva; *(fig peg: apatico)* zombie; **essere (ridotto a) una** ~ *(fig)* to be a shadow of one's former self.

lasagna |la'zaɲɲa| *sf* pasta sheet; ~**e al forno** baked lasagna *sg*.

lasciapassare |laʃʃapas'sare| *sm inv* pass, permit.

lasciare |laʃ'ʃare| **1** *vt* **(a)** *(gen)* to leave; ~ **qc a qn** to leave sb sth *o* sth to sb; **ha lasciato Roma nel '76** he left Rome in 1976; **ho lasciato i soldi a casa** I've left my money at home; **devo** ~ **l'università** I have to leave university, I have to give up university; **ha lasciato la scuola a 16 anni** he left school at 16; ~ **la porta aperta** to leave the door open; ~ **qn solo (a casa)** to leave sb (at home) alone; **ha lasciato la moglie** he's left his wife; **lascia la moglie e 2 bambini** he leaves a wife and 2 children; ~ **qn erede** to make sb one's heir; ~ **qn perplesso/confuso** *etc* to leave sb perplexed/confused *etc*.

(b) *(permettere)*: ~ **qn fare qc** *o* **che qn faccia qc** to let sb do sth, allow sb to do sth; **lascia fare a me** let me do it; **lascia stare** *o* **correre** *o* **perdere** let it drop, forget it.

(c) *(deporre: cose)* to leave, deposit; *(: persone)* to leave, drop (off); **ti lascio all'angolo** I'll drop you off at the corner.

(d) *(dare, concedere)* to give, let have; **mi puoi** ~ **la macchina oggi** can you let me have the car today?; **lasciami il tempo di farlo** give me time to do it.

(e) *(omettere)* to leave out, forget; **non** ~ **tutti i particolari interessanti** don't leave out all the interesting bits.

(f) *(serbare)* to leave, keep; **lasciami un po' di vino** leave some wine for me.

(g): ~ **stare qn** to let sb be, leave sb alone; ~ **stare qc** to leave sth alone; **lascia stare quel povero gatto!** leave that poor cat alone!; **lascia stare, ci penso io** leave it, I'll see to it; **lascialo stare, non vale la pena di arrabbiarsi** just ignore him, it's not worth getting annoyed; **lascia stare, offro io** it's all right, I'm paying; **è meglio lasciar stare certi argomenti** it's better not to raise certain subjects; **volevo insistere ma poi ho lasciato stare** I was going to insist but then decided to let it go.

(h) *(fraseologia)*: ~ **in bianco** to leave blank; ~ **(molto) a desiderare** to leave much to be desired; ~ **detto** *o* **scritto (a qn)** to leave word (for sb); ~ **qn indifferente** to leave sb unmoved; **non lascia mai niente al caso** he never leaves anything to chance; **lasciami in pace** leave me alone *o* in peace; ~ **la presa** to lose one's grip; ~ **il segno (su qc)** to mark (sth); *(fig)* to leave one's mark (on sth); **ci ha lasciato la vita** it cost him his life.

2: ~**rsi** *vr* **(a)**: ~**rsi sfruttare** to let o.s. be exploited; ~**rsi andare** to let o.s. go.

(b) *(uso reciproco)* to part (from one another); *(coniugi)* to leave one another, split up; **si sono lasciati all'aeroporto** they left each other at the airport, they said goodbye at the airport.

lascito |'laʃʃito| *sm (Dir)* legacy, bequest.

lascivia |laʃ'ʃivja| *sf* lust, lasciviousness.

lascivo, a |laʃ'ʃivo| *ag* lascivious, wanton.

laser |'lazer| *sm inv* laser.

lassativo, a |lassa'tivo| *ag, sm* laxative.

lasso |'lasso| *sm*: ~ **di tempo** interval, lapse of time.

lassù |las'su| *av (in alto)* up there; *(in paradiso)* in heaven above.

lastra |'lastra| *sf* **(a)** *(di marmo, pietra)* slab; *(di vetro, ghiaccio)* sheet; *(di finestra)* pane; *(di metallo)* plate. **(b)** *(Fot)* plate; *(Med)* X-ray; **fare le** ~**e a qn** to X-ray sb.

lastricare |lastri'kare| *vt* to pave.

lastricato |lastri'kato| *sm* paving.

lastrico, chi *o* **ci** |'lastriko| *sm* paving; **essere sul** ~ *(fig)* to be penniless; **gettare qn sul** ~ to leave sb destitute.

lastrone |las'trone| *sm (Alpinismo)* sheer rock face.

latente |la'tente| *ag* latent.

laterale |late'rale| **1** *ag (gen)* side *attr*, lateral; *(uscita, ingresso etc)* side *attr*. **2** *sm (Sport)* half.

lateralmente |lateral'mente| *av* sideways.

laterizio |late'rittsjo| *sm* (perforated) brick.

latice |'latitʃe| *sm* latex.

latifondista, i, e |latifon'dista| *sm/f* large agricultural landowner.

latifondo |lati'fondo| *sm* large agricultural estate.

latinismo |lati'nizmo| *sm* Latinism.

latinista, i, e |lati'nista| *sm/f* Latin scholar, Latinist.

latino, a |la'tino| **1** *ag* Latin. **2** *sm (lingua)* Latin.

latitante |lati'tante| **1** *ag*: **essere** ~ to be in hiding *o* on the run; **darsi** ~ to go into hiding. **2** *sm/f* fugitive (from justice).

latitanza |lati'tantsa| *sf*: **darsi alla** ~ to go into hiding.

latitudine |lati'tudine| *sf* latitude.

lato¹ |'lato| *sm (gen)* side, part; *(Mat, Geom)* side; *(fig: di problema etc)* aspect; **da ogni** ~, **da tutti i** ~**i** from all sides; **dal** ~ **opposto (di)** from the other *o* opposite side (of); **da un** ~ ... **dall'altro** ~... on the one hand ... on the other hand...;

l'altro ~ **della medaglia** (*fig*) the other side of the coin; **d'altro** ~ (*d'altra parte*) on the other hand.

lato² ['lato] *ag*: **in senso** ~ broadly speaking.

latore, trice [la'tore] *sm/f* (*Comm*) bearer.

latrare [la'trare] *vi* to howl.

latrina [la'trina] *sf* (public) lavatory.

latta ['latta] *sf* (*sostanza*) tin; (*recipiente*) tin, can.

lattaio, a [lat'tajo] *sm/f* (*commerciante*) dairyman/woman; (*distributore*) milkman/woman; **vado dal** ~ I'm going to the dairy.

lattante [lat'tante] **1** *ag* breast-fed. **2** *sm/f* breast-fed baby.

latte ['latte] **1** *sm* milk; **al** ~ milk *attr*; **dare il** ~ (**a un bambino**) to breast-feed (a baby); **fratello di** ~ foster brother; **avere ancora il** ~ **alla bocca** (*fig*) to be still wet behind the ears; **tutto** ~ **e miele** (*fig*) all smiles. **2:** ~ **di bellezza** beauty lotion; ~ **di cocco** coconut milk; ~ **detergente** cleansing milk; ~ **di gallina** eggnog; ~ **intero** full-cream milk; ~ **magro** *o* **scremato** skimmed milk; ~ **materno** mother's milk, breast milk; ~ **in polvere** dried *o* powdered milk.

latteo, a ['latteo] *ag* (*di latte*) milk *attr*; (*colore*) milky(-white); **la Via L~a** the Milky Way.

latteria [latte'ria] *sf* dairy.

lattice ['lattitʃe] *sm* = latice.

latticino [latti'tʃino] *sm* dairy product.

lattico, a, ci, che ['lattiko] *ag* lactic.

lattiera [lat'tjɛra] *sf* milk jug.

lattiginoso, a [lattidʒi'noso] *ag* milky.

lattosio [lat'tɔzjo] *sm* (*Chim*) lactose.

lattuga, ghe [lat'tuga] *sf* lettuce.

laurea ['laurea] *sf* degree; **prendere** *o* **conseguire la laurea** to take *o* obtain one's degree, graduate; **ha preso la** ~ **in legge** he took a law degree.

laureando, a [laure'ando] **1** *ag* final year *attr*; (*Am*) senior. **2** *sm/f* final-year student, (*Am*) senior.

laureare [laure'are] **1** *vt* to confer a degree on. **2:** ~**rsi** *vr* to take *o* obtain one's degree, graduate; **si è laureato in legge** he took a law degree.

laureato, a [laure'ato] **1** *ag* graduate *attr*. **2** *sm/f* graduate.

lauto, a ['lauto] *ag* (*pranzo, mancia etc*) lavish; ~**i guadagni** handsome profits.

lava ['lava] *sf* lava.

lavabiancheria [lavabjanke'ria] *sf inv* washing machine.

lavabicchieri [lavabik'kjɛri] *sm inv* glass-washer (*machine*).

lavabo [la'vabo] *sm* washbasin.

lavabottiglie [lavabot'tiʎʎe] *sm inv* bottle-washer (*machine*).

lavacristallo [lavakris'tallo] *sm* (*Aut*) windscreen washer.

lavaggio [la'vaddʒo] *sm* (*gen*) washing; ~ **auto** car wash; ~ **a secco** dry cleaning; ~ **del cervello** (*fig*) brainwashing.

lavagna [la'vaɲɲa] *sf* (**a**) (*minerale*) slate. (**b**) (*nelle scuole*) blackboard; **scrivere alla** ~ to write on the blackboard; ~ **luminosa** overhead projector.

lavanda¹ [la'vanda] *sf* (*gen*) washing; (*Med*) lavage; **fare una** ~ **gastrica a qn** to pump sb's stomach.

lavanda² [la'vanda] *sf* (*Bot*) lavender.

lavandaia [lavan'daja] *sf* washerwoman; (*fig peg*) fishwife.

lavanderia [lavande'ria] *sf* (*di ospedale, caserma etc*) laundry; (*negozio*) launderette, (*Am*) laundromat; (: ~ **a secco**) dry-cleaner's.

lavandino [lavan'dino] *sm* (*del bagno*) washbasin; (*della cucina*) sink.

lavapiatti [lava'pjatti] **1** *sm/f inv* (*persona*) dish-washer. **2** *sf inv* (*macchina*) dishwasher, dishwashing machine.

lavare [la'vare] **1** *vt* (**a**) (*gen*) to wash; ~ **a mano** to wash by hand, handwash; ~ **i piatti** to wash the dishes, do the washing up; ~ **la testa a qn** to wash sb's hair; ~ **i panni sporchi in pubblico** (*fig*) to wash one's dirty linen in public. (**b**) (*fig: purificare*) to cleanse, purify. (**c**): ~**rsi le mani/i capelli** *etc* to wash one's hands/hair *etc*; **me ne lavo le mani** (*fig*) I wash my hands of it. **2:** ~**rsi** *vr* to wash o.s., have a wash.

lavasecco [lava'sekko] **1** *sm inv* (*negozio*) dry-cleaner's. **2** *sf inv* dry-cleaning machine.

lavastoviglie [lavasto'viʎʎe] *sf inv* dishwasher.

lavata [la'vata] *sf* wash; (*fig*): **dare una** ~ **di capo a qn** to give sb a good telling-off.

lavativo [lava'tivo] *sm* (**a**) (*clistere*) enema. (**b**) (*buono a nulla*) good-for-nothing, idler.

lavatoio [lava'tojo] *sm* public washhouse.

lavatrice [lava'tritʃe] *sf* washing machine.

lavatura [lava'tura] *sf* (**a**) (*atto*) washing. (**b**) (*liquido*) dirty water; ~ **di piatti** dishwater; **questa minestra è** ~ **di piatti** this soup is like dishwater.

lavello [la'vɛllo] *sm* (kitchen) sink.

lavico, a, ci che ['laviko] *ag* lava *attr*.

lavina [la'vina] *sf* snowslide.

lavorante [lavo'rante] *sm/f* worker.

lavorare [lavo'rare] **1** *vi* (**a**) (*persona*) to work; **andare a** ~ to go to work; **va a** ~! go and get on with your work!; ~ **duro** *o* **sodo** to work hard; ~ **in proprio** to work for o.s., be self-employed; ~ **a maglia/ad ago** to knit/do needlework; ~ **a qc** to work on sth; ~ **di fantasia** (*suggestionarsi*) to imagine things; (*fantasticare*) to let one's imagination run free. (**b**) (*funzionare: macchinari*) to work, run, operate; (: *negozi, uffici: far affari*) to do well, do good business; **quel bar non lavora molto** that bar isn't doing very well; **far** ~ **il cervello** to use one's brains.

2 *vt* (*creta, ferro*) to work; (*legno*) to carve; (*Culin: pane, pasta*) to work, knead; (: *burro*) to beat; (*Agr: terra*) to work, cultivate; ~**rsi qn** (*fig: convincere*) to work on sb.

lavorativo, a [lavora'tivo] *ag* (*giorno, capacità*) working *attr*; **attività** ~**a** occupation.

lavorato, a [lavo'rato] *ag* (*cuoio*) tooled; (*legno, pietra*) carved; (*metallo*) wrought; (: *oro*) worked; (*prodotto*) finished; (*terreno*) cultivated; ~ **a mano** handmade.

lavoratore, trice [lavora'tore] **1** *ag* working; **la classe** ~**trice** the working class. **2** *sm/f* worker.

lavorazione [lavorat'tsjone] *sf* (**a**) (*gen*) working; (*di legno, pietra*) carving; (*di film*) making; (*del terreno*) cultivation; (*di pane, pasta*) working, kneading; (*di prodotto*) manufacture; **un nuovo film è in** ~ a new film is being made; ~ **della carta** paper making; '~ **a mano**' 'handmade'; ~ **a macchina** machine production; ~ **in serie** mass production. (**b**) (*modo di esecuzione*) workmanship.

lavorio [lavo'rio] *sm* intense activity.

lavoro [la'voro] *sm* (**a**) (*attività*): **il** ~ work; ~ **manuale/dei campi** manual/farm work; **avere molto/poco** ~ to have a lot of/little work to do; **essere al** ~ (**su qc**) to be at work (on sth); **mettersi al** ~ to set to *o* get down to work.

(**b**) (*compito*) job, task; **è un** ~ **da specialisti** it's a specialist's job, it's work for a specialist; **sta svolgendo un** ~ **di ricerca** he is carrying out research work; **è un** ~ **da niente!** it's no job at all!; **eseguire** *o* **fare (bene/male) un** ~ to do a job (well/badly).

(c) *(posto, impiego)*: **il** ~ work; **un** ~ a job, an occupation; **avere un buon** ~ to have a good job; **essere senza** ~ to be out of work *o* unemployed; **incidente sul** ~ industrial accident, accident at work; **Ministero del L**~ Department of Employment, *(Am)* Department of Labor; ~ **a catena** assembly line work; ~ **d'équipe** teamwork; ~ **nero** moonlighting; ~ **straordinario** overtime.

(d): ~i *pl* work *sg*; ~i **scientifici/di ricerca** scientific/research work; ~i **pesanti/leggeri** heavy/light work *o* jobs; **(fare) i** ~**i di casa** (to do) the housework; **far fare** ~**i in casa** to have some work done in the house; **aprire/chiudere i** ~**i del parlamento** to open/close the parliamentary session; **il convegno conclude domani i suoi** ~**i** the conference comes to an end tomorrow; ~**i di scavo** *(Archeol)* excavation works; **Ministero dei L**~**i Pubblici** Ministry of Public Works; '~**i in corso'** 'work in progress'; *(Aut)* 'road works ahead'; ~**i forzati** hard labour *sg*; **questi** ~**i non si fanno!** such things just aren't done!

(e) *(opera)* piece of work; *(: artistica)* work.

(f) *(Econ)* labour.

(g) *(Fis)* work.

lazzaretto [laddza'retto] *sm* leper hospital.

lazzarone [laddza'rone] *sm* scoundrel.

lazzo ['laddzo] *sm* jest.

le[1] [le] *art det fpl vedi* **il**.

le[2] [le] *pron pers* **(a)** *(complemento oggetto)* them; *vedi anche* **lo**[2]. **(b)** *(complemento di termine: a lei)* (to) her; ~ **ho detto tutto** I told her everything; ~ **appartiene** it belongs to her. **(c)** *(forma di cortesia: anche:* **L**~: *complemento di termine)* (to) you; ~ **posso dire una cosa?** may I tell you something?; ~ **dispiace attendere?** would you mind waiting?; ~ **chiedo scusa** I beg your pardon.

leale [le'ale] *ag (fedele)* loyal, faithful; *(onesto)* fair, honest.

lealtà [leal'ta] *sf inv* **(a)** *(fedeltà)* loyalty, faithfulness. **(b)** *(onestà)* fairness, honesty; **comportarsi con** ~ to behave fairly.

leasing ['liːzin] *sm inv* leasing.

lebbra ['lebbra] *sf* leprosy.

lebbroso, a [leb'broso] **1** *ag* leprous. **2** *sm/f* leper.

lecca lecca ['lekka'lekka] *sm inv* lollipop.

leccapiedi [lekka'pjɛdi] *sm/f (peg)* bootlicker.

leccarda [lek'karda] *sf (Culin)* dripping pan.

leccare [lek'kare] **1** *vt (gen)* to lick; ~**rsi le labbra/le dita** to lick one's lips/fingers; ~**rsi le ferite** *(anche fig)* to lick one's wounds; ~ **(i piedi a) qn** *(fig)* to suck up to sb. **2**: ~**rsi** *vr (fig)* to preen o.s.

leccata [lek'kata] *sf* lick.

leccato, a [lek'kato] *ag* affected.

leccio ['lettʃo] *sm* holm oak, ilex.

leccornia [lekkor'nia] *sf* delicacy.

lecitamente [letʃita'mente] *av* rightly, correctly.

lecito, a ['letʃito] **1** *ag (gen)* allowed; *(Dir)* lawful, legal; **ti par** *o* **sembra** ~ **che...?** does it seem right to you that...?; **crede che tutto gli sia** ~ he thinks he can do whatever he likes; **mi sia** ~ **far presente che...** may I point out that...; **se mi è** ~ if I may. **2** *sm* (what is) right.

ledere ['lɛdere] *vt* to damage; ~ **gli interessi di qn** to prejudice sb's interests.

lega[1]**, ghe** ['lega] *sf* **(a)** *(Pol, Calcio)* league; **la L**~ **delle Nazioni** the League of Nations; ~ **doganale** customs union; **far** ~ **con qn contro qn/qc** to be in league with sb against sb/sth. **(b)** *(Chim)* alloy; **metallo di bassa** ~**a** base metal; **gente di bassa** ~ common *o* vulgar people.

lega[2]**, ghe** ['lega] *sf (misura)* league.

legaccio [le'gattʃo] *sm* lace, string.

legale [le'gale] **1** *ag (gen)* legal; **medicina** ~ foren-sic medicine; **studio** ~ lawyer's office; **corso** ~ **delle monete** official exchange rate. **2** *sm* lawyer.

legalità [legali'ta] *sf* lawfulness, legality.

legalizzare [legalid'dzare] *vt* **(a)** *(rendere legale)* to legalize. **(b)** *(autenticare)* to authenticate.

legalizzazione [legalid'dzattsjone] *sf (vedi vb)* legalization; authentication.

legame [le'game] *sm* **(a)** *(gen, fig)* tie, bond; ~ **di sangue** *o* **di parentela** family tie; ~ **di amicizia** bond of friendship; **rompere i** ~**i con qn/qc** to break one's ties with sb/sth. **(b)** *(rapporto logico)* link, connection. **(c)** *(Chim)* bond.

legare [le'gare] **1** *vt* **(a)** *(gen)* to bind, tie (up); *(Tip: libro)* to bind; ~ **le mani a qn** *(anche fig)* to tie sb's hands; **ho le mani legate** my hands are tied; **è pazzo da** ~ *(fam)* he should be locked up.

(b) *(persone: unire)* to bind (together), unite; *(vincolare)* to bind; **sono legati da amicizia** they are friends; **siamo legati da questioni di interesse** we have financial interests in common; **questo posto è legato ai ricordi della mia infanzia** this place is bound up with memories of my childhood; **è legata al ricordo di suo marito** she is very attached to her husband's memory.

(c) *(connettere)* to connect, link up; **questi due fatti sono strettamente legati** these two facts are closely linked *o* connected.

(d) *(Culin)* to bind.

2 *vi (persone)* to get on; *(metalli)* to alloy; *(Culin)* to bind; **non hanno mai legato** they've never got on.

3: ~**rsi** *vr (fig)*: ~**rsi (a qn)** to become attached (to sb); **legarsela al dito** to bear a grudge.

legato[1]**, a** [le'gato] *ag (inibito)* awkward; **essere** ~ **nei movimenti** to be stiff in one's movements.

legato[2] [le'gato] *sm*: ~ **pontificio** papal legate.

legato[3] [le'gato] *sm (Dir)* legacy, bequest.

legatore, trice [lega'tore] *sm/f* bookbinder.

legatoria [legato'ria] *sf (attività)* bookbinding; *(negozio)* bookbinder's.

legatura [lega'tura] *sf (di libri)* bookbinding; *(Tip, Mus)* ligature.

legazione [legat'tsjone] *sf* legation.

legenda [lɛ'dʒɛnda] *sf vedi* **leggenda b**.

legge ['leddʒe] *sf (gen)* law; *(Parlamento)* act; **a norma** *o* **termini di** ~ according to the law; **per** ~ by law; **la** ~ **è uguale per tutti** everybody is equal before the law; **la** ~ **del più forte** the law of survival of the fittest; **ogni suo desiderio è** ~ your wish is my command; **la sua parola è** ~ his word is law; **le** ~**i della società** the rules *o* laws of society; ~ **marziale** martial law.

leggenda [led'dʒɛnda] *sf* **(a)** *(mito)* legend; *(diceria)* old wives' tale. **(b)** *(iscrizione)* legend; *(chiave di lettura)* key.

leggendario, a [leddʒen'darjo] *ag* legendary.

leggere ['lɛddʒere] *vt (gen, Mus)* to read; *(discorso, comunicato)* to read (out); ~ **ad alta voce** to read aloud; **l'ho letto sul giornale** I read (about) it in the newspaper; ~ **nel futuro** *(chiromante)* to read the future; ~ **la mano a qn** to read sb's palm; ~ **qc negli occhi di qn** to see sth in sb's eyes; ~ **il pensiero di qn** to read sb's mind *o* thoughts; ~ **fra le righe** *(fig)* to read between the lines; **letto e approvato** read and approved.

leggerezza [leddʒe'rettsa] *sf* **(a)** *(gen)* lightness; *(di ballerina etc)* lightness, nimbleness. **(b)** *(sconsideratezza)* thoughtlessness; **con** ~ thoughtlessly.

leggero, a [led'dʒero] *ag (gen)* light; *(agile)* light, nimble; *(rumore, dolore)* slight; *(malattia, punizione)* mild, slight; *(cibo, vino)* light; *(curry)* mild;

(caffè, tè) weak; ~ **come una piuma** light as a feather; **avere il sonno** ~ to be a light sleeper; **a passi** ~**i** with a light step; **avere un** ~ **accento straniero** to have a slight foreign accent; **ha avuto la malattia in forma** ~**a** she had a mild form of the illness; **fanteria/cavalleria** ~**a** light infantry/cavalry; **una ragazza** ~**a** *(fig)* a flirtatious girl; **prendere le cose alla** ~**a** to take things lightly.

leggiadria [ledd3a'dria] *sf* loveliness, prettiness; ~ **di stile** elegance of style.

leggiadro, a [led'd3adro] *ag (gen)* lovely, pretty; *(stile, movimenti)* elegant, graceful.

leggibile [led'd3ibile] *ag (calligrafia)* legible; *(libro)* readable.

leggio [led'd3io] *sm (per libri)* bookrest; *(Mus)* music stand; *(in chiesa, Univ)* lectern.

legiferare [ledʒife'rare] *vi* to legislate.

legionario [ledʒo'narjo] *sm* legionnaire.

legione [le'dʒone] *sf (Mil)* legion; *(fig)* host, multitude.

legislativo, a [ledʒizla'tivo] *ag* legislative.

legislatore [ledʒizla'tore] *sm* legislator.

legislatura [ledʒizlas'tura] *sf* legislature.

legislazione [ledʒizlat'tsjone] *sf* legislation.

legittimare [ledʒitti'mare] *vt (figlio)* to legitimize; *(comportamento etc)* to justify.

legittimità [ledʒittimi'ta] *sf* legitimacy.

legittimo, a [le'dʒittimo] *ag* legitimate; *(rivendicazione)* legitimate, rightful; **per** ~**a difesa** in self-defence.

legna ['leɲɲa] *sf* (fire)wood; ~ **da ardere** firewood; **stufa a** ~ wood stove; **far** ~ to gather firewood; **mettere** ~ **al fuoco** to put wood on the fire.

legnaia [leɲ'ɲaja] *sf* woodshed.

legnaiolo [leɲɲa'jɔlo] *sm* woodcutter.

legname [leɲ'ɲame] *sm* timber, wood.

legnata [leɲ'ɲata] *sf* blow with a stick; **dare a qn un sacco di** ~**e** to give sb a good hiding.

legno ['leɲɲo] *sm* **(a)** *(gen)* wood; **di** ~ wood *attr*, wooden; **testa di** ~ *(fig)* blockhead; ~ **stagionato** seasoned wood; ~ **dolce/duro** soft/hardwood. **(b)** *(pezzo di legno)* piece of wood. **(c)** *(fig: nave)* sailing ship.

legnoso, a [leɲ'ɲoso] *ag (di legno)* woody; *(come legno: movimenti)* stiff, wooden.

legume [le'gume] *sm* pulse vegetable; ~**i** pulses.

leguminosa [legumi'nosa] *sf* leguminous plant.

lei[1] ['lɛi] **1** *pron pers f* **(a)** *(complemento: dopo prep, con valore enfatico)* her; **sono venuto con** ~ I came with her; **senza di** ~ without her; **se non fosse per** ~ if it were not for her; **hanno accusato** ~**, non me** they accused her, not me; **chiedilo a** ~ ask her; ~ **qui non la voglio** I don't want her here. **(b)** *(sog: al posto di 'ella', con valore enfatico)* she; ~ **è meglio di te** she is better than you; **prendetela, è** ~ catch her, she's the one; **è stata** ~ **a dirmelo** she told me herself, it was she who told me; **ha ragione** ~, **non tu** she's right, not you; **neanche** ~ **ha tutti i torti** even she isn't completely in the wrong. **(c)** *(nelle comparazioni: sog)* she, her; *(: complemento)* her; **ne so quanto** ~ I know as much as she does, I know as much as her.

2 *sf inv (scherz)*: **la mia** ~ my beloved.

lei[2] ['lɛi] **1** *pron pers* **1** *pron pers (forma di cortesia: anche:* L~) **(a)** *you;* ~ **per cortesia venga con noi** be so good as to come with us; **senza di** ~ without you; **riconosco** ~ **senz'altro** I certainly recognize you. **(b)** *(nelle comparazioni)* you; **farò come** ~ I'll do the same as you (do). **2** *sm*: **dare del** ~ **a qn** to address sb as 'lei'.

lembo ['lembo] *sm (orlo)* hem; *(striscia: di stoffa, fig: di terra)* strip.

lemma, i ['lɛmma] *sm* **(a)** *(di dizionario)* headword; *(di enciclopedia)* (main) entry. **(b)** *(Mat, Filosofia)* lemma.

lemme lemme ['lɛmme'lɛmme] *av (fam)* very slowly.

lena ['lena] *sf*: **di buona** ~ *(lavorare, camminare)* at a good pace.

lenire [le'nire] *vt* to soothe, relieve.

lente ['lɛnte] *sf (Ottica, Fot)* lens; ~**i a contatto** contact lenses; ~ **d'ingrandimento** magnifying glass.

lentezza [len'tettsa] *sf* slowness; *(di mente)* slow-wittedness; **con** ~ slowly.

lenticchia [len'tikkja] *sf (Bot)* lentil; **per un piatto di** ~**e** *(fig)* for nothing, for peanuts.

lentiggine [len'tiddʒine] *sf* freckle.

lentigginoso, a [lentiddʒi'noso] *ag* freckled.

lento, a ['lɛnto] *ag* **(a)** *(gen)* slow; ~ **a o nel fare qc** slow in doing sth; **a passi** ~**i** slowly, with a slow step; **il bambino è un po'** ~ *(fig)* the child is a bit slow(-witted). **(b)** *(allentato)* loose; *(: fune)* slack.

lenza ['lɛntsa] *sf* (fishing) line.

lenzuolo [len'tswɔlo] *sm (pl(m)* ~**i o pl(f** ~**a)** sheet; ~ **funebre** shroud.

leoncino [leon'tʃino] *sm* lion cub.

leone [le'one] *sm* lion; *(Astrologia)*: L~ Leo; **essere del** L~ to be Leo; **fare la parte del** ~ to take the lion's share; ~ **marino** sea-lion.

leonessa [leo'nessa] *sf* lioness.

leonino, a [leo'nino] *ag* lion's, leonine.

leopardo [leo'pardo] *sm* leopard.

leporino, a [lepo'rino] *ag (Med)*: **labbro** ~ harelip.

lepre ['lɛpre] *sf* hare.

leprotto [le'prɔtto] *sm* leveret.

lercio, a, ci, ce ['lɛrtʃo] *ag* filthy, foul.

lerciume [ler'tʃume] *sm* filth.

lesbica, che ['lɛzbika] *sf* lesbian.

lesbico, a, ci, che ['lɛzbiko] *ag* lesbian.

lesione [le'zjone] *sf* **(a)** *(danno)* damage; ~ **personale** *(Dir)* personal injury. **(b)** *(Med)* lesion; ~**i interne** internal injuries.

lesivo, a [le'zivo] *ag*: ~ **(di)** detrimental (to), damaging (to).

leso, a ['lezo] **1** *pp di* **ledere**. **2** *ag (Dir)*: **parte** ~**a** injured party; ~**a maestà** lese-majesty.

lessare [les'sare] *vt (Culin)* to boil.

lessicale [lessi'kale] *ag* lexical.

lessico, ci ['lɛssiko] *sm (Linguistica)* lexis, vocabulary; *(dizionario)* lexicon.

lessicografia [lessikogra'fia] *sf* lexicography.

lesso, a ['lɛsso] *(Culin)* **1** *ag* boiled. **2** *sm (gen)* boiled meat; *(manzo)* boiled beef.

lesto, a ['lɛsto] *ag* quick, fast; ~ **di mano** *(fig)* light-fingered.

lestofante [lesto'fante] *sm* swindler, con man.

letale [le'tale] *ag* lethal, deadly.

letamaio [leta'majo] *sm* manure heap, dung heap; *(fig)* pigsty.

letame [le'tame] *sm* manure, dung; *(fig)* filth, muck.

letargo [le'targo] *sm* **(a)** *(di animale)* hibernation; **essere/andare o cadere in** ~ to be in/go into hibernation. **(b)** *(di persona)* lethargy.

letizia [le'tittsja] *sf* joy, happiness.

letta ['letta] *sf*: **dare una** ~ **a qc** to glance o look through sth.

lettera ['lɛttera] **1** *sf* **(a)** *(dell'alfabeto)* letter; **scrivere qc con** ~**e maiuscole/minuscole** to write sth in capitals o capital letters/in small letters; **scrivere un numero in** ~**e** to write out a number in full; **prendere qc alla** ~ to take sth

literally; **eseguire qc alla** ~ *(legge, ordine)* to carry out sth to the letter; **restar** ~ **morta** *(consiglio, invito)* to go unheeded; **diventar** ~ **morta** *(legge)* to become a dead letter. **(b)** *(missiva)* letter; ~ **d'affari/d'amore** business/love letter. **(c)**: ~**e** *pl (letteratura)* letters; **fa** ~**e all'università** he is doing arts subjects at university; ~**e antiche** classics; **un uomo di** ~**e** a man of letters.
  2: ~ **di accompagnamento** accompanying letter; ~ **di cambio** *(Comm)* bill of exchange; ~ **di credito** *(Comm)* letter of credit; ~ **di presentazione** *o* **raccomandazione** letter of presentation; ~ **raccomandata/assicurata** recorded delivery/ registered letter.

letterale [lette'rale] *ag* literal.

letteralmente [lettera'mente] *av* literally.

letterario, a [lette'rarjo] *ag* literary.

letterato, a [lette'rato] **1** *ag* cultured, educated. **2** *sm/f* scholar.

letteratura [lettera'tura] *sf* literature.

lettiga, ghe [let'tiga] *sf(barella)* stretcher; *(portantina)* litter.

letto¹, **a** [l'etto] *pp di* **leggere**.

letto² [l'etto] *sm* **1** *(gen, di fiume, lago)* bed; ~ **a una piazza/due piazze** single/double bed; **essere a** ~ to be in bed; **andare a** ~, **mettersi a** ~ to go to bed; **(ri)fare il** ~ to make the bed; **andare a** ~ **con qn** to go to bed with sb, sleep with sb; **a** ~, **bambini!** bedtime, children! **figlio di primo/secondo** ~ child by one's first/second marriage; **sul** ~ **di morte** on one's deathbed. **2:** ~**i gemelli/a castello** twin/bunk beds; ~ **matrimoniale** double bed.

lettorato [letto'rato] *sm* **(a)** *(Univ)* lectorship, assistantship. **(b)** *(Rel)* lectorate.

lettore, trice [let'tore] *sm/f* **(a)** *(gen)* reader; **il pubblico dei** ~**i** the reading public. **(b)** *(Univ)* lector, assistant. **(c)** *(Rel)* lector.

lettura [let'tura] *sf* *(gen)* reading; **un libro di piacevole** ~ a very readable book; **un libro di facile** ~ a book which is easy to read; **libro di** ~ *(Scol)* reading book; ~**e obbligatorie** *(Scol)* set books.

leucemia [leutʃe'mia] *sf* leukaemia.

leva¹ ['lɛva] *sf(anche fig)* lever; **far** ~ **su qc** to lever sth up; **far** ~ **su qn/qc** *(fig)* to take advantage of sb/sth; ~ **di comando/del cambio** control/gear lever *o* stick.

leva² ['lɛva] *sf(Mil)* call-up; *(Am)* draft; **essere di** ~ to be due for call-up.

levante [le'vante] *sm (Geog)* east; *(vento)* east wind; **il L**~ the Levant.

levare [le'vare] **1** *vt* **(a)** *(gen: togliere)* to remove, take away; *(: coperchio)* to take off; *(: tassa)* to abolish; *(: dente)* to take out, remove; *(Mat)* to subtract, take away; ~ **la sete** to quench one's thirst; ~ **qn/qc di mezzo** *o* **di torno** to get rid of sb/sth; ~ **l'assedio** *(Mil)* to raise the siege; ~ **un divieto** to lift a ban; ~ **le tende** *(fig)* to pack up and leave. **(b)** *(sollevare: occhi, testa etc)* to lift (up), raise; ~ **l'ancora** *(Naut)* to lift *o* weigh anchor; ~ **un grido** to let out a cry. **(c):** ~**rsi qc** *(vestito)* to take sth off, remove sth; **si è levato le scarpe** he took off his shoes; ~**rsi il pensiero** to put one's mind at rest.
  2: ~**rsi** *vr (vento, burrasca)* to rise; *(persona: alzarsi)* to get up; **levati di mezzo** *o* **di lì** *o* **di torno!** get out of my way!; **puoi levarti dalla luce?** could you get out of my light?

levata [le'vata] *sf* **(a)** *(Mil etc)* getting-up time. **(b)** *(Posta)* collection.

levataccia, ce [leva'tattʃa] *sf* early rise; **fare una** ~ to get up very early.

levatoio [leva'tojo] *ag*: **ponte** ~ drawbridge.

levatrice [leva'tritʃe] *sf* midwife.

levatura [leva'tura] *sf* intellect, intellectual capacity.

levigare [levi'gare] *vt* *(gen)* to smooth; *(marmo)* to polish.

levigato, a [levi'gato] *ag* *(superficie)* smooth; *(fig: stile)* polished; *(: viso)* flawless.

levità [levi'ta] *sf* lightness.

levitare [levi'tare] *vi* to levitate.

levitazione [levitat'tsjone] *sf* levitation.

levriere [le'vrjere] *sm* greyhound.

lezione [let'tsjone] *sf (Scol)* lesson; *(Univ)* lecture; **ora di** ~ *(Scol)* period; ~ **privata** private lesson; **far** ~ **(a qn)** to teach (sb), give lessons (to sb); **una** ~ **di generosità** a lesson in generosity; **servire di** ~ **a qn** to be a lesson to sb; **fare le** ~**i** *(fam)* to do one's homework.

leziosità [lettsjosi'ta] *sf inv* affectation.

lezioso, a [let'tsjoso] *ag* affected.

lezzo ['lɛddzo] *sm* stink, stench.

li [li] *pron pers pl* them; *vedi anche* **lo**².

lì [li] *av* **(a)** there; **mettilo** ~ put it there; **eccolo** ~! there he *(o* it) is!; **è rimasto** ~ **dov'era** he stayed where he was; ~ **dentro/fuori/sopra/sotto** *etc* in/out/up/under *etc* there; **di** *o* **da** ~ from there; **da** ~ **non si entra** you can't come in that way; **di** ~ **a pochi giorni** a few days later; **la discussione è finita** ~ the discussion ended there; **fin** ~ **tutto sembrava normale** up until then everything seemed normal; *vedi anche* **quello**.
  (b) *(fraseologia):* ~ **per** ~ *(sul momento)* then and there; **è arrabbiato, tutto** ~ he's angry, that's all; **essere** ~ (~) **per fare** to be about to do, be on the point of doing; **e** ~ **baci e abbracci** and then hugs and kisses all round; **se non l'ha offeso apertamente siamo** ~ he may not have insulted him openly but that's what it amounts to; **ormai col dizionario siamo** ~ *(quasi finito)* we've nearly finished the dictionary.

libagione [liba'dʒone] *sf* libation.

libanese [liba'nese] *ag*, *sm/f* Lebanese.

Libano ['libano] *sm*: **il** ~ the Lebanon.

libbra ['libbra] *sf* pound.

libeccio [li'bettʃo] *sm* south-west wind.

libellista, i, e [libel'lista] *sm/f* libeller.

libello [li'bello] *sm* libel.

libellula [li'bellula] *sf* dragonfly.

liberale [libe'rale] *ag*, *sm/f* *(gen, Pol)* liberal.

liberalismo [libera'lizmo] *sm* liberalism.

liberalità [liberali'ta] *sf* generosity; **con** ~ generously.

liberalizzare [liberalid'dzare] *vt* to liberalize.

liberalizzazione [liberalid'dzattsjone] *sf* liberalization.

liberare [libe'rare] **1** *vt* **(a)** *(rendere libero: prigioniero)* to release; *(: popolo)* to liberate, free; ~ **qn su cauzione** *(Dir)* to release sb on bail; **liberaci dal male** *(Rel)* deliver us from evil. **(b)** *(sgombrare: passaggio etc)* to clear; *(: stanza)* to vacate. **(c)** *(produrre: energia)* to release. **2:** ~**rsi** *vr* **(a)** *(stanza etc)* to become vacant; *(telefono, posto)* to become free. **(b):** ~**rsi di qc/qn** to get rid of sth/sb; ~**rsi dagli impegni** to free o.s. from one's commitments; **se riesco a liberarmi per le 5...** if I can manage to be free by 5 o'clock... .

liberatore, trice [libera'tore] **1** *ag* liberating; **guerra** ~**trice** war of liberation. **2** *sm/f* liberator.

liberatorio, a [libera'tɔrjo] *ag (Fin)*: **pagamento** ~ payment in full; *(fig)*: **fu un pianto** ~ crying was a release.

liberazione [liberat'tsjone] *sf (vedi vt a)* release; liberation; freeing; **è stata una** ~ **per lui**

(sollievo) it was a release for him; **la ~ della donna** women's liberation.

libercolo [li'bɛrkolo] *sm (peg)* worthless book.

liberismo [libe'rizmo] *sm (Econ)* laissez-faire.

libero, a ['libero] **1** *ag* **(a)** *(senza costrizioni)* free; *(persona: non sposata)* unattached; **~ da** *(legami, preoccupazioni etc)* free of *o* from; **essere ~ di fare qc** to be free to do sth; **sei ~ di rifiutare** you're free *o* at liberty to refuse; **dar ~ corso a** to give free rein to; **dar ~ sfogo a** to give vent to; **~a discussione** free *o* open discussion; **'ingresso ~'** *(gratuito)* 'entrance free'; **una donna dai ~i costumi** a woman of loose morals.

(b) *(non occupato: gen)* free; *(: posto)* clear; *(: passaggio)* vacant, free; **non ha mai un momento ~** he never has a free moment; **cosa fai nel tuo tempo ~?** what do you do in your free *o* spare time?; **via ~a!** all clear!; **avere via ~a** to have a free hand; **dare via ~a a qn** to give sb the go-ahead.

2: **~ arbitrio** free will; **~a professione** self-employment; **~ professionista** self-employed person; **~ scambio** free trade; **~a uscita** *(Mil)* leave.

liberoscambismo [liberoskam'bizmo] *sm (Econ)* free trade.

libertà [liber'ta] *sf inv* **(a)** *(gen)* freedom, liberty; **combattere per la ~** to fight for freedom; **~ di stampa/di pensiero/di espressione** freedom of the press/of thought/of expression; **il ladro è ancora in ~** the thief is still at large; **nei momenti di ~** *(tempo libero)* in one's free time. **(b)** *(Dir)* freedom, liberty; **concedere la ~ a qn** to release sb; **rimettere qn in ~** to set sb free, release sb; **essere in ~ provvisoria** to be released without bail; **essere in ~ vigilata** to be on probation. **(c)** *(licenza)* liberty; **prendersi la ~ di** to take the liberty of; **prendersi delle ~** to take liberties.

libertino, a [liber'tino] *ag, sm/f* libertine.

liberty ['liberti] *ag inv, sm inv* art nouveau.

Libia ['libja] *sf* Libya.

libico, a, ci, che ['libiko] *ag, sm/f* Libyan.

libidine [li'bidine] *sf* lust, lechery.

libidinoso, a [libidi'noso] *ag* lustful, lecherous.

libido [li'bido] *sf inv (Psic)* libido.

libraio [li'brajo] *sm* bookseller.

librario, a [li'brarjo] *ag* book *attr.*

librarsi [li'brarsi] *vr* to hover; **~ in volo** to take flight.

libreria [libre'ria] *sf* **(a)** *(negozio)* bookshop. **(b)** *(mobile)* bookcase.

libretto [li'bretto] *sm* booklet; **~ degli assegni** cheque book; **~ di circolazione** *(Aut)* logbook; **~ d'istruzioni** user's manual; **~ di lavoro** employment card; **~ di risparmio** savings book; **~ universitario** university report card.

libro ['libro] *sm* **(a)** *(gen)* book; **~ bianco** *(Pol)* white paper; **~ di consultazione** reference book; **~ di cucina** cookery book; **~ giallo** detective story, thriller; **essere sul ~ nero di qn** *(fig)* to be in sb's bad books; **~ tascabile** paperback; **~ di testo** textbook; **essere un ~ chiuso** *(fig: persona)* to give nothing away. **(b)** *(registro)* book, register; **~ mastro** ledger; **~i contabili** (account) books; **tenere i ~i** to keep the books.

licantropo [li'kantropo] *sm* werewolf.

liceale [litʃe'ale] **1** *ag* secondary school *attr, (Am)* high school *attr.* **2** *sm/f* secondary school *o (Am)* high school pupil.

licenza [li'tʃɛntsa] *sf* **(a)** *(gen: permesso)* permission, leave; **chiedere/dare ~ di fare qc** to ask/give permission to do sth; **prendersi la ~ di**

fare qc to take the liberty of doing sth. **(b)** *(documento: gen)* licence, permit; *(: Mil)* pass; *(Scol)* school-leaving certificate; **~ di caccia/di pesca/ matrimoniale** hunting/fishing/marriage licence; **essere in ~** *(Mil)* to be on leave. **(c)** *(sfrenatezza)* licence; **~ poetica** poetic licence.

licenziamento [litʃentsja'mento] *sm* dismissal; *(per eccesso di personale)* redundancy; **~ in massa** mass dismissals *(o* redundancies).

licenziare [litʃen'tsjare] **1** *vt* to dismiss; *(per eccesso di personale)* to make redundant. **2: ~rsi** *vr (andare via)* to take one's leave; *(dal lavoro)* to resign, hand in one's notice.

licenziosità [litʃentsjosi'ta] *sf* licentiousness.

licenzioso, a [litʃen'tsjoso] *ag* licentious.

liceo [li'tʃɛo] *sm* ≈ secondary school, high school *(Am)*; **~ classico/scientifico** secondary school specializing in classics/scientific subjects.

lichene [li'kɛne] *sm (Bot)* lichen.

lido ['lido] *sm (spiaggia)* shore; **il ~ di Venezia** the Venice Lido.

lieto, a ['ljeto] *ag* glad, happy; **a ~ fine** with a happy ending; **~ evento** happy event; **molto ~ (di fare la sua conoscenza)** pleased to meet you.

lieve ['ljeve] *ag (tocco, brezza etc)* soft, light; *(ferita)* slight.

lievità [ljevi'ta] *sf inv* = **levità**.

lievitare [ljevi'tare] **1** *vi (aus essere) (pane, pasta)* to rise. **2** *vt* to leaven.

lievitazione [ljevitat'tsjone] *sf* rising.

lievito ['ljevito] *sm* yeast; **~ in polvere** baking powder; **~ di birra** brewer's yeast.

ligio, a, gi, gie *o* **ge** ['lidʒo] *ag*: **~ (a)** faithful (to), loyal (to); **~ al dovere** devoted to duty.

lignaggio [liɲ'naddʒo] *sm* descent, lineage.

ligneo, a ['liɲneo] *ag* wooden.

ligure ['ligure] *ag, sm/f* Ligurian; **la Riviera L~** the Italian Riviera.

lilla ['lilla] *ag inv, sm inv* lilac.

lima ['lima] *sf* file; **~ da unghie** nailfile.

limaccioso, a [limat'tʃoso] *ag* muddy.

limare [li'mare] *vt* to file; *(fig: scritti)* to polish, perfect.

limatura [lima'tura] *sf (azione)* filing (down); *(residuo)* filings *pl.*

limbo ['limbo] *sm (Rel, fig)* limbo.

limitare [limi'tare] **1** *vt* **(a)** *(circoscrivere)* to bound, mark the bounds of. **(b)** *(contenere)*: **~ (a)** to limit (to), restrict (to). **2: ~rsi** *vr*: **~rsi a qc/a fare qc** to limit *o* confine o.s. to sth/to doing sth; **~rsi nel fumare** to limit one's smoking; **mi limiterò a dire che...** all I'm prepared to say is that....

limitatamente [limita'mente] *av* to a limited extent; **~ alle mie possibilità** in so far as I am able.

limitatezza [limita'tettsa] *sf*: **~ di idee** narrow-mindedness.

limitativo, a [limita'tivo] *ag* limiting, restrictive.

limitato, a [limi'tato] *ag (ristretto)* limited; *(scarso)* scarce, limited; **persona di idee ~e** narrow-minded person.

limitazione [limitat'tsjone] *sf (gen)* limitation; **~ delle nascite** birth control; **~ degli armamenti** arms limitation *o* control.

limite ['limite] **1** *sm (gen, fig)* limit; *(confine)* boundary, limit; **c'è un ~ a tutto!, tutto ha un ~!** there are limits!; **senza ~ o ~i** boundless, limitless; **conoscere i propri ~i** to know one's limitations; **nei ~i del possibile** as far as possible; **passare il o ogni ~** to go too far; **entro certi ~i** within certain limits; **al ~** if the worst comes to the worst; **~ di tempo/età/velocità** time/age/

limite speed limit; ~ **di rottura** breaking point. **2** *ag inv:* **caso** ~ extreme case.

limitrofo, a [li'mitrofo] *ag* neighbouring.

limo ['limo] *sm* mud, slime; *(Geog)* silt.

limonata [limo'nata] *sf* lemonade.

limone [li'mone] *sm (frutto)* lemon; *(albero)* lemon (tree).

limpidezza [limpi'dettsa] *sf (di acqua, cielo)* clearness; *(di discorso)* clarity.

limpido, a ['limpido] *ag (acqua)* limpid, clear; *(cielo)* clear; *(fig: discorso)* clear, lucid.

lince ['lintʃe] *sf* lynx; **avere un occhio di** ~ to be eagle-eyed.

linciaggio [lin'tʃaddʒo] *sm* lynching.

linciare [lin'tʃare] *vt* to lynch.

lindo, a ['lindo] *ag* neat and tidy.

linea ['linea] *sf* **(a)** *(gen, Mat)* line; ~ **tratteggiata** broken *o* dotted line; **a grandi** ~**e** in outline; **in** ~ **di massima** on the whole; **in** ~ **d'aria** as the crow flies; **avere qualche** ~ **di febbre** to have a slight temperature; ~ **di confine** boundary line; ~ **laterale** *(Sport)* sideline; ~ **di partenza/d'arrivo** *(Sport)* starting/finishing line.

(b) *(fig: direzione)* line; ~ **d'azione/di condotta** line of action/of conduct; **rimanere in** ~ **col proprio partito** to toe the party line.

(c) *(figura: di persona)* figure; *(: Moda, Aut)* line; **mantenere la** ~ to keep one's figure; **la** ~ **Dior** *(collezione)* the Dior collection.

(d) *(Ferr, Aer)* line; ~ **d'autobus** *(percorso)* bus route; *(servizio)* bus service; **volo di** ~ scheduled flight; ~ **aerea** airline.

(e) *(Elettr)* line; ~**e di alta tensione** high tension cables; **in** ~ **diretta da** *(TV, Radio)* coming to you direct from.

(f) *(Telec)* line; **la** ~ **è occupata** the line is engaged; **è caduta la** ~ I *(o* you *etc)* have been cut off.

(g) *(Mil)* line; **essere in prima** ~ to be in the front line; ~ **di mira/tiro** line of sight/fire.

lineamenti [linea'menti] *smpl (di volto)* features; *(fig: elementi essenziali):* ~ **di fisica** introduction to physics.

lineare [line'are] *ag (Mat, disegno)* linear; *(fig)* consistent.

lineetta [line'etta] *sf* dash; *(in composti, a fine riga)* hyphen.

linfa ['linfa] *sf (Bot)* sap; *(Anat)* lymph; ~ **vitale** *(fig)* lifeblood.

linfatico, a, ci, che [lin'fatiko] *ag* lymphatic.

lingotto [lin'gotto] *sm* ingot.

lingua ['lingwa] *sf* **(a)** *(Anat, Culin, fig)* tongue; **mostrare la** ~ **a qn** to stick *o* put out one's tongue at sb; **avere qc sulla punta della** ~ *(fig)* to have sth on the tip of one's tongue; **avere la** ~ **sciolta** to have a ready tongue in one's head; **avere una** ~ **velenosa** *(fig)* to have a nasty tongue; **tenere a freno la** ~ to hold one's tongue; **avere la** ~ **lunga** *(fig)* to talk too much; **la** ~ **batte dove il dente duole** *(Proverbio)* it is human nature to dwell on one's misfortunes; ~ **di bue** *(Culin)* ox tongue; ~ **di fuoco** tongue of flame.

(b) *(linguaggio)* language; ~ **viva/morta** living/dead language; **la** ~ **italiana** the Italian language; **paesi di** ~ **inglese** English-speaking countries; ~ **madre** mother tongue; **non parliamo la stessa** ~ *(anche fig)* we don't talk the same language.

(c): ~ **di terra** spit of land.

linguaccia [lin'gwattʃa] *sf (peg: persona)* spiteful gossip.

linguacciuto, a [lingwat'tʃuto] **1** *ag* gossipy. **2** *sm/f* gossip.

linguaggio [lin'gwaddʒo] *sm* language; ~ **base** *(Inform)* basic language; ~ **infantile** baby talk.

linguetta [lin'gwetta] *sf (di scarpe)* tongue; *(di busta)* flap.

linguista, i, e [lin'gwista] *sm/f* linguist.

linguistica [lin'gwistika] *sf* linguistics *sg*.

linguistico, a, ci, che [lin'gwistiko] *ag* linguistic.

linimento [lini'mento] *sm* liniment.

lino ['lino] *sm (Bot)* flax; *(tessuto)* linen; **seme di** ~ linseed.

linoleum [li'nɔleum] *sm inv* linoleum.

liofilizzare [liofilid'dzare] *vt* to freeze-dry.

liofilizzati [liofilid'dzati] *smpl* freeze-dried foods.

liquame [li'kwame] *sm* liquid sewage.

liquefare [likwe'fare] **1** *vt* to liquefy. **2:** ~**rsi** *vr* to liquefy; *(burro, ghiaccio etc)* to melt.

liquefatto, a [likwe'fatto] *pp di* **liquefare.**

liquidare [likwi'dare] *vt* **(a)** *(debiti etc)* to settle, pay off; *(società)* to wind up, liquidate; *(merci)* to sell off; *(pensione)* to pay. **(b)** *(fig: sbarazzarsi di: persona)* to get rid of; *(: uccidere)* to kill, liquidate; ~ **una questione** to settle a matter once and for all.

liquidatore, trice [likwida'tore] *sm/f (Dir, Comm)* liquidator.

liquidazione [likwidat'tsjone] *sf* **(a)** *(pagamento)* settlement, payment; *(di società)* liquidation; *(di merci)* clearance; **vendita/prezzi di** ~ clearance sale/prices. **(b)** *(Amm)* severance pay *(on retirement, redundancy, or when taking up other employment)*.

liquidità [likwidi'ta] *sf inv* liquidity.

liquido, a ['likwido] **1** *ag (gen, Comm, Fonetica)* liquid; *(Culin)* runny; **denaro** ~ cash, ready money. **2** *sm (a) (corpo* ~*)* liquid, fluid. **(b)** *(Econ: denaro contante)* ready money, ready cash.

liquigas [likwi'gas] *sm inv* ® Calor gas ®.

liquirizia [likwi'rittsja] *sf* liquorice.

liquore [li'kwore] *sm (aromatizzato)* liqueur; ~**i** *(bevande alcoliche)* spirits.

liquoroso, a [likwo'roso] *ag:* **vino** ~ dessert wine.

lira[1] ['lira] *sf (unità monetaria italiana, turca etc)* lira; ~ **sterlina** pound sterling; **100** ~**e** 100 lire; **non vale una** ~ it's worthless; **non avere una** ~ to be penniless.

lira[2] ['lira] *sf* **(a)** *(Mus)* lyre. **(b)** *(Zool)* lyrebird.

lirica, che ['lirika] *sf* **(a)** *(genere di poesia)* lyric poetry; *(componimento)* lyric poem. **(b)** *(Mus)* opera.

lirico, a, ci, che ['liriko] **1** *ag* **(a)** *(poesia)* lyric. **(b)** *(Mus)* opera *attr;* **la stagione** ~**a** the opera season. **2** *sm* lyric poet.

lirismo [li'rizmo] *sm* lyricism.

lisca, sche ['liska] *sf* (fish)bone.

lisciare [liʃ'ʃare] **1** *vt (gen)* to smooth; *(fig: adulare)* to flatter; ~**rsi i capelli** to straighten one's hair. **2:** ~**rsi** *vr (fig)* to preen o.s.

liscio, a, sci, sce ['liʃʃo] *ag (pelo, capelli etc)* smooth; *(affare, faccenda)* simple, straightforward; *(liquore)* neat, straight; **avere i capelli** ~**sci** to have straight hair; **è andato tutto** ~ it all went off smoothly *o* without a hitch; **non la passerà** ~**a** he won't get away with it; **com'è andata?** — ~ **come l'olio** how did it go? — it went without a hitch.

liscivia [liʃ'ʃivja] *sf*, **lisciva** [liʃ'ʃiva] *sf* lye.

liseuse [li'zøz] *sf* bed jacket.

liso, a ['lizo] *ag* worn, threadbare.

lista ['lista] *sf* **(a)** *(gen: elenco)* list; *(menù)* menu; ~ **della spesa/degli invitati** shopping/guest list; **fare la** ~ **di qc** to make a list of sth; **mettersi in** ~ **per** to put one's name down for *o* on the list for; ~

elettorale electoral roll. **(b)** *(striscia)* strip.

listare [lis'tare] *vt:* ~ **(di)** to border (with), edge (with).

listello [lis'tɛllo] *sm (Archit)* listel, fillet.

listino [lis'tino] *sm* list; ~ **di borsa** *(Fin)* share index; ~ **dei cambi** *(Fin)* exchange list; ~ **dei prezzi** price list; **prezzo di** ~ list price.

litania [lita'nia] *sf (Rel)* litany; *(fig: di nomi, titoli etc)* string.

lite ['lite] *sf* **(a)** *(gen)* quarrel, argument; **attaccar** ~ **(con qn)** to pick a fight (with sb). **(b)** *(Dir)* lawsuit.

litigante [liti'gante] *sm/f (gen)* quarreller; *(Dir)* litigant.

litigare [liti'gare] *vi (gen)* to quarrel, argue; *(Dir)* to litigate.

litigio [li'tidʒo] *sm* quarrel, dispute.

litigioso, a [liti'dʒoso] *ag (gen)* quarrelsome; *(Dir)* litigious, contentious.

litografia [litogra'fia] *sf (metodo)* lithography; *(stampa)* lithograph; *(stabilimento)* lithographic printing works *sg*.

litografico, a, ci, che [lito'grafiko] *ag* lithographic.

litorale [lito'rale] *sm* coast.

litoraneo, a [lito'raneo] *ag* coastal.

litro ['litro] *sm* litre.

littorio, a [lit'tɔrjo] *ag (Storia romana)* lictorial; **fascio** ~ *(anche Fascismo)* fasces *pl*.

liturgia [litur'dʒia] *sf* liturgy.

liturgico, a, ci, che [li'turdʒiko] *ag* liturgical.

liuto [li'uto] *sm* lute.

livella [li'vella] *sf (Tecn)* level; ~ **a bolla d'aria** spirit level.

livellamento [livella'mento] *sm* levelling.

livellare [livel'lare] **1** *vt (anche fig)* to level. **2:** ~**rsi** *vr* to become level; *(fig)* to level out, balance out.

livellatore, trice [livella'tore] *ag* levelling.

livellatrice [livella'tritʃe] *sf* steamroller.

livello [li'vello] *sm* **(a)** *(di olio, acqua)* level; **allo stesso** ~ at the same level; **a** ~ **della strada** in street *o* ground level; **sotto il/sul** ~ **del mare** *(Geog)* below/above sea level. **(b)** *(grado)* standard; *(: intellettuale, sociale)* level; **un alto** ~ **di vita** a high standard of living; **una conferenza ad alto** ~ high-level *o* top-level talks; **contatti ad alto** ~ high-powered *o* high-ranking contacts; **non è al tuo** ~ he is not on the same plane as you; **a** ~ **di confidenza** confidentially, between you and me; **a** ~ **economico/politico** at an economic/a political level; ~ **impiegatizio** employment grading; ~ **occupazionale** level of employment.

livido, a ['livido] **1** *ag (bluastro)* livid; *(plumbeo: cielo)* leaden; **labbra livide dal freddo** lips blue with cold; **essere** ~ **di collera** *o* **rabbia** to be livid, be white with rage; ~ **di invidia** green with envy. **2** *sm* bruise.

livore [li'vore] *sm* venom.

Livorno [li'vorno] *sf* Livorno, Leghorn.

livrea [li'vrɛa] *sf (uniforme)* livery; *(di animale)* coat; *(di uccello)* plumage.

lizza ['littsa] *sf:* **entrare** *o* **scendere in** ~ *(anche fig)* to enter the lists; **essere in** ~ **per** *(fig)* to compete for; **rimanere in** ~ *(fig)* to be left in the running.

lo¹ [lo] *art det m vedi* **il**.

lo² [lo] *pron (dav vocale* **l'***)* **(a)** *(riferito a persona)* him; *(riferito ad animale)* it, him; *(riferito a cosa)* it; ~ **vuoi conoscere?, vuoi conoscer**~? would you like to meet him?; **guarda**~! look at him (*o* it)!; **Paolo** ~ **conosco bene, ma Giovanna no** I know Paolo well, but not Giovanna. **(b)** *(con valore neutro: spesso non tradotto)*: **vieni? — non** ~ **so** are you coming? — I don't know; **te** ~ **dicevo**

io! I told you so!; non ~ **vedi che stai sbagliando?** can't you see you're wrong?; **può sembrare innocuo ma non** ~ **è** he may look harmless but he's not.

lobbia ['lɔbbja] *sf* homburg.

lobo ['lɔbo] *sm (Anat, Bot)* lobe; ~ **dell'orecchio** ear lobe.

locale [lo'kale] **1** *ag* local. **2** *sm (stanza)* room; *(luogo pubblico)* place; **non si servono alcolici in questo** ~ no alcohol is served on the premises; ~ **caldaie** boiler room; ~ **(notturno)** nightclub.

località [lokali'ta] *sf inv* locality; ~ **balneare/di villeggiatura** seaside/holiday resort.

localizzare [lokalid'dzare] **1** *vt (individuare)* to locate; *(circoscrivere: epidemia, incendio)* to confine. **2:** ~**rsi** *vr:* ~**rsi in** to become localized in.

locanda [lo'kanda] *sf* inn.

locandiere, a [lokan'djɛre] *sm/f* innkeeper.

locandina [lokan'dina] *sf (Teatro)* poster.

locare [lo'kare] *vt (casa)* to rent out, let; *(macchina)* to hire out.

locatario, a [loka'tarjo] *sm/f (di casa, appartamento)* tenant; *(di camera)* lodger.

locativo, a [loka'tivo] *ag (Dir)* rentable.

locatore, trice [loka'tore] *sm/f* landlord/lady.

locazione [lokat'tsjone] *sf* **(a)** *(da parte del locatario)* renting; *(da parte del locatore)* renting out, letting; **dare in** ~ to rent out, let. **(b)** *(anche:* **contratto di** ~*)* lease; **canone di** ~ rent.

locomotiva [lokomo'tiva] *sf* locomotive, engine.

locomotore [lokomo'tore] *sm*, **locomotrice** [lokomo'tritʃe] *sf* locomotive, engine.

locomozione [lokomot'tsjone] *sf* locomotion; **mezzi di** ~ means of transport, vehicles.

loculo ['lɔkulo] *sm* burial recess.

locusta [lo'kusta] *sf* locust.

locuzione [lokut'tsjone] *sf* phrase, locution.

lodare [lo'dare] *vt* to praise; ~ **qn per qc/per aver fatto qc** to praise sb for sth/for having done sth; **sia lodato Dio!** God be praised!

lode ['lɔde] *sf* praise; **degno di** ~ praiseworthy; **tessere le lodi di qn** to sing sb's praises; **in** ~ **di** in praise of; **torna a sua** ~ it's to his credit; **laurearsi con la** ~ *(Univ)* ≃ to graduate with a first-class honours degree.

loden ['lɔdən] *sm inv (stoffa)* loden; *(cappotto)* loden overcoat.

lodevole [lo'devole] *ag* praiseworthy.

logaritmo [loga'ritmo] *sm* logarithm.

loggia, ge ['lɔddʒa] *sf (Archit)* loggia; *(Massoneria)* lodge.

loggione [lod'dʒone] *sm (Teatro):* **il** ~ the gods.

logica ['lɔdʒika] *sf* logic; **è nella** ~ **delle cose** it is in the nature of things; **a rigor di** ~ logically.

logicamente [lodʒika'mente] *av* naturally, obviously.

logicità [lodʒitʃi'ta] *sf* logicality.

logico, a, ci, che ['lɔdʒiko] *ag* logical.

logistica [lo'dʒistika] *sf* logistics *sg*.

logistico, a, ci, che [lo'dʒistiko] *ag* logistic.

logoramento [logora'mento] *sm (di vestiti etc)* wear.

logorante [logo'rante] *ag* exhausting.

logorare [logo'rare] **1** *vt (abiti, scarpe)* to wear out; *(scalini, pietra)* to wear away; *(occhi, salute)* to ruin; *(nervi, resistenza)* to wear down; *(persona)* to wear out, exhaust; *(volto)* to line, mark; ~**rsi l'anima, la vita su qc** *(fig)* to wear o.s. out over sth; ~**rsi la vista** to ruin one's eyesight. **2:** ~**rsi** *vr (abiti, scarpe)* to wear out; *(occhi)* to be ruined; *(nervi)* to go; *(persona)* to wear o.s. out.

logorio [logo'rio] *sm* wear and tear, strain; **il** ~

della vita moderna the stresses and strains of life today.

logoro, a ['lɔgoro] *ag (scarpe)* worn (out); *(abiti, tappeto)* worn out, threadbare; *(fig: occhi, vista)* ruined; *(: aspetto)* worn out, exhausted.

lombaggine [lom'baddʒine] *sf (Med)* lumbago.

Lombardia [lombar'dia] *sf* Lombardy.

lombardo, a [lom'bardo] *ag, sm/f* Lombard.

lombare [lom'bare] *ag (Anat, Med)* lumbar.

lombata [lom'bata] *sf (Culin)* loin.

lombo ['lombo] *sm (Anat)* loin.

lombrico, ci [lom'briko] *sm* earthworm.

londinese [londi'nese] **1** *ag* London *attr.* **2** *sm/f* Londoner.

Londra ['londra] *sf* London.

longanime [lon'ganime] *ag* forbearing.

longevità [londʒevi'ta] *sf* longevity.

longevo, a [lon'dʒɛvo] *ag* long-lived.

longilineo, a [londʒi'lineo] *ag* long-limbed.

longitudinale [londʒitudi'nale] *ag* longitudinal.

longitudine [londʒi'tudine] *sf* longitude.

long play ['lɔŋplei] *sm inv* long-playing record, L.P.

lontanamente [lontana'mente] *av* remotely; **non ci pensavo neppure** ~ it didn't even occur to me.

lontananza [lonta'nantsa] *sf (distanza)* distance; *(assenza)* absence; **in** ~ in the distance; **la** ~ **da casa lo faceva soffrire** being far away from home upset him.

lontano, a [lon'tano] **1** *ag* **(a)** *(nello spazio, nel tempo)* distant, faraway; *(di parentela)* distant; ~ **da** far from; **essere ben** ~ **dal pensare che...** to be far from thinking that...; **tenere qn** ~ to keep sb at a distance; **tenersi** ~ **da** to keep one's distance from; ~ **dagli occhi** ~ **dal cuore** *(Proverbio)* out of sight out of mind; **il giorno della sua partenza non era** ~ the day when he was due to leave was not far off *o* away; **amici** ~**i** absent friends; **siamo parenti alla** ~**a** we are distantly related; **i nostri ricordi più** ~**i** our earliest memories; **i tempi** ~**i dell'università** those far-off days at university; **terre** ~**e** far-away places; **il** ~ **Oriente** the Far East. **(b)** *(vago)* vague, slight.

2 *av* far; **più** ~ farther, further; **è meno** ~ **di quello che pensi** it's not as far as you think; **abita** ~ he lives a long way off *o* away; **è** ~ **10 chilometri** it's 10 kilometres away; **da** ~ from a distance; **vengo da** ~ I've come quite a distance; ~ **nel passato** far back in the past; ~ **nel futuro** in the distant future; **andar** ~ *(anche fig)* to go far; **mirare** ~ *(fig)* to aim high; **vedere** ~ *(fig)* to see far ahead.

lontra ['lontra] *sf* otter.

lonza ['lontsa] *sf (Culin)* loin of pork.

loquace [lo'kwatʃe] *ag* talkative, loquacious; *(fig: occhiata, gesto)* expressive, eloquent.

loquacità [lokwatʃi'ta] *sf* talkativeness, loquacity.

lordo, a ['lordo] *ag* **(a)** dirty, filthy; ~ **di sangue** bloody. **(b)** *(Comm: stipendio, peso)* gross.

loro¹ ['loro] *pron pers pl* **(a)** *(complemento)* them; **chiedi (a)** ~ ask them; **disse** ~ **che non sarebbe venuto** he told them he wouldn't be coming; **sono venuto con** ~ I came with them; **senza di** ~ without them; ~ **qui non li voglio** I don't want them here.

(b) *(sog: al posto di 'essi', 'esse', con valore enfatico)* they; ~ **sono meglio di te** they are better than you; **prendeteli, sono** ~ catch them, they're the ones; **sono stati** ~ **a dirmelo** they told me themselves, it was they who told me; **hanno ragione** ~, **non tu** they are right, not you; **nean-** che ~ **hanno tutti i torti** even they aren't completely in the wrong.

(c) *(nelle comparazioni: sog)* they, them; *(: complemento)* them; **ne so quanto** ~ I know as much as they do, I know as much as them.

loro² ['loro] *pron pers pl (forma di cortesia: anche:* **L**~*)* **(a)** you; ~ **capiscono quanto ciò sia penoso** you are aware of how distressing that is; **chiedo lor signori di seguirmi** be so good as to follow me, gentlemen. **(b)** *(nelle comparazioni)* you.

loro³ ['loro] **1** *ag poss inv:* **il(la)** ~, **i(le)** ~ **(a)** their; **i** ~ **amici** their friends; **un** ~ **amico** a friend of theirs. **(b)** *(forma di cortesia: anche:* **L**~*)* your. **2** *pron poss inv:* **il(la)** ~, **i(le)** ~ **(a)** theirs; **questi libri sono i** ~ those books are theirs. **(b)** *(forma di cortesia: anche:* **L**~*)* yours. **3** *sm inv:* **vivono del** ~ they live on what they have; **i** ~ *(famiglia)* their family; *(amici etc)* their own people; **siamo dei** ~, **stiamo dalla** ~ *(parte)* we're on their side, we're with them; **vogliono sempre dire la** ~ they've always got something to say; **ne hanno fatto un'altra delle** ~ they've (gone and) done it again.

losanga, ghe [lo'zanga] *sf* diamond, lozenge.

losco, a, schi, sche ['lɔsko] *ag* **(a)** *(occhiata, aspetto)* sullen, surly. **(b)** *(equivoco: persona, affare)* shady, suspicious; **qui c'è del** ~ I smell a rat.

loto ['lɔto] *sm* lotus.

lotta ['lɔtta] *sf (combattimento)* fight, struggle; *(conflitto)* conflict; *(Sport)* wrestling; **essere in** ~ **(con)** to be in conflict (with); **fare la** ~ **(con)** to wrestle (with); ~ **all'ultimo sangue** fight to the death; ~ **armata** armed combat; ~ **corpo a corpo** hand-to-hand combat; ~ **di classe** *(Pol)* class struggle; ~ **libera** *(Sport)* all-in wrestling; ~ **mortale** mortal combat; ~ **per la sopravvivenza** struggle for survival.

lottare [lot'tare] *vi:* ~ **(con** *o* **contro)** to fight (with *o* against), struggle (with *o* against); ~ **contro il sonno** to struggle to keep awake; ~ **con la morte** to battle against death.

lottatore, trice [lotta'tore] *sm/f* fighter; *(Sport)* wrestler.

lotteria [lotte'ria] *sf* lottery; *(di gara ippica)* sweepstake.

lottizzare [lottid'dzare] *vt* to divide into plots.

lottizzazione [lottiddzat'tsjone] *sf* division into plots.

lotto¹ ['lɔtto] *sm (gen)* lot; *(di terreno)* plot; ~ **fabbricabile** *o* **edificabile** building lot.

lotto² ['lɔtto] *sm (gioco)* lottery; **vincere un terno al** ~ *(anche fig)* to hit the jackpot.

lozione [lot'tsjone] *sf* lotion.

L.st. *abbr (= lire sterline)* £.

lubrificante [lubrifi'kante] **1** *ag* lubricating. **2** *sm* lubricant.

lubrificare [lubrifi'kare] *vt* to lubricate.

lubrificazione [lubrifikat'tsjone] *sf* lubrication.

lucano, a [lu'kano] *ag (of o* from) Lucania.

lucchetto [luk'ketto] *sm* padlock.

luccicare [luttʃi'kare] *vi (gen)* to sparkle; *(stella)* to twinkle; *(oro)* to glitter; *(occhi)* to glisten; **non è tutt'oro quel che luccica** all that glitters is not gold.

luccichio [luttʃi'kio] *sm (vedi vb)* sparkling; twinkling; glittering.

luccicone [luttʃi'kone] *sm:* **avere i** ~**i agli occhi** to have tears in one's eyes.

luccio ['luttʃo] *sm (Zool)* pike.

lucciola ['luttʃola] *sf* firefly, glow-worm; **prendere** ~**e per lanterne** *(fig)* to get hold of the wrong end of the stick.

luce ['lutʃe] *sf* (**a**) *(gen)* light; **alla ~ del giorno** in daylight; **~ del sole/della luna** sun/moonlight; **accendere/spegnere la ~** to turn *o* switch the light on/off; **fare ~ su qc** *(fig)* to shed *o* throw light on sth; **mettere in ~** *(fig)* to spotlight, highlight; **mettere qn in buona/cattiva ~** *(fig)* to put sb in a good/bad light; **fare qc alla ~ del sole** *(fig)* to do sth in the open; **dare alla ~** *(bambino)* to give birth to; **venire alla ~** *(fatto)* to come to light; *(bambino)* to come into the world; **alla ~ di questi fatti** *(fig)* in the light of this; **contro ~** against the light; **~i di posizione** *(Aut)* sidelights; **~i della ribalta** *(Teatro)* footlights. (**b**) *(Archit: di ponte, arco)* span; **negozio a una ~** shop with one window.

lucente [lu'tʃɛnte] *ag* shining.

lucentezza [lutʃen'tettsa] *sf* shine.

lucerna [lu'tʃɛrna] *sf* oil lamp.

lucernario [lutʃer'narjo] *sm* skylight.

lucertola [lu'tʃɛrtola] *sf* *(animale)* lizard; *(pellame)* lizardskin.

lucidare [lutʃi'dare] *vt* (**a**) *(mobili, scarpe, pavimenti)* to polish. (**b**) *(ricalcare: disegno)* to trace.

lucidatrice [lutʃida'tritʃe] *sf* floor polisher.

lucidatura [lutʃida'tura] *sf* polishing.

lucidità [lutʃidi'ta] *sf* lucidity.

lucido, a ['lutʃido] **1** *ag* (**a**) shining, bright; **occhi ~i di pianto/per la febbre** eyes bright with tears/ with fever; **fondo stradale ~** *(per la pioggia)* greasy road surface. (**b**) *(pavimento, argento, scarpe)* polished; **~ come uno specchio** as bright as a mirror. (**c**) *(mente, discorso)* lucid, clear; *(malato)* lucid. **2** *sm* (**a**) *(lucentezza)* shine, lustre; **perdere il ~** to lose its shine. (**b**) *(sostanza)* polish; **~ da scarpe** shoe polish. (**c**) *(disegno, ricalco)* tracing; **carta da ~** tracing paper.

lucignolo [lu'tʃiɲɲolo] *sm* wick.

lucrativo, a [lukra'tivo] *ag* lucrative; **a scopo ~** for gain.

lucro ['lukro] *sm* profit, gain; **a scopo di ~** for gain; **associazione a scopo di ~** profit-making organization.

lucroso, a [lu'kroso] *ag* lucrative, profitable.

luculliano, a [lukul'ljano] *ag* *(pasto)* sumptuous.

ludibrio [lu'dibrjo] *sm* (**a**) *(scherno)* mockery, scorn. (**b**) *(zimbello)* laughing stock.

lue ['lue] *sf* syphilis.

luglio ['luʎʎo] *sm* July; **nel mese di ~** in July *o* in the month of July; **il primo ~** the first of July; **arrivare il 2 ~** to arrive on the 2nd of July; **all'inizio/alla fine di ~** at the beginning/at the end of July; **durante il mese di ~** during July; **a ~ del prossimo anno** in July of next year; **ogni anno a ~** every July; **che fai a ~?** what are you doing in July?; **ha piovuto molto a ~ quest'anno** July was very wet this year.

lugubre ['lugubre] *ag* gloomy, dismal.

lui ['lui] **1** *pron pers m* (**a**) *(complemento: dopo prep, con valore enfatico)* him; **sono venuto con ~** I came with him; **senza di ~** without him; **se non fosse per ~** if it were not for him; **hanno accusato ~, non me** they accused him, not me; **chiedilo a ~** ask him; **~ qui non lo voglio** I don't want him here.

(**b**) *(sog: al posto di 'egli', con valore enfatico)* he; **~ è meglio di te** he is better than you; **prendetelo, è ~** catch him, he's the one; **è stato ~ a dirmelo** he told me himself, it was he who told me; **ha ragione ~, non tu** he's right, not you; **neanche ~ ha tutti i torti** even he isn't completely in the wrong.

(**c**) *(nelle comparazioni: sog)* he, him; *(: complemento)* him; **ne so quanto ~** I know as much as

he does, I know as much as him.

2 *sm inv* *(scherz)*: **il mio ~** my beloved.

lumaca, che [lu'maka] *sf* *(Zool)* slug; *(: chiocciola)* snail; *(fig)* slowcoach; **a passo di ~** at a snail's pace.

lumacone [luma'kone] *sm* (large) slug; *(fig)* slowcoach.

lume ['lume] *sm* (**a**) *(gen)* light; **a ~ di candela** by candlelight; **a ~ di naso** *(fig)* by rule of thumb; **perdere il ~ della ragione** *(fig)* to be blinded by rage. (**b**) *(lampada)* lamp; **~ a olio** oil lamp.

lumicino [lumi'tʃino] *sm* small *o* faint light; **essere (ridotto) al ~** *(fig)* to be at death's door.

lumiera [lu'mjɛra] *sf* chandelier.

luminare [lumi'nare] *sm* luminary.

luminescente [lumineʃ'ʃɛnte] *ag* luminescent.

luminescenza [lumineʃ'ʃɛntsa] *sf* luminescence.

lumino [lu'mino] *sm* small light; **~ da notte** nightlight; **~ per i morti** candle for the dead.

luminosità [luminosi'ta] *sf* *(vedi ag)* luminosity; radiance; *(anche TV)* brightness; **c'è una ~ diffusa sopra la città** there's a hazy glow over the city.

luminoso, a [lumi'noso] *ag* (**a**) *(gen)* luminous; *(sorgente) of* light, light *attr*; **insegna ~a** illuminated sign. (**b**) *(cielo, occhi, avvenire, idea)* bright; *(sorriso, viso)* bright, radiant.

luna ['luna] *sf* moon; **~ nuova/piena** new/full moon; **una notte di ~** a moonlit night; **~ di miele** honeymoon; **avere la ~** to be in a bad mood; **svegliarsi con la ~** *(fig)* to get out of bed on the wrong side; **chiedere la ~** to ask for the moon.

luna park ['luna 'park] *sm inv* amusement park, funfair.

lunare [lu'nare] *ag* lunar, moon *attr*.

lunario [lu'narjo] *sm* almanac; **sbarcare il ~** *(fig)* to make ends meet.

lunatico, a, ci, che [lu'natiko] **1** *ag* quirky, temperamental. **2** *sm/f* temperamental person.

lunedì [lune'di] *sm inv* Monday; *per uso vedi* **martedì.**

lunetta [lu'netta] *sf* *(Archit)* lunette.

lunga ['lunga] *sf vedi* **lungo 3.**

lungaggine [lun'gaddʒine] *sf* slowness; **~i della burocrazia** red tape *sg*.

lungamente [lunga'mente] *av* *(a lungo)* for a long time; *(estesamente)* at length; **un figlio ~ atteso** a long-awaited child.

lungarno [lun'garno] *sm* embankment along the Arno.

lunghezza [lun'gettsa] *sf* length; **il lungomare si estende per una ~ di 5 km** the promenade stretches for 5 km; **nel senso della ~** lengthways, along its length; **~ d'onda** wavelength; **vincere per una ~** *(cavallo)* to win by a length.

lungi ['lundʒi]: **~ da** *prep* far from; **da me l'idea di offenderti!** far be it from me to offend you!; **~ dall'essere** far from being.

lungimirante [lundʒimi'rante] *ag* far-sighted.

lungo, a, ghi, ghe ['lungo] **1** *ag* (**a**) *(gen)* long; *(persona)* tall; *(viaggio)* lengthy; **una fila di macchine ~a 2 km** a line of cars 2 km long; **amici da ~a data** long-standing *o* old friends; **lo conosco da ~ tempo** I've known him for a long time; **un discorso ~ 2 ore** a 2-hour speech.

(**b**) *(lento: persona)* slow; **essere ~ a o nel fare qc** to be slow at doing sth, take a long time to do sth; **essere ~ come la fame** to be a slowcoach. (**c**) *(diluito: caffè, brodo)* weak.

(**d**) *(fraseologia)*: **avere la barba ~a** to be unshaven; **avere le mani ~ghe** to be light-fingered; **fare il passo più ~ della gamba** to bite off more than one can chew; **cadere ~ disteso** to measure one's length; **fare la faccia ~a o il muso**

~ *o* il viso ~ to pull a long face; a ~a gittata *(Mil)* long-range; saperla ~a *(fam)* to know a thing or two, know what's what; a ~a scadenza long term; a ~ andare in the long run.

2 *sm* length; per il ~ along its length, lengthways; in ~ e in largo *(girare, cercare)* far and wide; a ~ *(aspettare)* for a long time; *(spiegare)* in great detail.

3 *sf:* di gran ~a far and away; è di gran ~a il migliore he's far and away the best, he's the best by far; andare per le ~ghe to drag on; alla ~a in the long run.

4 *prep (spazio)* along, beside; *(tempo)* during; camminare ~ il fiume to walk along *o* beside the river; ~ il corso dei secoli throughout the centuries, in the course of the centuries; ~ il viaggio during the journey.

lungofiume [lungo'fjume] *sm* embankment.

lungolago [lungo'lago] *sm* road round a lake.

lungomare [lungo'mare] *sm* promenade.

lungometraggio [lungome'tradd3o] *sm (Cine)* feature film.

lungotevere [lungo'tevere] *sm* embankment along the Tiber.

lunotto [lu'nɔtto] *sm (Aut)* rear *o* back window; ~ termico heated rear window.

luogo, ghi ['lwɔgo] 1 *sm* (a) *(gen)* place; in ogni ~ everywhere; in qualsiasi ~ anywhere; in qualsiasi ~ vada wherever you go; in nessun ~ nowhere; sul ~ on the spot; fuori ~ *(fig)* out of place, inopportune; uno del ~ a native, a local. (b) *(fraseologia):* aver ~ to take place; far ~ a to give way to, make room for; dar ~ a *(critiche, dubbi etc)* to give rise to; in ~ di in place of, instead of; in primo/secondo ~ in the first/second place. 2: ~ comune commonplace, cliché; ~ del delitto scene of the crime; ~ geometrico locus; ~ di nascita *(gen)* birthplace; *(Amm)* place of birth; ~ di origine, ~ di provenienza place of origin; ~ di pena penitentiary, prison; ~ pubblico public place.

luogotenente [lwogote'nɛnte] *sm (Mil, fig)* lieutenant.

lupa ['lupa] *sf* she-wolf.

lupacchiotto [lupak'kjɔtto] *sm (Zool)* (wolf) cub.

lupara [lu'para] *sf (fucile)* sawn-off shotgun.

lupetto [lu'petto] *sm (Zool)* (wolf) cub; *(negli scouts)* cub scout.

lupino [lu'pino] *sm (Bot)* lupin.

lupo ['lupo] 1 *sm* wolf; cane ~ alsatian; avere una fame da ~i to be ravenous *o* famished; gridare al ~ to cry wolf; tempo da ~i filthy weather; in bocca al ~! good luck! 2: ~ mannaro werewolf; ~ di mare *(fig)* old salt.

luppolo ['luppolo] *sm (Bot)* hop.

lurido, a ['lurido] *ag (anche fig)* filthy, foul.

luridume [luri'dume] *sm* filth.

lusco ['lusko] *sm:* tra il ~ e il brusco at dusk.

lusinga, ghe [lu'zinga] *sf* flattery; con la ~ di un lauto stipendio with the promise of a high salary; non mi convincerai con le ~ghe flattery will get you nowhere.

lusingare [luzin'gare] *vt (adulare)* to flatter; lusingatissimo! *(onorato)* I'm honoured!; si è fatto ~ dalle promesse di una brillante carriera he let himself be swayed by promises of a brilliant career.

lusinghiero, a [luzin'gjero] *ag* flattering.

lussare [lus'sare] *vt (Med)* to dislocate.

lussazione [lussat'tsjone] *sf (Med)* dislocation.

Lussemburgo [lussem'burgo] *sm* Luxembourg.

lusso ['lusso] *sm* luxury; di ~ *(macchina, appartamento)* luxury *attr*; *(prodotto)* de luxe *attr*; vivere nel ~ più sfacciato to live in unashamed luxury; non posso permettermi il ~ di una vacanza I can't afford the luxury of a holiday.

lussuoso, a [lussu'oso] *ag* luxurious.

lussureggiante [lussured'd3ante] *ag (vegetazione, pianta)* luxuriant; *(fig: stile)* profuse.

lussureggiare [lussured'd3are] *vi* to be luxuriant; ~ di *(fig)* to abound in.

lussuria [lus'surja] *sf* lust.

lussurioso, a [lussu'rjoso] *ag* lascivious, lustful.

lustrare [lus'trare] *vt (mobili, pavimenti, scarpe)* to polish, shine; ~ le scarpe a qn *(fig)* to lick sb's boots.

lustrascarpe [lustras'karpe] *sm/f inv* shoeshine.

lustrino [lus'trino] *sm* sequin.

lustro, a ['lustro] 1 *ag* shiny; *(pelliccia)* glossy. 2 *sm* (a) shine, gloss. (b) *(fig: gloria)* prestige, glory. (c) *(quinquennio)* five-year period.

lutto ['lutto] *sm (gen)* mourning; *(perdita)* loss, bereavement; essere in/portare il ~ to be in/wear mourning; un ~ nazionale an occasion for national mourning; è stato un ~ per il paese it was a great loss to the country.

luttuoso, a [luttu'oso] *ag* sad, mournful.

M

M, m ['ɛmme] *sf o m inv (lettera)* M, m.
m. *abbr di* mese; miglia; monte.

ma [ma] **1** *cong* but; *(tuttavia)* yet, still, but; *(comunque)* however; **è bella ~ stupida** she's beautiful but stupid; **mi piacerebbe venire ~ non posso** I would love to come but I can't; **non solo non beve più ~ ha anche smesso di fumare** not only has he given up drinking but he's given up smoking too; **hanno fatto quel che potevano ~ non sono riusciti a salvarlo** they did what they could, but still they couldn't save him; **non se lo merita ~ dovremmo cercare di capirlo** although he doesn't deserve it, we should try to understand him; **~ non se lo merita** he doesn't deserve it though; **incredibile ~ vero** unbelievable, yet true; **si può sapere che cosa vuoi?** just what do you want?; **~ smettila!** give over!; **~ va'?** *(dubitativo)* really?; **~ va'!** *(escl)* surely not!; **~ davvero?** really?; **~ sì!** *(certo)* but of course!
   2 *sm* but; **ci sono ancora dei ~** there are still some uncertainties; **non c'è ~ che tenga** but me no buts.

macabro, a ['makabro] *ag* macabre, gruesome.
macaco, chi [ma'kako] *sm (Zool)* macaque; *(fig fam)* clod.
macadam [maka'dam] *sm* macadam.
macché [mak'ke] *escl (fam)* certainly not!, you must be joking!; **avete finito il lavoro? — ~!, abbiamo appena incominciato!** have you finished the work? — you must be joking, we've hardly started!
maccheroni [makke'roni] *smpl* macaroni.
macchia¹ ['makkja] *sf* **(a)** *(chiazza)* mark; *(sulla pelle)* blotch, mark; *(sul pelo)* patch; *(di sporco)* stain, mark; **~e di colore** splashes of colour; **~ d'inchiostro** ink stain; *(su foglio)* (ink) blot; **~ di vino** wine stain; **~ di grasso** greasy mark, grease stain; **~ di sangue** bloodstain; **~e solari** *(Astron)* sunspots; **coprirsi di ~e** *(pelle)* to come out in a rash; **estendersi a ~ d'olio** *(fig)* to spread rapidly. **(b)** *(fig: su reputazione)* blot, stain.
macchia² ['makkja] *sf (boscaglia)* scrub; **darsi/vivere alla ~** *(fig)* to go into/live in hiding.
macchiare [mak'kjare] **1** *vt (tovaglia, camicia)* to stain, mark; *(con inchiostro: quaderno)* to blot; *(fig: reputazione)* to sully, tarnish; **hai macchiato la tovaglia di caffè** you've stained the tablecloth with coffee; **la birra non macchia** beer doesn't stain *o* leave a mark; **mi sono macchiata il vestito** I stained my dress. **2** **~rsi** *vr (persona)* to get stains *o* marks on one's clothes; *(tessuto)* to become stained *o* marked; **ti sei macchiato tutto!** you've got yourself all dirty!; **~rsi di un delitto** to be guilty of a crime.
macchiato, a [mak'kjato] *ag* **(a)** *(gen)*: **~ (di)** stained (with); **caffè ~** coffee with a dash of milk. **(b)** *(pelle, pelo)* spotted.
macchietta [mak'kjetta] *sf (disegno)* sketch, caricature; *(Teatro)* caricature; *(fig: persona)* character.

macchiettista, i, e [makkjet'tista] *sm/f* caricaturist.
macchina ['makkina] **1** *sf* **(a)** *(gen, fig)* machine; *(motore, locomotiva)* engine; **sala ~e** *(Naut)* engine room; **la ~ burocratica** the bureaucratic machinery. **(b)** *(automobile)* car; **salire in ~** to get into the car; **andare/venire in ~** to go/come by car. **2**: **~ automatica** slot machine; **~ da cucire** sewing machine; **~ diesel** diesel engine; **~ fotografica** camera; **~ lavastoviglie** dishwasher; **~ lavatrice** washing machine; **~ da scrivere** typewriter; **~ utensile** machine tool; **~ a vapore** steam engine.
macchinalmente [makkinal'mente] *av* mechanically.
macchinare [makki'nare] *vt* to plot.
macchinario [makki'narjo] *sm* machinery.
macchinazione [makkinat'tsjone] *sf* plot, machination.
macchinetta [makki'netta] *sf:* **~ per il caffè** percolator; **~ per le sigarette** cigarette machine *o* dispenser; **parlare come una ~** to talk nineteen to the dozen.
macchinista, i [makki'nista] *sm (di treno)* enginedriver; *(di nave)* engineer; *(Teatro)* stagehand.
macchinoso, a [makki'noso] *ag* complex, complicated.
macedonia [matʃe'dɔnja] *sf (Culin)* fruit salad.
macellaio [matʃel'lajo] *sm (anche fig)* butcher.
macellare [matʃel'lare] *vt (anche fig)* to slaughter, butcher.
macellazione [matʃellat'tsjone] *sf* slaughtering, butchering.
macelleria [matʃelle'ria] *sf* butcher's (shop).
macello [ma'tʃello] *sm* **(a)** *(mattatoio)* slaughterhouse, abattoir. **(b)** *(azione: anche)* slaughter; **mandare al ~** *(fig: soldati etc)* to send to their deaths. **(c)** *(fig fam: disordine)* mess; *(: disastro)* disaster.
macerare [matʃe'rare] **1** *vt (canapa, carta)* to macerate; *(Culin)* to marinate. **2** **~rsi** *vr (consumarsi)*: **~rsi nel rimorso** to be consumed with remorse.
macerazione [matʃerat'tsjone] *sf* maceration.
macerie [ma'tʃɛrje] *sfpl* rubble *sg*, debris *sg*.
macero [matʃero] *sm (operazione)* pulping; *(stabilimento)* pulping mill; **carta da ~** paper for pulping.
machiavellico, a, ci, che [makja'vɛlliko] *ag (anche fig)* Machiavellian.
macigno [ma'tʃinɲo] *sm (masso)* rock, boulder; **duro come un ~** as hard as rock.
macilento, a [matʃi'lɛnto] *ag* emaciated.
macina ['matʃina] *sf (pietra)* millstone; *(macchina)* grinder.
macinacaffè [matʃinakaf'fɛ] *sm inv* coffee grinder, coffee mill.
macinapepe [matʃina'pepe] *sm inv* pepper mill.
macinare [matʃi'nare] *vt (grano, caffè)* to grind; *(carne)* to mince; **~ i chilometri** *(fig)* ≃ to eat up the miles.

macinato [matʃi'nato] *sm* (a) (*cereali, farina*) meal. (b) (*carne*) mince, minced meat.

macinatura [matʃina'tura] *sf*, **macinazione** [matʃinat'tsjone] *sf* grinding.

macinino [matʃi'nino] *sm* (a) (*per caffè, pepe etc*) mill. (b) (*scherz: macchina*) old banger.

maciullare [matʃul'lare] *vt* (*canapa, lino*) to brake; (*fig: braccio etc*) to crush.

macro... ['makro] *pref* macro... .

macroscopico, a, ci, che [makros'kɔpiko] *ag* (*dimensione*) macroscopic; (*errore*) glaring.

maculato, a [maku'lato] *ag* (*pelo*) spotted.

madia ['madja] *sf* chest for the making and storage of bread.

madido, a ['madido] *ag*: ~ (**di**) wet *o* moist (with); ~ **di sudore** bathed in sweat.

madonna [ma'dɔnna] *sf* (*Rel*): **M**~ Our Lady; (*Arte*) madonna; (*letterario, Storia*) my lady, madam; ~! (*fam*) good God!

madonnina [madon'nina] *sf* (*Arte*) madonna.

madornale [mador'nale] *ag* enormous, huge.

madras [ma'dras] *sm inv* madras cotton.

madre ['madre] **1** *sf* (a) mother; **senza** ~ motherless; ~ **di famiglia** mother; ~ **superiore** (*Rel*) mother superior. (b) (*sedimento: di aceto*) sediment; (*: di vino*) sediment, dregs. (c) (*Amm: di ricevuta*) counterfoil; (*Tecn: di vite*) female screw. **2** *ag inv*: **casa** ~ (*Rel*) mother house; **ragazza** ~ unmarried mother; **regina** ~ queen mother; **scena** ~ (*Teatro*) principal scene; **ha fatto una scena** ~ (*fig*) she made a terrible scene.

madrelingua [madre'lingwa] *sf* mother tongue, native language.

madrepatria [madre'patrja] *sf* mother country, native land.

madreperla [madre'pɛrla] *sf* mother-of-pearl.

madreperlaceo, a [madreper'latʃeo] *ag* pearly.

Madrid [ma'drid] *sf* Madrid.

madrigale [madri'gale] *sm* madrigal.

madrileno, a [madri'lɛno] **1** *ag* of (*o* from) Madrid. **2** *sm/f* person from Madrid.

madrina [ma'drina] *sf* (*di bambino*) godmother; (*di nave*) christener.

maestà [maes'ta] *sf inv* (*gen*) majesty; **Sua M**~ **il Re** His Majesty the King; **Sua M**~ **la Regina** Her Majesty the Queen.

maestosità [maestosi'ta] *sf* majesty.

maestoso, a [maes'toso] *ag* majestic.

maestrale [maes'trale] *sm* northwest wind.

maestranze [maes'trantse] *sfpl* workforce *sg*, workers.

maestria [maes'tria] *sf* mastery, skill.

maestro, a [ma'ɛstro] **1** *sm/f* (a) (*anche*: ~ **di scuola**) (primary) teacher. (b) (*fig: esperto*) expert; è ~**a nella cucina** (*fig*) she's an expert cook; **è stato un colpo da** ~ (*fig*) that was a masterly move. **2** *sm* (a) (*artigiano*) master; **i M**~**i del Rinascimento** to the Masters of the Renaissance. (b) (*Mus*) maestro. (c) (*vento*) northwest wind. **3** *ag*: **albero** ~ (*Naut*) main mast; **muro** ~ main wall; **strada** ~**a** main road. **4**: ~ **d'asilo** nursery teacher; ~ **di cerimonia** master of ceremonies; ~ **d'orchestra** conductor; ~ **di piano** piano teacher; ~ **di scherma/ballo** fencing/dancing master; ~ **di sci** skiing instructor.

mafia ['mafja] *sf* Mafia.

mafioso, a [ma'fjoso] **1** *ag* mafia attr. **2** *sm/f* member of the Mafia.

maga, ghe ['maga] *sf* sorceress.

magagna [ma'gaɲɲa] *sf* (a) (*anche fig*) defect, flaw. (b) (*noia, guaio*) problem.

magari [ma'gari] **1** *escl* (*esprime desiderio*): ~ **fosse vero** if only it were true!; **ti piacerebbe andare in**

Italia? — ~! would you like to go to Italy? — and how! *o* you bet!; **hai avuto l'aumento?** — sì, ~! did you get the increase? — oh, I wish I had! **2** *av* (*anche*) even; (*forse*) perhaps; **saremo in 5,** ~ **in 6** there will be 5, or perhaps 6, of us; **a uscire tutto sudato** ~ **ti prendi un raffreddore** if you go out before you've cooled down you're likely to *o* you might catch a cold.

magazzinaggio [magaddzi'naddʒo] *sm*: (**spese di**) ~ storage charges, warehousing charges.

magazziniere [magaddzi'njɛre] *sm* warehouseman.

magazzino [magad'dzino] *sm* (a) (*deposito*) warehouse; **avere merci in** *o* **a** ~ to have goods in stock; **fondi di** ~ unsold stock; ~ **doganale** bonded warehouse. (b) (*negozio*): **grande** ~ department store.

maggese [mad'dʒese] *sm* (*Agr*) fallow field; **lasciare a** ~ to leave fallow.

maggio ['maddʒo] *sm* May; *per uso vedi* **luglio.**

maggiorana [maddʒo'rana] *sf* (*Bot*) (sweet) marjoram.

maggioranza [maddʒo'rantsa] *sf* (*gen*) majority; **partito di** ~ party in power; **eletto con una** ~ **di** elected by a majority of, **essere in** ~ to be in the majority; **nella** ~ **dei casi** in most cases; **la** ~ **degli Italiani** most Italians, the majority of Italians.

maggiorare [maddʒo'rare] *vt* (*Comm: prezzo, conto*): ~ (**di**) to increase (by).

maggiorazione [maddʒorat'tsjone] *sf* (*Comm*) rise, increase.

maggiordomo [maddʒor'dɔmo] *sm* butler.

maggiore [mad'dʒore] **1** *ag comp* (a) (*più grande*) bigger, larger; (*: di quantità*) greater; **le spese sono state** ~**i del previsto** expenses were higher than expected; **ha dimostrato maggior entusiasmo di te** he showed greater enthusiasm than you; **a maggior ragione dovresti parlargli tu** all the more reason for speaking to him yourself. (b) (*più importante*) more important; (*di notevole rilevanza*) major; **opere** ~**i** major works. (c) (*più anziano*) elder, older. (d) (*di grado*): **sergente** ~ sergeant major; **Stato M**~ (*Mil*) general staff. (e) (*Mus*) major; **do** ~ C major.

   2 *ag superl* (*vedi* **1a, b, c**) biggest, largest; greatest; most important; eldest, oldest; **la maggior parte della gente** most people, the majority (of people); **andare per la** ~ (*cantante, attore etc*) to be very popular, be 'in'.

   3 *sm/f* (a) (*grado: Mil*) major; (*: Aer*) squadron leader. (b) (*d'età: tra due*) older, elder; (*: tra più di due*) oldest, eldest.

maggiorenne [maddʒo'rɛnne] **1** *ag* of age. **2** *sm/f* person who has come of age; **diventare** ~ to come of age, reach one's majority.

maggioritario, a [maddʒori'tarjo] *ag* majority attr.

magia [ma'dʒia] *sf* magic; **come per** ~ as if by magic, like magic.

magico, a, ci, che ['madʒiko] *ag* magic; (*fig: serata, incontro*) magical; (*: sorriso*) charming; **pronunciare la formula** ~**a** to say the magic words.

magio ['madʒo] *sm* (*Rel*): **i re Magi** the Magi, the Three Wise Men.

magistero [madʒis'tero] *sm*: **Facoltà di M**~ ≃ teachers' training college.

magistrale [madʒis'trale] **1** *ag* (a) (*Scol*) primary teachers', primary teaching *attr*; **abilitazione** ~ teaching diploma for primary teachers; **istituto** ~ *secondary school for the training of primary teachers*. (b) (*abile: colpo, intervento*) masterly, skilful. **2**: ~**i** *sfpl* = **istituto** ~.

magistrato [madʒis'trato] *sm* magistrate.

magistratura [madʒistra'tura] *sf* magistracy.

maglia ['maʎʎa] *sf* **(a)** *(punto)* stitch; *(lavoro ai ferri)* knitting; **lavorare a ~, fare la ~** to knit; **avviare/calare le ~e** to cast on/off; **una ~ dritta, una rovescia** knit one, purl one. **(b)** *(indumento intimo)* vest; *(Sport, maglione)* jersey; **indossa la ~ iridata** *(Ciclismo)* he's the world cycling champion. **(c)** *(di catena, armatura)* link; *(di rete, Tecn)* mesh; **una rete a ~e fitte/grosse** a fine-/wide-mesh net; **passare per le ~e della rete** *(anche fig)* to slip through the net.

magliaia [maʎ'ʎaja] *sf* knitter.

maglieria [maʎʎe'ria] *sf* **(a)** *(indumenti)* knitwear; **macchina per ~** knitting machine. **(b)** *(negozio)* knitwear shop.

maglietta [maʎ'ʎetta] *sf* *(canottiera)* vest; *(con maniche)* T-shirt.

maglificio [maʎʎi'fitʃo] *sm* knitwear factory.

maglina [maʎ'ʎina] *sf* *(tessuto)* jersey.

maglio ['maʎʎo] *sm* *(martello)* mallet; *(Tecn: macchina)* power hammer.

maglione [maʎ'ʎone] *sm* jersey, sweater.

magnaccia [maɲ'ɲattʃa] *sm inv* *(peg)* pimp.

magnanimità [maɲɲanimi'ta] *sf* magnanimity.

magnanimo, a [maɲ'ɲanimo] *ag* magnanimous.

magnate [maɲ'ɲate] *sm* tycoon, magnate.

magnesia [maɲ'ɲezja] *sf* magnesia.

magnesio [maɲ'ɲezjo] *sm* magnesium; **al ~** *(lampada, flash)* magnesium *attr*.

magnete [maɲ'ɲete] *sm* *(calamita)* magnet; *(Elettr, Aut)* magneto.

magnetico, a, ci, che [maɲ'ɲɛtiko] *ag* *(anche fig)* magnetic.

magnetismo [maɲɲe'tizmo] *sm* *(anche fig)* magnetism.

magnetizzare [maɲɲetid'dzare] *vt* *(Fis)* to magnetize; *(fig)* to mesmerize.

magnetizzazione [maɲɲetiddzat'tsjone] *sf* *(Fis)* magnetization.

magnetofono [maɲɲe'tɔfono] *sm* tape recorder.

magnificamente [maɲɲifika'mente] *av* magnificently, extremely well.

magnificare [maɲɲifi'kare] *vt* *(celebrare)* to extol, praise; **~ i pregi di qn/qc** to sing the praises of sb/sth.

magnificenza [maɲɲifi'tʃɛntsa] *sf* magnificence.

magnifico, a, ci, che [maɲ'ɲifiko] *ag* **(a)** *(gen)* magnificent; *(serata)* marvellous, wonderful; *(tempo)* gorgeous, superb; **domani si parte — ~!** we're leaving tomorrow — terrific! **(b)** *(liberale: ospite)* generous; **fare il ~** *(fig)* to play the millionaire.

magnolia [maɲ'ɲɔlja] *sf* magnolia.

mago, ghi ['mago] *sm* *(stregone)* magician, wizard; *(illusionista)* magician; *(fam: persona abilissima)* wizard.

magra ['magra] *sf* **(a)** *(di fiume)* low water; **essere in ~** to be very low; **periodo di ~** *(fig)* lean times. **(b)** *(fam: brutta figura)*: **fare una ~** to blunder, make a blunder.

magrezza [ma'grettsa] *sf* *(di persona, corpo)* thinness; *(di risorse)* scarcity.

magro, a ['magro] **1** *ag* **(a)** *(persona, corpo)* thin, skinny *(peg)*; *(viso)* thin, lean. **(b)** *(latte)* skimmed; *(carne)* lean; *(formaggio)* low-fat. **(c)** *(stipendio, guadagno)* meagre, poor; *(profitti)* small, slim; *(annata, raccolto)* poor; *(scusa)* poor, lame; *(cena, pasto)* skimpy. **(d)** *(Rel)*: **giorno di ~** day of abstinence; **mangiare (di) ~** to eat no meat. **2** *sm* *(carne)* lean meat.

mah [ma] *escl* *(fam)* well!

mai ['mai] *av* **(a)** *(negativo)* never, not ... ever; **non**
esce **~** she never goes out; **non sono ~ stato in Russia** I've never *o* I haven't ever been to Russia; **non me ne dimenticherò ~** I shall never *o* shan't ever forget it; **non avrei ~ detto che...** I would never have said that...; **non le ha ~ più telefonato** he never phoned her again, he has never phoned her since; **non si sa ~** you never can tell; **~ e poi ~!** no way!; **~ più** never again; *(assolutamente no)* no way; **quasi ~** hardly ever, practically never; **ora o ~** it's now or never.

(b) *(con tempi indefiniti)* ever; **l'hai ~ visto prima?** have you ever seen him before?; **sei ~ in ufficio il sabato?** are you ever at the office on a Saturday?; **se ~ ne trovassi uno** *o* **lo farei sapere** if I ever *o* if ever I found one I would let you know; **i prezzi delle case sono più alti che ~** house prices are higher than ever; **caso ~ si mettesse a piovere** in case it starts raining, should it start to rain; **caso** *o* **se ~ direi che ha sbagliato lui** if anything, I would say that he was in the wrong; **caso ~ ti telefono domenica** I might well phone you on Sunday; **come ~ non ci hai avvisato?** why (on earth) didn't you let us know?; **che dici ~?** what (on earth) are you saying?; **quando ~ ho detto una cosa simile?** when did I ever say anything like that?

maiale [ma'jale] *sm* **(a)** *(Zool, fig peg)* pig; **mangiare come un ~** to eat like a pig. **(b)** *(Culin)* pork.

maiolica [ma'jɔlika] *sf* majolica.

maionese [majo'nese] *sf* mayonnaise.

mais ['mais] *sm* maize, corn *(Am)*.

maiuscola [ma'juskola] *sf* *(anche:* **lettera ~**) capital (letter).

maiuscolo, a [ma'juskolo] **1** *ag* capital. **2** *sm* capital letters; *(Tip)* upper case; **scrivere tutto (in) ~** to write everything in capitals *o* in capital letters.

mala ['mala] *sf* *(gergo)* underworld.

malaccorto, a [malak'kɔrto] *ag* rash, careless.

malafede [mala'fede] *sf* bad faith.

malaffare [malaf'fare]: **di ~** *ag* *(gente)* shady, dishonest; **donna di ~** prostitute.

malagevole [mala'dʒevole] *ag* difficult, hard.

malagrazia [mala'grattsja] *sf*: **con ~** with bad grace, impolitely.

malalingua [mala'lingwa] *sf, pl* **malelingue** gossip *(person)*.

malamente [mala'mente] *av* *(gen)* badly; *(sgarbatamente)* rudely; **finire ~** *(persona)* to come to a bad end.

malandato, a [malan'dato] *ag* *(persona: di salute)* in poor health, in a bad way; *(: di condizioni finanziarie)* badly off; *(cosa: trascurata)* dilapidated.

malandrino, a [malan'drino] **1** *ag* *(scherz: occhi, sguardo)* mischievous, roguish. **2** *sm/f* rogue, rascal.

malanimo [ma'lanimo] *sm* ill will; **di ~** unwillingly, grudgingly.

malanno [ma'lanno] *sm* **(a)** *(disgrazia)* misfortune. **(b)** *(malattia)* ailment; **mi devo essere preso un ~** I must have caught something.

malapena [mala'pena]: **a ~** *av* hardly, scarcely; **ti sento a ~** I can hardly hear you.

malaria [ma'larja] *sf* malaria.

malarico, a, ci, che [ma'lariko] *ag* malarial.

malasorte [mala'sɔrte] *sf* bad luck, ill luck.

malaticcio, a, ci, che [mala'tittʃo] *ag* sickly.

malato, a [ma'lato] **1** *ag* *(persona)* ill, sick, unwell; *(organo, pianta)* diseased; **ho una gamba ~a** I've got a sore leg; **essere ~ di cuore** to have heart trouble *o* a bad heart; **~ di mente** mentally ill; **tu sei ~ al cervello!** *(fig)* you're off your head!;

darsi ~ *(sul lavoro etc)* to go sick. **2** *smf (infermo)* sick person; *(paziente)* patient; **i** ~**i** the sick; **sa trattare con i** ~**i** he's got a good bedside manner; **un** ~ **grave** a person who is seriously ill.

malattia [malat'tia] *sf* **(a)** *(Med)* illness, disease; *(di pianta)* disease; ~**e nervose** nervous diseases; ~**e del lavoro** industrial diseases; **mettersi in** ~ to go on sick leave; **fare una** ~ **di qc** *(fig: disperarsi)* to get in a state about sth. **(b)** *(fissazione)* mania; **ha la** ~ **del gioco** he's an inveterate gambler, he's hooked on gambling.

malaugurato, a [malaugu'rato] *ag* ill-fated, unlucky.

malaugurio [malau'gurjo] *sm* ill omen; **uccello del** ~ bird of ill omen.

malavita [mala'vita] *sf* underworld; **darsi alla** ~ to turn to crime.

malavoglia [mala'vɔʎʎa]: **di** ~ *av* reluctantly, unwillingly.

Malaysia [ma'laizja] *sf* Malaysia.

malaysiano, a [malai'zjano] *ag, smf* Malaysian.

malcapitato, a [malkapi'tato] **1** *ag* unlucky, unfortunate. **2** *smf* unfortunate person.

malconcio, a, ci, ce [mal'kontʃo] *ag (abiti, persona)* in a sorry state; **uscire** ~ **da qc** *(fig)* to come out of sth badly.

malcontento, a [malkon'tento] **1** *ag*: ~ **(di)** dissatisfied (with). **2** *sm (sentimento)* discontent.

malcostume [malkos'tume] *sm* immorality.

maldestro, a [mal'destro] *ag (goffo)* clumsy, awkward; *(inesperto)* inexperienced.

maldicente [maldi'tʃɛnte] *smf* gossip.

maldicenza [maldi'tʃɛntsa] *sf* malicious gossip; **è solo una** ~, **sono solo** ~**e** it's just gossip.

maldisposto, a [maldis'posto] *ag*: ~ **(verso)** ill-disposed (towards).

male ['male] **1** *av* **(a)** *(in modo insoddisfacente)* badly; *(in modo errato)* badly, wrongly; ~**! non avresti dovuto farlo** that was wrong of you — you shouldn't have done it; **questa porta chiude** ~ this door shuts badly *o* doesn't shut properly; **scrivere/comportarsi** ~ to write/behave badly; **pronunciare** ~ **una parola** to pronounce a word wrongly; **rispondere** ~ *(in modo errato)* to answer wrongly *o* incorrectly; *(in modo sgarbato)* to answer back; **riuscire** ~ to turn out badly; **qui si mangia molto** ~ the food is very bad *o* poor here; **pensi che abbia fatto** ~ **ad andare?** do you think it was wrong of him to go?; **parlar** ~ **di qn** to speak ill of sb; **trattar** ~ **qn** to ill-treat sb. **(b)** *(di salute)*: **sentirsi/star** ~ to feel/be ill. **(c)** *(fraseologia)*: **gli è andata** ~ **di nuovo** he failed again; **per** ~ **che vada** however badly things go; **capire** ~ to misunderstand; **le cose si stanno mettendo** ~ things are taking a turn for the worse; **ha preso molto** ~ **la cosa** he took it very badly; **rimanere** ~ *(deluso)* to be disappointed; *(dispiaciuto)* to be sorry; *(offeso)* to be hurt *o* offended; **sta** ~ **comportarsi così** that's no way to behave; **quell'abito le sta proprio** ~ that dress just doesn't suit her, that dress looks terrible on her; **il giallo sta** ~ **con il rosa** yellow looks awful with pink; **la vedo** ~ she's got problems; **bene** *o* ~ **ce la farò** one way or the other I'll manage; **niente** ~ **quel ragazzo** that boy's not bad, that boy's a bit of alright *(fam)*; **di** ~ **in peggio** from bad to worse; **non faresti** ~ **a dirglielo** it wouldn't be a bad idea to tell him.
2 *sm* **(a)** *(ciò che è ingiusto, disonesto)* evil, ill; **il** ~ evil; **un** ~ **necessario** a necessary evil; **le forze del** ~ the forces of evil; **il minore dei due** ~**i** the lesser of two evils; ~**i sociali** social evils. **(b)** *(danno)* harm; **fare del** ~ **a qn** to harm *o*

hurt sb; **le sigarette fanno** ~ cigarettes are bad for you; **che c'è di** ~ **se esco con lui?** what harm is there in my going out with him?; **non ho fatto niente di** ~ I haven't done anything wrong, I haven't done any harm; **non sarebbe (un)** ~ **se gliene parlassi** it wouldn't do any harm to talk to him about it; **non farebbe (del)** ~ **a una mosca** he wouldn't hurt a fly; **non gli voglio** ~ I don't dislike him.
(c) *(dolore)* pain, ache; *(malattia)* illness, disease; **farsi** ~ to hurt o.s.; **fare (del)** ~ **a qn** to hurt sb; **mi fa** ~ **la gamba, ho** ~ **ad una gamba** my leg hurts, I've got a pain in my leg; **mi fa** ~ **it** hurts; **avere mal di testa/di stomaco** to have a headache/stomach ache; **aver mal di denti/d'orecchi/di gola** to have toothache/earache/a sore throat; **avere mal di cuore/di fegato** to have a heart/liver complaint; **mal d'auto** car-sickness; **mal di mare** seasickness; **avere il mal di mare** to be seasick; **avere un brutto** ~ *(euf: cancro)* to have cancer; **i** ~**i della vecchiaia** the infirmities of old age.
(d) *(fraseologia)*: **andare a** ~ *(carne, latte)* to go off *o* bad; **non avertene a** ~, **non prendertela a** ~ don't take it to heart; **come va?** — **non c'è** ~ how are you? — not bad *o* O.K. *(fam)*; **mal comune mezzo gaudio** a trouble shared is a trouble halved; **a** ~**i estremi, estremi rimedi** extreme situations call for extreme measures.

maledetto, a [male'detto] **1** *pp di* **maledire**. **2** *ag* **(a)** *(dannato)* accursed; *(nelle imprecazioni)* cursed; ~**a la guerra!** cursed be the war! **(b)** *(fig fam)* damned, blasted, confounded; **avere una fame** ~**a** to be damned hungry; **spegni quella** ~**a radio!** turn that blasted radio off!; **ho una paura** ~**a dei ragni** I'm scared stiff of spiders; **è stato un giorno** ~ it's been a bloody awful day; **non vedo l'ora di finire questo** ~ **lavoro** I can't wait to finish this wretched work.

maledire [male'dire] *vt* to curse.

maledizione [maledit'tsjone] *sf (condanna, imprecazione)* curse; ~**!** damn!; **devo avere la** ~ **addosso!** there must be a jinx on me!

maleducato, a [maledu'kato] **1** *ag (persona)* rude, ill-mannered. **2** *smf* ill-mannered person; **fare il** ~ to be rude.

maleducazione [maledukat'tsjone] *sf* rudeness; **è** ~ **fare così** it's bad manners to do that.

malefatta [male'fatta] *sf* misdeed.

maleficio [male'fitʃo] *sm* evil spell.

malefico, a, ci, che [ma'lɛfiko] *ag (influsso)* evil; *(clima, cibo)* harmful.

malese [ma'lese] **1** *ag, smf* Malay(an). **2** *sm (lingua)* Malay.

Malesia [ma'lesja] *sf* Malaya.

malessere [ma'lessere] *sm* **(a)** *(indisposizione)* ailment, indisposition; **ha avuto un** ~ he felt dizzy. **(b)** *(fig: disagio)* disquiet, uneasiness.

malevolenza [malevo'lɛntsa] *sf* malevolence.

malevolo, a [ma'lɛvolo] *ag* malevolent.

malfamato, a [malfa'mato] *ag* of ill repute.

malfatto, a [mal'fatto] *ag (lavoro)* badly done; *(oggetto)* badly made; *(persona, corpo)* malformed.

malfattore, trice [malfat'tore] *smf* wrongdoer; **è una banda di** ~**i!** they're a gang of reprobates!

malfermo, a [mal'fermo] *ag (voce, mano)* shaky; *(passo)* unsteady; *(salute)* poor, delicate; **essere** ~ **sulle gambe** to be unsteady on one's legs.

malformazione [malformat'tsjone] *sf* malformation.

malga, ghe ['malga] *sf* Alpine hut.

malgoverno [malgo'verno] *sm (gen)* mismanagement; *(Pol)* misrule.

malgrado [mal'grado] **1** *prep* in spite of; ~ **tutto le sono ancora amico** we are still friends in spite of *o* despite everything; **suo** ~ **ha dovuto fare il lavoro** he had to do the work in spite of himself. **2** *cong* even though; ~ **fosse tardi sono riuscito a prendere il treno** even though it was late I managed to get the train.

malia [ma'lia] *sf (incantesimo)* spell; *(fig: fascino)* charm.

maliardo, a [mali'ardo] **1** *ag (occhi, sorriso)* bewitching. **2** *sf* enchantress.

malignamente [malinɲa'mente] *av* maliciously.

malignare [maliɲ'ɲare] *vi:* ~ **su** to malign, speak ill of.

malignità [maliɲɲi'ta] *sf inv* **(a)** *(qualità)* malice, spite; **con** ~ spitefully, maliciously. **(b)** *(osservazione)* spiteful remark.

maligno, a [ma'liɲɲo] **1** *ag* **(a)** *(persona, parole)* malicious, malignant; **spirito** ~ evil spirit. **(b)** *(Med)* malignant. **2** *sm/f* malicious person.

malinconia [malinko'nia] *sf* melancholy.

malinconico, a, ci, che [malin'kɔniko] *ag* melancholy.

malincuore [malin'kwɔre]: **a** ~ *av* reluctantly, unwillingly.

malinformato, a [malinfor'mato] *ag* misinformed.

malintenzionato, a [malintentsjo'nato] *ag* ill-intentioned.

malinteso [malin'teso] *sm* misunderstanding.

malizia [ma'littsja] *sf* **(a)** *(cattiveria)* malice, spite; *(furbizia)* mischievousness; **con** ~ maliciously, spitefully; mischievously. **(b)** *(trucco)* trick.

malizioso, a [malit'tsjoso] *ag (cattivo)* malicious, spiteful; *(vivace, birichino)* mischievous.

malleabile [malle'abile] *ag* malleable.

malleolo [mal'lɛolo] *sm (Anat)* malleolus *(T)*.

mallevadore [malleva'dore] *sm* guarantor.

malleveria [malleve'ria] *sf* guarantee, surety.

mallo ['mallo] *sm (Bot)* husk.

malloppo [mal'lɔppo] *sm (fam: refurtiva)* loot.

malmenare [malme'nare] *vt* to beat up.

malmesso, a [mal'messo] *ag (persona)* in a difficult situation; *(: vestito male)* badly dressed; *(: economicamente)* badly off; *(casa, macchina)* in a poor state of repair.

malnutrito, a [malnu'trito] *ag* undernourished.

malnutrizione [malnutrit'tsjone] *sf* malnutrition.

malo, a ['malo] *ag:* **in** ~ **modo** badly; *(sgarbatamente)* rudely; **essere a mal partito** to be in an awkward situation; ~**a lingua = malalingua;** ~**a sorte = malasorte;** ~**a voglia = malavoglia.**

malocchio [ma'lɔkkjo] *sm* evil eye.

malora [ma'lora] *sf (fam):* **andare in** ~ to go to the dogs; **alla** ~**!** to the devil!; **va in** ~**!** go to the devil!; **è un tirchio della** ~**!** he's a bloody miser!

malore [ma'lore] *sm* sudden illness; **venire** *o* **essere colto da** ~ to be taken ill suddenly.

malpreparato, a [malprepa'rato] *ag* ill-prepared.

malridotto, a [malri'dotto] *ag (abiti, scarpe, persona)* in a sorry state; *(casa, macchina)* dilapidated, in a poor state of repair.

malsano, a [mal'sano] *ag* unhealthy.

malsicuro, a [malsi'kuro] *ag (scala, edificio)* unsafe.

Malta ['malta] *sf* Malta.

malta ['malta] *sf (Edil)* mortar.

maltempo [mal'tɛmpo] *sm* bad weather.

maltenuto, a [malte'nuto] *ag* badly looked after, badly kept.

maltese [mal'tese] *ag, sm/f, sm* Maltese.

malto ['malto] *sm* malt.

maltolto [mal'tɔlto] *sm* ill-gotten gains *pl*.

maltrattamento [maltratta'mento] *sm* ill

treatment; **subire** ~**i** to be ill-treated.

maltrattare [maltrat'tare] *vt* to ill-treat.

maluccio [ma'luttʃo] *av (di salute)* poorly; *(di esame, gara etc)* rather badly.

malumore [malu'more] *sm* bad temper, ill humour; **essere di** ~ to be in a bad mood.

malva ['malva] **1** *sf (Bot)* mallow. **2** *sm inv (colore)* mauve. **3** *ag inv* mauve.

malvagio, a, gi, gie [mal'vadʒo] **1** *ag (uomo, azione)* evil, wicked; **non è** ~ *(fig: vino, cibo)* it's not unpleasant *o* bad; *(: spettacolo, film)* it's not bad. **2** *sm/f* wicked person.

malvagità [malvadʒi'ta] *sf inv (qualità)* wickedness; *(azione)* wicked deed.

malvestito, a [malves'tito] *ag* badly dressed, ill-clad.

malvisto, a [mal'visto] *ag (persona, idea, proposta)* ~ **(da)** unpopular (with).

malvivente [malvi'vente] *sm/f* criminal.

malvolentieri [malvolen'tjeri] *av* unwillingly, reluctantly.

malvolere [malvo'lere] *vt:* **farsi** ~ **(da)** to make o.s. unpopular (with); **essere malvoluto da qn** to be disliked by sb; **prendere qn a** ~ to take a dislike to sb.

mamma ['mamma] *sf (fam)* mummy, mum; **come l'ha fatto** ~ in one's birthday suit; ~ **mia!** good heavens!

mammalucco, chi [mamma'lukko] *sm* dolt, idiot.

mammario, a [mam'marjo] *ag (Anat)* mammary.

mammella [mam'mella] *sf (di donna)* breast; *(di animale)* udder.

mammifero, a [mam'mifero] **1** *ag (Zool)* mammalian. **2** *sm (Zool)* mammal.

mammismo [mam'mizmo] *sm excessive attachment to one's mother.*

mammola ['mammola] *sf (Bot)* violet.

mammut [mam'mut] *sm inv (Zool)* mammoth.

manager [mæ'nidʒə] *sm inv* manager.

manageriale [manadʒe'rjale] *ag* managerial.

manata [ma'nata] *sf (colpo)* slap; *(quantità)* handful; **a** ~**e** by the handful.

manca ['manka] *sf* left (hand); **a destra e a** ~ left, right and centre, on all sides.

mancamento [manka'mento] *sm (di forze)* (feeling of) faintness, weakness.

mancanza [man'kantsa] *sf* **(a)**: ~ **di** *(assenza)* lack of; *(carenza)* shortage of, scarcity of; ~ **di rispetto** lack of respect; ~ **di soldi** lack (*o* shortage) of money; **in** ~ **di vino berremo acqua** as there is no wine we'll drink water; **in** ~ **d'altro/di meglio** for want of anything else/better; **per** ~ **di tempo** through lack of time; **sentire la** ~ **di qc/qn** to miss sth/sb; **sento la tua** ~ I miss you. **(b)** *(fallo)* fault; *(difetto)* failing, shortcoming; **commettere una** ~ to commit an error.

mancare [man'kare] **1** *vi* **(a)** *(aus* **essere)** *(far difetto)* to be lacking; **mancano i soldi** money is lacking, there's not enough money; **manca sempre il tempo** there's never enough time; **mi mancano le parole per esprimerti la mia gratitudine** I can't find the words to express my gratitude to you; **ci manca il pane** we've run out of bread, we don't have any bread; **fammi sapere se ti manca qualcosa** let me know if you need anything; **i suoi non gli fanno mancar niente** his family doesn't let him want for anything; **gli sono venuti a** ~ **i soldi** his money ran out, he ran out of money; **quanto manca all'arrivo del treno?** how long before the train arrives?

(b) *(aus* **essere)** *(non esserci)* to be missing, not to be there; *(persona: essere assente)* to be absent, be away; **mancano ancora 10.000 lire**

we're still 10,000 lire short; **quanti pezzi manca-no?** how many pieces are missing?; **mancavi solo tu** you were the only one missing; **mi manchi** I miss you; **mancano prove** there's not enough evidence; ~ **da casa** to be away from home; ~ **all'appello** to be absent from roll call.

(**c**) (*aus* **essere**) (*venir meno: coraggio, forze*) to fail; (*morire*) to die; **gli è mancato il coraggio** his courage failed him; **gli sono mancate le parole** words failed him; **sentirsi** ~ to feel faint; **gli sono venuti a** ~ **i genitori** his parents died, he lost his parents; **manca la luce** the electricity is off.

(**d**) (*essere in errore*) to be wrong, make a mistake; **mi dispiace se ho mancato** I'm sorry if I was wrong.

(**e**): ~ **di** (*coraggio, giudizio*) to lack, be lacking in; (*risorse, soldi*) to be short of, lack; ~ **di rispet-to a** *o* **verso qn** to be lacking in respect towards sb, be disrespectful towards sb; ~ **di parola** not to keep one's word, go back on one's word; **non mancherò di salutarlo da parte tua** I promise I'll give him your regards; **non mancherò** I won't forget, I'll make sure I do.

(**f**): ~ **a** (*doveri*) to neglect; (*parola*) to fail to keep; (*appuntamento*) to miss.

(**g**) (*fraseologia*): **ci mancherebbe altro!** of course I (*o* you *etc*) will!; **ci mancava solo questa!** that's all we need!; **c'è mancato poco** it was a near thing; **c'è mancato poco** *o* **poco è mancato che si facesse male** he very nearly hurt himself; **gli manca una rotella** (*fig*) he's got a screw loose; **a questo cane manca solo la parola** that dog is almost human.

2 *vt* (*bersaglio*) to miss; **ha mancato la presa ed è caduto** he lost his grip and fell.

mancato, a [man'kato] *ag* (*tentativo*) abortive, un-successful; (*appuntamento*) missed; (*occasione*) lost, wasted; (*artista*) failed; **è un dottore** ~ (*fallito*) he's a failure as a doctor; (*non realizzato*) he should have been a doctor; ~ **pagamento** non-payment; ~ **arrivo** failure to arrive.

manche [maʃ] *sf inv* (*Sport*) heat.

manchevole [man'kevole] *ag* (*insufficiente*) inad-equate, insufficient; **essere** ~ **ai propri impegni** to fail to carry out one's duties.

manchevolezza [mankevo'lettsa] *sf* (*scorrettezza*) fault, shortcoming.

mancia, ce ['mantʃa] *sf* tip; ~ **competente** reward; **dare una** ~ **a qn** to tip sb, give sb a tip.

manciata [man'tʃata] *sf* handful; **a** ~**e** by the handful.

mancina [man'tʃina] *sf* (*mano*) left hand; (*parte*) left, left-hand side.

mancino, a [man'tʃino] **1** *ag* (*persona*) left-handed; (*fig*): **tiro** ~ dirty trick. **2** *sm/f* left-handed person.

manco ['manko] *av* (*fam: nemmeno*) not even; ~ **per sogno!**, ~ **per idea!** not on your life!

mandante [man'dante] *sm/f* (*Dir*) principal; (*istiga-tore*) instigator.

mandarancio [manda'rantʃo] *sm* clementine.

mandare [man'dare] *vt* (**a**) (*gen*) to send; ~ **qc per posta/per via aerea** to send sth through the post/by air; ~ **a chiamare qn** to send for sb; ~ **a dire** (**a qn**) to send word (to sb); ~ **due righe a qn** to drop sb a line; ~ **qn in prigione** to send sb to prison; ~ **un bacio a qn** to blow sb a kiss; ~ **in pezzi** (*vaso, vetro etc*) to shatter; ~ **in rovina** to ruin; **che Dio ce la mandi buona!** God help us! (**b**): ~ **avanti** (*persona*) to send ahead; (*fig: famiglia*) to provide for; (*: ditta*) to look after, run; (*: pratica*) to attend to; ~ **giù** (*persona*) to send down; (*cibo, fig*)

to swallow; ~ **via** (*persona*) to send away; (*: licen-ziare*) to dismiss. (**c**) (*emettere: segnali*) to send out; (*: grido*) to give, utter, let out; ~ **in onda** (*Radio, TV*) to broadcast.

mandarino[1] [manda'rino] *sm* (*in Cina*) mandarin.

mandarino[2] [manda'rino] *sm* (*Bot*) mandarin (orange).

mandata [man'data] *sf* (**a**) (*quantità*) consignment. (**b**) (*di chiave*) turn; **chiudere a doppia** ~ to double-lock.

mandatario [manda'tarjo] *sm* (*Dir*) representa-tive, agent.

mandato [man'dato] *sm* (**a**) (*ordine, incarico*) man-date; (*durata dell'incarico*) term of office; **su** ~ **di** by order of. (**b**) (*Dir*) warrant; ~ **di cattura** warrant for arrest; ~ **di comparizione** summons *sg*; ~ **di perquisizione** search warrant. (**c**): ~ **di pagamento** money order.

mandibola [man'dibola] *sf* (*Anat*) jaw, mandible (*T*).

mandolino [mando'lino] *sm* (*Mus*) mandolin(e).

mandorla ['mandorla] *sf* (*frutto*) almond; **occhi a** ~ almond(-shaped) eyes.

mandorlato [mandor'lato] *sm* nut brittle.

mandorlo ['mandorlo] *sm* almond tree.

mandragola [man'dragola] *sm* (*Bot*) mandrake.

mandria ['mandrja] *sf* herd.

mandriano [mandri'ano] *sm* cowherd, herdsman.

mandrillo [man'drillo] *sm* (*Zool*) mandrill; (*fig*) lecher.

mandrino [man'drino] *sm* (*Tecn*) mandrel.

maneggevole [maned'dʒevole] *ag* easy to handle; **poco** ~ difficult to handle.

maneggiare [maned'dʒare] *vt* (*utensili, arnesi*) to handle, use; (*cera, creta*) to work; (*fig: persone, denaro, situazione*) to handle, deal with.

maneggio [ma'neddʒo] *sm* (**a**) (*Equitazione: scuo-la*) riding school; (*: pista*) ring. (**b**) (*di denaro, affari*) management, handling. (**c**) (*fig: manovra, intrigo*) scheme, ploy.

manesco, a, schi, sche [ma'nesko] *ag* ready with one's fists.

manette [ma'nette] *sfpl* handcuffs; **mettere le** ~ **a qn** to handcuff sb.

manganellare [manganel'lare] *vt* to club.

manganellata [manganel'lata] *sf* blow with a club *o* cudgel.

manganello [manga'nɛllo] *sm* club, cudgel; (*della polizia*) truncheon, night stick (*Am*).

manganese [manga'nese] *sm* manganese.

mangereccio, a, ci, ce [mandʒe'rettʃo] *ag* edible.

mangiabile [man'dʒabile] *ag* edible, eatable.

mangiadischi [mandʒa'diski] *sm inv* portable record player.

mangianastri [mandʒa'nastri] *sm inv* cassette-recorder.

mangiapane [mandʒa'pane] *sm/f:* ~ **a tradimento** scrounger.

mangiare [man'dʒare] **1** *vt* (**a**) (*gen*) to eat; ~ **di tutto** to eat everything; **qui si mangia bene/male** the food is good/bad here; **non avere da** ~ not to have enough to eat; **dare da** ~ **a qn** to give sb something to eat; **farsi qc da** ~ to make o.s. sth to eat; ~ **fuori** to eat out, have a meal out; **resta a** ~ **con noi** stay and have a bite with us; **allora, si mangia?** is it ready then?; **si mangiano questi funghi?** are these mushrooms edible?; ~ **per due/quattro** (*fig*) to eat enough for two/like a horse; ~ **come un uccellino** (*fig*) to pick *o* peck at one's food; ~ **alle spalle di qn** (*fig*) to live off sb; **sembrava volesse mangiarmi** (*fig*) he could have killed me; **questo mobile è mangiato dai tarli** this piece of furniture has woodworm; **esser mangiato vivo dalle zanzare** to be eaten alive by mosquitoes.

(b) *(Carte, Scacchi etc)* to take.

(c): ~**rsi** *(fig: patrimonio, fondi etc)* to squander; ~**rsi qn con gli occhi** to devour sb with one's eyes; ~**rsi il fegato** *(fig)* to eat one's heart out; **mi sarei mangiato le mani** I could have kicked myself; ~**rsi le parole** to mumble; ~**rsi le unghie** to bite one's nails.

2 *sm (cibo)* food; **senza** ~ without food; **essere difficile nel** ~ to be a fussy eater.

mangiasoldi [mandʒa'sɔldi] *ag inv (fam)*: **macchinetta** ~ one-armed bandit.

mangiata [man'dʒata] *sf*: **che** ~**!** what a huge meal!; **una** ~ **coi fiocchi** a slap-up meal.

mangiatoia [mandʒa'toja] *sf* (feeding-)trough.

mangiatore, trice [mandʒa'tore] *sm/f* eater.

mangime [man'dʒime] *sm (foraggio)* fodder; *(becchime)* birdseed.

mangione, a [man'dʒone] *sm/f (fam)* glutton.

mangiucchiare [mandʒuk'kjare] *vt* to nibble.

mango, ghi ['mango] *sm (albero, frutto)* mango.

mania [ma'nia] *sf (Psic)* mania; *(abitudine)* odd habit, queer habit; **gli è presa la** ~ **di grattarsi l'orecchio mentre parla** he has developed the odd habit of scratching his ear while he's talking; **gli è presa la** ~ **dei francobolli** his latest craze is stamp collecting; **una delle sue** ~**e** one of his funny habits; **ha la** ~ **della puntualità/della pulizia** he's obsessed by punctuality/cleanliness; **avere la** ~ **di fare qc** to have a habit of doing sth; ~ **di persecuzione** persecution complex *o* mania.

maniacale [mania'kale] *ag (Psic)* maniacal; *(fanatico)* fanatical; **è una forma** ~ **la tua!** *(fig)* it's an obsession with you!

maniaco, a, ci, che [ma'niako] **1** *ag (Med)* maniac, suffering from a mania; **essere** ~ **dell'ordine** *(fig)* to have an obsession about tidiness. **2** *sm/f (Med)* maniac; *(fanatico)* fanatic.

manica, che ['manika] *sf* **(a)** sleeve; **a** ~**che lunghe** long-sleeved; **senza** ~**che** sleeveless; **essere in** ~**che di camicia** to be in one's shirt sleeves; **essere di** ~ **larga** *(prodigo)* to be free with one's money; *(indulgente)* to be easy going; **una** ~ **di delinquenti** *(fig: banda)* a bunch of criminals. **(b)** *(Geog)*: **la M**~ the English Channel. **(c)**: ~ **a vento** *(Aer)* wind sock; *(Naut)* ventilator.

manicaretto [manika'retto] *sm* titbit.

manichetta [mani'ketta] *sf (Tecn)* hose.

manichino [mani'kino] *sm* dummy.

manico, ci o chi ['maniko] *sm (gen)* handle; *(lungo: di rastrello etc)* shaft; *(di strumento musicale)* neck; ~ **di scopa** broomstick.

manicomio [mani'kɔmjo] *sm* lunatic asylum; *(fig)* madhouse; **questo è da** ~**!** this is lunatic!

manicotto [mani'kɔtto] *sm (di pelliccia)* muff; *(Tecn)* sleeve.

manicure [mani'kure] **1** *sm o f inv* manicure; **farsi il** *o* **la** ~ to do one's nails, give o.s. a manicure. **2** *sf (persona)* manicurist.

maniera [ma'njɛra] *sf* **(a)** *(modo)* way, manner; ~ **di vivere/di parlare** way of life/of speaking; **fare qc alla propria** ~ to do sth one's own way; **in una** ~ **o nell'altra** one way or another; **in qualche** ~ somehow or other; **in** ~ **che** so that; **in** ~ **da** so as to; **fa' in** ~ **che sia tutto pronto per domani** see to it that everything's ready for tomorrow; **dobbiamo fare in** ~ **da non ripetere gli stessi errori** we must see to it that we don't make the same mistakes again; **in tutte le** ~**e** *(a tutti i costi)* at all costs; **usare le** ~**e forti** to use strong-arm

measures; **in nessuna** ~ in no way. **(b)** *(Arte, stile)* style, manner; **alla** ~ **di** in *o* after the style of; **è un Picasso prima** ~ it's an early Picasso. **(c)** *(comportamento)*: ~**e** manners; **usare buone** ~**e con qn** to be polite to sb; **non mi piacciono le sue** ~**e** I don't like the way he behaves.

manierato, a [manje'rato] *ag (affettato)* affected; *(Arte)* mannered.

maniero [ma'njɛro] *sm* manor.

manifattura [manifat'tura] *sf (stabilimento)* factory; *(fabbricazione)* manufacture.

manifatturiero, a [manifattu'rjɛro] *ag* manufacturing.

manifestante [manifes'tante] *sm/f* demonstrator.

manifestare [manifes'tare] **1** *vt (gen)* to show; *(opinioni, intenzioni)* to reveal; ~ **il desiderio di fare qc** to express a desire to do sth, indicate one's wish to do sth. **2** *vi (Pol)*: ~ **contro/a favore di** to demonstrate against/in favour of. **3**: ~**rsi** *vr (sintomi, malattia)* to appear; ~**rsi contrario a un progetto** to reveal one's opposition to a plan; ~**rsi amico/nemico** to prove to be a friend/an enemy; **si è manifestato per quello che è** he has shown his true colours.

manifestazione [manifestat'tsjone] *sf* **(a)** *(di opinione, sentimento)* expression; *(di affetto)* demonstration; *(di malattia: comparsa)* manifestation. **(b)** *(spettacolo)* event; *(Pol)* demonstration; ~ **sportiva** sporting event.

manifestino [manifes'tino] *sm* leaflet.

manifesto, a [mani'festo] **1** *ag (errore, verità)* obvious, self-evident; *(fatto)* well-known; **i giornali hanno reso** ~ **il suo rapporto con la mafia** the newspapers have uncovered his links with the Mafia. **2** *sm* **(a)** *(Letteratura, Arte, Pol)* manifesto. **(b)** *(cartellone)* poster, bill; ~ **pubblicitario** advertising poster.

maniglia [ma'niʎʎa] *sf (di porta, cassetta)* handle; *(nell'autobus)* strap; *(Naut)* shackle.

manigoldo [mani'goldo] *sm* scoundrel, ruffian.

manipolare [manipo'lare] *vt* **(a)** *(gen)* to manipulate, handle; *(creta, cera)* to work, fashion. **(b)** *(falsificare: conti, elezione)* to rig.

manipolazione [manipolat'tsjone] *sf (gen, Med)* manipulation; *(di conti)* rigging.

manipolo [ma'nipolo] *sm* **(a)** *(drappello)* handful. **(b)** *(Storia, Rel)* maniple.

maniscalco, chi [manis'kalko] *sm* blacksmith, farrier.

manna ['manna] *sf (Rel)* manna; **è una** ~ **del cielo!** *(fig)* it (o he etc) is a godsend!

mannaia [man'naja] *sf (del boia)* (executioner's) axe; *(per carne)* cleaver.

mannaro [man'naro] *ag*: **lupo** ~ werewolf.

mannequin [manə'kɛ̃] *sm inv* model.

mano, i ['mano] *sf* **(a)** hand; **dare la** ~ **a qn** to give sb one's hand; *(per salutare)* to shake hands with sb; **darsi la** ~ to hold hands; *(per salutarsi)* to shake hands; **tenersi per** ~ to hold hands; ~ **nella** ~ hand in hand; **battere le** ~ to clap (one's hands); ~**i in alto!** hands up!; **cadere nelle** ~**i di qn** *(fig)* to fall into sb's hands.

(b) *(locuzioni)*: **di seconda** ~ secondhand; **a portata di** ~ within reach; **sotto** ~ *(vicino)* to hand; *(furtivamente)* secretly; **ce l'hai sotto** ~**?** have you got it to hand?; **fuori** ~ out of the way; **in** ~**i fidate** in safe hands; **in buone** ~**i** in good hands; **a** ~**i vuote** empty-handed; **a piene** ~**i** *(fig)* generously; **rapina a** ~ **armata** armed robbery; **fatto a** ~ handmade; **cucito a** ~ hand-sewn; **bagaglio a** ~ hand luggage; **alla** ~ *(persona)* easy-going; **con i soldi alla** ~ cash in hand; **con i fatti alla** ~ with his (o her etc) facts at the ready;

a ~ a ~ **che, man** ~ **che** *(mentre)* as; **man** ~ *(gradualmente)* little by little, gradually.

(**c**) *(locuzioni verbali):* **andare contro** ~ *(Aut)* to go against the (stream of) traffic; **ho le** ~**i legate** *(fig)* my hands are tied; **avere le** ~**i bucate** to spend money like water; **avere** ~**i di fata** to have a light touch; **aver le** ~**i in pasta** to be in the know; **avere qc per le** ~**i** *(progetto, lavoro)* to have sth in hand; **alzare le** ~**i su qn** to take one's hand to sb; **dare una** ~ **a qn** to lend sb a hand; **gli dai una** ~ **e si prende il braccio** give him an inch and he'll take a mile; **fare man bassa di qc** to run off with sth; **forzare la** ~ to go too far; **è il caso di una** ~ **lava l'altra** it's a case of a joint effort; **mettere la** ~ **sul fuoco per qc** *(fig)* to stake one's life on sth; **mettere le** ~**i su qc** to lay one's hands on sth; **mettere** ~ **a qc** to have a hand in sth; **mettere le** ~**i avanti** to safeguard o.s.; **mettere le** ~**i addosso a qn** to lay hands on sb; *(molestare: donna)* to touch sb up; **mettersi una** ~ **sulla coscienza** to examine one's conscience; **ci preso la** ~ I've got the hang of it; **starsene con le** ~**i in** ~ to twiddle one's thumbs; **venire alle** ~**i** to come to blows.

(**d**) *(strato)* coat; **dare una** ~ **di vernice a qc** to give sth a coat of paint.

manodopera [mano'dɔpera] *sf* labour, manpower.

manomesso, a [mano'messo] *pp di* **manomettere**.

manometro [ma'nɔmetro] *sm* manometer.

manomettere [mano'mettere] *vt (alterare: documento, prove)* to tamper with; *(aprire indebitamente: lettera)* to open (without permission); *(: serratura)* to force; *(: cassaforte)* to break open.

manomissione [manomis'sjone] *sf (di prove etc)* tampering; *(di lettera)* opening.

manomorta [mano'mɔrta] *sf (Dir)* mortmain.

manopola [ma'nɔpola] *sf* (**a**) *(di armatura)* gauntlet; *(guanto)* mitten, mitt. (**b**) *(impugnatura)* hand-grip; *(di televisore, radio)* knob.

manoscritto, a [manos'kritto] 1 *ag* handwritten. 2 *sm* manuscript.

manovalanza [manova'lantsa] *sf* unskilled workers.

manovale [mano'vale] *sm* unskilled worker, labourer.

manovella [mano'vɛlla] *sf (gen)* handle; *(Tecn)* crank; ~ **d'avviamento** starting handle; **dare il primo giro di** ~ *(Cine)* to begin filming.

manovra [ma'nɔvra] *sf* (**a**) *(Mil, fig)* manoeuvre; ~ **di accerchiamento** encircling movement; **grandi** ~**e** army manoeuvres o exercises; ~**e di corridoio** palace intrigues. (**b**) *(Ferr)* shunting; *(Aut etc)*: **fare** ~ to manoeuvre; **fare** ~ **di parcheggio** to park. (**c**): ~**e** *pl (Naut)* rigging *sg*.

manovrabile [mano'vrabile] *ag (anche fig)* easy to manipulate.

manovrare [mano'vrare] 1 *vt (veicolo)* to manoeuvre; *(macchina)* to operate, work; *(fig: persona)* to manipulate. 2 *vi* to manoeuvre.

manovratore, trice [manovra'tore] *sm/f (di tram)* driver; *(di treno)* shunter.

manrovescio [manro'vɛʃʃo] *sm* slap *(with back of hand)*.

mansarda [man'sarda] *sf* attic.

mansione [man'sjone] *sf* duty, job; **non rientra nelle mie** ~**i** it's not part of my job; **svolgere** o **esplicare le proprie** ~**i** to carry out one's duties.

mansueto, a [mansu'ɛto] *ag (animale)* tame; *(persona)* gentle, docile.

mansuetudine [mansue'tudine] *sf (vedi ag)* tameness; gentleness, docility.

mantella [man'tɛlla] *sf* cloak.

mantellina [mantel'lina] *sf* cape.

mantello [man'tɛllo] *sm* (**a**) *(cappotto)* cloak; *(Zool)* coat; *(fig: di neve)* blanket, mantle. (**b**) *(Tecn: rivestimento)* casing, shell.

mantenere [mante'nere] 1 *vt* (**a**) *(gen)* to keep; *(decisione)* to stand by, abide by; *(promessa)* to keep, maintain; *(tradizione)* to maintain, uphold; *(edificio)* to maintain; ~ **l'equilibrio/la linea** to keep one's balance/one's figure; ~ **qn in vita** to keep sb alive; ~ **i prezzi bassi** to hold prices down; ~ **i contatti con qn** to keep in touch with sb; ~ **l'ordine** *(Polizia)* to maintain law and order; *(in assemblea etc)* to keep order. (**b**) *(famiglia)* to maintain, support. 2: ~**rsi** *vr* (**a**) *(conservarsi)*: ~**rsi calmo/giovane** to stay o keep o remain calm/young; **il tempo si mantiene bello** the weather is holding; ~**rsi bene** *(persona)* to look good for one's age; **questo formaggio si mantiene per poco** this cheese doesn't keep for long. (**b**) *(sostentarsi)* to keep o.s.; **si mantiene da anni** he has looked after himself financially for years; **lavora per** ~**rsi** he works for a living; **si mantiene facendo l'idraulico** he earns his living as a plumber.

mantenimento [manteni'mento] *sm (gen)* maintenance; **provvedere al** ~ **della famiglia** to provide for one's family.

mantenuta [mante'nuta] *sf (peg)* kept woman.

mantenuto [mante'nuto] *sm* gigolo.

mantice [man'titʃe] *sm* (**a**) bellows *pl*; **sbuffare** o **soffiare come un** ~ to puff like a grampus. (**b**) *(di carrozza, automobile)* hood.

mantide ['mantide] *sf*: ~ **religiosa** praying mantis.

manto ['manto] *sm (cappotto)* cloak; *(fig: di neve)* blanket, mantle; ~ **stradale** road surface.

mantovana [manto'vana] *sf (di tenda)* pelmet.

manuale [manu'ale] 1 *ag (lavoro)* manual. 2 *sm (libro)* manual, handbook; **un caso da** ~ *(fig)* a textbook example.

manualmente [manual'mente] *av* manually, by hand.

manubrio [ma'nubrjo] *sm (gen)* handle; *(di bicicletta)* handlebars *pl*; *(attrezzo da ginnastica)* dumbbell.

manufatto [manu'fatto] *sm* manufactured article; ~**i** manufactured goods.

manutenzione [manuten'tsjone] *sf (gen)* maintenance; *(di edifici, locali)* upkeep; *(d'impianti)* maintenance, servicing.

manzo ['mandzo] *sm (animale)* steer; *(carne)* beef.

maomettano, a [maomet'tano] *ag, sm/f* Mohammedan.

mappa ['mappa] *sf* map.

mappamondo [mappa'mondo] *sm (globo)* globe; *(carta)* map of the world.

marachella [mara'kɛlla] *sf* mischievous trick.

marameo [mara'mɛo]: **fare** ~ **a** to thumb one's nose at.

maraschino [maras'kino] *sm* maraschino.

marasma [ma'razma] *sm (fig)* decline; **un** ~ **generale** *(fig: disordine)* chaos.

maratona [mara'tona] *sf (Sport, fig)* marathon.

maratoneta, i [marato'nɛta] *sm (Sport)* marathon runner.

marca, che ['marka] *sf* (**a**) *(Comm: di sigarette, caffè)* brand; *(: di scarpe, vestito etc)* make; *(: marchio di fabbrica)* trademark; **prodotti di (gran)** ~ high-class products. (**b**) *(bollo)* stamp; ~ **da bollo** official stamp. (**c**) *(scontrino)* ticket, check.

marcare [mar'kare] *vt* (**a**) *(segnare)* to mark; *(animale a fuoco)* to brand; *(biancheria)* to label; ~ **visita** *(Mil)* to report sick. (**b**) *(accentuare)* to stress. (c) (*Sport: goal*) to score; (: *avversario*) to mark.

marcato, a [mar'kato] *ag (lineamenti, accento etc)* pronounced.

marchesa [mar'keza] *sf* marchioness.

marchese [mar'keze] *sm* marquis, marquess.

marchetta [mar'ketta] *sf* (a) *(Amm)* ≈ National Insurance Stamp. (b) *(fam)*: **fare ~e** *(prostituirsi)* to be on the game.

marchiano, a [mar'kjano] *ag (errore)* glaring, gross.

marchiare [mar'kjare] *vt (bestiame)* to mark; **~ a fuoco** to brand; **~ a vita** *(fig)* to brand for life.

marchigiano, a [marki'dʒano] *ag of (o from)* the Marches.

marchio ['markjo] *sm* (a) *(Comm)* mark; **~ di fabbrica** trademark; **~ depositato** registered trademark. (b) *(per bestiame: segno)* brand; (: *strumento*) branding iron; **ha il ~ di** *o* **del bugiardo** *(fig)* he has been branded a liar.

marcia, ce ['martʃa] *sf* (a) *(gen, Mil, Mus)* march; **~ forzata** forced march; **~ funebre** funeral march; **essere in ~ verso** to be marching towards. (b): **mettersi in ~** to get moving; **mettere in ~** *(veicolo)* to start (up); *(apparecchio)* to set going. (c) *(Aut)* gear; **cambiare ~** to change gear; **fare ~ indietro** to reverse; *(fig)* to backpedal, backtrack. (d) *(Sport)* walking.

marciapiede [martʃa'pjɛde] *sm (di strada)* pavement; *(Ferr)* platform.

marciare [mar'tʃare] *vi* (a) *(Mil)* to march; *(Sport)* to walk; **far ~ dritto qn** *(fig)* to make sb toe the line. (b) *(veicolo)* to go, travel; *(fig: funzionare)* to run; **il treno marcia a 70 km/h** the train goes *o* travels at 70 km/h; **la ditta marcia bene** the firm is running smoothly.

marciatore, trice [martʃa'tore] *sm/f (Sport)* walker.

marcio, a, ci ce ['martʃo] **1** *ag (uovo, legno)* rotten; *(foglie)* rotting; *(frutta)* rotten, bad; *(ferita, piaga)* festering; *(fig: corrotto)* corrupt; **avere torto ~** to be utterly wrong. **2** *sm (di frutto etc)* rotten *o* bad part; **c'è del ~ in questa storia** *(fig)* there's something fishy about this business.

marcire [mar'tʃire] **1** *vi (aus essere) (cibi, frutta)* to go rotten *o* bad; *(cadaveri, legno, foglie)* to rot; *(ferita)* to fester; **~ in prigione** *(fig)* to rot in prison. **2** *vt* to rot.

marcita [mar'tʃita] *sf* water meadow.

marciume [mar'tʃume] *sm* (a) *(parte guasta: di cibi etc)* rotten part, bad part. (b) *(di radice, pianta)* rot; *(fig: corruzione)* rottenness, corruption.

marco, chi ['marko] *sm (moneta)* mark.

marconiterapia [markonitera'pia] *sf (Med)* diathermy.

mare ['mare] *sm* **1** (a̧) *(gen)* sea; **~ interno** inland sea; **~ calmo/mosso/grosso** calm/rough/heavy sea; **per ~** by sea; **sul ~** *(barca)* on the sea; *(villaggio, località)* by *o* beside the sea; **una vacanza al ~** a holiday beside *o* by the sea, a seaside holiday; **andare al ~** to go to the seaside; **mettere in ~ una barca** to get a boat out; **mettersi in ~** to put out to sea; **c'è un po' di ~ oggi** there's a bit of a swell today; **uomo in ~!** man overboard!; **di ~** *(brezza, acqua, uccelli, pesce)* sea *attr*. (b) *(gran quantità: di lettere, lamentele etc)* flood; (: *di gente, problemi, difficoltà*) host; (: *di lavoro*) pile; **ho un ~ di cose da fare** I've got stacks of things to do; **essere in un ~ di guai** to be up to one's neck in problems; **essere in un ~ di lacrime** to be in floods of tears.

2: M~ del Nord/Mediterraneo North/Mediterranean Sea; **Mar Caspio/Morto/Rosso**

Caspian/Dead/Red Sea; **M~ della Tranquillità** *(sulla luna)* Sea of Tranquillity.

marea [ma'rɛa] *sf* (a) tide; **alta/bassa ~** high/low tide; **~ calante/montante** ebb/flood *o* rising tide. (b) *(fig)* flood; **una ~ di gente affollava la piazza** the square was flooded with people.

mareggiata [mared'dʒata] *sf* sea storm.

maremma [ma'remma] *sf (Geog)* maremma.

maremmano, a [marem'mano] *ag* (a) *(zona, macchia)* swampy. (b) *(della Maremma)* of *(o* from*)* the Maremma.

maremoto [mare'mɔto] *sm* seaquake.

maresciallo [mareʃ'ʃallo] *sm (Mil)* marshal; (: *sottufficiale*) warrant officer.

marezzato, a [mared'dzato] *ag (seta etc)* watered, moiré; *(legno)* veined; *(carta)* marbled.

margarina [marga'rina] *sf* margarine.

margherita [marge'rita] *sf* (a) *(Bot)* oxeye daisy, marguerite. (b) *(di stampante)* daisy wheel.

margheritina [margeri'tina] *sf (Bot)* daisy.

marginale [mardʒi'nale] *ag* marginal.

marginare [mardʒi'nare] *vt (foglio, pagina)* to set the margins for.

margine ['mardʒine] **1** *sm (gen)* margin; *(di bosco, via)* edge; **al ~ di** on the edge of; **ai ~i della società** on the fringes of society; **note in o a ~** notes in the margin; **avere un buon ~ di tempo/denaro** to have plenty of time/money. **2: ~ di errore** margin of error; **~ di guadagno o di utile** profit margin; **~ operativo** operating margin; **~ sul prezzo** mark-up; **~ di sicurezza** safety margin.

marijuana [mæri'waːnə] *sf* marijuana.

marina [ma'rina] *sf* (a) *(costa)* coast; *(quadro)* seascape. (b) *(Mil)* navy; **M~ Militare** *(abbr* **M. M.**) ≈ Royal Navy *(abbr* R.N.*) (Brit)*, Navy *(Am)*; **~ mercantile** merchant navy.

marinaio [mari'najo] *sm* sailor; **~ di acqua dolce** *(peg)* landlubber.

marinare [mari'nare] *vt* (a) *(Culin)* to marinade; **aringhe marinate** soused *o* pickled herring. (b) *(disertare)*: **~ la scuola** to play truant.

marinaresco, a, schi, sche [marina'resko] *ag* sailor's *attr*.

marinaro, a [mari'naro] *ag (tradizione, popolo)* seafaring; **borgo ~** district where fishing folk live; **alla ~a** *(vestito, cappello)* sailor *attr*; *(Culin)* with seafood.

marino, a [ma'rino] *ag (aria, fondali)* sea *attr*; *(fauna)* marine; *(città, colonia)* seaside *attr*.

mariolo [mari'ɔlo] *sm* rascal.

marionetta [marjo'netta] *sf* puppet, marionette; *(fig: persona debole)* puppet; **teatrino/spettacolo di ~e** puppet theatre/show.

maritare [mari'tare] **1** *vt* to marry off. **2: ~rsi** *vr*: **~rsi (a o con qn)** to get married (to sb), marry (sb).

maritato, a [mari'tato] *ag* married.

marito [ma'rito] *sm* husband; **prendere ~** to get married; **ragazza (in età) da ~** girl of marriageable age.

maritozzo [mari'tɔttso] *sm* type of currant bun.

marittimo, a [ma'rittimo] **1** *ag (gen)* maritime; *(città)* coastal; **linee ~e** shipping lines. **2** *sm* seaman.

marmaglia [mar'maʎʎa] *sf (gente ignobile)* riffraff; *(ragazzacci)* gang of kids.

marmellata [marmel'lata] *sf* jam; *(di agrumi)* marmalade.

marmista, i [mar'mista] *sm (operaio)* marble-cutter; *(artigiano)* marble worker.

marmitta [mar'mitta] *sf* (a) *(recipiente)* (cooking) pot. (b) *(Aut)* silencer. (c) *(Geol)* pothole.

marmittone [marmit'tone] *sm (recluta)* raw recruit, rookie *(Am)*.

marmo ['marmo] *sm* marble; **di** ~ marble *attr*, made of marble; **bianco come il** ~ *(fig)* as white as a sheet; **duro come il** ~ as hard as a brick; **avere un cuore di** ~ to have a heart of stone.

marmocchio [mar'mɔkkjo] *sm (fam)* (tiny) tot, (little) kid.

marmoreo, a [mar'mɔreo] *ag (di marmo)* marble *attr*.

marmotta [mar'mɔtta] *sf (Zool)* marmot; *(fig: persona lenta)* slowcoach.

marocchino, a [marok'kino] **1** *ag, sm/f* Moroccan; *(peg) derogatory term used by Northern Italians to describe Southern Italians.* **2** *sm (cuoio)* morocco (leather).

Marocco [ma'rɔkko] *sm* Morocco.

maroso [ma'roso] *sm* breaker.

marpione, a [mar'pjone] *sm/f (fam)* cunning old devil.

marra ['marra] *sf (Agr)* hoe; *(Naut)* fluke.

marrano [mar'rano] *sm (scherz)* boor.

marrone [mar'rone] **1** *ag inv* brown. **2** *sm* **(a)** *(colore)* brown. **(b)** *(Bot)* chestnut; ~**i canditi** marrons glacés.

marsala [mar'sala] *sm inv (vino)* Marsala.

marsc' [marʃ] *escl:* **(avanti)** ~**!** quick march!

marsina [mar'sina] *sf* tails *pl*, tail coat.

marsupiale [marsu'pjale] *sm* marsupial.

marsupio [mar'supjo] *sm (Zool)* pouch, marsupium *(T)*.

Marte ['marte] *sm (Astron, Mitologia)* Mars.

martedì [marte'di] *sm inv* Tuesday; **oggi è** ~ **3 aprile** (the date) today is Tuesday 3rd April; ~ **stavo male** I wasn't well on Tuesday; **ogni** ~, **tutti i** ~ every Tuesday, on Tuesdays; **di** ~ on Tuesdays; **un** ~ **sì un** ~ **no** every other Tuesday; ~ **scorso/prossimo** last/next Tuesday; **il** ~ **successivo, il** ~ **dopo** the following Tuesday; **2 settimane fa, di** ~ a fortnight ago on Tuesday; ~ **fra una settimana/quindici giorni** a week/fortnight on Tuesday, Tuesday week/fortnight; ~ **mattina/pomeriggio/sera** Tuesday morning/afternoon/evening; **il film del** ~ the Tuesday film; **il giornale di** ~ Tuesday's newspaper; ~ **grasso** Shrove Tuesday.

martellamento [martella'mento] *sm* hammering, pounding; **mi fu difficile far fronte al** ~ **delle sue domande** I could hardly withstand his constant questioning.

martellante [martel'lante] *ag (fig: dolore)* throbbing.

martellare [martel'lare] **1** *vt (gen)* to hammer; ~ **qn di domande** to fire questions at sb. **2** *vi (pulsare: tempie)* to throb; *(: cuore)* to thump.

martellata [martel'lata] *sf:* **dare una** ~ **a qn/qc** to hit sb/sth with a hammer.

martelletto [martel'letto] *sm (di pianoforte)* hammer; *(di macchina da scrivere)* typebar; *(di giudice, nelle vendite all'asta)* gavel; *(Med)* percussion hammer.

martellio [martel'lio] *sm* hammering.

martello [mar'tɛllo] *sm (gen, Sport, Anat)* hammer; **battere col** ~ to beat with a hammer, hammer; **piantare un chiodo col** ~ to hammer in a nail; ~ **pneumatico** pneumatic drill; **lancio del** ~ *(Sport)* hammer throw; **suonare a** ~ *(fig: campane)* to sound the tocsin.

martinetto [marti'netto] *sm (Tecn)* jack.

martingala [martin'gala] *sf (di giacca)* half-belt; *(di cavallo)* martingale.

martin pescatore [mar'tin peska'tore] *sm* kingfisher.

martire ['martire] *sm/f (anche fig)* martyr; **fare il** *o* **atteggiarsi a** ~ to play the martyr.

martirio [mar'tirjo] *sm* martyrdom; *(fig)* agony, torture; **vivere con quell'uomo è un** ~ living with that man is sheer torture.

martirizzare [martirid'dzare] *vt (Rel)* to martyr; *(persona, animali)* to torture.

martora ['martora] *sf* marten.

martoriare [marto'rjare] *vt* to torment, torture.

marxismo [mark'sizmo] *sm* Marxism.

marxista, i, e [mark'sista] *ag, sm/f* Marxist.

marzapane [martsa'pane] *sm* marzipan.

marziale [mar'tsjale] *ag* martial.

marziano, a [mar'tsjano] **1** *ag* Martian. **2** *sm/f* Martian; *(fam: persona non inserita)* loner.

marzo [martso] *sm* March; *per uso vedi* **luglio**.

marzolino, a [martso'lino] *ag* March *attr*.

mas [mas] *sm inv* motor torpedo boat.

mascalzonata [maskaltso'nata] *sf* dirty trick.

mascalzone [maskal'tsone] *sm (anche scherz)* rascal, scoundrel.

mascara [mas'kara] *sm inv* mascara.

mascarpone [maskar'pone] *sm soft cream cheese often used in desserts.*

mascella [maʃ'ʃɛlla] *sf (Anat)* jaw.

mascellare [maʃʃel'lare] *ag* jaw *attr*.

maschera ['maskera] **1** *sf* **(a)** *(gen)* mask; *(costume)* fancy dress; **in** ~ *(mascherato)* masked; **mettersi** *o* **vestirsi in** ~ to dress up; **ballo in** ~ fancy-dress ball; **gettare la** ~ *(fig)* to reveal o.s.; **giù la** ~**!** *(fig)* stop acting! **(b)** *(Cine)* usher/usherette. **(c)** *(Teatro)* stock character. **2:** ~ **antigas/subacquea** gas/diving mask; ~ **di bellezza** face pack.

mascherare [maske'rare] **1** *vt (viso)* to mask; *(entrata, fig: sentimenti etc)* to hide, conceal. **2:** ~**rsi** *vr:* ~**rsi (da)** *(travestirsi)* to disguise o.s. (as); *(per un ballo)* to dress up (as).

mascherata [maske'rata] *sf (anche fig)* masquerade.

mascherina [maske'rina] *sf* **(a)** *(piccola maschera)* mask; *(di animale)* patch; *(di scarpe)* toe-cap. **(b)** *(Aut)* radiator grille.

mascherone [maske'rone] *sm (grotesque)* mask.

maschietto [mas'kjetto] *sm* little boy.

maschile [mas'kile] **1** *sm (gen, Gram)* masculine; *(sesso, popolazione)* male; *(abiti)* men's; *(per ragazzi: scuola)* boys'. **2** *sm (Gram)* masculine.

maschio, a ['maskjo] **1** *ag (animale, figlio)* male; *(comportamento, atteggiamento)* male, masculine; *(volto, voce)* masculine. **2** *sm (gen, Tecn, Bio, Zool)* male; *(uomo)* man; *(ragazzo)* boy; *(figlio)* son; **hanno un** ~ **e una femmina** they have a boy and a girl; **il** ~ **del leone** the male lion; ~ **della vite** screw tap.

mascolinità [maskolini'ta] *sf* masculinity.

mascolino, a [masko'lino] *ag* masculine.

mascotte [mas'kɔt] *sf inv* mascot.

masochismo [mazo'kizmo] *sm* masochism.

masochista, i, e [mazo'kista] **1** *ag* masochistic. **2** *sm/f* masochist.

massa ['massa] *sf* **(a)** *(volume, Fis)* mass; ~ **d'acqua** body of water; **cerebrale** brain, cerebral mass. **(b)** *(Sociol):* **la** ~, **le** ~**e** the masses; **la** ~ **dei cittadini** the majority of the townspeople; **manifestazione/cultura di** ~ mass demonstration/culture. **(c):** **una** ~ **di** *(oggetti)* heaps of, loads of; *(persone)* crowds of; **siete una** ~ **di idioti!** *(fam)* you're a bunch of idiots! **(d): produzione in** ~ mass production; **produrre in** ~ to mass-produce; **esecuzioni in** ~ mass executions; **arrivare in** ~ to arrive en masse. **(e)** *(Elettr)* earth; **collegare** *o* **mettere a** ~ to earth.

massacrante [massa'krante] *ag* exhausting, gruelling.

massacrare [massa'krare] *vt (uccidere)* to massacre, slaughter; *(: animali)* to slaughter; *(fig: avversario)* to make mincemeat of; *(: brano musicale)* to murder.

massacro [mas'sakro] *sm* massacre, slaughter; *(fig)* disaster; **fare un ~** to cause a massacre; **all'esame i professori hanno fatto un ~** the lecturers were failing people right, left and centre at the exam.

massaggiare [massad'dʒare] *vt* to massage; **farsi ~** to have a massage.

massaggiatore, trice [massaddʒa'tore] *sm/f* masseur/masseuse.

massaggio [mas'saddʒo] *sm* massage.

massaia [mas'saja] *sf* housewife.

massaio [mas'sajo] *sm (di podere)* estate manager.

massello [mas'sɛllo] *sm (di oro etc)* ingot.

masseria [masse'ria] *sf* large farm.

masserizie [masse'rittsje] *sfpl* (household) furnishings.

massicciata [massit'tʃata] *sf (Ferr)* ballast; *(di strada)* roadbed.

massiccio, a, ci, ce [mas'sittʃo] **1** *ag* **(a)** *(mobile, edificio)* massive, solid; *(corporatura)* stout. **(b):** **oro/legno ~** solid gold/wood. **(c)** *(fig: attacco)* massive; *(: dose)* heavy, massive. **2** *sm (Geog)* massif.

massima ['massima] *sf* **(a)** *(motto)* maxim. **(b)** *(Meteor)* maximum temperature. **(c):** **in linea di ~** generally speaking.

massimo, a ['massimo] **1** *ag (superl di grande) (gen)* greatest; *(temperatura, livello, prezzo)* maximum, highest; *(importanza, cura)* utmost, greatest; **è della ~a importanza che tu ci sia** it is of the utmost importance *o* it is vital that you be there; **è il ~ poeta del secolo** he is the greatest poet of the century; **erano presenti le ~e autorità** all the most important dignitaries were there; **al ~ grado** to the highest degree; **stupido al ~ grado** stupid beyond belief; **ha la mia ~a stima/il mio ~ rispetto** he has my highest regard/my greatest respect; **ottenere il ~ effetto con la minima spesa** to get the best result for the least cost; **in ~a parte** for the most part, mainly; **arrivare entro il tempo ~** to arrive within the time limit; **il tempo ~ concesso** the maximum time allowed; **la velocità ~a che questa macchina può raggiungere è...** the top *o* maximum speed of this car is...; **la velocità ~a permessa nei centri abitati** the speed limit in built-up areas.

2 *sm (gen)* maximum; **è il ~ che io possa fare** it's the most I can do; **è il ~ della stupidità** *(persona)* he's stupidity personified; *(gesto)* it's the height of stupidity; **è il ~!** *(colmo)* that's the limit *o* end!; **costerà al ~ 5 sterline** it'll cost 5 pounds at (the) most; **lavorare al ~** to work flat out; **sfruttare qc al ~** to make full use of sth; **al ~ finiamo lunedì** if the worst comes to the worst we will finish on Monday; **arriverò al ~ alle 5** I'll arrive at 5 at the latest; **ottenere il ~ dei voti** *(Scol)* to get full marks; *(in votazione)* to be accepted unanimously; **il ~ della pena** *(Dir)* the maximum penalty.

massivo, a [mas'sivo] *ag (intervento)* en masse; *(emigrazione)* mass; *(emorragia)* massive.

masso ['masso] *sm* rock, boulder; **dormire come un ~** to sleep like a log.

massone [mas'sone] *sm* freemason.

massoneria [massone'ria] *sf* freemasonry.

massonico, a, ci, che [mas'sɔniko] *ag* masonic.

mastello [mas'tɛllo] *sm* tub.

masticare [masti'kare] *vt* to chew, masticate *(T)*; *(tabacco, gomma)* to chew; **~ le parole** to mumble; **~ una scusa** to mumble an excuse; **mastico un po' di inglese** I have a smattering of English.

mastice ['mastitʃe] *sm (resina)* mastic; *(per vetri)* putty.

mastino [mas'tino] *sm* mastiff.

mastodonte [masto'donte] *sm* mastodon; **è un ~** *(fig)* he's a hulking great brute.

mastodontico, a, ci, che [masto'dɔntiko] *ag (fig)* gigantic, colossal.

mastro ['mastro] *sm* **(a)** *(persona):* **~ falegname** master carpenter. **(b)** *(Comm):* **(libro) ~** ledger.

masturbare [mastur'bare] *vt*, **~rsi** *vr* to masturbate.

masturbazione [masturbat'tsjone] *sf* masturbation.

matassa [ma'tassa] *sf (gen)* skein, hank; **venire a capo della ~** *(fig)* to unravel the problem; **ingarbugliare** *o* **imbrogliare la ~** to make things more muddled.

matematica [mate'matika] *sf* mathematics *sg*.

matematico, a, ci, che [mate'matiko] **1** *ag* mathematical; **è ~ che ci riesce** he's bound to succeed; **avere la certezza ~ che** to be absolutely certain that. **2** *sm/f* mathematician.

materassino [materas'sino] *sm* mat; **~ gonfiabile** air bed.

materasso [mate'rasso] *sm* mattress; **~ a molle** spring *o* interior-sprung mattress; **~ di gommapiuma** foam mattress.

materia [ma'tɛrja] **1** *sf (gen, Filosofia)* matter; *(Scol, argomento)* subject; *(sostanza)* material, substance; **prima di entrare in ~...** before discussing the matter in hand...; **un esperto in ~** *(di musica etc)* an expert on the subject (of music *etc*); **sono ignorante in ~** I know nothing about it. **2:** **~ cerebrale** cerebral matter; **~ grassa** fat; **~ grigia** *(anche fig)* grey matter; **~e plastiche** plastics; **~e prime** raw materials.

materiale [mate'rjale] **1** *ag (interessi, necessità, danni etc)* material; **non ho avuto il tempo ~ di farlo** I simply haven't had the time to do it; **non ha avuto la possibilità ~ di evitarlo** he just couldn't avoid it. **2** *sm (gen)* material; **di che ~ è fatto?** what is it made of?; **hai il ~ per scrivere?** have you got something to write with?; **~ da costruzione** building materials *pl*; **~ bellico** war materiel; **~ di scarto** waste material; **~ rotabile** rolling stock.

materialismo [materja'lizmo] *sm* materialism.

materialista, i, e [materja'lista] **1** *ag* materialistic. **2** *sm/f* materialist.

materialistico, a, ci, che [materja'listiko] *ag* materialistic.

materializzarsi [materjalid'dzarsi] *vr* to materialize.

materialmente [materjal'mente] *av (fisicamente)* materially; *(economicamente)* financially; **è ~ impossibile farlo** it's a physical impossibility.

maternità [materni'ta] *sf inv* **(a)** *(condizione)* motherhood; **in (congedo di) ~** on maternity leave. **(b)** *(clinica)* maternity hospital; **reparto ~** maternity ward.

materno, a [ma'tɛrno] *ag (gen)* maternal; *(amore, cura etc)* motherly; *(lingua, terra)* mother *attr*; **scuola ~a** nursery school.

matinée [mati'ne] *sf inv (Cine, Teatro)* matinée, afternoon performance.

matita [ma'tita] *sf* pencil; **scrivere a ~** to write in pencil; **disegno a ~** pencil drawing; **~e colorate**

crayons; ~ **per gli occhi** eyeliner (pencil).

matriarcale [matriar'kale] *ag* matriarchal.

matriarcato [matriar'kato] *sm* matriarchy.

matrice [ma'tritʃe] *sf* **(a)** *(Bio, Mat, Tip, Tecn)* matrix; *(per duplicatore)* stencil. **(b)** *(Comm)* counterfoil. **(c)** *(fig: culturale)* background; **l'attentato è di chiara ~ fascista** the fascists are undoubtedly behind this bombing.

matricidio [matri'tʃidjo] *sm* matricide.

matricola [ma'trikola] *sf* **(a)** *(registro)* register. **(b)** *(anche:* **numero di ~)** registration number; *(: Mil)* regimental number; *(: Tecn)* part number. **(c)** *(fig: studente)* freshman, fresher.

matricolato, a [matriko'lato] *ag (ladro, bugiardo etc)* downright *attr*, out-and-out *attr*.

matrigna [ma'triɲɲa] *sf* stepmother.

matrimoniale [matrimo'njale] *ag (gen)* matrimonial; *(rapporto)* marital; *(vita)* married; *(anello)* wedding *attr*; **camera/letto ~** double room/bed; **pubblicazioni ~i** (marriage) banns.

matrimonio [matri'mɔnjo] *sm (unione)* marriage; *(cerimonia)* wedding; **dopo 5 anni di ~** after 5 years of marriage; **~ religioso/civile** religious/ civil wedding; **~ di convenienza** marriage of convenience.

matrona [ma'trɔna] *sf (fig)* matronly woman.

matronale [matro'nale] *ag* matronly.

matta [matta] *sf (Carte)* joker.

mattacchione, a [mattak'kjone] *sm/f* joker.

mattatoio [matta'tojo] *sm* abattoir, slaughterhouse.

mattatore [matta'tore] *sm (di spettacolo, fig)* star turn.

matterello [matte'rɛllo] *sm* rolling pin.

mattina [mat'tina] *sf* morning; **la o alla o di ~** in the morning; **di prima ~, la ~ presto** early in the morning; **la ~ prima/dopo** the previous/following morning; **la ~ prima di...** the morning before...; **dalla ~ alla sera** *(continuamente)* from morning to night; *(improvvisamente: cambiare)* overnight; **alle due di ~** at 2 a.m.

mattinata [matti'nata] *sf* **(a)** morning; **in ~** in the course of the morning; **sarà pronto in ~** it will be ready before noon; **nella ~** in the morning; **nella tarda ~** at the end of the morning; **nella tarda ~ di sabato** late on Saturday morning. **(b)** *(spettacolo)* matinée.

mattiniero, a [matti'njɛro] *ag:* **essere ~** to be an early riser.

mattino [mat'tino] *sm* morning; **di buon ~** early in the morning; **sul far del ~** at daybreak.

matto, a ['matto] **1** *ag* **(a)** *(gen, fig)* mad, crazy; *(Med)* insane; **diventare ~** to go mad; **far diventare ~ qn** to drive sb mad *o* crazy; **andare ~ per qc** to be crazy about sth; **~ da legare** as mad as a hatter; **~ dalla gioia** mad with joy; **avere una voglia ~a di** *(cibo, cioccolato etc)* to have a craving for; **ho una voglia ~a di incontrarlo** I'm dying to meet him, I can't wait to meet him. **(b)** *(falso):* **oro ~** imitation gold. **(c)** *(opaco)* matt. **2** *sm/f* madman/woman, lunatic; **ridere come un ~** to laugh hysterically; **fare il ~** to act the fool; **roba da ~i!** it's unbelievable!; **una gabbia di ~i** *(fig)* a madhouse.

mattoide [mat'tɔide] *ag (fam)* nutty, screwy.

mattone [mat'tone] *sm* **(a)** brick; **casa di ~i** brick house; **color ~, rosso ~** brick red. **(b)** *(fig):* **questo libro/film è un ~** this book/film is really heavy going; **ho un ~ sullo stomaco** I feel as though I've got a lead weight in my stomach.

mattonella [matto'nɛlla] *sf* **(a)** *(piastrella)* tile; **a ~e** tiled. **(b)** *(di carbone etc)* briquette. **(c)** *(del biliardo)* cushion.

mattutino, a [mattu'tino] *ag* morning *attr*.

maturando, a [matu'rando] *sm/f* ≃ G.C.E. A-level candidate.

maturare [matu'rare] **1** *vt (frutta)* to ripen; *(fig: persona)* to mature; **~ una decisione** to come to a decision. **2** *vi (aus essere)*, **~rsi** *vr (frutta)* to ripen; *(fig: persona, Econ: interessi, azioni etc)* to mature.

maturità [maturi'ta] *sf* **(a)** maturity; **giungere a ~** to come to maturity; *(decisione)* to be reached; **se avessi un minimo di ~** if you were a responsible adult. **(b)** *(Scol: anche:* **esame di ~)** ≃ G.C.E. A-levels.

maturo, a [ma'turo] *ag* **(a)** *(frutto)* ripe; **troppo ~** overripe. **(b)** *(persona)* mature; **è un uomo ~** he's middle-aged; **i tempi sono ~i per agire** the time is ripe for action.

matusa [ma'tuza] *sm/f inv (scherz)* old fogey.

mausoleo [mauzo'lɛo] *sm* mausoleum.

max. *abbr* (= **massimo**) max.

maxi... ['maksi] *pref* maxi....

mazza ['mattsa] *sf (bastone)* club; *(Mil)* baton; *(nelle cerimonie)* mace; *(Tecn: martello)* sledgehammer; **~ d'arme** mace; **~ da golf** (golf) club; **~ da baseball/cricket** baseball/cricket bat.

mazzata [mat'tsata] *sf (anche fig)* heavy blow.

mazzetta [mat'tsetta] *sf (di banconote etc)* bundle.

mazziere [mat'tsjere] *sm* **(a)** *(in processioni)* macebearer. **(b)** *(Carte)* dealer.

mazzo ['mattso] *sm* **(a)** *(di fiori, chiavi)* bunch. **(b)** *(di carte da gioco)* pack; **tenere il ~** to be dealer; **fare il ~** *(mescolare)* to shuffle the cards.

me [me] *pron pers* **(a)** *(dopo prep, accentato)* me; **parlavate di ~?** were you talking about me?; **vieni con ~?** are you coming with me?; **dietro di ~** behind me; **lo ha dato a ~, non a te** he gave it to me *o* ME, not to you; **vieni da ~?** are you coming to my place?; **l'ho fatto da ~** I did it (all) by myself; **pensavo tra ~ e ~ che...** I was thinking to myself that...; **se fossi in ~ cosa faresti?** what would you do if you were me? *o* if you were in my position? **(b)** *(nelle comparazioni)* I, me; *(in espressioni esclamative)* me; **è alta come ~** she's as tall as I am *o* as me; **fai come ~** do the same as me, do as I do; **è più giovane di ~** he's younger than I (am) *o* than me; **povero ~!** poor me! **(c)** *vedi* **mi.**

meandro [me'andro] *sm (di fiume)* meander; **si è perso nei ~i del palazzo** he lost his way in the building's maze of corridors; **i ~i del suo pensiero** the twists and turns of his mind.

M.E.C. [mɛk] *sm (abbr di* **Mercato Comune Europeo)** EEC.

mecca ['mekka] *sf (anche fig)* Mecca.

meccanica [mek'kanika] *sf* **(a)** *(scienza)* mechanics *sg*; **~ agraria** agricultural technology. **(b)** *(meccanismo: di orologio, congegno etc)* mechanism; **c'è qualcosa che non va nella ~ di questa macchina** there's something mechanically wrong with this car; **spiegami la ~ dei fatti** *o* **dell'accaduto** tell me how it happened.

meccanicamente [mekkanika'mente] *av* mechanically.

meccanico, a, ci, che [mek'kaniko] **1** *ag (anche fig)* mechanical; **officina ~a** garage. **2** *sm* mechanic.

meccanismo [mekka'nizmo] *sm* mechanism.

meccanizzare [mekkanid'dzare] *vt* to mechanize.

meccanizzazione [mekkaniddzat'tsjone] *sf* mechanization.

meccanografia [mekkanogra'fia] *sf* (mechanical) data processing.

meccanografico, a, ci, che [mekkano'grafiko] *ag:* **centro ~** comptometer department.

mecenate [metʃe'nate] *sm* patron.

mèche [mɛʃ] *sf inv* streak; **farsi le ~ to** have one's hair streaked.

medaglia [me'daʎʎa] *sf* (*gen*) medal; (*distintivo*) badge; **~ d'oro** (*oggetto*) gold medal; (*atleta*) gold medallist; **il rovescio della ~** (*fig*) the other side of the coin.

medaglietta [medaʎ'ʎetta] *sf* (small) medal; (*per cani*) name tag.

medaglione [medaʎ'ʎone] *sm* (a) (*Arte, Culin*) medallion. (b) (*gioiello*) locket.

medesimo, a [me'dezimo] 1 *ag* (a) (*identico, uguale*) same; **mi ha detto le ~e cose** he said the same things to me; **sono della ~a taglia** they are the same size. (b) (*enfatizzato*) very; **arrivò il ~ giorno in cui io dovevo partire** he arrived the very day I was due to leave; **è la stessa ~a cosa** it's the very same thing; **le regole ~e del gioco impongono ciò** the very rules of the game state that. (c): **io ~, tu ~** *etc* I myself, you yourself *etc*; **il presidente ~** the president himself. 2 *pron*: **il(la) ~(a)** the same one.

media ['mɛdja] *sf* (a) (*Mat*) mean; **~ aritmetica/ geometrica** arithmetic/geometric mean. (b) (*valore intermedio*) average; **al di sopra/sotto della ~** above/below average; **in ~** on average; **questa macchina fa in ~ i 120 km/h** this car has an average speed of 120 km/h; **viaggiare ad una ~ di...** to travel at an average speed of...; **riceve in ~ 700.000 lire al mese** he earns 700,000 lire per month on average, he has an average income of 700,000 lire per month; **fu promosso con la ~ del 7** (*Scol*) he passed with an average of 7 out of 10; **ha avuto una ~ molto bassa** (*Scol*) his average marks were very low, he had a very low average mark. (c): **~e** *pl* = **scuola media**.

medianico, a, ci, che [me'djaniko] *ag* (*poteri*) extrasensory.

mediano, a [me'djano] 1 *ag* (*Geom*) median. 2 *sm* (*Calcio*) half-back; **~ di mischia** (*Rugby*) scrum half. 3 *sf* (*Geom*) median.

mediante [me'djante] *prep* (*per mezzo di*) by (means of); (*grazie a*) thanks to.

mediare [me'djare] *vi* (*fare da mediatore*) to mediate, act as mediator.

mediato, a [me'djato] *ag* indirect.

mediatore, trice [medja'tore] *sm/f* (*gen, Pol*) mediator; (*Comm*) middleman, agent; **fare da ~ fra** to mediate between.

mediazione [medjat'tsjone] *sf* (*gen, Pol*) mediation; (*Industria*) arbitration; (*Comm: azione, compenso*) brokerage.

medicamento [medika'mento] *sm* medicament.

medicare [medi'kare] *vt* (*paziente*) to treat; (*ferita*) to dress.

medicato, a [medi'kato] *ag* (*garza, shampoo*) medicated.

medicazione [medikat'tsjone] *sf* (*di ferita*) dressing; **fare una ~ a qn** to dress sb's wounds; **togliere/cambiare la ~** to remove/change the dressings.

medicina [medi'tʃina] *sf* medicine; **~ legale** forensic medicine; **il tempo è la miglior ~** (*fig*) time is a great healer.

medicinale [meditʃi'nale] 1 *ag* medicinal. 2 *sm* medicine, drug.

medico, a, ci, che ['mɛdiko] 1 *ag* (*gen*) medical; (*sostanza, erba*) medicinal; **ricetta ~a** prescription. 2 *sm* (*gen*) doctor; (*di bordo*) ship's doctor; **~ chirurgo** surgeon; **chi è il tuo ~ curante?** who's your doctor?; (*in ospedale*) which doctor is in charge of your case?; **~ fiscale** *doctor who examines patients signed off sick for a lengthy*

period by their private doctor; **~ di famiglia** family doctor; **~ generico** general practitioner, G.P.; **~ legale** forensic scientist.

medievale [medje'vale] *ag* (*anche fig*) medieval.

medio, a ['mɛdjo] *ag* (*gen*) average; (*misura, corporatura*) average, medium; **persona di statura ~a** person of average *o* medium height; (*dito*) **~** (*Anat*) middle finger; **scuola ~a** *first three years of secondary school*.

mediocre [me'djɔkre] *ag* (*gen*) mediocre; (*qualità, stipendio*) poor; (*persona, impiego*) mediocre, second-rate.

mediocrità [medjokri'ta] *sf* (*vedi ag*) mediocrity; poorness.

Medioevo [medjo'ɛvo] *sm* Middle Ages *pl*.

medioleggero [medjoled'dʒero] *sm* welterweight.

mediomassimo [medjo'massimo] *sm* light heavyweight.

meditabondo, a [medita'bondo] *ag* meditative, thoughtful.

meditare [medi'tare] 1 *vt* to ponder over, meditate on; (*progettare*) to plan, think out; **~ di fare qc** to contemplate doing sth. 2 *vi*: **~ (su/intorno a)** to meditate (on/about).

meditativo, a [medita'tivo] *ag* meditative, thoughtful.

meditato, a [medi'tato] *ag* (*gen*) meditated; (*parole*) carefully-weighed; (*vendetta*) premeditated; **ben ~** (*di piano*) well worked-out, neat.

meditazione [meditat'tsjone] *sf* meditation; **dopo lunga ~ si risolse a partire** after much thought he decided to leave.

mediterraneo, a [mediter'raneo] 1 *ag* Mediterranean. 2 *sm*: **il (mare) M~** the Mediterranean (Sea).

medium ['mɛdjum] *sm/f inv* medium.

medusa [me'duza] *sf* (a) (*Zool*) jellyfish. (b) (*Mitologia*): **M~** Medusa.

megafono [me'gafono] *sm* megaphone.

megalomane [mega'lɔmane] *ag, sm/f* megalomaniac.

megalomania [megaloma'nia] *sf* megalomania.

megera [me'dʒɛra] *sf* (*peg: donna*) shrew.

meglio ['mɛʎʎo] (*comp, superl di* **bene**) 1 *av* (a) better; **sto ~** I feel better; **gioca ~ di lui** she plays better than he does; **è cambiato in ~** he has changed for the better, he has improved; **~ non passare per quella strada** it's better not to take that road. (b) (*con senso superlativo*) best; **i ~ allenati** the best trained; **sono le ragazze ~ vestite della scuola** they are the best dressed girls in the school. (c): **~ che mai** better than ever; **~ tardi che mai** better late than never; **faresti ~ ad andartene** you had better leave; **andare di bene in ~**, **andare sempre ~** to get better and better.

2 *ag inv* (a) better; **questa casa è ~ dell'altra** this house is better than the other one; **è ~ che tu te ne vada** it would be better if you left, it would be better for you to go; **è ~ non raccontargli niente** it would be better not to tell him anything *o* if you didn't tell him anything; **ha trovato di ~ da fare** he's got better things to do. (b): **alla ~**, **alla bell'e ~** as best one can, somehow or other.

3 *sm* best; **al ~ delle proprie possibilità** as best one can, to the best of one's ability; **è il ~ che io possa fare** it's the best I can do; **fare il proprio ~** to do one's best; **le cose si sono messe per il ~** things turned out for the best; **essere al ~ della forma** to be in the best of form.

4 *sf*: **avere la ~** to come off best; **avere la ~ su qn** to get the better of sb.

mela ['mela] 1 *sf* apple; **torta di ~e** apple tart; **~e**

cotte stewed apples. **2:** ~ **cotogna** quince; ~ **selvatica** crab apple.

melagrana [mela'grana] *sf* pomegranate.

melanconia [melanko'nia] *etc* = **malinconia** *etc*.

melanina [mela'nina] *sf* melanin.

melanzana [melan'dzana] *sf* aubergine, eggplant.

melassa [me'lassa] *sf (Culin)* treacle, molasses *sg (Am)*.

melenso, a [me'lɛnso] *ag* dull, stupid.

melissa [me'lissa] *sf* (lemon) balm.

mellifluo, a [mel'lifluo] *ag (peg)* sugary, honeyed.

melma ['melma] *sf* mud.

melmoso, a [mel'moso] *ag* muddy.

melo ['melo] *sm* apple tree.

melodia [melo'dia] *sf (Mus)* melody; *(aria)* melody, tune; **cantare una** ~ to hum a tune.

melodico, a, ci, che [me'lɔdiko] *ag* melodic.

melodioso, a [melo'djoso] *ag* melodious, tuneful.

melodramma, i [melo'dramma] *sm (Teatro, peg)* melodrama.

melodrammatico, a, ci, che [melodram'matiko] *ag (Teatro, peg)* melodramatic.

melograno [melo'grano] *sm* pomegranate tree.

melone [me'lone] *sm* (musk) melon.

membrana [mem'brana] *sf* membrane.

membro ['membro] *sm* **(a)** *(Anat: pl(f)* ~**a)** limb; **riposare le stanche** ~**a** to rest one's weary limbs. **(b):** ~ **virile** male sexual organ. **(c)** *(persona, Mat, Gram)* member; **diventare** ~ **di** to become a member of.

memorabile [memo'rabile] *ag* memorable.

memorandum [memo'randum] *sm inv* memorandum.

memore ['mɛmore] *ag:* ~ **di** *(ricordando)* mindful of; *(riconoscente)* grateful for.

memoria [me'mɔrja] *sf* **(a)** *(gen, Inform)* memory; **avere molta** ~ to have a good memory; **non avere** ~ to have a bad memory; **imparare/sapere qc a** ~ to learn/know sth by heart; **frugare nella** ~ to search one's memory; **mi è rimasto impresso nella** ~ it remained impressed in my memory; **se la** ~ **non m'inganna** if my memory serves me well. **(b)** *(ricordo)* recollection, memory; **non resta** ~ **di quel fatto** no one recalls that event; **fatto degno di** ~ memorable deed; **a** ~ **d'uomo** within living memory; *(da tempo immemorabile)* from time immemorial; **in** *o* **alla** ~ **di** in (loving) memory of; **medaglia alla** ~ commemorative medal. **(c):** ~**e** *pl* memoirs.

memoriale [memo'rjale] *sm (raccolta di memorie)* memoirs *pl*.

memorizzare [memorid'dzare] *vt (gen)* to memorize; *(Inform)* to store.

memorizzazione [memoriddzat'tsjone] *sf (vedi vb)* memorization; storage.

menadito [mena'dito]: **a** ~ *av* perfectly, thoroughly; **sapere** *o* **conoscere qc a** ~ to have sth at one's fingertips.

ménage [me'naʒ] *sm inv:* **un** ~ **tranquillo** a happy relationship; ~ **a tre** ménage à trois.

menagramo [mena'gramo] *sm/f inv* jinx, Jonah.

menare [me'nare] **1** *vt* **(a)** *(poet: condurre)* to take, lead; **qual buon vento ti mena?** what brings you here?; ~ **qn per il naso** *(fig)* to lead sb by the nose; ~ **il can per l'aia** *(fig)* to beat about the bush; ~ **qc per le lunghe** to drag sth out; ~ **vanto di qc** to boast about sth. **(b)** *(picchiare):* ~ **qn** to hit *o* beat sb; ~ **le mani** *(essere manesco)* to be free with one's fists; *(picchiarsi)* to come to blows; ~ **calci** to kick. **2** *vi (strada, sentiero):* ~ **a,** ~ **in** to lead to. **3:** ~**rsi** *vr (uso reciproco)* to come to blows.

menata [me'nata] *sf* **(a)** *(bastonata)* beating,

hiding. **(b)** *(fig fam)* lecture; **ma che** ~**e!** what a fuss!

mendace [men'datʃe] *ag (poet)* lying, mendacious.

mendicante [mendi'kante] *sm/f* beggar.

mendicare [mendi'kare] **1** *vt (anche fig)* to beg for; ~ **qc a qn** to beg sb for sth, to beg sth from sb. **2** *vi (anche fig)* to beg.

menefreghismo [menefre'gizmo] *sm (fam)* couldn't-care-less attitude; **il suo è** ~ **bello e buono!** he simply doesn't give a damn!

menefreghista, i, e [menefre'gista] **1** *ag* couldn't-care-less. **2** *sm/f* person who couldn't care less; **quella donna è una** ~ that woman couldn't care less about anything *o* doesn't give a damn about anything.

menestrello [menes'trɛllo] *sm* minstrel.

menhir [me'nir] *sm inv* menhir, standing stone.

meninge [me'nindʒe] *sf (Med)* meninx; **spremersi le** ~**i** to rack one's brains.

meningite [menin'dʒite] *sf (Med)* meningitis.

menisco [me'nisko] *sm (Anat, Mat, Fis)* meniscus.

meno ['meno] **1** *av* **(a)** less; ~ **caro** less expensive, cheaper; **è** ~ **alto di suo fratello/di quel che pensavo** he is not as tall as his brother/as I thought, he is less tall than his brother/than I thought; **dovresti mangiare** ~ you should eat less, you shouldn't eat so much; **ho speso (di)** ~ I spent less; **fumo più mangio** the less I smoke the more I eat; ~ **ne discutiamo, meglio è** the less we talk about it, the better; **ha due anni** ~ **di me** he's two years younger than me; **andare all'università diventa sempre** ~ **facile** going to university is becoming less and less easy; **deve avere non** ~ **di trent'anni** he must be at least thirty; **arrivo tra** ~ **di un'ora** I'll be there in less than *o* in under an hour.

(b) *(con senso superlativo)* least; **è il** ~ **dotato dei miei studenti** he's the least gifted of my pupils; **è quello che leggo** ~ **spesso** it's the one I read the least often.

(c) *(sottrazione: Mat)* minus; **5** ~ **2** 5 minus 2, 5 take away 2; **sono le cinque** ~ **dieci** it's ten to five; **ci sono** ~ **25°** it's minus 25°; **ha preso sette** ~ he got (a) B minus; **mi hai dato 2 carte di** ~ you gave me 2 cards too few; **ho una sterlina in** ~ I am one pound short.

(d) *(fraseologia):* **men che** ~ **gli Inglesi** least of all the English; **quanto** ~ **poteva avvertire** he could at least have let us know; **non mi piace come scrive e tanto** ~ **come parla** I don't like the way he writes and even less the way he talks; **fammi sapere se verrai o** ~ let me know if you are coming or not; **in** ~ **che non si dica** in less than no time, quick as a flash; ~ **male!** good!; ~ **male che sei arrivato** it's a good job that you have come; **non è da** ~ **di lui** she is (every bit) as good as he is; **non voglio essere da** ~ **di lui** I don't want to be outdone by him; **fare a** ~ **di qn/qc** to do *o* manage without sb/sth; **se non c'è zucchero ne faremo a** ~ if there isn't any sugar we'll do without.

2 *ag inv (acqua, lavoro, soldi)* less; *(persone, libri, gente)* fewer; ~ **tempo** less time; ~ **turisti** fewer tourists; ~ **bambini ci sono, meglio è** the fewer children there are, the better; ~ **storie!** less of this messing around!

3 *sm inv* **(a):** **era il** ~ **che ti potesse capitare** *(rimprovero)* you were asking for it; **parlare del più e del** ~ to talk about this and that; **per lo** ~ = **perlomeno**.

(b) *(Mat)* minus.

4 *prep (fuorché, eccetto che):* **ci siamo tutti** ~ **lui** we are all here except (for) him; **tutti** ~ **uno**

all but one; **a ~ che non faccia caldo** unless it is hot; **a ~ di prendere un giorno di ferie** unless I (*o* you *etc*) take a day off.

menomare [meno'mare] *vt* to maim, disable; **restò menomato di una gamba** he was left without the use of one leg.

menomato, a [meno'mato] **1** *ag (persona)* disabled. **2** *sm/f* disabled person.

menomazione [menomat'tsjone] *sf* disablement.

menopausa [meno'pauza] *sf* menopause.

mensa ['mensa] *sf* **(a)** *(locale)* canteen; *(: Mil)* mess; *(: nelle università)* refectory. **(b)** *(fig)* table; **i piaceri della ~** the pleasures of the table.

mensile [men'sile] **1** *ag* monthly. **2** *sm (periodico)* monthly (magazine); *(stipendio)* monthly salary.

mensilità [mensili'ta] *sf inv (stipendio)* monthly salary; **riscuotere due ~ arretrate** to get two months' back pay; **13ª/14ª/15ª ~** once-/twice-/thrice-yearly bonus.

mensilmente [mensil'mente] *av (ogni mese)* every month; *(una volta al mese)* monthly.

mensola ['mensola] *sf (supporto)* bracket; *(ripiano)* shelf; *(Archit)* corbel; **~ del camino** mantelpiece.

menta ['menta] *sf (Bot)* mint; *(caramella)* mint, peppermint; *(bibita)* peppermint cordial; **~ piperita** peppermint; **alla ~, di ~** mint *attr*.

mentale [men'tale] *ag* mental.

mentalità [mentali'ta] *sf inv* mentality.

mentalmente [mental'mente] *av* mentally.

mente ['mente] *sf* **(a)** *(gen, fig)* mind; **~ aperta/lucida** open/clear mind; **~ agile/acuta** quick/sharp brain, agile/sharp mind; **~ malata** sick mind; **malato di ~** mentally ill; **avevo la ~ altrove** my mind was elsewhere.

(b) *(fraseologia)*: **a ~ fredda** objectively; **rivedere qc a ~ fresca** to take another look at sth when one's mind is fresh; **a ~ serena** serenely; **avere in ~ qc/qn** to have sth/sb in mind; **lo ha sempre in ~** she's always thinking of him; **avere in ~ di fare qc** to intend to do sth; **lasciami fare ~ locale** let me think; **fare venire in ~ qc a qn** to remind sb of sth; **mettersi in ~ di fare qc** to make up one's mind to do sth; **mi è scappato di ciò che ti volevo dire** I've forgotten what I was going to say to you; **volevo farlo ma mi è scappato di ~** I meant to do it, but it went out of my head; **cosa ti passa per la ~?** what are you thinking of?; **tenere a ~ qc** to bear sth in mind; **toglitelo dalla ~** forget about it; **mi è tornato in ~ quell'indirizzo** that address has come back to me, I've remembered that address; **mi è venuto in ~ che...** it occurred to me that.... .

mentecatto, a [mente'katto] **1** *ag* half-witted. **2** *sm/f* half-wit, imbecile.

mentina [men'tina] *sf* peppermint.

mentire [men'tire] *vi:* **~ (a qn su qc)** to lie (to sb about sth); **non saper ~** to be a poor liar; **~ spudoratamente** to lie through one's teeth.

mentito, a [men'tito] *ag:* **sotto ~e spoglie** under false pretences.

mentitore, trice [menti'tore] *sm/f* liar.

mento ['mento] *sm* chin; **doppio ~** double chin.

mentolo [men'tɔlo] *sm* menthol.

mentre ['mentre] **1** *cong* **(a)** *(temporale)* while; **è successo ~ ero fuori** it happened while I was out; **l'ho incontrato ~ entravo nel negozio** I met him as I was going into the shop. **(b)** *(avversativo)* whereas, while; **lui è biondo ~ sua sorella è mora** he's blond whereas his sister is dark. **2** *sm:* **in quel ~** at that very moment.

menu [mə'ny] *sm inv* (set) menu; **~ turistico** standard *o* tourists' menu.

menzionare [mentsjo'nare] *vt* to mention.

menzione [men'tsjone] *sf* mention; **fare ~ di** to mention; **degno di ~** worthy of note.

menzogna [men'tsoɲɲa] *sf* lie, falsehood.

menzognero, a [mentsoɲ'ɲero] *ag* false, untrue.

meraviglia [mera'viʎʎa] *sf* **(a)** *(stupore)* amazement, wonder; **non ti nascondo la mia ~** you can imagine my surprise; **con mia (grande) ~** to my amazement; **suscitare gran ~** to cause quite a stir; **mi fa ~ che...** I'm amazed that...; **quest'abito ti sta a ~** you look wonderful in that dress; **tutto va a ~** everything's going perfectly. **(b)** *(persona, cosa)* marvel, wonder; **hai un bimbo che è una ~** what a lovely baby you've got; **le sette ~e del mondo** the seven Wonders of the World.

meravigliare [meraviʎ'ʎare] **1** *vt* to amaze, surprise; **sono rimasto meravigliato** I was amazed *o* astonished; **mi meraviglierebbe se...** I would be surprised if..., it would surprise me if... . **2:** **~rsi** *vr:* **~rsi (di *o* per)** to be amazed (at), be astonished (at); **mi meraviglio di te!** I'm surprised at you!; **non c'è da ~rsi** it's not surprising.

meraviglioso, a [meraviʎ'ʎoso] *ag* wonderful, marvellous.

mercante [mer'kante] *sm* dealer, trader; *(ant)* merchant; **~ d'arte** art dealer; **~ di cavalli** horse dealer; **~ di schiavi** slave trader.

mercanteggiare [merkanted'dʒare] **1** *vi* to bargain, haggle; **~ sul prezzo** to haggle over the price. **2** *vt (peg: onore, voto)* to sell.

mercantile [merkan'tile] **1** *ag (gen)* mercantile; *(marina, nave)* merchant *attr.* **2** *sm (nave)* merchantman.

mercantilismo [merkanti'lizmo] *sm* mercantilism.

mercanzia [merkan'tsia] *sf* merchandise, goods *pl.*

mercatino [merka'tino] *sm* **(a)** *(rionale)* local street market. **(b)** *(Econ)* unofficial stock market.

mercato [mer'kato] **1** *sm* **(a)** *(luogo)* market; **giorno di ~** market day; **~ ortofrutticolo/del pesce** fruit/fish market. **(b)** *(Econ, Fin)* market; **mettere *o* lanciare qc sul ~** to launch sth on the market; **a buon ~** *(ag)* cheap; *(av)* cheaply; **di ~** *(economia, prezzo, ricerche)* market *attr*; **~ interno *o* nazionale** domestic market; **~ al rialzo/al ribasso** sellers'/buyers' market; **~ dei cambi/capitali/valori** exchange/capital/stock market. **2:** **il M~ Comune (Europeo)** the (European) Common Market; **~ nero** black market.

merce ['mɛrtʃe] *sf* goods *pl*, merchandise *(no pl).*

mercé [mer'tʃe] *sf* mercy; **essere alla ~ di qn** to be at sb's mercy.

mercenario, a [mertʃe'narjo] *ag, sm* mercenary.

merceologia [mertʃeolo'dʒia] *sf* study *o* knowledge of commodities.

merceria [mertʃe'ria] *sf (bottega, articoli)* haberdashery.

merciaio, a [mer'tʃajo] *sm/f* haberdasher.

mercoledì [merkole'di] *sm inv* Wednesday; **~ delle Ceneri** Ash Wednesday; *per uso vedi* **martedì**.

Mercurio [mer'kurjo] *sm (Astron, Mitologia)* Mercury.

mercurio [mer'kurjo] *sm* mercury.

merda ['merda] *sf (fam!)* shit(!).

merdoso, a [mer'doso] *ag (fam!)* shitty(!).

merenda [me'rɛnda] *sf* afternoon snack; **far ~** to have an afternoon snack.

meridiana [meri'djana] *sf* sundial.

meridiano, a [meri'djano] **1** *ag (di mezzogiorno)* midday *attr*, noonday *attr.* **2** *sm (Geog: anche:* **~ terrestre**) meridian.

meridionale [meridjo'nale] **1** *ag (gen)* southern; *(dell'Italia)* Southern Italian. **2** *sm/f (gen)* Southerner; *(dell'Italia)* Southern Italian.

meridione [meri'djone] *sm*: **il M~** the South; *(dell'Italia)* the South of Italy, Southern Italy.

meringa, ghe [me'ringa] *sf* meringue.

meritare [meri'tare] **1** *vt* **(a)** *(premio, stima)* to deserve, merit; **(si) merita un premio/un ceffone** he deserves a prize/to be slapped; **si è meritato la stima di tutti** he earned everybody's respect; **è una persona che merita** he deserves our respect *(o affection etc)*. **(b)** *(richiedere)*: **~ attenzione/considerazione** to require *o* need attention/consideration. **(c)** *(valere)* to be worth; **questo pranzo non merita il prezzo** this meal's not worth the money. **2** *vb impers (valere la pena)*: **merita andare** it is worth going; **non merita neanche parlarne** it is not worth talking about; **per quel che merita** for what it's worth.

meritevole [meri'tevole] *ag*: **~ (di)** *(di lode, biasimo)* worthy (of).

merito ['merito] *sm* **(a)** *(gen)* merit; *(valore)* worth; **dare a qn il ~ di qc/di aver fatto qc** to give sb credit for sth/for doing sth; **è ~ mio se tu hai avuto quel lavoro** it's thanks to me that you got that job; **Dio ve ne renda ~**! may God reward you!; **finire a pari ~** to finish joint first *(o second etc)*; **le due squadre hanno finito a pari ~** the two teams tied; **medaglia al ~** *(Mil)* medal for bravery. **(b)** *(argomento)*: **entrare nel ~ di una questione** to go into a matter; **non so niente in ~** I don't know anything about it; **in ~ a ciò di cui si è parlato** with reference to what was discussed.

meritorio, a [meri'tɔrjo] *ag* praiseworthy.

merlatura [mɛrla'tura] *sf (Archit)* battlements *pl*.

merlettaia [merlet'taja] *sf* lacemaker.

merletto [mer'letto] *sm* lace.

merlo ['mɛrlo] *sm* **(a)** *(Zool)* blackbird. **(b)** *(Archit)* battlement.

merluzzo [mer'luttso] *sm* cod.

mero, a ['mɛro] *ag* mere, sheer; **per ~ caso** by mere *o* sheer chance.

mescere ['meʃʃere] *vt* to pour (out).

meschinità [meskini'ta] *sf (grettezza)* meanness, pettiness; *(spilorceria)* stinginess; **è stata una ~** it was a mean *o* petty trick.

meschino, a [mes'kino] **1** *ag (infelice)* wretched; *(avaro)* mean; *(: gretto)* narrow-minded, mean, petty; *(scarso: guadagno)* meagre; **fare una figura ~a** to cut a poor figure. **2** *sm/f (poveraccio)* wretch; **non fare il ~** *(gretto)* don't be so petty.

mescita ['meʃʃita] *sf* wine shop.

mesciuto, a [meʃ'ʃuto] *pp di* **mescere**.

mescolanza [mesko'lantsa] *sf (gen)* mixture; *(di ingredienti)* blend, mixture; **una ~ di gente/di idee** a mix of people/ideas.

mescolare [mesko'lare] **1** *vt (gen, Culin)* to mix; *(col cucchiaio)* to stir; *(vini, colori)* to blend; *(mettere in disordine: fogli, schede)* to mix up, muddle up; *(carte)* to shuffle. **2**: **~rsi** *vr (gen, Culin)* to mix; *(vini, colori)* to blend; *(fogli, schede)* to get mixed up; **~rsi alla folla** to mingle with the crowd.

mescolata [mesko'lata] *sf*: **dare una ~ a** *(Culin)* to stir; *(Carte)* to shuffle.

mese ['mese] *sm* month; **fra un ~** in a month('s time); **un ~ di vacanza** a month's holiday; **un ~ di sciopero** a month-long strike; **il ~ scorso** last month; **il corrente ~** this month; **guadagna un milione al ~** she earns a million lira a *o* per month; **tre ~i d'affitto** three months' rent; **un bambino di sei ~i** a six-month-old baby.

messa[1] ['messa] *sf (Rel)* mass; **andare a *o* alla ~** to go to mass.

messa[2] ['messa] *sf (il mettere)*: **~ in opera** installation; **~ a fuoco** focusing; **~ in moto** starting-up; **~ in orbita** launching; **~ in piega** *(Acconciatura)* set; **~ in posizione** installation; **~ a punto** *(Tecn)* adjustment; *(Aut)* tuning; *(di progetto)* finalization; **~ in scena** *(Teatro)* production; **~ a terra** earthing.

messaggerie [messaddʒe'rie] *sfpl (ditta: di distribuzione)* distributors; *(: di trasporto)* freight company.

messaggero, a [messad'dʒero] *sm/f* messenger.

messaggio [mes'saddʒo] *sm* message.

messale [mes'sale] *sm (Rel)* missal.

messe ['messe] *sf* harvest.

messia [mes'sia] *sm inv* messiah; **il M~** the Messiah.

messianico, a, ci, che [messi'aniko] *ag* Messianic.

messicano, a [messi'kano] *ag, sm/f* Mexican.

Messico ['messiko] *sm* Mexico.

messinscena [messin'ʃena] *sf inv (Teatro: anche:* **messa in scena)** production; *(fig)* performance; **è tutta una ~** it's all an act.

messo[1] ['messo] *sm* messenger.

messo[2], **a** ['messo] **1** *pp di* **mettere**. **2** *ag*: **essere ben/mal ~** *(economicamente)* to be well-/badly-off; *(di salute)* to be in good/bad health.

mestierante [mestje'rante] *sm/f (peg)* money-grubber; *(: scrittore)* hack.

mestiere [mes'tjɛre] *sm (gen: lavoro)* job; *(: manuale)* trade; *(: artigianale)* craft; *(: intellettuale)* profession; *(fig: abilità nel lavoro)* skill, technique; **di ~** by *o* to trade; **fa il ~ di calzolaio** he is a shoemaker; **imparare un ~** to learn a trade; **essere del ~** to be in the trade; *(fig)* to be an expert; **essere padrone del ~** to know one's job inside out.

mesto, a ['mesto] *ag* sad, melancholy.

mestolo ['mestolo] *sm* ladle.

mestruale [mestru'ale] *ag* menstrual.

mestruazione [mestruat'tsjone] *sf* menstruation; **avere le ~i** to have one's period.

mestruo ['mestruo] *sm (Anat)* menstrual fluid.

meta ['meta] *sf (a) (destinazione)* destination; *(fig: scopo)* aim, goal; **vagare senza ~** to wander aimlessly. **(b)** *(Rugby)* try.

metà [me'ta] *sf inv* **(a)** half; **dividere qc a ~** to divide sth in half *o* into two halves, halve sth; **facciamo a ~** let's go halves; **dammene la ~** give me half (of it); **ho impiegato la ~ del tempo** it only took me half the time; **siamo arrivati a ~ del concerto** we arrived halfway through the concert; **dire le cose a ~** to leave some things unsaid; **fare le cose a ~** to leave things half-done; **la mia dolce ~** *(fam scherz)* my better half; **a ~ prezzo** at half price, half-price; **a ~ strada** halfway, at the halfway mark. **(b)** *(punto di mezzo)* middle; **tagliare una pagina per ~** to cut a page down the middle; **a ~ settimana** mid-week; **verso la ~ del mese** halfway through the month, towards the middle of the month.

metabolismo [metabo'lizmo] *sm* metabolism.

metafisica [meta'fizika] *sf* metaphysics *sg*.

metafisico, a, ci, che [meta'fiziko] *ag* metaphysical.

metafora [me'tafora] *sf* metaphor; **parlare per ~e** to speak metaphorically; **fuor di ~** without beating about the bush.

metaforico, a, ci, che [meta'fɔriko] *ag* metaphorical.

metallico, a, ci, che [me'talliko] *ag (simile al metallo)* metallic; *(di metallo)* metal *attr*.

metallizzato, a [metallid'dzato] *ag (verniciatura)* metallic.

metallo [me'tallo] *sm* metal; **di** ~ metal *attr.*

metallurgia [metallur'dʒia] *sf* metallurgy.

metallurgico, a, ci, che [metal'lurdʒiko] **1** *ag* metallurgical; **l'industria** ~**a** the iron and steel industry. **2** *sm* metal-worker.

metalmeccanico, a, ci, che [metalmek'kaniko] **1** *ag* engineering *attr.* **2** *sm* engineering worker.

metamorfico, a, ci, che [meta'mɔrfiko] *ag* metamorphic.

metamorfosi [meta'mɔrfozi] *sf inv* metamorphosis.

metano [me'tano] *sm* methane.

meteora [me'tɛora] *sf* meteor; **quell'attore è passato come una** ~ that actor's success was short-lived.

meteorico, a, ci, che [mete'ɔriko] *ag* meteoric.

meteorite [meteo'rite] *sm* meteorite.

meteorologia [meteorolo'dʒia] *sf* meteorology.

meteorologico, a, ci, che [meteoro'lɔdʒiko] *ag (fenomeno)* meteorological; *(previsione, stazione, carta)* weather *attr.*

meteorologo, a, ghi, ghe [meteo'rɔlogo] *sm/f* meteorologist.

meticcio, a, ci, ce [me'tittʃo] *sm/f* half-caste, half-breed.

meticoloso, a [metiko'loso] *ag* meticulous.

metilico, a, ci, che [me'tiliko] *ag* methyl *attr*; **alcol** ~ methyl alcohol.

metodicità [metoditʃi'ta] *sf* methodicalness.

metodico, a, ci, che [me'tɔdiko] *ag* methodical.

metodismo [meto'dismo] *sm (Rel)* Methodism.

metodista, i, e [meto'dista] *ag, sm/f (Rel)* Methodist.

metodo ['mɛtodo] *sm* method; **fare qc con/senza** ~ to do sth methodically/unmethodically; **aver il proprio** ~ **per fare qc** to have one's own way *o* method of doing sth.

metodologia [metodolo'dʒia] *sf* methodology.

metraggio [me'traddʒo] *sm* **(a)** *(sartoria)* length. **(b)** *(Cine)* footage; **lungo** ~ feature film; **corto** ~ short film.

metratura [metra'tura] *sf* length.

metrico, a, ci, che ['mɛtriko] *ag* metric; *(Poesia)* metrical; **il sistema** ~ **decimale** the metric system.

metro ['mɛtro] *sm (gen)* metre; *(strumento: a nastro)* tape measure; *(: asta)* (metre) rule; ~ **cubo/quadrato** cubic/square metre; **i cento** ~**i** *(Sport)* the hundred metres (race).

metrò [me'trɔ] *sm inv* underground, subway *(Am).*

metronomo [me'trɔnomo] *sm inv* metronome.

metronotte [metro'nɔtte] *sm inv* night security guard.

metropoli [me'trɔpoli] *sf inv* metropolis.

metropolitana [metropoli'tana] *sf (anche:* **ferrovia** ~) underground, subway *(Am).*

metropolitano, a [metropoli'tano] *ag* metropolitan.

mettere ['mɛttere] **1** *vt* **(a)** *(porre)* to put; **dove hai messo la mia penna?** where did you put my pen?; **guarda dove metti i piedi** be careful where you step; **gli ha messo una mano sulla spalla** he put *o* laid a hand on his shoulder; ~ **qc diritto** to put *o* set sth straight; ~ **un bambino a letto** to put a child to bed; ~ **un annuncio sul giornale** to place an advert in the paper; ~ **il lavoro al di sopra di tutto** to put work before all else; **quando si mette una cosa in testa...** when he gets an idea into his head...; ~ **qn sulla strada giusta** *(fig)* to set sb right.

(b) *(infondere):* ~ **fame/allegria/malinconia a**

qn to make sb (feel) hungry/happy/sad.

(c) *(anche:* ~**rsi:** *abito: indossare)* to put on; *(: portare)* to wear; **non metto più quelle scarpe** I've stopped wearing those shoes; **mettigli il cappello** put his hat on (for him); **non so cosa mettermi** I don't know what to wear *o* what to put on; **ma che cosa ti sei messo?** what on earth have you got on?

(d) *(installare: telefono, gas, finestre)* to put in; *(acqua)* to lay on.

(e) *(sveglia, allarme)* to set; ~ **la sicura alla porta** *(Aut)* to lock the door.

(f): ~ **che** *(supporre):* **mettiamo che...** let's suppose *o* say that... .

(g): metterci: metterci molta cura/molto tempo to take a lot of care/a lot of time; **ci ho messo 3 ore per venire** it's taken me 3 hours to get here; **mettercela tutta** to do one's best.

(h) *(fraseologia):* ~ **a confronto** to compare; ~ **in conto** *(somma etc)* to put on account; ~ **qn contro qn** *(fig)* to turn sb against sb; ~ **dentro qn** *(fam: imprigionare)* to put sb inside; ~ **insieme** *(gen)* to put together; *(organizzare: spettacolo, gruppo)* to organize, get together; *(soldi)* to save; ~ **in luce** *(problemi, errori)* to stress, highlight; ~ **qn a sedere** to sit sb down; ~ **sotto** *(sopraffare)* to get the better of; ~ **su il caffè** to put the coffee on; ~ **su casa** to set up house; ~ **su un negozio** to start a shop; ~ **su pancia** to develop a paunch; ~ **su peso** to put on weight; ~ **a tacere qn/qc** to keep sb/sth quiet; ~ **via** to put away.

2: ~**rsi** *vr* **(a)** *(persona)* to put *o.s.*; *(oggetto)* to go; **non metterti là** *(seduto)* don't sit there; *(in piedi)* don't stand there; ~**rsi a sedere** to sit down; ~**rsi a letto** to go to bed; *(malato)* to take to one's bed; **dove si mette il caffè?** where does the coffee go?

(b) *(vestirsi):* ~**rsi in costume** to put on one's swimming things; **ti dispiace se mi metto in maniche di camicia?** do you mind if I take off my jacket?

(c) *(incominciare):* ~**rsi a piangere/ridere** to start crying/laughing, to start *o* begin to cry/laugh; ~**rsi a bere** to take to drink; ~**rsi al lavoro** to set to work; ~**rsi sotto** to get down to things.

(d) *(in gruppo):* ~**rsi in società** to set up in business; **si sono messi insieme** *(coppia)* they've started going out together; **ci si sono messi in due** the two of them joined forces.

(e) *(prendere un andamento):* **si mette al bello** *(tempo)* the weather's turning fine; ~**rsi bene/male** *(faccenda)* to turn out well/badly; **vediamo come si mettono le cose** let's see how things go.

mezza ['meddza] *sf (mezzogiorno e mezzo)* half-past twelve.

mezzadria [meddza'dria] *sf (Agr)* sharecropping.

mezzadro [med'dzadro] *sm (Agr)* sharecropper.

mezzala [med'dzala] *sf (Calcio)* inside forward.

mezzaluna [meddza'luna] *sf, pl* **mezzelune** half-moon; *(dell'islamismo)* crescent; *(coltello)* (semicircular) chopping knife.

mezzanino [meddza'nino] *sm* mezzanine (floor).

mezzano, a [med'dzano] **1** *ag (medio)* average, medium; *(figlio)* middle *attr*; *(vela)* mizzen *attr*. **2** *sm/f (intermedio)* go-between; *(ruffiano)* procurer. **3** *sf (Naut):* **albero di** ~**a** mizzen mast.

mezzanotte [meddza'nɔtte] *sf* midnight.

mezz'asta [med'dzasta] *sf:* **bandiera a** ~ flag (flying) at half-mast.

mezzeria [meddze'ria] *sf (di strada)* centre line.

mezzo¹ ['mɛddzo] *sm* **(a)** *(strumento)* means *etc*; *(metodo)* means, way; ~**i di trasporto/di produzione** means of transport/production; **per** ~ **di**

by means of, through; **a ~ corriere** by carrier; **cercherò di ottenere il posto con qualsiasi ~** I'll try to get the job by whatever means; **non c'è ~ di fermarlo** there's no way of stopping him; **ci siamo arrangiati con ~i di fortuna** we sorted things out by makeshift means; **~i di comunicazione di massa** mass media *pl*; **~i pubblici** public transport.

(b): **~i** *pl (finanziari)* means; **è una persona che ha molti ~i** he has a large income, he's very well off; **farcela con i propri ~i** to manage on one's own; **fare una vita al di sopra dei propri ~i** to live beyond one's means.

(c) *(Fis)* medium.

mezzo², **a** ['mɛddzo] **1** *ag* **(a)** half; **~a bottiglia di vino** half a bottle of wine; **una ~a bottiglia di vino** a half-bottle of wine; **una ~a dozzina di uova** half a dozen eggs; **ha lasciato ~ panino** he left half of his sandwich; **c'era ~a città al concerto** half the town was at the concert; **mi ha fatto una ~a promessa** he half-promised to me; **aver una ~a idea di fare qc** to have half a mind to do sth; **è venuto ~ mondo** just about everybody was there; **è stato un ~ scandalo** it almost caused a scandal; **me l'ha detto a ~a voce** he said it to me in an undertone; **non mi piacciono le ~e misure** *(fig)* I don't like half measures; **mezz'ora = mezzora**.

(b) *(medio)*: **di ~a età** middle-aged; **un soprabito di ~a stagione** a spring (*o* autumn) coat.

2 *av* half; **~ pieno/vuoto** *etc* half full/empty *etc*.

3 *sm* **(a)** *(metà)* half; **un kilo e ~** a kilo and a half, one and a half kilos; **è l'una e ~** it's half past one; **una volta e ~ più grande** one and a half times bigger.

(b) *(parte centrale)* middle; **nel ~ della piazza** in the middle of the square; **la porta di ~** the middle door; **in ~ a** in the middle of; *(folla etc)* in the midst of; **nel bel ~ (di)** right in the middle (of).

(c) *(fraseologia)*: **esserci di ~** *(ostacolo)* to be in the way; **quando ci sono di ~ i numeri non ci capisco più niente** when something involves numbers I get completely lost; **non voglio andarci di ~** I don't want to suffer for it; **mettersi di ~** to interfere; **non mettermi in ~!** don't drag me into it!; **è meglio non porre tempo in ~** it is better to act swiftly; **togliere di ~** *(persona, cosa)* to get rid of; *(fam: uccidere)* to bump off; **togliersi di ~** to get out of the way; **il giusto ~** the happy medium; **non c'è una via di ~** there's no middle course.

mezzodì [meddzo'di] *sm inv* midday, noon.

mezzofondista, **i**, **e** [meddzofon'dista] *sm/f* middle-distance runner.

mezzofondo [meddzo'fondo] *sm* middle-distance running.

mezzogiorno [meddzo'dʒorno] *sm* **(a)** *(ora)* midday, noon; **a ~** at 12 (o'clock) *o* midday *o* noon; **a ~ e mezzo** at half past twelve. **(b)** *(Geog)* south; **il ~ d'Italia** the South of Italy, Southern Italy.

mezzora [mɛd'dzora] *sf (anche:* **mezz'ora)** half-anhour; **ti aspetto una ~** I'll wait for you for half-an-hour; **la prima ~** the first half-hour.

mezzosoprano [meddzoso'prano] *sm, pl* **~i** *o* **mezzi soprani** mezzosoprano.

mezzuccio [med'dzuttʃo] *sm* mean trick.

mi¹ [mi] *pron pers (dav lo, la, li, le, ne diventa* **me) (a)** *(ogg diretto)* me; **~ aiuti?** will you help me? **(b)** *(complemento di termine)* (to) me; **~ dai il libro?** will you give the book to me?, will you give me the book?; **~ compri il libro?** will you buy me the

book?, will you buy the book for me?; **me ne ha parlato** he spoke to me about it, he told me about it. **(c)** *(riflessivo)* myself; **~ servo da solo** I'll help myself; **~ sono pettinato** I combed my hair.

mi² [mi] *sm (Mus)* E; *(: solfeggiando la scala)* mi.

miagolare [mjago'lare] *vi* to miaow, mew.

miagolio [mjago'lio] *sm* miaowing, mewing.

miao ['mjao] *escl, sm inv* miaow.

miasma, i [mi'azma] *sm* miasma.

mica¹ ['mika] *av*: **non ...** ~ not ... at all; **non ci credo ~!** I don't believe that for a minute!; **non andrei ~ via!** I wouldn't dream of leaving!; **non sono ~ stanco** I'm not at all tired; **~ male!** not bad (at all)!

mica² ['mika] *sf (Chim)* mica.

miccia, ce ['mittʃa] *sf* fuse.

micidiale [mitʃi'djale] *ag (letale)* fatal, deadly; *(fig: musica)* murderous; *(: liquore)* deadly; **fa un caldo ~ oggi** the heat's killing today.

micio, a, ci, cie ['mitʃo] *sm/f* pussy (cat).

micro... ['mikro] *pref* micro... .

microbiologia [mikrobiolo'dʒia] *sf* microbiology.

microbo ['mikrobo] *sm* microbe.

microcosmo [mikro'kozmo] *sm* microcosm.

microfilm [mikro'film] *sm inv* microfilm.

microfono [mi'krofono] *sm* microphone.

micron ['mikron] *sm inv* micron.

microonda [mikro'onda] *sf* microwave.

microorganismo [mikroorga'nizmo] *sm* microorganism.

microscopico, a, ci, che [mikros'kɔpiko] *ag* microscopic.

microscopio [mikros'kɔpjo] *sm* microscope.

microsolco, chi [mikro'solko] *sm (solco)* microgroove; *(disco: a 33 giri)* long-playing record, LP; *(: a 45 giri)* extended-play record, EP.

microspia [mikros'pia] *sf* hidden microphone, *(fam)* bug.

midollo [mi'dollo] *sm, pl* **~a** *(Anat)* marrow; *(Bot)* pith; **~ osseo** bone marrow; **~ spinale** spinal cord; **bagnarsi fino alle ~a** *o* **al ~** to get soaking wet *o* drenched.

mie ['mie], **miei** ['mjei] *vedi* **mio**.

miele ['mjele] *sm* honey; **color ~** honey-coloured.

mietere ['mjetere] *vt (Agr, fig)* to reap, harvest; **l'epidemia ha mietuto molte vittime** the epidemic has claimed many victims.

mietitrebbiatrice [mjetitrebbja'tritʃe] *sf* combine harvester.

mietitrice [mjeti'tritʃe] *sf (macchina)* harvester.

mietitura [mjeti'tura] *sf (raccolto)* harvest; *(lavoro)* harvesting; *(tempo)* harvest time.

migliaio [miʎ'ʎajo] *sm, pl* **~a** thousand; **un ~ (di)** about a thousand, a thousand or so; **a ~a** by the thousand, in thousands; **poche ~a di persone** a few thousand people; **centinaia di ~a di persone** hundreds of thousands of people.

miglio¹ ['miʎʎo] *sm, pl(f)* **~a** mile; **~ marino** *o* **nautico** nautical mile; **si vede lontano un ~ che è falso** you can see a mile off that it's a fake.

miglio² ['miʎʎo] *sm (Bot)* millet.

miglioramento [miʎʎora'mento] *sm* improvement.

migliorare [miʎʎo'rare] **1** *vt, vi (aus* **essere)** to improve. **2**: **~rsi** *vr* to improve o.s.

migliore [miʎ'ʎore] *(comp, superl di* **buono) 1** *ag (comparativo)* better; *(superlativo)* best; **~ (di)** better (than); **il ~ dei due** the better of the two; **il ~ della classe** the best in the class; **molto ~** much better; **rendere ~** to make better, improve; **i ~i auguri** best wishes; **la cosa sarebbe di partire subito** the best thing would be to leave immediately. **2** *sm/f*: **il/la ~** the best one.

miglioria [miʎʎo'ria] *sf* improvement; **fare** *o* **apportare delle ~e** to make *o* carry out improvements.

mignolo ['miɲnolo] *sm (di mano)* little finger, pinkie; *(di piede)* little toe.

mignon [mi'ɲɔ̃] *ag inv:* **bottiglia ~** miniature (bottle); **pasticceria ~** petit fours *pl.*

migrare [mi'grare] *vi (aus* **essere)** to migrate.

migratore, trice [migra'tore] **1** *ag* migratory. **2** *sm/f* migrant.

migratorio, a [migra'tɔrjo] *ag* migratory.

migrazione [migrat'tsjone] *sf* migration.

mila ['mila] *in combinazione con* **due, tre** *etc vedi* **mille.**

milanese [mila'nese] **1** *ag* Milanese; **cotoletta alla ~** Wiener schnitzel; **risotto alla ~** *risotto with saffron.* **2** *sm/f* person from Milan; **i ~i** the Milanese.

Milano [mi'lano] *sf* Milan.

miliardario, a [miljar'darjo] *ag, sm/f* millionaire, billionaire *(Am).*

miliardo [mi'ljardo] *sm* thousand million, billion *(Am);* **un ~ di lire** a thousand million lire.

miliare [mi'ljare] *ag:* **pietra ~** *(anche fig)* milestone.

milieu [mi'ljø] *sm inv* milieu.

milionario, a [miljo'narjo] *ag, sm/f* millionaire.

milione [mi'ljone] *sm* million; **un ~ di lire** a million lire.

milionesimo, a [miljo'nɛzimo] *ag, sm/f, sm* millionth.

militante [mili'tante] **1** *ag* militant; **è un critico d'arte ancora ~** he's still an active art critic. **2** *sm/f* militant.

militanza [mili'tantsa] *sf* militancy.

militare[1] [mili'tare] *vi:* **~ in** *(partito, gruppo etc)* to be active in.

militare[2] [mili'tare] **1** *ag* army *attr,* military. **2** *sm* serviceman; **~ di carriera** regular (soldier); **fare il ~** to do one's military service.

militaresco, a, schi, sche [milita'resko] *ag (portamento)* military *attr.*

militarizzare [militarid'dzare] *vt* to militarize.

milite ['milite] *sm (soldato)* soldier; **il M~ Ignoto** the Unknown Soldier *o* Warrior.

militesente [milite'zɛnte] *ag* exempt from military service.

milizia [mi'littsja] *sf* militia.

millantatore, trice [millanta'tore] *sm/f* boaster.

millanteria [millante'ria] *sf (qualità)* boastfulness; **queste sono ~e** that's just boasting.

mille ['mille] **1** *ag inv* a *o* one thousand; **duemila** two thousand; **tremila** three thousand; **milleuno** a *o* one thousand and one; **~ grazie** thanks a lot; **a ~ (a ~)** in their thousands. **2** *sm inv* a *o* one thousand; **nel ~ d.C.** in one thousand A.D.

millefoglie [mille'fɔʎʎe] *sm inv (Culin)* cream *o* vanilla slice.

millenario, a [mille'narjo] **1** *ag* millennial; *(fig: molto vecchio)* ancient; *(: dominazione)* age-old. **2** *sm (anniversario)* thousandth anniversary, millennium.

millennio [mil'lɛnnjo] *sm* millennium.

millepiedi [mille'pjedi] *sm inv* centipede.

millesimo, a [mil'lezimo] *ag, sm* thousandth.

milli... ['milli] *pref* milli... .

milligrammo [milli'grammo] *sm* milligram(me).

millimetro [mil'limetro] *sm* millimetre.

milza ['miltsa] *sf (Anat)* spleen.

mimare [mi'mare] *vt (Teatro)* to mime; *(fig: imitare)* to mimic, take off.

mimesi [mi'mɛzi] *sf* mimesis.

mimetico, a, ci, che [mi'mɛtiko] *ag (arte)* mimetic; **tuta ~a** *(Mil)* camouflage.

mimetismo [mime'tizmo] *sm (Bio, Mil)* camouflage.

mimetizzare [mimetid'dzare] **1** *vt* to camouflage. **2: ~rsi** *vr* to camouflage o.s.

mimica ['mimika] *sf* mime.

mimico, a, ci, che ['mimiko] *ag* miming; **arte ~a** mime.

mimo ['mimo] *sm* **(a)** *(attore, spettacolo)* mime. **(b)** *(Zool)* mocking bird.

mimosa [mi'mosa] *sf* mimosa.

min. *abbr (= minuto; minimo)* min.

mina ['mina] *sf* **(a)** *(galleria, ordigno)* mine. **(b)** *(di matita)* lead.

minaccia, ce [mi'nattʃa] *sf* threat; **avere una ~ di aborto** to have a threatened miscarriage; **è una grave ~ per la nazione** it is a serious threat to the nation; **in segno di ~** as a threat; **sotto la ~ di** under threat of.

minacciare [minat'tʃare] *vt* to threaten; **~ qn di morte** to threaten sb with death; **~ qn con una pistola** to threaten sb with a gun; **gli ho minacciato una punizione tremenda** I threatened him with serious punishment; **lo sciopero minaccia di durare** the strike looks set to continue; **ha minacciato di andarsene** he threatened to leave; **minaccia di piovere** it looks like rain; **minaccia tempesta** there's a storm brewing.

minaccioso, a [minat'tʃoso] *ag* threatening, menacing.

minare [mi'nare] *vt (ponte etc)* to mine; *(fig: salute, reputazione, ordine)* to undermine.

minareto [mina'reto] *sm* minaret.

minatore [mina'tore] *sm* miner.

minatorio, a [mina'tɔrjo] *ag* threatening.

minchione, a [min'kjone] **1** *ag (fam)* idiotic. **2** *sm/f (fam)* idiot.

minchioneria [minkjone'ria] *sf (fam: qualità)* stupidity; *(: azione)* foolish thing.

minerale [mine'rale] **1** *ag* mineral. **2** *sm* mineral; **~ di ferro** iron ore.

mineralogia [mineralo'dʒia] *sf* mineralogy.

mineralogico, a, ci, che [minera'lɔdʒiko] *ag* mineralogical.

minerario, a [mine'rarjo] *ag (delle miniere)* mining; *(dei minerali)* ore *attr.*

minestra [mi'nɛstra] *sf* soup; **~ di verdura** vegetable soup; **'~ e'** *(sul menu)* 'first course'; **è sempre la solita ~** *(fig)* it's always the same old story; **o mangi questa ~ o salti dalla finestra** you can take it or leave it.

minestrina [mines'trina] *sf* broth.

minestrone [mines'trone] *sm (Culin)* minestrone; *(fig)* mix-up, confusion.

mingherlino, a [minger'lino] *ag* thin, skinny.

mini... ['mini] *pref* mini... .

mini ['mini] *sf inv* **(a)** *(Moda)* miniskirt. **(b)** *(Aut)* mini ®.

miniatura [minja'tura] *sf (dipinto)* miniature; *(arte, genere)* miniature painting; **in ~** in miniature.

minibus ['minibus] *sm inv* minibus.

miniera [mi'njɛra] *sf* mine; **~ sotterranea** pit, mine; **~ a cielo aperto** open-cast mine; **~ di carbone** *(gen)* coalmine; *(impresa)* colliery; **una ~ di informazioni** *(fig)* a mine of information.

minigolf [mini'gɔlf] *sm inv* minigolf; *(campo da gioco)* minigolf course.

minigonna [mini'gonna] *sf* miniskirt.

minimizzare [minimid'dzare] *vt* to minimize.

minimo, a ['minimo] **1** *ag (il più piccolo)* least, slightest; *(piccolissimo)* very small, slight; *(il più basso)* lowest, minimum; **non c'è la ~a differenza** there isn't the slightest difference; **la diffe-**

renza è ~a the difference is minimal *o* very small *o* slight; **il prezzo ~ è 10.000 lire** the lowest *o* minimum price is 10,000 lire; **gli effetti collaterali della medicina sono ~i** the medicine's side effects are minimal; **non ne ho la ~a idea** I haven't the slightest idea; **ridurre un problema ai ~i termini** to describe a problem in the simplest terms; ~ **comun denominatore** least *o* lowest common denominator.

2 *sm* **(a)** minimum; **è il ~ che tu possa fare** it's the least you can do; **non ha un ~ di comprensione** he is totally lacking in understanding; **gli hanno dato il ~ della pena** they gave him the minimum sentence; **come ~ avrebbe potuto dirmelo** he could at least have told me; **il ~ indispensabile** the bare minimum. **(b)** *(Aut)*: **girare al ~** to idle; **questo motore ha il ~ basso** this engine keeps cutting out.

minio ['minjo] *sm* red lead.

ministero [minis'tɛro] *sm* **(a)** *(Pol)* ministry, department *(spec Am)*; **M~ degli Interni** Ministry of the Interior, ≃ Home Office *(Brit)*, Department of the Interior *(Am)*; **M~ della Pubblica Istruzione** ≃ Department of Education and Science *(Brit)*. **(b)** *(Dir)*: **Pubblico M~** State Prosecutor. **(c)** *(Rel)* ministry.

ministro [mi'nistro] *sm* **(a)** *(Pol)* minister, secretary *(spec Am)*; **M~ degli Interni** Minister of the Interior, ≃ Home Secretary *(Brit)*, Secretary of the Interior *(Am)*. **(b)** *(Rel)* minister.

minoranza [mino'rantsa] *sf (gen)* minority; *(gruppo)* minority (group); **essere in ~** to be in the minority.

minorato, a [mino'rato] **1** *ag* handicapped. **2** *sm/f* physically handicapped person; ~ **psichico** mentally handicapped person.

minorazione [minorat'tsjone] *sf* handicap.

minore [mi'nore] **1** *ag comp di piccolo* **(a)** less; *(più breve)* shorter; *(meno grave)* lesser; *(numero)* lower; **le spese sono state ~i del previsto** expenses were less *o* lower than expected; **questo è il male ~** this is the lesser evil; **vocabolario in edizione ~** shorter *o* concise edition of a dictionary; **in misura ~** to a lesser extent. **(b)** *(meno importante)* less important; *(di poco rilievo)* minor; **opere ~i** minor works; **di minor pregio** of inferior quality. **(c)** *(più giovane)* younger; **il fratello ~** the younger brother. **(d)** *(Mus)* minor; **do ~** C minor.

2 *ag superl di piccolo (vedi* **1 a, b, c)** least; shortest; lowest; least important; youngest.

3 *sm/f* **(a)** *(d'età: tra due)* younger; *(: tra più di due)* youngest. **(b)** *(minorenne)* minor, person under age; ~ **non accompagnato** unaccompanied minor.

minorenne ·[mino'rɛnne] **1** *ag* under age. **2** *sm/f* minor, person under age.

minorile [mino'rile] *ag* juvenile; **carcere ~** young offenders' institution; **delinquenza ~** juvenile delinquency.

minoritario, a [minori'tarjo] *ag* minority *attr*.

minuetto [minu'etto] *sm (Mus)* minuet.

minuscola [mi'nuskola] *sf (anche:* **lettera ~)** small letter.

minuscolo, a [mi'nuskolo] **1** *ag* **(a)** *(piccolissimo)* tiny, minuscule, minute. **(b)** *(lettera)* small. **2** *sm* small letters; *(Tip)* lower case; **scrivere tutto (in) ~** to write everything in small letters.

minuta [mi'nuta] *sf* rough copy, draft.

minuto¹, a [mi'nuto] *ag* tiny, minute; *(pioggia, sabbia)* fine; *(corporatura)* delicate, fine; *(lavoro, descrizione)* detailed; **spese ~e** minor expenses; **al**

~ retail; **comprare al ~** to buy at retail prices, to buy retail.

minuto² [mi'nuto] *sm (gen, Geom, fig)* minute; *(momento)* moment, minute; **all'ultimo ~** at the (very) last minute *o* moment; **a ~i, da un ~ all'altro** any second *o* minute now; **in un ~** in one minute; *(fig: rapidamente)* in a flash; **tra pochi ~i** in a few minutes (time); **avere i ~i contati** to have very little time.

minuzia [mi'nuttsja] *sf (cura)* meticulousness; *(particolare)* detail; **perdersi in ~e** to waste one's time with trifling details.

minuziosità [minuttsjosi'ta] *sf* meticulousness.

minuzioso, a [minut'tsjoso] *ag (persona, descrizione)* meticulous; *(esame)* minute.

mio, a ['mio], *pl* **miei, mie 1** *ag poss*: **il(la) ~(a)** *etc* my; **il ~ cane** my dog; **~a madre** my mother; **un ~ amico** a friend of mine; **è colpa ~a** it's my fault; **è casa ~a, è la ~a casa** it's my house; **per amor ~** for love of me.

2 *pron poss*: **il(la) ~(a)** *etc* mine, my own; **la sua barca è più lunga della ~a** his boat is longer than mine; **è questo il ~?** is this mine?; **il ~ è stato solo un errore** it was simply an error on my part.

3 *sm* **(a)**: **ho speso del ~** I spent my own money; **vivo del ~** I live on my own income. **(b)**: **i miei** *(genitori, famiglia)* my family; *(amici)* my own people, my side; **lui è dei miei** he is on my side.

4 *sf*: **la ~a** *(opinione)* my view; **è dalla ~a** she is on my side; **sono riuscita a dire la ~a** I managed to say my piece; **anch'io ho avuto le ~e** *(disavventure)* I've had my problems too; **ne ho fatta una delle ~e!** *(sciocchezze)* I've done it again!; **cerco di stare sulle ~e** I try to keep myself to myself.

miope ['miope] **1** *ag* short-sighted, myopic; *(fig)* short-sighted. **2** *sm/f* myopic *o* short-sighted person.

miopia [mio'pia] *sf* short-sightedness, myopia; *(fig)* short-sightedness.

mira ['mira] *sf (anche fig)* aim; **prendere la ~** to take aim; **prendere di ~ qn** to pick on sb; **avere una buona/cattiva ~** to be a good/bad shot.

mirabile [mi'rabile] *ag* admirable, wonderful.

mirabolante [mirabo'lante] *ag* astonishing, amazing.

miracolare [mirako'lare] *vt* to cure *o* heal miraculously.

miracolato, a [mirako'lato] *sm/f* miraculously-cured person.

miracolo [mi'rakolo] *sm (anche fig)* miracle; *(persona)* wonder, prodigy; ~ **economico** economic miracle; **fare ~i** to work *o* perform miracles; *(fig)* to work wonders; **sapere vita, morte e ~i di qn** to know everything there is to know about sb; **per ~** miraculously.

miracoloso, a [mirako'loso] *ag* miraculous, prodigious; **non c'è niente di ~** there's nothing extraordinary about it.

miraggio [mi'raddʒo] *sm (also fig)* mirage.

mirare [mi'rare] **1** *vi*: ~ **(a)** *(anche fig)* to aim (at); **ha sempre mirato a diventare presidente** he has always aimed at becoming president; ~ **al potere** to aspire to power. **2**: ~**rsi** *vr*: ~**rsi allo specchio** to look at o.s. in the mirror.

miriade [mi'riade] *sf* myriad.

mirino [mi'rino] *sm (di arma da fuoco, strumento ottico)* sight; *(Fot)* viewfinder, viewer.

mirra ['mirra] *sf* myrrh.

mirtillo [mir'tillo] *sm* bilberry, whortleberry.

mirto ['mirto] *sm* myrtle.

misantropia [mizantro'pia] *sf* misanthropy.

misantropico, a, ci, che [mizan'trɔpiko] *ag* misanthropic.

misantropo, a [mi'zantropo] **1** *ag* misanthropic. **2** *sm/f* misanthrope, misanthropist.

miscela [miʃ'ʃɛla] *sf (gen)* mixture; *(di caffè, tè, tabacco)* blend; *(per motori)* petrol and oil mixture.

miscelare [miʃʃe'lare] *vt (gen)* to mix; *(caffè, tè, tabacco)* to blend.

miscelatore, trice [miʃʃela'tore] *(vedi vt)* **1** *ag* mixing; blending. **2** *sm* **(a)** *(macchinario, operaio)* mixer; blender. **(b)** *(TV)* mixer.

miscellanea [miʃʃel'lanea] *sf* miscellany.

miscellaneo, a [miʃʃel'laneo] *ag* miscellaneous.

mischia ['miskja] *sf (rissa, zuffa)* scuffle, brawl; *(Rugby)* scrum, scrummage; *(Calcio)* scuffle.

mischiare [mis'kjare] **1** *vt (gen)* to mix; *(caffè, tè)* to blend; *(carte)* to shuffle. **2:** ~**rsi** *vr* **(a)** *(liquidi etc)* to mix, blend. **(b)** *(persone)* to mix, mingle; ~**rsi tra la folla** to mingle with the crowd.

misconoscere [misko'noʃʃere] *vt (qualità, coraggio etc)* to fail to appreciate; **non puoi ~ l'arte moderna solo perché non ti piace Picasso** you can't ignore modern art just because you don't like Picasso.

misconosciuto, a [miskonoʃ'ʃuto] *pp di* **misconoscere.**

miscredente [miskre'dɛnte] **1** *sm/f (Rel)* misbeliever; *(: incredulo)* unbeliever. **2** *ag* misbelieving; unbelieving.

miscuglio [mis'kuʎʎo] *sm (gen)* mixture; *(accozzaglia)* jumble, hotchpotch.

miserabile [mize'rabile] **1** *ag* **(a)** *(pietoso: vita, condizioni)* miserable, wretched, pitiful; *(: persona)* pitiful, wretched. **(b)** *(povero)* poor, destitute; **vivere in condizioni ~i** to live in abject poverty; **una somma ~** a miserable *o* paltry sum of money. **(c)** *(spregevole: azione, persona)* mean, wretched. **2** *sm/f (persona spregevole)* wretch.

miserando, a [mize'rando] *ag* pitiful.

miserevole [mize'revole] *ag* pitiful, wretched, miserable.

miseria [mi'zɛrja] *sf* **(a)** *(povertà)* (extreme) poverty, destitution; **cadere in ~** to become destitute; **ridursi in ~** to be reduced to poverty; **vivere nella ~ più nera** to live in dire poverty; **piangere ~** to plead poverty. **(b)** *(somma):* **comprare qc per una ~** to buy sth for next to nothing *o* for a song; **costare una ~** to cost next to nothing; **lo pagano una ~** they pay him a pittance. **(c):** ~**e** *pl (brutture):* **le ~e del mondo** the wretchedness of this world.

misericordia [mizeri'kɔrdja] *sf* mercy, pity; **avere ~ di qn** to have pity on sb; **~ di Dio** *o* **divina** Divine mercy; **invocare la ~ di qn** to beg sb for mercy; **~! my goodness!**

misericordioso, a [mizerikor'djoso] *ag* merciful.

misero, a ['mizero] *ag* **(a)** *(pietoso: vita, condizioni)* miserable, wretched, pitiful; *(: persona)* pitiful, wretched; **fare una ~a figura** to cut a poor figure. **(b)** *(povero)* poor, poverty-stricken; **una ~a somma** a miserable *o* paltry sum. **(c)** *(spregevole, meschino)* mean, wretched; **ho preso un ~ 22 all'esame** I got a measly 22 in the exam; **è un ~ impiegatuccio** he's a miserable pen-pusher; **una ~a scusa** a lame excuse.

misfatto [mis'fatto] *sm (cattiva azione)* misdeed; *(delitto)* crime.

misoginia [mizodʒi'nia] *sf* misogyny.

misogino, a [mi'zɔdʒino] **1** *ag* misogynous. **2** *sm* misogynist.

miss [mis] *sf inv (in concorso di bellezza)* beauty queen; **M~ Mondo** Miss World.

missaggio [mis'saddʒo] *sm (Cine, TV)* mixing.

missile ['missile] **1** *sm* missile; **~ cruise** *o* **di crociera** cruise missile; **~ terra-aria** land-to-air missile; **~ teleguidato** guided missile. **2** *ag* missile *attr.*

missino, a [mis'sino] *ag, sm/f (Pol)* (member) of the Movimento Sociale Italiano *(Italian neofascist party).*

missionario, a [missjo'narjo] *ag, sm/f* missionary.

missione [mis'sjone] *sf* mission; **essere/partire in ~** to be/leave on a mission.

missiva [mis'siva] *sf* missive.

mister ['mistə] *sm inv (in concorso di bellezza):* **M~ Universo** Mister Universe.

misterioso, a [miste'rjoso] **1** *ag* mysterious. **2** *sm:* **fare il ~** to act mysterious.

mistero [mis'tero] *sm* mystery; **fare ~ di qc** to make a mystery out of sth; **non se ne fa un ~** there's no mystery about it; **quanti ~i!** why all the mystery?

misticismo [misti'tʃizmo] *sm* mysticism.

mistico, a, ci, che ['mistiko] **1** *ag* mystic(al). **2** *sm* mystic.

mistificare [mistifi'kare] *vt* **(a)** *(dato, fatti)* to falsify. **(b)** *(ingannare)* to fool, take in.

mistificatore, trice [mistifika'tore] *sm/f:* **è un(a) ~(trice)** he *(o* she) is distorting the facts.

mistificazione [mistifikat'tsjone] *sf (di fatti)* falsification; *(di persona)* hoaxing.

misto, a ['misto] **1** *ag (tutti i sensi)* mixed; **~ a qc** mixed with sth; **un tessuto in ~ lino** a linen mix; **cane di razza ~a** a mixed breed of dog; **che gente c'era? — beh, una roba ~a** what sort of people were there? — oh, a mixed bag. **2** *sm* mixture.

mistura [mis'tura] *sf (miscuglio)* mixture.

misura [mi'zura] *sf* **(a)** *(Mat)* measure; **unità di ~** unit of measure; **~ di lunghezza/capacità** measure of length/capacity.

(b) *(dimensione)* measurement; *(taglia)* size; **prendere le ~e a qn** to take sb's measurements, measure sb; **prendere le ~e di qc** to measure sth; **di ~ grande/piccola** *(scarpe, abito)* in a large/ small size; **su ~** made to measure.

(c) *(proporzione):* **in ~ di** in accordance with, according to; **i prezzi aumenteranno in ~ del 5%** prices will increase by 5%.

(d) *(provvedimento)* measure, step; **~e di sicurezza/prevenzione** safety/precautionary measures; **ho preso le mie ~e** I've taken the necessary steps.

(e) *(Mus)* time; *(: gruppo di note)* bar.

(f) *(Poesia)* measure, metre.

(g) *(fraseologia):* **nella ~ in cui** inasmuch as, insofar as; **in ugual ~** equally, in the same way; **non ha il senso della ~** he doesn't know when to stop; **passare la ~** to overstep the mark, go too far; **bere senza ~** to drink to excess; **oltre ~** beyond measure, excessively; **in giusta ~** moderately; **vincere di stretta ~** to win by a narrow margin.

misurare [mizu'rare] **1** *vt* **(a)** *(gen)* to measure; *(vista, udito)* to test; *(valore)* to estimate; *(capacità)* to judge; **~ a occhio** to measure roughly, give a rough estimate; **~ a passi una stanza** to pace a room. **(b)** *(fig: limitare: spese, perdite)* to limit; **~ le parole** to weigh one's words. **(c)** *(provare):* **~ o ~rsi qc** *(abito, scarpe, cappotto)* to try sth on. **2** *vi* to measure; **quanto misura questa stanza?** how big is this room?, what are the measurements of this room? **3:** **~rsi** *vr* **(a)** *(contenersi, regolarsi):* **~rsi nel bere** to control one's drinking. **(b)**

(provare le proprie forze): ~**rsi con qn** to compete with sb, pit o.s. against sb.

misurato, a [mizu'rato] *ag (determinato)* measured; *(prudente)* cautious; *(moderato)* moderate.

misuratore [mizura'tore] *sm* **(a)** *(strumento)* gauge. **(b)** *(persona: di terreno)* surveyor.

misurazione [mizurat'tsjone] *sf* measuring, measurement; *(di terreno)* surveying.

misurino [mizu'rino] *sm (recipiente)* measure.

mite ['mite] *ag (tempo, persona)* mild; *(condanna)* lenient; *(animale)* meek.

mitezza [mi'tettsa] *sf (vedi ag)* mildness; leniency; meekness.

mitico, a, ci, che ['mitiko] *ag* mythical.

mitigare [miti'gare] **1** *vt (gen)* to mitigate; *(dolore)* to soothe, relieve; *(sapore)* to sweeten. **2**: ~**rsi** *vr (dolore)* to lessen; *(clima)* to become milder.

mitilo [mi'tilo] *sm* mussel.

mito ['mito] *sm* myth.

mitologia, gie [mitolo'dʒia] *sf* mythology.

mitologico, a, ci, che [mito'lɔdʒiko] *ag* mythological.

mitra[1] ['mitra] *sf (Rel)* mitre.

mitra[2] ['mitra] *sm inv (arma)* sub-machine gun.

mitraglia [mi'traʎʎa] *sf* **(a)** *(tipo di munizione)* grapeshot. **(b)** *(arma)* machine gun.

mitragliare [mitraʎ'ʎare] *vt* to machine gun; ~ **qn di domande** *(fig)* to fire questions at sb, bombard sb with questions.

mitragliatrice [mitraʎʎa'tritʃe] *sf* machine gun.

mitteleuropeo, a [mitteleuro'pɛo] *ag* Central European.

mittente [mit'tɛnte] *sm/f* sender.

mixer ['miksə] *sm inv (per cocktail, Cine)* mixer.

M.M. *abbr di* **Marina Militare.**

mnemonico, a, ci, che [mne'mɔniko] *ag (gen)* mnemonic; *(peg: studio, apprendimento)* mechanical.

mo' [mɔ]: **a ~ di** *prep* like; **a ~ di esempio** by way of example.

mobile ['mɔbile] **1** *ag* **(a)** *(gen)* mobile; *(parte di meccanismo)* moving; *(Rel: festa)* movable; **beni ~i** *(Fin)* movable goods. **(b)** *(sguardo, sorriso)* mobile. **2** *sm* **(a)** *(per arredamento)* piece of furniture; **~i** furniture *sg*; ~ **componibile** piece of sectional furniture. **(b)** *(Fin):* ~**i** *pl* movable goods, movables.

mobilia [mo'bilja] *sf* furniture.

mobiliare [mobi'ljare] *ag (Dir)* personal, movable.

mobiliere [mobi'ljɛre] *sm (fabbricante)* furniture-maker; *(commerciante)* furniture-seller.

mobilificio [mobili'fitʃo] *sm* furniture factory.

mobilio [mo'biljo] *sm* furniture.

mobilità [mobili'ta] *sf (gen)* mobility.

mobilitare [mobili'tare] **1** *vt (Mil, fig)* to mobilize; ~ **l'opinione pubblica** to rouse public opinion. **2**: ~**rsi** *vr:* ~**rsi per fare qc** to get together to do sth.

mobilitazione [mobilitat'tsjone] *sf* mobilization.

moca ['mɔka] **1** *sm inv (tipo di caffè)* mocha coffee. **2** *sf inv (macchina)* mocha coffee pot.

mocassino [mokas'sino] *sm* moccasin.

moccio ['mottʃo] *sm (fam: muco)* snot.

moccioso, a [mot'tʃoso] *sm/f (bambino piccolo)* little kid; *(peg)* snotty-nosed kid.

moccolo ['mɔkkolo] *sm* **(a)** *(di candela)* candle end; **reggere il ~** *(fig)* to play gooseberry. **(b)** *(fam: bestemmia):* **tirare** *o* **mandare un ~** to curse, swear. **(c)** *(fam: moccio)* snot.

moda ['mɔda] *sf (gen)* fashion; *(peg)* craze; **essere alla ~** *(persona)* to be fashionable; **seguire la ~** to follow fashion; **essere di ~, andare di ~** *(abbigliamento, acconciatura etc)* to be fashion-

able, be in fashion; **veste sempre all'ultima ~** she's always dressed in the latest style; **è tornata di ~ la mini** the mini is back in fashion; **non è più di ~, è fuori ~** it's old-fashioned; **è diventato una ~** it has become the fashion; **rivista di ~** fashion magazine.

modale [mo'dale] *ag (Gram)* modal.

modalità [modali'ta] *sf inv (procedura)* formality; ~ **di pagamento** method of payment; **seguire attentamente le ~ d'uso** to follow the instructions carefully.

modanare [moda'nare] *vt (Archit)* to decorate with mouldings.

modanatura [modana'tura] *sf (Archit)* moulding.

modella [mo'dɛlla] *sf* model.

modellare [model'lare] **1** *vt (creta, statua)* to model, mould; ~ **qc su qc** *(fig: opera, stile etc)* to model sth on sth. **2**: ~**rsi** *vr:* ~**rsi su qc** to model o.s. on sth, take sth as a model.

modellino [model'lino] *sm* model.

modellismo [model'lizmo] *sm* model-making.

modellista, i, e [model'lista] *sm/f (di cappelli, abiti)* designer.

modello [mo'dɛllo] **1** *sm* **(a)** *(gen, fig)* model; *(stampo)* mould; **un ~ in cera** a wax model; **ha comprato l'ultimo ~ della FIAT** he's bought the latest FIAT model; **prendere a ~** *(fig)* to take as one's model; ~ **di serie/in scala** production/scale model. **(b)** *(Sartoria)* model, style; *(: forma)* style; **gli ultimi ~i di Armani** the latest Armani models *o* styles. **(c)** *(Amm)* form. **2** *ag inv (madre, marito, fabbrica etc)* model *attr.*

moderare [mode'rare] **1** *vt (gen)* to moderate, curb; ~ **la velocità** to reduce speed; ~ **i termini** to weigh one's words. **2**: ~**rsi** *vr* to restrain o.s.; ~**rsi nel mangiare/nelle spese** to control one's appetite/one's spending.

moderatezza [modera'tettsa] *sf* moderation.

moderato, a [mode'rato] **1** *ag* **(a)** *(gen, Pol)* moderate. **(b)** *(Mus)* moderato. **2** *sm (Pol)* moderate.

moderatore, trice [modera'tore] *sm/f* **(a)** *(in una discussione etc)* moderator; **fare da ~** to act as moderator. **(b)** *(Fis)* moderator.

moderazione [moderat'tsjone] *sf (vedi vb)* moderation; restraint; **bere con ~** to drink in moderation; **usare ~** to show moderation.

modernità [moderni'ta] *sf* modernity.

modernizzare [modernid'dzare] **1** *vt* to bring up to date, modernize. **2**: ~**rsi** *vr* to get up to date.

moderno, a [mo'dɛrno] **1** *ag (gen)* modern; **una mamma ~a** an up-to-date young mother, a modern mum. **2** *sm (stile)* modern style; *(mobili)* modern furniture.

modestia [mo'dɛstja] *sf* modesty; ~ **a parte...** in all modesty..., though I say it myself...; **certo non pecca di ~** he's hardly what you'd call modest.

modesto, a [mo'dɛsto] *ag* modest.

modico, a, ci, che ['mɔdiko] *ag (gen)* low, modest; **prezzi ~ci** low prices.

modifica, che [mo'difika] *sf (a motore)* adjustment; *(ad abito)* alteration; *(a piano)* modification; **fare una ~** to carry out an adjustment *(o* alteration *o* modification); **subire delle ~che** to undergo some modifications.

modificabile [modifi'kabile] *ag* modifiable.

modificare [modifi'kare] **1** *vt* to modify, alter. **2**: ~**rsi** *vr* to alter, change.

modificazione [modifikat'tsjone] *sf (vedi* **modifica)** adjustment; alteration; modification.

modista [mo'dista] *sf* milliner.

modo ['mɔdo] *sm* **(a)** *(maniera)* way, manner; **allo stesso ~** in the same way; **in ~ strano** strangely, in a strange way; **a** *o* **in questo/quel ~** (in) this/

that way; **va fatto in questo** ~ it should be done this way o like this; **in nessun** ~ in no way; **fare a** ~ **proprio** to do as one likes; **lo farò a** ~ **mio** I'll do it my own way; **non è il** ~ **di comportarsi** this is no way to behave; **ha un** ~ **tutto suo di giocare a tennis** he has his own way of playing tennis; **un** ~ **di dire** a turn of phrase, an expression; **per** ~ **di dire** so to speak, as it were; **l'ha perdonata per** ~ **di dire** he's forgiven her in a manner of speaking; **non mi piace il suo** ~ **di fare** I don't like his manner; **non c'è** ~ **(né maniera) di convincerlo** there's no way I'll (o you'll etc) convince him; **c'è** ~ **e** ~ **di farlo** there's a right way and a wrong way of doing it; **aver** ~ **di fare qc** to have the opportunity o chance of doing sth; **trovare il** ~ **di fare qc** to find a way o the means of doing sth; **in** o **ad ogni** ~ anyway; **in qualche** ~ somehow or another; **in un certo qual** ~ in a way, in some ways; **in tutti i** ~**i** at all costs; (comunque sia) anyway; (in ogni caso) in any case; **in** ~ **che** so that; **lo sgriderò in** ~ **che capisca che deve studiare** I'll tell him off in such a way that he understands he's got to study; **dovrò fare in** ~ **che non mi vedano** I'll have to make sure they don't see me; **in** ~ **da so as to**, in such a way as to; **in** ~ **da non disturbarlo** so as not to disturb him; **fate in** ~ **di tornare per le 5** try and be back for 5 o'clock.

(b) (misura, regola): **oltre** ~ extremely; **fare le cose a** ~ to do things properly; **una persona a** ~ a well-mannered person.

(c): ~**i** pl manners; **ha dei** ~**i molto brutti** he has dreadful manners.

(d) (Gram) mood; ~ **congiuntivo/indicativo** subjunctive/indicative mood.

(e) (Mus) mode.

modulare[1] [modu'lare] vt (voce, Fis) to modulate.

modulare[2] [modu'lare] ag (Aer, Tecn) modular.

modulatore [modula'tore] sm (Fis) modulator; ~ **di frequenza/di luce** frequency/light modulator.

modulazione [modulat'tsjone] sf modulation; ~ **di frequenza** (abbr **FM**) frequency modulation (abbr **FM**).

modulo ['modulo] sm (a) (modello) form; ~ **d'iscrizione** enrolment form; ~ **di versamento** deposit slip; **riempire un** ~ to fill in a form. (b) (Archit, Aer) module; ~ **di comando/lunare** command/lunar module. (c) (Mat) modulus.

mogano ['mogano] sm mahogany.

moggio ['moddʒo] sm (unità di misura) bushel.

mogio, a, gi, ge o **gie** ['modʒo] ag down in the dumps, dejected; **se n'è andato** ~ ~ he went off with his tail between his legs.

moglie ['moʎʎe] sf wife; **prendere** ~ to get married, take a wife; **tra** ~ **e marito non mettere il dito** (Proverbio) never interfere between husband and wife.

mohair [mo'ɛr] sm mohair.

moine [mo'ine] sfpl (carezze) endearments; (lusinghe) flattery sg; (smancerie) affectation sg; **fare le** ~ **a qn** to cajole sb; **è una ragazza tutta** ~ she's a very affected girl; **non mi convincerai con le tue** ~ it'll take more than your cajoling to persuade me.

moka ['moka] sf = **moca**.

mola ['mola] sf (di mulino) millstone; (per utensili etc) grindstone.

molare[1] [mo'lare] vt to grind.

molare[2] [mo'lare] ag, sm (dente) molar.

molato, a [mo'lato] ag: **vetro** ~ cut glass.

molatrice [mola'tritʃe] sf grinder.

mole ['mole] sf (gen) massive shape; **una** ~ **di lavoro** masses of work; **una** ~ **di lavoro arretra-**

to a massive backlog of work; è comparso sulla porta in tutta la sua ~ his massive shape appeared at the door.

molecola [mo'lekola] sf molecule.

molecolare [moleko'lare] ag molecular.

molestare [moles'tare] vt to annoy, bother.

molestia [mo'lestja] sf (noia, fastidio) annoyance; (azione molesta): ~**e** trouble sg, bother sg; **recare** ~ **a qn** to annoy o bother sb.

molesto, a [mo'lesto] ag annoying.

molla ['molla] sf (a) (Tecn) spring; (fig: incentivo) motivating force; **materasso a** ~**e** spring mattress; ~ **di orologio** watch spring; **a** ~ (giocattolo) clockwork; **i soldi sono la** ~ **che lo spinge ad agire** he's motivated by money. (b) (per camino): ~**e** pl tongs; **prendere qn con le** ~**e** to treat sb with kid gloves.

mollare [mol'lare] **1** vt (gen) to let go; (far cadere) to drop; ~ **la presa** to let go; ~ **gli ormeggi** (Naut) to cast off; ~ **un pugno a qn** (figfam) to punch sb; ~ **uno schiaffo a qn** (figfam) to slap sb; **ha mollato il suo ragazzo** she's ditched her boyfriend; **ha mollato il pacco qua e se n'è andato** he dumped the parcel here and left. **2** vi (cedere, arrendersi) to give in.

molle ['molle] ag (a) (gen) soft; (muscoli) flabby. (b) (fig: debole) weak, feeble; **essere una pappa** ~ (fig) to be spineless.

molleggiare [molled'dʒare] **1** vt to spring. **2** vi (letto etc) to be springy. **3**: ~**rsi** vr: ~**rsi sulle gambe** (Ginnastica) to do knee-bends; (camminando) to have a spring in one's step.

molleggiato, a [molled'dʒato] ag (letto) sprung; (auto) with good suspension.

molleggio [mol'leddʒo] sm (a) (per veicoli) suspension; (per letti) springs pl. (b) (elasticità) springiness. (c) (Ginnastica) knee-bends pl.

molletta [mol'letta] sf (per capelli) hairgrip; (per panni) clothes peg; ~**e** (per zucchero, ghiaccio) tongs.

mollezza [mol'lettsa] sf (a) (fig: di carattere) weakness. (b): ~**e** pl (agi, comodità) luxury sg.

mollica, che [mol'lika] sf crumb.

molliccio, a, ci, ce [mol'littʃo] ag (a) (terreno, impasto) soggy; (frutta) soft. (b) (floscio: mano) limp; (: muscolo) flabby.

mollusco, schi [mol'lusko] sm (Zool) mollusc.

molo ['molo] sm jetty, pier; **attraccare al** ~ to dock.

molotov ['molotov] sf (anche: **bottiglia** ~) Molotov cocktail.

molteplice [mol'teplitʃe] ag (forma, struttura etc) complex; ~**i** pl (svariati: interessi, attività etc) numerous, various.

molteplicità [molteplitʃi'ta] sf multiplicity.

moltiplicare [moltipli'kare] **1** vt (anche fig) to multiply; ~ **5 per 3** to multiply 5 by 3. **2** vi, ~**rsi** vr (gen) to multiply; (spese, richieste) to increase.

moltiplicatore, trice [moltiplika'tore] sm (Tecn, Fis, Mat) multiplier.

moltiplicazione [moltiplikat'tsjone] sf multiplication.

moltitudine [molti'tudine] sf (a): **una** ~ **di** a multitude of, a vast number of. (b) (poet: folla) multitude.

molto, a ['molto] **1** av (a) a lot, (very) much, a great deal; **non legge** ~ he doesn't read much o a great deal; **ha viaggiato** ~ he has travelled a lot o a great deal; **ti è piaciuto?** — **sì,** ~ did you like it? — yes, very much; **questo libro è** ~ **meglio dell'altro** this book is a lot o much better than the other one; **ci vorranno a dir** ~ **3 giorni** it will take 3 days at the most. (b) (con aggettivi, avverbi) very; *(con participio passato)* (very) much; **gli voglio** ~ **bene** I am very fond of him; **sono** ~ **stanco** I'm very tired; ~ **lodato** highly *o* (very) much praised. **(c)** *(tempo, distanza)*: **non ho** ~ **tempo** I don't have much time; **ci vuole** ~ **(tempo)?** will it take long?; **non la vedo da** ~ **(tempo)** I haven't seen her for a while *o* for a long time; **arriverà fra non** ~ he'll arrive soon; **ne hai ancora per** ~ **(tempo)?** will you be much longer?; **c'è ancora** ~**a strada da fare** there's still a long way to go.

2 *ag (quantità)* a great deal of, a lot of, much; *(numero)* a lot of, many; **c'è** ~**a neve** there's a great deal of *o* a lot of snow; ~**a gente** a lot of people, many people; ~**i libri** a lot of books, many books; **non c'è** ~ **pane** there isn't a lot of bread, there isn't (very) much bread; **non c'era no** ~**i turisti** there weren't many tourists.

3 *pron* much, a lot; ~**i(e)** many, a lot; ~**i pensano che sia giusto** many (people) think it's right; ~**i di noi** many of *o* a lot of us; **c'è pane?** — **sì** ~ is there any bread? — yes, a lot *o* lots *(fam)*.

momentaneamente [momentanea'mente] *av* at the moment, at present.

momentaneo, a [momen'taneo] *ag (gioia, dolore)* momentary, passing; *(assenza, scarsità)* temporary; *(situazione)* present.

momento [mo'mento] *sm* **(a)** *(gen)* moment; **in questo** ~ at the moment, at present; **in questo** ~ **è al telefono** he's on the phone at the moment; **la situazione non è rosea in questo** ~ *o* **al** ~ things don't look too rosy at the moment *o* at present; **da un** ~ **all'altro** any moment now; **il tempo è cambiato da un** ~ **all'altro** the weather changed from one moment to the next; **per il** ~ for the time being; **sul** ~ there and then; **fino a questo** ~ up till now, until now; **in qualunque** ~ at any time; **un** ~ **prego!** just a moment, please!; **proprio in quel** ~ at that very moment, just at that moment; **non sta fermo un** ~ he can't keep still; **posso parlarti un** ~? may I have a word with you?; **dal** ~ **che** since, given that.

(b) *(contingenza)* time; *(occasione)* moment, opportunity; **sono** ~**i difficili, è un** ~ **difficile** it's a difficult period; **aspettare il** ~ **favorevole** to wait for the right moment *o* opportunity; **è successo al** ~ **sbagliato** it happened at the wrong time *o* moment; ~ **culminante** climax; **abbiamo passato** ~**i bellissimi insieme** we had some great times together; **verremo in un altro** ~ we'll come another time; **è l'attore del** ~ he's the actor of the moment; **non è il** ~ **di scherzare** this is no time to joke; **al** ~ **di pagare...** when it came to paying... .

(c): **a** ~**i** *(da un momento all'altro)* any time *o* moment now; *(quasi)* nearly; **arriverà a** ~**i** he should arrive any moment now; **a** ~**i cadevo** I nearly fell.

(d) *(Fis)* moment.

monaca, che ['mɔnaka] *sf (Rel)* nun; **farsi** ~ to become a nun.

monacale [mona'kale] *ag* monastic.

monaco, ci ['mɔnako] *sm* monk.

monarca, chi [mo'narka] *sm* monarch.

monarchia [monar'kia] *sf* monarchy.

monarchico, a, ci, che [mo'narkiko] **1** *ag (stato, autorità)* monarchic; *(partito, fede)* monarchist. **2** *sm/f* monarchist.

monastero [monas'tɛro] *sm (di monaci)* monastery; *(di monache)* convent.

monastico, a, ci, che [mo'nastiko] *ag* monastic.

moncherino [monke'rino] *sm* stump.

monco, a, chi, che ['monko] **1** *ag* maimed, mutilated; ~ **di un braccio** one-armed. **2** *sm/f* maimed *o* mutilated person.

moncone [mon'kone] *sm* stump.

mondanità [mondani'ta] *sf* **(a)** *(frivolezza)* worldliness. **(b)**: ~ *pl (piaceri)* pleasures of the world.

mondano, a [mon'dano] **1** *ag (Rel: terrestre)* worldly, earthly; *(riunione, cronaca, vita)* society *attr*; *(obblighi)* social. **2** *sm/f* society man/woman, socialite.

mondare [mon'dare] *vt (piselli)* to shell; *(frutta, patate)* to peel; *(grano)* to winnow; *(poet: anima)* to cleanse.

mondezzaio [mondet'tsajo] *sm* rubbish dump.

mondiale [mon'djale] *ag (gen)* world *attr*; *(crisi, successo)* world-wide; *(di fama* ~ world famous; **la prima guerra** ~ the First World War; **su scala** ~ on a world-wide scale.

mondo¹, a ['mondo] *ag (verdura)* cleaned; *(frutta, patate)* peeled.

mondo² ['mondo] *sm* **(a)** *(gen, fig)* world; **in tutto il** ~ all over the world, throughout the world; **il migliore del** ~ the best in the world; **nessuno al** ~ no-one in the world; **il** ~ **dell'aldilà** the next life, the after life.

(b) *(fraseologia)*: **ti faccio un** ~ **di auguri, ti auguro un** ~ **di bene** all the best; **ti voglio un** ~ **di bene** I'm terribly fond of you; **gli voglio tutto il bene di questo** ~ I think the world of him; **per niente al** ~, **per nessuna cosa al** ~ not for all the world; **da che** ~ **è** ~ since time *o* the world began; **(sono) cose dell'altro** ~! it's incredible!; **non è poi la fine del** ~ **se non vengo** it isn't the end of the world if I can't make it; **mettere/venire al** ~ to bring/come into the world; **com'è piccolo il** ~! it's a small world!; **saper stare al** ~ to know how to get by in this world; **così va il** ~ that's life; **vivere fuori dal** ~ to be out of touch with the real world; **ma in che** ~ **vivi?** where in the world have you been all this time?; **vive in un** ~ **tutto suo** he lives in a world of his own; **mandare qn all'altro** ~ to kill sb.

monelleria [monelle'ria] *sf* prank, trick; **fare una** ~ to play a trick *o* prank.

monello [mo'nello] *sm (ragazzo di strada)* urchin; *(ragazzaccio)* rascal, scoundrel.

moneta [mo'neta] *sf* **(a)** *(pezzo)* coin; **una** ~ **da 100 lire** a 100 lire coin *o* piece; **ripagare qn della stessa** ~ *(fig)* to pay sb back in his own coin. **(b)** *(denaro)* money; *(spiccioli)* (small) change; **non ho** ~ I have no change; ~ **cartacea** paper money. **(c)** *(valuta)* currency; ~ **legale** legal tender; ~ **corrente** currency; **il marco è** ~ **forte** the mark is a strong currency.

monetario, a [mone'tarjo] *ag* monetary.

mongolfiera [mongol'fjɛra] *sf* hot-air balloon.

mongolismo [mongo'lizmo] *sm (Med)* mongolism.

mongolo, a ['mɔngolo] *ag, sm/f* Mongolian, Mongol.

mongoloide [mongo'lɔide] *ag, sm/f (Med)* mongol.

monile [mo'nile] *sm (collana)* necklace; *(gioiello)* jewel.

monito ['mɔnito] *sm* warning; **che ti serva di** ~! let this be a lesson to you!

monoblocco, chi [mono'blɔkko] *sm (Aut)* cylinder block.

monocolo [mo'nɔkolo] *sm* monocle, eyeglass.

monocolore [monoko'lore] **1** *ag (Pol)*: **governo** ~ one-party government. **2** *sm (Pol)* one-party government.

monocromatico, a, ci, che [monokro'matiko] *ag* monochrome, monochromatic.

monofase [mono'faze] *ag (Elettr)* single-phase.

monogamia [monoga'mia] *sf* monogamy.

monogamo, a [mo'nɔgamo] **1** ag monogamous. **2** sm monogamist.

monografia [monogra'fia] sf monograph.

monogramma, i [mono'gramma] sm monogram.

monolingue [mono'lingwe] **1** ag monolingual. **2** sm (dizionario) monolingual dictionary.

monolito [mo'nɔlito] sm monolith.

monologo, ghi [mo'nɔlogo] sm (Teatro, Psic) monologue; (soliloquio) soliloquy.

monopattino [mono'pattino] sm scooter.

monopolio [mono'pɔljo] sm (Econ, fig) monopoly; ~ **di stato** government monopoly.

monopolizzare [monopolid'dzare] vt (Comm, fig) to monopolize.

monopolizzatore, trice [monopoliddza'tore] **1** ag monopolizing. **2** sm monopolizer.

monopolizzazione [monopoliddzat'tsjone] sf monopolization.

monoposto [mono'posto] ag inv, sm single-seater (attr).

monoscì [monoʃ'ʃi] sm inv water-ski.

monosillabico, a, ci, che [monosil'labiko] ag monosyllabic.

monosillabo, a [mono'sillabo] **1** ag monosyllabic. **2** sm monosyllable; **rispondere a** ~**i** (fig) to answer in monosyllables.

monotonia [monoto'nia] sf monotony, dullness.

monotono, a [mo'nɔtono] ag (gen) monotonous; (vita) humdrum; (lavoro) dull, monotonous.

monovalente [monova'lɛnte] ag (Chim) monovalent.

monsignore [monsiɲ'ɲore] sm **(a)** (titolo ecclesiastico) monsignor. **(b)** (titolo: parlando a arcivescovo, vescovo, duca) Your Grace; (: a principe) Your Highness; (: parlando di terzi) His Grace; His Highness.

monsone [mon'sone] sm monsoon.

monta ['monta] sf (accoppiamento) covering; **stazione di** ~ stud farm.

montacarichi [monta'kariki] sm inv hoist, goods lift, service elevator (Am).

montaggio [mon'taddʒo] sm **(a)** (di macchina, telaio, mobile) assembly; **scatola/catena di** ~ assembly kit/line. **(b)** (Cine) editing.

montagna [mon'taɲɲa] sf **(a)** (monte) mountain; **una** ~ **di** (fig: gran quantità) a mountain o pile o heap of; ~**e russe** (giostra) big dipper sg, roller coaster sg. **(b)** (zona, regione): **la** ~ the mountains pl; **andare in** ~ to go to the mountains; **casa di** ~ house in the mountains; **aria/strada di** ~ mountain air/road.

montagnoso, a [montaɲ'ɲoso] ag mountainous.

montanaro, a [monta'naro] **1** ag mountain attr. **2** sm/f (persona) mountain dweller; (fig peg: zotico) hillbilly.

montano, a [mon'tano] ag mountain attr.

montante [mon'tante] sm **(a)** (di porta) jamb; (di finestra) upright; (Calcio: palo) post. **(b)** (Pugilato) upper cut. **(c)** (Comm) total amount.

montare [mon'tare] **1** vi (aus essere) **(a)** (salire) to go (o come) up; ~ **in bicicletta/in macchina/sul treno** to get on a bicycle/into a car/on the train; ~ **su una scala** to climb a ladder; ~ **in cima a** to climb to the top of; ~ **su tutte le furie** (fig) to lose one's temper. **(b)** (cavalcare): ~ **bene/male** to ride well/badly; ~ **a cavallo** to mount o get on a horse. **(c)** (aumentare: vento, marea) to rise.

2 vt **(a)** (salire) to go (o come) up; ~ **le scale** to go upstairs, climb the stairs. **(b)** (cavallo) to ride. **(c)** (Zool) to cover. **(d)**: ~ **la guardia** (Mil) to mount guard. **(e)** (costruire: macchina, mobile etc) to assemble; (tenda) to pitch; (film) to edit; (gioielli) to mount, set; (fotografia) to mount; (Aut:

gomma) to put on. **(f)** (fig: esagerare) to blow up, exaggerate; ~ **una messinscena** (fig) to put on an act. **(g)** (fig): ~ **la testa a qn** to turn sb's head; ~**rsi la testa** to become bigheaded. **(h)** (Culin: panna) to whip; (: chiara d'uovo) to whisk; ~ **a neve** to whisk until stiff.

montatura [monta'tura] sf (di gioiello) mounting, setting; (di occhiali) frames pl; (fig: esagerazione) exaggeration; **una** ~ **pubblicitaria** (fig) a publicity stunt.

montavivande [montavi'vande] sm inv dumbwaiter.

monte ['monte] **1** sm mountain; **a** ~ **(di)** (fiume) upstream (from); (di vallata) at the head (of); **un** ~ **di** (gran quantità) a mountain o pile o heap of; **il problema è a** ~ (fig) the problem goes back to the early stages; **andare a** ~ (fig) to come to nothing; **mandare a** ~ (fig: piano, progetto) to upset; **fu quel fatto a mandare a** ~ **il matrimonio** that's what caused the wedding to be called off. **2**: **il M**~ **Bianco** Mont Blanc; **il M**~ **Everest** Mount Everest; ~ **di pietà** pawnbroker's, pawnshop; **portare qc al** ~ **di pietà** to pawn sth; ~ **premi** prize.

montgomery [mənt'gʌməri] sm inv duffle coat.

montone [mon'tone] sm **(a)** (Zool) ram; **carne di** ~ mutton. **(b)** (anche: **giacca di** ~) sheepskin (jacket).

montuosità [montuosi'ta] sf mountainous nature.

montuoso, a [montu'oso] ag mountainous.

monumentale [monumen'tale] ag monumental.

monumento [monu'mento] sm monument; **ti farei un** ~! (fig) you deserve a medal!

moquette [mɔ'kɛt] sf fitted carpet.

mora¹ ['mɔra] sf (Bot: di gelso) mulberry; (: di rovo) blackberry.

mora² ['mɔra] sf (Dir) **(a)** default. **(b)** (somma dovuta) arrears.

morale [mo'rale] **1** ag (gen) moral. **2** sf **(a)** (norme, consuetudini) morals pl; (Filosofia) moral philosophy; **la** ~ **corrente** current moral standards pl. **(b)** (insegnamento) moral; **la** ~ **della favola** the moral of the tale; **così, ~ della favola siamo rimasti a casa** and the result was that we stayed at home. **3** sm (stato d'animo) morale; **essere giù di** ~ to be feeling down; **aver il** ~ **alto/a terra** to be in good/low spirits; **bisogna tener alto il** ~ **delle truppe** we must keep the troops' morale high.

moralista, i, e [mora'lista] **1** ag moralistic. **2** sm/f moralist.

moralistico, a, ci, che [mora'listiko] ag moralistic.

moralità [morali'ta] sf **(a)** (norme di vita, morale) morality, morals pl, moral standards pl; **una persona di alta** ~ a person of high moral standards. **(b)** (di comportamento) morality.

moralizzare [moralid'dzare] vi: ~ **(su)** to moralize (on, about).

moralizzatore, trice [moraliddza'tore] **1** ag moralizing. **2** sm/f moralizer.

moralmente [moral'mente] av morally.

moratoria [mora'tɔrja] sf (Dir) moratorium.

morbidezza [morbi'dettsa] sf (vedi ag) softness; tenderness.

morbido, a ['mɔrbido] ag (gen) soft; (carne) tender.

morbillo [mor'billo] sm measles sg.

morbo ['mɔrbo] sm (Med) disease; (: epidemia) epidemic.

morbosità [morbosi'ta] sf morbidity.

morboso, a [mor'boso] ag (Med, fig) morbid.

morchia ['mɔrkja] sf sludge, oily deposit.

mordace [mor'datʃe] ag (fig: satira) pungent;

(: *persona, parole*) cutting.

mordente [mor'dɛnte] *sm* **(a)** (*Chim*) mordant. **(b)** (*fig: di satira, critica*) bite; (: *di persona*) drive.

mordere ['mordere] **1** *vt* (*sog: persona, cane, insetto*) to bite; (*addentare: mela, panino*) to bite into; ~ **la gamba a qn** to bite sb's leg, bite sb in the leg; ~**rsi le labbra** (*fig*) to bite one's lips; ~**rsi la lingua** (*anche fig*) to bite one's tongue; ~ **il freno** (*anche fig*) to champ at the bit; ~ **l'asfalto** (*Aut*) to grip the road; **can che abbaia non morde** (*Proverbio*) his (*o her etc*) bark is worse than his (*o her etc*) bite; **mi sarei morso le mani** I could have kicked myself. **2** *vi* to bite.

mordicchiare [mordik'kjare] *vt* (*gen*) to chew at; ~**rsi le labbra** to bite one's lips.

morena [mo'rena] *sf* (*Geol*) moraine.

morente [mo'rɛnte] **1** *ag* dying. **2** *sm/f* (*persona*) dying man/woman; ~ **i** the dying.

moresco, a, schi, sche [mo'resko] *ag* Moorish.

morfina [mor'fina] *sf* morphine.

morfologia [morfolo'dʒia] *sf* morphology.

morfologico, a, ci, che [morfo'lɔdʒiko] *ag* morphological.

moria [mo'ria] *sf* high mortality.

moribondo, a [mori'bondo] **1** *ag* (*persona*) dying, moribund. **2** *sm/f* dying man/woman.

morigerato, a [moridʒe'rato] *ag* (*persona, vita*) moderate, sober.

morire [mo'rire] *vi* (*aus* **essere**) **(a)** (*gen*) to die; ~ **di malattia** to die after an illness; ~ **di morte violenta/naturale** to die a violent/natural death; ~ **di stenti** to die from hardship; ~ **in guerra** to die in battle; ~ **assassinato** to be murdered; ~ **di dolore** to die of a broken heart; ~ **di fame** to starve to death; (*fig*) to be starving, be famished; ~ **di freddo** to freeze to death; (*fig*) to be frozen; ~ **di sete** (*anche fig*) to die of thirst.

(b) (*fig*): ~ **d'invidia** to be green with envy; ~ **di noia** to be bored to death *o* to tears; ~ **dalle risate** *o* **dal ridere** to kill o.s. laughing, die laughing; ~ **di sonno** to be dog tired; ~ **dalla voglia di fare qc** to be dying to do sth; **fa un caldo da** ~ it's terribly hot; **ho un caldo da** ~ I'm terribly hot; **mi fa male da** ~ **questo braccio** my arm is killing me; **bello da** ~ stunning.

(c) (*luce, giorno*) to fade, die; (*fiamma*) to die down; (*fuoco, tradizione*) to die out; **il blu sul nero muore un po'** blue is lost on a black background.

mormone [mor'mone] *sm* (*Rel*) Mormon.

mormorare [mormo'rare] **1** *vi* **(a)** (*gen*) to murmur; (*sussurrare: persona, vento*) to murmur, whisper; (*brontolare*) to grumble, mutter; **si mormora che...** it's rumoured that.... **(b)** (*parlare male*): ~ **sul conto di qn** to speak ill of sb; **la gente mormora** people are talking. **2** *vt* (*parole d'amore etc*) to whisper, murmur.

mormorio [mormo'rio] *sm* (*di persone, vento, acque*) murmur; (*di foglie, fronde*) rustling.

moro¹, a [ˈmɔro] **1** *ag* **(a)** (*razza*) Moorish. **(b)** (*persona: dai capelli scuri*) dark, dark-haired; (: *di carnagione scura*) dark, dark-skinned. **2** *sm/f* (*vedi ag*) Moor; dark-haired person; dark-skinned person.

moro² [ˈmɔro] *sm* mulberry tree.

moroso, a [mo'roso] *ag* (*Dir*) defaulting.

morra [ˈmɔrra] *sf game involving guessing how many fingers are held up*.

morsa [ˈmɔrsa] *sf* (*Tecn*) vice; (*fig: stretta*) grip; **stretto in una** ~ **d'acciaio** (*fig*) caught in a vice-like grip.

morsetto [mor'setto] *sm* (*Tecn*) clamp; (*Elettr*) terminal.

morsicare [morsi'kare] *vt* to bite.

morso, a [ˈmɔrso] **1** *pp di* **mordere**. **2** *sm* **(a)** (*gen*) bite; **dare un** ~ **a qc/qn** to bite sth/sb; **mi dai un** ~ **di panino?** can I have a bite of your sandwich?; **i** ~**i della fame** hunger pangs. **(b)** (*di cavallo*) bit.

mortadella [morta'dɛlla] *sf* (*Culin*) mortadella (*type of salted pork meat*).

mortaio [mor'tajo] *sm* mortar.

mortale [mor'tale] **1** *ag* (*vita, uomo*) mortal. **(b)** (*veleno*) deadly; (*ferita, incidente*) fatal; **un colpo** ~ a deadly *o* fatal blow; **peccato** ~ (*Rel*) mortal sin. **2** *sm* mortal.

mortalità [mortali'ta] *sf* **(a)** (*l'essere mortale*) mortality. **(b)** (*Statistica*) mortality, death rate; ~ **infantile** infant mortality.

mortaretto [morta'retto] *sm* firecracker.

morte [ˈmorte] *sf* **(a)** (*gen*) death; (*fig: fine, rovina*) death, end; **alla** ~ **di sua madre** on the death of his mother; **in punto di** ~ at death's door; **in punto di** ~ **ha confessato** he confessed on his deathbed; **essere tra la vita e la** ~ to be fighting for one's life; **ferito a** ~ (*soldato*) mortally wounded; (*in incidente*) fatally injured; **condannare** *o* **mandare qn a** ~ to sentence sb to death; **pena di/condanna a** ~ death penalty/sentence.

(b) (*fraseologia*): **è questione di vita o di** ~ it's a matter of life or death; **essere annoiato a** ~ to be bored to death *o* to tears; **avercela a** ~ **con qn** to be bitterly resentful of sb; **si odiano a** ~ they have an abiding hatred of one another; **avere la** ~ **nel cuore** to have a heavy heart; **così facendo ha firmato la sua condanna a** ~ by doing that he signed his own death warrant.

mortificare [mortifi'kare] **1** *vt* to mortify. **2:** ~**rsi** *vr* (*Rel*) to mortify o.s.; (*vergognarsi, spiacersi*) to feel mortified.

mortificato, a [mortifi'kato] *ag*: **essere** ~ (**per qc**) to be mortified (about sth).

mortificazione [mortifikat'tsjone] *sf* mortification.

morto, a [ˈmorto] **1** *pp di* **morire**. **2** *ag* (*gen, fig*) dead; **sono** ~ **di freddo** I'm frozen stiff; **sono stanco** ~ I'm dead tired; **l'inverno è una stagione** ~ **a per noi** winter is our slack season; ~ **e sepolto** (*fig*) dead and buried. **3** *sm* **(a)** dead man; **i** ~**i** the dead; **fare il** ~ (*in acqua*) to float on one's back; **un** ~ **di fame** (*fig peg*) a down-and-out; **sembri un** ~ **che cammina** you look like death warmed up; **le campane suonavano a** ~ the funeral bells were tolling; **giorno dei** ~**i** All Souls' Day; **il regno dei** ~**i** the world beyond the grave. **(b)** (*Carte*) dummy. **4** *sf* dead woman.

mortorio [mor'tɔrjo] *sm* (*fig: cerimonia, festa etc*): **quella festa è stata un** ~ that party was more like a funeral.

mosaico, ci [mo'zaiko] *sm* **(a)** (*Arte*) mosaic; **pavimento a** ~ mosaic floor. **(b)** (*fig: di lingue, di popoli*) mixture.

Mosca [ˈmoska] *sf* Moscow.

mosca [ˈmoska] **1** *sf, pl* ~**sche** **(a)** (*Zool, Pesca*) fly; ~ **della carne** bluebottle, blowfly; ~ **cavallina** horsefly; ~ **tse-tse** tsetse fly. **(b)** (*fraseologia*): **non farebbe male a una** ~ he wouldn't hurt a fly; **morire come** ~**sche** to die like flies; **non si sentiva volare una** ~ you could have heard a pin drop; **gli è saltata la** ~ **al naso** he lost his temper; **giocare a** ~ **cieca** to play blind-man's buff; **raro come una** ~ **bianca** a rarity; **rimanere** *o* **restare con un pugno di** ~**sche** (*fig*) to be left empty-handed. **(c)** (*barba*) goatee. **2** *ag inv* (*Pugilato*): **peso** ~ flyweight.

moscato, a [mos'kato] **1** *ag* (*uva*) muscat. **2** *sm* (*uva*) muscat grape; (*vino*) muscatel.

moscerino [moʃʃe'rino] *sm* midge, gnat.

moschea [mos'kεa] *sf* mosque.
moschettiere [mosket'tjεre] *sm* musketeer.
moschettone [mosket'tone] *sm (gancio)* spring clip; *(Alpinismo)* karabiner, snap ring.
moschicida, i, e [moski't∫ida] *ag* fly *attr*; **carta ~** flypaper.
moscio, a, sci, sce ['mo∫∫o] *ag* **(a)** *(cappello)* soft; *(fig: persona)* lifeless, dull. **(b): ha la 'r' ~a** he can't roll his 'r's.
moscone [mos'kone] *sm* **(a)** *(insetto)* bluebottle. **(b)** *(pattino)* pedalo; *(: a remi)* pedalo with oars. **(c)** *(corteggiatore)* suitor.
moscovita, i, e [mosko'vita] *ag, sm/f* Muscovite.
mossa ['mɔssa] *sf* **(a)** *(gen: movimento)* movement; **prendere le ~e da qc** to come about as the result of sth; **darsi una ~** *(fig)* to give o.s. a shake. **(b)** *(Scacchi, Dama, fig)* move; **fare una ~ sbagliata** *(anche fig)* to make a wrong move.
mosso, a ['mɔsso] **1** *pp di* **muovere. 2** *ag* **(a)** *(mare)* rough; *(capelli)* wavy; *(fotografia)* blurred. **(b)** *(Mus)* mosso.
mostarda [mos'tarda] *sf (Culin)* mustard.
mosto ['mosto] *sm* must.
mostra ['mostra] *sf* **(a)** *(di oggetti)* exhibition; *(di animali, fiori)* show; **fare una ~** to put on an exhibition *(o* a show); **essere in ~** to be on show; **~ d'arte** art exhibition; **~ di cani** dog show; **il negozio ha messo in ~ gli ultimi arrivi** the shop has put its latest stock on display. **(b)** *(locale)* exhibition hall. **(c)** *(fraseologia):* **fare ~ di sé** to show off; **fare ~ di fare qc** *(fingere)* to pretend to do sth; **mettersi in ~** to draw attention to o.s.; **mettere qc in bella ~** to show sth off.
mostrare [mos'trare] **1** *vt:* **~ (qc a qn)** to show (sb sth), show (sth to sb); **mi mostri come si fa?** will you show me how to do it?; **ha mostrato un notevole coraggio** he displayed great courage; **~ i denti** *(anche fig)* to bare one's teeth; **~ la lingua** to stick out one's tongue; **~ i pugni a qn** to shake one's fist at sb. **2** *vi:* **~ di** *(dare a vedere)* to pretend to; **ha mostrato di non conoscermi** he pretended not to know me. **3:** **~rsi** *vr* **(a)** *(dimostrarsi)* to appear; **si è mostrato felice** he appeared *o* looked happy. **(b)** *(comparire)* to appear, show o.s.; **~rsi in pubblico** to appear in public.
mostrina [mos'trina] *sf (Mil)* flash.
mostro ['mostro] *sm (anche fig)* monster; **sei un ~ (di bravura)!** you're a genius!
mostruosità [mostruosi'ta] *sf* monstrosity.
mostruoso, a [mostru'oso] *ag (anche fig)* monstrous; *(mente, intelligenza)* incredible.
mota ['mɔta] *sf* mud.
motel [mo'tεl] *sm inv* motel.
motivare [moti'vare] *vt* **(a)** *(giustificare)* to justify, to give reasons for. **(b)** *(causare)* to cause; *(Psic)* to motivate.
motivazione [motivat'tsjone] *sf (ragione)* justification; *(Psic)* motivation.
motivo [mo'tivo] *sm* **(a)** *(causa, ragione)* reason, grounds *pl*; **senza ~** for no reason; **qual'è il ~ del tuo ritardo?** what is the reason for your being late?; **avere un ~ valido per fare qc** to have a valid reason for doing sth; **per ~i di salute** for health reasons, on health grounds; **per questo ~** for this reason, therefore; **~i personali** personal reasons; **mia madre sta male, ~ per cui non potrò venire** my mother is ill so I won't be able to come. **(b)** *(Mus, Pittura)* motif; *(di opera letteraria)* theme.
moto¹ ['mɔto] *sm* **(a)** *(di mare, macchina, pianeti)* movement; *(Fis, Tecn)* motion; **verbi di ~** verbs of motion; **mettere in ~ qc** *(anche fig)* to set sth in

motion; *(motore, macchina)* to start; **mettersi in ~** *(macchina)* to start; *(persona)* to set off. **(b)** *(esercizio fisico)* exercise; **fare del ~** to do some exercise. **(c)** *(gesto)* movement; **fece ~ di andarsene** he made as if to leave; **un ~ d'impazienza** an impatient gesture. **(d)** *(rivolta)* rising, revolt.
moto² ['moto] *sf inv (fam)* motorbike.
motobarca, che [moto'barka] *sf* motorboat.
motocarro [moto'karro] *sm* three-wheeler van.
motocicletta [motot∫i'kletta] *sf* motorcycle.
motociclismo [motot∫i'klizmo] *sm* motorcycling, motorcycle racing.
motociclista, i, e [motot∫i'klista] *sm/f* motorcyclist.
motociclistico, a, ci, che [motot∫i'klistiko] *ag* motorcycle *attr*.
motociclo [moto't∫iklo] *sm* motorcycle, motorbike *(fam)*.
motocross [moto'krɔs] *sm* motocross.
motonautica [moto'nautika] *sf* speedboat racing.
motonautico, a, ci, che [moto'nautiko] *ag* motorboat *attr*, speedboat *attr*.
motonave [moto'nave] *sf* motor vessel.
motopeschereccio [motopeske'rett∫o] *sm* motor fishing vessel.
motore, trice [mo'tore] **1** *ag* **(a)** *(Anat: organo, nervo)* motor *attr*. **(b)** *(Tecn)* driving; **albero ~** driving shaft; **forza ~trice** driving force. **2** *sm* **(a)** *(Tecn)* engine, motor; *(di macchina, treno, nave)* engine; **a ~** power-driven, motor *attr*; **~ elettrico** electric motor; **~ a reazione** jet engine; **~ a scoppio** internal combustion engine; **~ a 2/4 tempi** 2-/4 ⬚stroke engine. **(b)** *(Filosofia)* mover; **il Primo M~** the Prime Mover.
motoretta [moto'retta] *sf* motor scooter.
motorino [moto'rino] *sm* **(a)** *(Aut):* **~ d'avviamento** starter. **(b)** *(fam: ciclomotore)* moped.
motorio, a [mo'tɔrjo] *ag (Anat)* motor *attr*.
motorizzare [motorid'dzare] **1** *vt (polizia, soldati)* to motorize. **2:** **~rsi** *vr (fam)* to get a car *(o* motorbike).
motorizzazione [motoriddzat'tsjone] *sf (ufficio tecnico e organizzativo):* **(ufficio della) ~** road traffic office.
motorscooter ['moutəsku:tə] *sm inv* motor scooter.
motoscafo [motos'kafo] *sm* motorboat.
motosega, ghe [moto'sega] *sf* electric saw.
motovedetta [motove'detta] *sf* motor patrol vessel.
motrice [mo'trit∫e] *sf (Tecn)* engine, motor.
motteggiare [motted'dʒare] *vt* to joke, banter.
mottetto [mot'tetto] *sm (Poesia)* witty poem.
motto ['mɔtto] *sm (detto arguto)* witty remark; *(massima)* motto, maxim.
mousse [mus] *sf inv (Culin)* mousse.
movente [mo'vεnte] *sm (Dir)* motive.
movenza [mo'vεntsa] *sf* movement; **sciolto nelle ~e** graceful in one's movements.
movimentare [movimen'tare] *vt*, **~rsi** *vr (festa, scena etc)* to liven up.
movimentato, a [movimen'tato] *ag (festa, partita)* lively; *(riunione)* animated; *(strada, vita)* busy; *(soggiorno)* eventful.
movimento [movi'mento] *sm (gen, Mus, Pol, Letteratura)* movement; **essere sempre in ~** to be always on the go; **è vietato salire sul treno quando è in ~** do not get on the train while it is in motion; **fare un ~ falso** to make an awkward movement; **fece un ~ all'indietro** he stepped back; **fare un po' di ~** *(esercizio fisico)* to do some exercise; **c'è molto ~ in città** the town is very

busy; ~ **di capitali** movement of capital; ~**i di truppe** troop movements.

moviola [mo'vjɔla] *sf* moviola; **rivedere qc alla ~** to see an action replay of sth.

mozione [mot'tsjone] *sf (Pol)* motion.

mozzafiato [mottsa'fjato] *ag inv* breathtaking.

mozzare [mot'tsare] *vt (testa)* to cut off; *(coda)* to dock; ~ **il fiato a qn** *(fig)* to take sb's breath away.

mozzarella [mottsa'rella] *sf* mozzarella *(a moist Neapolitan curd cheese)*.

mozzicone [mottsi'kone] *sm (di sigaretta)* stub, end; *(di candela)* end; *(di matita)* stub.

mozzo¹, a ['mottso] *ag (testa)* cut off; *(coda)* docked.

mozzo² ['mottso] *sm* **(a)** *(Naut)* ship's boy. **(b)** *(Agr):* ~ **di stalla** stable boy.

mozzo³ ['mɔddzo] *sm (Tecn)* hub.

mq *abbr* (= *metro quadro)* sq. m.

M.S.I. - D.N. *abbr di Movimento Sociale Italiano - Destra Nazionale.*

mucca, che ['mukka] *sf* cow.

mucchio ['mukkjo] *sm (gen)* heap, pile; **a ~i in** piles; **un ~ di** *(molto)* heaps of, piles of; **ha detto un ~ di sciocchezze** he came out with a load of rubbish.

muco ['muko] *sm (Med)* mucus.

mucosa [mu'kosa] *sf (Anat)* mucous membrane.

muffa ['muffa] *sf* mould, mildew; **fare la ~** to go mouldy; **avere odore di ~** to smell mouldy.

mugghiare [mug'gjare] *vi (fig: mare, tuono)* to roar; *(: vento)* to howl.

muggire [mud'dʒire] *vi (bovini)* to low; *(vacca)* to moo, low.

muggito [mud'dʒito] *sm (vedi vb)* lowing; mooing; **i ~i del bestiame** the lowing of the cattle.

mughetto [mu'getto] *sm* **(a)** *(Bot)* lily of the valley. **(b)** *(Med)* thrush.

mugnaio [muɲ'najo] *sm* miller.

mugolare [mugo'lare] **1** *vi (cane)* to whimper, whine; *(fig: persona):* ~ **(di)** to moan (in *o* with). **2** *vt (borbottare)* to mutter.

mugolio [mugo'lio] *sm (vedi vb)* whimpering, whining; moaning; muttering.

mugugnare [muguɲ'ɲare] *vi (fam)* to mutter, mumble.

mulattiera [mulat'tjɛra] *sf* mule track.

mulattiere [mulat'tjɛre] *sm* mule-driver.

mulatto, a [mu'latto] *ag, sm/f* mulatto.

muliebre [mu'ljebre] *ag* feminine, womanly.

mulinare [muli'nare] *vi* to whirl, spin (round and round).

mulinello [muli'nello] *sm* **(a)** *(di vento, acqua)* eddy. **(b)** *(Pesca)* reel. **(c)** *(Naut)* windlass.

mulino [mu'lino] *sm* mill; ~ **ad acqua** water mill; ~ **a vento** windmill; **lottare** *o* **combattere contro i ~i a vento** *(fig)* to tilt at windmills.

mulo ['mulo] *sm* mule; **testardo come un ~** as stubborn as a mule.

multa ['multa] *sf* fine; **fare** *o* **dare una ~ a qn** to fine sb; **ho preso una ~ di 5.000 lire** I was fined 5,000 lire, I got a 5,000 lire fine.

multare [mul'tare] *vt* to fine.

multicolore [multiko'lore] *ag* multicoloured.

multiforme [multi'forme] *ag (paesaggio, attività, interessi)* varied; *(ingegno)* versatile.

multimiliardario, a [multimiljar'darjo] *ag, sm/f* billionaire.

multimilionario, a [multimiljo'narjo] *ag, sm/f* multimillionaire.

multinazionale [multinattsjo'nale] *ag, sf* multinational.

multiplo, a ['multiplo] **1** *ag* multiple. **2** *sm (Mat):* ~

(di) multiple (of); **minimo comune ~** lowest common multiple.

mummia ['mummja] *sf* mummy; *(fig: persona)* old fogey.

mummificare [mummifi'kare] **1** *vt* to mummify. **2:** ~**rsi** *vr* to become mummified.

mungere ['mundʒere] *vt* to milk.

mungitrice [mundʒi'tritʃe] *sf (macchina)* milking machine.

mungitura [mundʒi'tura] *sf* milking.

municipale [munitʃi'pale] *ag (gen)* municipal; **palazzo ~** town hall; **autorità ~i** local authorities.

municipio [muni'tʃipjo] *sm (comune)* town council; *(palazzo)* town hall; **sposarsi in ~** ≈ to get married at the registry office.

munifico, a, ci, che [mu'nifiko] *ag* munificent, generous.

munire [mu'nire] **1** *vt:* ~ **di** *(fortificare: città, nave)* to fortify with; *(equipaggiare: persona, stanza etc)* to equip with; ~ **una nave di uomini** to man a ship; ~ **di firma** *(documento)* to sign. **2:** ~**rsi** *vr:* ~**rsi di** *(gen: di denaro, documenti etc)* to provide o.s. with; *(di armi)* to arm o.s. with; ~**rsi di coraggio/pazienza** to arm o.s. with courage/patience; **'si pregano i clienti di ~rsi di scontrino'** *(in bar)* 'customers must pay at the desk and obtain a receipt before being served'; **si è munito di berretto e guanti ed è uscito** he equipped himself with hat and gloves and off he went.

munizioni [munit'tsjoni] *sfpl* ammunition *sg.*

munto, a ['munto] *pp di* **mungere.**

muovere ['mwɔvere] **1** *vt* **(a)** *(gen)* to move; *(macchina, ruota)* to drive; **il cane muoveva festosamente la coda** the dog was wagging its tail happily; ~ **i primi passi** to take one's first steps; *(fig)* to be starting out; **mosse un passo verso di me** he took a step towards me; **non muove un passo senza interpellare la moglie** *(fig)* he never takes a decision without asking his wife; **non ha mosso un dito per aiutarmi** he didn't lift a finger to help me; ~ **mari e monti** to move heaven and earth.

(b) *(fig: sollevare):* ~ **un'accusa a** *o* **contro qn** to make an accusation about sb; ~ **causa a qn** *(Dir)* to take legal action against sb; ~ **guerra a** *o* **contro qn** to wage war against sb; ~ **un'obiezione** to raise an objection.

(c) *(commuovere):* ~ **a compassione** to move to pity; ~ **al pianto** to move to tears.

(d) *(Scacchi etc)* to move; **tocca a te ~** it's your move.

2 *vi (aus essere)* **(a)** *(gen)* to move; ~ **verso, ~ in direzione di** to move towards. **(b)** *(derivare):* ~ **da** to derive from; **le sue osservazioni muovono da una premessa errata** his comments derive from *o* are based on a wrong assumption.

3: ~**rsi** *vr* **(a)** to move; ~**rsi in aiuto di qn** to go to sb's aid; **non si muove dalle sue posizioni** *(fig)* he won't budge; **finalmente qualcosa si è mosso** *(fig)* at last things are moving.

(b) *(sbrigarsi)* to hurry up, get a move on; **muoviti, cammina!** hurry up and get moving!

(c) *(commuoversi):* ~**rsi a compassione** *o* **pietà** to be moved to pity.

muraglia [mu'raʎʎa] *sf* (high) wall; **la M~ Cinese** the Great Wall of China.

muraglione [muraʎ'ʎone] *sm* massive wall.

murale [mu'rale] **1** *ag* wall *attr*; *(Arte)* mural; **carta ~** wall map; **pittura ~** mural. **2** *sm (Arte)* mural.

murare [mu'rare] **1** *vt (porta, finestra)* to wall up; *(mensola)* to embed into a wall; ~ **qn vivo** to wall sb up. **2:** ~**rsi** *vr (fig: rinchiudersi)* to shut o.s. up.

murario, a [mu'rarjo] *ag (tecnica)* building *attr*;

arte ~a masonry; opera ~a piece of masonry work.

muratore [mura'tore] *sm (che costruisce con pietre)* mason; *(che costruisce con mattoni)* bricklayer.

muratura [mura'tura] *sf* **(a)** *(atto del murare)* walling (up). **(b)** *(lavoro murario)* masonry; **casa in** ~ *(di pietra)* stonebuilt house; *(di mattoni)* brick house.

murena [mu'rɛna] *sf* moray eel.

muro ['muro] *sm* **(a)** *(anche fig)* wall; ~ **di mattoni** brick wall; **armadio a** ~ built-in cupboard; **alzare un** ~ to build a wall; **attaccare qc al** ~ to hang sth on the wall; **chiudere qc con un** ~ *(campo, giardino)* to build a wall around sth; **hanno messo i prigionieri al** ~ the prisoners were lined up and shot; **è come parlare al** ~ it's like talking to a brick wall; **tra noi c'è un** ~ *(fig)* there's a barrier between us; **un** ~ **d'incomprensione** a total lack of understanding; ~ **di cinta** surrounding wall; ~ **divisorio** dividing wall; ~ **maestro** main wall; ~ **del suono** *(Fis)* sound barrier. **(b)**: ~**a** *sfpl (di città, castello)* walls; **chiudersi fra quattro** ~**a** *(fig)* to shut o.s. up at home.

musa ['muza] *sf (Mitologia)* Muse; *(fig)* muse, inspiration.

muschio[1] ['muskjo] *sm (profumo)* musk.

muschio[2] ['muskjo] *sm (Bot)* moss.

muscolare [musko'lare] *ag (Anat: tessuto, fascio)* muscular, muscle *attr*; **strappo** ~ torn muscle.

muscolatura [muskola'tura] *sf* muscle structure.

muscolo ['muskolo] *sm* **(a)** *(Anat)* muscle; **scaldare i** ~**i** to warm up; **è tutto** ~**i e niente cervello** *(fig)* he's all brawn and no brains. **(b)** *(Culin)* lean meat. **(c)** *(Zool)* mussel.

muscoloso, a [musko'loso] *ag (gamba, braccio)* muscular; *(persona)* brawny.

museo [mu'zɛo] *sm* museum; **un pezzo da** ~ *(fig)* a museum piece.

museruola [muze'rwɔla] *sf (per cani)* muzzle; **mettere la** ~ **a un cane** to muzzle a dog; **mettere la** ~ **a qn** *(fig)* to muzzle sb, shut sb up.

musica ['muzika] *sf (gen, fig)* music; ~ **leggera/da camera/di sottofondo** light/chamber/background music; **un pezzo o brano di** ~ a piece of music; **mettere in** ~ to set to music; **è sempre la stessa** ~ *(fig)* it's always the same old story; **è ora di cambiare** ~ *(fig)* it's time you changed your tune.

musicale [muzi'kale] *ag* musical; **avere orecchio** ~ to have an ear for music.

musicante [muzi'kante] *sm/f* musician.

musicare [muzi'kare] *vt* to set to music.

musicassetta [muzikas'setta] *sf* (pre-recorded) cassette.

musicista, i, e [muzi't∫ista] *sm/f* musician.

musivo, a [mu'zivo] *ag* mosaic *attr*.

muso ['muzo] *sm (di animale)* muzzle; *(fig: di persona)* face; *(: peg)* mug; *(: di aereo)* nose; *(: di macchina, moto)* front (end); **rompere il** ~ **a qn** to smash sb's face in; **mettere o fare il** ~ to pull a long face; **tenere il** ~ **a qn** to be in a huff with sb; **ha storto il** ~ **quando gliene ho parlato** he turned up his nose when I mentioned it; **gliel'ho detto**

sul ~ I told him so to his face.

musone, a [mu'zone] *sm/f* sulk.

mussola ['mussola] *sf* muslin.

mustacchi [mus'takki] *smpl* mustachio *sg*.

mus(s)ulmano, a [mus(s)ul'mano] *ag, sm/f* Muslim, Moslem.

muta[1] ['muta] *sf* **(a)** *(di animali: gen)* moulting; *(: di serpenti)* sloughing; **andare in** ~ to moult; to slough off. **(b)** *(di subacqueo)* wet suit.

muta[2] ['muta] *sf (di cani)* pack.

mutabile [mu'tabile] *ag* changeable.

mutamento [muta'mento] *sm* change.

mutande [mu'tande] *sfpl (da uomo)* (under)pants; *(da donna)* pants.

mutandine [mutan'dine] *sfpl (da donna, da bambino)* pants; ~ **da bagno** swimming trunks; ~ **di plastica** plastic pants.

mutare [mu'tare] **1** *vt* **(a)** *(gen)* to change; *(opinione, carattere)* to change, alter; ~ **qc in** to change sth into. **(b)** *(Zool: sog: rettili)* to slough; *(: animali):* ~ **il pelo** to moult. **2** *vi (aus essere)* to change; ~ **di colore** to change colour; **qualcosa è mutato in lui** something about him has changed; ~ **in meglio/in peggio** to change for the better/ for the worse; **appena lo seppe il riso mutò in pianto** as soon as he found out his laughter turned to tears. **3**: ~**rsi** *vr*: ~**rsi in** to change into, turn into; **il ghiaccio si mutò in acqua** the ice turned to water.

mutazione [mutat'tsjone] *sf* change, alteration; *(Bio)* mutation.

mutevole [mu'tevole] *ag* changeable.

mutilare [muti'lare] *vt (gen, fig)* to mutilate; *(persona)* to maim; *(statua)* to deface; **la fresatrice gli ha mutilato la mano** the milling machine chopped off his hand.

mutilato, a [muti'lato] **1** *ag (vedi vb)* mutilated; maimed; defaced. **2** *sm/f* disabled person, cripple; ~ **di guerra** disabled ex-serviceman; ~ **del lavoro** person disabled at work.

mutilazione [mutilat'tsjone] *sf (vedi vb)* mutilation; maiming; defacement.

mutismo [mu'tizmo] *sm* **(a)** *(Med)* muteness. **(b)** *(silenzio ostinato)* (stubborn) silence; **chiudersi in un** ~ **ostinato** to maintain a stubborn silence.

muto, a ['muto] **1** *ag (Med)* dumb; *(Linguistica)* silent, mute; *(Geog: cartina, atlante)* blank; **il cinema** ~ the silent cinema; ~ **per la vergogna** speechless with shame; **ha fatto scena** ~**a** he didn't utter a word; **giuro che sarò** ~ **come un pesce** I swear I won't open my mouth; **un** ~ **rimprovero** a silent reproach. **2** *sm/f (Med)* dumb person, mute.

mutua ['mutua] *sf (anche:* **cassa** ~*)* sickness benefit fund; **medico della** ~ ≈ National Health Service doctor.

mutuato [mutu'ato] *sm* person contributing to sickness benefit fund.

mutuo[1]**, a** ['mutuo] *ag (reciproco)* mutual; **società di** ~ **soccorso** mutual benefit society.

mutuo[2] ['mutuo] *sm (Dir)* (long-term) loan; **fare un** ~ **per comprare una casa** to take out a loan to buy a house; ~ **ipotecario** mortgage.

N

N, n[1] ['ɛnne] *sf o m inv (lettera)* N, n.
n[2] *abbr (= numero)* no.
N. *abbr (= nord)* N.
nababbo [na'babbo] *sm (anche fig)* nabob.
nacchere ['nakkere] *sfpl* castanets.
nadir [na'dir] *sm (Astron)* nadir.
nafta ['nafta] *sf (Chim)* naphtha; *(carburante)* diesel oil; **motore a ~** diesel engine.
naftalina [nafta'lina] *sf (Chim)* naphthalene; *(tarmicida)* mothballs *pl*.
naia ['naja] *sf (Mil fam)* national service, draft *(Am)*.
naïf [na'if] *ag inv* naïve.
nailon ['nailon] *sm inv* = **nylon**.
nanna ['nanna] *sf (fam)* beddy-byes, bye-byes; **andare a ~** to go bye-byes; **fare la ~** to sleep.
nano, a ['nano] **1** *ag* dwarf *attr*. **2** *sm/f* dwarf.
napoletana [napole'tana] *sf (macchinetta da caffè)* Neapolitan coffeepot.
napoletano, a [napole'tano] *ag, sm/f* Neapolitan.
Napoli ['napoli] *sf* Naples.
nappa ['nappa] *sf* **(a)** *(ornamento per tende etc)* tassel. **(b)** *(pelle)* nappa, soft leather.
narcisismo [nartʃi'zizmo] *sm* narcissism.
narciso [nar'tʃizo] *sm* narcissus.
narcosi [nar'kɔzi] *sf (Med)* general anaesthesia, narcosis; **essere sotto ~** to be under general anaesthetic.
narice [na'ritʃe] *sf* nostril.
narrare [nar'rare] **1** *vt* to tell, narrate. **2** *vi:* **~ di** to tell the story of.
narrativa [narra'tiva] *sf* fiction.
narrativo, a [narra'tivo] *ag* narrative.
narratore, trice [narra'tore] *sm/f* narrator.
narrazione [narrat'tsjone] *sf* **(a)** *(di fatto, avvenimento)* narration, account. **(b)** *(storia, racconto)* story, tale.
nasale [na'sale] **1** *ag (Anat, Fonetica)* nasal. **2** *sf* nasal consonant.
nascente [naʃ'ʃɛnte] *ag (sole, luna)* rising.
nascere ['naʃʃere] *vi (aus essere)* **(a)** *(persona, animale)* to be born; *(pianta)* to come up, spring up; **sono nato il 4 febbraio** I was born on the 4th of February; **l'uomo nasce libero** man is born free; **nascono più femmine che maschi** there are more girls born than boys; **è appena nato** he's just a new baby; **da genitori ricchi/poveri** to be born of rich/poor parents; **la sig.ra Rossi, nata Bianchi** Mrs Rossi, née Bianchi; **essere nato per qc/per fare qc** *(fig)* to be destined for sth/to do sth; **non sono nato ieri** *(fig)* I wasn't born yesterday.
(b) *(idea, speranza)* to be born; *(giorno)* to break; *(difficoltà, dubbio)* to arise; *(industria, movimento)* to start up; **il sole nasce ad oriente** the sun rises in the east; **far ~** *(industria)* to create; *(sospetto, desiderio)* to arouse; **l'odio che nasce da tali conflitti** the hatred which springs from such conflicts; **nasce spontanea la domanda...** the question which springs to mind is...; **da cosa nasce cosa** one thing leads to another.

nascita ['naʃʃita] *sf* birth; **di ~** by birth; **nobile di ~** of noble birth; **dalla ~** from birth; **è cieco dalla ~** he has been blind from birth, he was born blind.
nascituro, a [naʃʃi'turo] *sm/f* future child; **come si chiamerà il ~?** what's the baby going to be called?
nascondere [nas'kondere] **1** *vt (gen)* to hide, conceal; **~ il viso tra le mani** to bury one's face in one's hands; **~ qc alla vista di qn** to hide sth from sb; **~ la verità a qn** to hide *o* keep the truth from sb; **non nascondo che mi farebbe molto piacere** I make no secret of the fact that I would like that. **2:** **~rsi** *vr* to hide; **~rsi alla vista di qn** to hide from sb, hide from sb's view; **dove si è nascosto?** where is he hiding?; **dovresti nasconderti** you had better hide; *(fig)* you should be ashamed of yourself.
nascondiglio [naskon'diʎʎo] *sm* hiding place.
nascondino [naskon'dino] *sm:* **giocare a ~** to play hide-and-seek.
nascosto, a [nas'kɔsto] **1** *pp di* **nascondere**. **2** *ag* hidden; **tenere ~ qc** to keep sth hidden; **gli hanno tenuto ~ a la notizia** they concealed *o* kept the news from him; **fare qc di ~** to do sth secretly.
naso ['naso] *sm (gen)* nose; **parlare col ~** to talk through one's nose; **torcere *o* arricciare il ~ (di fronte a qc)** to turn up one's nose (at sth); **avere ~ per gli affari** to have a flair for business; **mettere il ~ negli affari altrui** to poke one's nose into other people's business; **son 2 settimane che non metto il ~ fuori di casa** it's 2 weeks since I last stuck my nose out of the door; **guarda, ce l'hai sotto il ~** look, you've got it right under your nose.
nastrino [nas'trino] *sm* ribbon.
nastro ['nastro] *sm (gen, di macchina da scrivere)* ribbon; *(Tecn)* tape; **~ adesivo/isolante/magnetico** adhesive/insulating/magnetic tape; **~ trasportatore** conveyor belt.
Natale [na'tale] *sm* Christmas; **albero di ~** Christmas tree; **Babbo ~** Father Christmas; **cosa fai a ~?** what are you doing at Christmas? *o* at Christmastime?; **Buon ~!** Merry Christmas!
natale [na'tale] **1** *ag (paese, città)* native, of one's birth. **2:** **~i** *smpl:* **di illustri/umili ~i** of noble/humble birth.
natalità [natali'ta] *sf* birth rate.
natalizio, a [nata'littsjo] *ag* Christmas *attr*.
natante [na'tante] *sm* craft *inv*, boat.
natica, che ['natika] *sf* buttock.
natio, a [na'tio] *ag* native.
Natività [nativi'ta] *sf (Rel)* Nativity.
nativo, a [na'tivo] *ag, sm/f (gen)* native.
nato, a ['nato] **1** *pp di* **nascere**. **2** *ag (artista etc)* born; **un poeta ~** a born poet. **3** *sm:* **un nuovo ~** a newborn child; **i ~i del *o* nel 1960** those born in 1960.
N.A.T.O. ['nato] *abbr f* NATO.
natura [na'tura] *sf* **(a)** *(mondo naturale):* **la ~**

nature; **il mondo della** ~ the world of nature; **vivere a contatto con la** ~ to live close to nature; **questa sostanza non esiste in** ~ this substance does not exist naturally; **contro** ~ unnatural. **(b)** *(carattere)* nature; **la** ~ **umana** human nature; **è nella** ~ **delle cose** it's in the nature of things; **è allegro di** ~ he's naturally cheerful; **non è nella sua** ~ **fare così** he's not the sort of person who would do that; **i nostri rapporti sono di** ~ **professionale** our relationship is of a professional nature. **(c)** *(tipo)* nature, kind; **scritti di varia** ~ writings of various kinds; **pagare in** ~ *(Fin)* to pay in kind. **(d)** *(Pittura)*: ~ **morta** still life.

naturale [natu'rale] **1** *ag (gen)* natural; **è** ~ **che sia così** it's natural that it should be so; **gli viene** ~ **comportarsi così** it comes naturally to him to behave like that; **(ma) è** ~! *(in risposte)* of course!; **a grandezza** ~ life-size; **figlio** ~ natural *o* illegitimate son; **acqua** ~ spring water; **i suoi capelli sono** ~**i** her hair is naturally that colour. **2** *sm*: **al** ~ *(alimenti)* served plain; *(ritratto)* life-size; **è più bella al** ~ *(senza trucco)* she's prettier without make-up.

naturalezza [natura'lettsa] *sf* naturalness; **con** ~ naturally.

naturalizzare [naturalid'dzare] **1** *vt* to naturalize. **2**: ~**rsi** *vr* to become naturalized; **si è naturalizzato italiano** he's become a naturalized Italian.

naturalmente [natural'mente] *av* naturally; **vieni?** — ~ are you coming? — of course *o* naturally.

naturismo [natu'rizmo] *sm* naturism, nudism.

naturista, i, e [natu'rista] *ag, sm/f* naturist, nudist.

naufragare [naufra'gare] *vi (nave)* to be wrecked; *(persona)* to be shipwrecked; *(fig: progetto, disegno)* to fall through; **tutte le nostre speranze naufragarono** all our hopes were dashed.

naufragio [nau'fradʒo] *sm* shipwreck; *(fig)* ruin, failure; **fare** ~ to be shipwrecked; *(fig)* to fail, fall through.

naufrago, a, ghi, ghe ['naufrago] *sm/f* shipwrecked person; *(su un'isola)* castaway.

nausea ['nauzea] *sf (Med)* nausea; **avere la** ~ to feel sick; **mi dai la** ~! *(fig)* you make me sick!; **fino alla** ~ ad nauseam; **ho bevuto fino alla** ~ I drank till I felt sick.

nauseabondo, a [nauzea'bondo] *ag*, **nauseante** [nauze'ante] *ag* nauseating, sickening.

nauseare [nauze'are] *vt* to nauseate, make (feel) sick; **ho mangiato tanti funghi che ora ne sono nauseato** I've eaten so many mushrooms that now I'm sick of them; **il suo comportamento mi ha nauseato** his behaviour sickened me.

nautica ['nautika] *sf* navigation, nautical science.

nautico, a, ci, che ['nautiko] *ag (gen)* nautical; **salone** ~ *(mostra)* boat show; **sci** ~ water-skiing.

navale [na'vale] *ag (gen)* naval; **battaglia** ~ naval battle; *(gioco)* battleships *pl*; **cantiere** ~ shipyard.

navata [na'vata] *sf*: ~ **(centrale)** nave; ~ **(laterale)** aisle.

nave ['nave] *sf* ship, vessel; ~ **ammiraglia** flagship; ~ **da carico** cargo ship, freighter; ~ **cisterna** tanker; ~ **da guerra** warship; ~ **di linea** liner; ~ **mercantile** merchant ship; ~ **passeggeri** passenger ship; ~ **scuola** training ship; ~ **spaziale** spaceship; ~ **da trasporto** cargo ship; ~ **a vapore** steamship; ~ **a vela** sailing ship.

navetta [na'vetta] *sf* **(a)** *(di telaio)* shuttle. **(b)** *(servizio di collegamento)* shuttle (service).

navicella [navi'tʃella] *sf* **(a)** *(di pallone, dirigibile)* gondola; ~ **spaziale** spaceship. **(b)** *(per l'incenso)* incense boat.

navigabile [navi'gabile] *ag (canale, fiume)* navigable.

navigante [navi'gante] *sm* sailor, seaman.

navigare [navi'gare] *vi* to sail; **suo marito naviga** her husband is a sailor; ~ **in cattive acque** *(fig)* to be in deep water.

navigato, a [navi'gato] *ag (fig: esperto)* experienced.

navigatore, trice [naviga'tore] *sm/f (gen)* navigator; ~ **solitario** single-handed sailor.

navigazione [navigat'tsjone] *sf (Naut, Aer)* navigation; ~ **aerea/interna/fluviale** air/inland/river navigation; **compagnia di** ~ shipping company; **durante la** ~ during the (sea *o* river) voyage; **dopo una settimana di** ~ after a week at sea.

nazionale [nattsjo'nale] **1** *ag* national. **2** *sf (squadra)* national team.

nazionalismo [nattsjona'lizmo] *sm* nationalism.

nazionalista, i, e [nattsjona'lista] *ag, sm/f* nationalist.

nazionalistico, a, ci, che [nattsjona'listiko] *ag* nationalist.

nazionalità [nattsjonali'ta] *sf inv* nationality.

nazionalizzare [nattsjonalid'dzare] *vt* to nationalize.

nazionalizzazione [nattsjonaliddzat'tsjone] *sf* nationalization.

nazionalsocialismo [nattsjonalsotʃa'lizmo] *sm* National Socialism, Nazism.

nazione [nat'tsjone] *sf* nation.

nazismo [nat'tsizmo] *sm* Nazism.

nazista, i, e [nat'tsista] *ag, sm/f* Nazi.

N.B., n.b. *abbr (= nota bene)* N.B.

ne [ne] **1** *pron* **(a)** *(di lui, lei, loro)* of him *(o* her *o* them); about him *(o* her *o* them); ~ **riconosco la voce** I recognize his *(o* her) voice; **non lo vedo da anni, parlamene** I haven't seen him for years, tell me about him.

(b) *(con valore quantitativo, indefinito)* of it; of them *(spesso omesso)*; ~ **voglio ancora** I want some more (of it *o* them); **dammene un po'** give me some; **hai dei libri?** — **sì,** ~ **ho** do you have any books? — yes, I do *o* yes, I have; **hai del pane?** — **no, non** ~ **ho** do you have any bread? — no, I don't *o* no, I haven't any; **quanti anni hai?** — ~ **ho 17** how old are you? — I'm 17.

(c) *(riguardo)* about it; about them; **non me** ~ **importa niente** I couldn't care less about it; **cosa** ~ **pensi?** what do you think (about it)?; **cosa** ~ **faremo?** what will we do with it *(o* them)?

(d) *(da ciò)*: ~ **deduco che l'avete trovato** I gather you've found it; ~ **consegue che...** it follows therefore that... .

2 *av (moto da luogo: da lì)* from there; *(: da qui)* from here; ~ **vengo ora** I've just come from there; **me** ~ **vado immediatamente** I'm leaving (here) right away; **siamo arrivati al teatro alle 7 e** ~ **siamo venuti via alle 10** we got to the theatre at 7 and left there at 10.

né [ne] *cong*: ~ ... ~ neither ... nor; ~ **mio padre** ~ **mia madre parla l'italiano** neither my father nor my mother speaks Italian; **non voglio discutere** ~ **con lui** ~ **con mio fratello** I don't want to speak to either him or my brother; **non l'ho più vista** ~ **sentita** I haven't seen or heard from her again; **non voglio** ~ **posso accettare** I neither wish to nor can accept; ~ **da una parte** ~ **dall'altra** on neither side; ~ **più** ~ **meno** no more no less; ~ **l'uno** ~ **l'altro** neither of them, neither the one nor the other; **non mi fa** ~ **caldo** ~ **freddo** it makes no odds to me.

neanche [ne'anke] **1** *av* not even; **non mi ha pagato** he didn't even pay me; **non ci vado** —

neanch'io I'm not going — neither am I; ~ **lui lo farebbe** not even he would do it, even he wouldn't do it; **non ho ~ un soldo** I haven't got a single penny; **non ci penso ~!** I wouldn't dream of it!; ~ **per idea!**, ~ **per sogno!** not on your life!; **se ne è partito senza ~ salutare** he went off without even saying goodbye; **non parlo spagnolo — e lui?** — ~ I don't speak Spanish — what about him? — he doesn't either o neither does he.

2 *cong* not even; **non lo sposerei ~ se fosse un re** I wouldn't marry him even if he were a king; **lui non è inglese e ~ sua moglie** he isn't English and neither is his wife; ~ **a pagarlo lo farebbe** he wouldn't do it even if you paid him.

nebbia ['nebbja] *sf (densa)* fog; *(foschia)* mist.

nebbioso, a [neb'bjoso] *ag (vedi sf)* foggy; misty.

nebulizzatore [nebuliddza'tore] *sm* atomizer.

nebulosa [nebu'losa] *sf* nebula.

nebulosità [nebulosi'ta] *sf* haziness.

nebuloso, a [nebu'loso] *ag (atmosfera, cielo)* hazy; *(fig)* hazy, vague.

nécessaire [nesc'sɛr] *sm inv:* ~ **da viaggio** overnight case; ~ **da toilette** beauty case.

necessariamente [netʃessarja'mente] *av* necessarily.

necessario, a [netʃes'sarjo] **1** *ag (gen)* necessary; *(persona)* indispensable; **è ~ che tu vada** you will have to go, you must go, it is necessary that you go; **non è ~ che ti fermi** you don't need to stay; **non ho avuto il tempo ~** I didn't have enough o sufficient time; **se ~** if need be, if necessary; **rendersi ~** *(persona)* to make o.s. indispensable; **si rende ~ partire** it has become necessary for me *(o* you *etc)* to leave; **portami i documenti ~i** bring me the necessary o required documents.

2 *sm*: **fare il ~** to do what is necessary; **lo stretto ~** the bare essentials *pl*; **hanno appena il ~ per vivere** they have barely enough to live on; **non ho con me il ~** I haven't got what I need with me; **hai tutto il ~ per scrivere?** have you got all your writing materials?; **lavorare/preoccuparsi più del ~** to work/worry more than is necessary o more than one has to.

necessità [netʃessi'ta] *sf inv* necessity, need; **per ~** out of need o necessity; **di ~** *(necessariamente)* of necessity; **in caso di ~** in case of need, if need be; **non vedo la ~ di andare tutti quanti** I don't see any necessity for us all to go; **trovarsi nella ~ di fare qc** to be forced o obliged to do sth, have to do sth; **fare di ~ virtù** to make a virtue of necessity.

necessitare [netʃessi'tare] **1** *vi (aus essere) (aiuto, intervento etc)* to be necessary, be needed, be required; **necessita il vostro aiuto** your help is needed o necessary o required; **necessita di un'attenzione maggiore** it requires greater attention o care; **prima di essere pronto necessita di molte altre cose** a lot of other things are needed before it will be ready. **2** *vt* to need, require.

necrologio [nekro'lɔdʒo] *sm (annuncio)* obituary notice; *(registro)* register of deaths.

necropoli [ne'krɔpoli] *sf inv* necropolis.

nefando, a [ne'fando] *ag* base, vile.

nefasto, a [ne'fasto] *ag (giorno)* fateful, fatal; *(segno, presagio)* inauspicious; *(fam: persona)* full of gloom and doom.

nefrite [ne'frite] *sf (Med)* nephritis.

negare [ne'gare] *vt (gen)* to deny; ~ **qc/di aver fatto qc** to deny sth/having done sth; ~ **a qn il permesso (di fare qc)** to refuse sb permission (to do sth); ~ **a qn la possibilità di fare qc** to deny sb the possibility of doing sth; **mi hanno negato un**

aumento they turned down my request for a rise; ~ **obbedienza a qn** to refuse to obey sb.

negativa [nega'tiva] *sf (Gram, Fot)* negative.

negativamente [negativa'mente] *av* negatively; **rispose ~** he replied in the negative.

negativo, a [nega'tivo] **1** *ag* negative. **2** *sm (Fot)* negative.

negato, a [ne'gato] *ag (persona)*: **essere ~ per** o **in qc** to be hopeless at sth, be no good at sth.

negazione [negat'tsjone] *sf* negation.

negletto, a [ne'gletto] *ag* neglected.

negli ['neʎʎi] *prep + art vedi* **in.**

négligé [negli'ʒe] *sm inv* negligee.

negligente [negli'dʒɛnte] *ag (gen)* negligent; *(non diligente)* careless.

negligenza [negli'dʒɛntsa] *sf (vedi ag)* negligence; carelessness.

negoziabile [negot'tsjabile] *ag* negotiable.

negoziante [negot'tsjante] *sm/f* shopkeeper.

negoziare [negot'tsjare] *vt, vi* to negotiate.

negoziato [negot'tsjato] *sm* negotiation.

negoziatore, trice [negottsja'tore] *sm/f* negotiator.

negozio [ne'gɔttsjo] *sm* **(a)** *(bottega)* shop; ~ **di scarpe** shoe shop. **(b)** *(Dir):* ~ **giuridico** legal transaction.

negro, a ['negro] **1** *ag (razza, popolo)* Negro, black. **2** *sm/f* Negro/Negress; **lavorare come un ~** *(fig)* to work like a black.

negromante [negro'mante] *sm/f* necromancer.

negromanzia [negroman'tsia] *sf* necromancy.

nei ['nei], **nel** [nel], **nella** ['nella], **nelle** ['nelle], **nello** ['nello] *prep + art vedi* **in.**

nemico, a, ci, che [ne'miko] **1** *sm/f* enemy. **2** *ag (Mil)* enemy *attr; (ostile)* hostile; **farsi ~ qn** to make an enemy of sb; **essere ~ di qc** to be opposed to sth; **il gelo è ~ delle piante** frost is harmful to plants.

nemmeno [nem'meno] = **neanche.**

nenia ['nɛnja] *sf (anche fig peg)* dirge; *(fig: discorso)* tale of woe.

neo ['nɛo] *sm* mole; *(sul viso)* beauty spot; *(fig: imperfezione)* (slight) flaw; *(: di persona)* slight defect.

neo... ['nɛo] *pref* neo... .

neoclassico, a, ci, che [neo'klassiko] **1** *ag (stile, epoca, artista)* neoclassical. **2** *sm (stile)* neoclassical; *(artista)* neoclassicist.

neofascismo [neofaʃ'fizmo] *sm* neofascism.

neofascista, i, e [neofaʃ'fista] *sm/f* neofascist.

neologismo [neolo'dʒizmo] *sm* neologism.

neolatino, a [neola'tino] *ag* Romance *attr.*

neon ['nɛon] *sm (Chim)* neon; *(lampadario)* neon lamp; **luce al ~** neon light.

neonato, a [neo'nato] **1** *ag* newborn. **2** *sm/f* newborn baby.

neorealismo [neorea'lizmo] *sm* neorealism.

neozelandese [neoddzelan'dese] **1** *ag* New Zealand *attr.* **2** *sm/f* New Zealander.

nepotismo [nepo'tizmo] *sm* nepotism.

neppure [nep'pure] *av, cong* = **neanche.**

nerbata [ner'bata] *sf (colpo)* blow; *(sferzata)* whiplash.

nerbo ['nɛrbo] *sm* whip; *(fig: di esercito etc)* backbone.

nerboruto, a [nerbo'ruto] *ag* brawny, muscular.

neretto [ne'retto] *sm* **(a)** *(carattere tipografico)* bold type. **(b)** *(articolo di giornale)* article in bold type.

nero, a ['nero] **1** *ag* **(a)** *(colore)* black; *(capelli, occhi)* dark; *(pelle: abbronzata)* tanned; **mettere qc ~ su bianco** to put sth down in black and white; ~ **come il carbone/la pece** as black as coal/pitch; **quel colletto è** ~ *(sporco)* that collar is black *o* filthy. **(b)** *(negro)* black, coloured; **l'Africa** ~**a** black Africa. **(c)** *(fig: disperazione, futuro)* black; *(: giornata)* awful; **essere di umore** ~, **essere** ~ to be in a filthy mood; **vedere tutto** ~ to look on the black side (of things); **vivono nella miseria più** ~**a** they live in utter *o* abject poverty. **2** *sm (colore)* black; **vestirsi di** *o* **in** ~ to dress in black. **3** *sm/f (negro)* black, black man/woman.

nerofumo [nero'fumo] *sm* lampblack.

nervatura [nerva'tura] *sf (Anat)* nerves *pl*; *(Bot)* veining; *(Archit, Tecn)* rib.

nervo ['nɛrvo] *sm* nerve; ~ **ottico** optic nerve; **avere i** ~**i** to be nervy, be very irritable; **avere i** ~**i a fior di pelle** to be on edge, be nervy; **ho i** ~**i scossi** my nerves are shattered; **far venire i** ~**i a qn** to get on sb's nerves; **tenere/avere i** ~**i saldi** to keep/be calm; **che** ~**i!** damn it!

nervosismo [nervo'sizmo] *sm (Psic)* nervousness; *(irritazione)* irritability; **farsi prendere dal** ~ to let one's nerves get the better of one.

nervoso, a [ner'voso] **1** *ag* **(a)** *(tensione, sistema)* nervous; *(centro)* nerve *attr*; **esaurimento** ~ nervous breakdown. **(b)** *(agitato)* nervous, tense; *(irritabile)* irritable, touchy. **(c)** *((gambe, corpo)* sinewy. **2** *sm*: **fare venire il** ~ **a qn** to get on sb's nerves; **farsi prendere dal** ~ to let o.s. get irritated.

nespola ['nɛspola] *sf* medlar.

nespolo ['nɛspolo] *sm* medlar tree.

nesso ['nɛsso] *sm* connection, link.

nessuno, a [nes'suno] **1** *ag* **(nessun** *davanti a sm che non inizi per gn, pn, ps, s impura, x, z;* **nessun'** *davanti a sf che inizi per vocale)* **(a)** *(non uno)* no, not any; **nessun uomo è immortale** no man is immortal; **nessun altro ti crederà** no one else will believe you; **non ho nessun dubbio** I have no doubts; **non c'è nessun bisogno** there's no need, there isn't any need; **in nessun caso** under no circumstances; **in nessun luogo** nowhere; **per** ~**a cosa nel mondo** not for anything in the world. **(b)** *(qualche)* any; ~**a obiezione?** any objections?

2 *pron* **(a)** *(non uno)* no one, nobody; *(: cosa)* none; ~ **di** *(riferito a persone, cose)* none of; ~ **mi crede** no one believes me; ~ **si muova!** nobody move!; **non c'era** ~ there was no one there, there wasn't anyone there; ~ **di loro/dei presenti** none of them/of those present; **ha molti libri ma non me ne piace** ~ he has lots of books but I don't like any of them; **non ne ho letto** ~ I haven't read any of them, I have read none of them. **(b)** *(qualcuno)* anyone, anybody; **ha telefonato** ~? did anyone phone?

3 *sm (peg: nullità)* nobody, nonentity; **e io chi sono,** ~? and who am I then, nobody?; **con tutte quelle arie resta comunque un** ~ despite his airs and graces, he's still a nobody.

nettare[1] [net'tare] *vt* to clean.

nettare[2] ['nɛttare] *sm* nectar.

nettezza [net'tettsa] *sf* **(a)** *(pulizia)* cleanness, cleanliness; ~ **urbana** cleansing department. **(b)** *(chiarezza)* clarity.

netto, a ['nɛtto] **1** *ag* **(a)** *(pulito)* clean. **(b)** *(contorni, immagine)* clear, sharp; *(rifiuto, vittoria)* clear, definite; **tagliare qc di** ~ to cut sth clean off; **taglio** ~ clean cut; **taglio** ~ **col passato** *(fig)* clean break with the past. **(c)** *(stipendio, peso)* net; ~ **di tasse** after tax, net of tax. **2** *av*: **chiaro e** ~ plainly.

netturbino [nettur'bino] *sm* dustman.

neurochirurgia [neurokirur'dʒia] *sf* neurosurgery.

neurologia [neurolo'dʒia] *sf* neurology.

neurologico, a, ci, che [neuro'lɔdʒiko] *ag* neurological.

neurologo, a, gi, ghe [neu'rɔlogo] *sm/f* neurologist.

neurosi [neu'rɔzi] *sf* = **nevrosi**.

neutrale [neu'trale] *ag*, *sm* neutral.

neutralità [neutrali'ta] *sf* neutrality.

neutralizzare [neutralid'dzare] *vt (gen, Chim)* to neutralize.

neutro, a ['nɛutro] **1** *ag (gen)* neutral; *(Gram, Zool)* neuter. **2** *sm (Gram)* neuter.

neutrone [neu'trone] *sm* neutron.

nevaio [ne'vajo] *sm* snowfield.

neve ['neve] *sf* snow; **c'era un tempo da** ~ it was snowy; ~ **carbonica** dry ice; **montare a** ~ *(Culin)* to whip up.

nevicare [nevi'kare] *vb impers* to snow, be snowing.

nevicata [nevi'kata] *sf* snowfall.

nevischio [ne'viskjo] *sm* sleet.

nevoso, a [ne'voso] *ag (montagna)* snow-covered; *(tempo, inverno)* snowy.

nevralgia [nevral'dʒia] *sf* neuralgia.

nevralgico, a, ci, che [ne'vraldʒiko] *ag*: **punto** ~ *(Med)* nerve centre; *(fig)* crucial point; **è un punto** ~ **del traffico** it is one of the main areas of traffic congestion.

nevrastenico, a, ci, che [nevras'tɛniko] **1** *ag (Med)* neurasthenic; *(fig)* hot-tempered. **2** *sm/f (vedi ag)* neurasthenic; hot-tempered person.

nevrosi [ne'vrɔzi] *sf inv* neurosis.

nevrotico, a, ci, che [ne'vrɔtiko] *ag*, *sm/f (anche fig)* neurotic.

nibbio ['nibbjo] *sm (Zool)* kite.

nicchia ['nikkja] *sf (gen, fig)* niche; *(naturale: in montagna)* cavity, hollow.

nicchiare [nik'kjare] *vi* to shilly-shally, hesitate.

nichel ['nikel] *sm* nickel.

nichilismo [niki'lizmo] *sm* nihilism.

nicotina [niko'tina] *sf* nicotine.

nidiata [ni'djata] *sf (di uccelli, fig: di bambini)* brood; *(di altri animali)* litter.

nidificare [nidifi'kare] *vi* to nest.

nido ['nido] **1** *sm (Zool)* nest; *(fig: casa)* nest, home; **a** ~ **d'ape** *(tessuto, ricamo)* honeycomb *attr*. **2** *ag inv*: **asilo** ~ day nursery, crèche.

niente ['njɛnte] **1** *pron (nessuna cosa)* nothing; *(qualcosa)* anything; **non ...** ~ nothing, not ... anything; ~ **lo fermerà** nothing will stop him; **non ho visto** ~ I saw nothing, I didn't see anything; **ti serve** ~? do you need anything?; ~ **di grave/nuovo** nothing serious/new; **non gli va bene** ~ he's never satisfied; **un uomo da** ~ **a** nobody, a nonentity; **una cosa da** ~ a trivial thing; **non fa** ~! it doesn't matter!; **fa** ~ **se non vengo?** does it matter if I don't come?; **non mi sono fatto** ~ I haven't hurt myself at all; **la cura non gli ha fatto** ~ the treatment hasn't done anything for him; **non ho** ~ **a che fare con lui** I have nothing to do with him; **ha** ~ **in contrario se ...?** would you object if...?; **come se** ~ **fosse** as if nothing had happened; ~ **al mondo** nothing on earth *o* in the world; **nessuno fa** ~ **per** ~ no one does anything for nothing; **ho parlato per** ~ I spoke to no purpose; **sono venuto per** ~ there was no point in my coming; **si arrabbia per** ~ he gets annoyed at the slightest thing; **nient'altro** nothing else; **nient'altro?** *(in negozio etc)* is that all?, is there anything else?; **so poco o** ~ **di lui** I know next to nothing about him; **non so** ~ **di** ~ I know nothing at all; **quel brodo non sa di ~** that soup is tasteless; **~ meno = nientemeno.**

2 *ag:* **non ho ~ voglia di farlo** I have no desire whatsoever to do it; **~ paura!** never fear!; **e ~ scuse!** don't try to make excuses!; **~ male!** not bad at all!

3 *sm* nothing; **si è fatto dal ~** he's a self-made man; **il mondo è stato creato dal ~** the world was created out of nothing; **un bel ~** absolutely nothing; **basta un ~ per farla piangere** the slightest thing is enough to make her cry; **si è ridotta al ~** she has lost everything; **si è ridotta a un ~** she's just skin and bone.

4 *av (in nessuna misura):* **non ... ~** not ... at all; **non è ~ buono** it's not good at all; **~ affatto** not at all; **non si è visto per ~** he hasn't been seen at all; **non è per ~ vero** it's not true at all.

nientedimeno [njentedi'meno], **nientemeno** [njente'meno] **1** *av (addirittura)* actually, even; **è diventato ~ che segretaria del direttore** she has become secretary to the managing director, no less. **2** *escl* really!, you don't say!

Nigeria [ni'dʒɛrja] *sf* Nigeria.

nigeriano, a [nidʒe'rjano] *ag, sm/f* Nigerian.

night [nait] *sm inv,* **night-club** ['naitklʌb] *sm inv* nightclub.

Nilo ['nilo] *sm:* **il ~** the Nile.

nimbo ['nimbo] *sm* halo.

ninfa ['ninfa] *sf* nymph.

ninfea [nin'fɛa] *sf* water lily.

ninfomane [nin'fomane] *sf* nymphomaniac.

ninfomania [ninfoma'nia] *sf* nymphomania.

ninnananna [ninna'nanna] *sf* lullaby.

ninnolo ['ninnolo] *sm (gingillo)* knick-knack.

nipote [ni'pote] *sm/f (di nonni)* grandson/daughter, grandchild; *(di zii)* nephew/niece.

nipponico, a, ci, che [nip'poniko] *ag* Japanese, Nipponese.

nitidezza [niti'dettsa] *sf (gen)* clearness; *(di stile)* clarity; *(Fot, TV: di immagine)* sharpness.

nitido, a ['nitido] *ag (gen)* clear; *(immagine)* sharp, well-defined.

nitrato [ni'trato] *sm* nitrate.

nitrico, a, ci, che ['nitriko] *ag* nitric.

nitrire [ni'trire] *vi* to neigh.

nitrito[1] [ni'trito] *sm (di cavallo)* neigh; **~i** neighing *sg.*

nitrito[2] [ni'trito] *sm (Chim)* nitrite.

nitroglicerina [nitroglitʃe'rina] *sf* nitroglycerine.

niveo, a ['niveo] *ag* snow-white, snowy.

no [nɔ] **1** *av* **(a)** no; **vieni? — ~** are you coming? — no (I'm not); **la conosce? — ~** does he know her? — no (he doesn't); **lo conosciamo? — tu ~ ma io sì** do we know him? — you don't but I do; **verrai, ~?** you'll come, won't you?; **ha detto di ~** he said no. **(b)** *(con avverbio, congiunzione)* not; **perché ~?** why not?; **~ di certo!** certainly not!; **vieni? — come — ~!** are you coming? — of course! — or certainly!; **come ~?** what do you mean, no?; **simpatico o ~ lo devo sopportare** (whether he's) nice or not, I'll have to put up with him. **(c): credo di ~** I think not, I don't think so; **spero di ~** I hope not; **sembra di ~** apparently not; **direi di ~** I don't think so.

2 *sm no;* **da lui un ~ non me l'aspettavo** I didn't expect him to say no; **ci sono stati molti ~** *(voti, pareri contrari)* there were a lot of votes against, there were a lot of noes.

nobildonna [nobil'dɔnna] *sf* noblewoman.

nobile ['nɔbile] **1** *ag* noble; **di animo ~** noble-hearted. **2** *sm/f* noble, nobleman/woman; **i ~i** the nobility.

nobiliare [nobi'ljare] *ag* noble.

nobilitare [nobili'tare] **1** *vt (anche fig)* to ennoble. **2**: **~rsi** *vr (rendersi insigne)* to distinguish o.s.

nobiltà [nobil'ta] *sf (condizione, classe sociale)* nobility; *(fig: di azione, animo etc)* nobleness.

nobiluomo [nobi'lwomo] *sm, pl* **-uomini** nobleman.

nocca, che ['nɔkka] *sf* knuckle.

nocciola [not'tʃola] **1** *sf* hazelnut. **2** *ag inv (anche:* **color ~)** hazel, light brown.

nocciolina [nottʃo'lina] *sf (anche:* **~ americana)** peanut.

nocciolo[1] ['nɔttʃolo] *sm (di frutto)* stone; *(fig)* heart, core; **veniamo al ~!** let's get to the point!

nocciolo[2] [not'tʃolo] *sm (albero)* hazel.

noce ['notʃe] **1** *sm (albero)* walnut (tree); *(legno)* walnut. **2** *sf (frutto)* walnut; **~ di cocco** coconut; **~ moscata** nutmeg; **una ~ di burro** *(Culin)* a knob of butter.

nocepesca, sche [notʃe'pɛska] *sf* nectarine.

nocivo, a [no'tʃivo] *ag (gen)* harmful; *(fumi)* noxious; **insetti ~i** pests.

nodo ['nɔdo] *sm* **(a)** *(gen, del legname)* knot; *(fig: legame)* bond, tie; *(: punto centrale)* heart, crux; *(Bot)* node; **~ scorsoio** slipknot; **~ d'amore** love knot; **fare/sciogliere un ~** to tie/untie a knot; **avere i capelli pieni di ~i** to have tangles in one's hair; **avere un ~ alla gola** *(fig)* to have a lump in one's throat; **fare un ~ al fazzoletto** *(fig)* to tie a knot in one's handkerchief; **tutti i ~i vengono al pettine** *(Proverbio)* your sins catch up with you sooner or later. **(b)** *(incrocio: ferroviario, stradale)* junction. **(c)** *(Naut)* knot.

nodoso, a [no'doso] *ag (tronco, mani)* gnarled.

nodulo ['nodulo] *sm (Anat, Bot)* nodule.

noi ['noi] *pron pers* **(a)** *(soggetto)* we; **~ andiamo** we're going; **tutti ~ pensiamo che sia giusto** we all think it's right, all of us think it's right; **~ italiani** we Italians; **siamo stati ~ a dirglielo** it was us who told him, we were the ones to tell him; **~ accettare?, non sia mai detto!** us accept that?, never!

(b) *(oggetto: per dare rilievo, con preposizione)* us; **vuol vedere proprio ~** it's us he wants to see; **dice a ~?** is he talking to us?; **tocca a ~?** is it our turn?; **da ~** *(nel nostro paese)* in our country, where we come from; *(a casa nostra)* at our house.

(c) *(comparazioni)* we, us; **vanno veloce come ~** they are going as fast as we are, they are going as fast as us; **fate come ~** do as we do, do the same as us; **sono più giovani di ~** they are younger than we are *o* than us.

noia ['nɔja] *sf (tedio)* boredom; *(disturbo)* bother, trouble; *(fastidio)* nuisance; **morire di ~** to die of boredom; **mi è venuto a ~** I'm tired of it; **dare ~ a qn** to bother *o* annoy sb; **avere (delle) ~e con la polizia** to have trouble with the police; **che ~!** what a bore!; *(fastidio)* what a nuisance!

noialtri [no'jaltri] *pron pers* we.

noioso, a [no'joso] *ag (tedioso)* boring; *(fastidioso)* annoying, tiresome.

noleggiare [noled'dʒare] *vt (auto, bicicletta: prendere a noleggio)* to hire; *(: dare a noleggio)* to hire out; *(aereo, nave)* to charter.

noleggiatore, trice [noleddʒa'tore] *sm/f (vedi vb)* hirer; charterer.

noleggio [no'leddʒo] *sm (di auto, bicicletta)* hire; *(di nave, barca)* charter; **prendere/dare a ~** to hire/hire (out); **c'è un ~ di biciclette?** is there a place where you can hire bikes?

nolente [no'lente] *ag:* **volente o ~** whether one likes it or not, willy-nilly.

nolo ['nɔlo] *sm (di auto)* hire (charge); *(di nave)* charter (fee); *(per trasporto merci)* freight (charge); **prendere/dare a ~ qc** to hire/hire (out) sth.

nomade ['nɔmade] **1** *ag* nomadic. **2** *sm/f* nomad.

nome ['nome] **1** *sm (gen)* name; **a ~ di** on behalf of; **un uomo di ~ Giovanni** a man by the name of John, a man called John; **solo di ~** in name only; **in ~ della legge** in the name of the law; **in ~ del cielo!** in heaven's name!; **sotto il ~ di** under the name of; **sotto falso ~** under an assumed name *o* alias; **chiamare qn per ~** to call sb by name; **posso chiamarti per ~?** can I call you by your first name?; **li conosce tutti per ~** she knows them all by name; **lo conosco solo di ~** I know him only by name; **fare il ~ di qn** to name sb; **faccia pure il mio ~** feel free to mention my name; **farsi un buon/cattivo ~** to get a good/bad name; **ormai si è fatto un ~** he has made a name for himself now; **porta** *o* **gli hanno dato il ~ di suo nonno** he is named after his grandfather; **senza ~** nameless.

2: **~ d'arte** stage name; **~ astratto/proprio/comune** *(Gram)* abstract/proper/common noun; **~ di battaglia** nom de guerre; **~ di battesimo** Christian name; **~ da ragazza** maiden name; **~ da sposata** married name.

nomea [no'mɛa] *sf* notoriety.

nomenclatura [nomenkla'tura] *sf* nomenclature.

nomignolo [no'miɲɲolo] *sm* nickname.

nomina ['nɔmina] *sf* appointment; **conferire una ~ a qn** to appoint sb; **ottenere la ~ a presidente** to be appointed president.

nominale [nomi'nale] *ag (gen)* nominal; *(Gram)* noun *attr*; **valore ~** face *o* nominal value.

nominare [nomi'nare] *vt* to name; *(citare)* to mention; *(eleggere)* to appoint; **non l'ho mai sentito ~** I've never heard of it *(o* him); **l'hanno nominato segretario generale** he has been appointed secretary-general.

nominativo, a [nomina'tivo] **1** *ag (Gram)* nominative; *(Fin)* registered. **2** *sm* **(a)** *(Gram)* nominative (case). **(b)** *(Comm, Amm: nome)* name.

non [non] **1** *av* **(a)** not; **~ sono inglesi** they are not *o* aren't English; **~ ne ho** I do not *o* don't have any, I haven't any; **~ devi farlo** you must not *o* mustn't do it; **~ puoi venire** you cannot *o* can't come; **~ vieni?** aren't you coming?; **~ parli francese?** don't you speak French?; **~ è venuto nessuno** nobody came; **~ l'ho mai visto** I have never seen it; **~ lo capisco affatto** I do not *o* don't understand him at all; **~ più di 5 minuti** no more than 5 minutes; **~ oltre il 15 luglio** no later than 15th July; **grazie — ~ c'è di che** thank you — don't mention it.

(b) *(con sostantivo, aggettivo, pronome, avverbio)* not; **un guadagno ~ indifferente** a not inconsiderable gain; **~ pochi sono d'accordo** not a few are in agreement, many are in agreement; **~ uno dei presenti si è alzato** not one of those present stood up.

(c) *(pleonastico)*: **~ puoi ~ vederlo** you can't not see him, you'll have to see him; **finché ~ torno** until I get back; **per poco ~ cadevo in acqua** I almost fell into the water.

2 *pref* non-, un...; **politica di ~ intervento** policy of non-intervention; **i ~ credenti** the unbelievers; **i ~ abbienti** the have-nots; **i paesi ~ allineati** the non-aligned countries.

nonché [non'ke] *cong (tanto più, tanto meno)* let alone; **è inutile scrivergli, ~ telefonargli** it's pointless writing to him, let alone telephoning him. **(b)** *(e inoltre)* as well as; **lo ricorderò a lui, ~ a suo fratello** I'll remind him as well as his brother.

nonconformista, i, e [nonkonfor'mista] *ag, sm/f* nonconformist.

noncurante [nonku'rante] *ag*: **~ (di)** indifferent (to), careless (of); **con fare ~** with a nonchalant air.

noncuranza [nonku'rantsa] *sf* carelessness, indifference; **assumere un'aria di ~** to take on a nonchalant air.

nondimeno [nondi'meno] *cong (tuttavia)* however; *(nonostante)* nevertheless.

nonno, a ['nɔnno] *sm/f* grandfather/mother; *(in senso più familiare)* grandpa/grandma; **~i** *smpl* grandparents.

nonnulla [non'nulla] *sm inv*: **un ~** nothing, a trifle.

nono, a ['nɔno] *ag, sm/f, sm* ninth; *per uso vedi* **quinto.**

nonostante [nonos'tante] **1** *prep* in spite of, notwithstanding. **2** *cong* even though, in spite of the fact that; **~ fosse notte fonda** in spite of the fact that it was late at night; **~ che piovesse** even though *o* in spite of the fact that it was raining.

non plus ultra ['nonplus'ultra] *sm*: **il ~ (di)** the last word (in).

nonsenso [non'sɛnso] *sm* absurdity.

nontiscordardimé [nontiskordardi'me] *sm inv (Bot)* forget-me-not.

nord [nɔrd] **1** *sm* north; **a ~ (di)** north (of); **esposto a ~** facing north; **verso ~** northward(s); **il mare del N~** the North Sea; **l'America del N~** North America. **2** *ag inv (gen)* north; *(regione)* northern; **è partito in direzione ~** he set off northwards *o* in a northward direction.

nordest [nor'dest] *sm* north-east; **vento di ~** north-easterly wind.

nordico, a, ci, che ['nɔrdiko] **1** *ag* Nordic. **2** *sm/f* Northern European.

nordista, i, e [nor'dista] *ag, sm/f* Yankee.

nordovest [nor'dovest] *sm* north-west; **vento di ~** north-westerly wind.

norma ['nɔrma] *sf (principio)* norm; *(regola)* regulation, rule; *(consuetudine)* custom, rule; **scostarsi dalla ~** to diverge from the norm; **al di sopra della ~** above average, above the norm; **di ~** normally; **a ~ di legge** in accordance with the law; **per tua ~ e regola** for your information; **~e di sicurezza** safety regulations; **~e per l'uso** instructions for use; **proporsi una ~ di vita** to set o.s. rules to live by.

normale [nor'male] **1** *ag* normal; *(solito)* usual, normal; **ma tu non sei ~!** there must be something wrong with you!; **è ~ che sia così** it is quite normal for it to be like that. **2** *sm*: **più alto del ~** taller than average; **ha un'intelligenza al di sopra del ~** he is of above average intelligence. **3** *sf (Mat)* normal.

normalità [normali'ta] *sf* normality.

normalizzare [normalid'dzare] **1** *vt* to bring back to normal; *(Pol, Mat)* to normalize. **2**: **~rsi** *vr* to return to normal.

Normandia [norman'dia] *sf* Normandy.

normanno, a [nor'manno] *ag, sm/f* Norman.

normativa [norma'tiva] *sf* regulations *pl*.

normativo, a [norma'tivo] *ag* normative.

norvegese [norve'dʒese] *ag, sm, sm/f* Norwegian.

Norvegia [nor'vedʒa] *sf* Norway.

nosocomio [nozo'kɔmjo] *sm* hospital.

nostalgia [nostal'dʒia] *sf (di casa, paese)* homesickness; *(del passato)* nostalgia; **soffrire di ~** to be homesick; **aver ~ di casa** to be homesick.

nostalgico, a, ci, che [nos'taldʒiko] **1** *ag (vedi sf)* homesick; nostalgic. **2** *sm/f (Pol)* person who hopes for the return of Fascism.

nostrano, a [nos'trano] *ag (gen)* local; *(pianta, frutta)* home-grown.

nostro, a ['nɔstro] **1** *ag poss*: il(la) ~(a) *etc* our; il ~ **giardino** our garden; ~a **madre** our mother; **un** ~ **amico** a friend of ours; è **colpa** ~a it's our fault; **a casa** ~a at our house, at home.

2 *pron poss*: il(la) ~(a) *etc* ours, our own; **la vostra barca è più lunga della** ~a your boat is longer than ours; **il** ~ **è stato solo un errore** it was simply an error on our part.

3 *sm* **(a): abbiamo speso del** ~ we've spent our own money; **viviamo del** ~ we live on our own income. **(b): i** ~**i** *(famiglia)* our family; *(amici etc)* our own people, our side; **è dei** ~**i** he's one of us.

4 *sf*: **la** ~**a** *(opinione)* our view; **è dalla** ~**a** *(parte)* he's on our side; **anche noi abbiamo avuto le** ~**e** *(disavventure)* we've had our problems too; **alla** ~**a!** *(brindisi)* to us!

nostromo [nos'trɔmo] *sm* boatswain.

nota ['nɔta] *sf* **(a)** *(gen, Mus)* note; **prendere** ~ **di** qc to note, make a note of sth, write sth down; *(fig: fare attenzione)* to note, take note of sth; **degno di** ~ noteworthy, worthy of note; **una** ~ **di tristezza/allegria** a note of sadness/happiness; ~**e a piè di pagina** footnotes; ~**e caratteristiche** *(di carattere, stile)* distinguishing features; ~ **fondamentale** *(Mus)* tonic. **(b)** *(fattura)* bill; *(elenco)* list; ~ **spese** list of expenses; ~ **delle spese** shopping list.

notabile [no'tabile] **1** *ag* notable. **2** *sm* prominent citizen.

notaio [no'tajo] *sm* notary (public).

notare [no'tare] *vt (osservare)* to notice; *(rilevare)* to note; *(segnare)* to note (down); **hai notato com'era strano?** did you notice how strange he was?; **vi faccio** ~ **che...** I would have you note that...; ~ **qc a margine** to write sth in the margin; **farsi** ~ to get o.s. noticed.

notarile [nota'rile] *ag*: **studio** ~ notary's office; **atto** ~ legal document *(authorized by a notary)*.

notazione [notat'tsjone] *sf (Mus)* notation.

notevole [no'tevole] *ag (degno di nota)* notable, remarkable; *(rilevante)* considerable.

notifica, che [no'tifika] *sf* notification.

notificare [notifi'kare] *vt (Dir)*: ~ **qc a qn** to notify sb of sth, give sb notice of sth.

notificazione [notifikat'tskjone] *sf* notification.

notizia [no'tittsja] *sf* (piece of) news *sg*; *(informazione)* piece of information; ~**e** news *sg*; information *sg*; **avere una bella/brutta** ~ to have some good/bad news; **aver** ~**e di** qn to hear from sb; **fammi avere tue** ~**e!** keep in touch!

notiziario [notit'tsjarjo] *sm (Radio, TV, Stampa)* news *sg*.

noto, a ['nɔto] **1** *ag* well-known; ~ **a tutti** (well) known to everybody; **rendere** ~ qc to make sth known. **2** *sm*: **il** ~ **e l'ignoto** the known and the unknown.

notorietà [notorje'ta] *sf* fame; *(peg)* notoriety.

notorio, a [no'tɔrjo] *ag* well-known; *(peg)* notorious.

nottambulo, a [not'tambulo] *sm/f* night-bird.

nottata [not'tata] *sf* night; **ho passato la** ~ **in piedi** I was up all night.

notte ['nɔtte] *sf* night; *(oscurità)* darkness, night; *(periodo)* night, night-time; **camicia da** ~ nightgown; **portiere di** ~ night porter; **è meglio non uscire di** ~ it's better not to go out at night; **è successo di** ~ it happened during the night; **la** ~ **è meglio dormire** it's better to sleep at night; **la** ~ **di sabato, sabato** ~ (on) Saturday night; **questa** ~ *(passata)* last night; *(che viene)* tonight;

rientrare prima di ~ to come back home before dark; **col favore della** ~ under cover of darkness; **nella** ~ **dei tempi** in the mists of time; **come va?** — **peggio che andare di** ~ how are things? — worse than ever; ~ **bianca** sleepless night.

nottetempo [notte'tempo] *av* during the night.

nottola ['nɔttola] *sf (Zool)* noctule.

notturno, a [not'turno] **1** *ag (locale, servizio, guardiano)* night *attr*; *(Zool, fig)* nocturnal. **2** *sm (Mus)* nocturne. **3** *sf (Sport)* evening fixture.

nova ['nɔva] *sf (Astron)* nova.

novanta [no'vanta] *ag inv, sm inv* ninety; *per uso vedi* **cinquanta**.

novantenne [novan'tenne] *ag, sm/f* ninety-year-old; *per uso vedi* **cinquantenne**.

novantesimo, a [novan'tezimo] *ag, sm/f, sm* ninetieth; *per uso vedi* **quinto**.

novantina [novan'tina] *sf* about ninety; *per uso vedi* **cinquantina**.

nove ['nɔve] *ag inv, sm inv* nine; *per uso vedi* **cinque**.

novecentesco, a, schi, sche [novetʃen'tesko] *ag* twentieth-century.

novecento [nove'tʃento] **1** *ag inv* nine hundred. **2** *sm inv* nine hundred; *(secolo)*: **il N**~ the twentieth century.

novella [no'vɛlla] *sf (Letteratura)* short story.

novellino, a [novel'lino] *sm/f* beginner, greenhorn.

novellista, i, e [novel'lista] *sm/f* short-story writer.

novellistica [novel'listika] *sf (arte)* short-story writing; *(insieme di racconti)* short stories *pl*.

novello, a [no'vello] *ag (piante, patate)* new; *(insalata, verdura)* early; *(sposo)* newly-married; **pollo** ~ spring chicken.

novembre [no'vɛmbre] *sm* November; *per uso vedi* **luglio**.

novembrino, a [novem'brino] *ag* November *attr*.

novennale [noven'nale] *ag (che dura 9 anni)* nine-year *attr*; *(ogni 9 anni)* nine-yearly.

novilunio [novi'lunjo] *sm* new moon.

novità [novi'ta] *sf inv* **(a)** *(originalità)* novelty; *(cosa)* new thing; *(libro)* new publication; **questa è una** ~! that's new!; **le** ~ **della moda francese** the latest French fashions. **(b)** *(notizia)* (piece of) news *sg*; **che** ~ **ci sono?** what's the news?

noviziato [novit'tsjato] *sm (Rel)* novitiate; *(tirocinio)* apprenticeship.

novizio, a [no'vittsjo] *sm/f (Rel)* novice; *(tirocinante)* beginner, apprentice.

nozione [not'tsjone] *sf* notion, idea; **ho perso la** ~ **del tempo** I've lost all notion of time; **le prime** ~**i di matematica** the first elements of mathematics; **non ha che alcune** ~**i di filosofia** he only has a vague notion of philosophy.

nozionismo [nottsjo'nizmo] *sm* superficial knowledge.

nozionistico, a, ci, che [nottsjo'nistiko] *ag* superficial.

nozze ['nɔttse] *sfpl* wedding *sg*; **regalo di** ~ wedding present; **viaggio di** ~ honeymoon; ~ **d'argento/d'oro** silver/golden wedding.

ns. *abbr commerciale di* **nostro**.

nube ['nube] *sf (anche fig)* cloud.

nubifragio [nubi'fradʒo] *sm* cloudburst.

nubile ['nubile] **1** *ag (donna)* unmarried, single. **2** *sf* single *o* unmarried woman; *(meno giovane)* spinster.

nuca, che [nuka] *sf* nape (of the neck).

nucleare [nukle'are] *ag* nuclear.

nucleo ['nukleo] *sm (Bio, Fis)* nucleus; *(fig: parte centrale)* core, nucleus; *(gruppo)* unit, group;

(Mil, Polizia) unit, squad; **il ~ familiare** the family unit.

nudismo [nu'dizmo] *sm* nudism.

nudista, i, e [nu'dista] *sm/f* nudist.

nudità [nudi'ta] *sf inv (di persona)* nudity, nakedness; *(di paesaggio)* bareness; **le proprie ~** one's nakedness.

nudo, a ['nudo] **1** *ag (persona)* bare, naked; *(albero, parete, montagna)* bare; *(verità)* plain, naked; **mezzo/tutto ~** half-/stark naked; **a piedi ~i** barefoot; **a occhio ~** to the naked eye; **gli ha detto ~ e crudo che...** he said to him bluntly that...; **questa è la verità ~a e cruda** this is the plain truth; **mettere a ~** *(cuore, verità)* to lay bare. **2** *sm (Arte)* nude.

nugolo ['nugolo] *sm:* **un ~ di** a whole host of.

nulla ['nulla] **1** *pron, av* = **niente. 2** *sm* **(a)** nothing, nothingness; **Dio creò il mondo dal ~** God created the world out of nothing; **svanire nel ~** to vanish into thin air. **(b)** *(minima quantità)*: **basta un ~ per farlo arrabbiare** he gets annoyed over the slightest thing; **te lo cedo per (un) ~** I am giving it to you for a song *o* for next to nothing.

nullaosta [nulla'ɔsta] *sm inv* authorization, permission.

nullatenente [nullate'nɛnte] **1** *ag:* **essere ~** to own nothing. **2** *sm/f* person with no property.

nullità [nulli'ta] *sf inv* **(a)** *(Dir)* nullity; *(di idea, ragionamento)* invalidity. **(b)** *(persona)* nonentity.

nullo, a ['nullo] *ag (Dir)* null (and void); **scheda ~a** *(Pol)* spoiled vote; **l'incontro è stato dichiarato ~** *(Sport)* the match was declared invalid.

numerale [nume'rale] *ag, sm* numeral.

numerare [nume'rare] *vt* to number.

numeratore [numera'tore] *sm* **(a)** *(Mat)* numerator. **(b)** *(macchina)* numbering machine.

numerazione [numerat'tsjone] *sf* numbering; **~ araba/romana** arabic/roman numerals *pl*.

numerico, a, ci, che [nu'mɛriko] *ag* numerical.

numero ['numero] *sm* **(a)** *(gen)* number; *(arabo, romano)* numeral; **dodici di ~** twelve in number; **~ chiuso** *(Univ)* selective entry system; **~ civico** house number; **abito al ~ 6** I live at number 6; **~ legale** quorum; **che ~ di scarpe porti?** what size of shoe do you take?; **fare un ~** *(Telec)* to dial a number; **ha tutti i ~i per riuscire** he's got what it takes to succeed; **dare i ~i** *(farneticare)* not to be all there; **tanto per fare ~ invitiamo anche lui** why don't we invite him to make up the numbers?; **che ~ tuo fratello!** your brother is a real character! **(b)** *(di giornale, rivista)* issue, number; **~ arretrato** back number. **(c)** *(Teatro)* act, turn.

numeroso, a [nume'roso] *ag* **(a)** numerous, many; **le personalità sono intervenute ~e** celebrities were present in large numbers. **(b)** *(folla, famiglia)* large.

nunzio ['nuntsjo] *sm (Rel)* nuncio.

nuocere ['nwɔtʃere] *vi:* **~ a** to harm, damage; **il tentar non nuoce** *(Proverbio)* there's no harm in trying.

nuociuto, a [nwo'tʃuto] *pp di* **nuocere.**

nuora ['nwɔra] *sf* daughter-in-law.

nuotare [nwo'tare] **1** *vi* to swim; **~ a rana/sul dorso** to do the breast-stroke/back-stroke; **~ nell'oro** to be rolling in money; **nuotavo nel sudore** the sweat was pouring off me. **2** *vt* to swim.

nuotata [nwo'tata] *sf* swim.

nuotatore, trice [nwota'tore] *sm/f* swimmer.

nuoto ['nwɔto] *sm* swimming; **attraversare la Manica a ~** to swim (across) the Channel.

nuova ['nwɔva] *sf* news *sg*; **nessuna ~ buona ~** no news is good news; **che ~e ci sono?** is there any news?

nuovamente [nwɔva'mente] *av* again.

Nuova Zelanda [,nwɔvaddze'landa] *sf* New Zealand.

nuovo, a ['nwɔvo] **1** *ag* **(a)** *(gen)* new; *(originale: idea)* novel, new; *(: metodo)* new, up-to-date; **~ fiammante, ~ di zecca** brand-new; **il ~ presidente** the new *o* newly-elected president; **sono ~ del mestiere** I am new to this job; **sono ~ di questo posto/di Glasgow** I am new here/to Glasgow; **il suo volto non mi è ~** I know his face; **come ~** as good as new; **sembra ~** it looks like new.

(b) *(altro, secondo)* new, fresh; *(diverso)* new, different; **usa un foglio ~** take a fresh sheet of paper; **hai letto il suo ~ libro?** have you read his new *o* latest book?; **fino a ~ ordine** until further notice; **c'è stata una ~a serie di scosse** there has been a new *o* further series of tremors; **fare un ~ tentativo** to make another attempt; **anno ~, vita ~a!** it's time to turn over a new leaf!

(c): **di ~** again; **di ~ tu?** (is that) you again? **2** *sm:* **che c'è di ~?** what's the news?, what's new?; **non c'è niente di ~** there's no news *o* nothing new; **rimettere a ~** *(cosa, macchina)* to do up like new; **questa cura mi ha rimesso a ~** this treatment has given me a new lease of life.

nutrice [nu'tritʃe] *sf* wet-nurse.

nutriente [nutri'ɛnte] *ag* nutritious, nourishing; **crema ~** *(Cosmetica)* nourishing cream.

nutrimento [nutri'mento] *sm* nourishment.

nutrire [nu'trire] **1** *vt* to feed; *(fig: sentimenti)* to feel; **nutrivo profonda stima per lui** I felt great respect for him. **2** *vi (cibo)* to be nourishing. **3**: **~rsi** *vr:* **~rsi di** to feed on, eat.

nutritivo, a [nutri'tivo] *ag* nutritional.

nutrito, a [nu'trito] *ag* **(a)**: **ben/mal ~** well/poorly fed. **(b)** *(numeroso)* large; *(fitto)* heavy.

nutrizione [nutrit'tsjone] *sf (atto)* feeding, nutrition; *(dieta)* nutrition; **una scarsa ~** a poor diet.

nuvola ['nuvola] *sf* cloud; **avere la testa fra le ~e** to have one's head in the clouds; **cascare dalle ~e** to be astounded, be taken aback.

nuvolo, a ['nuvolo] *ag* cloudy.

nuvolosità [nuvolosi'ta] *sf* cloudiness; **~ persistente** persistent cloud cover.

nuvoloso, a [nuvo'loso] *ag (tempo)* cloudy; *(cielo)* cloudy, overcast.

nuziale [nut'tsjale] *ag* wedding *attr*, nuptial.

nylon ['nailən] *sm inv* ® nylon.

O

O, o¹ |ɔ| *sf o m inv (lettera)* O, o.

o² |o| *(dav vocale talvolta* **od)** *cong* **(a)** *(gen)* or; ~ **meglio** or rather; **due ~ tre volte** two or three times; **oggi ~ domani** (either) today or tomorrow; **lo farò ~ oggi ~ domani** I'll do it either today or tomorrow; **(~) l'uno ~ l'altro** either (of them); **sono decisa: ~ lui ~ nessuno** I've made up my mind: it's him or nobody. **(b)** *(altrimenti)* (or) else; **sbrigati ~ faremo tardi** hurry up or (else) we'll be late.

o³, oh |o| *escl* **(a)** oh! **(b)** *(fam: per chiamare)* hey!

O. *abbr (= ovest)* W.

oasi |'ɔazi| *sf inv (anche fig)* oasis.

obbediente |obbe'djɛnte| *etc* = **ubbidiente** *etc.*

obbiettare |obbjet'tare| *etc vedi* **obiettare** *etc.*

obbligare |obbli'gare| **1** *vt:* ~ **qn a fare qc** *(sog: circostanze, persona)* to force o oblige sb to do sth; *(legalmente)* to require sb to do sth; **sono obbligato (a farlo)** I have to (do it); **e chi ti obbliga?** who's forcing you (to do it)?; **la mia coscienza mi obbligò a tacere** I was bound by conscience to remain silent; **l'influenza lo obbliga a letto** he's confined to bed with flu. **2:** ~**rsi** *vr* **(a)** *(Dir):* ~**rsi per qn** to stand surety for sb, act as guarantor for sb. **(b)** *(impegnarsi):* ~**rsi a fare** to undertake to do.

obbligato, a |obbli'gato| *ag* **(a)** *(riconoscente):* ~ **verso qn** obliged o indebted to sb; **le sono molto ~!** I'm much obliged! **(b)** *(imposto):* **percorso ~** set o fixed route; **passaggio ~** *(fig)* essential requirement.

obbligatorio, a |obbliga'tɔrjo| *ag* compulsory, obligatory; *(clausola)* (legally) binding.

obbligazione |obbligat'tsjone| *sf* **(a)** *(gen, Dir)* obligation. **(b)** *(Fin)* bond, debenture; ~ **dello Stato** government bond.

obbligazionista, i, e |obbligattsjo'nista| *sm/f* bondholder.

obbligo, ghi |'ɔbbligo| *sm* obligation; *(dovere)* obligation, duty; **avere degli ~ghi con o verso qn** to be under an obligation to sb, be indebted to sb; **sentire/avere l'~ di fare** to feel/be obliged to do, feel/be under an obligation to do; **mi sono sentito in ~ (di farlo)** I felt obliged to (do it); **i libri vengono dati in prestito con l'~ di restituirli entro 15 giorni** books are lent on condition that they are returned within a fortnight; **essere d'~** *(discorso, applauso)* to be called for; **fare una visita d'~** to make a duty call; **le formalità d'~** the necessary formalities; **complimenti d'~** civilities; **'è d'~ l'abito scuro'** 'black tie'; ~**ghi militari** compulsory military service *sg.*

obbrobrio |ob'brɔbrjo| *sm* **(a)** disgrace, shame. **(b)** *(fig)* mess, eyesore; **quel palazzo è un ~** that building's an eyesore.

obbrob.ioso, a |obbrobrj'oso| *ag* disgraceful, shameful; *(fig)* ghastly.

obelisco, schi |obe'lisko| *sm* obelisk.

oberato, a |obe'rato| *ag:* ~ **di** *(lavoro)* overloaded o overburdened with; *(debiti)* crippled with.

obesità |obesi'ta| *sf* obesity.

obeso, a |o'bɛso| *ag* obese.

obiettare |objet'tare| *vt:* ~ **che** to object that; **non ho nulla da ~** I have no objection (to make); **ha obiettato che non aveva tempo** he pleaded lack of time.

obiettivamente |objettiva'mɛnte| *av* objectively.

obiettività |objettivi'ta| *sf* objectivity.

obiettivo, a |objet'tivo| **1** *ag* objective. **2** *sm* **(a)** *(Mil, fig)* objective. **(b)** *(Ottica, Fot)* lens, objective; ~ **grandangolare/a fuoco fisso** wide-angle/fixed-focus lens.

obiettore |objet'tore| *sm:* ~ **di coscienza** conscientious objector.

obiezione |objet'tsjone| *sf* objection; **fare o muovere o sollevare un'~** to make o raise an objection, object; ~ **accolta/respinta** *(Dir)* objection sustained/overruled.

obitorio |obi'tɔrjo| *sm* mortuary, morgue.

oblio |o'blio| *sm* oblivion; **cadere in ~** to sink into oblivion.

obliquità |oblikwi'ta| *sf* obliqueness.

obliquo, a |o'blikwo| *ag* *(gen, Mat)* oblique; *(calligrafia, raggi)* slanting.

obliterare |oblite'rare| *vt (francobollo)* to cancel; *(biglietto)* to stamp.

obliteratrice |oblitera'tritʃe| *sf (anche:* **macchina ~:** *vedi vb)* cancelling machine; stamping machine.

oblò |o'blɔ| *sm inv (Naut)* porthole.

oblungo, a, ghi, ghe |o'blungo| *ag* oblong.

oboe |'ɔboe| *sm* oboe.

obsoleto, a |obso'leto| *ag* obsolete.

obsolescenza |obsoleʃ'ʃɛntsa| *sf* obsolescence.

oca |'ɔka| *sf, pl* **oche** *(Zool)* goose; *(fig pej)* silly goose; ~ **maschio** gander; **il gioco dell'~** ≃ snakes and ladders.

ocaggine |okad'dʒine| *sf* silliness, stupidity.

occasionale |okkazjo'nale| *ag (incontro)* chance; *(cliente, guadagni)* casual, occasional.

occasione |okka'zjone| *sf* **(a)** *(opportunità)* chance, opportunity; **sarebbe l'~ buona per fare...** it would be an ideal opportunity to do...; **avere ~ di fare qc** to have the chance o opportunity of doing sth; **alla prima ~** at the first opportunity); **all'~** should the need arise. **(b)** *(circostanza)* occasion; **in ~ di** on the occasion of; **a seconda delle o secondo le ~i** depending on circumstances o on the situation. **(c)** *(motivo, pretesto)* occasion, cause; **dare ~ a** to cause, give rise to. **(d)** *(buon affare)* bargain; **d'~** *(economico: prezzi)* bargain *attr; (di seconda mano)* secondhand.

occhiacci |ok'kjattʃi| *smpl:* **fare gli ~ a qn** to scowl at sb.

occhiaia |ok'kjaja| *sf* **(a)** *(orbita)* eye socket. **(b):** ~**e** *sfpl:* **avere le ~e** to have shadows under one's eyes.

occhiali |ok'kjali| *smpl* glasses, spectacles; *(di protezione)* goggles; ~ **da ghiacciaio** snow goggles; ~ **da sole** sunglasses.

occhiata |ok'kjata| *sf* look, glance; **dare un'~ a** to have a look at, glance at; *(badare)* to keep an eye on; **un'~ d'intesa** a knowing look o glance.

occhieggiare [okkjed'dʒare] *vi (fiori)* to appear here and there, peep out.

occhiello [ok'kjɛllo] *sm* **(a)** buttonhole; *(di scarpe etc)* eyelet. **(b)** *(Tip)* half-title.

occhio ['ɔkkjo] *sm* **(a)** *(Anat)* eye; **avere gli ~i blu** to have blue eyes; **dagli ~i castani** brown-eyed; **avere ~i buoni** to have good eyesight; **logorarsi gli ~i** to strain one's eyes; **a ~ nudo** with the naked eye.

(b) *(sguardo, espressione)* look; **alzò gli ~i dal libro** he looked up from *o* raised his eyes from his book; **cercare qn con gli ~i** to look *o* glance around for sb; **ha l'~ smorto oggi** he's looking rather bleary-eyed today.

(c) *(accortezza, capacità di giudicare)*: **avere ~** to have a good eye; **ci vuole ~ per fare questo lavoro** this job requires a good eye; **vedere di buon/mal ~ qn/qc** to view sb/sth favourably/unfavourably.

(d) *(attenzione)*: **~!** look out!, watch out!; **~ alla borsa!** watch your bag!, keep an eye on your bag!; **essere tutt'~i** to be all eyes.

(e)*(cosa a forma d'~: di ciclone, patata etc)* eye.

(f) *(fraseologia)*: **a ~ (e croce)** roughly, approximately; **tieni gli ~ aperti per...** keep an eye out for...; **non riuscivo a tener gli ~i aperti** I could hardly keep my eyes open; **non ho chiuso ~ stanotte** I didn't sleep a wink last night; **chiudere un ~ (su)** *(fig)* to turn a blind eye (to); **a ~i chiusi** *(anche fig)* with one's eyes shut; **co-stare un ~ della testa** to cost a fortune; **darei un ~ per sapere** I'd give my eyeteeth to know; **dare nell'~** to attract attention; *(vestito, colore)* to be loud *o* gaudy; **fare l'~ a qc** to get used to sth; **fare gli ~i dolci a qn** to make sheep's eyes at sb; **guardare con tanto d'~i** to gaze wide-eyed at; **lasciare gli ~i su qc** to set one's heart on sth; **a quattr'~i** privately, in private; **ce l'hai sotto gli ~i** you've got it in front of you; **mi è capitato sott'~ un articolo interessante** I happened to see an interesting article; **tenere d'~ qn/qc** to keep an eye on sb/sth.

occhiolino [okkjo'lino] *sm*: **fare l'~ a qn** to wink at sb.

occidentale [ottʃiden'tale] **1** *ag (Geog)* western, west; *(: vento)* westerly; *(cultura, paesi)* Western. **2** *sm/f* westerner.

occidente [ottʃi'dɛnte] *sm* west; **a ~ di** (to the) west of; **il sole tramonta a ~** the sun sets in the west; **l'O~** *(Pol)* the West.

occipite [ot'tʃipite] *sm (Anat)* back of the head, occiput *(T)*.

occludere [ok'kludere] *vt (Med)* to occlude.

occlusione [okklu'zjone] *sf (Med)* occlusion.

occluso, a [ok'kluzo] *pp di* occludere.

occorrente [okkor'rɛnte] **1** *ag* necessary. **2** *sm*: **porta con te tutto l'~** bring everything you need; **l'~ per scrivere/disegnare** writing/drawing materials *pl*.

occorrenza [okkor'rɛntsa] *sf* **(a)** *(evenienza)* eventuality. **(b)** *(bisogno)* necessity, need; **all'~** if need be, if necessary.

occorrere [ok'korrere] *(aus* **essere)** **1** *vi (essere necessario)* to be needed, be required; **mi occorrono 2 milioni di lire** I need 2 million lire; **mi occorre un'ora per arrivarci** it takes me *o* I need an hour to get there. **2** *vb impers*: **occorre farlo** it must be done; **occorre far presto** we'll *(o* you'll *etc)* have to hurry; **non occorre che gli scriva subito** there's no need to write to him at once.

occorso, a [ok'korso] *pp di* occorrere.

occultamento [okkulta'mento] *sm* concealment.

occultare [okkul'tare] **1** *vt* to hide, conceal. **2**: **~rsi**

vr: **~rsi (a)** to hide (from), conceal o.s. (from).

occulto, a [ok'kulto] *ag (segreto)* hidden, secret; *(arcano)* occult; **le scienze ~e** the occult sciences, the occult.

occupante [okku'pante] **1** *ag (Mil)* occupying. **2** *sm/f (di casa)* occupier, occupant; **~ abusivo** squatter.

occupare [okku'pare] **1** *vt (gen, Mil)* to occupy; *(spazio, tempo)* to occupy, take up; *(casa)* to live in; *(carica)* to hold; *(manodopera)* to employ; **la casa è stata occupata (abusivamente)** the house has been taken over by squatters; **l'insegnamento occupa tutte le mie mattinate** teaching takes up all my mornings; **l'esercito ha occupato il paese** the army has occupied *o* taken over the country. **2**: **~rsi** *vr*: **~rsi di** *(interessarsi)* to be interested in; *(prendersi cura)* to take care of, look after; *(impicciarsi)* to interfere in, meddle in; **si occupa di assicurazione** he's in insurance; **occupati dei fatti tuoi!** mind your own business!

occupato, a [okku'pato] *ag (telefono, gabinetto)* engaged; *(posto)* taken, occupied; *(zona, fabbrica)* occupied; *(persona)* busy; **essere ~ a fare qc** to be busy doing sth.

occupazionale [okkupattsjo'nale] *ag* employment *attr*, of employment.

occupazione [okkupat'tsjone] *sf* **(a)** *(Mil, di fabbrica)* occupation; *(di casa)* occupancy, occupation; *(interesse, attività)* occupation; **~ abusiva** squatting. **(b)** *(lavoro)* employment; *(un lavoro)* job, occupation; **la piena ~** full employment.

oceanico, a, ci, che [otʃe'aniko] *ag* oceanic, ocean *attr*; *(fig: immenso)* vast, huge.

oceano [o'tʃeano] *sm* ocean.

ocra ['ɔkra] *sf* ochre.

O.C.S.E. *sf (abbr di* Organizzazione per la Cooperazione e lo Sviluppo Economico) OECD.

oculare [oku'lare] *ag (bulbo, lenti)* ocular, eye *attr*; **testimone ~** eyewitness.

oculatezza [okula'tettsa] *sf (vedi ag)* caution; shrewdness.

oculato, a [oku'lato] *ag* cautious, prudent; *(avveduto)* shrewd.

oculista, i, e [oku'lista] *sm/f* eye specialist, oculist.

od [od] *cong (dav vocale) vedi* **o**[2].

ode ['ɔde] *sf* ode.

odiare [o'djare] *vt* to hate, detest, loathe.

odierno, a [o'djɛrno] *ag (di oggi)* today's, of today; *(attuale)* present, current; **in data ~a** *(frm)* today.

odio ['ɔdjo] *sm* hatred, hate; **avere in ~ qc/qn** to hate *o* detest sth/sb; **prendere in ~ qc/qn** to take a strong dislike to sth/sb.

odioso, a [o'djoso] *ag* hateful, odious; *(antipatico)* unpleasant, obnoxious; **rendersi ~ (a)** to make o.s. unpopular (with).

odissea [odis'sɛa] *sf* odyssey.

odontoiatra, i, e [odonto'jatra] *sm/f* dentist, dental surgeon.

odontoiatria [odontoja'tria] *sf* dentistry.

odontoiatrico, a, ci, che [odonto'jatriko] *ag* dental.

odontotecnico, ci [odonto'tɛkniko] *sm* dental technician.

odorare [odo'rare] **1** *vt (anche fig)* to smell. **2** *vi (anche fig)* to smell; **questi fiori non odorano** these flowers don't have any smell *o* perfume; **~ di pulito/fresco** to smell clean/fresh; **~ di muffa/d'aglio** to smell mouldy/of garlic.

odorato [odo'rato] *sm* sense of smell.

odore [o'dore] *sm* **(a)** *(gen)* smell, odour; *(fragranza)* scent, fragrance; **senza ~** odourless; **sentire ~ di qc** to smell sth; **avere buon/cattivo ~** to smell nice/bad, have a nice/bad smell; ~ **di cucina** smell of cooking. (**b**): ~**i** *smpl (Culin)* herbs.

odoroso, a [odo'roso] *ag* sweet-smelling.

offendere [of'fɛndere] **1** *vt* (**a**) *(persona, morale pubblica, senso estetico)* to offend; *(far male a: vista etc)* to hurt; ~ **qn nell'onore** to offend sb's honour; ~ **la vista** *(fig)* to offend the eye. (**b**) *(insultare)* to insult, offend. (**c**) *(violare: libertà, diritti)* to violate; *(: legge)* to break; ~ **i diritti di qn** to infringe on sb's rights. **2**: ~**rsi** *vr*: ~**rsi (per)** to take offence (at), be offended (by).

offensivo, a [offen'sivo] **1** *ag (armi)* offensive; *(parole)* offensive, insulting. **2** *sf* offensive; **passare all'**~**a** to take the offensive.

offensore [offen'sore] *sm* aggressor.

offerente [offe'rɛnte] **1** *p presente di* **offrire**. **2** *sm/f (ad un'asta)* bidder; **il miglior** ~ the highest bidder.

offerta [of'fɛrta] *sf* (**a**) *(gen)* offer; *(per appalti)* tender; *(ad un'asta)* bid; *(Econ)* supply; **fare un'**~ to make an offer; *(per appalto)* to tender; *(ad un'asta)* to bid; ~**e d'impiego** *(Stampa)* situations vacant; **ci sono poche** ~**e d'impiego** there aren't many jobs advertised. (**b**) *(donazione)* offering, donation.

offerto, a [of'fɛrto] *pp di* **offrire**.

offertorio [offer'tɔrjo] *sm (Rel)* offertory.

offesa [of'fesa] *sf* (**a**) *(insulto)* offence, insult; **fare o recare** ~ **a qn** to give offence to sb. (**b**) *(trasgressione)* offence.

offeso, a [of'feso] **1** *pp di* **offendere**. **2** *ag* (**a**) *(nei sentimenti)* offended, hurt; *(fisicamente)* hurt, injured; **sei ancora** ~ **con me?** are you still annoyed with me? (**b**) *(Dir)*: **la parte** ~**a** the plaintiff. **3** *sm/f* offended party; **guarda, ora fa l'**~! look, now he's going all huffy!

officina [offi'tʃina] *sf* workshop; ~ **meccanica** *(Aut)* garage.

offrire [of'frire] **1** *vt* (**a**) *(sigaretta, lavoro, merce, aiuto etc)* to offer; *(preghiere, messa)* to offer (up); *(ad un'asta)* to bid; **ti offro da bere** I'll buy you a drink; **mi offri una sigaretta?** can I have a cigarette? (**b**) *(regalare)*: ~ **a** to give to; ~ **qc in dono a qn** to present sb with sth. (**c**) *(opportunità, vantaggio)* to offer. **2**: ~**rsi** *vr* (**a**) *(essere disposto)*: ~**rsi di fare qc** to volunteer to do sth. (**b**) *(presentarsi: occasione)* to present itself, arise. (**c**) *(Pubblicità)*: **'offresi posto di segretaria'** 'secretarial vacancy', 'vacancy for secretary'; **'segretaria offresi'** 'secretary seeks post'.

offuscare [offus'kare] **1** *vt* to darken, obscure; *(fig: gloria)* to obscure; *(: mente)* to dim. **2**: ~**rsi** *vr (vedi vt)* to darken, grow dark; to become obscured; to grow dim; *(fig: sguardo)* to cloud over.

oftalmico, a, ci, che [of'talmiko] *ag* ophthalmic.

oggettivare [oddʒetti'vare] **1** *vt* to objectify. **2**: ~**rsi** *vr* to become concrete.

oggettività [oddʒettivi'ta] *sf* objectivity.

oggettivo, a [oddʒet'tivo] *ag* objective; **proposizione** ~**a** *(Gram)* object clause.

oggetto [od'dʒɛtto] *sm* (**a**) *(cosa, articolo)* object, thing; ~**i preziosi** valuables, articles of value; ~**i smarriti** lost property *sg*. (**b**) *(di disputa, discorso, studio)* subject; *(di sogni, pensieri)* object; **essere** ~ **di** *(critiche, controversia)* to be the subject of; *(odio, pietà etc)* to be the object of; **essere** ~ **di scherno** to be a laughing-stock; **essere** ~ **di persecuzione** to be subjected to persecution. (**c**) *(di attività, contratto)* object, purpose. (**d**) *(in lettere commerciali)*: ~... re...; **in** ~ **a quanto**

detto as regards the matter mentioned above. (**e**) *(Gram, Filosofia)* object.

oggi ['ɔddʒi] **1** *av* today; *(al presente, al giorno d'oggi)* today, nowadays; ~ **stesso** today, this very day; ~ **nel pomeriggio** this afternoon; ~ (**a**) **otto** a week today, today week; **quanti ne abbiamo** ~? what is today's date?; ~ **come** ~ at present, as things stand; ~ **qui, domani là** *(fig)* here today, gone tomorrow; ~ **o domani** *(fig)* sooner or later; ~ **a me, domani a te** *(fig)* your day will come; **dagli** ~, **dagli domani** in the long run, over time. **2** *sm* today; **dall'**~ **al domani** from one day to the next; **a tutt'**~ up till now, till today; **le spese a tutt'**~ **sono...** expenses to date are... .

oggigiorno [oddʒi'dʒorno] **1** *av* nowadays, these days. **2** *sm* today.

ogiva [o'dʒiva] *sf* ogive, pointed arch.

ogni ['oɲɲi] *ag* (**a**) *(ciascuno)* every, each; *(tutti)* all; ~ **passeggero** every o each passenger; ~ **cosa** everything; ~ **uomo è mortale** all men are mortal; ~ **sorta di articoli** all sorts of goods. (**b**) *(qualsiasi)* any, all; **ad** ~ **costo** at any price, at all costs; **gente d'**~ **tipo** people of all sorts. (**c**) *(con valore distributivo)* every; ~ **due giorni** every two days, every other day; **l'autobus passa** ~ **20 minuti** the bus comes past every 20 minutes; **una persona** ~ **cento** one person in every hundred. (**d**) *(fraseologia)*: **in** ~ **caso** at any rate, in any case; **in** ~ **luogo** everywhere; **da** ~ **parte** from everywhere; **in o ad** ~ **modo** anyway, anyhow; ~ **tanto** every so often, every now and then; ~ **volta che** every time (that), whenever.

Ognissanti [oɲɲis'santi] *sm* All Saints' Day.

ognuno [oɲ'ɲuno] *pron (tutti)* everybody, everyone; *(ciascuno)* each (one); ~ **di noi sa quello che vuole** each of us knows what he wants, we all know what we want.

oh [ɔ, o] *escl* = **o**[3].

ohi ['ɔi] *escl* oh!; *(esprime dolore)* ow!; ~ **là!** hey there!

ohimè [oi'mɛ] *escl* oh dear!

Olanda [o'landa] *sf* Holland.

olandese [olan'dese] **1** *ag* Dutch. **2** *sm/f* Dutchman/ woman; **gli O**~**i** the Dutch. **3** *sm* (**a**) *(lingua)* Dutch. (**b**) *(formaggio)* Dutch cheese.

oleandro [ole'andro] *sm* oleander.

oleario, a [ole'arjo] *ag* oil *attr.*

oleato, a [ole'ato] *ag*: **carta** ~**a** greaseproof paper.

oleificio, ci [olei'fitʃo] *sm* oil mill.

oleodotto [oleo'dɔtto] *sm* (oil) pipeline.

oleoso, a [ole'oso] *ag* oily; *(che contiene olio)* oil *attr.*

olfatto [ol'fatto] *sm* sense of smell.

oliare [o'ljare] *vt* to oil, lubricate; *(Culin)* to grease.

oliatore [olja'tore] *sm* oilcan.

oliera [o'ljɛra] *sf* oil and vinegar cruet.

Olimpiadi [olim'piadi] *sfpl* Olympics, Olympic games.

olimpico, a, ci, che [o'limpiko] *ag* Olympic.

olimpionico, a, ci, che [olim'pjoniko] **1** *ag* Olympic. **2** *sm/f* competitor in the Olympics; *(campione)* Olympic champion.

olio ['ɔljo] *sm* (**a**) oil; **tonno/funghi sott'**~ tuna/ mushrooms in oil; ~ **d'oliva/di fegato di merluzzo** olive/cod-liver oil; ~ **da tavola** salad oil; ~ **di lino** linseed oil; ~ **di semi** vegetable oil; ~ **solare** suntan oil; ~ **lubrificante** lubricating oil; **il mare è un** ~ the sea is like a millpond; **gettare** ~ **sul fuoco** *(fig)* to add fuel to the flames. (**b**) *(Rel)*: ~ **santo** holy oil; **dare l'**~ **santo a qn** to give sb Extreme Unction. (**c**) *(Pittura)*: **un (quadro a)** ~ an oil painting; **dipingere a** ~ to paint in oils.

oliva [o'liva] **1** *sf* olive. **2** *ag inv (colore)* olive(-green).

olivastro, a [oli'vastro] *ag (colore)* olive-greenish; *(carnagione)* olive, sallow.

oliveto [oli'veto] *sm* olive grove.

olivo [o'livo] *sm* olive tree.

olmo ['olmo] *sm* elm.

olocausto [olo'kausto] *sm (Rel, fig)* sacrifice; *(Rel ebrea)* holocaust.

oltraggiare [oltrad'dʒare] *vt* to offend, insult.

oltraggio, gi [ol'traddʒo] *sm* **(a)** *(insulto)* insult, offence; **fare un ~ a** to offend, insult; **subire un ~** to suffer an affront. **(b)** *(Dir)*: **~ al pudore** indecent behaviour; **accusato di ~ a pubblico ufficiale** charged with insulting a public official. **(c)** *(danno)*: **gli ~gi del tempo** the ravages of time.

oltraggioso, a [oltrad'dʒoso] *ag (offensivo)* insulting, offensive.

oltralpe [ol'tralpe] *av* on the other side of the Alps; **un paese d'~** a country beyond the Alps.

oltranza [ol'trantsa] *sf*: **a o ad ~** to the (bitter) end, to the death; **sciopero ad ~** all-out strike.

oltranzismo [oltran'tsismo] *sm (Pol)* extremism.

oltranzista, i, e [oltran'tsista] *sm/f (Pol)* extremist.

oltre ['oltre] **1** *av* **(a)** *(di luogo)* further, farther; **andare troppo ~** *(fig)* to go too far. **(b)** *(di tempo)*: **non ... ~** no more, no longer; **non posso aspettare ~** I can't wait any longer, I can wait no longer. **(c)** *(di età)* over. **2** *prep* **(a)** *(di luogo)* on the other side of, beyond; **sono passati ~ i confini** they crossed the border. **(b)** *(di tempo, quantità)* more than, over; **sono ~ 3 mesi che non ti vedo** I haven't seen you in more than *o* in over 3 months; **non ~ il 10 febbraio** not later than 10th February. **(c)** *(in aggiunta a)*: **~ a/che** besides, as well as; **~ che piovere fa freddo** it's cold as well as wet. **(d)** *(all'infuori di, eccetto)*: **~ a** besides, apart from; **~ a tutto** on top of all that.

oltrecortina [oltrekor'tina] *av* behind the Iron Curtain; **paesi d'~** Iron Curtain countries.

oltremanica [oltre'manika] *av* across the Channel.

oltremare [oltre'mare] *av* overseas; **paesi d'~** overseas countries.

oltremarino, a [oltrema'rino] *ag (colore)* ultramarine.

oltremodo [oltre'modo] *av* extremely, greatly.

oltreoceano [oltreo'tʃeano] *av* overseas; **paesi d'~** overseas countries.

oltrepassare [oltrepas'sare] *vt (varcare)* to cross, go beyond; *(superare)* to exceed, go over; **~ i limiti** *(fig)* to go too far.

oltretomba [oltre'tomba] *sm*: **l'~** the hereafter.

omaggio, gi [o'maddʒo] **1** *sm* **(a)** *(segno di rispetto)* homage, tribute; **rendere ~ a qn** to pay homage *o* tribute to sb. **(b)** *(Comm, Stampa etc)*: **fare ~ di un libro** to give a presentation copy of a book; **copia in ~** presentation *o* complimentary copy; **biglietto in ~** complimentary ticket; **è un ~ della ditta** it's a present from the firm; **'in ~'** 'free gift'. **(c)**: **~gi** *smpl (ossequi)* respects, regards; **presentare i propri ~gi a qn** *(frm)* to pay one's respects to sb. **2** *ag inv* free.

ombelicale [ombeli'kale] *ag* umbilical; **cordone** *m* **~** umbilical cord.

ombelico, chi [ombe'liko] *sm* navel.

ombra ['ombra] **1** *sf* **(a)** *(zona non assolata)* shade; *(sagoma)* shadow; *(oscurità)* darkness; **sedersi all'~ (di)** to sit in the shade (of); **dare ~ a qn** *(fig)* to put sb in the shade; **essere l'~ di se stesso** to be a shadow of one's former self. **(b)** *(fantasma)* shade, ghost; **è uno che vede ~e dappertutto** he's the jittery sort. **(c)** *(fig: oscurità)* obscurity; **nell'~** *(tramare, agire)* secretly; **restare nell'~** *(persona)* to remain in obscurity. **(d)** *(parvenza,*

traccia): **non c'è ~ di verità in quello che dice** there isn't a grain of truth in what he says; **senza ~ di dubbio** without the shadow of a doubt; **un'~ di burro** a hint *o* touch of butter. **2** *ag inv*: **bandiera ~** flag of convenience; **governo ~** *(Pol)* shadow cabinet; **scrittore ~** ghostwriter.

ombreggiare [ombred'dʒare] *vt* to shade.

ombreggiatura [ombreddʒa'tura] *sf* shading.

ombrello [om'brɛllo] *sm* umbrella; **~ da sole** parasol, sunshade.

ombrellone [ombrel'lone] *sm (di caffè etc)* sunshade; **~ da spiaggia** beach umbrella.

ombretto [om'bretto] *sm* eyeshadow.

ombrosità [ombrosi'ta] *sf (vedi ag)* shadiness; skittishness; touchiness.

ombroso, a [om'broso] *ag* **(a)** *(bosco, viale etc)* shady. **(b)** *(fig: cavallo)* skittish; *(: persona)* touchy.

omelette [ɔmə'lɛt] *sf inv* omelette.

omelia [ome'lia] *sf* homily, sermon.

omeopatia [omeopa'tia] *sf* homoeopathy.

omeopatico, a, ci, che [omeo'patiko] **1** *ag* homoeopathic. **2** *sm* homoeopath.

omero ['ɔmero] *sm (Anat)* humerus.

omertà [omer'ta] *sf* conspiracy of silence.

omesso, a [o'messo] *pp di* **omettere.**

omettere [o'mettere] *vt* to leave out, omit; **~ di fare qc** to neglect *o* omit to do sth.

ometto [o'metto] *sm (fig: bambino)* little fellow.

omiciattolo [omi'tʃattolo] *sm* wretch.

omicida, i, e [omi'tʃida] **1** *ag* homicidal, murderous. **2** *sm/f* murderer/murderess.

omicidio [omi'tʃidjo] *sm* murder, *(Am)* homicide; **~ colposo** *(Dir)* manslaughter; **~ premeditato** *(Dir)* murder.

omissione [omis'sjone] *sf* omission; **reato d'~** criminal negligence; **~ di soccorso** failure to stop and give assistance.

omnibus ['ɔmnibus] *sm inv (Storia)* omnibus.

omogeneità [omodʒenei'ta] *sf* homogeneity.

omogeneizzare [omodʒeneid'dzare] *vt* to homogenize.

omogeneizzato, a [omodʒeneid'dzato] **1** *ag* homogenized. **2** *sm (per bambini)* tin *(o* jar) of baby food.

omogeneo, a [omo'dʒɛneo] *ag (gen)* homogeneous; *(fig: insieme di colori etc)* harmonious.

omologare [omolo'gare] *vt (Dir)* to approve, confirm; *(ratificare)* to ratify; **macchina omologata per 5 persone** car authorized to carry 5 people.

omologo, a, ghi, ghe [o'mɔlogo] *ag* homologous, corresponding.

omonimo, a [o'mɔnimo] **1** *ag (persone)* with the same name. **2** *sm/f (persona)* namesake. **3** *sm (Gram)* homonym.

omosessuale [omosessu'ale] *ag, sm/f* homosexual.

omosessualità [omosessuali'ta] *sf* homosexuality.

O.M.S. *sf (abbr di Organizzazione Mondiale della Sanità)* WHO.

omuncolo [o'munkolo] *sm = omiciattolo.*

oncia, ce ['ontʃa] *sf* ounce.

onda ['onda] *sf* **(a)** *(flutto, fig)* wave; **~ lunga** roller; **un'~ di commozione** a wave *o* surge of excitement; **capelli a ~e** wavy hair; **l'~ verde** *(Aut)* synchronized traffic lights *pl.* **(b)** *(Fisica)* wave; **~e corte/medie/lunghe** short/medium/long waves; **andare in ~** *(Radio, TV)* to go on the air, be broadcast; **mettere o mandare in ~** *(Radio, TV)* to broadcast.

ondata [on'data] *sf (anche fig)* wave; **~ di turisti** influx of tourists; **~ di entusiasmo** wave *o* surge of enthusiasm; **a ~e** *(muovere, avanzare)* in waves; ~ **di caldo** heatwave; ~ **di freddo** cold spell *o* snap.

onde ['onde] *cong (frm)* in order to, so as to.

ondeggiare [onded'dʒare] *vi (acqua, superficie, grano)* to ripple; *(bandiera)* to flutter; *(muoversi sulle onde: barca)* to rock; *(fig: folla, alberi, edificio)* to sway; *(: persona: essere incerto)* to waver, hesitate.

ondoso, a [on'doso] *ag (moto)* of the waves.

ondulare [ondu'lare] *vt (capelli)* to wave.

ondulato, a [ondu'lato] *ag (capelli)* wavy; *(terreno)* undulating; **cartone** ~ corrugated paper; **lamiera** ~**a** sheet of corrugated iron.

ondulatorio, a [ondula'torjo] *ag (movimento)* undulating; *(Fis)* undulatory, wave *attr.*

ondulazione [ondulat'tsjone] *sf* undulation; *(di capelli)* wave.

onerato, a [one'rato] *ag:* ~ **di** burdened with, loaded with.

onere ['onere] *sm (peso)* burden; *(responsabilità)* responsibility; ~**i fiscali** taxes.

oneroso, a [one'roso] *ag (compito)* onerous; *(tasse, pena)* heavy; *(condizioni: di contratto etc)* hard.

onestà [ones'ta] *sf (vedi ag)* honesty; fairness; virtue, chastity.

onestamente [onesta'mente] *av (vedi ag)* honestly; fairly; virtuously; *(in verità)* honestly, frankly.

onesto, a [o'nesto] *ag (retto)* honest; *(giusto: persona, prezzi)* fair; *(virtuoso, pudico)* virtuous, chaste; **con intenzioni poco** ~**e** with dubious intentions.

onice ['onitʃe] *sf* onyx.

onirico, a, ci, che [o'niriko] *ag* dreamlike, dream *attr.*

onnipotente [onnipo'tente] **1** *ag* omnipotent, all-powerful; **Dio** ~ Almighty God. **2** *sm:* **l'O**~ *(Rel)* the Almighty.

onnipresente [onnipre'zente] *ag* omnipresent; *(scherzoso)* ubiquitous.

onnisciente [onniʃ'ʃente] *ag* omniscient.

onnivoro, a [on'nivoro] *ag* omnivorous.

onomastico, ci [ono'mastiko] *sm* name day.

onomatopea [onomato'pea] *sf* onomatopoeia.

onoranze [ono'rantse] *sfpl* honours.

onorare [ono'rare] **1** *vt (gen)* to honour; *(far onore a)* to be a credit to; ~ **qn con** *o* **di qc** to honour sb with sth. **2:** ~**rsi** *vr:* ~**rsi di qc/di fare qc** to be *(o* feel) honoured by sth/to do sth.

onorario, a [ono'rarjo] **1** *ag* honorary. **2** *sm* fee.

onore [o'nore] *sm* **(a)** *(reputazione, integrità)* honour; **giuro sul mio** ~ **che...** I swear on my honour that.... **(b)** *(omaggio)* honour; **rendere** ~ **a qn/qc** to honour sb/sth. **(c)** *(privilegio)* honour, privilege; **aver l'**~ **di** to have the honour of; **posto d'**~ place of honour. **(d)** *(merito)* credit; **fare** ~ **ai genitori** to be a credit to one's parents; **si è fatto** ~ **agli esami** he performed very creditably in the exams, he distinguished himself in the exams. **(e):** ~**i smpl** *(onorificenze)* honours. **(f)** *(Carte)* honour (card). **(g)** *(fraseologia):* **in** ~ **di** in honour of; **a onor del vero** to tell the truth; **fare** ~ **alla tavola** *o* **alla cena** *etc* to do justice to the dinner *etc;* **fare gli** ~**i di casa** to do the honours (of the house).

onorevole [ono'revole] **1** *ag* honourable; *(Pol: titolo):* **l'**~... the Honourable.... **2** *sm/f:* **O**~ Member of Parliament.

onorificenza [onorifi'tʃentsa] *sf* honour.

onorifico, a, ci, che [ono'rifiko] *ag* honorary.

onta ['onta] *sf* **(a)** *(vergogna)* shame, disgrace; *(affronto)* insult, affront. **(b): ad** ~ **di** despite, notwithstanding.

ontano [on'tano] *sm* alder.

O.N.U. ['onu] *sf abbr di* **Organizzazione delle Nazioni Unite.**

opacità [opatʃi'ta] *sf (vedi ag)* opaqueness, opacity; matt quality; dullness.

opaco, a, chi, che [o'pako] *ag (vetro, corpo)* opaque; *(carta)* matt; *(sguardo, colore, fig: voce, mente)* dull.

opale [o'pale] *sm o f* opal.

opera ['opera] *sf* **(a)** *(attività, lavoro)* work; **mettersi/essere all'**~ to get down to/be at work; **vedere qn all'**~ to see sb in action; **abbiamo ottenuto quell'aumento per** ~ **sua** it was thanks to him that we got the rise; **fare** ~ **di persuasione presso qn** to try to convince sb; **fare** ~**e buone** *o* **di carità** to do good works *o* works of charity. **(b)** *(lavoro materiale)* work, piece of work; ~**e pubbliche** *(Amm)* public works; ~**e di restauro/di scavo** restoration/excavation work *sg.* **(c)** *(produzione artistica: nell'insieme)* works *pl; (: libro, quadro etc)* work; ~ **d'arte** work of art. **(d)** *(ente)* foundation; ~ **pia** religious charity. **(e)** *(Mus)* opus; *(: melodramma)* opera; *(: teatro)* opera (house); ~ **buffa** comic opera; ~ **lirica** (grand) opera.

operaio, a [ope'rajo] **1** *ag* **(a)** *(classe)* working *attr; (movimento, partito)* workers'; *(prete)* worker *attr.* **(b)** *(Zool: ape, formica)* worker *attr.* **2** *sm* worker, workman; ~ **di fabbrica** factory worker; ~ **a giornata** day labourer; ~ **specializzato/qualificato** skilled/semi-skilled worker. **3** *sf* female worker.

operare [ope'rare] **1** *vt* **(a)** *(riforma)* to carry out; *(effetto)* to produce; ~ **miracoli** to work wonders. **(b)** *(Med)* to operate on; **il chirurgo ha operato Mario di appendicite/allo stomaco** the surgeon operated on Mario for appendicitis/operated on Mario's stomach; ~ **qn d'urgenza** to perform an emergency operation on sb. **2** *vi* **(a)** *(agire)* to act, work; *(Mil, Comm)* to operate. **(b)** *(Med)* to operate. **3:** ~**rsi** *vr (verificarsi)* to take place, occur. **(b)** *(Med)* to have an operation; ~**rsi d'ernia** to have a hernia operation.

operativo, a [opera'tivo] *ag* operative, operating; **piano** ~ *(Mil)* plan of operations.

operato, a [ope'rato] **1** *sm (comportamento)* actions *pl.* **2** *sm/f (Med)* patient *(who has undergone an operation).* **3** *ag (tessuto)* diapered; *(carta)* embossed; *(cuoio)* tooled.

operatore, trice [opera'tore] *sm/f (a) ag)* operator; ~ **turistico** tour operator; **gli** ~**i turistici della zona** the local tourist trade; **aperto solo agli** ~**i** *(Comm)* open to the trade only; ~ **cinematografico** projectionist; ~ **di presa** *(Cine, TV)* cameraman; ~ **del suono** sound recordist. **(b)** *(Econ)* agent; ~ **di borsa** dealer on the stock exchange; **gli** ~**i economici del settore** those with commercial interests in that sector.

operatorio, a [opera'torjo] *ag (Med)* operating.

operazione [operat'tsjone] *sf (gen, Med, Mil, Mat)* operation; *(Econ)* transaction.

operetta [ope'retta] *sf* operetta, light opera.

operistico, a, ci, che [ope'ristiko] *ag* opera *attr.*

operosità [operosi'ta] *sf* industry.

operoso, a [ope'roso] *ag (attivo)* industrious, hardworking.

opificio [opi'fitʃo] *sm* factory, works *pl.*

opinabile [opi'nabile] *ag (discutibile)* debatable, questionable; **è** ~ it is a matter of opinion.

opinione [opi'njone] *sf* opinion; **secondo la mia** ~ in my opinion; **avere il coraggio delle proprie** ~**i** to have the courage of one's convictions; **l'**~ **pubblica** public opinion.

op là [op'la] *escl (per far saltare)* hup!; *(a bimbo che è caduto)* upsy-daisy!

oppio ['ɔppjo] *sm* opium.

oppiomane [op'pjɔmane] *sm/f* opium addict.

opponente [oppo'nɛnte] **1** *sm/f* opponent. **2** *ag* opposing.

opporre [op'porre] **1** *vt* (a) *(ragioni, argomenti)* to put forward; *(resistenza)* to put up, offer; ~ **un netto rifiuto a** to give a clear-cut refusal to. (b) *(obiettare)* to object; **non ho nulla da** ~ I have no objection. **2**: **opporsi** *vr* (a) *(fare opposizione)*: **opporsi a** *(nemico, proposta)* to oppose; **mi oppongo alla sua idea** I am opposed to o against his idea. (b) *(obiettare)* to object.

opportunismo [opportu'nizmo] *sm* opportunism.

opportunista, i, e [opportu'nista] *sm/f* opportunist.

opportunistico, a, ci, che [opportu'nistiko] *ag* opportunist.

opportunità [opportuni'ta] *sf inv* (a) *(convenienza)* opportuneness, timeliness; **avere il senso dell'**~ to have a sense of timing. (b) *(occasione)* opportunity; **avere l'**~ **di fare qc** to have the opportunity of doing sth.

opportuno, a [oppor'tuno] *ag (adatto, conveniente)* opportune, timely; *(giusto)* right, appropriate; **a tempo** ~ at the right o appropriate time; **ritengo** ~ **che gli scriva** I think you should write to him, I think it would be advisable for you to write to him.

oppositore, trice [oppozi'tore] **1** *sm/f* opponent. **2** *ag* opposing.

opposizione [oppozit'tsjone] *sf* (a) *(resistenza)* opposition; *(Pol)*: **l'O**~ the Opposition; **fare** ~ **a qn/qc** to oppose sb/sth. (b) *(contrasto)* opposition; **essere in netta** ~ *(idee, opinioni)* to clash, be in complete opposition. (c) *(Dir)* objection.

opposto, a [op'posto] **1** *pp di* **opporre**. **2** *ag* (a) *(direzione, lato)* opposite; **il palazzo** ~ **al museo** the building opposite o facing the museum. (b) *(contrario: idee, vedute)* opposite, conflicting; **le sue idee sono** ~**e alle mie** his ideas conflict with mine, his ideas are the opposite of mine. **3** *sm*: **l'**~ the opposite, the reverse; **all'**~ on the contrary; **io, all'**~ **di te, non li approvo** unlike you, I don't approve of them.

oppressione [oppres'sjone] *sf (Pol etc)* oppression; *(fisica, morale)* feeling of oppression.

oppressivo, a [oppres'sivo] *ag* oppressive.

oppresso, a [op'prɛsso] **1** *pp di* **opprimere**. **2** *ag* oppressed. **3**: **gli** ~**i** *smpl* the oppressed.

oppressore [oppres'sore] **1** *sm* oppressor. **2** *ag* oppressive.

opprimente [oppri'mɛnte] *ag (caldo, noia)* oppressive; *(persona)* tiresome; *(: deprimente)* depressing.

opprimere [op'primere] *vt* (a) *(sog: caldo, afa etc)* to suffocate, oppress; **cibo che opprime lo stomaco** food that lies heavy on the stomach. (b) *(sog: ansia, lavoro)* to weigh down, weigh heavily on; **il lavoro/mia moglie mi opprime** my work/my wife is getting me down. (c) *(popoli, libertà)* to oppress.

oppugnare [oppuɲ'ɲare] *vt (fig: dottrina etc)* to refute.

oppure [op'pure] *cong (o invece)* or; *(altrimenti)* otherwise, or (else).

optare [op'tare] *vi*: ~ **per** *(scegliere)* to opt for, decide upon; *(Borsa)* to take (out) an option on.

optimum ['ɔptimum] *sm inv* optimum.

opulento, a [opu'lɛnto] *ag (paese, società, persona)* rich, wealthy, affluent; *(vita, stile letterario)* opulent.

opulenza [opu'lɛntsa] *sf (vedi ag)* richness, wealth, affluence; opulence.

opuscolo [o'puskolo] *sm (letterario, scientifico)* booklet, pamphlet; *(pubblicitario)* brochure, leaflet.

opzionale [optsjo'nale] *ag* optional.

opzione [op'tsjone] *sf (gen, Comm)* option; **diritto di** ~ *(Borsa)* (right of) option.

ora ['ora] **1** *sf* (a) *(unità di tempo, durata)* hour; **durante le** ~**e d'ufficio** during office hours; **è a un'**~ **di cammino/d'auto dalla stazione** it's an hour's walk/drive from the station, it's an hour away from the station on foot/by car; **pagare a** ~**e** to pay by the hour; **mi pagano 2000 lire all'**~ they pay me 2000 lire an hour.

(b) *(parte della giornata)*: **che** ~ **è?, che** ~**e sono?** — **sono le 4** what time is it? — it's 4 (o'clock); **che** ~ **fai?** what time do you make it?; **a che** ~ **ci vediamo?** what time o when shall we meet?; ~ **estiva** o **legale** summer time; ~ **locale** local time.

(c) *(momento)* time; **domani a quest'**~ this time tomorrow; **l'**~ **di pranzo** lunchtime; **l'**~ **dei pasti** mealtimes; **è** ~ **di partire** it's time to go; **era** ~! about time too!; **le notizie dell'ultima** ~ the latest news; ~ **di punta** rush hour; **l'**~ **X** zero hour.

(d) *(fraseologia)*: **non vedo l'**~ **di finire** I can't wait to finish, I'm looking forward to finishing; **fare le** ~**e piccole** to stay up till the early hours (of the morning); **di buon'**~ early; **alla buon'**~! at last!; **di** ~ **in** ~ hourly, hour by hour.

2 *av* (a) *(adesso)* now; ~ **non posso uscire** I can't go out (just) now; **d'**~ **in avanti** o **in poi** from now on; ~ **come** ~ right now, at present.

(b) *(poco fa)*: **è uscito (proprio)** ~ he's just gone out; **or** ~ just now, a moment ago; **10 anni or sono** 10 years ago.

(c) *(tra poco)* in a moment, presently; ~ **arrivo** I'm just coming, I'll be right there.

(d) *(correlativo)*: ~ ... ~ now ... now; ~ **qui** ~ **lì** now here now there; ~ **piange** ~ **ride** one minute he's crying, the next he's laughing.

3 *cong* now; ~ **che** now (that).

oracolo [o'rakolo] *sm* oracle.

orafo ['ɔrafo] **1** *sm* goldsmith. **2**: ~, **a** *ag (arte etc)* goldsmith's, of a goldsmith.

orale [o'rale] *ag, sm* oral.

oralmente [oral'mɛnte] *av* orally.

oramai [ora'mai] *av* = **ormai**.

orango, ghi [o'rango] *sm*, **orangutan** [orangu'tan] *sm inv* orang-utan.

orario, a [o'rarjo] **1** *ag (cambiamento, media)* hourly; *(fuso, segnale)* time *attr*; **in senso** ~ clockwise; **velocità** ~**a** a speed per hour; **disco** ~ parking disc. **2** *sm* (a) *(di ufficio, visite etc)* hours, time(s *pl*); **fare l'**~ **ridotto** to be on short time; **in** ~ on time; ~ **elastico** o **flessibile** *(Industria)* flexitime; ~ **di lavoro/d'ufficio** working/office hours; ~ **di apertura/chiusura** opening/closing time. (b) *(tabella)* timetable, schedule; ~ **ferroviario** railway timetable.

orata [o'rata] *sf* sea bream.

oratore, trice [ora'tore] *sm/f* (public) speaker, orator.

oratorio, a [ora'tɔrjo] **1** *ag* oratorical. **2** *sm* (a) *(cappella)* oratory. (b) *(Mus)* oratorio. **3** *sf (arte)* oratory.

orazione [orat'tsjone] *sf* (a) *(preghiera)* prayer. (b) *(discorso)* oration, speech; ~ **funebre** funeral oration.

orbene [or'bɛne] *cong* well (then), so.

orbita ['ɔrbita] *sf* (a) *(Anat)* (eye-)socket; **aveva gli**

occhi fuori dalle ~**e** *(fig)* his eyes were popping out of his head. **(b)** *(Astron, Fis)* orbit; **mettere in** ~ to put into orbit. **(c)** *(fig: ambito d'influenza)* sphere of influence; **si muove nell'**~ **dell'ambasciata** he moves in embassy circles.

orbitale [orbi'tale] *ag* orbital.

orbitare [orbi'tare] *vi* to orbit.

orbo, a ['ɔrbo] *ag (scherz)* blind; **e giù botte da** ~**i** and the fists were flying.

orca, che ['ɔrka] *sf (Zool)* killer whale.

orchestra [or'kɛstra] *sf (complesso di musicisti, strumenti musicali)* orchestra; *(: da ballo, jazz)* band; *(Teatro: spazio)* orchestra pit.

orchestrale [orkes'trale] **1** *ag* orchestral. **2** *sm/f* member of an orchestra.

orchestrare [orkes'trare] *vt (Mus)* to orchestrate; *(fig: campagna)* to organize.

orchestrazione [orkestrat'tsjone] *sf (vedi vb)* orchestration; organization.

orchidea [orki'dɛa] *sf* orchid.

orcio ['ortʃo] *sm* jug, pitcher.

orco, chi ['ɔrko] *sm (mostro, fig)* ogre.

orda ['ɔrda] *sf (Storia, fig)* horde.

ordigno [or'diɲɲo] *sm*: ~ **esplosivo** explosive device.

ordinale [ordi'nale] **1** *ag* ordinal. **2** *sm* ordinal (number).

ordinamento [ordina'mento] *sm (organizzazione)* order, arrangement; *(regolamento)* regulations *pl*, rules *pl*; ~ **scolastico/giuridico** educational/legal system.

ordinanza [ordi'nantsa] *sf* **(a)** *(Dir)* order. **(b)** *(Amm: decreto)* decree; ~ **municipale** by(e)-law. **(c)** *(Mil)* order; *(: prescrizione)* regulation; *(: attendente)* batman; **d'**~ *(pistola, divisa)* regulation *attr*; **ufficiale d'**~ orderly.

ordinare [ordi'nare] **1** *vt* **(a)** *(schede, concetti, vita)* to organize, put in order. **(b)** *(comandare)* to order; *(Med: cura, medicina)* to prescribe; *(merce, pranzo)* to order; ~ **che** to order that; ~ **a qn di fare qc** to order sb to do sth. **(c)** *(Rel: sacerdote)* to ordain. **2**: ~**rsi** *vr (disporsi)*: ~**rsi in fila/in colonna** *etc* to line up/form a column *etc*.

ordinario, a [ordi'narjo] **1** *ag* **(a)** *(consueto, normale)* ordinary, usual; *(: tariffa, spedizione, seduta)* ordinary; **di statura** ~**a** of average height. **(b)** *(rozzo: persona)* common, coarse; *(scadente: materiale, stoffa)* of poor quality. **(c)** *(Univ: professore, assistente)* permanent. **2** *sm* **(a)**: **l'**~ the ordinary; **d'**~ usually, as a rule; **fuori dall'**~ out of the ordinary. **(b)** *(Univ)* (full) professor.

ordinata [ordi'nata] *sf (Mat)* ordinate, y-axis.

ordinativo, a [ordina'tivo] **1** *ag* governing, regulating. **2** *sm (Comm)* order.

ordinato, a [ordi'nato] *ag (casa, ragazzo, mente)* tidy, orderly; *(vita)* well-ordered; *(impiegato)* methodical; *(corteo)* orderly.

ordinazione [ordinat'tsjone] *sf* **(a)** *(Comm)* order; **fare un'**~ **di qc** to put in an order for sth, to order sth; **eseguire qc su** ~ to make sth to order. **(b)** *(Rel)* ordination.

ordine ['ordine] *sm* **(a)** *(disposizione, sequenza)* order; **in** ~ **alfabetico** in alphabetical order; **in** ~ **di anzianità/importanza** in order of seniority/importance; **in** ~ **di battaglia** *(Mil)* in battle order; **ritirarsi in buon** ~ *(Mil)* to retreat in good order; *(fig)* to back down gracefully; **ciò è nell'**~ **naturale delle cose** it's in the nature of things.

(b) *(di persona, camera)* tidiness, orderliness; **in** ~ *(documenti)* in order; *(casa)* tidy, orderly; **mettere in** ~ to tidy (up); **mettersi in** ~ to tidy (o.s.) up; **tenere in** ~ to keep in order.

(c) *(categoria: Archit, Bio etc)* order.

(d) *(associazione)* association, order; *(: Rel)* order; **l'**~ **dei medici** ≃ the Medical Association; **l'**~ **degli avvocati** ≃ the Bar.

(e) *(natura)*: **questioni di** ~ **pratico/generale** questions of a practical/general nature; **un affare dell'**~ **di 20 milioni** a deal worth in the order of 20 million; **di prim'**~ *(albergo, merce)* first-class; **non rientra nel mio** ~ **di idee** that's not the way I see things.

(f) *(principio d'organizzazione)* order; **l'**~ **costituito** the established order; **l'**~ **pubblico** law and order; **le forze dell'**~ the forces of law and order; **richiamare all'**~ to call to order.

(g): ~**i** *smpl (Rel)* (Holy) Orders.

(h) *(comando)* order, command; **dare (l')**~ **di fare qc** to give the order to do sth; **essere agli** ~**i di qn** *(Mil)* to be under sb's command; *(fig)* to be at sb's beck and call; **per** ~ **del governo** by order of the government; **fino a nuovo** ~ until further orders.

(i) *(Comm, Fin)* order; **pagabile all'**~ **di** payable to the order of.

(j): **l'**~ **del giorno** *(in riunioni etc)* the agenda; *(Mil)* the order of the day; **essere all'**~ **del giorno** *(di riunione etc)* to be on the agenda; *(fig)*: **gli scioperi sono ormai all'**~ **del giorno** strikes are now the order of the day, strikes are now an everyday affair.

ordire [or'dire] *vt (Industria tessile)* to warp; *(fig)*: ~ **una congiura** *o* **una trama** to hatch a plot, to plot.

ordito [or'dito] *sm (Industria tessile)* warp.

orecchiabile [orek'kjabile] *ag (canzone)* catchy.

orecchietta [orek'kjetta] *sf (Anat)* auricle.

orecchino [orek'kino] *sm* earring.

orecchio [o'rekkjo] *sm* **(a)** *(Anat: pl(f)* **orecchie)** ear; **mi fischiano le** ~**e** my ears are singing; *(fig)* my ears are burning; **essere tutto** ~**i** to be all ears; **venire all'**~ **di qn** to come to sb's attention; **te lo dico in un** ~ this is for your ears only; **tapparsi** *o* **turarsi le** ~**e** to put one's fingers in one's ears; **fare** ~**e da mercante (a)** to turn a deaf ear (to); **tirare le** ~**e a qn** to tweak sb's ears; *(fig)* to tell sb off, give sb an earful. **(b)** *(udito)* hearing; **essere debole d'**~ to be hard of hearing; **avere** ~ to have a good ear (for music); **cantare/suonare a** ~ to sing/play by ear. **(c)**: ~**e** *sfpl*: **fare le** ~**e a un libro** to dog-ear a book.

orecchioni [orek'kjoni] *smpl*: **gli** ~ (the) mumps.

orefice [o'refitʃe] *sm (negoziante)* jeweller.

oreficeria [orefitʃe'ria] *sf (negozio)* jeweller's (shop); *(arte)* goldsmith's (*o* silversmith's) craft; *(gioielli)* jewellery.

orfano, a ['ɔrfano] **1** *ag* orphan(ed). **2** *sm/f* orphan; **restare** ~ **di madre** to be left motherless, to have lost one's mother.

orfanotrofio [orfano'trɔfjo] *sm* orphanage.

organetto [orga'netto] *sm* barrel organ, street organ.

organico, a, ci, che [or'ganiko] **1** *ag (Chim, Med, Dir etc)* organic. **2** *sm (personale)* staff, personnel; *(: Mil)* cadre; **essere nell'**~ to be on the permanent staff.

organigramma, i [organi'gramma] *sm (diagramma gerarchico)* organization chart; *(Inform)* computer flow chart.

organismo [orga'nizmo] *sm (vegetale, animale)* organism; *(Anat, complesso amministrativo)* body, organism.

organista, i, e [orga'nista] *sm/f* organist.

organizzare [organid'dzare] **1** *vt* to organize, arrange. **2**: ~**rsi** *vr* to organize o.s., get (o.s.) organized.

organizzativo, a [organiddza'tivo] *ag* organizational.

organizzatore, trice [organiddza'tore] **1** *ag* organizing. **2** *sm/f* organizer.

organizzazione [organiddzat'tsjone] *sf* **(a)** *(azione)* organizing, organization, arranging; *(risultato)* organization, arrangement. **(b)** *(associazione)* organization; **O~ delle Nazioni Unite** *(abbr* **O.N.U.)** United Nations Organization *(abbr* UNO).

organo ['ɔrgano] *sm (Anat, Mus, pubblicazione)* organ; *(Amm)* organ, body; **~i di comando** *(Tecn)* controls; **~i di trasmissione** *(Tecn)* transmission (unit) *sg.*

orgasmo [or'gazmo] *sm* **(a)** *(Fisiologia)* orgasm, climax. **(b)** *(agitazione, ansia)* anxiety; **essere/ mettersi in ~** to be/get in a state.

orgia, ge ['ɔrdʒa] *sf* orgy; **un'~ di** a profusion *o* riot of; **un'~ di colori** an orgy of colour.

orgoglio [or'goʎʎo] *sm* pride.

orgoglioso, a [orgoʎ'ʎoso] *ag* proud; **sono ~ di te** I'm proud of you.

orientale [orjen'tale] **1** *ag (paese, regione)* eastern; *(civiltà, lingua, tappeti)* oriental. **2** *sm/f* Oriental.

orientamento [orjenta'mento] *sm* **(a)** *(azione: vedi vt)* positioning; orientation; directing. **(b)** *(direzione)* direction; **senso di** *o* **dell'~** sense of direction; **perdere l'~** to lose one's bearings. **(c)** *(tendenza: di partito, rivista)* tendencies *pl,* leanings *pl;* (: *di scienze*) trends *pl;* (: *di ricerche*) direction; **~ professionale** careers guidance.

orientare [orjen'tare] **1** *vt* **(a)** *(disporre: antenna, ventilatore)* to position. **(b)** *(carta, bussola)* to orientate. **(c)** *(dirigere: ricerche, persona)* to direct; **hanno orientato la conversazione su un tema d'attualità** they steered the conversation round to a topical subject. **2**: **~rsi** *vr* **(a)** *(viaggiatore)* to find one's bearings; *(fig: raccapezzarsi)* to find one's way; **in questa faccenda non riesco a ~rmi** I can't make head nor tail of this business. **(b)**: **~rsi per** *o* **verso** *(fig: indirizzarsi)* to take up, go in for; (: *propendere*) to lean towards, tend towards; **mi sto orientando verso l'acquisto di una casa** I'm coming round to the idea of buying a house.

orientativo, a [orjenta'tivo] *ag* indicative, for guidance; **a scopo ~** for guidance.

oriente [o'rjɛnte] *sm (levante)* east; **l'O~** the East, the Orient; **a ~** in the east; **il Medio/l'Estremo O~** the Middle/Far East.

orificio [ori'fitʃo] *sm,* **orifizio** [ori'fittsjo] *sm (apertura)* opening; (: *di tubo*) mouth; *(Anat)* orifice.

origano [o'rigano] *sm (Bot)* oreganum.

originale [oridʒi'nale] **1** *ag (gen)* original; *(nuovo)* new, original; *(strambo)* eccentric, odd. **2** *sm (opera, documento, Radio, TV etc)* original. **3** *sm/f* eccentric; **il tuo amico è un bell'~!** your friend is a real character!

originalità [oridʒinali'ta] *sf inv* **(a)** *(vedi ag)* originality; eccentricity, oddness. **(b)** *(atto da originale)* eccentric behaviour.

originare [oridʒi'nare] *vt* to cause, give rise to.

originario, a [oridʒi'narjo] *ag* **(a)**: **~ di** *(animale, pianta)* native to, indigenous to; **è ~ di Roma** he is a native of Rome, he was born in Rome. **(b)** *(primitivo, originale)* original.

origine [o'ridʒine] *sf (gen)* origin; *(provenienza: di persona, famiglia)* origin, extraction; (: *di cosa*) origin, provenance; *(di fiume)* source; *(causa)* origin, cause; **luogo/paese d'~** place/country of origin; **di ~ italiana** of Italian extraction *o* origin; **risalire alle ~i** *o* **all'~ di qc** to go back to the origins *o* the beginning of sth; **cominciare dalle**

~i to start at the beginning; **dare ~ a** to give rise to; **avere ~ da** to originate from.

origliare [oriʎ'ʎare] *vi* to eavesdrop.

orina [o'rina] *sf* urine.

orinale [ori'nale] *sm* chamberpot.

orinare [ori'nare] **1** *vi* to pass water, urinate. **2** *vt:* **~ sangue** to pass blood.

orinatoio [orina'tojo] *sm* (public) urinal.

oriundo, a [o'rjundo] **1** *ag:* **essere ~ di Milano** *etc* to be of Milanese *etc* extraction *o* origin. **2** *sm/f* person of foreign extraction *o* origin; **negli Stati Uniti ci sono molti ~i italiani** in the United States there are many people of Italian extraction *o* origin. **3** *sm (Sport: in Italia)* foreign player of Italian extraction.

orizzontale [oriddzon'tale] **1** *ag* horizontal. **2** *sf (cruciverba)* clue *(o word)* across.

orizzontarsi [oriddzon'tarsi] *vr (viaggiatore)* to get one's bearings; *(fig: raccapezzarsi)* to find one's way.

orizzonte [orid'dzonte] *sm* **(a)** horizon; **all'~** *(apparire)* on the horizon; *(sparire)* below the horizon. **(b)** *(fig: prospettiva)* horizon; **l'~ politico** the political scene; **fare un giro d'~** (*di situazione etc*) to examine the main aspects.

orlare [or'lare] *vt* to hem; *(con cordoncini etc)* to edge, trim.

orlatura [orla'tura] *sf* hemming.

orlo ['orlo] *sm* **(a)** edge; *(di tazza, vaso etc)* rim, brim; *(di precipizio)* brink; **pieno fino all'~** full to the brim, brimfull; **sull'~ della pazzia/della rovina** on the brink *o* verge of madness/ruin. **(b)** *(ripiegatura: di vestiti etc)* hem; **~ a giorno** hemstitch.

orma ['orma] *sf (di persona)* footprint; *(di animale)* track; *(fig: impronta, traccia)* trace, mark; **seguire** *o* **calcare le ~e di qn** to follow in sb's footsteps.

ormai [or'mai] *av* **(a)** *(riferito al presente)* by now; (: *a questo punto*) now; **~ è tardi** it's late now; **~ dovrebbe essere partito** he must have left by now. **(b)** *(allora)* by then. **(c)** *(riferito al futuro)* almost, nearly; **~ siamo arrivati** we're nearly *o* almost there.

ormeggiare [ormed'dʒare] *vt,* **~rsi** *vr* to moor.

ormeggio [or'meddʒo] *sm* mooring; **~i** *(cavi e catene)* moorings; **le navi erano all'~** the ships were at their moorings; **posto d'~** berth.

ormone [or'mone] *sm* hormone.

ornamentale [ornamen'tale] *ag* ornamental.

ornamento [orna'mento] *sm (gen)* ornament; *(azione)* adornment, decoration; *(Archit, Arte)* embellishment; **privo di ~i** *(stile, vestito, stanza)* plain, unadorned.

ornare [or'nare] **1** *vt* **(a)** *(stanza, vestito):* **~ (di con)** to decorate (with), adorn (with); *(fig: discorso):* **~ di** *o* **con** to embellish with. **(b)** *(sog: affresco, statua)* to adorn, decorate. **2**: **~rsi** *vr:* **~rsi di** to deck o.s. (out) with.

ornato, a [or'nato] **1** *ag* **(a)** *(adorno):* **~ di** adorned with, decorated with; **un cappello ~ di piume** a hat trimmed with feathers. **(b)** *(stile)* ornate, florid. **2** *sm (Archit)* embellishment.

ornitologia [ornitolo'dʒia] *sf* ornithology.

ornitologo, a, gi *o* **ghi, ghe** [orni'tɔlogo] *sm/f* ornithologist.

ornitorinco, chi [ornito'rinko] *sm* (duck-billed) platypus.

oro ['ɔro] *sm* **(a)** gold; **bracciale in ~** *o* **d'~** gold bracelet; **~ zecchino** pure gold. **(b)**: **~i** *smpl (oggetti d'~)* gold *sg; (gioielli)* jewellery *sg; (Carte)* suit in Neapolitan pack of cards. **(c)**: **d'~** *(oggetto)* gold; *(di colore: capelli, spighe etc)* golden; *(persona)* marvellous, wonderful; **un'occasione d'**~ a golden opportunity; **un affare d'**~ a real bargain; **fare affari d'**~ to do excellent business; **avere un cuore d'**~ to have a heart of gold; **nuotare nell'**~ to be rolling in money; **prendere qc per** ~ **colato** to take sth as gospel (truth); **per tutto l'**~ **del mondo** for all the money in the world; **quell'uomo vale tanto** ~ **quanto pesa** that man is worth his weight in gold; **non è tutt'**~ **quel che luccica** all that glitters is not gold.

orologeria [orolodʒe'ria] *sf (arte, industria)* watchmaking; *(negozio)* watchmaker's (shop); *(meccanismo)* clockwork; **bomba a** ~ time bomb.

orologiaio [orolo'dʒajo] *sm* watchmaker.

orologio [oro'lɔdʒo] *sm (da muro, a pendolo etc)* clock; *(da polso etc)* watch; ~ **da polso/tasca** wrist-/pocket-watch; ~ **solare** sundial; **il mio** ~ **va avanti/indietro** my watch is fast/slow; **una mezz'ora di** ~ exactly half an hour; **andare o funzionare come un** ~ *(meccanismo etc)* to run like clockwork.

oroscopo [o'rɔskopo] *sm* horoscope.

orrendo, a [or'rɛndo] *ag (spaventoso)* horrible, horrendous; *(brutto)* hideous; *(cattivo)* awful, terrible, dreadful; *(ripugnante)* revolting.

orribile [or'ribile] *ag* horrible; *(pessimo)* awful, dreadful; *(ripugnante)* revolting.

orrido, a [ˈɔrrido] *ag* horrid, dreadful.

orripilante [orripi'lante] *ag* horrifying, hair-raising.

orrore [or'rore] *sm (gen)* horror; *(ribrezzo)* disgust, loathing; **avere** ~ **di qc** to loathe *o* detest sth; **avere in** ~ **qn/qc** to loathe *o* detest sb/sth; **i ragni mi fanno** ~ I have a horror of spiders, I loathe spiders; **gli** ~**i della guerra** the atrocities of war; **che** ~! how awful *o* dreadful!; **quel quadro è un** ~ that painting is hideous.

orsa [ˈorsa] *sf* she-bear; **l'O**~ **maggiore/minore** Ursa Major/Minor, the Great/Little Bear.

orsacchiotto [orsak'kjɔtto] *sm* bear cub; *(giocattolo)* teddy bear.

orso [ˈorso] *sm (Zool, fig)* bear; ~ **bruno/bianco** brown/polar bear.

orsù [or'su] *escl* come now!

ortaggio [or'taddʒo] *sm* vegetable.

ortensia [or'tɛnsja] *sf* hydrangea.

ortica, che [or'tika] *sf* (stinging) nettle.

orticaria [orti'karja] *sf* nettlerash.

orticoltura [ortikol'tura] *sf* horticulture.

orto [ˈɔrto] *sm* vegetable garden, kitchen garden; *(Agr)* market garden; ~ **botanico** botanical garden(s *pl*).

ortodossia [ortodos'sia] *sf* orthodoxy.

ortodosso, a [orto'dɔsso] *ag, sm/f* orthodox.

ortofrutticolo, a [ortofrut'tikolo] *ag* fruit and vegetable *attr.*

ortografia [ortogra'fia] *sf* spelling, orthography; **errori di** ~ spelling mistakes.

ortografico, a, ci, che [orto'grafiko] *ag* spelling *attr*, orthographical.

ortolano, a [orto'lano] *sm/f (negoziante)* greengrocer; *(coltivatore)* market gardener.

ortopedia [ortope'dia] *sf* orthopaedics *sg.*

ortopedico, a, ci, che [orto'pɛdiko] **1** *ag* orthopaedic. **2** *sm/f* orthopaedist.

orzaiolo [ordza'jɔlo] *sm (Med)* sty(e).

orzata [or'dzata] *sf (bevanda)* barley water; *(sciroppo)* almond-based cordial.

orzo [ˈɔrdzo] *sm* barley.

osanna [o'zanna] *sm inv* hosanna.

osannare [ozan'nare] *vt (lodare)* to applaud, acclaim.

osare [o'zare] *vt* **(a)**: ~ **(fare)** to dare (do), dare (to do); **non osava domandargli** he didn't dare (to) ask him; **oserei dire che...** I dare say that...; **come osi?** how dare you? **(b)** *(tentare)* to attempt; *(arrischiare)* to risk.

oscenità [oʃʃeni'ta] *sf inv* obscenity.

osceno, a [oʃ'ʃɛno] *ag (indecente)* obscene; *(bruttissimo)* dreadful, awful.

oscillare [oʃʃil'lare] *vi (Fis)* to oscillate; *(pendolo)* to swing; *(fiamma)* to flicker; *(prezzi, temperatura)*: ~ **(fra)** to fluctuate (between); *(persona: essere indeciso)*: ~ **(fra)** to waver (between).

oscillazione [oʃʃillat'tsjone] *sf (vedi vb)* oscillation; fluctuation.

oscuramento [oskura'mento] *sm* **(a)** *(vedi vb)* darkening; obscuring; dimming. **(b)** *(in tempo di guerra)* blackout.

oscurare [osku'rare] **1** *vt* **(a)** *(rendere scuro)* to darken; *(offuscare: sole, veduta)* to obscure; *(schermare: lampada)* to shade. **(b)** *(fig)* to obscure. **2**: ~**rsi** *vr* **(a)** *(cielo)* to cloud over, darken. **(b)** *(vista, mente)* to dim, grow dim; **si oscurò in volto** his face clouded (over).

oscurità [oskuri'ta] *sf (vedi ag)* darkness; obscurity; gloominess; **sono nell'**~ **più completa per quanto riguarda i loro progetti** I am completely in the dark about their plans.

oscuro, a [os'kuro] **1** *ag* dark; *(fig: incomprensibile, sconosciuto)* obscure; *(: triste: pensiero)* gloomy, sombre; *(: umile: vita, natali)* humble, obscure; **è morto in circostanze** ~**e** he died in mysterious circumstances. **2** *sm* darkness; **tenere qn/essere all'**~ **di qc** to keep sb/be in the dark about sth.

ospedale [ospe'dale] *sm* hospital; ~ **da campo** field hospital.

ospedaliero, a [ospeda'ljɛro] **1** *ag* hospital *attr.* **2** *sm* hospital worker.

ospedalizzare [ospedalid'dzare] *vt* to hospitalize.

ospitale [ospi'tale] *ag (gente)* hospitable; *(casa, paese)* friendly.

ospitalità [ospitali'ta] *sf* hospitality.

ospitare [ospi'tare] *vt* **(a)** *(dare alloggio)* to put up; *(: sog: albergo)* to accommodate. **(b)** *(accogliere: mostre, gare, avvenimenti)* to hold; *(: Sport)* to play at home to; **il Milan ospiterà la Juventus domenica prossima** Milan will play at home to Juventus next Sunday.

ospite [ˈɔspite] **1** *sm/f (padrone di casa)* host/hostess; *(invitato, in albergo)* guest. **2** *ag:* **squadra** ~ *(Calcio)* visiting team.

ospizio [os'pittsjo] *sm (istituto di ricovero)* home; *(per viaggiatori, pellegrini)* hospice; ~ **per vecchi** old folks' home.

ossa [ˈɔssa] *sfpl vedi* **osso.**

ossatura [ossa'tura] *sf (di corpo)* bone structure, frame; *(di edificio, ponte, romanzo)* framework.

osseo, a [ˈɔsseo] *ag (Anat, Med)* bone *attr.*

ossequiente [osse'kwjɛnte] *ag:* ~ **alle leggi** law-abiding.

ossequio [os'sɛkwjo] *sm* **(a)** respect; **in** ~ **a** out of respect for. **(b)**: ~**i** *smpl (saluto)* respects, regards; ~**i alla signora!** (give my) regards to your wife!; **porgere i propri** ~**i a qn** *(frm)* to pay one's respects to sb; **i miei** ~**i** *(in una lettera)* sincere regards.

ossequioso, a [osse'kwjoso] *ag (rispettoso)* respectful; *(servile)* obsequious.

osservante [osser'vante] *ag (Rel)* practising.

osservanza [osser'vantsa] *sf* observance.

osservare [osser'vare] *vt* **(a)** *(guardare)* to observe; *(: attentamente: nemico etc)* to watch; *(: al microscopio)* to examine. **(b)** *(notare)* to notice; *(far notare)* to point out, remark, observe;

far ~ qc a qn to point sth out to sb; **ha osservato che...** he remarked that...; *(ha obiettato)* he objected *o* made the objection that...; **non ho nulla da ~** I have no objections. **(c)** *(rispettare: legge etc)* to observe; ~ **il digiuno** to fast, keep the fast.

osservatore, trice [osserva'tore] **1** *ag* observant. **2** *sm/f* observer.

osservatorio [osserva'tɔrjo] *sm (Astron, Meteor)* observatory; *(Mil)* observation *o* look-out post.

osservazione [osservat'tsjone] *sf* **(a)** observation; **tenere qn in** *o* **sotto ~** *(Med)* to keep sb under observation. **(b)** *(nota, giudizio)* comment, observation, remark; *(obiezione)* objection; *(rimprovero)* criticism; **fare un'~** to make a remark; to raise an objection; **fare un'~ a qn** to criticise sb; **fare ~ a qn** to reprimand sb. **(c)** *(ubbidienza, rispetto)* observance.

ossessionante [ossessjo'nante] *ag (vedi vb)* obsessive, haunting; troublesome.

ossessionare [ossessjo'nare] *vt* to obsess, haunt; *(infastidire)* to trouble, bother.

ossessione [osses'sjone] *sf* **(a)** obsession; **aveva l'~ del denaro** he was obsessed with money. **(b)** *(seccatura)* nuisance.

ossessivo, a [osses'sivo] *ag (vedi vb)* obsessive, haunting; troublesome; **ma sei proprio ~!** you really are a pest!

ossesso, a [os'sɛsso] **1** *ag* possessed. **2** *sm/f* person possessed; *(fig)*: **urlare come un ~** to shout like a madman.

ossia [os'sia] *cong (cioè)* that is, to be precise; *(o meglio)* or rather.

ossibuchi [ossi'buki] *smpl di* **ossobuco.**

ossidante [ossi'dante] *sm* oxidizer.

ossidare [ossi'dare] *vt*, **~rsi** *vr* to oxidize.

ossidazione [ossidat'tsjone] *sf* oxidization, oxidation.

ossido ['ɔssido] *sm* oxide; **~ di carbonio** carbon monoxide.

ossificare [ossifi'kare] *vt*, **~rsi** *vr* to ossify.

ossigenare [ossidʒe'nare] *vt* **(a)** *(Chim)* to oxygenate; **~ i capelli** to bleach one's hair. **(b)** *(fig)* to inject new life into; **~ i polmoni** to get some fresh air.

ossigeno [os'sidʒeno] *sm* oxygen; **dare l'~ a qn** to give sb oxygen; **dare ~ a qn/qc** *(fig)* to give sb/sth a new lease of life.

osso ['ɔsso] *sm, pl(f)* **~a** *o talvolta pl(m)* **~i (a)** bone; **d'~** *(bottone, manica)* bone *attr*; **carne senza ~** boneless *o* boned meat; **~ di balena** whalebone; **~ di seppia** cuttle-bone. **(b)** *(fam: di pesca etc)* stone. **(c)** *(fraseologia)*: **avere le ~a rotte** to be dead *o* dog tired; **bagnato fino all'~** soaked to the skin; **rompersi l'~ del collo** to break one's neck; **rimetterci l'~ del collo** *(fig)* to ruin o.s., lose everything; **essere ridotto all'~** *(fig: magro)* to be just skin and bone; *(: senza soldi)* to be in dire straits; **non riesco a farci le ~a** I can't get used to it; **un ~ duro** *(persona, impresa)* a tough number.

ossobuco [osso'buko], *pl* **ossibuchi** *sm (Cuc)* marrowbone; *(: piatto) stew made with knuckle of veal in tomato sauce.*

ossuto, a [os'suto] *ag (persona, viso)* angular; *(animale)* scraggy; *(mano)* bony.

ostacolare [ostako'lare] *vt* to obstruct; *(persona, piano)* to hinder.

ostacolista, i, e [ostako'lista] **1** *sm/f (atleta)* hurdler. **2** *sm (cavallo)* steeplechaser.

ostacolo [os'takolo] *sm* **(a)** *(anche fig)* obstacle; **essere di ~ a qn/qc** *(fig)* to stand in the way of sb/sth. **(b)** *(Atletica)* hurdle; *(Equitazione)* jump, fence.

ostaggio [os'taddʒo] *sm* hostage; **prendere/tenere qn in ~** to take/keep sb hostage.

oste, essa ['ɔste] **1** *sm/f* innkeeper, landlord/lady. **2** *sf* landlord's wife.

osteggiare [osted'dʒare] *vt* to oppose.

ostello [os'tɛllo] *sm*: **~ della gioventù** youth hostel.

ostentare [osten'tare] *vt (ricchezze, bravura)* to show off, flaunt; *(distacco, indifferenza)* to feign.

ostentazione [ostentat'tsjone] *sf* ostentation; **con ~** ostentatiously.

osteria [oste'ria] *sf* inn.

ostessa [os'tessa] *sf vedi* **oste.**

ostetricia [oste'tritʃa] *sf* obstetrics *sg.*

ostetrico, a, ci, che [os'tetriko] **1** *ag* obstetric(al); **clinica ~a** maternity home. **2** *sm/f (medico)* obstetrician. **3** *sf (levatrice)* midwife.

ostia ['ɔstja] *sf (Rel)* host; *(cialda)* wafer.

ostico, a, ci, che ['ɔstiko] *ag* difficult, tough.

ostile [os'tile] *ag*: **~ (a)** hostile (to *o* towards).

ostilità [ostili'ta] *sf inv (stato, atteggiamento)* hostility; *(atto)* act of hostility; *(Mil)*: **le ~** hostilities.

ostinarsi [osti'narsi] *vr* **(a)** *(impuntarsi)*: **~ su** *o* **in qc** to insist on sth, dig one's heels in about sth; **~ a voler fare qc** to be determined to do sth. **(b)** *(persistere)*: **~ a fare qc** to persist in doing sth.

ostinato, a [osti'nato] **1** *ag (persona, resistenza)* obstinate, stubborn; *(fatica, tosse, pioggia)* persistent. **2** *sm/f* obstinate *o* stubborn person.

ostinazione [ostinat'tsjone] *sf* obstinacy, stubbornness; **~ a fare qc** obstinate *o* stubborn determination to do sth.

ostracismo [ostra'tʃizmo] *sm* ostracism; **dare l'~ a qn** to ostracize sb.

ostrica, che ['ɔstrika] *sf* oyster; **~ perlifera** pearl oyster.

ostruire [ostru'ire] **1** *vt* to obstruct, block. **2**: **~rsi** *vr* to become obstructed *o* blocked.

ostruzione [ostrut'tsjone] *sf* **(a)** obstruction, blocking. **(b)** *(effetto, cosa che ostruisce)* obstruction, blockage; *(Sport)* obstruction.

ostruzionismo [ostruttsjo'nizmo] *sm (Pol)* obstructionism; *(Sport)* obstruction; **fare dell'~ a** *(progetto, legge)* to obstruct.

ostruzionista, i, e [ostruttsjo'nista] *ag, sm/f* obstructionist.

ostruzionistico, a, ci, che [ostruttsjo'nistiko] *ag* obstructionist.

otite [o'tite] *sf* ear infection.

otorino(laringoiatra), i, e [oto'rino(laringo-'jatra)] *sm/f* ear, nose and throat specialist.

otre ['otre] *sm* leather bag *o* bottle.

ottagonale [ottago'nale] *ag* octagonal, eight-sided.

ottagono [ot'tagono] *sm* octagon.

ottano [ot'tano] *sm* octane; **numero di ~i** octane rating; **benzina ad alto numero di ~i** high-octane petrol.

ottanta [ot'tanta] *ag inv, sm inv* eighty; *per uso vedi* **cinquanta.**

ottantenne [ottan'tɛnne] **1** *ag* eighty-year-old; *per uso vedi* **cinquantenne 2** *sm/f* octogenarian.

ottantesimo, a [ottan'tɛzimo] *ag, sm/f, sm* eightieth; *per uso vedi* **quinto.**

ottantina [ottan'tina] *sf* about eighty; *per uso vedi* **cinquantina.**

ottavo, a [ot'tavo] **1** *ag, sm/f* eighth; *per uso vedi* **quinto. 2** *sm* **(a)** *(frazione)* eighth. **(b)** *(Tip)* octavo; **edizione in ~** octavo edition. **(c)** *(Sport)*: **entrare negli ~i di finale** to get into the last sixteen; **superare gli ~i di finale** to reach the quarterfinals. **3** *sf (Poesia, Mus, Rel)* octave.

ottemperanza [ottempe'rantsa] *sf*: **in ~ a** *(Amm)* in accordance with, in compliance with.

ottemperare [ottempe'rare] *vi*: **~ a** to comply with, obey.

ottenebrare [ottene'brare] **1** vt (anche fig) to cloud; (sole) to hide, obscure. **2**: ~**rsi** vr to cloud (over).

ottenere [otte'nere] vt **(a)** (risposta, laurea, permesso) to obtain; ~ **una promozione** to get promotion; **ha ottenuto di parlargli lunedì** he managed to arrange a meeting with him for Monday; **ha ottenuto che il ragazzo venisse ricoverato** he managed to get the boy admitted to hospital. **(b)** (totale) to reach, arrive at; (risultato) to achieve, obtain; (premio, approvazione, fiducia) to gain, win; ~ **un buon successo** to have great success; **aggiungendo il giallo al blu si ottiene il verde** green is obtained by adding yellow to blue.

ottetto [ot'tetto] sm (Mus) octet; (Inform) byte.

ottico, a, ci, che ['ɔttiko] **1** ag (nervo) optic; (fenomeno, strumento) optical. **2** sm optician. **3** sf (Fis, tecnica) optics sg; (insieme di lenti) optics pl; (fig: punto di vista) point of view, viewpoint.

ottimale [otti'male] ag optimal, optimum.

ottimamente [ottima'mente] av very well.

ottimismo [otti'mizmo] sm optimism.

ottimista, i, e [otti'mista] **1** ag optimistic. **2** sm/f optimist.

ottimistico, a, ci, che [otti'mistiko] ag optimistic.

ottimo, a ['ɔttimo] **1** ag (superl di **buono**) very good, excellent. **2** sm (di produzione, carriera etc) peak.

otto ['ɔtto] **1** ag inv eight. **2** sm inv (numero, Canottaggio) eight; (tracciato) figure of eight; **oggi (a)** ~ **in** a week's time, today week; ~ **volante** switchback; per uso vedi **cinque**.

ottobre [ot'tobre] sm October; per uso vedi **luglio**.

ottobrino, a [otto'brino] ag October attr.

ottocentesco, a, schi, sche [ottotʃen'tesko] ag nineteenth-century.

ottocentista, i, e [ottotʃen'tista] sm/f **(a)** (studioso) nineteenth-century scholar o specialist; (artista, scrittore etc) nineteenth-century artist (o writer etc). **(b)** (Sport) eight hundred metres runner.

ottocento [otto'tʃento] **1** ag inv eight hundred. **2** sm inv eight hundred; (secolo): **l'O**~ the nineteenth century.

ottomila [otto'mila] ag inv, sm inv eight thousand.

ottone [ot'tone] sm brass; **di** o **in** ~ brass attr; **gli** ~**i** (Mus) the brass.

ottuagenario, a [ottuadʒe'narjo] ag, sm/f octogenarian.

otturare [ottu'rare] **1** vt (chiudere: falla, apertura) to stop up, seal; (bloccare: lavandino) to block (up); (riempire: dente) to fill. **2**: ~**rsi** vr (bloccarsi) to become o get blocked (up).

otturatore [ottura'tore] sm (Fot) shutter; (nelle armi) breechblock; (Tecn) valve.

otturazione [otturat'tsjone] sf **(a)** (vedi vb) stopping up, sealing; blocking; filling. **(b)** (di dente) filling; **fare un'**~ **a qn** to give sb a filling.

ottusità [ottuzi'ta] sf obtuseness.

ottuso, a [ot'tuzo] ag (anche fig) obtuse; (suono) muffled.

ouverture [uver'tyr] sf inv (Mus) overture.

ovaia [o'vaja] sf, **ovaio** [o'vajo] sm ovary.

ovale [o'vale] ag, sm oval.

ovatta [o'vatta] sf (per medicazione) cotton wool; (per imbottiture) padding.

ovattare [ovat'tare] vt **(a)** (imbottire) to pad; **ambiente ovattato** (fig) cocoon-like environment. **(b)** (fig: smorzare) to muffle.

ovest ['ɔvest] **1** sm west; **a** ~ **(di)** west (of); **verso** ~ westward(s). **2** ag inv (gen) west; (regione) western; **è partito in direzione** ~ he set off westwards o in a westward direction.

ovile [o'vile] sm (sheep)fold; **tornare all'**~ (fig) to return to the fold.

ovino, a [o'vino] ag (Zool) ovine (T); (mercato, allevamento) sheep attr.

O.V.N.I. ['ɔvni] sm (abbr di oggetto volante non identificato) UFO.

ovulazione [ovulat'tsjone] sf ovulation.

ovulo ['ɔvulo] sm (Anat) ovum; (Bot) ovule.

ovunque [o'vunkwe] av = **dovunque**.

ovvero [ov'vero] cong or (rather).

ovviare [ovvi'are] vi: ~ **a** to remedy; ~ **all'inconveniente (di)** to get round the problem (of).

ovvio, a ['ɔvvjo] ag obvious; **è** ~ **che**... obviously..., it is obvious o clear that... .

oziare [ot'tsjare] vi to laze around.

ozio ['ɔttsjo] sm **(a)** (peccato) sloth; (inattività) idleness; **stare in** ~ to be idle; **l'**~ **è il padre dei vizi** (Proverbio) the Devil finds work for idle hands. **(b)** (riposo): **ore d'**~ leisure o spare time.

ozioso, a [ot'tsjoso] **1** ag **(a)** (sfaccendato) idle; (inattivo: persona, giornata) lazy; (: per malattia) inactive. **(b)** (fig: discorsi) idle; (: domanda) pointless. **2** sm/f layabout, idler.

ozono [od'dzono] sm ozone.

P

P, p¹ [pi] *sf o m inv (lettera)* P, p.

p² *abbr (= pagina)* p.

pacatezza [paka'tettsa] *sf (vedi ag)* placidness; quietness, calmness.

pacato, a [pa'kato] *ag (carattere)* placid; *(voce, tono)* quiet, calm.

pacca, che ['pakka] *sf* slap.

pacchetto [pak'ketto] *sm (confezione)* parcel; *(: di sigarette)* packet; ~ **azionario** *(Fin)* shareholding.

pacchia ['pakkja] *sf (fam)*: **è stata una** ~! *(divertimento)* we had a great time!; *(di esame etc: molto facile)* it was a piece of cake!; **che** ~! what fun!

pacchiano, a [pak'kjano] *ag (colori)* garish; *(abiti, arredamento)* vulgar, garish; **ha un gusto veramente** ~ she has extremely vulgar taste.

pacco, chi ['pakko] *sm* **(a)** package; ~ **postale** parcel; **carta da** ~**chi** brown paper, wrapping paper. **(b)** *(involto)* bundle.

paccottiglia [pakkot'tiʎʎa] *sf* trash, junk.

pace ['patʃe] *sf (gen)* peace; **trattato di** ~ peace treaty; **firmare la** ~ to sign a peace treaty; **fare (la)** ~ **con qn** to make it up with sb; **far fare (la)** ~ **a due persone** to make peace between two people; **non si dà** ~ **per quello che è successo** she can't stop thinking about what happened; **non mi dà un momento di** ~ he doesn't give me a moment's peace; **mettersi l'animo in** ~ to resign o.s.; **lasciare qn in** ~ to leave sb alone; **riposare in** ~ to rest in peace; **santa** ~! for heaven's sake!; ~ **all'anima sua!** *(anche scherz)* may he rest in peace!; ~! *(fa niente)* never mind!

pachiderma, i [paki'dɛrma] *sm* pachyderm.

paciere, a [pa'tʃɛre] *sm/f* peacemaker.

pacificare [patʃifi'kare] *vt (due persone)* to reconcile, make peace between; **riuscì a** ~ **gli animi** he managed to mollify everyone.

pacifico, a, ci, che [pa'tʃifiko] **1** *ag* **(a)** *(persona, carattere)* peaceable; *(vita)* peaceful. **(b)** *(ovvio)*: **è** ~ **che resterà in carica** it is obvious *o* it goes without saying that he will stay in office. **(c)** *(Geog)* Pacific. **2** *sm*: **il P~, l'Oceano P~** the Pacific (Ocean).

pacifismo [patʃi'fizmo] *sm* pacifism.

pacifista, i, e [patʃi'fista] *sm/f* pacifist.

padano, a [pa'dano] *ag* of the Po; **la pianura** ~**a** the Lombardy plain.

padella [pa'della] *sf* **(a)** *(Culin)* frying pan; **cucinare in** ~ to fry; **cadere dalla** ~ **nella brace** *(fig)* to jump out of the frying pan into the fire. **(b)** *(per malati)* bedpan.

padiglione [padiʎ'ʎone] *sm* **(a)** *(di mostra, ospedale)* pavilion; ~ **di caccia** hunting lodge. **(b)** *(Anat)* ~ **auricolare** auricle, pinna.

Padova ['padova] *sf* Padua.

padovano, a [pado'vano] *ag* of *(o* from) Padua.

padre ['padre] *sm* **(a)** father; ~ **di famiglia** father; **Rossi,** ~ Rossi senior; **di** ~ **in figlio** from father to son; **per parte di** ~ on my *(o* his *etc)* father's side. **(b)**: ~**i** *pl (antenati)* forefathers, ancestors. **(c)** *(Rel)* father; **P~ mio** Father; **il Santo P~**

(il Papa) the Holy Father.

Padreterno [padre'tɛrno] *sm*: **il** ~ God the Father; **si crede un p**~ *(fig)* he thinks he is God Almighty.

padrino [pa'drino] *sm (di battesimo)* godfather; *(di cresima)* sponsor; *(di duello)* second.

padronale [padro'nale] *ag (scala, entrata)* main, principal; **casa** ~ country house.

padronanza [padro'nantsa] *sf (dominio)* command, mastery; ~ **di sé** self-control; **avere una buona** ~ **della lingua inglese** to have a good command of the English language.

padronato [padro'nato] *sm*: **il** ~ the ruling class.

padrone, a [pa'drone] *sm/f* **(a)** *(dominatore: anche fig)* master/mistress; *(proprietario)* owner; ~**/a di casa** master/mistress of the house; *(ospite)* host/hostess; *(di casa in affitto)* landlord/landlady; **essere** ~ **di sé** to be self-possessed; **non era più** ~ **di sé** he had lost his self-control; **sono** ~ **di fare ciò che voglio** I am my own master; **si crede** ~ **del mondo** he thinks he is God Almighty; **essere** ~ **di una lingua** to have mastered a language; **essere** ~ **della situazione** to be master of the situation, have the situation in hand; **farla da** ~ to play the lord and master; **non sono più** ~ **in casa mia** I am no longer master in my own home. **(b)** *(datore di lavoro)* employer, boss *(fam)*; **essere sotto** ~ to be an employee.

padroneggiare [padroned'dʒare] **1** *vt (istinti)* to control; *(lingua)* to master. **2**: ~**rsi** *vr* to control o.s.

paesaggio [pae'zaddʒo] *sm (panorama, Arte)* landscape; *(aspetto di un luogo)* scenery.

paesaggista, i, e [paezad'dʒista] *sm/f (pittore)* landscape painter.

paesano, a [pae'zano] **1** *ag* country *attr.* **2** *sm/f* **(a)** *(campagnolo)* peasant, rustic. **(b)** *(concittadino)* fellow countryman/countrywoman.

paese [pa'eze] **1** *sm* **(a)** *(nazione)* country, nation; **i** ~**i in via di sviluppo** the developing countries *o* nations; **l'Iraq è il** ~ **d'origine della mia famiglia** my family comes from Iraq. **(b)** *(terra)* country, land; **vorrei visitare** ~**i lontani** I should like to visit distant lands *o* far away places; **la Francia è un** ~ **fertile** France is a fertile country *o* land. **(c)** *(villaggio)* village; **gente di** ~ village people. **(d)** *(fraseologia)*: ~ **che vai usanze che trovi** when in Rome do as the Romans do; **tutto il mondo è** ~ people are the same the world over; **mandare qn a quel** ~ *(fam)* to tell sb to get lost. **2**: **i P~i Bassi** the Netherlands.

paffuto, a [paf'futo] *ag* plump, chubby.

paga, ghe ['paga] *sf (gen)* pay; *(di operaio)* wages *pl*; *(fig: ricompensa)* reward, recompense; **giorno di** ~ payday.

pagabile [pa'gabile] *ag* payable; ~ **alla consegna/a vista** payable on delivery/on demand.

pagaia [pa'gaja] *sf* paddle.

pagamento [paga'mento] *sm* payment; ~ **in contanti** cash payment; ~ **alla consegna** payment on delivery; ~ **anticipato** payment in advance; **non**

lo faccio nemmeno a ~ I won't do it even if they pay me.

paganesimo [paga'nezimo] *sm* paganism.

pagano, a [pa'gano] *ag, sm/f* pagan.

pagare [pa'gare] *vt* **(a)** *(somma, conto, operaio)* to pay; *(debito)* to pay, settle; ~ **una cambiale** to pay *o* honour a bill; ~ **in contanti** to pay cash.

(b) *(merce, lavoro)* to pay for; **quanto l'hai pagato?** how much did you pay for it?; ~ **una casa/una macchina 20 milioni** to pay 20 million lire for a house/a car; **me l'ha fatto ~ duemila lire** he charged me two thousand lire for it; **l'ho pagato caro/poco** I paid a lot/very little for it; **l'ho pagata cara** *(fig)* I paid dearly for it; ~ **qc salato** *o* **un occhio della testa** to pay through the nose for sth; **te la farò ~!** *(fig)* I'll make you pay for it!; **ha pagato con la vita** *(fig)* it cost him his life; ~ **di persona** *(fig)* to suffer the consequences; ~ **qc di tasca propria** to pay for sth out of one's own pocket; *(fig)* to learn sth to one's cost; **quanto non pagherei per sapere!** what wouldn't I give to know!

(c) *(offrire)*: **ti pago da bere** let me buy you a drink; **pago io** this is on me; **pago io questo giro** this is my round.

pagella [pa'dʒɛlla] *sf (Scol)* report.

paggio ['paddʒo] *sm* page(boy).

pagherò [page'rɔ] *sm inv* IOU.

pagina ['padʒina] *sf* page; **a ~ 5** on page 5; **le più belle ~e del Manzoni** Manzoni's finest passages.

paglia ['paʎʎa] *sf* straw; **cappello di ~** straw hat; **tetto di ~** thatched roof; **avere la coda di ~** *(fig)* to have a guilty conscience; **fuoco di ~** *(fig)* flash in the pan.

pagliaccetto [paʎʎat'tʃetto] *sm (per bambini)* rompers *pl*; *(per signora)* camiknickers *pl*.

pagliacciata [paʎʎat'tʃata] *sf* (piece of) buffoonery.

pagliaccio [paʎ'ʎattʃo] *sm* clown; **fare il ~** *(fig)* to play the fool.

pagliaio [paʎ'ʎajo] *sm* haystack.

pagliericcio [paʎʎe'rittʃo] *sm* straw mattress.

paglierino, a [paʎʎe'rino] *ag: giallo ~* pale yellow.

paglietta [paʎ'ʎetta] *sf* **(a)** *(cappello per uomo)* (straw) boater. **(b):** ~ **di ferro** *(per tegami)* steel wool.

pagliuzza [paʎ'ʎuttsa] *sf* (blade of) straw; *(di oro etc)* tiny particle, speck.

pagnotta [paɲ'ɲɔtta] *sf* round loaf.

pago, a, ghi, ghe ['pago] *ag:* **essere ~ di** to be satisfied with.

pagoda [pa'gɔda] *sf* pagoda.

paillette [pa'jɛt] *sf inv* sequin.

paio ['pajo] *sm, pl(f)* **paia** *(coppia)* pair; **un ~ di** *(due o più)* a couple of; *(guanti, scarpe etc)* a pair of; **un ~ di occhiali** a pair of glasses; **fra un ~ di settimane** in a couple of weeks; **fanno il ~** they are two of a kind; **è un altro ~ di maniche** *(fig)* that's another kettle of fish; **dare un ~ di schiaffi a qn** to box sb's ears.

paiolo [pa'jɔlo] *sm* copper pot.

Pakistan [pakis'tan] *sm* Pakistan.

pakistano, a [pakis'tano] *ag, sm/f* Pakistani.

pala ['pala] *sf* **(a)** shovel; *(di remo, ventilatore, elica)* blade; *(di ruota)* paddle. **(b)** *(Rel):* ~ **d'altare** altar piece.

paladino [pala'dino] *sm (Storia)* paladin; *(fig: difensore)* champion.

palafitta [pala'fitta] *sf* **(a)** *(abitazione)* pile-dwelling. **(b)** *(Edil: sostegno)* piles *pl*.

palandrana [palan'drana] *sf (scherz: abito lungo e largo)* tent.

palata [pa'lata] *sf (contenuto)* shovelful; **fa soldi a**

~**e** *(fig)* he is making a mint.

palatale [pala'tale] *ag, sf* palatal.

palato [pa'lato] *sm (Anat)* palate; *(gusto)* palate, (sense of) taste; **gradevole al ~** palatable; **avere un ~ fine** to have a good palate.

palazzina [palat'tsina] *sf (dimora signorile)* villa.

palazzo [pa'lattso] *sm (reggia)* palace; *(edificio)* building; ~ **dei congressi** conference centre; ~ **di giustizia** law courts *pl*; ~ **dello sport** sports stadium.

palco, chi ['palko] *sm* **(a)** *(tavolato)* platform; *(tribuna)* stand. **(b)** *(Teatro)* box.

palcoscenico [palkoʃ'ʃeniko] *sm (Teatro)* stage.

palermitano, a [palermi'tano] *ag* of *(o* from*)* Palermo.

palesare [pale'zare] **1** *vt* to reveal, disclose. **2:** ~**rsi** *vr* to reveal o.s.

palese [pa'leze] *ag* clear, evident; **rendere ~i le proprie intenzioni** to make one's intentions clear.

Palestina [pales'tina] *sf* Palestine.

palestinese [palesti'neze] *ag, sm/f* Palestinian.

palestra [pa'lestra] *sf (luogo)* gymnasium, gym; **devo fare un po' di ~** I must take a bit of exercise; **la scuola è ~ di vita** *(fig)* school is a preparation for life.

paletot [pal'to] *sm inv* = paltò.

paletta [pa'letta] *sf (giocattolo)* spade; *(per il focolare)* shovel; *(del capostazione)* signalling disc.

paletto [pa'letto] *sm (picchetto)* stake, peg; *(chiavistello per porte)* bolt.

palio ['paljo] *sm (Storia: drappo)* (prize) banner; **il P~ di Siena** horse race in which the different districts of Siena compete; **mettere qc in ~** *(fig)* to offer sth as a prize.

palissandro [palis'sandro] *sm* rosewood.

palizzata [palit'tsata] *sf* palisade.

palla ['palla] **1** *sf* ball; ~ **da tennis/golf** tennis/golf ball; ~ **di neve** snowball; **giocare a ~** to play (with a) ball; **sei una ~ al piede!** you are a drag!; **prendere la ~ al balzo** *(fig)* to seize one's opportunity; **rompere le ~e a qn** *(fam!)* to be a bloody nuisance to sb.

pallacanestro [pallaka'nestro] *sf* basketball.

pallamano [palla'mano] *sf* handball.

pallanuoto [palla'nwɔto] *sf* water polo.

pallavolo [palla'volo] *sf* volleyball.

palleggiare [palled'dʒare] **1** *vi (Calcio)* to practise with the ball; *(Tennis)* to knock up. **2:** ~**rsi** *vr:* **si stanno palleggiando le responsabilità** each is trying to shift the responsibility onto the other.

palleggio [pal'leddʒo] *sm (gen)* practising with a ball; *(prima di una partita)* warm-up; *(Tennis)* knock-up.

palliativo [pallja'tivo] *sm (Med)* palliative; *(fig)* stopgap measure.

pallido, a ['pallido] *ag (gen)* pale; *(malaticcio)* pallid; *(ricordo)* faint; *(sorriso)* faint, wan; **è diventata ~a** she paled, she turned pale; **non ho la più ~a idea** I haven't the faintest *o* foggiest (idea).

pallina [pal'lina] *sf (bilia)* marble.

pallino [pal'lino] *sm* **(a)** *(Biliardo)* cue ball; *(Bocce)* jack. **(b)** *(proiettile)* pellet. **(c)** *(pois)* dot; **bianco a ~i blu** white with blue dots. **(d)** *(idea fissa)* craze, obsession; **avere il ~ di** to be crazy about; **ha il ~ della matematica** he has a passion for mathematics.

pallonata [pallo'nata] *sf* blow (from a ball).

palloncino [pallon'tʃino] *sm (giocattolo)* balloon.

pallone [pal'lone] *sm* **(a)** *(palla)* ball; *(Calcio)* football; **gioco del ~** football; **essere un ~ gonfiato** *(fig)* to be full of o.s. **(b)** *(aerostato)* balloon; ~ **sonda** weather balloon.

pallonetto [pallo'netto] *sm (Calcio, Tennis)* lob.

pallore [pal'lore] *sm* pallor, paleness.

pallottola [pal'lɔttola] *sf* **(a)** *(di carta)* ball; **c'erano delle** ~e **di carta nel cestino** there were some bits of screwed-up paper in the bin. **(b)** *(proiettile)* bullet.

pallottoliere [pallotto'ljere] *sm* abacus.

palma[1] ['palma] *sf (Anat)* = **palmo**.

palma[2] ['palma] *sf (Bot)* palm; ~ **da datteri** date palm; **riportare/vincere la** ~ *(fig)* to walk off with/win the prize.

palmato, a [pal'mato] *ag (Zool: piede)* webbed; *(Bot)* palmate.

palmeto [pal'meto] *sm* palm grove.

palmipede [pal'mipede] *ag* web-footed.

palmizio [pal'mittsjo] *sm (palma)* palm tree; *(ramo)* palm.

palmo ['palmo] *sm (Anat)* palm; **restare con un** ~ **di naso** *(fig)* to be disappointed; **essere alto un** ~ *(fig)* to be tiny.

palo ['palo] *sm (legno appuntito)* stake; *(sostegno)* pole; *(Calcio)* goalpost; **fare da** *o* **il** ~ *(fig)* to act as look out; **saltare di** ~ **in frasca** *((fig)* to jump from one topic to another.

palombaro [palom'baro] *sm* (deep-sea) diver.

palombo [pa'lombo] *sm (pesce)* dogfish; *(colombo)* wood pigeon.

palpabile [pal'pabile] *ag (differenza, errore)* palpable.

palpare [pal'pare] *vt (tastare)* to feel, finger; *(Med)* to palpate.

palpebra ['palpebra] *sf* eyelid.

palpitante [palpi'tante] *ag:* ~ **di** *(paura)* trembling with; *(emozione)* quivering with.

palpitare [palpi'tare] *vi (cuore)* to pound; *(tempie)* to throb; ~ **di paura** to tremble with fear; ~ **di gioia** to quiver with delight.

palpitazione [palpitat'tsjone] *sf (Med):* **avere le** ~i to have palpitations.

palpito ['palpito] *sm (del cuore)* beat; *(fig: d'amore)* throb.

paltò [pal'tɔ] *sm inv* overcoat.

palude [pa'lude] *sf* marsh, swamp.

paludoso, a [palu'doso] *ag* swampy, marshy.

palustre [pa'lustre] *ag* marsh *attr*, swamp *attr*.

pampa ['pampa] *sf* pampas *sg o pl*.

pampino ['pampino] *sm* vine leaf.

panacea [pana'tʃɛa] *sf* panacea.

Panama ['panama] *sf* Panama; **il canale di** ~ the Panama Canal.

panama ['panama] *sm inv (cappello)* panama (hat).

panamense [pana'mɛnse] *ag, sm/f* Panamanian.

panca, che ['panka] *sf* bench.

pancetta [pan'tʃetta] *sf (Culin)* bacon.

panchina [pan'kina] *sf* garden seat; *(di giardino pubblico)* park bench.

pancia, ce ['pantʃa] *sf* belly, stomach; **aver mal di** ~ to have a stomach ache; **mettere su** ~ to develop a paunch; **non star lì a grattarti la** ~! don't sit (*o* stand) there doing nothing!

panciata [pan'tʃata] *sf* belly flop.

panciera [pan'tʃɛra] *sf* corset.

panciolle [pan'tʃɔlle] *av:* **stare in** ~ to lounge about.

panciotto [pan'tʃɔtto] *sm* waistcoat.

pancreas ['pankreas] *sm* pancreas.

panda ['panda] *sm inv* panda.

pandemonio [pande'mɔnjo] *sm* pandemonium.

pandoro [pan'dɔro] *sm type of sponge cake eaten at Christmas.*

pane ['pane] **1** *sm (gen)* bread; *(di cera)* bar; *(di burro)* block; **il** ~ **quotidiano** one's daily bread; **guadagnarsi il** ~ to earn one's living; **mangiare**

il ~ **a tradimento** to sponge, scrounge; **rendere pan per focaccia** to give tit for tat; **dire** ~ **al** ~, **vino al vino** to call a spade a spade; **essere buono come il** ~ to have a heart of gold; **quella ragazza non è** ~ **per i tuoi denti** that girl's not for you; **per un pezzo di** ~ *(comprare, vendere)* for a song. **2**: ~ **bianco** white bread; ~ **casereccio** homemade bread; ~ **a cassetta** sliced bread; ~ **integrale**, ~ **nero** wholemeal bread; ~ **di segale** rye bread; **pan di Spagna** sponge cake.

panegirico, ci [pane'dʒiriko] *sm* panegyric; **fare un** ~ **di qn** to sing sb's praises.

panetteria [panette'ria] *sf (forno)* bakery; *(negozio)* baker's (shop), bakery.

panettiere, a [panet'tjere] *sm/f* baker.

panetto [pa'netto] *sm (di burro)* block.

panettone [panet'tone] *sm a kind of brioche with sultanas, eaten at Christmas.*

panfilo ['panfilo] *sm* yacht.

panforte [pan'fɔrte] *sm Sienese nougat-type delicacy.*

pangrattato [pangrat'tato] *sm* breadcrumbs *pl*.

panico [pa'niko] *sm* panic; **essere in preda al** ~ to be panic-stricken; **lasciarsi prendere dal** ~ to panic.

paniere [pa'njere] *sm* basket.

panificare [panifi'kare] *vi* to make bread.

panificio [pani'fitʃo] *sm (forno)* bakery; *(negozio)* baker's (shop), bakery.

panino [pa'nino] *sm* roll; ~ **imbottito** filled roll, sandwich.

panna ['panna] *sf* cream; ~ **montata** whipped cream.

panne ['pan] *sf (Aut)* breakdown; **la macchina è in** ~ the car has broken down; **restare in** ~ to break down.

panneggio [pan'neddʒo] *sm* drapery.

pannello [pan'nɛllo] *sm* panel.

panno ['panno] *sm* **(a)** *(tessuto, straccio)* cloth. **(b)**: ~i *pl (vestiti)* clothes; ~i **da lavare** laundry, washing; **mettiti nei miei** ~i *(fig)* put yourself in my shoes; **non stava più nei suoi** ~i **dalla gioia** *(fig)* he was beside himself with joy.

pannocchia [pan'nɔkkja] *sf* corncob.

pannolino [panno'lino] *sm (per bambini)* nappy, diaper (*Am*); *(assorbente)* sanitary towel.

panorama, i [pano'rama] *sm* panorama.

panoramica, che [pano'ramika] *sf* **(a)** *(strada)* scenic route. **(b)** *(Cine)* pan shot; *(Fot)* panorama; **fare una** ~ **di qc** *(fig)* to outline sth.

panoramico, a, ci, che [pano'ramiko] *ag (gen)* panoramic; **strada** ~a scenic route; **rassegna** ~a overall view.

panpepato [panpe'pato] *sm type of gingerbread.*

pantaloni [panta'loni] *smpl* trousers.

pantano [pan'tano] *sm* marsh, bog.

pantera [pan'tɛra] *sf* **(a)** *(Zool)* panther. **(b)** *(auto della polizia)* (high-speed) police car.

pantofola [pan'tɔfola] *sf* slipper.

pantomima [panto'mima] *sf* pantomime.

panzana [pan'tsana] *sf* fib, tall story.

paonazzo, a [pao'nattso] *ag* purple.

papa, i ['papa] *sm* pope; **ad ogni morte di** ~ *(fig)* once in a blue moon.

papà [pa'pa] *sm inv* daddy, dad; **figlio di** ~ spoilt young man.

papale [pa'pale] *ag* papal.

papalina [papa'lina] *sf* skullcap.

paparazzo [papa'rattso] *sm* paparazzo.

papato [pa'pato] *sm* papacy.

papavero [pa'pavero] *sm* poppy.

papera ['papera] *sf (errore)* slip of the tongue; **ha**

fatto una ~ that was a slip of the tongue on his *(o her)* part.

papero, a ['papero] *sm/f (Zool)* gosling.

papillon [papi'jɔ̃] *sm inv* bow tie.

papiro [pa'piro] *sm* papyrus.

pappa ['pappa] *sf (per bambini)* baby food; *(peg: poltiglia)* mush; **~ reale** royal jelly; **hai sempre avuto la ~ pronta** *(fig)* you've never had to stand on your own two feet.

pappagallesco, a, schi, sche [pappagal'lesko] *ag* parrot-like *attr.*

pappagallo [pappa'gallo] *sm (Zool)* parrot; *(fig: uomo)* wolf; **ripetere tutto come un ~** *(fig)* to repeat everything parrot-fashion.

pappagorgia, ge [pappa'gordʒa] *sf* double chin.

pappardella [pappar'della] *sf (Culin)* wide strip of pasta; *(fig):* **che ~ il suo discorso!** what a bore his speech was!

pappare [pap'pare] *vt (fam: mangiare)* to gobble up; *(: appropriarsi di: soldi)* to walk off with.

paprica ['paprika] *sf* paprika.

para ['para] *sf:* **suole di ~** crêpe (rubber) soles.

parà [pa'ra] *sm inv (abbr di* **paracadutista)** para.

parabola[1] [pa'rabola] *sf (Mat)* parabola.

parabola[2] [pa'rabola] *sf (Rel)* parable.

parabolico, a, ci, che [para'bɔliko] *ag* parabolic.

parabrezza [para'breddza] *sm inv (Aut)* windscreen.

paracadutare [parakadu'tare] *vt,* **~ rsi** *vr* to parachute.

paracadute [paraka'dute] *sm inv* parachute.

paracadutismo [parakadu'tizmo] *sm* parachuting.

paracadutista, i, e [parakadu'tista] *sm/f* parachutist; *(Mil)* paratrooper.

paracarro [para'karro] *sm* roadside post.

paradigma, i [para'digma] *sm* paradigm.

paradisiaco, a, ci, che [paradi'ziako] *ag* heavenly.

paradiso [para'dizo] *sm (anche fig)* paradise, heaven; **il P~ terrestre** the Garden of Eden, the Earthly Paradise; **~ fiscale** tax haven; **~i artificiali** drug-induced fantasies; **sentirsi in ~** to be in seventh heaven.

paradossale [parados'sale] *ag* paradoxical.

paradosso [para'dɔsso] *sm* paradox.

parafango, ghi [para'fango] *sm* mudguard.

paraffina [paraf'fina] *sf* paraffin, paraffin wax.

parafrasare [parafra'zare] *vt* to paraphrase.

parafrasi [pa'rafrazi] *sf inv* paraphrase.

parafulmine [para'fulmine] *sm* lightning conductor.

paraggi [pa'raddʒi] *smpl:* **nei ~ (di)** in the vicinity (of), in the neighbourhood (of); **in questi ~** in this neighbourhood, somewhere around here.

paragonabile [parago'nabile] *ag:* **~ (a)** comparable (to).

paragonare [parago'nare] **1** *vt:* **~ a, ~ con** to compare to, compare with. **2: ~rsi** *vr:* **~rsi a, ~rsi con** to compare o.s. to, compare o.s. with.

paragone [para'gone] *sm* comparison; **a ~ di** as compared to, in comparison with; **il ~ non regge** the two just can't be compared; **non regge al ~** it doesn't stand *o* bear comparison; **senza ~** incomparable, peerless.

paragrafo [pa'ragrafo] *sm (Gram, fig)* paragraph.

paralisi [pa'ralizi] *sf inv (Med, fig)* paralysis.

paralitico, a, ci, che [para'litiko] *ag, sm/f* paralytic.

paralizzare [paralid'dzare] *vt (Med, fig)* to paralyze.

paralizzato, a [paralid'dzato] *ag* paralyzed.

parallela [paral'lɛla] *sf (Geom)* parallel (line); **~e** *(Sport)* parallel bars.

parallelepipedo [parallele'pipedo] *sm* parallelepiped.

parallelo, a [paral'lɛlo] **1** *ag* parallel. **2** *sm (Geog, fig)* parallel; **fare un ~ tra** to draw a parallel between.

parallelogramma, i [parallelo'gramma] *sm* parallelogram.

paralume [para'lume] *sm* lampshade.

paramenti [para'menti] *smpl (Rel)* vestments.

parametro [pa'rametro] *sm* parameter.

paramilitare [paramili'tare] *ag* paramilitary.

paranco, chi [pa'ranko] *sm* hoist.

paranoia [para'nɔja] *sf* paranoia.

paranoico, a, ci, che [para'nɔiko] *ag, sm/f* paranoid.

paranormale [paranor'male] *ag* paranormal.

paraocchi [para'ɔkki] *smpl (anche fig)* blinkers.

parapetto [para'petto] *sm* parapet.

parapiglia [para'piʎʎa] *sm* uproar, commotion.

parapsicologia [parapsikolɔ'dʒia] *sf* parapsychology.

parare [pa'rare] **1** *vt* **(a)** *(addobbare)* to adorn, deck (out). **(b)** *(schermare: occhi)* to shield. **(c)** *(scansare: colpo: anche fig)* to parry; *(: goal, tiro)* to save. **2** *vi:* **dove vuoi andar a ~?** what are you driving at? **3: ~rsi** *vr (presentarsi)* to appear.

parascolastico, a, ci, che [parasko'lastiko] *ag (attività)* extracurricular.

parasole [para'sole] *sm inv* parasol.

parassita, i [paras'sita] **1** *ag* parasitic. **2** *sm* parasite.

parassitario, a [parassi'tarjo] *ag* parasitic.

parastatale [parasta'tale] *ag* state-controlled.

parata[1] [pa'rata] *sf (Sport)* save.

parata[2] [pa'rata] *sf (Mil)* review, parade.

paratia [para'tia] *sf (Naut)* bulkhead.

parati [pa'rati] *smpl* hangings *pl;* **carta da ~** wallpaper.

paraurti [para'urti] *sm inv (Aut)* bumper.

paravento [para'vento] *sm* folding screen; **fare da ~ a qn** *(fig)* to shield sb.

parcella [par'tʃella] *sf* fee.

parcheggiare [parked'dʒare] *vt* to park.

parcheggio [par'keddʒo] *sm (luogo)* car park; *(singolo posto)* parking space; **'divieto di ~'** 'no parking'.

parchimetro [par'kimetro] *sm* parking meter.

parco[1], **chi** ['parko] *sm* **(a)** *(giardino)* park; **~ giochi** amusement park; **~ nazionale** national park. **(b)** *(insieme di veicoli):* **~ macchine** car fleet; **~ rotabile** *(Ferr)* rolling stock.

parco[2], **a, chi, che** ['parko] *ag:* **~ (in)** *(sobrio)* moderate (in); *(avaro)* sparing (with).

parecchio, a [pa'rekkjo] **1** *ag indef* **(a)** quite a lot of; **c'è ~ vino** there is quite a lot of wine; **c'era ~a gente** there were quite a lot of *o* several people; **ho ~a fame** I am quite hungry; **non lo vedo da ~ tempo** I haven't seen him for ages *o* for a long time; **è ~ tempo che ti aspetto** I have been waiting for you for ages; **~ tempo fa** a long time ago, long ago. **(b):** **~i(e)** several; **~e persone/volte/cose** several *o* a number of people/ times/things; **ho avuto ~i guai** I have had a lot of trouble.

2 *pron indef* quite a lot; **~i(e)** several; **c'è del pane? — ~** is there any bread? — yes, a lot; **quanto tempo hai aspettato? — ~** how long did you wait? — quite a long time *o* quite a while; **ci ho pensato ~** I gave it a lot of thought; **~i dicono...** several people *o* a number of people say...; **eravamo in ~** there were several of us; **~i di noi** several of us.

3 *av* **(a)** *(seguito da ag)* quite; **è ~ intelligente**

he is quite intelligent. (b) *(seguito da vb)* a lot; **mangia** ~ he eats a lot; **è dimagrito** ~ he has lost a lot of weight.

pareggiare [pared'dʒare] **1** *vt (gen)* to make equal; *(terreno)* to level, make level; *(bilancio, conti)* to balance. **2** *vi (Sport: durante la partita)* to equalize; *(: risultato)* to draw.

pareggio [pa'reddʒo] *sm (Econ)* balance; *(Sport)* draw.

parentado [paren'tado] *sm* relatives *pl*, relations *pl*; **alla festa c'era tutto il** ~ the whole family was at the party.

parente [pa'rɛnte] *smf* relative, relation.

parentela [paren'tela] *sf (vincolo di sangue, fig)* relationship; *(insieme dei parenti)* relatives *pl*, relations *pl*.

parentesi [pa'rɛntezi] *sf inv (segno grafico)* bracket, parenthesis; *(digressione)* digression; **tra** ~ in brackets; *(fig)* incidentally; **fare una** ~ *(fig)* to digress; **dopo la** ~ **estiva** *(fig)* after the summer break.

parere[1] [pa'rere] *sm (opinione)* opinion; **a mio** ~ in my opinion.

parere[2] [pa'rere] *vi (aus essere)* (a) *(apparire)* to look, seem, appear; **pare onesto** he looks *o* seems *o* appears honest; **pare impossibile ma è così** it doesn't seem possible and yet it's true; **pare di sì/no** it appears/doesn't appear so; **non mi pare vero!** I can scarcely believe it!; **pare che** it seems that; **a quanto pare se n'è andato** he seems to have left, he has apparently left. (b) *(essere dell'opinione)*: **mi pare che** I think (that), it seems to me (that); **mi pare di sì/no** I think/don't think so; **che te ne pare di quella ragazza?** what do you think of that girl?; **che te ne pare di andare al cinema?** how about going to the cinema?, how do you fancy going to the cinema?; **è ora di andare, non ti pare?** don't you think it's time we left?; **disturbo?** — **ma le pare!** am I disturbing you? — not at all!; **fai come ti pare!** do what *o* as you like!

parete [pa'rete] *sf (muro)* wall; *(di montagna)* face; **fra le** ~**i domestiche** at home, within one's own four walls.

pari[1] ['pari] **1** *ag inv* (a) *(uguale)* equal, (the) same; **essere** ~ **a qn in qc** to be equal to sb in sth; **essere** ~ **di grado** to have the same rank; **essere** ~ **in bellezza/intelligenza** to be equally beautiful/intelligent; **essere intelligente al** ~ **di qn** to be as intelligent as sb; **comportarsi al** ~ **di qn** to behave like sb; **andare di** ~ **passo (con)** to proceed at the same rate (as); **copiato** ~ ~ **dal libro** copied word for word from the book; **ragazza alla** ~ au pair.

(b) *(piano)* level; **una superficie** ~ **a** level *o* an even surface; **saltare qc a piè** ~ *(fig: omettere)* to skip sth.

(c) *(Mat: numero)* even.

(d) *(Sport)*: **la partita è** ~ the match is a draw; **siamo** ~, **vuoi la rivincita?** it's a draw, do you want a decider?; **siamo** ~ *(fig)* we are quits *o* even.

2 *smf* peer, equal.

pari[2] ['pari] *sm inv (Pol Brit)* peer.

paria ['parja] *sm inv (anche fig)* pariah.

parificare [parifi'kare] *vt (scuola)* to recognize officially.

parificato, a [parifi'kato] *ag*: **scuola** ~**a** *officially recognized private school.*

Parigi [pa'ridʒi] *sf* Paris.

parigino, a [pari'dʒino] *ag, sm/f* Parisian.

pariglia [pa'riʎʎa] *sf* (a) *(tiro di cavalli)* pair. (b): **rendere la** ~ *(fig)* to give tit for tat.

parità [pari'ta] *sf* parity, equality; **a** ~ **di condi-**

zioni all things being equal; **trattamento di** ~ equal treatment; **un risultato di** ~ *(Sport)* a draw.

paritetico, a, ci, che [pari'tɛtiko] *ag*: **rapporto** ~ equal relationship; **commissione** ~**a** joint committee.

parlamentare[1] [parlamen'tare] **1** *ag* parliamentary. **2** *sm/f* member of parliament.

parlamentare[2] [parlamen'tare] *vi* to negotiate, parley.

parlamento [parla'mento] *sm* parliament.

parlante [par'lante] *ag (bambola, pappagallo)* talking; **ritratto** ~ *(fig)* lifelike painting.

parlantina [parlan'tina] *sf* talkativeness; **avere una buona** ~ to have the gift of the gab.

parlare [par'lare] **1** *vi* (a) *(facoltà)* to talk; *(modo)* to talk, speak; **il bambino non sa ancora** ~ the baby can't talk yet; **si parlavano a gesti** they were using sign language; **parla piano/più forte** talk *o* speak quietly/louder; **non riusciva a** ~ **per la gioia** he was speechless with joy; **parla bene!** talk properly!; ~ **tra i denti** to mutter; ~ **come un libro stampato** to talk like a book; **ha occhi che parlano** *(fig)* he has expressive eyes.

(b) *(esprimere il proprio pensiero)* to speak; ~ **chiaro** to speak one's mind; ~ **a caso** *o* **a vanvera** to ramble on; ~ **male di qn/qc** to speak ill of sb/sth; **fallo** *o* **lascialo** ~ give him a chance to speak, let him have his say; **con rispetto parlando** with respect; **i dati parlano** *(fig)* the facts speak for themselves.

(c) *(conversare)* to talk; ~ **a/con qn di qc** to talk *o* speak to/with sb about *o* of sth; **non ci parliamo più** we're not on speaking terms; ~ **del più e del meno** to talk of this and that; **è come** ~ **al vento** *o* **a un muro** it's like talking to a brick wall; **senti, ne parliamo a quattrocchi** look, we'll discuss it *o* talk about it in private; **non parliamone più** let's just forget about it; **non ne voglio più sentir** ~ let's hear no more about it; **far** ~ **di sé** to speak o.s. talked about; **parlano di matrimonio** they are talking about getting married, they are discussing marriage; **per ora non se ne parla** there's nothing doing for the moment.

(d) *(Telec)*: **sta parlando al telefono** he's on the phone; **pronto? chi parla?** hello, who's speaking?; **parla Bianchi** Bianchi here *o* speaking; **posso** ~ **con il Sig. Rossi?** can I speak to Mr Rossi?

(e): ~ **di** *(far cenno a)* to mention; *(trattare di: argomento)* to be about, deal with; **ne ho sentito** ~ I have heard it mentioned; **ne parlano tutti i giornali** all the newspapers mention it; **il libro parla del problema della droga** the book deals with the drug problem; **di cosa parla il suo ultimo romanzo?** what is his latest book about?

(f) *(confessare)* to talk; **far** ~ **un prigioniero** to make a prisoner talk.

2 *vt (una lingua)* to speak; **sai** ~ **l'inglese?** can you speak English?; **per me parla arabo** *(fig)* it's all Greek to me.

3 *sm (dialetto)* dialect.

parlata [par'lata] *sf (dialetto)* dialect.

parlato, a [par'lato] *ag* spoken.

parlatore, trice [parla'tore] *sm/f (oratore)* speaker.

parlatorio [parla'tɔrjo] *sm (di carcere etc)* visiting room; *(di collegio)* parlour.

parlottare [parlot'tare] *vi* to mutter.

parlottio [parlot'tio] *sm* muttering.

parmigiano, a [parmi'dʒano] **1** *ag* Parma *attr*, of *(o* from*)* Parma; **alla** ~**a** *(Culin)* with Parmesan cheese. **2** *sm (grana)* Parmesan (cheese).

parodia [paro'dia] *sf* parody.

parola [pa'rɔla] *sf* (a) *(facoltà)* speech; **ha perso il bene della parola** he's lost the power of speech; **a quel cane manca solo la ~** that dog is almost human; **avere la ~ facile** to have the gift of the gab.

(b) *(vocabolo)* word; **rimanere senza ~e** to be speechless; **rivolgere la ~ a qn** to speak to sb; **mi hai tolto la ~ di bocca** you have taken the words right out of my mouth; **mettere una buona ~ per qn** to put in a good word for sb; **non è detta l'ultima ~** that's not the end of the matter; **non farne ~ a nessuno!** don't breathe a word to anyone!; **è una ~!** it's easier said than done!; **non ho ~e per ringraziarti** I don't know how to thank you; **passare dalle ~e ai fatti** to get down to business; **~ d'ordine** *(Mil)* password; **~e incrociate** crossword (puzzle) *sg*.

(c): **~e** *(di canzone)* words, lyrics.

(d) *(promessa)* word; **dare la propria ~ a qn** to give sb one's word; **mantenere la ~** to keep one's word; **è una persona di ~** he is a man of his word; **rimangiarsi la ~** to go back on one's word; **~ d'onore** word of honour.

(e) *(in dibattiti)*: **diritto di ~** the right to speak; **chiedere la ~** to ask permission to speak; **prendere la ~** to take the floor; **dare la ~ a qn** to call on sb to speak.

parolaccia, ce [paro'lattʃa] *sf* bad word, swearword.

parolaio, a [paro'lajo] *sm/f (peg)* windbag.

paroliere [paro'ljɛre] *sm* lyricist.

parolina [paro'lina] *sf*: **dire una ~ a qn** *(di rimprovero)* to have a few words with sb; *(d'amore)* to whisper sweet nothings to sb.

parossismo [paros'sizmo] *sm (Med)* paroxysm; *(fig: di amore, odio)* height; **amare/odiare fino al ~** to be beside o.s. with love/hate.

parquet [par'kɛ] *sm* parquet (flooring).

parricida, i, e [parri'tʃida] *sm/f* parricide.

parricidio [parri'tʃidjo] *sm* parricide.

parrocchia [par'rɔkkja] *sf (suddivisione)* parish; *(chiesa)* parish church.

parrocchiale [parrok'kjale] *ag* parish *attr*.

parrocchiano, a [parrok'kjano] *sm/f* parishioner.

parroco, ci ['parroko] *sm* parish priest.

parrucca, che [par'rukka] *sf* wig.

parrucchiera [parruk'kjɛra] *sf* hairdresser.

parrucchiere [parruk'kjɛre] *sm (per uomo)* barber; *(per signora)* hairdresser.

parsimonia [parsi'mɔnja] *sf* parsimony, frugality, thrift.

parsimonioso, a [parsimo'njoso] *ag* frugal, thrifty.

parso, a ['parso] *pp di* **parere**.

partaccia, ce [par'tattʃa] *sf*: **fare una ~ a qn** to give sb a telling-off.

parte ['parte] *sf* (a) *(gen)* part; *(porzione)* share; **~ del libro non mi è piaciuta** I didn't like some *o* part of the book; **una ~ di noi** some of us; **gran *o* la maggior ~ degli spettatori** most of the audience; **in ~** in part, partly; **fare le ~i di qc** to divide sth up; **fare la ~ del leone** to take the lion's share.

(b) *(partecipazione)*: **fare ~ di qc** to belong to sth; **prendere ~ a qc** *(dibattito, conversazione)* to take part in, participate in; *(lutto)* to share in; **mettere qn a ~ di qc** to inform sb of sth, tell sb about sth.

(c) *(lato: anche fig)* side; *(direzione)* direction; **la ~ destra del corpo** the right-hand side of the body; **da ~ di madre** on his *(o her etc)* mother's side; **dall'altra ~ della strada** on the other side of the road; **veniva dall'altra ~** he was coming

from the opposite direction; **essere dalla ~ della ragione** to be in the right; **non sapeva da che ~ voltarsi** *(fig)* he didn't know which way to turn; **stare dalla ~ di qn** to be on sb's side; **prendere le ~i di qn** to take sb's side; **mettere/prendere da ~** to put/take aside.

(d) *(luogo, regione)*: **da qualche ~** somewhere; **da ogni ~** everywhere; **da nessuna ~** nowhere; **dalle mie ~i** where I come from; **abita dalle mie ~i** he lives in the same area as I do; **dalle ~i di Glasgow Street** in the vicinity of Glasgow Street.

(e) *(fazione, partito)* group, faction; *(Dir)* party; **uomo di ~** partisan; **da partigiano; da nessuna ~** to associate in an action with the public prosecutor against sb; **le ~i in causa** the parties concerned.

(f) *(Teatro)* part, role; **avere una ~ secondaria** to have a minor role; **fare la ~ dello stupido/della vittima** *(fig)* to act the fool/the martyr.

(g) *(fraseologia)*: **a ~** *(ag)* separate; *(av)* separately; **fatto a ~** done separately; **scherzi a ~** joking aside; **a ~ ciò** apart from that; **d'altra ~** on the other hand; **da ~ di** *(per conto di)* on behalf of; **da un anno a questa ~** for about a year now.

partecipante [partetʃi'pante] **1** *ag*: **~ a** taking part in, participating in. **2** *sm/f*: **~** (a) *(a riunione, dibattito)* participant (in); *(a gara sportiva)* competitor (in); *(a concorso)* entrant (to); **i ~i alla cerimonia** those taking part in the ceremony.

partecipare [partetʃi'pare] **1** *vi*: **~ a** to take part in, participate in; *(utili etc)* to share in; *(spese etc)* to contribute to; *(dolore, successo di qn)* to share (in). **2** *vt*: **~ le nozze (a)** to announce one's wedding (to).

partecipazione [partetʃipat'tsjone] *sf* (a): **~** (a) *(dibattito, cerimonia)* participation (in); *(spettacolo)* appearance (in); *(complotto)* involvement (in); **~ a banda armata** *(Dir)* belonging to an armed gang; **~i di nozze** *wedding announcement card.* (b) *(Econ)*: **~ agli utili** profit-sharing.

partecipe [par'tetʃipe] *ag* participating; **essere ~ della gioia/del dolore di qn** to share in sb's joy/sorrow.

parteggiare [parted'dʒare] *vi*: **~ per** to side with.

partenza [par'tentsa] *sf* (a) *(gen)* departure; **dopo la mia ~ si deciderà** things will be decided after I leave *o* after my departure; **essere in ~** *(treno, aereo, nave)* to be about to leave; **prenderò il primo treno in ~ per Milano** I'll catch the first train for Milan; **'il treno per Roma è in ~ dal binario 15'** 'the Rome train is leaving from platform 15'; **passeggeri in ~ per** passengers travelling to; **siamo tornati al punto di ~** *(fig)* we are back where we started. (b) *(Sport)* start; **segnale di ~** start, starting signal; **linea di ~** start, starting line; **falsa ~** *(anche fig)* false start; **tutti sulla linea di ~!** take your places please!

particella [parti'tʃella] *sf (Gram, Fis)* particle.

participio [parti'tʃipjo] *sm (Gram)* participle.

particolare [partiko'lare] **1** *ag* (a) *(specifico)* particular; *(caratteristico)* distinctive; **in questo caso ~** in this particular case, in this specific instance; **ha un sapore ~** it has a distinctive flavour; **in ~** in particular, particularly. (b) *(strano)* peculiar, odd. (c) *(insolito)* unusual; **l'ho fatto con cura ~** I took particular care over it; **amicizie ~i** homosexual relationships. (d) *(privato: udienza, ragioni)* private. **2** *sm* detail; **raccontare un fatto in tutti i ~i** to give all the details *o* particulars of an occurrence; **entrare nei ~i** to go into details.

particolareggiato [partikolared'dʒato] *ag* (extremely) detailed.

particolarità [partikolari'ta] *sf inv* (a) *(carattere eccezionale)* peculiarity; **data la ~ del caso** given the peculiarity of the case. (b) *(dettaglio)* detail, particularity. (c) *(caratteristica specifica)* distinctive feature.

partigiano, a [parti'dʒano] **1** *ag* partisan. **2** *sm (fautore)* supporter; *(Mil)* partisan.

partire [par'tire] *vi (aus* essere*)* (a) *(gen)* to go; *(lasciare un luogo)* to leave; *(mettersi in cammino)* to set off, set out; *(allontanarsi)* to go away, go off; **~ da/per** to leave from/for; **~ in treno/in macchina** to go by train/car; **~ come una freccia** to be off like a shot; **non dargli troppo da bere perché lui parte subito** *(fam)* don't give him too much to drink because it goes straight to his head.

　(b) *(cominciare: Sport, fig)*: **~ (da)** to start (from); **la corsa parte dal nord della città** the race starts *o* leaves from the north of the town; **la loro è una storia partita male** theirs is a story which began badly.

　(c) *(motore)* to start; *(aereo)* to take off; *(treno)* to leave; **il volo parte da Linate** the flight leaves from Linate; **~ in quarta** to drive off at top speed; *(fig)* to be very enthusiastic; **far ~ la macchina** to start (up) the car.

　(d) *(colpo di arma da fuoco)* to go off; *(tappo)* to pop out, shoot out.

　(e): **a ~ da** from; **a ~ da oggi** from today onwards; **a ~ da ora** from now on; **la seconda a ~ da destra** the second from the right; **a ~ da 5000 lire** from 5000 lire.

partita [par'tita] *sf* (a) *(Comm)* lot, consignment. (b) *(Contabilità)* entry, item; **~ IVA** VAT registration number; **~ semplice/doppia** single-/double-entry bookkeeping. (c) *(Carte)* game; *(Sport)* match, game; **~ amichevole** friendly (match); **facciamo una ~ a tennis** let's have a game of tennis; **dare ~ vinta** to admit defeat. (d) *(escursione)*: **~ di caccia** hunting party.

partitura [parti'tura] *sf* score.

partner ['paːtnə] *sm/f inv* partner.

parto ['parto] *sm (Med)* labour; **durante il ~** during labour; **i dolori del ~** labour pains; **sala ~** labour room; **~ prematuro** premature birth *o* delivery; **al momento del ~ il bambino stava bene** at birth the child was in good health; **morire di ~** to die in childbirth.

partoriente [parto'rjɛnte] *sf* woman in labour.

partorire [parto'rire] *vt* to give birth to; *(fig: invenzione)* to produce.

part time ['paːt 'taim] *av, ag inv* part-time.

party ['paːti] *sm inv* party.

parure [pa'ryr] *sf inv (di biancheria)* set of underwear; *(di gioielli)* (set of) jewellery.

parvenza [par'vɛntsa] *sf* semblance.

parziale [par'tsjale] *ag (limitato)* partial; *(non obiettivo)* biased, partial.

parzialità [partsjali'ta] *sf* (a): **~ (a favore di qn)** partiality (for sb), bias (towards sb); **~ (contro qn)** bias (against sb). (b) *(azione)* unfair action.

pascere ['paʃʃere] **1** *vi* to graze. **2** *vt (brucare)* to graze on; **~ le mucche** to lead the cows to pasture. **3**: **~rsi** *vr*: **~rsi di** *(erba, illusioni)* to feed on.

pascià [paʃ'ʃa] *sm* pasha; **fare il ~, stare come un ~** *(fig)* to live like a lord.

pasciuto, a [paʃ'ʃuto] **1** *pp di* pascere. **2** *ag*: **ben ~** plump.

pascolare [pasko'lare] *vt, vi* to graze.

pascolo ['paskolo] *sm (luogo)* pasture; **diritto di ~** grazing rights.

Pasqua ['paskwa] *sf* Easter; **la domenica di ~** Easter Sunday; **essere contento come una ~** to be as happy as a sandboy.

pasquale [pas'kwale] *ag* Easter *attr*.

pasquetta [pas'kwetta] *sf* Easter Monday.

passabile [pas'sabile] *ag* fairly good, passable.

passaggio [pas'saddʒo] **1** *sm* (a) *(atto del passare)* passing, passage; **aspettare il ~ dell'autobus** to wait for the bus to go by; **l'autobus fa 4 ~i al giorno** the bus goes by 4 times a day; **guardare il ~ degli uccelli** to watch the birds fly past; **sono qui solo di ~** I'm just passing through.

　(b) *(trasferimento: di poteri, diritti, calciatore)* transfer; **il ~ dall'infanzia all'adolescenza** the transition from childhood to adolescence; **il ~ dal giorno alla notte** the change from day to night.

　(c) *(luogo)* passage; *(cammino)* way, passage; *(itinerario)* route; **impedire il ~ a qn** to block *o* stand in sb's way.

　(d) *(traffico)*: **c'è molto ~** there's a lot of traffic; **luogo di ~** thoroughfare.

　(e) *(Naut)* passage; *(Aut)* lift; **prenotarsi un ~ per Napoli** to book one's passage to Naples; **dare un ~ a qn** to give sb a lift.

　(f) *(brano)* passage.

　(g) *(Calcio)* pass.

　2: **~ a livello** level crossing; **~ sotterraneo** subway, underpass; **~ pedonale** pedestrian crossing.

passamaneria [passamane'ria] *sf* braid, trimming.

passamano [passa'mano] *sm* braid.

passamontagna [passamon'taɲɲa] *sm inv* balaclava.

passante [pas'sante] **1** *sm/f* passer-by. **2** *sm (di cintura)* loop.

passaporto [passa'pɔrto] *sm* passport.

passare [pas'sare] **1** *vi (aus* essere*)* (a) *(persona, macchina, treno)* to go by, pass (by); **l'autobus passa davanti a casa nostra** the bus goes past our house; **siamo passati davanti a casa tua** we went past your house, we walked (*o* drove) past your house; **~ dall'altra parte della strada** to cross (over) to the other side of the street.

　(b) *(fare una breve sosta)* to call in; *(: presso amico)* to call in, drop in; **~ a casa di qn *o* da qn** to drop in on sb; **~ a trovare/salutare qn** to drop by to see/say 'hello' to sb; **~ a prendere qc/qn** to come by and pick sth/sb up; **~ in banca/ufficio** to call in at the bank/office.

　(c) *(filtrare attraverso: aria, sole, luce)* to pass, get through; *(: acqua)* to seep through.

　(d) *(trasferirsi)*: **~ da ... a** to pass from ... to; **~ di mano in mano** to be passed *o* handed round; **~ da un argomento ad un altro** to go from one subject to another; **~ ad altro** to change the subject; *(in una riunione)* to discuss the next item; **passiamo ad altro!** let's go on!; **~ al nemico** to go over to the enemy; **~ alla storia** to pass into history; *(fig)* to become a legend; **~ a miglior vita** *(euf)* to pass away.

　(e) *(tempo)* to pass, go by; **col ~ degli anni** *(riferito al presente)* as time goes by; *(riferito al* *passato)* as time passed *o* went by; **30 anni e passa** well over 30 years ago.

(f) *(allontanarsi: temporale, dolore, voglia etc)* to pass, go away; **il peggio è passato** the worst is over; **far ~ a qn la voglia di qc/di fare qc** to stifle sb's desire for sth/to do sth; **gli passerà!** he'll get over it!

(g) *(essere accettato: proposta di legge, candidato)* to pass; **~ di grado** to be promoted.

(h) *(Culin):* **~ di cottura** to be overdone.

(i) *(Carte)* to pass.

(j) *(esistere):* **ci passa una bella differenza tra i 2 quadri** there's a big difference between the 2 pictures.

(k): **~ per uno stupido/un genio** to be taken for a fool/a genius; **~ per buono** to be taken as valid, be accepted; **~ inosservato** to go unnoticed; **farsi ~ per** to pass o.s. off as, pretend to be.

(l): cosa ti passa per la testa? *(a che pensi?)* what is going through your mind?; **(come puoi pensarlo?)** what are you thinking of!; **per dove si passa per arrivare in centro?** which way do I *(o* we) go to get into town?; **far ~ qn per** *o* **da** to let sb in *(o* out) by; **~ sotto/sopra/attraverso** to pass below/above/through; **far ~ avanti qn** to let sb get past *o* by; **non dobbiamo farci ~ avanti dagli altri** we mustn't be overtaken by the others; **questa volta non ci passa sopra** I'm not prepared to overlook it this time.

2 *vt* **(a)** *(attraversare)* to cross.

(b) *(esame)* to pass; *(dogana)* to go through, clear; *(visita medica)* to have.

(c) *(trafiggere):* **~ qn/qc da parte a parte** to pass right through sb/sth.

(d) *(trascorrere)* to spend, pass; **~ le vacanze in montagna** to spend one's holidays in the mountains; **non passerà la notte** he *(o* she) won't survive the night; **non passa giorno che lui non ne combini una delle sue** hardly a day goes by without him getting up to something.

(e) *(andare oltre ai limiti)* to exceed; **ha passato la quarantina** he *(o* she) is over 40; **c'erano 100 persone e passa** there were well over a 100 people.

(f) *(dare: oggetto)* to pass, give, hand; *(Calcio: pallone)* to pass; **i miei genitori mi passano 100.000 lire al mese** my parents give me 100,000 lire a month; **mi passi Maria?** *(al telefono)* could you put Maria on?; **le passo il signor Rossi** here's Mr Rossi.

(g) *(brodo, verdura etc)* to strain.

(h): **~ lo straccio per terra** to give the floor a wipe; **~ l'aspirapolvere** to hoover; **~ una mano di vernice su qc** to give sth a coat of paint.

(i) *(fraseologia):* **passarsela bene/male** to get on well/badly; *(economicamente)* to manage well/badly; **come te la passi?** how are you getting on?; **passarla liscia** *(fam)* to get away with it; **ne ha passate tante** he's been through a lot, he's had some difficult times.

passata [pas'sata] *sf* **(a)** *(occhiata)* glance, look; **dare una ~ al giornale** to skim through *o* have a glance at the paper. **(b): dare una ~ a qc** *(con lo straccio)* to dust sth quickly; *(con lo straccio bagnato)* to give sth a wipe; *(con il ferro da stiro)* to give sth a quick iron.

passatempo [passa'tempo] *sm* pastime, hobby; **per ~** as a hobby.

passato, a [pas'sato] **1** *ag* **(a)** *(scorso)* last; **l'anno ~** last year; **nel corso degli anni ~i** over the past years. **(b)** *(finito: gloria, generazioni)* past; *(usanze)* out of date; **~ di moda** out of fashion; **sono**

cose ormai **~e** that's all over now; **nei tempi ~i** in the past; **è acqua ~a** *(fig)* it's over and done with. **(c)** *(superato):* **sono le 8 ~e** it's past *o* after 8 o'clock; **ha 40 anni ~i** he's over 40. **2** *sm* **(a)** past; **ha un ~ di droga e furti** he has a history of drugs and theft. **(b)** *(Gram)* past (tense); **~ prossimo** present perfect; **~ remoto** past historic. **(c)** *(Culin):* **~ di verdura** vegetable purée.

passatoia [passa'toja] *sf (di scale)* stair carpet; *(di corridoio)* hall carpet.

passatutto [passa'tutto] *sm inv*, **passaverdura** [passaver'dura] *sm inv* vegetable mill.

passeggero, a [passed'dʒero] **1** *ag (malessere, nuvola, temporale)* passing; *(bellezza, benessere)* transient. **2** *sm/f* passenger; **~ in arrivo/in partenza/in transito** arriving/departing/transit passenger.

passeggiare [passed'dʒare] *vi* to stroll, walk; **passeggiava nervosamente nel corridoio** he was pacing nervously up and down the corridor.

passeggiata [passed'dʒata] *sf* **(a)** *(a piedi)* walk; *(in macchina)* drive; **fare una ~** to go for a walk *(o* drive). **(b)** *(luogo):* **~ a mare** promenade.

passeggiatrice [passeddʒa'tritʃe] *sf (euf)* streetwalker.

passeggino [passed'dʒino] *sm* pushchair.

passeggio [pas'seddʒo] *sm* walk, stroll; **andare a ~** to go for a walk *o* a stroll; **guardare il ~** to watch people out for a stroll.

passe-partout ['pas par'tu] *sm inv* **(a)** *(chiave)* skeleton key, master key. **(b)** *(per cornici)* passepartout.

passera ['passera] *sf (uccello)* hedge sparrow.

passerella [passe'rella] *sf (gen)* footbridge; *(di nave)* gangway; *(pedana)* catwalk.

passero ['passero] *sm* sparrow.

passibile [pas'sibile] *ag:* **~ di** liable to; **~ di aumento** liable to go up *o* increase.

passino [pas'sino] *sm* sieve, strainer.

passionale [passjo'nale] *ag (temperamento)* passionate; **delitto ~** crime of passion.

passione [pas'sjone] *sf* passion; **aver la ~ di** *o* **per** to have a passion for.

passivante [passi'vante] *ag (Gram):* **il si ~** the passive 'si' .

passività [passivi'ta] *sf* **(a)** *(qualità)* passivity, passiveness. **(b)** *(Comm)* liability.

passivo, a [pas'sivo] **1** *ag* passive. **2** *sm* **(a)** *(Gram)* passive. **(b)** *(Econ)* debit; *(: complesso dei debiti)* liabilities *pl*.

passo¹ ['passo] *sm* **(a)** *(gen)* step; *(rumore)* footstep; *(orma)* footprint; **a due ~i da qui** a stone's throw from here; **~ ~** step by step; **seguire qn ~** to follow close on sb's heels; **fare i primi ~i** *(anche fig)* to take one's first steps; **fare due *o* quattro ~i** to go for a short walk; **fare un ~ avanti/indietro** *(fig)* to take a step forward/back; **ha fatto ~i da gigante in spagnolo** *(fig)* his Spanish has improved by leaps and bounds; **fare il gran ~** *(fig)* to take the plunge; **fare un ~ falso** *(fig)* to make the wrong move; **fare i ~i necessari** *(fig)* to take the necessary steps; **fare il ~ più lungo della gamba** *(fig)* to bite off more than one can chew; **tornare sui propri ~i** to retrace one's steps; **non ho intenzione di tornare sui miei ~i** I have no intention of starting all over again.

(b) *(andatura)* pace; *(: Mil, danza)* step; **fare il ~ dell'oca** to goose-step; **allungare il ~** to quicken one's pace; **di buon ~** at a good *o* brisk pace; **marciare al ~** to march; **mettere il cavallo al ~** to walk one's horse; **'a ~ d'uomo'** *(Aut)* 'dead slow'; **le macchine andavano a ~ d'uomo** the cars were crawling along; **andare al ~ coi tempi**

to keep up with the times; **di questo** ~ *(fig)* at this rate. **(c)** *(brano)* passage. **(d)** *(Cine)* gauge.

passo[2] ['passo] *sm* **(a)** *(passaggio)*: **cedere il** ~ **a qn** to give way to sb; **sbarrare il** ~ **a qn** to bar sb's way; '~ **carrabile**', '~ **carraio**' 'keep clear'; **uccelli di** ~ birds of passage, migratory birds. **(b)** *(valico)* pass.

pasta ['pasta] *sf* **(a)** *(Culin: impasto: per pane)* dough; *(: per crostate)* pastry; *(pastasciutta)* pasta; *(dolcino)* cake, pastry; **lavorare la** ~ to knead the dough; **spianare la** ~ to roll pastry; **hai le mani di** ~ **frolla!** what a butterfingers you are!; ~ **fatta in casa** home-made pasta; ~ **frolla** short crust pastry; ~ **sfoglia** puff pastry. **(b)** *(sostanza pastosa)* paste; ~ **di acciughe** anchovy paste; ~ **di mandorle** almond paste; ~ **dentifricia** toothpaste. **(c)** *(fig: indole)* nature; **siamo tutti della stessa** ~ we are all cast in the same mould.

pastasciutta [pastaʃ'ʃutta] *sf* pasta.

pasteggiare [pasted'dʒare] *vi*: ~ **a vino/champagne** to have wine/champagne with one's meal.

pastella [pas'tɛlla] *sf* batter.

pastello [pas'tɛllo] *ag inv*, *sm* pastel *(attr)*.

pastetta [pas'tetta] *sf (Culin)* = **pastella**.

pasticca, che [pas'tikka] *sf* = **pastiglia**.

pasticceria [pastittʃe'ria] *sf* **(a)** *(pasticcini)* pastries *pl*, cakes *pl*. **(b)** *(negozio)* cake shop. **(c)** *(arte)* confectionery.

pasticciare [pastit'tʃare] **1** *vt* to mess up, make a mess of. **2** *vi* to make a mess.

pasticciere, a [pastit'tʃere] *sm/f* pastry cook, confectioner.

pasticcino [pastit'tʃino] *sm* petit four.

pasticcio [pas'tittʃo] *sm* **(a)** *(Culin)* pie. **(b)** *(lavoro disordinato, imbroglio)* mess; **cacciarsi nei** ~**i** to get into trouble.

pasticcione, a [pastit'tʃone] **1** *ag* bungling, clumsy. **2** *sm/f* bungler, clumsy idiot.

pastificio [pasti'fitʃo] *sm* pasta factory.

pastiglia [pas'tiʎʎa] *sf (Med)* pastille, lozenge; ~**e per la gola** throat lozenges *o* pastilles; ~**e per la tosse** cough drops *o* pastilles.

pastina [pas'tina] *sf* small pasta shapes used in soup.

pastinaca, che [pasti'naka] *sf* parsnip.

pasto ['pasto] *sm* meal; **saltare i** ~**i** to skip meals; **da prendersi prima dei** ~**i** to be taken before meals; **non mangiare fuori** ~ *o* **fuori dei** ~**i** don't eat between meals; **vino da** ~ table wine; **la notizia fu data in** ~ **al pubblico** *(fig)* the news was made common knowledge; **lo diedero in** ~ **ai leoni** *(anche fig)* he was thrown to the lions.

pastone [pas'tone] *sm (per polli, maiali)* mash; *(peg: cibo)* overcooked stodge.

pastorale [pasto'rale] **1** *ag (gen)* pastoral. **2** *sf* **(a)** *(Rel: lettera del vescovo)* pastoral (letter). **(b)** *(Mus)* pastoral(e). **3** *sm (Rel: bastone)* crook, crosier.

pastore [pas'tore] **1** *sm (anche Rel)* shepherd; *(sacerdote)* minister, pastor; **cane** *m* **da** ~ sheepdog. **2:** ~ **scoʒzese** collie; ~ **tedesco** Alsatian.

pastorizia [pasto'rittsja] *sf* sheep-rearing, sheep farming.

pastorizzare [pastorid'dzare] *vt* to pasteurize; **latte pastorizzato** pasteurized milk.

pastoso, a [pas'toso] *ag* **(a)** *(miscuglio)* doughy. **(b)** *(colore, voce)* mellow, soft; *(vino)* mellow.

pastrano [pas'trano] *sm* greatcoat.

patacca, che [pa'takka] *sf* **(a)** *(distintivo)* medal, decoration. **(b)** *(fig: macchia)* grease spot, grease mark.

patata [pa'tata] *sf* potato; *(fig peg: persona)* stupid

oaf; ~ **dolce** sweet potato, yam; **che spirito di** ~! some joke that! *(iro)*.

patatina [pata'tina] *sf*: ~**e fritte** chips, French fries *(Am)*; *(confezionate)* crisps.

patatrac [pata'trak] *sm inv (fig: disastro)* disaster; *(: dissesto economico)* crash.

pâté [pa'te] *sm inv* pâté; ~ **di fegato d'oca** pâté de foie gras.

patella [pa'tɛlla] *sf (Zool)* limpet.

patema, i [pa'tɛma] *sm*: ~ **(d'animo)** anxiety; **è inutile farsi tanti** ~**i (d'animo)** there's no point in getting so upset.

patentato, a [paten'tato] *ag* **(a)** *(munito di patente)* licensed, certified. **(b)** *(fig scherz: qualificato)* utter, thorough; **un cretino** ~ an utter fool; **un ladro** ~ an out and out thief.

patente [pa'tɛnte] *sf* licence, permit; ~ **(di guida)** driving licence.

patentino [paten'tino] *sm* temporary licence.

paternale [pater'nale] *sf* rebuke, reprimand; **fare una** ~ **a qn** to rebuke *o* reprimand sb.

paternalistico, a, ci, che [paterna'listiko] *ag* paternalistic.

paternità [paterni'ta] *sf* fatherhood, paternity.

paterno, a [pa'tɛrno] *ag* paternal; *(benevolo)* fatherly; **lasciare la casa** ~**a** to leave one's father's house.

patetico, a, ci, che [pa'tɛtiko] **1** *ag (gen, Anat, peg)* pathetic. **2** *sm* sentimentalism; **cadere nel** ~ to become (over)sentimental.

pathos ['patos] *sm* pathos.

patibolo [pa'tibolo] *sm* scaffold, gallows *pl*; **pare che vada al** ~! *(fig)* you'd think his hour had come!

patimento [pati'mento] *sm* suffering.

patina ['patina] *sf (gen)* patina; *(su medaglie)* coat; *(sulla lingua)* fur, coating.

patio ['patjo] *sm inv* patio.

patire [pa'tire] **1** *vt (ingiurie, offese)* to suffer; *(fame, sete)* to suffer (from); *(ingiustizie)* to endure. **2** *vi*: ~ **(di)** to suffer (from); ~ **di cuore** to have a weak heart; **la carne patisce al caldo** meat goes bad in the heat; **ha finito di** ~ his sufferings are over.

patito, a [pa'tito] **1** *ag (sofferente)* run-down; *(: volto)* wan. **2** *sm/f*: **essere un(a)** ~**(a) di** *(musica, sport etc)* to be a fan *o* lover of; **è un** ~ **di Mozart** he is very keen on Mozart.

patologia [patolo'dʒia] *sf (Med)* pathology.

patologico, a, ci, che [pato'lɔdʒiko] *ag (Med, fig)* pathological.

patologo, a, gi, ghe [pa'tɔlogo] *sm/f (Med)* pathologist.

patria ['patrja] *sf (paese)* homeland, fatherland; *(fig: città o luogo natale)* birthplace; **Vienna, la** ~ **del walzer** Vienna, the home of the waltz; **tornare in** ~ to return to one's own country; **amor di** ~ patriotism.

patriarca, chi [patri'arka] *sm* patriarch.

patriarcale [patriar'kale] *ag* patriarchal.

patrigno [pa'triɲɲo] *sm* stepfather.

patrimoniale [patrimo'njale] *ag* patrimonial; **rendita** ~ income from property.

patrimonio [patri'mɔnjo] *sm* **(a)** estate, property; ~ **pubblico** public property; **mi è costato un** ~ *(fig)* it cost me a fortune, I paid a fortune for it. **(b)** *(fig)*: ~ **ereditario** hereditary characteristics *pl*; ~ **spirituale/culturale** spiritual/cultural heritage.

patrio, a, ii, ie ['patrjo] *ag* **(a)** *(di patria)* native, of one's country; **amor** ~ love of one's country. **(b)** *(Dir)*: ~**a potestà** parental authority.

patriota, i, e [patri'ɔta] *sm/f* patriot.

patriottico, a, ci, che [patri'ɔttiko] *ag* patriotic.
patriottismo [patriot'tizmo] *sm* patriotism.
patrocinare [patrotʃi'nare] *vt (Dir)* to defend; *(fig: candidatura)* to support.
patrocinio [patro'tʃinjo] *sm* patronage.
patronato [patro'nato] *sm* **(a)** *(patrocinio)* patronage. **(b)** *(istituzione benefica)* charitable institution; ~ **scolastico** charitable foundation for schools.
patrona [pa'trɔna] *sf (Rel)* patron saint.
patronessa [patro'nessa] *sf* patroness.
patrono [pa'trɔno] *sm* **(a)** *(benefattore)* patron. **(b)** *(Rel)* patron saint.
patta[1] ['patta] *sf (di tasca)* flap; *(dei pantaloni)* fly.
patta[2] ['patta] *sf (pareggio)* draw, tie; **essere pari e** ~ *(fig)* to be even *o* all square.
patteggiare [patted'dʒare] **1** *vt (negoziare: resa, tregua)* to negotiate. **2** *vi:* ~ **con qn** *(scendere a patti)* to negotiate with sb; *(scendere a compromessi)* to come to a compromise with sb.
pattinaggio [patti'naddʒo] *sm* skating; **fare del** ~ to go skating; ~ **artistico** figure skating; ~ **a rotelle** roller skating; ~ **sul ghiaccio** ice skating.
pattinare [patti'nare] *vi* **(a)** *(Sport)* to skate; ~ **sul ghiaccio/a rotelle** to ice-/roller-skate. **(b)** *(Aut: scivolare)* to skid.
pattinatore, trice [pattina'tore] *sm/f* skater.
pattino ['pattino] *sm* **(a)** *(Sport)* skate; ~**i** *(da ghiaccio)* (ice) skates; ~**i a rotelle** roller skates. **(b)** *(Tecn)* sliding block; *(Aer)* skid; *(di slitta)* runner.
patto ['patto] *sm* **(a)** *(accordo)* pact, agreement; **fare un** ~ to make a pact *o* an agreement; ~ **di non aggressione** non-aggression pact. **(b)** *(condizione)* condition; **a nessun** ~ under no circumstances; **venire** *o* **scendere a** ~**i (con)** to come to terms (with); **a** ~ **che** on condition that.
pattuglia [pat'tuʎʎa] *sf* patrol; **essere di** ~ to be on patrol.
pattugliare [pattuʎ'ʎare] *vt* to patrol.
pattuire [pattu'ire] *vt* to reach an agreement on.
pattume [pat'tume] *sm* rubbish, garbage.
pattumiera [pattu'mjɛra] *sf* (dust)bin.
paura [pa'ura] *sf* fear; **avere** ~ **di qc/qn** to be afraid *o* frightened of sth/sb; **fare** *o* **mettere** ~ **a qn** to frighten sb; **era morto di** ~ he was scared to death *o* frightened out of his wits; **ho** ~ **di sì/no** I am afraid so/not; **ha** ~ **di ingrassare** she's afraid of *o* worried about putting on weight; **ho** ~ **che non venga** *o* **che non verrà** I am afraid he won't come; **non aver** ~, **tutto si risolverà** don't worry, everything will work out in the end; **niente** ~, **ci penso io** don't worry, I'll see to it; **parlava piano per** ~ **di svegliarlo** he spoke quietly so as not to wake him; **è magro da far** ~ he is frightfully *o* terribly thin; **ha una faccia da far** ~ he looks terrible; **piove da far** ~ it's bucketing down.
pauroso, a [pau'roso] *ag* **(a)** *(che incute paura)* frightening; *(fig: straordinario)* awful, dreadful, frightful. **(b)** *(timoroso)* timid, fearful.
pausa ['pauza] *sf (sosta)* break; *(nel parlare, Mus)* pause; **fare una** ~ **di 10 minuti** to have a 10-minute break; **fece una** ~ **poi riprese a parlare** he paused then began speaking again.
pavese[1] [pa'vese] *sm (bandiere)* bunting.
pavese[2] [pa'vese] *ag* of *(o* from) Pavia.
pavido, a ['pavido] *ag (poet)* fearful.
pavimentare [pavimen'tare] *vt (stanza)* to floor; *(strada)* to pave.
pavimentazione [pavimentat'tsjone] *sf (vedi vb)* flooring; paving.
pavimento [pavi'mento] *sm* floor.
pavone [pa'vone] *sm* peacock.

pavoneggiarsi [pavoned'dʒarsi] *vr* to strut about, show off.
pazientare [pattsjen'tare] *vi* to be patient.
paziente [pat'tsjɛnte] **1** *ag* patient. **2** *sm/f (Med)* patient.
pazienza [pat'tsjɛntsa] *sf* patience; **aver** ~ to be patient; **perdere la** ~ to lose (one's) patience; ~! never mind!; **santa** ~! (God) give me patience!
pazzamente [pattsa'mente] *av* madly; **essere** ~ **innamorato** to be madly in love.
pazzerellone, a [pattserel'lone] *sm/f* madcap.
pazzesco, a, schi, sche [pat'tsesko] *ag (assurdo: persona, comportamento)* crazy, daft; *(incredibile: scena)* incredible; **ad una velocità** ~**a** at breakneck speed; **ha una cultura** ~**a** he's incredibly knowledgeable; ~! incredible!
pazzia [pat'tsia] *sf (Med, fig)* madness, lunacy; **dar segni di** ~ to show signs of madness; **mi sento in vena di far** ~**e** I feel like doing something crazy; **è stata una** ~! it was sheer madness!
pazzo, a ['pattso] **1** *ag (persona, idea etc)* mad, crazy, insane; **essere** ~ **da legare** to be raving mad *o* a raving lunatic; **essere** ~ **di gioia/dolore** to be beside o.s. with joy/grief; **essere** ~ **di gelosia** to be insanely jealous; **essere innamorato** ~ to be madly in love; **è** ~ **di lei** he's crazy about her; **va** ~ **per il cioccolato** he adores chocolate; **prova un gusto** ~ **a prendere in giro la gente** he thoroughly enjoys taking people for a ride; **andava a** ~**a velocità** he was going at breakneck speed. **2** *sm/f* lunatic, madman/ woman; **urlava come un** ~ he was shouting his head off, he was shouting like a lunatic.
pazzoide [pat'tsɔide] **1** *ag* crazy. **2** *sm/f* madcap, nutcase *(fam)*.
P.C.I. *abbr di Partito Comunista Italiano.*
pecca, che ['pekka] *sf* defect, flaw.
peccaminoso, a [pekkami'noso] *ag* sinful, wicked.
peccare [pek'kare] *vi* **(a)** *(Rel)* to sin; ~ **di superbia** *(anche fig)* to be guilty of pride; ~ **per troppa bontà** to be too kind. **(b)** *(difettare)*: ~ **di** to lack, be lacking in; ~ **di modestia** to be lacking in modesty; **quel romanzo pecca nella struttura** that novel lacks structure.
peccato [pek'kato] *sm (Rel)* sin; ~ **mortale/veniale** mortal/venial sin; ~ **di gola** gluttony; **un** ~ **di gioventù** *(fig)* a youthful error *o* indiscretion; **che** ~! what a pity!, what a shame!; **è un** ~ **che sia finita così** it's a shame that it had to end like that.
peccatore, trice [pekka'tore] *sm/f* sinner.
pece ['petʃe] *sf* pitch.
pechinese [peki'nese] **1** *ag, sm/f* Pekin(g)ese *(inv)*. **2** *sm (anche: cane* ~) Pekin(g)ese inv, Peke.
pecora ['pɛkora] *sf (gen, fig)* sheep *inv; (femmina)* ewe; ~ **nera** *(fig)* black sheep.
pecoraio [peko'rajo] *sm* shepherd.
pecorella [peko'rella] *sf* lamb; **la** ~ **smarrita** the lost sheep; **cielo a** ~**e** *(fig: nuvole)* mackerel sky.
pecorino [peko'rino] *sm (anche: formaggio* ~) sheep's milk cheese.
pecorone [peko'rone] *sm (fig peg)* spineless creature.
peculato [peku'lato] *sm (Dir)* embezzlement.
peculiare [peku'ljare] *ag:* ~ **di** peculiar to.
peculiarità [pekuljari'ta] *sf* peculiarity.
pecuniario, a [peku'njarjo] *ag* financial, monetary.
pedaggio, gi [pe'daddʒo] *sm* toll.
pedagogia [pedago'dʒia] *sf* pedagogy, pedagogics *sg*.
pedagogico, a, ci, che [peda'gɔdʒiko] *ag* pedagogic(al).

pedalare [peda'lare] *vi* to pedal.

pedalata [peda'lata] *sf* push on the pedals.

pedale [pe'dale] *sm (gen)* pedal; *(di macchina da cucire)* treadle.

pedana [pe'dana] *sf* **(a)** *(gen)* footboard; ~ della cattedra platform, dais. **(b)** *(Sport: nel salto)* springboard; *(: Scherma)* piste; *(: nel lancio del disco etc)* throwing circle.

pedante [pe'dante] **1** *ag* pedantic. **2** *sm/f* pedant, pedantic person.

pedanteria [pedante'ria] *sf* pedantry.

pedata [pe'data] *sf* kick; **dare una** ~ **a qn** to kick sb, give sb a kick.

pederasta, i [pede'rasta] *sm* pederast.

pedestre [pe'dɛstre] *ag* pedestrian.

pediatra, i, e [pe'djatra] *sm/f* pediatrician.

pediatria [pedja'tria] *sf* pediatrics *sg*.

pediatrico, a, ci, che [pe'djatriko] *ag* pediatric, children's *attr*; **clinica** ~ **a** children's hospital.

pedicure [pedi'kure] *sm/f* chiropodist.

pediluvio [pedi'luvjo] *sm* footbath.

pedina [pe'dina] *sf (Dama)* draughtsman; *(fig)* pawn.

pedinare [pedi'nare] *vt* to shadow, tail; **far** ~ **qn** to have sb followed, put a tail on sb.

pedissequo, a [pe'dissekwo] *ag (imitatore)* servile; *(traduzione)* literal.

pedonale [pedo'nale] *ag (passaggio, isola, traffico etc)* pedestrian *attr*.

pedone [pe'done] *sm* **(a)** *(persona)* pedestrian. **(b)** *(Scacchi)* pawn.

peggio ['pɛddʒo] *(comp, superl di* **male)** **1** *av* **(a)** *(con senso comparativo)* worse; **gioca** ~ **di lui** she plays worse than he does, she's a worse player than he is; **senza occhiali vedo** ~ I don't see as well without my glasses, my eyesight is worse without my glasses; **andare** ~ to be worse; **gli affari vanno** ~ **che mai** business is worse than ever; **cambiare in** ~ to get *o* become worse, change for the worse; **si comporta sempre** ~ his behaviour gets worse and worse; ~ **per te!** so much the worse for you!; ~ **di così si muore** things couldn't be worse; **è** ~ **che andar di notte!** it's worse than ever!; **non c'è niente di** ~ **che...** there's nothing worse than.... .

(**b**) *(con senso superlativo)* worst; **i** ~ **allenati** the worst trained; **sono le ragazze** ~ **vestite della scuola** they are the worst dressed girls in the school.

2 *ag inv* **(a)** *(con senso comparativo)* worse; **è** ~ **di suo fratello** he's worse than his brother.

(**b**): **tirare avanti alla meno** ~ to get along as best one can; **alla** ~ if the worst comes to the worst.

3 *sm* worst; **il** ~ **è che...** the worst thing *o* the worst of it is that... .

4 *sf*: **avere la** ~ to come off worse, get the worst of it.

peggioramento [peddʒora'mento] *sm (gen)* worsening; *(di malattia, rapporti)* worsening, deterioration; **portare un** ~ **in, portare ad un** ~ **di** to worsen, lead to a worsening in; **ci sarà un** ~ *(Meteor)* the weather will deteriorate *o* become worse.

peggiorare [peddʒo'rare] **1** *vt* to worsen, make worse. **2** *vi (aus* **essere)** to worsen, become worse.

peggiorativo, a [peddʒora'tivo] *ag* pejorative.

peggiore [ped'dʒore] **1** *ag (comparativo)* worse; *(superlativo)* worst; ~ **(di)** worse (than); **il** ~ **dei due** the worse of the two; **il** ~ **della classe** the worst in the class; **molto** ~ much worse; **nel peggior dei casi** if the worst comes to the worst;

le cose non potevano concludersi in modo ~ things couldn't have come to a worse end; **ho conosciuto tempi** ~ **i** I've been through worse. **2** *sm/f*: **il/la** ~ the worst one.

pegli ['peʎʎi] *forma desueta*: = **per + gli**.

pegno ['peɲɲo] *sm* **(a)** *(Dir)* pledge, security; **dare qc in** ~ to pawn sth; **banco dei** ~**i** pawnshop. **(b)** *(fig: segno)* token, pledge; **un** ~ **d'amore** a love token; **in** ~ **d'amicizia** as a token of friendship.

pei ['pei] *forma desueta*: = **per +i**.

pel [pel] *forma desueta*: = **per +il**.

pelame [pe'lame] *sm (di animale)* coat, fur.

pelandrone [pelan'drone] *sm* loafer, idler.

pelapatate [pelapa'tate] *sm inv* potato peeler.

pelare [pe'lare] **1** *vt (pollo)* to pluck; *(coniglio)* to skin; *(frutta, patate)* to peel; **ti hanno pelato!** *(di capelli)* they've scalped you!; **in quel negozio ti pelano** they make you pay through the nose in that shop. **2**: ~**rsi** *vr (diventar calvo)* to go bald.

pelata [pe'lata] *sf (calvizie parziale)* bald patch.

pelato, a [pe'lato] **1** *ag* **(a)** *(sbucciato)* peeled; **pomodori** ~**i** peeled tomatoes. **(b)** *(calvo)* bald. **2**: ~**i** *smpl (pomodori)* peeled tomatoes.

pella ['pella] *forma desueta*: = **per +la**.

pellaccia, ce [pel'lattʃa] *sf (fig: persona)*: **essere una** ~ to be tough.

pellame [pel'lame] *sm* hides *pl*, skins *pl*.

pelle[1] ['pɛlle] *sf* **(a)** *(gen)* skin; **avere la** ~ **grassa** to have greasy skin. **(b)** *(di animale)* skin, hide; *(di rettile)* skin; *(conciato)* leather; ~ **di camoscio** suede (leather); ~ **di montone** sheepskin; **borsa di** ~ leather handbag. **(c)** *(buccia)* skin, peel. **(d)** *(fraseologia)*: **avere la** ~ **dura** *(fig)* to be tough; **avere la** ~ **d'oca** to have goose pimples; **mi ha fatto venire la** ~ **d'oca** *(paura, disgusto)* it made my flesh creep; **avere i nervi a fior di** ~ to be edgy; **essere** ~ **ed ossa** to be skin and bone; **non stare più nella** ~ **dalla gioia** to be beside o.s. with delight; **lasciarci la** ~ to lose one's life; **salvare la** ~ to save one's skin; **vendere cara la** ~ to put up a fierce struggle; **amici per la** ~ firm *o* close friends.

pelle[2] ['pelle] *forma desueta*: = **per +le**.

pellegrinaggio [pellegri'naddʒo] *sm* pilgrimage; **andare in** ~ to go on a pilgrimage.

pellegrino [pelle'grino] *sm* pilgrim.

pellerossa [pelle'rossa] *sm/f, pl* **pellirosse** redskin.

pelletteria [pellette'ria] *sf* **(a)** *(industria)* leather trade, leather industry. **(b)** *(negozio)* leather goods shop; **articoli di** ~ leather goods.

pellicano [pelli'kano] *sm* pelican.

pellicceria [pellittʃe'ria] *sf* **(a)** *(pellicce)* furs *pl*. **(b)** *(negozio)* furrier's (shop).

pelliccia, ce [pel'littʃa] *sf* **(a)** *(mantello di animale)* fur. **(b)** *(indumento)* fur (coat); ~ **di visone** mink coat.

pellicciaio [pellit'tʃajo] *sm* furrier.

pellicola [pel'likola] *sf* **(a)** *(membrana)* film, layer. **(b)** *(Fot, Cine)* film.

pello ['pello] *forma desueta*: = **per +lo**.

pelo ['pelo] *sm* **(a)** *(gen)* hair; **ho tanti** ~**i sulle gambe** I've got a lot of hair *o* hairs on my legs; **non aver** ~**i sulla lingua** *(fig)* to speak one's mind; **cercare il** ~ **nell'uovo** *(fig)* to pick holes, split hairs; **per un** ~: **l'ha mancato per un** ~ he just missed it; **per un** ~ **non s'ammazzava** he almost *o* nearly killed himself; **è un** ~ **più grande** *(un po')* it's slightly bigger.

(**b**) *(di animale: pelame)* coat, fur; *(pelliccia)* fur; **il gatto ha un** ~ **morbido** the cat has soft fur *o* a soft coat; **impermeabile con l'interno di** ~ fur-lined raincoat; **pelliccia a** ~ **lungo** long-haired fur coat; **fare il** ~ **e il contropelo a qn** to give sb a good dressing-down; **il lupo perde il ~ ma non il vizio** (Proverbio) the leopard cannot change its spots.

(**c**) (di tappeto) pile; (di tessuto) pile, nap; **tappeto a ~ lungo** thick pile carpet.

(**d**) (superficie): **il ~ dell'acqua** the surface of the water.

peloso, a [pe'loso] ag hairy.

peltro ['peltro] sm pewter.

peluche [pǝ'lyʃ] sm plush; **giocattoli di ~** soft toys; **un cane di ~** a fluffy dog.

peluria [pe'lurja] sf down.

pelvico, a, ci, che ['pɛlviko] ag pelvic.

pena ['pena] sf (**a**) (dolore) sorrow; (angoscia) worry, anxiety; **essere** o **stare in ~ (per qc/qn)** to worry o be anxious (about sth/sb); **le ~e dell'inferno** the torments of hell; **ha passato le ~e dell'inferno** (fig) she went through hell.

(**b**) (pietà) pity; **mi fa ~** I'm sorry for him; **fa ~ vederlo così** it is pitiful to see him like this; **quel cappello fa ~** (fig) that hat is a disgrace.

(**c**) (Dir) sentence; (: punizione) penalty, punishment; **fu condannato ad una ~ di 5 anni** he was sentenced to 5 years' imprisonment; **scontare una ~** to serve a term of imprisonment; **~ capitale** capital punishment; **~ di morte** death sentence; **~ pecuniaria** fine.

(**d**) (fatica, disturbo): **darsi la ~ di fare qc** to take the trouble to do sth; **vale la ~ farlo** it is worth doing; **non ne vale la ~** it's not worth the effort.

penale [pe'nale] 1 ag (Dir) criminal, penal; **codice ~** penal code; **causa ~** criminal trial; **diritto ~** criminal law. 2 sf (anche: **clausola ~**) penalty clause; **pagare la ~** to pay the penalty.

penalista, i, e [pena'lista] sm/f (avvocato) criminal lawyer.

penalità [penali'ta] sf inv penalty.

penalizzare [penalid'dzare] vt to penalize.

penalizzazione [penaliddzat'tsjone] sf (Sport) penalty.

penare [pe'nare] vi to suffer; **ha finito di ~** his sufferings are over; **~ a fare qc** to have difficulty in doing sth; **lo fecero senza ~ troppo** they did it without too much difficulty.

pendaglio [pen'daʎʎo] sm (ciondolo) pendant; **~ da forca** (fig) gallows bird.

pendente [pen'dɛnte] 1 ag (Dir: causa, lite) pending. 2 sm (pendaglio) pendant; (orecchino) drop earring.

pendenza [pen'dɛntsa] sf (**a**) slope; **essere in leggera ~** to slope (down) gently; **in ~** (tetto) sloping; (strada, terreno) on a slope; **una strada con una ~ del 20%** a road with a 1 in 5 gradient. (**b**) (Dir) pending suit. (**c**) (Comm) outstanding account.

pendere ['pendere] vi (**a**) (essere appeso): **~ (da)** to hang (from); **~ dalle labbra di qn** to hang on sb's every word. (**b**) (essere sospeso: causa) to be pending. (**c**) (essere inclinato: superficie) to slope, slant; (: nave) to list; **~ da una parte** to slope to one side; **~ dalla parte di qn** (fig) to be inclined to take sb's part; **la bilancia pende in suo favore** (fig) things are in his favour.

pendio, ii [pen'dio] sm (**a**) (luogo in pendenza) slope. (**b**) (pendenza) slope, slant.

pendolare [pendo'lare] 1 ag (moto) pendular, pendulum attr. 2 sm/f (lavoratore) commuter.

pendolo ['pendolo] sm pendulum; **orologio a ~** pendulum clock.

pene ['pɛne] sm (Anat) penis.

penetrante [pene'trante] ag (freddo) biting, piercing; (odore) penetrating; (sguardo) penetrating, piercing.

penetrare [pene'trare] 1 vi (**a**) (gen): **~ (in qc)** to penetrate (sth); **penetrò in casa di nascosto** he entered the house by stealth, he stole into the house. (**b**) (aria, freddo) to get in, come in; (liquido) to soak in; **~ nella parete** (chiodo) to penetrate the wall; (acqua) to soak into the wall; **il sole penetrò nella stanza** the sun shone into the room; **il freddo mi penetrava nelle ossa** the cold went right through me; **far ~** (aria, luce etc) to let in. 2 vt (gen, fig) to penetrate; **~ un mistero** to get to the bottom of a mystery.

penetrazione [penetrat'tsjone] sf penetration.

penicillina [penitʃil'lina] sf penicillin.

peninsulare [peninsu'lare] ag peninsular; **l'Italia ~** mainland Italy.

penisola [pe'nizola] sf peninsula; **la ~ italiana** the Italian mainland.

penitente [peni'tɛnte] sm/f penitent.

penitenza [peni'tɛntsa] sf (**a**) (Rel: pentimento) repentance, penitence; (: pena) penance; **far ~** to do penance. (**b**) (nei giochi) forfeit.

penitenziario [penitɛn'tsjarjo] sm prison, penitentiary (Am).

penna ['penna] sf (**a**) (di uccello) feather; **mettere le ~e** to grow feathers, fledge; **lasciarci** o **rimetterci le ~e** (fig) to get one's fingers burnt; **le ~e nere** (Mil) the Italian Alpine troops. (**b**) (per scrivere) pen; **~ biro** biro; **~ d'oca** quill; **~ a sfera** ball-point (pen); **~ stilografica** fountain pen. (**c**) (Culin): **~e** pl type of pasta. (**d**) (Mus) plectrum.

pennacchio [pen'nakkjo] sm (ornamento) plume; **un ~ di fumo** (fig) a plume o spiral of smoke.

pennarello [penna'rɛllo] sm felt(-tip) pen.

pennellare [pennel'lare] vi to paint.

pennellata [pennel'lata] sf (di vernice) brush stroke; **dare le ultime ~e a qc** (anche fig) to give the finishing touches to sth.

pennello [pen'nɛllo] sm (gen) brush; (di pittore, imbianchino) paintbrush; **quest'abito ti sta a ~** this dress fits you like a glove.

pennino [pen'nino] sm (pen) nib.

pennone [pen'none] sm (**a**) (bandiera) banner, standard. (**b**) (Naut) yard.

pennuto, a [pen'nuto] 1 ag feathered. 2 sm bird.

penombra [pe'nombra] sf half-light, dim light.

penoso, a [pe'noso] ag (doloroso: esperienza, compito) painful; (angoscioso: attesa) anxious; (sgradevole: lavoro, viaggio) difficult; (patetico: scena, scusa) pathetic; **un ~ silenzio** a painful silence.

pensante [pen'sante] 1 ag thinking. 2 sm/f: **ben ~** = **benpensante.**

pensare [pen'sare] 1 vt (**a**) to think; **~ a qc/qn** to think about sth/sb; **a chi stai pensando?** who are you thinking about?; **pensava al tempo passato** he was remembering days gone by; **vorrei pensarci su** I would like to think it over o give it some thought; **penso di sì** I think so; **penso di no** I don't think so; **a pensarci bene...** on second thoughts...; **~ con la propria testa** to think for o.s.; **pensa a come sarebbe bello** think how lovely it would be; **prima di parlare pensa** think before you speak; **se solo ci avessi pensato** if only I had thought about it; **non voglio nemmeno pensarci** I don't even want to think about it; **ciò mi dà da ~** that gives me something to think about; **~ bene/male di qn** to think well/badly of sb, have a good/bad opinion of sb; **ma pensa un po'!** just think of that!

(**b**) (provvedere): **~ a qc** to see to sth, take care of sth; **ci penso io** I'll see to o take care of it;

ha altro a cui ~ ora he's got other *o* more important things to think about now; **pensa ai fatti tuoi!** mind your own business!

2 *vt* **(a)** *(gen)* to think; **che stai pensando?** what are you thinking?; **cosa ne pensi?** what do you think of it?, how do you feel about it?; **penso che sia colpa sua** I think it is his fault *o* that he is to blame; **non avrei mai pensato finisse così** I would never have believed it would end like this; **ti pensavo più furbo** I thought you were more intelligent; **chi l'avrebbe mai pensato?** who would have thought it?; **e ~ che...** and to think that... .

(b) *(prendere in considerazione)* to realize; **devi ~ che ha appena iniziato** you must realize *o* remember that he's only just started; **non pensa che quello che fa può danneggiare gli altri** he doesn't realize that what he does may harm others.

(c) *(avere intenzione)*: **~ di fare qc** to think of doing sth; **pensavo di invitare anche lui** I was thinking of inviting him too; **penso di partire in serata** I'm thinking of leaving in the course of the evening.

(d) *(escogitare)*: **ne pensa sempre una nuova** he's always got something new up his sleeve; **l'ha pensata bella** he had a bright idea; **una ne fa e cento ne pensa** he's always up to something.

3: ~rsi *vr* to think o.s.; **si pensa più furbo di quello che è** he thinks he's more intelligent than he is; **chi ti pensi di essere?** just who do you think you are?

pensata [pen'sata] *sf (trovata)* idea, thought; **ma che bella ~!** what a good idea!

pensatore, trice [pensa'tore] *sm/f* thinker.

pensierino [pensje'rino] *sm* **(a)** *(pensiero)*: **ci farò un ~** I'll think about it. **(b)** *(dono)* little gift.

pensiero [pen'sjɛro] *sm* **(a)** thought; **riandare col ~ a** to remember, think back to; **leggere il ~ di qn** to read sb's thoughts *o* mind; **essere assorto nei propri ~i** to be deep *o* lost in thought; **un ~ gentile** *(anche fig: dono etc)* a kind thought; **libertà di ~** freedom of thought. **(b)** *(preoccupazione)* worry; **ha tanti ~i** he has so many worries; **stare in ~ per qc/qn** to be worried about sth/sb; **darsi ~ per qc** to worry about sth; **è un tipo senza ~i** he's a carefree chap. **(c)** *(dottrina)* thinking; **il ~ di Hegel** Hegelian thinking.

pensieroso, a [pensje'roso] *ag* pensive.

pensile ['pensile] *ag* hanging, suspended; **giardino ~** hanging garden.

pensilina [pensi'lina] *sf* projecting roof; *(di stazione)* platform roof.

pensionabile [pensjo'nabile] *ag* pensionable.

pensionamento [pensjona'mento] *sm* retirement.

pensionante [pensjo'nante] *sm/f* lodger; *(in albergo)* resident.

pensionato¹ [pensjo'nato] *sm (istituto)* hostel.

pensionato², a [pensjo'nato] *sm/f* pensioner.

pensione [pen'sjone] *sf* **(a)** *(rendita)* pension; **~ di guerra** war pension; **~ per la vecchiaia** old age pension. **(b)** *(albergo)* boarding house; *(alloggio e vitto)* board and lodging; **essere a ~ da qn** to board with sb; **tenere a ~ qn** to have sb as a lodger.

pensionistico, a, ci, che [pensjo'nistiko] *ag* pension *attr*.

pensoso, a [pen'soso] *ag* thoughtful, pensive.

pentagono [pen'tagono] *sm* **(a)** *(Geom)* pentagon. **(b)** *(Pol)*: **il P~** the Pentagon.

pentagramma, i [penta'gramma] *sm (Mus)* staff, stave.

pentat(h)lon ['pentatlon] *sm inv* pentathlon.

Pentecoste [pente'kɔste] *sf* Whit Sunday, Pentecost.

pentimento [penti'mento] *sm* repentance; *(rimpianto)* regret.

pentirsi [pen'tirsi] *vr (Rel)* to repent; **~ di qc/di aver fatto qc** to repent of sth/of having done sth; *(rimpiangere)* to regret sth/having done sth; **se segui i miei consigli, non te ne pentirai** if you follow my advice you won't regret it.

pentola ['pentola] *sf (recipiente)* pot; *(contenuto)* pot(ful); **~ a pressione** pressure cooker; **qualcosa bolle in ~** *(fig)* there's something brewing.

pentolino [pento'lino] *sm* small saucepan; **~ del latte** milk pan.

penultimo, a [pe'nultimo] **1** *ag* penultimate, last but one. **2** *sm/f*: **il(la) ~(a)** the last but one.

penuria [pe'nurja] *sf* shortage.

penzolare [pendzo'lare] *vi (pendere)* to hang, dangle.

penzoloni [pendzo'loni] *av (anche:* **a ~)** hanging, dangling; **se ne stava con le braccia ~** he stood there with his arms dangling.

peonia [pe'ɔnja] *sf (Bot)* peony.

pepare [pe'pare] *vt* to pepper.

pepato, a [pe'pato] *ag* **(a)** *(condito con pepe)* peppery, hot. **(b)** *(fig: pungente)* sharp.

pepe ['pepe] *sm* pepper; **~ in grani** whole pepper, peppercorns; **~ macinato** ground pepper; **~ della Giamaica** allspice; **è tutto ~** *(fig)* he's full of life.

peperonata [pepero'nata] *sf (Culin)* stewed peppers, tomatoes and onions.

peperoncino [peperon'tʃino] *sm* chili pepper.

peperone [pepe'rone] *sm*: **~ (verde)** green pepper, capsicum; **~ (rosso)** red pepper, capsicum; **~i ripieni** stuffed peppers; **rosso come un ~** as red as a beetroot.

pepita [pe'pita] *sf* nugget.

per [per] *prep* **(a)** *(direzione)* for, to; **quando parti ~ Parigi?** when are you leaving for *o* are you off to Paris?; **l'autobus ~ Milano** the Milan bus, the bus for *o* to Milan; **proseguire ~ Londra** to go on to London; **il suo grande amore ~ la sorella** his great love for *o* of his sister; **ha una passione ~ la musica** he is passionately fond of music.

(b) *(moto attraverso luogo)* through; **i ladri sono passati ~ la finestra** the thieves got in *(o* out) through the window; **sono passato ~ Roma** I came through *o* via Rome; **l'ho incontrato ~ le scale** I met him on the stairs; **l'ho cercato ~ tutta la casa** I searched the whole house *o* all over the house for it; **ti ho cercato ~ mari e ~ monti** I looked everywhere for you; **il maestro è passato ~ i banchi** the teacher went along the (rows of) desks.

(c) *(stato in luogo)*: **seduto/sdraiato ~ terra** sitting/lying on the ground.

(d) *(tempo)* for; **~ anni/lungo tempo** for years/a long time; **~ giorni e giorni** for days on end; **giorno ~ giorno** day by day; **è piovuto ~ tutta la settimana/giornata** it has rained all week/all day long; **~ tutta l'estate** all through *o* throughout the summer, all summer long; **sarò di ritorno ~ le 3/Natale** I'll be back by 3 o'clock/ Christmas; **dobbiamo finirlo ~ lunedì/la prossima settimana** we must get it finished by *o* for Monday/next week; **ci rivedremo ~ Pasqua** we'll see one another again at Easter.

(e) *(mezzo, maniera)* by; **~ lettera/ferrovia** by letter/rail *o* train; **~ via aerea** by air; **~ vie legali** through legal channels; **chiamare qn ~ nome** to call sb by name; **l'ha presa ~ mano** he took her by the hand; **non mi piace parlare ~ telefono** I don't like using the phone *o* speaking on the phone; **l'ha fatto ~ gioco** *o* **scherzo** he did it as a joke.

(f) *(causa, scopo)* for; **condannato ~ omicidio** convicted of murder; **processato ~ rapina a mano armata** tried for armed robbery; **~ motivi di salute** for health reasons; **chiuso ~ malattia** closed because of *o* on account of illness; **è morto ~ avvelenamento** he died from poisoning; **~ un errore** through *o* by error; **~ abitudine** out of *o* from habit; **non l'ha fatto ~ pigrizia** he didn't do it out of laziness; **non stare in pena ~ lui** don't worry about him; **le tende ~ la cucina** the kitchen curtains, the curtains for the kitchen; **pastiglie ~ il mal di gola** throat pastilles *o* lozenges; **~ il freddo** because of the cold; **questo lavoro non fa ~ me** this isn't the right job for me.

(g) *(prezzo, misura)* for; **l'ho comprato ~ un milione** I bought it for a million lire; **lo vendo ~ poco** I'm selling it for very little, I'm selling it cheap; **assicurato ~ 10 milioni** insured for 10 million lire; **il terreno si estende ~ molti chilometri** the property extends for several kilometres; **~ miglia e miglia non si vedeva nulla** you couldn't see anything for miles.

(h) *(limitazione)* for; **è troppo difficile ~ lui** it's too hard for him; **~ questa volta ci passerò sopra** I'll forget about it this time; **~ quel che mi riguarda** as far as I'm concerned; **~ me è come una madre** she's like a mother to me.

(i) *(distributivo)*: **due mila lire ~ persona** two thousand lire per person *o* a head *o* apiece; **in fila ~ tre!** line up in threes!; **entrate uno ~ volta** come in one at a time; **vi interrogo uno ~ uno** I'll question you one by one; **ce n'è uno ~ parte** there's one on each side; **un interesse del 5 ~ cento** 5 per cent interest; **moltiplicare/dividere ~ 10** to multiply/divide by 10; **2 ~ 3 fa 6** 2 times 3 equals 6.

(j) *(in qualità di)* as; *(al posto di)* for; **ha avuto suo padre ~ professore** he had his father as one of his teachers, he was taught by his father; **me l'hanno venduto ~ lana** they sold it to me as if it were wool; **prendere qn ~ uno sciocco** to take sb for a fool; **ti ho preso ~ tuo fratello** I mistook you for your brother; **lo hanno dato ~ morto** he was given up for dead; **te lo dico ~ certo** I tell you it's gospel.

(k) *(introduce proposizione finale)* to, in order to; **l'ho fatto ~ aiutarti** I did it to help you; **dicevo così ~ scherzare** I said it as a joke *o* in fun.

(l) *(introduce proposizione causale)* for; **è stato punito ~ aver picchiato suo fratello** he was punished for hitting his brother; **è morta ~ aver ingerito troppi barbiturici** she died from *o* of an overdose of barbiturates.

(m) *(introduce proposizione concessiva)*: **~ poco che sia** however little it is, little though it is; **~ quanto si dia da fare...** however hard he tries...; **~ quanto io sappia** as far as I know.

pera ['pera] *sf* **(a)** *(frutto)* pear; **~e cotte** stewed pears; **cadere come una ~ cotta** *(fig: innamorarsi)* to fall head over heels in love. **(b)**: **~ di gomma** *(Med: per clistere)* rubber syringe; **farsi una ~** *(fig fam)* to give o.s. a fix.

peraltro [pe'raltro] *av* *(per di più)* moreover, what's more; *(comunque)* however.

perbacco [per'bakko] *escl* by Jove!

perbene [per'bɛne] **1** *ag inv* *(ammodo)* respectable, decent. **2** *av* *(accuratamente)* well, properly.

perbenismo [perbe'nizmo] *sm* (so-called) respectability.

percento [per'tʃento] *sm inv* percentage.

percentuale [pertʃentu'ale] **1** *ag* percentage *attr.* **2** *sf* percentage; **percepisce una ~ del 20% su ciò che vende** he receives a commission of 20% on what he sells.

percepire [pertʃe'pire] *vt* **(a)** *(sentire, intuire)* to perceive. **(b)** *(ricevere: somma, compenso)* to receive.

percettibile [pertʃet'tibile] *ag* perceptible; **un suono appena ~** a barely audible sound.

percezione [pertʃet'tsjone] *sf* perception.

perché [per'ke] **1** *av* why; **~ no?** why not?; **~ non vuoi andarci?** why don't you want to go?; **spiegami ~ l'hai fatto** tell me why you did it; **vorrei sapere ~ non te ne vai** I'd like to know why you don't leave.

2 *cong* **(a)** *(causale: poiché)* because; **non posso uscire ~ ho da fare** I can't go out because *o* as I've a lot to do. **(b)** *(finale: affinché)* so (that), in order that; **te lo do ~ tu lo legga** I'm giving it to you so you can read it. **(c)** *(consecutivo: cosicché)*: **l'ostacolo era troppo alto ~ si potesse scavalcarlo** the obstacle was too high to climb over; **è troppo forte ~ si possa vincerlo** he's too strong to be beaten *o* for anyone to beat him.

3 *sm inv* *(motivo)* reason; **non c'è un vero ~** there's no real reason for it; **vorrei sapere il ~ di un simile atteggiamento** I'd like to know the reason for his attitude; **i ~ sono tanti** there are many reasons for it; **voglio sapere il ~ e il percome** I want to know the whys and wherefores.

perciò [per'tʃɔ] *cong* therefore, so.

percorrere [per'korrere] *vt* *(distanza, circuito, territorio)* to cover; *(strada)* to follow; **~ un paese in lungo e in largo** to travel all over a country.

percorso, a [per'korso] **1** *pp di* **percorrere. 2** *sm* *(distanza)* distance; *(tragitto)* journey; *(itinerario)* route; *(Sport)* course; **~ obbligato** *(Sport)* set course; **~ netto** *(Ippica)* clear round.

percossa [per'kɔssa] *sf* blow.

percosso, a [per'kɔsso] *pp di* **percuotere.**

percuotere [per'kwɔtere] *vt* *(gen)* to beat; **~rsi il petto** to beat one's breast.

percussione [perkus'sjone] *sf* percussion; **strumenti a ~** *(Mus)* percussion instruments.

perdente [per'dɛnte] **1** *ag* losing. **2** *sm/f* loser.

perdere ['perdere] **1** *vt* **(a)** *(gen)* to lose; *(abitudine)* to get out of; **~ di vista qn** *(anche fig)* to lose sight of sb; **~ la speranza/l'appetito/la vista** to lose hope/one's appetite/one's sight; **~ i capelli** to lose one's hair, go bald; **gli alberi perdono le foglie** the trees are shedding their leaves; **~ al gioco** to lose money gambling; **saper ~** to be a good loser; **lascia ~!** *(non insistere)* forget it!; *(non ascoltarlo)* don't listen to him!; **non ho niente da ~** *(fig)* I've got nothing to lose.

(b) *(lasciar sfuggire: treno, autobus)* to miss; **è un'occasione da non ~** it's a marvellous opportunity; *(affare)* it's a great bargain.

(c) *(sprecare: tempo, danaro)* to waste; **ho perso l'intera giornata a cercarlo** I wasted the whole day looking for it; **è fatica persa** it's a waste of effort.

(d) *(lasciar uscire: sangue)* to lose; **il rubinetto perde** *(acqua)* the tap leaks; **la stufa perde gas** the gas fire is leaking.

(e) *(rimetterci)*: **hanno alzato i prezzi per non perderci** they put up their prices so as not to make a loss; **non hai perso niente a non vedere quel film** you haven't missed anything by not seeing that film; **ci perdi a non venire** you are missing out by not coming.

2 *vi*: **~ di** *(diminuire)*: **~ di autorità/**

importanza to lose authority/importance; ~ **di valore** to go down in value.

3: ~**rsi** vr (a) (smarrirsi) to lose one's way, get lost; ~**rsi in un bicchiere d'acqua** to be unable to cope with the slightest problem; ~**rsi in chiacchiere** to waste time talking; ~**rsi dietro a qn** to waste one's time with sb; **non perderti in queste sciocchezze** don't waste your time with this nonsense.

(b) (scomparire: oggetto) to disappear; (: suono) to fade away; ~**rsi alla vista** to disappear from sight.

(c) (uso reciproco): ~**rsi di vista** to lose sight of each other; (fig) to lose touch.

perdifiato [perdi'fjato]: **a** ~ av (correre) at breathtaking speed; (gridare) at the top of one's voice.

perdigiorno [perdi'dʒorno] sm/f inv idler, loafer.

perdinci [per'dintʃi] escl for goodness' sake!

perdio [per'dio] escl for God's sake!

perdita ['perdita] sf (a) (gen) loss; (di persona: morte) loss, death; **è una grave** ~ it's a great loss; **a** ~ **d'occhio** (fig) as far as the eye can see. (b) (Econ) loss, deficit; **siamo in** ~ we are running at a loss. (c) (spreco) waste; **è una** ~ **di tempo** it's a waste of time. (d) (spandimento: di rubinetto etc) leak; (: di sangue) loss; **le** ~**e bianche** (Med) the whites.

perditempo [perdi'tempo] sm/f inv waster, idler.

perdizione [perdit'tsjone] sf (Rel) perdition, damnation; **luogo di** ~ place of ill repute.

perdonare [perdo'nare] **1** vt (a) to forgive, pardon; ~ **a qn qc/di aver fatto qc** to forgive sb for sth/for doing o having done sth; **mi perdoni?** will you forgive me?; **per farsi** ~ in order to be forgiven; **non gliel'ha mai perdonata** he has never forgiven him for that; **non me lo perdonerò mai** I'll never forgive myself. (b) (scusare): **perdona la domanda** may I ask you a question?; **vogliate** ~ **il (mio) ritardo** my apologies for being late; **perdona la mia ignoranza** forgive my ignorance; **bisogna** ~ **la sua giovane età** you must make allowances for his youth.

2 vi to forgive; **un male che non perdona** an incurable disease; **un uomo che non perdona** an unforgiving man.

perdono [per'dono] sm (gen) forgiveness; (Dir) pardon; **chiedere** ~ **a qn (per)** to ask for sb's forgiveness (for); (scusarsi) to apologize to sb (for); **l'ho urtata? chiedo** ~ was that you I hit? I do beg your pardon o I do apologise.

perdurare [perdu'rare] vi to persist; **il cattivo tempo perdura** the bad weather continues; ~ **nei propositi di vendetta** to persist in seeking revenge.

perdutamente [perduta'mente] av: **amare** ~ **qn** to be desperately in love with sb.

perduto, a [per'duto] **1** pp di **perdere**. **2** ag (gen) lost; **sentirsi** o **vedersi** ~ (fig) to realize the hopelessness of one's position; **una donna** ~**a** (fig) a fallen woman.

peregrinare [peregri'nare] vi to wander, roam.

peregrinazione [peregrinat'tsjone] sf (anche fig) peregrination.

perenne [pe'renne] ag (anche Bot) perennial; (gloria, ricordo) everlasting; **nevi** ~**i** perpetual snow sg.

perentorio, a [peren'tɔrjo] ag (tono, ordine) peremptory.

perequazione [perekwat'tsjone] sf (Amm) equal distribution.

perfettamente [perfetta'mente] av perfectly; **sai** ~ **che...** you know perfectly well that.... .

perfetto, a [per'fetto] ag (gen) perfect; (silenzio,

accordo) complete, total; **è un** ~ **cretino** he's an utter o a perfect idiot.

perfezionamento [perfettsjona'mento] sm (vedi vb): ~ **(di)** perfection (of), improvement (in); **corso di** ~ proficiency course.

perfezionare [perfettsjo'nare] **1** vt (rendere perfetto) to perfect; (migliorare) to improve. **2:** ~**rsi** vr (cosa) to improve; (persona) to improve o.s.; ~**rsi in inglese** to improve one's English.

perfezione [perfet'tsjone] sf perfection; **alla** o **a** ~ to perfection.

perfezionismo [perfettsjo'nizmo] sm perfectionism.

perfezionista, i, e [perfettsjo'nista] sm/f perfectionist.

perfidia [per'fidja] sf perfidy.

perfido, a ['perfido] ag perfidious.

perfino [per'fino] av even; ~ **lui si è commosso** even he was moved; **è un peccato** ~ **pensarlo** you should be ashamed to even think of such a thing.

perforare [perfo'rare] vt (gen) to pierce; (Med) to perforate; (schede) to punch; (Tecn) to drill; **ulcera perforata** (Med) perforated ulcer.

perforatore, trice [perfora'tore] **1** sm/f (Inform: persona) punch-card operator. **2** sm (macchina) perforator; (: Inform) card punch. **3** sf (Inform: macchina) card punch.

perforazione [perforat'tsjone] sf (a) (di sottosuolo) boring, drilling; (Inform: atto) punching; (: foro) punch. (b) (Med) perforation.

pergamena [perga'mena] sf parchment.

pergola ['pergola] sf, **pergolato** [pergo'lato] sm pergola.

pericolante [periko'lante] ag (muro, edificio) unsafe; (fig: economia) shaky, precarious.

pericolo [pe'rikolo] sm danger; **essere/trovarsi in** ~ to be/find o.s. in danger; **mettere in** ~ to endanger, put in danger; **essere fuori** ~ to be out of danger; (Med) to be off the danger list; '~ **di morte'** ≃ 'danger: high voltage'; **è un** ~ **pubblico** (fig: persona) he's a public menace; **non c'è** ~ **che rifiuti** (iro) there's no chance of his refusing, there's no fear that he'll refuse.

pericoloso, a [periko'loso] ag (gen) dangerous; (impresa) hazardous, risky; **zona** ~**a** danger zone.

periferia [perife'ria] sf (perimetro) periphery; (di città) outskirts pl, suburbs pl; **vivere in** ~ to live on the outskirts o in the suburbs.

periferico, a, ci, che [peri'feriko] ag (Anat, Inform) peripheral; (zona) outlying.

perifrasi [pe'rifrazi] sf inv circumlocution.

perimetro [pe'rimetro] sm (gen, Mat) perimeter.

periodico, a, ci, che [peri'ɔdiko] **1** ag periodic(al). **2** sm (pubblicazione) periodical.

periodo [pe'riodo] sm (gen) period; ~ **di prova** trial period; **durante il** ~ **elettorale** at election time; **durante il** ~ **estivo** during the summer (period).

peripezie [peripet'tsie] sfpl vicissitudes, ups and downs.

periplo ['periplo] sm circumnavigation.

perire [pe'rire] vi (aus essere) to perish.

periscopio [peris'kɔpjo] sm periscope.

perito [pe'rito] sm (esperto) expert; (: Edil) surveyor, **è** ~ **chimico/agrario** (Scol) he has a qualification o diploma in chemistry/agriculture.

peritonite [perito'nite] sf peritonitis.

perizia [pe'rittsja] sf (a) (maestria) skill, ability; **un lavoro fatto con** ~ a skilful piece of work. (b) (Dir: giudizio, esame) expert opinion; (scritta) report; ~ **psichiatrica** psychiatrist's report.

perla ['perla] **1** sf pearl; **una collana di** ~**e** a pearl necklace; ~ **coltivata** cultured pearl; **Venezia, la**

~ **dell'Adriatico** (*fig*) Venice, the jewel of the Adriatic; **una ~ di marito** (*fig*) a gem of a husband. **2** *ag inv* (*colore*) pearl *attr*; **grigio** ~ pearl grey.

perlaceo, a [per'latʃeo] *ag* pearly.

perlomeno [perlo'meno] *av* (*almeno*) at least.

perlopiù [perlo'pju] *av* (*quasi sempre*) in most cases, usually.

perlustrare [perlus'trare] *vt* to patrol, reconnoitre.

perlustrazione [perlustrat'tsjone] *sf* patrol, reconnaissance; **andare in** ~ to go on patrol.

permalosità [permalosi'ta] *sf* touchiness.

permaloso, a [perma'loso] **1** *ag* touchy. **2** *sm/f* touchy person.

permanente [perma'nɛnte] **1** *ag* (*gen*) permanent; (*esercito, commissione*) standing. **2** *sf* (*acconciatura*) permanent wave, perm.

permanenza [perma'nɛntsa] *sf* (**a**) (*continuità*) continuation. (**b**) (*soggiorno*) stay, sojourn; **buona ~!** enjoy your stay!

permanere [perma'nere] *vi* (*aus essere*) (*rimanere*) to remain.

permeabile [perme'abile] *ag* permeable.

permeare [perme'are] *vt* (*anche fig*): ~ (**di**) to permeate (with).

permesso, a [per'messo] **1** *pp di* **permettere. 2** *sm* (**a**) (*autorizzazione*) permission; **chiedere il ~ di fare qc** to ask permission to do sth. (**b**) (*Amm, Mil: licenza*) leave (of absence); **andare in** ~ to go on leave. (**c**) (*documento*) permit; (*: Mil*) pass; ~ **di lavoro/soggiorno** work/residence permit.

permettere [per'mettere] *vt* (**a**) (*gen: consentire*) to allow, permit; ~ **a qn di fare qc** (*autorizzare*) to allow *o* permit sb to do sth, let sb do sth; (*dare la possibilità*) to enable sb to do sth; (*dare il diritto*) to entitle sb to do sth; **crede che tutto gli sia permesso** he thinks he can do just as he likes; **i miei impegni non me lo permettono** I'm too busy to be able to do it; **ci andremo, tempo permettendo** we'll go, weather permitting; **non permetto che mi si tratti così** I will not tolerate being treated in this way.

(**b**): **~rsi qc/di fare qc** (*concedersi*) to allow o.s. sth/to do sth; (*avere la possibilità*) to afford sth/to do sth; **non possono ~rsi una casa più grande** they can't afford a bigger house; **non posso permettermi di perdere neanche un minuto** I can't afford to waste any time; **sai cosa si è permessa di dire?** do you know what she dared to say?

(**c**) (*fraseologia*): **è permesso?** may I?; **se permetti avrei un'obiezione** if you don't mind I wish to object; **mi sia permesso di sottolineare che...** may I take the liberty of pointing out that...; **permettete che mi presenti** let me introduce myself, may I introduce myself?

permissivo, a [permis'sivo] *ag* permissive.

permuta ['permuta] *sf* (*Dir*) transfer; **valore di** ~ (*di macchina etc*) trade-in value; **accettare qc in** ~ to take sth as a trade-in.

pernacchia [per'nakkja] *sf* (*fam*) raspberry; **fare una** ~ to blow a raspberry.

pernice [per'nitʃe] *sf* partridge.

pernicioso, a [perni'tʃoso] *ag* pernicious.

perno ['perno] *sm* (*anche fig*) pivot; **fare** ~ **su qc** to pivot on sth.

pernottamento [pernotta'mento] *sm* overnight stay.

pernottare [pernot'tare] *vi* to spend the night.

pero ['pero] *sm* (*Bot*) pear (tree).

però [pe'rɔ] *cong* (*ma*) (and) yet, but (nevertheless); (*tuttavia*) nevertheless, however; ~ **non è**

giusto che... and yet *o* but nevertheless it's not fair that...; ~ **avresti potuto dirmelo** you could have told me nevertheless; **sono stanco, non tanto ~ da non poter finire** I'm tired, but not so tired as to be unable to finish.

perorare [pero'rare] *vt* (*Dir, fig*): ~ **la causa di qn** to plead sb's case.

perpendicolare [perpendiko'lare] **1** *ag* perpendicular. **2** *sf* (*Mat*) perpendicular (line).

perpendicolo [perpen'dikolo] *sm*: **a ~** perpendicularly.

perpetrare [perpe'trare] *vt* to commit, perpetrate.

perpetuare [perpetu'are] *vt* to perpetuate.

perpetuo, a [per'pɛtuo] *ag* (*gen*) perpetual; (*rendita, carcere*) life *attr*.

perplessità [perplessi'ta] *sf inv* perplexity.

perplesso, a [per'plesso] *ag* perplexed, puzzled; **lasciare qn** ~ to perplex *o* puzzle sb.

perquisire [perkwi'zire] *vt* to search.

perquisizione [perkwizit'tsjone] *sf* search; **mandato di** ~ search warrant; **fare una** ~ (**di**) to carry out a search (of).

persecutore, trice [perseku'tore] *sm/f* persecutor.

persecuzione [persekut'tsjone] *sf* persecution; **mania di** ~ (*Psic*) persecution complex.

perseguibile [perse'gwibile] *ag* (*Dir*): **essere ~ per legge** to be liable to prosecution.

perseguire [perse'gwire] *vt* (**a**) (*scopo, intento*) to pursue. (**b**) (*Dir*) to prosecute.

perseguitare [persegwi'tare] *vt* (*anche fig*) to persecute; **essere perseguitato dalla sfortuna** to be dogged by ill luck.

perseguitato, a [persegwi'tato] *sm/f* victim of persecution.

perseveranza [perseve'rantsa] *sf* perseverance.

perseverare [perseve'rare] *vi*: ~ **in qc/nel fare qc** to persevere in sth/in doing sth.

Persia ['persja] *sf* Persia.

persiana [per'sjana] *sf* shutter.

persiano, a [per'sjano] **1** *ag, sm/f* Persian. **2** *sm* (**a**) (*Zool: gatto*) Persian (cat). (**b**) (*pelliccia*) Persian lamb.

persico, a, ci, che ['pɛrsiko] *ag*: **il Golfo P~** the Persian Gulf; **pesce** ~ perch.

persino [per'sino] *av* = **perfino.**

persistente [persis'tɛnte] *ag* persistent.

persistenza [persis'tɛntsa] *sf* persistence.

persistere [per'sistere] *vi* to persist; ~ **in qc/a fare qc** to persist in sth/in doing sth; **persiste nella sua opinione** he sticks to his opinion.

persistito, a [persis'tito] *pp di* **persistere.**

perso, a ['pɛrso] **1** *pp di* **perdere. 2** *ag* (*smarrito: anche fig*) lost; (*sprecato*) wasted; **questo è tempo** ~ this is a waste of time; **fare qc a tempo** ~ to do sth in one's spare time; ~ **per** ~ I've (*o* we've *etc*) got nothing further to lose; **dare per** ~ to give up for lost.

persona [per'sona] *sf* (**a**) (*essere umano*) person; **tre ~e** three people, three persons (*Am*); **per** ~ (*a testa*) per head *o* person; **per interposta** ~ through an intermediary *o* a third party; ~ **di servizio** domestic help; ~ **giuridica** (*Dir*) legal person.

(**b**) (*corpo*): **aver cura della propria** ~ to look after o.s.; **in ~, di** ~ in person; **ci andrò di** ~ I'll go there personally *o* in person; **è l'onestà in** ~ he is honesty personified.

(**c**) (*Gram*) person; **alla terza** ~ **singolare** in the third person singular; **vivere qc in prima** ~ to experience sth personally.

(**d**) (*qualcuno*) somebody; **c'era una** ~ **che ti cercava** somebody was looking for you.

personaggio [perso'naddʒo] *sm* (**a**)*(celebrità)* personage; *(scherz: individuo)* character, individual. (**b**) *(di romanzo)* character; *(di quadro)* figure.

personale [perso'nale] **1** *ag* personal. **2** *sf (mostra)* one-man exhibition. **3** (**a**) *sm (complesso di dipendenti)* personnel, staff. (**b**) *(corpo, figura)* build; **quella ragazza ha un bel** ~ that girl's got a lovely figure.

personalità [personali'ta] *sf inv (tutti i sensi)* personality.

personalmente [personal'mente] *av* personally.

personificare [personifi'kare] *vt (rappresentare)* to personify; *(essere simbolo)* to personify, embody.

personificazione [personifikat'tsjone] *sf (figurazione concreta)* personification, embodiment; **essere la** ~ **della gentilezza** to be kindness itself.

perspicace [perspi'katʃe] *ag* discerning, shrewd.

perspicacia [perspi'katʃa] *sf* perspicacity, shrewdness.

persuadere [persua'dere] **1** *vt* to persuade, convince; ~ **qn di qc** to persuade *o* convince sb of sth; **lasciarsi** ~ to let o.s. be convinced; **ne sono persuaso** I'm quite sure *o* convinced (of it). **2**: ~**rsi** *vr* to convince o.s.

persuasione [persua'zjone] *sf (gen)* persuasion; *(credenza)* conviction, belief.

persuasivo, a [persua'zivo] *ag* persuasive, convincing.

persuaso, a [persu'azo] *pp di* **persuadere**.

persuasore [persua'zore] *sm*: ~ **occulto** hidden persuader.

pertanto [per'tanto] *cong* therefore, so.

pertica, che ['pɛrtika] *sf (bastone)* pole, rod; *(Sport)* pole; *(fig: persona alta e magra)* beanpole.

pertinace [perti'natʃe] *ag* pertinacious.

pertinacia [perti'natʃa] *sf* pertinacity.

pertinente [perti'nɛnte] *ag*: ~ (**a**) pertinent (to), relevant (to).

pertinenza [perti'nɛntsa] *sf* (**a**) *(attinenza)* pertinence, relevance. (**b**) *(competenza)*: **essere di** ~ **di qn** to be sb's business; **è di** ~ **del tribunale di Napoli** it comes under the jurisdiction of the Naples courts.

pertosse [per'tosse] *sf (Med)* whooping cough.

pertugio [per'tudʒo] *sm* hole.

perturbare [pertur'bare] **1** *vt* to upset, disturb. **2**: ~**rsi** *vr* to become *o* get upset.

perturbazione [perturbat'tsjone] *sf (Meteor, Astron)* disturbance.

Perù [pe'ru] *sm* Peru.

peruviano, a [peru'vjano] *ag, sm/f* Peruvian.

pervadere [per'vadere] *vt* to pervade, permeate.

pervaso, a [per'vazo] *pp di* **pervadere**.

pervenire [perve'nire] *vi (aus* **essere**): ~ **a** to reach, arrive at, come to; **far** ~ **qc a qn** to have sth sent to sb; **ci sono pervenute migliaia di lettere** we have received thousands of letters.

pervenuto, a [perve'nuto] *pp di* **pervenire**.

perversione [perver'sjone] *sf* perversion.

perversità [perversi'ta] *sf* perversity.

perverso, a [per'vɛrso] *ag* perverted.

pervertire [perver'tire] *vt* to pervert, corrupt.

pervertito, a [perver'tito] **1** *ag* perverted. **2** *sm/f* pervert.

pervicace [pervi'katʃe] *ag* stubborn, obstinate.

pervicacia [pervi'katʃa] *sf* stubbornness, obstinacy.

p.es. *abbr* (= *per esempio*) e.g.

pesa ['pesa] *sf (azione)* weighing; *(luogo)* weigh-house; *(apparecchiatura)* weighing machine.

pesante [pe'sante] *ag (gen, fig)* heavy; *(cibo)* heavy, rich; *(sonno)* heavy, deep; *(stile)* ponderous; *(fig:*

persona) tedious; **questo libro è** ~ *(fig)* this book is heavy reading; **il film era un po'** ~ I found the film heavy going; **ho gli occhi** ~ I I can't keep my eyes open; **è andata giù** ~ *(ha esagerato)* she was rather heavy-handed; **artiglieria** ~ heavy artillery; **atletica** ~ weightlifting and wrestling.

pesantezza [pesan'tettsa] *sf (anche fig)* heaviness; **avere** ~ **di stomaco** to feel bloated.

pesapersone [pesaper'sone] *ag inv*: (**bilancia**) ~ (weighing) scales *pl*; *(automatica)* weighing machine.

pesare [pe'sare] **1** *vt* to weigh; *(fig: valutare)* to weigh (up); ~ **i pro e i contro** to weigh up the pros and cons; ~ **le parole** to weigh one's words.

2 *vi* (**a**) *(gen)* to weigh; **quanto pesi?** how much do you weigh?; **come pesa!** how heavy it is!; ~ **sulla coscienza/sullo stomaco** to lie heavy on one's conscience/on one's stomach; **tutta la responsabilità pesa su di lui** all the responsibility rests on his shoulders; **la responsabilità gli pesa** the responsibility weighs heavy on him; **ha sempre pesato sui genitori** he has always been dependent on his parents; **è molto gentile ma lo fa** ~ he is very kind but he makes sure it doesn't go unnoticed; **le ha sempre fatto** ~ **il fatto che viene da una famiglia povera** he has always made her aware of her humble origins.

(**b**) *(dispiacere)*: **mi pesa partire** I don't want to leave; **mi pesa dirti di no** I regret having to say no; **è una situazione che mi pesa** it's a difficult situation for me.

(**c**) *(contare)* to count for; **il suo parere pesa molto** his opinion counts for a lot.

pesca[1] ['pɛska] *sf (frutto)* peach.

pesca[2] ['pɛska] *sf* (**a**) *(Sport)* fishing; **andare a** ~ to go fishing; ~ **subacquea** underwater fishing; ~ **con l'amo** angling. (**b**) *(pesce pescato)* catch; **avete fatto una buona** ~? did you get a good catch? (**c**) *(lotteria)*: ~ **di beneficenza** lucky dip.

pescaggio [pes'kaddʒo] *sm (Naut)* draught.

pescare [pes'kare] **1** *vt (essere pescatore di)* to fish for; *(prendere)* to catch; (: *molluschi)* to gather; **ma dove le vai a** ~ **queste idee?** where on earth do you get hold of such ideas?; **dove hai pescato questo cappello?** where on earth did you get that hat?; **l'hanno pescato con le mani nel sacco** they caught him red-handed. **2** *vi (gen)* to go fishing; *(con l'amo)* to go angling.

pescatore [peska'tore] *sm (persona)* fisherman; (: *con l'amo)* angler.

pesce ['peʃʃe] **1** *sm* (**a**) *fish*; **c'erano molti** ~**i** there were a lot of fish *o* fishes; **ti piace il** ~? do you like fish? (**b**) *(Astrologia)*: **P**~**i** Pisces; **essere dei P**~**i** to be Pisces. (**c**) *(Tip)* omission. (**d**) *(fraseologia)*: ~ **d'aprile** *(burla)* April Fool; **sano come un** ~ as fit as a fiddle; **buttarsi a** ~ **su un'offerta** to jump at an offer; **sentirsi un** ~ **fuor d'acqua** to feel like a fish out of water; **prendere qn a** ~ **in faccia** to treat sb like dirt; **non saper che** ~**i prendere** not to know which way to turn; **hanno preso solo i** ~**i piccoli** *(fig)* they only caught the small fry; **chi dorme non piglia** ~**i** *(Proverbio)* the early bird catches the worm.

2: ~ **gatto** catfish; ~ **martello** hammerhead; ~ **ragno** weever; ~ **rosso** goldfish; ~ **spada** swordfish.

pescecane [peʃʃe'kane] *sm*, *pl* ~**i** *o* **pescicani** *(Zool)* shark; *(fig: profittatore)* shark, profiteer.

peschereccio, a, ci, ce [peske'rettʃo] *sm* fishing boat.

pescheria [peske'ria] *sf* fishmonger's (shop).

peschiera [pes'kjɛra] *sf* fish farm.

pescivendolo [peʃʃi'vendolo] *sm* fishmonger;

(negozio) fishmonger's (shop).
pesco, schi ['pesko] *sm (Bot)* peach (tree).
pescoso, a [pes'koso] *ag* teeming with fish.
peseta [pe'zɛta] *sf* peseta.
pesista, i, e [pe'sista] *sm/f (Sport)* weightlifter.
peso ['peso] **1** *sm* **(a)** *(gen)* weight; **comprare a ~** to buy by weight; **rubare sul ~** to give short weight; **eccesso di ~** excess weight; **metter su ~** to put on weight; **piegarsi sotto il ~ di** *(sog: trave)* to bend under the weight of; *(fig: dispiaceri etc)* to be weighed down by; **lo portarono via di ~** they carried him away bodily; **avere due ~i e due misure** *(fig)* to have double standards.
(b) *(fig: onere)* weight; **il ~ degli anni** the weight of years; **avere un ~ sullo stomaco** to have something lying heavy on one's stomach; **mi sono liberato di un ~** *(preoccupazione)* that's a load off my mind; **togliersi un ~ dalla coscienza** to take a load off one's conscience; **essere di ~ a qn** to be a burden to sb.
(c) *(fig: importanza)* weight, importance; **una questione di un certo ~** a matter of some weight *o* importance; **dar ~ a qc** to attach importance to sth.
(d) *(Sport)*: **lancio del ~** putting the shot; **sollevamento ~i** weightlifting.
2: ~ lordo/netto *(Comm)* gross/net weight; **~ piuma/mosca/gallo/medio/massimo** *(Pugilato)* feather/fly/bantam/middle/heavyweight; **~ morto** dead load; **~ specifico** *(Fis)* specific gravity.
pessimismo [pessi'mizmo] *sm* pessimism.
pessimista, i, e [pessi'mista] **1** *ag* pessimistic. **2** *sm/f* pessimist.
pessimistico, a, ci, che [pessi'mistiko] *ag* pessimistic.
pessimo, a ['pessimo] *ag (superl di cattivo)* **(a)** *(gen)* awful, dreadful; **abbiamo fatto un ~ viaggio** we had a dreadful *o* an awful *o* an appalling journey; **c'è un ~ odore in questa stanza** there's an awful *o* a dreadful smell in this room; **ha fatto un tempo ~** the weather has been rotten *o* dreadful; **è un ~ insegnante** he *(o* she*)* is a very poor teacher; **di ~a qualità** of very poor quality, shoddy; **essere di ~ umore** to be in a foul mood; **hai un ~ aspetto** *o* **una ~a cera** you look awful *o* dreadful; **quello scherzo è di ~ gusto** that joke is in very bad taste. **(b)** *(molto riprovevole)* very wicked, nasty.
pestare [pes'tare] *vt* **(a)** *(calpestare)* to tread on; **~ i piedi** to stamp one's feet; **~ i piedi a qn** *(anche fig)* to tread on sb's toes; **~ qn** *(picchiarlo)* to beat sb up. **(b)** *(frantumare: aglio, pepe etc)* to crush.
peste ['peste] *sf (Med)* plague; *(fig: persona)* pest, nuisance; **dire ~ e corna di qn** to tear sb to bits.
pestello [pes'tɛllo] *sm* pestle.
pestifero, a [pes'tifero] *ag (anche fig)* pestilential, pestiferous; *(odore)* noxious.
pestilenza [pesti'lɛntsa] *sf (peste)* plague, pestilence; *(fetore)* stench.
pestilenziale [pestilen'tsjale] *ag (odore)* noxious.
pesto, a ['pesto] **1** *ag*: **occhio ~** black eye; **avere gli occhi ~i** *(per la stanchezza)* to have bags under one's eyes; **era buio ~** it was pitch-black. **2** *sm (Culin)* sauce made from oil, basil and garlic.
petalo ['petalo] *sm* petal.
petardo [pe'tardo] *sm* firecracker; *(Ferr)* detonator, torpedo *(Am)*.
petizione [petit'tsjone] *sf (Dir)* petition; **fare una ~ a** to petition.
peto ['peto] *sm (fam)* fart.
petrolchimica [petrol'kimika] *sf* petrochemical industry.

petrolchimico, a, ci, che [petrol'kimiko] *ag* petrochemical.
petroliera [petro'ljɛra] *sf* (oil) tanker *(ship)*.
petroliere [petro'ljɛre] *sm* **(a)** *(tecnico)* worker in the oil industry. **(b)** *(industriale)* oilman.
petroliero, a [petro'ljɛro] *ag* oil *attr*.
petrolifero, a [petro'lifero] *ag (industria, pozzo etc)* oil *attr*.
petrolio [pe'trɔljo] *sm* oil, petroleum; **~ grezzo** crude oil; **lume a ~** oil *o* paraffin lamp.
pettegolare [pettego'lare] *vi* to gossip.
pettegolezzo [pettego'leddzo] *sm* piece of gossip; **non mi piacciono questi ~i** I don't like gossip.
pettegolo, a [pet'tegolo] **1** *ag* gossipy; **è ~a di carattere** she is given to gossip. **2** *sm/f* gossip.
pettinare [petti'nare] **1** *vt (capelli)* to comb; *(tessuto)* to comb, tease. **2: ~rsi** *vr* to comb one's hair, do one's hair.
pettinata [petti'nata] *sf* comb, combing; **darsi una ~** to give one's hair a comb.
pettinato, a [petti'nato] **1** *ag (capelli)* combed; *(persona)* with one's hair combed; *(tessuto)* carded, combed. **2** *sm* worsted.
pettinatura [pettina'tura] *sf* **(a)** *(acconciatura)* hairstyle, hairdo. **(b)** *(d. tessuto)* carding, combing.
pettine ['pɛttine] *sm* **(a)** comb. **(b)** *(Zool)* scallop.
pettirosso [petti'rosso] *sm* robin.
petto ['pɛtto] *sm* **(a)** *(Anat)* chest; *(: seno)* breast; **giacca a doppio ~** double-breasted jacket; **essere debole di ~** to have a weak chest; **battersi** *o* **picchiarsi il ~** to beat one's breast; **mettersi una mano sul ~** *(fig)* to put one's hand on one's heart; **prendere qn/qc di ~** to face up to sb/sth. **(b)** *(Culin)* breast; **~ di pollo** chicken breast; **punta di ~** brisket. **(c)** *(Mus)*: **voce f di ~** chest voice.
pettorale [petto'rale] *ag* pectoral.
pettoruto, a [petto'ruto] *ag (uomo)* broad-chested; *(donna)* full-breasted.
petulante [petu'lante] *ag* petulant.
petulanza [petu'lantsa] *sf* petulance.
petunia [pe'tunja] *sf* petunia.
pezza ['pɛttsa] *sf* **(a)** *(rotolo di tessuto)* bolt of cloth. **(b)** *(toppa)* patch; *(cencio)* rag; **bambola di ~** rag doll; **mettere una ~ su qc** *(vestito etc)* to patch sth; **trattare qn come una ~ da piedi** to treat sb like a doormat. **(c)** *(Amm)*: **~ d'appoggio** *o* **giustificativa** voucher.
pezzato, a [pet'tsato] **1** *ag* piebald. **2** *sm (anche: cavallo ~)* piebald (horse).
pezzente [pet'tsɛnte] *sm/f (accattone)* beggar, wretch; *(fig: tirchio)* miser.
pezzo ['pɛttso] *sm* **(a)** *(gen)* piece; *(frammento)* piece, bit; **andare in ~i** to shatter; **fare a ~i qc** to pull sth to pieces; **essere a ~i** *(oggetto)* to be in pieces *o* bits; *(fig: persona)* to be shattered; **ha i nervi a ~i** his nerves are shattered; **ne vuoi ancora un ~?** *(di torta, pane etc)* would you like a bit more *o* another piece?; **ci ha accompagnato per un bel ~ di strada** he came quite a long way with us.
(b) *(oggetto, negli scacchi)* piece; *(Mil)* gun; **vendersi al ~** to be sold separately *o* individually; **1000 lire al ~** 1000 lire each *o* apiece; **un due ~i** *(costume)* a two-piece suit; **un servizio da 24 ~i** *(piatti)* a 24-piece dinner service.
(c) *(Tecn)* part; **~ di ricambio** spare part; **smontare qc ~ per ~** to dismantle sth piece by piece *o* bit by bit.
(d) *(brano: Mus)* piece; *(: scritto)* piece, passage; **~ forte** pièce de résistance.
(e) *(tempo)*: **è qui da un ~** he's been here for quite a while; **resterà per un bel ~** he'll stay for

quite a long time; **è un ~ che non lo vedo** I haven't seen him for a while.

(f) *(fraseologia)*: **un ~ grosso** a big shot; **un ~ d'uomo** a fine figure of a man; **essere tutto d'un ~** to be a man (*o* woman) of integrity; **che ~ di ragazza!** she's a bit of all right!; **~ di cretino** stupid idiot.

piacente [pja'tʃɛnte] *ag* attractive.

piacere¹ [pja'tʃere] *sm* **(a)** *(gen)* pleasure; **i ~i della vita** the pleasures of life; **fare qc per il ~ di farlo** to do sth for the sake of doing it; **ho il ~ di annunciare che...** it gives me great pleasure to tell you that...; **mi fa ~ per lui** I am pleased for him; **è un ~ averti qui** it's a pleasure to have you here; **che ~ vederti!** how nice to see you!; **~, è un ~ conoscerla** pleased to meet you; **mi farebbe ~ rivederlo** I would like to see him again; **se ti fa ~** if you like; **con ~** with pleasure; **fare qc con ~** to be happy *o* glad to do sth; **ho saputo con ~ che ti sposi** I was delighted to hear you're getting married; **un viaggio di ~** a pleasure trip; **potevi averne a ~** *(volontà)* you could take as many as you wanted; **tanto ~!** so what?

(b) *(favore)* favour; **fare un ~ a qn** to do sb a favour; **mi fai il ~ di smetterla?** would you kindly stop that?; **per ~, potresti...?** could you please...?; **su mangia la minestra, fammi il ~** come on, eat your soup like a good boy (*o* girl); **ma fammi il ~!** for heaven's sake!

piacere² [pja'tʃere] *vi (aus essere) (persona)*: **~ a qn** to be liked by sb; **mi piace** *(lavoro, film)* I like *o* enjoy it; *(progetto)* it suits me; *(sport, attività)* I enjoy it; **mi piace molto questo quadro** I like this picture very much; **non credo gli piaccia** I don't think he likes it; **mi piace di più così** I like it better this way; **mi piace di più così** I like it better this way; **mi gusto che piace** a pleasant *o* agreeable flavour; **il suo discorso è piaciuto molto** his speech was well received; **che ti piaccia o no, ti piaccia o non ti piaccia** whether you like it or not; **che cosa ti piacerebbe fare?** what would you like to do?, what do you fancy doing?; **mi sarebbe piaciuto andarci** I would have liked to have gone; **fa' come ti pare e piace** do as you please *o* like; **a Dio piacendo** God willing.

piacevole [pja'tʃevole] *ag* pleasant, nice.

piacimento [pjatʃi'mento] *sm*: **a ~** *(a volontà)* as much as one likes, at will; **lo farà a suo ~** he'll do it when it suits him.

piaciuto, a [pja'tʃuto] *pp di* **piacere²**.

piaga, ghe ['pjaga] *sf* **(a)** *(Med)* sore; **mettere un dito sulla ~** *(fig)* to touch a sore point; **le ~ghe d'Egitto** the plagues of Egypt. **(b)** *(fig peg: persona)* nuisance, pain in the neck.

piagnisteo [pjaɲɲis'teo] *sm* wailing, whining.

piagnucolare [pjaɲɲuko'lare] *vi* to whine, whimper.

piagnucolio, ii [pjaɲɲuko'lio] *sm* whimpering.

piagnucolone [pjaɲɲuko'lone] *sm* whiner, moaner.

piagnucoloso, a [pjaɲɲuko'loso] *ag* whiny, whimpering, moaning.

pialla ['pjalla] *sf* plane.

piallare [pjal'lare] *vt* to plane.

piallatore [pjalla'tore] *sm (operaio)* planer.

piallatrice [pjalla'tritʃe] *sf* planing machine.

piallatura [pjalla'tura] *sf (lavorazione)* planing.

piana ['pjana] *sf (Geog)* plain.

pianeggiante [pjaned'dʒante] *ag* flat, level.

pianerottolo [pjane'rɔttolo] *sm* landing.

pianeta¹, i [pja'neta] *sm (Astron)* planet.

pianeta² [pja'neta] *sf (Rel)* chasuble.

piangere ['pjandʒere] **1** *vi (gen)* to cry, weep; **~ di gioia** to weep for joy; **~ a calde lacrime** to cry

one's heart out; **mi piange il cuore** my heart bleeds; **mi piange il cuore a buttare via tanta roba** I could weep at having to throw away so much stuff; **è inutile ~ sul latte versato** it's no use crying over spilt milk. **2** *vt* **(a)** to cry, weep.

(b) *(lamentare)*: **~ la morte di qn** to mourn sb's death; **~ miseria** to moan about money.

pianificare [pjanifi'kare] *vt* to plan.

pianificazione [pjanifikat'tsjone] *sf (Econ)* planning.

pianista, i, e [pja'nista] *sm/f* pianist.

pianistico, a, ci, che [pja'nistiko] *ag* piano *attr*.

piano¹, a ['pjano] **1** *ag (piatto)* flat; *(senza asperità)* smooth; **geometria ~a** plane geometry; **corsa ~a** *(Sport)* flat race.

2 *av (lentamente)* slowly; *(con cautela)* carefully; *(a basso volume)* quietly; **la macchina andava ~** the car was travelling slowly; **vai ~!** *(in macchina)* drive slowly!; *(fig: non esagerare: nel bere)* take it easy with that!; *(: nelle minacce)* calm down!; *(: nel lodarsi)* come off it!; **attento, fai ~!** *(fare meno rumore)* don't make so much noise!; *(stare attento)* watch out!, be careful!; **parla più ~** *(lentamente)* speak more slowly; *(a bassa voce)* lower your voice; **pian pianino** *o* **pian ~ siamo arrivati** slowly but surely we got there; **pian pianino** *o* **pian ~ ha acquistato una certa esperienza** he gradually acquired experience.

3 *sm* **(a)** *(Geom)* plane; *(superficie)* top, surface; *(fig: livello)* level; **~ inclinato** inclined plane; **~ di lavoro** *(in cucina)* worktop; **~ stradale** road surface; **~ di coda** *(Aer)* empennage; **mettere tutto sullo stesso ~** to lump everything together, give equal importance to everything; **consideralo su un altro ~** look at it from another point of view; **quei due alunni sono sullo stesso ~** those two pupils are at the same level *o* are on a par.

(b) *(di edificio)* floor, storey; *(di autobus: superiore)* top (deck); *(: inferiore)* lower deck; **una casa di 3 ~i** a 3-storey house; **al ~ di sopra/di sotto** on the floor above/below; **all'ultimo ~** on the top floor; **al ~ terra** on the ground floor; **un autobus a due ~i** a double-decker.

(c) *(Fot, Cine, Arte etc)*: **primo ~** foreground; **secondo ~** background; **in primo/secondo ~** in the foreground/background; **fare un primo ~** *(Cine, Fot)* to take a close-up; **in primissimo ~** right in the foreground; **uno scrittore di primo ~** *(fig)* a major author; **mettere qc in secondo ~** to consider sth of secondary importance; **un fattore di secondo ~** a secondary *o* minor factor; **passare in secondo ~** to become less important.

piano² ['pjano] **1** *sm (progetto: anche Mil)* plan; *(: industriale)* design; **facciamo un ~** let's draw up a plan; **non era nei nostri ~i** we hadn't intended to do it, we hadn't planned on doing so; **tutto secondo i ~i** all according to plan. **2:** **~ di battaglia** *(Mil)* plan of battle; **~ di guerra** *(Mil)* plan of campaign; **~ di studi** *(Univ)* programme, schedule; **~ regolatore** *(Urbanistica)* town-planning scheme.

piano³ ['pjano] *sm* = **pianoforte**.

pianoforte [pjano'fɔrte] *sm* piano, pianoforte.

pianola [pja'nɔla] *sf* player piano, Pianola ®.

pianoterra [pjano'tɛrra] *sm inv* ground floor; **al ~** on the ground floor.

pianta ['pjanta] *sf* **(a)** *(Bot)* plant; **~ d'appartamento** house plant; **~ grassa** succulent (plant). **(b)** *(di piede, scarpa)* sole. **(c)** *(disegno)* plan; *(cartina topografica)* map, plan; **~ stradale** street map. **(d)** *(fraseologia)*: **l'ha inventato di sana ~** he made the whole thing up; **essere**

assunto in ~ **stabile** to be taken on as a permanent employee; **ormai è qui da noi in ~ stabile** *(fig)* he seems to have taken up residence at our place.

piantagione [pjanta'dʒone] *sf* plantation.

piantagrane [pjanta'grane] *sm/f inv* troublemaker.

piantare [pjan'tare] **1** *vt* **(a)** *(pianta)* to plant, put in. **(b):** ~ **(in)** *(chiodo)* to hammer in(to), knock in(to); *(paletto)* to drive in(to); *(ago)* to stick in(to); ~ **grane** *(fig)* to cause trouble. **(c)** *(fig: lasciare: moglie, figli)* to leave, abandon; **ha piantato il suo ragazzo** she has left her boyfriend; ~ **qn in asso** to leave sb in the lurch; **piantala!** stop it! **2:** ~**rsi** *vr* **(a)** *(proiettile)*: ~**rsi** in to enter; **mi si è piantata una scheggia nel dito** I've got a splinter in my finger. **(b)** *(persona)*: **mi si piantò davanti, si piantò davanti a me** he planted himself in front of me. **(c)** *(uso reciproco)* to leave each other.

piantato, a [pjan'tato] *ag*: **ben** ~ *(persona)* well-built.

piantatore [pjanta'tore] *sm* planter.

pianterreno [pjanter'reno] *sm* ground floor.

pianto [a [pjanto] **1** *pp di* **piangere. 2** *sm* crying, weeping; **scoppiò in un** ~ **dirotto** he burst into tears; **è uno che ha il** ~ **facile** he cries easily.

piantonare [pjanto'nare] *vt* to guard, watch over.

piantone [pjan'tone] *sm* **(a)** *(Mil)* orderly. **(b)** *(Aut)* steering column.

pianura [pja'nura] *sf (Geog)* plain.

piastra ['pjastra] *sf* **(a)** *(di metallo)* sheet, plate; *(di marmo, cemento)* slab; *(Elettr, Fot, di rivestimento)* plate; *(di fornello)* hotplate; ~ **di registrazione** tape deck. **(b)** *(moneta)* piastre.

piastrella [pjas'trɛlla] *sf* tile.

piastrellare [pjastrel'lare] *vt* to tile.

piastrina [pjas'trina] *sf* **(a)** *(Anat)* platelet. **(b):** ~ **di riconoscimento** *(Mil)* name tag, identification tag.

piattaforma [pjatta'forma] *sf, pl* **piatteforme** *(gen, fig, Pol)* platform; *(per tuffi)* board; ~ **continentale** *(Geog)* continental shelf; ~ **girevole** *(Tecn)* turntable; ~ **di lancio** *(Mil)* launching pad o platform; ~ **rivendicativa** document prepared by the unions in an industry to put forward their claims.

piattello [pjat'tello] *sm* clay pigeon; **tiro al** ~ clay pigeon shooting.

piattino [pjat'tino] *sm (di tazza)* saucer.

piatto, a [a [pjatto] **1** *ag (gen)* flat; *(fig: scialbo)* flat, dreary, dull. **2** *sm* **(a)** *(recipiente)* dish, plate; *(quantità)* plate(ful); ~ **fondo** soup plate; **un** ~ **di minestra** a plate of soup. **(b)** *(Culin)* course; **primo/secondo** ~ first/second course; ~ **forte** main course; ~ **del giorno** dish of the day, plat du jour. **(c)** *(Tecn)* plate; ~ **della bilancia** scale pan; ~ **del giradischi** turntable. **(d):** ~**i** *pl (Mus)* cymbals.

piazza ['pjattsa] *sf* **(a)** *(Archit)* square; ~ **del mercato** market place; **scendere in** ~ *(fig)* to take to the streets, demonstrate; **vendere sulla pubblica** ~ to sell in the market place; **fare** ~ **pulita** *(fig)* to make a clean sweep; **mettere in** ~ *(fig: rendere pubblico)* to make public. **(b)** *(Mil)*: ~ **d'armi** parade ground. **(c)** *(di letto, lenzuolo)*: **a una** ~ single; **a due** ~ double.

piazzaforte [pjattsa'forte] *sf, pl* **piazzeforti** *(Mil)* fortified town; *(fig)* stronghold.

piazzale [pjat'tsale] *sm (piazza)* open square; *(di autostrada, stazione)* service area.

piazzamento [pjattsa'mento] *sm (Sport)* place, placing.

piazzare [pjat'tsare] **1** *vt* **(a)** *(mettere: gen)* to place, put; *(: colpo)* to land, place. **(b)** *(Comm: vendere)*

to place, sell. **2:** ~**rsi** *vr* **(a)** *(Sport)*: ~**rsi bene** to finish with the leaders o in a good position; ~**rsi male** to do badly (in a race). **(b)** *(fig: piantarsi)*: **si è piazzato di fronte a me** he planted himself in front of me; **si è piazzato a casa mia e non si vuole più muovere** he's moved in at my place and refuses to budge.

piazzista, i, e [pjat'tsista] *sm/f (Comm)* salesman/woman, sales representative.

piazzola [pjat'tsɔla] *sf* **(a)** *(Aut)* lay-by. **(b)** *(Mil)* (gun) emplacement.

picca, che ['pikka] *sf (arma)* pike; *(Carte)*: ~**che** spades; **rispondere** ~**che a qn** *(fig)* to give sb a flat refusal.

piccante [pik'kante] *ag (sapore)* spicy, hot; *(fig: sconcio: barzelletta)* risqué; *(: dettaglio)* titillating, spicy.

piccarsi [pik'karsi] *vr* **(a)** *(pretendere)*: ~ **di fare qc** to claim to do sth. **(b)** *(impermalirsi)* to take offence.

picchettaggio [pikket'taddʒo] *sm* picketing.

picchettare [pikket'tare] *vt* **(a)** *(piantare paletti)* to stake out. **(b)** *(fare picchettaggio)* to picket.

picchetto [pik'ketto] *sm* **(a)** *(paletto)* stake, peg. **(b)** *(Mil)* picket; **essere di** ~ to be on picket duty; **ufficiale di** ~ orderly officer. **(c)** *(di scioperanti)* picket.

picchiare [pik'kjare] **1** *vt* **(a)** *(persona: colpire)* to hit; *(: dar botte a)* to beat (up), thrash; **lo picchiarono selvaggiamente** they gave him a savage beating; ~ **qn a sangue** to beat sb black and blue. **(b)** *(battere)* to beat; *(sbattere)* to bang, knock; ~ **i pugni sul tavolo** to bang o beat one's fists on the table; **ho picchiato la testa contro il muro** I banged my head against o off the wall. **2** *vi* **(a)** *(bussare)*: ~ **a** to knock on, knock at. **(b)** *(colpire)*: **ha picchiato sodo** he hit out hard; **il sole picchiava forte** the sun was beating down; ~ **in testa** *(Aut)* to knock; **picchia e ripicchia** by dint of perseverance.

picchiata [pik'kjata] *sf (Aer)* (nose-)dive; **scendere in** ~ to (nose-)dive.

picchiettare [pikkjet'tare] **1** *vi (gen)* to tap; *(pioggia)* to patter. **2** *vt (punteggiare)* to spot, dot, fleck.

picchio ['pikkjo] *sm (Zool)* woodpecker.

piccino, a [pit'tʃino] **1** *ag* little, small, tiny. **2** *sm/f (bambino)* small child, little boy/girl.

picciolo [pit'tʃɔlo] *sm (Bot)* stalk.

piccionaia [pittʃo'naja] *sf* **(a)** pigeon loft. **(b)** *(soffitta)* loft. **(c)** *(Teatro: loggione)*: **la** ~ the gods *sg*.

piccione [pit'tʃone] *sm* pigeon; **pigliare due** ~**i con una fava** to kill two birds with one stone.

picco, chi ['pikko] *sm (cima)* peak, summit; **una roccia a** ~ **sul mare** a rock rising straight from the sea; **colare a** ~ *(Naut, fig)* to sink.

piccolezza [pikko'lettsa] *sf* **(a)** *(dimensione)* smallness; *(fig: grettezza)* meanness, pettiness. **(b)** *(fig: inezia)* trifle; **è inutile che ti arrabbi per delle** ~**e simili** there's no point in getting annoyed over such trifles.

piccolo, a ['pikkolo] **1** *ag* **(a)** *(oggetto, misura etc)* small; *(vezzeggiativo)* little; **è** ~ **di statura** he is small, he is of small stature; **è più** ~ **di me** he is smaller than me; **com'è** ~ **il mondo!** it's a small world! **(b)** *(giovane)* young, small; *(vezzeggiativo)* little; **bambini** ~**i** young children; **mio fratello più** ~ my younger o little brother. **(c)** *(trascurabile: difetto)* slight; *(: regalo)* little; *(: dettaglio)* minor. **(d)** *(breve: viaggio, lettera)* short, little. **(e)** *(modesto)* small; *(: peg: meschino)* petty, mean; ~ **possidente** smallholder; ~**a borghesia** lower middle-classes, *(peg)* the petty bourgeoisie; **farsi** ~ *(umile)* to make o.s. small, to cower.

2 *sm/f (bambino)* (small) child, small boy/girl; **da** ~ as a child.

3 *sm*: **la gatta e i suoi** ~**i** the cat and her kittens; **la volpe e i suoi** ~**i** the vixen and her young *o* cubs; **nel mio** ~ in my own small way; **mi sembra il Colosseo in** ~ it's like a smaller scale version of the Colosseum.

piccone [pik'kone] *sm* pick(axe).

piccozza [pik'kɔttsa] *sf* ice-axe.

pick-up ['pikʌp] *sm inv (Elettr, di giradischi)* pick-up.

picnic [pik'nik] *sm inv* picnic.

pidocchio [pi'dɔkkjo] *sm* **(a)** *(Zool)* louse; **pieno di** ~**i** crawling with lice. **(b)** *(fig: persona gretta)* mean person.

pidocchioso, a [pidok'kjoso] *ag* **(a)** *(infestato)* lousy. **(b)** *(fig: taccagno)* mean, stingy, tight.

piè [pjɛ] *sm inv*: **a ogni** ~ **sospinto** *(fig)* at every step; **saltare a** ~ **pari** *(omettere)* to skip; **a** ~ **di pagina** at the foot of the page; **note a** ~ **di pagina** footnotes.

pied-à-terre [pjeta'tɛːr] *sm inv* pied-à-terre.

pied-de-poule ['pjɛdə'pul] *sm inv (tessuto)* hound's-tooth cloth.

piede ['pjɛde] *sm* **(a)** *(gen)* foot; **a** ~**i nudi** barefoot; **avere i** ~**i piatti** to have flat feet, be flat-footed; **andare/essere a** ~**i** to go/be on foot; **essere** *o* **stare in** ~**i** to stand, be standing; **alzarsi in** ~**i** to rise to one's feet, stand up; **rimanere a** ~**i** to be without transport; **ai** ~**i della montagna/del letto** at the foot *o* bottom of the mountains/of the bed; **da capo a** ~**i** from head to foot, from top to toe.

(b) *(di tavolo etc)* leg; *(di lampada)* base.

(c): ~ **di porco** *(Culin)* pig's trotter; *(Tecn)* crowbar; *(per forzare serrature)* jemmy.

(d) *(Metrica)* foot.

(e) *(fraseologia)*: **avere tutti ai propri** ~**i** to have the world at one's feet; **essere sul** ~ **di guerra** to be ready for action; **fare qc con i** ~**i** *(fig)* to do sth badly; **fuori dai** ~**i!** get out of the way!; **levarsi** *o* **togliersi dai** ~**i** to get out from under sb's feet; **è sempre tra i** ~**i** he's always in the way; **a** ~ **libero** *(Dir)* on bail; **io non ci ho mai messo** ~ I've never set foot in there; **mettere i** ~**i in testa a qn** *(fig)* to walk all over sb; **mettere qn sotto i** ~**i** to push sb around; **mettere qc in** ~**i** *(azienda etc)* to set sth up; **prender** ~ *(teoria, tendenza)* to gain ground; **puntare i** ~**i** *(fig)* to dig one's heels in; **ragionare con i** ~**i** to reason like a fool; **sentirsi mancare la terra sotto i** ~**i** to feel lost; **su due** ~**i** *(rispondere, accettare)* on the spot; **tenere in** ~**i** *(persona)* to keep on his *(o* her) feet; *(fig: ditta etc)* to keep going; **tenersi in** ~**i** to stand; **non sta in** ~**i** *(persona)* he can't stand; *(fig: scusa etc)* it doesn't hold water.

piedistallo [pjedis'tallo] *sm (anche fig)* pedestal.

piega, ghe ['pjɛga] *sf* **(a)** *(gen, Geol)* fold; *(Cucito)* pleat; *(della pelle)* (skin) fold; *(grinza)* crease; ~ **dei pantaloni** trouser crease; **è tutto pieno di** ~**ghe** *(spiegazzato)* it's all creased; **prendere una brutta** *o* **cattiva** ~ *(fig: persona)* to get into bad ways; *(: situazione)* to take a turn for the worse; **non fa una** ~ *(fig: ragionamento)* it's faultless; **non ha fatto una** ~ *(fig: persona)* he didn't bat an eyelid. **(b)** *(acconciatura)* set; **farsi (fare) la messa in** ~ to have one's hair set.

piegamento [pjega'mento] *sm* **(a)** *(vedi vt)* folding; bending. **(b)**: ~ **sulle gambe** *(Ginnastica)* knee-bend.

piegare [pje'gare] **1** *vt* **(a)** *(ripiegare: vestito, tovagliolo, foglio)* to fold (up); *(: sedia, tavola)* to fold up. **(b)** *(curvare: ramo, schiena)* to bend; ~ **il capo**

di fronte a qn *(fig)* to bow to sb; ~ **qn alla propria volontà** to bend sb to one's will. **2**: ~**rsi** *vr* **(a)** *(sedia, tavolo)* to fold (up). **(b)** *(curvarsi: persona)* to bend (over); *(: asse, superficie)* to sag; ~**rsi sotto il peso degli anni** to become bent with age; ~**rsi ai voleri di qn** to give in to sb's wishes; ~**rsi in due dalle risate/dal dolore** to double up with laughter/with pain.

piegatura [pjega'tura] *sf* **(a)** *(vedi vt)* folding; bending. **(b)** *(piega)* fold.

pieghettare [pjeget'tare] *vt* to pleat.

pieghevole [pje'gevole] *ag* **(a)** *(flessibile)* pliable, bendable; *(fig)* pliable, yielding. **(b)** *(ripiegabile)* folding; **sedia** ~ folding chair.

Piemonte [pje'monte] *sm* Piedmont.

piemontese [pjemon'tese] *ag, sm/f* Piedmontese.

piena ['pjɛna] *sf* **(a)** *(di corso d'acqua)* flood, spate; **essere in** ~ to be in flood *o* in spate. **(b)** *(fig: calca)* crowd, throng.

pienezza [pje'nettsa] *sf* fullness.

pieno, a ['pjɛno] **1** *ag* **(a)** *(gen)* full; *(giornata, vita)* full, busy; ~ **di** *(gen)* full of; *(idee)* bursting with; *(macchie)* covered in *o* with; **un bicchiere** ~ **d'acqua** a glass full of water *o* filled with water; **avere la pancia** ~**a** to be full; **il cinema era** ~ **zeppo (di gente)** the cinema was packed; **luna** ~**a** full moon.

(b) *(completo: successo, fiducia)* total, complete; **a tempo** ~ full-time; **avere** ~**i poteri** to have full powers; **nel** ~ **possesso delle sue facoltà** in full possession of his faculties.

(c) *(muro, parete)* solid.

(d) *(fraseologia)*: **a** ~**e mani** abundantly; **è una persona che dà a** ~**e mani** he (*o* she) is very generous; **a** ~**i voti** unanimously; **essere** ~ **di lavoro** to have a lot of work to do; **essere in** ~**a forma** to be in top form; ~ **come un uovo** full to overflowing; **in** ~ *(completamente: sbagliare)* completely; *(colpire, centrare)* bang *o* right in the middle; **in** ~ **inverno** in the depths of winter; **in** ~ **giorno** in broad daylight; **in** ~**a stagione** at the height of the season.

2 *sm* **(a)**: **fare il** ~ *(Aut)* to fill up; **il** ~ **per favore** fill her up, please.

(b) *(colmo)* height; **arrivò nel** ~ **della festa** he arrived when the party was in full swing.

pienotto, a [pje'nɔtto] *ag* plump, chubby.

pietà [pje'ta] *sf (gen)* pity, compassion; *(Rel)* piety; **sentire** *o* **provare** ~ **per qn** to pity sb, feel pity for sb; **muovere qn a** ~ to move sb to pity; **senza** ~ *(agire)* ruthlessly; *(persona)* pitiless, ruthless; **far** ~ to arouse pity; **come pianista fa** ~ he's a useless *o* terrible pianist.

pietanza [pje'tantsa] *sf* course, dish.

pietoso, a [pje'toso] *ag* **(a)** *(che prova pietà)* compassionate. **(b)** *(che fa pietà)* pitiful; **essere ridotto in uno stato** ~ to be reduced to a pitiful *o* sorry state; **ho fatto una figura** ~**a** I made an awful fool of myself.

pietra ['pjɛtra] **1** *sf* stone; **di** ~ stone *attr*; **avere un cuore di** ~ to be hard-hearted; **porre la prima** ~ *(fig: fondare)* to set up; **scagliare la prima** ~ *(fig)* to cast the first stone; **mettiamoci una** ~ **sopra** let bygones be bygones. **2**: ~ **dura** semiprecious stone; ~ **focaia** flint(stone); ~ **di paragone** *(fig)* touchstone; ~ **pomice** pumice stone; ~ **preziosa** precious stone, gem; ~ **dello scandalo** *(fig)* cause of scandal.

pietraia [pje'traja] *sf (mucchio)* pile of stones; *(terreno)* stony ground; *(cava)* stone quarry.

pietrificare [pjetrifi'kare] **1** *vt (anche fig)* to petrify. **2**: ~**rsi** *vr (anche fig)* to be petrified, be turned to stone.

pietrisco, schi [pje'trisko] *sm* crushed stone, road metal.

pietroso, a [pje'troso] *ag* stony.

pieve ['pjɛve] *sf* parish church.

pifferaio [piffe'rajo] *sm* piper.

piffero ['piffero] *sm* fife, pipe.

pigiama, i [pi'dʒama] *sm* pyjamas *pl.*

pigia pigia ['pidʒa 'pidʒa] *sm* throng, crowd.

pigiare [pi'dʒare] *vt (pulsante)* to press; *(uva)* to tread.

pigiatrice [pidʒa'tritʃe] *sf* wine press.

pigione [pi'dʒone] *sf* rent.

pigliare [piʎ'ʎare] *vt (fam)* = **prendere.**

piglio[1] ['piʎʎo] *sm*: **dar di ~ a qc** *(fig: incominciare)* to get to grips with sth.

piglio[2] ['piʎʎo] *sm (aspetto)* look, countenance.

pigmentazione [pigmentat'tsjone] *sf* pigmentation.

pigmento [pig'mento] *sm* pigment.

pigmeo, a [pig'mɛo] *ag, sm/f* pigmy.

pigna ['piɲɲa] *sf (Bot)* pine cone.

pignatta [piɲ'ɲatta] *sf* pot.

pignoleria [piɲɲole'ria] *sf* fastidiousness, fussiness.

pignolo, a [piɲ'ɲɔlo] **1** *ag* fussy, pernickety. **2** *sm/f* fussy person.

pignorare [piɲɲo'rare] *vt (Dir)* to distrain.

pigolare [pigo'lare] *vi* to cheep, chirp.

pigolio [pigo'lio] *sm* cheeping, chirping.

pigrizia [pi'grittsja] *sf* laziness.

pigro, a ['pigro] *ag (persona)* lazy, idle; *(mente)* slow; *(andatura)* lazy; *(stomaco)* sluggish; **in un ~ pomeriggio d'agosto** on a lazy August afternoon.

pila ['pila] *sf* **(a)** *(mucchio)* pile. **(b)** *(Elettr)* battery; **a ~, a ~e** battery-operated; **~ atomica** nuclear reactor. **(c)** *(fam: torcia)* torch.

pilastro [pi'lastro] *sm (Archit)* pillar, pilaster; *(fig: sostegno)* pillar, mainstay.

pillola ['pillola] *sf* pill; **la ~ (anticoncezionale)** the pill; **prendere la ~** to be on the pill.

pilone [pi'lone] *sm* **(a)** *(Elettr)* pylon; *(di ponte)* pier. **(b)** *(Rugby)* prop.

pilota, i, e [pi'lɔta] **1** *sm/f (Naut, Aer)* pilot; *(Aut)* driver; **~ automatico** automatic pilot; **secondo ~** co-pilot. **2** *ag inv* pilot *attr.*

pilotaggio [pilo'taddʒo] *sm*: **cabina di ~** flight deck.

pilotare [pilo'tare] *vt (Aer, Naut)* to pilot; *(Aut)* to drive.

piluccare [piluk'kare] *vt* to nibble at; **smettila di ~** stop nibbling (at) your food.

pimento [pi'mento] *sm* pimento, allspice.

pimpante [pim'pante] *ag* lively, full of beans.

pinacoteca, che [pinako'tɛka] *sf* art gallery.

pineta [pi'neta] *sf* pinewood.

ping-pong [ping 'pɔng] *sm* table tennis.

pingue ['pingwe] *ag (grasso)* fat; *(fertile)* rich, fertile; *(fig: abbondante: guadagno etc)* huge.

pinguedine [pin'gwedine] *sf (adiposità)* fatness.

pinguino [pin'gwino] *sm* **(a)** *(Zool)* penguin. **(b)** *(gelato)* chocolate-coated ice cream on a stick.

pinna ['pinna] *sf* **(a)** *(Zool)* fin; *(di cetacei)* flipper. **(b)** *(per nuotare)* flipper. **(c)** *(Naut)* stabilizer; *(Aer)* fin. **(d)** *(Anat)*: **~ nasale** ala of the nose.

pinnacolo [pin'nakolo] *sm* pinnacle.

pino ['pino] *sm (albero)* pine (tree); *(legno)* pine(wood).

pinolo [pi'nɔlo] *sm (seme)* pine seed.

pinta ['pinta] *sf* pint.

pinza ['pintsa] *sf* **(a)** *(gen)* pliers *pl*; *(tanaglia)* pincers *pl*; *(molle)* tongs *pl.* **(b)** *(Med)* forceps *pl.* **(c)** *(di granchio etc)* pincer.

pinzette [pin'tsette] *sfpl* tweezers.

pio, a ['pio] *ag (devoto)* pious, devout; *(misericordioso)* charitable.

pioggerella [pjoddʒe'rɛlla] *sf* drizzle.

pioggia, ge ['pjɔddʒa] *sf* **(a)** rain; **sorpreso dalla ~** caught in the rain; **sotto la ~** in the rain; **~ fine** drizzle; **~ scrosciante** driving rain. **(b)** *(fig: di regali, fiori)* shower; *(di insulti)* hail.

piolo [pi'ɔlo] *sm* peg, stake; *(di scala)* rung; **scala a ~i** ladder.

piombare[1] [pjom'bare] *vi (aus essere)* **(a)**: **~ su** *(sog: tigre, leone)* to pounce on; *(: rapaci)* to swoop (down) on; *(: esercito nemico)* to swoop down on, pounce on; **il falco piombò sulla preda** the hawk swooped (down) on its prey; **gli sono piombati addosso** they swooped down on him, they pounced on him; **piombò nella più cupa disperazione** he plunged *o* sank into blackest despair. **(b)** *(arrivare)* to arrive unexpectedly, turn up; **è piombato qui alle 2 di mattina** he turned up here at 2 in the morning.

piombare[2] [pjom'bare] *vt (pacco)* to seal (with lead); *(dente)* to fill.

piombatura [pjomba'tura] *sf* **(a)** *(vedi piombare*[2]*)* sealing; filling. **(b)** *(sigillo)* seal; *(di dente)* filling.

piombino [pjom'bino] *sm (sigillo)* (lead) seal; *(Pesca)* sinker (weight).

piombo ['pjombo] **1** *sm* **(a)** *(metallo)* lead; *(Pesca)* sinker; *(Tip)* type; **di ~** *(tubo etc)* lead *attr*; *(fig: cielo)* leaden; **soldatino di ~** tin soldier. **(b)** *(fraseologia)*: **a ~** *(muro etc)* plumb; **non essere a ~** to be out of plumb; **cadere di ~** to fall suddenly; **andare con i piedi di ~** to tread carefully; **avere/sentirsi addosso una cappa di ~** to have/ feel a great weight on one's shoulders; **riempire qn di ~** *(fig: di proiettili)* to fill sb with lead. **2** *ag inv* leaden, lead-coloured; **grigio ~** lead grey.

pioniere, a [pjo'njere] *sm/f* pioneer.

pioppo ['pjɔppo] *sm* poplar.

piovano, a [pjo'vano] *ag*: **acqua ~a** rainwater.

piovere ['pjɔvere] **1** *vb impers* to rain; **piove** it's raining; **piove a dirotto** *o* **a catinelle** it's pouring; **non ci piove sopra** *(fig)* there's no doubt about it. **2** *vi (aus essere)* *(fig: lettere, regali)* to pour in; *(: persona: arrivare all'improvviso)* to turn up, arrive unexpectedly.

piovigginare [pjoviddʒi'nare] *vb impers* to drizzle.

piovigginoso, a [pjoviddʒi'noso] *ag* drizzly.

piovosità [pjovosi'ta] *sf (Meteor)* rainfall.

piovoso, a [pjo'voso] *ag* rainy, wet.

piovra ['pjɔvra] *sf* octopus.

pipa ['pipa] *sf* pipe; *(quantità di tabacco)* pipe(ful); **fumare la ~** to smoke a pipe.

pipetta [pi'petta] *sf* pipette.

pipì [pi'pi] *sf (fam)* wee (wee), pee (pee); **fare (la) ~** to pee, to have a wee (wee).

pipistrello [pipis'trɛllo] *sm* **(a)** *(Zool)* bat. **(b)** *(mantello)* cloak.

piramide [pi'ramide] *sf* pyramid; **a ~** pyramid-shaped.

pirata, i [pi'rata] **1** *sm* pirate; *(fig: ladro)* swindler, shark; **~ dell'aria** hijacker; **~ della strada** hit-and-run driver. **2** *ag inv* pirate *attr.*

pirateria [pirate'ria] *sf* piracy; *(atto)* act of piracy.

pirex ['pireks] *sm*® pyrex®.

pirico, a, ci, che ['piriko] *ag*: **polvere** *f* **~a** gunpowder.

pirite [pi'rite] *sf* pyrite.

piroetta [piro'etta] *sf* pirouette.

piroettare [piroet'tare] *vi* to pirouette.

pirofila [pi'rɔfila] *sf (materiale)* heat-resistant glass; *(tegame)* heat-resistant dish.

pirofilo, a [pi'rɔfilo] *ag* heat-resistant.

piroga, ghe [pi'rɔga] *sf* dugout canoe.

piromane [pi'rɔmane] *sm/f* pyromaniac.

piromania [piroma'nia] *sf* pyromania.

piroscafo [pi'rɔskafo] *sm* steamship, steamer.

pirotecnica [piro'tɛknika] *sf* pyrotechnics *sg*.

pirotecnico, a, ci, che [piro'tɛkniko] *ag* pyrotechnical.

piscia ['piʃʃa] *sf (fam)* piss.

pisciare [piʃ'ʃare] *vi (fam)* to piss.

pisciatoio [piʃʃa'tojo] *sm (fam)* public loo.

piscina [piʃ'ʃina] *sf* swimming pool; *(pubblica, comunale)* (swimming) baths *pl*.

piscio ['piʃʃo] *sm (fam)* piss.

pisello [pi'sɛllo] *sm (Bot)* pea.

pisolino [pizo'lino] *sm* nap, snooze; **fare un** ~ to have a nap.

pista ['pista] **1** *sf* **(a)** *(traccia)* track, trail; **siamo su una buona** ~ we are on the right track; ~! get out of the way! **(b)** *(Radio)* (sound)track; **registrato a doppia** ~ double-tracked. **(c)** *(Ippica)* course; *(di stadio)* track; *(Pattinaggio)* rink; *(Sci)* (ski) run; *(di circo)* ring. **2:** ~ **(da ballo)** (dance) floor; ~ **di lancio** launching pad; ~ **di rullaggio** *(Aer)* taxiway; ~ **di volo** *(Aer)* runway; ~ **ciclabile** cycle track.

pistacchio [pis'takkjo] *sm (albero)* pistachio (tree); *(seme)* pistachio (nut).

pistillo [pis'tillo] *sm (Bot)* pistil.

pistola [pis'tɔla] *sf* pistol, gun; ~ **automatica** automatic (pistol); ~ **a spruzzo** *(per vernice)* spray gun; ~ **a tamburo** revolver.

pistolettata [pistolet'tata] *sf* pistol shot.

pistone [pis'tone] *sm (Tecn)* piston; *(Mus)* valve.

pitagorico, a, ci, che [pita'gɔriko] *ag* Pythagorean.

pitoccare [pitok'kare] *vi, vt* to beg.

pitocco, a, chi, che [pi'tɔkko] **1** *ag* mean, stingy. **2** *sm/f* miser, skinflint.

pitone [pi'tone] *sm* python.

pittore, trice [pit'tore] *sm/f* **(a)** *(artista)* painter. **(b)** *(imbianchino)* (house) painter, decorator.

pittoresco, a, schi, sche [pitto'resko] *ag* picturesque; *(modo di parlare)* colourful, vivid.

pittorico, a, ci, che [pit'tɔriko] *ag* pictorial, painting *attr*, of painting; **scuola** ~ a school of painting.

pittura [pit'tura] *sf* **(a)** *(arte)* painting; *(dipinto)* painting, picture; ~ **murale** mural. **(b)** *(vernice)* paint; ~ **fresca** wet paint.

pitturare [pittu'rare] **1** *vt* to paint; ~**rsi le labbra** to put on lipstick; ~**rsi le unghie** to paint one's nails. **2:** ~**rsi** *vr (fam: truccarsi)* to make up.

più [pju] **1** *av* **(a)** *(tempo)*: **non ...** ~ no longer, not ... any more; **non lavora** ~ he doesn't work any more, he no longer works; **non ha** ~ **detto una parola** he didn't say another word; **non c'è** ~ **bisogno che...** there's no longer any need for...; **non riesco** ~ **a sopportarla** I can't stand her any more *o* longer; **non ne posso** ~! I can't take any more!; **non ritornerò mai** ~ I'll never come back; **non è** ~ **così giovane** he is not as young as he was.

(b) *(quantità)*: **non ...** ~ no more; **non abbiamo** ~ **vino/soldi** we have no more wine/money, we haven't got any wine/money (left); **non ce n'è** ~ there isn't any left; **non ce n'è quasi** ~ there's hardly any; **non c'è** ~ **nessuno** there's no one left; **non c'è** ~ **niente da fare** there's nothing else to do.

(c) *(uso comparativo)* more; **noi lavoriamo** ~ **di loro** we work more *o* harder than they do; **mi piace** ~ **di ogni altra cosa al mondo** I like it better *o* more than anything else in the world;

non guadagna ~ **di me** he doesn't earn any more than me; **è** ~ **intelligente di te** he is more intelligent than you (are); **è** ~ **povero di te** he is poorer than you; **cammina** ~ **veloce di me** she walks more quickly than me *o* than I do; **ne voglio di** ~ I want some more; **due volte** ~ **grande del mio** twice as big as mine; **si fa sempre** ~ **difficile** it is getting more and more difficult; **è** ~ **furbo che capace** he's cunning rather than able; **è** ~ **che intelligente** he's clever to say the least; **parla** ~ **forte!** speak up!; **non ce n'erano** ~ **di 15** there were no more than 15; **ha** ~ **di 70 anni** he is over 70; **è a** ~ **di 10 km da qui** it's more than *o* over 10 km from here; ~ **di uno gli ha detto che...** several people have told him that...; **e chi** ~ **ne ha,** ~ **ne metta!** and so on and so forth!

(d): **in** ~, **di** ~ more; **ci sono 3 persone in** *o* **di** ~ there are 3 more *o* extra people; **mi ha dato 3 pacchetti in** ~ he gave me 3 more *o* extra packets; *(troppi)* he gave me 3 packets too many; **e in** ~ **fa anche...** and in addition to *o* on top of that he also...; **una volta di** ~ once more.

(e) *(uso superlativo)* most; **la** ~ **bella del mondo** the most beautiful in the world; **è il** ~ **bravo di tutta la classe** he's the best in the class; **è ciò che ho di** ~ **caro** it's the thing I hold dearest; **è il programma che guardo** ~ **spesso** it's the programme I watch most often; **fare qc il** ~ **in fretta possibile** to do sth as quickly as possible; **è quello che mi piace di** ~ it's the one I like the most *o* best; **ciò che mi ha colpito di** ~ the thing that struck me most.

(f) *(Mat)* plus; ~ **due** *(gradi)* plus two, two degrees above freezing; **2** ~ **2 fa 4** 2 plus 2 equals 4.

(g) *(fraseologia)*: ~ **o meno** more or less; **avrà** ~ **o meno 30 anni** he must be about 30; **sarò lì** ~ **o meno alle 4** I'll be there about 4 o'clock; **minuto** ~ **minuto meno** give or take a minute; **chi** ~ **chi meno hanno tutti contribuito** everybody made a contribution of some sort; **né** ~ **né meno come sua madre** just like her mother; ~ **che mai** more than ever; ~ **che altro** above all; **e per di** ~ and what's more; **tanto** ~ **che non sai neppure parlare l'inglese** all the more so as you can't even speak English; **urlava a** ~ **non posso** she was shouting at the top of her voice.

2 *ag* **(a)** *(comparativo)* more; *(superlativo)* the most; **ci vuole** ~ **sale** it needs more salt; **ci sono** ~ **macchine** there are more cars; **chi ha** ~ **francobolli di tutti?** who has the most stamps?; ~ **gente viene meglio è** the more the merrier.

(b) *(molto, parecchio)* several; **abbiamo discusso per** ~ **ore** we argued for several hours.

3 *prep* plus; **i parenti,** ~ **i figli** parents plus *o* and their children.

4 *sm* **(a)** *(Mat)* plus (sign).

(b): **il** ~ **ormai è fatto** the worst is over, most of it is already done; **il** ~ **delle volte** more often than not, generally; **ottenere il** ~ **possibile** to get the best possible; **tutt'al** ~ *o* **al** ~ **possiamo andare al cinema** if the worst comes to the worst we can always go to the cinema; **per lo** ~ = **perlopiù**.

(c): **i** ~ **the majority; i** ~ **pensano così** most people have the same opinion; **la reazione dei** ~ the reaction of the majority.

piuccheperfetto [piukkeper'fɛtto] *sm* past perfect (tense), pluperfect (tense).

piuma ['pjuma] *sf (di uccello)* feather; *(ornamento)* feather, plume; ~**e** *sfpl* down *sg*; *(piumaggio)* plumage, feathers *pl*; **leggero/morbido come una** ~ light/soft as a feather; **guanciale di** ~**e**

feather pillow; **cappello con le** ~**e** plumed hat.
piumaggio [pju'maddʒo] *sm* plumage, feathers *pl*.
piumato, a [pju'mato] *ag* plumed.
piumino [pju'mino] *sm (per letto)* eiderdown; *(: tipo danese)* duvet; *(giacca)* quilted jacket *(with goose-feather padding)*; *(per cipria)* powder puff; *(per spolverare)* feather duster.
piuttosto [pjut'tɔsto] *av* **(a)** *(preferibilmente)* rather; **prenderei** ~ **un'aranciata** I'd rather have an orangeade; ~ **che studiare farebbe di tutto** he'd do anything rather than study; **qui piove in primavera** ~ **che in autunno** here it rains in the spring rather than *o* instead of in the autumn; ~ **la morte!** I'd rather die! **(b)** *(alquanto)* quite, rather; **fa** ~ **freddo** it's rather *o* fairly cold; **sono** ~ **stanco** I'm quite *o* rather tired; **siamo** ~ **indietro con il lavoro** we're rather *o* somewhat behind with the work.
pivello [pi'vɛllo] *sm (fam)* greenhorn.
pizza ['pittsa] *sf* **(a)** *(Culin)* pizza; *(fig: persona o cosa noiosa)* bore; **che** ~**!** what a bore! **(b)** *(Cine)* reel.
pizzaiola [pittsa'jɔla] *sf (Culin)*: **alla** ~ *with tomato and oregano sauce.*
pizzeria [pittse'ria] *sf* pizzeria.
pizzicagnolo, a [pittsi'kaɲɲolo] *sm/f* specialist grocer.
pizzicare [pittsi'kare] **1** *vt* **(a)** *(con pinze etc)* to pinch; *(sog: ape)* to sting; *(: zanzara, pulce)* to bite; *(: sostanza)* to sting; **gli ho pizzicato un braccio** I pinched his arm; **ha un sapore che ti pizzica la gola** the taste makes your mouth tingle; **mi sono pizzicato un dito** I've nipped my finger. **(b)** *(fig: acciuffare)* to nab, pinch; *(: rubare)* to pinch. **(c)** *(Mus)* to pluck. **2** *vi* **(a)** *(prudere)* to itch, be itchy; **mi pizzica il naso** my nose is itching. **(b)** *(essere piccante)* to be spicy, be hot.
pizzicato [pittsi'kato] *sm (Mus)* pizzicato.
pizzicheria [pittsike'ria] *sf* delicatessen (shop).
pizzico, chi ['pittsiko] *sm (pizzicotto)* pinch, nip; *(piccola quantità)* pinch, dash; *(puntura: di ape etc)* sting; *(: di zanzara)* bite; **un** ~ **di sale** a pinch of salt; **non ha un** ~ **di pudore** he hasn't an ounce of common decency.
pizzicotto [pittsi'kɔtto] *sm* pinch, nip.
pizzo ['pittso] *sm* **(a)** *(merletto)* lace. **(b)** *(barbetta)* goatee (beard). **(c)** *(cima)* peak.
placare [pla'kare] **1** *vt* **(a)** *(persona)* to calm down, pacify; *(desiderio)* to placate, assuage; *(dolore, eccitazione)* to soothe; *(coscienza)* to salve; *(scrupoli)* to allay; ~ **la fame** to satisfy one's hunger; ~ **la sete** to quench one's thirst; ~ **gli animi** to appease the crowd. **2**: ~**rsi** *vr (rivolta, tempesta)* to die down; *(persona)* to calm down.
placca, che ['plakka] *sf* **(a)** *(gen, Elettr)* plate; *(con iscrizione)* plaque. **(b)** *(Med)*: ~ **dentaria** (dental) plaque.
placcare [plak'kare] *vt* **(a)** to plate; **placcato in oro/argento** gold/silver plated. **(b)** *(Rugby)* to tackle, bring down.
placenta [pla'tʃɛnta] *sf* placenta.
placidità [platʃidi'ta] *sf* calm, peacefulness.
placido, a ['platʃido] *ag (persona)* placid, calm; *(acque, vento, sera)* calm.
plafoniera [plafo'njɛra] *sf* ceiling light.
plagiare [pla'dʒare] *vt* **(a)** *(copiare)* to plagiarize. **(b)** *(Dir: influenzare)* to coerce.
plagio ['pladʒo] *sm* **(a)** *(letterario)* plagiarism. **(b)** *(Dir)* duress.
plaid [plɛd] *sm inv* (travelling) rug.
planare [pla'nare] *vi (Aer)* to glide.
plancia, ce ['plantʃa] *sf* **(a)** *(Naut)* bridge; *(: passerella)* gangway. **(b)** *(Aut: cruscotto)* dashboard.

plancton ['plankton] *sm* plankton.
planetario, a [plane'tarjo] **1** *ag* planetary. **2** *sm* **(a)** *(Astron)* planetarium. **(b)** *(Aut)* crown wheel.
plasma ['plazma] *sm* plasma.
plasmare [plaz'mare] *vt (anche fig)* to mould, shape.
plastica, che ['plastika] *sf* **(a)** *(materiale)* plastic; **di** ~ plastic. **(b)** *(Med)* plastic surgery. **(c)** *(Arte)* plastic art.
plastico, a, ci, che ['plastiko] **1** *ag* plastic; **in materiale** ~ plastic. **2** *sm* **(a)** *(Topografia)* plastic model. **(b)** *(esplosivo)* plastic explosive; **bomba al** ~ plastic bomb.
plastificare [plastifi'kare] *vt* to coat with plastic.
plastilina [plasti'lina] *sf* ® plasticine ®.
platano ['platano] *sm* plane tree.
platea [pla'tea] *sf* **(a)** *(Teatro)* stalls *pl*, orchestra *(Am)*; *(pubblico)* audience. **(b)** *(Geol)* shelf.
plateale [plate'ale] *ag (gesto, atteggiamento)* theatrical.
platino ['platino] *sm* platinum.
platonico, a, ci, che [pla'tɔniko] **1** *ag* platonic. **2** *sm* Platonist.
plausibile [plau'zibile] *ag* plausible.
plauso ['plauzo] *sm (fig)* approbation.
plebaglia [ple'baʎʎa] *sf* rabble, riffraff.
plebe ['plɛbe] *sf* common people; *(peg)* rabble, riffraff.
plebeo, a [ple'bɛo] *ag, sm/f* plebeian.
plebiscito [plebiʃ'ʃito] *sm* plebiscite.
plenario, a [ple'narjo] *ag* plenary.
plenilunio [pleni'lunjo] *sm* full moon.
plenipotenziario, a [plenipoten'tsjarjo] *ag, sm* plenipotentiary.
pleonasmo [pleo'nazmo] *sm* pleonasm.
plettro ['plɛttro] *sm* plectrum.
pleurite [pleu'rite] *sf* pleurisy.
P.L.I. *abbr di Partito Liberale Italiano.*
plico, chi ['pliko] *sm (pacco)* parcel; **in** ~ **a parte** under separate cover.
plotone [plo'tone] *sm (Mil)* platoon; ~ **d'esecuzione** firing squad.
plumbeo, a ['plumbeo] *ag (colore, cielo)* leaden.
plurale [plu'rale] **1** *ag* plural. **2** *sm* plural; **mettere al** ~ to put into the plural, pluralize.
pluralismo [plura'lizmo] *sm* pluralism.
pluralità [plurali'ta] *sf* plurality; *(maggioranza)* majority.
plusvalore [plusva'lore] *sm (Econ)* surplus value.
plutocrate [plu'tɔkrate] *sm/f* plutocrat.
plutonio [plu'tɔnjo] *sm* plutonium.
pluviale [plu'vjale] *ag* rain attr.
pluviometro [plu'vjɔmetro] *sm* rain gauge.
po' [pɔ] *sm vedi* **poco.**
pochezza [po'kettsa] *sf* insufficiency, shortage; *(fig: meschinità)* meanness, smallness.
poco, a, chi, che ['pɔko] **1** *av* **(a)** *(piccola quantità)* little, not much; *(numero limitato)* few, not many; **guadagna** ~ he doesn't earn much, he earns little; **si accontenta di** ~ he's easily satisfied; **dorme troppo** ~ he doesn't get enough sleep; **c'è** ~ **da ridere** there's nothing to laugh about.
(b) *(con ag, av)* (a) little, not very; **è** ~ **socievole** he's not very sociable; **è** ~ **più vecchia di lui** she's a little *o* slightly older than him; **sta** ~ **bene** he's not very well; **è** ~ **probabile** it's unlikely.
(c) *(tempo)*: ~ **dopo** shortly after(wards); ~ **fa** a short while ago; **il film dura** ~ the film doesn't last long; **manca** ~ **alla fine** it's almost *o*

nearly *o* more or less finished; **ci vediamo ~** we hardly ever see each other.

(d): **un po'** a little, a bit; **è un po' corto** it's a little *o* a bit short; **zoppica un po'** he limps a bit *o* slightly, he has a slight limp; **arriverà fra un po'** he'll arrive shortly *o* in a little while; **un po' prima del solito** a little earlier than usual; **fammi un po' vedere** let me have a look; **ha dormito un bel po'** he slept for quite a while.

(e) *(fraseologia)*: **a dir ~** to say the least; **eravamo in 30 a dir ~** there were at least 30 of us; **ha vinto di ~** he only just won; **~ a ~** bit by bit, little by little; **per ~ non cadevo** I almost fell; **~ male** never mind, it doesn't matter; **è una cosa da ~** it's nothing, it's of no importance; **una persona da ~** a worthless individual.

2 *ag indef* **(a)** *(quantità)* little, not much; *(numero)* few, not many; **~ denaro/vino** little *o* not much money/wine; **~che persone/idee** few *o* not many people/ideas; **c'era ~a gente** there were only a few people; **con ~a spesa** for a small outlay; **a ~ prezzo** at a low price, cheap; **è un tipo di ~che parole** he's a man of few words.

(b) *(in espressioni ellittiche: tempo)* a short time, a little while; *(: quantità)* **(a)** little; **ci vediamo fra ~** see you soon *o* shortly; **ne abbiamo ancora per ~** we'll only be a little longer; **l'ha comprato per ~** he bought it cheap; **basta ~ per farlo contento** it doesn't take much to make him happy.

3 *pron* **(a)** **(a)** little; **c'è chi ha molto tempo e chi ne ha ~** there are those who have a lot of time and those who have little.

(b): **~chi** *pl* few (people); **~chi la pensano come lui** few people think as he does; **~chi di noi** few of us.

4 *sm* **(a)** little; **vive del ~ che ha** she lives on the little she has.

(b): **un po'** a little; **un po' di zucchero** a little sugar; **un po' di silenzio!** let's have a bit of quiet!; **ha un po' di mal di testa** he has a slight headache; **ha un po' di influenza** he has a touch of flu; **un bel po' di denaro** quite a lot of money, a tidy sum; **facciamo un po' per uno** let's do a bit each; **quel po' po' di ladro!** that thieving rascal!

podere [po'dere] *sm (Agr)* farm.

poderoso, a [pode'roso] *ag* powerful.

podestà [podes'ta] *sm inv (nel fascismo)* mayor, podestà.

podio ['pɔdjo] *sm* podium, dais.

podismo [po'dizmo] *sm (Sport: marcia)* walking; *(: corsa)* running.

podista, i, e [po'dista] *sm/f (vedi sm)* walker; runner.

poema, i [po'ema] *sm* poem; **conciato così sei un ~** *(iro)* you look a pretty sight like that; **è tutto un ~!** *(complicato)* it's a real palaver!

poesia [poe'zia] *sf (Arte, produzione poetica)* poetry; *(singolo componimento)* poem; *(fig: di incontro etc)* magic; **scrivere ~e** to write poetry.

poeta, i [po'eta] *sm* poet.

poetare [poe'tare] *vi* to write poetry, write verse.

poetessa [poe'tessa] *sf* poet(ess).

poetica [po'etika] *sf* poetics *sg.*

poetico, a, ci, che [po'etiko] *ag* poetic(al); **la produzione ~a di Dante** Dante's poetical works.

poggiare [pod'dʒare] **1** *vt* to lean, rest; *(mettere)* to put; **non ~ i gomiti sulla tavola** don't put your elbows on the table. **2** *vi (anche fig)* to stand, rest.

poggiatesta [poddʒa'tɛsta] *sm inv (Aut)* headrest.

poggio ['pɔddʒo] *sm* hill, hillock.

poi ['pɔi] **1** *av* **(a)** *(gen)* then; *(più tardi)* later (on); **e ~, cos'è successo?** and then, what happened?; **e**

~ *(inoltre)* and besides; **non ne ho voglia e ~ sono stanco** I don't feel like it and what's more I'm tired; **devi ~ sapere che...** you should also know that...; **prima o ~** sooner or later; **~ te lo dico** I'll tell you later (on); **a ~** till later; **d'ora in ~** from now on; **da domani in ~** from tomorrow onwards.

(b) *(enfatico)*: **lui, ~, non c'entra proprio** he simply doesn't come into it, it's nothing at all to do with him; **questo ~ non me lo aspettavo** I just wasn't expecting this at all; **questa ~ è bella!** *o* **grossa!** that's a good one!

2 *sm*: **il ~** the future; **pensare al ~** to think of the future.

poiché [poi'ke] *cong* since, as.

pois [pwa] *sm inv* dot; **a ~** spotted, dotted; **bianco a ~ rossi** white with red dots.

poker ['pɔker] *sm* poker; **un ~ d'assi** four aces.

polacco, a, chi, che [po'lakko] **1** *ag* Polish. **2** *sm/f (persona)* Pole. **3** *sm (lingua)* Polish.

polare [po'lare] *ag* polar; **la stella ~** the Pole Star.

polarità [polari'ta] *sf* polarity.

polarizzare [polarid'dzare] **1** *vt (Fis)* to polarize; *(fig: attrarre)* to attract; **~ la propria attenzione su** to focus one's attention on. **2**: **~rsi** *vr*: **~rsi su** *(fig: attenzione, sguardo)* to focus on.

polca, che ['pɔlka] *sf* polka.

polemica, che [po'lɛmika] *sf* controversy, argument, polemic; **fare ~che** to be contentious.

polemico, a, ci, che [po'lɛmiko] *ag (gen)* controversial; *(peg)* contentious.

polemista, i, e [pole'mista] *sm/f* polemicist; *(peg)* contentious person.

polemizzare [polemid'dzare] *vi*: **~ (su qc)** to argue (about sth).

polenta [po'lɛnta] *sf (Culin)* sort of thick porridge made with maize flour; *(fig: persona lenta)* slowcoach.

polentone, a [polen'tone] *sm/f* slowcoach.

poliambulatorio [poliambula'tɔrjo] *sm (Med)* ≃ health centre.

policlinico, ci [poli'kliniko] *sm (Med)* general hospital, polyclinic.

policromo, a [po'likromo] *ag* many-coloured, polychrome.

poliestere [poli'ɛstere] *sm* polyester.

polifase [poli'faze] *ag (Elettr)* multiphase.

poligamia [poliga'mia] *sf* polygamy.

poligamo, a [po'ligamo] **1** *ag* polygamous. **2** *sm/f* polygamist.

poliglotto, a [poli'glɔtto] *ag, sm/f* polyglot.

poligono [po'ligono] *sm* **(a)** *(Mat)* polygon. **(b)**: **~ di tiro** rifle range.

polimero [po'limero] *sm* polymer.

poliomielite [poljomie'lite] *sf (Med)* polio(myelitis).

polipo ['pɔlipo] *sm (Zool, Med)* polyp.

polistirolo [polisti'rɔlo] *sm* polystyrene.

politecnico, a, ci, che [poli'tɛkniko] **1** *ag* polytechnic. **2** *sm* institution for further education providing courses in the physical sciences, technology and engineering.

politica, che [po'litika] *sf* **(a)** *(scienza, carriera)* politics *sg*; **fare ~** *(militante)* to be a political activist; *(come professione)* to be in politics; **darsi alla ~** to go into politics. **(b)** *(linea di condotta)* policy; *(modo di governare)* policies *pl*; **~ estera** foreign policy; **la ~ del governo** the government's policies; **~ aziendale** company policy; **~ dei prezzi** prices policy; **~ dei redditi** incomes policy.

politicante [politi'kante] *sm/f (peg)* petty politician.

politicizzare [politit∫id'dzare] *vt* to politicize.

politico, a, ci, che [po'litiko] **1** *ag* political; **uomo ~** politician; **scienze ~che** political sciences; **elezioni ~che** parliamentary election(s). **2** *sm* politician.

polivalente [poliva'lɛnte] *ag* polyvalent.

polizia [polit'tsia] *sf* **(a)** *(Amm)* police (force); *(poliziotti)* police *pl*; **agente di ~** policeman; **~ stradale** traffic police; **~ sanitaria/tributaria** health/tax inspectorate. **(b)** *(commissariato)* police station.

poliziesco, a, schi, sche [polit'tsjesko] *ag (indagine etc)* police *attr*; *(film, libro)* detective *attr*; *(peg: modi, maniere)* bullying.

poliziotto [polit'tsjɔtto] **1** *sm* policeman. **2** *ag inv*: **donna ~** policewoman; **cane ~** police dog.

polizza ['pɔlittsa] *sf* **(a)** *(Assicurazione)* policy; **~ d'assicurazione** insurance policy. **(b)** *(Comm)* bill, voucher; **~ di carico** bill of lading; **~ di pegno** pawn ticket.

pollaio [pol'lajo] *sm (edificio)* henhouse; *(recinto)* chicken run.

pollaiolo, a [polla'jɔlo] *sm/f* poulterer.

pollame [pol'lame] *sm* poultry.

pollastro [pol'lastro] *sm* young cock; *(fig: persona ingenua)* sucker *(fam)*.

polleria [pɔlle'ria] *sf* poulterer's (shop).

pollice ['pɔllit∫e] *sm* **(a)** *(Anat)* thumb; **avere il ~ verde** *(fig)* to have green fingers. **(b)** *(unità di misura)* inch.

polline ['pɔlline] *sm* pollen.

pollivendolo, a [polli'vendolo] *sm/f* poulterer.

pollo ['pollo] *sm* **(a)** chicken; *(fig: persona ingenua)* sucker *(fam)*. **(b)** *(fraseologia):* **conoscere i propri ~i** to know who one is dealing with; **far ridere i ~i** *(situazione, persona)* to be utterly ridiculous.

polmonare [polmo'nare] *ag* lung *attr*, pulmonary.

polmone [pol'mone] *sm* lung; **~ d'acciaio** iron lung; **avere buoni ~i** to have a good pair of lungs; **gridare a pieni ~i** to shout at the top of one's voice; **respirare a pieni ~i** to take deep breaths, breathe deeply.

polmonite [polmo'nite] *sf (Med)* pneumonia.

polo¹ ['pɔlo] *sm (Fis, Mat, Geog)* pole; **P~ sud/nord** South/North Pole; **abitiamo ai ~i opposti della città** we live at opposite ends of the city.

polo² ['pɔlo] *sm (sport)* polo.

Polonia [po'lɔnja] *sf* Poland.

polpa ['polpa] *sf* **(a)** *(di frutto)* pulp, flesh. **(b)** *(di carne)* lean meat.

polpaccio [pol'patt∫o] *sm (Anat)* calf.

polpastrello [polpas'trɛllo] *sm* fingertip.

polpetta [pol'petta] *sf (in tegame)* meatball; *(fritta)* rissole; **far ~e di qn** to make mincemeat of sb.

polpettone [polpet'tone] *sm (Culin)* meat loaf; **questo film/libro è un ~** this film/book is far too long and involved.

polpo ['polpo] *sm* octopus.

polposo, a [pol'poso] *ag* fleshy.

polsino [pol'sino] *sm* cuff.

polso ['polso] *sm* **(a)** *(Anat)* wrist; *(di camicia)* cuff; *(Med)* pulse. **(b)** *(fraseologia):* **avere ~** *(fig)* to be strong; **un uomo di ~** a man of nerve; **orologio da ~** wristwatch; **con le manette ai ~i** in handcuffs.

poltiglia [pol'tiʎʎa] *sf (miscuglio)* paste; *(di sassi e cotto)* mush, pulp; *(di fango e neve)* slush; **il riso si era ridotto in ~** the rice had cooked to a mush; **ridurre qn in ~** to make mincemeat of sb.

poltrire [pol'trire] *vi (rimanere a letto)* to have a long lie(-in); *(oziare)* to loaf about, idle.

poltrona [pol'trona] *sf* armchair; *(Teatro)* seat in the stalls; **starsene in ~** *(fig)* to laze about; **aspi-**

rare alla ~ di direttore generale to aspire to the managing directorship.

poltroncina [poltron't∫ina] *sf (Teatro)* seat in the back stalls.

poltrone, a [pol'trone] **1** *sm/f* loafer, idler. **2** *ag* lazy, idle.

polvere ['polvere] **1** *sf (gen)* powder; *(pulviscolo)* dust; **caffè in ~** powdered coffee; **sapone in ~** soap powder; **fare ~** to raise clouds of dust; **ridurre in ~** to pulverize; **buttare o gettare la ~ negli occhi a qn** *(fig)* to pull the wool over sb's eyes; **far mangiare la ~ a qn** *(fig)* to leave sb far behind. **2: ~ di ferro** iron filings *pl*; **~ d'oro** gold dust; **~ pirica o da sparo** gunpowder; **~ di stelle** stardust.

polveriera [polve'rjera] *sf (Mil)* (gun)powder magazine; *(fig: zona calda)* powder keg.

polverificio [polveri'fit∫o] *sm* explosives factory.

polverina [polve'rina] *sf (gen, Med)* powder; *(gergo: cocaina)* snow.

polverizzare [polverid'dzare] **1** *vt (legno, ferro, fig: nemico)* to pulverize; *(liquido)* to spray; *(record)* to smash. **2: ~rsi** *vr* to turn to dust.

polverone [polve'rone] *sm* thick cloud of dust.

polveroso, a [polve'roso] *ag* dusty, covered with dust.

pomata [po'mata] *sf* ointment.

pomello [po'mɛllo] *sm* **(a)** *(impugnatura)* knob. **(b)** *(gota)* cheek.

pomeridiano, a [pomeri'djano] *ag* afternoon *attr*; **nelle ore ~e** in the afternoon.

pomeriggio [pome'riddʒo] *sm* afternoon; **il ~, di ~** in the afternoon; **nel primo/tardo ~** in the early/late afternoon; **alle 2 di ~** at 2 o'clock in the afternoon, at 2 pm; **tutti i ~i** every afternoon; **tutte le domeniche ~** every Sunday afternoon; **domani/sabato ~** tomorrow/Saturday afternoon.

pomice ['pomit∫e] *sf*: **(pietra) ~** pumice (stone).

pomiciare [pomi't∫are] *vi (fam: sbaciucchiarsi)* to neck.

pomo ['pomo] *sm (frutto)* apple; *(oggetto sferico)* knob; *(di sella)* pommel; **~ d'Adamo** *(Anat)* Adam's apple; **~ della discordia** *(Mitologia)* apple of discord; *(fig)* bone of contention.

pomodoro [pomo'dɔro] *sm (frutto)* tomato; *(pianta)* tomato plant; **spaghetti al ~** spaghetti with tomato sauce.

pompa¹ ['pompa] *sf* **(a)** *(fasto)* pomp; **mettersi in ~ magna** *(fig)* to get all dressed up. **(b):** **(impresa di) ~e funebri** undertaker's, funeral parlour.

pompa² ['pompa] *sf (Tecn)* pump; **~ antincendio** fire hose; **~ di benzina** petrol pump; *(distributore)* petrol station.

pompare [pom'pare] *vt* to pump; *(estrarre)* to pump out; *(gonfiare d'aria)* to pump up; *(fig: esagerare)* to exaggerate, blow up.

pompelmo [pom'pɛlmo] *sm (albero)* grapefruit (tree); *(frutto)* grapefruit.

pompiere [pom'pjere] *sm* fireman; **chiamare i ~i** to call the fire brigade.

pompon [pɔ̃'pɔ̃] *sm inv* pompon.

pomposo, a [pom'poso] *ag (cerimonia)* full of pomp (and circumstance); *(fig: discorso, atteggiamento)* pompous.

ponderare [ponde'rare] *vt* to ponder (over), think over; **~ i pro ed i contro** to weigh up the pros and cons; **fu una decisione ben ponderata** it was a carefully considered decision.

ponderazione [ponderat'tsjone] *sf* thought, consideration.

ponente [po'nɛnte] *sm (direzione)* west; *(vento)* west wind.

ponte ['ponte] **1** *sm* (*Edil, Med, Mil*) bridge; (*Naut*) deck; (*: anche:* ~ **di comando**) bridge; (*Aut*) axle; **vivere sotto i** ~**i** to be a tramp; **tagliare** *o* **rompere i** ~**i con qn** to break off relations with sb; **fare il** ~ to make a long weekend of it; **abbiamo fatto un** ~ **di 3 giorni** we had 3 days off. **2:** ~ **aereo** airlift; ~ **di barche** (*Mil*) pontoon bridge; ~ **di coperta** (*Naut*) upper deck; ~ **levatoio** drawbridge; ~ **radio** radio link; ~ **sospeso** suspension bridge. **3** *ag inv:* **governo** ~ caretaker government; **legge** ~ interim law.

pontefice [pon'tefitʃe] *sm* pontiff.

ponticello [ponti'tʃɛllo] *sm* (*di occhiali, Mus*) bridge.

pontificare [pontifi'kare] *vi* (*anche fig*) to pontificate.

pontificato [pontifi'kato] *sm* (*Rel*) papacy.

pontificio, a, ci, cie [ponti'fitʃo] *ag* pontifical; **Stato P**~ Papal State.

pontile [pon'tile] *sm* jetty.

popeline ['pɔpelin] *sm* poplin.

popò [po'pɔ] *sm* (*linguaggio infantile: sedere*) botty.

popolano, a [popo'lano] **1** *ag* of the people; **saggezza** ~**a** popular lore. **2** *sm/f* man/woman of the people.

popolare[1] [popo'lare] **1** *vt* to populate. **2:** ~**rsi** *vr* (*diventare popolato*) to become populated; ~**rsi di** (*affollarsi*) to become crowded with.

popolare[2] [popo'lare] *ag* (*gen, fig*) popular; (*quartiere*) working-class; **canzone** ~ folk song; **case** ~**i** council houses; **manifestazione** ~ mass demonstration; **repubblica** ~ people's republic.

popolarità [popolari'ta] *sf* popularity.

popolazione [popolat'tsjone] *sf* population.

popolino [popo'lino] *sm* (*peg*): **il** ~ the masses, the common people.

popolo ['pɔpolo] *sm* (*gen*) people; (*classe*): **il** ~ the (common) people; **il** ~ **italiano** the Italian people, the Italians; **a furor di** ~ by popular acclaim.

popoloso, a [popo'loso] *ag* heavily populated, populous.

popone [po'pone] *sm* melon.

poppa[1] ['pɔppa] *sf* (*Anat*) breast.

poppa[2] ['pɔppa] *sf* (*Naut*) stern; **a** ~ aft, astern; **andare col vento in** ~ to sail before the wind.

poppante [pop'pante] *sm/f* unweaned infant; (*fig: inesperto*) whippersnapper.

poppare [pop'pare] *vt* to suck.

poppata [pop'pata] *sf* (*allattamento*) feed; **l'ora della** ~ feeding time.

poppatoio [poppa'tojo] *sm* baby's bottle.

porcaio [por'kajo] *sm* (*anche fig*) pigsty.

porcaro [por'karo] *sm* swineherd.

porcellana [portʃel'lana] *sf* porcelain, china; (*oggetto*) piece of porcelain.

porcellino [portʃel'lino] *sm* piglet; ~ **d'India** guinea pig.

porcello, a [por'tʃɛllo] **1** *sm* (*Zool*) piglet. **2** *sm/f* (*peg*) pig.

porcellone, a [portʃel'lone] *sm/f* (*peg*) pig.

porcheria [porke'ria] *sf* (*gen*) dirt, muck, filth; (*azione disonesta*) dirty trick; (*cosa fatta male*) (load of) rubbish *o* trash; **mangia un sacco di** ~ he eats a lot of rubbish; **non si fanno queste** ~**e!** you shouldn't behave like that!

porchetta [por'ketta] *sf* (*Culin*) roast sucking pig.

porcile [por'tʃile] *sm* (*anche fig*) pigsty.

porcino, a [por'tʃino] **1** *ag:* **occhi** ~**i** piggy eyes. **2** *sm* (*anche: fungo* ~) boletus.

porco, a, ci, che ['pɔrko] **1** *sm* (*Zool*) pig; (*Culin*) pork. **2** *sm/f* (*peg*) pig; **un vecchio** ~ a dirty old man. **3** *ag:* ~**a miseria!**, ~ **Giuda!** (*fam*) bloody hell!

porcospino [porkos'pino] *sm* porcupine; (*fig: persona*): **è chiuso come un** ~ he doesn't come out of his shell easily.

porgere ['pɔrdʒere] *vt* to hand, give; (*tendere*) to hold out; ~ **la mano a qn** to hold out one's hand to sb; (*fig*) to give sb a helping hand, lend sb a hand; ~ **l'altra guancia** (*fig*) to turn the other cheek; ~ **orecchio** *o* **ascolto** to pay attention, listen.

pornografia [pornogra'fia] *sf* pornography.

pornografico, a, ci, che [porno'grafiko] *ag* pornographic.

poro ['pɔro] *sm* (*Anat*) pore; (*forellino*) hole.

poroso, a [po'roso] *ag* porous.

porpora ['pɔrpora] **1** *ag, sm* (*colore*) crimson. **2** *sf* (*stoffa, simbolo*) purple.

porre ['porre] **1** *vt* **(a)** (*mettere*) to put; (*collocare*) to place; (*posare*) to lay (down), put (down); ~ **le fondamenta di** (*edificio*) to lay the foundations of; ~ **le basi di** (*fig*) to lay the foundations of, establish; **abbiamo posto le basi per una futura collaborazione** we have laid the foundations for future cooperation; **fu posto al comando del reggimento** he was placed in command of the regiment; ~ **la propria fiducia in qn** to place one's trust in sb; ~ **fine** *o* **termine a qc** to put an end *o* a stop to sth; ~ **lo sguardo** *o* **gli occhi su** to look at.
  (b) (*condizioni*) to lay down, set out, state; (*problema*) to pose; (*questione*) to raise; ~ **una domanda (a qn)** to ask sb a question, put a question to sb.
  (c) (*supporre*) to suppose; **poniamo che...** let's suppose that...; **posto che...** supposing that..., on the assumption that... .
  2: porsi *vr:* **porsi in cammino** to set out *o* forth; **porsi al lavoro** to get down to work; **porsi a sedere** to sit down; **porsi in salvo** to save o.s.

porro ['porro] *sm* **(a)** (*Bot*) leek. **(b)** (*Med*) wart.

porta ['pɔrta] **1** *sf* (*gen*) door; (*soglia*) doorstep; (*apertura*) doorway; (*di fortezza, città, Sci*) gate; (*Calcio, Rugby etc*) goal; **a** ~**e chiuse** (*processo*) in camera; **abitare** ~ **a** ~ **con qn** to live right next door to sb; **vendere** ~ **a** ~ to sell from door to door; **indicare la** ~ **a qn** (*fig*) to show sb the door; **mettere qn alla** ~ to throw sb out; **prendere la** ~ **ed andarsene** (*fig*) to walk out the door; **sbattere** *o* **chiudere la** ~ **in faccia a qn** (*anche fig*) to slam the door in sb's face; **suonare alla** ~ to ring the (door)bell; **suonano alla** ~ there's somebody at the door; **trovare tutte le** ~**e chiuse** (*fig*) to find the way barred; **cacciamo questo problema dalla** ~ **e rientra dalla finestra** there's no getting rid of this problem; **esce dalla** ~ **e rientra dalla finestra** there's no getting rid of him; **l'inverno è alle** ~**e** (*fig*) winter is upon us; **tirare in** ~ (*Sport*) to take a shot at goal.
  2: ~ **di sicurezza** emergency exit; ~ **di servizio** tradesmen's entrance; ~ **stagna** watertight door.

portabagagli [portaba'gaʎʎi] *sm inv* **(a)** (*facchino*) porter. **(b)** (*Aut*) boot, trunk (*Am*); (*: sul tetto*) roof rack; (*in treno, corriera: retina*) luggage rack.

portabandiera [portaban'djera] *sm/f inv* (*anche fig*) standard bearer.

portabottiglie [portabot'tiʎʎe] *sm inv* (*scaffale*) bottle rack; (*per trasporto*) bottle carrier.

portacarte [porta'karte] *sm inv* paper holder, paper rack.

portacenere [porta'tʃenere] *sm inv* ashtray.

portachiavi [porta'kjavi] *sm/f inv* (*anello*) key ring; (*astuccio*) key case.

portacipria [porta'tʃipria] *sm inv* (powder) compact.

portaerei [porta'ɛrei] *sf inv* (*Naut*) aircraft carrier.

portafiammiferi [portafjam'miferi] *sm inv* match holder.

portafinestra [portafi'nɛstra] *sf, pl* **portefinestre** French window.

portafiori [porta'fjori] *sm inv* flower stand.

portafoglio [porta'fɔʎʎo] *sm* (a) *(per soldi)* wallet; **mettere mano al ~** *(fig)* to put one's hand in one's pocket. (b) *(Fin, Pol)* portfolio.

portafortuna [portafor'tuna] **1** *sm inv* lucky charm. **2** *ag inv* lucky.

portagioie [porta'dʒɔje] *sm inv*, **portagioielli** [portadʒo'jɛlli] *sm inv* jewel box.

portale [por'tale] *sm (Archit)* portal.

portalettere [porta'lettere] *sm/f inv* postman/woman, mailman *(Am)*.

portamento [porta'mento] *sm* bearing, carriage.

portamonete [portamo'nete] *sm inv* purse.

portante [por'tante] *ag (muro)* loadbearing, supporting.

portantina [portan'tina] *sf* (a) *(sedia)* sedan chair. (b) *(barella)* stretcher.

portaombrelli [portaom'brɛlli] *sm inv* umbrella stand.

portapacchi [porta'pakki] *sm inv (di moto, bicicletta)* luggage rack.

portapenne [porta'penne] *sm inv* pen holder; *(astuccio)* pencil case.

portare [por'tare] **1** *vt* (a) *(trasportare)* to carry; **portava il pacco sottobraccio** he was carrying the parcel under his arm; **questa macchina porta 4 persone** this car can carry 4 people; **puoi portarmi la valigia?** can you carry my case for me?; **si porta dietro un sacco di roba** he carries masses of stuff round with him; **~ via** to take away; *(rubare)* to take; **leggere queste bozze porta via molto tempo** reading these proofs takes (up) a lot of time; **porta bene i suoi anni** he's wearing well; **ognuno ha la propria croce da ~** we each have our cross to bear.
(b) *(consegnare, recare)* to take; **porta il libro in cucina!** *(vicino a chi parla)* bring the book into the kitchen!; *(lontano da chi parla)* take the book into the kitchen!; **portami un bicchiere!** bring me a glass!; **posso portarli a casa?** can I bring (o take) them home?; **~ qc alla bocca** to lift o put sth to one's lips; **il suo intervento ha portato dei vantaggi** his intervention has brought certain advantages; **~ fortuna/sfortuna** *o* **male a qn** to bring (good) luck/bad luck to sb.
(c) *(condurre)* to take; *(sog: strada)* to take, lead; *(fig: indurre)*: **~ qn a (fare) qc** to lead sb to (do) sth; **dove porta questa strada?** where does this road lead?; **where does this road take you?**; **~ i bambini a spasso** to take the children for a walk; **il vento ci sta portando al largo** the wind is carrying us out to sea; **dove ti porterà tutto questo?** where will all this lead you?; **~ qn alla disperazione** to lead sb to despair; **stiamo portando avanti il discorso sul disarmo** we are pursuing the topic of disarmament.
(d) *(indossare: scarpe, vestito)* to wear, have on; **non porto più queste scarpe** I don't wear these shoes any more; **porta i capelli lunghi** he wears his hair long, he has long hair.
(e) *(avere: nome, firma)* to have, bear; **porta il nome di suo nonno** he is called after his grandfather; **il documento porta la tua firma** the document has o bears your signature; **Firenze porta ancora i segni dell'alluvione** Florence still bears the signs of the flood; **non gli porto rancore** I don't bear him a grudge.
2: **~rsi** *vr (recarsi)* to go; **la polizia si è portata sul luogo del disastro** the police went to the scene of the disaster.

portariviste [portari'viste] *sm inv* magazine rack.

portasapone [portasa'pone] *sm inv* soap dish.

portasigarette [portasiga'rette] *sm inv* cigarette case.

portaspazzolino [portaspattso'lino] *sm inv* toothbrush holder.

portaspilli [portas'pilli] *sm inv* pin cushion.

portata [por'tata] *sf* (a) *(Culin)* course; **un pranzo di 7 ~e** a 7-course lunch. (b) *(di veicolo)* load capacity, carrying capacity. (c) *(di missile)* range; **a ~ di mano** within reach; **essere alla ~ di tutti** *(conoscenza)* to be within everybody's grasp; *(prezzo)* to be within everybody's means. (d) *(fig: importanza)* importance, significance; **di grande ~** of great importance. (e) *(di fiume)* (rate of) flow.

portatile [por'tatile] *ag* portable.

portato, a [por'tato] *ag*: **essere ~ per** *(studio, matematica etc)* to have a bent for.

portatore, trice [porta'tore] *sm/f* (a) *(di messaggio, assegno)* bearer; **pagabile al ~** payable to the bearer. (b) *(Med)*: **~ (sano)** carrier.

portatovagliolo [portatovaʎ'ʎɔlo] *sm* napkin ring.

portauova [porta'wɔva] *sm inv*, **portauovo** [porta'wɔvo] *sm inv* egg cup; *(scatola)* egg box.

portavoce [porta'votʃe] *sm/f inv* spokesman/woman.

portello [por'tɛllo] *sm (di portone)* door; *(Naut)* hatch.

portento [por'tɛnto] *sm* wonder, marvel.

portentoso, a [porten'toso] *ag* wonderful, marvellous.

porticato [porti'kato] *sm* portico.

portico ['portiko] *sm (Archit)* porch, portico; *(riparo)* lean-to.

portiera [por'tjɛra] *sf (Aut)* door.

portiere, a [por'tjɛre] *sm/f* (a) *(portinaio)* concierge, caretaker; *(di hotel)* porter. (b) *(Sport)* goalkeeper.

portinaio, a [porti'najo] *sm/f* concierge, caretaker.

portineria [portine'ria] *sf* caretaker's lodge.

porto[1] ['porto] **1** *sm* port, harbour; **andare** *o* **giungere in ~** *(fig)* to come to a successful conclusion; **condurre qc in ~** to bring sth to a successful conclusion; **questa casa è un ~ di mare** people are always coming and going in this house. **2**: **~ fluviale** river port; **~ franco** free port; **~ marittimo** seaport; **~ militare** naval base; **~ di scalo** port of call.

porto[2] ['porto] *sm* (a) *(Comm: trasporto)* carriage; **franco di ~** carriage free. (b): **~ d'armi** licence to carry firearms.

porto[3] ['porto] *sm inv (vino)* Port.

porto[4], **a** ['porto] *pp di* **porgere**.

Portogallo [porto'gallo] *sm* Portugal.

portoghese [porto'gese] *ag, sm/f, sm* Portuguese *(inv)*.

portone [por'tone] *sm* entrance.

portuale [portu'ale] **1** *ag* port *attr*, dock *attr*; **lavoratori ~i** dockers, dock workers. **2** *sm* docker, dock worker.

porzione [por'tsjone] *sf (gen)* portion, share; *(Culin)* helping.

posa ['pɔsa] *sf* (a) *(atteggiamento)* pose; *(: affettato)* posing; **teatro di ~** photographic studio; **mettersi in ~** to pose; **assumere ~e da grandonna** to act the lady; **è tutta una ~** *(fig)* it's just an act. (b) *(Fot)* exposure. (c) *(riposo)*: **lavorare senza ~** to work without a break. (d) *(collocazione)* laying, placing.

posacenere [posa'tʃenere] *sm inv* ashtray.

posare [po'sare] **1** *vt (gen)* to put (down); *(piatto,* *vassoio etc)* to lay (down), put (down); *(fondamenta, cavo)* to lay; ~ **gli occhi su** to look at; **posalo contro il muro** stand *o* put it against the wall. **2** *vi* **(a)** *(ponte, edificio, teoria):* ~ **su** to rest on. **(b)** *(Fot, Arte)* to pose, sit; *(atteggiarsi)* to pose; **posa a grande scrittore** *(fig)* he poses as a great writer. **3:** ~**rsi** *vr (uccello)* to alight; *(aereo)* to land, touch down; *(sguardo)* to settle, fix.

posata [po'sata] *sf* piece of cutlery; ~**e** cutlery *sg*.

posatezza [posa'tettsa] *sf (di persona)* composure; *(di discorso)* balanced nature.

posato, a [po'sato] *ag (persona)* steady, level-headed; *(comportamento)* steady, sober; *(discorso)* balanced.

poscritto [pos'kritto] *sm* postscript.

positiva [pozi'tiva] *sf (Fot)* (positive) print.

positivo, a [pozi'tivo] *ag, sm* positive.

posizione [pozit'tsjone] *sf (gen, fig)* position; **prendere** ~ **a favore di/contro** to take up a position in favour of/against; **devi prendere una** ~ you must take a stand; **farsi una** ~ to make one's way in the world; **è arrivato in prima/seconda** ~ *(Sport)* he arrived first/second; **luci di** ~ *(Aut)* sidelights.

posologia [pozolo'dʒia] *sf* dosage, directions *pl* for use.

posporre [pos'porre] *vt* **(a)** *(rimandare)* to postpone, put off. **(b)** *(subordinare)* to subordinate, place after.

posposto, a [pos'posto] *pp di* **posporre**.

possedere [posse'dere] *vt (gen)* to have; *(fortuna, qualità)* to possess; *(casa, terreno)* to own; *(diploma)* to hold; *(lingua etc: conoscere a fondo)* to have a thorough knowledge of; **era posseduto dal demone** he was possessed by the devil.

possedimento [possedi'mento] *sm* **(a)** *(proprietà terriera)* property, estate. **(b)** *(di uno Stato: territorio)* possession.

posseditrice [possedi'tritʃe] *sf vedi* **possessore**.

possente [pos'sɛnte] *ag* strong, powerful.

possessivo, a [posses'sivo] *ag (gen, Gram)* possessive.

possesso [pos'sɛsso] *sm* **(a)** *(gen, Dir)* possession; **essere in** ~ **di qc** to be in possession of sth; **prendere** ~ **di qc** to take possession of sth; **entrare in** ~ **dell'eredità** to come into one's inheritance. **(b):** ~**i** *pl (possedimenti)* property *sg*.

possessore, posseditrice [posses'sore, possedi'tritʃe] *smf* possessor, owner; *(di carica, diploma)* holder.

possibile [pos'sibile] **1** *ag (gen)* possible; *(progetto, piano)* feasible; **non mi sarà** ~ **farlo** I can't *o* won't be able to do it; **è** ~ **che arrivi più tardi** he may *o* might arrive later; **cerca di venir presto, se** ~ try to come early, if possible *o* if you can; **ha trovato tutte le scuse** ~**i e immaginabili per non venire** he came up with every excuse imaginable for not coming; **vieni prima** ~ come as soon as possible; **fallo meglio** ~ do it as best you can; **porta meno roba** ~ bring as little as possible; **non è** ~**!** *(irrealizzabile)* it's not possible!; *(falso)* that can't be true!; ~**?** *(sorpresa)* well I never! **2** *sm*: **fare il** ~ to do everything possible *o* everything in one's power; **nei limiti del** ~ as far as possible.

possibilità [possibili'ta] *sf inv (gen)* possibility; **c'è sempre la** ~ **che cambi idea** there's always the possibility *o* chance that he'll change his mind; **avere la** ~ **di fare qc** to be able to do sth; **non ha** ~ **di salvezza** there's no hope of escape for him; **nella mia posizione non ho avuto la** ~ **di aiutarlo** in my position I couldn't assist him *o* I had no

means of assisting him. **(b):** ~ *pl (mezzi)* means; **vivere secondo le proprie** ~ *(finanziarie)* to live according to one's means; **nei limiti delle nostre** ~ in so far as we can.

possibilmente [possibil'mente] *av* if possible; **ti telefono** ~ **domani** I'll phone you tomorrow if I can.

possidente [possi'dente] *smf* property owner.

post... [pɔst] *pref* post... .

posta ['pɔsta] *sf* **(a)** *(lettere)* mail; *(servizio)* postal service, mail service; *(ufficio)* post office; **c'è** ~ **per me?** are there any letters for me?, is there any mail for me?; **perché non lo mandi per** ~**?** why don't you send it by post?; **ministro delle P**~**e e Telecomunicazioni** Postmaster General; **impiegato delle P**~**e** post office clerk; ~ **aerea** airmail; **piccola** ~ *(su giornale)* letters to the editor, letters page. **(b)** *(Giochi: somma in palio)* stake(s); **la** ~ **in gioco è troppo alta** *(fig)* there's too much at stake. **(c)** *(Caccia)* hide; **fare la** ~ **a qn** *(fig)* to lie in wait for sb. **(d):** **a bella** ~ *(apposta)* on purpose.

postagiro [posta'dʒiro] *sm* postal giro.

postale [pos'tale] **1** *ag (servizio, vaglia)* postal; *(casella, impiegato)* post office *attr; (nave, treno)* mail *attr;* **cassetta** ~ letter box; **timbro** ~ postmark. **2** *sm (treno)* mail train; *(nave)* mail boat; *(furgone)* mail van.

postazione [postat'tsjone] *sf (Mil)* emplacement.

postbellico, a, ci, che [post'bɛlliko] *ag* postwar *attr.*

postdatare [postda'tare] *vt* to postdate.

posteggiare [posted'dʒare] *vt* to park.

posteggiatore, trice [posteddʒa'tore] *smf* car-park attendant.

posteggio [pos'teddʒo] *sm* **(a)** *(di taxi)* rank; *(parcheggio custodito)* attended car park. **(b)** *(di rivenditore)* pitch.

postelegrafonico, a, ci, che [postelegra'fɔniko] *ag* postal, telegraphic and telephonic.

posteri ['pɔsteri] *smpl* posterity *sg;* **i nostri** ~ our descendants.

posteriore [poste'rjore] **1** *ag* **(a)** *(parte: di oggetto)* back *attr,* rear; *(zampe)* hind. **(b)** *(tempo)* later; **questi avvenimenti sono** ~**i alla mia partenza** these events occurred after my departure. **2** *sm (euf: sedere)* behind, bottom.

posterità [posteri'ta] *sf* posterity.

posticcio, a, ci, ce [pos'tittʃo] *ag (capelli, barba)* false.

posticipare [postitʃi'pare] *vt:* ~ **(di)** to postpone (by).

postilla [pos'tilla] *sf* marginal note.

postino, a [pos'tino] *smf* postman/woman, mailman *(Am).*

posto¹, a ['posto] *pp di* **porre**.

posto² ['posto] *sm* **(a)** *(luogo)* place; **non è un** ~ **adatto ad una ragazza** it's no place for a girl; **un** ~ **di villeggiatura** a holiday *o* tourist spot, a resort; **i pompieri sono accorsi sul** ~ the firemen rushed to the spot; **lo faremo sul** ~ *o* **quando saremo sul** ~ we'll do it when we get there. **(b)** *(spazio)* room, space; **non c'è più** ~ **in macchina** there's no more room in the car; **fate** ~**!** make way!; ~ **(a sedere)** seat; **prender** ~ to take a seat; ~ **in piedi** *(Teatro, in autobus)* standing room; **ci sono 20** ~**i letto in quell'albergo** they can sleep 20 in that hotel; **vai pure al** ~ *(scolaro)* go and sit down; **mi tieni il** ~ **in fila?** will you keep my place in the queue?; **una macchina a 5** ~**i** a 5-seater car. **(c)** *(impiego)* job, post; ~ **di lavoro** job; **ha un** ~ **di segretaria** she works as *o* has a job as a secretary, she has a secretarial post.

(d) *(posizione)*: primo/secondo ~ *(in classifica)* first/second place; **è arrivato al primo** ~ he arrived first.

(e) *(Mil)* post; ~ **di blocco** *(alla frontiera)* frontier post; *(di polizia)* roadblock; **ognuno ai** ~**i di combattimento!** action stations!

(f) *(fraseologia)*: **al** ~ **tuo ci andrei** I'd go if I were in your shoes; **l'hanno assunto al** ~ **tuo** they employed him instead of you; **essere a** ~ *(in ordine: stanza)* to be tidy; *(: persona)* to be neat and tidy; **è gente a** ~ they are very respectable (people); **mettere a** ~ *(riordinare)* to tidy (up), put in order; *(faccende: sistemare)* to straighten out; **mettere a** ~ **qn** *(fig)* to sort sb out; **sa stare al suo** ~ *(fig)* he knows his place; **tenere la lingua a** ~ to hold one's tongue; **tieni le mani a** ~! keep your hands to yourself!; **per me non ha la testa tanto a** ~! I don't think he's all there!; **è ora che metti la testa a** ~ it's time you got yourself sorted out.

postoperatorio, a [postopera'tɔrjo] *ag (Med)* postoperative.

postribolo [pos'tribolo] *sm (poet)* brothel.

postscriptum [post'skriptum] *sm inv* postscript.

postulato [postu'lato] *sm (Mat, Filosofia)* postulate.

postumo, a ['pɔstumo] **1** *ag* posthumous. **2**: ~**i** *smpl* consequences, after-effects; **soffrire i** ~**i della sbornia** to have a hangover.

potabile [po'tabile] *ag* drinkable; **acqua** ~ drinking water.

potare [po'tare] *vt (albero da frutta)* to prune; *(siepe)* to trim.

potassio [po'tassjo] *sm* potassium.

potatura [pota'tura] *sf* pruning.

potente [po'tente] **1** *ag (gen)* powerful; *(efficace: medicina, veleno)* potent; *(argomenti)* potent, forceful; **è** ~ **all'interno dell'azienda** he has a lot of influence in the company. **2** *sm*: **i** ~**i** the mighty, the powerful.

potenza [po'tentsa] *sf* **(a)** *(potere, influenza)* power, influence; *(forza: fisica, di sentimenti)* strength; *(efficacia: di medicina, veleno)* potency; *(di argomenti, onde, pugni, armi)* force; **la** ~ **della stampa** the power of the press; ~ **militare** military might *o* strength; **le Grandi P**~**e** the Great Powers. **(b)** *(Fis, Mat)* power; **all'ennesima** ~ to the nth degree; **è un idiota all'ennesima** ~ he's a complete and utter idiot.

potenziale [poten'tsjale] *ag, sm* potential.

potenziamento [potentsja'mento] *sm* development.

potenziare [poten'tsjare] *vt* to develop.

potere[1] [po'tere] *sm (gen)* power; **non ho nessun** ~ **su di lui** I have no power *o* influence over him; **avere il** ~ **di fare qc** *(capacità)* to have the power *o* ability to do sth; *(autorità)* to have the authority *o* power to do sth; **ha il** ~ **di rovinare sempre tutto** he always manages to ruin everything; **essere al** ~ *(Pol)* to be in power *o* in office; **il quarto** ~ the fourth estate, the press; ~ **d'acquisto** purchasing power; ~ **esecutivo** executive power.

potere[2] [po'tere] **1** *vb aus (nei tempi composti prende l'ausiliare del verbo che accompagna)* **(a)** *(possibilità, capacità)* can, to be able to; **non posso venire** I can't come; **non è potuto venire** he couldn't come, he was unable to come; **non potrà mai farlo da solo** he'll never be able to do it alone; **non ho potuto farlo** I couldn't *o* wasn't able *o* was unable to do it; **come hai potuto fare una cosa simile?** how could you do a thing like that?; **a più**

non posso *(correre)* as fast as one can; *(urlare)* as loud as one can.

(b) *(permesso)* can, may; **posso entrare?** can *o* may I come in?; **potrei parlarti?** could *o* may I speak to you?; **si può sapere dove sei stato?** where on earth have you been?

(c) *(eventualità)*: **può anche esser vero** it may *o* might *o* could even be true; **potrebbe avere trent'anni** he must be about thirty; **può accadere di tutto** anything can happen; **si può fare** it can be done; **può darsi che** *o* **può essere che non venga** he may not *o* might not come.

(d) *(augurio)*: **potessimo trovare un po' di pace!** if only we could get a little peace!

(e) *(suggerimento)*: **potresti almeno ringraziare!** you could at least say thank you!

2 *vt* can; **puoi molto per me** you can do a lot for me; **non ha potuto niente** he could do nothing; **non ne posso più!** I can't take any more!

potestà [potes'ta] *sf (Dir)* power, authority.

poveraccio, a, ci, ce [pove'rattʃo] *sm/f* poor devil.

povero, a ['pɔvero] **1** *ag* **(a)** *(gen)* poor; *(stile, scusa)* weak; *(raccolto)* poor, scanty; *(vegetazione)* sparse; **minerale** ~ **di ferro** ore with a low iron content, ore poor in iron; **aria** ~**a di ossigeno** air low in oxygen; **paese** ~ **di risorse** country short of *o* lacking in resources. **(b)** *(fraseologia)*: **essere** ~ **in canna** to be as poor as a church mouse; ~ **illuso!** poor fool!; ~ **piccolo!** poor little thing!; **sei un** ~ **stupido!** you're a stupid fool!; ~ **me!** poor me!; **in parole** ~**e** in plain language; ~ **di spirito** half-wit; ~ **te se lo fai!** just you dare!; **il mio** ~ **marito** my poor late husband. **2** *sm/f* poor man/woman; **i** ~**i** the poor.

povertà [pover'ta] *sf (vedi ag)* poverty; weakness; scantiness; sparseness.

pozione [pot'tsjone] *sf* potion.

pozza ['pottsa] *sf (pozzanghera)* puddle; **una** ~ **di sangue** a pool of blood.

pozzanghera [pot'tsangera] *sf* puddle.

pozzetto [pot'tsetto] *sm* **(a)** *(di fognatura)* shaft. **(b)** *(Naut)* well-deck.

pozzo ['pottso] *sm (di acqua, petrolio)* well; *(di miniera)* shaft; ~ **nero** cesspit; **essere un** ~ **di scienza** to be a walking encyclopaedia *o* a mine of information; **essere un** ~ **senza fondo** *(ghiottone)* to be a bottomless pit.

prammatica [pram'matika] *sf* custom; **essere di** ~ to be customary.

prammatico, a, ci, che [pram'matiko] *ag* pragmatic.

pranzare [pran'dzare] *vi* to (have) lunch; **siamo andati a** ~ **fuori** we went out for lunch.

pranzo ['prandzo] *sm* lunch; ~ **di nozze** wedding breakfast.

prassi ['prassi] *sf* normal procedure.

prateria [prate'ria] *sf* prairie.

pratica, che ['pratika] *sf* **(a)** *(attività)* practice; **mettere in** ~ **qc** to put sth into practice; **ho messo in** ~ **i tuoi consigli** I have acted on your advice; **in** ~ in practice. **(b)** *(esperienza)* (practical) experience; **far** ~ **presso un avvocato** to be articled to a solicitor; **acquistare** ~ to gain experience; **ha fatto** ~ **presso un altro falegname** he was trained by another carpenter; **non ho** ~ **di queste cose** I have no experience of this. **(c)** *(Amm)* file, dossier; **fare le** ~**che per** to do the paperwork for. **(d)** *(usanza)* practice; ~**che illecite** *(abortive)* dishonest practices; ~**che religiose** religious practices.

praticabile [prati'kabile] *ag* practicable.

praticamente [pratika'mente] *av* **(a)** *(in modo*

pratico) in a practical way, practically. **(b)** *(quasi)* practically, almost.

praticante [prati'kante] *ag* practising.

praticare [prati'kare] *vt* **(a)** *(esercitare: arte, medicina)* to practise, practice *(Am)*; *(calcio, tennis)* to play; *(nuoto, scherma etc)* to go in for, do. **(b)** *(frequentare: persona)* to associate with, mix with; *(: luogo)* to frequent. **(c)** *(apertura, incisione)* to make; *(buco)* to pierce, bore; ~ **uno sconto** to give a discount.

praticità [pratitʃi'ta] *sf* practicality, practicalness; **per** ~ for practicality's sake.

pratico, a, ci, che ['pratiko] *ag* **(a)** *(non teorico, realista)* practical; **avere senso** ~ to be practical; **all'atto** ~ in practice. **(b)** *(comodo: gen)* practical; *(: strumento)* handy; **mi è più ~ venire di pomeriggio** it's more convenient for me to come in the afternoon; **è ~ avere i negozi così vicino** it's handy o convenient to have the shops so near. **(c): essere** ~ **di** *(motori etc)* to be good with; **è ~ del mestiere** he knows his trade; **è ~ del luogo** he knows the place well.

prato ['prato] *sm* meadow; ~ **all'inglese** lawn.

preallarme [preal'larme] *sm* warning (signal).

prealpino, a [preal'pino] *ag* of the Pre-Alps.

preambolo [pre'ambolo] *sm* preamble; **senza tanti** ~**i** without beating about the bush.

preannunciare [preannun'tʃare] *etc* = **preannunziare** *etc*.

preannunziare [preannun'tsjare] *vt* to give advance notice of; **le nubi preannunziavano la tempesta** the clouds heralded the storm.

preannunzio [prean'nuntsjo] *sm* advance warning.

preavvisare [preavvi'zare] *vt* to give advance notice of.

preavviso [preav'vizo] *sm* (advance) notice; *(Dir)* notice; **senza** ~ without notice; **3 giorni di** ~ 3 days' notice.

prebellico, a, ci, che [pre'bɛlliko] *ag* prewar *attr*.

precarietà [prekarje'ta] *sf* precariousness.

precario, a [pre'karjo] **1** *ag* **(a)** *(gen)* precarious; *(salute)* shaky; **in** ~**e condizioni economiche** in a precarious financial state. **(b)** *(Scol)* temporary, without tenure. **2** *sm/f (Scol)* temporary member of staff.

precauzionale [prekauttsjo'nale] *ag* precautionary.

precauzione [prekaut'tsjone] *sf* **(a)** *(cautela)* caution, care. **(b)** *(misura)* precaution; **prendere** ~**i** to take precautions.

precedente [pretʃe'dɛnte] **1** *ag* previous; **il giorno** ~ the previous day, the day before; **la pagina** ~ the previous o preceding page. **2** *sm* precedent; **senza** ~**i** unprecedented; ~**i penali** *(Dir)* criminal record.

precedenza [pretʃe'dɛntsa] *sf (gen)* priority; **dare** ~ **assoluta a qc** to give sth top priority; **dare la** ~ *(Aut)* to give way; **avere la** ~ *(Aut)* to have right of way.

precedere [pre'tʃedere] *vt* to precede, go *(o come)* before.

precettare [pretʃet'tare] *vt (Mil)* to call up, draft *(Am)*.

precetto [pre'tʃɛtto] *sm (gen)* precept; *(Mil)* call-up notice, draft notice *(Am)*.

precettore [pretʃet'tore] *sm* tutor.

precipitare [pretʃipi'tare] **1** *vt (gettare)* to hurl down, throw down; *(affrettare)* to hasten; ~ **una decisione** to make a hasty decision; **non precipitiamo le cose** let's not rush o precipitate things. **2** *vi (aus essere)* **a** *(cadere)* to fall; *(: aereo)* to crash; ~ **da una rupe/in un burrone** to fall off a

cliff/down a ravine; **la situazione sta precipitando** *(fig)* the situation is getting out of control. **(b)** *(Chim)* to precipitate. **3:** ~**rsi** *vr (affrettarsi)* to rush.

precipitato, a [pretʃipi'tato] **1** *ag* hasty. **2** *sm (Chim)* precipitate.

precipitazione [pretʃipitat'tsjone] *sf* precipitation; **con** ~ hastily.

precipitevolmente [pretʃipitevol'mente] *av* hastily.

precipitoso, a [pretʃipi'toso] *ag (partenza, decisione, passo)* hasty; *(fuga)* headlong.

precipizio [pretʃi'pittsjo] *sm* precipice; **scogli a** ~ **sul mare** cliffs rising sheer from the sea; **essere sull'orlo del** ~ *(fig)* to be on the edge of a precipice.

precipuo, a [pre'tʃipuo] *ag* main, principal.

precisamente [pretʃiza'mente] *av (gen)* precisely; *(con esattezza)* exactly.

precisare [pretʃi'zare] *vt* to clarify, make clear; **vi preciseremo la data in seguito** we'll let you know the exact date later; **ci tengo a** ~ **che...** I must point out that....

precisazione [pretʃizat'tsjone] *sf* clarification; **mi dai delle** ~**i riguardo al giorno del tuo arrivo?** can you give me some more information about when you'll be arriving?

precisione [pretʃi'zjone] *sf* precision; **strumenti di** ~ precision instruments.

preciso, a [pre'tʃizo] **1** *ag (esatto)* precise, accurate; *(ordine, idee, piano)* precise, definite; **in quel** ~ **istante** at that very moment; **queste sono le sue** ~**e parole** these were his very words; **sono le 4** ~**e** it's exactly 4 o'clock; **il tuo cappello è** ~ **al mio** your hat is exactly the same as o identical to mine. **2** *av* exactly, precisely.

precludere [pre'kludere] *vt* to preclude.

precluso, a [pre'kluzo] *pp di* **precludere.**

precoce [pre'kɔtʃe] *ag (morte)* premature, untimely; *(decisione)* hasty, premature; *(bambino)* precocious.

precocità [prekotʃi'ta] *sf (di morte)* untimeliness; *(di bambino)* precociousness, precocity.

preconcetto [prekon'tʃɛtto] **1** *ag* preconceived. **2** *sm* preconceived idea, prejudice.

preconizzare [prekonid'dzare] *vt* to predict, foretell.

precorrere [pre'korrere] *vt* to anticipate; ~ **i tempi** to be ahead of one's time.

precorritore, trice [prekorri'tore] *sm/f* precursor, forerunner.

precorso, a [pre'korso] *pp di* **precorrere.**

precursore [prekur'sore] *sm* precursor, forerunner.

preda ['prɛda] *sf* prey; **uccello da** ~ bird of prey; **essere in** ~ **a** *(paura, terrore etc)* to become o fall prey to; **era in** ~ **all'ira** he was beside himself with rage; **era in** ~ **al panico** he was in a panic.

predare [pre'dare] *vt* to plunder.

predatore, trice [preda'tore] **1** *ag* predatory. **2** *sm/f (Zool)* predator; *(predone)* plunderer.

predecessore, a [predetʃes'sore] *sm/f* predecessor.

predella [pre'dɛlla] *sf (di cattedra)* platform; *(di altare)* predella.

predellino [predel'lino] *sm (di vettura)* step, footboard.

predestinare [predesti'nare] *vt* to predestine.

predestinazione [predestinat'tsjone] *sf* predestination.

predetto, a [pre'detto] **1** *pp di* **predire. 2** *ag* aforesaid, aforementioned.

predica, che ['prɛdika] *sf (Rel)* sermon; *(fig)*

lecture, talking-to; **fare una** ~ to preach a sermon; **fare una** ~ **a qn** (*fig*) to give sb a lecture *o* a talking-to.

predicare [predi'kare] 1 *vt* to preach. 2 *vi* (*anche fig*) to preach; **predica bene e razzola male** he doesn't practise what he preaches.

predicativo, a [predika'tivo] *ag* predicative.

predicato [predi'kato] *sm* predicate.

predicatore [predika'tore] *sm* preacher.

predicazione [predikat'tsjone] *sf* preaching.

predicozzo [predi'kɔttso] *sm* lecture, talking-to; **fare un** ~ **a qn** to lecture sb.

prediletto, a [predi'letto] 1 *pp di* **prediligere**. 2 *ag* (*figlio, allievo*) favourite; (*amico*) best, closest. 3 *sm* favourite; **il** ~ **della mamma** mummy's pet.

predilezione [predilet'tsjone] *sf* partiality, predilection.

prediligere [predi'lidʒere] *vt* to prefer, have a predilection for.

predire [pre'dire] *vt* (*gen*) to predict; (*Meteor*) to forecast; ~ **il futuro** to tell *o* predict the future.

predisporre [predis'porre] 1 *vt* to get ready, prepare; ~ **qn a qc** to prepare sb for sth. 2: **predisporsi** *vr*: **predisporsi a qc** to prepare o.s. for sth.

predisposizione [predisposit'tsjone] *sf* (*Med*) predisposition; (*attitudine*) bent, aptitude; **avere** ~ **alla musica** to have a bent for music.

predisposto, a [predis'posto] *pp di* **predisporre**.

predizione [predit'tsjone] *sf* prediction.

predominante [predomi'nante] *ag* predominant.

predominare [predomi'nare] *vi* (*prevalere*) to predominate; (*eccellere*) to excel.

predominio [predo'minjo] *sm* (*il prevalere*) predominance; (*dominio*) domination; (*: fig*) sway; **avere il** ~ (*prevalere*) to be predominant.

predone [pre'done] *sm* marauder.

preesistente [preezis'tɛnte] *ag* pre-existent.

preesistenza [preezis'tɛntsa] *sf* pre-existence.

preesistere [pree'zistere] *vi* (*aus* **essere**) to pre-exist.

preesistito, a [preezis'tito] *pp di* **preesistere**.

prefabbricato, a [prefabbri'kato] 1 *ag* prefabricated. 2 *sm* prefab, prefabricated house.

prefazione [prefat'tsjone] *sf* preface, foreword.

preferenza [prefe'rɛntsa] *sf* preference; **di** ~ preferably, by preference; **a** ~ **di** rather than; **dare la** ~ **a qn/qc** to prefer sb/sth; **non ho** ~**e** I have no preferences either way, I don't mind; **qui non si fanno** ~**e** there is no favouritism here.

preferenziale [preferen'tsjale] *ag* preferential; **corsia** ~ (*Aut*) bus and taxi lane.

preferibile [prefe'ribile] *ag*: ~ **(a)** preferable (to), better (than); **sarebbe** ~ **andarsene** it would be better to go.

preferibilmente [preferibil'mente] *av* preferably.

preferire [prefe'rire] *vt* to prefer; **preferisco la città alla campagna** I prefer the town to the countryside; **preferirei non farlo** I'd rather not do it, I'd prefer not to do it; **preferirei morire piuttosto che...** I'd rather die than...; **cosa preferisci, tè o caffè?** what would you like, tea or coffee?

preferito, a [prefe'rito] *ag, sm/f* favourite.

prefettizio, a [prefet'tittsjo] *ag* prefectorial.

prefetto [pre'fetto] *sm* prefect.

prefettura [prefet'tura] *sf* prefecture.

prefiggersi [pre'fiddʒersi] *vr*: ~ **qc** (*scopo, meta*) to set o.s. sth.

prefigurare [prefigu'rare] *vt* (*simboleggiare*) to foreshadow; (*prevedere*) to foresee.

prefigurazione [prefigurat'tsjone] *sf* prefiguration.

prefisso, a [pre'fisso] 1 *pp di* **prefiggere**. 2 *sm* (*Gram*) prefix; (*Telec*) code.

pregare [pre'gare] 1 *vt* (*Rel*) to pray to; (*supplicare*) to beg; **l'ho pregato di venire** I asked him to come; **i passeggeri sono pregati di...** passengers are requested to...; **non si fa** ~ **due volte** he doesn't wait to be asked twice; **si fa** ~ **un po' troppo** he plays hard to get; **ti prego, lasciami in pace** please leave me alone; **la prego, stia comodo** please don't get up. 2 *vi* to pray.

pregevole [pre'dʒevole] *ag* (*persona, azione*) praiseworthy; (*oggetto, opera*) valuable.

preghiera [pre'gjɛra] *sf* (*Rel*) prayer; (*richiesta*) request; (*supplica*) plea, entreaty.

pregiarsi [pre'dʒarsi] *vr* (*frm*): ~ **di fare qc** to be honoured to do sth; **mi pregio di farle sapere che...** I am pleased *o* honoured to inform you that... .

pregiato, a [pre'dʒato] *ag* (*opera*) valuable; (*tessuto*) fine; (*valuta*) strong; **vino** ~ vintage wine; **Pregiatissimo Signor G. Agnelli** (*sulle buste*) G. Agnelli Esquire.

pregio ['prɛdʒo] *sm* (*di persona*) worth; (*di oggetto*) value; **avere molti** ~**i** (*persona*) to have a lot of good qualities; **i** ~**i artistici di un'opera** the artistic merit of a work; **il** ~ **di questo sistema è...** the merit of this system is...; **oggetto di** ~ valuable object.

pregiudicare [predʒudi'kare] *vt* (*compromettere*): ~ **qc** to jeopardize sth, put sth in jeopardy; ~ **la propria salute** to endanger one's health.

pregiudicato, a [predʒudi'kato] *sm/f* (*Dir*) previous offender; **ci sono troppi** ~**i in giro** there are too many criminals around.

pregiudizio [predʒu'dittsjo] *sm* (*opinione errata*) prejudice; (*superstizione*) superstition; **avere dei** ~**i contro** *o* **nei confronti di qn** to be prejudiced *o* biased against sb; **è un** ~ **largamente diffuso** it's a widely held superstition.

pregno, a ['prɛɲɲo] *ag* (*fig*): ~ **di** (*odio, passione*) filled with.

prego ['prɛgo] *escl* (*a chi ringrazia*) don't mention it!, you're welcome!, not at all!; (*invitando qn ad accomodarsi*) please sit down!; (*invitando qn ad andare prima*) after you!; ~, **si accomodi** (*entri*) come in please; (*si sieda*) take a seat please; **posso prenderlo?** — ~! can I take it? — please do!; — ~? pardon?, sorry?

pregustare [pregus'tare] *vt* to look forward to; **pregustava il piacere della vendetta** he savoured the idea of vengeance.

preistoria [preis'tɔrja] *sf* prehistory; **fin dalla** ~ from time immemorial.

preistorico, a, ci, che [preis'tɔriko] *ag* prehistoric; (*fig scherz*) antediluvian.

prelato [pre'lato] *sm* prelate.

prelavaggio [prela'vaddʒo] *sm* prewash.

prelazione [prelat'tsjone] *sf* (*Dir*) pre-emption; **avere il diritto di** ~ **su qc** to have the first option on sth.

prelevamento [preleva'mento] *sm* (*Banca*) withdrawal; (*di merce*) picking up, collection.

prelevare [prele'vare] *vt* (*Banca*) to withdraw; (*campione: di sangue etc*) to take; (*merce*) to collect, pick up; (*pregiudicato*) to pick up.

prelibato, a [preli'bato] *ag* delicious.

prelievo [pre'ljɛvo] *sm* (*Banca*) withdrawal; (*di merce*) collection; (*di tasse*) levying; **fare un** ~ **di sangue** to take a blood sample.

preliminare [prelimi'nare] 1 *ag* preliminary. 2 *sm*: ~**i** *pl* preliminaries; **i** ~**i della pace** the preliminaries to peace.

preludere [pre'ludere] *vi*: ~ **a (a)** (*preannunciare*:

crisi, guerra, temporale) to herald, be a sign of. **(b)** *(introdurre: dibattito etc)* to introduce, be a prelude to.

preludio [pre'ludjo] *sm (Mus, fig)* prelude; *(introduzione)* introduction.

preluso, a [pre'luzo] *pp di* **preludere.**

pré-maman [pre ma'mã] **1** *ag inv* maternity *attr.* **2** *sm inv* maternity dress.

prematrimoniale [prematrimo'njale] *ag* premarital.

prematuro, a [prema'turo] **1** *ag (gen)* premature; *(morte)* untimely. **2** *sm/f* premature baby.

premeditare [premedi'tare] *vt* to premeditate, plan; **omicidio premeditato** premeditated murder.

premeditazione [premeditat'tsjone] *sf* premeditation.

premere ['prɛmere] **1** *vt (gen)* to press; ~ **il grilletto** to pull the trigger; **premi forte!** press hard! **2** *vi* **(a):** ~ **su** *(gen)* to press on; *(pedale)* to press down on. **(b)** *(fig: stare a cuore)*: **è una faccenda che mi preme molto** it's a matter which I am very concerned about; **gli premeva (di) terminare il lavoro** he was anxious to finish the job.

premessa [pre'messa] *sf (introduzione)* introduction; *(Filosofia)* premise; **fare una** ~ to make an introductory statement; **mancano le** ~**e per una buona riuscita** we lack the basis for a successful outcome.

premesso, a [pre'messo] *pp di* **premettere.**

premettere [pre'mettere] *vt* **(a)** *(dire prima)* to start by saying, state first; **vorrei** ~ **alcune considerazioni di carattere generale** I should like to begin by making a few general points; **premetto che...** I must say first of all that...; **premesso che...** given that...; **ciò premesso...** that said.... **(b)** *(porre prima)* to put before; ~ **una prefazione ad un'opera** to preface a work.

premiare [pre'mjare] *vt (atleta, studente)* to give a prize to, award a prize to; *(libro, film)* to award a prize to; *(fig: merito, onestà)* to reward; **è stato premiato con una medaglia** he was awarded a medal.

premiato, a [pre'mjato] **1** *ag* prizewinning. **2** *sm/f* prizewinner.

premiazione [premjat'tsjone] *sf* prize-giving.

premier ['premjə] *sm inv (Pol)* premier.

première [prə'mjɛr] *sf inv (Teatro, Cine)* première, first performance.

preminente [premi'nɛnte] *ag* prominent.

preminenza [premi'nɛntsa] *sf* pre-eminence, superiority.

premio ['premjo] **1** *sm* **(a)** *(gen)* prize; *(ricompensa)* reward; ~ **d'ingaggio** *(Sport)* signing-on fee; ~ **Nobel** Nobel prize; **in** ~ **per** as a prize *(o* reward) for. **(b)** *(Fin, Assicurazione)* premium. **(c)** *(indennità speciale)* bonus; ~ **di produzione** productivity bonus. **2** *ag inv:* **ottenere una vacanza** ~ *(impiegato)* to win an all expenses paid holiday; *(studente)* to be given a free school trip.

premonitore, trice [premoni'tore] *ag* premonitory.

premonizione [premonit'tsjone] *sf* premonition.

premunire [premu'nire] **1** *vt:* ~ **(contro)** *(nemico, influenza)* to protect (against); ~ **qn contro i rischi della droga** to make sb aware of the dangers of drugs. **2:** ~**rsi** *vr:* ~**rsi (di** *o* **con)** to arm o.s. (with); ~**rsi (contro)** to protect o.s. (from), guard o.s. (against).

premura [pre'mura] *sf* **(a)** *(fretta):* **aver** ~ to be in a hurry; **far** ~ **a qn** to hurry sb; **fatto di** ~ done hurriedly. **(b)** *(cura)* attention; **usare ogni** ~ **nei**

riguardi di qn, circondare qn di ~**e** to be very attentive to sb.

premuroso, a [premu'roso] *ag* attentive, thoughtful.

prenatale [prena'tale] *ag* antenatal, prenatal.

prendere ['prɛndere] **1** *vt* **(a)** *(gen)* to take; *(andare a* ~: *cosa)* to get, fetch; *(: persona)* to pick up, fetch; **ha preso il libro dal tavolo** he picked up *o* took the book from the table; **l'ho preso nel cassetto** I took *o* got it out of the drawer; **l'ha preso per mano** he took his hand *o* took him by the hand; ~ **qc in spalla** to shoulder sth; ~ **qc per il manico** to take sth by the handle; **vieni a prendermi alla stazione** come and pick me up *o* fetch me from the station; **vai a prendermi le sigarette** go and get my cigarettes; **abbiamo preso una casa** *(affittare)* we have taken *o* rented a house; *(comprare)* we have bought a house.

(b) *(afferrare)* to seize, grab; ~ **qn per i capelli** to grab sb by the hair; **essere preso dai rimorsi** *(fig)* to be full of remorse; **essere preso dal panico** *(fig)* to be panic-stricken; **che cosa ti prende adesso?** *(fig)* now what's got into you!; **quel film mi ha preso** *(fig)* that film caught my imagination.

(c) *(catturare: ladro, pesce)* to catch; *(: fortezza)* to take; **è stato preso dalla polizia** he was caught by the police; **l'ho preso mentre tentava di scappare** I caught him trying to escape; **la cintura mi è rimasta presa nella porta** I caught *o* trapped my belt in the door, my belt got caught in the door.

(d) *(direzione, scorciatoia, mezzo pubblico)* to take; **non so che strada** ~ I don't know which road to take; **ha preso il treno** he took the train, he went by train; **ha preso il treno delle 10** he took *o* caught the 10 o'clock train; **preferisco** ~ **l'aereo anziché il treno** I prefer to go by plane rather than by train; **la nave ha preso il largo** the ship put out to sea.

(e) *(registrare)* to take (down); ~ **le misure di qn** to take sb's measurements; ~ **le generalità di qn** to take down sb's particulars; ~ **nota di** to take note of.

(f) *(guadagnare)* to get, earn; *(chiedere: denaro)* to charge; **prende un milione al mese** he makes a million lire a month; **quanto prende per un taglio di capelli?** how much do you charge for a haircut?

(g) *(ricevere: colpi, schiaffi, sgridata)* to get; *(subire: malattia)* to catch; **le ha prese** he got a good hiding; **ho preso uno spavento** I got such a fright; **ho preso freddo** I've caught a chill; **non so come la prenderà** I don't know how he'll take the news.

(h) *(ingoiare: pasto, panino, tè)* to have; *(: medicina)* to take; **non prendo nulla fuori pasto** I don't eat between meals; **prendi qualcosa?** would you like something to eat *(o* drink)?; **prendi pure** help yourself.

(i) *(assumere: operai)* to take on, hire; *(: responsabilità)* to take on, assume; *(: tono, aria)* to put on; *(: colore)* to take on; *(decisione)* to take, make, come to; ~**rsi un impegno** to take on a commitment; **ha preso uno strano odore** it smells funny; ~ **l'abitudine di** to get into the habit of.

(j) *(scambiare):* **ti avevo preso per mio fratello** I mistook you for *o* I thought you were my brother; **ha preso le mie parole per** *o* **come un'offesa** he took offence at my words; **per chi mi prendi?** who do you think I am?, what do you take me for?

(k) *(trattare: persona)* to handle; ~ **qn per il verso giusto** to handle sb the right way; ~ **qn con le buone/cattive** to handle sb tactfully/rudely.

(l) *(occupare: spazio, tempo)* to take up; **il tavolo prende poco posto** the table doesn't take up much room; **questo lavoro mi sta prendendo troppo tempo** this work is taking up too much of my time.

(m): ~ **a fare qc** to begin to do sth, start doing sth.

(n): prendersela *(adirarsi)* to get annoyed; *(preoccuparsi)* to get upset, worry; **prendersela a male** to take offence; **prendersela con qn** to get angry with sb; **perché te la prendi sempre con me?** why do you always pick on me?; **prendersela comoda** to take it easy.

(o) *(fraseologia):* ~ **da qn** *(assomigliare)* to take after sb; ~ **a calci qn** to kick sb; ~ **qn per fame** to starve sb into submission; ~ **o lasciare** take it or leave it; ~**rsi la soddisfazione (di)** to have the satisfaction (of); ~**rsi una vacanza** to take a holiday; ~**rsi cura di qn** to look after sb; ~**rsi gioco di qn** to mock sb.

2 *vi* **(a)** *(far presa: cemento, colla)* to set; *(: piante)* to take root; *(: fuoco)* to catch.

(b) *(andare):* ~ **a destra** to go *o* turn right; ~ **per i campi** to go across the fields.

(c) *(fraseologia):* **mi è preso un colpo** I got such a fright; **mi è preso freddo** I started feeling cold; **mi è presa la voglia di andare al mare** I feel like going to the seaside.

3: ~**rsi** *vr (uso reciproco: afferrarsi)* to grab each other, seize each other; ~**rsi a pugni** to come to blows; ~**rsi a calci** to kick each other.

prendisole [prendi'sole] *sm inv* sundress.

prenotare [preno'tare] **1** *vt (posto)* to book, reserve; *(camera)* to book. **2:** ~**rsi** *vr:* ~**rsi per qc** to put one's name down for sth.

prenotazione [prenotat'tsjone] *sf* booking, reservation.

prensile ['prɛnsile] *ag* prehensile.

preoccupante [preokku'pante] *ag* worrying.

preoccupare [preokku'pare] **1** *vt (impensierire)* to worry; **ciò che mi preoccupa è il viaggio** what's worrying *o* bothering me is the journey; **Giovanna mi preoccupa, sono preoccupato per Giovanna** I am worried about Giovanna; **la sua salute mi preoccupa** I'm concerned *o* anxious about his health; **me ne preoccupo io** I'll take care of it. **2:** ~**rsi** *vr:* ~**rsi (per)** to worry (about); **non preoccuparti** don't worry.

preoccupazione [preokkupat'tsjone] *sf (problema)* worry; *(inquietudine)* anxiety, worry; **è pieno di** ~**i** he has lots of worries *o* problems; **la sua unica** ~ **è vestirsi bene** her only concern *o* preoccupation is to dress well.

preordinato, a [preordi'nato] *ag* preordained.

preparare [prepa'rare] **1** *vt* **(a)** *(gen)* to prepare; *(pranzo, letto)* to make; *(tavola)* to lay; *(valigia)* to get ready, pack; *(esame)* to prepare for, study for; ~ **il terreno** *(anche fig)* to prepare the ground; **chissà cosa ci prepara il futuro!** who knows what the future has in store for us! **(b):** ~ **qn a** *(esame)* to prepare *o* coach sb for; *(notizia)* to prepare sb for; ~ **qn per un intervento** to get sb ready for an operation. **2:** ~**rsi** *vr:* ~**rsi a qc/a fare qc** to get ready for sth/to do sth; *(atleta)* to train for sth/to do sth; ~**rsi ad un esame** to prepare for *o* study for an exam.

preparativi [prepara'tivi] *smpl:* ~ **(per)** preparations (for).

preparato, a [prepa'rato] **1** *ag (gen)* prepared; *(pronto)* ready; **un allievo molto** ~ a well-

prepared student. **2** *sm (prodotto)* preparation.

preparatorio, a [prepara'tɔrjo] *ag* preparatory.

preparazione [preparat'tsjone] *sf (gen)* preparation; *(Sport)* training; **iniziare la** ~ **per gli esami** to begin preparation for the exams; **non ha la necessaria** ~ **per svolgere questo lavoro** he lacks the qualifications necessary for the job.

prepensionamento [prepensjona'mento] *sm* early retirement.

preponderante [preponde'rante] *ag* predominant.

preponderanza [preponde'rantsa] *sf (prevalenza)* preponderance; *(superiorità)* superiority; **erano in** ~ **cinesi** the majority were Chinese.

preporre [pre'porre] *vt* **(a)** *(porre innanzi)* to place before; *(fig: preferire)* to prefer, put before. **(b)** *(mettere a capo):* ~ **qn a qc** to put sb in charge of sth; **l'ufficiale preposto al comando del reggimento** the officer in command of the regiment.

preposizione [preposit'tsjone] *sf (Gram)* preposition.

preposto, a [pre'posto] *pp di* **preporre**.

prepotente [prepo'tɛnte] **1** *ag (persona)* overbearing, arrogant; *(fig: desiderio, bisogno)* overwhelming; **un** ~ **desiderio di qc/di fare qc** an overwhelming desire for sth/to do sth; **quel bambino è molto** ~ that child is a real bully. **2** *sm/f* bully.

prepotenza [prepo'tɛntsa] *sf (arroganza)* arrogance; **agire con** ~ to behave arrogantly; **è stata una** ~ **da parte tua** it was very high-handed of you.

prepuzio [pre'puttsjo] *sm (Anat)* foreskin.

prerogativa [preroga'tiva] *sf* **(a)** *(privilegio)* prerogative. **(b)** *(peculiarità)* property, quality.

presa ['prɛsa] **1** *sf* **(a)** *(gen)* grip; *(appiglio)* hold; *(Lotta)* grip, hold; **avere una** ~ **forte** to have a strong grip; **venire alle** ~**e con qc** *(fig)* to come to grips with sth; **a** ~ **rapida** *(cemento)* quick-setting; **far** ~ *(colla)* to set; **ha fatto** ~ **sul pubblico** *(fig)* it caught the public's imagination. **(b)** *(conquista)* taking, capture; *(Carte)* taking. **(c)** *(pizzico: di sale, tabacco)* pinch. **(d): macchina da** ~ *(Cine)* cine camera. **2:** ~ **dell'acqua** water (supply) point; ~ **d'aria** air inlet *o* intake; ~ **di corrente** *(Elettr)* socket; ~ **del gas** gas (supply) point; ~ **di posizione** stand; ~ **di possesso** taking possession; ~ **diretta** *(Aut)* direct drive; ~ **in giro** leg-pull.

presagio [pre'zadʒo] *sm* omen, sign; *(presentimento)* premonition, presentiment.

presagire [preza'dʒire] *vt (prevedere)* to predict, foresee; *(presentire)* to have a premonition of.

presago, a, ghi, ghe [pre'zago] *ag:* **essere** ~ **di qc** to have a premonition *o* presentiment of sth.

presalario [presa'larjo] *sm (Univ)* grant.

presbiopia [prezbio'pia] *sf* long-sightedness.

presbite ['prɛzbite] *ag* long-sighted.

presbiteriano, a [prezbite'rjano] *ag, sm/f* Presbyterian.

presbiterio [prezbi'tɛrjo] *sm* presbytery.

prescegliere [preʃ'ʃeʎʎere] *vt* to select, choose.

prescelto, a [preʃ'ʃelto] *pp di* **prescegliere**.

prescindere [preʃ'ʃindere] *vi:* ~ **da** to leave aside; **prescindendo da, a** ~ **da** leaving aside, apart from.

prescolastico, a, ci, che [presko'lastiko] *ag* pre-school *attr*; **bambini in età** ~**a** children not yet of school age.

prescritto, a [pres'kritto] *pp di* **prescrivere**.

prescrivere [pres'krivere] *vt (Med, Dir)* to prescribe; ~ **una medicina a qn** to prescribe medicine for sb.

prescrizione [preskrit'tsjone] *sf (Med, Dir)* prescription; *(norma)* rule, regulation; **cadere in ~** *(Dir)* to become statute-barred.

presentare [prezen'tare] **1** *vt* **(a)** *(gen)* to present; *(documento)* to present, show, produce; *(proposta, conti, bilancio)* to present, submit; *(domanda, reclamo)* to put in.

(b) *(spettacolo, nuovo modello)* to present; *(persona)* to introduce; **~ qn in società** to introduce sb into society; **~ qc in una esposizione** to show *o* display sth at an exhibition.

(c) *(dono)* to present, give; *(omaggi)* to present, pay; **~ le armi** *(Mil)* to present arms.

2: **~rsi** *vr* **(a)** *(recarsi, farsi vedere)* to present o.s., appear; **~rsi davanti al tribunale** to appear before the court; **è così che ti presenti?** is this any way to be seen?; **~rsi bene/male** to have a good/poor appearance.

(b) *(farsi conoscere)* to introduce o.s.

(c) *(candidato)* to come forward; **~rsi come cameriere** to apply for a job as a waiter; **~rsi a** *(elezione)* to stand for, run for *(Am)*; *(concorso)* to enter for; *(esame)* to sit, take.

(d) *(capitare: occasione, caso strano)* to occur, arise; **se mi si presenterà una simile occasione** should a similar opportunity occur *o* arise; **~rsi alla mente** *(idea)* to come *o* spring to mind.

(e) *(apparire)* to look, seem; **la situazione si presenta difficile** things aren't looking too good, things look a bit tricky.

presentatore, trice [prezenta'tore] *sm/f (Radio, TV)* introducer, presenter; **~ di quiz** quiz master.

presentazione [prezentat'tsjone] *sf (gen)* presentation; *(di persona)* introduction; **fare le ~i** to make the introductions.

presente¹ [pre'zɛnte] **1** *ag (gen)* present; **essere ~ a una riunione** to be present at *o* attend a meeting; **avere ~ qn/qc** *(fig)* to remember sb/sth; **tener ~ qn/qc** to keep sb/sth in mind. **2** *sm/f* person present; **i ~i** those present; **esclusi i ~i** present company excepted. **3** *sm (Gram)* present tense; *(tempo attuale):* **il ~** the present; **per il ~** for the present; **al ~** at present. **4** *sf (Comm: lettera):* **con la ~ vi comunico...** this is to inform you that.... .

presente² [pre'zɛnte] *sm (regalo)* present, gift.

presentimento [presenti'mento] *sm* premonition, presentiment; **ho uno strano ~ che...** I have a strange feeling that.... .

presentire [presen'tire] *vt* to have a presentiment of; **come presentivo non si è fatto più sentire** as I thought *o* foresaw he hasn't called since; **presentivo che sarebbe andata a finire così** I thought *o* had a feeling that it would end like that.

presenza [pre'zɛntsa] *sf (gen)* presence; *(Scol)* attendance; **fare atto di ~** to put in an appearance; **di ~** in person, personally; **in ~ di** in (the) presence of; **di bella ~** of good appearance; **~ di spirito** presence of mind; **conta 18 ~e in nazionale** *(Sport)* he's won 18 caps, he's played in the national team 18 times.

presenziare [prezen'tsjare] *vi:* **~ a** to be present at, attend.

presepio [pre'zɛpjo] *sm* crib.

preservare [preser'vare] *vt* to protect; **~ qn da qc** to protect sb from *o* against sth; **~ la salute** to protect one's health.

preservativo [preserva'tivo] *sm (profilattico)* sheath.

preservazione [preservat'tsjone] *sf* preservation, protection.

preside ['prɛside] *sm/f (Scol)* headmaster/ mistress; **~ di facoltà** *(Univ)* dean of faculty.

presidente [presi'dɛnte] *sm (di paese, club)* president; *(di assemblea, riunione, società commerciale) (Dir)* chairman; *(Dir)* presiding judge *o* magistrate; **il P~ della Camera** *(Parlamento)* ≃ the Speaker; **~ della commissione** *(Scol)* chief examiner; **P~ del Consiglio (dei Ministri)** Prime Minister.

presidentessa [presiden'tessa] *sf (vedi presidente)* president; chairwoman; *(moglie del presidente)* president's wife.

presidenza [presi'dɛntsa] *sf* **(a)** *(vedi presidente)* presidency; chairmanship; **essere alla ~** to be president *(o* chairman); **assumere la ~** to become president; to take the chair; **candidato alla ~** presidential candidate; candidate for the chairmanship. **(b)** *(di preside: carica)* headmastership; *(: ufficio)* headmaster's office *o* study.

presidenziale [presi'dɛntsjale] *ag* presidential.

presidiare [presi'djare] *vt (Mil)* to garrison; *(casa, fabbrica)* to guard.

presidio [pre'sidjo] *sm (Mil: guarnigione)* garrison; *(: comando territoriale)* command; *(: ufficio)* area recruitment office.

presiedere [pre'sjɛdere] **1** *vt (assemblea, riunione etc)* to preside over, chair; **presiede la Camera dei Deputati** *(Parlamento)* ≃ he *(o* she) is Speaker of the House of Commons. **2** *vi:* **~ a** *(discussione, riunione etc)* to preside over, chair.

preso, a ['preso] *pp di* **prendere**.

pressa ['prɛssa] *sf (Tecn)* press; **mettere** *o* **passare sotto la ~** to press.

pressante [pres'sante] *ag (bisogno, richiesta)* urgent, pressing.

pressappoco [pressap'pɔko] *av* about, roughly, approximately; **sono ~ uguali** they are more or less the same; **~ ha 40 anni** he's about 40.

pressare [pres'sare] *vt (Tecn)* to press.

pressione [pres'sjone] *sf* **(a)** *(gen, Fis, Med)* pressure; **mettere sotto ~** *(Tecn)* to pressurize; **~ atmosferica/sanguigna** atmospheric/blood pressure; **avere la ~ alta/bassa** *(Med)* to have high/low blood pressure; **pentola a ~** pressure cooker; **la macchina del caffè non è ancora in ~** there isn't enough steam in the espresso machine yet. **(b)** *(fig: insistenza)* pressure; **fare ~ su qn** to put pressure on sb; **subire forti ~i** to be under strong pressure; **sotto ~** under pressure.

presso ['prɛsso] **1** *av* **(a)** nearby, near; **abitava lì ~** he lived nearby, he lived near there. **(b):** **da ~**, **~ (incalzare)** closely; **da ~ (esaminare)** closely; **a un di ~** about, approximately.

2 *prep* **(a)** *(vicino)* close to, near (to); **~ a near** (to), by; **stava ~ la finestra** he was standing near the window. **(b)** *(in casa di, nella ditta di):* **abita ~ i genitori** he lives with his parents; **'~'** *(sulle buste)* 'care of', 'c/o'; **lavora ~ di noi** he works for us; **ambasciatore ~ la Santa Sede** ambassador to the Holy See. **(c)** *(nell'ambiente di)* among; **diffuso ~ le popolazioni primitive** common among primitive peoples; **ha avuto grande successo ~ i giovani** it has been a hit with young people.

3 *smpl:* **nei ~i** near, in the vicinity of; **nei ~i di Londra** near London.

pressoché [presso'ke] *av* nearly, almost.

pressurizzare [pressurid'dzare] *vt* to pressurize.

pressurizzazione [pressuriddzat'tsjone] *sf* pressurization.

prestabilire [prestabi'lire] *vt* to arrange beforehand, arrange in advance; **era già tutto prestabi-**

lito everything had already been arranged.

prestanome [presta'nome] *sm/f inv (Dir)* nominee; *(peg)* front man.

prestante [pres'tante] *ag* good-looking.

prestanza [pres'tantsa] *sf* (robust) good looks *pl.*

prestare [pres'tare] **1** *vt* to lend; ~ **qc a qn** to lend sb sth, lend sth to sb; **farsi** ~ **qc da qn** to borrow sth from sb; **aiuto a qn** to give sb a helping hand; ~ **soccorso a** to give assistance to; ~ **attenzione a** to pay attention to; ~ **fede a qc/qn** to give credence to sth/sb; ~ **giuramento** to take an oath; ~ **ascolto a** to listen to. **2:** ~**rsi** *vr* **(a)** *(offrirsi):* ~**rsi a fare qc** to agree to do sth; **si presta sempre volentieri** he's always willing to lend a hand. **(b)** *(essere adatto):* ~**rsi per o a** to lend itself to, be suitable for; **la frase si presta a molteplici interpretazioni** the phrase lends itself to numerous interpretations; **quel vestito non si presta all'occasione** that dress isn't suitable for the occasion.

prestazione [prestat'tsjone] *sf* **(a)** *(Tecn, Sport)* performance. **(b):** ~**i** *pl (opera, servizio)* services.

prestigiatore, trice [prestidʒa'tore] *sm/f* conjurer.

prestigio [pres'tidʒo] *sm* **(a)** *(fama, autorità)* prestige; **di** ~ prestigious. **(b):** **gioco di** ~ conjuring trick.

prestigioso, a [presti'dʒoso] *ag* prestigious.

prestito ['prestito] *sm* loan; **prendere qc in** ~ **da qn** to borrow sth from sb; **dare qc in** ~ **a qn** to lend sth to sb, lend sb sth; **mi fai un** ~? can I borrow some money from you?; ~ **bancario** bank loan; ~ **pubblico** public borrowing.

presto ['presto] *av* **(a)** *(fra poco)* soon; **ci rivedremo** ~ we'll see one another soon; ~ **o tardi** sooner or later; **arrivederci a** ~! goodbye for now!, see you soon!; **il più** ~ **possibile** as soon as possible; **se non la smette,** ~ **avrà dei guai** if he doesn't stop that he'll be for it.

(b) *(in fretta)* quickly, fast; **fai** ~! be quick about it!; **fai** ~ **che è già buio** be quick about it as it's already dark; **più** ~ **che puoi** as quickly *o* fast as you can; **ha fatto** ~ **a sbrigare quel lavoro** he got through that job quickly; **è** ~ **detto** it's easier said than done; **si fa** ~ **a criticare** it's easy to criticize.

(c) *(di buon'ora)* early; **mi alzo** ~ I get up early; **sono arrivato troppo** ~ **all'appuntamento** I arrived too early for the appointment; **è ancora** ~ **per decidere** it's still too early *o* too soon to decide.

presumere [pre'zumere] *vt* **(a)** *(ritenere, credere):* ~ **che** to presume that, imagine that; **presumo che venga** I presume *o* imagine he'll come. **(b)** *(pretendere, avere la presunzione di)* to presume; **presumi di potermi criticare** you have the nerve to think you can criticize me; **presume di sapere più degli altri** he presumes to know more than everybody else.

presumibile [prezu'mibile] *ag (dati, risultati)* likely; **è** ~ **che tu voglia vedere tua madre** presumably you want to see your mother.

presunto, a [pre'zunto] **1** *pp di* **presumere. 2** *ag:* **il** ~ **colpevole** the alleged culprit.

presuntuoso, a [prezuntu'oso] **1** *ag* presumptuous, conceited. **2** *sm:* **fare il** ~ to be cocksure.

presunzione [prezun'tsjone] *sf* **(a)** *(congettura)* presumption. **(b)** *(immodestia)* presumptuousness; **peccare di** ~ to be presumptuous.

presupporre [presup'porre] *vt* **(a)** *(immaginare, prevedere)* to assume, suppose. **(b)** *(implicare)* to presuppose.

presupposto, a [presup'posto] **1** *pp di* **presupporre. 2** *sm (premessa)* supposition, premise; **partendo dal** ~ **che...** assuming that...; **mancano i** ~**i necessari** the necessary conditions are lacking.

prêt-à-porter ['prɛt a pɔr'te] *sm* ready-to-wear (clothes).

prete ['prɛte] *sm* priest; **scherzo da** ~ *(fig fam)* nasty trick.

pretendente [preten'dɛnte] *sm/f* **(a)** *(aspirante):* ~ **(a)** pretender (to). **(b)** *(corteggiatore)* suitor.

pretendere [pre'tɛndere] *vt* **(a)** *(esigere)* to demand; *(aspettarsi)* to expect; **pretendo un po' di rispetto** I demand some respect; **pretendo la mia parte** I demand *o* claim my share; **pretende di essere pagato** he expects to be paid; **pretendi troppo da lui** you expect too much of him. **(b)** *(sostenere, presumere)* to claim; **pretende sempre di aver ragione** he always claims he is right.

pretenzioso, a [preten'tsjoso] *ag* pretentious.

preterintenzionale [preterintentsjo'nale] *ag (Dir):* **omicidio** ~ manslaughter.

pretesa [pre'tesa] *sf* **(a)** *(richiesta, esigenza)* claim, demand; **avanzare una** ~ to put forward a claim *o* demand; **un uomo di poche** ~**e** a man who is easily pleased *o* who doesn't ask much in life; **è pieno di** ~**e** he's difficult to please, he expects too much; **senza** ~**e** *(persona, casa, arredamento)* unpretentious, modest; *(abito)* simple. **(b)** *(presunzione)* pretension; **hai la** ~ **di criticarmi!** you've got the nerve to criticize me!; **non avrai la** ~ **di farmelo credere** you don't really expect me to believe that; **non ho la** ~ **di essere bella** I have no pretensions to beauty, I don't pretend to be good-looking.

preteso, a [pre'teso] *pp di* **pretendere.**

pretesto [pre'tɛsto] *sm* excuse, pretext; **con il** ~ **di** on the pretext of; **mi ha fornito il** ~ **per agire** he has provided me with a pretext for taking action.

pretore [pre'tore] *sm (Dir)* magistrate.

pretura [pre'tura] *sf (Dir: sede)* magistrate's court; *(: insieme dei pretori)* magistracy.

prevalente [preva'lɛnte] *ag* prevalent, prevailing.

prevalenza [preva'lɛntsa] *sf* predominance; **in** ~ predominantly, mainly.

prevalere [preva'lere] **1** *vi* to prevail; ~ **su tutti per intelligenza** to surpass everyone in intelligence. **2:** ~**rsi** *vr:* ~**rsi di** to avail o.s. of, take advantage of.

prevalso, a [pre'valso] *pp di* **prevalere.**

prevaricare [prevari'kare] *vi (abusare del potere)* to abuse one's power.

prevaricazione [prevarikat'tsjone] *sf (abuso di potere)* abuse of power.

prevedere [preve'dere] *vt* **(a)** *(avvenimento, conseguenza)* to foresee, anticipate; *(tempo)* to forecast; ~ **il futuro** to foretell the future; **era da** ~ it was to be expected; **non si sarebbe potuto** ~ that couldn't have been foreseen; **nulla lasciava** ~ **che...** there was nothing to suggest *o* to make one think that...; **non possiamo** ~ **tutto** we can't think of everything; **come previsto** as expected; **spese previste** anticipated expenditure; **tempo previsto per domani** weather forecast for tomorrow.

(b) *(programmare)* to plan; ~ **di fare qc** to plan to do sth; **avevamo previsto di partire oggi** we had planned to leave today; **all'ora prevista** at the appointed *o* scheduled time; **previsto per martedì** scheduled for Tuesday.

(c) *(sog: contratto, legge)* to make provision for, provide for; **questo caso non è previsto dalla legge** the law makes no provision for such a case.

prevedibile [preve'dibile] *ag* predictable; **non era assolutamente ~ che...** no one could have foreseen that... .

prevenire [preve'nire] *vt* (a) *(domanda)* to anticipate; *(obiezione)* to forestall. (b) *(preavvertire)* to inform in advance; *(mettere sull'avviso)* to forewarn; **ti hanno prevenuto contro di me** they have already warned you about me. (c) *(malattia, disgrazia)* to prevent; **gli incidenti si possono ~** accidents can be prevented.

preventivare [preventi'vare] *vt* (Comm: spesa) to estimate; (: mettere in bilancio) to budget for; **non avevamo preventivato un figlio** we hadn't reckoned on having a child.

preventivo [preven'tivo] **1** *ag* (intervento, cura) preventive; **carcere ~** custody *(pending trial)*; **bilancio ~** *(Comm)* budget. **2** *sm* (Comm) estimate; **fare un ~** to give an estimate.

prevenuto, a [preve'nuto] **1** *pp di* **prevenire. 2** *ag* *(mal disposto)*: **~** (contro qc/qn) prejudiced (against sth/sb).

prevenzione [preven'tsjone] *sf* (a) prevention; **~ degli infortuni** prevention of accidents. (b) *(preconcetto)* prejudice; **avere ~i contro qc/qn** to be prejudiced against sth/sb.

previdente [previ'dɛnte] *ag* prudent.

previdenza [previ'dɛntsa] *sf* prudence, foresight; **~ sociale** social security; **istituto di ~** provident institution.

previo, a ['prevjo] *ag (Comm)*: **~ avviso** upon notice; **~ pagamento** upon payment.

previsione [previ'zjone] *sf (gen)* prediction; *(attesa)* expectation; **tutto è andato secondo le ~i** everything went according to expectation(s); **in ~ di** in anticipation of; **~i del tempo** weather forecast.

previsto, a [pre'visto] **1** *pp di* **prevedere. 2** *sm*: **più/meno del ~** more/less than expected; **prima del ~** earlier than expected.

prezioso, a [pret'tsjoso] **1** *ag (gen)* precious; *(documento)* valuable; *(testimonianza, aiuto, consiglio)* invaluable. **2** *sm* (a) *(gioiello)* jewel; **le hanno rubato tutti i ~** they stole all her valuables. (b) *(fig: persona)*: **fare il ~** to play hard to get; **fa il ~ perché è diventato importante** he puts on airs and graces because he has become important.

prezzemolo [pret'tsemolo] *sm (Bot)* parsley; **essere come il ~** *(fig)* to turn up everywhere.

prezzo ['prɛttso] **1** *sm* price; **a buon ~** cheaply, at a good price; **a ~ di costo** at cost price; **a metà ~** at half price; **menu a ~ fisso** set price menu; **il ~ pattuito è 1.000.000 di lire** the agreed price is 1,000,000 lire; **tirare sul ~** to bargain, haggle; **ti faccio un ~ d'amico** *o* **di favore** I'll let you have it at a reduced price; **pagare qc a caro ~** *(fig)* to pay dearly for sth; **la libertà non ha ~** you can put no price on freedom; **è una cosa di poco ~** it's of little value, it's not worth much. **2**: **~ d'acquisto** purchase price; **~ di fabbrica** factory price; **~ di mercato** market price; **~ di vendita** selling price.

prigione [pri'dʒone] *sf (luogo)* prison, jail; *(pena)* imprisonment; **andare/mettere in ~** to go/send to prison; **scontare un anno di ~** to serve one year's imprisonment, spend a year in prison.

prigionia [pridʒo'nia] *sf* imprisonment.

prigioniero, a [pridʒo'njero] **1** *ag* captive; **essere ~** to be a prisoner; **essere ~ di un ricordo** *(fig)* to be tormented by a memory. **2** *sm* prisoner; **fare/tenere qn ~** to take/hold sb prisoner.

prima[1] ['prima] **1** *av* (a) *(in precedenza)* before; *(una volta)* once, formerly; **~ non lo sapevo** I didn't know that before; **due giorni ~** two days

before *o* earlier; **ne so quanto ~** I know as much as I did before, I'm none the wiser; **allora, amici come ~!** all right, let's make it up *o* let's be friends again!; **~ non si faceva così** people used not to do that; **usanze di ~** former customs; **non è più la stessa di ~** she's not the same as she was.

(b) *(in anticipo)* beforehand, in advance; **un'altra volta dimmelo ~** next time let me know in advance *o* beforehand.

(c) *(più presto)* sooner; **~ o poi** sooner or later; **credevo di fare ~** I thought I'd be finished sooner *o* earlier; **~ lo fai ~ sarai libero di uscire** the sooner you do it the sooner you can go out; **chi arriva ~, comperi i biglietti** whoever arrives first gets the tickets.

(d) *(innanzi)* before; *(in primo luogo)* first; **~ la famiglia** family first; **~ il dovere e poi il piacere** duty before pleasure.

2: **~ di** *prep (tempo, spazio)* before; **~ del suo arrivo** before his arrival; **sono andati via ~ di noi** they left before us; **~ d'ora** before now; **c'è un cinema ~ del semaforo** there's a cinema before the lights.

3: **~ di, ~ che** *cong* before; **~ di fare/che tu faccia** before doing/you do; **pensaci ~ che sia troppo tardi** give it some thought before it is too late.

prima[2] ['prima] *sf* (a) *(gen)* first; *(Teatro)* opening night; *(Cine)* première; *(Ferr)* first class; *(Aut)* first gear; **viaggiare in ~** to travel first class; **ingranare la ~** to engage first gear. (b) *(Scol: elementare)* primary one; *(: media)* first year at secondary school; *(: superiore)* fourth year at secondary school.

primario, a [pri'marjo] **1** *ag* (a) *(funzione, motivo, scopo)* main, chief, primary. (b) *(Geol)*: **roccia ~a** primary rock. **2** *sm/f (medico)* head physician, chief physician.

primate [pri'mate] *sm (Rel)* primate.

primatista, i, e [prima'tista] *sm/f (Sport)* record holder.

primato [pri'mato] *sm* (a) *(in campo industriale, artistico etc)* supremacy; **l'Italia ha il ~ nel campo della moda** Italy is the leader *o* holds the lead in the world of fashion. (b) *(Sport)* record.

primavera [prima'vera] *sf* spring.

primaverile [primave'rile] *ag* spring *attr*.

primeggiare [primed'dʒare] *vi*: **~ (in)** to excel (in).

primitivo, a [primi'tivo] **1** *ag (società, popolazione, usanza)* primitive; *(significato)* original. **2** *sm (della preistoria, arcaico)* primitive man; *(fig: zotico)* uncivilized person.

primizia [pri'mittsja] *sf* (a) *(Agr)*: **~e** *pl* early fruit and vegetables. (b) *(notizia)*: **ho una ~ per il tuo giornale** I've got a scoop for your paper; **articolo pieno di ~e** article full of the latest news.

primo, a ['primo] **1** *ag* (a) *(gen)* first; *(impressione)* first, initial; *(infanzia)* early; **Carlo ~** Charles the First; **le ~e 20 pagine** the first 20 pages; **dalla ~a all'ultima pagina** from beginning to end; **in ~a pagina** *(Stampa)* on the front page; **i suoi ~i quadri** his early paintings; **questo quadro è ~ Michelangelo** this is an early Michelangelo; **questo film è di Fellini ~a maniera** this film is in Fellini's early style; **di ~a mattina** early in the morning; **posare la ~a pietra** to lay the foundation stone; **ai ~i freddi** at the first sign of cold weather; **ustioni di ~ grado** first-degree burns.

(b) *(in un ordine)* first; **preferisco il ~ pittore al secondo** I prefer the former painter to the latter; **essere ~ in classifica** to be placed first, be in first place; **essere in ~a posizione** to be in the lead; **sul ~ scaffale in alto/in basso** on the top/bottom shelf; **di ~a qualità** top quality; **è un attore di prim'ordine** he is a first-rate actor.

(c) *(prossimo)* first, next; **prendi la ~a (strada) a destra** take the first *o* next (street) on the right; **scendo alla ~a fermata** I am getting off at the next stop.

(d) *(principale)* main, principal; **il ~ attore** the leading man; **la ~a ragione** the main reason.

(e) *(fraseologia)*: **per ~a cosa** firstly; **in ~ luogo** in the first place; **in un ~ tempo** *o* **momento** at first; **fin dal ~ momento** from the very first; **amore a ~a vista** love at first sight; **fare i ~i passi** to take one's first steps; **fare il ~ passo** *(fig)* to make the first move.

2 *sm/f* first (one); **è stata la ~a a farlo** she was the first to do it; **era fra i ~i ad arrivare** he was among the first to arrive; **è la ~a della classe** she is the top of the class; **non sposerò il ~ venuto** I won't marry just anyone.

3 *sm (gen)* first; *(piano)* first floor; *(Culin)* first course; **il ~ luglio** the first of July; **il ~ d'Aprile** April Fools' Day; **il ~ dell'anno** New Year's Day; **i ~i del Novecento** the early twentieth century; **ai ~i del mese** at the beginning of the month.

primogenito, a [primo'dʒenito] 1 *sm/f* first child, eldest child. 2 *ag* firstborn.

primordiale [primor'djale] *ag (era, scienza)* primordial.

primordi [pri'mɔrdi] *smpl* beginnings; **ai ~ della storia** at the dawn of history.

primula ['primula] *sf (Bot)* primula.

principale [printʃi'pale] 1 *ag (strada, motivo)* main; *(opera)* major; **proposizione ~** *(Gram)* main clause; **sede ~** head office. 2 *sm (fam)* boss.

principalmente [printʃipal'mente] *av* mainly, principally.

principato [printʃi'pato] *sm (titolo nobiliare)* princedom; *(Stato)* principality.

principe ['printʃipe] *sm (titolo nobiliare)* prince; **~ ereditario** crown prince; **~ consorte** prince consort; **stare come un ~** *(fig)* to live like a lord; **~ azzurro** *(fig)* prince charming.

principesco, a, schi, sche [printʃi'pesko] *ag (anche fig)* princely.

principessa [printʃi'pessa] *sf* princess.

principiante [printʃi'pjante] *sm/f* beginner; **un lavoro da ~i** *(peg)* an amateur job.

principiare [printʃi'pjare] 1 *vt (discorso, trattative, lavoro)* to start, begin. 2 *vi (persona: aus* avere; *tempo etc: aus* essere): **a ~ fare qc** to begin *o* start doing *o* to do sth; **a ~ da oggi/domani** starting from today/tomorrow; **a ~ da te/noi** *etc* starting with you/us *etc*.

principio [prin'tʃipjo] *sm* (a) *(inizio)* beginning, start; **ricominciare dal ~** to start from the beginning again; **fin dal ~** right from the start; **in o al ~** at first, at the beginning; **dal ~ alla fine** from beginning to end, from start to finish. (b) *(morale)* principle; **essere senza ~i** to have no principles; **una persona di sani ~i morali** a person of sound moral principles; **una questione di ~** a matter of principle; **per ~** on principle. (c) *(Mat)* principle. (d) *(causa, origine)* cause, origin.

priore [pri'ore] *sm (Rel, Storia)* prior.

priorità [priori'ta] *sf* priority; **avere la ~ (su)** to have priority (over).

prisma ['prizma] *sm* prism.

privacy ['praivəsi] *sf* privacy.

privare [pri'vare] 1 *vt:* **~ qn di qc** to deprive sb of sth; **~ qn della vita** to take sb's life; **non mi ha privato di niente** he didn't deny me anything. 2:

~rsi *vr:* **~rsi di qc** to do *o* go without sth; **non ~rsi di niente** to deny o.s. nothing.

privatista, i, e [priva'tista] *sm/f (studente)* private student; **studiare da o come ~** to study privately; **fare un esame da o come ~** to be an external candidate at an exam.

privativa [priva'tiva] *sf (Econ)* monopoly.

privativo, a [priva'tivo] *ag (Gram)* privative.

privato, a [pri'vato] 1 *ag (gen)* private; **diritto ~** *(Dir)* civil law; **~ cittadino** private citizen; **ritirarsi a vita ~a** to withdraw from public life; **discutere o parlare in ~** to talk in private. 2 *sm* (a) *(cittadino)* private citizen; *(persona singola)* member of the public; **il commercio è in mano ai ~i** commerce is in private hands; **'non vendiamo a ~i'** 'wholesale only'. (b) *(vita privata)* private life.

privazione [privat'tsjone] *sf* (a) *(di diritti, genitori)* loss. (b) *(sacrificio: spec pl)* hardship, privation.

privilegiare [privile'dʒare] *vt* to favour.

privilegiato, a [privile'dʒato] 1 *ag* (a) *(individuo, classe)* privileged; *(trattamento)* preferential. (b) *(Comm: credito)* preferential; **azioni ~e** preference shares. 2 *sm/f* privileged person.

privilegio [privi'lɛdʒo] *sm* privilege; **godere di/concedere un ~** to enjoy/grant a privilege; **avere il ~ di fare** to have the privilege of doing, be privileged to do.

privo, a ['privo] *ag:* **~ di** *(senza)* without; *(carente in)* lacking in; **~ di scrupoli** without scruples; **~ di coraggio** lacking in courage; **parole ~e di significato** meaningless words.

pro¹ [prɔ] 1 *prep (in favore di)* for, in favour of; **~ patria** patriotic; **raccolta ~ bambini spastici** collection on behalf of spastic children; **sei ~ o contro?** are you for or against? 2 *sm inv:* **il ~ e il contro, i ~ e i contro** the pros and cons; **valutare i ~ e i contro** to weigh up the pros and cons.

pro² [prɔ] *sm (vantaggio)* good; **a che ~?** what's the use?; **a che ~ l'hai fatto?** why did you do it?; **tutta questa fatica, e a che ~?** all this work, and for what?; **tornerà a tuo buon ~** it will stand you in good stead; **buon ~ ti faccia!** much good may it do you!

probabile [pro'babile] *ag* likely, probable; **è ~ che venga** he will probably come, he is likely to come.

probabilità [probabili'ta] *sf inv* (a) probability, likelihood; *(possibilità)* chance; **quali o che ~ ci sono?** what chances are there?; **c'è una ~ su mille** there's a one in a thousand chance; **con molta ~** very probably, in all probability. (b) *(Mat)* probability.

probabilmente [probabil'mente] *av* probably; **~ verrà** he'll probably come.

probante [pro'bante] *ag* convincing.

problema, i [pro'blema] *sm (gen, Mat)* problem; *(questione)* issue.

problematica [proble'matika] *sf* problems *pl*.

problematico, a, ci, che [proble'matiko] *ag* problematic; *(incerto)* doubtful; **vieni stasera? — è un po'~** are you coming tonight? — it is difficult to say.

proboscide [pro'bɔʃʃide] *sf (di elefante)* trunk; *(di insetto)* proboscis.

procacciare [prokat'tʃare] *vt* to get; **~rsi un lavoro** to get o.s. a job; **~rsi il pane o da vivere** to earn one's living.

procace [pro'katʃe] *ag (donna, aspetto)* provocative.

procedere [pro'tʃɛdere] *vi* (a) *(aus* essere) *(avanzare)* to advance, proceed; *(continuare)* to proceed, to go on; **~ oltre** to go on ahead; **prima di ~**

oltre before going any further; ~ **con lentezza** *(veicolo)* to drive along slowly; *(trattative)* to proceed slowly; **procediamo con ordine** let's do this in an orderly fashion; **gli affari procedono bene** business is going well; **procede nella ricerca scientifica** he is continuing his scientific research.

(b) *(passare a)*: ~ **a** to start, begin; **procediamo alla discussione** let's begin the discussion.

(c) *(agire)* to proceed; *(comportarsi)* to behave; **non mi piace il suo modo di** ~ I don't like the way he behaves; **bisogna** ~ **con cautela** we have to proceed cautiously.

(d) *(Dir)*: ~ **contro qn** to start *o* take proceedings against sb; **non luogo a** ~ nonsuit.

procedimento [protʃedi'mento] *sm* (a) *(svolgimento)* course. (b) *(metodo)* procedure; *(: industriale)* process; **il** ~ **usato per la fabbricazione** the manufacturing process. (c) *(Dir)* proceedings *pl*; ~ **penale** criminal proceedings.

procedura [protʃe'dura] *sf (gen, Dir)* procedure; **seguire** *o* **osservare la** ~ to follow procedure.

processare [protʃes'sare] *vt (Dir)*: ~ **qn (per)** to try sb (for).

processione [protʃes'sjone] *sf (gen)* procession.

processo [pro'tʃesso] *sm* (a) *(gen, Chim, Med, Tecn)* process; *(di malattia)* course; ~ **di fabbricazione** manufacturing process. (b) *(Dir: civile)* (legal) proceedings *pl*, (court) action, lawsuit; *(: penale)* trial; **essere sotto** ~ to be on trial; **mettere sotto** ~ *(anche fig)* to put on trial; **fare il** ~ **alle intenzioni di qn** to question sb's motives.

processuale [protʃessu'ale] *ag (Dir)*: **atti** ~**i** records of a trial; **spese** ~**i** legal costs.

procinto [pro'tʃinto] *sm*: **in** ~ **di** about to, on the point of; **ero in** ~ **di partire** I was about to leave *o* on the point of leaving.

procione [pro'tʃone] *sm (Zool)* raccoon.

proclama, i [pro'klama] *sm (bando, appello)* proclamation.

proclamare [prokla'mare] *vt (legge)* to promulgate; *(stato d'assedio, guerra, pace)* to declare; ~ **qn vincitore** to declare sb the winner; ~ **la propria innocenza** to proclaim one's innocence.

proclamazione [proklamat'tsjone] *sf (dichiarazione)* declaration.

procrastinare [prokrasti'nare] *vt (data)* to postpone; *(pagamento)* to defer.

procreare [prokre'are] *vt* to procreate.

procreazione [prokreat'tsjone] *sf* procreation.

procura [pro'kura] *sf (Dir)* (a) proxy, power of attorney; **per** ~ by proxy. (b): **la P~ della Repubblica** the Public Prosecutor's office.

procurare [proku'rare] *vt* (a): ~ **qc a qn** to obtain sth for sb, provide sb with sth; ~ **danni** to cause damage; ~ **noie a qn** to cause sb trouble; ~**rsi delle noie con la polizia** to get into trouble with the police. (b) *(fare in modo di)*: ~ **di fare qc** to try to do sth.

procuratore, trice [proku'ratore] *sm/f (Dir)* (a) *(chi è munito di procura)* holder of power of attorney. (b): ~ **legale** = solicitor; **P~ della Repubblica** = public prosecutor; **P~ Generale** = Attorney General.

prode ['prɔde] **1** *ag* valiant, brave. **2** *sm* brave man.

prodezza [pro'dettsa] *sf (qualità)* valour, bravery; *(atto: anche fig)* feat, exploit.

prodigare [prodi'gare] **1** *vt (lodi, affetto)* to lavish; **gli prodiga tutte le sue cure** she lavishes all her care on him. **2**: ~**rsi** *vr* to do one's best, do all one can.

prodigio [pro'didʒo] **1** *sm (miracolo)* wonder, marvel; *(fig: persona)* prodigy; **i** ~**i della tecnica/**

scienza the wonders of technology/science; **fare** ~**i** to work wonders. **2** *ag inv*: **bambino** ~ child prodigy.

prodigioso, a [prodi'dʒoso] *ag* wonderful, marvellous.

prodigo, a, ghi, ghe ['prɔdigo] *ag*: **essere** ~ **(di)** *(consigli, attenzioni)* to be lavish (with); *(denaro)* to be extravagant (with); **il figliol** ~ *(Rel)* the prodigal son.

prodotto, a [pro'dotto] **1** *pp di* **produrre**. **2** *sm (gen, Mat)* product; *(fig: risultato)* result, fruit, product; ~**i agricoli** agricultural produce *sg*; ~**i alimentari** foodstuffs; ~**i di bellezza** cosmetics; ~**i chimici** chemicals.

produrre [pro'durre] *vt* (a) *(gen, Cine)* to produce; *(calore)* to generate; *(fabbricare)* to manufacture, make, produce; ~ **in serie** to mass-produce. (b) *(causare: angoscia, timori etc)* to cause, give rise to.

produttività [produttivi'ta] *sf* productivity.

produttivo, a [produt'tivo] *ag (lavoro, investimento)* productive; *(metodo, ciclo)* of production, production *attr*.

produttore, trice [produt'tore] **1** *sm/f (gen, Cine, Agr)* producer. **2** *ag (gen, Agr)* producing *attr*; **paese** ~ **di petrolio** oil-producing country.

produzione [produt'tsjone] *sf* (a) *(gen, Cine, TV etc)* production; ~ **in serie** mass production; **articolo di** ~ **italiana** article of Italian manufacture. (b) *(quantità prodotta)* production, output; *(Agr)* production, yield.

proemio [pro'ɛmjo] *sm* introduction, preface.

Prof. *abbr (= professore)* Prof.

profanare [profa'nare] *vt (Rel)* to profane, desecrate; *(tomba)* to violate; *(fig: nome, ricordo)* to defile.

profanazione [profanat'tsjone] *sf (vedi vb)* profanation, desecration; violation; defilement.

profano, a [pro'fano] **1** *ag (non sacro)* profane, secular; *(fig: orecchio, occhio)* untrained. **2** *sm/f (gen)* layman, lay person. **3** *sm*: **il** ~ the profane, the secular.

proferire [profe'rire] *vt (parola, nome)* to utter; *(giudizio, desiderio)* to express.

professare [profes'sare] *vt (opinione, dottrina)* to profess; ~**rsi innocente** to declare o.s. innocent.

professionale [professjo'nale] *ag (gen)* professional; *(malattia)* occupational; **scuola** ~ training college.

professione [profes'sjone] *sf (gen)* occupation; *(manuale)* trade; **libera** ~ profession; ~ **di fede** *(Rel, fig)* profession of faith; **fare qc di** ~ to do sth for a living; **di** ~ professional, by profession.

professionista, i, e [professjo'nista] *sm/f (gen, Sport)* professional; **libero** ~ professional man/woman.

professore, essa [profes'sore] *sm/f (Scol)* teacher; *(Univ)* = lecturer; *(: titolare di cattedra)* professor; ~ **d'orchestra** member of an orchestra.

profeta, i [pro'feta] *sm* prophet.

profetessa [profe'tessa] *sf* prophetess.

profetico, a, ci, che [pro'fetiko] *ag* prophetic.

profetizzare [profetid'dzare] *vt* to prophesy.

profezia [profet'tsia] *sf* prophecy.

proficuo, a [pro'fikuo] *ag* profitable, useful.

profilare [profi'lare] **1** *vt* (a) *(descrivere in breve)* to outline. (b) *(Cucito)* to edge. (c) *(Tecn: barra metallica)* to shape. **2**: ~**rsi** *vr (figura)* to stand out, be outlined; *(soluzione, problemi)* to emerge; ~**rsi all'orizzonte** *(anche fig)* to appear on the horizon.

profilassi [profi'lassi] *sf (Med)* preventive treatment, prophylaxis.

profilato [profi'lato] *sm (Tecn: trave)* section.

profilattico, a, ci, che [profi'lattiko] *(Med)* **1** *ag* prophylactic. **2** *sm (anticoncezionale)* sheath, condom.

profilo [pro'filo] *sm (gen, fig)* profile; **di** ~ in profile; **mettersi di** ~ to turn sideways (on).

profittare [profit'tare] *vi:* ~ **di** *(situazione)* to profit by *o* from; *(: peg: persona)* to take advantage of.

profitto [pro'fitto] *sm (gen, Econ)* profit; **ricavare un** ~ **da** to make a profit from *o* out of; **vendere con** ~ to sell at a profit; **conto** ~**i e perdite** profit and loss account; **trarre** ~ **da** *(lezione, esperienza)* to profit *o* benefit from; *(dei problemi altrui)* to take advantage of; *(invenzione etc)* to turn to good account; *(tempo libero)* to make the most of.

profondersi [pro'fondersi] *vr:* ~**rsi in** *(scuse, ringraziamenti)* to be profuse in.

profondità [profondi'ta] *sf inv* depth; **scavare in** ~ to dig deep; **avere 10 metri di** ~, **avere una** ~ **di 10 metri** to be 10 metres deep *o* in depth; **le** ~ **del mare** the depths of the sea. **(b)** *(di persona, osservazione)* profundity; *(di sentimento, rispetto)* depth. **(c)** *(Cine, Fot):* ~ **di campo** depth of field; **dare il senso della** ~ to give an impression of depth.

profondo, a [pro'fondo] **1** *ag* **(a)** *(gen)* deep; **poco** ~ shallow; ~ **5 metri** 5 metres deep. **(b)** *(fig: notte, colore, voce)* deep; *(: sospiro)* deep, heavy; *(: sonno)* deep, sound; *(: silenzio, mistero)* deep, profound; *(: interesse, sentimento)* profound; *(: inchino)* deep, low; *(: causa, significato)* underlying, deeper; *(: tendenza)* deep-seated, underlying. **2** *sm:* **nel** ~ **del mare** in the depths of the sea, at the bottom of the sea; **dal** ~ **del cuore** from the bottom of one's heart; **nel** ~ **del cuore** *o* **dell'animo** in one's heart of hearts.

proforma [pro'forma] **1** *ag* routine *attr.* **2** *av:* **fare qc** ~ to do sth as a formality. **3** *sm inv* formality.

profugo, a, ghi, ghe ['profugo] *sm/f* refugee.

profumare [profu'mare] **1** *vt* **(a)** *(sog: fiori)* to perfume, scent; *(fazzoletto)* to put perfume *o* scent on; **l'aroma del caffè profumava l'aria** the smell of coffee filled the air. **(b):** ~**rsi** *(pelle, capelli)* to put perfume *o* scent on. **2** *vi* to smell good; ~ **di pulito/fresco** to smell clean/fresh. **3:** ~**rsi** *vr* to put perfume on, put scent on.

profumatamente [profumata'mente] *av:* **pagare qc** ~ to pay through the nose for sth.

profumato, a [profu'mato] *ag (fiore, aria)* fragrant; *(fazzoletto, saponetta)* scented; *(pelle)* sweet-smelling; *(persona)* with perfume on.

profumeria [profume'ria] *sf (gen)* perfumery; *(negozio)* perfume shop.

profumo [pro'fumo] *sm (sostanza)* perfume, scent; *(odore)* scent, fragrance; *(di caffè)* aroma; **avere un buon** ~ to smell nice; **senti che** ~! what a lovely smell!

profusione [profu'zjone] *sf* profusion; **a** ~ **in** plenty.

profuso, a [pro'fuzo] *pp di* **profondersi.**

progenitore, trice [prodʒeni'tore] *sm/f* ancestor.

progesterone [prodʒeste'rone] *sm* progesterone.

progettare [prodʒet'tare] *vt (ponte, casa etc)* to plan, design; *(vacanza, fuga, rapina)* to plan; ~ **di fare qc** to plan to do sth.

progettazione [prodʒettat'tsjone] *sf* planning; **in corso di** ~ at the planning stage.

progettista, i, e [prodʒet'tista] *sm/f* designer.

progetto [pro'dʒetto] *sm* **(a)** *(gen, Archit)* plan; **fare il** ~ **di una casa** to design a house; **fare** ~**i per il futuro** to make plans for the future; **avere**

in ~ **di fare qc** to be planning to do sth. **(b)** *(Dir):* ~ **di legge** bill.

prognosi ['proɲɲozi] *sf (Med)* prognosis; **essere in** ~ **riservata** to be on the danger list; **sciogliere la** ~ **su qn** to take sb off the danger list.

programma, i [pro'gramma] *sm* **(a)** *(Econ, TV, Radio, Pol)* programme, program *(Am)*; *(Inform)* program. **(b)** *(progetto)* plan; **fare** ~**i** to plan; **avere in** ~ **di fare qc** to be planning to do sth; **hai qualcosa in** ~ **per la serata?** do you have anything planned for this evening?; **a causa dello sciopero vi trasmettiamo fuori** ~ **un documentario** due to the strike we are now broadcasting a documentary instead of the scheduled programme. **(c)** *(Scol: di materia)* syllabus; **libri in** ~ set texts.

programmare [program'mare] *vt (gen)* to plan; *(Inform)* to program; *(Cine: avere in programma)* to plan to show; ~ **di fare qc** to plan to do sth.

programmatore, trice [programma'tore] *sm/f (Inform)* (computer) programmer.

programmazione [programmat'tsjone] *sf (vedi vb)* planning; programming.

progredire [progre'dire] *vi (persona: aus* avere; *cosa: aus* essere) *(migliorare)* to progress; ~ **in qc** to make progress in sth.

progressione [progres'sjone] *sf* progression.

progressista, i, e [progres'sista] *ag, sm/f* progressive.

progressivo, a [progres'sivo] *ag* progressive.

progresso [pro'gresso] *sm (gen)* progress; **fare** ~**i** to make progress.

proibire [proi'bire] *vt* **(a)** *(gen)* to forbid; *(per legge, regola)* to prohibit; ~ **a qn di fare qc** to forbid sb to do sth; **gli fu proibito di entrare** he was refused admission. **(b)** *(impedire):* ~ **a qn di fare qc** to prevent sb from doing sth.

proibitivo, a [proibi'tivo] *ag* prohibitive.

proibito, a [proi'bito] *ag:* **'è** ~ **l'accesso'** 'no admittance'; **'è** ~ **fumare'** 'no smoking'; **sogni** ~**i** impossible dreams; **frutto** ~ *(Rel, fig)* forbidden fruit.

proibizione [proibit'tsjone] *sf* prohibition.

proiettare [projet'tare] *vt* **(a)** *(gen, Cine, Geom)* to project; *(ombra, luce)* to cast, throw, project; **stanno proiettando un nuovo film** they're showing *o* screening a new film. **(b)** *(gettare)* to throw (out); **furono proiettati fuori dalla vettura** they were thrown out of the car.

proiettile [pro'jettile] *sm (corpo lanciato in aria)* projectile; *(pallottola)* bullet; **a prova di** ~ bulletproof.

proiettore [projet'tore] *sm* **(a)** *(Cine, Fot)* projector. **(b)** *(in stadio etc)* floodlight; *(Aut)* headlight.

proiezione [projet'tsjone] *sf (gen, Cine, Geom)* projection; **cabina di** ~ *(Cine)* projection room.

prole ['prɔle] *sf* children *pl*; **senza** ~ childless.

proletariato [proleta'rjato] *sm* proletariat.

proletario, a [prole'tarjo] *ag, sm/f* proletarian.

proliferare [prolife'rare] *vi (anche fig)* to proliferate.

prolifico, a, ci, che [pro'lifiko] *ag* prolific.

prolisso, a [pro'lisso] *ag* verbose.

prologo, ghi ['prɔlogo] *sm* prologue.

prolunga, ghe [pro'lunga] *sf* extension.

prolungamento [prolunga'mento] *sm (gen)* extension; *(di strada)* continuation.

prolungare [prolun'gare] **1** *vt (gen)* to prolong; *(biglietto)* to extend; *(strada, muro)* to extend, continue; *(vacanza)* to prolong, extend. **2:** ~**rsi** *vr (film, discussione etc)* to go on; *(effetto)* to last; **la vacanza si è prolungata di alcuni giorni** we *(o* they *etc*) extended our (*o* their *etc*) holiday by a few days.

promemoria [prome'mɔrja] *sm inv* memorandum, memo.

promessa [pro'messa] *sf* promise; **fare/mantenere una ~** to make/keep a promise; **gli ha fatto la ~ di tornare** she promised him that she would come back; **è una giovane ~ del teatro** he (*o* she) is a promising young actor (*o* actress); **ogni ~ è debito!** I'll hold you to that!

promesso, a [pro'messo] **1** *pp di* **promettere**. **2** *ag*: **terra ~a** (*Rel, fig*) promised land; **sposi ~i** betrothed couple *sg*. **3** *sm/f (fidanzato)* betrothed.

promettente [promet'tɛnte] *ag* promising.

promettere [pro'mettere] **1** *vt (gen, fig)* to promise; **te lo prometto** I promise (you); **ha promesso di venire** *o* **che sarebbe venuto** he promised to come *o* that he would come; **~ mari e monti a qn** to promise sb the earth. **2** *vi*: **~ (bene)** *(tempo)* to be promising; *(studente, attore etc)* to show promise, be very promising; **il tempo promette male** *o* **non promette niente di buono** the weather doesn't look very promising.

prominente [promi'nɛnte] *ag* prominent.

prominenza [promi'nɛntsa] *sf* protuberance.

promiscuità [promiskui'ta] *sf* promiscuity.

promiscuo, a [pro'miskuo] *ag* **(a)**: **matrimonio ~** mixed marriage. **(b)** *(Gram)*: **nome ~** common-gender noun.

promontorio [promon'tɔrjo] *sm (Geog)* promontory, headland.

promosso, a [pro'mɔsso] *pp di* **promuovere**.

promotore, trice [promo'tore] **1** *sm/f (di iniziativa, campagna)* promoter; *(di festa)* organizer. **2** *ag (vedi s)* promoting; organizing.

promozionale [promottsjo'nale] *ag* promotional.

promozione [promot'tsjone] *sf (gen, Comm, Sport)* promotion; **avere la ~ a** to be promoted to; **~ delle vendite** sales promotion.

promulgare [promul'gare] *vt* to promulgate.

promulgazione [promulgat'tsjone] *sf* promulgation.

promuovere [pro'mwɔvere] *vt (gen)* to promote; **~ qn (a)** to promote sb (to); **lo studente è stato promosso** the student passed (his exams).

pronipote [proni'pote] *sm/f* great-grandchild; **~i** *(discendenti)* déscendants.

pronome [pro'nome] *sm* pronoun.

pronominale [pronomi'nale] *ag* pronominal.

pronosticare [pronosti'kare] *vt* to predict, forecast, foretell.

pronostico, ci [pro'nɔstiko] *sm* forecast.

prontezza [pron'tettsa] *sf (vedi ag a, b)* readiness; quickness, promptness; **~ di spirito/mente** readiness of wit/mind; **~ di riflessi** quick reflexes.

pronto, a ['pronto] *ag* **(a)** *(gen)* ready; **essere ~ a tutto** to be ready for anything; **essere ~ a fare qc** to be ready to do sth; **tienti ~ a partire** be ready to leave; **~i! attenti! via!** ready! steady! go! **(b)** *(intervento)* quick, prompt; **ha sempre la risposta ~a** he's always got an answer; **squadre di ~ intervento** emergency services; **~ soccorso** first aid; **~a consegna** *(Comm)* prompt delivery; **a ~ cassa** *(Comm)* cash on delivery. **(c)** *(Telec)* hello.

prontuario [prontu'arjo] *sm* manual, handbook.

pronuncia [pro'nuntʃa] *etc* = **pronunzia** *etc*.

pronunzia [pro'nuntsja] *sf* pronunciation; **difetto di ~** speech defect.

pronunziare [pronun'tsjare] **1** *vt (gen)* to pronounce; *(nome)* to utter; **~ male qc** to mispronounce sth; **~ una sentenza** *(Dir)* to pronounce

sentence. **2**: **~rsi** *vr*: **~rsi (su qc)** *(dare un'opinione)* to give one's opinion (on sth); **~rsi a favore/contro** to pronounce o.s. in favour of/against; **non mi pronuncio** I don't want to commit myself.

pronunziato, a [pronun'tsjato] *ag* **(a)** *(accento, tendenza)* pronounced, marked. **(b)** *(lineamenti)* prominent; *(mento)* protruding.

propaganda [propa'ganda] *sf* propaganda; **fare ~ per qn/qc** to push sb/sth.

propagandare [propagan'dare] *vt (idea)* to propagandize; *(prodotto, invenzione)* to push, plug *(fam)*.

propagandista, i, e [propagan'dista] *sm/f* propagandist.

propagandistico, a, ci, che [propagan'distiko] *ag* propaganda *attr*.

propagare [propa'gare] **1** *vt (fede, idea)* to propagate; *(notizia, malattia)* to spread. **2**: **~rsi** *vr (gen)* to spread; *(Fis: onde)* to be propagated; *(Bio: specie)* to propagate.

propagatore, trice [propaga'tore] *sm/f* propagator.

propagazione [propagat'tsjone] *sf (vedi vb)* propagation; spreading.

propaggine [pro'paddʒine] *sf (Bot)* layer; *(fig: diramazione)* offshoot.

propano [pro'pano] *sm* propane.

propedeutico, a, ci, che [prope'dɛutiko] *ag (corso, trattato)* introductory.

propellente [propel'lɛnte] *ag, sm* propellent.

propendere [pro'pɛndere] *vi*: **~ per** to favour; **~ a fare qc** to be inclined to do sth; **~ per il sì** to be in favour; **~ per il no** not to be in favour.

propensione [propen'sjone] *sf* **(a)** inclination; **avere ~ a credere che...** to be inclined to think that.... **(b)** *(disposizione)* bent; **avere ~ per la matematica** to have a bent for mathematics.

propenso, a [pro'penso] **1** *pp di* **propendere**. **2** *ag*: **essere ~ a qc** to be in favour of sth; **essere ~ a fare qc** to be inclined to do sth.

propinare [propi'nare] *vt (scherz: pietanza)* to serve up; **~ veleno a qn** to slip poison to sb; **ci ha propinato tutte le foto di famiglia** he dragged out all the family photographs for us.

propiziare [propit'tsjare] *vt*: **~ qn**, **~rsi qn** to gain sb's favour; **~ gli dei** to propitiate the gods.

propiziatorio, a [propittsja'tɔrjo] *ag* propitiatory.

propizio, a [pro'pittsjo] *ag*: **~ (per)** *(gen)* favourable (to); *(momento)* opportune (for).

proponimento [proponi'mento] *sm* resolution; **fare il ~ di fare qc** to resolve to do sth; **nonostante i miei ~i** in spite of my good intentions.

proporre [pro'porre] **1** *vt* **(a)** *(suggerire)* to suggest, propose; *(soluzione, candidato)* to put forward; **~ qc a qn** to suggest *o* propose sth to sb; **~ di fare qc** to suggest *o* propose doing sth; **gli ho proposto di venire** I suggested that he should come, I suggested to him to come along. **(b)** *(offrire: aiuto, prezzo)* to offer; **~ di fare** to offer to do; **~ qc a qn** to offer sth to sb, offer sb sth. **(c)**: **proporsi qc** *(obiettivo, meta)* to set o.s. sth; **proporsi di fare qc** to resolve to do sth. **2**: **proporsi** *vr*: **proporsi come candidato** to put o.s. forward as a candidate.

proporzionale [proportsjo'nale] *ag* proportional; **~ a** proportional to, proportionate to.

proporzionato, a [proportsjo'nato] *ag*: **~ a** proportionate to, proportional to; **ben ~** well-proportioned.

proporzione [propor'tsjone] *sf (gen, Mat)* proportion; **in ~ (a)** in proportion (to); **in ~ diretta/inversa** in direct/inverse proportion *o* ratio;

mancare di ~ to be out of proportion; **un movimento di grandi** ~**i** (fig) an important movement.

proposito [pro'pɔzito] sm (a) (intenzione) intention; **avere il** ~ **di fare qc** to intend to do sth; **fare qc di** ~ to do sth on purpose o deliberately; **essere pieno di buoni** ~**i** to be full of good intentions. (b) (argomento): **a questo** ~ on this subject; **a quale** ~ **voleva vedermi?** what did he want to see me about?; **a** ~ **della tua ragazza...** talking of your girlfriend...; **le scrivo a** ~ **dell'inserzione** I am writing to you with reference to the advertisement; **a** ~, **sai dirmi...** by the way, can you tell me...; **capitare** o **arrivare a** ~ to turn up at the right time.

proposizione [propozit'tsjone] sf (a) (Gram) sentence; ~ **semplice/composta** simple/compound sentence; ~ **principale** principal clause. (b) (Mat) proposition.

proposta [pro'posta] sf (gen) proposal; (suggerimento) suggestion; **fare una** ~ to put forward a proposal; to make a suggestion; ~ **di legge** (Pol) bill; ~ **di matrimonio** proposal of marriage; **fare una** ~ **di matrimonio a qn** to propose to sb.

proposto, a [pro'posto] pp di **proporre.**

propriamente [proprja'mente] av (correttamente) properly, correctly; (in modo specifico) specifically; ~ **detto** in the strict sense of the word; **subito dopo l'ingresso** ~ **detto** immediately beyond the hall itself.

proprietà [proprje'ta] sf inv (a) (caratteristica, qualità) property. (b) (possedimento: casa) property; (: terreno) property, land; **avere delle** ~ to own property; ~ **privata** private property; **essere di** ~ **di qn** to belong to sb. (c) (nel parlare, scrivere) correctness; ~ **di linguaggio** correct use of language.

proprietario, a [proprje'tarjo] sm/f (gen) owner; (di pensione) landlord/lady; (di albergo) proprietor/tress; ~ **terriero** landowner.

proprio, a ['prɔprjo] 1 ag (a) (poss) own; **l'ho visto con i miei** ~**i occhi** I saw it with my own eyes; **per motivi miei** ~**i** for my own o for personal reasons; **fare qc per conto** ~ to do sth for o.s. (b) (tipico, caratteristico): ~ **di** peculiar to, characteristic of; **è** ~ **dei mammiferi** it's peculiar to o characteristic of mammals; **è un atteggiamento** ~ **di quel tipo di persona** it's an attitude characteristic o typical of that kind of person. (c) (esatto) proper, exact; **senso** ~ **di un termine** exact o proper meaning of a term; **è stata una vera e** ~**a sciocchezza** it was pure foolishness. (d) (Gram): **nome** m ~ proper noun.
2 pron one's own; **ognuno si prenda il** ~ everybody take their own.
3 sm: **mettersi in** ~ to set up on one's own; **perderci del** ~ to be out of pocket.
4 av (a) (precisamente) exactly, just; **le cose sono andate** ~ **così** things went just o exactly like this. (b) (veramente) really; **oggi mi sento** ~ **bene** I feel really fit today; **ma sei** ~ **certo?** are you really sure?, are you a hundred per cent certain?; **quel tipo non mi piace** ~ I really can't stand that man; **non voleva** ~ **farlo** he really didn't want to do it, he didn't want to do it at all.

propugnare [propuɲ'nare] vt to support.

propulsione [propul'sjone] sf (Tecn, Aer, Naut) propulsion; **a** ~ **atomica** atomic-powered.

propulsore [propul'sore] sm (Tecn) propeller.

prora ['prɔra] sf (Naut: prua) bow, bows, prow; **vento di** ~ head wind.

proroga, ghe ['prɔroga] sf (vedi vb) extension; deferment.

prorogare [proro'gare] vt (durata) to extend; (scadenza, termine) to defer, put back.

prorompente [prorom'pɛnte] ag (fiume, torrente) gushing; **il suo entusiasmo era** ~ he was overflowing with enthusiasm.

prorompere [pro'rompere] vi (fiume, torrente): ~ **dagli argini** to burst its banks; ~ **in pianto/in una risata** to burst into tears/out laughing.

prorotto, a [pro'rotto] pp di **prorompere.**

prosa ['prɔza] sf (a) (Letteratura) prose; **scrivere in** ~ to write in prose; **opera in** ~ prose work. (b) (Teatro): **la stagione della** ~ theatre season; **attore di** ~ theatre actor; **compagnia di** ~ theatrical company.

prosaico, a, ci, che [pro'zaiko] ag prosaic, mundane.

prosatore, trice [proza'tore] sm/f prose writer.

prosciogliere [proʃ'ʃɔʎʎere] vt: ~ **qn (da)** (obbligo, giuramento) to release sb (from); (Dir: da accusa) to acquit sb (of).

prosciolto, a [proʃ'ʃɔlto] pp di **prosciogliere.**

prosciugamento [proʃʃuga'mento] sm (naturale) drying up; (artificiale) draining; (bonifica) reclamation.

prosciugare [proʃʃu'gare] 1 vt (asciugare: naturalmente) to dry up; (: artificialmente) to drain; (bonificare) to reclaim. 2: ~**rsi** vr to dry up.

prosciutto [proʃ'ʃutto] sm ham; ~ **affumicato** smoked ham.

proscritto, a [pros'kritto] 1 pp di **proscrivere.** 2 sm/f (fuorilegge) outlaw; (esule) exile.

proscrivere [pros'krivere] vt (Storia) to proscribe; (esiliare) to exile, banish; (fig: abolire) to ban.

proscrizione [proskrit'tsjone] sf (vedi vb) proscription; banishment; banning.

prosecuzione [prosekut'tsjone] sf continuation.

proseguimento [prosegwi'mento] sm (gen) continuation; **buon** ~! all the best!; (per viaggio) enjoy the rest of your journey!

proseguire [prose'gwire] 1 vt (studi, viaggio) to continue; (lavoro) to continue with; ~ **il cammino** to continue on one's way; **proseguì dicendo che...** he went on to say that...; **proseguì la lettura del libro** he carried on reading the book. 2 vi (lavoro, viaggio, strada) to continue; ~ **negli studi** to continue o pursue one's studies; **come prosegue?** (lavoro etc) how is it coming along?; **la polizia prosegue nelle ricerche** the police are pursuing their inquiries.

proselito [pro'zɛlito] sm (Rel, Pol) convert.

prosperare [prospe'rare] vi (commercio, salute) to flourish; (finanze) to thrive; (paese, commerciante) to prosper.

prosperità [prosperi'ta] sf prosperity.

prospero, a ['prɔspero] ag (commercio, salute) flourishing; (finanze) thriving; (paese, commerciante) prosperous, affluent.

prosperoso, a [prospe'roso] ag (vedi **prospero**) flourishing; thriving; prosperous, affluent; **una ragazza** ~**a** a buxom girl.

prospettare [prospet'tare] 1 vt (possibilità) to indicate; (affare) to outline; (ipotesi) to advance. 2: ~**rsi** vr (possibilità) to present itself; (situazione, futuro) to look, seem; **la vacanza si prospetta bene** it looks like being an enjoyable holiday.

prospettiva [prospet'tiva] sf (a) (Disegno) perspective; **in** ~ in perspective. (b) (fig: previsione, possibilità) prospect; **che** ~**e hai?** what are your prospects?

prospetto [pros'petto] sm (a) (Disegno) elevation; (veduta) view; **guardare qc di** ~ to get a front view of sth. (b) (facciata) front, façade. (c) (tabella) table, schedule; (sommario) summary;

~ **delle lezioni** timetable; ~ **dei verbi** verb table.

prospiciente [prospi'tʃɛnte] *ag:* ~ **a** *o* **verso** *(casa)* looking on to; *(terrazza)* overlooking.

prossimamente [prossima'mente] *av* soon; '~ **su questi schermi'** *(Cine)* 'coming shortly to your screens'.

prossimità [prossimi'ta] *sf* proximity; **in** ~ **di** near (to), close to; **in** ~ **delle feste natalizie** as Christmas approaches.

prossimo, a ['prɔssimo] **1** *ag* **(a)** *(successivo: in tempo, spazio)* next; **nei** ~**i giorni** in the next few days; **scendo alla** ~**a fermata** I get off at the next stop; **la** ~**a volta stai attento!** next time be careful! **(b)** *(vicino: gen)* near; *(: parente)* close; **in un** ~ **futuro** in the near future; **essere** ~ **alla laurea** *o* **a laurearsi** to be about to graduate; **è** ~ **alla fine** *(fig: morte)* he is close to death. **(c)** *(Gram)*: **passato** ~ present perfect; **trapassato** ~ pluperfect. **2** *sm* **(a)** *(Rel)* neighbour, fellow man. **(b)**: **avanti il** ~**!** *(a sportello etc)* next please!

prostata ['prɔstata] *sf (Anat)* prostate (gland).

prosternarsi [proster'narsi] *vr:* ~ **davanti a qn** to prostrate o.s. before sb, bow down before sb.

prostituire [prostitu'ire] **1** *vt* to prostitute. **2:** ~**rsi** *vr* to prostitute o.s.

prostituta [prosti'tuta] *sf* prostitute.

prostituzione [prostitut'tsjone] *sf* prostitution.

prostrare [pros'trare] **1** *vt* *(sog: malattia)* to seriously debilitate; **prostrato dal dolore** overcome *o* prostrate with grief. **2:** ~**rsi** *vr* to prostrate o.s.; ~**rsi ai piedi di qn/davanti a qn** to bow down at sb's feet/before sb.

prostrazione [prostrat'tsjone] *sf* prostration.

protagonista, i, e [protago'nista] *sm/f* protagonist.

proteggere [pro'teddʒere] **1** *vt* *(gen)* to protect; *(moralmente)* to guard, shield; *(fig: artista, arte)* to be a patron of. **2:** ~**rsi** *vr* to protect o.s.

proteico, a, ci, che [pro'tɛiko] *ag* protein *attr*; **altamente** ~ high in protein.

proteina [prote'ina] *sf* protein.

protendere [pro'tɛndere] **1** *vt* to stretch out. **2:** ~**rsi** *vr* to stretch forward; ~**rsi dalla finestra** to lean out of the window.

protesi ['prɔtezi] *sf inv (Med)* prosthesis; ~ **dentaria** dentures *pl*.

proteso, a [pro'teso] *pp di* **protendere**.

protesta [pro'tɛsta] *sf* protest; **di** ~ *(marcia, sciopero etc)* protest *attr*; **fare una** ~ **contro** to protest against.

protestante [protes'tante] *ag, sm/f* Protestant.

protestantesimo [protestan'tezimo] *sm* Protestantism.

protestare [protes'tare] **1** *vt* to protest; ~ **la propria innocenza,** ~**rsi innocente** to protest one's innocence. **2** *vi* to protest.

protesto [pro'tɛsto] *sm (Dir)* protest; **mandare una cambiale in** ~ to dishonour a bill.

protettivo, a [protet'tivo] *ag* protective.

protetto, a [pro'tɛtto] **1** *pp di* **proteggere**. **2** *sm/f* protégé(e); *(fig: favorito)* favourite.

protettorato [protetto'rato] *sm (Pol)* protectorate.

protettore, trice [protet'tore] **1** *sm/f (difensore)* protector, guardian; *(di artista, arte)* patron. **2** *sm (di prostituta)* pimp. **3** *ag* **(a)** *(Rel)*: **santo** ~ patron saint. **(b)**: **società** ~**trice degli animali** animal protection society; **società** ~**trice dei consumatori** consumer protection society.

protezione [protet'tsjone] *sf (difesa)* protection; *(di arte, artista)* patronage; **misure di** ~ protective measures; ~ **della natura** preservation *o* protection of the countryside; **prendere qn sotto la propria** ~ to give sb one's patronage; ~ **civile** civil defence.

protezionismo [protettsjo'nizmo] *sm* protectionism.

protezionista, i, e [protettsjo'nista] *ag, sm* protectionist.

protocollare [protokol'lare] **1** *vt (Amm)* to register. **2** *ag* of protocol.

protocollo [proto'kɔllo] **1** *sm* **(a)** *(registro)* register; **numero di** ~ reference number. **(b)** *(accordo internazionale, cerimoniale)* protocol. **2** *ag inv*: **foglio** ~ foolscap.

protone [pro'tone] *sm* proton.

prototipo [pro'tɔtipo] *sm* prototype; **il** ~ **dell'americano** *(fig)* your typical American.

protrarre [pro'trarre] **1** *vt* to prolong; **ha deciso di** ~ **il suo soggiorno di un mese** he decided to stay on a month longer. **2:** **protrarsi** *vr* to go on, continue.

protratto, a [pro'tratto] *pp di* **protrarre**.

protuberanza [protube'rantsa] *sf (Geol)* protuberance; *(Anat)* swelling.

prova ['prɔva] *sf* **(a)** *(esperimento)* test, trial; **sottoporre ad una** ~ to test; **essere in** ~ *(persona: per lavoro)* to be on trial; **assumere in** ~ *(per lavoro)* to take on on a trial basis; **mettere alla** ~ to put to the test; **sta mettendo a dura** ~ **la mia pazienza** he is trying my patience severely; **circuito/volo di** ~ test track/flight; **giro di** ~ *(Sport)* trial run; **a** ~ **di bomba** bombproof; *(fig)* indestructible; **a** ~ **di proiettile** bulletproof; **la** ~ **del fuoco** *(fig)* the crucial test.

(b) *(tentativo)* attempt, try; **fare una** ~ to make an attempt, have a try.

(c) *(Scol)* exam, test; ~ **orale/scritta** oral/written exam.

(d) *(dimostrazione: anche Mat)* proof *no pl*; *(Dir)* proof *no pl*, evidence *no pl*; **dare** ~ **di** to give proof of; **hai le** ~**e di ciò che dici?** can you prove what you're saying?; **avevo ragione e tutto ciò ne è la** ~ I was right and this all goes to prove it; **una** ~ *(Dir)* a piece of evidence; ~ **a carico/a discarico** *(Dir)* evidence for the prosecution/for the defence; **assolto per insufficienza di** ~**e** acquitted due to lack of evidence; **fino a** ~ **contraria** until it's proved otherwise; **fino a** ~ **contraria questa è casa mia!** until such time as circumstances change this is my house!; ~ **del nove** *(Mat)* casting out nines; *(fig)* crucial test.

(e) *(Teatro)* rehearsal; ~ **generale** dress rehearsal; **fare le** ~**e** to rehearse.

(f) *(Tip)* proof.

provare [pro'vare] **1** *vt* **(a)** *(tentare)* to try; *(nuova medicina, macchina, freni)* to try out, test; *(scarpe, abito)* to try on; ~ **a fare qc** to try to do sth; **prova tu se ci riesci!** you try and see if you can do it!; ~**rsi una gonna** to try on a skirt. **(b)** *(dare le prove di: verità, teoria, Dir)* to prove. **(c)** *(mettere alla prova: coraggio etc)* to put to the test; **è molto provato da quell'esperienza** the experience has left its mark on him. **(d)** *(sentimento)* to feel; *(sensazione)* to experience. **(e)** *(Teatro)* to rehearse. **2:** ~**rsi** *vr:* ~**rsi a fare qc** to try to do sth; **provati e vedrai!** just you try it!

provenienza [prove'njentsa] *sf (origine)* origin; *(fonte)* source; **luogo di** ~ place of origin.

provenire [prove'nire] *vi (aus essere)*: ~ **da** *(per nascita etc)* to come from; *(essere causato)* to be due to, be the result of.

proventi [pro'vɛnti] *smpl* revenue *sg*.

provenuto, a [prove'nuto] *pp di* **provenire**.

provenzale [proven'tsale] *ag, sm* Provençal.

proverbiale [prover'bjale] *ag* proverbial.

proverbio [pro'vɛrbjo] *sm* proverb; **come dice il** ~ as the proverb says, as the saying goes.

provetta [pro'vetta] *sf (Chim)* test tube; **bambino in ~** test-tube baby; **fare un figlio in ~** to have a test-tube baby.

provetto, a [pro'vetto] *ag* skilled, experienced.

provincia, ce *o* **cie** [pro'vintʃa] *sf* province; **gente/vita di ~** provincial people/life; **venire dalla ~** to come from the provinces.

provinciale [provin'tʃale] **1** *ag (anche peg)* provincial; **strada ~** main road. **2** *sm/f (anche peg)* provincial.

provino [pro'vino] *sm (Cine)* screen test; **fare un ~** to have a screen test.

provocante [provo'kante] *ag* provocative.

provocare [provo'kare] *vt (incidente, rivolta, risata)* to cause; *(persona)* to provoke; *(collera, curiosità)* to arouse.

provocatore, trice [provoka'tore] **1** *sm/f (di rivolta etc)* agitator. **2** *ag:* **agente ~** agent provocateur.

provocatorio, a [provoka'tɔrjo] *ag* provocative.

provocazione [provokat'tsjone] *sf* provocation.

provvedere [provve'dere] **1** *vi* **(a): ~ a** *(famiglia)* to provide for. **(b)** *(prendere provvedimenti)* to take steps; **hanno provveduto a mandare rinforzi** they arranged for reinforcements to be sent. **(c): ~ a** *(occuparsi di)* to look after. **2** *vt:* **~ qc a qn** to supply sth to sb; **~ qn di qc** to provide *o* supply sb with sth.

provvedimento [provvedi'mento] *sm* measure, step; *(di previdenza)* precaution; **~ disciplinare** disciplinary measure.

provveditorato [provvedito'rato] *sm (Amm):* **~ agli studi** divisional education offices *pl.*

provveditore [provvedi'tore] *sm (Amm):* **~ agli studi** divisional director of education.

provvidenza [provvi'dɛntsa] *sf (divina)* providence; **un dono della ~** a godsend; **ti ha mandato la ~!** you're a godsend!

provvidenziale [provviden'tsjale] *ag (arrivo, pioggia)* providential; **il tuo arrivo è stato ~!** your coming here was a godsend!

provvigione [provvi'dʒone] *sf (Comm)* commission; **lavoro/stipendio a ~** job/salary on a commission basis.

provvisorietà [provvizorje'ta] *sf (vedi ag)* temporary nature; provisional nature.

provvisorio, a [provvi'zɔrjo] *ag (riparo, lavoro)* temporary; *(governo)* temporary, provisional.

provvista [prov'vista] *sf* supply, stock; **fare ~ di** to stock up with; **fare ~e** to take in supplies; **~e alimentari** provisions.

provvisto, a [prov'visto] *pp di* **provvedere.**

prua [prua] *sf (Naut)* bow, bows, prow.

prudente [pru'dɛnte] *ag (attento)* cautious, prudent; *(saggio)* wise, sensible; **sarebbe ~ che tu lo facessi** you would be well advised to do it; **non è ~** it's not advisable; **è più ~** it's wiser *o* safer; **sii ~!** be careful!, take care!

prudenza [pru'dɛntsa] *sf (vedi ag)* caution, prudence; wisdom; **per ~** as a precaution, to be on the safe side; **ha avuto la ~ di non dire niente** he had the good sense *o* he was wise enough to keep quiet.

prudere ['prudere] *vi* to be itchy, itch; **mi prude un orecchio** my ear is itchy.

prugna ['pruɲɲa] *sf (Bot)* plum; **~e secche** prunes.

pruno ['pruno] *sm (Bot: cespuglio)* blackthorn; *(: spina)* thorn.

pruriginoso, a [pruridʒi'noso] *ag* itchy.

prurito [pru'rito] *sm (anche fig)* itch; **ho ~ alla mano** my hand is itchy.

prussiano, a [prus'sjano] *ag, sm/f* Prussian.

P.S. *abbr* **(a)** *(= postscriptum)* P.S. **(b)** *abbr di* **Pubblica Sicurezza.**

pseudonimo [pseu'dɔnimo] *sm* assumed name; *(di scrittore)* pen name; *(di attore)* stage name.

P.S.I. *abbr di Partito Socialista Italiano.*

psicanalisi [psika'nalizi] *sf* psychoanalysis.

psicanalista, i, e [psikana'lista] *sm/f* psychoanalyst.

psicanalitico, a, ci, che [psikana'litiko] *ag* psychoanalytic(al).

psicanalizzare [psikanalid'dzare] *vt* to psychoanalyse.

psiche ['psike] *sf* psyche.

psichedelico, a, ci, che [psike'dɛliko] *ag (Psic, luci)* psychedelic.

psichiatra, i, e [psi'kjatra] *sm/f* psychiatrist.

psichiatria [psikja'tria] *sf* psychiatry.

psichiatrico, a, ci, che [psi'kjatriko] *ag (caso)* psychiatric; *(reparto, ospedale)* psychiatric, mental.

psichico, a, ci, che ['psikiko] *ag* psychological.

psicofarmaco, ci [psiko'farmako] *sm (Med)* drug used in treatment of mental conditions.

psicologia [psikolo'dʒia] *sf* psychology.

psicologico, a, ci, che [psiko'lɔdʒiko] *ag* psychological.

psicologo, a, gi, ghe [psi'kɔlogo] *sm/f* psychologist.

psicopatico, a, ci, che [psiko'patiko] **1** *ag* psychopathic. **2** *sm/f* psychopath.

psicosi [psi'kɔzi] *sf inv (Med)* psychosis; *(fig)* obsessive fear.

psicosomatico, a, ci, che [psikoso'matiko] *ag* psychosomatic.

P.T. *abbr (= Posta e Telegrafi)* P.O.

pubblicare [pubbli'kare] *vt* to publish.

pubblicazione [pubblikat'tsjone] *sf* **(a)** *(gen)* publication; **~ periodica** periodical. **(b)** *(di matrimonio):* **~i** *pl* banns; **fare le ~i** to publish the (marriage) banns.

pubblicista, i, e [pubbli'tʃista] *sm/f* **(a)** *(giornalista)* freelance journalist. **(b)** *(Dir)* expert in public law.

pubblicità [pubblitʃi'ta] *sf inv* **(a)** *(Comm: professione)* advertising; **fare ~ a qc** to advertise sth; **lavora nella ~** he works in advertising. **(b)** *(annuncio su giornali)* advertisement; **c'è troppa ~ su quella rivista** there are too many advertisements in that magazine. **(c)** *(rivelazione)* publicity; **fare molta ~ a qc** to give sth a lot of publicity.

pubblicitario, a [pubblitʃi'tarjo] **1** *ag (campagna, agenzia)* advertising; *(film, trovata)* publicity *attr;* **cartello ~** advertising poster; **annuncio** *o* **avviso ~** advertisement. **2** *sm* advertising agent.

pubblico, a, ci, che ['pubbliko] **1** *ag (gen)* public; **scuola ~a** state school; **~che relazioni** public relations. **2** *sm (gen)* public; *(Teatro, Cine)* audience, public; *(di partita)* spectators *pl;* **il ~ dei lettori** the reading public; **un libro destinato al grande ~** a book written for the general public.

pube ['pube] *sm (Anat)* pubis.

pubertà [puber'ta] *sf* puberty.

pudicizia [pudi'tʃittsja] *sf* modesty.

pudico, a, ci, che [pu'diko] *ag* modest.

pudore [pu'dore] *sm (sense of)* modesty; *(vergogna)* shame; *(riservatezza)* discretion; **falso ~** false modesty; **oltraggio al ~** *(Dir)* indecent behaviour.

puericultrice [puerikul'tritʃe] *sf* paediatric nurse.

puericultura [puerikul'tura] *sf* paedology.

puerile [pue'rile] *ag (anche peg)* childish, puerile.

puerilità [puerili'ta] *sf* childishness, puerility.

puerpera [pu'ɛrpera] *sf* woman who has just given birth.

pugilato [pudʒi'lato] *sm* boxing.

pugile ['pudʒile] *sm* boxer.

pugnalare [puɲɲa'lare] *vt* to stab; ~ **alle spalle** (*anche fig*) to stab in the back.

pugnalata [puɲɲa'lata] *sf* (*ferita*) stab wound; (*fig: colpo*) severe blow; **dare una** ~ **a qn** to stab sb; **una** ~ **alle spalle** (*anche fig*) a stab in the back.

pugnale [puɲ'ɲale] *sm* dagger; **colpo di** ~ stab; **uccidere con un** ~ to stab to death.

pugno ['puɲɲo] *sm* **(a)** (*mano*) fist; **a** ~**i stretti** with clenched fists; **con la pistola in** ~ with one's gun in one's hand; **scrivere qc di proprio** ~ to write sth in one's own hand; **mostrare i** ~**i a qn** to shake one's fist at sb; **ormai ha la vittoria in** ~ he now has victory within his grasp; **tenere la situazione in** ~ to have control of the situation; **avere qn in** ~ to have sb in the palm of one's hand; **ormai lo abbiamo in** ~ (*con ricatto, minacce etc*) we've got him in our power now; (*criminale*) we've got him now.

(b) (*colpo*) punch; **dare un** ~ **a qn** to punch sb; **gli ha dato un** ~ **in un occhio** he punched him in the eye; **fare a** ~**i** to fight; (*fig: colori*) to clash; ~ **di ferro** knuckleduster; **essere un** ~ **in un occhio** (*fig*) to be an eyesore.

(c) (*manciata*): **un** ~ **di** a handful of; **un** ~ **di uomini** a handful of men; **rimanere con un** ~ **di mosche in mano** (*fig*) to be left empty-handed.

pula ['pula] *sf* chaff.

pulce ['pultʃe] *sf* flea; **mercato delle** ~**i** flea market; **il gioco della** ~ tiddlywinks *sg*; **mi hai messo una** ~ **nell'orecchio** (*fig: insospettire*) you've aroused my suspicions.

Pulcinella [pultʃi'nɛlla] *sm* (*maschera*) Punch; **segreto di** ~ (*fig*) open secret.

pulcino [pul'tʃino] *sm* (*Zool*) chick; (*vezzeggiativo*) pet; **timido come un** ~ as shy as a mouse.

puledra [pu'ledra] *sf* filly.

puledro [pu'ledro] *sm* colt.

puleggia, ge [pu'leddʒa] *sf* (*Tecn*) pulley.

pulire [pu'lire] **1** *vt* **(a)** (*gen*) to clean; (*giardino*) to clear; (*cassetto*) to clear out; (*lucidare*) to polish; ~ **a secco** to dry-clean; **far** ~ **qc** to have sth cleaned; ~ **il piatto** (*fig*) to clear one's plate. **(b)**: ~**rsi** (*mani, sedere etc*) to clean; (*naso, bocca*) to wipe; ~**rsi i denti** to brush *o* clean one's teeth; **pulisciti i piedi** wipe your feet. **2**: ~**rsi** *vr* to clean o.s. (up).

pulita [pu'lita] *sf* quick clean; **dare una** ~ **a qc** to give sth a quick clean.

pulito, a [pu'lito] *ag* (*gen*) clean; (*fig: lavoro, persona*) honest; **una ragazza dalla faccia** ~**a** (*fig*) an innocent-looking girl; **avere la coscienza** ~**a** to have a clear conscience.

pulitura [puli'tura] *sf* cleaning; ~ **a secco** dry cleaning.

pulizia [pulit'tsia] *sf* **(a)** (*condizione*) cleanliness. **(b)** (*atto*) cleaning; **fare le** ~**e** (*gen*) to do the cleaning; **fare le** ~**e di primavera** to spring-clean; **far** ~ (*fig: portarsi via tutto*) to make a clean sweep.

pullman ['pulman] *sm inv* (*gen*) bus; (*per escursioni etc*) coach.

pullover [pul'lover] *sm inv* pullover, sweater.

pullulare [pullu'lare] *vi* (*pesci*) to teem; (*insetti*) to swarm; **il fiume pullula di pesci** the river is teeming with fish; **la piazza pullulava di turisti** the square was swarming with tourists; **esempi di questo tipo pullulano** there are many examples of this kind.

pulmino [pul'mino] *sm* minibus.

pulpito ['pulpito] *sm* pulpit; **senti da che** ~ **viene la predica!** (*fig*) look who's talking!

pulsante [pul'sante] *sm* (push) button.

pulsare [pul'sare] *vi* (*cuore*) to beat, pulsate; (*vena*) to throb.

pulsazione [pulsat'tsjone] *sf* (*di cuore*) beat; (*di vena*) throbbing; (*Fis*) pulsation.

pulviscolo [pul'viskolo] *sm* (fine) dust; ~ **atmosferico** specks *pl* of dust.

puma ['puma] *sm inv* puma.

pungente [pun'dʒɛnte] *ag* (*frutto, arbusto, spina*) prickly; (*fig: freddo, vento*) biting; (: *ironia, critica*) biting, pungent.

pungere ['pundʒere] **1** *vt* **(a)** (*sog: spina, ago*) to prick; (: *ortica, insetto*) to sting; ~ **qn sul vivo** (*fig*) to cut sb to the quick; **essere punto dal rimorso** to be stricken with remorse. **(b)**: ~**rsi un dito/ una mano** to prick one's finger/one's hand. **2**: ~**rsi** *vr* (*con ago, spina*) to prick o.s.

pungiglione [pundʒiʎ'ʎone] *sm* sting.

pungolare [pungo'lare] *vt* (*fig: spingere*): ~ **qn a fare qc** to goad sb into doing sth.

pungolo ['pungolo] *sm* (*per animali*) goad; (*fig: stimolo*) spur; **il** ~ **dell'ambizione** the spur of ambition.

punire [pu'nire] *vt* to punish.

punitivo, a [puni'tivo] *ag* punitive.

punizione [punit'tsjone] *sf* punishment; (*Sport*) penalty; **dare una** ~ **a qn** to punish sb; **dare una** ~ **esemplare a qn** to make an example of sb; **per** ~ as a punishment.

punta¹ ['punta] *sf* **(a)** (*di matita, ago, coltello*) point; (*di trapano*) drill; (*di perforatrice*) bit; (*di naso, piede, dito, lingua*) tip; (*di campanile, albero*) top; (*di monte*) top, peak; **fare la** ~ **a una matita** to sharpen a pencil; **le** ~**e degli alberi** the treetops; **camminare in** ~ **di piedi** to walk on tiptoe, tiptoe; **ballare sulle** ~**e** (*Danza*) to dance on points; **avere qc sulla** ~ **delle dita/della lingua** (*fig*) to have sth at one's fingertips/on the tip of one's tongue; **prendere qc di** ~ (*fig*) to meet sth head on; **uomo di** ~ (*Sport, Pol*) front-ranking man.

(b) (*fig: pizzico: di zucchero, farina*) touch; (: *di sale*) pinch; (: *d'invidia, rancore*) touch, hint; **c'è una** ~ **d'acido nel latte** the milk tastes slightly sour.

(c) (*Geog*) promontory.

(d) (*massima frequenza o intensità*) peak; **ore di** ~ peak hours; **il traffico delle ore di** ~ rush-hour traffic; ~ **massima/minima** highest/ lowest level.

punta² ['punta] *sf*: **cane da** ~ pointer.

puntare [pun'tare] **1** *vt* **(a)** (*arma*) to point, aim; (*cannocchiale, dito*) to point; ~ **un fucile contro qn** to point a gun at sb; ~ **il dito verso qn/qc** to point (one's finger) at sb/sth; ~ **l'attenzione su qn/qc** to turn one's attention to sb/sth; ~ **gli occhi su qn** to fix one's eyes on sb. **(b)** (*gomiti*) to plant; ~ **i piedi** (*fig*) to dig one's heels in. **(c)** (*nei giochi*): ~ **su** to bet on. **(d)** (*sog: cane*) to point. **2** *vi* **(a)**: ~ **su,** ~ **verso** (*aereo, nave etc*) to make for, head for; ~ **a qc/a fare qc** (*mirare*) to aim for sth/at doing sth. **(b)** (*contare*): ~ **su qn/qc** to rely on sb/sth, count on sb/sth.

puntaspilli [puntas'pilli] *sm inv* = **portaspilli**.

puntata¹ [pun'tata] *sf* **(a)** (*in scommessa, gioco*) bet; **fare una** ~ to place a bet. **(b)** (*fig: breve visita*): **fare una** ~ **a casa** to pop home; **farò una** ~ **a Parigi** I'll pay a flying visit to Paris.

puntata² [pun'tata] *sf* (*di romanzo*) instalment; (*di sceneggiato*) episode; **romanzo a** ~**e** serial.

punteggiare [punted'dʒare] *vt* to punctuate.

punteggiatura [punteddʒa'tura] *sf* punctuation.

punteggio [pun'teddʒo] *sm* (*in gara*) score; (*in esame*) mark; **totalizzare un ~ di 50 punti** to score 50 points.

puntellare [puntel'lare] *vt* (*ponte, muro*) to shore (up); (*porta, finestra*) to prop up; (*fig: ipotesi*) to back up, support.

puntello [pun'tɛllo] *sm* prop, support.

punteruolo [punte'rwɔlo] *sm* (*Tecn*) punch; (*: per stoffa*) bodkin.

puntiglio [pun'tiʎʎo] *sm* (*ostinazione*) obstinacy; **fare qc per ~** to do sth out of sheer obstinacy.

puntiglioso, a [puntiʎ'ʎoso] *ag* punctilious.

puntina [pun'tina] *sf* (a) (*da disegno*) drawing pin. (b) (*del giradischi*) stylus. (c) (*Aut*): **~e** *pl* points.

puntino [pun'tino] *sm* (*di punteggiatura*) dot; **~i di sospensione** suspension points; **mettere i ~i sulle 'i'** (*fig*) to dot the i's and cross the t's; **fare le cose a ~** to do things perfectly; **arrivare a ~** to arrive just at the right moment; **cotto a ~** cooked to a turn.

punto¹, a ['punto] *pp di* pungere.

punto² ['punto] **1** *sm* (a) (*gen*) point; (*luogo*) point, spot, place; (*grado*) point, stage; **la casa è in un bel ~** the house is in a nice spot; **a questo ~, al ~ in cui siamo** at this stage; **a che ~ sei?** (*con lavoro etc*) where have you got to?; (*nel prepararsi*) how are you getting on?; **ad un certo ~** at a certain point; **ad un certo ~ uno si chiede…** there comes a time when one asks oneself…; **fino ad un certo ~** (*fig*) to a certain extent; **non si può essere ingenui fino a questo o tal ~** one cannot be as naïve as that; **era a tal ~ arrabbiato che…** he was so angry that…; **lo odia al ~ tale che…** she hates him so much that…; **passiamo al prossimo ~** (*in discorso ecc*) let's move on to the next item *o* point; **su questo ~ siamo d'accordo** we agree on this point; **siamo sempre allo stesso ~** we're still at the same stage; **essere a buon ~** to have reached a satisfactory stage; **aver raggiunto il ~ in cui…** to have reached the stage where…; **venire al ~** to come to the point; **cotto al ~ giusto** cooked to a turn; **di ~ in bianco** (*improvvisamente*) all of a sudden; (*inaspettatamente*) out of the blue; **sono le 5 in ~** it's 5 o'clock sharp; **vestito di tutto ~** all dressed up.

(b) (*Aer, Naut: posizione*) position; **fare il ~** to take one's position; **fare il ~ della situazione** (*analisi*) to take stock of the situation; (*riassunto*) to sum up the situation.

(c) (*in alfabeto, morse, su 'i'*) dot; (*punteggiatura*) full stop; **~ esclamativo/interrogativo** exclamation/question mark; **due ~i** colon; **~ e virgola** semi-colon; **~ e a capo** new paragraph; **~ e basta!** that's it!, that's enough!

(d) (*Cucito, Maglia, Med*) stitch.

(e) (*Tecn*): **mettere a ~** (*gen*) to adjust; (*motore*) to tune; (*fig: questione*) to define; (*progetto*) to finalize.

2: **~ d'arrivo** arrival point; **~ caldo** (*Mil*) trouble spot; (*d'attualità*) major issue; **~ cardinale** cardinal point; **~ critico** (*anche fig*) critical point; **~ debole** weak spot; **~ di ebollizione** boiling point; **~ d'incontro** meeting place; **~ d'incontro di due rette** point where two lines meet; **~ morto** standstill; **~ nero** (*Anat*) blackhead; **~ nevralgico** (*anche fig*) nerve centre; **~ d'onore** point of honour; **~ di partenza** (*anche fig*) starting point; **~ di vista** point of view.

puntuale [puntu'ale] *ag* punctual; **essere ~** to be punctual, be on time; **arrivare ~** to arrive on time; **essere ~ nei pagamenti** to pay on time.

puntualità [puntuali'ta] *sf* punctuality.

puntualizzare [puntualid'dzare] *vt* to make clear.

puntualmente [puntual'mente] *av* (*gen*) on time; (*iro: al solito*) as usual.

puntura [pun'tura] *sf* (a) (*di insetto*) sting; (*di zanzara, ragno*) bite; (*di spillo*) prick. (b) (*Med*) injection; **~ lombare** lumbar puncture; **fare una ~ a qn** to give sb an injection.

punzecchiare [puntsek'kjare] **1** *vt* (*fig: molestare*) to tease. **2**: **~rsi** *vr* (*uso reciproco*) to tease one another.

punzonare [puntso'nare] *vt* (*Tecn*) to stamp.

punzone [pun'tsone] *sm* stamp.

pupa ['pupa] *sf* (a) (*bambola, fam: ragazza*) doll. (b) (*Zool*) pupa.

pupazzo [pu'pattso] *sm* puppet; **~ di neve** snowman.

pupilla [pu'pilla] *sf* (*Anat*) pupil.

pupillo, a [pu'pillo] *sm/f* (*Dir*) ward; (*fig*) favourite, pet.

purché [pur'ke] *cong* (*a patto che*) as long as, provided that, on condition that; **verrò con te ~ non ci sia molto da aspettare** I'll come with you as long as we don't have to wait long; **~ sia vero!** if only it were true!

pure ['pure] **1** *cong* (a) (*tuttavia, nondimeno*) but, and yet; **non è facile, ~ bisogna riuscirci** it's not easy and yet we have to succeed; **è giovane, ~ ha buon senso** he's young but he's sensible. (b) (*anche se, sebbene*) even though; **pur non volendo, ho dovuto farlo** I had to do it even though I didn't want to; **pur essendo fuori mano** even though it is out of the way. (c): **~ di vederlo contento farebbe di tutto** she would do anything to make him happy.

2 *av* (a) too, as well; (*in proposizioni negative*) either; **viene suo fratello e ~ sua sorella** his brother is coming as is his sister, his brother is coming and his sister is too *o* as well; **siamo stati a Zurigo e ~ a Lucerna** we went to Zurich and to Lucerne as well; **~ lei non lo sa fare** she can't do it either. (b) (*con valore concessivo*): **fai ~!** please do!, by all means!; **te l'avevo pur detto di non andarci** I did tell you not to go.

purè [pu're] *sm inv* (*Culin*) purée; **~ di patate** mashed potatoes.

purezza [pu'rettsa] *sf* (*gen*) purity; (*di colore*) clarity.

purga, ghe ['purga] *sf* purge.

purgante [pur'gante] **1** *sm* purge, purgative. **2** *ag* (*Med*) purgative.

purgare [pur'gare] **1** *vt* (*Med: malato*) to purge, give a purgative to; (*: sangue, aria*) to purify; (*fig: testo, discorso*) to expurgate. **2**: **~rsi** *vr* (*fig*): **~rsi dei peccati** to purge o.s. of one's sins.

purgativo, a [purga'tivo] *ag* (*Med*) purgative.

purgatorio [purga'tɔrjo] *sm* (*Rel, fig*) purgatory.

purificare [purifi'kare] **1** *vt* (*gen*) to purify, cleanse; (*metalli*) to refine. **2**: **~rsi** *vr* to cleanse o.s.

purificazione [purifikat'tsjone] *sf* (*vedi vb*) purification, cleansing; refinement.

puritanesimo [purita'nezimo] *sm* puritanism.

puritano, a [puri'tano] **1** *ag* (*Rel*) puritan; (*fig*) puritanical. **2** *sm/f* (*Rel*) Puritan; (*fig*) puritan.

puro, a ['puro] *ag* (*gen*) pure; (*acqua*) clear, limpid; (*aria*) pure, clean; (*fig: ragazza*) chaste, pure; **di razza ~a** thoroughbred; **è pazzia ~a** it's sheer madness; **è la ~a verità** that's the simple truth; **per ~ caso** by sheer chance, purely by chance.

purosangue [puro'sangwe] **1** *ag inv* (*cavallo*) thoroughbred; **un inglese ~** a full-blooded Englishman. **2** *sm/f inv* (*cavallo*) thoroughbred.

purtroppo [pur'trɔppo] *av* unfortunately.

purulento, a [puru'lɛnto] *ag (Med)* purulent, festering.

pus [pus] *sm (Med)* pus; **fare ~** to ooze pus.

pusillanime [puzil'lanime] **1** *ag* cowardly. **2** *sm/f* coward.

pustola ['pustola] *sf (Med)* pustule; *(foruncolo)* pimple.

putacaso [puta'kazo] *av* just supposing, suppose; **metti, ~, che arrivi anche lui** just supposing *o* suppose he comes too.

putativo, a [puta'tivo] *ag* putative.

putiferio [puti'fɛrjo] *sm* row, rumpus; **fare un ~** to kick up a row.

putrefarsi [putre'farsi] *vr* to putrefy, rot.

putrefatto, a [putre'fatto] **1** *pp di* **putrefarsi**. **2** *ag (carne, legno)* rotten; *(cadavere)* putrid, decayed.

putrefazione [putrefat'tsjone] *sf* putrefaction.

putrido, a ['putrido] *ag (acqua)* putrid; *(carne)* rotten.

puttana [put'tana] *sf (fam)* whore.

putto ['putto] *sm* cupid.

puzza ['puttsa] *sf* = **puzzo**.

puzzare [put'tsare] *vi:* **~ (di)** to smell (of), stink (of); **gli puzza l'alito** his breath stinks, he's got very bad breath; **la faccenda puzza (d'imbroglio)** there's something fishy about the matter; **mi puzza!** *(fig)* it smells fishy to me!

puzzle [pazl] *sm inv* jigsaw puzzle.

puzzo ['puttso] *sm* stink, foul smell; **~ di bruciato** smell of burning; **~ di fritto** stink of fried food; **sento ~** there's a horrible smell; **c'è ~ d'imbroglio** it smells fishy.

puzzola ['puttsola] *sf (Zool)* polecat.

puzzolente [puttso'lɛnte] *ag* smelly, stinking.

Q

Q, q[1] [ku] *sf o m inv (lettera)* Q, q.
q[2] *abbr di* **quintale.**
Q.I. *abbr di* **quoziente d'intelligenza.**
qua [kwa] *av* **(a)** here; **eccomi** ~**!** here I am!; ~ **dentro/sotto** in/under here; **da** *o* **di** ~ **non mi muovo!** I'm not budging from here!; **da** *o* **di** ~ **la vista è stupenda** the view is fantastic from here; **(al) di** ~ **del fiume** on this side of the river; **passavo (per) di** ~ I was passing this way; **(per) di** ~ **non si passa** you can't get through here *o* this way; **vieni più in** ~ come closer.
  (b) *(temporale)*: **da un anno in** ~ since last year; **da quando in** ~**?** since when?
  (c) *(fraseologia)*: **ecco** ~ **cosa succede a non fare attenzione!** just look what happens when you don't pay attention!; **prendi** ~ **questi soldi** here, take this money; **(dammi)** ~**, ci penso io!** just give it to me, I'll see to it!; **dammi** ~**, è mio** give it here, it's mine; **guarda** ~ **che confusione!** just look at this mess!; ~ **la mano** let's shake on it; **che diavolo vuole questo** ~**?** what on earth does he want?
quacchero, a ['kwakkero] *sm/f* Quaker.
quaderno [kwa'dɛrno] *sm (per scuola)* exercise book; ~ **a righe** lined exercise book; ~ **a quadretti** arithmetic exercise book.
quadrangolo [kwa'drangolo] *sm (Geom)* quadrangle.
quadrante [kwa'drante] *sm* **(a)** *(dell'orologio)* face. **(b)** *(Naut, Geom)* quadrant.
quadrare [kwa'drare] **1** *vt (Mat)* to square. **2** *vi (essere esatto: conti)* to tally, balance; *(fig: corrispondere)*: ~ **(con)** to correspond (with); **far** ~ **il bilancio** to balance the books; **qui c'è qualcosa che non quadra** something is amiss here; **quel tipo non mi quadra** *(fam)* I don't like that fellow at all.
quadrato, a [kwa'drato] **1** *ag* **(a)** *(Mat, tavolo, casa, superficie)* square; **metro/chilometro** ~ square metre/kilometre; **radice** ~**a** *(Mat)* square root. **(b)** *(maturo)* sensible, level-headed; *(peg)* square. **2** *sm* **(a)** *(gen, Mat)* square; **elevare al** ~ *(Mat)* to square; **6 al** ~ 6 squared. **(b)** *(Pugilato)* ring.
quadratura [kwadra'tura] *sf (Mat)* squaring; **la** ~ **del cerchio** the squaring of the circle.
quadrettato, a [kwadret'tato] *ag (foglio)* squared; *(tessuto)* checked.
quadretto [kwa'dretto] *sm* **(a)** *(fig: scena, spettacolo)* picture; **siete un bel** ~**!** you make a lovely picture! **(b)**: **a** ~**i** *(stoffa)* checked; *(foglio)* squared.
quadriennale [kwadrien'nale] *ag (che dura 4 anni)* four-year *attr*; *(che avviene ogni 4 anni)* four-yearly.
quadrifoglio [kwadri'fɔʎʎo] *sm* **(a)** *(Bot)* four-leaf clover. **(b)** *(Aut)* cloverleaf.
quadrigetto [kwadri'dʒetto] *sm* four-engined jet.
quadriglia [kwa'driʎʎa] *sf (danza)* quadrille.
quadrilatero, a [kwadri'latero] *ag, sm* quadrilateral.

quadrimestrale [kwadrimes'trale] *ag* **(a)** *(carica, durata)* four-month *attr*, of four months. **(b)** *(rivista, esame)* four-monthly.
quadrimestre [kwadri'mɛstre] *sm (periodo)* four-month period; *(Scol)* term.
quadrimotore [kwadrimo'tore] *sm (Aer)* four-engined plane.
quadripartito, a [kwadripar'tito] **1** *sm (Pol)* four-party government. **2** *ag (Pol: governo)* four-party *attr*; *(: alleanza, conferenza)* four-power *attr*.
quadro[1]**, a** ['kwadro] *ag (quadrato)* square; **parentesi** ~**a** square bracket.
quadro[2] ['kwadro] *sm* **(a)** *(Pittura)* picture, painting; **dipingere un** ~ to paint a picture, to do a painting; ~ **a olio** oil painting.
  (b) *(quadrato)* square; **a** ~**i** *(disegno)* checked.
  (c) *(fig: descrizione)* outline, description; **fare un** ~ **della situazione** to outline the situation; **questo ci fornisce un** ~ **completo della situazione** this gives us a complete picture of the situation; ~ **clinico** *(Med)* anamnesis.
  (d) *(Tecn)* panel, board; ~ **di comando** control panel; ~ **degli strumenti** instrument panel; ~ **di distribuzione** *(Elettr)* switchboard.
  (e) *(fig: tabella di dati)* table, chart.
  (f) *(Teatro)* scene; ~**i viventi** tableaux vivants; ~**!** *(Cine)* focus!
  (g): ~**i** *pl (Mil, di partito, organizzazione)* upper echelons; *(Comm)* managerial staff.
  (h): ~**i** *(Carte)* diamonds.
quadrupede [kwa'drupede] **1** *sm (Zool)* quadruped. **2** *ag (animale)* four-footed.
quadruplicare [kwadrupli'kare] *vt*, ~**rsi** *vr* to quadruple, increase fourfold.
quadruplice [kwa'druplitʃe] *ag* quadruple; **in** ~ **copia** in four copies.
quadruplo, a ['kwadruplo] **1** *ag* quadruple; **il lavoro è** ~ **rispetto a quello iniziale** the work is four times as much as it was at the beginning. **2** *sm (Mat)* quadruple; **vorrei il** ~ **del denaro che ho ora** I would like four times as much money as I have now.
quaggiù [kwad'dʒu] *av (gen)* down here; *(al sud)* here in the south; *(sulla terra)* in this life.
quaglia ['kwaʎʎa] *sf* quail.
qualche ['kwalke] **1** *ag indef* **(a)** *(alcuni, non molti)* a few; **per** ~ **giorno** for a few days; **ho visto** ~ **amico ieri** I saw some *o* a few friends yesterday; **fra** ~ **mese** in a few months; ~ **volta** sometimes; **l'ho incontrato** ~ **volta** I've met him a few times *o* once or twice.
  (b) *(con valore indet: in frasi affermative)* some; *(: in frasi negative e domande)* any; **l'ho già visto da** ~ **parte** I've already seen him somewhere; **in** ~ **modo** somehow; **hai** ~ **sigaretta?** have you any cigarettes?; **hai** ~ **soldo da prestarmi?** can you lend me some money?; **sai se passa** ~ **autobus da questa parte?** do you know if any buses go this way?
  (c) *(un certo)* some; **ci vuole** ~ **tempo per abituarsi** it takes some *o* a little time to get used

to it; **non senza ~ esitazione** not without some hesitation; **c'è ~ fondamento di verità** there's an element of truth in it; **ci dev'essere una ~ spiegazione** there must be some explanation.

2 *av* some, about; **ho camminato ~ 9 chilometri** I walked some *o* about 9 kilometres.

qualcheduno [kwalke'duno] *pron indef* = **qualcuno**.

qualcosa [kwal'kɔsa] *pron indef (in frasi affermative)* something; *(in domande)* anything; **ci dev'essere ~ che non va** there must be something wrong *o* the matter; **è già ~** that's something; **ho ~ da parte** *(soldi)* I've got a little something put aside; **~ mi dice che...** something tells me that...; **è medico, o ~ di simile** *o* **del genere** he's a doctor or something like that; **bevi ~?** would you like something to drink?; **posso fare ~ per te?** can I do anything for you?; **c'è qualcos'altro che desideri?** do you want anything else?; **posso chiederti qualcos'altro?** can I ask you something else?; **~ di meglio** something better; **la scena era ~ di grande** it was a really grand scene; **spera di diventare ~ nella vita** he hopes to become somebody in life.

qualcuno [kwal'kuno] *pron indef* **(a)** *(in frasi affermative)* somebody, someone; *(in domande, in proposizioni condizionali e dubitative)* anybody, anyone; **ho visto ~ là fuori** I saw somebody out there; **aspetti ~?** are you waiting for somebody?; **c'è ~ in casa?** is anybody at home?

(b) *(con valore partitivo: affermazioni)* some; *(: domande)* any; **~ di noi** some of us; **~ di voi vuol venire?** do any of you want to come?; **se ti piacciono, prendine ~ in più** if you like them, take some *o* a few more; **qualcun'altro** somebody *o* someone else; **viene qualcun'altro?** is anybody else coming?; **ce n'è rimasto ~?** are there any left?

(c) *(persona importante, di prestigio)* somebody; **diventerà ~ nella vita** he'll become somebody, he'll make something of his life.

quale ['kwale] **1** *ag* **(a)** *(interrog)* what; **~i sono i tuoi programmi?** what are your plans?; **a ~ conclusione è giunta?** what conclusion did she reach?; **per ~ ragione?** why?; **per ~ data conti di finire?** when do you hope to finish by?; **in ~ giorno vi siete incontrati?** when did you meet?

(b) *(scegliendo tra due o più cose o persone)* which; **~ stanza preferisci?** which room do you prefer?

(c) *(escl)* what; **~ sfortuna!** what bad luck!

(d): **è tale e ~ suo padre** he's just *o* exactly like his father; **è (tale) ~ l'avevo lasciato** it's just *o* exactly as I left it.

(e) *(con valore relativo: qualunque)*: **~ che** whatever; **accetterò ~i che siano le condizioni** I'll accept whatever the conditions.

(f) *(fraseologia)*: **in un certo qual modo** in some way or other, somehow or other; **per la qual cosa** for which reason.

2 *pron interrog (scegliendo tra due o più cose o persone)* which; **~ dei due scegli?** which of the two do you want?

3 *pron rel* **(a)** *(sog: persona)* who; *(: cosa)* which, that; **suo padre, il ~ è avvocato, ...** his father, who is a lawyer, ...; **a tutti coloro i ~i fossero interessati...** to whom it may concern...; **quel negozio, il ~ fu aperto nel 1910** that shop, which was opened in 1910.

(b) *(con prep)*: **il signore con il ~ parlavi** the gentleman to whom you were talking; **la signora alla ~ appartiene la casa** the lady to whom the house belongs; **la ragione per la ~ sono qui** the

reason why I am here; **l'albergo al ~ ci siamo fermati** the hotel where we stayed *o* which we stayed at; **la collina della ~ si vede la cima** the hill whose summit you can see.

(c) *(in elenchi)* such as, like; **piante ~i l'edera e le rose** plants such as *o* like ivy and roses; **pittori ~i Raffaello e Leonardo** painters such as *o* like Raphael and Leonardo.

(d): **per la ~** *(fam)*: **è stata una festa proprio per la ~** it was all a party should be; **non mi sembra una persona troppo per la ~** he doesn't inspire me with confidence.

4 *av (in veste di)* as; **~ legale della signora** as the lady's lawyer; **lo hanno assunto ~ direttore** they employed him as manager.

qualifica, che [kwa'lifika] *sf* qualification; **sono stato assunto con la ~ di meccanico** I was taken on as a mechanic; **ha la ~ di insegnante** he has a teaching qualification, he is a qualified teacher.

qualificare [kwalifi'kare] **1** *vt* **(a)** *(giudicare: persona, lavoro)* to judge. **(b)** *(definire)* to define, describe; **un'azione del genere non si può ~** such an action is beyond description; **il suo gesto lo qualifica per quello che è** his action labels him for what he is. **2**: **~rsi** *vr* **(a)** *(presentarsi)*: **~rsi come** to describe o.s. as. **(b)** *(ottenere una qualifica)*: **~rsi a un concorso** to pass a competitive exam; *(Sport)*: **~rsi per le semifinali** to qualify for the semifinals.

qualificativo, a [kwalifika'tivo] *ag (Gram)* **aggettivo ~** qualifying adjective.

qualificato, a [kwalifi'kato] *ag (dotato di qualifica)* qualified; *(esperto, abile)* skilled; **operaio ~** skilled worker; **è un medico molto ~** he is a very distinguished doctor; **non mi ritengo ~ per questo lavoro** I don't think I am qualified for this job.

qualificazione [kwalifikat'tsjone] *sf* **(a)** *(qualifica)* qualification. **(b)** *(Sport: anche: gara di ~)* qualifying event; **lottare per la ~** to fight to qualify.

qualità [kwali'ta] *sf inv* **(a)** *(gen)* quality; *(di suolo, clima)* nature; **di ottima o prima ~** top quality; **prodotto di ~** quality product; **un vino di pessima ~** a very poor wine; **controllo (di) ~** quality control; **ci interessa la ~ non la quantità** we are interested in quality not quantity. **(b)** *(dote, pregio)* quality; **ha molte ~** she has many good qualities. **(c)** *(genere, tipo)* kind, type; **fiori di varie ~** flowers of various kinds; **abbiamo sigarette di ogni ~** we have cigarettes of every kind; **articoli di ogni ~** all sorts of goods. **(d)** *(veste, carica)*: **in ~ di avvocato** in my *(o* your *etc)* capacity as a lawyer; **in ~ di amica** as a friend.

qualitativo, a [kwalita'tivo] *ag* qualitative.

qualora [kwa'lora] *cong*: **~ tu cambiassi idea** should you *(happen to)* change your mind.

qualsiasi [kwal'siasi] *ag indef* **(a)** *(tra molti)* any; **in ~ momento** at any time; **~ cosa** anything; **per lui farei ~ cosa** I'd do anything for him; **a prezzo di ~ sacrificio** at any cost, whatever the sacrifice. **(b)** *(tra due)* either; **prendine uno ~** take either of them. **(c)** *(peg)* ordinary; **non è uno ~** he's not just anybody; **non voglio un vino ~** I don't want any old wine; **quale vuoi?** — **uno ~** which do you want? — whichever, any old one. **(d)** *(rel)* whatever; **~ cosa dica** whatever he says; **~ favore tu mi chieda** whatever you ask of me.

qualunque [kwa'lunkwe] *ag indef* = **qualsiasi**.

qualunquista, i, e [kwalun'kwista] *sm/f person indifferent to politics.*

quando ['kwando] **1** *av* when; **~ arriverà?** when is he arriving?, when will he arrive?; **da ~?** since when?; **da ~ sono arrivato** (ever) since I arrived; **di** ~ **in** ~ from time to time; ~ **mai avrei detto una cosa del genere?** whenever did I say anything of the kind?; **quand'anche tu volessi parlargli...** even if you wanted to speak to him...; **fino a** ~ **continuerà così?** how long will it continue like this?

2 *cong* when; **ti raggiungo** ~ **ho finito** I'll join you when I've finished; **piange sempre** ~ **parto** she always cries when I leave, she cries whenever I leave; **ha voluto farlo** ~ **era meglio che non lo facesse** he insisted on doing it even though it would have been better had he not done so; ~ **te lo dico devi credermi** when I tell you something you should believe me.

quantità [kwanti'ta] *sf inv* **(a)** quantity, amount. **(b)** *(gran numero)*: **una** ~ **di** *(denaro, acqua)* a great deal of, a lot of; *(gente, cose)* a great many, a lot of, a great number of; **ho una** ~ **di cose da fare** I have a lot of things to do; **frutta in** ~ fruit in plenty. **(c)** *(Mat, Poesia)* quantity.

quantitativo, a [kwantita'tivo] **1** *ag* quantitative. **2** *sm* *(Comm: di merce)* amount, quantity.

quanto[1], a ['kwanto] **1** *ag* **(a)** *(interrog: quantità)* how much; *(: numero)* how many; ~**a stoffa ti serve?** how much material do you need?; ~**i metri desideri?** how many metres would you like?; ~ **tempo?** how long?; ~**e volte?** how often?, how many times?; ~ **tempo ci metti da qui all'ufficio?** how long does it take you from here to the office?; ~**i soldi ti hanno chiesto?** how much did they ask for it?

(b) *(escl)*: ~**e storie!** what a lot of nonsense!; ~ **tempo sprecato!** what a waste of time!

(c) *(rel: quantità)* as much as; *(: numero)* as many as; **ti darò** ~ **denaro ti serve** I'll give you as much money as you need; **prendi** ~**i libri vuoi** take as many books as you want; **fermati** ~ **tempo vuoi** stay as long as you want; **spende tanto denaro** ~**ne guadagna** he spends all that *o* every penny he earns, he spends as much as he earns.

2 *pron* **(a)** *(interrog: quantità)* how much; *(: numero)* how many; ~**i ne desidera?** how many do you want?; ~**i di loro?** how many of them?; **so che devo prendere della carne, ma non so** ~**a** I know I must get some meat, but I don't know how much; ~**i ne abbiamo oggi?** what's the date today?; ~ **stai via?** how long will you be away?; ~ **è da qui al negozio?** how far is it from here to the shop?; ~ **credi costerà?** how much do you think it will cost?

(b) *(escl)*: **vedi** ~**i hanno accettato!** see how many have accepted!; ~**e me ne ha dette!** *(insulti)* how he insulted me!; *(bugie)* what a lot of lies he told!

(c) *(rel: quantità)* as much as; *(: numero)* as many as; **faremo** ~ **potremo per aiutarti** we'll do all we can *o* as much as we can to help you; **gli darò** ~ **chiede** I'll give him what *o* as much he asks for; **fanne venire** ~**i vuoi** get as many as you like to come; **saranno scelti** ~**i hanno fatto la richiesta in tempo** all those whose applications arrived in time will be selected; **era (tanto) felice** ~ **non lo era stato mai** he was happier than he had ever been; **per** ~ **ne so io** as far as I know; **a** ~ **dice lui** according to him; **in risposta a** ~ **esposto nella sua lettera...** in answer to the points raised in your letter...; **è** ~ **di meglio potessi trovare** it's the best you could find.

quanto[2] ['kwanto] *av* **(a)** *(quantità)* how much; *(numero)* how many; ~ **fumi al giorno?** how many (cigarettes) do you smoke a day?; ~ **pesi?** how much do you weigh?; ~ **sono felice!** how happy I am!; **sapessi** ~ **abbiamo camminato!** if you knew how far we have walked!; **Dio solo sa** ~ **mi sono arrabbiato!** God only knows how angry I was!

(b) *(nella misura o quantità che)* as much as; **dovrai aspettare** ~ **è necessario** you'll have to wait as long as is necessary; **aggiungere brodo** ~ **basta** add sufficient *o* enough stock, add as much stock as is necessary; **strillava** ~ **poteva** she was shouting at the top of her voice *o* as loud as she could.

(c) *(come)*: **siamo ricchi** ~ **loro** we are as rich as they are; **è tanto sciocco** ~ **cafone** he is as stupid as he is uneducated, he is both stupid and uneducated; ~ **è vero Iddio...!** I swear to God...!; **mi sono riposato** ~ **mai in questi ultimi tempi** I've had more rest than ever in this period; **è una ragazza** ~ **mai semplice** she's a very unsophisticated girl; **è famoso non tanto per i romanzi** ~ **per le poesie** he's famous not so much for his novels as for his poetry.

(d): **in** ~ *(in qualità di)* as; *(perché, per il fatto che)* as, since; **in** ~ **a** *(per ciò che riguarda)* as far as; **in** ~ **insegnante** as a teacher; **non ho suonato in** ~ **temevo di svegliarti** I didn't ring as *o* since I was afraid I would wake you; **in** ~ **ai soldi che mi devi...** as for the money you owe me..., as far as the money you owe me is concerned... .

(e): **per** ~ *(nonostante, anche se)* however; *(tuttavia)* although; **per** ~ **si sforzi, non riesce** however hard he tries he can't do it; **per** ~ **sembri complicato** however complicated it may seem; **cercherò di fare qualcosa per lui, per** ~ **non se lo meriti** I'll try and do something for him although *o* even though he doesn't deserve it.

(f): ~ **più/meno** the more/less; ~ **più mi sforzo di ricordare tanto meno ci riesco** the harder I try *o* the more I try to remember the less I succeed; ~ **meno uno insiste tanto più gli viene offerto** the less one demands the more one is offered; ~ **più presto potrò** as soon as I can; **verrò** ~ **prima** I'll come as soon *o* as early as possible.

quantunque [kwan'tunkwe] *cong* *(sebbene)* although, even though; ~ **mi piaccia non ci andrei mai** even though I like it I would never go; **accetto** ~ **non convinto del tutto** I accept although *o* even though I'm not totally convinced.

quaranta [kwa'ranta] *ag inv, sm inv* forty; *per uso vedi* **cinquanta.**

quarantena [kwaran'tɛna] *sf* quarantine; **fare la** ~ to be in quarantine.

quarantenne [kwaran'tɛnne] *ag, smf* forty-year-old; *per uso vedi* **cinquantenne.**

quarantennio [kwaran'tɛnnjo] *sm* (period of) forty years.

quarantesimo, a [kwaran'tɛzimo] *ag, sm/f, sm* fortieth; *per uso vedi* **quinto.**

quarantina [kwaran'tina] *sf* about forty; *per uso vedi* **cinquantina.**

quarantotto [kwaran'tɔtto] **1** *ag inv* forty-eight. **2** *sm inv* forty-eight; **fare un** ~ *(fam)* to raise hell.

quaresima [kwa'rɛzima] *sf* (Rel) Lent; **osservare** *o* **fare la** ~ to keep Lent.

quarta ['kwarta] *sf (gen)* fourth; *(Aut)* fourth gear; *(Scol: elementare)* primary four; *(: superiore)* seventh year at secondary school; **mettere la** ~ to go into fourth (gear); **partire in** ~ *(fig)* to take off at top speed.

quartetto [kwar'tetto] *sm (Mus)* quartet; **fanno un bel** ~ they make a nice foursome.

quartiere [kwar'tjɛre] *sm* **(a)** *(di città)* district, area; **la gente del** ~ the local people; ~ **residenziale** residential area o district; **i** ~**i alti** the smart districts. **(b)** *(Mil)*: ~**i** *pl* quarters; ~ **generale** headquarters *pl*.

quartina [kwar'tina] *sf (Poesia)* quatrain.

quartino [kwar'tino] *sm* **(a)** *(di vino)* quarter litre; **andiamo a bere un** ~ let's go and have a glass of wine. **(b)** *(Mus: strumento)* small clarinet.

quarto, a ['kwarto] **1** *ag*, *sm/f* fourth; *per uso vedi* **quinto. 2** *sm* **(a)** *(frazione)* quarter; **un** ~ **di vino** a quarter-litre bottle of wine; **un** ~ **di pollo** a quarter chicken; **primo/ultimo** ~ *(della luna)* first/last quarter; ~**i di finale** *(Sport)* quarter-finals; **un chilo e un** ~ a kilo and a quarter. **(b)** *(ora)*: **un** ~ **d'ora** a quarter of an hour; **tre** ~**i d'ora** three quarters of an hour; **tre ore e un** ~ three and a quarter hours; **le sei e un** ~ (a) quarter past six; **le otto e tre** ~**i, le nove meno un** ~ (a) quarter to nine; **passare un brutto** ~ **d'ora** *(fig)* to have a bad o nasty time of it. **(c)** *(Naut)* watch; **il primo** ~ the first watch. **(d)** *(Tip)* quarto.

quartultimo, a [kwar'tultimo] *ag*, *sm/f* last but three, fourth from last.

quarzo ['kwartso] *sm* quartz; **orologio al** ~ quartz watch.

quasi ['kwazi] **1** *av (gen)* almost, nearly; *(restrittivo)* hardly, scarcely; **ha** ~ **30 anni** he's almost o nearly 30 (years old); ~ **niente** hardly o scarcely anything; ~ **mai** hardly ever; ~ **cadevo** I almost o nearly fell; **è** ~ **un fratello per me** he's like a brother to me; **oserei** ~ **dire che...** I'd almost say that...; ~ ~ **me ne vado** I've half a mind to leave; ~ ~ **è meglio così** it may even be better this way. **2** *cong (come se)* as if; **urla** ~ **fosse lui il padrone** he shouts as if he were the boss; **non si è fatto vivo,** ~ **sospettasse qualcosa** he hasn't been seen, as if he suspected something.

quassù [kwas'su] *av* up here.

quatto, a ['kwatto] *ag*: **stare** ~ ~ to keep as quiet as a mouse; **entrare** ~ ~ **in una stanza** to creep stealthily into a room; **uscire** ~ ~ to slip away.

quattordicenne [kwattordi'tʃɛnne] *ag*, *sm/f* fourteen-year-old.

quattordicesimo, a [kwattordi'tʃɛzimo] *ag*, *sm/f* fourteenth; *per uso vedi* **quinto.**

quattordici [kwat'torditʃi] *ag inv*, *sm inv* fourteen; *per uso vedi* **cinque.**

quattrino [kwat'trino] *sm*: **non avere un** ~ o il **becco di un** ~ *(fam)* to be penniless o broke; **fare** ~**i** to make money; **essere pieno di** ~**i** to be rolling in money; ~**i a palate** piles of money; **costare fior di** ~**i** to cost a fortune.

quattro ['kwattro] **1** *ag inv* four; **ho messo via** ~ **soldi** I put a little money aside; **c'erano** ~ **gatti allo spettacolo** there was only a handful of people at the show; **fare** ~ **passi** to take a stroll; **fare** ~ **salti** to go dancing; **fare** ~ **chiacchiere** to have a chat. **2** *sm inv* four; **farsi in** ~ **per qn** to go out of one's way for sb, put o.s. out for sb; **fare il diavolo a** ~ to kick up a rumpus; **in** ~ **e quattr'otto** in less than no time; **dirne** ~ **a qn** to give sb a piece of one's mind; *per uso vedi* **cinque.**

quattrocchi [kwat'trɔkki] **1** *sm inv (fig fam: persona con occhiali)* four eyes. **2: a** ~ *av (tra 2 persone)* face to face; *(privatamente)* in private.

quattrocentesco, a, schi, sche [kwattrotʃen'tesko] *ag* fifteenth-century *attr*.

quattrocento [kwattro'tʃɛnto] **1** *ag inv* four hundred. **2** *sm inv* four hundred; *(secolo)*: **il Q**~ the fifteenth century.

quello, a ['kwello] *(dav a sm* **quel** + *consonante,* **quell'** +*vocale,* **quello** + *s impura, gn, pn, ps, x, z; pl*

quei + *consonante,* **quegli** + *vocale o s impura, gn, pn, ps, x, z; dav a sf* **quella** + *consonante,* **quell'** + *vocale; pl* **quelle)** **1** *ag dimostr* **(a)** that; those *pl*; **mi passi quel libro?** could you pass me that book?; **dove hai comprato quei quadri?** where did you buy those paintings?; **voglio** ~**a camicia** lì o **là** I want that shirt.

(b) *(seguito da proposizione rel)*: **con quel poco che abbiamo** with what o the little we have; **dov'è quel maglione che mi dicevi?** where's the jumper you were telling me about?

(c) *(enfatico)*: **ho una di** ~**e paure!** I'm scared stiff!; **è uno di quei bastardi** *(fam)* he's one of those bastards; **ne ha fatte di** ~**e!** *(sciocchezze)* he did some really foolish things!; **in** ~ **stesso istante** at that very moment.

2 *pron dimostr* **(a)** that (one); those (ones) *pl*; ~ **cos'è?** and what is that?; **chi è** ~ **lì?** who is that person?; **prendiamo** ~ **là** we'll take that one there; **quale vuoi?** — ~ **bianco** which do you want? — the white one; ~**e sono le mie scarpe** those are my shoes; **il tuo nome e** ~ **di Riccarda** your name and Riccarda's; ~ **di Giovanna è il voto migliore** Giovanna's is the best mark, Giovanna has the best mark; **ho incontrato** ~**i della festa** I met the people we saw at the party; **a che ora viene** ~ **del latte?** when does the milkman come?

(b) *(in proposizione rel)*: ~**(a) che** *(persona)* the one (who); *(cosa)* the one (which), the one (that); ~**i(e) che** *(persone)* those who; *(cose)* those which; ~ **che hai comprato tu è più bello** the one (which) you bought is nicer; ~ **che hai visto è il padre** the person o the one you saw is the father; ~**a che hai incontrato è la seconda moglie** the one o woman you met is his second wife; **chiedi a** ~**i che l'hanno conosciuto** ask those who knew him.

(c) *(egli)* he; *(ella)* she; *(essi, esse)* they; **gliel'ho chiesto e** ~ **ha risposto che lui non c'entra** I asked him about it and he said that he had nothing to do with it; **sarebbe un'occasione d'oro e** ~**i non vogliono accettare** it's a golden opportunity but they don't want to accept.

(d): ~ **che** what; *(tutto)* all (that), everything; **ho detto** ~ **che sapevo** I've told you all I know; **nega, e quel che è peggio, ci scherza sopra** he denies it, and what is worse, jokes about it; **da** ~ **che ho sentito** from what I've heard.

(e) *(fraseologia)*: **in quel di Milano** in the Milan area o region; **in quel mentre** at that very moment.

quercia, ce ['kwɛrtʃa] *sf (albero)* oak (tree); *(legno)* oak; **forte come una** ~ as strong as an ox.

querela [kwe'rɛla] *sf (Dir)* (legal) action; **sporgere** ~ **contro qn** to bring an action against sb.

querelare [kwere'lare] *vt (Dir)* to bring an action against.

quesito [kwe'sito] *sm* question, query; **porre un** ~ **(a)** to put a question (to).

questi ['kwesti] *pron dimostr (poet)* this person.

questionario [kwestjo'narjo] *sm* questionnaire.

questione [kwes'tjone] *sf* **(a)** *(problema, faccenda)* question, matter; *(controversia)* issue; **si tratta di una** ~ **delicata/personale** it's a delicate/personal matter; **è una** ~ **politica** it's a political question o matter; **è una** ~ **di vita o di morte** it's a question o matter of life and death; **il nocciolo della** ~ the heart of the matter; **qui sta la** ~ this is the point; **non conosco i termini della** ~ I don't know the details of the matter; **ne ha fatto una** ~ he made an issue out of it; **è sorta una** ~ **in merito** they made an issue out of it; **comporre una** ~ *(Dir)* to settle an issue; **il caso in** ~ the matter at hand; **la persona in** ~ the person involved; **non voglio essere chiamato in** ~ I don't want to be dragged into the argument; **non faccio** ~**i di soldi** it's not a question of money; **litigare per** ~**i di eredità, essere in** ~ **per l'eredità** to be in dispute over an inheritance; **la Q**~ **Meridionale** the Southern Question.

(b) *(dubbio)*: **la sua promozione è ancora in** ~ his promotion is still in doubt; **mettere qc in** ~ to question sth; **è fuori** ~ it's out of the question.

questo, a ['kwesto] **1** *ag dimostr* **(a)** this; these *pl*; ~ **libro qui** *o* **qua** this book; **ti piace** ~ **maglione?** do you like this jumper?; ~**a sera** this evening; ~ **lunedì** this Monday; **in** ~**i ultimi giorni** these last few days; **di** ~**i tempi** in times like these; **quest'oggi** nowadays.

(b) *(enfatico)*: **non fatemi più prendere** ~**e paure** don't give me such a fright again; **non ti presenterai con** ~**i voti!** how dare you turn up with such bad marks *o* with marks like these!; **con** ~ **caldo** in this heat.

2 *pron dimostr* **(a)** this (one); these (ones) *pl*; ~ **è il tuo posto** this is your place; ~ **cosa significa?** what does this mean?; **prendo** ~ **qui** *o* **qua** I'll take this one; ~ **è troppo!** this is too much *o* the limit!; ~ **mi fa piacere** I am pleased about that.

(b) *(egli)* he; *(ella)* she; *(essi, esse)* they; **e** ~ **mi guarda e ride!** and this one just looks at me and laughs; **una tale occasione, e** ~**i che fanno?** — **rifiutano** such a great opportunity, and what do they do? — they refuse.

(c): ~ **...** **quello** *(il primo ... il secondo)* the former ... the latter; *(l'uno ... l'altro)* the one ... the other; ~**i ... quelli** some ... others; **Maria e Pietro sono entrambi all'università,** ~**a fa legge, quello fa lettere** Maria and Pietro are both at university, the former is studying law and the latter arts; **preferisci** ~ **o quello?** do you prefer this one or that one?; ~**i gridavano, quelli ridevano** some were shouting, others were laughing.

(d) *(fraseologia)*: **e con** ~? so what?; **e con** ~ **se n'è andato** and with that he left; **con tutto** ~ in spite of this, despite all this; ~ **poi!** as if that weren't enough!; ~ **sì che è il colmo!** this is the limit!; ~ **è quanto** that's all; ~**a non me la dovevi fare** you shouldn't have done this to me; **è per** ~ **che sono venuto** this is why I came.

questore [kwes'tore] *sm (Polizia)* ≃ chief constable.

questua ['kwɛstua] *sf* collection (of alms).

questura [kwes'tura] *sf (organo)* police force; *(edificio)* police headquarters *pl*.

questurino [kwestu'rino] *sm (fam: poliziotto)* cop.

qui [kwi] *av* = **qua**.

quiescente [kwjeʃ'ʃɛnte] *ag* dormant.

quiescenza [kwjeʃ'ʃɛntsa] *sf* **(a)** dormancy. **(b)** *(Amm)*: **porre qn in** ~ to retire sb.

quietanza [kwje'tantsa] *sf (Comm)* receipt.

quietare [kwje'tare] **1** *vt* to soothe, calm. **2**: ~**rsi** *vr (mare)* to become calm; *(vento)* to die down; *(bambino)* to calm down; **il dolore s'è quietato** the pain has eased.

quiete ['kwjɛte] *sf* **(a)** *(della notte)* quiet, stillness; *(della mente)* peace; **la** ~ **prima della tempesta** the calm before the storm; **aver bisogno di** ~ *(riposo)* to need peace and quiet; **la** ~ **della campagna** the tranquillity *o* peace of the countryside; **turbare la** ~ **pubblica** *(Dir)* to disturb the peace. **(b)** *(Fis)*: **stato di** ~ state of rest.

quieto, a ['kwjɛto] *ag (gen)* quiet; *(notte)* quiet, still; *(mare)* calm; *(cane)* tame; **l'ho fatto per il** ~ **vivere** I did it for a quiet life.

quindi ['kwindi] **1** *cong (perciò)* therefore, so. **2** *av (in seguito)* then; **devi continuare diritto,** ~ **girare a destra** you should carry straight on, then turn right.

quindicenne [kwindi'tʃɛnne] *ag, sm/f* fifteen-year-old; *per uso vedi* **cinquantenne.**

quindicennio [kwindi'tʃɛnnjo] *sm* (period of) fifteen years.

quindicesimo, a [kwindi'tʃɛzimo] *ag, sm/f* fifteenth; *per uso vedi* **quinto.**

quindici ['kwinditʃi] **1** *ag inv* fifteen; **oggi a** ~ **a** fortnight *o* two weeks today; **tra** ~ **giorni** in a fortnight *o* two weeks. **2** *sm inv* fifteen; *per uso vedi* **cinque.**

quindicina [kwindi'tʃina] *sf* about fifteen; **(fra) una** ~ **di giorni** (in) a fortnight; **la seconda** ~ **di marzo** the second half of March; *per uso vedi* **cinquantina.**

quindicinale [kwinditʃi'nale] **1** *ag* fortnightly. **2** *sm (rivista)* fortnightly magazine.

quinquennale [kwinkwen'nale] *ag (che dura 5 anni)* five-year; *(che avviene ogni 5 anni)* five-yearly.

quinquennio [kwin'kwennjo] *sm* (period of) five years, quinquennial.

quinta ['kwinta] *sf* **(a)** *(ge..)* fifth; *(Aut)* fifth gear; *(Scol: elementare)* primary five; *(: superiore)* last year at secondary school. **(b)**: **le** ~**e** *(Teatro)* the wings; **tra** *o* **dietro le** ~**e** *(fig)* behind the scenes.

quintale [kwin'tale] *sm* quintal *(= 100 kg)*; **pesa un** ~ *(fig)* it weighs a ton.

quintessenza [kwintes'sɛntsa] *sf* quintessence.

quintetto [kwin'tetto] *sm (Mus)* quintet.

quinto, a ['kwinto] **1** *ag* fifth; **la** ~**a parte di** a fifth of; **la** ~**a volta** the fifth time; **al** ~ **piano** on the fifth floor; **essere al** ~ **posto in classifica** to be fifth in the championship; **in** ~**a pagina** on the fifth page, on page five; **Carlo** ~ Charles the Fifth; ~**a colonna** *(fig)* fifth column. **2** *sm/f* fifth; **sei la** ~**a a cui faccio la domanda** you are the fifth person I have asked; **il** ~ **da destra** the fifth from the right; **arrivare** ~ to come in fifth; **il** ~ **arrivato vincerà una macchina** whoever comes fifth will win a car. **3** *sm (frazione)* fifth; **un** ~ **della popolazione** a fifth of the population; **tre** ~**i** three fifths.

quintultimo, a [kwin'tultimo] *ag, sm/f* last but four, fifth from last.

quintuplicare [kwintupli'kare] *vt*, ~**rsi** *vr* to increase fivefold.

qui pro quo ['kwiprɔ'kwɔ] *sm inv* misunderstanding.

quiz [kwidz] *sm inv* **(a)** *(domanda)* question; **risolvere un** ~ to answer a question. **(b)** *(anche: gioco a* ~*)* quiz game; ~ **televisivo** television quiz.

quorum ['kwɔrum] *sm inv* quorum.

quota ['kwɔta] *sf* **(a)** *(parte)* quota, share; **la sua** ~ **di azioni** his quota of shares; ~ **di immigrazione** immigration quota; ~ **fissa** fixed amount *o* sum; ~ **d'iscrizione** *(Univ)* enrolment fee; *(ad una gara)* entry fee; *(ad un club)* membership fee; ~ **imponibile** taxable income; **le** ~**e del totalizzatore** *(Ippica)* the odds. **(b)** *(altitudine)* altitude, height; **di alta** ~ high-altitude *attr*; **a** ~ **zero** at sea level; **a** ~ **750 metri** 750 metres above sea level; **prendere/perdere** ~ *(Aer)* to gain/lose height *o* altitude.

quotare [kwo'tare] *vt* **(a)** *(Fin, Borsa)* to quote; **il dollaro è quotato a 1700 lire** the dollar is quoted at 1700 lire; **queste azioni sono quotate in Borsa** these shares are quoted on the Stock Exchange. **(b)** *(valutare: anche fig)* to value; **questo quadro è stato quotato 15 milioni di lire** this painting was valued at 15 million lire; **è un pittore molto quotato** he is rated highly as a painter.

quotazione [kwotat'tsjone] *sf (Fin)* quotation; *(fig: di persona)* rating.

quotidianamente [kwotidjana'mente] *av* daily, every day.

quotidiano, a [kwoti'djano] *ag* **1** *(di ogni giorno)*

daily; *(banale)* everyday. **2** *sm (giornale)* daily (paper).

quoto ['kwɔto] *sm (Mat)* quotient.

quoziente [kwot'tsjɛnte] *sm* **(a)** *(Mat)* quotient. **(b)** *(tasso)* rate; ~ **di crescita zero** zero growth rate; ~ **d'intelligenza** *(abbr* Q.I.*)* intelligence quotient *(abbr* IQ*)*.

R

R, r |'ɛrrɛ| *sf o m inv (lettera)* R, r.
rabarbaro |raˈbarbaro| *sm (Bot)* rhubarb; *(liquore)* rhubarb liqueur.
rabberciare |rabberˈtʃare| *vt (anche fig)* to patch up.
rabbia |'rabbja| *sf* **(a)** *(ira)* anger, rage; *(fig: di onde, vento)* fury; **essere fuori di sé dalla ~** to be beside o.s. with rage; **farsi prendere dalla ~** to fly into a rage; **fare qc con ~** to do sth angrily; **mi fai una ~!** you make me so angry!; *(scherz: invidia)* you make me so jealous!; **che ~!** what a damned nuisance! **(b)** *(Med: idrofobia)* rabies *sg*.
rabbino |rabˈbino| *sm* rabbi.
rabbioso, a |rabˈbjoso| *ag* **(a)** *(discorso, tono, sguardo)* furious, angry; *(fig: vento, odio)* raging, furious. **(b)** *(Med)* rabid.
rabbonire |rabboˈnire| *vt*, **~rsi** *vr* to calm down.
rabbrividire |rabbriviˈdire| *vi (aus essere) (per il freddo)* to shiver, shudder; *(fig: per paura etc)* to shudder; **~ al solo pensiero di qc/di fare qc** to shudder at the mere thought of sth/of doing sth.
rabbuffo |rabˈbuffo| *sm* reprimand.
rabbuiare |rabbuˈjare| *vi (aus essere)*, **~rsi** *vr* to grow dark, darken; **si rabbuiò in viso** his (*o* her) face darkened.
rabdomante |rabdoˈmante| *sm* water diviner.
raccapezzarsi |rakkapetˈtsarsi| *vr*: **non ~** to be at a loss; **c'è tanta confusione che non mi raccapezzo più** things are in such a mess that I can't make head nor tail of anything.
raccapricciante |rakkapritˈtʃante| *ag* horrifying.
raccapriccio |rakkaˈprittʃo| *sm* horror.
raccattapalle |rakkattaˈpalle| *sm inv (Tennis)* ballboy.
raccattare |rakkatˈtare| *vt (raccogliere)* to pick up; *(fig: notizie)* to gather (up).
racchetta |rakˈketta| *sf (da tennis etc)* racket; *(da ping-pong)* bat; **~ da neve** snowshoe; **~ da sci** ski stick.
racchio, a |'rakkjo| *ag (fam)* ugly.
racchiudere |rakˈkjudere| *vt* to contain.
racchiuso, a |rakˈkjuso| *pp di* **racchiudere**.
raccogliere |rakˈkɔʎʎere| **1** *vt* **(a)** *(raccattare)* to pick up; **puoi ~ i tuoi giocattoli?** can you pick up your toys?; **l'istituto raccoglie molti bambini abbandonati** the institution takes in many abandoned children; **non ha raccolto il guanto** *(fig)* he didn't take up the gauntlet; **non ha raccolto** *(allusione)* he didn't take the hint; *(frecciata)* he took no notice of it.
(b) *(frutta, fiori)* to pick, pluck; *(Agr)* to harvest; *(fig: onori, successo)* to reap; **~ il grano** to harvest the wheat; **~ l'uva** to pick grapes; **~ i frutti del proprio lavoro** *(fig)* to reap the benefits of one's work.
(c) *(radunare: persone)* to assemble; *(: amici)* to bring together; *(notizie, denaro, firme)* to gather, collect; **ho raccolto le mie cose e me ne sono andata** I took my things and went; **~ le idee** *(fig)* to gather *o* collect one's thoughts.
(d) *(collezionare: francobolli etc)* to collect.

(e) *(ripiegare: ali)* to fold; *(: gambe)* to draw up; *(: vele)* to furl; *(: capelli)* to put up.
2: **~rsi** *vr* **(a)** *(radunarsi)* to gather.
(b) *(fig: concentrarsi)* to collect *o* gather one's thoughts.
raccoglimento |rakkoʎʎiˈmento| *sm* meditation.
raccoglitore |rakkoʎʎiˈtore| *sm (cartella)* folder, binder; *(: per francobolli)* album; **~ a fogli mobili** loose-leaf binder.
raccolta |rakˈkɔlta| *sf (gen)* collection; **fare la ~ di qc** to collect sth; **fare la ~ della frutta** to pick fruit. **(b)** *(di persone)* gathering; **chiamare a ~** to gather together.
raccolto, a |rakˈkɔlto| **1** *pp di* **raccogliere**. **2** *ag* **(a)** *(persona: assorto)* thoughtful; **~ in preghiera** absorbed in prayer. **(b)** *(luogo: appartato)* secluded, quiet. **(c)** *(gambe)* drawn up; **~ su se stesso** curled up. **3** *sm (Agr)* crop, harvest; *(: periodo)* harvest time.
raccomandabile |rakkomanˈdabile| *ag* (highly) commendable; **è un tipo poco ~** he is not to be trusted.
raccomandare |rakkomanˈdare| **1** *vt* **(a)** *(consigliare)* to recommend; *(esortare)*: **~ a qn di non fare qc** to tell *o* warn sb not to do sth; **ti raccomando questo libro/di leggere questo libro** I recommend this book to you/that you read this book; **ti raccomando di non fare tardi** now remember, don't come in late. **(b)** *(affidare)*: **~ qn a qn/alle cure di qn** to entrust sb to sb/to sb's care. **(c)** *(appoggiare)* to recommend; **~ qn per un lavoro** to recommend sb for a job. **2**: **~rsi** *vr*: **~rsi a qn** to implore sb's help; **~rsi alla pietà di qn** to implore sb's pity; **mi raccomando!** **non perderlo** please, don't lose it!; **mi raccomando! studia bene** be sure and study hard!
raccomandata |rakkomanˈdata| *sf (anche:* **lettera ~)** recorded-delivery letter; **~ con ricevuta di ritorno** *recorded-delivery letter with advice of receipt*.
raccomandato, a |rakkomanˈdato| **1** *ag* **(a)** *(lettera, pacco)* recorded-delivery. **(b)** *(candidato)* recommended. **2** *sm/f*: **essere un(a) ~(a) di ferro** to have friends in high places.
raccomandazione |rakkomandatˈtsjone| *sf* **(a)** *(appoggio)* recommendation; **lettera di ~** letter of introduction; **qui ci vuole la ~ di qualcuno** we need somebody to pull a few strings here. **(b)** *(esortazione)* piece of advice; **mi ha fatto mille ~i** he gave me lots of advice.
raccomodare |rakkomoˈdare| *vt (riparare)* to repair, mend.
raccontare |rakkonˈtare| *vt (storia, bugie)* to tell; *(avventure)* to tell about; **~ qc a qn** to tell sb sth; **non raccontarlo a nessuno** don't tell anyone about it; **raccontano che sia fuggito** they say that he escaped; **nel libro racconta delle sue avventure** in the book he tells of his adventures; **raccontami tutto** tell me the whole story; **a me non la racconti** don't try and kid me; **raccontala a qualcun altro!** try and pull the wool over

somebody else's eyes!; **a me lo vieni a** ~! don't tell me!; **se ne raccontano delle belle su di lui** I've heard a few stories about him; **cosa mi racconti di nuovo?** what's new?

racconto [rak'konto] *sm* (**a**) *(narrazione)* account; **il suo** ~ **dell'avventura** his account of the adventure. (**b**) *(genere letterario)* short story; ~**i per bambini** children's stories; ~**i di fate** fairy tales.

raccorciare [rakkor'tʃare] **1** *vt* to shorten. **2**: ~**rsi** *vr* to become shorter; **le giornate si stanno raccorciando** the days are drawing in.

raccordare [rakkor'dare] *vt (collegare)* to link up, join (up).

raccordo [rak'kɔrdo] *sm (Tecn: giunzione)* joint, connection; *(di autostrada)* junction; *(Ferr)* siding; ~ **anulare** *(Aut)* ring road.

rachitico, a, ci, che [ra'kitiko] **1** *ag (Med)* rickety; *(fig: pianta)* spindly. **2** *sm/f* person who suffers from rickets.

rachitismo [raki'tizmo] *sm (Med)* rickets *sg*.

racimolare [ratʃimo'lare] *vt (denaro)* to scrape together; *(fig: notizie)* to glean.

rada ['rada] *sf* (natural) harbour.

radar ['radar] *sm* radar.

raddolcire [raddol'tʃire] **1** *vt (persona, carattere)* to soften. **2**: ~**rsi** *vr (tempo)* to grow milder; *(persona)* to soften, mellow.

raddoppiamento [raddoppja'mento] *sm (gen)* doubling.

raddoppiare [raddop'pjare] *vt, vi,* ~**rsi** *vr* to double.

raddoppio [rad'doppjo] *sm (gen)* doubling; *(Biliardo)* double; *(Equitazione)* gallop.

raddrizzamento [raddrittsa'mento] *sm* straightening.

raddrizzare [raddrit'tsare] **1** *vt* (**a**) *(mettere dritto)* to straighten; *(fig: correggere)* to put straight, correct. (**b**) *(Elettr)* to rectify. **2**: ~**rsi** *vr (persona)* to straighten (o.s.) up; *(strada)* to straighten out.

radere ['radere] **1** *vt* (**a**) *(barba)* to shave off; *(mento)* to shave. (**b**) *(fig: sfiorare)* to graze, skim. (**c**) *(abbattere)*: ~ **al suolo** to raze to the ground. **2**: ~**rsi** *vr* to shave.

radiale [ra'djale] *ag, sm (Anat, Geom, Aut)* radial.

radiante [ra'djante] *ag (calore, energia)* radiant.

radiare [ra'djare] *vt (da scuola, società)* to expel; *(dall'esercito)* to dismiss.

radiatore [radja'tore] *sm* radiator.

radiazione [radjat'tsjone] *sf* (**a**) *(Fis)* radiation; ~ **nucleare** nuclear radiation. (**b**) *(cancellazione)* striking-off; *(espulsione)* expulsion.

radicale [radi'kale] **1** *ag (gen, Pol)* radical; *(Linguistica)* root *attr*. **2** *sm/f (Pol)* radical. **3** *sm (Mat, Chim)* radical; *(Linguistica)* root.

radicare [radi'kare] **1** *vi (aus essere) (Bot)* to take root. **2**: ~**rsi** *vr (fig)* to take root.

radicato, a [radi'kato] *ag (pregiudizio, credenza)* deep-seated, deeply-rooted.

radicchio [ra'dikkjo] *sm* chicory.

radice [ra'ditʃe] *sf (gen, Mat, Anat, fig)* root; **segno di** ~ *(Mat)* radical sign; ~ **quadrata** *(Mat)* square root; **colpire alla** ~ *(fig)* to strike at the root; **mettere** ~**i** *(idee, odio etc)* to take root; *(persona)* to put down roots.

radio¹ ['radjo] *sf inv* (**a**) *(apparecchio)* radio (set); ~ **ricevente/trasmittente** receiver/transmitter; ~ **a transistor** transistor (radio). (**b**) *(radiodiffusione)*: **la** ~ (the) radio; **trasmettere via** ~ **a qn** *(messaggio)* to radio to sb; **trasmettere per** ~ to broadcast; **stazione/ponte** ~ radio station/link.

radio² ['radjo] *sm (Anat)* radius.

radio³ ['radjo] *sm (Chim)* radium.

radioabbonato, a [radjoabbo'nato] *sm/f* radio subscriber.

radioamatore, trice [radjoama'tore] *sm/f* amateur radio operator, ham *(fam)*.

radioascoltatore, trice [radjoaskolta'tore] *sm/f (radio)* listener.

radioattività [radjoattivi'ta] *sf* radioactivity.

radioattivo, a [radjoat'tivo] *ag* radioactive.

radiocollegamento [radjokollega'mento] *sm* radio link.

radiocomandare [radjokoman'dare] *vt* to operate by remote control.

radiocomandato, a [radjokoman'dato] *ag* remote-controlled.

radiocomando [radjoko'mando] *sm* remote control.

radiocomunicazione [radjokomunikat'tsjone] *sf* radio message.

radiocronaca, che [radjo'krɔnaka] *sf* radio commentary.

radiocronista, i, e [radjokro'nista] *sm/f* radio commentator.

radiodiffusione [radjodiffu'zjone] *sf* radio broadcasting.

radiofonico, a, ci, che [radjo'fɔniko] *ag* radio *attr*.

radiofrequenza [radjofre'kwentsa] *sf* (radio) frequency.

radiografare [radjogra'fare] *vt* to X-ray.

radiografia [radjogra'fia] *sf* X-ray.

radiografico, a, ci, che [radjo'grafiko] *ag* X-ray *attr*.

radiolina [radjo'lina] *sf* portable radio, transistor.

radiologia [radjolo'dʒia] *sf* radiology.

radiologo, a, gi, ghe [ra'djɔlogo] *sm/f* radiologist.

radioricevente [radjoritʃe'vɛnte] *sf (anche:* **apparecchio** ~) receiver.

radioso, a [ra'djoso] *ag (anche fig)* radiant.

radiostazione [radjostat'tsjone] *sf* radio station.

radiosveglia [radjoz'veʎʎa] *sf* radio alarm.

radiotecnica [radjo'tɛknika] *sf* radio engineering.

radiotecnico, a, ci, che [radjo'tɛkniko] **1** *ag* radio engineering *attr*. **2** *sm* radio engineer.

radiotelegrafista, i, e [radjotelegra'fista] *sm/f* radiotelegrapher.

radiotrasmesso, a [radjotraz'messo] *pp di* **radiotrasmettere**.

radiotrasmettere [radjotraz'mettere] *vt* to broadcast (by radio).

radiotrasmittente [radjotrazmit'tente] **1** *ag* (radio) broadcasting *attr*. **2** *sf* (radio) broadcasting station.

rado, a ['rado] *ag (capelli)* sparse, thin; *(visite)* infrequent; **di** ~ rarely; **non di** ~ not uncommonly.

radunare [radu'nare] **1** *vt (persone)* to gather, assemble; *(Mil: truppe)* to rally; *(cose)* to collect, gather together. **2**: ~**rsi** *vr* to gather, assemble.

radunata [radu'nata] *sf (Mil)* muster.

raduno [ra'duno] *sm* gathering, meeting.

radura [ra'dura] *sf* clearing.

rafano ['rafano] *sm (Bot)* horseradish.

raffazzonare [raffattso'nare] *vt* to patch up.

raffermo, a [raf'fermo] *ag* stale.

raffica, che ['raffika] *sf (Meteor)* gust (of wind); *(scarica di colpi)* burst of gunfire; ~ **di insulti** *(fig)* avalanche of insults; **il vento soffiava a** ~ the wind was very blustery.

raffigurare [raffigu'rare] *vt (rappresentare)* to depict, represent; *(simboleggiare)* to represent, symbolize; **non riesco a raffigurarmelo** I can't picture it.

raffinare [raffi'nare] **1** *vt (zucchero, petrolio, fig)* to refine. **2**: ~**rsi** *vr (fig)* to become refined.

raffinatezza [raffina'tettsa] *sf* refinement; **arredato con** ~ tastefully furnished.

raffinato, a [raffi'nato] **1** *ag (anche fig)* refined; *(modi)* polished, sophisticated; *(astuzia, malizia)* refined, subtle. **2** *sm/f* refined person.

raffinazione [raffinat'tsjone] *sf (di zucchero, petrolio)* refining.

raffineria [raffine'ria] *sf* refinery.

rafforzamento [raffortsa'mento] *sm* reinforcement.

rafforzare [raffor'tsare] **1** *vt (gen, Mil)* to reinforce. **2**: ~**rsi** *vr (Mil)*: ~**rsi su una posizione** to reinforce one's position; **i miei dubbi su di lui si sono rafforzati** my doubts about him have grown.

rafforzativo, a [raffortsa'tivo] *(Gram)* **1** *ag* intensifying. **2** *sm* intensifier.

raffreddamento [raffredda'mento] *sm (anche fig)* cooling; ~ **ad aria** air cooling; **c'è stato un** ~ **dei rapporti** *(fig)* the relationship has cooled.

raffreddare [raffred'dare] **1** *vi* to cool, cool down; **lascia** ~ **la minestra** leave the soup to cool *o* cool down; **mettere il vino a** ~ to chill the wine. **2** *vt* to cool down; *(fig: entusiasmo)* to have a cooling effect on, dampen. **3**: ~**rsi** *vr* **(a)** *(caffè, minestra etc)* to cool down; *(aria)* to become cooler, become colder; *(fig: entusiasmo, relazione)* to cool; **non lasciare che la minestra si raffreddi** don't let the soup get cold; **aspetta che si raffreddi** wait till it cools down. **(b)** *(prendere un raffreddore)* to catch a cold.

raffreddato, a [raffred'dato] *ag (Med)*: **essere** ~ to have a cold.

raffreddore [raffred'dore] *sm (Med)* cold; ~ **da fieno** hay fever; **prendere/avere il** ~ to catch/ have a cold.

raffrontare [raffron'tare] *vt* to compare.

raffronto [raf'fronto] *sm* comparison.

rafia ['rafja] *sf* raffia.

raganella [raga'nɛlla] *sf (Zool)* tree frog.

ragazza [ra'gattsa] *sf (gen)* girl; *(fidanzata)* girlfriend; **brava** ~ nice girl, good sort; **nome da** ~ maiden name; **da** ~ **faceva la commessa** when she was younger she worked as a shop assistant; ~ **madre** unmarried mother; ~ **squillo** call girl.

ragazzata [ragat'tsata] *sf* childish action.

ragazzo [ra'gattso] *sm* **(a)** *(gen)* boy; *(fidanzato)* boyfriend; *(garzone)* boy, shop boy; **fin da quando era** ~ since he was a boy; ~ **padre** unmarried father; ~ **di strada** street urchin. **(b)**: ~**i** *pl (bambini, figli)* children; *(amici)* folks *(fam)*; **andiamo** ~**i!** let's go children *(o* folks*)!*; **film/libro per** ~**i** children's film/book.

raggelare [raddʒe'lare] **1** *vi (aus essere)*, ~**rsi** *vr* to freeze; **si sentì** ~ **all'idea** his blood froze *o* ran cold at the idea. **2** *vt* to freeze; ~ **una conversazione** to stop a conversation dead.

raggiante [rad'dʒante] *ag (sorriso, espressione)* beaming, radiant; **era** ~ **di gioia** she was beaming *o* radiant with joy.

raggiare [rad'dʒare] *vi* **(a)** *(splendere)* to shine. **(b)** *(Fis)* to radiate.

raggiera [rad'dʒɛra] *sf (di ruota)* spokes *pl*; **a** ~ with a sunburst pattern.

raggio ['raddʒo] *sm* **(a)** *(gen, Fis, fig)* ray, beam; **un** ~ **di sole** *(anche fig)* a ray of sunshine; ~ **di luna** moonbeam; ~ **di speranza** *(fig)* ray *o* gleam of hope; ~**i X** X-rays; ~ **laser** laser beam. **(b)** *(di ruota)* spoke. **(c)** *(Mat, fig)* radius; **nel** ~ **di 20 km** within a radius of 20 km *o* a 20-km radius; ~ **d'azione** *(di proiettile)* range; *(fig)* range, scope; **a largo** ~ *(esplorazione, incursione)* wide-ranging.

raggirare [raddʒi'rare] *vt* to deceive; **si è lasciato** ~ **dai suoi discorsi** he was taken in by his arguments.

raggiro [rad'dʒiro] *sm* trick, swindle; **non farti invischiare nei suoi** ~**i** don't let yourself get mixed up in his schemes.

raggiungere [rad'dʒundʒere] *vt* **(a)** *(persona)*: ~ **qn** to catch sb up, catch up with sb; *(: telefonicamente)* to get in touch with sb, reach sb; **li abbiamo raggiunti per strada/alla stazione** we caught up with them on the way/at the station; **vi raggiungo più tardi** I'll see you later, I'll catch you up later; **nella ricerca nucleare l'Italia non ha ancora raggiunto la Francia** *o* **il livello della Francia** Italy still hasn't caught up with France in nuclear research.

(b) *(luogo, oggetto posto in alto)* to reach; *(obiettivo)* to reach, achieve; *(bersaglio)* to hit; ~ **il proprio scopo** to reach one's goal, achieve one's aim; ~ **un accordo** to come to *o* reach an agreement.

raggiunto, a [rad'dʒunto] *pp di* **raggiungere**.

raggomitolare [raggomito'lare] **1** *vt (avvolgere)* to wind up. **2**: ~**rsi** *vr (fig: rannicchiarsi)* to curl up.

raggranellare [raggranel'lare] *vt (soldi)* to scrape together.

raggrinzare [raggrin'tsare] **1** *vt* to crease. **2**: ~**rsi** *vr (stoffa)* to wrinkle (up); *(viso, pelle)* to become wrinkled.

raggrumare [raggru'mare] *vt*, ~**rsi** *vr (sangue, latte)* to clot.

raggruppamento [raggruppa'mento] *sm* **(a)** *(azione)* grouping. **(b)** *(gruppo)* group; *(: Mil)* unit.

raggruppare [raggrup'pare] **1** *vt (in un unico gruppo)* to group (together); *(in molti gruppi)* to organize into groups. **2**: ~**rsi** *vr (in un unico gruppo)* to group (together); *(in molti gruppi)* to form into groups; ~**rsi intorno a qn** to gather around sb.

ragguagliare [raggwaʎ'ʎare] *vt* **(a)** *(confrontare)*: ~ **qc a qc** to compare sth to *o* with sth. **(b)** *(informare)*: ~ **(su)** to inform (about).

ragguaglio [rag'gwaʎʎo] *sm (informazione)*: **fare un** ~ **di qc** to give a report on sth; **fornire** ~**i su qc** to provide information about sth.

ragguardevole [raggwar'devole] *ag (successo, persona)* remarkable, notable; *(somma)* considerable, sizeable.

ragia ['radʒa] *sf*: **acqua** ~ = **acquaragia**.

ragià [ra'dʒa] *sm inv* rajah.

ragionamento [radʒona'mento] *sm (facoltà)* reasoning; *(argomentazione)* argument, reasoning; **ci sono arrivato con il** ~ I got there through reasoning; **è un** ~ **logico** it's a logical argument; **il tuo** ~ **fila** your argument makes sense; **è inutile perdersi in futili** ~**i** it's pointless getting involved in futile arguments.

ragionare [radʒo'nare] *vi* **(a)** *(pensare)* to reason, think; **ragionaci su!** think about it!, think it over!; **cerca di** ~ try and be reasonable. **(b)** *(discutere)*: ~ **di** to discuss, talk over.

ragionato, a [radʒo'nato] *ag (discorso)* reasoned.

ragione [ra'dʒone] **1** *sf* **(a)** *(facoltà)* reason; **perdere il lume della** ~ to lose one's reason, take leave of one's senses.

(b) *(motivo)* reason; **non è una buona** ~**!** that's no excuse *o* reason!; ~ **di più per fare così** all the more reason for doing so; ...**ragion per cui sarebbe meglio partire** ...that's why it would be better to leave; **a maggior** ~ **dovresti fare qualcosa** all the more reason why you should do something; **a ragion veduta** after due consideration; *(intenzionalmente)* deliberately; **senza** ~ for no reason; **per** ~**i di famiglia** for family

reasons; **a** ~ with good reason, rightly; **a torto o a** ~ rightly or wrongly.
  (c) (*Mat*) proportion, ratio; **in** ~ **di 20.000 lire per articolo** at the rate of 20,000 lire per item.
  (d) (*fraseologia*): **aver** ~ **(a fare)** to be right (in doing *o* to do); **aver** ~ **di qn/qc** to get the better of sb/sth; **dare** ~ **a qn** (*sog: persona*) to side with sb; (: *fatto*) to prove sb right; **farsi una** ~ **di qc** to accept sth, come to terms with sth; **picchiare qn di santa** ~ to give sb a good hiding.
  2: ~ **d'essere** raison d'être; ~ **sociale** (*Comm*) corporate name; **ragion di stato** reason of State.
ragioneria [radʒone'ria] *sf* (*scienza*) accountancy; (*ufficio*) accounts department.
ragionevole [radʒo'nevole] *ag* **(a)** (*sensato: persona*) reasonable, sensible; (: *consiglio*) sensible, sound. **(b)** (*giusto: prezzo*) reasonable, fair. **(c)** (*fondato: timore, sospetto*) well-founded.
ragioniere, a [radʒo'njɛre] *sm/f* accountant.
ragliare [raʎ'ʎare] *vi* to bray.
raglio ['raʎʎo] *sm* bray.
ragnatela [raɲɲa'tela] *sf* (spider's) web; **la casa era piena di** ~**e** the house was full of cobwebs.
ragno ['raɲɲo] *sm* spider; **non cavare un** ~ **dal buco** (*fig*) to draw a blank.
ragù [ra'gu] *sm inv* (*Culin*) meat sauce (*for pasta*).
RAI-TV ['raiti'vu] *abbr f di Radio Televisione Italiana.*
rallegramenti [rallegra'menti] *smpl* congratulations.
rallegrare [ralle'grare] **1** *vt* (*persona*) to cheer up; (*stanza, atmosfera*) to brighten up. **2**: ~**rsi** *vr* **(a)** (*diventare allegro*) to cheer up; (*provare allegrezza*) to rejoice; **si rallegrò solo a vederlo** he was glad just to see him. **(b)** (*congratularsi*): ~**rsi con qn per qc** to congratulate sb on sth.
rallentamento [rallenta'mento] *sm* (*di produzione etc*) slowing down, slackening; **subire un** ~ to slow down, slacken.
rallentare [rallen'tare] **1** *vt* (*gen*) to slow down; ~ **il ritmo** to slow down; ~ **il passo** to slacken one's pace. **2** *vi* to slow down.
rallentatore [rallenta'tore] *sm* (*Cine*) slow-motion camera; **al** ~ (*anche fig*) in slow motion.
rally ['ræli] *sm inv* (car) rally.
ramanzina [raman'dzina] *sf* lecture; **fare una bella** ~ **a qn** to give sb a good lecture.
ramare [ra'mare] *vt* **(a)** (*superficie*) to copper, coat with copper. **(b)** (*Agr: vite*) to spray with copper sulphate.
ramarro [ra'marro] *sm* green lizard.
ramato, a [ra'mato] *ag* (*oggetto: rivestito di rame*) copper-coated, coppered; (*capelli, barba*) coppery, copper-coloured.
rame ['rame] *sm* copper; **di** ~ copper *attr*; **incisione su** ~ copperplate.
ramificare [ramifi'kare] **1** *vi* (*Bot*) to put out branches. **2**: ~**rsi** *vr* (*diramarsi*) to branch out; (*Med: tumore, vene*) to ramify; ~**rsi in** (*biforcarsi*) to branch into.
ramificazione [ramifikat'tsjone] *sf* ramification.
ramingo, a, ghi, ghe [ra'mingo] *ag* (*poet*): **andare** ~ to go wandering, wander.
ramino [ra'mino] *sm* (*Carte*) rummy.
rammaricare [rammari'kare] **1** *vt* to grieve. **2**: ~**rsi** *vr*: ~**rsi di** *o* **per qc** (*dispiacersi*) to regret sth, be sorry about sth; (*lamentarsi*) to complain about sth; **è inutile** ~**rsi** there is no point in feeling sorry.
rammarico, chi [ram'mariko] *sm* regret.
rammendare [rammen'dare] *vt* to mend, darn.
rammendo [ram'mɛndo] *sm* darn, mend; **fare un** ~ to darn, mend.

rammentare [rammen'tare] **1** *vt* to remember, recall; ~ **qc a qn** to remind sb of sth. **2**: ~**rsi** *vr*: ~**rsi (di qc)** to remember (sth).
rammollire [rammol'lire] **1** *vt* to soften. **2**: ~**rsi** *vr* to soften, grow soft.
rammollito, a [rammol'lito] **1** *ag* weak. **2** *sm/f* weakling.
ramo ['ramo] *sm* (*gen, fig*) branch; (*branca: di una scienza*) branch; (: *di commercio*) field; **non è il mio** ~ it's not my field *o* line.
ramoscello [ramoʃ'ʃɛllo] *sm* twig.
rampa ['rampa] *sf* (*breve salita*) slope; (~ *d'accesso*) ramp; ~ **(di scale)** flight (of stairs); ~ **d'accesso** (*Aut*) slip road; ~ **di lancio** (*Aer*) launching pad.
rampante [ram'pante] *ag* (*Araldica*) rampant.
rampicante [rampi'kante] **1** *ag* (*Bot*) climbing. **2** *sm* (*Bot*) creeper, climber.
rampino [ram'pino] *sm* (*gancio*) hook; (*Naut*) grapnel.
rampollo [ram'pollo] *sm* (*di acqua*) spring; (*Bot: germoglio*) shoot; (*fig: discendente*) descendant.
rampone [ram'pone] *sm* (*fiocina*) harpoon; (*Alpinismo*) crampon.
rana ['rana] *sf* frog; **nuotare a** ~ to do the breaststroke; **uomo** ~ frogman.
ranch [rantʃ] *sm inv* ranch.
rancido, a ['rantʃido] **1** *ag* rancid. **2** *sm*: **odore di** ~ rank odour; **sa di** ~ it smells rancid.
rancio ['rantʃo] *sm* (*Mil*) mess; **ora del** ~ mess time.
rancore [ran'kore] *sm* rancour, resentment; **senza** ~? no hard feelings?; **portare** ~ **a qn, provare** ~ **per** *o* **verso qn** to bear sb a grudge.
randagio, a, gi, gie *o* **ge** [ran'dadʒo] *ag* (*gatto, cane*) stray.
randellare [randel'lare] *vt* to cudgel.
randello [ran'dello] *sm* cudgel, club.
rango, ghi ['rango] *sm* **(a)** (*grado*) rank; (*condizione sociale*) station, social standing; **avere il** ~ **di** to hold the rank of; **gli alti** ~**ghi** the upper ranks; **persone di** ~ **inferiore** people of lower standing. **(b)** (*Mil: schiera*) rank; (: *fila*) line; **rientrare nei** ~**ghi** to fall in; (*fig*) to fall into line; **uscire dai** ~**ghi** to fall out; (*fig*) to step out of line.
rannicchiare [rannik'kjare] **1** *vt* (*gambe*) to tuck up. **2**: ~**rsi** *vr* to crouch, huddle.
rannuvolamento [rannuvola'mento] *sm* clouding over.
rannuvolare [rannuvo'lare] **1** *vt* to darken. **2**: ~**rsi** *vr* (*cielo*) to cloud over, become overcast; (*fig: viso*) to darken.
ranocchio [ra'nɔkkjo] *sm* frog.
rantolare [ranto'lare] *vi* (*respirare affannosamente*) to wheeze; **si sentiva il moribondo** ~ you could hear the man's death rattle.
rantolio [ranto'lio] *sm* (*il respirare affannoso*) wheezing; (: *di agonizzante*) death rattle.
rantolo ['rantolo] *sm* (*respiro affannoso*) wheeze; (: *di agonizzante*) death rattle.
ranuncolo [ra'nunkolo] *sm* (*Bot*) buttercup.
rapa ['rapa] *sf* turnip; **cime di** ~ turnip tops; **testa di** ~ (*fig*) fathead, idiot; **è come voler cavar sangue da una rapa** it's like trying to draw blood from a stone.
rapace [ra'patʃe] **1** *ag* (*animale*) predatory; (*fig: avido*) rapacious, grasping. **2** *sm* bird of prey.
rapare [ra'pare] **1** *vt* (*capelli*) to crop, cut very short; **ti hanno rapato (i capelli) a zero** they have scalped you. **2**: ~**rsi** *vr*: ~**rsi (i capelli) a zero** to be scalped.
rapide ['rapide] *sfpl* (*di fiume*) rapids.
rapidità [rapidi'ta] *sf* speed, rapidity; **ha colpito**

con ~ he was quick to strike.

rapido, a ['rapido] **1** *ag (gen)* quick, rapid; **è ~ nell'agire** he is quick to act. **2** *sm (Ferr)* express (train) *(on which supplement must be paid)*.

rapimento [rapi'mɛnto] *sm* **(a)** *(di persona)* kidnapping, abduction. **(b)** *(Rel)* ecstasy; **fu preso da ~** he went into ecstasy *o* raptures.

rapina [ra'pina] *sf* robbery; **~ a mano armata** armed robbery; **~ in banca** bank robbery.

rapinare [rapi'nare] *vt* to rob.

rapinatore, trice [rapina'tore] *sm/f* robber.

rapire [ra'pire] *vt* **(a)** *(persona)* to kidnap, abduct. **(b)** *(avvincere)* to captivate; **~ l'attenzione del pubblico** to captivate one's audience.

rapito, a [ra'pito] **1** *ag* **(a)** *(persona)* kidnapped. **(b)** *(fig: in estasi)*: **ascoltare ~ qn** to be captivated by sb's words; **guardava ~ il quadro** he gazed at the painting, entranced. **2** *sm/f* kidnapped person.

rapitore, trice [rapi'tore] *sm/f* kidnapper.

rappacificare [rappatʃifi'kare] **1** *vt (riconciliare)* to reconcile. **2**: **~rsi** *vr (uso reciproco)* to be reconciled, make it up *(fam)*.

rappacificazione [rappatʃifikat'tsjone] *sf* reconciliation.

rappezzare [rappet'tsare] *vt* to patch; **~ un discorso** *(fig)* to throw together a speech.

rapportare [rappor'tare] **1** *vt* **(a)**: **~ qc a** *(confrontare)* to compare sth with; *(riferire)* to relate sth to. **(b)** *(riprodurre: disegno)*: **~ su scala più grande** to reproduce on a larger scale. **2**: **~rsi** *vr*: **~ rsi a** to be related to.

rapporto [rap'pɔrto] *sm* **(a)** *(legame)* connection, relationship, link; **non avere alcun ~ con qc** to have nothing to do with sth, be unrelated to sth; **in ~ a quanto è successo** with regard to *o* in relation to what happened.

(b) *(relazione)* relationship; **~ coniugale** marital relationship; **~i d'affari/di lavoro** business relations; **~i sessuali** (sexual) intercourse; **abbiamo un ottimo ~** we have a very good relationship; **i ~i tra di loro sono piuttosto tesi** they are not on very good terms; **essere in buoni/cattivi ~i con qn** to be on good/bad terms with sb; **l'Italia ha troncato i ~i con la Libia** Italy has broken off diplomatic relations with Libya.

(c) *(resoconto)* report; **fare ~ a qn su qc** to report sth to sb; **chiamare qn a ~** *(Mil)* to summon sb; **andare a ~ da qn** to report to sb.

(d) *(Mat, Tecn)* ratio; *(di bicicletta)* gear; **in ~ di 1 a 10** in a ratio of 1 to 10; **~ di compressione** pressure ratio; **~ di trasmissione** gear.

rapprendersi [rap'prɛndersi] *vr (sangue)* to coagulate, clot; *(latte)* to curdle.

rappresaglia [rappre'saʎʎa] *sf* reprisal, retaliation; **per ~** in reprisal *o* retaliation.

rappresentante [rapprezen'tante] *sm/f (gen, Pol, Comm)* representative; **~ di commercio** sales representative, sales rep *(fam)*; **~ sindacale** union delegate *o* representative.

rappresentanza [rapprezen'tantsa] *sf* **(a)** *(gen, Pol)* representation; *(gruppo)* delegation, deputation; **in ~ di qn** on behalf of sb; **spese di ~** entertainment expenses; **macchina di ~** official car. **(b)** *(Comm)* agency; **avere la ~ di** to be the agent for; **~ esclusiva** sole agency; **avere la ~ eclusiva** to be sole agent.

rappresentare [rapprezen'tare] *vt* **(a)** *(sog: pittore, romanziere, quadro)* to depict, portray; *(: fotografia)* to show; **non riesco a rappresentarmelo** I can't picture it.

(b) *(simboleggiare, significare)* to represent; **ciò rappresenta un grave pericolo per la nazione** this represents a serious threat to the nation;

quella ragazza non rappresenta più niente per me that girl no longer means anything to me.

(c) *(Teatro: recitare)* to perform, play; *(: mettere in scena)* to perform, put on; **hanno intenzione di ~ la Carmen** they intend to stage *o* put on Carmen.

(d) *(agire per conto di)* to represent; **farsi ~ dal proprio legale** to be represented by one's lawyer.

rappresentativa [rapprezenta'tiva] *sf (di partito, sindacale)* representative group; *(Sport: squadra)* representative (team).

rappresentativo, a [rapprezenta'tivo] *ag (gen)* representative; *(tipico)* typical.

rappresentazione [rapprezentat'tsjone] *sf* **(a)** *(raffigurazione)* representation; *(: di società, paesaggio)* portrayal. **(b)** *(Teatro)* performance; **prima ~ assoluta** world première; **sacra ~** religious play.

rappreso, a [rap'preso] *pp di* **rapprendersi.**

rapsodia [rapso'dia] *sf* rhapsody.

raptus ['raptus] *sm inv*: **~ di follia** fit of madness; **~ di ispirazione** flash of inspiration.

raramente [rara'mente] *av* seldom, rarely.

rarefare [rare'fare] *vt*, **~rsi** *vr* to rarefy.

rarefatto, a [rare'fatto] **1** *pp di* **rarefare. 2** *ag* rarefied.

rarefazione [rarefat'tsjone] *sf* rarefaction.

rarità [rari'ta] *sf inv* **(a)** *(scarsezza: di oggetto, malattia)* rarity; *(: di visite etc)* infrequency. **(b)** *(oggetto)* rarity; *(avvenimento)* rare occurrence, unusual occurrence.

raro, a ['raro] *ag* **(a)** *(poco comune)* rare; **è un caso molto ~** it's a very unusual *o* rare case; **è una bestia ~a** *(fig)* he's a rare breed. **(b)** *(poco numeroso)* few, rare; **le ~e persone che passavano** the few people that went by; **c'era qualche ~a nuvola** there was the odd cloud; **i clienti sono diventati ~i** customers have become scarce *o* few and far between.

rasare [ra'sare] **1** *vt (barba)* to shave off. **2**: **~rsi** *vr* to shave.

rasato, a [ra'sato] *ag (erba)* trimmed, cut; *(tessuto)* smooth; **avere la barba ~a** to be clean-shaven.

rasatura [rasa'tura] *sf* shave.

raschiamento [raskja'mento] *sm (Med)* curettage; **~ uterino** D and C.

raschiare [ras'kjare] **1** *vi* to clear one's throat. **2** *vt* to scrape; **~ (via) qc** to scrape sth off.

raschietto [ras'kjetto] *sm* scraper.

raschio ['raskjo] *sm (in gola)* irritation.

rasentare [razen'tare] *vt (muro)* to hug, keep close to; *(fig: sfiorare)* to border on; **questo rasenta la pazzia!** this is bordering on insanity!; **~ la cinquantina** to be getting on for fifty (years of age).

rasente [ra'zɛnte] *prep*: **~ (a)** close to, very near; **camminare ~ il** *o* **al muro** to hug the wall.

raso, a ['raso] **1** *pp di* **radere. 2** *ag* **(a)** *(liscio)*: **a pelo ~** *(pelliccia)* short-haired; *(tessuto)* smooth. **(b)** *(con misure di capacità)* level *attr*; *(pieno: bicchiere)* full to the brim. **3** *prep*: **~ terra** close to the ground; **volare ~ terra** to hedgehop. **4** *sm (tessuto)* satin.

rasoio [ra'sojo] *sm* razor; **~ elettrico** electric shaver *o* razor; **~ radi e getta** throwaway razor.

raspare [ras'pare] **1** *vt (levigare)* to rasp. **(b)** *(grattare: sog: gallina)* to scratch; *(: cavallo)* to paw. **2** *vi* to scrape, scratch.

raspo ['raspo] *sm (di uva)* grape stalk.

rassegna [ras'seɲɲa] *sf* **(a)** *(Mil)* inspection, review; **passare in ~** *(Mil, fig)* to review. **(b)** *(resoconto)* review, survey; *(rivista)* review; *(mostra)* exhibition.

rassegnare [rasseɲ'ɲare] **1** vt: ~ **le dimissioni** to resign, hand in one's resignation. **2**: ~**rsi** vr to resign o.s.; **bisogna** ~**rsi all'idea** we (o you etc) will have to accept o get used to the idea; **devo rassegnarmi di fronte all'evidenza dei fatti** I'll have to accept the facts; **mai rassegnarsi!** never give up!

rassegnazione [rasseɲɲat'tsjone] sf resignation; **accettare qc con** ~ to resign o.s. to sth.

rasserenamento [rasserena'mento] sm brightening up.

rasserenare [rassere'nare] **1** vb impers (Meteor) to clear up, brighten up. **2** vt (persona) to cheer up. **3**: ~**rsi** vr (Meteor) to brighten up, clear up; (persona) to cheer up.

rassettare [rasset'tare] **1** vt to tidy up. **2**: ~**rsi** vr to tidy o.s. up.

rassicurante [rassiku'rante] ag reassuring.

rassicurare [rassiku'rare] **1** vt to reassure. **2**: ~**rsi** vr to take heart, recover one's confidence.

rassicurazione [rassikurat'tsjone] sf reassurance.

rassodamento [rassoda'mento] sm (di muscoli) hardening, strengthening; (di tessuti) firming.

rassodare [rasso'dare] **1** vt (muscoli) to harden, strengthen; (tessuti) to firm (up); (fig: amicizia) to strengthen, consolidate. **2**: ~**rsi** vr to harden, strengthen; (tessuti) to firm (up).

rassomigliante [rassomiʎ'ʎante] ag: **questa foto è molto** ~ this photo is a good likeness.

rassomiglianza [rassomiʎ'ʎantsa] sf resemblance.

rassomigliare [rassomiʎ'ʎare] **1** vi: ~ **a** to resemble, look like. **2**: ~**rsi** vr (uso reciproco) to look alike, resemble each other.

rastrellamento [rastrella'mento] sm (di erba, fieno) raking; (Mil, di polizia) (thorough) search; **stanno facendo un** ~ **nella zona** they are combing the area.

rastrellare [rastrel'lare] vt (erba, fieno) to rake; (fig: perlustrare) to comb.

rastrelliera [rastrel'ljera] sf (per fieno) hayrack; (per fucili, biciclette) rack.

rastrello [ras'trello] sm rake.

rastremarsi [rastre'marsi] vr to taper.

rata ['rata] sf instalment; **pagare a** ~**e** to pay by instalments; **comprare/vendere a** ~**e** to buy/sell on hire purchase.

rateale [rate'ale] ag: **pagamento** ~ payment by instalments; **vendita** ~ hire-purchase sale.

rateare [rate'are] vt to divide into instalments.

rateazione [rateat'tsjone] sf division into instalments.

rateizzare [rateid'dzare] vt = **rateare.**

rateo ['rateo] sm (Econ) accrual.

ratifica, che [ra'tifika] sf ratification.

ratificare [ratifi'kare] vt (gen) to approve, ratify; (Amm, Dir) to ratify.

ratificazione [ratifikat'tsjone] sf = **ratifica.**

ratto[1] ['ratto] sm (Storia, Dir) abduction; **il** ~ **delle Sabine** the rape of the Sabines.

ratto[2] ['ratto] sm (Zool) rat.

rattoppare [rattop'pare] vt to patch.

rattoppo [rat'tɔppo] sm patch; **fare un** ~ **a** o **su qc** to patch sth.

rattrappire [rattrap'pire] **1** vt (piedi, mani) to make numb. **2**: ~**rsi** vr to become numb.

rattristare [rattris'tare] **1** vt (addolorare) to sadden. **2**: ~**rsi** vr to grow sad.

raucedine [rau'tʃɛdine] sf hoarseness; **ho un po' di** ~ I am a little hoarse.

rauco, a, chi, che ['rauko] ag hoarse.

ravanello [rava'nɛllo] sm radish.

ravioli [ravi'ɔli] smpl (Culin) ravioli sg.

ravvedersi [ravve'dersi] vr to mend one's ways.

ravviare [ravvi'are] vt (capelli) to tidy; ~**rsi i capelli** to tidy one's hair.

ravviata [ravvi'ata] sf tidying up.

ravvicinamento [ravvitʃina'mento] sm (tra persone) reconciliation; (Pol: tra paesi etc) rapprochement.

ravvicinare [ravvitʃi'nare] **1** vt (oggetti) to bring closer together; (fig: persone) to reconcile. **2**: ~**rsi** vr to be reconciled; **si è ravvicinato alla famiglia** he is now reconciled with his family.

ravvisare [ravvi'zare] vt (riconoscere) to recognize; (: errore) to spot.

ravvivare [ravvi'vare] **1** vt (fuoco, sentimento) to revive, rekindle; (fig: rallegrare) to brighten up. **2**: ~**rsi** vr (fuoco, sentimento) to be rekindled, be revived; (persona, ambiente) to brighten up.

ravvolgere [rav'vɔldʒere] **1** vt (coperta, lenzuolo) to roll up; ~ **qn in una coperta** to wrap a blanket round sb. **2**: ~**rsi** vr (coprirsi): ~**rsi in qc** to wrap o.s. up in sth.

ravvolto, a [rav'vɔlto] pp di **ravvolgere.**

ravvoltolare [ravvolto'lare] **1** vt: ~ **qn in qc** to wrap sb up in sth. **2**: ~**rsi** vr: ~**rsi in qc** to wrap o.s. up in sth.

raziocinio [rattsjo'tʃinjo] sm (facoltà di ragionare) reasoning; (buon senso) common sense; **essere dotato di** ~ to be able to reason, possess the faculty of reason.

razionale [rattsjo'nale] **1** ag (gen, Mat) rational; (funzionale) functional; **un** ~ **sfruttamento dello spazio** an intelligent use of space. **2** sm: **il** ~ the rational.

razionalità [rattsjonali'ta] sf rationality; (buon senso) common sense; **con** ~ rationally.

razionalizzare [rattsjonalid'dzare] vt to rationalize.

razionamento [rattsjona'mento] sm rationing.

razionare [rattsjo'nare] vt to ration.

razione [rat'tsjone] sf (gen) ration; (di soldato) rations pl; (fig: porzione) share.

razza ['rattsa] sf **(a)** (etnica) race; (Zool) breed; **di** ~ (gen) pedigree, purebred; (cavallo) thoroughbred; **essere di buona** ~ to come of good stock. **(b)** (specie, tipo) sort, kind; **tu e quelli della tua** ~ you and those like you; **che** ~ **di discorso è?** what sort of argument is that?; **che** ~ **di mascalzone!** what a scoundrel!

razzia [rat'tsia] sf raid; **fare una** ~ to carry out a raid; **fare** ~ **in un pollaio** to raid a henhouse.

razziale [rat'tsjale] ag racial; **pregiudizio** ~ racial prejudice.

razziare [rattsi'are] vt (bestiame) to raid; (città: saccheggiare) to plunder, ravage.

razzismo [rat'tsizmo] sm racism, racialism.

razzista, i, e [rat'tsista] ag, sm/f racist, racialist.

razzo ['raddzo] sm rocket; ~ **di segnalazione** flare; **veloce come un** ~ as quick as lightning; **partire come un** ~ to be off like a shot.

razzolare [rattso'lare] vi (galline) to scratch (about).

re[1] [re] sm inv (gen) king; (fig: magnate) tycoon, magnate; **i R**~ **Magi** the Three Wise Men, the Magi; **Cristo R**~ Christ the King; **fare una vita da** ~ (fig) to live like a king.

re[2] [rɛ] sm (Mus) D; (: solfeggiando) re.

reagente [rea'dʒɛnte] sm (Chim) reagent. **2** sm reagent.

reagire [rea'dʒire] vi (gen, Chim) to react; ~ **(a/contro)** to react (to/against).

reale[1] [re'ale] **1** ag (gen, Mat) real; (piacere, miglioramento) real, genuine; (Fin: valore, salario) real, actual; **nella vita** ~ in real life. **2** sm: **il** ~ reality.

reale[2] [re'ale] **1** ag (di, da re) royal; (fig: ottimo, *splendido)* regal, kingly. **2** *smpl*: **i R~i** the Royal family.

realismo [rea'lizmo] *sm* realism; **con ~** realistically.

realista¹, i, e [rea'lista] **1** *ag (gen)* realistic; *(Arte, Letteratura)* realist. **2** *sm/f* realist.

realista², i, e [rea'lista] *ag, sm/f* royalist.

realistico, a, ci, che [rea'listiko] *ag* realistic.

realizzabile [realid'dzabile] *ag (fattibile)* feasible; **questo abito è ~ in diversi tessuti** this dress can be made in various materials.

realizzare [realid'dzare] **1** *vt* **(a)** *(opera, progetto)* to carry out; *(scopo)* to achieve; *(sogno, desiderio)* to achieve, fulfil. **(b)** *(fig: capire)* to realize. **(c)** *(Fin: capitale)* to realize; **abbiamo realizzato 2.000.000 dalla vendita della macchina** we made 2,000,000 lire from the sale of the car. **(d)** *(Sport: goal)* to score. **2**: **~rsi** *vr (sogno, speranza)* to come true; *(persona)* to fulfil o.s.; **non mi sento realizzata nel mio lavoro** I don't feel fulfilled in my job.

realizzazione [realiddzat'tsjone] *sf* **(a)** *(di libro, opera)* realization; *(di sogno)* fulfilment; *(di persona)* self-fulfilment. **(b)** *(opera, creazione)* achievement *(Cine, Teatro)* production; **~ scenica** stage production. **(c)** *(Fin)* realization.

realizzo [rea'liddzo] *sm* **(a)** *(conversione in denaro)* conversion into cash. **(b)** *(vendita forzata)* clearance sale.

realmente [real'mente] *av (in realtà)* really; *(effettivamente)* actually.

realtà [real'ta] *sf inv* reality; **la dura ~** harsh reality; **il suo sogno è divenuto ~** his dream has become **(a)** reality *o* has come true; **in ~** *(in effetti)* in fact; *(a dire il vero)* really.

reame [re'ame] *sm* kingdom, realm; *(fig)* realm.

reato [re'ato] *sm (Dir)* offence, crime.

reattore [reat'tore] *sm (Aer)* jet engine; *(Fis nucleare)* reactor.

reazionario, a [reattsjo'narjo] *ag, sm/f* reactionary.

reazione [reat'tsjone] *sf* **(a)** *(gen)* reaction; **~ a catena** *(anche fig)* chain reaction; **motore m/aereo a ~** jet engine/plane. **(b)** *(Pol)* reaction, repression; **forze della ~** reactionary forces.

rebbio ['rebbjo] *sm* prong.

rebus ['rɛbus] *sm inv* rebus; *(fig: persona)* enigma; *(: situazione, comportamento etc)* puzzle.

recapitare [rekapi'tare] *vt* to deliver.

recapito [re'kapito] *sm* **(a)** *(indirizzo)* address; **ha un ~ telefonico?** do you have a telephone number where you can be reached? **(b)** *(consegna)* delivery; **~ a domicilio** home delivery (service).

recare [re'kare] **1** *vt* **(a)** *(portare)* to bear, carry; *(contenere)* to bear; **le recò in dono un anello** he brought her a ring as a gift; **il telegramma reca la data di ieri** the telegram bears yesterday's date. **(b)** *(causare, arrecare: gioia, piacere)* to give, bring; *(: danno)* to cause; **non voglio recarvi disturbo** I don't want to cause any inconvenience to you, I don't want to disturb you; **~ danno a qn** to harm sb, cause harm to sb. **2**: **~rsi** *vr* to go; **~rsi in città/a scuola** to go into town/to school.

recedere [re'tʃedere] *vi (ritirarsi: Dir, fig)*: **~ (da)** to withdraw (from).

recensione [retʃen'sjone] *sf* review; **fare la ~ di qc, scrivere una ~ su qc** to review sth.

recensire [retʃen'sire] *vt* to review.

recensore, a [retʃen'sore] *sm/f* reviewer.

recente [re'tʃɛnte] *ag* recent; **più ~** latest, most recent; **di ~** recently.

recentissime [retʃen'tissime] *sfpl (TV, Radio)* latest news; *(Stampa)* stop press.

recepire [retʃe'pire] *vt* to understand, take in.

recessione [retʃes'sjone] *sf* recession.

recesso [re'tʃɛsso] *sm* **(a)** *(azione)* recession, receding; *(Dir)* withdrawal. **(b)** *(luogo)* recess; **i ~i della mente** *(fig)* the recesses of the mind.

recidere [re'tʃidere] *vt* to cut off, chop off.

recidivo, a [retʃi'divo] *sm/f (Dir)* recidivist.

recintare [retʃin'tare] *vt* to enclose, fence off.

recinto [re'tʃinto] *sm* **(a)** *(gen)* enclosure; *(per animali)* pen; *(per cavalli)* paddock. **(b)** *(staccionata)* fence; *(in muratura)* surrounding wall.

recinzione [retʃin'tsjone] *sf* **(a)** *(azione)* enclosure, fencing-off. **(b)** *(recinto: di legno)* fence; *(: di mattoni)* wall; *(: reticolato)* wire fencing; *(: a sbarre)* railings *pl*.

recipiente [retʃi'pjɛnte] *sm* container.

reciprocità [retʃiproʃi'ta] *sf* reciprocity.

reciproco, a, ci, che [re'tʃiproko] **1** *ag (gen)* reciprocal; *(sentimento, interesse)* mutual. **2** *sm (Mat)* reciprocal.

reciso, a [re'tʃizo] **1** *pp di* **recidere**. **2** *ag (risposta)* sharp, curt.

recita ['retʃita] *sf (Teatro)* performance; *(di poesie)* recital.

recital [retʃi'tal] *sm inv* recital.

recitare [retʃi'tare] **1** *vi (Teatro, fig)* to act. **2** *vt (dramma)* to perform; *(poesia, lezione)* to recite; *(ruolo)* to play, act.

recitazione [retʃitat'tsjone] *sf (di poesia)* recitation; *(modo di recitare: di attore)* acting; **scuola di ~** drama school.

reclamare [rekla'mare] **1** *vi*: **~ (contro/presso qn)** to complain (about/to sb). **2** *vt (diritto)* to demand; **~ giustizia** to demand justice.

réclame [re'klam] *sf inv (annuncio)* advertisement, ad(vert) *(fam)*; **fare la ~ di qc, fare ~ a qc** to advertise sth.

reclamistico, a, ci, che [rekla'mistiko] *ag* advertising *attr*, publicity *attr*.

reclamizzare [reklamid'dzare] *vt* to advertise.

reclamo [re'klamo] *sm* complaint; **sporgere ~ a** to complain to, make a complaint to.

reclinabile [rekli'nabile] *ag (sedile)* reclining.

reclinare [rekli'nare] *vt (capo)* to bow, lower; *(sedile)* to tilt.

reclusione [reklu'zjone] *sf (Dir)* imprisonment.

recluso, a [re'kluzo] **1** *ag (in prigione)* imprisoned; *(in manicomio)* confined; **~ in prigione** shut away in prison. **2** *sm/f (prigioniero)* prisoner.

recluta ['rekluta] *sf (Mil, fig)* recruit.

reclutamento [rekluta'mento] *sm* recruitment; **ufficio (di) ~** recruiting office.

reclutare [reklu'tare] *vt (Mil, fig)* to recruit.

recondito, a [re'kɔndito] *ag (luogo)* hidden; *(fig: significato)* secret, hidden.

record ['rekord] **1** *ag inv* record *attr*; **in tempo ~, a tempo di ~** in record time. **2** *sm inv* record; **~ mondiale** world record; **detenere il ~ di** to hold the record for.

recriminare [rekrimi'nare] *vi*: **~ (su qc)** to complain (about sth).

recriminazione [rekriminat'tsjone] *sf* recrimination.

recrudescenza [rekrudeʃ'ʃentsa] *sf (di malattia)* fresh outbreak; *(fig: di violenza, scontri)* fresh wave.

recuperare [rekupe'rare] *vt =* **ricuperare**.

redarguire [redar'gwire] *vt* to rebuke, reproach.

redatto, a [re'datto] *pp di* **redigere**.

redattore, trice [redat'tore] *sm/f (Stampa)* editor; *(: di articolo)* writer; *(di dizionario, enciclopedia)* compiler; ~ **capo** chief editor.

redazione |rcdat'tsjonc| *sf* **(a)** *(Stampa)* editing; *(: di articolo)* writing. **(b)** *(redattori)* editorial staff; *(ufficio)* editorial office. **(b)** *(versione di testo)* version.

redditizio, a |rcddi'tittsjo| *ag* profitable.

reddito |'rcddito| *sm (privato)* income; *(statale)* revenue; *(di capitale)* yield; ~ **imponibile** taxable income; ~ **fisso** fixed income; ~ **nazionale** national income; ~ **pubblico** public revenue.

redento, a |rc'dcnto| **1** *pp di* **redimere**. **2** *smpl:* **i** ~**i** the redeemed.

redentore, trice |rcdcn'torc| **1** *ag* redeeming. **2** *sm:* **il R**~ the Redeemer.

redenzione |rcdcn'tsjonc| *sf* redemption.

redigere |rc'didʒerc| *vt (lettera, articolo)* to write; *(contratto, verbale)* to draft, draw up; *(dizionario)* to compile.

redimere |rc'dimcrc| **1** *vt (Rel, fig)* to redeem. **2:** ~**rsi** *vr (Rel, fig)* to redeem o.s.

redini |'rcdini| *sfpl (anche fig)* reins; **tenere le** ~ to hold the reins.

redivivo, a |rcdi'vivo| *ag:* **sei tua madre** ~**a** you're the living image of your mother; **è un Picasso** ~ he is another Picasso.

reduce |'rcdutʃe| **1** *ag (gen, Mil):* ~ **da** returning from, back from; **essere** ~ **da** *(esame, colloquio)* to have been through; *(malattia)* to be just over. **2** *sm* survivor; *(veterano)* veteran.

refe |'rcfe| *sm (filo)* thread; *(: più grosso)* yarn.

referendum |refe'rcndum| *sm inv* referendum.

referenza |rcfe'rcntsa| *sf* reference; **avere buone** ~**e** *(impiegato etc)* to have good references.

referto |re'fcrto| *sm* medical report.

refettorio |rcfet'torjo| *sm (in convento)* refectory; *(Scol)* dining hall.

refezione |rcfct'tsjonc| *sf (Scol)* school meal.

refrain |rə'frɛ| *sm inv* refrain.

refrattario, a |rcfrat'tarjo| *ag (materiale, Med)* refractory; *(fig: persona):* ~ **(a)** indifferent (to); **essere** ~ **alla matematica** to have no aptitude for mathematics.

refrigerante |refridʒe'rante| **1** *ag (Tecn)* cooling, refrigerating; *(bevanda)* refreshing. **2** *sm (Chim: fluido)* coolant; *(Tecn: apparecchio)* refrigerator.

refrigerare |refridʒe'rarc| *vt* to refrigerate.

refrigeratore |refridʒera'torc| *sm (Tecn)* refrigerator.

refrigerazione |refridzerat'tsjonc| *sf* refrigeration; *(Tecn)* cooling; ~ **ad acqua** *(Aut)* watercooling.

refrigerio |refri'dʒerjo| *sm:* **trovare** ~ to find somewhere cool.

refurtiva |rcfur'tiva| *sf* stolen goods *pl*.

regalare |rega'larc| *vt:* ~ **qc** to give sth (as a present), make a present of sth; *(fig: vendere a poco prezzo)* to give sth away; **cosa gli regali per il compleanno?** what are you giving him for his birthday?; **penso che mi regalerò una vacanza** I think I'll treat myself to a holiday.

regale |re'gale| *ag* royal; *(fig: portamento)* regal.

regalità |regali'ta| *sf (fig: di portamento, dimora)* regality.

regalo |rc'galo| **1** *sm* present, gift; **'articoli da** ~' 'gifts'; **fare un** ~ **a qn** to give sb a present; **'con bagno schiuma in** ~' 'with a free gift of bubble bath'. **2** *ag inv:* **libro** ~ free book; **confezione** ~ gift pack.

regata |re'gata| *sf* regatta.

reggente |red'dʒcnte| **1** *ag* **(a)** *(sovrano)* reigning. **(b)** *(Gram: proposizione)* main. **2** *sm/f* regent. **3** *sf (Gram)* main clause.

reggenza |red'dʒcntsa| *sf* regency.

reggere |'rcddʒcrc| **1** *vt* **(a)** *(tenere: persona)* to hold up; *(: pacco, valigia, timone)* to hold; **le gambe non lo reggevano più** his legs could carry him no longer. **(b)** *(sopportare: peso)* to bear; *(: fig: situazione)* to stand, bear; ~ **l'alcool** to hold one's drink; **non lo reggo più** *(fig: persona)* I can't put up with him any more. **(c)** *(Gram: sog: proposizione)* to govern; ~ **il dativo** to take the dative. **(d)** *(essere a capo di: Stato)* to govern; *(: ditta)* to run.

2 *vi* **(a)** *(resistere)* to hold on; ~ **a** *(peso, pressione)* to bear; *(urto)* to stand up to; ~ **alla tentazione** to resist temptation; **non regge al paragone** it *(o he etc)* doesn't stand comparison; **non ha retto a tali minacce** he was unable to hold out against such threats. **(b)** *(durare: bel tempo, situazione)* to last. **(c)** *(fig: stare in piedi: teoria etc)* to hold up, hold water; **è un discorso che non regge** the argument doesn't hold water.

3: ~**rsi** *vr* **(a)** *(stare dritto)* to stand; *(tenersi):* ~**rsi a** to hold on to; *(fig: ipotesi):* ~**rsi su** to be based on; **non si reggeva in piedi** he could barely stand; **non mi reggo più dalla stanchezza** I'm so tired that I can barely stand; **reggiti a me** hold on to me; **reggiti forte** hold on tight. **(b)** *(uso reciproco):* ~**rsi a vicenda** to support one another.

reggia, ge |'rcddʒa| *sf* royal palace; *(fig)* palace.

reggicalze |rcddʒi'kaltsc| *sm inv* suspender belt.

reggimentale |rcddʒimcn'talc| *ag* regimental.

reggimento |rcddʒi'mcnto| *sm* regiment.

reggipetto |rcddʒi'pctto| *sm*, **reggiseno** |rcddʒi'seno| *sm* bra.

regia, gie |rc'dʒia| *sf (Teatro)* production; *(TV, Cine)* direction.

regime |rc'dʒimc| *sm* **(a)** *(Pol, anche peg)* regime. **(b)** *(regola):* ~ **dietetico** diet; ~ **vegetariano** vegetarian diet. **(c)** *(di fiume, torrente)* flow. **(d)** *(Tecn):* ~ **di giri** *(di motore)* revs *pl* per minute.

regina |rc'dʒina| *sf (Pol, Scacchi, Carte, fig)* queen; **la** ~ **Elisabetta** Queen Elizabeth; **la** ~ **madre** the Queen Mother; **la** ~ **della festa** the belle of the ball.

reginetta |redʒi'netta| *sf:* ~ **di bellezza** beauty queen.

regio, a, gi, gie |'rcdʒo| *ag* royal.

regionale |redʒo'nalc| *ag* regional.

regionalismo |redʒona'lizmo| *sm* regionalism.

regione |rc'dʒonc| *sf (gen)* region; *(fig: zona)* area, region.

regista, i, e |rc'dʒista| *sm/f (Teatro)* producer; *(TV, Cine)* director.

registrare |redʒis'trare| *vt* **(a)** *(Amm: nascita, morte, veicolo)* to register; *(Comm: fattura, ordine)* to enter; ~ **i bagagli** *(Aer)* to check in one's luggage. **(b)** *(notare, constatare)* to report, note; *(sog: termometro, apparecchio)* to record, register; **è stato registrato un aumento della domanda** an increase in demand has been reported. **(c)** *(su nastro)* to (tape-)record; *(su disco)* to record. **(d)** *(Tecn):* ~ **i freni** to adjust the brakes.

registratore |redʒistra'torc| *sm* recorder, recording machine; ~ **a cassette** cassette recorder; ~ **di cassa** till, cash register; ~ **di volo** *(Aer)* black box.

registrazione |redʒistrat'tsjonc| *sf (vedi vb)* registration; entry; check-in; reporting; recording; adjustment.

registro |rc'dʒistro| *sm* **(a)** *(gen)* register; *(Comm):* ~ **(di cassa)** ledger; ~ **di classe** class register; ~ **di bordo** logbook. **(b)** *(Amm):* **ufficio del** ~ registrar's office. **(c)** *(Tecn: di orologio)* regulator; *(: di treno)* adjuster. **(d)** *(Mus: di voce)* range, register; *(: di strumento)* register.

regnante [reɲ'ɲante] **1** ag reigning, ruling. **2** sm/f ruler.

regnare [reɲ'ɲare] vi (anche fig) to reign; (predominare) to rule; **regnava il silenzio** silence reigned.

regno ['reɲɲo] sm (a) (reggenza) reign; **durante il ~ di** during the reign of. (b) (luogo) kingdom; **il R~ Unito** the United Kingdom; **il ~ animale/vegetale** the animal/plant kingdom; **il ~ della fantasia** the realm of fantasy.

regola ['regola] sf (a) (gen) rule; **di ~** as a rule; **essere in ~** (dipendente) to be a registered employee; (fig: essere pulito) to be clean; **proporsi una ~ di vita** to set o.s. rules to live by; **le ~e del gioco** (anche fig) the rules of the game; **a ~ d'arte** (lavoro etc) expert, professional; **per tua (norma e) ~** for your information; **avere le carte in ~** (gen) to have one's papers in order; (fig: essere adatto) to be the right person; (: avere la coscienza a posto) to have a clear conscience; **fare le cose in ~** to do things properly; **un'eccezione alla ~** an exception to the rule. (b) (Rel) rule.

regolabile [rego'labile] ag adjustable.

regolamentare [regolamen'tare] **1** ag (distanza, velocità) regulation attr, proper; (disposizione) statutory; **entro il tempo ~** within the time allowed, within the prescribed time. **2** vt (gen) to control.

regolamento [regola'mento] sm (a) (norme) regulations pl; **~ scolastico** school rules pl. (b) (atto del regolare: di debito) settlement; **un ~ di conti** (fig) a settling of scores.

regolare[1] [rego'lare] ag (a) (senza variazioni: gen, Gram, Mat) regular; (: velocità) steady; (: superficie) even; (: passo) steady, even. (b) (in regola: documento, permesso) in order; **presentare ~ domanda** to apply through the proper channels; **esercito ~** regular army; **è tutto ~!** everything is in order!; **tutto ciò non è ~** that's entirely irregular.

regolare[2] [rego'lare] **1** vt (gen) to regulate; (questione, debito, conto) to settle; (apparecchio) to adjust, regulate; (orologio) to set; **~ i conti** (fig) to settle old scores. **2**: **~rsi** vr (a) (limitarsi): **~rsi nel bere/nel mangiare** to watch one's drinking habits/one's eating habits. (b): **non so come regolarmi** I don't know what to do; (nell'usare ingredienti) I don't know what quantities to add; **cerca di regolarti** try to work it out.

regolarità [regolari'ta] sf (a) (vedi ag a) regularity; steadiness; evenness. (b) (nel pagare) punctuality.

regolarizzare [regolarid'dzare] vt (posizione) to regularize; (debito) to settle.

regolatezza [regola'tettsa] sf (ordine) orderliness; (moderazione) moderation.

regolato, a [rego'lato] ag (ordinato) orderly; (moderato) moderate.

regolatore, trice [regola'tore] **1** ag (principio, mente) controlling. **2** sm (Tecn) regulator; **~ di frequenza/di volume** frequency/volume control.

regolo ['regolo] sm ruler; **~ calcolatore** slide rule.

regredire [regre'dire] vi (aus essere) to regress; **~ negli studi** to fall behind in one's studies.

regressione [regres'sjone] sf regression.

regresso [re'gresso] sm (fig: declino) decline.

reietto, a [re'jetto] ag, sm/f outcast.

reincarnare [reinkar'nare] **1** vt to reincarnate. **2**: **~rsi** vr to be reincarnated.

reincarnazione [reinkarnat'tsjone] sf reincarnation.

reintegrare [reinte'grare] vt (produzione) to restore; (energie) to recover; **~ un dipendente al suo posto** to reinstate an employee.

reintegrazione [reintegrat'tsjone] sf (di produzione) restoration; (di dipendente) reinstatement.

reiterare [reite'rare] vt to reiterate.

relais [rə'lɛ] sm (Elettr) relay.

relativamente [relativa'mente] av relatively; **~ a** as regards.

relatività [relativi'ta] sf relativity.

relativo, a [rela'tivo] ag (gen, Gram, Mat) relative; (attinente) relevant; (rispettivo) respective; **~ a** (che concerne) relating to, concerning; (proporzionato) in proportion to.

relatore, trice [rela'tore] sm/f (gen) spokesman/woman; (Univ: di tesi) supervisor.

relax [re'laks] sm relaxation.

relazione [relat'tsjone] sf (a) (legame, nesso) relationship; **non c'è ~ tra le due cose** there's no connection between the two, the two things are in no way related; **essere in ~** to be connected; **mettere in ~** (fatti, elementi) to make the connection between; **in ~ a quanto detto prima** with regard to what has already been said. (b) (rapporto: con persone) relationship; **essere in buone ~i con qn** to be on good terms with sb; **~ (sentimentale)** love affair. (c) (resoconto) report, account; **fare una ~** to make a report, give an account.

relegare [rele'gare] vt to banish; (fig) to relegate.

relegazione [relegat'tsjone] sf (vedi vb) banishment; relegation.

religione [reli'dʒone] sf (gen, fig) religion; (fede) religious faith; **~ di Stato** state religion; **non c'è più ~!** (fig) what's the world coming to!

religioso, a [reli'dʒoso] **1** ag (gen) religious; (arte) sacred; (scuola, matrimonio, musica) church attr; **in ~ silenzio** in reverent silence. **2** sm/f monk/nun.

reliquia [re'likwja] sf (Rel, fig) relic; **tenere qc come una ~** (fig) to treasure sth.

relitto [re'litto] sm (gen, fig) wreck; (persona) down-and-out.

remainder [ri'meində] sm inv (libro) remainder.

remare [re'mare] vi to row.

rematore, trice [rema'tore] sm/f oarsman/woman.

reminiscenze [reminiʃ'ʃentse] sfpl reminiscences.

remissione [remis'sjone] sf (a) (di peccato, debito) remission; **~ di querela** (Dir) withdrawal of an action. (b) (sottomissione) submissiveness, compliance.

remissività [remissivi'ta] sf submissiveness.

remissivo, a [remis'sivo] ag submissive, compliant.

remo ['rɛmo] sm oar; **barca a ~i** rowing boat; **tirare i ~i in barca** (anche fig) to rest on one's oars.

remora ['rɛmora] sf (poet: indugio) hesitation. (b) (Gram): **passato ~** past definite; **trapassato ~** pluperfect.

remoto, a [re'mɔto] ag (lontano) remote. (b) (Gram): **passato ~** past definite; **trapassato ~** pluperfect.

remunerare [remune'rare] etc = **rimunerare** etc.

rena ['rena] sf sand.

renale [re'nale] ag kidney attr.

rendere ['rendere] **1** vt (a) (ridare) to give back, return; **potresti rendermi la penna?** could you give me back my pen?; **quanto prima gli sarà resa la libertà** he will be released as soon as possible; **~ la visita** to pay a return visit; **a buon ~!** (anche iro) my turn next time!; **~ l'anima a Dio** (euf) to breathe one's last.

(b) (dare): **~ grazie a qn** to thank sb; **~ omaggio a qn** to honour sb; **~ un servizio a qn** to do sb a service; **~ una testimonianza** to give evidence.

(c) *(fruttare)* to yield; ~ **il 10%** to yield 10%.

(d) *(esprimere, tradurre)* to render; ~ **l'idea** to give the idea; **non so se rendo l'idea!** I don't know if I make myself clear!

(e) *(+ ag: far diventare)* to make; **il suo intervento ha reso possibile l'affare** his intervention made the whole affair possible; **l'hai resa felice** you made her happy; ~ **la vita impossibile a qn** to make life impossible for sb.

2 *vi (fruttare: ditta)* to be profitable; *(: investimento, campo)* to yield, be productive; **una ditta che non rende** an unprofitable firm.

3: ~**rsi** *vr (+ ag: apparire)* to make o.s.; ~**rsi antipatico/ridicolo** to make o.s. unpleasant/ridiculous.

rendiconto [rendi'konto] *sm (resoconto)* report, account; *(Amm, Comm)* statement (of accounts).

rendimento [rendi'mento] *sm (di manodopera)* efficiency; *(di industria: produttività)* productivity; *(di motore)* performance; *(di podere)* yield; **avere un buon** ~ *(atleta)* to perform well; *(studente)* to do well.

rendita ['rendita] *sf (di individuo)* private o unearned income; *(Comm)* revenue; **vivere di** ~ to have private means; *(fig: studente)* to survive on one's past results; ~ **annua** annuity.

rene ['rɛne] *sm* kidney.

reni ['rɛni] *sfpl (schiena)* back *sg*; **spezzare le ~ a qn** *(fig)* to annihilate sb.

renitente [reni'tɛnte] **1** *ag* unwilling, reluctant. **2** *sm*: **essere un** ~ **(alla leva)** *(Mil)* to fail to report for military service.

renna ['rɛnna] *sf* reindeer *inv;* **giacca di** ~ reindeer skin jacket.

Reno ['rɛno] *sm*: **il** ~ the Rhine.

reo, a ['rɛo] **1** *ag*: ~ **(di)** guilty (of). **2** *sm/f (Dir)* offender; ~ **confesso** confessed criminal.

reparto [re'parto] *sm (di ospedale)* ward; *(di ufficio, negozio)* department; *(Mil: di esercito)* unit; ~ **uomo** *(in negozio)* men's department; ~ **d'attacco** *(Mil)* assault unit.

repellente [repel'lɛnte] *ag* **(a)** *(che ripugna)* repulsive. **(b)** *(Chim: insettifugo)*: **liquido** ~ (liquid) repellent.

repentaglio [repen'taʎʎo] *sm*: **mettere a** ~ to put at risk, jeopardize.

repentino, a [repen'tino] *ag (gesto, movimento)* sudden, unexpected.

reperibile [repe'ribile] *ag (articolo, prodotto)* available; **non è** ~ *(persona)* he can't be reached.

reperire [repe'rire] *vt* to find, trace.

reperto [re'pɛrto] *sm (Archeol)* find; *(anche:* ~ **giudiziario)** exhibit; *(Med)* report.

repertorio [reper'tɔrjo] *sm (Teatro)* repertoire, repertory; *(: di canzoni, fig)* repertoire.

replica, che ['rɛplika] *sf (a) (risposta: gen, Pol)* reply, answer; *(: obiezione)* objection. **(b)** *(ripetizione: gen)* repetition; *(: Teatro, Cine)* repeat performance; **avere molte** ~**che** to have a long run. **(c)** *(copia)* replica.

replicare [repli'kare] *vt* **(a)** *(rispondere)* to reply, answer. **(b)** *(Teatro, Cine)* to repeat.

reportage [rapɔr'taʒ] *sm inv* report.

reporter [re'pɔrter] *sm inv* reporter.

repressione [repres'sjone] *sf* repression.

repressivo, a [repres'sivo] *ag* repressive.

represso, a [re'prɛsso] **1** *pp di* **reprimere**. **2** *ag* repressed.

reprimere [re'primere] *vt (gen)* to suppress, repress; *(sommossa)* to put down, suppress; *(sentimenti)* to repress, hold back.

repubblica, che [re'pubblika] *sf* republic.

repubblicano, a [repubbli'kano] *ag, sm/f* republican.

repulsione [repul'sjone] *sf* **(a)** *(Fis)* repulsion. **(b)** *(fig)* = **ripulsione.**

reputare [repu'tare] **1** *vt* to consider, judge; ~ **qn intelligente** to consider o judge sb (to be) intelligent; **reputo che si possa fare** I think it can be done; **se lo reputerai opportuno** if you think it advisable. **2**: ~**rsi** *vr* to consider o.s.

reputazione [reputat'tsjone] *sf (gen)* reputation; *(buon nome)* reputation, good name; **avere una buona/cattiva** ~ to have a good/bad reputation; **farsi una cattiva** ~ to get o.s. a bad name.

requie ['rɛkwje] *sf* rest; **dare** ~ **a qn** to give sb some peace; **non dare** ~ **a qn** to give sb no quarter; **senza** ~ unceasingly.

requisire [rekwi'zire] *vt* to requisition.

requisito [rekwi'zito] *sm (gen)* requirement; **avere i** ~**i necessari per un lavoro** to have the necessary qualifications for a job.

requisitoria [rekwizi'tɔrja] *sf (Dir)* closing speech (for the prosecution).

requisizione [rekwizit'tsjone] *sf* requisition.

resa ['resa] *sf* **(a)** *(l'arrendersi)* surrender. **(b)** *(rendimento: di podere)* yield; *(: di operaio)* productivity. **(c)** *(fig)*: **è venuto il momento della** ~ **dei conti** the day of reckoning has arrived.

rescindere [reʃ'ʃindere] *vt (Dir)* to rescind, annul.

rescissione [reʃʃis'sjone] *sf (Dir)* rescission, annulment.

rescisso, a [reʃ'ʃisso] *pp di* **rescindere.**

residente [resi'dɛnte] *ag, sm/f* resident.

residenza [resi'dɛntsa] *sf* **(a)** *(soggiorno)* stay. **(b)** *(indirizzo, sede)* residence; **cambiare** ~ to change one's address.

residenziale [residen'tsjale] *ag* residential.

residuo, a [re'siduo] **1** *ag (rimanente)* remaining; *(Chim)* residual. **2** *sm (gen)* remainder; *(Chim, fig)* residue; ~**i industriali** industrial waste *sg*.

resina ['rezina] *sf* resin.

resinoso, a [rezi'noso] *ag* resinous.

resistente [resis'tɛnte] *ag (persona, oggetto)* strong, tough; *(pianta)* hardy; *(tessuto)* strong, hardwearing; *(colore)* fast; *(metallo)* strong, resistant; ~ **all'acqua** waterproof; ~ **al calore** heat-resistant; ~ **al fuoco** fireproof; ~ **al gelo** frost-resistant.

resistenza [resis'tɛntsa] *sf* **(a)** *(gen)* resistance; *(fisica)* stamina, endurance; *(mentale)* endurance, resistance; **opporre** ~ (a) to offer o put up resistance (to); *(decisione, scelta)* to show opposition (to); ~ **passiva** passive resistance; **prova di** ~ endurance test. **(b)** *(Elettr, Tecn, Fis)* resistance; *(Elettr: apparecchio)* resistor; ~ **di attrito** frictional resistance; **coefficiente** *m* **di** ~ drag coefficient. **(c)** *(Pol)*: **la R~** the Resistance.

resistere [re'sistere] *vi*: ~ **a** *(gen)* to resist; *(fatica, siccità)* to stand up to, withstand; *(peso)* to take; *(dolore)* to stand; *(tortura)* to endure; *(attacco)* to hold out against; ~ **al calore** to be heat-resistant; ~ **al fuoco** to be fireproof; ~ **alla prova del tempo** to stand the test of time; ~ **alla corrente di un fiume** to hold one's own against the current of a river; **colori che resistono al lavaggio** colours which are fast in the wash; ~ **al peso della responsabilità** to cope with the responsibility; **non ho resistito e gliel'ho detto** I couldn't contain myself any longer and I told him; **non resisterà molto in quell'ufficio** he won't last long in that office; **nessuno sa resistergli, nessuno sa** ~ **al suo fascino** everybody succumbs to his charm.

resistito, a [resis'tito] *pp di* **resistere.**

reso, a ['reso] *pp di* **rendere.**

resoconto [reso'konto] *sm (gen)* account; *(di giornalista)* report, account; *(di seduta, assemblea)* minutes *pl;* **fare il ~ di** to give an account of; to give a report of; to take the minutes of.

respingente [respin'dʒɛnte] *sm (Ferr)* buffer.

respingere [res'pindʒere] *vt* **(a)** *(attacco, nemico)* to drive back, repel; **~ la palla** *(Calcio)* to kick the ball back; *(Pallavolo etc)* to return the ball. **(b)** *(rifiutare: pacco, lettera)* to return; *(: invito)* to refuse; *(: proposta)* to reject, turn down; *(: persona)* to reject. **(c)** *(Scol: studente)* to fail.

respinto, a [res'pinto] **1** *pp di* **respingere. 2** *sm/f (Scol)* failed candidate.

respirare [respi'rare] **1** *vi (gen)* to breathe; *(fig: distendersi)* to get one's breath back; *(: rassicurarsi)* to breathe again; **non respiri!** *(dal medico)* hold your breath! **2** *vt:* **~ un po' d'aria fresca** *(anche fig)* to get a breath of fresh air; **si respira un'aria di rinnovamento** there is a feeling of renewal in the air.

respiratore [respira'tore] *sm (Med)* respirator; *(di subacqueo)* breathing apparatus.

respiratorio, a [respira'tɔrjo] *ag* respiratory.

respirazione [respira'tsjone] *sf* breathing; **~ artificiale** artificial respiration; **~ bocca a bocca** mouth-to-mouth resuscitation, kiss of life *(fam)*.

respiro [res'piro] *sm* breath; **avere il ~** **pesante** to breathe heavily; **trattenere il ~** to hold one's breath; **esalare l'ultimo ~** to breathe one's last; **godere di un momento di ~** to enjoy a moment's rest; **lavorare senza ~** to work non-stop; **dammi un'attimo di ~** give me a break; **di ampio ~** *(opera, lavoro)* far-reaching.

responsabile [respon'sabile] **1** *ag* **(a)** *(gen, fig):* **~ (di)** responsible (for); *(danni)* liable (for), responsible (for); **sentirsi ~ di fronte a qn** *(moralmente)* to feel responsible to sb, hold o.s. accountable to sb. **(b)** *(incaricato):* **~ (di)** responsible (for), in charge (of). **2** *sm/f* **(a): ~ (di)** *(danni, delitto etc)* person responsible (for). **(b): ~ (di)** *(sezione, ufficio etc)* person in charge (of), manager (of).

responsabilità [responsabili'ta] *sf inv:* **~ (di)** *(gen)* responsibility (for); *(Dir)* liability (for); **assumere la ~ di** to take on the responsibility for; **affidare a qn la ~ di qc** to make sb responsible for sth; **avere la ~ di** to be responsible for, have responsibility for; **fare qc sotto la propria ~** to do sth on one's own responsibility; **~ civile** civil liability.

responsabilizzare [responsabilid'dzare] **1** *vt:* **~ qn** to make sb feel responsible. **2: ~rsi** *vr* to become responsible.

responso [res'pɔnso] *sm (poet)* answer, reply; *(Dir)* verdict.

ressa ['rɛssa] *sf* crowd, throng; **quanta ~!** what a crush!; **far ~ intorno a qn** to throng round sb.

resta ['rɛsta] *sf (fig):* **partire con la lancia in ~** to be ready for battle.

restante [res'tante] **1** *ag (rimanente)* remaining. **2** *sm (resto):* **il ~** the remainder *no pl*, the rest *no pl*.

restare [res'tare] *vi (aus essere)* **(a)** *(in luogo)* to stay, remain; **~ a casa** to stay *o* remain at home; **~ a letto** to stay *o* remain in bed; **~ a cena** to stay for dinner; **~ a guardare la televisione** to stay and watch television; **che resti tra di noi** *(fig: segreto)* this is just between ourselves.

(b) *(in una condizione)* to stay, remain; **~ zitto** to remain *o* keep *o* stay silent; **~ sorpreso** to be surprised; **~ orfano** to become *o* be left an orphan; **~ cieco** to become blind; **~ in piedi** *(non sedersi)* to remain standing; *(non coricarsi)* to

stay up; **~ amici** to remain friends; **~ in buoni rapporti** to remain on good terms; **~ senza parole** to be left speechless.

(c) *(sussistere)* to be left, remain; **non restano che poche pietre** there are only a few stones left; **è l'unico parente che le resta** he's her only remaining relative; **coi pochi soldi che mi restano** with what little money I have left; **restano da fare 15 km** there are still 15 km to go; **ne resta ancora un po'** there's still some left; **resta ancora molto da fare** there's still a lot to do; **non ti resta altro (da fare) che accettare** all you can do is accept; **mi resti solo tu** you're all I have left; **mi resta ben poco da dire se non...** I've little left to say except... .

restaurare [restau'rare] *vt* to restore.

restauratore, trice [restaura'tore] *sm/f* restorer.

restaurazione [restaurat'tsjone] *sf (Pol)* restoration.

restauro [res'tauro] *sm (Archit, Arte)* restoration; **in ~** under repair; **sotto ~** *(dipinto)* being restored; **chiuso per ~i** closed for repairs.

restio, a, ii, ie [res'tio] *ag (riluttante):* **~ a** reluctant to.

restituibile [restitu'ibile] *ag* returnable.

restituire [restitu'ire] *vt:* **~ qc (a)** *(gen)* to return sth (to), give sth back (to); *(colore, forma, forza)* to restore sth (to); **mi ha restituito i soldi oggi** he paid me back today; **~ un favore** to return a favour.

restituzione [restitut'tsjone] *sf (gen)* return; *(di soldi)* repayment.

resto ['rɛsto] *sm* **(a)** *(gen)* rest; *(di soldi)* change; *(Mat)* remainder; **'il ~ alla prossima puntata'** to be continued'; **del ~** besides, moreover. **(b):** **~i** *pl (di cibo)* leftovers; *(di civiltà)* remains; **~i mortali** (mortal) remains.

restringere [res'trindʒere] **1** *vt (strada)* to narrow; *(abito, gonna)* to take in; *(: col lavaggio)* to shrink. **2: ~rsi** *vr (contrarsi)* to contract; *(farsi più stretto: strada, fiume)* to narrow; *(: tessuto)* to shrink; **il campo si restringe** *(fig: di ipotesi, possibilità)* the field has narrowed.

restrittivo, a [restrit'tivo] *ag* restrictive.

restrizione [restrit'tsjone] *sf* restriction.

resurrezione [resurret'tsjone] *sf* = **risurrezione.**

resuscitare [resuʃʃi'tare] *vt, vi* = **risuscitare.**

retata [re'tata] *sf (Pesca)* haul, catch; **fare una ~ di** *(fig: persone)* to round up.

rete ['rete] *sf* **(a)** *(tessuto, Pesca)* net; *(di equilibristi)* safety net; *(per bagagli)* (luggage) rack; *(di ragno)* web; *(maglia metallica, di plastica)* mesh; **~ del letto** (sprung) bed base; **~ metallica** *(attorno campo)* wire netting; **~ da pesca** fishing net; **finire nella ~** *(fig: trappola)* to be caught in the trap. **(b)** *(sistema)* network; **~ ferroviaria/stradale/di distribuzione** railway/road/distribution network; **~ (televisiva)** channel; **~ elettrica** *(nazionale)* (electricity) grid; **~ di spionaggio** spy network. **(c)** *(Sport)* net; **segnare una ~** *(Calcio)* to score a goal; **tirare in ~** *(Calcio)* to take a shot at goal.

reticente [reti'tʃɛnte] *ag* reticent.

reticenza [reti'tʃɛntsa] *sf* reticence; **parlare senza ~** to speak out.

reticolato [retiko'lato] *sm (gen)* grid; *(recinto)* wire netting; *(Mil)* barbed wire (fence).

reticolo [re'tikolo] *sm* network; **~ geografico** grid.

retina¹ ['rɛtina] *sf (Anat)* retina.

retina² [re'tina] *sf (per capelli)* hairnet.

retore ['rɛtore] *sm* rhetorician.

retorica [re'tɔrika] *sf (anche fig)* rhetoric.

retorico, a, ci, che [re'tɔriko] *ag* rhetorical; **domanda** ~a rhetorical question; **figura** ~a rhetorical device.

retribuire [retribu'ire] *vt (gen)* to pay; ~ **il lavoro di qn** to pay sb for his *(o her)* work; **un lavoro mal retribuito** a poorly-paid job.

retributivo, a [retribu'tivo] *ag* pay *attr.*

retribuzione [retribut'tsjone] *sf (stipendio)* pay, remuneration.

retrivo, a [re'trivo] *ag, sm/f* reactionary.

retro ['retro] *sm (gen)* back; *(di auto)* rear, back; 'vedi ~' 'see over(leaf)'.

retroattivo, a [retroat'tivo] *ag (Dir: legge)* retroactive; *(Amm: salario)* backdated.

retrobottega, ghe [retrobot'tega] *sf* back shop.

retrocedere [retro'tʃɛdere] **1** *vt (Mil)* to degrade, demote; *(Sport)* to relegate. **2** *vi (aus essere) (gen)* to move back; *(esercito)* to retreat; *(fig: di fronte a minacce)* to back down; ~ **in serie B** *(Calcio)* to be relegated to the second division.

retrocessione [retrotʃes'sjone] *sf (Mil, di impiegato)* demotion; *(Sport)* relegation.

retrocesso, a [retro'tʃɛsso] *pp di* **retrocedere.**

retrodatare [retroda'tare] *vt* to backdate.

retrogrado, a [re'trɔgrado] *ag (moto)* retrograde, backward; *(fig: idee)* reactionary, retrograde.

retroguardia [retro'gwardja] *sf (anche fig)* rearguard.

retromarcia [retro'martʃa] *sf (Aut)* reverse (gear); **inserire la** ~ to go into reverse gear; **andare in** ~, **fare** ~ to reverse.

retroscena [retroʃ'ʃɛna] *sm inv (Teatro)* backstage; *(fig)*: ~ *pl* behind-the-scenes activity *sg.*

retrospettivo, a [retrospet'tivo] **1** *ag* retrospective. **2** *sf (Arte)* retrospective exhibition.

retrostante [retros'tante] *ag*: ~ **(a)** at the back (of).

retroterra [retro'tɛrra] *sm* hinterland.

retrovia [retro'via] *sf (Mil)* zone behind the front; **mandare nelle** ~**e** to send to the rear.

retrovisore [retrovi'zore] *sm (Aut: anche:* **specchietto** ~) driving mirror.

retta ['rɛtta] *sf* **(a)** *(Geom)* straight line. **(b)** *(di collegio, convitto)* fee. **(c)** *(fig: ascolto)*: **dare** ~ **a qn** to pay attention to sb.

rettangolare [rettango'lare] *ag* rectangular.

rettangolo, a [ret'tangolo] **1** *ag* right-angled. **2** *sm* rectangle.

rettifica, che [ret'tifika] *sf* correction, rectification.

rettificare [rettifi'kare] *vt* **(a)** *(gen)* to rectify, correct. **(b)** *(Chim, Elettr, Mat)* to rectify.

rettificazione [rettifikat'tsjone] *sf* rectification.

rettile ['rɛttile] *sm* reptile.

rettilineo, a [retti'lineo] **1** *ag (gen, Mat)* rectilinear; *(strada)* straight. **2** *sm (di strada)* straight; **in** ~ on the straight; ~ **d'arrivo** *(Sport)* home straight.

rettitudine [retti'tudine] *sf* rectitude, uprightness.

retto, a ['rɛtto] **1** *pp di* **reggere. 2** *ag* **(a)** *(gen, linea)* straight; **angolo** ~ right angle. **(b)** *(fig: onesto)* honest, upright; **abbandonare la** ~**a via** *(fig)* to stray from the path of righteousness. **3** *sm (Anat)* rectum.

rettore [ret'tore] *sm* **(a)** *(Rel)* rector. **(b)** *(Univ)* ≈ chancellor.

reumatico, a, ci, che [reu'matiko] *ag* rheumatic.

reumatismo [reuma'tizmo] *sm* rheumatism.

reverendo, a [reve'rɛndo] *ag, sm* reverend.

reverente [reve'rɛnte] *ag* = **riverente.**

reverenza [reve'rɛntsa] *sf* = **riverenza.**

reversibile [rever'sibile] *ag (gen)* reversible; *(Dir)* revertible.

revisionare [revizjo'nare] *vt (Aut)* to service, overhaul; *(Fin: conti)* to audit.

revisione [revi'zjone] *sf (di contratto, processo, sentenza)* review; *(di macchina)* servicing; *(di conti)* auditing; *(di testo)* revision; ~ **di bozze** proofreading.

revisore [revi'zore] *sm*: ~ **di bozze** proofreader; ~ **ufficiale dei conti** auditor.

revoca, che ['rɛvoka] *sf (Dir)* repeal, revocation.

revocare [revo'kare] *vt (gen)* to revoke, repeal; *(licenza)* to revoke.

revocatorio, a [revoka'tɔrjo] *ag* revocatory, revocative.

revolver [re'vɔlver] *sm inv* revolver.

revolverata [revolve'rata] *sf* revolver shot.

riabbassare [riabbas'sare] *vt* to lower again.

riabbottonare [riabbotto'nare] *vt* to button up again.

riabilitare [riabili'tare] **1** *vt (gen)* to rehabilitate; **quel gesto lo ha riabilitato ai miei occhi** his action restored my good opinion of him. **2**: ~**rsi** *vr* to be rehabilitated; ~**rsi agli occhi di qn** to redeem o.s. in sb's eyes.

riabilitazione [riabilitat'tsjone] *sf* rehabilitation.

riaccendere [riat'tʃɛndere] **1** *vt (sigaretta, fuoco, gas)* to light again; *(luce, radio, TV)* to switch on again; *(fig: sentimenti, interesse)* to rekindle, revive. **2**: ~**rsi** *vr (fuoco)* to catch again; *(luce, radio, TV)* to come back on again; *(fig: sentimenti)* to revive, be rekindled.

riacceso, a [riat'tʃeso] *pp di* **riaccendere.**

riacquistare [riakkwis'tare] *vt (gen)* to buy again; *(ciò che si era venduto)* to buy back; *(fig: buonumore, sangue freddo, libertà)* to regain; ~ **la salute** to recover (one's health); ~ **le forze** to regain one's strength.

riadattare [riadat'tare] **1** *vt (abito)* to alter; *(locale)* to convert. **2**: ~**rsi** *vr*: ~**rsi a qc/a fare qc** to readjust to sth/to doing sth.

riaddormentare [riaddormen'tare] **1** *vt* to put to sleep again. **2**: ~**rsi** *vr* to fall asleep again.

rialzare [rial'tsare] **1** *vt* to raise, lift; *(fondo stradale, superficie)* to make higher, raise; *(prezzi)* to increase, put up, raise. **2** *vi (aus essere) (prezzi, azioni, febbre)* to rise, go up. **3**: ~**rsi** *vr (persona)* to get up.

rialzista, i [rial'tsista] *sm (Borsa)* bull.

rialzo [ri'altso] *sm* **(a)** *(Econ)*: ~ **(di)** rise (in), increase (in); **essere in** ~ *(azioni, prezzi)* to be up; **giocare al** ~ *(Borsa)* to bull. **(b)** *(rilievo: di terreno)* rise.

riandare [rian'dare] *vi (aus essere)*: ~ **(in)**, ~ **(a)** to go back (to), return (to); ~ **con la memoria a qc** *(fig)* to reminisce about sth.

rianimare [riani'mare] **1** *vt (Med)* to resuscitate; *(fig: rallegrare)* to cheer up; *(: dar coraggio)* to give heart to; ~ **una festa** to liven up a party. **2**: ~**rsi** *vr (vedi vt)* to recover consciousness; to cheer up; to take heart; to liven up.

rianimazione [rianimat'tsjone] *sf (Med)* resuscitation; **centro di** ~ intensive care unit.

riaperto, a [ria'pɛrto] *pp di* **riaprire.**

riapertura [riaper'tura] *sf* reopening.

riapparire [riappa'rire] *vi (aus essere)* to reappear.

riapparso, a [riap'parso] *pp di* **riapparire.**

riaprire [ria'prire] *vt,* ~**rsi** *vr* to reopen, open again.

riarmare [riar'mare] *vt,* ~**rsi** *vr* to rearm.

riarmo [ri'armo] *sm* rearmament.

riarso, a [ri'arso] *ag (terreno)* arid; *(gola)* parched; *(labbra)* dry.

riassetto [rias'sɛtto] *sm (di stanza)* rearrangement; *(Pol: di sistema)* reorganization.

riassumere [rias'sumere] *vt* **(a)** *(operaio, impiega-*

to, domestico) to re-employ. **(b)** (*riprendere: attività, funzione*) to resume. **(c)** (*ricapitolare: storia, racconto*) to summarize.

riassuntivo, a [riassun'tivo] *ag* summarizing, recapitulatory.

riassunto, a [rias'sunto] **1** *pp di* **riassumere. 2** *sm* summary.

riattaccare [riattak'kare] *vt* **(a)** (*attaccare di nuovo*): ~ **(a)** (*manifesto, francobollo*) to stick back (on); (*bottone*) to sew back (on); (*quadro, chiavi*) to hang back up (on); ~ (**il telefono** *o* **il ricevitore**) to hang up (the receiver). **(b)** (*riprendere*): ~ **discorso con qn** to begin talking to sb again; ~ **a fare qc** to begin doing sth again.

riattivare [riatti'vare] *vt* **(a)** (*strada, linea ferroviaria*) to reopen. **(b)** (*Med, fig: stimolare*) to stimulate; ~ **la circolazione sanguigna** to get the circulation going again. **(c)** (*macchina, motore*) to start up again.

riavere [ria'vere] **1** *vt* **(a)** (*gen*) to have again; **oggi ho riavuto la nausea** I felt sick again today. **(b)** (*recuperare: soldi, libro etc*) to get back; **far** ~ **qn** (*da svenimento*) to bring sb round. **2**: ~**rsi** *vr* (*da svenimento, stordimento*) to come round; ~**rsi dallo stupore** to recover from one's surprise.

riavvicinare [riavvitʃi'nare] **1** *vt*: ~ **qc a qc** to put sth near sth again; **riavvicinò la sedia al tavolo** he drew the chair up to the table again; **riavvicina i due quadri** put the two pictures next to one another again. **2**: ~**rsi** *vr*: ~**rsi a** to approach again.

ribadire [riba'dire] *vt* to reaffirm.

ribalta [ri'balta] *sf* **(a)** (*Teatro: proscenio*) front of the stage; (*: apparecchio d'illuminazione*) footlights *pl*; **essere/venire alla** ~ (*fig*) to be in/come into the limelight; **tornare alla** ~ (*personaggio*) to make a comeback; (*problema*) to come up again. **(b)** (*piano, sportello*) flap; (*mobile*) bureau.

ribaltabile [ribal'tabile] *ag* (*sedile*) tip-up *attr*.

ribaltare [ribal'tare] **1** *vt* (*rovesciare*) to overturn; (*fig: situazione*) to reverse; (*: questione*) to turn round. **2** *vi* (*aus* essere), ~**rsi** *vr* to overturn.

ribassare [ribas'sare] **1** *vt* (*prezzi*) to lower, bring down. **2** *vi* (*aus* essere) to fall, come down.

ribassista, i [ribas'sista] *sm* (*Borsa*) bear.

ribasso [ri'basso] *sm* (*Econ*): ~ (**di**) fall (in); **essere in** ~ (*azioni, prezzi*) to be down; (*fig: popolarità*) to be on the decline; **giocare al** ~ (*Borsa*) to bear.

ribattere [ri'battere] *vt* **(a)** (*battere di nuovo*) to beat again; (*con macchina da scrivere*) to type again; ~ (**una palla**) to return a ball. **(b)** (*controbattere a: accuse etc*) to refute; ~ **che** to retort that.

ribellarsi [ribel'larsi] *vr*: ~ (**a** *o* **contro**) to rebel (against).

ribelle [ri'belle] **1** *ag* (*soldati, truppe*) rebel; (*carattere, figlio*) rebellious; (*capelli*) unruly. **2** *sm/f* rebel.

ribellione [ribel'ljone] *sf*: ~ (**a** *o* **contro**) rebellion (against).

ribes ['ribes] *sm inv* (*Bot*) currant; ~ **rosso** redcurrant; ~ **nero** blackcurrant.

ribollire [ribol'lire] *vi* (*liquido*) to bubble; (*mare*) to seethe; (*vino*) to ferment; **scene che fanno** ~ **il sangue** (*fig*) scenes which make one's blood boil.

ribrezzo [ri'breddzo] *sm* disgust, repugnance; **avere** *o* **provare** ~ **di qc** to be disgusted at *o* by sth; **far** ~ **a qn** to disgust sb.

ributtante [ribut'tante] *ag* disgusting, revolting.

ributtare [ribut'tare] **1** *vt* **(a)** (*buttare di nuovo*) to throw back. **(b)** (*vomitare*) to bring up, throw up. **2**: ~**rsi** *vr* to throw o.s. back; ~**rsi a letto** to jump back into bed.

ricacciare [rikat'tʃare] *vt* (*respingere*) to drive back; ~ **qn fuori** to throw sb out.

ricadere [rika'dere] *vi* (*aus* essere) **(a)** (*cadere di nuovo*) to fall again; (*fig*): ~ **nel vizio** to fall back into bad habits; ~ **nell'errore** to lapse into error. **(b)** (*riversarsi: responsabilità, colpa*): ~ **su** to fall on. **(c)** (*scendere*) to fall, drop; **i capelli le ricadevano sulle spalle** her hair hung down over her shoulders.

ricaduta [rika'duta] *sf* **(a)** (*Med, fig*) relapse. **(b)** (*Fis*): ~ **radioattiva** fallout.

ricalcare [rikal'kare] *vt* (*Disegno*) to trace; (*fig: imitare*) to follow closely; ~ **le orme di qn** (*fig*) to follow in sb's footsteps.

ricalcitrare [rikaltʃi'trare] *vi* (*cavalli, asini, muli*) to kick; (*fig: persona*): ~ (**di fronte a**) to be recalcitrant (to).

ricamare [rika'mare] *vt* (*anche fig*) to embroider; **ci ha ricamato su** (*fig*) he's exaggerated it.

ricambiare [rikam'bjare] *vt* to return.

ricambio [ri'kambjo] *sm* **(a)** (*di biancheria, abiti*) change; **una camicia di** ~ a spare shirt; **pezzi di** ~ (*Tecn*) spare parts. **(b)** (*Med*) metabolism.

ricamo [ri'kamo] *sm* embroidery; **da** ~ embroidery *attr*; **senza** ~**i** (*fig*) without frills.

ricapitolare [rikapito'lare] *vt* to recapitulate, recap, sum up; **ricapitolando..., per** ~... to sum up..., to recap... .

ricapitolazione [rikapitolat'tsjone] *sf* recapitulation, summary.

ricaricare [rikari'kare] *vt* (*arma, macchina fotografica*) to reload; (*penna*) to refill; (*orologio, giocattolo*) to rewind; (*Elettr*) to recharge.

ricattare [rikat'tare] *vt* to blackmail.

ricattatore, trice [rikatta'tore] *sm/f* blackmailer.

ricatto [ri'katto] *sm* blackmail; **fare un** ~ **a qn** to blackmail sb; **subire un** ~ to be blackmailed.

ricavare [rika'vare] *vt* **(a)** (*estrarre*): ~ (**da**) to extract (from). **(b)** (*ottenere*): ~ (**da**) to get (from), obtain (from); ~ **una gonna da un taglio di stoffa** to make a skirt out of a piece of material; ~ **un profitto** to make a profit; **cosa ne ricavo io?** what do I get out of it?

ricavato [rika'vato] *sm* (*di vendite*) proceeds *pl*.

ricavo [ri'kavo] *sm* (*gen*) proceeds *pl*; (*Contabilità*) revenue.

ricchezza [rik'kettsa] *sf* **(a)** (*di persona, paese*) wealth; (*di terreno, colori*) richness; (*fig: abbondanza*) abundance; **con** ~ **di particolari** in great detail; **in questa zona c'è** ~ **di carbone** there's an abundance of coal in this area. **(b)**: ~**e** *pl* (*averi*) wealth *sg*; (*tesori*) treasures; ~**e naturali** natural resources.

riccio¹, a, ci, ce ['rittʃo] **1** *ag* (*capelli*) curly; (*persona*) curly-headed, with curly hair. **2** *sm* (*da di capelli*) curl; **farsi i** ~**ci** to curl one's hair. **(b)** (*di legno, metallo*) shaving; (*di burro*) curl.

riccio² [ri'ttʃo] *sm* **(a)** (*Zool*) hedgehog; ~ **di mare** sea urchin. **(b)** (*Bot*) chestnut husk.

ricciolo ['rittʃolo] *sm* curl.

ricciuto, a [rit'tʃuto] *ag* (*testa*) curly; (*persona*) curly-headed.

ricco, a, chi, che ['rikko] **1** *ag* **(a)** (*gen, fig*) rich; (*facoltoso*) rich, wealthy; (*fertile: terra*) rich, fertile; **è di famiglia** ~**a** he comes from a rich family; **essere** ~ **sfondato** to be rolling in money; **un piatto molto** ~ a very rich dish; **una** ~**a mancia** a large tip; **una** ~**a documentazione** a wealth of documentation. **(b)**: ~ **di** (*illustrazioni, idee*) full of; (*fauna, risorse, proteine, calorie*) rich in; **alimento** ~ **di vitamine** food rich in vitamins; **un ragazzo** ~ **di fantasia** a boy with a fertile imagination. **2** *sm/f* rich man/woman; **i ~chi** the rich, the wealthy.

ricerca, che [ri'tʃerka] *sf* (a): ~ **(di)** *(gen)* search (for); *(piacere, gloria)* pursuit (of); *(perfezione)* quest (for); **mettersi alla** ~ **di** to go in search of, look *o* search *o* hunt for; **essere alla** ~ **di** to be searching for, be looking for; **fare delle ~che** *(inchiesta)* to make inquiries; **dopo anni di ~che hanno ritrovato il bambino** after years of searching they found the child; ~ **di mercato** market research. **(b)** *(Univ):* **la** ~ research; **lavoro di** ~ piece of research; **fare delle ~che su un argomento** to do *o* carry out research into a subject.

ricercare [ritʃer'kare] *vt (onore, gloria)* to seek; *(successo, piacere)* to pursue, *(motivi, cause)* to look for, try to determine; **è ricercato dalla polizia** he's wanted by the police.

ricercatezza [ritʃerka'tettsa] *sf (raffinatezza)* refinement; *(: peg)* affectation.

ricercato, a [ritʃer'kato] **1** *ag* **(a)** *(molto richiesto)* in great demand, much sought-after. **(b)** *(raffinato: qualità, gusti, stile)* refined; *(peg: affettato)* affected; *(: stile)* studied. **2** *sm/f (criminale)* wanted man/woman.

ricercatore, trice [ritʃerka'tore] *sm/f (Univ)* researcher.

ricetrasmettitore [ritʃetrazmetti'tore] *sm* transceiver.

ricetta [ri'tʃetta] *sf* **(a)** *(Med)* prescription; *(fig: antidoto):* ~ **contro** remedy for. **(b)** *(Culin)* recipe.

ricettacolo [ritʃet'takolo] *sm (peg: luogo malfamato)* den.

ricettario [ritʃet'tarjo] *sm* **(a)** *(Med)* prescription pad. **(b)** *(Culin)* recipe book.

ricettatore, trice [ritʃetta'tore] *sm/f* receiver (of stolen goods).

ricettazione [ritʃettat'tsjone] *sf* receiving (stolen goods).

ricettivo, a [ritʃet'tivo] *ag* receptive.

ricevente [ritʃe'vɛnte] **1** *ag (Radio, TV)* receiving. **2** *sm/f (Comm)* receiver.

ricevere [ri'tʃevere] *vt* **(a)** *(gen)* to receive, get; *(voto)* to get; ~ **uno schiaffo** to get *o* be given a slap; ~ **un rifiuto** to meet with a refusal; **'confermiamo di aver ricevuto tale merce'** *(Comm)* 'we acknowledge receipt of these goods'. **(b)** *(accogliere)* to welcome, receive; *(ammettere alla propria presenza)* to see, receive; ~ **visite** to have visitors; **il dottore riceve il venerdì** the doctor has his surgery on Fridays; **il dottore la riceverà subito** the doctor will see you at once; **mi hanno ricevuto in salotto** they showed me into the living room. **(c)** *(TV, Radio)* to pick up, receive.

ricevimento [ritʃevi'mento] *sm* **(a)** *(il ricevere)* receipt; **al** ~ **della merce** on receipt of the goods. **(b)** *(festa)* reception; ~ **di nozze** wedding reception; **dare un** ~ to hold a reception *o* party.

ricevitore [ritʃevi'tore] *sm* **(a)** *(Telec, Radio, Tecn)* receiver. **(b)** *(Fisco):* ~ **(delle imposte)** tax collector.

ricevitoria [ritʃevito'ria] *sf* **(a)** *(Fisco):* ~ **(delle imposte)** Inland Revenue office. **(b):** ~ **del lotto** lottery office.

ricevuta [ritʃe'vuta] *sf (gen, Comm)* receipt; ~ **di versamento** receipt of payment; **accusare** ~ **di qc** *(Comm)* to acknowledge receipt of sth.

ricezione [ritʃet'tsjone] *sf (Radio, TV)* reception.

richiamare [rikja'mare] *vt* **(a)** *(gen, al telefono)* to call back; *(Mil)* to call up; ~ **qn indietro** to call sb back; ~ **le truppe** to withdraw the troops; ~ **qn alla realtà** to bring sb back to earth; ~ **in vita** to

bring back to life. **(b)** *(attrarre: folla)* to attract; **desidero** ~ **la vostra attenzione su...** I would like to draw your attention to.... **(c)** *(ricordare):* ~ **qc alla memoria di qn** *(sog: avvenimento etc)* to remind sb of sth; **è un colore che richiama il verde** it's a greenish colour. **(d)** *(rimproverare)* to reprimand; ~ **qn all'ordine** to call sb to order. **2:** ~**rsi vr:** ~**rsi a** to refer to.

richiamo [ri'kjamo] *sm* **(a)** *(di truppe etc)* recall. **(b)** *(voce, segno)* call; **il** ~ **della foresta/della natura** the call of the wild/of nature; **uccello da** ~ decoy; **servire da** ~ *(fig: attrazione)* to act as a decoy. **(c)** *(ammonimento)* reprimand; ~ **all'ordine** call to order. **(d)** *(Med: di vaccinazione)* booster. **(e)** *(rimando)* cross-reference.

richiedente [rikje'dɛnte] *sm/f* applicant.

richiedere [ri'kjɛdere] *vt* **(a)** *(chiedere: di nuovo)* to ask again; ~ *(in restituzione)* to ask for sth back. **(b)** *(chiedere: prestito, aiuto)* to ask for; **hanno richiesto il suo intervento** they asked him to intervene; **tutto ciò non è richiesto** all that is not necessary; **il tuo intervento non era richiesto** no-one asked you to intervene; **essere molto richiesto** to be in great demand. **(c)** *(necessitare)* to need, require; **tutto ciò richiede tempo e pazienza** all this requires time and patience.

richiesta [ri'kjɛsta] *sf* **(a)** *(gen):* ~ **(di)** request (for); *(impiego, documenti, congedo)* application (for); *(salario migliore, condizioni migliori)* demand (for); ~ **di matrimonio** marriage proposal; **su** *o* **a** ~ on request; **a** ~ **generale** by general request; **programma a** ~ *(Radio, TV)* request programme. **(b)** *(Comm, Econ)* demand.

richiesto, a [ri'kjɛsto] *pp di* **richiedere.**

richiudere [ri'kjudere] **1** *vt (porta, finestra, cassetto)* to close again, shut again; **quando esci, richiudi per piacere** when you go out please close the door behind you. **2:** ~**rsi vr (porta etc)** to close again; *(ferita)* to close up.

richiuso, a [ri'kjuso] *pp di* **richiudere.**

riciclare [ritʃi'klare] *vt (vetro, carta, bottiglie)* to recycle; *(fig: personale)* to retrain.

ricino ['ritʃino] *sm (Bot)* castor-oil plant; **olio di** ~ castor oil.

ricognitore [rikoɲɲi'tore] *sm (Aer)* reconnaissance aircraft.

ricognizione [rikoɲɲit'tsjone] *sf (Mil)* reconnaissance; **uscire in** ~ to reconnoitre.

ricollegare [rikolle'gare] **1** *vt* **(a)** *(collegare nuovamente: gen)* to join again, link again. **(b)** *(connettere: fatti):* ~ **(a, con)** to connect (with). **2:** ~**rsi vr:** ~**rsi a** *(sog: fatti: connettersi)* to be connected to; *(: persona: riferirsi)* to refer to.

ricolmare [rikol'mare] *vt:* ~ **qn di** *(fig: regali, gentilezze)* to shower sb with.

ricolmo, a [ri'kolmo] *ag:* ~ **(di)** *(bicchiere)* full to the brim (with); *(stanza, braccia)* full (of); **un cuore** ~ **di gioia** a heart overflowing with joy.

ricominciare [rikomin'tʃare] **1** *vt* to start again, begin again; ~ **a fare qc** to begin doing *o* to do sth again, start doing *o* to do sth again; **ha ricominciato a fumare** he's started smoking again; **ricomincia a piovere** it's raining again. **2** *vi (riprendere)* to start again, begin again; **ah, si ricomincia!** *(iro)* here we go again!; **ha ricominciato con la mania dei francobolli** he's off on his stamp craze again. **(b)** *(aus essere)* *(spettacolo)* to start, begin; **è ricominciato l'inverno** winter is here again.

ricompensa [rikom'pensa] *sf* reward.

ricompensare [rikompen'sare] *vt* to reward.

ricomporre [rikom'porre] **1** *vt* **(a)** *(viso, lineamenti)* to recompose. **(b)** *(Tip)* to reset. **2: ricom-**

porsi *vr* to compose o.s., regain one's composure.

ricomposto, a [rikom'posto] *pp di* **ricomporre**.

riconciliare [rikontʃi'ljare] **1** *vt* to reconcile. **2**: ~**rsi** *vr* (**a**): ~**rsi con qn** to make it up with sb, make one's peace with sb. (**b**) *(uso reciproco)* to be reconciled; *(: amici)* to make friends again, make it up again.

riconciliazione [rikontʃiliat'tsjone] *sf* reconciliation.

ricondotto, a [rikon'dotto] *pp di* **ricondurre**.

ricondurre [rikon'durre] *vt (gen)* to bring *(o* take*)* back.

riconferma [rikon'ferma] *sf* reconfirmation.

riconfermare [rikonfer'mare] *vt* to reconfirm.

ricongiungere [rikon'dʒundʒere] **1** *vt* to join together; *(persone)* to reunite. **2**: ~**rsi** *vr* (**a**): ~**rsi a** *(famiglia etc)* to be reunited with. (**b**) *(uso reciproco: eserciti)* to reunite.

ricongiunto, a [rikon'dʒunto] *pp di* **ricongiungere**.

riconoscente [rikonoʃ'ʃente] *ag* grateful.

riconoscenza [rikonoʃ'ʃentsa] *sf* gratitude.

riconoscere [riko'noʃʃere] **1** *vt* (**a**) *(identificare)* to recognize; **l'ho riconosciuto dalla voce** I recognized him by his voice; **per non farsi** ~ so as not to be recognized. (**b**) *(ammettere: gen)* to recognize; *(: errore, torto)* to admit; *(: superiorità)* to acknowledge; **devo** ~ **che hai ragione** I must admit you're right; ~ **i propri limiti** to recognize one's own limitations; ~ **a qn il diritto di fare qc** to acknowledge sb's right to do sth. (**c**) *(Dir)*: ~ **un figlio** to acknowledge a child; ~ **qn colpevole** to find sb guilty. **2**: ~**rsi** *vr* (**a**) *(ammettere)*: ~**rsi colpevole** to admit one's guilt; **si riconobbe sconfitto** he admitted he was beaten. (**b**) *(uso reciproco)* to recognize each other.

riconoscibile [rikonoʃ'ʃibile] *ag* recognizable.

riconoscimento [rikonoʃʃi'mento] *sm (gen, di diritti)* recognition; *(Dir: di figlio)* acknowledgement; *(Dir: di figlio)* acknowledgement; **documento di** ~ means of identification; **come** ~ **dei servizi resi** in recognition of services rendered; **segno di** ~ distinguishing mark.

riconosciuto, a [rikonoʃ'ʃuto] *pp di* **riconoscere**.

riconquista [rikon'kwista] *sf (di territorio perduto)* reconquest; *(di libertà)* recovery.

riconquistare [rikonkwis'tare] *vt (Mil)* to reconquer; *(libertà, stima)* to win back.

riconsegna [rikon'seɲɲa] *sf (seconda consegna)* redelivery; *(restituzione)* handing back.

riconsegnare [rikonseɲ'ɲare] *vt (restituire)* to hand back, give back.

riconsiderare [rikonside'rare] *vt* to reconsider.

ricoperto, a [riko'perto] **1** *pp di* **ricoprire**. **2** *sm (gelato)*: **un** ~ **(al cioccolato)** choc-ice on a stick.

ricopiare [riko'pjare] *vt* to copy; ~ **qc in bella copia** to make a fair copy of sth.

ricoprire [riko'prire] **1** *vt* (**a**) *(gen)*: ~ **(di)** to cover (with); *(divano, poltrona)* to re-cover (with); *(fig: persona: di gentilezze etc)* to shower (with); ~ **un dente** *(carica)* to hold. **2**: ~**rsi** *vr*: ~**rsi di** *(polvere etc)* to become covered in; **il cielo si è ricoperto di nuvole** the sky clouded over; **il prato si è ricoperto di fiori** the field is covered with flowers.

ricordare [rikor'dare] *vt* (**a**) *(nome, persona, fatto)*: ~ **qc**, ~**rsi (di) qc** to remember sth; ~ *o* ~**rsi di fare qc** to remember to do sth; ~ *o* ~**rsi di aver fatto qc** to remember having done sth; **se ben (mi) ricordo** if I remember rightly; **ti ricordi di me?** do you remember me?; **non si è più ricordato di darmi il libro** he forgot to give me the book. (**b**) *(far presente ad altri)*: ~ **a qn qc/di fare qc** to remind sb of sth/to do sth; **ti ricordo che**

c'ero prima io I'd like to remind you that I was here first; **scene che ricordano il passato** scenes which recall the past; **mi ricorda molto suo padre** he reminds me a lot of his father. (**c**) *(menzionare)* to mention. (**d**) *(commemorare)* to commemorate.

ricordino [rikor'dino] *sm* souvenir.

ricordo [ri'kɔrdo] *sm* (**a**) *(memoria)* memory; **non ho che un vago** ~ **di quella giornata** I have only a vague recollection of that day, I only remember that day vaguely; **vivere di** ~**i** to live in the past. (**b**) *(oggetto)* keepsake; *(: turistico)* souvenir; **un** ~ **di famiglia** a family heirloom; **prendere/dare qc per** *o* **in** ~ to take/give sth as a keepsake.

ricorrente [rikor'rente] **1** *ag* recurring, recurrent. **2** *sm/f (Dir)* plaintiff.

ricorrenza [rikor'rentsa] *sf* (**a**) *(il ricorrere)* recurrence. (**b**) *(anniversario)* anniversary.

ricorrere [ri'korrere] *vi (aus* **essere**) (**a**) *(ripetersi periodicamente)* to recur; **oggi ricorre il 5° anniversario di...** today is the 5th anniversary of...; **è un elemento che ricorre in tutta la sua poesia** it's a recurring element in all his poetry. (**b**) *(rivolgersi a)*: ~ **a** *(persona)* to turn to; *(polizia)* to call in; *(forza, stratagemma)* to resort to; ~ **alle vie legali** to take legal action. (**c**) *(Dir)*: ~ **contro una sentenza** to appeal against a sentence; ~ **in appello** to lodge an appeal.

ricorso, a [ri'korso] **1** *pp di* **ricorrere**. **2** *sm* (**a**): **fare** ~ **a** *(persona)* to turn to; *(mezzo, cosa)* to resort to; **dovette far** ~ **a tutto il suo coraggio** he had to summon up all his courage. (**b**) *(Dir)* appeal; **fare** ~ **(contro)** to appeal (against). (**c**) *(il ricorrere)* recurrence; **questo è un tipico esempio dei corsi e** ~**i della storia** this is a typical example of history repeating itself.

ricostituente [rikostitu'ente] **1** *ag (Med)*: **cura** ~ tonic treatment. **2** *sm (Med)* tonic.

ricostituire [rikostitu'ire] **1** *vt (società)* to build up again; *(governo, partito)* to re-form. **2**: ~**rsi** *vr (gruppo etc)* to re-form.

ricostruire [rikostru'ire] *vt (edificio)* to rebuild, reconstruct; *(testo, fatti, delitto)* to reconstruct.

ricostruzione [rikostrut'tsjone] *sf* reconstruction.

ricotta [ri'kɔtta] *sf* soft white unsalted cheese.

ricotto, a [ri'kɔtto] *pp di* **ricuocere**.

ricoverare [rikove'rare] *vt (Med)*: ~ **qn in ospedale/in manicomio** to admit sb to hospital/to a mental hospital; **far** ~ **qn in ospedale** to have sb admitted to hospital.

ricoverato, a [rikove'rato] *sm/f* patient.

ricovero [ri'kovero] *sm* (**a**) *(rifugio)* shelter; *(Mil)*: ~ **antiaereo** air-raid shelter. (**b**) *(Med)* admission.

ricreare [rikre'are] **1** *vt* (**a**) *(creare di nuovo)* to recreate. (**b**) *(fig: rallegrare)* to cheer; ~ **lo spirito** to restore one's spirits; ~ **la vista** to gladden the eye. **2**: ~**rsi** *vr (fig: svagarsi, divertirsi)* to enjoy o.s.

ricreativo, a [rikrea'tivo] *ag* recreational.

ricreazione [rikreat'tsjone] *sf* (**a**) *(svago)* recreation, entertainment. (**b**) *(Scol)* break; *(alle elementari)* break, playtime.

ricredersi [ri'kredersi] *vr*: ~ **(su qc/qn)** to change one's mind (about sth/sb).

ricrescere [ri'kreʃʃere] *vi (aus* **essere**) to grow again.

ricresciuto, a [rikreʃ'ʃuto] *pp di* **ricrescere**.

ricucire [riku'tʃire] *vt (vestito, colletto)* to stitch again; *(strappo, buco)* to mend; *(Med: ferita, gamba)* to stitch up, sew up; *(fam: paziente)* to stitch back up.

ricuocere [ri'kwɔtʃere] vt (Culin) to recook, cook again.

ricuperare [rikupe'rare] vt **(a)** (gen) to recover; (soldi) to get back; (peso) to put back on; ~ **il tempo perduto** to make up for lost time; ~ **la salute/le forze** to recover (one's health)/one's strength; ~ **lo svantaggio** (Sport) to close the gap. **(b)** (da naufragio, incendio: persone) to rescue; (: salme) to recover; (: oggetti, relitto) to salvage. **(c)** (disadattato, delinquente) to rehabilitate. **(d)** (usare di nuovo: cascami, rottami) to re-use; (Chim) to recover.

ricupero [ri'kupero] sm (gen) recovery; (di relitto etc) salvaging; **capacità di** ~ resilience; **partita di** ~ (Sport) replay; **minuti di** ~ (Sport) injury time.

ricurvo, a [ri'kurvo] ag (linea) curved; **avere le spalle** ~**e** to be round-shouldered; **stava** ~ **sul proprio lavoro** he was bent over his work.

ricusare [riku'zare] vt (offerta, carica) to decline.

ridacchiare [ridak'kjare] vi to snigger.

ridanciano, a [ridan'tʃano] ag (persona) jolly, fun-loving; (storiella) funny, amusing.

ridare [ri'dare] vt (oggetto) to give back, return; (salute, felicità) to restore.

ridente [ri'dɛnte] ag (occhi, volto) smiling; (paesaggio) delightful.

ridere ['ridere] **1** vi (gen) to laugh; ~ **di qc/qn** to laugh at sth/sb; ~ **alle spalle di qn**, ~ **dietro a qn** to laugh behind sb's back; ~ **in faccia a qn** to laugh in sb's face; **cerchiamo di riderci sopra** let's try and see the funny side of it; ~ **di cuore** to laugh heartily; ~ **fino alle lacrime** to laugh till one cries; **non c'è niente da** ~, **c'è poco da** ~ it's not a laughing matter; **lo ha detto per** ~ he was only joking, he said it in fun; **si fa così per** ~ we're just joking; **è roba da** ~ (facile) it's nothing; **che** ~! what a laugh!; **quasi soffocava dal gran** ~ he laughed so much he nearly choked; **c'è da morire dal** ~! it's hilarious!, it's really funny!; **se la rideva** he had a laugh to himself; **le ridevano gli occhi** her eyes sparkled; **ride bene chi ride ultimo** (Proverbio) he who laughs last laughs best.
2: ~**rsi** vr: ~**rsi di qc** (non curarsene) to laugh at sth; ~**rsi di qn** (beffarlo) to make fun of sb.

ridestare [rides'tare] **1** vt (fig: ricordi, passioni) to reawaken. **2**: ~**rsi** vr (fig: odio) to be roused again; (amore, speranza) to be rekindled.

ridetto, a [ri'detto] pp di **ridire**.

ridicolaggine [ridiko'laddʒine] sf (di situazione) absurdity; (cosa detta o fatta) nonsense no pl.

ridicolizzare [ridikolid'dzare] vt to ridicule.

ridicolo [ri'dikolo] **1** ag (gen) ridiculous; **rendersi** ~ to make a fool of o.s. **2** sm: **il** ~ **della situazione** the absurdity of the situation; **il** ~ **della storia era che...** the ridiculous o absurd thing about it was...; **cadere nel** ~ to become ridiculous; **mettere in** ~ to ridicule; **coprirsi di** ~ to make a laughing stock of o.s.

ridimensionamento [ridimensjona'mento] sm reorganization; (di fatto storico) reappraisal.

ridimensionare [ridimensjo'nare] **1** vt (ditta, industria) to reorganize; (fig: problema, autore, fatto storico) to put in perspective. **2**: ~**rsi** vr (persona) to get things into perspective; (sogni, ambizioni) to become more realistic.

ridire [ri'dire] vt **(a)** (ripetere, riferire) to repeat. **(b)** (criticare): **trovare da** ~ (su qc/qn) to find fault (with sth/sb); **che c'è da** ~? what's your objection?

ridonare [rido'nare] vt (salute, allegria) to restore, give back.

ridondante [ridon'dante] ag redundant.

ridosso [ri'dɔsso] sm: **a** ~ **di** (dietro) behind; (contro) against; **costruire una casa a** ~ **di una montagna** to build a house in the shelter of a mountain.

ridotto, a [ri'dotto] **1** pp di **ridurre**. **2** sm (Teatro) foyer.

ridurre [ri'durre] **1** vt **(a)** (gen, Mat) to reduce; (prezzo) to reduce, cut, bring down; (pressione) to lessen; (produzione) to cut (back), lower; (spese) to cut down on, cut back on. **(b)** (opera letteraria: per la radio, TV) to adapt; (brano musicale) to arrange. **(c)** (fraseologia): ~ **qc in cenere** to reduce sth to ashes; ~ **qn in poltiglia** (fig) to make mincemeat of sb; **guarda come hai ridotto quella gonna!** look at the state of your skirt!; **è proprio ridotto male** o **mal ridotto** (oggetto) it's really in bad condition; (persona) he's really in a bad way.
2: **ridursi** vr **(a)** (quantità, spese): **ridursi (a)** to be reduced (to); (fig: questione, problema) to come down (to); **il livello si è ridotto di un decimo** the level dropped by a tenth. **(b)** (persona): **ridursi male** to be in a bad state; **ridursi pelle e ossa** to be reduced to skin and bone; **ridursi a uno straccio** to be washed out; **si è ridotto a mendicare** he was reduced to begging; **come ti sei ridotto!** what a state you're in!

riduttore [ridut'tore] sm (Tecn, Chim, Elettr) reducer.

riduzione [ridut'tsjone] sf **(a)** (diminuzione: di salario, personale etc): ~ **(di)** reduction (in), cut (in). **(b)** (sconto) reduction, discount; **una** ~ **del 10%** a 10% reduction o discount. **(c)** (adattamento: di opera letteraria) adaptation; ~ **televisiva a cura di...** adapted for television by.... **(d)** (Mat, Chim, Med) reduction.

riecheggiare [rieked'dʒare] vi (aus essere) to re-echo; **in questi versi riecheggiano motivi leopardiani** in these lines we find echoes of Leopardi.

rieducare [riedu'kare] vt (persona) to re-educate; (malato) to rehabilitate; (arto) to re-educate.

rieducazione [riedukat'tsjone] sf (vedi vb) re-education; rehabilitation; **centro di** ~ rehabilitation centre.

rieleggere [rie'lɛddʒere] vt to re-elect.

rieletto, a [rie'letto] pp di **rieleggere**.

riempimento [riempi'mento] sm filling (up).

riempire [riem'pire] **1** vt (gen, fig): ~ **(di)** to fill (with); (Culin: farcire) to stuff (with); ~ **un modulo** to fill in a form; ~**rsi le tasche di** to fill one's pockets with; **si è riempito la testa di sciocchezze** he has filled his head with nonsense. **2**: ~**rsi** vr (gen): ~**rsi (di)** to fill (up) (with); (cibo) to stuff o.s. (with); **quel quadro si è riempito di polvere** that painting is covered in dust.

riempitivo [riempi'tivo] sm: **fare da** ~ (fam) to make up the numbers.

rientrante [rien'trante] ag (Archit) receding.

rientranza [rien'trantsa] sf (di costruzione) recess; (di costa) indentation.

rientrare [rien'trare] vi (aus essere) **(a)** (entrare di nuovo) to come (o go) back in. **(b)** (ritornare) to return, get back; ~ **(a casa)** to get back home; ~ **alla base** (Mil) to return to base; ~ **in sé** (dopo svenimento) to come round; (riacquistare controllo) to regain control of o.s.; ~ **in possesso di qc** to regain possession of sth. **(c)** (fig: far parte di, essere incluso): ~ **in** to be included among, form part of; **non rientra nei miei doveri** it isn't my duty; **non rientriamo nelle spese** we are not within our budget. **(d)** (superficie, linea) to curve inwards; *(costa)* to be indented.

rientro [ri'entro] *sm (gen: ritorno)* return; *(di astronave)* re-entry; **l'ora del ~** *(dal lavoro)* the rush hour; **è cominciato il grande ~ (dalle vacanze)** everyone is coming back from holiday.

riepilogare [riepilo'gare] **1** *vt (discorso, fatti)* to summarize. **2** *vi* to recapitulate.

riepilogo, ghi [rie'pilogo] *sm* recapitulation; **fare un ~ di qc** to summarize sth.

riesame [rie'zame] *sm* re-examination.

riesaminare [riezami'nare] *vt* to re-examine.

riessere [ri'essere] *vi (aus essere)*: **ci risiamo!** *(fam)* we're back to this again!

rievocare [rievo'kare] *vt (passato)* to recall; *(commemorare: figura, meriti)* to commemorate.

rifacimento [rifatʃi'mento] *sm (di film)* remake; *(di opera letteraria)* rehashing.

rifare [ri'fare] **1** *vt (ricominciare)* to redo, do again; *(ricostruire)* to make again; *(nodo)* to tie again, do up again; **è tutto da ~!** it will have to be completely redone!; **~rsi la bocca** *(anche fig)* to take away a bad taste; **~rsi i denti** to get false teeth; **~ il letto** to make the bed; **~rsi gli occhi** to look at something pleasant for a change; **~ una stanza** to tidy up a room; **~rsi il trucco** to touch up one's make-up; **~rsi una vita** to make a new life for o.s.
2: **~rsi** *vr* **(a)** *(ridiventare)* to become again. **(b)** *(ricuperare)*: **~rsi di** *(perdita, spesa)* to recover from; **~rsi di qc su qn** *(vendicarsi)* to get one's own back on sb for sth, get even with sb for sth. **(c)** *(riferirsi)*: **~rsi a** *(periodo, fenomeno storico)* to go back to; *(stile, autore)* to follow.

rifatto, a [ri'fatto] *pp di* **rifare.**

riferimento [riferi'mento] *sm* reference; **in ~ a, facendo ~ a, con ~ a** with reference to; **far ~ a** to refer to; **punto di ~** *(anche fig)* point of reference.

riferire [rife'rire] **1** *vt* **(a)** *(raccontare, riportare)* to report; **andare a ~ qc a qn** to go and tell sb sth; **riferirò** I'll pass on the message. **(b)** *(attribuire)* to attribute. **2** *vi*: **~ (su qc)** to make a report (on sth). **3**: **~rsi** *vr*: **~rsi a** to refer to.

rifilare [rifi'lare] *vt* **(a)** *(tagliare a filo)* to trim. **(b)** *(fam: affibbiare)*: **~ qc a qn** to palm sth off on sb; **gli ho rifilato un ceffone** I gave him a slap.

rifinire [rifi'nire] *vt (lavoro)* to finish off; *(opera d'arte, vestito)* to put the finishing touches to.

rifinitura [rifini'tura] *sf (gen)* finishing touch; *(di mobile, auto)*: **~e** finish *sg.*

rifiorire [rifjo'rire] *vi (aus essere) (anche fig: persona)* to bloom again; *(fig: studi, arti)* to flourish again, thrive again.

rifiutare [rifju'tare] *vt (gen)* to refuse; *(invito, offerta)* to turn down, decline; *(pretendente)* to turn down; **~ qc a qn** to deny sb sth; **~ o ~rsi di fare qc** to refuse to do sth.

rifiuto [ri'fjuto] *sm* **(a)** *(diniego)* refusal; **opporre un ~** to refuse. **(b)** *(scarto)* waste; **~i** *pl (immondizie)* rubbish *sg*; **i ~i della società** *(fig)* the dregs of society.

riflessione [rifles'sjone] *sf* **(a)** *(meditazione)* reflection, meditation; *(osservazione)* observation; **dopo matura ~** after due consideration; **ha fatto delle interessanti ~i** he made some interesting observations. **(b)** *(Fis)* reflection.

riflessivo, a [rifles'sivo] *ag* **(a)** *(persona)* thoughtful. **(b)** *(Gram)* reflexive.

riflesso, a [ri'flesso] **1** *pp di* **riflettere. 2** *ag (immagine)* reflected; *(azione, movimento)* reflex *attr.* **3** *sm* **(a)** *(di luce, rispecchiamento)* reflection; *(su capelli)* light; *(fig)* effect; **di ~** automatically. **(b)** *(Fisiologia)* reflex; **~ condizionato** conditioned

reflex; **avere i ~i pronti** to have quick reflexes.

riflettente [riflet'tɛnte] *ag (Fis)* reflective.

riflettere [ri'flɛttere] **1** *vi*: **~ (su qc)** *(meditare)* to reflect (upon sth); *(pensare)* to think (over sth); **se ti fermi a ~** if you stop and think; **agire senza ~** to act without thinking; **riflettendoci su...** on reflection... . **2** *vt (Fis, fig)* to reflect. **3**: **~rsi** *vr* **(a)** *(rispecchiarsi, anche fig)* to be reflected. **(b)** *(ripercuotersi)*: **~rsi su** to have repercussions on.

riflettore [riflet'tore] *sm* **(a)** *(Fis, Elettr)* reflector; *(Teatro, TV)* spotlight; *(in campo di calcio)* floodlight. **(b)** *(telescopio)* reflecting telescope.

rifluire [riflu'ire] *vi (aus essere) (scorrere: nuovamente)* to flow again; *(: indietro)* to flow back; *(marea)* to go out.

riflusso [ri'flusso] *sm (gen: di sangue)* flow; *(: di acqua, marea)* ebb; **flusso e ~** ebb and flow.

rifocillarsi [rifotʃil'larsi] *vr (poet)* to take refreshment.

rifondere [ri'fondere] *vt* **(a)** *(metalli, cera)* to remelt, melt down again. **(b)** *(risarcire: spese)* to refund, reimburse; **~ le spese a qn** to refund sb's expenses; **~ i danni a qn** to compensate sb for damages.

riforma [ri'forma] *sf* **(a)** *(gen)* reform; *(Rel)*: **la R~** the Reformation. **(b)** *(Mil: di recluta)* declaration of unfitness for service; *(: di soldato)* discharge.

riformare [rifor'mare] **1** *vt* **(a)** *(formare di nuovo)* to form again, re-form. **(b)** *(Rel, Pol etc)* to reform; *(Mil: recluta)* to declare unfit for military service; *(: soldato)* to discharge, invalid out. **2**: **~rsi** *vr (formarsi di nuovo)* to form again, re-form.

riformato, a [rifor'mato] *sm (Rel)* Protestant; *(Mil: recluta)* recruit unfit for military service; *(: soldato)* discharged soldier.

riformatore, trice [riforma'tore] **1** *ag* reforming. **2** *sm/f* reformer.

riformatorio [riforma'tɔrjo] *sm* approved school.

riformista, i, e [rifor'mista] *ag, sm/f* reformist.

rifornimento [riforni'mento] *sm* **(a)** *(operazione)* supplying, providing; *(di carburante)* refuelling; **fare ~ di** *(viveri)* to stock up with; *(benzina)* to fill up with; **posto di ~** filling station. **(b)**: **~i** *pl (scorte)* stocks, supplies.

rifornire [rifor'nire] **1** *vt*: **~ di** to supply with, provide with. **2**: **~rsi** *vr*: **~rsi di** to get in a supply of, stock up with.

rifrangere [ri'frandʒere] **1** *vt (Fis)* to refract. **2**: **~rsi** *vr* to be refracted.

rifratto, a [ri'fratto] *pp di* **rifrangere.**

rifrazione [rifrat'tsjone] *sf (Fis)* refraction.

rifuggire [rifud'dʒire] *vi (aus essere)*: **~ da qc** to be averse to sth, shun sth; **~ da fare qc** to be reluctant to do sth.

rifugiarsi [rifu'dʒarsi] *vr*: **~ in, ~ a** *(gen, fig)* to take refuge in; *(: da pioggia, freddo)* to (take) shelter in.

rifugiato, a [rifu'dʒato] *sm/f* refugee.

rifugio [ri'fudʒo] *sm (gen)* shelter, refuge; *(in montagna)* shelter; *(fig)* refuge; **cercare ~ in qc/presso qn** to seek refuge in sth/with sb; **~ antiaereo** air-raid shelter.

rifulgere [ri'fuldʒere] *vi (anche fig)*: **~ (di)** to shine (with), glow (with).

rifusione [rifu'zjone] *sf (Tecn)* remelting.

rifuso, a [ri'fuzo] *pp di* **rifondere.**

riga, ghe [ri'ga] *sf* **(a)** *(linea)* line; *(striscia)* stripe; **a ~ghe** *(foglio)* lined; *(tessuto)* striped. **(b)** *(scritta)* line; **buttare giù due ~ghe** *(note)* to jot down a few notes; **mandami due ~ghe appena arrivi** drop me a line as soon as you arrive. **(c)** *(Mil, Scol: fila)* line, row; *(Sport)* line; **mettersi in ~** to line up; **mettere qn in ~** *(fig)* to make sb toe the line; **rimettersi in** ~ *(fig)* to get back into line; **mettersi in** ~ **con qn** *(fig)* to come into line with sb; **rompete le ~ghe! break ranks! (d)** *(righello)* ruler. **(e)** *(nei capelli)* parting; **farsi la** ~ **in mezzo/da una parte** to put one's hair in a middle parting/side parting.

rigaglie [ri'gaʎʎe] *sfpl (Culin)* giblets.

rigagnolo [ri'gaɲɲolo] *sm* rivulet.

rigare [ri'gare] **1** *vt (pagina, foglio)* to rule; *(superficie: sfregiare)* to score; **col volto rigato di lacrime** with a tear-stained face. **2** *vi (fig)*: ~ **dritto** to toe the line.

rigatoni [riga'toni] *smpl (Culin)* short, ridged pasta shapes.

rigattiere [rigat'tjɛre] *sm* junk dealer, secondhand dealer.

rigatura [riga'tura] *sf (di pagina, quaderno)* lining, ruling; *(di fucile)* rifling.

rigenerare [ridʒene'rare] **1** *vt (gen, Tecn)* to regenerate; *(forze)* to restore; *(gomma)* to retread; **gomma rigenerata** retread. **2**: ~**rsi** *vr (gen)* to regenerate; *(ramo, tumore)* to regenerate, grow again.

rigenerativo, a [ridʒenera'tivo] *ag (processo)* regenerating.

rigenerazione [ridʒenerat'tsjone] *sf* regeneration.

rigettare [ridʒet'tare] **1** *vt* **(a)** *(gettare: di nuovo)* to throw again; *(: indietro)* to throw back. **(b)** *(respingere: proposta)* to reject, turn down; *(: Bio, Med)* to reject. **(c)** *(vomitare)* to throw up. **2**: ~**rsi** *vr*: ~**rsi in acqua** to jump back into the water; **si è rigettato in politica** he's launched himself back into politics.

rigetto [ri'dʒetto] *sm (gen, Med)* rejection.

righello [ri'gɛllo] *sm* ruler.

rigidezza [ridʒi'dettsa] *sf*, **rigidità** [rigidi'ta] *sf (gen)* rigidity; *(di membra)* stiffness; *(fig: di clima)* harshness, severity; *(: severità)* severity, strictness.

rigido, a ['ridʒido] *ag (gen)* rigid; *(membra, berretto, colletto)* stiff; *(fig: clima, inverno)* harsh, severe; *(: disciplina, principi)* strict.

rigirare [ridʒi'rare] **1** *vt (gen)* to turn; ~ **il discorso** to change the subject; ~ **qc tra le mani** to turn sth over in one's hands. **2**: ~**rsi** *vr (voltarsi: di nuovo)* to turn round; **girarsi e** ~**rsi nel letto** to toss and turn in bed.

rigo, ghi ['rigo] *sm (Mus)* staff, stave.

rigoglio [ri'goʎʎo] *sm (di piante)* luxuriance.

rigoglioso, a [rigoʎ'ʎoso] *ag (pianta, giardino)* luxuriant; *(fig: studi, commercio, sviluppo)* thriving.

rigonfiamento [rigonfja'mento] *sm (Anat)* swelling; *(su legno, intonaco etc)* bulge.

rigonfiare [rigon'fjare] *vt* to blow up (again).

rigonfio, a [ri'gonfjo] *ag (Anat)* swollen; *(vela)* full; *(grembiule, sporta)*: ~ **di** bulging with.

rigore [ri'gore] *sm* **(a)** *(di sentenza, legge)* severity; *(di disciplina)* strictness, severity; *(di clima)* severity, harshness; **punire qn con** ~ to punish sb severely; **'è di** ~ **l'abito da sera'** 'evening dress'; **a rigor di termini** strictly speaking; **i** ~**i dell'inverno** the rigours of winter. **(b)** *(Calcio)* penalty; **area/calcio di** ~ penalty area/kick.

rigorosità [rigorosi'ta] *sf (precisione: di conclusioni)* rigour; *(severità: di costumi)* strictness.

rigoroso, a [rigo'roso] *ag (definizione, logica)* rigorous, exact; *(punizione)* severe, harsh; *(ordine)* strict.

rigovernare [rigover'nare] *vt (piatti, stoviglie)* to wash (up); **non ho ancora rigovernato** I haven't done the washing-up yet.

riguadagnare [rigwadaɲ'ɲare] *vt* **(a)** *(guadagnare* *di nuovo)* to earn again. **(b)** *(recuperare: velocità)* to make up, regain; *(: terreno)* to regain; *(: stima, affetto)* to win back; ~ **il tempo perduto** to make up for lost time.

riguardare [rigwar'dare] **1** *vt* **(a)** *(guardare di nuovo)* to look at again, take another look at; *(controllare)* to check. **(b)** *(concernere)* to concern; **per quel che mi riguarda** as far as I'm concerned; **è un libro che riguarda la vita dei contadini** it's a book which deals with o looks at the life of country people; **sono affari che non ti riguardano** it's none of your business. **(c)** *(curare, tenere da conto)* to look after, take care of. **2**: ~**rsi** *vr (aver cura di sé)* to look after o.s., take care of o.s.; **ti devi** ~ **dalle correnti d'aria** you should stay out of draughts.

riguardo [ri'gwardo] *sm* **(a)** *(rispetto, considerazione)* regard, respect; **per** ~ **a** out of respect for; **trattare qn col massimo** ~ to treat sb with the greatest respect; **mancare di** ~ **verso qn** to be disrespectful towards sb; **ospite/persona di** ~ very important guest/person; **aver** ~ **delle cose altrui** to respect other people's property. **(b)**: ~ **a** *(a proposito di)* regarding, as regards; ~ **a me** as far as I'm concerned.

riguardoso, a [rigwar'doso] *ag (rispettoso)* respectful; *(premuroso)* considerate, thoughtful.

rigurgitare [rigurdʒi'tare] **1** *vi (liquido: aus essere)*: ~ **da** to gush out from; *(recipiente: traboccare)*: ~ **di** to overflow with. **2** *vt* to bring up.

rigurgito [ri'gurdʒito] *sm (Med)* regurgitation; *(fig: ritorno, risveglio)* revival.

rilanciare [rilan'tʃare] *vt (lanciare di nuovo: gen)* to throw again; *(: moda)* to bring back; *(: prodotto)* to re-launch; *(Carte)* to raise; ~ **un'offerta** *(asta)* to make a higher bid.

rilancio [ri'lantʃo] *sm (Carte, di offerta)* raising.

rilasciare [rilaʃ'ʃare] **1** *vt* **(a)** *(Amm: passaporto, certificato)* to issue; *(intervista)* to give; ~ **delle dichiarazioni** to make a statement. **(b)** *(persona, prigioniero)* to release. **(c)** *(muscoli, tensione, nervi)* to relax. **2**: ~**rsi** *vr* to relax.

rilascio [ri'laʃʃo] *sm (di documento)* issue; *(di prigioniero)* release.

rilassamento [rilassa'mento] *sm (gen, Med)* relaxation.

rilassare [rilas'sare] **1** *vt (distendere: nervi, muscoli)* to relax; *(: persona)* to help to relax. **2**: ~**rsi** *vr (gen)* to relax; *(fig: disciplina)* to become slack.

rilassatezza [rilassa'tettsa] *sf (fig: di costumi, disciplina)* laxity.

rilassato, a [rilas'sato] *ag (persona, muscoli)* relaxed; *(disciplina, costumi)* lax.

rilegare [rile'gare] *vt (libro, volume)* to bind.

rilegatore, trice [rilega'tore] *sm/f* bookbinder.

rilegatura [rilega'tura] *sf* binding.

rileggere [ri'leddʒere] *vt (leggere di nuovo)* to read again, reread; *(: per correggere)* to read over; **l'ho letto e riletto cento volte** I've read it over and over again.

rilento [ri'lɛnto]: **a** ~ *av* slowly; **gli affari vanno a** ~ business is slow.

riletto, a [ri'lɛtto] *pp di* **rileggere**.

rilevamento [rileva'mento] *sm (Topografia)* survey; *(Naut)* bearing.

rilevante [rile'vante] *ag* remarkable, considerable.

rilevare [rile'vare] *vt* **(a)** *(levare di nuovo)* to take off again. **(b)** *(notare)* to notice; **dai sintomi non si rileva alcun pericolo immediato** going by the symptoms, there is no immediate danger; **rilevo con soddisfazione che...** I note with satisfaction that...; **far** ~ **a qn che...** to point out to sb that... .

(c) *(raccogliere: dati)* to gather, collect; *(Topografia)* to survey; *(Naut: posizione)* to plot; **la polizia non ha potuto ~ alcun indizio** the police have been unable to find any evidence. **(d)** *(Comm: negozio, ditta)* to take over. **(e)** *(Mil: sentinella)* to relieve.

rilevazione [rilevat'tsjone] *sf* survey.

rilievo [ri'ljɛvo] *sm* **(a)** *(gen, Arte, Geog)* relief; **alto/basso ~** high/bas-relief; **i ~i alpini** the Alps. **(b): in ~** *(gen)* in relief; *(ricamo)* raised; **carta in ~** relief map; **dare ~ a qc, mettere in ~ qc** *(fig)* to stress o highlight sth; **di poco/nessun ~** *(fig)* of little/no importance; **un personaggio di ~** an important person. **(c)** *(Topografia, Statistica)* survey.

rilucente [rilu'tʃɛnte] *ag* bright, shining.

riluttante [rilut'tante] *ag* reluctant; **essere ~ a fare qc** to be reluctant to do sth.

riluttanza [rilut'tantsa] *sf (gen)* reluctance; **con ~** reluctantly.

riluttare [rilut'tare] *vi*: **~ a fare qc** to be reluctant to do sth.

rima ['rima] *sf (gen)* rhyme; *(verso)* verse; **far ~ con** to rhyme with; **mettere in ~** to put into rhyme; **~e alternate** alternate rhymes; **rispondere a qn per le ~e** to give sb tit for tat.

rimandare [riman'dare] *vt* **(a)** *(mandare: di nuovo)* to send again; *(: indietro)* to send back, return; **~ qn a** *(fig: far riferimento)* to refer sb back to. **(b)** *(posporre: partenza, appuntamento)*: **~ a** to put off until, postpone until; **non ~ a domani quel che puoi fare oggi** *(Proverbio)* don't put off till tomorrow what you can do today. **(c)** *(Scol)*: **~ qn (a settembre)** to make sb resit (in September); **è stato rimandato in matematica** he has a resit in Maths.

rimando [ri'mando] *sm (in testo)* cross-reference.

rimaneggiare [rimaned'dʒare] *vt (testo)* to reshape, recast; *(ministero)* to reshuffle.

rimanente [rima'nɛnte] **1** *ag* remaining. **2** *sm (resto)*: **il ~** the rest, the remainder; **i (o le) ~i** *(persone)* the rest (of them), the others.

rimanenza [rima'nɛntsa] *sf (gen)* rest, remainder; **~e di magazzino** *(Comm)* left-over stock *sg*.

rimanere [rima'nere] *vi* = **restare**.

rimangiare [riman'dʒare] *vt* to eat again; **~rsi la parola/una promessa** *(fig)* to go back on one's word/one's promise.

rimare [ri'mare] *vt, vi* to rhyme.

rimarginare [rimardʒi'nare] *vt, vi (aus* **essere***)*, **~rsi** *vr* to heal.

rimasto, a [ri'masto] *pp di* **rimanere**.

rimasuglio [rima'suʎʎo] *sm (di stoffa)* remnant; *(di cibo)*: **~i** left-overs.

rimbalzare [rimbal'tsare] *vi*: **~ (su)** *(pavimento)* to bounce (off); *(muro etc)* to rebound (off); *(sog: proiettile)* to ricochet (off); **far ~ una palla** to bounce a ball.

rimbalzo [rim'baltso] *sm (di palla)* bounce; *(di proiettile)* ricochet; **di ~** on the rebound; *(fig)* automatically.

rimbambire [rimbam'bire] *vi (aus* **essere***)*, **~rsi** *vr* to grow foolish; **~ o ~rsi con l'età** to grow senile.

rimbambito, a [rimbam'bito] *ag* senile, gaga *(fam)*; **un vecchio ~** a doddering old man.

rimbeccare [rimbek'kare] *vt (persona)* to answer back; *(offesa)* to return.

rimbecillire [rimbetʃil'lire] **1** *vt*: **~ qn** to make sb stupid. **2** *vi (aus* **essere***)*, **~rsi** *vr* to become stupid.

rimboccare [rimbok'kare] *vt (orlo)* to turn up; *(coperta)* to tuck in; *(pantaloni)* to roll up, turn up;

~rsi le maniche *(anche fig)* to roll up one's sleeves.

rimbombante [rimbom'bante] *ag (vedi vb)* roaring, rumbling; thundering.

rimbombare [rimbom'bare] *vi (tuono)* to roar, rumble; *(cannonata)* to roar, thunder.

rimborsare [rimbor'sare] *vt (persona)* to pay back, reimburse; *(spese, biglietto)* to refund, reimburse; **~ qc a qn** to reimburse sb for sth.

rimborso [rim'borso] *sm* repayment, reimbursement; *(di spese, biglietto)* refund; **~ fiscale** tax rebate.

rimboschimento [rimboski'mento] *sm* reafforestation.

rimboschire [rimbos'kire] *vt* to reafforest.

rimbrottare [rimbrot'tare] *vt* to reproach.

rimbrotto [rim'brotto] *sm* reproach; **fare un ~ a qn** to reproach sb.

rimediare [rime'djare] **1** *vi (con)* to remedy; **~ a qc** to remedy sth; **e adesso come si rimedia?** what can we do about it now?; **ha cercato di ~ al male fatto** he tried to make amends for the wrong he had done. **2** *vt (fam: procurarsi)* to scrape up; **~ da vivere** to scrape a living.

rimedio [ri'mɛdjo] *sm (gen)* remedy; *(cura)* remedy, cure; **un ~ per tutti i mali** a panacea; **porre ~ a qc** to remedy sth; **non c'è ~** there's no way out, there's nothing to be done about it; **è una situazione senza ~** it's a situation which cannot be remedied.

rimescolare [rimesko'lare] *vt* to mix well, stir well; *(carte)* to shuffle; **sentirsi ~ il sangue** *(per paura)* to feel one's blood run cold; *(per rabbia)* to feel one's blood boil.

rimescolio [rimesko'lio] *sm (trambusto)* bustle; *(turbamento)* shock.

rimessa [ri'messa] *sf* **(a)** *(per veicoli)* garage; *(per aerei)* hangar. **(b)** *(Comm: di merce)* shipment; *(: di denaro)* remittance. **(c)** *(Tennis)* return; **~ in gioco laterale** *(Calcio)* throw-in; *(Rugby)* lineout; **~ in gioco dal fondo** *(Calcio)* goal kick; *(Rugby)* drop-out.

rimesso, a [ri'messo] *pp di* **rimettere**.

rimestare [rimes'tare] *vt (mescolare)* to mix well, stir well; *(fig: passato)* to drag up again.

rimettere [ri'mettere] **1** *vt* **(a)** *(mettere: di nuovo)* to put back; *(indossare)* to put back on; **~ mano a qc** to take up sth again; **~ a nuovo** *(casa etc)* to do up. **(b)** *(demandare: decisione)*: **~ a qn** to refer to sb, leave to sb; **~ l'anima a Dio** to entrust one's soul to God. **(c)** *(perdonare: peccato)* to forgive; *(Dir: pena)* to quash; *(: debito)* to remit; **~ qn dei suoi peccati** to forgive sb's sins. **(d)** *(inviare: merce)* to deliver; *(: somma)* to remit. **(e)** *(Sport: pallone)* to throw in; *(Tennis)* to return. **(f)** *(perdere: anche:* **rimetterci***)* to lose; **rimetterci di tasca propria** to be out of pocket; **rimetterci la salute** to ruin one's health; **rimetterci la pelle** to lose one's life; **cosa ci rimetti?** what have you got to lose?

2: **~rsi** *vr* **(a)** *(mettersi di nuovo)*: **~rsi a fare qc** to start doing sth again; **~rsi in cammino** to set off again; **~rsi al lavoro** to start working again; **~rsi a dormire** to go back to sleep; **~rsi con qn** to get back together with sb. **(b)** *(affidarsi)*: **~rsi a** to trust. **(c)** *(riprendersi)* to recover; **~rsi in forze** to regain o recover one's strength; **~rsi da uno shock** to recover from a shock; **il tempo si è rimesso al bello** the weather has cleared up. **(d)** *(uso reciproco)*: **~rsi insieme** to get back together.

rimmel ['rimmel] *sm inv* ® mascara.

rimodernamento [rimoderna'mento] *sm* modernization.

rimodernare [rimoder'nare] vt (gen) to modernize; (vestito) to remodel.

rimonta [ri'monta] sf (Sport, gen) recovery; **fare una ~ in classifica** to climb back up the league.

rimontare [rimon'tare] 1 vt (a) (montare di nuovo: meccanismo) to reassemble, put back together again; (: tenda) to put up again. (b) (risalire): **~ la corrente** to go upstream. 2 vi (aus essere) (a): **~ in** (macchina, carrozza) to get back into; **~ a cavallo, ~ in sella** to remount; **~ su una bici** to get back on a bike. (b) (Sport) to close the gap.

rimorchiare [rimor'kjare] vt (veicolo) to tow; **~ qn** (dare un passaggio) to give sb a lift; (ragazza) to pick sb up.

rimorchiatore [rimorkja'tore] sm (Naut) tug.

rimorchio [ri'mɔrkjo] sm (a) (operazione) towing; **cavo da ~** towrope; **andare a ~** to be towed; **prendere a ~** to tow. (b) (veicolo trainato) trailer; **autocarro con ~** articulated lorry.

rimordere [ri'mɔrdere] vt (fig: tormentare) to torment; **non ti rimorde la coscienza?** isn't your conscience bothering you?

rimorso, a [ri'mɔrso] 1 pp di **rimordere.** 2 sm remorse; **essere preso dai ~i** to be stricken with remorse; **avere il ~ di aver fatto qc** to deeply regret having done sth.

rimosso, a [ri'mɔsso] pp di **rimuovere.**

rimostranza [rimos'trantsa] sf protest, complaint; **fare le proprie ~e a qn** to remonstrate with sb.

rimovibile [rimo'vibile] ag removable.

rimozione [rimot'tsjone] sf (a) (gen) removal; (di veicolo) towing away; **'~ forzata'** 'illegally parked vehicles will be removed at owner's expense'. (b) (da incarico) dismissal. (c) (Psic) repression.

rimpastare [rimpas'tare] vt (a) (pasta lievitata) to knead again; (cemento) to mix again. (b) (Pol: ministero) to reshuffle.

rimpasto [rim'pasto] sm: **~ ministeriale** cabinet reshuffle.

rimpatriare [rimpa'trjare] 1 vt to repatriate. 2 vi to return to one's country.

rimpatrio [rim'patrio] sm repatriation; **ottenere il ~** to be repatriated.

rimpetto [rim'petto]: **di ~** av, prep vedi **dirimpetto.**

rimpiangere [rim'pjandʒere] vt (gen) to regret; (passato, giovinezza) to look back on with regret; **~ di (non) aver fatto qc** to regret (not) having done sth.

rimpianto, a [rim'pjanto] 1 pp di **rimpiangere.** 2 ag (persona, periodo) sadly missed. 3 sm regret; **non aver ~i** to have no regrets.

rimpiattino [rimpjat'tino] sm (gioco) hide-and-seek.

rimpiazzare [rimpjat'tsare] vt to replace.

rimpicciolire [rimpittʃo'lire] 1 vt to make smaller. 2 vi (aus essere), **~rsi** vr to become smaller.

rimpinzare [rimpin'tsare] 1 vt (fam): **~ (di)** to stuff (with). 2: **~rsi** vr: **~rsi di** to stuff o.s. (with).

rimpolpare [rimpol'pare] vt (ingrassare) to fatten (up); (fig: articolo, discorso, finanze) to pad out, fill out.

rimproverare [rimprove'rare] vt (figlio, scolaro) to scold, tell off; (dipendente) to reproach, reprimand; **~ qc a qn** to reproach sb with sth; **non ho niente da rimproverarmi** I've nothing to reproach myself with.

rimprovero [rim'prɔvero] sm reproach; **fare un ~ a qn** to reproach sb; (bambino) to tell sb off; **di ~** (tono, occhiata) reproachful; (parole) of reproach.

rimuginare [rimudʒi'nare] vt: **~ qc** to turn sth over in one's mind; **che starà rimuginando?** what

can he be brooding over o about?

rimunerare [rimune'rare] vt (retribuire) to remunerate; (ricompensare: sacrificio etc) to reward; **un lavoro ben rimunerato** a well-paid job.

rimunerativo, a [rimunera'tivo] ag (lavoro, attività) remunerative, profitable.

rimunerazione [rimunerat'tsjone] sf (retribuzione) remuneration; (ricompensa) reward.

rimuovere [ri'mwɔvere] vt (a) (gen, Med) to remove; (fig: dubbio) to remove, eliminate; (: sospetto) to eliminate; (: ostacolo) to get rid of; **~ qn da una carica** to dismiss sb; **~ qn da un proposito** to deter sb from a purpose. (b) (Psic) to repress.

rinascere [ri'naʃʃere] vi (aus essere) (persona) to be born again; (pianta) to sprout again; (fig: speranza, interesse etc) to be revived; **sentirsi ~** to feel a new man (o woman).

rinascimentale [rinaʃʃimen'tale] ag Renaissance attr, of the Renaissance.

Rinascimento [rinaʃʃi'mento] sm: **il ~** the Renaissance.

rinascita [ri'naʃʃita] sf (fig) rebirth, revival.

rinato, a [ri'nato] pp di **rinascere.**

rincalzare [rinkal'tsare] vt (palo, albero) to prop up; (coperte, lenzuola) to tuck in.

rincalzo [rin'kaltso] sm (a) (sostegno) prop, support; (: fig) support. (b) (Sport: giocatore) reserve; (Mil): **~i** reserves.

rincarare [rinka'rare] 1 vt (prezzi) to raise; (prodotto) to raise the price of; **~ la dose** (fig) to pile it on. 2 vi (aus essere) (prezzo) to go up; (prodotto) to go up in price.

rincaro [rin'karo] sm: **~ (di)** (prezzi, costo della vita) increase (in); (prodotto) increase in the price (of).

rincasare [rinka'sare] vi (aus essere) to return home.

rinchiudere [rin'kjudere] 1 vt: **~ (in)** (gen) to shut up (in); (persona: in prigione, manicomio) to lock up (in). 2: **~rsi** vr: **~rsi (in)** (stanza) to shut o.s. up (in); (: a chiave) to lock o.s. up (in); **~rsi in un convento/in un monastero** to withdraw into a convent/monastery; **~rsi in se stesso** to withdraw into o.s.

rinchiuso, a [rin'kjuso] pp di **rinchiudere.**

rincitrullire [rintʃitrul'lire] vi (aus essere), **~rsi** vr to grow foolish, lose one's marbles (fam).

rincivilire [rintʃivi'lire] = **incivilire.**

rincominciare [rinkomin'tʃare] = **ricominciare.**

rincorrere [rin'korrere] 1 vt to chase, run after; (fig: sogno, chimere) to pursue. 2: **~rsi** (uso reciproco) to run after each other; **giocare a ~rsi** to play tag.

rincorso, a [rin'korso] pp di **rincorrere.**

rincrescere [rin'kreʃʃere] vi (aus essere): **mi rincresce (che)** I regret (that), I am sorry (that); **gli rincresce di non poterlo aiutare** he regrets being unable to help him.

rincrescimento [rinkreʃʃi'mento] sm regret; **con mio grande ~** much to my regret.

rincresciuto, a [rinkreʃ'ʃuto] pp di **rincrescere.**

rinculare [rinku'lare] vi (arma) to recoil; (veicolo) to reverse.

rinculo [rin'kulo] sm (di arma) recoil.

rinfacciare [rinfat'tʃare] vt: **~ qc a qn** to cast sth up at sb.

rinfocolare [rinfoko'lare] vt (fig: odio, passioni) to rekindle; (: risentimento, rabbia) to stir up.

rinforzare [rinfor'tsare] 1 vt (muro, argomento, gruppo) to reinforce; (muscoli, posizione, amicizia, prestigio) to strengthen; (presa, nodo) to tighten. 2: **~rsi** vr (persona) to become stronger;

(amicizia, legame) to strengthen.

rinforzo [rin'fortso] *sm* **(a)**: **mettere un ~ a** *(gen)* to strengthen; **di ~** *(asse, sbarra)* strengthening; *(esercito)* supporting; *(personale)* extra, additional. **(b)** *(Mil)*: **~i** *pl* reinforcements.

rinfrancare [rinfran'kare] **1** *vt (persona)* to encourage, reassure; *(spirito)* to cheer. **2**: **~rsi** *vr* to be reassured.

rinfrescante [rinfres'kante] *ag (bibita)* refreshing.

rinfrescare [rinfres'kare] **1** *vt (gen)* to cool; *(aria)* to cool, freshen; *(fig: pareti, soffitto, abiti)* to freshen up; **~rsi la gola** to quench one's thirst; **~rsi il viso** to splash one's face; **~ la memoria a qn** to refresh sb's memory. **2** *vi (aus essere)* to get cooler. **3**: **~rsi** *vr (persona: con bibita)* to have sth to drink; *(: con bagno)* to freshen up.

rinfresco, schi [rin'fresko] *sm* **(a)** *(ricevimento)* reception; *(festa)* party. **(b)**: **~schi** *pl (cibi e bevande)* refreshments.

rinfusa [rin'fuza] *sf*: **alla ~** higgledy-piggledy.

ringalluzzire [ringallut'tsire] *(scherz)* **1** *vt* to make cocky. **2**: **~rsi** *vr* to get cocky.

ringhiare [rin'gjare] *vi* to growl, snarl.

ringhiera [rin'gjera] *sf (di balcone)* railing; *(di scale)* banisters *pl*.

ringhio ['ringjo] *sm* growl, snarl.

ringhioso, a [rin'gjoso] *ag* growling, snarling.

ringiovanire [rindʒova'nire] **1** *vt*: **~ qn** *(sog: vestito, acconciatura)* to make sb look younger; *(: vacanze)* to rejuvenate sb. **2** *vi (aus essere)*, **~rsi** *vr* to look younger; **sembra ringiovanita di dieci anni** she looks ten years younger.

ringraziamento [ringrattsja'mento] *sm* thanks *pl*; **gli ho mandato i miei ~i** I sent him my thanks; **lettera/biglietto di ~** thank you letter/card.

ringraziare [ringrat'tsjare] *vt* to thank; **~ qn di qc/per aver fatto qc** to thank sb for sth/for doing sth; **ti ringrazio** thank you; **non so come ringraziarti** I don't know how to thank you; **se n'è andato senza neppure ~** he left without even saying thank you *o* without as much as a thank you; **sia ringraziato il Cielo!** thank heavens!

rinnegare [rinne'gare] *vt (fede, idee, partito)* to renounce; *(famiglia, figlio, origini)* to disown.

rinnegato, a [rinne'gato] *ag, sm/f* renegade.

rinnovamento [rinnova'mento] *sm (morale, civile)* renewal; *(economico)* revival.

rinnovare [rinno'vare] **1** *vt (gen, fig)* to renew; **~ l'arredamento** to buy new furnishings; **l'intero personale è stato rinnovato** the entire staff has been replaced. **2**: **~rsi** *(ripetersi: fenomeno, occasione)* to be repeated.

rinnovatore, trice [rinnova'tore] *ag* renewing.

rinnovo [rin'nɔvo] *sm (di contratto)* renewal; **'chiuso per ~ (dei) locali'** *(negozio)* 'closed for alterations'.

rinoceronte [rinotʃe'ronte] *sm* rhinoceros.

rinomato, a [rino'mato] *ag (specialista, ristorante)* renowned, famous; *(marca)* well-known.

rinsaldare [rinsal'dare] **1** *vt (fig: vincoli, amicizia)* to strengthen. **2**: **~rsi** *vr* to get stronger, be strengthened.

rinsanire [rinsa'nire] *vi (aus essere)* to become sane again.

rinsavire [rinsa'vire] *vi (aus essere) (anche fig)* to come to one's senses.

rinsecchito, a [rinsek'kito] *ag (vecchio, albero)* thin, gaunt.

rintanarsi [rinta'narsi] *vr (animale)* to go into its den; *(persona: nascondersi)* to hide; **~ in casa** to shut o.s. up in the house.

rintoccare [rintok'kare] *vi (campana)* to toll; *(ora, orologio)* to strike.

rintocco, chi [rin'tokko] *sm* toll; **i ~chi della campana** the tolling of the bell; **suonare a ~chi** to toll.

rintracciare [rintrat'tʃare] *vt (selvaggina, ladro, persona assente)* to track down; *(persona scomparsa, documento)* to trace.

rintronare [rintro'nare] **1** *vt (fam: cervello)* to stun; *(: orecchi)* to deafen. **2** *vi (tuono, cannone)* to boom, roar; **la casa rintronava sotto i colpi** the blows echoed round the house.

rintuzzare [rintut'tsare] *vt (ribattere)* to refute.

rinuncia, ce [ri'nuntʃa] *sf (gen, Rel)* renunciation; **~ a** *(carica)* resignation from; *(eredità)* relinquishment of; **~ agli atti del giudizio** *(Dir)* abandonment of a claim; **una vita di ~ce** a life of sacrifice.

rinunciare [rinun'tʃare] *vi*: **~ a** to give up; *(incarico)* to turn down; *(trono, eredità)* to renounce; **~ a fare qc** to give up doing sth; **rinunciò a presentarsi come candidato** he decided not to stand as a candidate; **~ alle speranze** to give up hope; **ci rinuncio!** I give up!

rinunzia [ri'nuntsja] *sf* = **rinuncia.**

rinunziare [rinun'tsjare] *vi* = **rinunciare.**

rinvenimento [rinveni'mento] *sm* **(a)** *(ritrovamento)* recovery; *(scoperta)* discovery. **(b)** *(Metallurgia)* tempering.

rinvenire [rinve'nire] **1** *vt (trovare)* to discover; *(: oggetto smarrito)* to recover. **2** *vi (aus essere) (persona)* to come round, regain consciousness; *(fiori)* to revive; **far ~** *(funghi secchi etc)* to reconstitute.

rinvenuto, a [rinve'nuto] *pp di* **rinvenire.**

rinverdire [rinver'dire] *vi (aus essere) (bosco, ramo)* to become green again.

rinviare [rinvi'are] *vt* **(a)** *(mandare indietro: pacco)* to send back, return; *(: persona)* to send away; *(Sport: pallone)* to return. **(b)** *(differire)*: **~ (a/di)** *(partenza, manifestazione)* to put off (till/for), postpone (till/for); *(seduta)* to adjourn (till/for); **~ una ▓unione ad altra data** to put off *o* postpone a meeting till a later date. **(c)** *(in testo, regolamento)*: **~ qn a** to refer sb to.

rinvigorire [rinvigo'rire] **1** *vt* to reinvigorate, strengthen. **2** *vi (aus essere)*, **~rsi** *vr* to regain strength.

rinvio, ii [rin'vio] *sm* **(a)** *(gen, Sport)* postponement; *(Dir)* adjournment. **(b)** *(in testo: rimando)* cross-reference.

rioccupare [riokku'pare] *vt* to reoccupy.

rionale [rio'nale] *ag (mercato, cinema)* local, district *attr*.

rione [ri'one] *sm* district.

riordinamento [riordina'mento] *sm (di ente, azienda)* reorganization.

riordinare [riordi'nare] *vt (armadio, casa, scaffali)* to tidy up; *(finanze, amministrazione)* to reorganize.

riorganizzare [riorganid'dzare] **1** *vt* to reorganize. **2**: **~rsi** *vr* to reorganize o.s.

riorganizzazione [riorganiddzat'tsjone] *sf* reorganization.

riottoso, a [riot'toso] *ag (attaccabrighe)* quarrelsome; *(indocile)* unruly.

ripagare [ripa'gare] *vt* **(a)** *(pagare di nuovo)* to pay again. **(b)** *(ricompensare)* to repay; **~ qn di qc** to repay sb for sth.

riparare [ripa'rare] **1** *vt* **(a)** *(aggiustare)* to repair; **portare qc a ~** to take sth to be repaired; **far ~ qc** to have sth repaired. **(b)** *(proteggere)*: **~ (da)** to protect (from); **~rsi gli occhi dalla luce** to shield one's eyes from the light. **(c)** *(rimediare)*: **~ (a)** *(offesa, gaffe)* to make up (for). **2** *vi (aus* *essere)*, **~rsi** *vr (rifugiarsi)* to take shelter; **~rsi dalla pioggia** to shelter from the rain.

riparato, a [ripa'rato] *ag (posto)* sheltered; **stare** *o* **tenersi ~** to shelter.

riparazione [riparat'tsjone] *sf* **(a)** *(di guasto etc)* repairing; *(: risultato)* repair. **(b)**: **~ (di)** *(di torto, offesa)* reparation (for); *(di danno)* compensation (for). **(c)** *(Scol):* **esame** *m* **di ~** resit.

riparlare [ripar'lare] *vi:* **~ di qc** to talk about sth again; **ne riparleremo!** *(in litigio)* you haven't heard the last of this!

riparo [ri'paro] *sm (gen)* shelter; **al ~ da** *(sole, vento)* sheltered from; **ormai siamo al ~** *(al sicuro)* we're safe now; **mettersi al ~** to take shelter; **sparano, mettiti al ~!** they're shooting, take cover!; **correre ai ~i** *(fig)* to take remedial action.

ripartire[1] [ripar'tire] *vi (aus essere) (partire di nuovo: persona)* to leave again; *(: motore, macchina)* to start again; **quando riparti?** when are you leaving?; **non riesco a far ~ la macchina** I can't get the car to start.

ripartire[2] [ripar'tire] *vt (dividere):* **~ (in)** *(somma, lavoro)* to divide up (into); **~ (tra)** to share out (among), distribute (among); **~ la posta** to sort the mail; **si sono ripartiti il lavoro** they shared out the work.

ripartizione [ripartit'tsjone] *sf* **(a)** *(vedi vt)* division; sharing out, distribution. **(b)** *(Amm: dipartimento)* department.

ripassare [ripas'sare] **1** *vt* **(a)** *(varcare di nuovo: confine)* to cross again. **(b)** *(passare di nuovo: gen)* to pass again; **mi puoi ~ Francesco?** *(al telefono)* can I speak to Francesco again? **(c)** *(stirare):* **~ qc** to give sth a quick iron. **(d)** *(lezione)* to revise, go over again. **2** *vi (aus essere) (ritornare)* to call again; **ripasserò da lui più tardi** I'll call on him again later; **pensavo di ~ in quel negozio** I was thinking of calling in at that shop again; **ripassiamo per Pisa?** are we passing through Pisa again?; **può ~ più tardi?** can you call back later?

ripassata [ripas'sata] *sf:* **dare una ~ a** *(pantaloni)* to give a quick iron; *(lezione)* to have another look through; *(fig: persona: sgridare)* to give a telling-off.

ripasso [ri'passo] *sm (di lezione)* revision.

ripensamento [ripensa'mento] *sm* second thoughts *pl*, change of mind; **avere un ~** to have second thoughts, change one's mind.

ripensare [ripen'sare] *vi* **(a)** *(riflettere):* **~ a qc** to think sth over; **ripensaci!** think it over!; **a ripensarci...** on thinking it over.... **(b)** *(ricordare):* **~ a qc** to recall sth. **(c)** *(cambiare idea):* **ripensarci** to change one's mind.

ripercorrere [riper'korrere] *vt (itinerario)* to travel over again; *(strada)* to go along again; *(fig: ricordi, passato)* to go back over.

ripercorso, a [riper'korso] *pp di* **ripercorrere**.

ripercosso, a [riper'kɔsso] *pp di* **ripercuotersi**.

ripercuotersi [riper'kwɔtersi] *vr (luce)* to be reflected; *(suono)* to reverberate; *(fig: avere effetto):* **~ su** to have repercussions on.

ripercussione [riperkus'sjone] *sf (di luce)* reflection; *(di suono)* reverberation; *(fig)* repercussions *pl;* **avere una ~ su, avere delle ~i su** to have repercussions on.

ripescare [ripes'kare] *vt (pesce)* to catch again; *(persona, cosa)* to fish out; *(fig: ritrovare)* to dig out; **~ qn a fare qc** *(fig: sorprendere)* to catch sb doing sth again.

ripetente [ripe'tente] *sm/f* student repeating the year.

ripetere [ri'petere] **1** *vt (parole, tentativo etc)* to

repeat; **gliel'ho ripetuto cento volte!** I've told him dozens of times!; **non se l'è fatto ~ due volte** he didn't have to be told twice; **dopo ripetuti tentativi** after repeated attempts; **scusi, può ~?** excuse me, could you repeat that?; **continua a ~ le stesse cose** he keeps repeating the same things; **~ qc a memoria** to recite sth by heart; **~ una lezione** *(studiarla)* to go over a lesson. **2**: **~rsi** *vr (persona)* to repeat o.s.; *(avvenimento, fenomeno)* to recur; **che non si ripeta più!** don't let this happen again!

ripetitore [ripeti'tore] *sm (Radio, TV)* relay.

ripetizione [ripetit'tsjone] *sf* **(a)** *(gen)* repetition; **fucile a ~** repeating rifle. **(b)** *(Scol: ripasso)* revision; *(: lezioni private):* **dare** *o* **fare ~i a qn** to give sb private lessons; **andare a ~ da qn** to take private lessons from sb.

ripetutamente [ripetuta'mente] *av* repeatedly, again and again.

ripiano [ri'pjano] *sm (di mobile)* shelf.

ripicca [ri'pikka] *sf:* **per ~** out of spite.

ripidezza [ripi'dettsa] *sf* steepness.

ripido, a ['ripido] *ag* steep.

ripiegamento [ripjega'mento] *sm (Mil)* retreat.

ripiegare [ripje'gare] **1** *vt* **(a)** *(piegare: di nuovo)* to fold (again); *(: più volte)* to fold up. **(b)** *(reclinare: capo)* to lower. **2** *vi (Mil)* to retreat, fall back; **~ su** *(fig)* to make do with, fall back on. **3**: **~rsi** *vr (ramo etc)* to bend.

ripiego, ghi [ri'pjego] *sm* expedient; **una soluzione di ~** a makeshift solution.

ripieno, a [ri'pjeno] *ag:* **~ (di)** full (of); *(panino)* filled (with); *(farcito)* stuffed (with); **panino ~** filled roll *(o* sandwich). **2** *sm (Culin)* stuffing; *(di cuscino, materasso)* filling.

ripigliare [ripiʎ'ʎare] *vt (pigliare: di nuovo)* to take back again; *(: indietro)* to take back; *(fig: forza, vigore)* to recover, get back; **~ fiato** to catch one's breath; *(fig)* to have a breather.

ripopolare [ripopo'lare] **1** *vt (gen)* to repopulate; **~ un fiume di pesci** to restock a river with fish. **2**: **~rsi** *vr (zona)* to be repopulated.

riporre [ri'porre] *vt* to put away; **~ qc al suo posto** to put sth where it belongs; **~ la propria fiducia/ le proprie speranze in qn** to place *o* put one's trust/hope in sb.

riportare [ripor'tare] **1** *vt* **(a)** *(portare di nuovo: gen)* to take back; *(: verso chi parla)* to bring back; **mi ha riportato a casa** he took me back home; **riportalo in cucina** take it back to the kitchen; **la scena lo riportò col pensiero all'infanzia** the scene took him back to his childhood. **(b)** *(ottenere)* to receive, get; *(: vittoria)* to carry off; *(: successo)* to have; **ha riportato gravi ferite** he was seriously injured; *(soldato)* he was seriously wounded; **ha riportato una frattura al braccio** he received a fracture to his arm; **la casa ha riportato gravi danni** the house has suffered serious damage, the house has been seriously damaged. **(c)** *(riferire: gen, Radio, TV)* to report; *(citare)* to quote. **(d)** *(Mat)* to carry (forward); **scrivo 5 e riporto 3** put down 5 and carry 3.

2: **~rsi** *vr* **(a)** *(ritornare)* to go back. **(b)** *(riferirsi):* **~rsi a** to refer to.

riporto [ri'porto] *sm* **(a)** *(Mat)* amount carried forward. **(b)** *(Calzoleria, Sartoria)* appliqué.

riposante [ripo'sante] *ag (gen)* restful; *(musica, colore)* soothing.

riposare [ripo'sare] **1** *vt* **(a)** *(posare di nuovo)* to put down again. **(b)** *(dare sollievo a: occhi, membra)* to rest; **per ~ un po' la mente** to give one's mind a rest. **2** *vi* **(a)** *(gen)* to rest; *(dormire)* to sleep; **è andato a ~** he's having a rest; *(a letto)* he has gone to lie down; **riposi in pace** *(defunto)* may he rest in peace; **qui riposa...** *(su tomba)* here lies... . **(b)** *(Culin: pasta, liquido)* to stand; *(vino)* to settle; *(terra)* to lie fallow. **3:** ~**rsi** *vr* to rest; *(dormire)* to sleep; **vado a riposarmi** I'm going to have a rest; *(a letto)* I'm going to lie down; **cerca di riposarti un po'** try to rest.

riposato, a [ripo'sato] *ag* *(viso, aspetto)* rested; *(mente)* fresh.

riposo [ri'pɔso] *sm* **(a)** rest; **eterno** ~ *(morte)* eternal rest; **prendersi un giorno/un mese di** ~ *(da lavoro)* to take a day/a month off; **buon** ~! I sleep well!; **senza un attimo di** ~ without a moment's rest; ~! *(Mil, Sport)* at ease!; **'oggi** ~' *(Cine, Teatro)* 'no performance today'; *(ristorante)* 'closed today'. **(b)** *(pensione)*: **andare a** ~ to go into retirement; **generale a** ~ retired general. **(c)** *(Mus)* rest.

ripostiglio [ripos'tiλλo] *sm* *(stanzino)* lumber room.

riposto, a [ri'posto] **1** *pp di* **riporre. 2** *ag (fig: senso, significato)* hidden.

riprendere [ri'prɛndere] **1** *vt* **(a)** *(prendere di nuovo: gen)* to take again; *(: prigioniero)* to recapture; *(: città)* to retake; *(: impiegato)* to take on again; *(: raffreddore)* to catch again; *(: velocità)* to pick up again; *(: quota)* to regain; ~ **moglie** to get married again; ~ **i sensi** to recover consciousness; ~ **sonno** to go back to sleep; **fu ripreso dal desiderio di vederla** again he felt the desire to see her; **fu ripreso dai dubbi** he began to have doubts again.

(b) *(riavere)* to get back; *(ritirare: oggetto riparato)* to collect; **riprenditi le tue cose** take your things; **passo a** ~ **Francesco/l'impermeabile più tardi** I'll call by to pick up Francesco/the raincoat later; **si è ripreso le sue fotografie** he took his photos back.

(c) *(ricominciare: viaggio, lavoro)* to resume, start again; ~ **a fare qc** to start doing sth again; ~ **il cammino** to set off again; ~ **una conversazione** to continue a conversation; **riprendi tutta la storia dall'inizio** start your story all over again; **'dunque', riprese, 'dove eravamo?'** 'so', he continued, 'where were we?'.

(d) *(Cine, TV)* to shoot; ~ **un attore in primo piano** to shoot a close-up of an actor; **questa foto li riprende in un atteggiamento affettuoso** this photo shows them in an affectionate pose.

(e) *(rimproverare)* to reprimand.

(f) *(Sport: raggiungere)* to catch up with.

2: ~**rsi** *vr* **(a)** *(riaversi)* to recover; *(: pianta)* to revive; **era emozionato ma si è ripreso** he was nervous but he pulled himself together.

(b) *(correggersi)* to correct o.s.

ripresa [ri'presa] *sf* **(a)** *(di attività, trattative)* resumption; **fare qc a più** ~**e** to do sth in stages. **(b)** *(Calcio)* second half; *(Pugilato)* round. **(c)** *(Cine, TV, Fot)* shot; *(: azione)* shooting *no pl*; **in** ~ **diretta** live. **(d)** *(ricupero: di persona, paese)* recovery; ~ **economica** economic recovery. **(e)** *(Aut)* acceleration; **quest'auto non ha** ~ this car's got no acceleration.

ripresentare [riprezen'tare] **1** *vt* *(certificato)* to submit again; *(domanda)* to put forward again; *(persona)* to introduce again. **2:** ~**rsi** *vr* *(ritornare: persona)* to come back; *(: occasione)* to arise again; ~**rsi a** *(esame)* to sit again; *(concorso)* to enter again; ~**rsi come candidato** *(Pol)* to stand again (as a candidate).

ripreso, a [ri'preso] *pp di* **riprendere.**

ripristinare [ripristi'nare] *vt* *(gen)* to restore; *(tradizione)* to revive, bring back into use;

(legge) to bring back into force.

ripristino [ri'pristino] *sm (gen)* restoration; *(di tradizioni)* revival.

riprodotto, a [ripro'dotto] *pp di* **riprodurre.**

riprodurre [ripro'durre] **1** *vt* to reproduce. **2:** **riprodursi** *vr* *(moltiplicarsi)* to reproduce; *(ripetersi: situazione, fenomeno)* to occur again.

riproduttivo, a [riprodut'tivo] *ag* reproductive.

riproduttore, trice [riprodut'tore] **1** *ag* *(organo)* reproductive. **2** *sm:* ~ **acustico** pick-up.

riproduzione [riprodut'tsjone] *sf* *(gen)* reproduction; '~ **vietata'** 'all rights reserved'.

ripromesso, a [ripro'messo] *pp di* **ripromettersi.**

ripromettersi [ripro'mettersi] *vt* **(a)** *(aspettarsi)*: ~ **qc da** to expect sth from. **(b)** *(intendere)*: ~ **di fare qc** to intend to do sth.

riproporre [ripro'porre] *vt* **(a)** *(soluzione)* to put forward again; *(legge)* to propose again; ~ **di fare qc** to suggest doing sth again. **(b):** **riproporsi di fare qc** to intend to do sth; **si è riproposto una lunga vacanza** he's thinking of having a long holiday.

riproposto, a [ripro'posto] *pp di* **riproporre.**

riprova [ri'prɔva] *sf* confirmation; **a** ~ **di** as confirmation of.

riprovare[1] [ripro'vare] **1** *vt* *(provare di nuovo: gen)* to try again; *(: vestito)* to try on again; *(: sensazione)* to experience again. **2** *vi (tentare)*: ~ **(a fare qc)** to try (to do sth) again; **riproverò più tardi** I'll try again later; **guai a lui se ci si riprova!** God help him if he tries that again!

riprovare[2] [ripro'vare] *vt* *(biasimare)* to disapprove of.

riprovevole [ripro'vevole] *ag* reprehensible.

ripudiare [ripu'djare] *vt* *(moglie, marito)* to repudiate; *(famiglia, patria)* to disown; *(principi, idee)* to reject.

ripudio [ri'pudjo] *sm (vedi vb)* repudiation; disowning; rejection.

ripugnante [ripuɲ'ɲante] *ag* repulsive, disgusting.

ripugnanza [ripuɲ'ɲantsa] *sf* repugnance, disgust; **provare** ~ **per qc/qn** to loathe sth/sb; **avere** ~ **a fare qc** to loathe doing sth.

ripugnare [ripuɲ'ɲare] *vi:* ~ **a qn** to repel sb, disgust sb; **la sola idea mi ripugna** I find the very idea of it disgusting; **non ti ripugna fare una cosa del genere?** don't you loathe doing such a thing?

ripulire [ripu'lire] **1** *vt* **(a)** *(pulire: di nuovo)* to clean again; *(: a fondo)* to clean up; ~ **il giardino dalle foglie secche** to clear the garden of dead leaves; **ha ripulito il frigorifero** *(fig)* he finished off *o* polished off everything in the fridge; **gli hanno ripulito le tasche** *(fig)* they cleaned him out. **(b)** *(perfezionare)* to polish, refine. **2:** ~**rsi** *vr* to clean o.s. up.

ripulsione [ripul'sjone] *sf (Fis, fig)* repulsion.

riquadro [ri'kwadro] *sm (gen, spazio)* square; *(di parete, soffitto, mobile)* panel.

risacca, che [ri'sakka] *sf* backwash.

risaia [ri'saja] *sf* paddy field.

risalire [risa'lire] **1** *vt (salire di nuovo: gen)* to go up again; *(scale)* to climb again; ~ **la corrente** to go upstream. **2** *vi (aus* **essere) (a)** *(gen, livello, prezzi)* to go up again, rise again; ~ **a cavallo** to remount; ~ **in macchina** to get back into the car; ~ **al piano di sopra** to go back upstairs; ~ **in cima alla classifica** to climb back (up) to the top of the league. **(b):** ~ **a** *(data, periodo)* to date back to. **(c)** *(ritornare):* ~ **a** to go back to; ~ **alle fonti** to go back to source material.

risalita [risa'lita] *sf:* **mezzi di** ~ *(Sci)* ski lifts.

risaltare [risal'tare] *vi (anche fig):* ~ **(su/fra)** to stand out (against/among); *(colore)* to show up (against/among).

risalto [ri'salto] *sm (rilievo)* prominence; *(enfasi)* emphasis; **dar ~ a qc** to give prominence to sth; to lay emphasis on sth; **mettere qc/qn in ~ to** make sth/sb stand out.

risanamento [risana'mento] *sm* **(a)** *(economico)* improvement; **~ del bilancio** reorganization of the budget. **(b)** *(bonifica)* reclamation; **~ edilizio** urban redevelopment.

risanare [risa'nare] **1** *vt* **(a)** *(economia)* to improve; *(bilancio)* to reorganize. **(b)** *(palude)* to reclaim; *(quartiere)* to redevelop. **2** *vi (aus essere)*, **~rsi** *vr (guarire, anche fig)* to heal.

risapere [risa'pere] *vt* to come to know of; **sono venuto a ~ l'accaduto** I heard about what happened.

risaputo, a [risa'puto] *ag*: **è ~ che...** everyone knows that..., it's common knowledge that...; **sono cose ~e** it's common knowledge.

risarcimento [risartʃi'mento] *sm*: **~ (di)** compensation (for); **chiedere il ~** to claim compensation; **aver diritto al ~ dei danni** to be entitled to damages.

risarcire [risar'tʃire] *vt (compensare)*: **~ qn di qc** to compensate sb for sth; **~ i danni a qn** to pay sb damages.

risata [ri'sata] *sf* laugh; **che ~e!** what a laugh!, how we laughed!; **farsi una bella ~** to have a good laugh.

riscaldamento [riskalda'mento] *sm* heating; **~ centrale** central heating.

riscaldare [riskal'dare] **1** *vt* **(a)** *(scaldare: stanza, acqua)* to heat; *(: mani)* to warm; **~rsi le mani/i piedi** to warm one's hands/feet. **(b)** *(scaldare di nuovo)* to heat up, reheat. **2**: **~rsi** *vr (persona)* to get warm, warm o.s. up; *(fig: infervorarsi)* to get elated.

riscattare [riskat'tare] **1** *vt (Dir, Comm, fig)* to redeem; *(prigioniero)* to ransom. **2**: **~rsi** *vr (fig)* to redeem o.s.

riscatto [ris'katto] *sm (Dir, Comm, fig)* redemption; *(di rapimento)* ransom.

rischiarare [riskja'rare] **1** *vt (gen)* to light up; **~rsi la voce** to clear one's throat. **2** *vi (aus essere)*, **~rsi** *vr (cielo)* to clear; *(liquido)* to become clear; **si rischiarò in volto** his face lit up; **rischiara, si sta rischiarando** *(Meteor)* it's clearing up.

rischiare [ris'kjare] **1** *vt* to risk; **~ il tutto per tutto** to risk everything. **2** *vi*: **~ di fare qc** to risk doing sth, run the risk of doing sth; **ha rischiato di cadere** he nearly fell.

rischio ['riskjo] *sm* risk; **a ~ di fare qc** at the risk of doing sth; **a proprio ~ e pericolo** at one's own risk; **correre il ~ di fare qc** to run the risk of doing sth; **mettere a ~ qc** to put sth at risk; **c'è il ~ che questo viaggio non si possa fare** there is a danger that we *(o you etc)* won't be able to make this trip.

rischioso, a [ris'kjoso] *ag* risky, dangerous.

risciacquare [riʃʃak'kware] *vt (panni, stoviglie)* to rinse; **~rsi la bocca** to rinse one's mouth out.

risciacquo [riʃ'ʃakkwo] *sm* rinse.

riscontrare [riskon'trare] *vt* **(a)** *(confrontare)* to compare; *(controllare: conti, motore)* to check; **~ la copia con l'originale** to compare the copy to the original; *(Tip)* to read against copy. **(b)** *(rilevare)* to notice; **non ho riscontrato errori** I haven't found *o* noticed any mistakes.

riscontro [ris'kontro] *sm* **(a)** *(confronto)* comparison; *(controllo)* check; **mettere a ~**, **fare il ~ di** to compare; to check; **fare il ~ della copia con l'originale** to compare the copy to the origi-

nal; *(Tip)* to read against copy; **un avvenimento che non ha avuto ~ in passato** an event which had no parallel in the past. **(b)** *(conferma)* confirmation; **le sue osservazioni non trovano ~ nella realtà** his remarks are not borne out by the reality of the situation. **(c)** *(Comm: risposta)* reply; **in attesa di un vostro cortese ~** we look forward to your reply.

riscoperto, a [risko'pɛrto] *pp di* **riscoprire**.

riscoprire [risko'prire] *vt* to rediscover.

riscossa [ris'kɔssa] *sf (riconquista)* recovery, reconquest.

riscossione [riskos'sjone] *sf* collection.

riscosso, a [ris'kɔsso] *pp di* **riscuotere**.

riscritto, a [ris'kritto] *pp di* **riscrivere**.

riscrivere [ris'krivere] **1** *vt* to rewrite. **2** *vi (in risposta)* to write back.

riscuotere [ris'kwɔtere] **1** *vt (stipendio, pensione)* to draw; *(tasse, affitto)* to collect; *(fig: applausi, approvazione, successo)* to win, earn; **~ un assegno** to cash a cheque. **2**: **~rsi** *vr*: **~rsi (da)** *(fig)* to rouse o.s. (from).

risentimento [risenti'mento] *sm* resentment; **provare** *o* **avere del ~ verso** *o* **contro qn** to feel resentful towards sb.

risentire [risen'tire] **1** *vt (sentire di nuovo)* to hear again; *(disco)* to listen to again. **2** *vi*: **~ di** *(esperienza, trauma)* to feel the effects of; *(: portarne i segni)* to show the effects of; **~ dell'influenza di** to show traces of the influence of; **questa pianta risente della benefica azione del sole** this plant benefits from exposure to sunshine. **3**: **~rsi** *vr (offendersi)*: **~rsi (di** *o* **per qc)** to take offence (at sth).

riserbo [ri'sɛrbo] *sm* reserve; **è una persona di grande ~** he's a very reserved person; **senza ~** unreservedly.

riserva [ri'sɛrva] *sf* **(a)** *(provvista, scorta)* reserve; **fare ~ di** *(acqua, cibo)* to get in a supply of; **tenere di ~** to keep in reserve; **~ aurea** gold reserves *pl*; **entrare in ~**, **essere in ~** *(Aut)* to be nearly out of petrol. **(b)** *(Mil, Sport)* reserve; **(giocatore di) ~** reserve (player); **truppe della ~** reserves. **(c)** *(limitazione: anche: ~ mentale)* reservation; **con le dovute ~e** with certain reservations; **ha accettato con la ~ di potersi ritirare** he accepted with the proviso that he could pull out. **(d)** *(territorio)*: **~ di caccia/pesca** hunting/fishing preserve; **~ indiana** Indian reservation.

riservare [riser'vare] **1** *vt* **(a)** *(tenere da parte)* to keep aside; *(mettere da parte)* to put aside; **~rsi il diritto di fare qc** to reserve the right to do sth; **~ una sorpresa a qn** to have a surprise in store for sb; **cosa ci riserva il destino?** what has destiny in store for us? **(b)** *(prenotare)* to book, reserve; **ti sei fatto ~ un tavolo?** have you booked *o* reserved a table? **2**: **~rsi** *vr*: **~rsi di fare qc** to intend to do sth.

riservatezza [riserva'tettsa] *sf (vedi ag* **a)** confidential nature; reserve; discretion.

riservato, a [riser'vato] *ag* **(a)** *(lettera, informazione)* confidential; *(persona, carattere)* reserved; *(: discreto)* discreet. **(b)** *(prenotato)* reserved.

risiedere [ri'sjedere] *vi* **(a)** *(vivere)*: **~ in** *o* **a** to reside in. **(b)** *(consistere, stare)*: **~ in** to lie in; **la causa del suo successo risiede nel suo senso dell'humour** the reason for his success is his sense of humour.

risma ['rizma] *sf* **(a)** *(di carta)* ream. **(b)** *(fig peg: tipo)* kind, sort; **essere della stessa ~** to be all of a kind.

riso¹, a ['riso] **1** *pp di* **ridere**. **2** *sm, pl(f)* ~**a** *(il ridere)* laughter; *(risata)* laugh; **uno scoppio di** ~**a** a burst of laughter; **non riusciva a trattenere il** ~ he couldn't help laughing; **sbellicarsi** *o* **crepare dalle** ~**a** *(fam)* to split one's sides laughing; **il** ~ **fa buon sangue** laughter is the best medicine there is.

riso² ['riso] *sm (Bot)* rice; ~ **in brodo** consommé with rice; ~ **in bianco** boiled rice.

risolare [riso'lare] *vt (scarpe)* to resole.

risolino [riso'lino] *sm (di scherno, ironico)* snigger.

risollevare [risolle'vare] **1** *vt (sollevare di nuovo: testa)* to raise again, lift up again; *(fig: questione)* to raise again, bring up again; *(: morale)* to raise; ~ **le sorti di qc** to improve the chances of sth. **2**: ~**rsi** *vr (da terra)* to rise again; *(fig: da malattia)* to recover.

risolto, a [ri'solto] *pp di* **risolvere**.

risolubile [riso'lubile] *ag* = **risolvibile**.

risolutezza [risolu'tettsa] *sf* decisiveness, resolution.

risolutivo, a [risolu'tivo] *ag (determinante)* decisive; *(che risolve)*: **arrivare ad una formula** ~**a** to come up with a formula to resolve a situation.

risoluto, a [riso'luto] *ag* resolute; **essere** ~ **a fare qc** to be determined to do sth.

risoluzione [risolut'tsjone] *sf* **(a)** *(soluzione, Mat)* solution. **(b)** *(decisione)* resolution. **(c)** *(Dir: di contratto)* annulment, cancellation. **(d)** *(Chim)* resolution.

risolvere [ri'solvere] **1** *vt* **(a)** *(problema, Mat)* to solve, work out; *(mistero, indovinello)* to solve; *(difficoltà, faccenda)* to resolve, sort out; **cosa risolvi facendo così?** what do you solve by doing that? **(b)** *(decidere)* to decide, resolve; **abbiamo risolto di partire al più presto** we've decided *o* resolved to leave as soon as possible. **(c)** *(Dir: contratto)* to annul, cancel. **(d)** *(Chim)* to break down. **2**: ~**rsi** *vr* **(a)** *(problema)* to be solved; *(malattia)* to clear up; **l'operazione si è risolta in un fiasco** the operation turned out to be a disaster. **(b)**: ~**rsi a fare qc** to make up one's mind to do sth.

risolvibile [risol'vibile] *ag* solvable.

risonante [riso'nante] *ag* resonant.

risonanza [riso'nantsa] *sf (Fis)* resonance; *(fig: eco)* interest; **entrare in** ~ *(Fis)* to resonate; **suscitare una vasta** ~ to arouse great interest.

risonare [riso'nare] = **risuonare**.

risorgere [ri'sordʒere] *vi (aus* **essere)** *(Rel, fig)* to rise again; **risorgeva in lui la speranza** his hopes were revived.

risorgimentale [risordʒimen'tale] *ag* of the Risorgimento.

risorgimento [risordʒi'mento] *sm (di arte, cultura)* revival; **il R**~ the Risorgimento.

risorsa [ri'sorsa] *sf (gen)* resource; **un uomo pieno di** ~**e** a very resourceful man; **è l'ultima** ~ it's the last resort.

risorto, a [ri'sorto] *pp di* **risorgere**.

risotto [ri'sotto] *sm (Culin)* risotto.

risparmiare [rispar'mjare] **1** *vt* **(a)** *(denaro, cibo, tempo)* to save; *(gas, elettricità)* to economize on, save on; ~ **fatica/fiato** to save one's energy/breath; **risparmiati il disturbo** *o* **la fatica** *(anche iro)* save yourself the trouble; ~ **qc a qn** *(fig: evitare)* to spare sb sth; **ti risparmio i particolari** I'll spare you the details. **(b)** *(non uccidere, non colpire)* to spare; ~ **la vita a qn** to spare sb's life. **2** *vi* to save; ~ **su qc** to economize on sth, save on sth.

risparmiatore, trice [risparmja'tore] *sm/f* saver.

risparmio [ris'parmjo] *sm* **(a)** *(azione)* saving; **ci**

riuscimmo con un ~ **di tempo e denaro** we succeeded and saved time and money into the bargain; **senza** ~ **di forze** sparing no effort. **(b)** *(denaro risparmiato)*: ~**i** savings.

rispecchiare [rispek'kjare] **1** *vt* to reflect. **2**: ~**rsi** *vr* to be reflected; **è così lucido che ti ci puoi** ~ it's so shiny that you can see your face in it.

rispedire [rispe'dire] *vt* to send back; ~ **qc a qn** to send sth back to sb.

rispettabile [rispet'tabile] *ag* **(a)** *(persona)* respectable. **(b)** *(considerevole: somma)* sizeable, considerable.

rispettabilità [rispettabili'ta] *sf* respectability.

rispettare [rispet'tare] **1** *vt (persona, idea)* to respect, have respect for; *(legge)* to obey, comply with, abide by; *(promessa)* to keep; **farsi** ~ **da qn** to command sb's respect; **far** ~ **la legge** to enforce the law; ~ **l'ordine alfabetico** to maintain alphabetical order; **bisogna** ~ **i tempi stabiliti dall'editore** we must stick to the publisher's schedule; ~ **le distanze** to keep one's distance. **2**: ~**rsi** *vr* to respect o.s.; **ogni medico che si rispetti** every self-respecting doctor.

rispettivamente [rispettiva'mente] *av* respectively.

rispettivo, a [rispet'tivo] *ag* respective.

rispetto [ris'petto] *sm* **(a)**: ~ **(di** *o* **per)** *(gen)* respect (for); *(norme, leggi)* observance (of), compliance (with); **portare** ~ **a qn/qc** to have *o* feel respect for sb/sth; **mancare di** ~ **a qn** to be disrespectful to sb; **non ha alcun** ~ **per le cose altrui** she has no respect *o* consideration *o* regard for other people's property; **con** ~ **parlando** if you will excuse my saying so. **(b)**: ~**i** *pl* *(omaggi)*: **(porga) i miei** ~**i alla signora** my regards to your wife. **(c)** *(riguardo, relazione)*: ~ **a** *(in confronto)* compared to, in comparison with; *(riguardo a)* as regards, with respect to, regarding; **sotto questo** ~ from this point of view; **sotto ogni** ~ in every respect.

rispettoso, a [rispet'toso] *ag* respectful; **essere** ~ **verso qn** to be respectful to sb, show respect to sb; **essere** ~ **di qc** to have respect for sth.

risplendente [risplen'dente] *ag (giornata, sole)* bright, shining; *(occhi)* sparkling.

risplendere [ris'plendere] *vi (gen)* to shine; *(luccicare)* to sparkle, glitter.

rispondente [rispon'dente] *ag*: ~ **a** in accordance with, in keeping with.

rispondenza [rispon'dentsa] *sf* correspondence.

rispondere [ris'pondere] **1** *vt*: ~ **che** to answer that, reply that; **cosa vuoi che ti risponda?** what can I say?

2 *vi* **(a)**: ~ **a** *(domanda)* to reply to, answer; *(persona)* to answer; *(invito)* to reply to; ~ **al telefono** to answer the telephone; ~ **di sì/di no** to say yes/no; ~ **bene** to give the right *o* correct answer; ~ **male** *(sgarbatamente)* to answer back; *(in modo errato)* to give the wrong answer; ~ **al nome di** to answer to the name of.

(b) *(rimbeccare)*: ~ **(a qn)** to answer (sb) back.

(c) *(reagire: veicolo etc)* to respond; **la macchina non risponde** the car isn't responding.

(d) *(corrispondere)*: ~ **a** to correspond to; ~ **alle esigenze di** to meet the needs of; **tutto risponde alle nostre speranze** everything is as we had hoped.

(e) *(garantire)*: ~ **di qn** to answer for sb, be responsible for sb, vouch for sb; *(essere responsabile)*: ~ **a qn di qc** to be answerable to sb for sth; **non rispondo più di me stesso** *o* **delle mie azioni** I can't answer for my actions.

(f) *(Carte)* to follow, reply.

risposarsi [rispo'zarsi] *vr* to get married again, remarry.

risposta [ris'posta] *sf* **(a)** *(a domanda, lettera etc)* answer, reply; **dare una ~** to give an answer; **in ~ a** in reply to, in answer to; **diamo ~ alla vostra lettera del...** in reply to your letter of...; **per tutta ~ mi ha sbattuto la porta in faccia** his only answer was to slam the door in my face. **(b)** *(replica)* reply, retort. **(c)** *(Carte)* reply.

risposto, a [ris'posto] *pp di* **rispondere**.

rissa ['rissa] *sf* fight, brawl.

rissoso, a [ris'soso] *ag* quarrelsome.

ristabilire [ristabi'lire] **1** *vt* **(a)** *(gen)* to re-establish; *(servizio)* to put back in operation; *(ordine, istituzione)* to restore. **(b)** *(persona: rafforzare, guarire)* to restore to health. **2**: **~rsi** *vr* *(persona)* to recover, get better; **~rsi da** to recover from.

ristagnare [ristaɲ'ɲare] *vi* *(acqua)* to be stagnant; *(sangue)* to cease flowing; *(fig: persona, industria)* to stagnate.

ristagno [ris'taɲɲo] *sm* *(anche fig)* stagnation; **c'è un ~ delle vendite** business is slack.

ristampa [ris'tampa] *sf* *(il ristampare)* reprinting; *(opera ristampata)* reprint.

ristampare [ristam'pare] *vt* to reprint.

ristorante [risto'rante] *sm* restaurant; **~ della stazione** station buffet.

ristorare [risto'rare] **1** *vt* to revive, refresh; **~ le forze** to restore one's strength. **2**: **~rsi** *vr* *(riposarsi)* to rest, have a rest; *(mangiare etc)* to have something to eat and drink.

ristoratore, trice [ristora'tore] *ag* refreshing, reviving.

ristoro [ris'tɔro] *sm* *(bevanda, cibo)* refreshment; **posto di ~** *(Ferr)* refreshment bar, buffet; **servizio di ~** *(Ferr)* refreshments *pl*.

ristrettezza [ristret'tettsa] *sf* **(a)** *(scarsità)* shortage, lack; **~ di idee** narrow-mindedness. **(b)**: **~e** *pl* poverty *sg*, straitened circumstances; **vivere nelle ~e** to live in poverty *o* in straitened circumstances.

ristretto, a [ris'tretto] **1** *pp di* **restringere**. **2** *ag* **(a)** *(limitato)* limited, restricted; **~ a** restricted to; **di idee ~e** *(fig)* narrow-minded. **(b)** *(concentrato: brodo)* thick; *(: caffè)* extra strong.

ristrutturare [ristruttu'rare] *vt* *(azienda)* to reorganize; *(edificio)* to restore; *(appartamento)* to alter.

ristrutturazione [ristrutturat'tsjone] *sf* *(vedi vb)* reorganization; restoration; alteration.

risucchiare [risuk'kjare] *vt* *(sog: vortice etc)* to swallow up.

risucchio [ri'sukkjo] *sm* *(di acqua)* undertow, pull; *(di aria)* suction.

risultante [risul'tante] **1** *sm* *(Mat)* resultant. **2** *sf* *(fig)* result, effect.

risultare [risul'tare] *vi* *(aus essere)* **(a)** *(rivelarsi)* to prove to be, turn out to be; *(essere accertato)* to be clear, emerge; *(essere noto)* to appear, seem; **le mie previsioni sono risultate errate** my forecasts proved to be wrong; **dalle analisi è risultato affetto da diabete** it is clear from the tests that he is suffering from diabetes; **risulta appartenere ad un determinato gruppo politico** he's known to belong to a specific political group; **è risultato vincitore** he emerged as the winner. **(b)**: **mi risulta che...** I understand that..., as far as I know...; **(ne) risulta che...** it follows that...; **non mi risulta** not as far as I know; **ti risulta che sia ancora qui?** do you know if he's still here?

risultato [risul'tato] *sm* *(gen, Mat, Sport)* result; **~i parziali** *(Sport)* half-time results.

risuonare [riswo'nare] **1** *vt* *(suonare di nuovo: musica)* to play again; *(: campanello)* to ring again. **2** *vi* **(a)** *(gen)* to resound; **un grido risuonò nel silenzio** a scream pierced the silence; **mi risuonano nella mente le sue parole** his words still echo in my mind. **(b)** *(Fis)* to resonate.

risurrezione [risurret'tsjone] *sf* *(Rel)* resurrection.

risuscitare [risuʃʃi'tare] **1** *vt* to resuscitate, restore to life; *(fig)* to revive; **~ qn dalla morte** to raise sb from the dead. **2** *vi* *(aus* **essere***)* to rise from the dead; *(fig: riprendere vigore)* to revive.

risvegliare [rizveʎ'ʎare] **1** *vt* *(gen)* to wake up, waken; *(fig: dall'inerzia etc)*: **~ qn (da)** to rouse sb (from); *(fig: interesse)* to stir up, arouse; *(: curiosità)* to arouse; **~ l'appetito** to whet one's appetite; **~ i ricordi** to bring back old memories. **2**: **~rsi** *vr* to wake up, awaken; *(fig: interesse, curiosità)* to be aroused; **il vulcano si è risvegliato** the volcano has become active again.

risveglio [riz'veʎʎo] *sm* *(azione)* awakening, waking up; *(fig: di arte, cultura)* revival; *(: di interesse)* arousal; **al ~** when he *(o* she *etc)* woke up.

risvolto [riz'vɔlto] *sm* **(a)** *(di giacca)* lapel; *(di manica)* cuff; *(di pantaloni)* turn-up; *(di tasca, libro)* flap. **(b)** *(fig: aspetto secondario)* implication.

ritagliare [ritaʎ'ʎare] *vt* *(tagliare via)*: **~ (da)** to cut out (of).

ritaglio [ri'taʎʎo] *sm* *(di giornale)* cutting, clipping; *(di stoffa)* remnant; **nei ~i di tempo** in one's spare time.

ritardare [ritar'dare] **1** *vt* **(a)** *(differire)* to delay, hold up; **~ il pagamento** to defer payment. **(b)** *(rallentare: sviluppo, processo)* to slow down. **2** *vi* *(persona, treno)* to be late; *(orologio)* to be slow; **~ a fare qc** to be late in doing sth; **~ di un quarto d'ora** to be fifteen minutes late.

ritardatario, a [ritarda'tarjo] *sm/f* latecomer.

ritardato, a [ritar'dato] **1** *pp di* **ritardare**. **2** *ag* *(Psic)* retarded.

ritardo [ri'tardo] *sm* **(a)** *(di treno, posta)* delay; *(di persona)* lateness; **essere in ~** to be late; **un ~ di 2 ore** a 2-hour delay; **arrivò con 2 ore di ~** it *(o* he *etc)* arrived 2 hours late; **scusa il ~** sorry I'm late. **(b)** *(Psic)* retardation; **un ~ dello sviluppo mentale** a retarded mental development.

ritegno [ri'teɲɲo] *sm* restraint; **abbi un po' di ~!** restrain yourself!

ritemprare [ritem'prare] *vt* *(forze, spirito)* to restore.

ritenere [rite'nere] **1** *vt* **(a)** *(considerare)* to think, believe; **lo ritengo un ottimo insegnante** I think he's an excellent teacher; **~ opportuno fare qc** to think it opportune to do sth; **ho ritenuto che fosse opportuno fare così** I felt it opportune to do so; **ritengo di sì** I think so; **ritengo di no** I don't think so; **si ritiene che l'uomo sia fuggito in macchina** they think that the man escaped by car. **(b)** *(trattenere: denaro)* to withhold; *(: nozioni, concetti)* to retain; **gli hanno ritenuto due giorni di paga** they withheld 2 days' pay; **ho una memoria così labile che non riesco a ~ nulla** my memory is so poor that I can't seem to retain anything. **(c)** *(umidità, liquidi)* to retain. **2**: **~rsi** *vr* to consider o.s.; **si ritiene un genio** he thinks he's a genius.

ritentare [riten'tare] *vt* to try again, make another attempt at.

ritenuta [rite'nuta] *sf* deduction; **~ sulla paga** deduction from one's pay; **~ d'acconto** *advance tax deduction*.

ritenzione [riten'tsjone] *sf (Med)* retention.

ritirare [riti'rare] 1 *vt* (a) *(tirare di nuovo)* to pull again; *(lanciare di nuovo)* to throw again. (b) *(mano, braccio)* to pull back; *(soldi, candidatura)* to withdraw; *(certificato, bagaglio)* to collect, pick up; *(bucato)* to bring in; ~ **il passaporto a qn** to withdraw sb's passport; **gli hanno ritirato la patente** they disqualified him from driving; **ritiro quello che ho detto** I take back what I said. 2: **~rsi** *vr* (a) *(Mil)* to retreat, withdraw; *(persona: appartarsi)* to withdraw, retire; **si ritirò nella sua stanza** he withdrew *o* retired to his room; **~rsi** *(da un'attività)* to retire; **~rsi a vita privata** to withdraw from public life. (b) *(retrocedere: acque)* to recede, subside. (c) *(tessuto)* to shrink.

ritirata [riti'rata] *sf* (a) *(Mil)* retreat, withdrawal; *(: in caserma)* tattoo; **suonare la** ~ to sound the retreat; to sound the tattoo. (b) *(latrina)* lavatory.

ritirato, a [riti'rato] *ag* secluded; **fare vita** ~a to live in seclusion.

ritiro [ri'tiro] *sm* (a) *(il ritirare: di truppe, candidatura, soldi)* withdrawal; *(: di biglietti, pacchi)* collection; *(: di passaporto)* confiscation; **la ricevuta vi verrà consegnata al momento del** ~ **della merce** you will be given the receipt on collection of the goods; **'per il** ~ **dei vaglia postali rivolgersi a...'** 'postal orders are issued at...'. (b) *(il ritirarsi: Mil)* withdrawal, retreat; *(: di acque)* subsidence; **dopo il suo** ~ **dal mondo dello spettacolo** after retiring from show business; **dopo il suo** ~ **dalla gara** after withdrawing from the competition. (c) *(luogo appartato: anche Rel)* retreat; **fare quindici giorni di** ~ to go on a fortnight's retreat.

ritmare [rit'mare] *vt*: ~ **il passo**, ~ **la corsa** to keep the rhythm, keep in rhythm.

ritmato, a [rit'mato] *ag* rhythmic(al).

ritmica ['ritmika] *sf (Mus)* rhythmics *sg*.

ritmico, a, ci, che ['ritmiko] *ag* rhythmic(al).

ritmo ['ritmo] *sm* (a) *(gen)* rhythm; **ballare al** ~ **di valzer** to waltz. (b) *(fig: velocità)* speed, rate; **al** ~ **di** at a speed *o* rate of; **a questo** ~ at this rate.

rito ['rito] *sm (Rel)* rite; *(cerimonia)* ritual; **di** ~ customary, usual.

ritoccare [ritok'kare] *vt (disegno, trucco etc)* to touch up; *(testo, prezzi)* to alter.

ritocco, chi [ri'tokko] *sm (di disegno, trucco etc)* touching-up; *(di testo)* alteration; **dare un** ~ **a qc** to touch sth up; to alter sth.

ritorcere [ri'tortʃere] *vt (filato)* to twist; *(fig: accusa, insulto)* to throw back. 2: **~rsi** *vr (tornare a danno di)*: **~rsi contro** to turn against.

ritornare [ritor'nare] 1 *vi (aus essere)* = **tornare**. 2 *vt (restituire)*: ~ **qc a qn** to return sth to sb, give sth back to sb.

ritornello [ritor'nello] *sm (Mus, Poesia)* refrain; *(fig: storia)* story; **è sempre il solito** ~ it's always the same old story.

ritorno [ri'torno] *sm* (a) *(gen)* return; **essere di** ~ to be back; **far** ~ to return; **durante il *(viaggio di)*** ~ on the return trip, on the way back; **al** ~ *(tornando)* on the way back; **al mio/tuo** ~ on my/your return; **avere un** ~ **di fiamma** *(Aut)* to backfire; **hanno avuto un** ~ **di fiamma** *(fig)* they're back in love again. (b) *(in restituzione)*: **fammelo avere di** ~ **entro la fine del mese** let me have it back by the end of the month.

ritorsione [ritor'sjone] *sf (rappresaglia)* retaliation.

ritorto, a [ri'torto] 1 *pp di* **ritorcere**. 2 *ag (cotone, corda)* twisted.

ritrarre [ri'trarre] 1 *vt* (a) *(Pittura, fig)* to portray,
depict. (b) *(tirare indietro)* to withdraw. 2: **ritrarsi** *vr* to move back.

ritrattabile [ritrat'tabile] *ag (dichiarazione, accusa)* retractable.

ritrattare [ritrat'tare] *vt* (a) *(dichiarazione)* to retract, withdraw. (b) *(trattare nuovamente)* to deal with again, cover again.

ritrattista, i, e [ritrat'tista] *sm/f* portrait painter.

ritratto, a [ri'tratto] 1 *pp di* **ritrarre**. 2 *sm* portrait; **essere il** ~ **della salute** to be the picture of health; **è il** ~ **di suo padre** he's his father's image.

ritrosia [ritro'sia] *sf (riluttanza)* reluctance, unwillingness; *(timidezza)* shyness.

ritroso, a [ri'troso] 1 *ag* (a) *(restio)*: ~ **a fare qc** reluctant to do sth. (b) *(timido)* shy, bashful. 2: **a** ~ *av (indietro)* backwards.

ritrovamento [ritrova'mento] *sm (di cadavere, oggetto smarrito etc)* finding; *(oggetto ritrovato)* find.

ritrovare [ritro'vare] 1 *vt* (a) *(ricuperare: oggetto, persona)* to find; *(pace, forza)* to find again, recover. (b) *(rincontrare)* to meet again; *(: per caso)* to run into. 2: **~rsi** *vr* (a) *(finire)* to end up; **si ritrovò solo/a fare i lavori più umili** he ended up alone/doing the most meniial tasks; **mi sono ritrovato con 5000 lire in più** I found myself with 5000 lire extra; **ci ritrovammo al punto di partenza** we ended up where we started. (b) *(incontrarsi)*: **~rsi con** *(amici etc)* to meet.

ritrovato, a [ritro'vato] *sm* discovery.

ritrovo [ri'trovo] *sm (anche: **luogo di** ~)* meeting place; ~ **notturno** nightclub.

ritto, a ['ritto] *ag (in piedi: persona)* upright, on one's feet; **aveva i capelli** ~i **in testa** his hair was standing on end.

rituale [ritu'ale] 1 *ag (di rito)* ritual; *(fig: solito)* customary, usual. 2 *sm (Rel)* ritual.

riunione [riu'njone] *sf (adunanza)* meeting; *(riconciliazione)* reunion; ~ **familiare** family gathering; **il presidente è in** ~ the president is at a meeting.

riunire [riu'nire] 1 *vt* (a) *(mettere insieme: oggetti)* to gather together, collect; *(: persone)* to assemble, get together; *(: fig: riconciliare)* to bring together, reunite; **siamo qui riuniti per festeggiare il vostro anniversario** we are gathered here to celebrate your anniversary. (b) *(ricongiungere)* to put together, join together. 2: **~rsi** *vr (radunarsi)* to meet; *(fig)* to come together again, be reunited.

riuscire [riuʃ'ʃire] *vi (aus essere)* (a) *(aver successo)*: ~ **(in qc/a fare qc)** to succeed (in sth/in doing sth), be successful (in sth/in doing sth); **il tentativo non è riuscito** the attempt was unsuccessful; ~ **negli studi** to do well at school *(o* at university *etc)*. (b) *(essere capace)* to be able, manage; ~ **a fare qc** to be able to do sth; **non riesco a farlo** I can't do it, I am unable to do it; **non mi riesce di farlo** I can't (manage to) do it; **non ci riesco** I can't. (c) *(essere, risultare)* to be, prove (to be); **ti riuscirà più facile dopo un po' di pratica** it'll be easier *o* you'll find it easier after a bit of practice; **mi riesce antipatico** I don't like him; **mi riesce difficile** I find it difficult; **la festa è riuscita male** the party wasn't a success. (d) *(uscire di nuovo)* to go out again.

riuscita [riuʃ'ʃita] *sf (esito)* result, outcome; *(buon esito)* success; **fare** *o* **avere una buona** ~ to be a success, be successful.

riutilizzare [riutilid'dzare] *vt* to use again.

riva ['riva] *sf (di mare, lago)* shore; *(di fiume)* bank; **in** ~ **al mare** on the (sea) shore.

rivale [ri'vale] 1 *ag* rival *attr*. 2 *sm/f* rival; **non**

avere ~i *(anche fig)* to be unrivalled.

rivaleggiare [rivaled'dʒare] *vi* to compete, vie; ~ con qn per qc to vie with sb for sth; **nessuno può** ~ **con lui** he is unrivalled.

rivalità [rivali'ta] *sf inv* rivalry.

rivalsa [ri'valsa] *sf* **(a)** *(risarcimento)* compensation. **(b)** *(rivincita)* revenge; **prendersi una** ~ **su qn** to take revenge on sb.

rivalutare [rivalu'tare] *vt (Econ)* to revalue; *(fig)* to re-evaluate.

rivalutazione [rivalutat'tsjone] *sf (Econ)* revaluation; *(fig)* re-evaluation.

rivangare [rivan'gare] *vt (ricordi etc)* to dig up (again).

rivedere [rive'dere] **1** *vt* **(a)** *(vedere di nuovo: film etc)* to see again; *(: persona)* to see again, meet again; **guarda chi si rivede!** look who it is! **(b)** *(verificare, correggere)* to revise; ~ **le bozze** to proofread. **2**: ~**rsi** *vr (uso reciproco)* to see each other again, meet (again).

rivedibile [rive'dibile] *ag (Mil) temporarily unfit for service.*

rivelare [rive'lare] **1** *vt (svelare)* to reveal; *(: segreto)* to disclose, reveal; *(dimostrare: capacità)* to reveal, display; **quella commedia lo rivelò al grande pubblico** that play revealed him to the public at large. **2**: ~**rsi** *vr (tendenza, talento)* to be revealed, reveal itself; *(Rel)* to reveal o.s.; **si è rivelato molto bravo** he proved to be very good.

rivelatore, trice [rivela'tore] **1** *ag* revealing. **2** *sm (Tecn)* detector; *(Fot)* developer.

rivelazione [rivelat'tsjone] *sf (gen)* revelation; *(di segreto, notizia)* disclosure; **quell'attore è stato la** ~ **dell'anno** that actor was the discovery of the year.

rivendere [ri'vendere] *vt (vendere: di nuovo)* to resell, sell again; *(: al dettaglio)* to retail, sell retail.

rivendicare [rivendi'kare] *vt* to claim.

rivendicazione [rivendikat'tsjone] *sf* claim; ~**i salariali** wage claims.

rivendita [ri'vendita] *sf (negozio)* retailer's (shop); ~ **di tabacchi** tobacconist's shop.

rivenditore, trice [rivendi'tore] *sm/f* retailer; ~ **autorizzato** authorized dealer.

riverberare [riverbe'rare] *vt (luce, calore)* to reflect; *(suono)* to reverberate.

riverbero [ri'verbero] *sm (vedi vb)* reflection; reverberation.

riverente [rive'rente] *ag,* reverent, respectful.

riverenza [rive'rentsa] *sf* **(a)** *(rispetto)* reverence, respect. **(b)** *(inchino)* bow; **fece una profonda** ~ he bowed low.

riverire [rive'rire] *vt* to revere, respect; **la riverisco, professore** *(salutando)* my respects, professor.

riversare [river'sare] **1** *vt (versare)* to pour; *(: di nuovo)* to pour again; *(fig: amore, affetto)*: ~ **su** to shower on, lavish on; **ha riversato tutte le sue energie in quel lavoro** he threw himself into that job. **2**: ~**rsi** *vr* to pour (out); **la folla si riversò nelle strade** the crowd poured into the streets.

rivestimento [rivesti'mento] *sm (azione, materiale)* covering; *(strato: di vernice)* coating, veneer.

rivestire [rives'tire] **1** *vt* **(a)** *(vestire di nuovo)* to dress again. **(b)** *(ricoprire: gen)*: ~ **(di)** to cover (with); *(: con vernice)* to coat (with); ~ **l'interno di una scatola in stoffa** to line a box with material; ~ **di piastrelle** to tile. **(c)** *(carica)* to hold; ~ **un grado elevato** to be high-ranking. **2**: ~**rsi** *vr* to get dressed (again).

rivetto [ri'vetto] *sm (Tecn)* rivet.

riviera [ri'vjera] *sf* coast; **la R**~ **Ligure** the Italian Riviera.

rivincita [ri'vintʃita] *sf (Sport)* return match; *(Carte)* return game; *(fig)* revenge; **prendersi la** ~ **(su qn)** to take o get one's revenge (on sb).

rivissuto, a [rivis'suto] *pp di* rivivere.

rivista [ri'vista] *sf* **(a)** *(periodico)* magazine; *(: letterario)* review; *(Tecn, Med)* journal. **(b)** *(Teatro, TV)* revue, variety show. **(c)** *(Mil)* inspection; **passare in** ~ to review.

rivisto, a [ri'visto] *pp di* rivedere.

rivitalizzare [rivitalid'dzare] *vt* to revitalize.

rivivere [ri'vivere] **1** *vt (avventura, esperienza)*: ~ **qc** to live through sth again. **2** *vi (aus essere)* *(vivere di nuovo)* to live again; *(prendere vigore)* to come to life again; *(tradizioni)* to be revived; **far** ~ *(resuscitare)* to bring back to life; *(rinvigorire)* to revive, put new life into; *(epoca, modu)* to revive; **sentirsi** ~ to feel a new man *(o woman)*.

rivo ['rivo] *sm (di lava, lacrime)* stream.

rivolere [rivo'lere] *vt (volere: indietro)* to want back; *(: di nuovo)* to want again.

rivolgere [ri'voldʒere] **1** *vt (indirizzare: attenzione, sguardo, proiettore)* to turn, direct; *(: parole)* to address; ~ **un'arma contro qn** to point a weapon at sb; ~ **lo sguardo verso qn** to turn *o* direct one's gaze towards sb; **le rivolse uno sguardo di rimprovero** he gave her a disapproving look; ~ **un'accusa/una critica a qn** to accuse/criticize sb; ~ **la propria attenzione a un problema** to turn one's attention to a problem; ~ **la parola a qn** to talk to sb, address sb; **non si rivolgono più la parola** they are no longer on speaking terms; ~ **un saluto a qn** to greet sb.

2: ~**rsi** *vr* **(a)**: ~**rsi a** *(per informazioni)* to go and see, go and speak to; ~**rsi all'ufficio competente** to apply to the office concerned; **non mi rivolgevo a te** I wasn't talking to you; **si rivolse a lei dicendo...** he turned to her and said.... **(b)**: ~**rsi verso** *(girarsi)* to turn to.

rivolgimento [rivoldʒi'mento] *sm* upheaval.

rivolta [ri'volta] *sf* revolt, rebellion; **in** ~ **(contro)** in revolt (against).

rivoltante [rivol'tante] *ag* revolting, disgusting.

rivoltare [rivol'tare] **1** *vt* **(a)** *(voltare: di nuovo)* to turn again; *(: pagine, carte etc)* to turn over again; *(: vestito)* to turn inside out; *(: bistecca, frittata)* to turn (over). **(b)** *(disgustare)* to revolt, disgust; **una scena che fa** ~ **lo stomaco** a scene which turns one's stomach. **2**: ~**rsi** *vr* **(a)** *(rigirarsi)* to turn; ~**rsi nel letto** to toss and turn (in bed). **(b)** *(ribellarsi)* to revolt, rebel.

rivoltella [rivol'tella] *sf (gen)* pistol; *(: a tamburo)* revolver.

rivoltellata [rivoltel'lata] *sf (vedi rivoltella)* (pistol) shot; (revolver) shot.

rivolto, a [ri'volto] *pp di* rivolgere.

rivoltoso, a [rivol'toso] **1** *ag* rebellious. **2** *sm/f* rebel.

rivoluzionare [rivoluttsjo'nare] *vt (anche fig)* to revolutionize; *(fig: mettere sottosopra)* to turn upside down.

rivoluzionario, a [rivoluttsjo'narjo] *ag, sm/f* revolutionary.

rivoluzione [rivolut'tsjone] *sf (gen, Pol, Mat, Astron)* revolution; *(fig: disordine)* mess.

rizzare [rit'tsare] **1** *vt (palo)* to erect; *(tenda)* to pitch; *(coda)* to raise, lift; *(orecchie)* to prick up; **è roba da far** ~ **i capelli (in testa)** it's enough to make your hair stand on end. **2**: ~**rsi** *vr* to stand up; ~**rsi in piedi** to stand up, get to one's feet; ~**rsi a sedere** to sit up; **gli si sono rizzati i capelli in testa** his hair stood on end.

roba ['roba] *sf* **(a)** *(gen)* things *pl*, stuff; *(cose proprie)* belongings *pl*, things *pl*, possessions *pl*; ~

da lavare washing; ~ **da mangiare** food; ~ **da stirare** ironing; ~ **usata** secondhand goods; ~ **di valore** valuables; **ho un sacco di** ~ **da fare** I've got a lot to do; **ha ancora qui tutta la sua** ~? has he still got all his things here?; **che** ~ **è questa?** what is this?; **e chiami whisky questa** ~? and you call this stuff whisky? **(b)** *(faccenda, affare)* affair, matter; **non è** ~ **che ti riguarda** this doesn't concern you. **(c)** *(fraseologia):* **bella** ~! *(iro: che gran cosa!)* so what!; *(: che mascalzonata!)* that's nice, isn't it!; ~ **da matti** *o* **pazzi!** it's sheer madness!

robivecchi [robi'vɛkki] *sm/f inv* junk dealer.

robot ['rɔbot] *sm inv* robot.

robustezza [robus'tettsa] *sf (di persona, pianta)* robustness, sturdiness; *(di edificio, ponte)* soundness.

robusto, a [ro'busto] *ag (persona, pianta)* robust, sturdy; *(euf: persona: grasso)* well-built; *(edificio, ponte)* sound, solid; *(corda, catena)* strong; *(appetito)* healthy; *(vino)* full-bodied; *(voce)* powerful; *(fede)* great, strong.

rocambolesco, a, schi, sche [rokambo'lesko] *ag* fantastic, incredible.

rocca, che ['rɔkka] *sf* fortress.

roccaforte [rokka'fɔrte] *sf, pl* **roccheforti** *(anche fig)* stronghold.

rocchetto [rok'ketto] *sm* **(a)** *(di filo)* spool. **(b)** *(Cine)* reel. **(c)** *(Elettr)* coil.

roccia, ce [rottʃa] *sf (gen, Geol)* rock; *(sport)* rock climbing; **fare** ~ to go rock climbing.

rocciatore, trice [rottʃa'tore] *sm/f* rock climber.

roccioso, a [rot'tʃoso] *ag* rocky; **le Montagne R~e** the Rocky Mountains.

rock [rɔk] *ag, sm (Mus)* rock.

roco, a, chi, che ['rɔko] *ag* hoarse.

rodaggio [ro'daddʒo] *sm (Aut)* running in; **la macchina è ancora in** ~ the car is still being run in; **periodo di** ~ *(fig)* period of adjustment.

Rodano ['rɔdano] *sm:* **il** ~ the Rhone.

rodare [ro'dare] *vt (Aut, Tecn)* to run in.

rodeo [ro'deo] *sm* rodeo.

rodere ['rodere] **1** *vt (rosicchiare)* to gnaw; *(corrodere)* to corrode; **~rsi il fegato** *(fig)* to torment o.s. **2:** **~rsi** *vr:* **~rsi dal rimorso/dall'invidia** to be consumed with remorse/with envy.

Rodi ['rodi] *sf* Rhodes.

roditore [rodi'tore] *sm (Zool)* rodent.

rododendro [rodo'dɛndro] *sm (Bot)* rhododendron.

rogito ['rɔdʒito] *sm (Dir)* (notary's) deed.

rogna ['rɔɲɲa] *sf (Med)* scabies; *(di animale)* mange; *(fig: guaio)* trouble, bother; **ha avuto ~e con la polizia** he got into trouble with the police.

rognone [roɲ'ɲone] *sm (Culin)* kidney.

rognoso, a [roɲ'ɲoso] *ag (persona)* scabby; *(animale)* mangy; *(fig)* troublesome.

rogo, ghi ['rɔgo] *sm (funebre)* funeral pyre; *(supplizio):* **il** ~ the stake; **mandare qn al** ~ to condemn sb to be burned at the stake; **la casa era ormai un** ~ the house was now a mass of flames.

rollare [rol'lare] *vi (Naut, Aer)* to roll.

rollio, ii [rol'lio] *sm (Naut, Aer)* roll, rolling.

Roma ['rɔma] *sf* Rome.

romanesco, a, schi, sche [roma'nesko] **1** *ag* Roman. **2** *sm* Roman dialect.

Romania [roma'nia] *sf* Rumania.

romanico, a, ci, che [ro'maniko] *ag, sm (Arte)* Romanesque.

romanità [romani'ta] *sf (Storia):* **la R~** the Roman world; *(fig: spirito)* Roman spirit.

romano, a [ro'mano] **1** *ag* Roman; **la Chiesa ~a** the Roman Catholic Church. **2** *sm/f* Roman.

romanticheria [romantike'ria] *sf* sentimentality.

romanticismo [romanti'tʃizmo] *sm* romanticism.

romantico, a, ci, che [ro'mantiko] *ag, sm/f* romantic.

romanza [ro'mandza] *sf (Mus, Letteratura)* romance.

romanzare [roman'dzare] *vt* to romanticize.

romanzesco, a, schi, sche [roman'dzesko] **1** *ag (stile, personaggi)* fictional; *(fig: amori, vicende)* fantastic. **2** *sm:* **avere del** ~ to sound like something out of fiction.

romanziere, a [roman'dzjɛre] *sm/f* novelist.

romanzo [ro'mandzo] *sm (gen)* novel; ~ **d'amore** love story; ~ **d'appendice** serial novel; ~ **d'avventure** adventure story; ~ **cavalleresco** tale of chivalry; ~ **di fantascienza** science-fiction novel *o* story; ~ **fiume** saga; ~ **poliziesco**, ~ **giallo** detective story; ~ **rosa** romantic novel; ~ **sceneggiato** novel adapted for television.

rombare [rom'bare] *vi* to roar.

rombo¹ ['rombo] *sm (rumore)* roar.

rombo² ['rombo] *sm (Mat)* rhombus.

rombo³ ['rombo] *sm (Zool)* turbot.

romeno, a [ro'mɛno] *ag, sm, sm/f* Rumanian.

rompere ['rompere] **1** *vt (gen, fig)* to break; *(sfasciare)* to smash up; *(scarpe, calzoni)* to split; *(fidanzamento, negoziati)* to break off; ~ **qc in testa a qn** to break sth over sb's head; **il fiume ha rotto gli argini** the river burst its banks; ~ **un contratto** to break a contract; ~ **il silenzio/il ghiaccio** to break the silence/the ice; ~ **le scatole a qn** *(fam)* to get on sb's wick; **hai proprio rotto (le scatole)!** *(fam)* knock it off!; **un rumore che rompe i timpani** a deafening noise; **~rsi una gamba/l'osso del collo** to break a leg/one's neck; **~rsi la testa** *(fig)* to rack one's brains; **~rsi la schiena** *(fig)* to work hard. **2:** **~rsi** *vr (gen)* to break; *(macchina)* to break down.

rompiballe [rompi'balle] *sm/f inv (fam!)* pain in the arse (!).

rompicapo [rompi'kapo] *sm (problema)* worry, headache; *(gioco enigmistico)* brain-teaser, puzzle.

rompicollo [rompi'kɔllo] *sm* daredevil.

rompighiaccio [rompi'gjattʃo] *sm* ice-breaker.

rompimento [rompi'mento] *sm (fig fam)* nuisance, bother.

rompipalle [rompi'palle] *sm/f inv (fam!)* = **rompiballe**.

rompiscatole [rompis'katole] *sm/f inv (fam)* nuisance, pain in the neck.

ronda ['ronda] *sf (Mil)* rounds *pl; (Polizia)* beat, patrol, rounds; *(pattuglia)* patrol; **fare la** ~ to be on one's rounds (*o* on patrol); **essere di** ~ to be on patrol duty.

rondella [ron'della] *sf (Tecn)* washer.

rondine ['rondine] *sf (Zool)* swallow; **una** ~ **non fa primavera** *(Proverbio)* one swallow doesn't make a summer.

rondone [ron'done] *sm (Zool)* swift.

ronfare [ron'fare] *vi (russare)* to snore.

ronzare [ron'dzare] *vi* to buzz, hum; ~ **intorno a qn** *(fig)* to hang about sb; **quell'idea continuava a ronzargli in testa** that idea was still buzzing around in his head; **mi ronzano le orecchie** my ears are buzzing.

ronzino [ron'dzino] *sm* nag.

ronzio, ii [ron'dzio] *sm (di insetti)* buzzing, humming; *(del motore)* humming; *(di orecchie)* buzzing, ringing.

rosa ['rɔza] **1** *ag inv (colore)* pink; *(peg: letteratura, romanzo)* romantic; **vedere tutto** ~ to see everything through rose-coloured spectacles. **2** *sf* **(a)**

(Bot) rose; ~ **canina** dog rose; ~ **di Natale** Christmas rose; **non è tutto** ~**e e fiori** *(fig)* it's not all a bed of roses; **se son** ~**e fioriranno** *(fig)* the proof of the pudding is in the eating; **non c'è** ~ **senza spine** *(Proverbio)* there's no rose without a thorn. **(b)** *(fig: gruppo)*: ~ **dei candidati** group of candidates. **(c)**: ~ **dei venti** wind rose. **3** *sm inv (colore)* pink.

rosaio [ro'zajo] *sm* rosebed.

rosario [ro'zarjo] *sm (Rel)* rosary.

rosato, a [ro'zato] **1** *ag (colore)* pinkish, rosy; *(vino)* rosé. **2** *sm (vino)* rosé.

rosbif ['rɔzbif] *sm* roast beef.

roseo, a ['rɔzeo] *ag (colorito)* pinkish, rosy; *(fig: ottimistico)* rosy, bright.

roseto [ro'zeto] *sm* rose garden.

rosetta [ro'zetta] *sf* **(a)** *(diamante)* rose-cut diamond. **(b)** *(Tecn: rondella)* washer. **(c)** *(pane)* kind of roll.

rosicchiare [rosik'kjare] *vt (rodere)* to gnaw at; *(mangiucchiare)* to nibble at; ~**rsi le unghie** to bite one's nails.

rosmarino [rozma'rino] *sm (Bot)* rosemary.

roso, a ['roso] *pp di* **rodere**.

rosolare [rozo'lare] *vt (Culin)* to brown.

rosolia [rozo'lia] *sf (Med)* German measles *sg*.

rosone [ro'zone] *sm (finestra: su chiese etc)* rose window; ~ **da soffitto** ceiling rose.

rospo ['rɔspo] *sm (Zool)* toad; **è un** ~ *(peg: persona)* she *(o* he) is hideous; **mandar giù** *o* **ingoiare un** *o* **il** ~ *(fig)* to swallow a bitter pill; **sputa il** ~! out with it!

rosseggiare [rossed'dʒare] *vt* to redden, turn red.

rossetto [ros'setto] *sm (per labbra)* lipstick; *(per guance)* rouge.

rossiccio, a, ci, ce [ros'sittʃo] *ag* reddish.

rosso, a ['rosso] **1** *ag* **(a)** *(gen)* red; **diventare** ~ **(per la vergogna)** to go red *o* blush (with *o* for shame); ~ **come un gambero** *(per la vergogna)* as red as a beetroot; *(per il sole)* as red as a lobster; **l'Armata R**~**a** the Red Army. **(b)** *(Geog)*: **il Mar R**~ the Red Sea. **2** *sm (colore)* red; *(di roulette)* rouge, red; *(di semaforo)* red light; *(vino)* red wine; ~ **d'uovo** egg yolk; ~ **di sera bel tempo si spera** *(Proverbio)* red sky at night shepherd's delight; ~ **di mattina brutto tempo s'avvicina** *(Proverbio)* red sky at dawning shepherd's warning. **3** *sm/f (che ha i capelli* ~**i)** redhead; *(fig Pol)* Red.

rossore [ros'sore] *sm (attorno a occhi, ferita)* redness; *(delle guance)* flush; *(: per vergo)* blush; **sentirsi salire il** ~ **alle guance** *(per vergogna, pudore)* to begin to blush, feel one's cheeks go red.

rosticceria [rostittʃe'ria] *sf* shop selling roast meat and other prepared food.

rostro ['rɔstro] *sm (di rapace)* beak.

rotabile [ro'tabile] *ag*: **strada** ~ carriageway; **materiale** *m* ~ *(Ferr)* rolling stock.

rotaia [ro'taja] *sf (Ferr)* rail.

rotare [ro'tare] *vt, vi* to rotate.

rotativa [rota'tiva] *sf* rotary press.

rotativo, a [rota'tivo] *ag* rotating, rotation *attr*.

rotatorio, a [rota'tɔrjo] *ag* rotary.

rotazione [rotat'tsjone] *sf* rotation.

roteare [rote'are] **1** *vt (spada, bastone)* to whirl; *(occhi)* to roll. **2** *vi (aus* **essere)** *(uccello rapace)* to circle.

rotella [ro'tɛlla] *sf (gen)* small wheel; *(di pattini)* roller; *(di mobili)* castor; *(ingranaggio)* cog wheel; **gli manca una** ~, **non ha tutte le** ~**e a posto** *(fig fam)* he's got a screw loose.

rotocalco, chi [roto'kalko] *sm (Tip)* rotogravure;

(rivista) illustrated magazine.

rotolare [roto'lare] **1** *vt, vi (aus* **essere)** to roll. **2**: ~**rsi** *vr*: ~**rsi per terra** to roll about on the floor; ~**rsi nell'erba** to roll (about) on the grass; ~**rsi (per terra) dalle risate** to roll about laughing.

rotolio [roto'lio] *sm* rolling.

rotolo ['rɔtolo] *sm (di carta, stoffa)* roll; *(di corda)* coil; *(di documenti)* scroll; **andare a** ~**i** *(fig)* to go to rack and ruin; **mandare a** ~**i** *(fig)* to ruin.

rotonda [ro'tonda] *sf (Archit)* rotunda; *(terrazza)* round terrace.

rotondeggiante [rotonded'dʒante] *ag* roundish.

rotondità [rotondi'ta] *sf inv* **(a)** roundness, rotundity. **(b)**: ~ *pl (scherz: di donna)* curves.

rotondo, a [ro'tondo] *ag (circolare)* round; *(paffuto: viso, mento)* round, full.

rotore [ro'tore] *sm* rotor.

rotta[1] ['rotta] *sf (Aer, Naut)* route, course; **essere in** ~ **per** to be en route for; **fare** ~ **su** *o* **per** *o* **verso** to head for *o* towards; **cambiare** ~ *(anche fig)* to change course; **in** ~ **di collisione** on a collision course; **ufficiale** *m* **di** ~ navigator, navigating officer.

rotta[2] ['rotta] *sf* **(a)** *(fig: rottura)*: **essere in** ~ **con qn** *(fig)* to be on bad terms with sb; **a** ~ **di collo** at breakneck speed. **(b)** *(disfatta)*: **mettere in** ~ **il nemico** to rout the enemy.

rottame [rot'tame] *sm* **(a)** *(pezzo di ferro)* piece of scrap iron; ~**i di ferro** scrap iron *sg*; ~**i** *pl (di nave, auto, aereo)* wreckage *sg*. **(b)** *(fig peg: persona, macchina)* wreck.

rotto, a ['rotto] **1** *pp di* **rompere**. **2** *ag (gen)* broken; *(braccio, gamba)* broken, fractured; *(macchina)* broken down; **avere le ossa** ~**e** *(fig)* to ache all over; **è** ~ **ad ogni esperienza** *(fig)* he's seen it all, he's been through it all. **3** *sm*: **per il** ~ **della cuffia** by the skin of one's teeth. **4** *smpl*: **trentamila lire e** ~**i** 30,000 odd lire.

rottura [rot'tura] *sf (azione)* breaking; *(di rapporti)* breaking off; *(di negoziati)* breakdown; *(di contratto)* breach; **è una tale** ~! *(fam: persona)* he's such a pain (in the neck)!; *(: situazione)* it's such a drag *o* bore!

roulette [ru'lɛt] *sf inv* roulette; ~ **russa** Russian roulette.

roulotte [ru'lɔt] *sf inv* caravan.

round [raund] *sm inv (Sport)* round.

routine [ru'tin] *sf inv* routine.

rovente [ro'vente] *ag (ferro, carbone)* red-hot; *(fig: sabbia, sole)* burning.

rovere [ro'vere] *sf (Bot)* English oak.

rovesciare [rovej'ʃare] **1** *vt (far cadere: gen)* to knock over; *(: liquido)* to pour; *(: accidentalmente)* to spill; *(capovolgere: barca)* to capsize; *(fig: situazione)* to reverse; *(: governo)* to overthrow; ~ **qc addosso a qn** to pour sth over sb; **ha rovesciato tutto il latte per terra** she spilled all the milk on the floor; ~ **la testa all'indietro** to throw one's head back. **2**: ~**rsi** *vr (sedia, macchina)* to overturn; *(barca)* to capsize; *(liquido)* to spill; *(fig: situazione)* to be reversed; **si è rovesciato tutto per terra** everything fell to the floor; *(liquido)* it all spilled on to the floor; **la folla si rovesciò nella piazza** the crowd poured into the square.

rovescio, a, sci, sce [ro'veʃʃo] **1** *ag (Maglia)* purl *attr*. **2** *sm* **(a)** *(lato: di stoffa, indumento)* wrong side; *(: di medaglia)* reverse side; **il** ~ **della medaglia** *(fig)* the other side of the coin. **(b)** *(Meteor)* downpour, heavy shower. **(c)** *(fig)*: ~ **di fortuna** setback. **(d)** *(Maglia)* purl stitch. **(e)** *(Tennis)* backhand. **3**: **a** ~, **alla** ~**a** *av (con il davanti dietro)* back to front; *(sottosopra)* upside down; *(con* *l'esterno all'interno)* inside out; **oggi mi va tutto alla ~a** everything is going wrong (for me) today; **capisce sempre tutto alla ~a** he always gets things the wrong way round.

rovina [ro'vina] *sf (gen, fig)* ruin; **in ~** *(palazzo)* in ruins; **~ finanziaria** financial ruin; **mandare qc/qn in ~** to ruin sth/sb; **sull'orlo della ~** on the brink of ruin; **sarà la sua ~** it *(o* she *etc)* will be the ruination of him.

rovinare [rovi'nare] 1 *vt (oggetto, persona: anche fig)* to ruin; *(fig: atmosfera, festa etc)* to ruin, spoil; **si è rovinata il vestito** she has ruined her dress. 2 *vi (aus essere) (crollare)* to collapse, fall down; *(precipitare)* to fall. 3: **~rsi** *vr* to be ruined, ruin o.s.; **mi voglio ~!** *(fig: sog: venditore etc)* I'm giving it away!

rovinato, a [rovi'nato] *ag* ruined, damaged; *(fig: persona)* ruined.

rovinoso, a [rovi'noso] *ag* ruinous.

rovistare [rovis'tare] *vt* to rummage through, search thoroughly; **~ ogni angolo** to search every corner.

rovo ['rovo] *sm (Bot)* blackberry bush, bramble bush; *(cespugli spinosi)* briar.

royalty ['rɔiəlti] *sf inv (percentuale)* royalty.

rozzezza [rod'dzettsa] *sf (vedi ag)* roughness; coarseness.

rozzo, a ['roddzo] *ag (gen)* rough; *(persona, modi)* uncouth, coarse.

ruba ['ruba] *sf:* **andare a ~** to sell like hot cakes.

rubacchiare [rubak'kjare] *vt* to pilfer.

rubacuori [ruba'kwori] *sm inv* ladykiller.

rubare [ru'bare] *vt:* **~ (qc a qn)** *(gen)* to steal (sth from sb); *(fig: idea, affetti, posto)* to steal (sth from sb), take (sth from sb); **gli hanno rubato tutto** they robbed him of everything; **~ il mestiere a qn** to do sb out of a job; **posso rubarti un minuto?** can I steal a minute of your time?; **mi hai rubato le parole di bocca** you've taken the words right out of my mouth.

rubicondo, a [rubi'kondo] *ag* ruddy.

rubinetto [rubi'netto] *sm* tap, faucet *(Am)*.

rubino [ru'bino] *sm* ruby.

rubizzo, a [ru'bittso] *ag* lively, sprightly.

rublo ['rublo] *sm* rouble.

rubrica, che [ru'brika] *sf (a) (quaderno)* index notebook; *(: per indirizzi)* address book; *(: per numeri di telefono)* telephone book. **(b)** *(di giornale: colonna)* column; *(: pagina)* page; **~ sportiva** sports page. **(c)** *(Radio, TV: parte di un programma)* spot, time; **'~ sportiva'** 'sports time'.

rude ['rude] *ag (duro, brusco)* tough; *(rozzo)* rough, coarse.

rudere ['rudere] *sm (rovina)* ruins *pl*; *(fig: persona)* wreck.

rudimentale [rudimen'tale] *ag* rudimentary, basic.

rudimenti [rudi'menti] *smpl (di disciplina)* rudiments; *(di teoria)* principles.

ruffianeria [ruffjane'ria] *sf* pandering.

ruffiano, a [ruf'fjano] *sm/f* pander; *(fig: leccapiedi)* bootlicker.

ruga, ghe ['ruga] *sf* wrinkle.

rugby ['rugbi] *sm* rugby (football).

ruggente [rud'dʒɛnte] *ag* roaring; **gli anni ~i** the roaring twenties.

ruggine ['ruddʒine] 1 *sf (Chim, Bot, colore)* rust; *(fig: rancore):* **fra di loro c'è della vecchia ~** there's bad blood between them. 2 *ag inv (colore)* rust, rust-coloured.

rugginoso, a [ruddʒi'noso] *ag* rusty.

ruggire [rud'dʒire] *vi* to roar.

ruggito [rud'dʒito] *sm* roar.

rugiada [ru'dʒada] *sf* dew.

rugoso, a [ru'goso] *ag (pieno di rughe)* wrinkled; *(scabro: superficie etc)* rough.

rullare [rul'lare] 1 *vt (spianare con il rullo)* to roll. 2 *vi* **(a)** *(tamburo)* to roll. **(b)** *(Aer)* to taxi.

rullino [rul'lino] *sm (Fot)* roll of film, spool.

rullio, ii [rul'lio] *sm (di tamburi)* roll.

rullo ['rullo] *sm* **(a)** *(di tamburo)* roll. **(b)** *(Tecn, Tip)* roller; *(Cine)* reel; **~ compressore** steamroller.

rum [rum] *sm inv* rum.

rumba ['rumba] *sf* rumba.

rumeno, a [ru'mɛno] *ag, sm, sm/f =* **romeno, a.**

ruminante [rumi'nante] *sm (Zool)* ruminant.

ruminare [rumi'nare] *vt (Zool)* to ruminate; *(fig)* to ruminate on *o* over, chew over.

rumore [ru'more] *sm (gen)* noise; *(di treno)* rumble; *(di motore)* sound; *(di piatti, stoviglie)* clatter; **un ~ sordo** a thud; **un ~ stridente** a shrill noise; **un ~ di passi** the sound of footsteps; **il ~ di sottofondo** the background noise; **fare ~** to make a noise; **senza ~** quietly; **non si sentiva alcun ~** not a sound could be heard; **la notizia ha fatto molto ~** *(fig)* the news aroused great interest.

rumoreggiare [rumored'dʒare] *vi (tuono etc)* to rumble; *(fig: folla)* to clamour.

rumoroso, a [rumo'roso] *ag (gen)* noisy; *(voce, risata)* loud, noisy.

ruolo ['rwɔlo] *sm* **(a)** *(gen, Cine, Teatro)* role; **avere un ~ di primo piano in qc** *(anche fig)* to play a leading role *o* part in sth. **(b)**: **di ~** *(personale, insegnante)* permanent; **professore di ~** *(Univ)* = lecturer with tenure; **fuori ~** *(personale, insegnante)* temporary.

ruota ['rwɔta] *sf (gen)* wheel; *(di ingranaggio)* cog (wheel); **fare la ~** *(Ginnastica)* to do a cartwheel; **gonna a ~** flared skirt; **veicolo a due ~e** two-wheeled vehicle; **~ di scorta** spare wheel; **~ del timone** (steering) wheel; **la ~ della fortuna** the wheel of fortune; **andare a ~ libera** to free-wheel; **parlare a ~ libera** *(fig)* to speak freely; **essere l'ultima ~ del carro** *(fig)* to count for nothing.

rupe ['rupe] *sf* cliff, rock.

rupestre [ru'pɛstre] *ag* rocky.

rurale [ru'rale] *ag* rural, country *attr.*

ruscello [ruʃ'ʃello] *sm* stream, brook.

ruspa ['ruspa] *sf* excavator.

ruspante [rus'pante] *ag (pollo)* free-range.

ruspare [rus'pare] *vi* to scratch about, peck about.

russare [rus'sare] *vi* to snore.

Russia ['russja] *sf* Russia.

russo, a ['russo] *ag, sm, sm/f* Russian.

rustico, a, ci, che ['rustiko] 1 *ag* country *attr*, rural; *(arredamento)* rustic; *(fig: modi)* rough. 2 *sm (fabbricato: per attrezzi)* shed; *(per abitazione)* farm labourer's cottage.

ruta ['ruta] *sf (Bot)* rue.

ruttare [rut'tare] *vi* to belch.

rutto ['rutto] *sm* belch; **fare un ~** to belch.

ruttore [rut'tore] *sm (Elettr)* contact breaker.

ruvido, a ['ruvido] *ag (gen, fig)* rough, coarse.

ruzzolare [ruttso'lare] *vi (aus essere)* to roll down, tumble down.

ruzzolone [ruttso'lone] *sm* tumble, fall; **un gran ~** a heavy fall; **ha fatto le scale a ~i** he tumbled down the stairs.

S

S, s ['esse] *sf o m inv (lettera)* S, s.
S. *abbr* **(a)** *(= sud)* S. **(b)** *(= santo)* St.
sabato ['sabato] *sm inv* Saturday; *(Rel)* sabbath;
  S~ **Santo** *(Rel)* Holy Saturday; *per uso vedi* **martedì.**
sabba ['sabba] *sm* witches' sabbath.
sabbatico, a, ci, che [sab'batiko] *ag* sabbatical.
sabbia ['sabbja] *sf* sand; ~**e mobili** quicksand *sg.*
sabbiatura [sabbja'tura] *sf* **(a)** *(Med)* sand bath;
  fare le ~**e** to take sand baths. **(b)** *(Tecn)* sand-blasting.
sabbioso, a [sab'bjoso] *ag* sandy.
sabotaggio [sabo'taddʒo] *sm (Mil, Pol, fig)* sabotage; *(: atto)* act of sabotage.
sabotare [sabo'tare] *vt* to sabotage.
sabotatore, trice [sabota'tore] *sm/f* saboteur.
sacca ['sakka] *sf* **(a)** *(borsa)* bag; ~ **da viaggio** duffle bag. **(b)** *(di fiume)* inlet. **(c)** *(di pus etc)* pocket; ~ **d'aria** air pocket.
saccarina [sakka'rina] *sf* saccharin.
saccente [sat'tʃɛnte] **1** *ag* presumptuous, conceited. **2** *sm/f* know-all.
saccheggiare [sakked'dʒare] *vt (Mil)* to sack, plunder; *(fig)* to raid.
saccheggiatore [sakkeddʒa'tore] *sm* plunderer.
saccheggio [sak'keddʒo] *sm* sacking, plundering.
sacchetto [sak'ketto] *sm* **(a)** *(piccolo sacco)* small bag; ~ **di carta/di plastica** paper/plastic bag. **(b)** *(quantità)* bagful.
sacco ['sakko] *sm* **(a)** *(tessuto)* sacking. **(b)** *(contenitore)* sack, bag; *(quantità)* sackful; *(fig):* **un** ~ **di** a lot of; **un** ~ **di gente** lots of people; **colazione** *f* **al** ~ packed lunch; ~ **da montagna** rucksack; ~ **a pelo** sleeping bag; **cogliere** *o* **prendere qn con le mani nel** ~ to catch sb red-handed; **vuotare il** ~ to confess, spill the beans *(fam)*; **mettere qn nel** ~ to cheat sb. **(c)** *(Anat, Bio)* sac. **(d)** *(saccheggio)* sacking, plundering.
sacerdotale [satʃerdo'tale] *ag* priestly.
sacerdote, essa [satʃer'dɔte] *sm/f* priest/priestess.
sacerdozio [satʃer'dɔttsjo] *sm* priesthood.
sacrale [sa'krale] *ag* holy, sacred.
sacramentale [sakramen'tale] *ag* sacramental.
sacramento [sakra'mento] *sm (Rel)* sacrament.
sacrario [sa'krarjo] *sm* memorial chapel.
sacrestano [sakres'tano] *sm* = **sagrestano.**
sacrestia [sakres'tia] *sf* = **sagrestia.**
sacrificare [sakrifi'kare] **1** *vt (gen)* to sacrifice. **2:** ~**rsi** *vr* to sacrifice o.s.
sacrificato, a [sakrifi'kato] *ag (gen, Rel)* sacrificed; *(fig: sprecato, sciupato)* wasted.
sacrificio [sakri'fitʃo] *sm (Rel, fig)* sacrifice; **fare un** ~ to make a sacrifice.
sacrilegio [sakri'lɛdʒo] *sm (Rel, fig)* sacrilege; **fare** ~, **commettere un** ~ to commit a sacrilege.
sacrilego, a, ghi, ghe [sa'krilego] *ag (Rel)* sacrilegious.
sacrista [sa'krista] *sm* = **sagrestano.**
sacro, a ['sakro] **1** *ag* **(a)** *(Rel)* holy, sacred; *(: arte, diritto)* sacred; **musica** ~**a** church music. **(b)**

(Anat): osso ~ sacrum. **2** *sm:* **il** ~ the sacred.
sacrosanto, a [sakro'santo] *ag* sacrosanct.
sadico, a, ci, che ['sadiko] **1** *ag* sadistic. **2** *sm/f* sadist.
sadismo [sa'dizmo] *sm* sadism.
saetta [sa'etta] *sf (fulmine)* thunderbolt; **essere (veloce come) una** ~ to be as quick as lightning.
safari [sa'fari] *sm inv* safari.
saga, ghe ['saga] *sf* saga.
sagace [sa'gatʃe] *ag* sagacious, shrewd.
sagacia [sa'gatʃa] *sf* sagacity, shrewdness.
saggezza [sad'dʒettsa] *sf* wisdom.
saggiare [sad'dʒare] *vt (metalli preziosi)* to assay; *(fig: mettere alla prova)* to test.
saggio[1], a, gi, ge ['saddʒo] **1** *ag* wise. **2** *sm* wise man; *(Antichità)* sage.
saggio[2] ['saddʒo] *sm* **(a)** *(prova: di abilità, forza etc)* proof; **dare** ~ **di** to give proof of; ~ **di ginnastica** gymnastics display; ~ **di musica** recital. **(b)** *(campione)* sample; *(di libro)* sample copy. **(c)** *(scritto: letterario)* essay; *(: Scol)* written test. **(d)** *(di metalli preziosi)* assay.
saggista, i, e [sad'dʒista] *sm/f* essayist.
saggistica, che [sad'dʒistika] *sf (attività)* essay writing; *(produzione)* essays *pl.*
Sagittario [sadʒit'tarjo] *sm* Sagittarius; **essere del** ~ to be Sagittarius.
sagoma ['sagoma] *sf (profilo, linea)* outline; *(forma)* shape, form; *(modello in cartone, legno)* template; *(nel tiro al bersaglio)* target; *(fig: persona)* character; **è una** ~! he's a scream!
sagra ['sagra] *sf* festival, feast.
sagrato [sa'grato] *sm* church yard.
sagrestano [sagres'tano] *sm* sexton.
sagrestia [sagres'tia] *sf*, **sagristia** [sagris'tia] *sf* sacristy.
sahariana [saa'rjana] *sf* bush jacket.
saio ['sajo] *sm (Rel)* habit; **prendere** *o* **vestire il** ~ to take the habit.
sala ['sala] **1** *sf (gen)* room; *(molto grande)* hall; *(salotto)* living room. **2:** ~ **d'aspetto** *o* **d'attesa** waiting room; ~ **da ballo** dance hall; ~ **da biliardo** *(pubblica)* billiard hall; *(privata)* billiard room; ~ **(dei) comandi** control room; ~ **dei concerti** concert hall; ~ **per conferenze** *(Univ)* lecture hall; *(in aziende)* conference room; ~ **da gioco** gaming room; ~ **macchine** *(Naut)* engine room; ~ **operatoria** *(Med)* operating theatre; ~ **da pranzo** dining room; ~ **professori** staff room; ~ **per ricevimenti** banqueting hall; ~ **delle udienze** *(Dir)* courtroom.
salace [sa'latʃe] *ag (spinto, piccante)* salacious, saucy; *(mordace)* cutting, biting.
salamandra [sala'mandra] *sf* salamander.
salame [sa'lame] *sm (cibo)* salami, salami sausage; *(fig: persona sciocca)* dope, clot.
salamelecchi [salame'lɛkki] *smpl (peg)* bowing and scraping; **fare** ~ to bow and scrape; **senza tanti** ~ without ceremony.
salamoia [sala'mɔja] *sf (Culin)* brine.
salare [sa'lare] *vt* **(a)** *(condire)* to salt, add salt to.

(b) *(mettere sotto sale: senza acqua)* to salt; *(: con acqua)* to brine.

salariale [sala'rjale] *ag* wage *attr*, pay *attr*; **aumento** ~ wage *o* pay increase.

salariato, a [sala'rjato] **1** *ag* wage-earning. **2** *sm/f* wage-earner.

salario [sa'larjo] *sm* pay, wage(s).

salassare [salas'sare] *vt* (*Med*) to bleed.

salasso [sa'lasso] *sm* (*Med*) bleeding, bloodletting; *(fig: forte spesa)* drain.

salatino [sala'tino] *sm* cracker, salted biscuit.

salato, a [sa'lato] *ag (sapore, cibo)* salty; *(acqua)* salt *attr; (burro)* salted; *(fig: costoso)* expensive, costly; *(: prezzo)* stiff; *(: mordace: discorso etc)* sharp, cutting; **pagare** ~ *(acquisto)* to pay through the nose for; **l'ha pagata** ~**a** *(fig)* he paid dearly for it.

saldare [sal'dare] **1** *vt* **(a)** *(Tecn, gen)* to join; *(con saldatore)* to solder; *(con saldatura autogena)* to weld. **(b)** *(conto)* to settle; *(fattura, debito)* to pay; ~ **un conto (con qn)** to settle an account (with sb); *(fig)* to settle a score (with sb). **2:** ~**rsi** *vr (ferita)* to heal.

saldatore [salda'tore] *sm (operaio: vedi vt)* solderer; welder; *(utensile)* soldering iron.

saldatrice [salda'tritʃe] *sf (macchina)* welder, welding machine; ~ **ad arco** arc welder.

saldatura [salda'tura] *sf (vedi vt: azione)* soldering; welding; *(: punto saldato)* soldered joint; weld; ~ **ad arco** arc welding; ~ **autogena** welding; ~ **dolce** soft soldering.

saldezza [sal'dettsa] *sf* firmness, strength.

saldo¹, a [saldo] *ag (gen)* steady, firm; *(fig: rapporto)* steady; *(: principi)* sound.

saldo² ['saldo] *sm* **(a)** *(pagamento)* settlement, payment; *(somma residua da pagare)* balance; **pagare a** ~ to pay in full; ~ **attivo** credit; ~ **passivo** deficit. **(b)** *(svendita)* sale.

sale ['sale] **1** *sm* **(a)** *(gen)* salt; **conservare sotto** ~ to salt; **sotto** ~ salted; ~**i e tabacchi** tobacconist's (shop); **restare di** ~ *(fig)* to be dumbfounded; **avere molto** ~ **in zucca** to have a lot of good sense; **non ha molto** ~ **in zucca** he doesn't have much sense. **(b):** ~**i** *pl (Med: da annusare)* smelling salts. **2:** ~ **da cucina,** ~ **grosso** cooking salt; ~ **da tavola,** ~ **fino** table salt; ~**i da bagno** bath salts; ~**i minerali** mineral salts.

salgemma [sal'dʒemma] *sm* rock salt.

salice ['salitʃe] *sm (Bot)* willow; ~ **piangente** weeping willow.

saliente [sa'ljɛnte] *ag* salient, main.

saliera [sa'ljɛra] *sf* saltcellar.

salina [sa'lina] *sf* **(a)** *(serie di vasche)* saltworks *pl*. **(b)** *(deposito naturale)* salt pan. **(c)** *(miniera di salgemma)* salt mine.

salino, a [sa'lino] *ag* saline.

salire [sa'lire] **1** *vt (scale, pendio)* to climb, go (*o* come) up.
2 *vi (aus essere)* **(a)** *(gen)* to go (*o* come) up; *(aereo etc)* to climb, go up; **sali tu o vengo giù io?** are you coming up or shall I come down?; **salimmo a piedi/con la bicicletta fino in cima** we walked/cycled up to the top; **la strada sale per 2 km** the road climbs for 2 km; **salì sull'albero** he climbed the tree; ~ **in quota** *(Aer)* to gain altitude.
(b): ~ **in macchina** to get into the car; ~ **sull'autobus/sul treno** to get on the bus/on the train; ~ **a bordo di** to (get on) board; ~ **a cavallo** to mount; ~ **su una o in bicicletta** to get on a bicycle; ~ **in sella** to get into the saddle.
(c) *(prezzo, temperatura)* to rise, go up;

(marea) to come in; *(fumo)* to rise.
(d) *(fraseologia):* ~ **in cielo** *o* **paradiso** to go to heaven; ~ **al potere** to rise to power; ~ **al trono** to ascend the throne; ~ **alle stelle** *(prezzi)* to rocket; ~ **nella stima di qn** to rise in sb's estimation.

saliscendi [saliʃ'ʃendi] *sm inv* latch.

salita [sa'lita] *sf* **(a)** *(azione)* climb, ascent. **(b)** *(strada)* hill, slope; **in** ~ *av, ag* uphill; **strada in** ~ road going uphill.

saliva [sa'liva] *sf* saliva.

salivare¹ [sali'vare] *ag* salivary.

salivare² [sali'vare] *vi* to salivate.

salma ['salma] *sf* body, remains *pl*.

salmastro, a [sal'mastro] **1** *ag (acqua)* salt *attr; (sapore)* salty. **2** *sm (sapore)* salty taste; *(odore)* salty smell.

salmì [sal'mi] *sm inv (Culin)* salmi.

salmo ['salmo] *sm (Rel)* psalm.

salmone [sal'mone] *sm* salmon.

salmonella [salmo'nɛlla] *sf* salmonella.

salmonellosi [salmonel'lɔzi] *sf* salmonellosis.

salnitro [sal'nitro] *sm (Chim)* saltpetre.

salone [sa'lone] *sm* **(a)** *(stanza)* sitting room, lounge; *(di ricevimento)* reception room; *(su nave)* lounge, saloon. **(b)** *(mostra)* show, exhibition; ~ **dell'automobile** motor show. **(c)** *(negozio: di parrucchiere)* hairdresser's (salon); ~ **di bellezza** beauty salon.

saloon [sa'lu:n] *sm inv* saloon.

salottiero, a [salot'tjero] *ag* mundane.

salotto [sa'lɔtto] *sm* **(a)** *(stanza)* sitting room, lounge; *(mobilio)* lounge suite. **(b)** *(circolo letterario etc)* salon; **chiacchiere da** ~ *(fig)* society gossip.

salpare [sal'pare] *(Naut)* **1** *vt:* ~ **l'ancora** to weigh anchor. **2** *vi (aus essere)* to set sail.

salsa ['salsa] *sf* sauce; ~ **di pomodoro** tomato sauce; **in tutte le** ~**e** *(fig)* in all kinds of ways.

salsedine [sal'sedine] *sf (del mare, vento)* saltiness; *(incrostazione)* (dried) salt.

salsiccia, ce [sal'sittʃa] *sf* sausage.

salsiera [sal'sjera] *sf* sauceboat.

saltare [sal'tare] **1** *vt (siepe, ostacolo)* to jump; *(fig: capitolo, pasto)* to skip, miss (out); ~ **la corda** to skip.
2 *vi* **(a)** *(gen)* to jump, leap; *(saltellare)* to hop, skip; ~ **su/sopra qc** to jump on/over sth; ~ **giù** to jump down; ~ **giù da qc** to jump off sth, jump down from sth; ~ **addosso a qn** *(aggredire)* to attack sb; **salta su!** *(in macchina)* jump up!; *(su moto, bici)* jump on!; **è saltato su e mi ha detto che...** he jumped up and told me that...; ~ **a terra** to jump down; ~ **dal letto/dalla finestra** to jump out of bed/out of the window; ~ **al collo di qn** *(in segno di affetto)* to throw one's arms round sb's neck; ~ **da un argomento all'altro** to jump from one subject to another; ~ **dalla gioia** to jump for joy; **salta agli occhi** it's obvious; **ma che ti salta in mente?** what are you thinking of?; **far** ~ **un bimbo sulle ginocchia** to bounce a child on one's knees.
(b) *(bottone)* to pop off; *(bomba)* to explode; *(ponte)* to blow up; *(fusibile)* to blow; *(fig: impiegato)* to be fired; *(: corso)* to be cancelled; ~ **in aria** to blow up.
(c): **far** ~ *(treno, ponte)* to blow up; *(fusibile)* to blow; *(mina)* to explode; *(serratura: forzare)* to break; *(: con esplosivo)* to blow; *(lezione, appuntamento)* to cancel; **far** ~ **il banco** *(Gioco)* to break the bank; **farsi** ~ **le cervella** to blow one's brains out.
(d): ~ **fuori** *(apparire improvvisamente)* to

jump out, leap out; *(venire trovato)* to turn up; *(dire improvvisamente)*: ~ **fuori con** to come out with; **dall'auto sono saltati fuori due ladri** two thieves jumped *o* leaped out of the car; **quel libro è finalmente saltato fuori** that book finally turned up; **da dove salti fuori?** where did you spring from?
(e) *(Culin)* to sauté.

saltatore [salta'tore] *sm (Sport: persona)* jumper; *(: cavallo)* steeplechaser.

saltellare [saltel'lare] *vi* to hop, skip.

saltello [sal'tɛllo] *sm* hop, little jump.

saltimbanco, a, chi, che [saltim'banko] *sm/f* acrobat; *(peg)* charlatan, fraud.

saltimbocca [saltim'bokka] *sm inv (Culin)* rolled veal and ham.

salto ['salto] *sm* **(a)** *(gen)* jump, leap; **fare un** ~ to jump; *(per la paura)* to start; **fare un** ~ **a Milano** to pop over to Milan; **fare un** ~ **da un amico** to drop in on a friend; **fare i** ~**i dalla gioia** to jump for joy; **un** ~ **nel buio** *(fig)* a leap in the dark. **(b)** *(Sport)*: ~ **in lungo/triplo** long/triple jump; ~ **con l'asta** pole vault; ~ **mortale** somersault; **ho fatto i** ~**i mortali per arrivare qui in tempo** I almost killed myself trying to get here on time. **(c)** *(dislivello)* drop; **un** ~ **di qualità** a difference in quality; *(miglioramento: nel lavoro, in condizioni)* a step up the ladder.

saltuario, a [saltu'arjo] *ag* occasional.

salubre [sa'lubre] *ag* healthy.

salubrità [salubri'ta] *sf* healthiness.

salumeria [salume'ria] *sf* ≃ delicatessen.

salumi [sa'lumi] *smpl* cured pork meats.

salumiere, a [salu'mjɛre] *sm/f* ≃ delicatessen owner.

salumificio [salumi'fitʃo] *sm* cured pork meat factory.

salutare[1] [salu'tare] *ag* healthy.

salutare[2] [salu'tare] *vt* **(a)** *(incontrandosi)* to greet; *(congedandosi)* to say goodbye to; *(trasmettere i saluti)* to give one's regards to, send one's regards to; **mi saluti sua moglie** my regards to your wife; **salutami Lucia se la vedi** if you see Lucia tell her I was asking after her. **(b)** *(Mil)* to salute.

salute [sa'lute] **1** *sf* health; **la** ~ **pubblica** public welfare; **godere di buona** ~ to be healthy, enjoy good health; **avere una** ~ **di ferro** to have an iron constitution. **2** *escl (a chi starnutisce)* bless you!; *(bevendo)* your health!, cheers!

saluto [sa'luto] *sm* **(a)** *(incontrandosi)* greeting; *(congedandosi)* goodbye, farewell; **rivolgere il** ~ **a qn** to greet sb; **gli ha tolto il** ~ he no longer says hello to him; **tanti** ~**i** best regards; **cordiali** ~**i, distinti** ~**i** yours truly, yours faithfully; **i miei** ~**i alla sua signora** my regards to your wife. **(b)** *(gesto: del capo)* nod; *(: con la mano)* wave; **mi fece un cenno di** ~ he nodded to me; he waved to me. **(c)** *(Mil)* salute.

salva ['salva] *sf* salvo; **sparare a** ~ to fire a salute.

salvacondotto [salvakon'dotto] *sm (Mil)* pass.

salvadanaio [salvada'najo] *sm* moneybox, piggy bank.

salvagente [salva'dʒɛnte] *sm* **(a)** *(Naut: ciambella)* life buoy, life belt; *(: giubbotto)* life jacket. **(b)** *(stradale)* traffic island.

salvaguardare [salvagwar'dare] *vt* to safeguard, protect.

salvaguardia [salva'gwardja] *sf* safeguard; **a** ~ **di** for the safeguard of.

salvare [sal'vare] **1** *vt (gen)* to save; *(portare soccorso)* to rescue; **lo salvarono da morte sicura** they saved him from certain death; **hanno salvato**

poche persone dal naufragio they rescued few people from the shipwreck; ~ **la vita a qn** to save sb's life; **mi hai salvato!** *(anche fig)* you saved me!; **hanno salvato poche cose dall'incendio** they salvaged very few items from the fire; ~ **la faccia** to save face; ~ **le apparenze** to keep up appearances; ~ **capra e cavoli** to have the best of both worlds; **Dio salvi la regina!** God save the Queen! **2**: ~**rsi** *vr (salvare la propria vita)* to save o.s.; **nessuno si è salvato dal disastro** nobody escaped the disaster; **si salvi chi può** every man for himself; **non si è salvato nulla** everything was destroyed.

salvataggio [salva'taddʒo] *sm* rescue; **cintura di** ~ lifebelt.

salvatore, trice [salva'tore] *sm/f* rescuer; *(Rel)*: **il S**~ the Saviour.

salvazione [salvat'tsjone] *sf (Rel)* salvation.

salve ['salve] *escl (ciao)* hello!, hi!; *(a chi starnutisce)* bless you!

salvezza [sal'vettsa] *sf* salvation; **cercare** ~ **nella fuga** to seek safety in flight.

salvia ['salvja] *sf (Bot)* sage.

salvietta [sal'vjetta] *sf* napkin, serviette.

salvo[1]**, a** [salvo] **1** *ag (persona)* safe, unhurt, unharmed; *(: fuori pericolo)* safe, out of danger; **uscir** ~ **da qc** to come out of sth safely; **avere** ~**a la vita** to have one's life spared. **2** *sm*: **essere in** ~ *(persona, cosa)* to be safe; **mettere qc in** ~ to put sth in a safe place; **mettersi in** ~ to reach safety; **portare qn in** ~ to lead sb to safety.

salvo[2] ['salvo] *prep (a)* *(eccetto)* except; *(a meno che)* unless; **è aperto tutti i giorni** ~ **il lunedì** it's open every day with the exception of *o* except Monday; **vennero tutti** ~ **lui** everybody came except him; ~ **errori, la somma ammonta a...** unless I am *(o* we are *etc)* mistaken, it amounts to...; ~ **imprevisti** barring accidents; ~ **errori e omissioni** errors and omissions excepted; ~ **contrordini** barring instructions to the contrary. **(b)**: ~ **che** *(eccetto che)* except (that); *(a meno che)* unless; **sono soddisfatto** ~ **che per una cosa** I'm quite satisfied except for one thing; **lo farò** ~ **che tu non voglia farlo** I'll do it unless you would rather do it.

sambuco, chi [sam'buko] *sm* elder (tree).

sanare [sa'nare] *vt* to heal, cure; *(economia)* to cure, put right, restore.

sanatorio [sana'tɔrjo] *sm* sanatorium.

San Bernardo ['san ber'nardo] *sm inv (cane)* Saint Bernard.

sancire [san'tʃire] *vt* to sanction; *(ratificare)* to ratify.

sandalo ['sandalo] *sm* **(a)** *(Bot)* sandalwood. **(b)** *(calzatura)* sandal.

sangue ['sangwe] *sm* blood; **animale a** ~ **caldo/ freddo** warm-/cold-blooded animal; ~ **freddo** *(fig)* sangfroid; **uccidere a** ~ **freddo** to kill in cold blood; **all'ultimo** ~ *(duello, lotta)* to the death; **il** ~ **gli salì alla testa** the blood rushed to his head; **non corre buon** ~ **tra di loro** there's bad blood between them; **ha la musica nel** ~ music is in his blood; **sentirsi gelare il** ~ **nelle vene** to feel one's blood run cold; **farsi cattivo** ~ **per qc** to get worked up about sth; **buon** ~ **non mente!** blood will out!

sanguigno, a [san'gwiɲɲo] *ag (gruppo, pressione, vaso)* blood *attr*; *(color rosso intenso)* blood-red.

sanguinante [sangwi'nante] *ag* bleeding.

sanguinare [sangwi'nare] *vi* to bleed.

sanguinario, a [sangwi'narjo] *ag* bloodthirsty.

sanguinoso, a [sangwi'noso] *ag* bloody.

sanguisuga, ghe [sangwi'suga] *sf (Zool, fig)* leech.

sanità [sani'ta] *sf* **(a)** *(gen)* health; ~ **mentale** sanity; **Ministero della S~** Ministry of Health. **(b)** *(Mil)* army medical corps.

sanitario, a [sani'tarjo] **1** *ag (servizio, misure)* health *attr*; *(condizioni)* sanitary; **Ufficiale S~** Health Officer; **(impianti)** ~**i** bathroom *o* sanitary fittings. **2** *sm (Amm: medico)* doctor.

sano, a ['sano] *ag (persona, clima)* healthy; *(fisico, denti)* healthy, sound; *(alimento)* healthy, wholesome; *(frutto)* sound; *(fig: politica, ambiente)* sound, good; ~ **e salvo** safe and sound; ~ **di mente** sane; **di** ~**i principi** of sound principles; **una** ~**a educazione** a good education; **una** ~**a sgridata** a good telling-off.

sanscrito, a ['sanskrito] *ag, sm* Sanskrit.

santificare [santifi'kare] *vt* to sanctify, hallow; *(feste)* to observe.

santino [san'tino] *sm* holy picture.

santissimo, a [san'tissimo] *ag* **(a):** **il S~ Sacramento** the Holy Sacrament; **il Padre S~** *(papa)* the Holy Father. **(b)** *(fig)*: **fammi il** ~ **piacere di star zitto!** do me a favour and keep quiet!

santità [santi'ta] *sf (Rel)* sanctity, holiness; *(fig)* sanctity; **Sua S~** His *(o* Your) Holiness.

santo, a ['santo] **1** *ag* **(a)** *(sacro)* holy; **Venerdì S~** Good Friday; ~ **cielo!** good heavens!; **Dio** ~! good God! **(b)** *(seguito da sm:* **san** + *consonante,* **sant'** + *vocale,* ~ + *s impura, gn, pn, ps, x, z; seguito da sf:* ~**a** + *consonante,* **sant'** + *vocale)* saint; **San Pietro** *(apostolo)* Saint Peter; *(chiesa)* Saint Peter's. **(c):** **è una** ~**a donna** she's a saint; **quel sant'uomo di tuo nonno** *(defunto)* your sainted grandfather; **parole** ~**e!** very true!; **vuoi farmi il** ~ **piacere di uscire?** would you do me a favour and get out?; **tutto il** ~ **giorno** the whole blessed day, all day long. **2** *sm/f (anche fig)* saint; **non sono una** ~**a** I'm no saint; **qualche** ~ **provvederà** something will turn up; **non c'è** ~ **che tenga!** that's no excuse!; **quella** ~**a di sua moglie** his wife, saint that she is. **3:** ~**i** *smpl:* **i S~i, tutti i S~i** All Saints' Day.

santone [san'tone] *sm* holy man.

santuario [santu'arjo] *sm* sanctuary.

sanzionare [santsjo'nare] *vt* to sanction.

sanzione [san'tsjone] *sf* **(a)** *(approvazione)* sanction, approval. **(b)** *(punizione)* sanction, penalty.

sapere [sa'pere] **1** *vt* **(a)** *(conoscere: lezione, nome)* to know; *(venire a sapere: notizia)* to hear; **sai dove abita?** do you know where he lives?; **sai se torna?** do you know if *o* whether he is coming back?; **lo so** I know; **non ne so nulla** I don't know anything about it; **sa quattro lingue** he knows *o* can speak four languages; **non ne vuole più** ~ **di lei** he doesn't want to have anything more to do with her; **come l'ha saputo?** how did he find out *o* hear about it?; **ho saputo che ti sei sposato** I hear you got married; **vuoi** ~ **la verità?** do you want to know *o* hear the truth?; **far** ~ **qc a qn** to let sb know about sth; **venir a** ~ **qc (da qn)** to find out *o* hear about sth (from sb).

(b) *(essere capace di)* to know how to; **non sa far niente** he can't do anything; **sai nuotare?** do you know how to swim?, can you swim?; **sa (come) cavarsela** he can manage.

(c) *(rendersi conto)* to know; **non sa cosa dice** he doesn't know *o* realize what he's saying; **sa quello che fa** he knows what he's doing; **so com'è difficile parlargli** I know how difficult it is to talk to him; **senza saperlo** without realizing it, unwittingly.

(d) *(fraseologia)*: **è difficile, e io ne so qualcosa** it's difficult and I know it; **e chi lo sa?** who knows?; **si sa che...** it's well known that..., everybody knows that...; **non si sa mai** you never know; **non saprei** I don't *o* wouldn't know; **non saprei dire** I couldn't say; **mi dispiace, non so che farci** I'm sorry, I don't see what I can do about it; **averlo saputo!** had I *(o* we *etc)* known!; **ci sa fare con le donne/macchine** he has a way with women/cars; **lui sì che ci sa fare** he's very good at it.

2 *vi* **(a):** ~ **di** *(aver sapore)* to taste of; *(aver odore)* to smell of; *(fig)* to smack of, resemble; **è un film che non sa di niente** it's a very dull film.

(b): **mi sa che...** *(credo)* I think (that)...; **mi sa che non viene** I don't think he's coming.

3 *sm* knowledge.

sapiente [sa'pjɛnte] **1** *ag (dotto)* learned; *(che rivela abilità)* masterly; **con mano** ~ with a skilful hand. **2** *sm/f* scholar.

sapientone, a [sapjen'tone] *sm/f (peg)* know-all.

sapienza [sa'pjɛntsa] *sf (saggezza)* wisdom; *(conoscenza)* knowledge, learning.

saponata [sapo'nata] *sf (acqua)* soapy water; *(schiuma)* (soap)suds *pl.*

sapone [sa'pone] *sm* soap; ~ **da bucato** washing soap; ~ **da barba** shaving soap; ~ **liquido** liquid soap; ~ **in scaglie** soapflakes *pl.*

saponetta [sapo'netta] *sf* bar of soap.

sapore [sa'pore] *sm (anche fig)* flavour; **non ha alcun** ~ it hasn't any flavour, it doesn't taste of anything; **è ciò che dà** ~ **alla vita** this is what makes life worth living; **parole di** ~ **amaro** words with a bitter ring to them.

saporito, a [sapo'rito] *ag (cibo)* tasty; *(fig: battuta)* witty; **poco** ~ tasteless; **farsi una dormita** ~**a** to sleep soundly.

saporoso, a [sapo'roso] *ag* tasty.

saputello, a [sapu'tɛllo] *sm/f* know-all.

sarabanda [sara'banda] *sf (fig)* uproar.

saracinesca, sche [saratʃi'neska] *sf* rolling shutter.

sarcasmo [sar'kazmo] *sm* sarcasm; **fare del** ~ to be sarcastic, make sarcastic remarks.

sarcastico, a, ci, che [sar'kastiko] *ag* sarcastic.

sarchiare [sar'kjare] *vt (Agr)* to hoe.

sarchiatrice [sarkja'tritʃe] *sf (Agr)* hoeing machine.

sarcofago, gi *o* **ghi** [sar'kɔfago] *sm* sarcophagus.

Sardegna [sar'deɲɲa] *sf* Sardinia.

sardina [sar'dina] *sf* sardine; **pigiati come** ~**e** *(fig)* packed like sardines.

sardo, a ['sardo] *ag, sm/f* Sardinian.

sardonico, a, ci, che [sar'dɔniko] *ag* sardonic.

sari ['sari] *sm inv* sari.

sarta ['sarta] *sf* dressmaker.

sartia ['sartja] *sf (Naut)* stay.

sartiame [sar'tjame] *sm (Naut)* stays *pl.*

sarto ['sarto] *sm* tailor; ~ **da donna** ladies' tailor; ~ **d'alta moda** couturier.

sartoria [sarto'ria] *sf* **(a)** *(Arte: di sarto)* tailoring; *(: di sarta)* dressmaking; ~ **d'alta moda** haute couture. **(b)** *(locale: di sarto)* tailor's; *(: di sarta)* dressmaker's; ~ **d'alta moda** couturier's.

sassaia [sas'saja] *sf (terreno)* stony ground; *(lungo argini etc)* (stone) dyke.

sassata [sas'sata] *sf* blow with a stone; **infranse il vetro con una** ~ he broke the pane with a stone; **tirare una** ~ **contro** *o* **a qc/qn** to throw a stone at sth/sb.

sasso ['sasso] *sm (pietra)* stone; *(ciottolo)* pebble; *(roccia)* rock; **restare** *o* **rimanere di** ~ to be dumbfounded; **è una cosa da far piangere i** ~**i** *(fig: penoso)* it's pitiful.

sassofonista, i, e [sassofo'nista] *sm/f* saxophonist.

sassofono [sas'sɔfono] *sm* saxophone.

sassone ['sassone] *ag*, *sm/f*, *sm* Saxon.

sassoso, a [sas'soso] *ag* stony.

Satana ['satana] *sm* Satan.

satanasso [sata'nasso] *sm* (*fig: persona*) devil.

satanico, a, ci, che [sa'taniko] *ag* satanic; (*fig*) diabolical, devilish.

satellite [sa'tɛllite] *sm*, *ag inv* (*anche fig*) satellite.

satin [sa'tɛ̃] *sm inv* satin.

satinato, a [sati'nato] *ag* with a satin finish.

satira ['satira] *sf* satire; **fare la ~ di qc/qn** to satirize sth/sb.

satireggiare [satired'dʒare] **1** *vt* to satirize. **2** *vi* (*fare della satira*) to be satirical; (*scrivere satire*) to write satires.

satirico, a, ci, che [sa'tiriko] *ag* satirical.

satollarsi [satol'larsi] *vr* to eat one's fill.

satollo, a [sa'tollo] *ag* full, replete.

saturare [satu'rare] **1** *vt* (*Fis, Chim*) to saturate. **2:** **~rsi** *vr* to become saturated.

saturazione [saturat'tsjone] *sf* (*Fis, Chim*) saturation; **aver raggiunto il punto di ~** to have reached saturation point; (*fig*) to have had more than enough *o* as much as one can take.

saturo, a [ˈsaturo] *ag* (*gen*) saturated; (*fig*): **~ (di)** full (of); **~ d'acqua** (*terreno*) waterlogged.

S.A.U.B. ['saub] *abbr f* ≈ N.H.S.

sauna ['sauna] *sf* sauna; **fare la ~** to have *o* take a sauna.

savana [sa'vana] *sf* savannah.

savio, a ['savjo] **1** *ag* wise, sensible. **2** *sm* wise man.

Savoia [sa'voja] *sf* Savoy.

savoiardo, a [savo'jardo] **1** *ag* of Savoy, Savoyard. **2** *sm* (*Culin*) sponge finger.

savoir-faire [sa'vwar'fɛr] *sm* savoir-faire, know-how.

saziare [sat'tsjare] **1** *vt* (*anche fig*) to satisfy. **2:** **~rsi** *vr* to eat one's fill; (*fig*): **non si sazia di guardarla** he's never tired of looking at her.

sazietà [sattsje'ta] *sf* satiety, satiation; **mangiare a ~** to eat one's fill; **ce ne sono a ~** there are more than enough.

sazio, a ['sattsjo] *ag*: **~ (di)** sated (with), full (of); **no, grazie, sono ~** no thanks, I've had enough; **sono ~ di questi discorsi** I'm fed up with this talk.

sbaciucchiare [zbatʃuk'kjare] *vt*, **~rsi** *vr* (*uso reciproco*) to kiss and cuddle.

sbadataggine [zbada'taddʒine] *sf* (*sventatezza*) carelessness; (*azione*) oversight.

sbadato, a [zba'dato] *ag* careless.

sbadigliare [zbadiʎ'ʎare] *vi* to yawn.

sbadiglio [zba'diʎʎo] *sm* yawn; **fare uno ~** to yawn.

sbafare [zba'fare] *vt* (*mangiare*) to devour, wolf (down); (*fig: scroccare*) to sponge, scrounge.

sbafo ['zbafo] *sm*: **a ~** at somebody else's expense.

sbagliare [zbaʎ'ʎare] **1** *vt* (*gen*) to make a mistake in, get wrong; (*bersaglio*) to miss; **ha sbagliato tutto** he got everything wrong; **ha sbagliato tutto (nella vita)** he has made a mess of his life; **~ strada** to go the wrong way; **~ treno** to get *o* take the wrong train; **scusi, ho sbagliato numero** (*Telec*) sorry, I've got the wrong number; **per me ha sbagliato mestiere** in my opinion he is in the wrong job; **sbagliò porta** he opened the wrong door; **sbagli tattica** you're going the wrong way about it; **~ una mossa** (*al gioco*) to make a wrong move.

2 *vi* to make a mistake; **hai sbagliato a dirle tutto** it was a mistake to tell her everything; **ha sbagliato nel ricopiare il numero** he made a mistake in *o* when copying down the number;

potrei ~ ma... I might be mistaken but...; **ha sbagliato nei suoi confronti** he behaved badly towards her; **ho sbagliato di pochi centimetri** I miscalculated by a few centimetres, I was a few centimetres out (in my calculations).

3: **~rsi** *vr* (*fare errori*) to make a mistake (*o* mistakes); (*ingannarsi*) to be wrong; **si è sbagliato nel ricopiare** he made a mistake in *o* when copying; **non c'è da ~rsi** there can be no mistake.

sbagliato, a [zbaʎ'ʎato] *ag* (*gen*) wrong; (*compito*) full of mistakes; (*conclusione*) erroneous.

sbaglio ['zbaʎʎo] *sm* mistake, error; **fare uno ~** to make a mistake; **ci deve essere uno ~** there must be some mistake; **ha pagato per lo ~ commesso** he's paid for his mistake.

sbalestrare [zbales'trare] *vt* (*scagliare*) to fling, hurl.

sbalestrato, a [zbales'trato] *ag* (*persona: scombussolato*) unsettled.

sballare [zbal'lare] **1** *vt* (*merce*) to unpack. **2** *vi* (*aus essere*) **(a)** (*Carte*) to go out. **(b)** (*fam*) to talk nonsense.

sballato, a [zbal'lato] *ag* (*calcolo*) wrong; (*fam: ragionamento, persona*) screwy.

sballottare [zballot'tare] *vt* to toss (about), throw (about).

sbalordire [zbalor'dire] *vt* to stun, amaze, astound.

sbalorditivo, a [zbalordi'tivo] *ag* amazing, astounding.

sbalzare[1] [zbal'tsare] **1** *vt* (*scaraventare*) to throw; **è stato sbalzato a 10 metri di distanza** he was thrown 10 metres. **2** *vi* (*aus essere*) (*temperatura: alzarsi bruscamente*) to jump, rise; (: *abbassarsi bruscamente*) to fall, plummet.

sbalzare[2] [zbal'tsare] *vt* (*Arte*) to emboss.

sbalzo ['zbaltso] *sm* (*sussulto*) start; **procedere a ~i** (*macchina*) to jolt along; **uno ~ di temperatura** a sudden change in temperature.

sbancare[1] [zban'kare] *vt* (*nei giochi*) to break the bank; (*fig*) to ruin, bankrupt.

sbancare[2] [zban'kare] *vt* (*Edil*) to excavate.

sbandamento [zbanda'mento] *sm* (*di veicolo*) skid; (*Naut*) list; (*fig: di persona*) confusion; **ha avuto un periodo di ~** he went off the rails for a bit.

sbandare [zban'dare] **1** *vi* (*Aut*) to skid; (*Naut*) to list. **2:** **~rsi** *vr* (*folla*) to disperse; (*truppe*) to scatter; (*fig: famiglia*) to break up.

sbandata [zban'data] *sf* (*Aut*) skid; (*Naut*) list; **prendere una ~ per qn** (*fig*) to fall for sb.

sbandato, a [zban'dato] *sm/f* mixed-up person.

sbandierare [zbandje'rare] *vt* (*bandiere*) to wave; (*fig: ostentare*) to show off, flaunt.

sbaraccare [zbarak'kare] *vt* (*libri, piatti etc*) to clear (up); **sarà meglio ~** (*fam*) it's time we cleared out.

sbaragliare [zbaraʎ'ʎare] *vt* to rout.

sbaraglio [zba'raʎʎo] *sm*: **andare o buttarsi allo ~** (*soldati*) to throw o.s. into the fray; (*fig: rischiare*) to risk everything.

sbarazzare [zbarat'tsare] **1** *vt* to clear. **2:** **~rsi** *vr*: **~rsi di qn/qc** to get rid of sb/sth.

sbarazzino, a [zbarat'tsino] **1** *ag* impish, cheeky. **2** *sm* scamp, imp.

sbarbare [zbar'bare] *vt*, **~rsi** *vr* to shave.

sbarbatello [zbarba'tɛllo] *sm* novice, greenhorn.

sbarcare [zbar'kare] **1** *vt* (*merci*) to unload; (*passeggeri: da nave, aereo*) to disembark, land; (: *da autobus, macchina*) to put down. **2** *vi* (*aus essere*): **~ (da un aereo), ~ (da una nave)** to land, disembark; **~ (da un treno)** to get off (a train), alight (from a train).

sbarco, chi ['zbarko] *sm* (*vedi vb*) unloading;

disembarkation, landing; putting down; **allo** ~ on landing; **forza da** ~ *(Mil)* landing party; **testa di** ~ beachhead.

sbarra ['zbarra] *sf* **(a)** *(gen, Sport)* bar; *(di passaggio a livello)* barrier; *(di timone)* tiller; **dietro le** ~**e** *(fig: in prigione)* behind bars; **presentarsi alla** ~ *(Dir: in tribunale)* to appear in court. **(b)** *(Ortografia)* stroke.

sbarramento [zbarra'mento] *sm (di strada, passaggio etc)* barrier; *(diga)* dam, barrage; *(Mil)* barrage.

sbarrare [zbar'rare] *vt* **(a)** *(bloccare)* to block, bar; ~ **la strada a qn** *(anche fig)* to bar sb's way. **(b)** *(spalancare: occhi)* to open wide. **(c)** *(cancellare)* to cross out, strike out; ~ **un assegno** to cross a cheque.

sbarrato, a [zbar'rato] *ag* **(a)** *(porta)* barred; *(passaggio)* blocked, barred; *(strada)* blocked, obstructed. **(b)** *(occhi)* staring. **(c)** *(assegno)* crossed.

sbatacchiare [zbatak'kjare] **1** *vt (porta)* to slam, bang; *(ali)* to flap. **2** *vi* to bang.

sbattere ['zbattere] **1** *vt* **(a)** *(gen)* to beat; *(uova)* to beat, whisk; *(panna)* to whip; *(ali)* to beat, flap; *(porta)* to slam, bang; ~ **un ginocchio contro qc** to knock one's knee against sth; ~ **un pugno sul tavolo** to thump the table; ~ **la porta in faccia a qn** *(anche fig)* to slam the door in sb's face; **non sapevo dove** ~ **la testa** *(fig)* I didn't know which way to turn; ~ **la testa contro un muro** *(fig)* to hit one's head against a brick wall; **finché non ci sbatte la testa da solo non capirà ragione** he'll find out the hard way. **(b)** *(buttare)* to throw; ~ **qc per terra** to throw sth to the ground; ~ **qn fuori/in galera** to throw sb out/into prison; ~ **via** to throw away *o* out; **sbattilo pure lì** just throw it over there. **(c)** *(fam!: avere rapporti sessuali)* to fuck(*!*). **2** *vi* **(a)** *(porta, finestra)* to bang; *(vele)* to flap; ~ **contro qc** to knock against sth. **(b)** *(fam)*: **sbattersene** not to give a damn; **me ne sbatto! I** don't give a damn!

sbattuto, a [zbat'tuto] *ag* **(a)** *(uovo)* beaten. **(b)** *(fig: persona)* worn out; **avere un'aria** ~**a** to look worn out.

sbavare [zba'vare] **1** *vi* **(a)** *(gen)* to dribble. **(b)** *(colore)* to run; *(rossetto, inchiostro)* to smudge. **2** *vt*: ~ **qc** to dribble over sth. **3**: ~**rsi** *vr* to dribble down o.s.

sbavatura [zbava'tura] *sf (di persone)* dribbling; *(di lumache)* slime; *(di rossetto, vernice)* smear.

sbeccare [zbek'kare] *vt* to chip.

sbellicarsi [zbelli'karsi] *vr*: ~ **dalle risa** to split one's sides laughing.

sberla ['zberla] *sf* slap; **dare una** ~ **a qn** to slap *o* hit sb.

sberleffo [zber'leffo] *sm*: **fare uno** ~ **a qn** to make a face at sb; **fare gli** ~**i** to make faces, grimace.

sbiadire [zbja'dire] **1** *vi (aus essere)* to fade. **2** *vt* to (cause to) fade; **ricordi sbiaditi dal tempo** memories which have faded with time.

sbiadito, a [zbja'dito] *ag (scolorito)* faded; *(fig: stile)* colourless, dull.

sbiancare [zbjan'kare] **1** *vt* to whiten. **2** *vi (aus essere)*, ~**rsi** *vr (persona)*: ~ *o* ~**rsi in viso** to pale, blanch.

sbieco, chi ['zbjɛko] **1** *ag (muro)* at an angle; *(pavimento)* sloping, slanting; **tagliare una stoffa di** ~ to cut material on the bias; **guardare qn di** ~ *(fig)* to look askance at sb. **2** *sm (Cucito)* bias.

sbigottimento [zbigotti'mento] *sm* dismay, consternation.

sbigottire [zbigot'tire] **1** *vt* to dismay, dumbfound.

2 *vi (aus essere)*, ~**rsi** *vr* to be dismayed, be dumbfounded.

sbilanciare [zbilan'tʃare] **1** *vt* to throw off balance. **2**: ~**rsi** *vr* to lose one's balance, overbalance; *(fig: compromettersi)* to compromise o.s.

sbilancio [zbi'lantʃo] *sm (Econ)* deficit.

sbilenco, a, chi, che [zbi'lenko] *ag (persona)* crooked, misshapen; *(fig: idea, ragionamento)* twisted.

sbirciare [zbir'tʃare] *vt* to peep at.

sbirciata [zbir'tʃata] *sf*: **dare una** ~ **a qc** to glance at sth, have a look at sth.

sbirro ['zbirro] *sm (peg)* cop.

sbizzarrirsi [zbiddzar'rirsi] *vr (sfogare i propri desideri)* to indulge o.s.; *(fare pazzie)* to go wild; ~ **a fare qc** to indulge o.s. in doing sth.

sbloccare [zblok'kare] **1** *vt (gen)* to unblock; *(passaggio, strada)* to clear, unblock; *(affitti)* to free from controls; ~ **la situazione** to get things moving again. **2**: ~**rsi** *vr (gen)* to become unblocked; *(passaggio, strada)* to clear, become unblocked; **la situazione si è sbloccata** things are moving again.

sblocco, chi ['zblɔkko] *sm (vedi vt)* unblocking; clearing; **dopo lo** ~ **degli affitti** after rents were freed from controls.

sboccare [zbok'kare] **1** *vi (aus essere)*: ~ **in** *(fiume)* to flow into; *(strada)* to lead to; *(valle)* to open into; *(persona)* to emerge into. **2** *vt (rompere: vaso, brocca)* to chip.

sboccato, a [zbok'kato] *ag (fig: persona)* foulmouthed; *(: linguaggio)* coarse.

sbocciare [zbot'tʃare] *vi (aus essere) (fiori)* to bloom, flower; *(fig: nascere)* to blossom.

sbocco, chi ['zbokko] *sm* **(a)** *(di fiume)* mouth; *(di tubazione)* outlet; *(di strada)* end; **una strada senza** ~ a dead end; **siamo in una situazione senza** ~ *o* ~**chi** there's no way out of this for us. **(b)** *(Comm)* outlet.

sbocconcellare [zbokkontʃel'lare] *vt*: ~ **(qc)** to nibble (at sth).

sbollentare [zbollen'tare] *vt (Culin)* to parboil.

sbollire [zbol'lire] *vi (aus essere) (fig: calmarsi)* to cool (down).

sbolognare [zboloɲ'ɲare] *vt*: ~ **qc/qn** to get rid of sth/sb.

sbornia ['zbɔrnja] *sf (fam)*: **prendersi una** ~ to get plastered.

sborsare [zbor'sare] *vt* to fork out.

sbottare [zbot'tare] *vi (aus essere) (fig: persona)*: ~ **in una risata** to burst out laughing; **sono sbottato** I couldn't contain myself.

sbottonare [zbotto'nare] **1** *vt* to unbutton. **2**: ~**rsi** *vr* to undo one's buttons; *(fig: confessare)* to unburden o.s.

sbozzare [zbot'tsare] *vt (gen)* to sketch out; *(scultura)* to rough-hew.

sbracciarsi [zbrat'tʃarsi] *vr* to wave (one's arms about).

sbracciato, a [zbrat'tʃato] *ag (persona)* with bare arms; *(indumento: senza maniche)* sleeveless; *(: a maniche corte)* short-sleeved.

sbraitare [zbrai'tare] *vi* to shout, yell.

sbranare [zbra'nare] **1** *vt* to tear to pieces. **2**: ~**rsi** *vr (uso reciproco: anche fig)* to tear one another to pieces.

sbriciolare [zbritʃo'lare] *vt*, ~**rsi** *vr* to crumble.

sbrigare [zbri'gare] **1** *vt (lavoro, pratiche)* to deal with, get through; *(clienti)* to attend to, see to; ~ **le faccende domestiche** to do the housework; **se la sa** ~ **da solo** he can manage *o* do it by himself. **2**: ~**rsi** *vr (fare in fretta)* to hurry up, get a move on.

sbrigativo, a [zbriga'tivo] *ag (persona, modi)* quick, expeditious; *(: peg)* abrupt, brusque; **è un piatto ~** it's a quick dish.

sbrigliare [zbriʎ'ʎare] *vt (fig: fantasia)* to give free rein to.

sbrinamento [zbrina'mento] *sm* defrosting.

sbrinare [zbri'nare] *vt* to defrost.

sbrinatore [zbrina'tore] *sm* defroster.

sbrindellato, a [zbrindel'lato] *ag* tattered, in tatters.

sbrodolare [zbrodo'lare] **1** *vt* to stain, dirty. **2:** **~rsi** *vr* to stain o.s., dirty o.s.; **ti sei tutto sbrodolato** *(mangiando)* you've spilt food all down yourself.

sbrogliare [zbroʎ'ʎare] **1** *vt (filo, matassa)* to unravel; *(vele)* to unfurl; *(fig: problema)* to solve, find a solution to; **è riuscito a sbrogliarsela** he has managed to sort things out. **2:** **~rsi** *vr (fig: persona)* to disentangle o.s., free o.s.

sbronza ['zbrontsa] *sf (fam)* = **sbornia.**

sbronzarsi [zbron'tsarsi] *vr (fam)* to get sozzled.

sbronzo, a ['zbrontso] *ag (fam)* sozzled.

sbruffone, a [zbruf'fone] *sm/f* boaster, braggart.

sbucare [zbu'kare] *vi (aus essere):* **~ da** to pop out of, pop out from; **~ fuori** to pop out; **da dove sbuca quel libro?** where did that book spring from?

sbucciapatate [zbuttʃapa'tate] *sm inv* potato peeler.

sbucciare [zbut'tʃare] *vt (gen)* to peel; *(piselli)* to shell; **~rsi un ginocchio** to graze one's knee.

sbucciatura [zbuttʃa'tura] *sf* graze.

sbudellare [zbudel'lare] **1** *vt* to disembowel. **2:** **~rsi** *vr:* **~rsi dalle risate** to split one's sides laughing.

sbuffare [zbuf'fare] *vt (gen)* to puff; *(: con impazienza)* to snort, fume.

sbuffo ['zbuffo] *sm (di vento)* gust. **(b): maniche a ~** puff(ed) sleeves.

sbullonare [zbullo'nare] *vt* to unbolt.

scabbia ['skabbja] *sf (Med)* scabies *sg.*

scabro, a ['skabro] *ag (superficie)* rough; *(fig: conciso)* concise, terse.

scabrosità [skabrosi'ta] *sf (vedi ag)* thorniness; embarrassing nature; indecency.

scabroso, a [ska'broso] *ag (fig: difficile)* difficult, thorny; *(: imbarazzante)* embarrassing; *(sconcio)* indecent.

scacchiera [skak'kjɛra] *sf (Scacchi)* chessboard; *(Dama)* draughtsboard.

Scacchiere [skak'kjɛre] *sm (Brit)* Exchequer.

scacchiere [skak'kjɛre] *sm (Mil)* sector.

scacchista, i, e [skak'kista] *sm/f* chessplayer.

scacciacani [skattʃa'kani] *sm o f inv* pistol with blanks.

scacciapensieri [skattʃapen'sjɛri] *sm inv (Mus)* jew's-harp.

scacciare [skat'tʃare] *vt (mandar via)* to drive away, chase away; *(buttar fuori)* to throw out,turn out; *(fig: malinconia, noia)* to overcome; *(: sospetto, dubbio)* to dispel; **~ qn di casa** to turn sb out of the house.

scacco, chi ['skakko] *sm* **(a)** *(pezzo del gioco)* chess piece, chessman; *(riquadro)* square; **~chi** *pl* chess *sg;* **giocare a ~chi** to play chess; **dare ~ al re** to check the king; **~ matto** checkmate; **dare ~ matto a qn** *(anche fig)* to checkmate sb; **subire uno ~** *(fig: sconfitta)* to suffer a setback. **(b)** *(quadretto)* square, check; **tessuto a ~chi** check(ed) material.

scadente [ska'dɛnte] *ag (qualità)* poor; *(voto)* unsatisfactory; *(prodotto)* poor quality *attr; (film, libro)* poor.

scadenza [ska'dɛntsa] *sf* expiry; **data di ~** expiry date; **con ~ il 24 maggio** *(pagamento)* (which falls) due on the 24th of May; *(permesso, licenza)* expiring on the 24th of May; **a breve/lunga ~** *(progetto, piano)* short/long term.

scadere [ska'dere] *vi (aus essere)* **(a)** *(perdere valore, stima)* to decline, go down; **~ agli occhi di qn, ~ nella stima di qn** to go down in sb's estimation. **(b)** *(perdere validità: documento)* to expire; *(: cambiale, termine di pagamento)* to fall due.

scafandro [ska'fandro] *sm (di palombaro)* diving suit.

scaffalatura [skaffala'tura] *sf* shelving, shelves *pl.*

scaffale [skaf'fale] *sm (ripiano)* shelf; *(mobile)* set of shelves.

scafo ['skafo] *sm (Naut)* hull.

scagionare [skadʒo'nare] **1** *vt* to exonerate, free from blame. **2:** **~rsi** *vr* to exonerate o.s., free o.s. from blame.

scaglia ['skaʎʎa] *sf (Zool)* scale; *(di metallo, pietra)* splinter, chip.

scagliare [skaʎ'ʎare] **1** *vt* to throw, hurl, fling. **2:** **~rsi** *vr:* **~rsi contro qn, ~rsi addosso a qn** to fling o.s. at sb, hurl o.s. at sb.

scaglionamento [skaʎʎona'mento] *sm (Mil)* arrangement in echelons.

scaglionare [skaʎʎo'nare] *vt (truppe)* to echelon; *(pagamenti)* to space out, spread out.

scaglione [skaʎ'ʎone] *sm (Mil)* echelon; **a ~i** *(fig)* in groups.

scagnozzo [skaɲ'ɲottso] *sm (peg)* lackey, hanger-on.

scala ['skala] *sf* **(a)** *(gen)* stairs *pl,* staircase; **salire/scendere le ~e** to go upstairs/downstairs, go up/down the stairs; **fece le ~e in fretta** he hurried up (*o* down) the stairs; **una ~ di marmo** a marble staircase; **~ a chiocciola** spiral staircase; **~ mobile** escalator, moving staircase; **~ di servizio** backstairs; **~ di sicurezza** *(antincendio)* fire escape.

   (b) *(anche:* **~ a pioli)** ladder; **~ di corda** rope ladder; **~ a libretto** stepladder.

   (c) *(Econ, Fis, Mat, Geog etc)* scale; **~ mobile** *(Econ)* sliding scale; **~ mobile (dei salari)** index-linked pay scale; **~ termometrica** scale of temperatures; **~ di misure** system of weights and measures; **~ Celsius/Fahrenheit** Celsius/Fahrenheit scale; **riproduzione in ~** reproduction to scale; **in ~ di 1 a 100.000** on a scale of 1 cm to 1 km; **su larga/piccola ~** on a large/small scale; **su ~ nazionale/mondiale** on a national/worldwide scale.

   (d) *(Mus)* scale; **~ maggiore/minore** major/minor scale.

   (e) *(Carte)* straight; **~ reale** straight flush.

scalare [ska'lare] *vt (Alpinismo, muro)* to climb, scale. **(b)** *(ridurre):* **~ un debito** to pay off a debt in instalments; **questa somma vi viene scalata dal prezzo originale** this sum is deducted from the original price. **(c)** *(capelli)* to layer.

scalata [ska'lata] *sf* **(a)** *(azione)* scaling, climbing. **(b)** *(arrampicata,fig)* climb; **~ al potere** climb to power.

scalatore, trice [skala'tore] *sm/f* climber.

scalcagnato, a [skalkaɲ'ɲato] *ag (logoro)* worn; *(persona)* shabby.

scalciare [skal'tʃare] *vi* to kick.

scalcinato, a [skaltʃi'nato] *ag (fig peg)* shabby.

scaldabagno [skalda'baɲɲo] *sm* water-heater.

scaldaletto [skalda'letto] *sm* warming pan.

scaldare [skal'dare] **1** *vt (latte, stanza etc)* to heat (up); **~rsi le mani/i piedi** to warm one's hands/

feet; ~ **la sedia** *(fig)* to twiddle one's thumbs. **2:** ~**rsi** *vr* to warm up; *(fig: arrabbiarsi)* to get excited, get worked up; ~**rsi al fuoco** to warm o.s. by the fire.

scaldavivande [skaldavi'vande] *sm inv* dishwarmer.

scaldino [skal'dino] *sm (per mani)* hand-warmer; *(per piedi)* foot-warmer; *(per letto)* bed-warmer.

scalfire [skal'fire] *vt* to scratch; *(fig: sicurezza etc)* to undermine.

scalfittura [skalfit'tura] *sf* scratch.

scalinata [skali'nata] *sf (interna)* staircase, (flight of) stairs; *(esterna)* (flight of) steps.

scalino [ska'lino] *sm (gen, fig)* step; *(di scala a pioli)* rung.

scalmana [skal'mana] *sf* (hot) flush.

scalmanarsi [skalma'narsi] *vr (affaticarsi)* to rush about, rush around; *(agitarsi, darsi da fare)* to get all hot and bothered; *(arrabbiarsi)* to get excited, get steamed up; **non scalmanarti a cercarlo** don't wear yourself out trying to find him.

scalmanato, a [skalma'nato] *sm/f* hothead.

scalmiera [skal'mjɛra] *sf* rowlock, oarlock *(Am)*.

scalo ['skalo] *sm* **(a)** *(per varo)* slipway, slips *pl.* **(b)** *(fermata: Naut, Aer)* stop; **fare** ~ **a** *(Naut)* to call at, put in at; *(Aer)* to make a stopover at; **volo senza** ~ non-stop flight. **(c)** *(luogo: Naut)* port of call; *(: Aer)* stopover. **(d)** *(Ferr)*: ~ **merci** goods yard, freight yard.

scalogna [ska'loɲɲa] *sf (fam)* bad luck.

scalognato, a [skaloɲ'ɲato] *ag (fam)* unlucky.

scalogno [ska'loɲɲo] *sm (Bot)* shallot.

scaloppina [skalop'pina] *sf (Culin)* escalope.

scalpellare [skalpel'lare] *vt* to chisel.

scalpellino [skalpel'lino] *sm* stone-cutter.

scalpello [skal'pello] *sm (gen)* chisel; *(Med)* scalpel; *(per pozzi)* drill.

scalpiccio [skalpit'tʃio] *sm (rumore)* shuffling (noise).

scalpitare [skalpi'tare] *vi (cavallo)* to paw the ground; *(persona)* to stamp one's feet.

scalpitio [skalpi'tio] *sm (vedi vb)* pawing; stamping.

scalpo ['skalpo] *sm* scalp.

scalpore [skal'pore] *sm* sensation; **fare** *o* **suscitare** ~ to cause a sensation.

scaltrezza [skal'trettsa] *sf (vedi ag)* shrewdness, astuteness; slyness, cunning.

scaltrire [skal'trire] **1** *vt*: ~**qn** to sharpen sb's wits. **2:** ~**rsi** *vr* to become shrewder.

scaltro, a ['skaltro] *ag* shrewd, astute; *(peg)* sly, cunning.

scalzacane [skaltsa'kane] *sm* **(a)** *(malvestito)* down-and-out. **(b)** *(incompetente)* bungler, blunderer.

scalzare [skal'tsare] **1** *vt (pianta)* to bare the roots of; *(muro, fig)* to undermine. **2:** ~**rsi** *vr* to take off one's shoes and socks.

scalzo, a ['skaltso] *ag* barefoot(ed).

scambiare [skam'bjare] *vt* **(a)** *(confondere)*: ~ **qn/qc per** to take *o* mistake sb/sth for; **scusa, l'ho scambiato per il mio** sorry, I thought it was mine. **(b)** *(barattare)*: ~ **qc per** to exchange sth for; **si sono scambiati i cappelli** they swapped hats; ~ **due parole** to exchange a few words; ~**rsi gli auguri di Natale** to wish each other a Happy Christmas; **si scambiarono un'occhiata** they exchanged looks.

scambievole [skam'bjevole] *ag* mutual, reciprocal.

scambio ['skambjo] *sm* **(a)** *(di persone, cose)* exchange; **fare (uno)** ~ to make a swap. **(b)** *(Comm)* trade; **libero** ~ free trade; ~**i con**

l'estero foreign trade. **(c)** *(Ferr)* points *pl.*

scamiciato, a [skami'tʃato] **1** *ag* in one's shirt sleeves. **2** *sm* pinafore (dress).

scamosciato, a [skamoʃ'ʃato] *ag* suede.

scampagnata [skampaɲ'ɲata] *sf* trip to the country, outing to the country; **fare una** ~ to go on an outing to the country.

scampanare [skampa'nare] **1** *vi* to peal. **2** *vt (gonna)* to flare.

scampanato, a [skampa'nato] *ag* flared.

scampanellare [skampanel'lare] *vi* to ring loudly.

scampanellata [skampanel'lata] *sf* loud ringing.

scampanio [skampa'nio] *sm* peal.

scampare [skam'pare] **1** *vt (pericolo)* to escape; ~ **la morte** to escape death; **scamparla bella** to have a lucky *o* narrow escape; **Dio ci scampi e liberi!** God forbid! **2** *vi (aus essere)*: ~ **a** *(pericolo, morte)* to escape; **pochi scamparono alla strage** few escaped (from) the massacre; **pochi scamparono al disastro** few people were untouched *o* unaffected by the disaster.

scampo[1] ['skampo] *sm* escape, way out; **non c'è (via di)** ~ there's no way out.

scampo[2] ['skampo] *sm (Zool)* prawn.

scampolo ['skampolo] *sm* remnant.

scanalatura [skanala'tura] *sf* grooving; *(Archit)* fluting.

scandagliare [skandaʎ'ʎare] *vt (mare)* to sound, fathom; *(fig: indagare)* to sound out.

scandaglio [skan'daʎʎo] *sm (Naut: azione)* sounding, fathoming; *(: strumento)* sounding line.

scandalistico, a, ci, che [skanda'listiko] *ag (settimanale etc)* sensational.

scandalizzare [skandalid'dzare] **1** *vt* to scandalize, shock. **2:** ~**rsi** *vr* to be scandalized, be shocked.

scandalo ['skandalo] *sm* scandal; **il loro comportamento è motivo di** ~ their behaviour is scandalous; **dare** ~ to cause a scandal.

scandaloso, a [skanda'loso] *ag* scandalous, shocking, outrageous.

Scandinavia [skandi'navja] *sf* Scandinavia.

scandinavo, a [skandi'navo] *ag, sm/f* Scandinavian.

scandire [skan'dire] *vt (versi)* to scan; *(parole)* to articulate, pronounce clearly.

scannare [skan'nare] *vt* to butcher, slaughter.

scanno ['skanno] *sm* seat, bench.

scansafatiche [skansafa'tike] *sm/f inv* idler, loafer.

scansare [skan'sare] **1** *vt* **(a)** *(spostare)* to move, shift. **(b)** *(evitare: colpo)* to dodge; *(: pericolo)* to avoid. **2:** ~**rsi** *vr (spostarsi)* to get out of the way, move out of the way; *(: per evitare un colpo)* to dodge; *(ritirarsi)* to draw back.

scansia [skan'sia] *sf (ripiano)* shelf; *(mobile)* bookcase.

scanso ['skanso] *sm*: **a** ~ **di** in order to avoid, as a precaution against; **a** ~ **di equivoci** to avoid (any) misunderstanding.

scantinato [skanti'nato] *sm* basement.

scantonare [skanto'nare] *vi* **(a)** *(per non essere visto)* to duck round the corner. **(b)** *(fig)* to become irrelevant.

scanzonato, a [skantso'nato] *ag* easy-going.

scapaccione [skapat'tʃone] *sm* clout, slap; **dare uno** ~ **a qn** to clout sb; **prendere qn a** ~**i** to slap sb about.

scapestrato, a [skapes'trato] **1** *ag* loose-living, dissolute. **2** *sm/f* dissolute.

scapigliare [skapiʎ'ʎare] *vt*: ~ **qn** to dishevel sb's hair.

scapigliato, a [skapiʎ'ʎato] *ag* dishevelled; *(fig: scapestrato)* dissolute.

scapito ['skapito] *sm*: **a** ~ **di** to the detriment of.

scapola ['skapola] *sf (Anat)* shoulder blade.

scapolo ['skapolo] *sm* bachelor.

scappamento [skappa'mento] *sm (Aut)* exhaust; **tubo di** ~ exhaust pipe.

scappare [skap'pare] *vi (aus essere)* **(a)** *(gen)*: ~ **(di)** to escape (from); ~ **di casa** to run away from home; **scappar via** to run away, escape; ~ **all'estero** to flee the country; **scusa, devo** ~ I'm sorry, but I must dash; ~ **a gambe levate** to take to one's heels. **(b)** *(sfuggire)*: **mi è scappato di mano** it slipped out of my hands; **mi è scappato l'autobus** I missed the bus; **mi è scappato di mente** it has slipped my mind; **mi è scappato da ridere** I couldn't contain my laughter; **mi scappa la pipì** I'm bursting. **(c)**: **lasciarsi** ~ *(occasione, affare)* to miss, let go by; *(dettaglio)* to overlook; *(parola)* to let slip; *(prigioniero)* to let escape.

scappata [skap'pata] *sf (breve visita)*: **fare una** ~ **da qn** to call o drop o pop in and see sb; **farò una** ~ **a Parigi/a casa tua** I'll pop over to Paris/to your place; **faccio una** ~ **in centro** I'm just going to pop into town.

scappatella [skappa'tɛlla] *sf* escapade.

scappatoia [skappa'toja] *sf (gen)* way out; *(nella burocrazia)* loophole.

scappellotto [skappel'lɔtto] *sm* clout, slap; **dare uno** ~ **a qn** to clout sb.

scarabeo [skara'bɛo] *sm (Zool)* scarab (beetle).

scarabocchiare [skarabok'kjare] *vt* to scribble, doodle; *(scrivere svogliatamente)* to scribble off.

scarabocchio [skara'bɔkkjo] *sm (sgorbio)* scribble, scrawl; *(disegno)* doodle; *(fig peg: quadro)* daub; *(macchia d'inchiostro)* blot.

scarafaggio [skara'faddʒo] *sm (Zool)* cockroach.

scaramanzia [skaraman'tsia] *sf*: **per** ~ for luck.

scaramuccia, ce [skara'muttʃa] *sf* skirmish.

scaraventare [skaraven'tare] **1** *vt* to fling, hurl. **2**: ~**rsi** *vr*: ~**rsi contro qc/qn** to fling o.s. at sth/sb.

scarcerare [skartʃe'rare] *vt* to release (from prison).

scarcerazione [skartʃerat'tsjone] *sf* release (from prison).

scardinare [skardi'nare] *vt* to take off its hinges.

scarica, che ['skarika] *sf* **(a)** *(di arma)* shot; *(fig: di insulti)* flood; *(: di pugni, sassi)* hail; **una** ~ **di mitra** a burst of machine-gun fire. **(b)** *(Elettr)*: ~ **(elettrica)** discharge (of electricity).

scaricabarili [skarikaba'rili] *sm*: **fare a** ~ *(fig)* to blame each other.

scaricare [skari'kare] **1** *vt (merce, veicolo)* to unload; *(batteria)* to cause to run down, cause to go flat; *(fig: coscienza)* to unburden; *(sog: fabbrica, materiale di scarto)*: ~ **in** to discharge into; **il canale scarica i rifiuti in mare** the canal deposits the rubbish in the sea; ~ **un'arma** *(togliendo la carica)* to unload a gun; *(sparando)* to discharge a gun; ~ **le proprie responsabilità su qn** to off-load one's responsibilities onto sb; ~ **la colpa addosso a qn** to blame sb else; ~ **la tensione** *(fig: rilassarsi)* to unwind; *(: sfogarsi)* to let off steam.

2: ~**rsi** *vr (molla, orologio)* to wind down, stop; *(batteria)* to go flat; *(fig: persona)* to unwind; *(: sfogarsi)* to let off steam; **la batteria si è scaricata** the battery is flat; **il fulmine si scaricò sull'albero** the lightning struck the tree; ~**rsi di ogni responsabilità** to relieve o.s. of all responsibilities; **piangendo si è scaricata** she had a good cry and felt better for it.

scaricatore [skarika'tore] *sm*: ~ **di porto** docker.

scarico¹, a, chi, che ['skariko] *ag (fucile)* unloaded, empty; *(orologio)* wound down; *(batteria)* run down, flat.

scarico², chi ['skariko] *sm (di merci, materiali)* unloading; *(di immondizie)* dumping, tipping; *(: luogo)* rubbish dump; *(Tecn: deflusso)* draining; *(: dispositivo)* drain; ~ **del lavandino** waste outlet.

scarlattina [skarlat'tina] *sf* scarlet fever.

scarlatto, a [skar'latto] *ag, sm* scarlet.

scarmigliare [skarmiʎ'ʎare] **1** *vt* to dishevel. **2**: ~**rsi** *vr* to be dishevelled.

scarnificare [skarnifi'kare] *vt* to strip the flesh from.

scarno, a ['skarno] *ag (persona)* lean, bony; *(volto)* gaunt; *(mano)* thin, bony; *(fig: insufficiente)* meagre; *(: spoglio: stile)* bare.

scarpa ['skarpa] *sf* shoe; **un paio di** ~**e** a pair of shoes; ~**e di gomma** rubber shoes; ~**e da ginnastica** gym shoes, plimsolls; ~**e coi tacchi (alti)** high-heeled shoes; ~**e col tacco basso** low-heeled shoes; ~**e senza tacco** flat shoes; **fare le** ~**e a qn** *(fig)* to double-cross sb.

scarpata [skar'pata] *sf* escarpment.

scarpiera [skar'pjɛra] *sf* shoe rack.

scarpinata [skarpi'nata] *sf (fam)* trek; **abbiamo fatto una** ~ it was some trek.

scarpone [skar'pone] *sm* boot; ~**i da montagna** climbing boots; ~**i da sci** ski boots.

scarrozzare [skarrot'tsare] *vt* to drive around.

scarseggiare [skarsed'dʒare] *vi (viveri, risorse)* to be scarce; ~ **di qc** to lack sth, be short of sth.

scarsezza [skar'settsa] *sf* shortage, lack.

scarsità [skarsi'ta] *sf* shortage.

scarso, a ['skarso] *ag (raccolto)* poor, lean; *(risorse)* meagre; *(qualità)* poor; *(alunno, voto)* mediocre; **è un chilo/metro** ~ it's just under the kilo/metre; **ha dimostrato** ~**a maturità/intelligenza** he showed little maturity/intelligence.

scartabellare [skartabel'lare] *vt* to skim through, glance through.

scartafaccio [skarta'fattʃo] *sm* notebook.

scartamento [skarta'mento] *sm (Ferr)* gauge; **a** ~ **ridotto** narrow-gauge.

scartare¹ [skar'tare] *vt (regalo, caramella)* to unwrap.

scartare² [skar'tare] *vt (Carte)* to discard; *(fig: possibilità)* to reject.

scartare³ [skar'tare] **1** *vi (deviare)* to swerve; ~ **a sinistra** to swerve to the left. **2** *vt (Calcio)* to dodge (past).

scarto¹ [skar'to] *sm* **(a)** *(prodotto, oggetto scartato)* reject. **(b)** *(Carte)* discard.

scarto² ['skarto] *sm* **(a)** *(movimento brusco)* swerve; **fare uno** ~ to swerve. **(b)** *(differenza)* gap, difference.

scartocciare [skartot'tʃare] *vt (gen)* to unwrap; *(mais)* to husk.

scartoffie [skar'tɔffje] *sfpl (peg)* papers *pl*.

scassare [skas'sare] **1** *vt (fam: rompere)* to wreck, smash. **2**: ~**rsi** *vr (rompersi)* to be wrecked.

scassinare [skassi'nare] *vt* to force, break.

scassinatore, trice [skassina'tore] *sm/f (di case)* housebreaker, burglar; *(di banche)* bank robber; *(di casseforti)* safe-cracker.

scasso ['skasso] *sm (Dir)* breaking and entering; **furto con** ~ burglary.

scatenare [skate'nare] **1** *vt (reazione, rabbia)* to provoke; *(rivolta)* to spark off; *(guai)* to stir up. **2**: ~**rsi** *vr (temporale)* to break; *(rivolta)* to break out; *(persona)*: ~**rsi contro qn** to rage at sb.

scatenato, a [skate'nato] *ag* wild.

scatola ['skatola] **1** *sf (gen)* box; *(di latta)* tin, can; **cibo in** ~ tinned o canned food; **una** ~ **di sardine** a tin of sardines; **una** ~ **di cioccolatini** a box of chocolates; **comprare qc a** ~ **chiusa** to buy sth sight unseen; **accettare qc a** ~ **chiusa** to accept sth blindly; **avere le** ~**e piene (di qc/qn)** *(fam)* to be fed up to the back teeth (with sth/sb); **rompere le ~e a qn** *(fam)* to get on sb's nerves. **2: ~ di cartone** cardboard box; **~ cranica** cranium; **~ di fiammiferi** *(vuota)* matchbox; *(piena)* box of matches; **~ nera** *(Aer)* black box.

scatolame [skato'lame] *sm* tinned food; *(insieme di scatole)* tins *pl*, cans *pl*.

scattante [skat'tante] *ag* quick off the mark.

scattare [skat'tare] **1** *vi (aus* **essere)** *(molla)* to be released; *(grilletto, interruttore)* to spring back; *(serratura: aprirsi)* to click open; *(: chiudersi)* to click shut; **far ~** to release; **~ in piedi** to spring o leap to one's feet; **~ sull'attenti** to spring o leap to attention; **scatta per niente** *(si arrabbia)* he flies off the handle at the slightest provocation. **2** *vt (Fot)*: **~ una foto** to take a photograph.

scatto ['skatto] *sm* **(a)** *(congegno)* release; *(: di arma da fuoco)* trigger mechanism; *(rumore)* click; **~ automatico** automatic release; *(Fot)* (automatic) timer; **serratura a ~** spring lock; **ho sentito lo ~ della serratura** I heard the lock click. **(b)** *(Telec)* unit. **(c)** *(Sport)* spurt. **(d)** *(di persona)* jump, start; **muoversi a ~i** to move jerkily; **ha avuto uno ~ (d'ira)** he flew off the handle; **si alzò di ~** he sprang o leapt to his feet. **(e)** *(aumento)*: **~ di stipendio** increment; **~ d'anzianità** long service bonus.

scaturire [skatu'rire] *vi (aus* **essere)** *(liquido)*: **~ (da)** to well (out of), flow (from); *(fig: avere origine)* to derive (from).

scavalcare [skaval'kare] *vt (ostacolo: anche fig)* to pass *(o climb)* over; *(fig: concorrenti)* to overtake; *(: collega)* to be promoted over (the head of).

scavare [ska'vare] *vt (gen)* to dig; *(trincea, Archeol)* to dig, excavate; *(pozzo, galleria)* to bore; *(tronco, pietra: renderlo cavo)* to hollow (out); **~rsi la fossa** *(fig)* to dig one's own grave; **un volto scavato dalla stanchezza** a haggard face; **~ nell'animo di qn** to search sb's soul; **~ nel passato di qn** to dig into sb's past.

scavatore [skava'tore] *sm (macchina, persona)* digger.

scavatrice [skava'tritʃe] *sf (macchina)* excavator.

scavezzacollo [skavettsa'kɔllo] *sm* daredevil.

scavo ['skavo] *sm (gen)* excavation; **fare degli ~i in una zona** to excavate an area.

scazzottare [skattsot'tare] *(fam)* **1** *vt* to beat up, give a thrashing to. **2: ~rsi** *vr (uso reciproco)* to beat one another up.

scazzottata [skattsot'tata] *sf (fam)* fight, punch-up.

scegliere ['ʃeʎʎere] *vt (gen)* to choose; *(prodotto, candidato)* to select, choose; **~ di fare qc** to choose to do sth; **~ il campo** *(Sport)* to toss for ends.

sceicco, chi [ʃe'ikko] *sm* sheik.

scelleratezza [ʃellera'tettsa] *sf (qualità)* wickedness; *(azione)* wicked deed, crime.

scellerato, a [ʃelle'rato] **1** *ag* wicked. **2** *sm/f* villain.

scellino [ʃel'lino] *sm (Brit)* shilling; *(Austria)* schilling.

scelta ['ʃelta] *sf (gen)* choice; *(selezione)* selection, choice; **fare una ~** to make a choice, choose; **non avere ~** to have no choice o option; **potete avere frutta o formaggio a ~** you have the choice of fruit or cheese; **di prima ~** top grade o quality; **c'è un'ampia ~ di prodotti** there's a wide selection o choice of products.

scelto, a ['ʃelto] **1** *pp di* **scegliere. 2** *ag (gruppo)* carefully selected; *(frutta, verdura)* top-quality, choice; **brani ~i** selected passages; **una compagnia ~a** a distinguished company; **pubblico ~** select audience.

scemare [ʃe'mare] *vi (aus* **essere)** *(rumore, applausi, interesse)* to lessen; *(forze)* to decline; *(vento)* to drop, abate.

scemenza [ʃe'mentsa] *sf* stupidity; **dire ~e** to talk nonsense o rubbish; **ha fatto una ~** he behaved foolishly o stupidly; **è stata una ~** it was sheer stupidity.

scemo, a ['ʃemo] **1** *ag* stupid, foolish. **2** *sm/f* idiot, fool; **fare lo ~** to play the fool.

scempio ['ʃempjo] *sm (strage)* massacre, slaughter; *(deturpazione)* destruction; **fare ~ di qc** to destroy sth.

scena ['ʃena] *sf* **(a)** *(gen, Teatro, Cine)* scene; **nella prima ~** in the first scene, in scene one; **la ~ si svolge a Parigi** the action takes place in Paris, the scene is set in Paris; **cambiamento di ~** scene change; **una ~ di caccia** a hunting scene; **sulla ~ internazionale** on the international scene; **ho assistito a tutta la ~** I was present at o during the whole scene; **fare una ~** *(fig)* to make a scene; **fu una ~ orribile** it was a horrible sight; **ha fatto ~ muta** *(fig)* he didn't open his mouth. **(b)** *(palcoscenico)* stage; **entrare in ~** to come on stage; *(fig)* to come on the scene; **uscire di ~** to leave the stage; *(fig)* to leave the scene; **mettere in ~** *(personaggio)* to present on the stage; *(commedia)* to stage, direct.

scenario [ʃe'narjo] *sm (Teatro)* scenery, set; *(fig: sfondo)* backdrop.

scenata [ʃe'nata] *sf* row, scene; **fare una ~ (a qn)** to make a scene.

scendere ['ʃendere] **1** *vt (scale, sentiero)* to go (o come) down, descend.

2 *vi (aus* **essere)** **(a)** *(gen)* to go *(o come)* down, descend; *(fiume, torrente)* to flow down; *(strada)* to slope down, descend; *(aereo)* to come down, descend; **~ con l'ascensore** to go *(o come)* down in the lift; **~ in città** to go into town; **~ in strada** to go down into the street; **~ in piazza** *(folla, manifestanti)* to take to the streets; **~ a piedi/correndo** to walk/run down; **scendo ad aprirgli il portone** I'll go down and open the door for him; **scendo subito!** I'm just coming!; **siamo scesi in mezz'ora** *(da collina etc)* we got down in half an hour; **quando i Longobardi scesero in Italia** when the Longobards descended on Italy; **i capelli le scendevano sulle spalle** her hair fell to her shoulders; **~ a terra** *(sbarcare)* to go ashore; **~ ad un albergo** to put up o stay at a hotel.

(b): **~ da** *(macchina, treno)* to get out of; *(nave)* to disembark from, get off; *(aereo, autobus, bici)* to get off; **~ da cavallo** to dismount; **~ dal letto** to get out of bed; **~ dalle scale** to go down the stairs; **scendo alla prossima fermata** I'm getting off at the next stop; **scendi da quell'albero!** come down from that tree!; **l'acqua scendeva dal rubinetto** the water was coming o running out of the tap.

(c) *(prezzi, temperatura)* to fall, drop; *(livello)* to fall, drop, go down; *(marea)* to go out; *(notte, oscurità)* to fall; *(sole)* to go down; *(nebbia)* to come down.

scendiletto [ʃendi'letto] *sm inv* bedside rug.

sceneggiare [ʃened'dʒare] *vt* to dramatize.

sceneggiatore, trice [ʃeneddʒa'tore] *sm/f* scriptwriter.

sceneggiatura [ʃeneddʒa'tura] *sf (Teatro)* scenario; *(Cine)* screenplay, scenario.

scenico, a, ci, che ['ʃeniko] *ag* stage *attr*.

scenografia [ʃenogra'fia] *sf (Teatro)* stage design; *(Cine)* set design; *(elementi scenici)* scenery.

scenografico, a, ci, che [ʃeno'grafiko] *ag* stage *attr*, set *attr*.

scenografo, a [ʃe'nɔgrafo] *sm/f* set designer.

sceriffo [ʃe'riffo] *sm* sheriff.

scervellarsi [ʃervel'larsi] *vr*: ~ **(su qc)** to rack one's brains (over sth).

scervellato, a [ʃervel'lato] *sm/f* half-wit, idiot.

sceso, a ['ʃeso] *pp di* **scendere**.

scetticismo [ʃetti'tʃizmo] *sm* scepticism.

scettico, a, ci, che ['ʃettiko] **1** *ag* sceptical. **2** *sm/f* sceptic.

scettro ['ʃettro] *sm* sceptre.

scevro, a ['ʃevro] *ag (poet)*: ~ **di** free from, devoid of.

scheda ['skɛda] *sf (di schedario)* index card; *(di elezioni)* ballot paper; ~ **perforata** punch card.

schedare [ske'dare] *vt (scrivere su schede)* to card-index; *(Dir)* to put on record.

schedario [ske'darjo] *sm* card index; *(mobile)* filing cabinet.

schedato, a [ske'dato] **1** *ag* with a (police) record. **2** *sm/f* person with a (police) record.

schedina [ske'dina] *sf* pools coupon.

scheggia, ge ['skeddʒa] *sf (gen)* splinter, chip; *(di porcellana)* chip.

scheggiare [sked'dʒare] *vt*, ~**rsi** *vr (gen)* to splinter, chip; *(porcellana)* to chip.

scheggiatura [skeddʒa'tura] *sf (vedi vb)* **(a)** *(azione)* splintering; chipping. **(b)** *(punto scheggiato)* chip.

scheletrico, a, ci, che [ske'lɛtriko] *ag* skeleton-like.

scheletrito, a [skele'trito] *ag (persona)* skeleton-like, all skin and bone; *(ramo, stile)* bare.

scheletro ['skɛletro] *sm (Anat)* skeleton; *(fig: struttura)* frame, framework; *(: di trama)* outline; **essere ridotto a uno** ~ to be reduced to skin and bone.

schema, i ['skɛma] *sm* **(a)** *(gen)* outline; *(diagramma)* diagram, sketch; ~ **riassuntivo** outline of the main points; ~ **di legge** bill. **(b)** *(fig: modello)*: **ribellarsi agli** ~**i** to rebel against traditional values; **secondo gli** ~**i tradizionali** in accordance with traditional values.

schematico, a, ci, che [ske'matiko] *ag* schematic.

schematizzare [skematid'dzare] *vt* to schematize.

scherma ['skɛrma] *sf (sport)* fencing; **tirare di** ~ to fence.

schermaglia [sker'maʎʎa] *sf (fig)* skirmish.

schermare [sker'mare] *vt* to screen.

schermire [sker'mire] **1** *vt* to protect, shield. **2**: ~**rsi** *vr* to defend o.s., protect o.s.

schermitore, trice [skermi'tore] *sm/f (Sport)* fencer.

schermo ['skermo] *sm (gen)* screen; **il piccolo/grande** ~ *(TV/Cine)* the small/large screen; **divo dello** ~ screen star; **farsi** ~ **con la mano** *(per proteggersi dalla luce)* to shield one's eyes with one's hand.

schermografia [skermogra'fia] *sf* X-rays *pl*.

schermografico, a, ci, che [skermo'grafiko] *ag* X-ray *attr*.

schernire [sker'nire] *vt* to mock, sneer at.

scherno ['skerno] *sm* scorn; **farsi** ~ **di** to sneer at; **essere oggetto di** ~ to be a laughing stock; **di** ~ *(parole)* scornful, sneering; *(gesto)* scornful.

scherzare [sker'tsare] *vi (gen)* to joke; **stavo scherzando** I was only joking o kidding; **è meglio non** ~ **su queste cose** it's better not to joke about these things; **quello è un tipo che non scherza** he is not a man to be trifled with; **c'è poco da** ~! it's no laughing matter!, it's no joke!; ~ **con i sentimenti altrui** to trifle with other people's feelings; **non** ~ **col fuoco!** *(fig)* you shouldn't play with fire!

scherzo ['skertso] *sm (gen)* joke; *(burla)* (practical) joke, prank; **fare uno** ~ **a qn** to play a (practical) joke o prank o trick on sb; **per** ~ as a joke, for a laugh, for fun; **fare un brutto** ~ **a qn** to play a nasty trick on sb; **neppure per** ~ not even in fun; **non sa stare allo** ~ he can't take a joke; ~**i a parte** seriously, joking apart; **...e niente** ~**i!** ...and no funny business!; **uno** ~ **da prete** a dirty trick; **è uno** ~! *(facile)* it's child's play!; ~**i di luce** effects of the light; ~**i d'acqua** waterworks.

scherzoso, a [sker'tsoso] *ag (tono, gesto)* playful; *(osservazione)* facetious; **è un tipo** ~ he likes o is fond of a joke.

schiaccianoci [skjattʃa'notʃi] *sm inv* nutcracker.

schiacciante [skjat'tʃante] *ag* overwhelming.

schiacciapatate [skjattʃapa'tate] *sm inv* potato masher.

schiacciare [skjat'tʃare] **1** *vt* **(a)** *(gen)* to squash, crush; *(patate)* to mash; *(aglio)* to crush; *(noce)* to crack; *(mozzicone)* to stub out; ~ **la palla** *(Tennis etc)* to smash the ball; ~ **un sonnellino** to take a nap; ~**rsi un dito nella porta** to shut one's finger in the door. **(b)** *(pulsante)* to press; *(pedale)* to stand on. **(c)** *(fig: opposizione, nemico)* to crush; *(: squadra avversaria)* to hammer; **quella prova l'ha schiacciato** that piece of evidence did for o nailed him; **era schiacciato da un senso di colpa** he was weighed down by feelings of guilt. **2**: ~**rsi** *vr* to get squashed, get crushed.

schiacciasassi [skjattʃa'sassi] *sm inv* steamroller.

schiacciata [skjat'tʃata] *sf (Tennis etc)* smash.

schiacciato, a [skjat'tʃato] *ag (naso)* flat; **ha una forma** ~**a** it's flat.

schiaffare [skjaf'fare] **1** *vt* to throw, chuck; **lo hanno schiaffato dentro** *(fam: in prigione)* they threw him in the cooler, they put him away. **2**: ~**rsi** *vr* to throw o.s.

schiaffeggiare [skjaffed'dʒare] *vt* to smack, slap.

schiaffo ['skjaffo] *sm* slap (in the face); **dare uno** ~ **a qn** to slap sb; **prendere qn a** ~**i** to slap sb's face; **uno** ~ **morale** a slap in the face, a rebuff; **avere una faccia da** ~**i** to look impudent.

schiamazzare [skjamat'tsare] *vi (galline, oche)* to squawk, cackle; *(fig: persone)* to make a din, make a racket.

schiamazzo [skja'mattso] *sm (fig: chiasso)* din, racket.

schiantare [skjan'tare] **1** *vt (spezzare)* to break; **il fulmine ha schiantato l'albero** the lightning split the tree. **2**: ~**rsi** *vr (macchina)*: ~**rsi contro** to crash into; *(aereo)*: ~**rsi al suolo** to crash (to the ground).

schianto ['skjanto] *sm (rumore)* crash; **di** ~ *(improvvisamente)* all of a sudden; **essere uno** ~ *(fig fam: bello)* to be a smasher, be fantastic.

schiappa ['skjappa] *sf*: **essere una** ~ **in qc** to be a washout at sth.

schiarimento [skjari'mento] *sm (del cielo)* clearing up, brightening; *(fig: delucidazione)* clarification, explanation.

schiarire [skja'rire] **1** *vt (gen)* to lighten; *(Fot)* to make brighter; *(tende, tessuto: far sbiadire)* to fade; ~**rsi la gola** to clear one's throat. **2** *vi (aus essere)*, ~**rsi** *vr (cielo, tempo)* to clear up; *(colore)* to become lighter; *(: sbiadire)* to fade.

schiarita [skja'rita] *sf (Meteor)* bright spell; *(fig)* improvement, turn for the better.

schiattare [skjat'tare] *vi (aus essere)* to burst; ~ **d'invidia** to be green with envy; ~ **di rabbia** to be beside o.s. with rage.

schiavismo [skja'vizmo] *sm* slavery; *(Pol)* support of slavery, anti-abolitionism.

schiavista, i, e [skja'vista] **1** *ag* slave *attr*. **2** *sm/f* *(trafficante)* slave trader, slaver; *(Pol)* supporter of slavery, anti-abolitionist; *(fig)* slave driver.

schiavitù [skjavi'tu] *sf* slavery; **ridurre in ~ to** subject, subjugate.

schiavo, a ['skjavo] **1** *ag* enslaved; **essere ~ delle proprie abitudini** to be a slave to habit. **2** *sm/f* slave.

schiena ['skjɛna] *sf* back; **soffrire di mal di ~ to** have a bad back; **avere mal di ~, avere la ~ a pezzi** to have backache, have a pain in one's back; **avere la ~ curva** *(con le spalle curve)* to be round-shouldered; *(con la spina dorsale curva)* to have a stoop; **voltare la ~ a qn** to turn one's back on sb; **rompersi la ~** to break one's back; *(fig: lavorare sodo)* to work one's fingers to the bone; **visto di ~** seen from behind *o* from the back; **a ~ di mulo** *(ponte)* humpback; *(strada)* steeply cambered.

schienale [skje'nale] *sm* **(a)** *(di poltrona, sedia)* back. **(b)** *(di animale macellato)* saddle.

schiera ['skjɛra] *sf* *(Mil: linea)* rank; **le ~e dei nemici** the enemy forces; **una ~ di persone a** crowd of people; **arrivarono a ~e** they arrived in their hundreds.

schieramento [skjera'mento] *sm* *(Mil)* (rank) formation; *(Sport)* formation; *(fig)* alliance.

schierare [skje'rare] **1** *vt* *(Mil)* to draw up. **2: ~rsi** *vr* *(Mil)* to draw up; *(fig):* **~rsi con** *o* **dalla parte di/contro qn** to side with/against sb.

schiettezza [skjet'tettsa] *sf* *(fig)* frankness, straightforwardness.

schietto, a ['skjetto] *ag* *(fig)* frank, straightforward.

schifare [ski'fare] **1** *vt* to disgust. **2: ~rsi** *vr* to be disgusted.

schifezza [ski'fettsa] *sf:* **essere una ~** *(cibo, bibita etc)* to be disgusting; *(film, libro)* to be dreadful; **mangia un sacco di ~e** he eats a lot of rubbish.

schifiltoso, a [skifil'toso] *ag* fussy, difficult; **fare lo ~** to be fussy.

schifo ['skifo] *sm* *(sensazione)* disgust; **è uno ~!** it's disgusting!; **fare ~** *(cibo, insetto)* to be disgusting; *(libro, film)* to be dreadful *o* awful; **mi fai ~** you make me sick; **la nostra squadra ha fatto ~** our team was useless.

schifoso, a [ski'foso] *ag* *(che fa ribrezzo)* disgusting; *(pessimo)* dreadful, awful; **hai avuto una fortuna ~a** you've been terribly lucky.

schioccare [skjok'kare] *vt* *(frusta)* to crack; *(dita)* to snap, click; *(lingua)* to click; *(labbra)* to smack; **le schioccò un bacio** he gave her a smacker *(fam)*.

schiocco, chi ['skjɔkko] *sm* *(di frusta)* crack; *(di dita)* snap, click; *(di lingua)* click; *(di labbra)* smack.

schiodare [skjo'dare] *vt* to unnail.

schioppettata [skjoppet'tata] *sf* gunshot.

schioppo ['skjɔppo] *sm* rifle, gun; **essere a un tiro di ~ da** to be a stone's throw from.

schiudere ['skjudere] **1** *vt* to open. **2: ~rsi** *vr* *(fiore)* to open, come out.

schiuma ['skjuma] *sf* *(gen)* foam; *(di bevande)* froth; **avere la ~ alla bocca** *(fig: arrabbiato)* to be foaming at the mouth.

schiumaiola [skjuma'jɔla] *sf* *(Culin)* skimmer.

schiumare [skju'mare] *vt* to skim.

schiumoso, a [skju'moso] *ag* foamy, frothy.

schiuso, a ['skjuso] *pp di* **schiudere**.

schivare [ski'vare] *vt* *(colpo, proiettile)* to dodge; *(persona, pericolo)* to avoid; *(domanda)* to evade.

schivo, a ['skivo] *ag* *(ritroso)* reserved; *(timido)* shy.

schizofrenia [skiddzofre'nia] *sf* schizophrenia.

schizofrenico, a, ci, che [skiddzo'frɛniko] *ag, sm/f* schizophrenic.

schizzare [skit'tsare] **1** *vt* **(a)** *(gen)* to squirt; *(inzuppare)* to splash; *(macchiare)* to spatter; **mi ha schizzato d'acqua** he splashed water over me, he splashed me with water; **ha schizzato inchiostro sulla tovaglia** he spattered ink on the tablecloth, he spattered the tablecloth with ink. **(b)** *(Disegno)* to sketch. **2** *vi* *(aus essere)* *(liquido)* to squirt; *(: con violenza)* to gush, spurt; **~ via** *(animale, persona)* to dart away; *(macchina, moto)* to accelerate away; **~ fuori** *(persona)* to dash out; **~ fuori dal letto** to leap *o* jump out of bed; **gli occhi gli schizzarono dalle orbite** *(fig)* his eyes nearly popped out of his head.

schizzinoso, a [skittsi'noso] **1** *ag* fussy, difficult. **2** *sm/f* fussy person, difficult person; **non fare lo ~!** don't be so fussy!

schizzo ['skittso] *sm* **(a)** *(di liquido)* squirt, splash; *(macchia)* stain, spot. **(b)** *(abbozzo)* sketch.

sci [ʃi] *sm inv* *(Sport: attività)* skiing; *(: attrezzo)* ski; **un paio di ~** a pair of skis; **fare dello ~** to ski; **~ nautico** water-skiing; **~ di fondo** cross-country skiing.

scia ['ʃia] *sf* *(di imbarcazione)* wake; *(fig: di fumo, profumo etc)* trail.

scià [ʃa] *sm inv* shah.

sciabola ['ʃabola] *sf* sabre.

sciabolata [ʃabo'lata] *sf* sabre cut.

sciabordio [ʃabor'dio] *sf* lapping.

sciacallo [ʃa'kallo] *sm* *(Zool)* jackal; *(fig peg: profittatore)* shark, profiteer; *(: ladro)* looter.

sciacquare [ʃak'kware] *vt* *(mani, capelli)* to rinse; *(panni)* to rinse (out); **~rsi la bocca** to rinse one's mouth.

sciacquatura [ʃakkwa'tura] *sf* *(azione)* rinsing; *(acqua)* rinsing water; *(: di piatti, anche peg)* dishwater.

sciacquo ['ʃakkwo] *sm* *(azione)* rinsing of the mouth; *(prodotto)* mouthwash; **fare degli ~i** to rinse one's mouth (with mouthwash).

sciagura [ʃa'gura] *sf* disaster, calamity; **una ~ aerea** an air disaster.

sciagurato, a [ʃagu'rato] **1** *ag* wretched. **2** *sm/f* wretch.

scialacquare [ʃalak'kware] *vt* to squander.

scialacquatore, trice [ʃalakkwa'tore] *sm/f* squanderer.

scialare [ʃa'lare] *vi* to spend money extravagantly; **c'è poco da ~** there's little money to spare.

scialbo, a ['ʃalbo] *ag* pale, dull; *(fig: persona)* dull, colourless.

scialle ['ʃalle] *sm* shawl.

scialo ['ʃalo] *sm* squandering, waste; **fare ~ di qc** to squander sth (away).

scialuppa [ʃa'luppa] *sf* *(Naut)* sloop; **~ di salvataggio** lifeboat.

sciamare [ʃa'mare] *vi* to swarm.

sciame ['ʃame] *sm* swarm; *(fig: di persone)* crowd, swarm.

sciancato, a [ʃan'kato] *ag* *(persona)* crippled, lame; *(fig: mobile)* rickety.

sciangai [ʃan'gai] *sm* *(gioco)* pick-up-sticks *sg*.

sciarada [ʃa'rada] *sf* charades *pl*.

sciare [ʃi'are] *vi* to ski; **andare a ~** to go skiing.

sciarpa ['ʃarpa] *sf* scarf.

sciatica ['ʃatika] *sf* *(Med)* sciatica.

sciatico, a, ci, che ['ʃatiko] *ag* *(Med)* sciatic.

sciatore, trice [ʃia'tore] *sm/f* skier.

sciattezza [ʃat'tettsa] *sf* slovenliness.

sciatto, a ['ʃatto] *ag* *(persona)* slovenly, unkempt; *(lavoro)* sloppy.

sciattone, a [ʃat'tone] *sm/f* sloven.

scibile ['ʃibile] *sm* knowledge.

sciccheria [ʃikke'ria] *sf* stylishness, chic; **che ~!** how chic!; **questo vestito è una ~** this dress is very chic.

scientifico, a, ci, che [ʃen'tifiko] *ag (gen)* scientific; *(materia, insegnamento)* science *attr;* **la (polizia)** ~**a** the forensic department.

scienza ['ʃɛntsa] *sf* **(a)** *(gen)* science; ~**e naturali/ occulte** natural/occult sciences; ~**e** *(Scol)* science *sg;* ~**e politiche** political science. **(b)** *(conoscenza)* knowledge, learning.

scienziato, a [ʃen'tsjato] *sm/f* scientist.

sciistico, a, ci, che [ʃi'istiko] *ag* skiing *attr.*

scimmia ['ʃimmja] *sf (Zool)* monkey; *(: più grande)* ape; *(fig: persona brutta)* horror; **avere la ~** *(fam: dipendenza da droga)* to have a monkey on one's back.

scimmiesco, a, schi, sche [ʃim'mjesko] *ag* monkey-like, ape-like.

scimmiottare [ʃimmjot'tare] *vt (beffeggiare)* to mock, make fun of; *(imitare)* to mimic, ape.

scimpanzé [ʃimpan'tse] *sm inv* chimpanzee.

scimunito, a [ʃimu'nito] **1** *ag* idiotic, stupid. **2** *sm/f* fool, idiot.

scindere ['ʃindere] **1** *vt* to split (up), divide. **2:** ~**rsi** *vr* to split up, break up; ~**rsi in** to split into.

scintilla [ʃin'tilla] *sf (anche fig)* spark; **fare ~e** to give off sparks, spark.

scintillare [ʃintil'lare] *vi* to give off sparks; *(fig)* to sparkle, glitter; **gli occhi le scintillavano di gioia** her eyes were sparkling with joy.

scintillio [ʃintil'lio] *sm* sparkling, glittering.

scioccare [ʃok'kare] *vt* to shock.

sciocchezza [ʃok'kettsa] *sf (qualità)* foolishness, silliness; **fare una ~** to do something silly; **è stata una ~** it was really foolish; **per me ha fatto una ~** I think it was very foolish *o* silly of him to do that; **ha detto un sacco di ~e** he talked a load of nonsense; **l'ho pagato una ~** I hardly paid anything for it; **è solo una ~** *(regalo)* it's only a trifle; ~**e!** rubbish!

sciocco, a, chi, che [ʃ'ɔkko] **1** *ag* silly, foolish. **2** *sm/f* fool.

sciogliere ['ʃɔʎʎere] **1** *vt* **(a)** *(liquefare)* to melt; *(nell'acqua: zucchero etc)* to dissolve; *(neve)* to melt, thaw; ~ **il ghiaccio** *(fig)* to break the ice. **(b)** *(disfare: nodo)* to undo, untie; *(: capelli)* to loosen. **(c)** *(slegare: persona, animale)* to set free, release; *(fig: persona: da obbligo)* to absolve, release; *(: contratto)* to cancel, annul; *(: parlamento, matrimonio)* to dissolve; *(: riunione)* to break up, bring to an end; *(: società)* to dissolve, wind up; ~ **le vele** *(Naut)* to set sail; ~ **i muscoli** to limber up; **(far) ~ la lingua a qn** to loosen sb's tongue; ~ **un mistero** to solve *o* unravel a mystery.

2: ~**rsi** *vr* **(a)** *(vedi vt* a*)* to melt; to dissolve; to thaw; **questa carne si scioglie in bocca** this meat melts in the mouth; ~**rsi in lacrime** to burst into tears. **(b)** *(liberarsi)* to free o.s., release o.s.; ~**rsi dai legami** *(fig)* to free o.s. from all ties. **(c)** *(assemblea, corteo, duo)* to break up.

scioltezza [ʃol'tettsa] *sf (agilità)* agility, nimbleness; *(disinvoltura)* ease, smoothness; *(: nel parlare)* fluency, ease.

sciolto, a [ʃ'ɔlto] **1** *pp di* **sciogliere. 2** *ag* **(a)** *(persona: agile)* agile, nimble; *(: disinvolto)* easygoing; **essere ~ nei movimenti** to be supple; **avere la lingua ~a** to have the gift of the gab. **(b)** *(Comm: sfuso)* loose.

scioperante [ʃope'rante] **1** *ag* on strike. **2** *sm/f* striker.

scioperare [ʃope'rare] *vi (fare sciopero)* to strike; *(entrare in sciopero)* to go on strike.

scioperato, a [ʃope'rato] **1** *ag* idle, lazy. **2** *sm/f* idler, loafer.

sciopero ['ʃopero] *sm* strike; **essere in ~, fare ~** to be on strike; **entrare in ~** to go on *o* come out on strike; ~ **bianco** work-to-rule; ~ **della fame** hunger strike; ~ **selvaggio** = wildcat strike; ~ **a singhiozzo** on-off strike; ~ **di solidarietà** sympathy strike.

sciorinare [ʃori'nare] *vt* **(a)** *(ostentare)* to show off, display. **(b)** *(dire con disinvoltura: consigli, citazioni)* to rattle off; ~ **bugie** to tell one lie after another.

sciovia [ʃio'via] *sf* ski lift.

sciovinismo [ʃovi'nizmo] *sm* chauvinism.

sciovinista, i, e [ʃovi'nista] *sm/f* chauvinist.

sciovinistico, a, ci, che [ʃovi'nistiko] *ag* chauvinistic.

scipito, a [ʃi'pito] *ag* insipid.

scippare [ʃip'pare] *vt:* ~ **qn** to snatch sb's bag.

scippatore [ʃippa'tore] *sm* bag-snatcher.

scippo ['ʃippo] *sm* bag-snatching.

scirocco [ʃi'rɔkko] *sm* sirocco.

sciroppare [ʃirop'pare] *vt (frutta)* to put in syrup; ~**rsi qc/qn** *(fig fam)* to put up with sth/sb.

sciroppato, a [ʃirop'pato] *ag* in syrup.

sciroppo [ʃi'rɔppo] *sm* syrup; ~ **per la tosse** cough syrup, cough mixture.

sciropposo, a [ʃirop'poso] *ag* syrupy.

scisma, i ['ʃizma] *sm (Rel, Pol)* schism.

scismatico, a, ci, che [ʃiz'matiko] *ag, sm* schismatic.

scissione [ʃis'sjone] *sf (Fis, Bio)* fission; *(di gruppo, partito)* splitting (up), division.

scisso, a ['ʃisso] *pp di* **scindere.**

sciupare [ʃu'pare] **1** *vt* **(a)** *(rovinare)* to ruin, spoil. **(b)** *(sprecare: denaro)* to waste, throw away; *(: occasione)* to miss. **2:** ~**rsi** *vr (rovinarsi)* to get ruined, get spoiled; **l'ho vista molto sciupata** she looked very run down when I saw her.

scivolare [ʃivo'lare] *vi (aus essere) (cadere)* to slip; ~ **sul ghiaccio** *(persona)* to slip on the ice; *(: per gioco)* to slide on the ice; *(: macchina)* to skid on the ice; **è scivolato giù dalle scale** he slipped and fell down the stairs; **attenta, si scivola** be careful, it's slippery; **il vaso gli scivolò dalle mani** the vase slipped out of his hands; **scivolò via non visto** he slipped away unseen; **l'uomo scivolò silenziosamente nella stanza** the man slipped silently into the room; **gli fece ~ il biglietto in tasca** he slipped the note into his pocket; ~ **nel ridicolo** to lapse into absurdity.

scivolata [ʃivo'lata] *sf (anche Aer)* slip; **fare una ~** to slip.

scivolo ['ʃivolo] *sm* slide; *(Tecn)* chute.

scivolone [ʃivo'lone] *sm* tumble, fall; **fare uno ~** to take a tumble.

scivoloso, a [ʃivo'loso] *ag* slippery.

scisso, a ['ʃisso] *pp di* **scindere.**

sclerosi [skle'rɔzi] *sf* sclerosis.

scoccare [skok'kare] **1** *vt* **(a)** *(freccia)* to shoot. **(b)** *(ore)* **l'orologio scoccò le 8** the clock struck 8. **2** *vi (aus essere)* **(a)** *(freccia)* to shoot out. **(b)** *(ore)* to strike; **scoccavano le 11** it was striking 11.

scocciare [skot'tʃare] **1** *vt* to annoy; **mi hai scocciato** *(stufato)* I'm fed up with you; *(seccato)* I'm annoyed with you; **se non ti scoccia** if it doesn't bother you; **ti scoccia se...?** do you mind if...?; **e ancora faceva lo scocciato** and he still wasn't happy. **2:** ~**rsi** *vr (stufarsi)* to get fed up; *(seccarsi)* to get annoyed.

scocciatore, trice [skottʃa'tore] *sm/f* nuisance, pest *(fam)*.

scocciatura [skottʃa'tura] *sf* nuisance, bore; **che ~!** what a nuisance!

scodella [sko'dɛlla] *sf (ciotola)* bowl; *(piatto fondo)* soup plate.

scodellare [skodel'lare] *vt* to dish out, dish up.

scodinzolare [skodintso'lare] *vi (cane)* to wag its tail.

scogliera [skoʎ'ʎɛra] *sf* rocks *pl*, reef; *(rupe)* cliff.

scoglio ['skɔʎʎo] *sm* rock; *(fig: ostacolo)* difficulty, stumbling block.

scoglioso, a [skoʎ'ʎoso] *ag* rocky.

scoiattolo [sko'jattolo] *sm (Zool)* squirrel; *(fig):* **agile come uno ~** agile as a monkey.

scolapasta [skola'pasta] *sm inv* colander.

scolapiatti [skola'pjatti] *sm inv* draining board; *(rastrelliera)* plate rack.

scolare [sko'lare] **1** *vt* to drain; **si è scolato una bottiglia!** he's drained *o* downed a bottle! **2** *vi (aus essere)* to drip.

scolaresca, sche [skola'reska] *sf* schoolchildren *pl*, pupils *pl*.

scolaro [sko'laro] *sm/f* schoolboy/girl, pupil; *(discepolo)* disciple, follower.

scolastico, a, ci, che [sko'lastiko] *ag (gen)* scholastic; *(libro, anno, divisa)* school *attr*; *(peg)* schoolish.

scoliosi [sko'ljɔzi] *sf (Med)* scoliosis.

scollacciato, a [skollat'tʃato] *ag (vestito)* low-cut, with a low neckline; *(donna)* in a low-necked dress *(o blouse etc)*.

scollare [skol'lare] **1** *vt* to unstick, unglue. **2:** **~rsi** *vr* to come unstuck, come off.

scollato, a [skol'lato] *ag (vestito)* low-cut, low-necked; *(donna)* wearing a low-cut dress *(o blouse etc)*.

scollatura [skolla'tura] *sf*, **scollo** ['skɔllo] *sm* neckline, neck.

scolo ['skolo] *sm* **(a)** *(condotto)* drainage; *(sbocco)* drain; **canale** *m* **di ~** drain; **tubo di ~** drainpipe. **(b)** *(acqua)* waste water.

scolorare [skolo'rare], **scolorire** [skolo'rire] **1** *vt* to discolour; *(sbiadire)* to fade. **2: ~rsi** *vr (vedi vt)* to become discoloured; to fade, become faded.

scolpare [skol'pare] **1** *vt* to free from blame, exonerate. **2: ~rsi** *vr* to free o.s. from blame, exonerate o.s.

scolpire [skol'pire] *vt (pietra)* to sculpt, sculpture; *(legno)* to carve; *(metallo)* to engrave; **quelle parole rimasero scolpite nella sua memoria** those words remained impressed on his memory.

scombinare [skombi'nare] *vt (scomporre)* to mess up, ruin; *(mandare a monte)* to break off, cancel.

scombinato, a [skombi'nato] *ag* confused, muddled.

scombussolare [skombusso'lare] *vt (persona)* to upset, disturb; *(piani)* to upset, mess up.

scommessa [skom'messa] *sf (azione)* bet; *(somma)* bet, stake; **fare una ~** to bet.

scommesso, a [skom'messo] *pp di* **scommettere.**

scommettere [skom'mettere] *vt* to bet; **~ 10.000 lire** to bet *o* wager 10,000 lire; **~ su un cavallo** to bet on a horse; **scommettiamo?** do you want to take a bet on it?; **non ci scommetterei** I wouldn't bet on it; **ci avrei scommesso!** I would have put money on it!; **puoi scommetterci** you can count on it; **quanto scommettiamo che...?** what's the betting that...?

scomodare [skomo'dare] **1** *vt* to disturb, bother. **2: ~rsi** *vr* to bother, trouble (o.s.).

scomodità [skomodi'ta] *sf inv (di sedia, letto etc)*

scomodo, a ['skɔmodo] *ag (sedia, letto, posizione)* uncomfortable; *(orario, turno)* inconvenient; **stare ~** to be uncomfortable; **mi è scomodo venire la sera** it's inconvenient for me to come in the evening; **è ~ da portare** it's difficult to carry, it's cumbersome.

scompaginare [skompadʒi'nare] **1** *vt* to upset, throw into disorder. **2: ~rsi** *vr* to be thrown into disorder.

scomparire [skompa'rire] *vi (aus essere) (sparire)* to disappear, vanish; *(fig: non risaltare)* to look insignificant.

scomparsa [skom'parsa] *sf (sparizione)* disappearance; *(fig: morte)* passing away, death.

scomparso, a [skom'parso] *pp di* **scomparire.**

scompartimento [skomparti'mento] *sm* **(a)** *(sezione)* division. **(b)** *(Ferr)* compartment.

scomparto [skom'parto] *sm* division.

scompenso [skom'pɛnso] *sm* imbalance, lack of balance; *(Med)* decompensation.

scompigliare [skompiʎ'ʎare] *vt* to mess up, muddle up; *(capelli)* to mess up, ruffle; *(fig: piani)* to upset; *(: idee)* to mess up, confuse.

scompiglio [skom'piʎʎo] *sm* confusion, chaos; **portare lo ~ in** to cause confusion in.

scomporre [skom'porre] **1** *vt (parola, numero)* to break up; *(Chim)* to decompose. **2: scomporsi** *vr* **(a)** *(Chim)* to decompose. **(b)** *(turbarsi)* to lose one's composure; **senza scomporsi** unperturbed.

scompostezza [skompos'tettsa] *sf* unseemliness.

scomposto, a [skom'posto] **1** *pp di* **scomporre. 2** *ag* **(a)** *(persona: sguaiato)* unseemly. **(b)** *(capelli etc: in disordine)* dishevelled, in a mess.

scomunica, che [sko'munika] *sf (Rel)* excommunication.

scomunicare [skomuni'kare] *vt (Rel)* to excommunicate.

scomunicato, a [skomuni'kato] *sm/f* excommunicate.

sconcertante [skontʃer'tante] *ag* disconcerting.

sconcertare [skontʃer'tare] **1** *vt* to disconcert, bewilder. **2: ~rsi** *vr* to be disconcerted.

sconcertato, a [skontʃer'tato] *ag* disconcerted.

sconcezza [skon'tʃettsa] *sf* obscenity, indecency; **è una ~!** it's a disgrace!

sconcio, a, ci, ce ['skontʃo] **1** *ag (osceno)* obscene, indecent; *(: parole)* rude, dirty. **2** *sm (cosa mal fatta)* disgrace.

sconclusionato, a [skonkluzjo'nato] *ag* incoherent, illogical.

scondito, a [skon'dito] *ag (minestra)* unseasoned; *(insalata)* without dressing.

sconfessare [skonfes'sare] *vt* to renounce, retract.

sconfiggere [skon'fiddʒere] *vt (gen, Pol, Sport)* to defeat.

sconfinamento [skonfina'mento] *sm (di frontiera)* border violation; *(di proprietà)* trespassing.

sconfinare [skonfi'nare] *vi* to cross the border; *(da proprietà)* to trespass; *(: involontariamente)* to stray; *(fig: uscire dai limiti fissati):* **~ da** *(verità, sentiero)* to stray from; *(tema, argomento)* to digress from.

sconfinato, a [skonfi'nato] *ag* limitless, boundless.

sconfitta [skon'fitta] *sf (gen, Pol, Sport)* defeat; **subire** *o* **riportare una ~** to be defeated.

sconfitto, a [skon'fitto] *pp di* **sconfiggere.**

sconfortante [skonfor'tante] *ag* discouraging, disheartening.

sconfortare [skonfor'tare] **1** *vt* to discourage, dishearten. **2: ~rsi** *vr* to become discouraged, become disheartened, lose heart.

sconfortato, a [skonfor'tato] *ag* dejected.

sconforto [skon'fɔrto] *sm* dejection; **essere in preda allo** ~ to be dejected.

scongelare [skondʒe'lare] *vt* to defrost.

scongiurare [skondʒu'rare] *vt* **(a)** *(supplicare)* to beg, implore. **(b)** *(evitare)* to avert, avoid.

scongiuro [skon'dʒuro] *sm (esorcismo)* exorcism; *(formula)* spell, charm; **fare gli** ~**i** to touch wood.

sconnesso, a [skon'nesso] *ag (staccato)* disconnected; *(fig: sconclusionato)* incoherent, disconnected.

sconosciuto, a [skonoʃ'ʃuto] **1** *ag* unknown; **una gioia** ~**a** a strange joy; **il suo viso mi è** ~ his face is new to me. **2** *sm/f* unknown (person), stranger.

sconquassare [skonkwas'sare] *vt* to shatter, smash.

sconquasso [skon'kwasso] *sm (danno)* damage; *(fig)* confusion.

sconsacrare [skonsa'krare] *vt (Rel)* to deconsecrate.

sconsideratezza [skonsidera'tettsa] *sf* lack of consideration, thoughtlessness.

sconsiderato, a [skonside'rato] **1** *ag* thoughtless, inconsiderate. **2** *sm/f* thoughtless person, inconsiderate person.

sconsigliare [skonsiʎ'ʎare] *vt*: ~ **qc a qn** to advise sb against sth; **ti sconsiglio di provarci** I advise you against trying; **quel ristorante? te lo sconsiglio!** that restaurant? I wouldn't recommend it!; **volevo andare ma mi hanno sconsigliato** I wanted to go but they advised me not to.

sconsolato, a [skonso'lato] *ag* disconsolate.

scontare [skon'tare] *vt* **(a)** *(Comm: detrarre)* to deduct, discount; ~ **una cambiale** to discount a bill of exchange; ~ **un debito** to pay off a debt in instalments. **(b)** *(peccato, colpa)* to pay for; *(Dir: pena)* to serve; ~ **5 anni di prigione** to serve 5 years in prison.

scontato, a [skon'tato] *ag* **(a)** *(prezzo, merce)* discounted, at a discount. **(b)** *(previsto)* foreseen, taken for granted; **era** ~ **che finisse così** it was bound to end that way; **dare qc per** ~ to take sth for granted.

scontentare [skonten'tare] *vt* to displease, dissatisfy.

scontentezza [skonten'tettsa] *sf* displeasure, dissatisfaction.

scontento, a [skon'tento] **1** *ag* dissatisfied, displeased; **essere** ~ **di qc** to be displeased *o* dissatisfied with sth. **2** *sm* discontent, dissatisfaction.

sconto ['skonto] *sm (Comm)* discount; **fare** *o* **concedere uno** ~ to give a discount; **uno** ~ **del 10%** a 10% discount.

scontrarsi [skon'trarsi] *vr* **(a)** *(veicolo, persona)*: ~ **con** to collide with. **(b)** *(uso reciproco: veicoli, persone)* to collide; *(Mil, fig: opinioni)* to clash.

scontrino [skon'trino] *sm (biglietto)* ticket, check *(Am)*; *(di cassa)* receipt.

scontro ['skontro] *sm (di veicoli)* collision, crash; *(Mil)* clash, engagement; *(fig: litigio)* disagreement; **ci sono stati** ~**i tra polizia e dimostranti** there were clashes between police and demonstrators, police and demonstrators clashed; ~ **a fuoco** shoot-out.

scontrosità [skontrosi'ta] *sf* surliness.

scontroso, a [skon'troso] *ag* surly.

sconveniente [skonve'njɛnte] *ag* **(a)** *(comportamento, modi)* unseemly; *(osservazione, proposta)* improper. **(b)** *(prezzo)* disadvantageous, unattractive.

sconvenienza [skonve'njɛntsa] *sf (vedi ag)* unseemliness; impropriety; unattractiveness.

sconvolgente [skonvol'dʒɛnte] *ag (notizia, brutta esperienza)* upsetting, disturbing; *(bellezza)* amazing; *(passione)* overwhelming.

sconvolgere [skon'vɔldʒere] **1** *vt (persona)* to upset, disturb; *(piani)* to upset; ~ **l'opinione pubblica** to shock o shake public opinion; **la notizia ha sconvolto il mondo intero** the news shook the whole world; **la zona sconvolta dal terremoto** the area hit *o* affected by the earthquake; **le campagne sconvolte dall'alluvione** the flooded countryside, the countryside affected *o* devastated by the floods. **2**: ~ **rsi** *vr* to become upset, become disturbed.

sconvolgimento [skonvoldʒi'mento] *sm (scompiglio)* confusion; *(devastazione)* devastation.

sconvolto, a [skon'vɔlto] **1** *pp di* **sconvolgere**. **2** *ag (persona)* distraught, very upset; ~ **dal dolore** beside o.s. with grief.

scopa¹ ['skopa] *sf* broom; **sembra un manico di** ~ he's as thin as a rake.

scopa² ['skopa] *sf* kind of card game.

scopare [sko'pare] **1** *vt* **(a)** *(spazzare)* to sweep. **(b)** *(fam!)* to screw(!). **2** *vi (fam!)* to screw(!).

scopata [sko'pata] *sf* **(a)** sweep; **dare una** ~ **a qc** to give sth a sweep, sweep sth out; **dare una** ~ **a qn** to hit sb with a broom. **(b)** *(fam!)* screw(!).

scoperchiare [skoper'kjare] *vt (pentola, vaso)* to take the lid off, uncover; *(casa)* to take the roof off.

scoperta [sko'pɛrta] *sf* discovery; **bella** ~**!** *(iro)* what a revelation!

scoperto, a [sko'pɛrto] **1** *pp di* **scoprire**. **2** *ag* **(a)** *(pentola)* uncovered, with the lid off; *(macchina)* open; *(spalle, braccia)* bare; **a capo** ~ bareheaded; **dormire** ~ to sleep uncovered; **giocare a carte** ~**e** *(anche fig)* to put one's cards on the table. **(b)**: **assegno** ~ uncovered cheque; **conto** ~ overdrawn account; **avere un conto** ~ to be overdrawn. **3** *sm*: **allo** ~ *(dormire etc)* out in the open; **è uscito allo** ~ *(fig)* he came out into the open.

scopiazzare [skopjat'tsare] *vt (peg)* to copy.

scopino [sko'pino] *sm (spazzino)* street sweeper.

scopo ['skopo] *sm* aim, purpose; **allo** ~ **di fare qc** in order to do sth; **cercare uno** ~ **nella vita** to look for an aim *o* purpose in life; **senza** ~ *(fare, cercare)* pointlessly; **la sua vita è senza** ~ his life is pointless; **a** ~ **di lucro** for gain *o* money; **adatto allo** ~ fit for its purpose.

scopone [sko'pone] *sm* kind of card game.

scoppiare [skop'pjare] *vi (aus essere)* **(a)** *(bomba, serbatoio etc)* to explode; *(pneumatico, palloncino)* to burst; *(fig: rivolta, guerra, epidemia)* to break out; **la notizia fece** ~ **lo scandalo** the news caused a scandal. **(b)** *(fraseologia)*: ~ **dal caldo** to be boiling; ~ **dall'invidia** to be dying of envy; ~ **a piangere** *o* **in lacrime** to burst into tears; ~ **a ridere** to burst out laughing; ~ **di salute** to be the picture of health; ~ **dalla voglia di fare qc** to be dying *o* longing to do sth; **a quel punto sono scoppiato** *(dalla rabbia, dal ridere)* at that point I couldn't contain myself any longer.

scoppiettare [skoppjet'tare] *vi (fuoco)* to crackle; *(motore)* to chug.

scoppiettio [skoppjet'tio] *sm* crackling.

scoppio ['skɔppjo] *sm (esplosione)* explosion; *(di pneumatico)* bang; *(fig: di rivolta, guerra, epidemia)* outbreak; **bomba a** ~ **ritardato** delayed-action bomb; **reazione a** ~ **ritardato** delayed *o* slow reaction; **uno** ~ **di risa** a burst of laughter; **uno** ~ **di collera** an explosion of anger.

scoprire [sko'prire] **1** *vt* **(a)** *(trovare)* to discover; *(causa, verità)* to discover, find out; ~ **che/come**

to find out *o* discover that/how; **ha scoperto di avere uno zio in India** he found out *o* discovered he has an uncle in India; **hai scoperto l'America!** *(iro)* you mean you've only just found out about it! **(b)** *(pentola)* to take the lid off; *(statua)* to unveil; *(rovine, cadaveri)* to uncover; *(spalle, braccia)* to bare, uncover; **una camicetta che scopre la schiena** a blouse with a low-cut back; **~rsi il capo** to take off one's hat, bare one's head; **~rsi il fianco** *(fig)* to leave one's flank exposed.
 2: ~rsi *vr (esporsi: Sport, fig)* to expose o.s.; *(fig: rivelare le proprie idee)* to betray o.s.; **non scoprirti che fa freddo** keep well wrapped up because it's cold; **il bambino si è scoperto durante la notte** the child threw off the bedclothes during the night.

scopritore, trice [skopri'tore] *sm/f* discoverer.

scoraggiamento [skoraddʒa'mento] *sm* discouragement, dejection.

scoraggiare [skorad'dʒare] **1** *vt* to discourage. **2: ~rsi** *vr* to become discouraged, become disheartened.

scorbutico, a, ci, che [skor'butiko] *ag (fig)* peevish, cantankerous.

scorbuto [skor'buto] *sm* scurvy.

scorciare [skor'tʃare] *vt* = **accorciare**.

scorciatoia [skortʃa'toja] *sf (anche fig)* short cut.

scorcio [skor'tʃo] *sm* **(a)** *(Arte)* foreshortening. **(b)** *(di paesaggio)* glimpse; **~ panoramico** vista.

scordare[1] [skor'dare] **1** *vt (gen)* to forget; *(appuntamento, preoccupazione)* to forget (about); **~ di fare qc** to forget to do sth; **avevo scordato di avertelo già chiesto** I had forgotten that I had already asked you. **2: ~rsi** *vr:* **~rsi di qc/di fare qc** to forget sth/to do sth.

scordare[2] [skor'dare] **1** *vt (Mus)* to put out of tune. **2: ~rsi** *vr* to go out of tune.

scoreggia, ge [sko'reddʒa] *sf (fam)* fart.

scoreggiare [skored'dʒare] *vi (fam)* to fart.

scorfano [skor'fano] *sm (Zool)* scorpion fish; *(fig: persona brutta)* fright.

scorgere [skor'dʒere] *vt* to see, catch sight of; *(fig: accorgersi di)* to become aware of, realize; **senza farsi ~** unnoticed, without being seen.

scoria [sko'rja] *sf (di metalli)* slag; *(vulcanica)* scoria; **~e radioattive** *(Fis)* radioactive waste *sg.*

scornare [skor'nare] *vt (fig)* to humiliate.

scornato, a [skor'nato] *ag (fig)* humiliated.

scorno [sko'rno] *sm* humiliation.

scorpacciata [skorpat'tʃata] *sf* big feed; **farsi una ~ (di qc)** to stuff o.s. (with sth).

scorpione [skor'pjone] *sm* **(a)** *(Zool)* scorpion. **(b)** *(Astrologia):* **S~** Scorpio; **essere dello S~** to be Scorpio.

scorrazzare [skorrat'tsare] *vi* to run about, romp about.

scorrere [skor'rere] **1** *vi (aus essere) (liquido, fiume)* to run, flow; *(fune)* to run; *(cassetto, porta)* to slide easily; *(tempo)* to pass (by); **lascia ~ l'acqua** let the water run, leave the water running; **il tempo scorre lento** time passes slowly; **ha uno stile che scorre** he *(o* it *etc)* has a flowing style. **2** *vt (leggere)* to glance through, run one's eye over.

scorreria [skorre'ria] *sf* raid, incursion.

scorrettezza [skorret'tettsa] *sf (vedi ag)* incorrectness; lack of politeness, rudeness; unfairness; **~ al gioco** foul play; **con ~** *(sgarbatamente)* rudely, impolitely; **è stata una ~ da parte sua** it was rude of him, it was bad manners on his part; **commettere una ~** *(essere sleale)* to be unfair.

scorretto, a [skor'retto] *ag (traduzione, uso)* incorrect; *(persona: sgarbato)* impolite, rude; *(: sleale)* unfair; *(: gioco)* foul.

scorrevole [skor'revole] *ag (porta)* sliding; *(nastro)* moving; *(fig: stile)* flowing.

scorrevolezza [skorrevo'lettsa] *sf (fig: di stile)* fluency.

scorribanda [skorri'banda] *sf* raid, incursion.

scorsa ['skorsa] *sf* glance, quick look; **dare una ~ a qc** to glance over *o* through sth.

scorso, a [skorso] **1** *pp di* **scorrere. 2** *ag* last; **lo ~ mese** last month.

scorsoio, a [skor'sojo] *ag:* **nodo ~** slipknot.

scorta ['skorta] *sf* **(a)** *(gen, Mil)* escort; **fare la ~ a qn** to escort sb; **sotto la ~ di due agenti** escorted by two policemen. **(b)** *(provvista)* supply; **fare ~ di** to stock up with, get in a supply of; **di ~** *(materiali)* spare; **ruota di ~** spare wheel.

scortare [skor'tare] *vt* to escort.

scortese [skor'tese] *ag* impolite, discourteous, rude.

scortesia [skorte'zia] *sf (qualità)* impoliteness, discourtesy, rudeness; *(azione)* discourtesy.

scorticare [skorti'kare] *vt (animali)* to skin, flay; **~rsi un gomito** to skin *o* graze one's elbow.

scorto, a ['skorto] *pp di* **scorgere**.

scorza ['skordza] *sf (di albero)* bark; *(di agrumi)* peel, skin; **avere la ~ dura** *(fig: persona)* to be thick-skinned; **sotto la ~ c'è un animo gentile** he's kind-hearted beneath his crusty exterior.

scosceso, a [skoʃ'ʃeso] *ag* steep.

scossa ['skossa] *sf (sobbalzo)* jolt, jerk; *(elettrica)* shock; **procedere a ~e** to jolt *o* jerk along; **dare una ~ a qn** *(fig)* to shake sb; **~ elettrica** electric shock; **prendere la ~** to get an electric shock; **~ di terremoto** earth tremor.

scosso, a ['skosso] **1** *pp di* **scuotere. 2** *ag (persona)* shaken; **ho i nervi ~i** my nerves are shattered.

scossone [skos'sone] *sm:* **dare uno ~ a qn** to give sb a shake; **procedere a ~i** to jolt *o* jerk along.

scostante [skos'tante] *ag (persona, modi)* off-putting, unpleasant.

scostare [skos'tare] **1** *vt* to push aside, move aside; **scosta la poltrona dal muro** move the armchair away from the wall. **2: ~rsi** *vr* to move aside; **scostati dal muro** move away from the wall.

scostumato, a [skostu'mato] **1** *ag (immorale)* immoral, dissolute; *(maleducato)* bad-mannered, boorish. **2** *sm (vedi ag)* dissolute person; boor.

scotennare [skoten'nare] *vt (animale)* to skin; *(persona)* to scalp.

scottante [skot'tante] *ag (fig: urgente)* pressing; *(: delicato)* delicate.

scottare [skot'tare] **1** *vt (gen)* to burn; *(con liquido, vapore)* to scald, burn; *(Culin: in acqua)* to scald; *(: friggendo)* to sear; **~rsi una mano** to burn one's hand; **sono già stato scottato una volta** *(fig)* I've already burnt my fingers once. **2** *vi (gen)* to be very hot; *(sole, sabbia)* to be burning, be scorching; **è roba che scotta** *(fig: refurtiva etc)* it's hot; **sono argomenti che scottano** *(fig: delicati)* these are delicate issues; **gli scotta il terreno sotto ai piedi** *(fig)* he's itching to be off. **3: ~rsi** *vr* to burn o.s.; *(con liquido, vapore)* to scald o.s., burn o.s.

scottata [skot'tata] *sf (Culin):* **dare una ~ a qc** *(in acqua)* to scald sth; *(friggendo)* to sear sth.

scottatura [skotta'tura] *sf (gen)* burn; *(con liquido, vapore)* scald, burn.

scotto[1], **a** ['skotto] *ag (Culin)* overcooked, overdone.

scotto[2] ['skotto] *sm (fig: punizione):* **pagare lo ~** to pay the consequences.

scovare [sko'vare] *vt (Caccia)* to put up; *(fig)* to unearth, find.

Scozia ['skɔttsja] sf Scotland.

scozzese [skot'tsese] **1** ag (gen) Scottish; (whisky) Scotch; **tessuto** ~ tartan; **gonna** ~ kilt. **2** sm/f Scot, Scotsman/woman; **gli** S~**i** the Scots.

screanzato, a [skrean'tsato] **1** ag ill-mannered. **2** sm/f boor.

screditare [skredi'tare] **1** vt to discredit. **2**: ~**rsi** vr to be discredited.

scremare [skre'mare] vt to skim.

scremato, a [skre'mato] ag skimmed.

screpolare [skrepo'lare] **1** vt (pelle, labbra) to chap, crack; (mani) to chap; (intonaco) to crack. **2**: ~**rsi** (vedi vt) to chap; to crack.

screpolatura [skrepola'tura] sf (su pelle, labbra, mani) chap; (su intonaco) crack.

screziato, a [skret'tsjato] ag (striato) streaked.

screzio ['skrɛttsjo] sm friction; **hanno avuto degli** ~**i** there was some friction between them.

scribacchiare [skribak'kjare] vt to scribble.

scribacchino [skribak'kino] sm (peg: impiegato) penpusher; (: scrittore) hack.

scricchiolare [skrikkjo'lare] vi to creak.

scricchiolio [skrikkjo'lio] sm creaking.

scricciolo ['skrittʃolo] sm (Zool) wren; **lei è uno** ~ (fig: persona gracile) she's like a little bird.

scrigno ['skriɲɲo] sm casket.

scriminatura [skrimina'tura] sf (di capelli) parting.

scriteriato [skrite'rjato] **1** ag scatterbrained. **2** sm/f scatterbrain.

scritta ['skritta] sf (iscrizione) inscription; (avviso) notice; **cosa dice la** ~ **sul cartello?** what does the (writing on the) sign say?

scritto, a ['skritto] **1** pp di **scrivere**. **2** ag (lingua, esame etc) written. **3** sm **(a)** (lettera) letter. **(b)** (opera) work; **gli** ~**i di** the work(s) o the writings of.

scrittoio [skrit'tojo] sm (writing-)desk.

scrittore, trice [skrit'tore] sm/f writer, author.

scrittura [skrit'tura] sf **(a)** (calligrafia) (hand)writing; **avere una bella/brutta** ~ to have good/bad handwriting. **(b)** (Rel): **la Sacra** S~ the Scriptures pl. **(c)** (Cine, Teatro, TV) contract. **(d)** (Dir) document; ~ **privata** parol, contract.

scritturare [skrittu'rare] vt (Cine, Teatro, TV) to engage, sign on.

scrivania [skriva'nia] sf (writing-)desk.

scrivano [skri'vano] sm (amanuense) scribe; (impiegato) clerk.

scrivere ['skrivere] vt (gen) to write; ~ **qc a qn** to write sth to sb; ~ **qc a macchina** to type sth; ~ **a penna/matita** to write in pen/pencil; ~ **qc maiuscolo/minuscolo** to write sth in capital/small letters; ~ **alla lavagna** to write on the blackboard; **come si scrive questa parola?** how do you write o spell this word?; **era scritto che dovesse succedere** (fig) it was fated o bound to happen.

scroccare [skrok'kare] vt (fam) to scrounge, cadge.

scrocco[1] ['skrokko] sm: **vivere a** ~ (fam) to be a sponger.

scrocco[2]**, chi** ['skrokko] sm **(a)** (rumore) click. **(b)**: **coltello a** ~ jack-knife.

scroccone [skrok'kone] sm (fam) scrounger, sponger.

scrofa ['skrɔfa] sf (Zool) sow; (fig peg: donna) cow.

scrollare [skrol'lare] **1** vt **(a)** to shake; ~ **la testa** to shake one's head; ~ **le spalle** to shrug one's shoulders. **(b)**: ~**rsi qc di dosso** to shake sth off; (fig: malinconia, stanchezza) to shrug sth off. **2**: ~**rsi** vr to shake o.s.; (fig) to stir o.s., give o.s. a shake.

scrollata [skrol'lata] sf shake; **dare una** ~ **a qc** to

scrosciante [skroʃ'ʃante] ag (pioggia) pouring; (fig: applausi) thunderous.

scrosciare [skroʃ'ʃare] vi (pioggia) to pelt down; **gli applausi scrosciavano** there was thunderous applause.

scroscio ['skrɔʃʃo] sm (di torrente, cascata) roar; (di applausi) thunder; **sentivamo lo** ~ **della pioggia** we could hear the rain pelting down.

scrostare [skros'tare] **1** vt (vernice, intonaco) to scrape off, strip off; (tubo) to descale; ~ **una ferita** to remove the scab (from a wound). **2**: ~**rsi** vr (vernice, intonaco) to peel off.

scroto ['skrɔto] sm (Anat) scrotum.

scrupolo ['skrupolo] sm (morale) scruple; (diligenza) care, conscientiousness; ~ **morale**, ~ **di coscienza** scruple; **essere senza** ~**i** to be unscrupulous; **non farti tanti** ~**i con lui** I wouldn't have any scruples about him if I were you; **lavoro fatto con** ~ a conscientious piece of work; **è onesto fino allo** ~ he's scrupulously honest.

scrupolosità [skrupolosi'ta] sf (vedi ag) scrupulousness; conscientiousness.

scrupoloso, a [skrupo'loso] ag (onesto) scrupulous; (diligente) conscientious.

scrutare [skru'tare] vt (orizzonte, vallata) to scan; (cielo, volto) to search; (persona) to scrutinize.

scrutatore, trice [skruta'tore] **1** ag (sguardo) searching. **2** sm/f scrutineer.

scrutinare [skruti'nare] vt to scrutinize.

scrutinatore, trice [skrutina'tore] sm/f scrutineer.

scrutinio [skru'tinjo] sm **(a)** (votazione) ballot; (insieme delle operazioni) poll; ~ **segreto** secret ballot. **(b)** (Scol) end-of-term (o end-of-year) assessment.

scucire [sku'tʃire] **1** vt to unstitch, unpick; (fam: soldi) to fork out. **2**: ~**rsi** vr to come unstitched.

scuderia [skude'ria] sf (Ippica) stable; (Aut) team.

scudetto [sku'detto] sm (Sport) shield; **hanno vinto lo** ~ they won the national championship.

scudiero [sku'djero] sm squire.

scudiscio [sku'diʃʃo] sm (riding) crop, (riding) whip.

scudo ['skudo] sm (gen) shield; **farsi** ~ **di** o **con qc** to shield o.s. with sth; ~ **aereo/missilistico** air/missile defence; ~ **termico** heat shield.

sculacciare [skulat'tʃare] vt to spank.

sculacciata [skulat'tʃata] sf spanking; **dare una** ~ **a qn** to spank sb, give sb a spanking.

sculaccione [skulat'tʃone] sm = **sculacciata**.

sculettare [skulet'tare] vi to sway one's hips, wiggle one's hips.

scultore, trice [skul'tore] sm/f sculptor/tress; (di legno) woodcarver.

scultoreo, a [skul'tɔreo] ag of sculpture, sculptural; **arte** ~**a** sculpture.

scultura [skul'tura] sf sculpture; (di legno) woodcarving.

scuola ['skwɔla] sf **(a)** (istituzione, edificio) school; **andare a** ~ to go to school; **non c'è** ~ **domani** there's no school tomorrow; **ci vediamo dopo la** ~ see you after school; ~ **privata/pubblica** private/state school; ~ **dell'obbligo** compulsory education; ~ **guida** driving school; **nave** ~ training ship. **(b)** (Arte) school; **un artista che ha fatto** ~ an artist who has developed a following.

scuolabus ['skwɔlabus] sm inv school bus.

scuotere ['skwɔtere] **1** vt **(a)** (anche fig) to shake; ~ **la testa** to shake one's head; ~ **le spalle** to shrug one's shoulders; **cercò di scuoterlo dalla sua apatia** he tried to shake him out of o rouse him from his apathy. **(b):** ~**rsi di dosso qc** to shake sth off; *(fig: malinconia, stanchezza)* to shrug sth off. **2:** ~**rsi** to shake o.s.; *(fig)* to stir o.s.; ~**rsi dall'apatia** to rouse o.s. from one's apathy.

scure ['skure] *sf* axe.

scurire [sku'rire] **1** *vt* to darken, make darker. **2** *vi (aus essere)*, ~**rsi** *vr* to darken, become dark, grow dark.

scuro¹, a ['skuro] **1** *ag (colore, vestito, capelli etc)* dark; **avere una faccia** ~ **a** to have a grim expression on one's face. **2** *sm (colore)* dark colour; **vestire di** ~ to wear dark colours.

scuro² ['skuro] *sm (di finestra)* shutter.

scurrile [skur'rile] *ag* scurrilous.

scusa ['skuza] *sf* **(a)** *(gen)* apology; **vi prego di accettare le mie** ~**e** please accept my apologies; **chiedere** ~ **a qn per qc** to apologize for sth; **chiedo** *o* **domando** ~ I apologize, I beg your pardon; **fare/presentare le proprie** ~**e** to make/ give one's apologies. **(b)** *(pretesto)* excuse; **cercare una** ~/**delle** ~**e** to look for an excuse/ excuses; **questa è una** ~ **bella e buona!** that's some excuse!; **non ci sono** ~**e che tengano!** there's no possible excuse!

scusare [sku'zare] **1** *vt (gen)* to excuse; *(perdonare)* to forgive; ~ **qn di** *o* **per qc** to forgive sb for sth; **scusami, scusa, mi scusi** (I'm) sorry; *(più formale)* I beg your pardon; **scusa il ritardo** I'm sorry I'm late; **tutto questo non ti scusa** this is no excuse; **scusi, sa dirmi dove...?** excuse me, can you tell me where...? **2:** ~**rsi** *vr* to apologize; ~**rsi con qn di** *o* **per qc** to apologize to sb for sth; **si è scusato del ritardo** he apologized for being late; **potresti almeno scusarti** you could at least say you're sorry; **non so come scusarmi** I don't know how to apologize; **non cercare di scusarti!** don't look for excuses!

sdaziare [zdat'tsjare] *vt* to pay customs duties on.

sdebitarsi [zdebi'tarsi] *vr:* ~**rsi (con qn di** *o* **per qc)** *(anche fig)* to repay (sb for sth).

sdegnare [zdeɲ'ɲare] **1** *vt (disprezzare)* to scorn. **2:** ~**rsi** *vr (arrabbiarsi):* ~**rsi (con)** to get angry (with).

sdegnato, a [zdeɲ'ɲato] *ag* indignant, angry.

sdegno ['zdeɲɲo] *sm (disprezzo)* scorn, disdain; *(indignazione)* indignation.

sdegnosità [zdeɲɲosi'ta] *sf* scorn, disdain.

sdegnoso, a [zdeɲ'ɲoso] *ag* scornful, contemptuous, disdainful.

sdentare [zden'tare] **1** *vt (sega etc)* to break the teeth of. **2:** ~**rsi** *vr* to lose one's teeth.

sdentato, a [zden'tato] *ag (senza denti: persona)* toothless; *(: sega)* without teeth.

sdilinquirsi [zdilin'kwirsi] *vr (illanguidirsi)* to become sentimental.

sdoganare [zdoga'nare] *vt (Comm)* to clear through customs.

sdolcinato, a [zdoltʃi'nato] *ag (persona)* gushing; *(parole)* sugary; *(modi)* affected; *(film, libro)* oversentimental.

sdoppiamento [zdoppja'mento] *sm (Chim: di composto)* splitting; *(Psic):* ~ **della personalità** split personality.

sdoppiare [zdop'pjare] **1** *vt* to split in two, divide in two. **2:** ~**rsi** *vr* to split in two, divide in two.

sdraiare [zdra'jare] **1** *vt* to lay down; ~ **qn a terra/ sul letto** to lay sb down on the ground/on the bed. **2:** ~**rsi** *vr* to lie down; ~**rsi a terra/sul letto** to lie down on the ground/on the bed; ~**rsi al sole** to stretch out in the sun.

sdraiato, a [zdra'jato] *ag* lying down; **mettersi** ~ to lie down.

sdraio ['zdrajo] *sf (anche:* **sedia a** ~**)** deckchair.

sdrammatizzare [zdrammatid'dzare] *vt* to play down, minimize.

sdrucciolare [zdruttʃo'lare] *vi (persona)* to slip, slide.

sdrucciolevole [zdruttʃo'levole] *ag* slippery.

sdrucciolo, a ['zdruttʃolo] **1** *ag (Linguistica)* proparoxytone. **2** *sm* trisyllabic verse.

sdrucito, a [zdru'tʃito] *ag (strappato)* torn; *(logoro)* threadbare.

se¹ [se] **1** *cong* **(a)** *(condizionale, concessiva)* if; ~ **nevica non vengo**, ~ **nevicherà non verrò** I won't come if it snows; ~ **fosse più furbo verrebbe** if he were smarter he would come; ~ **fosse stato interessato sarebbe venuto** if he had been interested he would have come; ~ **fossi in te** if I were you; **deve essere così** ~ **lo dice lui** it must be so if he says so; ~ **invece preferisci questo...** should you *o* if you prefer this one... .

(b) *(dubitativa, in domande indirette)* whether, if; **mi chiedevo** ~ **avesse capito** I wondered whether he had understood; **non sapevo** ~ **veniva o meno** I didn't know whether he would come; **guarda lì** ~ **c'è** look and see whether *o* if it's there.

(c) *(ottativa)* if only; ~ **(solo) me l'avesse detto prima!** if only he had told me earlier!; ~ **ci fosse ancora lui!** if only he were still here!

(d) *(fraseologia):* ~ **no** *(altrimenti)* or (else), otherwise; **non fiatare,** ~ **no vedi!** don't breathe a word, or else!; **mangia,** ~ **no non reggi fino a stasera** eat up, otherwise *o* or else you'll be starving by this evening; **scappo** ~ **no perdo l'autobus** I must dash or I'll miss the bus; ~ **non** *(anzi)* if not; *(tranne)* except; **costa lo stesso,** ~ **non meno** it costs the same, if not less; **non lo darò a nessuno** ~ **non a lui** I won't give it to anybody except *o* other than him; ~ **non altro** if nothing else, at least; ~ **non altro non disturba** at least he's no trouble; ~ **poi decidesse di restare** should he decide *o* were he to decide to stay; ~ **mai passassi per di qua** should you ever *o* if ever you pass this way; **lascialo in atrio** ~ **mai** leave it in the hall if necessary; **siamo noi** ~ **mai che le siamo grati** it is we who should be grateful to you; **come** ~ as if; **come** ~ **non lo sapesse!** as if he didn't know!; **e** ~ **poi se ne accorge?** and what if he notices?; **e** ~ **andassimo in montagna?** how about going to the mountains?; **ma** ~ **l'ho visto io!** but I saw it myself!; **lo so io** ~ **mi manca** know how much I miss him; ~ **pure** = **seppure**.

2 *sm* if; **c'è solo un grosso** ~ there's just one big if.

se² [se] *vedi* **si¹.**

sé [se] *pron riflessivo (gen)* oneself; *(maschile)* himself; *(femminile)* herself; *(neutro)* itself; *(pl)* themselves; **l'ha fatto da** ~ he did it (all) by himself; **lo portò con** ~ he took it with him; **pensa solo a** ~ *o* **se stesso** he thinks only of himself; **è piena di** ~ she's very full of herself; **di per** ~ **non è un problema** it's no problem in itself; **parlare tra** ~ **e** ~ to talk to oneself; **tornare in** ~ to come to (one's senses); **va da** ~ **che...** it goes without saying that..., it's obvious that..., it stands to reason that...; **è un caso a** ~ *o* **a se stante** it's a special case; **si chiude da** ~ *(porta)* it closes automatically; **un uomo che s'è fatto da** ~ a self-made man; **chi fa da** ~ **fa per tre** it's quicker to do things oneself.

sebbene [seb'bene] *cong* (even) though, although; ~ **non sia colpa sua...** although *o* (even) though it is not his fault...; **lo farò,** ~ **mi pesi molto** I'll do it even though I'm not very happy about it.

sebo ['sɛbo] *sm* sebum.

sec. *abbr* (= *secolo*) c.

secante [se'kante] *sf (Mat)* secant.

secca, che ['sekka] *sf (Naut)* bank, shallow; **andare in** ~ to run aground.

seccante [sek'kante] *ag* tiresome, annoying.

seccare [sek'kare] **1** *vt* **(a)** *(gen)* to dry; *(prosciugare)* to dry (up); *(fiori: appassire)* to wither. **(b)** *(infastidire)* to annoy, bother; **questa volta mi hai proprio seccato** I've had enough of you this time; **ti secca se aspetto qui?** do you mind if I wait here?; **se ti secca chiederlo lo faccio io** if you don't like to ask him I'll do it; **mi secca fare tutta questa fila** it annoys me having to queue like this. **2** *vi (aus* **essere)** to dry (up). **3:** ~**rsi** *vr* **(a)** *(diventar secco)* to dry (up); *(pelle)* to become dry; *(fiori)* to wither. **(b)** *(infastidirsi)* to become annoyed; **si è seccato molto** he was very annoyed.

seccato, a [sek'kato] *ag (fig: infastidito)* bothered, annoyed; *(: stufo)* fed up.

seccatore, trice [sekka'tore] *sm/f* nuisance, bother.

seccatura [sekka'tura] *sf* nuisance, bother; **che** ~! what a nuisance!

secchia ['sekkja] *sf* bucket.

secchiata [sek'kjata] *sf* bucket(ful).

secchiello [sek'kjɛllo] *sm (per bambini)* pail, bucket.

secchio ['sekkjo] *sm* bucket, pail; ~ **della spazzatura** *o* **delle immondizie** dustbin.

secchione, a [sek'kjone] *sm/f (fam peg)* swot.

secco, a, chi, che ['sekko] **1** *ag* **(a)** *(gen)* dry; *(terreno)* arid, dry; *(uva, fichi)* dried; *(fig: risposta)* sharp; **avere la gola** ~**a** to feel dry, be parched; **un no** ~ a curt no; **un colpo** ~ a sharp blow. **(b)** *(persona: magro)* thin; ~ **come un chiodo** as thin as a rake. **(c)** *(fraseologia)*: **fare** ~ **qn** to knock sb off; **ci è rimasto** ~ *(fig: morto)* it killed him. **2** *sm* **(a)** *(di clima)* dryness; *(siccità)* drought. **(b)** *(fraseologia)*: **lavare a** ~ to dry-clean; **tirare a** ~ *(barca)* to beach; **essere a** ~ **(di soldi)** to be broke; **rimanere a** ~ **di benzina** to run out of petrol.

secentesco, a, schi, sche [setʃen'tesko] *ag* seventeenth-century.

secernere [se'tʃɛrnere] *vt* to secrete.

secessione [setʃes'sjone] *sf (Pol)* secession.

secolare [seko'lare] *ag* **(a)** *(antico)* centuries-old, age-old. **(b)** *(laico)* secular, lay; **clero** ~ lay clergy.

secolo ['sɛkolo] *sm* **(a)** century; *(epoca)* century, age; **nel terzo** ~ **a.C.** in the third century B.C.; **nel nostro** ~ this century; **l'avvenimento del** ~ the event of the century; **il** ~ **della Ragione** the Age of Reason; **per tutti i** ~**i dei** ~**i** *(Rel)* forever and ever; **Giovanni Paolo II, al** ~ **Carol Wojtyla** John Paul II, whose original name was Carol Wojtyla. **(b)** *(fig)*: **è un** ~ **che non ti vedo** I haven't seen you in ages; **è un** ~ **che aspetto** I've been waiting for you.

seconda [se'konda] **1** *sf* **(a)** *(Aut)* second (gear). **(b)** *(Scol: elementare)* second year of primary school; *(: media)* second year at secondary school; *(: superiore)* fifth year at secondary school. **(c)** *(Ferr)* second class; **viaggiare in** ~ to travel second class; **un biglietto di** ~ a second-class ticket. **(d)**: **comandante m in** ~ second-in-command. **2: a** ~ **di** *prep* according to.

secondariamente [sekondarja'mente] *av* secondly.

secondario, a [sekon'darjo] *ag* secondary, minor; **di importanza** ~**a** of secondary *o* minor importance; **scuola/istruzione** ~**a** secondary school/education.

secondino [sekon'dino] *sm* prison officer, warder.

secondo¹, a [se'kondo] **1** *ag (gen)* second; **in** ~**a fila** in the second row; **in** ~ **luogo** in the second place; **si è classificato al** ~ **posto** he came second; **figlio di** ~**e nozze** son by a second marriage; **passare a** ~**e nozze** to remarry, marry for a second time; **elevare alla** ~**a potenza** *(Mat)* to raise to the power of two; **Carlo S**~ Charles the Second; ~ **piatto** main course, second course; **è un** ~ **Picasso** he's another *o* a second Picasso; **un albergo di second'ordine** a second-class hotel. **2** *sm* **(a)** *(tempo)* second; **aspetta un** ~! wait a moment! **(b)** *(piatto)* main course, second course. **3** *sm/f* second (person); **sei il** ~ **che me lo dice** you're the second person to tell me that.

secondo² [se'kondo] *prep* **(a)** *(in base a, nell'opinione di)* according to; *(nel modo prescritto da, stando a)* in accordance with; ~ **me** in my opinion; ~ **le mie possibilità** according to my means; **il Vangelo** ~ **Matteo** the Gospel according to St Matthew; ~ **la legge/quanto si era deciso** in accordance with the law/the decision taken; **agire** ~ **coscienza** to follow one's conscience. **(b)** *(in direzione di: vento, corrente)* with; *(: linea)* along.

secondogenito, a [sekondo'dʒenito] *sm/f* second-born.

secrezione [sekret'tsjone] *sf (Bio)* secretion.

sedano ['sɛdano] *sm* celery; ~ **rapa** celeriac.

sedare [se'dare] *vt* **(a)** *(dolore)* to soothe. **(b)** *(rivolta)* to put down, suppress.

sedativo, a [seda'tivo] *ag, sm (Med)* sedative.

sede ['sɛde] *sf* **(a)** *(luogo di residenza)* (place of) residence; **prendere** ~ to take up residence; **cambiare** ~ to change one's residence.

(b) *(di società: principale)* head office; *(: secondaria)* branch (office); *(di partito)* headquarters *pl*; *(di governo, parlamento)* seat; *(Rel)* see; **un'azienda con diverse** ~**i in città** a firm with several branches in the city; ~ **centrale** head office; ~ **sociale** registered office; **il presidente è fuori** ~ the chairman is not in the office.

(c) *(località)* site; **Londra sarà** ~ **di un'importante mostra** London will be the site of an important exhibition.

(d): **in** ~ **di** *(in occasione di)* during; **in** ~ **d'esame** during the exam; **in** ~ **di discussione** during the discussion; **in** ~ **legislativa** in legislative sitting; **in altra** ~ on another occasion.

sedentario, a [seden'tarjo] *ag* sedentary.

sedere¹ [se'dere] **1** *vi (aus* **essere)** **(a)** *(essere seduto)* to be sitting, be seated; **sedeva a terra/a tavola** he was sitting on the ground/at table; **posto a** ~ seat; **siede in Parlamento** he has a seat in Parliament. **(b)** *(mettersi seduto)* to sit (down); **siedi qui** sit here; **mettiti a** ~ sit down, take a seat; **sieda per cortesia** please sit down, please take a seat; **mettersi seduto** *(da posizione orizzontale)* to sit up. **2:** ~**rsi** *vr* to sit (down); **siediti qui** sit down (here).

sedere² [se'dere] *sm (Anat)* bottom; **lo ha spedito fuori a calci nel** ~ he kicked him out.

sedia ['sɛdja] *sf* chair; ~ **elettrica** electric chair; ~ **a rotelle** wheelchair.

sedicenne [sedi'tʃɛnne] *ag, sm/f* sixteen-year-old; *per uso vedi* **cinquantenne**.

sedicente [sedi'tʃɛnte] *ag* self-styled.

sedicesimo, a [sedi'tʃɛzimo] *ag, sm/f, sm* sixteenth; *per uso vedi* **quinto**.

sedici ['seditʃi] *ag inv, sm inv* sixteen; *per uso vedi* **cinque**.

sedile [se'dile] *sm (in automezzi)* seat; *(panchina)* bench.

sedimentare [sedimen'tare] *ag* sedimentary.

sedimento [sedi'mento] *sm* sediment.

sedizione [sedit'tsjone] *sf* uprising, insurrection.

sedizioso, a [sedit'tsjoso] **1** *ag* seditious. **2** *sm/f* insurrectionist.

sedotto, a [se'dotto] *pp di* **sedurre.**

seducente [sedu't∫ɛnte] *ag* seductive.

sedurre [se'durre] *vt* **(a)** *(abusare di)* to seduce. **(b)** *(affascinare)* to charm, captivate; *(: sog: idea)* to appeal to.

seduta [se'duta] *sf (gen)* session, sitting; **essere in** ~ to be in session, be sitting; ~ **spiritica** séance; ~ **stante** *(fig: immediatamente)* straight away.

seduttore, trice [sedut'tore] *sm/f* seducer/seductress.

seduzione [sedut'tsjone] *sf (vedi vb)* seduction; charm; appeal.

sega, ghe ['sega] *sf (Tecn)* saw; ~ **circolare** circular saw; ~ **a mano** handsaw.

segala ['segala] *sf*, **segale** ['segale] *sf (Bot)* rye.

segare [se'gare] *vt* to saw; *(in più parti)* to saw up; ~ **via** to saw off; ~ **in due** to saw in two; **le corde le segavano i polsi** the ropes were cutting into her wrists.

segatura [sega'tura] *sf* sawdust.

seggio ['sɛddʒo] *sm* **(a)** *(gen)* seat. **(b):** ~ **elettorale** polling station.

seggiola ['sɛddʒola] *sf* chair.

seggiolone [sɛddʒo'lone] *sm (per bambini)* highchair.

seggiovia [sɛddʒo'via] *sf* chair lift.

segheria [sege'ria] *sf* saw mill.

seghettato, a [seget'tato] *ag* serrated.

seghetto [se'getto] *sm* hacksaw.

segmento [seg'mento] *sm* segment.

segnalare [seɲɲa'lare] **1** *vt (essere segno di)* to indicate, be a sign of; *(avvertire)* to signal; *(menzionare)* to indicate; *(: fatto, risultato, aumento)* to report; *(: errore, dettaglio)* to point out; ~ **una svolta a sinistra** *(Aut)* to indicate *o* signal a left turn; ~ **la posizione di una nave** to signal the position of a ship; **niente da** ~ nothing to report; ~ **qn a qn** *(per lavoro etc)* to bring sb to sb's attention. **2:** ~**rsi** *vr (distinguersi)* to distinguish o.s.

segnalazione [seɲɲalat'tsjone] *sf* **(a)** *(azione)* signalling; *(segnale)* signal; ~**i acustiche** acoustic *o* sound signals. **(b)** *(annuncio)* report; *(raccomandazione)* recommendation.

segnale [seɲ'ɲale] *sm (gen)* signal; **ad un suo** ~ **tutti uscirono** when he gave the signal *o* sign everybody went out; ~ **acustico** acoustic *o* sound signal; ~ **d'allarme** alarm; ~ **luminoso** light signal; ~ **orario** time signal; ~ **stradale** road sign.

segnaletica [seɲɲa'lɛtika] *sf:* ~ **(stradale)** road signs *pl*, traffic signs *pl*.

segnalibro [seɲɲa'libro] *sm* bookmark(er).

segnapunti [seɲɲa'punti] *sm/f inv* scorer.

segnare [seɲ'ɲare] **1** *vt* **(a)** *(fare un segno: gen)* to mark; *(scalfire)* to score, mark, cut into; *(graffiare)* to scratch; ~ **il passo** *(Mil)* to mark time; **è molto segnato da quell'esperienza** that experience has left its mark on him; **aveva il volto segnato dalla stanchezza** his face was drawn and tired. **(b)** *(scrivere)* to make a note of, jot down; **segna quanto ti devo** make a note of what I owe you. **(c)** *(indicare)* to show, indicate; **un orologio serve a** ~ **le ore** a watch tells *o* shows *o* indicates the time; **il mio orologio segna le 5** my watch says 5 o'clock; ~ **a dito** to point at; **essere**

segnato a dito *(fig)* to be talked about. **(d)** *(Sport)* to score. **2:** ~**rsi** *vr (Rel)* to cross o.s., make the sign of the cross.

segno ['seɲɲo] **1** *sm* **(a)** *(gen)* sign; *(traccia)* mark, sign; *(graffio)* scratch; *(indizio)* sign, indication; **lasciare un** ~ *(anche fig)* to leave a mark; **non c'erano** ~**i di vita** there was no sign of life; **non ha dato** ~**i di vita** he gave no sign of life; **è brutto** ~ it's a bad sign; **in** *o* **come** ~ **d'amicizia** as a mark *o* token of friendship; **diede** ~ **di voler andare** he indicated that he wanted to leave; **perdere il** ~ *(leggendo)* to lose one's place; **il** ~ **dei suoi passi** his footprints; **fare** ~ **di sì** to nod; **fare** ~ **di no** to shake one's head; **fare** ~ **con la mano** to make a sign with one's hand; **mi fece** ~ **di spostarmi/avvicinarmi** he made a sign to me to move/come nearer; **essere del** ~ **dell'Acquario** *etc* to be an Aquarian *etc*.

(b) *(bersaglio)* target; **tiro a** ~ target shooting; **colpire nel** ~ to hit the target; *(fig)* to hit the bullseye *o* the nail on the head.

2: il ~ **della croce** *(Rel)* the sign of the cross; ~ **meno/più** *(Mat)* minus/plus sign; ~ **zodiacale** sign of the zodiac; '~**i particolari'** *(su documento etc)* 'distinguishing marks'.

segregare [segre'gare] **1** *vt (gen)* to segregate; *(pazzo)* to confine. **2:** ~**rsi** *vr (fig: isolarsi)*: ~**rsi in casa** to shut o.s. up in the house.

segregazione [segregat'tsjone] *sf* segregation.

segreta [se'greta] *sf* dungeon.

segretariato [segreta'rjato] *sm* secretariat.

segretario, a [segre'tarjo] *sm/f (gen)* secretary; ~ **di direzione** personal assistant; ~ **del partito** party leader; **S**~ **di Stato** *(Am)* Secretary of State.

segreteria [segrete'ria] *sf* **(a)** *(ufficio)* secretary's office; *(in enti)* secretarial offices *pl*. **(b)** *(Pol: carica)* secretaryship; *(: segretariato)* secretariat. **(c):** ~ **telefonica** answering service.

segretezza [segre'tettsa] *sf* secrecy; **notizie della massima** ~ confidential information; **in tutta** ~ in secret; *(confidenzialmente)* in confidence.

segreto, a [se'greto] **1** *ag (gen)* secret; *(documenti)* confidential, secret; **tenere** ~ **qc** to keep sth secret; **passaggio** ~ hidden *o* secret passage. **2** *sm (gen)* secret; **in** ~ in secret; *(in confidenza)* in confidence; **mantenere** *o* **tenere un** ~ to keep a secret; **il** ~ **professionale** professional secrecy; **un** ~ **professionale** a professional secret; **il** ~ **di Pulcinella** an open secret; **il** ~ **del successo** the secret *o* key to success; **nel** ~ **dell'animo** in the depths of one's soul, deep down; **nel** ~ **del cuore** in one's innermost heart, deep down.

seguace [se'gwat∫e] *sm (Rel, gen)* disciple, follower.

seguente [se'gwɛnte] *ag* following, next; **il giorno** ~ the next *o* following day; **i** ~**i candidati sono pregati di farsi avanti** would the following candidates please come forward; **nel modo** ~ as follows, in the following way.

segugio [se'gudʒo] *sm* **(a)** *(Zool)* hound, hunting dog. **(b)** *(fig)* private eye, sleuth.

seguire [se'gwire] **1** *vt* **(a)** *(gen)* to follow; ~ **qn come un'ombra** to follow sb about like a shadow; **segui quella macchina!** follow that car!; **ha fatto** ~ **la moglie** he had his wife followed; **mi segua, la prego** this way *o* follow me, please; **segui la statale per 15 km** follow *o* keep to the main road for 15 km; ~ **una cura** to follow a course of treatment; ~ **i consigli di qn** to follow *o* take sb's advice; ~/**far** ~ **una dieta** to be/put on a diet; **le cose seguono il loro corso** things are taking *o* running their course; ~ **un programma alla TV**

to watch a programme on TV; ~ **un alunno** (fig) to follow the progress of a pupil; ~ **gli avvenimenti di attualità** to follow o keep up with current events.

(b) (capire: persona, argomento) to follow; **scusa, non ti seguo** I'm sorry, I don't follow o I'm not with you.

(c) (corso, lezione: gen) to follow, take; (: essere presente a) to attend, go to; ~ **un corso per corrispondenza** to follow o take a correspondence course; **non è obbligatorio** ~ **le lezioni** attendance at lessons is not compulsory.

2 vi (aus essere) **(a)** (venir dopo, fig: derivare) to follow; **come segue** as follows; **a Pio XI seguì Pio XII** Pius XI was succeeded by Pius XII; **a ciò seguì un aumento dei prezzi** this was followed by a rise in prices.

(b) (continuare) to continue; '**segue**' 'to be continued'.

seguitare [segwi'tare] **1** vt to continue, carry on with; ~ **a fare qc** to continue doing sth. **2** vi to continue, carry on.

seguito ['segwito] sm **(a)** (di persone) retinue, suite; **essere al** ~ **di qn** to be among sb's suite, be one of sb's retinue. **(b)** (continuazione: di film etc) sequel; (: nuovo episodio) continuation; (resto) remainder, rest; **il** ~ **la settimana prossima** to be continued next week; **manca il** ~ the rest is missing. **(c)** (conseguenze): **non aver** ~ to have no repercussions; **il suo tentativo non ha avuto** ~ there was no follow-up to his attempt. **(d)**: **in** ~ then; **in** ~ **a** following; **facciamo** ~ **alla lettera del...** further to o in answer to your letter of... .

sei ['sɛi] ag inv, sm inv six; per uso vedi **cinque**.

seicentesco, a, schi, sche [seitʃen'tesko] ag seventeenth-century.

seicento [sei'tʃɛnto] **1** ag inv six hundred. **2** sm inv six hundred; (secolo): **il S**~ the seventeenth century.

selce ['seltʃe] sf flint, flintstone.

selciato [sel'tʃato] sm cobbled surface; **si sentirono i suoi passi sul** ~ you could hear his footsteps on the cobbles.

selettività [selettivi'ta] sf selectivity.

selettivo, a [selet'tivo] ag selective.

selettore [selet'tore] sm (Tecn) selector.

selezionare [selettsjo'nare] vt to select, choose.

selezione [selet'tsjone] sf selection, choice; **fare una** ~ to make a selection o choice; ~ **naturale** natural selection.

sella ['sella] sf saddle; **montare in** ~ to mount, get into the saddle.

sellare [sel'lare] vt to saddle, put a saddle on.

selleria [selle'ria] sf saddlery.

sellino [sel'lino] sm saddle.

seltz [selts] sm inv soda (water).

selva ['selva] sf (bosco) wood; (foresta) forest; (fig: di gente, capelli) mass.

selvaggina [selvad'dʒina] sf game.

selvaggio, a [sel'vaddʒo] **1** ag (gen) wild; (tribù) savage, primitive; (peg: omicidio) savage, ferocious; (: torture) brutal, cruel. **2** sm savage.

selvatico, a, ci, che [sel'vatiko] **1** ag (animali, fiori) wild; (fig: persona: timido) unsociable. **2** sm (di selvaggina): **sapere di** ~ to taste gamy; **puzzare di** ~ to smell high o gamy.

semaforo [se'maforo] sm (Aut) traffic lights pl; (Ferr) signal.

semantica [se'mantika] sf semantics sg.

semantico, a, ci, che [se'mantiko] ag semantic.

sembiante [sem'bjante] sm (poet: aspetto) appearance; (: volto) countenance.

sembianza [sem'bjantsa] sf (poet) **(a)** (aspetto)

appearance. **(b)**: ~**e** pl (lineamenti) features; (fig: falsa apparenza) semblance.

sembrare [sem'brare] (aus essere) **1** vi (gen) to seem; **sembra simpatico** he seems o appears (to be) nice; **sembrava più giovane** he seemed o looked younger; **sembra suo padre** he looks like his father; **sembra caffè** it tastes like coffee; **al tocco sembrava seta** it felt like silk; **sembra odore di bruciato** it smells as if something is burning.

2 vb impers: **sembra che** it seems that; **mi sembra che** (ho l'impressione) it seems to me that, it looks to me as though; (penso) I think that, I have a feeling that; **ti sembra giusto?** do you think it's fair?; **non gli sembrava onesto farlo** he didn't think it was honest to do it; **le sembra di sapere tutto** she thinks she knows everything; **fai come ti sembra** do as you please o as you see fit; **non mi sembra vero!** I can't believe it!

seme ['seme] sm **(a)** (gen) seed; (di agrumi, mela, pera etc) pip; (di ciliegia, pesca) stone; **gettare il** ~ **della discordia** to sow the seeds of discord. **(b)** (Anat: sperma) semen. **(c)** (Carte) suit.

semente [se'mente] sf seed.

semestrale [semes'trale] ag (che dura 6 mesi) six-month attr; (che avviene ogni 6 mesi) six-monthly.

semestre [se'mestre] sm (gen) six months, six-month period, half year; (Scol) semester; **nel primo** ~ **dell'anno** in the first half of the year.

semi... ['semi] pref semi... .

semiaperto, a [semia'perto] ag half-open.

semibreve [semi'breve] sf (Mus) semibreve (Brit), whole note (Am).

semicerchio [semi'tʃerkjo] sm semicircle.

semicircolare [semitʃirko'lare] ag semicircular.

semiconduttore [semikondut'tore] sm semiconductor.

semicroma [semi'krɔma] sf (Mus) semiquaver (Brit), sixteenth note (Am).

semifinale [semifi'nale] sf (Sport) semifinal.

semifinalista, i, e [semifina'lista] sm/f semifinalist.

semifreddo [semi'freddo] sm (Culin) chilled dessert made with ice cream.

semilavorato, a [semilavo'rato] ag semifinished.

semina ['semina] sf (Agr) sowing; **periodo della** ~ sowing time.

seminale [semi'nale] ag (Anat) seminal, sperm attr.

seminare [semi'nare] vt **(a)** (Agr) to sow; **chi semina raccoglie** as you sow, so shall you reap. **(b)** (inseguitore) to lose, shake off.

seminario [semi'narjo] sm **(a)** (Rel) seminary. **(b)** (Scol) seminar.

seminato [semi'nato] sm: **uscire dal** ~ (fig) to wander off the point.

seminatore [semina'tore] sm sower.

seminatrice [semina'tritʃe] sf (macchina) seeder.

seminfermità [seminfermi'ta] sf (Med) partial infirmity.

seminterrato [seminter'rato] sm basement; (appartamento) basement flat.

seminudo, a [semi'nudo] ag half-naked.

semiologia [semjolo'dʒia] sf semiology.

semioscurità [semioskuri'ta] sf half-light, semi-darkness.

semiserio, a [semi'sɛrjo] ag half-serious.

semitico, a, ci, che [se'mitiko] ag Semitic.

semmai [sem'mai] = **se mai**; vedi **se**[1].

semola ['semola] sf bran; ~ **di grano duro** durum wheat.

semolato [semo'lato] ag: **zucchero** ~ castor sugar.

semolino [semo'lino] sm semolina.

semovente [semo'vɛnte] ag self-propelled.

semplice ['semplitʃe] *ag* **(a)** *(gen: non complicato)* simple; *(persona, modi etc: non affettato)* simple, unaffected; *(: ingenuo)* simple, ingenuous; **è ~ da capire** it's easy *o* simple to understand; **una visione della vita un po' ~** a simplistic view of life; **è una ~ formalità** it's a mere formality; **è una ~ questione d'orgoglio** it's simply a matter of pride; **è pazzia pura e ~** it's sheer madness; **acqua ~** tap water. **(b)** *(Gram)* simple. **(c)** *(Mil)*: **marinaio ~** ordinary seaman; **soldato ~** private.

semplicemente [semplitʃe'mente] *av* **(a)** *(in maniera semplice)* simply, in a simple way; **parla ~ e lentamente** speak slowly and simply. **(b)** *(solamente)* only, merely, simply; **desidero ~ la verità** I merely want the truth; **è ~ ridicolo** it's simply ridiculous. **(c)** *(con modestia)* simply, modestly; **vive molto ~** he lives very simply.

semplicione [sempli'tʃone] *sm (fam)* simpleton.

semplicistico, a, ci, che [sempli'tʃistiko] *ag* simplistic.

semplicità [semplitʃi'ta] *sf* simplicity, simpleness.

semplificare [semplifi'kare] *vt* to simplify.

semplificazione [semplifikat'tsjone] *sf* simplification; **fare una ~ di** to simplify.

sempre ['sempre] *av* **(a)** *(continuità)* always; *(eternamente)* always, forever; **viene ~ alle 5** he always comes at 5 o'clock; **crede di aver ~ ragione** she thinks she's always right; **ti amerò ~** I'll always love you, I'll love you for ever; **è la persona di ~** he's the same as ever, he's his usual self; **sei il cretino di ~, sei ~ il solito cretino** you are as daft as ever; **per ~** for ever; **una volta per ~** once and for all; **arriva ~ a disturbare** he's always *o* forever coming to disturb me *(o us etc)*; **ha nevicato ~** it snowed all the time; **è un abito che puoi indossare ~** it's a dress you can wear any time *o* on any occasion; **è rimasto ~ lí, fermo** he stayed there, immobile.

(b) *(ancora, comunque)* still; **esci ~ con lui?** are you still going out with him?; **c'è ~ la possibilità che...** there's still a chance that..., there's always the possibility that...; **ha una certa età ma è ~ bella** she is getting on but is still very attractive; **è (pur) ~ tuo fratello** he is still your brother (however); **è ~ meglio che niente** it's better than nothing.

(c): **~ che** as long as, provided that; **~ che non piova** as long as *o* provided that it doesn't rain, unless it rains; **~ che tu non cambi idea** as long as you don't change your mind, unless you change your mind.

(d) *(rafforzativo)*: **~ più** more and more; **~ meno** less and less; **va ~ meglio** things are getting better and better; **è ~ più giovane** she gets younger and younger.

sempreverde [sempre'verde] *ag, sm of* evergreen.

senape ['senape] **1** *sf (Bot, Culin)* mustard. **2** *ag inv (colore)* mustard-coloured.

senato [se'nato] *sm* senate.

senatore, trice [sena'tore] *sm/f* senator.

senile [se'nile] *ag* senile.

senilità [senili'ta] *sf* senility.

senno ['senno] *sm* judgment, good sense; **uscire di ~** to lose one's mind *o* wits; **col ~ di poi** with hindsight; **del ~ di poi son piene le fosse** it's easy to be wise after the event.

sennò [sen'nɔ] **= se no**; *vedi* **se**[1].

seno[1] ['seno] *sm* **(a)** *(Anat)* bosom; *(: mammella)* breast; *(: grembo)* womb; **portare un figlio in ~** to carry a child (in one's womb); **in ~ alla famiglia** in the bosom of the family; **in ~ al partito/all'organizzazione** within the party/the organization. **(b)** *(Anat, Zool)* sinus.

seno[2] ['seno] *sm (Mat)* sine.

sensale [sen'sale] *sm (Comm)* agent.

sensatezza [sensa'tettsa] *sf* good sense, good judgment.

sensato, a [sen'sato] *ag* sensible.

sensazionale [sensattsjo'nale] *ag* sensational, exciting.

sensazione [sensat'tsjone] *sf* feeling, sensation; **ho la ~ di averlo già visto** I have a feeling I've seen him before; **fare ~** *(interesse, stupore)* to cause a sensation; **essere a caccia di nuove ~i** to be after new thrills *o* experiences.

sensibile [sen'sibile] *ag* **(a)** *(gen)* sensitive; **ha un animo ~** he's tender-hearted; **essere ~ a** *(freddo, caldo)* to be sensitive to; *(: complimenti, adulazioni, fascino)* to be susceptible to. **(b)** *(progresso, differenze)* appreciable, noticeable.

sensibilità [sensibili'ta] *sf* sensitivity, sensitiveness.

sensibilizzare [sensibilid'dzare] *vt (fig)* to make aware, awaken; **~ le masse ai problemi del paese** to make the people aware of the country's problems.

sensitivo, a [sensi'tivo] **1** *ag* **(a)** *(Anat)* sensory, sensorial; **percezioni ~e** sensory perception. **(b)** *(persona)* sensitive, susceptible. **2** *sm/f* sensitive person; *(medium)* medium.

senso ['senso] *sm* **(a)** *(istinto, coscienza)* sense; **i 5 ~i** the 5 senses; **perdere/riprendere i ~i** to lose/regain consciousness; **~ d'orientamento** sense of direction; **avere ~ pratico** to be practical; **~ del dovere/dell'umorismo** sense of duty/humour; **avere un sesto ~** to have a sixth sense.

(b) *(sensazione)* feeling, sense; **un ~ di angoscia** a feeling *o* sense of anxiety; **provare un ~ di inquietudine** to feel anxious; **fare ~ (a qn)** *(ribrezzo)* to disgust (sb), repel (sb).

(c) *(significato)* meaning, sense; **nel ~ letterale/figurato** in the literal/figurative sense *o* meaning; **senza** *o* **privo di ~** meaningless; **in un certo ~ ha ragione lui** in a way *o* sense he's right; **nel ~ che** in the sense that; **che ~ ha?** where's the sense in that?; **(per me) non ha ~** it doesn't make (any) sense (to me); **nel vero ~ della parola** in the true sense of the word.

(d) *(direzione)* direction; **in ~ opposto** in the opposite direction; **nel ~ della lunghezza** lengthwise, lengthways; **nel ~ della larghezza** widthwise; **io venivo nel ~ contrario** I was coming from the opposite direction; **in ~ orario** clockwise; **in ~ antiorario** anticlockwise, counterclockwise *(Am)*; **ho dato disposizioni in quel ~** I've given instructions to that end *o* effect.

(e) *(Aut)*: **a ~ unico** *(strada)* one-way; **'~ vietato'** 'no entry'.

sensuale [sensu'ale] *ag* sensual.

sensualità [sensuali'ta] *sf* sensuality, sensuousness.

sentenza [sen'tɛntsa] *sf* **(a)** *(Dir)* sentence; **pronunciare una ~** di morte a qn to sentence sb to death. **(b)**: **sputar ~e** *(peg)* to moralize.

sentenziare [senten'tsjare] *vt (Dir)*: **~ che** to rule that; **~ la pena di morte** to pass the death sentence.

sentenzioso, a [senten'tsjoso] *ag* sententious.

sentiero [sen'tjɛro] *sm* path.

sentimentale [sentimen'tale] **1** *ag (gen)* sentimental; *(peg)* soppy; **vita ~** love life. **2** *sm/f* sentimentalist.

sentimento [senti'mento] *sm (gen)* feeling; **una persona di nobili ~i** a person of noble sentiments; **urtare i ~i di qn** to hurt sb's feelings.

sentinella [senti'nɛlla] *sf (Mil)* sentry, guard;

essere di ~ to be on guard o sentry duty.

sentire [sen'tire] **1** vt (**a**) (percepire: gen, al tatto) to feel; ~ **freddo/caldo** to feel cold/hot; ~ **dolore** to feel pain; **sento un gran male qui** I've got a terrible pain here; **senti quanto pesa** feel how heavy it is; **non sento niente** I can't feel a thing; **il caldo si fa** ~ the heat is oppressive o is really making itself felt; **la sua assenza si fa** ~ his absence is noticeable.

(**b**) (emozione) to feel; ~ **un profondo affetto per qn** to feel deep affection for sb; **non sento niente per lui** I don't feel anything for him; ~ **la mancanza di qn** to miss sb; **sento che succederà qualcosa** I sense that something is going to happen; **sento che mente** I can sense that he is lying; **sento che mi vuoi lasciare** I can sense that you want to leave me; **dice sempre quello che sente** he always says what he feels.

(**c**) (al gusto) to taste; (all'olfatto) to smell; **senti se ti piace questa salsa** taste this sauce to see if you like it; **senti se ti piace questo profumo** smell this perfume to see if you like it; **ho il raffreddore e non sento gli odori/i sapori** I've got a cold and I can't smell/taste anything.

(**d**) (udire) to listen to; (ascoltare) to listen to; **sento dei passi** I can hear footsteps; **mi piace ~ la musica** I like listening to music; **stare a ~** to listen; **hai sentito l'ultima?** have you heard the latest?; **senti, mi presti quel disco?** listen, will you lend me that record?; **ho sentito dire che...** I have heard that...; **stammi bene a ~!** just you listen to me!; **a ~ lui...** to hear him talk...; **farsi ~** to make o.s. heard; **fatti ~** keep in touch; **non ci sente** (sordo) he's deaf, he can't hear; **non ci sente da quell'orecchio** (fig) he always turns a deaf ear to things like that; **senti quello che ti dice l'avvocato** go and ask your lawyer for advice; **intendo ~ il mio legale/il parere di un medico** I'm going to consult my lawyer/a doctor; **senti cosa vuole** see what he wants; **ma senti un po'!** just fancy that!; **senti questa!** just listen to this!; **si sente che è straniero** you can tell he's a foreigner; **per sentito dire** by hearsay.

2: ~**rsi** vr (**a**) (gen) to feel; ~**rsi bene/male** to feel well/ill; **come ti senti?** how are you?; ~**rsi svenire** to feel faint.

(**b**) (essere disposto): ~**rsi di fare qc** to feel like doing sth; **sentirsela: non me la sento** I don't feel like it; **proprio non se la sente di continuare** he doesn't feel like carrying on.

(**c**) (uso reciproco) to hear from one another; **si sono sentiti di recente** they were in touch (with one another) recently.

sentitamente [sentita'mente] av sincerely; **ringraziare ~** to thank sincerely.

sentito, a [sen'tito] ag (ringraziamenti, condoglianze) sincere, deep.

sentore [sen'tore] sm rumour, talk; **c'è ~ di un aumento di stipendio** there's talk of a pay rise; **aver ~ di qc** to hear about sth.

senza ['sɛntsa] **1** prep without; **uscì ~ ombrello** he went out without his umbrella; **non so cosa farei ~ il suo aiuto** I don't know what I'd do without his help; **mangiare ~ (la) forchetta** to eat without a fork; **non ~ alcune riserve** not without some reservations; **non posso stare ~ di te** I can't live without you; **siamo rimasti ~ zucchero/tè** we've run out of sugar/tea, we have no sugar/tea left; **forza, ~ tante chiacchiere** come on, stop the talking and let's get on with it; ~ **casa** homeless; ~ **padre** fatherless; ~ **preoccupazioni** carefree; ~ **impegno** without obligation; **un dettato ~ errori** an error-free dictation; **un**

discorso ~ senso a meaningless speech.

2 cong without; ~ **batter ciglio** without batting an eyelid; **ho trascorso tutta la notte ~ chiudere occhio** I didn't sleep a wink all night, I didn't close my eyes all night; ~ **dire niente** without saying a thing; **parlò ~ riflettere** he spoke without thinking; ~ **che tu lo sapessi** without your knowing about it; ~ **dire che...** not to mention the fact that...; ~ **contare che...** without considering that... .

senzatetto [sentsa'tetto] **1** sm/f inv homeless person; **i ~** the homeless. **2** ag inv homeless.

separare [sepa'rare] **1** vt (gen) to separate; (litiganti) to pull apart, part; (aspetti, problemi) to distinguish between; **le Alpi separano la Svizzera dall'Italia** the Alps divide o separate Italy from Switzerland; ~ **il bene dal male** to distinguish between good and evil; **solo pochi chilometri lo separavano da casa** only a few kilometres separated him from home o stood between him and home.

2: ~**rsi** vr (**a**) (lasciare): ~**rsi da** (persona) to leave; (oggetto) to part with; **gli dispiaceva ~rsi dai propri cari/da quegli oggetti cari** he didn't want to leave his dear ones/to part with those dear objects; **si è separata dal marito** she has left her husband. (**b**) (staccarsi): ~**rsi da** to split off from, separate off from. (**c**) (uso reciproco: gen) to part; (: coniugi, soci) to part, split up, separate; **dopo 2 ore di cammino si separarono** after 2 hours' walk they parted (company).

separatamente [separata'mente] av separately.

separatismo [separa'tizmo] sm separatism.

separatista, i, e [separa'tista] ag, sm/f separatist.

separato, a [sepa'rato] ag (gen) separate; **in ~a sede** (privatamente) in private; **vivono ~i** (coniugi) they have separated.

separazione [separat'tsjone] sf (gen, Dir) separation; **dopo la ~** (di coniugi) after they parted; ~ **dei beni** division of property.

séparé [sepa're] sm inv screen.

sepolcrale [sepol'krale] ag sepulchral.

sepolcro [se'polkro] sm sepulchre; **il Santo S~** the Holy Sepulchre.

sepolto, a [se'polto] **1** pp di **seppellire**. **2** ag (gen, fig) buried; ~ **vivo** buried alive; **morto e ~** (anche fig) dead and buried; ~ **nel profondo del cuore** buried deep in one's heart.

sepoltura [sepol'tura] sf burial; **dare ~ a qn** to bury sb.

seppellire [seppel'lire] **1** vt (gen) to bury; (fig: passato, ricordi) to bury, forget; **il villaggio era sepolto dalla neve** the village was buried under the snow; ~ **antichi rancori** to bury the hatchet, let bygones be bygones. **2:** ~**rsi** vr (fig: isolarsi) to shut o.s. off, cut o.s. off; ~**rsi tra i libri** to bury o.s. in one's books.

seppia ['seppja] sf (Zool) cuttlefish; **nero di ~** sepia.

seppure [sep'pure] cong even if.

sequela [se'kwɛla] sf (di avvenimenti) series, sequence; (di offese, ingiurie) string.

sequenza [se'kwɛntsa] sf sequence.

sequestrare [sekwes'trare] vt (**a**) (gen) to confiscate; (Dir) to sequestrate. (**b**) (rapire) to kidnap.

sequestro [se'kwɛstro] sm (**a**) (Dir) sequestration. (**b**) (anche: ~ di persona) kidnapping.

sequoia [se'kwɔja] sf sequoia.

sera ['sera] sf evening; **si fa ~** it's getting dark, night is falling; **di ~** in the evening; **alle 6 di ~** at 6 o'clock in the evening, at 6 p.m.; **alle 11 di ~** at 11 o'clock at night, at 11 p.m.; **questa ~** this evening, tonight; **dalla mattina alla ~** from morning to night.

serafico, a, ci, che [se'rafiko] *ag* seraphic.

serale [se'rale] *ag* evening *attr*; **scuola ~** evening classes *pl*, night school.

serata [se'rata] *sf* **(a)** *(sera)* evening. **(b)** *(ricevimento)* evening party, soirée; **~ danzante** dance. **(c)** *(Teatro)* evening performance; **~ di gala/d'addio** gala/farewell performance.

serbare [ser'bare] *vt (tenere)* to keep; *(mettere da parte)* to put aside, keep; **~ rancore a qn** to bear *o* harbour a grudge against sb.

serbatoio [serba'tojo] *sm (gen)* tank; *(cisterna)* cistern; **~ (della benzina)** *(Aut)* (petrol) tank.

serbo[1] ['sɛrbo] *sm*: **in ~** *(sorpresa etc)* in store; **te lo tengo in ~** I'll set it aside for you.

serbo[2], **a** ['sɛrbo] **1** *ag* Serbian. **2** *sm/f* Serbian, Serb. **3** *sm (lingua)* Serbian.

serenata [sere'nata] *sf* serenade; **fare la ~ a qn** to serenade sb, sing sb a serenade.

serenità [sereni'ta] *sf* peace, tranquillity, serenity; **~ d'animo** peace of mind.

sereno, a [se'reno] **1** *ag (tempo, cielo)* clear, serene; *(volto, persona)* calm, serene; *(giudizio)* dispassionate; *(vita)* quiet; **un fulmine a ciel ~** *(fig)* a bolt from the blue. **2** *sm (tempo)* good weather.

sergente [ser'dʒente] *sm (Mil)* sergeant; **~ maggiore** sergeant major.

sericoltura [serikol'tura] *sf* sericulture.

serie ['sɛrje] *sf inv* **(a)** *(gen)* series *inv*; *(di numeri)* series, sequence; *(di chiavi)* set; **tutta una ~ di problemi** a whole string of problems. **(b)** *(Sport)* division; **~ A/B** ≈ first/second division. **(c)** *(Comm)*: **produzione in ~** mass production; **produrre in ~** to mass-produce; **modello di ~/fuori ~** *(Aut)* standard/custom-built model.

serietà [serje'ta] *sf (vedi ag)* seriousness; earnestness; reliability.

serio, a ['sɛrjo] **1** *ag (gen)* serious; *(persona, conversazione)* serious, earnest; *(persona, ditta: affidabile)* reliable; **restare ~** to keep a straight face; **sii ~!** be serious!; **aveva una faccia ~a** he looked serious; **è una ragazza ~a** *(per bene)* she's a respectable girl. **2** *sm*: **sul ~** seriously; **sul ~ ti ha invitato?** did he really invite you?; **non facevo sul ~, non dicevo sul ~** I wasn't serious; **faccio sul ~** I mean it; **prendere qc/qn sul ~** to take sth/sb seriously.

sermone [ser'mone] *sm (Rel)* sermon; *(fig)* lecture, sermon; **fare un ~ a qn** *(fig)* to give sb a lecture *o* sermon.

serpe ['sɛrpe] *sf* snake; *(fig peg)* viper; **scaldare una ~ in seno** to nurse a viper in one's bosom.

serpeggiante [serped'dʒante] *ag* winding, twisting.

serpeggiare [serped'dʒare] *vi (strada, fiume)* to wind, snake, twist; *(fig: malcontento, rivolta)* to spread (insidiously).

serpente [ser'pɛnte] *sm* **(a)** *(Zool)* snake, serpent; **~ a sonagli** rattlesnake. **(b)** *(pelle)* snakeskin.

serpentina [serpen'tina] *sf*: **a ~** *(strada)* winding.

serra[1] ['sɛrra] *sf (Agr)* greenhouse; *(: riscaldata)* hothouse.

serra[2] ['sɛrra] *sf (Geog)* sierra.

serraglio [ser'raʎʎo] *sm* **(a)** *(di animali)* menagerie. **(b)** *(di sultano)* harem.

serramanico [serra'maniko] *sm*: **coltello a ~** jackknife.

serranda [ser'randa] *sf* (rolling) shutter.

serrare [ser'rare] *vt (chiudere)* to close, shut; *(stringere)* to shut tightly; **~ i pugni/i denti** to clench one's fists/one's teeth; **~ le file** *(anche fig)*

to close ranks; **~ il nemico** to close in on the enemy.

serrata [ser'rata] *sf (Industria)* lockout.

serrato, a [ser'rato] *ag* **(a)** *(porta, finestra)* closed, shut; *(pugni, denti)* clenched; *(occhi)* tightly closed. **(b)** *(stringato)* logical, coherent. **(c)** *(veloce)*: **a ritmo ~** quickly, fast.

serratura [serra'tura] *sf* lock.

serva ['serva] *sf vedi* **servo.**

servigio [ser'vidʒo] *sm* favour, service.

servile [ser'vile] *ag* **(a)** *(gen, fig)* servile. **(b)** *(Gram: verbo)* modal.

servire [ser'vire] **1** *vt* **(a)** *(essere al servizio di)* to serve; **~ qn** *(in negozio)* to attend to *o* serve sb; *(al ristorante)* to wait on *o* serve sb; **gli piace farsi ~** he likes to be waited on; **in cosa posso servirla?** *(negozio)* can I help you?; **adesso ti servo io!** *(iro)* now I'll show you!; **grazie — per servirla** thank you — at your service; **~ la Messa/la Patria** to serve Mass/one's country. **(b)** *(piatto)* to serve; **~ qc a qn** to serve sb with sth, help sb to sth; **'~ ghiacciato'** 'serve chilled'; **~ a tavola** to wait on table; **~ da bere a qn** to serve a drink to sb; **il pranzo è servito** dinner is served. **(c)** *(Carte)* to deal.

2 *vi* **(a)** *(aus* **essere***)*: **~ a (fare) qc** *(essere utile)* to be used for (doing) sth; **~ a qn** to be of use to sb; **a cosa serve questo aggeggio?** what is this gadget (used) for?; **serve a tagliare la frutta** it's for cutting fruit; **questa stanza serve da studio** this room is used as a study; **che ti serva da lezione** let that be a lesson to you; **ha insistito ma non è servito (a niente)** he insisted but to no purpose; **mi serve un paio di forbici** I need a pair of scissors; **non mi serve più** I don't need it any more; **te lo presto, se ti serve** I'll lend it to you, if you need it; **piangere non serve a niente** it's no use crying, crying doesn't help; **a che serve lamentarsi?** what would be the point of complaining? **(b)** *(Tennis)* to serve.

3: **~rsi** *vr* **(a)** *(fare uso)*: **~rsi di** to make use of, use. **(b)** *(a tavola)* to help o.s. **(c)**: **~rsi da** *(negoziante)* to shop at.

servitore, trice [servi'tore] *sm/f* servant.

servitù [servi'tu] *sf* **(a)** *(condizione)* slavery, bondage; **~ della gleba** *(Storia)* serfdom. **(b)** *(domestici)* servants *pl*, domestic staff.

servizievole [servit'tsjevole] *ag* obliging, helpful.

servizio [ser'vittsjo] *sm* **(a)** *(lavoro)* duty; **essere di *o* in ~** to be on duty; **prendere ~** to come on duty; **avere 20 anni di ~** to have completed 20 years' service; **non bevo in ~** I don't drink on duty.

(b) *(come domestico)* (domestic) service; **andare/essere a ~** to go into/be in service; **entrata di ~** service *o* tradesman's entrance.

(c) *(Mil)*: **il ~ militare** military service; **prestare ~ militare** to do one's military *o* national service; **~ segreto** secret service; **~ armato** combatant service; **~ d'ordine** *(Polizia)* police patrol; *(di manifestanti)* team of stewards *(responsible for crowd control)*.

(d) *(istituzioni pubbliche)* service; **~ postale/ telefonico** postal/telephone service.

(e) *(funzionamento)* service; **fuori ~** out of order; **rimettere in ~** to put *o* bring back into service.

(f) *(favore)* service, favour; *(prestazioni)*: **~i** services; **offrire i propri ~i a qn** to offer sb one's services; **bel ~ mi hai fatto!** *(iro)* you've been a real help!; **sono al suo ~** I am at your service.

(g) *(al ristorante)* service; *(sul conto)* service (charge); **~ compreso/escluso** service included/ not included.

(h) *(TV, Radio, Stampa)* report; ~ **fotografico** *(Stampa)* photo feature; ~ **in diretta** live coverage.

(i) *(Rel)* service.

(j) *(Tennis)* service; **al** ~ **Borg** Borg to serve.

(k) *(insieme di oggetti)*: ~ **da tè** tea set; ~ **di cristallo** set of crystal glassware.

(l): **i** ~**i** *pl (di casa)* kitchen and bathroom; **casa con doppi** ~**i** house with two bathrooms.

servo, a ['servo] *sm/f* servant, man/maidservant.

servofreno [servo'freno] *sm (Aut)* servo brake.

servosterzo [servos'tɛrtso] *sm (Aut)* power steering.

sesamo ['sɛzamo] *sm (Bot)* sesame.

sessanta [ses'santa] *ag inv, sm inv* sixty; *per uso vedi* **cinquanta.**

sessantenne [sessan'tɛnne] *ag, sm/f* sixty-year-old; *per uso vedi* **cinquantenne.**

sessantesimo, a [sessan'tɛzimo] *ag, sm/f, sm* six-tieth; *per uso vedi* **quinto.**

sessantina [sessan'tina] *sf* about sixty; *per uso vedi* **cinquantina.**

sessione [ses'sjone] *sf* session.

sesso ['sɛsso] *sm* sex; **il** ~ **debole/forte** the weaker/ stronger sex.

sessuale [sessu'ale] *ag (gen)* sexual; *(vita, organo, educazione)* sex *attr*, sexual.

sessualità [sessuali'ta] *sf* sexuality.

sestante [ses'tante] *sm (Naut)* sextant.

sestetto [ses'tetto] *sm (Mus)* sextet.

sesto¹ ['sɛsto] *ag, sm/f, sm (numerale)* sixth; *per uso vedi* **quinto.**

sesto² ['sɛsto] *sm (Archit)*: **arco a** ~ **acuto** pointed arch; **arco a tutto** ~ rounded arch.

sesto³ ['sɛsto] *sm*: **rimettere in** ~ *(aggiustare)* to put back in order; *(fig: persona)* to put back on his *(o her)* feet; **rimettersi in** ~ *(riprendersi)* to recover, get well; *(riassettarsi)* to tidy o.s. up.

set [set] *sm inv* set.

seta ['seta] *sf* silk.

setacciare [setat'tʃare] *vt (farina etc)* to sift, sieve; *(fig: zona)* to search, comb.

setaccio [se'tattʃo] *sm* sieve; **passare al** ~ *(fig)* to search, comb.

sete ['sete] *sf (anche fig)* thirst; **avere** ~ to be thirsty; **soffrire la** ~ to suffer from thirst; **morire di** ~ to die of thirst; ~ **di potere** thirst for power.

setificio [seti'fitʃo] *sm* silk factory.

setola ['setola] *sf* bristle.

setta ['sɛtta] *sf (Rel)* sect.

settanta [set'tanta] *ag inv, sm inv* seventy; *per uso vedi* **cinquanta.**

settantenne [settan'tɛnne] *ag, sm/f* seventy-year-old; *per uso vedi* **cinquantenne.**

settantesimo, a [settan'tɛzimo] *ag, sm/f, sm* seven-tieth; *per uso vedi* **cinquantesimo.**

settantina [settan'tina] *sf* about seventy; *per uso vedi* **cinquantina.**

settario, a [set'tarjo] *ag, sm* sectarian.

settarismo [setta'rizmo] *sm* sectarianism.

sette ['sɛtte] *ag inv, sm inv* seven; *per uso vedi* **cinque.**

settecentesco, a, schi, sche [settetʃen'tesko] *ag* eighteenth-century.

settecento [sette'tʃɛnto] **1** *ag inv* seven hundred. **2** *sm inv* seven hundred; *(secolo)*: **il S~** the eighteenth century.

settembre [set'tɛmbre] *sm* September; *per uso vedi* **luglio.**

settentrionale [settentrjo'nale] **1** *ag* northern; **Italia** ~ Northern Italy; **vento** ~ north *o* northerly wind. **2** *sm/f* northerner, person from the north.

settentrione [setten'trjone] *sm* north; **del** ~ north(ern), of the north; *(vento)* north(erly).

setter ['setter] *sm inv (Zool)* setter.

setticemia [settitʃe'mia] *sf* blood poisoning, septi-caemia.

settico, a, ci, che ['settiko] *ag* septic.

settimana [setti'mana] *sf* **(a)** week; **una volta/due volte alla** ~ once/twice a week; **questa** ~ this week; **la** ~ **scorsa/prossima** last/next week; **a metà** ~ in the middle of the week; **2** ~**e fa** 2 weeks ago; **fra 2** ~**e** in 2 weeks' time; **prendere 3** ~**e di ferie** to take 3 weeks' holiday; ~ **dopo** ~ week after week, week in, week out; **una** ~ **sì, una no** every other week; ~ **lavorativa** working week; ~ **santa** Holy Week. **(b)** *(paga)* week's pay, wages *pl*; *(per bambini)* weekly allowance, pocket money.

settimanale [settima'nale] **1** *ag* weekly. **2** *sm (rivista)* weekly (publication).

settimino [setti'mino] *sm (neonato) baby born two months' premature.*

settimo, a [set'timo] *ag, sm/f, sm* seventh; *per uso vedi* **quinto.**

setto ['setto] *sm (Anat)* septum.

settore [set'tore] *sm (Econ, Geom, Mil)* sector; *(fig)* area.

severità [severi'ta] *sf (vedi ag)* severity; strictness.

severo, a [se'vero] *ag (gen)* severe; *(padre, insegnante, giudice)* strict.

sevizie [se'vittsje] *sfpl* torture *sg*.

seviziare [sevit'tsjare] *vt (torturare)* to torture; *(picchiare)* to beat up.

sezionare [settsjo'nare] *vt (gen)* to divide up, cut up; *(Med)* to dissect.

sezione [set'tsjone] *sf (gen, Geom, Archit, Tecn)* section; *(di ufficio)* department; *(a scuola)* stream.

sfaccendato, a [sfattʃen'dato] **1** *ag* lazy, idle. **2** *sm/f* idler, loafer.

sfaccettare [sfattʃet'tare] *vt (pietre preziose)* to cut, facet.

sfaccettatura [sfattʃetta'tura] *sf (azione)* faceting; *(parte sfaccettata, fig)* facet.

sfacchinare [sfakki'nare] *vi (fam)* to toil, drudge.

sfacchinata [sfakki'nata] *sf (fam)* toil, drudgery.

sfacciataggine [sfattʃa'taddʒine] *sf* insolence, cheek; **ma che** ~**!** what a cheek *o* nerve!; **avere la** ~ **di fare qc** to have the nerve *o* cheek to do sth.

sfacciato, a [sfat'tʃato] *ag* insolent, cheeky.

sfacelo [sfa'tʃelo] *sm (fig: di famiglia, organizzazione)* break-up; **andare in** ~ *(costruzione)* to fall to pieces; *(piani)* to be ruined.

sfaldarsi [sfal'darsi] *vr (rocce)* to exfoliate.

sfalsare [sfal'sare] *vt* to stagger, offset.

sfamare [sfa'mare] **1** *vt (nutrire)* to feed; *(soddisfare la fame):* ~ **qn** to satisfy sb's hunger. **2:** ~**rsi** *vr* to satisfy one's hunger, fill o.s. up.

sfare [sfare] **1** *vt* = **disfare. 2:** ~**rsi** *vr (neve)* to melt.

sfarfallare [sfarfal'lare] *vi* **(a)** *(fig: persona)* to flutter about. **(b)** *(Cine, TV)* to flicker.

sfarfallio [sfarfal'lio] *sm (Cine, TV)* flickering.

sfarzo ['sfartso] *sm* pomp, splendour, magnificence.

sfarzoso, a [sfar'tsoso] *ag* splendid, magnificent.

sfasamento [sfaza'mento] *sm (Elettr)* phase displacement; *(fig)* confusion, bewilderment.

sfasato, a [sfa'zato] *ag (Elettr, motore)* out of phase; *(fig: persona)* confused, bewildered.

sfasciare¹ [sfaʃ'ʃare] *vt (togliere una fascia)* to un-bandage.

sfasciare² [sfaʃ'ʃare] **1** *vt (macchina)* to smash, wreck; *(vaso)* to smash, shatter; *(letto, sedia)* to wreck, break. **2:** ~**rsi** *vr (macchina)* to be smashed, be wrecked; *(vaso)* to shatter; *(letto, sedia)* to fall to pieces.

sfatare [sfa'tare] *vt (leggenda, mito)* to explode.

sfaticato, a [sfati'kato] **1** *ag* lazy, idle. **2** *sm/f* idler, loafer.

sfatto, a ['sfatto] **1** *pp di* sfare. **2** *ag (letto)* unmade; *(orlo etc)* undone; *(gelato, neve)* melted; *(frutta)* overripe; *(riso, pasta etc)* overdone, overcooked; *(fam: persona, corpo)* flabby.

sfavillante [sfavil'lante] *ag (vedi vb)* sparkling; flickering.

sfavillare [sfavil'lare] *vi (diamante, occhi)* to sparkle; *(fiamma)* to flicker.

sfavillio [sfavil'lio] *sm (vedi vb)* sparkling; flickering.

sfavore [sfa'vore] *sm* disfavour, disapproval.

sfavorevole [sfavo'revole] *ag* unfavourable.

sfebbrare [sfeb'brare] *vi (aus essere)*: **entro qualche giorno sfebbrerà** his temperature will go down in a few days.

sfegatato, a [sfega'tato] *ag (anche peg)* fanatical.

sfera ['sfera] *sf (anche fig)* sphere.

sferico, a, ci, che ['sferiko] *ag* spherical.

sferragliare [sferra'ʎʎare] *vi* to rattle, clatter.

sferrare [sfer'rare] *vt (attacco)* to launch; ~ **un colpo a qn** to hit out at sb, lash out at sb (with one's fist); ~ **un calcio a qn** to kick out at sb, lash out at sb (with one's foot).

sferruzzare [sferrut'tsare] *vi* to knit away.

sferza ['sfertsa] *sf* whip, lash.

sferzante [sfer'tsante] *ag (critiche, parole)* stinging.

sferzare [sfer'tsare] *vt (gen)* to whip; *(sog: vento)* to lash; *(: onde)* to lash against, break on.

sferzata [sfer'tsata] *sf* whipping; *(fig)* lashing.

sfiancare [sfjan'kare] **1** *vt* to wear out, exhaust. **2:** ~**rsi** *vr* to exhaust o.s., wear o.s. out.

sfiatare [sfja'tare] *vi* to allow air *(o gas etc)* to escape.

sfiatatoio [sfjata'tojo] *sm* **(a)** *(Zool)* blowhole. **(b)** *(Tecn)* vent.

sfibrante [sfi'brante] *ag* exhausting, energy-sapping.

sfibrare [sfi'brare] *vt* to exhaust, enervate.

sfibrato, a [sfi'brato] *ag* exhausted, worn out.

sfida ['sfida] *sf* challenge; **lanciare una** ~ **a qn** to challenge sb.

sfidante [sfi'dante] **1** *ag* challenging. **2** *sm/f* challenger.

sfidare [sfi'dare] **1** *vt* **(a)** to challenge; ~ **qn a duello** to challenge sb to a duel; ~ **qn a fare qc** to challenge sb to do sth. **(b)** *(fig: affrontare)* to defy; ~ **la morte** to defy death; ~ **un pericolo** to brave a danger. **(c)** *(fraseologia)*: **sfido io!** I dare say!; **sfido che...** I dare say (that).... . **2:** ~**rsi** *vr (uso reciproco)* to challenge one another.

sfiducia [sfi'dutʃa] *sf* distrust; **avere** ~ **in qn/qc** to distrust sb/sth; **voto di** ~ *(Pol)* vote of no confidence.

sfigurare [sfigu'rare] **1** *vt* to disfigure. **2** *vi* to make a bad impression, cut a poor figure.

sfilacciare [sfilat'tʃare] *vt, vi (aus essere)*, ~**rsi** *vr* to fray.

sfilare [sfi'lare] **1** *vt* **(a)** *(orlo, tessuto)* to pull the threads out of; *(perle)* to unstring; *(ago)* to unthread. **(b)** *(togliere: stivali, scarpe)* to take off; **gli sfilò il portafoglio** he pinched *o* lifted his wallet; ~**rsi il vestito/le scarpe** to take one's dress/shoes off. **2** *vi (truppe)* to parade, march past; *(manifestanti)* to march; *(modelle)* to parade. **3:** ~**rsi** *vr (orlo, tessuto)* to fray; *(calza)* to ladder, run.

sfilata [sfi'lata] *sf (Mil)* parade; *(di manifestanti)* march; ~ **(di moda)** fashion show.

sfilza ['sfiltsa] *sf (di case)* row; *(di errori)* series *inv*.

sfinge ['sfindʒe] *sf* sphinx.

sfinimento [sfini'mento] *sm* exhaustion.

sfinire [sfi'nire] **1** *vt* to exhaust, wear out. **2:** ~**rsi** *vr* to wear o.s. out, exhaust o.s.

sfinito, a [sfi'nito] *ag* exhausted, worn out.

sfintere [sfin'tere] *sm (Anat)* sphincter.

sfiorare [sfjo'rare] *vt (acqua, cime di alberi etc)* to skim (over); **il proiettile l'ha solo sfiorato** the bullet only grazed him; ~ **un argomento** to touch on a subject; **è un'idea che non mi sfiora nemmeno** it's an idea which hasn't even crossed my mind; **non ti ha mai sfiorato il dubbio che possa rifiutare?** has it never occurred to you *o* has it never crossed your mind that he might refuse?; ~ **la velocità di 150 km/h** to touch 150 km/h.

sfiorire [sfjo'rire] *vi (aus essere) (fiore, pianta)* to wither, fade; *(fig: bellezza)* to fade.

sfitto, a ['sfitto] *ag* vacant, empty.

sfizio ['sfittsjo] *sm* whim, fancy; **togliersi lo** ~ **di fare qc** to satisfy one's whim to do sth.

sfocare [sfo'kare] *vt* to blur.

sfocato, a [sfo'kato] *ag* blurred, out of focus.

sfociare [sfo'tʃare] *vi (aus essere) (fiume)*: ~ **in** to flow into; **il malcontento sfociò in una rivolta** the discontent developed into open rebellion.

sfoderare [sfode'rare] *vt* **(a)** *(spada, pugnale)* to draw, unsheathe; *(pistola)* to draw; *(fig: ostentare: cultura etc)* to parade, show off; ~ **un sorriso** to give a smile. **(b)** *(togliere la fodera a)* to remove the lining from.

sfoderato, a [sfode'rato] *ag (vestito)* unlined.

sfogare [sfo'gare] **1** *vt (gioia, tristezza etc)* to give vent to; *(energia)* to work off; ~ **la propria rabbia su qn** to vent one's anger on sb. **2** *vi (aus essere) (liquido)* to flow out; *(gas)* to escape; *(malattia, febbre)* to run its course. **3:** ~**rsi** *vr (persona)* to give vent to one's feelings; *(: liberarsi di un peso)* to get a load off one's chest; ~**rsi con qn** *(confidarsi)* to unburden o.s. *o* open one's heart to sb; **pianse e finalmente si sfogò** she had a good cry and felt better for it; **non sfogarti su di me!** don't take it out on me!

sfoggiare [sfod'dʒare] *vt* to show off.

sfoggio ['sfoddʒo] *sm* show, display; **fare** ~ **di** to show off, display.

sfoglia ['sfoʎʎa] *sf (gen)* thin layer; *(Culin)* sheet of pasta dough; **pasta** ~ puff pastry.

sfogliare[1] [sfoʎ'ʎare] *vt (fiore)* to pluck the petals off.

sfogliare[2] [sfoʎ'ʎare] *vt (libro, rivista)* to leaf through.

sfogliata[1] [sfoʎ'ʎata] *sf (scorsa)* glance, look; **dare una** ~ **a** to leaf through.

sfogliata[2] [sfoʎ'ʎata] *sf (Culin)* puff.

sfogo, ghi ['sfogo] *sm* **(a)** *(di liquido, gas)* outlet; *(di aria)* vent; *(di prodotto)* outlet, market; *(fig: di rabbia etc)* outburst; **dare** ~ **a** to give vent to. **(b)** *(Med)* rash.

sfolgorante [sfolgo'rante] *ag (luce)* blazing; *(fig: vittoria)* brilliant.

sfolgorare [sfolgo'rare] *vi* to blaze.

sfolgorio [sfolgo'rio] *sm* blaze, glare.

sfollagente [sfolla'dʒente] *sm inv* truncheon.

sfollamento [sfolla'mento] *sm (vedi vt)* clearing, emptying; evacuation.

sfollare [sfol'lare] **1** *vt (piazza, strada)* to clear, empty; *(edificio)* to evacuate, empty. **2** *vi (aus essere) (gente, dimostranti)* to disperse; ~ **da una città** to evacuate a town.

sfollato, a [sfol'lato] **1** *ag* evacuated. **2** *sm/f* evacuee.

sfoltire [sfol'tire] *vt*, ~**rsi** *vr* to thin (out).

sfoltita [sfol'tita] *sf* thinning; **dare una** ~ **a qc** to thin sth.

sfondamento [sfonda'mento] *sm (di porta)* breaking (down); *(di parete)* knocking down; *(Mil)* breaking through, breach.

sfondare [sfon'dare] **1** *vt (porta)* to break down; *(parete)* to break down, knock down; *(pavimento)* to break through; *(scarpe)* to wear through; *(sedia, barca)* to knock the bottom out of; *(scatola)* to burst, knock the bottom out of; ~ **le linee nemiche** *(Mil)* to break through the enemy lines. **2** *vi (fig: attore etc: avere successo)* to make a name for o.s. **3**: ~**rsi** *vr (porta, sedia, pavimento)* to give way; *(parete)* to fall down; *(scarpe)* to wear out; *(scatola)* to burst.

sfondato, a [sfon'dato] *ag (scarpe)* worn out; *(scatola)* burst; *(sedia)* broken, damaged; **essere ricco** ~ to be rolling in it.

sfondo ['sfondo] *sm (gen, Pittura, Fot)* background; *(di film, libro)* background, setting; **sullo** ~ **in the** background.

sforbiciata [sforbi'tʃata] *sf* **(a)** *(taglio)* snip, cut. **(b)** *(Sport)* scissor kick.

sformare [sfor'mare] **1** *vt* to put out of shape, knock out of shape. **2**: ~**rsi** *vr* to lose shape, get out of shape.

sformato¹, a [sfor'mato] *ag (che ha perso forma)* shapeless.

sformato² [sfor'mato] *sm (Culin) type of soufflé.*

sfornare [sfor'nare] *vt (Culin)* to take out of the oven; *(fig: libri, film etc)* to churn out.

sfornito, a [sfor'nito] *ag*: ~ **di** lacking in, without; *(negozio)* out of.

sfortuna [sfor'tuna] *sf* bad luck, misfortune; **avere** ~ to be unlucky; **per** ~**!** unfortunately!; **che** ~**!** how unfortunate!

sfortunato, a [sfortu'nato] *ag* unlucky.

sforzare [sfor'tsare] **1** *vt (gen)* to force; *(voce, occhi)* to strain; ~ **qn a fare qc** to force sb to do sth. **2**: ~**rsi** *vr*: ~**rsi (a fare qc)** *(costringersi)* to force o.s. (to do sth); *(fare uno sforzo)* to make an effort (to do sth).

sforzo ['sfortso] *sm (gen)* effort; *(Tecn)* stress, strain; **fare uno** ~ to make an effort; **essere sotto** ~ *(motore, macchina, fig: persona)* to be under stress.

sfottere ['sfottere] *vt (fam)* to tease.

sfracellare [sfratʃel'lare] **1** *vt* to smash. **2**: ~**rsi** *vr* to smash; ~**rsi al suolo** to crash to the ground.

sfrattare [sfrat'tare] *vt* to evict.

sfrattato, a [sfrat'tato] **1** *ag* evicted. **2** *sm/f* evicted person.

sfratto ['sfratto] *sm* eviction; **dare lo** ~ **a qn** to give sb notice to quit.

sfrecciare [sfret'tʃare] *vi (aus essere)* to shoot past, flash past.

sfregare [sfre'gare] *vt (strofinare)* to rub; *(graffiare)* to scratch; ~ **un fiammifero** to strike a match; ~**rsi le mani** to rub one's hands.

sfregiare [sfre'dʒare] *vt* to slash.

sfregio ['sfredʒo] *sm* **(a)** *(cicatrice)* scar; *(graffio)* scratch. **(b)** *(fig: offesa)* affront.

sfrenato, a [sfre'nato] *ag (persona)* wild, uncontrolled; *(: dissoluto)* dissolute; *(passioni)* unbridled, unrestrained; *(bambino)* unruly; **essere** ~ **nel bere/nel mangiare** to drink/eat excessively; **vivere in un lusso** ~ to live in unrestrained luxury.

sfrigolare [sfrigo'lare] *vi (olio)* to sizzle; *(legno)* to crackle.

sfrondare [sfron'dare] *vt (albero)* to prune, thin out; *(fig: discorso, scritto)* to prune (down).

sfrontatezza [sfronta'tettsa] *sf* impudence, cheek;

avere la ~ di fare qc to have the cheek to do sth.

sfrontato, a [sfron'tato] *ag* impudent, cheeky.

sfruttamento [sfrutta'mento] *sm* exploitation.

sfruttare [sfrut'tare] *vt (anche peg)* to exploit; *(occasione, momento)* to make the most of, take advantage of.

sfruttatore, trice [sfrutta'tore] *sm/f* exploiter.

sfuggente [sfud'dʒente] *ag (fig: sguardo)* elusive; *(mento)* receding.

sfuggire [sfud'dʒire] *vi (aus essere) (gen)* to escape; ~ **alla polizia** to escape from the police; ~ **alla morte/alla cattura** to escape death/capture; **il sapone mi è sfuggito di mano** the soap slipped out of my hands; **mi sfugge il nome** his name escapes me; **mi è sfuggito di mente** it has slipped my memory; **si è lasciato** ~ **il nome** he let the name slip; **non ti sfugge niente** nothing escapes you, you don't miss a thing; **lasciarsi** ~ **un'occasione** to let an opportunity go by; ~ **al controllo** *(macchina)* to go out of control; *(situazione)* to be no longer under control.

sfuggita [sfud'dʒita] *sf*: **di** ~ *(notare, salutare)* in passing; **vedere di** ~ to catch a glimpse of.

sfumare [sfu'mare] **1** *vt (colore: schiarire)* to soften, shade off; *(suono)* to fade out; *(capelli)* to taper. **2** *vi (aus essere) (colore)*: ~ **in** to fade into, shade off into; *(fig: speranza)* to vanish, disappear.

sfumato, a [sfu'mato] *ag (colore)* soft, mellow.

sfumatura [sfuma'tura] *sf* **(a)** *(azione: vedi vt)* softening, shading off; fading out; tapering. **(b)** *(di colore)* shade; **diverse** ~**e di significato** different shades of meaning, different nuances; **una** ~ **d'ironia** a hint of irony.

sfuriata [sfu'rjata] *sf* outburst of rage, fit of rage; **fare una** ~ **a qn** to give sb a good telling off.

sfuso, a ['sfuso] *ag (caramelle etc)* loose, unpacked; *(vino)* unbottled; *(birra)* draught.

sgabello [zga'bɛllo] *sm* stool.

sgabuzzino [zgabud'dzino] *sm* lumber room.

sgambettare [zgambet'tare] *vi* to kick (one's legs); *(bambino)* to toddle.

sgambetto [zgam'betto] *sm*: **fare lo** ~ **a qn** to trip sb up; *(fig)* to oust sb.

sganasciarsi [zganaʃ'ʃarsi] *vr*: ~ **dalle risate** *o* **dal ridere** to roar with laughter.

sganciamento [zgantʃa'mento] *sm (gen)* unhooking; *(Ferr)* uncoupling; *(di bombe)* dropping.

sganciare [zgan'tʃare] **1** *vt (gen)* to unhook; *(chiusura)* to unfasten, undo; *(treno)* to uncouple; *(bombe)* to drop, release; *(fig fam: soldi)* to fork out. **2**: ~**rsi** *vr (gen)* to come unhooked; *(chiusura)* to come unfastened, come undone; *(treno)* to come uncoupled; ~**rsi da** *(fig: persona)* to get away from.

sgangherare [zgange'rare] **1** *vt (porta)* to unhinge; *(cassa, baule: sfasciare)* to smash. **2**: ~**rsi** *vr*: ~**rsi dalle risate** to split one's sides laughing.

sgangherato, a [zgange'rato] *ag (porta)* unhinged, off its hinges; *(auto)* ramshackle, rickety; *(risata)* wild, boisterous.

sgarbatezza [zgarba'tettsa] *sf (qualità)* rudeness, impoliteness, bad manners *pl*; **è stata una** ~ **arrivare tardi** it was rude to arrive late.

sgarbato, a [zgar'bato] *ag* rude, ill-mannered, impolite.

sgarbo ['zgarbo] *sm*: **fare uno** ~ **a qn** to be rude to sb.

sgargiante [zgar'dʒante] *ag* gaudy, showy.

sgarrare [zgar'rare] *vi (persona)* to step out of line; *(orologio: essere avanti)* to gain; *(: essere indietro)* to lose; **e guarda di non** ~**!** watch your step!; **l'orologio sgarra di 2 minuti** the clock is 2 minutes fast *(o* slow).

sgattaiolare [zgattajo'lare] *vi:* ~ **fuori** to slip out, sneak out; ~ **via** to sneak off.

sgelare [zdʒe'lare] *vi (aus essere)*, ~**rsi** *vr* to melt, thaw.

sghembo, a ['zgembo] *ag (storto)* crooked; **di** ~ *(storto)* crookedly; *(obliquamente)* on the slant.

sghignazzare [zgiɲɲat'tsare] *vi* to laugh scornfully.

sghignazzata [zgiɲɲat'tsata] *sf* scornful laugh.

sghimbescio [zgim'beʃʃo] *sm:* **a** *o* **di** ~ *(storto)* crookedly; *(obliquamente)* on the slant.

sghiribizzo [zgiri'biddzo] *sm (fam: capriccio)* whim, fancy; **avere lo** ~ **di** *(fare)* **qc** to fancy (doing) sth.

sgobbare [zgob'bare] *vi (fam: lavorare)* to slog, slave; *(: a scuola)* to swot; ~ **sui libri** to swot over one's books.

sgobbata [zgob'bata] *sf (fam: lavoro)* slog, grind.

sgobbone [zgob'bone] *sm (fam)* slogger; *(: secchione)* swot.

sgocciolare [zgottʃo'lare] **1** *vt (acqua)* to drip; *(cosa immersa in un liquido)* to drain. **2** *vi (aus essere)* to drip.

sgocciolatura [zgottʃola'tura] *sf* **(a)** dripping. **(b)** *(gocce)* drops *pl; (di pittura)* runs *pl,* streaks *pl.*

sgoccioli ['zgottʃoli] *smpl:* **essere agli** ~ *(lavoro, provviste etc)* to be nearly finished; *(periodo)* to be nearly over; **siamo agli** ~ we've nearly finished, the end is in sight.

sgolarsi [zgo'larsi] *vr* to become hoarse; *(fig: parlare inutilmente)* to waste one's breath.

sgomberare [zgombe'rare] **1** *vt (stanza, aula, strada)* to clear; *(alloggio)* to move out of, vacate; *(zona: evacuare)* to evacuate. **2** *vi (traslocare)* to move.

sgombero ['zgombero] *sm (di strada, stanze etc)* clearing; *(di città)* evacuation; *(trasloco)* moving.

sgombrare [zgom'brare] *vt* = **sgomberare.**

sgombro¹, a ['zgombro] **1** *ag (gen)* clear, empty. **2** *sm* = **sgombero.**

sgombro² ['zgombro] *sm (Zool)* mackerel.

sgomentare [zgomen'tare] **1** *vt* to dismay, alarm. **2:** ~**rsi** *vr* to be dismayed, be alarmed.

sgomento, a [zgo'mento] **1** *ag* dismayed, alarmed. **2** *sm* dismay, alarm; **farsi prendere dallo** ~ to be filled with dismay, be alarmed.

sgominare [zgomi'nare] *vt (nemico)* to rout; *(avversario)* to defeat; *(fig: epidemia)* to overcome.

sgonfiare [zgon'fjare] **1** *vt (gen)* to deflate, let the air out of; *(fig: persona)* to bring down a peg or two. **2:** ~**rsi** *vr* **(a)** *(gen)* to deflate; *(pneumatico)* to go flat. **(b)** *(Med)* to go down.

sgonfio, a ['zgonfjo] *ag* **(a)** *(pneumatico, pallone)* flat. **(b)** *(Med)* no longer inflamed.

sgorbio ['zgɔrbjo] *sm (macchia)* blot; *(scarabocchio)* scrawl, scribble; *(peg: quadro etc)* daub; *(fam: persona brutta)* fright.

sgorgare [zgor'gare] *vi (aus essere) (gen)* to gush (out), spurt (out); *(lacrime)* to pour, flow; **il sangue sgorgava dalla ferita** the blood gushed *o* spurted from the wound.

sgozzare [zgot'tsare] *vt* to cut the throat of; *(anche fig: macellare)* to slaughter.

sgradevole [zgra'devole] *ag* unpleasant.

sgradito, a [zgra'dito] *ag* unwelcome.

sgraffignare [zgraffiɲ'ɲare] *vt (fam)* to pinch, swipe.

sgrammaticato, a [zgrammati'kato] *ag* ungrammatical.

sgranare [zgra'nare] *vt (fagioli)* to shell; *(pannocchia)* to remove the corn from; ~ **gli occhi** to open one's eyes wide.

sgranchire [zgran'kire] *vt* to stretch; ~**rsi le gambe** to stretch one's legs.

sgranocchiare [zgranok'kjare] *vt* to munch, crunch.

sgrassare [zgras'sare] *vt* to remove the grease from.

sgravare [zgra'vare] **1** *vt:* ~ **qn/qc (di)** *(peso, anche fig)* to relieve sb/sth (of). **2:** ~**rsi** *vr (partorire)* to give birth.

sgravio ['zgravjo] *sm:* ~ **fiscale** tax relief.

sgraziato, a [zgrat'tsjato] *ag* ungraceful, awkward.

sgretolamento [zgretola'mento] *sm (vedi vb)* splitting; flaking off; crumbling.

sgretolare [zgreto'lare] **1** *vt (roccia)* to split; *(intonaco)* to cause to flake off. **2:** ~**rsi** *vr (muro, creta, gesso)* to crumble; *(roccia)* to split.

sgridare [zgri'dare] *vt:* ~ **qn** to tell sb off, scold sb.

sgridata [zgri'data] *sf* telling off, scolding.

sgrossare [zgros'sare] *vt (marmo, legno)* to roughhew; *(fig: modi)* to polish, refine.

sguaiato, a [zgwa'jato] *ag* coarse; **una risata** ~**a** a guffaw.

sguainare [zgwai'nare] *vt* to draw, unsheathe.

sgualcire [zgwal'tʃire] **1** *vt* to crumple, crease. **2:** ~**rsi** *vr* to become crumpled, become creased.

sgualdrina [zgwal'drina] *sf* trollop.

sguardo ['zgwardo] *sm* **(a)** *(occhiata)* glance, look; **dare uno** ~ **a** to glance at sth, cast a glance *o* an eye over sth; **lanciare uno** ~ **di rimprovero a qn** to give sb a reproachful look.

(b) *(espressione)* look, expression; **avere lo** ~ **fisso** to have a fixed expression; **ha uno** ~ **intelligente** he has an intelligent expression.

(c) *(occhi):* **alzare** *o* **sollevare lo** ~ to raise one's eyes, look up; **abbassare lo** ~ to lower one's eyes, look down; **cercare qc/qn con lo** ~ to look round for sth/sb; **distogliere lo** ~ **da qc/qn** to take one's eyes off sth/sb; **fissare lo** ~ **su qc/qn** to stare at sth/sb; **soffermarsi con lo** ~ **su qc/qn** to rest one's eyes on sth/sb; **volgere lo** ~ **altrove** to look elsewhere; **attirare gli** ~**i** *(fig: attenzione)* to attract people's attention.

sguarnire [zgwar'nire] *vt* **(a)** *(togliere la guarnizione)* to take the trimming off. **(b)** *(Mil: lasciare indifeso)* to leave undefended.

sguarnito, a [zgwar'nito] *ag (vedi vb)* untrimmed; undefended.

sguattera ['zgwattera] *sf* scullery maid.

sguattero ['zgwattero] *sm* scullery boy.

sguazzare [zgwat'tsare] *vi (in acqua)* to splash (about); *(nel fango)* to wallow; ~ **nell'oro** to be rolling in money.

sguinzagliare [zgwintsaʎ'ʎare] *vt (cane)* to unleash; *(fig: persona):* ~ **qn dietro a qn** to set sb on sb.

sgusciare¹ [zguʃ'ʃare] *vt (uovo, piselli)* to shell.

sgusciare² [zguʃ'ʃare] *vi (aus essere)* to slip; ~ **di mano** to slip out of one's hand; ~ **via** *(scappare)* to slip away, escape.

shaker ['ʃeikə] *sm inv* (cocktail) shaker.

shampoo [ʃæm'pu:] *sm inv* shampoo.

sherry ['ʃeri] *sm inv* sherry.

shoccare [ʃok'kare] *vt* = **scioccare.**

shock [ʃɔk] *sm inv (gen, Med)* shock; **sotto** ~ in a state of shock.

si¹ [si] *pron (dav* **lo, la, li, le, ne** *diventa* **se)** **(a)** *(in verbi riflessivi: impers)* oneself; *(: maschile)* himself; *(: femminile)* herself; *(: neutro)* itself; *(: pl)* themselves; **lavarsi** to wash (oneself); **sporcarsi** to get dirty; **pettinarsi** to comb one's hair; **digli di sbrigarsi** tell him to hurry up; **si nascosero** they hid; **si è tagliato** he's cut himself; **si**

guardava allo specchio he was looking at himself in the mirror; **si crede importante** he (o she) thinks a lot of himself (o herself); ~ **è dimenticato di me** he has forgotten me; **se ne è dimenticata** she forgot about it; **l'orologio** ~ **è fermato** the clock has stopped; ~ **è rotto** it has broken.

(b) (in verbi riflessivi: con complemento oggetto): **lavarsi le mani** to wash one's hands; ~ **è tolto il cappello** he took off his hat; ~ **è sporcato i pantaloni** he got his trousers dirty; ~ **godette la vacanza** he (o she) enjoyed his (o her) holiday; **se l'è ricordato** he remembered it.

(c) (uso reciproco) each other, one another; ~ **odiano** they hate each other o one another; ~ **baciarono** they kissed; ~ **incontrarono alle 5** they met at 5 o'clock.

(d) (passivo): ~ **ripara facilmente** it can easily be repaired; ~ **vende al chilo** it is sold by the kilo; **dove** ~ **parla russo** where Russian is spoken, where they speak Russian.

(e) (impersonale): ~ **dice che...** it is said that..., people say that...; **non** ~ **risponde così!** that's no way to answer somebody!; **mi** ~ **dice che...** I am told that...; ~ **vede che è nuovo** one (o you) can tell it's new; **non** ~ **sa mai** you never can tell.

si² [si] sm (Mus) B; (: solfeggiando la scala) ti.

sì¹ [si] **1** av **(a)** yes; **hai finito?** — ~ **have you finished?** — yes (I have); **sei sicuro?** — ~ **certo** are you sure? — yes, of course (I am); **ma** ~! yes, of course!, I should say so!; ~ **e no** yes and no; **avrà** ~ **e no 10 anni** he must be about 10 years old; **saranno stati** ~ **e no in 20** there must have been about 20 of them; **uno** ~ **e uno no** every other one; **un giorno** ~ **e uno no** every other day; ~ **domani!**, ~ **proprio!** you'll be lucky!, fat chance of that! **(b)** (rafforzativo): **allora vieni,** ~ **o no?** well, are you coming or not?; **questa** ~ **è bella!** that's a good one! **(c):** **dire di** ~ to say yes; **spero/penso di** ~ I hope/think so; **forse (che)** ~, **forse (che) no** maybe or maybe not; **fece di** ~ **col capo** he nodded (his head); **vieni? se** ~ **ci vediamo dopo** are you coming? if so I'll see you later; **e** ~ **che...** and to think that... .

2 sm yes; **non mi aspettavo un** ~ I didn't expect him (o her etc) to say yes; **sono tra il** ~ **e il no** I'm uncertain, I can't make up my mind; **per me è** ~ I should think so, I expect so.

sì² [si] av = **così.**

sia ['sia] cong **(a):** ~ ... ~, ~, ... che (tanto ... quanto) both ... and; ~ **Franco** ~ **Mario hanno accettato,** ~ **Franco che Mario hanno accettato** both Franco and Mario have accepted. **(b):** ~ **che ...** ~ **che** (o ... o) whether ... or; ~ **che accetti** ~ **che non accetti** whether he accepts or not.

siamese [sia'mese] **1** ag Siamese; **gatto** ~ Siamese (cat); **fratelli** ~**i** Siamese twins. **2** sm/f Siamese inv.

sibilante [sibi'lante] **1** ag (suono) hissing; (Fonetica) sibilant. **2** sf (Fonetica) sibilant.

sibilare [sibi'lare] vi (serpente) to hiss; (vento) to whistle.

sibilo ['sibilo] sm (di serpente) hiss(ing); (di vento) whistling.

sicario [si'karjo] sm hired assassin, hired killer.

sicché [sik'ke] cong (così che) so (that), therefore; (allora) (and) so.

siccità [sittʃi'ta] sf drought.

siccome [sik'kome] cong since, as.

Sicilia [si'tʃilja] sf Sicily.

siciliano, a [sitʃi'ljano] ag, sm/f Sicilian.

sicomoro [siko'mɔro] sm sycamore.

siculo, a ['sikulo] ag, sm/f Sicilian.

sicura [si'kura] sf (di arma, spilla) safety catch; (di portiera) safety lock.

sicurezza [siku'rettsa] sf **(a)** (immunità) safety; ~ **stradale** road safety; **di** ~ (dispositivo, margine) safety attr. **(b)** (salvaguardia di diritti etc) security; **per la** ~ **nazionale** for national security; **(forze di) Pubblica S**~ police (force). **(c)** (certezza) certainty; **avere la** ~ **di qc** to be sure o certain of sth; **lo so con** ~ I am quite certain. **(d)** (fiducia, tranquillità) confidence; **ha risposto con molta** ~ he answered very confidently.

sicuro, a [si'kuro] **1** ag **(a)** (senza pericolo) safe; (ben difeso) safe, secure; **non è** ~ **qui** it isn't safe here; **sentirsi** ~ to feel safe. **(b)** (certo) certain, sure; **essere** ~ **di/che** to be sure of/that; **ne ero** ~! I knew it!; **la vittoria è** ~**a** victory is assured; **ne sei proprio** ~? are you sure o certain? **(c)** (fiducioso, tranquillo) (self-)confident, sure of o.s.; **essere** ~ **di sé** to be self-confident, be sure of o.s. **(d)** (attendibile) reliable, sure; (: rimedio) sure, safe; **da fonte** ~**a** from reliable sources. **(e)** (saldo) firm, steady; **con mano** ~**a** with a steady hand.

2 av of course, certainly; **di** ~ certainly.

3 sm **(a)** (cosa certa): **dare qc per** ~ to be sure about sth; **dare per** ~ **che** to be sure that. **(b)** (luogo sicuro): **essere al** ~ to be safe, be in a safe place; **mettersi al** ~ to take cover; **mettere qc al** ~ to put sth away (in a safe place). **(c)** (non rischiare): **andare sul** ~ to play safe.

siderurgia [siderur'dʒia] sf iron and steel industry.

siderurgico, a, ci, che [side'rurdʒiko] ag iron and steel attr.

sidro ['sidro] sm cider.

siepe ['sjɛpe] sf hedge; (Sport) hedge, hurdle.

siero ['sjɛro] sm serum; ~ **antivipera** snake bite serum; ~ **della verità** truth serum o drug; ~ **del latte** whey.

sierra ['sjɛrra] sf (Geog) sierra.

siesta ['sjɛsta] sf siesta, (afternoon) nap; **fare la** ~ to have a nap o siesta.

sifilide [si'filide] sf syphilis.

sifone [si'fone] sm (Tecn) siphon; (per seltz) (soda) siphon.

Sig. abbr (= signore) Mr.

sigaretta [siga'retta] sf cigarette.

sigaro ['sigaro] sm cigar.

Sigg. abbr (= signori) Messrs.

sigillare [sidʒil'lare] vt to seal.

sigillo [si'dʒillo] sm seal; **mettere o porre i** ~**i a qc** to seal sth, put seals on sth; **anello con** ~ signet ring.

sigla ['sigla] sf **(a)** (abbreviazione) acronym, abbreviation; (iniziali) initials pl; (monogramma) monogram; ~ **automobilistica** abbreviation of province on vehicle number plate. **(b):** ~ **musicale** signature tune.

siglare [si'glare] vt to initial.

Sig.na abbr (= signorina) Miss.

significare [siɲɲifi'kare] vt **(a)** (aver senso) to mean; **cosa significa?** what does this mean?; **cosa significa questa parola?** what does this word mean? **(b)** (avere importanza) to mean, matter; **tu significhi molto per me** you mean a lot to me.

significativo, a [siɲɲifika'tivo] ag significant.

significato [siɲɲifi'kato] sm meaning, sense; (valore, importanza) importance; **senza** ~ meaningless; **non ha alcun** ~ **per me** it doesn't mean anything to me.

signora [siɲ'nora] sf **(a)** (donna) lady; (moglie) wife; **ti cercava una** ~ there was a lady looking for you; **è una vera ~** she's a real lady; **vive da ~** she leads a life of luxury; **le presento la mia ~** may I introduce my wife?; **S~e e Signori!** Ladies and Gentlemen!; **nostra S~** (Rel) Our Lady. **(b)** (rivolgendosi a qualcuno): **buon giorno ~** good morning; (deferente) good morning Madam; (quando si conosce il nome) good morning Mrs X; **~!** (Scol) please Mrs X!, please Miss!; **~ Presidentessa** Madam chairman. **(c)** (parlando di qualcuno): **la ~ Rossi sta male** Mrs Rossi is ill; **lo dirò alla ~** I'll let Mrs X know. **(d)** (in lettere): **Gentile S~** Dear Madam; **Gentile S~ Rossi** Dear Mrs Rossi; **Cara S~** Dear Mrs X; **Gentile S~ Anna Rossi** (sulle buste) Mrs Anna Rossi.

signore [siɲˈɲore] sm **(a)** (uomo) gentleman; **c'è un ~ che ti cerca** there's a gentleman looking for you; **è un vero ~** he's a real gentleman; **fa una vita da (gran) ~** he lives like a lord; **fanno una vita da ~i** they lead a life of luxury; **il S~** (Rel) the Lord; **oh S~!** oh Lord!, oh God! **(b)** (rivolgendosi a qualcuno): **buon giorno ~** good morning; (deferente) good morning Sir; (quando si conosce il nome) good morning Mr X; **signor maestro!** (Scol) please Mr X!, please Sir!; **signor Presidente** Mr chairman. **(c)** (parlando di qualcuno): **il signor Rossi sta male** Mr Rossi is ill; **lo dirò al ~** I'll let Mr X know. **(d)** (in lettere): **Gentile S~** Dear Sir; **Gentile (o Caro) Signor Rossi** Dear Mr Rossi; **Gentile Signor Paolo Rossi** (sulle buste) Mr Paolo Rossi.

signoria [siɲɲoˈria] sf (Storia) seignory, signoria.

signorile [siɲɲoˈrile] ag (distinto) refined, distinguished; (: quartiere) exclusive; (da signore) gentlemanly, gentlemanlike; (da signora) ladylike.

signorilità [siɲɲoriliˈta] sf (raffinatezza) refinement; (eleganza) elegance.

signorina [siɲɲoˈrina] sf **(a)** (giovane donna) young woman; **ormai sei una ~!** (complimento) how grown up you are!; (rimprovero) you're not a child any more!; **rimanere ~** to remain a spinster. **(b)** (rivolgendosi a qualcuno): **buon giorno ~** good morning; (deferente) good morning Madam; (quando si conosce il nome) good morning Miss X; **~!** (Scol) please Miss X!, please Miss! **(c)** (parlando di qualcuno): **la ~ Rossi sta male** Miss Rossi is ill. **(d)** (in lettere): **Gentile ~** Dear Madam; **Gentile ~ Rossi** Dear Miss Rossi; **Cara S~** Dear Miss X; **Gentile S~ Anna Rossi** (sulle buste) Miss Anna Rossi.

signorino [siɲɲoˈrino] sm young master.

Sig.ra abbr (= signora) Mrs.

silenziatore [silentsjaˈtore] sm (di arma, Tecn) silencer.

silenzio [siˈlɛntsjo] sm **(a)** (gen) silence; **fare ~** to be quiet, stop talking; **restare in ~** to keep quiet; **in ~** in silence; **far passare qc sotto ~** to keep quiet about sth, hush sth up. **(b)** (calma, pace) silence, still(ness), quiet; **nel ~ della notte** in the still of the night. **(c)** (Mil) lights out.

silenzioso, a [silenˈtsjoso] ag (gen) silent, quiet; (motore) quiet.

silice [ˈsilitʃe] sf silica.

silicone [siliˈkone] sm silicone.

sillaba [ˈsillaba] sf syllable; **dividere in ~e** to divide into syllables; **non ho capito una ~ di quello che hai detto** I haven't understood a single word of what you've said; **senza mutare una ~** word for word.

sillabare [sillaˈbare] vt to divide into syllables.

sillabario [sillaˈbarjo] sm spelling book.

sillabico, a, ci, che [silˈlabiko] ag syllabic.

silo [ˈsilo] sm silo.

silografia [silograˈfia] sf wood engraving, xylography.

siluramento [siluraˈmento] sm (Mil) torpedoing.

silurare [siluˈrare] vt (Mil, fig: legge) to torpedo; (: persona di comando) to remove from power.

siluro [siˈluro] sm (Mil) torpedo.

silvestre [silˈvɛstre] ag woodland attr.

simbiosi [simbiˈɔzi] sf (Bio, fig) symbiosis.

simboleggiare [simboledˈdʒare] vt to symbolize, represent.

simbolico, a, ci, che [simˈbɔliko] ag symbolic.

simbolismo [simboˈlizmo] sm symbolism.

simbolista, i, e [simboˈlista] **1** ag symbolist attr. **2** sm/f symbolist.

simbolo [ˈsimbolo] sm (gen, Mat, Chim) symbol; **~ di successo** status symbol.

similare [simiˈlare] ag similar.

simile [ˈsimile] **1** ag **(a)** (gen) similar; **~ a** like, similar to; **hai la gonna ~ alla mia** you've got a skirt like mine; **avevo un vestito ~ una volta** I had a dress like that once; **abbiamo gusti ~i** we have similar tastes. **(b)** (peg: tale) such; **una cosa ~** such a thing; **un uomo ~** such a man. **(c): di ~: non ho mai visto niente di ~** I've never seen anything of the sort o like that; **è insegnante o qualcosa di ~** he's a teacher or something like that. **2** sm (persona) fellow man; **vendono vasi e ~i** they sell vases and things like that.

similitudine [similiˈtudine] sf **(a)** (Retorica) simile. **(b)** (Mat) similarity.

simmetria [simmeˈtria] sf symmetry.

simmetrico, a, ci, che [simˈmetriko] ag symmetric(al).

simpatia [simpaˈtia] sf (qualità) pleasantness; (inclinazione) liking; **è di una ~!** she's extremely nice o pleasant!; **con ~** (su lettera etc) with much affection; **avere o provare ~ per qn** to like sb; **prendere qn in ~** to take (a liking) to sb; **guadagnarsi la ~ di qn** to gain sb's affection; **avere una ~ per qn** (esserne attratto) to feel attracted to sb.

simpatico¹, a, ci, che [simˈpatiko] ag **(a)** (persona) nice, pleasant, likeable; (appartamento, albergo etc) nice, pleasant; **mi è molto ~** I like him very much; **non è ~ quando succedono queste cose** it's not very nice when these things happen; **un modo di fare ~** friendly manners. **(b): inchiostro ~** invisible ink.

simpatico² [simˈpatiko] sm (Anat) sympathetic nervous system.

simpatizzante [simpatidˈdzante] sm/f sympathizer.

simpatizzare [simpatidˈdzare] vi: **~ con** to take a liking to.

simposio [simˈpɔzjo] sm symposium.

simulare [simuˈlare] vt (gen, Tecn) to simulate; (sentimento) to fake, feign; **~ uno svenimento** to pretend to faint; **~ una malattia** to pretend to be ill, feign o fake illness.

simulatore [simulaˈtore] sm (Tecn) simulator.

simulazione [simulatˈtsjone] sf (vedi vb) simulation; faking, feigning; **fu tutta una ~** it was all a pretence.

simultaneità [simultaneiˈta] sf simultaneity.

simultaneo, a [simulˈtaneo] ag simultaneous.

sinagoga [sinaˈgoga] sf synagogue.

sinceramente [sintʃeraˈmente] av (gen) sincerely; (francamente) honestly, sincerely.

sincerarsi [sintʃeˈrarsi] vr: **~ (di qc)** to make sure (of sth).

sincerità [sintʃeriˈta] sf (vedi ag) sincerity; genuineness; **con tutta ~** in all sincerity, honestly.

sincero, a [sinˈtʃero] ag **(a)** (onesto) sincere,

honest; **essere ~ con qn** to be honest with sb; **per essere ~** to be honest, honestly. **(b)** *(genuino)* real, genuine, true; **un amico ~** a real friend.

sincopato, a [sinko'pato] *ag (Mus)* syncopated.

sincope ['sinkope] *sf (Med, Linguistica)* syncope; *(Mus)* syncopation.

sincronico, a, ci, che [sin'krɔniko] *ag* synchronic.

sincronizzare [sinkronid'dzare] *vt* to synchronize.

sincronizzato, a [sinkronid'dzato] *ag* synchronized; *(Aut):* **marce ~e** syncromesh (gears).

sincronizzatore [sinkroniddza'tore] *sm* synchronizer.

sincronizzazione [sinkroniddzat'tsjone] *sf* synchronization.

sindacale [sinda'kale] *ag (legge, lotta, riunione)* (trade) union *attr; (dottrina)* unionist.

sindacalismo [sindaka'lizmo] *sm* (trade) unionism.

sindacalista, i, e [sindaka'lista] *sm/f* trade unionist.

sindacare [sinda'kare] *vt* **(a)** *(controllare)* to inspect. **(b)** *(fig: criticare)* to criticize.

sindacato [sinda'kato] *sm (di lavoratori)* trade union; *(di datori di lavoro)* union, syndicate.

sindaco, ci ['sindako] *sm* mayor.

sindone ['sindone] *sf (Rel):* **la Sacra S~** the Holy Shroud.

sindrome ['sindrome] *sf (Med)* syndrome.

sinfonia [sinfo'nia] *sf* symphony.

sinfonico, a, ci, che [sin'fɔniko] *ag* symphonic; *(orchestra)* symphony *attr.*

singhiozzare [singjot'tsare] *vi* to sob.

singhiozzo [sin'gjottso] *sm* **(a)** *(Med)* hiccup; **avere il ~** to have hiccups; **la macchina andava a ~** the car jolted *o* jerked along. **(b)** *(di pianto)* sob; **scoppiare in ~i** to burst into tears; **addormentarsi tra i ~i** to sob o.s. to sleep.

singolare [singo'lare] **1** *ag* **(a)** *(Gram)* singular; **1ª persona ~** 1st person singular. **(b)** *(insolito, particolare)* remarkable, singular; *(strano)* strange, peculiar. **2** *sm* **(a)** *(Gram)* singular; **al ~** in the singular. **(b)** *(Tennis):* **un ~** a singles (match).

singolarmente [singolar'mente] *av* **(a)** *(separatamente)* individually, one at a time. **(b)** *(in modo strano)* strangely, peculiarly, oddly.

singolo, a ['singolo] **1** *ag (gen)* single; **ogni ~ caso** every single case, each case; **ogni ~ individuo** each individual; **camera ~a** single room. **2** *sm* **(a)** *(individuo)* individual. **(b)** *(Tennis):* **un ~** a singles (match).

sinistra [si'nistra] *sf* **(a)** *(mano)* left hand. **(b)** *(parte)* left, left-hand side; **a ~** *(stato in luogo)* on the left; *(moto a luogo)* to the left; **a ~ di** to the left of; **corsia di ~** left-hand lane; **guida a ~** left-hand drive; **tenere la ~** to keep to the left. **(c)** *(Pol):* **la ~** the left; **di ~** left-wing.

sinistrato, a [sinis'trato] *ag* damaged; **zona ~a** disaster area.

sinistro, a [si'nistro] **1** *ag* **(a)** *(mano, piede)* left; *(parte, lato)* left(-hand). **(b)** *(bieco)* sinister. **2** *sm* **(a)** *(incidente)* accident. **(b)** *(Pugilato)* left; *(Calcio):* **tirare di ~** to kick with one's left foot.

sinistroide [sinis'trɔide] *ag, sm/f (peg)* leftist.

sino ['sino] *prep* = **fino.**

sinonimo [si'nɔnimo] *sm* synonym; **un nome che è ~ di qualità** a name which is synonymous with good quality.

sintassi [sin'tassi] *sf* syntax.

sintattico, a, ci, che [sin'tattiko] *ag* syntactic.

sintesi [sintezi] *sf* **(a)** *(Chim, Filosofia)* synthesis. **(b)** *(riassunto)* summary, résumé; **fare la ~ di qc** to make a summary of sth; **in ~** in brief, in short.

sintetico, a, ci, che [sin'tɛtiko] *ag* **(a)** *(conciso)*

brief, concise. **(b)** *(fibre, materiale)* synthetic.

sintetizzare [sintetid'dzare] *vt (Bio, Chim etc)* to synthesize; *(riassumere: testo etc)* to summarize.

sintetizzatore [sintetiddza'tore] *sm (Mus)* synthesizer.

sintomatico, a, ci, che [sinto'matiko] *ag (Med, fig)* symptomatic.

sintomo ['sintomo] *sm (Med, fig)* symptom; **presentare i ~i di** to show symptoms of.

sintonia [sinto'nia] *sf (Radio)* tuning; **essere in ~ con qn** *(fig)* to be on the same wavelength as sb.

sintonizzare [sintonid'dzare] **1** *vt* to tune (in). **2:** **~rsi** *vr:* **~rsi su** to tune in to.

sintonizzatore [sintoniddza'tore] *sm* tuner.

sintonizzazione [sintoniddzat'tsjone] *sf* tuning.

sinuosità [sinuosi'ta] *sf inv (di strada, fiume)* winding; *(di corpo)* curve.

sinuoso, a [sinu'oso] *ag (gen)* sinuous; *(fiume, strada)* winding, sinuous.

sinusite [sinu'zite] *sf* sinusitis.

sionismo [sio'nizmo] *sm* Zionism.

sionista, i, e [sio'nista] *ag, sm/f* Zionist.

sipario [si'parjo] *sm (Teatro)* curtain.

sire ['sire] *sm (al re):* **S~** Sire.

sirena [si'rena] *sf* **(a)** *(Mitologia, fig)* mermaid, siren. **(b)** *(segnale: di polizia, ambulanza, pompieri)* siren; *(: di fabbrica)* hooter; **~ d'allarme** *(per incendio)* fire alarm; *(per furto)* burglar alarm.

Siria ['sirja] *sf* Syria.

siriano, a [si'rjano] *ag, sm/f* Syrian.

siringa, ghe [si'ringa] *sf* **(a)** *(Med)* syringe. **(b)** *(Culin)* ≃ piping bag, forcing bag.

siringare [sirin'gare] *vt (Med)* to syringe.

sisma, i ['sizma] *sm* earthquake.

sismico, a, ci, che ['sizmiko] *ag (gen)* seismic; *(zona)* earthquake *attr.*

sismografo [siz'mɔgrafo] *sm* seismograph.

sismologia [sizmolo'dʒia] *sf* seismology.

sismologo, gi [siz'mɔlogo] *sm* seismologist.

sissignore [sissiɲ'nore] *av (a un superiore)* yes, sir; *(enfatico)* yes indeed, of course.

sistema, i [sis'tɛma] *sm* **(a)** *(Anat, Mat, Filosofia etc)* system; **~ nervoso/solare** nervous/solar system; **~ di sicurezza** security system; **abbasso il ~!** *(Pol)* down with the system! **(b)** *(metodo)* method; *(procedimento)* process; **è meglio seguire questo ~** it's better to follow this method; **il suo ~ di vita** his way of life; **trovare il ~ per fare qc** to find a way to do sth; **non è questo il ~ di lavorare!** this is no way to work!; **ti suggerisco di cambiare ~** I suggest you go about things in a different way; **bel ~ di trovare la soluzione!** *(iro)* that's some solution! **(c)** *(Totocalcio etc)* system.

sistemare [siste'mare] **1** *vt* **(a)** *(mettere a posto: stanza etc)* to tidy up, put in order; *(: arredamento)* to arrange; **mi piace come hai sistemato la casa** I like the way you've arranged the house; **~rsi i capelli** to tidy one's hair; **~rsi i vestiti** to straighten one's clothes. **(b):** **~ qn** *(trovargli lavoro)* to fix sb up with a job; *(trovare marito o moglie)* to marry sb off; *(fare i conti con)* to fix sb; **~ qn in un albergo** to fix sb up with a hotel; **l'abbiamo sistemato da noi** we put him up; **~ qn per le feste** to beat sb up. **(c)** *(questione, faccenda)* to settle; **sistemo tutto io** I'll see to everything.

2: **~rsi** *vr (problema, questione)* to be settled; *(persona: trovare alloggio)* to find accommodation; *(: trovare lavoro)* to find a job; *(: sposarsi)* to get married; **è ora che ti sistemi** it's time you settled down; **si è sistemato in un albergo** he found a room in a hotel, he fixed himself up with a hotel; **si sistemò sul divano** he slept on the sofa.

sistematico, a, ci, che [siste'matiko] *ag* systematic, methodical.

sistemazione [sistemat'tsjone] *sf* **(a)** *(di stanza, casa etc: assetto)* tidying up; *(: disposizione)* arrangement, layout. **(b): cercare una ~** *(alloggio)* to look for accommodation; *(lavoro)* to look for work *o* employment. **(c)** *(di problema, questione)* settlement.

sito, a ['sito] **1** *ag (Amm)* situated. **2** *sm (poet)* place.

situare [situ'are] *vt (casa)* to site, situate, locate; to place; *(film, romanzo etc)* to set; **la casa è situata su una collina/in riva al mare** the house is situated on a hill/on the coast.

situazione [situat'tsjone] *sf* situation; **vista la tua ~ familiare** given your family situation *o* circumstances; **nella tua ~** in your position *o* situation; **mi trovo in una ~ critica** I'm in a very difficult situation *o* position.

skai ['skai] *sm* ® Leatherette ®.

sketch [sketʃ] *sm inv (Teatro)* sketch.

slabbrare [zlab'brare] **1** *vt (tazza)* to chip the rim of; *(ferita)* to open. **2: ~rsi** *vr (orlo)* to become chipped; *(ferita)* to open.

slacciare [zlat'tʃare] **1** *vt (nodo)* to untie, undo; *(scarpa)* to unlace; *(bottoni)* to unbutton; *(abito, cravatta, cappotto)* to undo. **2: ~rsi** *vr (vedi vt)* to come untied; to come undone; to come unlaced; to come unbuttoned.

slalom ['zlalom] *sm (Sci)* slalom; **~ gigante** giant slalom.

slanciare [zlan'tʃare] **1** *vt* to hurl, fling, throw. **2: ~rsi** *vr* to throw o.s., hurl o.s.; **~rsi contro qn** to throw o.s. on sb; **~rsi nella mischia** to throw o.s. into the fray.

slanciato, a [zlan'tʃato] *ag (persona)* slender, slim; *(colonna)* slender.

slancio ['zlantʃo] *sm* dash, leap; *(fig)* surge; **darsi** *o* **prendere lo ~** to spring up; *(correndo)* to bound forward; **in uno ~ d'affetto** in a burst *o* rush of affection; **abbracciare qn con ~** to hug sb enthusiastically; **agire di ~** to act impetuously; **uno ~ di generosità** a surge of generosity.

slavato, a [zla'vato] *ag (colore)* washed out, faded; *(persona)* mousy.

slavina [zla'vina] *sf* snowslide.

slavo, a ['zlavo] **1** *ag* Slav, Slavonic. **2** *sm/f* Slav. **3** *sm (lingua)* Slavic.

sleale [zle'ale] *ag (persona: non leale)* disloyal; *(concorrenza)* unfair; **essere ~ con** to be disloyal towards; **gioco ~** *(Sport)* foul play; **essere ~ al gioco** to cheat.

slealtà [zleal'ta] *sf (vedi ag)* unfairness; disloyalty.

slegare [zle'gare] **1** *vt (gen)* to untie; *(liberare)* to free, release. **2: ~rsi** *vr (vedi vt)* to untie o.s.; to free o.s.

slegato, a [zle'gato] *ag (animale)* loose; *(fig: discorso, stile)* disconnected.

slip [zlip] *sm inv (mutandine)* briefs *pl*; *(da bagno: per uomo)* (swimming) trunks *pl*; *(: per donna)* bikini briefs *pl*.

slitta ['zlitta] *sf (gen)* sledge; *(trainata)* sleigh.

slittamento [zlitta'mento] *sm (vedi vb)* slipping; skidding; sliding; fall; postponement.

slittare [zlit'tare] *vi (automobile)* to slip, slide; *(automobile)* to skid; *(fig: partito etc)* to slide; *(: valuta)* to fall; *(: incontro, conferenza)* to be put off, be postponed.

slogan ['zlɔgan] *sm inv* slogan.

slogare [zlo'gare] *vt (Med)* to dislocate; *(: caviglia, polso)* to sprain.

slogatura [zloga'tura] *sf (di spalla)* dislocation; *(di caviglia, polso)* sprain.

sloggiare [zlod'dʒare] **1** *vt:* **~ (da)** *(nemico)* to dislodge (from); *(inquilino)* to turn out (of). **2** *vi:* **~ (da)** to move out (of); **sloggia!** *(fam)* shove off!, clear off!

smacchiare [zmak'kjare] *vt* to remove stains from.

smacchiatore [zmakkja'tore] *sm* stain remover.

smacco, chi ['zmakko] *sm* humiliating defeat.

smagliante [zmaʎ'ʎante] *ag (anche fig)* dazzling.

smagliare [zmaʎ'ʎare] **1** *vt (catena, rete)* to break; *(calze)* to ladder. **2: ~rsi** *vr (calze)* to ladder.

smagliatura [zmaʎʎa'tura] *sf* **(a)** *(su calza)* ladder. **(b)** *(Med: sulla pelle)* stretch mark.

smagrito, a [zma'grito] *ag:* **essere ~** to have lost a lot of weight.

smaliziare [zmalit'tsjare] **1** *vt:* **~ qn** to teach sb a thing or two. **2: ~rsi** *vr* to learn a thing or two.

smaliziato, a [zmalit'tsjato] *ag* shrewd, cunning.

smaltare [zmal'tare] *vt* to enamel; *(ceramica)* to glaze; **~rsi le unghie** to varnish one's nails.

smaltire [zmal'tire] *vt* **(a)** *(cibo)* to digest; *(fig: peso)* to lose; *(: rabbia)* to get over; **~ la sbornia** to get over one's hangover; *(: dormendo)* to sleep it off. **(b)** *(merce)* to sell off. **(c)** *(acque di scarico)* to drain away, drain off.

smalto ['zmalto] *sm* **(a)** *(per metalli)* enamel; *(per ceramica)* glaze; **~ per le unghie** nail polish, nail varnish; **mettersi lo ~** to varnish one's nails. **(b)** *(Anat: di denti)* enamel.

smammare [zmam'mare] *vi (fam)* to shove off, clear off.

smancerie [zmantʃe'rie] *sfpl* mawkishness *sg*.

smania ['zmanja] *sf (agitazione)* agitation, restlessness; *(fig: di potere, ricchezze):* **~ di** craving for, thirst for; **ha una gran ~ di andarsene** he's desperate to leave.

smaniare [zma'njare] *vi* to be agitated, be restless; **~ di fare qc** *(fig)* to long to do sth.

smanioso, a [zma'njoso] *ag* eager; **essere ~ di fare qc** to long to do sth; **sono ~ di rivederla** I'm dying *o* longing to see her again.

smantellamento [zmantella'mento] *sm* dismantling.

smantellare [zmantel'lare] *vt (gen)* to dismantle; *(demolire)* to demolish.

smargiasso [zmar'dʒasso] *sm* show-off; **fare lo ~** to show off.

smarrimento [zmarri'mento] *sm* **(a)** *(perdita)* loss. **(b)** *(fig: turbamento)* confusion, bewilderment; **avere un attimo di ~** to be momentarily nonplussed *o* bewildered.

smarrire [zmar'rire] **1** *vt (perdere)* to lose; **~ la strada** to lose one's way. **2: ~rsi** *vr* to get lost, lose one's way.

smarrito, a [zmar'rito] *ag* **(a)** *(oggetto)* lost; **ufficio oggetti ~i** lost property office. **(b)** *(fig: confuso: persona)* bewildered, nonplussed; *(: sguardo)* bewildered.

smascherare [zmaske'rare] **1** *vt (colpevole)* to unmask; *(intrigo, complotto)* to uncover. **2: ~rsi** *vr* to give o.s. away.

smembrare [zmem'brare] **1** *vt (gruppo, partito etc)* to split. **2: ~rsi** *vr* to split up.

smemorataggine [zmemora'taddʒine] *sf* absent-mindedness.

smemorato, a [zmemo'rato] **1** *ag* forgetful, absent-minded. **2** *sm/f* forgetful person, absent-minded person.

smentire [zmen'tire] **1** *vt (notizie)* to deny; *(testimonianza)* to refute; **smentisco quello che afferma il testimone** I refute what the witness is saying; **i fatti smentiscono le sue parole** the facts belie his words; **ha smentito la sua fama di dongiovanni** it gave the lie to his reputation of being a Don Juan. **2:** ~**rsi** *vr* to be inconsistent; **non ti smentisci mai** you're always the same; **ancora una volta non si è smentita** once again she was true to herself.

smentita [zmen'tita] *sf (di notizie)* denial; *(di testimonianza)* refutation.

smeraldo [zme'raldo] *sm, ag inv* emerald.

smerciare [zmer'tʃare] *vt (gen)* to sell; *(rimanenze)* to sell off; *(droga)* to push.

smercio ['zmɛrtʃo] *sm* sale; **avere poco/molto** ~ to have poor/good sales.

smerigliato, a [zmeriʎ'ʎato] *ag:* **carta** ~**a** emery paper; **vetro** ~ frosted glass.

smeriglio [zme'riʎʎo] *sm* emery.

smerlare [zmer'lare] *vt (Cucito)* to scallop.

smerlo ['zmerlo] *sm:* **punto (a)** ~ scallop stitch.

smesso, a ['zmesso] **1** *pp di* **smettere**. **2** *ag:* **abiti** *mpl* ~**i** cast-offs.

smettere ['zmettere] **1** *vt (gen)* to stop; *(studi)* to give up; *(vestiti)* to stop wearing; **smettila!** stop it!; **smettila di urlare!** stop shouting! **2** *vi (interrompersi)* to stop; ~ **di fare qc** to stop doing sth; ~ **di fumare** to stop *o* give up smoking; **smise di piovere** it stopped raining; **a che ora smetti stasera?** *(di lavorare)* when do you stop this evening?

smidollato, a [zmidol'lato] **1** *ag (fig: persona)* spineless. **2** *sm/f* spineless person.

smilitarizzare [zmilitarid'dzare] *vt* to demilitarize.

smilitarizzazione [zmilitariddzat'tsjone] *sf* demilitarization.

smilzo, a ['zmiltso] *ag* thin, lean.

sminuire [zminu'ire] **1** *vt (fig)* to belittle, run down; ~ **l'importanza di qc** to play sth down. **2:** ~**rsi** *vr (fig)* to run o.s. down, belittle o.s.

sminuzzare [zminut'tsare] *vt (pane)* to crumble; *(carta)* to tear into small pieces.

smistamento [zmista'mento] *sm (di posta)* sorting; *(Ferr)* shunting.

smistare [zmis'tare] *vt (posta)* to sort; *(Ferr)* to shunt; **hanno smistato gli alunni in varie classi** they sorted the pupils into different classes.

smisurato, a [zmizu'rato] *ag* enormous, immense; *(eccessivo)* excessive; *(senza limiti)* boundless.

smitizzare [zmitid'dzare] *vt* to debunk.

smobilitare [zmobili'tare] *vt* to demobilize.

smobilitazione [zmobilitat'tsjone] *sf* demobilization.

smoccolare [zmokko'lare] *vi (fam)* to swear.

smodato, a [zmo'dato] *ag* excessive, unrestrained.

smoderato, a [zmode'rato] *ag (gen)* immoderate; ~ **nel bere** intemperate.

smoking ['smoukiŋ] *sm inv* dinner jacket, tuxedo *(Am)*.

smontare [zmon'tare] **1** *vt (gen)* to take to pieces; *(macchina, mobile)* to dismantle; *(motore)* to take down; *(fig: persona: scoraggiare)* to discourage. **2** *vi (aus essere)*: ~ **(da)** *(bicicletta, treno)* to get off; *(sedia)* to get down (from); *(macchina)* to get out (of); ~ **da cavallo** to dismount; **a che ora smonti?** *(fig: da lavoro)* when do you knock off? **3:** ~**rsi** *vr (fig: persona: scoraggiarsi)* to lose heart.

smorfia ['zmɔrfja] *sf (gen)* grimace; **fare una** ~ **di dolore** to grimace with pain; **fare** ~**e** *(boccacce)* to make faces.

smorfioso, a [zmor'fjoso] **1** *ag* simpering. **2** *sm/f:* **non fare lo** ~ stop simpering *o* whining; **fare la** ~**a con qn** *(ragazza: civettare)* to flirt with sb.

smorto, a ['zmɔrto] *ag (viso)* pale, wan; *(colore, stile)* dull.

smorzare [zmor'tsare] **1** *vt (suoni)* to muffle; *(colori)* to tone down; *(luce)* to dim; *(sete)* to quench; *(entusiasmo)* to dampen. **2:** ~**rsi** *vr (suoni)* to die down, fade; *(luce)* to fade; *(entusiasmo)* to dampen.

smosso, a ['zmɔsso] *pp di* **smuovere**.

smottamento [zmotta'mento] *sm* landslide.

smottare [zmot'tare] *vi (aus essere)* to slide.

smunto, a ['zmunto] *ag* haggard, pinched.

smuovere ['zmwɔvere] **1** *vt (oggetto)* to move, shift; *(fig: persona: scuotere)* to rouse, stir; *(: dissuadere)*: ~ **qn da qc** to dissuade *o* deter sb from sth. **2:** ~**rsi** *vr (fig: persona: scuotersi)* to rouse o.s.; *(: dissuadersi)*: ~**rsi da qc** to change one's mind about sth.

smussare [zmus'sare] **1** *vt (angolo)* to round off, smooth down; *(lama)* to blunt; *(fig: carattere)* to soften. **2:** ~**rsi** *vr (lama)* to become blunt; *(fig: carattere)* to soften.

snaturare [znatu'rare] *vt (intenzioni, idee)* to distort, misrepresent.

snaturato, a [znatu'rato] *ag* cruel, heartless.

snazionalizzare [znattsjonalid'dzare] *vt* to denationalize.

snellimento [znelli'mento] *sm (di traffico)* speeding up; *(di procedura)* streamlining.

snellire [znel'lire] **1** *vt (persona)* to make slim; *(traffico)* to speed up; *(procedura)* to streamline. **2:** ~**rsi** *vr (persona)* to (get) slim; *(traffico)* to speed up.

snello, a ['znɛllo] *ag* slim, slender.

snervante [zner'vante] *ag (attesa, lavoro)* exasperating.

snervare [zner'vare] *vt* to exasperate, wear out.

snidare [zni'dare] *vt (selvaggina, anche fig)* to drive out; *(: uccelli)* to flush (out).

snob [znɔb] **1** *ag* snobbish *inv*. **2** *sm/f inv* snob.

snobbare [znob'bare] *vt* to snub.

snobismo [zno'bizmo] *sm* snobbery.

snocciolare [znottʃo'lare] *vt (frutta)* to stone; *(fig: bugie, lamentele)* to rattle off.

snodabile [zno'dabile] *ag (lampada)* adjustable; *(tubo, braccio)* hinged; **rasoio con testina** ~ swivel-head razor.

snodare [zno'dare] **1** *vt (nodo)* to untie, undo; *(membra)* to loosen (up), limber up. **2:** ~**rsi** *vr (tubatura etc)* to be hinged; *(fig: strada)* to wind.

soave [so'ave] *ag (voce, maniere)* gentle; *(volto)* delicate, sweet; *(musica)* soft, sweet; *(profumo)* delicate.

soavità [soavi'ta] *sf (vedi ag)* gentleness; delicacy; sweetness; softness.

sobbalzare [sobbal'tsare] *vi (veicolo)* to bump, jolt; *(persona: trasalire)* to jump, start.

sobbalzo [sob'baltso] *sm (vedi vb)* bump, jolt; jump, start.

sobbarcarsi [sobbar'karsi] *vr:* ~ **a** to undertake, take on.

sobborgo, ghi [sob'borgo] *sm* suburb.

sobillare [sobil'lare] *vt* to stir up, incite.

sobillatore, trice [sobilla'tore] *sm/f* instigator.

sobrietà [sobrje'ta] *sf (vedi ag)* sobriety; moderation; simplicity.

sobrio, a ['sɔbrjo] *ag (persona)* sober, moderate; *(: non ubriaco)* sober; *(colore, stile)* sober, simple; *(vita)* moderate, simple; **vestire in modo** ~ to dress soberly.

socchiudere [sok'kjudere] *vt (occhi)* to half-close; *(porta, finestra)* to leave ajar.

socchiuso, a [sok'kjuso] **1** *pp di* **socchiudere**. **2** *ag (porta, finestra)* ajar; *(occhi)* half-closed.

soccombere [sok'kombere] *vi (aus essere)* to succumb, give way.

soccorrere [sok'korrere] *vt* to help, assist.

soccorritore, trice [sokkorri'tore] *smf* rescuer.

soccorso, a [sok'korso] **1** *pp di* **soccorrere. 2** *sm (gen)* help, assistance; *(di vittime di terremoto etc)* rescue; **organizzare ~i per i terremotati** to organize relief *o* aid for the earthquake victims; **prestare ~ a qn** to help *o* assist sb; **venire in ~ di qn** to help sb, come to sb's aid; **operazioni di ~** rescue operations; **~ stradale** breakdown service.

socialdemocratico, a, ci, che [sotʃaldemo-'kratiko] **1** *ag* Social Democratic. **2** *smf* Social Democrat.

socialdemocrazia [sotʃaldemokrat'tsia] *sf* Social Democracy.

sociale [so'tʃale] *ag* **(a)** *(gen)* social; **la realtà ~** the reality of life. **(b)** *(di ditta, società)* company *attr.*

socialismo [sotʃa'lizmo] *sm* Socialism.

socialista, i, e [sotʃa'lista] *ag, smf* socialist.

socializzare [sotʃalid'dzare] *vi* to socialize.

società [sotʃe'ta] *sf inv* **(a)** *(comunità)* society; **vivere in ~** to live in society; **l'alta ~** high society; **la buona ~** polite society; **giochi di ~** parlour games. **(b)** *(associazione)* association, club, society; **una ~ segreta** a secret society; **~ sportiva** sports club. **(c)** *(Comm)* company, firm; **~ per azioni** *(abbr S.p.A.)* limited company *(abbr Ltd)*; **~ a responsabilità limitata** *(abbr S.r.l.)* joint-stock company; **in ~ con qn** in partnership with sb; **mettersi in ~ con qn** to go into business with sb.

socievole [so'tʃevole] *ag* sociable.

socievolezza [sotʃevo'lettsa] *sf* sociability.

socio ['sɔtʃo] *sm* **(a)** *(Comm)* partner, associate *(Am)*; **'Black e ~i'** 'Black & Co'. **(b)** *(membro)* member; *(di società scientifiche)* fellow; **farsi ~ di un circolo** to become a member of a club.

sociologia [sotʃolo'dʒia] *sf* sociology.

sociologico, a, ci, che [sotʃo'lɔdʒiko] *ag* sociological.

sociologo, a, gi, ghe [so'tʃɔlogo] *smf* sociologist.

soda ['sɔda] *sf* **(a)** *(Chim)* soda. **(b)** *(per bevande)* soda (water).

sodalizio [soda'littsjo] *sm* association, society.

soddisfacente [soddisfa'tʃɛnte] *ag* satisfactory.

soddisfare [soddis'fare] *vt (gen)* to satisfy; *(impegno)* to fulfil; *(richiesta)* to comply with.

soddisfatto, a [soddis'fatto] **1** *pp di* **soddisfare. 2** *ag* satisfied, pleased; **essere ~ di** to be satisfied *o* pleased with; **mostrarsi ~** to show one's satisfaction.

soddisfazione [soddisfat'tsjone] *sf (gen, di offesa)* satisfaction; **avere la ~ di** to have the satisfaction of; **dare la ~ a qn di** to give sb the satisfaction of; **la vita mi ha dato tante ~i!** life has given me so much satisfaction!

sodio ['sɔdjo] *sm (Chim)* sodium.

sodo, a ['sɔdo] **1** *ag (terreno)* hard; *(corpo)* firm; **uova ~e** hard-boiled eggs. **2** *sm*: **venire al ~** to come to the point. **3** *av*: **picchiare ~** to hit hard; **dormire ~** to sleep soundly; **lavorare ~** to work hard.

sodomia [sodo'mia] *sf* sodomy.

sodomita, i [sodo'mita] *sm* sodomite.

sofà [so'fa] *sm inv* sofa.

sofferente [soffe'rɛnte] *ag* suffering.

sofferenza [soffe'rɛntsa] *sf* **(a)** *(gen)* suffering; **dopo anni di ~e** *(povertà, stenti)* after years of hardship. **(b)** *(Comm)*: **in ~** unpaid.

soffermare [soffer'mare] *vt*: **soffermò lo sguardo su...** his eyes lingered on.... **2**: **~rsi** *vr*:

~rsi su *(argomento, punto)* to dwell on.

sofferto, a [sof'fɛrto] **1** *pp di* **soffrire. 2** *ag (vittoria)* hard-fought; *(distacco)* painful; **ha un viso ~** she has the face of someone who has suffered.

soffiare [sof'fjare] **1** *vt* **(a)** *(gen)* to blow; **~rsi il naso** to blow one's nose. **(b)** *(fig fam: rubare)*: **~ qc/qn a qn** to steal sth/sb from sb, pinch sth/sb from sb. **2** *vi (gen)* to blow; *(sbuffare)* to puff (and blow); **~ sul fuoco** *(fig)* to fan the flames.

soffiata [sof'fjata] *sf (fam)* tip-off; **fare una ~ alla polizia** to tip off the police.

soffice ['sɔffitʃe] *ag* soft.

soffietto [sof'fjetto] *sm* **(a)** *(Mus, per fuoco)* bellows *pl.* **(b)**: **porta a ~** folding door.

soffio ['sɔffjo] *sm* **(a)** *(di aria, vento)* breath; **in un ~** *(fig)* in a flash. **(b)** *(Med)* murmur; **~ al cuore** heart murmur.

soffione[1] [sof'fjone] *sm (Geol)*: **~ boracifero** fumarole.

soffione[2] [sof'fjone] *sm (Bot)* dandelion.

soffitta [sof'fitta] *sf (solaio)* attic, loft; *(appartamento)* attic flat.

soffitto [sof'fitto] *sm* ceiling.

soffocamento [soffoka'mento] *sm* suffocation; **è morto per ~** he died of suffocation.

soffocante [soffo'kante] *ag (caldo, atmosfera)* suffocating, stifling; *(fig: persona)*: **ma sei proprio ~!** you're stifling me!

soffocare [soffo'kare] *vt (gen)* to suffocate; *(fiamme)* to smother, put out; *(fig: sommossa)* to suppress; *(sentimento)* to stifle, repress; *(sbadiglio)* to stifle; **qui dentro si soffoca** it's stifling in here; **~ qn di baci/d'affetto** to smother sb with kisses/with affection.

soffocazione [soffokat'tsjone] *sf (gen)* suffocation; *(di sommossa)* suppression.

soffriggere [sof'friddʒere] *vt, vi* to fry lightly.

soffrire [sof'frire] **1** *vt* **(a)** *(patire)* to suffer; **~ la fame/sete** to suffer (from) hunger/thirst; **~ le pene dell'inferno** *(fig)* to suffer *o* go through hell. **(b)** *(sopportare)* to stand, bear; **non lo posso ~** I can't stand him. **2** *vi* **(a)** *(gen)* to suffer; **la tua vita privata ne soffrirà** your private life will suffer. **(b)** *(Med)*: **~ di qc** to suffer from sth.

soffritto, a [sof'fritto] **1** *pp di* **soffriggere. 2** *sm (Culin)* fried mixture of herbs, bacon and onions.

sofisticare [sofisti'kare] *vt (vino etc)* to adulterate.

sofisticato, a [sofisti'kato] *ag* **(a)** *(vino)* adulterated. **(b)** *(macchina, persona)* sophisticated.

sofisticazione [sofistikat'tsjone] *sf (di vino etc)* adulteration.

soggettista, i, e [soddʒet'tista] *smf (Cine, TV)* scriptwriter.

soggettività [soddʒettivi'ta] *sf* subjectivity.

soggettivo, a [soddʒet'tivo] *ag* subjective.

soggetto[1]**, a** [sod'dʒetto] *ag*: **~ a subject to; ~ a tassa** taxable; **andare *o* essere ~ a frequenti mal di testa** to be prone to frequent headaches.

soggetto[2] [sod'dʒetto] *sm* **(a)** *(argomento)* subject, topic; **recitare a ~** *(Teatro)* to improvise. **(b)** *(Gram)* subject. **(c)** *(persona: Med)* subject; *(: peg)* sort; **è un cattivo ~** *(peg)* he's a bad sort.

soggezione [soddʒet'tsjone] *sf* **(a)** *(imbarazzo, disagio)* uneasiness; **incutere ~ a qn, mettere qn in ~** to make sb feel uneasy; **avere ~ di qn** to feel uneasy with sb. **(b)** *(sottomissione)* subjection.

sogghignare [soggiɲ'ɲare] *vi* to sneer.

sogghigno [sog'giɲɲo] *sm* sneer.

soggiacere [soddʒa'tʃere] *vi*: **~ a** to be subjected to.

soggiogare [soddʒo'gare] *vt* to subdue, subjugate.

soggiornare [soddʒor'nare] *vi* to stay.

soggiorno [sod'dʒorno] *sm* **(a)** *(permanenza)* stay;

luogo di ~ holiday resort; **fare un** ~ **di un mese alle Bahamas** to go on a month's holiday to the Bahamas. **(b)** *(stanza)* sitting room, lounge.

soggiungere [sod'dʒundʒere] *vt* to add.

soggiunto, a [sod'dʒunto] *pp di* **soggiungere**.

soglia ['sɔʎʎa] *sf* threshold; **varcare la** ~ to cross the threshold; **essere sulla** ~ **della vecchiaia** to be on the threshold of old age.

sogliola ['sɔʎʎola] *sf (Zool)* sole.

sognante [soɲ'ɲante] *ag* dreamy.

sognare [soɲ'ɲare] **1** *vt:* ~ **qc** to dream of o about sth; **ha sempre sognato una casa così/di avere una casa così** he has always dreamt of a house like that/of having a house like that. **2** *vi* to dream; ~ **a occhi aperti** to daydream. **3:** ~**rsi** *vr:* ~**rsi di qc/di fare qc** to dream of sth/of doing sth; **non me lo sogno nemmeno!** I wouldn't dream of it!

sognatore, trice [soɲɲa'tore] *sm/f* dreamer.

sogno ['soɲɲo] *sm* dream; **fare un** ~ to have a dream; **un** ~ **ad occhi aperti** a daydream; **la donna dei suoi** ~**i** the woman of his dreams; **quella ragazza è un** ~ that girl is gorgeous; **una crociera/casa di** ~ a dream cruise/house; **nemmeno** o **neanche per** ~! not on your life!

soia ['sɔja] *sf (Bot)* soya.

sol [sɔl] *sm inv (Mus)* G; *(: solfeggiando la scala)* so(h).

solaio [so'lajo] *sm* attic, loft.

solamente [sola'mente] *av* only.

solare [so'lare] *ag (Astron, Astrologia)* solar; *(crema)*, sun *attr;* **energia** ~ solar energy; **luce** ~ sunlight.

solcare [sol'kare] *vt (terreno, fig: mari)* to plough.

solco, chi ['solko] *sm (di aratro)* furrow; *(di ruota)* track; *(di nave)* wake; *(su disco)* groove; *(sulla fronte)* wrinkle, furrow.

soldatesca [solda'teska] *sf* soldiers *pl*, troops *pl*.

soldatino [solda'tino] *sm* toy soldier.

soldato [sol'dato] *sm* soldier; **fare il** ~ to serve in the army; **andare (a fare il)** ~ to enlist (in the army); ~ **semplice** private; ~ **di leva** conscript; ~ **di carriera** professional soldier.

soldo ['sɔldo] *sm* **(a)** *(quattrino, moneta)* penny, cent *(Am);* **non ho un** ~ I haven't got a penny; **non vale un** ~ **bucato** it isn't worth a penny; **per quattro** ~**i** for next to nothing; **è roba da pochi** ~**i** it's cheap stuff. **(b):** ~**i** *pl (denaro)* money *sg;* **fare** ~**i** to make money; **essere pieno di** ~**i** to have lots of money; **buttare via i** ~**i** to throw one's money away.

sole ['sole] *sm (astro)* sun; *(luce)* sunlight, sun; *(calore)* sunshine, sun; **c'è il** ~ the sun is shining; **una giornata di** ~ a sunny day; **prendere il** ~ to sunbathe; **al calar del** ~ at sunset; **occhiali da** ~ sunglasses, dark glasses.

soleggiato, a [soled'dʒato] *ag* sunny.

solenne [so'lɛnne] *ag* solemn; *(scherz: ceffone etc)* almighty, sound.

solennità [solenni'ta] *sf inv* **(a)** *(di cerimonia)* solemnity. **(b)** *(festività)* holiday, feast day.

solere [so'lere] **1** *vt:* ~ **fare qc** to be in the habit of doing sth; **soleva raccontare lunghe storie della guerra** he used to tell long stories about the war. **2** *vb impers (aus essere):* **come suole accadere as** is usually the case, as usually happens; **come si suol dire** as they say.

solerte [so'lɛrte] *ag* diligent.

solerzia [so'lɛrtsja] *sf* diligence.

soletta [so'letta] *sf* **(a)** *(per scarpe)* insole. **(b)** *(di sci)* running surface.

solfa ['sɔlfa] *sf:* **è sempre la solita** ~ it's always the same old story.

solfatara [solfa'tara] *sf (Geol)* solfatara.

solfato [sol'fato] *sm (Chim)* sulphate; ~ **di rame** copper sulphate.

solfeggio [sol'feddʒo] *sm (Mus)* solfeggio.

solforico, a, ci, che [sol'foriko] *ag (Chim)* sulphuric; **acido** ~ sulphuric acid.

solfuro [sol'furo] *sm (Chim)* sulphur.

solidale [soli'dale] *ag* in agreement; **essere** ~ **con qn** *(essere d'accordo)* to be in agreement with sb; *(appoggiare)* to be behind sb.

solidarietà [solidarje'ta] *sf* solidarity.

solidarizzare [solidarid'dzare] *vi:* ~ **con** to express one's solidarity with.

solidificare [solidifi'kare] *vt, vi (aus essere),* ~**rsi** *vr* to solidify.

solidificazione [solidifikat'tsjone] *sf* solidification.

solidità [solidi'ta] *sf (vedi ag)* solidity; firmness; strength; soundness; reliability.

solido, a ['sɔlido] **1** *ag* **(a)** *(non liquido)* solid. **(b)** *(robusto: oggetto, muscoli, fede)* firm, strong; *(nervi, salute)* sound, strong; *(amicizia, matrimonio)* sound, solid; *(società)* reliable, sound. **2** *sm (Mat)* solid.

soliloquio [soli'lɔkwjo] *sm (Teatro)* soliloquy; *(discorso tra sé e sé)* monologue.

solista, i, e [so'lista] **1** *ag* solo. **2** *sm/f* soloist.

solitamente [solita'mente] *av* usually, generally, as a rule.

solitaria [soli'tarja] *sf (Naut):* **in** ~ single-handed.

solitario, a [soli'tarjo] **1** *ag (gen)* solitary; *(passante, navigatore)* lone, solitary; *(luogo, strada)* lonely, deserted, secluded; *(vita)* lonely, secluded; **è un tipo** ~ he is a loner. **2** *sm/f (persona)* solitary person, loner. **3** *sm* **(a)** *(brillante)* solitaire. **(b)** *(Carte)* patience.

solito, a ['sɔlito] **1** *ag* usual; **essere** ~ **fare** to be in the habit of doing; **è** ~ **mangiare alle otto** he usually eats at eight o'clock, he is in the habit of eating at eight o'clock; **era** ~ **passeggiare di notte** he used to go for walks during the night; **è sempre la** ~**a storia!** it's always the same old story!; **siamo alle** ~**e!** *(fam)* here we go again! **2** *sm:* **di** ~ usually, generally, as a rule; **(come) al** ~ as usual; **più tardi del** ~ later than usual.

solitudine [soli'tudine] *sf* **(a)** *(tranquillità)* solitude; *(l'essere solo)* loneliness; *(di posto)* loneliness. **(b)** *(luogo solitario)* solitude.

sollazzare [sollat'tsare] **1** *vt* to entertain. **2:** ~**rsi** *vr* to amuse o.s.

sollecitare [solletʃi'tare] *vt* **(a)** *(affrettare: pratica, lavoro, telefonata)* to speed up; *(: persona)* to urge on; *(chiedere con insistenza)* to press for; ~ **qn perché faccia qc** to urge sb to do sth. **(b)** *(stimolare: fantasia)* to stimulate, rouse. **(c)** *(Tecn)* to stress.

sollecitazione [solletʃitat'tsjone] *sf* **(a)** *(richiesta)* request; *(fig: stimolo)* stimulus; **lettera di** ~ *(Comm)* reminder. **(b)** *(Tecn)* stress.

sollecito, a [sol'letʃito] **1** *ag* prompt, quick; **essere** ~ **nel fare qc** to be prompt in doing sth. **2** *sm (Comm)* reminder; ~ **di pagamento** payment reminder.

sollecitudine [solletʃi'tudine] *sf* promptness, speed.

solleone [solle'one] *sm (periodo estivo)* dog days *pl;* *(gran caldo)* summer heat.

solleticare [solleti'kare] *vt (gen)* to tickle; *(fig: curiosità)* to arouse; *(: fantasia)* to excite; *(: appetito)* to whet.

solletico [sol'letiko] *sm* tickling; **fare il** ~ **a qn** to tickle sb; **soffrire il** ~ to be ticklish.

sollevamento [solleva'mento] *sm* **(a)** *(gen)*

raising, lifting; **c'è stato un ~ del terreno** *(Geol)* the ground has risen; **~ pesi** *(sport)* weightlifting. **(b)** *(rivolta)* revolt, rebellion.

sollevare [solle'vare] **1** *vt* **(a)** *(peso, occhi, testa)* to lift, raise; *(polvere, sabbia)* to raise; *(con argani etc)* to hoist; **~ da terra** to lift up, lift off the ground; **il motoscafo sollevò delle onde** the motorboat made waves; **~ un'obiezione** *(fig)* to raise an objection. **(b)** *(fig: dar conforto)* to comfort, cheer up; **~ il morale a qn** to raise sb's morale; **~ qn da un peso** *(fig)* to take a load off sb's mind. **(c)** *(fig: folla)* to rouse, stir up.

2: ~rsi *vr* **(a)** *(persona)* to get up; **sollevati un po'** *(dal letto)* sit up a little; *(da una sedia)* stand up a minute; **~rsi da terra** *(persona)* to get up from the ground; *(aereo)* to take off. **(b)** *(vento, polvere)* to rise; *(nebbia)* to lift, clear; **si sollevarono onde enormi** the sea became very rough. **(c)** *(fig: riprendersi)* to feel better, recover; **~rsi da qc** *(malattia, spavento)* to get over sth; **sentirsi sollevato** to feel relieved. **(d)** *(fig: truppe, popolo)* to rise up, rebel.

sollievo [sol'ljɛvo] *sm* relief; **con mio grande ~** to my great relief; **un sospiro di ~** a sigh of relief.

sollucchero [sol'lukkero] *sm:* **andare in ~** *(fig)* to go into ecstasy.

solo, a ['solo] **1** *ag* **(a)** *(senza compagnia)* alone, on one's *(o* it's *etc)* own, by oneself *(o* itself *etc)*; *(isolato)* lonely; **da ~** *(senza aiuti)* by oneself *(o* himself *etc)*; **entra pure, sono ~** please come in, I'm alone *o* there's no-one with me; **vive (da) ~** he lives on his own; **è tanto ~** he's very lonely; **riesci a farlo da ~?** can you do it by yourself?; **parlare da ~** to talk to oneself.

(b) *(senza altri):* **finalmente ~i!** alone at last!; **vogliono stare ~e** they want to be alone; **possiamo vederci da ~i?** can I see you in private?

(c) *(seguito da sostantivo)* only; **il ~ motivo** the only *o* sole reason; **c'è un ~ libro** there is only one book; **ha un ~ figlio** she has only one son; **è il ~ proprietario** he's the sole proprietor; **essi sono una persona ~a** they are as one; **non si vive di ~ pane** man does not live by bread alone; **l'incontrò due ~e volte** he only met twice; **la ~a idea mi fa tremare** the very *o* mere thought of it is enough to make me tremble; **la mia ~a speranza è che...** my only hope is that...; **non un ~ istante ho creduto che...** I didn't believe for a single moment that... .

2 *av* *(soltanto)* only; **resto ~ un giorno** I'm only staying one day; **mancavi ~ tu** only you were missing, you were the only one missing; **non ~ ha negato, ma...** not only did he deny it, but... .

3: ~ che but; **l'ho visto, ~ che non son riuscito a parlargli** I saw him, but I didn't get a chance to speak to him.

4 *sm/f:* **sono il ~ a poter giudicare** I'm the only one who can judge; **è la ~a che ha chiesto notizie** she was the only one to ask for news.

5: a ~ *sm* *(Mus)* solo.

solstizio [sol'stittsjo] *sm* solstice.

soltanto [sol'tanto] **1** *av* *(gen)* only; **c'era ~ lui** there was only him; **restano qui ~ 2 giorni** they are only staying 2 days; **sono arrivato ~ ieri** I only arrived yesterday; **chiedo ~ questo!** that's all I ask! **2** *cong* but, only; **vorrei, ~ (che) non posso** I would like to, but I can't; **ha la macchina, ~ non funziona, temo** he has a car, only *o* but I don't think it's working.

solubile [so'lubile] *ag* soluble; **caffè ~** instant coffee.

solubilità [solubili'ta] *sf* *(Chim)* solubility.

soluzione [solut'tsjone] *sf* *(gen, Mat, Chim)* solution;

(di indovinello) answer; **non c'è altra ~!** there's no alternative!; **senza ~ di continuità** uninterruptedly.

solvente [sol'vɛnte] **1** *ag* *(Chim, Comm)* solvent. **2** *sm* *(Chim)* solvent; **~ per vernici** paint remover; **~ per unghie** nail varnish remover.

solvenza [sol'vɛntsa] *sf* *(Comm)* solvency.

soma ['soma] *sf* burden, load; **bestia da ~** pack animal.

Somalia [so'malja] *sf* Somalia.

somalo, a ['somalo] **1** *ag, sm/f* Somalian. **2** *sm* *(lingua)* Somali.

somaro [so'maro] *sm* *(Zool)* donkey, ass; *(fig)* dunce.

somatico, a, ci, che [so'matiko] *ag* *(Bio)* somatic.

sombrero [som'brero] *sm inv* sombrero.

somigliante [somiʎ'ʎante] *ag* similar; **essere ~ a qc** to be similar to *o* like sth; **essere ~ a qn** to look like sb; **sono molto ~i** they are very alike; **è un ritratto molto ~** it's a very good likeness.

somiglianza [somiʎ'ʎantsa] *sf* *(tra cose)* similarity; *(tra persone)* resemblance.

somigliare [somiʎ'ʎare] **1** *vi:* **~ a** to resemble, look like; **somiglia a sua sorella** she looks like *o* resembles her sister; **somiglia al mio** it looks like mine. **2: ~rsi** *vr* *(uso reciproco)* to be alike, resemble each other; **non si somigliano affatto** they don't look at all like each other.

somma ['somma] *sf* **(a)** *(Mat)* addition; *(: risultato)* sum; *(fig: sostanza)* conclusion; **sai fare le ~e?** can you add?; **tirare le ~e** *(fig)* to sum up; **tirate le ~e** *(fig)* all things considered. **(b)** *(di denaro)* sum, amount.

sommare [som'mare] **1** *vt* *(Mat)* to add up, add together; *(aggiungere)* to add; **tutto sommato** *(fig)* all things considered. **2** *vi* *(ammontare):* **~ a** to add up to, to amount to.

sommario, a [som'marjo] **1** *ag* **(a)** *(esame)* brief; *(lavoro)* rough; **racconto ~** brief summary. **(b)** *(Dir)* summary. **2** *sm* *(breve riassunto)* summary; *(compendio)* compendium; **~ del telegiornale** *(TV)* news headlines *pl.*

sommergere [som'mɛrdʒere] *vt* *(barca)* to submerge; **le onde hanno sommerso la barca** the waves swamped the boat; **~ qn di** *(doni, gentilezze)* to overwhelm sb with; *(baci)* to smother sb with.

sommergibile [sommer'dʒibile] **1** *ag* submersible. **2** *sm* *(Naut)* submarine.

sommergibilista, i [sommerdʒibi'lista] *sm* submariner.

sommerso, a [som'mɛrso] **1** *pp di* **sommergere. 2** *ag* *(tesori, città)* sunken; **il mondo ~** the underwater world.

sommesso, a [som'messo] *ag* soft, low.

somministrare [somminis'trare] *vt* to give, administer.

somministrazione [somministrat'tsjone] *sf* giving, administration.

sommità [sommi'ta] *sf inv* summit, top; *(fig)* peak.

sommo, a ['sommo] **1** *ag* *(grado, livello)* highest; *(rispetto etc)* highest, greatest; *(poeta, artista)* great, outstanding; **il S~ Pontefice** the Supreme Pontiff; **per ~i capi** in short, in brief. **2** *sm* *(fig)* peak.

sommossa [som'mɔssa] *sf* uprising, revolt.

sommozzatore [sommottsa'tore] *sm* (deep-sea) diver; *(Mil)* frogman.

sonagliera [sonaʎ'ʎera] *sf* bell-collar.

sonaglio [so'naʎʎo] *sm* *(di mucche etc)* bell; *(per bambini)* rattle.

sonante [so'nante] *ag:* **denaro** *o* **moneta ~** (ready) cash.

sonare [so'nare] *etc* = **suonare** *etc*.

sonata [so'nata] *sf (Mus)* sonata.

sonda ['sonda] **1** *sf (Med, Meteor, Aer)* probe; *(Mineralogia)* drill. **2** *ag inv*: **pallone** *m* ~ weather balloon.

sondaggio [son'daddʒo] *sm (vedi vb)* sounding; drilling, boring; probing; survey; ~ **d'opinione** opinion poll.

sondare [son'dare] *vt (Naut)* to sound; *(Mineralogia)* to drill, bore; *(Meteor, Med)* to probe; *(fig: opinione etc)* to survey, poll.

sonetto [so'netto] *sm* sonnet.

sonnacchioso, a [sonnak'kjoso] *ag* sleepy.

sonnambulismo [sonnambu'lizmo] *sm* somnambulism, sleepwalking.

sonnambulo, a [son'nambulo] *sm* somnambulist, sleepwalker.

sonnecchiare [sonnek'kjare] *vi* to doze, drowse.

sonnellino [sonnel'lino] *sm* nap.

sonnifero [son'nifero] *sm (pillola)* sleeping pill; *(gocce etc)* sleeping draught.

sonno ['sonno] *sm* **(a)** *(il dormire)* sleep; **avere il** ~ **pesante/leggero** to be a heavy/light sleeper; **prendere** ~ to fall asleep; **ho perso 4 ore di** ~ I lost 4 hours' sleep; **il** ~ **eterno** eternal rest. **(b)** *(bisogno di dormire)* sleepiness, sleep; **avere** ~ to be sleepy; **cascare dal** ~ to be asleep on one's feet; **far venire** ~ **a qn** *(fig)* to send sb to sleep.

sonnolento, a [sonno'lɛnto] *ag* sleepy, drowsy; *(movimenti)* sluggish.

sonnolenza [sonno'lɛntsa] *sf* sleepiness, drowsiness.

sonorità [sonori'ta] *sf* sonority, resonance.

sonoro, a [so'nɔro] **1** *ag* **(a)** *(ambiente)* resonant; *(voce)* sonorous; *(schiaffo, risata)* loud; *(fig: parole)* high-flown, high-sounding. **(b)** *(Cine)* sound *attr*; **colonna** ~ **a di un film** soundtrack of a film; **il cinema** ~ the talkies. **(c)** *(Linguistica)* voiced. **2** *sm*: **il** ~ *(Cine)* the talkies.

sontuosità [sontuosi'ta] *sf* sumptuousness.

sontuoso, a [sontu'oso] *ag* sumptuous.

soperchieria [soperkje'ria] *sf* = **soverchieria**.

sopire [so'pire] *vt (fig: dolore, tensione)* to soothe.

sopore [so'pore] *sm* drowsiness.

soporifero, a [sopo'rifero] *ag* soporific; *(fig: discorso)* tedious, soporific.

sopperire [soppe'rire] *vi*: ~ **a** to provide for; ~ **alla mancanza di qc** to make up for the lack of sth.

soppesare [soppe'sare] *vt* to weigh (in one's hand), feel the weight of; ~ **i pro e i contro** to weigh up the pros and cons.

soppiantare [soppjan'tare] *vt* to supplant.

soppiatto [sop'pjatto] *av*: **di** ~ secretly, furtively; **se n'è andato di** ~ he stole off *o* away.

sopportabile [soppor'tabile] *ag* tolerable, bearable.

sopportare [soppor'tare] *vt* **(a)** *(peso)* to support, bear. **(b)** *(subire: perdita, spese)* to bear, sustain; *(: conseguenze, disagi)* to bear, suffer. **(c)** *(tollerare: persona, comportamento)* to stand, put up with, bear; *(: temperatura, sforzo etc)* to take, stand; **non sopporto il pesce/il giallo** I can't stand fish/yellow; **non sopporto le persone disoneste!** I can't stand dishonest people!; **non sopporterò più questo comportamento!** I won't put up with this behaviour any longer!

sopportazione [sopportat'tsjone] *sf* patience; **avere spirito di** ~, **avere capacità di** ~ to be long-suffering; **la mia** ~ **ha un limite** there is a limit to my patience; **ho raggiunto il limite della** ~ I am at the end of my tether.

soppressione [soppres'sjone] *sf* **(a)** *(di legge)* abolition; *(di linea ferroviaria etc)* closure; *(di*

servizio) withdrawal. **(b)** *(uccisione)* elimination, liquidation.

soppresso, a [sop'presso] *pp di* **sopprimere**.

sopprimere [sop'primere] *vt* **(a)** *(privilegi, carica etc)* to do away with, abolish; *(servizio)* to withdraw; *(giornale)* to suppress; *(clausola)* to cut out, delete. **(b)** *(uccidere)* to eliminate, liquidate.

sopra ['sopra] **1** *prep* **(a)** *(gen)* over; **c'era un lampadario** ~ **il tavolo** there was a candelabra over the table; **indossava un golf** ~ **la camicetta** she was wearing a jumper over her blouse; **mettiti il cappotto** ~ **le spalle** put your coat over your shoulders; **costruirono un ponte** ~ **il fiume** they built a bridge over the river; **guadagna** ~ **i 2 milioni al mese** he earns over 2 million lire a month; **pesa** ~ **il chilo** it weighs over *o* more than a kilo; **persone** ~ **i 30 anni** people over 30 (years of age); **pensaci** ~ think it over; **passar** ~ **a qc** *(anche fig)* to pass over sth; ~ **pensiero** = **soprappensiero**.

(b) *(più in su di)* above; **l'aereo volava** ~ **le nuvole** the plane was flying above the clouds; **100 metri** ~ **il livello del mare** 100 metres above sea level; **5 gradi** ~ **lo zero** 5 degrees above zero; ~ **l'orizzonte** above the horizon; ~ **l'equatore** north of *o* above the equator; **un paesino** ~ **Napoli** a village north of Naples; **abitano** ~ **di noi** they live above us; **ha un appartamento** ~ **il negozio** he has a flat over the shop; **essere al di** ~ **di ogni sospetto** to be above suspicion; **amare qn** ~ **ogni cosa** to love sb above all else.

(c) *(a contatto con)* on; *(moto)* on(to); *(in cima a)* on (top of); **il libro è** ~ **il tavolo** the book is on the table; **il gatto è salito** ~ **il tavolo** the cat climbed onto the table; **mettilo** ~ **l'armadio** put it on (top of) the cupboard; **si buttò** ~ **di lui** he threw himself on him.

(d) *(intorno a, riguardo a)* about, on; **un dibattito** ~ **la riforma carceraria** a debate about *o* on prison reform; **chiedere un parere** ~ **qc** to ask for an opinion about *o* on sth.

2 *av* **(a)** *(su)* up; *(in superficie)* on top; **metti tutto lì o là** ~ put everything up there; ~ **è un po' rovinato** *(libro, borsa etc)* it's a bit damaged on top; **una torta con** ~ **la panna** a cake topped with cream; **un disegno con** ~ **la firma** a signed drawing.

(b): *(al piano) di* ~ upstairs; **abitano di** ~ they live upstairs; **vado di** ~ **a chiudere le finestre** I'm just going upstairs to close the windows; **la tua è la stanza di** ~ yours is the upstairs room.

(c) *(prima)* above; **per i motivi** ~ **illustrati** for the above-mentioned reasons, for the reasons shown above; **vedi/come** ~ see/as above; **mettilo nel cassetto** ~ put it in the drawer above.

3 *sm* top; **il** ~ **del tavolo è in mogano** the top of the table is mahogany; **la parte di** ~ the top, the upper part.

soprabito [so'prabito] *sm* overcoat.

sopraccennato, a [soprattʃen'nato] *ag* above-mentioned.

sopracciglio [soprat'tʃiʎʎo] *sm, pl(m)* ~ **i** *o pl(f)* ~ **a** eyebrow.

sopracciliare [soprattʃi'ljare] *ag* eyebrow *attr*.

sopraccoperta [soprakko'perta] **1** *sf* bedspread. **2** *av (Naut)* on deck.

sopraddetto, a [soprad'detto] *ag* aforesaid.

sopraffare [sopraf'fare] *vt* to overwhelm, overpower.

sopraffatto, a [sopraf'fatto] *pp di* **sopraffare**.

sopraffazione [sopraffat'tsjone] *sf* overwhelming, overpowering.

sopraffino, a [sopraf'fino] *ag (olio)* extra fine; *(burro etc)* best-quality *attr; (pranzo, gusto)* excellent; *(fig: astuzia, mente)* masterly.

sopraggiungere [soprad'dʒundʒere] *vi (aus essere) (persone, rinforzi)* to arrive (unexpectedly); *(fig: difficoltà, complicazioni)* to arise (unexpectedly).

sopraggiunto, a [soprad'dʒunto] *pp di* **sopraggiungere.**

sopralluogo, ghi [sopral'lwɔgo] *sm (di esperti)* inspection; *(di polizia)* on-the-spot investigation.

soprammobile [sopram'mɔbile] *sm* ornament.

soprannaturale [soprannatu'rale] *ag, sm* supernatural.

soprannome [sopran'nome] *sm* nickname.

soprannominare [soprannomi'nare] *vt* to nickname.

soprannumero [sopran'numero] *av:* in ~ in excess; **in questa classe siamo in** ~ there are too many in this class.

soprano [so'prano] *sm/f, pl(m)* ~**i**, *pl(f) inv (Mus)* soprano.

soprappensiero ['soprappen'sjɛro] *av* lost in thought.

soprappiù [soprap'pju] *sm* surplus, extra; **in** ~ extra, surplus; *(per giunta)* besides, in addition; **l'offerta è in** ~ **rispetto alla domanda** there is more supply than demand.

soprassalto [sopras'salto] *sm:* **di** ~ with a jump, with a start.

soprassedere [soprasse'dere] *vi:* ~ **a** to put off, postpone.

soprattassa [soprat'tassa] *sf (Fin)* surtax.

soprattutto [soprat'tutto] *av* **(a)** *(anzitutto)* above all. **(b)** *(specialmente)* especially, particularly.

sopravvalutare [sopravvalu'tare] *vt (persona, capacità)* to overestimate.

sopravvenire [sopravve'nire] *vi (aus essere) (persone, macchine, rinforzi)* to arrive suddenly; *(difficoltà, complicazioni)* to arise, occur.

sopravvento [soprav'vɛnto] **1** *sm:* **avere/prendere il** ~ **su qn** to have/get the upper hand over sb. **2** *av* windward; **essere/mettersi** ~ to be/get on the windward side.

sopravvenuto, a [sopravve'nuto] *pp di* **sopravvenire.**

sopravvissuto, a [sopravvis'suto] **1** *pp di* **sopravvivere.** **2** *sm/f* survivor.

sopravvivenza [sopravvi'vɛntsa] *sf* survival.

sopravvivere [soprav'vivere] *vi (aus essere):* ~ **a** *(incidente, guerra)* to survive; *(persona)* to outlive, survive.

soprelevata [soprele'vata] *sf (di strada, ferrovia)* elevated section.

soprelevato, a [soprele'vato] *ag* elevated, raised.

soprelevazione [soprelevat'tsjone] *sf (Edil)* raising; *(parte soprelevata)* raised part.

soprintendente [soprinten'dɛnte] *sm/f (gen)* superintendent, supervisor; *(statale: di Belle Arti etc):* ~ **(a)** keeper (of).

soprintendenza [soprinten'dɛntsa] *sf* **(a)** superintendence, supervision. **(b)** *(ente statale):* ~ **alle Belle Arti** *branch of Department of the Environment responsible for monuments and artistic treasures.*

soprintendere [soprin'tɛndere] *vi:* ~ **a** to superintend, supervise.

soprinteso, a [soprin'teso] *pp di* **soprintendere.**

sopruso [so'pruzo] *sm* abuse (of power); **subire un** ~ to be abused; **questo è un** ~**!** this is an outrage!

soqquadro [sok'kwadro] *sm:* **mettere a** ~ to turn upside down.

sorbettiera [sorbet'tjɛra] *sf* ice-cream churn.

sorbetto [sor'betto] *sm* sorbet.

sorbire [sor'bire] **1** *vt* to sip. **2:** ~**rsi** *vr (fig):* ~**rsi qc** to put up with sth, suffer sth.

sorcio ['sortʃo] *sm* mouse; **far vedere i** ~**i verdi a qn** *(fig)* to give sb a rough time.

sordido, a ['sɔrdido] *ag (locale, appartamento)* sordid, squalid; *(fig: affare, storia)* sordid; *(fig: gretto)* mean.

sordina [sor'dina] *sf (Mus)* mute; **mettere la** ~ to mute; **cantare in** ~ to hum softly; **andarsene in** ~ *(fig)* to sneak off.

sordità [sordi'ta] *sf* deafness.

sordo, a ['sordo] **1** *ag* **(a)** *(persona)* deaf; **essere** ~ **da un orecchio** to be deaf in one ear; **essere** ~ **come una campana** to be as deaf as a post; ~ **ai consigli** deaf to advice. **(b)** *(rumore, colpo)* muffled; *(dolore)* dull; *(odio, rancore)* veiled; *(lotta)* silent, hidden. **(c)** *(Fonetica)* voiceless. **2** *sm/f* deaf person; **i** ~**i** the deaf; **non fare il** ~ don't pretend you didn't hear me.

sordomuto, a [sordo'muto] **1** *ag* deaf and dumb. **2** *sm/f* deaf-mute.

sorella [so'rɛlla] **1** *sf (gen, Rel)* sister; **è come una** ~ **per me** she's like a sister to me. **2** *ag (organizzazione, nave)* sister *attr.*

sorellastra [sorel'lastra] *sf* stepsister.

sorgente [sor'dʒɛnte] *sf (fonte)* spring; *(: di fiume, fig)* source; ~ **termale** thermal spring; **acqua di** ~ spring water; ~ **di calore** source of heat.

sorgere ['sordʒere] **1** *vi (aus essere) (gen)* to rise; *(fig: difficoltà)* to arise; **mi sorge il dubbio che...** I am beginning to suspect that...; **mi sorge un dubbio, forse ho lasciato il gas acceso** I wonder, did I leave the gas on? **2** *sm:* **al** ~ **del sole** at sunrise.

soriano, a [so'rjano] *ag, sm/f* tabby.

sormontare [sormon'tare] *vt (fig: ostacoli, difficoltà)* to overcome, surmount.

sornione, a [sor'njone] **1** *ag* sly, crafty. **2** *sm/f* sly one.

sorpassare [sorpas'sare] *vt (oltrepassare)* to go past; *(: Aut)* to overtake; *(fig)* to surpass; *(rivali)* to surpass, outdo; ~ **qn in intelligenza** to be more intelligent o brighter than sb; **l'ha sorpassato in altezza** she has grown taller than him.

sorpassato, a [sorpas'sato] *ag (metodo, moda)* outmoded, old-fashioned; *(macchina)* obsolete.

sorpasso [sor'passo] *sm (Aut)* overtaking; **fare un** ~ to overtake.

sorprendente [sorpren'dɛnte] *ag* surprising; *(eccezionale, inaspettato)* astonishing, amazing.

sorprendere [sor'prɛndere] **1** *vt* **(a)** *(cogliere di sorpresa)* to catch; *(: ladro)* to surprise, catch in the act; **l'ha sorpreso a fumare** she caught him smoking; **furono sorpresi dalla bufera** they were caught in the storm. **(b)** *(fig: stupire)* to surprise; **non mi sorprenderebbe affatto!** I wouldn't be at all surprised! **2:** ~**rsi** *vr* **(a)** *(meravigliarsi):* ~**rsi di qc** to be surprised about o at sth. **(b)** *(trovarsi):* ~**rsi a pensare a qn** to catch o find o.s. thinking of sb.

sorpresa [sor'presa] *sf (gen)* surprise; **fare una** ~ **a qn** to give sb a surprise; **attaccare di** ~ to make a surprise attack; **prendere qn di** ~ to take sb by surprise o unawares; **risultato a** ~ surprise result.

sorpreso, a [sor'preso] *pp di* **sorprendere.**

sorreggere [sor'rɛddʒere] *vt (malato, bambino)* to support, hold up; *(fig: sog: fede, speranza)* to sustain.

sorretto, a [sor'retto] *pp di* **sorreggere.**

sorridere [sor'ridere] *vi* to smile; ~ **a qn** to smile at sb, give sb a smile; **la vita ti sorride** life smiles on you; **mi sorride l'idea di rivederlo** the idea of seeing him again appeals to me.

sorriso, a [sor'riso] **1** *pp di* **sorridere. 2** *sm* smile; **mi ha fatto un** ~ he gave me a smile, he smiled at me; **un accenno di** ~ a faint smile.

sorsata [sor'sata] *sf* gulp; **bere a** ~**e** to gulp.

sorseggiare [sorsed'dʒare] *vt* to sip.

sorso ['sorso] *sm* sip; **ne ho bevuto solo un** ~ I only had a sip; **d'un** ~, **in un** ~ **solo** at one gulp.

sorta ['sorta] *sf* sort, kind; **ogni** ~ **di** all sorts of; **di ogni** ~ of every kind; **non voglio regali di** ~ I want no presents whatsoever.

sorte ['sorte] *sf (fato)* fate, destiny; *(caso)* chance; **decidere della** ~ **di qn** to decide sb's fate; **tentare la** ~ to try one's luck; **tirare a** ~ to draw lots.

sorteggiare [sorted'dʒare] *vt* to draw for.

sorteggio [sor'teddʒo] *sm* draw.

sortilegio [sorti'ledʒo] *sm* spell; **fare un** ~ **a qn** to cast a spell on sb.

sortire [sor'tire] *vt (ottenere)* to produce.

sortita [sor'tita] *sf (Mil)* sortie; *(fig: battuta)* witty remark.

sorto, a ['sorto] *pp di* **sorgere.**

sorvegliante [sorveʎ'ʎante] *sm/f (di carcere)* warder; *(di fabbrica etc)* supervisor.

sorveglianza [sorveʎ'ʎantsa] *sf (controllo)* supervision; *(: Polizia, Mil)* surveillance; **fare** ~ **agli esami** to invigilate (at) the exams.

sorvegliare [sorveʎ'ʎare] *vt (detenuto, bambino, bagaglio)* to watch, keep an eye on; *(casa)* to watch, keep watch on; *(operai, lavori)* to supervise, oversee; *(malato)* to watch over.

sorvolare [sorvo'lare] *vi:* ~ **su,** *vt* to fly over; *(fig: argomento, dettagli)* to pass over, skim over; **sorvoliamo!** let's skip it!

S.O.S. *abbr m* SOS.

sosia ['sɔzja] *sm inv* double.

sospendere [sos'pɛndere] *vt* **(a)** *(appendere)* to hang. **(b)** *(interrompere: gen)* to suspend; *(: vacanze, trasmissione)* to interrupt; *(seduta)* to adjourn. **(c)** *(funzionario)* to suspend; ~ **qn dal suo incarico** to suspend sb from office.

sospensione [sospen'sjone] *sf (gen, Aut, Chim)* suspension; *(rinvio: di processo etc)* adjournment; *(: di partita etc)* postponement; **puntini di** ~ *(Tip)* suspension points.

sospeso, a [sos'peso] **1** *pp di* **sospendere. 2** *ag (mano, braccio)* raised; **ponte** ~ suspension bridge; **col fiato** ~ with bated breath; **tenere qn col fiato** ~ to keep sb in suspense; **in** ~ *(pratica)* pending; *(discorso)* unfinished; *(conto)* outstanding.

sospettare [sospet'tare] **1** *vt* to suspect; ~ **qn di qc** *(furto, omicidio)* to suspect sb of sth; ~ **che** to suspect (that); **lo sospettavo!** I suspected as much! **2** *vi:* ~ **(di qn)** to suspect (sb); *(diffidare)* to be suspicious (of sb); **non sospetta di niente** he doesn't suspect a thing.

sospetto[1], a [sos'pɛtto] *ag (individuo)* suspicious; *(affermazione)* suspect.

sospetto[2] [sos'pɛtto] *sm* suspicion; **destare i** ~**i di qn** to arouse sb's suspicions; **destare** ~**i** to give rise to suspicion; **avere dei** ~**i** to have one's suspicions; **ho il** ~ **che** I suspect (that); **guardare qn con** ~ to look suspiciously at sb.

sospettoso, a [sospet'toso] *ag* suspicious.

sospingere [sos'pindʒere] *vt* to push; *(fig: incitare)* to urge, impel; **il vento li sospinse al largo** the wind drove them out to sea.

sospinto, a [sos'pinto] *pp di* **sospingere.**

sospirare [sospi'rare] **1** *vi* to sigh. **2** *vt* to yearn for, long for; **fare** ~ **qc a qn** to keep sb waiting *o* hanging around for sth.

sospiro [sos'piro] *sm* sigh; ~ **di sollievo** sigh of relief; **fare** *o* **mandare un** ~ to sigh, heave a sigh.

sosta ['sɔsta] *sf (fermata)* stop, halt; *(pausa, interruzione)* pause, break; **'divieto di** ~**'** *(Aut)* 'no parking'; **senza** ~ without a break, non-stop; **avere un attimo di** ~ to have a moment's rest.

sostantivato, a [sostanti'vato] *ag (Gram):* **aggettivo** ~ adjective used as a noun.

sostantivo [sostan'tivo] *sm (Gram)* noun, substantive; ~ **in funzione di aggettivo** noun used as an adjective.

sostanza [sos'tantsa] *sf* **(a)** substance; **badare alla** ~ **delle cose** to pay attention to essentials; **la** ~ **del discorso** the essence of the speech; **in** ~ in short, to sum up. **(b):** ~**e** *pl (ricchezze)* wealth; *(beni)* property *sg*, possessions.

sostanziale [sostan'tsjale] *ag* substantial.

sostanzioso, a [sostan'tsjoso] *ag (cibo, pasto)* nourishing, substantial; *(fig: patrimonio, resoconto)* substantial; **un libro** ~ a book of substance.

sostare [sos'tare] *vi (fermarsi)* to stop; *(: macchina)* to stop, park; *(fare una pausa)* to take a break; *(pernottare: in un albergo)* to stay; *(: in una città)* to stop over; ~ **in preghiera/raccoglimento** to pause in prayer/in thought.

sostegno [sos'teɲɲo] *sm* support; **a** ~ **di** in support of; **muro di** ~ supporting wall.

sostenere [soste'nere] **1** *vt* **(a)** *(gen: tenere su)* to support, hold up; *(con medicina etc)* to sustain; ~ **il peso di** *(anche fig)* to bear the weight of.

(b) *(candidato, partito)* to support, back; *(famiglia)* to support; ~ **qn** *(moralmente)* to be a support to sb; *(difendere)* to stand up for sb, take sb's part.

(c) *(attacco, shock)* to stand up to, withstand; *(sguardo)* to bear, stand; *(sforzo)* to keep up, sustain; *(esame)* to take; ~ **il confronto** to stand comparison; ~ **delle spese** to meet *o* incur expenses; ~ **un'ingente spesa** to have a large outlay.

(d) *(teoria)* to maintain, uphold; *(diritti)* to assert; *(innocenza)* to maintain; ~ **la tesi** *(Univ)* to attend one's viva; **la tesi da lui sostenuta è che...** he maintains that....

(e) *(Teatro, Cine):* ~ **una parte** to play a role; ~ **la parte di** to play the part of.

2: ~**rsi** *vr* **(a)** *(tenersi su: con medicine etc)* to keep o.s. going, keep one's strength up; ~**rsi al muro** *(appoggiarsi)* to hold on to the wall, lean on the wall.

(b) *(uso reciproco)* to hold each other up; *(fig: moralmente)* to stand by each other, support each other.

sostenibile [soste'nibile] *ag (tesi)* tenable; *(spese)* bearable.

sostenitore, trice [sosteni'tore] *sm/f (di partito, candidato)* supporter, backer; *(di tesi)* upholder, supporter.

sostentamento [sostenta'mento] *sm* sustenance; **mezzi di** ~ means of support.

sostenuto, a [soste'nuto] **1** *ag (stile)* elevated; *(velocità, ritmo)* sustained; *(prezzo)* high. **2** *sm:* **fare il** ~ to be standoffish, keep one's distance.

sostituire [sostitu'ire] **1** *vt* **(a):** ~ **(a/con)** to substitute (for/by). **(b)** *(prendere il posto di: persona)* to replace, take the place of; *(: temporaneamente)* to stand in for; *(: cosa)* to take the place of. **2:** ~**rsi** *vr:* ~**rsi a qn** to replace sb, take the place of sb.

sostitutivo, a [sostitu'tivo] *ag (Amm: documento, certificato)* equivalent.

sostituto, a [sosti'tuto] *sm/f* substitute, deputy; ~

procuratore della Repubblica *(Dir)* ≃ deputy public prosecutor.

sostituzione [sostitut'tsjone] *sf* substitution; **in ~ di** in place of, as a substitute for.

sottaceti [sotta'tʃeti] *smpl (Culin)* pickles.

sottaceto [sotta'tʃeto] *(Culin)* **1** *ag inv* pickled. **2** *av:* **mettere ~** to pickle.

sottana [sot'tana] *sf (sottoveste)* petticoat; *(gonna)* skirt; *(Rel)* cassock, soutane; **correre dietro alle ~e** *(fig)* to run after women; **stare sempre attaccato alla ~ della mamma** *(fig)* to be tied to one's mother's apron-strings.

sottecchi [sot'tekki] *av:* **guardare di ~** to steal a glance at.

sotterfugio [sotter'fudʒo] *sm* subterfuge.

sotterramento [sotterra'mento] *sm* burial, interment.

sotterraneo, a [sotter'raneo] **1** *ag* underground. **2** *sm* vault.

sotterrare [sotter'rare] *vt (oggetto)* to bury; *(morto)* to bury, inter; **mi sotterrerei per la vergogna!** *(fig fam)* I wish the ground would open up and swallow me!

sottigliezza [sottiʎ'ʎettsa] *sf* **(a)** *(di spessore)* thinness; *(fig: acutezza)* subtlety. **(b):** **~e** *pl:* **perdersi in ~e** to get bogged down in details; **non bado a certe ~e** I don't care about such niceties.

sottile [sot'tile] **1** *ag* **(a)** *(fetta, corda, viso)* thin; *(figura, caviglia)* slim, slender; *(capelli)* fine; *(profumo)* delicate. **(b)** *(fig: vista)* sharp, keen; *(: mente, ragionamento, significato, ironia)* subtle; *(differenza)* slight. **2** *sm:* **non andare per il ~** not to mince matters.

sottilizzare [sottilid'dzare] *vi* to split hairs.

sottintendere [sottin'tɛndere] *vt (implicare)* to imply; **è sottinteso che** it is understood that, it goes without saying that; **lasciare ~ che** to let it be understood that; **il soggetto è sottinteso** *(Gram)* the subject is understood.

sottinteso, a [sottin'teso] **1** *pp di* **sottintendere. 2** *sm* insinuation; **smetti di parlare per ~i, parla senza ~i** speak plainly, speak your mind.

sotto ['sotto] **1** *prep* **(a)** *(posizione)* under, beneath, underneath; **dov'era? — ~ il giornale** where was it? — under *o* beneath *o* underneath the newspaper; **si riparò ~ un albero** he sheltered under *o* beneath *o* underneath a tree; **~ la superficie** under *o* beneath the surface; **si nascose ~ il letto** he hid under *o* underneath the bed; **~ il soprabito indossava un vestito verde** she was wearing a green dress under her coat; **portare qc ~ il braccio** to carry sth under one's arm; **vieni ~ l'ombrello** come under the umbrella; **dormire ~ la tenda** to sleep under canvas *o* in a tent; **tutti quelli ~ i 18 anni** all those under 18 (years of age); **camminare ~ la pioggia** to walk in the rain; **finire ~ un treno** to be run over by a train; **infilarsi ~ le lenzuola** to get in between the sheets; **c'incontriamo ~ casa** we'll meet outside my house; **~ le mura** *(di città)* beneath the walls.

(b) *(più in basso di)* below; *(a sud di)* south of, below; **~ il livello del mare** below sea level; **~ zero** below zero; **quest'anno le gonne si portano ~ il ginocchio** this year skirts are being worn below the knee; **Palermo è ~ Napoli** Palermo is south of *o* below Naples; **~ il chilo** under *o* less than a kilo; **abita ~ di noi** he lives below us.

(c) *(durante il governo di)* under; **l'Italia ~ Vittorio Emanuele** Italy under Victor Emmanuel; **~ l'impero romano** under the Roman empire; **~ il regno di** during the reign of.

(d) *(soggetto a)* under; **ha 5 impiegati ~ di sé** he has 5 clerks under him; **~ l'effetto dell'alcool**

under the influence of alcohol; **~ anestesia** under anaesthetic; **tenere qn ~ la propria protezione** to keep sb under one's wing; **tenere qn/qc sott'occhio** to keep an eye on sb/sth; **~ l'alto patronato di** under the patronage of.

(e) *(tempo: in prossimità di)* near; **siamo ~ Natale/Pasqua** it's nearly Christmas/Easter.

(f) *(da):* **analizzare qc ~ un altro aspetto** to examine sth from another point of view; **~ un certo punto di vista** in a sense.

(g) *(fraseologia):* **~ forma di** in the form of; **~ falso nome** under a false name; **non c'è niente di nuovo ~ il sole** there is nothing new under the sun; **avere qc ~ il naso/gli occhi** to have sth under one's nose/before one's eyes.

2 *av* **(a)** *(giù)* down; *(nella parte inferiore)* underneath; **qui/lì ~** down here/there; **~ c'è uno strato di cioccolato** underneath there's a layer of chocolate; **~, la scatola è rossa** underneath, the box is red.

(b): *(al piano) di* **~** downstairs; **ti aspetto (di) ~** I'll wait for you downstairs; **quelli di ~** the people who live downstairs.

(c) *(oltre)* below; **vedi ~** see below; **la riga ~** the line below.

(d) *(addosso)* underneath; **cos'hai ~?** what have you got on underneath?

3 *sm inv* bottom; **il ~ della pentola** the bottom of the pan.

sottobanco [sotto'banko] *av (di nascosto: vendere, comprare)* under the counter; *(agire)* in an underhand way; **passare una notizia ~** to hush up a piece of news.

sottobicchiere [sottobik'kjɛre] *sm* mat, coaster.

sottobosco, schi [sotto'bɔsko] *sm* undergrowth *no pl*.

sottobraccio [sotto'brattʃo] *av* by the arm; **prendere qn ~** to take sb by the arm; **camminare ~ a qn** to walk arm in arm with sb.

sottocchio [sot'tɔkkjo] *av* in front of one, to hand; **non l'ho ~** *(pratica etc)* I haven't got it in front of me *o* to hand.

sottoccupazione [sottokkupat'tsjone] *sf* underemployment.

sottochiave [sotto'kjave] *av* under lock and key.

sottocoperta [sottoko'perta] *av (Naut)* below deck.

sottocosto [sotto'kɔsto] *av* below cost (price).

sottocutaneo, a [sottoku'taneo] *ag* subcutaneous.

sottoesporre [sottoes'porre] *vt (Fot)* to underexpose.

sottoesposto, a [sottoes'posto] **1** *pp di* **sottoesporre. 2** *ag (fotografia, pellicola)* underexposed.

sottofondo [sotto'fondo] *sm* background; **~ musicale** background music.

sottogamba [sotto'gamba] *av:* **prendere qc ~** not to take sth seriously; **prendere qn ~** not to take sb seriously; *(sottovalutare)* to underestimate sb.

sottogonna [sotto'gonna] *sf* underskirt.

sottogruppo [sotto'gruppo] *sm* subgroup; *(di partito)* faction.

sottolineare [sottoline'are] *vt* to underline; *(fig)* to underline, emphasize, stress.

sottolineatura [sottolinea'tura] *sf* underlining.

sott'olio [sot'tɔljo] *av, ag inv* in oil.

sottomano [sotto'mano] *av* **(a)** *(a portata di mano)* within reach, to hand; **ho un affare ~** I have some business in hand. **(b)** *(di nascosto)* secretly.

sottomarino, a [sottoma'rino] **1** *ag (flora, paesaggio)* submarine; *(cavo, galleria)* underwater *attr*. **2** *sm (Naut)* submarine.

sottomesso, a [sotto'messo] **1** *pp di* **sottomettere. 2** *ag* submissive.

sottomettere [sotto'mettere] **1** *vt (gen)* to subject;

(popolo, nemico) to subjugate, subdue; ~ **qn alla propria volontà** to impose one's will on sb. **2:** ~**rsi** *vr* to submit; ~**rsi alla volontà di qn** to bow to sb's will.

sottomissione [sottomis'sjone] *sf* submission.

sottopassaggio [sottopas'saddʒo] *sm (Aut)* underpass; *(pedonale)* subway, underpass.

sottoporre [sotto'porre] **1** *vt* **(a)** *(costringere):* ~ **qn/qc a** to subject sb/sth to; ~ **ad un esame** to subject to an examination. **(b)** *(fig: presentare):* ~ **qc a qn** *o* **all'attenzione di qn** to submit sth to sb, put sth to sb. **2: sottoporsi** *vr:* **sottoporsi a** *(volontà)* to submit to; *(operazione)* to undergo.

sottoposto, a [sotto'posto] *pp di* **sottoporre**.

sottoprodotto [sottopro'dotto] *sm* by-product.

sottoproduzione [sottoprodut'tsjone] *sf* underproduction.

sottoproletariato [sottoproleta'rjato] *sm:* **il** ~ the underprivileged class.

sottoproletario, a [sottoprole'tarjo] *sm/f:* **i** ~**i** the underprivileged.

sottordine [sot'tordine] *av:* **passare in** ~ to become of minor importance.

sottoscala [sotto'skala] *sm inv (ripostiglio)* cupboard under the stairs; *(stanza)* room under the stairs.

sottoscritto, a [sottos'kritto] **1** *pp di* **sottoscrivere**. **2** *sm/f:* **io** ~, **il** ~ the undersigned.

sottoscrivere [sottos'krivere] **1** *vt (firmare: atto, petizione)* to sign. **2** *vi* **(a):** ~ **a** *(programma)* to adhere to. **(b)** *(contribuire):* ~ **per diecimila lire** to contribute ten thousand lire.

sottoscrizione [sottoskrit'tsjone] *sf* **(a)** *(firma)* signing. **(b)** *(raccolta di adesioni)* subscription; **è iniziata la** ~ **per il referendum** signatures in favour of a referendum are now being collected.

sottosegretario, a [sottosegre'tarjo] *sm/f (Pol)* undersecretary.

sottosopra [sotto'sopra] *av (capovolto)* upside down, topsy-turvy; **mettere tutto** ~ to turn everything upside down; **sentirsi** ~, **avere lo stomaco** ~ to feel queasy; **sentirsi** ~ *(turbato)* to be in a whirl.

sottospecie [sottos'pɛtʃe] *sf inv (Bot, Zool)* subspecies *inv;* **è una** ~ **di musica** *(peg)* it's hardly what you would call music.

sottostante [sottos'tante] *ag (piani)* lower; *(zona)* underlying; **la valle** ~ the valley below.

sottostare [sottos'tare] *vi (aus essere):* ~ **a** *(assoggettarsi a)* to submit to; *(: richieste)* to give in to; *(subire: prova)* to undergo.

sottosterzante [sottoster'tsante] *ag (Aut):* **questa macchina è** ~ this car understeers.

sottosuolo [sotto'swɔlo] *sm* subsoil.

sottosviluppato, a [sottozvilup'pato] *ag* underdeveloped.

sottosviluppo [sottozvi'luppo] *sm* underdevelopment.

sottotenente [sottote'nɛnte] *sm (Mil)* second lieutenant.

sottoterra [sotto'terra] *av* underground.

sottotetto [sotto'tetto] *sm* attic.

sottotitolo [sotto'titolo] *sm* subtitle.

sottovalutare [sottovalu'tare] **1** *vt (persona, prova)* to underestimate, underrate. **2:** ~**rsi** *vr* to underrate o.s.

sottovaso [sotto'vazo] *sm* flowerpot saucer.

sottovento [sotto'vɛnto] *(Naut)* **1** *av* leeward(s). **2** *ag inv (lato)* leeward, lee.

sottoveste [sotto'vɛste] *sf* petticoat, slip.

sottovoce [sotto'votʃe] *av* in a low voice, softly.

sottovuoto [sotto'vwɔto] **1** *av:* **confezionare** ~ to

vacuum-pack. **2** *ag:* **prodotto confezionato** ~ vacuum-packed product.

sottrarre [sot'trarre] **1** *vt* **(a)** *(Mat)* to subtract; *(dedurre)* to deduct; **sottratte le spese** once expenses have been deducted. **(b)** *(portar via):* ~ **a** to take away from; *(liberare):* ~ **a** *o* **da** to save from, rescue from; *(rubare):* ~ **da** to remove from, steal from; **gli hanno sottratto il portafoglio** they stole his wallet; ~ **qc/qn alla vista di qn** to remove sth/sb from sb's sight. **2: sottrarsi** *vr:* **sottrarsi a** *(sfuggire)* to escape; *(evitare)* to avoid.

sottratto, a [sot'tratto] *pp di* **sottrarre**.

sottrazione [sottrat'tsjone] *sf (Mat)* subtraction; *(furto)* removal.

sottufficiale [sottuffi'tʃale] *sm (Mil)* non-commissioned officer; *(Naut)* petty officer.

soubrette [su'brɛt] *sf inv* showgirl.

soufflé [su'fle] *sm inv (Culin)* soufflé.

souvenir [suvə'nir] *sm inv* souvenir.

sovente [so'vɛnte] *av* often.

soverchiare [sover'kjare] *vt* to overpower, overwhelm.

soverchieria [soverkje'ria] *sf (prepotenza)* abuse (of power).

soviet [so'vjɛt] *sm inv* soviet.

sovietico, a, ci, che [so'vjɛtiko] **1** *ag* Soviet. **2** *sm/f* Soviet citizen.

sovrabbondante [sovrabbon'dante] *ag* overabundant.

sovrabbondanza [sovrabbon'dantsa] *sf* overabundance; **in** ~ in excess.

sovraccaricare [sovrakkari'kare] *vt* to overload; ~ **qn di lavoro** to overload *o* overburden sb with work.

sovraccarico, a, chi, che [sovrak'kariko] **1** *ag:* ~ **(di)** overloaded (with); ~ **di lavoro** overworked. **2** *sm* excess load.

sovraesporre [sovraes'porre] *vt (Fot)* to overexpose.

sovraesposizione [sovraespozit'tsjone] *sf (Fot)* overexposure.

sovraesposto, a [sovraes'posto] *pp di* **sovraesporre**.

sovraffollato, a [sovraffol'lato] *ag* overcrowded.

sovranità [sovrani'ta] *sf* sovereignty; *(fig: superiorità)* supremacy.

sovrannaturale [sovrannatu'rale] = **soprannaturale**.

sovrano, a [so'vrano] **1** *ag* sovereign *attr; (fig: sommo)* supreme. **2** *sm/f* sovereign.

sovrappopolare [sovrappopo'lare] *vt* to overpopulate.

sovrappopolazione [sovrappopolat'tsjone] *sf* overpopulation.

sovrapporre [sovrap'porre] **1** *vt* to place on top of, put on top of; *(Fot, Geom)* to superimpose; **sovrapponili** place *o* put them one on top of the other. **2: sovrapporsi** *vr (fig: aggiungersi)* to be added; *(Fot)* to be superimposed.

sovrapposizione [sovrapposit'tsjone] *sf* superimposition.

sovrapposto, a [sovrap'posto] *pp di* **sovrapporre**.

sovrapproduzione [sovrapprodut'tsjone] *sf* overproduction.

sovrastare [sovras'tare] *vt* **(a)** *(sog: montagna, fortezza)* to dominate; *(: nube)* to hang over; **è così alto che sovrasta gli altri** he's so tall that he towers over the others; **un'epidemia sovrasta la città** an epidemic threatens the city. **(b)** *(fig: superare)* to surpass.

sovrastruttura [sovrastrut'tura] *sf* superstructure.

sovreccitare [sovrettʃi'tare] *vt* to overexcite.

sovreccitazione [sovrettʃitat'tsjone] *sf* overexcitement.

sovrimpressione [sovrimpres'sjone] *sf (Fot, Cine)* superimposition; *(: per errore)* double exposure; **immagini in** ~ superimposed images.

sovrintendente [sovrinten'dɛnte] *etc* = **soprintendente** *etc*.

sovrumano, a [sovru'mano] *ag* superhuman.

sovvenire [sovve'nire] *vi (aus essere) (venire in mente):* ~ **a** to occur to; **mi sovvenne che** it occurred to me that.

sovvenzionare [sovventsjo'nare] *vt* to subsidize.

sovvenzione [sovven'tsjone] *sf* subsidy, grant.

sovversione [sovver'sjone] *sf* subversion.

sovversivo, a [sovver'sivo] *ag* subversive.

sovvertimento [sovverti'mento] *sm* subverting, undermining.

sovvertire [sovver'tire] *vt (Pol: ordine, stato)* to subvert, undermine.

sovvertitore, trice [sovverti'tore] *sm/f* subverter.

sozzo, a ['sottso] *ag* filthy.

sozzura [sot'tsura] *sf* filth.

S.p.A. *abbr di* **società per azioni**.

spaccalegna [spakka'leɲɲa] *sm inv* woodcutter.

spaccare [spak'kare] **1** *vt (rompere)* to break, split; *(legna)* to chop; **ti spacco il muso!** I'll bash your face in!; **o la va o la spacca** it's all or nothing; **quest'orologio spacca il minuto** this watch keeps perfect time; **c'è un sole che spacca le pietre** it's hot enough to fry an egg. **2:** ~**rsi** *vr (rompersi)* to break, split.

spaccata [spak'kata] *sf (Ginnastica):* **fare una** ~ to do the splits.

spaccato, a [spak'kato] **1** *ag*: **è un cretino** ~ he's a complete idiot, he's an idiot through and through; **è sordo** ~ he is as deaf as a post; **è geloso** ~ he's mad with jealousy; **sei tuo padre** ~ you're the spitting image of your father. **2** *sm (Archit)* section.

spaccatura [spakka'tura] *sf (gen, fig)* split; *(in un muro)* crack; *(nel terreno)* crack, fissure.

spacciare [spat'tʃare] **1** *vt (merce rubata)* to traffic in; *(droga)* to peddle, push; *(denaro falso)* to pass; ~ **per** *(far passare per)* to pass off as; **l'ha spacciata per sua moglie** he passed her off as his wife. **2:** ~**rsi** *vr:* ~**rsi per** to pass o.s. off as, pretend to be.

spacciato, a [spat'tʃato] *ag (fam: malato, fuggiasco):* **essere** ~ to be done for.

spacciatore, trice [spattʃa'tore] *sm/f (di droga)* pusher.

spaccio ['spattʃo] *sm* **(a):** ~ **(di)** *(merce rubata)* trafficking (in); *(denaro falso)* passing (of); ~ **di droga** drugpushing. **(b)** *(negozio)* shop.

spacco, chi ['spakko] *sm* **(a)** *(incrinatura)* crack; *(strappo)* tear. **(b)** *(di gonna)* slit; *(di giacca)* vent.

spaccone [spak'kone] *sm (fam)* boaster, braggart.

spada ['spada] *sf* **(a)** sword. **(b):** ~**e** *pl (Carte)* suit in Neapolitan pack of cards.

spadaccino, a [spadat'tʃino] *sm/f* swordsman/woman.

spadino [spa'dino] *sm* dress sword.

spadroneggiare [spadroned'dʒare] *vi* to swagger; **pensa di poter** ~ he thinks he can boss everyone about; **non ti permetto di** ~ **a casa mia** I won't allow you to lord it in my house.

spaesato, a [spae'zato] *ag* lost; **mi sentivo** ~ **tra di loro** I felt lost *o* out of my depth in their company.

spaghettata [spaget'tata] *sf* spaghetti meal.

spaghetti [spa'getti] *smpl (Culin)* spaghetti *sg*.

Spagna ['spaɲɲa] *sf* Spain.

spagnoletta [spaɲɲo'letta] *sf* spool.

spagnolo, a [spaɲ'ɲɔlo] **1** *ag* Spanish. **2** *sm/f (abitante)* Spaniard; **gli S~i** the Spanish. **3** *sm (lingua)* Spanish.

spago, ghi ['spago] *sm* string, twine; **un rotolo di** ~ a ball of string; **dare** ~ **a qn** *(fig)* to let sb have his *(o* her) way.

spaiato, a [spa'jato] *ag (calza, guanto)* odd.

spalancare [spalan'kare] **1** *vt* to open wide; **spalancò la porta** he flung the door open; **a braccia spalancate** with open arms. **2:** ~**rsi** *vr* to open wide.

spalare [spa'lare] *vt (terra, neve)* to shovel.

spalatore [spala'tore] *sm* shoveller.

spalatrice [spala'tritʃe] *sf* mechanical shovel.

spalla ['spalla] *sf* **(a)** *(Anat)* shoulder; **questa giacca mi sta grande di** ~**e** this jacket is too big across the shoulders; **avere le** ~**e larghe** *(anche fig)* to have broad shoulders; **portare qc/qn in** *o* **a** ~ to carry sth/sb on one's shoulders; **alzare le** ~**e** to shrug one's shoulders; **avere la famiglia sulle** ~**e** *(fig)* to have a family to support; **vivere alle** ~**e di qn** *(fig)* to live off sb, live at sb's expense.

(b): ~**e** *pl (schiena)* back; **di** ~**e** from behind; **seduto alle mie** ~**e** sitting behind me; **voltare le** ~**e a qn/qc** *(fig)* to turn one's back on sb/sth; **ridere alle** ~**e di qn** *(fig)* to laugh behind sb's back; **prendere/colpire qn alle** ~**e** to take/hit sb from behind; **mettere qn con le** ~**e al muro** *(fig)* to put sb with his *(o* her) back to the wall.

(c) *(Teatro)* stooge; **fare da** ~ **a qn** to act as sb's stooge.

spallata [spal'lata] *sf* push with the shoulder.

spalleggiare [spalled'dʒare] *vt* to support, back up.

spalletta [spal'letta] *sf* parapet.

spalliera [spal'ljɛra] *sf (di sedia, poltrona)* back; *(di letto: alla testa)* head(board); *(: ai piedi)* foot(board); *(Ginnastica)* wall bars; *(Agr)* espalier.

spallina [spal'lina] *sf* **(a)** *(Mil)* epaulette. **(b)** *(di sottoveste, maglietta)* strap; **senza** ~**e** strapless.

spalluccia, ce [spal'luttʃa] *sf:* **fare** ~**ce** to shrug.

spalmare [spal'mare] **1** *vt* to spread; ~ **il burro sul pane,** ~ **il pane di burro** to butter one's bread, spread butter on one's bread; ~ **una crema sulla pelle** to rub a cream into one's skin. **2:** ~**rsi** *vr:* ~**rsi di** to cover o.s. with.

spalti ['spalti] *smpl (di stadio)* terraces.

spanciarsi [span'tʃarsi] *vr (fig fam):* ~ **dalle risate** *o* **dal ridere** to split one's sides laughing.

spanciata [span'tʃata] *sf* belly flop.

spandere ['spandere] **1** *vt* **(a)** *(distendere: cera, crema)* to spread. **(b)** *(spargere: liquido)* to spill; *(: polvere)* to scatter; *(: calore, profumo)* to give off; *(: fig: notizie)* to spread; ~ **lacrime** to shed tears. **2:** ~**rsi** *vr* to spread.

spanto, a ['spanto] *pp di* **spandere**.

spappolare [spappo'lare] **1** *vt (ossa, gamba etc)* to crush; **non far** ~ **le patate** *(cuocere troppo)* don't reduce the potatoes to mush. **2:** ~**rsi** *vr (ossa, gamba etc)* to be crushed; *(patate)* to become mushy.

sparare [spa'rare] **1** *vt (arma, colpo)* to fire; ~ **a bruciapelo** to shoot at point-blank range; ~ **fandonie** *(fig)* to talk nonsense; **spararle grosse** *(fig)* to exaggerate; **ha sparato un prezzo assurdo** he came out with a ridiculous price; ~ **calci** to kick out. **2** *vi (arma)* to fire; *(soldato, persona)* to shoot, fire; ~ **a qn/qc** to shoot sb/sth, fire at sb/sth.

sparata [spa'rata] *sf (fig)* tall tale.

sparato [spa'rato] *sm (di camicia)* dicky.

sparatore, trice [spara'tore] *sm/f* gunman/woman.

sparatoria [spara'tɔrja] *sf (tra polizia e malviventi)* exchange of shots; *(tra malviventi)* shoot-out.

sparecchiare [sparek'kjare] *vt:* ~ **(la tavola)** to clear the table.

spareggio [spa'reddʒo] *sm (Sport)* play-off.

spargere ['spardʒere] **1** *vt* **(a)** *(sparpagliare)* to scatter. **(b)** *(versare: vino)* to spill; *(: sangue, lacrime)* to shed. **(c)** *(diffondere: notizia)* to spread; *(: luce)* to give out. **2:** ~**rsi** *vr (persone)* to scatter; *(voce, notizia)* to spread; **si è sparsa una voce sul suo conto** there is a rumour going round about him.

spargimento [spardʒi'mento] *sm:* ~ **di sangue** bloodshed.

sparire [spa'rire] *vi (aus essere)* to disappear, vanish; **la nave sparì all'orizzonte** the ship disappeared over the horizon; ~ **dalla circolazione** *(fig fam)* to lie low, keep a low profile; **far** ~ *(fig: rubare)* to steal, pinch; *(: mangiare)* to devour, put away; **sparisci!** *(fig fam)* scram!, beat it!

sparizione [sparit'tsjone] *sf* disappearance.

sparlare [spar'lare] *vt:* ~ **di qn/qc** to speak ill of sb/sth, run sb/sth down.

sparo ['sparo] *sm* shot.

sparpagliare [sparpaʎ'ʎare] *vt,* ~**rsi** *vr* to scatter.

sparso, a ['sparso] **1** *pp di* **spargere. 2** *ag (fogli)* scattered; *(capelli)* loose; **in ordine** ~ *(Mil)* in open order.

spartano, a [spar'tano] *ag (fig)* spartan.

spartiacque [sparti'akkwe] *sm (Geog)* watershed.

spartineve [sparti'neve] *sm inv* snowplough.

spartire [spar'tire] *vt* **(a)** *(denaro, eredità)* to share out; **non ho nulla da** ~ **con lui** *(fig)* I have no dealings whatever with him; **ci siamo spartiti il bottino** we split up the loot. **(b)** *(separare: avversari)* to separate; *(: capelli)* to part.

spartito [spar'tito] *sm (Mus)* score.

spartitraffico [sparti'traffiko] **1** *sm inv (Aut: banchina: in città)* traffic island; *(: su autostrada)* central reservation, median strip *(Am)*. **2** *ag inv (vedi sm):* **aiuola** ~ traffic island; central reservation, median strip *(Am)*.

spartizione [spartit'tsjone] *sf* division; **la** ~ **dell'eredità** the dividing up of the inheritance.

sparuto, a [spa'ruto] *ag (scarno: viso)* lean, haggard; *(esiguo: gruppo)* small, thin.

sparviero [spar'vjero] *sm (Zool)* sparrowhawk.

spasimante [spazi'mante] *sm* suitor.

spasimare [spazi'mare] *vi* to be in agony; ~ **di fare qc** *(fig)* to long to do sth, be dying to do sth; ~ **per qn** to be madly in love with sb.

spasimo ['spazimo] *sm* pang; **morire tra atroci** ~**i** to die in agony.

spasmo ['spazmo] *sm (Med)* spasm; *(spasimo)* pang.

spasmodico, a, ci, che [spaz'mɔdiko] *ag (Med)* spasmodic; *(fig: attesa, ricerca)* agonizing; **il ritmo** ~ **della vita moderna** the hectic pace of modern life.

spassarsela [spas'sarsela] *vi* to enjoy o.s., have a good time.

spassionato, a [spassjo'nato] *ag (parere, consiglio)* impartial, dispassionate.

spasso ['spasso] *sm* **(a)** *(divertimento)* amusement, enjoyment; **per** ~ for amusement; **sei uno** ~! you're a scream! **(b)** *(passeggiata):* **andare a** ~ to go for a walk; **portare qn a** ~ to take sb out; **essere a** ~ *(fig)* to be unemployed *o* out of work; **mandare qn a** ~ *(fig)* to give sb the sack.

spassoso, a [spas'soso] *ag* amusing, entertaining.

spastico, a, ci, che ['spastiko] *ag, sm/f* spastic.

spatola ['spatola] *sf (Med)* spatula; *(di muratore)* trowel; *(di decoratore)* putty knife.

spauracchio [spau'rakkjo] *sm* scarecrow; *(fig)* bogey, bugbear.

spaurito, a [spau'rito] *ag* frightened, terrified.

spavalderia [spavalde'ria] *sf* boldness, arrogance.

spavaldo, a [spa'valdo] *ag* bold, arrogant.

spaventapasseri [spaventa'passeri] *sm inv* scarecrow.

spaventare [spaven'tare] **1** *vt* to frighten, scare. **2:** ~**rsi** *vr* to become frightened, become scared.

spavento [spa'vento] *sm* fear, fright; **fare** *o* **mettere** ~ **a qn** to frighten *o* scare sb, give sb a fright; **morire di** ~ *(fig)* to be scared to death; **è uno** ~, **è brutto da far** ~ he is frightfully ugly.

spaventoso, a [spaven'toso] *ag (sogno, avventura)* frightening; *(incidente, delitto)* horrifying, terrible; *(fig fam: incredibile)* incredible; *(: tempesta, prezzi)* terrible, frightening; **ho una fame** ~**a** I'm ravenous; **ho fatto una figura** ~**a** I made an awful fool of myself.

spaziale [spat'tsjale] *ag* **(a)** *(volo, nave, tuta)* space *attr.* **(b)** *(Archit, Geom)* spatial.

spaziare [spat'tsjare] **1** *vi:* ~ **in,** ~ **per** to range over; ~ **col pensiero** to let one's thoughts wander. **2** *vt (Tip: parole, lettere)* to space (out).

spaziatura [spattsja'tura] *sf (Tip)* spacing.

spazientirsi [spattsjen'tirsi] *vr* to lose one's patience.

spazio ['spattsjo] *sm (gen, Fis, Mus, Tip)* space; *(posto)* room, space; **fare** ~ **per qc/qn** to make room for sth/sb; **ci manca lo** ~ we are short of room *o* space; **lo** ~ **tra le file** the space *o* gap between the rows; **nello** ~ **di un'ora** within an hour, in the space of an hour; ~ **vitale** living space; **dare** ~ **a** *(fig)* to make room for.

spazioso, a [spat'tsjoso] *ag (casa, macchina)* spacious, roomy; *(strada)* wide.

spazzacamino [spattsaka'mino] *sm* chimney sweep.

spazzaneve [spattsa'neve] *sm inv (spartineve, Sci)* snowplough.

spazzare [spat'tsare] *vt (pavimento, strada)* to sweep; *(foglie, polvere etc)* to sweep up; ~ **via** to sweep away; *(fig: cibo)* to put away.

spazzatura [spattsa'tura] *sf (immondizia)* rubbish.

spazzino, a [spat'tsino] *sm/f* roadsweeper, street sweeper.

spazzola ['spattsola] *sf* brush; ~ **per abiti** clothes brush; ~ **per capelli** hairbrush; ~ **da scarpe** shoebrush; ~ **di ferro** wire brush; **capelli a** ~ crewcut.

spazzolare [spattso'lare] *vt* to brush.

spazzolata [spattso'lata] *sf* brush, brushing.

spazzolino [spattso'lino] *sm* (small) brush; ~ **da denti** toothbrush; ~ **per unghie** nailbrush.

spazzolone [spattso'lone] *sm* scrubbing brush; *(per lucidare)* floor polisher.

speaker ['spiːkə] *sm inv (Radio, TV)* announcer; *(: Sport)* commentator.

specchiarsi [spek'kjarsi] *vr* to look at o.s. in a mirror; **si specchia in tutte le vetrine** she looks at herself in all the shop windows; **il pavimento è così pulito che ti ci puoi specchiare** the floor is so clean that you can see yourself in it; **le montagne si specchiano nel lago** the mountains are reflected in the lake.

specchiera [spek'kjera] *sf* **(a)** *(specchio)* large mirror. **(b)** *(mobile)* dressing table.

specchietto[1] [spek'kjetto] *sm:* ~ **retrovisore** *(Aut)* rear-view mirror; ~ **da borsetta** pocket mirror.

specchietto[2] [spek'kjetto] *sm (tabella)* table, chart.

specchio¹ ['spɛkkjo] *sm* mirror; **la sua casa è uno** ~ her house is as clean as a new pin; **il mare è uno** ~ the sea is as smooth as glass; **uno** ~ **d'acqua** a sheet of water.

specchio² ['spɛkkjo] *sm (tabella)* table, chart.

speciale [spe't∫ale] *ag (gen)* special; *(specifico)* particular; *(singolare)* peculiar, singular; **hai qualche motivo** ~ **per sospettare di lui?** do you have any particular reason to suspect him?; **ha un modo tutto** ~ **di parlare** he has a highly individual way of speaking; **questo arrosto è** ~ this roast is delicious; **in special modo** especially; **inviato** ~ *(Radio, TV, Stampa)* special correspondent; **offerta** ~ special offer; **treno** ~ special *o* extra train; **poteri/leggi** ~**i** *(Pol)* emergency powers/legislation.

specialista, i, e [spet∫a'lista] *sm/f (gen)* expert, specialist; *(Med)* specialist.

specialistico, a, ci, che [spet∫a'listiko] *ag (conoscenza, preparazione)* specialized; **devo fare una visita** ~**a** *(Med)* I have to see a specialist.

specialità [spet∫ali'ta] *sf inv (a) (prodotto tipico)* speciality. **(b)** *(branca di studio)* special field, specialism.

specializzare [spet∫alid'dzare] **1** *vt (industria)* to make more specialized. **2:** ~**rsi** *vr:* ~**rsi in** *(studio, professione)* to specialize in; **mi sono specializzato in torte** I'm a dab hand at cakes.

specializzato, a [spet∫alid'dzato] *ag (manodopera)* skilled; **operaio non** ~ unskilled worker; **essere** ~ **in** to be a specialist in.

specializzazione [spet∫aliddzat'tsjone] *sf* specialization; **prendere la** ~ **in** to specialize in.

specialmente [spet∫al'mente] *av* especially, particularly.

specie ['spɛt∫e] **1** *sf inv (a) (Bio, Bot, Zool)* species *sg;* **la** ~ **umana** mankind. **(b)** *(tipo)* sort, kind, variety; **una** ~ **di** a kind of; **gente di ogni** ~ all kinds of people; **mi fa** ~ it surprises me. **2** *av* especially, particularly.

specifica, che [spe't∫ifika] *sf* specification.

specificare [spet∫ifi'kare] *vt* to specify, state clearly.

specificazione [spet∫ifikat'tsjone] *sf* **(a)** *(gen)* specification; **non c'è bisogno di** ~**i!** there's no need to go into details! **(b)** *(Gram):* **complemento di** ~ possessive case.

specifico, a, ci, che [spe't∫ifiko] *ag* specific; **mi ha rivolto accuse** ~**che** his accusations were very specific; **nel caso** ~ in this particular case; **peso** ~ specific gravity.

speculare¹ [speku'lare] *vi* **(a)** *(Comm)* to speculate; *(fig: approfittare):* ~ **su** to take advantage of; ~ **in Borsa** to speculate on the Stock Exchange. **(b)** *(Filosofia):* ~ **(su)** to speculate (on *o* about).

speculare² [speku'lare] *ag (immagine, scrittura)* mirror *attr.*

speculativo, a [spekula'tivo] *ag (Filosofia, Comm)* speculative.

speculatore, trice [spekula'tore] *sm/f (Comm)* speculator.

speculazione [spekulat'tsjone] *sf* speculation.

spedire [spe'dire] *vt* to send, dispatch; *(Comm)* to dispatch, forward; ~ **per posta** to post; ~ **per mare** to ship; ~ **qn all'altro mondo** *(fig)* to send sb to meet his *(o* her) maker.

speditamente [spedita'mente] *av (lavorare)* quickly; *(parlare: veloce)* quickly; *(: con sicurezza)* fluently; **camminare** ~ to walk at a brisk pace.

spedito, a [spe'dito] **1** *ag (gen)* quick; **con passo** ~ at a brisk pace; **ha una pronuncia** ~**a** he has a fluent manner of speaking. **2** *av* = **speditamente.**

spedizione [spedit'tsjone] *sf* **(a)** *(atto)* sending;

posting; *(Comm)* forwarding; shipping; *(collo, merce)* consignment, shipment; **agenzia di** ~ forwarding agency; **spese di** ~ postal charges; *(Comm)* forwarding charges; **fare una** ~ to send a consignment. **(b)** *(scientifica, Mil)* expedition; **una** ~ **punitiva** a punitive raid.

spedizioniere [spedittsjo'njere] *sm* forwarding agent, shipping agent.

spegnere ['speɲɲere] **1** *vt (fuoco, sigaretta)* to put out, extinguish; *(apparecchio elettrico)* to turn off, switch off; *(luce)* to put out, turn off, switch off; *(gas)* to turn off; *(fig: suoni, passioni)* to stifle; *(: debito)* to pay off, extinguish. **2:** ~**rsi** *vr* **(a)** *(fuoco, sigaretta)* to go out; *(apparecchio elettrico, luce)* to go off; *(fig: passioni, suoni)* to be stifled; *(: ricordo)* to fade. **(b)** *(euf: morire)* to pass away.

spegnimento [speɲɲi'mento] *sm (di sigaretta, debito)* extinguishing; *(di luce, apparecchio elettrico)* switching off.

spelacchiato, a [spelak'kjato] *ag (gatto, cane)* mangy; *(coperta, tappeto)* threadbare, worn-out; *(pelliccia, animale di pezza)* shabby.

spelarsi [spe'larsi] *vr (animali)* to moult; *(pelliccia)* to lose hair.

speleologia [speleolo'dʒia] *sf (studio)* speleology; *(pratica)* potholing.

speleologo, a, gi, ghe [spele'ɔlogo] *sm/f (vedi sf)* speleologist; potholer.

spellare [spel'lare] **1** *vt* **(a)** *(coniglio)* to skin; *(fam: ginocchio)* to graze; **mi sono spellato il ginocchio** I grazed my knee. **(b)** *(fig: cliente)* to fleece. **2:** ~**rsi** *vr (rettile)* to shed its skin; *(persona: per il troppo sole)* to peel; *(: escoriarsi)* to graze o.s.

spelonca, che [spe'lonka] *sf* cave, cavern; *(fig: casa squallida)* hovel.

spendaccione, a [spendat't∫one] *sm/f* spendthrift.

spendere ['spendere] *vt (denaro, tempo)* to spend; **quanto ti hanno fatto** ~? how much did they charge you?; **quanto hai speso?** how much did you spend?; **quanto hai speso per quella pelliccia?** how much did you spend on *o* pay for that fur coat?; ~ **un occhio della testa** *(fig)* to spend a fortune; ~ **una buona parola per qn** *(fig)* to put in a good word for sb; ~ **e spandere** to squander one's money; ~ **la vita sui libri** to spend one's life studying.

spennacchiare [spennak'kjare] **1** *vt (gallina)* to pluck. **2:** ~**rsi** *vr* to moult, lose its feathers.

spennare [spen'nare] **1** *vt (gallina)* to pluck; *(fig: cliente)* to fleece. **2:** ~**rsi** *vr* to moult, lose its feathers.

spennellare [spennel'lare] **1** *vi* to paint. **2** *vt (Med):* ~ **una ferita con la tintura di iodio** to dab a wound with iodine; *(Culin):* ~ **un dolce con l'uovo** to brush some egg on a cake.

spennellata [spennel'lata] *sf* brush-stroke.

spensieratezza [spensjera'tettsa] *sf* carefreeness, lightheartedness.

spensierato, a [spensje'rato] *ag* carefree, lighthearted.

spento, a ['spento] **1** *pp di* **spegnere. 2** *ag (luce, fuoco, sigaretta)* out; *(colore)* dull, faded; *(vulcano)* extinct; *(persona, sguardo, festa)* lifeless; *(suono)* muffled.

speranza [spe'rantsa] *sf* hope; **nella** ~ **di rivederti** hoping to see *o* in the hope of seeing you again; **avere la** ~ **che/di** to be hopeful that/of; **hai qualche** ~ **di vincere?** have you any hope *o* chance of winning?; **pieno di** ~**e** hopeful; **senza** ~ *(situazione)* hopeless; *(amare)* without hope; **quel giovane è una** ~ **dell'atletica** that boy is a promising athlete.

speranzoso, a [speran'tsoso] *ag* hopeful.

sperare [spe'rare] **1** *vt*: ~ qc/di fare qc to hope for sth/to do sth; **spero di sì** I hope so; **spero di no** I hope not; **speriamo bene!** let's hope so!; **lo spero** I hope so; **non speravo più che venissi** I no longer expected you to come. **2** *vi*: ~ **in** (*successo etc*) to hope for; ~ **in Dio** to trust in God; **spero in te per risolvere la situazione** I'm counting on you to save the situation; **tutto fa** ~ **per il meglio** everything leads one to hope for the best; **speriamo in una pronta guarigione** we hope the patient recovers soon.

sperduto, a [sper'duto] *ag* (*isolato: casa, villaggio*) out-of-the-way; (*persona: smarrito*) lost; (: *a disagio*) ill at ease.

spergiurare [sperdʒu'rare] *vi* to commit perjury, perjure o.s.

spergiuro, a [sper'dʒuro] **1** *ag* faithless. **2** *sm/f* perjurer. **3** *sm* perjury.

spericolato, a [speriko'lato] **1** *ag* (*gen*) fearless, daring; (*guidatore*) reckless. **2** *sm/f* daredevil.

sperimentale [sperimen'tale] *ag* experimental; **scuola** ~ pilot school; **fare qc in via** ~ to try sth out.

sperimentare [sperimen'tare] *vt* (a) (*nuovo farmaco*) to experiment with, test; (*motore*) to test; (*metodo*) to try out, test out; ~ **qc sugli animali** to try sth out on *o* test sth on animals. (b) (*fig: tentare*) to try; (: *mettere alla prova*) to test, put to the test.

sperimentatore, trice [sperimenta'tore] *sm/f* experimenter.

sperimentazione [sperimentat'tsjone] *sf* experimentation.

sperma ['sperma] *sm* sperm, semen.

spermatozoo, i [spermatod'dzɔo] *sm* spermatozoon.

speronare [spero'nare] *vt* (*nave*) to ram.

sperone [spe'rone] *sm* (*di stivali, Geog*) spur; (*Naut: rostro*) ram; (*Archit*) buttress.

sperperare [sperpe'rare] *vt* (*denaro*) to squander.

sperpero ['sperpero] *sm* (*di denaro*) squandering, waste; (*di cibo, materiali*) waste.

sperso, a ['sperso] *ag* (*persona: smarrito*) lost; (: *a disagio*) ill at ease.

spersonalizzare [spersonalid'dzare] **1** *vt* (*persona, quadro*) to deprive of individuality; (*stile, narrazione*) to depersonalize. **2:** ~**rsi** *vr* (*persona*) to lose one's individuality.

spesa ['spesa] *sf* (a) (*soldi spesi*) expense; (*uscita*) outlay, expenditure; (*costo*) cost; **la** ~ **è di 200.000 lire** it will cost 200,000 lire; **con la modica** ~ **di un milione di lire** for the modest sum *o* outlay of one million lire; **ridurre le** ~**e** (*gen*) to cut down; (*Comm*) to reduce expenditure; **a** ~**e della ditta** at the firm's expense; **a mie** ~**e** (*fig*) at my expense; **fare le** ~**e di qc** (*fig*) to pay the price for sth; ~ **pubblica** public expenditure; ~**e d'impianto** (*Comm*) initial outlay; ~**e generali** (*Comm*) overheads; ~**e legali** legal costs; ~**e di manutenzione** maintenance costs; ~**e postali** postage *o* postal charges; ~**e di viaggio** travelling expenses. (b) (*acquisto*) buy; (*fam: compere*) shopping; **fare la** ~ to do the shopping; **fare delle** ~**e** to go shopping.

spesare [spe'sare] *vt*: **sono spesato dalla società** the company pays my expenses; **viaggio tutto spesato** an all-expenses-paid trip.

speso, a ['speso] *pp di* **spendere**.

spesso ['spesso] *av* often; **andiamo** ~ **al cinema** we often go to the cinema; **anche troppo** ~ all too often; ~ **e volentieri** very often.

spessore [spes'sore] *sm* thickness; **ha uno** ~ **di 20 cm** it is 20 cm thick.

Spett. *abbr di* **spettabile**.

spettabile [spet'tabile] *ag* (*Comm*): ~ **ditta X** Messrs X and Co; **avvertiamo la** ~ **clientela...** we inform our customers... .

spettacolare [spettako'lare] *ag* spectacular.

spettacolarità [spettakolari'ta] *sf* spectacular nature.

spettacolo [spet'takolo] *sm* (a) (*Cine, TV, Teatro etc*) show, performance; **mettere su uno** ~ to put on a show; **gli** ~**i iniziano alle 20** performances begin at 8 pm; **primo/secondo** ~ (*Cine*) first/second showing. (b) (*vista, scena*) sight; **dare** ~ **di sé** to make an exhibition *o* a spectacle of o.s.

spettacoloso, a [spettako'loso] *ag* spectacular; (*fig*) amazing, incredible.

spettanza [spet'tantsa] *sf* (*frm*) (a) (*competenza*) concern; **non è di mia** ~ it's no concern of mine. (b): ~**e** *pl* (*somma dovuta*) amount due; **non ho ancora avuto le mie** ~**e** I haven't yet received what is owing to me.

spettare [spet'tare] *vi* (*aus* **essere**): ~ **a** (*decisione*) to be up to; (*stipendio*) to be due to; **spetta a te decidere** it's up to you to decide; **mi spetta una parte del bottino** I'm due a share of the loot.

spettatore, trice [spetta'tore] *sm/f* (*Cine, TV, Teatro*) spectator; (*di avvenimento*) bystander, onlooker; **è stato** ~ **di un incidente** he witnessed an accident.

spettegolare [spettego'lare] *vi* to gossip.

spettinare [spetti'nare] **1** *vt*: ~ **qn** to ruffle sb's hair. **2:** ~**rsi** *vr* to get one's hair in a mess.

spettrale [spet'trale] *ag* (*gen*) spectral, ghostly.

spettro ['spettro] *sm* (a) (*fantasma*) spectre, ghost. (b) (*Fis*) spectrum.

spezie ['spettsje] *sfpl* (*Culin*) spices.

spezzare [spet'tsare] **1** *vt* (*rompere*) to break; (*fig: interrompere*) to break up; ~ **la legna** to chop wood; ~ **il cuore a qn** (*fig*) to break sb's heart; ~ **un fiore** to break off a flower; ~ **il viaggio** to break one's journey; **mi spezza la giornata** it breaks up my day. **2:** ~**rsi** *vr* to break.

spezzatino [spettsa'tino] *sm* (*Culin*) stew.

spezzato, a [spet'tsato] **1** *ag* (*unghia, ramo, braccio*) broken; **fare orario** ~ to work a split shift. **2** *sm* (*abito maschile*) coordinated jacket and trousers.

spezzettamento [spettsetta'mento] *sm* breaking up.

spezzettare [spettset'tare] *vt* to break up into small pieces; ~ **pane** to crumble bread; ~ **legno** to chop wood into small pieces; ~ **il lavoro in più giorni** to divide work up over several days.

spezzone [spet'tsone] *sm* (*Cine*) clip.

spia ['spia] *sf* (a) (*gen*) spy; (*confidente della polizia*) informer; **non fare la** ~ don't give me (*o* us *etc*) away; (*di bambini*) don't be a telltale. (b) (*Elettr: anche*: ~ **luminosa**) warning light; (*di porta*) spyhole, peephole; (*fig: sintomo*) sign, indication; ~ **dell'olio** (*Aut*) oil warning light.

spiaccicare [spjattʃi'kare] *vt* (*fam: schiacciare*) to squash, crush; **ti spiaccico al muro** I'll flatten you.

spiacente [spja'tʃɛnte] *ag* sorry; **siamo** ~**i di non poter accettare** we regret being unable to accept, we are sorry we cannot accept; **siamo** ~**i di quanto è successo** we regret what happened, we are sorry about what happened; **siamo** ~**i di dovervi annunciare che...** we regret to announce that...; **sono molto** ~ **ma...** I am extremely sorry, but... .

spiacere [spja'tʃere] = **dispiacere 2, 3**.

spiacevole [spja'tʃevole] *ag* unpleasant, disagreeable.

spiaggia, ge ['spjaddʒa] *sf* beach.

spianare [spja'nare] vt (terreno) to level, make level; (palazzo, città) to raze to the ground; (pasta) to roll out; (cuciture) to press, iron; ~ il **fucile** to level one's gun; ~ **il terreno** (fig) to prepare o clear the ground.

spianata [spja'nata] sf clearing.

spiano ['spjano]: **a tutto** ~ av (lavorare) non-stop, without a break; (spendere) lavishly; **comprare a tutto** ~ to go on a shopping spree; **piove a tutto** ~ it's bucketing down.

spiantato, a [spjan'tato] **1** ag penniless. **2** sm pauper.

spiare [spi'are] vt (gen) to spy on; (momento, occasione) to watch for, wait for; ~ **le mosse di qn** to spy on sb's movements; ~ **da dietro la porta** to spy at the door; ~ **attraverso il buco della serratura** to spy through the keyhole.

spiata [spi'ata] sf tip-off.

spiattellare [spjattel'lare] vt (fam: verità, segreto) to blurt out; ~ **tutto** to spill the beans.

spiazzo ['spjattso] sm open space; (radura) clearing.

spiccare [spik'kare] **1** vt (a): ~ **un balzo** to jump, leap; ~ **il volo** to fly off, take wing; (fig) to spread one's wings. (b) (Dir, Comm: mandato, assegno) to issue. **2** vi (risaltare) to stand out.

spiccato, a [spik'kato] ag (senso del dovere, dell'umorismo) marked, strong; (gusto) definite, marked; (accento) broad; **ha una** ~**a simpatia per lui** she is very fond of him.

spicchio ['spikkjo] sm (di agrumi) segment; (di aglio) clove; **fare** o **tagliare a** ~**i** to divide into segments.

spicciare [spit'tʃare] **1** vt (lavoro, faccenda) to finish off; (cliente) to attend to. **2**: ~**rsi** vr to hurry up, get a move on.

spiccicare [spittʃi'kare] **1** vt (adesivo, francobollo) to unstick, detach; **non ha spiccicato parola** he didn't utter a word. **2**: ~**rsi** vr (francobollo etc) to come unstuck, come off.

spiccio, a, ci, ce ['spittʃo] **1** ag (a) (faccenda) quick; **andare per le** ~**ce** to be quick off the mark, waste no time. **(b): denaro** ~, **moneta** ~**a** (small) change. **2** smpl: ~**ci** (moneta) (small) change sg.

spicciolata [spittʃo'lata] av: **alla** ~ in dribs and drabs, a few at a time.

spicciolo, a, ci, ce ['spittʃolo] **1** ag: **denaro** ~, **moneta** ~**a** (small) change. **2** sm: **non ho uno** ~ I'm penniless; **hai degli** ~**i?** have you got any (small) change?

spicco ['spikko] sm: **fare** ~ to stand out; **di** ~ outstanding, prominent; (tema) main, principal.

spider ['spaidə] sm o f inv (Aut) two-seater convertible sports car.

spidocchiare [spidok'kjare] **1** vt to delouse. **2**: ~**rsi** vr to delouse o.s.

spiedino [spje'dino] sm (a) (utensile) skewer. (b) (Culin: di carne, pesce etc) kebab.

spiedo ['spjɛdo] sm (Culin) spit; **allo** ~ on a spit.

spiegamento [spjega'mento] sm (Mil): ~ **di forze** deployment of forces.

spiegare [spje'gare] **1** vt (a) (significato, mistero etc) to explain; **farsi** ~ **qc** to get o have sth explained; ~ **qc a qn** to explain sth to sb. (b) (tovaglia) to unfold; (vele) to unfurl; **a voce spiegata** (fig) at the top of one's voice; **a sirene spiegate** with sirens wailing. (c) (Mil) to deploy. **2**: ~**rsi** vr (farsi capire) to explain o.s., make o.s. clear; (capire) to understand; **mi spiego?** do I make myself clear?; **non so se mi spiego!** need I say more!; **spieghiamoci una volta per tutte!** let's get things straight once and for all!; **non mi**

spiego come... I can't understand how...; **ora si spiega tutto!** now everything is clear!

spiegazione [spjegat'tsjone] sf explanation; **avere una** ~ **con qn** to have it out with sb.

spiegazzare [spjegat'tsare] vt to crease, crumple.

spietato, a [spje'tato] ag (persona) ruthless, pitiless; (guerra) cruel, bitter; (fig: concorrenza) fierce; **fare una corte** ~**a a qn** to chase (after) sb.

spifferare [spiffe'rare] vt (fam) to blurt out.

spiffero ['spiffero] sm draught.

spiga, ghe ['spiga] sf (Bot: di grano) ear.

spigato, a [spi'gato] ag (tessuto) herringbone.

spigliatezza [spiʎʎa'tettsa] sf ease, self-confidence.

spigliato, a [spiʎ'ʎato] ag (persona) self-confident, self-possessed; (modi) (free and) easy.

spigolare [spigo'lare] vt (anche fig) to glean.

spigolatura [spigola'tura] sf (anche fig) gleaning.

spigolo ['spigolo] sm (di mobile, muro) corner, edge; (Geom) edge; **smussare gli** ~**i** (fig) to knock off the rough edges.

spigoloso, a [spigo'loso] ag (mobile) angular; (persona, carattere) difficult.

spilla ['spilla] sf brooch; ~ **di sicurezza** o **da balia** safety pin.

spillare [spil'lare] vt (a) (botte, vino, fig) to tap; ~ **denaro/notizie a qn** to tap sb for money/information. (b) (fogli) to clip together.

spillo ['spillo] sm (gen) pin; (da cappello) hatpin; (da cravatta) tiepin; **tacco a** ~ stiletto heel; **valvola a** ~ needle valve.

spillone [spil'lone] sm hatpin.

spilluzzicare [spilluttsi'kare] vt (cibo) to nibble, peck at.

spilorceria [spilortʃe'ria] sf meanness, stinginess; **questa è una** ~! that's really mean o stingy!

spilorcio, a, ci, ce [spi'lortʃo] **1** ag mean, stingy, tight-fisted. **2** sm/f miser, stingy person.

spilungone, a [spilun'gone] sm/f beanpole.

spina ['spina] sf (a) (Bot: di rosa etc) thorn; **avere una** ~ **nel cuore** (fig) to have a thorn in one's flesh o side; **stare sulle** ~**e** (fig) to be on tenterhooks. (b) (Zool) spine, prickle; (: di pesce) bone; ~ **dorsale** (Anat) backbone. (c) (Elettr) plug. (d) (di botte) bunghole; **birra alla** ~ draught beer.

spinacio [spi'natʃo] sm (Bot) spinach; (Culin): ~**i** spinach sg.

spinale [spi'nale] ag (Anat) spinal.

spinato, a [spi'nato] ag (a): **filo** ~ barbed wire. (b) (tessuto) herringbone attr.

spinello [spi'nello] sm (gergo) joint (cigarette).

spingere ['spindʒere] **1** vt (a) (gen) to push; (premere) to press, push; **non spingete** don't push o shove; '~' 'push'; **mi spingi?** (sull'altalena) can you give me a push?; ~ **il motore** (Aut) to drive hard; **le onde ci hanno spinto contro gli scogli** the waves drove us on to the rocks; ~ **le cose all'eccesso** to take o carry things too far o to extremes; ~ **lo sguardo lontano** to look into the distance. (b) (fig: stimolare): ~ **qn a fare qc** to urge o press sb to do sth; ~ **qn al delitto/suicidio** to drive sb to crime/suicide; **spinto dalla fame/disperazione** driven by hunger/despair; **che cosa ti spinge a continuare?** what drives you on? **2** vi to push. **3**: ~**rsi** vr: ~**rsi troppo lontano** (anche fig) to go too far; **ci siamo spinti fino al faro** we ventured as far as the lighthouse.

spino ['spino] sm (Bot) thorn bush.

spinone [spi'none] sm (cane) griffon.

spinoso, a [spi'noso] ag (anche fig) thorny, prickly.

spinta ['spinta] sf (gen) push; (urto) push, shove;

(Fis) thrust; *(fig: stimolo)* incentive, spur; *(fig: raccomandazione)*: **ho bisogno di una** ~ I need someone to pull strings for me.

spintarella [spinta'rella] *sf (fig: raccomandazione)*: **ha avuto una** ~ someone pulled strings for him.

spinterogeno [spinte'rɔdʒɛno] *sm (Aut)* coil ignition.

spinto, a ['spinto] **1** *pp di* **spingere**. **2** *ag (film, barzelletta)* risqué.

spintone [spin'tone] *sm* push, shove.

spionaggio [spio'naddʒo] *sm* espionage, spying.

spioncino [spion'tʃino] *sm* peephole, spyhole.

spione, a [spi'one] *sm/f (peg)* sneak, telltale.

spionistico, a, ci, che [spio'nistiko] *ag (organizzazione)* spy *attr*; **rete** ~**a** spy ring.

spiovente [spjo'vɛnte] **1** *ag (tetto)* sloping; **palla** *o* **tiro** ~ *(Calcio)* drop shot. **2** *sm (Calcio)* drop shot.

spiovere[1] ['spjɔvere] *vi (Meteor)* to stop raining.

spiovere[2] ['spjɔvere] *vi (aus* **essere***) (scorrere)* to flow down.

spira ['spira] *sf (gen)* coil; *(di fumo)* curl.

spiraglio [spi'raʎʎo] *sm (fessura)* chink; *(raggio di luce: anche fig)* glimmer, gleam; **uno** ~ **di speranza** a glimmer of hope, a faint hope.

spirale [spi'rale] *sf* **(a)** spiral; **a** ~ spiral(-shaped); **molla a** ~ *(di orologio)* hairspring. **(b)** *(contraccettivo)* coil.

spirare[1] [spi'rare] *vi (vento)* to blow; *(odore: emanare)*: ~ **da** to come from; **spira aria di burrasca** *(fig)* there's trouble brewing.

spirare[2] [spi'rare] *vi (aus* **essere***) (morire)* to expire, pass away.

spiritato, a [spiri'tato] **1** *ag (occhi, espressione)* wild. **2** *sm/f* person possessed by a devil; **come uno** ~ like one possessed.

spiritico, a, ci, che [spi'ritiko] *ag* spiritualist; **seduta** ~**a** séance.

spiritismo [spiri'tizmo] *sm* spiritualism.

spiritista, i, e [spiri'tista] *sm/f* spiritualist.

spirito ['spirito] *sm* **(a)** *(gen)* spirit; *(fantasma)* spirit, ghost; **lo S**~ **Santo** the Holy Ghost; **valori dello** ~ spiritual values; **aver paura degli** ~**i** to be afraid of ghosts.

(b) *(intelletto)* mind; **uno dei più grandi** ~**i della storia** one of the greatest minds in history.

(c) *(disposizione d'animo)* spirit, disposition; *(significato: di legge, epoca, testo)* spirit; **per sollevarti lo** ~ to raise your spirits; **in buone condizioni di** ~ in the right frame of mind; ~ **di classe** class consciousness; ~ **materno** motherly instinct; **non ha** ~ **di parte** he never takes sides; ~ **di squadra** team spirit; **ha detto di no per** ~ **di contraddizione** he said no for the sake of being argumentative.

(d) *(arguzia)* wit; *(umorismo)* humour; **battuta di** ~ joke; **è una persona di** ~ he has a sense of humour; **non fare dello** ~ don't try to be witty.

(e) *(Chim)* spirit, alcohol.

spiritosaggine [spirito'saddʒine] *sf* witticism; *(peg)* wisecrack.

spiritoso, a [spiri'toso] **1** *ag* witty. **2** *sm/f* witty person; **non fare lo** ~! don't try and be funny!

spirituale [spiritu'ale] *ag (gen, Filosofia, Rel)* spiritual.

spiritualità [spirituali'ta] *sf* spirituality.

spiritualizzare [spiritualid'dzare] *vt* to spiritualize.

spiritualmente [spiritual'mente] *av* spiritually.

spizzicare [spittsi'kare] *vt* to nibble, peck at.

splendente [splen'dɛnte] *ag (giornata)* bright, sunny; *(occhi)* shining; *(pavimento)* shining, gleaming.

splendere ['splɛndere] *vi* to shine.

splendido, a ['splɛndido] *ag (gen)* magnificent, splendid; *(carriera)* brilliant; **una giornata** ~**a** a glorious day.

splendore [splen'dore] *sm* splendour; *(luce intensa)* brilliance, brightness; **gli** ~**i dell'antica Roma** the splendour of ancient Rome; **che** ~ **di ragazza!** what a beautiful girl!

spodestare [spodes'tare] *vt (sovrano)* to depose, dethrone; ~ **da** to oust from.

spoetizzare [spoetid'dzare] *vt (momento, fatto)* to take the beauty out of.

spoglia ['spɔʎʎa] *sf* **(a)** *(di animale)* skin; *(di rettile)* slough. **(b)**: ~**e** *pl (poet: salma)* remains. **(c)**: ~**e** *pl (bottino)* spoils, booty *sg*.

spogliare [spoʎ'ʎare] **1** *vt* **(a)** *(svestire)* to undress; *(: con la forza)* to strip; *(fig: privare: di autorità)* to divest, strip; *(: di tesori)* to strip; ~ **qn di qc** *(derubare)* to strip *o* rob sb of sth. **(b)** *(fare lo spoglio: di schede elettorali)* to count. **2**: ~**rsi** *vr (persona)* to undress, strip; *(serpente)* to shed its skin; *(albero)* to shed its leaves; ~**rsi di** *(fig: ricchezze)* to strip o.s. of; *(: pregiudizi)* to get rid of.

spogliarellista, i, e [spoʎʎarel'lista] *sm/f* striptease artist, stripper.

spogliarello [spoʎʎa'rello] *sm* striptease.

spogliatoio [spoʎʎa'tojo] *sm (di casa)* dressing room; *(di scuola etc)* cloakroom; *(Sport)* changing room.

spoglio[1]**, a** ['spɔʎʎo] *ag (stanza)* empty, bare; *(terreno, albero)* bare; *(stile)* simple.

spoglio[2] ['spɔʎʎo] *sm*: ~ **dei voti** counting of the votes.

spola ['spɔla] *sf (Cucito: bobina)* spool; *(: navetta)* shuttle; **fare la** ~ **fra** *(sog: autobus, persona)* to go to and fro between.

spoletta [spo'letta] *sf (Cucito: bobina)* spool; *(di bomba)* fuse.

spoliticizzare [spolitit'ʃid'dzare] **1** *vt* to make nonpolitical. **2**: ~**rsi** *vr* to become nonpolitical.

spolmonarsi [spolmo'narsi] *vr* to shout o.s. hoarse.

spolpare [spol'pare] *vt (pollo etc)* to strip the flesh off; *(fig: al gioco)* to skin; **ci hanno spolpato con queste tasse** they have bled us white with these taxes.

spolverare[1] [spolve'rare] **1** *vt (mobile etc)* to dust; *(fig: mangiare)* to polish off. **2** *vi* to dust.

spolverare[2] [spolve'rare] *vt (Culin)*: ~ **(di)** to sprinkle (with), dust (with).

spolverata[1] [spolve'rata] *sf* (quick) dust(ing).

spolverata[2] [spolve'rata] *sf (di neve)* light fall; **dare una** ~ **di zucchero a qc** to sprinkle sth with sugar.

spolverino [spolve'rino] *sm (indumento)* dust coat.

sponda ['sponda] *sf* **(a)** *(di fiume)* bank; *(di mare, lago)* shore. **(b)** *(bordo: di letto, carro)* side.

spontaneità [spontanei'ta] *sf* spontaneity.

spontaneo, a [spon'taneo] *ag (gen)* spontaneous; *(affetto, persona)* natural; *(vegetazione)* wild; **di sua** ~**a volontà** of his own free will; **viene** ~**a la domanda...** the question springs to mind...; **sii** ~ **quando ti fanno una foto!** try to be natural when you're having your photo taken!

spopolamento [spopola'mento] *sm* depopulation.

spopolare [spopo'lare] **1** *vt* to depopulate. **2** *vi (cantante, attore)* to draw the crowds. **3**: ~**rsi** *vr* to become depopulated.

spora ['spɔra] *sf* spore.

sporadicità [sporadit'ʃi'ta] *sf* sporadic nature.

sporadico, a, ci, che [spo'radiko] *ag* sporadic.

sporcaccione, a [sporkat'tʃone] *(peg)* **1** *ag* filthy, disgusting. **2** *sm/f* pig, filthy person.

sporcare [spor'kare] **1** *vt* to dirty, make dirty;

(macchiare) to stain; *(fig: reputazione)* to sully, soil; ~**rsi le mani** *(anche fig)* to dirty one's hands; ~**rsi la reputazione** to sully one's reputation; ~**rsi la fedina penale** to get a police record. **2:** ~**rsi** *vr* to get dirty.

sporcizia [spor'tʃittsja] *sf (sudiciume)* filth, dirt; *(polvere)* dirt; **c'era tanta di quella** ~ **per le strade** the streets were really filthy *o* dirty; **vivere nella** ~ to live in squalor.

sporco, a, chi, che ['sporko] **1** *ag* dirty, filthy; *(macchiato)* stained; *(fig: immorale)* dirty; *(: losco: politica, faccenda)* shady; *(: denaro)* dirty; **il fazzoletto è** ~ **di inchiostro/sangue** there is ink/blood on the handkerchief; **hai le scarpe** ~**che di fango** there is mud on your shoes, your shoes are muddy; **avere la coscienza** ~**a** to have a guilty conscience; **avere la fedina penale** ~**a** to have a police record; ~ **bastardo!** *(fam)* filthy bastard!; **farla** ~**a** *(fig: farla grossa)* to behave disgracefully. **2** *sm* dirt, filth.

sporgente [spor'dʒɛnte] *ag (occhi)* protuberant, bulging; *(denti)* prominent, protruding; *(mento)* prominent; **ha le ossa** ~**i** his bones stick out.

sporgenza [spor'dʒɛntsa] *sf (su scogli, rocce)* projection; *(su parete)* bulge.

sporgere ['spordʒere] **1** *vt* **(a)** *(braccio, testa)*: ~ **da** to put out of. **(b)** *(Dir)*: ~ **querela contro qn** to take legal action against sb. **2** *vi (aus essere) (venire in fuori)* to stick out; *(protendersi: massi)* to jut out. **3:** ~**rsi** *vr*: ~**rsi da** to lean out of.

sport [sport] *sm inv* sport; **fare dello** ~ to do sport; **che** ~ **fai?** what sports do you play?; **per** ~ for fun.

sporta ['sporta] *sf (borsa)* shopping bag; **dirne un sacco e una** ~ **a qn** to tell sb a load of rubbish; *(insultare)* to give sb a mouthful.

sportello [spor'tello] *sm* **(a)** *(di veicolo, mobile)* door. **(b)** *(di banca, ufficio)* counter, window.

sportività [sportivi'ta] *sf* sportsmanship.

sportivo, a [spor'tivo] **1** *ag (gara, giornale, auto)* sports *attr*; *(persona, spirito, atteggiamento)* sporting; *(abito)* casual; **giacca** ~**a** sports jacket; **un atteggiamento molto poco** ~ a very unsporting attitude; **campo** ~ playing field. **2** *sm/f* sportsman/woman.

sporto, a ['sporto] *pp di* **sporgere**.

sposa ['spoza] *sf* bride; *(moglie)* wife; **abito** *o* **vestito da** ~ wedding dress; **dare qn in** ~ **a** to give sb in marriage to.

sposalizio [spoza'littsjo] *sm* wedding (ceremony).

sposare [spo'zare] **1** *vt (gen)* to marry; *(sog: genitori)* to marry off; *(fig: idea, fede, causa)* to embrace, espouse. **2:** ~**rsi** *vr* to get married, marry; ~**rsi con qn** to marry sb, get married to sb.

sposo ['spozo] *sm* bridegroom; *(marito)* husband; **gli** ~**i** the newlyweds.

spossante [spos'sante] *ag* exhausting.

spossare [spos'sare] *vt* to exhaust, wear out.

spossatezza [spossa'tettsa] *sf* exhaustion.

spossato, a [spos'sato] *ag* exhausted, worn-out.

spostamento [sposta'mento] *sm* movement, change of position.

spostare [spos'tare] **1** *vt* **(a)** *(gen)* to move; *(mobile)* to move, shift. **(b)** *(cambiare: orario, data)* to change; **hanno spostato la partenza di qualche giorno** they postponed *o* put off their departure by a few days. **2:** ~**rsi** *vr* to move.

spostato, a [spos'tato] *sm/f* misfit.

spranga, ghe ['spranga] *sf (barra)* bar; *(catenaccio)* bolt.

sprangare [spran'gare] *vt (vedi sf)* to bar; to bolt.

sprazzo ['sprattso] *sm (di luce, sole etc)* flash; *(fig: di*

gioia) burst; *(: di intelligenza)* flash.

sprecare [spre'kare] **1** *vt (gen, fig)* to waste; *(denaro)* to waste, squander; **è fatica sprecata!** it's a waste of effort!; **è fiato sprecato!** it's a waste of breath!; **sei sprecato qui!** your talents are wasted here! **2:** ~**rsi** *vr (persona)* to waste one's energy; **non sprecarti!** *(iro: non affaticarti)* don't strain yourself!; **si sono sprecati!** *(iro)* they certainly didn't break the bank!

spreco, chi ['sprɛko] *sm* waste; **che** ~! what a waste!; *(scherz)* you *(o* they *etc)* really went to a lot of trouble *o* bother!

sprecone, a [spre'kone] *sm/f* spendthrift.

spregevole [spre'dʒevole] *ag* contemptible, despicable.

spregiare [spre'dʒare] *vt* to despise, be contemptuous of.

spregiativo, a [spredʒa'tivo] **1** *ag* pejorative, derogatory. **2** *sm (Gram)* pejorative.

spregio ['spredʒo] *sm (disprezzo)* contempt, scorn, disdain.

spregiudicatezza [spredʒudika'tettsa] *sf* lack of scruples.

spregiudicato, a [spredʒudi'kato] *ag (senza scrupoli)* unscrupulous; *(sfacciato)* unrestrained.

spremere ['spremere] *vt (agrumi)* to squeeze; *(olive)* to press; ~ **denaro** *a o* **da qn** to squeeze money out of sb; ~**rsi le meningi** *(fig)* to rack one's brains.

spremiagrumi [spremia'grumi] *sm* lemon squeezer.

spremuta [spre'muta] *sf* fresh fruit juice; ~ **d'arancia** fresh orange juice.

spretarsi [spre'tarsi] *vr* to abandon the priesthood.

sprezzante [spret'tsante] *ag (sguardo, modi, parole)* contemptuous, scornful, disdainful; ~ **del pericolo** scornful of danger.

sprezzo ['sprettso] *sm* contempt, scorn, disdain.

sprigionare [spridʒo'nare] **1** *vt (calore, odore)* to give off, emit; *(potenza nucleare, gas tossici)* to release; *(fig: energia)* to unleash. **2:** ~**rsi** *vr*: ~**rsi da** *(sog: calore)* to emanate from, be given off by; *(: con impeto: gas)* to burst from; *(: petrolio, acqua)* to gush out from.

sprizzare [sprit'tsare] **1** *vi (aus essere)* to spurt. **2** *vt* to spurt; *(fig: gioia, vitalità)* to be bursting with; **sprizza salute da tutti i pori** he's bursting with health.

sprizzo ['sprittso] *sm (zampillo)* spurt; *(fig: di allegria)* burst.

sprofondare [sprofon'dare] **1** *vi (casa, tetto)* to collapse; *(pavimento, terreno)* to subside, settle; *(nave)* to sink; **la terra sprofondava sotto il peso del carro** the ground sank under the weight of the cart; **i suoi piedi sprofondavano nella neve** his feet sank into the snow; **sprofondò in un buco** he fell into a hole; **sprofondò nel dolore** he was overcome with grief. **2:** ~**rsi** *vr*: ~**rsi in** *(poltrona)* to sink into; *(fig: studio, lavoro)* to become engrossed in.

sproloquio [spro'lɔkwjo] *sm* rambling speech.

spronare [spro'nare] *vt (cavallo)* to spur (on); *(fig: persona)* to spur on, encourage; ~ **qn a fare qc** to encourage sb to do sth.

sprone ['sprone] *sm (sperone)* spur; *(fig)* spur, incentive; **fuggire a spron battuto** to take to one's heels.

sproporzionato, a [sproportsjo'nato] *ag* disproportionate, out of all proportion; *(prezzo)* exorbitant; *(condanna)* excessive; ~ **(rispetto) a** out of proportion to.

sproporzione [spropor'tsjone] *sf* disproportion.

spropositato, a [spropozi'tato] *ag* excessive.

sproposito [spro'pɔzito] *sm (azione sconsiderata)* blunder; **ho fatto uno ~** *(pazzia)* I did something silly; **per quella donna farei uno ~** I'd do anything for that woman; **non dire ~i** don't talk rubbish; **non farmi dire uno ~** don't make me say something I'll regret; **pesa uno ~!** it weighs a ton!; **costa uno ~!** it costs a fortune!; **arrivare a ~** to arrive at the wrong time; **parlare a ~** to talk out of turn.

sprovveduto, a [sprovve'duto] *ag* inexperienced, naïve.

sprovvisto, a [sprov'visto] *ag* **(a): ~ di** lacking in; **passeggeri ~i di passaporto** passengers without a passport; **siamo ~i di bicchieri** we haven't enough glasses; **ne siamo ~i** *(negozio)* we are out of it (*o* them). **(b): prendere qn alla ~a** to catch sb unawares.

spruzzare [sprut'tsare] *vt (a nebulizzazione)* to spray; *(aspergere)* to sprinkle; *(inzaccherare)* to splash.

spruzzata [sprut'tsata] *sf (di acqua)* splash; *(di profumo)* spray; *(di neve)* light fall; **dare una ~ di zucchero a qc** to sprinkle sth with sugar.

spruzzatore [spruttsa'tore] *sm (per profumi)* spray, atomizer; *(per biancheria)* sprinkler, spray.

spruzzo ['spruttso] *sm* splash; **verniciatura a ~** spray painting.

spudoratezza [spudora'tettsa] *sf* shamelessness.

spudorato, a [spudo'rato] *ag* shameless; **è stato così ~ da venirmi a chiedere aiuto** he had the cheek to come and ask me for help.

spugna ['spuɲɲa] *sf (Zool)* sponge; *(tessuto)* terry towelling, terry cloth; **bere come una ~** to drink like a fish; **gettare la ~** *(Pugilato, fig)* to throw in the sponge.

spugnatura [spuɲɲa'tura] *sf* sponging, sponge down.

spugnoso, a [spuɲ'ɲoso] *ag* spongy.

spulciare [spul'tʃare] *vt (animali)* to rid of fleas; *(fig: testo, compito)* to examine thoroughly.

spuma ['spuma] *sf (schiuma)* foam; *(bibita)* fizzy drink.

spumante [spu'mante] *sm* sparkling wine.

spumeggiante [spumed'dʒante] *ag (vino, fig)* sparkling; *(mare)* foaming.

spumeggiare [spumed'dʒare] *vi (vino)* to sparkle; *(mare)* to foam.

spumone [spu'mone] *sm (gelato)* soft ice cream made with whipped cream.

spuntare[1] [spun'tare] **1** *vt (lapis, coltello)* to break the point of; *(capelli, baffi)* to trim; **spuntarla** *(fig: vincere)* to succeed, win (through); *(: averla vinta)* to get one's own way. **2** *vi (aus* **essere***) (nascere: germogli)* to sprout; *(: capelli)* to begin to grow; *(: dente)* to come through; *(apparire: sole)* to rise; *(: giorno)* to dawn; **gli è spuntato un dente** he has cut a tooth; **è spuntato da chissà dove** *(fig)* he turned up from out of the blue. **3: ~rsi** *vr* to lose its point, become blunt. **4** *sm:* **allo ~ del sole** at sunrise; **allo ~ del giorno** at daybreak.

spuntare[2] [spun'tare] *vt (elenco)* to tick off.

spuntino [spun'tino] *sm* snack; **fare uno ~** to have a snack.

spunto ['spunto] *sm (Mus, Teatro)* cue; *(fig: base)* starting point; *(: idea)* idea; **dare** *o* **fornire lo ~ a qc** *(polemiche)* to give rise to sth; **ciò mi ha dato lo ~ per iniziare a dipingere** it started me painting; **prendere ~ da qc** to take sth as one's starting point.

spurgare [spur'gare] *vt (fogna, canale)* to clear, clean; *(Med)* to clean; *(Aut: freni)* to bleed.

spurgo, ghi ['spurgo] *sm* **(a)** *(vedi vb)* clearing; cleaning; bleeding; **valvola di ~** bleeder. **(b)** *(Med)* discharge.

sputacchiare [sputak'kjare] *vi* to spit.

sputacchiera [sputak'kjera] *sf* spittoon.

sputare [spu'tare] **1** *vt* to spit (out); **mi ha fatto sputar sangue** *(fig)* he made me sweat blood; **~ veleno** *(fig)* to talk spitefully; **sputa fuori!** *(anche fig)* spit it out!; **sputa l'osso!** *(fig)* out with it!; **è suo padre sputato** *(fam)* he's the spitting image of his father. **2** *vi* to spit; **~ in faccia a qn** *(fig)* to spit in sb's face; **~ addosso a qn** *(fig)* to despise sb; **non ci sputerei sopra** *(fig)* I wouldn't turn my nose up at it; **non ~ nel piatto in cui mangi** don't bite the hand that feeds you.

sputasentenze [sputasen'tɛntse] *sm/f inv* know-all.

sputo ['sputo] *sm* spittle, spit; **questo libro deve essere appiccicato con lo ~** this book just comes apart in your hands.

sputtanare [sputta'nare] *(fam)* **1** *vt* to run down. **2: ~rsi** *vr* to disgrace o.s.

squadra[1] ['skwadra] *sf (strumento)* (set) square; **a ~ at right angles**; **essere fuori ~** to be crooked; *(fig: persona)* to be out of sorts.

squadra[2] ['skwadra] *sf (gruppo)* team, squad; *(di operai)* gang, squad; *(Sport)* team; *(Mil)* squad; *(: Aer, Naut)* squadron; **lavoro a ~e** teamwork; **~ mobile/del buon costume** *(Polizia)* flying/vice squad.

squadrare [skwa'drare] *vt* to square; **~ qn da capo a piedi** *(fig)* to look sb up and down.

squadriglia [skwa'driʎʎa] *sf (Aer)* flight.

squadrone [skwa'drone] *sm (Mil)* squadron.

squagliare [skwaʎ'ʎare] **1** *vt* to melt. **2: ~rsi** *vr* to melt; **~rsi, squagliarsela** *(fig fam)* to sneak off.

squalifica, che [skwa'lifika] *sf* disqualification.

squalificare [skwalifi'kare] **1** *vt (gen, Sport)* to disqualify; *(fig: screditare)* to bring discredit on. **2: ~rsi** *vr* to bring discredit on o.s.

squallido, a ['skwallido] *ag (luogo)* wretched, bleak; *(vita)* miserable; *(vicenda)* squalid, sordid.

squallore [skwal'lore] *sm (vedi ag)* wretchedness, bleakness; misery; squalor.

squalo ['skwalo] *sm* shark.

squama ['skwama] *sf (scaglia)* scale; **ho delle ~e sulla pelle** my skin is flaking off.

squamare [skwa'mare] **1** *vt* to scale. **2: ~rsi** *vr* to flake (off); *(Med)* to desquamate.

squarciagola [skwartʃa'gola] *av:* **a ~** at the top of one's voice.

squarciare [skwar'tʃare] **1** *vt (muro, corpo)* to rip open; *(tessuto)* to rip; *(fig: tenebre, silenzio)* to split; *(: nuvole)* to pierce. **2: ~rsi** *vr (vedi vt)* to rip open; to rip; *(nuvole)* to part.

squarcio ['skwartʃo] *sm* **(a)** *(ferita)* gash; *(in lenzuolo, abito)* rip; *(in un muro)* breach; *(in una nave)* hole; **uno ~ di sole** a burst of sunlight. **(b)** *(brano)* passage, excerpt.

squartare [skwar'tare] *vt* to quarter, cut up.

squattrinato, a [skwattri'nato] **1** *ag* penniless. **2** *sm/f* pauper.

squilibrare [skwili'brare] **1** *vt* to unbalance; *(psicologicamente)* to derange, unbalance; **~ qn finanziariamente** to upset sb's bank balance. **2: ~rsi** *vr* to lose one's balance.

squilibrato, a [skwili'brato] **1** *ag (alimentazione)* unbalanced; *(mente)* deranged, unbalanced. **2** *sm/f (anche:* **~ mentale***)* deranged person.

squilibrio [skwi'librjo] *sm* **(a)** *(Psic: anche:* **~ mentale***)* derangement. **(b)** *(Econ: differenza)* imbalance.

squillante [skwil'lante] *ag (suono)* shrill, sharp; *(voce)* shrill; *(fig: colore)* loud.

squillare [skwil'lare] *vi (campanello, telefono)* to ring (out); *(tromba)* to blare.

squillo ['skwillo] **1** *sm (di campanello etc)* ring; *(di tromba)* blast; **ti avverto con tre ~i di telefono** I'll let the phone ring three times to warn you. **2** *sf inv (anche:* **ragazza ~)** call girl.

squinternato, a [skwinter'nato] **1** *ag* crazy. **2** *sm/f* loony *(fam)*.

squisitezza [skwizi'tettsa] *sf (di sentimenti, gusto)* refinement; *(di modi)* considerateness; **questo pollo è una ~** this chicken is exquisite.

squisito, a [skwi'zito] *ag (gen)* lovely, exquisite; *(gusto, gioiello)* exquisite; *(persona)* delightful; *(modi)* considerate; *(cibo)* delicious.

squittire [skwit'tire] *vi (uccello)* to squawk; *(topo)* to squeak.

sradicare [zradi'kare] *vt (albero)* to uproot; *(erba)* to root out; *(fig: vizio)* to eradicate; **sentirsi sradicato** *(fig)* to feel uprooted.

sragionare [zradʒo'nare] *vi (vaneggiare)* to rave; *(fare discorsi sconnessi)* to talk nonsense.

sregolatezza [zregola'tettsa] *sf (nel mangiare, bere)* lack of moderation; *(di vita)* dissoluteness, dissipation; **le sue ~e gli costeranno care** his excesses will cost him dear.

sregolato, a [zrego'lato] *ag (vita: senza ordine)* disorderly; *(: dissoluto)* dissolute; **è ~ nel mangiare** he has irregular eating habits.

S.r.l. *abbr di* **società a responsabilità limitata.**

srotolare [zroto'lare] *vt, ~rsi vr* to unroll.

stabbio ['stabbjo] *sm (a) (recinto)* pen, fold; *(: di maiali)* pigsty. **(b)** *(letame)* manure.

stabile ['stabile] **1** *ag (gen)* stable; *(fondamenta)* solid; *(impiego)* steady, permanent; *(carattere)* firm; **la scala non è ~** the ladder is shaky; **il ponte non è ~** the bridge is unstable; **essere ~ nei propri propositi** to stick to one's decisions, keep to one's plans; **compagnia ~** *(Teatro)* resident company; **teatro ~** civic theatre. **2** *sm* **(a)** *(edificio)* building. **(b)** *(anche:* **teatro ~)** civic theatre. **3** *sf (Teatro)* resident company.

stabilimento [stabili'mento] **1** *sm (fabbrica)* plant, factory. **2: ~ balneare** bathing establishment; **~ carcerario** prison; **~ tessile** textile mill.

stabilire [stabi'lire] **1** *vt (gen)* to establish; *(fissare: prezzi, data)* to fix; *(decidere)* to decide; **hanno stabilito la chiusura di tutte le scuole** they decided to close all the schools; **~ un aumento dei prezzi** to decide on a price increase; **~ un collegamento** to establish contact; **resta stabilito che...** it is agreed that.... **2: ~rsi vr** *(prendere dimora)* to settle; **mi vorrei ~ in un posto** I would like to settle down somewhere.

stabilità [stabili'ta] *sf* stability.

stabilizzare [stabilid'dzare] **1** *vt* to stabilize. **2: ~rsi vr** *(situazione economica, malato)* to become stable; *(tempo)* to become settled.

stabilizzatore, trice [stabiliddza'tore] **1** *ag* stabilizing. **2** *sm (Aer, Naut, Chim)* stabilizer; *(Elettr)*: **~ di tensione** voltage regulator.

stabilizzazione [stabiliddzat'tsjone] *sf* stabilization.

staccanovista, i, e [stakkano'vista] *sm/f (iro)* eager beaver.

staccare [stak'kare] **1** *vt* **(a)** *(togliere)*: **~ (da)** to remove (from), take (from); *(quadro)* to take down (from); *(foglio, pagina)* to tear out (of), remove (from); **stacca quel tavolo dalla parete** pull that table out from the wall; **~ la televisione/il telefono** to disconnect the television/ the phone; **~ un assegno** to write a cheque; **non riusciva a ~ gli occhi da quella scena** he could not take his eyes off the scene before him.

(b) *(separare: anche fig)* to separate, divide; *(: buoi)* to unyoke; *(: cavalli)* to unharness; **~ la locomotiva dal treno** to uncouple the locomotive from the train; **~ le parole** to pronounce one's words clearly; **~ le note** *(Mus)* to play staccato.

(c) *(Sport: distanziare)* to leave behind.

2 *vi* **(a)** *(risaltare)* to stand out.

(b) *(fam: finire di lavorare)* to knock off.

3: ~rsi vr (a) *(venir via: bottone)* to come off; *(: foglio)* to come out; *(sganciarsi)* to break loose.

(b): ~rsi da *(allontanarsi)* to move away from; *(: dalla famiglia)* to leave; **non si staccano mai** they never leave each other; **non si stacca mai dalla televisione** he's always glued to the television.

staccato, a [stak'kato] **1** *ag (foglio)* loose; *(fascicolo)* separate. **2** *sm (Mus)* staccato.

staccionata [stattʃo'nata] *sf (gen)* fence; *(Ippica)* hurdle.

stacco, chi ['stakko] *sm* **(a)** *(intervallo)* gap; *(: tra due scene)* break; *(differenza)* difference; **fare uno ~ tra una parola e l'altra** to articulate one's words; **c'è troppo ~ tra i due colori** there's too much of a difference between the two colours; **fare ~ su** to stand out against. **(b)** *(Sport: nel salto)* takeoff.

stadera [sta'dera] *sf* lever scales *pl*.

stadio ['stadjo] *sm* **(a)** *(Sport)* stadium. **(b)** *(periodo, fase)* stage; **a due/tre ~i** two-/three-stage *attr*.

staffa ['staffa] *sf* **(a)** *(gen, Tecn, Edil)* stirrup; **perdere le ~e** *(fig)* to fly off the handle; **tenere il piede in due ~e** *(fig)* to run with the hare and hunt with the hounds. **(b)** *(Anat)* stirrup bone.

staffetta [staf'fetta] *sf* **(a)** *(messo)* courier, runner. **(b)** *(Sport)* relay race.

stafilococco, chi [stafilo'kɔkko] *sm* staphylococcus.

stagflazione [stagflat'tsjone] *sf (Econ)* stagflation.

stagionale [stadʒo'nale] **1** *ag* seasonal; **'apertura ~'** 'open during the tourist season'. **2** *sm/f* seasonal worker.

stagionare [stadʒo'nare] *vt, vi (aus essere)*, **~rsi vr** *(legno)* to season; *(formaggio, vino)* to mature.

stagionato, a [stadʒo'nato] *ag (vedi vb)* seasoned; matured; *(scherz: attempato)* getting on in years.

stagionatura [stadʒona'tura] *sf (vedi vb)* seasoning; maturing.

stagione [sta'dʒone] *sf* season; **la bella ~** the summer months; **la ~ delle piogge** the rainy season; **in questa ~** at this time of year; **frutta di ~** seasonal fruit; **saldi di fine ~** end-of-season sales; **vestiti di mezza ~** clothes for spring and autumn; **alta/bassa ~** *(Turismo)* high/low *o* off-season.

stagliarsi [staʎ'ʎarsi] *vr*: **~ contro** *o* **su** to stand out against, be silhouetted against.

stagnante [staɲ'ɲante] *ag (anche fig)* stagnant.

stagnare[1] [staɲ'ɲare] *vt* **(a)** *(ricoprire di stagno)* to tin-plate; *(saldare)* to solder. **(b)** *(rendere ermetico)* to make watertight.

stagnare[2] [staɲ'ɲare] **1** *vi (acqua, Econ)* to stagnate; **l'aria stagnava nella stanza** the air in the room was stale. **2** *vt (sangue)* to stop.

stagnatura [staɲɲa'tura] *sf* tinning, tin-plating.

stagnino [staɲ'ɲino] *sm* tinsmith.

stagno[1] ['staɲɲo] *sm (Chim)* tin; *(per saldare)* solder.

stagno[2] ['staɲɲo] *sm (acquitrino)* pond.

stagno[3]**, a** ['staɲɲo] *ag (a tenuta d'acqua)* watertight; *(a tenuta d'aria)* airtight.

stagnola [staɲ'ɲɔla] *sf (anche:* **carta ~)** tinfoil.

stalagmite [stalag'mite] *sf* stalagmite.

stalattite [stalat'tite] *sf* stalactite.

stalla ['stalla] *sf (per bovini)* cowshed; *(per cavalli)* stable; *(fig: casa)* pigsty; **passare dalle stelle alle** ~**e** *(fig)* to go downhill.

stalliere [stal'ljɛre] *sm* groom, stableboy.

stallo ['stallo] *sm* **(a)** stall, seat. **(b)** *(Scacchi)* stalemate; *(Aer)* stall; **situazione di** ~ *(fig)* stalemate.

stallone [stal'lone] *sm* stallion.

stamani [sta'mani] *av*, **stamattina** [stamat'tina] *av* this morning.

stambecco, chi [stam'bekko] *sm* ibex.

stamberga, ghe [stam'bɛrga] *sf* hovel.

stampa ['stampa] *sf* **(a)** *(Tip, Fot: tecnica)* printing; *(: riproduzione, copia)* print; *(insieme dei quotidiani, giornalisti):* **la** ~ the press; **andare in** ~ to go to press; **il libro è in** ~ the book is being printed; **fuori** ~ out of print; **dare un'opera alle** ~**e** to have a work published; **mandare in** ~ to pass for press; **errore di** ~ printing error; **prova di** ~ print sample; **libertà di** ~ freedom of the press; '~**e**' 'printed matter'. **(b)** *(Tecn: di plastica)* moulding; *(: di metallo)* pressing; *(: di tessuto)* printing.

stampaggio [stam'paddʒo] *sm (di plastica)* moulding; *(di metalli)* pressing.

stampante [stam'pante] *sf (Inform)* printer.

stampare [stam'pare] **1** *vt* **(a)** *(gen, Tip, Fot)* to print; *(denaro)* to strike, coin; *(pubblicare)* to publish; ~ **nella memoria a qn** *(fig)* to impress upon sb's memory; ~ **qc in testa a qn** *(fig)* to din sth into sb's head; **gli ha stampato un bacio in fronte** she planted a kiss on his forehead; **non li stampo mica i soldi** I am not made of money. **(b)** *(Tecn: plastica)* to mould; *(: metalli)* to press; *(: tessuti)* to print. **2:** ~**rsi** *vr:* ~**rsi nella mente** *o* **nella memoria** to be imprinted in one's memory.

stampatello [stampa'tɛllo] *sm* block capitals *pl*, block letters *pl*; **scrivere in** *o* **a** ~ to write in block capitals *o* letters.

stampato, a [stam'pato] **1** *ag* printed. **2** *sm (opuscolo)* leaflet; *(modulo)* form; ~**i** printed matter.

stampatore, trice [stampa'tore] **1** *sm/f* printer. **2** *sf (Cine, Fot)* printing machine.

stampella [stam'pɛlla] *sf* crutch.

stamperia [stampe'ria] *sf (di libri)* printing works *sg*, printing house; *(di tessuti)* printworks *sg*.

stampigliare [stampiʎ'ʎare] *vt* to stamp.

stampigliatura [stampiʎʎa'tura] *sf (atto)* stamping; *(marchio)* stamp.

stampino [stam'pino] *sm (normografo)* stencil; *(punteruolo)* punch.

stampo ['stampo] *sm (gen, Culin)* mould; *(Tecn)* mould, die; *(fig: indole)* type, kind, sort; **di** ~ **antico** old-fashioned; **essere fatto con lo** ~ *(fig)* to be cast in the same mould.

stanare [sta'nare] *vt* to drive out.

stancare [stan'kare] **1** *vt (spossare)* to tire; *(annoiare)* to bore; *(infastidire)* to annoy. **2:** ~**rsi** *vr* to get tired, tire o.s. out; ~**rsi (di)** *(stufarsi)* to grow tired (of), get fed up (with).

stanchezza [stan'kettsa] *sf (fisica)* fatigue, tiredness; *(mentale)* tiredness, weariness; *(fig: noia)* weariness, boredom; **dare segni di** ~ to show signs of tiredness; **che** ~!, **ho una** ~ **addosso!** I am dead beat!

stanco, a, chi, che ['stanko] *ag* tired; ~ **morto** dead tired; **con una voce** ~**a disse...** he said wearily...; ~ **(di)** *(stufo)* tired (of), fed up (with); ~ **di vivere** tired of life; **nato** ~ *(fig)* bone idle.

stand [stænd] *sm inv (padiglione, tribuna)* stand.

standard ['standard] **1** *ag inv* standard. **2** *sm inv* standard; ~ **di vita** standard of living.

standardizzare [standardid'dzare] *vt* to standardize.

standardizzazione [standardiddzat'tsjone] *sf* standardization.

standista, i, e [stan'dista] *sm/f (in una fiera etc)* person responsible for a stand.

stanga, ghe ['stanga] *sm* bar; *(di carro)* shaft; *(fig fam: persona)* beanpole.

stangare [stan'gare] *vt (colpire)* to beat, thrash; *(fig: far pagare troppo)* to sting; *(: bocciare)* to give a poor mark to.

stangata [stan'gata] *sf (gen, fig)* blow; *(Calcio)* shot; **prendere una** ~ *(fam: pagare troppo)* to get stung; *(: agli esami)* to fail miserably.

stanghetta [stan'getta] *sf (di occhiali)* leg. **(b)** *(Mus, di scrittura)* bar.

stanotte [sta'nɔtte] *av* tonight; *(notte passata)* last night.

stante ['stante] **1** *ag:* **a sé** ~ *(appartamento, casa)* independent, separate; **seduta** ~ *(fig: subito)* on the spot. **2** *prep* owing to, because of.

stantio, a, ii, e [stan'tio] *ag (anche fig)* stale; *(burro)* rancid; **sapere di** ~ to taste stale *(o* rancid*)*; **idee** ~**e** old-fashioned ideas.

stantuffo [stan'tuffo] *sm* piston.

stanza ['stantsa] *sf* **(a)** *(vano)* room; ~ **da bagno** bathroom; ~ **da letto** bedroom; ~ **dei bottoni** control room. **(b)** *(Poesia)* stanza. **(c)** *(dimora):* **prendere** ~ **in** to take up residence in; **essere di** ~ **a** *(Mil)* to be stationed in.

stanziamento [stantsja'mento] *sm* allocation.

stanziare [stan'tsjare] **1** *vt* to allocate. **2:** ~**rsi** *vr (gen)* to settle; *(Mil)* to be stationed.

stanzino [stan'tsino] *sm (ripostiglio)* storeroom; *(spogliatoio)* changing room.

stappare [stap'pare] *vt* to uncork; *(tappo a corona)* to uncap.

star [sta:] *sf inv (diva)* star.

stare ['stare] *vi (aus essere)* **(a)** *(rimanere)* to stay, be; ~ **in piedi** to stand; ~ **fermo** to keep *o* stay still; ~ **seduto** to sit, be sitting; ~ **disteso** to lie; ~ **zitto** to keep quiet; **stai dove sei!** stay where you are!; **starò a Roma per qualche giorno** I'll stay *o* be in Rome for a few days; ~ **a casa** to be *o* stay at home; **è stato su tutta la notte** he stayed *o* was up all night; ~ **in equilibrio** to keep one's balance.

(b) *(abitare: temporaneamente)* to stay; *(: permanentemente)* to live; **sta con i suoi** he lives with his parents; **sta da solo** he lives on his own; **sta in via Rossetti 5** he lives at No. 5 via Rossetti; **al momento sta con degli amici** he's staying with friends at the moment.

(c) *(essere, trovarsi)* to be; **la casa sta in cima al colle** the house is at the top of the hill; **stando così le cose** given the situation; **le cose stanno così** this is the situation; **non voglio** ~ **da solo** I don't want to be on my own; **sono stato dal dentista** I've been to the dentist; ~ **bene/male** *(di salute)* to be well/ill; **sta bene!** *(d'accordo così)* that's fine!; **non sta bene che un uomo della tua posizione si comporti così** it doesn't become a man in your position to behave like this; **quel vestito ti sta bene/male** that dress suits/doesn't suit you; **gli sta bene!** *(così impara)* it serves him right!; **stai sicuro che non la passerà liscia!** rest assured he won't get away with it!; ~ **al banco** *(cameriere etc)* to serve at the bar; ~ **alla cassa** to work at the till; ~ **a dieta** to be on a diet.

(d) *(seguito da gerundio):* **stavo andando a casa** I was going home; **cosa stai facendo?** what are you doing?; **stava piovendo** it was raining.

(e): ~ **per fare qc** to be on the point of doing

sth, be about to do sth; **stavo per dirgli tutto ma il telefono squillò** I was on the point of telling him everything when the phone rang; **stavi per rovinare tutto** you nearly spoiled *o* ruined everything.

(f): ~ **a sentire** to listen; ~ **ad insistere** to insist; **sta' a sentire** listen a minute; **è inutile che stai a dirmi tutte queste cose** there's no good *o* use telling me all this; **sta a te decidere** it's up to you to decide; **stando a ciò che dice lui** according to him *o* to his version; **stando ai fatti, sembrerebbe che...** the facts would seem to indicate that...; **stiamo a vedere cosa succede** let's wait and see (what happens); **stai a vedere che aveva ragione lei!** you'll see that she was right!

(g): starci *(considerazione): contenuto):* **ci sta ancora qualcosa lì dentro?** is there room for anything else?; **non credo ci stia tutta quella pasta** I don't think there's room for all that pasta; **non ci stanno più di 4 persone in quella macchina** there is only room for 4 in that car; **il 5 nel 25 ci sta 5 volte** 5 goes into 25 5 times; **1 sta a 2 come 3 sta a 6** 1 is to 2 as 3 is to 6.

(h): starci *(essere d'accordo):* **ci stai se andiamo** *o* **ad andare fuori a cena?** do you want to go out for a meal?; **ha detto che non ci sta** he said he didn't agree, he said he was against the idea; **OK, ci sto** OK, that's fine.

(i): starsene: se ne stava lì in un angolo he was over in the corner; **se n'è stato zitto** he never opened his mouth; **non startene lì seduto, fa' qualcosa** don't just sit there, do something; **stasera me ne sto a casa** I'll be staying in tonight.

starnazzare [starnat'tsare] *vi* to squawk.

starnutire [starnu'tire] *vi* to sneeze.

starnuto [star'nuto] *sm* sneeze; **fare uno** ~ to sneeze.

starter ['starter] *sm inv (Aut, Sport)* starter.

stasera [sta'sera] *av* this evening, tonight.

stasi ['stazi] *sf (Med, fig)* stasis.

statale [sta'tale] **1** *ag* government *attr*, state *attr*; **bilancio** ~ national budget; **impiegato** ~ state employee; **strada** ~ ≃ trunk *o* main road. **2** *sm/f (impiegato)* civil servant. **3** *sf (strada)* ≃ trunk road, main road.

statalizzare [statalid'dzare] *vt* to nationalize, put under state control.

statica, che ['statika] *sf* statics *sg*.

statico, a, ci, che ['statiko] *ag (Elettr, fig)* static.

statino [sta'tino] *sm (Univ)* examination ticket.

statista, i [sta'tista] *sm* statesman.

statistico, a, ci, che [sta'tistiko] **1** *ag* statistical. **2** *sf* statistics *sg*; **fare una** ~**a** to carry out a statistical examination.

stato¹, a ['stato] *pp di* **essere, stare.**

stato² ['stato] **1** *sm* **(a)** *(condizione: gen)* state; *(di paziente)* condition; ~ **d'animo** mood; ~ **(di salute)** state of health; **guarda in quale** ~ **si è ridotto!** look at the state it *(o* he) is in!; **vivere allo** ~ **selvaggio** to live in the wild. **(b)** *(fraseologia):* **essere in** ~ **d'accusa** to have been charged with an offence; **essere in** ~ **d'arresto** to be under arrest; **essere in** ~ **d'assedio** to be under siege; **essere in** ~ **d'emergenza** to be in a state of emergency; **essere in** ~ **interessante** to be pregnant; **allo** ~ **liquido/gassoso** in the liquid/ gaseous state.

2: ~ **civile** marital status; ~ **di famiglia** *certificate giving details of a household and its dependents;* ~ **patrimoniale** statement of assets and liabilities; **S**~ **Maggiore** *(Mil)* general staff.

stato³ ['stato] *sm (Pol)* state; **di** ~ state *attr*; **gli S**~**i**

Uniti **(d'America)** the United States (of America).

statua ['statua] *sf* statue.

statuario, a [statu'arjo] *ag (fig: bellezza, posa)* statuesque.

statunitense [statuni'tɛnse] **1** *ag* United States *attr*, of the United States. **2** *sm/f* American citizen, citizen of the United States.

statura [sta'tura] *sf* height; **essere alto/basso di** ~ to be tall/short *o* small; **un uomo politico della sua** ~ a politician of his stature.

status ['status] *sm inv* status.

statutario, a [statu'tarjo] *ag* statutory.

statuto [sta'tuto] *sm* statute; **regione a** ~ **speciale** *Italian region with political autonomy in certain matters.*

stavolta [sta'vɔlta] *av* this time.

stazionamento [stattsjona'mento] *sm (Aut)* parking; *(: sosta)* waiting; **freno di** ~ handbrake.

stazionare [stattsjo'nare] *vi (veicoli)* to be parked.

stazionario, a [stattsjo'narjo] *ag (fig: immutato)* stable, unchanged.

stazione [stat'tsjone] *sf* **(a)** *(gen, Radio etc)* station; ~ **ferroviaria/degli autobus** train/coach station; ~ **di servizio** service *o* petrol *o* filling station; ~ **meteorologica** weather station; ~ **radio** radio station; ~ **trasmittente** *(Radio, TV)* transmitting station. **(b)** *(località):* ~ **balneare** seaside resort; ~ **climatica** health resort; ~ **invernale** winter sports resort; ~ **termale** (thermal) spa.

stazza ['stattsa] *sf* tonnage.

stecca, che ['stekka] *sf (gen)* stick; *(di ombrello)* rib; *(da biliardo)* cue; *(Med)* splint; *(di sigarette)* carton; **prendere una** ~ *(fig: stonatura: cantando)* to sing a wrong note; *(: suonando)* to play a wrong note.

steccare [stek'kare] *vt (Med)* to splint.

steccato [stek'kato] *sm* fence.

stecchetto [stek'ketto] *sm (fam):* **tenere qn a** ~ to keep sb on short rations.

stecchino [stek'kino] *sm* toothpick.

stecchire [stek'kire] *vt (fam: ammazzare)* to kill (stone dead).

stecchito, a [stek'kito] *ag (ramo)* dried up; **morto** ~ stone dead; **lasciare qn** ~ *(fig: sorpreso)* to leave sb flabbergasted.

stecco, chi ['stekko] *sm (ramo)* twig; *(bastoncino)* stick; *(fig: persona magra)* beanpole.

stele ['stele] *sf inv* stele.

stella ['stella] *sf* star; ~ **cadente** *o* **filante** shooting star; ~ **polare** pole *o* north star; ~ **alpina** *(Bot)* edelweiss; ~ **di mare** starfish; ~**e filanti** *(per carnevale etc)* streamers; **senza** ~**e** starless; **alla luce delle** ~**e** by starlight; **dormire sotto le** ~**e** to sleep out under the stars; **vedere le** ~**e** *(per il dolore)* to see stars; **ringrazia la tua buona** ~ thank your lucky stars; **nascere sotto una buona/ cattiva** ~ to be born under a lucky/an unlucky star; **i prezzi sono andati** *o* **saliti alle** ~**e** prices have gone sky-high; **una** ~ **del cinema** a cinema star; **la sua** ~ **sta tramontando** his star is waning.

stellare [stel'lare] *ag* stellar; **luce** ~ starlight.

stellato, a [stel'lato] *ag (cielo, notte)* starry.

stelletta [stel'letta] *sf* **(a)** *(Mil)* star; **guadagnarsi/ rimetterci le** ~**e** to be promoted/demoted. **(b)** *(Tip)* asterisk.

stelo ['stɛlo] *sm (Bot)* stem; *(asta)* rod.

stemma, i ['stɛmma] *sm* coat of arms.

stemperare [stempe'rare] *vt (calce, colore)* to dissolve.

stempiarsi [stem'pjarsi] *vr* to develop a receding hairline.

stempiato, a [stem'pjato] *ag* with a receding hairline.

stendardo [sten'dardo] *sm* standard.

stendere ['stɛndere] **1** *vt* **(a)** *(braccia, gambe)* to stretch (out); *(tovaglia)* to spread (out); *(bucato)* to hang out; *(mettere a giacere)* to lay (down); *(spalmare)* to spread; *(pasta)* to roll out. **(b)** *(persona: far giacere)* to lay (down); *(: gettare a terra, fig: vincere)* to floor; *(: uccidere)* to kill. **(c)** *(lettera, verbale etc)* to draw up. **2:** ~**rsi** *vr* **(a)** *(persona)* to lie down; ~**rsi a terra/sul letto** to lie down on the ground/on the bed. **(b)** *(pianura, vallata)* to extend, stretch.

stendibiancheria [stendibjanke'ria] *sm inv* clothes horse.

stenditoio [stendi'tojo] *sm (locale)* drying room; *(stendibiancheria)* clothes horse.

stenodattilografia [stenodattilogra'fia] *sf* shorthand typing.

stenodattilografo, a [stenodatti'lɔgrafo] *sm/f* shorthand typist.

stenografare [stenogra'fare] *vt* to take down in shorthand.

stenografia [stenogra'fia] *sf* shorthand.

stenografico, a, ci, che [steno'grafiko] *ag* shorthand *attr*.

stenografo, a [ste'nɔgrafo] *sm/f* stenographer.

stenotipia [stenoti'pia] *sf* stenotype.

stentare [sten'tare] *vi:* ~ **a fare qc** to have difficulty in doing sth, find it hard to do sth; **stento a crederci** I find it hard to believe.

stentato, a [sten'tato] *ag (compito, stile)* laboured; *(sorriso)* forced; **con passo** ~ stiffly.

stento ['stɛnto] *sm* **(a): una vita di** ~**i** a life of hardship *o* privation; **vivere tra gli** ~**i** to live a life of hardship *o* privation. **(b): a** ~ with difficulty; **capire qc a** ~ to understand sth with difficulty.

steppa ['steppa] *sf* steppe.

sterco ['sterko] *sm* dung.

stereo ['stɛreo] *ag inv, sm inv* stereo.

stereofonia [stereofo'nia] *sf* stereophony.

stereofonico, a, ci, che [stereo'fɔniko] *ag* stereo(phonic).

stereoscopico, a, ci, che [stereos'kɔpiko] *ag* stereoscopic.

stereoscopio [stereos'kɔpjo] *sm* stereoscope.

stereotipato, a [stereoti'pato] *ag (anche fig)* stereotyped.

stereotipia [stereoti'pia] *sf (Tecn, Psic)* stereotypy; *(Tip)* stereotype print.

stereotipo [stere'ɔtipo] *sm* stereotype; **pensare per** ~**i** to think in clichés.

sterile ['stɛrile] *ag (terreno)* arid; *(persona)* sterile; *(fig: polemica)* fruitless; *(: vita)* empty.

sterilità [sterili'ta] *sf (vedi ag)* aridity; sterility; fruitlessness; emptiness.

sterilizzare [sterilid'dzare] *vt* to sterilize.

sterilizzazione [steriliddzat'tsjone] *sf* sterilization.

sterlina [ster'lina] *sf* pound (sterling).

sterminare [stermi'nare] *vt* to exterminate, wipe out.

sterminato, a [stermi'nato] *ag* immense, endless.

sterminio [ster'minjo] *sm* extermination; **campo di** ~ death camp.

sterno ['stɛrno] *sm (Anat)* breastbone, sternum *(T)*.

sterpaglia [ster'paʎʎa] *sf* brushwood.

sterpo ['stɛrpo] *sm* dry twig.

sterrare [ster'rare] *vt* to excavate.

sterratore [sterra'tore] *sm* navvy.

sterzare [ster'tsare] *vi (Aut)* to steer; *(: bruscamente)* to swerve; ~ **a destra/a sinistra** to steer *(o* swerve*)* right/left.

sterzata [ster'tsata] *sf (Aut)* turn of the wheel; *(: brusca)* swerve; **fare** *o* **dare una** ~ to steer; *(bruscamente)* to swerve.

sterzo ['stertso] *sm* steering wheel.

steso, a ['steso] *pp di* **stendere.**

stesso, a ['stesso] **1** *ag* **(a)** *(medesimo, identico)* same; **aveva lo** ~ **vestito** she had the same dress; **ha i tuoi** ~**i anni** he's the same age as you; **abbiamo gli** ~**i gusti** we have the same tastes; **al tempo** ~ at the same time; **è sempre la** ~**a storia** it's always the same old thing.

(b) *(esatto, preciso)* very; **in quello** ~ **istante** at that very moment; **quello** ~ **giorno** that very day; **oggi** ~ today.

(c) *(rafforzativo: dopo sostantivo):* **lo** ~ **medico lo sconsiglia** even the doctor *o* the doctor himself advised against it; **è venuto il ministro** ~ **ad inaugurarlo** the minister himself came to inaugurate it.

(d) *(rafforzativo: dopo pron pers sog):* **l'ho visto io** ~ I saw him myself; **voi** ~**i sapete bene che...** you (yourselves) know very well that...; **lei** ~**a è venuta a dirmelo** she came and told me herself, she herself came and told me.

(e) *(rafforzativo: dopo pron rifl):* **me** ~ myself; **te** ~ yourself; **se** ~ himself; *(neutro)* itself; *(indef)* oneself; **se** ~**a** herself; **noi** ~**i** ourselves; **voi** ~**i** yourselves; **loro** ~**i** themselves; **ama solo se** ~ he only loves himself; **di per se** ~ **non ha un gran valore** it's not worth a lot in itself.

(f) *(proprio)* own; **l'ho visto con i miei** ~**i occhi** I saw it with my own eyes; **l'ha fatto con le sue** ~**e mani** he did it with his own hands.

2 *pron dimostr:* **lo(la)** ~**(a)** the same one; **è lo** ~ **di sempre** he *(o* it*)* is just the same as always; **chi canta?** — **lo** ~ **di prima** who's singing? — the same singer as before; **per me fa lo** ~ it's all the same to me.

3: lo ~ *av (comunque)* all the same, even so; **parto lo** ~ I'm going all the same; **lo** ~ **non doveva comportarsi così** all the same *o* even so he shouldn't have behaved like that.

stesura [ste'sura] *sf (azione)* drawing up; *(documento)* draft.

stetoscopio [stetos'kɔpjo] *sm* stethoscope.

stia ['stia] *sf* hutch.

stigma, i ['stigma] *sm* stigma.

stigmate ['stigmate] *sfpl (Rel)* stigmata *pl.*

stigmatizzare [stigmatid'dzare] *vt* to stigmatize.

stilare [sti'lare] *vt* to draw up, draft.

stile ['stile] *sm (gen)* style; *(classe)* style, class; *(Sport):* ~ **libero** free style; **mobili in** ~ period furniture; **in grande** ~ in great style; **è proprio nel suo** ~ *(fig)* it's just like him; **non è nel suo** ~ *(fig)* it's not like him.

stiletto [sti'letto] *sm* stiletto.

stilista, i, e [sti'lista] *sm/f (Moda)* designer.

stilistico, a, ci, che [sti'listiko] *ag* stylistic.

stilizzare [stilid'dzare] *vt* to stylize.

stilizzato, a [stilid'dzato] *ag* stylized.

stillare [stil'lare] *vt, vi (aus essere) (gocciolare)* to drip; *(trasudare)* to ooze.

stillicidio [stilli'tʃidjo] *sm (fig)* continual pestering *(o* moaning *etc).*

stilografica, che [stilo'grafika] *sf (anche:* **penna** ~*)* fountain pen.

stima ['stima] *sf* **(a)** *(buona opinione)* respect; **avere** ~ **di qn** to have respect for sb; **godere della** ~ **di qn** to enjoy sb's respect. **(b)** *(Econ, Fin)* estimate, valuation; **fare la** ~ **di qc** to estimate the value of sth.

stimare [sti'mare] *vt* **(a)** *(persona)* to respect. **(b)** *(Econ, Fin)* to assess the value of, estimate the value of, value.

stimolante [stimo'lante] **1** *ag* stimulating. **2** *sm* stimulant.

stimolare [stimo'lare] *vt (gen)* to stimulate; ~ **qn a fare qc** *(incitare)* to spur sb on to do sth.

stimolazione [stimolat'tsjone] *sf* stimulation.

stimolo ['stimolo] *sm (anche fig)* stimulus.

stinco, chi ['stinko] *sm (Anat)* shinbone, shin; **non essere uno ~ di santo** to be no saint.

stingere ['stindʒere] *vt, vi (aus essere)*, ~**rsi** *vr* to fade.

stinto, a ['stinto] **1** *pp di* **stingere. 2** *ag* faded.

stipare [sti'pare] **1** *vt* to cram, pack. **2:** ~**rsi** *vr (accalcarsi):* ~**rsi in** to crowd into.

stipendiare [stipen'djare] *vt (pagare)* to pay (a salary to).

stipendiato, a [stipen'djato] **1** *ag* salaried. **2** *sm/f* salaried worker.

stipendio [sti'pendjo] *sm* salary.

stipite ['stipite] *sm (di porta, finestra)* jamb.

stipulare [stipu'lare] *vt (accordo, contratto)* to draw up.

stipulazione [stipulat'tsjone] *sf (di contratto: stesura)* drafting; *(: firma)* signing.

stiracalzoni [stirakal'tsoni] *sm inv* trouser press.

stiracchiare [stirak'kjare] **1** *vt (fig: significato di una parola)* to stretch, force. **2:** ~**rsi** *vr (persona)* to stretch.

stiracchiato, a [stirak'kjato] *ag (sforzato)* forced.

stiramento [stira'mento] *sm (Med)* sprain.

stirare [sti'rare] **1** *vt* **(a)** *(con ferro da stiro)* to iron. **(b)** *(distendere)* to stretch. **2:** ~**rsi** *vr* to stretch (o.s.).

stiratrice [stira'tritʃe] *sf (donna)* laundry worker; *(macchina)* laundry press.

stiratura [stira'tura] *sf* **(a)** *(con ferro da stiro)* ironing. **(b)** *(Med)* sprain.

stiro ['stiro] *sm* ironing; **ferro da ~** iron; **asse** *o* **tavolo da ~** ironing board.

stirpe ['stirpe] *sf* **(a)** *(schiatta):* **di nobile ~** of noble descent. **(b)** *(discendenti)* descendants *pl.*

stitichezza [stiti'kettsa] *sf* constipation.

stitico, a, ci, che ['stitiko] *ag* constipated.

stiva ['stiva] *sf (di nave)* hold.

stivale [sti'vale] *sm* boot; **ma quel medico dei miei ~i!** *(peg)* that apology for a doctor!; ~ **da birra** boot-shaped beer glass.

stivaletto [stiva'letto] *sm* ankle boot.

stivare [sti'vare] *vt* to stow, load.

stizza ['stittsa] *sf* anger, vexation.

stizzire [stit'tsire] **1** *vt* to irritate. **2:** ~**rsi** *vr* to become irritated, become vexed.

stizzoso, a [stit'tsoso] *ag (persona)* irascible; *(risposta)* angry.

stoccafisso [stokka'fisso] *sm* stockfish, dried cod.

stoccata [stok'kata] *sf (Scherma)* thrust; *(Calcio)* shot; *(fig: allusione)* gibe.

stock [stɔk] *sm inv (Comm)* stock.

stoffa ['stɔffa] *sf* material; **avere della ~** *(fig)* to have what it takes; **avere la ~ per diventare qc** to have the makings of sth.

stoicismo [stoi'tʃizmo] *sm* stoicism.

stoico, a, ci, che ['stɔiko] *ag, sm/f (anche fig)* stoic.

stoino [sto'ino] *sm* doormat.

stola ['stɔla] *sf (gen, Rel)* stole.

stoltezza [stol'tettsa] *sf* stupidity; *(azione)* foolish action.

stolto, a ['stolto] **1** *ag* stupid, foolish. **2** *sm/f* blockhead.

stomacare [stoma'kare] **1** *vt (nauseare)* to nauseate. **2:** ~**rsi** *vr:* ~**rsi di qc** to become nauseated by sth.

stomachevole [stoma'kevole] *ag* disgusting.

stomaco, chi ['stɔmako] *sm* stomach; **dare di ~** to vomit, be sick; **avere qc sullo ~** to have sth lying on one's stomach; **quel tipo mi sta sullo ~** I can't put up with that character; **mi fa rivoltare lo ~** it makes me sick; **bisogna avere dello ~ per fare quel lavoro** you need a strong stomach to do that kind of work.

stomatite [stoma'tite] *sf (Med)* stomatitis.

stonare [sto'nare] **1** *vt (cantando)* to sing out of tune; *(suonando)* to play out of tune. **2** *vi* to be out of tune, to sing *(o* play) out of tune; *(fig: colori etc)* to clash.

stonato, a [sto'nato] *ag (persona)* off-key; *(strumento)* off-key, out of tune; **c'era una nota ~a** *(fig)* something didn't ring true.

stonatura [stona'tura] *sf (suono)* false note.

stop [stɔp] *sm inv* **(a)** *(Telegrafia)* stop. **(b)** *(Aut: fanalino)* brake light; *(: segnale stradale)* stop sign.

stoppa ['stoppa] *sf* tow; **come ~** *(capelli)* towcoloured, towy; **essere come un pulcino nella ~** to look lost and helpless.

stoppare [stop'pare] *vt (Calcio)* to stop.

stoppata [stop'pata] *sf (Calcio)* action of stopping the ball.

stoppia ['stoppja] *sf* stubble.

stoppino [stop'pino] *sm (di candela)* wick; *(miccia)* fuse.

stopposo, a [stop'poso] *ag* towy.

storcere ['stortʃere] **1** *vt (gen)* to twist; ~ **il naso** *(fig)* to turn up one's nose; ~**rsi la caviglia** to twist one's ankle. **2:** ~**rsi** *vr* to writhe, twist.

stordimento [stordi'mento] *sm (gen)* dizziness; *(da droga)* stupefaction.

stordire [stor'dire] **1** *vt (sog: colpo, notizia, droga)* to stun, daze. **2:** ~**rsi** *vr (fig):* ~**rsi col bere** to dull one's senses with drink.

stordito, a [stor'dito] *ag* dazed, stunned.

storia ['storja] *sf* **(a)** *(scienza, materia, opera)* history; **libro di ~** history book; **passare alla ~** to go down in history. **(b)** *(racconto)* story; *(bugia)* story, fib; **mi ha raccontato un sacco di ~e** he told me a lot of rubbish; **sono tutte ~e!** it's all lies! **(c)** *(faccenda)* business; **non voglio saperne più di questa ~** I don't want to hear any more about this business; **è sempre la solita ~** it's always the same old story. **(d):** ~**e** *pl (smorfie)* fuss *sg;* **non ha fatto ~e** he didn't make a fuss; **senza tante ~e!** don't make such a fuss!

storicità [storitʃi'ta] *sf* historical authenticity.

storico, a, ci, che ['stɔriko] **1** *ag* historical; *(memorabile)* historic. **2** *sm/f* historian.

storiella [sto'rjɛlla] *sf (storia divertente)* funny story; *(frottola)* story, fib.

storiografia [storjogra'fia] *sf* historiography.

storione [sto'rjone] *sm (Zool)* sturgeon.

stormire [stor'mire] *vi* to rustle.

stormo ['stormo] *sm (di uccelli)* flock.

stornare [stor'nare] *vt* **(a)** *(Comm)* to transfer. **(b)** *(fig: evitare: pericolo etc)* to avert.

stornello [stor'nɛllo] *sm* kind of folk song.

storno ['storno] *sm* **(a)** *(Zool)* starling. **(b)** *(Comm)* transfer.

storpiare [stor'pjare] **1** *vt (persona)* to cripple, maim; *(fig: parole)* to mangle; *(: significato)* to twist. **2:** ~**rsi** *vr* to become crippled.

storpiatura [storpja'tura] *sf (fig: di parola)* twisting, distortion.

storpio, a ['storpjo] **1** *ag* crippled, maimed. **2** *sm/f* cripple.

storta ['storta] *sf (distorsione)* sprain; **prendere una ~ al piede** to sprain one's foot.

storto, a ['storto] **1** *pp di* **storcere. 2** *ag (tubo,* *chiodo)* twisted, bent; *(ruota)* buckled, warped; *(manubrio, quadro)* crooked; **avere le gambe ~e** to have crooked legs; **avere gli occhi ~i** to have a squint, be cross-eyed. **3** *av:* **guardare ~ qn** *(fig)* to look askance at sb.

stoviglie [sto'viʎʎe] *sfpl* dishes, crockery *sg;* **lavare le ~** to wash the dishes.

strabico, a, ci, che ['strabiko] *ag (occhi)* squint; *(persona):* **essere ~** to have a squint.

strabiliante [strabi'ljante] *ag* astonishing, amazing.

strabiliare [strabi'ljare] *vi* to astonish, amaze.

strabismo [stra'bizmo] *sm* squinting.

strabuzzare [strabud'dzare] *vt:* **~ gli occhi** to open one's eyes wide.

stracarico, a, chi, che [stra'kariko] *ag* overloaded.

stracchino [strak'kino] *sm type of soft cheese.*

stracciare [strat'tʃare] **1** *vt* to tear up, rip up; **~ gli avversari** *(fig)* to wipe the floor with one's opponents. **2: ~rsi** *vr* to tear, rip.

straccio, a, ci, ce ['strattʃo] **1** *ag:* **carta ~a** waste paper. **2** *sm (gen)* rag; *(per pulire)* cloth, duster; *(fig: persona)* wretch; **non ho uno ~ di vestito** I haven't got a thing to wear; **non ha nemmeno uno ~ di marito** she doesn't have a husband of any description.

straccione, a [strat'tʃone] *sm/f* ragamuffin.

straccivendolo [strattʃi'vendolo] *sm* ragman.

stracco, a, chi, che ['strakko] *ag:* **~ (morto)** exhausted, dead tired.

stracotto, a [stra'kɔtto] **1** *pp di* **stracuocere. 2** *ag* overcooked. **3** *sm (Culin)* beef stew.

stracuocere [stra'kwɔtʃere] *vt* to overdo, overcook.

strada ['strada] *sf* **(a)** *(gen)* road; *(di città)* street; **andare fuori ~** *(Aut)* to go off the road; **~ principale** main road; **~ ferrata** railway; **~ a senso unico** one-way street; **~ senza uscita** dead end, cul-de-sac; **l'uomo della ~** *(fig)* the man in the street; **donna di ~** *(fig peg)* streetwalker; **ragazzo di ~** *(fig peg)* child of the streets.

(b) *(percorso)* way; **qual'è la ~ per andare al cinema?** which is the way to the cinema?, how does one get to the cinema?; **mostrare la ~ a qn** to show the way to sb, show sb the way; **c'è tanta ~ da fare?** is it a long way?; **tre ore di ~ (a piedi)/(in macchina)** three hours' walk/drive; **non è sulla mia ~** it's not on my way; **facciamo la ~ insieme?** shall we go along together?; **~ facendo** on the way.

(c) *(fig)* path, way, road; **essere sulla buona ~** *(nella vita)* to be on the right road *o* path; *(Polizia etc)* to be on the right track; **essere fuori ~** *(Polizia etc)* to be on the wrong track; **portare qn sulla cattiva ~** to lead sb astray.

(d): **fare ~** *(fig: persona)* to get on in life; **farsi ~ tra la folla** to make one's way through the crowd; **trovarsi in mezzo ad una ~** to find o.s. out on the street; **tagliare la ~ a qn** to cut across in front of sb; **fare ~ a qn** to show sb the way.

stradale [stra'dale] **1** *ag (gen)* road *attr;* *(polizia, regolamento)* traffic *attr.* **2** *sf (polizia)* traffic police.

stradario [stra'darjo] *sm* street guide.

stradino [stra'dino] *sm* road worker.

stradone [stra'done] *sm* wide road.

strafalcione [strafal'tʃone] *sm (errore)* howler *(fam).*

strafare [stra'fare] *vi* to overdo it.

strafatto, a [stra'fatto] *pp di* **strafare.**

straforo [stra'foro] *av:* **di ~** *(di nascosto)* on the sly.

strafottente [strafot'tɛnte] **1** *ag* arrogant. **2** *sm/f* arrogant person.

strafottenza [strafot'tɛntsa] *sf* arrogance.

strage ['stradʒe] *sf* massacre, slaughter; **fare una ~** to carry out a massacre *o* slaughter; **fare ~ di** *(animali etc)* to slaughter; **fare strage di cuori** to be a heartbreaker.

stragrande [stra'grande] *ag:* **la ~ maggioranza** the overwhelming majority.

stralciare [stral'tʃare] *vt* to remove.

stralcio ['straltʃo] **1** *sm: (Comm)* **vendere in ~** to sell off (at bargain prices), clear. **2** *ag inv:* **legge ~** abridged version of an act.

stralunato, a [stralu'nato] *ag (occhi)* wide open, staring; *(persona)* dazed, thunderstruck.

stramaledetto, a [stramale'detto] **1** *pp di* **stramaledire. 2** *ag (fam)* damned.

stramaledire [stramale'dire] *vt (fam)* to curse.

stramazzare [stramat'tsare] *vi (aus essere)* to collapse; **~ al suolo** to crash to the floor.

stramberia [strambe'ria] *sf* eccentricity.

strambo, a ['strambo] *ag* strange, queer.

strampalato, a [strampa'lato] *ag* odd, eccentric.

stranezza [stra'nettsa] *sf (qualità)* strangeness; *(atto):* **le sue ~e mi preoccupano** his strange behaviour worries me.

strangolamento [strangola'mento] *sm (atto)* strangling; *(effetto)* strangulation.

strangolare [strango'lare] *vt* to strangle.

straniero, a [stra'njero] **1** *ag* foreign; *(Amm)* alien. **2** *sm/f* foreigner; *(Amm)* alien; **liberarsi dallo ~** to rid o.s. of the enemy.

stranito, a [stra'nito] *ag* dazed.

strano, a ['strano] *ag (gen)* strange; *(bizzarro)* strange, odd, queer; **è ~ che...** it is odd that...; **e cosa ~a...** strangely enough... .

straordinario, a [straordi'narjo] **1** *ag (gen)* extraordinary; *(treno, imposta)* special; *(impiegato)* temporary; **lavoro ~** overtime. **2** *sm (impiegato)* temporary employee; *(lavoro)* overtime.

strapagare [strapa'gare] *vt* to overpay.

strapazzare [strapat'tsare] **1** *vt (maltrattare: persona, oggetto)* to handle roughly; *(affaticare)* to tire out; **uova strapazzate** scrambled eggs. **2: ~rsi** *vr* to tire o.s. out.

strapazzata [strapat'tsata] *sf (gran fatica)* strain; **dare una ~ a qn** *(sgridarlo)* to tear a strip off sb.

strapazzo [stra'pattso] *sm* strain; **da ~** *(fig peg: persona)* third-rate.

strapieno, a [stra'pjɛno] *ag* overflowing, absolutely full up.

strapiombo [stra'pjombo] *sm (roccia)* overhanging rock; **a ~** overhanging.

strapotere [strapo'tere] *sm* excessive power.

strappalacrime [strappa'lakrime] *ag inv (fam):* **romanzo** *(o film etc)* **~** tear-jerker.

strappare [strap'pare] **1** *vt (gen)* to tear, rip; *(pagina etc)* to tear off, tear out; *(erbacce)* to pull up; *(bottone)* to pull off; **~ qc di mano a qn** to snatch sth out of sb's hand; **si strappò la gonna** she tore *o* ripped her skirt; **~rsi i capelli** to tear one's hair; **~rsi i vestiti di dosso** to rip one's clothes off; **~rsi un muscolo** to tear a muscle; **~ una promessa a qn** to extract a promise from sb; **~ un segreto a qn** to wring a secret from sb; **~ gli applausi del pubblico** to win the audience's applause; **~ qn dal suo ambiente** to take sb away from his *(o* her) own environment; **una scena che strappa il cuore** a heartrending scene. **2: ~rsi** *vr (lacerarsi)* to tear, rip.

strappo ['strappo] *sm* **(a)** *(lacerazione)* tear; **~ (muscolare)** *(Med)* strain, tear. **(b)** *(strattone)* tug; **dare uno ~ a qc** to give sth a tug; **fare uno ~**

alla regola (fig) to make an exception to the rule. **(c)** (fig fam: passaggio) lift; **puoi darmi uno ~ (fino) in centro?** can you give me a lift into town?

strapuntino [strapun'tino] sm (sedile) foldaway seat, jump seat.

straricco, a, chi, che [stra'rikko] ag extremely rich.

straripamento [straripa'mento] sm overflowing.

straripare [strari'pare] vi (fiume) to overflow, burst its banks.

strascicare [straʃʃi'kare] **1** vt (trascinare): **~ qc per terra** to drag sth along the ground, trail sth along the ground; **~ i piedi** to drag one's feet, trail one's heels; **~ le parole** to drawl; **~ un lavoro** to drag o draw out a piece of work; **~ una malattia** to be unable to shake off an illness. **2** vi to trail. **3: ~rsi** vr (trascinarsi) to drag o.s. (along); (bambino) to crawl.

strascico, chi ['straʃʃiko] sm **(a)** (di abito) train; **reggere lo ~ a qn** to carry sb's train. **(b):** rete a **~** trawl (net); **pesca a ~** trawling. **(c)** (fig: conseguenza) after-effect.

strascinare [straʃʃi'nare] **1** vt to drag. **2: ~rsi** vr to drag o.s. (along); (fig: lavoro etc) to drag on.

stratagemma, i [strata'dʒɛmma] sm (Mil, fig) stratagem.

stratega, ghi [stra'tega] sm strategist.

strategia, gie [strate'dʒia] sf (Mil, fig) strategy.

strategico, a, ci, che [stra'tɛdʒiko] ag (Mil, fig) strategic.

stratificare [stratifi'kare] **1** vt to stratify. **2: ~rsi** vr to become stratified.

stratificazione [stratifikat'tsjone] sf stratification.

stratiforme [strati'forme] ag stratiform.

strato ['strato] sm (gen) layer; (di vernice) coat; (Meteor) stratus; (Geol) stratum; **~ sociale** social stratum; **i vari ~i della società** the various strata of society.

stratosfera [stratos'fera] sf stratosphere.

strattone [strat'tone] sm tug, jerk; **dare uno ~ a qc** to tug o jerk sth, give sth a tug o jerk.

stravagante [strava'gante] ag eccentric.

stravaganza [strava'gantsa] sf eccentricity.

stravecchio, a [stra'vekkjo] ag (gen) very old; (vino) mellow; (formaggio) very mature.

stravedere [strave'dere] vi: **~ per qn** to dote on sb.

stravincere [stra'vintʃere] vt to win easily; **~ qn** to beat sb hollow.

stravinto, a [stra'vinto] pp di **stravincere**.

stravisto, a [stra'visto] pp di **stravedere**.

stravizio [stra'vittsjo] sm excess; **darsi agli ~i** to lead a dissolute life.

stravolgere [stra'vɔldʒere] vt (persona) to upset; (organizzazione, sistema) to shake, rock; (significato) to twist, distort.

stravolto, a [stra'vɔlto] **1** pp di **stravolgere**. **2** ag (persona: per stanchezza etc) in a terrible state; (: per sofferenza) distraught; **aveva il volto ~** he looked terrible.

straziante [strat'tsjante] ag (scena) harrowing; (urlo) bloodcurdling; (dolore) excruciating.

straziare [strat'tsjare] vt (carni, corpo) to torment, torture; **~ il cuore a qn** to break sb's heart; **una musica che strazia le orecchie** an excruciating piece of music.

strazio ['strattsjo] sm (di torture) torment; **fare ~ di** (corpo, vittima) to mutilate; **la scena era uno ~** it was a harrowing scene; **questo libro è uno ~!** this book is appalling!; **che ~!** (compito etc) what a mess!; (spettacolo etc) what a disaster!

strega, ghe ['strega] sf (anche fig: donna malvagia) witch; (peg: donna brutta) old hag, old witch.

stregare [stre'gare] vt (anche fig) to bewitch.

stregone [stre'gone] sm (in tribù) witch doctor; (mago) sorcerer.

stregoneria [stregone'ria] sf (pratica) witchcraft; (incantesimo) spell; **fare una ~** to cast a spell.

stregua ['stregwa] sf: **alla (stessa) ~ di** on a par with; **trattare tutti alla stessa ~** to treat everybody in the same manner.

stremare [stre'mare] vt to exhaust.

stremo ['stremo] sm: **essere allo ~ (delle forze)** to be at the end of one's tether.

strenna ['strenna] sf: **~ natalizia** (regalo) Christmas present; (libro) book published for the Christmas market.

strenuo, a ['strenuo] ag (valoroso) brave, courageous; (infaticabile) tireless.

strepitare [strepi'tare] vi to yell and shout.

strepito ['strepito] sm (di voci, folla) clamour; (di catene) clanking, rattling.

strepitoso, a [strepi'toso] ag (anche fig) resounding.

streptococco, chi [strepto'kɔkko] sm streptococcus.

stress [strɛs] sm inv stress.

stressare [stres'sare] vt to put under stress.

stressato, a [stres'sato] ag under stress.

stretta ['stretta] sf (gen) grip, firm hold; **una ~ di mano** a handshake; **dare ~ di mano a qn** to shake hands with sb, shake sb's hand; **una ~ di spalle** a shrug (of one's shoulders); **una ~ al cuore** a sudden sadness; **essere alle ~e** to be in a tight corner; **mettere qn alle ~e** to put sb in a tight corner; **~ creditizia** (Econ) credit squeeze.

strettamente [stretta'mente] av **(a)** (in modo stretto) tightly. **(b)** (fig: rigorosamente) strictly, closely; **attenersi ~ alle regole** to keep strictly to the rules, stick closely to the rules.

strettezza [stret'tettsa] sf **(a)** (gen) narrowness; (di scarpe, vestito) tightness. **(b): ~e** pl poverty sg, straitened circumstances.

stretto, a ['stretto] **1** pp di **stringere**. **2** ag **(a)** (corridoio, stanza, limiti) narrow; (gonna, scarpe, nodo) tight; (curva) tight, sharp; **questa gonna mi è ~a** this skirt is tight on me; **stavamo ~i in macchina** we were packed tight in the car; **tienti ~!** hold on tight!; **tenere ~ qc/qn** to hold sth/sb tight; **a denti ~i** with clenched teeth. **(b)** (parente, amico) close. **(c)** (preciso, esatto: significato) precise, strict; (: osservanza) strict. **3** sm (di mare) strait.

strettoia [stret'toja] sf bottleneck.

striato, a [stri'ato] ag streaked.

striatura [stria'tura] sf (atto) streaking; (effetto) streaks pl.

stricnina [strik'nina] sf strychnine.

strida ['strida] sfpl screaming sg.

stridente [stri'dɛnte] ag (rumore) strident; (colori) clashing.

stridere ['stridere] vi (porta) to squeak; (animale) to screech, shriek; (colori) to clash.

stridio, ii [stri'dio] sm screeching.

stridore [stri'dore] sm screeching.

stridulo, a ['stridulo] ag (voce) shrill.

striglia ['striʎʎa] sf curry-comb.

strigliare [striʎ'ʎare] vt (cavallo) to curry.

strigliata [striʎ'ʎata] sf (di cavallo) currying; (fig): **dare una ~ a qn** to give sb a scolding.

strillare [stril'lare] **1** vi (gridare) to scream; **non ~!** (parla piano) don't shout! **2** vt: **~ aiuto** to cry for help; **strillò arrivederci** he shouted goodbye.

strillo ['strillo] sm scream, shriek; **fare uno ~** to let out a scream.

strillone [stril'lone] sm news vendor.

striminzito, a [strimin'tsito] *ag (misero)* shabby; *(molto magro)* skinny.

strimpellare [strimpel'lare] *vt (chitarra)* to strum away on; *(pianoforte)* to plonk away on.

stringa, ghe ['stringa] *sf* lace.

stringare [strin'gare] *vt (fig: discorso)* to condense.

stringatezza [stringa'tettsa] *sf* concision, terseness.

stringato, a [strin'gato] *ag (fig)* concise.

stringere ['strindʒere] **1** *vt* **(a)** *(con la mano)* to grip, hold tight; ~ **il braccio di qn** to clasp sb's arm; ~ **la mano a qn** *(afferrarla)* to squeeze *o* press sb's hand; *(salutando)* to shake sb's hand, shake hands with sb; **si strinsero la mano** they shook hands; ~ **qn alla gola** to grab sb by the throat.

(b) *(pugno, mascella)* to clench; *(labbra)* to compress; **una scena che stringe il cuore** a scene which brings a lump to one's throat; ~ **i denti** to clench one's teeth; *(fig)* to grit one's teeth.

(c) *(gonna etc: fare più stretto)* to take in.

(d) *(vite)* to tighten; *(rubinetto)* to turn tight; *(cintura, nodo)* to tighten, pull tight.

(e) *(avvicinare: oggetti)* to close up, put close together; *(: persone)* to squeeze up, squeeze together.

(f) *(fraseologia)*: ~ **qn tra le braccia** to clasp sb in one's arms; ~ **amicizia con qn** to make friends with sb; ~ **un patto** to conclude a treaty; ~ **un'alleanza** to form an alliance; **stringi stringi** in conclusion; **stringi!** get to the point!; ~ **qn in curva** *(Aut)* to cut in on sb on a bend.

2 *vi (essere stretto)* to be tight; *(fig: arrivare al dunque)* to come to the point; **il tempo stringe** time is short.

3: ~**rsi** *vr (persona)*: ~**rsi a** *(muro, parete)* to press o.s. up against; **si strinse a lui** she drew close to him; **mi si stringe il cuore** it brings a lump to my throat.

strip-tease [strip'tiːz] *sm inv* striptease; **fare lo** ~ to do a striptease.

striscia, sce ['striʃʃa] *sf (di tessuto, carta, fumetto)* strip; *(riga)* stripe; **a** ~**sce** striped; ~**sce pedonali** zebra crossing *sg*.

strisciante [striʃ'ʃante] *ag* **(a)** *(fig peg)* unctuous. **(b)** *(Econ: inflazione)* creeping.

strisciare [striʃ'ʃare] **1** *vt (piedi)* to drag; *(muro, macchina)* to scrape. **2** *vi (gen)* to crawl; ~ **contro un muro** to sidle along a wall; ~ **con la macchina contro il muro** to scrape one's car against the wall; **lo farò** ~ **ai miei piedi** I'll make him crawl at my feet.

strisciata [striʃ'ʃata] *sf (segno)* scratch.

striscio ['striʃʃo] *sm* **(a)** *(segno)* scratch; **colpire di** ~ to graze. **(b)** *(Med: esame)* smear test.

striscione [striʃ'ʃone] *sm* banner.

stritolamento [stritola'mento] *sm* crushing.

stritolare [strito'lare] *vt (anche fig)* to crush.

strizzare [strit'tsare] *vt (panni)* to wring (out); ~ **l'occhio (a qn)** to wink (at sb).

strizzata [strit'tsata] *sf*: **dare una** ~ **a qc** to give sth a wring; **una** ~ **d'occhio** a wink.

strofa ['strɔfa] *sf*, **strofe** ['strɔfe] *sf inv* strophe.

strofinaccio [strofi'nattʃo] *sm (gen)* duster, cloth; *(per piatti)* dishcloth; *(per pavimenti)* floorcloth.

strofinare [strofi'nare] **1** *vt (gen)* to rub; *(lucidare)* to polish; *(pavimento)* to wipe; ~**rsi gli occhi/le mani** to rub one's eyes/one's hands. **2**: ~**rsi** *vr*: ~**rsi (contro)** to rub o.s. (against).

strofinio, ii [strofi'nio] *sm (continual)* rubbing.

strombazzare [strombat'tsare] **1** *vt (divulgare)* to proclaim; ~ **i propri meriti** to blow one's own trumpet; ~ **qc ai quattro venti** to proclaim sth to

the four winds. **2** *vi (fam: suonare il clacson)* to hoot.

strombettare [strombet'tare] *vi (con tromba)* to blare away; *(con clacson)* to hoot.

stroncare [stron'kare] *vt (ramo etc)* to break off; *(fig: rivolta)* to put down; *(: libro, film)* to pan; **fu stroncato da un infarto** he was carried off by a heart attack.

stronzio ['strontsjo] *sm (Chim)* strontium.

stronzo ['strontso] *sm (sterco)* turd; *(fig fam!: persona)* shit(!), turd(!).

stropicciare [stropit'tʃare] *vt* **(a)** *(strofinare)* to rub; ~**rsi gli occhi** to rub one's eyes. **(b)** *(spiegazzare)* to crease.

strozzare [strot'tsare] **1** *vt (persona)* to choke, strangle; *(sog: cibo)* to choke; *(conduttura)* to narrow. **2**: ~**rsi** *vr* to choke.

strozzatura [strottsa'tura] *sf (di conduttura)* narrowing; *(di strada, Econ)* bottleneck.

strozzinaggio [strottsi'naddʒo] *sm* usury.

strozzino, a [strot'tsino] *sm/f (usuraio)* usurer; *(fig)* shark.

struccare [struk'kare] **1** *vt* to remove make-up from. **2**: ~**rsi** *vr* to remove one's make-up.

strudel ['strudel] *sm (Culin)* strudel.

struggere ['struddʒere] **1** *vt (sog: amore etc)* to consume. **2**: ~**rsi** *vr*: ~**rsi d'amore per qn** to be consumed with love for sb; ~**rsi dal dolore** to be consumed with grief.

struggimento [struddʒi'mento] *sm (desiderio)* yearning.

strumentale [strumen'tale] *ag (gen, Mus)* instrumental.

strumentalizzare [strumentalid'dzare] *vt* to exploit, use to one's own ends.

strumentare [strumen'tare] *vt (Mus)* to orchestrate.

strumentazione [strumentat'tsjone] *sf* **(a)** *(Mus)* orchestration. **(b)** *(Tecn)* instrumentation.

strumentista, i, e [strumen'tista] *sm/f (Mus)* instrumentalist.

strumento [stru'mento] *sm* **(a)** *(arnese)* tool; ~**i di bordo** *(Aer)* flight instruments; *(Naut)* ship instruments; ~**i di precisione** precision instruments; **essere lo** ~ **di qn** *(fig: persona)* to be sb's tool. **(b)** *(Mus)* instrument.

strusciare [struʃ'ʃare] **1** *vt (piedi)* to slide; *(gomiti)* to rub. **2**: ~**rsi** *vr*: ~**rsi contro qc** to rub o.s. against sth; **gli si strusciava addosso** she was all over him.

strutto¹, a ['strutto] *pp di* **struggere**.

strutto² ['strutto] *sm (Culin)* lard.

struttura [strut'tura] *sf* structure.

strutturale [struttu'rale] *ag (gen, Gram)* structural.

strutturare [struttu'rare] *vt* to structure.

struzzo ['struttso] *sm* ostrich; **piume di** ~ ostrich feathers; **fare lo** ~, **fare la politica dello** ~ to bury one's head in the sand; **avere lo stomaco di uno** ~ to have a cast-iron stomach.

stuccare [stuk'kare] *vt (muro)* to plaster; *(vetro)* to putty; *(decorare con stucchi)* to stucco.

stuccatore, trice [stukka'tore] *sm/f* plasterer; *(artista)* stucco worker.

stuccatura [stukka'tura] *sf (vedi vb)* plastering; puttying; stuccoing.

stucchevole [stuk'kevole] *ag (fig)* tedious, boring.

stucco, chi ['stukko] *sm (per muro)* plaster; *(per vetri)* putty; *(ornamentale)* stucco; **rimanere di** ~ *(fig)* to be dumbfounded, be left speechless.

studente, essa [stu'dente] *sm/f (gen)* student; *(scolaro)* pupil, schoolboy/girl; *(Univ)* student, undergraduate.

studentesco, a, schi, sche [studen'tesko] *ag* student *attr*.

studiacchiare [studjak'kjare] *vt, vi* to study fitfully.

studiare [stu'djare] **1** *vt (gen)* to study; *(lezione)* to learn; ~ **un sistema per fare qc** to try to find a way of doing sth; **una persona che studia i gesti/le parole** a person of studied manners/speech. **2** *vi* to study. **3:** ~**rsi** *vr* **(a)** *(osservarsi)* to examine o.s. **(b)** *(uso reciproco)* to eye one another.

studiato, a [stu'djato] *ag (modi, sorriso)* affected.

studio ['studjo] *sm* **(a)** *(gen: azione)* studying, study; **una giornata di** ~ a day's studying; **mantenersi agli** ~**i** to pay one's way through college *(o* university *etc)*; **fare** ~**i letterari/scientifici** to study arts/science; **alla fine degli** ~**i** at the end of one's course (of studies).

(b) *(lavoro, ricerca, disegno)* study; **fare uno** ~ **o degli** ~**i su qn/qc** to do research on sb/sth, make a study of sb/sth; **secondo recenti** ~**i, appare che...** recent research indicates that...; **uno** ~ **critico** a critical study; **uno** ~ **dal vero** a life study.

(c) *(progettazione)* project; **la proposta è allo** ~ the proposal is under consideration.

(d) *(stanza)* study; ~ **legale** lawyer's office; **lo** ~ **di un fotografo** a photographer's studio; **lo** ~ **di un medico** a doctor's surgery.

(e) *(TV, Cine)* studio; **trasmettiamo dagli** ~**i di Roma** we are broadcasting from our Rome studios.

studioso, a [stu'djoso] **1** *ag* studious, hardworking. **2** *sm/f* scholar.

stufa ['stufa] *sf (gen)* stove; *(elettrica)* heater; ~ **a legna/carbone** wood-burning/coal stove.

stufare [stu'fare] **1** *vt* **(a)** *(Culin)* to stew. **(b)** *(fig fam)* to bore, weary; **mi avete proprio stufato con il vostro comportamento** I am really fed up with your behaviour; **mi hai proprio stufato** I am really fed up with you. **2:** ~**rsi** *vr:* ~**rsi (di)** to grow weary (of); **si è stufato di ascoltarlo** he got fed up listening to him.

stufato [stu'fato] *sm (Culin)* stew.

stufo, a ['stufo] *ag (fam):* **essere** ~ **(di)** to be fed up (with), be sick and tired (of).

stuoia ['stwɔja] *sf* mat; *(tessuto)* rush matting.

stuolo ['stwɔlo] *sm* crowd, host.

stupefacente [stupefa'tʃɛnte] **1** *ag* amazing. **2** *sm* drug, narcotic.

stupefare [stupe'fare] *vt* to stun, astound.

stupefatto, a [stupe'fatto] *pp di* **stupefare**.

stupendo, a [stu'pɛndo] *ag* marvellous, wonderful.

stupidaggine [stupi'daddʒine] *sf (qualità)* stupidity, foolishness; *(atto, discorso):* **dire** ~ to say something stupid; **dire** ~**i** to talk nonsense; **fare una** ~ to do something stupid; **ti ho preso una** ~ *(regaletto)* I bought you a little something.

stupidità [stupidi'ta] *sf inv (qualità)* stupidity; *(atto, discorso):* **non dire** ~ don't talk nonsense.

stupido, a ['stupido] **1** *ag* stupid. **2** *sm/f* fool, idiot.

stupire [stu'pire] **1** *vt* to amaze, stun. **2** *vi (aus* **essere)**, ~**rsi** *vr* to be amazed, be stunned; **non c'è da** ~**rsi** that's not surprising.

stupore [stu'pore] *sm* amazement, astonishment.

stuprare [stu'prare] *vt* to rape.

stupro ['stupro] *sm* rape.

sturare [stu'rare] *vt (lavandino)* to unblock; *(bottiglia)* to uncork; **sturati le orecchie!** *(fig)* clean your ears out!

stuzzicadenti [stuttsika'dɛnti] *sm inv* toothpick; *(fig: persona magra)* beanpole.

stuzzicante [stuttsi'kante] *ag (gen)* stimulating;

(appetitoso) appetizing; **che idea** ~ what a good idea.

stuzzicare [stuttsi'kare] *vt (ferita etc)* to poke (at), prod (at); *(fig: persona)* to tease; *(: appetito)* to whet; *(: curiosità)* to stimulate.

su [su] **1** *prep (su + il =* **sul,** *su + lo =* **sullo,** *su + l' =* **sull',** *su + la =* **sulla,** *su + i =* **sui,** *su + gli =* **sugli,** *su + le =* **sulle) (a)** *(gen)* on; *(moto)* on(to); *(in cima a)* on (top of); **il libro è sul tavolo** the book is on the table; **mettilo sulla scrivania** put it on the desk; **è salito sul tavolo** he got up on(to) the table; **gettarsi sulla preda** to throw o.s. on one's prey; **la marcia** ~ **Roma** the march on Rome; **fecero rotta** ~ **Palermo** they set out towards Palermo; **ricamo** ~ **seta** embroidery on silk; **basare un argomento** ~ to base an argument on sth; **conto** ~ **di te/sul tuo aiuto** I'm counting on you/on your help; **puntare una somma** ~ **un cavallo** to bet a sum on a horse; **procedi sulla sinistra** keep on *o* to the left; **è sulla destra** it's on the right; **fece fuoco sulla folla** he fired on the crowd; **la finestra dà sul giardino** the window looks onto the garden; **non è mai stato** ~ **un aereo** he's never been in a plane; **l'ho visto sul giornale** I saw it in the paper; **fa errori** ~ **errori** he makes one mistake after another; **sta sulle sue** to keep to himself.

(b) *(addosso)* over; **buttati uno scialle sulle spalle** throw a shawl over *o* round your shoulders; **sul vestito indossava un golf rosso** she was wearing a red jumper over her dress.

(c) *(da una parte all'altra)* over; **un ponte sul fiume** a bridge over the river; **un aereo passò sulle nostre teste** an aeroplane flew over our heads.

(d) *(autorità, dominio etc)* over; **non ha alcun potere** ~ **di lui** he has no power over him.

(e) *(più in alto di)* above; **100 metri sul livello del mare** 100 metres above sea level.

(f) *(argomento)* about, on; **discutere** ~ **un argomento** to discuss a subject; **un articolo sulla prima guerra mondiale** an article on *o* about the first world war; **una conferenza sulla pace nel mondo** a conference on *o* about world peace.

(g) *(circa)* about; **c'erano sulle 100 persone** there were about 100 people; **sarà sulla sessantina** he must be about sixty; **è costato sui trenta milioni** it cost about thirty million lire.

(h) *(proporzione)* out of, in; **50** ~ **100 hanno votato contro** 50 out of 100 voted against it; **2 giorni** ~ **3** 2 days out of 3, 2 days in 3; **5** ~ **10** *(voto)* 5 out of 10.

(i) *(causa):* **scarpe** ~ **misura** handmade shoes; **spedire qc** ~ **richiesta** to send sth on request.

2 *av* **(a)** *(in alto, verso l'alto)* up; *(al piano superiore)* upstairs; **guarda** ~ look up; **qui/lì** ~ up here/there; ~ **le mani!** hands up!; **era** ~ **che ci aspettava** he was waiting for us upstairs.

(b) *(in poi)* onwards; **dal numero 39 in** ~ from number 39 onwards; **dai 20 anni in** ~ from the age of 20 onwards.

(c) *(addosso)* on; **cos'hai** ~? what have you got on?; **posso metterlo** ~? can I put it on?; **aveva** ~ **una tunica** she had a strange tunic on.

(d) *(fraseologia):* ~ **coraggio!** come on, cheer up!; ~ **smettila!** come on, that's enough of that!; ~ **svelto!** come on, hurry up!; ~ ~ **non fare così!** now, now, don't behave like that!; **andare** ~ **e giù** to go up and down; **andava** ~ **e giù per il corridoio** he paced up and down the corridor; **venir** ~ **dal niente** to rise from nothing; ~ **per giù** approximately.

sua ['sua] *vedi* **suo.**

suadente [sua'dɛnte] *ag* persuasive.

sub [sub] *sm/f inv* skindiver.

subacqueo, a [su'bakkweo] **1** *ag* underwater *attr.* **2** *sm* skindiver.

subaffittare [subaffit'tare] *vt* to sublet.

subaffitto [subaf'fitto] *sm (contratto)* sublet.

subalterno, a [subal'tɛrno] *ag, sm* subordinate; *(Mil)* subaltern.

subappaltare [subappal'tare] *vt* to subcontract.

subappalto [subap'palto] *sm* subcontract.

subbuglio [sub'buʎʎo] *sm* confusion, turmoil; **essere/mettere in ~** to be in/throw into a turmoil.

subconscio, a [subkɔnʃo] *ag, sm,* **subcosciente** [subkoʃ'ʃɛnte] *ag, sm* subconscious.

subdolo, a ['subdolo] *ag* sneaky, underhand.

subentrare [suben'trare] *vi (aus essere):* **è subentrato a suo padre nella direzione della ditta** he took over from his father as director of the firm; **alla sorpresa subentrò la paura** surprise gave way to fear; **sono subentrati altri problemi** other problems arose.

subequatoriale [subekwato'rjale] *ag* subequatorial.

subire [su'bire] *vt (gen)* to suffer; *(operazione, interrogatorio)* to undergo; **~ un interrogatorio** to undergo an interrogation, be interrogated; **~ una tortura** to be tortured; **ha dovuto ~ e tacere** he had to suffer in silence; **per quanto ancora dobbiamo ~ questo despota?** for how long must we put up with this despot?

subissare [subis'sare] *vt:* **~ qn di** *(doni, lodi)* to shower sb with.

subitaneo, a [subi'taneo] *ag* sudden.

subito ['subito] *av* immediately, at once, straightaway; **torno ~** I'll be right back; **è ~ fatto** it's easily done.

sublimare [subli'mare] *vt (Rel, fig)* to exalt; *(Psic)* to sublimate; *(Chim)* to sublime.

sublimazione [sublimat'tsjone] *sf (Rel, fig)* exaltation; *(Psic, Chim)* sublimation.

sublime [su'blime] *ag, sm* sublime.

sublocare [sublo'kare] *vt* to sublease.

sublocazione [sublokat'tsjone] *sf* sublease.

subnormale [subnor'male] **1** *ag* subnormal. **2** *sm/f* mentally handicapped person.

subodorare [subodo'rare] *vt (insidia etc)* to smell, suspect.

subordinare [subordi'nare] *vt* to subordinate.

subordinata [subordi'nata] *sf (Gram)* subordinate clause.

subordinato, a [subordi'nato] *ag (gen, Gram)* subordinate; *(dipendente):* **~ a** dependent on, subject to.

subordinazione [subordinat'tsjone] *sf* subordination.

subordine [su'bordine] *sm:* **in ~** secondarily.

subtropicale [subtropi'kale] *ag* subtropical.

suburbano, a [subur'bano] *ag* suburban.

succedaneo, a [suttʃe'daneo] *ag, sm* substitute *(attr).*

succedere [sut'tʃedere] **1** *vi (aus essere)* **(a)** *(accadere)* to happen; **sapessi cosa mi è successo!** wait till you hear what happened to me!; **cosa ti succede?** what's the matter with you?; **sono cose che succedono** these things happen. **(b):** **~ a** *(seguire: persona)* to succeed; **~ al trono** to succeed to the throne. **2:** **~rsi** *vr* to follow each other; **i mesi si succedevano lenti** the months dragged on.

succeditrice [suttʃedi'tritʃe] *vedi* **successore.**

successione [suttʃes'sjone] *sf* succession.

successivo, a [suttʃes'sivo] *ag (continuo)* successive; *(che segue)* following; **il giorno ~** the

following day; **in un momento ~** subsequently.

successo, a [sut'tʃɛsso] **1** *pp di* **succedere. 2** *sm (gen)* success; *(disco)* hit; *(libro)* bestseller; *(film)* box-office success, hit; **arrivare al ~** to become a success; **avere ~** *(persona)* to be successful; *(idea)* to be well received; **non ho avuto ~** I was unsuccessful; **ho provato, ma senza ~** I tried, but without success, I tried in vain; **di ~** *(attore, cantante etc)* successful; **canzone di ~** hit (song).

successore, succeditrice [suttʃes'sore] **1** *ag* successive. **2** *sm/f* successor.

succhiare [suk'kjare] *vt (gen)* to suck; **~ il sangue a qn** *(fig)* to bleed sb.

succhiello [suk'kjɛllo] *sm* gimlet.

succhiotto [suk'kjɔtto] *sm* dummy.

succinto, a [sut'tʃinto] *ag (discorso)* succinct; *(abito)* brief.

succo, chi ['sukko] *sm (Anat, di frutto)* juice; **~ di frutta** fruit juice; **~ di pomodoro** tomato juice; **il ~ del discorso** *(fig)* the essence of the speech.

succoso, a [suk'koso] *ag* juicy; *(fig)* pithy.

succube ['sukkube] *sm/f* victim; **essere ~ di qn** to be dominated by sb.

succulento, a [sukku'lɛnto] *ag (pietanza)* succulent; *(gustoso: pranzo, cibo)* tasty.

succursale [sukkur'sale] *sf* branch (office).

sud [sud] **1** *sm* south; **a ~ (di)** south (of); **esposto a ~** facing south; **verso ~** south, southwards; **i mari del S~** the South Seas; **l'Italia del S~** Southern Italy; **America del S~** South America. **2** *ag inv (gen)* south; *(regione)* southern; **partirono in direzione ~** they set off southwards o in a southerly direction, they headed south.

sudare [su'dare] **1** *vi* to perspire, sweat; **ho dovuto ~ per finire quella traduzione** *(fig)* to work hard to finish that translation; **mi ha fatto ~** *(fig)* he made me work hard; **~ freddo** *(anche fig)* to come out in a cold sweat. **2** *vt* to work hard for; **~rsi il pane** to earn one's bread by the sweat of one's brow.

sudario [su'darjo] *sm* shroud.

sudata [su'data] *sf (anche fig)* sweat; **ho fatto una bella ~ per finire in tempo** it was a real sweat to finish in time.

sudaticcio, a, ci, ce [suda'tittʃo] *ag* sweaty, damp.

sudato, a [su'dato] *ag (persona, mani)* sweaty; *(fig: denaro)* hard-earned; **una vittoria ~a** a hard-won victory.

suddetto, a [sud'detto] *ag* above-mentioned *attr,* mentioned above.

sudditanza [suddi'tantsa] *sf* subjection; *(cittadinanza)* citizenship.

suddito, a ['suddito] *sm/f* subject.

suddividere [suddi'videre] *vt* to subdivide.

suddivisione [suddivi'zjone] *sf* subdivision.

suddiviso, a [suddi'vizo] *pp di* **suddividere.**

sudest [su'dɛst] *sm* south-east; **vento di ~** southeasterly wind.

sudiceria [suditʃe'ria] *sf (qualità)* filthiness, dirtiness; *(cosa sporca)* dirty thing; **libro pieno di ~e** filthy o obscene book.

sudicio, a, ci, ce ['suditʃo] **1** *ag* dirty, filthy; *(fig: indecente)* dirty, indecent; *(: disonesto)* dirty. **2** *sm (anche fig)* dirt, filth.

sudicione, a [sudi'tʃone] *sm/f (anche fig)* filthy person, pig *(fam).*

sudiciume [sudi'tʃume] *sm (anche fig)* dirt, filth.

sudore [su'dore] *sm* perspiration, sweat; **col ~ della propria fronte** with the sweat of one's brow.

sudovest [su'dɔvest] *sm* south-west; **vento di ~** south-westerly wind.

sue ['sue] *vedi* **suo.**

Suez ['suez] *sm*: **canale** *m* **di** ~ Suez Canal.

sufficiente |suffi'tʃɛnte| **1** *ag (adeguato)* sufficient; *(abbastanza)* enough; *(voto)* satisfactory; **questo fu ~ a farlo tacere** that was enough to shut him up; **non c'è spazio ~ per tutti** there is not enough space for everyone; **credi sia ~?** do you think that will do?; **è più che ~** it is more than enough. **2** *sm*: **avere il ~ per vivere** to have enough to live on.

sufficienza [suffi'tʃentsa] *sf* **(a): ne ho a ~** I have got plenty; **ne ho avuto a ~!** *(sono stufo)* I've had enough of this!; **ce ne sono a ~** there are enough; **con un'aria di ~** *(fig)* with a condescending air. **(b)** *(Scol)* pass mark.

suffisso [suf'fisso] *sm (Gram)* suffix.

suffragetta [suffra'dʒetta] *sf* suffragette.

suffragio [suf'fradʒo] *sm (a) (Pol: voto)* vote; **~ universale** universal suffrage. **(b)** *(Rel)* intercession; **messa di ~** mass for somebody's soul.

suggellare [suddʒel'lare] *vt (anche fig)* to seal.

suggello [sud'dʒello] *sm (anche fig)* seal.

suggerimento [suddʒeri'mento] *sm* suggestion; **dietro suo ~** on his advice.

suggerire [suddʒe'rire] *vt (gen)* to suggest; *(soluzione)* to suggest, put forward; *(Teatro)* to prompt; **suggerisco che ci si trovi lì** I suggest that we meet there; **~ a qn di fare qc** to suggest to sb that he *(o* she*)* do sth; **mi ha suggerito un periodo di riposo** he advised me to take time off; **non ~!** *(Scol)* don't whisper the answer!

suggeritore, trice [suddʒeri'tore] *sm/f (Teatro)* prompter.

suggestionare [suddʒestjo'nare] **1** *vt* to influence; **non lasciarti ~ da quello che dice** don't let yourself be influenced by what he says. **2: ~rsi** *vr* to be influenced.

suggestione [suddʒes'tjone] *sf (Psic)* suggestion; *(fascino)* fascination.

suggestivo, a [suddʒes'tivo] *ag (paesaggio)* evocative; *(veduta)* enchanting.

sughero ['sugero] *sm (gen)* cork; *(albero)* cork oak; **tappo di ~** cork.

sugli ['suʎʎi] *prep + art vedi* **su**.

sugna ['suɲɲa] *sf* lard.

sugo, ghi ['sugo] *sm (succo)* juice; *(di carne)* gravy; *(per pastasciutta)* sauce.

sugoso, a [su'goso] *ag (frutto)* juicy; *(fig: articolo etc)* pithy.

sui ['sui] *prep + art vedi* **su**.

suicida, i, e [sui'tʃida] **1** *ag* suicidal. **2** *sm/f* suicide.

suicidarsi [suitʃi'darsi] *vr* to commit suicide.

suicidio [sui'tʃidjo] *sm* suicide.

suino, a [su'ino] **1** *ag*: **carne ~a** pork. **2** *sm* pig; **i ~i** swine *pl*.

sul [sul] *prep + art vedi* **su**.

sulfamidico, a, ci, che [sulfa'midiko] *ag*, *sm* sulphonamide *(attr)*.

sulfureo, a [sul'fureo] *ag* sulphur *attr*.

sulla ['sulla], **sulle** ['sulle], **sullo** ['sullo] *prep + art vedi* **su**.

sultanina [sulta'nina] *sf*: **(uva)** ~ sultana.

sultano, a [sul'tano] *sm/f* sultan/sultana.

sunnominato, a [sunnomi'nato] *ag* aforesaid *attr*.

sunto ['sunto] *sm* summary; **fare il ~ di qc** to summarize sth.

suo[1], a ['suo], *pl* **suoi, sue 1** *ag poss*: **il(la) ~(a)** *etc (maschile)* his; *(femminile)* her; *(neutro)* its; **il ~ giardino** his *(o* her*)* garden; **~a madre** his *(o* her*)* mother; **~ padre** his *(o* her*)* father; **un ~ amico** a friend of his *(o* hers*)*; **è colpa ~a** it's his *(o* her*)* fault; **è casa ~a**, **la ~a casa** it's his *(o* her*)* house; **per amor ~** for love of him *(o* her*)*; **Sua Altezza** His *(o* Her*)* Highness.

2 *pron poss*: **il(la) ~(a)** *etc (maschile)* his, his own; *(femminile)* hers, her own; *(neutro)* its, its own; **la mia barca è più lunga della ~a** my boat is longer than his *(o* hers*)*; **il ~ è stato solo un errore** it was simply an error on his *(o* her*)* part.

3 *sm* **(a): ha speso del ~** he *(o* she*)* spent his *(o* her*)* own money; **vive del ~** he *(o* she*)* lives on his *(o* her*)* own income. **(b): i suoi** *(genitori, famiglia)* his *(o* her*)* family; *(amici)* his *(o* her*)* own people, his *(o* her*)* side; **lui è dei suoi** he is on his *(o* her*)* side.

4 *sf*: **la ~a** *(opinione)* his *(o* her*)* view; **è dalla ~a** *(parte)* he's on his *(o* her*)* side; **anche lui ha avuto le ~e** *(disavventure)* he's had his problems too.

suo[2], a ['suo], *pl* **suoi, sue** *(forma di cortesia: anche:* S~*)* **1** *ag poss*: **il(la) ~(a)** *etc* your; **il ~ ombrello, signore!** your umbrella, sir!; **Sua Altezza** Your Highness; **~ devotissimo** *(in lettere)* your devoted servant. **2** *pron poss*: **il(la) ~(a)** *etc* yours, your own; **la ~a è pura scortesia** that's sheer discourtesy on your part. **3** *sm*: **ha speso del ~?** did you spend your own money? **4** *sf*: **la ~a** *(opinione)* your view; **è dalla ~a** he's on your side; **alla ~a!** your very good health!

suocera ['swɔtʃera] *sf* mother-in-law.

suocero ['swɔtʃero] *sm* father-in-law; **~i** father-and mother-in-law.

suoi ['swɔi] *vedi* **suo**.

suola ['swɔla] *sf (di scarpa)* sole; **rifare le ~e alle scarpe** to have one's shoes resoled.

suolo ['swɔlo] *sm (terreno)* ground; *(terra)* soil; **cadde al ~** he fell to the ground; **in ~ italiano** on Italian soil.

suonare [swo'nare] **1** *vt (strumento, pezzo musicale)* to play; *(campana, campanello)* to ring; *(clacson, allarme, ritirata)* to sound; **l'orologio ha suonato le cinque** the clock struck five; **ha suonato il clacson** he sounded the horn; **gliele ho suonate** *(fam)* I gave him a thrashing. **2** *vi (musicista)* to play; *(campane, campanello, telefono)* to ring; *(ore)* to strike; *(fig: discorso)* to sound, ring; **le campane suonano a morto** the bells are sounding a death knell; **il piano suona male** the piano doesn't have a nice sound; **mi suona strano** *(fig)* it sounds strange to me.

suonato, a [swo'nato] *ag* **(a)** *(compiuto)*: **ha cinquant'anni ~i** he is well over fifty. **(b)** *(Pugilato)* punch-drunk; *(fig fam: rimbambito)* soft in the head.

suonatore, trice [swona'tore] *sm/f* player; **~ ambulante** street musician.

suoneria [swone'ria] *sf* alarm.

suono ['swɔno] *sm (gen)* sound; *(di campane)* sound, ringing; **ballare al ~ di un'orchestra** to dance to the music of an orchestra; **lo accolsero a suon di fischi** they booed and jeered him as he arrived.

suora ['swɔra] *sf (Rel)* nun; **Suor Maria** Sister Maria.

super ['super] **1** *ag inv*: **(benzina)** ~ ≈ four-star (petrol), premium *(Am)*. **2** *pref* super...; over...; **~affollato, a** *ag* overcrowded; **~allenamento** *sm* overtraining; **~petroliera** *sf* supertanker.

superalimentazione [superalimentat'tsjone] *sf* overfeeding.

superamento [supera'mento] *sm (di ostacolo)* overcoming; *(di montagna)* crossing; **arrivare al ~ di** *(idee, dottrine)* to move on from.

superare [supe'rare] *vt (limite, aspettative)* to exceed; *(traguardo, montagne)* to cross; *(esame)* to pass; *(muro)* to get over; *(fig: ostacolo, malattia, paura)* to overcome; *(: rivale)* to surpass, outdo; *(Aut: sorpassare)* to overtake; **~ i limiti di**

velocità to exceed the speed limit; ~ **qn in altezza/peso** to be taller/heavier than sb; **ha superato la cinquantina** he's over fifty; **stavolta ha superato se stesso** this time he has surpassed himself.

superato, a [supe'rato] *ag* outmoded.

superbia [su'pɛrbja] *sf* pride.

superbo, a [su'pɛrbo] *ag* **(a)** *(persona)* proud, haughty. **(b)** *(fig: grandioso, splendido)* superb, magnificent.

superdonna [super'dɔnna] *sf (iro)* superwoman.

superdotato, a [superdo'tato] **1** *ag* highly gifted. **2** *sm/f* highly gifted person.

super-ego ['super 'ɛgo] *sm* superego.

superficiale [superfi'tʃale] **1** *ag (gen)* superficial; **acque** ~**i** surface water *sg.* **2** *sm/f* superficial person.

superficialità [superfitʃali'ta] *sf* superficiality.

superficie [super'fitʃe] *sf* **(a)** *(di muro, specchio)* surface; ~ **terrestre** surface of the earth; **tornare in** ~ *(a galla)* to return to the surface; *(fig: problemi etc)* to resurface; **non va mai oltre la** ~ **delle cose** *(fig)* he has a superficial approach. **(b)** *(area)* surface area; ~ **alare** *(Aer)* wing area; ~ **velica** *(Naut)* sail area.

superfluo, a [su'pɛrfluo] **1** *ag (gen)* superfluous; *(spese)* unnecessary; **peli** ~**i** unwanted hair *sg.* **2** *sm* surplus.

super-io ['supe'rio] *sm* superego.

superiora [supe'rjora] *sf (Rel: anche:* **madre** ~) mother superior.

superiore [supe'rjore] **1** *ag* **(a)** *(intelligenza, qualità)* superior; *(numero)* greater; *(quantità, somma)* larger; **intelligenza** ~ **alla media** above-average intelligence; **è** ~ **alle mie forze** it's beyond me; **sono** ~ **a queste cose** I don't let these things worry me. **(b)** *(che sta più in alto: rami, classe)* upper; *(livello)* higher; **il corso** ~ **di un fiume** the upper reaches of a river; **al piano** ~ on the upper floor; *(di edificio a più piani)* on the floor above; **scuola** ~, **scuole** ~**i** ≃ senior comprehensive school; **istruzione** ~ higher education; **per ordine** ~ on orders from above. **2** *sm* superior. **3** *sfpl:* **le** ~**i** *(Scol)* ≃ senior comprehensive school.

superiorità [superjori'ta] *sf* superiority; **ha dimostrato una netta** ~ **sull'avversario** he was clearly superior to his opponent; **aria di** ~ air of superiority.

superlativo, a [superla'tivo] *ag, sm (gen, Gram)* superlative.

superlavoro [superla'voro] *sm* overwork.

supermercato [supermer'kato] *sm* supermarket.

supernova, ae [super'nɔva] *sf (Astron)* supernova.

superpotenza [superpo'tɛntsa] *sf (Pol)* superpower.

supersonico, a, ci, che [super'sɔniko] *ag* supersonic.

superstite [su'pɛrstite] **1** *ag* surviving. **2** *sm/f* survivor.

superstizione [superstit'tsjone] *sf* superstition.

superstizioso, a [superstit'tsjoso] **1** *ag* superstitious. **2** *sm/f* superstitious person.

superstrada [super'strada] *sf* ≃ expressway.

superuomo [supe'rwɔmo] *sm, pl* **-uomini** superman.

supervisione [supervi'zjone] *sf* supervision.

supervisore [supervi'zore] *sm* supervisor.

supino, a [su'pino] *ag* supine; **dormire** ~ to sleep on one's back; **accettazione** ~**a** *(fig)* blind acceptance.

suppellettili [suppel'lettili] *sfpl (gen)* ornaments; *(Archeol)* grave goods.

suppergiù [supper'dʒu] *av* more or less, roughly.

supplementare [supplemen'tare] *ag (gen)* extra; *(entrate)* additional; *(treno)* relief *attr;* **attività** ~**i** additional activities.

supplemento [supple'mento] *sm* supplement.

supplente [sup'plɛnte] **1** *ag (insegnante)* supply *attr.* **2** *sm/f* supply teacher.

supplenza [sup'plɛntsa] *sf (Scol):* **ha avuto una** ~ **di un anno** he's been asked to do a year's supply teaching; **fare** ~ to do supply teaching, supply.

suppletivo, a [supple'tivo] *ag (gen)* supplementary; *(sessione d'esami)* extra.

supplì [sup'pli] *sm inv (Culin)* rice croquette.

supplica, che [sup'plika] *sf (Rel, fig)* petition, supplication; **con un tono di** ~ in an imploring voice.

supplicare [suppli'kare] *vt* to implore, beseech; **ti supplico, non andartene** don't go, I beg you.

supplichevole [suppli'kevole] *ag* imploring.

supplire [sup'plire] **1** *vt* to stand in for, replace temporarily. **2** *vi:* ~ **a** *(difetto, mancanza)* to make up for, compensate for.

supplizio [sup'plittsjo] *sm (tortura)* torture; *(fig)* torment; **fu condotto al** ~ *(a morte)* he was led to execution.

supporre [sup'porre] *vt (gen)* to suppose; **supponiamo che...** let's o just suppose that...; **suppongo che sia lo stesso** I imagine it's the same; **suppongo di sì/di no** I suppose so/not.

supporto [sup'pɔrto] *sm (sostegno)* support; *(struttura)* stand, holder.

supposizione [suppozit'tsjone] *sf* supposition; **le mie sono solo** ~**i** I'm only guessing; **è una** ~ **infondata** it's a groundless assumption.

supposta [sup'posta] *sf (Med)* suppository.

supposto, a [sup'posto] **1** *pp di* **supporre**. **2:** ~ **che** *cong* supposing that.

suppurare [suppu'rare] *vi* to suppurate.

suppurazione [suppurat'tsjone] *sf* suppuration.

supremazia [supremat'tsia] *sf* supremacy.

supremo, a [su'prɛmo] *ag (gen)* supreme; **con** ~ **disprezzo** with the utmost contempt; **l'ora** ~**a** *(fig)* one's last hour; **il giudizio** ~ *(Rel)* the Last Judgement.

surclassare [surklas'sare] *vt* to outclass.

surgelamento [surdʒela'mento] *sm* (deep-)freezing.

surgelare [surdʒe'lare] *vt* to (deep-)freeze.

surgelato, a [surdʒe'lato] **1** *ag* (deep-)frozen. **2** *smpl:* ~**i** frozen food *sg.*

surmenage [syrmə'naʒ] *sm (fisico)* overwork; *(mentale)* mental strain; *(Sport)* overtraining.

surplus [syr'ply] *sm inv (Econ)* surplus.

surreale [surre'ale] *ag* surrealistic.

surriscaldamento [surriskalda'mento] *sm (gen, Tecn)* overheating.

surriscaldare [surriskal'dare] *vt,* ~**rsi** *vr (gen, Tecn)* to overheat.

surrogato, a [surro'gato] *ag, sm* substitute *attr.*

suscettibile [suʃʃet'tibile] *ag* **(a)** *(permaloso)* touchy, sensitive. **(b):** ~ **di** *(miglioramento)* open to; *(cambiamento)* subject to.

suscettibilità [suʃʃettibili'ta] *sf* touchiness; **urtare la** ~ **di qn** to hurt sb's feelings.

suscitare [suʃʃi'tare] *vt (provocare)* to cause, provoke; *(destare: ira)* to arouse; ~ **uno scroscio di applausi** to provoke thunderous applause.

susina [su'sina] *sf* plum.

susino [su'sino] *sm* plum (tree).

suspense [sɔs'pɛns] *sf* suspense.

susseguire [susse'gwire] **1** *vt* to follow, come after. **2** *vi (aus essere)* to follow; **da ciò segue che...** it follows that.... **3:** ~**rsi** *vr (uso reciproco)* to succeed one another; **le sorprese continuavano a**

~rsi there was a continual succession of surprises.

sussidiario, a [sussi'djarjo] *ag (gen)* subsidiary; *(treno)* relief *attr; (fermata)* extra.

sussidio [sus'sidjo] *sm* **(a)** *(aiuto)* aid; **~i didattici/ audiovisivi** teaching/audiovisual aids; **mandare truppe in ~ a qn** to send reinforcements to sb. **(b)** *(sovvenzione)* subsidy; **~ di disoccupazione** unemployment benefit.

sussiego [sus'sjɛgo] *sm* haughtiness; **con aria di ~** haughtily.

sussistenza [sussis'tɛntsa] *sf* **(a)** *(esistenza)* existence. **(b)** *(sostentamento)* subsistence; **mezzi di ~** means of substinence. **(c)** *(Mil)* provisioning.

sussistere [sus'sistere] *vi (aus essere) (esistere)* to exist; *(essere fondato: motivi etc)* to be valid, be sound.

sussultare [sussul'tare] *vi (di spavento etc)* to start; **~ di gioia** to jump for joy.

sussulto [sus'sulto] *sm* start; **dare** *o* **avere un ~** to give a start, start.

sussurrare [sussur'rare] **1** *vt* to whisper; **gli sussurrò qualcosa all'orecchio** he whispered something in his ear; **si sussurra che...** it's rumoured that... . **2** *vi (fronde)* to rustle; *(acque)* to murmur.

sussurro [sus'surro] *sm (vedi vb)* whisper; rustle; murmur.

sutura [su'tura] *sf (Med)* suture.

suturare [sutu'rare] *vt* to stitch up, suture.

suvvia [suv'via] *escl* come on!

svagare [zva'gare] **1** *vt (divertire)* to amuse; *(distrarre)*: **~ qn** to take sb's mind off things. **2: ~rsi** *vr (divertirsi)* to enjoy o.s.; *(distrarsi)* to take one's mind off things.

svago, ghi ['zvago] *sm (riposo)* relaxation; *(passatempo)* pastime; **l'ho fatto per ~** I did it just to pass the time.

svaligiare [zvali'dʒare] *vt (banca)* to rob; *(casa)* to burgle.

svaligiatore, trice [zvalidʒa'tore] *sm/f (di banca)* robber; *(di casa)* burglar.

svalutare [zvalu'tare] **1** *vt (Econ)* to devalue; *(fig)* to belittle. **2: ~rsi** *vr (Econ)* to be devalued.

svalutazione [zvalutat'tsjone] *sf (Econ)* devaluation.

svampito, a [zvam'pito] **1** *ag* absent-minded. **2** *sm/f* absent-minded person.

svanire [zva'nire] *vi (aus essere) (anche fig)* to disappear, vanish; *(rumore)* to fade; **~ nel nulla** to disappear *o* vanish completely.

svanito, a [zva'nito] **1** *ag (fig: persona)* absentminded. **2** *sm/f* absent-minded person.

svantaggiato, a [zvantad'dʒato] *ag* at a disadvantage.

svantaggio [zvan'taddʒo] *sm* disadvantage; *(inconveniente)* drawback, disadvantage; **tornerà a tuo ~** it will work against you; **sono in ~ rispetto a te** you have an advantage over me; **essere in ~ di due gol** *(Sport)* to be two goals down; **essere in ~ di due minuti** *(Sport)* to be two minutes behind.

svantaggioso, a [zvantad'dʒoso] *ag* disadvantageous; **è un'offerta ~a per me** it is not in my interest to accept this offer; **è un prezzo ~** it is not an attractive price.

svaporare [zvapo'rare] *vi (aus essere)* to evaporate.

svariato, a [zva'rjato] *ag (numeroso)* various; *(vario, diverso)* varied; **di questa macchina esistono ~i modelli** this car comes in a variety of models.

svasare [zva'zare] *vt* **(a)** *(pianta)* to repot. **(b)** *(Cucito: gonna)* to flare.

svastica, che ['zvastika] *sf* swastika.

svedese [zve'dese] **1** *ag* **(a)** *(della Svezia)* Swedish. **(b): (fiammiferi) ~i** *mpl* safety matches. **2** *sm/f* Swede. **3** *sm (lingua)* Swedish.

sveglia ['zveʎʎa] *sf (a) (azione)* waking up; *(Mil)* reveille; **la ~ è alle 7** we have to get up at 7; **mi può dare la ~ alle 9?** would you wake me up at 9?; **suonare la ~** *(Mil)* to sound the reveille. **(b)** *(orologio)* alarm (clock); **~ telefonica** alarm call.

svegliare [zveʎ'ʎare] **1** *vt (persona)* to wake (up), waken; *(sentimenti etc)* to awaken, rouse; **la camminata ha svegliato il suo appetito** the walk gave him an appetite. **2: ~rsi** *vr* to wake up; *(fig)* to waken o.s. up.

sveglio, a ['zveʎʎo] *ag (gen)* awake; *(fig: attento, pronto)* quick-witted; *(: furbo)* smart; **sei ~?** are you awake?; **non è molto ~** *(fig)* he's not very bright.

svelare [zve'lare] **1** *vt (segreto)* to reveal; *(mistero)* to uncover. **2: ~rsi** *vr* to show o.s.; **con quell'azione si è svelato per quello che è** that action has shown him up for what he is.

sveltezza [zvel'tettsa] *sf (gen)* speed; *(mentale)* quick-wittedness.

sveltire [zvel'tire] **1** *vt (ɡen)* to speed up; *(procedura)* to streamline; **~ il traffico** to speed up the flow of traffic; **~ il passo** to quicken one's pace. **2: ~rsi** *vr (fig: persona)* to waken o.s. up.

svelto, a ['zvelto] *ag (gen)* quick; *(passo)* brisk; *(fig: persona: sveglio)* quick-witted; **essere ~ di mano** *(rubare)* to be light-fingered; *(picchiare)* to be free with one's hands *o* fists; **facciamo alla ~a** let's get a move on.

svenare [zve'nare] **1** *vt* to slash the veins of; *(fig: privare di tutto)* to bleed dry. **2: ~rsi** *vr* to slash one's wrists; *(fig)* to reduce o.s. to poverty.

svendere ['zvendere] *vt* to sell off, clear.

svendita ['zvendita] *sf (Comm)* (clearance) sale.

svenevole [zve'nevole] *ag* mawkish.

svenimento [zveni'mento] *sm* fainting fit, faint; **avere uno ~** to faint.

svenire [zve'nire] *vi (aus essere)* to faint, pass out.

sventare [zven'tare] *vt* to foil, thwart.

sventatezza [zventa'tettsa] *sf (qualità: distrazione)* absent-mindedness; *(: mancanza di prudenza)* rashness; **è stata una ~ da parte sua fare...** it was rash of him to do... .

sventato, a [zven'tato] **1** *ag (distratto)* scatterbrained; *(imprudente)* rash. **2** *sm/f* scatterbrain.

sventola ['zventola] *sf* **(a)** *(fig: sberla)* slap; **mollare una ~ a qn** to slap sb. **(b): ha le orecchie a ~** his *(o* her) ears stick out.

sventolare [zvento'lare] **1** *vt (bandiera etc)* to wave. **2** *vi* to flutter.

sventrare [zven'trare] *vt (animale)* to disembowel; *(fig: persona)* to rip open; **stanno sventrando il quartiere** they are demolishing the heart of the district.

sventura [zven'tura] *sf (sorte avversa)* misfortune; *(disgrazia)* mishap; **per colmo di ~** to crown it all; **è stata una ~** it was a piece of ill luck; **compagno di ~** *(scherz)* fellow sufferer.

sventurato, a [zventu'rato] **1** *ag* unlucky, unfortunate. **2** *sm/f* unlucky person; *(scherz)* poor unfortunate.

svenuto, a [sve'nuto] *pp di* **svenire**.

sverginare [zverdʒi'nare] *vt* to deflower.

svergognare [zvergoɲ'ɲare] *vt* to shame.

svergognato, a [zvergoɲ'ɲato] **1** *ag (privo di pudore)* shameless, brazen; *(privo di ritegno)* impudent. **2** *sm/f (vedi ag)* shameless person; impudent person.

svernare [zver'nare] *vi* to winter.

svestire [zves'tire] 1 *vt* to undress. 2: ~**rsi** *vr* to get undressed.

Svezia ['zvɛtsja] *sf* Sweden.

svezzamento [zvettsa'mento] *sm (anche fig)* weaning.

svezzare [zvet'tsare] *vt* to wean.

sviare [zvi'are] *vt (sospetti)* to divert; *(attenzione)* to distract; *(colpo)* to ward off; ~ **le indagini della polizia** to put the police off the track; ~ **il discorso** to change the subject.

svicolare [zviko'lare] *vi* to slip down an alley; *(fig)* to sneak off.

svignarsela [zviɲ'ɲarsela] *vr* to slip away, sneak off.

svilimento [zvili'mento] *sm* debasement.

svilire [zvi'lire] *vt* to debase.

sviluppare [zvilup'pare] 1 *vt (gen, Fot, Mat)* to develop; *(commercio)* to expand; *(incendio)* to cause; *(gas)* to emit. 2: ~**rsi** *vr (gen)* to develop; *(città)* to expand, grow; *(commercio)* to develop, expand; **si sviluppano dei gas** there is a build-up of gas.

sviluppatrice [zviluppa'tritʃe] *sf (Fot, Chim)* developer.

sviluppo [zvi'luppo] *sm (gen, Fot, Mat, Econ)* development; *(di città)* development, growth; *(di concetto, tema)* development, treatment; *(di industria)* expansion; **gli ~i della situazione** the developments in the situation; **in via di ~** in the process of development; **paesi in via di ~** developing countries.

svincolare [zvinko'lare] 1 *vt (da vincolo)* to free, release; *(Comm: merce)* to clear. 2: ~**rsi** *vr* to free o.s.

svincolo ['zvinkolo] *sm* (a) *(Comm)* clearance. (b) *(Aut)* motorway intersection.

sviolinata [zvioli'nata] *sf (fam)* fawning.

sviscerare [zviʃʃe'rare] *vt (fig: argomento)* to examine in depth.

sviscerato, a [zviʃʃe'rato] *ag (amore, odio)* passionate.

svista ['zvista] *sf* oversight, slip.

svitare [zvi'tare] *vt* to unscrew.

svitato, a [zvi'tato] *(fam)* 1 *ag (persona)* unhinged, nutty. 2 *sm/f* screwball.

Svizzera ['zvittsera] *sf* Switzerland.

svizzero, a ['zvittsero] *ag, sm/f* Swiss.

svogliatezza [zvoʎʎa'tettsa] *sf (vedi ag)* listlessness; indolence.

svogliato, a [zvoʎ'ʎato] 1 *ag* listless; *(pigro)* lazy, indolent. 2 *sm/f* lazybones *sg*.

svolazzare [zvolat'tsare] *vi* to flutter about.

svolazzo [zvo'lattso] *sm (fig: di scrittura)* flourish.

svolgere ['zvɔldʒere] 1 *vt (rotolo)* to unroll; *(gomitolo)* to unwind; *(fig: argomento, tema)* to discuss; *(: piano, programma)* to carry out; **quale professione svolge?** what is your occupation? 2: ~**rsi** *vr (filo)* to unwind; *(vita, eventi: procedere)* to go on; *(fig: aver luogo: scena, film)* to be set; **ecco come si sono svolti i fatti** this was the sequence of events; **tutto si è svolto secondo i piani** everything went according to plan.

svolgimento [zvoldʒi'mento] *sm (di tema)* discussion; *(di programma)* carrying out; **lo ~ dei fatti** the sequence of events.

svolta ['zvɔlta] *sf (curva)* turn; *(fig: mutamento)* turning point; ~ **continua** *(Aut)* filter lane; **è proibita la ~ a sinistra** no left turn; **prendi la prima ~ a destra** take the first turning on your right; ~ **a destra/a sinistra** *(Pol)* swing to the right/to the left; **essere ad una ~ nella propria vita** to be at a crossroads in one's life.

svoltare [zvol'tare] *vi* to turn.

svolto, a ['zvɔlto] *pp di* **svolgere**.

svuotamento [zvwota'mento] *sm* emptying.

svuotare [zvwo'tare] *vt (vuotare)* to empty (out); *(: fig)*: ~ **di** to deprive of.

T

T, t [ti] *sf o m inv (lettera)* T, t.
tabaccaio, a [tabak'kajo] *sm/f* tobacconist.
tabaccheria [tabakke'ria] *sf* tobacconist's (shop).
tabacchiera [tabak'kjɛra] *sf* snuffbox.
tabacco, chi [ta'bakko] *sm* tobacco.
tabella [ta'bella] *sf (tavola)* table; *(cartellone)* board; ~ **dei prezzi** price list; ~ **di marcia** schedule.
tabellone [tabel'lone] *sm (per pubblicità)* billboard; *(per informazioni)* notice board; *(: in stazione)* timetable board.
tabernacolo [taber'nakolo] *sm* tabernacle.
tabù [ta'bu] *ag inv, sm inv* taboo.
tabula rasa ['tabula'raza] *sf* tabula rasa; **fare ~** *(fig)* to make a clean sweep; **ha fatto ~ di tutti i dolci** he polished off all the cakes.
tabulare [tabu'lare] *vt* to tabulate.
tabulato [tabu'lato] *sm (Inform)* printout.
tabulatore [tabula'tore] *sm* tabulator.
tabulatrice [tabula'tritʃe] *sf (Inform)* printer.
tacca, che ['takka] *sf (gen)* notch; *(meno profondo)* nick; **di mezza ~** *(fig peg)* mediocre.
taccagneria [takkaɲɲe'ria] *sf* meanness, stinginess.
taccagno, a [tak'kaɲɲo] *ag* mean, stingy.
taccheggiare [takked'dʒare] *vt* to shoplift.
taccheggiatore, trice [takkeddʒa'tore] *sm/f* shoplifter.
taccheggio [tak'keddʒo] *sm (furto)* shoplifting.
tacchetto [tak'ketto] *sm (di scarpa)* low heel; *(Sport)* stud.
tacchino [tak'kino] *sm* turkey.
tacciare [tat'tʃare] *vt:* ~ **qn di** *(vigliaccheria etc)* to accuse sb of.
tacco, chi ['takko] *sm* **(a)** *(di scarpe)* heel. **(b)** *(cuneo per fermare le ruote)* chock.
taccuino [takku'ino] *sm* notebook.
tacere [ta'tʃere] **1** *vi (stare in silenzio)* to be silent, be quiet; *(smettere di parlare)* to fall silent; **continuava a ~** he remained silent; **taci!** keep quiet!; **fatelo ~** make him keep quiet; **tutto taceva** all was silent *o* quiet; **i cannoni tacquero** the cannons fell silent; **mettere a ~ qc** to hush sth up. **2** *vt (colpa, accaduto)* to keep silent about; ~ **la verità** to hold back the truth.
tachicardia [takikar'dia] *sf (Med)* tachycardia.
tachimetro [ta'kimetro] *sm* speedometer.
tacito, a ['tatʃito] *ag* silent; *(sottinteso)* tacit, unspoken.
taciturno, a [tatʃi'turno] *ag* taciturn.
taciuto, a [ta'tʃuto] *pp di* **tacere.**
tafano [ta'fano] *sm* horsefly.
tafferuglio [taffe'ruʎʎo] *sm* brawl, scuffle.
taffettà [taffet'ta] *sm* taffeta.
taglia ['taʎʎa] *sf* **(a)** *(misura: di abito etc)* size; **che ~ porti?** what size do you wear *o* take? **(b)** *(su criminale)* reward; **c'è una ~ sulla sua testa** there is a price on his head.
tagliaboschi [taʎʎa'bɔski] *sm inv* woodcutter.
tagliacarte [taʎʎa'karte] *sm inv* paperknife.
taglialegna [taʎʎa'leɲɲa] *sm inv* woodcutter.

tagliando [taʎ'ʎando] *sm* coupon, voucher.
tagliare [taʎ'ʎare] **1** *vt* **(a)** *(gen)* to cut; *(torta, salame)* to cut, slice; *(arrosto)* to carve; *(siepe)* to trim; *(fieno, prato)* to mow; *(grano)* to reap; *(albero)* to fell, cut down; ~ **qc in due/in più parti** to cut sth in two/into several pieces; ~ **la gola a qn** to cut *o* slit sb's throat; **mi tagli una fetta di torta?** would you cut me a slice of cake?; ~**rsi le unghie** to cut one's nails; **farsi ~ i capelli** to have one's hair cut; **una lama che taglia** a sharp blade.
(b) *(articolo, scritto, scena)* to cut; *(acqua, telefono, gas)* to cut off; **mio padre mi ha tagliato i viveri** my father is refusing to support me any more.
(c) *(curva)* to cut; *(traguardo)* to cross; *(Tennis: palla)* to put a spin on; ~ **la strada a qn** to cut across in front of sb.
(d) *(fraseologia):* ~ **la testa al toro** *(fig)* to settle things once and for all; ~ **le gambe a qn** *(fig)* to make it impossible for sb to act; **un vino che taglia le gambe** a very strong wine; ~ **i panni addosso a qn** *(fig)* to tear sb to pieces.
2 *vi:* ~ **per i campi** to cut across the fields; **tagliamo per di là** let's cut across that way.
tagliatelle [taʎʎa'tɛlle] *sfpl* tagliatelle *sg.*
tagliato, a [taʎ'ʎato] *ag:* **essere ~ per qc** *(fig)* to be cut out for sth.
tagliatrice [taʎʎa'tritʃe] *sf (Tecn)* cutter.
tagliaunghie [taʎʎa'ungje] *sm inv* nail clippers *pl.*
taglieggiare [taʎʎed'dʒare] *vt* to exact a tribute from.
tagliente [taʎ'ʎɛnte] *ag (lama)* sharp; *(fig: tono, parole)* cutting, sharp.
tagliere [taʎ'ʎɛre] *sm* chopping board; *(per il pane)* bread board.
taglierini [taʎʎe'rini] *smpl (Culin)* thin soup noodles.
taglio ['taʎʎo] *sm* **(a)** *(gen: atto)* cutting, cut; *(di capelli)* (hair)cut; *(di fieno, erba)* mowing; *(di vini)* blending; **dare un ~ a qc** *(fig)* to make a clean break in sth; ~ **cesareo** *(Med)* Caesarean section; **vino da ~** blending wine.
(b) *(effetto)* cut; **farsi un ~ al dito** to cut one's finger; ~ **netto** clean cut; **c'erano dei ~i nel film/nel libro** cuts were made in the film/in the book.
(c) *(pezzo: di carne)* piece; *(: di stoffa)* length; **banconote di piccolo/grosso ~** small-/high-denomination notes.
(d) *(stile: di abito)* cut, style; *(: di capelli)* (hair)style; *(: di pietra preziosa)* cut; **di ~ classico** with a classic cut; **scuola di ~** dressmaking school.
(e) *(di lama)* cutting edge, edge.
(f) *(Tennis)* spin; **colpire la palla di ~** to put a spin on the ball.
tagliola [taʎ'ʎɔla] *sf* trap, snare.
taglione [taʎ'ʎone] *sm:* **la legge del ~** the concept of an eye for an eye and a tooth for a tooth.
tagliuzzare [taʎʎut'tsare] *vt* to cut into small pieces.

tailandese [tailan'dese] *ag, sm/f, sm* Thai.

Tailandia [tai'landja] *sf* Thailand.

tailleur [ta'jœr] *sm inv* (tailored) costume.

talamo ['talamo] *sm (poet)* marriage bed.

talco, chi ['talko] *sm* talc, talcum powder.

tale ['tale] **1** *ag dimostr* **(a)** *(simile, così grande)* such; **non avevo mai visto un ~ disordine** I had never seen such a mess; **è di una ~ arroganza** he is so arrogant; **~i discorsi non si possono accettare** such talk is not acceptable; **e con ~i scuse è riuscito ad evitare la punizione** and with similar excuses he managed to escape punishment; **cosa ti fa credere che nutra ~i sentimenti?** what makes you think he feels like that?; **~ articolo è in vendita presso le nostre filiali** the above-mentioned article is on sale at our branches.

(b) *(nelle similitudini)*: **~ ... ~** like ... like; **~ padre ~ figlio** like father like son; **è ~ quale suo nonno** he's exactly like his grandfather; **hanno riportato una vittoria ~, quale non avevano sperato** they won an even greater victory than they had expected.

2 *ag indef* **(a)** *(certo)* one; **ti cercava una ~ Giovanna** somebody called Giovanna was looking for you; **ha detto che vedeva un amico, un tal Rossi** he said he was meeting a friend, a certain Rossi; **quella ~ persona desidera parlarti** that man (*o* woman) wants to see you.

(b) *(persona o cosa indeterminata)* such-and-such; **gli ho detto di venire il giorno ~ all'ora ~** I told him to come on such-and-such a day, at such-and-such a time.

3 *pron indef* **(a)** *(una certa persona)* that person, that man/woman; **ha telefonato di nuovo quel ~** that man phoned again; **l'hai più visto quel ~ di cui mi dicevi?** did you ever see that person *o* chap you were telling me about again?

(b): **il tal dei ~i** whats-his-name; **la tal dei ~i** whats-her-name; **diciamo che l'ho saputo dal tal dei ~i** let's just say I had it from you know who.

talea [ta'lea] *sf (Giardinaggio)* cutting.

taleggio [ta'leddʒo] *sm type of soft cheese.*

talento [ta'lento] *sm (capacità)* talent; *(persona)* talented person; **essere privo/pieno di ~** to be untalented/very talented.

talismano [taliz'mano] *sm* talisman.

tallonare [tallo'nare] *vt (inseguire)* to follow (hot) on the heels of, pursue; *(Sport)* to pursue; **~ il pallone** *(Calcio, Rugby)* to heel the ball.

talloncino [tallon'tʃino] *sm (cedola)* voucher; **~ del prezzo** *(di medicinali)* tear-off tag.

tallone [tal'lone] *sm* heel; **~ di Achille** *(fig)* Achilles' heel.

talmente [tal'mente] *av (così tanto)* so; **sono ~ contento!** I'm so happy!; **ero ~ emozionato che...** I was so moved that...; **è stato ~ ingenuo da cascarci** he was so naïve as to fall for it.

talora [ta'lora] *av* = **talvolta.**

talpa ['talpa] *sf (Zool, fig)* mole; **cieco come una ~** as blind as a bat.

talvolta [tal'vɔlta] *av* sometimes, at times.

tamarindo [tama'rindo] *sm* tamarind.

tamburellare [tamburel'lare] *vi (pioggia)* to drum; **~ con le dita** to drum one's fingers.

tamburello [tambu'rɛllo] *sm (Mus)* tambourine.

tamburino [tambu'rino] *sm* drummer boy.

tamburo [tam'buro] *sm* **(a)** *(Mus: strumento)* drum; *(: suonatore)* drummer; **a ~ battente** *(fig)* immediately, at once. **(b)** *(Tecn, Aut)* drum; *(di armi)* cylinder; *(di orologio)* barrel; **freni a ~** drum brakes; **pistola a ~** revolver.

Tamigi [ta'midʒi] *sm*: **il ~** the Thames.

tamponamento [tampona'mento] *sm (Aut)* collision; **~ a catena** pile-up.

tamponare [tampo'nare] *vt* **(a)** *(otturare)* to plug. **(b)** *(urtare: macchina)* to crash into, ram into.

tampone [tam'pone] *sm* **(a)** *(Med: gen)* plug; *(: di cotone)* wad; *(: per pulire una ferita)* swab; *(: per stendere un liquido)* pad; *(assorbente interno)* tampon. **(b)** *(cuscinetto: per timbri)* inkpad; *(: di carta assorbente)* blotter.

tamtam [tam'tam] *sm inv* tomtom.

tana ['tana] *sf (gen)* lair, den; *(di conigli)* burrow; *(fig: nascondiglio)* den, hideout.

tanca ['tanka] *sf (tanica)* jerry can; *(Naut: serbatoio)* tank.

tandem ['tandem] *sm inv (bicicletta)* tandem.

tanfo ['tanfo] *sm* stench.

tangente [tan'dʒente] **1** *ag (Geom)*: **~ (a)** tangential (to). **2** *sf* **(a)** *(Geom)* tangent; **filare per la ~** *(fig: svignarsela)* to make one's getaway; **partire per la ~** *(fig: divagare)* to go off at a tangent. **(b)** *(Comm: quota)* share; *(denaro estorto)* rake-off *(fam)*, cut.

tangenza [tan'dʒɛntsa] *sf (Geom)* tangency; *(Aer)* ceiling.

tangenziale [tandʒen'tsjale] **1** *ag (Geom)* tangential; **retta ~** tangent. **2** *sf (strada)* bypass.

tanghero ['tangero] *sm (peg)* bumpkin.

tangibile [tan'dʒibile] *ag* tangible.

tango, ghi ['tango] *sm* tango.

tanica, che ['tanika] *sf* jerry can.

tannino [tan'nino] *sm* tannin.

tantino [tan'tino] **1**: **un ~** *av* a little, a bit; *(alquanto)* rather. **2** *sm*: **un ~ di** a little bit of; *(di liquidi)* a drop of.

tanto, a ['tanto] **1** *ag indef* **(a)** *(molto: quantità)* a lot of, much; *(: numero)* a lot of, many; *(così ~: quantità)* so much, such a lot of; *(: numero)* so many, such a lot of; **~e volte** so many times, so often; **c'è ancora ~a strada da fare!** there's still a long way to go!; **~e persone, ~e opinioni diverse** there are as many different opinions as there are people; **ogni ~i giorni/chilometri** every so many days/kilometres; **~i saluti da parte di mia madre** my mother sends her regards; **ti faccio ~i auguri** all the best; **~e grazie** many thanks.

(b) *(rafforzativo)* such; **l'ha detto con ~a gentilezza** he said it with such kindness *o* so kindly; **ho aspettato per ~ tempo** I waited so long *o* for such a long time.

(c): **~ ... quanto** *(quantità)* as much ... as; *(numero)* as many ... as; **ha ~i amici quanti nemici** he has as many friends as he has enemies; **ho ~i libri quanti ne ha lui** I have as many books as him *o* as he has; **ho ~a pazienza quanto ne hai tu** I am as patient as you are, I have as much patience as you (have).

2 *pron indef* **(a)** *(molto)* much, a lot; *(così ~)* so much, such a lot; **~i(e)** many, a lot; so many, such a lot; **credevo ce ne fosse ~** I thought there was (such) a lot, I thought there was plenty; **se cerchi un bicchiere, lassù ce ne sono ~i** if you are looking for a glass, there are a lot *o* lots up there; **è una ragazza come ~e** she's like any other girl; **~i credono sia semplice farlo** many people believe it is easy to do; **è solo uno dei ~i che...** he's just one of the many who... .

(b) *(altrettanto)*: **~ quanto** *(denaro)* as much as; *(cioccolatini etc)* as many as; **denaro? ne ho ~ quanto basta** money? I have as much as I need.

(c) *(con valore indeterminato)*: **della somma che ho a disposizione ~ andrà per il vitto, ~ per l'alloggio** of the sum at my disposal so much will go on board and so much on lodging; **nell'anno millecinquecento e ~i** in the year fifteen hundred and something; **riceve un ~ al mese** he receives so much a month; **costa un ~ al metro** it costs so much a metre.

(d) *(fraseologia)*: **di ~ in ~, ogni ~** every so often, now and again; **~ vale che...** you may *o* might as well...; **se ~ mi dà ~** oh well, if that's the case...; **~ di guadagnato!, ~ meglio così!** so much the better!; **ascoltava con ~ d'orecchie** he was all ears; **me ne ha dette ~e!** he gave me a real mouthful!; **lo guardò con ~ d'occhi** she gazed at him in wonder *(o* astonishment *etc)*; **è rimasto con ~ di naso** he was left feeling disappointed; **c'era una cameriera con ~ di grembiule bianco** there was a waitress with an enormous white apron.

3 *av* **(a)** *(così, in questo modo: con vb)* so much; *(: con av, ag)* so; **non lavorare ~!** don't work so hard!; **perché piangeva ~?** why was she crying so (much)?; **stanno ~ bene insieme!** they go so well together!; **~ ... che** so ... (that); **è ~ bello che sembra finto** it's so beautiful (that) it seems unreal; **~ ... da** so ... as; **saresti ~ gentile da prendermi una tazza?** would you be so kind as to pass me a cup?; **è stato ~ idiota da crederci** he was so stupid as to believe it.

(b) *(nei comparativi)*: **~ ... quanto** as ... as; **è ~ gentile quanto discreto** he is as kind as he is discreet; **non è poi ~ difficile quanto sembra** it is not as difficult as it seems after all; **mi piace non ~ per l'aspetto quanto per il suo carattere** I like her not so much for her looks as for her character.

(c) *(molto)* very; **vengo ~ volentieri** I'd be very glad to come; **non è poi ~ giovane** he is not all that young; **l'ho visto ~ giù** he seemed very fed up to me; **non ci vuole ~ a capirlo** it doesn't take much to understand it; **scusami ~** I'm very sorry, do excuse me; **sono ~ ~ contento di vederti** I'm so very happy to see you.

(d) *(a lungo)* (for) long; **starai via ~?** will you be away long?; **un'ora a dir ~** an hour at the most; **non stare fuori ~** don't stay out for long.

(e) *(solamente)* just; **parla ~ per parlare** he talks just for the sake of talking; **~ per cambiare** *(anche iro)* just for a change; **~ per fare due risate** just for a laugh; **una volta ~ potresti farlo** you could do it just for once.

(f): **~ più lo vedo ~ meno mi piace** the more I see him the less I like him; **~ più insisti, ~ più non mollerà** the more you insist the more stubborn he'll be.

4 *cong* after all; **lo farò, ~ non mi costa niente** I'll do it, after all it won't cost me anything; **fanne a meno, ~ a me non importa** do without then, I don't care; **è inutile che urli, ~ nessuno ti può sentire** there's no point in shouting, after all nobody can hear you.

tapioca [ta'pjɔka] *sf* tapioca.

tapiro [ta'piro] *sm* tapir.

tappa ['tappa] *sf* **(a)** *(luogo di sosta, fermata)* stop, halt. **(b)** *(Sport: parte di percorso)* stage, leg; *(fig: stadio)* stage; **a ~e** in stages; **bruciare le ~e** *(fig)* to be a whizz kid.

tappabuchi [tappa'buki] *sm inv* stopgap; **fare da ~** to act as a stopgap.

tappare [tap'pare] **1** *vt (otturare)* to plug, stop up; *(: bottiglia)* to cork; **~ un buco** *(fig)* to provide a short term remedy; **~ la bocca a qn** *(fig)* to shut sb up; **~rsi il naso** to hold one's nose; **~rsi le orecchie/gli occhi** to turn a deaf ear/a blind eye. **2: ~rsi** *vr*: **~rsi in casa** to shut o.s. up at home.

tapparella [tappa'rɛlla] *sf* rolling shutter.

tappeto [tap'peto] *sm* carpet; *(piccolo)* rug; *(stuoia)* mat; *(per tavoli)* cloth; **~ verde** green baize (cloth); *(tavolo da gioco)* gaming table; **~ erboso** lawn; **bombardamento a ~** carpet bombing; **andare al ~** *(Pugilato, fig)* to be floored; **mandare qn al ~** *(fig)* to floor sb; **mettere sul ~** *(fig: questione)* to table.

tappezzare [tappet'tsare] *vt (pareti)* to paper; *(divano, sedia)* to cover; **~ una stanza di manifesti** to cover a room with posters.

tappezzeria [tappettse'ria] *sf (arredamento)* soft furnishings *pl*; *(carta da parati)* wallpaper; *(di automobile)* upholstery; **fare da ~** *(fig)* to be a wallflower.

tappezziere, a [tappet'tsjere] *sm/f* upholsterer.

tappo ['tappo] *sm (di bottiglia: in sughero)* cork; *(: in vetro, plastica)* stopper; *(di barattolo, serbatoio, radiatore)* cap; *(di penna)* top; *(di vasca, lavandino)* plug; **~ a corona** bottle top; **~ a vite** screw top; **sei un ~!** *(scherz)* you're very tubby!

tara ['tara] *sf* **(a)** *(peso)* tare. **(b)** *(Med)* hereditary defect; *(difetto)* flaw.

tarantella [taran'tella] *sf (danza)* tarantella.

tarantola [ta'rantola] *sf* tarantula.

tarare [ta'rare] *vt (Comm)* to tare; *(Tecn)* to calibrate.

tarato, a [ta'rato] *ag* **(a)** *(Comm)* tared; *(Tecn)* calibrated. **(b)** *(Med)* with a hereditary defect; **ma tu sei ~!** *(scherz)* you're touched in the head.

taratura [tara'tura] *sf (Comm)* taring; *(Tecn)* calibration.

tarchiato, a [tar'kjato] *ag* stocky, thickset.

tardare [tar'dare] **1** *vi* to be late; **ha tardato molto** he was very late. **2** *vt* to delay; **~ a fare qc** to be late in doing sth.

tardi ['tardi] **1** *av* late; **svegliarsi ~** to wake up late, oversleep; **arrivare ~** to arrive late; **lavorare fino a ~** to work late; **ieri sera ho fatto ~** I stayed up late last night; **meglio ~ che mai** better late than never; **a più ~!** see you later!; **presto o ~** sooner or later; **sarò lì alle 9 al più ~** I'll be there by 9 at the latest; **si è fatto ~** it is late. **2** *sm*: **ci siamo incontrati sul ~** we met quite late.

tardivo, a [tar'divo] *ag (primavera, fioritura, sviluppo)* late; *(rimedio, pentimento)* belated, tardy.

tardo, a ['tardo] *ag (lento, ottuso)* slow; *(avanzato: mattinata, primavera)* late; *(tardivo: pentimento)* tardy.

tardona [tar'dona] *sf (peg)*: **essere una ~** to be mutton dressed as lamb.

tardone [tar'done] *sm* slowcoach.

targa, ghe ['targa] *sf (gen)* plate; *(su una porta)* nameplate; *(Aut)* number plate; *(placca)* plaque.

targare [tar'gare] *vt (Aut)* to register.

tariffa [ta'riffa] *sf (gen)* rate, tariff; *(di trasporti)* fare; **~e doganali** customs rates *o* tariff; **~e postali/telefoniche** postal/telephone charges; **~ normale/ridotta** standard/reduced rate; *(su mezzi di trasporto)* full/concessionary fare.

tariffario, ii [tarif'farjo] **1** *ag*: **aumento ~** increase in charges *o* rates. **2** *sm* tariff, table of charges.

tarlare [tar'lare] *vi (aus essere)*, **~rsi** *vr (legno)* to have woodworm; *(tessuto)* to be moth-eaten.

tarlo ['tarlo] *sm* woodworm; **il ~ del dubbio lo assillava** doubts gnawed at him; **~ della gelosia** pangs of jealousy.

tarma ['tarma] *sf* moth.

tarmare [tar'mare] *vi (aus essere)*, **~rsi** *vr* to be moth-eaten.

tarmicida, i [tarmi'tʃida] *ag, sm* moth-killer.

tarocco, chi [ta'rɔkko] *sm* tarot card; **~chi** *(gioco)* tarot *sg*.

tarpare [tar'pare] *vt (fig):* ~ **le ali a qn** to clip sb's wings.

tarso ['tarso] *sm (Anat)* tarsus.

tartagliare [tartaʎ'ʎare] **1** *vi* to stutter, stammer. **2** *vt* to mutter.

tartaro, a ['tartaro] **1** *ag (Storia)* Tartar; *(Culin)* tartar(e); **bistecca alla** ~**a** steak tartare. **2** *sm/f* Tartar.

tartaruga, ghe [tarta'ruga] *sf* tortoise; *(di mare)* turtle; *(materiale)* tortoiseshell; **zuppa di** ~ turtle soup; **essere lento come una** ~ to be a slowcoach.

tartassare [tartas'sare] *vt (fam):* ~ **qn** to give sb the works; ~ **qn a un esame** to give sb a grilling at an exam; **smettila di** ~ **quel piano!** stop thumping on that piano!

tartina [tar'tina] *sf* canapé.

tartufo [tar'tufo] *sm* truffle.

tasca, sche ['taska] *sf* pocket; *(scomparto: di valigia etc)* compartment; *(Zool, Anat)* pouch; ~ **dei pantaloni** trouser pocket; **da** ~ pocket *attr;* **non ho un soldo in** ~ *(al momento)* I haven't any money on me; *(essere al verde)* I'm broke; **riempirsi le** ~**sche di qc** to fill one's pockets with sth; **non startene con le mani in** ~ *(fig)* don't just stand there with your hands in your pockets; **non me ne viene niente in** ~ *(fig)* I get nothing out of it; **che cosa me ne viene in** ~? *(fig)* what do I stand to gain from that?; **fare i conti in** ~ **a qn** *(fig)* to meddle in sb's affairs; **conosco Roma come le mie** ~**sche** I know Rome like the back of my hand; **averne le** ~**sche piene di** *(fig)* to be fed up with.

tascabile [tas'kabile] **1** *ag (libro)* pocket *attr.* **2** *sm* ≃ paperback.

tascapane [taska'pane] *sm inv* haversack.

taschino [tas'kino] *sm* breast pocket.

tassa ['tassa] *sf (imposta)* tax; *(doganale)* duty; *(Scol, Univ)* fee; ~ **di circolazione/di soggiorno** road/tourist tax; **soggetto a** ~**e** taxable.

tassametro [tas'sametro] *sm* taximeter.

tassare [tas'sare] **1** *vt (gen)* to tax; *(sog: Dogana)* to levy a duty on. **2:** ~**rsi** *vr:* ~**rsi per** to chip in, contribute.

tassativo, a [tassa'tivo] *ag* peremptory.

tassazione [tassat'tsjone] *sf* taxation; **soggetto a** ~ taxable.

tassello [tas'sɛllo] *sm (pezzetto di legno, pietra etc)* plug; *(per vestiti)* gusset; *(assaggio: di formaggio, cocomero etc)* wedge.

tassì [tas'si] *sm inv* = **taxi.**

tassista, i, e [tas'sista] *sm/f* taxi driver, cab driver.

tasso[1] ['tasso] *sm (di natalità, d'interesse etc)* rate; ~ **di cambio/di interesse** rate of exchange/of interest.

tasso[2] ['tasso] *sm (Bot)* yew.

tasso[3] ['tasso] *sm (Zool)* badger.

tastare [tas'tare] *vt* to feel; ~ **il polso a qn** to feel sb's pulse; ~ **il terreno** to probe the ground; *(fig)* to see how the land lies.

tastiera [tas'tjɛra] *sf (gen, Mus, Inform)* keyboard; *(di strumenti a corda)* fingerboard.

tasto ['tasto] *sm (gen, Tecn, Mus)* key; *(tatto)* touch, feel; *(fig: argomento)* topic, subject; **toccare un** ~ **delicato** *(fig)* to touch on a delicate subject; **toccare il** ~ **giusto** *(fig)* to strike the right note.

tastoni [tas'toni] *av:* **procedere (a)** ~ to grope one's way forward.

tatticismo [tatti'tʃizmo] *sm* use of tactics.

tattico, a, ci, che ['tattiko] **1** *ag* tactical. **2** *sf* tactics *pl.*

tattile ['tattile] *ag* tactile.

tatto ['tatto] *sm (senso)* touch; *(fig: diplomazia)* tact;

duro al ~ hard to the touch; **aver** ~ *(fig)* to be tactful, have tact.

tatuaggio [tatu'addʒo] *sm* tattoo.

tatuare [tatu'are] **1** *vt* to tattoo. **2:** ~**rsi** *vr* to have o.s. tattooed.

taurino, a [tau'rino] *ag* bull-like; **ha un collo** ~ he is bullnecked.

taverna [ta'vɛrna] *sf (osteria)* tavern.

tavola ['tavola] **1** *sf* **(a)** *(mobile)* table; **a** ~! come and eat!; **essere a** ~ to be having a meal, be at table; **preparare la** ~ to lay *o* set the table; **sedersi a** ~ to sit down to eat, sit down at the table; **ama i piaceri della** ~ he enjoys his food. **(b)** *(asse)* plank, board; **il mare è una** ~ the sea is like a millpond. **(c)** *(tabella)* table; *(illustrazione)* plate; *(quadro su legno)* painting; ~**e pitagoriche** multiplication tables. **2:** ~ **calda** snack bar; ~ **rotonda** *(anche fig)* round table; ~ **reale** *(gioco)* backgammon.

tavolata [tavo'lata] *sf* company at table.

tavolato [tavo'lato] *sm* **(a)** planking; *(di palco, palcoscenico)* boards *pl.* **(b)** *(Geog)* plateau.

tavoletta [tavo'letta] *sf (di cioccolata)* bar; **andare a** ~ *(Aut)* to go flat out.

tavolino [tavo'lino] *sm (gen)* small table; *(scrittoio, banco)* desk; ~ **da tè/gioco** coffee/card table; **mettersi a** ~ to get down to work; **decidere qc a** ~ *(fig)* to decide sth on a theoretical level.

tavolo ['tavolo] **1** *sm* table; *(scrittoio)* desk. **2:** ~ **da disegno** drawing board; ~ **da lavoro** desk; *(Tecn)* workbench; ~ **operatorio** operating table; ~ **da stiro** ironing board.

tavolozza [tavo'lɔttsa] *sf (Arte)* palette.

taxi ['taksi] *sm inv* taxi.

tazza ['tattsa] *sf* cup; *(contenuto)* cupful; *(di gabinetto)* (lavatory) pan; ~ **da caffè** coffee cup; ~ **da tè** teacup; **una** ~ **di tè** a cup of tea.

tazzina [tat'tsina] *sf* coffee cup.

te [te] *pron pers* **(a)** *(dopo prep, accentato)* you; **lo ha dato a** ~, **non a me** he gave it to you *o* YOU, not to me; **parlavamo di** ~ we were talking about you; **vengo con** ~ I'm coming with you; **dietro di** ~ behind you; **verrò da** ~ I'll come round to your place, I'll drop in and see you; **fallo da** ~ do it yourself; **se fossi in** ~ if I were you; **povero** ~! poor you! **(b)** *(nelle comparazioni)* you; **è alto come** ~ he's as tall as you (are); **parla come** ~ she speaks like you (do); **è più giovane di** ~ he's younger than you (are). **(c)** *vedi* **ti.**

tè [te] *sm inv* tea; *(pianta)* tea plant; *(trattenimento)* tea party; **da** ~ tea *attr;* **vuoi un** ~? would you like a cup of tea?

teatrale [tea'trale] *ag (spettacolo)* theatrical, stage *attr;* *(attore)* stage *attr;* *(stagione, compagnia)* theatre *attr;* *(fig: gesto, atteggiamento)* theatrical; **siamo andati a vedere uno spettacolo** ~ we went to the theatre.

teatralità [teatrali'ta] *sf (anche fig)* theatricality.

teatro [te'atro] *sm* **(a)** *(edificio)* theatre, playhouse; *(pubblico)* house, audience; *(fig: luogo)* scene; **andare a** ~ to go to the theatre; **il** ~ **era pieno** there was a full house; ~ **di posa** film studio; **il** ~ **delle operazioni** *(Mil)* the theatre of operations; **la sua casa è stata** ~ **di un orrendo delitto** his house was the scene of a hideous crime. **(b)** *(genere)* theatre; *(professione)* theatre, stage; **il** ~ **classico** the classical theatre, classical drama; ~ **comico** comedy; ~ **lirico** opera; **il** ~ **di Pirandello** Pirandello's plays *o* dramatic works, the theatre of Pirandello; **interessarsi di** ~ to be interested in drama *o* the theatre; **uomo di** ~ man of the theatre *o* stage.

teca, che ['tɛka] *sf (Rel)* reliquary.

technicolor [tekni'kɔlor] *sm* ® Technicolor®.

tecnica, che ['tɛknika] *sf (scienza)* technology; *(metodo)* technique.

tecnicismo [tekni'tʃizmo] *sm* **(a)** *(predominio dell'aspetto tecnico)* excessive attention to technical details. **(b)** *(termine tecnico)* technical term.

tecnico, a, ci, che ['tɛkniko] **1** *ag* technical. **2** *sm/f* technician; *(esperto)* expert; ~ **del suono/della televisione** sound/television engineer.

tecnicolor [tekni'kɔlor] *sm* = **technicolor**.

tecnocrate [tek'nɔkrate] *sm/f* technocrat.

tecnocrazia [teknokrat'tsia] *sf* technocracy.

tecnologia, gie [teknolo'dʒia] *sf (scienza)* technology; *(tecnica)* technique.

tecnologico, a, ci, che [tekno'lɔdʒiko] *ag* technological.

tedesco, a, schi, sche [te'desko] *ag, sm/f, sm* German.

tediare [te'djare] *vt (infastidire)* to bother, annoy; *(annoiare)* to bore.

tedio ['tɛdjo] *sm* tedium, boredom.

tedioso, a [te'djoso] *ag* tedious, boring.

Teflon ['teflon] *sm* ® Teflon®.

tegame [te'game] *sm (Culin)* (frying) pan; *(contenuto)* panful; **al** ~ fried.

teglia ['teʎʎa] *sf (Culin: per dolci)* (baking) tin; *(: per arrosti)* (roasting) tin.

tegola ['tegola] *sf* (roofing) tile.

tegumento [tegu'mento] *sm (Bio)* integument.

teiera [te'jɛra] *sf* teapot.

tek ['tek] *sm inv* teak.

tela ['tela] *sf* **(a)** *(tessuto)* cloth; **di** ~ *(lenzuolo)* linen; *(pantaloni)* (heavy) cotton *attr*; *(scarpe, borsa)* canvas *attr*; **rilegato in** ~ clothbound; ~ **cerata** oilcloth; ~ **di ragno** spider's web. **(b)** *(Pittura: supporto)* canvas; *(: dipinto)* canvas, painting.

telaio [te'lajo] *sm (per tessere)* loom; *(struttura)* frame; *(Aut)* chassis; ~ **da ricamo** embroidery frame.

tele ['tɛle] *sf inv (fam)* telly.

teleabbonato [teleabbo'nato] *sm* television licence holder.

telecamera [tele'kamera] *sf* television camera.

telecomandare [telekoman'dare] *vt* to operate by remote control.

telecomando [teleko'mando] *sm* remote control; *(dispositivo)* remote-control device.

telecomunicazioni [telekomunikat'tsjoni] *sfpl* telecommunications.

telecronaca, che [tele'krɔnaka] *sf* television report.

telecronista, i, e [telekro'nista] *sm/f* (television) commentator.

teleferica, che [tele'fɛrika] *sf* cableway.

telefilm [tele'film] *sm inv* television film.

telefonare [telefo'nare] **1** *vi* to (tele)phone, ring; *(fare una chiamata)* to make a phone call; ~ **a qn** to telephone sb, phone *o* ring *o* call sb (up); **sta telefonando** he is on the phone. **2** *vt* to (tele)phone.

telefonata [telefo'nata] *sf* (telephone) call; ~ **a carico del destinatario** reverse charge call; ~ **con preavviso** person-to-person call; ~ **urbana/interurbana** local/long-distance call; ~ **in teleselezione** STD call.

telefonia [telefo'nia] *sf* telephony.

telefonico, a, ci, che [tele'fɔniko] *ag* (tele)phone *attr*.

telefonista, i, e [telefo'nista] *sm/f* telephonist; *(di impresa)* switchboard operator.

telefono [te'lefono] *sm (sistema)* telephone; *(apparecchio)* telephone, phone; **avere il** ~ to be

on the (tele)phone; ~ **pubblico** public phone, call box; ~ **interno** internal phone; ~ **a gettoni** pay phone.

telegiornale [teledʒor'nale] *sm* television news (programme).

telegrafare [telegra'fare] *vt, vi* to telegraph, cable.

telegrafia [telegra'fia] *sf* telegraphy.

telegrafico, a, ci, che [tele'grafiko] *ag* telegraph *attr*; *(fig: stile)* telegraphic.

telegrafista, i, e [telegra'fista] *sm/f* telegraphist, telegraph operator.

telegrafo [te'lɛgrafo] *sm* telegraph; *(ufficio)* telegraph office.

telegramma, i [tele'gramma] *sm* telegram.

telematica [tele'matika] *sf* data transmission.

teleobiettivo [teleobjet'tivo] *sm* telephoto lens *sg*.

telepatia [telepa'tia] *sf* telepathy.

telepatico, a, ci, che [tele'patiko] *ag* telepathic.

telequiz [tele'kwits] *sm inv* television quiz.

teleschermo [teles'kermo] *sm* television screen.

telescopico, a, ci, che [teles'kɔpiko] *ag* telescopic.

telescopio [teles'kɔpjo] *sm* telescope; **a** ~ telescopic.

telescrivente [teleskri'vɛnte] **1** *ag* teleprinting. **2** *sf* teleprinter.

teleselettiva, a [teleselet'tivo] *ag*: **prefisso** ~ STD code, dialling code.

teleselezione [teleselet'tsjone] *sf* ≃ subscriber trunk dialling *(abbr* STD).

telespettatore, trice [telespetta'tore] *sm/f* (television) viewer.

teletaxe [tele'taks] *sm inv* ® telephone meter.

teletrasmesso, a [teletraz'messo] *pp di* **teletrasmettere**.

teletrasmettere [teletraz'mettere] *vt* to televise.

televisione [televi'zjone] *sf (gen)* television; *(televisore)* television (set); **alla** ~ on television.

televisivo, a [televi'zivo] *ag* television *attr*.

televisore [televi'zore] *sm* television set.

telex ['tɛleks] **1** *ag inv* telex *attr*. **2** *sm inv* telex.

telo ['telo] *sm* length of cloth.

telone [te'lone] *sm* **(a)** *(per merci etc)* tarpaulin. **(b)** *(sipario)* drop curtain.

tema, i ['tɛma] *sm* **(a)** *(argomento)* theme; *(: di conversazione)* subject, topic; *(Mus)* theme, motif; *(Scol)* essay, composition; ~ **libero** *(Scol)* free composition; **andare fuori** ~ to go off the subject. **(b)** *(Linguistica)* theme, stem.

tematica [te'matika] *sf* basic themes *pl*.

tematico, a, ci, che [te'matiko] *ag (tutti i sensi)* thematic.

temerarietà [temerarje'ta] *sf* recklessness, rashness.

temerario, a [teme'rarjo] **1** *ag* reckless, rash. **2** *sm/f* reckless person.

temere [te'mere] **1** *vt* to be afraid of, fear; **temo il pericolo** I am afraid of danger; **temo che non venga** I am afraid he won't come; **temo di non farcela** I am afraid I won't make it; ~ **il peggio** to fear the worst; ~ **una brutta sorpresa** to expect a nasty surprise; ~ **il freddo** *(pianta)* to be sensitive to cold. **2** *vi* to fear; ~ **per** to fear for; **non** ~! don't be afraid!; *(non preoccuparti)* don't worry!

tempaccio [tem'pattʃo] *sm* bad weather.

tempera ['tɛmpera] *sf* **(a)** *(Arte: colore, tecnica)* tempera; *(: dipinto)* painting in tempera; **colori a** ~ tempera; **dipingere a** ~ to paint in tempera. **(b)** *(Tecn)* = **tempra**.

temperalapis [tempera'lapis] *sm inv*, **temperamatite** [temperama'tite] *sm inv* pencil sharpener.

temperamento [tempera'mento] *sm (carattere)* temperament, character; **è nervoso di** ~ he has a nervous temperament o disposition o character; **lo fa per** ~ it's just his nature; **manca di** ~ he's weak-willed.

temperante [tempe'rante] *ag* moderate.

temperare [tempe'rare] *vt* **(a)** *(matita)* to sharpen. **(b)** *(metalli)* to temper.

temperato, a [tempe'rato] *ag* **(a)** *(moderato)* moderate, temperate; *(clima)* temperate. **(b)** *(acciaio)* tempered.

temperatura [tempera'tura] *sf* temperature; ~ **ambiente** room temperature.

temperino [tempe'rino] *sm* penknife.

tempesta [tem'pesta] *sf* storm; ~ **di sabbia/neve** sand/snowstorm; **il mare era in** ~ the sea was stormy.

tempestare [tempes'tare] *vt* **(a)**: ~ **qn di colpi** to rain blows on sb; ~ **qn di domande** to bombard sb with questions. **(b)** *(ornare)* to stud.

tempestività [tempestivi'ta] *sf* timeliness.

tempestivo, a [tempes'tivo] *ag* timely, well-timed.

tempestoso, a [tempes'toso] *ag* stormy.

tempia ['tɛmpja] *sf (Anat)* temple.

tempio ['tɛmpjo] *sm (anche fig)* temple.

tempismo [tem'pizmo] *sm* sense of timing.

tempista, i, e [tem'pista] *sm/f* **(a)** *(fig)* person with a good sense of timing. **(b)** *(Sport: cronometrista)* timekeeper.

tempo ['tɛmpo] *sm* **(a)** *(gen)* time; **il ~ e lo spazio** time and space; **il ~ vola!** time flies!; **il ~ stringe** time is short; **ci vuole** ~ it takes time; **abbiamo** ~ **3 giorni** we have 3 days; **c'è** o **abbiamo** ~ there is plenty of time; **c'è sempre** ~ there is still time; **non c'è** ~ **da perdere** there is no time to lose; **perdere** ~ to waste time; **trovare il** ~ **di fare qc** to find the time to do sth; **con l'andare del** ~ with the passing of time; **a** ~ **di record** in record time; **un impiego a** ~ **pieno** a full-time job; **nei ritagli di** ~, **a** ~ **perso** in one's spare moments; ~ **libero** free o spare time.

(b) *(periodo)* time; **da** ~ for a long time now; **da quanto** ~? since when?; ~ **fa** some time ago; **poco** ~ **dopo** not long after; **per qualche** ~ for a while; **dove sei stato tutto questo** ~? where have you been all this time?; **a** ~ **e luogo** at the right time and place; **a suo** ~ in due course, at the appropriate time; **ogni cosa a suo** ~ we'll (o you'll *etc*) deal with it in due course; **in** ~ **utile** in due time o course; **al** ~ **stesso** at the same time; **fare in** ~ **a fare qc** to manage to do sth; **farai in** ~ **a prendere il treno?** will you be in time for the train?, will you manage to catch the train?; **arrivare/essere in** ~ to arrive/be in time; **per** ~ in good time; **un** ~ once.

(c) *(durata di un'operazione)* time; *(fase)* stage; ~ **di cottura** cooking time; ~**i di lavorazione** *(Industria)* throughput time; **rispettare i** ~**i** to keep to the timetable; **stringere i** ~**i** to speed things up.

(d) *(stagione)* season; **quando arriva il** ~ **delle ciliege** when the cherries ripen.

(e) *(epoca)* time; **al** ~ **della Rivoluzione Culturale** at the time of o in the days of the Cultural Revolution; ~**i duri** hard times; **altri** ~**i!** those were the days!; **con i** ~**i che corrono** these days; **andare al passo con i** ~**i** to keep pace with the times; **nella notte dei** ~**i** in the dim and distant past; **in** ~ **di pace** in peace time; **in questi ultimi** ~**i** of late; **ai miei** ~**i** in my day; **quel maglione ha fatto il suo** ~ that pullover has had its day.

(f) *(condizioni atmosferiche)* weather; **che** ~ **fa?** what's the weather like?; **fa bel/brutto** ~ the weather's fine/bad; **con questo** ~**!** in this weather!; **previsioni** *fpl* **del** ~ weather forecast *sg*.

(g) *(Mus)* time; *(: grado di velocità)* tempo; *(: movimento)* movement; **andare a** ~ to keep time; **essere fuori** ~ to be out of time; **battere** o **segnare il** ~ to mark time; **in tre** ~**i** in triple time.

(h) *(Gram)* tense; ~ **presente** present tense.

(i) *(di film)* part; *(di incontro sportivo)* half; ~**i supplementari** extra time *sg*.

(j) *(di motore a scoppio)* stroke; **motore a due** ~**i** two-stroke engine.

(k) *(fraseologia)*: **dare** ~ **al** ~ to let matters take their course; **chi ha** ~ **non aspetti** ~ there's no time like the present; **fare il bello e il cattivo** ~ to rule the roost; **il tuo rimprovero lascia il** ~ **che trova** I don't care what you think; **prendiamo** ~ let's play for time; **senza** ~ timeless.

temporale¹ [tempo'rale] *sm* (thunder)storm.

temporale² [tempo'rale] **1** *ag (gen)* temporal; **avverbi** ~**i** adverbs of time. **2** *sf (Gram)* time clause.

temporalesco, a, schi, sche [tempora'lesko] *ag* stormy.

temporaneità [temporanei'ta] *sf* temporariness, provisional nature.

temporaneo, a [tempo'raneo] *ag* temporary.

temporeggiamento [tempored dʒa'mento] *sm* playing for time, temporizing.

temporeggiare [tempored'dʒare] *vi* to play for time, temporize.

temporeggiatore, trice [tempored dʒa'tore] *sm/f* temporizer.

tempra ['tempra] *sf* **(a)** *(Tecn: atto)* tempering, hardening; *(: effetto)* temper. **(b)** *(fig: costituzione fisica)* constitution; *(: intellettuale)* temperament.

temprare [tem'prare] **1** *vt (gen, Tecn)* to temper; *(fig)* to strengthen, toughen. **2**: ~**rsi** *vr (anche fig)* to become stronger, become tougher.

tenace [te'natʃe] *ag (filo, colla)* strong; *(fig: odio, amicizia)* lasting; *(: persona)* tenacious.

tenacia [te'natʃa] *sf* tenacity.

tenacità [tenatʃi'ta] *sf (Tecn)* toughness.

tenaglie [te'naʎʎe] *sfpl (arnese, chele)* pincers *pl*; *(del dentista)* forceps *pl*.

tenda ['tɛnda] *sf* **(a)** *(riparo: di negozio, terrazza)* awning; *(di finestra)* curtain; **tirare le** ~**e** to draw the curtains. **(b)** *(Mil, da campeggio etc)* tent; **la** ~ **del circo** the big top; **piantare le** ~**e** to pitch one's tent; *(fig)* to settle down; **è ora di levar le** ~**e** *(fig)* it's time to hit the trail; ~ **a ossigeno** oxygen tent.

tendaggio [ten'daddʒo] *sm* curtaining, curtains *pl*.

tendenza [ten'dentsa] *sf (gen)* tendency; *(inclinazione)* inclination; *(orientamento: Pol, Econ)* trend; **ha la** ~ **a ingrassare** she tends to put on weight; **avere una** ~ **per qc** to have a bent for sth; **con** ~ **al bello** *(Meteor)* tending to fair; ~ **al rialzo/ribasso** upward/downward trend.

tendenziosità [tendentsjosi'ta] *sf* tendentiousness.

tendenzioso, a [tenden'tsjoso] *ag* tendentious, biased.

tendere ['tɛndere] **1** *vt* **(a)** *(mettere in tensione: corda)* to tighten, pull tight; *(: elastico, muscoli)* to stretch; *(: tessuto)* to stretch, pull tight, draw tight; ~ **una trappola a qn** to set a trap for sb. **(b)** *(sporgere: collo)* to crane; *(: mano)* to hold out; *(: braccio)* to stretch out; ~ **la mano** to hold out one's hand; *(fig: chiedere l'elemosina)* to beg; *(: aiutare)* to lend a helping hand; ~ **le orecchie** *(fig)* to prick up one's ears.

2 *vi*: ~ **a fare qc** *(aver la tendenza)* to tend to do sth; ~ **a qc/a fare qc** (mirare a) to aim at sth/to do sth; **era chiaro che tendeva a restare in casa** it was clear that he intended to remain at home; **tutti i nostri sforzi sono tesi a...** all our efforts are geared towards...; **tende al pessimismo** he tends to be pessimistic; ~ **a sinistra** (Pol) to have left-wing tendencies; **la situazione tende a migliorare** the situation is improving; **il tempo tende al bello** the weather is improving; **un blu che tende al verde** a greenish blue.

tendina [ten'dina] sf curtain.

tendine ['tendine] sm tendon, sinew.

tendone [ten'done] sm (di circo) big top.

tendopoli [ten'dɔpoli] sf inv (large) camp.

tenebre ['tɛnebre] sfpl darkness sg, gloom.

tenebroso, a [tene'broso] ag dark, gloomy; (fig) mysterious.

tenente [te'nɛnte] sm lieutenant.

tenere [te'nere] **1** vt (a) (reggere: in mano) to hold; (: in posizione) to hold, keep; (: in alto) to keep; **tieni!** (prendilo) here!; ~ **qn per mano** to hold sb by the hand; ~ **una pentola per il manico** to hold a pan by the handle; **tieni la porta aperta** hold the door open; **tengono sempre la porta aperta** they always keep their door open; **tiene sempre la camicia sbottonata** he always has his shirt unbuttoned; ~ **le mani in tasca** to keep one's hands in one's pockets; **tieni gli occhi chiusi** keep your eyes shut o closed; **un cappotto che tiene caldo** a warm coat; **tiene la casa molto bene** her house is always tidy; ~ **la rotta** (Naut) to stay on course; **il nemico teneva la città** the enemy had the city under its control o held the city; ~ **la destra/la sinistra** (Aut) to keep to the right/the left.

(b) (dare: conferenza, corso etc) to give; (organizzare: riunione, assemblea) to hold.

(c) (occupare: spazio) to take up; ~ **il posto a qn** to keep sb's seat.

(d) (contenere: sog: recipiente) to hold.

(e) (resistere a): **che tiene l'acqua** (tessuto) waterproof; (contenitore) watertight; ~ **il mare** (Naut) to be seaworthy; ~ **la strada** (Aut) to hold the road.

(f) (considerare): ~ **conto di qn/qc** to take sb/sth into account o consideration; ~ **in gran conto** o **considerazione qn** to have a high regard for sb, think highly of sb.

2 vi (a) (resistere) to hold out, last; (: chiusura, nodo) to hold; **tiene quella scatola?** is that box strong enough?; **questa vite non tiene** this screw is loose; **non ci sono scuse che tengano** I'll take no excuses.

(b) (parteggiare): ~ **per qn/qc** to support sb/sth; **io tengo per lui** I am on his side.

(c): ~ **a** (reputazione, persona, vestiario) to attach great importance to; **tiene molto all'educazione** he is a great believer in education.

(d): **tenerci: tenerci a** to attach great importance to; **ci tengo ad ottenere la presidenza** I aim to become chairman; **ci tenevo ad andare** I was keen on going; **ci tiene che lo sappia** he wants him to know; **non ci tengo** I don't care about it, it's not that important to me; **se ci tieni proprio!** if you really want!

3: ~**rsi** vr (a) (reggersi): ~**rsi a qn/qc** to hold onto sb/sth; ~**rsi per la mano** (uso reciproco) to hold hands; ~**rsi in piedi** to stay on one's feet; **non si teneva più dal ridere** (fig) he couldn't help laughing, he couldn't keep from laughing.

(b) (mantenersi) to keep, be; ~**rsi pronto (a fare qc)** to be ready (to do sth); ~**rsi vicino al/lontano dal muro** to keep close to/away from the wall; ~**rsi sulla corsia di destra** to stay in the right-hand lane; ~**rsi a destra/sinistra** to keep right/left.

(c) (attenersi): ~**rsi a** to comply with, stick to.

tenerezza [tene'rettsa] sf tenderness; **che ~ che mi fa questo piccolino!** what a lovely little baby!; **non sono abituato a tutte queste ~e** I am not used to all this attention.

tenero, a ['tɛnero] **1** ag (a) (carne, verdura) tender; (pietra, cera, colore) soft; **grano ~** soft wheat; **erba ~a** young grass; **è morto in ~a età** he died young; **alla sua ~a età** (scherz) at his tender age. (b) (indulgente) soft, tender; (che esprime tenerezza) tender; **un ~ padre** a loving father; **avere il cuore ~** to be tender-hearted; **che ~!** how lovely! **2** sm (a) (parte tenera) tender part. (b) (affetto): **tra quei due c'è del ~** there's a romance budding between those two.

tenia ['tenja] sf tapeworm.

tennis ['tɛnnis] sm tennis; **giocare a ~** to play tennis; **da ~** tennis attr; ~ **da tavolo** table tennis.

tennista, i, e [ten'nista] sm/f tennis player.

tennistico, a, ci, che [ten'nistiko] ag tennis attr.

tenore [te'nore] sm (a) (tono) tone; **il ~ della sua lettera** the tone of his letter; ~ **di vita** standard of living. (b) (Mus) tenor.

tensione [ten'sjone] sf (gen) tension; (Elettr) tension, voltage; ~ **arteriosa** arterial tension; **ad alta ~** (Elettr) high-voltage attr, high-tension attr; **c'è un po' di ~** (fig) things are rather tense.

tentacolo [ten'takolo] sm (anche fig) tentacle.

tentare [ten'tare] vt (a) (provare): ~ **qc/di fare qc** to attempt o try sth/to do sth; **ho tentato l'esame, ma non l'ho passato** I attempted the exam but I didn't pass it; ~ **il suicidio** to attempt suicide, try to commit suicide; ~ **un nuovo metodo** (sperimentare) to try out a new method; **le ho tentate tutte** I have tried them all; (per convincere qn) I have tried every way; ~ **la sorte** to try one's luck; **il tentar non nuoce** there's no harm in trying. (b) (cercare di corrompere, allettare) to tempt; (mettere alla prova) to test.

tentativo [tenta'tivo] sm attempt; **fa' ancora un ~** try again; ~ **di suicidio** suicide attempt.

tentatore, trice [tenta'tore] **1** ag tempting. **2** sm/f tempter/temptress.

tentazione [tentat'tsjone] sf temptation; **aver la ~ di fare** to be tempted to do.

tentennamento [tentenna'mento] sm (fig) hesitation, wavering; **dopo molti ~i** after much hesitation.

tentennare [tenten'nare] **1** vi (persona) to totter, stagger; (fig) to hesitate; **il vecchio uscì tentennando** the old man staggered out. **2** vt: ~ **il capo** to shake one's head.

tentoni [ten'toni] av (anche fig): **a ~** gropingly; **andare (a) ~** to grope one's way.

tenue ['tenue] ag (a) (colore) soft; (voce) feeble; (sole) faint; (fig: speranza) slender, slight. (b) (Anat): **intestino ~** small intestine.

tenuta [te'nuta] sf (a) (capacità) capacity; **a ~ d'aria** airtight; ~ **di strada** (Aut) roadholding. (b) (divisa) uniform; **in ~ da lavoro** in one's working clothes; **in ~ da sci** in a skiing outfit; **in ~ da calciatore** in a football strip. (c) (podere) estate.

tenutaria [tenu'tarja] sf brothel madam.

teologia [teolo'dʒia] sf theology.

teologico, a, ci, che [teolo'dʒiko] ag theological.

teologo, gi [te'ɔlogo] sm theologian.

teorema, i [teo'rema] sm (Mat) theorem.

teoretico, a, ci, che [teo'retiko] ag theoretical.

teoria [teo'ria] *sf* theory; **in** ~ in theory, theoretically.

teorico, a, ci, che [te'ɔriko] **1** *ag* theoretical; **a livello** ~, **in linea** ~**a** theoretically. **2** *sm* theorist, theoretician.

teorizzare [teorid'dzare] *vt* to theorize.

tepido, a ['tɛpido] *ag* = **tiepido**.

tepore [te'pore] *sm* warmth.

teppa ['teppa] *sf* mob, hooligans *pl*.

teppaglia [tep'paʎʎa] *sf* hooligans *pl*.

teppismo [tep'pizmo] *sm* hooliganism.

teppista, i, e [tep'pista] *sm/f* hooligan.

terapeutico, a, ci, che [tera'pɛutiko] *ag* therapeutic.

terapia [tera'pia] *sf* (*Med*) therapeutics *sg*, therapy; (*: cura*) therapy, treatment; ~ **del sonno** sleep therapy.

terapista, i, e [tera'pista] *sm/f* therapist.

tergicristallo [terdʒikris'tallo] *sm* windscreen wiper.

tergiversare [terdʒiver'sare] *vi* to beat about the bush.

tergo, ghi ['tergo] *sm* back; (*di moneta*) reverse; **a** ~ behind; **vedi a** ~ please turn over.

terital ['terital] *sm inv* ® Terylene®.

termale [ter'male] *ag* thermal; **sorgente** *f* ~ hot spring; **stazione** *f* ~ spa.

terme ['terme] *sfpl* (thermal) baths.

termico, a, ci, che ['tɛrmiko] *ag* (*Fis*) thermic; **centrale** ~**a** thermal power station; **trattamento** ~ heat treatment.

terminal ['tɔ:minl] *sm inv* (*gen*) terminal; (*Aer*) city-centre terminal.

terminale [termi'nale] **1** *ag* (*fase, parte*) final; (*Med*) terminal; **tratto** ~ (*di fiume*) lower reaches. **2** *sm* terminal.

terminare [termi'nare] **1** *vt* to end; (*lavoro*) to finish; (*cibo, provviste*) to be out of; **dopo aver terminato l'università** after finishing university. **2** *vi* (*aus* **essere**) to end; ~ **a punta** to end in a point; ~ **in consonante** to end in *o* with a consonant; **la pioggia è terminata** the rain stopped; **dove termina la valle c'è un lago** there is a lake at the end of the valley.

terminazione [terminat'tsjone] *sf* (*fine*) end; (*Gram*) ending; ~**i nervose** (*Anat*) nerve endings.

termine ['tɛrmine] *sm* (**a**) (*confine*) boundary, limit; (*punto estremo*) end; **al** ~ **della strada** at the end of the road; **porre** ~ **a qc** to put an end to sth; **avere** ~ to end; **portare a** ~ **qc** to bring sth to a conclusion. (**b**) (*spazio di tempo*) stipulated period; (*scadenza*) deadline; **entro un** ~ **di tre ore** within three hours; **fissare un** ~ to set a deadline; **entro il** ~ **convenuto** within the stipulated period; **a breve/lungo** ~ short/long term; **contratto a** ~ fixed-term contract. (**c**): ~**i** (*condizioni*) terms; (*limiti*) limits; **ai** ~**i di legge** by law; **questo contratto non è valido ai** ~**i di legge** this contract is not valid under law; **fissare i** ~**i della questione** to define the problem; **la questione sta in questi** ~**i** this is how the matter stands; **lasciarsi in buoni** ~**i** to part on good terms. (**d**) (*Gram, Mat*) term; **ridurre ai minimi** ~**i** (*Mat*) to reduce to the lowest terms; ~**i di paragone** terms of comparison; **in altri** ~**i** in other words; **modera i** ~**i!** moderate your language!; **parlare senza mezzi** ~**i** not to mince one's words.

terminologia [terminolo'dʒia] *sf* terminology.

termite ['tɛrmite] *sf* termite.

termocoperta [termoko'pɛrta] *sf* electric blanket.

termodinamica [termodi'namika] *sf* thermodynamics *sg*.

termodinamico, a, ci, che [termodi'namiko] *ag* thermodynamic.

termometro [ter'mɔmetro] *sm* (*anche fig*) thermometer.

termonucleare [termonukle'are] *ag* thermonuclear.

termos ['tɛrmos] *sm inv* = **thermos**.

termosifone [termosi'fone] *sm* radiator; (*riscaldamento* **a**) ~ central heating.

termostato [ter'mɔstato] *sm* thermostat.

terna ['tɛrna] *sf* set of three; (*lista di tre nomi*) list of three candidates.

ternario, a [ter'narjo] *ag* (*Poesia: verso*) three-syllable *attr*; (*Chim*) ternary.

terno ['tɛrno] *sm* (*al lotto etc*) (set of) three winning numbers; **vincere un** ~ **al lotto** (*fig*) to hit the jackpot.

terra ['tɛrra] **1** *sf* (**a**): **la** ~ (*pianeta*) the earth; (*fig: mondo*) the world; **sulla faccia della** ~ on the face of the earth; **i piaceri di questa** ~ the pleasures of this world. (**b**) (*terreno, suolo*) ground; (*sostanza*) soil, earth; (*argilla*) clay; **per** ~ (*appoggiare*) on the ground; (*cadere*) to the ground; **il tesoro è sotto** ~ the treasure is buried; **scavare sotto** ~ to dig a hole; **il fiume passa sotto** ~ the stream runs underground; **strada in** ~ **battuta** dirt track. (**c**) (*distesa, campagna*) land; **un pezzo di** ~ a piece of land; (*fabbricabile, per orto*) a plot of land; **una lingua di** ~ a strip of land; **le sue** ~**e** (*possedimento*) his estate. (**d**) (*terraferma*) land; **scendere a** ~ to go ashore; **via** ~ (*viaggiare*) by land, overland. (**e**) (*paese, regione*) land, country; **in** ~ **straniera** in foreign parts; **è della mia** ~ he is a fellow countryman; **la T~ Promessa** the Promised Land. (**f**) (*Elettr*) earth, ground; **mettere a** ~ to earth. (**g**) (*fraseologia*): **avere una gomma a** ~ to have a flat tyre; **essere a** ~ (*fig: depresso*) to be at rock bottom; ~ ~ (*fig: persona, argomento*) prosaic, pedestrian; **cercare qc/qn per mare e per** ~ to look high and low for sth/sb; **non sta né in cielo né in** ~ it is quite unheard of; **stare con i piedi sulla** ~ (*fig*) to have both feet on the ground. **2:** ~ **di nessuno** no-man's-land; **la T~ Santa** the Holy Land; ~ **di Siena** sienna.

terracotta [terra'kɔtta] *sf, pl* **terrecotte** terracotta; **di** ~ terracotta *attr*; **vasellame** *m* **di** ~ earthenware.

terracqueo, a [ter'rakkweo] *ag* = **terraqueo**.

terraferma [terra'ferma] *sf* dry land, terra firma; (*continente*) mainland; **avvistare la** ~ to sight land.

terraglia [ter'raʎʎa] *sf* (**a**) pottery. (**b**): ~**e** *pl* (*oggetti*) crockery *sg*, earthenware *sg*.

terrapieno [terra'pjeno] *sm* embankment, bank.

terraqueo, a [ter'rakweo] *ag*: **il globo** ~ the globe.

terrazza [ter'rattsa] *sf* (*gen, Agr*) terrace.

terrazzare [terrat'tsare] *vt* (*gen, Agr*) to terrace.

terrazzato, a [terrat'tsato] *ag* (*gen, Agr*) terraced.

terrazzo [ter'rattso] *sm* (*gen, Agr, Geog*) terrace; (*balcone*) balcony.

terremotato, a [terremo'tato] **1** *ag* (*zona*) devastated by an earthquake. **2** *sm/f* earthquake victim.

terremoto [terre'mɔto] *sm* earthquake; (*fig scherz: bambino*) terror.

terreno, a [ter'reno] **1** *ag* (**a**) (*vita, beni*) earthly. (**b**) (*a livello della strada*): **piano** ~ ground floor.

2 *sm* **(a)** *(gen)* ground; *(suolo)* soil, ground; **un ~ montuoso** a mountainous terrain; **~ alluvionale** *(Geol)* alluvial soil; **dissodare il ~** to till the soil; **tastare il ~** *(fig)* to check the lie of the land. **(b)** *(area coltivabile)* land; *(area edificabile)* land, plot; **ho comprato un ~** I bought a piece *o* a plot of land; **una casa con 500 ettari di ~** a house with 500 hectares of land. **(c)** *(Mil: teatro di operazioni)* field; *(: guadagnato, perduto)* ground; **perdere ~** *(anche fig)* to lose ground. **(d)** *(Sport)*: **~ di gioco** field; **partita sospesa a causa del ~ pesante** match postponed due to heavy ground conditions.

terreo, a ['tɛrreo] *ag (viso, colorito)* wan.

terrestre [ter'rɛstre] **1** *ag (della terra: superficie etc)* of the earth; *(: magnetismo)* terrestrial; *(di terra: battaglia, animale)* land *attr*; **il globo ~** the globe. **2** *sm* earthling.

terribile [ter'ribile] *ag (orribile)* terrible, dreadful; *(: nemico)* terrible; *(: visione)* fearful; *(: forza)* tremendous; *(fam: formidabile)* terrific, tremendous; **ho una fame ~** I am terribly hungry.

terriccio [ter'rittʃo] *sm* soil.

terrier [te'rje] *sm inv (cane)* terrier.

terriero, a [ter'rjɛro] *ag*: **proprietà ~a** landed property; **proprietario ~** landowner.

terrificante [terrifi'kante] *ag* terrifying.

terrina [ter'rina] *sf (zuppiera)* tureen.

territoriale [territo'rjale] *ag* territorial.

territorio [terri'tɔrjo] *sm* territory; *(di comune)* precinct; *(di giudice)* jurisdiction.

terrone, a [ter'rone] *sm/f* derogatory term used by Northern Italians to describe Southern Italians.

terrore [ter'rore] *sm (anche fig)* terror; **il T~** *(Storia)* the Reign of Terror; **incutere ~ a qn** to strike terror into sb's heart; **avere il ~ di qc** to be terrified of sth; **con ~** in terror.

terrorismo [terro'rizmo] *sm* terrorism.

terrorista, i, e [terro'rista] *sm/f* terrorist.

terroristico, a, ci, che [terro'ristiko] *ag* terrorist *attr*.

terrorizzare [terrorid'dzare] *vt (gen)* to terrify; *(popolazione)* to terrorize; **l'idea di viaggiare in aereo lo terrorizza** he is terrified of flying.

terroso, a [ter'roso] *ag (acqua)* muddy; *(mani, funghi etc)* covered with earth; *(Chim: metallo)* earth *attr*.

terso, a ['tɛrso] *ag (acqua)* clear.

terza ['tɛrtsa] *sf (gen)* third; *(Aut)* third gear; *(Scol: elementare)* primary three; *(: media)* third year at secondary school; *(: superiore)* sixth year at secondary school; *(di trasporti)* third class.

terzetto [ter'tsetto] *sm (Mus)* trio, terzetto; *(di persone)* trio.

terziario, a [ter'tsjarjo] **1** *ag (Geol, Econ)* tertiary. **2** *sm (Geol)* tertiary period. **3** *sm/f (Rel)* tertiary.

terzina [ter'tsina] *sf (Letteratura)* tercet; *(Mus)* triplet.

terzino [ter'tsino] *sm (Calcio)* fullback, back.

terzo, a ['tɛrtso] **1** *ag* third; **~, in ~ luogo** thirdly, in the third place; **di terz'ordine** third-rate; **il ~ mondo** the Third World; **la ~a età** old age. **2** *sm/f* **(a)** third. **(b)**: **~i** *pl (altri)* others; *(Dir)* third party *sg*; **agire per conto di ~i** to act on behalf of a third party; **assicurazione contro i ~i** third-party insurance. **3** *sm (frazione)* third; *per uso* **vedi quinto.**

terzultimo, a [ter'tsultimo] *ag, sm/f* third from last, last but two.

tesa ['tesa] *sf (di cappello)* brim; **a larghe ~e** wide-brimmed.

tesaurizzare [tezaurid'dzare] *vt, vi (anche fig)* to hoard.

teschio ['teskjo] *sm* skull.

tesi ['tɛzi] *sf inv (gen)* thesis; *(Univ)* dissertation, thesis; **~ di laurea** degree thesis; **sostenere una ~** to uphold a theory.

teso, a ['teso] **1** *pp di* **tendere. 2** *ag (corda)* taut, tight; *(nervi, volto)* tense; *(rapporti)* strained; *(braccia)* outstretched; **è molto ~ in questi giorni** he's very tense these days; **con la mano ~a** with hand outstretched; **stava lì con le orecchie tese** he was all ears.

tesoreria [tezore'ria] *sf* treasury.

tesoriere [tezo'rjɛre] *sm* treasurer.

tesoro [te'zɔro] *sm* **(a)** *(gen, fig)* treasure; **~i** riches; *(ricchezze naturali)* resources; **far ~ dei consigli di qn** to take sb's advice to heart; **sei un ~!** how nice of you!; **che ~ di ragazza** what a nice girl; **grazie ~!** thank you darling! **(b)** *(Fin)* exchequer; **il Ministero del T~** the Treasury; **Buono del T~** Treasury Bond.

tessera ['tɛssera] *sf* **(a)** *(di socio)* (membership) card; *(di giornalista)* pass; *(di abbonato)* season ticket; **ha la ~ del partito** he's a party member. **(b)** *(di mosaico)* tessera.

tesserare [tesse'rare] *vt (iscrivere)* to give a membership card to.

tesserato, a [tesse'rato] *sm/f (di società sportiva etc)* (fully paid-up) member; *(Pol)* (card-carrying) member.

tessere ['tɛssere] *vt* to weave; *(fig: inganni, tradimenti)* to plan, plot; **~ le lodi di qn** *(fig)* to sing sb's praises.

tessile ['tɛssile] **1** *ag* textile. **2** *sm/f* textile worker.

tessitore, trice [tessi'tore] *sm/f* weaver.

tessitura [tessi'tura] *sf (operazione)* weaving; *(impianto)* weaving mill *o* factory.

tessuto, a [tes'suto] *sm* **(a)** material, fabric; *(di lana)* cloth, material; **~i** textiles. **(b)** *(Bio)* tissue.

testa ['tɛsta] *sf* **(a)** *(gen, Anat)* head; **a ~ alta** with one's head held high; **a ~ bassa** *(correre)* headlong; *(con aria dimessa)* with head bowed; **gettarsi in qc a ~ bassa** to rush headlong into sth; **cadere a ~ in giù** to fall head first; **dalla ~ ai piedi** from head to foot; **5.000 lire a ~** 5,000 lire apiece *o* a head *o* per person; **vincere di mezza ~** to win by half a head; **una ~ d'aglio** a bulb of garlic.

(b) *(fig: cervello)* head, brain, brains; **~ di rapa** *(fig)* blockhead; **avere la ~ dura** to be stubborn; **avere la ~ vuota** to be empty-headed; **avere la ~ tra le nuvole** to have one's head in the clouds; **non avere ~** to be scatterbrained; **usare la ~** to use one's head *o* brains; **ma dove hai la ~?** whatever are you thinking of?; **ha poca ~ per la matematica** he hasn't got much of a head for maths; **fare qc di ~ propria** to do as one pleases; **far entrare qc in ~ a qn** to din sth into sb's head; **mettersi in ~ di fare qc** to take it into one's head to do sth; **che cosa gli hai messo in ~?** what ideas have you been putting into his head?; **non so che cosa gli sia passato per la ~** I don't know what's come over him.

(c) *(parte anteriore: di treno, processione)* front, head; *(: di colonna militare)* head; *(: di pagina, lista)* top, head; **le carrozze di ~** *(Ferr)* the front of the train; **essere in ~** *(corridore)* to be in the lead, be the leader; **essere in ~ alla classifica** *(corridore)* to be number one; *(squadra)* to be at the top of the league table; *(disco)* to be top of the charts; **essere alla ~ di qc** *(società)* to be the head of; *(esercito)* to be at the head of; **~ di serie** *(Sport)* seeded player.

(d) *(fraseologia)*: **avere la ~ sulle spalle** to

have one's head screwed on; **dare alla ~** to go to one's head; **montarsi la ~** to become big-headed; **perdere la ~ per qn** to lose one's head over sb; **perdere la ~** *(per ira)* to lose one's head; **ci scommetterei la ~** I'd bet my boots; **tener ~ a qn** to hold sb off; **lavata di ~** telling-off, ticking-off; **~ o croce?** heads or tails?; **fare a ~ o croce to** toss up.

testa-coda ['tɛsta 'koda] *sm inv (Aut)* spin.

testamentario, a [testamen'tarjo] *ag (Dir)* testamentary; **le sue disposizioni ~e** the provisions of his will.

testamento [testa'mento] *sm (Dir)* will, testament; **fare ~** to make one's will; **l'Antico/il Nuovo T~** *(Rel)* the Old/New Testament; **~ spirituale** *(fig)* spiritual testament.

testardaggine [testar'daddʒine] *sf* stubbornness, obstinacy.

testardo, a [tes'tardo] **1** *ag* stubborn, obstinate. **2** *sm/f* stubborn *o* obstinate person.

testata [tes'tata] *sf* **(a)** *(di letto)* headboard; *(di giornale)* heading. **(b)** *(Aut)* (cylinder) head; *(Aer: di missile)* head; **missile m a ~ nucleare** missile with a nuclear warhead. **(c)** *(colpo)* bang on the head; **dare una ~ contro qc** to bang one's head on sth.

teste ['tɛste] *sm/f (Dir)* witness.

testicolo [tes'tikolo] *sm* testicle.

testiera [tes'tjɛra] *sf* **(a)** *(del letto)* headboard. **(b)** *(di cavallo)* headpiece.

testimone [testi'mɔne] **1** *sm/f* witness; **~ oculare** eye witness; **fare da ~ alle nozze di qn** to be a witness at sb's wedding; **queste rovine sono ~i della grandezza di Roma** these ruins bear witness to the former greatness of Rome. **2** *sm (Sport)* baton.

testimonianza [testimo'njantsa] *sf (atto)* deposition; *(effetto)* evidence; *(fig: prova)* proof; **accusare qn di falsa ~** to accuse sb of perjury; **rilasciare una ~** to give evidence; **ne fanno ~ altri autori contemporanei** *(fig)* other contemporary authors testify to it; **ha dato ~ di grande fedeltà** he proved his great loyalty.

testimoniare [testimo'njare] **1** *vt*: **~ che** to testify that; **~ il vero** to tell the truth; **~ il falso** to perjure us; **le impronte testimoniano la sua colpevolezza** the fingerprints are proof of his guilt. **2** *vi* to testify, give evidence; **~ a favore di/contro qn** to testify for/against sb; **non ha voluto ~ sull'accaduto** he didn't want to give evidence on *o* about what happened; **è stato chiamato a ~** he was called upon to give evidence.

testina [tes'tina] *sf (di giradischi, registratore)* head.

testo ['tɛsto] *sm (gen)* text; *(originale di traduzione)* original text; **libro di ~** *(Scol)* textbook; **fare ~** *(opera, autore)* to be authoritative; **questo libro non fa ~** this book is not essential reading; **le sue parole fanno ~** his words carry weight.

testone [tes'tone] *sm/f (ostinato)* pig-headed person; *(stupido)* blockhead, dunderhead.

testuale [testu'ale] *ag* textual; **parole ~i** actual words.

testuggine [tes'tuddʒine] *sf (Zool)* tortoise; *(: marina)* turtle.

tetano ['tɛtano] *sm (Med)* tetanus.

tête-à-tête ['tɛta'tɛt] *sm inv* tête-à-tête.

tetro, a ['tɛtro] *ag* gloomy, dismal; *(fig: umore)* gloomy; **era di umore ~** he was gloomy *o* glum.

tetta ['tɛtta] *sf (fam)* boob, tit.

tettarella [tetta'rɛlla] *sf* teat.

tetto ['tɛtto] *sm (gen)* roof; *(di veicolo)* roof, top; *(fig)* house, home; **~ a cupola** dome; **restare**

senza ~ to be homeless *o* without a roof over one's head; **i senza ~** the homeless; **abbandonare il ~ coniugale** to desert one's family.

tettoia [tet'toja] *sf (gen)* canopy; *(di stazione)* roof.

teutonico, a, ci, che [teu'tɔniko] *ag* Teutonic.

Tevere ['tevere] *sm*: **il ~** the Tiber.

thermos ['tɛrmos] *sm inv* ® Thermos®.

thriller ['θrilə] *sm inv*, **thrilling** ['θrilin] *sm inv (libro, film)* thriller.

ti [ti] *(dav lo, la, li, le, ne diventa te) pron pers* **(a)** *(ogg diretto)* you; **non ~ ascolta mai** he never listens to you; **non ~ ho visto stamattina** I didn't see you this morning. **(b)** *(complemento di termine)* (to) you; **~ dirò tutto** I'll tell you everything; **te lo ha dato?** did he give it to you? **(c)** *(riflessivo)* yourself; **~ sei lavata?** have you washed?; **~ sei pettinato?** have you combed your hair?; **quando ~ prendi una vacanza?** when are you going to have yourself a holiday?

tiara ['tjara] *sf* tiara.

tibia ['tibja] *sf (Anat)* tibia, shinbone.

tic [tik] *sm inv* **(a)** *(di orologio)* tick. **(b)** *(Med)* twitch, tic.

ticchettio [tikket'tio] *sm (di macchina da scrivere)* clicking; *(di orologio)* ticking; *(di pioggia)* pattering.

ticchio ['tikkjo] *sm (tic)* twitch, tic; *(fig: capriccio)* whim; **mi è preso il ~ di andar in Africa** I've taken a notion to visit Africa.

ticket ['tikit] *sm inv (Med)* prescription charge.

tictac [tik'tak] *sm inv* tick-tock.

tiepido, a ['tjɛpido] *ag* lukewarm, tepid; *(fig: accoglienza)* lukewarm; *(: fede etc)* half-hearted.

tifare [ti'fare] *vi*: **~ per** to be a fan of, support.

tifo ['tifo] *sm* **(a)** *(Med)* typhus. **(b)** *(Sport)*: **fare il ~ per** to be a fan of, support.

tifoidea [tifoi'dɛa] *sf* typhoid.

tifone [ti'fone] *sm (Meteor)* typhoon.

tifoso, a [ti'foso] **1** *ag*: **essere ~ di** to be a fan of. **2** *sm/f (Sport etc)* fan.

tight ['tait] *sm inv* morning suit.

tiglio ['tiʎʎo] *sm* lime (tree).

tigna ['tiɲɲa] *sf (Med)* ringworm.

tignola [tiɲ'ɲɔla] *sf (Zool)* moth.

tigrato, a [ti'grato] *ag* striped.

tigre ['tigre] *sf* tiger/tigress.

tilde ['tilde] *sm o f* tilde.

timballo [tim'ballo] *sm (Culin)* timbale.

timbrare [tim'brare] *vt* to stamp; *(annullare: francobolli)* to postmark; **~ il cartellino** to clock in.

timbratura [timbra'tura] *sf (vedi vb)* stamping; postmarking.

timbro ['timbro] *sm* **(a)** *(strumento)* (rubber) stamp; *(su documento etc)* stamp; *(su francobollo)* postmark; **mettere il ~ su qc** to stamp sth. **(b)** *(Mus)* tone, timbre.

timidezza [timi'dettsa] *sf* shyness, timidity.

timido, a ['timido] **1** *ag (persona, animale)* shy, timid; *(tentativo)* bashful. **2** *sm/f* shy person.

timo¹ ['timo] *sm (Bot)* thyme.

timo² ['timo] *sm (Anat)* thymus.

timone [ti'mone] *sm (Naut)* helm; *(: parte sommersa)* rudder; *(Aer)* rudder; *(di carro)* shaft; **barra del ~** *(Naut)* tiller; **ruota del ~** *(Naut)* wheel; **essere al ~** *(anche fig)* to be at the helm; **prendere il ~** *(anche fig)* to take the helm.

timoniere [timo'njɛre] *sm (Naut)* helmsman; *(Canottaggio)* cox.

timorato, a [timo'rato] *ag* conscientious; **~ di Dio** God-fearing.

timore [ti'more] *sm (paura)* fear, dread; *(preoccupazione)* fear; *(rispetto)* awe; **avere ~ di qc/qn** *(paura)* to be afraid of sth/sb; **ho il ~ che non ci**

arriveremo I fear we won't make it; **non aver ~, arriverà in tempo** don't worry, he'll get here in time; **ha un ~ reverenziale di suo padre** he stands in awe of his father.

timoroso, a [timo'roso] *ag (pauroso)* frightened, afraid; *(preoccupato)* worried, afraid.

timpano ['timpano] *sm* **(a)** *(Anat)* tympanum, eardrum. **(b)** *(Mus)* kettledrum; **i ~i** the timpani.

tinello [ti'nɛllo] *sm* small dining room.

tingere ['tindʒere] **1** *vt (stoffa, capelli)* to dye; *(labbra)* to colour, paint; **il tramonto tingeva il cielo di rosso** the sunset was reddening the sky *o* was turning the sky red. **2:** ~**rsi** *vr:* **il cielo si è tinto di rosso** the sky turned red.

tino ['tino] *sm* vat.

tinozza [ti'nɔttsa] *sf* tub.

tinta ['tinta] *sf* **(a)** *(colore)* colour; **una stoffa di ~ scura** a dark material. **(b)** *(per muri etc)* paint; **dare una mano di ~ a qc** to give sth a coat of paint; **dipingere qc a ~e fosche** *(fig)* to paint a gloomy picture of sth.

tintarella [tinta'rɛlla] *sf* (sun)tan; **prendere la ~** to get a tan.

tintinnare [tintin'nare] *vi* to tinkle; *(bicchieri)* to clink, tinkle.

tintinnio [tintin'nio] *sm* tinkling.

tinto, a ['tinto] *pp di* tingere.

tintore [tin'tore] *sm (di tessuti)* dyer.

tintoria [tinto'ria] *sf* dry cleaner's (shop).

tintura [tin'tura] *sf* **(a)** *(operazione)* dyeing; *(soluzione colorante)* dye. **(b)** *(Med)* tincture; ~ **di iodio** tincture of iodine.

tipa ['tipa] *sf (donna originale)* character.

tipico, a, ci, che ['tipiko] *ag* typical.

tipo ['tipo] **1** *sm* **(a)** *(genere)* kind, sort, type; **vestiti di tutti i ~i** all kinds of clothes; **sul ~ di questo** of this sort. **(b)** *(modello)* type, model. **(c)** *(persona originale)* character; **chi era quel ~?** who was that character?; **sei un bel ~!** you're a fine one! **2** *ag inv* average, typical.

tipografia [tipogra'fia] *sf* typography.

tipografico, a, ci, che [tipo'grafiko] *ag* typographical.

tipografo [ti'pɔgrafo] *sm* typographer.

tipologia [tipolo'dʒia] *sf* typology.

tip tap [tip tap] *sm* tap dancing.

tiraggio [ti'raddʒo] *sm* draught, draw.

tiranneggiare [tiranned'dʒare] *vt* to tyrannize.

tirannia [tiran'nia] *sf* tyranny.

tirannico, a, ci, che [ti'ranniko] *ag* tyrannical.

tirannide [ti'rannide] *sf* tyranny.

tiranno, a [ti'ranno] **1** *sm* tyrant. **2** *ag* tyrannical.

tirante [ti'rante] *sm (Naut, di tenda etc)* guy; *(Edil)* brace.

tirapiedi [tira'pjɛdi] *sm/f inv* hanger-on.

tirare [ti'rare] **1** *vt* **(a)** *(gen)* to pull; *(slitta)* to pull, drag; *(rimorchio)* to tow; ~ **qn per la manica** to tug at sb's sleeve; ~ **qn da parte** to take *o* draw sb aside; ~ **gli orecchi a qn** to tweak sb's ears; ~ **qn per i capelli** to pull sb's hair; *(fig)* to force sb; ~ **qc per le lunghe** to drag sth out; ~ **le somme** *(fig)* to draw a conclusion; ~ **un sospiro (di sollievo)** to heave a sigh (of relief); **una parola tira l'altra** one thing *o* word leads to another; ~ **fuori** to pull out; ~ **giù** to pull down; ~ **su qc/qn** to pull sth/sb up; ~ **su qn** *(fig: rallegrare)* to cheer sb up; *(: allevare)* to bring sb up.

(b) *(chiudere: tende)* to draw, close; ~ **la porta** to close the door, pull the door to.

(c) *(tracciare, disegnare)* to draw.

(d) *(gettare: sasso, palla)* to throw, fling; *(: fig: bestemmie, imprecazioni)* to hurl, let fly; **gli ho tirato un pugno** I punched him; **gli ho tirato uno**

schiaffo I slapped him; ~ **calci** to kick; ~ **il pallone** *(Calcio)* to kick the ball.

(e): ~**rsi:** ~**rsi dietro qn** to bring *o* drag sb along; ~**rsi su i capelli** to put one's hair up; ~**rsi addosso qc** to pull sth down on top of o.s.; *(fig)* to bring sth upon o.s.

2 *vi:* ~ **avanti** *(fig)* to get by; ~ **diritto** to keep right on going; ~ **col fucile/con l'arco** to shoot with a rifle/with a bow and arrow; **tirava un forte vento** a strong wind was blowing; **che aria tira?** *(fig)* what are things like in there?; ~ **a campare** to keep going as best one can; ~ **a indovinare** to take a guess; ~ **sul prezzo** to bargain; ~ **di scherma** to fence; ~ **in porta** *(Calcio)* to shoot (at goal).

3: ~**rsi** *vr:* ~**rsi indietro** to draw *o* move back; *(fig)* to back out; ~**rsi su** to pull o.s. up; *(fig)* to cheer o.s. up.

tirata [ti'rata] *sf* **(a)** *(strattone)* pull, tug; ~ **d'orecchi** *(fig)* telling-off, ticking-off. **(b)** *(di sigaretta)* drag, puff. **(c)** *(svolgimento ininterrotto):* **abbiamo fatto tutta una ~** we did it all in one go; **l'ho letto in una ~** I read it at one go. **(d)** *(discorso polemico)* tirade.

tiratore, trice [tira'tore] *sm/f* shot; ~ **scelto** marksman; **franco ~** *(Mil)* irregular; *(: cecchino)* sniper.

tiratura [tira'tura] *sf (di giornali)* circulation; *(di libri)* edition.

tirchieria [tirkje'ria] *sf* meanness, stinginess.

tirchio, a ['tirkjo] **1** *ag* mean, stingy. **2** *sm/f* miser.

tiremmolla [tirem'mɔlla] *sm inv* hesitation, shilly-shallying *no pl.*

tiritera [tiri'tɛra] *sf* drivel, hot air.

tiro ['tiro] **1** *sm* **(a)** *(di cavalli, buoi)* team; ~ **a quattro** coach and four. **(b)** *(di pistola, freccia, Calcio etc)* shooting; *(: colpo)* shot; **è stato un buon ~** that was a good shot; **essere a ~** to be in range; *(fig)* to be within reach; **se mi capita** *o* **viene a ~** if I get my hands on him *(o* her*)*!; **a un ~ di schioppo** a stone's throw away. **(c)** *(lancio)* throwing; *(: effetto)* throw. **(d)** *(fig):* **giocare un brutto ~** *o* **un ~ mancino a qn** to play a dirty trick on sb. **2:** ~ **con l'arco** archery; ~ **al bersaglio,** ~ **a segno** target shooting; ~ **alla fune** tug-of-war; ~ **al piattello** clay pigeon shooting, skeat shooting *(Am);* ~ **al piccione** pigeon shooting.

tirocinante [tirotʃi'nante] *(vedi* **tirocinio***)* **1** *ag* apprentice *attr;* trainee *attr.* **2** *sm/f* apprentice, trainee.

tirocinio [tiro'tʃinjo] *sm:* ~ **(in)** *(di mestiere)* apprenticeship (in); *(di professione)* training (in); **fare il proprio ~** to serve one's apprenticeship; to do one's training.

tiroide [ti'rɔide] *sf (Anat)* thyroid (gland).

tirolese [tiro'lese] *ag, sm/f* Tyrolean.

Tirolo [ti'rɔlo] *sm:* **il ~** the Tyrol.

tirrennico, a, ci, che [tir'rɛnniko] *ag* Tyrrhenian.

Tirreno [tir'rɛno] *sm:* **il (mar)** ~ the Tyrrhenian Sea.

tisana [ti'zana] *sf* herb tea, tisane.

tisi ['tizi] *sf (Med)* consumption.

tisico, a, ci, che ['tiziko] **1** *ag (Med)* consumptive; *(fig: gracile)* frail. **2** *sm/f (Med)* consumptive (person).

titanico, a, ci, che [ti'taniko] *ag* gigantic, enormous.

titanio [ti'tanjo] *sm (Chim)* titanium.

titano [ti'tano] *sm (Mitologia, fig)* titan.

titillare [titil'lare] *vt* to tickle, titillate.

titolare [tito'lare] **1** *ag (gen)* appointed; *(Univ)* with a full-time appointment; *(sovrano, vescovo)* titular. **2** *sm/f (gen)* holder; *(proprietario)* owner, proprietor; *(Sport: in un club)* regular first-team player; *(: a livello nazionale)* regular member of the national squad; ~ **di cattedra** *(Univ)* full professor.

titolato, a [tito'lato] *ag (persona)* titled.

titolo ['titolo] *sm* **(a)** *(di libro etc)* title; *(di giornale)* headline; ~**i di testa** *(Cine)* credits. **(b)** *(Fin: gen)* security; *(: azione)* share, stock; ~**i esteri** foreign securities; ~ **obbligazionario** bond; ~ **di credito** document of credit; ~ **al portatore** bearer bond. **(c)** *(qualifica: nobiliare, Sport)* title; *(: di studio)* qualification; ~ **mondiale** *(Sport)* world title. **(d)** *(fig: motivo)*: **a che** ~ **sei venuto?** why *o* for what reason have you come?; **a** ~ **di amicizia** for *o* out of friendship; **a** ~ **di curiosità** out of curiosity; **a** ~ **di prestito/favore** as a loan/favour; **a** ~ **di cronaca** for your information.

titubante [titu'bante] *ag* hesitant, undecided; **è** ~ **per natura** he is irresolute by nature.

titubanza [titu'bantsa] *sf* hesitation, indecision.

tivù [ti'vu] *sf inv (fam)* telly, TV.

tizio, a ['tittsjo] *sm/f* character, individual; **chi era quel** ~**?** who was that bloke?; **chi era quella** ~**a?** who was that girl?; **T**~, **Caio e Sempronio** Tom, Dick and Harry.

tizzone [tit'tsone] *sm (di legno)* brand; *(di carbone)* live coal.

to' [tɔ] *escl* **(a)** *(eccoti)* here you are!; ~, **tieni!** here, take this! **(b)** *(guarda un po')*: ~! **chi si vede** look who's here!; ~! **questa è bella** *(iro)* well, that's very nice!

toast ['toust] *sm inv* toasted sandwich.

toccante [tok'kante] *ag (commovente)* touching, moving.

toccare [tok'kare] **1** *vt* **(a)** *(gen)* to touch; *(fig: sfiorare: argomento, tema)* to touch on; **non** ~ **la mia roba** don't touch my things; **non ha toccato cibo** he hasn't touched his food; **non voglio** ~ **i miei risparmi** I don't want to touch my savings; ~ **un tasto delicato** *(fig)* to touch a sore point; **hai toccato il mio punto debole** *(fig)* you have hit on my weak point; ~ **con mano** *(fig)* to find out for o.s.

(b) *(raggiungere)* to touch, reach; **si tocca?** *(in acqua)* can you touch the bottom?; ~ **il fondo** to touch the bottom; *(fig)* to touch rock bottom; ~ **terra** *(Naut)* to reach land; *(Aer)* to touch down; **abbiamo toccato diverse città** we stopped at a number of towns; **abbiamo toccato diversi porti** we put in at various ports; **ha appena toccato la cinquantina** he has just turned fifty.

(c) *(commuovere)* to touch; *(ferire)* to hurt; **le tue allusioni non mi toccano** your remarks don't bother me; ~ **qn sul vivo** to cut sb to the quick; **la vicenda ci tocca da vicino** the matter concerns *o* affects us closely.

2 *vi (aus essere)* **(a)** *(capitare)*: **mi è toccata una bella fortuna** I have had great good fortune; **perché toccano sempre a me queste cose?** why is it always me who has to do these things?; **a chi tocca, tocca** that's life.

(b) *(essere costretto)*: **mi toccava andare** I have to go; **che cosa mi tocca sentire!** what's this I hear?; **sai che cosa mi è toccato fare?** do you know what I had to do?

(c) *(spettare)*: ~ **a** to be the turn of; **a chi tocca?** whose turn *o* go is it?; **tocca a me** it's my turn *o* go; **non tocca a me giudicare** it is not for me to judge.

3: ~**rsi** *vr* to touch; **gli estremi si toccano** *(fig)* extremes meet.

toccasana [tokka'sana] *sm inv* cure-all, panacea.

toccata [tok'kata] *sf* touch; *(Mus)* toccata.

toccato, a [tok'kato] *ag*, **tocco**[1], **a, chi, che** ['tokko] *ag* mad, touched.

tocco[2], **chi** ['tokko] *sm* **(a)** *(gen, Mus)* touch; **gli ultimi** ~**chi** the finishing touches. **(b)** *(colpo: di campana, orologio, pennello)* stroke.

tocco[3], **chi** ['tokko] *sm (di pane, formaggio)* piece, chunk; **che** ~ **di ragazza!** what a terrific-looking girl!

toeletta [toe'letta] *sf* = **toilette**.

toga, ghe ['toga] *sf (di magistrato)* gown, robe; *(Storia)* toga.

togato, a [to'gato] *ag (fig)*: **giudice** *m* ~ magistrate.

togliere ['tɔʎʎere] **1** *vt* **(a)** *(gen)* to take off, take away, remove; **togli il quadro dal muro** take the picture off the wall; ~ **le mani di tasca** to take one's hands out of one's pockets; ~ **qn di mezzo** to get rid of sb; *(fig)* to bump sb off *(fam)*; ~ **la parola a qn** to interrupt sb; ~ **la parola di bocca a qn** to take the words out of sb's mouth; ~ **il saluto a qn** to ignore sb, snub sb; **mi hai tolto un peso** you took a weight off my mind; **volevo togliermi un peso (dalla coscienza)** I wanted to get it off my chest; ~**rsi la vita** to take one's (own) life, commit suicide; ~**rsi i guanti/il vestito/il trucco** to take off one's gloves/suit/make-up; ~**rsi una voglia** to satisfy an urge *o* whim; ~**rsi la soddisfazione di** to have the satisfaction of; **ciò non toglie che...** that doesn't alter the fact that...

(b) *(Mat)* to take away, subtract; ~ **3 da 7** to take 3 away from 7.

2: ~**rsi** *vr* to get out of the way; **togliti (di mezzo** *o* **dai piedi)!** get out of the way!

toilette [twa'let] *sf inv*, **toletta** [to'letta] *sf* **(a)** *(gabinetto)* toilet. **(b)** *(cosmesi)* make-up; **fare** ~ to get made up, make o.s. beautiful. **(c)** *(abbigliamento)* gown, dress. **(d)** *(mobile)* dressing table.

tollerante [tolle'rante] *ag* tolerant.

tolleranza [tolle'rantsa] *sf (gen)* tolerance; *(Rel)* toleration; **non ha un minimo di** ~ he is completely intolerant; **casa di** ~ brothel.

tollerare [tolle'rare] *vt* **(a)** *(sopportare: ingiustizia, offese)* to tolerate, put up with; *(: liquori, freddo etc)* to take; *(: persona)* to put up with, bear, stand; **non tollero le lunghe camminate** I am unable to go for long walks; ~ **il freddo/caldo** to stand *o* take the cold/the heat. **(b)** *(ammettere)* to tolerate, allow; **non tollero repliche** I won't stand for objections; **non sono tollerati i ritardi** lateness will not be tolerated.

tolto, a ['tɔlto] **1** *pp di* **togliere. 2** *prep (eccetto)* except for. **3** *sm*: **mal** ~ = **maltolto**.

tomaia [to'maja] *sf (di scarpa)* upper.

tomba ['tomba] *sf* grave; *(cappella sotterranea)* tomb; **è una** ~ *(fig: persona)* he won't give anything away; **nelle strade c'era un silenzio di** ~ it was as silent as the grave in the streets; **lo accolsero con un silenzio di** ~ he was greeted with a deathly hush; **avere un piede nella** ~ to have one foot in the grave.

tombale [tom'bale] *ag*: **pietra** ~ tombstone, gravestone.

tombino [tom'bino] *sm* manhole; *(coperchio)* manhole cover.

tombola ['tombola] *sf* **(a)** *(gioco)* bingo *(played at home)*. **(b)** *(fam: caduta)* tumble.

tombolo ['tombolo] *sm* **(a)** *(cuscino)* lace pillow; **merletto a** ~ bobbin lace. **(b)** *(persona grassoccia)* podge *(fam)*.

tomo ['tɔmo] *sm* **(a)** *(volume)* volume, tome. **(b)** *(persona)* queer fish.

tonaca, che ['tɔnaka] *sf (Rel)* habit; **indossare la** ~

(frate) to take the habit; *(monaca)* to take the veil.

tonale [to'nale] *ag (Mus)* tonal, tone *attr; (Pittura)* tonal.

tonante [to'nante] *ag (voce)* loud, booming.

tonare [to'nare] *vi* = **tuonare.**

tondeggiante [tonded'dʒante] *ag* roundish.

tondo, a ['tondo] **1** *ag (circolare)* round; **fare cifra ~a** to round up *(o* down); **tre mesi ~i** exactly three months; **gli ho detto chiaro e ~** I told him very clearly *o* bluntly. **2** *sm (cerchio)* circle; **scultura a tutto ~** full-relief sculpture.

tonfo ['tonfo] *sm* thud, thump; *(nell'acqua)* plop; **fare un ~** *(cadere)* to take a tumble.

tonico, a, ci, che ['tɔniko] **1** *ag* tonic. **2** *sm* **(a)** *(Med)* tonic. **(b)** *(cosmetico)* toner.

tonificante [tonifi'kante] *ag* invigorating, bracing.

tonificare [tonifi'kare] *vt (gen)* to invigorate; *(pelle)* to tone (up).

tonnara [ton'nara] *sf* tuna-fishing nets *pl.*

tonnato, a [ton'nato] *ag (Culin)*: **vitello ~** veal with tuna fish sauce.

tonnellaggio [tonnel'laddʒo] *sm (Naut)* tonnage.

tonnellata [tonnel'lata] *sf* ton.

tonno ['tonno] *sm* tuna.

tono ['tɔno] *sm (gen, Mus)* tone; *(di colore)* tone, shade; **parlare con ~ minaccioso** to speak in a threatening tone *o* threateningly; **abbassa il ~ della voce!** lower your tone (of voice)!; **il ~ della lettera/del discorso** the tone of the letter/ speech; **se la metti su questo ~...** if that's the way you want to put it...; **rispondere a ~** *(a proposito)* to answer to the point; *(nello stesso modo)* to answer in kind; *(per le rime)* to answer back; **essere giù di ~** to be off-colour; **cercava di darsi un ~** she tried to affect refined manners.

tonsilla [ton'silla] *sf (Med)* tonsil; **operarsi di ~e** to have one's tonsils out.

tonsillite [tonsil'lite] *sf (Med)* tonsillitis.

tonsura [ton'sura] *sf* tonsure.

tonto, a ['tonto] **1** *ag* stupid, silly, dumb. **2** *sm/f* blockhead, dunce; **fare il finto ~** to play dumb.

topaia [to'paja] *sf (di topo)* mousehole; *(di ratto)* rat's nest; *(fig: casa etc)* hovel, dump.

topazio [to'pattsjo] *sm* topaz.

topicida, i [topi'tʃida] *sm* rat poison.

topless ['tɔplis] *sm inv* topless bathing costume.

topo ['tɔpo] *sm (Zool)* mouse; *(ratto)* rat; **~ d'albergo** *(fig)* hotel thief; **~ di biblioteca** *(fig)* bookworm.

topografia [topogra'fia] *sf* topography.

toppa ['tɔppa] *sf* **(a)** *(di stoffa)* patch. **(b)** *(serratura)* keyhole.

torace [to'ratʃe] *sm (Anat)* thorax, chest; *(Zool)* thorax.

toracico, a, ci, che [to'ratʃiko] *ag* chest *attr;* **gabbia ~a** rib cage.

torba ['torba] *sf* peat.

torbidezza [torbi'dettsa] *sf (vedi ag)* cloudiness; muddiness; darkness.

torbido, a ['torbido] **1** *ag (liquido)* cloudy; *(: fiume)* muddy; *(fig: pensieri)* dark, sinister. **2** *sm*: **qui c'è del ~** there is something fishy going on here; **pescare nel ~** to fish in troubled waters.

torcere ['tɔrtʃere] **1** *vt* **(a)** to twist; *(biancheria)* to wring; **~ un braccio a qn** to twist sb's arm; **non ~ un capello a qn** not to hurt a hair of sb's head; **dare del filo da ~ a qn** to make life *o* things difficult for sb. **(b)** *(piegare)* to bend. **2: ~rsi** *vr* to writhe; **~rsi dal dolore** to writhe in pain; **~rsi dalle risa** to double up laughing.

torchiare [tor'kjare] *vt (olive)* to press; *(fig fam: persona)* to grill.

torchiatura [torkja'tura] *sf (di olive)* pressing.

torchio ['tɔrkjo] *sm* press; **mettere qn sotto il ~** *(fig fam: interrogare)* to grill sb.

torcia, ce ['tɔrtʃa] *sf* torch.

torcicollo [tortʃi'kɔllo] *sm:* **avere il ~** to have a stiff neck.

tordo ['tordo] *sm* thrush.

torero [to'rɛro] *sm* bullfighter, toreador.

torinese [tori'nese] **1** *ag* of *(o* from) Turin. **2** *sm/f* person from Turin.

Torino [to'rino] *sf* Turin.

torma ['torma] *sf* crowd, throng.

tormalina [torma'lina] *sf* tourmaline.

tormenta [tor'menta] *sf* snowstorm, blizzard.

tormentare [tormen'tare] **1** *vt (gen)* to torment; *(fig: infastidire)* to bother, pester. **2: ~rsi** *vr* to worry, torture o.s.

tormento [tor'mento] *sm* **(a)** *(dolore fisico, morale)* torment, agony; *(tortura)*: **~i** torture *sg*; **morire fra atroci ~i** to die in terrible agony. **(b)** *(fastidio: di zanzare, caldo)* torment; *(: fam: persona)* pest.

tornaconto [torna'konto] *sm* advantage, benefit; **pensa solo al proprio ~** he thinks only of his own interest.

tornado [tor'nado] *sm* tornado.

tornante [tor'nante] *sm* hairpin bend.

tornare [tor'nare] **1** *vi (aus essere)* **(a)** to return, go *(o* come) back; **~ a casa** to go *(o* come) home; **~ da scuola** to come home from school; **un'occasione così non torna più** such an opportunity won't repeat itself, you won't get another chance like this; **non torniamo più sull'argomento** let's drop the subject; **continua a ~ sull'argomento** *(peg)* he harps on about it; **è tornato alla carica con la sua idea di...** he's gone back to the old idea of...; **è tornato a dire/a fare...** he's back to saying/ doing...; **mi è tornato alla mente** I've just remembered; **~ al punto di partenza** to start again; **siamo tornati al punto di partenza** we are back where we started; **~ in sé** to regain consciousness, come to one's senses, come round; **~ su** to come up; **la cipolla mi torna su** onions repeat on me.

(b) *(ridiventare)* to become again; **~ di moda** to become *o* be fashionable again; **il cielo è tornato sereno** it's cleared up again.

(c) *(quadrare)* to be right, be correct; **i conti tornano** the accounts balance; **qualcosa non torna in questa storia** there's something not quite right about this business.

(d) *(essere, risultare)* to (turn out to) be; **~ utile/vantaggioso** to be useful/advantageous; **tornerà a tuo danno** it will come home to roost; **~ a onore di qn** to be a credit to sb, do sb credit.

2 *vt:* **~ qc a qn** to return sth to sb, give sth back to sb.

tornasole [torna'sole] *sm* litmus.

torneo [tor'nɛo] *sm (Storia)* tournament; *(Sport)* tournament, competition.

tornio ['tɔrnjo] *sm* lathe.

tornire [tor'nire] *vt (Tecn)* to turn (on a lathe); *(fig)* to shape, polish.

tornito, a [tor'nito] *ag (gambe, caviglie)* well-shaped.

tornitore [torni'tore] *sm (Tecn)* (lathe-)turner.

tornitura [torni'tura] *sf (Tecn)* **(a)** *(Tecn)* turning; *(di legno)* wood turning. **(b)** *(trucioli)* wood shavings.

torno ['torno] **1** *sm*: **di ~**: **levati di ~!** clear off! **2** *av:* **~ ~** around; **mi girava ~ ~** he was hanging round me.

toro ['tɔro] *sm* **(a)** *(Zool, fig)* bull; **essere forte come un ~** to be as strong as an ox; **prendere il ~ per le corna** *(fig)* to take the bull by the horns. **(b)**

(Astron, Astrologia): **T~** Taurus; **essere del T~** to be Taurus.

torpedine [tor'pɛdine] *sf* (**a**) *(Zool)* stingray. (**b**) *(Mil: mina)* torpedo.

torpediniera [torpedi'njɛra] *sf (Naut)* torpedo boat.

torpedo [tor'pɛdo] *sf inv (Aut)* tourer.

torpedone [torpe'done] *sm* (tourist) coach.

torpido, a ['tɔrpido] *ag* torpid; *(fig)* dull, sluggish.

torpore [tor'pore] *sm* torpor.

torre ['torre] *sf* (**a**) *(di città, castello)* tower; **~ di controllo** *(Aer)* control tower. (**b**) *(Scacchi)* rook, castle.

torrefare [torre'fare] *vt (caffè)* to roast.

torrefatto, a [torre'fatto] *pp di* **torrefare**.

torrefazione [torrefat'tsjone] *sf (del caffè)* (coffee) roasting; *(negozio)* coffee shop.

torreggiare [torred'dʒare] *vi*: **~ (su)** to tower (over).

torrente [tor'rɛnte] *sm* torrent; *(fig)* flood, stream.

torrentizio, a [torren'tittsjo] *ag* torrential.

torrenziale [torren'tsjale] *ag* torrential.

torretta [tor'retta] *sf (gen, Mil)* turret; *(Naut)* tower; **~ di comando** *(Naut)* conning tower.

torrido, a ['tɔrrido] *ag* scorching, torrid.

torrione [tor'rjone] *sm (torre)* keep, tower; *(Naut)* conning tower.

torrone [tor'rone] *sm (Culin)* kind of nougat.

torsione [tor'sjone] *sf (gen)* twisting; *(Tecn)* torsion; *(Ginnastica)* twist.

torso ['torso] *sm (Anat, Arte)* torso; *(di frutta)* core; **a ~ nudo** bare-chested.

torsolo ['torsolo] *sm (di cavolo etc)* stump; *(di frutta)* core.

torta ['torta] *sf (Culin)* cake; *(: crostata)* tart; **spartirsi la ~** *(fig)* to split the loot.

tortellini [tortel'lini] *smpl (Culin)* tortellini.

tortiera [tor'tjɛra] *sf* cake tin.

tortino [tor'tino] *sm (Culin)* savoury pie.

torto¹, a ['tɔrto] *pp di* **torcere**.

torto² ['tɔrto] *sm (ingiustizia)* wrong; *(colpa)* fault; **fare un ~ a qn** to wrong sb; **ricevere un ~** to be wronged; **avere ~** to be wrong; **hai ~ marcio** you're dead wrong; **a ~** wrongly, unjustly; **a ~ o a ragione** rightly or wrongly; **quest'azione ti fa ~** this action is unworthy of you; **gli ho dato ~** I said he was wrong; **essere/passare dalla parte del ~** to be/put o.s. in the wrong; **lui non ha tutti i ~i** there's something in what he says.

tortora ['tortora] **1** *sf (Zool)* turtledove. **2** *ag inv*: **grigio ~** dove-grey.

tortuosità [tortuosi'ta] *sf (vedi ag)* winding nature; convolution; tortuosity.

tortuoso, a [tortu'oso] *ag (gen)* winding; *(fig: discorso, ragionamento)* convoluted; *(: politica)* tortuous; **esprimersi in modo ~** to express o.s. in a convoluted way.

tortura [tor'tura] *sf* torture; *(fig)* torment, torture; **sottoporre qn alla ~** to torture sb.

torturare [tortu'rare] **1** *vt* to torture; *(fig)* to torment, torture; **~rsi il cervello** to rack one's brains. **2**: **~rsi** *vr* to torment o.s.

torvo, a ['torvo] *ag (occhi, sguardo)* surly; **era ~ in viso** he looked grim; **guardare qn con occhi ~i** to give sb a surly look.

tosaerba [toza'ɛrba] *sm o f inv* lawn mower.

tosare [to'zare] *vt (pecore)* to shear; *(cani)* to clip; *(siepi)* to trim, clip; **ti hanno tosato** *(scherz)* they have cropped you.

tosasiepi [toza'sjɛpi] *sm o f inv* hedge clippers *pl*.

tosatrice [toza'tritʃe] *sf (per capelli)* clippers *pl*; *(per pecore)* electric shears *pl*.

tosatura [toza'tura] *sf (di pecore)* shearing; *(di cani)*

clipping; *(di siepi)* trimming, clipping.

Toscana [tos'kana] *sf* Tuscany.

toscano, a [tos'kano] **1** *ag, sm/f* Tuscan. **2** *sm (anche:* **sigaro ~**) strong Italian cigar.

tosse ['tosse] *sf* cough; **avere la ~** to have a cough; **prenderla la ~** to get a cough.

tossicchiare [tossik'kjare] *vi* to cough.

tossicità [tossitʃi'ta] *sf* toxicity.

tossico, a, ci, che ['tɔssiko] *ag* toxic.

tossicodipendente [tossikodipen'dɛnte] *sm/f* drug addict.

tossicomane [tossi'kɔmane] *sm/f* drug addict.

tossicomania [tossikoma'nia] *sf* drug addiction.

tossina [tos'sina] *sf* toxin.

tossire [tos'sire] *vi* to cough.

tostapane [tosta'pane] *sm inv* toaster.

tostare [tos'tare] *vt (pane)* to toast; *(caffè)* to roast.

tostatura [tosta'tura] *sf (di pane)* toasting; *(di caffè)* roasting.

tosto¹ ['tɔsto] *av* at once, immediately; **~ che** as soon as.

tosto², a ['tɔsto] *ag*: **che faccia ~a!** what cheek!; **hai una bella faccia ~a!** you've got a real cheek!

tot ['tɔt] **1** *ag* so many, X; **ci vediamo il giorno ~ all'ora** **~** see you on such a day at such a time; **diciamo che costa ~ milioni** let's say it costs so many *o* X million. **2** *sm*: **un ~** so much; **mi dà un ~ al mese** he gives me so much a month.

totale [to'tale] **1** *ag (gen)* total; **anestesia ~** general anaesthetic. **2** *sm* total. **3** *sf (Med)* general anaesthetic.

totalità [totali'ta] *sf* totality, entirety; **nella ~ dei casi** in all cases; **la ~ dei presenti** all of those present.

totalitario, a [totali'tarjo] *ag (Pol)* totalitarian; *(totale)* complete, total; **adesione ~a** complete support.

totalitarismo [totalita'rizmo] *sm (Pol)* totalitarianism.

totalizzare [totalid'dzare] *vt* to total, make a total of; *(Sport: punti)* to score.

totalizzatore [totaliddza'tore] *sm (Tecn)* totalizator; *(Ippica)* totalizator, tote *(fam)*.

totem ['tɔtem] *sm inv* totem (pole).

totocalcio [toto'kaltʃo] *sm* (football) pools *pl*; **giocare al ~** to do the pools.

toupet [tu'pɛ] *sm inv* toupée, hair piece.

tour de force ['turdə'fɔrs] *sm inv (fig)* tremendous effort.

tournée [tur'ne] *sf* tour; **essere in ~** to be on tour.

tovaglia [to'vaʎʎa] *sf* tablecloth.

tovagliolo [tovaʎ'ʎɔlo] *sm* napkin, serviette; **~ di carta** paper napkin.

tozzo¹, a ['tɔttso] *ag (persona)* stocky, thickset; *(cosa)* squat.

tozzo² ['tɔttso] *sm* piece, morsel; **per un ~ di pane** *(fig)* for a song.

tra [tra] *prep* (**a**) *(fra due)* between; *(fra più di due)* among, amongst; **c'è un giardino ~ le due case** there's a garden between the two houses; **era ~ gente sconosciuta** he was among strangers; **~ i presenti c'era anche il sindaco** the mayor was also among those present; **~ casa mia e casa loro ci sono 10 minuti di strada** it's 10 minutes walk between my house and theirs; **esitare ~ il sì e il no** to hesitate between yes and no; **avrà ~ i 15 e i 20 anni** he must be between 15 and 20 years old; **costerà ~ le venti e le venticinque mila lire** it'll cost between twenty and twenty-five thousand lire; **sia detto ~ noi...** between you and me...; **mi raccomando, che resti ~ noi** remember, that's between you and me; **scomparire ~ la folla/gli alberi** to disappear into the crowd/among the trees; ~ **una cosa e l'altra** what with one thing and another; ~ **vitto e alloggio fanno 150.000 lire** board and lodging together come to 150,000 lire.

(b) *(attraverso)* through; **il sole filtrava ~ le persiane** the sun filtered through the shutters; **una strada ~ i campi** a road through the fields; **farsi strada ~ la folla** to make one's way through the crowd.

(c) *(in)* in; **la prese ~ le braccia** he took her in his arms; ~ **venti chilometri c'è un'area di servizio** there's a service area in twenty kilometres.

(d) *(tempo)* in; **torno ~ un'ora** I'll be back in an hour; ~ **qualche giorno** in a few days; **sarà qui ~ poco** he'll be here soon *o* shortly; ~ **breve** soon, shortly.

(e): ~ **l'altro** *(inoltre)* besides which, what is more; ~ **tutti non saranno più di venti** there won't be more than twenty in all; ~ **tutto sono 5000 lire** that's 5000 lire in all.

traballante [trabal'lante] *ag (mobile)* shaky.

traballare [trabal'lare] *vi (persona)* to stagger; *(mobile, fig: governo etc)* to be shaky.

trabiccolo [tra'bikkolo] *sm (peg: auto)* old banger, jalopy.

traboccare [trabok'kare] *vi* **(a)** *(aus essere) (liquido):* ~ **(da)** to overflow (from). **(b)** *(contenitore):* ~ **(di)** to overflow (with); **il teatro traboccava di gente** the theatre was full to bursting; ~ **di felicità** to bubble over with happiness.

trabocchetto [trabok'ketto] **1** *sm* trap door; *(fig)* trap; **tendere un ~ a qn** to set a trap for sb. **2** *ag inv* trap *attr*; **domanda ~** trick question.

tracagnotto, a [trakaɲ'ɲɔtto] **1** *ag* dumpy. **2** *sm/f* dumpy person.

tracannare [trakan'nare] *vt* to down, gulp down.

traccia, ce ['trattʃa] *sf* **(a)** *(gen, fig: segno)* mark; *(di aereo, lumaca, fig)* trace; *(di ruota)* track; *(di animale)* tracks *pl*; *(di persona)* footprints *pl*; **essere sulle ~ce di qn** to be on sb's trail; **perdere le ~ce di qn** to lose track of *o* lose the trail of sb; **seguire le ~ce di qn** to follow sb's footprints *o* tracks; *(fig)* to follow in sb's footsteps; **la polizia sta seguendo una ~ sbagliata** the police are on the wrong track; **è sparito senza lasciare ~ce** he vanished without trace.

(b) *(quantità residua, vestigia di civilizzazione)* trace; *(indizio)* sign; **nella sua voce non c'è ~ di accento straniero** he speaks without a trace of a foreign accent; **hanno fatto sparire ogni ~ della loro presenza** they removed all sign of their presence.

(c) *(schema)* outline.

tracciare [trat'tʃare] *vt* **(a)** *(percorso, strada)* to mark out; *(confini)* to map out; *(rotta)* to plot. **(b)** *(disegnare)* to sketch, draw; ~ **una linea** to draw a line; ~ **un arco** to describe a curve. **(c)** *(fig)* to sketch out, outline; ~ **un quadro della situazione** to outline the situation.

tracciato [trat'tʃato] *sm* layout, plan; **strada dal ~ irregolare** winding road; ~ **di gara** *(Sport)* race route.

trachea [tra'kɛa] *sf* windpipe, trachea.

tracolla [tra'kɔlla] *sf* shoulder strap; **portare qc a ~** to carry sth over one's shoulder; **borsa a ~** shoulder bag.

tracollo [tra'kɔllo] *sm (fig)* collapse, ruin; ~ **finanziario** crash; **avere un ~** *(Med)* to have a setback; *(Fin)* to slip, fall.

tracotante [trako'tante] **1** *ag* arrogant, overbearing. **2** *sm/f* arrogant person.

tracotanza [trako'tantsa] *sf* arrogance.

tradimento [tradi'mento] *sm (gen)* betrayal; *(Dir, Mil)* treason; **a ~** by surprise; **mangiare pane a ~**

to live off other people; **alto ~** high treason.

tradire [tra'dire] **1** *vt* **(a)** *(gen)* to betray; *(moglie, marito)* to cheat on, betray, be unfaithful to; ~ **la fiducia di qn** to betray sb's trust; **ha tradito le attese di tutti** he let everyone down; **se la memoria non mi tradisce** if my memory serves me well. **(b)** *(rivelare: segreto)* to reveal, let out; *(: pensiero)* to reveal, show, betray. **2:** ~**rsi** *vr* to give o.s. away.

traditore, trice [tradi'tore] **1** *sm/f* traitor. **2** *ag* treacherous.

tradizionale [tradittsjo'nale] *ag* traditional.

tradizione [tradit'tsjone] *sf* tradition; **secondo la ~** traditionally, according to tradition.

tradotta [tra'dotta] *sf (Mil)* troop train.

tradotto, a [tra'dotto] *pp di* **tradurre.**

tradurre [tra'durre] *vt (gen)* *(testo, autore)* to translate; ~ **dall'inglese in italiano** to translate from English into Italian; ~ **alla lettera** to translate literally; ~ **parola per parola** to translate word for word. **(b)** *(esprimere)* to render, convey; ~ **in parole povere** to explain simply; ~ **in cifre** to put into figures; ~ **in atto** *(fig)* to put into effect. **(c)** *(Dir):* ~ **qn in carcere/tribunale** to take sb to prison/court; ~ **qn davanti al giudice** to bring sb before the court.

traduttore, trice [tradut'tore] *sm/f* translator.

traduzione [tradut'tsjone] *sf* **(a)** *(di testo)* translation. **(b)** *(Dir)* transfer.

trafelato, a [trafe'lato] *ag* breathless, out of breath.

trafficante [traffi'kante] *sm/f (peg)* trafficker; *(: di droga)* pusher; *(: di merce rubata)* fence.

trafficare [traffi'kare] *vi* **(a)** *(commerciare)* to deal, trade; *(in droga etc)* to traffic, trade (illicitly). **(b)** *(affaccendarsi)* to be busy.

trafficato, a [traffi'kato] *ag (strada, zona)* busy.

traffico ['traffiko] *sm* **(a)** *(peg: commercio)* traffic; ~ **di droga** drug trafficking. **(b)** *(movimento)* traffic; ~ **aereo/ferroviario** air/rail traffic; ~ **stradale** traffic; **regolare il ~** *(Aut)* to control *o* regulate the traffic; **chiudere una strada al ~** *(Aut)* to close a road to traffic.

trafiggere [tra'fiddʒere] *vt (ferire)* to run through; *(: fig)* to pierce.

trafila [tra'fila] *sf* procedure; **bisognerà seguire la solita ~** we'll have to go through the usual routine.

trafiletto [trafi'letto] *sm (di giornale)* short article.

trafitto, a [tra'fitto] *pp di* **trafiggere.**

traforare [trafo'rare] *vt (gen)* to pierce; *(montagna)* to tunnel through, make a tunnel through; *(legno, metallo)* to drill; **il proiettile gli ha traforato il cuore** the bullet pierced his heart.

traforo [tra'foro] *sm* **(a)** *(operazione: vedi vb)* piercing; tunnelling; drilling. **(b)** *(galleria)* tunnel. **(c):** **lavoro di ~** *(su metallo, legno)* fretwork.

trafugamento [trafuga'mento] *sm* purloining; ~ **di tesori/opere d'arte** purloining of treasures/works of art; ~ **di salme** body snatching.

trafugare [trafu'gare] *vt* to purloin.

tragedia [tra'dʒɛdja] *sf (Teatro, fig: disastro)* tragedy; ~ **greca/latina** Greek/Latin tragedy; **non farne una ~** *(fig iro)* don't make a fuss about it.

traghettare [traget'tare] *vt (fiume)* to ferry across; *(persone)* to ferry.

traghettatore, trice [tragetta'tore] *sm/f* ferryman/woman.

traghetto [tra'getto] **1** *sm (trasporto)* ferrying; *(luogo)* ferry; *(mezzo)* ferry(boat). **2** *ag inv* ferry *attr*.

tragicità [tradʒitʃi'ta] *sf* tragedy.

tragico, a, ci, che ['tradʒiko] **1** *ag* tragic. **2** *sm* *(tragediografo)* tragedian; **non fare il** ~ *(fig)* don't make a song and dance over it; **prendere tutto sul** ~ *(fig)* to take everything far too seriously; **il** ~ **della faccenda è che…** *(fig)* the worst thing about it is… .

tragicomico, a, ci, che [tradʒi'kɔmiko] *ag* tragicomic.

tragicommedia [tradʒikom'medja] *sf* tragicomedy.

tragitto [tra'dʒitto] *sm* **(a)** *(viaggio)* journey; **durante il** ~ on the journey. **(b)** *(tratto di strada)* way; **durante il** ~ on the way; **ti accompagno per un breve** ~ I'll go with you part of the way.

traguardo [tra'gwardo] *sm (Sport)* finish, finishing post; *(: linea)* finishing line; *(fig)* aim, goal; **tagliare il** ~ to cross the line; **raggiungere il** ~ to reach the finish; *(fig)* to reach one's goal.

traiettoria [trajet'tɔrja] *sf* trajectory.

trainare [trai'nare] *vt (carro)* to draw, pull; *(auto)* to tow.

traino ['traino] *sm* **(a)** *(operazione)* drawing, pulling; *(: di auto)* towing. **(b)** *(cosa trainata)* trailer load.

tralasciare [tralaʃ'ʃare] *vt* **(a)** *(trascurare: studi)* to neglect. **(b)** *(omettere)* to leave out; **tralasciamo i particolari** let's skip the details.

tralcio ['traltʃo] *sm* shoot.

traliccio [tra'littʃo] *sm (pilone)* pylon.

tralice [tra'litʃe]: **in** ~ *av*: **guardare qn in** ~ to look askance at sb.

tram [tram] *sm inv* tram.

trama ['trama] *sf* **(a)** *(filo)* weft, woof. **(b)** *(di opera)* plot; *(inganno)* plot, conspiracy; **ordire una** ~ **ai danni di qn** to weave a plot against sb.

tramandare [traman'dare] *vt* to hand down.

tramare [tra'mare] *vt* to plot, scheme; ~ **un complotto** to plot.

trambusto [tram'busto] *sm (rumore)* racket; *(disordine)* turmoil.

tramestio, ii [trames'tio] *sm* bustle, bustling.

tramezzino [tramed'dzino] *sm* sandwich.

tramezzo [tra'meddzo] *sm* partition, dividing wall.

tramite ['tramite] **1** *sm* means *pl*; **agire/fare da** ~ to act as/be a go-between. **2** *prep (per mezzo di: cosa)* by means of; *(: persona)* through.

tramontana [tramon'tana] *sf (Meteor)* north wind; **perdere la** ~ *(fig)* to lose one's bearings.

tramontare [tramon'tare] *vi (aus essere) (astri)* to go down, set; *(fig: bellezza, gloria)* to fade.

tramonto [tra'monto] *sm (Astron)* setting; *(: del sole)* sunset; **è sul viale del** ~ *(fig: attore)* he has passed his peak.

tramortire [tramor'tire] **1** *vt* to knock out, knock unconscious. **2** *vi (aus essere)* to pass out, faint, lose consciousness; **essere tramortito** to be unconscious.

trampolino [trampo'lino] *sm (Sport: per tuffi)* springboard; *(: in muratura)* diving board; *(: Sci)* ski jump; **servire da** ~ *(fig)* to serve as a springboard.

trampolo ['trampolo] *sm* stilt.

tramutare [tramu'tare] **1** *vt*: ~ **in** to change into, turn into. **2**: ~**rsi** *vr*: ~**rsi in** to change into, turn into.

trance ['traːns] *sf inv* trance; **in stato di** ~ **in a** (state of) trance; **cadere in** ~ to fall into a trance.

trancia, ce ['trantʃa] *sf* **(a)** *(Tecn)* shears *pl*. **(b)** *(fetta)* slice; ~ **di salmone** *(Culin)* salmon cutlet; **a** ~**ce** in slices.

tranciare [tran'tʃare] *vt (Tecn)* to shear.

trancio ['trantʃo] *sm* = **trancia b**.

tranello [tra'nello] *sm* trap; **tendere un** ~ **a qn** to set a trap for sb; **cadere in un** ~ to fall into a trap.

trangugiare [trangu'dʒare] *vt* to gulp down; *(fig: amarezze)* to swallow.

tranne ['tranne] **1** *prep (eccetto)* except; **c'erano tutti** ~ **lui** they were all there except *o* but him; **tutti i giorni** ~ **il venerdì** every day except *o* with the exception of Friday; **va d'accordo con tutti** ~ **che con me** he gets on with everybody except *o* but me. **2**: ~ **che** *cong* unless; **non si accetteranno variazioni** ~ **che non siano seriamente motivate** no changes will be accepted unless there are good reasons for them.

tranquillante [trankwil'lante] *sm (Med)* tranquillizer.

tranquillità [trankwilli'ta] *sf (di luogo, animo)* tranquillity; **è ritornata la** ~ the situation has returned to normal; **per amore della** ~ for the sake of peace and quiet; **amo la mia** ~ I am fond of my privacy; **per la mia** ~ to set my mind at ease.

tranquillizzare [trankwillid'dzare] **1** *vt* to reassure. **2**: ~**rsi** *vr* to calm down.

tranquillo, a [tran'kwillo] *ag* **(a)** *(luogo)* calm, peaceful; **il mare è** ~ the sea is calm. **(b)** *(persona)* calm; *(: sicuro)* sure, confident; **dormire sonni** ~**i** to sleep easy *o* peacefully; **avere la coscienza** ~**a** to have an easy conscience; **stai** ~ **che ce la fa!** don't worry — he'll do it alright!

transalpino, a [transal'pino] *ag* transalpine.

transatlantico, a, ci, che [transat'lantiko] **1** *ag* transatlantic. **2** *sm (Naut)* transatlantic liner.

transatto, a [tran'satto] *pp di* **transigere**.

transazione [transat'tsjone] *sf (Dir)* settlement; *(Comm)* transaction.

transenna [tran'senna] *sf (cavalletto)* barrier.

transetto [tran'setto] *sm* transept.

transfert ['transfert] *sm inv (Psic)* transference.

transiberiano, a [transibe'rjano] *ag* trans-Siberian.

transigere [tran'sidʒere] *vi* to compromise; **è uno che non transige** he is intransigent; **in fatto di sincerità io non transigo** I won't put up with insincerity.

transistor [tran'sistor] *sm inv (Elettr)* transistor; *(Radio)* transistor (radio).

transitabile [transi'tabile] *ag* passable, practicable.

transitare [transi'tare] *vi (aus essere)* to pass.

transitivo, a [transi'tivo] *ag* transitive.

transito ['transito] *sm* transit; **'divieto di** ~**'** 'no entry'; **stazione** *f* **di** ~ transit station; **'**~ **interrotto'** 'road closed'.

transitorio, a [transi'tɔrjo] *ag (temporaneo)* provvedimento) temporary, provisional; *(: gloria etc)* transitory, fleeting.

transizione [transit'tsjone] *sf* transition; **età/periodo di** ~ age/period of transition.

tran tran [tran 'tran] *sm* routine; **il solito** ~ the same old routine.

tranvia [tran'via] *sm inv* tram.

tranviario, a [tran'vjarjo] *ag* tram *attr*; **linea** ~**a** tramline.

tranviere [tran'vjɛre] *sm (conducente)* tram driver; *(bigliettaio)* tram conductor.

trapanare [trapa'nare] *vt (Tecn)* to drill.

trapanazione [trapanat'tsjone] *sf* drilling; ~ **del cranio** *(Med)* trepanation.

trapano ['trapano] *sm* drill.

trapassare [trapas'sare] **1** *vt* to go through, pierce. **2** *vi (aus essere) (fig: morire)* to pass away.

trapassato, a [trapas'sato] *sm (Gram)* past perfect.

trapasso [tra'passo] *sm* **(a)** *(Dir: passaggio)*: ~ **di proprietà** *(di case)* conveyancing; *(di auto etc)* legal transfer. **(b): l'ora del** ~ *(poet)* one's final hour.

trapelare [trape'lare] *vi* (*aus* **essere**) (*luce*) to filter through; (*fig: segreto*) to leak; **dal suo viso trapelava tutta la sua gioia** his face shone with joy.

trapezio [tra'pɛttsjo] *sm* (**a**) (*Mat*) trapezium. (**b**) (*Sport*) trapeze. (**c**) (*Anat*) trapezius.

trapezista, i, e [trapet'tsista] *sm/f* trapeze artist.

trapiantare [trapjan'tare] **1** *vt* (**a**) (*Bot, Med*) to transplant; (*fig: moda etc*) to introduce. **2**: ~**rsi** *vr* to move; **ormai si sono trapiantati in Kenia** they have now settled in Kenya.

trapianto [tra'pjanto] *sm* (*Bot*) transplanting; (*Med*) transplant.

trappola ['trappola] *sf* (**a**) (*anche fig*) trap; **prendere qn/qc in** ~ (*anche fig*) to catch sb/sth in a trap; **cadere in** ~ (*anche fig*) to fall into a trap; **tendere una** ~ **a qn** to set a trap for sb. (**b**) (*peg: catorcio*) old wreck.

trapunta [tra'punta] *sf* quilt.

trarre ['trarre] **1** *vt* (**a**) to draw, pull; **la sua aria innocente trae in inganno** her innocent appearance is misleading *o* deceptive; **sono stato tratto in inganno dal suo modo di fare** I was misled *o* deceived by his manner; ~ **qn d'impaccio** to get sb out of an awkward situation; ~ **in salvo** to rescue. (**b**) (*estrarre*) to pull out, draw; ~ **un sospiro di sollievo** to heave a sigh of relief. (**c**) (*derivare*) to obtain, get; ~ **guadagno** to make a profit; ~ **beneficio** *o* **profitto da qc** to benefit from sth; ~ **esempio da qn** to follow sb's example; ~ **un film da un libro** to make a film adaptation of a book, make a film from a book; ~ **le conclusioni** to draw one's own conclusions.
2: trarsi *vr*: **trarsi da** to get (o.s.) out of; **stai tranquillo che sa trarsi d'impaccio da solo** don't worry, he knows how to look after himself.

trasalire [trasa'lire] *vi* to jump, give a start; **fare** ~ **qn** to make sb jump *o* start.

trasandato, a [trazan'dato] *ag* (*persona, abito*) scruffy; **è** ~ **nel vestire** he is a sloppy dresser.

trasbordare [trazbor'dare] **1** *vt* to transfer. **2** *vi* (*Naut*) to change ship; (*Aer*) to change plane; (*Ferr*) to change (trains).

trasbordo [traz'bordo] *sm* transfer.

trascendentale [traʃʃenden'tale] *ag* (*Filosofia*) transcendental; (*fig*): **non è niente di** ~ it (*o* he *etc*) is nothing exceptional.

trascendente [traʃʃen'dɛnte] *ag* (*Filosofia*) transcendent; (*Mat*) transcendental.

trascendere [traʃ'ʃɛndere] *vt* (*Filosofia, Rel*) to transcend; (*fig: superare*) to surpass, go beyond.

trasceso, a [traʃ'ʃeso] *pp di* **trascendere**.

trascinare [traʃʃi'nare] **1** *vt* (*gen*) to drag; ~ **i piedi** to drag one's feet; **trascina una gamba** he has a stiff leg; ~ **qn in tribunale** to take sb to court; **sa** ~ **la folla** (*fig*) he knows how to carry the crowd; **la sua musica ti trascina** his music is enthralling; ~ **qn sulla via del male** to lead sb astray. **2**: ~**rsi** *vr* (*strisciare*) to drag o.s.; (*fig: durare*) to drag on.

trascolorare [traskolo'rare] *vi* (*aus* **essere**): **trascolorò in volto** his face changed colour.

trascorrere [tras'korrere] **1** *vt* (*vacanze, giorni*) to spend, pass. **2** *vi* (*aus* **essere**) (*passare: ore, mesi, giorni*) to pass; **le ore trascorrevano lente** the hours dragged by; **sono trascorsi sei giorni da allora** six days have passed since then.

trascorso, a [tras'korso] **1** *pp di* **trascorrere**. **2** *ag* past. **3** *sm* mistake; **non voglio conoscere i suoi** ~**i** I don't want to know about his past.

trascritto, a [tras'kritto] *pp di* **trascrivere**.

trascrivere [tras'krivere] *vt* (**a**) (*citazioni, frasi, idee*) to write down, copy down. (**b**) (*traslitterare*) to transliterate; (: *sistema fonetico e delle note*

musicali) to transcribe.

trascrizione [traskrit'tsjone] *sf* (*gen*) writing down, copying down; (*di discorso*) transcript; (*traslitterazione*) transliteration; (: *nel sistema fonetico e delle note musicali*) transcription.

trascurare [trasku'rare] **1** *vt* (**a**) (*studio, lavoro, famiglia*) to neglect. (**b**) (*omettere*) to omit, skip, leave out. (**c**) (*non tener conto di*) to ignore, overlook. **2**: ~**rsi** *vr* to neglect o.s.

trascuratezza [traskura'tettsa] *sf* carelessness, neglect; (*disordine*) untidiness.

trascurato, a [trasku'rato] *ag* (**a**) (*sciatto*) slovenly. (**b**) (*non curato*) neglected; **sentirsi** ~ to feel neglected; **un'influenza** ~ **a può portare alla polmonite** if you neglect a bout of flu it can develop into pneumonia.

trasecolare [traseko'lare] *vi* to be dumbfounded.

trasferimento [trasferi'mento] *sm* (**a**) (*cambiamento di sede*) transfer; **ha chiesto il** ~ he requested a transfer. (**b**) (*Dir: di titoli*) transfer; (: *di proprietà*) conveyancing.

trasferire [trasfe'rire] **1** *vt* (**a**) (*sede, potere*) to transfer. (**b**) (*Dir: titoli*) to transfer; (: *proprietà*) to transfer, convey. **2**: ~**rsi** *vr* to move.

trasferta [tras'fɛrta] *sf* (**a**) (*di funzionario etc*) temporary transfer; **essere in** ~ to be on temporary transfer. (**b**) (*anche: indennità di* ~) travel allowance, travel expenses *pl*. (**c**) (*Sport*) away game; **giocare in** ~ to play away (from home).

trasfigurare [trasfigu'rare] **1** *vt* to transfigure. **2**: ~**rsi** *vr* to be transfigured.

trasfigurazione [trasfigurat'tsjone] *sf* transfiguration.

trasformare [trasfor'mare] **1** *vt* (**a**) (*gen*) to change, alter; (*radicalmente*) to transform; **hanno trasformato la stalla in un ristorante** they converted the stable into a restaurant; **la strega ha trasformato il principe in un albero** the witch turned the prince into a tree; **quel vestito ti trasforma** that dress changes you completely *o* transforms you. (**b**) (*Rugby*) to convert; ~ **un rigore** (*Calcio*) to score from a penalty. **2**: ~**rsi** *vr* (*embrione, larva*) to be transformed, transform itself; (*energia*) to be converted; (*persona, paese*) to change, alter; (: *radicalmente*) to be transformed.

trasformatore [trasforma'tore] *sm* (*Elettr*) transformer.

trasformazione [trasformat'tsjone] *sf* (*vedi vb*) change, alteration; transformation; conversion.

trasfusione [trasfu'zjone] *sf* (*Med*) transfusion.

trasgredire [trazgre'dire] *vt, vi*: ~ **a** (*legge, regola*) to break, infringe; (*ordini*) to disobey.

trasgressione [trazgres'sjone] *sf* (*vedi vb*) breaking, infringement; disobeying.

trasgressore, trasgreditrice [trazgres'sore, trazgredi'tritʃe] *sm/f* (*Dir*) transgressor.

traslato, a [traz'lato] **1** *ag* metaphorical, figurative. **2** *sm* metaphor.

traslazione [trazlat'tsjone] *sf* (**a**) (*gen, Fin*) transfer. (**b**) (*Fis*) translation.

traslocare [trazlo'kare] *vt, vi* to move.

trasloco, chi [traz'lɔko] *sm* move.

traslucido, a [traz'lutʃido] *ag* translucent.

trasmesso, a [traz'messo] *pp di* **trasmettere**.

trasmettere [traz'mettere] **1** *vt* (**a**) (*usanza, diritto, titolo*) to pass on; (*lettera, telegramma, notizia*) to send. (**b**) (*Telec*) to transmit; (*Radio, TV*) to broadcast; ~ **una partita in diretta** to broadcast a match live; **trasmettono un western** (*TV*) they're showing a western. **2**: ~**rsi** *vr* (*usanza* *etc)* to be passed on; *(Med)* to be spread, be transmitted.

trasmettitore, trice |trazmetti'torc| **1** *ag* transmitting. **2** *sm* transmitter.

trasmigrazione |trazmigrat'tsjonc| *sf (di anime)* transmigration.

trasmissione |trazmis'sjonc| *sf* **(a)** *(gen)* transmission; *(di titolo, eredità)* passing on, handing down; **albero di** ~ *(Aut)* transmission shaft. **(b)** *(Radio, TV: programma)* transmission, broadcast, programme; **le** ~**i riprenderanno domani** programmes will resume tomorrow.

trasmittente |trazmit'tente| **1** *ag* transmitting. **2** *sf* transmitter.

trasognato, a |trasoɲ'ɲato| *ag* dreamy.

trasparente |traspa'rente| **1** *ag (anche fig)* transparent; *(sottile)* wafer-thin. **2** *sm* transparency.

trasparenza |traspa'rentsa| *sf* transparency; **guardare qc in** ~ to look at sth against the light.

trasparire |traspa'rirc| *vi (aus essere)* **(a)** to shine through; **lasciare** ~ **la luce** to let the light shine through. **(b)** *(vedersi)* to be visible; **sotto il vestito traspare la sottoveste** her slip shows *o* can be seen through her dress; **dal suo volto traspariva la gioia** his face shone with joy.

traspirare |traspi'rarc| *vi (aus essere)* to perspire; *(fig: trapelare)* to leak out.

traspirazione |traspirat'tsjonc| *sf* perspiration.

trasporre |tras'porrc| *vt* to transpose.

trasportare |traspor'tarc| *vt* **(a)** *(gen, fig)* to carry; *(con veicolo)* to carry, transport; **lo hanno trasportato d'urgenza in ospedale** they rushed him to hospital; **questo libro ci trasporta al Rinascimento** this book transports us to the Renaissance. **(b):** **lasciarsi** ~ **dall'ira** to lose one's temper; **lasciarsi** ~ **dalla gioia** to become carried away with delight. **(c)** *(trascinare)* to carry off; **l'hanno trasportato in questura** they carried him off to the police station.

trasportatore, trice |trasporta'torc| **1** *ag* transport *attr*. **2** *sm* **(a)** *(persona)* transporter, carrier; *(: per strada)* haulier. **(b)** *(macchina)* conveyor.

trasporto |tras'porto| *sm* **(a)** *(gen)* transport; **danneggiato durante il** ~ damaged in transit; ~ **marittimo/aereo** sea/air transport; ~ **stradale** (road) haulage; ~ **(funebre)** funeral procession; **mezzi di** ~ means of transport; **nave** *f*/**aereo da** ~ transport ship/aircraft; **compagnia di** ~ carriers *pl*; *(per strada)* hauliers *pl*; **i** ~**i** transport *sg*; **i** ~**i pubblici** public transport. **(b)** *(fig)* rapture, passion; **con** ~ passionately; **un** ~ **d'ira** a fit of anger.

trasposizione |traspozit'tsjone| *sf (Linguistica)* transposition.

trasposto, a |tras'posto| *pp di* **trasporre**.

trastullare |trastul'larc| **1** *vt (bambino)* to play with. **2:** ~**rsi** *vr (divertirsi)*: ~**rsi con qc** to amuse o.s. with sth; *(gingillarsi)* to fritter away one's time.

trastullo |tras'tullo| *sm* game.

trasudare |trasu'darc| **1** *vt* to ooze. **2** *vi* **(a)** *(aus essere: filtrare)* to ooze (out). **(b)** *(traspirare)* to sweat.

trasversale |trazver'salc| *ag (taglio, sbarra)* cross *attr*; *(retta)* transverse; **via** ~ side street; **una camicia a righe** ~**i** a shirt with horizontal stripes.

tratta |'tratta| *sf* **(a)** *(traffico)* trade; **la** ~ **dei negri** *o* **degli schiavi** the slave trade; **la** ~ **delle bianche** the white slave trade. **(b)** *(Fin)* draft.

trattamento |tratta'mento| *sm* **(a)** *(gen)* treatment; *(servizio in ristorante etc)* service; ~ **di riguardo** special treatment; **ricevere un buon**

~ *(cliente)* to get good service; **fare un** ~ **di favore** to give special treatment. **(b)** *(Tecn, Med)* treatment; **essere sotto** ~ to be under treatment.

trattare |trat'tarc| **1** *vt* **(a)** *(discutere: tema, questione)* to deal with, discuss; *(negoziare: pace, resa)* to negotiate; **non ho trattato l'affare** I didn't deal with the matter. **(b)** *(comportarsi con)* to treat; ~ **bene/male qn** to treat sb well/badly. **(c)** *(Comm: vendere)* to deal in, handle. **(d)** *(Tecn, Med)* to treat.

2 *vi* **(a)** *(libro, film)*: ~ **di** to deal with, be about. **(b)** *(avere relazioni)*: ~ **con** to deal with; **stanno ancora trattando** they are still negotiating.

3: ~**rsi** *vb impers*: **si tratta di sua moglie** it's about his wife; **si tratta di pochi minuti** it will only take a few minutes; **si tratterebbe solo di poche ore** it would just be a matter of a few hours; **di che si tratta?** what's it about?; **si tratta di vita o di morte** it's a matter of life or death.

4: ~**rsi** *vr* to look after o.s.

trattativa |tratta'tiva| *sf* negotiation; **essere in** ~**e con qn** to negotiate with sb.

trattato |trat'tato| *sm* **(a)** *(Dir: accordo)* treaty; **firmare/ratificare un** ~ to sign/ratify a treaty; ~ **di pace** peace treaty; ~ **commerciale** trade agreement. **(b)** *(opera)* treatise.

trattazione |trattat'tsjone| *sf* **(a)** *(di argomento etc)* treatment. **(b)** *(opera)* treatise.

tratteggiare |tratted'dʒarc| *vt (ombreggiare)* to hatch; *(abbozzare)* to sketch; *(fig: descrivere)* to outline; **linea trattegiata** dotted line.

tratteggio |trat'teddʒo| *sm (Disegno)* hatching.

trattenere |tratte'nerc| **1** *vt* **(a)** *(fermare)* to keep back; *(: in ospedale, carcere)* to detain; ~ **qn dal fare qc** to restrain sb *o* hold sb back from doing sth; ~ **in osservazione** to detain for observation; **ho cercato di trattenerlo** I tried to hold him back; **sono stato trattenuto in ufficio** I was delayed at the office; **mi hanno trattenuto a pranzo** they had me stay for lunch. **(b)** *(lacrime, riso)* to hold back, keep back, restrain; *(respiro)* to hold. **(c)** *(detrarre)* to withhold, keep back. **2:** ~**rsi** *vr (fermarsi)* to stay; **mi sono trattenuto in ufficio** I stayed on at the office; **mi sono trattenuto a cena** I stayed for dinner; ~**rsi dal fare qc** to keep *o* stop o.s. from doing sth; **non sono più riuscito a trattenermi** I just couldn't stop myself.

trattenimento |tratteni'mento| *sm* party; ~ **danzante** dance.

trattenuta |tratte'nuta| *sf (anche:* ~ **sullo stipendio)** deduction.

trattino |trat'tino| *sm (nelle parole composte)* hyphen; *(per iniziare il discorso diretto)* dash.

tratto¹, a |'tratto| *pp di* **trarre**.

tratto² |'tratto| *sm* **(a)** *(di penna)* stroke; **disegnare a grandi** ~**i** to sketch; **descrivere qc a grandi** ~**i** to give an outline of sth. **(b):** ~**i** *pl (caratteristiche)* features; *(modo di fare)* manners, ways; **ha i** ~**i molto marcati** he has very prominent features; **i** ~**i essenziali del periodo/del suo carattere** the essential features of the period/his character; **una persona dai** ~**i gentili** a kind person. **(c)** *(segmento)* part, section; *(: di mare)* stretch; **dobbiamo fare ancora un bel** ~ **a piedi** we still have quite a long way to walk; **alcuni** ~**i del suo romanzo** some parts of his novel. **(d)** *(spazio di tempo)* time, period; **a** ~**i** at times; **(tutto) ad un** ~ all at once.

trattore |trat'torc| *sm* tractor.

trattoria |tratto'ria| *sf (small)* restaurant.

trauma, i |'trauma| *sm (Med: anche:* ~ **psichico)** trauma; ~ **cranico** concussion; **la morte di suo padre è stata un** ~ his father's death was a

traumatic experience for him.
traumatico, a, ci, che [trau'matiko] *ag* traumatic.
traumatizzare [traumatid'dzare] *vt* (*Med*) to traumatize; (*fig: impressionare*) to shock.
travagliare [travaʎ'ʎare] **1** *vt* (*affliggere*) to trouble, afflict; (*fig: tormentare*) to torment; **ha avuto un'esistenza travagliata** he has had a difficult life. **2** *vi* (*poet*) to suffer.
travaglio [tra'vaʎʎo] *sm* (*sofferenza: mentale*) anguish, distress; (*: fisica*) pain, suffering; ~ **del parto** (*Med*) labour.
travasare [trava'zare] *vt* (*liquidi*) to pour; (*: vino*) to decant.
travaso [tra'vazo] *sm* (*vedi vb*) pouring; decanting.
travatura [trava'tura] *sf* beams *pl*.
trave ['trave] *sf* beam.
traveggole [tra'veggole] *sfpl*: **avere le** ~ to be seeing things.
traversa [tra'vɛrsa] *sf* (**a**) (*trave trasversale*) crossbeam, crosspiece; (*Ferr*) sleeper; (*Calcio*) crossbar. (**b**) (*lenzuolo*) drawsheet. (**c**) (*via*) side road; **prendi la seconda** ~ **a destra** take the second right.
traversare [traver'sare] *vt* (*attraversare*) to cross; ~ **un fiume a nuoto** to swim across a river.
traversata [traver'sata] *sf* (*gen, Naut*) crossing; (*Aer*) flight, trip.
traversie [traver'sie] *sfpl* hardships.
traversina [traver'sina] *sf* (*Ferr*) sleeper.
traverso, a [tra'vɛrso] **1** *ag* cross attr, transverse; **via** ~**a** side road; **ottenere qc per vie** ~**e** (*fig*) to obtain sth in an underhand way. **2: di** ~ *av*: **camminare di** ~ to walk sideways (on); **andare di** ~ (*cibo*) to go down the wrong way; **guardare qn di** ~ to give sb a nasty look; **avere la luna di** ~ to be in a bad mood; **messo di** ~ sideways on.
travertino [traver'tino] *sm* travertine.
travestimento [travesti'mento] *sm* disguise; (*per carnevale*) costume.
travestire [traves'tire] **1** *vt* (*camuffare*) to disguise; (*in costume*) to dress up; ~ **da donna** to dress up as a woman. **2:** ~**rsi** *vr* (*vedi vt*) to disguise o.s.; to dress up.
travestito [traves'tito] *sm* transvestite.
traviare [travi'are] **1** *vt* to lead astray. **2:** ~**rsi** *vr* to go off the straight and narrow.
travisare [travi'zare] *vt* to distort, misrepresent.
travolgente [travol'dʒɛnte] *ag* overwhelming.
travolgere [tra'vɔldʒere] *vt* (*sog: piena, valanga*) to sweep away; (*fig*) to overwhelm; **è stato travolto da un'auto** he was run over by a car; **si è lasciato** ~ **dalla passione** he was overwhelmed by passion.
travolto, a [tra'vɔlto] *pp di* **travolgere**.
trazione [trat'tsjone] *sf* (*Med, Tecn*) traction; (*Aut*) drive; ~ **anteriore/posteriore** (*Aut*) front-wheel/rear-wheel drive.
tre [tre] **1** *ag inv* three; ~ **volte** three times, thrice. **2** *sm inv* three; **non c'è due senza** ~ it never rains but it pours; *per uso vedi* **cinque**.
trealberi [tre'alberi] *sm inv* (*Naut*) three-master.
trebbia ['trebbja] *sf* (*Agr: operazione*) threshing; (*: stagione*) threshing season.
trebbiare [treb'bjare] *vt* (*Agr*) to thresh.
trebbiatrice [trebbja'tritʃe] *sf* (*Agr*) threshing machine.
treccia, ce ['trettʃa] *sf* (*gen*) braid; (*di capelli*) plait, braid.
trecentesco, a, schi, sche [tretʃen'tesko] *ag* fourteenth-century.
trecento [tre'tʃɛnto] **1** *ag inv* three hundred. **2** *sm inv* three hundred; (*secolo*): **il T**~ the fourteenth century.

tredicenne [tredi'tʃɛnne] *ag, sm/f* thirteen-year-old; *per uso vedi* **cinquantenne**.
tredicesima [tredi'tʃɛzima] *sf Christmas bonus of a month's pay*.
tredicesimo, a [tredi'tʃɛzimo] *ag, sm/f, sm* thirteenth; *per uso vedi* **quinto**.
tredici ['treditʃi] **1** *ag inv* thirteen. **2** *sm inv* thirteen; **fare** ~ (*Totocalcio*) to win the pools; *per uso vedi* **cinque**.
tregua ['tregwa] *sf* (*Mil, Pol*) truce; (*fig*) rest, respite; **il dolore non gli dà** ~ the pain gives him no peace, he is in constant pain; **senza** ~ non-stop, without stopping, uninterruptedly.
tremante [tre'mante] *ag* trembling, shaking.
tremare [tre'mare] *vi* (**a**) (*gen*) to tremble, shake; (*fig: temere*) to be afraid; ~ **di freddo** to shiver; ~ **di paura** to tremble with fear; ~ **come una foglia** to shake like a leaf; **mi tremano le gambe** my legs are shaking; ~ **per la sorte di qn** to fear for sb; **faceva** ~ **gli studenti** he made the students tremble with fear. (**b**) (*oscillare: vetri etc*) to vibrate; (*: terra*) to shake; (*: voce*) to shake, tremble; (*: luce, candela*) to flicker; **mi trema la vista** I can't see straight.
tremarella [trema'rɛlla] *sf* shivers *pl*; **ho la** ~ I have got the shivers; **mi ha fatto venire la** ~ it gave me the shivers.
tremendo, a [tre'mɛndo] *ag* (*in tutti i sensi*) terrible, awful, dreadful; **avere una fame** ~**a** to be awfully o very hungry, be famished; **faceva un caldo** ~ it was dreadfully o terribly hot.
trementina [tremen'tina] *sf* turpentine.
tremito ['trɛmito] *sm* trembling; **mi è venuto un** ~ I started to tremble.
tremolante [tremo'lante] *ag* (*vedi vb*) trembling, shaking; flickering; twinkling.
tremolare [tremo'lare] *vi* (*gen*) to tremble, shake; (*luci, candele*) to flicker; (*stelle*) to twinkle.
tremolio [tremo'lio] *sm* (*gen*) trembling, shaking; (*di luci*) flickering.
tremore [tre'more] *sm* trembling, shaking.
tremulo, a ['trɛmulo] *ag* (*gen*) trembling, shaking; (*stelle*) twinkling; (*luci*) flickering.
trend [trend] *sm inv* (*Econ*) trend.
trenette [tre'nette] *sfpl* (*Culin*) long, flat noodles.
trenino [tre'nino] *sm* (*giocattolo*) toy train.
treno ['trɛno] *sm* (**a**) (*Ferr*) train; ~ **merci/viaggiatori** goods/passenger train; ~ **locale/diretto/espresso** local/fast/express train; ~ **rapido** express (train) (*for which supplement must be paid*); ~ **straordinario** special train; **prendere/perdere il** ~ to catch/miss the train; **salire in/scendere dal** ~ to get on/get off the train; **andare/viaggiare in** ~ to go/travel by train. (**b**) (*Aut*): ~ **di gomme** set of tyres.
trenta ['trenta] **1** *ag inv* thirty. **2** *sm inv* (**a**) thirty. (**b**) (*Univ*): ~ **su** ~ full marks; ~ **e lode** full marks plus distinction o cum laude; *per uso vedi* **cinque**.
trentenne [tren'tenne] *ag, sm/f* thirty-year-old; *per uso vedi* **cinquantenne**.
trentennio [tren'tennjo] *sm* period of thirty years.
trentesimo, a [tren'tɛzimo] *ag, sm/f, sm* thirtieth; *per uso vedi* **quinto**.
trentina [tren'tina] *sf* about thirty; *per uso vedi* **cinquantina**.
trepidante [trepi'dante] *ag* anxious.
trepidare [trepi'dare] *vi* to be anxious; ~ **per qn** to be anxious about sb; **trepidava nell'attesa** she waited in trepidation.
trepido, a ['trɛpido] *ag* anxious.
treppiede [trep'pjede] *sm* tripod.

trequarti [tre'kwarti] *sm inv* three-quarter-length coat.

tresca, sche ['treska] *sf (fig)* intrigue, plot; ~ (amorosa) (love) affair.

trespolo ['trespolo] *sm* trestle; *(per uccelli)* perch.

triangolare [triango'lare] *ag* triangular.

triangolo [tri'angolo] *sm (gen, fig, Mat, Mus)* triangle; *(Aut)* warning triangle; ~ **ottusangolo/ rettangolo** obtuse-angled/right-angled triangle.

tribolare [tribo'lare] *vi (patire)* to suffer; *(fare fatica)* to have a lot of trouble; **ha finito di** ~ *(euf: è morto)* death has put an end to his suffering; **ha tribolato parecchio per ottenerlo** he went to a lot of trouble to get it.

tribolazione [tribolat'tsjone] *sf* tribulation, suffering; **quel figlio è la mia** ~ that son of mine brings me nothing but suffering; **una vita di** ~**i** a life of trials and tribulations.

tribordo [tri'bordo] *sm (Naut)* starboard.

tribù [tri'bu] *sf inv* tribe.

tribuna [tri'buna] *sf* **(a)** *(per oratore)* platform. **(b)** *(per il pubblico)* gallery; *(: di stadio)* stand; *(: di ippodromo)* grandstand; ~ **della stampa/riservata al pubblico** press/public gallery. **(c)** *(TV, Radio)*: ~ **politica** party political broadcast.

tribunale [tribu'nale] *sm (Dir)* court; **chiamare in** ~ to take to court; **presentarsi** *o* **comparire in** ~ to appear in court; ~ **supremo** supreme court; ~ **militare** military tribunal.

tribuno [tri'buno] *sm (Storia)* tribune.

tributare [tribu'tare] *vt*: ~ **gli onori dovuti a qn** to pay tribute to sb.

tributario, a [tribu'tarjo] *ag* **(a)** *(Fisco)* tax *attr*, fiscal. **(b)** *(Geog)*: **fiume** ~ tributary.

tributo [tri'buto] *sm (imposta)* tax; *(Storia, fig)* tribute.

tricheco, chi [tri'kɛko] *sm* walrus.

triciclo [tri'tʃiklo] *sm* tricycle.

tricolore [triko'lore] **1** *ag* three-coloured. **2** *sm (bandiera)* tricolour; **il T~** the Italian flag.

tridente [tri'dɛnte] *sm* trident; *(per fieno)* pitchfork.

tridimensionale [tridimensjo'nale] *ag* three-dimensional.

triennale [trien'nale] *ag (che dura 5 anni)* three-year *attr*; *(che avviene ogni 5 anni)* five-yearly.

triennio [tri'ɛnnjo] *sm* period of three years.

triestino, a [tries'tino] *ag (o* from*)* Trieste.

trifase [tri'faze] *ag (Elettr)* three-phase.

trifoglio [tri'fɔʎʎo] *sm* clover.

trifolato, a [trifo'lato] *ag (Culin)* cooked in oil, garlic and parsley.

trigemino, a [tri'dʒemino] **1** *ag* **(a)** *(Med)*: **avere un parto** ~ to give birth to triplets. **(b)** *(Anat)* trigeminal. **2** *sm (Anat)* trigeminal (nerve).

triglia ['triʎʎa] *sf* mullet; **fare gli occhi di** ~ **a qn** to make sheep's eyes at sb.

trigonometria [trigonome'tria] *sf* trigonometry.

trilione [tri'ljone] *sm* trillion.

trillare [tril'lare] *vi (Mus)* to trill; *(campanello)* to ring.

trillo ['trillo] *sm (Mus)* trill; *(di campanello etc)* ring.

trimestrale [trimes'trale] *ag (periodo, abbonamento)* three-month *attr*; *(scadenza, pubblicazione)* quarterly.

trimestre [tri'mɛstre] *sm* **(a)** *(periodo)* three months, quarter; *(: Scol)* term. **(b)** *(rata)* quarterly payment.

trimotore [trimo'tore] *sm (Aer)* three-engined plane.

trina ['trina] *sf* lace.

trincare [trin'kare] *vt (vino, birra etc)* to knock

back; **trinca come una spugna** he drinks like a fish.

trincea [trin'tʃɛa] *sf (Mil)* trench; **guerra di** ~ trench warfare.

trinceramento [trintʃera'mento] *sm (Mil)* entrenchment.

trincerare [trintʃe'rare] **1** *vt (Mil)* to entrench. **2**: ~**rsi** *vr (Mil)* to entrench o.s.; ~**rsi nel silenzio più assoluto** *(fig)* to take refuge in silence; ~**rsi dietro un pretesto** to hide behind an excuse.

trincetto [trin'tʃetto] *sm* cobbler's knife.

trinciapollo [trintʃa'pollo] *sm inv* poultry shears *pl*.

trinciare [trin'tʃare] *vt* **(a)** to cut up. **(b)** *(fig)*: ~ **giudizi su qn/qc** to make rash judgments about sb/sth; ~ **i panni addosso a qn** to tear sb to pieces.

trinità [trini'ta] *sf* trinity; **la (santissima) T~** the (Holy) Trinity.

trio ['trio] *sm (Mus, fig)* trio.

trionfale [trion'fale] *ag (arco, entrata)* triumphal; *(successo)* triumphant.

trionfante [trion'fante] *ag* triumphant.

trionfare [trion'fare] *vi* **(a)** *(gen, Mil)* to triumph; *(commedia, film)* to be a great success; ~ **sui nemici** to triumph over one's enemies. **(b)** *(esultare)* to rejoice; ~ **per qc** to rejoice at *o* over sth.

trionfatore, trice [trionfa'tore] **1** *ag (truppe)* triumphant, victorious. **2** *sm/f* victor.

trionfo [tri'onfo] *sm (gen)* triumph; *(morale)* (moral) victory; **in** ~ in triumph.

tripartitico, a, ci, che [tripar'titiko] *ag*, **tripartito, a** [tripar'tito] *ag (Pol)* tripartite, three-party *attr*.

triplicare [tripli'kare] *vt*, ~**rsi** *vr* to treble, triple.

triplice ['triplitʃe] *ag* triple; **in** ~ **copia** in triplicate; **la T~ Alleanza** the Triple Alliance.

triplo, a ['triplo] **1** *ag* triple, treble; **salto** ~ *(Sport)* triple jump; **la spesa è** ~**a** it costs three times as much; **mi occorre uno stipendio** ~ I need treble *o* three times the salary. **2** *sm*: **mi occorre il** ~ I need three times as much; **lavorare il** ~ to work three times as hard.

tripode ['tripode] *sm* tripod.

trippa ['trippa] *sf (Culin)* tripe; *(fig: pancia)* paunch.

tripudio [tri'pudjo] *sm* triumph, jubilation; *(fig: di colori)* galaxy.

tris [tris] *sm inv (Carte)*: ~ **d'assi/di re** *etc* three aces/kings *etc*.

triste ['triste] *ag (gen)* sad; *(persona, destino)* unhappy, sad; *(sguardo)* sorrowful, sad; *(spettacolo, condizioni)* miserable; *(luogo)* gloomy, dismal; *(esperienza)* painful.

tristezza [tris'tettsa] *sf (gen)* sadness; *(dolore)* sorrow; *(di paesaggio)* bleakness, dreariness; **che** ~! how sad!

tristo, a ['tristo] *ag (poet: cattivo)* wicked, evil; *(: meschino)* poor, mean.

tritacarne [trita'karne] *sm inv* mincer.

tritaghiaccio [trita'gjattʃo] *sm inv* ice crusher.

tritare [tri'tare] *vt (carne)* to mince; *(verdura, cipolla)* to chop.

tritatutto [trita'tutto] *sm inv* mincer.

trito, a ['trito] **1** *ag (carne)* minced; ~ **e ritrito** *(idee, argomenti, frasi)* trite, hackneyed. **2** *sm*: **fare un** ~ **di cipolla** to chop an onion finely.

tritolo [tri'tɔlo] *sm* trinitrotoluene.

tritone [tri'tone] *sm (Zool)* newt.

trittico, ci ['trittiko] *sm* triptych.

triturare [tritu'rare] *vt* to grind.

triunvirato [triunvi'rato] *sm* triumvirate.

trivella [tri'vɛlla] *sf (Falegnameria)* auger; *(per miniera, pozzi etc)* drill.

trivellare [trivel'lare] *vt* to drill.

trivellazione [trivellat'tsjone] *sf* drilling; **torre** *f* **di** ~ derrick.

triviale [tri'vjale] *ag (volgare)* coarse, crude.

trivialità [trivjali'ta] *sf inv (volgarità)* coarseness, crudeness; *(: osservazione)* coarse *o* crude remark.

trofeo [tro'fɛo] *sm* trophy.

troglodita, i, e [troglo'dita] *sm/f* troglodyte, cave dweller; *(fig)* barbarian.

trogolo ['trɔgolo] *sm* trough.

troia ['trɔja] *sf (Zool)* sow; *(fig peg)* whore.

troiaio [tro'jajo] *sm (fam: luogo sporco)* pigsty.

tromba ['tromba] *sf* **(a)** *(Mus)* trumpet; *(Aut)* horn; **partire in** ~ *(fig)* to be off like a shot. **(b)** *(suonatore)* trumpeter; *(: Mil)* bugler. **(c):** ~ **delle scale** *(Archit)* stairwell; ~ **marina** *(Meteor)* waterspout; ~ **d'aria** *(Meteor)* whirlwind; ~ **d'Eustachio/di Falloppio** *(Anat)* Eustachian/fallopian tube.

trombetta [trom'betta] *sf* toy trumpet.

trombettiere [trombet'tjɛre] *sm (Mil)* bugler.

trombettista, i, e [trombet'tista] *sm/f* trumpeter, trumpet (player).

trombone [trom'bone] *sm* **(a)** *(Mus: strumento)* trombone; *(: suonatore)* trombonist, trombone (player). **(b)** *(fig: persona)* windbag. **(c)** *(Bot)* daffodil.

trombosi [trom'bɔzi] *sf* thrombosis.

troncamento [tronka'mento] *sm* **(a)** *(vedi vb* **a)** breaking off; cutting off. **(b)** *(Linguistica)* apocope.

troncare [tron'kare] *vt* **(a)** *(spezzare)* to break off; *(con cesoie, ascia etc)* to cut off; ~ **il capo a qn** to behead sb. **(b)** *(Linguistica)* to apocopate. **(c)** *(amicizia, relazione)* to break off; *(carriera)* to ruin, cut short; **una salita che tronca le gambe** a tiring climb.

tronchese [tron'kese] *sm o f* clippers *pl*.

tronco¹, a, chi, che ['tronko] *ag (colonna, parola)* truncated.

tronco², chi ['tronko] *sm (Bot, Anat)* trunk; *(tronco d'albero tagliato)* log; *(fig: tratto: di strada, ferrovia)* section; ~ **di cono** *(Geom)* truncated cone; **licenziare qn in** ~ *(fig)* to sack *o* fire sb on the spot.

troneggiare [troned'dʒare] *vi* **(a)** *(sovrastare):* ~ **su qn/qc** to tower over *o* dominate sb/sth. **(b)** *(imporsi all'attenzione):* ~ **in mezzo a qc** to dominate sth; **un grosso brillante troneggiava al centro della vetrina** a large diamond dominated the window display.

tronfio, a ['tronfjo] *ag* conceited, pompous.

trono ['trɔno] *sm* throne; **salire** *o* **ascendere al** ~ to come to *o* ascend the throne.

tropicale [tropi'kale] *ag* tropical.

tropico, ci ['trɔpiko] *sm* tropic; ~ **del Cancro/Capricorno** Tropic of Cancer/Capricorn; **i** ~**i** the tropics.

troppo, a ['trɔppo] **1** *ag indef (quantità: tempo, acqua)* too much; *(numero: persone, promesse)* too many; **c'era** ~ **a gente** there were too many people; **non vorrei causarvi** ~ **disturbo** I wouldn't like to put you to too much trouble.

2 *pron indef* **(a)** *(quantità eccessiva)* too much; *(numero eccessivo)* too many; **ne vorrei ancora un po', ma non** ~ I'd like a little more, but not too much though; **hai detto anche** ~ you've said far too much *o* quite enough; **non ne prendo più, ne ho fin** ~**i** I won't take any more, I've got far too many. **(b):** ~**i** too many (people); ~**i la pensano come lui** too many (people) think like him; **eravamo in** ~**i** there were too many of us.

3 *av* **(a)** *(dav ag, av)* too; *(con verbo: gen)* too much; *(: aspettare, durare)* too long; **fa** ~ **caldo** it's too hot; **è** ~ **bello per essere vero** it's too good to be true; **è fin** ~ **furbo!** he's too clever by half!; **fidarsi** ~ **di qn** to trust sb too much; **sei arrivato** ~ **tardi** you arrived too late; **ho aspettato** ~ I've waited too long; ~ **poco** too little. **(b)** *(rafforzativo)* too, so (very); ~ **buono da parte tua!** *(anche iro)* you're too kind!; **non esserne** ~ **sicuro!** don't be too *o* so sure of that!; **non ci sarebbe** ~ **da stupirsi se decidesse così** it wouldn't be so very *o* all that surprising if he were to decide to do that; **non** ~ **volentieri** none too willingly. **(c):** **di** ~ too much; **essere di** ~ to be in the way.

trota ['trɔta] *sf* trout.

trottare [trot'tare] *vi (cavallo, cavaliere)* to trot; *(aus essere: bambino, cucciolo)* to trot along.

trottata [trot'tata] *sf* trot.

trotterellare [trotterel'lare] *vi (cavallo)* to jog along; *(aus essere: bambino, cucciolo)* to trot along.

trotto ['trɔtto] *sm* trot; **andare al** ~ to trot; **corse** *fpl* **al** ~ trotting races.

trottola ['trɔttola] *sf* (spinning) top.

troupe [trup] *sf inv* troupe, company.

trovare [tro'vare] **1** *vt* **(a)** *(gen)* to find; *(per caso)* to find, come upon, come across; *(difficoltà)* to come up against, meet with; ~ **lavoro/casa** to find work *o* a job/a house; **non trovo le scarpe** I can't find my shoes; **andare/venire a** ~ **qn** to go/come and see sb; ~ **la morte** to meet one's death.

(b): ~ **da ridire (su tutto)** to find sth to criticize (in everything); ~ **da dormire** to find somewhere to sleep.

(c) *(giudicare):* ~ **che** to find *o* think that; **lo trovo un po' invecchiato** I think he has aged a bit; **ti trovo dimagrito** you look thinner; **trovi?** do you think so?; **trovo giusto/sbagliato che...** I think/don't think it's right that...; **lo trovo bello** *o* **buono** I like it.

(d) *(cogliere)* to find, catch; **la notizia ci trovò impreparati** the news found *o* caught us unawares; ~ **qn sul fatto** to catch sb in the act.

2: ~**rsi** *vr* **(a)** *(essere situato)* to be; **dove si trova la stazione?** where is the station?

(b) *(capitare)* to find o.s.; **ci siamo trovati a Napoli** we found ourselves in Naples.

(c) *(essere)* to be; ~**rsi bene/male** to get on well/badly; ~**rsi in pericolo/smarrito** to be in danger/lost; ~**rsi nell'impossibilità di rispondere** to be unable to answer; ~**rsi d'accordo con qn** to be in agreement with sb; ~**rsi a disagio** to feel ill at ease; ~**rsi solo** to find o.s. alone; ~**rsi nei pasticci** to find o.s. in trouble; ~**rsi con un pugno di mosche in mano** *(fig)* to be left empty-handed.

(d) *(uso reciproco: incontrarsi)* to meet; **si sono trovati in piazza** they met (each other) in the square.

trovata [tro'vata] *sf (idea)* brainwave, stroke of genius; ~ **pubblicitaria** gimmick, publicity stunt.

trovatello, a [trova'tɛllo] *sm/f* foundling.

truccare [truk'kare] **1** *vt* **(a)** *(Sport: partita, incontro)* to fix, rig; *(carte da gioco)* to mark; *(dadi)* to load; *(Aut: motore)* to soup up. **(b)** *(attore, viso, occhi)* to make up; ~**rsi** *vr* **(a)** *(gen, Teatro, Cine)* to make o.s. up; ~**rsi da** to make o.s. up as. **(b)** *(travestirsi):* ~**rsi da** to disguise o.s. as.

truccatore, trice [trukka'tore] *sm/f* make-up artist.

trucco, chi ['trukko] *sm* **(a)** *(cosmesi)* make-up.

(b) *(artificio)* trick; *(Cine)* effect, trick; **i ~chi del mestiere** the tricks of the trade.

truce ['trutʃe] *ag (viso, sguardo)* grim, cruel; *(tiranno)* cruel.

trucidare [trutʃi'dare] *vt* to slay, massacre.

truciolo ['trutʃolo] *sm (di legno, metallo)* shaving; **~i di paglia/carta** straw/paper packing material.

truculento, a [truku'lɛnto] *ag (persona, espressione)* truculent, grim.

truffa ['truffa] *sf (Dir)* fraud; *(imbroglio)* swindle.

truffare [truf'fare] *vt* to swindle.

truffatore, trice [truffa'tore] *sm/f* swindler, cheat.

truppa ['truppa] *sf* **(a)** *(Mil)* troop; *(soldati semplici)* troops *pl*. **(b)** *(fig: di amici etc)* group, band, troop.

trust [trʌst] *sm inv (Econ)* trust; **~ di cervelli** *(fig)* brains trust.

tse-tse [tset'tse] *ag inv*: **mosca ~** tsetse fly.

tu [tu] **1** *pron pers* you; **~ è meglio che taci!** you'd do better to keep quiet!; **questo lo dici ~**! that's what you say!; **proprio ~ lo dici!** you're a right one to talk!; **sei ~ quello che fa sempre storie** you're the one who always causes a fuss. **2** *sm*: **dare del ~ a qn** to address sb as 'tu', ≃ be on first-name terms with sb; **trovarsi a ~ per ~ con qn** to find o.s. face to face with sb; **perché non gli parli a ~ per ~?** why don't you have a word with him in private?

tua ['tua] *vedi* **tuo**.

tuba ['tuba] *sf* **(a)** *(Mus)* tuba. **(b)** *(Anat)* tube. **(c)** *(cappello)* top hat.

tubare [tu'bare] *vi (colombi etc)* to coo; *(fig: innamorati)* to bill and coo.

tubatura [tuba'tura] *sf*, **tubazione** [tubat'tsjone] *sf* pipes *pl*, piping.

tubercolosi [tuberko'lɔzi] *sf* tuberculosis.

tubero ['tubero] *sm* tuber.

tubetto [tu'betto] *sm (di dentifricio etc)* tube.

tubino [tu'bino] *sm* **(a)** *(cappello)* bowler. **(b)** *(abito da donna)* sheath dress.

tubo ['tubo] *sm (gen)* tube; *(per condutture)* pipe; **~ digerente** *(Anat)* digestive tract; **~ elettronico** *(Tecn)* electron tube; **~ di scappamento** *(Aut)* exhaust (pipe); **~ di scarico** waste pipe; **non me ne importa un ~** *(fig fam)* I couldn't care less, I don't give a damn.

tubolare [tubo'lare] **1** *ag* tubular; **elastico ~** elastic thread. **2** *sm* tubeless tyre.

tue ['tue] *vedi* **tuo**.

tuffare [tuf'fare] **1** *vt (immergere)* to plunge; *(intingere)* to dip. **2**: **~rsi** *vr (gen)* to dive; **~rsi in mare** to dive *o* plunge into the sea; **~rsi nella mischia** *(fig)* to rush *o* dive into the fray; **~rsi nello studio** *(fig)* to bury *o* immerse o.s. in one's studies; **~rsi a capofitto in qc** *(fig)* to throw o.s. into sth.

tuffatore, trice [tuffa'tore] *sm/f (Sport)* diver.

tuffo ['tuffo] *sm* dive; **~i** *(Sport)* diving *sg*; **fare un ~** to dive; **ho provato un ~ al cuore** *(fig)* my heart skipped *o* missed a beat.

tugurio [tu'gurjo] *sm (peg)* hovel.

tulipano [tuli'pano] *sm* tulip.

tumefatto, a [tume'fatto] *ag* swollen.

tumefazione [tumefat'tsjone] *sf* swelling.

tumido, a ['tumido] *ag (gonfio)* swollen; *(carnoso: labbra)* thick.

tumore [tu'more] *sm* tumour; **~ benigno/maligno** benign/malignant tumour.

tumulazione [tumulat'tsjone] *sf* burial.

tumulo ['tumulo] *sm* tumulus.

tumulto [tu'multo] *sm* **(a)** *(di folla: rumore)* commotion, uproar; *(: agitazione)* turmoil, tumult; *(ribellione)* riot. **(b)** *(fig: di pensieri, desideri)* turmoil; **avere l'animo in ~** to be in a turmoil.

tumultuoso, a [tumultu'oso] *ag (folla)* turbulent, rowdy; *(assemblea)* stormy, turbulent; *(fiume)* turbulent; *(passione)* tumultuous, turbulent.

tundra ['tundra] *sf* tundra.

tungsteno [tung'stɛno] *sm* tungsten.

tunica, che ['tunika] *sf* tunic.

Tunisia [tuni'zia] *sf* Tunisia.

tunisino, a [tuni'zino] *ag, sm/f* Tunisian.

tunnel ['tunnel] *sm inv* tunnel.

tuo, a ['tuo], *pl* **tuoi, tue** **1** *ag poss*: **il(la) ~(a)** *etc* your; **il ~ cane** your dog; **~ padre** your father; **una ~a amica** a friend of yours; **è colpa ~a** it's your fault; **è casa ~a, è la ~a casa** it's your house; **per amor ~** for love of you.

2 *pron poss*: **il(la) ~(a)** *etc* yours, your own; **la nostra barca è più lunga della ~a** our boat is longer than yours; **è questo il ~?** is this yours?; **il ~ è stato solo un errore** it was simply an error on your part.

3 *sm* **(a): hai speso del ~?** did you spend your own money?; **vivi del ~?** do you live on your own income? **(b): i tuoi** *(genitori, famiglia)* your family; *(amici)* your own people, your side; **è dei tuoi** he is on your side.

4 *sf*: **la ~a** *(opinione)* your view; **è dalla ~a** he is on your side; **anche tu hai avuto le ~e** *(disavventure)* you've had your problems too; **alla ~a!** *(brindisi)* your health!

tuoi ['twɔi] *vedi* **tuo**.

tuonare [two'nare] **1** *vi (fig: armi, voce)* to thunder, boom; **~ contro qc/qn** *(inveire)* to rage against sth/sb. **2** *vb impers*: **sta tuonando** there is thunder.

tuono ['twɔno] *sm (anche fig)* thunder.

tuorlo ['twɔrlo] *sm* yoke.

turacciolo [tu'rattʃolo] *sm (tappo)* stopper; *(di sughero)* cork.

turare [tu'rare] *vt (buco, falla)* to stop, plug; *(bottiglia)* to cork; **~rsi il naso** to hold one's nose; **~rsi le orecchie** to stop one's ears.

turba ['turba] *sf* **(a)** *(folla)* crowd, throng; *(: peg)* mob. **(b): ~e** *pl* disorder(s); **soffrire di ~e psichiche** to suffer from a mental disorder.

turbamento [turba'mento] *sm* anxiety; **provò un profondo ~** he was extremely upset.

turbante [tur'bante] *sm* turban.

turbare [tur'bare] **1** *vt* to disturb, trouble; **~ la quiete pubblica** *(Dir)* to disturb the peace; **~ l'opinione pubblica** to upset public opinion. **2**: **~rsi** *vr* to get upset.

turbina [tur'bina] *sf* turbine.

turbinare [turbi'nare] *vi (anche fig)* to whirl.

turbine ['turbine] *sm* whirlwind; **~ di neve** gust *o* swirl of snow; **~ di polvere** dust storm; **il ~ della danza** the whirl of the dance.

turbinoso, a [turbi'noso] *ag (vento, danza etc)* whirling.

turbolento, a [turbo'lɛnto] *ag (ragazzo)* boisterous; *(Meteor, tempi)* turbulent.

turbolenza [turbo'lɛntsa] *sf (vedi ag)* boisterousness; turbulence.

turboreattore [turboreat'tore] *sm* turbojet engine.

turchese [tur'kese] *ag, sm, sf* turquoise.

turchino, a [tur'kino] *ag, sm* deep blue.

Turchia [tur'kia] *sf* Turkey.

turco, a, chi, che ['turko] **1** *ag* Turkish; **bagno ~** *(anche fig: di stanza)* Turkish bath; **ho fatto un bagno ~** I sweated like a pig *(fam)*; **caffè alla ~a** Turkish coffee. **2** *sm* **(a)** *(abitante)* Turk; **fumare**

come un ~ *(fig)* to smoke like a chimney; **bestemmiare come un** ~ *(fig)* to swear like a trooper. **(b)** *(lingua)* Turkish; **parlare in** ~ *(fig)* to talk double-dutch. **3** *sf* Turkish woman.

turgido, a ['turdʒido] *ag* swollen.

turibolo [tu'ribolo] *sm* thurible, censer.

turismo [tu'rizmo] *sm* tourism.

turista, i, e [tu'rista] *sm/f* tourist.

turistico, a, ci, che [tu'ristiko] *ag* tourist *attr.*

turlupinare [turlupi'nare] *vt* to cheat.

turnista, i, e [tur'nista] *sm/f* shift worker.

turno ['turno] *sm (volta)* turn; *(di lavoro)* shift; **essere di** ~ *(soldato, medico, custode)* to be on duty; ~ **di notte** nightshift; **qual'è la farmacia di** ~ **domenica?** which chemist will be open on Sunday?; **rispondere a** ~ to answer in turn; **aspettare il proprio** ~ to await one's turn; **fare a** ~ **a fare qc** to take it in turns to do sth; ~ **di guardia** *(Mil)* sentry *o* guard duty.

turpe ['turpe] *ag (voglia)* filthy; *(accusa)* foul, vile; *(persona)* vile, repugnant.

turpiloquio [turpi'lɔkwjo] *sm* obscene language.

turrito, a [tur'rito] *ag* turreted.

tuta ['tuta] *sf* overalls *pl*; *(Sport)* tracksuit; ~ **spaziale** spacesuit; ~ **mimetica** *(Mil)* camouflage clothing; ~ **subacquea** wetsuit.

tutela [tu'tɛla] *sf* **(a)** *(Dir)* guardianship; **essere sotto la** ~ **di qn** to be sb's ward; ~ **di un minore** guardianship of a minor. **(b)** *(protezione)* protection; **fare qc a** ~ **dei propri interessi** to do sth to protect one's interests.

tutelare[1] [tute'lare] **1** *vt* to protect, defend. **2**: ~**rsi** *vr* to protect o.s.

tutelare[2] [tute'lare] *ag (Dir)*: **giudice** ~ *judge with responsibility for guardianship cases.*

tutore, trice [tu'tore] *sm/f (Dir)* guardian; *(protettore)* protector, defender. **2** *sm (Agr)* support.

tuttavia [tutta'via] *cong* nevertheless, yet.

tutto, a ['tutto] **1** *ag* **(a)** *(intero)* all (of), the whole (of); ~ **il**, ~**a la** the whole (of the), all (the); ~**a l'Europa** the whole of *o* all Europe; **ha letto** ~ **Dante** he has read all (of) Dante; ~**a la verità** the whole truth; **sarò qui** ~**a la settimana** I'll be here all week *o* the whole week; **ha studiato** ~ **il giorno** he studied the whole day *o* all day long; **rimanere sveglio** ~**a la notte** to stay awake all night (long); **famoso in** ~ **il mondo** world-famous, famous the world over; **si diffuse in** ~ **il paese** it spread through the whole country; **ho** ~**a la sua fiducia** I have his complete confidence.

(b) *(proprio)*: **è** ~**a sua madre** she's just *o* exactly like her mother; **è** ~ **l'opposto di...** it's the exact opposite of...; **è tutt'altra cosa, è** ~**a un'altra cosa** *(è ben diverso)* that's quite another thing; **viaggiare in aereo è tutt'altra cosa** *(è meglio)* travelling by plane is altogether different.

(c) *(completamente)*: **è** ~**a presa dal suo lavoro** she's completely *o* entirely taken up by her work; **tremava** ~**a** she was trembling all over; **era** ~**a vestita di nero** she was dressed all in black; **era** ~**a contenta** she was overjoyed; **era** ~**a sorrisi e sorrisetti** she was all smiles; **è** ~ **naso** he's got a big nose; **è** ~**a gambe e braccia** she's all arms and legs; **essere tutt'occhi/orecchi** *(fig)* to be all eyes/ears.

(d) *(pl, collettivo)* all; ~**i gli uomini/animali** all men/animals; ~**e queste cose** all these things; ~**i i posti erano occupati** all the seats were *o* every seat was occupied; **in** ~**e le direzioni** in all

directions, in every direction; **con** ~**i i pensieri che ho** worried as I am, with all my worries; ~**i e quattro** all four of them; ~**i e due** both of them; **una volta per** ~**e** once and for all.

(e) *(qualsiasi)* all; **telefona a** ~**e le ore** she phones at all hours; **a** ~**i i costi** at all costs; **in** ~**i i modi** *(a qualsiasi costo)* at all costs; *(comunque)* anyway.

(f) *(ogni)*: ~**i gli anni** every year; ~**i i santi giorni** every blessed day; ~**i i venerdì** every Friday.

(g) *(fraseologia)*: **la sua fedeltà è a** ~**a prova** his loyalty is unshakeable *o* will stand any test; **con** ~ **il cuore** *o* ~**a l'anima** wholeheartedly; **con** ~**a la mia buona volontà, non posso aiutarti** however much I may want to, I can't help you; **a** ~**a velocità** at full speed; **per me è tutt'uno** it's all one and the same to me.

2 *pron* **(a)** *(ogni cosa)* everything, all; *(qualunque cosa)* anything; ~ **è in ordine** everything's in order; **dimmi** ~ tell me everything; **questo è** ~ **quello che ho** this is all I have; ~ **dipende da lui** everything *o* it all depends on him; ~ **sta a vedere se...** it all depends on whether or not...; ~ **sta nel cominciare** the essential *o* important thing is to get started; **ha fatto (un po') di** ~ he's done (a bit of) everything; **essere capace di** ~ to be capable of anything; **mangia di** ~ he eats anything; **farebbe di** ~ **per ferirti** he would do anything to hurt you.

(b): ~**i(e)** *(ognuno)* all, everybody; **erano** ~**i presenti** they were all present; **vengono** ~**i** they are all coming, everybody's coming; ~**i quanti** all and sundry.

(c) *(fraseologia)*: **questo è** ~, **ecco** ~ that's all (I have to say); **e non è** ~ and that's not all; **prima di** *o* **innanzi** ~ first of all; **in** ~ *(complessivamente)* in all; **in** ~ **sono 8000 lire** that's 8000 lire in all; **in** ~ **e per** ~ *(completamente)* entirely, completely; **dipende in** ~ **e per** ~ **dai suoi** he is entirely *o* completely dependent on his parents; **con** ~ **che** *(malgrado)* although; ...**che è** ~ **dire** ...and that's saying a lot; ~ **compreso** inclusive, all-in.

3 *av* **(a)** entirely, quite; **non sono del** ~ **convinto/sicuro** I'm not entirely convinced/ sure; **è** ~ **il contrario** it's quite *o* exactly the opposite; **è** ~ **il contrario** *o* **l'opposto di ciò che credi** it's not what you think at all; **fa** ~ **il contrario di quello che gli dico** he does the exact opposite of what I tell him to do.

(b) *(fraseologia)*: **tutt'intorno** all around; ~ **d'un colpo** all of a sudden, suddenly; **saranno stati tutt'al più una cinquantina** there were about fifty of them at (the very) most; **tutt'al più possiamo prendere un treno** if the worst comes to the worst we can catch a train.

4 *sm* **(a)** *(insieme)* whole; **il** ~ **costa 300.000 lire** the whole thing *o* lot costs 300,000 lire; **vi manderemo il** ~ **nel corso della settimana** we'll send you the (whole) lot during the course of the week.

(b): **il** ~ **si è risolto in bene** everything turned out for the best; **rischiare il** ~ **per** ~ to risk everything.

tuttofare [tutto'fare] **1** *ag inv*: **domestica** ~ general maid; **ragazzo** ~ office boy. **2** *sm/f inv* handyman/woman.

tuttora [tut'tora] *av* still.

tutù [tu'tu] *sm inv* tutu, ballet skirt.

TV [ti'vu] *sf inv (abbr di televisione)* TV.

U

U, u [u] *sf o m inv (lettera)* U, u; **inversione** *f* **ad U** U-turn.

ubbidiente [ubbi'djɛnte] *ag* obedient.

ubbidienza [ubbi'djɛntsa] *sf* obedience; *(al sovrano)* allegiance; ~ **ai genitori/alla legge** obedience to one's parents/the law; **ridurre all'**~ to reduce to a state of submission.

ubbidire [ubbi'dire] *vi*: ~ **a** to obey; ~ **alla legge** to obey the law; ~ **alle leggi della natura** *(fig)* to obey nature's laws; **farsi** ~ to enforce *o* compel obedience.

ubicazione [ubikat'tsjone] *sf* site, location.

ubiquità [ubikwi'ta] *sf* ubiquity; **non ho il dono dell'**~! I can't be everywhere at once!

ubriacare [ubria'kare] **1** *vt (sog: persona)* to get drunk; *(: bevanda)* to make drunk, intoxicate; *(con discorsi, promesse)* to intoxicate sb, make sb's head spin. **2**: ~**rsi** *vr* to get drunk.

ubriacatura [ubriaka'tura] *sf*: **prendersi una solenne** ~ to get blind *o* roaring drunk *(fam)*.

ubriachezza [ubria'kettsa] *sf* drunkenness; **guidare in stato di** ~ to drive under the influence of alcohol.

ubriaco, a, chi, che [ubri'ako] **1** *ag* drunk; **essere** ~ **marcio** *o* **fradicio** to be blind *o* roaring drunk *(fam)*; ~ **di stanchezza** reeling from tiredness; ~ **di gelosia** beside o.s. with jealousy. **2** *sm/f* drunkard, drunk.

ubriacone [ubria'kone] *sm* drunkard.

uccellagione [uttʃella'dʒone] *sf* bird catching.

uccellatore [uttʃella'tore] *sm* bird catcher.

uccelliera [uttʃel'ljɛra] *sf* aviary.

uccello [ut'tʃello] *sm (Zool)* bird; ~ **del malaugurio** *(fig)* bird of ill omen; **essere uccel di bosco** *(fig)* to be one's own man, be free of ties.

uccidere [ut'tʃidere] **1** *vt (gen)* to kill; *(assassinare)* to murder, kill; *(sog: malattia)* to carry off, kill; ~ **con arma da fuoco** to shoot dead; ~ **a coltellate** to stab to death; ~ **con il veleno** to poison; **è rimasto ucciso in un incidente** he was killed in an accident; **l'alcool uccide** alcohol is a killer; ~ **un uomo morto** *(fig)* to kick a man when he's down. **2**: ~**rsi** *vr* **(a)** *(suicidarsi)* to kill o.s.; ~**rsi col gas** to gas o.s. **(b)** *(uso reciproco)* to kill one another.

uccisione [uttʃi'zjone] *sf (gen)* killing; *(assassinio)* murder.

ucciso, a [ut'tʃizo] **1** *pp di* **uccidere**. **2** *sm/f* person killed, victim; **gli** ~**i** the dead.

uccisore [uttʃi'zore] *sm* killer.

udibile [u'dibile] *ag* audible.

udienza [u'djɛntsa] *sf (gen)* audience; *(Dir)* hearing; **dare** ~ **a** to grant an audience to; ~ **a porte chiuse** hearing in camera.

udire [u'dire] *vt (gen)* to hear; **l'abbiamo udita piangere** we heard her crying.

uditivo, a [udi'tivo] *ag* auditory.

udito [u'dito] *sm* (sense of) hearing.

uditore, trice [udi'tore] *sm/f (Univ)* unregistered student *(attending lectures)*.

uditorio [udi'tɔrjo] *sm* audience.

ufficiale [uffi'tʃale] **1** *ag (gen)* official. **2** *sm* **(a)** *(Mil, Naut)* officer; ~ **di marina** naval officer; **primo** ~ *(Naut)* first mate. **(b)** *(Amm)* official; ~ **sanitario** health inspector; **pubblico** ~ public official; ~ **di stato civile** registrar; ~ **giudiziario** *(Dir)* clerk of the court.

ufficio [uf'fitʃo] *sm* **(a)** *(luogo: gen)* office; *(organo)* office, bureau, agency; *(reparto)* department; **recarsi** *o* **andare in** ~ to go to the office; ~ **di collocamento** employment office; ~ **postale** post office; ~ **vendite/del personale** sales/ personnel department; ~ **informazioni** information bureau.

(b) *(incarico)* office; *(dovere)* duty; *(mansione)* function; **l'**~ **di direttore generale** the office *o* position of general manager; **coprire/accettare un** ~ to hold/accept a position; **provvedere d'**~ to act officially.

(c) *(Dir)*: **difensore** *m o* **avvocato d'**~ court-appointed counsel for the defence; **convocare d'**~ to summons.

(d) *(intervento)*: **grazie ai suoi buoni** ~**i** thanks to his good offices.

(e) *(Rel)* office.

ufficioso, a [uffi'tʃoso] *ag* unofficial.

ufo[1] ['ufo] *sm inv* UFO.

ufo[2] ['ufo]: **a** ~ *av*: **mangiare a** ~ to sponge a meal.

ufologia [ufolo'dʒia] *sf* ufology.

ugello [u'dʒello] *sm* nozzle.

uggia ['uddʒa] *sf (noia)* boredom; *(fastidio)* bore; **avere/prendere qn in** ~ to dislike/take a dislike to sb.

uggiolare [uddʒo'lare] *vi* to whine.

uggiolio [uddʒo'lio] *sm* whine.

uggioso, a [ud'dʒoso] *ag (gen)* tiresome; *(tempo)* dull, dreary.

ugola ['ugola] *sf* uvula.

uguaglianza [ugwaʎ'ʎantsa] *sf (gen)* equality; *(Mat)* identity; **su una base di** ~ on an equal footing, on equal terms; **segno di** ~ *(Mat)* equals sign.

uguagliare [ugwaʎ'ʎare] **1** *vt* **(a)** *(livellare: persone, stipendi)* to make equal; *(: siepe)* to straighten. **(b)** *(raggiungere, essere uguale a)* to equal; ~ **qn in bellezza/bravura** to equal sb *o* be equal to sb in beauty/skill; ~ **un record** *(Sport)* to equal a record; **in lui l'intelligenza uguaglia la bontà** he is as intelligent as he is good. **2**: ~**rsi** *vr* to be equal.

uguale [u'gwale] **1** *ag* **(a)** *(avente il medesimo valore)* equal; *(identico)* identical; **di peso/valore** ~ of equal weight/value; **a** ~ **distanza da** equidistant from; **abbiamo stipendi** ~**i** our salaries are the same; **quei gemelli sono proprio** ~**i** those twins are identical; **siamo alti** ~**i** we are the same height; **il tuo maglione è** ~ **al mio** your sweater is the same as mine. **(b)** *(liscio, piano: superficie)* even, level; *(uniforme: andatura)* even; *(: voce)* steady. **2** *av*: **costano** ~ they cost the same. **3** *sm/f* equal; **non ha** ~**i per ostinazione** when it comes to stubbornness there's no-one like him.

460

ugualmente [ugwal'mente] *av* **(a)** *(allo stesso modo)* equally. **(b)** *(lo stesso)* all the same, just the same; **lo farò** ~ I'm going to do it anyway.
ulcera ['ultʃera] *sf* ulcer; **avere l'**~ to have an ulcer.
ulcerazione [ultʃerat'tsjone] *sf* ulceration.
uliva [u'liva] *etc* = **oliva** *etc*.
ulteriore [ulte'rjore] *ag* further.
ultimamente [ultima'mente] *av* lately, of late.
ultimare [ulti'mare] *vt* to finish, complete.
ultimatum [ulti'matum] *sm inv* ultimatum.
ultimissime [ulti'missime] *sfpl* latest news *sg*.
ultimo, a ['ultimo] **1** *ag* **(a)** *(di serie: gen)* last; *(: piano)* top; *(: fila)* back; *(: mano di vernice)* last, final; **l'**~ **scalino** *(in basso)* the bottom step; *(in alto)* the top step; **le** ~**e 20 pagine** the last 20 pages; **in** ~**a pagina** *(di giornale)* on the back page; **entrare/uscire per** ~ to come in/go out last.

(b) *(tempo: gen)* last; *(: più recente)* latest; *(: finale)* final; **negli** ~**i tempi** recently; **gli** ~**i giorni prima di partire** the last days before leaving; **l'**~**a volta che l'ho visto** the last time I saw him; **all'**~ **momento** at the last minute; **le** ~**e notizie** the latest news; **all'**~**a moda** in the latest fashion; **rispondiamo alla vostra lettera del 7 aprile** ~ **scorso** we reply to your letter of April the 7th last.

(c) *(estremo: speranza, risorsa)* last, final; *(: più lontano)* farthest; **l'**~ **lembo di terra italiana** the farthest tip of Italy; **spendere fino all'**~ **centesimo** to spend down to one's last cent; **dare un'**~**a occhiata a qc** to have one last look at sth.

(d) *(per importanza)* last; **è l'**~ **film che vorrei andare a vedere** that's the last film I would want to go and see; **qual'è l'**~ **prezzo (che mi può fare)?** what's the lowest you'll go?

(e) *(Filosofia)* ultimate.

(f) *(fraseologia)*: **in** ~**a analisi** in the final *o* last analysis; **in** ~ **luogo** finally; **avere** *o* **dire l'**~**a parola** to have the last word; **le** ~**e parole famose!** famous last words!; **esalare** *o* **rendere l'**~ **respiro** to breathe one's last.

2 *sm/f* last (one); **l'**~ **nato** youngest (child); **l'**~ **ad entrare** the last (person) to come in; **gli** ~**i arrivati** the last ones to arrive; **è l'**~**a della classe** she's at the bottom of the class; **questa è l'**~**a delle mie preoccupazioni** that's the least of my worries; **è l'**~ **degli** ~**i** he's the lowest of the low; **quest'**~ *(tra due)* the latter; *(tra più di due)* this last, the last-mentioned.

3 *sm*: **l'**~ **del mese/dell'anno** the last day of the month/year; **arrivare in** ~ to arrive at the last minute; **all'**~ **ho deciso di restare** in the end I decided to stay; **fino all'**~ to the last, till the end; **in** ~ at the end; **da** ~ finally; **essere all'**~ *o* **agli** ~**i** to be at death's door.

4 *sf* *(notizia, birichinata)*: **hai sentito l'**~**a?** have you heard the latest?; **questa è l'**~**a (che mi combini)** that's the last time you'll play that trick on me.
ultramoderno, a [ultramo'derno] *ag* ultramodern.
ultrarapido, a [ultra'rapido] *ag* (*Fot*) high-speed.
ultrasensibile [ultrasen'sibile] *ag* ultrasensitive.
ultrasinistra [ultrasi'nistra] *sf* (*Pol*) extreme left.
ultrasonico, a, ci, che [ultra'sɔniko] *ag* ultrasonic.
ultrasuono [ultra'swɔno] *sm* ultrasound; **fare gli** ~**i** (*Med*) to undergo ultrasound therapy.
ultraterreno, a [ultrater'reno] *ag*: **la vita** ~**a** the afterlife.
ultravioletto, a [ultravio'letto] *ag* ultraviolet.
ululare [ulu'lare] *vi* to howl.

ululato [ulu'lato] *sm* *(urlo)* howl; *(l'ululare)* howling.
umanamente [umana'mente] *av* *(con umanità)* humanely; *(nei limiti delle capacità umane)* humanly; **è** ~ **impossibile** it's not humanly possible.
umanità [umani'ta] *sf* *(gen)* humanity; **l'**~ humanity, mankind.
umanitario, a [umani'tarjo] *ag* humanitarian.
umanizzare [umanid'dzare] *vt* to humanize.
umano, a [u'mano] **1** *ag* *(gen)* human; *(comprensivo)* humane; **essere** *o* **mostrarsi** ~ **(con qn)** to show humanity (towards sb), act humanely (towards sb); **errare è** ~ to err is human; **un essere** ~ a human being; **è** ~ **che si comporti così** it's quite normal to behave like that. **2** *sm* human.
umbilico [umbi'liko] *sm* = **ombelico**.
umettare [umet'tare] *vt* *(labbra)* to moisten.
umidiccio, a, ci, ce [umi'dittʃo] *ag* *(terreno)* damp; *(mano)* moist, clammy.
umidificare [umidifi'kare] *vt* to humidify.
umidificatore [umidifika'tore] *sm* humidifier.
umidità [umidi'ta] *sf* *(vedi ag)* dampness; moistness, clamminess; humidity; **proteggere qc dall'**~ to protect sth from damp.
umido, a [u'mido] **1** *ag* *(gen)* damp; *(mano)* moist, clammy; *(clima: caldo)* humid; *(: freddo)* damp; **aveva gli occhi** ~**i di pianto** her eyes were moist with tears. **2** *sm* **(a)** *(umidità)* dampness. **(b)** *(Culin)*: **carne in** ~ meat stew.
umile ['umile] **1** *ag* *(gen)* humble; **i lavori più** ~**i** the most menial tasks.
umiliante [umi'ljante] *ag* humiliating.
umiliare [umi'ljare] **1** *vt* *(gen)* to humiliate; ~ **la carne** to mortify the flesh. **2**: ~**rsi** *vr*: ~**rsi (davanti a)** to humiliate *o* humble o.s. (before).
umiliazione [umiljat'tsjone] *sf* humiliation.
umiltà [umil'ta] *sf* humility; **con** ~ humbly.
umore [u'more] *sm* **(a)** *(indole)* temper, temperament; *(momentaneo)* mood, humour; **un vecchio d'**~ **irascibile** an irascible *o* bad-tempered old man; **essere di buono/cattivo** ~ to be in a good/bad mood *o* humour. **(b)** *(Bio)* humour.
umorismo [umo'rizmo] *sm* humour; **avere il senso dell'**~ to have a sense of humour.
umorista, i, e [umo'rista] *sm/f* humorist.
umoristico, a, ci, che [umo'ristiko] *ag* *(battuta, racconto)* humorous, funny; **senso** ~ sense of humour.
un [un], **un'** [un], **una** ['una] *vedi* **uno**.
unanime [u'nanime] *ag* unanimous.
unanimità [unanimi'ta] *sf* unanimity; **all'**~ unanimously.
una tantum ['una 'tantum] **1** *ag* one-off *attr*. **2** *sf* *(imposta)* one-off tax.
uncinare [untʃi'nare] *vt* to hook.
uncinato, a [untʃi'nato] *ag* *(amo)* barbed; *(ferro)* hooked; **croce** *f* ~**a** swastika.
uncinetto [untʃi'netto] *sm* crochet hook; **lavorare all'**~ to crochet; **lavoro all'**~ crochet work.
uncino [un'tʃino] *sm* hook.
undicenne [undi'tʃenne] *ag, sm/f* eleven-year-old; *per uso vedi* **cinquantenne**.
undicesimo, a [undi'tʃezimo] *ag, sm/f, sm* eleventh; *per uso vedi* **quinto**.
undici ['unditʃi] *ag inv, sm inv* eleven; *per uso vedi* **cinque**.
ungere ['undʒere] **1** *vt* *(macchina)* to oil, lubricate; *(teglia)* to grease; *(Rel)* to anoint; *(fig)* to flatter. **2**: ~**rsi** *vr* *(macchiarsi)* to get covered in grease; ~**rsi con la crema** to put cream on; ~**rsi le mani/la pelle** to rub cream into one's hands/skin.
ungherese [unge'rese] *ag, sm/f, sm* Hungarian.

Ungheria [unge'ria] *sf* Hungary.

unghia ['ungja] *sf* **(a)** *(Anat)* nail; *(di animale)* claw; *(di rapace)* talon; *(di cavallo, bue etc)* hoof; **le ~e delle mani** the fingernails; **le ~e dei piedi** the toenails; **difendersi con le ~e e con i denti** to defend o.s. tooth and nail; **tirar fuori le ~e** *(anche fig)* to show one's claws; **pagare sull'~** *(fig)* to pay on the nail. **(b)** *(di temperino)* groove. **(c)** *(dimensione):* **ce ne vuole un'~ di più/di meno** a fraction more/less is needed.

unghiata [un'gjata] *sf* scratch.

unguento [un'gwɛnto] *sm* ointment.

unicamente [unika'mente] *av* only.

unicamerale [unikame'rale] *ag (Pol)* unicameral.

unicità [unitʃi'ta] *sf* uniqueness.

unico, a, ci, che ['uniko] **1** *ag* **(a)** *(solo)* only; *(esclusivo)* sole; **è la mia ~a speranza** it's my only hope; **la mia ~a speranza è che...** my one *o* only hope is that...; **è figlio ~** he's an only child; **è l'~ esemplare in Italia** it's the only one of its kind in Italy; **due aspetti di un ~ problema** two aspects of one and the same problem; **atto ~** *(Teatro)* one-act play; **agente** *m* **~** *(Comm)* sole agent; **binario ~** *(Ferr)* single track; **numero ~** *(di giornale)* special issue; **senso ~** *(Aut)* one way. **(b)** *(eccezionale)* unique; **~ nel suo genere** unique of its kind; **~ al mondo** absolutely unique, the only one of its kind in the world; **sei ~!** you're priceless!; **è un tipo più ~ che raro** he's one of a kind.

2 *sm/f* the only one; **fu l'~ a capire** he was the only one who understood *o* to understand.

3 *sf* only thing to do; **l'~a è aspettare** the only thing to do is to wait, we can only wait.

unicorno [uni'kɔrno] *sm* unicorn.

unificare [unifi'kare] *vt (stato, leggi)* to unify; *(standardizzare: prodotto)* to standardize.

unificazione [unifikat'tsjone] *sf (vedi vb)* unification; standardization.

uniformare [unifor'mare] **1** *vt (terreno, superficie)* to level; **~ qc a** to adjust *o* relate sth to. **2: ~rsi** *vr:* **~rsi a** to conform to.

uniforme[1] [uni'forme] *ag (gen)* uniform; *(superficie)* even.

uniforme[2] [uni'forme] *sf (divisa)* uniform; **in ~** in uniform; **alta ~** dress uniform.

uniformità [uniformi'ta] *sf (vedi ag)* uniformity; evenness.

unigenito [uni'dʒɛnito] *ag (Rel)* **figlio ~ del Padre** God's only-begotten son.

unilaterale [unilate'rale] *ag* unilateral; *(fig)* one-sided.

unilateralità [unilaterali'ta] *sf (arbitrarietà)* one-sidedness.

uninominale [uninomi'nale] *ag (Pol):* **collegio ~** single-member constituency

unione [u'njone] **1** *sf (alleanza, matrimonio)* union; *(di colori)* combination, blending; *(di elementi)* cohesion; **l'~ fa la forza** strength through unity. **2: ~ sindacale** trade union; **U~ Sovietica** Soviet Union.

unionista, i, e [unjo'nista] *sm/f* unionist.

unire [u'nire] **1** *vt* **(a)** *(associare):* **~ (a)** to unite (with); **~ in matrimonio** to unite *o* join in matrimony; **il sentimento che li unisce** the feeling which binds them together *o* unites them. **(b)** *(congiungere: città, linee)* to join, link; *(mescolare: ingredienti)* to mix. **(c)** *(colori, suoni)* to combine. **2: ~rsi** *vr:* **~rsi contro/a** to unite against/with; **~rsi in matrimonio** to get married; **~rsi a un gruppo** to join a group.

unisex ['uniseks] *ag inv* unisex.

unisono [u'nisono] *sm* unison; **all'~** *(Mus, fig)* in unison.

unità [uni'ta] *sf inv* **(a)** *(unione)* unity. **(b)** *(Mat, Comm: elemento)* unit; **~ di misura** unit of measure; **~ monetaria** monetary unit. **(c)** *(Mil)* unit; *(Naut)* (war)ship; *(Aer)* aeroplane.

unitario, a [uni'tarjo] *ag (gen)* unitary; *(Pol, Rel)* unitarian; **prezzo *o* costo ~** unit price.

unito, a [u'nito] *ag* **(a)** *(gen)* united; *(amici, coppia)* close; *(famiglia)* close(-knit), united. **(b)** *(colore)* plain; **in tinta ~a** plain, self-coloured.

universale [univer'sale] *ag (gen)* universal; *(plauso, consenso)* general; *(mente, genio)* wide-ranging; **il giudizio ~** *(Rel)* the Last Judgment; **suffragio ~** *(Pol)* universal suffrage.

universalità [universali'ta] *sf* universality.

universalizzare [universalid'dzare] *vt* to make universal.

universalmente [universal'mente] *ag* universally.

università [universi'ta] *sf inv* university.

universitario, a [universi'tarjo] **1** *ag (gen)* university *attr; (studi)* university, academic. **2** *sm/f (docente)* academic, university lecturer; *(studente)* university student.

universo [uni'vɛrso] *sm* universe.

univoco, a, ci, che [u'nivoko] *ag* unambiguous.

uno, a ['uno] *(dav a sm* **un**+*consonante, vocale,* **uno**+*s impura, gn, pn, ps, x, z; dav a sf* **un'**+*vocale,* **una**+*consonante).* **1** *ag (gen)* one; **ho passato un mese in Italia** I spent one month in Italy; **ho comprato ~a mela e due pere** I bought one apple and two pears; **non ha ~a lira** he hasn't a penny, he's penniless.

2 *art indet* **(a)** a, an *(+vocale);* **ho visto un uomo** I saw a man; **~ zingaro** a gypsy; **era ~a giornata splendida** it was a beautiful day; **un giorno gli ho telefonato** I called him one day; **dammene uno po'** give me some.

(b) *(intensivo):* **ho ~a paura!** I'm terrified!; **~a noia!** such a bore!; **ma questo è un porcile!** it's an absolute pigsty in here!

(c) *(circa):* **costerà un 5000 lire** it'll cost round about 5000 lire; **disterà un 10 km** it's round about 10 km away.

3 *pron* **(a)** one; **me ne dai ~?** will you give me one (of them)?; **ne ho comprato ~ stamattina** I bought one this morning; **è ~ dei più veloci** it's one of the fastest; **~ dei tanti** one of the many; **~ di noi** one of us; **facciamo metà per ~** let's go halves; **abbiamo fatto un po' per ~** we each did a bit.

(b) *(un tale)* somebody, someone; **ho incontrato ~ che ti conosce** I met someone who knows you; **c'era ~a al telefono** there was a woman on the phone; **è ~a del mio paese** she's from the same village as I am.

(c) *(in costruzione impers)* one, you; **se ~ vuole** if one wants, if you want; **se ~ ha i soldi** if one has the money.

(d) *(con art det):* **l'~** one; **non confondere gli uni con gli altri** don't confuse one lot with the other; **abbiamo visto l'~ e l'altro** we've seen both of them; **sono entrati l'~ dopo l'altro** they came in one after the other; **si amano l'un l'altro** they love each other.

4 *sm, sf (gen)* one; **~ più ~ fa due** one plus one equals two; **a ~ a ~** one by one; **incontrarlo e fuggire con lui fu tutt'~** as soon as I saw him I immediately wanted to run away with him.

5 *sf* **(a)** *(ora)* one o'clock; **è l'~a** it's one (o'clock).

(b): ne ha detta ~a! you should have heard what he said!; **ne hai combinata ~a delle tue!** you've done it again, haven't you!; **ne vuoi sentire ~a?** do you want to hear a good one?; **non me**

ne va mai bene ~a nothing ever goes right for me.

unto, a ['unto] **1** *pp di* **ungere. 2** *ag* greasy, oily; ~ **e bisunto** filthy dirty. **3** *sm* grease.

untume [un'tume] *sm (peg)* grease.

untuosità [untuosi'ta] *sf* greasiness; *(fig: servilismo)* unctuousness.

untuoso, a [untu'oso] *ag (pelle)* greasy; *(cibo)* oily; *(fig: persona)* unctuous, smooth.

unzione [un'tsjone] *sf:* **l'Estrema U~** *(Rel)* Extreme Unction.

uomo ['wɔmo], *pl* **uomini** ['wɔmini] **1** *sm (gen)* man; *(specie umana):* **l'~** mankind, humanity; **abiti/ calzature da** *o* **per** ~ men's clothes/shoes, clothes/shoes for men; **parlare da** ~ **a** ~ to have a man-to-man talk; **a memoria d'~** since the world began; **a passo d'~** at walking pace; ~ **avvisato mezzo salvato** forewarned is forearmed. **2:** ~ **d'affari** businessman; ~ **d'azione** man of action; ~ **delle caverne** caveman; ~ **d'equipaggio: una nave con 30 uomini d'equipaggio** a ship with a crew of 30 men; ~ **di fatica** workhand; ~ **di fiducia** right-hand man; **è un** ~ **finito** he's finished; ~ **del gas/latte** gas/ milkman; ~ **di mondo** man of the world; ~ **di paglia** stooge; ~ **rana** frogman; **l'~ della strada** the man in the street.

uopo ['wɔpo] *sm:* **all'~** if necessary, in case of need; **è d'~ far così** it is necessary to do this.

uovo ['wɔvo] *sm, pl(f)* **uova (a)** egg; ~ **fresco** new-laid *o* fresh egg; ~ **à la coque/sodo** soft-/hard-boiled egg; ~ **al tegame** *o* **all'occhio di bue** fried egg; ~**a affogate** *o* **in camicia** poached eggs; ~**a strapazzate** scrambled eggs; ~ **di Pasqua** Easter egg. **(b)** *(fraseologia):* **è l'~ di Colombo!** *(fig)* it's as plain as the nose on your face!; **essere pieno come un** ~ to be full (up); **cercare il pelo nell'~** *(fig)* to split hairs; **rompere le** ~**a nel paniere a qn** *(fig)* to upset sb's plans; **meglio un** ~ **oggi che una gallina domani** *(Proverbio)* a bird in the hand is worth two in the bush.

uragano [ura'gano] *sm* hurricane; *(fig: di applausi)* storm.

uranio [u'ranjo] *sm* uranium.

urbanesimo [urba'nezimo] *sm* urbanization.

urbanista, i, e [urba'nista] *sm/f* town planner.

urbanistica [urba'nistika] *sf* town planning.

urbanistico, a, ci, che [urba'nistiko] *ag* urban, town *attr.*

urbanità [urbani'ta] *sf* urbanity.

urbanizzare [urbanid'dzare] *vt* to urbanize.

urbanizzazione [urbaniddzat'tsjone] *sf* urbanization.

urbano, a [ur'bano] *ag* **(a)** *(gen: sviluppo etc)* urban, city *attr.* **(b)** *(gentile: modi, risposta)* urbane.

urgente [ur'dʒɛnte] *ag* urgent.

urgenza [ur'dʒɛntsa] *sf (di decisione, situazione)* urgency; **non c'è** ~ **there's** no hurry; **fare qc d'~** to do sth as a matter of urgency; **trasportare qn d'~ all'ospedale** to rush sb to hospital; **il direttore l'ha convocato d'~** the director requested to see him urgently *o* immediately; **questo lavoro va fatto con** ~ this work is urgent; **chiamata d'~** emergency call.

urgere ['urdʒere] *vi* to be needed urgently; **urge che si faccia qualcosa** something needs to be done urgently.

urina [u'rina] *sf* urine.

urinare [uri'nare] *vi* to urinate.

urlare [ur'lare] **1** *vi (persona)* to scream, yell; *(animale, vento)* to howl; **non** ~ **che ti sento benissimo** there's no need to shout, I can hear you perfectly well; ~ **di dolore** to scream with pain.

2 *vt:* ~ **qc (a qn)** to scream *o* yell sth (at sb); ~ **a qn di fare qc** to scream at sb to do sth; **gliene ho urlate dietro di tutti i colori** I hurled abuse at him.

urlatore, trice [urla'tore] *ag* howling, shrieking.

urlo ['urlo] *sm (di persona)* scream; *(di animale, vento)* howl; *(di sirena)* wail; **lanciare un** ~ **(di)** to scream (with).

urna ['urna] *sf* **(a)** *(vaso)* urn. **(b)** *(Pol):* ~ **(elettorale)** ballot box; **andare alle** ~**e** to vote, go to the polls.

urrà [ur'ra] *escl* hurrah!

U.R.S.S. *sf (abbr di Unione delle Repubbliche Socialiste Sovietiche):* **l'~** the USSR.

urtante [ur'tante] *ag (comportamento)* irritating, annoying.

urtare [ur'tare] **1** *vt* **(a)** *(persona, ostacolo)* to bump into, knock against; *(gomito, testa)* to knock, bump. **(b)** *(fig: irritare)* to annoy, irritate; ~ **i nervi a qn** to get on sb's nerves. **2** *vi:* ~ **contro** *(auto, barca)* to bump into; *(persona)* to bump into, knock against. **3:** ~**rsi** *vr* **(a)** *(uso reciproco)* to collide. **(b)** *(irritarsi)* to get annoyed, get irritated.

urto ['urto] *sm (collisione)* crash, collision; *(colpo)* knock, bump; *(fig: contrasto)* clash; *(Mil)* attack; **nell'~ si è rotto il vetro** the impact of the crash broke the glass; **essere in** ~ **con qn per qc** *(fig)* to clash with sb over sth; **terapia d'~** *(Med)* shock treatment; **dose** *f* **d'~** *(Med)* massive dose; **contingente** *m* **d'~** *(Mil)* shock troops *pl.*

U.S.A. *mpl (abbr di Stati Uniti d'America):* **gli** ~ the USA.

usanza [u'zantsa] *sf (costume)* custom; **è l'~** it's the custom, it's what's done; **secondo l'~** according to custom, as is customary.

usare [u'zare] **1** *vt* **(a)** *(adoperare)* to use; **posso** ~ **la tua macchina?** may I use your car?; **grazie per il tavolo, l'ho usato molto** thank you for the table, I got a lot of use out of it; **sai** ~ *o* **come si usa la lavatrice?** do you know how to use the washing machine?; **non** ~ **tutta l'acqua** *(consumare)* don't use (up) all the water; **cerca di** ~ **il cervello!** try to use your head!; **usa gli occhi/le orecchie!** use your eyes/ears!; ~ **la forza** to use force; ~ **le mani** *(picchiare)* to use one's fists; ~ **la massima cura nel fare qc** to exercise great care when doing sth; **dovresti** ~ **un po' di comprensione** you should show a little understanding; **potresti usarmi la cortesia di spegnere la radio?** would you be so kind as to switch off the radio? **(b)** *(aver l'abitudine):* ~ **fare qc** to be in the habit of doing sth, be accustomed to doing sth; **a casa nostra si usa fare così** this is how we do things at home.

2 *vi* **(a)** *(essere di moda)* to be fashionable; **usano di nuovo i tacchi alti** high heels are fashionable again *o* are back in fashion. **(b):** ~ **di** *(servirsi di)* to use; *(: diritto)* to exercise.

3 *vb impers* to be customary; **da queste parti usa così** it's the custom round here, this is customary round here.

usato, a [u'zato] **1** *ag* **(a)** *(logoro)* worn (out). **(b)** *(di seconda mano)* used, second-hand. **2** *sm* second-hand goods *pl;* **il mercato dell'~** the second-hand market.

uscente [uʃ'ʃɛnte] *ag (Amm)* outgoing.

usciere [uʃ'ʃɛre] *sm* usher.

uscio ['uʃʃo] *sm* door; **sull'~** on the doorstep.

uscire [uʃ'ʃire] *vi (aus essere)* **1a** *(persona: andare fuori)* to go out, leave; *(: venire fuori)* to come out, leave; *(: a piedi)* to walk out; *(: a spasso, la sera)* to go out; ~ **a prendere il giornale** to go out

for the paper; **lasciatemi** *o* **fatemi** ~! let me out!;
uscite! get out!; ~ **da** *(posto)* to go *(o* come) out
of, leave; *(: carcere)* to get out of; **è uscito dalla
porta di servizio/per la finestra** he left by the
tradesman's entrance/got out through the window; **da dove sei uscito?** where did you spring
from?; ~ **dall'acqua/ dal letto** to get out of the
water/of bed.

(**b**) *(oggetto: gen)* to come out; *(disco, film)* to
be released; *(numero alla lotteria)* to come up; **la
merce che esce dal paese dev'essere dichiarata**
goods leaving *o* going out of the country must be
declared.

(**c**) *(sporgere: vite, puntina)* to stick out.

(**d**) *(andar fuori, sconfinare)*: ~ **dagli argini**
(fiume) to overflow its banks; ~ **dai binari** *(treno)*
to leave the rails; ~ **di strada** *(auto)* to leave the
road; **l'acqua sta uscendo dalla vasca** the bath is
overflowing; ~ **dall'ordinario** *(fig)* to be out of
the ordinary.

(**e**) *(passare da una condizione a un'altra)*: ~
dall'adolescenza to leave adolescence behind; ~
da una brutta malattia to get over *o* recover from
a bad illness; **è uscito bene da quella storia** he
came out of that business well; **è uscito illeso
dall'incidente** he emerged from the accident
unscathed.

(**f**) *(fraseologia)*: **chissà cosa uscirà da tutta
questa storia?** who knows what will come of all
this?; **se ne uscì con una delle sue** he came out
with one of his typical remarks; ~ **dai gangheri**
(fig) to fly off the handle; **mi è uscito di mente** it
slipped my mind; ~ **vincitore** to come out *o*
emerge as the winner.

uscita [uʃˈʃita] *sf* (**a**) *(azione: di persona)* leaving,
exit; **è l'ora dell'~ degli scolari** school's over for
the day, the children are coming out of school;
un'~ veloce a quick exit; **ho la libera** ~ *(Mil)* I'm
off duty. (**b**) *(porta, passaggio)* exit; ~ **di sicurezza** emergency exit; **vietata l'~** no exit. (**c**) *(passeggiata)* outing; *(Mil)* foray; **è la sua prima** ~
dopo la malattia it's his first day out since his
illness. (**d**) *(fig: battuta)* witty remark; **ha di
quelle ~e** he comes out with some odd remarks.
(**e**) *(Comm)* outlay; **entrate ed** ~**e** income and
expenditure. (**f**) *(Elettr)* output.

usignolo [uziɲˈɲɔlo] *sm* nightingale.

uso[1] [ˈuzo] *sm* (**a**) *(gen)* use; *(di parola)* usage; *(Dir)*
exercise; **a** ~ **di** for, for the use of; **testo a** ~ **delle
elementari** book for use in primary schools; **per**
~ **esterno** *(Med)* for external use only; **per** ~
personale for one's own use; **fare buono/cattivo**
~ **di qc** to make good/bad use of sth; **istruzioni
per l'~** instructions; **fuori** ~ out of use; **fare** ~ **di
qc** to use sth; **perdere l'~ della ragione** to go out
of one's mind. (**b**) *(esercizio)* practice; **con l'~**
with practice. (**c**) *(abitudine)* usage, custom; **essere in** ~ to be in common *o* current use; **gli** ~**i e
costumi dei Romani** Roman customs.

uso[2]**, a** [ˈuzo] *ag (poet)*: ~ **a qc/a fare qc** accustomed to sth/to doing sth.

ustionare [ustjoˈnare] **1** *vt* to burn. **2**: ~**rsi** *vr* to
burn o.s.

ustione [usˈtjone] *sf* burn; ~**i di terzo grado** third-
degree burns.

usuale [uzuˈale] *ag (espressione)* everyday attr; *(oggetto)* everyday, ordinary.

usufruire [uzufruˈire] *vi*: ~ **di** *(giovarsi di)* to take
advantage of, make use of.

usufrutto [uzuˈfrutto] *sm (Dir)* usufruct.

usufruttuario [uzufruttuˈarjo] *sm (Dir)* usufruc-
tuary.

usura[1] [uˈzura] *sf* usury; **prestare a** ~ to lend at
exorbitant interest.

usura[2] [uˈzura] *sf (logoramento)* wear (and tear); ~
dei freni wear on the brakes.

usuraio, a [uzuˈrajo] *sm/f* usurer.

usurpare [uzurˈpare] *vt (trono, potere)* to
usurp.

usurpatore, trice [uzurpaˈtore] *sm/f* usurper.

usurpazione [uzurpatˈtsjone] *sf* usurpation.

utensile [utenˈsile] **1** *ag*: **macchina** ~ machine tool.
2 *sm* tool, implement; ~**i da cucina** kitchen utensils.

utensileria [utensileˈria] *sf* (**a**) *(utensili)* tools pl.
(**b**) *(reparto)* tool room.

utente [uˈtente] *sm/f (gen)* user; *(di gas etc)* consumer; *(del telefono)* subscriber.

utenza [uˈtentsa] *sf* (**a**) *(di servizi pubblici)* use. (**b**)
(vedi **utente**) users pl; consumers pl; subscribers
pl.

uterino, a [uteˈrino] *ag* uterine.

utero [ˈutero] *sm* uterus, womb.

utile [ˈutile] **1** *ag (gen)* useful; *(consiglio, persona)*
helpful; **mi è stato molto** ~ *(oggetto)* it came in
very handy, it was very useful; **questo ti sarà** ~
this will be of use to you; **posso esserle** ~? can I
help you?, can I be of help?; **posso esserti** ~? can
I do anything for you?; **in tempo** ~ **per** in time
for; **rendersi** ~ to be helpful. **2** *sm* (**a**): **badare
solo all'**~ to think only of what is useful; **unire
l'**~ **al dilettevole** to combine business with
pleasure. (**b**) *(vantaggio)* advantage, benefit;
(Econ) profit; **partecipare agli** ~**i** to share in the
profits; **non ha saputo trarne alcun** ~ *(fig)* he
couldn't get anything out of it.

utilità [utiliˈta] *sf* usefulness; **senza** ~ **pratica**
without practical application, of no real use;
essere di grande ~ to be very useful.

utilitaria [utiliˈtarja] *sf (Aut)* runabout.

utilitario, a [utiliˈtarjo] *ag* utilitarian.

utilitarista, i, e [utilitaˈrista] *sm/f* utilitarian.

utilitaristico, a, ci, che [utilitaˈristiko] *ag* utilitarian.

utilizzare [utilidˈdzare] *vt* to use, make use of.

utilizzazione [utiliddzatˈtsjone] *sf* use.

utilizzo [utiˈliddzo] *sm (Amm)* utilization; *(Banca:
di credito)* availment.

utilmente [utilˈmente] *av* usefully, profitably.

utopia [utoˈpia] *sf* utopia; **è pura** ~ that's sheer
utopianism.

uva [ˈuva] *sf* grapes pl; ~ **passa** raisins pl; ~ **spina**
gooseberry.

uvetta [uˈvetta] *sf* raisins pl.

uxoricida, i, e [uksoriˈtʃida] *sm/f*: **essere** ~ to have
killed one's own husband/wife.

V

V, v [vu, vi] *sf o m inv (lettera)* V, v.
v. *abbr (= vedi)* v.
vacante [va'kante] *ag* vacant.
vacanza [va'kantsa] *sf* **(a)** holiday, vacation *(Am)*;
le ~e di Pasqua the Easter holidays; **essere/
andare in ~** to be/go on holiday; **prendersi una ~**
to take a holiday; **un giorno/mese di ~** a day's/
month's holiday; **far ~** to have a holiday. **(b)** *(di
cattedra etc)* vacancy.
vacca, che ['vakka] *sf (anche peg)* cow; **tempo delle
~che grasse/magre** *(fig)* fat/lean years.
vaccinare [vattʃi'nare] *vt (Med)*: **~ qn contro qc** to
vaccinate sb against sth; **farsi ~** to have a vaccination, get vaccinated; **ormai sono vaccinato
contro le delusioni amorose** I am immune to
disappointments in love now.
vaccinazione [vattʃinat'tsjone] *sf* vaccination.
vaccino, a [vat'tʃino] **1** *ag*: **latte m ~** cow's milk. **2**
sm vaccine; **fare un ~** to have a vaccination; **fare
un ~ a qn** to vaccinate sb.
vacillante [vatʃil'lante] *ag (edificio, vecchio)* shaky,
unsteady; *(fiamma)* flickering; *(salute, memoria)*
shaky, failing; **camminava con passo ~** he was
walking shakily *o* unsteadily.
vacillare [vatʃil'lare] *vi* **(a)** *(edificio, muro, ubriaco)*
to sway (to and fro); **~ per la stanchezza** to reel
with tiredness; **camminare vacillando** *(vecchio)*
to totter along; *(ubriaco, persona stanca)* to stagger along; **il pugno lo fece ~** the punch made him
reel. **(b)** *(fiamma)* to flicker; *(salute, memoria)* to
be shaky, be failing; *(trono, governo)* to be
unstable; *(fede)* to waver, be shaky; *(coraggio)* to
falter, waver.
vacuità [vakui'ta] *sf* vacuity, vacuousness.
vacuo, a ['vakuo] *ag* vacuous.
va e vieni ['va e v'vjeni] *sm inv (di persone)* coming
and going.
vagabondaggio [vagabon'daddʒo] *sm* wandering,
roaming; *(Dir)* vagrancy.
vagabondare [vagabon'dare] *vi* to roam, wander;
~ per to roam *o* wander about.
vagabondo, a [vaga'bondo] **1** *ag (gente, vita)*
wandering; *(fig: fannullone)* idle. **2** *sm/f (gen)* vagrant, tramp, vagabond; *(fig)* layabout, loafer.
vagare [va'gare] *vi*: **~ per** *(persona)* to wander
about, roam about; *(animale)* to roam; **~ con la
mente** *(fig)* to let one's mind wander; **~ con la
fantasia** *(fig)* to give free rein to one's imagination.
vagheggiare [vaged'dʒare] *vt (fig: desiderare)* to
long for, dream of.
vaghezza [va'gettsa] *sf* vagueness.
vagina [va'dʒina] *sf* vagina.
vaginale [vadʒi'nale] *ag* vaginal.
vagire [va'dʒire] *vi (bambino)* to cry, wail.
vagito [va'dʒito] *sm* cry, wailing.
vaglia ['vaʎʎa] *sm inv (Comm)* money order; **~
bancario** bank draft; **~ (postale)** postal order.
vagliare [vaʎ'ʎare] *vt (sabbia)* to riddle, sift;
(grano) to sift; *(fig: proposta, problema)* to weigh
up.

vaglio ['vaʎʎo] *sm* sieve; **passare al ~** *(fig)* to
examine closely.
vago, a, ghi, ghe ['vago] **1** *ag (gen)* vague;
(sguardo) vacant, empty. **2** *sm* **(a)** vagueness;
tenersi nel ~ to keep it all rather vague, stick to
generalities. **(b)** *(Anat)* vagus (nerve).
vagone [va'gone] *sm (per merci)* truck, wagon,
freight car *(Am)*; *(per passeggeri)* carriage, car
(Am); **~ letto** sleeping car; **~ ristorante** restaurant *o* dining car.
vaiolo [va'jɔlo] *sm* smallpox.
valanga, ghe [va'langa] *sf* avalanche; *(fig)* flood; **a
~** *(fig)* headlong.
valente [va'lɛnte] *ag* able, talented.
valenza [va'lɛntsa] *sf (Chim)* valency.
valere [va'lere] **1** *vi (aus essere)* **(a)** *(persona: contare)* to be worth; **come medico non vale molto** he
isn't worth much as a doctor, he's not much of a
doctor; **far ~ le proprie ragioni** to make o.s.
heard; **farsi ~** to make o.s. appreciated *o*
respected.
  (b) *(avere efficacia: documento)* to be valid;
(: legge) to be in force.
  (c) *(essere regolamentare: partita)* to be valid,
count; **non vale!** that's not fair!
  (d) *(giovare)* to be of use; **i suoi sforzi non
sono valsi a niente** his efforts came to nought; **i
tuoi consigli sono valsi a fargli cambiare idea**
your advice convinced him to change his
mind.
  (e) *(equivalere)* to be equal to; *(essere compa-
rabile a)* to be worth; *(significare)* to amount to;
l'uno vale l'altro the one is as good as the other,
they amount to the same thing; **non vale la pena**
it's not worth the effort; **vale a dire** that is to say;
quel che hai detto vale una critica what you have
said amounts to a criticism.
  (f) *(cosa: avere pregio)* to be worth; **vale 2
milioni (di lire)** it's worth 2 million lire; **non vale
niente** it's worthless.
  2 *vt (procurare)*: **ciò gli è valso un esaurimento**
that was what brought on *o* caused his nervous
breakdown.
  3: **~rsi** *vr*: **~rsi di** to use, make use of; **~rsi
dei consigli di qn** to take *o* act upon sb's advice.
valevole [va'levole] *ag* valid.
valicare [vali'kare] *vt (catena montuosa)* to cross.
valico, chi ['valiko] *sm* pass.
validità [validi'ta] *sf* validity; **ha una ~ di tre mesi**
it is valid for three months.
valido, a ['valido] *ag* **(a)** *(gen)* valid; **l'incontro non
è ~ per la finale** the match doesn't count for the
final; **non è ~!** *(in giochi etc)* that doesn't count!
  (b) *(efficace: resistenza, rimedio)* effective; *(: aiuto)* real; *(: contributo)* substantial; **essere di ~
aiuto a qn** to be a great help to sb. **(c)** *(persona:
bravo)* worthwhile.
valigeria [validʒe'ria] *sf (assortimento)* leather
goods *pl*; *(negozio)* leather goods shop.
valigia, gie *o* **ge** [va'lidʒa] *sf* (suit)case; **fare/
disfare le ~gie** to pack/unpack (one's bags); **~**

diplomatica *(Pol)* diplomatic bag; *(da uomo d'affari)* executive briefcase.

vallata [val'lata] *sf* valley.

valle ['valle] *sf* **(a)** valley; **a** ~ downhill; **a** ~ **di** *(su corso d'acqua)* downriver from. **(b)** *(tipo di laguna)*: ~i *pl* marshes.

valletta [val'letta] *sf (TV)* assistant.

valletto [val'letto] *sm* **(a)** *(domestico)* valet. **(b)** *(TV)* assistant.

valligiano, a [valli'dʒano] *sm/f* inhabitant of a valley.

vallo ['vallo] *sm (fortificazione)* wall; **il** ~ **Adriano** Hadrian's Wall.

valore [va'lore] *sm* **(a)** *(pregio: di merce)* value, worth; *(Fin: di moneta, titolo)* value, price; **il** ~ **della merce** the value of the goods; **crescere/diminuire di** ~ to go up/down in value, gain/lose in value; **è di gran** ~ it's worth a lot, it's very valuable; **privo di** ~ worthless.

(b): ~**i** *pl (titoli)* securities; *(oggetti preziosi)* valuables; **Borsa V**~**i** Stock Exchange; ~**i mobiliari** transferable securities; ~**i bollati** (revenue) stamps.

(c) *(di persona)* worth, merit; *(di opera)* merit, value; *(di vita, amicizia etc)* value; **artista di** ~ artist of considerable merit; ~**i morali/estetici** moral/aesthetic values; **scala dei** ~**i** scale of values; **per te l'amicizia non ha alcun** ~ friendship means nothing to you.

(d) *(significato)* meaning; *(funzione)* value; **le sue parole hanno** ~ **di una promessa** what he said amounts to *o* is tantamount to a promise; **il** ~ **di un vocabolo** the exact meaning of a word; **qui il participio ha** ~ **di aggettivo** the participle acts as *o* is used as an adjective here.

(e) *(coraggio)* courage, valour; **difendersi/combattere con gran** ~ to defend o.s./fight with great courage; **medaglia al** ~ **militare** medal for gallantry; **atti di** ~ acts of bravery *o* gallantry.

(f) *(Dir: validità)*: **questo documento non ha** ~ **legale** this document has no value in law.

valorizzare [valorid'dzare] *vt* **(a)** *(terreno, immobile)* to enhance the value of. **(b)** *(fig: mettere in risalto)* to set off, make the most of; **quel trucco valorizza i suoi occhi** that make-up makes the most of her eyes *o* accentuates her eyes.

valoroso, a [valo'roso] *ag* courageous, valorous.

valso, a ['valso] *pp* di **valere.**

valuta [va'luta] *sf* **(a)** *(Fin: moneta)* currency; ~ **estera** foreign currency; ~ **cartacea** paper money. **(b):** ~ **primo gennaio** interest to run from January the first.

valutare [valu'tare] *vt* **(a)** *(Econ: stimare: casa, gioiello etc)* to value; *(: danni, costo)* to assess, evaluate; *(: approssimativamente)* to estimate; *(fig: capacità etc)* to appreciate. **(b)** *(vagliare)* to weigh (up); ~ **il pro e il contro** to weigh up the pros and cons.

valutario, a [valu'tarjo] *ag (Fin: norme)* currency *attr.*

valutazione [valutat'tsjone] *sf (vedi vb a)* valuation; assessment, evaluation; estimate; **stando alle prime** ~**i, ...** going by initial estimates, ...

valva ['valva] *sf (Zool, Bot)* valve.

valvola ['valvola] *sf (gen)* valve; *(Elettr: fusibile)* fuse; ~ **a farfalla del carburatore** *(Aut)* throttle; ~ **di sicurezza** safety valve.

valzer ['valtser] *sm inv* waltz.

vamp [vamp] *sf inv* vamp.

vampa ['vampa] *sf (del sole)* burning heat; *(fiamma)* flame; *(fig: rossore: per calore, ira etc)* flush; *(: per vergogna)* blush.

vampata [vam'pata] *sf (fiammata)* blaze; *(di calore)* blast; *(fig: al viso)* flush.

vampiro [vam'piro] *sm (gen)* vampire; *(Zool)* vampire bat.

vanagloria [vana'glɔrja] *sf* boastfulness.

vanaglorioso, a [vanaglo'rjoso] *ag* boastful.

vandalico, a, ci, che [van'daliko] *ag* vandal *attr;* **atto** ~ act of vandalism.

vandalismo [vanda'lizmo] *sm* vandalism.

vandalo ['vandalo] *sm* vandal.

vaneggiamento [vaneddʒa'mento] *sm* raving, delirium.

vaneggiare [vaned'dʒare] *vi* to rave, be delirious; **ma tu vaneggi!** you must be mad!

vanesio, a [va'nezjo] *ag* vain, conceited.

vanga, ghe ['vanga] *sf* spade.

vangare [van'gare] *vt* to dig.

vangelo [van'dʒelo] *sm (Rel,fig)* gospel; **per me è** ~ *(fig)* it's gospel as far as I'm concerned.

vaniglia [va'niʎʎa] *sf* vanilla.

vanigliato, a [vaniʎ'ʎato] *ag* vanilla *attr.*

vaniloquio [vani'lɔkwjo] *sm (discorso futile)* nonsense, twaddle *(fam).*

vanità [vani'ta] *sf* **(a)** *(vanagloria)* vanity, pride, conceit. **(b)** *(futilità: di promessa)* emptiness, vanity; *(: di sforzo)* futility, fruitlessness.

vanitoso, a [vani'toso] **1** *ag* vain, conceited. **2** *sm/f* vain person.

vano, a ['vano] **1** *ag* **(a)** *(illusione, promessa)* vain, empty; *(fatiche)* vain, futile, fruitless; *(proteste, minacce)* idle, useless; **riuscire** ~ to come to nothing. **(b)** *(vanitoso)* vain, conceited. **2** *sm* **(a)** *(spazio vuoto)* space; **il** ~ **della porta** the doorway; **il** ~ **portabagagli** *(Aut)* the boot, the trunk *(Am).* **(b)** *(stanza)* room; **un appartamento di quattro** ~**i** a four-roomed flat.

vantaggio [van'taddʒo] *sm* **(a)** *(gen)* advantage; **avere il** ~ **(di)** to have the advantage (of). **(b)** *(profitto)* benefit, advantage; **tornerà a tuo** ~ it will be to your advantage; **trarre** ~ **da qc** to benefit from sth; **non trarre alcun** ~ **da qc** to get nothing out of sth. **(c)** *(distacco)* start; *(: Sport)* lead; *(: Tennis)* advantage; **hanno un** ~ **di 3 ore su di noi** they have a 3-hour start on us; *(Sport)* they have a 3-hour lead over us; **portarsi in** ~ *(Sport)* to take the lead; **ha 2 punti di** ~ **sull'avversario** he has a 2-point lead over his opponent.

vantaggioso, a [vantad'dʒoso] *ag* advantageous, favourable.

vantare [van'tare] **1** *vt* **(a)** *(lodare: persona, cosa, prodotto)* to speak highly of; *(avere: qualità)* to boast, have. **(b)** *(andare fiero di)* to boast of *o* about, vaunt. **2:** ~**rsi** *vr:* ~**rsi di qc/di aver fatto qc** to boast *o* brag about sth/about having done sth; **non faccio per vantarmi** without false modesty, without wishing to boast *o* brag.

vanteria [vante'ria] *sf (qualità)* boasting; *(atto, detto)* boast.

vanto ['vanto] *sm* **(a)** *(atto)*: **menar** ~ **di** to boast *o* brag about. **(b)** *(merito)* merit, virtue. **(c)** *(orgoglio)* pride; **è il** ~ **di sua madre** he's his mother's pride and joy.

vanvera ['vanvera] *sf*: **a** ~ haphazardly; **parlare a** ~ to talk nonsense.

vapore [va'pore] *sm (Chim, Fis)* vapour; *(dell'alcool)*: ~**i** fumes; ~ **acqueo** steam, (water) vapour; **ferro/locomotiva a** ~ steam iron/engine; **al** ~ *(Culin)* steamed; **andare a tutto** ~ *(fig: persona, macchina)* to go at full speed.

vaporetto [vapo'retto] *sm* steamer.

vaporizzare [vaporid'dzare] *vt* to vaporize; *(Cosmesi)* to steam.

vaporizzatore [vaporiddza'tore] *sm* spray.

vaporizzazione [vaporiddzat'tsjone] *sf* vaporization.

vaporosità [vaporosi'ta] *sf (vedi ag)* filminess; fullness.

vaporoso, a [vapo'roso] *ag (tessuto)* filmy; *(capelli)* full.

varare [va'rare] *vt (Naut, fig)* to launch; *(Dir)* to pass.

varcare [var'kare] *vt* to cross; **~ i limiti** to overstep *o* exceed the limits; **ha varcato l'ottantina** he's just over eighty.

varco, chi ['varko] *sm* passage; **aprirsi un ~ tra la folla** to push one's way through the crowd; **aspettare qn al ~** *(fig)* to lie in wait for sb.

varechina [vare'kina] *sf* bleach.

variabile [va'rjabile] **1** *ag (gen)* variable; *(tempo)* changeable, unsettled; *(umore)* changeable. **2** *sf (Mat, Econ)* variable.

variabilità [varjabili'ta] *sf (vedi ag)* variability; changeableness.

variante [va'rjante] *sf (gen)* variation, change; *(Linguistica)* variant; *(Sport)* alternative route.

variare [va'rjare] **1** *vt* to vary. **2** *vi (sog: persona: aus avere; sog: cosa: aus essere)* to vary.

variato, a [va'rjato] *ag* varied.

variazione [varjat'tsjone] *sf (gen)* variation, change; *(Mat, Mus)* variation; **una ~ di programma** a change of plan.

varice [va'ritʃe] *sf* varicose vein.

varicella [vari'tʃella] *sf* chickenpox.

varicoso, a [vari'koso] *ag*: **vena ~a** varicose vein.

variegato, a [varje'gato] *ag* variegated.

varietà [varje'ta] **1** *sf inv (gen)* variety. **2** *sm inv:* **(spettacolo di) ~** variety show.

vario, a ['varjo] **1** *ag* **(a)** *(diversificato: stile, paesaggio)* varied. **(b)** *(differente: oggetti, argomenti)* various; **avere ~e cose da fare** to have quite a few things to do; **~e volte** several times. **(c)** *(instabile: tempo)* changeable, unsettled; *(: umore)* uncertain. **2** *pron pl:* **~i** several people. **3** *sfpl:* **~e ed eventuali** *(nell'ordine del giorno)* any other business.

variopinto, a [varjo'pinto] *ag* multicoloured.

varo ['varo] *sm (Naut)* launch, launching.

vasaio, a [va'zajo] *sm/f* potter.

vasca, sche ['vaska] *sf* **(a)** *(gen)* tub; *(per pesci)* tank; *(cisterna)* water butt; **~ da bagno** bath(tub). **(b)** *(piscina)* (swimming) pool; *(: lunghezza della ~)* length; **fare una ~** to swim a length.

vascello [vaʃ'ʃello] *sm (Naut)* vessel, ship; **capitano di ~** captain; **tenente di ~** lieutenant.

vaschetta [vas'ketta] *sf (per gelato)* tub; *(per sviluppare fotografie)* basin.

vascolare [vasko'lare] *ag* vascular.

vaselina [vaze'lina] *sf* vaseline, petroleum jelly.

vasellame [vazel'lame] *sm (stoviglie)* crockery; *(: di porcellana)* china; *(: d'oro, d'argento)* plate.

vaso ['vazo] *sm* **(a)** *(recipiente: per fiori)* vase; *(: ornamentale)* vase, pot; *(: per conserve)* jar, pot; **~ da fiori** flowerpot; **~ da notte** chamber pot; **~ piccolo, unguento prezioso** *(fig)* it's the quality, not the quantity, that matters. **(b)** *(Anat, Bot, Fis)* vessel; **~i sanguigni/comunicanti** blood/communicating vessels.

vassoio [vas'sojo] *sm* tray.

vastità [vasti'ta] *sf* vastness.

vasto, a ['vasto] *ag (gen)* vast, huge, immense; *(fig: idee)* ambitious; **di ~e proporzioni** *(incendio)* huge; *(fenomeno, rivolta)* widespread; **su ~a scala** on a vast *o* huge scale; **di ~a cultura** widely read.

vaticano, a [vati'kano] **1** *ag* Vatican *attr.* **2**: **il V~** the Vatican; **la Città del V~** the Vatican City.

vattelappesca [vattelap'peska] *escl*: **come si chiama? — ~!** what's his name? — who knows?

ve [ve] *pron, av vedi* **vi.**

vecchia ['vekkja] *sf* old woman; **la mia ~** *(fam)* my old woman.

vecchiaia [vek'kjaja] *sf* old age; **sarai il bastone della mia ~** *(fig)* you'll support me in my old age.

vecchio, a ['vekkjo] **1** *ag* **(a)** *(gen)* old; **è più ~ di me** he is older than me; **è una ~a storia** it's an old story; **è un mio ~ amico** he's an old friend of mine; **è un uomo ~ stile** *o* **~a stampa** he's an old-fashioned man; **è ~ del mestiere** he's an old hand at the job; **~a volpe** *(fig)* cunning *o* wily old fox; **~ come il mondo** as old as the hills. **(b)** *(precedente)* old, former; **il ~ sindaco** the old *o* former mayor; **la sua ~a macchina** his old car. **(c)** *(stagionato: legno)* weathered; *(: vino, formaggio)* mature; *(stantìo: pane)* stale.
2 *sm* **(a)** *(persona)* old; **il contrasto tra il ~ e il nuovo** the contrast between old and new. **(b)** *(persona)* old man; **i ~i** the old *o* aged, old *o* elderly people, old folk; **come stanno i tuoi ~i?** *(genitori)* how are your folks?; **il ~** the *o* my old man; **~ mio!** old man!, old chap!

vecchiume [vek'kjume] *sm (peg: cose)* old rubbish, old junk; **il ~ delle sue idee** his old-fashioned ideas.

vece ['vetʃe] *sf (funzione)* place, stead; **firma del padre o di chi ne fa le ~i** signature of the father or guardian; **in ~ mia/tua** in my/your place *o* stead.

vedere [ve'dere] **1** *vt* **(a)** to see; **senza occhiali, non ci vedo** I can't see without my glasses; **non ci si vede, non si vede niente** you can't see a thing; **~ qn fare qc** to see sb do sth; **è una partita da ~** it'll be a match worth seeing; **l'ho visto nascere** *(fig)* I've known him since he was born; **ho visto costruire questa casa** I saw this house being built.

(b) *(raffigurarsi)* to see; **~ tutto nero** to take a bleak view of things; **non vedo una via d'uscita** I can see no way out; **modo di ~** outlook, view of things; **vorrei ~ te al posto suo!** I would like to see you in his place!; **lo vedo male questo progetto** I can't see this project working.

(c) *(esaminare: libro, prodotto)* to see, look at; *(: conti)* to go over, check; **vedi pagina 8** see page 8; **mi fai ~ il nuovo dizionario?** let me see *o* have a look at the new dictionary.

(d) *(scoprire)* to see, find out; **vai a ~ cos'è successo** go and see *o* find out what has happened; **voglio ~ come vanno le cose/che possibilità ci sono** I want to see how things are going/find out what opportunities there are; **vediamo se funziona** let's see if it works; **è da ~ se...** it remains to be seen whether... .

(e) *(incontrare)* to see, meet; **guarda chi si vede!** look who it is!; **fatti ~ ogni tanto** come and see us *(o me etc)* from time to time; **non farsi più ~ in giro** to disappear from the scene; **non si è più fatto ~** he hasn't shown his face since; **non la posso proprio ~** *(fig)* I can't stand her.

(f) *(visitare: museo, mostra)* to visit; *(consultare: medico, avvocato)* to see, consult; **farsi ~ da un medico** to go and see a doctor.

(g) *(capire)* to see, grasp; **ho visto subito che...** I soon realized that...; **non vedo la ragione di farlo** I can't see any reason to do it; **è triste ma non lo dà a ~** he is sad but he isn't letting it show *o* he is hiding it; **ci vedo poco chiaro in questa faccenda** I can't quite understand this business.

(h) *(fare in modo)*: **~ di fare qc** to see (to it)

that sth is done, make sure that sth is done; **vedi di non arrivare in ritardo** see you don't arrive late; **adesso vedi tu se lo puoi fare** now see what you can do; **vedi tu** (*decidi tu*) it's up to you.

(**i**) (*fraseologia*): **essere ben/mal visto da qn** to be/not to be well thought of by sb; **non ~ qn di buon occhio** to disapprove of sb; **non avere niente a che ~ con qn/qc** to have nothing to do with sb/sth; **~ le stelle** to see stars; **vederci doppio** to see double; **non vederci più dalla rabbia** to be beside o.s. with rage; **non vederci più dalla fame** to be ravenous; **non ~ l'ora di fare qc** to look forward to doing sth; **non vedo l'ora che arrivino** I can't wait for them to arrive; **a vederlo si direbbe che...** by the look of him you'd think that...; **in vita mia ne ho viste di tutti i colori** I've been through a lot in my time; **ti faccio ~ io!** I'll show you!

2: **~rsi** vr (**a**) (*specchiarsi, raffigurarsi*) to see o.s.

(**b**): **si era visto perduto** he realized (that) he was lost; **si era visto negare l'ingresso** he was refused admission; **si era visto costretto a...** he found himself forced to... .

(**c**) (*essere visibile*) to show; **non si vede** it doesn't show, you can't see it; **si vede!** that's obvious!

(**d**) (*uso reciproco*) to see each other, meet; **ci vedremo da mio cugino** I'll see you at my cousin's; **chi s'è visto s'è visto!** (*fig*) and that's that!

(**e**): **vedersela**: **vedetevela voi** you see to it; **se l'è vista brutta** he thought his last hour had come.

vedetta [ve'detta] sf (**a**) (*Mil: luogo, guardia*) lookout; **essere** o **stare di ~** to be on lookout duty. (**b**) (*Naut*) patrol ship.

vedette [vɔ'dɛt] sf inv (*attrice*) star.

vedova ['vedova] sf vedi **vedovo**.

vedovanza [vedo'vantsa] sf widowhood.

vedovo, a ['vedovo] **1** ag widowed. **2** sm/f widower/ widow; **rimaner ~** to be widowed.

veduta [ve'duta] sf (**a**) (*panorama, rappresentazione di paesaggio*) view. (**b**): **~e** sfpl (*fig*) views, opinions; **di larghe** o **ampie ~e** broad-minded; **di ~e limitate** narrow-minded.

veemente [vee'mɛnte] ag (*discorso, azione*) vehement; (*assalto*) vigorous; (*passione, desiderio*) overwhelming.

veemenza [vee'mɛntsa] sf vehemence; **con ~** vehemently; **la ~ dell'attacco** the force of the attack.

vegetale [vedʒe'tale] **1** ag (*gen*) vegetable attr; (*organismo*) plant attr; **regno ~** plant o vegetable kingdom. **2** sm: **i ~i** plants.

vegetare [vedʒe'tare] vi (**a**) (*piante*) to grow. (**b**) (*fig: persona*) to vegetate.

vegetariano, a [vedʒeta'rjano] ag, sm/f vegetarian.

vegetativo, a [vedʒeta'tivo] ag vegetative.

vegetazione [vedʒetat'tsjone] sf vegetation.

vegeto, a ['vedʒeto] ag (*piante*) thriving; (*persona*) strong, robust; **vivo e ~** hale and hearty.

veggente [ved'dʒɛnte] sm/f (*indovino*) clairvoyant.

veglia ['veʎʎa] sf (**a**) (*atto*) vigil, watch; **fare la ~ a qn** to watch over sb; **~ funebre** wake. (**b**): **ha passato ore di ~ sui libri** he spent many hours awake over his books; **tra la ~ e il sonno** half awake. (**c**) (*festicciola*) all-night party; **~ danzante** all-night dance.

vegliare [veʎ'ʎare] **1** vt (*malato, morto*) to watch over, sit up with. **2** vi (**a**) (*stare sveglio*) to stay up, sit up; **~ al capezzale di qn** to sit up with sb, watch by sb's bedside; **~ pregando** to pass the

night in prayer. (**b**) (*prendersi cura*): **~ su qn** to watch over sb.

veglione [veʎ'ʎone] sm ball, dance; **~ di Capodanno** New Year's Eve dance.

veicolo [ve'ikolo] sm (**a**) (*Tecn*) vehicle; **~ spaziale** spacecraft. (**b**) (*mezzo di diffusione: di idee, suoni*) vehicle, medium; (: *di malattia*) carrier.

vela ['vela] sf (**a**) (*Naut*) sail; **issare/spiegare/ammainare le ~e** to hoist/unfurl/strike the sails; **tutto va a gonfie ~e** (*fig*) everything is going perfectly. (**b**) (*Sport*) sailing; **andare a ~** to go sailing.

velare[1] [ve'lare] **1** vt (*anche fig*) to veil, cover; **~rsi il volto** to cover one's face; **le lacrime gli velarono gli occhi** his eyes were dimmed with tears. **2**: **~rsi** vr: **gli occhi le si velarono di pianto** o **crime** her eyes filled with tears; **lo sguardo le si velò** her eyes grew dim; **l'acqua si velò di ghiaccio** ice formed on the water.

velare[2] [ve'lare] ag (*Linguistica*) velar.

velato, a [ve'lato] ag (*anche fig: accenno*) veiled; **occhi ~i di lacrime** eyes filled with tears; **sorriso ~ di tristezza** smile tinged with sadness; **con la voce ~a per l'emozione** in a voice thick with emotion; **calze ~e** transparent o sheer stockings.

velatura [vela'tura] sf (*Naut*) sails pl.

veleggiare [veled'dʒare] vi (**a**) (*Naut*) to sail. (**b**) (*aliante, deltaplano*) to soar.

veleno [ve'leno] sm (*sostanza tossica*) poison; (*di serpente*) venom; **l'alcool è un ~ per il fegato** alcohol poisons your liver; **parole piene di ~** venomous words; **sputa sempre ~ su tutti** he is always making spiteful remarks about everybody.

velenoso, a [vele'noso] ag (*sostanza, fungo, animale*) poisonous; (*persona, lingua, risposta*) venomous.

veletta [ve'letta] sf (*di cappello*) veil.

velico, a, ci, che ['vɛliko] ag (*regata*) sailing attr; **superficie ~a** sail area.

veliero [ve'ljɛro] sm (*Naut*) sailing ship.

velina [ve'lina] sf (*anche*: **carta ~**: *per impacchettare*) tissue paper; (: *per copie*) flimsy paper; (: *copia*) carbon.

velista, i, e [ve'lista] sm/f yachtsman/woman.

velivolo [ve'livolo] sm aircraft.

velleità [vellei'ta] sfpl vain ambitions.

velleitario, a [vellei'tarjo] ag (*aspirazione*) fanciful, unrealistic; (*politica, tentativo*) unrealistic.

vello ['vello] sm (*di pecora, montone*) fleece; (*di altro animale*) skin.

vellutato, a [vellu'tato] ag (*stoffa, petalo, pesca, colore*) velvety; (*voce*) mellow.

velluto [vel'luto] sm (*stoffa*) velvet; **~ di cotone/seta** cotton/silk velvet; **~ a coste** corduroy.

velo ['velo] sm (**a**) (*gen*) veil; (*strato sottile*) film, layer; (: *di nebbia*) layer, veil; **~ nuziale** o **da sposa** bridal veil; **prendere il ~** (*Rel*) to take the veil; **un ~ di ghiaccio** a film of ice; **nel suo sorriso c'era un ~ di tristezza** there was a hint o touch of sadness in his smile. (**b**) (*tessuto*) voile. (**c**) (*Anat*): **~ palatino** soft palate.

veloce [ve'lotʃe] **1** ag (*gen*) quick, rapid; (*veicolo, cavallo, corridore*) fast; **il ~ scorrere del tempo** the swift o quick passage of time; **~ come un razzo** as quick as lightning; **più ~ della luce** (*fig*) as quick as a flash. **2** av fast.

velocipede [velo'tʃipede] sm velocipede.

velocista, i, e [velo'tʃista] sm/f (*Sport*) sprinter.

velocità [velotʃi'ta] sf inv (**a**) (*gen, Fis*) speed, velocity; **la sua ~ nel reagire** the swiftness of his response; **a grande ~** very quickly o fast; (*di* *veicolo)* at high speed; **a tutta** ~ at full speed; ~ **di crociera** cruising speed; **aumentare la** ~ to accelerate; **diminuire** *o* **ridurre la** ~ to reduce speed; **prendere** ~ to gain speed; **viaggiava alla** ~ **di 130 chilometri all'ora** it *(o* he) was travelling at a speed of 130 kilometres an hour. **(b)** *(Sport)*: **gara** *o* **corsa di** ~ sprint, dash.

velodromo [ve'lɔdromo] *sm* velodrome.

vena ['vena] *sf* **(a)** *(Anat)* vein; *(aurifera, di piombo etc)* vein, lode; *(di carbone)* seam; *(d'acqua)* spring; *(venatura: di marmo)* vein, streak; *(: di legno)* grain; **una** ~ **di tristezza** *(fig)* a hint of sadness. **(b)** *(estro)* inspiration; *(disposizione)* mood; **essere/sentirsi in** ~ **di fare qc** to be/feel in the mood to do sth; **non sono in** ~ **di scherzi** I'm not in the mood for jokes, I'm not in a joking mood.

venale [ve'nale] *ag* **(a)** *(Comm: valore)* market *attr*; *(: prezzo)* selling, market *attr*; **cose** ~**i** *(fig)* material things. **(b)** *(fig: persona)* venal; **ma come sei** ~! how mercenary you are!

venalità [venali'ta] *sf* venality.

venato, a [ve'nato] *ag (marmo)* veined, streaked; *(legno)* grained.

venatorio, a [vena'tɔrjo] *ag* hunting; **la stagione** ~**a** the hunting season.

venatura [vena'tura] *sf (di marmo)* vein, streak; *(di legno)* grain; **le** ~**e del legno** the grain of the wood.

vendemmia [ven'demmja] *sf* grape harvest, vintage; **fare la** ~ to pick *o* harvest the grapes.

vendemmiare [vendem'mjare] **1** *vi* to pick the grapes, harvest the grapes. **2** *vt (uva)* to pick, harvest.

vendemmiatore, trice [vendemmja'tore] *sm/f* grape-picker.

vendere ['vendere] **1** *vt (anche fig)* to sell; ~ **qc a qn** to sell sb sth, sell sth to sb; ~ **qc a** *o* **per 20 sterline** to sell sth for £20; ~ **all'ingrosso/al dettaglio** *o* **minuto** to sell wholesale/retail; ~ **a rate** to sell by instalments; **'non si vende a credito'** 'no credit given'; ~ **all'asta** to sell by auction; ~ **a buon mercato** to sell cheaply *o* at a good price; ~ **cara la pelle** *(fig)* to sell one's life dearly; ~ **l'anima al diavolo** to sell one's soul to the devil; **averne da** ~ *(fig)* to have enough and to spare. **2:** ~**rsi** *vr* **(a)** *(merce)*: **questi articoli si vendono bene/male** these articles sell well/don't sell well; ~**rsi al minuto** to be sold retail. **(b)** *(prostituirsi)* to prostitute o.s., sell o.s.

vendetta [ven'detta] *sf* revenge, vengeance; **prendersi la** ~ to take one's revenge, wreak vengeance; **essere assetato di** ~ to thirst for revenge.

vendicare [vendi'kare] **1** *vt* to avenge, revenge. **2:** ~**rsi** *vr*: ~**rsi (di qc)** to avenge *o* revenge o.s. (for sth); ~**rsi su qn** to avenge *o* revenge o.s. on sb.

vendicativo, a [vendika'tivo] *ag (persona, carattere)* vindictive.

vendicatore, trice [vendika'tore] **1** *ag (furia)* avenging. **2** *sm* avenger.

vendita ['vendita] *sf* sale; **contratto di** ~ sales agreement; **reparto** ~**e** sales department; ~ **all'ingrosso** wholesale; ~ **al minuto** *o* **dettaglio** retail; **mettere in** ~ to put on sale; **in** ~ **presso** on sale at; ~ **all'asta** auction (sale).

venditore, trice [vendi'tore] *sm/f* seller, vendor; ~ **ambulante** hawker, pedlar.

venduto, a [ven'duto] *ag (peg)* corrupt.

venefico, a, ci, che [ve'nɛfiko] *ag* poisonous; *(fig: insinuazione)* poisonous, venomous.

venerabile [vene'rabile] *ag*, **venerando, a** [vene'rando] *ag* venerable.

venerare [vene'rare] *vt* to venerate, revere.

venerazione [venerat'tsjone] *sf* veneration, reverence.

venerdì [vener'di] *sm inv* Friday; **V~ Santo** Good Friday; **gli manca qualche** ~ *(fig)* he's got a screw loose; *per uso vedi* **martedì.**

Venere ['venere] *sf, sm* Venus.

venereo, a [ve'nɛreo] *ag* venereal; **malattia** ~**a** venereal disease *(abbr* V.D.).

veneto, a ['vɛneto] *ag, sm/f* Venetian.

Venezia [ve'nettsja] *sf* Venice.

veneziana [venet'tsjana] *sf (tenda)* venetian blind.

veneziano, a [venet'tsjano] *ag, sm/f* Venetian.

veniale [ve'njale] *ag (Rel: peccato)* venial.

venire [ve'nire] **1** *vi (aus* essere) **(a)** to come; **verremo a salutarti/trovarti** we'll come and say goodbye/see you; **è venuto in macchina/treno** he came by car/train; **sono venuto a piedi** I came on foot; **vieni di corsa** come quickly; **vengo!** I'm coming!, just coming!

(b) *(giungere)* to come, arrive; *(cadere: festa)* to fall; **non è ancora venuto** he hasn't come *o* arrived yet; **prendere le cose come vengono** to take things as they come; **fallo come viene viene** do it any old how; ~ **a patti/alle mani** to come to an agreement/to blows; ~ **a capo di qc** to unravel sth, sort sth out; ~ **a sapere qc** to learn sth; ~ **al dunque** *o* **nocciolo** *o* **fatto** to come to the point; **questo lavoro/quel tipo mi è venuto a noia** I'm fed up with this work/with him; ~ **è venuto il momento di** the time has come to; **negli anni a** ~ in the years to come, in future; **sono cose di là da** ~ these things are still a long way off; **mi è venuta un'idea** I've had an idea; **ma che ti viene in mente?** whatever are you thinking of?; **gli era venuto il dubbio** *o* **sospetto che...** he began to suspect that...; **mi è venuto un dubbio** I began to have doubts; **mi è venuto il raffreddore** I've got a cold; **mi viene da vomitare/ridere** I feel sick/like laughing.

(c) *(provenire)*: ~ **da** to come from.

(d) *(riuscire: lavoro)* to turn out; ~ **bene/male** to turn out well/badly; **il maglione viene troppo lungo/stretto** the jumper is going to end up too long/tight; **non mi viene** *(problema, operazione, calcolo)* I can't get it to come out right.

(e) *(costare)* to cost; **quanto viene?** how much is it *o* does it cost?

(f) *(essere sorteggiato)* to come up.

(g) *(con av)*: ~ **fuori con** *(battuta)* to come out with; ~ **meno** *(persona)* to feel faint; ~ **meno a** *(promessa)* to break; *(impegno, dovere)* not to fulfil; ~ **su** *(crescere: persona)* to grow (up); *(: pianta)* to come up; **il bambino sta venendo su molto robusto** the baby's growing very strong; ~ **via** *(macchia)* to come off.

(h): **far** ~ *(medico)* to call, send for; **mi hai fatto** ~ **per niente** you got me to come *o* you made me come for nothing; **mi fa** ~ **il vomito** *(anche fig)* it makes me sick.

(i) *(con participio passato)*: ~ **stimato da tutti** to be respected by everybody; **verrà giudicato in base al suo punteggio** he will be judged on his marks.

2: venirsene *vr*: **venirsene via** to come away; **venirsene verso casa** to come home.

3 *sm*: **tutto quell'andare e** ~ **mi rendeva nervoso** all that coming and going made me irritable.

venoso, a [ve'noso] *ag* venous.

ventaglio [ven'taʎʎo] *sm* fan; **a** ~ fan-shaped; **disporsi a** ~ to fan out.

ventata [ven'tata] *sf (folata)* gust; **come una** ~ **d'aria fresca** *(fig)* like a breath of fresh air.

ventennale [venten'nale] *ag (che dura 20 anni)* twenty-year *attr; (che ricorre ogni 20 anni)* which takes place every twenty years.

ventenne [ven'tɛnne] *ag, sm/f* twenty-year-old; *per uso vedi* **cinquantenne.**

ventennio [ven'tɛnnjo] *sm* period of twenty years; **il ~ fascista** the Fascist period.

ventesimo, a [ven'tezimo] *ag, sm/f, sm* twentieth; *per uso vedi* **quinto.**

venti ['venti] *ag inv, sm inv* twenty; *per uso vedi* **cinque.**

ventilare [venti'lare] *vt* **(a)** *(Agr)* to winnow. **(b)** *(stanza)* to air, ventilate; *(fig: idea, proposta)* to air.

ventilato, a [venti'lato] *ag (camera, zona)* airy; **poco ~** airless; **una zona troppo ~a** a windy area.

ventilatore [ventila'tore] *sm* fan, ventilator.

ventilazione [ventilat'tsjone] *sf* ventilation.

ventina [ven'tina] *sf* about twenty; *per uso vedi* **cinquantina.**

ventiquattro [venti'kwattro] **1** *ag inv* twenty-four; **~ ore su ~** around the clock, 24 hours a day. **2** *sm inv* twenty-four; *per uso vedi* **cinque.**

ventiquattr'ore [ventikwat'trore] **1** *sfpl (periodo)* twenty-four hours. **2** *sf inv* **(a)** *(valigetta)* overnight case. **(b)** *(Sport)* twenty-four-hour race.

ventitré [venti'tre] **1** *ag inv, sm inv* twenty-three; *per uso vedi* **cinque. 2: portava il cappello sulle ~** he wore his hat at a jaunty angle.

vento ['vɛnto] *sm* wind; **un ~ caldo** a warm wind; **c'è ~** it's windy; **un colpo di ~** a gust of wind; **contro ~** against the wind; **~ contrario** *(Naut)* headwind; **c'è una barca sopra/sotto ~** *(Naut)* there is a boat to wind/leeward of us; **con i capelli al ~** with windswept hair; **fatica buttata al ~** wasted effort; **parlare al ~** to waste one's breath; **non andare a dirlo ai quattro ~i** don't go spreading it around; **un ~ di rivolta** a wind of revolt; **qual buon ~ ti porta?** to what do I (*o* we) owe the pleasure of seeing you?

ventola ['vɛntola] *sf (Aut, Tecn)* fan.

ventosa [ven'tosa] *sf (di gomma)* suction cap; *(Zool)* sucker; **funziona a ~** it works by suction.

ventoso, a [ven'toso] *ag* windy.

ventotto [ven'tɔtto] *ag inv, sm inv* twenty-eight; *per uso vedi* **cinque.**

ventre ['vɛntre] *sm* **(a)** *(addome)* stomach, tummy *(fam);* **avere dolori al ~** to have a stomach *o* tummy ache; **sdraiato sul ~** lying on one's stomach *o* front. **(b)** *(utero)* womb; **il ~ della terra** *(fig)* the depths of the earth.

ventricolare [ventriko'lare] *ag (Anat)* ventricular.

ventriglio [ven'triʎʎo] *sm (Zool)* gizzard.

ventriloquo, a [ven'trilokwo] *sm/f* ventriloquist.

ventuno [ven'tuno] *ag inv, sm inv* twenty-one; *per uso vedi* **cinque.**

ventura [ven'tura] *sf* fortune, chance; **andare alla ~** to trust to luck; **soldato di ~** mercenary; **compagnia di ~** company of mercenaries.

venturo, a [ven'turo] *ag* next.

venuta [ve'nuta] *sf* coming, arrival; **per la ~ della regina hanno organizzato un ricevimento** they have organized a reception for the queen's visit.

venuto, a [ve'nuto] **1** *pp di* **venire. 2** *sm/f:* **il(la) primo(a) ~(a)** the first person who comes along.

vera ['vera] *sf* wedding ring.

verace [ve'ratʃe] *ag (testimone)* truthful; *(testimonianza)* accurate, veracious; *(cibi)* real, genuine.

veracità [veratʃi'ta] *sf (vedi ag)* truthfulness, accuracy, veracity; genuineness; **nessuno mette in dubbio la ~ delle sue parole** nobody doubts the truth of what he said.

veramente [vera'mente] *av (realmente)* really; **~?**

really?; **è ~ cretino** he's a real idiot; **io, ~, al posto tuo...** frankly, in your place, I...; **~, non ne sapevo niente** actually, I didn't know anything about it.

veranda [ve'randa] *sf* veranda(h).

verbale [ver'bale] **1** *ag* **(a)** *(orale)* verbal, spoken; **accordo ~** verbal agreement. **(b)** *(Gram)* verbal. **2** *sm (di riunione)* minutes *pl;* *(Dir)* record; **le faccio il verbale** *(Polizia)* I'll have to report this; **mettere a ~** to place in the minutes *o* on record.

verbena [ver'bɛna] *sf (Bot)* vervain, verbena.

verbo ['vɛrbo] *sm* **(a)** *(Gram)* verb. **(b)** *(parola)* word; **il V~** *(Rel)* the Word.

verbosità [verbosi'ta] *sf* wordiness, verbosity.

verboso, a [ver'boso] *ag* wordy, verbose.

verdastro, a [ver'dastro] *ag* greenish.

verdazzurro, a [verdad'dzurro] *ag* bluish green.

verde ['verde] **1** *ag* **(a)** *(colore)* green; **~ bottiglia/oliva** bottle-/olive-green; **~ dalla bile** *(fig)* livid *o* white with rage. **(b)** *(acerbo: frutta)* green, unripe; *(: legna)* green; **gli anni ~i** *(fig)* youth. **2** *sm* **(a)** *(colore)* green; **essere al ~** *(fig)* to be broke. **(b)** *(vegetazione)* greenery; **c'è molto ~ in questa città** this city is very green; **una casa immersa nel ~** a house surrounded by greenery; **ho bisogno di un po' di ~** I feel in need of country air. **(c)** *(semaforo)* green (light).

verdeggiante [verded'dʒante] *ag* green, verdant.

verdeggiare [verded'dʒare] *vi:* **una distesa di prati verdeggiava davanti a noi** green fields spread out before us; **qualcosa verdeggiava in lontananza** there was something green in the distance.

verdemare [verde'mare] *ag, sm* sea-green.

verderame [verde'rame] *sm (Chim)* verdigris.

verdetto [ver'detto] *sm (Dir, med)* verdict.

verdognolo, a [ver'doɲɲolo] *ag* greenish.

verdone [ver'done] *sm (Zool)* greenfinch.

verdura [ver'dura] *sf (Culin)* vegetables *pl.*

verecondia [vere'kondja] *sf* modesty.

verecondo, a [vere'kondo] *ag* modest.

verga, ghe ['verga] *sf (canne, rod; (di pastore)* crook; **~ d'oro** gold bar; **percuotere qn con la ~** to cane sb.

vergare [ver'gare] *vt* **(a)** *(scrivere)* to write; *(rigare):* **carta vergata** lined paper. **(b)** *(percuotere)* to cane, beat.

vergatina [verga'tina] *sf (per macchina da scrivere)* flimsy.

verginale [verdʒi'nale] *ag* virginal, virgin *attr.*

vergine ['verdʒine] **1** *ag* **(a)** *(gen)* virgin; **la V~** the Virgin Mary *o* Mother. **(b)** *(Astrologia):* **V~** Virgo; **essere della V~** to be Virgo. **2** *ag (persona, terra)* virgin *attr;* **foresta ~** virgin forest; **pura lana ~** pure new wool; **olio ~ d'oliva** pure *o* virgin olive oil.

verginità [verdʒini'ta] *sf* virginity; **fare voto di ~** *(Rel)* to take one's vow of chastity.

vergogna [ver'goɲɲa] *sf* **(a)** *(gen)* shame; *(timidezza)* shyness; *(imbarazzo)* embarrassment; **prova-va ~ per ciò che era successo** he felt ashamed about what had happened; **provo ~ davanti a lui** he makes me feel shy; **vincere la propria ~** to overcome one's shyness; **non avere ~ di nessuno** to be shameless; **sprofondare per la ~** to be overcome by embarrassment. **(b)** *(onta, disonore)* disgrace; **è una ~ che non abbiano fatto niente** the fact that they haven't done anything is a disgrace; **è la ~ della famiglia** he is a disgrace to his family.

vergognarsi [vergoɲ'ɲarsi] *vr (vedi sf* **a)** to feel ashamed; to feel shy; to feel embarrassed; **vergognati!** you should be ashamed of yourself!

vergognoso, a [vergoɲ'ɲoso] *ag (che è timido)* timid, shy; *(che provoca vergogna)* shameful; *(che provoca disonore)* disgraceful.

veridico, a, ci, che [ve'ridiko] *ag* truthful.

verifica, che [ve'rifika] *sf* **(a): fare una ~ di** *(freni, testimonianza, firma)* to check. **(b)** *(Fin):* **~ contàbile** audit. **(c)** *(Scol)* test; **questo lavoro è una continua ~ delle proprie capacità** *(fig)* this work is a continual test of one's abilities.

verificabile [verifi'kabile] *ag* verifiable.

verificare [verifi'kare] **1** *vt* **(a)** *(controllare: verità etc)* to check, verify. **(b)** *(Fin)* to audit. **(c)** *(Mat: teoria, postulato)* to prove. **2:** **~rsi** *vr (accadere)* to happen, occur, take place.

verità [veri'ta] *sf inv (gen)* truth; **la pura ~** the absolute truth; **la ~ nuda e cruda** the plain unvarnished truth; **è una ~ sacrosanta** it's gospel; **travisare la ~** to distort the truth; **a dire la ~, per la ~** truth to tell, actually. **(b)** *(assioma)* truth; **le ~ scientifiche** scientific truths.

veritiero, a [veri'tjero] *ag* true, accurate.

verme ['verme] *sm (gen, fig)* worm; *(di frutto, formaggio)* maggot; **~ solitario** tapeworm; **nudo come un ~** stark naked; **mi sento un ~!** *(fig)* I could die!, I feel awful!

vermicelli [vermi'tʃelli] *smpl (pasta)* vermicelli *sg*.

vermifugo, a [ver'mifugo] *ag, sm* vermifuge.

vermiglio, a [ver'miʎʎo] *ag, sm* vermilion.

vermouth [ver'mut] *sm inv*, **vermut** ['vermut] *sm inv* vermouth.

vernacolo, a [ver'nakolo] *ag, sm* vernacular.

vernice [ver'nitʃe] *sf* **(a)** varnish; *(pittura: lucida)* gloss (paint); *(: opaca)* matt (paint); **'~ fresca'** 'wet paint'. **(b): scarpe/borsa di ~** patent leather shoes/bag.

verniciare [verni'tʃare] *vt* to varnish; *(pitturare)* to paint.

verniciatore [vernitʃa'tore] *sm* **(a)** *(operaio)* varnisher. **(b)** *(dispositivo):* **~ a spruzzo** spray gun.

verniciatura [vernitʃa'tura] *sf* painting; *(con vernice trasparente)* varnishing.

vernissage [verni'saʒ] *sm inv (Arte)* preview.

vero, a ['vero] **1** *ag (gen)* true; *(reale)* real; *(autentico)* genuine; **è una storia ~a** it is a true story; **incredibile ma ~** incredible but true; **il suo ~ nome è Giovanni** his real *o* true name is Giovanni; **ma è ~ questo Modigliani?** is this a genuine *o* real Modigliani?; **perle ~e** real pearls; **quei fiori sembrano ~i** those flowers look real; **il ~ problema è...** the real problem is...; **fosse ~!** if only it were true!; **nulla di più ~!** you've said it!, how true!; **non mi pare ~!** it doesn't seem possible!; **come è ~ Dio** I swear to God; **tant'è ~ che...** so much so that...; **~?** isn't that right?; **hai il mio libro, ~?** you've got my book, haven't you?; **sei italiano, ~?** you're Italian, aren't you?; **è andata stamattina, ~?** she went this morning, didn't she?; **vorresti andare, ~?** you'd like to go, wouldn't you?

2 *sm* truth; **c'è del ~ in ciò che dice** there is some truth in what he says; **sto dicendo il ~** I am telling the truth; **a onor del ~, a dire il ~** to tell the truth; **è una copia dal ~** *(disegno)* it's a copy from life.

verosimiglianza [verosimiʎ'ʎantsa] *sf (vedi ag)* likelihood, probability; plausibility.

verosimile [vero'simile] *ag (racconto, ipotesi)* likely, probable; *(trama)* plausible, convincing; **poco ~** *(racconto)* improbable, unlikely; *(trama)* implausible.

verro ['verro] *sm (Zool)* boar.

verruca, che [ver'ruka] *sf (Med, Bot)* verruca, wart.

versaccio [ver'sattʃo] *sm:* **fare i ~i** to make faces.

versamento [versa'mento] *sm* **(a)** *(gen)* payment; *(deposito in banca)* deposit. **(b)** *(Med)* effusion.

versante [ver'sante] *sm (Geog)* side.

versare[1] [ver'sare] **1** *vt* **(a)** *(liquido, polvere)* to pour; *(servire: caffè)* to pour (out); **~ la minestra** to serve (up) the soup. **(b)** *(spargere: liquidi, polvere)* to spill; *(: lacrime, sangue)* to shed; **mi sono versato il caffè addosso** I've spilt coffee over myself; **~ acqua sul fuoco** *(fig)* to pour oil on troubled waters. **(c):** **il Po versa le proprie acque nell'Adriatico** the Po flows into the Adriatic. **(d)** *(Econ: pagare)* to pay; *(: depositare)* to deposit, pay in; **ho versato la somma sul mio conto** I paid the sum into my account, I deposited the sum in my account; **~ una cauzione** to pay a deposit.

2: **~rsi** *vr* **(a)** to spill; **il latte si è versato sul fuoco** the milk has boiled over. **(b):** **~rsi in** *(sog: fiume)* to flow into; *(: folla)* to pour into.

versare[2] [ver'sare] *vi:* **~ in gravi difficoltà** to find o.s. with serious problems; **~ in fin di vita** to be dying.

versatile [ver'satile] *ag* versatile.

versatilità [versatili'ta] *sf* versatility.

versato, a [ver'sato] *ag:* **~ in** (well-)versed in.

verseggiare [versed'dʒare] **1** *vt* to put into verse. **2** *vi* to write verse, write poetry. **3** *sm* verse, poetry.

versetto [ver'setto] *sm (di poesia)* line; *(Rel)* verse.

versione [ver'sjone] *sf* **(a)** *(gen)* version; **in ~ originale** *(libro)* in the original (version); *(film)* in the original language *o* version; **la ~ cinematografica del suo ultimo libro** the film of his latest book; **~ lusso** *(Aut)* luxury model. **(b)** *(traduzione)* translation.

verso[1] ['verso] *sm (di pagina)* verso; *(di moneta)* reverse.

verso[2] ['verso] *sm* **(a)** *(di animali, uccelli)* call, cry; **qual'è il ~ del gatto?** what noise *o* sound does a cat make?; **~ di richiamo** call; **Maria ha fatto un ~ di dolore** Maria cried out in pain *o* gave a cry of pain; **smettila di fare tutti quei ~i** stop making those noises; **rifare il ~ a qn** *(imitare)* to take sb off.

(b) *(riga: di poesia)* line, verse; **~i sciolti** blank verse *sg*; **in ~i** in verse.

(c) *(direzione, Mat)* direction; *(di legno, stoffa)* grain; **prendere qn/qc per il ~ giusto** to approach sb/sth the right way; **non c'è ~ di convincerlo** it is impossible to persuade him; **per un ~ o per l'altro** one way or another; **chi per un ~, chi per un altro tutti hanno deciso di partire** for one reason or another they all decided to leave.

verso[3] ['verso] *prep* **(a)** *(in direzione di)* toward(s), to; **andando ~ la stazione** going towards the station; **veniva ~ di me** he was coming towards me; **~ l'alto** upwards; **~ il basso** downwards; **guardare ~ il cielo** to look heavenwards *o* skywards; **navigare ~ sud** to sail south(wards). **(b)** *(nei pressi di)* near, around (about); **abito ~ il centro** I live near the centre. **(c)** *(in senso temporale)* about, around; **arrivi ~ che ora?** around *o* about what time will you arrive?; **~ sera** towards evening; **~ la fine dell'anno** towards the end of the year.

vertebra ['vertebra] *sf* vertebra.

vertebrale [verte'brale] *ag* vertebral; **colonna ~** spinal column, spine.

vertebrato, a [verte'brato] *ag, sm* vertebrate.

vertenza [ver'tentsa] *sf (lite)* lawsuit, case; *(sindacale)* dispute.

vertere ['vertere] *vi:* **~ su** to deal with, be about.

verticale [verti'kale] **1** *ag* vertical. **2** *sf* **(a)** *(linea)* vertical. **(b)** *(Ginnastica: sulle mani)* handstand; *(: sulla testa)* headstand; **fare la** ~ to do a handstand *(o headstand)*. **(c)** *(nei cruciverba)* clue *(o word)* down.

vertice ['vɛrtitʃe] *sm* **(a)** *(Geom)* vertex. **(b)** *(vetta)* summit, peak; *(fig: punto più alto)* peak, height; **il** ~ **della carriera** the peak of one's career. **(c)** *(Pol)* summit; **incontro al** ~ summit meeting.

vertigine [ver'tidʒine] *sf* giddiness, dizziness; *(Med)* vertigo; **mi fa venire le** ~**i** it makes my head spin; **cifre da** ~ incredible sums *o* amounts.

vertiginoso, a [vertidʒi'noso] *ag* *(altezza)* dizzy, giddy; *(velocità)* breakneck *attr;* *(danza)* breathless; *(cifra)* exorbitant; *(scollatura)* plunging; **il ritmo** ~ **della vita moderna** the frenetic pace of modern life.

verve [vɛrv] *sf* verve.

verza ['vɛrdza] *sf* Savoy cabbage.

vescica, che [veʃ'ʃika] *sf* **(a)** *(Anat)* bladder. **(b)** *(Med: bolla)* blister.

vescovado [vesko'vado] *sm* *(Rel: diocesi)* bishopric; *(: sede)* bishop's palace.

vescovile [vesko'vile] *ag* episcopal.

vescovo ['veskovo] *sm* bishop.

vespa¹ ['vɛspa] *sf* *(Zool)* wasp.

vespa² ['vɛspa] *sf* ® (motor) scooter.

vespaio [ves'pajo] *sm* wasps' nest; **suscitare un** ~ *(fig)* to stir up a hornets' nest.

vespasiano [vespa'zjano] *sm* urinal.

vespro ['vɛspero] *sm* *(poet: sera)* evening; *(Rel)* vespers *pl.*

vessare [ves'sare] *vt* to oppress.

vessazione [vessat'tsjone] *sf* oppression.

vessillo [ves'sillo] *sm* *(Mil)* standard; *(fig)* banner, ensign; **il** ~ **della libertà** the banner of freedom.

vestaglia [ves'taʎʎa] *sf* dressing gown.

vestale [ves'tale] *sf* vestal virgin.

veste ['veste] *sf* **(a)** *(da donna)* dress; *(di monaco, suora)* habit; ~**i** clothes; ~ **da camera** dressing gown. **(b)** *(fig: di libro):* ~ **editoriale** layout. **(c)** *(funzione)* capacity; *(fig: apparenza)* appearance; **in** ~ **di** (in one's capacity) as; **in** ~ **ufficiale** in an official capacity; **si è presentato in** ~ **di amico** he passed himself off as a friend.

vestiario [ves'tjarjo] *sm* wardrobe, clothes *pl;* **capo di** ~ article of clothing, garment.

vestibolo [ves'tibolo] *sm* (entrance) hall.

vestigia [ves'tidʒa] *sfpl* **(a)** *(tracce)* vestiges, traces. **(b)** *(rovine)* ruins, remains.

vestire [ves'tire] **1** *vt* **(a)** *(gen):* ~ **(di)** to dress (in); *(mascherare):* ~ **da** to dress up as. **(b)** *(provvedere degli indumenti necessari)* to clothe; **Valentino veste le attrici più famose** Valentino makes *o* designs clothes for all the famous actresses. **(c)** *(indossare: stato)* to wear; *(: atto)* to put on.

2 *vi* *(indossare)* to wear; *(abbigliarsi)* to dress; ~ **di bianco/a lutto** to wear white/mourning; ~ **con eleganza** to dress smartly; **questa giacca veste bene** this is a well-cut jacket.

3: ~**rsi** *vr* *(gen)* to dress, get dressed; *(abbigliarsi)* to dress; ~**rsi da** *(negozio)* to buy *o* get one's clothes at; *(sarto)* to have one's clothes made at; ~**rsi da indiano/Peter Pan** to dress up as an Indian/Peter Pan; ~**rsi a festa** to wear one's Sunday best *o* one's best clothes; ~**rsi bene/con gusto** to dress well/tastefully; **come mi devo** ~ **stasera?** what should I wear this evening?

vestito¹, a [ves'tito] *ag* dressed; ~ **da** *(in maschera)* dressed up as; ~ **di tutto punto** all dressed up; **dormire** ~ to sleep in one's clothes.

vestito² [ves'tito] *sm* *(abito: da donna)* dress; *(com-*

pleto da uomo, tailleur) suit; ~**i** clothes; **cambiare** ~**i** to change one's clothes; **farsi fare un** ~ to have a dress *(o* suit) made.

Vesuvio [ve'zuvjo] *sm:* **il** ~ Vesuvius.

veterano, a [vete'rano] **1** *sm* *(Mil)* veteran. **2** *sm/f* *(fig)* veteran, old hand.

veterinaria [veteri'narja] *sf* veterinary medicine.

veterinario, a [veteri'narjo] **1** *ag* veterinary. **2** *sm* veterinary surgeon, vet *(fam).*

veto ['veto] *sm* *(Dir, fig)* veto; **diritto di** ~ right of veto; **porre il** ~ **a qc** to veto sth.

vetraio [ve'trajo] *sm* *(gen)* glazier, glass-worker; *(chi soffia il vetro)* glass-blower.

vetrata [ve'trata] *sf* glass door *(o* window); *(di chiesa)* stained-glass window.

vetrato, a [ve'trato] *ag* glass *attr;* **carta** ~**a** sandpaper.

vetreria [vetre'ria] *sf* *(fabbrica)* glassworks *sg.*

vetrificare [vetrifi'kare] **1** *vt* to vitrify; *(ceramica)* to glaze. **2:** ~**rsi** *vr* to vitrify.

vetrina [ve'trina] *sf* **(a)** *(di negozio)* (shop) window; **in** ~ in the window; **allestire una** ~ to dress a window; **andare a guardare le** ~**e** to go window-shopping. **(b)** *(mobile: di museo)* showcase, display cabinet; *(: di negozio)* display cabinet.

vetrinista, i, e [vetri'nista] *sm/f* window dresser.

vetrino [ve'trino] *sm* slide.

vetriolo [vetri'ɔlo] *sm* vitriol.

vetro ['vetro] *sm* **(a)** *(materiale)* glass; *(frammento)* piece of glass; *(scheggia)* splinter of glass; ~ **blindato** bulletproof glass; ~ **di sicurezza** safety glass; ~ **infrangibile** shatterproof glass; **lana di** ~ glass fibre; **fibra di** ~ fibreglass; **mettere qc sotto** ~ to put sth under glass. **(b)** *(di finestra, porta)* (window) pane; *(di orologio)* watch glass; **devo pulire i** ~**i** I have to clean the windows; **porta a** ~**i** glass door. **(c)** *(oggetto):* **i** ~**i di Murano** Murano glassware *sg.*

vetroso, a [ve'troso] *ag* vitreous.

vetta ['vetta] *sf* *(di montagna)* top, summit; **toccare le più alte** ~**e del successo** to reach the top of the ladder.

vettore [vet'tore] **1** *sm* **(a)** *(Mat, Fis)* vector. **(b)** *(trasportatore)* carrier. **2** *ag:* **razzo** ~ booster rocket.

vettovaglie [vetto'vaʎʎe] *sfpl* provisions.

vettovagliamento [vettovaʎʎa'mento] *sm* provisioning.

vettura [vet'tura] *sf* **(a)** *(carrozza)* coach, carriage; ~ **di piazza** hackney carriage. **(b)** *(Ferr)* coach, carriage, car *(Am);* **in** ~! all aboard! **(c)** *(auto)* car, automobile *(Am).*

vetturino [vettu'rino] *sm* coach driver, coachman.

vezzeggiamento [vettseddʒa'mento] *sm* caressing.

vezzeggiare [vettsed'dʒare] **1** *vt* to make a fuss of. **2:** ~**rsi** *vr* *(fare il vezzoso)* to simper; **smettila di vezzeggiarti davanti allo specchio** stop simpering at *o* admiring yourself in the mirror.

vezzeggiativo, a [vettseddʒa'tivo] **1** *ag* of endearment. **2** *sm* form of endearment.

vezzo ['vettso] *sm* **(a)** *(abitudine)* (affected) habit; **avere il** ~ **di fare qc** to have the habit of doing sth. **(b)** *(gesto affettuoso)* caress. **(c):** ~**i** *pl* *(moine)* affected ways; *(grazia)* charm *sg.*

vezzosità [vettsosi'ta] *sf* affected ways *pl,* affectation.

vezzoso, a [vet'tsoso] **1** *ag* **(a)** *(leggiadro)* pretty, charming. **(b)** *(lezioso)* affected. **2** *sm/f:* **fare il(la)** ~**(a)** to turn on the charm.

vi [vi] *(dav* **lo, la, li, le, ne** *diventa* **ve) 1** *pron pers* **(a)** *(ogg diretto)* you; ~ **stavo cercando** I was looking for you; **vorrei aiutarvi** I'd like to help you. **(b)**

(complemento di termine) (to) you; **ve l'hanno dato** they gave it to you; ~ **darò un consiglio** I'll give you some advice. **(c)** *(riflessivo)* yourselves; *(reciproco)* each other; **vestitevi** get dressed; **divertitevi** enjoy yourselves; **ve ne pentirete** you'll regret it; ~ **conoscete?** do you know each other? **2** *pron dimostr* = **ci. 3** *av (in questo luogo)* here; *(in quel luogo)* there; **non ~ erano che pochi turisti** there were only a few tourists there; ~ **sono molti modi di farlo** there are many ways of doing it.

via[1] ['via] *sf* **(a)** *(strada)* road; *(: di città)* street, road; *(cammino)* way; *(percorso)* route; **abito in ~ Cairoli 14** I live at number 14 Via Cairoli; **la V~ Crucis** the Way of the Cross; **la V~ Lattea** the Milky Way; **~e di comunicazione** communication routes; ~ **commerciale** trade route; **che ~ fai di solito?** what route do you usually take?; **sulla ~ di casa** on one's way home; **hai ~ libera** *(a un incrocio)* the road is clear; **dare ~ libera a qc** *(fig)* to give free rein to sth; **allontanarsi dalla retta ~** *(fig)* to stray from the straight and narrow; **in ~ di guarigione** *(fig)* on the road to recovery; **la ~ italiana al socialismo** the Italian road to socialism; **la sua laurea gli apre molte ~e** his degree offers him many possibilities.

(b) *(mezzo)* way, means; *(fig: modo)* way; **tentare tutte le ~e** to try everything possible; **per ~e traverse** by underhand means; **non avevo altra ~** I had no alternative; **non c'è ~ di scampo** *o* **d'uscita** there's no way out; **scegliere la ~ di mezzo** to compromise; **glielo dico in ~ privata** *o* **confidenziale** I'm telling you in confidence; *(ufficiosamente)* I'm telling you unofficially; **in ~ eccezionale** as an exception; **in ~ amichevole** in a friendly manner; **comporre una disputa in ~ amichevole** *(Dir)* to settle a dispute out of court; **le ~e del Signore** the ways of the Lord; **passare alle ~e di fatto** to resort to violence; **per ~ aerea** by air; ~ **satellite** by satellite; ~ **Dover** via Dover; **per ~ di** because of.

(c) *(Anat)* tract; **le ~e respiratorie** the respiratory tracts; **per ~ orale** *(Med)* orally.

via[2] ['via] **1** *av* **(a)** *(allontanamento)* away; *(: temporaneo)* away; **buttare** *o* **gettare ~ qc** to throw sth away; **tagliare ~** to cut off *o* away; **dare ~ qc** to give sth away; **è andato ~** *(di casa)* he has gone out; *(di città)* he has gone away; **sono stato ~ per 3 settimane** I was away for three weeks; **vai ~!** go away!, clear off! *(fam)*; **questa macchia non va ~** this mark won't come out. **(b)** *(eccetera)* **e così ~** and so on; **e ~ dicendo, e ~ di questo passo** and so on (and so forth). **(c):** ~ ~ *(pian piano)* gradually; ~ ~ **che** *(man mano)* as.

2: ~ **da** *prep* away from; **non andare ~ da me** don't leave me.

3 *escl (orsù)* come on!; *(allontanati)* go away!; *(: a un animale)* shoo!; **pronti, ~!** ready, steady, go!

4 *sm (Sport)* (signal to) start; **dare il ~ to** start the race; **dare il ~ a un progetto** to give the green light to a project; **hanno dato il ~ ai lavori** they've begun *o* started work.

viabilità [viabili'ta] *sf (percorribilità)* practicability; **per migliorare la ~ del centro** in order to improve traffic circulation in the centre.

viadotto [via'dotto] *sm* viaduct.

viaggiare [viad'dʒare] *vi (gen)* to travel; **a me piace ~** I like travelling; **la macchina viaggiava a 50 chilometri all'ora** the car was travelling at (a speed of) 50 kilometres per hour; **il treno viaggia con 50 minuti di ritardo** the train is running 50 minutes late; **le merci viaggiano via mare** the

goods go *o* are sent by sea; **viaggio per una ditta di tessuti** I travel in textiles.

viaggiatore, trice [viaddʒa'tore] **1** *ag* travelling; **piccione** *m* ~ carrier pigeon; **commesso** ~ travelling salesman. **2** *sm/f (gen)* traveller; *(passeggero)* passenger.

viaggio [vi'addʒo] *sm* journey, trip; *(in aereo)* flight; *(via mare)* voyage; **è in ~** he's away; **spese di ~** travelling expenses; ~ **d'affari** business trip; ~ **di nozze** honeymoon; ~ **organizzato** package tour *o* holiday; **ho dovuto fare due ~i per portar su i libri** I had to make two trips to bring the books up; **fare il ~ a vuoto** to make a wasted journey; **mi hanno rimborsato il ~** they gave me my travelling expenses.

viale [vi'ale] *sm* **(a)** *(del parco)* path, walk. **(b)** *(della città)* avenue.

viandante [vian'dante] *sm/f* vagrant.

viavai [via'vai] *sm* coming and going, bustle.

vibrante [vi'brante] *ag (membrana)* vibrating; *(voce, suono)* vibrant, resonant; ~ **di** vibrant with.

vibrare [vi'brare] **1** *vt (poet: arma)* to brandish; ~ **un colpo a qn** to strike sb. **2** *vi* **(a)** *(gen, Fis)* to vibrate; *(voce)* to quiver, be vibrant; **il suo cuore vibrava di emozione** her heart throbbed with emotion. **(b)** *(risuonare)* to resound, ring.

vibrato [vi'brato] *sm (Mus)* vibrato.

vibratore, trice [vibra'tore] **1** *ag* vibrating. **2** *sm* vibrator.

vibratorio, a [vibra'tɔrjo] *ag* vibratory.

vibrazione [vibrat'tsjone] *sf* vibration.

vicario [vi'karjo] *sm (Rel)* vicar.

vice ['vitʃe] *sm/f* deputy.

vice- ['vitʃe] *pref* vice...; **~ammiraglio** vice-admiral.

vicedirettore, trice [vitʃediret'tore] *sm/f (gen)* deputy manager/manageress; *(di giornale etc)* deputy editor; *(di scuola)* deputy headmaster.

vicenda [vi'tʃenda] **1** *sf* **(a)** *(episodio)* event. **(b):** **~e** *pl (sorte)* fortunes; **con alterne ~e** with mixed fortunes. **2: a ~** *av* **(a)** *(reciprocamente)* each other, one another. **(b)** *(alternativamente)* in turns.

vicendevole [vitʃen'devole] *ag* mutual, reciprocal.

vicepreside [vitʃe'preside] *sm/f* deputy headmaster/mistress.

vicepresidente [vitʃepresi'dɛnte] *sm* vice-president, vice-chairman.

viceré [vitʃe're] *sm inv* viceroy.

viceversa [vitʃe'versa] *av* vice versa.

vichingo, a, ghi, ghe [vi'kingo] *ag, sm/f* Viking.

vicinanza [vitʃi'nantsa] *sf* **(a)** *(prossimità)* proximity, closeness. **(b):** ~**e** *pl (paraggi)* vicinity *sg*; **nelle ~e ci sono due panettieri** there are two bakers in the vicinity *o* in the area.

vicinato [vitʃi'nato] *sm (zona)* neighbourhood; *(vicini)* neighbours *pl*; **avere rapporti di buon ~** to get on well with one's neighbours.

vicino, a [vi'tʃino] **1** *ag* **(a)** *(a poca distanza)* near, nearby; *(: paese)* neighbouring, nearby; ~ **a** near, close to; **la stazione è ~a** the station is near, the station is close (by); **dov'è il ristorante più vicino?** where is the nearest restaurant?; **quei quadri sono troppo ~i** those pictures are too close (to one another); **abbiamo idee molto ~e** we hold very similar views; **mi sono stati molto ~i** *(fig)* they were very supportive towards me.

(b) *(accanto)* next; **la mia stanza è ~a alla tua** my room is next to yours.

(c) *(nel tempo)* near, close at hand; **la fine è ~a** the end is near *o* imminent; **siamo ~i alla fine**

we've almost *o* nearly finished; **le vacanze sono** ~**e** the holidays are approaching; **è** ~**a ai trent'anni** she's almost thirty.

2 *av* **(a)** *(a poca distanza)* near, nearby, close (by); *(: nel tempo)* near, close; **vieni più** ~ come closer; **abitiamo qui** ~ we live near here; **stai** ~! stay close to me!

(b): **da** ~ close to; *(esaminare)* closely; *(sparare)* at close quarters; **da** ~ **è più bella** she's much prettier when you see her close up; **fai la fotografia da** ~ take the photograph close up.

(c): ~ **a** close to, near (to); *(accanto a)* beside, next to; **vivono** ~ **al mare** they live close to *o* near the sea; **era seduto** ~ **a me** he was sitting near me; *(accanto a)* he was sitting next to *o* beside me; **state** ~ **a vostro padre** *(anche fig)* stay close to your father; **ci sono andato** ~ *(fig: quasi indovinato)* I almost got it.

3 *sm/f* neighbour; **i nostri** ~**i di casa** our next-door neighbours; **il mio** ~ **di banco** the person at the desk next to mine.

vicissitudine [vitʃissi'tudine] *sf* vicissitude; **le** ~**i della vita** the ups and downs of life.

vicolo ['vikolo] *sm* alley; ~ **cieco** blind alley.

video ['video] *sm (TV: schermo)* screen; **ci sono dei disturbi al** ~ the picture is not very good.

videocassetta [videokas'setta] *sf* videocassette.

videogioco, chi [video'dʒɔko] *sm* video game.

videoregistratore [videoredʒistra'tore] *sm (apparecchio)* video (recorder).

vidimare [vidi'mare] *vt (Amm)* to authenticate.

vidimazione [vidimat'tsjone] *sf (Amm)* authentication.

Vienna ['vjenna] *sf* Vienna.

vietare [vje'tare] *vt (proibire)* to forbid; *(Amm: importazione, sosta etc)* to prohibit, ban; *(: libro)* to ban; ~ **a qn di fare qc** to forbid sb to do sth; **il dottore mi ha vietato gli alcolici** the doctor has forbidden me to take alcohol; **hanno vietato il passaggio dei camion in centro** lorries have been banned from *o* prohibited in the centre; **nulla ti vieta di farlo** there is nothing to prevent *o* stop you doing it; **nulla vieta che io lo faccia** there is nothing to stop me; **e chi te lo vieta?** who's stopping you?

vietato, a [vje'tato] *ag (vedi vb)* forbidden; prohibited; banned; **'~ calpestare le aiuole'** 'keep off the grass'; **'~ fumare'** 'no smoking'; **'senso** ~**'** *(Aut)* 'no entry'; **'sosta** ~**a'** *(Aut)* 'no parking'; ~ **ai minori di 14/18 anni** prohibited to children under 14/18.

Vietnam [vjet'nam] *sm* Vietnam.

vietnamita, i, e [vjetna'mita] *ag, sm/f, sm* Vietnamese.

vigente [vi'dʒente] *ag (Dir: legge)* in force; *(fig)* current, in use.

vigere ['vidʒere] *vi (difettivo: si usa solo alla terza persona)*: **in Italia vige ancora l'obbligo del servizio militare** in Italy national service is still in force; **in casa mia vige l'abitudine di**... at home we are in the habit of....

vigilante [vidʒi'lante] **1** *ag* vigilant, watchful. **2** *sm/f* guard.

vigilanza [vidʒi'lantsa] *sf (sorveglianza: di operai, alunni)* supervision; *(: di sospetti, criminali)* surveillance; ~ **notturna** night-watchman service.

vigilare [vidʒi'lare] *vt* **(a)** *(sorvegliare: operai, studenti)* to supervise; *(: sospetti, criminali)* to keep under surveillance. **(b)** *(provvedere a)*: ~ **che** to make sure that, see to it that.

vigilato, a [vidʒi'lato] *sm/f (Dir)* person under police surveillance.

vigilatrice [vidʒila'tritʃe] *sf*: ~ **d'infanzia** nursery-

school teacher; ~ **scolastica** school health officer.

vigile ['vidʒile] **1** *ag (persona, occhio)* vigilant, watchful; *(cura)* vigilant. **2** *sm (anche:* ~ **urbano)** (traffic) policeman; ~ **del fuoco** fireman.

vigilessa [vidʒi'lessa] *sf* (traffic) policewoman.

vigilia [vi'dʒilja] *sf* **(a)** *(giorno antecedente)* eve; **alla** ~ **degli esami** on the eve of the exams. **(b)** *(veglia)* vigil.

vigliaccheria [viʎʎakke'ria] *sf* cowardice; **è stata una** ~ **da parte sua** it was contemptible of him.

vigliacco, a, chi, che [viʎ'ʎakko] **1** *ag (persona, azione)* cowardly; *(: spregevole)* contemptible. **2** *sm/f* **(a)** *(codardo)* coward. **(b)** *(profittatore)* rogue, scoundrel.

vigna ['viɲɲa] *sf* vineyard.

vigneto [viɲ'ɲeto] *sm* (large) vineyard.

vignetta [viɲ'ɲetta] *sf (disegno)* illustration; *(umoristica)* cartoon.

vignettista, i, e [viɲɲet'tista] *sm/f* illustrator; *(di vignette umoristiche)* cartoonist.

vigogna [vi'goɲɲa] *sf* vicuña.

vigore [vi'gore] *sm* **(a)** *(gen)* vigour, strength; *(fig: forza)* vigour, force; **nel suo pieno** ~ in his prime, in the prime of life; **perdere** ~ *(persona)* to lose strength; *(campagna elettorale)* to lose impetus; *(discorso, stile)* to become less vigorous *o* energetic. **(b)** *(Dir)*: **essere in** ~ to be in force; **entrare in** ~ to come into force *o* effect; **non è più in** ~ it is no longer in force, it no longer applies.

vigorosità [vigorosi'ta] *sf* vigour, strength.

vigoroso, a [vigo'roso] *ag (gen)* vigorous; *(braccio)* strong, powerful; *(stile)* vigorous, energetic; *(resistenza)* vigorous, strenuous; **una** ~**a stretta di mano** a firm handshake.

vile ['vile] **1** *ag (vigliacco)* cowardly; *(spregevole)* contemptible, base; ~ **menzogna** wicked lie; **il** ~ **denaro** filthy lucre; **di** ~**i natali** of humble origins. **2** *sm/f* coward.

vilipendere [vili'pendere] *vt* to despise, scorn.

vilipendio [vili'pendjo] *sm* contempt, scorn; *(Dir)*: ~ **alla bandiera** contempt for the national flag.

vilipeso, a [vili'peso] *pp di* **vilipendere**.

villa ['villa] *sf (in città)* detached house; *(in campagna)* country house; *(sulla riviera)* villa.

villaggio [vil'laddʒo] *sm* village; ~ **turistico** holiday village; ~ **residenziale** commuter town; ~ **olimpico** Olympic village.

villanata [villa'nata] *sf* rude act, impolite act.

villania [villa'nia] *sf (sgarbataggine)* rudeness, bad manners *pl*; **è stata una** ~ **da parte sua** it was very rude of him.

villano, a [vil'lano] **1** *ag* rude, ill-mannered; **modi** ~**i** bad manners. **2** *sm/f* **(a)** *(poet: contadino)* peasant. **(b)** *(peg: persona sgarbata)* lout, boor.

villanzone, a [villan'tsone] *sm/f* ill-bred person, boor.

villeggiante [villed'dʒante] *sm/f* holiday-maker.

villeggiare [villed'dʒare] *vi* to holiday, spend one's holidays, vacation *(Am)*.

villeggiatura [villeddʒa'tura] *sf*: **andare/essere in** ~ to go/be on holiday *o* vacation *(Am)*; **luogo di** ~ (holiday) resort.

villetta [vil'letta] *sf*, **villino** [vil'lino] *sm* small (detached) house.

villoso, a [vil'loso] *ag* hairy.

viltà [vil'ta] *sf* cowardice; **atto di** ~ act of cowardice.

viluppo [vi'luppo] *sm* tangle.

vimine ['vimine] *sm (Bot)* osier; **di** ~**i** *(sedia etc)* wicker *attr*, wickerwork *attr*.

vinaio [vi'najo] *sm* wine merchant.

vincente [vin't∫εnte] *ag* winning; **carta** ~ winning card; *(fig)* trump card.

vincere ['vint∫ere] **1** *vt* **(a)** *(gen)* to win; ~ **una causa** *(Dir)* to win a case *o* suit; ~ **un premio** to win a prize. **(b)** *(sconfiggere: nemico)* to defeat, vanquish; *(: avversario)* to beat; ~ **qn a tennis** to beat sb at tennis. **(c)** *(superare: sentimenti)* to overcome; *(avere ragione di)* to get the better of, outdo; **fu vinto dalla stanchezza** tiredness overcame him; **lasciarsi** ~ **dalla tentazione** to succumb *o* yield to temptation; ~ **qn in** *(abilità)* to outdo *o* surpass sb in; *(bellezza)* to surpass sb in; **vuole sempre averla vinta** he always wants to have the upper hand.

2 *vi* **(a)** *(in gioco, battaglia)* to win; **vinca il migliore** may the best man win. **(b)** *(prevalere)* to win, prevail.

3: ~**rsi** *vr* to control o.s.

vincita ['vint∫ita] *sf (il vincere)* win, victory; *(cosa vinta)* winnings *pl.*

vincitore, trice [vint∫i'tore] **1** *ag* winning, victorious. **2** *sm/f (in gara)* winner; *(in battaglia)* victor, winner.

vincolante [vinko'lante] *ag* binding.

vincolare [vinko'lare] *vt* **(a)** *(Dir)* to bind; *(sog: famiglia, lavoro)* to tie down. **(b)** *(Fin)*: ~ **una somma in banca** to place a sum on fixed deposit.

vincolato, a [vinko'lato] *ag (vedi vb)* bound; tied down; **deposito** ~ fixed deposit.

vincolo ['vinkolo] *sm (gen)* bond, tie; *(di sangue)* tie; *(Dir)* encumbrance; **libero da ogni** ~ free from all ties; *(Dir)* unencumbered.

vinicolo, a [vi'nikolo] *ag* wine *attr*; **regione** ~a wine-producing area.

vinificazione [vinifikat'tsjone] *sf* wine-making.

vino ['vino] *sm* wine; **lista dei** ~**i** wine list; ~ **bianco/rosso/rosato** white/red/rosé wine; **buon** ~ **fa buon sangue** *(Proverbio)* good wine makes good cheer.

vinto, a ['vinto] **1** *pp di* **vincere**. **2** *ag* **(a)** *(sconfitto)* defeated, beaten. **(b)** *(oggetto)*: **i soldi** ~**i al gioco** money won gambling; **darla** ~**a a qn** to let sb have his way; **darsi per** ~ to give up, give in; **vuol sempre aver partita** ~**a** he always wants to have the upper hand. **3** *sm/f (gen)* loser; **i** ~**i** *(Mil)* the defeated (side), the vanquished.

viola¹ [vi'ɔla] **1** *sf (Bot)* violet; ~ **del pensiero** pansy. **2** *sm inv (colore)* violet.

viola² [vi'ɔla] *sf (Mus)* viola.

violacciocca, che [violat't∫ɔkka] *sf (Bot)* stock.

violare [vio'lare] *vt (gen)* to violate; *(legge)* to violate, infringe, break; *(promessa)* to break; *(domicilio)* to break into; *(tempio)* to desecrate; *(donna)* to rape; ~ **la privacy di qn** to invade sb's privacy.

violazione [violat'tsjone] *sf (vedi vb)* violation; infringement, breach; breaking; breaking into; desecration; ~ **di domicilio** *(Dir)* breaking and entering.

violentare [violen'tare] *vt (sessualmente)* to assault (sexually); *(fig: coscienza)* to outrage; **in questo modo violenti la sua volontà** you are forcing him to do it against his will

violento, a [vio'lento] **1** *ag (gen)* violent; *(suono)* loud; *(colore)* loud, garish; *(incendio)* raging; **usare un tono** ~ to express o.s. with violence; **usare modi** ~**i** to use violence; **rimedi** ~**i** drastic remedies. **2** *sm/f* violent person.

violenza [vio'lentsa] *sf (gen)* violence; *(di vento, temporale)* violence, force; ~ **carnale** (sexual) assault; **ricorrere alla/far uso della** ~ to resort to/use violence; **ottenere qc con la** ~ to obtain sth by violent means *o* the use of violence.

violetta [vio'letta] *sf (Bot)* violet.

violetto, a [vio'letto] *ag, sm (colore)* violet.

violinista, i, e [violi'nista] *sm/f* violinist.

violino [vio'lino] *sm* violin; **essere teso come una corda di** ~ to be very tense; **primo** ~ first violin; **chiave di** ~ treble clef.

violoncellista, i, e [violont∫el'lista] *sm/f* cellist, cello player.

violoncello [violon't∫ello] *sm* violoncello, cello.

viottolo [vi'ɔttolo] *sm* path, track.

vipera ['vipera] *sf (Zool)* viper; *(fig)* catty person; **è una lingua di** ~ she has a vicious tongue.

viperino, a [vipe'rino] *ag (Zool)* viper attr, viper's; *(fig)* venomous.

viraggio [vi'radd3o] *sm* **(a)** *(Naut)* coming about; *(Aer)* turn. **(b)** *(Fot)* toning.

virago [vi'rago] *sf, pl* **viragini** Amazon.

virale [vi'rale] *ag* viral.

virare [vi'rare] *vi* **(a)** *(Naut)* to come about; *(Aer)* to turn; ~ **di bordo** to change course. **(b)** *(Fot)* to tone.

virata [vi'rata] *sf (vedi vb* **a***)* coming about; turning; change of course; *(Sport: nuoto)* turn.

virgola ['virgola] *sf (nella punteggiatura)* comma; *(Mat)* (decimal) point; **sette** ~ **cinque** seven point five; **non c'è una** ~ **fuori posto** *(scritto)* it's an excellent piece of work; **non cambiare una** ~ *(fig)* don't change a thing; **punto e** ~ semicolon.

virgoletta [virgo'letta] *sf* inverted comma, quotation mark; **tra** ~**e** in inverted commas *o* quotation marks.

virgulto [vir'gulto] *sm (Bot)* shoot; *(fig: discendente)* scion.

virile [vi'rile] *ag (aspetto, voce)* masculine; *(atteggiamento, lineamenti)* manly, virile; *(bellezza)* male; *(stile)* vigorous, virile; *(linguaggio)* firm; **età** ~ manhood.

virilità [virili'ta] *sf (vedi ag)* masculinity; manliness; virility; vigour; firmness.

virologia [virolo'd3ia] *sf* virology.

virtù [vir'tu] *sf inv* **(a)** *(Rel)* virtue; *(pregio, qualità)* virtue, quality; *(virtuosità, castità)* virtuousness; **un modello di** ~ a paragon of virtue; **fare di necessità** ~ to make a virtue of necessity. **(b)** *(capacità: di persona)* ability; *(proprietà: di erbe etc)* property; **in** ~ **di questa legge** by virtue of this law; **in** ~ **della nostra amicizia** for friendship's sake.

virtuale [virtu'ale] *ag (gen)* potential; *(Fis)* virtual.

virtuosismo [virtuo'sizmo] *sm (abilità)* virtuosity; **esibirsi in inutili** ~**i** to show off.

virtuoso, a [virtu'oso] **1** *ag* virtuous. **2** *sm/f (del violino, del pennello etc)* virtuoso, master.

virulento, a [viru'lento] *ag* virulent.

virulenza [viru'lentsa] *sf* virulence.

virus ['virus] *sm inv* virus.

visagista, i, e [viza'd3ista] *sm/f* beautician.

vis-à-vis [viz a 'vi] *av:* **eravamo seduti** ~ we were sitting opposite each other.

viscerale [vi∫∫e'rale] *ag (Med)* visceral; *(fig)* profound, deep-rooted.

viscere [vi∫∫ere] **1** *sm (Anat)* internal organ. **2** *sfpl (fig)* depths; **nelle** ~ **della terra** in the bowels of the earth.

vischio ['viskjo] *sm* **(a)** *(Bot)* mistletoe. **(b)** *(pania)* birdlime.

vischiosità [viskjosi'ta] *sf (collosità)* stickiness; *(Fis, Chim)* viscosity.

vischioso, a [vis'kjoso] *ag (colloso)* sticky; *(viscoso)* viscous.

viscidità [vi∫∫idi'ta] *sf (vedi ag)* sliminess; smarminess.

viscido, a ['viʃʃido] *ag (lumaca, pelle)* slimy; *(persona)* smarmy.

visconte [vis'konte] *sm* viscount.

viscosa [vis'kosa] *sf* viscose.

viscosità [viskosi'ta] *sf* viscosity.

viscoso, a [vis'koso] *ag* viscous.

visibile [vi'zibile] *ag (gen)* visible; *(imbarazzo)* obvious, evident, visible; *(progresso)* clear, perceptible.

visibilio [vizi'biljo] *sm:* **andare in** ~ **(per qc)** to go into ecstasies *o* raptures (over sth).

visibilità [vizibili'ta] *sf* visibility.

visiera [vi'zjɛra] *sf (di cappello)* peak; *(di armatura)* visor; *(Scherma)* fencing mask.

visionare [vizjo'nare] *vt (gen)* to look at, examine; *(Cine)* to screen.

visionario, a [vizjo'narjo] *ag, sm/f* visionary.

visione [vi'zjone] *sf (a) (gen, Rel)* vision; *(scena)* sight; *(idea, concetto)* view; **ma tu hai le** ~**i!** you must be seeing things!; **avere una** ~ **limitata della realtà** to have a narrow view of reality. **(b)** *(atto del vedere)* vision, sight; **prendere** ~ **di qc** to have a look at sth; **mandare qc in** ~ **(Comm)** to send sth on approval; **cinema di prima** ~ **cinema** *where films are shown on first release.*

visita ['vizita] *sf (a) (gen)* visit; *(di amico, rappresentante)* visit, call; **far** ~ **a qn, andare in** ~ **da qn** to visit sb, pay sb a visit; **in** ~ **ufficiale in Italia** on an official visit to Italy; ~ **sanitaria** sanitary inspection; ~ **a domicilio** house call; **il dottore sta facendo il giro delle** ~**e** the doctor is doing his rounds; **orario di** ~**e** *(ospedale)* visiting hours; **biglietto da** ~ (visiting) card; **abbiamo** ~**e** we have visitors *o* guests.

(b) *(turistica: di città)* tour; *(: di museo)* tour, visit; ~ **guidata** guided tour; **la** ~ **del castello dura 2 ore** the tour of the castle takes 2 hours, it takes 2 hours to go round the castle.

(c) *(Med: esame)* medical examination; **orario di** ~**e** surgery hours; ~ **di controllo** checkup; ~ **di leva** *(Mil)* medical checkup for national service; **marcare** ~ *(Mil)* to report sick.

visitare [vizi'tare] *vt (a) (andare in visita)* to visit, call on, go and see; *(rappresentante)* to call on; **andare a** ~ **qn** to go and see *o* visit sb. **(b)** *(museo)* to visit, go round; **ci ha fatto** ~ **la casa/il castello** he showed us round the house/castle. **(c)** *(Med)* to examine; ~ **i pazienti a casa** to see patients at home; **il dottore sta visitando** the doctor is seeing *o* receiving patients now; **il dottore visita solo il giovedì** the doctor only sees patients on Thursdays; **bisogna che mi faccia** ~ I must go and have a medical *o* a checkup.

visitatore, trice [vizita'tore] *sm/f (a) (ospite)* visitor, guest. **(b)** *(turista)* visitor, tourist.

visivo, a [vi'zivo] *ag* visual; **memoria** ~**a** visual memory; **gli organi** ~**i** the eyes.

viso ['vizo] *sm* face; **crema per il** ~ face *o* facial cream; **guardare in** ~ **qn** to look sb in the face, look straight at sb; **fare buon** ~ **a cattivo gioco** to make the best of things; **a** ~ **aperto** openly; ~ **pallido** *(uomo bianco)* paleface.

visone [vi'zone] *sm (Zool)* mink; *(pelliccia)* mink (coat).

visore [vi'zore] *sm (Fot)* viewer.

vispo, a ['vispo] *ag (persona)* lively; *(mente)* lively, quick.

vissuto, a [vis'suto] **1** *pp di* **vivere**. **2** *ag* **(a):** **storia di vita** ~**a** a story from real life. **(b)** *(persona)* experienced, who has had many experiences.

vista ['vista] *sf (a) (gen)* sight; *(capacità visiva)* eye(sight); **avere la** ~ **buona** to have good eyesight; **avere la** ~ **corta/lunga** to be short-/long-sighted; *(fig)* to be short-/far-sighted; **ho avuto un improvviso abbassamento della vista** my eyesight suddenly got worse; **esame della** ~ eye test; **occhiali da** ~ glasses; **sottrarsi alla** ~ **di qn** to disappear from sb's sight; **mettersi in** ~ to draw attention to o.s.; *(peg)* to show off; **essere in** ~ *(persona)* to be in the public eye; **terra in** ~! land ahoy!; **a prima** ~ at first sight; **conoscere qn di** ~ to know sb by sight; **in** ~ **di qc** in view of sth; **sparare a** ~ to shoot on sight; **pagabile a** ~ payable on demand; **avere in** ~ **qc** to have sth in view; **a** ~ **d'occhio** before one's very eyes; **perdere qn di** ~ *(anche fig)* to lose sight of sb.

(b) *(veduta)* view; **con** ~ **sul lago** with a view over the lake.

vistare [vis'tare] *vt* to approve; *(Amm: passaporto)* to visa.

visto, a ['visto] **1** *pp di* **vedere**. **2** *sm* **(a)** *(segno)* tick; *(Amm: approvazione)* approval. **(b)** *(Amm)* visa; ~ **d'ingresso/di transito** entry/transit visa; ~ **permanente/di soggiorno** permanent/tourist visa.

vistosità [vistosi'ta] *sf* gaudiness, showiness.

vistoso, a [vis'toso] *ag (che si nota)* gaudy, showy; *(ingente)* enormous, huge.

visuale [vizu'ale] **1** *ag* visual. **2** *sf (gen)* view; *(Ottica)* line of vision; *(nel tiro)* line of sight; ~ **la visuale a qn** to block sb's view.

visualizzare [vizualid'dzare] *vt* to visualize.

vita¹ ['vita] *sf (a) (gen)* life; **essere in** ~ to be alive; **perdere la** ~ to lose one's life; **far ritornare in** ~ to bring sb back to life; **dare la** ~ **per qn/qc** to give one's life for sb/sth; **pieno di** ~ full of life; **ha portato la** ~ **in casa** he brought a bit of life into the house.

(b) *(modo di vivere)* life, lifestyle; **nella** ~ **quotidiana** *o* **di ogni giorno** in everyday life; **la** ~ **da studente** life as a student; **la** ~ **in Scozia** life in Scotland; **la** ~ **degli animali** animal life; **condurre una** ~ **attiva** to lead an active life; **avere una doppia** ~ to lead a double life; **cambiare** ~ to change one's way of life *o* one's lifestyle.

(c) *(mezzi di sussistenza)* living; **guadagnarsi la** ~ to earn one's living; **il costo della** ~ the cost of living; **la** ~ **è cara a Parigi** life is expensive in Paris, it's expensive to live in Paris.

(d) *(durata)* life, lifetime; **ti amerò per tutta la** ~ I'll love you for ever *o* all my life; **ho lavorato per tutta la** ~ I've worked all my life; **capita una volta sola nella** ~ it only happens once in a lifetime; **membro a** ~ life member; **essere condannato a** ~ to be sentenced to life imprisonment; **avere sette** ~**e** to have nine lives; **non basterebbe una** ~ **per spiegartelo** it would take a lifetime *o* ages to explain it to you; ~ **media** average life expectancy.

(e) *(biografia)* life (story); **mi ha raccontato tutta la sua** ~ she told me her life story *o* the story of her life.

(f) *(fraseologia):* **l'altra** ~ the hereafter; **o la borsa o,la** ~! your money or your life!; **ci metti una** ~! you are taking ages!; **è la** ~! that's life!; **è una** ~ **da cani!** it's a dog's life!; **è una ragazza di** ~ she's a prostitute; **fare la bella** ~ to lead the good life *o* a life of pleasure; **finché c'è** ~ **c'è speranza** while there's life there's hope; **pena la** ~ on pain of death; **rendere la** ~ **difficile a qn** to make life difficult for sb; **sapere** ~**, morte e miracoli di qn** to know all the ins and outs of sb's life, know all there is to know about sb.

vita² ['vita] *sf (Anat, Sartoria)* waist; **abito a** ~ **alta/bassa** dress with a high/low waist; **punto di** ~ waist; **su con la** ~! *(fig)* cheer up.

vitale [vi'tale] *ag* **(a)** *(gen)* vital; *(vivace: persona, bambino)* lively, vital; **spazio** ~ living space. **(b)** *(che può vivere)* viable.

vitalità [vitali'ta] *sf* vitality, vigour.

vitalizio [vita'littsjo] *sm (Dir)* life annuity.

vitamina [vita'mina] *sf* vitamin.

vitaminico, a, ci, che [vita'miniko] *ag* vitamin *attr;* **biscotto** ~ vitamin-enriched biscuit.

vitaminizzare [vitaminid'dzare] *vt* to enrich with vitamins.

vite[1] ['vite] *sf (Bot)* (grape)vine.

vite[2] ['vite] *sf (Tecn)* screw; ~ **senza fine** endless screw; **giro di** ~ *(anche fig)* turn of the screw; **tappo a** ~ screw(-on) cap *o* top.

vitella [vi'tɛlla] *sf* **(a)** *(Zool)* calf; ~ **da latte** suckling calf. **(b)** *(Culin)* veal.

vitello [vi'tɛllo] *sm* **(a)** *(Zool)* calf. **(b)** *(Culin)* veal. **(c)** *(pelle)* calf(skin).

vitellone [vitel'lone] *sm* **(a)** *(Zool)* bullock. **(b)** *(Culin)* tender young beef. **(c)** *(fig)* loafer.

viticcio [vi'tittʃo] *sm (Bot)* tendril.

viticoltore [vitikol'tore] *sm* vine grower.

viticoltura [vitikol'tura] *sf* vine growing.

vitreo, a ['vitreo] *ag (sostanza)* vitreous; *(occhio, sguardo)* glossy.

vittima ['vittima] *sf (gen)* victim; *(di incidente)* casualty, victim; **fare la** ~ to play the martyr.

vittimismo [vitti'mizmo] *sm* self-pity.

vitto ['vitto] *sm (cibo)* food; *(in pensioni)* board; ~ **e alloggio** room and board.

vittoria [vit'tɔrja] *sf* victory; **cantar** ~ to crow (over one's victory).

vittoriano, a [vitto'rjano] *ag* Victorian.

vittorioso, a [vitto'rjoso] *ag* victorious, triumphant.

vituperare [vitupe'rare] *vt* to berate, rail against.

vituperio [vitu'perjo] *sm* insult.

viuzza [vi'uttsa] *sf (in città)* alley.

viva ['viva] *escl* long live; ~ **il re!** long live the king!; ~ **il Milan!** three cheers for Milan!

vivacchiare [vivak'kjare] *vi* to scrape a living.

vivace [vi'vatʃe] *ag* **(a)** *(gen)* lively; *(intelligenza)* lively, keen; *(colore)* vivid, brilliant. **(b)** *(Mus)* vivace.

vivacità [vivatʃi'ta] *sf (vedi ag)* liveliness; keenness; vividness, brilliance.

vivacizzare [vivatʃid'dzare] *vt* to liven up.

vivaio [vi'vajo] *sm (di piante)* nursery; *(di pesci)* fish farm; *(fig)* breeding ground.

vivamente [viva'mente] *av (commuoversi)* deeply, profoundly; *(ringraziare etc)* sincerely, warmly.

vivanda [vi'vanda] *sf* food *no pl.*

vivente [vi'vente] **1** *ag* living; **è il ritratto** ~ **del nonno** he is the spitting image of his grandfather; **l'autore è ancora** ~ the author is still alive; **è il massimo poeta** ~ he is the greatest living poet; **sembri un cadavere** ~ you look like death warmed up. **2** *smpl:* **i** ~**i** the living.

vivere ['vivere] **1** *vi (aus essere)* **(a)** *(gen)* to live; *(essere vivo)* to live, be alive; ~ **fino a 100 anni** to live to be 100; **non gli resta molto da** ~ he hasn't long to live; **ha cessato di** ~ he is dead; **finché vivrò** as long as I live; **chi vivrà vedrà** only time will tell; **vivi e lascia** ~ live and let live; ~ **fuori dalla realtà** to live in another world, be out of touch with reality.

(b) *(abitare)* to live; **vivo in campagna** I live in the country; **viviamo insieme** we live together.

(c) *(sostentarsi):* ~ **(di)** to live (on); *(cibarsi):* ~ **di** to live on, feed on; **io vivo di poco o niente** I live on little or nothing; **ho giusto di che** ~ I have just enough to live on; **guadagnarsi da** ~ **con le traduzioni** *o* **facendo traduzioni** to earn one's

living by doing translations; ~ **di sospetti** to feed on one's suspicions; ~ **d'aria e d'amore** to live on wine and roses; ~ **alla giornata** to live from day to day; ~ **di stenti** to live in utter poverty; ~ **da signore** to live like a lord; ~ **nel lusso** to live a life of luxury.

(d) *(comportarsi)* to live; **devi ancora imparare a** ~ you've still got a lot to learn about life.

(e) *(Tip):* **vive stet.**

2 *vt (vita)* to live; *(avvenimento, fatto)* to live through, go through; ~ **una vita tranquilla** to lead a quiet life; ~ **giorni di dolore** to live through a sad period; **ha vissuto la scuola come una punizione** he hated his school days.

3 *sm* life; **lo faccio per il quieto** ~! anything for a quiet life!

viveri ['viveri] *smpl* provisions, supplies.

viveur [vi'vœr] *sm inv* pleasure-seeker.

vivido, a ['vivido] *ag (ricordo)* vivid, very clear; *(luce)* bright, brilliant; *(colori)* bright, vivid; **di** ~ **ingegno** quick-witted, bright.

vivificare [vivifi'kare] *vt (materia)* to give life to; *(ravvivare: piante)* to revive, refresh; *(fig: racconto)* to bring to life.

viviparo, a [vi'viparo] *ag* viviparous.

vivisezionare [vivisettsjo'nare] *vt* to vivisect.

vivisezione [viviset'tsjone] *sf* vivisection.

vivo, a ['vivo] **1** *ag* **(a)** *(in vita)* alive, living; *(in uso: espressione, tradizione)* living; **è ancora** ~ he is still alive *o* living; **esperimenti su animali** ~**i** experiments on live *o* living animals; **lingua** ~**a** living language; **non c'era anima** ~**a** there wasn't a (living) soul there; **me lo mangerei** ~! *(fig)* I could eat him alive!, I could murder him!; **essere più morto che** ~ to be more dead than alive.

(b) *(intenso: ricordo)* vivid, very clear; *(: emozione)* intense; *(: luce)* brilliant, bright; *(: colore)* bright, vivid; **occhi** ~**i** bright *o* sparkling eyes; ~**a commozione** intense emotion; **con** ~ **rammarico** with deep regret; **congratulazioni vivissime** sincerest congratulations; **con i più** ~**i ringraziamenti** with deepest *o* warmest thanks; **cuocere a fuoco** ~ to cook on a high flame *o* heat.

(c) *(vivace: persona)* lively, vivacious; *(: città, strada, discussione)* lively, animated; **ha un'intelligenza molto** ~**a** he has a lively mind.

(d) *(fraseologia):* **farsi** ~ *(mettersi in contatto con)* to get in touch with sb; **spese** ~**e** immediate *o* out-of-pocket expenses; **spigolo** ~ sharp edge; **l'ho sentito dalla sua** ~**a voce** I heard it from the horse's mouth *o* from his own lips.

2 *sm* living; **il** ~ the living; **registrazione dal** ~ live recording; **cogliere** *o* **colpire qn nel** ~ to cut sb to the quick; **entrare nel** ~ **di una questione** to get to the heart of a matter.

viziare [vit'tsjare] **1** *vt* **(a)** *(persona)* to spoil. **(b)** *(Dir)* to invalidate; *(rovinare: rapporti, ragionamento)* to ruin, spoil. **2:** ~**rsi** *vr* to become spoilt.

viziato, a [vit'tsjato] *ag* **(a)** *(persona)* spoilt. **(b)** *(Dir)* invalid, invalidated; *(rapporti, ragionamento)* ruined, spoiled. **(c)** *(aria)* stale, foul.

vizio ['vittsjo] *sm* **(a)** *(morale)* vice; *(cattiva abitudine)* bad habit; **vivere nel** ~ to live a life of vice. **(b)** *(Dir)* flaw, defect; *(Gram)* error, fault; ~ **di forma** legal flaw *o* irregularity; ~ **procedurale** procedural error.

vizioso, a [vit'tsjoso] **1** *ag* **(a)** *(corrotto)* depraved; **vita** ~**a** life of vice. **(b)** *(difettoso)* incorrect, wrong; **circolo** ~ vicious circle. **2** *sm/f* depraved person.

vizzo, a ['vittso] *ag (Bot)* withered; *(fig: pelle,*

guance, carni) withered, wrinkled.

V.le *abbr di* viale.

vocabolario [vokabo'larjo] *sm (dizionario)* dictionary; *(lessico personale)* vocabulary.

vocabolo [vo'kabolo] *sm* word.

vocale[1] [vo'kale] *ag (Anat, Mus)* vocal.

vocale[2] [vo'kale] *sf* vowel.

vocalico, a, ci, che [vo'kaliko] *ag* vowel *attr*, vocalic.

vocalizzare [vokalid'dzare] *vi, vt* to vocalize.

vocativo, a [voka'tivo] *ag, sm* vocative.

vocazione [vokat'tsjone] *sf (anche Rel)* vocation; *(inclinazione naturale)* bent; **non ho ~ per la matematica** I'm not cut out to study Maths, I have no gift for Maths.

voce ['votʃe] *sf (a) (gen)* voice; **ho avuto un abbassamento di ~** I lost my voice; **la ~ della coscienza** the voice of conscience; **parlare a alta/bassa ~** to speak in a loud/low *o* soft voice; **con un fil di ~** in a weak voice; **dar ~ a qc** to voice *o* give voice to sth; **dare una ~ a qn** to call sb, give sb a call; **fare la ~ grossa** to raise one's voice; **a gran ~** in a loud voice, loudly; **l'hanno acclamato a gran ~** they greeted him with thunderous applause; **me l'ha detto a ~** he told me himself *o* in person; **te lo dico a ~** I'll tell you when I see you; **a una ~** unanimously.

(b) *(opinione)* opinion; *(indiscrezione)* rumour; **avere ~ in capitolo** to have a say in the matter; **circolano delle ~i secondo cui il governo si dimetterà** it is rumoured *o* rumour has it that the government will resign; **~i di corridoio** rumours.

(c) *(Mus)* voice; **cantare a due ~i** to sing in two parts.

(d) *(Gram)* voice.

(e) *(vocabolo)* word; *(di elenco)* item; *(di dizionario)* entry; **è una ~ antiquata** it is an obsolete term *o* word.

vociare [vo'tʃare] **1** *vi* to shout. **2** *sm* shouting.

vocio [vo'tʃio] *sm* shouting.

vodka ['vɔdka] *sf inv* vodka.

voga[1] ['voga] *sf (Naut)* rowing.

voga[2] ['voga] *sf*: **essere in ~** *(abito)* to be fashionable; *(canzone)* to be popular.

vogare [vo'gare] *vi* to row.

vogata [vo'gata] *sf (colpo di remi)* stroke; **farsi una ~** to go for a row, go rowing.

vogatore, trice [voga'tore] **1** *sm/f* oarsman/woman. **2** *sm* rowing machine.

voglia ['vɔʎʎa] *sf (a) (desiderio)* wish, desire; *(di donna incinta)* craving; **avere ~ di fare qc** to want to do *o* feel like doing sth; **morire dalla ~ di fare qc/di qc** to be dying *o* longing to do sth/for sth; **e chi ne ha ~?** I don't feel like it at the moment. **(b)** *(disposizione)* will; **di buona ~** willingly; **contro ~, di mala ~** unwillingly. **(c)** *(Med: macchia)* birthmark.

voglioso, a [voʎ'ʎoso] *ag (sguardo)* longing.

voi ['voi] *pron pers (a) (soggetto)* you; **~ tutti lo sapete** all of you know, you all know; **che ne dite, ~?** what do you think?; **~ italiani** you Italians; **siete stati ~ a dirglielo** it was you who told him, you were the ones to tell him. **(b)** *(oggetto: per dare rilievo, con preposizione)* you; **vuol vedere proprio ~** it's you he wants to see; **parlo a ~, non a lui** I'm talking to you, not to him; **tocca a ~** it's your turn; **da ~** *(nel vostro paese)* where you come from, in your country; *(a casa vostra)* at your house. **(c)** *(comparazioni)* you; **sono alti come ~** they are as tall as you (are); **faremo come ~** we'll do as you do, we'll do the same as you; **siamo più giovani di ~** we are younger than you.

voialtri, e ['vojaltri] *pron pers* you.

voile [vwal] *sm* voile.

volano [vo'lano] *sm (a) (Sport)* shuttlecock. **(b)** *(Tecn)* flywheel.

volant [vɔ'lã] *sm inv* frill.

volante[1] [vo'lante] **1** *ag (gen)* flying; *(foglio)* loose; *(indossatrice)* freelance. **2** *sf (Polizia: anche:* **squadra ~***)* flying squad.

volante[2] [vo'lante] *sm (Aut)* steering wheel; **essere al ~** to drive, be at the wheel.

volantinaggio [volanti'naddʒo] *sm* handing out of leaflets.

volantino [volan'tino] *sm (foglietto)* leaflet, pamphlet.

volare [vo'lare] *vi (aus essere, avere) (a) (aereo, uccello, passeggero)* to fly; **far ~ un aquilone** to fly a kite. **(b)** *(fig: tempo)* to fly, go by very quickly; *(: notizie)* to spread quickly; *(: pugni, insulti)* to fly; **sembra che i soldi volino** money just seems to disappear; **quando ho sentito la notizia sono volato da lei** when I heard the news I rushed round to her place; **il pallone è volato fuori dal campo** the ball flew off the pitch. **(c)** *(allontanarsi)*: **~ via** *(cappello, fogli)* to blow away, fly away; *(fig: tempo)* to fly; *(cadere)*: **~ giù** *(vaso, persona)* to fall.

volata [vo'lata] *sf (a) (di uccello, freccia etc)* flight. **(b)** *(fig: corsa)*: **faccio una ~ a casa** I am just going to pop home; **passare di ~ da qn** to drop in on sb briefly. **(c)** *(Ciclismo)* final sprint; **vincere in ~** to sprint home to win.

volatile [vo'latile] **1** *ag (Chim)* volatile. **2** *sm (uccello)* bird, winged creature.

volatilizzare [volatilid'dzare] **1** *vt (Chim)* to volatilize. **2: ~rsi** *vr (Chim)* to volatilize; *(fig)* to vanish, disappear.

vol-au-vent ['vɔlovã] *sm inv (Culin)* vol-au-vent.

volente [vo'lente] *ag*: **verrai ~ o nolente** you'll come whether you like it or not, you'll come willy-nilly.

volenteroso, a [volente'roso] *ag* willing, keen.

volentieri [volen'tjeri] *av* willingly, gladly; **spesso e ~** frequently, very often.

volere [vo'lere] **1** *vt (nei tempi composti prende l'ausiliare del verbo che accompagna) (a) (gen)* to want; **voglio una risposta da voi** I want an answer from you; **voglio che ti lavi le mani** I want you to wash your hands; **che tu lo voglia o no** whether you like it or not; **vuol venire a tutti i costi** he wants to come at all costs; **quanto vuole per quel quadro?** how much does he want for that painting?

(b) *(desiderare)*: **vorrei del pane** I would like some bread; **vorrei farlo/che tu lo facessi** I would like to do it/you to do it; **mi vorrebbero vedere sposato** they would like to see me married, they would like me to marry; **se volete, possiamo partire subito** if you like *o* want, we can leave right away; **come vuoi** as you like; **volevo parlartene** I meant to talk to you about it; **se volesse potrebbe farcela** he could do it if he wanted to.

(c) *(con funzione di richiesta o offerta)*: **vuole** *o* **vorrebbe essere così gentile da...?** would you be so kind as to...?; **vuoi chiudere la finestra?** would you mind closing the window?; **non vuole accomodarsi?** won't you sit down?; **vogliamo sederci?** shall we sit down?; **prendine quanto vuoi** help yourself, take as many (*o* much) as you like; **ne vuoi ancora?** would you like some more?; **vuoi che io faccia qualcosa?** would you like me to do something?, shall I do something?; **ma vuoi star zitto!** oh, do be quiet!

(d) (*consentire*): **se la padrona di casa vuole, ti posso ospitare** if my landlady agrees I can put you up; **ho chiesto di parlargli, ma non ha voluto ricevermi** I asked to have a word with him but he wouldn't see me; **la macchina non vuole partire** the car won't start; **parla bene l'inglese quando vuole** he can speak English well when he has a mind to *o* when he feels like it.

(e) (*aspettarsi*) to want, expect; (*richiedere*) to want, require; **vuole troppo dai suoi studenti** he expects too much of his students; **che cosa vuoi da me?** what do you want from me?, what do you expect of me?; **la tradizione vuole che...** custom requires that...; **la leggenda vuole che...** legend has it that...; **il verbo transitivo vuole il complemento oggetto** transitive verbs require a direct object.

(f): **volerne a qn** to have sth against sb, have a grudge against sb; **me ne vuole ancora per quello che gli ho fatto** he still bears me a grudge for what I did to him; **non me ne ~** don't hold it against me.

(g): **voler dire** (*significare*) to mean; **se non puoi oggi vorrà dire che ci vediamo domani** if you can't make it today, I'll see you tomorrow; **vuoi dire che non parti più?** do you mean that you're not leaving after all?; **voglio dire...** (*per correggersi*) I mean...; **volevo ben dire!** I thought as much!

(h) (*ritenere*) to think; **si vuole che anche lui sia coinvolto nella faccenda** he is also thought to be involved in the matter.

(i): **volerci** (*essere necessario: materiale, attenzione*) to need; (*: tempo*) to take; **quanta farina ci vuole per questa torta?** how much flour do you need to make this cake?; **ci vorrebbe un bel caffè** a nice cup of coffee is just what's needed; **è quel che ci vuole** it's just what is needed; **ce ne vuole per farglielo entrare in testa** it's not easy to get it into his thick skull; **ci vuol ben altro per farmi arrabbiare** it'll take a lot more than that to make me angry; **ci vuole un'ora per andare a Parigi** it takes an hour to get to Paris.

(j) (*fraseologia*): **voler bene a qn** (*amore*) to love sb; (*affetto*) to be fond of sb, like sb very much; **voler male a qn** to dislike sb; **chi troppo vuole nulla stringe** (*Proverbio*) don't ask for too much or you may come away empty-handed; **qui ti voglio** I was hoping you would mention that *o* bring that up; **senza ~** unwittingly; **te la sei voluta** you asked for it; **~ è potere** where there's a will there's a way; **se Dio vuole** God willing; **volesse il cielo che...** God grant that...; **voglio vedere se rifiuta** I bet she doesn't refuse; **vorrei proprio vedere!** I'm not at all surprised!, that doesn't surprise me in the slightest!; **sembra che voglia piovere** it looks like rain; **sembra che voglia mettersi al bello** the weather seems to be clearing up; **vuoi ... vuoi...** either ... or....

2: **~rsi** vr (*uso reciproco*): **~rsi bene** (*amore*) to love each other; (*affetto*) to be fond of *o* like each other.

3 sm will, wish(es); **contro il ~ di** against the wishes of; **per ~ del padre** in obedience to his father's will *o* wishes.

volgare [vol'gare] **1** ag **(a)** (*del popolo*) common, popular. **(b)** (*grossolano*) vulgar, coarse. **2** sm vernacular.

volgarità [volgari'ta] sf vulgarity.

volgarizzare [volgarid'dzare] vt to translate into the vernacular; (*fig*) to popularize.

volgarmente [volgar'mente] av **(a)** (*in modo volgare*) vulgarly, coarsely. **(b)** (*del popolo*) commonly, popularly.

volgere ['vɔldʒere] **1** vi: **~ a (a)** (*piegare verso*) to turn to *o* towards, bend round to *o* towards; **la strada volge a destra** the road bends round to the right. **(b)** (*avvicinarsi a*): **le vacanze volgono al termine** the holidays are coming to an end; **il giorno volge al termine** the day is drawing to its close; **il tempo volge al bello** the weather is setting fair; **la situazione volge al peggio** the situation is deteriorating; **azzurro che volge al verde** blue which is verging on green.

2 vt **(a)** (*voltare*) to turn; **~ le spalle a qn** (*anche fig*) to turn one's back on sb. **(b)** (*trasformare*) to turn; **volge sempre tutto in tragedia** he always turns everything into a tragedy.

3: **~rsi** vr to turn; **si volse e mi guardò** he turned round and looked at me; **si volse verso di lui** he turned to *o* towards him; **la sua ira si volse contro di noi** he turned his anger on us.

volgo, ghi ['volgo] sm (*anche peg*) common people.

voliera [vo'ljera] sf aviary.

volitivo, a [voli'tivo] **1** ag wilful; (*persona*) wilful, strong-willed. **2** sm/f strong-willed person.

volo ['volo] sm **(a)** (*gen*) flight; **il tuo ~ è alle tre** your flight leaves at three o'clock; **ci sono due ore di ~ da Londra a Milano** it is a two-hour flight between London and Milan; **velocità/ condizioni di ~** flying speed/conditions; **~ di linea** scheduled flight; **essere in ~** (*uccello*) to be in flight; (*Aer*) to be flying; **colpire un uccello in ~** to shoot a bird on the wing *o* in flight; **~ a vela** gliding.

(b) (*fraseologia*): **capire qc al ~** to grasp sth straight away; **prendere al ~** (*autobus, treno*) to catch at the last possible moment; (*palla*) to catch as it flies past; (*occasione*) to seize; **prendere il ~** (*aereo*) to take off; (*uccello*) to fly away; (*fig: giovane*) to leave home; (*: cosa: sparire*) to vanish; **ha fatto un ~ dalla scala** (*cadere*) he went flying down the stairs; **veduta a ~ d'uccello** bird's-eye view.

volontà [volon'ta] sf inv **(a)** (*capacità di volere*) will; **ha molta ~** he has a very strong will; **non ha ~** he is weak-willed; **contro la sua ~** against his will; **di sua spontanea ~** of his own free will; **riuscire a forza di ~** to succeed through sheer willpower *o* determination. **(b)** (*desiderio*): **manifestare la ~ di fare qc** to show one's desire to do sth; **ci ho messo tutta la mia buona ~** I did it to the best of my ability; **ce ne sono a ~** there are more than enough of them; **prendine a ~** help yourself, take as much (*o* many) as you like; **'zuccherare a ~'** 'sugar to taste'. **(c)**: **ultime ~** pl (*testamento*) last will and testament sg; **quali sono le sue ultime ~?** what are his last wishes?

volontariamente [volontarja'mente] av voluntarily.

volontariato [volonta'rjato] sm **(a)** (*Mil*) voluntary service. **(b)** (*lavoro gratuito*) voluntary work.

volontario, a [volon'tarjo] **1** ag (*gen*) voluntary; (*Mil*) volunteer attr; **esilio ~** voluntary exile. **2** sm/f (*gen, Mil*) volunteer; (*di organizzazione*) voluntary worker.

volpe ['volpe] sf (*Zool*) fox; (*: femmina*) vixen; (*pelliccia*) fox; (*fig*) sly fox, crafty person; (*: ironico*) clever person, bright spark.

volpino, a [vol'pino] **1** ag (*pelo, coda*) fox's; (*aspetto, astuzia*) fox-like. **2** sm (*cane*) Pomeranian.

volpone, a [vol'pone] sm/f old fox, crafty dog.

volt [vɔlt] sm inv (*Elettr*) volt.

volta¹ ['vɔlta] sf **(a)** time; **una ~** once; **due ~e** twice; **tre ~e** three times; **una ~ ogni due**

settimane once every two weeks; **9 ~e su 10** 9 times out of 10; **la prima/l'ultima ~ che l'ho visto** the first/last time I saw him; **per questa ~ passi** I'll let you off this time; **ci ho pensato due ~e prima di decidere** I thought twice about it before making a decision; **tutto in una ~** all at once; **ti decidi una buona ~** make up your mind once and for all; **una ~ tanto** just for once; **una ~ per tutte** once and for all; **di ~ in ~** from time to time; **delle** *o* **alle** *o* **certe ~e, a ~e** sometimes, at times; **una ~ o l'altra** one of these days; **te le darò ~ per ~** *(istruzioni)* I'll give them to you a bit at a time.

(b) *(tempo, occasione)*: **c'era una ~** once upon a time there was; **una ~** *(un tempo)* once, in the past; **le cose di una ~** the things of the past; **una ~ che sei partito** once *o* when you have left; **ti ricordi quella ~ che...** do you remember (the time) when...; **pensa a tutte le ~e che...** think of all the occasions on which...; **lo facciamo un'altra ~** we'll do it another time *o* some other time.

(c) *(Mat)*: **3 ~e 2** 3 times 2; **4 ~e di più** 4 times as much.

(d) *(fraseologia)*: **a sua ~** *(turno)* in (his *o* her *etc*) turn; **partire alla ~ di** to set off for; **ti ha dato di ~ il cervello?** have you gone out of your mind?

volta² ['vɔlta] *sf (Archit, Anat)* vault; **la ~ celeste** the vault of heaven.

voltafaccia [volta'fattʃa] *sm inv* about-turn, volte-face.

voltagabbana [voltagab'bana] *sm/f inv* turn-coat.

voltaggio [vol'taddʒo] *sm* voltage.

voltare [vol'tare] **1** *vt* to turn; **~ pagina** *(fig)* to turn over a new leaf; **~ le spalle a qn** to turn one's back on sb. **2** *vi* to turn. **3: ~rsi** *vr* to turn; **non sapere da che parte ~rsi** *(fig)* not to know which way to turn.

voltastomaco [voltas'tɔmako] *sm* nausea; *(fig)* disgust.

volteggiare [volted'dʒare] *vi* **(a)** *(volare girando: uccello, piuma)* to circle; **la ballerina volteggiava nella stanza** the dancer twirled *o* spun around the room. **(b)** *(Ginnastica)* to vault.

volto¹, a ['vɔlto] **1** *pp di* **volgere**. **2** *ag*: **~ a (a)** *(rivolto verso: casa)* facing. **(b)** *(inteso a)*: **il mio discorso è ~ a spiegare...** in my speech I intend to explain...; **il corso è ~ a introdurre gli studenti all'analisi matematica** the course is intended to introduce students to calculus.

volto² ['volto] *sm (faccia)* face; *(fig)* face, nature.

volubile [vo'lubile] *ag (persona)* changeable, fickle; *(tempo)* changeable, variable.

volubilità [volubili'ta] *sf (di persona)* fickleness, inconstancy; *(di tempo)* variability.

volume [vo'lume] *sm (gen)* volume; **fa ~** *(oggetto)* it takes up a lot of space, it is very bulky.

volumetrico, a, ci, che [volu'metriko] *ag* volumetric.

voluminoso, a [volumi'noso] *ag* bulky, voluminous.

voluta [vo'luta] *sf (gen)* spiral; *(Archit)* volute.

voluto, a [vo'luto] *ag* **(a)** *(intenzionale)* deliberate, intentional; **era ~** it was intentional; **un errore ~** a deliberate mistake. **(b)** *(desiderato: bambino)* wanted; *(: somma)* desired.

voluttà [volut'ta] *sf inv* sensual pleasure.

voluttuario, a [voluttu'arjo] *ag* unnecessary, non-essential.

voluttuosità [voluttuosi'ta] *sf* voluptuousness.

voluttuoso, a [voluttu'oso] *ag* voluptuous, sensual.

vomere ['vɔmere] *sm (Agr)* ploughshare.

vomitare [vomi'tare] **1** *vt* to vomit, throw up; **~ ingiurie** *(fig)* to spew out insults; **questo quadro mi fa ~** this painting makes me sick. **2** *vi* to be sick, vomit, throw up.

vomito ['vɔmito] *sm* vomit; **ho il ~** I feel sick; **mi fa venire il ~** *(anche fig)* it makes me sick.

vongola ['vongola] *sf (Zool)* clam.

vorace [vo'ratʃe] *ag (appetito)* voracious; **è un bambino ~** this child has a voracious appetite.

voracità [voratʃi'ta] *sf* voracity, voraciousness.

voragine [vo'radʒine] *sf* chasm, abyss.

vorticare [vorti'kare] *vi* to whirl, swirl.

vortice ['vɔrtitʃe] *sm* whirl, vortex; *(fig)* whirl; **~ di vento** whirlwind.

vorticoso, a [vorti'koso] *ag* whirling.

vostro, a ['vɔstro] **1** *ag poss*: **il(la) ~(a)** *etc* your; **il ~ cane** your dog; **un ~ conoscente** an acquaintance of yours; **~a zia** your aunt; **è colpa ~a** it's your fault; **a casa ~a** at your house. **2** *pron poss*: **il(la) ~(a)** *etc* yours, your own; **la nostra casa è più lontana della ~a** our house is further away than yours; **la ~a è stata una brutta storia** your story is an unpleasant one. **3** *sm* **(a)**: **ci potreste rimettere del ~ in quell'affare** you could well lose money in that business. **(b)**: **i ~i** *(famiglia)* your family; **è dei ~i** he's on your side. **4** *sf*: **la ~a** *(opinione)* your view; **è dalla ~a** *(parte)* he's on your side; **l'ultima ~a** *(Comm: lettera)* your most recent letter; **alla ~a!** *(brindisi)* here's to you!, your health!

votante [vo'tante] *sm/f* voter.

votare [vo'tare] **1** *vi* to vote. **2** *vt* **(a)** *(gen)* to vote for; *(approvare)* to pass. **(b)**: **~ a** *(vita)* to devote to, dedicate to. **3: ~rsi** *vr*: **~rsi a** to devote o.s. to.

votazione [votat'tsjone] *sf* **(a)** *(gen, Pol: atto)* voting; **alle ~i** at the elections. **(b)** *(Scol)* mark; **~ finale** results *pl*.

votivo, a [vo'tivo] *ag* votive.

voto ['voto] *sm* **(a)** *(Scol)* mark. **(b)** *(Pol)* vote; **~ di fiducia** vote of confidence. **(c)** *(Rel)* vow; **prendere i ~i** to take one's vows.

vs. *abbr commerciale di* **vostro**.

vulcanico, a, ci, che [vul'kaniko] *ag* volcanic; **ha una fantasia ~a** he has a fertile imagination.

vulcanismo [vulka'nizmo] *sm* volcanism.

vulcanizzazione [vulkaniddzat'tsjone] *sf (Tecn)* vulcanization.

vulcano [vul'kano] *sm* volcano; **quel ragazzo è un ~ di idee** *(fig)* that boy is bursting with ideas.

vulnerabile [vulne'rabile] *ag* vulnerable.

vulnerabilità [vulnerabili'ta] *sf* vulnerability.

vulva ['vulva] *sf (Anat)* vulva.

vuotare [vwo'tare] **1** *vt (bicchiere, stanza)* to empty; *(vasca, piscina)* to drain, empty; **~ il sacco** to confess, spill the beans *(fam)*; **i ladri mi hanno vuotato la casa** the burglars cleaned out my house. **2: ~rsi** *vr* to empty.

vuoto, a ['vwɔto] **1** *ag* **(a)** *(gen)* empty; **a stomaco ~** on an empty stomach. **(b)** *(non occupato: posto)* vacant, free; *(: spazio)* empty. **(c)** *(fig: pensiero, persona)* shallow, superficial. **2** *sm* **(a)** *(spazio)* void; *(Fis)* vacuum; **è rimasto sospeso nel ~** *(scalatore)* he was left hanging in mid-air; **aver paura del ~** to be afraid of heights; **guardare nel ~** to gaze into space; **ha lasciato un ~ fra di noi** he has left a real gap; **ho un ~ allo stomaco** my stomach feels empty; **un ~ d'aria** *(Aer)* an air pocket; **sotto** ~ = **sottovuoto.** (**b**): **a** ~ : **ho fatto un viaggio a** ~ I have had a wasted journey; **parlare a** ~ to waste one's breath; **assegno a** ~ dud cheque; **girare a** ~ *(Aut)* to idle. (**c**) *(bottiglia)* empty; '~ **a rendere**' 'returnable'; '~ **a perdere**' 'no deposit'.

W

W, w |'dɔppjo vu| *sf o m inv (lettera)* W, w.
wafer |'vafer| *sm inv (Culin, Elettr)* wafer.
wagon-lit |vagɔ'li| *sm inv (Ferr)* sleeping car.
walkie-talkie |'wɔːki'tɔːki| *sm inv* walkie-talkie.
water closet |'wɔːtə 'klɔzɪt| *sm inv* toilet, lavatory.
watt |vat| *sm inv (Elettr)* watt.
wattora |vat'tora| *sm inv (Elettr)* watt-hour.

WC *abbr (= water closet)* W.C.
week-end |'wiːkɛnd| *sm inv* weekend.
western |'wɛstɛrn| **1** *ag (Cine)* cowboy *attr.* **2** *sm inv (Cine)* western, cowboy film; ~ **all'italiana** spaghetti western.
whisky |'wiski| *sm inv* whisky.
würstel |'vyrstəl| *sm inv* frankfurter.

X

X, x |iks| *sf o m inv (lettera)* X, x.
xenofobia |ksɛnofo'bia| *sf* xenophobia.
xenofobo, a |ksɛ'nɔfobo| **1** *ag* xenophobic. **2** *sm/f* xenophobe.
xerocopia |ksɛro'kɔpja| *sf* xerox, photocopy.

xerocopiare |ksɛroko'pjarɛ| *vt* to photocopy.
xerografia |ksɛrogra'fia| *sf* xerography.
xilofono |ksi'lɔfono| *sm* xylophone.
xilografia |ksilogra'fia| *sf* = **silografia**.

Y

Y, y |'ipsilon| *sf o m inv (lettera)* Y, y.
yacht |jɔt| *sm inv* yacht.
yankee |'jæŋki| *sm/f inv* Yank, Yankee.

yiddish |'jidiʃ| *ag inv, sm inv* Yiddish.
yoga |'jɔga| *ag inv, sm* yoga *(attr)*.
yogurt |'jɔgurt| *sm inv* yog(h)urt.

Z

Z, z ['dzɛta] *sf o m inv (lettera)* Z, z.
zabaione [dzaba'jone] *sm dessert made of egg yolks, sugar and marsala.*
zaffata [tsaf'fata] *sf (di odore)* stench, stink.
zafferano [dzaffe'rano] *sm* saffron.
zaffiro [dzaf'firo] *sm* sapphire.
zagara ['dzagara] *sf* orange blossom.
zaino ['dzaino] *sm* rucksack.
zampa ['tsampa] *sf (Zool: gamba)* leg; *(: piede: di animale con artigli)* paw; *(: di elefante, uccello)* foot; ~**e di gallina** *(calligrafia)* scrawl; *(rughe)* crow's feet; **calzoni a** ~ **d'elefante** bell-bottom trousers, bell-bottoms; **camminare a quattro** ~**e** to go on all fours; **giù le** ~**e!** *(fam)* hands off!
zampata [tsam'pata] *sf (di cane, gatto)* blow with a paw.
zampettare [tsampet'tare] *vi* to scamper.
zampillare [tsampil'lare] *vi* to gush, spurt.
zampillo [tsam'pillo] *sm* gush, spurt.
zampino [tsam'pino] *sm* paw; ~ **di coniglio** *(portafortuna)* lucky rabbit's foot; **qui c'è sotto il suo** ~ *(fig)* he's had a hand in this.
zampirone [dzampi'rone] *sm* mosquito repellent.
zampogna [tsam'poɲɲa] *sf* Italian bagpipes *pl.*
zampognaro [tsampoɲ'ɲaro] *sm* Italian bagpipes' player.
zampone [tsam'pone] *sm stuffed pig's trotter.*
zangola ['tsangola] *sf* churn.
zanna ['tsanna] *sf (di elefante, cinghiale etc)* tusk; *(di cani, lupi etc)* fang.
zanzara [dzan'dzara] *sf* mosquito.
zanzariera [dzandza'rjɛra] *sf* mosquito net.
zappa ['tsappa] *sf (Agr)* hoe; **tirarsi la** ~ **sui piedi** *(fig)* to cut one's own throat.
zappare [tsap'pare] *vt (Agr)* to hoe.
zappatore [tsappa'tore] *sm (Agr)* hoer; *(Mil)* sapper.
zappatrice [tsappa'tritʃe] *sf (Agr: macchina)* mechanical hoe.
zappatura [tsappa'tura] *sf (Agr)* hoeing.
zar [tsar] *sm* tsar.
zarina [tsa'rina] *sf* tsarina.
zattera ['tsattera] *sf* raft.
zavorra [dza'vɔrra] *sf (Naut, Aer)* ballast; *(fig)* junk; **gettare la** ~ to dump ballast.
zazzera ['tsattsera] *sf* shock of hair, mop.
zebra ['dzɛbra] *sf (Zool)* zebra; *(Aut)* zebra crossing.
zebrato, a [dze'brato] *ag* with black and white stripes; **strisce** ~**e, attraversamento** ~ *(Aut)* zebra crossing.
zecca¹, che [ts'tsekka] *sf (Zool)* tick.
zecca² ['tsekka] *sf (officina)* mint; **nuovo di** ~ brand-new.
zecchino [tsek'kino] *sm* gold coin; **oro** ~ pure gold.
zefiro ['dzɛfiro] *sm (vento)* zephyr.
zelante [dze'lante] *ag* zealous.
zelo ['dzelo] *sm* zeal; **mostrare troppo** ~ to be overzealous.
zenit ['dzɛnit] *sm (Astron)* zenith.
zenzero ['dzendzero] *sm* ginger.

zeppa ['tseppa] *sf (di mobili)* wedge; *(di scarpe)* platform.
zeppo, a ['tseppo] *ag:* ~ *o* **pieno** ~ **(di)** jam-packed (with).
zerbino [dzer'bino] *sm* (door)mat.
zerbinotto [dzerbi'nɔtto] *sm* dandy, fop.
zero ['dzɛro] **1** *sm* **(a)** *(gen, Scol, Mat)* zero, nought; *(in un numero di telefono)* O; ~ **virgola cinque** (nought) point five; **2 gradi sopra** ~ 2 degrees above freezing point *o* above zero; ~ **in condotta** *(Scol)* bad marks for behaviour; **ridursi a** ~ *(fig)* to have nothing left, be at rock-bottom; **capelli tagliati a** ~ close-cropped hair. **(b)** *(Calcio)* nil; *(Tennis)* love. **2** *ag inv* zero *attr*; **l'ora** ~ zero hour.
zeta ['dzɛta] *sm o f, pl(f) inv o* ~**e, pl(m) inv (lettera)** zed, zee *(Am).*
zia ['tsia] *sf* aunt.
zibaldone [dzibal'done] *sm (Letteratura)* author's notebook.
zibellino [dzibel'lino] *sm* sable.
zibibbo [dzi'bibbo] *sm* kind of muscat grape.
zigano, a [tsi'gano] *ag, sm/f* gypsy.
zigomo ['dzigomo] *sm* cheekbone; ~**i sporgenti** high cheekbones.
zigrinare [dzigri'nare] *vt (gen)* to knurl; *(pellame)* to grain; *(monete)* to mill.
zig zag [dzig'dzag] *sm inv* zigzag; **camminare a** ~ to zigzag.
zigzagare [dzigdza'gare] *vi* to zigzag.
zimarra [dzi'marra] *sf* long shabby coat.
zimbello [tsim'bɛllo] *sm (Zool)* decoy (bird); *(fig)* laughing stock.
zincare [tsin'kare] *vt* to galvanize, coat with zinc.
zinco ['tsinko] *sm* zinc.
zingaresco, a, schi, sche [tsinga'resko] *ag* gypsy *attr.*
zingaro, a ['tsingaro] *ag, sm/f* gypsy.
zio ['tsio] *sm* uncle; ~ **d'America** *(fig)* rich uncle.
zipolo ['tsipolo] *sm (di botte)* bung.
zircone [dzir'kone] *sm* zircon.
zirlare [dzir'lare] *vi* to sing (like a thrush).
zirlo ['dzirlo] *sm* thrush's song.
zitella [tsi'tella] *sf* spinster, old maid *(peg).*
zitellone [tsitel'lone] *sm* (elderly) bachelor.
zittire [tsit'tire] **1** *vt* to silence, hush *o* shut up. **2** *vi* to hiss.
zitto, a ['tsitto] *ag* quiet, silent; ~**!** be quiet!, shut up! *(fam);* **stare** ~ to keep quiet, shut up *(fam);* ~ *(di nascosto)* on the quiet.
zizzania [dzid'dzanja] *sf (Bot)* darnel; *(fig)* discord; **gettare** *o* **seminare** ~ to sow discord.
zoccolo ['tsɔkkolo] *sm* **(a)** *(Zool)* hoof. **(b)** *(calzatura)* clog. **(c)** *(Archit)* plinth; *(di parete)* skirting (board); *(di armadio)* base (support).
zodiacale [dzodia'kale] *ag* of the zodiac, zodiac *attr*; **segno** ~ sign of the zodiac.
zodiaco [dzo'diako] *sm* zodiac.
zolfanello [tsolfa'nello] *sm* (sulphur) match.
zolfatara [tsolfa'tara] *sf* sulphur mine.
zolfo ['tsolfo] *sm* sulphur.
zolla ['dzolla] *sf* turf.

zolletta [dzol'letta] *sf (di zucchero)* lump, cube.

zona ['dzɔna] *sf (gen)* area, zone; *(regione)* area, region; *(di città)* area, district; ~ **disco** *(Aut)* ≃ meter zone; ~ **di guerra** war zone; ~ **notte** *(di casa)* sleeping area; ~ **verde** *(Aut)* restricted parking zone *o* area; *(Urbanistica)* green area.

zonale [dzo'nale] *ag* district *attr*, area *attr*.

zonzo ['dzondzo]: **a** ~ *av*: **andare a** ~ to wander about.

zoo ['dzɔo] *sm inv* zoo.

zoologia [dzoolo'dʒia] *sf* zoology.

zoologico, a, ci, che [dzoo'lɔdʒiko] *ag* zoological; **giardino** ~ zoological garden(s), zoo.

zoologo, a, gi, ghe [dzo'ɔlogo] *sm/f* zoologist.

zoom [zuːm] *sm inv (Fot)* zoom (lens).

zoosafari [dzoosa'fari] *sm inv* safari park.

zootecnico, a, ci, che [dzoo'tɛkniko] *ag* zootechnical; **il patrimonio** ~ **di un paese** a country's livestock resources.

zoppicante [tsoppi'kante] *ag (persona)* limping; *(fig)* shaky, weak.

zoppicare [tsoppi'kare] *vi (persona)* to have a limp, walk with a limp; *(: essere zoppo)* to be lame; **zoppica in matematica** *(fig)* he's weak in maths, maths isn't his strong point.

zoppo, a ['tsɔppo] **1** *ag (persona)* lame; *(mobile)* rickety, wobbly. **2** *sm/f* lame person.

zotico, a ['dzɔtiko] *sm/f* lout, boor.

zuava [dzu'ava] *sf*: **pantaloni** *mpl* **alla** ~ knickerbockers.

zucca ['tsukka] *sf (Bot)* pumpkin; *(scherz)* head;

avere sale in ~ to be sensible, have sense; **non gli entra in** ~ it won't enter his thick skull.

zuccherare [tsukke'rare] *vt* to put sugar in, add sugar to.

zuccherato, a [tsukke'rato] *ag* sweet, sweetened.

zuccheriera [tsukke'rjɛra] *sf* sugar bowl.

zuccherificio [tsukkeri'fitʃo] *sm* sugar refinery.

zuccherino, a [tsukke'rino] **1** *ag* sweet, sugary. **2** *sm* piece of sugar, lump of sugar.

zucchero ['tsukkero] *sm* sugar; ~ **di canna** cane sugar; ~ **caramellato** caramel; ~ **filato** candy floss, cotton candy *(Am)*; ~ **a velo** icing sugar.

zuccheroso, a [tsukke'roso] *ag* sweet, sugary.

zucchetto [tsuk'ketto] *sm* skull cap.

zucchina [tsuk'kina] *sf*, **zucchino** [tsuk'kino] *sm* courgette.

zuccone, a [tsuk'kone] **1** *ag* dull, dense, slow(-witted). **2** *sm/f* dunce, blockhead.

zuccotto [tsuk'kɔtto] *sm* ice-cream sponge.

zuffa ['tsuffa] *sf* fight, brawl.

zufolare [tsufo'lare] *vt, vi* to whistle.

zufolio [tsufo'lio] *sm* whistling.

zufolo ['tsufolo] *sm (Mus)* flageolet.

zuppa ['tsuppa] *sf* soup; ~ **inglese** ≃ trifle; **se non è** ~ **è pan bagnato** *(fig)* it's six of one and half a dozen of the other.

zuppiera [tsup'pjɛra] *sf* (soup) tureen.

zuppo, a ['tsuppo] *ag*: ~ **(di)** soaked (with).

zuzzurullone [dzuddzurul'lone] *sm/f (fam)* overgrown schoolboy/schoolgirl.

A

A, a¹ [eɪ] *n* **(a)** *(letter)* A, a *f or m inv;* **to know sth from A to Z** sapere *or* conoscere qc dall'a alla zeta. **(b)** *(Mus)* la *m.*

a² [eɪ, ə] *indef art (before vowel or silent h:* **an**) **(a)** un (uno + *s impure, gn, pn, ps, x, z*), *f* una (un' + *vowel*); ~ **mirror** uno specchio; **an apple** una mela; **half an hour** mezz'ora; **I haven't got** ~ **car** non ho la macchina; ~ **drink would be nice** berrei volentieri qualcosa; **he's** ~ **doctor** è medico, fa il medico; **as** ~ **young man** da giovane; **what** ~ **surprise!** che sorpresa!; **they are of** ~ **size** sono della stessa misura; ~ **child is full of curiosity** i bambini sono molto curiosi; ~ **Mr Smith called to see you** è venuto un certo signor Smith che voleva vederla.
   (b) *(each)* a, per; **£4** ~ **person** 4 sterline per *or* a persona; **£4** ~ **pound** 4 sterline alla libbra; **2 apples** ~ **head** 2 mele a testa *or* (per) ciascuno; **50 kilometres an hour** 50 chilometri all'ora; **3 times** ~ **month** 3 volte al mese.

AA *n* **(a)** *(abbr of Automobile Association)* ≈A.C.I. *f.* **(b)** *abbr of Alcoholics Anonymous.*

aback [ə'bæk] *adv:* **to be taken** ~ essere colto(a) *or* preso(a) alla sprovvista, rimanere sconcertato(a).

aban·don [ə'bændən] **1** *vt* **(a)** *(desert)* abbandonare; **to** ~ **ship** abbandonare la nave. **(b)** *(give up: plan, hope, game etc)* abbandonare, rinunciare a; **to** ~ **o.s. to sth** abbandonarsi a qc, lasciarsi andare a qc. **2** *n:* **with** ~, **in gay** ~ sfrenatamente, spensieratamente.

aban·doned [ə'bændənd] *adj (child, house etc)* abbandonato(a); *(unrestrained: manner)* disinvolto(a), spontaneo(a).

abase [ə'beɪs] *vt* umiliare, mortificare; **to** ~ **o.s. (so far as to do...)** umiliarsi *or* abbassarsi (al punto di fare...).

abashed [ə'bæʃt] *adj* imbarazzato(a).

abate [ə'beɪt] *vi (anger, enthusiasm, storm)* placarsi, calmarsi, calare; *(pain)* calmarsi; *(fever)* abbassarsi, calare; *(flood)* abbassarsi; *(noise)* diminuire, affievolirsi.

abate·ment [ə'beɪtmənt] *n (of pollution, noise)* soppressione *f,* eliminazione *f;* **noise** ~ **society** associazione *f* per la lotta contro i rumori.

ab·at·toir ['æbətwɑːr] *n* macello, mattatoio.

ab·bey ['æbɪ] *n* abbazia.

ab·bot ['æbət] *n* abate *m.*

ab·bre·vi·ate [ə'briːvɪeɪt] *vt* abbreviare.

ab·bre·via·tion [ə,briːvɪ'eɪʃən] *n* abbreviazione *f.*

ab·di·cate ['æbdɪkeɪt] **1** *vt (throne)* abdicare a; *(responsibility)* rinunciare a. **2** *vi* abdicare.

ab·di·ca·tion [,æbdɪ'keɪʃən] *n (of monarch)* abdicazione *f.*

ab·do·men ['æbdəmen] *n* addome *m.*

ab·domi·nal [æb'dɒmɪnl] *adj* addominale.

ab·duct [æb'dʌkt] *vt* rapire.

ab·duc·tion [æb'dʌkʃən] *n* rapimento, sequestro di persona.

ab·duc·tor [æb'dʌktər] *n* rapitore/trice.

ab·er·rant [ə'bɛrənt] *adj (Bio)* aberrante.

ab·er·ra·tion [,æbə'reɪʃən] *n* aberrazione *f;* **in a moment of mental** ~ in un momento di aberrazione mentale; **a youthful** ~ una follia *or* un errore giovanile.

abet [ə'bɛt] *vt see* **aid.**

abey·ance [ə'beɪəns] *n:* **to be in** ~ *(law, custom)* essere in disuso; *(matter, plan)* essere in sospeso.

ab·hor [əb'hɔːr] *vt* aborrire, provare orrore per.

ab·hor·rence [əb'hɒrəns] *n* avversione *f,* orrore *m;* **to have an** ~ **of sth** detestare qc.

ab·hor·rent [əb'hɒrənt] *adj:* **to be** ~ **to sb** ripugnare a qn.

abide [ə'baɪd] *pt, pp* **abode** *or* **abided** *vt (only neg)* sopportare, soffrire; **I can't** ~ **him** non lo posso soffrire *or* sopportare.

♦ **abide by** *vi + prep (rules)* attenersi a, rispettare; *(consequences)* accettare; *(promise)* tener fede a, rispettare.

abil·ity [ə'bɪlɪtɪ] *n* capacità *f inv,* abilità *f inv;* **abilities** doti *fpl;* **a person of many abilities** una persona molto dotata; **to the best of my** ~ con il massimo impegno.

ab·ject ['æbdʒɛkt] *adj (poverty)* abietto(a); *(apology)* umiliante; *(coward)* indegno(a), vile.

ablaze [ə'bleɪz] *adv* in fiamme; **the house was** ~ **with light** *(fig)* la casa era tutta illuminata *or* risplendeva di luci.

able ['eɪbl] **1** *adj (person)* capace, bravo(a); *(piece of work)* abile, intelligente; **to be** ~ **to do sth** poter fare qc, essere in grado di fare qc; **he's not** ~ **to walk** non può *or* non è in grado di *or* non è in condizione di camminare; *(child)* non sa camminare; **those who are** ~ **to pay** coloro che sono in condizione di *or* possono permettersi di pagare. **2** *cpd:* ~(**-bodied**) **seaman** *see* **able-bodied.**

able-bodied [,eɪbl'bɒdɪd] *adj* robusto(a), valido(a); ~ **citizen** cittadino idoneo *or* abile (al servizio militare); ~ **seaman** marinaio scelto.

ab·nor·mal [æb'nɔːml] *adj* anormale.

ab·nor·mal·ity [,æbnɔː'mælɪtɪ] *n (condition)* anormalità; *(instance)* anomalia.

ab·nor·mal·ly [æb'nɔːməlɪ] *adv* in modo anormale; *(exceptionally)* insolitamente, stranamente.

aboard [ə'bɔːd] **1** *adv (Naut, Aer)* a bordo; **to go** ~ salire a bordo; **all** ~! *(Rail)* (signori) in carrozza *or* in vettura!; *(Naut)* tutti a bordo! **2** *prep:* ~ **the ship** a bordo (della nave), sulla nave; ~ **the train** in *or* sul treno.

abode [ə'bəʊd] **1** *pt, pp of* **abide. 2** *n (old)* dimora; *(Law)* domicilio, dimora; **of no fixed** ~ senza fissa dimora.

abol·ish [ə'bɒlɪʃ] *vt* abolire.

abo·li·tion [æbəʊ'lɪʃən] *n* abolizione *f.*

abomi·nable [ə'bɒmɪnəbl] *adj (detestable)* abominevole; *(unpleasant)* pessimo(a), orrendo(a), orribile.

abomi·nably [ə'bɒmɪnəblɪ] *adv* disgustosamente, **to be** ~ **rude to sb** essere terribilmente maleducato con qn.

abomi·na·tion [ə,bɒmɪ'neɪʃən] *n (feeling)* avversione *f,* disgusto; *(detestable act, thing)* azione *f (or* cosa) orrenda; **to hold sth in** ~ detestare qc.

abo·rigi·nal [,æbə'rɪdʒɪnl] *adj* aborigeno(a), indigeno(a).

abo·rigi·ne [,æbə'rɪdʒɪnɪ] *n* aborigeno/a.

abort [ə'bɔːt] **1** *vi (Med)* abortire; *(fig: plans, space mission)* fallire (prematuramente). **2** *vt (Med):* **to** ~ **a baby, a pregnancy** interrompere una gravidanza; *(fig)* sospendere, rinunciare a portare a termine.

abor·tion [ə'bɔːʃən] *n (Med)* aborto; **to have an** ~

avere un aborto, abortire.

abor·tive [ə'bɔːtɪv] *adj (fig: plan)* fallito(a), mancato(a); *(attempt)* vano(a), infruttuoso(a).

abound [ə'baʊnd] *vi (exist in great quantity)* abbondare; *(have in great quantity)*: **to ~ in** *or* **with** abbondare di, essere ricco(a) di.

about [ə'baʊt] **1** *adv* **(a)** *(place)* qua e là, in giro; **they left all their things lying ~** hanno lasciato tutta la loro roba in giro; **to run ~** correre qua e là; **to walk ~** camminare; **to look ~** guardarsi intorno; **to be ~ again** *(after illness)* essere di nuovo in piedi; **we were ~ early** eravamo in piedi presto; **is Paul ~?** hai visto Paul in giro?; **there's a lot of measles ~** c'è molto morbillo in giro; **it's the other way ~** è rivolto dalla parte opposta; *(fig)* è il contrario, è viceversa.

(b) *(approximately)* circa, quasi, pressappoco; **~ 50 people** una cinquantina di persone; **she's ~ the same age as you** ha pressappoco la tua età; **~ 2 o'clock** verso le 2; **it is ~ 2 o'clock** sono circa le 2; **it's just ~ finished** è quasi finito; **that's ~ right** è più o meno giusto.

(c): **to be ~ to do sth** stare per fare qc; **they were ~ to fire when...** erano sul punto di *or* lì lì per sparare quando...; **I'm not ~ to do all that for nothing** non ho intenzione di fare tutto questo per niente.

2 *prep* **(a)** *(place)* intorno a; **her clothes were scattered ~ the room** i suoi vestiti erano sparsi *or* in giro per tutta la stanza; **the fields ~ the house** i campi intorno alla casa; **somewhere ~ here** qui intorno da qualche parte; **to wander ~ the town** andare in giro per la città; **to do jobs ~ the house** fare lavori per la casa; **he looked ~ him** si è guardato intorno.

(b) *(relating to)* su, a proposito di, riguardo a; **what is it ~?** di che si tratta?; **we talked ~ it** ne abbiamo parlato; **a book ~ travel** un libro sui viaggi; **do something ~ it!** fai qualcosa!; **there's something interesting ~ him** ha qualcosa di interessante; **there's something ~ a soldier which...** c'è qualcosa nei soldati che...; **how ~ me?** e io?; **how ~ coming with us?** che ne dici *or* diresti di venire con noi?; **how ~ a drink?** che ne diresti di bere qualcosa?, e se bevessimo qualcosa?; **what ~ it?** *(what do you say)* che te ne pare?, cosa ne pensi?; *(what of it)* e allora?

(c) *(occupied with):* **while you're ~ it...** già che ci sei... .

about-face [ə‚baʊt'feɪs] *n*, **about-turn** [ə‚baʊt'tɜːn] *n (Mil, fig)* dietro front *m*.

above [ə'bʌv] **1** *adv* di sopra, al di sopra; *(in text)* prima, sopra; **the flat ~** l'appartamento di sopra *or* al piano di sopra; **from ~** dall'alto; **the clouds ~** le nuvole sovrastanti; **all the players are 6 feet or ~** tutti i giocatori sono alti 6 piedi o più; **children of 7 years or ~** ragazzi dai 7 anni in su *or* a partire dai 7 anni; **orders from ~** ordini superiori *or* (che vengono) dall'alto; **the address ~** l'indirizzo di cui sopra.

2 *prep* sopra; **~ the clouds** al di sopra delle nuvole; **the Thames ~ London** il Tamigi a monte di Londra; **2000 metres ~ sea level** 2000 metri sopra il livello del mare; **he is ~ me in rank** ha un grado superiore al mio; **I couldn't hear ~ the din** non riuscivo a sentire in mezzo a *or* attraverso tutto quel frastuono; **he's ~ that sort of thing** è superiore a queste cose; **he's not ~ a bit of blackmail** non rifuggirebbe dal ricatto; **it's ~ me** è troppo complicato per me; **to get ~ o.s.** montarsi la testa; **she can't count ~ 10** non sa contare oltre il 10; **children ~ 7 years of age** ragazzi al di sopra dei 7 anni (di età).

above·board [ə‚bʌv'bɔːd] *adj* leale, onesto(a); **are you sure this is ~?** sei sicuro che sia una faccenda pulita?

above-mentioned [ə'bʌv'menʃənd] *adj* sopra menzionato(a).

abra·sion [ə'breɪʒən] *n* abrasione *f*; *(injury)* escoriazione *f*, abrasione *f*.

abra·sive [ə'breɪsɪv] **1** *adj* abrasivo(a); *(fig: person, personality)* caustico(a); *(: voice)* stridente. **2** *n* abrasivo.

abreast [ə'brest] *adv* di fianco, fianco a fianco; **to march 4 ~** marciare in riga per 4; **to come ~ of** affiancarsi a; **to keep ~ of the news/times** tenersi aggiornato.

abridged [ə'brɪdʒd] *adj* ridotto(a).

abroad [ə'brɔːd] *adv (in foreign parts)* all'estero; **to go ~** andare all'estero; **there is a rumour ~ that...** si sente dire in giro che..., circola la voce che...; **how did the news get ~?** come si è sparsa *or* diffusa la notizia?

ab·rupt [ə'brʌpt] *adj (halt, person, slope)* brusco(a); *(style)* discontinuo(a), sconnesso(a).

ab·rupt·ly [ə'brʌptlɪ] *adv* bruscamente.

ab·scess ['æbsɪs] *n* ascesso.

ab·scond [əb'skɒnd] *vi* fuggire, scappare.

ab·sence ['æbsəns] *n (of person)* assenza; *(of thing)* mancanza; **in the ~ of** *(person)* in assenza di; *(thing)* in mancanza di; **in my ~** in mia assenza; **in the ~ of any evidence** non essendoci prove; **~ of mind** distrazione *f*.

ab·sent ['æbsənt] *adj (person)* assente; *(thing)* assente, mancante; *(fig: ~-minded)* assente, distratto(a).

ab·sen·tee [‚æbsən'tiː] *n* assente *m/f*.

ab·sen·tee·ism [‚æbsən'tiːɪzəm] *n* assenteismo.

ab·sent·ly ['æbsəntlɪ] *adv* distrattamente.

absent-minded [‚æbsənt'maɪndɪd] *adj* distratto(a).

ab·so·lute ['æbsəluːt] *adj (gen)* assoluto(a); *(support)* totale, completo(a), senza riserve; *(proof)* inconfutabile; *(denial)* categorico(a); *(lie)* bello(a) e buono(a); **he's an ~ idiot** è un perfetto idiota; **it's an ~ scandal** è un autentico scandalo.

ab·so·lute·ly ['æbsəluːtlɪ] *adv* completamente, assolutamente; **oh yes, ~!** oh sì, altro che!

ab·so·lu·tion [‚æbsə'luːʃən] *n (Rel)* assoluzione *f*.

ab·solve [əb'zɒlv] *vt:* **to ~ (from)** *(obligation etc)* sciogliere (da); *(sins)* assolvere (da).

ab·sorb [əb'sɔːb] *vt (also fig)* assorbire; *(costs)* ammortizzare; *(information)* assimilare; **she was ~ed in a book** era immersa *or* assorta nella lettura di un libro.

ab·sorb·ent [əb'sɔːbənt] *adj* assorbente; **~ cotton** *(Am)* cotone *m* idrofilo.

ab·sorb·ing [əb'sɔːbɪŋ] *adj* avvincente, molto interessante.

ab·stain [əb'steɪn] *vi (not vote):* **to ~ (from)** astenersi (da); *(not drink)* astenersi dal bere.

ab·stain·er [əb'steɪnəʳ] *n (teetotaller)* astemio/a.

ab·ste·mi·ous [əb'stiːmɪəs] *adj (person)* moderato(a); *(meal)* frugale.

ab·sten·tion [əb'stenʃən] *n* astensione *f*.

ab·sti·nence ['æbstɪnəns] *n* astinenza.

ab·stract ['æbstrækt] **1** *adj* astratto(a). **2** *n (summary)* riassunto, sommario; *(work of art)* opera astratta; **in the ~** in teoria, in astratto. **3** [æb'strækt] *vt (remove)* estrarre; *(summarize)* riassumere.

ab·surd [əb'sɜːd] *adj* assurdo(a); *(appearance, hat)* ridicolo(a).

ab·surd·ity [əb'sɜːdɪtɪ] *n* **(a)** *(no pl: see adj)* assurdità, assurdo; ridicolaggine *f*, assurdità. **(b)** *(thing etc)* assurdità *f inv*.

abun·dance [ə'bʌndəns] *n* abbondanza, gran quantità; **in** ~ in abbondanza, in gran quantità.

abun·dant |ə'bʌndənt| *adj (crop, supply)* abbondante; *(proof)* ampio(a); ~ **in** ricco di.

abun·dant·ly |ə'bʌndəntlı| *adv* in grande abbondanza; **he made it** ~ **clear to me that...** mi ha fatto abbondantemente capire che... .

abuse |ə'bjuːs| **1** *n* **(a)** *(insults)* insulti *mpl*, ingiurie *fpl*, improperi *mpl*; **to heap** ~ **on sb** coprire qn di insulti. **(b)** *(misuse)* abuso; ~ **of power** abuso di potere; **open to** ~ che si presta ad abusi. **2** |ə'bjuːz| *vt* **(a)** *(revile)* insultare. **(b)** *(misuse)* abusare di, fare cattivo uso di; **to** ~ **one's health** rovinarsi la salute.

abu·sive |əb'juːsıv| *adj (insulting)* villano(a); (: *language)* offensivo(a), ingiurioso(a).

abys·mal |ə'bızməl| *adj (ignorance)* abissale, spaventoso(a); *(result, food)* pessimo(a); *(weather, job)* da cani; ~ **poverty** la povertà più nera.

abyss |ə'bıs| *n* abisso, baratro.

aca·dem·ic |,ækə'demık| **1** *adj (Univ)* accademico(a), universitario(a); *(intellectual)* intellettuale; ~ **life** vita universitaria; ~ **subjects** materie *fpl* umanistiche; ~ **year** *(Univ)* anno accademico; **that's rather** ~ **now** ormai è un po' superfluo al lato pratico. **2** *n* docente *m/f* universitario(a).

acad·emy |ə'kædəmı| *n* accademia; ~ **of music** *(Brit)* conservatorio.

ac·cede |æk'siːd| *vi*: **to** ~ **to** *(throne etc)* salire a; *(request)* aderire a.

ac·cel·er·ate |æk'seləreıt| **1** *vt* accelerare, affrettare. **2** *vi (Aut)* accelerare.

ac·cel·era·tion |æk,selə'reıʃən| *n (Aut)* accelerazione *f*.

ac·cel·era·tor |æk'seləreıtəʳ| *n (Aut)* acceleratore *m*.

ac·cent |'æksənt| *n (all senses)* accento.

ac·cen·tu·ate |æk'sentjueıt| *vt (syllable)* accentuare; *(need, difference etc)* accentuare, mettere in risalto *or* in evidenza.

ac·cept |ək'sept| *vt (gen, Comm)* accettare; *(acknowledge)* ammettere; **I can't** ~ **that he's really in financial difficulties** mi rifiuto di credere che abbia davvero delle difficoltà economiche; **he refused to** ~ **defeat** non ha voluto ammettere la sconfitta; **it's the** ~**ed thing** è un'usanza comunemente accettata.

ac·cept·able |ək'septəbl| *adj* accettabile; *(gift)* gradito(a); **tea is always** ~ un tè è sempre ben accetto, un tè lo si beve sempre volentieri.

ac·cept·ance |ək'septəns| *n* accettazione *f*; *(of person: by others)* accoglienza (favorevole); **to meet with general** ~ incontrare il favore *or* il consenso generale.

ac·cess |'ækses| **1** *n* accesso; **to have/gain** ~ **to sb/sth** avere/ottenere libero accesso presso qn/a qc; **we don't have easy** ~ **to a good sports complex** ci è difficile raggiungere un buon centro sportivo; **the burglars gained** ~ **through a window** i ladri sono riusciti a penetrare da *or* attraverso una finestra. **2** *vt (Computers)* accedere a. **3** *cpd*: ~ **road** *n* strada d'accesso; *(to motorway)* raccordo di entrata.

ac·ces·sible |æk'sesəbl| *adj (place)* accessibile, che si può raggiungere facilmente; *(person, information)* facilmente reperibile.

ac·ces·sion |æk'seʃən| *n (addition)* aggiunta; *(to library)* accessione *f*, acquisto; *(of king)* ascesa *or* salita al trono.

ac·ces·so·ry |æk'sesərı| *n* **(a)** *(gen pl: Dress, Comm etc)* accessorio; **toilet accessories** articoli *mpl* da toletta. **(b)** *(Law)* complice *m/f*.

ac·ci·dent |'æksıdənt| *n (harmful)* incidente *m*, disgrazia; *(unexpected)* (puro) caso; ~**s at work**

infortuni *mpl* sul lavoro; **road** ~ incidente stradale; **by** ~ *(by chance)* per caso; *(unintentionally)* senza volere, per sbaglio; ~**s will happen** sono cose che capitano *or* succedono; **to meet with** *or* **to have an** ~ avere un incidente.

ac·ci·den·tal |,æksı'dentl| *adj (by chance)* fortuito(a), casuale; *(unintentional)* involontario(a); ~ **death** morte *f* accidentale.

ac·ci·den·tal·ly |,æksı'dentəlı| *adv (by chance)* per caso; *(unintentionally)* senza volere, inavvertitamente.

ac·cident-prone |'æksıdənt,prəun| *adj* predisposto(a) agli incidenti.

ac·claim |ə'kleım| **1** *vt* acclamare. **2** *n (approval)* acclamazioni *fpl*, consensi *mpl*; *(applause)* applauso.

ac·cla·ma·tion |,æklə'meıʃən| *n (approval)* acclamazione *f*; *(applause)* applauso; **by** ~ per acclamazione.

ac·cli·ma·tize |ə'klaımətaız| *vt*, *(Am)* **ac·cli·mate** |ə'klaımət| *vt* acclimatare; **to** ~ **o.s. (to)** acclimatarsi (a), adattarsi (a).

ac·com·mo·date |ə'kɒmədeıt| *vt* **(a)** *(lodge, have room for: person)* ospitare, alloggiare; (: *thing)* ospitare; **this car** ~**s 4 people comfortably** quest'auto può trasportare comodamente 4 persone. **(b)** *(wishes etc)* venire incontro a. **(c)** *(differences)* conciliare.

ac·com·mo·dat·ing |ə'kɒmədeıtıŋ| *adj (easy to deal with)* accomodante, conciliante; *(willing to help)* gentile, premuroso(a).

ac·com·mo·da·tion |ə,kɒmə'deıʃən| **1** *n (place to live)* sistemazione *f*, alloggio; *(space)* posto; '~ **to let'** 'camere in affitto'; **have you any** ~ **available?** avete posto?; **seating** ~ posti a sedere. **2** *cpd*: ~ **bureau** *n* agenzia immobiliare.

ac·com·pa·ni·ment |ə'kʌmpənımənt| *n (also Mus)* accompagnamento.

ac·com·pa·nist |ə'kʌmpənıst| *n (Mus)* accompagnatore/trice.

ac·com·pa·ny |ə'kʌmpənı| *vt (gen)* accompagnare; *(Mus)*: **to** ~ **(on)** accompagnare (a).

ac·com·plice |ə'kʌmplıs| *n*: ~ **(in)** complice *m/f* (di).

ac·com·plish |ə'kʌmplıʃ| *vt (task, mission)* compiere, portare a termine; *(one's design)* realizzare; *(purpose)* ottenere.

ac·com·plished |ə'kʌmplıʃt| *adj (pianist etc)* esperto(a).

ac·com·plish·ment |ə'kʌmplıʃmənt| *n (completion)* realizzazione *f*, completamento; *(thing achieved)* risultato, impresa; *(skill)* dote *f*, talento.

ac·cord |ə'kɔːd| **1** *n (harmony)* accordo; **of his own** ~ spontaneamente, di sua iniziativa; **with one** ~ all'unanimità, di comune accordo; **to be in** ~ **with** essere d'accordo con. **2** *vt* accordare. **3** *vi*: **to** ~ **(with)** andare d'accordo (con), accordarsi (con).

ac·cord·ance |ə'kɔːdəns| *n*: **in** ~ **with** secondo, in conformità di a.

ac·cord·ing |ə'kɔːdıŋ| *prep*: ~ **to** secondo, stando a; ~ **to what he says** stando a quanto dice; **they will be punished** ~ **to the seriousness of their crimes** saranno puniti a seconda della gravità dei loro delitti; ~ **to him** secondo lui; **it went** ~ **to plan** è andata secondo il previsto.

ac·cord·ing·ly |ə'kɔːdıŋlı| *adv (all senses)* di conseguenza.

ac·cor·di·on |ə'kɔːdıən| *n* fisarmonica.

ac·cost |ə'kɒst| *vt* abbordare.

ac·count |ə'kaunt| **1** *n* **(a)** *(report)* resoconto, relazione *f*; **to give an** ~ **of sth** fare un resoconto di *or* una relazione su qc; **to keep an** ~ **of** tenere nota di; **to bring sb to ~ for sth/for having done sth** chiedere a qn di render conto di qc/per aver fatto qc; **by all ~s** a detta di tutti, secondo l'opinione generale; **to give a good ~ of o.s.** farsi onore, dare un'ottima prova di sé.

(b) *(consideration)* considerazione *f*, conto; *(importance)* importanza, conto; **it's of no ~** non importa; **on no ~** per nessuna ragione, per nessun motivo, in nessun caso; **on his ~** *(on his behalf)* per conto di lui; *(for him)* per lui, a causa di lui; **on ~** a causa di; **to take ~ of sth, take sth into ~** tener conto di qc, prendere in considerazione qc; **to turn sth to good ~** trarre profitto da qc.

(c) *(at shop, bank, Comm)* conto; **to open an ~ (with)** aprire un conto (presso); **they have the Pirelli ~** la Pirelli è fra i loro clienti; **your ~ is still outstanding** il tuo conto non è ancora stato saldato; **to get £50 on ~** ricevere 50 sterline come *or* in *or* di acconto, ricevere un acconto di 50 sterline; **to put £50 down on ~** versare un acconto di 50 sterline; **to buy sth on ~** comprare qc a credito.

(d) *(Comm)*: **~s** *pl* conti *mpl*; **to keep the ~s** tenere i conti.

2 *cpd*: **~ number** *n* numero di conto; **~s department** *n* ufficio contabilità.

♦ **account for** *vi + prep (explain)* spiegare; *(give reckoning of: actions, expenditure)* render conto di, rispondere di; *(destroy, kill)* uccidere; **that ~s for it** questo spiega tutto; **all the children were ~ed for** nessun ragazzo mancava all'appello; **there's no ~ing for taste** tutti i gusti son gusti.

ac·count·able [ə'kaυntəbl] *adj*: **to be ~ (for sth/to sb)** essere responsabile (di qc/verso qn).

ac·count·an·cy [ə'kaυntənsı] *n* ragioneria, contabilità.

ac·count·ant [ə'kaυntənt] *n* ragioniere/a, contabile *m/f*.

ac·count·ing [ə'kaυntıŋ] *n* contabilità; **~ period** esercizio finanziario.

ac·cred·ited [ə'krɛdıtıd] *adj* accreditato(a).

ac·crue [ə'kru:] *vi (mount up)* aumentare; *(: interest)* maturare; **to ~ to** derivare a; **the notoriety that ~d to him** la notorietà che gliene è derivata.

ac·cu·mu·late [ə'kju:mjυleıt] **1** *vt* accumulare. **2** *vi* accumularsi.

ac·cu·mu·la·tion [ə,kju:mjυ'leıʃən] *n (amassing)* accumulo; *(mass, heap)* mucchio, cumulo.

ac·cu·ra·cy ['ækjυrəsı] *n (see adj)* esattezza; accuratezza; precisione *f*; fedeltà.

ac·cu·rate ['ækjυrıt] *adj (description, report, assessment)* accurato(a), esatto(a), preciso(a); *(observation, estimate)* accurato(a); *(answer)* corretto(a), esatto(a); *(shot, instrument, worker)* preciso(a); *(copy)* fedele.

ac·cu·rate·ly ['ækjυrıtlı] *adv (see adj)* accuratamente; con esattezza; con precisione; correttamente; fedelmente.

ac·cu·sa·tion [,ækjυ'zeıʃən] *n* accusa.

ac·cuse [ə'kju:z] *vt*: **to ~ sb (of)** accusare qn (di).

ac·cused [ə'kju:zd] *n (Law)* accusato/a, imputato/a.

ac·cus·ing·ly [ə'kju:zıŋlı] *adv* con fare d'accusa.

ac·cus·tom [ə'kʌstəm] *vt*: **to ~ sb to sth/to doing sth** abituare qn a qc/a fare qc; **to be ~ed to sth** essere abituato(a) a qc; **to get ~ed to sth/to doing sth** abituarsi *or* adattarsi a qc/a fare qc; **to ~ o.s. to sth** abituarsi a qc.

ace [eıs] *n (Cards, fig: of sportsman etc)* asso; **to be within an ~ of** essere a un pelo da; **to keep an ~ up one's sleeve** avere un asso nella manica.

ache [eık] **1** *n (pain)* dolore *m*; **stomach ~** mal *m* di stomaco; **I've got stomach ~** ho mal di stomaco;

I'm full of ~s and pains mi fa male dappertutto, sono pieno di dolori. **2** *vi (hurt)* far male; **his head ~s** gli fa male la testa; **it makes my head ~** mi fa venire *or* mi dà il mal di testa; **I'm aching all over** sono tutto indolenzito; **it made her heart ~ to see...** le piangeva il cuore vedere.... **3** *vt (yearn)*: **to ~ to do sth** morire dalla voglia di fare qc.

achieve [ə'tʃi:v] *vt (attain)* raggiungere; *(accomplish)* realizzare.

achieve·ment [ə'tʃi:vmənt] *n (act)* realizzazione *f*, raggiungimento; *(thing achieved)* risultato; **that's quite an ~** è una bella impresa, è un bel successo.

acid ['æsıd] **1** *n* acido. **2** *adj (Chem)* acido(a); *(sour)* acido(a), acidulo(a); *(fig: wit, remark)* caustico(a); *(person)* acido(a).

acid·ity [ə'sıdıtı] *n* acidità.

ac·knowl·edge [ək'nɒlıdʒ] *vt (mistake)* riconoscere, ammettere; *(truth etc)* riconoscere; *(claim)* prendere atto di; *(letter: also ~ receipt of)* accusare ricevuta di; *(help, present)* manifestare la propria gratitudine per; *(greeting)* rispondere a, ricambiare; **I smiled at him but he didn't even ~ me** gli ho sorriso ma lui non ha nemmeno dato segno di accorgersi di me; **to ~ sb as leader** riconoscere qn come capo; **to ~ o.s. beaten** ammettere la propria sconfitta.

ac·knowl·edge·ment [ək'nɒlıdʒmənt] *n (admission)* ammissione *f*, riconoscimento; *(of letter etc)* conferma (di aver ricevuto), riscontro; **~s** *(in book)* ringraziamenti *mpl*; **in ~ of** in riconoscimento di.

acme ['ækmı] *n* culmine *m*, acme *m*.

acne ['æknı] *n (Med)* acne *f*.

aco·lyte ['ækəυlaıt] *n* accolito.

acorn ['eıkɔ:n] *n (Bot)* ghianda.

acous·tic [ə'ku:stık] *adj* acustico(a).

acous·tics [ə'ku:stıks] *n (sg or pl)* acustica.

ac·quaint [ə'kweınt] *vt* **(a)** *(inform)*: **to ~ sb with sth** informare qn di qc, mettere qn al corrente di qc; **he's already ~ed with the facts** è già informato *or* a conoscenza dei fatti; **to ~ o.s. with sth** familiarizzarsi con qc, impratichirsi su qc. **(b)** *(with person)*: **to be ~ed with sb** conoscere (personalmente) qn; **to become ~ed with sb** fare la conoscenza di qn; **we became ~ed in Paris** ci siamo conosciuti a Parigi.

ac·quaint·ance [ə'kweıntəns] *n* **(a)** *(with person, subject etc)*: **~ (with)** conoscenza (di); **to make sb's ~** fare la conoscenza di qn; **it improves on ~** più lo si conosce e più lo si apprezza. **(b)** *(person)* conoscente *m/f*, conoscenza; **a business ~** una conoscenza di lavoro; **an ~ of mine** un mio conoscente.

ac·qui·esce [,ækwı'ɛs] *vi (agree)*: **to ~ (in)** acconsentire (a).

ac·qui·es·cence [,ækwı'ɛsns] *n* acquiescenza, consenso.

ac·quire [ə'kwaıə'] *vt (possessions, territory, knowledge)* acquisire; *(language etc)* imparare; *(habit)* contrarre, prendere; *(reputation)* farsi; **to ~ a name for honesty** guadagnarsi la fama di essere onesto; **to ~ a taste for** prender gusto a.

ac·quired [ə'kwaıəd] *adj (Psych)* acquisito(a); **an ~ taste** una cosa che si impara ad apprezzare.

ac·qui·si·tion [,ækwı'zıʃən] *n* acquisto.

ac·quisi·tive [ə'kwızıtıv] *adj (person)* a cui piace accumulare oggetti.

ac·quit [ə'kwıt] *vt* **(a)** *(Law)*: **to ~ sb (of)** assolvere qn (da). **(b)**: **to ~ o.s. (well/badly)** comportarsi (bene/male).

ac·quit·tal [ə'kwıtl] *n* assoluzione *f*.

acre ['eıkə'] *n* acro, ≈ mezzo ettaro.

ac·rid ['ækrɪd] *adj (smell)* acre, pungente; *(fig)* pungente.

ac·ri·mo·ni·ous [,ækrɪ'məʊnɪəs] *adj (remark)* astioso(a), malevolo(a); *(argument)* aspro(a).

ac·ro·bat ['ækrəbæt] *n* acrobata *m/f*.

ac·ro·bat·ics [,ækrəʊ'bætɪks] *npl* acrobazie *fpl*.

across [ə'krɒs] **1** *prep* **(a)** *(from one side to other of)* attraverso; **to go ~ a bridge** attraversare un ponte; **there was a motif printed ~ the front of his tee-shirt** c'era un disegno stampato sul davanti della sua maglietta. **(b)** *(on the other side of)* dall'altra parte di, al di là di; **the shop ~ the road** il negozio sull'altro lato *or* dall'altra parte della strada; **~ the street from our house** di fronte *or* dirimpetto a casa nostra. **(c)** *(crosswise over)* di traverso a.

2 *adv* **(a)** *(direction)* dall'altra parte; **to jump ~** saltare dall'altra parte, attraversare con un salto; **I helped the old man ~** ho aiutato il vecchio ad attraversare; **don't go round, go ~** non fare il giro, attraversa *or* passa nel mezzo; **to cut sth ~** tagliare qc per *or* di traverso; **~ from** di fronte a; **3 ~** *(in crosswords)* 3 orizzontale; **to get sth ~ to sb** *(fig)* far capire qc a qn. **(b)** *(measurement)*: **the lake is 12 km ~** il lago ha una larghezza di 12 km *or* è largo 12 km.

act [ækt] **1** *n* **(a)** *(deed)* atto; **an ~ of kindness** un atto di gentilezza; **~ of God** calamità *f* inv naturale; **an ~ of folly** una pazzia, una follia; **I was in the ~ of writing to him** stavo (proprio) scrivendo a lui; **to catch sb in the ~** cogliere qn in flagrante *or* sul fatto; **I caught him in the ~ of stealing** l'ho sorpreso a rubare. **(b)** *(also: ~ of Parliament)* legge *f*. **(c)** *(Theatre: of play)* atto; *(in circus etc)* numero; *(fig: pretence)* scena, messinscena; **it's only an ~** è tutta scena, è solo una messinscena.

2 *vt (play)* rappresentare, mettere in scena; *(part)* recitare, interpretare; **to ~ the fool** *(fig)* fare lo stupido *or* il cretino.

3 *vi* **(a)** *(Theatre, Cine)* recitare; **he's only ~ing** sta solo facendo finta *or* recitando. **(b)** *(function: thing, person)*: **to ~ as** fungere da, fare da; *(: drug)* agire; **he ~s as my assistant** mi fa da assistente; **~ing in my capacity as chairman, I...** in qualità di presidente, io...; **it ~s as a deterrent** serve da deterrente; **to ~ for sb** agire in nome *or* per conto di qn; **who is ~ing for the defendant?** chi è l'avvocato difensore? **(c)** *(behave)* comportarsi; **to ~ like a fool** fare lo stupido, comportarsi come uno stupido; **she ~ed as if she was upset** si era mostrata contrariata. **(d)** *(take action)* agire; **he ~ed to stop it** è intervenuto per fermarlo.

♦ **act out** *vt + adv (event)* ricostruire; *(fantasies)* dare forma concreta a.

♦ **act up** *vi + adv (fam: person)* fare i capricci; *(: injury)* farsi sentire; *(: machine)* fare degli scherzi.

♦ **act (up)on** *vi + prep (advice)* seguire; *(order)* eseguire.

act·ing ['æktɪŋ] **1** *adj*: **he is the ~ manager** fa le veci del direttore. **2** *n* recitazione *f*.

ac·tion ['ækʃən] **1** *n* **(a)** *(doing)* azione *f*; *(deed)* fatto, azione; *(movement: of horse, athlete)* stile *m*; *(effect: of acid, drug etc)* azione, effetto; *(Mil)* azione, combattimento; *(Tech: of clock, machine)* meccanismo; **to take ~** passare all'azione, agire; **to put a plan into ~** realizzare un piano; **to be out of ~** *(Tech)* non funzionare, essere fuori uso; **killed in ~** *(Mil)* ucciso in combattimento. **(b)** *(Law)* azione *f* legale; **to bring an ~ against sb** intentare causa contro qn. **2** *cpd*:

~ replay *n (TV)* replay *m* inv.

ac·ti·vate ['æktɪveɪt] *vt* attivare.

ac·tive ['æktɪv] *adj (gen, Gram, volcano)* attivo(a); **to play an ~ part in** partecipare attivamente a, prendere parte attiva in; **to be on ~ service** *(Mil)* prestar servizio in zona di operazioni; **we are giving it ~ consideration** lo stiamo considerando attentamente.

ac·tive·ly ['æktɪvlɪ] *adv* attivamente; **to be ~ involved in** prendere parte attiva in.

ac·tiv·ist ['æktɪvɪst] *n* attivista *m/f*.

ac·tiv·ity [æk'tɪvɪtɪ] *n (gen)* attività *f* inv; *(of scene)* animazione *f*, movimento; **social activities** attività ricreative.

ac·tor ['æktəʳ] *n* attore *m*.

ac·tress ['æktrɪs] *n* attrice *f*.

ac·tual ['æktjʊəl] *adj (amount, result)* reale, effettivo(a); *(example)* concreto(a); **in ~ fact** in realtà; **what were his ~ words?** cosa ha detto esattamente?

ac·tu·al·ly ['æktjʊəlɪ] *adv (really)* veramente, davvero; *(even)* addirittura, perfino; **he ~ expected us to put him up for the whole holiday** si aspettava sul serio che lo ospitassimo per tutta la vacanza!; **that's not true, ~** questo non è proprio vero; **I wasn't ~ there** a *or* per dire la verità io non c'ero.

ac·tu·ary ['æktjʊərɪ] *n* attuario/a.

ac·tu·ate ['æktjʊeɪt] *vt* spingere; **~d by** animato da.

acu·men ['ækjʊmɛn] *n* acume *m*, perspicacia; **business ~** fiuto negli affari.

acu·punc·ture ['ækjʊpʌŋktʃəʳ] *n* agopuntura.

acute [ə'kju:t] *adj (eyesight, accent, angle, deafness)* acuto(a); *(hearing, smell etc)* fine; *(pain, anxiety, joy)* intenso(a); *(crisis, shortage)* grave; *(person, mind)* perspicace, dotato(a) di acume.

acute·ly [ə'kju:tlɪ] *adv (intensely)* intensamente; *(shrewdly)* con perspicacia.

A.D. *abbr (= Anno Domini)* d.C.

ad [æd] *n abbr (fam) of* advertisement.

Adam ['ædəm] *n*: **I don't know him from ~** non ho idea di chi sia; **~'s apple** pomo d'Adamo.

ada·mant ['ædəmənt] *adj (fig)* inflessibile, irremovibile.

adapt [ə'dæpt] **1** *vt (machine)* modificare, fare delle modifiche a; *(building)* trasformare; *(text)* adattare; **to ~ o.s. to sth** adattarsi a qc. **2** *vi*: **to ~ (to)** adattarsi (a).

adapt·able [ə'dæptəbl] *adj (vehicle etc)* versatile; *(person)* adattabile, che sa adattarsi; **he's very ~** si adatta facilmente.

ad·ap·ta·tion [,ædæp'teɪʃən] *n* adattamento.

adapt·er, adap·tor [ə'dæptəʳ] *n (Elec)* presa multipla; *(: for 2- pin to 3- pin system)* riduttore *m*.

add [æd] **1** *vt*: **to ~ (to)** aggiungere (a); *(Math)* sommare (a), addizionare (a); **he ~ed that...** ha soggiunto *or* ha aggiunto che...; **~ed to which...** e per giunta..., e per di più...; **to ~ insult to injury** aggiungere al danno anche le beffe. **2** *vi (count)* fare le addizioni *or* le somme, addizionare.

♦ **add to** *vi + prep* aumentare, accrescere.

♦ **add up 1** *vt + adv (figures)* addizionare, sommare; *(advantages etc)* mettere insieme. **2** *vi + adv*: **it ~s up to 25** la somma è 25; **it doesn't ~ up to much** *(fig)* non vuol dire molto, non ha molto senso; **it doesn't ~ up** *(fig fam)* non quadra, non ha senso; **it's all beginning to ~ up** *(fig fam)* si comincia a capire *or* a spiegare tutto.

ad·der ['ædəʳ] *n* vipera.

ad·dict ['ædɪkt] *n* drogato/a, tossicomane *m/f*; *(fig)* fanatico/a; **heroin ~** eroinomane *m/f*; **television ~** fanatico della televisione.

ad·dicted [ə'dıktıd] *adj*: ~ **(to)** *(drugs etc)* dipendente (da); *(fig)* fanatico(a) (di), maniaco(a) (di); **to become** ~ **to cocaine** diventare cocainomane.

ad·dic·tion [ə'dıkʃən] *n* assuefazione *f*; **drug** ~ tossicodipendenza; **an** ~ **to chocolate** un debole per il cioccolato.

ad·dic·tive [ə'dıktıv] *adj* che dà assuefazione.

ad·di·tion [ə'dıʃən] *n* aggiunta; *(Math)* addizione *f*; **if my** ~ **is correct** se ho fatto bene i conti; **there has been an** ~ **to the family** la famiglia si è accresciuta; **in** ~ **to** oltre a, in aggiunta a; **in** ~, ... inoltre, ...

ad·di·tion·al [ə'dıʃənl] *adj* supplementare.

ad·di·tive ['ædıtıv] *n* additivo.

ad·dress [ə'dres] **1** *n* **(a)** *(of house etc)* indirizzo, recapito; *(on envelope)* indirizzo. **(b)** *(speech)* discorso, allocuzione *f*. **(c):** **form of** ~ *(gen)* formula di cortesia; *(in letters)* formula d'indirizzo *or* di intestazione; **the correct form of** ~ **for a bishop** la maniera corretta di rivolgersi ad un vescovo.

2 *vt* **(a)** *(direct: letter)* indirizzare; *(: write name etc on envelope)* mettere *or* scrivere l'indirizzo su; *(remarks etc)* rivolgere; **this letter is wrongly** ~**ed** l'indirizzo su questa lettera è sbagliato; **please** ~ **your complaints to the manager** per i reclami si rivolga al direttore; **to** ~ **o.s. to sth** indirizzare le proprie energie verso qc. **(b)** *(person)* rivolgersi a; *(meeting)* parlare a; **she** ~**ed him as 'Your Lordship'** si rivolse a lui chiamandolo 'Sua Eccellenza'; **the judge** ~**ed the jury** il giudice si è rivolto alla giuria.

ad·enoids ['ædınɔıdz] *npl* adenoidi *fpl*.

adept ['ædept] **1** *adj*: ~ **in** *or* **at** **sth/at doing sth** abile in qc/nel fare qc, bravissimo(a) in qc/a fare qc. **2** *n*: ~ **(in, at)** esperto(a) (in).

ad·equate ['ædıkwıt] *adj (amount, supply)*: ~ **(for/ to do sth)** sufficiente (a/per fare qc); *(reward, description)*: ~ **(for)** adeguato(a) (a); *(tool)*: ~ **(to)** adatto(a) (a); *(essay, performance)* discreto(a); *(person)* all'altezza; **to feel** ~ **to a task** sentirsi all'altezza di un compito.

ad·equate·ly ['ædıkwıtlı] *adv (heated, paid)* adeguatamente, sufficientemente; *(perform, answer)* convenientemente; **will he do it** ~? sarà all'altezza?

ad·here [əd'hıə'] *vi* aderire.

♦ **adhere to** *vi* + *prep (party, policy)* aderire a; *(belief)* rimanere fedele a; *(promise)* mantenere; *(rule)* attenersi a.

ad·her·ent [əd'hıərənt] *n (person)* aderente *m/f*.

ad·he·sive [əd'hiːzıv] **1** *adj* adesivo(a); ~ **tape** nastro adesivo. **2** *n* adesivo.

ad hoc [,æd'hɒk] *adj (decision)* ad hoc *inv*; *(committee)* apposito(a).

ad·ja·cent [ə'dʒeısənt] *adj*: ~ **(to)** adiacente (a).

ad·jec·tive ['ædʒektıv] *n* aggettivo.

ad·join [ə'dʒɔın] *vt* essere contiguo(a) *or* attiguo(a).

ad·join·ing [ə'dʒɔınıŋ] *adj* contiguo(a), attiguo(a).

ad·journ [ə'dʒɜːn] **1** *vt (suspend)* aggiornare, rinviare; *(Am: end)* sospendere; **to** ~ **a meeting till the following week** aggiornare *or* rinviare un incontro alla settimana seguente; **to** ~ **a meeting for a month** rinviare un incontro di un mese. **2** *vi* sospendere la seduta; *(Parliament)* sospendere i lavori; **they** ~**ed to the pub** *(fam)* si sono trasferiti al pub.

ad·journ·ment [ə'dʒɜːnmənt] *n (period: see vb)* rinvio, aggiornamento; sospensione *f*.

ad·ju·di·cate [ə'dʒuːdıkeıt] *vt (contest)* giudicare; *(claim)* decidere su.

ad·just [ə'dʒʌst] **1** *vt (instrument, tool, speed)* rego-

lare; *(wages, prices)* modificare; *(aim, tie, dress)* aggiustare. **2** *vi*: **to** ~ **(to)** adattarsi (a).

ad·just·able [ə'dʒʌstəbl] *adj* regolabile.

ad·just·ment [ə'dʒʌstmənt] *n (of instrument)* regolazione *f*; *(of wages, prices)* modifica; *(of person)* adattamento; **to make an** ~ **to one's plans** modificare i propri piani.

ad lib [æd'lıb] **1** *adv* a piacere, a volontà. **2 ad-lib** *adj* improvvisato(a), estemporaneo(a). **3 ad-lib** *vt, vi* improvvisare.

ad·min·is·ter [əd'mınıstə'] *vt* **(a)** *(manage: company)* dirigere, gestire; *(: fund)* amministrare. **(b)** *(dispense: medicine)* somministrare; *(: justice, laws)* amministrare; **to** ~ **an oath to sb** far prestare giuramento a qn.

ad·min·is·tra·tion [əd,mınıs'treıʃən] *n* **(a)** *(see vb)* direzione *f*, gestione *f*; amministrazione *f*; somministrazione *f*. **(b)** *(Pol)* governo.

ad·min·is·tra·tive [əd'mınıstrətıv] *adj* amministrativo(a).

ad·min·is·tra·tor [əd'mınıstreıtə'] *n* amministratore/trice.

ad·mi·rable ['ædmərəbl] *adj* ammirevole.

ad·mi·ral ['ædmərəl] *n* ammiraglio.

ad·mi·ra·tion [,ædmə'reıʃən] *n* ammirazione *f*.

ad·mire [əd'maıə'] *vt* ammirare; **she was admiring herself in the mirror** si rimirava allo *or* davanti allo specchio.

ad·mis·sible [əd'mısəbl] *adj* ammissibile.

ad·mis·sion [əd'mıʃən] *n* **(a)** *(entry: to society, school etc)* ammissione *f*; *(: to building)* entrata, ingresso; *(price)* prezzo del biglietto (d'ingresso); '~ **free**' 'ingresso gratuito'. **(b)** *(confession)* ammissione *f*, confessione *f*; **it would be an** ~ **of defeat** sarebbe come dichiararsi sconfitto; **by his own** ~ per sua ammissione.

ad·mit [əd'mıt] *vt* **(a)** *(allow to enter)* lasciar entrare; *(: air, light)* lasciar passare; **children not** ~**ted** vietato l'ingresso ai bambini; **this ticket** ~**s two** questo biglietto è valido per due persone; **he was** ~**ted to hospital** è stato ricoverato all'ospedale. **(b)** *(acknowledge)* ammettere, riconoscere; *(: crime)* ammettere *or* confessare (di aver compiuto); **it is hard, I** ~ è duro, lo ammetto *or* devo ammetterlo; **I must** ~ **that...** devo ammettere *or* confessare che... .

ad·mit·tance [əd'mıtəns] *n* ingresso; **they refused me** ~ mi hanno rifiutato il permesso di entrare; **to gain** ~ riuscire a entrare; '**no** ~' 'vietato l'ingresso'.

ad·mit·ted·ly [əd'mıtıdlı] *adv* bisogna ammettere (che), va detto (che).

ad·mon·ish [əd'mɒnıʃ] *vt (reprimand)*: **to** ~ **sb (for)** riprendere qn (per).

ad nau·seam [,æd'nɔːsıæm] *adv* fino alla nausea, a non finire.

ado·les·cence [,ædəʊ'lɛsns] *n* adolescenza.

ado·les·cent [,ædəʊ'lɛsnt] *adj, n* adolescente *(m/f)*.

adopt [ə'dɒpt] *vt (child, method)* adottare; *(report, suggestion)* approvare; *(Pol: candidate)* scegliere.

adop·tion [ə'dɒpʃən] *n (see vb)* adozione *f*; approvazione *f*; scelta.

ador·able [ə'dɔːrəbl] *adj* adorabile.

ado·ra·tion [,ædə'reıʃən] *n* adorazione *f*.

adore [ə'dɔː'] *vt* adorare.

adorn [ə'dɔːn] *vt* abbellire, ornare.

adrena·lin [ə'drɛnəlın] *n* adrenalina.

Adri·at·ic (Sea) [,eıdrı'ætık('siː)] *n (mare m)* Adriatico.

adrift [ə'drıft] *adv (esp Naut)* alla deriva; **to come** ~ *(boat)* andare alla deriva; *(wire, rope etc)* essersi staccato(a) *or* sciolto(a).

adroit [ə'drɔıt] *adj* abile.

adu·la·tion [,ædjʊ'leɪʃən] n adulazione f.

adult ['ædʌlt] **1** adj (person, animal) adulto(a); (behaviour) da adulto; (film, book) per adulti; ~ education scuola per adulti. **2** n adulto/a; '~s only' 'vietato ai minori di 18 anni'.

adul·ter·ate [ə'dʌltəreɪt] vt adulterare.

adul·tery [ə'dʌltərɪ] n adulterio.

ad·vance [əd'vɑːns] **1** n (a) (Mil) avanzata; (fig: progress) passo avanti, progresso; **the** ~ **of old age** l'avanzare dell'età or degli anni; **recent** ~**s in technology** i recenti progressi della tecnica; **to make** ~**s to sb** (gen) fare degli approcci a qn; (amorously) fare delle avances a qn; **in** ~ in anticipo; **to arrive in** ~ **of sb** arrivare in anticipo su qn or prima di qn; **to be in** ~ **of one's time** essere in anticipo sul proprio tempo; **to send sth a week in** ~ spedire qc con una settimana di anticipo. **(b)** (loan): ~ **(on)** anticipo (su).

2 vt **(a)** (move forward: time, date) anticipare; (further: plan, knowledge; Mil: troops) far avanzare; (promote: interests) favorire; (: person: in career) promuovere. **(b)** (idea, suggestion, claim) avanzare. **(c)** (money) anticipare; **she wants him to** ~ **her a loan** vuole che lui le faccia un prestito.

3 vi (move forward) avanzare; (Mil) fare l'avanzata; (science, technology) fare dei progressi, progredire; (person, pupil etc) migliorare, fare dei progressi; **to** ~ **on sb** (threateningly) avanzare contro qn.

4 cpd (payment) anticipato(a); (copy of book) distribuito(a) in anticipo; ~ **notice** n preavviso; ~ **party** n pattuglia di punta.

ad·vanced [əd'vɑːnst] adj (gen: ideas, civilization etc) progredito(a), avanzato(a); (student) di livello più avanzato; (studies) superiore; (class) avanzato(a); ~ **in years** avanti negli anni.

ad·van·tage [əd'vɑːntɪdʒ] n vantaggio; **he has the** ~ **of youth** ha il vantaggio di essere giovane; **the plan has many** ~**s** il progetto presenta molti vantaggi; **it's to our** ~ è nel nostro interesse, torna a nostro vantaggio; **to have an** ~ **over sb** avere un vantaggio su qn; **to take** ~ **of** (opportunity) approfittare di, sfruttare; **to take** ~ **of sb** (unfairly) approfittarsi di qn; (sexually) approfittare di qn.

ad·van·ta·geous [,ædvən'teɪdʒəs] adj: ~ **(to)** vantaggioso(a) (per).

ad·vent ['ædvənt] n (arrival) avvento; (Rel): **A**~ l'Avvento.

ad·ven·ture [əd'ventʃə^r] **1** n avventura. **2** cpd (story, film) di avventure.

ad·ven·tur·ous [əd'ventʃərəs] adj avventuroso(a).

ad·verb ['ædvɜːb] n avverbio.

ad·ver·sary ['ædvəsərɪ] n avversario/a, antagonista m/f.

ad·verse ['ædvɜːs] adj (criticism, decision, effect) sfavorevole; (wind) contrario(a); ~ **weather conditions** condizioni atmosferiche avverse.

ad·vert ['ædvɜːt] n abbr of **advertisement**.

ad·ver·tise ['ædvətaɪz] **1** vt (Comm etc) fare pubblicità or réclame a, reclamizzare; **to** ~ **a flat for sale** mettere un annuncio per vendere un appartamento. **2** vi fare (della) pubblicità or (della) réclame; **to** ~ **for** mettere un annuncio or inserire (sul giornale) per; **to** ~ **on television** fare della pubblicità in televisione.

ad·ver·tise·ment [əd'vɜːtɪsmənt] n réclame f inv, pubblicità f inv; (in classified ads) inserzione f, annuncio; **to put an** ~ **in the paper** mettere un annuncio sul giornale; **an** ~ **for soap** la réclame or la pubblicità di un sapone.

ad·ver·tis·er ['ædvətaɪzə^r] n azienda che reclamizza un prodotto; inserzionista m/f.

ad·ver·tis·ing ['ædvətaɪzɪŋ] **1** n pubblicità (commerciale); (advertisements collectively) pubblicità, réclame f inv; **my brother's in** ~ mio fratello lavora nel settore pubblicitario. **2** cpd: ~ **agency** n agenzia pubblicitaria or di pubblicità; ~ **campaign** n campagna pubblicitaria.

ad·vice [əd'vaɪs] n consiglio, consigli mpl; **a piece of** ~ un consiglio; **legal** ~ consulenza legale; **to ask (sb) for** ~ chiedere il consiglio (di qn), chiedere un consiglio (a qn); **to take sb's** ~ seguire il consiglio or i consigli di qn.

ad·vis·able [əd'vaɪzəbl] adj consigliabile, raccomandabile; **I do not think it** ~ **for you to come** non le consiglio di venire.

ad·vise [əd'vaɪz] vt **(a)** (counsel): **to** ~ **sb** (on or about sth) consigliare qn (a proposito di qc); **to** ~ **sb to do sth** consigliare a qn di fare qc; **to** ~ **sb against sth/against doing sth** sconsigliare qc a qn/a qn di fare qc; **he** ~**s the President on foreign affairs** è il consigliere del Presidente in materia di affari esteri; **you would be well/ill** ~**d to go** faresti bene/male ad andare. **(b)** (inform): **to** ~ **sb of sth** avvisare qn di qc.

ad·vis·er [əd'vaɪzə^r] n (in politics) consigliere/a; (in business) consulente m/f, consigliere/a.

ad·vi·so·ry [əd'vaɪzərɪ] adj (body) consultivo(a); **in an** ~ **capacity** in veste di consulente.

ad·vo·cate 1 n (Scot Law) avvocato (difensore); (fig) sostenitore/trice. **2** ['ædvəkeɪt] vt sostenere la validità di.

aeon ['iːən] n eternità f inv.

aer·ate ['ɛəreɪt] vt (liquid) gassare; (blood) ossigenare.

aer·ial ['ɛərɪəl] **1** adj aereo(a); ~ **photograph** fotografia aerea, aerofotogramma m; ~ **railway** teleferica, funivia. **2** n (Brit Radio, TV) antenna.

aero... ['ɛərəʊ] pref aero....

aero·bat·ics ['ɛərəʊ'bætɪks] npl acrobazia aerea sg; (stunts) acrobazie fpl aeree.

aero·bics [ɛə'rəʊbɪks] nsg aerobica.

aero·drome ['ɛərədrəʊm] n (esp Brit) aerodromo.

aero·dy·nam·ics ['ɛərəʊdaɪ'næmɪks] nsg aerodinamica.

aero·naut·ics [,ɛərə'nɔːtɪks] nsg aeronautica.

aero·plane ['ɛərəplɛɪn] n (esp Brit) aeroplano.

aero·sol ['ɛərəsɒl] n (can) aerosol m inv.

aero·space ['ɛərəʊspeɪs] adj attr: ~ **industry** industria aerospaziale.

aes·thet·ic [iːs'θetɪk] adj estetico(a).

aes·thet·ics [iːs'θetɪks] nsg estetica.

afar [ə'fɑː^r] adv lontano; **from** ~ da lontano.

af·fable ['æfəbl] adj affabile.

af·fair [ə'fɛə^r] n (event) faccenda, affare m; (love ~) relazione f, avventura; ~**s** (business) affari; **foreign** ~**s** affari esteri; ~**s of state** affari di stato; **it will be a big** ~ sarà un avvenimento; **the Watergate** ~ il caso Watergate; **that's my** ~ sono affari or fatti miei; **it's a bad state of** ~**s** è una brutta situazione.

af·fect [ə'fɛkt] vt **(a)** (have an effect on) influire su, incidere su; (concern) riguardare, concernere; (harm: health etc) danneggiare; **it did not** ~ **my decision** non ha influito sulla mia decisione, non ha influenzato la mia decisione. **(b)** (move emotionally) colpire; **he seemed much** ~**ed** sembrava molto colpito.

af·fec·ta·tion [,æfɛk'teɪʃən] n affettazione f; ~**s** modi mpl affettati, leziosaggini fpl.

af·fect·ed [ə'fɛktɪd] adj affettato(a).

af·fec·tion [ə'fɛkʃən] n affetto.

af·fec·tion·ate [ə'fɛkʃənɪt] adj affezionato(a).

af·fi·da·vit [,æfɪ'deɪvɪt] n (Law) affidavit m inv.

af·fili·ated [ə'fɪlɪeɪtɪd] adj: ~ **(to or with)** affiliato(a) (a), associato(a) (a); ~ **company** filiale *f*.

af·filia·tion [ə‚fɪlɪ'eɪʃən] *n* affiliazione *f*; **to have ~s with** essere affiliato a.

af·fin·ity [ə'fɪnɪtɪ] *n* (*relationship*) affinità *f inv*; (*liking*) simpatia.

af·firm [ə'fɜːm] *vt* affermare, asserire.

af·firma·tive [ə'fɜːmətɪv] *adj* affermativo(a); **to answer in the ~** rispondere affermativamente *or* di sì.

af·fix [ə'fɪks] *vt* (*signature etc*) apporre; (*stamp*) attaccare.

af·flict [ə'flɪkt] *vt* affliggere.

af·flic·tion [ə'flɪkʃən] *n* (*suffering*) disagio, sofferenza; (*bodily*) infermità *f inv*.

af·flu·ence ['æfluəns] *n* (*wealth*) ricchezza; (*plenty*) abbondanza.

af·flu·ent ['æfluənt] *adj* ricco(a); **the ~ society** la società del benessere.

af·ford [ə'fɔːd] *vt* (**a**): **to ~ sth/to do sth** permettersi qc/di fare qc; **can we ~ a car?** possiamo permetterci un'automobile?; **I can't ~ the time** non ho proprio il tempo; **I can't ~ not to do it** non mi posso permettere di non farlo; **an opportunity you cannot ~ to miss** un'occasione che non puoi lasciarti sfuggire. (**b**) (*frm: provide: opportunity*) offrire, fornire.

af·fray [ə'freɪ] *n* rissa.

af·front [ə'frʌnt] **1** *n* affronto. **2** *vt* fare un affronto a; **to be ~ed (by)** offendersi (per).

afield [ə'fiːld] *adv*: **far ~** lontano, distante.

afloat [ə'fləʊt] *adv* a galla; **to keep ~** (*also fig*) rimanere a galla.

afoot [ə'fʊt] *adv* in preparazione, in corso; **there's trouble ~** ci sono guai in vista.

afore·men·tioned [ə‚fɔː'mɛnʃənd] *adj*, **aforesaid** [ə'fɔːsɛd] *adj* suddetto(a).

afraid [ə'freɪd] *adj*: **to be ~** aver paura; **to be ~ for sb** temere per qn, preoccuparsi per qn; **to be ~ of sb/sth** aver paura di qn/qc; **I was ~ to ask** avevo paura di *or* non osavo domandare; **I'm ~ of hurting her** ho paura di *or* temo di farle male; **I'm ~ he's out** (*regret*) mi rincresce *or* dispiace, ma è fuori; **I'm ~ I have to go now** mi dispiace ma adesso devo proprio andare; **I'm ~ so!** ho paura di sì!, temo proprio di sì!; **I'm ~ not** no mi dispiace, purtroppo no.

afresh [ə'freʃ] *adv* da capo, di nuovo; **to start ~** ricominciare (tutto) da capo.

Af·ri·ca ['æfrɪkə] *n* Africa.

Af·ri·can ['æfrɪkən] *adj, n* africano(a) (*m/f*).

Afro-American ['æfrəʊə'mɛrɪkən] *adj* afroamericano(a).

aft [ɑːft] *adv* (*Naut*) a *or* verso poppa.

af·ter ['ɑːftə'] **1** *adv* (*afterwards*) dopo; **the day ~** il giorno dopo *or* seguente.

  2 *prep* (**a**) (*time, order, place*) dopo; **day ~ day** giorno dopo giorno; **for kilometre ~ kilometre** per chilometri e chilometri; **you tell me lie ~ lie** mi stai dicendo una bugia dopo l'altra; **time ~ time** tantissime volte; **~ dinner** dopo cena; **the day ~ tomorrow** dopodomani; **soon ~ eating it** poco dopo averlo mangiato; **~ all** dopotutto, malgrado tutto; **half ~ two** (*Am*) le due e mezzo; **one ~ the other** uno dopo l'altro, uno per uno; **shut the door ~ you** chiudi la porta dietro di te; **~ you!** prima lei! (**b**) (*in pursuit*) dietro; **he ran ~ me** mi è corso dietro, mi ha rincorso; **the police are ~ him** è ricercato dalla polizia; **what is he ~?** (*fam*) (che) cosa vuole?

  3 *conj* dopo che; **~ what has happened** dopo quello che è successo; **~ he had eaten he went out** dopo aver mangiato uscì, dopo che ebbe mangiato uscì.

after·birth ['ɑːftəbɜːθ] *n* placenta.

after·care ['ɑːftəkɛə'] *n* (*Med*) assistenza medica post-degenza.

after-effect ['ɑːftərɪfɛkt] *n* (*of events*) ripercussione *f*, conseguenza; (*of drug*) reazione *f*; (*of illness*) postumo.

after·life ['ɑːftəlaɪf] *n* vita dell'al di là.

after·math ['ɑːftəmæθ] *n* conseguenze *fpl*.

after·noon ['ɑːftə'nuːn] *n* pomeriggio; **in the ~** nel *or* di pomeriggio; **at 3 o'clock in the ~** alle 3 del pomeriggio; **good ~!** buon giorno!

after-sales ser·vice [‚ɑːftə'seɪlz,sɜːvɪs] *n* servizio assistenza clienti.

after-shave (lo·tion) ['ɑːftə‚ʃeɪv(‚ləʊʃən)] *n* dopobarba *m inv*.

after·taste ['ɑːftəteɪst] *n* sapore *m* che rimane in bocca.

after·thought ['ɑːftəθɔːt] *n* ripensamento; **it was very much an ~** è un'idea che mi è venuta più tardi; **we added it as an ~** l'abbiamo aggiunto solo più tardi; **I had ~s about it** ho avuto dei ripensamenti.

after·wards ['ɑːftəwədz] *adv* dopo, più tardi, in seguito; **soon ~** poco dopo.

again [ə'gɛn] *adv* ancora, di nuovo, un'altra volta; **try ~** riprova, prova ancora *or* un'altra volta; **come ~ soon** torna presto; **~ and ~** ripetutamente, tante volte; **I've told him ~ and ~** gliel'ho detto e ripetuto; **never ~!** mai più!; **now and ~** di tanto in tanto, a volte; **as much ~** due volte tanto; **then ~** (*on the other hand*) d'altra parte; (*moreover*) inoltre.

against [ə'gɛnst] *prep* (**a**) (*in contact with*) a, contro; **I was leaning ~ the desk** ero appoggiato alla scrivania; **he leaned the ladder ~ the wall** appoggiò la scala al *or* contro il muro. (**b**) (*in opposition to*) contro; **he was ~ going** era contrario ad andare; **what have you got ~ me?** cos'hai contro di me?; **it's ~ the law** è contrario alla *or* contro la legge; **to run ~ sb** (*Pol*) contrapporre la propria candidatura a quella di qn. (**c**) (*in contrast to*): **~ the light** controluce; **to stand out ~ a background** spiccare su uno sfondo. (**d**) (*in comparisons*): (**as**) **~** in confronto a, contro.

age [eɪdʒ] **1** *n* (**a**) età *f inv*; (*of thing*) anni *mpl*; **old ~** vecchiaia; **what ~ is he?, what's his ~?** quanti anni ha?; **when I was your ~** quando avevo la tua età; **she doesn't look her ~** non dimostra la sua età *or* i suoi anni; **at the ~ of** all'età di; **to come of ~** diventare maggiorenne, raggiungere la maggiore età; **under ~** minorenne. (**b**) (*period*) epoca, era; **the Iron A~** l'età del ferro. (**c**) (*fam: long time*): **we waited (for) ~s** abbiamo aspettato per ore; **it's an ~ since I saw him** sono secoli che non lo vedo. **2** *vt* fare invecchiare. **3** *vi* invecchiare. **4** *cpd*: **~ group** *n*: **the 40 to 50 ~ group** le persone fra i 40 e i 50 anni; **~ limit** *n* limite *m* di età.

aged ['eɪdʒɪd] **1** *adj* (**a**) (*old*) anziano(a). (**b**) [eɪdʒd] dell'età di; **a boy ~ 10** un ragazzo di 10 anni. **2** *npl*: **the ~** gli anziani, i vecchi.

age·less ['eɪdʒlɪs] *adj* (*eternal*) eterno(a); (*always young*) senza età.

agen·cy ['eɪdʒənsɪ] *n* (**a**) (*office*) agenzia; (*distributorship*) rappresentanza; **travel ~** agenzia di viaggi. (**b**) (*instrumentality*): **through the ~ of** grazie a, per mezzo *or* per opera di.

agen·da [ə'dʒɛndə] *n* ordine *m* del giorno; **on the ~** all'ordine del giorno.

agent ['eɪdʒənt] *n* (**a**) (*Comm, Police, Theatre etc*) agente *m*; (*representative*) rappresentante *m/f*; **to be sole ~ for** avere la rappresentanza esclusiva per; **he is not a free ~** (*fig*) non è padrone di fare quel che vuole. (**b**) (*Chem*) agente *m*.

ag·gra·vate ['ægrəveɪt] vt aggravare, peggiorare; (annoy) esasperare, irritare.

ag·gra·vat·ing ['ægrəveɪtɪŋ] adj esasperante, irritante.

ag·gre·gate ['ægrɪgɪt] 1 n (a) (total) insieme m; in the ~ nel complesso. (b) (Geol) aggregato; (Constr) inerti mpl. 2 adj complessivo(a).

ag·gres·sion [ə'grɛʃən] n aggressione f.

ag·gres·sive [ə'grɛsɪv] adj aggressivo(a); (salesman, approach etc) intraprendente.

ag·grieved [ə'griːvd] adj: ~ (at, by) offeso(a) (da).

ag·hast [ə'gɑːst] adj: ~ (at) sbigottito(a) (a); (terrified) inorridito(a) (a), atterrito(a) (a).

ag·ile ['ædʒaɪl] adj agile, svelto(a).

agi·tate ['ædʒɪteɪt] 1 vt (perturb) turbare, mettere in (uno stato di) agitazione; (shake) agitare. 2 vi (Pol): to ~ (for) agitarsi or fare un'agitazione (per).

agi·tated ['ædʒɪteɪtɪd] adj agitato(a), inquieto(a).

agi·ta·tion [,ædʒɪ'teɪʃən] n agitazione f.

agi·ta·tor ['ædʒɪteɪtəʳ] n (Pol) agitatore/trice.

AGM abbr of **annual general meeting.**

ag·nos·tic [æg'nɒstɪk] adj, n agnostico(a) (m/f).

ag·nos·ti·cism [æg'nɒstɪsɪzəm] n agnosticismo.

ago [ə'gəʊ] adv: **a week** ~ una settimana fa; **long** ~ molto tempo fa; **as long** ~ **as 1960** già nel 1960; **how long** ~? quanto tempo fa?; **how long** ~ **was it?** quanto tempo è passato da quella volta?, da quanto tempo è successo?

agog [ə'gɒg] adj: (all) ~ (for) ansioso(a) (di), impaziente (di); ~ **with excitement** emozionato(a), eccitato(a).

ago·nize ['ægənaɪz] vi: to ~ (over) angosciarsi (per).

ago·ny ['ægənɪ] 1 n (pain) dolore m atroce; (: mental) angoscia; **I was in** ~ avevo dei dolori atroci, soffrivo atrocemente; **to suffer agonies of doubt** avere dei dubbi atroci. 2 cpd: ~ **column** n posta del cuore.

agree [ə'griː] 1 vi (a) (be in agreement): to ~ (with) essere d'accordo (con), essere della stessa opinione (di); **I quite** ~ sono perfettamente d'accordo; **don't you** ~? non sei d'accordo? (b) (come to terms): to ~ (on sth) mettersi d'accordo (su qc). (c) (consent): to ~ to sth accettare qc, acconsentire a qc. (d) (be in harmony: things) andare d'accordo, concordare; (: persons: get on together) andare or trovarsi d'accordo; (Gram) concordare. (e) (food): **garlic doesn't** ~ **with me** non riesco a digerire l'aglio, l'aglio mi rimane sullo stomaco.
2 vt (a) (come to agreement): to ~ (that) essere d'accordo (sul fatto che); **it was** ~**d that...** è stato deciso (di comune accordo) che...; **are we all** ~**d?** siamo tutti d'accordo?; **is that** ~**d?** (siamo) d'accordo?; to ~ **to differ** rimanere ognuno della propria idea. (b) (consent): to ~ **to do sth** accettare di fare qc, acconsentire a fare qc.

agree·able [ə'griːəbl] adj (pleasing) piacevole; (willing): to be ~ to sth/to doing sth essere ben disposto(a) a qc/a fare qc; **if you are** ~ se sei d'accordo.

agree·ment [ə'griːmənt] n (gen) accordo; (consent) consenso; **by mutual** ~ di comune accordo; **to come to an** ~ venire a un accordo, accordarsi; **to be in** ~ **with sb** essere or trovarsi d'accordo con qn.

ag·ri·cul·tur·al [,ægrɪ'kʌltʃərəl] adj (gen) agricolo(a); (college, studies) agrario(a); ~ **expert** agronomo/a, agrario/a.

ag·ri·cul·ture ['ægrɪkʌltʃəʳ] n agricoltura.

aground [ə'graʊnd] adv (Naut) in secca; **to run** ~ arenarsi, incagliarsi.

ahead [ə'hɛd] adv (a) (in space) avanti, davanti; **to go** ~ andare avanti; (fig): **go** ~! fai pure!, prego!; **to get** ~ **of sb** superare qn. (b) (in time: book, plan) in anticipo; **Italy is one hour** ~ **of Britain at the moment** attualmente l'Italia è un'ora avanti or avanti di un'ora rispetto all'Inghilterra; **he finished half an hour** ~ **of the others** ha finito con mezz'ora di anticipo sugli or rispetto agli altri, ha finito mezz'ora prima degli altri; **to look** ~ (fig) pensare all'avvenire; **to be** ~ **of one's time** precorrere i propri tempi.

ahoy [ə'hɔɪ] excl ehi!; **ship** ~! ehi della nave!

aid [eɪd] 1 n aiuto, assistenza; **economic** ~ aiuti economici mpl, assistenza economica; **with the** ~ **of** con l'aiuto di; **in** ~ **of** a favore di; **what's all this in** ~ **of?** (fam) a cosa serve tutto questo?; **to come to the** ~ **of** venire in aiuto a. 2 vt (person): **to** ~ **sb (to do sth)** aiutare qn (a fare qc); (progress, recovery) contribuire a; **to** ~ **and abet sb** (Law) essere complice di qn.

aide [eɪd] n (Mil) aiutante m di campo, addetto (militare); (Pol) consigliere/a, addetto.

ail·ment ['eɪlmənt] n indisposizione f.

aim [eɪm] 1 n (of weapon) mira; (fig: purpose, object) scopo, proposito; **his** ~ **is bad** non ha una buona mira; **to have no** ~ **in life** non avere un preciso scopo nella vita; **to take** ~ prendere la mira, mirare; **to take** ~ **at sth/sb** mirare a qc/qn. 2 vt: **to** ~ **(at)** (gun) puntare (su or contro); (blow) tirare a(a); (remark, criticism) dirigere a(a), rivolgere (a); **to** ~ **to do sth** aspirare a fare qc; (less formal) avere l'intenzione di fare qc. 3 vi prendere la mira, mirare; **to** ~ **at sth** (also fig) mirare a qc; **to** ~ **for the goal** (Ftbl etc) tirare in porta.

aim·less ['eɪmlɪs] adj senza scopo.

ain't [eɪnt] (incorrect) = **am not, is not, are not; has not, have not.**

air [ɛəʳ] 1 n (a) (gen) aria; **in the open** ~ all'aria aperta, all'aperto; **by** ~ (travel) in aereo; (Post) per via or posta aerea; **to get some fresh** ~ andare a prendere una boccata d'aria (fresca); **to clear the** ~ (fig) chiarire la situazione; **there's something in the** ~ (fig) c'è qualcosa nell'aria; **our plans are up in the** ~ i nostri progetti sono ancora campati in aria. (b) (Radio, TV): **to be on the** ~ (programme) essere in onda; (station) trasmettere; (person) parlare alla radio (or alla televisione); **we're now going off the** ~ la trasmissione si conclude qui. (c) (appearance) aria, aspetto; **with a guilty** ~ con aria colpevole; **she had an** ~ **of mystery about her** aveva una certa aria di mistero; **to give o.s.** ~**s** darsi delle arie.
2 vt (room, bed) arieggiare; (clothes) far prendere aria a; (idea, grievance) esprimere pubblicamente, manifestare; (views) far conoscere.
3 cpd (current, bubble) d'aria; (cushion, mattress) gonfiabile; (pressure) atmosferico(a); (brake, gun) ad aria compressa; (Mil: base, attack etc) aereo(a); ~ **bed** n materassino; ~ **conditioning** n aria condizionata; ~ **force** n aviazione f; ~ **hostess** n hostess f inv; ~ **lane** n corridoio aereo; ~ **letter** n aerogramma m; ~ **pocket** n vuoto d'aria; ~ **raid** n incursione f aerea; ~ **terminal** n air-terminal m inv; ~ **traffic control** n controllo del traffico aereo; ~ **traffic controller** n controllore m del traffico aereo.

air·borne ['ɛəbɔːn] adj (troops) aerotrasportato(a), aviotrasportato(a); (aircraft): **as soon as the plane was** ~ appena l'aereo ebbe decollato; **suddenly we were** ~ in un attimo avevamo già preso quota.

air-conditioned ['ɛəkən,dɪʃnd] adj con or ad aria condizionata.

air-cooled ['ɛəku:ld] adj raffreddato(a) ad aria.
air-craft ['ɛəkrɑ:ft] **1** n, pl inv aeromobile m. **2** cpd:
~ **carrier** n portaerei f inv.
air-drome ['ɛədrəum] n (Am) = **aerodrome.**
air-field ['ɛəfi:ld] n campo d'aviazione.
air-ing ['ɛərɪŋ] **1** n: **to give an** ~ **to** (linen) far
prendere aria a; (room) arieggiare; (fig: ideas etc)
ventilare. **2** cpd: ~ **cupboard** n armadio riscaldato
per asciugare panni.
air-less ['ɛəlɪs] adj (room) senz'aria; (day) senza un
filo di vento.
air-lift ['ɛəlɪft] n ponte m aereo.
air-line ['ɛəlaɪn] n linea or compagnia aerea, avio-
linea.
air-lock ['ɛəlɒk] n (in pipe) bolla d'aria; (in spacecraft etc) cassa d'aria, camera di equilibrio.
air-mail ['ɛəmeɪl] n posta aerea; **by** ~ per via or
posta aerea.
air-plane ['ɛəpleɪn] n (Am) = **aeroplane.**
air-port ['ɛəpɔ:t] n aeroporto.
air-sea res-cue [,ɛəsi:'rɛskju:] n salvataggio aereo
in mare.
air-ship ['ɛəʃɪp] n dirigibile m, aeronave f.
air-sick ['ɛəsɪk] adj: **to be** ~ soffrire di mal d'aria
or d'aereo.
air-space ['ɛəspeɪs] n spazio aereo.
air-strip ['ɛəstrɪp] n pista d'atterraggio.
air-tight ['ɛətaɪt] adj (container) a chiusura ermetica; (seal, cap) ermetico(a).
air-worthy ['ɛəwɜ:ðɪ] adj in condizione di poter
volare.
airy ['ɛərɪ] adj (**-ier, -iest**) (place) arieggiato(a);
(room) arioso(a); (remark etc) superficiale; (manner) spensierato(a).
aisle [aɪl] n (of church) navata; (of theatre, train,
coach) corridoio; (in supermarket) passaggio; **it
had them rolling in the** ~**s** li ha fatti rotolare
(per terra) dalle risate.
ajar [ə'dʒɑ:'] adv socchiuso(a).
ala-bas-ter ['æləbɑ:stə'] n alabastro.
à la carte [,ɑ:lɑ:'kɑ:t] adv alla carta.
alac-rity [ə'lækrɪtɪ] n: **with** ~ con prontezza.
alarm [ə'lɑ:m] **1** n (warning, signal) allarme m; (~
clock) sveglia; **to raise the** ~ dare l'allarme;
there's no need for any ~ non c'è bisogno di
allarmarsi. **2** vt allarmare, spaventare; **to be
~ed (at)** essere preoccupato (per) or allarmato
(da).
alarm-ing [ə'lɑ:mɪŋ] adj allarmante, preoccupante.
alarm-ist [ə'lɑ:mɪst] n allarmista m/f.
alas [ə'læs] excl ohimè!, ahimè!
Al-ba-nia [æl'beɪnɪə] n Albania.
al-ba-tross ['ælbətrɒs] n albatro.
al-bi-no [æl'bi:nəʊ] adj, n albino(a) (m/f).
al-bum ['ælbəm] n album m inv; **photograph** ~
album di or delle fotografie; (new) album per
fotografie.
al-che-my ['ælkɪmɪ] n alchimia.
al-co-hol ['ælkəhɒl] n alcool m; **I never touch** ~ non
bevo (mai) alcolici.
al-co-hol-ic [,ælkə'hɒlɪk] **1** adj alcolico(a). **2** n al-
colizzato/a.
al-co-hol-ism ['ælkəhɒlɪzəm] n alcolismo.
al-cove ['ælkəʊv] n alcova.
ale [eɪl] n birra.
alert [ə'lɜ:t] **1** adj (acute, wide-awake) sveglio(a);
(mind) pronto(a), agile, vivace; (expression) intelligente; (guard) vigile. **2** n allarme m; **to be on the**
~ (person) stare all'erta; (troops) essere in stato
di allarme. **3** vt: **to** ~ **sb (to sth)** avvisare qn (di
qc), avvertire qn (di qc); **to** ~ **sb to the dangers
of sth** mettere qn in guardia contro qc.

al-fal-fa [æl'fælfə] n erba medica.
al-fres-co [æl'freskəʊ] adj, adv all'aperto.
al-gae ['ældʒi:] npl alghe fpl.
al-ge-bra ['ældʒɪbrə] n algebra.
Al-ge-ria [æl'dʒɪərɪə] n Algeria.
ali-as ['eɪlɪæs] **1** n nome m falso, pseudonimo. **2** adv
alias, altrimenti detto(a).
ali-bi ['ælɪbaɪ] n alibi m inv.
al-ien ['eɪlɪən] **1** adj (very different): ~ **to** estra-
neo(a) a, alieno(a) da; (of foreign country) stra-
niero(a), forestiero(a). **2** n (foreign) straniero/a,
forestiero/a; (extra-terrestrial) extraterrestre
m/f, alieno/a.
al-ien-ate ['eɪlɪəneɪt] vt alienare; **her behaviour
has ~d her friends** il suo comportamento ha
fatto allontanare gli amici.
al-iena-tion [,eɪlɪə'neɪʃən] n (estrangement) alienazione f; (of friend) allontanamento.
alight[1] [ə'laɪt] adj: **to be** ~ (building) essere in
fiamme; (fire) essere acceso(a).
alight[2] [ə'laɪt] vi (from vehicle): **to** ~ **(from)** scendere (da); (bird): **to** ~ **(on)** posarsi (su).
align [ə'laɪn] vt allineare; **to** ~ **o.s. with** allinearsi
con, schierarsi dalla parte di.
align-ment [ə'laɪnmənt] n (Tech, Pol) allineamento; **out of** ~ **(with)** non allineato (con); **a new** ~ **of
political forces** un nuovo schieramento delle
forze politiche.
alike [ə'laɪk] **1** adj pred simile, uguale; **to be** ~
assomigliarsi; **you're all** ~! siete tutti uguali! **2**
adv allo stesso modo; **winter and summer** ~ sia
d'estate che d'inverno.
ali-men-ta-ry [,ælɪ'mentərɪ] adj alimentare; ~
canal tubo digerente.
ali-mo-ny ['ælɪmənɪ] n (Law) alimenti mpl.
alive [ə'laɪv] adj (living) vivo(a), in vita, vivente;
(fig: lively) vivace, sveglio(a); **to stay** ~ sopravvivere; **he was buried** ~ è stato sepolto vivo; **it's
good to be** ~ esser vivi è una bella cosa; **he's the
best footballer** ~ è il miglior calciatore vivente
or esistente; **to keep a tradition** ~ mantener viva
or in vita una tradizione; **to come** ~ (fig) risve-
gliarsi, rianimarsi; **to be** ~ **with** (insects etc)
brulicare or pullulare di; ~ **to** (danger, honour)
conscio di.
al-ka-li ['ælkəlaɪ] n alcali m inv.
all [ɔ:l] **1** adj tutto(a); ~ **day** tutto il giorno; ~ **men**
tutti gli uomini; ~ **three** tutti e tre; ~ **three
books** tutti e tre i libri; ~ **the country** tutto il
paese; ~ **the books** tutti i libri; **for** ~ **their
efforts** nonostante tutti i loro sforzi.
2 pron **(a)** tutto(a); ~ **is lost** tutto è perduto;
he ate it ~ l'ha mangiato tutto; **is that** ~? non c'è
altro?; (in shop) basta così?; **if that's** ~ **then it's
not important** se è tutto lì allora non ha importanza; ~ **of it** tutto. **(b)** (pl) tutti(e); ~ **of the girls**
tutte le ragazze; ~ **of us** tutti c'eravamo noi; **we** ~
sat down ci sedemmo tutti quanti, noi tutti ci
sedemmo. **(c)** (in phrases): **above** ~ più di tutto;
after ~ dopotutto; **not at** ~ per niente, (niente)
affatto; (answer to thanks) prego!, s'immagini! si
figuri!; **I'm not at** ~ **tired** non sono affatto or per
niente stanco; ~ **in** ~ tutto sommato; **for** ~ **I
know** per quel che ne so io, per quanto ne so; **50
men in** ~ 50 uomini in tutto; **most of** ~ (more than
anybody) più di chiunque altro, soprattutto;
(more than anything) più di qualsiasi altra cosa,
soprattutto.
3 adv tutto; **dressed** ~ **in black** vestito tutto di
nero; **it's** ~ **dirty** è tutto sporco; **it's not as bad as**
~ **that** non è poi così cattivo; **things aren't** ~ **that
good/bad** le cose non vanno poi così bene/male;
~ **but** quasi; **the score is two** ~ il punteggio è di

due a due; **to be/feel ~ in** *(fam)* essere/sentirsi sfinito *or* distrutto; **to go ~ out** mettercela tutta; **he was going ~ out down the motorway** stava andando a tutto gas sull'autostrada.
4 *cpd*: **A~ Saints' Day** *n* Ognissanti *m inv; see* **over, right, alone** *etc*.

Allah ['ælə] *n* Allah *m*.

al·lay [ə'leɪ] *vt* dissipare.

al·le·ga·tion [,ælɪ'geɪʃən] *n* accusa *(ancora da provarsi)*, asserzione *f*.

al·lege [ə'ledʒ] *vt* asserire, dichiarare; **he is ~d to have said...** avrebbe detto che...; **the ~d crime** il presunto delitto.

al·le·giance [ə'liːdʒəns] *n* fedeltà, lealtà; **to swear ~ to** fare giuramento di fedeltà a.

al·le·go·ry ['ælɪgərɪ] *n* allegoria.

al·ler·gic [ə'lɜːdʒɪk] *adj*: **~ to** allergico(a) a.

al·ler·gy ['ælədʒɪ] *n* allergia.

al·le·vi·ate [ə'liːvɪeɪt] *vt* alleviare.

al·ley ['ælɪ] *n (between buildings)* vicolo; *(in garden, park)* vialetto; **blind ~** vicolo cieco.

al·li·ance [ə'laɪəns] *n (Pol)* alleanza.

al·li·ga·tor ['ælɪgeɪtər] *n* alligatore *m*.

all-important [,ɔːlɪm'pɔːtənt] *adj* cruciale, fondamentale.

all-in [,ɔːl'ɪn] *adj (price, charge)* tutto compreso *inv*; **I'll let you have them at an ~ price** te li farò avere a un prezzo forfettario; **~ wrestling** lotta libera.

al·lit·era·tion [ə,lɪtə'reɪʃən] *n* allitterazione *f*.

all-night [,ɔːl'naɪt] *adj (café, garage)* aperto(a) tutta la notte; *(vigil, party)* che dura *(or* è durato *etc)* tutta la notte.

al·lo·cate ['æləʊkeɪt] *vt (allot)*: **to ~ (to)** assegnare (a); *(: in budget: money)* stanziare (per); *(distribute)*: **to ~ (among)** ripartire (fra), distribuire (fra).

al·lot [ə'lɒt] *vt (task, share, time)*: **to ~ (to)** assegnare (a); **in the ~ted time** nel tempo fissato *or* prestabilito.

al·lot·ment [ə'lɒtmənt] *n (Brit: land)* piccolo lotto di terreno *(dato in affitto per coltivazioni ad uso familiare)*.

all-out [,ɔːl'aʊt] *adj (attack)* con tutti i mezzi a disposizione; **to make an ~ effort to do sth** impegnare tutte le proprie energie per fare qc.

al·low [ə'laʊ] *vt* **(a)** *(permit)*: **to ~ sb to do sth** permettere a qn di fare qc, autorizzare qn a fare qc; **smoking is not ~ed** è vietato fumare, non è permesso fumare; **he's not ~ed alcohol** gli hanno proibito l'alcool; **to ~ sb in/out** *etc* lasciare entrare/uscire *etc* qn; **~ me!** mi permetta!, se mi permette!, prego! **(b)** *(make provision for)* tener conto di, calcolare; **we must ~ 3 days for the journey** dobbiamo calcolare 3 giorni per il viaggio; **~ 5 cm for the hem** lasciare 5 cm in più per il bordo. **(c)** *(grant: money, rations)* concedere, accordare; *(Law: claim, appeal)* riconoscere, ammettere; *(Sport: goal)* convalidare.
♦ **allow for** *vi + prep* tener conto di, prendere in considerazione.

al·low·ance [ə'laʊəns] *n (payment)* assegno; *(for travelling, accommodation)* indennità *f inv*; *(ration)* razione *f*; *(Tax)* detrazione *f* d'imposta; *(discount)* riduzione *f*, sconto; **monthly clothing ~** cifra mensile per il vestiario; **family ~** assegni *mpl* familiari; **to make ~(s) for** *(person)* scusare; *(allow for: shrinkage etc)* tener conto di.

al·loy ['ælɔɪ] *n* lega.

all-rounder [,ɔːl'raʊndər] *n*: **to be a good ~** essere bravo(a) in tutto.

all·spice ['ɔːlspaɪs] *n* pepe *m* della Giamaica.

all-time ['ɔːl'taɪm] *adj (record)* senza precedenti.

al·lude [ə'luːd] *vi*: **to ~ to** alludere a, fare allusione a.

al·lus·ion [ə'luːʒən] *n* accenno, allusione *f*; *(Literature)* riferimento.

al·lu·vial [ə'luːvɪəl] *adj* alluvionale.

ally ['ælaɪ] **1** *n* alleato/a. **2** *vt*: **to ~ o.s. with** allearsi con.

al·ma·nac ['ɔːlmənæk] *n* almanacco.

al·mighty [ɔːl'maɪtɪ] **1** *adj* onnipotente; *(fam)* enorme, colossale. **2** *n*: **the A~** l'Onnipotente.

al·mond ['ɑːmənd] *n (nut)* mandorla; *(~ tree)* mandorlo.

al·most ['ɔːlməʊst] *adv* quasi; **he ~ fell** per poco non è caduto.

alms [ɑːmz] *n or npl* elemosina; **to give ~** fare l'elemosina.

aloft [ə'lɒft] *adv* in alto; *(Naut)* sull'alberatura.

alone [ə'ləʊn] *adj, adv* solo(a), da solo(a); **all ~** tutto(a) solo(a); **am I ~ in thinking so?** sono il solo a pensarla così?; **leave me ~!** lasciami in pace!, lasciami stare!; **to let** *or* **leave sth ~** *(object)* lasciar stare qc; *(business, scheme)* non immischiarsi in qc; **let ~...** figuriamoci poi..., tanto meno...; **he can't read, let ~ write** non sa leggere, figuriamoci scrivere; **you can't do it ~** non puoi farlo da solo; **the travel ~ cost £600** il viaggio da solo è costato 600 sterline.

along [ə'lɒŋ] **1** *adv*: **take it ~** prendilo con te; **come ~ with me** vieni con me; **are you coming ~?** vieni anche tu?; **move ~ there!** muovetevi, avanti!; *(said by policeman)* circolare!; **~ with the others** con gli altri, insieme agli altri; **I knew all ~** sapevo fin dall'inizio. **2** *prep* lungo; **to walk ~ the street** camminare lungo la strada; **the trees ~ the path** gli alberi lungo il sentiero; **~ here** per di qua; **somewhere ~ the way** *(also fig)* da qualche parte lungo la strada.

along·side [ə'lɒŋ'saɪd] **1** *adv (Naut)* sottobordo; **we brought our boat ~** *(of a pier/shore etc)* abbiamo accostato la barca (al molo/alla riva *etc)*. **2** *prep (along)* lungo; *(beside)* accanto a; **the railway runs ~ the beach** la ferrovia costeggia la spiaggia; **to come ~ the quay** accostare al molo.

aloof [ə'luːf] *adj* riservato(a), distante; **to stand ~ (from)** tenersi a distanza (da) *or* in disparte (da).

aloud [ə'laʊd] *adv* ad alta voce, a voce alta.

al·pha·bet ['ælfəbet] *n* alfabeto.

al·pha·beti·cal [,ælfə'betɪkəl] *adj* alfabetico(a); **in ~ order** in ordine alfabetico.

al·pine ['ælpaɪn] *adj (too)* alpino(a); *(plant, pasture)* alpestre; **~ hut** rifugio alpino.

Alps [ælps] *npl*: **the ~** le Alpi.

al·ready [ɔːl'redɪ] *adv* già.

Al·sa·tian [æl'seɪʃən] *n (Brit: dog)* pastore *m* tedesco, *(cane m)* lupo.

also ['ɔːlsəʊ] *adv* **(a)** *(too)* anche, pure; **her cousin ~ came** è venuto anche suo cugino. **(b)** *(moreover)* inoltre, anche; **~, I must explain...** **(e)** inoltre devo spiegare..., devo anche spiegare... .

also-ran ['ɔːlsəʊ,ræn] *n (Sport)* (cavallo) non piazzato; *(fam: person)* perdente *m/f*.

al·tar ['ɒltər] *n* altare *m*; **high ~** altar maggiore.

al·ter ['ɒltər] **1** *vt (gen)* modificare, cambiare; *(opinion)* far cambiare, mutare; *(Sewing)* fare una modifica *(or* delle modifiche) a; **to ~ one's opinion** cambiare opinione. **2** *vi* cambiare.

al·tera·tion [,ɒltə'reɪʃən] *n (act: see vb)* modifica, cambiamento; *(in appearance)* cambiamento, trasformazione *f*; **~s** *(Sewing, Archit)* modifiche *fpl*; **to make ~s in sth** apportare delle modifiche a qc; **timetable subject to ~** orario soggetto a variazioni.

al·ter·nate [ɒl'tɜːnɪt] **1** *adj (alternating: layers)* alternato(a); *(every other: days)* alterni(e), uno(a) sì e uno(a) no. **2** ['ɒltɜːneɪt] *vi:* **to ~ (with/between)** alternarsi (a/fra), avvicendarsi (a/fra). **3** *vt (crops)* alternare, avvicendare.

al·ter·nat·ing cur·rent ['ɒltəneɪtɪŋ'kʌrənt] *n* corrente *f* alternàta.

al·ter·na·tive [ɒl'tɜːnətɪv] **1** *adj* alternativo(a). **2** *n* alternativa; **you have no ~ but to go** non hai altra alternativa che andare; **there are several ~s** ci sono diverse alternative *or* possibilità; **there is no ~** non c'è altra alternativa *or* scelta.

al·ter·na·tive·ly [ɒl'tɜːnətɪvlɪ] *adv* come alternativa.

al·ter·na·tor ['ɒltɜːneɪtə^r] *n (Elec, Aut)* alternatore *m*.

al·though [ɔːl'ðəʊ] *conj* benché + *sub*, sebbene + *sub*.

al·ti·tude ['æltɪtjuːd] *n* altitudine *f*, altezza, quota; **at these ~s** a questa altezza; **to gain/lose ~** *(Aer)* prendere/perdere quota.

alto ['æltəʊ] *n (instrument)* contralto; *(male)* contraltino; *(female)* contralto.

al·to·geth·er [ˌɔːltə'geðə^r] *adv* **(a)** *(in all)* tutto sommato, in complesso, nell'insieme; **~ it was rather unpleasant** tutto sommato *or* in complesso è stato piuttosto spiacevole; **how much is that ~?** quant'è in tutto? **(b)** *(entirely)* del tutto, completamente; **I'm not ~ sure** non sono del tutto *or* proprio sicuro.

al·tru·ism ['æltrʊɪzəm] *n* altruismo.

alu·min·ium [ˌæljʊ'mɪnɪəm] *n*, *(Am)* **alu·mi·num** [ə'luːmɪnəm] *n* alluminio.

al·ways ['ɔːlweɪz] *adv* sempre; **as ~** come sempre; **you can ~ go by train** puoi sempre prendere il treno.

am [æm] *1st pers sg present of* be.

a.m. *abbr (= ante meridiem)* del mattino.

amal·gam·ate [ə'mælgəmeɪt] **1** *vt* amalgamare, fondere. **2** *vi* amalgamarsi, fondersi.

amass [ə'mæs] *vt* accumulare, ammassare.

ama·teur ['æmətə^r] **1** *n* dilettante *m/f*. **2** *adj (painter, player)* dilettante; *(activity)* dilettantistico(a), per dilettanti; **~ dramatics** filodrammatica.

ama·teur·ish ['æmətərɪʃ] *adj (pej)* dilettantesco(a).

amaze [ə'meɪz] *vt* stupire, sbalordire; **to be ~d (at)** essere sbalordito (da).

amaze·ment [ə'meɪzmənt] *n* stupore *m*, meraviglia; **to my ~...** con mia gran sorpresa...; **he looked at me in ~** mi guardò stupito.

amaz·ing [ə'meɪzɪŋ] *adj* sorprendente, sbalorditivo(a); *(bargain, offer)* sensazionale.

amaz·ing·ly [ə'meɪzɪŋlɪ] *adv* incredibilmente, sbalorditivamente.

am·bas·sa·dor [æm'bæsədə^r] *n* ambasciatore/trice.

am·ber ['æmbə^r] **1** *n* ambra. **2** *adj (colour)* ambra *inv*, ambrato(a); *(traffic light)* giallo(a).

am·bi·dex·trous [ˌæmbɪ'dekstrəs] *adj* ambidestro(a).

am·bi·gu·ity [ˌæmbɪ'gjʊɪtɪ] *n* ambiguità *f inv*.

am·bigu·ous [æm'bɪgjʊəs] *adj* ambiguo(a).

am·bi·tion [æm'bɪʃən] *n* ambizione *f*, aspirazione *f*; **he has no ~** non ha nessuna ambizione; **to achieve one's ~** realizzare le proprie aspirazioni *or* ambizioni.

am·bi·tious [æm'bɪʃəs] *adj* ambizioso(a); **to be ~ for one's children** avere delle ambizioni per i propri figli.

am·ble ['æmbl] *vi (person)* camminare senza fretta; **he ~d up to me** mi è venuto incontro senza fretta.

am·bu·lance ['æmbjʊləns] **1** *n* ambulanza, autoam-

bulanza. **2** *cpd:* **~ driver** *n* guidatore *m* d'ambulanza.

am·bush ['æmbʊʃ] **1** *n (attack)* imboscata, agguato; *(place)* agguato; **to lie in ~** stare in agguato; **to lie on ~ for sb** tendere un'imboscata qn. **2** *vt* fare un'imboscata a.

ame·ba [ə'miːbə] *n (Am)* = **amoeba.**

amen ['ɑː'men] *excl* così sia, amen.

ame·nable [ə'miːnəbl] *adj* conciliante; **~ to flattery** sensibile all'adulazione; **~ to reason** ragionevole.

amend [ə'mend] *vt (law etc)* emendare.

amend·ment [ə'mendmənt] *n* emendamento.

amends [ə'mendz] *npl:* **to make ~ (to sb) for sth** *(apologize)* farsi perdonare (da qn) per qc; *(compensate)* risarcire *or* indennizzare (qn) per qc.

amen·ity [ə'miːnɪtɪ] *n (gen)* amenità, piacevolezza; *(pleasant thing: usu pl):* **amenities** attrezzature *fpl* ricreative e culturali; **a house with all amenities** una casa con tutte le comodità.

Ameri·ca [ə'merɪkə] *n* America.

Ameri·can [ə'merɪkən] *adj*, *n* americano(a) *(m/f)*.

ameri·can·ize [ə'merɪkənaɪz] *vt* americanizzare.

am·ethyst ['æmɪθɪst] *n* ametista.

ami·able ['eɪmɪəbl] *adj* affabile.

ami·cable ['æmɪkəbl] *adj* amichevole.

amid(st) [ə'mɪd(st)] *prep (frm, poet)* in mezzo a, tra.

amiss [ə'mɪs] *adj*, *adv:* **there's something ~** c'è qualcosa che non va; **don't take it ~, will you?** non te la prenderai (a male), spero.

am·mo·nia [ə'məʊnɪə] *n* ammoniaca.

am·mu·ni·tion [ˌæmjʊ'nɪʃən] **1** *n* munizioni *fpl*; *(fig)* arma. **2** *cpd:* **~ dump** *n* deposito di munizioni.

am·ne·sia [æm'niːzɪə] *n* amnesia.

am·nes·ty ['æmnɪstɪ] *n* amnistia; **to grant an ~ to** concedere l'amnistia a, amnistiare.

amoe·ba [ə'miːbə] *n* ameba.

amok [ə'mɒk] *adv* = **amuck.**

among(st) [ə'mʌŋ(st)] *prep* tra, in mezzo a; **he is ~ those who...** fa parte di quelli che..., è uno di quelli che...; **share it ~ yourselves** dividetevelo tra (di) voi.

amor·al [eɪ'mɒrəl] *adj* amorale.

amo·rous ['æmərəs] *adj* amoroso(a); *(stronger)* appassionato(a).

amor·phous [ə'mɔːfəs] *adj* amorfo(a).

amount [ə'maʊnt] *n (sum of money)* somma, cifra; *(of invoice, bill etc)* importo; *(quantity)* quantità *f inv*; **in small ~s** poco per volta; **the total ~** *(of money)* l'importo totale; *(of things)* la quantità totale; **he has any ~ of time/money** ha tutto il tempo/tutti i soldi che vuole.

♦ **amount to** *vi* + *prep* ammontare a; *(fig)* equivalere a, non essere altro che; **this ~s to a refusal** questo equivale a un rifiuto; **he'll never ~ to much** non conterà mai nulla.

amp [æmp] *n*, **am·père** ['æmpeə^r] *n* ampère *m inv*; **a 13 ~ plug** una spina con fusibile da 13 ampère.

am·phib·ian [æm'fɪbɪən] *n (Bio, vehicle)* anfibio.

am·phibi·ous [æm'fɪbɪəs] *adj* anfibio(a).

am·phi·thea·tre, *(Am)* **am·phi·thea·ter** ['æmfɪˌθɪətə^r] *n* anfiteatro.

am·ple ['æmpl] *adj* (-er, -est) **(a)** *(large: boot of car, garment)* ampio(a). **(b)** *(more than enough: money)* in abbondanza; *(: space, means, resources)* abbondante, ampio(a); **we have ~ reason to believe that...** abbiamo abbondanti ragioni per credere che...; **we have ~ time to finish it** abbiamo tutto il tempo (necessario) per finirlo; **that should be ~** *(time, money etc)* dovrebbe essere più che sufficiente.

am·pli·fi·er ['æmplɪfaɪə^r] *n* amplificatore *m*.

am·pli·fy ['æmplɪfaɪ] vt (sound) amplificare; (statement etc) ampliare.

am·ply ['æmplɪ] adv ampiamente.

am·pu·tate ['æmpjʊteɪt] vt amputare.

am·pu·ta·tion [,æmpjʊ'teɪʃən] n amputazione f.

amuck [ə'mʌk] adv: **to run** ~ essere in preda a furia or furore omicida, scatenarsi.

amuse [ə'mjuːz] vt (cause mirth) divertire, far ridere; (entertain) (far) divertire; **to be** ~**d** at essere divertito da; **to** ~ **o.s. with sth/by doing sth** divertirsi con qc/a fare qc; **run along and** ~ **yourselves** andate a divertirvi.

amuse·ment [ə'mjuːzmənt] **1** n **(a)** divertimento; **much to my** ~ con mio grande spasso; **a look of** ~ un'aria divertita. **(b)** (entertainment) divertimento, svago; **they do it for** ~ **only** lo fanno solo per divertirsi or per svago. **2** cpd: ~ **arcade** n sala giochi (solo con macchinette a gettoni); ~ **park** n luna park m inv.

amus·ing [ə'mjuːzɪŋ] adj divertente.

an [æn, ən, n] indef art see **a**.

anach·ro·nism [ə'nækrənɪzəm] n anacronismo.

anaemia [ə'niːmɪə] n anemia.

anaemic [ə'niːmɪk] adj anemico(a).

an·aes·thet·ic [,ænɪs'θetɪk] n anestetico; **under** ~ sotto anestesia; **local/general** ~ anestesia locale/totale.

anaes·the·tist [æ'niːsθɪtɪst] n anestetista m/f.

ana·gram ['ænəgræm] n anagramma m.

ana·log, ana·logue ['ænəlɒg] **1** n cosa analoga. **2** cpd: ~ **computer** n calcolatore m analogico.

analo·gous [ə'næləgəs] adj: ~ **(to, with)** analogo(a) (a), affine (a).

anal·ogy [ə'nælədʒɪ] n analogia; **to draw an** ~ **between** fare un'analogia tra.

ana·lyse ['ænəlaɪz] vt analizzare, fare l'analisi di.

analy·sis [ə'næləsɪs] n, pl **analyses** [ə'nælɪsiːz] analisi f inv; (Psych) psicanalisi f inv; **in the last** ~ in ultima analisi.

ana·lyst ['ænəlɪst] n analista m/f; (also: **psycho**~) psicanalista m/f.

ana·lyt·ic(al) [,ænə'lɪtɪk(əl)] adj analitico(a).

ana·lyze ['ænəlaɪz] vt (Am) = **analyse**.

an·ar·chist ['ænəkɪst] n anarchico/a.

an·ar·chy ['ænəkɪ] n anarchia.

anath·ema [ə'næθɪmə] n (Rel) anatema m; **it was** ~ **to him** non ne voleva neanche sentir parlare.

anato·my [ə'nætəmɪ] n anatomia.

an·ces·tor ['ænsɪstə'] n antenato/a, avo/a.

an·ces·tral [æn'sestrəl] adj ancestrale, atavico(a); ~ **home** casa avita.

an·ces·try ['ænsɪstrɪ] n stirpe f, lignaggio.

an·chor ['æŋkə'] **1** n ancora; (fig) ancora di salvezza; **to drop** ~ gettare l'ancora. **2** vt (also fig) ancorare. **3** vi ancorarsi.

an·cho·vy ['æntʃəvɪ] n acciuga, alice f.

an·cient ['eɪnʃənt] adj (old, classical) antico(a); (fam: person) decrepito(a); (: object) vecchio(a) come il cucco; ~ **monument** monumento storico; ~ **Rome** l'antica Roma.

and [ænd, ənd, nd, ən] conj e (often ed before vowel); **one** ~ **a half** uno e mezzo; **three hundred** ~ **ten** trecentodieci; **richer** ~ **richer** sempre più ricco; **without shoes** ~ **socks** senza scarpe né calze; **there are lawyers** ~ **lawyers!** ci sono avvocati e avvocati!; **he talked** ~ **talked** (e) parlava (e) parlava; **try** ~ **do it** prova a farlo; **wait** ~ **see** aspetta e vedrai.

An·des ['ændiːz] npl: **the** ~ le Ande.

an·ec·dote ['ænɪkdəʊt] n aneddoto.

anemia [ə'niːmɪə] etc = **anaemia** etc.

anemo·ne [ə'nemənɪ] n (Bot) anemone m; (sea ~) anemone m di mare, attinia.

an·es·thet·ic [,ænɪs'θetɪk] etc = **anaesthetic** etc.

anew [ə'njuː] adv (poet) di nuovo; **to begin** ~ ricominciare.

an·gel ['eɪndʒəl] n angelo; **be an** ~ **and fetch my gloves** se mi vai a prendere i guanti sei proprio un angelo.

an·gel·ic [æn'dʒelɪk] adj angelico(a).

an·ger ['æŋgə'] **1** n rabbia, collera; **red with** ~ rosso per or dalla rabbia; **in** ~ nell'impeto della collera. **2** vt far arrabbiare; **he is easily** ~**ed** si arrabbia facilmente.

an·gi·na (pec·to·ris) [æn'dʒaɪnə ('pektərɪs)] n (Med) angina pectoris.

an·gle¹ ['æŋgl] n (Math) angolo; (fig) punto di vista; **right** ~ angolo retto; **at right** ~**s to** ad angolo retto con, perpendicolare a; **at an** ~ **of 80°** a un angolo di 80°; **at an** ~ di sbieco; **to cut sth at an** ~ tagliare qc di traverso; **to look at sth from a different** ~ (fig) considerare qc da un altro punto di vista or sotto un altro aspetto.

an·gle² ['æŋgl] vi (for fish) pescare (con l'amo); **to** ~ **for** (fig) cercare di avere.

an·gler ['æŋglə'] n pescatore m (con la lenza).

An·gli·can ['æŋglɪkən] adj anglicano(a).

an·gli·cize ['æŋglɪsaɪz] vt anglicizzare.

an·gling ['æŋglɪŋ] n pesca (con la lenza).

Anglo- ['æŋgləʊ] pref anglo-; ~**Italian** italobritannico(a).

an·gri·ly ['æŋgrɪlɪ] adv con rabbia.

an·gry ['æŋgrɪ] adj (-ier, -iest) (gen) arrabbiato(a); (annoyed) irritato(a); (wound) infiammato(a); (sky) minaccioso(a); **to be** ~ **with sb/about, at sth** essere arrabbiato or in collera con qn/per qc; **to get** ~ arrabbiarsi; **to make sb** ~ far arrabbiare qn; **you won't be** ~, **will you?** non ti arrabbi però?; **he was** ~ **at being treated so badly** era arrabbiato perché lo avevano trattato così male.

an·guish ['æŋgwɪʃ] n angoscia.

an·gu·lar ['æŋgjʊlə'] adj angoloso(a), spigoloso(a); (measurement etc) angolare.

ani·mal ['ænɪməl] **1** adj animale. **2** n animale m; (pej: person) bestia, bruto.

ani·mate ['ænɪmɪt] **1** adj (animal, plants) vivente; (capable of movement) animato(a). **2** ['ænɪmeɪt] vt animare.

ani·mat·ed ['ænɪmeɪtɪd] adj animato(a); **to become** ~ animarsi; ~ **cartoon** cartone m animato.

ani·ma·tion [,ænɪ'meɪʃən] n animazione f.

ani·mos·ity [,ænɪ'mɒsɪtɪ] n animosità f inv.

ani·seed ['ænɪsiːd] n semi mpl di anice.

an·kle ['æŋkl] **1** n caviglia. **2** cpd: ~ **socks** npl calzini mpl.

an·nals ['ænəlz] npl annali mpl.

an·nex [ə'neks] vt (territory): **to** ~ **(to)** annettere (a).

an·nex(e) ['æneks] n (edificio) annesso.

an·ni·hi·late [ə'naɪəleɪt] vt annientare, annichilire; (argument) demolire.

an·ni·ver·sa·ry [,ænɪ'vɜːsərɪ] n anniversario.

an·no·tate ['ænəʊteɪt] vt annotare.

an·nounce [ə'naʊns] vt (gen) annunciare; **to** ~ **the marriage/death of sb** partecipare le nozze/il lutto di qn; **he** ~**d that he wasn't going to** ha dichiarato che non (ci) sarebbe andato.

an·nounce·ment [ə'naʊnsmənt] n (declaration) comunicazione f, annuncio; (official, through media) comunicato; (private: in newspaper) annuncio; **I'd like to make an** ~ ho una comunicazione da fare.

an·nounc·er [ə'naʊnsə'] n (Radio, TV: reading news etc) annunciatore/trice; (: introducing people) presentatore/trice.

an·noy [ə'nɔɪ] vt dare fastidio a, infastidire, dare

noia a; **to be ~ed about sth** essere seccato per qc, essere contrariato *or* irritato da qc; **to be ~ed (at sth/with sb)** essere seccato *or* irritato (per qc/ con qn); **he's just trying to ~ you** sta solo cercando di stuzzicarti.

an·noy·ance [ə'nɔɪəns] *n (state)* fastidio, irritazione *f*; *(cause of ~)* seccatura, noia; **to her ~** con suo gran dispetto.

an·noy·ing [ə'nɔɪɪŋ] *adj (person, habit, noise)* irritante, seccante; **it's ~ to have to wait** è (una cosa) seccante dover aspettare.

an·nual ['ænjʊəl] **1** *adj (income)* annuo(a); *(event, plant)* annuale; **~ general meeting** *(abbr* **AGM)** assemblea generale. **2** *n (book)* pubblicazione *f* annuale, annuario; *(children's comic book)* almanacco; *(Bot)* pianta annuale.

an·nu·ity [ə'nju:ɪtɪ] *n* annualità *f inv*, rendita annuale; *(for life)* vitalizio.

an·nul [ə'nʌl] *vt* annullare.

an·nul·ment [ə'nʌlmənt] *n* annullamento.

An·nun·cia·tion [ə,nʌnsɪ'eɪʃən] *n* Annunciazione *f*.

an·ode ['ænəʊd] *n* anodo.

anoint [ə'nɔɪnt] *vt (Rel)* ungere; **to ~ sb king** consacrare qn re.

anoma·lous [ə'nɒmələs] *adj* anomalo(a).

anoma·ly [ə'nɒməlɪ] *n* anomalia.

ano·nym·ity [,ænə'nɪmɪtɪ] *n* anonimato.

anony·mous [ə'nɒnɪməs] *adj* anonimo(a); **to remain ~** mantenere l'anonimato.

ano·rak ['ænəræk] *n* giacca a vento (con cappuccio).

ano·rexia [ænə'rɛksɪə] *n* anoressia.

an·oth·er [ə'nʌðə^r] **1** *adj (additional)* un altro(un'altra), ancora un(a); *(different)* un altro(un'altra); *(second)* un altro(un'altra), un(a) secondo(a); **~ 10 coffees** ancora 10 caffè, altri 10 caffè; **~ drink?** ancora qualcosa da bere?; **in ~ 5 years** fra altri 5 anni; **without ~ word** senza aggiungere una sola *or* nemmeno una parola; **that's quite ~ matter** è tutt'un'altra cosa; **he's ~ Shakespeare** è un nuovo *or* altro Shakespeare. **2** *pron* un altro(un'altra); **from one town to ~** da una città all'altra; **they love one ~** si vogliono bene.

an·swer ['ɑ:nsə^r] **1** *n* **(a)** *(reply)* risposta; **in ~ to your question** in risposta *or* per rispondere alla tua domanda; **to know all the ~s** *(fig)* saper tutto, saperla lunga. **(b)** *(solution)* soluzione *f*; *(Math etc)* soluzione, risposta; **there is no easy ~** non è un problema facile da risolvere. **2** *vt* **(a)** *(reply to)* rispondere a; **our prayers have been ~ed** le nostre preghiere sono state esaudite; **to ~ the door** andare ad aprire (la porta). **(b)** *(fulfil: needs)* rispondere a, soddisfare; *(: expectations)* corrispondere a, rispondere a; *(: purpose)* servire a, rispondere a. **3** *vi* rispondere.

♦ **answer back** *vi + adv*: **to ~ (sb) back** rispondere male (a qn).

♦ **answer for** *vi + prep (sb's safety)* rispondere di; *(truth of sth)* garantire; **he's got a lot to ~ for** ci sono molte cose di cui deve render conto.

♦ **answer to** *vi + prep (name, description)* rispondere a.

an·swer·able ['ɑ:nsərəbl] *adj* **(a)** *(responsible)* responsabile; **to be ~ to sb for sth** dover rispondere *or* render conto a qn di qc. **(b)** *(question)* (a) cui si può rispondere.

an·swer·ing ['ɑ:nsərɪŋ] *adj*: **~ machine** *n* segreteria (telefonica) automatica; **~ service** *n* servizio di segreteria (telefonica) automatica.

ant [ænt] *n* formica.

an·tago·nism [æn'tægənɪzəm] *n* antagonismo.

an·tago·nist [æn'tægənɪst] *n* antagonista *m/f*.

an·tago·nize [æn'tægənaɪz] *vt* provocare l'ostilità di, inimicarsi; **I don't want to ~ her** non voglio inimicarmene.

Ant·arc·tic [ænt'ɑ:ktɪk] **1** *adj* antartico(a); **the ~ Circle** il circolo polare antartico; **the ~ Ocean** l'Oceano antartico. **2** *n*: **the ~** l'Antartico.

Ant·arc·ti·ca [ænt'ɑ:ktɪkə] *n* Antartide *f*.

ante... ['æntɪ] *pref* anti..., ante..., pre...; **~chamber** *n* anticamera.

ant·eater ['ænt,i:tə^r] *n (Zool)* formichiere *m*.

ante·ced·ent [,æntɪ'si:dənt] *n* antecedente *m*, precedente *m*; **~s** *(past history)* antecedenti, precedenti; *(ancestors)* antenati *mpl*.

ante·date ['æntɪ'deɪt] *vt* **(a)** *(precede)* precedere. **(b)** *(cheque etc)* retrodatare.

ante·lope ['æntɪləʊp] *n* antilope *f*.

ante·na·tal ['æntɪ'neɪtl] *adj* prenatale; **~ clinic** clinica ostetrica *(per assistenza preparto)*.

an·ten·na [æn'tenə] *n, pl* **antennae** [æn'tɛni:] antenna.

ante·room ['æntɪrʊm] *n* anticamera.

an·them ['ænθəm] *n* inno.

an·thol·ogy [æn'θɒlədʒɪ] *n* antologia.

an·thra·cite ['ænθrəsaɪt] *n* antracite *f*.

an·thro·poid ['ænθrəʊpɔɪd] *adj* antropoide.

an·thro·polo·gist [,ænθrə'pɒlədʒɪst] *n* antropologo/a.

an·thro·pol·ogy [,ænθrə'pɒlədʒɪ] *n* antropologia.

anti... ['æntɪ] *pref* anti...; **he's ~ everything** è un bastian contrario.

anti·aircraft ['æntɪ'ɛəkrɑ:ft] *adj (gun)* contraereo(a), antiaereo(a).

anti·bi·ot·ic ['æntɪbaɪ'ɒtɪk] *n* antibiotico.

anti·body ['æntɪ,bɒdɪ] *n* anticorpo.

an·tici·pate [æn'tɪsɪpeɪt] *vt* **(a)** *(expect: trouble)* prevedere, aspettarsi; *(: pleasure)* pregustare, assaporare in anticipo; **this is worse than I ~d** è peggio di quel che immaginavo *or* pensavo; **to ~ that...** prevedere che...; **I ~ seeing him tomorrow** presumo *or* mi immagino che lo vedrò domani; **as ~d** come previsto. **(b)** *(forestall: person)* prevenire, precedere; *(foresee: event)* prevedere; *(: question, objection, wishes)* prevenire.

an·tici·pa·tion [æn,tɪsɪ'peɪʃən] *n (expectation)*: **in ~ (of)** in previsione *or* attesa (di); *(excitement)*: **we waited in great ~** abbiamo aspettato con grande impazienza; **in ~ of a fine week** pregustando una bella settimana; **thanking you in ~** ringraziandola anticipatamente.

anti·cli·max ['æntɪ'klaɪmæks] *n* delusione *f*; **the game came as an ~** la partita si rivelò una delusione.

anti·clock·wise ['æntɪ'klɒkwaɪz] *adv* in senso antiorario.

an·tics ['æntɪks] *npl (of clown etc)* lazzi *mpl*, buffonerie *fpl*; *(of child, animal etc)* buffe acrobazie *fpl*; *(pej)* scherzetto.

anti·cy·clone ['æntɪ'saɪkləʊn] *n* anticiclone *m*.

anti·dote ['æntɪdəʊt] *n* antidoto.

anti·freeze ['æntɪ'fri:z] *n* antigelo, anticongelante *m*.

anti·his·ta·mine [,æntɪ'hɪstəmɪn] *n* antistaminico.

an·tipa·thy [æn'tɪpəθɪ] *n* antipatia.

an·tipo·des [æn'tɪpədi:z] *npl*: **the ~** gli antipodi.

anti·quat·ed ['æntɪkweɪtɪd] *adj (pej)* antiquato(a), sorpassato(a).

an·tique [æn'ti:k] **1** *adj (furniture etc)* antico(a), d'epoca. **2** *n* oggetto antico, pezzo d'antiquariato; **he deals in ~s** commercia in antiquariato; **'~s'** *(sign)* 'antichità'. **3** *cpd*: **~ dealer** *n* antiquario/a; **~ shop** *n* bottega *or* negozio di antiquario.

an·tiq·uity [æn'tɪkwɪtɪ] n antichità f; **of great ~** molto antico.

anti-semitic ['æntɪsɪ'mɪtɪk] adj antisemitico(a), antisemita.

anti-semitism ['æntɪ'sɛmɪtɪzəm] n antisemitismo.

anti·sep·tic [ˌæntɪ'sɛptɪk] **1** adj antisettico(a). **2** n antisettico.

anti·so·cial ['æntɪ'səʊʃəl] adj (behaviour, tendency) antisociale; (unsociable) scorbutico(a), asociale.

an·tith·esis [æn'tɪθɪsɪs] n, pl antitheses [æn'tɪθɪsiːz] antitesi f inv; (contrast) carattere m antitetico.

ant·ler ['æntlə'] n palco; **~s** corna fpl.

an·to·nym ['æntənɪm] n contrario, antonimo.

anus ['eɪnəs] n ano.

an·vil ['ænvɪl] n incudine f.

anxi·ety [æŋ'zaɪətɪ] n (a) ansia, ansietà; **I have no anxieties about them** non sono in ansia per loro; **it is a great ~ to me** è una grossa preoccupazione per me. (b) (eagerness): **~ (to do sth)** smania (di fare qc); **in his ~ to be gone he forgot his case** nella furia or fretta di andarsene si è dimenticato la borsa.

anx·ious ['æŋkʃəs] adj (a) (worried) preoccupato(a), in ansia, inquieto(a); **I'm very ~ about you** sono molto preoccupato or in pensiero per te; **with an ~ glance** con uno sguardo pieno d'ansia. (b) (causing worry: moment) angoscioso(a). (c) (eager): **~ for sth/to do sth** impaziente di qc/di fare qc; **I am ~ that he should do it** ci tengo moltissimo che lo faccia; **he is ~ for success** ha un grande desiderio di successo; **I'm not very ~ to go** ho poca voglia di andarci.

anx·ious·ly ['æŋkʃəslɪ] adv ansiosamente, con ansia.

any ['ɛnɪ] **1** adj (a) (in questions etc): **is there ~ meat?** c'è (della) carne?; **are there ~ others?** ce ne sono (degli) altri?; **have you ~ money?** hai (dei) soldi?, hai qualche soldo?; **if there are ~ tickets left** se ci sono ancora (dei) biglietti, se c'è ancora qualche biglietto.

(b) (with negative): **I haven't ~ money/bread/work** non ho soldi/pane/lavoro, sono senza soldi/pane/lavoro; **I don't see ~ cows** non vedo alcuna or nessuna mucca, non vedo mucche; **without ~ difficulty** senza (nessuna or alcuna) difficoltà.

(c) (no matter which) uno(a) qualsiasi, uno(a) qualunque; (every) ogni inv; **~ excuse will do** (una) qualunque or qualsiasi scusa andrà bene, una scusa qualunque or qualsiasi andrà bene; **wear ~ hat (you like)** mettiti un cappello qualsiasi or qualunque; **~ farmer will tell you** qualunque or qualsiasi agricoltore te lo dirà, ogni agricoltore te lo dirà.

2 pron (a) (negative, question etc): **are there ~?** ce ne sono?; **are ~ of them coming?** viene qualcuno di loro?; **there aren't ~ left** non ce ne sono più; (emphatic) **there isn't ~ left** non è rimasto nemmeno uno; **I haven't ~ (of them)** non ne ho.

(b): **take ~ of those books (you like)** prendi qualsiasi libro; **few, if ~** pochi, sempre che ce ne siano.

3 adv: **are you feeling ~ better?** ti senti un po' meglio?; **do you want ~ more tea?** vuoi ancora un po' di tè?, vuoi ancora del tè?; **I can't hear him ~ more** non lo sento più; **don't wait ~ longer** non aspettare più.

any·body ['ɛnɪbɒdɪ] pron (a) (in questions) qualcuno, nessuno; **did you see ~?** hai visto qualcuno? or nessuno? (b) (negative) nessuno; **I can't see ~** non vedo nessuno; **without ~ seeing him** senza che nessuno lo vedesse, senza esser visto da nessuno. (c) (no matter who) chiunque; **~ will tell you the same** chiunque ti dirà la stessa cosa;

~ else would have laughed chiunque altro avrebbe riso; **she's not going to marry just ~** non sposerà il primo che le capita or uno qualunque.

any·how ['ɛnɪhaʊ] adv (a) (at any rate) ad or in ogni modo, comunque; **I shall go ~** ci andrò lo stesso or comunque. (b) (haphazard) come capita; **do it ~ you like** fallo come ti pare; **I finished it ~** in qualche modo l'ho finito; **he leaves things just ~** lascia tutto come (gli) capita.

any·one ['ɛnɪwʌn] pron = anybody.

any·place ['ɛnɪpleɪs] pron (Am fam) = anywhere.

any·thing ['ɛnɪθɪŋ] pron (a) (in questions, negative etc) niente, qualcosa; **are you doing ~ tonight?** fai qualcosa stasera?; **~ else?** basta (così)?, nient'altro?, altro?; **is there ~ else you want to tell me?** hai qualcos'altro or nient'altro da dirmi?; **it wasn't ~ serious** non era niente di serio; **I saw hardly ~** non ho visto quasi niente; **can't ~ be done?** (non) si può fare qualcosa? or niente?; **it can cost ~ between £15 and £20** può costare qualcosa come 15 o 20 sterline. (b) (no matter what) qualsiasi cosa, qualunque cosa; **you can say ~ you like** puoi dire quello che vuoi; **~ but that** tutto tranne questo; **they'll eat ~** mangiano qualsiasi cosa or di tutto.

any·way ['ɛnɪweɪ] adv = anyhow (a).

any·where ['ɛnɪweə'] adv (a) (in questions) da qualche parte, in qualche posto; **do you see him ~?** lo vedi da qualche parte?; **~ else?** da qualche or nessun'altra parte?, in qualche or nessun altro posto? (b) (negative) da nessuna parte, in nessun posto; **they never go ~ else** non vanno mai da nessun'altra parte. (c) (no matter where) da qualsiasi or qualunque parte, in qualunque or qualsiasi posto, dovunque, **~ in the world** dovunque nel mondo; **put the books down ~** metti i libri dove ti capita.

aor·ta [eɪ'ɔːtə] n aorta.

apart [ə'pɑːt] adv (a) (in pieces) a pezzi; **to fall ~** cadere a pezzi, sfasciarsi; **to take sth ~** smontare qc. (b) (separated) a distanza; **we live 3 miles ~** abitiamo a 3 miglia di distanza (l'uno dall'altro); **their birthdays are two days ~** i loro compleanni sono a distanza di due giorni l'uno dall'altro; **he stood ~ from the others** se ne stava or rimase in disparte; **to live ~** vivere separati; **he lives ~ from his wife** vive separato da sua moglie; **I can't tell them ~** non li distinguo l'uno dall'altro; **joking ~** scherzi a parte, a parte gli scherzi; **these problems ~** a parte questi problemi; **~ from a parte;** **~ from the fact that a** parte il fatto che.

apart·heid [ə'pɑːteɪt] n apartheid f.

apart·ment [ə'pɑːtmənt] **1** n (Am: flat) appartamento; (Brit: room) sala. **2** cpd: **~ house** n (Am) stabile m, caseggiato.

apa·thet·ic [ˌæpə'θɛtɪk] adj apatico(a), indifferente.

apa·thy ['æpəθɪ] n apatia, indifferenza.

ape [eɪp] **1** n (esp anthropoid) scimmia. **2** vt scimmiottare.

Ap·en·nines ['æpənaɪnz] npl Appennini mpl.

ape·ri·tif [ə'pɛrɪtɪv] n aperitivo.

ap·er·ture ['æpətʃjʊə'] n fessura; (Phot) apertura.

apex ['eɪpɛks] n (Geom) vertice m; (fig) vertice, apice m.

apho·rism ['æfərɪzəm] n aforisma.

aph·ro·dis·i·ac [ˌæfrəʊ'dɪzɪæk] n afrodisiaco.

apiece [ə'piːs] adv ciascuno(a); **he gave them £1 ~** ha dato loro una sterlina (per) ciascuno; **these pens sell at 10p ~** queste penne si vendono a 10 pence ciascuna.

aplomb [ə'plɒm] n disinvoltura; **with great ~** senza scomporsi.

Apoca·lypse [ə'pɒkəlɪps] n Apocalisse f.

Apoc·ry·pha [ə'pɒkrɪfə] npl libri mpl apocrifi.

apoc·ry·phal [ə'pɒkrɪfəl] adj apocrifo(a).

apo·liti·cal [ˌeɪpə'lɪtɪkəl] adj apolitico(a).

apolo·get·ic [əˌpɒlə'dʒɛtɪk] adj (look, remark) di scusa; **he was very ~ about it/for not coming** si è scusato moltissimo di ciò/per or di non essere venuto.

apolo·geti·cal·ly [əˌpɒlə'dʒɛtɪkəlɪ] adv per scusarsi.

apolo·gize [ə'pɒlədʒaɪz] vi: **to ~ (to sb for sth)** scusarsi (con qn per or di qc), chiedere scusa (a qn per or di qc); **they ~d for being late** si sono scusati per il ritardo; **there's no need to ~** non è il caso di scusarsi.

apol·ogy [ə'pɒlədʒɪ] n scuse fpl; **I demand an ~** esigo delle scuse; **please accept my apologies** la prego di accettare le mie scuse; **an ~ for a stew** (pej) un tentativo mal riuscito di stufato.

apo·plec·tic [ˌæpə'plɛktɪk] adj (Med) apoplettico(a); (fam): **~ with rage** livido(a) per la rabbia.

apo·plexy ['æpəplɛksɪ] n apoplessia.

apos·tle [ə'pɒsl] n apostolo.

ap·os·tol·ic [ˌæpəs'tɒlɪk] adj apostolico(a).

apos·tro·phe [ə'pɒstrəfɪ] n (Gram: sign) apostrofo.

ap·pal [ə'pɔːl] vt sconvolgere, sgomentare.

ap·pal·ling [ə'pɔːlɪŋ] adj (ignorance, conditions, destruction) spaventoso(a), impressionante; (fam: film, taste etc) pessimo(a), spaventoso(a); **she's an ~ cook** è un disastro come cuoca.

ap·pa·rat·us [ˌæpə'reɪtəs] n (for heating etc) impianto; (for filming, camping, in gym) attrezzatura; (Anat) apparato; (system) sistema m.

ap·par·ent [ə'pærənt] adj (seeming) apparente; (clear) evidente, ovvio(a); **to become ~** manifestarsi, rivelarsi; **it is ~ that** è evidente che.

ap·par·ent·ly [ə'pærəntlɪ] adv a quanto pare.

ap·pa·ri·tion [ˌæpə'rɪʃən] n fantasma m.

ap·peal [ə'piːl] **1** n (a) (call) appello; **an ~ for funds** una richiesta di aiuti economici or di fondi; **he made an ~ for calm** ha fatto appello alla calma. (b) (Law) appello, ricorso (legale); **right of ~** diritto d'appello. (c) (attraction) attrattiva, fascino; **a book of general ~** un libro di interesse generale.

2 vi (a) (call, beg): **to ~ (to sb)** implorare (qn); supplicare (qn); **he ~ed for silence** ha invitato al silenzio; **he ~ed to them for help** si è rivolto a loro per un aiuto; **she ~ed to her attacker for mercy** ha supplicato il suo assalitore di avere pietà; **to ~ for funds** lanciare un appello per ottenere dei fondi. (b) (Law): **to ~ (against sth/to sb)** appellarsi (contro qc/presso qn), ricorrere in appello (contro qc/presso qn). (c) (attract) attirare, attrarre; **it ~s to the imagination** stimola la fantasia.

ap·peal·ing [ə'piːlɪŋ] adj (moving) commovente; (attractive) attraente.

ap·pear [ə'pɪəʳ] vi (a) (gen) apparire, comparire; (ghost) apparire; **he ~ed from nowhere** è saltato fuori all'improvviso. (b) (in public) esibirsi; (Theatre) recitare; (book etc) uscire; **to ~ on TV** apparire in televisione. (c) (Law) comparire, presentarsi; **who is ~ing for the defendant?** chi è l'avvocato difensore? (d) (seem) sembrare, parere; **she ~s to want to leave** sembra che voglia andarsene; **the house ~s to be empty** la casa sembra vuota; **he ~s tired** sembra stanco, ha l'aria stanca; **it ~s that...** a quanto pare...; **so it would ~** pare proprio di sì, così pare.

ap·pear·ance [ə'pɪərəns] n (a) (act) apparizione f; (Theatre) comparsa, apparizione; (of book etc) uscita, pubblicazione f; **in order of ~** in ordine di apparizione; **to make one's first ~** fare il proprio debutto, debuttare; **to put in an ~** fare atto di presenza. (b) (look) aspetto; **in ~ a vedersi; he was rather sickly in ~** aveva un aspetto malaticcio or un'aria malaticcia; **~s can be deceptive** non bisogna fidarsi delle apparenze, le apparenze ingannano; **to all ~s** a giudicar dalle apparenze; **to keep up ~s** salvare le apparenze.

ap·pease [ə'piːz] vt (pacify) placare; (satisfy: hunger, curiosity) appagare, soddisfare.

ap·pease·ment [ə'piːzmənt] n (Pol) appeasement m.

ap·pend [ə'pɛnd] vt (frm: add: signature) apporre; (: attach) allegare.

ap·pend·age [ə'pɛndɪdʒ] n appendice f.

ap·pen·di·ci·tis [əˌpɛndɪ'saɪtɪs] n appendicite f.

ap·pen·dix [ə'pɛndɪks] n, pl **appendices** [ə'pɛndɪsiːz] (a) (Anat) appendice f; **to have one's ~ out** operarsi or farsi operare di appendicite. (b) (to book etc) appendice f.

ap·pe·tite ['æpɪtaɪt] n: **~ (for)** appetito (per); (fig) voglia (di), desiderio (di); **that walk has given me an ~** la passeggiata mi ha messo or fatto venire l'appetito; **to have a good ~** godere di or avere un ottimo appetito.

ap·pe·tiz·er ['æpɪtaɪzəʳ] n (food) stuzzichino; (drink) aperitivo.

ap·pe·tiz·ing ['æpɪtaɪzɪŋ] adj appetitoso(a), invitante.

ap·plaud [ə'plɔːd] **1** vt applaudire; (fig) lodare, approvare. **2** vi applaudire.

ap·plause [ə'plɔːz] n applauso; (fig) lode f, elogio.

ap·ple ['æpl] **1** n (fruit) mela; **the ~ of one's eye** (fam) la pupilla dei propri occhi. **2** cpd: **~ pie** n crostata di mele (ricoperta di pasta); **~ tree** n melo.

ap·pli·ance [ə'plaɪəns] n apparecchio; **electrical ~s** elettrodomestici mpl.

ap·pli·cable [ə'plɪkəbl] adj applicabile; **the law is ~ from January** la legge entrerà in vigore in gennaio; **to be ~ to** essere valido per.

ap·pli·cant ['æplɪkənt] n (for a post etc) candidato/a; (Admin: for benefit etc) chi ha fatto domanda or richiesta.

ap·pli·ca·tion [ˌæplɪ'keɪʃən] **1** n (a) (act of applying) applicazione f; **for external ~ only** (Med) (solo) per uso esterno. (b) (request) domanda; **~ for a job** domanda di assunzione; **further details may be had on ~ to X** per informazioni più dettagliate rivolgersi a X. (c) (diligence) applicazione f, impegno. **2** cpd: **~ form** n modulo di domanda.

ap·plied [ə'plaɪd] adj applicato(a); **~ linguistics** linguistica applicata.

ap·ply [ə'plaɪ] **1** vt: **to ~ (to)** (ointment) applicare (su), spalmare (su); (elastoplast) mettere (su), applicare (su); (paint) dare (a), stendere (su); (rule, law) applicare (a); **to ~ one's knowledge to sth** servirsi delle proprie nozioni per qc; **to ~ one's mind to a problem** concentrarsi su un problema; **to ~ o.s. (to one's studies)** applicarsi (nello studio); **to ~ a match to sth** dare fuoco a qc con un fiammifero; **to ~ the brakes** azionare i freni.

2 vi (a) (be applicable): **to ~ (to)** applicarsi (a), essere valido(a) (per); **the law applies to everybody** la legge è valida or vale per tutti. (b) (request) fare or presentare domanda; **to ~ for a job** fare domanda d'impiego; **to ~ for a visa** chiedere un visto; **to ~ to sb for sth** rivolgersi a qn per qc.

ap·point [ə'pɔɪnt] vt **(a)** (nominate) nominare; **they ~ed him chairman** lo hanno nominato presidente; **they ~ed a new teacher** hanno assunto un nuovo insegnante. **(b)** (frm: time, place) fissare, stabilire; **at the ~ed time** all'ora stabilita. **(c):** **a well-~ed house** una casa ben attrezzata.

ap·point·ment [ə'pɔɪntmənt] n **(a)** (to a job) nomina; (job) posto, carica; (Press): **'~s (vacant)'** 'offerte di impiego'. **(b)** (engagement) appuntamento; **by ~** su or per appuntamento; **have you an ~?** (to caller) ha l'appuntamento?; **to keep an ~** non mancare a un appuntamento; **she won't be able to keep the ~** non potrà venire all'appuntamento; **to make an ~ with sb** prendere un appuntamento con qn.

ap·por·tion [ə'pɔːʃən] vt attribuire.

ap·prais·al [ə'preɪzəl] n valutazione f, stima; (fig) giudizio.

ap·praise [ə'preɪz] vt (value) valutare, fare una stima di; (fig) dare or esprimere un giudizio su; (: situation etc) fare il bilancio di.

ap·pre·ci·able [ə'priːʃəbl] adj apprezzabile.

ap·pre·ci·ate [ə'priːʃɪeɪt] **1** vt **(a)** (be grateful for) apprezzare, essere grato(a) per; **I ~d your help** ti sono grato per l'aiuto. **(b)** (value) apprezzare; **I am not ~d here** qui nessuno mi apprezza abbastanza. **(c)** (understand: problem, difference) rendersi conto di; **yes, I ~ that** certo, me ne rendo conto. **2** vi (property etc) aumentare di valore.

ap·pre·cia·tion [ə,priːʃɪ'eɪʃən] n **(a)** (understanding) comprensione f; (praise) apprezzamento; (gratitude) riconoscimento; (Art: critique) critica; **he showed no ~ of my difficulties** non ha dimostrato di rendersi conto delle mie difficoltà; **as a token of my ~** in segno della mia gratitudine; **he has no ~ of good music** non apprezza la buona musica. **(b)** (rise in value) aumento.

ap·pre·cia·tive [ə'priːʃɪətɪv] adj (look) di ammirazione; (comment) di elogio; (audience) caloroso(a); **he was very ~ of what I had done** mi era molto grato di or ha dimostrato di apprezzare molto quello che avevo fatto.

ap·pre·hend [,æprɪ'hend] vt (arrest: frm) arrestare.

ap·pre·hen·sion [,æprɪ'henʃən] n **(a)** (arrest) arresto. **(b)** (fear) apprensione f, inquietudine f; **my chief ~ is...** la mia paura più grande è... .

ap·pre·hen·sive [,æprɪ'hensɪv] adj in apprensione.

ap·pren·tice [ə'prentɪs] **1** n apprendista m/f; **an ~ plumber, a plumber's ~** un apprendista idraulico. **2** vt: **to ~ to** mettere come apprendista presso; **to be ~d to** lavorare come apprendista presso.

ap·pren·tice·ship [ə'prentɪsʃɪp] n apprendistato, tirocinio; **to serve one's ~** fare il proprio apprendistato or tirocinio.

ap·prise [ə'praɪz] vt (frm): **to ~ sb of sth** mettere qn a conoscenza di qc, informare qn di qc.

ap·proach [ə'prəʊtʃ] **1** vt **(a)** (come near: animal, person) avvicinarsi a; (: place) stare per arrivare a, avvicinarsi a; (fig: subject etc) impostare, affrontare; **I ~ it with an open mind** considero la cosa senza pregiudizi; **he's ~ing 50** si avvicina ai 50, va per i 50; **no other painter ~es him** (fig) nessun altro pittore lo uguaglia. **(b)** (with request etc): **to ~ sb about sth** rivolgersi a qn per qc.
2 vi avvicinarsi; **the ~ing elections** le imminenti elezioni.
3 n **(a)** (act) avvicinarsi m; **at the ~ of night** all'avvicinarsi della notte. **(b)** (to problem, subject) modo di affrontare, approccio; **a new ~ to maths** un nuovo approccio alla matematica. **(c)**

(access) accesso; **the northern ~es to the city** le vie d'accesso a nord della città. **(d)** (advance) proposta; (: to committee, department) presa di contatto; **to make ~es to sb** fare degli approcci or delle avances a qn; **to make an ~ to sb** contattare qn.
4 cpd: **~ road** n strada d'accesso.

ap·proach·able [ə'prəʊtʃəbl] adj (person) avvicinabile, accessibile.

ap·pro·ba·tion [,æprə'beɪʃən] n approvazione f, benestare m.

ap·pro·pri·ate [ə'prəʊprɪɪt] **1** adj (moment, name, remark) adatto(a), opportuno(a); (word) giusto(a), adatto(a); (authority) competente; **~ for** or **to** adatto a, appropriato a, adeguato a; **it would not be ~ for me to comment** non sta a me fare dei commenti; **whichever seems more ~** ciò che sembra più adatto; **he is the ~ person to ask** è lui il competente in materia. **2** [ə'prəʊprɪeɪt] vt (steal) appropriarsi di.

ap·pro·pri·ate·ly [ə'prəʊprɪɪtlɪ] adv in modo adatto; **he was ~ insured** era assicurato in modo adeguato or convenientemente.

ap·prov·al [ə'pruːvəl] n (consent) approvazione f, assenso; **on ~** (Comm) in prova, in esame; **to meet with sb's ~** soddisfare qn, essere di gradimento di qn.

ap·prove [ə'pruːv] vt approvare.
♦ **approve of** vi + prep approvare; **I don't ~ of boys going to pubs** non approvo or disapprovo che i ragazzi vadano al pub; **she doesn't ~ of me** disapprova il mio modo di essere.

ap·proxi·mate [ə'prɒksɪmɪt] **1** adj approssimativo(a), approssimato(a). **2** [ə'prɒksɪmeɪt] vi: **to ~ to** essere un'approssimazione di, avvicinarsi a.

ap·proxi·mate·ly [ə'prɒksɪmətlɪ] adv approssimativamente, pressappoco.

apri·cot ['eɪprɪkɒt] n (fruit) albicocca.

April ['eɪprəl] **1** n aprile m; for usage see July. **2** cpd: **~ Fool!** pesce d'aprile!; **~ Fools' Day** n il primo d'aprile.

apron ['eɪprən] n (gen, workman's) grembiule m; (Aer) area di stazionamento; **tied to his mother's/wife's ~ strings** attaccato alle sottane di sua madre/moglie.

apse [æps] n (Archit) abside f.

apt [æpt] adj (-er, -est) **(a)** (suitable: remark) appropriato(a), pertinente; (: description) felice, indovinato(a), giusto(a). **(b)** (liable): **to be ~ to do sth** avere (la) tendenza a fare qc; **I am ~ to be out on Mondays** generalmente di lunedì non ci sono; **we are ~ to forget that...** tendiamo a dimenticare che... . **(c)** (pupil etc) dotato(a).

ap·ti·tude ['æptɪtjuːd] **1** n (ability) abilità f inv. **2** cpd: **~ test** n test m inv attitudinale.

apt·ly ['æptlɪ] adv appropriatamente, in modo adatto; **she was ~ dressed for the occasion** aveva un vestito adatto all'occasione.

aqua·lung ['ækwəlʌŋ] n autorespiratore m.

aquar·ium [ə'kwɛərɪəm] n acquario.

Aquar·ius [ə'kwɛərɪəs] n Acquario; **to be ~** essere dell'Acquario.

aquat·ic [ə'kwætɪk] adj acquatico(a).

aque·duct ['ækwɪdʌkt] n acquedotto.

aqui·line ['ækwɪlaɪn] adj aquilino(a).

Arab ['ærəb] **1** adj arabo(a). **2** n (person) arabo/a; (horse) cavallo arabo.

ara·besque [,ærə'besk] n arabesco.

Ara·bian [ə'reɪbɪən] adj arabo(a), dell'Arabia; (sea, desert) arabico(a); **the ~ Nights** le Mille e una Notte.

Ara·bic ['ærəbɪk] **1** adj arabo(a); **~ numerals**

numeri arabi, numerazione f araba. **2** n *(language)* arabo.

ar·able ['ærəbl] *adj* arabile.

ar·bi·trary ['ɑːbɪtrərɪ] *adj* arbitrario(a).

ar·bi·trate ['ɑːbɪtreɪt] *vi* fare da arbitro.

ar·bi·tra·tion [,ɑːbɪ'treɪʃən] n arbitrato; **the dispute went to** ~ la controversia è stata sottoposta ad arbitrato.

ar·bi·tra·tor ['ɑːbɪtreɪtə'] n arbitro.

arc [ɑːk] n arco.

ar·cade [ɑː'keɪd] n *(Archit)* portico; *(round public square)* porticato, portici mpl; *(with shops)* galleria.

arch¹ [ɑːtʃ] **1** n **(a)** *(Archit)* arco, arcata. **(b)** *(of foot)* arco or arcata plantare. **2** vt *(back, body etc)* arcuare, inarcare; *(eyebrows)* inarcare.

arch² [ɑːtʃ] *adj attr* grande *(before n)*; **an** ~ **villain** un grande criminale; **the** ~ **villain** il cattivo per eccellenza.

ar·chaeo·logi·cal [,ɑːkɪə'lɒdʒɪkəl] *adj* archeologico(a).

ar·chae·olo·gist [,ɑːkɪ'ɒlədʒɪst] n archeologo/a.

ar·chae·ol·ogy [,ɑːkɪ'ɒlədʒɪ] n archeologia.

ar·cha·ic [ɑː'keɪɪk] *adj* arcaico(a).

arch·angel ['ɑːk,eɪndʒəl] n arcangelo.

arch·bishop ['ɑːtʃ'bɪʃəp] n arcivescovo.

arched [ɑːtʃt] *adj* arcuato(a), ad arco.

arch-enemy [,ɑːtʃ'ɛnɪmɪ] n nemico per eccellenza.

ar·che·ol·ogy [,ɑːkɪ'ɒlədʒɪ] *etc (Am)* = **archaeology** *etc*.

arch·er ['ɑːtʃə'] n arciere m.

ar·chery ['ɑːtʃərɪ] n tiro con l'arco.

ar·che·typ·al ['ɑːkɪtaɪpəl] *adj* tipico(a).

ar·che·type ['ɑːkɪtaɪp] n *(original)* archetipo; *(epitome)* prototipo.

archi·pela·go [,ɑːkɪ'pɛlɪgəʊ] n arcipelago.

archi·tect ['ɑːkɪtɛkt] n architetto.

archi·tec·tur·al [,ɑːkɪ'tɛktʃərəl] *adj* architettonico(a).

archi·tec·ture ['ɑːkɪtɛktʃə'] n architettura.

ar·chives ['ɑːkaɪvz] npl archivio, archivi mpl.

arch·way ['ɑːtʃweɪ] n *(passage)* (passaggio a) volta; *(arch)* arco, arcata.

arc·tic ['ɑːktɪk] **1** *adj* artico(a); *(fig: very cold)* polare; **the A**~ **Circle** il circolo polare artico; **the A**~ **Ocean** l'Oceano artico. **2** n: **the A**~ l'Artico.

ar·dent ['ɑːdənt] *adj (supporter)* ardente, fervente; *(desire, lover)* ardente.

ar·dour, *(Am)* **ardor** ['ɑːdə'] n ardore m.

ar·du·ous ['ɑːdjʊəs] *adj* arduo(a).

are [ɑː', ə'] *2nd pers sg, 1st, 2nd and 3rd pers pl present of* **be**.

area ['ɛərɪə] **1** n **(a)** *(surface extent)* area, superficie f. **(b)** *(region)* zona; **the London** ~ la zona di Londra; **in the** ~ **of £5000** sulle or intorno alle 5000 sterline. **(c)** *(fig: of knowledge)* campo, settore m; *(: of responsibility etc)* sfera; **matters outside my** ~ **of responsibility** questioni che esulano dalla mia competenza. **2** cpd: ~ **code** n *(Am Telec)* prefisso m.

arena [ə'riːnə] n arena.

aren't [ɑːnt] = **are not**.

Ar·gen·ti·na [,ɑːdʒən'tiːnə] n Argentina.

Ar·gen·tin·ian [,ɑːdʒən'tɪnɪən] *adj* argentino(a).

ar·gu·able ['ɑːgjʊəbl] *adj (rather doubtful)* discutibile; *(capable of being argued for)*: **it is** ~ **that...** si può sostenere che...; **it is** ~ **whether** è una cosa discutibile se + *sub*.

ar·gu·ably ['ɑːgjʊəblɪ] *adv*: **it is** ~**...** si può sostenere che è... .

ar·gue ['ɑːgjuː] **1** vi **(a)** *(dispute)* litigare; **to** ~ **about sth (with sb)** litigare per or a proposito di

qc (con qn); **don't** ~! senza tante discussioni!, non discutere! **(b)** *(reason)* ragionare; **to** ~ **against/for** portare degli argomenti contro/in favore di. **2** vt *(debate: case, matter)* dibattere, discutere; *(persuade)*: **to** ~ **sb into doing sth** persuadere or convincere qn a fare qc; *(maintain)*: **to** ~ **that...** sostenere or affermare che... .

ar·gu·ment ['ɑːgjʊmənt] n **(a)** *(reason)* argomento, ragione f, motivo; ~ **for/against** argomento a or in favore di/contro; **I don't follow your** ~ non ti seguo. **(b)** *(discussion)* discussione f, dibattito; *(quarrel)* litigio; **to hear both sides of the** ~ ascoltare entrambe le versioni.

ar·gu·men·ta·tive [,ɑːgjʊ'mɛntətɪv] *adj* polemico(a).

arid ['ærɪd] *adj* arido(a); *(fig)* piatto(a).

Aries ['ɛəriːz] n Ariete m; **to be** ~ essere dell'Ariete.

arise [ə'raɪz] *pt* **arose,** *pp* **arisen** [ə'rɪzn] vi **(a)** *(occur)* presentarsi, offrirsi; *(result)*: **to** ~ **(from)** derivare (da); **difficulties have arisen** sono insorte or sorte delle difficoltà; **should the need** ~ dovesse presentarsi la necessità, in caso di necessità; **a storm arose** si scatenò una tempesta; **the question does not** ~ la questione non si pone. **(b)** *(old: get up)* levarsi, alzarsi.

ar·is·toc·ra·cy [,ærɪs'tɒkrəsɪ] n aristocrazia.

aris·to·crat ['ærɪstəkræt] n aristocratico/a, nobile m/f.

aris·to·crat·ic [,ærɪstə'krætɪk] *adj* aristocratico(a).

arith·me·tic [ə'rɪθmətɪk] n aritmetica; **mental** ~ calcolo mentale.

arith·meti·cal [,ærɪθ'mɛtɪkəl] *adj* aritmetico(a).

ark [ɑːk] n *(Bible)* arca; **Noah's A**~ l'arca di Noè.

arm [ɑːm] **1** n **(a)** *(Anat)* braccio; *(of chair)* bracciolo; ~ **in** ~ a braccetto, sottobraccio; **with open** ~**s** *(fig)* a braccia aperte; **within** ~**'s reach** a portata di mano; **to keep sb at** ~**'s length** *(fig)* tenere qn a distanza; **to put one's** ~ **round sb** mettere un braccio intorno alle spalle di qn. **(b)**: ~**s** *(Mil)* armi fpl; *(coat of* ~*s)* stemma m; **the** ~**s race** la corsa agli armamenti; **to be up in** ~**s** *(fig)* essere furibondo(a). **2** vt *(person, ship)* armare; **she was** ~**ed with all the facts** aveva in mano tutti i fatti; **he** ~**ed himself with some good arguments** si è armato di validi argomenti.

ar·ma·ments ['ɑːməmənts] npl *(weapons)* armamenti mpl.

arm·chair ['ɑːm,tʃɛə'] n poltrona.

armed [ɑːmd] *adj* armato(a); **the** ~ **forces** le forze armate; ~ **robbery** rapina a mano armata.

arm·ful ['ɑːmfʊl] n bracciata.

ar·mi·stice ['ɑːmɪstɪs] n armistizio.

ar·mour, *(Am)* **ar·mor** ['ɑːmə'] n *(of knight)* armatura; *(Mil:* ~*-plating)* corazza, blindatura.

ar·moured car ['ɑːməd 'kɑː'] n *(Mil)* autoblinda.

arm·pit ['ɑːm,pɪt] n ascella.

arm·rest ['ɑːm,rɛst] n bracciolo.

army ['ɑːmɪ] n *(Mil, fig)* esercito; **to join the** ~ arruolarsi.

aro·ma [ə'rəʊmə] n aroma m.

aro·mat·ic [,ærəʊ'mætɪk] *adj* aromatico(a).

arose [ə'rəʊz] *pt of* **arise**.

around [ə'raʊnd] **1** adv **(a)** *(place)* attorno, intorno; **for miles** ~ nel raggio di molte miglia; **he must be somewhere** ~ dev'essere qui in giro or nei paraggi. **(b)** *(approximately)* all'incirca, circa; ~ **10 o'clock** verso le 10; ~ **50** circa 50. **2** prep intorno a; **it's just** ~ **the corner** è appena girato l'angolo.

arouse [ə'raʊz] vt *(awaken)* svegliare; *(fig)* eccitare, stimolare.

ar·range [ə'reɪndʒ] 1 vt (a) (put into order: books, thoughts, furniture) sistemare, ordinare, disporre; (hair) fare un'acconciatura a; (flowers etc) sistemare. (b) (Mus) adattare, arrangiare. (c) (decide on: meeting) combinare, organizzare; (: date, programme) stabilire, fissare; to ~ a time for stabilire or fissare una data per; everything is ~d è tutto a posto; it was ~d that... è stato deciso or stabilito che...; what did you ~ with him? per or su che cosa siete rimasti d'accordo?; to ~ to do sth mettersi d'accordo per fare qc.

2 vi mettersi d'accordo, combinare; to ~ for sth/for sb to do sth organizzare or predisporre qc/che qn faccia qc; we have ~d for a taxi to pick you up la faremo venire a prendere da un taxi; I have ~d for you to go ho combinato che tu vada.

ar·range·ment [ə'reɪndʒmənt] n (a) (order, act of ordering) sistemazione f, disposizione f; (Mus) arrangiamento; a flower ~ una composizione floreale. (b) (agreement) accordo; to come to an ~ (with sb) venire a un accordo (con qn), mettersi d'accordo or accordarsi (con qn); by ~ su richiesta; by ~ with the tour operator secondo gli accordi con l'operatore turistico; by ~ with La Scala con l'autorizzazione del Teatro della Scala. (c) (plan) piano, programma m; ~s (plans) piani, programmi; (preparations) preparativi mpl; I'll make ~s for you to be met darò disposizioni or istruzioni perché ci sia qualcuno ad incontrarla; we must make ~s to help dobbiamo organizzarci per aiutare; all the ~s for the party are made tutto è pronto per la festa.

ar·ray [ə'reɪ] n (of troops, police etc) schieramento; in battle ~ in ordine di battaglia; a fine ~ of hats/cakes etc tanti cappelli/tante torte etc in bella mostra.

ar·rears [ə'rɪəz] npl (of money) arretrati mpl; ~ of filing pratiche fpl arretrate da archiviare; in ~ in arretrato.

ar·rest [ə'rest] 1 n arresto; to be under ~ essere in (stato di) arresto; to place sb under ~ mettere qn in stato di arresto, arrestare qn. 2 vt (criminal) arrestare; (attention, interest) fermare, attirare; (halt: progress, decay etc) arrestare, bloccare.

ar·rest·ing [ə'restɪŋ] adj (fig) che colpisce.

ar·ri·val [ə'raɪvəl] n (gen) arrivo; (person) arrivato/a; a new ~ un nuovo venuto; (baby) un neonato; on ~ all'arrivo.

ar·rive [ə'raɪv] vi (gen) arrivare; (day, time) arrivare, giungere.

♦ **arrive at** vi + prep (place, price) arrivare a; (decision, solution) arrivare a, giungere a.

ar·ro·gance ['ærəgəns] n arroganza.

ar·ro·gant ['ærəgənt] adj arrogante.

ar·row ['ærəʊ] n freccia.

arse [ɑːs] n (fam!) culo(!).

ar·senal ['ɑːsɪnl] n arsenale m.

ar·senic ['ɑːsnɪk] n arsenico.

ar·son ['ɑːsn] n incendio doloso.

art [ɑːt] 1 n (a) arte f; (Scol: subject) disegno e storia dell'arte; the ~s le belle arti; ~s and crafts artigianato; to study ~ fare degli studi artistici; work of ~ opera d'arte. (b): ~s (Univ) lettere fpl, studi mpl umanistici; Faculty of A~s facoltà di Lettere. 2 cpd: ~ collection n collezione f d'arte; ~ gallery n (shop) galleria d'arte; (museum) museo d'arte, galleria d'arte; ~ school n scuola d'arte; A~s degree n laurea in lettere.

ar·te·fact ['ɑːtɪfækt] n manufatto.

ar·te·rial [ɑː'tɪərɪəl] adj (Anat) arterioso(a); (road etc) di grande comunicazione; ~ roads le (grandi) or principali) arterie.

ar·te·rio·sclero·sis [ɑː'tɪərɪəʊsklɪ'rəʊsɪs] n arteriosclerosi f.

ar·tery ['ɑːtərɪ] n (Anat, fig) arteria.

art·ful ['ɑːtful] adj (person) furbo(a), abile; (trick) abile.

ar·thrit·ic [ɑː'θrɪtɪk] adj artritico(a).

ar·thri·tis [ɑː'θraɪtɪs] n artrite f.

ar·ti·choke ['ɑːtɪtʃəʊk] n (globe ~) carciofo; (Jerusalem ~) topinambur m inv.

ar·ti·cle ['ɑːtɪkl] n (Admin, Law, Comm, Gram etc) articolo; (object) oggetto; ~s of clothing indumenti mpl; ~s (Law, Admin) contratto di tirocinio; to be in ~s fare il tirocinio.

ar·ticu·late [ɑː'tɪkjʊlɪt] 1 adj (account, diction) chiaro(a); (person) che si esprime bene. 2 [ɑː'tɪkjʊleɪt] vt (words) articolare, pronunciare. 3 cpd: ~d lorry n autoarticolato.

ar·ticu·la·tion [ɑː,tɪkjʊ'leɪʃən] n (of sounds) articolazione f; (of speech) dizione f.

ar·ti·fact ['ɑːtɪfækt] n = artefact.

ar·ti·fice ['ɑːtɪfɪs] n (cunning) abilità, destrezza; (trick) artificio.

ar·ti·fi·cial [,ɑːtɪ'fɪʃəl] adj (synthetic) artificiale; (fig pej: smile, manner) studiato(a), affettato(a); (: tears, situation) falso(a); ~ respiration/ insemination respirazione f/fecondazione f artificiale.

ar·til·lery [ɑː'tɪlərɪ] n artiglieria.

ar·ti·san ['ɑːtɪzæn] n artigiano/a.

art·ist ['ɑːtɪst] n artista m/f.

ar·tis·tic [ɑː'tɪstɪk] adj artistico(a); to be ~ avere una sensibilità artistica.

art·ist·ry ['ɑːtɪstrɪ] n (skill) arte f, abilità artistica.

art·less ['ɑːtlɪs] adj ingenuo(a), semplice.

as [æz, əz] conj (a) (time) mentre; as a child... da bambino...; he came in ~ I was leaving è arrivato nel momento in cui or quando stavo per andarmene; ~ from tomorrow (a partire or a cominciare) da domani; ~ I get older, I... con l'età io... .

(b) (because) visto che, dal momento che, siccome.

(c) (although): stupid ~ he is per quanto sia stupido, anche se è stupido; much ~ I like them, ... per quanto mi siano simpatici, ...; try ~ he would, he couldn't do it malgrado i suoi sforzi, non ha potuto farlo.

(d) (in comparisons: also adv): this car will go ~ fast ~ 120 m.p.h. questa macchina raggiunge le 120 miglia all'ora; I didn't know it could go ~ fast ~ that non sapevo che fosse così veloce; twice ~ old due volte più vecchio; ~ tall ~ him alto come lui; ~ quickly ~ possible il più rapidamente possibile; ~ pale ~ death pallido come un morto; you've got ~ much ~ she has ne hai (tanto) quanto ne ha lei.

(e) (way, manner: also prep) come; do ~ you wish fa' come vuoi; leave things ~ they are lascia tutto così com'è; you've got plenty ~ it is ne hai già abbastanza; ~ I've said before... come ho già detto...; disguised ~ a nun travestito da suora; he succeeded ~ a politician come politico ha avuto successo.

(f) (concerning): ~ for, ~ regards, ~ to per quanto or quello che riguarda, quanto a; ~ to that per quanto or quello non ti so dire; ~ for the children, they were exhausted quanto ai bambini, erano sfiniti.

(g): ~ if, ~ though come se +sub; he fought ~ if his life depended on it si è battuto come se ne andasse della sua vita; he got up ~ if to leave si alzò come per andarsene; he looked ~ if he was ill aveva l'aria di star male; see be, same, such, so etc.

a.s.a.p. *abbr of* **as soon as possible.**

as·bes·tos [æz'bɛstəs] *n* amianto, asbesto.

as·cend [ə'sɛnd] **1** *vt (frm: stairs)* salire; *(mountain)* scalare; *(throne)* salire a, ascendere a. **2** *vi* salire.

as·cend·ancy [ə'sɛndənsɪ] *n* ascendente *m*.

as·cend·ant [ə'sɛndənt] *n*: **to be in the ~** essere in auge.

as·cen·sion [ə'sɛnʃən] *n*: **the A~** *(Rel)* l'Ascensione *f*.

as·cent [ə'sɛnt] *n (of mountain)* ascensione *f*, scalata; *(in plane)*: **we made a rapid ~ to our cruising altitude** siamo saliti rapidamente fino alla quota di crociera.

as·cer·tain [ˌæsə'teɪn] *vt* accertare; **have you ~ed her real name yet?** hai accertato quale sia il suo vero nome?

as·cet·ic [ə'sɛtɪk] **1** *adj* ascetico(a). **2** *n* asceta *m/f*.

as·ceti·cism [ə'sɛtɪsɪzəm] *n* ascetismo.

as·cribe [ə'skraɪb] *vt*: **to ~ sth to** attribuire qc a.

ash¹ [æʃ] *n (Bot)* frassino.

ash² [æʃ] **1** *n* cenere *f*; **~es** *pl (of fire)* cenere *f*; *(of dead)* ceneri *fpl*; **burnt to ~es** carbonizzato(a). **2** *cpd*: **A~ Wednesday** *n* mercoledì *m inv* delle Ceneri.

ashamed [ə'ʃeɪmd] *adj* pieno(a) di vergogna; **to be** *or* **feel ~ (of o.s.)** vergognarsi; **to be ~ of sb/sth/ to do sth** vergognarsi di qn/qc/di fare qc; **you ought to be ~ of yourself!** dovresti vergognarti!, vergognati!; **it's nothing to be ~ of** non è una cosa di cui ci si debba vergognare.

ashore [ə'ʃɔːʳ] *adv* a terra; **to go ~** scendere a terra.

ash·tray ['æʃtreɪ] *n* portacenere *m inv*.

Asia ['eɪʃə] *n* Asia.

Asian ['eɪʃn] *adj, n*, **Asi·at·ic** [ˌeɪʃɪ'ætɪk] *adj, n* asiatico(a) *(m/f)*.

aside [ə'saɪd] **1** *adv* da parte. **2** *prep*: **~ from** *(as well as)* oltre a; *(except for)* a parte, salvo, eccetto. **3** *n (esp Theatre)* a parte *m inv*.

ask [ɑːsk] **1** *vt* **(a)** *(inquire)*: **to ~ sb sth** domandare qc a qn, chiedere qc a qn; **she ~ed him about his father** lei gli domandò (notizie) di suo padre; **to ~ sb a question** fare una domanda a qn; **to ~ sb the time** chiedere l'ora a qn; **don't ~ me!** *(fam)* non domandarlo a me!, a me lo chiedi? **(b)** *(request)*: **to ~ sb for sth/sb to do sth** chiedere qc a qn/a qn di fare qc; **to ~ sb a favour** chiedere un piacere *or* un favore a qn; **how much are they ~ing for it?** quanto chiedono per quello?; **the ~ing price** il prezzo di partenza; **that's ~ing a lot!** questo è pretendere un po' troppo! **(c)** *(invite)*: **to ~ sb to sth/to do sth** invitare qn a qc/a fare qc; **to ~ sb out** invitare qn fuori; **to ~ sb to dinner** invitare qn a pranzo.

2 *vi (inquire)* chiedere; *(request)* richiedere; **to ~ about sth** informarsi su *or* di qc; **you should ~ at the information desk** dovresti rivolgerti all'ufficio informazioni; **it's yours for the ~ing** non hai che da chiederlo.

♦ **ask after** *vi + prep* domandare *or* chiedere (notizie) di, informarsi di.

♦ **ask for** *vi + prep (person)* chiedere di, cercare; *(help, information, money)* chiedere, domandare; **I ~ed him for help** gli ho chiesto aiuto *or* di aiutarmi; **it's just ~ing for trouble** è proprio (come) andarsele a cercare.

askance [ə'skɑːns] *adv*: **to look ~ at sb/sth** guardare qn/qc storto *or* di traverso.

askew [ə'skjuː] *adv* di traverso.

asleep [ə'sliːp] *adj* addormentato(a); **to be fast ~** dormire profondamente; **to fall ~** addormentarsi; **my foot's ~** mi si è addormentato *or* intorpidito il piede.

as·para·gus [əs'pærəgəs] *n (plant)* asparago; *(food)* asparagi *mpl*.

as·pect ['æspɛkt] *n* **(a)** *(of person, situation etc)* aspetto; **to study all ~s of a question** esaminare una questione sotto tutti gli aspetti. **(b)** *(of building etc)* esposizione *f*; **a house with a northerly ~** una casa esposta a nord.

as·phalt ['æsfælt] *n* asfalto.

as·phyxia [æs'fɪksɪə] *n* asfissia.

as·phyxi·ate [æs'fɪksɪeɪt] *vt, vi* asfissiare.

as·pic ['æspɪk] *n*: **chicken in ~** aspic *f* di pollo.

as·pi·ra·tion [ˌæspə'reɪʃən] *n* aspirazione *f*.

as·pire [əs'paɪəʳ] *vi*: **to ~ to** aspirare a, ambire a.

as·pi·rin ['æsprɪn] *n* aspirina.

ass¹ [æs] *n (Zool)* asino, somaro; *(fig fam)* scemo/a; **to make an ~ of o.s.** rendersi ridicolo.

ass² [æs] *n (Am fam!)* culo(!).

as·sail [ə'seɪl] *vt*: **to ~ (with)** assalire (di).

as·sail·ant [ə'seɪlənt] *n* assalitore/trice.

as·sas·sin [ə'sæsɪn] *n* assassino/a.

as·sas·si·nate [ə'sæsɪneɪt] *vt* assassinare.

as·sas·si·na·tion [ə,sæsɪ'neɪʃən] *n* assassinio.

as·sault [ə'sɔːlt] **1** *n (Mil)*: **~ (on)** assalto (a); *(Law)* aggressione *f*; **~ and battery** *(Law)* vie *fpl* di fatto. **2** *vt (Mil)* assaltare, assalire; *(Law)* aggredire; *(sexually)* violentare.

as·sem·ble [ə'sɛmbl] **1** *vt (objects, ideas)* radunare, raccogliere; *(people)* radunare, riunire; *(Tech)* montare, assemblare. **2** *vi* radunarsi, riunirsi.

as·sem·bly [ə'sɛmblɪ] **1** *n (meeting)* assemblea; *(Tech)* assemblaggio, montaggio; **right of ~** libertà di riunione. **2** *cpd*: **~ line** *n* catena di montaggio.

as·sent [ə'sɛnt] **1** *n* benestare *m*; **by common ~** di comune accordo. **2** *vi*: **to ~ (to sth)** approvare (qc).

as·sert [ə'sɜːt] *vt (declare)* affermare, asserire; *(insist on: rights)* far valere; **to ~ o.s.** farsi valere.

as·ser·tion [ə'sɜːʃən] *n* affermazione *f*, asserzione *f*.

as·ser·tive [ə'sɜːtɪv] *adj* che sa imporsi.

as·sess [ə'sɛs] *vt (gen)* valutare; *(rateable property, tax)* accertare l'imponibile di; *(damages)* valutare; *(fig: situation etc)* giudicare.

as·sess·ment [ə'sɛsmənt] *n (see vb)* valutazione *f*; accertamento; *(judgment)*: **~ (of)** giudizio (su).

as·set ['æsɛt] *n (useful quality)* bene *m*, qualità; *(person)* elemento prezioso; **~s** *(Fin: of individual)* beni *mpl*; *(: of company)* attivo, attività *fpl*.

asset-stripping ['æsɛt,strɪpɪŋ] *n (Comm)* acquisto di una società in fallimento con lo scopo di rivenderne le attività.

as·sidu·ous [ə'sɪdjʊəs] *adj* assiduo(a).

as·sign [ə'saɪn] *vt*: **to ~ (to)** *(allot: task, room)* assegnare (a); *(reason)* dare (a), attribuire (a); *(Law: property)* cedere (a), trasferire (a); *(appoint)*: **to ~ sb to** dare a qn l'incarico di; **to ~ a date to sth** fissare la data di qc.

as·sig·na·tion [ˌæsɪg'neɪʃən] *n (of lovers)* convegno galante.

as·sign·ment [ə'saɪnmənt] *n (task)* incarico.

as·simi·late [ə'sɪmɪleɪt] *vt* assimilare.

as·sist [ə'sɪst] **1** *vt*: **to ~ sb (to do** *or* **in doing sth)** aiutare qn (a fare qc), assistere qn (a *or* nel fare qc); **we ~ed him with his car** lo abbiamo aiutato a raggiungere la sua macchina. **2** *vi (help)*: **to ~ in sth** aiutare in qc, essere di aiuto in qc.

as·sis·tance [ə'sɪstəns] *n* aiuto, assistenza; **can I be of any ~?** posso esserle utile (in qualcosa)?; *(in shop)* desidera?; **to come to sb's ~** venire in aiuto a qn.

as·sis·tant [ə'sɪstənt] **1** *n* aiutante *m/f*, assistente *m/f*, aiuto. **2** *cpd* aiuto *inv*; **~ headmaster** *n* vicepreside *m*; ~ **librarian** *n* aiuto bibliotecario/a; ~ **manager** *n* vicedirettore *m*.

as·so·ci·ate [ə'səʊʃɪɪt] **1** *adj (company)* consociato(a), associato(a); *(member)* aggregato(a), aggiunto(a). **2** *n (colleague)* collega *m/f*; *(accomplice)* complice *m/f*; *(member: of club)* socio(a) aggregato(a), (: *of learned society)* membro aggregato. **3** [ə'səʊʃɪeɪt] *vt* associare, collegare; **to ~ o.s. with** associarsi a, unirsi a; **I don't wish to be ~d with it** non voglio che si pensi che io abbia a che fare con la cosa. **4** [ə'səʊʃɪeɪt] *vi*: **to ~ with sb** frequentare qn.

as·so·ci·a·tion [ə,səʊsɪ'eɪʃən] *n (most senses)* associazione *f*; **his ~ with her family** i suoi legami con la famiglia di lei; **in ~ with** in collaborazione con; **full of historic ~s** ricco di reminiscenze storiche; **the name has unpleasant ~s** il nome è associato a qualcosa di spiacevole.

as·sort·ed [ə'sɔːtɪd] *adj* assortito(a); **in ~ sizes** in diverse taglie; **ill-/well-~** mal/ben assortito.

as·sort·ment [ə'sɔːtmənt] *n (mixture: Comm)* assortimento; **there was a strange ~ of guests** c'era uno strano miscuglio di invitati.

as·suage [ə'sweɪdʒ] *vt (feelings, pain)* attenuare; *(appetite)* placare.

as·sume [ə'sjuːm] *vt* **(a)** *(suppose)* supporre, presumere, presupporre; **assuming that...** supponendo che.... **(b)** *(power, control, attitude etc)* assumere; **to ~ responsibility for** assumersi la responsabilità di; **under an ~d name** sotto falso nome.

as·sump·tion [ə'sʌmpʃən] *n* **(a)** *(supposition)* supposizione *f*, ipotesi *f inv*; **on the ~ that** partendo dal presupposto che; **to work on the ~ that** partire dal presupposto che. **(b)**: **the A~** *(Rel)* l'Assunzione *f*.

as·sur·ance [ə'ʃʊərəns] *n* **(a)** *(guarantee)* assicurazione *f*, garanzia; **I can give you no ~s** non posso assicurare *or* garantirle niente. **(b)** *(confidence)* sicurezza, convinzione *f*; *(self-confidence)* fiducia in se stesso(a), sicurezza di sé; **he spoke with ~** ha parlato con convinzione. **(c)** *(Brit: insurance)* assicurazione *f*.

as·sure [ə'ʃʊəʳ] *vt (make certain)*: **to ~ sb (of sth)** assicurare qn (di qc); **I ~d him of my support** gli ho assicurato il mio appoggio; **success was ~d** il successo era garantito *or* assicurato.

as·ter·isk ['æstərɪsk] *n* asterisco.

astern [ə'stɜːn] *adv* a poppa.

as·ter·oid ['æstərɔɪd] *n* asteroide *m*.

asth·ma ['æsmə] *n* asma.

asth·mat·ic [æs'mætɪk] *adj* asmatico(a).

astig·ma·tism [æs'tɪgmətɪzəm] *n* astigmatismo.

aston·ish [ə'stɒnɪʃ] *vt* stupire, meravigliare; **you ~ me!** mi fa l'avrebbe mai detto!

aston·ish·ing [ə'stɒnɪʃɪŋ] *adj* sorprendente, stupefacente; **I find it ~ that...** mi stupisce che... .

aston·ish·ly [ə'stɒnɪʃɪŋlɪ] *adv* straordinariamente, incredibilmente.

aston·ish·ment [ə'stɒnɪʃmənt] *n* stupore *m*, meraviglia; **he gave me a look of ~** mi ha lanciato uno sguardo stupito; **to my ~** con mia gran meraviglia, con mio grande stupore.

astound [ə'staʊnd] *vt* sbalordire; **he was ~ed to hear...** è rimasto stupefatto *or* allibito nel sentire... .

astray [ə'streɪ] *adv*: **to go ~** perdere la strada, perdersi; *(morally)* mettersi su una cattiva strada; **to go ~ in one's calculations** sballare i calcoli; **to lead sb ~** *(fig)* portare qn su una brutta strada.

astride [ə'straɪd] *prep (fence)* a cavalcioni di; *(animal)* a cavallo di; *(horse)* in sella a.

as·trin·gent [əs'trɪndʒənt] *adj, n* astringente *(m)*.

as·trolo·ger [əs'trɒlədʒəʳ] *n* astrologo/a.

as·trol·ogy [əs'trɒlədʒɪ] *n* astrologia.

as·tro·naut ['æstrənɔːt] *n* astronauta *m/f*.

as·trono·mer [əs'trɒnəməʳ] *n* astronomo/a.

as·tro·nomi·cal [,æstrə'nɒmɪkəl] *adj (also fig)* astronomico(a).

as·trono·my [əs'trɒnəmɪ] *n* astronomia.

as·tro·phys·ics ['æstrəʊ'fɪzɪks] *nsg* astrofisica.

as·tute [əs'tjuːt] *adj* astuto(a), accorto(a).

asy·lum [ə'saɪləm] *n* **(a)** *(refuge)* asilo, rifugio; **to seek political ~** chiedere asilo politico. **(b)** *(lunatic ~)* manicomio.

asym·met·ric(al) [,eɪsɪ'mɛtrɪk(əl)] *adj* asimmetrico(a).

at [æt] *prep* **(a)** *(position)* a; *(direction)* verso; **~ the desk** al banco; **~ home/school** a casa/scuola; **~ John's** da John, a casa di John; **to stand ~ the door** stare sulla porta; **to look ~** sth guardare qc. **(b)** *(time)*: **~ 4 o'clock** alle quattro; **~ a time like this** in un momento come questo; **~ night** di notte; **~ Christmas** a *or* per Natale. **(c)** *(rate)* a; **~ 50p each** a 50 pence l'uno; **two ~ a time** due alla *or* per volta. **(d)** *(activity)*: **to be ~ work** essere al lavoro, stare lavorando; **to play ~ cowboys** giocare ai cowboy; **to be good ~ sth** riuscire bene in qc, essere bravo in qc *or* a fare qc; **while you're ~ it** *(fam)* già che ci sei; **she's ~ it again** *(fam)* eccola che ricomincia, ci risiamo; **he's always (on) ~ me** *(fam)* mi sta sempre alle costole. **(e)** *(manner)*: **~ full speed** a tutta velocità; **~ 50 km/h** a 50 km/h; **~ peace** in pace; **~ a run** di corsa, correndo. **(f)** *(cause)*: **~ his suggestion** dietro suo consiglio; **I was shocked/surprised ~ the news** sono rimasto colpito/sorpreso dalla notizia; **annoyed ~** arrabbiato per.

ate [ɛt, *(Am)* eɪt] *pt of* eat.

athe·ism ['eɪθɪɪzəm] *n* ateismo.

athe·ist ['eɪθɪɪst] *n* ateo/a.

Ath·ens ['æθɪnz] *n* Atene *f*.

ath·lete ['æθliːt] *n* atleta *m/f*.

ath·let·ic [æθ'lɛtɪk] *adj (meeting etc)* di atletica, atletico(a); *(person)* atletico(a); (: *sporty)* sportivo(a).

ath·let·ics [æθ'lɛtɪks] *nsg* atletica.

At·lan·tic [ət'læntɪk] *adj* dell'Atlantico; **the ~ (Ocean)** l'Atlantico, l'Oceano Atlantico.

at·las ['ætləs] *n* atlante *m*.

at·mos·phere ['ætməsfɪəʳ] *n (Geog, fig)* atmosfera; *(air)* aria.

at·mos·pher·ics [,ætməs'fɛrɪks] *npl (Radio)* disturbi *mpl* (dovuti *or* scariche elettriche).

atom ['ætəm] **1** *n* atomo; *(fig)*: **not an ~ of truth** nemmeno un pizzico di verità. **2** *cpd*: **~ bomb** *n* bomba atomica.

atom·ic [ə'tɒmɪk] *adj* atomico(a).

atone [ə'təʊn] *vi*: **to ~ for** *(crime, sins)* espiare; *(mistake, rudeness)* riparare a.

atone·ment [ə'təʊnmənt] *n* espiazione *f*; *(Rel)* redenzione *f*; **to make ~ for a mistake** riparare ad un errore.

atro·cious [ə'trəʊʃəs] *adj* atroce.

atroc·ity [ə'trɒsɪtɪ] *n* atrocità *f inv*.

at·ro·phy ['ætrəfɪ] **1** *n* atrofia. **2** *vi* atrofizzarsi.

at·tach [ə'tætʃ] *vt*: **to ~ (to)** **(a)** *(fasten, stick)* attaccare (a); *(tie)* legare (a); *(join)* annettere (a), attaccare (a); **the ~ed letter** la lettera acclusa *or* allegata; **to be ~ed to sb** *(fig)* essere attaccato *or* affezionato a qn; **he ~ed himself to us** si è appiccicato a noi; **he's ~ed** *(fam: married etc)* è impegnato. **(b)** *(attribute: importance, value)* at-

tribuire (a), dare (a). **(c)** *(assign)* assegnare (a).
at·ta·ché [ə'tæʃeɪ] **1** *n* addetto (di ambasciata), attaché *m inv;* **cultural** ~ addetto culturale. **2** *cpd:* ~ **case** *n* valigetta (diplomatica).
at·tach·ment [ə'tætʃmənt] *n* **(a)** *(device)* accessorio. **(b)** *(affection):* ~ **(to)** attaccamento (per).
at·tack [ə'tæk] **1** *n* **(a)** *(Mil, fig)* attacco; *(on individual)* aggressione *f;* **surprise** ~ attacco di sorpresa; ~ **on sb's life** attentato alla vita di qn; **to be under** ~ **(from)** essere attaccato (da); **to launch an** ~ *(Mil, fig)* sferrare un attacco. **(b)** *(Med)* attacco, accesso. **2** *vt (Mil, Med, fig)* attaccare; *(person)* aggredire, assalire; *(tackle: job, problem)* affrontare.
at·tack·er [ə'tækəʳ] *n* aggressore *m,* assalitore/trice.
at·tain [ə'teɪn] *vt (ambition)* realizzare; *(age, rank, happiness)* raggiungere, arrivare a.
at·tain·ment [ə'teɪnmənt] *n (see vb)* realizzazione *f;* raggiungimento; *(achievement)* risultato ottenuto; **linguistic** ~s cognizioni *fpl* linguistiche.
at·tempt [ə'tɛmpt] **1** *n (try)* tentativo; **he made no** ~ **to help** non ha (neanche) tentato *or* cercato di aiutare; **to make an** ~ **on sb's life** attentare alla vita di qn. **2** *vt:* **to** ~ **sth/to do sth** tentare qc/di fare qc; **he** ~**ed the exam** ha tentato l'esame; ~**ed murder** tentato omicidio.
at·tend [ə'tɛnd] **1** *vt* **(a)** *(be present at: meeting etc)* andare a, assistere a, essere presente a; *(regularly: school, church)* frequentare; *(: course, classes)* seguire, frequentare; **the lecture was well** ~**ed** c'era molta gente alla conferenza. **(b)** *(subj: bridesmaid, lady-in-waiting)* accompagnare; *(: doctor)* avere in cura, curare. **2** *vi (be present)* essere presente, esserci; *(pay attention to)* prestare attenzione, stare attento(a).
♦ **attend to** *vi + prep (lesson, speech)* prestare attenzione a; *(work, customer)* occuparsi di; **are you being** ~**ed to?** *(in shop)* la stanno servendo?
at·tend·ance [ə'tɛndəns] *n (act):* ~ **(at)** presenza (a); *(: regular)* frequenza (a); *(those present)* persone *fpl* presenti; **what was the** ~ **at the meeting?** quanti erano i presenti alla riunione?
at·tend·ant [ə'tɛndənt] *n (in carpark, museum etc)* custode *m/f;* *(servant)* attendente *m/f.*
at·ten·tion [ə'tɛnʃən] *n* **(a)** attenzione *f;* **to call sb's** ~ **to sth** richiamare qc all'attenzione di qn; **it has come to my** ~ **that...** sono venuto a conoscenza (del fatto) che...; **to pay** ~ **(to)** stare attento (a), fare attenzione (a); **for the** ~ **of** all'attenzione di. **(b)** *(Mil):* ~! attenti!; **to come to/stand at** ~ mettersi/stare sull'attenti. **(c):** ~s *pl* attenzioni *fpl,* premure *fpl.*
at·ten·tive [ə'tɛntɪv] *adj (heedful)* attento(a); *(polite, kind)* premuroso(a).
at·test [ə'tɛst] **1** *vt* attestare; *(signature)* autenticare. **2** *vi:* **to** ~ **to** testimoniare.
at·tic ['ætɪk] *n* soffitta, solaio; *(room)* mansarda.
at·tire [ə'taɪəʳ] **1** *n (frm)* tenuta. **2** *vt (frm):* **to** ~ **(in)** abbigliare (di, con).
at·ti·tude ['ætɪtjuːd] *n (gen)* atteggiamento; *(opinion):* ~ **(towards)** punto di vista (nei confronti di); ~ **of mind** modo di pensare; **if that's your** ~ se la prendi così.
at·tor·ney [ə'tɜːnɪ] *n (Am: lawyer)* avvocato/essa; *(representative)* procuratore *m;* **power of** ~ procura; **A**~ **General** *(Brit)* ≈ Procuratore *m* Generale; *(Am)* ≈ Ministro di grazia e giustizia, guardasigilli *m inv.*
at·tract [ə'trækt] *vt (subj: magnet etc)* attirare, attrarre; *(fig: interest, attention etc)* attirare, suscitare.
at·trac·tion [ə'trækʃən] *n* attrazione *f,* fascino; **city**

life **has no** ~ **for me** la vita di città non mi attira affatto; **one of the** ~**s was a free car** uno dei vantaggi era quello di una macchina gratis.
at·trac·tive [ə'træktɪv] *adj (person, dress, place)* attraente, affascinante; *(idea, offer, price)* allettante, interessante.
at·trac·tive·ly [ə'træktɪvlɪ] *adv* in modo attraente.
at·trib·ute ['ætrɪbjuːt] **1** *n* attributo. **2** [ə'trɪbjuːt] *vt:* **to** ~ **(to)** attribuire (a).
at·tribu·tive [ə'trɪbjʊtɪv] *adj (Gram)* attributivo(a).
at·tri·tion [ə'trɪʃən] *n* usura (per attrito); **war of** ~ guerra di logoramento.
auber·gine ['əʊbəʒiːn] *n (esp Brit)* melanzana.
auburn ['ɔːbən] *adj (hair)* ramato(a).
auc·tion ['ɔːkʃən] **1** *n* asta. **2** *vt* vendere all'asta. **3** *cpd:* ~ **room** *n* sala dell'asta; ~ **sale** *n* vendita all'asta.
auc·tion·eer [ˌɔːkʃə'nɪəʳ] *n* banditore/trice.
auda·cious [ɔː'deɪʃəs] *adj (bold)* audace; *(impudent)* sfrontato(a).
audac·ity [ɔː'dæsɪtɪ] *n (see adj)* audacia; sfacciataggine *f,* sfrontatezza.
audible ['ɔːdɪbl] *adj* udibile, percettibile; **there was** ~ **laughter** si è chiaramente sentita una risata; **he was hardly** ~ si riusciva a malapena a sentirlo.
audibly ['ɔːdɪblɪ] *adv* in modo che si senta, in modo chiaro.
audi·ence ['ɔːdɪəns] *n* **(a)** *(gathering)* pubblico; *(Radio)* ascoltatori *mpl;* *(TV)* telespettatori *mpl;* *(of speaker)* uditorio; **there was a big** ~ **at the theatre** c'erano molti spettatori *or* c'era un gran pubblico al teatro. **(b)** *(interview)* udienza.
audio-visual [ˌɔːdɪəʊ'vɪzjʊəl] *adj* audiovisivo(a); ~ **aids** sussidi *mpl* audiovisivi.
audit ['ɔːdɪt] **1** *n* revisione *f* dei conti, verifica (ufficiale) dei conti. **2** *vt* fare una revisione *or* un controllo di.
audi·tion [ɔː'dɪʃən] **1** *n (Theatre)* audizione *f;* *(Cine)* provino. **2** *vt* fare un'audizione *(or* un provino) a. **3** *vi* fare un'audizione *(or* un provino).
audi·tor ['ɔːdɪtəʳ] *n* revisore *m* dei conti.
audi·to·rium [ˌɔːdɪ'tɔːrɪəm] *n* sala, auditorio.
aug·ment [ɔːg'mɛnt] *vt* arrotondare.
August ['ɔːgəst] *n* agosto; *for usage see* **July.**
august [ɔː'gʌst] *adj (frm)* augusto(a).
aunt [ɑːnt] *n* zia; **my** ~ **and uncle** i miei zii, mia zia e mio zio.
auntie, aunty ['ɑːntɪ] *n (fam)* zietta; ~ **Jane** zia Jane.
au pair (girl) ['əʊ'pɛəʳ (ˌgɜːl)] *n* ragazza alla pari.
aura ['ɔːrə] *n* aura.
aus·pices ['ɔːspɪsɪz] *npl:* **under the** ~ **of** sotto gli auspici *or* l'auspicio di.
aus·pi·cious [ɔːs'pɪʃəs] *adj (sign)* di buon augurio, di buon auspicio; *(occasion)* propizio(a), favorevole; **to make an** ~ **start** iniziare sotto buoni auspici.
aus·tere [ɒs'tɪəʳ] *adj* austero(a).
aus·ter·ity [ɒs'tɛrɪtɪ] *n* austerità *f inv.*
Aus·tralia [ɒs'treɪlɪə] *n* Australia.
Aus·tral·ian [ɒs'treɪlɪən] *adj, n* australiano(a) *(m/f).*
Aus·tria ['ɒstrɪə] *n* Austria.
Aus·trian ['ɒstrɪən] *adj, n* austriaco(a) *(m/f).*
authen·tic [ɔː'θɛntɪk] *adj* autentico(a).
au·then·tic·ity [ˌɔːθɛn'tɪsɪtɪ] *n* autenticità.
author ['ɔːθəʳ] *n* autore/trice.
authori·tar·ian [ˌɔːθɒrɪ'tɛərɪən] *adj* autoritario(a).
authori·ta·tive [ɔː'θɒrɪtətɪv] *adj* autorevole.
author·ity [ɔː'θɒrɪtɪ] *n (power)* autorità; *(permission)* autorizzazione *f;* **those in** ~ i dirigenti, i governanti; **the authorities** le autorità; **the**

health authorities l'autorità sanitaria; **to be in ~ over** dare gli ordini a; **to have ~ to do sth** avere l'autorizzazione a fare *or* il diritto di fare qc; **he's an ~ (on)** è un'autorità (in materia di); **I have it on good ~ that...** so da fonte sicura *or* autorevole che... .

authori·za·tion [ˌɔːθəraɪˈzeɪʃən] *n* autorizzazione *f*.

author·ize [ˈɔːθəraɪz] *vt*: **to ~ sth/sb (to do sth)** autorizzare qc/qn (a fare qc).

autis·tic [ɔːˈtɪstɪk] *adj* autistico(a).

auto [ˈɔːtəʊ] *n (Am)* auto *f inv*.

auto... [ˈɔːtəʊ] *pref* auto... .

auto·bi·og·ra·phy [ˌɔːtəʊbaɪˈɒgrəfɪ] *n* autobiografia.

auto·crat·ic [ˌɔːtəʊˈkrætɪk] *adj* autocratico(a).

auto·graph [ˈɔːtəgrɑːf] **1** *n* autografo. **2** *vt* firmare.

auto·mat [ˈɔːtəmæt] *n (Am)* tavola calda fornita esclusivamente di distributori automatici.

auto·mat·ic [ˌɔːtəˈmætɪk] **1** *adj* automatico(a); **on ~ pilot** con pilota automatico. **2** *n (pistol)* (pistola) automatica; *(car)* automobile *f* con cambio automatico; *(washing machine)* lavatrice *f* automatica.

auto·mati·cal·ly [ˌɔːtəˈmætɪkəlɪ] *adv* automaticamente.

auto·ma·tion [ˌɔːtəˈmeɪʃən] *n* automazione *f*.

automa·ton [ɔːˈtɒmətən] *n, pl* **-ta** automa *m*.

auto·mo·bile [ˈɔːtəməbiːl] *n (Am)* automobile *f*.

autono·my [ɔːˈtɒnəmɪ] *n* autonomia.

autop·sy [ˈɔːtɒpsɪ] *n* autopsia.

autumn [ˈɔːtəm] **1** *n* autunno. **2** *adj* autunnale.

aux·ilia·ry [ɔːgˈzɪlɪərɪ] **1** *adj* ausiliario(a); *(Gram)* ausiliare. **2** *n (assistant)* assistente *m/f*, aiuto; *(verb)* ausiliare *m;* **auxiliaries** *(Mil)* truppe *fpl* ausiliarie.

Av., Ave. *abbr of* **avenue.**

avail [əˈveɪl] **1** *n*: **of no ~** inutile; **to no ~** invano, inutilmente. **2** *vt*: **to ~ o.s. of** *(opportunity)* approfittare di; *(rights)* (av)valersi di.

avail·abil·ity [əveɪləˈbɪlɪtɪ] *n* disponibilità.

avail·able [əˈveɪləbl] *adj* disponibile; **to make sth ~ to sb** mettere qc a disposizione di qn; **is the manager ~?** è libero il direttore?

ava·lanche [ˈævəlɑːnʃ] *n* valanga.

avant-garde [ˈævɑ̃ŋˈgɑːd] **1** *n* avanguardia. **2** *adj* d'avanguardia.

ava·rice [ˈævərɪs] *n* avarizia.

ava·ri·cious [ˌævəˈrɪʃəs] *adj* avaro(a).

avenge [əˈvendʒ] *vt* vendicare; **to ~ o.s. (on sb)** vendicarsi (di qn).

av·enue [ˈævənjuː] *n* viale *m;* *(fig)* strada, via.

av·er·age [ˈævərɪdʒ] **1** *adj* medio(a); *(pej)* qualsiasi *inv*, ordinario(a). **2** *n* media; **on ~** in media; **above ~** al di sopra della media. **3** *vt* **(a)** *(find the ~ of: also: ~ out)* fare *or* calcolare la media fra; *(reach an ~ of)* fare una media di. **(b)** *(also: ~ out at)* aggirarsi in media su, essere in media di.

averse [əˈvɜːs] *adj*: **~ to** *(opposed)* (contrario(a) (a); *(disinclined)* restio(a) (a); **I'm not ~ to an occasional drink** non mi dispiace bere un bicchierino ogni tanto.

aver·sion [əˈvɜːʃən] *n (dislike)*: **~ (for, to)** avversione *f* (per); **spiders are his ~** ha la fobia dei ragni; **my pet ~** ciò che detesto di più; **to have an ~ to sb/sth** avere *or* nutrire un'avversione nei confronti di qn/qc.

avert [əˈvɜːt] *vt (turn away: eyes, thoughts)*: **to ~ (from)** distogliere (da), allontanare (da); *(prevent: accident, danger etc)* evitare.

aviary [ˈeɪvɪərɪ] *n* voliera, uccelliera.

avia·tion [ˌeɪvɪˈeɪʃən] *n* aviazione *f*.

avid [ˈævɪd] *adj*: **~ (for)** desideroso (di), insa-

ziabile (di); **an ~ reader** un accanito *or* appassionato lettore.

avo·ca·do [ˌævəˈkɑːdəʊ] *n* avocado.

avoid [əˈvɔɪd] *vt (obstacle)* scansare, schivare, evitare; *(argument etc)* evitare; *(danger)* sfuggire a; **to ~ doing sth** evitare di fare qc; **try to ~ being seen** cerca di non farti vedere; **are you trying to ~ me?** stai cercando di evitarmi *or* di sfuggirmi?

avoid·able [əˈvɔɪdəbl] *adj* evitabile.

avow [əˈvaʊ] *vt (frm: declare)* dichiarare apertamente.

avowed [əˈvaʊd] *adj* dichiarato(a).

await [əˈweɪt] *vt* aspettare, attendere; **long ~ed** tanto atteso.

awake [əˈweɪk] *(vb: pt* **awoke** *or* **~d,** *pp* **awoken** *or* **~d)* **1** *adj* sveglio(a); **to lie ~** rimanere sveglio a letto; **coffee keeps me ~** il caffè mi fa star sveglio; **to be ~ to** *(fig)* essere cosciente *or* conscio di. **2** *vt* svegliare; *(fig)* destare, svegliare; *(: memories)* risvegliare, ridestare. **3** *vi* svegliarsi; *(fig)*: **to ~ to sth** rendersi conto di qc, aprire gli occhi su qc.

awak·en [əˈweɪkən] *vt, vi* = **awake 2, 3.**

award [əˈwɔːd] **1** *n (prize)* premio; *(scholarship)* borsa di studio; *(Law: decision)* sentenza arbitrale; *(: sum)* ricompensa, risarcimento. **2** *vt*: **to ~ sb sth, to ~ sth to sb** *(prize)* assegnare qc a qn; *(medal)* conferire qc a qn; *(damages)* concedere a qn il risarcimento di qc.

aware [əˈwɛəˈ] *adj*: **to be ~ of** *(conscious)* rendersi conto di; *(informed)* essere al corrente di; **not that I am ~ of** non che io sappia; **I am fully ~ that** mi rendo perfettamente conto che; **to make sb ~ of sth** rendere qn consapevole di qc; **to be politically/socially ~** aver coscienza politica/sociale.

aware·ness [əˈwɛənɪs] *n* coscienza.

awash [əˈwɒʃ] *adj*: **~ (with)** inondato(a) (di).

away [əˈweɪ] *adv* **(a)** lontano; **far ~ from home** molto lontano da casa; **the village is 3 miles ~** il paese è a 3 miglia di distanza *or* è lontano 3 miglia; **~ in the distance** in lontananza. **(b)** *(absent)*: **to be ~** essere via; **he's ~ in Milan** è (andato) a Milano; **go ~!** va' via (di qui)!, via di qui! **(c)**: **to turn ~** girarsi, voltarsi; **to die ~** *(sound)* spegnersi in lontananza; **the snow melted ~** la neve si è completamente sciolta; **to play ~** *(Sport)* giocare in trasferta *or* fuori casa; **to talk ~** parlare in continuazione; **to work ~** continuare a lavorare.

awe [ɔː] **1** *n* timore *m* reverenziale; **to stand in ~ of** aver soggezione di. **2** *vt* intimidire.

awe-inspiring [ˈɔːɪnˌspaɪərɪŋ] *adj*, **awe·some** [ˈɔːsəm] *adj* imponente.

aw·ful [ˈɔːfəl] *adj (fam)* terribile, orribile; **an ~ lot of** *(people, cars, dogs)* un numero incredibile di; *(jam, flowers)* una quantità incredibile di; **how ~!** che orrore!

aw·ful·ly [ˈɔːflɪ] *adv (fam)* terribilmente; **thanks ~** mille grazie; **I'm ~ sorry** sono terribilmente spiacente.

awk·ward [ˈɔːkwəd] *adj* **(a)** *(difficult: problem, question, situation, task)* delicato(a), difficile; *(silence)* imbarazzante; *(time, moment)* poco opportuno(a); *(tool)* poco maneggevole, scomodo(a); *(shape)* difficile, *(Aut: corner)* difficile; **you've caught me at an ~ time** mi hai pescato in un momento poco opportuno; **Friday is ~ for me** venerdì mi riesce scomodo; **he's being ~ about it** sta rendendo la cosa un po' difficile; **he's an ~ customer** è un tipo difficile. **(b)** *(clumsy: person)* goffo(a); *(: gesture, movement)* impacciato(a);

(style, phrasing) contorto(a); **the ~ age** l'età difficile.

awl [ɔːl] *n* punteruolo.

awn·ing ['ɔːnɪŋ] *n (of shop etc)* tenda, tendone *m*.

awoke [ə'wəuk] *pt of* **awake; ~n** [ə'wəukən[*pp of* **awake.**

axe, *(Am)* **ax** [æks] **1** *n* ascia, scure *f;* **to have an ~ to grind** *(fig)* fare i propri interessi *or* il proprio tornaconto. **2** *vt (fig: expenditure)* ridurre dra-

sticamente; *(: person)* liquidare *(per ragioni economiche).*

axi·om ['æksɪəm] *n* assioma *m*.

axio·mat·ic [,æksɪəu'mætɪk] *adj* assiomatico(a).

axis ['æksɪs] *n, pl* **axes** ['æksiːz] asse *m (Geom etc).*

axle ['æksl] *n (of wheel)* semiasse *m; (~-tree)* asse *m.*

azalea [ə'zeɪlɪə] *n* azalea.

az·ure ['eɪʒəʳ] **1** *adj* azzurro(a). **2** *n* azzurro.

B

B, b [biː] *n* **(a)** *(letter)* B, b f *or m inv.* **(b)** *(Mus)* si *m.*
B.A. *abbr see* **bachelor.**
bab·ble ['bæbl] **1** *n (of voices)* mormorio; *(of baby)*
balbettio; *(of stream)* gorgoglio. **2** *vi (indistinctly)*
farfugliare; *(chatter)* parlare a vanvera; *(baby)*
balbettare; *(stream)* gorgogliare.
ba·boon [bə'buːn] *n* babbuino.
baby ['beɪbɪ] **1** *n (human)* bambino/a, bimbo/a; *(of
animal)* piccolo; *(fam: as address: to woman)* piccola, bimba mia; *(: to man)* piccolo, bello; **the ~
of the family** il piccolino *or* il pupo di casa; **don't
be such a ~!** non fare il bambino!; **to throw the ~
out with the bathwater** *(fig)* buttar tutto a mare;
the new system was his ~ *(fam)* il nuovo sistema
era la sua creatura; **I was left holding the ~**
(fam) mi hanno piantato lì a sbrogliarmela da
solo. **2** *cpd (clothes etc)* da bambino; **~ bird** *n*
uccellino; **~ boy** *n* maschietto; **~ carriage** *n*
carrozzina; **~ girl** *n* femminuccia; **~ grand
(piano)** *n* pianoforte *m* a mezza coda; **~ rabbit** *n*
coniglietto.
ba·by·hood ['beɪbɪhʊd] *n* prima infanzia.
ba·by·ish ['beɪbɪɪʃ] *adj* puerile, infantile.
baby-minder ['beɪbɪ,maɪndəʳ] *n* bambinaia *(che
tiene i bambini mentre la madre lavora).*
baby-sit ['beɪbɪsɪt] *vi:* **to ~ (for sb)** guardare i
bambini (a qn), fare il(la) baby-sitter (per qn).
baby-sitter ['beɪbɪ,sɪtəʳ] *n* baby-sitter *m/f inv.*
bach·elor ['bætʃələʳ] *n* scapolo; **B~ of Arts/
Science** *(abbr* **B.A./B.Sc.)** *(Univ: degree)* laurea in
lettere/scienze; *(: person)* dottore/essa in lettere/
scienze.
ba·cil·lus [bə'sɪləs] *n, pl* **bacilli** [bə'sɪlaɪ] bacillo.
back [bæk] **1** *n* **(a)** *(of person)* schiena; *(of animal)*
dorso, schiena; **he fell on his ~** è caduto di
schiena; **I don't like to sit with my ~ to the
engine** *(in train)* preferisco sedermi nel senso di
marcia; **with one's ~ to the light** con le spalle
alla luce; **seen from the ~** visto di spalle; **~ to ~**
di spalle (uno contro l'altro); **behind sb's ~** alle
spalle di qn; *(fig)* alle spalle *or* dietro le spalle di
qn; **to break one's ~** rompersi la schiena; **to
break the ~ of a job** fare il grosso *or* il peggio di
un lavoro; **to put one's ~ into it** *(fam)* mettercela
tutta; **to have one's ~ to the wall** *(fig)* essere *or*
trovarsi con le spalle al muro; **to put sb's ~ up**
(fam) far irritare qn; **to get off sb's ~** *(fam)*
lasciare qn in pace; **I was glad to see the ~ of him**
(fam) quando se n'è andato ho tirato un respiro di
sollievo.
  (b) *(as opposed to front)* dietro; *(of cheque, envelope, medal)* retro, rovescio; *(of head)* nuca; *(of
hand)* dorso; *(of hall, room)* fondo; *(of house, car)*
parte *f* posteriore, dietro; *(of chair)* spalliera,
schienale *m;* **at the ~ of the classroom** in fondo
alla classe; **~ to front** all'incontrario; **at the ~ of
my mind was the thought that...** sotto sotto pensavo che...; **it's always there at the ~ of my mind**
è sempre lì, non riesco a togliermelo dalla mente; **I know Naples like the ~ of my hand** conosco
Napoli come il palmo della mia mano *or* come le

mie tasche; **at the ~ of beyond** *(fam)* in capo al
mondo; **he's at the ~ of all this trouble** c'è lui
dietro a questa storia.
  2 *adj attr* **(a)** *(rear)* di dietro; *(: wheel, seat)*
posteriore; **~ garden/room** giardino/stanza sul
retro (della casa); **~ cover** retro della copertina;
~ page ultima pagina; **to take a ~ seat** *(fig)*
restare in secondo piano; **he's a ~ seat driver** sta
sempre a criticare chi guida; **~ street** vicolo; **he
grew up in the ~ streets of Glasgow** è cresciuto
nei bassifondi di Glasgow.
  (b) *(overdue: rent, etc)* arretrato(a); *(past:
number: of magazine etc)* arretrato(a), vecchio(a);
~ payments arretrati *mpl.*
  3 *adv* **(a)** *(again, returning):* often 'ri' + *verb:* **to
go ~** (ri)tornare; **to be ~** essere tornato; **when
will you be ~?** quando torni?; **30 km there and ~**
30 km fra andata e ritorno; **put it ~ on the shelf**
rimettilo sullo scaffale; **she kissed him ~** gli
restituì il bacio, lo baciò a sua volta.
  (b) *(in distance)* indietro; **stand ~!** indietro!;
~ and forth avanti e indietro; **set ~ from the
road** un po' indietro rispetto alla strada.
  (c) *(in time):* **some months ~** mesi fa *or* addietro; **as far ~ as the 13th century** già nel
duecento.
  4 *vt* **(a)** *(car):* **to ~ (into)** far entrare a marcia
indietro (in).
  (b) *(support: plan, person)* appoggiare, sostenere, spalleggiare; *(: financially)* finanziare.
  (c) *(bet on: horse)* puntare su.
  5 *vi (move: person)* indietreggiare; *(in car)* fare
marcia indietro; **she ~ed into me** ha fatto un
passo indietro e mi è venuta addosso; *(in car)* mi
è venuta addosso a marcia indietro.
♦ **back away** *vi + adv:* **to ~ away (from)** indietreggiare (davanti a), tirarsi indietro (da).
♦ **back down** *vi + adv (fig)* abbandonare, arrendersi.
♦ **back on to** *vi + prep:* **the house ~s on to the golf
course** il retro della casa dà sul campo da golf.
♦ **back out** *vi + adv (fig)* tirarsi indietro; **to ~ out
of sth** *(duty)* sottrarsi a; *(deal)* ritirarsi da.
♦ **back up 1** *vt + adv* **(a)** *(support: person)* appoggiare, sostenere; *(claim, theory)* confermare, avvalorare. **(b)** *(car):* **to ~ the car up** far marcia
indietro. **2** *vi + adv* **(a)** *(in car)* far marcia indietro. **(b)** *(Am: be congested)* ingorgarsi.
back·ache ['bæk,eɪk] *n* mal *m* di schiena.
back·bencher ['bæk'bentʃəʳ] *n* deputato/essa,
semplice parlamentare *m/f.*
back·bone ['bækbəʊn] *n (also fig)* spina dorsale;
the ~ of the organization l'anima dell'organizzazione.
back·chat ['bæk,tʃæt] *n* impertinenza.
back·cloth ['bæk,klɒθ] *n* fondale *m.*
back·comb ['bæk,kəʊm] *vt* cotonare.
back·date [,bæk'deɪt] *vt* retrodatare; **~d payrise**
aumento retroattivo.
back·drop ['bæk,drɒp] *n* = **backcloth.**
back·er ['bækəʳ] *n (supporter)* sostenitore/trice,

fautore/trice; *(Comm)* finanziatore/trice.

back·fire ['bæk'faɪəʳ] *vi (Aut)* avere un ritorno di fiamma; *(fig)* avere effetto contrario; **to ~ on sb** ritorcersi contro qn.

back·gam·mon [bæk'gæmən] *n* backgammon *m*, tavola reale.

back·ground ['bækgraʊnd] **1** *n* **(a)** *(gen)* sfondo; *(fig)* sfondo, scenario; **in the ~** sullo sfondo; *(fig)* nell'ombra; **on a red ~** su sfondo rosso. **(b)** *(of person: social)* ambiente *m*; *(: cultural)* formazione *f*; *(of problem, event)* retroscena *m*; **she comes from a wealthy ~** è di famiglia ricca. **2** *cpd (music, noise)* di fondo; **~ reading** *n* letture *fpl* sull'argomento.

back·hand ['bæk,hænd] *n (Sport)* rovescio.

back·hand·er ['bæk,hændəʳ] *n (bribe)* bustarella.

back·ing ['bækɪŋ] *n* **(a)** *(support)* appoggio, sostegno; *(Comm)* finanziamento. **(b)** *(Mus)* accompagnamento. **(c)** *(paper etc protecting the back)* rivestimento, strato protettivo.

back·lash ['bæk,læʃ] *n (fig)* reazione *f* (violenta).

back·log ['bæk,lɒg] *n (of work)* cumulo di lavoro arretrato; **the strike resulted in a ~ of orders** a causa dello sciopero si sono accumulate le ordinazioni.

back·pack ['bæk,pæk] *n* zaino.

back·side [,bæk'saɪd] *n (fam)* didietro *m inv*, sedere *m*.

back·slide [,bæk'slaɪd] *vi* ricadere.

back·space ['bæk,speɪs] *vi (in typing)* battere il tasto di ritorno.

back·stage [,bæk'steɪdʒ] *adv* nel retroscena.

back·street ['bæk,striːt] *adj attr* secondario(a); **a ~ cafe** un bar d'infima categoria; **~ abortionist** praticante *m/f* di aborti clandestini.

back·stroke ['bæk,strəʊk] *n (Swimming)* dorso.

back·up ['bækʌp] **1** *adj (train, plane)* supplementare. **2** *n (Am: congestion)* ingorgo.

back·ward ['bækwəd] *adj* **(a)** *(motion, glance)* all'indietro. **(b)** *(pupil)* lento(a); *(country)* arretrato(a). **(c)** *(reluctant):* **~ (in doing sth)** restio(a) (a fare qc).

back·ward(s) ['bækwəd(z)] *adv* indietro; **to walk ~** camminare all'indietro; **~ and forwards** avanti e indietro; **to bend over ~ to do sth** *(fam)* farsi in quattro per fare qc; **to know sth ~** *(fam)* sapere qc a menadito.

back·water ['bæk,wɔːtəʳ] *n* acqua stagnante; *(fig pej)* buco, angolo sperduto; **this town is a cultural ~** questa città è un deserto culturale.

back·yard [,bæk'jɑːd] *n* cortile *m*.

ba·con ['beɪkən] *n* pancetta; **~ and eggs** uova *fpl* con la pancetta.

bac·te·ria [bæk'tɪərɪə] *npl* batteri *mpl*.

bac·te·rial [bæk'tɪərɪəl] *adj* batterico(a).

bac·te·ri·ol·ogy [bæk,tɪərɪ'ɒlədʒɪ] *n* batteriologia.

bad [bæd] *adj (comp* **worse,** *superl* **worst) (a)** *(gen)* cattivo(a); *(habit, news, weather)* brutto(a); *(workmanship, film)* scadente, brutto(a); *(mistake, illness, cut)* brutto(a), grave; **~ language** parolacce *fpl*; **~ debt** credito difficile da recuperare; **you ~ boy!** (brutto) cattivo!; **he's ~ at tennis/at keeping appointments** non sa giocare a tennis/tenere un impegno; **smoking is ~ for you** il fumo fa male alla salute; **not ~** *(quite good)* non male; *(less enthusiastic)* così così; **how are you feeling? — not ~** come si sente? — non c'è male; **not ~, eh?** mica male, eh?; **that wouldn't be a ~ thing** non sarebbe una cattiva idea; **that's too ~** *(sympathetic)* che peccato; *(indignant)* tanto peggio per te *(or lei etc)*; **it's too ~ of you** è poco carino da parte tua; **business is ~** gli affari vanno male; **from ~ to worse** di male in peggio;

to have a ~ time of it passarsela male; **to be in a ~ way** *(in difficulties)* essere nei guai; *(ill)* stare molto male.

(b) *(rotten: food)* guasto(a); *(: smell)* cattivo(a); *(: tooth)* cariato(a), guasto(a); **to go ~** andare a male.

(c): to have a ~ back/stomach *etc* avere dei problemi alla schiena/allo stomaco *etc*; **to feel ~** *(sick)* sentirsi male; **I feel ~ about it** *(guilty)* mi sento un po' in colpa; **there's no need for you to feel ~ about it** non c'è bisogno di prendersela.

bade [bæd, beɪd] *pt of* **bid.**

badge [bædʒ] *n (gen, Scol)* distintivo; *(Mil)* scudetto; *(stick-on)* adesivo.

badg·er ['bædʒəʳ] **1** *n* tasso. **2** *vt (fig)* tormentare.

bad·ly ['bædlɪ] *adv (comp* **worse,** *superl* **worst) (a)** male; **a ~ behaved child** un bambino maleducato; **things are going ~** le cose vanno male; **to treat sb ~** trattar male qn. **(b)** *(seriously: wounded)* gravemente; **he was ~ hurt** ha riportato gravi ferite. **(c)** *(very much):* **I need it ~** ne ho assolutamente bisogno; **I want it ~** lo voglio ad ogni costo; **it ~ needs painting** ha proprio bisogno di una mano di vernice; **he ~ needs help** ha urgente bisogno di aiuto.

bad-mannered [,bæd'mænəd] *adj* maleducato(a), sgarbato(a).

bad·min·ton ['bædmɪntən] *n* badminton *m*.

bad-tempered [,bæd'tempəd] *adj* irascibile, di brutto carattere; *(in bad mood)* di malumore.

baf·fle ['bæfl] *vt* lasciare perplesso(a), confondere; **it ~s me how he does it** non riesco a capire come faccia.

baf·fling ['bæflɪŋ] *adj* sconcertante.

bag [bæg] *n (gen)* borsa; *(paper ~, carrier ~)* sacchetto; *(hand~)* borsa, borsetta; *(suitcase)* valigia; **to pack one's ~s** fare le valigie; **it's in the ~** *(fam)* ce l'ho *(or* ce l'hai *etc)* in tasca, è cosa fatta; **~s under the eyes** borse sotto gli occhi; **~s of** *(fam: lots)* un sacco di.

bag·gage ['bægɪdʒ] **1** *n* bagaglio, bagagli *mpl*. **2** *cpd:* **~ claim** *n* ritiro bagagli.

bag·gy ['bægɪ] *adj* largo(a), sformato(a).

bag·pipes ['bæg,paɪps] *npl (in Scotland)* cornamusa; *(in Italy)* zampogna.

bag-snatcher ['bæg,snætʃəʳ] *n* scippatore/trice.

Ba·ha·mas [bə'hɑːməz] *npl:* **the ~** le Bahama.

bail[1] [beɪl] *n (Law)* cauzione *f*; **he was granted ~** ha ottenuto la libertà provvisoria su cauzione; **to stand ~ for sb** rendersi garante di *or* per qn; **to be released on ~** essere rilasciato su cauzione.

♦ **bail out** *vt + adv (Law)* far mettere in libertà provvisoria su cauzione; *(fig)* tirare fuori dai guai.

bail[2] [beɪl] *vt, vi see* **bale out 1, 2(a).**

bail·iff ['beɪlɪf] *n (Law)* ufficiale *m* giudiziario; *(on estate)* amministratore *m*, fattore *m*.

bait [beɪt] **1** *n (also fig)* esca; **he didn't rise to the ~** *(fig)* non ha abboccato (all'amo). **2** *vt (hook)* innescare; *(trap)* munire di esca; *(torment: person, animal)* stuzzicare, tormentare.

baize [beɪz] *n* panno.

bake [beɪk] *vt (bread, cake)* cuocere (al forno); *(bricks)* cuocere; **she ~d a cake today** ha fatto un dolce oggi; **~d beans** fagioli *mpl* in umido; **~d potatoes** patate *fpl* al forno.

bak·er ['beɪkəʳ] *n* fornaio, panettiere *m*; **~'s (shop)** panetteria; **at the ~'s** dal fornaio.

bak·ery ['beɪkərɪ] *n* panificio, forno.

bak·ing ['beɪkɪŋ] **1** *n* cottura (al forno); **Monday is her day for doing the ~** lunedì fa il pane (e/o i dolci). **2** *adj (fam: hot):* **it's ~ in here** qui dentro è un forno. **3** *cpd:* **~ dish** *n* pirofila; **~ powder** *n* lievito in polvere; ~ **soda** n bicarbonato di soda; ~ **tin** n stampo, tortiera.

bala·cla·va (**hel·met**) [ˌbælə'klɑːvə('hɛlmɪt)] n passamontagna m inv.

bal·ance ['bæləns] **1** n (a) (equilibrium) equilibrio; **to lose one's** ~ perdere l'equilibrio; **to throw sb off** ~ far perdere l'equilibrio a qn; (fig) sconcertare qn, far mancare la terra sotto i piedi a qn; ~ **of power** equilibrio di potere; **to strike the right** ~ trovare il giusto mezzo; **on** ~ (fig) a conti fatti, tutto sommato; **a nice** ~ **of humour and pathos** un'armoniosa combinazione di humour e pathos. **(b)** (scales) bilancia; **to hang in the** ~ (fig) essere incerto or in bilico. **(c)** (Comm) bilancio; (: difference) saldo; (: remainder) resto; **a healthy bank** ~ un buon conto in banca; ~ **carried forward** saldo riportato or da riportare; ~ **of payments** bilancia dei pagamenti; ~ **of trade** bilancia commerciale.

2 vt **(a)** tenere in equilibrio or in bilico; (Aut: wheel) fare l'equilibratura di; (fig: compare) soppesare, valutare; (make up for) compensare; **the two things** ~ **each other** out le due cose si compensano; **this must be** ~**d against that** nel considerare questo fattore bisogna tener presente l'altro. **(b)** (Comm: account) saldare; (: budget) pareggiare; **to** ~ **the books** fare il bilancio.

3 vi **(a)** tenersi in equilibrio. **(b)** (accounts) quadrare, essere in pareggio.

4 cpd: ~ **sheet** n bilancio (di esercizio).

bal·anced ['bælənst] adj (views) moderato(a); (personality, diet) equilibrato(a).

bal·co·ny ['bælkənɪ] n balcone m; (Theatre) prima galleria, balconata.

bald [bɔːld] adj (person) calvo(a); (tyre) liscio(a); (statement) asciutto(a); (style) spoglio(a); **to go** ~ perdere i capelli.

bald·ly ['bɔːldlɪ] adv senza tanti complimenti.

bald·ness ['bɔːldnɪs] n (of person) calvizie f; (of tyre) stato di logoramento.

bale[1] [beɪl] n (of cloth, hay) balla.

bale[2] [beɪl] vt, vi see **bale out** 1, 2(a).

♦ **bale out 1** vt + adv (Naut: water) vuotare; (: boat) sgottare. **2** vi + adv **(a)** (Naut) saltare in acqua. **(b)** (Aer) gettarsi col paracadute.

Bal·ear·ic [ˌbælɪ'ærɪk] adj: **the** ~ **Islands** le (isole) Baleari.

bale·ful ['beɪlfʊl] adj (look) minaccioso(a).

balk [bɔːk] vi: **to** ~ (**at the idea of**) (person) recalcitrare (all'idea di); (horse) recalcitrare or impennarsi (di fronte a).

Bal·kan ['bɔːlkən] **1** adj balcanico(a). **2** n: **the** ~**s i** Balcani.

ball[1] [bɔːl] **1** n (gen) palla; (inflated: Ftbl etc) pallone m; (of wool, string) gomitolo; **a glass** ~ un globo di vetro; **he rolled the paper into a** ~ ha appallottolato la carta; **the** ~ **of the foot** la punta del piede; **the** ~ **of the thumb** il polpastrello del pollice; **to be on the** ~ (fig: competent) essere in gamba; (: alert) stare all'erta; **to play** ~ (**with sb**) giocare a palla (con qn); (fig) stare al gioco (di qn); **to start the** ~ **rolling** (fig) fare la prima mossa; **to keep the** ~ **rolling** (fig) mandare avanti le cose; **the** ~ **is in your court** (fig) tocca a te. **2** cpd: ~ **bearing** n cuscinetto a sfere.

ball[2] [bɔːl] n (dance) ballo.

bal·lad ['bæləd] n ballata.

bal·last ['bæləst] n zavorra.

ball·cock ['bɔːl,kɒk] n galleggiante m.

bal·le·ri·na [ˌbælə'riːnə] n ballerina.

bal·let ['bæleɪ] **1** n balletto; (art) danza classica. **2** cpd: ~ **dancer** n ballerino/a.

bal·lis·tic [bə'lɪstɪk] adj balistico(a); **interconti-**

nental ~ **missile** missile m a gettata intercontinentale.

bal·lis·tics [bə'lɪstɪks] nsg balistica.

bal·loon [bə'luːn] n (toy) palloncino; (Aer) pallone m aerostatico, mongolfiera; (in comic strip) fumetto.

bal·loon·ist [bə'luːnɪst] n aeronauta m/f.

bal·lot ['bælət] **1** n votazione f (a scrutinio segreto); **on the first** ~ alla prima votazione. **2** vt (members) consultare tramite votazione. **3** cpd: ~ **box** n urna (elettorale); ~ **paper** n scheda (elettorale).

ball·park ['bɔːl,pɑːk] n (Am) stadio di baseball.

ball·point (**pen**) ['bɔːl,pɔɪnt('pɛn)] n penna a sfera.

ball·room ['bɔːl,rʊm] **1** n sala da ballo. **2** cpd: ~ **dancing** n ballo moderno.

balm [bɑːm] n balsamo.

balmy ['bɑːmɪ] adj **(a)** (breeze, air) balsamico(a). **(b)** (fam) = **barmy.**

bal·sa (**wood**) ['bɔːlsə(ˌwʊd)] n (legno di) balsa.

Bal·tic ['bɔːltɪk] adj baltico(a); **the** ~ (**Sea**) il Mar Baltico.

bal·us·trade [ˌbæləs'treɪd] n balaustrata.

bam·boo [bæm'buː] n bambù m.

bam·boo·zle [bæm'buːzl] vt (fam) abbindolare.

ban [bæn] **1** n divieto, bando; **to put a** ~ **on sth** proibire qc. **2** vt (pt, pp ~**ned**) (person) sospendere, espellere; (alcohol, book, film) proibire; **he was** ~**ned from driving** gli hanno tolto la patente.

ba·nal [bə'nɑːl] adj banale.

ba·nal·ity [bə'nælɪtɪ] n banalità.

ba·na·na [bə'nɑːnə] n (fruit) banana; (tree) banano.

band[1] [bænd] n (gen) banda, striscia; (of hat, cigar) nastro.

band[2] [bænd] n **(a)** (Mus) banda (musicale); (jazz ~, pop ~) complesso; (Mil) fanfara. **(b)** (group of people) banda.

♦ **band together** vi + adv mettersi in gruppo.

band·age ['bændɪdʒ] **1** n fascia, benda. **2** vt fasciare, bendare.

ban·dan(n)a [bæn'dænə] n fazzolettone m.

ban·dit ['bændɪt] n bandito, brigante m.

band·stand ['bænd,stænd] n palco dell'orchestra.

band·wagon ['bænd,wægən] n: **to jump** or **climb on the** ~ buttarcisi.

ban·dy ['bændɪ] vt (jokes, insults) scambiarsi; **to** ~ **sb's name about** sparlare di qn.

bandy-legged ['bændɪ'lɛgɪd] adj dalle or con le gambe storte.

bane [beɪn] n: **it** (or he etc) **is the** ~ **of my life** è la mia rovina.

bang[1] [bæŋ] **1** n (noise: of explosion, gun) scoppio, colpo; (: of sth falling) tonfo; (blow) botta, colpo; **he closed the door with a** ~ ha sbattuto la porta; **it went with a** ~ (fam) è stato una bomba. **2** adv: **to go** ~ esplodere, fare bang; **to be** ~ **on time** (fam) spaccare il secondo; ~ **went £10** mi (or gli etc) sono volate 10 sterline. **3** vt (thump) battere, picchiare; (hit, knock, slam) sbattere; **he** ~**ed the receiver down** ha sbattuto giù il telefono. **4** vi (explode) scoppiare, esplodere; (slam: door) sbattere; **to** ~ **at/on sth** picchiare a/su qc; **to** ~ **into sth** sbattere contro qc.

bang[2] [bæŋ] n (fringe) frangetta.

bang·er ['bæŋə'] n (fam) **(a)** (sausage) salsiccia. **(b)** (firework) mortaretto. **(c)** (old car) macinino.

ban·gle ['bæŋgl] n braccialetto.

ban·ish ['bænɪʃ] vt: **to** ~ (**from**) (person) bandire (da), esiliare (da); (thought, fear) bandire (da).

ban·is·ters ['bænɪstəz] npl ringhiera.

ban·jo ['bændʒəʊ] n banjo m inv.

bank [bæŋk] **1** *n* **(a)** *(of river etc)* sponda, riva; *(: embankment)* argine *m*; *(of road, racetrack)* terrapieno. **(b)** *(heap: of earth, mud)* mucchio; *(: of snow)* cumulo; *(: of clouds, sand)* banco. **(c)** *(Fin, Med)* banca; *(Gambling)* banco. **(d)** *(Aer)* virata. **2** *vt (money)* depositare in banca. **3** *vi* servirsi di una banca; **where do you ~?** qual'è la sua banca? **4** *cpd:* **~ account** *n* conto in banca; **~ card** *n* carta assegni; **~ charges** *npl* spese *fpl* bancarie; **~ draft** *n* assegno circolare *or* bancario; **~ holiday** *n* festa nazionale, giorno di festa; **~ loan** *n* prestito bancario; **~ manager** *n* direttore di banca; **~ rate** *n* tasso bancario.

♦ **bank on** *vi* + *prep (fam)* far conto su.

bank·book ['bæŋk,bʊk] *n* libretto di banca.

bank·er ['bæŋkə'] *n* banchiere *m*; **~'s card** carta assegni.

bank·ing ['bæŋkɪŋ] *n* attività bancaria; **to study ~** fare studi bancari *or* di tecnica bancaria.

bank·note ['bæŋk,nəʊt] *n* banconota.

bank·rupt ['bæŋkrʌpt] **1** *adj* fallito(a); *(fam: broke)* senza una lira; **to go ~** fallire, fare fallimento *or* bancarotta. **2** *n* fallito/a. **3** *vt* portare al fallimento.

bank·rupt·cy ['bæŋkrəptsɪ] *n* fallimento, bancarotta.

ban·ner ['bænə'] *n* stendardo; *(with slogan)* striscione *m*.

ban·nis·ters ['bænɪstəz] *npl* = **banisters.**

banns [bænz] *npl* pubblicazioni *fpl* matrimoniali; **to put up the ~** fare le pubblicazioni.

ban·quet ['bæŋkwɪt] *n* banchetto.

ban·tam ['bæntəm] *n* gallo 'bantam'.

bantam·weight ['bæntəm,weɪt] *n (Sport)* peso gallo.

ban·ter ['bæntə'] *n* scherzi *mpl* bonari.

bap·tism ['bæptɪzəm] *n* battesimo.

Bap·tist ['bæptɪst] *adj, n (Rel)* battista *(m/f)*; **St John the ~** San Giovanni Battista.

bap·tize [bæp'taɪz] *vt* battezzare.

bar¹ [baː'] **1** *n* **(a)** *(piece: of wood, metal etc)* sbarra; *(of chocolate)* tavoletta; *(of electric fire)* elemento; **~ of soap** saponetta. **(b)** *(of window, cage etc)* sbarra; *(on door)* spranga; *(fig: obstacle)*: **~ (to)** barriera (a), ostacolo (a); **behind ~s** dietro le sbarre. **(c)** *(pub)* bar *m inv*; *(counter)* banco. **(d)** *(Law: in court)*: **the prisoner at the ~** l'imputato; **to be called** *or (Am)* **admitted to the B~** essere ammesso all'Ordine degli Avvocati. **(e)** *(Mus)* battuta. **2** *vt (obstruct: way)* sbarrare; *(fasten: door, window)* sbarrare, sprangare; *(ban: person)* escludere; *(: activity, thing)* proibire.

bar² [baː'] *prep* ad esclusione di, tranne; **~ none** nessuno escluso.

barb [baːb] *n (of hook, arrow)* punta.

Bar·ba·dos [baː'beɪdɒs] *n* Barbados *fpl*.

bar·bar·ian [baː'bɛərɪən] *n* barbaro/a.

bar·bar·ic [baː'bærɪk] *adj*, **bar·ba·rous** ['baːbərəs] *adj (culture, cruelty)* barbaro(a); *(splendour)* barbarico(a).

bar·becue ['baːbɪkjuː] **1** *n (grill)* barbecue *m inv*; *(party)* grigliata all'aperto. **2** *vt* cuocere alla brace.

barbed wire ['baːbd'waɪə'] *n* filo spinato.

bar·ber ['baːbə'] *n* barbiere *m*; **at the ~'s (shop)** dal barbiere.

bar·bi·tu·rate [baː'bɪtjʊrɪt] *n* barbiturico.

bard [baːd] *n (old)* bardo.

bare [bɛə'] **1** *adj* **(a)** *(gen)* nudo(a); *(arms, legs, head)* nudo(a), scoperto(a); *(landscape)* spoglio(a), brullo(a); *(ground, tree, room)* nudo(a), spoglio(a); *(cupboard)* vuoto(a); *(Elec: wire)* scoperto(a); **there's a ~ patch in the carpet** il tap-

peto è spelacchiato in quel punto; **with his ~ hands** con le sue stesse mani; **to lay ~** *(fig)* mettere a nudo. **(b)** *(meagre: majority etc)* minimo(a); **to earn/scrape a ~ living** guadagnare/racimolare appena da vivere; **there's just a ~ possibility he'll agree** c'è una vaga possibilità che accetti; **the ~ essentials** il minimo indispensabile; *(information)* l'essenziale *m*; **the ~ necessities** lo stretto necessario. **2** *vt* scoprire; *(teeth)* mostrare; **to ~ one's heart** *(fig)* mettere il proprio animo a nudo.

bare·back ['bɛə,bæk] *adv* senza sella.

bare·faced ['bɛə,feɪst] *adj* sfacciato(a), spudorato(a).

bare·foot(ed) ['bɛə,fʊt.,bɛə'fʊtɪd] *adj* scalzo(a), a piedi nudi.

bare·headed [,bɛə'hɛdɪd] *adj* a capo scoperto.

bare·ly ['bɛəlɪ] *adv* appena; **they had ~ enough money** i soldi gli bastavano appena; **it was ~ warm enough to sunbathe** faceva appena abbastanza caldo da stendersi al sole.

bar·gain ['baːgɪn] **1** *n* **(a)** *(transaction)* affare *m*; **to make a ~ with sb** fare un patto con qn; *(business)* concludere un affare con qn; **it's a ~!** affare fatto!; **you drive a hard ~** lei mi pone delle condizioni difficili; **into the ~** *(fig)* per giunta, per di più. **(b)** *(cheap thing)* affare *m*, occasione *f*; *(in January sales etc)* occasione; **to get a ~** fare un affare; **it's a real ~** è un vero affare, è un'occasione. **2** *vi* contrattare; *(in market etc)* tirare sul prezzo.

♦ **bargain for** *vi* + *prep (fam)*: **to ~ for sth** aspettarsi qc; **he got more than he ~ed for** gli è andata peggio di quel che si aspettasse *or* che avesse calcolato.

barge [baːdʒ] **1** *n* chiatta, barcone *m*; *(ceremonial)* lancia. **2** *cpd:* **~ pole** *n*: **I wouldn't touch it with a ~ pole** *(fam: revolting)* non lo toccherei nemmeno con un dito; *(: risky)* girerei alla larga.

♦ **barge in** *vi* + *adv (enter)* precipitarsi dentro; *(interrupt)* intromettersi.

♦ **barge into** *vi* + *prep (knock)* andare a sbattere contro; *(enter)* piombare in; *(interrupt)* intromettersi in.

bari·tone ['bærɪtəʊn] *n* baritono.

bar·ium meal [,bɛərɪəm'miːl] *n* (pasto di) bario.

bark¹ [baːk] *n (of tree)* corteccia.

bark² [baːk] **1** *n (of dog)* latrato, abbaiare *m*; **his ~ is worse than his bite** abbaia ma non morde. **2** *vi*: **to ~ (at)** abbaiare (a); **to be ~ing up the wrong tree** essere sulla strada sbagliata, sbagliarsi di grosso.

♦ **bark out** *vt* + *adv (order)* urlare.

bar·ley ['baːlɪ] **1** *n* orzo. **2** *cpd:* **~ sugar** *n* zucchero d'orzo.

bar·maid ['baː,meɪd] *n* cameriera, ragazza del bar.

bar·man ['baːmən] *n, pl* **~men** barista *m*.

bar·my ['baːmɪ] *adj (fam)* toccato(a), suonato(a).

barn [baːn] *n* fienile *m*; *(for animals)* stalla; *(for tools)* rimessa.

bar·na·cle ['baːnəkl] *n* cirripede *m*.

barn·yard ['baːn,jaːd] *n* aia.

ba·rom·eter [bə'rɒmɪtə'] *n* barometro.

bar·on ['bærən] *n* barone *m*; *(fig)* magnate *m*; **the press ~s** i baroni della stampa.

ba·roque [bə'rɒk] *adj* barocco(a).

bar·racks ['bærəks] *npl* caserma; **confined to ~** consegnato in caserma.

bar·rage ['bæraːʒ] *n (dam)* (opera di) sbarramento; *(Mil)* sbarramento; **a ~ of questions** un raffica di *or* un fuoco di fila di domande.

bar·rel ['bærəl] **1** *n* barile *m; (of gun)* canna. **2** *cpd:* ~ **organ** *n* organetto.

bar·ren ['bærən] *adj (soil)* arido(a), povero(a); *(plant)* infruttuoso(a); *(animal)* sterile.

bar·ri·cade [ˌbærɪ'keɪd] **1** *n* barricata. **2** *vt* barricare.

bar·ri·er ['bærɪəʳ] **1** *n* barriera; *(crash* ~*)* guardrail *m inv; (Rail: in station)* cancello; *(fig)* barriera, ostacolo. **2** *cpd:* ~ **cream** *n* crema protettiva.

bar·ring ['baːrɪŋ] *prep* = **bar**[2].

bar·ris·ter ['bærɪstəʳ] *n (Brit)* avvocato/essa *(con diritto di parlare davanti a tutte le corti).*

bar·row ['bærəʊ] *n (wheel*~*)* carriola; *(market stall)* carretto, carrettino.

bar·tender ['baːˌtɛndəʳ] *n* barista *m.*

bar·ter ['baːtəʳ] **1** *vt:* **to** ~ **sth (for sth)** barattare qc (con qc). **2** *vi:* **to** ~ **with sb (for sth)** barattare (qc) con qn.

base[1] [beɪs] **1** *n (gen, Mil)* base *f.* **2** *vt (troops):* **to** ~ **at** mettere di stanza a; *(opinion, relationship):* **to** ~ **on** basare su, fondare su; **I'm** ~**d in London** sono di base *or* ho base a Londra; **the job is** ~**d in London** è un lavoro con base a Londra. **3** *cpd:* ~ **camp** *n* campo *m* base *inv;* ~ **line** *n (Tennis)* linea di fondo; *(Baseball)* linea di base.

base[2] [beɪs] *adj (action, motive)* basso(a); *(behaviour)* ignobile; *(metal)* vile.

base·ball ['beɪsˌbɔːl] *n* baseball *m.*

-based [beɪst] *adj ending in cpds:* **coffee**~ a base di caffè; **a London**~ **company** una società con sede a Londra.

base·ment ['beɪsmənt] *n* seminterrato, scantinato; *(in shop)* sottosuolo, sotterraneo.

bases (a) ['beɪsiːz] *pl of* **basis. (b)** ['beɪsɪz] *pl of* **base.**

bash [bæʃ] *(fam)* **1** *n* botta; **the car has had a** ~ **la** macchina ha preso una botta; **I'll have a** ~ **(at it)** ci proverò. **2** *vt* sbattere; *(person)* picchiare, menare.

♦ **bash in** *vt* + *adv (fam)* sfondare; **to** ~ **sb's head in** spaccare la testa a qn.

♦ **bash up** *vt* + *adv (fam: car)* sfasciare; *(: person)* riempire di *or* prendere a botte.

bash·ful ['bæʃfʊl] *adj* timido(a).

ba·sic ['beɪsɪk] *adj (fundamental: reason, problem)* fondamentale, base *inv; (rudimentary: knowledge)* rudimentale; *(: equipment)* primitivo(a); *(elementary: principles, precautions, rules)* elementare; *(salary)* base *inv (after n);* '**B**~ **Italian**' 'Italiano elementare'.

ba·si·cal·ly ['beɪsɪklɪ] *adv* fondamentalmente, sostanzialmente.

bas·il ['bæzl] *n* basilico.

ba·sin ['beɪsn] *n (for food)* terrina; *(wash*~*)* lavabo, lavandino; *(Geog)* bacino.

ba·sis ['beɪsɪs] *n, pl* **bases** *(foundation)* base *f,* fondamento; **on the** ~ **of what you've said** in base alle tue asserzioni.

bask [baːsk] *vi:* **to** ~ **in the sun** crogiolarsi al sole; **to** ~ **in sb's favour** godere del favore di qn.

bas·ket ['baːskɪt] *n (gen, bread* ~, *wastepaper* ~*)* cestino; *(large)* cesta, cesta; *(shopping* ~*)* sporta; *(at supermarket)* cestello; *(wicker* ~*)* paniere *m; (Basketball)* canestro.

basket·ball ['baːskɪtˌbɔːl] **1** *n* pallacanestro *f,* basket *m.* **2** *cpd:* ~ **player** *n* cestista *m/f.*

bass [beɪs] *(Mus)* **1** *adj* basso(a); ~ **clef** chiave *f* di basso. **2** *n (voice)* voce *f* di basso; *(singer)* basso.

bas·soon [bə'suːn] *n* fagotto.

bas·tard ['baːstəd] *n* bastardo/a; *(fam pej)* figlio di puttana.

baste [beɪst] *vt (Culin)* ungere, inumidire col suo sugo; *(Sewing)* imbastire.

bat[1] [bæt] *n (Zool)* pipistrello.

bat[2] [bæt] **1** *n (Cricket, Baseball)* mazza; *(Table-tennis)* racchetta; **off one's own** ~ *(fam)* di testa propria. **2** *vi (Sport)* battere. **3** *vt:* **he didn't** ~ **an eyelid** *(fam)* non ha battuto ciglio.

batch [bætʃ] *n (of applicants, letters)* gruppo; *(of work)* sezione *f; (of goods)* partita, lotto; *(of recruits)* contingente *m; (of bread)* infornata.

bat·ed ['beɪtəd] *adj:* **with** ~ **breath** con il fiato sospeso.

bath [baːθ] **1** *n, pl* ~**s** [baːðz] **(a)** *(wash)* bagno; *(esp Brit:* ~*tub)* (vasca da) bagno; **room with** ~ camera con bagno; **to have a** ~ fare *or* farsi un bagno. **(b)** *(esp pl:* swimming ~*s)* piscina. **2** *vt* fare il bagno a. **3** *vi* fare *or* farsi un bagno.

bath·chair ['baːθˌtʃɛəʳ] *n* poltrona a rotelle.

bathe [beɪð] **1** *n* bagno. **2** *vt* **(a)** *(wound etc)* lavare. **(b)** *(Am) see* **bath 2**. **3** *vi* **(a)** *(swim)* fare i bagni, bagnarsi; **to go bathing** andare a fare il bagno *or* a nuotare. **(b)** *(Am)* = **bath 3**.

bath·er ['beɪðəʳ] *n* bagnante *m/f.*

bath·ing cap ['beɪðɪŋˌkæp] *n* cuffia da bagno.

bath·ing cos·tume ['beɪðɪŋˌkɒstjuːm] *n* costume *m* da bagno.

bath·ing trunks ['beɪðɪŋˌtrʌŋks] *npl* pantaloncini *mpl or* costume *m* da bagno.

bath·mat ['baːθˌmæt] *n* tappetino da bagno.

bath·robe ['baːθˌrəʊb] *n* accappatoio.

bath·room ['baːθrʊm] *n* (stanza da) bagno.

bath·towel ['baːθˌtaʊəl] *n* asciugamano da bagno.

bath·tub ['baːθˌtʌb] *n* (vasca da) bagno.

bat·man ['bætmæn] *n (Mil)* attendente *m.*

ba·ton ['bætən] *n (Mus)* bacchetta; *(Mil)* bastone *m* di comando; *(of policeman)* sfollagente *m inv,* manganello; *(in race)* testimone *m.*

bat·tal·ion [bə'tælɪən] *n* battaglione *m.*

bat·ter[1] ['bætəʳ] *n (Culin)* pastella.

bat·ter[2] ['bætəʳ] *vt (person)* ridurre in cattivo stato; *(wife, baby)* maltrattare; *(subj: wind, waves)* colpire violentemente.

♦ **batter down** *vt* + *adv* abbattere, buttare giù.

bat·tered ['bætəd] *adj* malridotto(a); ~ **baby/wife** bambino/moglie maltrattato(a) *or* vittima di maltrattamenti.

bat·ter·ing ram ['bætərɪŋˌræm] *n* ariete *m.*

bat·tery ['bætərɪ] **1** *n (Elec)* pila; *(Aut, Mil)* batteria; *(large number: of lights, tests)* batteria; *(: of questions)* pioggia, raffica. **2** *cpd:* ~ **charger** *n* caricabatterie *m inv;* ~ **farming** *n* allevamento intensivo.

bat·tle ['bætl] **1** *n (Mil)* battaglia, combattimento; *(fig)* lotta, battaglia; **killed in** ~ ucciso in combattimento; **I had quite a** ~ **to get permission** è stata una battaglia ottenere il permesso; **a** ~ **of wits** una gara d'ingegno; **that's half the** ~ *(fam)* è già una mezza vittoria; **to fight a losing** ~ *(fig)* battersi per una causa persa. **2** *vi (fig):* **to** ~ **(for)** lottare (per), combattere (per); **he** ~**d to retain his self-control** dovette fare uno sforzo per controllarsi; **to** ~ **against the wind** lottare con *or* contro il vento.

battle·field ['bætlˌfiːld] *n,* **battle·ground** ['bætlˌgraʊnd] *n* campo di battaglia.

bat·tle·ments ['bætlmənts] *npl* bastioni *mpl.*

battle·ship ['bætlˌʃɪp] *n* nave *f* da guerra.

bau·ble ['bɔːbl] *n* ninnolo.

baulk [bɔːlk] *vi* = **balk.**

baux·ite ['bɔːksaɪt] *n* bauxite *f.*

bawdy ['bɔːdɪ] *adj* piccante, spinto(a), salace; ~ **song** canzonaccia.

bawl [bɔːl] *vi (cry)* strillare; *(shout)* urlare, sbraitare; **don't** ~ **at me!** non urlare!

♦ **bawl out** *vt* + *adv* **(a)** urlare (a squarciagola).

(b) *(fam)*: **to ~ sb out** fare una sfuriata *or* una lavata di testa a qn.

bay¹ [beɪ] *n (Geog)* baia; **the B~ of Biscay** il golfo di Biscaglia.

bay² [beɪ] **1** *n (for parking)* piazzola di sosta; *(for loading)* piazzale *m* di (sosta e) carico. **2** *cpd*: **~ window** *n* bovindo.

bay³ [beɪ] **1** *vi (hound)* abbaiare, latrare. **2** *n (bark)* latrato; **to keep sb/sth at ~** *(fig)* tenere a bada qn/qc.

bay⁴ [beɪ] *adj (horse)* baio(a).

bay leaf [ˈbeɪˌliːf] *n* foglia d'alloro.

bayo·net [ˈbeɪənɪt] **1** *n* baionetta. **2** *vt* infilzare con la baionetta.

ba·zaar [bəˈzɑːʳ] *n (sale of work)* vendita di beneficenza; *(Oriental market)* bazar *m inv*.

b.&b., B.&B. *abbr see* bed.

B.B.C. *n abbr of British Broadcasting Corporation.*

B.C. *abbr (= before Christ)* a. C.

be [biː] *present* **am, is, are;** *pt* **was, were;** *pp* **been 1** *vi* **(a)** *(exist)* essere, esistere; **to ~ or not to ~** essere o non essere; **the best singer that ever was** il miglior cantante mai esistito; **leave it as it is** lascialo così; **~ that as it may** sia come sia, comunque sia; **so ~ it** sia pure, e sia; **let me ~!** lasciami in pace!; **how much was it?** quanto è costato?, quant'era?; **his wife to ~** la sua futura moglie.

(b) *(place)* essere, trovarsi; **he won't ~ here tomorrow** non ci sarà domani; **Edinburgh is in Scotland** Edimburgo è *or* si trova in Scozia; **it's on the table** è *or* sta sul tavolo; **we've been here for ages** sono secoli che siamo qui.

(c): **there is** c'è; **there are** ci sono; **there were 3 of us** eravamo in 3; **there was once a house here** c'era una volta una casa qua; **there will ~ dancing** si ballerà; **let there ~ light** sia la luce.

(d) *(presenting, pointing out)*: **here is, here are** ecco; **there is, there are** ecco; **here you are** (take it) ecco qua (prendi); **there's the church** ecco la chiesa.

(e) *(movement)*: **I've been to China** sono stato in Cina; **where have you been?** dove sei stato?

2 *copulative vb* **(a)** *(essere)*; **he's a pianist** è (un) pianista; **2 and 2 are 4** 2 più 2 fa 4; **the book is in French** il libro è in francese; **I'm not Sue, I'm Mary** non sono Sue, sono Mary; **he's tall** è alto; **they're English** sono inglesi; **~ good!** sii buono!

(b) *(health)* stare; **how are you?** come stai (*or* sta)?; **I'm better now** ora sto meglio.

(c) *(age)*: **how old is she?** — **she's 9** quanti anni ha? — ne ha 9 *or* ha 9 anni.

3 *impers vb* **(a):** **it is said that...** si dice che... + *sub*; **it is possible that...** può darsi *or* essere che... + *sub*.

(b) *(time)* essere; **it's 8 o'clock** sono le 8; **it's the 3rd of May** è il 3 (di) maggio.

(c) *(measurement)*: **it's 5 km to the village** da qui al paese sono 5 km.

(d) *(weather)* fare; **it's too hot** fa troppo caldo.

(e) *(emphatic)*: **it's only me** sono solo io.

4 *aux vb* **(a)** *(with prp: forming continuous tenses)*: **what are you doing?** che fai?, che stai facendo?; **he's always grumbling** brontola sempre, non fa che brontolare; **they're coming tomorrow** vengono domani; **I'll ~ seeing you** ci vediamo; **I've been waiting for her for 2 hours** l'aspetto da 2 ore.

(b) *(with pp: forming passives)* essere; **to ~ killed** essere *or* venire ucciso; **the box had been opened** la scatola era stata aperta; **he is nowhere to ~ found** non lo si trova da nessuna parte; **what's to ~ done?** che fare?

(c) *(in tag questions)*: **he's handsome, isn't he?** è un bell'uomo, vero?; **it was fun, wasn't it?** è stato bello, no?; **he's back again, is he?** così è tornato, eh?

(d) *(+ to + infin)*: **the car is to ~ sold** abbiamo (*or* hanno *etc*) intenzione di vendere la macchina; **he was to have come yesterday** sarebbe dovuto venire ieri; **he's to ~ congratulated on his work** dobbiamo fargli i complimenti per il suo lavoro; **am I to understand that...?** devo dedurre che...?; **you're to put on your shoes** devi metterti le scarpe; **he's not to open it** non deve aprirlo per nessuna ragione.

(e) *(modal)*: **if it was** *or* **were to snow...** (se) dovesse nevicare...; **if I were you...** se fossi in te... .

beach [biːtʃ] **1** *n* spiaggia. **2** *cpd*: **~ buggy** *n* dune buggy *f inv*.

beach·ball [ˈbiːtʃˌbɔːl] *n* pallone *m* da mare *or* da spiaggia.

beach·comber [ˈbiːtʃˌkəʊməʳ] *n* vagabondo *(che s'aggira sulla spiaggia)*.

beach·wear [ˈbiːtʃˌwɛəʳ] *n* abbigliamento da mare.

bea·con [ˈbiːkən] *n (fire)* fuoco di segnalazione; *(light)* faro, fanale *m*; *(radio ~)* radiofaro.

bead [biːd] *n* perlina; *(of rosary)* grano; *(of dew, sweat)* goccia; **~s** *(necklace)* collana; *(also:* **rosary ~s**) corona (del rosario), rosario.

beady-eyed [ˈbiːdɪˈaɪd] *adj* dagli occhi piccoli e penetranti.

beak [biːk] *n* becco.

beak·er [ˈbiːkəʳ] *n* coppa; *(Chem)* becher *m inv*, bicchiere *m*.

beam [biːm] **1** *n* **(a)** *(Archit)* trave *f*. **(b)** *(of light, sunlight)* raggio; *(of torch)* fascio (di luce); *(Radio)* fascio (d'onde); **to drive on full** *or* **main ~** guidare con gli abbaglianti accesi. **(c)** *(smile)* sorriso raggiante. **2** *vt (Radio)* trasmettere con antenna direzionale. **3** *vi (smile)* sorridere radiosamente; **to ~ at sb** fare un largo sorriso a qn.

bean [biːn] *n* fagiolo; *(broad ~)* fava; *(runner ~)* fagiolino; *(of coffee)* grano, chicco; **full of ~s** *(fam: child)* vivacissimo(a); *(: adult)* in gran forma.

bean·shoots [ˈbiːnˌʃuːts] *npl*, **bean·sprouts** [ˈbiːnˌsprauts] *npl* germogli *mpl* di soia.

bear¹ [bɛəʳ] *n* orso/a.

bear² [bɛəʳ] *pt* **bore,** *pp* **borne 1** *vt* **(a)** *(carry: burden, signature, date, name)* portare; *(: news, message)* recare; *(: traces, signs)* mostrare; **to ~ some resemblance to** somigliare a; **he bore himself like a soldier** *(of posture)* aveva un portamento militare; *(of behaviour)* si comportò da soldato; **the love he bore her** l'amore che le portava; **to ~ sb ill will** portare *or* serbare rancore a qn.

(b) *(support: weight)* reggere, sostenere; *(: cost)* sostenere; *(: responsibility)* assumere; *(: comparison)* reggere (a); **the roof couldn't ~ the weight of the snow** il tetto non ha retto il *or* al peso della neve.

(c) *(endure: pain)* sopportare; *(stand up to: inspection, examination)* reggere a; **it won't ~ close examination** non bisogna guardarlo troppo da vicino; **I can't ~ him** non lo posso soffrire *or* sopportare; **I can't ~ to look** non ho il coraggio di guardare; **it doesn't ~ thinking about** non ci si può neanche pensare.

(d) *(produce: fruit)* produrre, dare; *(: young)* partorire; *(: child)* generare, dare alla luce; *(Fin: interest)* fruttare.

2 *vi* **(a)** *(move)*: **to ~ right/left** andare a destra/sinistra.

(b): to bring sth to ~ (on) *(influence, powers of persuasion)* esercitare qc (su); **to bring pressure to ~ on sb** fare pressione su qn; **to bring one's mind to ~ on sth** concentrarsi su qc.

♦ **bear down** *vi + adv:* **to ~ down (on)** *(ship)* venire dritto (contro); *(person)* stare per piombare addosso (a).

♦ **bear out** *vt + adv (theory, suspicion)* confermare, convalidare; *(person)* dare il proprio appoggio a.

♦ **bear up** *vi + adv* farsi coraggio; **he bore up well under the strain** ha sopportato bene lo stress.

♦ **bear with** *vi + prep (sb's moods, temper)* sopportare (con pazienza); **if you'll ~ with me...** se ha la cortesia *or* la pazienza di aspettare... .

bear·able ['bɛərəbl] *adj* sopportabile.

beard [bɪəd] **1** *n* barba. **2** *vt:* **to ~ the lion in his den** *(hum)* affrontare il nemico in casa sua.

beard·ed ['bɪədɪd] *adj* barbuto(a).

bear·er ['bɛərər] *n (of news, cheque)* portatore *m; (of passport)* titolare *m/f.*

bear·ing ['bɛərɪŋ] *n* **(a)** *(of person)* portamento. **(b)** *(relevance):* **~ (on)** attinenza (con). **(c)** *(Tech)* cuscinetto. **(d)** *(position):* **to take a compass ~** effettuare un rilevamento con la bussola; **to take a ship's ~s** fare il punto nave; **to find one's ~s** *(fig)* orientarsi; **to lose one's ~s** *(fig)* perdere l'orientamento.

beast [biːst] *n (animal, fam: disagreeable person)* bestia, animale *m; (cruel person)* bruto; **~ of burden** bestia da soma; **it's a ~ of a job** *(fam)* è un lavoraccio.

beast·ly ['biːstlɪ] *adj (fam: person, behaviour)* insopportabile; *(: weather, party)* orrendo(a).

beat [biːt] *(vb: pt* **beat***, pp* **beaten***)* **1** *n* **(a)** colpo; *(of drum: single ~)* colpo; *(: repeated ~ing)* rullo; *(of heart)* battito; *(Mus: rhythm)* ritmo; *(: measure)* battuta; **to give the ~** dare il tempo. **(b)** *(of policeman)* giro d'ispezione a piedi; **on the beat** che sta facendo il suo giro.

2 *vt* **(a)** *(hit)* battere, picchiare; *(person: as punishment)* picchiare; *(: with stick)* bastonare; *(carpet)* battere, sbattere; *(drum)* suonare; **the bird ~ its wings** l'uccello batteva le ali; **to ~ time** *(Mus)* battere il tempo; **~ it!** *(fam)* fila!, fuori dai piedi! **(b)** *(defeat: team, army)* battere, sconfiggere; *(: record)* battere; **I ~ him to it** *(fam)* ci sono arrivato prima di lui; **coffee ~s tea any day** *(fam)* il tè sarà anche buono, ma non c'è niente che batta il caffè; **that ~s everything!** *(fam)* questo è il colmo!; **it's got me ~(en)** *(fam)* devo arrendermi. **(c)** *(Culin)* sbattere.

3 *vi (heart)* battere, palpitare; *(drums)* rullare; **to ~ on a door** picchiare a una porta; **the rain was ~ing against the windows** la pioggia batteva contro le finestre; **don't ~ about the bush** non menare il can per l'aia.

4 *adj* **(a)** *(pred: fam: tired)* sfinito(a). **(b)** *(usu attr: group, music)* beat *inv.*

♦ **beat back** *vt + adv* respingere.

♦ **beat down 1** *vt + adv (door)* abbattere, buttare giù; *(price)* far abbassare; *(seller)* far scendere. **2** *vi + adv (rain)* scrosciare; *(sun)* picchiare.

♦ **beat off** *vt + adv* respingere.

♦ **beat out** *vt + adv (flames)* spegnere (battendo); *(dent)* ribattere, martellare; *(rhythm)* battere.

♦ **beat up** *vt (fam: person)* pestare.

beat·en ['biːtn] **1** *pp of* **beat**. **2** *adj (metal)* battuto(a); **off the ~ track** fuori mano.

beat·er ['biːtər] *n (Culin)* frullino; *(carpet ~)* batti-panni *m inv.*

be·ati·fy [biːˈætɪfaɪ] *vt* beatificare.

beat·ing ['biːtɪŋ] *n* **(a)** *(punishment)* botte *fpl;* **to give sb a ~** riempire qn di botte. **(b)** *(defeat)*

sconfitta; **to take a ~** prendere una (bella) batosta.

beat·nik ['biːtnɪk] *n* beatnik *m/f inv.*

beat-up [ˌbiːtˈʌp] *adj (fam)* scassato(a).

beau·ti·ful ['bjuːtɪfʊl] *adj* bello(a), splendido(a).

beau·ti·ful·ly ['bjuːtɪflɪ] *adv* splendidamente, magnificamente.

beau·ti·fy ['bjuːtɪfaɪ] *vt* abbellire.

beau·ty ['bjuːtɪ] **1** *n (concept)* bello; *(of person, thing)* bellezza; **~ is in the eye of the beholder** non è bello ciò che è bello, ma è bello ciò che piace; **the ~ of it is that...** il bello è che...; **his car's a ~!** *(fam)* ha una macchina che è una meraviglia *or* una bellezza! **2** *cpd (contest, salon etc)* di bellezza; **~ queen** *n* miss *f inv*, reginetta di bellezza; **you need your ~ sleep** *(hum)* hai bisogno di fare una buona dormita; **~ spot** *n (on face)* neo; *(in country)* luogo di particolare bellezza.

bea·ver ['biːvər] *n* castoro; **to work like a ~** lavorare come matti.

be·calmed [bɪˈkɑːmd] *adj:* **to be ~** avere bonaccia.

be·came [bɪˈkeɪm] *pt of* become.

be·cause [bɪˈkɒz] *conj (gen)* perché; **all the more surprising ~** ancora più sorprendente dal momento che *or* poiché; **~ of** a causa di.

beck·on ['bɛkən] *vt, vi:* **to ~ to sb** chiamare qn con un cenno; **he ~ed me in/over** mi ha fatto cenno di entrare/di avvicinarmi.

be·come [bɪˈkʌm] *pt* **became***, pp* **become 1** *vi* diventare, divenire; **to ~ famous** diventare famoso; **to ~ angry** arrabbiarsi; **to ~ accustomed to sth** abituarsi a qc; **to ~ a doctor** diventare medico; **it became known that** si è venuto a sapere che. **2** *impers vb:* **what has ~ of him?** che ne è stato di lui?; **whatever can have ~ of that book?** dove sarà mai finito quel libro? **3** *vt:* **it does not ~ her** *(dress etc)* non le sta bene; *(behaviour)* non le si addice.

be·com·ing [bɪˈkʌmɪŋ] *adj (clothes)* grazioso(a); *(conduct)* adatto(a).

bed [bɛd] **1** *n* **(a)** letto; **to go to ~** andare a letto; **to go to ~ with sb** andare a letto con qn; **to get out of ~** alzarsi dal letto; **to get out of ~ on the wrong side** alzarsi col piede sbagliato; **to make the ~** (ri)fare il letto; **to put sb to ~** mettere qn a letto; **I was in ~** ero a letto; **could you give me a ~ for the night?** puoi tenermi a dormire per stanotte?; **his life's not a ~ of roses** la sua vita non è tutta rose e fiori. **(b)** *(of sea, lake)* fondo; *(of river)* letto. **(c)** *(flower ~)* aiuola; **oyster ~** banco di ostriche; **vegetable ~** orticello. **(d)** *(layer: of coal, ore)* strato; *(: in road-building)* massicciata. **2** *cpd:* **~ and breakfast** *(abbr* **b.& b.***)* ≃ pensione *f* familiare; **to book in for ~ and breakfast** prenotare una camera con prima colazione.

♦ **bed down** *vi + adv* sistemarsi (per dormire).

♦ **bed out** *vt + adv (plants)* piantare a intervalli regolari.

bed·bath ['bɛdˌbɑːθ] *n:* **to give sb a ~** lavare qn a letto.

bed·clothes ['bɛdˌkləʊðz] *npl* coperte e lenzuola *fpl.*

bed·ding ['bɛdɪŋ] *n* coperte e lenzuola *fpl; (for animal)* lettiera.

be·dev·il [bɪˈdɛvl] *vt (person)* affliggere; *(plans)* intralciare.

bed·fellow ['bɛdˌfɛləʊ] *n:* **they are strange ~s** *(fig)* fanno una coppia ben strana.

bed·lam ['bɛdləm] *n* baraonda.

bed·pan ['bɛdˌpæn] *n* padella.

be·drag·gled [bɪˈdrægld] *adj (person, clothes)* sbrindellato(a); *(hair)* scompigliato(a); *(wet)* bagnato(a).

bed·rid·den ['bɛd,rɪdən] *adj* costretto(a) *or* inchiodato(a) a letto.

bed·room ['bɛdrʊm] **1** *n* camera (da letto), stanza da letto. **2** *cpd:* ~ **farce** *n (Theatre)* pochade *f inv;* ~ **slipper** *n* pantofola.

bed·side ['bɛdsaɪd] **1** *n:* **at his** ~ al suo capezzale. **2** *cpd:* ~ **lamp** *n* lampada da comodino; **to have a good** ~ **manner** *(doctor)* saper trattare i pazienti; ~ **rug** *n* scendiletto; ~ **table** *n* comodino.

bed·sit(ter) ['bɛd,sɪt(ə^r)] *n*, **bed-sitting room** [,bɛd'sɪtɪŋrʊm] *n* monolocale *m*.

bed·spread ['bɛd,sprɛd] *n* copriletto.

bed·time ['bɛdtaɪm] **1** *n:* **it's** ~ è ora di andare a letto; **it's past your** ~ a quest'ora dovresti già essere a letto; **John's** ~ **is 8.00 pm** John va a letto alle 8. **2** *cpd:* **will you tell me a** ~ **story?** mi racconti una storia prima di dormire?

bed-wetting ['bɛd,wɛtɪŋ] *n* incontinenza notturna.

bee [biː] *n* ape *f;* **to have a** ~ **in one's bonnet (about sth)** avere la fissazione (di qc).

beech [biːtʃ] *n* faggio.

beef [biːf] *n (Culin)* manzo; **roast** ~ arrosto di manzo.

beef·bur·ger ['biːf,bɜːgə^r] *n* hamburger *m inv*.

beef·eater ['biːf,iːtə^r] *n* guardia della Torre di Londra.

bee·hive ['biː,haɪv] *n* alveare *m*.

bee·line ['biː,laɪn] *n:* **to make a** ~ **for sb/sth** andare diretto(a) verso qn/qc.

been [biːn] *pp of* **be.**

beer [bɪə^r] **1** *n* birra. **2** *cpd:* ~ **can** *n* lattina di birra; ~ **glass** *n* boccale *m*, bicchiere *m* da birra.

bees·wax ['biːz,wæks] *n* cera d'api.

beet [biːt] *n* barbabietola.

bee·tle ['biːtl] *n (Zool)* coleottero, *(: scarab)* scarabeo; *(: black* ~*)* scarafaggio.

beetle-browed ['biːtl,braʊd] *adj* dalle folte sopracciglia.

beet·root ['biːt,ruːt] *n* barbabietola.

be·fall [bɪ'fɔːl] *pt* **befell** [bɪ'fɛl], *pp* **befallen** [bɪ'fɔːlən] *vt* accadere a.

be·fit·ting [bɪ'fɪtɪŋ] *adj* adatto(a); **it's hardly** ~ **for a lady** si addice poco a una signora.

be·fore [bɪ'fɔː^r] **1** *prep* **(a)** *(in time)* prima di; ~ **7 o'clock** prima delle 7; **the day** ~ **last** *or* **yesterday** due giorni fa, l'altro ieri, ieri l'altro; ~ **Christ** avanti Cristo; ~ **long** fra poco, fra non molto. **(b)** *(in place, rank, in the presence of)* davanti a; **a new life lay** ~ **him** una nuova vita si apriva davanti a lui; **to appear** ~ **a judge** comparire davanti *or* dinanzi a un giudice; **the question** ~ **us** la questione di cui ci dobbiamo occupare; ~ **my very eyes** proprio sotto ai miei occhi; **ladies** ~ **gentlemen** prima le signore, la precedenza alle signore; **to put death** ~ **dishonour** preferire la morte al disonore.

2 *adv* prima; **the day** ~ il giorno prima *or* precedente; **I have read it** ~ l'ho già letto; **I knew long** ~ **that...** sapevo da molto tempo che... .

3 *conj (time)* prima di + *infin*, prima che + *sub; (rather than)* piuttosto che; ~ **doing it you...,** ~ **you do it, you...** prima di farlo, tu..., prima che tu lo faccia, tu...; **he will die** ~ **he betrays his friends** morirebbe piuttosto che tradire gli amici.

before·hand [bɪ'fɔːhænd] *adv* prima; **let me know your plans** ~ fammi sapere i tuoi piani in anticipo.

be·friend [bɪ'frɛnd] *vt* prendersi a cuore.

be·fud·dled [bɪ'fʌdld] *adj* confuso(a).

beg [bɛg] **1** *vt* **(a)** *(entreat)* supplicare; *(subj: beggar: food, money)* mendicare; **he** ~**ged me for mercy** mi supplicava di aver pietà; **he** ~**ged me**

to help him mi ha supplicato *or* pregato di aiutarlo; **to** ~ **forgiveness** implorare perdono; **I** ~ **your pardon** *(apologising)* mi scusi; *(not hearing)* scusi?; **I** ~ **to differ** mi permetto di non essere d'accordo. **(b):** **this** ~**s the question** questo presuppone che il problema sia già risolto. **2** *vi (entreat):* **to** ~ **for** implorare; *(beggar)* chiedere l'elemosina *or* la carità; **it's going** ~**ging** *(fam)* non lo vuole proprio nessuno.

be·gan [bɪ'gæn] *pt of* **begin.**

beg·gar ['bɛgə^r] **1** *n* mendicante *m/f;* **lucky** ~! *(fam)* che fortuna sfacciata!; **poor** ~! *(fam)* povero diavolo!; ~**s can't be choosers** o mangiar questa minestra *o* saltar dalla finestra. **2** *vt (ruin)* ridurre sul lastrico *or* in miseria; **it** ~**s description** è indescrivibile.

be·gin [bɪ'gɪn] *pt* **began,** *pp* **begun 1** *vt (gen)* cominciare, incominciare, iniziare; *(originate: fashion)* lanciare; *(: custom)* inaugurare; *(: war)* scatenare; *(: rumour)* spargere; **to** ~ **doing sth, to** ~ **to do sth** incominciare *or* iniziare a fare qc; **it began to rain** ha cominciato *or* si è messo a piovere; **this skirt began life as an evening dress** questa gonna in origine era un abito da sera; **it doesn't** ~ **to compare with...** non c'è nemmeno da paragonarlo con...; **I can't** ~ **to thank you** non so proprio come ringraziarti.

2 *vi* incominciare, cominciare; *(river, fashion, custom)* nascere; *(rumour)* spargersi; **to** ~ **with sth/by doing sth** cominciare con qc/col fare qc; **to** ~ **on sth** cominciare qc; **let me** ~ **by saying...** permettetemi di cominciare col dire...; **to** ~ **with, I'd like to know...** tanto per cominciare vorrei sapere...; **to** ~ **with there were only two of us** all'inizio eravamo solo in due; ~**ning from Monday** a partire da lunedì; **the service began at 9 a.m.** la funzione ha avuto inizio alle 9.

be·gin·ner [bɪ'gɪnə^r] *n* principiante *m/f*.

be·gin·ning [bɪ'gɪnɪŋ] *n* inizio, principio; **at the** ~ **of the century** all'inizio *or* al principio del secolo; **right from the** ~ fin dal primo momento, fin dall'inizio; **start at the** ~ **and tell me all about it** raccontami tutto (cominciando *or* a partire) dall'inizio; **the** ~ **of the end** il principio della fine; **to make a** ~ cominciare; **the** ~ **of the world** le origini del mondo; **Buddhism had its** ~**s...** il buddismo nacque *or* ebbe origine... .

be·gonia [bɪ'gəʊnɪə] *n* begonia.

be·grudge [bɪ'grʌdʒ] *vt* = **grudge.**

be·guile [bɪ'gaɪl] *vt (enchant)* incantare.

be·gun [bɪ'gʌn] *pp of* **begin.**

be·half [bɪ'hɑːf]: **on** ~ **of,** *(Am)* **in** ~ **of** *prep* per conto di; *(thank, accept)* a nome di; **don't worry on my** ~ non preoccuparti per me.

be·have [bɪ'heɪv] *vi (also:* ~ **o.s.:** *conduct o.s.)* comportarsi; *(: conduct o.s. well)* comportarsi bene; **you** ~**d very wisely** hai agito saggiamente; **to** ~ **well towards sb** comportarsi bene nei confronti di qn; ~ **yourself!** comportati bene!

be·hav·iour, *(Am)* **be·hav·ior** [bɪ'heɪvjə^r] *n* comportamento; **to be on one's best** ~ sforzarsi di comportarsi bene.

be·hav·io(u)r·ism [bɪ'heɪvjərɪzəm] *n* comportamentismo.

be·head [bɪ'hɛd] *vt* decapitare.

be·held [bɪ'hɛld] *pt of* **behold.**

be·hest [bɪ'hɛst] *n:* **at his** ~ su ordine suo.

be·hind [bɪ'haɪnd] **1** *prep* dietro; **look** ~ **you!** guarda dietro di te!; **what's** ~ **all this?** *(fig)* cosa c'è sotto?; **we're** ~ **them in technology** *(fig)* siamo più indietro *or* più arretrati di loro nella tecnica; **his family is** ~ **him** *(fig)* ha l'appoggio della famiglia. **2** *adv* dietro; **to stay** ~ **(to do sth)**

fermarsi (a fare qc); **to leave sth ~** dimenticare di prendere qc; **to be ~ with sth** essere indietro con qc; *(payments)* essere in arretrato con qc. **3** *n (fam)* didietro *m inv.*

be·hold [bɪˈhəʊld] *pt, pp* **beheld** *vt (old, poet)* scorgere, vedere.

be·hove [bɪˈhəʊv] , *(Am)* **be·hoove** [bɪˈhuːv] *impers vt (frm):* **to ~ sb to do sth** stare a qn di fare qc.

beige [beɪʒ] *adj, n* beige *(m) inv.*

be·ing [ˈbiːɪŋ] *n* **(a)** *(existence)* essere *m*, esistenza; **to come into ~** nascere, cominciare a esistere; **to bring sth into ~** creare qc. **(b)** *(creature)* essere *m.*

be·la·bour, *(Am)* **be·la·bor** [bɪˈleɪbəʳ] *vt (beat)* bastonare; *(fig):* **to ~ with** *(questions)* tartassare di; *(insults)* bombardare di.

be·lat·ed [bɪˈleɪtɪd] *adj* in ritardo; **his ~ arrival** il suo ritardo.

belch [bɛltʃ] **1** *n* rutto. **2** *vi* ruttare. **3** *vt (also:* **~ out:** *smoke)* sputare (fuori); *(: flames)* vomitare.

be·lea·guered [bɪˈliːgəd] *adj (city, fig)* assediato(a); *(army)* accerchiato(a).

bel·fry [ˈbɛlfrɪ] *n* campanile *m.*

Bel·gian [ˈbɛldʒən] *adj, n* belga *(m/f).*

Bel·gium [ˈbɛldʒəm] *n* Belgio.

be·lie [bɪˈlaɪ] *vt (prove false)* smentire; *(give false impression of)* nascondere.

be·lief [bɪˈliːf] *n (faith)* fede *f*; *(trust)* fiducia; *(tenet, doctrine)* convinzione *f*; **~ in God** fede in Dio; **it's a ~ held by all Christians** è credenza comune a tutti i cristiani; **it's beyond ~** è incredibile; **rich beyond ~** incredibilmente ricco; **a man of strong ~s** un uomo dalle ferme convinzioni; **it is my ~ that** sono convinto che; **in the ~ that** nella convinzione che.

be·lieve [bɪˈliːv] **1** *vt (story, person)* credere a; *(be of the opinion that):* **to ~ (that)** credere (che); **I don't ~ he'll come** non credo che verrà *or* che venga; **don't you ~ it!** non crederci!; **I don't ~ a word of it!** non credo a una parola di tutto questo!; **he is ~d to be abroad** si pensa (che) sia all'estero. **2** *vi* credere; **to ~ in** *(God)* credere in; *(ghosts)* credere a; *(method)* avere fiducia in; **I don't ~ in corporal punishment** sono contrario alle punizioni corporali.

be·liev·er [bɪˈliːvəʳ] *n (Rel)* credente *m/f.*

be·lit·tle [bɪˈlɪtl] *vt* sminuire.

bell [bɛl] **1** *n (gen)* campanello; *(church ~)* campana; *(on cats, harness)* sonaglio; *(on cow)* campanaccio; *(of telephone)* soneria; **that rings a ~** *(fig)* mi ricorda qualcosa. **2** *cpd:* **~ jar** *n* campana di vetro; **~ push** *n* pulsante *m or* bottone *m* del campanello; **~ tower** *n* torre *f* campanaria.

bell-bottomed [ˈbɛlˌbɒtəmd] *adj (trousers)* a zampa d'elefante.

bell·boy [ˈbɛlˌbɔɪ] *n*, **bell·hop** [ˈbɛlˌhɒp] *n (Am)* ragazzo d'albergo, fattorino d'albergo.

belle [bɛl] *n:* **the ~ of the ball** la regina della festa.

bel·li·cose [ˈbɛlɪkəʊs] *adj* bellicoso(a).

bel·lig·er·ent [bɪˈlɪdʒərənt] *adj* belligerante; *(fig)* bellicoso(a).

bel·low [ˈbɛləʊ] **1** *n (of bull etc)* muggito; *(of person)* urlo. **2** *vi (see n)* muggire; urlare (a squarciagola). **3** *vt (also:* **~ out:** *order, song)* urlare (a squarciagola).

bel·lows [ˈbɛləʊz] *npl (of forge, organ)* mantice *m*; *(for fire)* soffietto.

bell-shaped [ˈbɛlˌʃeɪpt] *adj* a campana.

bel·ly [ˈbɛlɪ] *n* pancia.

belly·ache [ˈbɛlɪˌeɪk] **1** *n* mal di pancia. **2** *vi (fam)* mugugnare.

be·long [bɪˈlɒŋ] *vi* **(a): to ~ to sb/sth** *(be the property of)* appartenere a qn/qc; **who does this ~ to?**

questo di chi è?; **to ~ to a club** essere socio di un club. **(b)** *(have rightful place):* **put it back where it ~s** rimettilo al suo posto; **it ~s on the shelf** va sullo scaffale; **I felt I didn't ~** mi sentivo estraneo.

be·long·ings [bɪˈlɒŋɪŋz] *npl* ciò che si possiede; **he lost all his ~** ha perso tutto ciò che possedeva; **personal ~** effetti personali.

be·lov·ed [bɪˈlʌvɪd] *adj, n* adorato(a) *(m/f).*

be·low [bɪˈləʊ] **1** *prep* sotto; **temperatures ~ normal** temperature al di sotto del normale; **they live in the flat ~ us** abitano nell'appartamento sotto al nostro. **2** *adv* sotto; **the mountains ~** le montagne sottostanti; **the flat ~** l'appartamento al piano di sotto; **see ~** *(on page)* vedi oltre.

belt [bɛlt] **1** *n (gen)* cintura; *(of trousers)* cintura, cinghia; *(Tech)* cinghia; *(Geog: zone)* zona, regione *f*; **industrial ~** zona industriale; **to tighten one's ~** *(fig)* tirare la cinghia; **that was below the ~** *(fig)* è stato un colpo basso. **2** *vt (thrash)* usare la cinghia con; **he ~ed me one** *(fam)* mi ha mollato un pugno. **3** *vi (rush):* **to ~ in/out** *etc* entrare/uscire *etc* di gran corsa; **he was ~ing up the motorway at 100 mph** filava sull'autostrada a 100 miglia all'ora.

♦ **belt out** *vt + adv (song)* cantare a squarciagola.

♦ **belt up** *vi + adv (fam: be quiet)* chiudere la boccaccia; **~ up!** chiudi quella boccaccia!

be·moan [bɪˈməʊn] *vt* lamentare.

be·mused [bɪˈmjuːzd] *adj* perplesso(a), stupito(a).

bench [bɛntʃ] *n (seat: with back)* panchina; *(: without back)* panca; *(in tiers, work~)* banco; **to be on the B~** *(Law)* essere giudice.

bend [bɛnd] *(vb: pt, pp* **bent**) **1** *n (in road)* curva; *(in river)* ansa, gomito; *(in arm, knee)* piega; *(in pipe)* gomito; **he drives me round the ~!** *(fam)* mi fa diventare matto! **2** *vt (wire etc)* curvare, piegare; *(knee)* flettere, piegare; *(arm)* piegare; *(head)* piegare, chinare. **3** *vi* piegarsi, curvarsi; *(road)* fare una curva; *(river)* fare un gomito; *(person)* chinarsi.

♦ **bend down** *vi + adv* chinarsi (a terra).

♦ **bend over** *vi + adv* chinarsi, piegarsi.

bends [bɛndz] *npl* embolia.

be·neath [bɪˈniːθ] **1** *prep* sotto; **it is ~ my notice** non è degno della mia attenzione; **it is ~ him to do such a thing** non si degnerebbe mai di fare una cosa del genere. **2** *adv* sotto; **the flat ~** l'appartamento al piano di sotto.

ben·edic·tion [ˌbɛnɪˈdɪkʃən] *n* benedizione *f.*

ben·efac·tor [ˈbɛnɪfæktəʳ] *n* benefattore/trice.

ben·efi·cial [ˌbɛnɪˈfɪʃəl] *adj* benefico(a); **~ to che** giova a.

bene·fi·ciary [ˌbɛnɪˈfɪʃərɪ] *n (Law)* beneficiario/a.

ben·efit [ˈbɛnɪfɪt] **1** *n* **(a)** vantaggio; **the ~s of a good education** i vantaggi di una buona educazione; **it might be of some ~ to you** potrebbe giovarti; **for the ~ of one's health** per la propria salute; **to give sb the ~ of the doubt** concedere a qn il beneficio del dubbio. **(b)** *(allowance)* indennità *f inv*, sussidio; **unemployment ~** indennità di disoccupazione. **2** *vi* trarre vantaggio *or* profitto da. **3** *vt* giovare a, far bene a; **the holiday ~ed his health** la vacanza gli ha giovato alla salute.

Bene·lux [ˈbɛnɪlʌks] *adj:* **the ~ countries** i paesi del Benelux.

be·nevo·lence [bɪˈnɛvələns] *n* benevolenza.

be·nevo·lent [bɪˈnɛvələnt] *adj* benevolo(a).

be·nign [bɪˈnaɪn] *adj* benevolo(a); *(Med)* benigno(a).

bent [bɛnt] **1** *pt, pp of* **bend. 2** *adj* **(a)** *(wire, pipe)* piegato(a), storto(a); *(pej fam: dishonest)* losco(a); (: *homosexual*) invertito(a). **(b): to be ~ on sth/on doing sth** (*fig: determined*) essere deciso(a) a qc/a fare qc; **to be ~ on a quarrel** voler proprio litigare. **3** *n* (*aptitude*) inclinazione *f*, disposizione *f*; **to follow one's ~** seguire la propria inclinazione.

bent·wood ['bɛntwʊd] *adj* di legno ricurvo.

be·queath [bɪ'kwi:ð] *vt*: **to ~ sth to sb** lasciare qc in eredità a qn.

be·quest [bɪ'kwɛst] *n* lascito.

be·rate [bɪ'reɪt] *vt* rimproverare, redarguire.

be·reaved [bɪ'ri:vd] **1** *adj* in lutto. **2: the ~** *npl* i familiari in lutto.

be·reave·ment [bɪ'ri:vmənt] *n* lutto.

be·reft [bɪ'rɛft] *adj*: **to be ~ of sth** essere privo(a) di qc.

be·ret ['bɛreɪ] *n* berretto.

Ber·lin [bɜː'lɪn] *n* Berlino *f*; **East/West ~** Berlino Est/Ovest.

Ber·mu·da [bɜː'mjuːdə] *n* Bermude *fpl*; **~ shorts** bermuda *m inv*.

ber·ry ['bɛrɪ] *n* bacca; **brown as a ~** abbronzatissimo.

ber·serk [bə'sɜːk] *adj*: **to go ~** diventare pazzo(a) furioso(a); (*with anger*) andare su tutte le furie.

berth [bɜːθ] **1** *n* (*on ship, train*) cuccetta; (*Naut: place at wharf*) ormeggio; **to give sb a wide ~** (*fig*) tenersi alla larga da qn. **2** *vi* ormeggiare.

be·seech [bɪ'siːtʃ] *pt, pp* **besought** *vt* implorare.

be·set [bɪ'sɛt] *pt, pp* **beset** *vt* (*person*) assillare; **a policy ~ with dangers** una politica irta *or* piena di pericoli.

be·set·ting [bɪ'sɛtɪŋ] *adj*: **his ~ sin** il suo più grande difetto.

be·side [bɪ'saɪd] *prep* (*at the side of*) accanto a, vicino a; (*compared with*) rispetto a, in confronto a; **to be ~ o.s. (with)** (*anger, joy etc*) essere fuori di sé (da); **that's ~ the point** non c'entra.

be·sides [bɪ'saɪdz] **1** *prep* (*in addition to*) oltre a; (*apart from*) all'infuori di, a parte; **~ which...** per di più.... **2** *adv* (*in addition*) inoltre; (*anyway*) poi, del resto, per di più; **and more ~** e altri ancora.

be·siege [bɪ'siːdʒ] *vt* (*Mil, fig*) assediare, assalire; **we were ~ed with inquiries** siamo stati tempestati di domande.

be·sot·ted [bɪ'sɒtɪd] *adj*: **~ with sb** perso(a) (d'amore) per qn.

be·sought [bɪ'sɔːt] *pt, pp of* **beseech**.

be·spat·tered [bɪ'spætəd] *adj*: **~ with** schizzato(a) di.

be·spec·ta·cled [bɪ'spɛktɪkld] *adj* occhialuto(a).

be·spoke [bɪ'spəʊk] *adj* (*garment*) su misura; **~ tailor** sarto.

best [bɛst] **1** *adj* (*superl of* **good**) migliore; **to be ~** essere il(la) migliore; **the ~ pupil in the class** il primo(la prima) della classe; **in her ~ dress** vestita del suo abito migliore; **my ~ friend** il mio migliore amico; **the ~ thing about her is...** ciò che di meglio ha è...; **the ~ thing to do is...** la cosa migliore da fare *or* farsi è...; **for the ~ part of the year** per la maggior parte dell'anno; **may the ~ man win!** vinca il migliore!

2 *adv* (*superl of* **well**) meglio; **the ~ liked** il più ben voluto; **the ~ dressed** il più elegante; **as ~ I could** meglio che ho potuto; **you know ~** tu sai meglio di chiunque; **John came off ~** John ha avuto la meglio; **you had ~ leave now** faresti meglio ad andartene ora.

3 *n* il(la) migliore; **she's the ~ at drawing** disegna meglio di tutti; **he deserves the ~** si merita quanto c'è di meglio; **at ~** nella migliore delle ipotesi; **he wasn't at his ~** non era in vena *or* in piena forma; **he's not exactly patient at the**

~ of times non è mai molto paziente; **I acted for the ~** ho agito per il meglio; **let's hope for the ~** speriamo che tutto vada per il meglio; **to the ~ of my knowledge** per quel che ne so io; **to the ~ of my ability** come meglio posso; **to do one's ~** fare del proprio meglio; **to look one's ~** (*person*) essere più bello che mai; (*house etc*) essere più splendente che mai; **to make the ~ of a bad job** far buon viso a cattivo gioco; **she can dance with the ~ of them** è una ballerina di prima classe.

4 *cpd*: **~ man** *n* testimone *m* dello sposo.

bes·tial ['bɛstɪəl] *adj* bestiale.

be·stow [bɪ'stəʊ] *vt*: **to ~ sth on sb** (*title*) conferire qc a qn; (*honour, affections*) accordare qc a qn.

best·seller [,bɛst'sɛlə'] *n* bestseller *m inv*.

bet [bɛt] (*vb: pt, pp* **bet** *or* **betted**) **1** *n* scommessa; **to put a ~ on** fare una puntata; **it's a safe ~** (*fig*) è molto probabile. **2** *vi*: **to ~ (on)** scommettere (su); **to ~ on a horse** scommettere *or* puntare su un cavallo; **are you going? — you ~!** (*fam*) ci vai? — ci puoi giurare!; **I'm not a ~ting man** non sono uno scommettitore. **3** *vt* scommettere; **he ~ £5 on the favourite** ha giocato *or* puntato 5 sterline sul favorito; **I ~ you a pound that...** scommettiamo una sterlina che...; **I ~ he doesn't come** (*fam*) scommetto che non viene; **you can ~ your life that...** (*fam*) puoi scommetterci la testa che... .

be·tray [bɪ'treɪ] *vt* (*also fig*) tradire; **to ~ sb to the enemy** consegnare qn nelle mani del nemico; **his face ~ed his surprise** il suo viso tradiva la sorpresa.

be·tray·al [bɪ'treɪəl] *n* tradimento.

be·troth·al [bɪ'trəʊðəl] *n* fidanzamento.

bet·ter ['bɛtə'] **1** *adj* (*comp of* **good**) migliore; **I'm ~ at German than French** riesco meglio in tedesco che in francese; **he's ~ than his brother at mending cars** è più bravo di suo fratello ad aggiustare le macchine; **are you ~ now?** (*in health*) adesso stai meglio?; **to get ~** migliorare; (*Med*) star meglio, rimettersi; **that's ~!** così va meglio!; **it couldn't be ~** non potrebbe andar meglio (di così); **it would be ~ to go now** sarebbe meglio andare adesso; **he's no ~ than a thief** non è né più né meno che un ladro; **it lasted the ~ part of a year** è durato quasi un anno.

2 *adv* (*comp of* **well**) meglio; **he speaks French ~ than Italian/his brother** parla il francese meglio dell'italiano/di suo fratello; **~ known** meglio *or* più conosciuto; **so much the ~, all the ~** tanto meglio, meglio così; **he was all the ~ for it** ci ha guadagnato, gli ha fatto molto bene; **they are ~ off than we are** stanno meglio di noi; **you'd be ~ off staying where you are** faresti meglio a restare dove sei; **I had ~ go** dovrei andare; **hadn't you ~ ask him?** non sarebbe meglio se lo chiedessi a lui? (*fam*); **to think ~ of it** cambiare idea.

3 *n*: **a change for the ~** un cambiamento in meglio; **for ~ or worse** nella buona e nella cattiva sorte; **to get the ~ of sb** avere la meglio su qn; **one's ~s** i propri superiori.

4 *vt* migliorare; **to ~ o.s.** migliorare la propria condizione.

bet·ting shop ['bɛtɪŋ,ʃɒp] *n* (ufficio di) allibratore *m*.

be·tween [bɪ'twiːn] **1** *prep* (*gen*) tra, fra; **the road ~ here and London** la strada da qui a Londra; **a village ~ Florence and Pisa** un paese tra Firenze e Pisa; **~ now and next week we must...** da qui alla settimana prossima dobbiamo...; **I sat (in) ~ John and Sue** ero seduto (in mezzo) tra John e Sue; **it's ~ 5 and 6 metres long** è lungo fra i 5 e i 6 metri; **we shared it ~ us** ce lo siamo diviso tra di noi; **just ~ you and me...**, **just ~ ourselves...** sia detto tra me e te..., sia detto tra noi (due)...; **we only had £5 ~ us** fra tutti e due avevamo solo 5 sterline. **2** adv (also: **in ~**: of place) in mezzo; (: of time) nel frattempo; **few and far ~** rarissimi.

bev·elled ['bevld] adj: **~ edge** profilo smussato.

bev·er·age ['bevərɪdʒ] n bevanda.

bevy ['bevɪ] n banda.

be·wail [bɪ'weɪl] vt lamentare.

be·ware [bɪ'weər] vi: **to ~ of sb/sth** stare attento(a) a qn/qc, guardarsi da qn/qc; **you must ~ of falling** devi stare attento a non cadere; **~ of the dog!** attenti al cane!

be·wil·der [bɪ'wɪldər] vt sconcertare, disorientare.

be·wil·dered [bɪ'wɪldəd] adj disorientato(a).

be·wil·der·ing [bɪ'wɪldərɪŋ] adj sconcertante, sbalorditivo(a).

be·wil·der·ment [bɪ'wɪldəmənt] n perplessità, sbalordimento.

be·witch [bɪ'wɪtʃ] vt stregare; (fig) affascinare, ammaliare.

be·yond [bɪ'jɒnd] **1** prep (in place, time) al di là di; (: further than) più in là di; (exceeding) al di là di, al di sopra di; (apart from) oltre a; **~ my reach** fuori della mia portata; **we talked till ~ 5 pm** abbiamo parlato fino a oltre le 5; **it's almost ~ belief** è al limite del credibile; **that job is ~ him** quel lavoro è al di sopra delle sue capacità; **it's ~ me why...** (fam) non arriverò mai a capire perché; **that's ~ a joke** questo non è più uno scherzo. **2** adv più oltre, più in là, più avanti.

bi... [baɪ] pref bi... .

bi·an·nual [baɪ'ænjʊəl] adj semestrale.

bias ['baɪəs] **1** n (a) (inclination): **~ (towards** or **in favour of)** tendenza (verso); (prejudice): **~ (against)** pregiudizio (contro); **a right-wing ~** una tendenza di destra. **(b)** (of material) sbieco; **to cut sth on the ~** tagliare qc in sbieco. **2** vt: **to ~ sb towards** influenzare qn nei confronti di; **to ~ sb against** prevenire qn contro; **to be ~(s)ed** essere parziale; **to be ~(s)ed against** essere prevenuto contro. **3** cpd: **~ binding** n (Sewing) fettuccia in sbieco.

bib [bɪb] n (for child) bavaglino; (on dungarees) pettorina.

Bi·ble ['baɪbl] n bibbia.

bib·li·cal ['bɪblɪkəl] adj biblico(a).

bib·li·og·ra·phy [,bɪblɪ'ɒgrəfɪ] n bibliografia.

bi·car·bo·nate of soda [baɪ'kɑːbənɪtəv'səʊdə] n bicarbonato (di sodio).

bi·cen·tenary [,baɪsɛn'tiːnərɪ] n, (Am) **bi·cen·ten·nial** [baɪsɛn'tɛnɪəl] n bicentenario.

bi·ceps ['baɪsɛps] nsg bicipite m.

bick·er ['bɪkər] vi bisticciare.

bi·cy·cle ['baɪsɪkl] **1** n bicicletta; **to ride a ~** andare in bicicletta. **2** cpd: **~ parts** npl ricambi mpl per bicicletta; **~ path** n sentiero ciclabile; **~ pump** n pompa della bicicletta; **~ race** n gara ciclistica.

bid [bɪd] **1** n offerta; (Comm: tender) offerta (di appalto); (attempt) tentativo; (Cards) dichiarazione f; **a suicide ~** un tentativo di suicidio; **to make a ~ for freedom/power** fare un tentativo per ottenere la libertà/per impadronirsi del potere. **2** vt (a) (pt, pp bid) offrire; **to ~ £10 for** offrire 10 sterline per. **(b)** (pt bade, pp bidden: old, poet: order): **to ~ sb to do sth** ingiungere a qn di fare qc. **(c)** (pt bade, pp bidden): **to ~ sb good morning/farewell** dare il buon giorno/l'addio a qn, dire buon giorno/addio a qn. **3** vi (a) (pt, pp bid) (gen): **to ~ (for)** fare un'offerta (per); (Cards) dichiarare; **to ~ against sb** gareggiare

contro qn. **(b)** (pt bade, pp bidden): **to ~ fair to be/do sth** promettere di essere/fare qc.

bid·den ['bɪdn] pp of bid.

bid·der ['bɪdər] n offerente m/f; (Cards) chi fa la dichiarazione; **the highest ~** il miglior offerente.

bid·ding ['bɪdɪŋ] n (a) (at auction) offerte fpl; (Cards) dichiarazioni fpl; **the ~ opened at £5** le offerte sono partite dalle 5 sterline. **(b): I did his ~** ho fatto ciò che voleva.

bide [baɪd] vt: **to ~ one's time** aspettare il momento giusto.

bi·det ['biːdeɪ] n bidè m inv.

bi·en·nial [baɪ'ɛnɪəl] **1** adj biennale. **2** n (pianta) biennale f.

bier [bɪər] n (for coffin) catafalco; (for corpse) feretro.

biff [bɪf] n (Brit fam) botta.

bi·fo·cals [baɪ'fəʊkəlz] npl occhiali mpl bifocali.

big [bɪg] **1** adj (-ger, -gest) **(a)** (in height, age: building, tree, person) grande; (in bulk, amount: parcel, lie, increase) grosso(a); (important) grande, importante; **my ~ brother** mio fratello maggiore. **(b): to make the ~ time** sfondare; **to earn ~ money** guadagnare forte; **~ business** grossi affari mpl; **pop music is ~ business** la musica pop è un grosso affare; **to have ~ ideas** avere delle grandi idee; **to do things in a ~ way** fare le cose in grande; **he's too ~ for his boots** (fam) ha delle belle pretese; **why don't you keep your ~ mouth shut!** (fam) ma perché non tieni quella boccaccia chiusa?; **that's ~ of you!** (iro) che generosità!; **~ deal!** (fam) bella roba!

2 adv (fam): **to talk ~** dirne tante; **to think ~** avere delle grandi idee.

3 cpd: **~ dipper** n montagne fpl russe, otto m inv volante; **~ end** n (Aut) testa di biella; **~ game hunting** n caccia grossa; **~ noise** or **shot** n (fam) pezzo grosso; **~ toe** n alluce m; **~ top** n (circus) circo; (main tent) tendone m del circo; **~ wheel** n (at fair) ruota (panoramica); (Am) = **~ noise**.

biga·mist ['bɪgəmɪst] n bigamo/a.

biga·my ['bɪgəmɪ] n bigamia.

big·head ['bɪghɛd] n (fam) montato/a.

big-headed [bɪg'hɛdɪd] adj (fam) che si dà un sacco di arie.

big·ot ['bɪgət] n fanatico/a.

big·ot·ed ['bɪgətɪd] adj fanatico(a).

big·ot·ry ['bɪgətrɪ] n fanatismo.

big·wig ['bɪgwɪg] n (fam) pezzo grosso.

bike [baɪk] n (fam) bici f inv.

bi·ki·ni [bɪ'kiːnɪ] n bikini m inv.

bi·lat·er·al [baɪ'lætərəl] adj bilaterale.

bil·berry ['bɪlbərɪ] n mirtillo.

bile [baɪl] n (Med, fig) bile f.

bi·lin·gual [baɪ'lɪŋgwəl] adj bilingue.

bili·ous ['bɪlɪəs] adj (Med) biliare; (fig: irritable) collerico(a); **~ attack** attacco di bile.

bill[1] [bɪl] **1** n (of bird) becco. **2** vi: **to ~ and coo** tubare.

bill[2] [bɪl] **1** n **(a)** (account) fattura; (: in hotel, restaurant) conto; (: for gas, electricity) bolletta, conto; **may I have the ~ please?** posso avere il conto per piacere? **(b)** (Parliament) progetto di legge; **~ of rights** dichiarazione f dei diritti. **(c)** (Am: banknote) banconota, biglietto. **(d)** (notice) avviso; **'post no ~s'** 'divieto di affissione'; **that fits the ~** (fig) quello va proprio al caso mio (or tuo etc); **~ of fare** lista delle vivande, menù m inv. **(e)** (Theatre) cartellone m, manifesto; (: smaller) locandina; **to top the ~** essere in cima al cartellone. **(f)** (esp Comm, Fin) cambiale f; **~ of exchange** cambiale, tratta; **~ of lading** polizza di

carico; ~ **of sale** atto di vendita.
2 vt **(a)** *(Theatre)* essere in cartellone. **(b)** *(customer)*: **to ~ sb for sth** mandare la fattura di qc a qn.
bill·board ['bɪl,bɔːd] n tabellone m.
bil·let ['bɪlɪt] **1** n acquartieramento. **2** vt: **to ~ sb (on sb)** acquartierare qn (presso qn).
bill·fold ['bɪl,fəʊld] n *(Am)* portafoglio.
bil·liards ['bɪljədz] nsg biliardo.
bill·ing ['bɪlɪŋ] n *(Theatre)*: **to get top ~** figurare in testa al cartellone.
bil·lion ['bɪljən] n *(Brit)* bilione m; *(Am)* miliardo.
bil·low ['bɪləʊ] **1** n *(of smoke)* nuvola; *(of sail)* rigonfiamento. **2** vi *(smoke)* alzarsi in volute; *(sail)* gonfiarsi.
bil·ly(-goat) ['bɪlɪ(,gəʊt)] n caprone m, becco.
bin [bɪn] n *(for coal, rubbish)* bidone m; *(for bread)* cassetta; *(dust~)* pattumiera; *(litter~)* cestino.
bi·na·ry ['baɪnərɪ] adj binario(a).
bind [baɪnd] *(pt, pp* **bound)** **1** vt **(a)** *(tie together, make fast)* legare; *(: fig)* legare, unire; *(Culin)* legare; **bound hand and foot** legato mani e piedi. **(b)** *(encircle)* avvolgere; *(: wound, arm etc)* fasciare, bendare; *(Sewing: material, hem)*: **to ~ (with)** orlare (di); *(book)* rilegare. **(c)** *(oblige)*: **to ~ sb to sth/to do sth** obbligare qn a qc/a fare qc. **2** n *(fam: nuisance)* scocciatura.
♦ **bind over** vt + adv *(Law)* dare la condizionale a.
♦ **bind together** vt + adv *(sticks etc)* legare (insieme); *(fig)* unire.
♦ **bind up** vt + adv *(wound)* fasciare, bendare; **to be bound up in** *(work, research etc)* essere completamente assorbito da; **to be bound up with** *(person)* dedicarsi completamente a.
bind·er ['baɪndə'] n **(a)** *(Agr)* mietilegatrice f. **(b)** *(file)* classificatore m.
bind·ing ['baɪndɪŋ] **1** n *(of book)* rilegatura; *(Sewing)* fettuccia, bordo; *(on skis)* attacco. **2** adj *(agreement, contract)* vincolante; **to be ~ on sb** essere vincolante per qn.
bin·go ['bɪŋgəʊ] n tombola pubblica.
bin·ocu·lars [bɪ'nɒkjʊləz] npl binocolo.
bio·chem·ist ['baɪəʊ'kɛmɪst] n biochimico/a.
bio·chem·is·try ['baɪəʊ'kɛmɪstrɪ] n biochimica.
bio·degrad·able ['baɪəʊdɪ'greɪdəbl] adj biodegradabile.
bi·og·raph·er [baɪ'ɒgrəfə'] n biografo/a.
bio·graphi·cal [,baɪəʊ'græfɪkəl] adj biografico(a).
bi·og·ra·phy [baɪ'ɒgrəfɪ] n biografia.
bio·logi·cal [,baɪə'lɒdʒɪkəl] adj biologico(a).
bi·olo·gist [baɪ'ɒlədʒɪst] n biologo/a.
bi·ol·ogy [baɪ'ɒlədʒɪ] n biologia.
bio·phys·ics [,baɪəʊ'fɪzɪks] nsg biofisica.
birch [bɜːtʃ] n *(tree, wood)* betulla; *(for whipping)* frusta (di betulla).
bird [bɜːd] **1** n uccello; *(fam: girl)* tipa; **have you put the ~ in the oven?** hai messo il pollo *(or il tacchino etc)* nel forno?; **~ of prey** uccello rapace *or* da preda; **a little ~ told me** *(hum)* me l'ha detto l'uccellino; **the early ~ catches the worm** chi dorme non piglia pesci; **a ~ in the hand is worth two in the bush** è meglio un uovo oggi che una gallina domani; **~s of a feather flock together** chi si assomiglia si piglia; **to kill two ~s with one stone** prendere due piccioni con una fava. **2** cpds: **~ cage** n gabbia per uccelli; **~ sanctuary** n riserva per uccelli; **~'s-eye view** n vista panoramica; **~ watcher** n ornitologo/a dilettante.
birth [bɜːθ] **1** n *(also fig)* nascita; *(childbirth)* parto; **it was a difficult ~** è stato un parto difficile; **at ~** alla nascita; **Italian by ~** italiano di nascita; **place of ~** luogo di nascita; **to give ~ to** dare alla

luce; *(fig)* dare inizio a. **2** cpd: **~ certificate** n certificato *or* atto di nascita; **~ control** n controllo delle nascite; **~ place** n luogo di nascita; *(town)* città natale; **~ rate** n *(tasso di)* natalità.
birth·day ['bɜːθdeɪ] **1** n compleanno. **2** cpd *(present, party, cake)* del *or* di compleanno.
birth·mark ['bɜːθ,maːk] n voglia.
birth·right ['bɜːθ,raɪt] n *(fig)* diritto di nascita.
bis·cuit ['bɪskɪt] n *(Brit)* biscotto; *(Am)* panino al latte.
bi·sect [baɪ'sɛkt] vt tagliare in due (parti); *(Math)* bisecare.
bish·op ['bɪʃəp] n vescovo; *(Chess)* alfiere m.
bi·son ['baɪsn] n bisonte m.
bit¹ [bɪt] n *(tool)* punta.
bit² [bɪt] n **(a)** *(piece)* pezzo; *(smaller)* pezzetto; **a ~ of** *(paper, wood, cake)* un pezzo di; *(wine, sunshine, peace)* un po' di; **a ~ too much** un po' troppo; **a ~ bigger/smaller** un po' più grande/più piccolo; **a little ~ dearer** un pochino più caro; **a good ~ cheaper** molto più a buon mercato; **a ~ of news** una notizia; **a ~ of advice** un (piccolo) consiglio; **a ~ of luck** una fortuna; **they have a ~ of money** hanno un po' di soldi; **it was a ~ of a shock** è stato un po' un colpo; **that's not a ~ of help** questo non aiuta affatto; **to come to ~s** *(break)* andare a pezzi; *(be dismantled)* essere smontabile; **in ~s (and pieces)** *(broken)* a pezzi; *(dismantled)* smontato; **bring all your ~s and pieces** porta tutte le tue cose; **to do one's ~** fare la propria parte; **when it comes to the ~** quando si arriva al dunque.
(b) *(short time)*: **a ~** un momento, un attimo. **(c)** *(considerable sum)*: **a ~** un bel po'. **(d)** *(Am: 12½ cents)* ottavo di dollaro.
bit³ [bɪt] pt of **bite.**
bitch [bɪtʃ] **1** n **(a)** *(of canines)* femmina; *(of dog)* cagna; **a terrier ~** un terrier femmina. **(b)** *(fam: woman)* stronza; *(fam: complain)* mugugnare.
bite [baɪt] *(vb: pt* **bit,** *pp* **bitten)** **1** n **(a)** *(act)* morso; *(wound: of dog, snake etc)* morsicatura; *(: of insect)* puntura; **to take a ~ at** dare un morso a, addentare. **(b)** *(of food)* boccone m; **there's not a ~ to eat** non c'è niente da mettere sotto i denti; **do you fancy a ~ (to eat)?** non vorresti mangiare qualcosa? **(c)** *(Fishing)*: **he didn't get a single ~** non un solo pesce ha abboccato.
2 vt *(gen)* mordere; *(subj: dog)* morsicare, mordere; *(subj: insect)* pungere; **to ~ one's nails** mangiarsi le unghie; **once bitten twice shy** *(fig)* una volta scottati...; **to ~ the hand that feeds you** *(fig)* sputare nel piatto in cui si mangia; **to ~ the dust** *(die)* lasciarci la pelle.
3 vi **(a)** *(dog etc)* mordere; *(insect)* pungere. **(b)** *(fish)* abboccare. **(c)** *(fig: cuts, inflation etc)* farsi sentire.
♦ **bite into** vi + prep *(subj: person)* addentare, dare un morso a; *(: acid)* intaccare.
♦ **bite off** vt + adv staccare con un morso; **to ~ off more than one can chew** *(fig)* fare il passo più lungo della gamba; **to ~ sb's head off** *(fig)* saltare in testa a qn.
♦ **bite through** vt + adv tagliare con i denti.
bit·ing ['baɪtɪŋ] adj *(cold, wind)* pungente; *(criticism, sarcasm)* pungente, mordace; *(remark)* caustico(a).
bit·ten ['bɪtn] pp of **bite.**
bit·ter ['bɪtə'] **1** adj **(a)** *(taste: gen)* amaro(a); *(: of fruit)* aspro(a); **a ~ pill to swallow** *(fig)* un boccone amaro da ingoiare; **~ lemon** *(drink)* limonata amara. **(b)** *(icy: weather)* gelido(a). **(c)** *(enemy, hatred)* acerrimo(a); *(quarrel)* aspro(a); *(disappointment)* amaro(a); *(person)* amareggia-

to(a); **to the ~ end** fino all'ultimo. **2** *n (Brit: beer)* birra inglese amara.

bit·ter·ly ['bɪtəlɪ] *adv (disappoint, complain, weep)* amaramente; *(oppose, criticise)* aspramente; *(jealous)* profondamente; **it's ~ cold** fa un freddo gelido.

bit·ter·ness ['bɪtənɪs] *n (gen)* amarezza; *(of fruit, fig: of quarrel)* asprezza.

bitter·sweet ['bɪtə,swiːt] *adj (taste)* agrodolce; *(love affair)* dolce-amaro(a).

bit·ty ['bɪtɪ] *adj (fam)* frammentario(a).

bi·tu·men ['bɪtjʊmɪn] *n* bitume *m*.

bivou·ac ['bɪvʊæk] *(vb: pt, pp ~ked)* **1** *n* bivacco. **2** *vi* bivaccare.

bi·zarre [bɪ'zɑːʳ] *adj* bizzarro(a).

blab [blæb] **1** *vt (also: ~ out)* spifferare. **2** *vi (chatter)* cianciare; *(to police etc)* vuotare il sacco.

black [blæk] **1** *adj* **(a)** nero(a); *(in darkness)* buio(a); *(fig: gloomy: prospects)* poco allegro(a); *(: despair)* nero(a), cupo(a): *(: future)* poco promettente; *(: wicked: thought, deed)* malvagio(a); **things look pretty ~** *(fig)* c'è poco da star allegri; **he looked as ~ as thunder** *(fig)* aveva un'aria furiosa; **~ coffee** caffè *m inv* nero; **~ and blue** pieno di lividi; **to beat sb ~ and blue** riempire qn di lividi. **(b)** *(negro)* negro(a).

2 *n* **(a)** *(colour)* nero; **dressed in ~** vestito di *or* in nero; **there it is in ~ and white** *(fig)* eccolo nero su bianco; **in the ~** *(Fin)* in attivo. **(b)** *(person)* negro/a.

3 *vt (Industry: goods, firm)* boicottare.

4 *cpd*: **~ box** *n (Aer)* scatola nera; **~ eye** *n* occhio nero; **~ humour** *n* umorismo nero; **~ magic** *n* magia nera; **~ mark** *n (fig)* marchio; **~ market** *n* mercato nero; *(in wartime)* borsa nera; **on the ~ market** al mercato nero; alla borsa nera; **~ pudding** *n* sanguinaccio; **B~ Sea** *n* Mar *m* Nero; **~ sheep** *n* pecora nera; **~ spot** *n (Aut)* luogo famigerato per gli incidenti. **'~ tie'** *(on invitations)* 'abito scuro'.

♦ **black out 1** *vt + adv* **(a)** *(obliterate)* cancellare. **(b)** *(in wartime)* oscurare; *(subj: power cut)* piombare nell'oscurità. **2** *vi + adv (faint)* svenire.

black·berry ['blækbərɪ] *n* mora (di rovo); *(~ bush)* cespuglio di more.

black·bird ['blækbɜːd] *n* merlo.

black·board ['blækbɔːd] *n* lavagna.

black·cur·rant [,blæk'kʌrənt] *n* ribes *m inv* nero.

black·en ['blækən] **1** *vi* annerirsi; *(sky)* oscurarsi. **2** *vt* annerire; *(fig: reputation)* sporcare.

black·head ['blækhed] *n* punto nero, comedone *m*.

black·jack ['blæk,dʒæk] *n (Cards)* ventuno; *(at casino)* blackjack *m*.

black·leg ['blækleg] *n (Brit)* crumiro/a.

black·list ['blæklɪst] **1** *n* lista nera. **2** *vt* mettere sulla lista nera.

black·mail ['blækmeɪl] **1** *n* ricatto. **2** *vt* ricattare; **to ~ sb into doing sth** ricattare qn affinché faccia qc.

black·ness ['blæknɪs] *n (colore m)* nero; *(darkness)* buio, oscurità.

black·out ['blækaʊt] *n* **(a)** *(of lights)* interruzione *f* di corrente (elettrica); *(during war)* oscuramento; *(TV)* interruzione delle trasmissioni. **(b)** *(Med)* svenimento.

black·shirt ['blæk,ʃɜːt] *n (Pol)* camicia nera.

black·smith ['blæk,smɪθ] *n* fabbro ferraio.

blad·der ['blædəʳ] *n (Anat)* vescica.

blade [bleɪd] *n (cutting edge)* lama; *(: of safety razor)* lametta; *(of propeller)* pala; *(of grass etc)* filo.

blame [bleɪm] **1** *n (responsibility)* colpa, responsabilità; *(censure)* biasimo; **to lay the ~ on sb** attribuire la responsabilità di qc a qn, dare la colpa

di qc a qn. **2** *vt* **(a)** *(hold responsible)*: **to ~ sb for sth** dare la colpa a qn di qc, ritenere qn responsabile di qc; **to be to ~ for** essere responsabile di; **I'm not to ~** non è colpa mia; **you have only yourself to ~** puoi ringraziare solo te stesso. **(b)** *(reproach)* criticare, biasimare; **and I don't ~ him** e non gli do torto.

blame·less ['bleɪmlɪs] *adj* irreprensibile.

blanch [blɑːntʃ] **1** *vi (person)* sbiancare in viso. **2** *vt (Culin)* scottare.

bland [blænd] *adj (smile)* blando(a); *(character)* insulso(a); *(food)* poco condito(a).

blan·dish·ments ['blændɪʃmənts] *npl* lusinghe *fpl*.

blank [blæŋk] **1** *adj (paper, space etc)* bianco(a); *(wall)* cieco(a); *(empty: expression etc)* vacuo(a); **a look of ~ amazement** uno sguardo allibito; **my mind went ~** ho avuto un vuoto. **2** *n (void)* vuoto; *(in form)* spazio in bianco; *(cartridge)* cartuccia a salve; **his mind was a ~** si sentiva la testa vuota; **to draw a ~** *(fig)* non aver nessun risultato. **3** *cpd*: **~ cartridge** *n* cartuccia a salve; **~ cheque** *n* assegno in bianco; **~ verse** *n* versi *mpl* sciolti *or* liberi.

blan·ket ['blæŋkɪt] **1** *n* coperta; *(fig: of snow, fog)* coltre *f*; *(of smoke)* cappa. **2** *cpd (statement, agreement)* globale; **to give ~ cover** *(subj: insurance policy)* coprire tutti i rischi.

blare [bleəʳ] **1** *n (of trumpet, car horn)* strombettio; *(of siren)* urlo; *(of radio)* frastuono. **2** *vt (also: ~ out)* far risuonare. **3** *vi (see n)* strombettare; urlare; *(radio)* suonare a tutto volume.

blasé ['blɑːzeɪ] *adj* blasé *inv*.

blas·pheme [blæs'fiːm] *vi* bestemmiare.

blas·phem·er [blæs'fiːməʳ] *n* bestemmiatore/trice.

blas·phe·mous ['blæsfɪməs] *adj* blasfemo(a).

blas·phe·my ['blæsfɪmɪ] *n* bestemmia.

blast [blɑːst] **1** *n* **(a)** *(of air, steam)* getto; *(of wind)* raffica; **(at) full ~** *(also fig)* a tutta forza. **(b)** *(sound: of trumpet)* squillo; *(: of car horn, siren etc)* colpo; **(at) full ~** *(radio etc)* a tutto volume. **(c)** *(shock wave: of explosion, furnace etc)* spostamento d'aria; *(noise)* esplosione *f*. **2** *vt (tear apart: with explosives)* far saltare; *(: by lightning)* bruciare; *(fig: hopes, future)* distruggere. **3** *excl (fam)* mannaggia!; **~ him!** mannaggia a lui! **4** *cpd*: **~ furnace** *n* altoforno.

♦ **blast off** *vi + adv (spacecraft etc)* essere lanciato(a).

blast·ed ['blɑːstɪd] *adj (fam)* maledetto(a).

blast·ing ['blɑːstɪŋ] *n (Tech)* brillamento; **'~ in progress'** 'attenzione: sparo di mine'.

blast-off ['blɑːst,ɒf] *n (of rockets)* lancio.

bla·tant ['bleɪtənt] *adj* sfacciato(a).

bla·tant·ly ['bleɪtəntlɪ] *adv* sfacciatamente; **it's ~ obvious** è lampante.

blaze¹ [bleɪz] **1** *n (fire: of buildings etc)* incendio; *(glow: of fire, sun etc)* bagliore *m*; *(of gems, beauty)* splendore *m*; **a ~ of colour** un'esplosione di colori; **a ~ of anger** un impeto d'ira; **in a ~ of publicity** circondato da grande pubblicità; **go to ~s!** *(fam)* va al diavolo!; **like ~s** *(fam)* come un matto. **2** *vi (fire)* ardere; *(conflagration)* divampare; *(building)* essere in fiamme; *(sun)* sfolgorare; *(light)* risplendere; *(eyes)*: **to ~ with anger** fiammeggiare dalla rabbia; **to ~ with passion** ardere di passione.

♦ **blaze away** *vi + adv*: **to ~ away (at)** continuare a far fuoco (su).

♦ **blaze up** *vi + adv* fare una fiammata; *(fig: feelings)* accendersi.

blaze² [bleɪz] **1** *n (mark: on horse)* stella; *(: on tree)* segno. **2** *vt (tree)* segnare; **to ~ a trail**

(also fig) aprire una nuova via.

blaz·er ['bleɪzəʳ] *n* blazer *m inv.*

blaz·ing ['bleɪzɪŋ] *adj (building etc)* in fiamme; *(fire)* ardente; *(sun)* infuocato(a); *(light)* sfolgorante; *(jewel)* sfavillante; *(eyes)* fiammeggiante; *(colour, quarrel, anger)* acceso(a).

bleach [bliːtʃ] **1** *n* decolorante *m; (liquid ~)* acqua ossigenata; *(household ~)* candeggina, varechina. **2** *vt (material)* candeggiare; *(bones)* sbiancare; *(hair)* ossigenare.

bleach·ers ['bliːtʃəz] *npl (Am)* posti *mpl* di gradinata.

bleak [bliːk] *adj (landscape)* desolato(a); *(weather)* gelido(a), *(smile)* pallido(a); *(prospect, future)* tetro(a), deprimente; **the chances of your getting a job here are** ~ le probabilità che tu trovi un lavoro qui sono molto scarse.

bleary ['blɪərɪ] *adj (eyes)* appannato(a).

bleary-eyed ['blɪərɪ'aɪd] *adj:* **to be** ~ avere gli occhi appannati.

bleat [bliːt] **1** *n* belato. **2** *vi* belare; *(fig fam)* piagnucolare.

bleed [bliːd] *pt, pp* **bled** [blɛd] **1** *vi* sanguinare; **his nose is** ~**ing** gli sanguina il naso, gli esce il sangue dal naso; **to** ~ **to death** morire dissanguato; **my heart** ~**s for him** *(iro)* mi fa proprio compassione, poverino! **2** *vt* **(a)** salassare. **(b)** *(brakes, radiator)* spurgare.

bleed·ing ['bliːdɪŋ] **1** *adj* **(a)** *(wound, person)* sanguinante. **(b)** *(Brit fam)* dannato(a), maledetto(a); **you** ~ **idiot!** pezzo di cretino! **2** *n* perdita di sangue; *(serious)* emorragia.

bleep [bliːp] **1** *n (Radio, TV)* segnale *m* (acustico). **2** *vi* emettere dei segnali.

bleep·er ['bliːpəʳ] *n (of doctor etc)* cicalino.

blem·ish ['blɛmɪʃ] **1** *n* imperfezione *f; (on fruit)* ammaccatura; *(on reputation)* macchia. **2** *vt* deturpare.

blench [blɛntʃ] *vi (flinch)* sussultare; *(turn pale)* impallidire.

blend [blɛnd] **1** *n (gen)* mescolanza, miscuglio; *(of tea, whisky etc)* miscela; *(of tobacco)* mistura. **2** *vt (teas etc)* mischiare; *(colours)* mescolare, mischiare; *(Culin)* amalgamare. **3** *vi (harmonize):* **to** ~ **(with)** *(gen)* mescolarsi (a); *(sounds, perfumes)* confondersi (con); *(styles)* essere in armonia (con); *(opinions, races)* fondersi (con); *(colours)* fondersi (con); *(: go well together)* star bene insieme.

blend·er ['blɛndəʳ] *n (Culin)* frullatore *m.*

bless [blɛs] *vt* benedire; **God** ~ **the queen!** Dio benedica la regina!; ~ **you!** sei un angelo!; *(after sneezing)* salute!; **I'm** ~**ed if I know!** *(fam)* non ne so un accidente!

bless·ed ['blɛsɪd] *adj* **(a)** *(Rel: holy)* benedetto(a); *(: happy)* beato(a); **the B**~ **Sacrament** il Santissimo Sacramento; **the B**~ **Virgin** la Santa Vergine; **B**~ **Margaret Sinclair** Beata Margaret Sinclair. **(b)** *(fam euph)* benedetto(a); **every** ~ **day** tutti i santi giorni; **where's that** ~ **book?** dov'è quel benedetto libro?

bless·ing ['blɛsɪŋ] *n* **(a)** *(Rel)* benedizione *f.* **(b)** *(advantage)* vantaggio; **to count one's** ~**s** ringraziare Iddio, ritenersi fortunato; **what a** ~ **that...** meno male che...; **it was a** ~ **in disguise** in fondo è stato un bene.

blest [blɛst] *pp (poet)* of **bless.**

blew [bluː] *pt of* **blow.**

blight [blaɪt] **1** *n (of plants, fruit, trees)* carie *f; (of cereals)* carbonchio; *(fig)* piaga. **2** *vt (plants etc)* far avvizzire; *(fig: future, hopes)* rovinare, distruggere.

blind [blaɪnd] **1** *adj (person, corner, obedience, anger*

etc) cieco(a); ~ **in one eye** cieco da un occhio; ~ **as a bat** *(fam)* cieco come una talpa; **to go** ~ diventare cieco; **he was** ~ **to her faults** non vedeva i suoi difetti; **to turn a** ~ **eye to** chiudere un occhio su.

2 *n* **(a): the** ~ *pl* i ciechi; **it's a case of the** ~ **leading the** ~ è come mettere insieme uno storpio e uno sciancato. **(b)** *(shade)* tenda avvolgibile; **Venetian** ~ veneziana.

3 *adv (fly, land)* alla cieca; ~ **drunk** *(fam)* ubriaco fradicio.

4 *vt* accecare; **he was** ~**ed in the war** ha perso la vista in guerra; **his love** ~**ed him to her faults** il suo amore lo rendeva cieco ai suoi difetti.

5 *cpd:* ~ **date** *n* appuntamento con qualcuno che non si conosce; ~ **spot** *n (Anat)* punto cieco; *(Aut)* angolo morto; *(fig)* punto debole.

blind·fold ['blaɪndfəʊld] **1** *adj* con gli occhi bendati, bendato(a); **I could do it** ~ potrei farlo ad occhi bendati. **2** *n* benda. **3** *vt* bendare (gli occhi a).

blind·ly ['blaɪndlɪ] *adv* ciecamente.

blind·ness ['blaɪndnɪs] *n* cecità; ~ **to the realities of life** rifiuto di guardare in faccia la realtà.

blink [blɪŋk] **1** *n* battito di ciglia; **to be on the** ~ *(fam)* essere scassato. **2** *vt:* **to** ~ **one's eyes** sbattere le palpebre. **3** *vi* sbattere le palpebre; *(light)* lampeggiare.

blink·ered ['blɪŋkəd] *adj (fig: person)* che ha i paraocchi; **to have a** ~ **view of reality** vedere la realtà con i paraocchi.

blink·ers ['blɪŋkəz] *npl* paraocchi *mpl.*

bliss [blɪs] *n (Rel)* beatitudine *f; (happy state)* (immensa) felicità; **ignorance is** ~ *(Proverb)* beata l'ignoranza; **it's** ~! *(fam)* è meraviglioso!

bliss·ful ['blɪsfʊl] *adj* stupendo(a), meraviglioso(a); **in** ~ **ignorance** nella (più) beata ignoranza.

bliss·ful·ly ['blɪsfəlɪ] *adv (sigh, smile)* beatamente; ~ **happy** magnificamente felice.

blis·ter ['blɪstəʳ] **1** *n (on skin)* vescica; *(of paint)* bolla. **2** *vt (skin)* far venire le vesciche a; *(paint)* produrre delle bolle in. **3** *vi (skin)* riempirsi di bollicine; *(paint)* formare delle bolle.

blithe·ly ['blaɪðlɪ] *adv* allegramente.

blitz [blɪts] **1** *n (Mil)* attacco improvviso; **the B**~ il bombardamento aereo della Gran Bretagna; **to have a** ~ **on sth** *(fig)* prendere d'assalto qc. **2** *vt* bombardare.

bliz·zard ['blɪzəd] *n* bufera di neve.

bloat·ed ['bləʊtɪd] *adj (also fig):* ~ **(with)** gonfio(a) (di).

blob [blɒb] *n (drop)* goccia, *(stain, spot)* macchia; *(lump: of mud etc)* pallina.

bloc [blɒk] *n (Pol)* blocco.

block [blɒk] **1** *n* **(a)** *(of stone etc)* blocco; *(toy)* cubo *(per fare le costruzioni); (executioner's)* ceppo; **to knock sb's** ~ **off** *(fam)* rompere la zucca a qn. **(b)** *(building)* palazzo; *(esp Am: group of buildings)* isolato; *(of flats* caseggiato; **to walk around the** ~ fare il giro dell'isolato; **3** ~**s from here** a 3 isolati di distanza da qui. **(c)** *(section: of tickets)* blocchetto; *(: of shares)* pacchetto. **(d)** *(blockage: in pipe)* ingorgo; *(Med)* blocco; **mental** ~ blocco mentale. **2** *vt (gen)* bloccare; *(pipe)* ingorgare, bloccare; *(Ftbl)* stoppare; **to** ~ **sb's way** sbarrare la strada a qn; **to** ~ **sb's view** coprire la vista a qn. **3** *cpd:* ~ **booking** *n* prenotazione *f* in blocco; ~ **letters** *or* **capitals** *npl* stampatello; ~ **and tackle** *n (Tech)* paranco.

♦ **block out** *vt + adv (obscure: light)* escludere; *(obliterate: picture)* cancellare.

♦ **block up** *vt + adv (obstruct: passage)* bloccare;

(: pipe) ingorgare, intasare; *(fill in: gap)* tappare; *(: window, entrance)* murare; **my nose is ~ed up** ho il naso intasato.

block·ade [blɒˈkeɪd] **1** *n (Mil)* blocco. **2** *vt* bloccare.

block·age [ˈblɒkɪdʒ] *n (obstruction)* ingorgo; *(Med)* blocco.

bloke [bləʊk] *n (fam)* tipo, tizio.

blond [blɒnd] **1** *n (man)* biondo. **2** *adj* biondo(a).

blonde [blɒnd] **1** *n (woman)* bionda. **2** *adj* biondo(a).

blood [blʌd] **1** *n* sangue *m*; **to give ~** donare sangue; **of royal ~** di sangue reale; **there's bad ~ between them** corre cattivo sangue fra di loro; **new ~** *(fig)* nuova linfa; **it's like trying to get ~ out of a stone** è come cavar sangue dalle pietre; **in cold ~** a sangue freddo; **~ is thicker than water** *(Proverb)* la voce del sangue è più forte; **it's in the ~** ce l'ho *(or* l'hai *etc)* nel sangue; **he's after my ~** *(hum)* se mi prende m'ammazza; **my ~ ran cold** mi son sentito gelare il sangue.

2 *cpd*: **~ bank** *n* banca del sangue; **~ brother** *n* fratello di sangue; **~ donor** *n* donatore/trice di sangue; **~ group** *n* gruppo sanguigno; **~ heat** *n* temperatura corporea; **~ money** *n* denaro sporco; **~ orange** *n* arancia sanguigna; **~ pressure** *n* pressione *f* del sangue; **to have high/low ~ pressure** avere la pressione alta/bassa; **~ poisoning** *n* setticemia; **~ red** *adj* rosso sangue *inv*; **~ sports** *npl* sport *npl* cruenti; **~ stream** *n* (circolazione *f* del) sangue *m*; **~ test** *n* analisi *f inv* del sangue; **~ transfusion** *n* trasfusione *f* di sangue; **~ vessel** *n* vaso sanguigno.

blood-curdling [ˈblʌdˌkɜːdlɪŋ] *adj* raccapricciante, da far gelare il sangue.

blood·hound [ˈblʌdˌhaʊnd] *n* segugio.

blood·less [ˈblʌdlɪs] *adj (pale)* smorto(a), esangue; *(coup)* senza spargimento di sangue.

blood·shed [ˈblʌdˌʃed] *n* spargimento di sangue.

blood·shot [ˈblʌdˌʃɒt] *adj* iniettato(a) di sangue.

blood·stain [ˈblʌdˌsteɪn] *n* macchia di sangue.

blood·stained [ˈblʌdˌsteɪnd] *adj* insanguinato(a).

blood·thirsty [ˈblʌdˌθɜːstɪ] *adj* sanguinario(a).

bloody [ˈblʌdɪ] **1** *adj* **(a)** *(bleeding)* sanguinante, che sanguina; *(bloodstained)* insanguinato(a); *(cruel: battle etc)* sanguinoso(a), cruento(a). **(b)** *(Brit fam)* maledetto(a), dannato(a); **~ hell!** porca miseria!; **I'm a ~ genius!** madonna, che genio che sono! **2** *adv (Brit fam)*: **that's no ~ good!** questo non serve a un cavolo!; **he runs ~ fast!** cavoli, se corre veloce!

bloody-minded [ˌblʌdɪˈmaɪndɪd] *adj (Brit fam)* indisponente.

bloody-minded·ness [ˌblʌdɪˈmaɪndɪdnɪs] *n (Brit fam)* dispetto.

bloom [bluːm] **1** *n (flower)* fiore *m*; *(on fruit)* lanugine *f*; *(on complexion)* colorito roseo; **in ~** *(flower)* sbocciato; *(tree)* in fiore; **in full ~** in piena fioritura; **in the full ~ of youth** nel fiore della giovinezza. **2** *vi (flower)* aprirsi; *(tree)* sfiorire.

bloom·ers [ˈbluːməz] *npl* mutandoni *mpl* a sbuffo.

blos·som [ˈblɒsəm] **1** *n* fiori *mpl*; *(single flower)* fiore *m*; **apple ~** fiori di melo. **2** *vi (also:* **~ out)** fiorire; **to ~ into** *(fig)* diventare.

blot [blɒt] **1** *n* macchia; **to be a ~ on the landscape** rovinare il paesaggio. **2** *vt* **(a)** *(spot with ink)* macchiare d'inchiostro; **to ~ one's copy book** *(fig)* farla grossa. **(b)** *(dry: ink, writing)* asciugare.

♦ **blot out** *vt* + *adv (words, memories)* cancellare; *(sun, view)* offuscare.

blotch [blɒtʃ] *n (of ink, colour)* macchia, chiazza; *(on skin)* chiazza.

blot·ter [ˈblɒtər] *n* tampone *m* (di carta assorbente).

blot·ting pa·per [ˈblɒtɪŋˌpeɪpər] *n* carta assorbente, carta asciugante.

blouse [blaʊz] *n* camicetta.

blow[1] [bləʊ] *n (gen)* colpo; *(with fist)* pugno; **a ~ with a hammer** un colpo di martello; **at one ~** in un colpo (solo); **to come to ~s** venire alle mani; **the news came as a great ~ to her** la notizia fu un duro colpo per lei.

blow[2] [bləʊ] *pt* **blew**, *pp* **blown 1** *vt* **(a)** *(subj: wind: ship)* spingere; *(: hair)* far svolazzare; **a gale blew the ship off course** una bufera ha fatto uscire di rotta la nave. **(b)** *(trumpet, horn)* suonare; **to ~ a whistle** fischiare; **to ~ one's own trumpet** cantare le proprie lodi. **(c)** *(bubbles)* fare; *(glass)* soffiare; *(kiss)* mandare; **to ~ one's nose** soffiarsi il naso. **(d)** *(fuse, safe)* far saltare; **to ~ money on sth** *(fam)* buttare via dei soldi per qc; **to ~ a secret** spifferare un segreto; **to ~ one's top** *(fam)* esplodere, andare su tutte le furie; **~ the expense!** crepi l'avarizia!

2 *vi* **(a)** *(wind, person)* soffiare; *(leaves etc)* svolazzare; *(flag)* sventolare; **to ~ on one's fingers** scaldarsi le mani soffiando; **to ~ on one's soup** soffiare sulla minestra; **to see which way the wind ~s** *(fig)* vedere che aria tira; **his hat blew out of the window** il suo cappello è volato fuori dalla finestra; **the door blew open/shut** un colpo di vento ha spalancato/chiuso la porta. **(b)** *(make sound: trumpet etc)* suonare. **(c)** *(fuse etc)* saltare; *(tyre)* scoppiare.

♦ **blow away 1** *vi* + *adv* volare via. **2** *vt* + *adv* soffiare via; *(hat)* portare via.

♦ **blow down 1** *vi* + *adv* essere abbattuto(a) *(dal vento)*. **2** *vt* + *adv* abbattere.

♦ **blow in** *vi* + *adv (window)* sfasciarsi; *(enter: leaves, dust)* volar dentro; **look who's just ~n in!** *(fam)* ma guarda chi è arrivato!

♦ **blow off 1** *vi* + *adv (hat)* volar via. **2** *vt* + *adv (hat)* portare via; **to ~ off steam** *(fig fam)* sfogarsi.

♦ **blow out** *vt* + *adv (candle)* spegnere; *(swell out: cheeks)* gonfiare.

♦ **blow over 1** *vt* + *adv (tree)* abbattere. **2** *vi* + *adv (tree etc)* rovesciarsi; *(storm, fig: dispute)* passare.

♦ **blow up 1** *vt* + *adv (bridge etc)* far saltare; *(tyre etc)* gonfiare; *(photo)* ingrandire; *(event etc)* esagerare. **2** *vi* + *adv (bomb, fig: person)* esplodere; *(row etc)* scoppiare; *(wind)* alzarsi; *(storm: gather)* arrivare.

blow-by-blow [ˈbləʊbaɪˌbləʊ] *adj (account etc)* minuto per minuto.

blow-dry [ˈbləʊˌdraɪ] **1** *n (hairstyle)* messa in piega a föhn. **2** *vt* asciugare con il föhn.

blow·lamp [ˈbləʊˌlæmp] *n* lampada a benzina per saldare.

blown [bləʊn] *pp of* **blow**[2].

blow·out [ˈbləʊaʊt] *n (of tyre)* scoppio; *(of fuse)* corto circuito; *(fam: big meal)* abbuffata.

blow·pipe [ˈbləʊˌpaɪp] *n (weapon)* cerbottana.

blowy [ˈbləʊɪ] *adj* ventoso(a).

blowzy [ˈblaʊzɪ] *adj (woman)* sciatto(a).

blub·ber [ˈblʌbər] **1** *n (of whales)* grasso di balena. **2** *vi (weep)* frignare.

blue [bluː] **1** *adj* **(a)** *(light ~)* azzurro(a), celeste; *(darker)* blu *inv*; **~ with cold** livido dal freddo; **once in a ~ moon** a ogni morte di papa; **you can talk till you're ~ in the face** puoi parlare fino a domani; **to be in a ~ funk** *(fam)* avere una fifa nera. **(b)** *(obscene: film, book)* porno *inv*; *(: joke)* sporco(a), sconcio(a). **(c)** *(fam: sad)*: **to feel ~** sentirsi giù. **2** *n* **(a)** *(colour: see adj)* azzurro, celeste *m*; blu *m inv*; *(sky)*: **the ~** l'azzurro; **out of the ~** *(fig)* all'improvviso. **(b)**: **the ~s** *(Mus)* il blues; *(fam: feeling)*: **to have the ~s** essere a terra. **3** *cpd:* ~ **baby** *n* neonato cianotico; ~ **blood** *n* sangue *m* blu; ~ **cheese** *n* formaggio tipo gorgonzola.

blue·bell ['bluːˌbɛl] *n* giacinto dei boschi.

blue·berry ['bluːbərɪ] *n (Am)* mirtillo.

blue·bottle ['bluːˌbɒtl] *n* moscone *m*.

blue·collar ['bluːˌkɒləʳ] *adj* operaio(a).

blue·eyed ['bluːˈaɪd] *adj* dagli occhi azzurri; **~-eyed boy** *(fig)* favorito.

blue·print ['bluːˌprɪnt] *n* cianografia; *(fig):* ~ **(for)** formula (di).

bluff¹ [blʌf] *adj (person)* senza peli sulla lingua.

bluff² [blʌf] *n (cliff)* scogliera a picco.

bluff³ [blʌf] **1** *n* bluff *m inv;* **to call sb's ~** sfidare qn alla prova dei fatti. **2** *vt:* **to ~ it out** cavarsela bluffando. **3** *vi* bluffare.

blun·der ['blʌndəʳ] **1** *n* gaffe *f inv;* *(error)* abbaglio; **to make a ~** fare una gaffe; prendere un abbaglio. **2** *vi* **(a)** *(see n)* fare una gaffe; prendere un abbaglio. **(b)** *(move clumsily):* **to ~ about** andare *or* muoversi a tentoni; **to ~ into sb/sth** andare a sbattere contro qn/qc.

blunt [blʌnt] **1** *adj* **(a)** *(not sharp: edge)* non tagliente; *(: knife)* che non taglia; *(: point)* spuntato(a); **this pencil is ~** questa matita non ha più la punta; ~ **instrument** *(Dir)* corpo contundente. **(b)** *(outspoken)* brutale; *(manners)* brusco(a). **2** *vt (knife)* rendere meno tagliente; *(point)* spuntare; *(fig: nerves, feelings)* rendere insensibile.

blunt·ly ['blʌntlɪ] *adv (speak)* senza mezzi termini.

blunt·ness ['blʌntnɪs] *n (fig: outspokenness)* brutale franchezza.

blur [blɜːʳ] **1** *n (shape)* massa indistinta *or* confusa; **my mind was a ~** avevo la mente annebbiata. **2** *vt* **(a)** *(writing)* rendere (quasi) illeggibile; *(outline, sight, memory, judgment)* offuscare. **3** *vi (see vt)* diventare (quasi) illeggibile; offuscarsi; **her eyes ~red with tears** gli occhi le si annebbiarono di lacrime.

blurb [blɜːb] *n* trafiletto pubblicitario.

blurred [blɜːd] *adj (TV)* sfuocato(a); *(photo)* mosso(a).

blurt [blɜːt] *vt (also:* ~ **out)** lasciarsi scappare.

blush [blʌʃ] **1** *n* rossore *m;* **with a ~** arrossendo; **without a ~** senza neppure arrossire. **2** *vi:* **to ~ (with)** arrossire (per *o* da).

blus·ter ['blʌstəʳ] **1** *n* bravate *fpl.* **2** *vi (wind)* infuriare; *(person: boast)* fare lo spaccone; *(: rage)* dare in escandescenze.

blus·tery ['blʌstərɪ] *adj (wind)* a raffiche; *(day)* ventoso(a).

B.O. *n (abbr of body odour)* odori *mpl* sgradevoli *(del corpo).*

boa ['bəʊə] *n (snake: also:* ~ **constrictor)** (serpente *m)* boa *inv; (of feathers)* boa *m inv.*

boar [bɔːʳ] *n (male pig)* verro; *(wild ~)* cinghiale *m.*

board [bɔːd] **1** *n* **(a)** *(of wood)* asse *f,* tavola; *(for chess etc)* scacchiera; *(black~)* lavagna; **across the ~** *(fig: adv)* per tutte le categorie; *(: adj)* generale; **to go by the ~** *(fig)* andare a monte; **above ~** *(fig)* regolare. **(b)** *(provision of meals)* vitto; **half ~** mezza pensione *f;* **full ~** pensione completa; ~ **and lodging** vitto e alloggio. **(c)** *(Naut, Aer):* **on ~** a bordo; **to go on ~** salire a bordo. **(d)** *(group of officials)* commissione *f;* ~ **of directors** consiglio di amministrazione; ~ **of examiners** commissione esaminatrice *or* d'esame. **(e)** *(institution)* ente *m;* **B~ of Trade** *(Brit)* Ministero del Commercio.

2 *vt* **(a)** *(ship, plane)* imbarcarsi su, salire a bordo di; *(enemy ship)* andare all'abbordaggio di;

(bus, train) salire su *or* in. **(b)** *(also:* ~ **up:** *window)* chiudere con delle tavole.

3 *vi:* **to ~ with sb** essere a pensione da qn.

4 *cpd:* ~ **game** *n* gioco da tavolo; ~ **room** *n* sala del consiglio; ~ **meeting** *n* riunione *f* di consiglio.

board·er ['bɔːdəʳ] *n* pensionante *m/f; (Scol)* collegiale *m/f.*

board·ing card ['bɔːdɪŋˌkɑːd] *n,* **board·ing pass** ['bɔːdɪŋˌpɑːs] *n (Aer)* carta d'imbarco.

board·ing house ['bɔːdɪŋˌhaʊs] *n* pensione *f.*

board·ing school ['bɔːdɪŋˌskuːl] *n* collegio, convitto.

board·walk ['bɔːdˌwɔːk] *n (Am)* passeggiata a mare.

boast [bəʊst] **1** *n* vanteria; **it is his ~ that he's never lost a match** si fa vanto di non aver mai perso un incontro. **2** *vt* vantare. **3** *vi:* **to ~ (about** *or* **of)** vantarsi (di).

boast·ful ['bəʊstfʊl] *adj* pieno(a) di sé, che si vanta sempre.

boast·ing ['bəʊstɪŋ] *n* vanterie *fpl.*

boat [bəʊt] **1** *n (gen)* barca; *(ship)* nave *f;* **to go by ~** andare in barca *(or* in nave); **we're all in the same ~** *(fig fam)* siamo tutti nella stessa barca. **2** *cpd:* ~ **hook** *n* mezzo marinaio; ~ **race** *n* gara di canottaggio; ~ **train** *n* treno in coincidenza con il traghetto.

boat·er ['bəʊtəʳ] *n* paglietta, magiostrina.

boat·swain ['bəʊsn] *n* nostromo.

bob¹ [bɒb] **1** *n (curtsy)* riverenza, inchino. **2** *vi (also:* ~ **up and down)** andare su e giù.

♦ **bob up** *vi + adv (appear)* spuntare.

bob² [bɒb] *n* pettinatura alla paggio.

bob³ [bɒb] *n, pl inv (old: Brit fam)* scellino.

bob·bin ['bɒbɪn] *n* spoletta.

bob·ble ['bɒbl] *n (on hat)* pompon *m inv.*

bob·by ['bɒbɪ] *n (Brit fam)* poliziotto.

bob·cat ['bɒbˌkæt] *n (Am)* lince *f.*

bob·sleigh ['bɒbˌsleɪ] *n* bob *m inv.*

bod·ice ['bɒdɪs] *n (of dress)* corpino, corpetto.

bodi·ly ['bɒdɪlɪ] **1** *adj (comfort, needs)* materiale; *(pain)* fisico(a). **2** *adv (carry)* in braccio; *(lift)* di peso.

body ['bɒdɪ] *n* **(a)** *(of person, animal)* corpo; *(dead* ~*)* corpo, cadavere *m;* **to keep ~ and soul together** tirare avanti; **over my dead ~!** neanche se mi ammazzi! **(b)** *(main part: of structure)* corpo; *(: of car)* carrozzeria; *(: of plane)* fusoliera; *(: of ship)* scafo, corpo; *(: of speech, document)* parte *f* principale. **(c)** *(mass, collection: of facts)* massa, quantità; *(: of laws)* raccolta; *(: of people, water)* massa; *(: of troops)* grosso; **the student ~** gli studenti; **the ~ politic** lo Stato; **in a ~** in massa. **(d)** *(organization)* associazione *f,* organizzazione *f; (: legislative* ~ corpo legislativo; **ruling ~** direttivo. **(e)** *(of wine, hair)* corpo.

body·guard ['bɒdɪˌgɑːd] *n (person, group)* guardia del corpo.

body·work ['bɒdɪˌwɜːk] *n (Aut)* carrozzeria.

bog [bɒg] *n* palude *f; (Brit fam: toilet)* cesso.

♦ **bog down** *vt + adv:* **to get ~ged down (in)** impantanarsi (in).

bog·gle ['bɒgl] *vi (fam):* **his eyes ~ed at the sight** gli si sono spalancati gli occhi davanti a quella scena; **the mind ~s!** si stenta a immaginarlo!

bo·gus ['bəʊgəs] *adj (jewels, claim)* falso(a), fasullo(a); *(person, attitude)* finto(a).

boil¹ [bɔɪl] *n (Med)* foruncolo.

boil² [bɔɪl] **1** *n:* **to bring to the ~** portare a ebollizione; **on the ~** che bolle; **it's off the ~** ha smesso di bollire. **2** *vt (far)* bollire; *(potatoes, meat)* (far) bollire, (far) lessare; **~ed egg** uovo alla coque;

hard ~**ed egg** uovo sodo; ~**ed ham** prosciutto cotto; ~**ed potatoes** patate *fpl* bollite *or* lesse. **3** *vi (water etc)* bollire; **the kettle is** ~**ing** l'acqua bolle; **to let a saucepan** ~ **dry** far evaporare tutta l'acqua da una pentola; **to** ~ **with rage** *(fig)* bollire di rabbia.

♦ **boil down** *vi* + *adv (fig):* **to** ~ **down to** ridursi a.

♦ **boil over** *vi* + *adv* traboccare (bollendo).

boil·er ['bɔɪlə'] **1** *n (gen)* caldaia; *(for hot water)* scaldabagno, scaldaacqua *m inv.* **2** *cpd:* ~ **suit** *n* tuta (da lavoro).

boiler·maker ['bɔɪlə',meɪkə'] *n* operaio metallurgico.

boil·ing ['bɔɪlɪŋ] *adj (also fig)* bollente; **a** ~ **hot day** un giorno torrido; **I'm** ~ **(hot)** *(fam)* sto morendo di caldo; ~ **point** punto di ebollizione.

bois·ter·ous ['bɔɪstərəs] *adj (meeting)* turbolento(a); *(person)* chiassoso(a); *(party etc)* animato(a).

bold [bəʊld] *adj* **(a)** *(brave: person, attempt)* audace; *(fig: plan, move)* ardito(a). **(b)** *(forward: child, remark)* sfacciato(a). **(c)** *(striking: line, pattern)* vistoso(a), che salta all'occhio; ~ **type** *(Typ)* neretto, grassetto.

bold·ness ['bəʊldnɪs] *n (of person, plan)* audacia; *(impudence)* sfacciataggine *f.*

Bo·livia [bə'lɪvɪə] *n* Bolivia.

bol·lard ['bɒləd] *n* colonnina.

Bol·she·vik ['bɒlʃəvɪk] *adj, n* bolscevico(a) *(m/f).*

Bol·she·vism ['bɒlʃəvɪzəm] *n* bolscevismo.

bol·ster ['bəʊlstə'] **1** *n* capezzale *m.* **2** *vt (also:* ~ **up**) sostenere; **to** ~ **sb's courage** incoraggiare qn.

bolt [bəʊlt] **1** *n* **(a)** *(on door)* chiavistello, catenaccio; *(of lock)* catenaccio; *(Tech)* bullone *m; (of crossbow)* dardo; *(of cloth)* pezza; **he's shot his bolt** *(fig)* ha giocato la sua ultima carta. **(b)** *(dash):* **to make a** ~ **for the door** fare un balzo *or* schizzare verso la porta; **to make a** ~ **for it** darsela a gambe. **(c)** *(lightning)* fulmine *m;* **a** ~ **from the blue** *(fig)* un fulmine a ciel sereno. **2** *adv:* ~ **upright** diritto(a) come un fuso. **3** *vt* **(a)** *(door etc)* chiudere con il catenaccio *or* il chiavistello; *(Tech: also:* ~ **together)** imbullonare. **(b)** *(food: also:* ~ **down)** ingollare. **4** *vi (run away: person)* darsela a gambe; *(: horse)* imbizzarrirsi; *(rush)* svignarsela.

bomb [bɒm] **1** *n* bomba; **it went like a** ~ *(fam: party)* è andato a meraviglia; **it goes like a** ~ *(fam: car)* va come un razzo. **2** *vt (target)* bombardare. **3** *cpd:* ~ **disposal expert** *n* artificiere *m;* ~ **site** *n* luogo bombardato.

bom·bard [bɒm'bɑːd] *vt (Mil):* **to** ~ **(with)** bombardare (con); **I was** ~**ed with questions** sono stato bombardato di domande.

bom·bard·ment [bɒm'bɑːdmənt] *n* bombardamento.

bom·bas·tic [bɒm'bæstɪk] *adj* magniloquente.

bomb·er ['bɒmə'] *n (aircraft)* bombardiere *m; (terrorist)* dinamitardo/a.

bomb·shell ['bɒmʃel] *n (fig: of news, person)* bomba.

bona fide ['bəʊnə'faɪd] *adj (antique, excuse)* autentico(a); *(offer)* serio(a).

bo·nan·za [bə'nænzə] *n* cuccagna.

bond [bɒnd] **1** *n* **(a)** *(agreement)* impegno, accordo; **to enter into a** ~ **(to do sth)** impegnarsi (a fare qc); **his word is his** ~ ci si può fidare completamente della sua parola. **(b)** *(link)* legame *m,* vincolo; ~**s** *(chains etc)* catene *fpl.* **(c)** *(Fin)* obbligazione *f.* **(d)** *(Comm):* **in** ~ in attesa di sdoganamento. **(e)** *(adhesion)* aderenza. **2** *vt (bricks)* cementare; *(subj: glue)* far aderire, incollare.

bond·ed ['bɒndɪd] *adj:* ~ **warehouse** magazzino doganale.

bone [bəʊn] **1** *n (gen)* osso; *(of fish)* lisca, spina; **I feel it in my** ~**s** me lo sento, qualcosa me lo dice; **I have a** ~ **to pick with you** *(fam)* devo regolare un conto con te; **he made no** ~**s about saying what he thought** ci ha detto quello che pensava senza fare tante cerimonie. **2** *vt (meat)* disossare; *(fish)* diliscare, spinare. **3** *cpd (buttons etc)* d'osso; ~ **china** *n* porcellana fine; **to be** ~ **idle** *(fam)* essere un(a) fannullone(a); ~ **meal** *n* farina d'ossa.

bone-dry ['bəʊn'draɪ] *adj (fam)* asciuttissimo(a).

bon·fire ['bɒnfaɪə'] *n* falò *m inv.*

bon·net ['bɒnɪt] *n* **(a)** *(woman's, baby's)* cuffia; *(esp Scot: man's)* berretto. **(b)** *(Brit Aut)* cofano.

bon·ny ['bɒnɪ] *adj (esp Scot)* bello(a), carino(a).

bo·nus ['bəʊnəs] *n (on wages)* gratifica; *(insurance etc)* premio; *(fig)* sovrappiù *m;* **Christmas** ~ tredicesima.

bony ['bəʊnɪ] *adj* (**-ier, -iest**) *(having bones: tissue)* osseo(a); *(: fish)* pieno(a) di lische; *(: meat)* con parecchio osso; *(like bone)* simile a osso; *(thin: person)* ossuto(a), angoloso(a); *(: fingers)* ossuto(a).

boo [buː] **1** *excl* bu! **2** *n:* ~**s** fischi *mpl.* **3** *vt* fischiare; **he was** ~**ed off the stage** l'hanno cacciato di scena a suon di fischi.

boob [buːb] *n (fam: mistake)* gaffe *f inv; (: breast)* tetta.

boo·by prize ['buːbɪ,praɪz] *n* premio per il peggior contendere.

boo·by trap ['buːbɪ,træp] *n* trabocchetto; *(Mil etc)* trabocchetto (con ordigno esplosivo).

book [bʊk] **1** *n* **(a)** *(gen)* libro; *(notebook)* quaderno; *(of matches)* bustina; *(of tickets)* blocchetto; **the** ~**s** *(Comm)* i libri contabili; **to keep the** ~**s** tenere la contabilità; **to be in sb's bad** ~**s** essere nel libro nero di qn; **to bring sb to** ~ **(for sth)** costringere qn a render conto (di qc); **to throw the** ~ **at sb** incriminare qn seriamente *or* con tutte le aggravanti; **by the** ~ secondo le regole; **in my** ~ a mio avviso, a parer mio. **2** *vt* **(a)** *(reserve: ticket)* riservare, prendere; *(: seat, room)* prenotare, fissare, riservare. **(b)** *(Police: driver)* fare una contravvenzione a; *(Ftbl)* ammonire. **3** *vi (see vt a)* riservare; prenotare. **4** *cpd:* ~ **token** *n* buono *m* libri *inv.*

♦ **book in** *vi* + *adv (at hotel)* prendere una camera. **2** *vt* + *adv (person)* prenotare (una camera) per.

♦ **book up** *vt* + *adv* riservare, prenotare; **the hotel is** ~**ed up** l'albergo è al completo; **all seats are** ~**ed up** è tutto esaurito; **I'm fully** ~**ed up** *(fam)* sono occupatissimo.

book·case ['bʊk,keɪs] *n* libreria.

bookie ['bʊkɪ] *n (fam)* = **bookmaker.**

book·ing ['bʊkɪŋ] **1** *n (in hotel etc)* prenotazione *f.* **2** *cpd:* ~ **clerk** *n* impiegato della biglietteria; ~ **office** *n (Rail)* biglietteria, ufficio *m* prenotazioni *inv; (Theatre)* botteghino.

book·keeper ['bʊk,kiːpə'] *n* contabile *m/f.*

book·keeping ['bʊk,kiːpɪŋ] *n* contabilità.

book·let ['bʊklɪt] *n* opuscolo, libretto.

book·maker ['bʊk,meɪkə'] *n* bookmaker *m inv,* allibratore *m.*

book·mark ['bʊk,mɑːk] *n* segnalibro.

book·shop ['bʊk,ʃɒp] *n* libreria.

book·stall ['bʊk,stɔːl] *n (in station etc)* edicola, chiosco (dei giornali); *(in market, for secondhand books)* bancarella.

book·worm ['bʊk,wɜːm] *n (fig)* topo di biblioteca.

boom¹ [buːm] *n (Naut)* boma; *(of crane)* braccio;

(across harbour) sbarramento; *(of microphone)* giraffa.

boom² [buːm] **1** *n (of guns, thunder)* rombo, rimbombo; *(deeper)* boato; **sonic** ~ **bang** *m inv* sonico. **2** *vi (voice, radio, sea: also:* ~ **out)** rimbombare; *(gun)* tuonare. **3** *vt (also:* ~ **out)** urlare con voce tonante.

boom³ [buːm] **1** *n (in prices, shares)* forte incremento; *(of product)* boom *m inv*, improvvisa popolarità; *(of sales)* esplosione *f*; *(period of growth)* boom (economico). **2** *vi (trade)* andare a gonfie vele; *(sales)* aumentare vertiginosamente; *(industry, town)* avere una *or* essere in forte espansione, svilupparsi enormemente. **3** *cpd:* ~ **town** *n* città *f inv* in rapidissima espansione.

boom·er·ang ['buːməræŋ] **1** *n* boomerang *m inv*. **2** *vi (fig)* avere effetto contrario; **to** ~ **on sb** ritorcersi contro qn.

boon [buːn] *n (blessing)* salvezza, benedizione *f*.

boor [buəʳ] *n* bifolco, zotico.

boor·ish ['buərɪʃ] *adj (manners)* da zoticone, da bifolco.

boost [buːst] **1** *n* **(a)** *(encouragement)* spinta, sprone *m*; **to give a** ~ **to** *(morale)* tirar su; **it gave a** ~ **to his confidence** è stata per lui un'iniezione di fiducia. **(b)** *(upward thrust: to person)* spinta (in su); *(: to rocket)* spinta propulsiva. **2** *vt (increase: sales, production)* incentivare; *(fig: hopes)* rinforzare; *(promote: product)* promuovere (sul mercato); *(Elec: voltage)* elevare; *(radio signal)* amplificare; *(Space)* lanciare.

boost·er ['buːstəʳ] *n (TV)* amplificatore *m* di segnale; *(Elec)* amplificatore; *(also:* ~ **rocket)** razzo vettore; *(Med)* richiamo.

boot [buːt] **1** *n* **(a)** *(gen)* stivale *m*; *(ankle* ~*)* stivaletto; *(of soldier, skier, workman)* scarpone *m*; *(football* ~*)* scarpetta; **to give sb the** ~ *(fam)* mettere qn alla porta. **(b)** *(Brit Aut)* portabagagli *m inv*, bagagliaio. **2** *vt (fam: kick)* dare un calcio a; **to** ~ **sb out** buttar fuori *or* cacciar via qn (a pedate).

bootee [buːˈtiː] *n (baby's)* scarpetta; *(woman's)* stivaletto (da donna).

booth [buːð] *n (at fair)* bancarella; *(Telec, voting* ~*)* cabina.

boot·lace ['buːt,leɪs] *n* laccio, stringa.

boot·leg ['buːt,leg] *adj* di contrabbando; ~ **record** registrazione *f* pirata *inv*.

boot·leg·ger ['buːt,legəʳ] *n* spacciatore *m* di alcool.

boot-polish ['buːt,pɒlɪʃ] *n* lucido (da scarpe).

boo·ty ['buːtɪ] *n* bottino, refurtiva.

booze [buːz] *(fam)* **1** *n* alcool *m*; **bring your own** ~ portatevi da bere. **2** *vi* sbevazzare, alzare il gomito.

booz·er ['buːzəʳ] *n (fam: person)* beone *m*; *(Brit fam: pub)* osteria.

bor·der ['bɔːdəʳ] **1** *n* **(a)** *(edge: as decoration)* bordo, orlatura; *(: as boundary)* margine *m*, limite *m*. **(b)** *(frontier)* confine *m*. **(c)** *(in garden)* aiuola (laterale). **2** *vt (line, adjoin)* fiancheggiare, costeggiare.

♦ **border (up)on** *vi + prep* confinare con; *(fig: come close to being)* sfiorare, rasentare.

border·line ['bɔːdəlaɪn] **1** *n* linea di demarcazione. **2** *cpd:* ~ **case** *n* caso incerto; **he was a** ~ **failure** è stato bocciato per poco.

bore¹ [bɔːʳ] **1** *n (also:* ~ **hole)** foro di sonda; *(diameter)* diametro interno; *(: of gun)* calibro; **a 12-**~ **shotgun** un fucile calibro 12. **2** *vt (hole)* praticare; *(tunnel)* scavare. **3** *vi:* **to** ~ **for** perforare *or* trivellare alla ricerca di.

bore² [bɔːʳ] **1** *n (person)* noioso/a, noia; *(event)* noia,

barba; **the party/office** ~ l'attaccabottoni *m/f inv (di una festa/un ufficio).* **2** *vt* annoiare; **he's** ~**d to tears** *or* ~**d to death** *or* ~**d stiff** è annoiato a morte, si annoia da morire.

bore³ [bɔːʳ] *pt of* **bear**².

bore·dom ['bɔːdəm] *n* noia.

bor·ing ['bɔːrɪŋ] *adj (tedious)* noioso(a).

born [bɔːn] *adj* nato(a); **to be** ~ *(also fig)* nascere; **I was** ~ **in 1955** sono nato nel 1955; **the revolution was** ~ **of the workers' discontent** la rivoluzione scaturì dallo scontento degli operai; **to be** ~ **again** rinascere; **I wasn't** ~ **yesterday!** *(fam)* non sono nato ieri!; **a** ~ **actor/musician** un attore/musicista nato; **a** ~ **liar** un bugiardo matricolato; **a** ~ **fool** un cretino nato.

borne [bɔːn] *pp of* **bear**².

bor·ough ['bʌrə] *n* comune *m*, circoscrizione *f* amministrativa; *(in London)* distretto.

bor·row ['bɒrəu] *vt:* **to** ~ **(from)** prendere in *or* a prestito (da), farsi prestare (da); *(idea, word)* prendere (da); **may I** ~ **your car?** può prestarmi la macchina?

bor·row·er ['bɒrəuəʳ] *n (gen)* chi prende in prestito; *(in library)* lettore/trice.

bor·row·ing ['bɒrəuɪŋ] *n* prestito.

bor·stal ['bɔːstl] *n* riformatorio.

bos·om ['buzəm] **1** *n (of woman)* petto, seno; **in the** ~ **of the family** in seno alla famiglia. **2** *cpd:* ~ **friend** *n* amico/a del cuore.

boss [bɒs] *(fam)* **1** *n (employer, owner)* capo, padrone *m*, principale *m*; *(manager, of organization)* capo; *(of criminal organization)* boss *m inv*. **2** *vt (also:* ~ **about** *or* **around)** comandare a bacchetta; **stop** ~**ing everyone about!** smettila di dare ordini a tutti!

bossy ['bɒsɪ] *adj (person)* autoritario(a); **don't you get** ~ **with me!** non cominciare a darmi ordini!

bo·tan·ic(al) [bəˈtænɪk(əl)] *adj* botanico(a); ~ **gardens** orto botanico.

bota·nist ['bɒtənɪst] *n* botanico/a.

bota·ny ['bɒtənɪ] *n* botanica.

botch [bɒtʃ] **1** *n (of job)* pasticcio, macello. **2** *vt (also:* ~ **up:** *job)* raffazzonare; *(essay, chances)* fare un pasticcio *or* macello di, rovinare.

both [bəuθ] **1** *adj* tutti(e) e due, entrambi(e), ambedue *inv*; ~ **books/boys** tutti e due *or* entrambi *or* ambedue i libri/ragazzi.

2 *pron* tutti(e) e due, entrambi(e), ambedue *inv*; **they were** ~ **there,** ~ **of them were there** c'erano tutti e due; ~ **are to blame** la colpa è di tutti e due; ~ **of us agree** siamo d'accordo tutti e due; **come in** ~ **of you** entrate tutti e due; **she has 2 daughters;** ~ **are blonde** ha 2 figlie, bionde entrambe.

3 *adv:* **John and I** ~ **went** ci siamo andati sia John che io; ~ **this and that** non solo questo ma anche quello; ~ **you and I saw it** l'abbiamo visto sia tu che io; **she was** ~ **laughing and crying** piangeva e rideva a un tempo *or* allo stesso tempo; **he** ~ **plays and sings** oltre a suonare canta.

both·er ['bɒðəʳ] **1** *n (nuisance)* seccatura, noia; *(trouble)* fastidio, disturbo; **that's no** ~, **I'll see to it** non c'è problema, ci penso io; **the children were no** ~ **at all** i bambini non hanno dato nessun fastidio; **it wasn't any** ~ *(don't mention it)* si figuri!, s'immagini!; **he had a spot of** ~ **with the police** ha avuto delle noie con la polizia.

2 *vt (worry)* preoccupare; *(annoy)* seccare, infastidire, dar fastidio a; *(take trouble)* **to** ~ **to do sth** darsi la pena di fare qc; **I'm sorry to** ~ **you with my problems** non vorrei importunarti con i miei problemi; **I'm sorry to** ~ **you** mi dispiace disturbarti; **does the noise ~ you?** ti dà fastidio il rumore?; **don't ~ me!** non mi seccare!, lasciami in pace!; **I can't be ~ed going out** or **to go out** proprio non mi va di uscire; **his leg ~s him** gli fa un po' male la gamba; **he didn't even ~ to write** non si è nemmeno sprecato a scrivere due righe. **3** *vi*: **to ~ (about)** preoccuparsi (di or per); **please don't ~** non si scomodi. **4** *excl* uffa!, accidenti!

bot·tle ['bɒtl] **1** *n* bottiglia; *(of perfume, shampoo etc)* flacone *m*; *(baby's)* biberon *m inv*, poppatoio; **~ of wine/milk** bottiglia di vino/latte; **wine/milk ~** bottiglia da vino/del latte. **2** *vt (wine)* imbottigliare; *(fruit)* conservare (in vasetti). **3** *cpd*: **~ party** *n* festa a cui gli invitati portano da bere.
♦ **bottle up** *vt + adv (emotion)* soffocare, reprimere.

bottle-fed ['bɒtl,fɛd] *adj* allattato(a) artificialmente.

bottle·neck ['bɒtl,nɛk] *n* strozzatura.

bottle-opener ['bɒtl,əupnəʳ] *n* apribottiglie *m inv*.

bot·tom ['bɒtəm] **1** *n (gen)* fondo; *(of mountain, tree, hill)* piedi *mpl*; *(of shoe)* suola; *(of chair)* sedile *m*; *(of ship)* scafo; *(of person)* sedere *m*; **at the ~ of** *(hill, ladder)* ai piedi di; *(road, list)* in fondo a; **at the ~ of the page** in fondo alla pagina, a piè di pagina; **to be ~ of the class** essere l'ultimo della classe; **on the ~ (of)** *(shoe, case etc)* sotto; *(sea, lake etc)* sul fondo (di); **the boat floated ~ up** la barca galleggiava capovolta; **I fell flat on my ~** sono crollato a sedere; **at ~** in fondo; **from the ~ of my heart** con tutto il cuore, dal profondo del cuore; **to get to the ~ of sth** *(fig)* andare al fondo di or in fondo a qc; **he's at the ~ of it** *(fig)* qui ci dev'essere il suo zampino; **~s up!** *(fam)* cin-cin! **2** *cpd (lowest: shelf, step)* più basso(a), ultimo(a); *(part)* inferiore; **~ drawer** *n (fig)* dote *f*; **~ gear** *n (Aut)* prima; **~ half** *n (of box)* parte *f* inferiore; *(of list, class)* seconda metà.

bot·tom·less ['bɒtəmlis] *adj (pit)* senza fondo; *(supply)* interminabile, smisurato(a).

bot·tom·most ['bɒtəm,məust] *adj* ultimo(a) (in basso), più basso(a).

bough [bau] *n* ramo.

bought [bɔːt] *pt, pp of* **buy.**

boul·der ['bəuldəʳ] *n* masso, macigno.

bounce [bauns] **1** *n (of ball)* rimbalzo; *(springiness: of hair, mattress)* elasticità; **he's got plenty of ~** *(fig)* è molto esuberante. **2** *vt (ball)* far rimbalzare. **3** *vi (ball)* rimbalzare; *(fam: cheque)* essere scoperto(a); *(child)* saltare, balzare; **to ~ in** entrare di slancio or con foga.
♦ **bounce back** *vi + adv (person)* riprendersi.

bounc·er ['baunsəʳ] *n (fam)* buttafuori *m inv*.

bounc·ing ['baunsɪŋ] *adj*: **~ baby** bambino(a) pieno(a) di salute.

bouncy ['baunsɪ] *adj (ball)* che rimbalza bene; *(hair)* vaporoso(a); *(mattress)* (ben) molleggiato(a); *(person)* dinamico(a), esuberante.

bound¹ [baund] **1** *n*: **~s** limiti *mpl*; **out of ~s** vietato or proibito l'accesso; **within the ~s of modesty** nei limiti della decenza; **his ambition knows no ~s** la sua ambizione è senza limiti or non conosce limiti. **2** *vt*: **~ed by** limitato(a) da.

bound² [baund] **1** *n (jump)* salto, balzo. **2** *vi (person, animal)* saltare, balzare; **he ~ed out of bed** è saltato fuori or è balzato giù dal letto; **his heart ~ed with joy** il cuore gli balzò in petto dalla gioia.

bound³ [baund] **1** *pt, pp of* **bind.** **2** *adj* **(a)** *(prisoner)* legato(a); **~ hand and foot** legato mani e piedi. **(b)** *(book)* rilegato(a). **(c)**: **he's ~ to say yes** vedrai che dirà di sì; **it was ~ to happen** doveva

succedere, era da prevedersi. **(d)** *(obliged)*: **to be ~ to do sth** essere obbligato(a) a or tenuto(a) a fare qc; **I'm ~ to say that...** devo dire che.... .

bound⁴ [baund] *adj (destined)*: **~ for** *(person, train, ship etc)* diretto(a) a, in viaggio per; *(parcel)* indirizzato(a) a, diretto(a) a; **where are you ~ (for)?** dove sei diretto?; **California ~** diretto in California; **west~ traffic** traffico diretto verso ovest.

bounda·ry ['baundərɪ] *n* confine *m*.

bound·less ['baundlɪs] *adj (also fig)* illimitato(a), sconfinato(a).

boun·ti·ful ['bauntɪful] *adj (person)* munifico(a); *(God)* misericordioso(a); *(supply)* abbondante.

boun·ty ['bauntɪ] **1** *n (generosity)* liberalità, munificenza; *(reward)* taglia. **2** *cpd*: **~ hunter** *n* cacciatore *m* di taglie.

bou·quet ['bukeɪ] *n* bouquet *m inv*.

bour·bon ['buəbən] *n (Am: also: ~ whiskey)* bourbon *m inv*.

bour·geois ['buəʒwɑː] *adj, n* borghese *(m/f)*.

bour·geoi·sie [,buəʒwɑːˈziː] *n* borghesia.

bout [baut] *n* **(a)** *(of illness)* attacco, accesso; **a severe ~ of flu** una brutta influenza; **he's had several ~s of illness** è stato ammalato diverse volte; **a ~ of hard work** una buona tirata di lavoro; **he went on a drinking ~** gli è preso la voglia di bere. **(b)** *(boxing match)* incontro.

bou·tique [buːˈtiːk] *n* boutique *f inv*.

bow¹ [bəu] **1** *n* arco; *(Mus)* archetto; *(knot)* fiocco, nodo. **2** *cpd*: **~ tie** *n* (cravatta a) farfalla.

bow² [bau] **1** *n* inchino; **to take a ~** inchinarsi al pubblico or all'applauso del pubblico. **2** *vt (lower: head)* chinare; *(bend: back)* curvare, piegare; **~ed down by cares** schiacciato dalle preoccupazioni. **3** *vi*: **to ~ (to)** inchinarsi (a), fare un inchino (a); *(fig: yield)* inchinarsi (di fronte a); **to ~ to the inevitable** rassegnarsi all'inevitabile.
♦ **bow out** *vi + adv (fig)* uscire di scena.

bow³ [bau] *n (Naut: also: ~s)* prua; **on the port/starboard ~** di prua a sinistra/a destra.

bowd·ler·ize ['baudləraɪz] *vt* espurgare.

bow·els ['bauəlz] *npl* intestino, intestini *mpl*; **~s of the earth** viscere *fpl* della terra.

bowl¹ [bəul] *n* **(a)** *(for soup)* scodella, piatto fondo; *(for cereal, fruit)* coppetta; *(mixing ~)* terrina; *(for salad)* insalatiera; *(for washing up)* bacinella, catino; **~ of milk** ciotola di latte; **~ of soup** piatto di minestra. **(b)** *(hollow: of lavatory)* tazza; *(: of spoon)* incavo, cavo; *(: of pipe)* fornello. **(c)** *(Am: stadium)* stadio.

bowl² [bəul] **1** *n (ball)* boccia; **~s** *(game: Brit)* (gioco delle) bocce. **2** *vt (ball)* lanciare. **3** *vi (Cricket)* servire; *(Bowls)* tirare.
♦ **bowl over** *vt + adv* rovesciare (a terra); *(fig)* lasciare strabiliato(a).

bow-legged [,bəuˈlɛgɪd] *adj (person)* con le gambe storte.

bowl·er ['bəuləʳ] *n* **(a)** *(in cricket)* lanciatore/trice. **(b)** *(Brit: also: ~ hat)* bombetta.

bowl·ing ['bəulɪŋ] **1** *n (Brit)* gioco delle bocce; *(Am)* bowling *m*. **2** *cpd*: **~ alley** *n* bowling *m inv*; **~ green** *n* campo da bocce (di erba).

box¹ [bɒks] **1** *n* **(a)** *(gen)* scatola; *(crate; also for money)* cassetta; *(for jewels etc)* cofanetto; **the ~** *(fam: TV)* la tivù. **(b)** *(Theatre)* palco; *(Law: for witness, press etc)* banco. **2** *cpd*: **~ junction** *n (Brit Aut)* area d'incrocio; **~ number** *n (for advertisements)* casella; **~ office** *n* botteghino; **~ room** *n =* **boxroom.**
♦ **box in** *vt + adv (bath)* incassare; *(car)* incastrare; **to feel ~ed in** sentirsi imprigionato.

box² [bɒks] **1** *n*: **a ~ on the ear** uno scapaccione, un ceffone. **2** *vt*: **to ~ sb's ears** prendere qn a scapaccioni. **3** *vi (Sport)* fare il pugile; (: *fight)* combattere.

box·er ['bɒksə^r] *n (Sport)* pugile *m*, boxeur *m inv*; *(dog)* boxer *m inv*.

box·ing ['bɒksɪŋ] **1** *n* pugilato, boxe *f*. **2** *cpd*: **B~ Day** *n (Brit)* Santo Stefano; **~ gloves** *npl* guantoni *mpl* (da pugile *or* da boxe); **~ match** *n* incontro di pugilato; **~ ring** *n* ring *m inv*.

box·room ['bɒks,rʊm] *n (Brit)* ripostiglio, stanzino.

boy [bɔɪ] *n* ragazzo; *(small)* bambino; *(son)* figlio; **she had a ~** ha avuto un maschio; **school for ~s** scuola maschile; **when I was a ~** quand'ero piccolo; **~s will be ~s** che vuoi — sono maschi; **he's out with the ~s** è fuori con gli amici; **old ~** vecchio mio; **my dear ~** mio caro; **oh ~!** mamma mia!

boy·cott ['bɔɪkɒt] **1** *n* boicottaggio. **2** *vt* boicottare.

boy·friend ['bɔɪ,frɛnd] *n* ragazzo.

boy·hood ['bɔɪhʊd] *n* infanzia; *(as teenager)* adolescenza.

boy·ish ['bɔɪɪʃ] *adj (appearance, manner)* da ragazzo.

BR *n abbr of British Rail.*

bra [brɑː] *n* reggiseno, reggipetto.

brace [breɪs] **1** *n* **(a)** *(Constr)* rinforzo, sostegno; *(dental)* apparecchio (ortodontico); *(Typ)* graffa; **~ and bit** trapano a manubrio. **(b)** *(pl inv: pair: of animals etc)* coppia, paio. **2** *vt (strengthen: building)* rinforzare, puntellare; **to ~ o.s.** *(also fig)* tenersi forte.

brace·let ['breɪslɪt] *n* braccialetto.

braces ['breɪsɪz] *npl (Brit)* bretelle *fpl*.

brac·ing ['breɪsɪŋ] *adj (air)* tonificante, vivificante.

brack·en ['brækən] *n (plant)* felce *f*; *(mass of ~)* felci *pl*.

brack·et ['brækɪt] **1** *n* **(a)** *(support)* sostegno; (: *of metal, plastic)* mensola. **(b)** *(Typ etc: usu pl)* parentesi *f inv*; **round/square ~s** parentesi tonde/quadre; **in ~s** tra parentesi. **(c)** *(group)* categoria; **income ~** fascia di reddito. **2** *vt (Typ)* mettere tra parentesi; *(fig: also: ~ **together**)* mettere insieme.

brack·ish ['brækɪʃ] *adj (water)* salmastro(a).

brag [bræg] *vt, vi*: **to ~ (about/that)** vantarsi (di).

braid [breɪd] **1** *n (on dress)* spighetta; *(Mil, on dressing gown)* cordoncino; *(of hair)* treccia. **2** *vt (hair)* intrecciare.

Braille [breɪl] *n* braille *m*.

brain [breɪn] **1** *n* **(a)** *(Anat)* cervello; *(Culin)*: **~s** cervella *sg*; **to blow one's ~s out** farsi saltare le cervella; **he's got cars on the ~** ha il chiodo fisso delle macchine. **(b)** *(fig fam: intelligence)*: **~s** testa; **he's got ~s** è una bella testa; **he's the ~s of the family** è il cervellone di casa. **2** *vt (fam)* spaccare la testa a.

brain·child ['breɪn,tʃaɪld] *n* creatura, creazione *f*.

brain·less ['breɪnlɪs] *adj* deficiente, stupido(a).

brain·storm ['breɪn,stɔːm] *n (fig)* attacco di pazzia; *(Am)* = **brainwave**.

brain·wash ['breɪn,wɒʃ] *vt*: **to ~ sb (into doing sth)** fare il lavaggio del cervello a qn (per convincerlo a fare qc).

brain·wash·ing ['breɪn,wɒʃɪŋ] *n* lavaggio del cervello.

brain·wave ['breɪn,weɪv] *n (fam)* idea brillante.

brainy ['breɪnɪ] *adj (-ier, -iest) (fam)* geniale.

braise [breɪz] *vt (Culin)* brasare.

brake [breɪk] **1** *n* freno; **to put on** *or* **apply the ~s** *(Aut)* azionare i freni; **to put the ~s on sth** *(fig)* mettere un freno a qc. **2** *vi* frenare. **3** *cpd*: **~ light**

n (fanalino dello) stop *m inv*; **~ pedal** *n* pedale *m* del freno.

brak·ing ['breɪkɪŋ] **1** *n* frenatura. **2** *cpd (distance, power)* di frenatura.

bram·ble ['bræmbl] *n* rovo; *(fruit)* mora.

bran [bræn] *n* crusca.

branch [brɑːntʃ] **1** *n (also fig)* ramo; *(in road, railway, pipe)* diramazione *f*; *(Comm: of company, bank)* filiale *f*, succursale *f*. **2** *vi (road etc)* diramarsi, ramificarsi; *(also: ~ **off**)* biforcarsi. **3** *cpd*: **~ line** *n (Rail)* linea secondaria; **~ office** *n* filiale *f*, succursale *f*.

♦ **branch out** *vi + adv*: **to ~ out into** *(business)* intraprendere una nuova attività nel ramo di; *(person)* mettersi nel ramo di; **he's ~ed out on his own** si è messo in proprio.

brand [brænd] **1** *n* **(a)** *(Comm)* marca. **(b)** *(on cattle, prisoner)* marchio. **2** *vt (cattle, fig: person)* marchiare; **his name is ~ed on my memory** il suo nome è impresso indelebilmente nella mia memoria. **3** *cpd*: **~ name** *n* marca.

bran·dish ['brændɪʃ] *vt* brandire.

brand-new ['brænd'njuː] *adj* nuovo(a) di zecca, nuovo(a) fiammante.

bran·dy ['brændɪ] *n* brandy *m inv*.

brash [bræʃ] *adj (impudent)* insolente, sfrontato(a).

brass [brɑːs] **1** *n* ottone *m*; **the ~** *(Mus)* gli ottoni. **2** *adj (ornament etc)* d'ottone; **~ band** fanfara; **to get down to ~ tacks** *(fam)* venire al sodo.

bras·sière ['bræsiə^r] *n* reggiseno, reggipetto.

brat [bræt] *n (fam pej)* moccioso/a.

bra·va·do [brə'vɑːdəʊ] *n* spavalderia.

brave [breɪv] **1** *adj* coraggioso(a); **be ~** coraggio!, sii forte! **2** *n (Indian)* giovane guerriero pellerossa. **3** *vt (weather, death etc)* sfidare; **to ~ it out** affrontare la situazione.

brav·ery ['breɪvərɪ] *n* coraggio.

bra·vo ['brɑː'vəʊ] *excl* bravo!, bene!

brawl [brɔːl] **1** *n* rissa. **2** *vi* azzuffarsi.

brawn [brɔːn] *n* muscoli *mpl*; *(Culin)* coppa.

brawny ['brɔːnɪ] *adj* muscoloso(a).

bray [breɪ] **1** *n* raglio. **2** *vi* ragliare.

bra·zen ['breɪzn] **1** *adj (~-faced)* sfacciato(a). **2** *vt*: **to ~ it out** continuare con la massima faccia tosta.

bra·zi·er ['breɪzɪə^r] *n* braciere *m*.

Bra·zil [brə'zɪl] *n* Brasile *m*.

Bra·zil·ian [brə'zɪlɪən] *adj, n* brasiliano(a) *(m/f)*.

breach [briːtʃ] **1** *n* **(a)** *(violation: of law)* violazione *f*; *(of rules)* infrazione *f*; **~ of contract** inadempienza di contratto; **~ of the peace** reato contro l'ordine pubblico. **(b)** *(gap: in wall etc)* apertura, varco; *(Mil)* breccia; *(estrangement)* rottura. **2** *vt (defences)* far breccia in.

bread [brɛd] *n* pane *m*; *(fam: money)* grana; **~ and butter** pane e burro; **it's his ~ and butter** *(fig)* è il suo pane; **to earn one's daily ~** guadagnarsi il pane; **to know which side one's ~ is buttered on** saper fare i propri interessi.

bread·bin ['brɛd,bɪn] *n* cassetta *f* portapane *inv*.

bread·board ['brɛd,bɔːd] *n* tagliere *m (per il pane)*.

bread·crumb ['brɛd,krʌm] *n* briciola; **~s** *(Culin)* pangrattato; **fried in ~s** panato e fritto.

bread·knife ['brɛd,naɪf] *n, pl* **-knives** ['brɛd,naɪvz] coltello per il pane *or* da pane.

bread·line ['brɛd,laɪn] *n*: **to be on the ~** farcela a malapena a sbarcare il lunario.

breadth [brɛtθ] *n (also fig)* larghezza; **to be 2 metres in ~** misurare 2 metri di larghezza, essere largo 2 metri.

bread·winner ['brɛd,wɪnə^r] *n* chi mantiene la famiglia, chi porta i soldi a casa *(fam)*.

break [breɪk] (*vb: pt* **broke,** *pp* **broken**) **1** *n* **(a)** *(gen)* rottura; *(fracture)* fenditura; (: *in bone)* frattura; *(in wall, fence)* apertura; *(in line, row, electric circuit)* interruzione *f;* **with a ~ in her voice** con voce rotta *or* incrinata dall'emozione; **a ~ in the clouds** una schiarita; **a ~ in the weather** un cambiamento di tempo; **at ~ of day** allo spuntare del giorno, sul far del giorno; **to make a ~ for it** *(fam)* darsela a gambe. **(b)** *(in conversation)* pausa, interruzione *f; (rest, in journey)* sosta; *(tea ~)* intervallo; *(Scol)* ricreazione *f,* intervallo; *(holiday)* vacanza; **the Christmas ~** le vacanze di Natale; **to have** *or* **take a ~** *(few minutes)* fare una pausa; *(rest, holiday)* prendere un po' di riposo; **without a ~** senza una pausa. **(c)** *(fam: chance)* **a lucky ~** un colpo di fortuna; **give me a ~!** dammi questa possibilità!; *(leave me alone)* lasciami respirare!

2 *vt* **(a)** *(gen)* rompere; *(bone)* rompere, fratturare; *(skin)* lacerare; *(surpass: record)* battere; **to ~ one's back** rompersi la schiena; **to ~ surface** *(submarine, diver)* affiorare (alla superficie); **to ~ sb's heart** *(fig)* spezzare il cuore a *or* di qn; **to ~ the ice** *(fig)* rompere il ghiaccio. **(b)** *(law, rule)* violare; *(promise)* mancare a; *(vow)* rompere; *(appointment)* disdire, mandare all'aria; **to ~ the law** infrangere la legge. **(c)** *(resistance, spirits)* fiaccare, annientare; *(health)* rovinare; *(strike)* domare, stroncare; **I can't ~ the habit** non riesco a perdere il vizio; **to ~ sb** *(financially)* mandare in rovina qn. **(d)** *(silence, spell)* rompere; *(journey)* spezzare, interrompere; *(electrical circuit)* interrompere. **(e)** *(soften: force)* smorzare; (: *fall, blow)* attutire. **(f)** *(news):* **to ~ (to)** annunciare (a); **try to ~ it to her gently** cerca di dirglielo con tatto.

3 *vi* **(a)** *(gen)* rompersi; *(wave)* frangersi, infrangersi; *(fig: heart)* spezzarsi; **to ~ into tiny pieces** andare in frantumi *or* in mille pezzi; **the stick broke in two** il bastone si è spezzato in due; **to ~ even** *(in business)* coprire le spese; *(in gambling)* finire pari; **let's ~ for lunch** facciamo una sosta per pranzo; **to ~ with sb** *(fig)* rompere con qn. **(b)** *(dawn, day)* spuntare; *(storm)* scoppiare; *(news)* saltare fuori. **(c)** *(health, spirits)* cedere; *(weather)* cambiare; *(heatwave etc)* finire; *(voice: boy's)* cambiare; (: *in emotion)* rompersi.

◆ **break away** *vi + adv:* **to ~ away (from)** staccarsi (da); *(Ftbl etc)* scattare via (da).

◆ **break down 1** *vt + adv* **(a)** *(door etc)* buttare giù, abbattere; *(resistance)* stroncare. **(b)** *(analyse: figures)* analizzare; (: *substance)* scomporre. **2** *vi + adv (machine)* rompersi, guastarsi; *(Aut)* restare in panne, avere un guasto, rompersi; *(person: under pressure)* crollare; (: *from emotion)* scoppiare in lacrime; *(health)* cedere; *(talks etc)* arenarsi.

◆ **break in 1** *vt + adv* **(a)** *(door)* sfondare. **(b)** *(train: horse)* domare; **it'll take you a while to ~ yourself in** ti ci vorrà un po' per prenderci la mano *or* per ambientarti. **2** *vi* **(a)** *(burglar)* fare irruzione. **(b)** *(interrupt):* **to ~ in (on sb/sth)** interrompere (qn/qc).

◆ **break into** *vi + prep* **(a)** *(house)* fare irruzione in; *(safe)* scassinare, forzare; *(savings)* intaccare. **(b)** *(begin suddenly):* **to ~ into song/a trot** *etc* mettersi a cantare/trottare *etc.*

◆ **break off 1** *vt + adv (piece etc)* staccare, spezzare; *(talks, engagement)* rompere. **2** *vi + adv* **(a)** *(twig etc)* staccarsi, spezzarsi. **(b)** *(stop):* **to ~ off (from doing sth)** smettere (di fare qc); **to ~ off from work** interrompere il lavoro.

◆ **break out** *vi + adv* **(a)** *(prisoners):* **to ~ out (of)**

evadere (da). **(b)** *(war, fire, argument)* scoppiare; *(violence)* esplodere; **to ~ out in spots** coprirsi di macchie.

◆ **break through 1** *vi + adv (Mil)* aprirsi un varco, sfondare; **the sun broke through** il sole ha fatto capolino tra le nuvole. **2** *vi + prep (defences, barrier)* sfondare, penetrare in; *(crowd)* aprirsi un varco in *or* tra, aprirsi un passaggio in *or* tra.

◆ **break up 1** *vt + adv (rocks etc)* spaccare, fare a pezzi; *(marriage)* finire; *(crowd)* disperdere; *(fight)* far cessare. **2** *vi + adv (ship)* andare a *or* in pezzi, sfondarsi; *(ice)* spaccarsi, disintegrarsi; *(partnership, meeting)* sciogliersi; *(marriage)* andare in pezzi; *(crowd, clouds)* disperdersi; **the schools ~ up tomorrow** le scuole chiudono domani.

break·able ['breɪkəbl] **1** *adj* fragile. **2:** **~s** *npl* oggetti *mpl* fragili.

break·age ['breɪkɪdʒ] *n* danni *mpl;* **to pay for ~s** pagare i danni.

break·away ['breɪkə,weɪ] *adj (group etc)* scissionista, dissidente.

break·down ['breɪkdaʊn] **1** *n* **(a)** *(of machine)* guasto, rottura; *(in system)* interruzione *f,* sospensione *f* di servizio; (Aut) panne *f inv; (of talks, in relations)* rottura; *(in communications)* interruzione; *(Med)* collasso; (: *mental)* esaurimento nervoso. **(b)** *(of figures etc)* resoconto; *(Chem)* scomposizione *f.* **2** *cpd:* **~ van** *n* carro *m* attrezzi *inv.*

break·er ['breɪkəʳ] *n (wave)* frangente *m.*

break·fast ['brɛkfəst] **1** *n* (prima) colazione *f.* **2** *vi:* **to ~ (on)** fare colazione (con). **3** *cpd:* **~ cereal** *n* fiocchi *mpl* d'avena *(or* di mais *etc);* **~ time** *n* ora di colazione.

break-in ['breɪk,ɪn] *n* irruzione *f.*

break·ing ['breɪkɪŋ] **1** *n:* **~ and entering** *(Law)* violazione *f* di domicilio con scasso. **2** *adj:* **~ point** limite *m* di rottura; *(fig: of person)* limite (della sopportazione).

break·neck ['breɪk,nɛk] *adj:* **at ~ speed** a rotta di collo.

break-out ['breɪk,aʊt] *n* evasione *f.*

break·through ['breɪk,θruː] *n (in research etc)* scoperta decisiva; *(Mil)* breccia.

break-up ['breɪk,ʌp] *n (of partnership, marriage)* rottura.

break·water ['breɪk,wɔːtəʳ] *n* frangiflutti *m inv.*

breast [brɛst] **1** *n (Anat, Culin)* petto; *(of woman)* seno, mammella; **to make a clean ~ of it** *(fig)* vuotare il sacco. **2** *vt (finishing tape)* toccare.

breast·bone ['brɛst,bəʊn] *n* sterno.

breast-fed ['brɛst,fɛd] *adj* allattato(a) naturalmente.

breast-feed ['brɛst,fiːd] *pt, pp* **breast-fed** *vt* allattare (al seno).

breast·stroke ['brɛst,strəʊk] *n* (nuoto a) rana; **to swim** *or* **do the ~** nuotare a rana.

breath [brɛθ] *n* fiato, alito; *(act of breathing)* respiro; **he drew a deep ~** fece un respiro profondo; **bad ~** alito cattivo; **in the same ~** nello stesso istante; **out of ~** senza fiato; **under one's ~** sotto voce; **to go out for a ~ of air** andare a prendere una boccata d'aria; **to hold one's ~** trattenere il fiato *or* il respiro; **it took my ~ away** mi ha lasciato senza fiato, mi ha mozzato il respiro.

Breatha·lyz·er ['brɛθə,laɪzəʳ] *n*® *(Brit)* alcotest *m inv.*

breathe [briːð] **1** *vt (air)* respirare; *(sigh)* tirare; **he ~d garlic all over me** mi ha soffiato addosso il suo alito puzzolente d'aglio; **I won't ~ a word about it** non fiaterò; **to ~ new life into sb/sth** *(fig)* ridar vita a qn/qc. **2** *vi* respirare; **to ~ heavily**

ansimare, avere il fiato grosso; **now we can ~ again** (fig) adesso si respira.
♦ **breathe in 1** vi + adv inspirare. **2** vt + adv respirare.
♦ **breathe out** vt + adv, vi + adv espirare.
breath·er ['briːðəʳ] n (fam) attimo di respiro.
breath·ing ['briːðɪŋ] n respiro, respirazione f; **~ space** (fig) attimo di respiro.
breath·less ['brɛθlɪs] adj (exhausted) senza fiato; (with excitement) con il fiato sospeso; (silence) religioso(a); (anticipation, anxiety) vivissimo(a); **his asthma makes him ~** l'asma gli fa mancare il fiato.
breath-taking ['brɛθ,teɪkɪŋ] adj (sight) mozzafiato inv.
bred [brɛd] pt, pp of **breed.**
-bred [brɛd] suf: **to be well/ill~** essere ben educato(a)/maleducato(a).
breech [briːtʃ] n (of gun) culatta.
breeches ['brɪtʃɪz] npl (knee ~) calzoni mpl alla zuava; (riding ~) pantaloni mpl da cavallo.
breed [briːd] (vb: pt, pp **bred**) **1** n razza, varietà f inv; (fig) tipo, specie f inv. **2** vt allevare; (fig: hate, suspicion) generare, provocare. **3** vi (animals) riprodursi.
breed·er ['briːdəʳ] n (a) (person) allevatore/trice. (b) (Phys: also: ~ **reactor**) reattore m autofertilizzante.
breed·ing ['briːdɪŋ] n (of stock) allevamento m; (reproduction) riproduzione f; (of person: also: **good** ~) (buona) educazione f.
breeze [briːz] **1** n brezza, venticello. **2** vi: **to ~ in/out** etc entrare/andarsene allegramente come se niente fosse.
breezy ['briːzɪ] adj (day, weather) ventoso(a); (spot) ventilato(a), ventoso(a); (person's manner) brioso(a), gioviale; **she's so bright and ~** è così piena di brio.
breth·ren ['brɛðrɪn] npl (Rel) of **brother.**
brev·ity ['brɛvɪtɪ] n brevità.
brew [bruː] **1** n (of beer) fermentazione f; (of tea, herbs) infuso m; **a strong ~** (of beer) una qualità forte; (of tea) un tè forte. **2** vt (beer) mettere a fermentare; (tea) (mettere a) fare; (herbs) fare un infuso di; (fig: scheme, mischief) macchinare. **3** vi (beer) fermentare; (tea) farsi; (fig: storm) prepararsi; (: plot) ordirsi; **there's trouble ~ing** c'è aria di burrasca; **something's ~ing** qualcosa bolle in pentola.
brew·ery ['bruːərɪ] n fabbrica di birra.
bri·ar ['braɪəʳ] n (thorny bush) rovo; (wild rose) rosa selvatica.
bribe [braɪb] **1** n bustarella. **2** vt corrompere; **to ~ sb to do sth** pagare qn sottobanco perché faccia qc.
brib·ery ['braɪbərɪ] n corruzione f.
bric-à-brac ['brɪkəbræk] n (no pl) bric-à-brac m.
brick [brɪk] n (single) mattone m; (material) mattoni mpl; (toy) cubo; **building ~s** (gioco delle) costruzioni fpl; **he came down on me like a ton of ~s** (fig) ancora un po' e mi mangiava; **to drop a ~** (fig fam) fare una gaffe; **to beat** or **run one's head against a ~ wall** (fig) parlare al muro.
♦ **brick in, brick up** vt + adv murare.
brick·layer ['brɪk,leɪəʳ] n muratore m.
brid·al ['braɪdl] adj (veil, gown) da sposa, nuziale; (feast, procession) nuziale.
bride [braɪd] n sposa; **the ~ and groom** gli sposi, gli sposini.
bride·groom ['braɪd,gruːm] n sposo.
brides·maid ['braɪdz,meɪd] n damigella d'onore.
bridge¹ [brɪdʒ] **1** n (gen, Dentistry) ponte m; (Naut) ponte di comando, plancia; **~ of the nose** setto

nasale. **2** vt gettare un ponte su; **to ~ a gap** (fig: in knowledge) colmare una lacuna; (: in budget) colmare un disavanzo.
bridge² [brɪdʒ] n (Cards) bridge m.
bridge·head ['brɪdʒ,hɛd] n (Mil) testa di ponte.
bridg·ing ['brɪdʒɪŋ] adj: **~ loan** anticipazione f sul mutuo.
bri·dle ['braɪdl] **1** n briglia. **2** vt mettere le briglie a. **3** vi (in anger etc) adombrarsi, adontarsi. **4** cpd: **~ path** n sentiero (per cavalli).
brief [briːf] **1** adj (visit, period, speech) breve; (glimpse, moment) veloce, breve; **for a ~ moment I thought...** per un attimo ho creduto...; **I caught a ~ glimpse of the queen** ho intravisto per un attimo la regina; **in ~...** in breve..., a farla breve... . **2** n (a) (Law) dossier m inv. (b) (Mil, gen) istruzioni fpl; **that's outwith my ~** non è di mia competenza. (c): **~s** (man's) slip m inv; (woman's) mutandine fpl. **3** vt (Mil etc) dare istruzioni a; (person): **to ~ sb (about sth)** mettere qn al corrente (di qc); (Law) affidare una causa a.
brief·case ['briːf,keɪs] n cartella.
brief·ing ['briːfɪŋ] n briefing m inv.
brief·ly ['briːflɪ] adv (speak, visit) brevemente; (glimpse) di sfuggita.
bri·er ['braɪəʳ] n = **briar.**
bri·gade [brɪ'geɪd] n compagnia; (of troops) brigata.
briga·dier [,brɪgə'dɪəʳ] n generale m di brigata.
bright [braɪt] adj (a) (day, weather) sereno(a); (room) luminoso(a); (eyes, star, gem, surface) lucente, brillante; (sunshine) splendente; (light, lamp) forte; (fire, flame) vivo(a); (colour) vivace; **~ intervals** (Met) schiarite fpl; **~ red** rosso acceso. (b) (cheerful: person) vispo(a), allegro(a); (: expression) radioso(a), animato(a); (: future) brillante, radioso(a); **~ and early** di buon'ora, di buon mattino; **to look on the ~ side** vedere il lato positivo delle cose. (c) (clever: person) intelligente, dotato(a); (: idea, move) brillante, geniale.
bright·en ['braɪtn] **1** vt (also: ~ **up**) (colour) ravvivare; (television picture) alzare la luminosità di; (house) ravviare, rallegrare; (situation) migliorare; **a child will ~ up your life** un figlio allieterà la tua vita. **2** vi (also: ~ **up**) (person) rianimarsi, rallegrarsi; (eyes, expression) illuminarsi; (weather) schiarirsi.
bright·ly ['braɪtlɪ] adv (smile) radiosamente; (behave, talk) con animazione; (shine) vivamente, intensamente.
bright·ness ['braɪtnɪs] n (of room) luminosità; (of eyes, star) lucentezza; (of sunshine) splendore m; (of flame, colour) vivacità.
bril·liance ['brɪljəns] n (of light) intensità; (of colour) vivacità; (fig: of person) intelligenza scintillante.
bril·liant ['brɪljənt] adj (sunshine) sfolgorante; (light, idea, person, success) brillante.
brim [brɪm] **1** n (of cup) orlo; (of hat) tesa, falda. **2** vi: **to ~ (over)** with traboccare di; **eyes ~ming with tears** occhi colmi di lacrime.
brim·ful ['brɪm'ful] adj: **~ (of)** pieno(a) fino all'orlo (di), traboccante (di); **~ of confidence** traboccante di sicurezza.
bring [brɪŋ] pt, pp **brought** vt (gen) portare; (dissatisfaction, storm) provocare; (consequences) avere; **to ~ relief** dare sollievo; **to ~ luck** portare fortuna; **to ~ tears to sb's eyes** fare venire le lacrime agli occhi di qn; **to ~ sth to an end** mettere fine a qc; **to ~ sth on o.s.** (fig) tirarsi qc addosso; **to ~ a good price** vendersi bene, rendere bene; **I can't ~ myself to sack him** non so risolvermi a licenziarlo.

♦ **bring about** *vt + adv* **(a)** *(change, crisis)* causare, provocare. **(b): to ~ the boat about** virare.
♦ **bring back** *vt + adv (person, object)* riportare; *(souvenir)* portare (al ritorno); *(memories)* risvegliare; **she brought a friend back for dinner** ha portato un'amico a casa per cena.
♦ **bring down** *vt (lower: prices, temperature)* far scendere; *(opponent: also Ftbl, Rugby)* atterrare; *(enemy plane)* abbattere; *(government)* rovesciare, far cadere.
♦ **bring forward** *vt + adv* **(a)** *(person)* far venire avanti; *(chair)* spostare in avanti; *(witness, proof)* produrre. **(b)** *(advance time of: meeting)* anticipare. **(c)** *(Bookkeeping)* riportare.
♦ **bring in** *vt + adv* **(a)** *(person)* fare entrare; *(object)* portare; *(Parliament: bill)* presentare; *(: legislation)* introdurre; *(Law: verdict)* emettere. **(b)** *(produce: income)* rendere.
♦ **bring off** *vt + adv* **(a)** *(plan)* far riuscire, realizzare; *(deal)* concludere; **he didn't ~ it off** *(fam)* (il colpo) non gli è riuscito. **(b)** *(people from wreck)* portare in salvo.
♦ **bring on** *vt + adv* **(a)** *(illness, quarrel)* provocare, produrre; *(crops, flowers)* far spuntare. **(b)** *(Theatre: performer)* fare entrare; *(: object)* portare in scena; *(Sport: player)* mandare in sostituzione, far scendere in campo.
♦ **bring out** *vt + adv (meaning)* mettere in luce; *(colour, weaknesses)* far risaltare; *(qualities)* valorizzare, mettere in luce; *(new product)* lanciare; *(book)* pubblicare, fare uscire.
♦ **bring round** *vt + adv* **(a)** *(persuade)*: **to ~ sb round (to the idea of sth)** persuadere qn (a fare qc). **(b)** *(steer: conversation)*: **to ~ round to** portare su, far cadere su. **(c)** *(unconscious person)* far rinvenire, rianimare.
♦ **bring up** *vt + adv (person)* far salire; *(rear: child)* allevare; *(mention: question)* sollevare; *(: fact, problem)* far presente; *(vomit)* rimettere, rigurgitare; **well brought-up** ben educato.
brink [brɪŋk] *n* orlo; **on the ~ of doing sth** sul punto di fare qc; **she was on the ~ of tears** era lì lì per piangere.
brisk [brɪsk] *adj (person, tone)* spiccio(a), sbrigativo(a); *(: abrupt)* brusco(a); *(walk)* svelto(a); *(wind)* fresco(a); *(trade etc)* vivace, attivo(a); **business is ~** gli affari vanno bene; **at a ~ pace** di buon passo.
bris·tle [brɪsl] **1** *n (of beard, animal)* pelo; *(of boar, brush)* setola; **pure ~ brush** spazzola di pura setola; **brush with nylon ~s** spazzola di nylon. **2** *vi (also: ~ up)* rizzarsi; *(fig)*: **to ~ with** *(pins, difficulties)* essere irto(a) di; *(policemen)* brulicare di; **he ~d with anger** fremeva di rabbia.
bris·tly [brɪslɪ] *adj (chin)* ispido(a); *(beard, hair)* irsuto(a), setoloso(a).
Brit·ain [brɪtən] *n (also:* **Great ~**) Gran Bretagna.
Brit·ish [brɪtɪʃ] **1** *adj (economy, team)* inglese, britannico(a); *(ambassador)* inglese, della Gran Bretagna; **the ~ Commonwealth** il Commonwealth Britannico; **the ~ Isles** le Isole Britanniche. **2** *npl:* **the ~** gli inglesi.
Brit·on [brɪtən] *n* inglese *m/f*.
brit·tle [brɪtl] *adj* fragile.
broach [brəʊtʃ] *vt* **(a)** *(subject)* affrontare. **(b)** *(bottle of wine)* stappare.
broad [brɔːd] **1** *adj (street, smile)* largo(a); *(mind, view)* aperto(a); *(hint)* chiaro(a), esplicito(a); *(accent)* marcato(a); **3 metres ~** largo 3 metri; **the ~ outlines** le grandi linee; **in ~ daylight** in pieno giorno; **in the ~est sense** nel senso più ampio. **2** *n (Am fam)* bellona. **3** *cpd:* **~ bean** *n* fava.
broad·cast [brɔːdkɑːst] *(vb: pt, pp* **broadcast**) **1** *n*

(TV, Radio) trasmissione *f*. **2** *vt (TV)* (tele)trasmettere, mandare in onda; *(Radio)* (radio)trasmettere, mandare in onda; *(fig: news, rumour)* diffondere; **don't ~ it!** non spargerlo ai quattro venti! **3** *vi (station)* trasmettere; *(person)* fare una trasmissione.
broad·cast·er [brɔːdkɑːstəʳ] *n* personaggio televisivo *(or* radiofonico).
broad·cast·ing [brɔːdkɑːstɪŋ] **1** *n (TV)* televisione *f*; *(Radio)* radiodiffusione *f*; *(broadcasts)* trasmissioni *fpl*. **2** *cpd:* **~ station** *n* stazione *f* trasmittente.
broad·en [brɔːdn] **1** *vt (road)* allargare; **to ~ one's mind** allargare i propri orizzonti. **2** *vi (also: ~ out)* allargarsi.
broad·ly [brɔːdlɪ] *adv:* **~ speaking** parlando in senso lato, grosso modo.
broad-minded [ˌbrɔːdmaɪndɪd] *adj (person)* di mente aperta, di larghe vedute; *(attitude)* aperto(a).
broad-shouldered [ˌbrɔːdʃəʊldəd] *adj* largo(a) di spalle.
broad·side [brɔːdsaɪd] *n (Naut)* bordata; *(fig)* attacco massiccio.
bro·cade [brəʊkeɪd] *n* broccato.
broc·co·li [brɒkəlɪ] *n (Bot)* broccolo; *(Culin)* broccoli *mpl*.
bro·chure [brəʊʃjʊəʳ] *n* opuscolo, dépliant *m inv*.
brogue[1] [brəʊg] *n (shoe)* scarpone *m*.
brogue[2] [brəʊg] *n (accent)* accento irlandese.
broil [brɔɪl] *vt (Am Culin)* fare alla griglia.
broke [brəʊk] **1** *pt of* **break. 2** *adj (fam)* senza una lira, al verde; **to go ~** fare fallimento.
bro·ken [brəʊkən] **1** *pp of* **break. 2** *adj* **(a)** *(gen)* rotto(a); *(stick)* spezzato(a); *(fig: marriage)* fallito(a); *(: promise, vow)* spezzato(a); *(: appointment)* mancato(a); *(: health)* rovinato(a); *(: spirit)* a pezzi; *(: heart)* infranto(a); **he comes from a ~ home** i suoi sono divisi; **he's a ~ old man** è un vecchio finito. **(b)** *(uneven: surface, coastline)* irregolare; *(: road, ground)* accidentato(a); *(interrupted: line)* spezzato(a); *(: sleep)* agitato(a); *(: night)* insonne; **he speaks ~ English** parla un inglese stentato.
broken-down [brəʊkəndaʊn] *adj (car)* in panne, rotto(a); *(machine)* guasto(a), fuori uso; *(house)* abbandonato(a), in rovina.
broken-hearted [ˌbrəʊkənhɑːtɪd] *adj* affranto(a) dal dolore, col cuore spezzato.
bro·ker [brəʊkəʳ] *n (Comm)* mediatore/trice; *(stock ~)* agente *m* di cambio.
brol·ly [brɒlɪ] *n (Brit fam)* ombrello.
bro·mide [brəʊmaɪd] *n (Chem)* bromuro.
bron·chial [brɒŋkɪəl] *adj* bronchiale; **~ tubes** bronchi *mpl*.
bron·chi·tis [brɒŋkaɪtɪs] *n* bronchite *f*.
bronze [brɒnz] **1** *n* bronzo. **2** *adj (made of ~)* di bronzo; *(colour)* bronzeo(a), color del bronzo *inv*; **the B~ Age** l'età del bronzo. **3** *vi* abbronzarsi. **4** *vt (skin)* abbronzare.
bronzed [brɒnzd] *adj (person)* abbronzato(a).
brooch [brəʊtʃ] *n* spilla, fermaglio.
brood [bruːd] **1** *n (of chicks)* covata; *(of birds)* nidiata; *(hum: of children)* figliolanza, prole *f*. **2** *vi (bird)* covare; *(fig: person)* rimuginare, stare a pensare.
♦ **brood on** *vi + prep* rimuginare su, stare a pensare a.
broody [bruːdɪ] *adj:* **~ hen** chioccia.
brook[1] [brʊk] *n* ruscello.
brook[2] [brʊk] *vt (tolerate)* tollerare, ammettere.
broom [brʊm] *n (brush)* scopa; *(Bot)* ginestra.
Bros *abbr* (= **brothers**) F.lli.

broth [brɒθ] *n* minestra (in brodo), brodo.

broth·el ['brɒθl] *n* bordello.

broth·er ['brʌðəʳ] **1** *n* (*gen, Rel*) fratello; (*Trade Union etc*) compagno, fratello. **2** *cpd*: ~ **officers** *npl* compagni *mpl* d'armi; ~ **workers** *npl* compagni lavoratori.

brother·hood ['brʌðəhʊd] *n* fratellanza, fraternità; (*group*) confraternita.

brother-in-law ['brʌðərɪn,lɔː] *n* cognato.

broth·er·ly ['brʌðəlɪ] *adj* fraterno(a).

brought [brɔːt] *pt, pp of* bring.

brow [braʊ] *n* (*forehead*) fronte *f*; (*eye*~) sopracciglio; (*of hill*) cima; (: *on road*) dosso.

brow·beat ['braʊbiːt] *pt* browbeat, *pp* browbeaten *vt* intimidire; **to ~ sb into doing sth** costringere qn a fare qc con la prepotenza.

brown [braʊn] **1** *adj* (*gen*) marrone; (*hair*) castano(a); (*bronzed: skin*) scuro(a), abbronzato(a); **to go ~** (*person*) abbronzarsi; (*leaves*) ingiallire. **2** *n* marrone *m*. **3** *vt* (*Culin: meat*) rosolare; (: *onion*) dorare; **to be ~ed off (with sth)** (*fam*) essere stufo (di qc). **4** *vi* (*Culin*) rosolarsi. **5** *cpd*: ~ **ale** *n* birra scura; ~ **bread** *n* pane *m* integrale, pane nero; ~ **paper** *n* carta da pacchi *or* da imballaggio; ~ **rice** *n* riso greggio; ~ **sugar** *n* zucchero greggio.

Brownie ['braʊnɪ] *n* coccinella (*scout*).

brown·ish ['braʊnɪʃ] *adj* (*stain, mark*) marroncino(a); (*colour, eyes*) sul marrone.

browse [braʊz] **1** *vi* (*in bookshop*) curiosare; (*in other shop*) guardare in giro, curiosare; (*animal*) brucare; **to ~ through a book** sfogliare un libro. **2** *n*: **to have a ~ (around)** dare un'occhiata (in giro).

bruise [bruːz] **1** *n* (*on person*) livido; (*on fruit*) ammaccatura. **2** *vt* (*leg etc*) farsi un livido a; (*fruit*) ammaccare; (*fig: feelings*) urtare. **3** *vi*: **I ~ easily** mi vengono facilmente i lividi sulla pelle.

bru·nette [bruːˈnɛt] *n* bruna.

brunt [brʌnt] *n*: **to bear the ~ of sth** (*of attack*) sostenere l'urto di qc; (*of work, cost*) sostenere il peso di qc.

brush [brʌʃ] **1** *n* **(a)** (*gen*) spazzola; (*broom*) scopa; (*hearth* ~) scopettino, scopino; (: *scrubbing* ~) spazzola per pavimenti; (*paint* ~) pennello; **hair/shoe ~** spazzola per capelli/da scarpe; **tooth ~** spazzolino da denti. **(b)** (*act of ~ing*) spazzolata, colpo di spazzola. **(c)** (*argument*): **to have a ~ with sb** (*verbally*) avere uno scontro con qn; (*physically*) venire a diverbio *or* alle mani con qn; **to have a ~ with the police** avere delle noie con la polizia. **(d)** (*light touch*) lieve tocco; **he felt the ~ of her hair against his face** sentiva i capelli di lei che gli sfioravano il viso. **(e)** (*undergrowth*) boscaglia, sottobosco.

   2 *vt* **(a)** (*clean: floor*) scopare; (: *clothes, hair*) spazzolare; (: *shoes*) lucidare, spazzolare; (: *teeth*) lavarsi. **(b)** (*touch lightly*) sfiorare.

♦ **brush against** *vi* + *prep* sfiorare.

♦ **brush aside** *vt* + *adv* (*fig*) ignorare, rifiutare di ascoltare.

♦ **brush away** *vt* + *adv* (*dirt: on clothes*) togliere (con la spazzola); (: *on floor*) scopar via; (*tears*) asciugarsi; (*insects*) cacciare (via).

♦ **brush off** *vt* + *adv* (*mud*) levare con la spazzola; (*fig: suggestion*) scartare; (: *criticism, attentions*) ignorare.

♦ **brush past** *vi* + *prep* sfiorare (passando).

♦ **brush up** *vt* + *adv* **(a)** (*crumbs*) raccogliere (con la spazzola). **(b)** (*also:* ~ **up on:** *revise*) dare una spolverata *or* una ripassata a.

brushed [brʌʃt] *adj* **(a)** (*Tech: steel, chrome etc*) sabbiato(a). **(b)** (*nylon, denim etc*) pettinato(a).

brusque [bruːsk] *adj* (*person, manner*) brusco(a); (*tone*) secco(a).

brusque·ness ['bruːsknɪs] *n* modi *mpl* bruschi, asprezza.

Brus·sels ['brʌslz] *n* Bruxelles; ~ **sprouts** *npl* cavoletti *mpl* di Bruxelles.

bru·tal ['bruːtl] *adj* brutale.

bru·tal·ity [bruːˈtælɪtɪ] *n* brutalità *f inv*.

brute [bruːt] **1** *n* (*animal*) bestia; (*person*) bruto; **you ~!** mostro! **2** *adj* (*force, strength*) bruto(a); **by ~ force** con la forza, a viva forza.

B.Sc. *abbr see* bachelor.

bub·ble ['bʌbl] **1** *n* bolla, (*smaller*) bollicina; **soap ~** bolla di sapone. **2** *vi* ribollire, fare bollicine; (*champagne*) spumeggiare. **3** *cpd*: ~ **bath** *n* bagno schiuma; ~ **gum** *n* bubble-gum *m inv*.

♦ **bubble over** *vi* + *adv* traboccare; (*fig*): **to ~ over (with)** scoppiare (di *or* da), traboccare (di).

buck [bʌk] **1** *n* **(a)** (*Zool*) maschio. **(b)** (*Am fam: dollar*) dollaro. **(c)**: **to pass the ~** (*fam*) scaricare la responsabilità (*or* la colpa *etc*) sugli altri. **2** *vi* (*horse*) sgroppare. **3** *cpd*: ~ **teeth** *npl* denti *mpl* da coniglio.

♦ **buck up** (*fam*) **1** *vi* + *adv* (*cheer up*) tirarsi su; (*hurry up*) sbrigarsi, smuoversi. **2** *vt* + *adv* **(a)** (*make cheerful*) tirar su (il morale di). **(b)**: **to ~ one's ideas up** mettere la testa a partito.

buck·et ['bʌkɪt] **1** *n* secchio, (*large*) secchia. **2** *vi* (*fam*): **the rain is ~ing (down)** piove a catinelle.

buck·le ['bʌkl] **1** *n* fibbia, fermaglio. **2** *vt* **(a)** (*shoe, belt*) allacciare. **(b)** (*wheel, girder*) distorcere, piegare. **3** *vi* (*see vt*) allacciarsi, chiudersi con una fibbia; distorcersi, piegarsi.

♦ **buckle down** *vi* + *adv* mettersi sotto; **to ~ down to a job** mettersi a lavorare d'impegno *or* di buzzo buono.

buck·skin ['bʌk,skɪn] *n* pelle *f* di daino.

bud [bʌd] **1** *n* (*of flower*) bocciolo, boccio; (*on tree, plant*) gemma, germoglio; **to be in ~** (*flower*) essere in boccio; (*tree*) stare germogliando. **2** *vi* (*plant*) mettere i bocci; (*tree*) germogliare, mettere le gemme.

Buddha ['bʊdə] *n* Budda *m inv*.

Bud·dhism ['bʊdɪzəm] *n* buddismo.

Bud·dhist ['bʊdɪst] *adj, n* buddista (*m/f*).

bud·ding ['bʌdɪŋ] *adj* (*fig: talent*) in erba.

bud·dy ['bʌdɪ] *n* (*esp Am*) amico; **they've been buddies for years** sono amiconi da anni.

budge [bʌdʒ] **1** *vt* (*move*) spostare, smuovere; **I couldn't ~ him an inch** (*fig*) non sono riuscito a smuoverlo di un dito. **2** *vi* muoversi, spostarsi; (*fig*) smuoversi.

budg·eri·gar ['bʌdʒərɪgɑːʳ] *n* pappagallino.

budg·et ['bʌdʒɪt] **1** *n* bilancio (preventivo), preventivo; **I'm on a tight ~** devo contare la lira; **she works out her ~ every month** fa il preventivo delle spese ogni mese; **the B~** (*Brit*) il bilancio dello Stato. **2** *vi* fare un preventivo; (*household*) fare i propri conti.

♦ **budget for** *vi* + *prep* mettere in conto *or* in preventivo, preventivare.

budgie ['bʌdʒɪ] *n abbr of* budgerigar.

buff [bʌf] **1** *adj* (*colour*) color paglierino *inv*. **2** *vt* (*also:* ~ **up**) lucidare, lustrare.

buf·fa·lo ['bʌfələʊ] *n, pl* ~**es** (*wild ox*) bufalo/a; (*esp Am: bison*) bisonte *m*.

buff·er ['bʌfəʳ] **1** *n* (*for railway engine*) respingente *m*; (*fig*) cuscinetto. **2** *cpd*: ~ **state** *n* stato cuscinetto.

buf·fet[1] ['bʌfɪt] **1** *n* (*blow*) schiaffo; **the ~s of fate** (*fig*) i colpi della sorte. **2** *vt* (*ship, car etc*) sballottare; (*house*) sferzare.

buf·fet[2] ['bʊfeɪ] **1** *n* (*for refreshments*) buffet *m inv*, bar *m inv; (meal)* buffet, rinfresco. **2** *cpd:* ~ **car** *n (Brit Rail)* = servizio ristoro; ~ **lunch** *n* pranzo in piedi; ~ **supper** *n* cena fredda.

bug [bʌg] *(fam)* **1** *n* **(a)** *(insect)* insetto; *(germ)* infezione *f*, virus *m inv; (fig: obsession)* mania, passione *f*; **I've got the travel** ~ *(fig)* mi è presa la mania dei viaggi. **(b)** *(bugging device)* microfono (nascosto). **2** *vt* **(a)** *(telephone)* mettere sotto controllo; *(room)* installare microfoni-spia in. **(b)** *(annoy)* scocciare; **it really** ~s **me** mi fa una rabbia.

bug·bear [ˈbʌgˌbɛəʳ] *n* spauracchio, incubo.

bu·gle [ˈbjuːgl] *n* tromba.

build [bɪld] *(vb: pt, pp* **built) 1** *n (of person)* corporatura, fisico. **2** *vt (house)* costruire, fabbricare; *(ship, town, machine)* costruire; *(nest)* fare; *(fig: relationship, career)* costruire; *(empire)* edificare; **a new bridge is being built** è in costruzione un nuovo ponte.

♦ **build on 1** *vt + adv* aggiungere. **2** *vt + prep (fig)* fondare su, basare su.

♦ **build up 1** *vt + adv (establish: business)* costruire; *(: reputation)* fare, consolidare; *(increase: production)* allargare, incrementare; *(stocks etc)* accumulare; *(collection)* mettere insieme; *(spirits, morale)* tirar su; *(hopes)* far crescere; **don't** ~ **your hopes up too soon** non sperarci troppo; **to** ~ **up one's strength** rimettersi in forze. **2** *vi + adv (pressure)* salire; *(Fin: interest)* accumularsi; **the music built up to a crescendo** la musica aumentava in un crescendo continuo.

build·er [ˈbɪldəʳ] *n (contractor)* costruttore *m*, imprenditore *m (edile); (workman)* muratore *m; (fig)* creatore/trice.

build·ing [ˈbɪldɪŋ] **1** *n* **(a)** costruzione *f*, edificio; *(block)* palazzo. **(b)** *(no pl)* costruzione *f;* (~ *industry)* edilizia. **2** *cpd:* ~ **contractor** *n* costruttore *m*, imprenditore *m* (edile); ~ **industry** *n*, ~ **trade** *n* industria edilizia; ~ **site** *n* cantiere *m* di costruzione; ~ **society** *n* società *f inv* immobiliare.

build-up [ˈbɪldʌp] *n* **(a)** *(of pressure etc)* aumento, accumulo; *(Mil: of troops)* ammassamento; *(of traffic)* aumento di volume, intensificarsi *m inv; (fig: of tension etc)* aumento. **(b)** *(publicity)* campagna pubblicitaria; **to give sb/sth a good** ~ fare buona pubblicità a qn/qc.

built [bɪlt] *pt, pp* of **build.**

built-in [ˈbɪltˌɪn] *adj (furniture)* a muro; *(aerial)* incorporato(a).

built-up [ˈbɪltˌʌp] *adj:* ~ **area** abitato.

bulb [bʌlb] *n (Bot, of thermometer)* bulbo; *(Elec)* lampadina.

bulb·ous [ˈbʌlbəs] *adj* a forma di bulbo.

Bul·garia [bʌlˈgɛərɪə] *n* Bulgaria.

Bul·gar·ian [bʌlˈgɛərɪən] **1** *adj* bulgaro(a). **2** *n* **(a)** *(person)* bulgaro/a. **(b)** *(language)* bulgaro.

bulge [bʌldʒ] **1** *n* **(a)** *(in surface)* rigonfiamento; *(in plaster, metal)* bolla; *(curve: of thighs, hips)* curva; *(: of jug)* pancia. **(b)** *(in birth rate, sales)* punta, rapido aumento; **the postwar** ~ l'esplosione demografica del dopoguerra. **2** *vi (pocket etc):* **to** ~ **(with)** essere gonfio(a) (di); *(stomach, muscles)* sporgere.

bulk [bʌlk] *n (of thing)* volume *m*, massa; *(of person)* corporatura (pesante), massa del corpo; **the** ~ **of** la maggior parte di; **the** ~ **of the work** il grosso del lavoro; **to buy in** ~ comprare in grande quantità.

bulky [ˈbʌlkɪ] *adj (parcel)* voluminoso(a); *(person)* corpulento(a).

bull[1] [bʊl] *n* toro; *(male of elephant, seal)* maschio; **like a** ~ **in a china shop** come un elefante; **to take**

the ~ **by the horns** *(fig)* prendere il toro per le corna.

bull[2] [bʊl] *n (Rel)* bolla (papale).

bull·dog [ˈbʊldɒg] *n* bulldog *m inv.*

bull·doze [ˈbʊldəʊz] *vt* aprire *or* spianare col bulldozer; **I was** ~**d into doing it** *(fig fam)* mi ci hanno costretto con la prepotenza.

bull·doz·er [ˈbʊldəʊzəʳ] *n* bulldozer *m inv*, apripista *m inv.*

bul·let [ˈbʊlɪt] *n* proiettile *m*, pallottola; ~ **hole** *n* foro di proiettile.

bul·letin [ˈbʊlɪtɪn] *n (statement)* comunicato (ufficiale); *(journal)* bollettino.

bullet·proof [ˈbʊlɪtˌpruːf] *adj* a prova di proiettile; ~ **vest** giubbotto antiproiettile.

bull·fight [ˈbʊlfaɪt] *n* corrida.

bull·fighter [ˈbʊlˌfaɪtəʳ] *n* torero.

bul·lion [ˈbʊljən] *n* oro *(or* argento) in lingotti.

bull·ock [ˈbʊlək] *n* manzo.

bull·ring [ˈbʊlˌrɪŋ] *n* arena (per corride).

bull's-eye [ˈbʊlzaɪ] *n (of target)* centro (del bersaglio); **to hit the** ~ *(fig)* far centro, colpire nel segno.

bul·ly [ˈbʊlɪ] **1** *n* bullo, prepotente *m*. **2** *vt (also:* ~ **around)** fare il prepotente con; *(: subj: children)* fare le prepotenze a; **to** ~ **sb into doing sth** far fare qc a qn con la prepotenza.

bul·rush [ˈbʊlrʌʃ] *n* stiancia.

bul·wark [ˈbʊlwək] *n (Mil, fig)* baluardo, bastione *m; (Naut)* parapetto.

bum[1] [bʌm] *n (Brit fam: bottom)* culo.

bum[2] [bʌm] *(fam)* **1** *n (esp Am: idler)* fannullone/a; *(tramp)* barbone/a, vagabondo/a. **2** *adj* scadente; ~ **coin** patacca. **3** *vt (money, food)* scroccare.

♦ **bum around** *vi + adv* vagabondare.

bumble·bee [ˈbʌmblbiː] *n* bombo.

bumf [bʌmf] *n (fam: forms etc)* scartoffie *fpl.*

bump [bʌmp] **1** *n* **(a)** *(blow)* botta, colpo; *(noise)* botto; *(jolt of vehicle)* botta, urto. **(b)** *(swelling)* bernoccolo, bozzo, gonfiore *m; (: on skin)* gonfiore; *(: on road etc)* cunetta, bozzo. **2** *vt (car)* urtare, sbattere; **to** ~ **one's head** sbattere la testa. **3** *vi (also:* ~ **along)** avanzare a sbalzi e scossoni.

♦ **bump into** *vi + prep* **(a)** *(vehicle)* andare a sbattere contro. **(b)** *(fam: meet)* imbattersi in, incontrare per caso; **fancy** ~**ing into you!** ma guarda chi si vede!

♦ **bump off** *vt + adv (fam)* far fuori.

bump·er[1] [ˈbʌmpəʳ] *n (Brit Aut)* paraurti *m inv.*

bump·er[2] [ˈbʌmpəʳ] *adj (harvest)* eccezionale.

bumpy [ˈbʌmpɪ] *adj (surface, road)* accidentato(a), irregolare; *(journey, flight)* movimentato(a).

bun [bʌn] *n (Culin)* panino dolce; *(of hair)* chignon *m inv*, crocchia; **to wear one's hair in a** ~ portare lo chignon.

bunch [bʌntʃ] *n (of flowers)* mazzo, *(small)* mazzetto, mazzolino; *(of bananas)* casco; *(of grapes)* grappolo; *(of keys)* mazzo; *(set of people)* gruppo; **to wear one's hair in** ~**es** portare le codine; **the best of a bad** ~ il *(or* la *etc)* meno peggio.

♦ **bunch together 1** *vt + adv (objects)* ammucchiare. **2** *vi + adv (people)* ammucchiarsi.

bun·dle [ˈbʌndl] **1** *n (of clothes, rags)* fagotto, involto; *(of sticks)* fascina; *(of papers)* mucchio; *(of newspapers)* fascio. **2** *vt* **(a)** *(also:* ~ **up:** *clothes)* fare un fagotto di, raccogliere in un mucchio; *(: papers)* fare un fascio di. **(b)** *(put hastily)* nascondere, metter via in fretta; *(: person)* spingere, caricare in gran fretta; **he was** ~**d off to Australia** l'hanno spedito in fretta e furia in Australia.

bung [bʌŋ] **1** *n* tappo, turacciolo. **2** *vt (also:* ~ **up:**

pipe, hole) tappare, otturare; **my nose is ~ed up** *(fam)* ho il naso otturato.

bun·ga·low ['bʌŋgələʊ] *n* bungalow *m inv*, villetta a un piano.

bun·gle ['bʌŋgl] *(fam)* **1** *vt* fare un pasticcio di. **2** *vi* fare pasticci.

bun·ion ['bʌnjən] *n (Med)* cipolla.

bunk [bʌŋk] *n (Naut, Rail etc)* cuccetta; **~s** *(also: ~-beds)* letti *mpl* a castello.

bun·ker ['bʌŋkəʳ] *n (coal ~)* carbonaia; *(Mil, Golf)* bunker *m inv*.

bun·kum ['bʌŋkəm] *n (fam)* scempiaggini *fpl*.

bunt·ing ['bʌntɪŋ] *n (Naut)* gran pavese *m; (in street)* bandierine *fpl*.

buoy [bɔɪ] *n* boa, gavitello.

♦ **buoy up** *vt + adv (person, boat)* tenere a galla; *(fig: spirits)* tener su; (: *hopes)* alimentare.

buoy·ant ['bɔɪənt] *adj (ship, log)* che galleggia (bene), galleggiante; *(fig: person)* di ottimo umore, su di corda; (: *nature)* ottimista; *(Fin: market)* sostenuto(a); *(prices, currency)* stabile.

bur·den ['bɜːdn] **1** *n (load)* carico, peso; *(fig: of years)* peso; *(of taxes, payment)* onere *m;* **the ~ of proof lies with him** spetta a lui l'onere della prova; **to be a ~ to sb** essere di peso a qn. **2** *vt:* **to ~ (with)** *(cares etc)* opprimere (con); **~ed with debts** oberato di debiti.

bu·reau [bjʊəˈrəʊ] *n* **(a)** *(office)* ufficio, agenzia; *(government department)* dipartimento, sezione *f.* **(b)** *(Brit: desk)* secrétaire *m inv; (Am: chest of drawers)* cassettone *m.*

bu·reau·cra·cy [bjʊəˈrɒkrəsɪ] *n* burocrazia.

bu·reau·crat ['bjʊərəʊkræt] *n* burocrate *m/f.*

bu·reau·crat·ic [ˌbjʊərəʊˈkrætɪk] *adj* burocratico(a).

bur·glar ['bɜːgləʳ] **1** *n* ladro, scassinatore/trice. **2** *cpd:* **~ alarm** *n* antifurto *m inv.*

bur·glar·ize ['bɜːgləraɪz] *vt (Am)* svaligiare.

bur·gla·ry ['bɜːglərɪ] *n* furto (con scasso).

bur·gle ['bɜːgl] *vt (house, shop)* svaligiare; **I've been ~d** mi hanno svaligiato la casa *(or* il negozio *etc).*

bur·ial ['bɛrɪəl] *n* sepoltura, seppellimento.

bur·lesque [bɜːˈlɛsk] *n* parodia.

bur·ly ['bɜːlɪ] *adj* ben piantato(a).

Bur·ma ['bɜːmə] *n* Birmania.

Bur·mese [bɜːˈmiːz] *adj, n* birmano(a) *(m/f).*

burn [bɜːn] *(vb: pt, pp* burned *or* burnt) **1** *n (gen)* bruciatura; *(superficial)* scottatura; *(Med)* ustione *f.*

2 *vt (gen)* bruciare; *(set fire to)* incendiare; *(person, skin: also of sun)* bruciare, scottare; *(toast, meat etc)* (far) bruciare; *(use as fuel: boiler etc;* **the cigarette ~t a hole in her dress** si è fatta un buco nel vestito con la sigaretta; **to be ~t to death** morire tra le fiamme, morire bruciato *or* carbonizzato; *(at stake)* essere bruciato vivo; **I've ~t myself!** mi sono bruciato!; **to ~ one's boats** *or* **bridges** *(fig)* darsi la zappa sui piedi; **to ~ the candle at both ends** *(fig)* ridursi male (facendo le ore piccole).

3 *vi (gen)* bruciare; *(fire)* ardere; *(skin, person)* bruciarsi, scottarsi; *(meat, pastry etc)* bruciarsi; *(light, gas)* essere *or* rimanere acceso(a); *(fig):* **to ~ with anger** fremere di rabbia; **to ~ with fever** bruciare per la febbre; **to ~ to do sth** bruciare dalla voglia di fare qc.

♦ **burn down 1** *vt + adv (building)* bruciare, dare alle fiamme. **2** *vi + adv (house)* essere distrutto(a) dal fuoco, bruciarsi; *(candle, fire)* consumarsi, abbassarsi.

♦ **burn off** *vt + adv (paint etc)* togliere col fuoco.

♦ **burn out 1** *vt + adv (subj: writer etc):* **to ~ o.s. out** esaurirsi; *(subj: talent):* **to ~ itself out** esaurirsi; (: *enthusiasm)* spegnersi. **2** *vi (fuse)* saltare; *(candle, lamp)* spegnersi; *(flames)* estinguersi.

♦ **burn up 1** *vi (fire)* ravvivarsi, divampare. **2** *vt + adv (rubbish etc)* bruciare.

burn·er ['bɜːnəʳ] *n (on cooker)* fornello; *(Tech)* bruciatore *m*, becco (a gas).

burn·ing ['bɜːnɪŋ] **1** *n* bruciato; **I can smell ~** sento odore di bruciato. **2** *adj (building, forest)* in fiamme; *(coals)* acceso(a); *(flame)* vivo(a), ardente; *(fig: thirst, fever, desire)* bruciante, divorante; *(tears)* cocente; *(question, topic)* scottante.

bur·nish ['bɜːnɪʃ] *vt* brunire.

burnt [bɜːnt] *pt, pp of* **burn.**

burp [bɜːp] *(fam)* **1** *n* rutto; *(of baby)* ruttino. **2** *vi* ruttare, fare un rutto. **3** *vt (baby)* far fare il ruttino a.

bur·row ['bʌrəʊ] **1** *n (of rabbit etc)* tana, cunicolo. **2** *vt (hole)* scavare; **to ~ one's way (under/through** *etc)* scavarsi un tunnel (sotto/attraverso *etc).* **3** *vi (rabbits etc)* scavare gallerie; **he ~ed under the bedclothes** si è rintanato sotto le coperte.

bur·sar ['bɜːsəʳ] *n (Univ etc)* economo.

bur·sa·ry ['bɜːsərɪ] *n (Scot Scol)* borsa di studio.

burst [bɜːst] *(vb: pt, pp* burst) **1** *n (of shell etc)* scoppio, esplosione *f; (in pipe)* rottura; *(of shots)* raffica, scarica; **a ~ of applause** uno scroscio d'applausi; **a ~ of laughter/activity** uno scoppio di risa/attività; **a ~ of speed** uno scatto (di velocità).

2 *vt (gen)* far scoppiare; *(bag)* sfondare, spaccare; **the river has ~ its banks** il fiume ha rotto gli argini *or* ha straripato.

3 *vi (a) (gen)* scoppiare; *(tyre: blow out)* scoppiare; (: *puncture)* bucarsi; *(shell, firework)* scoppiare, esplodere; *(bag)* sfondarsi, spaccarsi; *(dam)* cedere; **the door ~ open** la porta si è spalancata di colpo; **filled to ~ing point** pieno da scoppiare; **to be ~ing at the seams** essere pieno(a) zeppo(a) (di), traboccare (di); **the room was ~ing at the seams** la stanza rigurgitava di persone; **to be ~ing with pride** sprizzare soddisfazione da tutti i pori; **I was ~ing to tell you** *(fam)* non ne potevo più *or* crepavo dalla voglia di dirtelo.

(b) *(start, go suddenly):* **to ~ into/out of the room** piombare nella/scappare precipitosamente dalla stanza; **to ~ into flames** prendere fuoco, andare in fiamme; **to ~ into tears** scoppiare a piangere; **the sun ~ through the clouds** è sbucato il sole; **to ~ out laughing** scoppiare a ridere; **~ out singing** mettersi (improvvisamente) a cantare.

bury ['bɛrɪ] *vt (body, treasure)* seppellire; *(plunge: claws, knife):* **to ~ (in)** affondare (in); **he buried his face in his hands** si copri il volto con le mani; **buried by an avalanche** travolto(a) da una valanga; **buried in thought** sprofondato(a) nei propri pensieri; **to ~ the hatchet** seppellire l'ascia di guerra.

bus [bʌs] **1** *n, pl* **~es** *or (Am)* **~ses** autobus *m inv;* **to go by ~** andare in autobus. **2** *cpd (driver, service, ticket)* d'autobus; **~ route** *n* percorso; **~ shelter** *n* pensilina, fermata coperta; **~ station** *n* stazione *f* delle autolinee, autostazione *f;* **~ stop** *n* fermata d'autobus.

bush [bʊʃ] *n* **(a)** cespuglio. **(b)** *(in Africa, Australia):* **the ~** la boscaglia.

bushy ['bʊʃɪ] *adj (plant, tail, beard)* folto(a); *(eyebrows)* irsuto(a).

busi·ly ['bɪzɪlɪ] *adv* con impegno, alacremente.

busi·ness ['bɪznɪs] **1** *n* **(a)** *(commerce)* affari *mpl*; **selling books is his** ~ di mestiere vende libri; **he's in the insurance** ~ lavora nel campo delle assicurazioni; **he's in the wool** ~ è nel commercio della lana; **I'm here on** ~ sono qui per affari; **to do** ~ **with sb** fare affari con qn; **let's get down to** ~ *(fam)* bando alle chiacchiere; ~ **is** ~ gli affari sono affari; **now we're in** ~! ci siamo!; **he means** ~ fa sul serio. **(b)** *(firm)* impresa; **to set up a** ~ metter su un'impresa; **it's a family** ~ è un'impresa familiare. **(c)** *(task, duty, concern)* affare *m*; **to make it one's** ~ **to do sth** incaricarsi di fare qc; **that's none of your** ~ non sono affari tuoi, non ti riguarda; **that's my** ~ (è) affar mio, (sono) affari miei; **it's his** ~ **to see that...** spetta a lui accertarsi che...; **you had no** ~ **to do that** non stava a te farlo; **mind your own** ~ pensa ai fatti tuoi, non t'impicciare. **(d)** *(fam: affair, matter)* storia, faccenda; **what an awful** ~ **it was!** che orrore che è stato!; **it's a nasty** ~ è una brutta faccenda, è un brutto affare.

2 *cpd* *(deal, quarter, trip, relationship)* d'affari; *(studies, college)* commerciale; ~ **address** *n* indirizzo di lavoro *or* d'ufficio; ~ **card** *n* biglietto da visita della ditta; ~ **expenses** *npl* spese *fpl*; **to claim for sth on** ~ **expenses** mettere qc in conto spese; ~ **sense** *n* senso degli affari.

business·like ['bɪznɪslaɪk] *adj (approach, transaction)* efficiente; *(firm)* serio(a); *(person, manner)* pratico(a), efficiente.

business·man ['bɪznɪsmæn] *n, pl* **-men** uomo d'affari.

business·woman ['bɪznɪswʊmən] *n, pl* **-women** donna d'affari.

busk·er ['bʌskəʳ] *n (Brit)* suonatore/trice ambulante.

bust[1] [bʌst] **1** *n (Art)* busto; *(bosom)* petto. **2** *cpd*: ~ **measurement** *n* giro *m* petto *inv*.

bust[2] [bʌst] *(fam)* **1** *adj (broken)* rotto(a), scassato(a); *(bankrupt)*: **to go** ~ fallire, fare fallimento. **2** *vt* **(a)** = **burst 2**. **(b)** *(Police: arrest)* pizzicare, beccare; *(: raid)* fare irruzione in. **(c)** *(break)* scassare.

bus·tle ['bʌsl] **1** *n* trambusto. **2** *vi (person: also:* ~ **about)** darsi da fare, affaccendarsi; *(place)* essere animatissimo(a).

busy ['bɪzɪ] **1** *adj* **(a)** *(occupied: person)* occupato(a); **he's a** ~ **man** *(normally)* è un uomo molto occupato; *(temporarily)* ha molto da fare, è molto occupato; **she's** ~ **studying/cooking** sta studiando/cucinando; **he's** ~ **at his work** sta lavorando, è molto preso dal lavoro; **let's get** ~ *(fam)* diamoci da fare. **(b)** *(active: day, time)* movimentato(a), intenso(a); *(: place, town)* animato(a); **Christmas is a** ~ **time of year** a Natale ci sono sempre mille cose da fare; **the roads are** ~ c'è molto traffico sulle strade. **(c)** *(esp Am: telephone, line)* occupato(a); ~ **signal** segnale *m* di occupato. **2** *vt*: **to** ~ **o.s. (doing sth/with sth)** darsi da fare (a fare qc/con qc).

busy·body ['bɪzɪbɒdɪ] *n* ficcanaso *m/f inv*, impiccione/a.

but [bʌt] **1** *conj (gen)* ma; **she was poor** ~ **she was honest** era povera ma onesta; **we never go out** ~ **it rains** non usciamo mai senza che ci metta a piovere; **never a week passes** ~ **she's ill** mai una settimana che non stia male.

2 *adv* solo, soltanto; **she's** ~ **a child** è solo una bambina, non è che una bambina; **had I** ~ **known** se solo l'avessi saputo; **I cannot help** ~ **think that...** non posso fare a meno di pensare che...; **you can** ~ **try** tentar non nuoce.

3 *prep* eccetto, tranne, meno; **he was nothing**

~ **trouble** non dava altro che guai; **no one** ~ **him** solo lui; **no one** ~ **him can do it** è l'unico che lo sappia fare; **the last** ~ **one** il(la) penultimo(a); **I live in the next street** ~ **one** abito due strade più in su *(or* giù); ~ **for you** se non fosse per te; **anything** ~ **that** tutto ma non questo.

4 *n*: **no** ~**s about it!** non c'è ma che tenga!

bu·tane ['bjuːteɪn] *n (also:* ~ **gas)** butano.

butch·er ['bʊtʃəʳ] **1** *n (also fig)* macellaio; ~**'s (shop)** macelleria; **at the** ~**'s** dal macellaio. **2** *vt* macellare.

but·ler ['bʌtləʳ] *n* maggiordomo.

butt[1] [bʌt] *n* botte *f*.

butt[2] [bʌt] *n (end)* fine *f*; *(of gun)* calcio; *(of cigar, cigarette)* mozzicone *m*.

butt[3] [bʌt] *n (Shooting, Archery)*: **the** ~**s** il campo *or* poligono di tiro; *(fig)* bersaglio, zimbello; **she's the** ~ **of his jokes** è il bersaglio dei suoi scherzi, è il suo zimbello.

butt[4] [bʌt] **1** *n (push with head)* testata; *(of goat)* cornata. **2** *vt* dare una testata *(or* cornata) a.

♦ **butt in** *vi + adv (interrupt)* interrompere; *(meddle)* immischiarsi.

but·ter ['bʌtəʳ] **1** *n* burro; **he looks as if** ~ **wouldn't melt in his mouth** ha una faccia d'angelo. **2** *vt (bread)* imburrare, spalmare di burro. **3** *cpd*: ~ **bean** *n* fagiolo bianco; ~ **dish** *n* burriera.

butter·cup ['bʌtəˌkʌp] *n* ranuncolo.

butter·fingers ['bʌtəˌfɪŋgəz] *n (fam)* mani *fpl* di ricotta.

butter·fly ['bʌtəflaɪ] *n* **(a)** farfalla; **I've got butterflies (in my stomach)** ho il batticuore. **(b)** *(swimming: also:* ~ **stroke)** (nuoto a) farfalla.

but·tock ['bʌtək] *n* natica.

but·ton ['bʌtn] **1** *n (on garment)* bottone *m*; *(on doorbell, machine)* pulsante *m*, bottone. **2** *vt (also:* ~ **up)** abbottonare. **3** *vi* abbottonarsi.

button·hole ['bʌtnhəʊl] **1** *n* asola, occhiello; **to wear a** ~ portare un fiore all'occhiello. **2** *vt (person)* attaccar bottone a *or* con.

but·tress ['bʌtrɪs] **1** *n* contrafforte *m*, sperone *m*. **2** *vt* armare di contrafforti, rafforzare (con speroni); *(fig)* tener su, tenere in piedi *(: argument)* avvalorare.

bux·om ['bʌksəm] *adj* ben in carne.

buy [baɪ] *(vb: pt, pp* **bought) 1** *n*: **a good/bad** ~ un buon/cattivo acquisto *or* affare *m*. **2** *vt* comprare, acquistare; *(tickets, petrol)* fare, prendere; *(Comm: company)* acquistare; *(fig: time)* guadagnare; **the victory was dearly bought** la vittoria è stata pagata a caro prezzo; **to** ~ **sb a drink** offrire da bere a qn; **he won't** ~ **that explanation** *(fam)* quella scusa non se la beve.

♦ **buy back** *vt + adv* riprendersi, prendersi indietro.

♦ **buy in** *vt + adv* far provvista di.

♦ **buy off** *vt + adv (fam: bribe)* comprare.

♦ **buy out** *vt + adv (business)* rilevare.

♦ **buy up** *vt + adv (property etc)* accaparrar(si).

buy·er ['baɪəʳ] *n (in store)* compratore/trice, acquirente *m/f*; ~**'s market** mercato favorevole ai compratori.

buzz [bʌz] **1** *n* ronzio; *(of conversation)* brusio; **to give sb a** ~ *(fam: telephone call)* dare un colpo a qn. **2** *vt (call on intercom)* chiamare al citofono; *(: with buzzer)* chiamare col cicalino; *(Aer: plane, building)* passare rasente. **3** *vi (insect, ears)* ronzare; **my head is** ~**ing** mi gira la testa.

♦ **buzz off** *vi + adv (Brit fam)* filare, levarsi di torno.

buz·zard ['bʌzəd] *n* poiana.

buzz·er ['bʌzəʳ] *n* cicalino; *(in factory etc)* sirena.

by [baɪ] **1** *adv* (lì) vicino; **close** *or* **hard** ~ vicinissimo, molto vicino; **to go** *or* **pass** ~ passare; **to rush** ~ passare correndo; **to put** *or* **lay sth** ~ mettere qc da parte; ~ **and** ~ *(in past)* poco dopo; *(in future)* fra breve; ~ **and large** nel complesso.

2 *prep* **(a)** *(close to)* vicino a, accanto a, presso; **the house** ~ **the river** la casa sul fiume; **a holiday** ~ **the sea** una vacanza al mare; **I've got it** ~ **me** ce l'ho a portata di mano *or* sottomano.

(b) *(via, through)* per; **we came** ~ **Dover** siamo venuti via Dover.

(c) *(past)* davanti a; **I go** ~ **the post office every day** passo davanti alla posta ogni giorno; **she walked** ~ **me** mi è passata accanto.

(d) *(during)*: ~ **day/night** di giorno/notte.

(e) *(not later than)* per; ~ **this time tomorrow** domani a quest'ora; ~ **the time I got there it was too late** quando sono arrivato era ormai troppo tardi; ~ **that time** *or* ~ **then I knew** ormai lo sapevo.

(f) *(amount)* a; ~ **the kilo/metre** a chili/metri; ~ **the hour** a ore; ~ **degrees** gradualmente; **one** ~ **one** uno per uno; **little** ~ **little** a poco a poco.

(g) *(agent, cause)* da; **killed** ~ **lightning** ucciso da un fulmine; **a painting** ~ **Picasso** un quadro di Picasso; **surrounded** ~ **enemies** circondato da nemici.

(h) *(method, manner, means)* per; ~ **bus/car** in autobus/macchina, con l'autobus/la macchina; ~ **rail** *or* **train** con il treno, in treno; ~ **land and** ~ **sea** per terra e per mare; ~ **force** con la forza; **to pay** ~ **cheque** pagare con (un) assegno; **made** ~ **hand** fatto a mano; **to lead sb** ~ **the hand** portare qn per mano; ~ **moonlight** al chiaro di luna; ~ **saving hard, he...** risparmiando molto, lui... .

(i) *(according to)* per; **to play** ~ **the rules** attenersi alle regole; **it's all right** ~ **me** per me va bene.

(j) *(measuring difference)* di; **it's broader** ~ **a metre** è un metro più largo; **it missed me** ~ **inches** non mi ha preso per un millimetro.

(k) *(Math, measure)*: **to divide/multiply** ~ dividere/moltiplicare per; **a room 3 metres** ~ **4** una stanza di 3 metri per 4.

(l) *(points of compass)*: **north** ~ **north-east** nord-nordest.

(m) *(in oaths)*: **I swear** ~ **Almighty God** giuro dinanzi a Dio *or* nel nome di Dio; ~ **heaven!** *(fam)* perdio!

(n): ~ **the way,** ~ **the by(e)** a proposito; **this wasn't my idea** ~ **the way** tra l'altro l'idea non era mia.

bye [baɪ] *excl (fam: also:* ~-~*)* ciao!

by(e)-election [ˈbaɪɪˌlɛkʃən] *n* elezioni *fpl* suppletive *(in un collegio uninominale)*.

by·gone [ˈbaɪgɒn] **1** *adj*: **in** ~ **days** una volta. **2** *n*: **let** ~**s be** ~**s** mettiamoci una pietra sopra.

by·law [ˈbaɪˌlɔː] *n* norma del regolamento comunale.

by·pass [ˈbaɪpɑːs] **1** *n (road)* circonvallazione *f*. **2** *vt (town)* (fare una deviazione per) evitare; *(fig: person)* scavalcare; *(difficulty)* aggirare.

by·product [ˈbaɪˌprɒdʌkt] *n (Chem etc)* sottoprodotto; *(fig)* conseguenza.

by·stander [ˈbaɪˌstændəʳ] *n* astante *m/f*.

by·way [ˈbaɪˌweɪ] *n* strada secondaria.

by·word [ˈbaɪˌwɜːd] *n*: **his name is a** ~ **for success** il suo nome è sinonimo di successo.

C

C, c [siː] n **(a)** (letter) C, c f or m inv. **(b)** (Mus) do.

c. abbr **(a)** (= century) sec. **(b)** (= circa) ca.

C.A. abbr of **chartered accountant**.

cab [kæb] n **(a)** (taxi) taxi m inv; **by** ~ in taxi. **(b)** (of lorry etc) cabina.

caba·ret ['kæbəreɪ] n cabaret m inv.

cab·bage ['kæbɪdʒ] n cavolo.

cab·in ['kæbɪn] **1** n (hut) capanna; (Naut, Aer) cabina. **2** cpd: ~ **cruiser** n cabinato.

cabi·net ['kæbɪnɪt] **1** n **(a)** (cupboard) armadietto; (with windows) vetrinetta. **(b)** (Pol: also: **C**~) Consiglio dei Ministri. **2** cpd: ~ **minister** n ministro (membro del Consiglio).

ca·ble ['keɪbl] **1** n (rope, Elec) cavo; (cablegram) cablogramma m. **2** vt (information) trasmettere per cablogramma; (person) mandare un cablogramma a. **3** cpd: ~ **television** n televisione f via cavo.

ca·ble·car ['keɪbl͵kɑːʳ] n funivia; (on rail) funicolare m.

ca·ble·gram ['keɪbl͵græm] n cablogramma m.

cache [kæʃ] n deposito segreto.

cack·le ['kækl] **1** n (of hen) coccodè m; (laugh) risolino (stridulo); (chatter) chiacchierio. **2** vi (hen) fare coccodè; (person: laugh) ridacchiare.

ca·copho·ny [kæ'kɒfənɪ] n cacofonia.

cac·tus ['kæktəs] n, pl ~es or **cacti** ['kæktaɪ] cactus m inv.

ca·dav·er [kə'deɪvəʳ] n (Med) cadavere m.

ca·dav·er·ous [kə'dævərəs] adj cadaverico(a).

cad·die, cad·dy[1] ['kædɪ] n (in golf) caddie m inv.

cad·dy[2] ['kædɪ] n (tea ~) barattolo del tè.

ca·dence ['keɪdəns] n cadenza.

ca·det [kə'dɛt] **1** n (Mil etc) cadetto; **police** ~ allievo poliziotto. **2** cpd: ~ **nurse** n allieva infermiera.

cadge [kædʒ] vt (fam: money, cigarette etc): **to** ~ **(from)** scroccare (a); **to** ~ **a lift from sb** scroccare un passaggio a qn.

cadg·er ['kædʒəʳ] n (fam) scroccone/a.

Cae·sar·ean [siː'zɛərɪən] n (also: ~ **section**) (taglio) cesareo.

café ['kæfeɪ] n caffè m inv, bar m inv (senza licenza per alcolici).

caf·eteria [͵kæfɪ'tɪərɪə] n self-service m inv; (in factory etc) mensa.

caf·fein(e) ['kæfiːn] n caffeina.

cage [keɪdʒ] **1** n (gen, in mine) gabbia. **2** vt mettere in gabbia.

cag·ey ['keɪdʒɪ] adj (fam) riservato(a); **to give a** ~ **answer** essere cauto nel rispondere; **to be** ~ **about doing sth** essere riluttante a fare qc.

ca·hoots [kə'huːts] npl (fam): **to be in** ~ **with sb** essere in combutta con qn.

cairn [kɛən] n tumulo (di pietre), cumulo (di pietre).

Cai·ro ['kaɪərəʊ] n il Cairo.

ca·jole [kə'dʒəʊl] vt (coax) convincere con le buone; (: deceitfully) convincere con lusinghe; **to** ~ **sb into doing sth** convincere qn a fare qc.

cake [keɪk] **1** n **(a)** (large) torta; (small) pasticcino; **piece of** ~ fetta di torta; **it's a piece of** ~ (fam) è una cosa da nulla; **driving is a piece of** ~ per guidare non ci vuole niente; **to sell like hot** ~**s** (fam) andare a ruba; **he wants to have his** ~ **and eat it** (fig) vuole la botte piena e la moglie ubriaca. **(b)** (of chocolate etc) tavoletta; ~ **of soap** saponetta. **2** vt: **to** ~ **(with)** incrostare (di). **3** vi (blood) aggrumarsi; (mud) incrostarsi. **4** cpd: ~ **shop** n pasticceria.

cala·mine ['kæləmaɪn] n (also: ~ **lotion**) tipo di lozione calmante.

ca·lam·ity [kə'læmɪtɪ] n calamità f inv.

cal·ci·fy ['kælsɪfaɪ] **1** vt calcificare. **2** vi calcificarsi.

cal·cium ['kælsɪəm] n calcio (Chim).

cal·cu·late ['kælkjʊleɪt] **1** vt (cost, distance etc) calcolare; (estimate: chances, effect) valutare; **to be** ~**d to do sth** essere fatto or studiato per fare qc. **2** vi (Math) fare (i) conti.

♦ **calculate on** vi + prep: **to** ~ **on sth/on doing sth** contare su qc/di fare qc; **he hadn't** ~**d on the arrival of the night watchman** non aveva fatto i conti con l'arrivo del guardiano notturno.

cal·cu·lat·ed ['kælkjʊleɪtɪd] adj (insult, action) calcolato(a), intenzionale; **a** ~ **risk** un rischio calcolato.

cal·cu·lat·ing ['kælkjʊleɪtɪŋ] **1** adj (scheming) calcolatore(trice). **2** cpd: ~ **machine** n (macchina) calcolatrice f.

cal·cu·la·tion [͵kælkjʊ'leɪʃən] n calcolo.

cal·cu·la·tor ['kælkjʊleɪtəʳ] n calcolatore m.

cal·cu·lus ['kælkjʊləs] n analisi f infinitesimale.

cal·en·dar ['kæləndəʳ] **1** n calendario; **the Church** ~ il calendario ecclesiastico. **2** cpd: ~ **month** n mese m (di calendario).

calf[1] [kɑːf] n, pl **calves (a)** (young cow) vitello/a; **seal/elephant** etc ~ piccolo di foca/elefante etc. **(b)** = **calfskin**.

calf[2] [kɑːf] n, pl **calves** (Anat) polpaccio.

calf·skin ['kɑːfskɪn] n vitello.

cali·brate ['kælɪbreɪt] vt (gun etc) calibrare; (scale of measuring instrument) tarare.

cali·bra·tion [͵kælɪ'breɪʃən] n (see vb) calibratura; taratura.

cali·bre, (Am) cali·ber ['kælɪbəʳ] n (also fig) calibro.

cali·co ['kælɪkəʊ] n tela grezza, cotone m grezzo.

cali·pers ['kælɪpəz] npl (Am) = **callipers**.

call [kɔːl] **1** n **(a)** (cry) richiamo, grido; (of bird) canto; **to give a** ~ lanciare un grido; **within** ~ a portata di voce; **please give me a** ~ **at 7** per piacere mi chiami alle 7; **whose** ~ **is it?** (Cards) a chi tocca (giocare)?

(b) (Telec) telefonata, chiamata; **long-distance** ~ chiamata interurbana; **to make a** ~ telefonare, fare una telefonata.

(c) (summons: for flight etc) chiamata; (fig: lure) richiamo; **to be on** ~ essere a disposizione; **the** ~ **of the sea** il richiamo del mare; **to answer the** ~ **of duty** fare il proprio dovere.

(d) (visit: also Med) visita; **port of** ~ (porto di)

53

scalo; **to pay a ~ on sb** fare (una) visita a qn.

(e) *(need):* **I've not much ~ for this jacket** non mi serve molto questa giacca; **there's not much ~ for these items** non c'è molta richiesta di questi articoli; **you had no ~ to say that** non c'era nessun bisogno di dirlo; **there is no ~ for alarm** non ci sono motivi di allarme.

(f) *(claim):* **there are many ~s on my time** sono molto preso, ho molti impegni.

2 *vt* **(a)** chiamare; *(Telec)* chiamare, telefonare a; *(announce: flight)* annunciare; *(meeting, strike)* indire, proclamare; *(waken)* svegliare, chiamare.

(b) *(name)* chiamare; *(describe as)* considerare; **can I ~ you by your first name?** posso chiamarti per nome?; **what are you ~ed?** come ti chiami?; **would you ~ Italian a difficult language?** diresti che l'italiano è una lingua difficile?; **I ~ it an insult** questo lo chiamo un insulto, lo considero un insulto; **are you ~ing me a liar?** mi stai dando del bugiardo?; **let's ~ it £50** facciamo 50 sterline; **let's ~ it a day** *(fam)* smettiamo, basta per oggi.

3 *vi* **(a)** *(shout: person)* chiamare; *(bird)* lanciare un richiamo; **to ~ to sb** gridare a qn.

(b) *(Telec):* **who is ~ing?** chi parla?; **London ~ing** *(Radio)* qui Londra.

(c) *(visit)* passare.

♦ **call aside** *vt + adv* chiamare da parte.

♦ **call at** *vi + prep (subj: ship)* fare scalo a; *(: train)* fermarsi a.

♦ **call away** *vt + adv:* **to be ~ed away on business** dovere andare via per lavoro.

♦ **call back 1** *vt + adv (Telec)* ritelefonare a, richiamare. **2** *vi + adv (Telec)* ritelefonare, richiamare; *(return)* ritornare.

♦ **call for** *vi + prep (summon: wine, the bill)* chiedere; *(demand: courage, action etc)* richiedere; *(collect: person)* passare a prendere; *(: goods)* ritirare; **this ~s for a drink!** qui ci vuole un brindisi!

♦ **call in 1** *vt + adv* **(a)** *(doctor, expert, police)* chiamare, far venire. **(b)** *(Comm etc: faulty goods)* riprendere; *(: currency)* mettere fuori corso. **2** *vi + adv* = **call 3c.**

♦ **call off** *vt + adv* **(a)** *(meeting, race)* disdire, revocare; *(deal)* cancellare; **the strike was ~ed off** lo sciopero è stato revocato. **(b)** *(dog)* richiamare.

♦ **call on** *vi + prep* **(a)** *(visit)* far visita a, andare a trovare. **(b)** *(invite):* **to ~ on sb to do sth** invitare qn a fare qc; **I now ~ on Mr Brown to speak** ora invito il signor Brown a parlare.

♦ **call out 1** *vt + adv (doctor, police, troops)* chiamare; **to ~ workers out on strike** invitare gli operai allo sciopero. **2** *vi + adv (in pain)* urlare; *(to person)* chiamare; **to ~ out for help** invocare aiuto.

♦ **call round** *vi + adv* passare; **to ~ round to see sb** passare da qn.

♦ **call up** *vt + adv* **(a)** *(Mil)* richiamare, mobilitare. **(b)** *(Telec)* chiamare, telefonare a. **(c)** *(fig: memories)* richiamare, evocare.

♦ **call upon** *vi + prep* = **call on.**

call·box ['kɔːl‚bɒks] *n (Brit)* cabina telefonica.

cal·ler ['kɔːlə'] *n (visitor)* visitatore/trice; *(Telec):* **hold the line, ~!** rimanga in linea, signore *(or signora)*!

cal·lig·ra·phy [kə'lɪgrəfɪ] *n* calligrafia.

call·ing ['kɔːlɪŋ] *n* vocazione *f.*

cal·li·pers [*Am*] **cali·pers** ['kælɪpəz] *npl (Med)* gambale *m;* *(Math)* calibro.

cal·lous ['kæləs] *adj (person)* insensibile; *(remark)*

indelicato(a).

cal·low ['kæləʊ] *adj* immaturo(a).

call-up ['kɔːl‚ʌp] *n (Mil)* chiamata (alle armi).

calm [kɑːm] **1** *adj (gen)* calmo(a); *(weather)* sereno(a); **~ and collected** padrone di sé; **keep ~!** sta' calmo! **2** *n* calma, pace *f;* **the ~ before the storm** *(also fig)* la calma che precede la tempesta. **3** *vt (also:* **~ down:** *person)* calmare; **~ yourself!** calmati!

♦ **calm down 1** *vt + adv =* **calm 3. 2** *vi + adv* calmarsi.

calm·ly ['kɑːmlɪ] *adv* tranquillamente, con calma.

calo·rie ['kælərɪ] *n* caloria; **low-~ product** prodotto a basso contenuto di calorie.

calo·rif·ic [‚kælə'rɪfɪk] *adj:* **~ value** *(Phys)* valore *m* calorico.

cal·um·ny ['kæləmnɪ] *n (frm)* calunnia.

calve [kɑːv] *vi* figliare.

calves [kɑːvz] *npl of* **calf**[1] *and* **calf**[2].

cam·ber ['kæmbə'] *n (in road)* curvatura.

Cam·bo·dia [kæm'bəʊdɪə] *n* Cambogia.

came [keɪm] *pt of* **come.**

cam·el ['kæməl] **1** *n* cammello. **2** *adj (colour)* color cammello *inv.* **3** *cpd:* **~ coat** *n* cappotto di cammello.

ca·mel·lia [kə'miːlɪə] *n* camelia.

cameo ['kæmɪəʊ] **1** *n* cammeo. **2** *cpd (ring, brooch etc)* con cammeo.

cam·era ['kæmərə] *n* **(a)** macchina fotografica; *(movie ~)* cinepresa; *(Cine, TV)* telecamera. **(b)** *(Law):* **in ~** a porte chiuse.

camera·man ['kæmərə‚mæn] *n, pl* **-men** cameraman *m inv.*

camou·flage ['kæməflɑːʒ] **1** *n* mimetizzazione *f.* **2** *vt* mimetizzare.

camp[1] [kæmp] **1** *n (gen)* accampamento, campo; *(holiday ~)* campeggio; *(Pol etc)* campo, schieramento. **2** *vi* accamparsi; **to go ~ing** andare in campeggio. **3** *cpd:* **~ bed** *n* branda; **~ follower** *(fig)* simpatizzante *m/f;* **~ site** *n* (zona di) campeggio.

♦ **camp out** *vi + adv* attendarsi, campeggiare.

camp[2] [kæmp] *adj (fam: theatrical)* melodrammatico(a); *(: effeminate, homosexual)* effeminato(a).

cam·paign [kæm'peɪn] **1** *n* campagna. **2** *vi (Mil, fig):* **to ~ (for/against)** fare una campagna (per/contro).

cam·paign·er [kæm'peɪnə'] *n (Mil):* **old ~** veterano, vecchio combattente *m;* **~ for** fautore/trice di; **~ against** oppositore/trice di.

camp·er ['kæmpə'] *n (person)* campeggiatore/trice; *(vehicle)* camper *m inv.*

cam·phor ['kæmfə'] *n* canfora.

cam·pus ['kæmpəs] *n* campus *m inv.*

cam·shaft ['kæmʃæft] *n* albero a camme.

can[1] [kæn] *modal aux vb (neg* **cannot, can't;** *cond and pt* **could)** **(a)** *(be able to)* potere; **he ~ do it if he tries** è capace di farlo se si sforza; **I ~'t** *or* **~not go any further** non posso andare oltre; **I'll tell you all I ~** ti dirò tutto quello che posso; **they couldn't help it** non potevano farci niente; **she ~ be very annoying** lei a volte è molto seccante, lei riesce ad essere molto seccante; **she was as happy as could be** più felice di così non poteva essere.

(b) *(know how to)* essere capace di, sapere; **he ~'t swim** non sa nuotare, non è capace di nuotare; **~ you speak Italian?** parli italiano?

(c) *(may)* potere; **~ I use your telephone?** posso usare il tuo telefono?; **could I have a word with you?** potrei parlarti un attimo?; **~'t I come too?** non posso venire anch'io?

(d) *(expressing disbelief, puzzlement etc):* **this**

~'t be true! non può essere vero!; you ~'t be serious! scherzi?; she ~'t possibly marry that creep! *(fam)* non è possibile che sposi quell'essere!; how could you lie to me! come hai potuto dirmi una bugia!; they ~'t have left already! non è possibile che siano già partiti!; what CAN he want? cosa può mai volere?

(e) *(expressing possibility, suggestion etc)*: they could have forgotten potrebbero essersene dimenticati; he could be in the library può darsi che sia in biblioteca; I could cry/scream! potrei piangere/urlare!

(f) *(not translated)*: I ~'t see you non ti vedo; ~ you hear me? mi senti?

can² [kæn] **1** n *(container: for foodstuffs)* scatola; *(: for oil, water etc)* latta; *(esp Am: garbage ~)* bidone m; a ~ of beer una lattina di birra; to carry the ~ *(fam)* prendere la colpa. **2** vt *(food)* inscatolare.

Ca·na·da ['kænədə] n Canada m.

Ca·na·dian [kə'neɪdɪən] adj, n canadese *(m/f)*.

ca·nal [kə'næl] n canale m.

ca·nary [kə'nɛərɪ] **1** n canarino. **2** cpd: ~ yellow adj, n giallo canarino inv.

can·cel ['kænsəl] vt **(a)** *(call off: holiday, booking)* cancellare, annullare, disdire; *(meeting, event)* cancellare, sospendere; *(annul: order, contract)* annullare. **(b)** *(obliterate: name)* cancellare, radiare; *(: stamp)* timbrare, annullare; *(: cheque)* annullare. **(c)** *(Math)* semplificare.

♦ **cancel out 1** vt + adv *(Math)* semplificare; *(fig)* annullare; they ~ each other out *(anche fig)* si annullano a vicenda. **2** vi *(Math)* semplificarsi.

can·cel·la·tion [,kænsə'leɪʃən] n *(see vt a, c)* cancellazione f; annullamento; disdetta; sospensione f; semplificazione f.

can·cer ['kænsər] **1** n *(Med)* cancro; *(Astron, Geog)*: C~ Cancro; to be ~ *(Astrology)* essere del Cancro. **2** cpd: ~ patient n malato/a di cancro; ~ research n ricerca sul cancro.

can·cer·ous ['kænsərəs] adj canceroso(a).

can·de·la·bra [,kændɪ'lɑːbrə] n candelabro.

can·did ['kændɪd] adj franco(a).

can·di·da·cy ['kændɪdəsɪ] n candidatura.

can·di·date ['kændɪdeɪt] n candidato/a.

can·di·da·ture ['kændɪdətʃər] n = **candidacy.**

can·dle ['kændl] n candela; *(in church)* cero.

candle·light ['kændl,laɪt] n lume m di candela.

candle·stick ['kændl,stɪk] n candeliere m.

can·dour, *(Am)* **can·dor** ['kændər] n candore m, franchezza.

can·dy ['kændɪ] **1** n *(sugar ~)* caramella; *(Am: sweets)* dolciumi mpl. **2** vt *(fruit)* candire; **candied peel** scorzette di frutta candita.

candy·floss ['kændɪ,flɒs] n zucchero filato.

cane [keɪn] **1** n *(Bot)* canna; *(for baskets, chairs etc)* bambù m; *(stick: for walking)* bastone m (da passeggio); *(: for punishment)* bacchetta, verga; to get the ~ *(Scol)* prenderle con la bacchetta. **2** vt *(pupil)* picchiare con la bacchetta. **3** cpd: ~ chair n poltroncina di vimini; ~ sugar n zucchero di canna.

ca·nine ['keɪnaɪn] **1** adj canino(a). **2** n *(~ tooth)* (dente m) canino.

can·is·ter ['kænɪstər] n *(for tea, coffee)* barattolo *(metallico)*; *(for gas)* candelotto.

can·na·bis ['kænəbɪs] n canapa indiana.

canned [kænd] **1** pt, pp of **can².** **2** adj *(food)* in scatola; *(fam: recorded: music)* registrato(a); *(fam: drunk)* sbronzo(a).

can·ni·bal ['kænɪbəl] n cannibale m/f.

can·ni·bal·ize ['kænɪbəlaɪz] vt *(car etc)* smontare *(per usare alcuni singoli pezzi)*.

can·non ['kænən] **1** n, pl ~ or ~s cannone m. **2** cpd: ~ fodder n carne f da macello.

cannon·ball ['kænən,bɔːl] n palla di cannone.

can·not ['kænɒt] negative of **can¹.**

ca·noe [kə'nuː] **1** n canoa. **2** vi andare in canoa.

ca·noe·ist [kə'nuːɪst] n canoista m/f.

can·on ['kænən] **1** n *(Rel, Mus etc)* canone m; *(cleric)* canonico. **2** cpd: ~ law n *(Rel)* diritto canonico.

can·on·ize ['kænənaɪz] vt canonizzare.

cano·py ['kænəpɪ] n *(above bed, throne)* baldacchino.

cant [kænt] n *(jargon)* gergo; *(hypocritical talk)* discorsi mpl ipocriti.

can't [kɑːnt] abbr of **cannot;** see **can¹.**

can·tan·ker·ous [kæn'tæŋkərəs] adj irascibile.

can·teen [kæn'tiːn] n **(a)** *(restaurant)* mensa. **(b)**: a ~ of cutlery un servizio di posate.

can·ter ['kæntər] **1** n piccolo galoppo. **2** vi andare al piccolo galoppo.

can·ti·lever ['kæntɪliːvər] **1** n mensola. **2** cpd: ~ bridge n ponte m a mensola.

can·ton ['kæntən] n cantone m.

can·vas ['kænvəs] n tela; under ~ *(in a tent)* in tenda; *(Naut)* a vele spiegate.

can·vass ['kænvəs] **1** vt *(Pol: district)* fare un giro elettorale di; *(: person)* fare propaganda elettorale a; *(Comm: district)* fare un'indagine di mercato in; *(: citizens, opinions)* fare un sondaggio di. **2** vi *(Pol)* raccogliere voti; *(Comm)* fare il piazzista.

can·vass·er ['kænvəsər] n *(Pol)* propagandista m/f *(elettorale)*; *(Comm)* agente m viaggiatore, piazzista m.

can·yon ['kænjən] n canyon m inv.

cap [kæp] **1** n **(a)** *(hat)* berretto; *(for swimming)* cuffia; ~ in hand *(fig)* umilmente; if the ~ fits wear it chi ha orecchie per intendere intenda; he's got his ~ for England *(Sport)* è stato scelto per la nazionale inglese. **(b)** *(of bottle, radiator etc)* tappo; *(of pen)* cappuccio; *(contraceptive)* diaframma m. **2** vt *(a)* *(bottle etc)* tappare; *(tooth)* ricoprire; *(surpass: story, joke)* superare, essere meglio di; **and to ~ it all, he...** e per completare l'opera, lui.... **(b)** *(Ftbl etc)*: he's been ~ped 15 times for England ha rappresentato l'Inghilterra 15 volte.

ca·pa·bil·ity [,keɪpə'bɪlətɪ] n *(no pl: competence)* capacità, competenza; *(potential ability)* possibilità f inv.

ca·pable ['keɪpəbl] adj **(a)** *(competent)* capace, abile. **(b)** *(able to)*: ~ of (doing) sth in grado di fare qc; your son's ~ of doing better at school suo figlio potrebbe riuscire meglio a scuola; she's quite ~ of letting someone else take the blame sarebbe capace di dar la colpa a un altro.

ca·pac·ity [kə'pæsɪtɪ] **1** n **(a)** *(Elec, Phys, of container etc)* capacità; **seating** ~ capienza; **filled to** ~ pieno zeppo; **to work at full** ~ *(factory etc)* lavorare a pieno ritmo. **(b)** *(position)* posizione f, funzione f; **in my** ~ **as chairman** nella mia veste di presidente; **in an advisory** ~ a titolo consultativo; **in his official** ~ nell'esercizio delle sue funzioni. **(c)** *(ability)* capacità; **this work is beyond my** ~ questo lavoro supera le mie possibilità. **2** cpd: ~ audience n sala piena.

cape¹ [keɪp] n *(Geog)* capo; C~ of Good Hope Capo di Buona Speranza.

cape² [keɪp] n *(garment)* cappa; *(of policeman, cyclist)* mantella.

ca·per¹ ['keɪpər] n *(Culin)* cappero.

ca·per² ['keɪpər] **1** n *(escapade)* scherzetto. **2** vi *(child)* saltellare.

ca·pil·lary [kə'pɪlərɪ] adj, n capillare *(m)*.

capi·tal ['kæpɪtl] 1 *adj* (a) *(letter)* maiuscolo(a). (b) *(Law)*: ~ **offence** delitto passibile di pena capitale; ~ **punishment** pena capitale. (c) *(old: idea)* meraviglioso(a), splendido(a). 2 *n (also:* ~ **letter)** *(lettera)* maiuscola; *(also:* ~ **city)** capitale *f; (Fin)* capitale *m;* **to make** ~ **out of sth** *(fig)* sfruttare qc. 3 *cpd:* ~ **assets** *npl* capitale *m* fisso; ~ **expenditure** *n* spese *fpl* in capitale; ~ **gains tax** *n* imposta sulla plusvalenza.

capi·tal·ism ['kæpɪtəlɪzəm] *n* capitalismo.

capi·tal·ist ['kæpɪtəlɪst] *adj, n* capitalista *(m/f)*.

capi·tal·ize ['kæpɪtəlaɪz] *vt* (a) *(Fin: provide with capital)* capitalizzare. (b) *(letter)* scrivere maiuscolo.

♦ **capitalize on** *vi + prep (fig)* trarre vantaggio da.

ca·pitu·late [kə'pɪtjʊleɪt] *vi* capitolare.

ca·price [kə'priːs] *n* capriccio.

ca·pri·cious [kə'prɪʃəs] *adj* capriccioso(a).

Cap·ri·corn ['kæprɪkɔːn] *n* Capricorno; **to be** ~ essere del Capricorno.

cap·size [kæp'saɪz] 1 *vt* ribaltare. 2 *vi* ribaltarsi.

cap·stan ['kæpstən] *n (Naut)* argano.

cap·sule ['kæpsjuːl] *n* capsula.

cap·tain ['kæptɪn] 1 *n* capitano; ~ **of industry** capitano d'industria. 2 *vt (team)* essere capitano di, capitanare; *(ship)* comandare.

cap·tion ['kæpʃən] *n (heading)* sottotitolo; *(to cartoon etc)* didascalia.

cap·ti·vate ['kæptɪveɪt] *vt* affascinare, incantare.

cap·tive ['kæptɪv] 1 *adj (person)* prigioniero(a); *(animal)* in cattività; **he had a** ~ **audience** il pubblico era ben obbligato ad ascoltarlo. 2 *n* prigioniero/a; **to hold sb** ~ tenere prigioniero qn.

cap·tiv·ity [kæp'tɪvɪtɪ] *n* prigionia; *(of animal)* cattività.

cap·tor ['kæptəʳ] *n (lawful)* chi ha catturato; *(unlawful)* rapitore *m;* **he managed to escape from his** ~**s** riuscì a sfuggire a quelli che l'avevano catturato.

cap·ture ['kæptʃəʳ] 1 *n (of animal, soldier, escapee)* cattura; *(of city etc)* presa; *(thing caught)* preda. 2 *vt (animal)* catturare; *(escapee, soldier)* catturare, far prigioniero; *(city etc)* prendere; *(fig: attention)* cattivare, attirare; *(Art: atmosphere etc)* cogliere, rendere.

car [kɑːʳ] 1 *n* (a) *(Aut)* macchina, automobile *f,* auto *f inv;* **by** ~ in macchina. (b) *(esp Am: in train)* carrozza; *(: in tram)* vettura. 2 *cpd:* ~ **ferry** *n* ferry-boat *m inv,* nave *f* traghetto *inv;* ~ **park** *n* parcheggio.

ca·rafe [kə'ræf] *n* caraffa.

cara·mel ['kærəməl] 1 *n* caramello; *(sweet)* caramella. 2 *cpd (custard, flavouring)* al caramello.

car·at ['kærət] *n* carato; **18** ~ **gold** oro a 18 carati.

cara·van ['kærəvæn] 1 *n* (a) *(gipsies')* carrozzone *m; (Brit Aut)* roulotte *f inv.* (b) *(in desert)* carovana. 2 *vi* viaggiare con la roulotte.

cara·way ['kærəweɪ] *n* cumino (dei prati).

car·bo·hy·drate ['kɑːbəʊ'haɪdreɪt] *n* carboidrato.

car·bol·ic [kɑː'bɒlɪk] *adj:* ~ **acid** acido fenico, fenolo.

car·bon ['kɑːbən] 1 *n (Chem)* carbonio; *(also:* ~ **paper)** carta carbone. 2 *cpd:* ~ **copy** *n (Typing)* copia (in carta carbone); *(fig)* copia carbone; **he's a** ~ **copy of his father** è tutto suo padre, è la copia carbone di suo padre; ~ **dioxide** *n* diossido di carbonio; ~ **monoxide** *n* monossido di carbonio.

car·bon·ated ['kɑːbəˌneɪtəd] *adj (drink)* gassato(a).

car·bon·ize ['kɑːbənaɪz] *vt* carbonizzare.

car·bun·cle ['kɑːbʌŋkl] *n (Med)* foruncolo.

car·bu·ret·tor [ˌkɑːbjʊ'retəʳ] *n* carburatore *m.*

car·cass, car·case ['kɑːkəs] *n (of animal)* carcassa.

car·cino·gen·ic [ˌkɑːsɪnə'dʒɛnɪk] *adj* cancerogeno(a).

card [kɑːd] 1 *n (greetings* ~, *visiting* ~ *etc)* biglietto; *(membership* ~) tessera; *(index* ~) scheda; *(playing* ~) carta (da gioco); *(thin cardboard)* cartoncino; **to play** ~**s** giocare a carte; **it's on the** ~**s** *(fig)* è probabile; **to lay one's** ~**s on the table** *(also fig)* mettere le carte in tavola; **to play one's** ~**s right** *(fig)* giocare bene le proprie carte. 2 *cpd:* ~ **game** *n* gioco di carte; ~ **index** *n* schedario; ~ **table** *n* tavolo da carte.

car·da·mom ['kɑːdəməm] *n* cardamomo.

card·board ['kɑːd,bɔːd] 1 *n* cartone *m.* 2 *cpd:* ~ **box** *n* (scatola di) cartone *m.*

car·di·ac ['kɑːdɪæk] *adj* cardiaco(a); ~ **arrest** arresto cardiaco.

car·di·gan ['kɑːdɪgən] *n* cardigan *m inv.*

car·di·nal ['kɑːdɪnl] *adj, n* cardinale *(m).*

care [kɛəʳ] 1 *n* (a) *(anxiety)* preoccupazione *f;* **he hasn't a** ~ **in the world** non ha preoccupazioni di sorta; **the** ~**s of State** i problemi di Stato. (b) *(carefulness)* attenzione *f; (charge)* cura, custodia; **'with** ~**'** *'fragile'*; **to take** ~ **to do sth** fare attenzione a *or* badare a fare qc; **take** ~! *(as warning)* (stai) attento!; *(as good wishes)* stammi bene!; **to take** ~ **of** *(details, arrangements)* occuparsi di; **to take** ~ **of sb** badare a qn, curare qn; **I'll take** ~ **of him!** *(fam)* ora se la vede con me!, adesso mi sente!; **she can take** ~ **of herself** si arrangia da sola; **take** ~ **not to drop it!** stai attento a non farlo cadere!; ~ **of** *(abbr* c/o: *on letter)* presso *(abbr* c/o); **I'm leaving it in your** ~ te lo affido; **the child has been taken into** ~ il bambino è stato preso in custodia.

2 *vi (be concerned):* **to** ~ **(about)** interessarsi (di), preoccuparsi (di); **I don't** ~ non m'importa; **to** ~ **deeply about** tenere molto a; **for all I** ~ per quello che mi interessa; **who** ~**s?** chi se ne importa?

3 *vt* (a) *(be concerned):* **I don't** ~ **what you think** non mi interessa quello che pensi; **I couldn't** ~ **less what people say** me ne infischio di quel che dice la gente. (b) *(frm: like)* volere, desiderare; **would you** ~ **to come this way?** vorrebbe venire da questa parte?; **I shouldn't** ~ **to meet him** non vorrei davvero a incontrarlo.

♦ **care for** *vi + prep* (a) *(look after)* curare. (b) *(like)* volere; **it's the most expensive model, but I don't** ~ **much for it** è il modello più costoso, ma non ci tengo ad averlo; **I don't** ~ **for coffee** non amo particolarmente il caffè; **would you** ~ **for a drink?** gradiresti qualcosa da bere?; **she no longer** ~**s for him** non le importa più niente di lui.

ca·reer [kə'rɪəʳ] 1 *n (occupation)* professione *f; (working life)* carriera. 2 *vi (also:* ~ **along)** sfrecciare. 3 *cpd (diplomat, soldier etc)* di carriera; ~ **girl** *n* donna dedita alla carriera; ~**s officer** *n* consulente *m/f* d'orientamento professionale.

care·free ['kɛəfriː] *adj* spensierato(a).

care·ful ['kɛəfʊl] *adj* (a) *(taking care, cautious)* attento(a); **(be)** ~! (stai) attento!; **to be** ~ **with sth** fare attenzione a qc; **he's very** ~ **with his money** bada molto alle spese; **be** ~ **what you say to him** stai attento a come gli parli; **he was** ~ **not to offend her** badava di non offenderla. (b) *(painstaking: work)* accurato(a); *(: writer, worker etc)* attento(a), diligente, zelante.

care·ful·ly ['kɛəfʊlɪ] *adv (see adj)* attentamente, con attenzione; accuratamente.

care·ful·ness ['kɛəfʊlnɪs] *n (see adj)* attenzione *f;* accuratezza.

care·less ['kɛəlɪs] *adj (worker, driver, driving)* distratto(a), disattento(a); *(work)* fatto(a) con poco impegno; *(thoughtless: remark)* senza tatto; ~ **mistake** errore *m* di distrazione.

care·less·ly ['kɛəlɪslɪ] *adv (see adj)* con disattenzione, distrattamente; con poco impegno; senza tatto.

care·less·ness ['kɛəlɪsnɪs] *n (see adj)* disattenzione *f*; mancanza d'impegno; mancanza di tatto.

ca·ress [kə'rɛs] **1** *n* carezza. **2** *vt* carezzare, accarezzare.

care·taker ['kɛə,teɪkə'] *n* **1** portinaio/a. **2** *cpd:* ~ **government** *n* governo *m* ponte *inv.*

care·worn ['kɛəwɔ:n] *adj* sciupato(a) *(dalle preoccupazioni).*

car·go ['kɑ:gəʊ] **1** *n* carico. **2** *cpd:* ~ **boat** *n* cargo.

Car·ib·bean [kærɪ'bi:ən] *adj, n:* **the** ~ **(Sea)** il mar dei Caraibi.

cari·ca·ture ['kærɪkətjʊə'] **1** *n* caricatura. **2** *vt* fare una caricatura di.

cari·es ['kɛərɪːz] *n (frm)* carie *f.*

car·nage ['kɑ:nɪdʒ] *n* carneficina.

car·nal ['kɑ:nl] *adj* carnale.

car·na·tion [kɑ:'neɪʃən] *n* garofano.

car·ni·val ['kɑ:nɪvəl] *n* carnevale *m.*

car·ni·vore ['kɑ:nɪvɔ:'] *n* carnivoro.

car·nivo·rous [kɑ:'nɪvərəs] *adj* carnivoro(a).

car·ol ['kærəl] *n* canto di Natale.

ca·rouse [kə'raʊz] *vi* far baldoria.

carou·sel [,kæru'sɛl] *n (Am)* giostra.

carp¹ [kɑ:p] *n (fish)* carpa.

carp² [kɑ:p] *vi (complain):* **to** ~ **at** avere da ridire su.

car·pen·ter ['kɑ:pɪntə'] *n* carpentiere *m.*

car·pen·try ['kɑ:pɪntrɪ] *n* carpenteria.

car·pet ['kɑ:pɪt] **1** *n* tappeto; *(fitted ~)* moquette *f inv.* **2** *vt (floor, house)* coprire di tappeti; *(: with fitted ~)* rivestire di moquette. **3** *cpd:* ~ **slippers** *npl* pantofole *fpl;* ~ **sweeper** *n* battitappeto *m inv.*

car·riage ['kærɪdʒ] *n* **(a)** *(Brit Rail)* carrozza, vagone *m; (horse-drawn)* carrozza; *(of typewriter)* carrello. **(b)** *(of person: bearing)* portamento. **(c)** *(Comm: transporting)* trasporto; *(cost of ~)* (spese *fpl* di) trasporto; ~ **free** franco di porto; ~ **paid** trasporto già pagato; ~ **return** *n (on typewriter)* leva *(or* tasto) del ritorno a capo.

carriage·way ['kærɪdʒ,weɪ] *n (Aut)* carreggiata.

car·ri·er ['kærɪə'] *n* **(a)** *(of goods: person)* corriere *m; (: company)* impresa di trasporti; **by** ~ per corriere. **(b)** *(Med: of disease)* portatore/trice. **(c)** *(aircraft ~)* portaerei *f inv;* **troop** ~ *(Aer/Naut)* aereo/nave *f* per trasporto truppe. **(d)** *(Brit: also:* ~ **bag)** sacchetto, borsa (di plastica).

car·ri·on ['kærɪən] *n* carogna.

car·rot ['kærət] *n* carota.

car·ry ['kærɪ] **1** *vt* **(a)** *(gen)* portare; *(have on one's person: money, documents)* portare, avere con sé; *(transport: goods)* trasportare; *(: passengers)* portare; *(message, news)* recare, portare; *(subj: pillar)* sostenere; **to** ~ **sth about with one** portarsi dietro qc; **the wind carried the sound to him** il vento gli portò il suono; **the offence carries a £50 fine** il reato prevede una multa di 50 sterline; **both papers carried the story** tutt'e due i giornali riportarono la storia; **he carries his drink well** regge bene l'alcool; **you're ~ing things too far!** *(fig)* stai esagerando!

(b) *(Comm: goods)* tenere.

(c) *(Math: figure)* riportare; *(Fin: interest)* avere; **this loan carries 10% interest** questo prestito è sulla base di un interesse del 10%.

(d) *(approve: motion)* approvare; *(win: election, point)* vincere; **to** ~ **the day** avere successo.

(e): **he carries himself like a soldier** ha il portamento di un militare; **she carries herself well** ha un bel portamento.

2 *vi (sound)* trasmettersi, diffondersi.

♦ **carry away** *vt + adv* portare via; **to get carried away by sth** *(fig)* farsi *or* lasciarsi prendere da qc.

♦ **carry back** *vt + adv (also fig: remind)* riportare.

♦ **carry forward** *vt + adv (Math, Fin)* riportare.

♦ **carry off** *vt + adv (seize, take away)* portare via; *(kidnap)* sequestrare; *(win: prize, medal)* vincere; **he carried it off very well** se l'è cavata molto bene.

♦ **carry on 1** *vt + adv (continue: tradition etc)* portare avanti, continuare; *(conduct: conversation)* continuare, proseguire; *(: business, trade)* mandare avanti. **2** *vi + adv* **(a)** *(continue)* continuare. **(b)** *(fam: make a fuss)* fare storie; **how you do ~ on!** quante storie fai! **(c)** *(fam: have an affair):* **to** ~ **on (with)** intendersela (con), filare (con).

♦ **carry out** *vt + adv (accomplish etc: plan)* realizzare; *(perform, implement: idea, threat)* mettere in pratica; *(: orders)* eseguire; *(: experiment, search, repairs)* effettuare.

♦ **carry through** *vt + adv (accomplish: task)* portare a termine, realizzare; *(sustain: person)* sostenere.

carry·cot ['kærɪkɒt] *n* porte-enfant *m inv.*

carry-on [,kærɪ'ɒn] *n (fam: fuss)* casino, confusione *f.*

car·sick ['kɑ:sɪk] *adj:* **to be** ~ soffrire il mal d'auto.

cart [kɑ:t] **1** *n* carretto; **to put the** ~ **before the horse** *(fig)* mettere il carro davanti ai buoi. **2** *vt (fam)* trascinare, scarrozzare.

carte blanche ['kɑ:t'blɑ̃ʃ] *n:* **to give sb** ~ dare carta bianca a qn.

car·tel [kɑ:'tɛl] *n (Comm)* cartello.

car·ti·lage ['kɑ:tɪlɪdʒ] *n* cartilagine *f.*

car·tog·ra·phy [kɑ:'tɒgrəfɪ] *n* cartografia.

car·ton ['kɑ:tən] *n (of milk, yogurt)* cartone *m; (of ice cream)* vaschetta; *(of cigarettes)* stecca.

car·toon [kɑ:'tu:n] *n (in newspaper etc)* vignetta; *(Cine, TV)* cartone *m* animato; *(sketch for fresco etc)* cartone *m.*

car·toon·ist [,kɑ:'tu:nɪst] *n (in newspaper etc)* vignettista *m/f; (Cine, TV)* autore *m* di cartoni animati.

car·tridge ['kɑ:trɪdʒ] **1** *n (for gun, pen)* cartuccia; *(for camera)* caricatore *m.* **2** *cpd:* ~ **paper** *n* carta da disegno (ruvida).

cart·wheel ['kɑ:t,wi:l] *n:* **to turn a** ~ *(Sport etc)* fare la ruota.

carve [kɑ:v] **1** *vt (Culin: meat)* tagliare; *(stone, wood)* scolpire; *(name on tree etc)* incidere; **to** ~ **out a career for o.s.** farsi una carriera. **2** *vi (Culin)* tagliare la carne.

♦ **carve up** *vt + adv (meat)* tagliare; *(fig: country)* suddividere.

carv·er ['kɑ:və'] *n,* **carv·ing knife** ['kɑ:vɪŋ,naɪf] *n* trinciante *m.*

cas·cade [kæs'keɪd] **1** *n* cascata. **2** *vi* scendere a cascata; **her hair** ~**d over her shoulders** i capelli le ricadevano sulle spalle.

case¹ [keɪs] *n* **(a)** *(suitcase)* valigia; *(packing ~)* cassa, cassetta; *(for camera)* custodia; *(for jewellery)* scatolina, astuccio; *(for spectacles etc)* custodia, astuccio; *(display ~)* vetrinetta; *(of watch)* cassa. **(b)** *(Typ):* **lower/upper** ~ (carattere *m)* minuscolo/maiuscolo.

case² [keɪs] **1** *n* **(a)** *(gen, Med, Gram)* caso; **the doctor has many** ~**s to see today** il dottore oggi deve vedere molti pazienti; **in any** ~ in ogni caso, comunque; **in that** ~ in quel caso; **(just) in** ~ non si sa mai; **I think she knows you're coming, but just in** ~**,** you'd better phone her penso che sappia che stai arrivando ma, per sicurezza *or* per ogni evenienza, faresti meglio a telefonarle; **in** ~ **of emergency** in caso di emergenza; **a** ~ **in point** un esempio tipico; **it's a clear** ~ **of murder** è un chiaro caso di omicidio; **in most** ~**s** nella maggior parte dei casi, in genere; **it's generally the** ~ **that people are selfish** di solito succede che la gente sia egoista; **as this was the** ~**,** we decided not to go stando così le cose, decidemmo di non andare; **if that is the** ~ quand'è così, se così è; **as the** ~ **may be** a seconda del caso.

(b) *(Law)* caso, causa; *(argument)* motivo, ragione *f;* **the** ~ **for the defence/prosecution** le ragioni *or* argomentazioni della difesa/dell'accusa; **to state one's** ~ perorare la propria causa; *(fig)* dire le proprie ragioni; **to have a good** ~ avere pretese legittime; **there's a strong** ~ **for reform** ci sono validi argomenti a favore della riforma.

2 *cpd:* ~ **history** *n (Med)* cartella clinica; ~ **law** *n* giurisprudenza basata su sentenze precedenti.

case·work ['keɪs,wɜːk] *n (Sociol)* assistenza sociale *(ristretto allo studio dei casi individuali)*.

cash [kæʃ] 1 *n* **(a)** *(coins, notes)* soldi *mpl*, denaro; **to pay (in)** ~ pagare in contanti; **ready** ~ *(fam)* (denaro) contante *m;* ~ **in hand** coi soldi in tasca. **(b)** *(immediate payment):* **to pay** ~ **down** pagare in contanti; ~ **on delivery** *(abbr* **C.O.D.**) pagamento alla consegna. **(c)** *(fam: money)* quattrini *mpl;* **he's got plenty of** ~ ha un sacco di quattrini; **to be short of** ~ essere a corto di soldi. 2 *vt (cheque)* riscuotere, incassare. 3 *cpd:* ~ **desk** *n* cassa; ~ **dispenser** *n* sportello automatico; ~ **flow** *n* cash-flow *m inv*, liquidità *f inv;* ~ **payment** *n* pagamento in contanti; ~ **prize** *n* premio in denaro; ~ **register** *n* registratore *m* di cassa; ~ **sale** *n* vendita per contanti.

♦ **cash in** 1 *vt + adv (insurance policy etc)* riscuotere, riconvertire. 2 *vi + adv:* **to** ~ **in on sth** sfruttare qc.

cash-and-carry ['kæʃənd'kærɪ] *n* cash and carry *m inv*.

cash·ew [kæ'ʃuː] *n (also:* ~ **nut)** anacardio.

cash·ier [kæ'ʃɪər] *n* cassiere/a.

cash·mere [kæʃ'mɪər] 1 *n* cachemire *m inv*. 2 *cpd* di cachemire.

cas·ing ['keɪsɪŋ] *n (Tech)* rivestimento; *(of tyre)* copertone *m*.

ca·si·no [kə'siːnəʊ] *n* casinò *m inv*.

cask [kɑːsk] *n* barile *m*, botte *f*.

cas·ket ['kɑːskɪt] *n (for jewels)* scrigno; *(Am: coffin)* bara.

cas·se·role ['kæsərəʊl] *n (utensil)* casseruola (a due manici); *(food):* **chicken/veal** ~ pollo/vitello in casseruola.

cas·sette [kæ'sɛt] 1 *n* cassetta. 2 *cpd:* ~ **deck** *n* piastra di registrazione; ~ **recorder** *n* registratore *m* a cassette.

cas·sock ['kæsək] *n* tonaca.

cast [kɑːst] *(vb: pt, pp* **cast)** 1 *n* **(a)** *(Fishing)* lancio. **(b)** *(mould)* stampo; *(Med: plaster* ~) gesso; ~ **of mind** mentalità *f inv*. **(c)** *(of play etc)* cast *m inv*. **(d)** *(Med: squint)* strabismo; **he has a** ~ **in his right eye** ha l'occhio destro strabico. 2 *vt* **(a)** *(also fig: throw)* gettare; *(fishing line)* lanciare; *(shadow, light)* gettare, proiettare; **to** ~ **doubts on sth** far sorgere dubbi su qc; **to** ~ **one's vote** votare; **to** ~ **one's eyes over sth** dare un'occhiata

a qc. **(b)** *(shed)* spogliarsi di; *(horseshoe)* perdere; **the snake** ~ **its skin** il serpente ha cambiato la pelle. **(c)** *(metal)* colare; *(plaster)* gettare; *(bronze etc statue)* fondere. **(d)** *(part)* affidare; *(actor)* scritturare; **he was** ~ **as Macbeth** gli affidarono il ruolo di Macbeth. 3 *cpd:* ~ **iron** *n* = cast-iron 2.

♦ **cast about for** *vi + prep* cercare di trovare.

♦ **cast aside** *vt + adv (reject)* mettere da parte.

♦ **cast away** *vt + adv (Naut):* **to be** ~ **away** naufragare.

♦ **cast down** *vt + adv:* **to be** ~ **down** essere giù (di corda), essere depresso(a).

♦ **cast off** 1 *vt + adv (Naut)* disormeggiare; *(Knitting)* diminuire, calare. 2 *vi + adv (Naut)* levare gli ormeggi; *(Knitting)* diminuire, calare.

♦ **cast on** *(Knitting)* 1 *vt + adv* avviare. 2 *vi + adv* avviare (le maglie).

♦ **cast up** *vt + adv:* **to** ~ **sth up (at sb)** rinfacciare qc (a qn).

cas·ta·nets [,kæstə'nɛts] *npl* castagnette *fpl*, nacchere *fpl*.

cast·away ['kɑːstəweɪ] *n* naufrago/a.

caste [kɑːst] 1 *n* casta. 2 *cpd* di casta.

cast·er ['kɑːstər] *n (wheel)* rotella.

cast·er sug·ar ['kɑːstər,ʃʊgər] *n* zucchero semolato.

cas·ti·gate ['kæstɪgeɪt] *vt (frm)* castigare, punire.

cast·ing vote ['kɑːstɪŋ'vəʊt] *n* voto decisivo.

cast-iron ['kɑːst,aɪən] 1 *adj* di ghisa; *(fig: will, alibi)* di ferro, d'acciaio; **the police had a** ~ **case against the drug smuggler** la polizia aveva prove schiaccianti contro lo spacciatore di droga. 2 [,kɑːst'aɪən] *n* ghisa.

cas·tle ['kɑːsl] *n* castello; *(Chess)* torre *f;* ~**s in the air** *(fig)* castelli in aria.

cast-off ['kɑːst,ɒf] 1 *adj (clothing etc)* smesso(a). 2 ['kɑːstɒf] *n (garment)* indumento *or* vestito smesso.

cas·tor ['kɑːstər] *n* = caster.

cas·tor oil ['kɑːstər'ɔɪl] *n* olio di ricino.

cas·trate [kæs'treɪt] *vt* castrare.

cas·ual ['kæʒjʊl] 1 *adj* **(a)** *(by chance: meeting)* fortuito(a), casuale; *(: walk, stroll)* senza meta precisa; *(: glance)* di sfuggita; *(: remark)* fatto(a) di sfuggita; **we're just** ~ **acquaintances** ci conosciamo solo di vista. **(b)** *(offhand: attitude, person)* noncurante, disinvolto(a); **he was very** ~ **about it** ci si è mostrato indifferente. **(c)** *(informal: discussion, tone etc)* informale; *(: clothing)* sportivo(a), casual *inv*. **(d)** *(irregular: labour)* saltuario(a); *(: worker)* saltuario(a), avventizio(a). 2: ~**s** *npl (shoes)* scarpe *fpl* sportive.

casu·al·ly ['kæʒjʊlɪ] *adv (see adj* **a, b, c)** casualmente; senza meta precisa; di sfuggita; con noncuranza, in modo informale; in modo sportivo.

casu·al·ty ['kæʒjʊltɪ] 1 *n (Mil: dead)* vittima, caduto; *(: wounded)* ferito; *(in accident)* vittima. 2 *cpd:* ~ **ward** *n* pronto soccorso.

cat [kæt] *n* gatto/a; *(species)* felino; **that's put the** ~ **among the pigeons!** ha suscitato un vespaio; **that's let the** ~ **out of the bag** questo non è più un segreto; **like a** ~ **on hot bricks** sulle spine, come un'anima in pena; **to fight like** ~ **and dog** essere come cane e gatto; **when the** ~**'s away the mice will play** quando il gatto non c'è i topi ballano.

cata·clysm ['kætəklɪzəm] *n* cataclisma *m*.

cata·combs ['kætəkuːmz] *npl* catacombe *fpl*.

cata·logue, *(Am)* **cata·log** ['kætəlɒg] 1 *n* catalogo. 2 *vt* catalogare.

cata·lyst ['kætəlɪst] *n* catalizzatore *m*.

cata·ma·ran [,kætəmə'ræn] *n* catamarano.

cata·pult ['kætəpʌlt] 1 *n (slingshot)* fionda, *(Mil,*

Aer) catapulta. **2** *vt* catapultare.
cata·ract ['kætərækt] *n (Geog, Med)* cateratta.
ca·tarrh [kə'tɑːʳ] *n* catarro.
ca·tas·tro·phe [kə'tæstrəfɪ] *n* catastrofe *f.*
cata·stroph·ic [ˌkætə'strɒfɪk] *adj* catastrofico(a).
cat·call ['kæt,kɔːl] **1** *n (at meeting etc)* fischio. **2** *vi* fischiare.
catch [kætʃ] *(vb: pt, pp* **caught**) **1** *n* **(a)** *(of ball etc)* presa; *(of trawler)* retata; **he spent all day fishing without a single** ~ passò tutta la giornata a pescare senza prendere niente; **he's a good** ~ *(fig)* è un buon partito.
(b) *(fastener: on suitcase, door etc)* gancio, fermo.
(c) *(trick, snag)* tranello, trabocchetto; **where's the** ~? dove sta l'inganno?
(d): with a ~ **in one's voice** con la voce spezzata *or* rotta.
2 *vt* **(a)** *(ball)* afferrare, prendere; *(fish)* prendere, pescare; *(thief)* prendere, acciuffare; *(bus, train etc)* prendere; **I caught my fingers in the door** ho chiuso le dita nella porta; **I caught my coat on that nail** mi si è impigliato il cappotto in quel chiodo; **to** ~ **sb's attention/eye** attirare l'attenzione/lo sguardo di qn.
(b) *(take by surprise)* cogliere, sorprendere; **to** ~ **sb doing sth** sorprendere qn a fare qc; **you won't catch me doing...** non mi vedrai mai fare...; **caught in the act** colto sul fatto; **caught in the rain** sorpreso dalla pioggia.
(c) *(hear, understand: remark)* sentire, cogliere; *(portray: atmosphere, likeness)* cogliere.
(d) *(disease)* contrarre, prendere; *(hit)* colpire; **to** ~ **cold** prendere freddo; **the punch caught him on the chin** è stato colpito al mento; **to** ~ **one's breath** *(from shock etc)* restare col fiato mozzato; *(after effort)* tirare il fiato; **you'll** ~ **it!** *(fam)* vedrai!
3 *vi* **(a)** *(get entangled)* impigliarsi, restare impigliato(a).
(b) *(fire, wood)* prendere, attaccare.
4 *cpd:* ~ **phrase** *n* slogan *m*, frase *f* di moda; ~ **question** *n* domanda *f* trabocchetto *inv.*
♦ **catch at** *vi + prep (object)* afferrare; *(opportunity)* cogliere.
♦ **catch on** *vi + adv* **(a)** *(become popular)* affermarsi, far presa. **(b)** *(understand)*: **to** ~ **on (to sth)** capire (qc).
♦ **catch out** *vt + adv (fig: with trick question)* cogliere in fallo; **to** ~ **sb out in a lie** dimostrare che qn mente.
♦ **catch up 1** *vt + adv (snatch up)* afferrare; **to** ~ **sb up** *(walking, working etc)* raggiungere qn. **2** *vi + adv:* **to** ~ **up with sb** raggiungere qn; **to** ~ **up on one's work** mettersi in pari col lavoro; **to** ~ **up with the news** aggiornarsi.
catch·ing ['kætʃɪŋ] *adj (Med, fig)* contagioso(a).
catch·ment area ['kætʃmənt,ɛərɪə] *n (Scol)* comprensorio, zona di competenza.
catch-22 ['kætʃ,twentɪ'tuː] *n*: **it's a** ~ **situation** non c'è via d'uscita.
catchy ['kætʃɪ] *adj (tune)* orecchiabile.
cat·echism ['kætɪkɪzəm] *n* catechismo.
cat·egori·cal [ˌkætɪ'gɒrɪkəl] *adj* categorico(a).
cat·ego·rize ['kætɪgəraɪz] *vt* catalogare, classificare.
cat·ego·ry ['kætɪgərɪ] *n* categoria.
ca·ter ['keɪtəʳ] *vi:* **to** ~ **for (a)** *(provide food)* provvedere alla ristorazione di. **(b)** *(Am:* ~ **to:** *fig)* provvedere a; **to** ~ **for sb's needs** provvedere ai bisogni di qn; **to** ~ **for all tastes** cercare di soddisfare tutti i gusti.

ca·ter·er ['keɪtərəʳ] *n* persona che si occupa di catering.
cat·er·pil·lar ['kætəpɪləʳ] **1** *n (Zool)* bruco; *(vehicle)* (veicolo) cingolato. **2** *cpd:* ~ **track** *n* cingolo.
ca·the·dral [kə'θiːdrəl] *n* cattedrale *f.*
cath·erine wheel ['kæθərɪn,wiːl] *n* girandola.
cath·ode ['kæθəʊd] *n* catodo.
cathode-ray tube ['kæθəʊd,reɪ'tjuːb] *n* tubo a raggi catodici.
Catho·lic ['kæθəlɪk] *(Rel)* **1** *adj (Roman* ~*)* cattolico(a); **the** ~ **Church** la Chiesa Cattolica. **2** *n* cattolico/a.
catho·lic ['kæθəlɪk] *adj (wide-ranging: taste, interests)* ampio(a), vasto(a).
Ca·tholi·cism [kə'θɒlɪsɪzəm] *n* Cattolicesimo.
cat·kin ['kætkɪn] *n (Bot)* amento, gattino.
cat's-eye ['kætsaɪ] *n (Brit Aut)* catarifrangente *m.*
cat·sup ['kætsəp] *n (Am)* ketchup *m inv.*
cat·tle ['kætl] *npl* bestiame *m.*
cat·ty ['kætɪ] *adj (-ier, -iest) (fam)* maligno(a), dispettoso(a).
cat·walk ['kæt,wɔːk] *n* passerella.
Cau·ca·sian [kɔː'keɪzɪən] *adj, n* caucasico(a) *m/f.*
cau·cus ['kɔːkəs] *n (Am Pol)* (riunione *f* del) comitato elettorale; *(Pol: group)* comitato di dirigenti.
caught [kɔːt] *pt, pp of* **catch.**
caul·dron ['kɔːldrən] *n* calderone *m.*
cau·li·flow·er ['kɒlɪflaʊəʳ] **1** *n* cavolfiore *m.* **2** *cpd:* ~ **cheese** *n (Culin)* cavolfiori *mpl* gratinati.
cause [kɔːz] **1** *n* **(a)** causa; *(reason)* motivo, ragione *f;* ~ **and effect** causa e effetto; **with good** ~ a ragione; **to be the** ~ **of** essere (la) causa di; **there's no** ~ **for alarm** non c'è motivo di allarme.
(b) *(purpose)* causa; **in the** ~ **of justice** per la (causa della) giustizia; **to make common** ~ **with** far causa comune con; **it's all in a good** ~ *(fam)* è tutto a fin di bene. **2** *vt* causare; **to** ~ **sth to be done** far fare qc; **to** ~ **sb to do sth** far fare qc a qn.
cause·way ['kɔːzweɪ] *n* strada rialzata.
caus·tic ['kɔːstɪk] **1** *adj* caustico(a). **2** *cpd:* ~ **soda** *n* soda caustica.
cau·ter·ize ['kɔːtəraɪz] *vt* cauterizzare.
cau·tion ['kɔːʃən] **1** *n (care)* attenzione *f*, prudenza; *(warning)* avvertimento, ammonizione *f.* **2** *vt:* **to** ~ **sb** *(subj: official)* ammonire qn; **to** ~ **sb against doing sth** diffidare qn dal fare qc.
cau·tion·ary ['kɔːʃənərɪ] *adj:* ~ **tale** storiella ammonitrice.
cau·tious [ˌkɔːʃəs] *adj* cauto(a), prudente.
cava·lier [ˌkævə'lɪəʳ] **1** *n (knight)* cavaliere *m.* **2** *adj (pej: offhand: person, attitude)* brusco(a).
cav·al·ry ['kævəlrɪ] *n* cavalleria.
cave [keɪv] **1** *n* grotta, caverna. **2** *vi:* **to go caving** fare speleologia.
♦ **cave in** *vi + adv (ceiling)* sfondarsi; *(ground)* franare, cedere.
cave·man ['keɪv,mæn] *n, pl* **-men** cavernicolo, uomo delle caverne.
cav·ern ['kævən] *n* caverna.
cav·ern·ous ['kævənəs] *adj (eyes, cheeks)* incavato(a), infossato(a); *(pit)* ampio(a) e profondo(a); *(darkness)* fitto(a).
cavi·ar(e) ['kævɪɑːʳ] *n* caviale *m.*
cav·il ['kævɪl] *pt, pp* ~**led**, *(Am)* ~**ed** *vi:* **to** ~ **(at)** cavillare (su).
cav·ity ['kævɪtɪ] **1** *n* cavità *f inv.* **2** *cpd:* ~ **wall insulation** *n* isolamento per pareti a intercapedine.
ca·vort [kə'vɔːt] *vi* far salti, saltellare.
caw [kɔː] **1** *n* gracchio. **2** *vi* gracchiare.
cay·enne ['keɪɛn] *n:* ~ **(pepper)** pepe *m* di Caienna.

CB abbr (= citizens' band): ~ **radio (set)** baracchino.

CBI abbr (= Confederation of British Industries) ≈ Confindustria.

cc abbr (= cubic centimetres) cc; (= carbon copy) copia (in carta carbone).

cease [si:s] 1 vt cessare, smettere. 2 vi cessare.

cease-fire [,si:s'faɪə'] n cessate il fuoco m inv.

cease·less ['si:slɪs] adj incessante, senza sosta.

ce·dar ['si:də'] 1 n cedro. 2 cpd di cedro.

cede [si:d] vt (territory) cedere; (argument) cedere su.

ce·dil·la [sɪ'dɪlə] n cediglia.

ceil·ing ['si:lɪŋ] n (of room etc) soffitto; (fig: upper limit) tetto, limite m massimo.

cel·ebrate ['selɪbreɪt] 1 vt (event, festival, birthday) celebrare, festeggiare; (mass) celebrare. 2 vi far festa.

cel·ebrat·ed ['selɪbreɪtɪd] adj celebre.

cel·ebra·tion [,selɪ'breɪʃən] n (act) celebrazione f; (festivity) celebrazione, festa.

ce·leb·rity [sɪ'lebrɪtɪ] n celebrità f inv.

ce·leri·ac [sə'lerɪæk] n sedano rapa m.

cel·ery ['selərɪ] n sedano; **head/stick of** ~ testa/gambo di sedano.

ce·les·tial [sɪ'lestɪəl] adj (also fig) celestiale.

celi·ba·cy ['selɪbəsɪ] n celibato.

celi·bate ['selɪbɪt] adj, n (man) celibe (m); (woman) nubile (f).

cell [sel] n (in prison, monastery etc) cella; (Bio) cellula; (Elec) elemento (della pila).

cel·lar ['selə'] n cantina.

cel·list ['tʃelɪst] n violoncellista m/f.

cel·lo ['tʃeləʊ] n violoncello.

cel·lo·phane ['seləfeɪn] n cellophane m.

cel·lu·lar ['seljʊlə'] adj (Bio) cellulare; ~ **blanket** coperta a tessitura rada.

cel·lu·loid ['seljʊlɔɪd] n celluloide f.

cel·lu·lose ['seljʊləʊs] n cellulosa.

Celsius ['selsɪəs] adj Celsius inv.

Celt [kelt, selt] n celta m/f.

Celt·ic ['keltɪk, 'seltɪk] adj celtico(a).

ce·ment [sə'ment] 1 n cemento; (glue) adesivo. 2 vt cementare. 3 cpd: ~ **mixer** n betoniera.

cem·etery ['semɪtrɪ] n cimitero, camposanto.

ceno·taph ['senətɑ:f] n cenotafio.

cen·sor ['sensə'] 1 n censore m. 2 vt censurare.

cen·sor·ship ['sensəʃɪp] n censura.

cen·sure ['senʃə'] 1 n censura, condanna. 2 vt censurare.

cen·sus ['sensəs] n censimento.

cent [sent] n (coin) centesimo; **I haven't a** ~ (Am) non ho una lira or un centesimo.

cen·te·nary [sen'ti:nərɪ] n centenario.

cen·ten·nial [sen'tenɪəl] 1 adj centennale. 2 n (Am) = centenary.

cen·ter ['sentə'] n (Am) = centre.

cen·ti·grade ['sentɪɡreɪd] adj centigrado(a); **30 degrees** ~ 30 gradi centigradi.

cen·ti·me·tre, (Am) **cen·ti·me·ter** ['sentɪ,mi:tə'] n centimetro.

cen·ti·pede ['sentɪpi:d] n millepiedi m inv.

cen·tral ['sentrəl] 1 adj centrale. 2 cpd: ~ **America/Europe** n America/Europa centrale; ~ **government** n governo centrale; ~ **heating** n riscaldamento centrale; ~ **nervous system** n sistema m nervoso centrale; ~ **reservation** n (Brit Aut) banchina f spartitraffico inv.

cen·tral·ize ['sentrəlaɪz] vt centralizzare, accentrare.

cen·tre, (Am) **cen·ter** ['sentə'] 1 n centro; **she is the** ~ **of attention** è al centro dell'attenzione; ~ **of gravity** baricentro, centro di gravità. 2 vt (a)

centrare, mettere al centro. (b) (concentrate): **to** ~ **(on)** concentrare (su); **a press article** ~**d round industry** un articolo di giornale focalizzato sull'industria; **her plans** ~ **on her child** i suoi progetti ruotano attorno al bambino. 3 vi centrare. 4 cpd: ~ **forward** n (Sport) centravanti m inv.

cen·trifu·gal [sen'trɪfjʊɡəl] adj centrifugo(a).

cen·tri·fuge ['sentrɪfju:ʒ] n centrifuga.

cen·tu·ri·on [sen'tjʊərɪən] n centurione m.

cen·tu·ry ['sentjʊrɪ] n secolo; (in cricket) cento punti; **in the twentieth** ~ nel ventesimo secolo.

ce·ram·ic [sɪ'ræmɪk] 1 adj in or di ceramica. 2: ~**s** npl ceramica.

ce·real ['sɪərɪəl] n (crop) cereale m; (breakfast ~) fiocchi mpl di cereali.

cer·ebral ['serɪbrəl] adj cerebrale.

cer·emo·nial [,serɪ'məʊnɪəl] 1 adj (rite) formale, solenne; (dress) da cerimonia. 2 n cerimoniale m; (rite) rito.

cer·emo·ni·ous [,serɪ'məʊnɪəs] adj formale; (slightly pej) cerimonioso(a).

cer·emo·ny ['serɪmənɪ] n (event) cerimonia; (no pl: formality) cerimonie fpl; **to stand on** ~ stare all'etichetta, fare complimenti.

cert [sɜ:t] n: **it's a dead** ~ non c'è alcun dubbio.

cer·tain ['sɜ:tən] adj (a) (sure) certo(a), sicuro(a); (inevitable: death, success) sicuro(a); (cure) infallibile, garantito(a); **he's** ~ **to leave his job** è certo che lui lascerà il lavoro; **it is** ~ **that...** è certo che...; **I am** ~ **of it** ne sono certo; **he is** ~ **to be there** lui ci sarà certamente; **I can't say for** ~ **that...** non posso dire con certezza che...; **be** ~ **to tell her** ricordati or non dimenticarti di dirglielo; **to make** ~ **of sth** accertarsi di qc. (b) (before n: particular) certo(a); **a** ~ **gentleman called** ha telefonato un signore.

cer·tain·ly ['sɜ:tənlɪ] adv certamente, certo; ~**!** (ma) certo!; ~ **not!** no di certo!; **I shall** ~ **be there** ci sarò senza fallo, ci sarò certamente.

cer·tain·ty ['sɜ:təntɪ] n certezza; **faced with the** ~ **of disaster** di fronte al sicuro disastro; **we know for a** ~ **that...** sappiamo per certo che... .

cer·ti·fi·able [,sɜ:tɪ'faɪəbl] adj (fact, claim) dimostrabile; (fam: mad) pazzo(a) da legare.

cer·tifi·cate [sə'tɪfɪkɪt] n (gen) certificato; (academic) diploma m.

cer·ti·fied ['sɜ:tɪfaɪd] 1 adj (cheque, translation) autenticato(a); (person: declared insane) pazzo(a), malato(a) di mente. 2 cpd: ~ **public accountant** n (Am) = commercialista m/f.

cer·ti·fy ['sɜ:tɪfaɪ] 1 vt (a) certificare, attestare; **the will has been certified** il testamento è stato autenticato. (b) (Med): **to** ~ **sb** dichiarare pazzo qn. 2 vi: **to** ~ **to sth** certificare qc, attestare qc.

cer·vi·cal ['sɜ:vɪkəl] adj: ~ **cancer** cancro della cervice; ~ **smear** Pap-test m inv.

cer·vix ['sɜ:vɪks] n, pl cervices [sə'vaɪsi:z] collo dell'utero.

Ce·sar·ean [si:'zeərɪən] n (Am) = **Caesarean**.

ces·sa·tion [se'seɪʃən] n (frm) cessazione f.

cess·pit ['sespɪt] n, **cess·pool** ['sespu:l] n pozzo nero.

cf. abbr (= compare) cf, cfr.

chafe [tʃeɪf] 1 vt (rub against: skin etc) sfregare contro. 2 vi (a) (become sore) irritarsi. (b) (fig): **to** ~ **(at)** irritarsi (per).

chaff [tʃɑ:f] n (husks) pula, loppa; (animal food) foraggio.

chaf·finch ['tʃæfɪntʃ] n fringuello.

cha·grin ['ʃæɡrɪn] n disappunto, dispiacere m.

chain [tʃeɪn] 1 n (gen) catena; **gold** ~ catenina d'oro. 2 vt incatenare. 3 cpd: ~ **mail** n cotta di maglia; ~ **reaction** n reazione f a catena; ~ **smoker** n fumatore m accanito; ~ **store** n grande magazzino (con varie succursali).

♦ **chain up** vt + adv (prisoner) incatenare; (dog) mettere alla catena.

chair [tʃɛəʳ] **1** n sedia, seggiola; (arm~) poltrona; (seat) posto (a sedere); (Univ) cattedra; (Am: electric ~): **the** ~ la sedia elettrica; **please take a** ~ prego, si accomodi; **to take the** ~ (at meeting) assumere la presidenza. **2** vt (meeting) presiedere. **3** cpd: ~ **lift** n seggiovia.

chair·man ['tʃɛəmən] n, pl -**men** presidente m.

chair·man·ship ['tʃɛəmənʃɪp] n presidenza.

chair·person ['tʃɛə,pɜːsn] n presidente/essa.

chair·woman ['tʃɛə,wumən] n, pl -**women** presidentessa.

cha·let ['ʃæleɪ] n (in mountains) chalet m inv; (in holiday camp etc) bungalow m inv.

chal·ice ['tʃælɪs] n calice m.

chalk [tʃɔːk] **1** n gesso; **a** (piece of) ~ un gesso, un gessetto; **not by a long** ~ (fam) proprio per niente, per niente affatto; **they are as different as** ~ **and cheese** sono diversi come il giorno e la notte. **2** vt (message) scrivere col gesso; (luggage) segnare col gesso.

♦ **chalk up** vt + adv scrivere col gesso; (fig: success) ottenere; (: victory) riportare.

chal·lenge ['tʃælɪndʒ] **1** n sfida; (of sentry) intimazione f; **to put out a** ~ lanciare una sfida; **to take up the** ~ raccogliere la sfida; **this task is a great** ~ questo compito è una grande sfida. **2** vt (to game, fight etc) sfidare; (subj: sentry) intimare l'alt etc a; (dispute: fact, point) contestare; **to** ~ **sb to a duel** sfidare qn a duello.

chal·leng·er ['tʃælɪndʒəʳ] n sfidante m/f.

chal·leng·ing ['tʃælɪndʒɪŋ] adj (remark, look) provocatorio(a); (book) stimolante; (situation, work) impegnativo(a).

cham·ber ['tʃeɪmbəʳ] **1** n (of parliament) camera; (old: esp bedroom) stanza; ~**s** (of judge, lawyer) studio; **the Upper/Lower C**~ (Pol) la Camera Alta/Bassa; ~ **of commerce** camera di commercio. **2** cpd: ~ **music** n musica da camera.

cham·ber·maid ['tʃeɪmbə,meɪd] n cameriera (in albergo).

cha·me·le·on [kə'miːliən] n camaleonte m.

cham·ois ['ʃæmwɑː] **1** n (Zool) camoscio. **2** cpd: ~ **leather** n (pelle f di) camoscio.

cham·pagne [ʃæm'peɪn] n champagne m inv.

cham·pi·on ['tʃæmpjən] **1** n (of cause) difensore m; (Sport) campione/essa; **boxing** ~ campione di boxe; **world** ~ campione/essa mondiale. **2** vt difendere, lottare per.

cham·pi·on·ship ['tʃæmpjənʃɪp] n (contest) campionato.

chance [tʃɑːns] **1** n **(a)** (luck) caso; **game of** ~ gioco d'azzardo; **by** ~ per caso; **do you by any** ~ **know each other?** per caso vi conoscete?; **to leave nothing to** ~ non affidare nulla al caso. **(b)** (opportunity) possibilità f inv, occasione f; **it's the** ~ **of a lifetime** è un'occasione unica; **he never had a** ~ **in life** non ha mai avuto nessuna possibilità nella vita; **to give sb a** ~ dare a qn la possibilità (di fare qc); **to have an eye to the main** ~ (pej) essere sempre pronto ad approfittare, non perdere occasioni. **(c)** (possibility) probabilità f inv; **the** ~**s are that...** probabilmente..., è probabile che... + sub; **he doesn't stand or he hasn't a** ~ **of winning** non ha nessuna possibilità di vincere. **(d)** (risk) rischio; **an element of** ~ una parte di fortuna; **to take a** ~ rischiare; **I'm taking no** ~**s** non voglio lasciare niente al caso.

2 vt (happen): **to** ~ **to do sth** (frm) fare per caso

qc; (risk): **I'll** ~ **it** ci provo, rischio.

3 cpd (meeting, remark, error) casuale, fortuito(a).

♦ **chance (up)on** vi + prep (person) incontrare per caso, imbattersi in; (thing) trovare per caso.

chan·cel ['tʃɑːnsəl] n coro.

chan·cel·lor ['tʃɑːnsələʳ] n cancelliere m; **C**~ **of the Exchequer** Cancelliere dello Scacchiere; ≈ Ministro del Tesoro.

chan·de·lier [,ʃændə'liəʳ] n lampadario.

change [tʃeɪndʒ] **1** n **(a)** cambiamento; **a** ~ **for the better/worse** un miglioramento/peggioramento, un mutamento per il meglio/peggio; **just for a** ~ tanto per cambiare; **he likes a** ~ gli piace cambiare; ~ **of address** cambio di indirizzo; ~ **of clothes** cambio (di vestiti); ~ **of heart** cambiare idea; **the** ~ **of life** (Med) la menopausa; **to have a** ~ **of scene** cambiare aria; **there's been a** ~ **in the weather** il tempo è cambiato. **(b)** (small coins) moneta; (money returned) resto; **small** or **loose** ~ spiccioli mpl; **can you give me** ~ **for £1?** mi può cambiare una sterlina?; **you don't get much** ~ **out of £5** non avanza molto da 5 sterline; **keep the** ~ tenga il resto.

2 vt **(a)** (by substitution) cambiare; **to** ~ **hands** cambiare padrone; **a sum of money** ~**d hands** c'è stato un movimento di denaro; **to** ~ **gear** (Aut) cambiare (marcia); **to** ~ **places** (2 people) scambiarsi di posto; **I** ~**d places with him** ho scambiato il mio posto con il suo; **to** ~ **trains/buses** (at) cambiare treno/autobus (a); **let's** ~ **the subject** cambiamo argomento. **(b)** (exchange: in shop) cambiare. **(c)** (alter: person, idea) cambiare; (transform: person) trasformare; (: thing) tramutare; **to** ~ **one's mind** cambiare idea. **(d)** (money) cambiare.

3 vi **(a)** (alter) cambiare, mutare; **you've** ~**d!** come sei cambiato! **(b)** (~ clothes) cambiarsi; **she** ~**d into an old skirt** si è cambiata e ha messo una vecchia gonna. **(c)** (Rail etc) cambiare; **all** ~! si cambia!

♦ **change down** vi + adv (Aut) scalare (la marcia).

♦ **change over** vi + adv (make complete change): **to** ~ **over from sth to sth** passare da qc a qc; (players etc) scambiarsi (di posto).

♦ **change up** vi + adv (Aut) cambiare, mettere una marcia superiore.

change·able ['tʃeɪndʒəbl] adj (person) mutevole; (weather) mutevole, variabile.

chang·ing ['tʃeɪndʒɪŋ] **1** adj (face, expression) mutevole. **2** n: **the** ~ **of the guard** il cambio della guardia.

chan·nel ['tʃænl] **1** n (all senses) canale m; **to go through the usual** ~**s** seguire la normale procedura; **the (English) C**~ la Manica. **2** vt (hollow out: course) scavare; (direct: river etc) far scorrere, convogliare; (fig: interest, energies): ~ **into** concentrare su, indirizzare verso. **3** cpd: **the C**~ **Islands** le Isole della Manica.

chant [tʃɑːnt] **1** n (Rel, Mus) canto; (of crowd) slogan m inv. **2** vt (Rel, Mus) cantare; (subj: crowd): **the demonstrators** ~**ed their disapproval** i dimostranti lanciavano slogan di protesta. **3** vi (see vt) cantare; lanciare slogan.

cha·os ['keɪɒs] n caos m; **to be in** ~ essere nel caos.

cha·ot·ic [keɪ'ɒtɪk] adj caotico(a), confuso(a).

chap¹ [tʃæp] n (on lip etc) screpolatura.

chap² [tʃæp] n (fam: man) tipo, tizio; **he's the sort of** ~ **everyone likes** è il tipo di persona che piace a tutti; **old** ~ vecchio mio; **poor little** ~ povero piccolo.

chap·el ['tʃæpəl] n (of church, school etc) cappella; (small church) chiesetta.

chap·er·one ['ʃæpərəʊn] **1** *n* accompagnatore/trice. **2** *vt* fare da accompagnatore (*or* accompagnatrice) a.

chap·lain ['tʃæplɪn] *n* cappellano.

chapped ['tʃæpt] *adj (lips, hands)* screpolato(a).

chap·ter ['tʃæptə'] *n* capitolo; **a ~ of accidents** una serie di imprevisti.

char[1] [tʃɑː'] *vt (burn black)* carbonizzare.

char[2] [tʃɑː'] **1** *n (charwoman)* donna a ore. **2** *vi* fare servizi a ore.

char·ac·ter ['kærɪktə'] **1** *n (most senses)* carattere *m*; *(in novel, play etc)* personaggio; **a man of ~** un uomo di polso; **a person of good ~** una persona a modo; **it's quite in/out of ~ for him to be rude** è/non è nella sua natura l'essere tanto maleducato; **he's quite a ~** è un (bel) tipo; **Gothic ~s** caratteri gotici. **2** *cpd:* **~ actor/actress** *n* caratterista *m/f.*

char·ac·ter·is·tic [,kærɪktə'rɪstɪk] **1** *adj* caratteristico(a), tipico(a); **~ of** tipico di; **it was ~ of him to ask for a lift home** era nel suo stile chiedere di essere accompagnato a casa. **2** *n* caratteristica.

char·ac·teri·za·tion [,kærɪktəraɪ'zeɪʃən] *n (in novel)* caratterizzazione *f.*

char·ac·ter·ize ['kærɪktəraɪz] *vt (be characteristic of)* caratterizzare; *(describe):* **to ~ (as)** descrivere (come).

cha·rade [ʃə'rɑːd] *n* finta.

char·coal ['tʃɑːkəʊl] *n* carbone *m*; *(for sketching)* carboncino.

charge [tʃɑːdʒ] **1** *n* **(a)** *(Law)* accusa, imputazione *f*; **to bring a ~ against sb** accusare qn, imputare qn; **he was arrested on a ~ of murder** fu arrestato sotto accusa di omicidio. **(b)** *(Mil)* carica. **(c)** *(fee)* tariffa; **free of ~** gratis, gratuito; **extra ~** supplemento. **(d)** *(control, responsibility):* **the person in ~** il responsabile; **who is in ~ here?** chi è il responsabile qui?; **to be in ~ of** essere responsabile di; **to take ~ (of)** assumere il controllo (di); **can you take ~ here?** se ne occupa lei?; **these children are my ~s** questi bambini sono affidati a me. **(e)** *(explosive ~, electrical ~)* carica.

2 *vt* **(a)** *(accuse):* **to ~ (with)** accusare (di). **(b)** *(Mil etc: attack)* attaccare. **(c)** *(price)* chiedere, far pagare; *(customer)* far pagare a; **what did they ~ you for it?** quanto te l'hanno fatto pagare?; **~ it to my account** lo metta *or* addebiti sul mio conto. **(d)** *(battery)* caricare.

3 *vi (Mil etc)* attaccare; *(fam: rush)* precipitarsi; **to ~ up/down the stairs** lanciarsi su/giù per le scale.

4 *cpd:* **~ account** *n (Am)* conto.

char·gé d'af·faires ['ʃɑːʒeɪdæ'feə'] *n* incaricato d'affari.

charg·er ['tʃɑːdʒə'] *n (Elec)* caricabatterie *m inv; (old: warhorse)* destriero.

chari·ot ['tʃærɪət] *n* cocchio, carro.

cha·ris·ma [kæ'rɪzmə] *n* carisma *m.*

chari·table ['tʃærɪtəbl] *adj (organization, society)* filantropico(a), di beneficenza; *(person)* caritatevole; *(deed)* buono(a), di carità; *(remark, view)* indulgente, caritatevole.

char·ity ['tʃærɪtɪ] *n* **(a)** carità; **out of ~** per carità *or* misericordia; **to live on ~** vivere di elemosine; **~ begins at home** *(Proverb)* il primo prossimo è la tua famiglia. **(b)** *(organization)* opera pia, associazione *f* benefica; **she gave all her money to ~** lasciò tutto il suo denaro in beneficenza.

charm [tʃɑːm] **1** *n (of person)* fascino; *(of object)* incanto; *(also fig: magic spell)* incanto, incantesimo; **it worked like a ~** *(fig)* ha funzionato

perfettamente. **2** *vt* affascinare; **to lead a ~ed life** essere nato con la camicia. **3** *cpd:* **~ bracelet** *n* braccialetto con ciondoli.

charm·ing ['tʃɑːmɪŋ] *adj* delizioso(a).

chart [tʃɑːt] **1** *n (table)* tabella, tavola; *(graph, Med)* grafico; *(Met: weather ~)* carta del tempo; *(Naut: map)* carta (nautica); **to be in the ~s** *(record, pop group)* essere nella Hit Parade. **2** *vt (plot: course)* tracciare; *(: sales, progress)* tracciare il grafico di.

char·ter ['tʃɑːtə'] **1** *n* **(a)** *(document)* carta; *(of city, organization)* statuto. **(b)** *(Naut, Aer etc: hire)* noleggio; **on ~** a nolo. **2** *vt (plane etc)* noleggiare. **3** *cpd:* **~ flight** *n* volo *m* charter *inv.*

char·tered ac·count·ant ['tʃɑːtəd'kaʊntənt] *n (Brit)* ≈ commercialista *m/f.*

char·woman ['tʃɑː,wʊmən] *n, pl* **-women** donna delle pulizie, donna a ore.

chary ['tʃɛərɪ] *adj* cauto(a), attento(a); **to be ~ of doing sth** esitare prima di fare qc.

chase [tʃeɪs] **1** *n* inseguimento; **the ~** *(Hunting)* la caccia; **to give ~** dare la caccia, mettersi all'inseguimento. **2** *vt* inseguire. **3** *vi:* **to ~ after** qn correre dietro a qn.

♦ **chase away, chase off** *vt* + *adv* cacciare via.

♦ **chase up** *vt* + *adv (information)* scoprire, raccogliere; *(person)* scovare.

chasm ['kæzəm] *n* crepaccio.

chas·sis ['ʃæsɪ] *n (Aut)* telaio.

chaste [tʃeɪst] *adj* casto(a).

chas·ten·ing ['tʃeɪsnɪŋ] *adj* che fa riflettere.

chas·tise [tʃæs'taɪz] *vt (punish)* punire, castigare.

chas·tity ['tʃæstɪtɪ] *n* castità.

chat [tʃæt] **1** *n* chiacchierata; **to have a ~** fare quattro chiacchiere. **2** *vi:* **to ~ (with *or* to)** chiacchierare (con). **3** *cpd:* **~ show** *n* conversazione *f* televisiva.

♦ **chat up** *vt* + *adv (fam: girl)* agganciare.

chat·tel ['tʃætl] *n see* **goods.**

chat·ter ['tʃætə'] **1** *n (talk)* parlottio, chiacchiere *fpl.* **2** *vi (person)* chiacchierare; *(birds)* cinguettare; **her teeth were ~ing** batteva i denti.

chatter·box ['tʃætəbɒks] *n (fam)* chiacchierone/a.

chat·ty ['tʃætɪ] *adj* ciarliero(a).

chauf·feur ['ʃəʊfə'] *n* autista *m.*

chau·vin·ism ['ʃəʊvɪnɪzəm] *n (male ~)* maschilismo; *(nationalism)* sciovinismo.

chau·vin·ist ['ʃəʊvɪnɪst] *n (male ~)* maschilista *m; (nationalist)* sciovinista *m/f;* **(male) ~ pig** *(fam pej)* sporco maschilista.

cheap [tʃiːp] **1** *adj (low cost: goods)* a buon prezzo, economico(a); *(reduced: ticket)* a prezzo ridotto(a); *(: fare)* ridotto(a); *(poor quality)* scadente; *(vulgar, mean: joke, behaviour, trick)* volgare, dozzinale; **it's ~ at the price** il prezzo è buono *or* conveniente. **2** *adv* a buon prezzo. **3** *n:* **on the ~** *(fam)* a prezzo stracciato.

cheap·en ['tʃiːpən] *vt:* **to ~ o.s.** screditarsi; *(woman: sexually)* degradarsi.

cheap·ly ['tʃiːplɪ] *adv* a buon prezzo, a buon mercato.

cheap·skate ['tʃiːpskeɪt] *n (fam)* taccagno/a.

cheat [tʃiːt] **1** *n* imbroglione/a. **2** *vt* imbrogliare, truffare; **to ~ sb out of sth** fregare qc a qn; **I was ~ed out of the job** mi è stato soffiato il lavoro. **3** *vi (at games)* barare, imbrogliare; *(in exam)* copiare; **he's been ~ing on his wife** ha tradito sua moglie.

check [tʃek] **1** *n* **(a)** *(control, restraint)* limitazione *f*; **to hold *or* keep sb/sth in ~** tenere qn/qc sotto controllo; **to act as a ~ on sth** fare da freno a qc. **(b)** *(Chess):* **in ~** in scacco; **~!** scacco (al re)! **(c)** *(inspection)* controllo; **to keep a ~ on sb/sth** con-

trollare qn/qc, fare attenzione a qn/qc. (d) (Am: bill) conto; (: receipt) scontrino. (e) (Am) = cheque. (f): ~s (pattern) quadretti mpl, scacchi mpl. 2 vt (a) (control, stop) bloccare, arrestare; to ~ o.s. frenarsi. (b) (examine: facts, figures) verificare; (: ticket, tyres, oil etc) controllare. (c) (Am: tick) spuntare. 3 vi controllare; to ~ with sb chiedere a qn; (official etc) informarsi presso qn.
♦ check in 1 vi + adv (at airport) fare il check-in; (at hotel: arrive) arrivare; (: register) firmare il registro. 2 vt + adv (luggage) registrare, fare il check-in di.
♦ check out 1 vi + adv (leave hotel) saldare il conto e partire. 2 vt + adv (a) (luggage) ritirare. (b) (investigate: story) controllare, verificare; (: person) prendere informazioni su.
♦ check up vi + adv controllare.
♦ check up on vi + prep (story) controllare, verificare; (person) controllare.
check·ered ['tʃɛkəd] adj (Am) = chequered.
check·ers ['tʃɛkəz] npl (Am) dama.
check-in ['tʃɛkɪn] n (also: ~ desk: at airport) check-in m inv, accettazione f (bagagli inv).
check·list ['tʃɛklɪst] n lista di controllo.
check·mate ['tʃɛk,meɪt] 1 n (in chess, fig) scacco matto. 2 vt dare scacco matto a; (fig) bloccare.
check·out ['tʃɛkaʊt] n (in supermarket) cassa.
check·point ['tʃɛk,pɔɪnt] n posto di blocco.
check·room ['tʃɛk,rʊm] n (Am: for coats etc) guardaroba m inv; (: for luggage) deposito m bagagli inv.
check·up ['tʃɛkʌp] n (Med) check-up m inv, (visita di) controllo.
ched·dar ['tʃɛdəʳ] n (also: ~ cheese) (formaggio) cheddar m inv.
cheek [tʃiːk] 1 n (a) (Anat) guancia; (: buttock) natica. (b) (fam: impudence) faccia tosta, sfacciataggine f; what a ~! che faccia tosta! 2 vt essere sfacciato(a) con.
cheeky ['tʃiːkɪ] adj sfacciato(a), impudente.
cheep [tʃiːp] 1 n (of bird) pigolio. 2 vi pigolare.
cheer [tʃɪəʳ] 1 n (applause) grido (di incoraggiamento), evviva m inv; three ~s for the winner! tre urrà per il vincitore!; ~s! (toast) alla salute!, cin cin!; (fam: thank you) grazie!, evviva!; (: goodbye) ciao! 2 vt (a) (applaud: winner etc) acclamare. (b) (also: ~ up: gladden) rallegrare. 3 vi acclamare.
♦ cheer on vt + adv (person etc) incitare.
♦ cheer up 1 vi + adv rallegrarsi; ~ up! coraggio!, su con la vita! 2 vt + adv = cheer 2b.
cheer·ful ['tʃɪəfʊl] adj allegro(a).
cheerio [,tʃɪərɪ'əʊ] excl (Brit fam) ciao!
cheery ['tʃɪərɪ] adj allegro(a).
cheese [tʃiːz] n formaggio; say ~! (Phot) sorridi!
cheese·board ['tʃiːz,bɔːd] n piatto del (or per il) formaggio.
cheese·cake ['tʃiːz,keɪk] n specie di torta di ricotta, a volte con frutta.
cheese·cloth ['tʃiːz,klɒθ] n tela indiana, garza.
chee·tah ['tʃiːtə] n ghepardo.
chef [ʃɛf] n chef m inv, capocuoco.
chemi·cal ['kɛmɪkəl] 1 adj chimico(a). 2 n prodotto chimico.
chem·ist ['kɛmɪst] n (scientist) chimico/a; (Brit: pharmacist) farmacista m/f; ~'s (shop) farmacia.
chem·is·try ['kɛmɪstrɪ] n chimica.
cheque, (Am) check [tʃɛk] 1 n assegno; a ~ for £20 un assegno di 20 sterline; to pay by ~ pagare per assegno or con un assegno. 2 cpd: ~ card n carta assegni.
cheque·book, (Am) check·book ['tʃɛk,bʊk] n libretto degli assegni.

cheq·uered, (Am) check·ered ['tʃɛkəd] adj a scacchi, a quadretti; a ~ career (fig) una carriera movimentata.
cher·ish ['tʃɛrɪʃ] vt (person) avere caro(a); (hope etc) nutrire.
cher·ry ['tʃɛrɪ] 1 n (fruit) ciliegia; (~ tree) ciliegio. 2 cpd (pie, jam) di ciliegie; ~ brandy n cherry brandy m inv; ~ red adj rosso ciliegia inv.
cher·ub ['tʃɛrəb] n cherubino.
chess [tʃɛs] n scacchi mpl.
chess·board ['tʃɛs,bɔːd] n scacchiera.
chess·man ['tʃɛs,mæn] n, pl -men pezzo (degli scacchi).
chest [tʃɛst] 1 n (a) (Anat) petto; to get sth off one's ~ (fam) sputare il rospo. (b) (box) baule m, cassapanca; ~ of drawers comò m inv, cassettone m. 2 cpd: ~ cold n: to catch a ~ cold prendere un colpo di freddo al petto; ~ measurement n giro m torace inv; ~ specialist n specialista m/f in malattie pulmonari.
chest·nut ['tʃɛsnʌt] 1 n (fruit) castagna; (~ tree) castagno; (colour) castano. 2 adj castano(a).
chesty ['tʃɛstɪ] adj di petto.
chew [tʃuː] vt masticare.
♦ chew over vt + adv rimuginare su.
♦ chew up vt + adv mangiucchiare.
chew·ing gum ['tʃuːɪŋ,gʌm] n chewing-gum m inv.
chic [ʃiːk] adj chic inv, elegante.
chick [tʃɪk] n (baby bird) piccolo, uccellino; (baby hen) pulcino.
chick·en ['tʃɪkɪn] n pollo; (fam: coward) coniglio; don't count your ~s before they're hatched (Proverb) non dire quattro finché non l'hai nel sacco.
♦ chicken out vi + adv (fam) avere fifa; to ~ out of sth tirarsi indietro da qc per fifa or paura.
chicken·pox ['tʃɪkɪn,pɒks] n varicella.
chick·pea ['tʃɪk,piː] n cece m.
chico·ry ['tʃɪkərɪ] n cicoria.
chief [tʃiːf] 1 adj (principal: reason etc) principale; (in rank) capo inv. 2 n capo; C~ of Staff (Mil) Capo di Stato Maggiore.
chief·ly ['tʃiːflɪ] adv soprattutto, più che altro.
chief·tain ['tʃiːftən] n capo.
chif·fon ['ʃɪfɒn] 1 n chiffon m. 2 cpd di chiffon.
chil·blain ['tʃɪlbleɪn] n gelone m.
child [tʃaɪld] 1 n, pl children (gen) bambino/a; (son/daughter) figlio/a, bambino/a; it's ~'s play è una cosa da nulla. 2 cpd: ~ benefit n ≃ assegni mpl familiari; ~ labour n lavoro minorile; ~ minder n bambinaia (che sorveglia i bambini a casa propria).
child-bearing ['tʃaɪld,bɛərɪŋ] 1 adj: of ~ age in età feconda. 2 n maternità; constant ~ gravidanze fpl ripetute.
child·birth ['tʃaɪld,bɜːθ] n parto; to die in ~ morire di parto.
child·hood ['tʃaɪldhʊd] n infanzia; from ~ fin dall'infanzia, fin da piccolo.
child·ish ['tʃaɪldɪʃ] adj infantile, puerile.
child·less ['tʃaɪldlɪs] adj senza figli.
child·like ['tʃaɪld,laɪk] adj ingenuo(a), innocente.
chil·dren ['tʃɪldrən] npl of child.
Chile ['tʃɪlɪ] n Cile m.
Chil·ean ['tʃɪlɪən] adj, n cileno(a) (m/f).
chill [tʃɪl] 1 adj (wind) freddo(a). 2 n freddo; (Med) infreddatura, colpo di freddo; there's a ~ in the air l'aria è fredda; to take the ~ off (a room) riscaldare un po' (una stanza); to catch a ~ (Med) prendere un colpo di freddo. 3 vt (wine, meat) mettere in fresco; to ~ sb's blood (fig) far gelare il sangue a qn; to be ~ed to the bone essere gelato fino al midollo.

chil(l)i ['tʃɪlɪ] *n* peperoncino.

chil·ly ['tʃɪlɪ] *adj (weather, room)* fresco(a), freddo(a); *(fig: person, look, reception)* freddo(a), gelido(a); **I feel** ~ ho *or* sento freddo.

chime [tʃaɪm] **1** *n* rintocco. **2** *vt, vi* suonare.

♦ **chime in** *vi* + *adv (fam: interrupt, join in)* intervenire; *(: echo)* far coro.

chim·ney ['tʃɪmnɪ] **1** *n* camino. **2** *cpd*: ~ **pot** *n* comignolo; ~ **sweep** *n* spazzacamino.

chim·pan·zee [,tʃɪmpæn'ziː] *n* scimpanzé *m inv*.

chin [tʃɪn] *n* mento; **(keep your)** ~ **up!** *(fam)* coraggio!

Chi·na ['tʃaɪnə] *n* Cina.

chi·na ['tʃaɪnə] **1** *n (porcelain)* porcellana; *(crockery)* porcellane *fpl*. **2** *cpd* di porcellana.

Chi·nese ['tʃaɪ'niːz] **1** *adj* cinese. **2** *n (person: pl inv)* cinese *m/f; (language)* cinese *m*.

chink¹ [tʃɪŋk] *n* fessura.

chink² [tʃɪŋk] **1** *n (sound)* tintinnio. **2** *vt* far tintinnare. **3** *vi* tintinnare.

chintz [tʃɪnts] *n* chintz *m inv*.

chip [tʃɪp] **1** *n* **(a)** *(piece)* frammento; *(: of china)* coccio; *(: of glass, wood, stone)* scheggia; **he's a** ~ **off the old block** *(fig)* è della stessa razza del padre; **he's got a** ~ **on his shoulder because...** gli è rimasto sullo stomaco il fatto che.... **(b)** *(Culin: Brit: French fry)* patatina fritta; *(: Am: crisp)* patatina. **(c)** *(in crockery, furniture)* scheggiatura; **there's a** ~ **in this cup** questa tazza è scheggiata. **(d)** *(in gambling)* fiche *f inv*; **when the** ~**s are down** *(fig)* al momento critico. **(e)** *(micro*~*)* chip *m inv*. **2** *vt* scheggiare. **3** *vi* scheggiarsi.

♦ **chip in** *vi* + *adv (fam: contribute)* contribuire; *(: interrupt)* intromettersi.

♦ **chip off 1** *vi* + *adv (paint etc)* scrostarsi. **2** *vt* + *adv (paint etc)* scrostare.

chip·board ['tʃɪp,bɔːd] *n* agglomerato.

chip·munk ['tʃɪpmʌŋk] *n* tamia *m* striato.

chi·ropo·dist [kɪ'rɒpədɪst] *n* callista *m/f*, pedicure *m/f*.

chi·ropo·dy [kɪ'rɒpədɪ] *n* mestiere *m* di callista.

chirp [tʃɜːp] **1** *n (of birds)* cinguettìo; *(of crickets)* cri cri *m*. **2** *vi (see n)* cinguettare; cantare, fare cri cri.

chir·rup ['tʃɪrəp] *n, vi* = **chirp**.

chis·el ['tʃɪzl] **1** *n* scalpello; *(smaller)* cesello; *(for engraving)* bulino. **2** *vt (pt, pp (Brit)* ~**led**, *(Am)* ~**ed**) *(also:* ~ **out)** scolpire; cesellare; incidere con il bulino.

chit¹ [tʃɪt] *n* nota *f* spese *inv*.

chit² [tʃɪt] *n*: **a** ~ **of a girl** una ragazzina.

chiv·al·rous ['ʃɪvəlrəs] *adj* cavalleresco(a).

chiv·al·ry ['ʃɪvəlrɪ] *n* cavalleria.

chives ['tʃaɪvz] *npl* erba cipollina.

chlo·ride ['klɔːraɪd] *n* cloruro.

chlo·rin·ate ['klɔrɪneɪt] *vt* clorare.

chlo·rine ['klɔːriːn] *n* cloro.

chlo·ro·form ['klɒrəfɔːm] *n* cloroformio.

chlo·ro·phyll ['klɒrəfɪl] *n* clorofilla.

choc-ice ['tʃɒkaɪs] *n* barretta di gelato ricoperto di cioccolato.

chock [tʃɒk] *n* zeppa.

chock-a-block ['tʃɒkə'blɒk] *adj*: ~ **(with)** pieno(a) zeppo(a) (di).

chock-full ['tʃɒk'fʊl] *adj*: ~ **(of)** pieno(a) zeppo(a) (di).

choco·late ['tʃɒklɪt] **1** *n* cioccolata, cioccolato; *(individual sweet)* cioccolatino; **hot** *or* **drinking** ~ cioccolata (calda). **2** *cpd (biscuit, cake, egg)* di cioccolato, al cioccolato; *(colour)* (color) cioccolato *inv*.

choice [tʃɔɪs] **1** *n* scelta; **he's not really my** ~ non è proprio quello che sceglierei io; **I did it by** *or* **from** ~ l'ho fatto di mia volontà *or* per mia scelta; **a wide** ~ un'ampia scelta; **it's Hobson's** ~ è una questione di prendere o lasciare; **he had no** ~ **but to go** non aveva altra scelta che andare; **take your** ~! scegli pure! **2** *adj (fruit, wine)* di prima scelta; *(hum: example, remark)* bello(a), adatto(a); *(: language)*: **his language was really** ~! il suo tono non era esattamente garbato!

choir ['kwaɪəʳ] *n* coro.

choir·boy ['kwaɪə,bɔɪ] *n* corista *m (ragazzo)*.

choke [tʃəʊk] **1** *n (Aut)* aria. **2** *vt (person)* soffocare; *(: strangle)* strangolare; *(also:* ~ **up:** *pipe etc)* intasare. **3** *vi* soffocare.

♦ **choke back** *vt* + *adv* ingoiare.

chok·er ['tʃəʊkəʳ] *n* collana a girocollo.

chol·era ['kɒlərə] *n* colera *m*.

cho·les·ter·ol [kə'lestərɒl] *n* colesterolo.

choose [tʃuːz] *pt* **chose,** *pp* **chosen 1** *vt* scegliere; **to** ~ **to do sth** scegliere *or* decidere di fare qc. **2** *vi* scegliere; **to** ~ **between** scegliere tra; **there is nothing to** ~ **between them** uno vale l'altro; **to** ~ **from** scegliere da *or* tra; **there were several to** ~ **from** vi era parecchia scelta; **as/when I** ~ come/quando voglio *or* decido io.

choosy ['tʃuːzɪ] *adj* **(-ier, -iest)** *(fam)* schizzinoso(a).

chop¹ [tʃɒp] **1** *n* **(a)** *(blow)* colpo secco; **to get the** ~ *(fam: project)* essere bocciato; *(: person: be sacked)* essere licenziato. **(b)** *(Culin)* costoletta. **2** *vt (wood)* tagliare, spaccare; *(meat, vegetables)* tagliare (a pezzetti).

♦ **chop down** *vt* + *adv* abbattere.

♦ **chop off** *vt* + *adv* tagliare (via).

chop² [tʃɒp] *vi*: **to** ~ **and change** cambiare continuamente parere.

chop·per ['tʃɒpəʳ] *n (of butcher)* mannaia; *(Aer fam)* elicottero.

chop·ping ['tʃɒpɪŋ] *adj*: ~ **board** tagliere *m;* ~ **knife** coltello (per tritare).

chop·py ['tʃɒpɪ] *adj* **(-ier, -iest)** *(lake)* agitato(a); *(wind)* variabile; ~ **sea** maretta.

chop·stick ['tʃɒpstɪk] *n* bastoncino.

cho·ral ['kɔːrəl] *adj* corale; ~ **society** coro, compagnia di canti.

chord [kɔːd] *n (gen)* corda; *(Mus)* accordo; **to touch the right** ~ *(fig)* toccare il tasto giusto.

chore [tʃɔːʳ] *n* faccenda; *(pej)* rottura; **to do the** ~**s** sbrigare le faccende di casa.

cho·reog·ra·pher [,kɒrɪ'ɒgrəfəʳ] *n* coreografo/a.

cho·reog·ra·phy [,kɒrɪ'ɒgrəfɪ] *n* coreografia.

chor·tle ['tʃɔːtl] *vi* ridacchiare, fare risolini.

cho·rus ['kɔːrəs] **1** *n* **(a)** *(musical work, people)* coro; **in** ~ in coro. **(b)** *(refrain)* ritornello. **2** *vt (answer)* rispondere in coro. **3** *cpd*: ~ **girl** *n* girl *f inv*.

chose [tʃəʊz] *pt of* **choose**.

cho·sen ['tʃəʊzn] **1** *pp of* **choose**. **2** *adj*: **the** ~ **(people)** gli eletti.

chow·der ['tʃaʊdəʳ] *n (esp Am)* zuppa di pesce.

Christ [kraɪst] *n* Cristo.

chris·ten ['krɪsn] *vt* battezzare.

chris·ten·ing ['krɪsnɪŋ] *n* battesimo.

Chris·tian ['krɪstɪən] **1** *adj* cristiano(a); *(also:* **c**~: *fig)* caritatevole; ~ **name** nome *m* (di battesimo). **2** *n* cristiano/a.

Chris·ti·an·ity [,krɪstɪ'ænɪtɪ] *n* cristianesimo.

Christ·mas ['krɪsməs] **1** *n* Natale *m;* **at** ~ a Natale; **happy** *or* **merry** ~! Buon Natale!; **Father** ~ Babbo Natale. **2** *cpd (tree, cake, present, party)* di Natale; ~ **card** *n* biglietto di Natale, cartolina di auguri natalizi; ~ **Day** *n* il giorno di Natale; ~ **Eve** *n* la vigilia di Natale.

Christ·mas·time ['krɪsməs,taɪm] n periodo natalizio or di Natale.

chro·mat·ic [krə'mætɪk] adj cromatico(a).

chrome [krəʊm] n metallo cromato.

chro·mium ['krəʊmɪəm] n cromo.

chro·mo·some ['krəʊməsəʊm] n cromosoma m.

chron·ic ['krɒnɪk] adj (invalid, disease) cronico(a); (fig: liar, smoker) incallito(a); (fam: weather, actor etc) allucinante.

chroni·cle ['krɒnɪkl] n cronaca.

chrono·logi·cal [,krɒnə'lɒdʒɪkəl] adj cronologico(a).

chro·nol·ogy [krə'nɒlədʒɪ] n cronologia.

chrysa·lis ['krɪsəlɪs] n crisalide f.

chry·san·themum [krɪ'sænθəməm] n crisantemo.

chub·by ['tʃʌbɪ] adj paffuto(a), grassoccio(a).

chuck [tʃʌk] vt (fam) (a) (also: ~ away) buttare, gettare. (b) (throw) gettare. (c) (also: ~ up, ~ in: job) buttare via; (: person) piantare.

♦ **chuck out** vt + adv (fam: useless article) buttare via; (: person) sbattere fuori.

chuck·le ['tʃʌkl] 1 n risolino. 2 vi ridacchiare; to ~ at or over ridere or ridacchiare per.

chuffed [tʃʌft] adj (fam) tutto(a) contento(a).

chug [tʃʌg] vi (a) (train) sbuffare, fare ciuf ciuf; (motor) sbuffare. (b) (also: ~ along: train) muoversi sbuffando.

chum [tʃʌm] n (fam) amicone/a.

chunk [tʃʌŋk] n bel pezzo.

chunky ['tʃʌŋkɪ] adj (-ier, -iest) (furniture etc) basso(a) e largo(a); (person) ben piantato(a); (knitwear) di lana grossa.

church [tʃɜːtʃ] n chiesa; the C~ of England la Chiesa anglicana; to go to ~ andare in chiesa; after ~ dopo la funzione; (for Catholics) dopo la messa; to enter the C~ prendere gli ordini.

church·goer ['tʃɜːtʃ,gəʊəʳ] n fedele m/f; his parents are regular ~s i suoi genitori vanno regolarmente in chiesa.

church·yard ['tʃɜːtʃ,jɑːd] n cimitero (attorno a una chiesa).

churl·ish ['tʃɜːlɪʃ] adj rozzo(a), sgarbato(a).

churn [tʃɜːn] 1 n (for butter) zangola; (Brit: for milk) bidone m per il latte. 2 vt (butter) fare (nella zangola); (fig: also: ~ up: water) agitare. 3 vi essere agitato(a).

♦ **churn out** vt + adv sfornare.

chute [ʃuːt] n scivolo.

chut·ney ['tʃʌtnɪ] n salsa piccante (di frutta, zucchero e spezie).

CIA n (abbr of Central Intelligence Agency) CIA f.

ci·ca·da [sɪ'kɑːdə] n cicala.

CID abbr of Criminal Investigation Department.

ci·der ['saɪdəʳ] n sidro.

C.I.F. abbr (= cost, insurance, freight) C.I.F.

ci·gar [sɪ'gɑːʳ] n sigaro.

ciga·rette [,sɪgə'ret] 1 n sigaretta. 2 cpd: ~ case n portasigarette m inv; ~ end n mozzicone m (di sigaretta), cicca; ~ lighter n accendino.

cinch [sɪntʃ] n (fam): it's a ~ (easy thing) è una cretinata or una sciocchezza; (sure thing) è una cosa sicura.

cin·der ['sɪndəʳ] 1 n tizzone m; burned to a ~ (fig: food etc) carbonizzato. 2 cpd: ~ track n (Sport) pista di cenere.

Cinderella [,sɪndə'relə] n Cenerentola.

cine cam·era ['sɪnɪ'kæmərə] n (Brit) cinepresa.

cin·ema ['sɪnəmə] n cinema m inv.

cin·na·mon ['sɪnəmən] n cannella.

ci·pher ['saɪfəʳ] n (code) codice m (cifrato); (Math) zero; in ~ in codice.

cir·cle ['sɜːkl] 1 n (gen) cerchio; (in theatre) galleria; to stand in a ~ mettersi in cerchio; she

moves in wealthy ~s frequenta l'alta società; the family ~ la cerchia familiare; to come full ~ (fig) ritornare al punto di partenza; to go round in ~s (fam) girare sempre attorno allo stesso punto. 2 vt (surround) accerchiare; (move round) girare attorno a; (draw round) segnare con un cerchio.

cir·cuit ['sɜːkɪt] n (journey around) giro; (of judge) distretto giudiziario; (Cine) rete f di distribuzione; (Sport, Elec) circuito.

cir·cui·tous [sɜː'kjuɪtəs] adj: to come by a ~ route prendere la strada più lunga.

cir·cu·lar ['sɜːkjʊləʳ] 1 adj circolare. 2 n (letter) circolare f; (as advertisement) volantino pubblicitario.

cir·cu·late ['sɜːkjʊleɪt] 1 vi (gen) circolare; (person: socially) girare e andare un po' da tutti. 2 vt far circolare.

cir·cu·la·tion [,sɜːkjʊ'leɪʃən] n (gen) circolazione f; (of news) diffusione f; (of newspaper etc) tiratura; she has poor ~ (Med) ha una cattiva circolazione; to withdraw sth from ~ togliere qc dalla circolazione; he's back in ~ (fam) è tornato in circolazione.

cir·cum·cise ['sɜːkəmsaɪz] vt circoncidere.

cir·cum·ci·sion [,sɜːkəm'sɪʒən] n circoncisione f.

cir·cum·fer·ence [sə'kʌmfərəns] n circonferenza.

cir·cum·flex ['sɜːkəmfleks] n accento circonflesso.

cir·cum·scribe ['sɜːkəmskraɪb] vt circoscrivere; (fig: limit) limitare.

cir·cum·spect ['sɜːkəmspekt] adj circospetto(a).

cir·cum·stance ['sɜːkəmstəns] n (usu pl) circostanza; in the ~s date le circostanze; under no ~s per nessun motivo; to be easy/poor ~s versare in buone/cattive acque.

cir·cum·stan·tial [,sɜːkəm'stænʃəl] adj (report, statement) circostanziato(a), dettagliato(a); ~ evidence prova indiziaria.

cir·cum·vent [,sɜːkəm'vent] vt (rule etc) aggirare.

cir·cus ['sɜːkəs] n (entertainment) circo; (usu C~: in place names) piazza (di forma circolare).

cir·rho·sis [sɪ'rəʊsɪs] n cirrosi f.

cis·sy ['sɪsɪ] n femminuccia.

cis·tern ['sɪstən] n serbatoio.

cita·del ['sɪtədl] n cittadella.

cite [saɪt] vt citare; he was ~d to appear in court (Law) fu citato in tribunale.

citi·zen ['sɪtɪzn] n (of state) cittadino/a; (of city) abitante m/f.

citi·zen·ship ['sɪtɪznʃɪp] n cittadinanza.

cit·ric ['sɪtrɪk] adj: ~ acid acido citrico.

cit·rus ['sɪtrəs] 1 n agrume m. 2 cpd: ~ fruits npl agrumi mpl.

city ['sɪtɪ] 1 n (grande) città f inv; the C~ (Fin) la City di Londra. 2 cpd: ~ centre n centro della città; ~ dweller n chi abita in città; ~ page n (Fin) pagina finanziaria; ~ slicker (pej fam) imbroglione m con l'aria da gentiluomo.

civ·ic ['sɪvɪk] adj civico(a); ~ centre (Brit) centro civico.

civ·il ['sɪvl] 1 adj (a) (war, law, marriage) civile. (b) (polite) educato(a), gentile. 2 cpd: ~ defence n protezione f civile; ~ disobedience n resistenza passiva; ~ engineering n ingegneria civile; ~ rights movement n movimento per i diritti civili; ~ servant n funzionario statale; ~ service n amministrazione f pubblica.

ci·vil·ian [sɪ'vɪlɪən] 1 adj (clothes, government) civile, borghese; (life) da civile, da borghese. 2 n civile m/f, borghese m/f.

ci·vil·ity [sɪ'vɪlɪtɪ] n gentilezza.

civi·li·za·tion [,sɪvɪlaɪ'zeɪʃən] n civiltà f inv.

civi·lize ['sıvılaız] *vt* civilizzare.

civi·lized ['sıvılaızd] *adj* civilizzato(a); *(behaviour, manner)* civile.

clad [klæd] *adj*: ~ **(in)** vestito(a) (di).

claim [kleım] **1** *n* **(a)** *(demand: to title, right)* pretesa; *(: for expenses, damages, increased pay)* richiesta; *(insurance ~)* domanda d'indennizzo; **the poor have a ~ to our sympathy** i poveri hanno diritto alla nostra comprensione; **there are many ~s on my time** sono molto preso; **to lay ~ to sth** avanzare pretese a qc; **to put in a ~ for sth** fare una richiesta di qc; **to put in a ~ for petrol expenses** chiedere il rimborso delle spese per la benzina. **(b)** *(assertion)* affermazione *f*, pretesa; **I make no ~ to be infallible** non pretendo di essere infallibile.

2 *vt* **(a)** *(rights, territory)* pretendere, rivendicare; *(expenses, damages)* richiedere; *(lost property)* reclamare; **something else ~ed her attention** qualcosa distolse la sua attenzione. **(b)** *(assert)* dichiarare, sostenere; **the new system ~s many advantages over the old one** il nuovo sistema afferma di avere molti vantaggi su quello vecchio; **he ~s to have seen her** sostiene di averla vista; **to ~ that...** affermare *or* sostenere che... .

3 *cpd*: ~ **form** *n (gen)* modulo di richiesta; *(for expenses)* modulo di rimborso spese.

claim·ant ['kleımənt] *n (in court)* citante *m/f*; *(to social benefit)* richiedente *m/f*; *(to throne etc)* pretendente *m/f*.

clair·voy·ant [klɛə'vɔıənt] *adj, n* chiaroveggente *(m/f)*.

clam [klæm] *n* vongola.

♦ **clam up** *vi + adv (fam)* azzittirsi.

clam·ber ['klæmbə'] *vi* arrampicarsi.

clam·my ['klæmı] *adj (-ier, -iest) (hands)* sudaticcio(a); *(weather)* appiccicoso(a).

clam·our, *(Am)* **clam·or** ['klæmə'] **1** *n (noise)* clamore *m*; *(protest)* protesta. **2** *vi*: **to ~ for sth** chiedere a gran voce qc.

clamp [klæmp] **1** *n* morsetto. **2** *vt* stringere con un morsetto.

♦ **clamp down** *vi + adv (fig)*: **to ~ down (on)** dare un giro di vite (a).

clan [klæn] *n* clan *m inv*.

clan·des·tine [klæn'destın] *adj* clandestino(a).

clang [klæŋ] **1** *n* rumore *m* metallico. **2** *vi* emettere un suono metallico; **the gate ~ed shut** il cancello si chiuse con fragore.

clang·er ['klæŋə'] *n (fam)* gaffe *f inv*; **to drop a ~** fare una gaffe.

clank ['klæŋk] **1** *n* rumore *m* metallico. **2** *vi* emettere un suono metallico.

clap [klæp] **1** *n (on shoulder)* pacca; *(of the hands)* battimano; *(usu pl: applause)* applauso; **a ~ of thunder** un tuono. **2** *vt (applaud)* applaudire; **to ~ one's hands** battere le mani; **to ~ a hand over sb's mouth** chiudere la bocca (con la mano) a qn; **they ~ped him in prison** *(fam)* lo sbatterono dentro. **3** *vi (applaud)* applaudire.

clap·ping ['klæpıŋ] *n* applauso.

clap·trap ['klæp,træp] *n (pej fam)* sciocchezze *fpl* (per fare colpo).

clar·et ['klærət] *n* chiaretto.

clari·fi·ca·tion [,klærıfı'keıʃən] *n* chiarificazione *f*, chiarimento.

clari·fy ['klærıfaı] *vt (statement etc)* chiarire.

clari·net [,klærı'net] *n* clarinetto.

clar·ity ['klærıtı] *n* chiarezza.

clash [klæʃ] **1** *n* **(a)** *(noise)* fragore *m*. **(b)** *(Mil, of personalities, interests)* scontro, conflitto; *(of dates, programmes)* conflitto; *(of colours)* contra-

sto, disarmonia; **a ~ with the police** uno scontro con la polizia; **a ~ of wills** uno scontro di idee. **2** *vt (cymbals)* far risuonare; *(swords)* far cozzare. **3** *vi*: **to ~ (with)** *(Mil, fig: have an argument)* scontrarsi (con); *(personalities, interests)* scontrarsi (con), essere in conflitto (con); *(colours)* stridere (con); *(dates, events)* coincidere (con).

clasp [klɑːsp] **1** *n* gancio, fermaglio. **2** *vt* afferrare; **to ~ one's hands (together)** stringere le mani; **to ~ sb in one's arms** stringere qn tra le braccia.

class [klɑːs] **1** *n (group, category)* tipo, categoria; *(social ~, Bio, Scol, Univ)* classe *f*; **to have ~** *(fam)* avere classe; **to be in a ~ of one's own** essere impareggiabile. **2** *vt*: **to ~ sb as sth** definire qn qc. **3** *cpd*: ~ **distinction** *n (Sociol)* distinzione *f* di classe; ~ **war(fare)** *n (Sociol)* lotta di classe.

class-conscious ['klɑːs,kɒnʃəs] *adj* classista.

clas·sic ['klæsık] **1** *adj* classico(a). **2** *n* classico; ~**s** *(Univ)* studi *mpl* umanistici.

clas·si·cal ['klæsıkəl] *adj* classico(a); ~ **scholar** studioso di lettere antiche; ~ **music** musica classica.

clas·si·fi·ca·tion [,klæsıfı'keıʃən] *n* classificazione *f*.

clas·si·fied ['klæsıfaıd] *adj (information)* segreto(a), riservato(a); ~ **advertisement** annuncio economico.

clas·si·fy ['klæsıfaı] *vt* classificare.

class·room ['klɑːs,rum] *n* classe *f*, aula.

classy ['klɑːsı] *adj (-ier, -iest) (fam)* di classe, chic *inv*.

clat·ter ['klætə'] **1** *n (of plates)* tintinnio; *(of hooves)* scalpitio. **2** *vi (metal object etc)* sferragliare; *(hooves)* scalpitare; **the gate ~ed behind her** il cancello sbattè con fragore dietro a lei; **to ~ in/out** correre fragorosamente dentro/fuori.

clause [klɔːz] *n (Gram)* proposizione *f*; *(in contract, law, will)* clausola.

claus·tro·pho·bia [,klɔːstrə'fəubıə] *n* claustrofobia.

claus·tro·pho·bic [,klɔːstrə'fəubık] *adj (person)* claustrofobico(a); *(atmosphere)* da claustrofobia.

claw [klɔː] **1** *n (of cat, small bird)* unghia; *(of lion, eagle etc)* artiglio; *(of lobster)* chela. **2** *vt* graffiare; **to ~ sth to shreds** dilaniare qc. **3** *vi*: **to ~ at** graffiare; *(prey)* ghermire.

clay [kleı] **1** *n (gen)* argilla; *(for pottery)* creta, argilla. **2** *cpd*: ~ **pigeon shooting** *n* tiro al piattello; ~ **pipe** *n* pipa di terracotta.

clean [kliːn] **1** *adj (gen)* pulito(a); *(sheet of paper)* nuovo(a); *(smooth, even: outline, movement, break)* netto(a); *(fair: fight)* leale, corretto(a); **to wipe sth ~** pulire qc; **to make a ~ sweep** fare piazza pulita; **the doctor gave me a ~ bill of health** il medico ha garantito che godo di ottima salute; **to make a ~ breast of sth** togliersi qc dalla coscienza; **a ~ record** *(Police)* una fedina penale pulita; **to have a ~ driving licence** non aver mai preso contravvenzioni.

2 *adv*: **he ~ forgot** si è completamente dimenticato; **he got ~ away** se l'è svignata senza lasciare tracce; **the ball went ~ through the window** la palla andò dritta dentro la finestra; **to come ~** *(fam: admit guilt)* confessare; *(: tell unpleasant truth)* dire veramente come sono le cose; **I'm ~ out of cigarettes** non ho neanche mezza sigaretta.

3 *n* pulita, ripulitura.

4 *vt (gen)* pulire; *(blackboard)* cancellare; *(shoes)* lucidare; **to ~ one's teeth** lavarsi i denti.

♦ **clean off** *vt + adv* togliere.

♦ **clean out** vt + adv (also fig) ripulire.

♦ **clean up 1** vt + adv (room, mess) pulire, ripulire; (fig: city etc) fare un po' di pulizia in; **to ~ o.s. up** darsi una ripulita. **2** vi + adv ripulire; (fig: make profit): **to ~ up on** fare una barca di soldi con.

clean·er ['kliːnə^r] n (person) uomo/donna delle pulizie; (substance) detergente m; ~**'s (shop)** tintoria.

clean·ing ['kliːnɪŋ] **1** n pulizia; **to do the ~** fare le pulizie. **2** cpd: ~ **lady** n donna delle pulizie.

clean·li·ness ['klɛnlɪnɪs] n pulizia.

clean·ness ['kliːnnɪs] n pulizia.

cleanse [klɛnz] vt pulire; (fig: soul etc) purificare.

cleans·er ['klɛnzə^r] n (detergent) detersivo; (cosmetic) latte m detergente.

clean-shaven ['kliːn'ʃeɪvn] adj senza barba.

clear [klɪə^r] **1** adj **(a)** (water) chiaro(a), limpido(a); (glass, plastic) trasparente; (air, sky, weather) sereno(a); (complexion) chiaro(a); (photograph, outline) nitido(a); (conscience) pulito(a); **on a ~ day** in una giornata limpida.

(b) (sound) chiaro(a), distinto(a); (impression, meaning, explanation) chiaro(a); (motive, consequence) ovvio(a); (understanding, proof) certo(a), sicuro(a); (profit, majority) netto(a); **a ~ case of murder** un chiaro caso di omicidio; **to make o.s. ~** spiegarsi bene; **to make it ~ to sb that...** far capire a qn che...; **it is ~ to me that** per me è evidente che; **as ~ as day** chiaro come il sole; **three ~ days** tre giorni interi; **to win by a ~ head** (horse) vincere di un'incollatura.

(c) (free: road, space) libero(a), sgombro(a); **I have a ~ day tomorrow** non ho impegni domani; **we had a ~ view** avevamo una buona visuale; **the ship was ~ of the rocks** la nave aveva superato il pericolo delle rocce; **we're ~ of the police now** ora siamo sufficientemente lontani dalla polizia; **all ~!** cessato pericolo!

2 adv **(a)** see **loud**.

(b) (completely) completamente; **to get ~ away** svignarsela senza lasciar tracce; **to keep ~ of sb/sth** tenersi lontano da qn/qc, stare alla larga da qn/qc; **to stand ~ of sth** stare lontano da qc.

3 n: **to be in the ~** (out of debt) essere in attivo; (out of suspicion) essere apposto; (out of danger) essere fuori pericolo.

4 vt **(a)** (place, surface, road, railway track) liberare, sgombrare; (site, woodland) spianare; (pipe) sbloccare; (Med: blood) purificare; **to ~ a space for sth/sb** fare posto per qc/qn; **he ~ed the path of leaves** ha sgombrato le foglie dal viale; **to ~ the table** sparecchiare (la tavola); **to ~ one's throat** schiarirsi la gola; **to ~ the air** (fig) chiarire le cose; **to ~ one's conscience** togliersi un peso dalla coscienza.

(b) (get over: fence etc) scavalcare; (get past: rocks etc) scansare; **to ~ 2 metres** (athlete etc) superare i 2 metri.

(c) (declare innocent) discolpare; (get permission for): **to ~ sth (with sb)** ottenere il permesso (di qn) per qc; **he was ~ed of murder** fu scagionato dall'accusa di omicidio; **to ~ o.s.** provare la propria innocenza; **he'll have to be ~ed by the security department** dovrà superare il controllo del dipartimento di sicurezza.

(d) (Comm etc: debt) liquidare, saldare; (: goods etc) svendere; (: cheque) fare la compensazione di; **to ~ a profit** avere un profitto netto.

5 vi (weather, sky) schiarirsi, rasserenarsi; (smoke, fog) dissolversi.

♦ **clear off 1** vt + adv (debt) saldare, liquidare. **2** vi

+ adv (fam: leave) svignarsela.

♦ **clear out 1** vt + adv liberare, sgombrare. **2** vi + adv = **clear off 2**.

♦ **clear up 1** vt + adv **(a)** (matter, mystery) chiarire. **(b)** (tidy: room etc) mettere in ordine, rassettare. **2** vi + adv **(a)** (weather) schiararsi, rasserenarsi. **(b)** (tidy up) fare ordine.

clear·ance ['klɪərəns] **1** n **(a)** (of road, room, surface) sgombero; (of site, woodland) spianamento; (of rubbish, litter) rimozione f; (space) spazio (libero). **(b)** (authorization) autorizzazione f; (: by customs) sdoganamento; ~ **for take-off** (Aer) permesso di decollo. **2** cpd: ~ **sale** n svendita, liquidazione f.

clear-cut ['klɪəkʌt] adj ben definito(a).

clear·ing ['klɪərɪŋ] **1** n (in wood) radura. **2** cpd: ~ **bank** n (Fin) banca (che fa uso della camera di compensazione); ~ **house** n (Fin) camera di compensazione.

clear·ly ['klɪəlɪ] adv chiaramente.

cleav·age ['kliːvɪdʒ] n: **she wore a dress which emphasised her ~** indossava un vestito con una profonda scollatura.

cleav·er ['kliːvə^r] n mannaia.

clef [klɛf] n (Mus) chiave f.

cleft [klɛft] **1** n crepa, fenditura. **2** cpd: ~ **palate** n (Med) palatoschisi f; ~ **stick** n: **in a ~ stick** (fig) in un vicolo cieco.

clem·en·cy ['klɛmənsɪ] n clemenza.

clench [klɛntʃ] vt stringere; **to ~ sth in one's hand** stringere in pugno qc.

cler·gy ['klɜːdʒɪ] n clero.

clergy·man ['klɜːdʒɪmən] n, pl -men ecclesiastico.

cleri·cal ['klɛrɪkəl] adj **(a)** (Comm: job) d'ufficio; ~ **worker** impiegato/a; ~ **error** svista. **(b)** (Rel) clericale.

clerk [klɑːk], (Am) [klɜːrk] n (Comm) impiegato/a; (Am: shop assistant) commesso/a; (Am: in hotel) impiegato di reception; **C~ of the Court** cancelliere m; ~ **of works** assessore m ai lavori pubblici.

clev·er ['klɛvə^r] adj (gen) intelligente; (smart: idea, person, invention etc) geniale; **to be ~ at sth** essere abile in qc; **he is very ~ with his hands** è molto abile nei lavori manuali; **he was too ~ for us** era più furbo di noi.

clev·er·ly ['klɛvəlɪ] adv intelligentemente.

clev·er·ness ['klɛvənɪs] n (see adj) intelligenza; genialità; abilità.

clew [kluː] n (Am) = **clue**.

cli·ché ['kliːʃeɪ] n frase f fatta.

click [klɪk] **1** n (of camera etc) scatto; (of heels) battito; (of tongue) schiocco. **2** vt (heels etc) battere; (tongue) fare schioccare. **3** vi (camera etc) scattare; (heels) battere; **the door ~ed shut** la porta si chiuse con uno scatto; **suddenly it all ~ed (into place)** (fig fam) improvvisamente mi fu chiarito tutto.

cli·ent ['klaɪənt] n cliente m/f.

cli·en·tele [ˌkliːɑːnˈtɛl] n clientela.

cliff [klɪf] n (sea ~) scogliera; (of mountain etc) dirupo.

cliff-hanger ['klɪfˌhæŋə^r] n (TV, fig) episodio (or situazione etc) ricco(a) di suspense.

cli·mate ['klaɪmɪt] n clima m; **the ~ of popular opinion** l'opinione pubblica.

cli·max ['klaɪmæks] n culmine m; (of play etc) momento più emozionante; (sexual ~) orgasmo.

climb [klaɪm] **1** n (gen) ascesa, salita; (of mountain) scalata; (Aer) ascesa. **2** vt (also: ~ **up:** tree, ladder etc) salire su, arrampicarsi su; (: staircase) salire; (: mountain, wall) scalare; **to ~ a rope** arrampicarsi su una corda. **3** vi (road, person) salire;

(plane) prendere quota; *(plant)* arrampicarsi; **the pilot ~ed into the cockpit** il pilota si è infilato nella cabina di pilotaggio; **to ~ over a wall** scavalcare un muro.

♦ **climb down 1** *vi + prep* scendere da. **2** *vi + adv* scendere; *(fig)* far marcia indietro.

climb·er ['klaɪməʳ] *n (rock ~)* alpinista *m/f; (Bot)* rampicante *m;* **social ~** arrampicatore/trice sociale.

climb·ing ['klaɪmɪŋ] *n (rock ~)* alpinismo; **to go ~** andare a far roccia.

clinch [klɪntʃ] **1** *n:* **in a ~** *(fam: embrace)* abbracciati stretti. **2** *vt (settle: deal etc)* concludere; **that ~es it** è fatta.

cling [klɪŋ] *pt, pp* **clung** *vi:* **to ~ to** *(gen, fig)* aggrapparsi a; **the smell clung to her clothes** l'odore le restava attaccato ai vestiti.

clin·ic ['klɪnɪk] *n (hospital, dental ~ etc)* clinica; *(for guidance etc)* centro.

clini·cal ['klɪnɪkəl] *adj* clinico(a); *(fig)* freddo(a), distaccato(a).

clink [klɪŋk] **1** *n* tintinnio. **2** *vt:* **to ~ glasses with sb** brindare *or* fare cin cin con qn. **3** *vi* tintinnare.

clip¹ [klɪp] **1** *n (Cine)* sequenza. **2** *vt (cut: gen)* tagliare; *(sheep, dog)* tosare; *(ticket)* forare; *(article from newspaper)* ritagliare; **to ~ sb's wings** *(fig)* tarpare le ali a qn.

clip² [klɪp] *n (paper ~)* clip *f inv; (bulldog ~)* fermafogli *m inv; (hair ~)* molletta; *(brooch)* spilla, fermaglio.

♦ **clip on** *vt + adv (brooch)* agganciare; *(document: with paper clip etc)* attaccare.

♦ **clip together** *vt + adv* attaccare (con una clip).

clip·board ['klɪp,bɔːd] *n* fermabloc *m inv.*

clipped [klɪpt] *adj:* **in a ~ voice** scandendo bene le sillabe.

clip·per ['klɪpəʳ] *n (Naut)* clipper *m inv.*

clip·pers ['klɪpəz] *npl (for nails)* tagliaunghie *m; (for hedge)* tosasiepi *m,* cesoie *fpl.*

clip·ping ['klɪpɪŋ] *n (from newspaper)* ritaglio.

clique [kliːk] *n* cricca.

cloak [kləʊk] *n* cappa, mantella; **under the ~ of darkness** *(fig)* sotto il manto dell'oscurità.

cloak-and-dagger [,kləʊkən'dægəʳ] *adj (film etc)* del mistero; *(activities)* misterioso(a).

cloak·room ['kləʊkrʊm] *n (for coats)* guardaroba *m inv; (Brit euph)* toilette *f inv.*

clock [klɒk] **1** *n (gen)* orologio; *(of taxi)* tassametro; **30,000 on the ~** *(Aut)* 30.000 sul contachilometri; **to sleep round the ~** dormire un giorno intero; **to work against the ~** lavorare in gara col tempo. **2** *vt (runner)* cronometrare; *(time)* registrare.

♦ **clock in, clock on** *vi + adv* timbrare il cartellino (all'entrata).

♦ **clock off, clock out** *vi + adv* timbrare il cartellino (all'uscita).

♦ **clock up** *vt + adv (Aut)* registrare, fare.

clock·wise ['klɒkwaɪz] *adv* in senso orario.

clock·work ['klɒkwɜːk] **1** *n:* **to go like ~** funzionare come un orologio. **2** *cpd (toy, train)* a molla.

clod [klɒd] *n* zolla.

clog [klɒg] **1** *n* zoccolo. **2** *vt (also: ~ up: pipe, drain)* ostruire, intasare; *(: machine, mechanism)* bloccare. **3** *vi (also: ~ up)* intasarsi, bloccarsi.

clois·ter ['klɔɪstəʳ] *n* chiostro.

clois·tered ['klɔɪstəd] *adj (life)* da recluso *(or* reclusa).

close¹ [kləʊs] **1** *adv* vicino; **~ by** qui *(or* lì) vicino; **to hold sb ~** tenere stretto qn; **~ together** vicino, attaccato; **stay ~ to me** stammi vicino; **to follow ~ behind** seguire da vicino.

2 *adj* **(a)** *(near)* vicino(a); *(: relative, connection, resemblance)* stretto(a); *(: friend)* intimo(a);

(almost equal: result) quasi pari; *(: fight, contest, election, race)* combattuto(a); **how ~ is Edinburgh to Glasgow?** quanto dista Edimburgo da Glasgow?; **they're very ~** *(in age)* sono molto vicini (come età); *(emotionally)* sono molto uniti; **at ~ quarters** da vicino; **~ combat** combattimento corpo a corpo; **that was a ~ shave** *(fig fam)* l'ho *(or* l'hai *etc)* scampata per un pelo.

(b) *(exact, detailed: examination, study)* accurato(a); *(: investigation, questioning)* approfondito(a); *(: surveillance, control)* stretto(a); **to pay ~ attention to sb/sth** stare ben attento a qn/qc; **to keep a ~ watch on sb** guardare qn a vista.

(c) *(handwriting, texture, weave)* fitto(a).

(d) *(stuffy: atmosphere, room)* soffocante; *(weather)* afoso(a); **it's rather ~ in here** qui c'è aria viziata.

close² [kləʊz] **1** *n (end)* fine *f,* chiusura; **to bring sth to a ~** terminare qc; **to draw to a ~** avvicinarsi alla fine. **2** *vi (shut)* chiudersi; *(end)* chiudersi, concludersi. **3** *vt* **(a)** *(shut: door, road, shop etc)* chiudere; **to ~ the gap between 2 things** *(fig)* colmare il divario tra 2 cose; **to ~ one's eyes to sth** *(fig)* ignorare qc. **(b)** *(end: discussion, meeting)* chiudere, concludere; *(: bank account)* chiudere, estinguere; *(: bargain, deal)* concludere.

♦ **close down 1** *vi + adv (business)* chiudersi, chiudere; *(TV, Radio)* terminare i programmi. **2** *vt + adv* chiudere.

♦ **close in** *vi + adv (hunters)* stringersi attorno; *(evening, night, fog)* calare; **the days are closing in** le giornate si accorciano; **to ~ in on sb** accerchiare qn.

♦ **close off** *vt + adv (area)* chiudere.

♦ **close round** *vi + prep* stringersi attorno a.

♦ **close up 1** *vi + adv (people in queue)* stringersi; *(wound)* rimarginarsi. **2** *vt + adv (shop, house, opening)* chiudere; *(wound)* chiudere, suturare.

closed [kləʊzd] *adj* chiuso(a); **sociology is a ~ book to me** per me la sociologia è un mistero; **~ shop** *(Industry)* ditta *(or* ente *m)* che assume solo lavoratori iscritti al sindacato.

closed-circuit tele·vi·sion ['kləʊzd,sɜːkɪt-'telɪ,vɪʒən] *n* televisione *f* a circuito chiuso.

close-down ['kləʊz,daʊn] *n (of shop, factory)* chiusura; *(TV, Radio)* fine *f* delle trasmissioni.

close·ly ['kləʊslɪ] *adv (guard)* strettamente; *(listen, follow, study)* attentamente; *(resemble)* molto; *(connected)* strettamente; **a ~ guarded secret** un assoluto segreto; **we are ~ related** siamo parenti stretti.

close·ness ['kləʊsnɪs] *n (nearness)* vicinanza; *(of friendship)* profondità; *(of room)* mancanza d'aria; **the ~ of the weather** il tempo afoso; **the ~ of the resemblance** la stretta somiglianza.

clos·et ['klɒzɪt] **1** *n (Am: cupboard)* armadio a muro. **2** *vt:* **to be ~ed with sb** essersi appartato(a) con qn.

close-up ['kləʊsʌp] *n* primo piano; **in ~** in primo piano.

clos·ing ['kləʊzɪŋ] *adj (stages, remarks)* conclusivo(a), finale; **~ speech** discorso di chiusura; **when is ~ time?** a che ora chiude?; **~ price** *(Stock Exchange)* prezzo di chiusura.

clo·sure ['kləʊʒəʳ] *n* chiusura.

clot [klɒt] **1** *n (gen, Med)* grumo; *(fam: fool)* scemo/a, zuccone/a. **2** *vi* coagularsi; **~ted cream** panna rappresa *(ottenuta scaldando il latte).*

cloth [klɒθ] *n (material)* tessuto, stoffa; *(for cleaning)* panno, straccio; *(table~)* tovaglia; **a man of the ~** *(Rel)* un religioso, un ecclesiastico.

clothe [kləʊð] *vt* vestire.

clothes [kləʊðz] 1 *npl* vestiti *mpl*, abiti *mpl*; **to put one's ~ on** vestirsi; **to take one's ~ off** togliersi i vestiti, svestirsi. 2 *cpd*: ~ **horse** *n* stendibiancheria *m inv*; ~ **line** *n* corda del bucato; ~ **peg** *n*, *(Am)* ~ **pin** *n* molletta (da bucato); ~ **shop** *n* negozio di abbigliamento.

cloth·ing [ˈkləʊðɪŋ] 1 *n* abbigliamento; **article of** ~.capo di vestiario. 2 *cpd*: ~ **allowance** *n* indennità *f inv* per gli abiti da lavoro.

cloud [klaʊd] 1 *n (Met)* nuvola, nube *f; (of dust, smoke, gas)* nube; *(of insects)* nugolo; **to be under a** ~ essere malvisto; **he has his head in the** ~**s** ha la testa tra le nuvole; **to be on** ~ **nine** essere al settimo cielo. 2 *vt (liquid)* intorbidire; *(mirror)* appannare; *(fig: memory)* confondere; *(: mind)* turbare; **a** ~**ed sky** un cielo nuvoloso; **to** ~ **the issue** distogliere dal problema.

♦ **cloud over** *vi* + *adv* rannuvolarsi; *(fig)* offuscarsi.

cloud·burst [ˈklaʊd,bɜːst] *n* acquazzone *m*.

cloud-cuckoo-land [ˌklaʊdˈkʊkuː,lænd] *n* mondo dei sogni.

cloud·less [ˈklaʊdlɪs] *adj* sereno(a), senza nubi.

cloudy [ˈklaʊdɪ] *adj (sky)* nuvoloso(a), coperto(a); *(liquid)* torbido(a).

clout [klaʊt] 1 *n (blow)* ceffone *m; (fig)* influenza. 2 *vt* colpire.

clove [kləʊv] *n* chiodo di garofano; ~ **of garlic** spicchio d'aglio.

clo·ver [ˈkləʊvəʳ] *n* trifoglio; **a four-leaved** ~ un quadrifoglio; **to be in** ~ *(fam)* nuotare nell'abbondanza.

clover·leaf [ˈkləʊvə,liːf] *n (Bot)* foglia di trifoglio; *(Aut)* raccordo (a quadrifoglio).

clown [klaʊn] 1 *n (in circus)* pagliaccio, clown *m inv; (fam)* buffone *m.* 2 *vi (also:* ~ **about** *or* **around)** fare il buffone *or* il pagliaccio.

club [klʌb] 1 *n* **(a)** *(stick)* randello; *(of caveman)* clava; *(golf* ~*)* mazza; *(Cards):* ~**s** fiori *mpl;* **he played a** ~ ha giocato una carta di fiori. **(b)** *(association)* circolo, club *m inv;* **tennis** ~ circolo di tennis; **join the** ~**!** *(fig)* non sei il solo! 2 *vt (person)* bastonare; ~**bed to death with sticks** ucciso a colpi di bastone. 3 *vi:* **to** ~ **together (to buy)** mettersi insieme (per comprare).

club·house [ˈklʌb,haʊs] *n* circolo.

cluck [klʌk] *vi* chiocciare.

clue [kluː] *n* indicazione *f; (in a crime etc)* indizio; *(of crossword)* definizione *f;* **I'll give you a** ~ ti metto sulla strada giusta; **I haven't a** ~ *(fam)* non ne ho la minima idea.

clued up [kluːdˈʌp] *adj (fam)* (ben) informato(a).

clue·less [ˈkluːlɪs] *adj (fam):* **to be** ~ non capirci niente.

clump[1] [klʌmp] *n (of trees, flowers etc)* gruppo; *(of grass)* ciuffo.

clump[2] [klʌmp] 1 *n* rumore *m* sordo. 2 *vi:* **to** ~ **(about)** camminare con passo pesante.

clum·sy [ˈklʌmzɪ] *adj (person, action, gesture)* goffo(a), maldestro(a); *(painting, forgery)* malfatto(a); *(tool)* poco pratico(a); *(remark)* maldestro(a); *(apology)* goffo(a).

clung [klʌŋ] *pt, pp of* **cling.**

clus·ter [ˈklʌstəʳ] 1 *n (of houses, people, trees)* gruppo; *(of grapes)* grappolo; *(of stars)* ammasso. 2 *vi (people, things):* **to** ~ **(round sb/sth)** raggrupparsi (intorno a qn/qc).

clutch [klʌtʃ] 1 *n* **(a)** *(Aut)* frizione *f; (pedal)* (pedale *m* della) frizione *f.* **(b): to fall into sb's** ~**es** cadere nelle grinfie di qn. 2 *vt (catch hold of)* afferrare; *(hold tightly)* tenere stretto(a), stringere forte. 3 *vi:* **to** ~ **at** cercare di afferrare; **to** ~ **at straws** *(fig)* crearsi delle illusioni.

clut·ter [ˈklʌtəʳ] 1 *n* confusione *f*, disordine *m;* **in a** ~ in disordine. 2 *vt (also:* ~ **up)** ingombrare; **to be** ~**ed up with sth** essere pieno zeppo di qc.

Co. (a) *(abbr of* **company)** C., C.ia. **(b)** *abbr of* **county.**

co- [kəʊ] *pref* co... .

c/o *abbr of* **care of.**

coach [kəʊtʃ] 1 *n* **(a)** *(bus)* corriera; *(: for excursions)* pullman *m inv; (Brit Rail)* carrozza, vettura; *(horse drawn)* carrozza; *(: stage~)* diligenza. **(b)** *(Sport)* allenatore/trice; *(tutor)* chi dà ripetizioni. 2 *vt (team)* allenare; *(student)* dare ripetizioni a.

co·agu·late [kəʊˈægjʊleɪt] 1 *vt* coagulare. 2 *vi* coagularsi.

coal [kəʊl] 1 *n* carbone *m;* **to carry** ~**s to Newcastle** *(fig)* portare acqua al mare. 2 *cpd (fire)* di carbone; *(industry)* del carbone; *(stove)* a carbone; ~ **cellar** *n*, ~ **shed** *n* carbonaia; ~ **scuttle** *n* secchio del carbone.

coal-black [ˈkəʊlˈblæk] *adj* nero(a) come il carbone.

coal·dust [ˈkəʊl,dʌst] *n* polvere *f* di carbone.

coal·face [ˈkəʊl,feɪs] *n* fronte *f*.

coal·field [ˈkəʊl,fiːld] *n* bacino carbonifero.

coa·li·tion [ˌkəʊəˈlɪʃən] *n (Pol)* coalizione *f.*

coal·man [ˈkəʊlmæn] *n*, *pl* **-men** carbonaio.

coal·mine [ˈkəʊl,maɪn] *n* miniera di carbone.

coal·miner [ˈkəʊl,maɪnəʳ] *n* minatore *m*.

coal·mining [ˈkəʊl,maɪnɪŋ] *n* estrazione *f* del carbone.

coarse [kɔːs] *adj (texture, skin, material)* ruvido(a); *(salt, sand)* grosso(a); *(sandpaper)* a grana grossa; *(vulgar: character, laugh, remark)* volgare.

coarse·ly [ˈkɔːslɪ] *adv (ground, woven)* grossolanamente; *(laugh, say)* volgarmente.

coars·en [ˈkɔːsn] 1 *vi (skin)* diventare ruvido(a); *(person, manners)* diventare grossolano(a). 2 *vt (see vi)* rendere ruvido(a); rendere grossolano(a).

coast [kəʊst] 1 *n* costa *f; (~ line)* litorale *m;* **the** ~ **is clear** *(fig)* la via è libera. 2 *vi (Aut)* andare in folle; *(Cycling)* andare a ruota libera.

coast·al [ˈkəʊstəl] *adj* costiero(a).

coast·er [ˈkəʊstəʳ] *n* **(a)** *(Naut)* nave *f* da cabotaggio. **(b)** *(for glass)* sottobicchiere *m*.

coast·guard [ˈkəʊst,gɑːd] *n (person)* guardacoste *m inv; (organisation)* guardia costiera.

coast·line [ˈkəʊst,laɪn] *n* litorale *m*.

coat [kəʊt] 1 *n* **(a)** *(garment)* cappotto, soprabito. **(b)** *(animal's)* pelo; *(horse's)* mantello. **(c)** *(layer)* strato; *(of paint)* mano *f.* **(d):** ~ **of arms** stemma *m*, blasone *m.* 2 *vt:* **to** ~ **sth with** ricoprire qc con uno strato di; *(paint)* dare a qc una mano di.

coat·hanger [ˈkəʊt,hæŋəʳ] *n* stampella, gruccia.

co-author [ˈkəʊ,ɔːθəʳ] *n* coautore/trice.

coax [kəʊks] *vt:* **to** ~ **sth out of sb** ottenere qc da qn (con le buone); **to** ~ **sb into/out of doing sth** convincere (con moine) qn a fare/non fare qc.

co·balt [ˈkəʊbɒlt] *n* cobalto.

cob·ble [ˈkɒbl] *n (also:* ~ **stone)** ciottolo.

cob·bled [ˈkɒbld] *adj:* ~ **street** strada pavimentata con ciottoli.

cob·bler [ˈkɒbləʳ] *n* calzolaio.

co·bra [ˈkəʊbrə] *n* cobra *m inv.*

cob·web [ˈkɒbweb] *n* ragnatela.

Coca-Cola [ˌkəʊkəˈkəʊlə] *n* ® coca-cola *f inv* ®.

co·caine [kəˈkeɪn] *n* cocaina.

cock [kɒk] 1 *n (cockerel)* gallo; *(other male bird)* maschio. 2 *vt (gun)* alzare il cane di; **to** ~ **(up) one's ears** *(also fig)* drizzare le orecchie; **to** ~ **a snook at** fare marameo a; *(fig)* burlarsi di.

cock-a-doodle-doo [ˌkɒkəˌduːdəl'duː] n chicchirichì m.

cock-a-hoop [ˌkɒkə'huːp] adj esultante, euforico(a).

cock-and-bull [ˌkɒkənd'bʊl] adj: ~ **story** frottola.

cocka·too [ˌkɒkə'tuː] n cacatoa m inv.

cock·crow ['kɒk,krəʊ] n: at ~ al primo canto del gallo.

cock·er·el ['kɒkərəl] n galletto.

cock·eyed [ˌkɒk'aɪd] adj (crooked) storto(a); (absurd) assurdo(a).

cock·le ['kɒkl] n (Zool) cardio.

cock·ney ['kɒknɪ] n (person) cockney m/f inv; (dialect) cockney m.

cock·pit ['kɒkpɪt] n (Aer) cabina di pilotaggio.

cock·roach ['kɒkrəʊtʃ] n scarafaggio.

cock·sure [ˌkɒk'ʃʊəʳ] adj troppo sicuro(a) di sé, baldanzoso(a).

cock·tail ['kɒkteɪl] 1 n (drink) cocktail m inv; **fruit** ~ macedonia di frutta; **prawn** ~ cocktail di gamberetti. 2 cpd: ~ **bar** n bar m inv (di un albergo); ~ **cabinet** n mobile m bar inv; ~ **party** n cocktail m inv.

cocky ['kɒkɪ] adj (fam pej) impertinente.

co·coa ['kəʊkəʊ] n cacao; (drink) cioccolato caldo.

coco·nut ['kəʊkənʌt] 1 n (fruit) noce f di cocco; (tree: also: ~ **palm**) palma di cocco; (substance) cocco. 2 cpd: ~ **matting** n stuoia (di fibra) di cocco.

co·coon [kə'kuːn] n bozzolo.

cod [kɒd] n merluzzo.

C.O.D. abbr of **cash on delivery.**

cod·dle ['kɒdl] vt (Culin: esp eggs) cuocere a fuoco lento; (also: **molly**~) coccolare.

code [kəʊd] 1 n codice m; **in** ~ in codice; ~ **of behaviour** regole fpl di condotta. 2 vt cifrare. 3 cpd: ~ **name** n nome m in codice.

co·deine ['kəʊdiːn] n codeina.

codi·cil ['kɒdɪsɪl] n codicillo.

cod-liver oil ['kɒdlɪvər'ɔɪl] n olio di fegato di merluzzo.

co-driver ['kəʊdraɪvəʳ] n (in race) copilota m; (of lorry) secondo autista m.

co-ed ['kəʊ'ɛd] (fam) 1 adj misto(a). 2 n (Am) studentessa di scuola mista.

co·edu·ca·tion ['kəʊˌɛdjʊ'keɪʃən] n (istruzione f in) scuole fpl miste.

co·erce [kəʊ'ɜːs] vt: **to** ~ **sb** (into doing sth) costringere qn (a fare qc).

co·er·cion [kəʊ'ɜːʃən] n forza; (Law) coercizione f.

co·ex·ist ['kəʊɪg'zɪst] vi coesistere.

co·ex·ist·ence ['kəʊɪg'zɪstəns] n coesistenza.

C. of E. n abbr of **Church of England.**

cof·fee ['kɒfɪ] 1 n caffè m inv; **black** ~ caffè nero; **two white** ~**s, please** due caffellatte, per favore. 2 cpd: ~ **bar** n caffè m inv; ~ **break** n pausa per il caffè; ~ **cup** n tazzina da caffè; ~ **table** n tavolino.

coffee·pot ['kɒfɪ,pɒt] n caffettiera.

cof·fin ['kɒfɪn] n bara.

cog [kɒg] n dente m; **a** ~ **in the wheel** (fig) una rotella in un grande ingranaggio.

co·gent ['kəʊdʒənt] adj convincente.

cogi·tate ['kɒdʒɪteɪt] vi meditare.

cog·nac ['kɒnjæk] n cognac m inv.

co·hab·it [kəʊ'hæbɪt] vi (frm): **to** ~ **(with sb)** coabitare (con qn).

co·her·ence [kəʊ'hɪərəns] n coerenza.

co·her·ent [kəʊ'hɪərənt] adj coerente.

co·he·sive [kəʊ'hiːsɪv] adj (fig) unificante, coesivo(a).

coil [kɔɪl] 1 n (a) (roll) rotolo; (single loop) giro; (of hair) ciocca; (of snake) spira; (of smoke) filo. (b)

(Aut, Elec) bobina. **(c)**: **the** ~ (contraceptive) la spirale. 2 vt avvolgere; **to** ~ **sth up** avvolgere qc (in un rotolo). 3 vi attorcigliarsi.

coin [kɔɪn] 1 n moneta. 2 vt (fam: money) fare soldi a palate; (fig: word etc) coniare; **to** ~ **a phrase** (hum) per così dire.

co·in·cide [ˌkəʊɪn'saɪd] vi: **to** ~ **(with)** coincidere (con).

co·in·ci·dence [kəʊ'ɪnsɪdəns] n (chance) coincidenza, combinazione f.

coin-operated [ˌkɔɪn'ɒpəreɪtɪd] adj (machine) (che funziona) a monete.

coke [kəʊk] n **(a)** (fuel) carbone m coke. **(b)** (fam: cocaine) coca. **(c)** (®: Coca-Cola) coca f inv.

col·an·der ['kʌləndəʳ] n colino, colapasta m inv.

cold [kəʊld] 1 adj (also fig) freddo(a); **it's a** ~ **day** fa freddo oggi; **I'm** ~ ho freddo; **my feet are** ~ ho freddo ai piedi; **to get** ~ (person) cominciare a sentire freddo; (food etc) raffreddarsi, diventare freddo; **it's getting** ~ (weather) comincia a far freddo; **the room's getting** ~ comincia a far freddo in questa stanza; **to be out** ~ (fam: unconscious) essere privo di sensi; **to knock sb (out)** ~ mettere qn fuori combattimento; **in** ~ **blood** a sangue freddo; **it leaves me** ~ (fam) non mi fa né caldo, né freddo; **to have** ~ **feet** (fig) avere fifa; **it's** ~ **comfort** è una magra consolazione; **to put sth into** ~ **storage** (food) mettere qc in cella frigorifera; (fig: project) accantonare qc.

2 n **(a)** (Met etc) freddo; **to feel the** ~ sentire il freddo; **to be left out in the** ~ (fig) essere lasciato in disparte. **(b)** (Med: also: **common** ~) raffreddore m; **to catch a** ~ prendere un raffreddore.

3 cpd: ~ **cream** n crema emolliente; ~ **sore** n febbre f, herpes m inv; **the** ~ **war** la guerra fredda.

cold-blooded [ˌkəʊld'blʌdɪd] adj (Zool) a sangue freddo; (fig) spietato(a).

cold-hearted [ˌkəʊld'hɑːtɪd] adj insensibile.

cold·ly ['kəʊldlɪ] adv (fig) freddamente.

cold-shoulder [ˌkəʊld'ʃəʊldəʳ] vt trattare con freddezza.

cole·slaw ['kəʊlslɔː] n (no pl) insalata di cavolo bianco.

col·ic ['kɒlɪk] n colica.

col·labo·rate [kə'læbəreɪt] vi: **to** ~ **(with sb in sth)** collaborare (con qn a or in qc).

col·labo·ra·tion [kəˌlæbə'reɪʃən] n collaborazione f.

col·labo·ra·tor [kə'læbəreɪtəʳ] n collaboratore/trice.

col·lapse [kə'læps] 1 n (gen) crollo; (of government) caduta; (of plans, scheme, business) fallimento; (Med) collasso. 2 vi (see n) crollare; cadere; fallire; (Med) avere un collasso; (fam: with laughter) piegarsi in due dalle risate.

col·laps·ible [kə'læpsəbl] adj pieghevole.

col·lar ['kɒləʳ] 1 n (gen) collo; (of shirt, blouse) colletto; (for dog) collare m; (Tech) anello, fascetta. 2 vt (fam: person, object) beccare.

collar·bone ['kɒlə,bəʊn] n clavicola.

col·late [kɒ'leɪt] vt collazionare.

col·lat·er·al [kɒ'lætərəl] n (Fin) garanzia.

col·league ['kɒliːg] n collega m/f.

col·lect [kə'lɛkt] 1 vt **(a)** (gen) raccogliere; (as hobby: stamps, valuables) fare collezione di; **to** ~ **o.s.** riprendersi; **to** ~ **one's thoughts** raccogliere le proprie idee; **the** ~**ed works of Shakespeare** l'opera completa di Shakespeare. **(b)** (call for, pick up: person) andare a prendere; (: post, ticket) ritirare; (: subscriptions, rent, taxes) riscuotere; (: rubbish) portare via, raccogliere; (: dust) accumulare. 2 vi (people) riunirsi, radunarsi; (water, *dust)* accumularsi; **to ~ for charity** fare una raccolta per beneficenza; **~ on delivery** *(Am)* pagamento alla consegna. **3** *adv (Am)*: **to call ~** *(Telec)* fare una chiamata a carico del destinatario.

col·lec·tion [kə'lɛkʃən] *n (of information etc)* raccolta; *(of taxes)* riscossione *f; (of refuse)* rimozione *f; (of stamps)* collezione *f*, raccolta; *(of miscellaneous objects, people)* miscuglio; *(Rel)* questua; *(for charity)* colletta, raccolta; *(Post)* levata.

col·lec·tive [kə'lɛktɪv] **1** *n* collettivo. **2** *adj* collettivo(a). **3** *cpd:* **~ bargaining** *n* trattative *fpl* (sindacali) collettive.

col·lec·tor [kə'lɛktə^r] *n (of taxes)* esattore *m; (of stamps etc)* collezionista *m/f;* **~'s item** *or* **piece** pezzo da collezionista.

col·lege ['kɒlɪdʒ] *n* **(a)** *(of technology, agriculture etc)* istituto superiore; *(Brit, Am Univ)* college *m inv;* **~ of art** scuola d'arte; **~ of music** conservatorio. **(b)** *(body)* collegio.

col·lide [kə'laɪd] *vi:* **to ~ (with)** scontrarsi (con).

col·lie ['kɒlɪ] *n (dog)* collie *m inv.*

col·liery ['kɒlɪərɪ] *n* miniera di carbone.

col·li·sion [kə'lɪʒən] *n* scontro, collisione *f;* **to be on a ~ course** *(also fig)* essere in rotta di collisione.

col·lo·quial [kə'ləʊkwɪəl] *adj (word, phrase)* familiare; *(style)* colloquiale.

col·lu·sion [kə'luːʒən] *n* collusione *f;* **in ~ with** in accordo segreto con.

co·logne [kə'ləʊn] *n (also:* **eau de ~)** acqua di colonia.

co·lon ['kəʊlən] *n* **(a)** *(Anat)* colon *m inv.* **(b)** *(Typ)* due punti *mpl.*

colo·nel ['kɜːnl] *n* colonnello.

co·lo·nial [kə'ləʊnɪəl] *adj* coloniale; *(architecture)* di stile coloniale.

colo·nist ['kɒlənɪst] *n* colonizzatore/trice.

colo·nize ['kɒlənaɪz] *vt* colonizzare.

colo·ny ['kɒlənɪ] *n* colonia.

col·or ['kʌlə^r] *etc (Am)* = **colour** *etc.*

co·los·sal [kə'lɒsl] *adj* colossale.

col·our, *(Am)* **col·or** ['kʌlə^r] **1** *n* **(a)** *(gen)* colore *m;* **what ~ is it?** di che colore è?; **I want to see the ~ of his money** voglio vederlo con i soldi in mano; **to change ~** cambiare colore. **(b)** *(complexion)* colore *m*, colorito; **to get one's ~ back** riprendere colore; **the ~ drained from his face** è impallidito; **to be off ~** essere giù di corda. **(c)** *(Mil, Naut, gen):* **~s** colori *mpl;* **to salute the ~s** salutare la bandiera; **to see sth in its true ~s** *(fig: usu pej)* vedere qc come veramente è; **to show one's true ~s** *(fig: usu pej)* rivelare la propria vera personalità; **to come through (sth) with flying ~s** *(fig)* fare un'ottima figura (a qc).

2 *vt (gen)* colorare; *(tint, dye)* tingere; *(fig: affect)* influenzare; **to ~ sth green** tingere qc di verde.

3 *vi (blush: also:* **~ up)** arrossire.

4 *cpd (film, slide, photograph)* a colori; **~ bar** *n* discriminazione *f* razziale; **~ scheme** *n* combinazione *f* di colori; **~ supplement** *n (Press)* supplemento a colori; **~ television** *n* televisione *f* a colori; **~ television (set)** *n* televisore *m* or televisione *f* a colori.

♦ colour in *vt + adv* colorare.

colour-blind ['kʌləblaɪnd] *adj* daltonico(a).

col·oured ['kʌləd] *adj* colorato(a); *(person, race)* di colore; **a straw-~ hat** un cappello color paglia; **highly-~** *(tale, account)* molto colorito.

col·our·ful ['kʌləfʊl] *adj (dress)* dai colori vivaci; *(picture)* ricco(a) di colore; *(person)* particolare; *(story)* avvincente.

col·our·ing ['kʌlərɪŋ] **1** *n* colorazione *f; (substance)*

colorante *m; (complexion)* colorito. **2** *cpd:* **~ book** *n* album *m inv* da colorare.

col·our·less ['kʌləlɪs] *adj* incolore; *(fig: dull)* scialbo(a).

colt [kəʊlt] *n* puledro.

col·umn ['kɒləm] *n (gen)* colonna; *(in newspaper)* colonna; *(: fashion* **~**, **sports ~** *etc)* rubrica; **the editorial ~** l'articolo di fondo; **the advertising ~s** gli annunci economici.

col·umn·ist ['kɒləmnɪst] *n* giornalista *m/f (che cura una rubrica).*

coma ['kəʊmə] *n (Med)* coma *m inv;* **to go into a ~** entrare in coma.

co·ma·tose ['kəʊmətəʊs] *adj* comatoso(a).

comb [kəʊm] **1** *n* pettine *m;* **to run a ~ through one's hair** darsi una pettinata. **2** *vt* **(a)** *(hair)* pettinare; **to ~ one's hair** pettinarsi. **(b)** *(search: countryside etc)* rastrellare, setacciare.

com·bat ['kɒmbæt] **1** *n* lotta, combattimento; *(Mil)* combattimento. **2** *vt (fig)* combattere, lottare contro.

com·bat·ant ['kɒmbətənt] *n* combattente *m/f.*

com·bi·na·tion [ˌkɒmbɪ'neɪʃən] **1** *n* combinazione *f.* **2** *cpd:* **~ lock** *n* serratura a combinazione.

com·bine [kəm'baɪn] **1** *vt:* **to ~ (with)** *(projects, proposals)* combinare (con); *(qualities)* unire (a); **our ~d incomes** i nostri stipendi messi insieme; **to ~ business with pleasure** unire l'utile al dilettevole; **to ~ forces with sb** unire le proprie forze con qn; **a ~d effort** uno sforzo collettivo; **a ~d operation** *(Mil)* operazione *f* combinata. **2** *vi* **(a)** unirsi, mettersi insieme; **to ~ with** unirsi a; **to ~ against sth/sb** unirsi contro qc/qn. **(b)** *(Chem):* **to ~ (with)** combinarsi (con). **3** ['kɒmbaɪn] *n* associazione *f; (Comm, Fin)* trust *m inv; (also:* **~ harvester)** mietitrebbia.

com·bus·tible [kəm'bʌstɪbl] *adj* combustibile.

com·bus·tion [kəm'bʌstʃən] *n* combustione *f.*

come [kʌm] *pt* **came,** *pp* **come** *vi* **(a)** *(gen)* venire; *(arrive)* venire, arrivare; *(have its place)* venire, trovarsi; **~ with me** vieni con me; **~ home** vieni a casa; **~ and see us soon** vieni a trovarci presto; **we have ~ to help you** siamo venuti ad aiutarti; **she has ~ from London** è venuta da Londra; **we've just ~ from Paris** siamo appena arrivati da Parigi; **this necklace ~s from Spain** questa collana viene dalla Spagna; **they have ~ a long way** vengono da lontano; *(fig)* hanno fatto molta strada; **people were coming and going all day** c'era gente che andava e veniva tutto il giorno; **to ~ running** venire di corsa; **to ~ for sb/sth** venire a prendere qn/qc; **we'll ~ after you** ti seguiamo; **coming!** vengo!, arrivo!; **we came to a village** siamo arrivati a un paese; **to ~ to a decision** arrivare *or* giungere a una decisione; **the water only came to her waist** l'acqua le arrivava solo alla vita; **it came to me that** *(idea: occur)* mi è venuto in mente che; **it may ~ as a surprise to you...** può sorprenderti...; **it came as a shock to her** è stato un colpo per lei; **when it ~s to choosing** dovendo scegliere; **when it ~s to mathematics** quanto alla matematica; **the time will ~ when...** verrà il giorno in cui...; **the new ruling ~s into force next year** il nuovo regolamento entrerà in vigore l'anno prossimo; **A ~s before B** A viene prima di B; **he came 3rd in the race** è arrivato 3° nella gara.

(b) *(happen)* accadere, succedere; **~ what may** qualunque cosa succeda; **no good will ~ of it** andrà a finire male; **nothing came of it** non è saltato fuori niente; **that's what ~s of being careless** ecco cosa succede a non far attenzione; **how does this chair ~ to be broken?** come mai

questa sedia è rotta?; **how ~?** *(fam)* come mai?
  (c) *(be, become)* diventare; **my dreams came true** i miei sogni si sono avverati; **the button has ~ loose** il bottone si è allentato; **my shoelaces have ~ undone** i lacci (delle scarpe) si sono sciolti; **your zip has ~ undone** ti si è aperta la chiusura lampo; **it ~s naturally to him** gli viene spontaneo; **it'll all ~ right in the end** tutto si accomoderà alla fine; **those shoes ~ in 2 colours** quelle scarpe sono disponibili in 2 colori; **I have ~ to like her** ho finito col trovarla simpatica; **now I ~ to think of it** ora che ci penso.
  (d) *(phrases):* **in (the) years to ~** negli anni futuri; **if it ~s to it** nella peggiore delle ipotesi; **~ to that... se è per questo...; ~ again?** *(fam)* come?; **he had it coming to him** ha avuto quello che si meritava; **I could see it coming** me lo aspettavo; **he's as daft as they ~** è scemo come ce ne sono pochi; **to ~ between 2 people** mettersi fra due persone.

♦ **come about** *vi + adv* succedere, accadere.
♦ **come across 1** *vi + adv* **(a)** *(gen)* attraversare. **(b)** *(fig):* **to ~ across well/badly** fare una buona/cattiva impressione; **she came across as a very nice person** ha dato l'impressione di essere una persona molto simpatica. **2** *vi + prep (find)* trovare.
♦ **come along** *vi + adv* **(a):** **~ along!** fa' presto!, sbrigati! **(b)** *(accompany)* venire. **(c)** *(progress)* far progressi, migliorare; **how's your arm coming along?** come va il tuo braccio?
♦ **come apart** *vi + adv* andare in pezzi; *(jacket, sleeve)* scucirsi.
♦ **come away** *vi + adv (leave)* venir via; *(become detached)* staccarsi; **~ away from there!** levati di lì!, vieni via da lì!
♦ **come back** *vi + adv* **(a)** *(return)* tornare; **to ~ back to what we were discussing...** per tornare all'argomento di prima.... . **(b)** *(reply: fam):* **can I ~ back to you on that one?** possiamo riparlarne più tardi? **(c)** *(return to mind):* **it's all coming back to me** mi sta tornando in mente.
♦ **come by** *vi + prep:* **to ~ by sth** procurarsi qc.
♦ **come down 1** *vi + prep* scendere. **2** *vi + adv (person):* **to ~ down (from/to)** scendere (da/a); *(buildings)* essere demolito(a); *(prices, temperature)* diminuire, calare; **to ~ down in the world** ridursi male; **she came down on him like a ton of bricks** gli ha fatto una sfuriata; **to ~ down with a cold** prendersi un raffreddore.
♦ **come forward** *vi + adv* farsi avanti.
♦ **come in** *vi + adv (person)* entrare; *(train)* arrivare; *(tide)* salire; *(in race)* arrivare; *(in election)* salire al potere; **~ in!** avanti!; **where do I ~ in?** dove entro in ballo io?; **to ~ in for criticism/praise** ricevere critiche/elogi; **they have no money** coming in non hanno entrate.
♦ **come into** *vi + prep (inherit)* ereditare; *(be involved):* **where do I ~ into it?** come vi entro io?; **money doesn't ~ into it** i soldi non c'entrano.
♦ **come off 1** *vi + adv* **(a)** *(button etc)* staccarsi; *(stain)* andare via. **(b)** *(event)* avere luogo; *(plans)* attuarsi; *(attempt, experiment)* riuscire. **(c)** *(acquit o.s.):* **to ~ off best/worst** avere la meglio/la peggio. **2** *vi + prep:* **a button came off my jacket** mi si è staccato un bottone dalla giacca; **she came off her bike** è caduta dalla bicicletta; **~ off it!** *(fam)* piantala!
♦ **come on** *vi + adv* **(a)** *(follow, progress)* = **come along a, c. (b)** *(start)* cominciare; **I feel a cold coming on** mi sta venendo un raffreddore; **winter is coming on now** l'inverno si avvicina. **(c)** *(Theatre)* entrare in scena.

♦ **come out** *vi + adv (person, object):* **to ~ out (of)** uscire (da); *(flowers)* sbocciare; *(sun, stars)* apparire; *(news: esp scandal)* essere divulgato(a); *(truth)* saltare fuori; *(book, film, magazine)* uscire, essere pubblicato(a); *(qualities: show)* rivelarsi, mostrarsi; *(stain)* andare via; **it's bound to ~ out in the newspapers** apparirà senz'altro sui giornali; **he came out in a rash** gli è venuto uno sfogo; **the dye has ~ out of your jumper** il tuo maglione ha lasciato giù il colore; **to ~ out on strike** fare sciopero; **to ~ out against sth** dichiararsi decisamente contrario a qc; **you never know what he's going to ~ out with next!** *(fam)* non si sa mai con cosa verrà fuori la prossima volta!
♦ **come over 1** *vi + adv* venire; **they came over to England for a holiday** sono venuti in Inghilterra per una vacanza; **you'll soon ~ over to my way of thinking** presto sarai anche tu della mia idea; **I came over all dizzy** mi è venuto un giramento di testa; **her speech came over very well** il suo discorso ha fatto una buona impressione. **2** *vi + prep:* **I don't know what's ~ over him!** non so cosa gli sia successo!; **a feeling of weariness came over her** un forte senso di stanchezza la assalì.
♦ **come round** *vi + adv* **(a)** passare, venire; **he is coming round to see us** passa da noi, viene a trovarci. **(b)** *(occur regularly)* ricorrere, venire; **Christmas seems to ~ round earlier every year** ogni anno sembra che il Natale venga prima. **(c)** *(make detour):* **to ~ round (by)** passare (per); **we came round by the longer route** abbiamo fatto la strada più lunga. **(d)** *(change one's mind)* cambiare idea; **she'll soon ~ round to your way of thinking** presto la penserà come te. **(e)** *(throw off bad mood):* **leave him alone, he'll soon ~ round** lascialo in pace, presto gli passerà. **(f)** *(regain consciousness)* riprendere conoscenza, rinvenire.
♦ **come through 1** *vi + adv* **(a)** *(survive)* sopravvivere, farcela. **(b)** *(telephone call):* **the call came through** ci hanno passato la telefonata. **2** *vi + prep (survive: war, danger)* superare, uscire indenne da.
♦ **come to 1** *vi + prep (amount):* **how much does it ~ to?** quanto costa?, quanto viene? **2** *vi + adv (regain consciousness)* riprendere conoscenza, rinvenire.
♦ **come together** *vi + adv (assemble)* riunirsi; *(meet)* incontrarsi.
♦ **come under** *vi + prep (heading)* trovarsi sotto; *(influence)* cadere sotto, subire.
♦ **come up 1** *vi + adv* **(a)** salire; **he came up to us with a smile** ci si avvicinò sorridendo. **(b)** *(matters for discussion)* essere sollevato(a); **to ~ up (before)** *(accused)* comparire (davanti a); *(lawsuit)* essere ascoltato(a) (da); **she came up against complete opposition to her proposals** le sue proposte hanno incontrato la più completa opposizione. **2** *vi + prep* salire.
♦ **come up to** *vi + prep* arrivare (fino) a; **the film didn't ~ up to our expectations** il film ci ha deluso.
♦ **come up with** *vi + prep (suggest: idea, plan)* suggerire, proporre; *(offer: money, suggestion)* offrire.
♦ **come upon** *vi + prep (object, person)* trovare per caso.

come-back ['kʌmbæk] *n (Theatre, Cine):* **to make a ~** tornare sulle scene; *(reaction)* reazione *f*; *(response)* risultato, risposta.
co·median [kə'miːdɪən] *n* (attore *m*) comico.
co·medi·enne [kə,miːdɪ'ɛn] *n* attrice *f* comica.

come·down ['kʌmdaʊn] n (no pl) umiliazione f.

com·edy ['kɒmɪdɪ] n (gen) commedia; (humour) lato comico.

com·er ['kʌmə'] n: **open to all** ~s aperto(a) a tutti; **the first** ~ il primo venuto.

com·et ['kɒmɪt] n cometa.

come·up·pance [,kʌm'ʌpəns] n: **she got her** ~ ha avuto quello che si meritava.

com·fort ['kʌmfət] **1** n **(a)** (solace) consolazione f, conforto; **you're a great** ~ **to me** mi sei di gran conforto. **(b)** (physical ~) comodità f inv; **to live in** ~ vivere nell'agiatezza; **that car was a bit too close for** ~ quella macchina è passata troppo vicino per i miei gusti. **2** vt confortare, consolare. **3** cpd: ~ **station** (Am) toilette f inv.

com·fort·able ['kʌmfətəbl] adj (house, chair, shoes, life) comodo(a); (income, majority) più che sufficiente; (temperature) piacevole; **to make o.s.** ~ mettersi a proprio agio; **are you** ~, **sitting there?** sta comodo, seduto lì?; **I don't feel very** ~ **about it** non mi sento molto tranquillo.

com·fort·ably ['kʌmfətəblɪ] adv (sit etc) comodamente; (live) bene; **to be** ~ **off** vivere agiatamente; **to win** ~ vincere senza problemi.

com·ic ['kɒmɪk] **1** adj comico(a). **2** n (person) comico; (paper) giornale m a fumetti. **3** cpd: ~ **opera** n opera buffa; ~ **relief** n parentesi f comica; ~ **strip** n fumetto; ~ **verse** n poesia umoristica.

comi·cal ['kɒmɪkəl] adj divertente, buffo(a).

com·ing ['kʌmɪŋ] **1** adj (next) prossimo(a); (future) futuro(a); **in the** ~ **weeks/election** nelle prossime settimane/elezioni. **2** n avvento; ~ **and going** andirivieni m inv.

com·ma ['kɒmə] n virgola.

com·mand [kə'mɑ:nd] **1** n (esp Mil: order) ordine m, comando; (: control) comando; **by** or **at the** ~ **of** per ordine di; **under the** ~ **of** sotto il comando di; **to be in** ~ **(of)** essere al comando (di); **to have/take** ~ **of** avere/prendere il comando di; **to have at one's** ~ (money, resources etc) avere a propria disposizione; **to have a good** ~ **of English** avere una buona padronanza dell'inglese.

    2 vt (order): **to** ~ **sb to do sth** ordinare or comandare a qn di fare qc; (lead: men, ship) essere al comando di; (have at one's disposal: resources) disporre di, avere a propria disposizione; (respect) ottenere; **that antique will** ~ **a high price** quell'oggetto di antiquariato sarà venduto ad un prezzo alto.

    3 cpd: ~ **module** n modulo di comando; ~ **performance** n ≈ serata di gala (su richiesta del capo di Stato); ~ **post** n posto di comando.

com·man·deer [,kɒmən'dɪə'] vt requisire.

com·mand·er [kə'mɑ:ndə'] n capo; (Mil) comandante m; ~ **in chief** comandante in capo.

com·mand·ing [kə'mɑ:ndɪŋ] adj (appearance) imponente; (voice, tone) autorevole; (lead, position) dominante; ~ **officer** comandante m.

com·mand·ment [kə'mɑ:ndmənt] n (Bible) comandamento.

com·man·do [kə'mɑ:ndəʊ] n (group) commando; (soldier) soldato appartenente ad un commando.

com·memo·rate [kə'mɛməreɪt] vt commemorare.

com·memo·ra·tion [kə,mɛmə'reɪʃən] n commemorazione f; **in** ~ **of** in memoria di.

com·memo·ra·tive [kə'mɛmərətɪv] adj commemorativo(a).

com·mence [kə'mɛns] **1** vt cominciare; **to** ~ **doing sth** cominciare a fare qc. **2** vi cominciare.

com·mence·ment [kə'mɛnsmənt] n inizio.

com·mend [kə'mɛnd] vt **(a)** (praise) lodare. **(b)** (recommend) raccomandare; **the proposal has**

little to ~ **it** la proposta dà poco affidamento. **(c)** (entrust): **to** ~ **(to)** affidare (a).

com·mend·able [kə'mɛndəbl] adj lodevole.

com·men·da·tion [,kɒmɛn'deɪʃən] n (for bravery etc) encomio.

com·men·su·rate [kə'mɛnʃərɪt] adj: ~ **with** proporzionato(a) a, commisurato(a) a.

com·ment ['kɒmɛnt] **1** n (remark: written or spoken) commento, osservazione f; (: critical) critica; **'no** ~' 'niente da dire'; **to cause** ~ provocare critiche. **2** vi: **to** ~ **(on)** fare commenti (su). **3** vt: **to** ~ **that** osservare che.

com·men·tary ['kɒmɛntərɪ] n **(a)** (Radio) radiocronaca; (TV) telecronaca. **(b)** (on text) commento.

com·men·tate ['kɒmɛnteɪt] vi commentare.

com·men·ta·tor ['kɒmɛnteɪtə'] n (Radio) radiocronista m/f; (TV) telecronista m/f.

com·merce ['kɒmɜːs] n commercio; ~ **between the two countries** scambi commerciali fra i due paesi.

com·mer·cial [kə'mɜːʃəl] **1** adj commerciale; **the** ~ **world** il mondo del commercio. **2** n (TV: advert) pubblicità f inv. **3** cpd: ~ **radio/television** n radio fpl/televisioni fpl private; ~ **traveller** n viaggiatore m di commercio; ~ **vehicle** n veicolo per il trasporto di merci.

com·mer·cial·ism [kə'mɜːʃəlɪzəm] n affarismo.

com·mer·cial·ize [kə'mɜːʃəlaɪz] vt commercializzare.

com·mis·er·ate [kə'mɪzəreɪt] vi: **to** ~ **with** partecipare al dolore di.

com·mis·sion [kə'mɪʃən] **1** n **(a)** (committee) commissione f; ~ **of inquiry** commissione d'inchiesta. **(b)** (order for work: esp of artist) incarico. **(c)** (for salesman) commissione f, provvigione f; **sell on** ~ vendere a provvigione; **I get 10%** ~ ricevo il 10% sulle vendite. **(d)** (Mil): **to get one's** ~ ricevere la nomina ad ufficiale. **(e)**: **out of** ~ (machine) fuori uso. **2** vt **(a)** (expert, consultant, artist): **to** ~ **sb to do sth** incaricare qn di fare qc; (painting etc): **to** ~ **sth from sb** commissionare qc a qn. **(b)** (Mil) nominare ufficiale; ~**ed officer** ufficiale m.

com·mis·sion·aire [kə,mɪʃə'nɛə'] n portiere m in livrea.

com·mis·sion·er [kə'mɪʃənə'] n membro di una commissione; ~ **of police** ≈ questore m.

com·mit [kə'mɪt] vt **(a)** (crime) commettere; **to** ~ **suicide** suicidarsi. **(b)** (consign): **to** ~ **sth to sb** affidare qc a qn; **to** ~ **to memory** imparare a memoria; **to** ~ **to writing** mettere per iscritto; **to** ~ **sb for trial** rinviare qn a giudizio. **(c)**: **to** ~ **o.s.** **(to)** impegnarsi (a); **a** ~**ted Christian** un cristiano convinto; **a** ~**ted writer** uno scrittore impegnato.

com·mit·ment [kə'mɪtmənt] n (gen) impegno; (devotion) dedizione f; **he refused to make any** ~ ha rifiutato d'impegnarsi in alcun modo.

com·mit·tee [kə'mɪtɪ] **1** n (takes sg or pl vb) comitato, commissione f; (Parliament) commissione; ~ **of inquiry** commissione d'inchiesta; **to be on a** ~ far parte di un comitato or di una commissione. **2** cpd: ~ **meeting** n riunione f di comitato or di commissione; ~ **member** n membro di un comitato or di una commissione.

com·mod·ity [kə'mɒdɪtɪ] n prodotto.

com·mon ['kɒmən] **1** adj **(a)** comune; **it's a** ~ **belief that...** si tende a credere che...; **it's a** ~ **occurrence** succede di frequente; **it's** ~ **knowledge that...** è risaputo che..., è notorio che...; **it's** ~ **courtesy** è una questione di semplice cortesia; **in** ~ **use** di uso comune; ~ **or**

garden ordinario; ~ **ground** (fig) punti mpl d'incontro; **the** ~ **man** l'uomo della strada; **the C**~ **Market** il Mercato Comune; **in** ~ **parlance** nel linguaggio corrente; **the** ~ **people** il popolo; ~ **sense** (n) buon senso; (adj) sensato. **(b)** (pej: vulgar) volgare, grossolano(a). **2** n **(a)** (land) parco comunale. **(b)** (Brit Pol): **the C**~**s** la Camera dei Comuni. **(c):** **we have a lot in** ~ abbiamo molto in comune.

com·mon·er ['kɒmənəʳ] n semplice cittadino/a.

common-law ['kɒmənlɔː] adj: ~ **wife** convivente f more uxorio.

com·mon·ly ['kɒmənlɪ] adv (see adj) comunemente; in modo volgare.

common·place ['kɒmənpleɪs] **1** adj comune; (pej) banale. **2** n (event) cosa di tutti i giorni; (statement) luogo comune.

common-room ['kɒmənrʊm] n (staff room) sala dei professori; (for students) sala di ritrovo.

common·wealth ['kɒmənwɛlθ] n: **the C**~ il Commonwealth.

com·mo·tion [kə'məʊʃən] n confusione f, trambusto.

com·mu·nal ['kɒmjuːnl] adj (facilities) in comune; (life) di comunità.

com·mune ['kɒmjuːn] **1** n (group) comune f. **2** [kə'mjuːn] vi: **to** ~ **with nature** comunicare con la natura.

com·mu·ni·cant [kə'mjuːnɪkənt] n (Rel) comunicante m/f.

com·mu·ni·cate [kə'mjuːnɪkeɪt] **1** vt: **to** ~ **sth (to sb)** (thoughts, information) comunicare qc (a qn); (frm: disease) trasmettere qc (a qn). **2** vi (speak etc): **to** ~ **(with)** comunicare (con), mettersi in contatto (con); **communicating rooms** stanze fpl intercomunicanti.

com·mu·ni·ca·tion [kə,mjuːnɪ'keɪʃən] **1** n comunicazione f; **to be in** ~ **with** (frm) essere in contatto con. **2** cpd: ~ **cord** n (Rail) segnale m d'allarme; ~**s network** n rete f delle comunicazioni; ~**s satellite** n satellite m per telecomunicazioni.

com·mu·ni·ca·tive [kə'mjuːnɪkətɪv] adj (gen) loquace; ~ **skills** (Scol) capacità f inv di esprimersi.

com·mun·ion [kə'mjuːnɪən] n (gen) comunione f; **to take** ~ ricevere la comunione.

com·mu·ni·qué [kə'mjuːnɪkeɪ] n comunicato, bollettino.

com·mun·ism ['kɒmjʊnɪzəm] n comunismo.

com·mun·ist ['kɒmjʊnɪst] adj, n comunista (m/f).

com·mu·nity [kə'mjuːnɪtɪ] **1** n (gen) comunità f inv; (of goods, interests) comunanza. **2** cpd: ~ **centre** n centro civico rionale; ~ **chest** n (Am) fondo di beneficenza; ~ **health centre** n centro sociosanitario; ~ **spirit** n spirito civico.

com·mute [kə'mjuːt] **1** vi fare il pendolare. **2** vt (payment): **to** ~ **for** or **into** commutare in; (Law: sentence): **to** ~ **(to)** commutare (a).

com·mut·er [kə'mjuːtəʳ] n pendolare m/f; **the** ~ **belt** (Brit) la fascia dei pendolari.

com·pact[1] [kəm'pækt] adj compatto(a); **this house is very** ~ questa casa è piccola ma funzionale.

com·pact[2] ['kɒmpækt] n **(a)** (agreement) patto, contratto. **(b)** (also: **powder** ~) portacipria m inv.

com·pan·ion [kəm'pænjən] **1** n compagno/a; (lady's) dama di compagnia; (book) manuale m, guida; (one of pair of objects) pendant m inv. **2** cpd: ~ **volume** n volume m complementare.

com·pan·ion·able [kəm'pænjənəbl] adj (person) di compagnia; **we sat in** ~ **silence** eravamo seduti tranquillamente in silenzio.

com·pan·ion·ship [kəm'pænjənʃɪp] n compagnia.

com·pan·ion·way [kəm'pænjən,weɪ] n (Naut) scala.

com·pa·ny ['kʌmpənɪ] **1** n (gen, Mil, Theatre etc) compagnia; (Comm, Fin) società f inv, compagnia; **he's good/poor** ~ è di buona/cattiva compagnia; **to keep sb** ~ tenere or fare compagnia a qn; **to get into bad** ~ farsi cattive amicizie; **to keep bad** ~ frequentare cattive compagnie; **to part** ~ **with sb** dividersi or separarsi da qn; **we have** ~ **this evening** abbiamo ospiti stasera; **Smith and C**~ Smith e soci. **2** cpd: ~ **car** n macchina di proprietà della ditta; ~ **secretary** n segretario/a generale.

com·pa·rable ['kɒmpərəbl] adj simile; ~ **to** or **with** paragonabile a.

com·para·tive [kəm'pærətɪv] **1** adj (freedom, luxury, cost) relativo(a); (Gram, study, literature) comparativo(a); **she's a** ~ **stranger** la conosco relativamente poco. **2** n (Gram) comparativo.

com·para·tive·ly [kəm'pærətɪvlɪ] adv (see adj) relativamente; comparativamente.

com·pare [kəm'pɛəʳ] **1** vt: **to** ~ **(with)** paragonare (a), mettere a confronto (con); ~**d with** or **to a paragone di, rispetto a; to** ~ **notes with sb** (fig) scambiare le proprie impressioni con qn. **2** vi: **to** ~ **(with)** essere paragonabile (a); **how do they** ~ **for speed?** che velocità fanno rispettivamente?; **how do the prices** ~? che differenza di prezzo c'è?; **it doesn't** ~ **with yours** non è paragonabile al tuo. **3** n: **beyond** ~ (poet: adj) senza confronto or paragone; (: adv) incomparabilmente.

com·pari·son [kəm'pærɪsn] n paragone m, confronto; **in** ~ **with, by** ~ **with** rispetto a, in confronto a; **by** ~ a confronto.

com·part·ment [kəm'pɑːtmənt] n comparto; (Brit Rail) scompartimento.

com·pass ['kʌmpəs] n **(a)** (Naut etc) bussola. **(b)** (Math): **(a pair of)** ~**es** compasso. **(c)** (fig: range) portata; **within the** ~ **of** entro i limiti di.

com·pas·sion [kəm'pæʃən] n compassione f.

com·pas·sion·ate [kəm'pæʃənɪt] adj (person) compassionevole; (leave) straordinario(a); **on** ~ **grounds** per motivi personali.

com·pat·ible [kəm'pætɪbl] adj: ~ **(with)** compatibile (con).

com·pat·ri·ot [kəm'pætrɪət] n compatriota m/f.

com·pel [kəm'pɛl] vt (force): **to** ~ **sb (to do sth)** forzare qn (a fare qc), costringere qn (a fare qc); (respect, obedience etc) esigere; ~**ling reasons** ragioni impellenti.

com·pen·dium [kəm'pɛndɪəm] n (summary) compendio, sommario; ~ **of games** (Brit) scatola di giochi vari.

com·pen·sate ['kɒmpənseɪt] **1** vt: **to** ~ **sb (for sth)** compensare qn (per qc); (financially) indennizzare qn (per qc). **2** vi: **to** ~ **(for)** compensare (per).

com·pen·sa·tion [,kɒmpən'seɪʃən] n (see vb) compenso; indennità; **in** ~ **(for)** come compenso (per); come indennizzo (per).

com·père ['kɒmpɛəʳ] **1** n presentatore/trice. **2** vt (show) presentare.

com·pete [kəm'piːt] vi competere; (Comm) essere in concorrenza; **to** ~ **with one another** farsi concorrenza.

com·pe·tence ['kɒmpɪtəns] n, **com·pe·ten·cy** ['kɒmpɪtənsɪ] n competenza.

com·pe·tent ['kɒmpɪtənt] adj competente; **this court is not** ~ **to deal with that** questa corte non è competente in materia.

com·pe·ti·tion [,kɒmpɪ'tɪʃən] n **(a)** (Comm) concorrenza; **in** ~ **with** in concorrenza con. **(b)** (gen,

Sport) gara, competizione *f;* **beauty** ~ concorso di bellezza.

com·peti·tive [kəm'pɛtɪtɪv] *adj* **(a)** *(sports)* agonistico(a); *(person)* che ha spirito di competizione; *(: in sport)* che ha spirito agonistico; ~ **exam** concorso. **(b)** *(Comm: price)* concorrenziale; *(: goods)* a prezzo concorrenziale.

com·peti·tor [kəm'pɛtɪtə^r] *n* concorrente *m/f.*

com·pile [kəm'paɪl] *vt* compilare.

com·pla·cen·cy [kəm'pleɪsnsɪ] *n* eccessivo compiacimento.

com·pla·cent [kəm'pleɪsənt] *adj* compiaciuto(a).

com·plain [kəm'pleɪn] *vi:* **to** ~ **(to sb about sth)** lamentarsi (con qn di qc), lagnarsi (con qn di qc); *(make a formal complaint)* fare un reclamo (a qn per qc); **to** ~ **of** lamentarsi di.

com·plaint [kəm'pleɪnt] *n* lamentela; *(to manager of shop etc)* reclamo; *(Med: illness)* disturbo, malattia.

com·ple·ment ['kɒmplɪmənt] **1** *n* **(a)** *(gen, Gram, Math)* complemento. **(b)** *(of staff)* effettivo. **2** ['kɒmplɪmɛnt] *vt* accompagnarsi bene a.

com·ple·men·tary [ˌkɒmplɪ'mɛntərɪ] *adj* complementare; **the food and wine were** ~ il cibo e il vino erano ben assortiti.

com·plete [kəm'pliːt] **1** *adj (whole)* completo(a); *(finished)* completo(a), finito(a); ~ **with** completo di; **it's a** ~ **disaster** è un vero disastro. **2** *vt (set, collection)* completare; *(piece of work)* finire, completare; *(fill up: form)* riempire; **and to** ~ **my misfortunes** e per colmo di sfortuna.

com·plete·ly [kəm'pliːtlɪ] *adv* completamente.

com·ple·tion [kəm'pliːʃən] *n* completamento; **to be nearing** ~ essere in fase di completamento; **on** ~ **of contract** alla firma del contratto.

com·plex ['kɒmplɛks] **1** *adj (all senses)* complesso(a). **2** *n* **(a)** *(Psych)* complesso; **he's got a** ~ **about his weight** ha il complesso del peso. **(b)** *(of buildings)* complesso; **sports/housing** ~ complesso sportivo/edilizio.

com·plex·ion [kəm'plɛkʃən] *n* carnagione *f; (fig):* **that puts a different** ~ **on it** allora cambia tutto.

com·plex·ity [kəm'plɛksɪtɪ] *n* complessità *f inv.*

com·pli·ance [kəm'plaɪəns] *n* **(a)** *(with rules etc):* **in** ~ **with** in conformità con. **(b)** *(submissiveness)* arrendevolezza.

com·pli·cate ['kɒmplɪkeɪt] *vt* complicare.

com·pli·cat·ed ['kɒmplɪkeɪtɪd] *adj* complicato(a), complesso(a).

com·pli·ca·tion [ˌkɒmplɪ'keɪʃən] *n* complicazione *f.*

com·pli·ment ['kɒmplɪmənt] **1** *n* **(a)** complimento; **to pay sb a** ~ **(on sth)** fare un complimento a qn (per qc). **(b):** ~**s** *npl (greetings)* auguri *mpl;* ~**s of the season** auguri; **with the** ~**s of Mr X** con gli omaggi del Signor X. **2** ['kɒmplɪmɛnt] *vt:* **to** ~ **sb (on sth/on doing sth)** congratularsi con qn (per qc/per aver fatto qc), complimentarsi con qn (per qc/per aver fatto qc). **3** *cpd:* ~**s slip** *n* cartoncino della società.

com·pli·men·tary [ˌkɒmplɪ'mɛntərɪ] *adj (remark etc)* lusinghiero(a); *(free: ticket)* (in) omaggio *inv.*

com·ply [kəm'plaɪ] *vi:* **to** ~ **with** *(rules etc)* attenersi a, osservare; *(wishes, request)* assecondare.

com·po·nent [kəm'pəʊnənt] *adj, n* componente *(m).*

com·pose [kəm'pəʊz] *vt* **(a)** *(music, poetry)* comporre; *(letter)* mettere insieme; **to be** ~**d of** essere composto di. **(b)** *(calm: thoughts)* riordinare; **to** ~ **o.s.** ricomporsi.

com·posed [kəm'pəʊzd] *adj* composto(a).

com·pos·er [kəm'pəʊzə^r] *n (Mus)* compositore/trice.

com·po·si·tion [ˌkɒmpə'zɪʃən] *n* composizione *f.*

com·posi·tor [kəm'pɒzɪtə^r] *n (Typ)* compositore *m.*

com·post ['kɒmpɒst] *n* concime *m.*

com·po·sure [kəm'pəʊʒə^r] *n* calma, padronanza di sé.

com·pote ['kɒmpəʊt] *n (Culin)* composta, conserva di frutta.

com·pound ['kɒmpaʊnd] **1** *n* **(a)** *(Chem)* composto; *(Gram)* parola composta. **(b)** *(enclosed area)* recinto. **2** *adj* composto(a); *(fracture)* esposto(a); ~ **substance** composto. **3** [kəm'paʊnd] *vt (fig: problem, difficulty)* peggiorare.

com·pre·hend [ˌkɒmprɪ'hɛnd] *vt* capire, comprendere.

com·pre·hen·sible [ˌkɒmprɪ'hɛnsəbl] *adj* comprensibile.

com·pre·hen·sion [ˌkɒmprɪ'hɛnʃən] *n (understanding)* comprensione *f; (Scol)* esercizio di comprensione.

com·pre·hen·sive [ˌkɒmprɪ'hɛnsɪv] **1** *adj (study)* esauriente; *(knowledge)* esteso(a); *(description)* dettagliato(a); *(report, review)* completo(a), esauriente; *(measures)* di vasta portata; *(insurance)* globale. **2** *n (Brit: also:* ~ **school)** scuola secondaria dagli 11 ai 18 anni.

com·press [kəm'prɛs] **1** *vt (substance)* comprimere; *(text etc)* condensare. **2** ['kɒmprɛs] *n (Med)* compressa.

com·pres·sion [kəm'prɛʃən] *n* compressione *f.*

com·pres·sor [kəm'prɛsə^r] *n* compressore *m.*

com·prise [kəm'praɪz] *vt (be made up of)* comprendere; *(make up)* costituire.

com·pro·mise ['kɒmprəmaɪz] **1** *n* compromesso. **2** *vi:* **to** ~ **(with sb over sth)** venire a un compromesso (con qn su qc). **3** *vt* compromettere. **4** *cpd (decision, solution)* di compromesso.

com·pul·sion [kəm'pʌlʃən] *n* **(a)** *(force):* **under** ~ sotto pressioni; **he is under no** ~ **(to do it)** nessuno lo costringe (a farlo). **(b)** desiderio incontrollabile.

com·pul·sive [kəm'pʌlsɪv] *adj (desire, behaviour)* incontrollabile; **she's a** ~ **liar** non può fare a meno di mentire; **he's a** ~ **eater/drinker/smoker** non riesce a controllarsi nel mangiare/nel bere/nel fumare.

com·pul·so·ry [kəm'pʌlsərɪ] **1** *adj* obbligatorio(a). **2** *cpd:* ~ **purchase** *n* espropriazione *f.*

com·punc·tion [kəm'pʌŋkʃən] *n* scrupolo; **to have no** ~ **about doing sth** non farsi scrupoli a fare qc.

com·pu·ta·tion [ˌkɒmpjʊ'teɪʃən] *n* calcolo.

com·pute [kəm'pjuːt] *vt* calcolare.

com·put·er [kəm'pjuːtə^r] **1** *n* elaboratore *m* elettronico, computer *m inv.* **2** *cpd (language)* da computer; *(program, programming etc)* del computer; ~ **science** *n* informatica.

com·put·eri·za·tion [kəm,pjuːtəraɪ'zeɪʃən] *n* computerizzazione *f.*

com·put·er·ize [kəm'pjuːtəraɪz] *vt* computerizzare.

com·rade ['kɒmrɪd] *n* compagno/a.

con[1] [kɒn] *(fam)* **1** *vt:* **to** ~ **sb into doing sth** indurre qn a fare qc con raggiri; **I've been** ~**ned!** mi hanno fregato! **2** *n* truffa. **3** *cpd:* ~ **man** *n* truffatore *m.*

con[2] [kɒn] *n (disadvantage) see* **pro.**

con·cave [kɒn'keɪv] *adj* concavo(a).

con·ceal [kən'siːl] *vt:* **to** ~ **(sth from sb)** nascondere (qc a qn); *(news)* tenere nascosto(a) (qc a qn); ~**ed lighting** illuminazione indiretta.

con·cede [kən'siːd] *vt (admit: point, defeat)* ammettere; *(: argument)* riconoscere la validità di; *(territory)* cedere; **to** ~ **victory** darla vinta.

con·ceit [kən'siːt] *n* vanità.

con·ceit·ed [kən'si:tɪd] *adj* pieno(a) di sé, vanitoso(a).

con·ceiv·able [kən'si:vəbl] *adj* concepibile; **it is ~ that...** può anche darsi che... .

con·ceiv·ably [kən'si:vəblɪ] *adv*: **he may ~ be right** può anche darsi che abbia ragione.

con·ceive [kən'si:v] **1** *vt (child, idea)* concepire. **2** *vi*: **to ~ of sth/of doing sth** immaginare qc/di fare qc.

con·cen·trate ['kɒnsəntreɪt] **1** *vt* concentrare; **to ~ one's thoughts on sth** concentrarsi in qc. **2** *vi* **(a)** *(pay attention)*: **to ~ (on)** concentrarsi (in *or* su); **~ on getting well** pensa soprattutto a guarire. **(b)** *(group closely)* concentrarsi. **3** *n (Chem)* concentrato.

con·cen·tra·tion [,kɒnsən'treɪʃən] **1** *n* concentrazione *f*. **2** *cpd*: **~ camp** *n* campo di concentramento.

con·cept ['kɒnsept] *n* concetto.

con·cep·tion [kən'sepʃən] *n* **(a)** *(of child)* concepimento. **(b)** *(idea)* idea, concetto.

con·cern [kən'sɜːn] **1** *n* **(a)**: **what ~ is it of yours?** non vedo come ti possa riguardare; **it's of no ~ to me, it's no ~ of mine** non mi riguarda. **(b)** *(anxiety)* ansietà, preoccupazione *f*; **it is a matter for ~ that...** è preoccupante che... . **(c)** *(firm)* impresa, ditta. **2** *vt* **(a)** riguardare, interessare; **this shouldn't ~ you** *(affect)* questo non dovrebbe cambiarti nulla; **'to whom it may ~'** 'a tutti gli interessati'; **as far as I am ~ed** per quanto mi riguarda; **the department ~ed** *(under discussion)* l'ufficio in questione; *(relevant)* l'ufficio competente; **to be ~ed with** occuparsi di; **to be ~ed in** interessarsi a; **to ~ o.s. with** occuparsi di. **(b)** *(worry)*: **to be ~ed at** *or* **by** *or* **about sth/for** *or* **about sb** preoccuparsi per qc/per qn, essere preoccupato per qc/per qn.

con·cern·ing [kən'sɜːnɪŋ] *prep* riguardo a.

con·cert ['kɒnsət] **1** *n (Mus)* concerto; **in ~** in concerto. **2** *cpd*: **~ hall** *n* sala dei concerti; **~ pianist** *n* concertista *m/f (che suona il piano)*; **~ ticket** *n* biglietto di concerto; **~ tour** *n* serie *f inv* di concerti.

con·cert·ed [kən'sɜːtɪd] *adj (effort, attack)* concertato(a).

con·cer·ti·na [,kɒnsə'ti:nə] **1** *n* piccola fisarmonica. **2** *vi* accartocciarsi.

con·cer·to [kən'tʃeətəu] *n* concerto.

con·ces·sion [kən'seʃən] *n* concessione *f*.

con·ces·sion·ary [kən'seʃənərɪ] *adj (ticket, fare)* a prezzo ridotto.

con·cili·ate [kən'sɪlɪeɪt] *vt (person)* placare; *(opposing view)* conciliare.

con·cilia·tory [kən'sɪlɪətərɪ] *adj* conciliante, conciliatorio(a).

con·cise [kən'saɪs] *adj* conciso(a).

con·clude [kən'klu:d] **1** *vt (all senses)* concludere. **2** *vi (events)* concludersi; *(speaker)* concludere.

con·clu·sion [kən'klu:ʒən] *n (all senses)* conclusione *f*; **in ~** in conclusione; **to come to the ~ that** concludere che, arrivare alla conclusione che.

con·clu·sive [kən'klu:sɪv] *adj* conclusivo(a).

con·coct [kən'kɒkt] *vt (food, drink)* mettere insieme; *(lie, story, excuse)* inventare; *(scheme)* architettare.

con·coc·tion [kən'kɒkʃən] *n (food, drink)* miscuglio.

con·cord ['kɒŋkɔːd] *n (harmony)* armonia, concordia; *(treaty)* accordo.

con·course ['kɒŋkɔːs] *n (of people)* folla; *(place)* luogo di assembramento; *(in station etc)* atrio.

con·crete ['kɒnkri:t] **1** *adj* **(a)** *(object, advantage etc)* concreto(a). **(b)** *(building)* di calcestruzzo. **2**

n (Constr) calcestruzzo. **3** *vt (path)* rivestire di calcestruzzo. **4** *cpd*: **~ mixer** *n* betoniera.

con·cur [kən'kɜː'] *vi* **(a)** *(agree)*: **to .~ (with)** *(opinions etc)* coincidere (con); *(person)* essere d'accordo (con). **(b)** *(happen at the same time)* coincidere.

con·cur·rent [kən'kʌrənt] *adj* simultaneo(a); **to be ~ with** coincidere con.

con·cussed [kən'kʌst] *adj*: **to be ~** avere una commozione cerebrale.

con·cus·sion [kən'kʌʃən] *n* commozione *f* cerebrale.

con·demn [kən'dem] *vt (person)* condannare; *(declare unfit: building)* dichiarare pericoloso(a); *(: food)* dichiarare immangiabile; **to ~ sb to death** condannare qn a morte.

con·dem·na·tion [,kɒndem'neɪʃən] *n* condanna.

con·den·sa·tion [,kɒnden'seɪʃən] *n* condensazione *f*.

con·dense [kən'dens] **1** *vt* condensare. **2** *vi* condensarsi.

con·dens·er [kən'densə'] *n* condensatore *m*.

con·de·scend [,kɒndɪ'send] *vi*: **to ~ to sb** mostrarsi accondiscendente con qn; **to ~ to do sth** degnarsi di fare qc.

con·de·scend·ing [,kɒndɪ'sendɪŋ] *adj* condiscendente.

con·di·ment ['kɒndɪmənt] *n* condimento.

con·di·tion [kən'dɪʃən] **1** *n* **(a)** *(circumstance)* condizione *f*; **on ~ that** a condizione che + *sub*; **under** *or* **in the present ~s** nelle attuali condizioni; **in good/poor ~** in buone/cattive condizioni; **to be in no ~ to do sth** non essere in condizione di fare qc; **to be out of ~** *(thing)* essere in cattivo stato; *(person)* essere fuori forma; **physical ~** *(of person)* condizioni fisiche; **physical ~s** condizioni ambientali; **weather ~s** condizioni meteorologiche. **(b)** *(disease)* malattia. **2** *vt* condizionare.

con·di·tion·al [kən'dɪʃənl] *adj* condizionale; **to be ~ upon** dipendere da.

con·di·tion·er [kən'dɪʃənə'] *n (for hair)* balsamo; *(for clothes)* ammorbidente *m*.

con·do·lences [kən'dəulənsɪz] *npl* condoglianze *fpl*.

con·dom ['kɒndəm] *n* preservativo.

con·do·min·ium [,kɒndə'mɪnɪəm] *n (Am)* condominio.

con·done [kən'dəun] *vt (forgive)* perdonare; *(overlook)* passare sopra a.

con·du·cive [kən'dju:sɪv] *adj*: **to be ~ to** favorire.

con·duct ['kɒndʌkt] **1** *n* condotta. **2** [kən'dʌkt] *vt (gen, Phys)* condurre; *(guide)* accompagnare; *(Law)* presentare; *(Mus)* dirigere; **to ~ o.s.** comportarsi; **~ed tour** giro organizzato; *(of building)* visita organizzata.

con·duc·tion [kən'dʌkʃən] *n* conduzione *f*.

con·duc·tiv·ity [,kɒndʌk'tɪvɪtɪ] *n* conduttività.

con·duc·tor [kən'dʌktə'] *n (Mus)* direttore/trice; *(of bus)* bigliettaio; *(Am Rail)* controllore *m*; *(Phys: of heat, electricity)* conduttore *m*.

con·duit ['kɒndɪt] *n (pipe)* conduttura.

cone [kəun] *n (gen, of ice cream)* cono; *(Bot)* pigna.

con·fab ['kɒnfæb] *n (fam)*: **to have a ~** fare una chiacchierata.

con·fec·tion·er [kən'fekʃənə'] *n* pasticciere *m*; **~'s (shop)** ≈ pasticceria.

con·fec·tion·ery [kən'fekʃənərɪ] *n (sweets)* dolciumi *mpl*.

con·fed·er·ate [kən'fedərɪt] **1** *adj* confederato(a). **2** *n (pej)* complice *m/f*; *(Am Hist)* confederato.

con·fed·era·tion [kən,fedə'reɪʃən] *n* confederazione *f*.

con·fer [kən'fɜː'] **1** *vt*: **to ~ sth on sb** conferire qc a qn. **2** *vi:* to ~ **(with sb about sth)** consultarsi (con qn su qc).

con·fer·ence ['kɒnfərəns] **1** *n (convention, meeting)* conferenza, convegno, congresso; *(participants)* partecipanti *mpl* alla conferenza *(or* al convegno *etc);* **to be in** ~ essere in riunione. **2** *cpd:* ~ **room** *n* sala *f* conferenze *inv.*

con·fess [kən'fɛs] **1** *vt* confessare; **to** ~ **o.s. guilty of** *(sin, crime)* confessare di essere colpevole di. **2** *vi (admit, also Rel):* **to** ~ **(to sth/to doing sth)** confessare (qc/di aver fatto qc).

con·fes·sion [kən'fɛʃən] *n* confessione *f;* **to go to** ~ andare a confessarsi; **to make one's** ~ confessarsi.

con·fes·sion·al [kən'fɛʃənl] *n* confessionale *m.*

con·fes·sor [kən'fɛsə'] *n* confessore *m.*

con·fet·ti [kən'fɛtiː] *n* coriandoli *mpl.*

con·fi·dant [ˌkɒnfɪ'dænt] *n* confidente *m.*

con·fi·dante [ˌkɒnfɪ'dænt] *n* confidente *f.*

con·fide [kən'faɪd] **1** *vt* confidare. **2** *vi:* **to** ~ **in sb (about sth)** confidarsi con qn (su qc).

con·fi·dence ['kɒnfɪdəns] **1** *n* **(a)** *(trust)* fiducia; **to have (every)** ~ **in sb** avere (piena) fiducia in qn; **to have (every)** ~ **that** essere assolutamente certo che; **motion of no** ~ mozione *f* di sfiducia. **(b)** *(self-confidence)* sicurezza; **to gain** ~ acquistare sicurezza. **(c)** *(secret)* confidenza; **to take sb into one's** ~ confidarsi con qn; **to tell sb sth in strict** ~ dire qc a qn in via strettamente confidenziale; **to write in** ~ **to sb** scrivere a qn con la massima riservatezza. **2** *cpd:* ~ **trick** *n* truffa.

con·fi·dent ['kɒnfɪdənt] *adj* sicuro(a); *(person)* sicuro(a) (di sé); **to be** ~ **of doing sth/that** essere sicuro di fare qc/che.

con·fi·den·tial [ˌkɒnfɪ'dɛnʃəl] *adj (letter, report, remark)* confidenziale; *(secretary)* particolare.

con·fi·den·tial·ly [ˌkɒnfɪ'dɛnʃəlɪ] *adv* in confidenza.

con·fine [kən'faɪn] *vt* **(a)** *(imprison, shut up)* rinchiudere; **~d to barracks** consegnato (in caserma); **~d to bed** costretto a letto. **(b)** *(limit)* limitare; **to** ~ **o.s. to doing sth** limitarsi a fare qc; **a ~d space** uno spazio ristretto.

con·fine·ment [kən'faɪnmənt] *n* **(a)** *(imprisonment)* reclusione *f.* **(b)** *(Med)* parto.

con·fines ['kɒnfaɪnz] *n (bounds)* confini *mpl.*

con·firm [kən'fɜːm] *vt (gen)* confermare; *(strengthen: belief)* rafforzare; *(Rel)* cresimare.

con·fir·ma·tion [ˌkɒnfə'meɪʃən] *n* conferma; *(Rel)* cresima.

con·firmed [kən'fɜːmd] *adj (smoker, habit etc)* incallito(a); *(bachelor)* impenitente; *(admirer)* fervente.

con·fis·cate ['kɒnfɪskeɪt] *vt:* **to** ~ **sth (from sb)** confiscare qc (a qn).

con·flict ['kɒnflɪkt] **1** *n* conflitto. **2** [kən'flɪkt] *vi:* **to** ~ **(with)** essere in conflitto (con).

con·flict·ing [kɒn'flɪktɪŋ] *adj (reports, evidence, opinions)* contraddittorio(a); *(opinions)* contrastante.

con·form [kən'fɔːm] *vi:* **to** ~ **(to)** conformarsi (a).

con·form·ity [kən'fɔːmɪtɪ] *n:* **in** ~ **with** in conformità a.

con·found [kən'faʊnd] *vt (confuse)* confondere; *(amaze)* sconcertare; ~ **it!** al diavolo!

con·front [kən'frʌnt] *vt* affrontare; *(defiantly)* fronteggiare; **to** ~ **sb with sth** mettere qn a confronto con qc; **the problems which** ~ **us** i problemi da affrontare.

con·fron·ta·tion [ˌkɒnfrʌn'teɪʃən] *n* scontro.

con·fuse [kən'fjuːz] *vt* confondere.

con·fused [kən'fjuːzd] *adj* confuso(a); **in a** ~ **state** in uno stato di confusione; **to get** ~ confondersi.

con·fus·ing [kən'fjuːzɪŋ] *adj* sconcertante.

con·fu·sion [kən'fjuːʒən] *n* confusione *f.*

con·geal [kən'dʒiːl] *vi* rapprendersi.

con·gen·ial [kən'dʒiːnɪəl] *adj (place, work, company)* piacevole; *(person)* simpatico(a).

con·geni·tal [kən'dʒɛnɪtl] *adj* congenito(a).

con·gest·ed [kən'dʒɛstɪd] *adj (gen, Med)* congestionato(a); *(telephone lines)* sovraccarico(a).

con·ges·tion [kən'dʒɛstʃən] *n (with traffic, Med)* congestione *f; (with people)* sovraffollamento.

con·glom·er·ate [kən'glɒmərɪt] *n (Comm, Geol)* conglomerato.

con·gratu·late [kən'grætjʊleɪt] *vt:* **to** ~ **sb (on sth/ on doing sth)** congratularsi con qn (per qc/per aver fatto qc).

con·gratu·la·tions [kən,grætjʊ'leɪʃənz] *npl:* ~ **(on)** congratulazioni *fpl* (per); ~**!** congratulazioni!, rallegramenti!; **to give sb one's** ~ fare le congratulazioni a qn.

con·gre·gate ['kɒŋgrɪgeɪt] *vi* radunarsi, raccogliersi.

con·gre·ga·tion [ˌkɒŋgrɪ'geɪʃən] *n (worshippers)* assemblea (dei fedeli); *(parishioners)* parrocchiani *mpl.*

con·gress ['kɒŋgrɛs] *n* congresso; *(Am):* **C~** il Congresso.

congress·man ['kɒŋgrɛsmən] *n, pl* **-men** *(Am)* membro del Congresso.

congress·woman ['kɒŋgrɛswʊmən] *n, pl* **-women** *(Am)* (donna) membro del Congresso.

coni·cal ['kɒnɪkəl] *adj* conico(a); ~ **hat** cappello a cono.

co·ni·fer ['kɒnɪfə'] *n* conifera.

co·nif·er·ous [kə'nɪfərəs] *adj (forest)* di conifere; *(tree)* conifero(a).

con·jec·ture [kən'dʒɛktʃə'] **1** *n* congettura. **2** *vt, vi (frm)* congetturare.

con·ju·gal ['kɒndʒʊgəl] *adj* coniugale.

con·ju·gate ['kɒndʒʊgeɪt] **1** *vt* coniugare. **2** *vi* coniugarsi.

con·ju·ga·tion [ˌkɒndʒʊ'geɪʃən] *n* coniugazione *f.*

con·junc·tion [kən'dʒʌŋkʃən] *n* **(a)** *(Gram)* congiunzione *f.* **(b): in** ~ **with** in accordo con, insieme con.

con·junc·ti·vi·tis [kən,dʒʌŋktɪ'vaɪtɪs] *n (Med)* congiuntivite *f.*

con·jure ['kʌndʒə'] *vi* fare giochi di prestigio; **a name to** ~ **with** un nome prestigioso *or* molto importante.

♦ **conjure up** *vt + adv (memories)* evocare; *(meal)* inventare, improvvisare.

con·jur·er, con·jur·or ['kʌndʒərə'] *n* prestigiatore/trice, prestidigitatore/trice.

con·jur·ing ['kʌndʒərɪŋ] **1** *n* prestidigitazione *f.* **2** *adj:* ~ **trick** gioco di prestigio.

conk out [ˌkɒŋk'aʊt] *vi + adv (fam: break down)* scassarsi.

conk·er ['kɒŋkə'] *n (Brit fam)* castagna (d'ippocastano).

con·nect [kə'nɛkt] **1** *vt* **(a)** *(gen)* collegare; *(Telec: caller):* **to** ~ **(with)** mettere in comunicazione (con); *(pipes, drains):* **to** ~ **(to)** collegare (con); *(install: cooker, telephone)* installare, allacciare; **I am trying to** ~ **you** *(Telec)* sto cercando di darle la linea; **to** ~ **sth (up) to the mains** *(Elec)* collegare qc con la rete. **(b)** *(associate):* **to** ~ **sb/sth (with)** associare qn/qc (con), collegare qn/qc (con); **the evidence clearly ~ed him with the crime** le prove dimostravano chiaramente che era implicato nel delitto; **to be ~ed (to, with)** *(language, family, species)* essere imparentato (con); *(event)* essere collegato (a, con); **these 2**

things are in no way ~**ed** non c'è alcun legame tra le 2 cose. **2** *vi* collegarsi; *(trains, planes)* essere in coincidenza.

con·nec·tion, con·nex·ion [kə'nɛkʃən] *n* **(a)** *(Tech, Elec, Telec, Rail etc)* collegamento; *(connecting point)* giuntura; **to miss/make a** ~ perdere/prendere una coincidenza. **(b)** *(relationship)* rapporto, collegamento; ~ **between/with** rapporto tra/con; **what is the** ~ **between them?** in che modo sono legati?; **in** ~ **with** con riferimento a, a proposito di; **in this** ~ riguardo a questo; **family** ~ legame *m* di parentela; *(person)* parente *m/f;* **she has many business** ~**s** ha molti rapporti d'affari; **she's got the right** ~**s** conosce le persone giuste.

con·ning tow·er ['kɒnɪŋ,tauəʳ] *n (of submarine)* torre *f* di comando.

con·niv·ance [kə'naɪvəns] *n* connivenza.

con·nive [kə'naɪv] *vi:* **to** ~ **at** *(pretend not to notice)* chiudere un occhio su; *(aid and abet)* essere connivente in.

con·nois·seur [,kɒnə'sɜːʳ] *n* conoscitore/trice, intenditore/trice.

con·no·ta·tion [,kɒnəʊ'teɪʃən] *n* connotazione *f.*

con·quer ['kɒŋkəʳ] *vt (territory, nation, castle)* conquistare; *(enemy)* vincere, battere; *(habit, feelings)* superare.

con·quer·ing ['kɒŋkərɪŋ] *adj* vincitore(trice).

con·quer·or ['kɒŋkərəʳ] *n* conquistatore *m.*

con·quest ['kɒŋkwɛst] *n* conquista.

con·science ['kɒnʃəns] *n* coscienza; **with a clear** ~ con la coscienza pulita *or* a posto; **to have sth on one's** ~ avere qc sulla coscienza; **in all** ~ onestamente, in coscienza.

conscience-stricken ['kɒnʃəns,strɪkən] *adj:* **to be** ~ avere dei rimorsi.

con·sci·en·tious [,kɒnʃɪ'ɛnʃəs] *adj* coscienzioso(a); ~ **objector** obiettore *m* di coscienza.

con·scious ['kɒnʃəs] *adj* **(a)** *(Med)* cosciente; **to become** ~ riprendere conoscenza. **(b)** *(aware):* ~ **(of sth/of doing)** consapevole (di qc/di fare), conscio(a) (di qc/di fare); **to become** ~ **of sth/that** rendersi conto di qc/che. **(c)** *(deliberate: insult, error)* intenzionale, voluto(a).

con·scious·ness ['kɒnʃəsnɪs] *n* **(a)** *(Med)* conoscenza; **to lose/regain** ~ perdere/riprendere i sensi *or* la conoscenza. **(b)** *(awareness):* ~ **(of)** consapevolezza (di).

con·script ['kɒnskrɪpt] **1** *n* coscritto. **2** [kən'skrɪpt] *vt* arruolare, chiamare sotto le armi.

con·scrip·tion [kən'skrɪpʃən] *n* arruolamento (obbligatorio).

con·se·crate ['kɒnsɪkreɪt] *vt* consacrare.

con·se·cra·tion [,kɒnsɪ'kreɪʃən] *n* consacrazione *f.*

con·secu·tive [kən'sɛkjʊtɪv] *adj* consecutivo(a); **on 3** ~ **occasions** 3 volte di fila.

con·sen·sus [kən'sɛnsəs] *n* consenso; **the** ~ **of opinion** l'opinione unanime *or* comune.

con·sent [kən'sɛnt] **1** *n* consenso, benestare *m;* **by mutual** ~ per mutuo consenso; **by common** ~ di comune accordo; **the age of** ~ l'età legale (per avere rapporti sessuali). **2** *vi:* **to** ~ **(to sth/to do sth)** acconsentire (a qc/a fare qc).

con·se·quence ['kɒnsɪkwəns] *n* **(a)** *(result)* conseguenza; **in** ~ di conseguenza. **(b)** *(importance)* importanza; **it is of no** ~ non ha nessuna importanza.

con·se·quent ['kɒnsɪkwənt] *adj* conseguente.

con·se·quent·ly ['kɒnsɪkwəntlɪ] *adv* di conseguenza, quindi.

con·ser·va·tion [,kɒnsə'veɪʃən] *n* conservazione *f,* tutela; *(of nature)* tutela dell'ambiente.

con·ser·va·tion·ist [,kɒnsə'veɪʃənɪst] *n* fautore/ trice della tutela dell'ambiente.

con·serva·tive [kən'sɜːvətɪv] **1** *adj* (Pol, person, style) conservatore(trice); *(estimate etc)* prudente, modesto(a). **2** *n* conservatore/trice.

con·serva·tory [kən'sɜːvətrɪ] *n (greenhouse)* serra; *(Mus)* conservatorio.

con·serve [kən'sɜːv] *vt* conservare; **to** ~ **one's strength** risparmiare le forze.

con·sid·er [kən'sɪdəʳ] *vt* **(a)** *(think about: problem, possibility)* considerare, prendere in considerazione; *(question, matter, subject)* valutare, studiare; **to** ~ **doing sth** considerare la possibilità di fare qc; **all things** ~**ed** tutto sommato *or* considerato; **it is my** ~**ed opinion that...** sono fermamente convinto che... . **(b)** *(take into account)* considerare, fare conto di. **(c)** *(be of the opinion)* ritenere, considerare; **his teacher** ~**s him too lazy to pass the exams** il suo insegnante lo considera *or* lo ritiene troppo pigro per superare gli esami; ~ **yourself lucky** puoi dirti fortunato.

con·sid·er·able [kən'sɪdərəbl] *adj* considerevole; **to a** ~ **extent** in gran parte, in misura notevole.

con·sid·er·ably [kən'sɪdərəblɪ] *adv* notevolmente, decisamente.

con·sid·er·ate [kən'sɪdərɪt] *adj* riguardoso(a), premuroso(a).

con·sid·era·tion [kən,sɪdə'reɪʃən] *n* **(a)** *(no pl: thought, reflection)* considerazione *f;* **to be under** ~ essere in esame; **after due** ~ dopo un attento esame; **to take sth into** ~ considerare qc; **taking everything into** ~ tutto considerato *or* sommato. **(b)** *(no pl: thoughtfulness)* attenzione *f,* premura; **out of** ~ **for** per riguardo a; **to show** ~ **for sb's feelings** avere riguardo per qn. **(c)** *(factor)* elemento; **my first** ~ **is my family** il mio primo pensiero è per la mia famiglia; **his age is an important** ~ la sua età è un fattore importante; **it's of no** ~ non ha nessuna importanza. **(d)** *(payment)* ricompensa; **for a** ~ dietro compenso.

con·sid·er·ing [kən'sɪdərɪŋ] **1** *prep:* ~ **(that)** se si considera (che). **2** *adv:* **he did very well,** ~ è stato molto bravo, tutto sommato.

con·sign [kən'saɪn] *vt (Comm: send)* consegnare, inviare; *(frm: commit, entrust)* affidare.

con·sign·ment [kən'saɪnmənt] **1** *n (of goods)* partita. **2** *cpd:* ~ **note** *n* nota di spedizione.

con·sist [kən'sɪst] *vi:* **to** ~ **of** consistere di; **to** ~ **in sth/in doing sth** consistere in qc/nel fare qc.

con·sist·en·cy [kən'sɪstənsɪ] *n* **(a)** *(of person, action)* coerenza. **(b)** *(density)* consistenza.

con·sist·ent [kən'sɪstənt] *adj (results, action, argument)* costante; *(person)* fermo(a), costante; **to be** ~ **with** essere coerente con.

con·sist·ent·ly [kən'sɪstəntlɪ] *adv (argue, behave, happen)* costantemente.

con·so·la·tion [,kɒnsə'leɪʃən] **1** *n* consolazione *f.* **2** *cpd:* ~ **prize** *n* premio di consolazione.

con·sole[1] [kən'səʊl] *vt:* **to** ~ **(sb for sth)** consolare (qn per qc).

con·sole[2] ['kɒnsəʊl] *n (control panel)* quadro di comando.

con·soli·date [kən'sɒlɪdeɪt] *vt* **(a)** *(position, influence)* consolidare. **(b)** *(combine)* unire, fondere.

con·soli·da·tion [kən,sɒlɪ'deɪʃən] *n (see vb)* consolidazione *f;* fusione *f,* unione *f.*

con·som·mé [kɒn'sɒmeɪ] *n* consommé *m inv,* brodo ristretto.

con·so·nant ['kɒnsənənt] *n* consonante *f.*

con·sort [kən'sɔːt] **1** *n* consorte *m/f;* **prince** ~ principe *m* consorte. **2** [kən'sɔːt] *vi (often pej):* **to** ~ **with sb** frequentare qn.

con·sor·tium [kən'sɔːtɪəm] *n* consorzio.

con·spicu·ous [kən'spɪkjʊəs] *adj (person, behaviour)* che si fa notare; *(clothes)* vistoso(a); *(sign, notice)* ben visibile; *(bravery, difference)* notevole, evidente; **a ~ lack of sth** una notevole mancanza di qc; **to make o.s. ~** farsi notare; **to be ~ by one's absence** farsi notare per la propria assenza.

con·spira·cy [kən'spɪrəsɪ] *n (plotting)* cospirazione *f; (plot)* congiura.

con·spira·tor [kən'spɪrətə^r] *n* cospiratore/trice.

con·spire [kən'spaɪə^r] *vi (people)*: **to ~ (with sb against sb/sth)** congiurare (con qn contro qn/qc), cospirare (con qn contro qn/qc); **to ~ to do sth** *(people)* cospirare *or* congiurare per fare qc; *(events)* congiurare per fare qc.

con·sta·ble [ˈkʌnstəbl] *n (Brit: also:* **police ~)** ≃ agente *m* di polizia.

con·stabu·lary [kən'stæbjʊlərɪ] *n* forze *fpl* dell'ordine.

con·stant [ˈkɒnstənt] *adj (interruptions etc)* continuo(a), incessante; *(use etc)* continuo(a), costante; *(speed, temperature, rhythm)* costante; *(affection)* costante, stabile; *(friend, love)* fedele.

con·stant·ly [ˈkɒnstəntlɪ] *adv* continuamente.

con·stel·la·tion [ˌkɒnstə'leɪʃən] *n* costellazione *f*.

con·ster·na·tion [ˌkɒnstə'neɪʃən] *n* costernazione *f*, orrore *m;* **filled with ~ (at)** costernato (per).

con·sti·pat·ed [ˈkɒnstɪpeɪtɪd] *adj* stitico(a).

con·sti·pa·tion [ˌkɒnstɪ'peɪʃən] *n* stitichezza.

con·stitu·en·cy [kən'stɪtjʊənsɪ] **1** *n (district)* collegio elettorale; *(people)* elettori *mpl* (del collegio). **2** *cpd*: **~ party** *n* sezione *f* locale (del partito).

con·stitu·ent [kən'stɪtjʊənt] **1** *n (component)* ingrediente *m*, componente *m; (Pol: voter)* elettore/ trice. **2** *adj* costitutivo(a).

con·sti·tute [ˈkɒnstɪtjuːt] *vt* costituire.

con·sti·tu·tion [ˌkɒnstɪ'tjuːʃən] *n* costituzione *f*.

con·sti·tu·tion·al [ˌkɒnstɪ'tjuːʃənl] *adj* costituzionale.

con·strain [kən'streɪn] *vt* costringere; **to feel/be ~ed to do sth** sentirsi/essere costretto a fare qc.

con·straint [kən'streɪnt] *n (no pl: compulsion)* costrizione *f; (restraint)* limitazione *f; (embarrassment)* imbarazzo, soggezione *f*.

con·strict [kən'strɪkt] *vt (gen)* costringere, restringere; *(movements)* impedire.

con·stric·tion [kən'strɪkʃən] *n* costrizione *f*; *(feeling)* oppressione *f*.

con·struct [kən'strʌkt] *vt* costruire.

con·struc·tion [kən'strʌkʃən] **1** *n (gen)* costruzione *f; (fig: interpretation)* interpretazione *f*; **under ~** in costruzione. **2** *cpd*: **~ industry** *n* edilizia, industria edile.

con·struc·tive [kən'strʌktɪv] *adj* costruttivo(a).

con·strue [kən'struː] *vt (interpret)* interpretare.

con·sul [ˈkɒnsəl] *n* console *m*.

con·su·lar [ˈkɒnsjʊlə^r] *adj* consolare.

con·su·late [ˈkɒnsjʊlɪt] *n* consolato.

con·sult [kən'sʌlt] **1** *vt*: **to ~ sb (about sth)** consultare qn *(su or* riguardo a qc). **2** *vi* consultarsi.

con·sul·tan·cy [kən'sʌltənsɪ] **1** *n* consulenza. **2** *cpd (fees, business)* di consulenza.

con·sult·ant [kən'sʌltənt] **1** *n* consulente *m/f; (Brit Med)* specialista *m/f*. **2** *cpd*: **~ paediatrician** *n* specialista *m/f* in pediatria.

con·sul·ta·tion [ˌkɒnsəl'teɪʃən] *n* consultazione *f; (Med)* consulto; **in ~ with** consultandosi con.

con·sume [kən'sjuːm] *vt (gen)* consumare; **to be ~d with** *(envy)* rodersi di; *(grief)* consumarsi di.

con·sum·er [kən'sjuːmə^r] **1** *n* consumatore/trice; *(of electricity, gas etc)* utente *m/f*. **2** *cpd*: **~ durables** *npl* prodotti *mpl* di consumo durevole; **~**

goods *npl* beni *mpl* di consumo; **a ~ organization** un'organizzazione di consumatori; **~ protection** *n* protezione *f* dei consumatori; **~ society** *n* società consumista *or* dei consumi.

con·sum·mate [kən'sʌmɪt] **1** *adj* consumato(a), abile; **with ~ ease** con estrema facilità. **2** [ˈkɒnsʌmeɪt] *vt (marriage)* consumare.

con·sump·tion [ˈkɒnsʌmpʃən] *n (of food, fuel)* consumo; *(old use: tuberculosis)* consunzione *f;* **not fit for human ~** non commestibile.

cont. *abbr (= continued)* segue.

con·tact [ˈkɒntækt] **1** *n (all senses)* contatto; **to be in ~ with sb/sth** essere in contatto con qn/qc; **to make ~ with sb** mettersi in contatto con qn; **to lose ~ (with sb)** perdere il contatto (con qn); **business ~s** contatti *mpl* d'affari. **2** *vt* mettersi in contatto con, contattare. **3** *cpd*: **~ adhesive** *n* adesivo istantaneo; **~ lenses** *npl* lenti *fpl* a contatto.

con·ta·gious [kən'teɪdʒəs] *adj* contagioso(a), infettivo(a).

con·tain [kən'teɪn] *vt* contenere; *(fire, disease)* arginare.

con·tain·er [kən'teɪnə^r] **1** *n (box, jug etc)* contenitore *m; (Comm: for transport)* container *m inv*. **2** *cpd (train, lorry, ship)* da container; *(dock, depot, transport)* per container.

con·tain·er·ize [kən'teɪnəraɪz] *vt* mettere in container.

con·tami·nate [kən'tæmɪneɪt] *vt* contaminare.

cont'd *abbr = cont.*

con·tem·plate [ˈkɒntəmpleɪt] *vt (gaze at, reflect upon)* contemplare; *(consider)*: **to ~ sth/doing sth** pensare a qc/di fare qc.

con·tem·pla·tion [ˌkɒntəm'pleɪʃən] *n* contemplazione *f*.

con·tem·pla·tive [kən'templətɪv] *adj* contemplativo(a).

con·tem·po·rary [kən'tempərərɪ] **1** *adj* contemporaneo(a). **2** *n* contemporaneo/a; *(of the same age)* coetaneo/a.

con·tempt [kən'tempt] *n* disprezzo, disdegno; **to hold sth/sb in ~** disprezzare qc/qn; **~ of court** *(Law)* oltraggio alla Corte; **it's beneath ~** è oltremodo vergognoso.

con·tempt·ible [kən'temptəbl] *adj* vergognoso(a), spregevole.

con·temp·tu·ous [kən'temptjʊəs] *adj (person)*: **~ (of)** sprezzante (di); *(manner, gesture)* sprezzante, altezzoso(a).

con·tend [kən'tend] **1** *vt*: **to ~ that** sostenere che, asserire che. **2** *vi (fig)*: **to ~ (with sb) for sth** contendere qc (con qn); **we have many problems to ~ with** dobbiamo lottare contro molti problemi; **you'll have me to ~ with** dovrai vedertela con me; **he has a lot to ~ with** ha un sacco di guai.

con·tend·er [kən'tendə^r] *n* contendente *m/f*.

con·tent^1 [kən'tent] **1** *adj*: **~ (with)** contento(a) *or* soddisfatto(a) (di); **to be ~ to do sth** accontentarsi di fare qc. **2** *n* contentezza; **to one's heart's ~** a volontà, a piacimento. **3** *vt* fare contento(a), soddisfare; **to ~ o.s. with sth/with doing sth** accontentarsi di qc/di fare qc.

con·tent^2 [ˈkɒntent] *n* contenuto; **~s** *(of box, case etc)* contenuto; **table of ~s** *(of book)* indice *m*.

con·tent·ed [kən'tentɪd] *adj*: **~ (with)** contento(a) (di), soddisfatto(a) (di).

con·ten·tion [kən'tenʃən] *n (strife)* contesa, disputa; *(assertion)* tesi *f inv*; **bone of ~** pomo della discordia.

con·tent·ment [kən'tentmənt] *n* contentezza, soddisfazione *f*.

con·test [ˈkɒntest] **1** *n (struggle)* gara, lotta;

(Boxing, Wrestling) incontro; *(competition)* gara, concorso. **2** [kən'tɛst] *vt (dispute: argument, right etc)* contestare, disputare; *(Law)* impugnare; *(election, seat)* essere in lizza per.

con·test·ant [kən'tɛstənt] *n (in competition)* concorrente *m/f; (Sport)* contendente *m/f;* ~ **for a title** aspirante *m/f* a un titolo.

con·text ['kɒntɛkst] *n* contesto; **in/out of** ~ nel/ fuori dal contesto.

con·ti·nent ['kɒntɪnənt] *n* **(a)** continente *m.* **(b)** *(Brit):* **the C**~ l'Europa (continentale); **on the C**~ in Europa.

con·ti·nen·tal [,kɒntɪ'nɛntl] *adj* continentale; *(drift)* dei continenti; *(Brit: European)* europeo(a), dell'Europa continentale; ~ **breakfast** colazione *f* all'europea; ~ **quilt** piumino.

con·tin·gen·cy [kən'tɪndʒənsɪ] **1** *n* contingenza, evenienza; **in certain contingencies** in certi frangenti. **2** *cpd:* ~ **funds** *npl* fondi *mpl* di previdenza; ~ **plans** *npl* piani *mpl* di emergenza.

con·tin·gent [kən'tɪndʒənt] **1** *adj:* **to be** ~ **upon** dipendere da. **2** *n (Mil)* contingente *m; (group)* gruppo.

con·tin·ual [kən'tɪnjuəl] *adj* continuo(a).

con·tin·al·ly [kən'tɪnjuəlɪ] *adv* continuamente, senza tregua.

con·tin·u·ance [kən'tɪnjuəns] *n (continuation)* continuazione *f; (duration)* durata.

con·tin·u·ation [kən,tɪnju'eɪʃən] *n* continuazione *f; (resumption)* ripresa; *(of serial story)* seguito.

con·tinue [kən'tɪnjuː] **1** *vt (gen):* **to** ~ **(to do sth)** continuare (a fare qc); *(resume)* riprendere, continuare; *(serial story):* **to be** ~**d** continua; ~**d on page 10** segue *or* continua a pagina 10. **2** *vi (gen)* continuare; *(resume)* riprendere, continuare; *(extend)* estendersi, proseguire; **to** ~ **on one's way** riprendere la strada.

con·ti·nu·ity [,kɒntɪ'njuːɪtɪ] **1** *n* continuità; *(Cine)* (ordine *m* della) sceneggiatura. **2** *cpd:* ~ **girl** *n (Cine)* segretaria di edizione.

con·tin·u·ous [kən'tɪnjuəs] *adj* continuo(a), ininterrotto(a); ~ **performance** *(Cine)* spettacolo continuato.

con·tin·u·ous·ly [kən'tɪnjuəslɪ] *adv (repeatedly)* continuamente; *(uninterruptedly)* ininterrottamente.

con·tort [kən'tɔːt] *vt* contorcere.

con·tor·tion [kən'tɔːʃən] *n* contorsione *f.*

con·tour ['kɒntuəʳ] **1** *n* contorno. **2** *cpd:* ~ **line** *n* isoipsa, curva di livello; ~ **map** *n* carta a curve di livello.

contra·band ['kɒntrəbænd] **1** *n* contrabbando. **2** *adj* di contrabbando.

contra·cep·tion [,kɒntrə'sɛpʃən] *n* contraccezione *f.*

contra·cep·tive [,kɒntrə'sɛptɪv] **1** *adj* contraccettivo(a), anticoncezionale. **2** *n* contraccettivo, anticoncezionale *m.*

con·tract ['kɒntrækt] **1** *n* contratto; **to enter into a** ~ **with sb to do sth/for sth** stipulare un contratto con qn per fare qc/per qc; **to be under** ~ **to do sth** aver stipulato un contratto per fare qc; **to put work out to** ~ dare del lavoro in appalto; **by** ~ per contratto; **there's a** ~ **out for him** *(fig fam)* c'è una taglia sul di lui. **2** *vt* [kən'trækt] *(all senses)* contrarre; **to** ~ **with sb to do sth** stipulare un contratto con qn per fare qc. **3** *vi* [kən'trækt] contrarsi; *(metal)* restringersi. **4** *cpd (price, date)* del contratto; *(work)* a contratto; ~ **bridge** *n (Cards)* bridge *m* contratto.

♦ **contract in** *vi + adv* impegnarsi (con un contratto).

♦ **contract out** *vi + adv:* **to** ~ **out (of)** ritirarsi

(da); **to** ~ **out of a pension scheme** cessare di pagare i contributi per una pensione.

con·trac·tion [kən'trækʃən] *n* contrazione *f; (of metal)* restringimento.

con·trac·tor [kən'træktəʳ] *n* appaltatore *m.*

con·trac·tual [kən'træktʃuəl] *adj* contrattuale.

contra·dict [,kɒntrə'dɪkt] *vt* contraddire.

contra·dic·tion [,kɒntrə'dɪkʃən] *n* contraddizione *f;* **to be in** ~ **with** discordare con; ~ **in terms** contraddizione.

contra·dic·tory [,kɒntrə'dɪktərɪ] *adj* contraddittorio(a); **to be** ~ **to** contraddire.

con·tral·to [kən'træltəu] *n* contralto.

con·trap·tion [kən'træpʃən] *n (fam)* aggeggio.

con·tra·ry ['kɒntrərɪ] **1** *adj* **(a):** ~ **(to)** contrario(a) (a), opposto(a) (a); ~ **to nature** contro natura; ~ **to what we thought** a differenza di *or* contrariamente a quanto pensavamo. **(b)** [kən'trɛərɪ] *(self-willed)* difficile, cocciuto(a). **2** *n* contrario; **on the** ~ al contrario; **unless you hear to the** ~ salvo contrordine.

con·trast ['kɒntrɑːst] **1** *n* contrasto; **in** ~ **to** *or* **with** a differenza di, contrariamente a. **2** *vt* [kən'trɑːst]: **to** ~ **(with)** mettere a confronto (con), opporre (a). **3** *vi* [kən'trɑːst]: **to** ~ **(with)** contrastare (con).

con·trast·ing [kən'trɑːstɪŋ] *adj* contrastante.

contra·vene [,kɒntrə'viːn] *vt* contravvenire a.

contra·ven·tion [,kɒntrə'vɛnʃən] *n:* ~ **(of)** contravvenzione *f* (a), infrazione *f* (di).

con·tre·temps ['kɒntrə,tɒŋ] *n* contrattempo.

con·trib·ute [kən'trɪbjuːt] **1** *vt (sum of money, help)* offrire; *(article to a newspaper)* contribuire con, collaborare con. **2** *vi:* **to** ~ **to** *(charity, collection, success)* contribuire a; *(discussion)* partecipare a; *(newspaper)* collaborare a *or* con; *(Admin)* pagare i contributi per.

con·tri·bu·tion [,kɒntrɪ'bjuːʃən] *n* **(a)** *(see vb)* offerta; contribuzione *f;* collaborazione *f.* **(b)** *(money, to discussion)* contributo; *(to journal)* intervento.

con·tribu·tor [kən'trɪbjutəʳ] *n (of money)* donatore/ trice; *(to journal)* collaboratore/trice.

con·tribu·tory [kən'trɪbjutərɪ] *adj (cause)* che contribuisce; **it was a** ~ **factor in...** quello ha contribuito a... .

con·trite ['kɒntraɪt] *adj* mortificato(a); *(Rel)* contrito(a).

con·tri·tion [kən'trɪʃən] *n (see adj)* mortificazione *f;* contrizione *f.*

con·triv·ance [kən'traɪvəns] *n (machine, device)* congegno.

con·trive [kən'traɪv] *vt (plan, scheme)* inventare, escogitare; **to** ~ **a means of doing sth** escogitare un sistema per fare qc; **to** ~ **to do sth** trovare un modo per fare qc.

con·trol [kən'trəul] **1** *n* **(a)** *(no pl: gen)* controllo; *(of traffic)* regolamentazione *f; (of pests)* eliminazione *f;* **the** ~ **of cancer** la lotta contro il cancro; **they have no** ~ **over their son** non riescono a controllare il loro bambino; **to keep sth/sb under** ~ tenere qc/qn sotto controllo; **to lose** ~ **of sth** perdere il controllo di qc; **to lose** ~ **of o.s.** perdere le staffe; **to be in** ~ **of** tenere sotto controllo; **to bring a fire under** ~ arginare *or* circoscrivere un incendio; **everything is under** ~ tutto è sotto controllo; **the car went out of** ~ la macchina non rispondeva ai comandi; **the class was quite out of** ~ la classe era in subbuglio; **circumstances beyond our** ~ circostanze che non dipendono da noi; **who is in** ~? chi è responsabile?; **wage** ~**s** limitazione *f* dei salari.

(b) *(Tech, TV, Radio)* comando; **to take over**

the ~s prendere i comandi.
(c) *(in experiment)* gruppo di controllo.
2 *vt (gen)* controllare; *(traffic)* dirigere, regolare; *(crowd)* tenere sotto controllo; *(disease, fire)* arginare, limitare; *(emotions)* controllare, frenare; **to** ~ **o.s.** controllarsi.
3 *cpd:* ~ **group** *n (Med, Psych etc)* gruppo di controllo; ~ **knob** *n (TV, Radio)* manopola (di comando); ~ **panel** *n (on aircraft, ship, TV etc)* quadro dei comandi; ~ **room** *n (Naut, Mil)* sala di comando; *(Radio, TV)* sala di regia; ~ **tower** *n (Aer)* torre *f* di controllo.

con·trolled [kən'trəʊld] *adj* **(a)** *(emotion)* contenuto(a); **she was very** ~ era padrona di sé. **(b)** *(Econ:)* ~ **economy** economia controllata.

con·trol·ler [kən'trəʊlə'] *n* controllore *m*.

con·trol·ling [kən'trəʊlɪŋ] *adj (factor)* dominante; ~ **interest** maggioranza delle azioni.

con·tro·ver·sial [ˌkɒntrə'vɜːʃəl] *adj (subject, speech, decision)* controverso(a), discusso(a); *(person, book)* discusso(a), che suscita polemiche.

con·tro·ver·sy [kən'trɒvəsɪ] *n* controversia; **it has caused a lot of** ~ ha causato molte controversie.

con·tu·sion [kən'tjuː:ʒən] *n* contusione *f*.

co·nun·drum [kə'nʌndrəm] *n* indovinello.

con·ur·ba·tion [ˌkɒnɜː'beɪʃən] *n* conurbazione *f*.

con·va·lesce [ˌkɒnvə'les] *vi* fare la convalescenza.

con·va·les·cence [ˌkɒnvə'lesəns] *n* convalescenza.

con·va·les·cent [ˌkɒnvə'lesənt] *adj, n* convalescente *(m/f)*; ~ **home** convalescenziario.

con·vec·tion [kən'vekʃən] *n* convezione *f*.

con·vec·tor [kən'vektə'] *n (also:* ~ **heater, convection heater)** convettore *m*.

con·vene [kən'viːn] **1** *vt (people)* convocare; *(meeting)* organizzare. **2** *vi* riunirsi, convenire.

con·ven·er [kən'viːnə'] *n (esp Brit)* presidente *m (di commissione etc)*.

con·veni·ence [kən'viːnɪəns] **1** *n* **(a)** *(of house, plan, person)* comodità; **at your earliest** ~ *(Comm)* appena possibile. **(b):** ~**s** *(amenities: of house)* comodità *fpl*. **2** *cpd:* ~ **foods** *npl* cibi *mpl* precotti.

con·veni·ent [kən'viːnɪənt] *adj (tool, size, place etc)* comodo(a); *(event, time, occasion)* adatto(a), opportuno(a); **the house is** ~ **for the shops** la casa è vicina ai *or* comoda per i negozi; **if it is** ~ **to you** se per lei va bene, se non la incomoda; **would tomorrow be** ~? andrebbe bene domani?; **is it** ~ **to call tomorrow?** potrei passare domani?

con·veni·ent·ly [kən'viːnɪəntlɪ] *adv (happen)* a proposito; *(situated)* in un posto comodo; **very** ~ **he arrived late** fortunatamente è arrivato tardi.

con·vent ['kɒnvənt] **1** *n* convento (di suore). **2** *cpd:* ~ **school** *n* scuola retta da suore.

con·ven·tion [kən'venʃən] *n (custom, agreement)* convenzione *f*; *(meeting)* congresso.

con·ven·tion·al [kən'venʃənl] *adj (person, style, weapons)* convenzionale; *(methods)* tradizionale.

con·verge [kən'vɜːdʒ] *vi:* **to** ~ **(on)** convergere (su).

con·ver·sa·tion [ˌkɒnvə'seɪʃən] **1** *n* conversazione *f*; **in** ~ **with** a colloquio con; **to have a** ~ **with sb** conversare con qn; **what was your** ~ **about?** di che cosa parlavate? **2** *cpd:* **it was a** ~ **piece** faceva parlare di sé; **that was a** ~ **stopper** *(fam)* quella cosa ha lasciato tutti a bocca aperta.

con·ver·sa·tion·al [ˌkɒnvə'seɪʃənl] *adj (style, tone)* colloquiale; ~ **Italian** italiano parlato.

con·ver·sa·tion·al·ist [ˌkɒnvə'seɪʃnəlɪst] *n* conversatore/trice.

con·verse¹ [kən'vɜːs] *vi:* **to** ~ **(with sb about sth)** conversare (con qn su qc).

con·verse² ['kɒnvɜːs] **1** *n* inverso, opposto. **2** *adj* opposto(a).

con·verse·ly [kɒn'vɜːslɪ] *adv* al contrario, per contro.

con·ver·sion [kən'vɜːʃən] *n (gen, Rel)* conversione *f*; *(house* ~) trasformazione *f*, rimodernamento; *(Rugby, Am Ftbl)* trasformazione.

con·vert ['kɒnvɜːt] **1** *n* convertito/a. **2** [kən'vɜːt] *vt* **(a)** *(Rel):* **to** ~ **(to)** convertire (a). **(b):** **to** ~ **(to, into)** *(gen)* convertire (in); *(house)* trasformare (in), convertire (in). **(c)** *(Rugby, Am Ftbl)* trasformare.

con·ver·ter [kən'vɜːtə'] *n (Elec)* convertitore *m*.

con·vert·ible [kən'vɜːtəbl] **1** *adj (currency)* convertibile; ~ **settee** divano letto. **2** *n (car)* auto *f* *inv* decappottabile.

con·vex ['kɒn'veks] *adj* convesso(a).

con·vey [kən'veɪ] *vt (goods, passengers)* trasportare; *(subj: pipeline)* convogliare; *(thanks, congratulations, sound, order)* trasmettere; *(meaning, ideas)* comunicare, esprimere; **to** ~ **to sb that** comunicare a qn che; **words cannot** ~... le parole non possono esprimere...; **the name** ~**s nothing to me** il nome non mi dice niente.

con·vey·ance [kən'veɪəns] *n (of goods)* trasporto; *(vehicle)* mezzo di trasporto.

con·vey·anc·ing [kən'veɪənsɪŋ] *n (Law)* redazione *f* di transazioni di proprietà.

con·vey·or belt [kən'veɪə',belt] *n* nastro trasportatore.

con·vict ['kɒnvɪkt] **1** *n* carcerato/a. **2** [kən'vɪkt] *vt:* **to** ~ **(of)** riconoscere colpevole (di); ~**ed murderer** persona riconosciuta colpevole di omicidio.

con·vic·tion [kən'vɪkʃən] *n* **(a)** *(Law)* condanna. **(b)** *(belief)* convinzione *f*; **it is my** ~ **that** sono convinto che; **to carry** ~ essere convincente.

con·vince [kən'vɪns] *vt:* **to** ~ **sb (of sth/that)** convincere qn (di qc/che), persuadere qn (di qc/che).

con·vinc·ing [kən'vɪnsɪŋ] *adj (gen)* convincente; *(win)* netto(a).

con·vinc·ing·ly [kən'vɪnsɪŋlɪ] *adv (see adj)* in modo convincente; nettamente.

con·viv·ial [kən'vɪvɪəl] *adj* allegro(a), gioviale.

con·vo·lut·ed ['kɒnvəluːtɪd] *adj (shape)* attorcigliato(a), avvolto(a); *(argument)* involuto(a).

con·voy ['kɒnvɔɪ] *n* convoglio; *(escort)* scorta; **in** ~ in convoglio; **under** ~ sotto scorta.

con·vulse [kən'vʌls] *vt* sconvolgere; **to be** ~**d with pain** contorcersi dal dolore; ~**d with laughter** piegato in due dalle risate.

con·vul·sion [kən'vʌlʃən] *n (fit, seizure)* convulsione *f*; **in** ~**s** *(fam: laughter)* piegato in due (dalle risate).

con·vul·sive [kən'vʌlsɪv] *adj (movement, laughter)* convulso(a); *(Med)* convulsivo(a).

coo [kuː] *vi (dove)* tubare; *(baby)* fare versetti.

cook [kʊk] **1** *n* cuoco/a. **2** *vt* **(a)** *(meal)* preparare; **shall I** ~ **you an omelette?** ti cucino *or* ti faccio un'omelette?; **to** ~ **sb's goose** *(fig fam)* rompere le uova nel paniere a qn; **to** ~ **one's own goose** *(fig fam)* darsi la zappa sui piedi. **(b)** *(fam: falsify: accounts)* falsificare, alterare. **3** *vi (food)* cuocere; *(person)* cucinare; **what's** ~**ing?** *(fig fam)* cosa bolle in pentola?

♦ **cook up** *vt + adv (fam: excuse, story)* improvvisare, inventare.

cook·book ['kʊkbʊk] *n (Am)* = **cookery book**.

cook·er ['kʊkə'] *n (stove)* cucina *(apparecchio)*; *(cooking apple)* mela da cuocere.

cook·ery ['kʊkərɪ] **1** *n* cucina *(attività)*. **2** *cpd:* ~ **book** *n* libro di ricette, ricettario.

cook·house ['kʊkhaʊs] *n (esp Am)* cucina (da campo).

cook·ie ['kʊkɪ] *n (Am: biscuit)* biscotto.

cook·ing ['kʊkɪŋ] **1** *n* cucina *(attività e cibo)*. **2** *cpd (apples, chocolate)* da cuocere; *(utensils, salt, foil)* da cucina.

cook·out ['kʊkaʊt] *n (Am)* pranzo (cucinato) all'aperto.

cool [kuːl] **1** *adj* (**-er, -est**) *(gen)* fresco(a); *(drink)* rinfrescante; *(dress)* fresco(a), leggero(a); *(calm)* calmo(a); *(unenthusiastic, unfriendly)* freddo(a); **it is ~** *(weather)* fa fresco; **to keep sth ~ or in a ~ place** tenere qc in fresco; **to keep sb ~** essere freddo con qn; **to keep ~** mantenersi fresco(a); *(fig)* conservare la calma; **keep ~!** calma!; **play it ~!** fa' finta di niente!; **to be as ~ as a cucumber** essere fresco come una rosa; *(fig)* essere imperturbabile; **he's a pretty ~ customer** *(fam)* ha un gran sangue freddo; *(pej)* ha una bella faccia tosta; **that was very ~ of you!** *(fam)* che sangue freddo!; **we paid a ~ £20,000 for that house** *(fam)* abbiamo pagato la bellezza di 20.000 sterline per quella casa.
   2 *n*: **in the ~ of the evening** nella frescura serale; **to keep sth in the ~** tenere qc in fresco; **to keep one's ~** *(fam)* conservare la calma; **to lose one's ~** *(fam)* perdere le staffe.
   3 *vt (air)* rinfrescare; *(food)* raffreddare; *(engine)* far raffreddare; **~ it!** *(fam)* calmati!; **to ~ one's heels** *(fam)* aspettare (a lungo).
   4 *vi (air, liquid)* raffreddarsi.
   5 *cpd*: **~ box** *n* borsa termica.

♦ **cool down 1** *vi + adv* raffreddarsi; *(fig: person, situation)* calmarsi. **2** *vt + adv* far raffreddare; *(fig)* calmare.

♦ **cool off** *vi + adv (become less angry)* calmarsi; *(lose enthusiasm, become less affectionate)* diventare più freddo(a).

cool·ant ['kuːlənt] *n (Tech)* refrigerante *m*.

cool·er ['kuːlə'] *n (for food)* ghiacciaia; *(fam: prison)*: **to send sb to the ~** mettere qn al fresco.

cool·ing ['kuːlɪŋ] *adj* rinfrescante; **~ tower** torre *f* di refrigerazione.

cooling-off pe·ri·od [,kuːlɪŋ'ɒf,pɪərɪəd] *n (Industry)* periodo di tregua.

cool·ly ['kuːlɪ] *adv (calmly)* con calma, tranquillamente; *(audaciously)* come se niente fosse; *(unenthusiastically)* freddamente.

cool·ness ['kuːlnɪs] *n (see adj)* freschezza *(also of drink)*; calma; freddezza; *(of weather)* frescura.

coop [kuːp] *n* stia.

♦ **coop up** *vt + adv* rinchiudere.

co-op ['kəʊ'ɒp] *n (abbr of* **cooperative***)* coop *f*.

co-oper·ate [kəʊ'ɒpəreɪt] *vi*: **to ~ (with sb in sth/to do sth)** cooperare (con qn in qc/per fare qc); **will he ~?** sarà disposto a collaborare?

co-opera·tion [kəʊ,ɒpə'reɪʃən] *n* cooperazione *f*.

co-opera·tive [kəʊ'ɒpərətɪv] **1** *adj* (**a**) *(person)* disposto a collaborare; **you're not very ~!** non sei di grande aiuto! (**b**) *(farm etc)* cooperativo(a). **2** *n* cooperativa.

co-opt [kəʊ'ɒpt] *vt*: **to ~ sb onto sth** cooptare qn per qc.

co·or·di·nate [kəʊ'ɔːdnɪt] **1** *n* coordinata. **2** [kəʊ'ɔːdɪneɪt] *vt* coordinare.

co·or·di·na·tion [kəʊ,ɔːdɪ'neɪʃən] *n* coordinazione *f*.

co·or·di·na·tor [kəʊ'ɔːdɪneɪtə'] *n* coordinatore/trice.

cop [kɒp] *(fam)* **1** *n* (**a**) *(policeman)* poliziotto. (**b**): **it's not much ~** non vale molto. **2** *vt*: **to ~ it** buscarle.

♦ **cop out** *vi + adv (fam)* piantare tutto; **to ~ out of sth** tirarsi indietro da qc.

cope [kəʊp] *vi* farcela; **to ~ with** *(task, child)* farcela con; *(situation, difficulties, problems: tackle)* affrontare; *(: solve)* risolvere; **he's coping pretty well** se la cava abbastanza bene; **leave it to me, I'll ~** lascia stare, ci penso io.

Co·pen·ha·gen [,kəʊpn'heɪgən] *n* Copenhagen *f*.

copi·er ['kɒpɪə'] *n (photo~)* (foto)copiatrice *f*.

co-pilot ['kəʊ'paɪlət] *n* secondo pilota *m*.

co·pi·ous ['kəʊpɪəs] *adj (harvest, tears)* copioso(a); *(notes, supply)* abbondante.

cop·per ['kɒpə'] **1** *n* (**a**) *(gen)* rame *m*; *(coin)* monetina; **~s** spiccioli *mpl.* (**b**) *(fam: policeman)* poliziotto. **2** *adj (wire, kettle)* di rame; *(colour)* (color) rame *inv*, ramato(a).

cop·pice ['kɒpɪs] *n*, **copse** [kɒps] *n* boschetto.

copu·late ['kɒpjʊleɪt] *vi* accoppiarsi.

copu·la·tion [,kɒpjʊ'leɪʃən] *n* copula, accoppiamento.

copy ['kɒpɪ] **1** *n* (**a**) *(gen)* copia; *(of painting)* copia, riproduzione *f*; **rough/fair ~** brutta/bella (copia). (**b**) *(material: for printing)* materiale *m*, testo; **to make good ~** *(fig)* fare notizia. **2** *vt (imitate)* imitare; *(make copy of, cheat)* copiare.

♦ **copy out** *vt + adv* ricopiare, trascrivere.

copy·ing ['kɒpɪɪŋ] *adj*: **~ ink** inchiostro copiativo.

copy·right ['kɒpɪraɪt] *n* diritti *mpl* d'autore, copyright *m*.

copy·writer ['kɒpɪ,raɪtə'] *n* copywriter *m inv*, redattore/trice (di testi pubblicitari).

cor·al ['kɒrəl] **1** *n* corallo. **2** *cpd (island, reef)* corallino(a); **~ necklace** *n* collana di corallo.

cord [kɔːd] *n* (**a**) *(gen)* corda; *(for pyjamas)* cintura; *(round parcel etc)* corda, spago; *(Elec)* filo. (**b**) *(material)* velluto a coste; **~s** *(trousers)* calzoni *mpl* (di velluto) a coste.

cor·dial ['kɔːdɪəl] **1** *adj* cordiale. **2** *n* cordiale *m*.

cor·don ['kɔːdn] *n* cordone *m*.

♦ **cordon off** *vt + adv* fare cordone attorno a.

cor·du·roy ['kɔːdərɔɪ] *n* velluto a coste.

core [kɔː'] **1** *n (of fruit)* torsolo; *(of cable)* centro; *(of earth, nuclear reactor)* nucleo; *(of problem etc)* cuore *m*, nocciolo; **a hard ~ of resistance** un forte nucleo di resistenza; **rotten to the ~** marcio fino al midollo; **English to the ~** inglese in tutto e per tutto. **2** *vt (fruit)* togliere il torsolo a.

co-respond·ent ['kəʊrɪs'pɒndənt] *n (Law)* correo/a *(di adulterio)*.

co·ri·an·der [,kɒrɪ'ændə'] *n* coriandolo.

cork [kɔːk] **1** *n (substance)* sughero; *(stopper)* tappo, turacciolo; **to pull the ~ out of a bottle** stappare una bottiglia. **2** *vt (bottle: also:* **~ up***)* tappare. **3** *cpd* di sughero; **~ oak** *n* quercia da sughero, sughera.

corked [kɔːkt] *adj (wine)* che sa di tappo.

cork·screw ['kɔːk,skruː] *n* cavatappi *m inv*.

corn[1] [kɔːn] **1** *n (Brit: wheat)* grano, frumento; *(Am: maize)* granturco, mais *m*; **~ on the cob** pannocchia. **2** *cpd*: **~ oil** *n* olio di mais.

corn[2] [kɔːn] **1** *n (Med)* callo. **2** *cpd*: **~ plaster** *n* callifugo.

cor·nea ['kɔːnɪə] *n* cornea.

corned beef ['kɔːnd'biːf] *n* carne *f* (di manzo) in scatola.

cor·ner ['kɔːnə'] **1** *n* (**a**) *(gen)* angolo; *(of table)* spigolo, angolo; **it's just around the ~** *(also fig)* è proprio dietro l'angolo; *(: in time)* è molto vicino; **to turn the ~** *(fig)* fare una svolta; **in odd ~s** nei posti più strani *or* impensati; **the four ~s of the world** i quattro angoli del mondo; **out of the ~ of one's eye** con la coda dell'occhio; **to drive sb into a ~** *(fig)* mettere qn con le spalle al muro; **to be in a**

(tight) ~ *(fig)* essere nei pasticci *or* guai; **to cut a** ~ *(Aut)* tagliare una curva; **to cut** ~**s** *(fig)* prendere una scorciatoia. **(b)** *(Ftbl)* corner *m inv*, calcio d'angolo.

2 *vt* **(a)** *(animal)* intrappolare; *(fugitive)* mettere in trappola; *(fig: person: catch to speak to)* bloccare. **(b)** *(Comm: market)* monopolizzare; *(: goods)* accaparrare.

3 *vi* **(Aut)** curvare.

4 *cpd (house, seat, table)* d'angolo; ~ **cupboard** *n* angoliera; ~ **shop** *n* negozio all'angolo.

corner·stone ['kɔːnə,stəʊn] *n (also fig)* pietra angolare.

cor·net ['kɔːnɪt] *n* **(a)** *(Mus)* cornetta. **(b)** *(Brit: ice cream)* cornetto, cono.

corn·field ['kɔːn,fiːld] *n (Brit)* campo di grano; *(Am)* campo di granturco.

corn·flakes ['kɔːn,fleɪks] *npl* fiocchi *mpl* di granturco.

corn·flour ['kɔːn,flaʊəʳ] *n* ≃ fecola di patate.

cor·nice ['kɔːnɪs] *n (Archit)* cornicione *m*; *(: interior)* cornice *f*.

Cor·nish ['kɔːnɪʃ] *adj* della Cornovaglia.

corn·starch ['kɔːn,stɑːtʃ] *n (Am)* = **cornflour**.

Corn·wall ['kɔːnwəl] *n* Cornovaglia.

corny ['kɔːnɪ] *adj* **(-ier, -iest)** *(fam)* banale.

cor·ol·lary [kə'rɒlərɪ] *n* corollario *m*.

coro·nary ['kɒrənərɪ] **1** *adj (artery)* coronario(a); *(disease)* coronarico(a). **2** *n (also:* ~ **thrombosis)** trombosi *f* coronarica.

coro·na·tion [,kɒrə'neɪʃən] *n* incoronazione *f*.

coro·ner ['kɒrənəʳ] *n* coroner *m inv (pubblico ufficiale che indaga la causa di morte in circostanze sospette)*.

coro·net ['kɒrənɪt] *n* coroncina; *(of peer)* corona nobiliare.

cor·po·ral ['kɔːpərəl] **1** *adj*: ~ **punishment** punizione *f* corporale. **2** *n (Mil)* caporale *m*.

cor·po·rate ['kɔːpərɪt] *adj (joint: action, effort)* congiunto(a), unitario(a); *(ownership, responsibility)* comune; ~ **body** corpo unico.

cor·po·ra·tion [,kɔːpə'reɪʃən] *n (Comm)* società *f inv*; *(: Am)* società di capitali; *(of city)* consiglio (comunale).

corps [kɔːʳ] *n, pl* **corps** [kɔːz] corpo; **press** ~ ufficio *m* stampa *inv*; ~ **de ballet** corpo di ballo.

corpse [kɔːps] *n* cadavere *m*.

cor·pu·lence ['kɔːpjʊləns] *n* corpulenza.

cor·pu·lent ['kɔːpjʊlənt] *adj* corpulento(a).

cor·pus·cle ['kɔːpʌsl] *n (of blood)* globulo.

cor·rect [kə'rekt] **1** *adj (answer)* corretto(a), esatto(a), giusto(a); *(temperature, time, amount, forecast)* esatto(a), giusto(a); *(behaviour)* corretto(a); *(dress)* adatto(a); *(procedure)* giusto(a), corretto(a); **you are** ~ ha ragione. **2** *vt (mistake, work, proofs)* correggere; **I stand** ~**ed** (ammetto che) ho torto.

cor·rec·tion [kə'rekʃən] *n* correzione *f*.

cor·rect·ly [kə'rektlɪ] *adv (accurately)* correttamente; *(properly)* correttamente, in modo corretto.

cor·re·late ['kɒrɪleɪt] **1** *vt* correlare, mettere in relazione. **2** *vi* essere in correlazione; **to** ~ **with** essere in rapporto con.

cor·re·la·tion [,kɒrɪ'leɪʃən] *n* correlazione *f*.

cor·re·spond [,kɒrɪs'pɒnd] *vi* **(a)** *(be in accordance)*: **to** ~ **(with)** corrispondere (a); *(be equivalent)*: **to** ~ **(to)** corrispondere (a), equivalere (a). **(b)** *(by letter)*: **to** ~ **(with sb)** corrispondere (con qn), essere in corrispondenza (con qn); **they** ~ si scrivono.

cor·re·spond·ence [,kɒrɪs'pɒndəns] **1** *n* **(a)** *(agreement)*: ~ **(between)** accordo (tra). **(b)** *(let-*

ters) corrispondenza; *(collection of letters)* carteggio. **2** *cpd*: ~ **column** *n* rubrica delle lettere (al direttore); ~ **course** *n* corso per corrispondenza.

cor·re·spond·ent [,kɒrɪs'pɒndənt] *n* corrispondente *m/f*.

cor·re·spond·ing [,kɒrɪs'pɒndɪŋ] *adj* corrispondente.

cor·ri·dor ['kɒrɪdɔːʳ] *n* corridoio.

cor·robo·rate [kə'rɒbəreɪt] *vt* corroborare.

cor·robo·ra·tion [kə,rɒbə'reɪʃən] *n* corroborazione *f*.

cor·rode [kə'rəʊd] **1** *vt* corrodere. **2** *vi* corrodersi.

cor·ro·sion [kə'rəʊʒən] *n* corrosione *f*.

cor·ro·sive [kə'rəʊzɪv] *adj* corrosivo(a).

cor·ru·gat·ed ['kɒrəgeɪtɪd] *adj* ondulato(a); ~ **iron** lamiera ondulata.

cor·rupt [kə'rʌpt] **1** *adj* corrotto(a); ~ **practices** *(dishonesty, bribery)* pratiche *fpl* illecite. **2** *vt* corrompere.

cor·rup·tion [kə'rʌpʃən] *n* corruzione *f*.

cor·set ['kɔːsɪt] *n (undergarment)* corsetto, busto; *(Med)* busto (ortopedico).

Cor·si·ca ['kɔːsɪkə] *n* Corsica *f*.

cor·tège [kɔː'teːʒ] *n* corteo.

cor·ti·sone ['kɔːtɪzəʊn] *n* cortisone *m*.

cosh [kɒʃ] *(Brit)* **1** *n* manganello. **2** *vt (fam)* pestare, manganellare.

cos·met·ic [kɒz'metɪk] **1** *adj (preparation)* cosmetico(a); *(surgery)* estetico(a). **2** *n* cosmetico, prodotto di bellezza.

cos·mic ['kɒzmɪk] *adj* cosmico(a).

cos·mo·naut ['kɒzmənɔːt] *n* cosmonauta *m/f*.

cos·mo·poli·tan [,kɒzmə'pɒlɪtən] *adj, n* cosmopolita *(m/f)*.

cos·mos ['kɒzmɒs] *n* cosmo.

cos·set ['kɒsɪt] *vt* coccolare.

cost [kɒst] **1** *n* costo; *(Law)*: ~**s** spese *fpl*; ~ **of living** costo della vita; **to bear the** ~ **of** sostenere la spesa di; *(fig)* fare le spese di; **at great** ~ a caro prezzo; **at** ~ **(price)** a prezzo di costo; **at all** ~**s, at any** ~ *(fig)* a tutti i costi, a ogni costo; **whatever the** ~ *(fig)* costi quel che costi; **to my** ~ a mie spese; **at the** ~ **of his life/health** pagando con la vita/la salute.

2 *vt* **(a)** *(pt, pp* **cost)** costare; **how much does it** ~? quanto costa?, quanto viene?; **what will it** ~ **to have it repaired?** quanto costerà farlo riparare?; **it** ~ **him a lot of money** gli è costato un sacco di soldi; **it** ~**s the earth** *(fam)* costa un occhio della testa; **it** ~ **him his life/job** gli è costato la vita/il lavoro; **it** ~ **me a great deal of time/effort** mi è costato molto tempo/molta fatica; **it** ~**s nothing to be polite** essere educati non costa nulla; **whatever it** ~**s** *(fig)* costi quel che costi. **(b)** *(pt, pp* ~**ed)** *(Comm)* stabilire il prezzo di.

3 *cpd*: ~ **analysis** *n* analisi *f inv* dei costi.

co-star ['kəʊstɑːʳ] *n* co-protagonista *m/f*.

cost-effective [,kɒstɪ'fektɪv] *adj (Comm)* redditizio(a); *(person)* conveniente, economico(a).

cost·ing ['kɒstɪŋ] *n* (determinazione *f* dei) costi *mpl*.

cost·ly ['kɒstlɪ] *adj* costoso(a).

cost-of-living [,kɒstəv'lɪvɪŋ] *adj*: ~ **allowance** indennità *f inv* di contingenza; ~ **index** indice *m* della scala mobile.

cos·tume ['kɒstjuːm] **1** *n (gen)* costume *m*; *(lady's suit)* tailleur *m inv*. **2** *cpd*: ~ **ball** *n* ballo in maschera *or* in costume; ~ **drama** *n* dramma *m* storico; ~ **jewellery** *n* bigiotteria.

cosy ['kəʊzɪ] **1** *adj* **(-ier, -iest)** *(room, atmosphere)* accogliente; *(clothes)* bello(a) caldo(a); **I'm very**

~ here sto proprio bene qui; **we had a ~ chat** abbiamo fatto una bella chiacchierata. **2** n (tea ~) copriteiera m inv; (egg ~) copriuovo.

cot [kɒt] n (Brit) lettino; (Am: folding bed) brandina.

cot·tage ['kɒtɪdʒ] **1** n villetta, cottage m inv. **2** cpd: **~ cheese** n fiocchi mpl di latte; **~ hospital** n ospedale m di campagna; **~ industry** n industria artigianale basata sul lavoro a cottimo.

cot·ton ['kɒtn] **1** n (cloth, plant) cotone m; (thread) (filo di) cotone. **2** cpd (shirt, dress) di cotone; **~ candy** n (Am) zucchero filato; **~ industry** n industria cotoniera; **~ mill** n cotonificio; **~ wool** n (Brit) cotone m idrofilo.

♦ **cotton on** vi + adv (fam): **to ~ on (to sth)** afferrare (qc).

couch [kaʊtʃ] **1** n (gen) divano; (in doctor's surgery) lettino. **2** vt esprimere.

cou·chette [ku:'ʃet] n cuccetta.

cough [kɒf] **1** n (single instance) colpo di tosse; (illness) tosse f. **2** vi tossire. **3** cpd: **~ drops** or **sweets** npl pasticche fpl per la tosse; **~ mixture** n sciroppo per la tosse.

♦ **cough up 1** vt + adv (blood, phlegm) sputare; (fig fam: money) tirare fuori. **2** vi + adv (fig fam) cacciare i soldi.

could [kʊd] pt, cond of **can**.

couldn't ['kʊdnt] = **could not**.

coun·cil ['kaʊnsl] **1** n consiglio; **city** or **town ~** consiglio municipale or comunale; **the Security C~ of the United Nations** il Consiglio di Sicurezza delle Nazioni Unite. **2** cpd: **~ house** n, **~ flat** n (Brit) casa popolare (gestita dal comune); **~ housing** n alloggio popolare; **~ housing estate** n complesso di case popolari; **~ meeting** n seduta del consiglio.

coun·cil·lor ['kaʊnsɪlə'] n consigliere m.

coun·sel ['kaʊnsəl] **1** n (a) (advice) consiglio; **to keep one's own ~** tenere le proprie opinioni per sé. **(b)** (Law: pl inv) avvocato/essa; **~ for the defence/the prosecution** avvocato difensore/di parte civile; **Queen's (or King's) C~** avvocato della Corona. **2** vt: **to ~ sth/sb to do sth** consigliare qc/a qn di fare qc; (caution) raccomandare qc/a qn di fare qc.

coun·sel·lor, (Am) **coun·se·lor** ['kaʊnslə'] n consigliere m; (adviser) consulente m/f; (Am: lawyer) avvocato/essa.

count[1] [kaʊnt] **1** n **(a)** conteggio; (of votes at election) spoglio; **to be out for the ~** (Boxing) essere fuori combattimento; (fam) essere knock out; **to keep ~ of sth** tenere il conto di qc; **you made me lose ~** mi hai fatto perdere il conto. **(b)** (Law): **he was found guilty on all ~s** è stato giudicato colpevole di tutti i capi di accusa.

2 vt **(a)** (gen) contare; (one's change etc) controllare; **don't ~ your chickens before they're hatched** non vendere la pelle dell'orso prima di averlo ucciso, non dir quattro se non l'hai nel sacco; **to ~ sheep** (fig) contare le pecore; **to ~ the cost of** calcolare il costo di; (fig) valutare il prezzo di; **without ~ing the cost** (also fig) senza badare al prezzo; **~ your blessings** considera la tua fortuna. **(b)** (include) contare; (consider): **to ~ sb among** annoverare qn tra; **not ~ing the children** senza contare i bambini; **10 ~ing him** 10 compreso lui; **~ yourself lucky** considerati fortunato; **will you ~ it against me?** te la prenderai con me?; **I ~ it an honour (to do/that)** mi ritengo onorato (a fare/che + sub).

3 vi **(a)** contare; **to ~ (up) to 10** contare fino a 10; **~ing from today** partendo da oggi, oggi compreso. **(b)** (be considered, be valid) valere, contare; **two children ~ as one adult** due bambini

valgono come un adulto; **that doesn't ~** quello non conta; **it will ~ against him** deporrà a suo sfavore; **it ~s for very little** non conta molto, non ha molta importanza.

♦ **count in** vt + adv comprendere nel conto; **~ me in!** (fam) ci sto anch'io!

♦ **count on** vi + prep contare su; **to ~ on doing sth** contare di fare qc.

♦ **count out** vt + adv **(a)** (Boxing): **to be ~ed out** essere dichiarato K.O. **(b)** (money, small objects) contare. **(c)** (fam): **~ me out!** non ci sto!

♦ **count up** vt + adv contare; (column of figures) sommare.

♦ **count upon** vi + prep = **count on**.

count[2] [kaʊnt] n (nobleman) conte m.

count·able ['kaʊntəbl] adj computabile; (Gram): **~ noun** un sostantivo numerabile.

count·down ['kaʊnt,daʊn] n conto alla rovescia.

coun·te·nance ['kaʊntɪnəns] (frm) **1** n (face) (espressione f del) volto; **to keep one's ~** restare impassibile. **2** vt (permit): **to ~ sth/sb doing sth** ammettere qc/che qn faccia qc.

count·er[1] ['kaʊntə'] n **(a)** (of shop, canteen) banco, bancone m; (position: in post office, bank) sportello; **to buy under the ~** (fig) comperare sottobanco. **(b)** (in game) gettone m. **(c)** (Tech) contatore m.

coun·ter[2] ['kaʊntə'] **1** adv: **~ to** contrariamente a; **to run ~ to** andare contro. **2** vt: **to ~ sth with sth/by doing sth** rispondere a qc con qc/facendo qc. **3** vi: **to ~ with** rispondere con; (words) ribattere con.

counter... ['kaʊntə'] pref contro...; **counteract** vt controbilanciare; (effect) neutralizzare; **counter-attack 1** n contrattacco. **2** vt, vi contrattaccare; **counterbalance 1** n contrappeso. **2** vt controbilanciare; **counter-clockwise** adv in senso antiorario; **counter-espionage** n controspionaggio.

counter·feit ['kaʊntəfɪt] **1** adj contraffatto(a), falsificato(a), falso(a); (money) falso(a). **2** n falso, contraffazione f; (coin) moneta falsa. **3** vt contraffare, falsificare.

counter·foil ['kaʊntəfɔɪl] n matrice f.

counter·in·tel·li·gence [,kaʊntərɪn'telɪdʒəns] n = **counter-espionage**.

counter·mand ['kaʊntəmɑ:nd] vt annullare.

counter·measure ['kaʊntə,meʒə'] n contromisura.

counter·offensive [kaʊntərə,fensɪv] n controffensiva.

counter·pane ['kaʊntəpeɪn] n copriletto.

counter·part ['kaʊntəpɑ:t] n equivalente m/f.

counter·productive [,kaʊntəprə'dʌktɪv] adj controproducente.

counter·sign ['kaʊntəsaɪn] vt controfirmare.

counter·sink ['kaʊntəsɪŋk] pt, pp **countersunk** ['kaʊntəsʌŋk] vt (hole) svasare; (screw) accecare.

coun·tess ['kaʊntɪs] n contessa.

count·less ['kaʊntlɪs] adj: **on ~ occasions** in mille occasioni; **~ numbers of** un'infinità di.

coun·try ['kʌntrɪ] **1** n **(a)** (gen) paese m; (fatherland) patria; **to go to the ~** (Pol) indire le elezioni; **to die for one's ~** morire per la patria. **(b)** (countryside) campagna; (terrain, land) territorio; **in the ~** in campagna; **there is some lovely ~ further south** ci sono delle campagne bellissime più a sud; **mountainous ~** territorio montagnoso; **unknown ~** terra sconosciuta; (fig) campo sconosciuto. **2** cpd (life, road) di campagna; **~ bumpkin** n (pej) burino/a; **~ cousin** n (fig) provinciale m/f; **~ dancing** n danza popolare; **~ dweller** n campagnolo/a; **~ house** n residenza in campagna; ~ **and western (music)** *n* musica country e western, country *m*.

country·man ['kʌntrɪmən] *n, pl* **-men** *(country dweller)* campagnolo/a; *(compatriot)* compatriota *m/f*, connazionale *m/f*.

country·side ['kʌntrɪsaɪd] *n* campagna.

country-wide ['kʌntrɪ,waɪd] *adj* (su scala) nazionale.

coun·ty ['kaʊntɪ] **1** *n* contea. **2** *cpd (boundary, court)* di contea; ~ **town** *n* capoluogo.

coup [kuː] *n (Pol: also:* ~ **d'état)** colpo di stato; *(triumph)* bel colpo.

cou·pé ['kuːpeɪ] *n (Aut)* coupé *n inv*.

cou·ple ['kʌpl] **1** *n (of animals, people)* coppia; *(two or three):* **a** ~ **of times/hours/books** un paio di volte/ore/libri. **2** *vt* **(a): to** ~ **with** associare con. **(b)** *(Tech):* **to** ~ **(on** *or* **up)** agganciare.

cou·pon ['kuːpɒn] *n (voucher)* buono; *(football pool* ~*)* schedina.

cour·age ['kʌrɪdʒ] *n* coraggio; **I haven't the** ~ **to refuse** non ho il coraggio di rifiutare; **to have the** ~ **of one's convictions** avere il coraggio delle proprie convinzioni *or* idee; **to take one's** ~ **in both hands** prendere il coraggio a due mani.

cou·ra·geous [kə'reɪdʒəs] *adj* coraggioso/a).

cour·gette [,kʊə'ʒet] *n* zucchina.

cou·ri·er ['kʊrɪər] *n (messenger)* corriere *m*; *(travel guide)* guida turistica.

course [kɔːs] **1** *n* **(a)** *(route: of ship)* rotta; *(: of river)* corso; *(: of planet)* orbita; **to set** ~ **for** *(Naut)* far rotta per; **to change** ~ *(Naut, fig)* cambiare rotta; **to go off** ~ deviare dalla rotta; **to hold one's** ~ seguire la rotta; **to take/follow a** ~ **of action** *(fig)* imboccare/seguire una politica; **we have no other** ~ **but to...** non possiamo far altro che...; **there are 2** ~**s open to us** abbiamo 2 possibilità; **the best** ~ **would be to...** la cosa migliore sarebbe...; **to let things/events take** *or* **run their** ~ lasciare le cose/gli eventi seguano il loro corso; **as a matter of** ~ come una cosa scontata.

(b) *(duration):* **in the** ~ **of** *(life, disease, events)* nel corso di; **in the** ~ **of time** col passare del tempo; **in the normal** *or* **ordinary** ~ **of events** normalmente; **in (the)** ~ **of construction** in (via di) costruzione; **in the** ~ **of the next few days** nel corso dei prossimi giorni.

(c): of ~ naturalmente, ovviamente; **yes, of** ~! sì, certo!; **(no) of** ~ **not!** certo che no!, no di certo!; **of** ~ **you can** certo che puoi; **of** ~ **I won't do it** certo che non lo farò.

(d) *(Scol, Univ)* corso; **to take a** ~ **in French** seguire un corso di francese; **a** ~ **of lectures on a subject** una serie di conferenze su un argomento; **a** ~ **of treatment** *(Med)* una cura.

(e) *(Sport): golf* ~*)* campo da golf; *(: race*~*)* pista.

(f) *(Culin)* piatto, portata; **a three-**~ **meal** un pasto di tre portate.

2 *vi (water, tears etc)* scorrere; **it sent the blood coursing through his veins** gli ha rimescolato il sangue nelle vene.

court [kɔːt] **1** *n* **(a)** *(Law)* corte *f*; *(: ~room)* aula; ~ **of appeal** corte d'appello; ~ **of inquiry** commissione *f* d'inchiesta; **to take sb to** ~ **(over sth)** citare in tribunale qn (per qc); **to settle a case out of** ~ conciliare una causa in via amichevole; **to rule out of** ~ dichiarare inammissibile; **he was brought before the** ~ **on a charge of theft** fu processato sotto accusa di furto. **(b)** *(Tennis)* campo. **(c)** *(royal)* corte *f*. **2** *vt (woman)* corteggiare, fare la corte a; *(fig: favour, popularity)* cercare di conquistare; *(: death, disaster)* sfiorare, rasentare. **3** *vi* corteggiarsi; **a** ~**ing couple** una

coppia di innamorati. **4** *cpd:* ~ **card** *n (Cards)* figura; ~ **shoe** *n* scarpa *f* décolleté *inv*.

cour·teous ['kɜːtɪəs] *adj* cortese.

cour·tesy ['kɜːtɪsɪ] **1** *n (politeness)* cortesia, gentilezza; *(polite act)* cortesia, piacere *m*; **by** ~ **of** per gentile concessione di; **you might have had the** ~ **to tell me** avresti potuto farmi la cortesia di dirmelo; **to exchange courtesies** scambiarsi convenevoli. **2** *cpd:* ~ **coach** *n* autobus *m inv* gratuito *(di hotel, aeroporto etc);* ~ **light** *n (Aut)* luce *f* interna; ~ **visit** *n* visita di cortesia.

court·house ['kɔːthaʊs] *n (Am)* tribunale *m*, palazzo di giustizia.

cour·ti·er ['kɔːtɪər] *n* cortigiano/a.

court-martial ['kɔːt'mɑːʃəl] **1** *n* corte *f* marziale. **2** *vt* processare in corte marziale.

court·ship ['kɔːtʃɪp] *n* corteggiamento.

court·yard ['kɔːtjɑːd] *n* cortile *m*.

cous·in ['kʌzn] *n* cugino/a.

cove [kəʊv] *n (piccola)* baia.

cov·enant ['kʌvɪnənt] **1** *n* **(a)** accordo (scritto). **(b)** *(Bible)* alleanza. **2** *vt:* **to** ~ **to do sth** impegnarsi (per iscritto) a fare qc; **to** ~ **£20 per year to a charity** impegnarsi a versare 20 sterline all'anno a un'organizzazione benefica.

Cov·en·try ['kɒvəntrɪ] *n:* **to send sb to** ~ *(fig)* dare l'ostracismo a qn.

cov·er ['kʌvər] **1** *n* **(a)** *(gen)* copertura; *(of dish, bowl, saucepan)* coperchio; *(of furniture, typewriter)* fodera; *(for merchandise, on vehicle)* telo, telone *m*; *(bedspread)* copriletto; *(often pl: blanket)* coperta; *(of book, magazine)* copertina; **under separate** ~ *(Comm)* a parte, in plico separato; **to read a book from** ~ **to** ~ leggere un libro dalla prima pagina all'ultima. **(b)** *(shelter)* riparo; *(covering fire)* copertura; **to take** ~ *(hide)* nascondersi; *(Mil, shelter)* ripararsi; **to break** ~ uscire allo scoperto; **under** ~ al coperto; *(hiding)* nascosto; **under** ~ **of darkness** protetto dall'oscurità. **(c)** *(Fin, Insurance, in espionage etc)* copertura; **without** ~ *(Fin)* senza copertura; **fire** ~ copertura contro l'incendio. **(d)** *(frm: at table)* coperto.

2 *vt* **(a)** *(gen):* **to** ~ **(with)** coprire (con); ~**ed with coperto di; *(fig):* ~**ed with confusion** tutto confuso; ~**ed with shame** pieno di vergogna; **to** ~ **o.s. with glory/disgrace** coprirsi di gloria/vergogna. **(b)** *(hide: facts, mistakes)* nascondere; *(: feeling)* nascondere, dissimulare; *(: noise)* coprire. **(c)** *(protect: Mil, Sport, Insurance)* coprire; **he only said that to** ~ **himself** lo disse solo per mettersi al sicuro; **I've got you** ~**ed!** sei sotto tiro! **(d)** *(be sufficient for, include)* coprire; **£10 will** ~ **everything** 10 sterline saranno sufficienti; **we must** ~ **all possibilities** dobbiamo prevedere tutte le possibilità. **(e)** *(distance)* coprire, percorrere; **to** ~ **a lot of ground** fare molta strada; *(fig)* combinare molto. **(f)** *(Press: report on)* fare un servizio su.

3 *vi:* **to** ~ **for sb** *(at work etc)* sostituire qn.

4 *cpd:* ~ **charge** *n (in restaurant)* coperto; ~ **girl** *n* cover girl *f inv*, ragazza-copertina; ~ **note** *n (Insurance)* polizza (di assicurazione) provvisoria.

♦ **cover over** *vt + adv* (ri)coprire.

♦ **cover up 1** *vt + adv (child, object):* **to** ~ **up (with)** coprire (di); *(fig: hide: truth, facts)* nascondere; **to** ~ **up one's tracks** *(also fig)* cancellare le tracce. **2** *vi + adv (warmly)* coprirsi; *(fig):* **to** ~ **up for sb** coprire qn.

cov·er·age ['kʌvərɪdʒ] *n (Press, TV, Radio):* **to give full** ~ **to an event** fare un ampio servizio su un avvenimento; **the visit got nationwide** ~ *(Radio,*

TV) la visita fu trasmessa su tutta la rete nazionale.

cover·alls ['kʌvərɔːlz] *npl (Am)* tuta.

cov·er·ing ['kʌvərɪŋ] **1** *n* copertura; *(of snow, dust etc)* strato. **2** *cpd:* ~ **letter** *n* nota esplicativa, lettera d'accompagnamento.

cov·ert ['kʌvət] *adj (gen)* nascosto(a); *(glance)* di sottecchi, furtivo(a).

cover·up ['kʌvərʌp] *n* occultamento (di informazioni).

cov·et ['kʌvɪt] *vt* concupire.

cov·et·ous ['kʌvɪtəs] *adj* avido(a), bramoso(a).

cow [kaʊ] **1** *n* mucca; *(fam pej: woman)* vacca. **2** *vt (person)* intimidire; **a ~ed look** un'aria da cane bastonato. **3** *cpd:* ~ **elephant** *n* elefantessa; ~ **seal** *n* foca femmina.

cow·ard ['kaʊəd] *n* vigliacco/a.

cow·ard·ice ['kaʊədɪs] *n*, **cow·ard·li·ness** ['kaʊədlɪnɪs] *n* vigliaccheria.

cow·ard·ly ['kaʊədlɪ] *adj* vigliacco(a).

cow·boy ['kaʊbɔɪ] *n* cowboy *m inv*.

cow·er ['kaʊəʳ] *vi* acquattarsi.

cow·hide ['kaʊhaɪd] *n* pelle *f* di mucca, vacchetta.

cowl [kaʊl] *n* cappuccio.

cow·man ['kaʊmən] *n, pl* **-men** vaccaro.

cow·shed ['kaʊʃed] *n* stalla.

cow·slip ['kaʊslɪp] *n (Bot)* primula (odorata).

cox [kɒks] **1** *n* timoniere *m*. **2** *vt* essere al timone di. **3** *vi* fare da timoniere.

coy [kɔɪ] *adj (-er, -est) (person)* che fa i (*or* la) vergognoso(a); *(smile)* da vergognoso(a); *(pej: woman: coquettish)* civettuolo(a).

cozy ['kəʊzɪ] *adj* = **cosy**.

crab [kræb] **1** *n* granchio. **2** *cpd:* ~ **apple** *n* mela selvatica.

crab·by ['kræbɪ] *adj (fam: also:* **crabbed**) acido(a), scontroso(a).

crack [kræk] **1** *n* **(a)** *(split, slit: in glass, pottery)* crepa, incrinatura; *(: in wall, plaster, ground, paint)* crepa, spaccatura; *(: in skin)* screpolatura; **through the ~ in the door** *(slight opening)* dalla fessura della porta; **at the ~ of dawn** alle prime luci dell'alba. **(b)** *(noise: of twigs)* scricchiolio, crepitio; *(: of whip)* schiocco; *(: of rifle)* colpo; *(: of thunder)* boato. **(c)** *(blow):* **a ~ on the head** una botta in testa. **(d)** *(fam: attempt):* **to have a ~ at sth** tentare qc. **(e)** *(fam: joke, insult)* battuta.

2 *vt* **(a)** *(break: glass, pottery, wood)* incrinare; *(: nut)* schiacciare; *(: egg)* rompere; *(fig fam: safe)* scassinare; *(: bottle)* stappare, aprire; **to ~ one's skull** spaccarsi la testa; **to ~ sb over the head** dare un colpo in testa a qn. **(b)** *(cause to sound: whip, finger joints)* far schioccare; **to ~ jokes** *(fam)* dire battute, scherzare. **(c)** *(case: solve)* risolvere; *(code)* decifrare.

3 *vi* **(a)** *(break: pottery, glass)* incrinarsi; *(: ground, wall, dry wood)* creparsi; *(skin)* screpolarsi; **to ~ under the strain** *(person)* non reggere alla tensione. **(b)** *(whip)* schioccare; *(dry wood)* scricchiolare; **to get ~ing** *(fam)* darsi una mossa.

4 *cpd (team etc)* scelto(a); **a ~ gymnast** un ginnasta di prim'ordine; **a ~ shot** un tiratore infallibile.

♦ **crack down** *vi + adv:* **to ~ down (on)** porre freno (a).

♦ **crack up** *(fam)* **1** *vi + adv* crollare. **2** *vt + adv:* **he's not all he's ~ed up to be** non è così meraviglioso come dicono.

cracked [krækt] *adj (fam: mad: also:* **crackers**) tocco(a), matto(a).

crack·er ['krækəʳ] *n* **(a)** *(firework)* petardo; *(Christ-*

mas ~) mortaretto natalizio (con sorpresa). **(b)** *(biscuit)* cracker *m inv*.

crack·le ['krækl] **1** *vi (twigs burning)* crepitare, scoppiettare; *(sth frying)* sfrigolare. **2** *n (see vb)* crepitio, scoppiettio; sfrigolio; *(on telephone)* disturbo.

crack·ling ['kræklɪŋ] *n* **(a)** *(Culin)* cotenna arrostita. **(b)** *(sound)* crepitio; *(of frying food)* sfrigolio; *(on radio, telephone)* disturbo.

cra·dle ['kreɪdl] **1** *n* culla; *(of telephone)* forcella; *(Constr)* gabbia. **2** *vt (child)* tenere fra le braccia; *(object)* reggere tra le braccia.

craft [krɑːft] *n* **(a)** *(trade)* arte *f; (handicraft)* mestiere *m; (skill)* abilità, maestria. **(b)** *(cunning: pej)* furbizia, astuzia. **(c)** *(boat: pl inv)* barca, imbarcazione *f*.

crafts·man ['krɑːftsmən] *n, pl* **-men** artigiano.

crafts·man·ship ['krɑːftsmənʃɪp] *n (skill)* abilità, maestria; **a piece of ~** un pezzo di artigianato.

crafty ['krɑːftɪ] *adj (-ier, -iest) (person)* furbo(a), astuto(a); *(action)* abile.

crag [kræg] *n* rupe *f*.

crag·gy ['krægɪ] *adj (-ier, -iest) (rock)* dirupato(a); *(features)* marcato(a); *(face)* dai tratti marcati.

cram [kræm] **1** *vt (stuff):* **to ~ into** infilare in; *(: people, passengers)* fare affollare in; *(fill):* **to ~ with** riempire di; **to ~ in** far stare, trovare posto per; **his head is ~med with strange ideas** ha la testa piena di strane idee; **the room was ~med with furniture/people** la stanza era stipata di mobili/affollata di gente; **she ~med her hat down over her eyes** si calcò il cappello sugli occhi; **to ~ o.s. with food** abbuffarsi. **2** *vi* **(a)** *(people):* **to ~ (into)** affollarsi (in). **(b)** *(pupil: for exam)* prepararsi (in gran fretta).

cramp [kræmp] **1** *n (Med):* ~ **(in)** crampo (in). **2** *vt* soffocare, impedire; **to ~ sb's style** *(fig fam)* tarpare le ali a qn.

cramped [kræmpt] *adj (room etc)* angusto(a); *(writing)* fitto(a); *(position)* rannicchiato(a); **we are very ~ for space** stiamo uno sopra l'altro.

cran·berry ['krænbərɪ] *n* bacca del muschio.

crane [kreɪn] **1** *n (Zool, Tech)* gru *f inv.* **2** *vt, vi:* **to ~ forward, to ~ one's neck** allungare il collo. **3** *cpd:* ~ **driver** *n* gruista *m*.

crank [kræŋk] **1** *n* **(a)** *(Tech)* gomito. **(b)** *(person)* eccentrico/a. **2** *vt (also:* ~ **up)** avviare a manovella.

crank·shaft ['kræŋkʃɑːft] *n* albero a gomiti.

cranky ['kræŋkɪ] *adj (-ier, -iest) (strange: ideas, people)* eccentrico(a); *(bad-tempered):* **to be ~** avere i nervi.

crap [kræp] *n (fam!)* merda(!); *(nonsense)* cazzate *fpl*(!).

crape [kreɪp] *n* = **crêpe**.

crash [kræʃ] **1** *n* **(a)** *(noise)* fragore *m*, fracasso *m; (of thunder)* colpo. **(b)** *(accident)* incidente *m;* **there has been a plane ~** un aereo è precipitato. **(c)** *(of business)* fallimento; *(Stock Exchange)* crollo.

2 *vt (smash: car)* avere un incidente con; **he ~ed the car into a wall** andò a sbattere contro un muro con la macchina; **the pilot ~ed the plane** il pilota ha fatto precipitare l'aereo.

3 *vi* **(a)** *(car)* avere un incidente; *(plane)* cadere, precipitare; *(collide: two vehicles)* scontrarsi; **to ~ into sth** scontrarsi con qc; **the plates came ~ing down** i piatti si sono fracassati al suolo. **(b)** *(business)* fallire; *(stock market)* crollare.

4 *cpd (diet, course)* intensivo(a), rapido(a); ~ **barrier** *n (Aut)* guardrail *m inv;* ~ **helmet** *n* casco (di protezione); ~ **landing** *n* atterraggio forzato.

crass [kræs] *adj* crasso(a).

crate [kreɪt] *n* cassa.
cra·ter ['kreɪtə^r] *n* cratere *m*.
cra·vat [krə'væt] *n (for men)* foulard *m inv*.
crave [kreɪv] 1 *vt* (a) *(desire)* desiderare disperatamente. (b) *(frm: pardon, permission)* implorare. 2 *vi*: to ~ for = 1 a.
crav·ing ['kreɪvɪŋ] *n (for food, cigarettes etc)* (gran) voglia; *(in pregnancy)* voglia; *(for affection, attention)* desiderio estremo.
craw·fish ['krɔːfɪʃ] *n* = **crayfish**.
crawl [krɔːl] 1 *n* (a) *(slow pace)* passo lento; **the traffic went at a** ~ il traffico procedeva a passo d'uomo. (b) *(Swimming)* crawl *m*; **to do the** ~ nuotare a crawl. 2 *vi* (a) *(drag o.s.)* trascinarsi, strisciare; *(child)* andare a gattoni; *(traffic)* procedere a passo d'uomo; *(time)* non passare mai; **to** ~ **in/out** *etc* trascinarsi dentro/fuori *etc* a carponi; **to be** ~**ing with ants** brulicare di formiche; **there was a fly** ~**ing up the wall** c'era una mosca che camminava sul muro. (b) *(fam: suck up)*: **to** ~ **to sb** arruffianarsi qn.
cray·fish ['kreɪfɪʃ] *n* gambero.
cray·on ['kreɪən] *n (chalk)* gessetto; *(wax)* pastello a cera; *(child's)* pastello.
craze [kreɪz] *n* mania.
crazed [kreɪzd] *adj (look, person)* folle, pazzo(a); *(pottery, glaze)* incrinato(a).
cra·zy ['kreɪzɪ] *adj* (**-ier, -iest**) (a) *(mad)* matto(a), folle; **to go** ~ uscir di senno, impazzire; ~ **with grief/anxiety** pazzo di dolore/ansia; **it was a** ~ **idea** era un'idea folle; **you were** ~ **to do it** sei stato un pazzo a farlo. (b) *(fam: keen)*: **to be** ~ **about sb** essere pazzo di qn; **to be** ~ **about sth** andare matto per qc. (c) *(angle, slope)* pericolante; ~ **paving** pavimentazione *f* a mosaico irregolare.
creak [kriːk] 1 *vi (wood, shoe etc)* scricchiolare; *(hinge etc)* cigolare. 2 *n (vedi vb)* scricchiolio; cigolio.
cream [kriːm] 1 *n* (a) *(Culin)* crema; *(: fresh)* panna; **whipped** ~ panna montata; **a chocolate** ~ *(a sweet)* un cremino al cioccolato; ~ **of tomato soup** crema di pomodoro; **the** ~ **of society** *(fig)* la crème della società. (b) *(lotion: for face, shoes etc)* crema. 2 *adj* (~-**coloured**) color crema *inv*, color panna *inv*; *(made with* ~*)* alla panna; ~ **cheese** formaggio fresco. 3 *vt (mix: also:* ~ **together**) amalgamare; ~**ed potatoes** purè *m* di patate.
♦ **cream off** *vi + prep (best talents, part of profits)* portarsi via.
creamy ['kriːmɪ] *adj* (**-ier, -iest**) *(taste, texture)* cremoso(a); *(colour)* crema *inv*, panna *inv*.
crease [kriːs] 1 *n (fold: in trousers)* piega; *(wrinkle: in cloth)* grinza; *(: in face)* ruga, grinza. 2 *vt* sgualcire, spiegazzare; **his face was** ~**d with laughter** aveva il volto contratto dalle risate. 3 *vi* sgualcirsi.
crease-re·sist·ant ['kriːsrɪˌzɪstənt] *adj* ingualcibile.
cre·ate [kriː'eɪt] *vt (gen)* creare; *(impression, fuss, noise)* fare; **he was** ~**d a peer by the Queen** fu nominato pari dalla Regina.
crea·tion [kriː'eɪʃən] *n* creazione *f*.
crea·tive [kriː'eɪtɪv] *adj* creativo(a).
crea·tiv·ity [ˌkriːeɪ'tɪvɪtɪ] *n* creatività.
crea·tor [krɪ'eɪtə^r] *n* creatore/trice.
crea·ture ['kriːtʃə^r] 1 *n (gen)* creatura; **the poor** ~ **had no home** il poverino era senza casa; **a** ~ **of habit** una persona abitudinaria. 2 *cpd*: ~ **comforts** *npl* comodità *fpl*.
crèche [kreɪʃ] *n* asilo *m* nido *inv*.
cre·den·tials [krɪ'denʃəlz] *npl (identifying papers,*

of diplomat) credenziali *fpl*; *(letters of reference)* referenze *fpl*.
cred·ibil·ity [ˌkrɛdə'bɪlɪtɪ] *n (see adj)* credibilità; attendibilità.
cred·ible ['krɛdɪbl] *adj (gen)* credibile; *(witness, source)* attendibile.
cred·it ['krɛdɪt] 1 *n* (a) *(Fin)* credito; **to give sb** ~ far credito a qn; **you have £10 to your** ~ lei ha 10 sterline a suo credito; **on** ~ a credito; **is his** ~ **good?** gli si può dare credito? (b) *(honour)* onore *m*; **it is to his** ~ **that...** bisogna riconoscergli che...; **he's a** ~ **to his family** fa onore alla sua famiglia; **to give sb** ~ **for (doing) sth** riconoscere a qn il merito di (aver fatto) qc; **I gave you** ~ **for more sense** ti reputavo più sensato; **it does you** ~ ti fa onore; **to take** ~ **for (doing) sth** attribuirsi il merito di (aver fatto) qc. (c) *(Cine)*: ~**s** titoli *mpl* di testa *(or* di coda). (d) *(Univ: esp Am)* certificato del compimento di una parte del corso universitario.
2 *vt* (a) *(believe)* credere. (b) *(attribute)* attribuire il credito a; **I** ~**ed him with more sense** credevo che avesse più cervello; **he** ~**ed them with the victory** attribuì a loro il merito della vittoria. (c) *(Comm)*: **to** ~ **£5 to sb, to** ~ **sb with £5** accreditare 5 sterline a qn.
3 *cpd (limit, agency etc)* di credito; ~ **card** *n* carta di credito; ~ **facilities** *npl* agevolazioni *fpl* creditizie; ~ **note** *n* nota di credito; ~ **rating** *n* affidabilità di credito; **on the** ~ **side** *(fig)* a suo favore; ~ **squeeze** *n* limitazione *f* dei crediti, stretta creditizia; ~ **terms** *npl* condizioni *fpl* di credito.
cred·it·able ['krɛdɪtəbl] *adj* lodevole.
credi·tor ['krɛdɪtə^r] *n* creditore/trice.
credit·worthy ['krɛdɪt,wɜːðɪ] *adj* autorizzabile al credito.
cre·du·lity [krɪ'djuːlɪtɪ] *n* credulità.
credu·lous ['krɛdjʊləs] *adj* credulo(a).
creed [kriːd] *n* credo.
creek [kriːk] *n (inlet)* insenatura.
creep [kriːp] *pt, pp* **crept** 1 *vi (animal)* strisciare; *(plant)* arrampicarsi; *(person: stealthily)* andare furtivamente; *(: slowly)* procedere lentamente; **to** ~ **in/out** entrare/uscire quatto quatto; **to** ~ **up on sb** avvicinarsi quatto quatto a qn; *(fig: old age etc)* cogliere qn alla sprovvista; **a feeling of peace crept over him** lo avvolse un senso di pace; **it made my flesh** ~ mi fece accapponare la pelle; **an error has crept in** ci è scappato un errore. 2 *n* (*fam*): **it gives me the** ~**s** mi fa venire la pelle d'oca; **he's a** ~ è un tipo viscido.
creep·er ['kriːpə^r] *n (Bot)* (pianta) rampicante *f*; ~**s** *npl (Am: rompers)* tutina.
creepy ['kriːpɪ] *adj* (**-ier, -iest**) che fa accapponare la pelle.
creepy-crawly ['kriːpɪ,krɔːlɪ] *n (fam)* bestiolina, insetto.
cre·mate [krɪ'meɪt] *vt* cremare.
cre·ma·tion [krɪ'meɪʃən] *n* cremazione *f*.
crema·to·rium [ˌkrɛmə'tɔːrɪəm] *n* crematorio.
creo·sote ['krɪəsəʊt] 1 *n* creosoto. 2 *vt* dare il creosoto a.
crêpe [kreɪp] 1 *n* (a) *(fabric)* crespo. (b) *(also:* ~ **rubber**) para. 2 *cpd*: ~ **bandage** *n* fascia elastica; ~ **paper** *n* carta crespa; ~ **sole** *n (on shoes)* suola di para.
crept [krɛpt] *pt, pp of* **creep**.
cre·scen·do [krɪ'ʃɛndəʊ] *n (Mus, fig)* crescendo.
cres·cent ['krɛsnt] 1 *adj (moon)* crescente; *(shape)* a mezzaluna. 2 *n (shape)* mezzaluna; *(street)* via *(a semicerchio)*.
cress [krɛs] *n* crescione *m*.

crest [krɛst] n (of bird, wave, mountain) cresta; (on helmet) pennacchio; (Heraldry) cimiero; **to be on the ~ of the wave** (fig) essere sulla cresta dell'onda.

crest·fallen ['krɛst,fɔːlən] adj abbattuto(a), depresso(a); **to look ~** avere un'aria mogia.

Crete [kriːt] n Creta.

cret·in ['krɛtɪn] n (fam pej) cretino/a.

cre·vasse [krɪ'væs] n crepaccio.

crev·ice ['krɛvɪs] n crepa, fessura.

crew[1] [kruː] **1** n (Naut, Aer) equipaggio; (Rowing etc: team) squadra; (Cine) troupe f inv; (gang) banda, compagnia. **2** vi (Sailing): **to ~ for sb** vogare per qn. **3** cpd: **~ cut** n: **to have a ~ cut** avere i capelli a spazzola.

crew[2] [kruː] pt of **crow**.

crib [krɪb] **1** n (a) (small cot) culla; (Rel) presepio; (manger) mangiatoia. **(b)** (plagiarism) plagio; (Scol: translation) traduzione f suggerita. **2** vt (Scol) copiare.

crick [krɪk] **1** n: **~ in the neck** torcicollo. **2** vt: **to ~ one's neck** prendere il torcicollo.

crick·et[1] ['krɪkɪt] n (Zool) grillo.

crick·et[2] ['krɪkɪt] **1** n (sport) cricket m; **that's not ~** (fig) questo non è leale. **2** cpd: **~ ball** n palla da cricket; **~ match** n partita di cricket.

crime [kraɪm] **1** n (in general) criminalità; (instance) crimine m, delitto; **it's a ~** (fig) è una vergogna. **2** cpd: **~ wave** n ondata di criminalità.

crimi·nal ['krɪmɪnl] **1** n criminale m/f. **2** adj criminale; (fig) vergognoso(a); **C~ Investigation Department** (abbr C.I.D.) polizia giudiziaria; **~ lawyer** (avvocato) penalista m; **to take ~ proceedings against sb** istruire una causa penale contro qn.

crimi·nol·ogy [,krɪmɪ'nɒlədʒɪ] n criminologia.

crim·son ['krɪmzn] adj, n cremisi (m) inv.

cringe [krɪndʒ] vi (shrink back): **to ~ (from)** acquattarsi ritraendosi (da); (fawn): **to ~ (before)** strisciare (davanti a); **the very thought of it makes me ~** solo a pensarci mi sento sprofondare.

crin·kle ['krɪŋkl] vt spiegazzare, sgualcire.

crin·kly ['krɪŋklɪ] adj (-ier, -iest) (hair) crespo(a); (paper etc) crespato(a).

crip·ple ['krɪpl] **1** n (lame) zoppo/a; (disabled) invalido/a; (maimed) mutilato/a. **2** vt (a) lasciare mutilato(a); **~d with arthritis** sciancato per l'artrite. **(b)** (ship, plane) avariare; (production, exports) rovinare; **crippling taxes** tasse fpl esorbitanti.

cri·sis ['kraɪsɪs] n, pl crises ['kraɪsiːz] crisi f inv; **to come to a ~** entrare in crisi.

crisp [krɪsp] **1** adj (-er, -est) (bread, biscuit, vegetables) croccante; (snow) fresco(a); (bank note) nuovo(a) di zecca; (linen) inamidato(a); (air) fresco(a), frizzante; (manner, tone, reply) secco(a), brusco(a); (style) conciso(a) e vivace. **2** n (Brit: potato ~) patatina.

criss·cross ['krɪskrɒs] adj (lines) intrecciati(e); (pattern) a linee intrecciate.

cri·teri·on [kraɪ'tɪərɪən] n, pl criteria [kraɪ'tɪərɪə] criterio.

crit·ic ['krɪtɪk] n critico/a.

criti·cal ['krɪtɪkəl] adj (all senses) critico(a); **to be ~ of sb/sth** criticare qn/qc, essere critico verso qn/qc; **a ~ success** (book, play etc) un successo di critica.

criti·cal·ly ['krɪtɪkəlɪ] adv criticamente; **to be ~ ill** versare in condizioni critiche.

criti·cism ['krɪtɪsɪzəm] n critica.

criti·cize ['krɪtɪsaɪz] vt criticare.

cri·tique [krɪ'tiːk] n critica, saggio critico.

croak [krəʊk] **1** n (of raven) gracchio; (of frog) gracidio, gracidare m. **2** vi (raven) gracchiare; (frog) gracidare; (person) dire con voce rauca.

cro·chet ['krəʊʃeɪ] **1** n uncinetto. **2** vt, vi lavorare all'uncinetto. **3** cpd: **~ hook** n uncinetto.

crock [krɒk] n coccio; (fam: person: also: **old ~**) rottame m; (: car etc) caffettiera, rottame.

crock·ery ['krɒkərɪ] n (earthenware) vasellame m (di terracotta); (plates, cups etc) stoviglie fpl.

croco·dile ['krɒkədaɪl] n coccodrillo; **~ tears** (fig) lacrime fpl di coccodrillo.

cro·cus ['krəʊkəs] n croco.

croft [krɒft] n (Scot) piccola fattoria.

croft·er ['krɒftə'] n (Scot) fattore m (di piccola fattoria).

crois·sant ['krwæsɒŋ] n croissant m inv, cornetto.

cro·ny ['krəʊnɪ] n (fam pej) amicone/a.

crook [krʊk] **1** n (a) (shepherd's) bastone m (da pastore); (bishop's) pastorale m. **(b): the ~ of one's arm** l'incavo del braccio. **(c)** (fam: thief) ladro/a. **2** vt (arm, finger) piegare.

crook·ed ['krʊkɪd] adj (stick, person, picture) storto(a); (path) tortuoso(a); (smile) forzato(a); (dishonest: deal, means, person) disonesto(a).

croon [kruːn] vt, vi canticchiare; (crooner) cantare.

croon·er ['kruːnə'] n cantante m melodico.

crop [krɒp] **1** n (a) (produce) coltivazione f; (amount produced: of fruit, vegetables) raccolto; (: of cereals) raccolto, messe f; (fig: of problems, applicants) serie f inv, gruppo. **(b)** (Ornithology) gozzo, ingluvie f. **(c)** (of whip) manico; (riding ~) frustino. **2** vt (cut: hair) tagliare, rapare; (subj: animals: grass) brucare. **3** cpd: **~ spraying** n spruzzatura di antiparassitari.

♦ **crop up** vi + adv (fig: arise) sorgere; **something must have ~ped up** dev'essere capitato or successo qualcosa.

cro·quet ['krəʊkeɪ] n croquet m.

cro·quette [krəʊ'kɛt] n (Culin) crocchetta.

cross [krɒs] **1** n (a) croce f; **we each have our ~ to bear** (fig) tutti dobbiamo portare la nostra croce. **(b)** (Zool, Bio) incrocio, ibrido; **it's a ~ between geography and sociology** è un misto di geografia e sociologia. **(c)** (bias): **cut on the ~** tagliato in sbieco.

2 adj (-er, -est) (angry) arrabbiato(a), seccato(a); **to be/get ~ with sb (about sth)** essere arrabbiato/arrabbiarsi con qn (per qc); **it makes me ~ when...** mi fa arrabbiare quando... .

3 vt (a) (gen) attraversare; (threshold, ditch) attraversare, varcare; **this road ~es the motorway** questa strada incrocia or interseca l'autostrada; **it ~ed my mind that...** mi è venuto in mente che...; **we'll ~ that bridge when we come to it** (fig) ogni cosa a tempo debito. **(b)** (cheque, letter t) sbarrare; **to ~ o.s.** fare il segno della croce, segnarsi; **~ my heart!** giuro (sulla mia vita)! **(c)** (arms) incrociare; (legs) accavallare, incrociare; **to keep one's fingers ~ed** (fig) fare gli scongiuri; **I've got a ~ed line** (Telec) c'è un'interferenza; **they've got their lines ~ed** (fig) si sono fraintesi. **(d)** (thwart: person, plan) contrastare, ostacolare. **(e)** (animals, plants) incrociare.

4 vi (a) (also: **~ over**) attraversare; **the boat ~es from Dieppe to Newhaven** la barca fa la traversata da Dieppe a Newhaven. **(b)** (roads) intersecarsi; (letters, people) incrociarsi.

♦ **cross off** vt + adv, **cross out** vt + adv cancellare (tirandoci un rigo sopra).

cross·bar ['krɒsbɑː'] n (of bicycle) canna; (of goal post) traversa.

cross·breed ['krɒsbriːd] *n* incrocio, ibrido.
cross-Channel [ˌkrɒs'tʃænl] *adj*: ~ **ferry** traghetto che attraversa la Manica.
cross-check [ˌkrɒs'tʃɛk] **1** *n* controprova. **2** *vt* fare una controprova di.
cross-country [ˌkrɒs'kʌntrɪ] *adj (race)* campestre; ~ **skiing** sci *m* di fondo.
cross-examina·tion ['krɒsɪgˌzæmɪ'neɪʃən] *n* controinterrogatorio.
cross-examine [ˌkrɒsɪg'zæmɪn] *vt* controinterrogare.
cross-eyed ['krɒsaɪd] *adj* strabico(a).
cross·fire ['krɒsˌfaɪəʳ] *n* fuoco incrociato.
cross·ing ['krɒsɪŋ] *n (esp by sea)* traversata; *(of equator)* attraversamento; *(road junction)* incrocio, crocicchio; *(pedestrian ~)* strisce *fpl* pedonali, passaggio pedonale; *(level ~)* passaggio a livello; **cross at the** ~ attraversare sulle strisce.
cross·legged [ˌkrɒs'lɛgɪd] *adv* a gambe incrociate.
cross·ly ['krɒslɪ] *adv* in tono arrabbiato, con rabbia.
cross·patch ['krɒspætʃ] *n (fam)* permaloso/a, musone/a.
cross-purposes [ˌkrɒs'pɜːpəsɪz] *npl*: **to be at** ~ **with sb** *(disagree)* essere in contrasto con qn; *(misunderstand)* fraintendere qn; **to talk at** ~ fraintendersi.
cross-reference [ˌkrɒs'rɛfərəns] *n* rinvio, rimando.
cross·road(s) ['krɒsrəʊd(z)] *nsg* incrocio, crocicchio.
cross-section ['krɒsˌsɛkʃən] *n (Bio etc)* sezione *f* trasversale; *(of population)* campione *m*.
cross·walk ['krɒsˌwɔːk] *n (Am)* strisce *fpl* pedonali, passaggio pedonale.
cross·wind ['krɒsˌwɪnd] *n* vento di traverso.
cross·word ['krɒsˌwɜːd] *n*: ~ **(puzzle)** parole *fpl* incrociate, cruciverba *m inv*.
crotch [krɒtʃ] *n* **(a)** *(of tree)* forcella, biforcazione *f*. **(b)** *(also:* **crutch**: *Anat)* inforcatura; *(: of garment)* cavallo.
crotch·et ['krɒtʃɪt] *n (Brit Mus)* seminimina.
crouch [kraʊtʃ] *vi (also:* ~ **down**: *person, animal)* accucciarsi, accovacciarsi.
croup [kruːp] *n (Med)* crup *m*.
crou·pi·er ['kruːpɪeɪ] *n* croupier *m inv*.
crou·ton ['kruːtɒn] *n (Culin)* crostino.
crow [krəʊ] **1** *n* **(a)** *(bird)* cornacchia; **as the** ~ **flies** in linea d'aria; ~'**s feet** *(wrinkles)* zampe *fpl* di gallina; ~'**s nest** *(Naut)* coffa. **(b)** *(noise: of cock)* canto, chicchirichì *m*; *(: of baby, person)* gridolino. **2** *vi* **(a)** *pt* **crowed** *or* **crew**, *pp* **crowed** *(cock)* cantare, fare chicchirichì. **(b)** *pt, pp* **crowed** *(child)* lanciare gridolini; *(fig):* **to** ~ **over** *or* **about sth** vantarsi di qc.
crow·bar ['krəʊbɑːʳ] *n* piede *m* di porco.
crowd [kraʊd] **1** *n* folla; ~**s of people** un sacco di gente; **the** ~ *(common herd)* il volgo, la massa; **I don't like that** ~ **at all** non mi piace affatto quella gente; **she is part of the university** ~ appartiene alla cricca dell'università; **to follow the** ~ *(fig)* seguire la massa. **2** *vt (place)* affollare, gremire; *(things):* **to** ~ **sth into** ammassare qc in. **3** *vi* affollarsi; **to** ~ **in** entrare in massa; **to** ~ **round sb/sth** affollarsi attorno a qn/qc. **4** *cpd:* ~ **scene** *n (Cine, Theatre)* scena di massa.
♦ **crowd out** *vt + adv (not let in)* escludere (dal proprio gruppo); **the bar was** ~**ed out** il bar era così pieno che non si poteva entrare.
crowd·ed ['kraʊdɪd] *adj (meeting, event, place etc)* affollato(a); *(town)* molto popolato(a); *(day)* pieno(a); *(profession)* inflazionato(a); ~ **with** pieno di.

crown [kraʊn] **1** *n* **(a)** corona; *(Law):* **the C~** ≈ il Pubblico Ministero. **(b)** *(top: of hat, head)* cocuzzolo; *(: of hill)* cima, vetta; *(: of road: raised centre)* centro; *(: of tooth)* corona; *(: artificial)* capsula. **2** *vt* **(a)** *(king etc, fig)* incoronare; *(tooth)* incapsulare; **and to** ~ **it all...** *(fig)* e per giunta..., e come se non bastasse.... **(b)** *(fam: hit)* dare una botta in testa; **I'll** ~ **you if you do that again!** se lo fai ancora ti do una botta in testa! **3** *cpd:* ~ **court** *n (Law)* ≈ corte *f* d'assise; ~ **jewels** *npl* gioielli *mpl* della corona; ~ **prince** *n* principe *m* ereditario.
crown·ing ['kraʊnɪŋ] *adj (achievement, glory)* supremo(a).
cru·cial ['kruːʃəl] *adj* cruciale; **his approval is** ~ **to the success of the project** la sua approvazione è essenziale per il successo del progetto.
cru·ci·ble ['kruːsɪbl] *n* crogiolo.
cru·ci·fix ['kruːsɪfɪks] *n* crocifisso.
cru·ci·fix·ion [ˌkruːsɪ'fɪkʃən] *n* crocifissione *f*.
cru·ci·fy ['kruːsɪfaɪ] *vt* crocifiggere; *(fig)* distruggere, fare a pezzi.
crude [kruːd] *adj (-r, -st)* **(a)** *(unprocessed)* grezzo. **(b)** *(clumsy, unsophisticated)* rozzo(a); *(light, colour)* violento(a); **to make a** ~ **attempt at doing sth** fare un rozzo tentativo di fare qc. **(c)** *(vulgar)* volgare, grossolano(a).
crude·ness ['kruːdnɪs] *n*, **crud·ity** ['kruːdɪtɪ] *n (see adj* **b, c**) rozzezza; violenza; volgarità.
cru·el ['kruəl] *adj (-ler, -lest):* ~ **(to** *or* **towards)** crudele (con *or* nei confronti di).
cru·el·ty ['kruəltɪ] *n* crudeltà.
cru·et ['kruːɪt] *n (bottle)* ampolla; *(stand)* ampolliera.
cruise [kruːz] **1** *n* crociera; **to go on a** ~ fare una crociera. **2** *vi (ship, fleet)* incrociare; *(holidaymakers)* fare una crociera; *(Aut):* **the car** ~**s at 100 kph** la macchina fa tranquillamente i 100 all'ora; **cruising speed** velocità di crociera. **3** *cpd:* ~ **missile** *n* missile *m* cruise *inv*.
cruis·er ['kruːzəʳ] *n (Naut)* incrociatore *m*.
crumb [krʌm] *n (of bread, cake etc)* briciola; *(inner part of bread)* mollica; *(fig):* **a** ~ **of comfort** un briciolo di conforto; ~**s of information** ben poche informazioni; ~**s!** *(fam)* accidenti!; **he's a** ~ *(fam)* è un buono a nulla.
crum·ble ['krʌmbl] **1** *vt* sbriciolare. **2** *vi (bread, earth)* sbriciolarsi; *(building etc)* andare in rovina; *(plaster, bricks)* sgretolarsi; *(fig: hopes, power)* crollare.
crum·pet ['krʌmpɪt] *n (Culin)* specie di frittella.
crum·ple ['krʌmpl] **1** *vt (also:* ~ **up**: *paper)* accartocciare; *(: clothes)* stropicciare, sgualcire. **2** *vi (see vt)* accartocciarsi; stropicciarsi, sgualcirsi.
crunch [krʌntʃ] **1** *n (of broken glass, gravel)* scricchiolio; **if it comes to the** ~ *(fig)* al momento cruciale. **2** *vt (with teeth)* sgranocchiare. **3** *vi (gravel etc)* scricchiolare.
crunchy ['krʌntʃɪ] *adj (-ier, -iest)* croccante.
cru·sade [kruː'seɪd] **1** *n* crociata. **2** *vi (fig):* **to** ~ **for/against** fare una crociata per/contro.
cru·sad·er [kruː'seɪdəʳ] *n (History)* crociato; *(fig)* sostenitore/trice.
crush [krʌʃ] **1** *n* **(a)** *(crowd)* ressa, calca. **(b)** *(fam: infatuation)* cotta; **to have a** ~ **on sb** avere una cotta per qn. **2** *vt (squash: also fig)* schiacciare; *(crumple: clothes, paper)* sgualcire; *(grind, break up: garlic, ice)* tritare; *(: grapes)* pigiare; *(: scrap metal)* pressare; *(: stones)* frantumare; **to be** ~**ed to a pulp** andare in poltiglia. **3** *vi (clothes)* sgualcirsi. **4** *cpd:* ~ **barrier** *n* transenna.
crush·ing ['krʌʃɪŋ] *adj (defeat, blow)* schiacciante; *(reply)* mordace.

crust [krʌst] *n* crosta; *(layer)* strato; **the Earth's ~** la crosta terrestre.

crus·ta·cean [krʌsˈteɪʃən] *n* crostaceo.

crusty [ˈkrʌstɪ] *adj* (**-ier, -iest**) *(loaf)* croccante; *(fam: person)* irritabile.

crutch [krʌtʃ] *n* **(a)** *(Med)* stampella, gruccia; *(support)* sostegno. **(b)** = **crotch b.**

crux [krʌks] *n*: **the ~ of the matter** il nodo della questione.

cry [kraɪ] **1** *n* **(a)** *(call, shout)* grido; *(of animal)* verso; **to give a ~** emettere un grido; **a ~ for help** un grido di aiuto; **it's a far ~ from...** *(fig)* è tutt'un'altra cosa da...; **'jobs, not bombs' was their ~** 'lavoro, non bombe' era il loro slogan. **(b)** *(weep)*: **she had a good ~** si è fatta un bel pianto.

2 *vi* **(a)** *(call out, shout)* gridare; **he cried (out) with pain** urlò di dolore; **to ~ for help** gridare aiuto; **to ~ for mercy** invocare pietà. **(b)** *(weep)* piangere; **what are you ~ing about?** perché piangi?; **the child was ~ing for his mother** il bambino piangeva perché voleva la mamma; **I laughed till I cried** risi fino alle lacrime; **I'll give him something to ~ about!** *(fam)* glielo darò ben io un motivo per piangere!; **it's no good ~ing over spilt milk** *(fig)* è inutile piangere sul latte versato.

3 *vt* **(a)** gridare. **(b)**: **to ~ o.s. to sleep** piangere fino ad addormentarsi.

♦ **cry off** *vi + adv* rinunciare, ritirarsi.

♦ **cry out 1** *vi + adv (call out, shout)* urlare, gridare; **this car is ~ing out to be resprayed** *(fam)* questa macchina ha un gran bisogno di essere ridipinta. **2** *vt + adv* **(a)** *(call)* gridare, urlare. **(b)**: **to ~ one's eyes** *or* **heart out** piangere tutte le proprie lacrime.

cry·ing [ˈkraɪɪŋ] **1** *adj (child)* in lacrime, piangente; *(fam: bad)* disperato(a); **it's a ~ shame** è una vera vergogna. **2** *n (weeping)* pianto.

crypt [krɪpt] *n* cripta.

cryp·tic [ˈkrɪptɪk] *adj* oscuro(a), enigmatico(a); **~ crossword** cruciverba *m* a crittogramma.

crys·tal [ˈkrɪstl] **1** *n (gen)* cristallo; *(watch glass)* vetro. **2** *adj (glass, vase)* di cristallo; *(clear: water, lake)* cristallino(a). **3** *cpd*: **~ ball** *n* sfera di cristallo.

crystal-clear [ˌkrɪstlˈklɪər] *adj (water, wine)* cristallino(a); *(fig)* chiaro(a) (come il sole).

crystal-gazing [ˈkrɪstl,ɡeɪzɪŋ] *n* predizione *f* del futuro.

crys·tal·lize [ˈkrɪstəlaɪz] **1** *vt (Chem)* cristallizzare; *(fig)* concretizzare, concretare; **~d fruits** frutta candita. **2** *vi (see vt)* cristallizzarsi; concretizzarsi, concretarsi.

cu. *abbr of* **cubic.**

cub [kʌb] *n* **(a)** cucciolo; **lion ~** leoncino; **wolf ~** lupetto. **(b)** *(also:* **~ scout)** lupetto.

Cuba [ˈkjuːbə] *n* Cuba; **in ~** a Cuba.

cubby·hole [ˈkʌbɪhəʊl] *n* angolo, cantuccio.

cube [kjuːb] **1** *n* cubo; *(of sugar)* cubetto. **2** *vt (Math)* elevare al cubo *or* alla terza potenza. **3** *cpd*: **~ root** *n* radice *f* cubica.

cu·bic [ˈkjuːbɪk] *adj (shape, volume)* cubico(a); *(metre, foot)* cubo(a); **~ capacity** *(Aut)* cilindrata.

cu·bi·cle [ˈkjuːbɪkəl] *n* cabina.

cuckoo [ˈkʊkuː] **1** *n* cuculo, cucù *m inv.* **2** *adj (fam)* tocco(a), matto(a). **3** *cpd*: **~ clock** *n* orologio a cucù.

cu·cum·ber [ˈkjuːkʌmbər] *n* cetriolo.

cud·dle [ˈkʌdl] **1** *n* abbraccio. **2** *vt* coccolare. **3** *vi*: **to ~ down** accoccolarsi; **to ~ up to sb** accoccolarsi contro qn.

cud·dly [ˈkʌdlɪ] *adj* (**-ier, -iest**) *(child, animal)* coccolone(a); *(toy)* morbido(a).

cudg·el [ˈkʌdʒəl] **1** *n (weapon)* manganello, randello; **to take up the ~s for sb/sth** *(fig)* mettersi a lottare per qn/qc. **2** *vt*: **to ~ one's brains** scervellarsi, spremere le meningi.

cue [kjuː] *n* **(a)** *(Billiards)* stecca. **(b)** *(Theatre: verbal, by signal)* segnale *m*, imbeccata; *(Mus: by signal)* segnale; **to take one's ~ from sb** *(fig)* prendere esempio da qn.

cuff¹ [kʌf] **1** *n* schiaffo. **2** *vt* dare uno schiaffo a.

cuff² [kʌf] **1** *n (of sleeve)* polsino; *(Am: of trousers)* risvolto; **off the ~** *(fig)* improvvisando. **2** *cpd*: **~ link** *n* gemello.

cui·sine [kwɪˈziːn] *n* cucina.

cul-de-sac [ˈkʌldəˈsæk] *n* vicolo cieco.

culi·nary [ˈkʌlɪnərɪ] *adj* culinario(a).

cull [kʌl] **1** *vt (select: fruit)* scegliere; *(kill selectively: animals)* selezionare e abbattere. **2** *n* selezione *f*; **seal ~** abbattimento selettivo delle foche.

cul·mi·nate [ˈkʌlmɪneɪt] *vi*: **to ~ in** culminare con.

cul·mi·na·tion [ˌkʌlmɪˈneɪʃən] *n* culmine *m.*

cu·lottes [kjuː(ː)ˈlɒts] *npl* gonna *f* pantalone *inv.*

cul·pable [ˈkʌlpəbl] *adj* colpevole.

cul·prit [ˈkʌlprɪt] *n* colpevole *m/f.*

cult [kʌlt] *n (Rel,fig)* culto; **to make a ~ of sth** avere un culto per qc; **a ~ figure** un idolo.

cul·ti·vate [ˈkʌltɪveɪt] *vt* coltivare.

cul·ti·va·tion [ˌkʌltɪˈveɪʃən] *n (Agr)* coltivazione *f*, coltura.

cul·tur·al [ˈkʌltʃərəl] *adj* culturale.

cul·ture [ˈkʌltʃər] *n* **(a)** *(the arts)* cultura; *(civilization)* civiltà *f inv.* **(b)** *(Bio, Agr)* coltura.

cul·tured [ˈkʌltʃəd] *adj (person, voice, mind)* colto(a); *(manners)* raffinato(a); *(pearl)* coltivato(a).

cum·ber·some [ˈkʌmbəsəm] *adj* pesante e ingombrante.

cum·in [ˈkʌmɪn] *n (spice)* cumino.

cu·mu·la·tive [ˈkjuːmjʊlətɪv] *adj* cumulativo(a).

cun·ning [ˈkʌnɪŋ] **1** *adj (pej: crafty)* furbo(a); *(clever: device, idea)* ingegnoso(a). **2** *n* furbizia.

cup [kʌp] **1** *n (for tea etc)* tazza; *(as prize, of brassière)* coppa; **a ~ of tea** una tazza di tè; **tea ~** tazza da tè; **it's not everyone's ~ of tea** *(fam)* non è una cosa che piace a tutti; **that's just not my ~ of tea** *(fam)* non è proprio il mio genere. **2** *vt (hands)* riunire (a coppa); **to ~ one's hands round sth** prendere qc fra le mani. **3** *cpd*: **~ final** *n (Ftbl)* finale *f* di coppa; **~ tie** *n (Ftbl)* partita eliminatoria.

cup·board [ˈkʌbəd] **1** *n* armadio. **2** *cpd*: **~ love** *n (Brit)* amore m interessato.

cu·rate [ˈkjʊərɪt] *n* curato.

cu·ra·tor [kjʊəˈreɪtər] *n* conservatore/trice (di museo).

curb¹ [kɜːb] **1** *n (fig)* freno. **2** *vt (fig: temper, impatience etc)* frenare; *(: expenditure)* limitare.

curb² [kɜːb] *n (Am)* = **kerb.**

curd [kɜːd] **1** *n (usu pl)*: **~s** latte *m* cagliato. **2** *cpd*: **~ cheese** *n* cagliata.

cur·dle [ˈkɜːdl] **1** *vt* far cagliare. **2** *vi* cagliarsi; **it made my blood ~** mi ha gelato il sangue nelle vene.

cure [kjʊər] **1** *n (remedy)* cura; *(recovery)* guarigione *f*; **to take a ~** fare una cura. **2** *vt* **(a)** *(Med: disease, patient)* guarire; *(fig: poverty, injustice, evil)* eliminare; **to be ~d of sth** essere guarito da qc; **to ~ sb of a habit** far perdere a qn un'abitudine. **(b)** *(preserve: in salt)* salare; *(: by smoking)* affumicare; *(: by drying)* seccare; *(: animal hide)* conciare.

cure-all ['kjʊərɔːl] n (also fig) panacea, toccasana m inv.

cur·few ['kɜːfjuː] n coprifuoco.

cu·rio ['kjʊərɪəʊ] n curiosità f inv.

cu·ri·os·ity [ˌkjʊərɪˈɒsɪtɪ] n curiosità f inv; ~ **killed the cat** la curiosità si paga cara.

cu·ri·ous ['kjʊərɪəs] adj (a) (inquisitive) curioso(a); **I'm ~ about him** m'incuriosisce; **I'd be ~ to know** sarei curioso di sapere. (b) (strange) strano(a), curioso(a).

cu·ri·ous·ly ['kjʊərɪəslɪ] adv (see adj) con curiosità; stranamente; ~ **enough,** ... per quanto possa sembrare strano, ...

curl [kɜːl] 1 n (of hair) ricciolo; (of smoke etc) anello. 2 vt (hair) arricciare; **she ~ed her lip in scorn** arricciò il labbro in segno di disprezzo. 3 vi (hair) arricciarsi.

♦ **curl up** vi + adv (leaves, paper) accartocciarsi; (cat) acciambellarsi; (person, dog) accoccolarsi; (fam: from shame) sprofondare (dalla vergogna); (with laughter) piegarsi in due (dalle risate).

curl·er ['kɜːlər] n bigodino.

cur·lew ['kɜːluː] n chiurlo.

curl·ing ['kɜːlɪŋ] 1 n (Sport) curling m. 2 adj: ~ **tongs** (for hair) arricciacapelli m inv.

curly ['kɜːlɪ] adj (-ier, -iest) (gen) riccio(a); (eyelashes) ricurvo(a).

cur·rant ['kʌrənt] 1 n (dried grape) uva passa; (bush, fruit) ribes m inv. 2 cpd: ~ **bun** n panino con l'uva.

cur·ren·cy ['kʌrənsɪ] n (a) moneta; **foreign** ~ valuta estera. (b) (fig: of ideas): **to gain** ~ acquistare credito.

cur·rent ['kʌrənt] 1 adj (fashion, opinion, year) corrente; (tendency, price, event) attuale; (phrase) di uso corrente; **in ~ use** in uso corrente, d'uso comune; ~ **account** (Bank) conto corrente; ~ **affairs** problemi mpl d'attualità; ~ **assets** (Fin) attivo realizzabile e disponibile; **the ~ issue of a magazine** l'ultimo numero di una rivista; **her ~ boyfriend** il suo attuale ragazzo. 2 n (of air, water, Elec, fig) corrente f; **direct/alternating** ~ corrente continua/alternata; **to go against the** ~ (fig) andare controcorrente.

cur·rent·ly ['kʌrəntlɪ] adv attualmente, al momento.

cur·ricu·lum [kəˈrɪkjʊləm] 1 n programma m. 2 cpd: ~ **vitae** n curriculum vitae m inv.

cur·ry¹ ['kʌrɪ] 1 n (spice) curry m; (dish): **beef/vegetable** ~ manzo/verdura al curry. 2 vt cucinare un curry. 3 cpd: ~ **powder** n curry m.

cur·ry² ['kʌrɪ] vt: **to ~ favour with sb** cercare di accattivarsi (il favore di) qn.

curse [kɜːs] 1 n (a) maledizione f; **to put a ~ on sb** maledire qn. (b) (bane) rovina, flagello; **the ~ of it is that...** il guaio è che... . (c) (swearword) imprecazione f; (blasphemous) bestemmia; ~**s!** (fam) maledizione! (d) (fam: menstruation): **she's got the** ~ ha le mestruazioni or le sue cose. 2 vt maledire; **to be ~d with** (fig) essere tormentato da. 3 vi bestemmiare.

cur·sory ['kɜːsərɪ] adj (glance) di sfuggita; **a ~ reading** una rapida scorsa.

curt [kɜːt] adj brusco(a); **with a ~ nod** con un breve cenno del capo.

cur·tail [kɜːˈteɪl] vt accorciare; (wages, expenditure) limitare.

cur·tain ['kɜːtn] 1 n tenda; (Theatre) sipario; **to draw the ~s** (together) chiudere or tirare le tende; (apart) aprire le tende; **it'll be ~s for you!** (fam) per te sarà la fine! 2 cpd: ~ **call** n (Theatre) chinata alla ribalta; ~ **hook** n gancio della tenda;

~ **ring** n anello della tenda; ~ **rod** n asta or bastone m della tenda.

♦ **curtain off** vt + adv separare con una tenda.

curt·s(e)y ['kɜːtsɪ] 1 n inchino. 2 vi fare un inchino.

cur·va·ceous [kɜːˈveɪʃəs] adj (fam: woman) formoso(a).

cur·va·ture ['kɜːvətʃər] n curvatura; (Med): ~ **of the spine** deviazione f della colonna vertebrale.

curve [kɜːv] 1 n (gen) curva; (of river) ansa; **a ~ in the road** una curva or svolta della strada. 2 vt curvare. 3 vi (road, river) fare una curva; (line, surface, arch) curvarsi.

curved [kɜːvd] adj curvo(a).

cush·ion ['kʊʃən] 1 n cuscino; (of billiard table) sponda (elastica). 2 vt (blow, fall) attutire; **to ~ sb against sth** proteggere qn da qc.

cushy ['kʊʃɪ] adj (-ier, -iest) (fam): **a ~ job** un lavoro di tutto riposo; **to have a ~ time** spassarsela.

cus·tard ['kʌstəd] 1 n crema pasticcera. 2 cpd: ~ **cream** n (biscuit) biscotto farcito alla crema; ~ **powder** n crema pasticcera in polvere; ~ **tart** n crostata di crema.

cus·to·dian [kʌsˈtəʊdɪən] n (gen) custode m/f; (of museum etc) soprintendente m/f.

cus·to·dy ['kʌstədɪ] n (Law: of children) custodia; (police ~) detenzione f (preventiva); **to take sb into** ~ mettere qn in detenzione preventiva; **in safe** ~ al sicuro; **in the ~ of** alla custodia di.

cus·tom ['kʌstəm] n (a) costume m, consuetudine f; **social ~s** convenzioni fpl sociali; **it is her ~ to go for a walk each evening** è sua consuetudine fare una passeggiata ogni sera. (b) (Comm): **to get sb's** ~ ottenere qn per cliente; **the shop has lost a lot of** ~ il negozio ha perso molti clienti. (c): ~**s** (also: **C~s**) see **customs**.

cus·tom·ary ['kʌstəmərɪ] adj consueto(a); **it is ~ to do it** è consuetudine fare.

custom-built ['kʌstəmbɪlt] adj fatto(a) su ordinazione.

cus·tom·er ['kʌstəmər] n cliente m/f; **he's an awkward** ~ (fam) è un tipo incontentabile; **ugly** ~ (fam) brutto tipo.

cus·toms ['kʌstəmz] 1 npl (also: **C~**) dogana; **to go through (the)** ~ passare la dogana. 2 cpd: ~ **duty** n tassa doganale; ~ **inspection** n ispezione f doganale; ~ **officer** n doganiere m.

cut [kʌt] (vb: pt, pp **cut**) 1 n (a) (gen) taglio; (Med) taglio, incisione f; (Cards) alzata; **the ~ and thrust of politics** i vivaci contrasti della politica; **he's a ~ above the others** è di gran lunga migliore degli altri.

(b) (reduction) riduzione f, taglio; (deletion) taglio; (Elec) interruzione f; **to take a ~ in salary** avere una riduzione dello stipendio.

(c) (of clothes, hair) taglia.

(d) (of meat: piece) taglio; (: slice) pezzo, parte f; (fam: share) parte.

2 adj (flowers) reciso(a); (glass) intagliato(a).

3 vt (a) (gen) tagliare; (Cards) alzare; **to ~ one's finger** tagliarsi un dito; **to ~ sth in half/in two** etc tagliare qc a metà/in due etc; **he is ~ting his own throat** (fig) si sta dando la zappa sui piedi; **to ~ to pieces** (army, fig) fare a pezzi, distruggere; **to ~ sth to size** ridurre qc (alla misura desiderata); **to ~ open** aprire con un coltello (or con le forbici etc); **I ~ my hand open on a tin** mi sono fatto un brutto taglio alla mano con una lattina; **to ~ sb free** liberare qn (tagliando qc); **it ~ me to the quick** or **the heart** (fig) mi ha ferito profondamente.

(b) (shape: gen, jewel) tagliare; (steps, channel)

scavare; *(key)* fare una copia di, riprodurre; *(glass)* lavorare; *(figure, statue)* scolpire; *(engrave)* incidere; *(record)* incidere, registrare; **to ~ one's way through** aprirsi la strada attraverso; **to ~ one's coat according to one's cloth** *(fig)* non fare il passo più lungo della gamba.

(c) *(clip, trim: hair, nails, hedge etc)* tagliare; **to get one's hair ~** farsi tagliare i capelli.

(d) *(reduce: wages, prices, production etc)* ridurre; *(expenses)* ridurre, limitare; *(speech, text, film)* tagliare; *(interrupt)* interrompere; **to ~ sb/ sth short** interrompere qn/qc; **to ~ 30 seconds off a record** *(Sport)* abbassare un record di 30 secondi.

(e) *(intersect)* intersecare.

(f) *(fam: avoid: class, lecture, appointment)* saltare; **to ~ sb dead** ignorare qn completamente.

4 *vi* **(a)** *(person, knife)* **she ~ into the melon** ha affondato il coltello nel melone; **it ~s both ways** *(fig)* è un'arma a doppio taglio; **to ~ and run** *(fam)* tagliare la corda; **to ~ loose (from sth)** *(fig)* staccarsi (da qc).

(b) *(hurry)*: **to ~ across country/through the lane** tagliare per la campagna/per il sentiero; **I must ~ along now** ora devo avviarmi.

(c) *(Cine)*: **the film ~ from the bedroom to the garden scene** la scena del film si è spostata dalla stanza da letto al giardino; **~! stop!**

(d) *(Cards)* tagliare il mazzo.

♦ **cut away** *vt + adv* tagliare via.

♦ **cut back** *vt + adv (plants)* tagliare; *(production, expenditure)* ridurre.

♦ **cut down 1** *vi + adv* **(a)** *(tree)* abbattere; *(enemy)* falciare. **(b)** *(reduce: consumption, expenses)* ridurre; *(: text)* tagliare; **to ~ sb down to size** *(fig)* sgonfiare *or* ridimensionare qn. **2** *vi + adv* limitarsi; **to ~ down on sth** ridurre qc, diminuire qc.

♦ **cut in** *vi + adv*: **to ~ in (on)** *(interrupt: conversation)* intromettersi (in); *(Aut)* tagliare la strada (a).

♦ **cut off** *vt + adv* **(a)** *(gen)* tagliare; **to ~ off one's nose to spite one's face** *(fam)* farsi dispetto. **(b)** *(disconnect: telephone, gas)* tagliare; *(engine)* spegnere; **we've been ~ off** *(Telec)* è caduta la linea. **(c)** *(isolate)* isolare; **they feel very ~ off** si sentono molto tagliati fuori; **to ~ o.s. off from sth/sb** allontanarsi *or* isolarsi da qc/qn; **to ~ off the enemy's retreat** tagliare la ritirata al nemico; **to ~ sb off without a penny** diseredare qn.

♦ **cut out 1** *vi + adv (engine)* spegnersi. **2** *vt + adv* **(a)** *(article, picture)* ritagliare; *(statue, shape)* scolpire; *(dress etc)* tagliare, ricavare; **to be ~ out for sth/to do sth** *(fig)* essere tagliato per qc/per fare qc; **you'll have your work ~ out for you** avrai un bel daffare. **(b)** *(delete)* eliminare, togliere. **(c)** *(stop, give up)* eliminare; **~ it out!** *(fam)* dacci un taglio!

♦ **cut up 1** *vt + adv* **(a)** *(gen)* tagliare; *(chop: food)* sminuzzare. **(b)** *(fam)*: **to be ~ up about sth** *(hurt)* rimanerci da cani per qc; *(annoyed)* essere arrabbiato per qc. **2** *vi + adv*: **to ~ up rough** *(fam)* perdere le staffe.

cut-and-dried [ˌkʌtənˈdraɪd] *adj (also:* **cut-and-dry**) *(fig)* assodato(a).

cut·back [ˈkʌtbæk] *n* **(a)** *(in expenditure, staff, production)* taglio, riduzione *f*. **(b)** *(Cine: flashback)* flashback *m inv*.

cute [kjuːt] *adj (fam: sweet)* carino(a); *(: clever)* furbo(a).

cu·ti·cle [ˈkjuːtɪkl] *n* cuticola, pellicina.

cut·lery [ˈkʌtlərɪ] *n* posate *fpl*.

cut·let [ˈkʌtlɪt] *n* cotoletta (senza osso).

cut·off [ˈkʌtɒf] **1** *n (also:* **~ point**) limite *m*. **2** *cpd*: **~ switch** *n* interruttore *m*.

cut·out [ˈkʌtaʊt] *n (paper, cardboard figure)* ritaglio; *(switch)* interruttore *m*.

cut-price [ˈkʌt,praɪs] *adj (goods)* scontato(a); *(shop)* che fa prezzi bassi.

cut-throat [ˈkʌtθrəʊt] **1** *n* assassino. **2** *adj (razor)* da barbiere; *(competition)* spietato(a).

cut·ting [ˈkʌtɪŋ] **1** *n* **(a)** *(of plant)* talea. **(b)** *(from newspaper)* ritaglio; *(Cine)* montaggio. **(c)** *(for road, railway)* scavo. **2** *adj* **(a)** *(knife)* tagliente; **the ~ edge** la lama. **(b)** *(cold: wind etc)* pungente; *(fig: remark)* tagliente, mordace. **(c)** *(Cine)*: **~ room** sala di montaggio.

cuttle·fish [ˈkʌtlfɪʃ] *n* seppia.

cwt *abbr of* **hundredweight**.

cya·nide [ˈsaɪənaɪd] *n* cianuro.

cy·ber·net·ics [ˌsaɪbəˈnɛtɪks] *n* cibernetica.

cyc·la·men [ˈsɪkləmən] *n* ciclamino.

cy·cle [ˈsaɪkl] **1** *n* **(a)** bicicletta. **(b)** *(of seasons, poems etc)* ciclo. **2** *vi* andare in bicicletta. **3** *cpd*: **~ path** *n* pista ciclabile; **~ race** *n* gara *or* corsa ciclistica; **~ rack** *n* portabiciclette *m inv*.

cy·cling [ˈsaɪklɪŋ] **1** *n* ciclismo. **2** *cpd*: **~ holiday** *n* vacanza in bicicletta.

cy·clist [ˈsaɪklɪst] *n* ciclista *m/f*.

cy·clone [ˈsaɪkləʊn] *n* ciclone *m*.

cy·clo·style [ˈsaɪkləstaɪl] *vt* ciclostilare.

cyg·net [ˈsɪgnɪt] *n* giovane cigno.

cyl·in·der [ˈsɪlɪndə*] **1** *n* cilindro; **a 6-~ engine** un motore a 6 cilindri. **2** *cpd*: **~ block** *n* monoblocco; **~ head** *n* testata; **~ head gasket** *n* guarnizione *f* della testata.

cy·lin·dri·cal [sɪˈlɪndrɪkəl] *adj* cilindrico(a).

cym·bal [ˈsɪmbəl] *n* cembalo.

cyn·ic [ˈsɪnɪk] *n* cinico/a.

cyni·cal [ˈsɪnɪkəl] *adj* cinico(a).

cyni·cism [ˈsɪnɪsɪzəm] *n* cinismo.

cy·press [ˈsaɪprɪs] *n* cipresso.

Cyp·ri·ot [ˈsɪprɪət] *adj, n* cipriota *(m/f)*.

Cy·prus [ˈsaɪprəs] *n* Cipro; **in ~** a Cipro.

cyst [sɪst] *n* cisti *f inv*.

cys·ti·tis [sɪsˈtaɪtɪs] *n* cistite *f*.

czar [zɑː*] *n* zar *m inv*.

cza·ri·na [zɑːˈriːnə] *n* zarina.

Czech [tʃɛk] **1** *adj* ceco(a). **2** *n (person)* ceco/a; *(language)* ceco.

Czecho·slo·va·kia [ˈtʃɛkəʊsləˈvækɪə] *n* Cecoslovacchia.

Czecho·slo·vak(ian) [ˈtʃɛkəʊsləˈvæk(ɪən)] **1** *adj* cecoslovacco(a). **2** *n (person)* cecoslovacco/a; *(language)* cecoslovacco.

D

D, d [diː] n (a) (letter) D, d for m inv. (b) (Mus) re m.

dab [dæb] 1 n (a) (light stroke) colpetto, tocco; (: of paint) pennellata. (b) (small amount) pochino, punta; (: of glue) goccio; a ~ of paint una pennellatina. 2 adj: to be a ~ hand at sth/at doing sth (fam) essere in gambissima in qc/a fare qc. 3 vt (touch lightly: also vi: ~ at) picchiettare lievemente; (wound) tamponare; (apply): to ~ sth on sth applicare qc con colpetti leggeri su qc.

dab·ble ['dæbl] 1 vt: to ~ one's hands/feet in the water sguazzare con le mani/i piedi nell'acqua. 2 vi (fig): to ~ in sth occuparsi di qc a tempo perso, dilettarsi di qc; to ~ in politics dilettarsi in politica.

dachs·hund ['dækshʊnd] n bassotto.

dad [dæd] n, **dad·dy** ['dædɪ] n (fam) papà m inv, babbo.

daddy-long-legs [ˌdædɪ'lɒŋlegz] n, pl inv zanzarone m.

daf·fo·dil ['dæfədɪl] n trombone m, giunchiglia.

daft [dɑːft] adj (-er, -est) (fam) sciocco(a); to be ~ about sb perdere la testa per qn; to be ~ about sth andare pazzo per qc.

dag·ger ['dægə'] n pugnale m, stiletto; (Typ) croce f; to be at ~s drawn (with sb) essere ai ferri corti (con qn); to look ~s at sb fare gli occhiacci a qn.

dago ['deɪgəʊ] n ≃ marocchino.

dahl·ia ['deɪlɪə] n dalia.

dai·ly ['deɪlɪ] 1 adj (routine, task, paper) quotidiano(a); (wage, output, consumption) giornaliero(a); he takes a ~ walk fa una passeggiata ogni giorno; our ~ bread il nostro pane quotidiano; the ~ grind il tran-tran quotidiano. 2 adv quotidianamente, ogni giorno, tutti i giorni; twice ~ due volte al giorno. 3 n (paper) quotidiano; (servant) donna di servizio.

dain·ty ['deɪntɪ] adj (-ier, -iest) (person, figure) minuto(a); (child, manners) aggraziato(a); (flowers, gesture, dishes, food) delicato(a); (dress, shoes) grazioso(a).

dairy ['dɛərɪ] 1 n (shop) latteria; (organization, on farm) caseificio. 2 cpd: ~ cow n mucca da latte; ~ farm n caseificio; ~ ice cream n gelato alla crema; ~ produce n latticini mpl.

dais ['deɪɪs] n pedana, palco.

dai·sy ['deɪzɪ] 1 n margherita; (wild) pratolina, margheritina. 2 cpd: ~ wheel n (on printer) margherita.

dale [deɪl] n valle f.

dal·ly ['dælɪ] vi (delay) dilungarsi; to ~ about perdere tempo; to ~ over sth gingillarsi con qc.

dal·ma·tian [dæl'meɪʃən] n (dog) dalmata m.

dam [dæm] 1 n (wall) diga, sbarramento; (reservoir) bacino artificiale. 2 vt (also: ~ up: river) sbarrare con una diga; (: lake) costruire una diga su; (: fig) arginare, frenare.

dam·age ['dæmɪdʒ] 1 n (a) danno, danni mpl; (fig) danno; ~ to property danni materiali; to suffer ~ riportare or subire danni; the fire did a lot of ~ l'incendio ha provocato danni ingenti; to do ~ to a relationship pregiudicare un rapporto; what's the ~? (fam: cost) quanto tocca sborsare? (b): ~s npl (Law) danni mpl; liable for ~s tenuto al risarcimento dei danni; to pay £5000 in ~s pagare 5000 sterline di indennizzo. 2 vt (furniture, crops, machine) danneggiare; (health, eyesight) rovinare; (hopes, reputation) compromettere; (relationship) guastare; (cause) minare, compromettere.

dam·ag·ing ['dæmɪdʒɪŋ] adj: ~ (to) nocivo(a) (a).

dame [deɪm] n (title, Am fam) donna; (Theatre) vecchia signora (ruolo comico di donna recitato da un uomo).

damn [dæm] 1 vt (Rel) dannare; (swear at) maledire; (condemn: film, book) condannare, stroncare; ~ it! (fam) accidenti!; ~ him/you! (fam) accidenti a lui/a te!; well I'll be ~ed! (fam) che mi venga un accidente!; I'll be ~ed if I will! (fam) (non lo faccio) manco morto! 2 n (fam): I don't give a ~ me ne infischio; it's not worth a ~ non vale un fico secco. 3 adj (fam: also: ~ed) maledetto(a), del diavolo. 4 adv (fam: also: ~ed): it's ~ hot fa un caldo del diavolo; he knew ~ well lo sapeva benissimo; ~ all un bel niente.

dam·nable ['dæmnəbl] adj (fam: behaviour) vergognoso(a); (: weather) schifoso(a).

dam·na·tion [dæm'neɪʃən] 1 n (Rel) dannazione f. 2 excl (fam) dannazione!, diavolo!

damned·est ['dæmdɪst] n: to do one's ~ to succeed fare tutto il possibile e l'immaginabile per riuscire.

damn·ing ['dæmɪŋ] adj (remarks, implications) fortemente negativo(a); ~ evidence prove fpl schiaccianti; ~ criticism stroncatura.

damp [dæmp] 1 adj (-er, -est) umido(a); ~ with perspiration madido di sudore; that was a ~ squib (fam) è stato un vero fiasco. 2 n (also: ~ness) umidità, umido. 3 vt (also: ~en) inumidire, bagnare leggermente; (: fig: enthusiasm) raffreddare; (: hopes) diminuire; (also: ~ down: fire) coprire; to ~ sb's courage scoraggiare qn; to ~ sb's spirits abbattere qn.

damp·course ['dæmpˌkɔːs] n strato isolante antiumido.

damp·en ['dæmpən] vt = damp 3.

damp·er ['dæmpə'] n (Mus) sordina; (of fire) valvola di tiraggio; to put a ~ on sth (fig: atmosphere) gelare; (: enthusiasm) far sbollire.

dam·son ['dæmzən] n (fruit) susina or prugna selvatica; (tree) susino selvatico.

dance [dɑːns] 1 n (movement) ballo; (traditional, in ballet) danza; (event) ballo, serata danzante; to lead sb a ~ (fig) far girare qn come una trottola. 2 vt (waltz, tango) ballare; to ~ attendance on sb girare intorno a qn. 3 vi ballare, danzare; (fig: flowers, boat on waves) danzare; will you ~ with me? vuole ballare (con me)?; to ~ about saltellare; to ~ for joy ballare dalla gioia or dalla contentezza. 4 cpd (band, music, hall) da ballo.

danc·er ['dɑːnsə'] n ballerino/a.

danc·ing ['dɑːnsɪŋ] n ballo, danza.

dan·de·lion ['dændɪlaɪən] n dente m di leone.

dan·druff ['dændrəf] n forfora.
dan·dy ['dændɪ] 1 n dandy m inv, elegantone m. 2 adj (Am fam) fantastico(a).
Dane [deɪn] n danese m/f.
dan·ger ['deɪndʒəʳ] 1 n pericolo; in ~ in pericolo; out of ~ fuori pericolo; to put one's life in ~ mettere a rischio la propria vita; to be in ~ of falling rischiare di cadere; there was no ~ that he would be caught non c'era pericolo che lo prendessero; '~! men at work' 'attenzione! lavori in corso'; '~! keep out' 'pericolo! vietato l'accesso'. 2 cpd: ~ list n (Med): on the ~ list in prognosi riservata; ~ money n indennità di rischio; ~ zone n area di pericolo.
dan·ger·ous ['deɪndʒrəs] adj (gen) pericoloso(a); (activity) rischioso(a); (illness) grave, pericoloso(a).
dan·ger·ous·ly ['deɪndʒrəslɪ] adv (gen) pericolosamente; (wounded) gravemente; ~ ill in pericolo di vita.
dan·gle ['dæŋgl] 1 vt (arm, leg) (far) dondolare; (object on string etc) far oscillare; (fig: tempting offer): to ~ sth in front of sb allettare qn con qc. 2 vi pendere, penzolare; with one's legs dangling con le gambe penzoloni.
Dan·ish ['deɪnɪʃ] 1 adj danese; ~ blue (cheese) formaggio tipo gorgonzola; ~ pastry dolce m di pasta sfoglia. 2 n danese m.
dank [dæŋk] adj freddo(a) e umido(a).
dap·per ['dæpəʳ] adj azzimato(a).
dap·pled ['dæpld] adj screziato(a); (horse) pomellato(a).
dare [dɛəʳ] 1 n sfida; I did it for a ~ l'ho fatto per scommessa. 2 vt (a) (challenge): to ~ sb to do sth sfidare qn a fare qc; I ~ you! ti sfido a farlo!; to ~ death/sb's anger sfidare la morte/l'ira di qn. (b) osare; to ~ (to) do sth osare fare qc; I ~n't tell him non oso dirglielo; how ~ you! come si permette!, come osa!; I ~ say he'll turn up immagino che spunterà; I ~ say! (iro) sarà!
dare·devil ['dɛəˌdevl] n scavezzacollo.
dar·ing ['dɛərɪŋ] 1 adj audace. 2 n audacia.
dark [dɑːk] 1 adj (-er, -est) (a) (room, night) scuro(a), buio(a); it is/is getting ~ è/si sta facendo buio; the ~ side of the moon l'altra faccia della luna. (b) (in colour) scuro(a); (complexion, hair) scuro(a), bruno(a); ~ blue/red etc blu/rosso etc scuro; ~ brown hair capelli castano scuro; ~ glasses occhiali scuri; ~ chocolate cioccolata amara. (c) (fig: sad, gloomy) nero(a); (: sinister: secret, plan, threat etc) oscuro(a); to keep sth ~ non far parola di qc; she's a ~ horse (fig) è un'incognita; the D~ Ages l'alto medioevo. 2 n: the ~ il buio, l'oscurità; in the ~ al buio; before ~ prima che faccia buio; after ~ col buio; until ~ fino a sera; to be in the ~ about sth (fig) essere all'oscuro di qc.
dark·en ['dɑːkən] 1 vt (sky) oscurare; (colour) scurire. 2 vi (room, sky) oscurarsi; (landscape) farsi buio(a); (colour) scurirsi.
dark-haired [ˌdɑːk'hɛəd] adj bruno(a), dai capelli scuri.
dark·ly ['dɑːklɪ] adv (gloomily) cupamente, con aria cupa; (sinisterly) minacciosamente.
dark·ness ['dɑːknɪs] n oscurità, buio; (of hair) colore m scuro; the house was in ~ la casa era immersa nel buio or nell'oscurità.
dark·room ['dɑːkrʊm] n camera oscura.
dark-skinned [ˌdɑːk'skɪnd] adj di pelle or carnagione scura.
dar·ling ['dɑːlɪŋ] 1 n beniamino/a, prediletto/a; he's a little ~ è un amore; be a ~... (fam) sii un angelo or un tesoro...; come here ~ vieni qui

tesoro. 2 adj (daughter, husband) caro(a); (dress, house) adorabile, delizioso(a).
darn [dɑːn] 1 n rammendo. 2 vt (socks, cloth) rammendare. 3 excl (fam) euph for damn.
darn·ing ['dɑːnɪŋ] 1 n rammendo; (items to be darned) roba da rammendare. 2 adj (needle, wool) da rammendo.
dart [dɑːt] 1 n (a) dardo, freccia; (Sport) freccetta; ~s (game) freccette. (b) (Sewing) pince f inv, ripresa. 2 vt (look) lanciare. 3 vi: to ~ in/out etc entrare/uscire etc come una freccia; to ~ away sfrecciar via; to ~ at sth lanciarsi verso qc.
dart·board ['dɑːtbɔːd] n bersaglio per freccette.
dash [dæʃ] 1 n (a) (small quantity: of liquid) goccio, goccino; (: of soda) spruzzo; (: of seasoning) pizzico; (: of colour) tocco. (b) (punctuation mark) lineetta, trattino; (Morse) linea. (c) (rush): to make a ~ (at, towards) lanciarsi (verso), scattare (verso); he had to make a ~ for it ha dovuto fare una corsa; the 100-metre ~ (Am) i 100 metri piani.
2 vt (a) (throw) scaraventare, gettare con violenza; to ~ sth to pieces mandare qc in frantumi; to ~ one's head against sth sbattere la testa contro qc. (b) (fig: spirits) abbattere; all his hopes were ~ed tutte le sue speranze sono naufragate.
3 vi (a) (smash: object, waves): to ~ against infrangersi su or contro. (b) (rush): to ~ away scappare (via); to ~ in/out entrare/uscire di corsa; I must ~ (fam) devo proprio scappare.
4 excl: ~ it (all)! al diavolo!
♦ **dash off** vt + adv (letter, drawing) buttar giù.
dash·board ['dæʃbɔːd] n cruscotto.
dash·ing ['dæʃɪŋ] adj brillante, affascinante.
data ['deɪtə] 1 npl dati mpl. 2 cpd: ~ bank n banca dei dati; ~ processing n elaborazione f dei dati.
date[1] [deɪt] 1 n (a) data; what's the ~ today? quanti ne abbiamo oggi?; ~ of birth data di nascita; closing ~ scadenza, termine m; to ~ fino a oggi; to be up to ~ (person, document, information) essere aggiornato; (person: fashionable) essere alla moda; (: with one's work) essere nei termini; (building) moderno; to bring up to ~ (correspondence, information) aggiornare; (method) modernizzare; to bring sb up to ~ aggiornare qn, mettere qn al corrente; to be out of ~ (information) non essere aggiornato; (document) essere scaduto; (person, style) essere fuori moda. (b) (fam: appointment) appuntamento; (: girlfriend, boyfriend) ragazzo/a; to make a ~ with sb fissare un appuntamento con qn; he asked her for a ~ le ha chiesto di uscire con lui.
2 vt (a) (letter) datare; (ruin, manuscript etc) attribuire una data a, datare; thank you for your letter ~d 5th July la ringrazio per la sua lettera in data 5 luglio; his style of dress ~s him il suo abbigliamento tradisce la sua età. (b) (fam: girl etc) uscire con.
3 vi (a): to ~ from risalire a. (b) (become old-fashioned) passare di moda.
4 cpd: ~ stamp n (on library book) timbro datario; (on fresh food) scadenza; (postmark) timbro.
date[2] [deɪt] n dattero; (also: ~ palm) palma da dattero.
dat·ed ['deɪtɪd] adj antiquato(a), fuori moda.
date-line ['deɪtlaɪn] n linea del cambiamento di data.
daub [dɔːb] vt: to ~ (with) imbrattare (di).
daugh·ter ['dɔːtəʳ] n figlia.
daughter-in-law ['dɔːtərɪnlɔː] n nuora.
daunt [dɔːnt] vt atterrire, scoraggiare; **nothing**

~ed... per nulla scoraggiato.... .

daunt·ing ['dɔ:ntɪŋ] *adj* non invidiabile.

daunt·less ['dɔ:ntlɪs] *adj* impavido(a).

daw·dle ['dɔ:dl] *vi (in walking)* ciondolare, bighellonare; **to ~ over one's work** gingillarsi con il lavoro.

dawn [dɔ:n] **1** *n* alba; *(fig: also:* **~ing**: *of civilization)* albori *mpl;* **at ~** all'alba; **from ~ to dusk** dall'alba al tramonto; **the ~ of a new age** lo schiudersi di una nuova era. **2** *vi (day)* spuntare. **3** *cpd:* **~ chorus** *n* coro mattutino degli uccelli.

♦ **dawn (up)on** *vi + prep:* **the truth gradually ~ed on us** poco a poco cominciammo a vederci chiaro; **the idea ~ed upon me that...** mi è balenata nella mente l'idea che...; **it suddenly ~ed on him that...** improvvisamente gli è venuto in mente che... .

day [deɪ] **1** *n* **(a)** *(24 hours)* giorno; **what ~ is it today?** che giorno è oggi?; **2** **~s ago** 2 giorni fa; **one ~** un giorno; **(on) the ~ that...** il giorno che *or* in cui...; **(on) that ~** quel giorno; **the ~ before yesterday** l'altroieri; **the ~ before his birthday** la vigilia del suo compleanno; **the ~ after, the following ~** il giorno dopo, il giorno seguente; **the ~ after tomorrow** dopodomani; **this ~ week** oggi a otto; **her mother died 3 years ago to the ~** oggi sono 3 anni che è morta sua madre; **he works 8 hours a ~** lavora 8 ore al giorno; **any ~ now** da un giorno all'altro; **every ~** ogni giorno; **every other ~** un giorno sì e uno no, ogni due giorni; **twice a ~** due volte al giorno; **one of these ~s** uno di questi giorni, un giorno o l'altro; **the other ~** l'altro giorno; **from one ~ to the next** da un giorno all'altro; **~ after ~, ~ in ~ out** un giorno dopo l'altro, tutti i santi giorni; **for ~s on end** per giorni e giorni; **~ by ~** giorno per giorno; **to live from ~ to ~** *or* **from one ~ to the next** vivere alla giornata; **it made my ~ to see him smile** *(fam)* mi ha fatto veramente felice vederlo sorridere; **he's fifty if he's a ~** *(fam)* ha cinquant'anni suonati; **that'll be the ~, when he offers to pay!** *(fam)* figuriamoci se offre di pagare!

(b) *(daylight hours)* giorno, giornata; *(working hours)* giornata; **to travel by ~** *or* **during the ~** viaggiare di giorno *or* durante il giorno; **to work all ~** lavorare tutto il giorno; **to work ~ and night** lavorare giorno e notte; **it's a fine ~** è una bella giornata; **to arrive on a fine/wet ~** arrivare col bel tempo/con la pioggia; **one summer's ~** un giorno d'estate; **a ~ off** un giorno libero; **to work an 8-hour ~** avere una giornata lavorativa di 8 ore; **it's all in a ~'s work** fa parte del mestiere; **paid by the ~** pagato a giornata; **to work ~s** fare il turno di giorno.

(c) *(period)* tempo, tempi *mpl,* epoca; **in this ~ and age** ai nostri tempi; **these ~s, in the present ~** di questi tempi, oggigiorno; **to this ~...** ancor oggi...; **in ~s to come** in futuro; **in those ~s a** quei tempi, a quell'epoca; **in the ~s when...** all'epoca in cui...; **in Queen Victoria's ~** ai tempi della Regina Vittoria; **he was famous in his ~** ai suoi tempi era famoso; **in his younger ~s** quand'era (più) giovane; **in the good old ~s** ai bei tempi; **the happiest ~s of your life** il periodo più felice della propria vita; **during the early ~s of the strike** nelle prime fasi dello sciopero; **it's had its ~** ha fatto il suo tempo.

2 *cpd:* **~ boy/girl** *n (Scol)* alunno(a) esterno(a); **~ nursery** *n* giardino d'infanzia; **~ release course** *n* corso di formazione professionale *(che si svolge durante un normale giorno lavorativo);* **~ return (ticket)** *n* biglietto giorna-

liero di andata e ritorno; **to go to ~ school** frequentare una scuola da esterno(a); **~ shift** *n* turno di giorno; **to be on ~ shift** fare il turno di giorno; **~ trip** *n* gita (di un giorno); **~ tripper** *n* gitante *m/f.*

day·break ['deɪbreɪk] *n:* **at ~** allo spuntar del giorno, all'alba.

day·dream ['deɪdri:m] **1** *n* sogno (ad occhi aperti). **2** *vi* sognare (ad occhi aperti).

day·light ['deɪlaɪt] **1** *n* luce *f* (del giorno); **at ~** *(dawn)* alle prime luci, all'alba; **in the ~, by ~** alla luce del giorno; **I am beginning to see ~** *(fig: understand)* ora comincio a vederci chiaro; *(: near the end of a job)* comincio a vedere uno spiraglio di luce. **2** *cpd:* **~ attack** *n* attacco di giorno; **~ hours** *npl* ore *fpl* diurne *or* del giorno; **it's ~ robbery!** *(fam)* è un furto!; **~-saving time** *n (Am)* ora legale.

day·time ['deɪtaɪm] **1** *n* giorno; **in the ~** di giorno. **2** *cpd* di giorno.

day-to-day ['deɪtə,deɪ] *adj (routine)* quotidiano(a); *(expenses)* giornaliero(a); **on a ~ basis** a giornata.

daze [deɪz] **1** *n:* **in a ~** stordito(a). **2** *vt* stordire.

daz·zle ['dæzl] *vt* abbagliare.

daz·zling ['dæzlɪŋ] *adj (light)* abbagliante; *(colour)* violento(a); *(smile)* smagliante.

D-day ['di:,deɪ] *n* giorno dello sbarco alleato in Normandia.

DDT *n abbr* D.D.T. *m.*

dea·con ['di:kən] *n* diacono.

dead [ded] **1** *adj* **(a)** *(person, animal, plant)* morto(a); *(matter)* inanimato(a); *(fingers)* intorpidito(a); **to fall** *or* **drop (down) ~** cadere *or* cascare morto; **he's been ~ for 2 years** è morto da due anni; **~ and buried** *(also fig)* morto e sepolto; **~ or alive** vivo o morto; **over my ~ body!** *(fam)* sono manco morto!; **I feel absolutely ~!** *(fig fam)* sono morto (di stanchezza)!

(b) *(volcano, cigarette)* spento(a); *(battery)* scarico(a); *(telephone line)* caduto(a); *(language, town, party)* morto(a); *(custom)* scomparso(a), estinto(a); **~ season** *(Tourism)* stagione *f* morta; **the line has gone ~** *(Telec)* è caduta la linea; **he was ~ to the world** *(fig)* era proprio partito.

(c) *(complete)* silence, calm) assoluto(a), totale; **to hit sth ~ centre** centrare qc in pieno; **to come to a ~ stop** fermarsi (del tutto); **it was a ~ heat** *(race etc)* è stata una vittoria a pari merito; **~ weight** peso morto; **to fall into a ~ faint** svenire; **it's a ~ loss** *(fam)* non vale niente.

2 *adv (completely):* **~ certain** assolutamente certo, sicurissimo; **he stopped ~** si è fermato di colpo; **~ ahead** sempre dritto; **it's ~ ahead of us** è proprio davanti a noi; **~ on time** in perfetto orario; **to land ~ on target** far centro; **~ slow** *(Aut)* a passo d'uomo; *(Naut)* avanti piano; **to be ~ set on doing sth** volere fare qc a tutti i costi; **to be ~ set against sth** *(fam)* essere assolutamente contrario a qc; **~ beat** *(fam)* sfinito; **~ broke** *(fam)* senza il becco di un quattrino; **~ drunk** *(fam)* ubriaco fradicio; **~ tired** *(fam)* stanco morto.

3 *n* **(a): the ~** *npl* i morti.

(b): at ~ of night nel cuore della notte; **in the ~ of winter** nel cuore dell'inverno.

4 *cpd:* **~ end 1** *n (also fig)* vicolo cieco; **2** *adj:* **a ~-end job** un lavoro senza sbocchi; **D~ Sea** *n* Mar *m* Morto.

dead·en ['dedn] *vt (noise, pain, blow)* attutire; *(nerve)* rendere insensibile.

dead·line ['dedlaɪn] *n* termine *m* (di consegna), scadenza; **to work to a ~** avere una scadenza.

dead·lock ['dɛdlɒk] n punto morto, impasse f inv.

dead·ly ['dɛdlɪ] **1** adj (-ier, -iest) (gen) mortale; (weapon, poison, aim) micidiale; (disease) letale; **they are ~ enemies** sono nemici mortali; **the seven ~ sins** i sette peccati capitali; **he is in ~ earnest** fa (or parla) sul serio, non scherza; **this book is ~** (fam: very boring) questo libro è un mattone. **2** adv: **~ dull** di una noia micidiale; **~ pale** mortalmente pallido.

dead·pan ['dɛd,pæn] adj (face) impassibile; (humour) all'inglese.

deaf [dɛf] **1** adj (-er, -est) sordo(a); **~ in one ear** sordo da un orecchio; **to be ~ to sth** non sentire qc; (fig) restare sordo a qc; **to turn a ~ ear to sth** fare orecchi da mercante a qc; **as ~ as a (door)post** sordo come una campana. **2** npl: **the ~** i sordi.

deaf-aid ['dɛfeɪd] n apparecchio acustico.

deaf-and-dumb ['dɛfən'dʌm] adj (person) sordomuto(a); (alphabet) dei sordomuti.

deaf·en ['dɛfn] vt assordare.

deaf·en·ing ['dɛfnɪŋ] adj assordante.

deaf-mute ['dɛfmjuːt] n sordomuto/a.

deaf·ness ['dɛfnɪs] n sordità.

deal[1] [diːl] n legno di pino (or di abete).

deal[2] [diːl] (vb: pt, pp **dealt**) **1** n **(a)** (agreement) accordo; **business ~** affare m; **to do a ~ with sb** fare un affare con qn; **perhaps we can do a ~?** forse ci si può aggiustare fra di noi?; **it's a ~!** (fam) affare fatto!; **a new ~** (Pol etc) un piano di riforme; **he got a bad/fair ~ from them** l'hanno trattato male/bene; **a fair ~ for working mothers** un trattamento equo per le madri che lavorano.

(b) (Cards) turno (nel dare le carte); **it's my ~ this time** adesso tocca a me dare le carte.

(c) (in expressions of quantity): **a good ~**, **a great ~** molto, parecchio; **to have a great ~ to do** avere molto da fare; **a great** or **good ~ of** una buona quantità or parte di; **that's saying a good ~** non è dire poco; **a great ~ cleverer** di gran lunga più intelligente; **he thinks a great ~ of his father** ha una grande stima di suo padre; **it means a great ~ to me** vuol dire molto per me; **there's a good ~ of truth in it** c'è molto di vero. **2** vt **(a)**: **to ~ sb a blow** assestare un colpo a qn.

(b) (Cards: also: **~ out**) distribuire, dare.

♦ **deal in** vi + prep (Comm) occuparsi di.

♦ **deal out** vt + adv (cards, money) distribuire; **to ~ out justice** far giustizia.

♦ **deal with** vi + prep **(a)** (Comm) trattare con, fare affari con. **(b)** (handle: person, task) occuparsi di; (: problem) affrontare; (: Comm: application) sbrigare; (: order) completare; **I'll ~ with you later!** con te facciamo i conti più tardi!; **to know how to ~ with sb** saper come prendere qn; **he's not easy to ~ with** è un tipo difficile. **(c)** (subj: book, film etc: be about) trattare di.

deal·er ['diːləʳ] n **(a)** (Comm): **~ (in)** commerciante m/f (di); **an antique ~** un antiquario. **(b)** (Cards) chi fa or dà le carte.

deal·ings ['diːlɪŋz] npl **(a)** (relationship) rapporti mpl; **to have ~ with sb** avere a che fare con qn. **(b)** (Comm, Stock Exchange) rapporti mpl d'affari; (in goods, shares) transazioni fpl.

dean [diːn] n (of college, university) preside m, (Rel) decano.

dear·[1] [dɪəʳ] **1** adj (-er, -est) **(a)** (loved, lovable) caro(a); **I hold it very ~** mi è molto caro; **my ~est wish** il mio più ardente desiderio; **what a ~ little boy!** che amore di bambino!; **a ~ little cottage** una casetta deliziosa. **(b)** (in letter writing): **D~**

Daddy/Peter caro papà/Peter; **D~ Sir** Egregio Signore; **D~ Mr/Mrs Smith** Gentile Signor/Signora Smith; **D~ Mr and Mrs Smith** Gentili Signori Smith. **(c)** (expensive) caro(a). **2** excl: **oh ~!** oh Dio!, mamma mia!; **~ me!** Dio mio! **3** n: **(my) ~** (mio(a)) caro(a); **my ~est** amor mio; **(you) poor ~!** poverino!; **he's a ~** (fam) è un tesoro; **post this letter for me, there's a ~** (fam) sii gentile, imbucami questa lettera. **4** adv caro; **he bought his freedom ~** la sua libertà gli è costata cara.

dear·ly ['dɪəlɪ] adv: **to love sb/sth ~** amare qn/qc teneramente; **I should ~ love to go there** mi piacerebbe infinitamente andarci; **to pay ~ for sth** (esp fig) pagar caro or a caro prezzo qc.

dearth [dɜːθ] n (of food, resources, money) scarsità, penuria; (of ideas) mancanza.

death [dɛθ] **1** n morte f; (Med, Law) decesso; (of plans, hopes) naufragio; **to be burnt to ~** morire carbonizzato; **to drink o.s. to ~** uccidersi a forza di bere; **to sentence sb to ~** condannare a morte qn; **to put sb to ~** mettere a morte qn, giustiziare qn; **a fight to the ~** un duello all'ultimo sangue; **to be at ~'s door** essere in punto di morte; **it will be the ~ of him** sarà la sua rovina; **you'll be the ~ of me** (fig) mi farai morire; **bored to ~** (fam) annoiato a morte; **I'm sick** or **tired of ~ of it** (fam) ne ho fin sopra i capelli. **2** cpd: **~ certificate** n certificato di morte; **~ duties** npl tassa di successione; **~ penalty** n pena di morte; **~ rate** n (indice m di) mortalità; **~ sentence** n condanna a morte; **~ wish** n desiderio di morte.

death·bed ['dɛθbɛd] **1** n letto di morte. **2** cpd (confession) in punto di morte.

death·blow ['dɛθbləʊ] n colpo di grazia.

death·ly ['dɛθlɪ] **1** adj (-ier, -iest) (pallor) mortale; (appearance) cadaverico(a); (silence) di morte. **2** adv: **~ pale** pallido/a come un cadavere.

death-trap ['dɛθtræp] n trappola mortale.

de·bar [dɪ'bɑːʳ] vt: **to ~ sb from sth** escludere qn da qc; **to ~ sb from doing sth** vietare a qn di fare qc.

de·base [dɪ'beɪs] vt (coinage) svilire; (person, relationship, word) degradare, svilire.

de·bat·able [dɪ'beɪtəbl] adj discutibile; **it is ~ whether...** è in dubbio se... .

de·bate [dɪ'beɪt] **1** vt discutere, dibattere; **we ~d whether to go or not** eravamo in dubbio se andare o no. **2** vi: **to ~ (with sb about sth)** discutere (con qn su qc); **to ~ with o.s. (about, (up)on sth)** essere in dubbio (su qc). **3** n dibattito, discussione f; **after much ~** dopo lunga discussione.

de·bat·ing so·ci·ety [dɪ'beɪtɪŋ sə'saɪətɪ] n (Scol, Univ) circolo che organizza dibattiti con votazione finale.

de·bauch [dɪ'bɔːtʃ] vt corrompere.

de·bauched [dɪ'bɔːtʃt] adj (taste, morals) dissoluto(a), vizioso(a); (person) debosciato(a).

de·bauch·ery [dɪ'bɔːtʃərɪ] n dissolutezza.

de·ben·ture [dɪ'bɛntʃəʳ] n (Fin) obbligazione f.

de·bil·i·tate [dɪ'bɪlɪteɪt] vt debilitare.

deb·it ['dɛbɪt] **1** n addebito. **2** vt: **to ~ sb/sb's account with a sum** addebitare una somma a qn/sul conto di qn. **3** cpd: **~ side** n colonna del dare; (fig): **on the ~ side is the fact that...** il lato negativo è che... .

de·bo·nair [,dɛbə'nɛəʳ] adj gioviale e disinvolto(a).

de·brief [,diː'briːf] vt chiamare a rapporto (a operazione ultimata).

de·bris ['dɛbriː] n detriti mpl.

debt [dɛt] **1** n debito; **~s of £5000** debiti per 5000 sterline; **bad ~** debito insoluto; **a ~ of honour/ gratitude** un debito d'onore/di gratitudine or di riconoscenza; **to be in** ~ **(to sb)** avere debiti (con qn); **I am £5 in** ~ sono in debito di 5 sterline; **to be in sb's** ~ *(fig)* essere in debito verso qn; **to get into** ~ far debiti, indebitarsi; **to be out of** ~ essere libero da debiti. **2** *cpd:* ~ **collector** *n* agente *m* di recupero crediti.

debt·or ['dɛtə^r] *n* debitore/trice.

de·bunk [‚diː'bʌŋk] *vt (fam: theory)* demistificare; *(: claim)* smentire; *(: person, institution)* screditare.

de·but ['deɪbjuː] *n* debutto; **to make one's** ~ debuttare, fare il proprio debutto; **to make one's stage/film** ~ debuttare sulle scene/sullo schermo.

dec·ade ['dɛkeɪd] *n* decennio.

deca·dence ['dɛkədəns] *n* decadenza.

deca·dent ['dɛkədənt] *adj* decadente.

de·camp [dɪ'kæmp] *vi (fam)* filarsela, levare le tende.

de·cant [dɪ'kænt] *vt (wine)* travasare.

de·cant·er [dɪ'kæntə^r] *n* bottiglia (di cristallo) *(per liquori o vini)*.

de·capi·tate [dɪ'kæpɪteɪt] *vt* decapitare.

de·cay [dɪ'keɪ] **1** *vi (vegetation)* decomporsi, putrefarsi; *(food)* deteriorarsi, andare a male; *(teeth)* cariarsi; *(building, urban area)* andare in rovina; *(fig: civilization)* decadere; *(: one's faculties)* deteriorarsi. **2** *n (see vb)* decomposizione *f*, putrefazione *f*; deterioramento; carie *f*; decadenza; *(of building, urban area)* stato di abbandono.

de·cease [dɪ'siːs] *n* decesso.

de·ceased [dɪ'siːst] **1** *adj* deceduto(a). **2** *n:* **the** ~ il(la) defunto(a).

de·ceit [dɪ'siːt] *n (quality)* disonestà; *(action)* inganno, truffa.

de·ceit·ful [dɪ'siːtfʊl] *adj (person)* falso(a), disonesto(a); *(words, behaviour)* menzognero(a), ingannatore(trice).

de·ceive [dɪ'siːv] *vt* ingannare; **she** ~**d me into thinking that...** mi ha ingannato facendomi credere che...; **unless my eyes are deceiving me** se gli occhi non m'ingannano; **don't be** ~**d by appearances** non ti fare ingannare dalle apparenze; **to** ~ **o.s.** illudersi, ingannarsi.

de·cel·er·ate [diː'sɛləreɪt] *vt* decelerare.

De·cem·ber [dɪ'sɛmbə^r] *n* dicembre *m; for usage see* **July.**

de·cen·cy ['diːsənsɪ] *n (propriety)* decenza, decoro; **he has no sense of** ~ non ha un minimo di pudore; **to have the** ~ **to do sth** avere la decenza di fare qc; **out of common** ~ per gentilezza se non altro.

de·cent ['diːsənt] *adj* **(a)** *(respectable: person, house)* per bene, ammodo *inv; (proper: clothes, behaviour, language)* decente. **(b)** *(kind)* gentile, bravo(a); **he was very** ~ **to me** si è comportato bene verso di me. **(c)** *(satisfactory: meal, house etc)* decente, discreto(a).

de·cent·ly ['diːsəntlɪ] *adv (respectably)* decentemente, convenientemente; *(kindly)* gentilmente.

de·cen·trali·za·tion [diː‚sɛntrəlaɪ'zeɪʃən] *n* decentramento.

de·cen·tral·ize [diː'sɛntrəlaɪz] *vt* decentrare.

de·cep·tion [dɪ'sɛpʃən] *n* inganno; **to practise** ~ **on sb** raggirare qn.

de·cep·tive [dɪ'sɛptɪv] *adj (liable to deceive)* ingannevole; *(meant to deceive)* ingannatore(trice).

de·cep·tive·ly [dɪ'sɛptɪvlɪ] *adv:* ~ **simple** *etc* (solo) apparentemente facile *etc*.

deci·bel ['dɛsɪbɛl] *n* decibel *m inv*.

de·cide [dɪ'saɪd] **1** *vt* decidere; **that** ~**d me** è stata la cosa che mi ha fatto decidere; **to** ~ **to do sth**

decidere di fare qc, decidersi a fare qc. **2** *vi* decidere; **to** ~ **for** *or* **in favour of sb** decidere a favore di qn; **to** ~ **on/against sth** optare per/contro qc; **to** ~ **on doing sth** decidere di fare qc; **to** ~ **against doing sth** decidere di non fare qc.

de·cid·ed [dɪ'saɪdɪd] *adj (person, tone, improvement)* deciso(a); *(opinion)* chiaro(a), preciso(a).

de·cid·ed·ly [dɪ'saɪdɪdlɪ] *adv* decisamente.

de·cid·ing [dɪ'saɪdɪŋ] *adj* decisivo(a).

de·cidu·ous [dɪ'sɪdjʊəs] *adj* deciduo(a).

deci·mal ['dɛsɪməl] **1** *adj* decimale; ~ **point** virgola *(in un numero decimale)*; **to 3** ~ **places** al terzo decimale. **2** *n* (numero) decimale *m*.

deci·mal·ize ['dɛsɪmǝlaɪz] *vt* convertire al sistema metrico decimale.

deci·mate ['dɛsɪmeɪt] *vt (also fig)* decimare.

de·ci·pher [dɪ'saɪfə^r] *vt* decifrare.

de·ci·sion [dɪ'sɪʒən] *n* decisione *f*; **to make a** ~ prendere una decisione.

de·ci·sive [dɪ'saɪsɪv] *adj (victory, factor)* decisivo(a); *(influence)* determinante; *(manner, person)* risoluto(a), deciso(a); *(reply)* deciso(a), categorico(a).

deck [dɛk] **1** *n* **(a)** *(Naut)* (ponte *m* di) coperta; **to go up on** ~ salire in coperta; **below** ~ sotto coperta. **(b)** *(of bus):* **top** *or* **upper** ~ piano di sopra; **bottom** *or* **lower** ~ piano di sotto. **(c)** *(of cards)* mazzo. **(d)** *(of record player)* piatto; **cassette** ~ piastra (di registrazione). **2** *vt (also:* ~ **out):** **to** ~ **(with)** decorare (di).

deck·chair ['dɛktʃɛə^r] *n* sedia a sdraio.

de·claim [dɪ'kleɪm] *vi* declamare.

dec·la·ma·tion [‚dɛklə'meɪʃən] *n* declamazione *f*.

dec·la·ra·tion [‚dɛklə'reɪʃən] *n* dichiarazione *f*.

de·clare [dɪ'klɛə^r] *vt (gen)* dichiarare; *(results)* annunciare; **have you anything to** ~? *(Customs)* ha niente da dichiarare?; **to** ~ **that** dichiarare che; **he** ~**ed that he was innocent** ha dichiarato di essere innocente, si è dichiarato innocente; **to** ~ **war (on** *or* **against sb)** dichiarare (la) guerra (a qn).

de·clas·si·fy [diː'klæsɪfaɪ] *vt* rendere accessibile al pubblico.

de·clen·sion [dɪ'klɛnʃən] *n (Gram)* declinazione *f*.

de·cline [dɪ'klaɪn] **1** *n (decrease):* ~ **(in)** calo (di); *(deterioration)* declino; ~ **in living standards** abbassamento del tenore di vita; **to be on the** ~ *(gen)* essere in diminuzione; *(prices)* essere in ribasso. **2** *vt* **(a)** *(refuse: invitation)* declinare; **to** ~ **to do sth** rifiutar(si) di fare qc. **(b)** *(Gram)* declinare. **3** *vi* **(a)** *(power, influence)* diminuire, declinare; *(empire)* decadere; *(health)* deteriorare; **in his declining years** sul declinare degli anni; **to** ~ **in importance** diminuire d'importanza. **(b)** *(Gram)* declinarsi.

de·clutch ['diː'klʌtʃ] *vi* premere la frizione.

de·code [‚diː'kəʊd] *vt* decodificare.

de·com·pose [‚diːkəm'pəʊz] **1** *vt* decomporre. **2** *vi* decomporsi.

de·com·po·si·tion [‚diːkɒmpə'zɪʃən] *n* decomposizione *f*.

de·com·pres·sion [‚diːkəm'prɛʃən] **1** *n* decompressione *f*. **2** *cpd:* ~ **chamber** *n* camera di decompressione.

de·con·gest·ant [‚diːkən'dʒɛstənt] *n* decongestionante *m*.

de·con·tami·nate [‚diːkən'tæmɪneɪt] *vt* decontaminare.

de·con·trol [‚diːkən'trəʊl] *vt (trade)* liberalizzare; *(prices)* togliere il controllo governativo a.

dé·cor ['deɪkɔː^r] *n* arredamento.

deco·rate ['dɛkəreɪt] *vt* **(a):** **to** ~ **(with)** *(adorn)* decorare (di *or* con). **(b)** *(paint: room, house)* pitturare (e tappezzare). **(c)** *(honour: soldier)* decorare.

deco·rat·ing ['dɛkəreɪtɪŋ] *n* decorazione *f;* **they are doing some** ~ stanno ripitturando.

deco·ra·tion [,dɛkə'reɪʃən] *n* decorazione *f.*

deco·ra·tive ['dɛkərətɪv] *adj* decorativo(a).

deco·ra·tor ['dɛkəreɪtəʳ] *n* decoratore/trice.

deco·rous ['dɛkərəs] *adj* decoroso(a).

de·co·rum [dɪ'kɔ:rəm] *n* decoro; **out of a sense of** ~ per rispetto alle convenienze; **a breach of** ~ una sconvenienza.

de·coy ['di:kɔɪ] *n (bird)* (uccello da) richiamo; *(fig: bait: thing)* tranello; *(: person)* esca; **police** ~ poliziotto in borghese *(usato come esca).*

de·crease ['di:kri:s] **1** *n:* ~ **(in)** *(amount, numbers, population, power)* diminuzione *f* (di); *(birth rate, value, production, enthusiasm)* calo (di); *(prices)* ribasso (di); *(strength, dose)* riduzione *f* (di); **to be on the** ~ essere in diminuzione. **2** [di:'kri:s] *vt (see n)* diminuire; far calare; ribassare; ridurre. **3** [di:'kri:s] *vi (see n)* diminuire; calare *(also prices); (Knitting)* calare (le maglie); **to** ~ **by 10%** diminuire del 10%.

de·creas·ing [di:'kri:sɪŋ] *adj* sempre meno *inv.*

de·cree [dɪ'kri:] **1** *n (Law etc)* decreto; *(municipal)* ordinanza; ~ **absolute/nisi** *(of divorce)* sentenza di divorzio definitiva/interlocutoria. **2** *vt:* **to** ~ **(that)** decretare (che + *sub).*

de·crep·it [dɪ'krɛpɪt] *adj (building)* cadente; *(person)* decrepito(a).

de·cry [dɪ'kraɪ] *vt* condannare, deplorare.

dedi·cate ['dɛdɪkeɪt] *vt (gen)* dedicare; **to** ~ **one's life** *or* **o.s. to sth/to doing sth** dedicare la propria esistenza a qc/a fare qc.

dedi·cat·ed ['dɛdɪkeɪtɪd] *adj* coscienzioso(a); *(Computers)* specializzato(a).

dedi·ca·tion [,dɛdɪ'keɪʃən] *n (in book)* dedica; *(devotion)* dedizione *f.*

de·duce [dɪ'dju:s] *vt:* **to** ~ **sth from sth/that** dedurre qc da qc/che.

de·duct [dɪ'dʌkt] *vt:* **to** ~ **(from)** *(gen)* dedurre (da); *(from wages)* trattenere (su); *(from price)* fare una riduzione (su); *(Scol: marks)* togliere (da).

de·duct·ible [dɪ'dʌktəbl] *adj* deducibile.

de·duc·tion [dɪ'dʌkʃən] *n* **(a)** *(act of deducing)* deduzione *f.* **(b)** *(act of deducting, amount deducted)* detrazione *f; (from wages)* trattenuta.

deed [di:d] *n* **(a)** azione *f,* atto; **brave** ~ impresa; **good** ~ buona azione; **in** ~ di fatto. **(b)** *(Law)* atto *(notarile);* ~ **of covenant** atto di donazione; **by** ~ **poll** con atto unilaterale.

deem [di:m] *vt (frm)* giudicare, ritenere; **to** ~ **it wise to do** ritenere prudente fare.

deep [di:p] **1** *adj* **(-er, -est) (a)** *(water, hole, wound)* profondo(a); *(snow)* alto(a); **the lake was 16 metres** ~ il lago era profondo 16 metri; **we were ankle-~/knee-~ in mud** il fango ci arrivava alle caviglie/ai ginocchi; **to be in** ~ **water** *(fig)* navigare in cattive acque; **the** ~ **end** *(of swimming pool)* la parte più profonda; **to be thrown in (at) the** ~ **end** *(fig fam)* avere il battesimo del fuoco; **to go off (at) the** ~ **end** *(fig fam: excited)* lanciarsi, buttarsi; *(: angry)* partire per la tangente.

(b) *(shelf, cupboard)* profondo(a); *(border, hem)* lungo(a); **these kitchen units are 30 cm** ~ questi mobili da cucina hanno una profondità di 30 cm.

(c) *(voice, note, sigh)* profondo(a); ~ **breathing exercises** esercizi *mpl* respiratori.

(d) *(feeling, sleep, writer, insight)* profondo(a); *(colour)* intenso(a), cupo(a); *(relief)* immenso(a); *(interest, concern)* vivo(a); **to be** ~ **in thought/**~

in a book essere immerso nei propri pensieri/ sprofondato in un libro.

2 *adv:* ~ **in her heart** in fondo al cuore; **the spectators were standing 6** ~ c'erano 6 file di spettatori in piedi; **don't go in too** ~ **if you can't swim** non andare dove non si tocca se non sai nuotare; **to dig** ~ scavare in profondità; ~ **in the forest** nel cuore della foresta; ~ **into the night** fino a tarda notte.

3 *n:* **the** ~ gli abissi marini.

deep·en ['di:pən] **1** *vt (hole, knowledge, understanding)* approfondire; *(sound, friendship, love)* rendere più profondo(a); *(colour)* scurire; *(interest)* ravvivare; *(sorrow)* aggravare. **2** *vi (gen)* diventare più profondo(a); *(colour)* diventare più intenso(a); *(mystery)* infittirsi.

deep·freeze [,di:p'fri:z] *n* congelatore *m.*

deep·fry [,di:p'fraɪ] *vt* friggere in olio abbondante.

deep·ly ['di:plɪ] *adv (breathe)* profondamente; *(dig)* in profondità; *(drink)* a gran sorsi; *(interested, concerned)* vivamente; *(moving)* estremamente; *(grateful, offended)* profondamente; **to regret sth** ~ rammaricarsi sinceramente di qc; **to go** ~ **into sth** approfondire qc.

deep·rooted [,di:p'ru:tɪd] *adj (prejudice)* profondamente radicato(a); *(affection)* profondo(a); *(habit)* inveterato(a).

deep·sea [,di:p'si:] *adj (creatures, plants)* pelagico(a), abissale; *(fisherman, fishing)* d'alto mare; ~ **diver** palombaro; ~ **diving** immersione *f* a grandi profondità.

deep·seated [,di:p'si:tɪd] *adj* radicato(a).

deep·set ['di:p,sɛt] *adj:* ~ **eyes** occhi *mpl* infossati.

deer [dɪəʳ] *n, pl inv* cervo/a; *(red* ~) cervo; *(roe* ~) capriolo; *(fallow* ~) daino; **the** ~ **family** la famiglia dei cervidi.

deer·skin ['dɪəskɪn] *n* pelle *f* di daino.

deer·stalker ['dɪə,stɔ:kəʳ] *n* berretto da cacciatore.

deer·stalking ['dɪə,stɔ:kɪŋ] *n* caccia al cervo a piedi.

de·face [dɪ'feɪs] *vt (wall, monument, countryside)* deturpare; *(work of art)* sfregiare; *(: statue)* mutilare; *(poster)* imbrattare.

defa·ma·tion [,dɛfə'meɪʃən] *n* diffamazione *f.*

de·fama·tory [dɪ'fæmətərɪ] *adj* diffamatorio(a).

de·fame [dɪ'feɪm] *vt* diffamare.

de·fault [dɪ'fɔ:lt] **1** *n:* **in** ~ **of** in mancanza di, per difetto di; **by** ~ *(Law)* in contumacia; *(Sport)* per abbandono dell'avversario. **2** *vi (Law: not appear)* non presentarsi in giudizio; *(: not pay)* risultare inadempiente; **to** ~ **on a debt** non onorare un debito.

de·feat [dɪ'fi:t] **1** *n (of army, team)* sconfitta; *(: more serious)* disfatta; *(of ambition, plan)* fallimento, insuccesso. **2** *vt (army, team, opponent)* sconfiggere, battere; *(plan, ambition, efforts)* frustrare; *(Pol: party)* sconfiggere; *(: bill, amendment)* respingere; **to** ~ **one's own ends** darsi la zappa sui piedi.

de·feat·ism [dɪ'fi:tɪzəm] *n* disfattismo.

de·feat·ist [dɪ'fi:tɪst] *n, adj* disfattista *(m/f).*

def·ecate ['dɛfəkeɪt] *vi (frm)* defecare.

de·fect ['di:fɛkt] **1** *n (gen)* difetto; **physical** ~ difetto fisico; **mental** ~ anomalia mentale; **moral** ~ difetto. **2** [dɪ'fɛkt] *vi (from political party)* defezionare; **to** ~ **from one country to another** fuggire da un paese a un altro per ragioni politiche.

de·fec·tion [dɪ'fɛkʃən] *n (see vi)* defezione *f;* fuga.

de·fec·tive [dɪ'fɛktɪv] *adj (machine, workmanship, eyesight)* difettoso(a); *(system, reasoning)* cattivo(a); *(Gram)* difettivo(a); **to be ~ in sth** mancare di qc.

de·fec·tor [dɪˈfɛktəʳ] *n* rifugiato(a) politico(a).

de·fence, *(Am)* **de·fense** [dɪˈfɛns] **1** *n* difesa; **in ~ of** in difesa di; **the Ministry of D~** il Ministero della Difesa; **in his ~** in sua difesa; **the case for the ~** la difesa; **witness for the ~** teste *m/f* a difesa; **the body's ~s against disease** le difese naturali dell'organismo contro la malattia; **as a ~ against** per ripararsi da. **2** *cpd (policy, strategy, mechanism)* di difesa; **~ spending** *n* spese *fpl* per gli armamenti a scopo difensivo.

de·fence·less [dɪˈfɛnslɪs] *adj* inerme, indifeso(a).

de·fend [dɪˈfɛnd] *vt (gen)* difendere; *(decision, action)* giustificare; *(opinion)* sostenere; **to ~ o.s. (against)** difendersi (da).

de·fend·ant [dɪˈfɛndənt] *n (Law)* imputato/a.

de·fend·ing [dɪˈfɛndɪŋ] *adj:* **~ champion** *(Sport)* campione/essa in carica; **~ counsel** *(Law)* avvocato difensore.

de·fense [dɪˈfɛns] *n (Am)* = defence.

de·fen·sive [dɪˈfɛnsɪv] **1** *adj* difensivo(a); *(person)* sulla difensiva. **2** *n* difensiva; **on the ~** sulla difensiva.

de·fer [dɪˈfɜːʳ] **1** *vt (gen)* rimandare, rinviare; *(Law: case)* aggiornare. **2** *vi (submit):* **to ~ to sb/sth** rimettersi a qn/qc; **to ~ to sb's (greater) knowledge** rimettersi alla scienza di qn.

def·er·ence [ˈdɛfərəns] *n* deferenza; **out of** *or* **in ~ to** per riguardo a.

def·er·en·tial [ˌdɛfəˈrɛnʃəl] *adj* deferente.

de·fer·ment [dɪˈfɜːmənt] *n* rinvio, differimento.

de·fi·ance [dɪˈfaɪəns] *n* (atteggiamento di) sfida; **in ~ of** a dispetto di; **in ~ of orders/the law** sfidando gli ordini/la legge.

de·fi·ant [dɪˈfaɪənt] *adj (person)* ribelle; *(tone, attitude)* di sfida; *(reply)* insolente.

de·fi·cien·cy [dɪˈfɪʃənsɪ] *n* **(a)** *(of goods)* mancanza, insufficienza; *(of vitamins etc)* carenza; **~ of the heart/liver** insufficienza cardiaca/epatica. **(b)** *(in system, plan etc)* carenza. **(c)** *(Fin)* ammanco.

de·fi·cient [dɪˈfɪʃənt] *adj:* **to be ~ in sth** mancare di qc.

defi·cit [ˈdɛfɪsɪt] *n (Fin etc)* deficit *m inv*.

de·file¹ [diːˈfaɪl] *vt (pollute)* deturpare.

de·file² [ˈdiːfaɪl] *n (passage)* passo.

de·fine [dɪˈfaɪn] *vt (all senses)* definire, precisare; **the skyscraper was clearly ~d against the sky** il grattacielo si stagliava nettamente contro il cielo.

defi·nite [ˈdɛfɪnɪt] *adj* **(a)** *(exact, clear: date, plan, intention)* preciso(a); *(: answer, agreement)* definitivo(a); *(positive, decided: sale, order)* sicuro(a); *(: tone, manner)* deciso(a); **is it ~ that...?** è sicuro che...? **(b)** *(clearly noticeable)* netto(a). **(c)** *(Gram):* **~ article** articolo determinativo; **past ~ tense** passato remoto.

defi·nite·ly [ˈdɛfɪnɪtlɪ] *adv (certainly)* di sicuro, certamente; *(emphatically: state)* categoricamente; *(appreciably: better)* decisamente; **~!** assolutamente!

defi·ni·tion [ˌdɛfɪˈnɪʃən] *n (gen, Phot, TV)* definizione *f*.

de·fini·tive [dɪˈfɪnɪtɪv] *adj* definitivo(a).

de·flate [diːˈfleɪt] *vt (tyre etc)* sgonfiare; *(pompous person)* fare abbassare la cresta a; *(Econ)* deflazionare.

de·fla·tion [diːˈfleɪʃən] *n (Econ)* deflazione *f*.

de·fla·tion·ary [diːˈfleɪʃənərɪ] *adj (Econ)* deflazionistico(a).

de·flect [dɪˈflɛkt] *vt (ball, bullet)* (far) deviare; *(fig: person):* **to ~ (from)** distogliere (da).

de·form [dɪˈfɔːm] *vt* deformare.

de·formed [dɪˈfɔːmd] *adj (person, limb, body)* deforme; *(structure)* deformato(a).

de·form·ity [dɪˈfɔːmɪtɪ] *n (of body)* deformità *f inv*.

de·fraud [dɪˈfrɔːd] *vt:* **to ~ (of)** defraudare (di).

de·fray [dɪˈfreɪ] *vt (frm: expenses)* coprire.

de·frost [diːˈfrɒst] *vt (refrigerator)* sbrinare; *(frozen food)* scongelare.

deft [dɛft] *adj* **(-er, -est)** abile.

de·funct [dɪˈfʌŋkt] *adj (company etc)* scomparso(a); *(scheme)* morto(a) e sepolto(a).

de·fuse [diːˈfjuːz] *vt (bomb)* disinnescare; *(fig)* distendere.

defy [dɪˈfaɪ] *vt* **(a)** *(challenge):* **to ~ sb (to do sth)** sfidare qn (a fare qc). **(b)** *(refuse to obey: person)* rifiutare di obbedire a; *(: authority, death, danger)* sfidare; *(resist: efforts)* resistere a; **it defies description** supera ogni descrizione.

de·gen·er·ate [dɪˈdʒɛnərɪt] **1** *adj (person)* degenere; *(morals, art)* degenerato(a). **2** *n* degenerato/a. **3** [dɪˈdʒɛnəreɪt] *vi:* **to ~ (into)** degenerare (in).

deg·ra·da·tion [ˌdɛɡrəˈdeɪʃən] *n* degradazione *f*.

de·grade [dɪˈɡreɪd] *vt* degradare.

de·grad·ing [dɪˈɡreɪdɪŋ] *adj* degradante, umiliante.

de·gree [dɪˈɡriː] *n* **(a)** *(gen, Math, Geog)* grado; **10 ~s below freezing** 10 gradi sotto zero. **(b):** **a high ~ of uncertainty** un largo margine d'incertezza; **a considerable ~ of risk** una grossa percentuale di rischio; **by ~s** gradualmente, a poco a poco; **to some ~, to a certain ~** fino a un certo punto, in certa misura. **(c)** *(Univ)* laurea; **first ~** laurea; **honorary ~** laurea ad honorem; **I'm taking a ~ in languages** sono iscritto a lingue.

de·hy·drate [ˌdiːˈhaɪdreɪt] *vt* disidratare.

de·hy·dra·ted [diːhaɪˈdreɪtɪd] *adj (person, vegetables)* disidratato(a); *(milk, eggs)* in polvere.

de·hy·dra·tion [ˌdiːhaɪˈdreɪʃən] *n* disidratazione *f*.

de·icer [ˈdiːˈaɪsəʳ] *n* sbrinatore *m*.

deign [deɪn] *vt:* **to ~ to do sth** degnarsi di fare qc.

de·ity [ˈdiːɪtɪ] *n* divinità *f inv*.

de·ject·ed [dɪˈdʒɛktɪd] *adj* abbattuto(a).

de·jec·tion [dɪˈdʒɛkʃən] *n* abbattimento.

de·lay [dɪˈleɪ] **1** *n* ritardo; **~s to traffic** inconvenienti *mpl* sulle strade; **without (further) ~** senza (ulteriore) indugio. **2** *vt (postpone)* rimandare, rinviare; *(payment)* differire; *(hold up: person)* trattenere; *(: traffic)* far rallentare; *(: action, event)* ritardare; **his train must have been ~ed** il suo treno avrà fatto ritardo; **~ed-action bomb** ordigno a scoppio ritardato. **3** *vi:* **to ~ (in doing sth)** ritardare (a fare qc); **don't ~!** non perdere tempo!

de·lec·table [dɪˈlɛktəbl] *adj* delizioso(a).

del·egate [ˈdɛlɪɡɪt] **1** *n:* **~ (to)** delegato/a (a). **2** [ˈdɛlɪɡeɪt] *vt:* **to ~ sth to sb/sb to do sth** delegare qc a qn/qn a fare qc.

del·ega·tion [ˌdɛlɪˈɡeɪʃən] *n* **(a)** *(of work etc)* delega. **(b)** *(group)* delegazione *f*.

de·lete [dɪˈliːt] *vt:* **to ~ (from)** *(item: from list, catalogue)* togliere (da); *(mistake, line)* cancellare (da).

de·letion [dɪˈliːʃən] *n* soppressione *f*, eliminazione *f*; *(sth deleted)* elemento soppresso.

de·lib·er·ate [dɪˈlɪbərɪt] **1** *adj (intentional: insult, action)* deliberato(a), premeditato(a); *(: mistake)* voluto(a); *(: lie)* calcolato(a); *(cautious, thoughtful)* ponderato(a); *(unhurried: manner, voice)* posato(a). **2** [dɪˈlɪbəreɪt] *vt (think about)* considerare, riflettere su; *(discuss)* discutere su. **3** [dɪˈlɪbəreɪt] *vi:* **to ~ (on)** deliberare (su).

de·lib·er·ate·ly [dɪˈlɪbərɪtlɪ] *adv (intentionally)* deliberatamente, volutamente; *(cautiously, slowly)* posatamente.

de·lib·era·tion [dɪ,lɪbə'reɪʃən] n (a) (consideration) riflessione f; (discussion) discussione f, deliberazione f; **after due** ~ dopo matura riflessione. (b) (slowness) ponderatezza, posatezza.

deli·ca·cy ['delɪkəsɪ] n (a) (see adj) delicatezza; finezza. (b) (special food) ghiottoneria.

deli·cate ['delɪkɪt] adj (gen) delicato(a); (workmanship, design) fine.

deli·cate·ly ['delɪkɪtlɪ] adv (gen) delicatamente; (act, express) con delicatezza.

deli·ca·tes·sen [,delɪkə'tesn] n ≃ salumeria.

de·li·cious [dɪ'lɪʃəs] adj delizioso(a), squisito(a).

de·light [dɪ'laɪt] 1 n (feeling of joy) piacere m, gioia; (pleasurable thing) delizia, piacere; **the ~s of good food** i piaceri della buona tavola; **to my** ~ con mia grande gioia. 2 vt riempire di gioia.

♦**delight in** vi + prep: **to** ~ **in sth/in doing sth** dilettarsi di qc/nel fare qc.

de·light·ed [dɪ'laɪtɪd] adj: ~ **(at, with sth)** contentissimo(a) (di qc), felice (di qc); **to be** ~ **to do sth/that** essere felice di fare qc/che + sub; **I'd be** ~ **con grande piacere**.

de·light·ful [dɪ'laɪtfʊl] adj (person, place, meal) delizioso(a); (manner, smile) incantevole.

de·lim·it [diː'lɪmɪt] vt delimitare.

de·lin·eate [dɪ'lɪnɪeɪt] vt delineare.

de·lin·quen·cy [dɪ'lɪŋkwənsɪ] n delinquenza.

de·lin·quent [dɪ'lɪŋkwənt] 1 adj delinquenziale, da delinquente. 2 n delinquente m/f.

de·liri·ous [dɪ'lɪrɪəs] adj (Med, fig) delirante, in delirio; **to be** ~ delirare; (fig) farneticare; ~ **with joy** pazzo di gioia.

de·liri·ous·ly [dɪ'lɪrɪəslɪ] adv: ~ **happy** fuori di sé dalla gioia.

de·lir·ium [dɪ'lɪrɪəm] n delirio.

de·liv·er [dɪ'lɪvə'] vt (a) (goods, message) consegnare; (letter, parcel) recapitare, consegnare; **he ~ed me home safely** mi ha portato a casa sano e salvo; **he ~ed the goods** (fam) ha fatto quel che doveva fare. (b) (old use: rescue): **to** ~ **(from)** liberare (da). (c) (speech, sermon, verdict) pronunciare; (lecture) tenere, fare; (uitimatum) dare; (blow, punch) tirare. (d) (subj: doctor: baby) far venire al mondo, far partorire.

de·liv·er·ance [dɪ'lɪvərəns] n liberazione f.

de·liv·ery [dɪ'lɪvərɪ] 1 n (of goods, parcels) consegna; (of mail) recapito; (of speaker) dizione f; (Med) parto; **there is no** ~ **on Sundays** (Post) non c'è posta la domenica. 2 cpd: ~ **boy** n fattorino; ~ **note** n bolla di consegna; ~ **van** n furgoncino (per le consegne).

del·ta ['deltə] n delta m inv.

de·lude [dɪ'luːd] vt illudere, ingannare; **to** ~ **sb into thinking that...** far credere a qn che...; **to** ~ **o.s.** illudersi, farsi (delle) illusioni.

del·uge ['deljuːdʒ] 1 n diluvio; **a** ~ **of protests** un diluvio di proteste. 2 vt (fig): **to** ~ **(with)** subissare (di), inondare (di).

de·lu·sion [dɪ'luːʒən] n illusione f; (Psych) fissazione f.

de luxe [dɪ'lʌks] adj di lusso.

delve [delv] vi frugare.

dema·gogue ['deməgɒg] n demagogo.

de·mand [dɪ'mɑːnd] 1 n (a) (request): ~ **(for)** (help, money) richiesta (di); (better pay etc) richiesta (di), rivendicazione f (di); **by popular** ~ a richiesta generale; **on** ~ a richiesta; **I have many ~s on my time** sono impegnatissimo. (b) (Comm): ~ **(for)** domanda (di); **to be in** ~ essere richiesto. 2 vt (ask for): **to** ~ **sth (from or of sb)** pretendere qc (da qn), esigere qc (da qn); (need) richiedere; **to** ~ **that...** richiedere che... + sub; **I**

~ **to see the manager** esigo di vedere il direttore.

de·mand·ing [dɪ'mɑːndɪŋ] adj (person) esigente; (work: physically) stancante; (: mentally) stressante.

de·mar·ca·tion [,diːmɑː'keɪʃən] 1 n demarcazione f. 2 cpd: ~ **dispute** n controversia settoriale (or di categoria); ~ **line** n linea di demarcazione.

de·mean·our, (Am) **de·mean·or** [dɪ'miːnə'] n contegno.

de·ment·ed [dɪ'mentɪd] adj pazzo(a).

demi- ['demɪ] pref semi...; ~**god** n semidio.

de·mili·ta·rize ['diː'mɪlɪtəraɪz] vt smilitarizzare.

de·mise [dɪ'maɪz] n (frm) decesso.

de·mist [dɪ'mɪst] vt (Aut) sbrinare.

de·mist·er [diː'mɪstə'] n (Aut) sbrinatore m.

demo ['deməʊ] n fam abbr of **demonstration**.

de·mo·bi·lize [diː'məʊbɪlaɪz] vt smobilitare.

de·moc·ra·cy [dɪ'mɒkrəsɪ] n democrazia.

demo·crat ['deməkræt] n democratico/a.

demo·crat·ic [,demə'krætɪk] adj democratico(a).

de·mog·ra·phy [dɪ'mɒgrəfɪ] n demografia.

de·mol·ish [dɪ'mɒlɪʃ] vt (gen) demolire; (hum: cake etc) far fuori.

demo·li·tion [,demə'lɪʃən] n demolizione f.

de·mon ['diːmən] n demonio; **he's a** ~ **for work** (fam) è uno stacanovista.

dem·on·strate ['demənstreɪt] 1 vt (a) (truth, ability) dimostrare; (emotion) manifestare. (b) (appliance etc) fare una dimostrazione di. 2 vi (Pol etc): **to** ~ **(for/against)** dimostrare (per/contro), manifestare (per/contro).

dem·on·stra·tion [,demən'streɪʃən] n (see vt) dimostrazione f; manifestazione f; **to hold a** ~ (Pol) tenere una manifestazione, fare una dimostrazione.

dem·on·stra·tive [dɪ'mɒnstrətɪv] adj (person) espansivo(a); (Gram) dimostrativo(a).

dem·on·stra·tor ['demənstreɪtə'] n (Pol) dimostrante m/f.

de·mor·al·ize [dɪ'mɒrəlaɪz] vt demoralizzare.

de·mote [dɪ'məʊt] vt degradare.

de·mur [dɪ'mɜː'] 1 vi (frm): **to** ~ **(at)** sollevare obiezioni (a or su). 2 n: **without** ~ senza obiezioni.

de·mure [dɪ'mjʊə'] adj (smile) contegnoso(a); (girl) pieno(a) di contegno.

den [den] n (wild animal's) tana, covo; (room) buco (fam); **a** ~ **of thieves** (fig) un covo di ladri.

de·na·tion·al·ize [diː'næʃnəlaɪz] vt snazionalizzare.

de·ni·al [dɪ'naɪəl] n (a) (of accusation, guilt) diniego, rifiuto; **the government issued an official** ~ il governo ha emesso una smentita ufficiale. (b) (refusal: of request) rifiuto; (: of rights) mancato riconoscimento.

den·ier ['denɪə'] n denaro (di filati, calze).

den·im ['denɪm] 1 n tessuto jeans; (heavier) (tessuto di) cotone m ritorto; ~**s blue jeans** mpl. 2 cpd: ~ **jacket** n giubbotto di jeans.

Den·mark ['denmɑːk] n Danimarca.

de·nomi·na·tion [dɪ,nɒmɪ'neɪʃən] n (Rel) confessione f; (of coin etc) valore m.

de·nomi·na·tor [dɪ'nɒmɪneɪtə'] n denominatore m.

de·note [dɪ'nəʊt] vt denotare, indicare; (subj: word) significare.

de·nounce [dɪ'naʊns] vt (accuse publicly): **to** ~ **sb (as a thief** etc) accusare pubblicamente qn (di essere un ladro etc); (to police etc) denunciare.

dense [dens] adj (-r, -st) (fog) denso(a), fitto(a); (forest, crowd) fitto(a); (fur) folto(a); (fam: person) tonto(a), ottuso(a).

den·sity ['densɪtɪ] n densità f inv.

dent [dɛnt] **1** *n (in metal)* ammaccatura, bozzo; *(in wood)* tacca, intaccatura; **the holiday left a ~ in our savings** la vacanza ha intaccato i nostri risparmi. **2** *vt (car, hat etc)* ammaccare.

den·tal ['dɛntl] *adj (surgery, care)* dentistico(a), odontoiatrico(a); *(appointment)* dal dentista; ~ **surgeon** medico dentista, odontoiatra *m/f*.

den·ti·frice ['dɛntɪfrɪs] *n* dentifricio.

den·tist ['dɛntɪst] *n* dentista *m/f*; ~**'s surgery** gabinetto dentistico.

den·tis·try ['dɛntɪstrɪ] *n* odontoiatria.

den·tures ['dɛntʃəz] *npl* dentiera.

de·nude [dɪ'njuːd] *vt*: **to ~ (of)** spogliare (di), denudare (di).

de·nun·cia·tion [dɪˌnʌnsɪ'eɪʃən] *n* denuncia; *(in public)* pubblica accusa.

deny [dɪ'naɪ] *vt* **(a)** *(possibility, truth of statement, charge)* negare; *(report)* smentire; **there's no ~ing it** è innegabile; **he denies having said it** nega di averlo detto. **(b)** *(refuse)*: **to ~ sb sth** negare qc a qn, rifiutare qc a qn; **to ~ o.s. sth** negarsi qc, privarsi di qc.

de·odor·ant [diː'əʊdərənt] *n* deodorante *m*.

de·part [dɪ'pɑːt] *vi*: **to ~ (from)** *(train)* partire (da); *(person)* andar via (da), allontanarsi (da); *(custom, truth etc)* deviare (da).

de·part·ed [dɪ'pɑːtɪd] **1** *adj (bygone: days, glory)* trascorso(a), passato(a); *(dead)* scomparso(a). **2** *npl*: **the ~** i defunti.

de·part·ment [dɪ'pɑːtmənt] **1** *n (Admin)* sezione *f*, reparto; *(in shop)* reparto; *(in government)* ministero; *(Univ)* istituto; **the English D~** *(Scol)* i professori d'inglese; **that's not my ~** *(also fig)* questo non è di mia competenza; **D~ of Employment** *(Brit)* Ministero del Lavoro; **D~ of State** *(Am)* Dipartimento di Stato. **2** *cpd*: ~ **store** *n* grande magazzino.

de·part·men·tal [ˌdiːpɑːt'mɛntl] *adj (dispute)* settoriale; *(meeting)* di sezione; ~ **manager** caporeparto.

de·par·ture [dɪ'pɑːtʃəʳ] **1** *n (gen)* partenza; *(fig: from custom, principle)*: ~ **(from)** abbandono (di), deviazione *f* (da); **a new** ~ *(fig)* una svolta (decisiva). **2** *cpd*: ~ **lounge** *n* sala d'attesa.

de·pend [dɪ'pɛnd] *vi* **(a)**: **to ~ (up)on** *(rely)* contare su; *(be dependent on)* dipendere (economicamente) da, essere a carico di; **you can ~ on it** sta pur certo, non dubitare. **(b)**: **to ~ (on)** *(be influenced by)* dipendere (da); **it (all) ~s on the weather** (tutto) dipende dal tempo; **it (all) ~s what you mean** dipende da che cosa vuoi dire; **that ~s** dipende.

de·pend·able [dɪ'pɛndəbl] *adj (person)* fidato(a), serio(a); *(machine, car)* affidabile.

de·pend·ant [dɪ'pɛndənt] *n* persona a carico.

de·pend·ence [dɪ'pɛndəns] *n*: ~ **(on)** dipendenza (da).

de·pend·ent [dɪ'pɛndənt] **1** *adj*: **to be ~ (on)** *(gen)* dipendere (da); *(child, relative)* essere a carico (di). **2** *n* = **dependant**.

de·pict [dɪ'pɪkt] *vt (in picture)* rappresentare; *(in words)* descrivere, dipingere.

de·pila·tory [dɪ'pɪlətərɪ] *n (also:* ~ **cream)** crema depilatoria.

de·plete [dɪ'pliːt] *vt* ridurre al minimo.

de·plor·able [dɪ'plɔːrəbl] *adj* deplorevole.

de·plore [dɪ'plɔːʳ] *vt* deplorare.

de·ploy [dɪ'plɔɪ] *vt (Mil)* schierare; *(fig: resources etc)* impiegare, far uso di.

de·popu·late [diː'pɒpjʊleɪt] *vt* spopolare.

de·popu·la·tion [ˈdiːˌpɒpjʊ'leɪʃən] *n* spopolamento.

de·port [dɪ'pɔːt] *vt* deportare.

de·por·ta·tion [ˌdiːpɔː'teɪʃən] **1** *n* deportazione *f*. **2** *cpd*: ~ **order** *n* foglio di via obbligatorio.

de·port·ment [dɪ'pɔːtmənt] *n (behaviour)* comportamento; *(carriage)* portamento.

de·pose [dɪ'pəʊz] *vt* deporre.

de·pos·it [dɪ'pɒzɪt] **1** *n* **(a)** *(in bank)* deposito; *(Comm: part payment)* acconto, caparra; *(: returnable security)* cauzione *f*; **to put down a ~ of £50** versare una caparra di 50 sterline. **(b)** *(Chem, Geol etc)* deposito; *(of ore, oil)* giacimento. **2** *vt* **(a)** *(put down)* posare; *(leave: luggage)* lasciare in deposito, depositare. **(b)** *(money: in bank)* depositare. **3** *cpd*: ~ **account** *n* libretto di risparmio.

de·posi·tor [dɪ'pɒzɪtəʳ] *n* depositante *m/f*.

de·pot ['dɛpəʊ] *n (storehouse)* magazzino, deposito *m* merci *inv*; *(bus garage etc)* deposito.

de·praved [dɪ'preɪvd] *adj* depravato(a).

de·prav·ity [dɪ'prævɪtɪ] *n* depravazione *f*.

dep·re·cate ['dɛprɪkeɪt] *vt (frm)* deprecare.

dep·re·cat·ing ['dɛprɪkeɪtɪŋ] *adj (disapproving)* di biasimo; *(apologetic)*: **a ~ smile** un sorriso di scusa.

de·pre·ci·ate [dɪ'priːʃɪeɪt] **1** *vi* deprezzarsi. **2** *vt* deprezzare.

de·pre·cia·tion [dɪˌpriːʃɪ'eɪʃən] *n* deprezzamento.

de·press [dɪ'prɛs] *vt* **(a)** *(person)* deprimere; *(spirits)* buttar giù. **(b)** *(trade)* ridurre; *(prices)* far scendere, abbassare. **(c)** *(frm: press down: lever)* abbassare.

de·pres·sant [dɪ'prɛsnt] *n (Med)* sedativo.

de·pressed [dɪ'prɛst] *adj* **(a)** *(area)* depresso(a); *(industry)* in crisi; *(Fin: market, trade)* stagnante, in ribasso. **(b)** *(person)* depresso(a); **to feel ~** sentirsi depresso(a); **to get ~** perdersi d'animo.

de·press·ing [dɪ'prɛsɪŋ] *adj* deprimente, demoralizzante.

de·pres·sion [dɪ'prɛʃən] *n (gen, Med, Econ, Met etc)* depressione *f*; **the economy is in a state of ~** è in atto una crisi economica; **the D~** la crisi del 1929.

dep·ri·va·tion [ˌdɛprɪ'veɪʃən] *n (act)* privazione *f*; *(state)* indigenza; *(Psych)* carenza affettiva.

de·prive [dɪ'praɪv] *vt*: **to ~ sb of sth** privare qn di qc; **to ~ o.s. of sth** privarsi di qc.

de·prived [dɪ'praɪvd] *adj* bisognoso(a).

depth [dɛpθ] *n (gen, of knowledge, thought)* profondità, *f inv*; *(of snow)* altezza, spessore *m*; *(of shelf)* profondità, larghezza; *(of colour, feeling)* intensità *f inv*; **at a ~ of 3 metres** a una profondità di 3 metri, a 3 metri di profondità; **the ~s of the sea** gli abissi del mare; **to be out of one's ~** *(swimmer)* essere dove non si tocca; *(fig)* non sentirsi all'altezza della situazione; **in the ~s of despair** *(fig)* in preda alla disperazione; **in the ~s of winter/the forest** nel cuore dell'inverno/della foresta; **to study sth in ~** studiare qc in profondità.

depu·ta·tion [ˌdɛpjʊ'teɪʃən] *n* deputazione *f*.

de·pute [dɪ'pjuːt] *vt*: **to ~ sth to sb** delegare qc a qn; **to ~ sb to do sth** deputare o delegare qn a fare qc.

depu·tize ['dɛpjʊtaɪz] *vi*: **to ~ (for sb)** fare le veci (di qn), sostituire (qn).

depu·ty ['dɛpjʊtɪ] **1** *n (replacement)* sostituto/a; *(second in command)* vice *m/f*. **2** *cpd*: ~ **head** *n* vicepreside *m/f*; ~ **leader** *n (Pol)* sottosegretario.

de·rail [dɪ'reɪl] *vt* far deragliare.

de·rail·ment [dɪ'reɪlmənt] *n* deragliamento.

de·ranged [dɪ'reɪndʒd] *adj (mind)* sconvolto(a); *(person)* squilibrato(a); **to be (mentally) ~** essere uno(a) squilibrato(a).

der·elict ['dɛrɪlɪkt] *adj (abandoned)* abbandonato(a); *(ruined)* cadente, fatiscente.

de·ride [dɪ'raɪd] *vt* deridere.

de·ri·sion [dɪ'rɪʒən] *n* derisione *f.*

de·ri·sive [dɪ'raɪsɪv] *adj (laughter)* di scherno, di derisione; *(smile)* beffardo(a).

de·ri·sory [dɪ'raɪsərɪ] *adj* **(a)** *(amount)* irrisorio(a). **(b)** = **derisive.**

deri·va·tion [ˌdɛrɪ'veɪʃən] *n* derivazione *f.*

de·riva·tive [dɪ'rɪvətɪv] **1** *adj (Chem, Gram)* derivato(a); *(literary work, style)* poco originale. **2** *n* derivato.

de·rive [dɪ'raɪv] **1** *vt:* **to ~ (from)** *(name)* derivare (da); *(origins)* trarre (da); *(profit, comfort, pleasure)* ricavare (da), trarre (da). **2** *vi:* **to ~ from** *(subj: word, language)* derivare da; *(: power, fortune)* provenire da.

der·ma·ti·tis [ˌdɜːmə'taɪtɪs] *n* dermatite *f.*

der·ma·tol·ogy [ˌdɜːmə'tɒlədʒɪ] *n* dermatologia.

de·roga·tory [dɪ'rɒgətərɪ] *adj (word)* spregiativo(a); *(remark)* denigratorio(a).

der·rick ['dɛrɪk] *n (in port)* albero di carico; *(above oil well)* derrick *m inv.*

derv [dɜːv] *n (Brit)* gasolio.

des·cant ['dɛskænt] *n (Mus)* discanto.

de·scend [dɪ'sɛnd] **1** *vt* **(a)** *(frm: stairs)* scendere. **(b): to be ~ed from sb** discendere da qn. **2** *vi* **(a)** *(go down):* **to ~ (from)** (di)scendere (da); *(road)* scendere (da); **in ~ing order of importance** in ordine decrescente d'importanza. **(b)** *(property, customs):* **to ~ from ... to** passare da ... a; **to ~ from generation to generation** tramandarsi di generazione in generazione.

♦ **descend on** *vi + prep (subj: enemy, angry person)* assalire, piombare su; *(: misfortune)* arrivare addosso a; *(fig: gloom, silence)* scendere su; **visitors ~ed (up)on us** ci sono arrivate visite tra capo e collo.

♦ **descend to** *vi + prep:* **to ~ to sth** scendere a qc; **to ~ to doing sth** abbassarsi a fare qc.

de·scend·ant [dɪ'sɛndənt] *n* discendente *m/f.*

de·scent [dɪ'sɛnt] *n (going down)* discesa; *(ancestry):* **~ (from)** origine *f* (da), discendenza (da).

de·scribe [dɪs'kraɪb] *vt* descrivere; **~ him for us** descrivicelo; **she ~s herself as a teacher** dice di essere insegnante.

de·scrip·tion [dɪs'krɪpʃən] *n (gen)* descrizione *f;* *(of event)* racconto; *(of suspect)* connotati *mpl,* descrizione; **beyond ~** oltre ogni dire; **he carried a gun of some ~** aveva un fucile di qualche tipo; **of every ~** di ogni genere e specie.

de·scrip·tive [dɪs'krɪptɪv] *adj* descrittivo(a).

des·ecrate ['dɛsɪkreɪt] *vt* profanare.

des·ert ['dɛzət] **1** *n* deserto. **2** [dɪ'zɜːt] *vt* abbandonare, lasciare; **his courage ~ed him** il coraggio l'ha abbandonato. **3** [dɪ'zɜːt] *vi (Mil):* **to ~ (from)** disertare (da); **to ~ (to)** passare (a). **4** *cpd (climate, region)* desertico(a); **~ island** *n* isola deserta.

de·sert·er [dɪ'zɜːtəʳ] *n (Mil)* disertore *m.*

de·ser·tion [dɪ'zɜːʃən] *n (Mil)* diserzione *f;* *(of spouse)* abbandono del tetto coniugale.

de·serts [dɪ'zɜːts] *npl:* **to get one's just ~** avere ciò che si merita.

de·serve [dɪ'zɜːv] *vt* meritare; **he ~s to win** merita di vincere; **he got what he ~d** ha avuto quel che si meritava.

de·serv·ed·ly [dɪ'zɜːvɪdlɪ] *adv* meritatamente, giustamente.

de·serv·ing [dɪ'zɜːvɪŋ] *adj (cause)* degno(a); *(action)* meritevole; *(person)* che merita aiuto; *(case)* meritorio(a).

des·ic·ca·ted ['dɛsɪkeɪtɪd] *adj* essiccato(a).

de·sign [dɪ'zaɪn] **1** *n* **(a)** *(plan, drawing: of building)*

progetto, disegno; *(: of dress, car)* modello; *(: of machine)* progettazione *f;* *(style)* linea; *(pattern)* disegno, motivo; *(art of ~)* design *m;* **industrial ~** disegno industriale; **dress with a floral ~** vestito a disegni floreali. **(b)** *(intention)* intenzione *f;* **by ~** intenzionalmente, di proposito; **to have ~s on sb/sth** avere delle mire su qn/qc. **2** *vt* **(a)** *(building etc)* disegnare; *(Industry)* progettare; *(perfect crime, scheme)* concepire, elaborare. **(b)** *(intend):* **to be ~ed for sb/sth** essere fatto espressamente per qn/qc; **a well ~ed house** una casa ben concepita.

des·ig·nate ['dɛzɪgneɪt] **1** *vt:* **to ~ (as/to do)** designare (come/a fare). **2** ['dɛzɪgnɪt] *adj (dopo il sostantivo)* designato(a).

des·ig·na·tion [ˌdɛzɪg'neɪʃən] *n (title)* titolo.

de·sign·er [dɪ'zaɪnəʳ] *n (of machines etc)* disegnatore/trice, progettista *m/f;* *(of furniture)* designer *m/f inv;* *(fashion ~)* disegnatore/trice di moda; *(of theatre sets)* scenografo/a.

de·sir·able [dɪ'zaɪərəbl] *adj (woman)* desiderabile; *(house, job)* attraente; *(offer)* vantaggioso(a); **it is ~ that** è opportuno che + *sub.*

de·sire [dɪ'zaɪəʳ] **1** *n:* **~ (for/to do sth)** desiderio (di/di fare qc); **I have no ~ to see him** non ho nessuna voglia di vederlo. **2** *vt (want):* **to ~ sth/to do sth/that** desiderare qc/di fare qc/che + *sub;* **it leaves much to be ~d** lascia molto a desiderare.

de·sir·ous [dɪ'zaɪərəs] *adj (frm):* **~ (of)** desideroso(a) (di).

de·sist [dɪ'zɪst] *vi:* **to ~ (from)** desistere (da).

desk [dɛsk] **1** *n (in office, study etc)* scrivania; *(Scol)* banco; *(in shop)* cassa; *(in hotel)* accettazione *f.* **2** *cpd:* **~ job** *n* lavoro d'ufficio.

deso·late ['dɛsəlɪt] *adj (place)* desolato(a), deserto(a); *(building)* abbandonato(a); *(outlook, future)* nero(a); *(person: grief-stricken)* affranto(a) (dal dolore), desolato(a); *(: friendless)* abbandonato(a) da tutti.

deso·la·tion [ˌdɛsə'leɪʃən] *n (of battlefield)* devastazione *f;* *(of landscape, person)* desolazione *f.*

des·pair [dɪs'pɛəʳ] **1** *n* disperazione *f;* **in ~** disperato(a). **2** *vi:* **to ~ (of)** disperare (di); **don't ~!** non disperare!

des·pair·ing [dɪs'pɛərɪŋ] *adj* disperato(a).

des·patch [dɪs'pætʃ] *n, vt* = **dispatch.**

des·pe·ra·do [ˌdɛspə'rɑːdəʊ] *n* disperato.

des·per·ate ['dɛspərɪt] *adj (gen)* disperato(a); *(criminal)* capace di tutto; *(measures)* estremo(a); **we are getting ~** siamo sull'orlo della disperazione; **to be ~ to do sth** volere disperatamente fare qc; **I'm ~ for money** *(fam)* ho un disperato bisogno di soldi.

des·per·ate·ly ['dɛspərɪtlɪ] *adv (say, look)* con disperazione; *(regret, fight etc)* disperatamente; *(extremely)* terribilmente, estremamente; **~ ill** in pericolo di vita; **~ in love** perdutamente innamorato.

des·pera·tion [ˌdɛspə'reɪʃən] *n* disperazione *f;* **an act of ~** un gesto disperato; **she drove him to ~** l'ha ridotto alla disperazione; **in (sheer) ~** per (pura) disperazione.

des·pic·able [dɪs'pɪkəbl] *adj* spregevole; *(behaviour)* vergognoso(a), ignobile.

des·pise [dɪs'paɪz] *vt (person)* disprezzare; *(sb's attentions, offer)* disdegnare.

de·spite [dɪs'paɪt] *prep* malgrado, nonostante.

de·spond·en·cy [dɪs'pɒndənsɪ] *n* abbattimento, avvilimento.

de·spond·ent [dɪs'pɒndənt] *adj:* **~ (about)** avvilito(a) (per), abbattuto(a) (per); **he is ~ about his future** quanto al suo futuro è molto demoralizzato.

de·spond·ent·ly [dɪs'pɒndəntlɪ] *adv* con aria avvilita *or* abbattuta.

des·pot ['dɛspɒt] *n* despota *m*.

des·pot·ism ['dɛspətɪzəm] *n* dispotismo.

des·sert [dɪ'zɜ:t] **1** *n* dessert *m inv*, dolce *m*. **2** *cpd*: ~ **wine** *n* vino da dessert.

dessert·spoon [dɪ'zɜ:tspu:n] *n* cucchiaino da dessert.

des·ti·na·tion [ˌdɛstɪ'neɪʃən] *n* destinazione *f*.

des·tined ['dɛstɪnd] *adj pred*: ~ **for sth/sb/to do sth** destinato(a) a qc/qn/a fare qc; **we were** ~ **to meet** eravamo destinati a incontrarci; ~ **for London** diretto a Londra, con destinazione Londra.

des·ti·ny ['dɛstɪnɪ] *n* destino, sorte *f*.

des·ti·tute ['dɛstɪtju:t] *adj* senza risorse, indigente.

de·stroy [dɪs'trɔɪ] *vt (gen)* distruggere; *(kill: injured horse)* abbattere; *(: pet)* sopprimere; *(: vermin)* sterminare; *(mood, appetite)* rovinare.

de·stroy·er [dɪs'trɔɪə^r] *n (Naut)* cacciatorpediniere *m*.

de·struc·tion [dɪs'trʌkʃən] *n (gen)* distruzione *f*; *(from war, fire)* danni *mpl*.

de·struc·tive [dɪs'trʌktɪv] *adj (person)* distruttore (trice); *(policy)* rovinoso(a); *(weapon)* di distruzione; *(action, power, criticism)* distruttivo(a).

des·ul·tory ['dɛsəltərɪ] *adj (reading)* disordinato(a); *(conversation)* sconnesso(a); *(contact)* saltuario(a), irregolare.

de·tach [dɪ'tætʃ] *vt* staccare.

de·tach·able [dɪ'tætʃəbl] *adj* staccabile.

de·tached [dɪ'tætʃt] *adj* **(a)** staccato(a), separato(a); ~ **house** villa. **(b)** *(impartial: opinion)* imparziale, obiettivo(a); *(unemotional: manner)* distaccato(a).

de·tach·ment [dɪ'tætʃmənt] *n* **(a)** *(see adj b)* imparzialità, obiettività; distacco. **(b)** *(Mil)* distaccamento.

de·tail ['di:teɪl] **1** *n* **(a)** *(gen)* particolare *m*, dettaglio; *(no pl: taken collectively)* particolari, dettagli; *(part of painting)* particolare; **his attention to** ~ la sua minuziosità; **in** ~ nei dettagli, nei particolari; **to go into** ~**(s)** scendere nei particolari. **(b)** *(Mil)* piccolo distaccamento. **2** *vt* **(a)** *(facts, story)* esporre dettagliatamente. **(b)** *(Mil)* distaccare.

de·tailed ['di:teɪld] *adj* dettagliato(a), particolareggiato(a).

de·tain [dɪ'teɪn] *vt* trattenere.

de·tect [dɪ'tɛkt] *vt (discover)* scoprire; *(: culprit)* individuare; *(perceive)* avvertire, notare.

de·tec·tion [dɪ'tɛkʃən] *n* scoperta; **crime** ~ indagini *fpl* criminali; **to escape** ~ *(criminal)* eludere le ricerche; *(mistake)* passare inosservato.

de·tec·tive [dɪ'tɛktɪv] **1** *n* investigatore/trice; *(private* ~*)* investigatore(trice) privato(a). **2** *cpd*: ~ **story** *n* romanzo poliziesco, (romanzo) giallo.

de·tec·tor [dɪ'tɛktə^r] *n* rivelatore *m*, detector *m inv*.

dé·tente ['deɪtɒnt] *n* distensione *f*.

de·ten·tion [dɪ'tɛnʃən] *n (of criminal, spy)* detenzione *f*; *(of schoolchild)* punizione *f*.

de·ter [dɪ'tɜ:^r] *vt*: **to** ~ **sb (from doing sth)** dissuadere qn (dal fare qc).

de·ter·gent [dɪ'tɜ:dʒənt] *n* detersivo, detergente *m*.

de·terio·rate [dɪ'tɪərɪəreɪt] *vi* deteriorarsi.

de·terio·ra·tion [dɪˌtɪərɪə'reɪʃən] *n* deterioramento.

de·ter·mi·na·tion [dɪˌtɜ:mɪ'neɪʃən] *n* **(a)** *(of person)*: ~ **(to do)** determinazione *f* (di fare). **(b)** *(of cause, position)* determinazione *f*, individuazione *f*.

de·ter·mine [dɪ'tɜ:mɪn] *vt* **(a)** *(gen)* determinare; *(sb's fate, character)* decidere, decidere di; *(resolve)*: **to** ~ **to do sth** decidere di fare qc; **to** ~ **sb to do sth** far decidere a qn di fare qc. **(b)** *(ascertain: cause, meaning)* determinare, stabilire.

♦ **determine on** *vi* + *prep* decidersi per.

de·ter·mined [dɪ'tɜ:mɪnd] *adj (person)* risoluto(a), deciso(a); **a** ~ **effort** uno sforzo di volontà; **to be** ~ **to do sth** essere determinato *or* deciso a fare qc.

de·ter·rent [dɪ'tɛrənt] *n* deterrente *m*; **to act as a** ~ funzionare da deterrente.

de·test [dɪ'tɛst] *vt* detestare.

de·test·able [dɪ'tɛstəbl] *adj* detestabile.

deto·nate ['dɛtəneɪt] **1** *vt* far detonare. **2** *vi* detonare.

deto·na·tor ['dɛtəneɪtə^r] *n* detonatore *m*.

de·tour ['di:ˌtuə^r] *n* giro più lungo, deviazione *f*; *(for traffic)* deviazione; **to make a** ~ **(through)** fare una deviazione (passando per).

de·tract [dɪ'trækt] *vi*: **to** ~ **from** *(value)* sminuire; *(reputation)* intaccare; *(pleasure)* attenuare.

det·ri·ment ['dɛtrɪmənt] *n* detrimento, danno; **to the** ~ **of** a *or* con detrimento di, a danno di; **without** ~ **to** senza danno a.

det·ri·men·tal [ˌdɛtrɪ'mɛntl] *adj*: ~ **(to)** dannoso(a) (a), nocivo(a) (a); **to be** ~ **to sth** pregiudicare qc.

deuce [dju:s] *n (Tennis)* quaranta pari *m inv*.

de·valu·a·tion [ˌdɪvælju'eɪʃən] *n (Fin)* svalutazione *f*.

de·value ['di:'vælju:] *vt (Fin)* svalutare.

dev·as·tate ['dɛvəsteɪt] *vt (place)* devastare; *(opponent, opposition)* sbaragliare, annientare; *(overwhelm: person)* annichilire.

dev·as·tat·ing ['dɛvəsteɪtɪŋ] *adj (flood, storm)* devastatore(trice); *(news, effect)* micidiale; *(beauty)* travolgente.

dev·as·tat·ing·ly ['dɛvəsteɪtɪŋlɪ] *adv (beautiful, funny)* da morire, irresistibilmente.

dev·as·ta·tion [ˌdɛvə'steɪʃən] *n* devastazione *f*.

de·vel·op [dɪ'vɛləp] **1** *vt* **(a)** *(gen, Phot)* sviluppare; *(mind)* allargare; *(interest)* coltivare. **(b)** *(acquire: habit)* prendere (a poco a poco); **to** ~ **a taste for sth** imparare a gustare qc; **she has** ~**ed an interest in politics** è sorto in lei un interesse per la politica. **(c)** *(resources)* sviluppare, valorizzare; *(region)* valorizzare, promuovere lo sviluppo di; **this land is to be** ~**ed** qui costruiranno. **2** *vi* **(a)** *(gen)* svilupparsi; *(person: mentally, emotionally)* maturare; *(baby)* crescere; *(plot, illness)* progredire; **the area has** ~**ed industrially** la zona si è sviluppata sotto il profilo industriale; **to** ~ **into** diventare. **(b)** *(come into being: symptoms, feelings)* comparire, manifestarsi; *(come about: situation, event)* verificarsi, prodursi; **it later** ~**ed that...** in seguito si è visto che... .

de·vel·op·er [dɪ'vɛləpə^r] *n (Phot)* sviluppatore *m*; *(property* ~*)* costruttore *m* (edile).

de·vel·op·ing [dɪ'vɛləpɪŋ] **1** *adj (country, industry)* in via di sviluppo; *(crisis, storm)* che sta per scoppiare, imminente. **2** *n (Phot)* sviluppo.

de·vel·op·ment [dɪ'vɛləpmənt] *n (gen)* sviluppo; **to await** ~**s** attendere ulteriori sviluppi; **the latest** ~**s** gli ultimi sviluppi (della situazione).

de·vi·ate ['di:vɪeɪt] *vi*: **to** ~ **(from)** deviare (da).

de·via·tion [ˌdi:vɪ'eɪʃən] *n*: ~ **(from)** deviazione *f* (da).

de·vice [dɪ'vaɪs] *n (gadget etc)* congegno, dispositivo; *(explosive* ~*)* ordigno esplosivo; *(scheme)* stratagemma *m;* **leave him to his own ~s** che si arrangi da solo.

dev·il ['dɛvl] *n* **(a)** *(evil spirit)* diavolo; **the D~** il Diavolo, il Demonio.

  (b) *(fam: person)* diavolo; **poor ~** povero diavolo!; **be a ~!** fai uno strappo!; **you little ~!** monellaccio!; **she is a ~ to work for** lavorare per lei è un inferno.

  (c) *(fam: as intensifier)*: **it's the ~ of a job** è un lavoraccio; **he had the ~ of a job to find it** ha sudato sette camicie per trovarlo; **I'm in the ~ of a mess** sono in un pasticcio del diavolo; **to work/ run like the ~** lavorare/correre come un dannato; **how/what/who the ~...?** come/che/chi diavolo...?; **there will be the ~ to pay** saranno guai.

  (d) *(phrases)*: **between the ~ and the deep blue sea** tra Scilla e Cariddi; **go to the ~!** *(fam)* vai al diavolo!; **speak** *or* **talk of the ~!** *(fam)* lupus in fabula!; **to play (the) ~'s advocate** fare l'avvocato del diavolo; **(to) give the ~ his due...** bisogna riconoscerglielo..., siamo giusti... .

dev·il·ish ['dɛvlɪʃ] **1** *adj (wicked)* diabolico(a); *(mischievous: child)* indiavolato(a); *(: mood)* infernale. **2** *adv (also: ~ly)* terribilmente.

de·vi·ous ['diːvɪəs] *adj (path, argument, methods, minds)* tortuoso(a); *(person)* subdolo(a); **by ~ means** per vie traverse.

de·vi·ous·ness ['diːvɪəsnɪs] *n* tortuosità.

de·vise [dɪ'vaɪz] *vt* escogitare, ideare.

de·void [dɪ'vɔɪd] *adj:* **~ of** privo(a) di, senza.

de·vo·lu·tion [ˌdiːvə'luːʃən] *n (Pol)* decentramento.

de·volve [dɪ'vɒlv] **1** *vt (power, responsibility)* devolvere. **2** *vi:* **to ~ (up)on** ricadere su; **it ~d on me to tell him** è stato compito mio dirglielo.

de·vote [dɪ'vəʊt] *vt:* **to ~ (to)** dedicare (a); **to ~ o.s. to** dedicarsi a; *(to cause)* consacrarsi a.

de·vot·ed [dɪ'vəʊtɪd] *adj* devoto(a); **to be ~ to sb** essere molto attaccato a qn.

devo·tee [ˌdevəʊ'tiː] *n* appassionato(a).

de·vo·tion [dɪ'vəʊʃən] *n:* **~ (to)** *(studies etc)* devozione *f* (a), dedizione *f* (a); *(friend etc)* attaccamento (a), fedeltà (a); **~s** *(Rel)* devozioni.

de·vour [dɪ'vaʊə^r] *vt (food)* divorare; **~ed by jealousy** divorato dalla gelosia.

de·vout [dɪ'vaʊt] *adj (person)* devoto(a), pio(a); *(prayer, hope)* devoto(a), fervido(a).

dew [djuː] *n* rugiada.

dew·drop ['djuːdrɒp] *n* goccia di rugiada.

dewy ['djuːɪ] *adj* bagnato(a) di rugiada.

dewy-eyed ['djuːaɪd] *adj* con gli occhi languidi.

dex·ter·ity [dɛks'tɛrɪtɪ] *n:* **~ (in doing sth)** *(of hands)* destrezza (a fare qc); *(of mind)* abilità (nel fare qc).

dex·t(e)rous ['dɛkstrəs] *adj (skilful)* destro(a), abile; *(: movement)* agile.

dia·be·tes [ˌdaɪə'biːtiːz] *n* diabete *m.*

dia·bet·ic [ˌdaɪə'bɛtɪk] **1** *adj (gen)* diabetico(a); *(chocolate, jam)* per diabetici. **2** *n* diabetico/a.

dia·boli·cal [ˌdaɪə'bɒlɪkəl] *adj* diabolico(a); *(fam: dreadful)* infernale, atroce.

dia·crit·ic [ˌdaɪə'krɪtɪk] *n* segno diacritico.

dia·dem ['daɪədɛm] *n* diadema *m.*

di·aer·esis [daɪ'ɛrɪsɪs] *n* dieresi *f inv.*

di·ag·nose ['daɪəgnəʊz] *vt* diagnosticare; **it was ~d as bronchitis** hanno diagnosticato una bronchite.

di·ag·no·sis [ˌdaɪəg'nəʊsɪs] *n, pl* **diagnoses** diagnosi *f inv.*

di·ag·nos·tic [ˌdaɪəg'nɒstɪk] *adj (gen)* diagnostico(a); *(probe, X-ray)* a scopo diagnostico.

di·ago·nal [daɪ'ægənl] *adj, n* diagonale *(f).*

di·ago·nal·ly [daɪ'ægənəlɪ] *adv (cut, fold)* in diago-

nale, diagonalmente; **to go ~ across** attraversare in senso *or* in direzione diagonale; **~ opposite** dall'altra parte in diagonale.

dia·gram ['daɪəgræm] *n* diagramma *m,* schema *m;* *(Math)* diagramma, grafico.

dial ['daɪəl] **1** *n (of clock, instrument)* quadrante *m;* *(of radio)* scala; *(of telephone)* disco (combinatore). **2** *vt (Telec: number)* fare, *(more formal)* comporre; **to ~ a wrong number** sbagliare numero; **can I ~ London direct?** si può chiamare Londra in teleselezione?; **to ~ 999** ≃ chiamare il 113. **3** *cpd:* **~ling code** *n* prefisso; **~ling tone** *n* segnale *m* di libero.

dia·lect ['daɪəlɛkt] **1** *n* dialetto; **the local ~** il dialetto del luogo. **2** *cpd:* **~ word** *n* termine *m* dialettale.

dia·logue ['daɪəlɒg] *n* dialogo.

di·aly·sis [daɪ'æləsɪs] *n* dialisi *f.*

di·am·eter [daɪ'æmɪtə^r] *n* diametro; **it is one metre in ~** misura un metro di diametro.

dia·met·ri·cal·ly [ˌdaɪə'mɛtrɪkəlɪ] *adv:* **~ opposed (to)** diametralmente opposto (a).

dia·mond ['daɪəmənd] **1** *n (stone)* diamante *m,* brillante *m; (shape)* rombo, losanga; *(in cards)* quadri *mpl;* **the Queen of ~s** la donna di quadri. **2** *cpd:* **~ jubilee** *n* sessantesimo anniversario; **~ neck·lace** *n* collana di diamanti *or* brillanti; **~ ring** *n* anello di brillanti; *(with one diamond)* anello con brillante; **~ wedding** *n* nozze *fpl* di diamante.

dia·per ['daɪəpə^r] *n (Am)* pannolino.

dia·phragm ['daɪəfræm] *n* diaframma *m.*

di·ar·rhoea [ˌdaɪə'riːə] *n* diarrea.

dia·ry ['daɪərɪ] *n* diario; *(for engagements)* agenda; **to keep a ~** tenere un diario.

dia·tribe ['daɪətraɪb] *n:* **~ (against)** diatriba (contro).

dice [daɪs] **1** *n, pl inv* dado; **to play ~** giocare a dadi. **2** *vt (vegetables)* tagliare a dadini. **3** *vi:* **to ~ with death** scherzare con la morte.

dicey ['daɪsɪ] *adj (fam)*: **it's a bit ~** è un po' un rischio.

di·choto·my [dɪ'kɒtəmɪ] *n* dicotomia.

Dic·ta·phone ['dɪktəfəʊn] *n* ® dittafono.

dic·tate [dɪk'teɪt] **1** *vt, vi (all senses)* dettare; **he decided to act as circumstances ~d** decise di agire come gli dettavano le circostanze. **2** ['dɪkteɪt]: **~s** *npl (of heart, fashion)* dettami *mpl.*

♦ **dictate to** *vi + prep (person)* dare ordini a, dettar legge a; **I won't be ~d to** non ricevo ordini.

dic·ta·tion [dɪk'teɪʃən] *n (to secretary etc)* dettatura; *(Scol)* dettato; **at ~ speed** a velocità di dettatura.

dic·ta·tor [dɪk'teɪtə^r] *n* dittatore *m.*

dic·ta·tor·ial [ˌdɪktə'tɔːrɪəl] *adj* dittatoriale, da dittatore.

dic·ta·tor·ship [dɪk'teɪtəʃɪp] *n* dittatura.

dic·tion ['dɪkʃən] *n* dizione *f.*

dic·tion·ary ['dɪkʃənrɪ] *n* vocabolario, dizionario.

did [dɪd] *pt of* **do.**

di·dac·tic [dɪ'dæktɪk] *adj* didattico(a).

did·dle ['dɪdl] *vt (fam)* infinocchiare; **to ~ sb out of sth** fregare qc a qn.

didn't ['dɪdənt] = **did not.**

die¹ [daɪ] *prp* **dying** *vi* **(a)** *(person, animal, plant)*: **to ~ (of** *or* **from)** morire (di); *(engine)* spegnersi, fermarsi; *(fig: friendship)* finire; *(: interest, enthusiasm)* spegnersi; **to be dying** star morendo; **to ~ a natural/ violent death** morire di morte naturale/violenta; **he ~d a hero** è morto da eroe; **the daylight was dying fast** si stava facendo buio in fretta; **never say ~** *(fig fam)* la speranza è l'ultima a morire; **I nearly ~d** *(laughing)* per poco non morivo (dal ridere); *(with embarrassment)*

avrei voluto sprofondare; **old habits ~ hard** il lupo perde il pelo ma non il vizio. **(b): to be dying for sth/to do sth** morire dalla voglia di qc/di fare qc.
♦ **die away** *vi + adv (sound, voice)* spegnersi.
♦ **die down** *vi + adv (fire)* spegnersi; *(flames)* abbassarsi, languire; *(storm, wind, emotion)* calmarsi.
♦ **die off** *vi + adv (plants, animals)* morire uno(a) dopo l'altro(a).
♦ **die out** *vi + adv* estinguersi, scomparire.
die² [daɪ] *n, pl* **dice: the ~ is cast** il dado è tratto.
die·hard ['daɪhɑːd] *n* reazionario/a.
die·sel ['diːzəl] **1** *n* diesel *m*. **2** *cpd:* ~ **engine** *n* motore *m* diesel *inv;* ~ **oil** *n,* ~ **fuel** *n* gasolio (per motori diesel); ~ **train** *n* (treno con) locomotiva diesel.
diet ['daɪət] **1** *n* **(a)** *(customary food)* alimentazione *f,* regime *m* alimentare; **to live on a ~ of** nutrirsi di. **(b)** *(restricted food)* dieta; **to be/go on a ~** essere/mettersi a dieta. **2** *vi* seguire una dieta.
di·eti·cian [ˌdaɪə'tɪʃən] *n* dietista *m/f.*
dif·fer ['dɪfəʳ] *vi* **(a)** *(be unlike):* **to ~ (from)** differire (da), essere diverso(a) (da). **(b)** *(disagree):* **to ~ (with sb on** *or* **over** *or* **about sth)** dissentire (da qn su qc), discordare (da qn su qc); **we ~ed over the matter** ci siamo trovati in disaccordo sulla questione.
dif·fer·ence ['dɪfrəns] *n* **(a):** ~ **(in/between)** differenza (di/tra); **that makes all the ~** è tutta un'altra cosa; **it makes no ~ to me** per me è lo stesso; **a car with a ~** una macchina diversa dalle altre; **the ~ in her is amazing** è incredibile com'è cambiata; **I'll make up the ~ later** *(of money)* ti do il resto dopo. **(b)** *(quarrel):* **a ~ of opinion** una divergenza di opinioni; **to settle one's ~s** risolvere la situazione.
dif·fer·ent ['dɪfrənt] *adj (not alike):* ~ **(from** *or* **to)** diverso(a) (da), differente (da); *(changed)* altro(a), diverso(a); *(various)* diverso(a), vario(a); **I feel a ~ person** mi sento un altro; **that's quite a ~ matter** è tutt'altra cosa, è una faccenda completamente diversa; **it comes in several ~ colours** è fatto in diversi *or* vari colori.
dif·fer·en·tial [ˌdɪfə'renʃəl] **1** *adj* differenziale. **2** *n (Econ)* scarto salariale; *(Math, Aut)* differenziale *m.*
dif·fer·en·ti·ate [ˌdɪfə'renʃɪeɪt] **1** *vt:* **to ~ (from)** *(tell the difference)* distinguere (fra); *(make the difference)* differenziare (da). **2** *vi:* **to ~ (between)** distinguere (tra), differenziare (tra); **to ~ between** *(people)* fare differenza tra.
dif·fer·ent·ly ['dɪfrəntlɪ] *adv* in modo diverso *or* differente, differentemente; **she thinks quite ~ now** la pensa diversamente adesso.
dif·fi·cult ['dɪfɪkəlt] *adj* difficile; ~ **to understand** difficile da capire; **I find her ~ to get on with** la trovo difficile di carattere; **I find it ~ to believe (that...)** mi pare impossibile (che...); **the ~ thing is to begin** il difficile sta nel cominciare.
dif·fi·cul·ty ['dɪfɪkəltɪ] *n* difficoltà *f inv;* **he has ~ in walking/breathing** ha difficoltà a camminare/di respirazione; **to have difficulties with** *(police, landlord etc)* avere noie con; **to get o.s. into ~** mettersi nei guai; **to be in ~** essere *or* trovarsi in difficoltà; **to be in (financial) difficulties** avere dei problemi finanziari.
dif·fi·dence ['dɪfɪdəns] *n* mancanza di sicurezza.
dif·fi·dent ['dɪfɪdənt] *adj (person)* poco sicuro(a) di sé; *(smile)* timido(a), imbarazzato(a); **to be ~ about doing sth** esitare a fare qc.
dif·fuse [dɪ'fjuːs] **1** *adj* diffuso(a). **2** [dɪ'fjuːz] *vt*

(light, heat) diffondere; *(smoke, gas, liquid)* spargere.
dif·fu·sion [dɪ'fjuːʒən] *n (see vb)* diffusione *f;* spargimento.
dig [dɪg] *(vb: pt, pp* **dug) 1** *n* **(a)** *(with elbow)* gomitata; **to give sb a ~ in the ribs** dare una gomitata nel fianco a qn. **(b)** *(fam: taunt)* frecciata, insinuazione *f;* **to have a ~ at sb/sth** lanciare una frecciata a qn/qc. **(c)** *(Archeol)* scavo, scavi *mpl.* **2** *vt* **(a)** *(ground, hole etc)* scavare; *(garden)* zappare, vangare. **(b)** *(poke, thrust):* **to ~ sth into sth** conficcare qc in qc. **(c)** *(fam: esp Am: enjoy):* ~ **that beat, man!** senti che forza quel ritmo!; **I don't ~ that kind of scene** quell'ambiente non mi va a genio; **he really ~s jazz** va pazzo per il jazz. **3** *vi (gen, Tech)* scavare; *(Archeol)* fare degli scavi; **to ~ for minerals** scavare alla ricerca di minerali; **to ~ into one's pockets for sth** frugarsi le tasche cercando qc.
♦ **dig in 1** *vi + adv* **(a)** *(fam: eat)* attaccare a mangiare; ~ **in!** dateci sotto! **(b)** *(also:* ~ **o.s. in:** *Mil)* trincerarsi; *(: fig)* insediarsi, installarsi. **2** *vt + adv (compost)* interrare; *(knife, claw)* affondare; **to ~ in one's heels** *(fig)* impuntarsi.
♦ **dig out** *vt + adv (survivors, car from snow)* tirar fuori (scavando), estrarre (scavando); *(fig)* scovare.
♦ **dig up** *vt + adv (vegetables)* scalzare, dissotterrare; *(weeds)* estirpare; *(treasure, body)* dissotterrare; *(fig fam: fact, information)* pescare.
di·gest [daɪ'dʒest] **1** *vt* digerire. **2** *vi* digerirsi. **3** ['daɪdʒest] *n (summary)* compendio.
di·gest·ible [dɪ'dʒestəbl] *adj* digeribile.
di·ges·tion [dɪ'dʒestʃən] *n* digestione *f.*
di·ges·tive [dɪ'dʒestɪv] *adj* digestivo(a); ~ **system** apparato digerente; ~ **(biscuit)** biscotto tipo frollino di farina integrale.
dig·it ['dɪdʒɪt] *n (Math)* cifra; *(finger)* dito.
digi·tal ['dɪdʒɪtl] *adj (clock, computer)* digitale.
dig·ni·fied ['dɪgnɪfaɪd] *adj* dignitoso(a), pieno(a) di dignità.
dig·ni·tary ['dɪgnɪtərɪ] *n* dignitario.
dig·nity ['dɪgnɪtɪ] *n* dignità; **that would be beneath my ~** non mi abbasserei mai a farlo.
di·gress [daɪ'gres] *vi:* **to ~ (from)** divagare (da), fare digressioni (da).
di·gres·sion [daɪ'greʃən] *n* digressione *f.*
digs [dɪgz] *npl (Brit fam):* **to be in ~** stare in camera ammobiliata; **I took him back to his ~** l'ho riportato a casa sua.
dike [daɪk] *n* = **dyke.**
di·lapi·da·ted [dɪ'læpɪdeɪtɪd] *adj (building etc)* in pessime condizioni; *(vehicle etc)* sgangherato(a), scassato(a).
di·lapi·da·tion [dɪˌlæpɪ'deɪʃən] *n* sfacelo, disfacimento.
di·late [daɪ'leɪt] **1** *vi* dilatarsi. **2** *vt* dilatare.
di·la·tion [daɪ'leɪʃən] *n* dilatazione *f.*
di·la·tory ['dɪlətərɪ] *adj (person)* lento(a); *(action, policy)* dilatorio(a).
di·lem·ma [daɪ'lemə] *n* dilemma *m;* **to be in a ~** essere di fronte a un dilemma.
dili·gence ['dɪlɪdʒəns] *n* diligenza.
dili·gent ['dɪlɪdʒənt] *adj (person)* diligente, attento(a); *(work, search)* accurato(a), diligente.
dill [dɪl] *n* aneto.
dilly-dally ['dɪlɪdælɪ] *vi* gingillarsi.
di·lute [daɪ'luːt] *vt (fruit juice, colour etc)* diluire, allungare; *(wine)* annacquare; *(fig: statement, concept)* diluire; '~ **to taste**' aggiungere acqua a piacere'.
dim [dɪm] **1** *adj* **(-mer, -mest)** *(light)* debole, fioco(a); *(sight)* debole; *(forest)* oscuro(a); *(room)* in

penombra; *(shape, outline, memory, sound)* indistinto(a); *(fam: person)* tonto(a); **to grow ~** *(light)* affievolirsi; *(eyesight)* indebolirsi; **to take a ~ view of sth** *(fam)* non vedere qc di buon occhio. **2** vt *(light)* abbassare; *(sound, memory, colour)* affievolire; *(shape, outline, beauty, glory)* offuscare; *(sight, senses)* annebbiare; *(metal)* annerire. **3** vi *(light, sight, memory)* affievolirsi; *(outline)* divenire indistinto(a).

dime [daɪm] n *(Am)* monetina da 10 cent.

di·men·sion [daɪ'mɛnʃən] n *(size)* dimensione f, proporzione f; *(Math, fig)* dimensione; **to add a new ~** to dare una dimensione nuova a.

-di·men·sion·al [daɪ'mɛnʃənl] adj suf: **two~** bidimensionale; **three~** tridimensionale.

di·min·ish [dɪ'mɪnɪʃ] **1** vt *(speed, authority etc)* diminuire, ridurre; *(value)* sminuire. **2** vi diminuire, ridursi; *(value)* scendere.

di·min·ished [dɪ'mɪnɪʃt] adj *(value, staff)* ridotto(a); **~ responsibility** *(Law)* incapacità d'intendere e di volere.

di·minu·tive [dɪ'mɪnjʊtɪv] **1** adj minuto(a). **2** n *(Gram)* diminutivo.

dim·ly ['dɪmlɪ] adv *(hear, remember)* vagamente; *(shine)* debolmente.

dim·ple ['dɪmpl] n *(on chin etc)* fossetta.

din [dɪn] **1** n *(in classroom, from people)* chiasso, baccano; *(from machine, factory, traffic)* rumore m infernale. **2** vt: **to ~ sth into sb** *(fam)* ficcare qc in testa a qn; **he tried to ~ it into her that...** ha cercato di ficcarle in testa che... .

dine [daɪn] vi *(frm)*: **to ~ (on)** pranzare (a base di); *(in the evening)* cenare (a base di); **to ~ out** pranzare *or* cenare fuori.

din·er ['daɪnə'] n *(person: in restaurant)* cliente m; *(Rail)* carrozza *or* vagone m ristorante; *(Am: eating place)* tavola calda.

din·ghy ['dɪŋɡɪ] n *(rubber ~)* gommone m; *(sailing ~)* dinghy m inv.

din·go ['dɪŋɡəʊ] n *(Zool)* dingo.

din·gy ['dɪndʒɪ] adj squallido(a).

din·ing ['daɪnɪŋ] adj: **~ car** carrozza *or* vagone m ristorante; **~ room** sala da pranzo; **~ table** tavola *or* tavolo da pranzo.

din·ner ['dɪnə'] **1** n *(evening meal)* cena; *(lunch)* pranzo; *(banquet)* banchetto; **school ~s** refezione f scolastica; **we're having people to ~** abbiamo gente a cena; **to go out to ~ in a restaurant/at friends** andare a cena fuori/da amici. **2** cpd: **~ jacket** n smoking m inv; **~ party** n cena (con amici); **~ plate** n piatto piano; **~ service** n servizio da tavola.

di·no·saur ['daɪnəsɔː'] n dinosauro.

dint [dɪnt] n: **by ~ of (doing) sth** a forza di (fare) qc.

dio·cese ['daɪəsɪs] n diocesi f inv.

di·ox·ide [daɪ'ɒksaɪd] n biossido; **carbon ~** anidride f carbonica.

dip [dɪp] **1** n **(a)** *(swim)* nuotatina; **to go for a ~** andare a fare una nuotatina. **(b)** *(slope)* pendenza, discesa; *(hollow)* cunetta. **(c)** *(Culin)* salsetta. **2** vt *(into liquid)* immergere, bagnare; *(hand: into bag)* infilare; *(sheep)* immergere nel disinfestante; **to ~ one's pen in ink** intingere la penna nell'inchiostro; **he ~ped his bread in his soup** ha intinto il pane nella minestra; **to ~ one's headlights** *(Brit Aut)* abbassare i fari. **3** vi *(slope down: road)* essere in pendenza, andare in discesa; *(move down: bird, plane)* abbassarsi; *(temperature, sun)* calare; **to ~ into one's pocket/savings** *(fig)* attingere al portafoglio/ai propri risparmi; **to ~ into a book** scorrere un libro; **to ~ into an author** leggere qualcosa di un autore.

diph·theria [dɪf'θɪərɪə] n difterite f.

diph·thong ['dɪfθɒŋ] n dittongo.

di·plo·ma [dɪ'pləʊmə] n diploma m.

di·plo·ma·cy [dɪ'pləʊməsɪ] n *(Pol, fig)* diplomazia.

dip·lo·mat ['dɪpləmæt] n diplomatico.

dip·lo·mat·ic [,dɪplə'mætɪk] adj *(also fig)* diplomatico(a); **~ corps** corpo diplomatico; **~ service** diplomazia; **to break off ~ relations** rompere le relazioni diplomatiche.

dip·so·ma·nia [,dɪpsəʊ'meɪnɪə] n dipsomania.

dip·so·ma·ni·ac [,dɪpsəʊ'meɪnɪæk] n dipsomane m/f.

dip·stick ['dɪpstɪk] n *(Aut)* asta dell'olio.

dip·switch ['dɪpswɪtʃ] n *(Aut)* levetta dei fari.

dire ['daɪə'] adj *(consequences)* disastroso(a); *(event)* terribile; *(poverty)* nero(a); **~ necessity** dura necessità; **in ~ straits** ridotto agli estremi.

di·rect [daɪ'rɛkt] **1** adj *(gen)* diretto(a); *(answer)* chiaro(a); *(refusal)* esplicito(a); *(manner, person)* franco(a), esplicito(a); **~ object** *(Gram)* complemento oggetto; **to be a ~ descendant of** discendere in linea diretta da; **the ~ opposite of** esattamente il contrario di; **to make a ~ hit** colpire in pieno.

2 adv *(go etc)* direttamente.

3 vt **(a)** *(aim: remark, gaze, attention)*: **to ~ at**, **to** dirigere a, rivolgere a; *(address: letter)*: **to ~ to** indirizzare a; **can you ~ me to the station?** può indicarmi la strada per la stazione? **(b)** *(control: traffic, business, group of actors)* dirigere; *(play, film, programme)* curare la regia di, dirigere. **(c)** *(instruct)*: **to ~ sb to do sth** dare direttive a qn di fare qc.

4 cpd: **~ current** n *(Elec)* corrente f continua.

di·rec·tion [daɪ'rɛkʃən] n **(a)** *(way)* direzione f; *(fig)* scopo, direzione; **in the ~ of** in direzione di; **sense of ~** senso dell'orientamento. **(b)** *(management: of business etc)* direzione f, amministrazione f; *(of play, film, programme)* regia. **(c)**: **~s** npl *(instructions: to a place)* indicazioni fpl; *(: for use)* istruzioni fpl; **to ask for ~s** chiedere la strada; **stage ~s** didascalie fpl.

di·rec·tive [dɪ'rɛktɪv] n direttiva, ordine m; **a government ~** una disposizione governativa.

di·rect·ly [dɪ'rɛktlɪ] **1** adv *(gen)* direttamente; *(at once)* subito; *(descended)* in linea diretta; *(frankly: speak)* con franchezza, senza peli sulla lingua; *(completely: opposite)* proprio. **2** conj *(non)* appena; **he'll come ~ he's ready** appena è pronto viene.

di·rect·ness [daɪ'rɛktnɪs] n *(of person, speech)* franchezza.

di·rec·tor [dɪ'rɛktə'] **1** n *(Comm etc)* dirigente m/f, direttore/trice (d'azienda); *(of play, film, TV programme)* regista m/f. **2** cpd: **D~ of Public Prosecutions** n ≈ Procuratore m della Repubblica.

di·rec·tor·ship [dɪ'rɛktəʃɪp] n direzione f.

di·rec·tory [dɪ'rɛktərɪ] n *(telephone ~)* elenco (telefonico); *(street ~)* stradario; *(trade ~)* repertorio del commercio. **2** cpd: **~ enquiries** n *(service)* servizio informazioni, informazioni fpl elenco abbonati.

dirge [dɜːdʒ] n nenia.

dirt [dɜːt] n *(on face, clothes etc)* sporco, sporcizia; *(earth)* terra; *(mud)* fango; **dog ~** bisogni mpl di un cane; **to treat sb like ~** *(fam)* trattare qn come uno straccio; **to spread the ~ about sb** *(fam)* sparlare di qn; **what's the latest ~ on...?** *(fam)* qual è l'ultimo pettegolezzo su...?

dirt-cheap ['dɜːt'tʃiːp] adj *(fam)* regalato(a).

dirti·ness ['dɜːtɪnɪs] n sporcizia, sudiciume m.

dirty ['dɜːtɪ] **1** adj **-ier, -iest** *(gen)* sporco(a); *(cut, wound)* infetto(a); *(indecent: novel, story, joke)* sporco(a), spinto(a); **to give sb a ~ look** (fam) lanciare un'occhiataccia a qn; **to play a ~ trick on sb** farla sporca a qn, fare un brutto scherzo a qn; **to have a ~ mind** pensare solo a quello; **a ~ old man** un vecchio sporcaccione; **~ word** parolaccia; **it's a ~ word these days** oggigiorno è un argomento tabù; **do your own ~ work!** non passare a me le tue gatte da pelare! **2** vt sporcare, insudiciare.

dis·abil·ity [ˌdɪsə'bɪlɪtɪ] **1** n (injury etc) menomazione f, infermità f inv; (state) invalidità f inv; (fig) handicap m inv. **2** cpd: **~ allowance** n pensione f d'invalidità.

dis·able [dɪs'eɪbl] vt (subj: illness, accident) rendere invalido(a); (tank, gun) mettere fuori uso; (Law: disqualify) rendere inabile.

dis·abled [dɪs'eɪbld] **1** adj (person) invalido(a). **2: the ~** npl gli invalidi.

dis·ad·vant·age [ˌdɪsəd'vɑːntɪdʒ] n svantaggio; **to be to sb's ~** tornare a svantaggio or sfavore di qn; **to be at a ~** essere svantaggiato, trovarsi in condizioni sfavorevoli.

dis·ad·van·taged [ˌdɪsəd'vɑːntɪdʒd] adj (person) svantaggiato(a).

dis·ad·van·ta·geous [ˌdɪsædvɑːn'teɪdʒəs] adj svantaggioso(a), sfavorevole.

dis·agree [ˌdɪsə'griː] vi **(a): to ~ (with sb on** or **about sth)** essere in disaccordo (con qn su qc), dissentire (da qn su qc); (quarrel) litigare; (view etc: conflict) essere discordante; **I ~ with you** non sono d'accordo con te. **(b)** (climate, food): **to ~ with** non fare bene a; **a hot climate ~s with me** il clima caldo non mi si confà; **onions ~ with me** la cipolla non mi va.

dis·agree·able [ˌdɪsə'griːəbl] adj (gen) spiacevole; (weather) brutto(a); (person) antipatico(a); (tone of voice etc) sgradevole.

dis·agree·ment [ˌdɪsə'griːmənt] n (with opinion) disaccordo; (quarrel) dissapore m; (between accounts etc) discrepanza, discordanza; **to have a ~ with sb** litigare con qn.

dis·al·low [ˈdɪsə'laʊ] vt respingere; (Ftbl: goal) annullare.

dis·ap·pear [ˌdɪsə'pɪər] vi scomparire, sparire; **he ~ed from sight** è scomparso alla vista; **to make sth ~** far sparire qc.

dis·ap·pear·ance [ˌdɪsə'pɪərəns] n scomparsa, sparizione f.

dis·ap·point [ˌdɪsə'pɔɪnt] vt deludere.

dis·ap·point·ed [ˌdɪsə'pɔɪntɪd] adj deluso(a).

dis·ap·point·ing [ˌdɪsə'pɔɪntɪŋ] adj deludente.

dis·ap·point·ment [ˌdɪsə'pɔɪntmənt] n (in dejection) disappunto; (cause of dejection) delusione f.

dis·ap·prov·al [ˌdɪsə'pruːvəl] n disapprovazione f.

dis·ap·prove [ˌdɪsə'pruːv] vi: **to ~ (of sb/sth)** disapprovare (qn/qc).

dis·ap·prov·ing [ˌdɪsə'pruːvɪŋ] adj di disapprovazione.

dis·arm [dɪs'ɑːm] **1** vt disarmare. **2** vi (Mil) disarmarsi.

dis·arma·ment [dɪs'ɑːməmənt] **1** n disarmo. **2** cpd: **~ talks** npl conferenza sul disarmo.

dis·arm·ing [dɪs'ɑːmɪŋ] adj (smile) disarmante.

dis·ar·ray [ˌdɪsə'reɪ] n: **in ~** (troops) in rotta; (thoughts) confuso(a); (clothes) in disordine.

dis·as·ter [dɪ'zɑːstər] **1** n (also fig) disastro. **2** cpd: **~ area** n zona disastrata.

dis·as·trous [dɪ'zɑːstrəs] adj disastroso(a).

dis·band [dɪs'bænd] **1** vt (army) congedare; (organization) sciogliere. **2** vi sciogliersi.

dis·be·lief [ˈdɪsbə'liːf] n incredulità; **in ~** incredulo.

dis·be·lieve [ˈdɪsbə'liːv] vt (person, story) non credere a, mettere in dubbio.

disc [dɪsk] **1** n (gen) disco; (identity ~: of dog) targhetta di riconoscimento; (: of soldier) piastrina di riconoscimento; (in computer) floppy disk m inv. **2** cpd: **~ brakes** npl (Aut) freni mpl a disco; **~ jockey** n disc-jockey m inv.

dis·card [dɪs'kɑːd] vt (gen) smettere; (idea, plan) scartare, abbandonare.

dis·cern [dɪ'sɜːn] vt distinguere, discernere.

dis·cern·ible [dɪ'sɜːnəbl] adj percepibile.

dis·cern·ing [dɪ'sɜːnɪŋ] adj (person) esperto(a); (look) penetrante; (taste) raffinato(a).

dis·cern·ment [dɪ'sɜːnmənt] n discernimento.

dis·charge ['dɪstʃɑːdʒ] **1** n **(a)** (of cargo) operazione f di scarico; (of gun) scarica. **(b)** (of worker) licenziamento; (of soldier) congedo; (of prisoner) rilascio; (of duty) adempimento; (of debt) estinzione f. **(c)** (Elec) scarica; (of gas, chemicals) emissione f; (Med: from wound) secrezione f; (: vaginal ~) perdite fpl (bianche). **2** [dɪs'tʃɑːdʒ] vt **(a)** (ship, load) scaricare; (shot) far partire; (subj: river) sfociare; (Med: pus etc) spurgare. **(b)** (dismiss: employee) licenziare; (: soldier) congedare; (: patient) dimettere; (: prisoner) rilasciare; (: defendant) prosciogliere; (settle: debt) pagare, estinguere; (complete: task, duty) assolvere, adempiere a. **3** [dɪs'tʃɑːdʒ] vi (wound, sore) spurgare.

dis·ci·ple [dɪ'saɪpl] n (also fig) discepolo/a.

dis·ci·pli·nary ['dɪsɪplɪnərɪ] adj disciplinare; **to take ~ action against sb** prendere un provvedimento disciplinare contro qn.

dis·ci·pline ['dɪsɪplɪn] **1** n disciplina; (punishment) punizione f, castigo; **to keep/maintain ~** tenere/mantenere la disciplina. **2** vt (punish) punire, castigare; **to ~ o.s. to do sth** imporsi di fare qc; **to ~ o.s.** darsi una regola.

dis·claim [dɪs'kleɪm] vt negare, smentire; **to ~ all knowledge of sth** negare di essere a conoscenza di qc.

dis·claim·er [dɪs'kleɪmər] n smentita; **to issue a ~** pubblicare una smentita.

dis·close [dɪs'kləʊz] vt (all senses) rivelare.

dis·clo·sure [dɪs'kləʊʒər] n rivelazione f.

dis·co ['dɪskəʊ] n (fam: place) discoteca; (: event) festa (con discoteca).

dis·col·our, (Am) **dis·col·or** [dɪs'kʌlər] vt sbiadire, scolorire.

dis·col·o(u)r·a·tion [dɪsˌkʌlə'reɪʃən] n scolorimento.

dis·com·fi·ture [dɪs'kʌmfɪtʃər] n disagio, imbarazzo.

dis·com·fort [dɪs'kʌmfət] n (lack of comfort) scomodità f inv; (uneasiness) disagio, imbarazzo; **his wound gave him some ~** la ferita gli dava fastidio.

dis·con·cert [ˌdɪskən'sɜːt] vt sconcertare.

dis·con·cert·ed [ˌdɪskən'sɜːtɪd] adj sconcertato(a).

dis·con·nect ['dɪskə'nekt] vt (pipe, television) staccare; (electricity, gas etc) sospendere (l'erogazione di); **I've been ~ed** (Telec: for non-payment) mi hanno tagliato il telefono; (: in mid-conversation) è caduta la linea, si è interrotta la comunicazione.

dis·con·so·late [dɪs'kɒnsəlɪt] adj sconsolato(a).

dis·con·tent [ˌdɪskən'tent] n scontentezza, dispiacere m; (Pol) malcontento, scontento.

dis·con·tent·ed [ˌdɪskən'tentɪd] adj: **~ (with, about)** scontento(a) (di), insoddisfatto(a) (di).

dis·con·tinue ['dɪskən'tɪnjuː] vt interrompere; (Comm): **~d line** articolo fuori produzione.

dis·cord ['dɪskɔːd] n disaccordo, discordia; (Mus) dissonanza.

dis·cord·ant [dɪs'kɔːdənt] adj non armonioso(a); (sound) dissonante, stonato(a).

dis·co·theque ['dɪskəʊtɛk] n discoteca.

dis·count ['dɪskaʊnt] 1 n (on article) sconto, riduzione f; at a ~ con uno sconto; **to give sb a ~ on sth** fare uno sconto a qn su qc; ~ **for cash** sconto cassa. 2 [dɪs'kaʊnt] vt (report etc) non badare a. 3 cpd: ~ **rate** n tasso di sconto; ~ **store** n negozio di vendita diretta.

dis·cour·age [dɪs'kʌrɪdʒ] vt (a) (dishearten) scoraggiare; **I don't want to ~ you, but...** non per scoraggiarti, ma.... (b) (dissuade, deter) tentare di dissuadere; **to ~ sb from doing sth** tentare di dissuadere qn dal fare qc.

dis·cour·age·ment [dɪs'kʌrɪdʒmənt] n (dissuasion) disapprovazione f; (depression) scoraggiamento; **to act as a ~ to** ostacolare.

dis·cour·ag·ing [dɪs'kʌrɪdʒɪŋ] adj scoraggiante, avvilente.

dis·cour·teous [dɪs'kɜːtɪəs] adj scortese.

dis·cour·tesy [dɪs'kɜːtɪsɪ] n scortesia.

dis·cov·er [dɪs'kʌvəʳ] vt (gen) scoprire; (after search) scovare, trovare; (notice: loss, mistake) scoprire, accorgersi di.

dis·cov·ery [dɪs'kʌvərɪ] n scoperta.

dis·cred·it [dɪs'krɛdɪt] 1 n discredito; **to bring ~ on sb/sth** far cadere qn/qc in discredito. 2 vt screditare.

dis·creet [dɪs'kriːt] adj discreto(a).

dis·crep·an·cy [dɪs'krɛpənsɪ] n discrepanza; **she pointed out a ~ in his argument** mise in evidenza una contraddizione nel suo discorso.

dis·cre·tion [dɪs'krɛʃən] n discrezione f; **at your/ his** etc ~ a tua/sua etc discrezione; **use your own ~** giudica tu.

dis·cre·tion·ary [dɪs'krɛʃənərɪ] adj (powers) discrezionale.

dis·crimi·nate [dɪs'krɪmɪneɪt] vi: **to ~ (between)** (gen) distinguere (tra); (pej) fare discriminazione (tra); **to ~ against/in favour of** fare discriminazioni ai danni di/a favore di.

dis·crimi·nat·ing [dɪs'krɪmɪneɪtɪŋ] adj (person) esigente; (judgment) acuto(a); (ear, taste) fine; (tax, duty) discriminante.

dis·crimi·na·tion [dɪs,krɪmɪ'neɪʃən] n **(a)** (prejudice): ~ **(against/in favour of)** discriminazione f (ai danni di/a favore di); **racial/sexual ~** discriminazione razziale/sessuale. **(b)** (good judgment) discernimento.

dis·cus ['dɪskəs] 1 n disco. 2 cpd: ~ **thrower** n lanciatore m di disco.

dis·cuss [dɪs'kʌs] vt (topic etc) discutere di; (problem, plan) discutere; **to ~ sth at length** dibattere qc a lungo.

dis·cus·sion [dɪs'kʌʃən] n discussione f; (meeting) colloquio, dibattito; **under ~** in discussione.

dis·dain [dɪs'deɪn] 1 n disdegno. 2 vt sdegnare; **to ~ to do sth** disdegnare di fare qc.

dis·ease [dɪ'ziːz] n malattia.

dis·eased [dɪ'ziːzd] adj malato(a).

dis·em·bark [,dɪsɪm'baːk] vi sbarcare.

dis·em·bar·ka·tion [,dɪsɛmbaː'keɪʃən] n sbarco.

dis·em·bod·ied ['dɪsɪm'bɒdɪd] adj incorporeo(a); (voice) etereo(a).

dis·en·chant·ed [,dɪsɪn'tʃaːntɪd] adj disincantato(a); ~ **(with)** deluso (da).

dis·en·gage [,dɪsɪn'geɪdʒ] vt (Aut: clutch) disinnestare.

dis·en·tan·gle ['dɪsɪn'tæŋgl] vt (string etc) sbrogliare; **to ~ o.s. from** (fig) districarsi da, sbrogliarsi da.

dis·fa·vour, (Am) **dis·fa·vor** [dɪs'feɪvəʳ] n disapprovazione f; **to fall into ~** cadere in disgrazia; **to be in ~ with sb** avere la disapprovazione di qn; **to look with ~ on** disapprovare.

dis·fig·ure [dɪs'fɪgəʳ] vt (person) sfigurare; (landscape) deturpare.

dis·fig·ure·ment [dɪs'fɪgəmənt] n: **to have a hideous ~** essere orribilmente sfigurato; **his ~ was caused by an accident** rimase sfigurato in un incidente.

dis·gorge [dɪs'gɔːdʒ] vt (subj: river) riversare; (: bus, lift etc) vomitare.

dis·grace [dɪs'greɪs] 1 n (state of shame) disonore m, vergogna; (shameful thing) vergogna; (disfavour) disgrazia; **he's a ~ to the school/family** è il disonore della scuola/della famiglia; **he's brought ~ upon himself** si è ricoperto di vergogna; **to be in ~** essere in disgrazia; (child, dog) essere in castigo; **it's a ~** è una vergogna. 2 vt (family, country) disonorare; **he ~d himself** ha fatto una pessima figura; **he was publicly ~d** fu svergognato pubblicamente.

dis·grace·ful [dɪs'greɪsfʊl] adj vergognoso(a), scandaloso(a).

dis·grun·tled [dɪs'grʌntld] adj (person) di malumore inv; (look) seccato(a).

dis·guise [dɪs'gaɪz] 1 n travestimento; **in ~** travestito. 2 vt (gen) travestire; (voice) contraffare; (feelings etc) mascherare; **to ~ o.s. as** travestirsi da; **there's no disguising the fact that...** non si può nascondere (il fatto) che... .

dis·gust [dɪs'gʌst] 1 n disgusto; **much to my ~** con mio profondo disgusto; **she left in ~** se n'è andata disgustata. 2 vt disgustare.

dis·gust·ing [dɪs'gʌstɪŋ] adj disgustoso(a).

dish [dɪʃ] n piatto; (food) piatto, pietanza; **to wash** or **do the ~es** lavare o fare i piatti.

♦ **dish out** vt + adv (food) servire; (advice) elargire; (money) tirare fuori; (exam papers) distribuire.

♦ **dish up** vt + adv (food) servire; (facts, figures) presentare.

dish·cloth ['dɪʃklɒθ] n strofinaccio dei piatti.

dis·heart·en [dɪs'haːtn] vt scoraggiare.

dis·heart·en·ing [dɪs'haːtnɪŋ] adj scoraggiante, deprimente.

di·shev·elled, (Am) **di·shev·eled** [dɪ'ʃevəld] adj (hair) arruffato(a); (clothes) tutto(a) in disordine.

dis·hon·est [dɪs'ɒnɪst] adj (person, action) disonesto(a); (means) sleale.

dis·hon·es·ty [dɪs'ɒnɪstɪ] n (see adj) disonestà; slealtà.

dis·hon·our, (Am) **dis·hon·or** [dɪs'ɒnəʳ] n disonore m; **to bring ~ on** gettare il disonore su, far disonore a.

dis·hon·our·able, (Am) **dis·honor·able** [dɪs'ɒnərəbl] adj disonorevole.

dish·towel ['dɪʃ,taʊəl] n strofinaccio dei piatti.

dish·washer ['dɪʃ,wɒʃəʳ] n (machine) lavastoviglie f inv; (person: in restaurant) lavapiatti m/f inv, sguattero/a.

dis·il·lu·sion [,dɪsɪ'luːʒən] 1 n delusione f, disinganno. 2 vt disilludere, disingannare; **to become ~ed (with)** perdere le illusioni (su).

dis·in·cen·tive [,dɪsɪn'sɛntɪv] n: **to act as a ~ (to)** agire da freno (su); **to be a ~ to** scoraggiare.

dis·in·cli·na·tion [,dɪsɪnklɪ'neɪʃən] n: ~ **(for/to do)** riluttanza (a/a fare).

dis·in·clined [,dɪsɪn'klaɪnd] adj: **to be ~ to do sth** essere poco propenso(a) a fare qc.

dis·in·fect [,dɪsɪn'fɛkt] vt disinfettare.

dis·in·fec·tant [,dɪsɪn'fɛktənt] n disinfettante m.

dis·in·her·it ['dɪsɪn'hɛrɪt] vt diseredare.

dis·in·te·grate [dɪs'ɪntɪgreɪt] vi disintegrarsi; *(fig: society, theory)* disgregarsi.

dis·in·te·gra·tion [dɪs,ɪntɪ'greɪʃən] n *(vedi vb)* disintegrazione f; disgregamento.

dis·in·ter·est·ed [dɪs'ɪntrɪstɪd] adj *(impartial)* disinteressato(a); *(strictly incorrect: uninterested)* non interessato(a), indifferente.

dis·joint·ed [dɪs'dʒɔɪntɪd] adj sconnesso(a), slegato(a).

disk [dɪsk] n = **disc.**

dis·like [dɪs'laɪk] 1 n: ~ (of) antipatia (per), avversione f (per); **to take a ~ to sb/sth** prendere in antipatia qn/qc. 2 vt *(thing, person):* **I ~ it** non mi piace; **I ~ the idea** l'idea non mi va; **I ~ her intensely** mi è fortemente antipatica.

dis·lo·cate ['dɪslaʊkeɪt] vt *(Med)* slogare, lussare; *(fig: plans)* scombussolare; **he ~d his shoulder** si è lussato una spalla.

dis·lodge [dɪs'lɒdʒ] vt *(gen)* rimuovere; *(enemy)* far sgomberare.

dis·loy·al ['dɪs'lɔɪəl] adj: ~ (to) sleale (verso).

dis·loy·al·ty ['dɪs'lɔɪəltɪ] n slealtà.

dis·mal ['dɪzməl] adj *(gloomy)* tetro(a), cupo(a); *(weather)* grigio(a); **it was a ~ failure** è stato un misero fallimento.

dis·man·tle [dɪs'mæntl] vt *(machine etc)* smontare; *(service, system)* smantellare.

dis·may [dɪs'meɪ] 1 n sgomento, costernazione f; **in ~** costernato; **much to my ~** con mio gran stupore. 2 vt costernare, sgomentare.

dis·miss [dɪs'mɪs] vt **(a)** *(worker)* licenziare; *(official)* destituire. **(b)** *(gen)* congedare; *(charge, accused)* prosciogliere; *(court case, matter)* chiudere; *(problem, possibility)* scartare; **class ~ed!** *(Scol)* potete andare!

dis·mis·sal [dɪs'mɪsəl] n *(see vb)* licenziamento; destituzione f; congedo; proscioglimento *(also of case).*

dis·mount [dɪs'maʊnt] 1 vi: **to ~ (from)** smontare (da), scendere (da). 2 vt *(rider)* disarcionare.

dis·obedi·ence [,dɪsə'biːdɪəns] n disubbidienza.

dis·obedi·ent [,dɪsə'biːdɪənt] adj disubbidiente.

dis·obey ['dɪsə'beɪ] vt *(person, order)* disubbidire a; *(rule)* trasgredire.

dis·oblig·ing ['dɪsə'blaɪdʒɪŋ] adj poco disponibile.

dis·or·der [dɪs'ɔːdə'] n **(a)** *(confusion)* confusione f, caos m; *(untidiness)* disordine m; *(Pol: rioting)* disordini, tumulto; **in ~** in disordine; **civil ~** disordini interni. **(b)** *(Med)* disturbi mpl.

dis·or·dered [dɪs'ɔːdəd] adj *(room)* disordinato(a), in disordine; *(life)* disordinato(a); *(thoughts)* disordinato(a), confuso(a); *(Med: mind)* turbato(a).

dis·or·der·ly [dɪs'ɔːdəlɪ] adj *(room)* disordinato(a); *(behaviour, crowd)* turbolento(a); *(meeting)* tumultuoso(a), burrascoso(a); **~ conduct** *(Law)* comportamento atto a turbare l'ordine pubblico.

dis·or·gan·ized [dɪs'ɔːɡənaɪzd] adj *(person, life)* disorganizzato(a); *(system, meeting)* male organizzato(a).

dis·own [dɪs'əʊn] vt rinnegare, ripudiare.

dis·par·age [dɪs'pærɪdʒ] vt *(person, achievements)* denigrare.

dis·par·ag·ing [dɪs'pærɪdʒɪŋ] adj *(comment etc)* denigratorio(a); **to be ~ about sb/sth** denigrare qn/qc.

dis·par·ity [dɪs'pærɪtɪ] n disparità f inv.

dis·pas·sion·ate [dɪs'pæʃənɪt] adj *(unbiased)* spassionato(a), imparziale; *(unemotional)* calmo(a).

dis·patch [dɪs'pætʃ] 1 n **(a)** *(sending: of person)* invio; *(: of goods)* spedizione f, invio. **(b)** *(Mil, Press: report)* dispaccio; **mentioned in ~es** *(Mil)* citato all'ordine del giorno. **(c)** *(promptness)* prontezza, rapidità. 2 vt *(send: letter, goods)* spe-

dire; *(: messenger, troops)* inviare; *(deal with: business)* sbrigare; *(old use: kill)* far fuori. 3 cpd: ~ **rider** n *(Mil)* corriere m, portaordini m inv.

dis·pel [dɪs'pel] vt dissipare.

dis·pen·sa·ry [dɪs'pensərɪ] n farmacia; *(clinic)* dispensario, ambulatorio.

dis·pen·sa·tion [,dɪspen'seɪʃən] n *(Law, Rel)* dispensa.

dis·pense [dɪs'pens] vt *(food, money)* dispensare, distribuire; *(justice)* amministrare; *(medicine)* preparare e dare; **to ~ prescriptions** preparare e dare medicine su ricetta.

♦ **dispense with** vi + prep *(do without)* fare a meno di; *(make unnecessary)* rendere superfluo(a).

dis·pens·er [dɪs'pensə'] n *(at chemist's)* farmacista m/f; *(container)* distributore m.

dis·pens·ing chem·ist [dɪ'spensɪŋ'kemɪst] n *(person)* farmacista m/f; *(shop)* farmacia.

dis·per·sal [dɪs'pɜːsəl] n dispersione f.

dis·perse [dɪs'pɜːs] 1 vt *(scatter)* disperdere; *(information etc)* mettere in giro. 2 vi *(crowd)* dispersi; *(mist)* dissiparsi.

dis·per·sion [dɪs'pɜːʃən] n = **dispersal.**

dis·pir·it·ed [dɪs'pɪrɪtɪd] adj abbattuto(a), scoraggiato(a); *(sigh)* di avvilimento.

dis·place [dɪs'pleɪs] vt *(move)* spostare; *(replace)* rimpiazzare, soppiantare; *(remove from office)* destituire; *(water: Naut)* dislocare; *(: Phys)* spostare; **~d person** profugo/a.

dis·place·ment [dɪs'pleɪsmənt] n *(see vb)* spostamento; rimpiazzo; destituzione f; dislocamento.

dis·play [dɪs'pleɪ] 1 n *(of goods for sale, paintings etc)* mostra, esposizione f; *(also: window ~)* mostra; *(of emotion)* manifestazione f; *(of strength, authority, force, interest)* dimostrazione f; *(ostentation)* sfoggio, ostentazione f; *(military ~)* parata *(militare)*; *(computer ~)* display m inv; **on ~** *(gen)* in mostra; *(goods)* in vetrina; *(results, art)* esposto. 2 vt *(gen)* esporre; *(ostentatiously)* ostentare, far sfoggio di; *(emotion, ignorance)* mostrare, manifestare; *(notice, results)* affiggere.

dis·please [dɪs'pliːz] vt dispiacere a, scontentare; **~d with** scontento di.

dis·pleas·ure [dɪs'pleʒə'] n: ~ (at) dispiacere (per).

dis·pos·able [dɪs'pəʊzəbl] adj *(not reusable: napkin etc)* da buttar via; *(available: income)* disponibile.

dis·pos·al [dɪs'pəʊzəl] n *(of rubbish)* eliminazione f; *(of property etc: by selling)* vendita; *(: by giving away)* cessione f; **to put sth at sb's ~** mettere qc a disposizione di qn; **to have at one's ~** avere a propria disposizione.

dis·pose [dɪs'pəʊz] vt **(a)** *(arrange: furniture)* disporre; *(troops)* disporre, schierare. **(b): to be ~d to do sth** essere disposto a fare qc; **to be well ~d towards sb/sth** essere ben disposto verso qn/qc.

♦ **dispose of** vi + prep *(get rid of: evidence, rubbish etc)* sbarazzarsi di, disfarsi di; *(: matter, problem)* eliminare; *(Comm: sell)* vendere.

dis·po·si·tion [,dɪspə'zɪʃən] n *(temperament)* indole f, temperamento.

dis·pos·sess ['dɪspə'zes] vt: **to ~ sb (of)** spossessare qn (di).

dis·pro·por·tion·ate [,dɪsprə'pɔːʃnɪt] adj: ~ (to) sproporzionato(a) (a or rispetto a).

dis·prove [dɪs'pruːv] vt confutare.

dis·put·able [dɪs'pjuːtəbl] adj discutibile, contestabile.

dis·pute [dɪs'pjuːt] 1 n *(quarrel)* disputa; *(controversy)* discussione f, controversia; *(legal)* lite f; **industrial ~** controversia sindacale; **beyond ~** fuori discussione; **to be in or under ~** *(matter)* essere in discussione; *(territory)* essere oggetto di contesa. **2** *vt (statement, claim)* contestare; **to ~ a victory** disputarsi una vittoria. **3** *vi (argue)*: **to ~ (about or over)** discutere (su).

dis·quali·fi·ca·tion [dɪsˌkwɒlɪfɪ'keɪʃən] *n (from competition)* squalifica; *(of member)* espulsione *f*; *(from driving)* ritiro della patente.

dis·quali·fy [dɪs'kwɒlɪfaɪ] *vt*: **to ~ sb (from)** squalificare qn (da); **to ~ sb from doing sth** impedire a qn di fare qc; **to ~ sb from driving** ritirare la patente a qn; **it disqualified him for the job** lo ha reso inabile al lavoro.

dis·qui·et [dɪs'kwaɪət] *n* inquietudine *f*.

dis·qui·et·ing [dɪs'kwaɪətɪŋ] *adj* inquietante, allarmante.

dis·re·gard ['dɪsrɪ'gɑːd] **1** *n (indifference)*: **~ (for)** *(feelings)* insensibilità (a), indifferenza *(verso)*; *(danger)* noncuranza (di); *(money)* disprezzo (di); *(non-observance: of law, rules)*: **~ (of)** inosservanza (di). **2** *vt (remark, feelings)* ignorare, non tenere conto di; *(duty)* trascurare; *(authority)* non curarsi di.

dis·re·pair ['dɪsrɪ'peəʳ] *n* cattivo stato; **to fall into ~** *(building)* andare in rovina; *(street)* deteriorarsi.

dis·repu·table [dɪs'rɛpjʊtəbl] *adj (person)* poco raccomandabile; *(clothing, behaviour)* indecente; *(area)* malfamato(a), poco raccomandabile.

dis·re·pute ['dɪsrɪ'pjuːt] *n* disonore *m*, vergogna; **to fall into ~** rovinarsi la reputazione; **to bring into ~** rovinare la reputazione di.

dis·re·spect ['dɪsrɪs'pɛkt] *n* mancanza di rispetto.

dis·re·spect·ful [ˌdɪsrɪs'pɛktfʊl] *adj (person)* poco rispettoso(a); *(comment)* irriverente; **to be ~** *or* **towards** mancare di rispetto a *or* verso.

dis·rupt [dɪs'rʌpt] *vt (meeting, lesson)* disturbare, interrompere; *(public transport)* creare scompiglio in; *(plans)* scombussolare.

dis·rup·tion [dɪs'rʌpʃən] *n (see vb)* interruzione *f*; scompiglio; scombussolamento.

dis·rup·tive [dɪs'rʌptɪv] *adj (influence)* negativo(a), deleterio(a); *(strike action)* paralizzante.

dis·sat·is·fac·tion ['dɪsˌsætɪs'fækʃən] *n*: **~ (with)** insoddisfazione *f* (per), scontento (per *or a* causa di).

dis·sat·is·fied ['dɪs'sætɪsfaɪd] *adj*: **~ (with)** insoddisfatto(a) (di), scontento(a) (di).

dis·sect [dɪ'sɛkt] *vt (animal)* dissecare; *(fig)* vivisezionare, sviscerare.

dis·sec·tion [dɪ'sɛkʃən] *n (see vb)* dissezione *f*; vivisezione *f*.

dis·sem·ble [dɪ'sɛmbl] *vt, vi* dissimulare.

dis·semi·nate [dɪ'sɛmɪneɪt] *vt* disseminare.

dis·sen·sion [dɪ'sɛnʃən] *n* dissenso.

dis·sent [dɪ'sɛnt] **1** *n* dissenso. **2** *vi (gen)*: **to ~ (from)** dissentire (da).

dis·sent·er [dɪ'sɛntəʳ] *n (Rel, Pol etc)* dissidente *m/f*.

dis·sent·ing [dɪ'sɛntɪŋ] *adj* dissenziente.

dis·ser·ta·tion [ˌdɪsə'teɪʃən] *n (Univ)* tesi *f inv*, dissertazione *f*.

dis·ser·vice ['dɪs'sɜːvɪs] *n*: **to do sb a ~** rendere un cattivo servizio a qn.

dis·si·dent ['dɪsɪdənt] *(Pol)* **1** *n* dissidente *m/f*. **2** *adj (speech, voice)* di dissenso; *(group)* dissidente.

dis·simi·lar ['dɪ'sɪmɪləʳ] *adj*: **~ (to)** dissimile (da), diverso(a) (da); **two very ~ cases** due casi molto dissimili l'uno dall'altro.

dis·simi·lar·ity [ˌdɪsɪmɪ'lærɪtɪ] *n*: **~ (between)** dissomiglianza (tra).

dis·si·pate ['dɪsɪpeɪt] *vt* dissipare.

dis·si·pat·ed ['dɪsɪpeɪtɪd] *adj (person, life)* dissipato(a); *(behaviour)* dissoluto(a).

dis·si·pa·tion [ˌdɪsɪ'peɪʃən] *n (gen)* dissipazione *f*; *(debauchery)* dissolutezza.

dis·so·ci·ate [dɪ'səʊʃɪeɪt] *vt*: **to ~ (from)** dissociare (da), separare (da); **to ~ o.s. from** dichiarare di non avere niente a che fare con; *(from political line)* dissociarsi da.

dis·so·lute ['dɪsəluːt] *adj* dissoluto(a).

dis·so·lu·tion [ˌdɪsə'luːʃən] *n (of partnership, Pol)* scioglimento; *(decay)* dissoluzione *f*.

dis·solve [dɪ'zɒlv] **1** *vt (gen)* dissolvere, sciogliere; *(partnership, business, Pol)* sciogliere. **2** *vi* dissolversi, sciogliersi; *(Pol)* sciogliersi; **it ~s in water** si scioglie in acqua; **she ~d into tears** si è sciolta in lacrime.

dis·suade [dɪ'sweɪd] *vt*: **to ~ (from doing)** dissuadere (dal fare), distogliere (dall'idea di fare).

dis·tance ['dɪstəns] *n (between 2 things)* distanza; *(far-off point)* distanza, lontananza; **the ~ between the houses** la distanza *or* lo spazio tra le case; **what ~ is it to London?** quanto dista Londra?; **it's a good ~** dista un bel po', è parecchio lontano; **it's within walking ~** ci si arriva a piedi; **at a ~ of 2 metres** a 2 metri di distanza; **in the ~** in lontananza; **from a ~** da lontano; **at this ~ in time** a tanto tempo di distanza; **to keep sb at a ~** tenere qn a distanza; **to keep one's ~** tenersi a distanza.

dis·tant ['dɪstənt] *adj (gen)* lontano(a); *(country)* distante, lontano(a); *(likeness)* vago(a), lontano(a); *(fig: aloof: manner, person)* distaccato(a); **the school is 2 km ~ from the church** la scuola dista *or* è distante 2 km dalla chiesa; **in the ~ past/future** nel lontano passato/futuro.

dis·tant·ly ['dɪstəntlɪ] *adv (smile, say)* freddamente, con distacco; *(resemble)* vagamente; **we are ~ related** siamo lontani parenti.

dis·taste ['dɪs'teɪst] *n*: **~ (for)** ripugnanza (per).

dis·taste·ful [dɪs'teɪstful] *adj* sgradevole; **the very idea is ~** la sola idea mi ripugna.

dis·tem·per¹ [dɪs'tɛmpəʳ] *n (paint)* tempera.

dis·tem·per² [dɪs'tɛmpəʳ] *n (of dogs)* cimurro.

dis·tend [dɪs'tɛnd] **1** *vt* gonfiare. **2** *vi* gonfiarsi.

dis·til, *(Am)* **dis·till** [dɪs'tɪl] *vt* distillare.

dis·till·ery [dɪs'tɪlərɪ] *n* distilleria.

dis·tinct [dɪs'tɪŋkt] *adj* **(a)** *(different: species etc)*: **~ (from)** diverso(a) (da), distinto(a) (da); **as ~ from** a differenza di. **(b)** *(clear: sound, shape)* chiaro(a), distinto(a); *(unmistakable: increase, change, feeling etc)* palese, netto(a).

dis·tinc·tion [dɪs'tɪŋkʃən] *n (difference)* distinzione *f*, differenza; *(mark of honour)* onorificenza; **a writer of ~** uno scrittore di notevoli qualità; **to draw a ~ between** fare distinzione tra; **he got a ~ in English** *(Scol)* ha avuto il massimo dei voti in inglese; *(Univ)* ha ottenuto la lode.

dis·tinc·tive [dɪs'tɪŋktɪv] *adj* tutto(a) particolare.

dis·tinct·ly [dɪs'tɪŋktlɪ] *adv (see, hear)* distintamente; *(promise)* chiaramente; *(prefer)* nettamente; *(friendly, better)* decisamente.

dis·tin·guish [dɪs'tɪŋgwɪʃ] **1** *vt* distinguere; **to ~ o.s. (as)** distinguersi (come); **he can't ~ red from green** non distingue il rosso dal verde; **he could just ~ the form of a man** riusciva a malapena a distinguere la sagoma di un uomo. **2** *vi*: **to ~ (between)** distinguere (tra).

dis·tin·guished [dɪs'tɪŋgwɪʃt] *adj (eminent: pianist)* eminente, noto(a); *(: scholar)* insigne; *(: career)* brillante; *(refined)* distinto(a), signorile.

dis·tort [dɪs'tɔːt] *vt (also fig)* distorcere; *(face)* deformare; *(account, news)* falsare; **a ~ed impression** una falsa impressione.

dis·tor·tion [dɪs'tɔːʃən] *n (gen)* distorsione *f*; *(of truth etc)* alterazione *f*; *(of facts)* travisamento.

dis·tract [dɪs'trækt] vt (person): **to ~ sb (from sth)** distrarre qn (da qc); **to ~ sb's attention (from sth)** distrarre or sviare l'attenzione di qn (da qc).

dis·tract·ed [dɪs'træktɪd] adj confuso(a); **to drive sb ~ far** impazzire qn.

dis·trac·tion [dɪs'trækʃən] n **(a)** (interruption) distrazione f; (entertainment) distrazione, diversivo. **(b)** (distress, anxiety): **to drive sb to ~ far** impazzire qn.

dis·traught [dɪs'trɔːt] adj stravolto(a), sconvolto(a).

dis·tress [dɪs'tres] 1 n **(a)** (pain) dolore m; (mental anguish) angoscia, pena; **to be in great ~** essere sconvolto or affranto dal dolore. **(b)** (poverty) bisogno. **(c)** (danger) pericolo; **in ~** (ship etc) in pericolo, in difficoltà. 2 vt addolorare. 3 cpd: **~ signal** n segnale m di soccorso.

dis·tress·ing [dɪs'tresɪŋ] adj penoso(a), doloroso(a).

dis·trib·ute [dɪs'trɪbjuːt] vt (leaflets, prizes, load) distribuire; (tasks) ripartire.

dis·tri·bu·tion [dɪstrɪ'bjuːʃən] n distribuzione f.

dis·tribu·tor [dɪs'trɪbjʊtəʳ] n **(a)** (Aut, Tech) distributore m. **(b)** (Comm) concessionario; (Cine) distributore m.

dis·trict ['dɪstrɪkt] 1 n (of country) regione f; (of town) quartiere m; (administrative area) distretto. 2 cpd: **~ attorney** n (Am) ≃ Procuratore m della Repubblica; **~ council** n consiglio distrettuale; **~ manager** n responsabile m di zona.

dis·trust [dɪs'trʌst] 1 n: **~ (of)** diffidenza (verso). 2 vt diffidare di, non fidarsi di.

dis·trust·ful [dɪs'trʌstfʊl] adj diffidente.

dis·turb [dɪs'tɜːb] vt (bother, interrupt) disturbare, importunare; (worry) turbare; (sleep, order, meeting etc) turbare, disturbare; (water) turbare; (papers) scompigliare; **sorry to ~ you** scusi se la disturbo; **'please do not ~'** 'non disturbare'.

dis·turb·ance [dɪs'tɜːbəns] n (social, political) disordini mpl; (in house) lite f; (in street) tafferuglio; (interruption) interruzione f; **~ of the peace** disturbo della quiete pubblica; **to cause a ~** provocare disordini; (Law) turbare l'ordine pubblico.

dis·turbed [dɪs'tɜːbd] adj turbato(a); **to be emotionally ~** (Psych) avere problemi emotivi; **to be mentally ~** (Psych) essere malato di mente.

dis·use ['dɪs'juːs] n: **to fall into ~** cadere in disuso.

dis·used ['dɪs'juːzd] adj abbandonato(a), in disuso.

ditch [dɪtʃ] 1 n fosso, fossa; (irrigation channel) fosso or canale m d'irrigazione. 2 vt (fam: get rid of: car) abbandonare, mollare; (: person) piantare.

dith·er ['dɪðəʳ] (fam) 1 n: **to be in a ~** essere in agitazione. 2 vi agitarsi; **to ~ over a decision** tentennare di fronte a una decisione.

dit·to ['dɪtəʊ] n (fam): **I'd like a coffee — ~ (for me)** per me caffè — per me idem.

dit·ty ['dɪtɪ] n canzoncina.

di·van [dɪ'væn] 1 n divano. 2 cpd: **~ bed** n divano letto.

dive [daɪv] 1 n **(a)** (of swimmer, goalkeeper) tuffo; (of submarine) immersione f; (Aer) picchiata. **(b)** (pej fam: club etc) bettola. 2 vi **(a)** (swimmer): **to ~ (into)** tuffarsi (in); (submarine) immergersi; (Aer) scendere in picchiata; (Ftbl) tuffarsi. **(b)** (fam: move quickly): **to ~ out** saltare fuori; **to ~ into** (doorway, hole) buttarsi dentro; (car, taxi) saltare su; **he ~d for cover** si è buttato al riparo; **he ~d into the crowd** si tuffò or si lanciò tra la folla; **he ~d for the exit** si è lanciato or precipitato verso l'uscita.

dive-bomb ['daɪvbɒm] vt (town etc) bombardare in picchiata.

div·er ['daɪvəʳ] n (swimmer) tuffatore/trice; (deep-sea ~) palombaro.

di·verge [daɪ'vɜːdʒ] vi divergere.

di·ver·gence [daɪ'vɜːdʒəns] n divergenza.

di·ver·gent [daɪ'vɜːdʒənt] adj divergente.

di·verse [daɪ'vɜːs] adj svariato(a), vario(a).

di·ver·si·fy [daɪ'vɜːsɪfaɪ] 1 vt rendere vario(a); (Comm) diversificare. 2 vi (Comm) diversificarsi.

di·ver·sion [daɪ'vɜːʃən] n (of traffic, river) deviazione f; (pastime) diversivo, distrazione f; **to create a ~** creare un'azione diversiva.

di·ver·sity [daɪ'vɜːsɪtɪ] n varietà f inv, diversità f inv.

di·vert [daɪ'vɜːt] vt **(a)** (traffic, river) deviare; (conversation, attention, person) sviare; (train, plane) dirottare. **(b)** (amuse) distrarre, divertire.

di·vest [daɪ'vest] vt: **to ~ of** spogliare di.

di·vide [dɪ'vaɪd] 1 vt: **to ~ (from/into)** dividere (da/in); **to ~ (between, among)** dividere (tra), ripartire (tra); **to ~ by 6** dividere 36 per 6; **40 ~d by 5** 40 diviso 5. 2 vi (road, river) dividersi, biforcarsi; (Math) essere divisibile.

♦ **divide off** vi + adv (road) separarsi, staccarsi. 2 vt + adv (land) separare.

♦ **divide out** vt + adv: **to ~ out (between, among)** (sweets etc) distribuire (tra); (tasks) distribuire or ripartire (tra).

♦ **divide up** vt + adv dividere.

di·vid·ed [dɪ'vaɪdɪd] adj (country, couple) diviso(a); (opinions) discordi; **to be ~ in one's mind about sth** essere indeciso su qc.

divi·dend ['dɪvɪdend] n (Fin) dividendo.

di·vid·ers [dɪ'vaɪdəz] npl compasso a punte fisse.

di·vine [dɪ'vaɪn] 1 adj (Rel, fig fam) divino(a); **what ~ weather!** che tempo favoloso! 2 vt (future) divinare, predire; (truth) indovinare; (water, metal) individuare tramite radioestesia.

div·ing ['daɪvɪŋ] 1 n tuffi mpl. 2 cpd: **~ board** n trampolino.

di·vin·ity [dɪ'vɪnɪtɪ] n divinità f inv; (as study) teologia.

di·vi·sible [dɪ'vɪzəbl] adj: **~ (by)** divisibile (per).

di·vi·sion [dɪ'vɪʒən] n (gen) divisione f; (Ftbl) serie f inv; **to call a ~** (Parliament) procedere alla votazione, passare ai voti; **~ of labour** divisione del lavoro.

di·vi·sive [dɪ'vaɪsɪv] adj che è causa di discordia.

di·vorce [dɪ'vɔːs] 1 n divorzio. 2 vt divorziare da; (fig) separare. 3 vi divorziare.

di·vor·cee [dɪˌvɔː'siː] n divorziato/a.

di·vulge [daɪ'vʌldʒ] vt divulgare; (evidence, information) rendere pubblico(a).

D.I.Y. abbr of **do-it-yourself.**

diz·zi·ness ['dɪzɪnɪs] n capogiro.

diz·zy ['dɪzɪ] adj (person) che soffre di capogiri; (height) vertiginoso(a); **I feel ~** mi gira la testa, ho il capogiro; **the view makes me ~** questa vista mi dà le vertigini.

D.J. abbr of disc jockey.

do [duː] 3rd pers sg present **does**; pt **did**; pp **done** 1 aux vb **(a)**: **~ you understand?** capisci?; **I don't understand** non capisco; **didn't you know?** non lo sapevi?; **didn't you ask?** non (l')hai chiesto?

(b) (for emphasis): ᴅᴏ **tell me!** su, dimmelo!; ᴅᴏ **come!** dai, vieni!; **I** ᴅᴏ **wish I could...** magari potessi...; ᴅᴏ **shut up!** ma sta zitto!; **but I** ᴅᴏ **like it!** mi piace proprio!; **so you** ᴅᴏ **know him!** dunque è vero che lo conosci!; ᴅᴏ **sit down** (polite) si accomodi la prego, prego si sieda; (annoyed) insomma siediti.

(c) *(used to avoid repeating vb)*: **you speak better than I** ~ parli meglio di me; **so does he** anche lui; **neither** ~ **we** nemmeno noi; **he doesn't like it and neither** ~ **we** a lui non piace e a noi nemmeno.

(d) *(in question tags)*: **he lives here, doesn't he?** abita qui, vero?; **I don't know him,** ~ **I?** non lo conosco, vero?

(e) *(in answers: replacing vb)*: ~ **you speak English?** — **yes, I** ~/no **I don't** parli inglese? — sì/no; **may I come in?** — ~! posso entrare? — certo!; **who made this mess?** — **I did** chi ha fatto questo macello? — io! *or* sono stato io!; **please** ~ so prego faccia pure; ~ **you really?** davvero?, ah sì?

2 *vt* **(a)** *(gen)* fare; **what are you** ~**ing tonight?** che fai stasera?; **I've got nothing to** ~ non ho niente da fare; **I shall** ~ **nothing of the sort** non farò niente del genere; **what does he** ~ **for a living?** cosa fa per vivere?; **what am I to** ~ **with you?** dimmi tu come devo fare con te!; **I'm going to** ~ **the washing up/washing** adesso faccio i piatti/il bucato; **I'm going to** ~ **the cooking** adesso mi metto a cucinare; **what's to be done?** che fare?; **I'll** ~ **all I can** farò tutto il possibile; **what can I** ~ **for you?** *(in shop)* desidera?; **it has to be done again** è tutto da rifare; **what's done cannot be undone** quello che è fatto è fatto; **well done!** bravo!, benissimo!; **that's done it!** *(fam)* ci mancava pure questa!

(b): **to** ~ **Shakespeare/Italian** *(Scol)* fare Shakespeare/italiano; **I'll** ~ **the flowers** ai fiori ci penso io; **who does your hair?** chi ti fa i capelli?; **to** ~ **one's nails** farsi le unghie; **to** ~ **one's teeth** pulirsi i denti; **this room needs** ~**ing** questa stanza è ancora da fare; **she does her guests proud** i suoi ospiti li tratta da principi.

(c) *(only as pt, pp: finish)*: **the job's done** il lavoro è fatto; **I haven't done telling you** *(fam)* non ho ancora finito la storia.

(d) *(visit: city, museum)* fare, visitare.

(e) *(Aut etc)* fare; **the car was** ~**ing 100** la macchina faceva i 100 all'ora; **we've done 200 km already** abbiamo già fatto 200 km.

(f) *(fam: be sufficient)* bastare; *(: be suitable)* andar bene; **that won't** ~ **him** questo non gli basta; **that'll** ~ **me nicely** per me va benissimo.

(g) *(play role of)* fare (la parte di); *(mimic)* imitare.

(h) *(fam: cheat)* imbrogliare, fargliela a; *(: rob)* ripulire; **I've been done!** mi hanno fregato!; **to** ~ **sb out of sth** fregare qc a qn; **he did her out of a job** le ha fregato *or* soffiato il posto.

(i) *(Culin: vegetables etc)* fare; **to** ~ **the cooking** cucinare; **how do you like your steak done?** come preferisci la bistecca?; **well done** ben cotto.

3 *vi* **(a)** *(act etc)* fare, agire; ~ **as I** ~ fai come me, fai come faccio io; **he did well to take your advice** ha fatto bene a seguire il tuo consiglio.

(b) *(get on, fare)* andare; **he's** ~**ing well/badly at school** va bene/male a scuola; **how do you** ~? piacere; **how are you** ~**ing?** *(fam)* come va?; **his business is** ~**ing well** gli affari gli vanno bene.

(c) *(finish: in past tenses only)*: **I've done** ho fatto, ho finito; **hasn't he done with that book yet?** ancora non ha finito con quel libro?; **have you done?** hai finito?, hai finito?; **the meat's done** la carne è fatta; **done to a turn** *(meat)* cotto a puntino.

(d) *(suit)* andare bene; **will it** ~? andrà bene?; **that will never** ~! non se ne parla nemmeno!; **this room will** ~ questa stanza va bene; **will it** ~

if I come back at 8? va bene se torno alle 8?; **it doesn't** ~ **to upset her** è meglio non agitarla; **this coat will** ~ **as a cover** questo cappotto potrà fare da coperta; **you'll have to make** ~ **with £10** dovrai arrangiarti con 10 sterline.

(e) *(be sufficient)* bastare; **will £5** ~? bastano *or* vanno bene 5 sterline?; **that'll** ~ basta così; **that'll** ~! *(in annoyance)* ora basta!

4 *n* *(fam)* **(a)** *(party)* festa; *(formal gathering)* occasione *f*; **it was rather a grand** ~ è stato un ricevimento piuttosto imponente; **we're having a little** ~ **on Saturday** facciamo una festicciola sabato.

(b) *(in phrases)*: **it's a poor** ~ è brutto segno; **the** ~**s and don'ts** le regole del gioco; **fair** ~**s!** *(be fair)* siamo giusti!; *(fair shares)* parti *fpl* uguali!

♦ **do away with** *vi* + *prep* *(kill)* far fuori; *(abolish)* abolire.

♦ **do by** *vi* + *prep*: **to** ~ **well/badly by sb** comportarsi bene/male con qn; **to be hard done by** essere *or* venire trattato male.

♦ **do for** *vi* + *prep* *(fam)* **(a)** *(clean for)* fare i servizi per; **to** ~ **for o.s.** fare da sé. **(b)** *(finish off: project)* mandare all'aria; *(: person)* spacciare; **he's done for!** è spacciato!

♦ **do in** *vt* + *adv* *(fam: kill)* far fuori.

♦ **do out** *vt* + *adv* *(room)* fare.

♦ **do up** *vt* + *adv* **(a)** *(dress, shoes)* allacciare; *(zip)* tirar su; *(buttons)* abbottonare; **books done up in paper** libri impacchettati. **(b)** *(renovate: house, room)* rimettere a nuovo, rifare; **to** ~ **o.s. up** farsi bello.

♦ **do with** *vi* + *prep* **(a)** *(with can, could: need)* avere bisogno di; **I could** ~ **with some help/a drink** un aiuto/un bicchierino non guasterebbe. **(b)**: **what has that got to** ~ **with it?** che c'entra?; **it has to** ~ **with...** ha a che vedere *or* fare con...; **money has a lot to** ~ **with it** è una questione di soldi; **that has nothing to** ~ **with you!** non sono affari tuoi!, **I won't have anything to** ~ **with it** non voglio aver niente a che farci. **(c)**: **what have you done with my slippers?** cosa hai fatto delle mie pantofole?; **what's he done with his hair?** che si è fatto ai capelli?

♦ **do without 1** *vi* + *prep* fare meno di. **2** *vi* + *adv* fare senza.

doc·ile ['dəʊsaɪl] *adj* docile.

dock¹ [dɒk] *n* *(Bot)* romice *m*.

dock² [dɒk] *vt* **(a)** *(tail)* mozzare. **(b)** *(pay etc)* decurtare.

dock³ [dɒk] **1** *n* *(Naut)* bacino; *(: wharf)* molo; *(: for repairs)* darsena; ~**s** dock *m inv*. **2** *vt* mettere in bacino. **3** *vi* entrare in bacino.

dock⁴ [dɒk] *n* *(in court)* banco degli imputati.

dock·er ['dɒkəʳ] *n* scaricatore *m* (di porto), portuale *m*.

dock·et ['dɒkɪt] *n* *(on parcel etc)* etichetta, cartellino.

dock·yard ['dɒkjɑːd] *n* cantiere *m* (navale).

doc·tor ['dɒktəʳ] **1** *n* **(a)** *(Med)* dottore/essa, medico; **D~ Brown** il Dottor Brown. **(b)** *(Univ)* dottore/essa. **2** *vt* **(a)** *(interfere with: food, drink)* adulterare; *(: text, document)* alterare, manipolare. **(b)** *(treat: cold)* curare. **(c)** *(fam: castrate: cat etc)* castrare.

doc·tor·ate ['dɒktərɪt] *n* ≃ dottorato di ricerca.

doc·tri·naire [,dɒktrɪ'neəʳ] *adj* dottrinario(a).

doc·tri·nal [dɒk'traɪnl] *adj* dottrinale.

doc·trine ['dɒktrɪn] *n* dottrina.

docu·ment ['dɒkjʊmənt] **1** *n* documento. **2** ['dɒkjʊmənt] *vt* documentare.

docu·men·tary [,dɒkjʊ'mentərɪ] **1** *adj* documentario(a); *(evidence)* documentato(a). **2** *n (Cine, TV)* documentario.

docu·men·ta·tion [,dɒkjʊmɛn'teɪʃən] *n* documentazione *f*.

dod·der ['dɒdə'] *vi* camminare a passi malfermi.

dod·der·ing ['dɒdərɪŋ] *adj*, **dod·dery** ['dɒdərɪ] *adj* malfermo(a) sulle gambe.

dodge [dɒdʒ] **1** *n (fam: trick)* espediente *m*, trucchetto; **a tax** ~ un trucchetto per evadere le tasse. **2** *vt (blow, ball)* schivare; *(pursuer, question, difficulty)* eludere; *(tax)* evadere; *(work, duty)* sottrarsi a; **to** ~ **the issue** menare il can per l'aia. **3** *vi* scansarsi; *(Sport)* fare una schivata; **to** ~ **out of the way** scansarsi; **to** ~ **through the traffic** destreggiarsi nel traffico; **to** ~ **behind a tree** nascondersi dietro un albero.

dodg·ems ['dɒdʒəmz] *npl (also:* **dodgem cars**) autoscontri *mpl*.

dodgy ['dɒdʒɪ] *adj* (**-ier, -iest**) *(fam)* dubbio(a); *(plan)* azzardato(a); **we're in a** ~ **situation** navighiamo in cattive acque.

doe [dəʊ] *n (deer)* femmina di daino; *(rabbit)* coniglia.

does [dʌz] *3rd pers sg present of* **do**.

doesn't ['dʌznt] = **does not**.

dog [dɒg] **1** *n* cane *m*, cagna; *(male fox, wolf)* maschio; **he's a lucky** ~ *(fam)* è nato con la camicia; **every** ~ **has its day** il momento buono viene per tutti; **he's a** ~ **in the manger** è semplicemente egoista; **to go to the** ~**s** *(person)* ridursi male, lasciarsi andare; *(nation etc)* andare in malora; **it's a** ~**'s life!** che vita da cani!; **he hasn't a** ~**'s chance** non ha la benché minima probabilità (di successo). **2** *vt (follow closely)* pedinare; *(fig: memory etc)* perseguitare; ~**ged by ill luck** perseguitato dalla scalogna; **he** ~**s my footsteps** mi sta alle costole, mi sta alle calcagna. **3** *cpd (breed, show)* canino(a); *(fox, wolf)* maschio; ~ **biscuit** *n* biscotto per cani; ~ **collar** *n* collare *m* da cani; *(fig)* collarina; ~ **food** *n* cibo per cani.

dog-eared ['dɒg,ɪəd] *adj (book)* con le orecchiette.

dog·ged ['dɒgɪd] *adj* tenace.

dog·ger·el ['dɒgərəl] *n* poesia di scarso valore.

dog·go ['dɒgəʊ] *adv (fam):* **to lie** ~ fare il morto.

dog·house ['dɒg,haʊs] *n:* **he's in the** ~ *(fam)* è in castigo.

dog·ma ['dɒgmə] *n* dogma *m*.

dog·mat·ic [dɒg'mætɪk] *adj (person, attitude)* dogmatico(a); *(tone)* autoritario(a).

do-gooder ['du:'gʊdə'] *n (fam pej):* **to be a** ~ fare il filantropo.

dogs·body ['dɒgzbɒdɪ] *n* factotum *m inv*.

dog-tired [,dɒg'taɪəd] *adj (fam)* stanco(a) morto(a).

do·ing ['du:ɪŋ] *n:* **this is your** ~ è opera tua, sei stato tu!; **that takes some** ~! accidenti che bravo!; ~**s** *npl* imprese *fpl*.

do-it-yourself ['du:ɪtjə'sɛlf] *n* il far da sé *m*, bricolage *m*.

dol·drums ['dɒldrəmz] *npl (fig):* **to be in the** ~ *(person)* essere giù di corda; *(business)* attraversare un momento difficile.

dole [dəʊl] *n (Brit fam)* sussidio di disoccupazione; **to be on the** ~ ricevere un sussidio di disoccupazione.

♦ **dole out** *vt + adv* distribuire.

dole·ful ['dəʊlfʊl] *adj (expression)* afflitto(a); *(song, prospect)* triste.

doll [dɒl] *n* bambola.

♦ **doll up** *vt + adv:* **to** ~ **o.s. up** *(fam)* farsi bello(a); **to get (all)** ~**ed up** mettersi in ghingheri.

dol·lar ['dɒlə'] *n* dollaro.

dol·lop ['dɒləp] *n (of jam etc)* cucchiaiata; *(of butter)* tocchetto.

dol·phin ['dɒlfɪn] *n* delfino.

dolt [dəʊlt] *n* imbecille *m/f*.

do·main [dəʊ'meɪn] *n (lands etc)* domini *mpl; (fig)* campo, sfera.

dome [dəʊm] *n* cupola.

domed [dəʊmd] *adj (roof)* a cupola; *(forehead)* bombato(a).

do·mes·tic [də'mɛstɪk] *adj (bliss, animal)* domestico(a); *(duty)* familiare; *(industry, flight)* nazionale; *(affairs, policy)* interno(a); *(news)* dall'interno; ~ **science** economia domestica; ~ **servant** domestico/a.

do·mes·ti·cate [də'mɛstɪkeɪt] *vt (animal)* addomesticare.

do·mes·ti·cat·ed [də'mɛstɪkeɪtɪd] *adj (animal)* addomesticato(a); *(person)* casalingo(a).

do·mes·ti·city [,dəʊmɛs'tɪsɪtɪ] *n* vita di famiglia.

domi·cile ['dɒmɪsaɪl] *n (frm)* domicilio.

domi·nant ['dɒmɪnənt] *adj (gen, Mus)* dominante; *(influence)* predominante.

domi·nate ['dɒmɪneɪt] *vt, vi* dominare.

domi·na·tion [,dɒmɪ'neɪʃən] *n* dominazione *f*.

domi·neer [,dɒmɪ'nɪə'] *vi:* **to** ~ **(over)** fare da tiranno (con).

domi·neer·ing [,dɒmɪ'nɪərɪŋ] *adj* dispotico(a), autoritario(a).

do·min·ion [də'mɪnɪən] *n (rule)* dominio, sovranità; *(territory)* dominio, possedimenti *mpl; (Brit Pol)* dominion *m inv*.

domi·no ['dɒmɪnəʊ] *n, pl* ~**es** domino.

don[1] [dɒn] *n (Brit Univ)* docente *m/f* universitario(a).

don[2] [dɒn] *vt (garment)* mettersi.

do·nate [dəʊ'neɪt] *vt* donare, far dono di.

do·na·tion [dəʊ'neɪʃən] *n* donazione *f*.

done [dʌn] *pp of* **do**.

don·key ['dɒŋkɪ] *n* asino/a; **I've known him for** ~**'s years** *(fam)* lo conosco da secoli.

donkey-work ['dɒŋkɪwɜ:k] *n (fam)* lavoro ingrato.

do·nor ['dəʊnə'] *n (gen, Med)* donatore/trice.

don't [dəʊnt] = **do not**.

do·nut ['dəʊnʌt] *n (Am)* = **doughnut**.

doo·dle ['du:dl] **1** *n* scarabocchio. **2** *vi* scarabocchiare.

doom [du:m] **1** *n (fate)* destino; *(ruin)* rovina; **impending** ~ disastro incombente. **2** *vt (destine):* **to** ~ **(to)** condannare (a); ~**ed to failure** votato al fallimento.

dooms·day ['du:mzdeɪ] *n:* **till** ~ *(fig)* fino al giorno del giudizio.

door [dɔ:'] *n* porta; *(of vehicle)* sportello, portiera; **at the** ~ alla porta; **'pay at the** ~**'** 'pagare all'entrata'; **back/front** ~ porta di servizio/principale; **3** ~**s down the street** 3 case più giù; **from** ~ **to** ~ di porta in porta.

door·bell ['dɔ:bɛl] *n* campanello.

door·keeper ['dɔ:,ki:pə'] *n*, **door·man** ['dɔ:,mæn] *n, pl* **-men** *(of hotel)* portiere *m; (of block of flats)* portinaio.

door·knob ['dɔ:nɒb] *n* pomo, maniglia.

door·mat ['dɔ:mæt] *n* stoino, zerbino; *(fig)* pezza da piedi.

door·nail ['dɔ:neɪl] *n:* **as dead as a** ~ morto(a) stecchito(a).

door·step ['dɔ:stɛp] *n* gradino della porta, soglia; **on our** ~ sulla porta di casa.

door·way ['dɔ:weɪ] *n* porta; **in the** ~ nel vano della porta.

dope [dəʊp] **1** *n* **(a)** *(fam: drugs)* roba; *(Sport)* droga; **he takes** ~ si droga. **(b)** *(fam: information)* dati *mpl;* **to give sb the** ~ **(on sth)** fare una soffiata a qn (su qc). **(c)** *(fam: stupid person)* tonto/a. **2** *vt (horse, person, drink)* drogare.

dopey ['dəʊpɪ] *adj* **(-ier, -iest)** *(drugged)* inebetito(a); *(sleepy, stupid)* addormentato(a).

dor·mant ['dɔ:mənt] *adj (Bot, volcano)* quiescente; *(energy)* latente; **to lie** ~ rimanere inattivo; *(fig)* rimanere latente.

dor·mer ['dɔ:mə`] *n (also:* ~ **window**) abbaino.

dor·mi·tory ['dɔ:mɪtrɪ] **1** *n* dormitorio; *(Am: hall of residence)* casa dello studente. **2** *cpd:* ~ **town** *n* città *f inv* dormitorio *inv*.

dor·mouse ['dɔ:maʊs] *n, pl* **dormice** ['dɔ:maɪs] ghiro.

dor·sal ['dɔ:sl] *adj* dorsale; ~ **fin** pinna dorsale.

dos·age ['dəʊsɪdʒ] *n (on medicine bottle)* posologia.

dose [dəʊs] **1** *n (of medicine)* dose *f; (of fever etc)* attacco; **a** ~ **of flu** una bella influenza; **in small** ~**s** *(fig)* a piccole dosi. **2** *vt:* **to** ~ **sb with sth** somministrare qc a qn.

doss [dɒs] *vi:* **to** ~ **(down)** *(fam)* sistemarsi (per la notte).

doss·house ['dɒshaʊs] *n (fam)* ≃ dormitorio pubblico.

dos·si·er ['dɒsɪeɪ] *n:* ~ **(on)** dossier *m inv* (su).

dot [dɒt] **1** *n (gen)* punto; *(on material)* pois *m inv; (in punctuation):* ~**s** puntini *mpl* di sospensione; *(morse):* ~**s and dashes** punti *mpl* e linee *fpl;* **on the** ~ *(fig)* in punto. **2** *vt (fig):* **to** ~ **one's i's and cross one's t's** mettere i puntini sulle i; **a field** ~**ted with flowers** un campo punteggiato di fiori; **they are** ~**ted about the country** sono disseminati per il paese; ~**ted line** linea punteggiata; **'tear along the** ~**ted line'** 'staccare seguendo la perforazione *or* i puntini'; **to sign on the** ~**ted line** firmare (nell'apposito spazio); *(fig)* accettare.

dot·age ['dəʊtɪdʒ] *n:* **to be in one's** ~ essere rimbambito(a).

dote [dəʊt] *vi:* **to** ~ **on** stravedere per.

dot·ing ['dəʊtɪŋ] *adj:* ~ **mother** madre *f* che stravede per i figli; ~ **husband** marito che stravede per la moglie.

dou·ble ['dʌbl] **1** *adj (gen)* doppio(a); *(room)* per due, doppio(a); *(bed)* matrimoniale, a due piazze; *(dual: purpose)* duplice; **with a** ~ **meaning** a doppio senso; **to lead a** ~ **life** avere una doppia vita; ~ **five two six (5526)** *(Telec)* cinque cinque due sei; **spelt with a** ~ **'l'** scritto con due elle *or* con doppia elle; ~ **bass** contrabbasso; ~ **bend** *(Aut)* doppia curva; ~ **chin** doppio mento; ~ **cream** doppia panna; ~ **glazing** doppi vetri *mpl.*

2 *adv (fold, bend)* in due; *(see)* doppio; *(twice):* ~ **the amount (of sth)** il doppio (di qc); ~ **quick** velocissimo.

3 *n (amount)* doppio; *(person)* sosia *m inv; (Cine)* controfigura; *(in tennis):* **a game of mixed/ladies'** ~**s** un doppio misto/femminile; **at the** ~ *(running)* a passo di corsa.

4 *vt* **(a)** *(increase twofold: money, quantity etc)* raddoppiare. **(b)** *(fold: also:* ~ **over)** piegare in due.

5 *vi* **(a)** *(quantity etc)* raddoppiare. **(b)** *(have two uses etc):* **to** ~ **as** funzionare *or* servire anche da; *(Theatre, Cinema)* fare anche la parte di.

♦ **double back 1** *vi + adv (person)* tornare sui propri passi. **2** *vt + adv (blanket)* ripiegare.

♦ **double up** *vi + adv* **(a)** *(bend over)* piegarsi in due; **he** ~**d up with laughter** si sbellicava dal ridere. **(b)** *(share bedroom)* dividere una stanza.

double-barrelled [,dʌbl'bærəld] *adj (gun)* a due canne, a doppia canna; *(Brit: surname)* cognome *m* doppio.

double-breasted [,dʌbl'brɛstɪd] *adj (jacket)* a doppio petto.

double-check [,dʌbl'tʃɛk] *vt, vi* ricontrollare.

double-cross [,dʌbl'krɒs] *vt (fam)* fare il doppio gioco con.

double-dealing [,dʌbl'di:lɪŋ] *n* doppio gioco.

double-decker [,dʌbl'dɛkə`] *n (also:* ~ **bus**) autobus *m inv* a due piani; *(also:* ~ **sandwich**) doppio tramezzino.

double-dutch [,dʌbl'dʌtʃ] *n (Brit fam)* turco, cinese *m.*

double-edged [,dʌbl'ɛdʒd] *adj (remark)* a doppio taglio.

double-park [,dʌbl'pɑ:k] *vi* parcheggiare in doppia fila.

double-talk ['dʌbl,tɔ:k] *n* acrobazie *fpl* verbali.

dou·bly ['dʌblɪ] *adv* doppiamente.

doubt [daʊt] **1** *n* dubbio; **to be in** ~ essere in dubbio; **without (a)** ~ senza dubbio; **beyond** ~ fuor di dubbio; **if in** ~ nell'incertezza, in caso di dubbio; **no** ~ **he will come** verrà senza dubbio; **there is no** ~ **of that** su questo non c'è dubbio; **I have my** ~**s about whether he'll come** ho i miei dubbi che venga. **2** *vt* **(a)** *(truth of statement etc)* dubitare di; **to** ~ **one's own eyes** non credere ai propri occhi; **I** ~ **it very much** ho i miei dubbi, nutro seri dubbi in proposito. **(b)** *(be uncertain):* **to** ~ **whether** *or* **if** dubitare che + *sub;* **I don't** ~ **that he will come** non dubito *or* non ho dubbi che verrà.

doubt·ful ['daʊtfʊl] *adj (undecided: person)* indeciso(a), poco convinto(a); *(: question, look)* dubbioso(a); *(: result, success)* dubbio(a), incerto(a); *(questionable: taste, reputation)* dubbio(a); *(: person, affair)* equivoco(a); **to be** ~ **about sth** avere dei dubbi su qc, non essere convinto di qc; **I'm a bit** ~ non ne sono sicuro; **it's** ~ **whether...** non è sicuro che... + *sub.*

doubt·ful·ly ['daʊtfəlɪ] *adv (unconvincedly)* con aria dubbiosa, senza convinzione.

doubt·less ['daʊtlɪs] *adv* senza dubbio, indubbiamente.

dough [dəʊ] *n* **(a)** impasto. **(b)** *(fam: money)* grana.

dough·nut ['dəʊnʌt] *n* krapfen *m inv.*

dour ['dʊə`] *adj (unfriendly)* arcigno(a).

douse [daʊs] *vt (with water)* infradiciare; *(flames)* spegnere.

dove [dʌv] *n* colombo/a.

dove·tail ['dʌvteɪl] **1** *n (also:* ~ **joint**) incastro a coda di rondine. **2** *vt (fig):* **to** ~ **with/into** connettere a/con. **3** *vi (fig)* combaciare, collimare.

dowa·ger ['daʊədʒə`] *n* vedova titolata.

dow·dy ['daʊdɪ] *adj* **(-ier, -iest)** scialbo(a).

down¹ [daʊn] *n (on bird, in quilts)* piume *fpl; (on person, fruit)* peluria, lanugine *f.*

down² [daʊn] *n (hill)* collina, collo.

down³ [daʊn] **1** *adv* **(a)** *(movement)* giù; *(to the ground)* giù, a terra; *(to dog):* ~! a cuccia!; **get** ~! scendi!; **to fall** ~ cadere; **to run** ~ correre giù; **he came** ~ **from Glasgow** è venuto giù da Glasgow; **from the year 1600** ~ **to the present day** dal 1600 fino ai giorni nostri; **from the biggest** ~ **to the smallest** dal più grande al più piccolo; ~ **with traitors!** abbasso i traditori!

(b) *(position)* giù; ~ **there** laggiù, là in fondo; ~ **here** quaggiù; ~ **under** agli antipodi *(Australia etc);* **the sun is** ~ il sole è tramontato; **the blinds are** ~ le tapparelle sono tirate giù *or* abbassate; **to kick a man when he's** ~ *(fig)* uccidere un uomo morto; **I'll be** ~ **in a minute** scendo tra un minuto; **I've been** ~ **with flu** sono stato a letto con l'influenza; **he lives** ~ **south** vive nel sud; **the tyres are** ~ le gomme sono sgonfie *or* a terra; **his**

temperature is ~ la febbre gli è scesa; **England is two goals** ~ l'Inghilterra sta perdendo per due goal; **the price of meat is** ~ il prezzo della carne è sceso; **write this** ~ scrivi; **I've got it** ~ **in my diary** ce l'ho sulla mia agenda; **you're** ~ **for the next race** sei iscritto alla prossima gara.

(c) *(as deposit)*: **to pay £2** ~ dare 2 sterline in acconto *or* di anticipo.

2 *prep (indicating movement)* giù per; *(at a lower point on)* più giù; **he ran his finger** ~ **the list** percorse la lista col dito; **he went** ~ **the hill** è andato giù per la collina; **he's** ~ **the hill** è in fondo alla collina; **he lives** ~ **the street** abita un po' più giù; **looking** ~ **this road, you can see...** se guardi in fondo alla strada, vedrai...; ~ **the ages** nel corso della storia; **he's gone** ~ **the pub/**~ **town** *(fam)* è andato al pub/in città.

3 *adj (train, line)* che parte dalla città; ~ **payment** acconto; **I'm feeling a bit** ~ *(fam)* mi sento un po' giù.

4 *vt (opponent)* atterrare; **to** ~ **tools** *(fig)* incrociare le braccia; **he** ~**ed a pint of beer** si è scolato una pinta di birra.

5 *n*: **to have a** ~ **on sb** *(fam)* avercela con qn.

down-and-out ['daʊnǝnd'aʊt] **1** *adj (destitute)* sul lastrico. **2** *n (tramp)* barbone *m*.

down·cast ['daʊnkɑːst] *adj (sad)* abbattuto(a), avvilito(a); *(eyes)* basso(a).

down·fall ['daʊnfɔːl] *n* rovina, caduta.

down·grade ['daʊngreɪd] *vt (job, hotel)* declassare; *(person)* degradare.

down·hearted [,daʊn'hɑːtɪd] *adj* scoraggiato(a), demoralizzato(a).

down·hill [,daʊn'hɪl] *adv*: **to go** ~ *(road)* andare in discesa; *(car)* andare giù per la discesa; *(fig: person)* lasciarsi andare; *(: business)* andare a rotoli.

down·pour ['daʊnpɔː^r] *n* acquazzone *m*, pioggia torrenziale.

down·right ['daʊnraɪt] **1** *adj (person, manner)* franco(a); *(lie, liar)* bell'e buono(a); *(refusal)* categorico(a). **2** *adv (rude, angry)* davvero; *(refuse)* categoricamente.

down·stairs ['daʊn'stɛəz] **1** *adj (on the ground floor)* al pianterreno, al piano terra; *(on the floor underneath)* al piano di sotto. **2** *adv* di sotto, giù; **to come** ~, **go** ~ scendere giù; **she lives** ~ abita al piano di sotto.

down·stream ['daʊn'striːm] *adv*: ~ **(from)** a valle (di).

down-to-earth ['daʊntʊ'ɜːθ] *adj (person)* coi piedi per terra, pratico(a); *(advice, approach)* pratico(a).

down·town ['daʊn'taʊn] **1** *adv (Am)* in città, in centro. **2** *adj*: ~ **San Francisco** il centro di San Francisco.

down·trod·den ['daʊn,trɒdn] *adj* oppresso(a).

down·ward ['daʊnwəd] *adj (curve, movement etc)* in giù, verso il basso; *(slope)* in discesa; **a** ~ **trend** una diminuzione progressiva; **a** ~ **trend in prices** una tendenza al ribasso dei prezzi.

down·ward(s) ['daʊnwəd(z)] *adv (go)* in giù; *(look)* verso il basso; **face** ~**s** *(person)* bocconi; *(object)* a faccia in giù; **from the President** ~**s** dal Presidente in giù.

dow·ry ['daʊrɪ] *n* dote *f*.

doz. *abbr of* **dozen**.

doze [dəʊz] **1** *n* sonnellino, pisolino. **2** *vi* sonnecchiare.

♦ **doze off** *vi* + *adv* appisolarsi.

doz·en ['dʌzn] *n* dozzina; **80p a** ~ 80 pence la dozzina; **a** ~ **eggs** una dozzina d'uova; ~**s of**

times centinaia *or* migliaia di volte; ~**s of people** decine di persone.

Dr *abbr of* **doctor; drive**.

drab [dræb] *adj* (**-ber, -best**) *(colour)* cupo(a); *(clothes)* triste; *(life)* grigio(a).

draft [drɑːft] **1** *n* (**a**) *(outline)* abbozzo, brutta; *(of contract, document)* minuta. (**b**) *(Mil: detachment)* distaccamento; **the** ~ *(Am Mil: conscription)* la leva. (**c**) *(Comm: also: banker's ~)* tratta. (**d**) *(Am)* = **draught. 2** *vt* (**a**) *(also:* ~ **out)** abbozzare; *(: plan)* tracciare; *(: document, report)* stendere (in versione preliminare). (**b**) *(Mil: for specific duty)* distaccare; *(Am Mil: conscript)* arruolare.

drag [dræg] **1** *n* (**a**) *(Aer: resistance)* resistenza (aerodinamica); *(fam: boring thing)* noia, strazio; **what a** ~**!** che scocciatura! (**b**) *(on cigarette)* tirata. (**c**) *(women's clothing)*: **in** ~ travestito (da donna). **2** *vt* (**a**) *(object)* trascinare, tirare; *(person)* trascinare; **to** ~ **one's feet over sth** *(fig)* farla lunga con qc. (**b**) *(sea bed, river etc)* dragare. **3** *vi (go very slowly: evening, conversation etc)* trascinarsi, non finire mai.

♦ **drag along** *vt* + *adv (person)* trascinare (controvoglia); *(object)* tirare.

♦ **drag away** *vt* + *adv*: **to** ~ **away (from)** tirare via (da).

♦ **drag down** *vt* + *adv* trascinare giù *or* in basso; **to** ~ **sb down to one's own level** *(fig)* far abbassare qn al proprio livello.

♦ **drag in** *vt* + *adv (subject)* tirare in ballo.

♦ **drag on** *vi* + *adv (meeting, conversation)* trascinarsi.

drag·on ['drægən] *n* drago.

dragon·fly ['drægənflaɪ] *n* libellula.

drain [dreɪn] **1** *n* (**a**) *(outlet)* scarico; *(: pipe)* tubatura di scarico; *(~ cover)* tombino; **the** ~**s** *(sewage system)* le fognature; **to throw one's money down the** ~ *(fig)* buttare i soldi dalla finestra. (**b**) *(fig: source of loss)*: **a** ~ **on** *(energies, resources)* un salasso per; **it has been a great** ~ **on her** l'ha veramente spossata. **2** *vt (land, lake)* prosciugare; *(marshes)* bonificare, drenare; *(vegetables, pasta)* scolare; *(glass, bottle of wine)* svuotare; *(radiator etc)* (far) svuotare; *(Med: wound etc)* drenare; **to feel** ~**ed (of energy)** *(fig)* sentirsi svuotato (di energie), sentirsi sfinito. **3** *vi (washed dishes, vegetables)* scolare; *(liquid, stream)*: **to** ~ **(into)** defluire (in).

♦ **drain away 1** *vt* + *adv (liquid)* far scolare. **2** *vi* + *adv (liquid)* scolare; *(strength)* esaurirsi.

♦ **drain off** *vt* + *adv (liquid)* far scolare.

drain·age ['dreɪnɪdʒ] *n (of land: natural)* scolo; *(: artificial)* drenaggio; *(of lake)* prosciugamento; *(sewage system)* fognature *fpl*.

drain·ing board ['dreɪnɪŋ,bɔːd] *n* piano del lavello.

drain·pipe ['dreɪnpaɪp] *n* tubo di scarico.

drake [dreɪk] *n* maschio dell'anatra.

dra·ma ['drɑːmɑ] **1** *n* dramma *m*. **2** *cpd*: ~ **critic** *n* critico teatrale; ~ **student** *n* studente/essa di arte drammatica.

dra·mat·ic [drə'mætɪk] *adj (art, event etc)* drammatico(a); *(criticism, effect, entrance)* teatrale; *(change)* spettacolare.

dra·mat·ics [drə'mætɪks] *npl* arte *f* drammatica.

drama·tist ['dræmətɪst] *n* drammaturgo/a.

drama·tize ['dræmətaɪz] *vt (events etc)* drammatizzare; *(adapt: novel: for TV)* ridurre *or* adattare per la televisione; *(: for cinema)* ridurre *or* adattare per lo schermo.

drank [dræŋk] *pt of* **drink**.

drape [dreɪp] **1** *n (Am)*: ~**s** tende *fpl*. **2** *vt*: **to** ~ **(with)** *(altar)* drappeggiare (con); *(shoulders)* avvolgere (in); **to ~ (over)** *(cloth, clothing)* avvolgere (intorno a).

drap·er ['dreɪpəʳ] *n* negoziante *m/f* di stoffe.

dra·pery ['dreɪpərɪ] *n (draper's shop)* negozio di tessuti; **draperies** *npl* tendaggi *mpl*.

dras·tic ['dræstɪk] *adj* drastico(a).

draught [drɑːft] **1** *n* **(a)** *(of air)* corrente *f* (d'aria), spiffero; *(for fire)* tiraggio; *(Naut)* pescaggio. **(b)** *(drink):* **he took a long ~ of beer** ha bevuto una lunga sorsata di birra; **on ~** alla spina. **(c):** **(game of) ~s** (gioco della) dama. **2** *cpd:* **~ beer** *n* birra alla spina.

draughts·man ['drɑːftsmən] *n, pl* **-men** *(in drawing office)* disegnatore(trice) (tecnico(a)).

draughty ['drɑːftɪ] *adj* **(-ier, -iest)** *(room)* pieno(a) di correnti *or* di spifferi; *(street corner)* ventoso(a).

draw [drɔː] *(vb: pt* **drew,** *pp* **drawn) 1** *n* **(a)** *(lottery)* lotteria, riffa; *(picking of ticket)* estrazione *f*, sorteggio; *(for sporting events)* sorteggio.

(b) *(equal score)* pareggio; **the match ended in a ~** la partita è finita con un pareggio.

(c) *(attraction)* attrazione *f*.

(d): to be quick on the ~ essere veloce con la pistola; *(fig)* avere i riflessi pronti.

2 *vt* **(a)** *(pull: bolt, curtains)* tirare; *(: caravan, trailer)* trainare, rimorchiare; *(: bow)* tendere la corda di; **he drew his finger along the table** ha passato il dito sul tavolo; **he drew his hat over his eyes** si è calato il cappello sugli occhi; **she drew him to one side** lo tirò da una parte.

(b) *(extract: from pocket, bag)* tirar fuori; *(: from well, tap)* attingere; *(: sword)* sguainare; *(: teeth, cork)* cavare; *(cheque)* cambiare, riscuotere; *(salary, money from bank)* ritirare; *(Culin: fowl)* pulire; **to ~ a bath** preparare un bagno; **to ~ blood** far uscir sangue; *(fig)* colpire nel vivo; **to ~ a card** estrarre una carta (dal mazzo); **to ~ a breath** tirare un respiro; **to ~ breath** (ri)prendere fiato; **to ~ comfort from sth** trovare conforto in qc; **to ~ a smile from sb** strappare un sorriso a qn.

(c) *(attract: attention, crowd, customer)* attrarre, attirare; **to feel ~n to sb** sentirsi attratto verso qn, provare attrazione per qn.

(d) *(sketch etc: picture, portrait)* fare; *(: object, person)* disegnare; *(: plan, line, circle)* tracciare; *(: map)* disegnare, fare; *(fig: situation)* fare un quadro di; *(: character)* disegnare; **I ~ the line at (doing)** that mi rifiuto (di farlo).

(e) *(formulate: conclusion):* **to ~ (from)** trarre (da), ricavare (da); *(: comparison, distinction):* **to ~ (between)** fare (tra).

(f) *(Ftbl etc):* **to ~ a match** pareggiare.

3 *vi* **(a)** *(move):* **to ~ (towards)** avvicinarsi (a), avanzare (verso); **he drew to one side** si è tirato da parte *or* in disparte; **the train drew into the station** il treno è entrato in stazione; **the car drew over to the kerb** la macchina si è accostata al marciapiede; **he drew ahead of the other runners** si è staccato dagli altri corridori; **to ~ level** affiancarsi; **to ~ near** avvicinarsi; **to ~ to an end** volgere alla fine.

(b) *(in cards):* **to ~ for trumps** scegliere il seme *or* la briscola.

(c) *(chimney etc)* tirare.

(d) *(be equal: two teams)* pareggiare; **the teams drew for second place** le due squadre sono arrivate seconde a pari merito.

(e) *(sketch)* disegnare.

♦ **draw back 1** *vt + adv (object, hand)* tirare indietro, ritirare; *(curtains)* tirare, aprire. **2** *vi + adv (move back):* **to ~ back (from)** indietreggiare (di

fronte a), tirarsi indietro (di fronte a).

♦ **draw in 1** *vi + adv* **(a)** *(car)* accostarsi; *(train)* entrare in stazione. **(b): the days are ~ing in** le giornate si accorciano. **2** *vt + adv (breath)* tirare; *(air)* aspirare; *(pull back in: claws)* ritirare; *(attract: crowds)* richiamare.

♦ **draw on** *vi + prep (resources)* attingere a; *(imagination, person)* far ricorso a.

♦ **draw out** *vt + adv* **(a)** *(take out: handkerchief)* tirar fuori; *(money from bank)* ritirare; **to ~ sb out (of his shell)** *(fig)* tirare qn fuori dal suo guscio. **(b)** *(prolong: meeting)* tirare per le lunghe.

♦ **draw up 1** *vt + adv* **(a)** *(formulate: will, contract)* stendere, formulare; *(: plans)* formulare. **(b)** *(chair)* avvicinare; *(troops)* schierare; **to ~ o.s. up (to one's full height)** raddrizzarsi (in tutta la persona). **2** *vi + adv (car etc):* **to ~ up (beside sth/sb)** accostarsi (a qc/qn).

draw·back ['drɔːbæk] *n* inconveniente *m*, svantaggio.

draw·bridge ['drɔːbrɪdʒ] *n* ponte *m* levatoio.

draw·er [drɔːʳ] *n* **(a)** *(in desk etc)* cassetto. **(b)** *(of cheque)* riscuotitore/trice.

draw·ing ['drɔːɪŋ] **1** *n (picture)* disegno; **I'm no good at ~** non so disegnare. **2** *cpd:* **~ board** *n* tavolo da disegno; **back to the ~ board!** *(fig)* ricominciamo da capo!; **~ pin** *n* puntina da disegno; **~ room** *n* salotto.

drawl [drɔːl] **1** *n* cadenza strascicata. **2** *vt* strascicare. **3** *vi* strascicare le parole.

drawn [drɔːn] **1** *pp* of **draw. 2** *adj (haggard: with tiredness)* tirato(a); *(: with pain)* contratto(a) (dal dolore).

dread [dred] **1** *n* terrore *m*. **2** *vt* avere il terrore di, tremare all'idea di.

dread·ful ['dredfʊl] *adj (crime, sight, suffering)* terribile, spaventoso(a); *(weather)* tremendo(a); **I feel ~!** *(ill)* mi sento uno straccio!; *(ashamed)* vorrei scomparire (dalla vergogna)!

dread·fully ['dredfəlɪ] *adv* terribilmente; **I'm ~ sorry** sono terribilmente spiacente.

dream [driːm] *(vb: pt, pp* **dreamed** *or* **dreamt) 1** *n* sogno; **to have a ~ about sb/sth** fare un sogno su qn/qc; **I had a bad ~** ho fatto un brutto sogno; **sweet ~s!** sogni d'oro!; **that museum is an archaeologist's ~** quel museo è il paradiso degli studiosi di archeologia; **it worked like a ~** ha funzionato a meraviglia; **she goes about in a ~** ha sempre la testa tra le nuvole; **rich beyond his wildest ~s** ricco come non si era mai sognato in vita sua; **isn't he a ~?** non è un sogno *or* un amore?

2 *vt* sognare; *(imagine)* sognarsi, credersi; **I didn't ~ that...** non mi sarei mai sognato che... + *sub.*

3 *vi* sognare; *(imagine)* sognarsi; **to ~ (of** *or* **about sb/sth)** sognare ((di) qn/qc); *(imagine)* sognarsi; **I shouldn't ~ of it!** non me lo sognerei neanche!; **I'm sorry, I was ~ing** mi scusi, stavo fantasticando; **there were more than I'd ever ~ed of** ce n'erano di più di quanto avessi mai immaginato.

♦ **dream up** *vt + adv (reason, excuse)* inventare; *(plan, idea)* escogitare.

dream·er ['driːməʳ] *n* sognatore/trice.

dreamt [dremt] *pt, pp* of **dream.**

dreamy ['driːmɪ] *adj* **(-ier, -iest)** *(person)* distratto(a), sognatore(trice); *(look, voice)* sognante; *(music, quality)* di sogno.

dreary ['drɪərɪ] *adj* **(-ier, -iest)** *(landscape)* tetro(a); *(weather)* deprimente; *(life)* squallido(a); *(work, book, speech)* noioso(a).

dredge [drɛdʒ] **1** *n* draga. **2** *vt* dragare.
♦ **dredge up** *vt* + *adv* tirare alla superficie; *(fig: unpleasant facts)* rivangare.
dredg·er ['drɛdʒə'] *n (ship)* draga.
dregs [drɛgz] *npl (also fig)* feccia.
drench [drɛntʃ] *vt* inzuppare, infradiciare; ~ed to the skin bagnato fino all'osso, bagnato fradicio.
dress [drɛs] **1** *n (frock)* vestito, abito; *(no pl: clothing)* abbigliamento; **in summer** ~ in abiti estivi. **2** *vt* **(a)** vestire; **to** ~ **o.s.**, **to get** ~ed vestirsi; ~ed **in green** vestito di verde. **(b)** *(Culin: salad)* condire; *(: chicken, crab)* preparare; *(wound)* medicare; *(shop window)* allestire. **3** *vi* vestirsi; **she** ~es **very well** veste molto bene. **4** *cpd:* ~ **circle** *n* prima galleria; ~ **designer** *n* disegnatore/trice di moda; ~ **rehearsal** *n* prova generale; ~ **shirt** *n* camicia da sera.
♦ **dress up** *vi* + *adv (in smart clothes)* mettersi elegante; *(in fancy dress)* mettersi in costume, mascherarsi. **2** *vt* + *adv (improve appearance of: facts etc)* presentare sotto una veste migliore.
dress·er ['drɛsə'] *n (in kitchen)* credenza; *(Am: dressing table)* toilette *f inv.*
dress·ing ['drɛsɪŋ] **1** *n (act)* il vestirsi; *(style)* (modo di) vestire; *(Med: bandage)* fasciatura; *(Culin: salad* ~*)* condimento. **2** *cpd:* ~ **gown** *n* vestaglia, veste *f* da camera; ~ **room** *n (in theatre)* camerino; *(Sport)* spogliatoio; ~ **table** *n* toilette *f inv.*
dress·maker ['drɛs,meɪkə'] *n* sarto/a.
dress·making ['drɛs,meɪkɪŋ] *n* sartoria; *(in school)* taglio e cucito.
dressy ['drɛsɪ] *adj* (-ier, -iest) *(fam)* elegante.
drew [druː] *pt of* **draw.**
drib·ble ['drɪbl] **1** *n (of saliva)* bava, filo di saliva; *(Ftbl)* dribbling *m.* **2** *vt (liquid)* sbrodolare. **3** *vi (baby)* sbavare; *(liquid)* sgocciolare; *(Ftbl)* dribblare, fare il dribbling; *(people):* **to** ~ **in/out** entrare/uscire alla spicciolata.
dried [draɪd] *adj (vegetables)* liofilizzato(a); *(fruit, beans, flowers, herbs)* secco(a); *(milk)* in polvere.
dri·er ['draɪə'] *n* = **dryer.**
drift [drɪft] **1** *n* **(a)** *(deviation from course)* deriva; *(direction: of current)* direzione *f*; *(: of events)* corso; *(: of conversation, opinion)* tendenza; *(meaning: of questions)* senso; **continental** ~ deriva dei continenti; **to catch sb's** ~ capire dove qn vuole arrivare. **(b)** *(mass of snow, sand)* cumulo, mucchio. **2** *vi (in wind, current)* andare alla deriva; *(clouds)* essere sospinto(a) dal vento; *(snow, sand)* accumularsi, ammucchiarsi; *(person)* vagare; *(events):* **to** ~ **(towards)** scivolare (verso); **to** ~ **downstream** venir portato a valle dalla corrente; **he** ~ed **into marriage** ha finito con lo sposarsi; **to let things** ~ lasciare che le cose vadano come vogliono; **to** ~ **apart** *(friends)* perdersi di vista; *(lovers)* allontanarsi l'uno dall'altro.
drift·er ['drɪftə'] *n* persona che fa una vita da zingaro.
drift·wood ['drɪftwʊd] *n* legno portato dalla corrente.
drill¹ [drɪl] **1** *n (for wood, metal, dentist's* ~*)* trapano; *(in mine, quarry)* perforatrice *f*; *(in oilfield)* trivella; *(pneumatic* ~*)* martello pneumatico. **2** *vt (wood etc)* forare, trapanare; *(tooth)* trapanare; *(oil well)* trivellare, scavare. **3** *vi:* **to** ~ **(for)** fare trivellazioni (alla ricerca di).
drill² [drɪl] **1** *n (Scol etc: exercises)* esercizi *mpl*; *(Mil)* esercitazione *f.* **2** *vt (soldiers)* esercitare, addestrare; *(pupils: in grammar)* fare esercitare, far fare esercizi a; **to** ~ **good manners into a child** fare entrare la buona educazione in testa a

un bambino. **3** *vi (Mil)* fare esercitazioni.
drill³ [drɪl] *n (fabric)* spesso tessuto di cotone.
drill·ing ['drɪlɪŋ] **1** *n (of metal, wood)* perforazione *f*; *(for oil)* trivellazione *f*; *(by dentist)* trapanazione *f.* **2** *cpd:* ~ **rig** *n (on land)* torre *f* di perforazione; *(at sea)* piattaforma (per trivellazioni subacquee).
dri·ly ['draɪlɪ] *adv* = **dryly.**
drink [drɪŋk] *(vb: pt* **drank,** *pp* **drunk) 1** *n* **(a)** *(liquid to* ~*)* bevanda, bibita; **there's food and** ~ **in the kitchen** c'è da mangiare e da bere in cucina; **may I have a** ~? posso avere qualcosa da bere?; **to give sb a** ~ dare qc da bere a qn. **(b)** *(glass of alcohol):* **a** ~ un bicchierino; **let's have a** ~ prendiamo un bicchierino; **I need a** ~ ho proprio bisogno di bere qualcosa; **to invite sb for** ~s invitare qn a bere qualcosa. **(c)** *(alcoholic liquor)* alcolici *mpl*; **he has a** ~ **problem** è uno che beve; **to take to** ~ darsi al bere; **to smell of** ~ puzzare d'alcool; **his worries drove him to** ~ le preoccupazioni lo hanno spinto al bere.
2 *vt (gen)* bere; *(soup)* mangiare; **would you like something to** ~? vuole qualcosa da bere?; **to** ~ **sb under the table** far finire qn sotto il tavolo (completamente ubriaco).
3 *vi (gen)* bere; **he doesn't** ~ non beve; **'don't** ~ **and drive'** 'non guidate in stato di ubriachezza'; **he** ~s **like a fish** beve come una spugna; **to** ~ **to sb/sth** bere alla salute di qn/a qc.
♦ **drink in** *vt* + *adv (subj: person: fresh air)* aspirare; *(: story)* ascoltare avidamente; *(: sight)* ammirare, bersi con gli occhi.
♦ **drink up 1** *vt* + *adv* bere tutto. **2** *vi* + *adv* finire di bere; ~ **up!** *(to child)* su, finiscilo!; *(in pub)* finisci il bicchiere!
drink·able ['drɪŋkəbl] *adj (not poisonous)* potabile; *(palatable)* bevibile.
drink·er ['drɪŋkə'] *n* bevitore/trice; **a heavy** ~ un forte bevitore.
drink·ing ['drɪŋkɪŋ] **1** *n (drunkenness)* il bere, alcoolismo. **2** *cpd:* ~ **fountain** *n* fontanella; ~ **water** *n* acqua potabile.
drip [drɪp] **1** *n* **(a)** *(droplet)* goccia; *(: of blood, dew)* stilla; *(sound: of water etc)* sgocciolio; *(fam: spineless person)* lavativo. **(b)** *(Med)* fleboclisi *f inv*; **he's on a** ~ gli stanno facendo la flebo. **2** *vt (liquid)* sbrodolare; **you're** ~ping **paint everywhere!** stai schizzando vernice dappertutto! **3** *vi (liquid)* gocciare, sgocciolare; *(tap etc)* perdere; **to be** ~ping **with sweat/blood** grondare sudore/sangue.
drip-dry ['drɪp'draɪ] *adj* che non si stira.
drip·ping ['drɪpɪŋ] **1** *n (Culin)* grasso (dell'arrosto). **2** *adj (tap)* che gocciola; *(washing, coat)* tutto(a) bagnato(a); ~ **wet** *(fam)* bagnato fradicio.
drive [draɪv] *(vb: pt* **drove,** *pp* **driven) 1** *n* **(a)** *(outing)* giro, passeggiata (in macchina); *(journey)* tragitto; **to go for a** ~ andare a fare un giro in macchina; **it's a long** ~ è un lungo viaggio; **it's 3 hours'** ~ **from London** è a 3 ore di macchina da Londra.
(b) *(private road)* viale *m* (d'accesso).
(c) *(Tennis)* dritto; *(Golf)* drive *m inv.*
(d) *(energy)* grinta; *(motivation)* spinta, stimolo; *(Psych)* impulso; **sex** ~ libido *f inv.*
(e) *(Comm, Pol)* campagna; **sales** ~ campagna di vendita, sforzo promozionale.
(f) *(Tech)* trasmissione *f*; *(Aut):* **front-/rear-wheel** ~ trazione *f* anteriore/posteriore; **left-hand** ~ guida a sinistra.
2 *vt* **(a)** *(cause to move: people, animals)* spingere; *(: clouds, leaves)* sospingere; **the gale drove the ship off course** la tempesta ha spinto la nave

fuori rotta; **to ~ sb hard** *(fig)* far sgobbare qn; **to ~ sb to (do) sth** spingere qn a (fare) qc; **I was driven to it** sono stato costretto a farlo; **he is driven by greed/ambition** la sua molla è il denaro/l'ambizione; **to ~ sb mad** far impazzire qn; **to ~ sb to despair** ridurre qn alla disperazione.

(b) *(vehicle)* guidare; *(passenger)* portare (in macchina *etc)*; **he ~s a taxi** fa il tassista; **he ~s a Mercedes** ha una Mercedes; **I'll ~ you home** ti porto a casa (in macchina).

(c) *(operate: machine)* azionare; **steam-driven train** treno a vapore; **machine driven by electricity** macchina che funziona a elettricità.

(d) *(nail, stake)*: **to ~ (into)** conficcare (in), piantare (in); **to ~ sth home** *(fig)* dimostrare qc in modo lampante.

3 *vi (Aut)* guidare; *(: travel)* andare in macchina; **to ~ away/back** partire/ritornare in macchina; **can you ~?** sai guidare?; **to ~ at 50 km an hour** guidare *or* andare a 50 km all'ora; **to ~ on the left** guidare a sinistra.

♦ **drive at** *vi + prep (fig: intend, mean)* mirare a, voler dire.

♦ **drive back** *vt + adv (person, army)* respingere, ributtare indietro.

♦ **drive off** *vt + adv (enemy etc)* cacciare.

♦ **drive on** **1** *vi + adv* proseguire, andare (più) avanti. **2** *vt + adv (incite, encourage)* sospingere, spingere.

♦ **drive up** *vi + adv (car)* sopraggiungere, arrivare; *(person)* arrivare (in macchina).

drive-in ['draɪv,ɪn] *adj (esp Am)*: **~ cinema** *(or* **café** *etc)* drive-in *m inv.*

driv·el ['drɪvl] *n (fam: nonsense)* ciance *fpl,* bubbole *fpl.*

driv·en ['drɪvn] *pt of* **drive.**

driv·er ['draɪvəʳ] *n (of car)* guidatore/trice; *(salaried: of car, lorry)* autista *m/f; (: of bus)* conducente *m; (of taxi)* tassista *m;* **to be in the ~'s seat** essere seduto nel posto del conducente; *(fig)* essere al timone; **he's a good ~** guida bene.

drive·way ['draɪv,weɪ] *n* viale *m* d'accesso.

driv·ing ['draɪvɪŋ] **1** *n (Aut)* guida. **2** *adj (force)* motore(trice); *(rain)* battente, sferzante. **3** *cpd:* **~ lesson** *n* lezione *f* di guida; **~ licence** *n* patente *f* (di guida); **~ mirror** *n* specchietto retrovisore; **~ school** *n* scuola guida; **~ test** *n* esame per la patente.

driz·zle ['drɪzl] **1** *n* pioggerella, acquerugiola. **2** *vi* piovigginare.

droll [drəʊl] *adj (humour)* bizzarro(a); *(expression)* buffo(a), strambo(a).

drom·edary ['drɒmɪdərɪ] *n* dromedario.

drone [drəʊn] **1** *n* **(a)** *(male bee)* fuco, pecchione *m.* **(b)** *(noise: of bees, aircraft)* ronzio; *(: of voices)* brusio. **2** *vi (bee, engine, aircraft)* ronzare; *(person: also:* **~ on**) continuare a parlare (in modo monotono); *(voice)* continuare a ronzare.

drool [dru:l] *vi (baby)* sbavare; **to ~ over sb/sth** *(fig)* andare in estasi per qn/qc.

droop [dru:p] *vi (head)* chinarsi; *(: with sleep)* cadere; *(shoulders)* piegarsi; *(flower)* appassire; *(person)* abbattersi; **she ~ed with tiredness** cascava di stanchezza; **his spirits ~ed** si è molto abbattuto, si è avvilito.

drop [drɒp] **1** *n* **(a)** *(gen)* goccia; *(of wine, tea etc)* goccio, goccino; **a ~ in the ocean** *(fig)* una goccia nel mare; **he's had a ~ too much** *(fam)* ha bevuto un bicchiere di troppo; **~s** *(Med)* gocce *fpl; (sweets)* confetti *mpl;* **cough ~s** pastiglie *fpl* per la tosse.

(b) *(fall: in price)* calo, ribasso; *(: in temperature)* abbassamento; *(: in salary)* riduzione *f,* ta-

glio; **a ~ of 10%** un calo del 10%; **at the ~ of a hat** in quattro e quattr'otto.

(c) *(steep incline)* salto, dislivello; *(fall)* salto; **a ~ of 10 metres** un salto di 10 metri.

(d) *(unloading by parachute: of supplies, arms)* lancio.

2 *vt* **(a)** *(let fall)* far *or* lasciar cadere; *(: bomb)* lanciare, sganciare; *(: liquid)* gocciolare; *(: stitch)* lasciar cadere; *(lower: hemline)* allungare; *(: eyes, voice, price)* abbassare; *(set down from car: object, person)* lasciare; *(from boat: cargo, passengers)* sbarcare; **to ~ anchor** gettare l'ancora.

(b) *(utter casually: remark, name, clue)* lasciar cadere; **to ~ a word in sb's ear** dire una parolina nell'orecchio a qn; **to ~ (sb) a hint about sth** far capire qc (a qn).

(c) *(postcard, note)* mandare, scrivere; **to ~ sb a line** mandare due righe a qn.

(d) *(omit: word, letter)* dimenticare; *(: intentionally: person)* escludere; *(: thing)* omettere.

(e) *(abandon: work, conversation)* lasciar cadere; *(: idea)* abbandonare; *(: candidate)* escludere; *(: boyfriend)* piantare; **let's ~ the subject** lasciamo perdere; **~ it!** *(fam: subject)* piantala!; *(: gun)* buttalo!

(f) *(lose: money, game)* perdere.

3 *vi (fall: object)* cadere, cascare; **I'm ready to ~** *(fam)* sto cascando (dal sonno *etc);* **~ dead!** *(fam)* va' al diavolo!

(b) *(decrease: wind, temperature, price, voice)* calare; *(: numbers, attendance)* diminuire.

♦ **drop back, drop behind** *vi + adv* restare indietro.

♦ **drop down** *vi + adv* cadere, cascare.

♦ **drop in** *vi + adv (fam: visit)*: **to ~ in (on)** fare un salto (da), passare (da).

♦ **drop off** **1** *vi + adv* **(a)** *(fall asleep)* addormentarsi. **(b)** *(decline: sales, interest)* calare, diminuire; *(: craze)* passare; *(: friends)* non farsi più vedere. **2** *vt + adv (from car)*: **to ~ sb off** far scendere qn; **to ~ sth off** lasciare qc.

♦ **drop out** *vi + adv (contents etc)* cascar fuori; *(fig: from competition etc)* ritirarsi; **to ~ out of society/university** abbandonare la società/gli studi universitari.

drop·let ['drɒplɪt] *n* gocciolina.

drop·out ['drɒpaʊt] *n (from society/from university)* chi ha abbandonato (la società/gli studi).

drop·per ['drɒpəʳ] *n (Med etc)* contagocce *m inv.*

drop·pings ['drɒpɪŋz] *npl (of bird, animal)* escrementi *mpl.*

dross [drɒs] *n (fig)* avanzi *mpl.*

drought [draʊt] *n* siccità.

drove [drəʊv] **1** *pt of* **drive.** **2** *n (of cattle)* mandria, branco; **~s of people** centinaia di persone; **they came in ~s** sono arrivati a frotte.

drown [draʊn] **1** *vt (people, animals)* affogare, annegare; *(land)* allagare; *(also:* **~ out:** *sound)* coprire. **2** *vi (also:* **to be ~ed**) annegare, affogare.

drowse [draʊz] *vi* sonnecchiare, essere mezzo assopito(a).

drowsy ['draʊzɪ] *adj* **(-ier, -iest)** *(sleepy: person, smile, look)* assonnato(a); *(soporific: afternoon, atmosphere)* sonnolento(a).

drudge [drʌdʒ] *n (person)* uomo/donna di fatica; *(job)* faticaccia.

drudg·ery ['drʌdʒərɪ] *n* fatica improba; **housework is sheer ~** le faccende domestiche sono alienanti.

drug [drʌg] **1** *n (Med)* medicina, medicinale *m; (addictive substance)* droga, stupefacente *m;* **he's on ~s** si droga; *(Med)* segue una cura. **2** *vt (person, wine etc)* drogare; **to be in a ~ged sleep**

dormire sotto l'effetto di narcotici. **3** cpd: ~ **addict** n tossicodipendente m/f, tossicomane m/f; ~ **peddler** n spacciatore/trice di droga; ~ **runner** n trafficante m/f di droga.

drug·gist ['drʌgɪst] n (Am) farmacista m/f.

drug·store ['drʌg,stɔːʳ] n (Am) negozio di generi vari e di articoli di farmacia e di profumeria con un bar.

drum [drʌm] **1** n (a) (Mus) tamburo; **the** ~**s** la batteria; **big** ~ grancassa. **(b)** (container: for oil) bidone m; (Tech: cylinder, machine part) tamburo. **(c)** (Anat: also: **ear**~) timpano. **2** vt: **to** ~ **one's fingers on the table** tamburellare con le dita sulla tavola; **to** ~ **sth into sb** (fig) ficcare qc in testa a qn. **3** vi (Mus) battere or suonare il tamburo; (tap: with fingers) tamburellare; **the noise was** ~**ming in my ears** il rumore mi martellava nel cervello.

♦ **drum up** vt + adv (enthusiasm, support) conquistarsi.

drum·mer ['drʌməʳ] n (in military band etc) tamburo; (in pop group) batterista m/f.

drum·stick ['drʌmstɪk] n (a) (Mus) bacchetta. **(b)** (chicken leg) coscia di pollo.

drunk [drʌŋk] **1** pp of **drink**. **2** adj ubriaco(a); (fig) ebbro(a), ubriaco(a); **to get** ~ ubriacarsi, prendere una sbornia; **to arrest sb for being** ~ **and disorderly** arrestare qn per ubriachezza molesta. **3** n (fam) ubriaco/a.

drunk·ard ['drʌŋkəd] n ubriacone/a, beone/a.

drunk·en ['drʌŋkən] adj (intoxicated) ubriaco(a); (: habitually) alcolizzato(a); (brawl, orgy) di ubriachi; (rage) provocato(a) dall'alcool; (voice) da ubriaco; ~ **driving** guida in stato di ebbrezza.

drunk·en·ness ['drʌŋknnɪs] n (state) ubriachezza; (habit, problem) abuso dell'alcool.

dry [draɪ] **1** adj (**-ier, -iest**) **(a)** (gen) secco(a); (clothes) asciutto(a); (day) senza pioggia; (battery) a secco; **on** ~ **land** sulla terraferma; **as** ~ **as a bone** completamente asciutto; **to be** ~ (thirsty) avere la gola secca; **the river ran** ~ il fiume è andato in secca. **(b)** (humour) asciutto(a); (uninteresting: lecture, subject) poco avvincente. **2** vt (subj: person: clothes, child) asciugare; (: herbs, figs, flowers) far seccare; (subj: sun, wind) seccare; **to** ~ **one's hands/hair/eyes** asciugarsi le mani/i capelli/gli occhi; **to** ~ **the dishes** asciugare i piatti; **to** ~ **o.s.** asciugarsi. **3** vi asciugarsi. **4** cpd: ~ **cleaner's** n lavasecco m or f inv, tintoria; ~ **dock** n (Naut) bacino di carenaggio; ~ **goods** npl (Comm) tessuti mpl e mercerie fpl; ~ **ice** n ghiaccio secco; ~ **run** n (fig) prova; ~ **ski slope** n pista artificiale.

♦ **dry off 1** vi + adv (clothes etc) asciugarsi. **2** vt + adv asciugare.

♦ **dry out 1** vi + adv seccarsi; (alcoholic) disintossicarsi. **2** vt + adv asciugare.

♦ **dry up** vi + adv (river, well) seccarsi, prosciugarsi; (moisture) asciugarsi; (source of supply) esaurirsi; (fig: imagination etc) inaridirsi. **(b)** (dry the dishes) asciugare i piatti. **(c)** (fall silent: speaker) azzittirsi; ~ **up!** (fam) chiudi il becco!

dry-clean [,draɪ'kliːn] vt pulire or lavare a secco; '~ **only**' (on label) 'pulire a secco'.

dry·er ['draɪəʳ] n (for hair) föhn m inv, asciugacapelli m inv; (for clothes) asciugabiancheria m inv.

dry·ness ['draɪnɪs] n (gen) secchezza; (of ground) aridità.

dual ['djʊəl] adj doppio(a), duplice; ~ **carriageway** (Brit) strada a doppia carreggiata; ~ **nationality** doppia nazionalità; ~ **purpose** a doppio uso.

dub [dʌb] vt (a) (Cine) doppiare. **(b):** **they** ~**bed him 'Shorty'** l'hanno ribattezzato or soprannominato 'Piccoletto'.

du·bi·ous ['djuːbɪəs] adj (gen) dubbio(a); (look, smile) dubbioso(a); (character, manner) ambiguo(a), equivoco(a); **to feel** ~ **about** or **as to what to do next** essere incerto sul da farsi; **I'm very** ~ **about it** ho i miei dubbi in proposito.

du·bi·ous·ly ['djuːbɪəslɪ] adv con esitazione.

duch·ess ['dʌtʃɪs] n duchessa.

duck [dʌk] **1** n anatra; **wild** ~ anatra selvatica; **he's taken to it like a** ~ **to water** ci sguazza dentro. **2** vt **(a)** (plunge in water: person, head) spingere sotto (acqua). **(b):** **to** ~ **one's head** abbassare la testa. **3** vi (also: ~ **down**) accucciarsi; (in fight) fare una schivata; (under water) tuffarsi sotto acqua.

♦ **duck out of** vi + prep (fam): **to** ~ **out of doing sth** svignarsela per evitare di fare qc.

duck·ling ['dʌklɪŋ] n anatroccolo.

duct [dʌkt] n (Tech, Anat) condotto.

duc·tile ['dʌktaɪl] adj (metal) duttile.

dud [dʌd] **1** adj (fam: shell, bomb) inesploso(a); (: not working: machine etc) inservibile; (: false: coin, note) falso(a); (: cheque) a vuoto. **2** n (thing) arnese m inservibile; (person) nullità f inv, zero.

dudg·eon ['dʌdʒən] n: **in high** ~ profondamente indegnato(a).

due [djuː] **1** adj **(a)** (owing: sum, money) dovuto(a); **the rent's** ~ **on the 30th** l'affitto scade il 30; our **thanks are** ~ **to him** un grazie gli è dovuto; **I am** ~ **6 days' leave** mi spettano 6 giorni di ferie. **(b)** (proper: care, respect) dovuto(a), debito(a); **with all** ~ **respect** con rispetto parlando; **after** ~ **consideration** dopo un attento esame; **in** ~ **course** a tempo debito. **(c)** (expected) atteso(a); **the train is** ~ **at 8** il treno è atteso per le 8; **she is** ~ **back tomorrow** dovrebbe essere di ritorno domani; **it is** ~ **to be demolished** è destinato alla demolizione. **(d):** ~ **to** (caused by) dovuto(a) a; (because of) a causa di; (thanks to) grazie a; **what's it** ~ **to?** a cosa è dovuto?

2 adv: ~ **west** di proprio a ovest di; **to go** ~ **north** andare dritto verso nord; **to face** ~ **south** guardare verso sud.

3 n **(a):** ~**s** pl (club, union fees) quota; **harbour** ~**s** diritti mpl di porto. **(b): to give him his** ~, **he did try hard** per essere onesti (nei suoi confronti), bisogna riconoscere che ce l'ha messa tutta.

duel ['djʊəl] **1** n duello. **2** vi battersi in duello, fare un duello.

duet [djuː'ɛt] n duetto.

duf·fel, duf·fle ['dʌfəl] adj: ~ **bag** sacca da viaggio di tela; ~ **coat** montgomery m inv.

dug [dʌg] pt, pp of **dig**.

duke [djuːk] n duca m.

dull [dʌl] **1** adj **(a)** (**-er, -est**) (sight, hearing) debole; (slow-witted: person, mind) ottuso(a); (: pupil) lento(a); (boring: book, evening) noioso(a); (: person, style) insulso(a); **as** ~ **as ditchwater** una vera pizza. **(b)** (dim: colour, eyes) spento(a); (metal) opaco(a); (overcast: weather, sky) cupo(a); (muffled: sound, thud) sordo(a); (Comm: trade, business) stagnante; (lacking spirit: person, mood) svogliato(a); (: humour) senza mordente. **2** vt (senses) ottundere; (blade) smussare; (impression, memory) offuscare; (pleasure, pain) attenuare; (mind) annebbiare; (sound, colour) smozzare; (mirror, metal) rendere opaco(a).

duly ['djuːlɪ] adv (properly) come si deve, debitamente; (as expected) come previsto, secondo le previsioni; **he** ~ **arrived at 3** è arrivato alle 3 come previsto; **everybody was** ~ **shocked** tutti sono rimasti giustamente scioccati.

dumb [dʌm] adj (**-er, -est**) **(a)** (Med) muto(a); (with surprise etc) senza parole, ammutolito(a); **a** ~

person un(a) muto(a); ~ **animals** gli animali; **to be struck** ~ *(fig)* ammutolire, restare senza parole. **(b)** *(fam: stupid)* stupido(a); **to act** ~ fare lo gnorri.

dumb·bell ['dʌmbɛl] *n (Sport)* manubrio, peso.

dumb·found [dʌm'faʊnd] *vt* sbigottire.

dumb·ness ['dʌmnɪs] *n* **(a)** *(Med)* mutismo. **(b)** *(fam: stupidity)* idiozia, stupidità.

dum·my ['dʌmɪ] **1** *adj (not real)* finto(a); ~ **run** giro di prova. **2** *n (Comm: sham object)* cosa finta, riproduzione *f*; *(for clothes)* manichino; *(ventriloquist's* ~*)* pupazzo; *(baby's teat)* tettarella, succhiotto; *(Ftbl)* finta; *(Bridge)* morto; *(fam: idiot)* scemo(a).

dump [dʌmp] **1** *n (pile of rubbish)* mucchio di immondizie; *(place for refuse)* discarica pubblica; *(Mil)* deposito; *(pej fam: town, hotel etc)* buco; *(: house)* catapecchia; **to be (down) in the** ~**s** *(fam)* essere giù di corda. **2** *vt* **(a)** *(get rid of: rubbish etc)* buttare; *(: Comm: goods)* svendere; *(fam: person, girlfriend)* piantare, scaricare. **(b)** *(put down: sand, load)* scaricare; *(: fam: parcel, passenger, coat)* mollare.

dump·ling ['dʌmplɪŋ] *n* gnocco di pasta.

dumpy ['dʌmpɪ] *adj* tracagnotto(a).

dun [dʌn] *adj* bigio(a), grigiastro(a).

dunce [dʌns] *n (Scol)* asino/a, somaro/a.

dune [dju:n] *n* duna.

dung [dʌŋ] *n (of horse etc)* sterco; *(as manure)* letame *m*.

dun·ga·rees [ˌdʌŋgə'ri:z] *npl (child's)* tutina; *(adult's)* salopette *f inv*; *(of workmen)* tuta.

dun·geon ['dʌndʒən] *n* segreta.

dunk [dʌŋk] *vt* intingere.

duo·denal [ˌdju:əʊ'di:nl] *adj (ulcer)* duodenale.

duo·denum [ˌdju:əʊ'di:nəm] *n* duodeno.

dupe [dju:p] **1** *n* zimbello/a; **to be sb's** ~ lasciarsi ingannare da qn. **2** *vt* ingannare; **to** ~ **sb into doing sth** ingannare qn per fargli fare qc.

du·plex ['dju:plɛks] *n (Am: also:* ~ **apartment)** appartamento su due piani.

du·pli·cate ['dju:plɪkeɪt] **1** *vt (document etc)* fare una doppia copia di; *(on machine)* ciclostilare, duplicare; *(repeat: action)* ripetere, riprodurre. **2** ['dju:plɪkɪt] *n (copy of letter etc)* duplicato; **in** ~ in doppia copia. **3** ['dju:plɪkɪt] *adj (copy)* conforme, esattamente uguale; ~ **key** duplicato (della chiave).

du·pli·cat·ing ma·chine ['dju:plɪkeɪtɪŋ mə'ʃi:n] *n*, **du·pli·ca·tor** ['dju:plɪkeɪtə'] *n* duplicatore *m*.

du·plic·ity [dju:'plɪsɪtɪ] *n* doppiezza, duplicità.

du·rabil·ity [ˌdjʊərə'bɪlɪtɪ] *n* durevolezza.

du·rable ['djʊərəbl] *adj (material)* resistente; *(Comm)* durevole; *(friendship)* duraturo(a).

du·ra·tion [djʊə'reɪʃən] *n* durata; **of 6 years'** ~ della durata di 6 anni.

du·ress [djʊə'rɛs] *n*: **under** ~ sotto costrizione, con la coercizione.

du·rex ['djʊərɛks] *n* ® preservativo.

dur·ing ['djʊərɪŋ] *prep* durante.

dusk [dʌsk] *n (twilight)* crepuscolo; *(gloom)* (semi)oscurità; **at** ~ sul far della sera, al crepuscolo.

dust [dʌst] **1** *n (on furniture etc)* polvere *f*. **2** *vt, vi* spolverare; **she** ~**ed the cake with sugar** ha spolverato il dolce di zucchero. **3** *cpd:* ~ **bowl** *n (Geog)* regione semi-arida soggetta a tempeste di polvere; ~ **cover** *n*, ~ **jacket** *n (of book)* sopraccoperta; ~ **sheet** *n* telo di protezione.

dust·bin ['dʌstbɪn] *n (Brit)* bidone *m*.

dust·cart ['dʌstkɑːt] *n* carro della nettezza urbana *or* delle immondizie.

dust·er ['dʌstə'] *n (for dusting)* straccio per la pol-

---

vere; *(for blackboard)* straccio per la lavagna.

dust·man ['dʌstmən] *n, pl* -**men** *(Brit)* netturbino.

dust·pan ['dʌstpæn] *n* pattumiera.

dust-up ['dʌstʌp] *n (fam)* zuffa.

dusty ['dʌstɪ] *adj* (-**ier, -iest**) polveroso(a); **to get** ~ impolverarsi.

Dutch [dʌtʃ] **1** *adj* olandese; **to give o.s.** ~ **courage** farsi coraggio con un bicchierino. **2** *n (language)* olandese *m*; **the** ~ *npl (people)* gli olandesi. **3** *adv:* **to go** ~ *or* **d**~ fare alla romana.

Dutch·man ['dʌtʃmən] *n* olandese *m*.

du·ti·able ['dju:tɪəbl] *adj* soggetto(a) a dazio.

du·ti·ful ['dju:tɪfʊl] *adj (child)* rispettoso(a); *(husband)* premuroso(a); *(employee)* coscienzioso(a).

duty ['dju:tɪ] **1** *n* **(a)** *(moral, legal)* dovere *m*; **to do one's** ~ **(by sb)** fare il proprio dovere (verso qn); **to make it one's** ~ **to do sth** assumersi l'obbligo di fare qc; **I am** ~ **bound to say that...** mi sento in dovere di affermare che.... **(b)** *(often pl: task, responsibility)* mansione *f*, funzione *f*; **on** ~ *(Med: in hospital)* di guardia; *(Mil)* di servizio; *(Admin, Scol)* di turno; **off** ~ *(gen)* fuori servizio; *(Mil)* in libera uscita. **(c)** *(tax)* tassa; *(: at customs)* dazio; **to pay** ~ **on sth** pagare il dazio su qc. **2** *cpd:* ~ **officer** *n (Mil etc)* ufficiale *m* di servizio.

duty-free [ˌdju:tɪ'fri:] *adj (goods etc)* esente da dogana; ~ **shop** duty free *m inv*.

du·vet ['du:veɪ] *n* piumino, piumone *m*.

dwarf [dwɔ:f] **1** *adj, n* nano(a) *(m/f)*. **2** *vt (subj: sky-scraper, person)* far scomparire; *(achievement)* eclissare.

dwell [dwɛl] *pt, pp* **dwelt** *vi (poet)* dimorare.

♦ **dwell (up)on** *vi + prep (think about)* soffermarsi su, rimuginare; *(talk about)* soffermarsi su; *(subj: conversation)* aggirarsi su; **don't let's** ~ **upon it** non insistiamo su questo punto.

dwell·er ['dwɛlə'] *n* abitante *m/f*; **city** ~ cittadino/a.

dwell·ing ['dwɛlɪŋ] **1** *n (frm, poet)* dimora. **2** *cpd:* ~ **house** *n (frm)* abitazione *f*.

dwelt [dwɛlt] *pt, pp of* **dwell**.

dwin·dle ['dwɪndl] *vi (numbers, supplies)* assottigliarsi; *(interest)* affievolirsi; **to** ~ **to** ridursi a.

dwin·dling ['dwɪndlɪŋ] *adj (strength, interest)* che si affievolisce; *(resources, supplies)* in diminuzione.

dye [daɪ] **1** *n* colore *m*; *(chemical)* colorante *m*, tintura; **hair** ~ tinta per capelli; **the** ~ **has run** si è stinto. **2** *vt (fabric)* tingere; **to** ~ **sth red** tingere qc di *or* in rosso; **to** ~ **one's hair blond** farsi biondo; ~**d hair** capelli tinti.

dy·ing ['daɪɪŋ] **1** *n (death)* morte *f*; **the** ~ *npl* i morenti. **2** *adj (man)* morente; *(custom, race)* in via di estinzione; **his** ~ **words were...** le sue ultime parole furono... .

dyke [daɪk] *n* **(a)** *(barrier)* diga, argine *m*; *(channel)* canale *m* di scolo; *(causeway)* sentiero rialzato. **(b)** *(fam: lesbian)* lesbica.

dy·nam·ic [daɪ'næmɪk] *adj* dinamico(a).

dy·nam·ics [daɪ'næmɪks] *nsg* dinamica.

dy·na·mism ['daɪnəmɪzəm] *n* dinamismo.

dy·na·mite ['daɪnəmaɪt] **1** *n* dinamite *f*; *(fig fam)* **he's** ~**!** è una bomba!; **the story is** ~ è una storia esplosiva. **2** *vt* far saltare con la dinamite.

dy·na·mo ['daɪnəməʊ] *n* dinamo *f inv*.

dyn·as·ty ['dɪnəstɪ] *n* dinastia.

d'you = **do you**.

dys·en·tery ['dɪsɪntrɪ] *n* dissenteria.

dys·lexia [dɪs'lɛksɪə] *n* dislessia.

dys·lex·ic [dɪs'lɛksɪk] *adj, n* dislessico(a) *(m/f)*.

dys·pep·sia [dɪs'pɛpsɪə] *n* dispepsia.

dys·tro·phy ['dɪstrəfɪ] *n* distrofia; **muscular** ~ distrofia muscolare.

E

E¹, e [iː] n (a) (letter) E, e f or m inv. (b) (Mus) mi m.
E² abbr (= east) E.
each [iːtʃ] **1** adj ogni inv, ciascuno(a); **in ~ hand** per mano, in ogni mano; **~ day** ogni giorno; **~ one of them** ciascuno or ognuno di loro. **2** pron (a) ognuno(a), ciascuno(a); **~ of us** ciascuno or ognuno di noi; **a little of ~ please** un po' di tutto per favore. (b): **~ other** l'un(a) l'altro(a); **they love ~ other** si amano; **people must help ~ other** ci si deve aiutare a vicenda or l'un l'altro; **separated from ~ other** separati l'uno dall'altro; **next to ~ other** uno accanto all'altro. **3** adv l'uno, per uno, ciascuno; **we gave them one apple ~** abbiamo dato una mela a ciascuno; **they cost £5 ~** costano 5 sterline l'uno.
eager [ˈiːgəʳ] adj (keen: pupil) appassionato(a), attento(a); (: supporter, search, desire) appassionato(a); (impatient): **to be ~ to do sth** essere impaziente or ansioso di fare qc; **to be ~ for** (knowledge, power) essere avido di; (affection) essere desideroso di; (happiness) desiderare ardentemente; **he gave me an ~ look** mi ha guardato con impazienza.
eager·ly [ˈiːgəlɪ] adv (listen, watch) attentamente; (speak, work) con entusiasmo; (wait) con impazienza.
eager·ness [ˈiːgənɪs] n (see adj) passione f; impazienza, ansia; (for happiness, affection) desiderio; (for knowledge, power) sete f.
eagle [ˈiːgl] n aquila.
eagle-eyed [ˈiːglˈaɪd] adj (person) dagli occhi di lince.
ear¹ [ɪəʳ] n orecchio; **~, nose and throat specialist** otorinolaringoiatra m/f; **to be all ~s** essere tutt'orecchi; **he could not believe his ~s** non credeva alle proprie orecchie; **your ~s must have been burning** non ti fischiavano le orecchie?; **it goes in one ~ and out the other** mi (or ti etc) entra da un orecchio e esce dall'altro; **up to the ~s in debt** nei debiti fino al collo; **to have a good ~ for music** avere molto orecchio; **to have a good ~ for languages** avere molto orecchio per le lingue; **to play sth by ~** (tune etc) suonare qc a orecchio; **I'll play it by ~** (fig) vedrò come si mettono le cose.
ear² [ɪəʳ] n (of corn etc) spiga.
ear·ache [ˈɪəreɪk] n mal m d'orecchi.
ear·drum [ˈɪədrʌm] n timpano.
earl [ɜːl] n conte m.
ear·ly [ˈɜːlɪ] **1** adj (-ier, -iest) (man) primitivo(a); (Christians, settlers) primo(a); (fruit, plant) precoce; (death) prematuro(a); (reply) pronto(a); **it's still ~** è ancora presto; **you're ~!** sei in anticipo!; **to be an ~ riser, to be an ~ bird** essere mattiniero; **at an ~ hour** presto; **in the ~ morning** al mattino presto; **~ in the morning/afternoon** nelle prime ore del mattino/del pomeriggio; **~ in the spring** all'inizio della primavera; **she's in her ~ forties** ha appena passato la quarantina; **from an ~ age** fin dall'infanzia; **his ~ youth** la sua prima giovinezza; **Shakespeare's ~ work** le prime opere di Shakespeare; **at your earliest convenience** (Comm) non appena possibile.
2 adv presto; **I came home ~** sono tornato a casa presto; **as ~ as possible** il più presto possibile; **he was 10 minutes ~** è arrivato con 10 minuti di anticipo; **to book ~** prenotare in anticipo; **I can't come any earlier** non posso venire prima; **earlier on** poco tempo prima.
ear·mark [ˈɪəmɑːk] vt: **to ~ (for)** (money) mettere da parte (per); (person, job) destinare (a).
earn [ɜːn] vt (money, salary) guadagnare; (interest) maturare; (praise) meritarsi; **to ~ one's living** guadagnarsi da vivere.
ear·nest [ˈɜːnɪst] **1** adj (person, character, request) serio(a); (wish) sincero(a). **2** n: **in ~** (with determination) con serietà, con coscienza; (without joking) sul serio.
ear·nest·ly [ˈɜːnɪstlɪ] adv (speak) con serietà; (work) con coscienza; (pray) con fervore.
earn·ings [ˈɜːnɪŋz] npl (of individual) guadagni mpl; (of company etc) proventi mpl.
ear·phones [ˈɪəfəʊnz] npl (Telec etc) cuffia sg.
ear·plugs [ˈɪəplʌgz] npl tappi mpl per le orecchie.
ear·ring [ˈɪərɪŋ] n orecchino.
ear·shot [ˈɪəʃɒt] n: **within ~** a portata di voce; **wait till he's out of ~ before you say anything** aspetta che si allontani prima di parlare.
earth [ɜːθ] **1** n (a) (the world) terra; **(the) E~** la Terra; **on ~** sulla terra; **the silliest man on ~** l'uomo più stupido del mondo; **she looks like nothing on ~ in that dress** (fam) quel vestito le sta malissimo; **it must have cost the ~!** (fam) deve essere costato un occhio della testa!; **where/who on ~...?** (fam) dove/chi diavolo...?; **what on ~...?** (fam) che diavolo...? (b) (ground) terra; (soil) terra, terreno; **to fall to ~** cadere a terra, cadere al suolo. (c) (of fox, badger) tana; **to run to ~** (animal) inseguire fino alla tana; (person) scovare. (d) (Elec) terra, massa. **2** vt (Elec: apparatus) mettere or collegare a terra.
earthen·ware [ˈɜːθənwɛəʳ] n terraglie fpl.
earth·ly [ˈɜːθlɪ] adj terreno(a); **~ paradise** paradiso terrestre; **there is no ~ reason to think...** non vi è ragione di pensare...; **it's of no ~ use** non serve assolutamente a nulla.
earth·quake [ˈɜːθkweɪk] n terremoto.
earth·ward(s) [ˈɜːθwəd(z)] adv verso terra.
earth·worm [ˈɜːθwɜːm] n lombrico.
earthy [ˈɜːθɪ] adj (a) (taste, smell) di terra. (b) (person) terra terra inv; (humour) grossolano(a).
ear·wig [ˈɪəwɪg] n forbicina.
ease [iːz] **1** n (a) disinvoltura, scioltezza; **with ~** senza difficoltà. (b) (freedom from worry) tranquillità; **a life of ~** una vita agiata; **to feel at ~/ill at ~** sentirsi a proprio agio/a disagio; **to put sb at his ~** mettere qn a suo agio; **stand at ~!** (Mil) riposo! **2** vt (task) facilitare; (pain) alleviare; (rope, strap, pressure) allentare; (collar) slacciare; **to ~ sb's mind** tranquillizzare or rassicurare qn; **to ~ in the clutch** (Aut) rilasciare la frizione

121

dolcemente. **3** *vi* *(situation)* allentarsi, distendersi.

♦ **ease off, ease up** *vi* + *adv* *(slow down: car)* rallentare; *(work, business)* diminuire; *(pressure, tension)* allentarsi; *(pain)* calmarsi; *(relax)* rilassarsi; ~ **up a bit!** rallenta un po'!

easel ['izzl] *n* cavalletto.

easi·ly ['izzlı] *adv* *(without effort: win, climb)* facilmente, agevolmente; **he may** ~ **change his mind** è facile che cambi idea; **it's** ~ **the best** è senza dubbio il migliore; **there were** ~ **500 at the meeting** c'erano almeno 500 persone alla riunione.

easi·ness ['izzɪnɪs] *n* **(a)** facilità, semplicità. **(b)** *(of manners)* disinvoltura.

east [izst] **1** *n* est *m*, oriente *m*; **the mysterious E**~ l'Oriente misterioso; **the E**~ *(Pol)* i Paesi dell'Est; **the wind is in the** ~, **the wind is from the** ~ il vento viene da est; **to the** ~ **of** a est di; **in the** ~ **of** nella parte orientale di. **2** *adj* *(side, coast)* orientale; *(wind)* da est, di levante; **E**~ **Africa** l'Africa orientale. **3** *adv* *(travel)* a est, verso est; ~ **of the border** a est della frontiera.

East·er ['izstə'] **1** *n* Pasqua; **at** ~ a Pasqua. **2** *cpd* *(holidays)* pasquale, di Pasqua; *(week)* di Pasqua; ~ **egg** *n* uovo di Pasqua; ~ **Monday** *n* Pasquetta; ~ **Sunday** *n* domenica di Pasqua.

east·er·ly ['izstəlı] *adj* *(point, aspect)* orientale; *(wind)* da est, di levante; **in an** ~ **direction** in direzione est.

east·ern ['izstən] *adj* orientale; **E**~ **Europe** l'Europa orientale; **the E**~ **bloc** *(Pol)* i Paesi dell'Est.

east·ward **1** *adj* *(direction)* est *inv*. **2** *adv* *(also:* ~**s)** a est, verso est.

easy ['izzı] **1** *adj* *(*-**ier,** -**iest)** **(a)** *(not difficult)* facile; **it is** ~ **to see that...** è facile comprendere che...; **he's** ~ **to get on with** ha un buon carattere; **he came in an** ~ **first** ha vinto di larga misura; **easier said than done** tra il dire e il fare c'è di mezzo il mare; ~ **money** facili guadagni *mpl*. **(b)** *(carefree: life)* agiato(a), tranquillo(a); *(: relationship)* cordiale; *(relaxed: manners, style)* disinvolto(a); **to feel** ~ **in one's mind** sentirsi tranquillo; **payment on** ~ **terms** *(Comm)* facilitazioni di pagamento; **I'm** ~ *(fam)* non ho problemi. **2** *adv:* ~ **does it!** piano!; **to take things** *or* **it** ~ prendere le cose con calma; **take it** ~! *(don't worry)* non prendertela!; *(don't rush)* calma!; **go** ~ **with the sugar** vacci piano con lo zucchero; **go** ~ **on him** non infierire su di lui. **3** *cpd:* ~ **chair** *n* poltrona.

easy-going [,izzı'gəʊɪŋ] *adj* *(person)* accomodante; *(attitude)* compiacente, condiscendente.

eat [izt] *pt* **ate,** *pp* **eaten** **1** *vt* *(food)* mangiare; **he's** ~**ing us out of house and home** *(fam)* è un mangiapane a tradimento; **to** ~ **one's fill** mangiare a sazietà; **he won't** ~ **you** *(fam)* non ti mangia mica; **what's** ~**ing you?** *(fam)* che cosa ti rode?; **to** ~ **one's words** *(fig)* ritrattare. **2** *vi* mangiare; **he** ~**s like a horse** mangia come un lupo; **I've got him** ~**ing out of my hand** pende dalle mie labbra, fa tutto quello che voglio io.

♦ **eat away** *vt* + *adv* *(subj: sea)* erodere; *(: acid)* corrodere; *(: mice)* rosicchiare.

♦ **eat into** *vi* + *prep* *(subj: acid)* corrodere; *(savings)* intaccare.

♦ **eat out** **1** *vi* + *adv* mangiare fuori. **2** *vt* + *adv:* **to** ~ **one's heart out** mangiarsi il cuore *or* il fegato, farsi il sangue amaro.

♦ **eat up** **1** *vt* + *adv* *(meal etc)* finire di mangiare; **it** ~**s up electricity** consuma un sacco di corrente; **this car** ~**s up the miles** questa macchina macina i chilometri. **2** *vi* + *adv:* ~ **up!** finisci di mangiare!

eat·able ['iːtəbl] *adj* *(fit to eat)* mangiabile; *(edible)* commestibile.

eat·en ['iːtn] *pp* of **eat.**

eat·er ['iːtə'] *n:* **a big** ~ un gran mangiatore.

eau de Co·logne ['əʊdəkə'ləʊn] *n* acqua di colonia.

eaves ['iːvz] *npl* gronda *sg*.

eaves·drop ['iːvzdrɒp] *vi* origliare; **to** ~ **on a conversation** tendere le orecchie per ascoltare una conversazione.

ebb [ɛb] **1** *n* *(of tide)* riflusso; ~ **and flow** flusso e riflusso; **to be at a low** ~ *(fig: person, spirits)* avere il morale a terra; *(: business)* andar male. **2** *vi* rifluire; *(fig)* diminuire; **his strength was** ~**ing fast** continuavano a venirgli meno le forze; **to** ~ **and flow** *(fig)* fluire e rifluire. **3** *cpd:* ~ **tide** *n* marea discendente.

eb·ony ['ɛbənı] *n* ebano.

ebul·lience [ı'bʌlıəns] *n* esuberanza.

ebul·lient [ı'bʌlıənt] *adj* esuberante.

ec·cen·tric [ık'sɛntrık] *adj, n* eccentrico(a) *(m/f)*.

ec·cen·tric·ity [,ɛksən'trısıtı] *n* eccentricità *f inv*.

ec·cle·si·as·ti·cal [ı,kliːzı'æstıkəl] *adj* ecclesiastico(a).

echo ['ɛkəʊ] **1** *n, pl* ~**es** eco *m or f*. **2** *vt* fare eco a. **3** *vi* *(sound)* echeggiare; **the room** ~**ed with their laughter** le loro risate risonavano nella stanza.

éclair ['eɪkleə'] *n* ≈ bignè *m inv*.

ec·lec·tic [ı'klɛktık] *adj* eclettico(a).

ec·lec·ti·cism [ı'klɛktısızəm] *n* eclettismo.

eclipse [ı'klıps] **1** *n* eclissi *f inv*. **2** *vt* eclissare.

eco·logi·cal [,iːkəʊ'lɒdʒıkəl] *adj* ecologico(a).

ecol·o·gist [ı'kɒlədʒıst] *n* ecologo/a.

ecol·ogy [ı'kɒlədʒı] *n* ecologia.

eco·nom·ic [,iːkə'nɒmık] *adj* **(a)** *(problems, development, geography)* economico(a). **(b)** *(profitable: price)* vantaggioso(a); *(: business)* che rende.

eco·nomi·cal [,iːkə'nɒmıkəl] *adj* *(person)* parsimonioso(a); *(method, appliance, car)* economico(a).

eco·nomi·cal·ly [,iːkə'nɒmıkəlı] *adv* **(a)** con economia. **(b)** *(regarding economics)* dal punto di vista economico.

eco·nom·ics [,iːkə'nɒmıks] *n* **(a)** *(sg: science)* economia. **(b)** *(pl: financial aspects)* aspetto *or* lato economico.

econo·mist [ı'kɒnəmıst] *n* economista *m/f*.

econo·mize [ı'kɒnəmaız] *vi:* **to** ~ **(on)** fare economia (di).

econo·my [ı'kɒnəmı] **1** *n* *(all senses)* economia; **we must make economies** dobbiamo fare economia. **2** *cpd:* ~ **class** *n* classe *f* turistica; ~ **drive** *n:* **to have an** ~ **drive** adottare una politica del risparmio; ~ **size** *n* confezione *f* economica.

ec·sta·sy ['ɛkstəsı] *n* *(Rel, fig)* estasi *f inv*; **to go into ecstasies over** andare in estasi per.

ec·stat·ic [ɛks'tætık] *adj* estatico(a).

Ecua·dor ['ɛkwədɔː'] *n* Ecuador *m*.

ecu·meni·cal [,iːkjuː'mɛnıkəl] *adj* ecumenico(a).

ec·ze·ma ['ɛksımə] *n* eczema *m*.

eddy ['ɛdı] **1** *n* *(of water, wind, air)* mulinello. **2** *vi* *(water)* far mulinelli; *(wind, air)* turbinare.

edge [ɛdʒ] **1** *n* *(in gen)* orlo, bordo; *(of cube, brick)* spigolo; *(of page)* bordo; *(of lake)* sponda; *(of road)* ciglio; *(of forest)* limitare *m*; *(of knife, razor)* taglio, filo; **on the** ~ **of the town** ai margini della città; **the trees are at the** ~ **of the road** gli alberi lungo il ciglio della strada; **a book with gilt** ~**s** un libro con i bordi dorati; **to be on** ~ *(fig)* essere nervoso, avere i nervi; **it sets my teeth on** ~ mi fa venire i brividi; **to be on the** ~ **of disaster** essere sull'orlo del disastro; **that took the** ~ **off my appetite** mi ha tolto la fame; **to have the** ~ **on**

sb/sth avere un leggero vantaggio su qn/qc. **2** *vt* **(a): to ~ (with)** *(garment)* spostare piano piano. **3** *vi:* **to ~ past** passar rasente; **to ~ forward** avanzare a poco a poco; **to ~ away from sb** allontanarsi piano piano da qn.

edge·ways ['ɛdʒweɪz] *adv* di fianco; **I couldn't get a word in ~** *(fam)* non sono riuscito a infilare neppure una parola.

edg·ing ['ɛdʒɪŋ] *n* bordo.

edgy ['ɛdʒɪ] *adj* nervoso(a), teso(a).

ed·ible ['ɛdɪbl] *adj (fit to eat)* mangiabile; *(produce, mushrooms)* commestibile.

edict ['iːdɪkt] *n* editto.

edi·fi·ca·tion [ˌɛdɪfɪ'keɪʃən] *n (often iro)* cultura.

edi·fice ['ɛdɪfɪs] *n* costruzione *f*.

edi·fy·ing ['ɛdɪfaɪɪŋ] *adj* edificante.

Ed·in·burgh ['ɛdɪnbərə] *n* Edimburgo.

edit ['ɛdɪt] *vt (newspaper, magazine)* dirigere; *(book, series)* curare; *(article, speech, text)* fare la revisione di; *(tape, film, TV: programme)* montare.

edi·tion [ɪ'dɪʃən] *n* edizione *f*.

edi·tor ['ɛdɪtəʳ] *n (of newspaper, magazine)* direttore/trice; *(publisher's ~: of series)* editore/trice; *(: of text)* redattore/trice; *(film ~)* responsabile *m/f* del montaggio.

edi·to·rial [ˌɛdɪ'tɔːrɪəl] **1** *adj* redazionale; **~ assistant** assistente *m/f* di redazione; **~ staff** redazione *f*. **2** *n (in newspaper)* editoriale *m*, articolo di fondo.

edu·cate ['ɛdjʊkeɪt] *vt (pupil)* istruire; *(the public, the mind)* educare; *(tastes)* affinare; **I was ~d abroad** ho fatto i miei studi all'estero.

edu·cat·ed ['ɛdjʊkeɪtɪd] *adj (person)* colto(a).

edu·ca·tion [ˌɛdjʊ'keɪʃən] *n* istruzione *f*; *(teaching)* insegnamento; *(knowledge, culture)* cultura; *(studies)* studi *mpl*; *(training)* formazione *f*; *(Univ: subject etc)* pedagogia; **Ministry of E~** Ministero della Pubblica Istruzione; **primary/secondary ~** scuola primaria/secondaria; **physical ~** educazione *f* fisica.

edu·ca·tion·al [ˌɛdjʊ'keɪʃənl] *adj (methods)* didattico(a); *(establishment, institution)* d'insegnamento; *(system)* dell'istruzione; *(film, visit, role)* educativo(a); *(experience, event)* istruttivo(a).

Ed·ward·ian [ɛd'wɔːdɪən] *adj* edoardiano(a).

EEC *n abbr of* **European Economic Community.**

eel [iːl] *n* anguilla.

eerie ['ɪərɪ] *adj* sinistro(a).

ef·face [ɪ'feɪs] *vt* cancellare.

ef·fect [ɪ'fɛkt] **1** *n* **(a)** *(result)* effetto; **to have an ~ on sb/sth** avere *or* produrre un effetto su qn/qc; **to have no ~** non avere *or* produrre alcun effetto; **to no ~** in vano; **to such good ~ that** con risultati così buoni che; **to recover from the ~s of an illness** riaversi dai postumi di una malattia; **to put into ~** *(rule)* rendere operativo; *(plan)* attuare; **to take ~** *(drug)* fare effetto; **to come into ~** *(Law)* entrare in vigore; **in ~** in realtà, di fatto, in effetti; **his letter is to the ~ that...** il contenuto della sua lettera è che...; **or words to that ~** o qualcosa di simile. **(b)** *(impression)* effetto, impressione *f*; **sound/special ~s** effetti sonori/speciali; **to create an ~** fare effetto; **he said it for ~** l'ha detto per far colpo. **(c)** *(property):* **~s** *npl* effetti *mpl*.
  2 *vt (bring about)* effettuare; *(: saving, transformation, reunion)* operare.

ef·fec·tive [ɪ'fɛktɪv] *adj* **(a)** *(efficient)* efficace; **to become ~** *(Law)* entrare in vigore. **(b)** *(striking: display, outfit)* che fa colpo. **(c)** *(actual)* effettivo(a).

ef·fec·tive·ly [ɪ'fɛktɪvlɪ] *adv (efficiently)*

efficacemente; *(strikingly)* ad effetto; *(in reality)* di fatto.

ef·fec·tive·ness [ɪ'fɛktɪvnɪs] *n* efficacia.

ef·fec·tual [ɪ'fɛktjʊəl] *adj* efficace.

ef·femi·nate [ɪ'fɛmɪnɪt] *adj* effeminato(a).

ef·fer·vesce [ˌɛfə'vɛs] *vi (also fig)* essere in effervescenza; **she ~d with excitement** sprizzava felicità da tutti i pori.

ef·fer·ves·cent [ˌɛfə'vɛsnt] *adj* effervescente.

ef·fi·ca·cious [ˌɛfɪ'keɪʃəs] *adj* efficace.

ef·fi·ca·cy ['ɛfɪkəsɪ] *n* efficacia.

ef·fi·cien·cy [ɪ'fɪʃənsɪ] *n (see adj)* efficienza; efficacia; rendimento.

ef·fi·cient [ɪ'fɪʃənt] *adj (person)* efficiente; *(remedy, product, system)* efficace; *(machine, car)* che ha un buon rendimento.

ef·fi·cient·ly [ɪ'fɪʃəntlɪ] *adv (see adj)* in modo efficiente; in modo efficace; **the new machine works ~** il nuovo macchinario ha un buon rendimento.

ef·fi·gy ['ɛfɪdʒɪ] *n* effigie *f*.

ef·flu·ent ['ɛflʊənt] *n* effluente *m*.

ef·fort ['ɛfət] *n* sforzo; **to make an ~ to do sth** sforzarsi di fare qc; **to make every ~ to do sth** fare il possibile per fare qc; **he made no ~ to be polite** non si è sforzato di essere gentile; **he won a prize for ~** gli è stato dato un premio per l'impegno dimostrato; **it's not worth the ~** non vale la pena; **that's a good ~** *(fam)* niente male; **his latest ~** *(fam)* la sua ultima fatica.

ef·fort·less ['ɛfətlɪs] *adj (success)* facile; *(movement)* disinvolto(a).

ef·fort·less·ly ['ɛfətlɪslɪ] *adv* senza sforzo.

ef·fron·tery [ɪ'frʌntərɪ] *n* sfrontatezza, sfacciataggine *f*.

ef·fu·sive [ɪ'fjuːsɪv] *adj (person)* espansivo(a); *(welcome, letter)* caloroso(a); *(thanks, apologies)* interminabile.

e.g. *abbr (= for example)* ad es.

egali·tar·ian [ɪˌgælɪ'tɛərɪən] *adj* egualitario(a).

egg [ɛg] **1** *n* uovo; *(Bio: seed)* ovulo; **don't put all your ~s in one basket** *(fig)* non giocare il tutto per tutto. **2** *cpd:* **~ cup** *n* portauovo *m inv;* **~ white** *n* albume *m*, bianco d'uovo; **~ yolk** *n* tuorlo, rosso (d'uovo).

♦ **egg on** *vt + adv:* **to ~ sb on (to do sth)** spingere qn (a fare qc).

egg·head ['ɛghɛd] *n (pej fam)* intellettuale *m/f*.

egg·plant ['ɛgplɑːnt] *n (esp Am)* melanzana.

egg·shell ['ɛgʃɛl] **1** *n* guscio d'uovo. **2** *cpd (paint)* guscio d'uovo *inv*.

ego ['iːgəʊ] **1** *n (Psych)* ego, io; *(pride)* amor proprio *m*. **2** *cpd:* **~ trip** *n (fam):* **to be on an ~ trip** fare lo spaccone.

ego·cen·tric(al) [ˌɛgəʊ'sɛntrɪk(əl)] *adj* egocentrico(a).

ego·ism ['ɛgəʊɪzəm] *n* egoismo.

ego·ist ['ɛgəʊɪst] *n* egoista *m/f*.

ego·tism ['ɛgəʊtɪzəm] *n* egotismo.

ego·tist ['ɛgəʊtɪst] *n* egotista *m/f*.

Egypt ['iːdʒɪpt] *n* Egitto.

Egyp·tian [ɪ'dʒɪpʃən] *adj, n* egiziano(a) *(m/f)*.

eider·down ['aɪdədaʊn] *n (quilt)* trapunta di piuma.

eight [eɪt] *adj, n* otto *(m) inv;* **he's had one over the ~** *(fam)* ha alzato troppo il gomito; *for usage see* **five.**

eight·een ['eɪ'tiːn] *adj, n* diciotto *(m) inv; for usage see* **five.**

eight·eenth ['eɪ'tiːnθ] **1** *adj* diciottesimo(a). **2** *n (in series)* diciottesimo/a; *(fraction)* diciottesimo; *for usage see* **fifth.**

eighth [eɪtθ] **1** *adj* ottavo(a). **2** *n (in series)* ottavo/a;

(fraction) ottavo; *for usage see* **fifth.**

eighti·eth ['eɪtɪəθ] **1** *adj* ottantesimo(a). **2** *n (in series)* ottantesimo/a; *(fraction)* ottantesimo; *for usage see* **fifth.**

eighty ['eɪtɪ] *adj, n* ottanta *(m) inv; for usage see* **five.**

Eire ['ɛərə] *n* Repubblica d'Irlanda.

either ['aɪðə^r] **1** *adj* **(a)** *(one or other)* l'uno(a) o l'altro(a); ~ **day would suit me** mi vanno bene tutti e due i giorni. **(b)** *(each)* entrambi(e); **on** ~ **side** su entrambi i lati; **in** ~ **hand** per mano. **2** *pron* l'uno(a) o l'altro(a); **which bus will you take?** — ~ **che autobus prendi?** — l'uno o l'altro; **I don't want** ~ **of them** non voglio né l'uno né l'altro; **give it to** ~ **of them** dallo a uno dei due. **3** *conj:* ~ ... **or** o ... o; *(after neg)* né ... né; ~ **come in or stay out** o entri o stai fuori; **I have never been to** ~ **Paris or Rome** non sono mai stato né a Parigi né a Roma. **4** *adv* neanche, nemmeno, neppure; **he can't sing** ~ non sa neppure cantare; **no, I haven't** ~ no, nemmeno io.

ejacu·late [ɪ'dʒækjʊleɪt] *vt, vi* **(a)** *(cry out)* esclamare. **(b)** *(semen)* eiaculare.

eject [ɪ'dʒɛkt] **1** *vt (bomb)* sganciare; *(flames)* emettere; *(cartridge)* far uscire; *(troublemaker)* espellere. **2** *vi (pilot)* catapultarsi.

ejec·tion [ɪ'dʒɛkʃən] *n (gen)* espulsione *f; (of bomb)* sganciamento.

ejec·tor seat [ɪ'dʒɛktə^r,siːt] *n (in plane)* seggiolino eiettabile.

eke [iːk] *vt:* **to** ~ **out** *(food, supplies, money)* far bastare; *(income)* integrare; **to** ~ **out a living** sbarcare il lunario.

elabo·rate [ɪ'læbərɪt] **1** *adj (design, pattern, hairstyle)* complicato(a), ricercato(a); *(style of writing)* elaborato(a); *(meal)* raffinato(a); *(plan)* complesso(a). **2** [ɪ'læbəreɪt] *vt (work out)* elaborare; *(describe)* illustrare. **3** [ɪ'læbəreɪt] *vi* entrare in dettagli; **to** ~ **on sth** approfondire qc.

elapse [ɪ'læps] *vi* trascorrere.

elas·tic [ɪ'læstɪk] **1** *adj* elastico(a). **2** *n (in garment)* elastico. **3** *cpd:* ~ **band** *n* elastico.

elas·tici·ty [,iːlæs'tɪsɪtɪ] *n* elasticità.

elat·ed [ɪ'leɪtɪd] *adj* esultante.

ela·tion [ɪ'leɪʃən] *n* esultanza.

el·bow ['ɛlbəʊ] **1** *n (Anat)* gomito; **at his** ~ **al** fianco. **2** *vt:* **to** ~ **sb aside** scostare qn a gomitate; **to** ~ **one's way through the crowd** farsi largo tra la folla a gomitate. **3** *cpd:* ~ **grease** *n (fam)* olio di gomito.

elbow·room ['ɛlbəʊrʊm] *n* spazio; **give me some** ~ fammi spazio.

el·der[1] ['ɛldə^r] **1** *adj (brother etc)* maggiore; ~ **statesman** illustre politico *(ritiratosi dall'attività politica)*. **2** *n:* **he is your** ~ è più anziano di te; ~**s** *(of tribe)* anziani *mpl;* **you should respect your** ~**s** devi rispettare chi è più anziano di te.

el·der[2] ['ɛldə^r] *n (Bot)* sambuco.

elder·berry ['ɛldəbɛrɪ] *n* bacca di sambuco.

el·der·ly ['ɛldəlɪ] *adj* anziano(a).

eld·est ['ɛldɪst] *adj* maggiore; **my** ~ **brother** il maggiore dei miei fratelli.

elect [ɪ'lɛkt] **1** *vt* **(a)** *(Pol etc):* **to** ~ **(to)** eleggere (a); **he was** ~**ed chairman** è stato eletto presidente. **(b)** *(choose)* scegliere, decidere; **he** ~**ed to remain** ha deciso di restare. **2** *adj* futuro(a); **the president** ~ il futuro presidente.

elec·tion [ɪ'lɛkʃən] **1** *n* elezione *f;* **to hold an** ~ indire un'elezione; **the** ~ **will be held next week** l'elezione avrà luogo la settimana prossima. **2** *cpd:* ~ **campaign** *n* campagna elettorale; ~ **day** *n* giorno delle elezioni.

elec·tion·eer [ɪ,lɛkʃə'nɪə^r] *vi* fare propaganda elettorale.

elec·tion·eer·ing [ɪ,lɛkʃə'nɪərɪŋ] *n* propaganda elettorale.

elec·tor [ɪ'lɛktə^r] *n* elettore/trice.

elec·tor·al [ɪ'lɛktərəl] **1** *adj* elettorale. **2** *cpd:* ~ **college** *n* collegio elettorale; ~ **roll** *n* registro elettorale.

elec·tor·ate [ɪ'lɛktərɪt] *n* elettorato.

elec·tric [ɪ'lɛktrɪk] **1** *adj* elettrico(a); **the atmosphere was** ~ *(fig)* c'era elettricità nell'aria. **2** *cpd:* ~ **blanket** *n* coperta termica; ~ **chair** *n* sedia elettrica; ~ **fire** *n* stufa elettrica; ~ **light** *n* luce *f* elettrica; ~ **shock** *n* scossa (elettrica); ~ **storm** *n* tempesta elettromagnetica.

elec·tri·cal [ɪ'lɛktrɪkəl] **1** *adj* elettrico(a). **2** *cpd:* ~ **engineer** *n* ingegnere *m* elettrotecnico; ~ **failure** *n* guasto all'impianto elettrico.

elec·tri·cian [ɪlɛk'trɪʃən] *n* elettricista *m*.

elec·tric·ity [ɪlɛk'trɪsɪtɪ] **1** *n* elettricità; **to switch on/off the** ~ attaccare/staccare la corrente. **2** *cpd:* ~ **board** *n (Brit)* ente *m* regionale per l'energia elettrica.

elec·tri·fy [ɪ'lɛktrɪfaɪ] *vt (railway system)* elettrificare; *(charge with electricity, fig)* elettrizzare.

elec·tri·fy·ing [ɪ'lɛktrɪfaɪɪŋ] *adj* elettrizzante.

electro... [ɪ'lɛktrəʊ] *pref* elettro...; ~**cardiogram** *n* elettrocardiogramma *m;* ~**convulsive:** ~**convulsive therapy** *n* elettroshockterapia.

elec·tro·cute [ɪ'lɛktrəkjuːt] *vt* fulminare (con la corrente elettrica).

elec·trode [ɪ'lɛktrəʊd] *n* elettrodo.

elec·tro·en·cepha·lo·gram [ɪ,lɛktrəʊen'sɛfələ,græm] *n* elettroencefalogramma *m*.

elec·troly·sis [ɪlɛk'trɒlɪsɪs] *n* elettrolisi *f*.

elec·tro·mag·net·ic [ɪ'lɛktrəʊmæg'nɛtɪk] *adj* elettromagnetico(a).

elec·tron [ɪ'lɛktrɒn] **1** *n* elettrone *m*. **2** *cpd:* ~ **microscope** *n* microscopio elettronico.

elec·tron·ic [ɪlɛk'trɒnɪk] *adj* elettronico(a).

elec·tron·ics [ɪlɛk'trɒnɪks] *nsg* elettronica.

elec·tro·plat·ed [ɪ'lɛktrəʊpleɪtɪd] *adj* galvanizzato(a).

elec·tro·shock treat·ment [ɪ'lɛktrəʊ,ʃɒk,triːtmənt] *n* elettroshockterapia.

el·egance ['ɛlɪgəns] *n* eleganza.

el·egant ['ɛlɪgənt] *adj* elegante.

el·egant·ly ['ɛlɪgəntlɪ] *adv* in modo elegante, con eleganza.

el·egy ['ɛlɪdʒɪ] *n* elegia.

el·ement ['ɛlɪmənt] *n (gen)* elemento; *(of surprise, luck etc)* componente *f; (Elec)* resistenza; **the** ~**s** *(weather)* gli elementi; **the** ~**s of mathematics** i fondamenti della matematica; **to be in one's** ~ essere nel proprio elemento *or* ambiente naturale.

el·emen·ta·ry [,ɛlɪ'mɛntərɪ] *adj* elementare; ~ **physics** i primi rudimenti di fisica.

el·ephant ['ɛlɪfənt] *n* elefante *m*.

el·evate ['ɛlɪveɪt] *vt (raise in rank)* promuovere; *(fig: mind etc)* elevare.

el·eva·tion [,ɛlɪ'veɪʃən] *n (gen)* elevazione *f; (altitude)* altitudine *f,* altezza; *(of style, thought)* alto livello.

el·eva·tor ['ɛlɪveɪtə^r] *n (Am: lift)* ascensore *m; (hoist)* montacarichi *m inv*.

elev·en [ɪ'lɛvn] **1** *adj* undici *inv*. **2** *n* undici *m inv; (Sport):* **the first** ~ la prima squadra; *for usage see* **five.**

elev·en·ses [ɪ'lɛvnzɪz] *npl (Brit fam)* caffè *m inv* a metà mattina *or* delle undici.

elev·enth [ɪ'lɛvnθ] **1** *adj* undicesimo(a); **at the** ~ **hour** *(fig)* all'ultimo minuto. **2** *n (in series)* undicesimo/a; *(fraction)* undicesimo; *for usage see* **fifth.**

elf [ɛlf] *n, pl* **elves** elfo.

elic·it [ɪ'lɪsɪt] *vt:* **to ~ sth (from sb)** *(truth, secret)* strappare qc (a qn); *(admission, reply)* ottenere qc (da qn).

eli·gibil·ity [ˌɛlɪdʒə'bɪlɪtɪ] *n (see adj)* idoneità; eleggibilità.

eli·gible ['ɛlɪdʒəbl] *adj (suitable):* **~ (for)** idoneo(a) (a); *(public office)* eleggibile (a); **to be ~ for a pension** essere pensionabile; **he's a very ~ young man** è un buon partito.

elimi·nate [ɪ'lɪmɪneɪt] *vt (gen)* eliminare; *(suspect, possibility)* scartare.

elimi·na·tion [ɪˌlɪmɪ'neɪʃən] *n* eliminazione *f;* **by process of ~** per eliminazione.

eli·sion [ɪ'lɪʒən] *n* elisione *f.*

élite [eɪ'liːt] *n* élite *f inv.*

élit·ist [eɪ'liːtɪst] *adj (pej)* elitario(a).

elix·ir [ɪ'lɪksəʳ] *n* elisir *m inv.*

Eliza·bethan [ɪˌlɪzə'biːθən] *adj* elisabettiano(a).

el·lipse [ɪ'lɪps] *n* ellisse *f inv.*

elm [ɛlm] *n* olmo.

elo·cu·tion [ˌɛlə'kjuːʃən] *n* dizione *f.*

elon·gate ['iːlɒŋgeɪt] *vt* allungare.

elope [ɪ'ləʊp] *vi* fuggire.

elope·ment [ɪ'ləʊpmənt] *n* fuga (romantica).

elo·quence ['ɛləkwəns] *n* eloquenza.

elo·quent ['ɛləkwənt] *adj* eloquente.

else [ɛls] *adv* **(a)** altro; **anybody ~ would have done it** chiunque altro l'avrebbe fatto; **is it anybody ~'s?** è di qualcun altro?; **I'd prefer anything ~ rather than...** preferirei qualsiasi altra cosa piuttosto che...; **is there anything ~ I can do?** posso fare qualcos'altro?; **anything ~, sir?** *(shop assistant)* desidera altro, signore?; **I'd go anywhere ~ but there** andrei ovunque fuorché lì; **have you tried anywhere ~?** hai provato da qualche altra parte?; **everyone ~** tutti gli altri; **everything ~** tutto il resto; **nobody ~** nessun altro; **nothing ~** nient'altro; **nothing ~, thank you** *(in shop)* è tutto, grazie; **nowhere ~** nessun altro posto; **I went nowhere ~** non sono andato in nessun altro posto; **somebody ~** qualcun altro; **is this somebody ~'s coat?** è di qualcun altro questo cappotto?; **something ~** qualcos'altro; **it's something ~!** *(fam)* è qualcosa di speciale!; **somewhere ~** da qualche altra parte; **who/what/where/how ~?** chi/che/dove/come altro?; **there is little ~ to be done** rimane ben poco da fare; **he said that, and much ~** ha detto così e molto ancora.

(b) *(otherwise):* **or ~** altrimenti; **keep quiet or ~ go away** stai zitto altrimenti vai via; **do as I say, or ~!** *(fam)* fai come ti dico, se no vedi!

else·where ['ɛls'wɛəʳ] *adv* altrove; **these flowers cannot be found ~** questi fiori non si trovano da nessun'altra parte.

elu·ci·date [ɪ'luːsɪdeɪt] *vt* delucidare.

elude [ɪ'luːd] *vt (arrest, pursuit, enemy, observation)* sfuggire a; *(question)* eludere; **success has ~d him** il successo non gli ha arriso.

elu·sive [ɪ'luːsɪv] *adj (prey, enemy)* inafferrabile; *(thoughts, word, success etc)* che sfugge; *(glance)* sfuggente; *(answer)* evasivo(a); **he is very ~** è proprio inafferrabile *or* irraggiungibile.

elves [ɛlvz] *npl of* **elf.**

ema·ci·at·ed [ɪ'meɪsɪeɪtɪd] *adj* emaciato(a).

ema·nate ['ɛməneɪt] *vi:* **to ~ from** provenire da.

eman·ci·pate [ɪ'mænsɪpeɪt] *vt (women, slaves)* emancipare; *(fig)* liberare.

eman·ci·pa·tion [ɪˌmænsɪ'peɪʃən] *n* emancipazione *f.*

em·balm [ɪm'bɑːm] *vt* imbalsamare.

em·bank·ment [ɪm'bæŋkmənt] *n (of path)* terrapieno; *(of railway)* massicciata; *(of canal, river)* argine *m.*

em·bar·go [ɪm'bɑːgəʊ] *n (Comm, Naut)* embargo; **to put an ~ on sth** mettere l'embargo su qc.

em·bark [ɪm'bɑːk] **1** *vt* imbarcare. **2** *vi (Naut, Aer)* imbarcarsi; **to ~ on sth** *(a journey)* intraprendere qc; *(business venture, explanation, discussion)* imbarcarsi in qc.

em·bar·ka·tion [ˌɛmbɑː'keɪʃən] **1** *n* imbarco. **2** *cpd:* **~ card** *n* carta d'imbarco.

em·bar·rass [ɪm'bærəs] *vt* mettere in imbarazzo; **to be ~ed** essere imbarazzato; **I was ~ed by the question** la domanda mi ha messo in imbarazzo; **to be financially ~ed** avere difficoltà economiche.

em·bar·rass·ing [ɪm'bærəsɪŋ] *adj* imbarazzante.

em·bar·rass·ment [ɪm'bærəsmənt] *n* imbarazzo; **to be an ~ to sb** essere fonte d'imbarazzo per qn; **financial ~s** difficoltà *fpl* economiche.

em·bas·sy ['ɛmbəsɪ] *n* ambasciata; **the Italian E~** l'ambasciata d'Italia.

em·bed [ɪm'bed] *vt (in wood, cement, rock)* incastrare; *(weapon, teeth)* conficcare; *(jewel)* incastonare; **it is ~ded in my memory** è impresso nella mia memoria.

em·bel·lish [ɪm'belɪʃ] *vt:* **to ~ (with)** *(decorate)* abbellire (con); *(fig: story, truth)* infiorare (con).

em·bers ['ɛmbəz] *npl* brace *f.*

em·bez·zle [ɪm'bezl] *vt* appropriarsi indebitamente di.

em·bez·zle·ment [ɪm'bezlmənt] *n* appropriazione *f* indebita.

em·bez·zler [ɪm'bezləʳ] *n* malversatore/trice.

em·bit·ter [ɪm'bɪtəʳ] *vt* inasprire; **~ed by constant failure** amareggiato dai continui fallimenti.

em·blem ['ɛmbləm] *n* emblema *m.*

em·bodi·ment [ɪm'bɒdɪmənt] *n* incarnazione *f,* personificazione *f.*

em·body [ɪm'bɒdɪ] *vt* **(a)** *(spirit, quality)* incarnare; *(thought, theory):* **to ~ (in)** esprimere (in). **(b)** *(include)* comprendere.

em·bo·lism ['ɛmbəlɪzəm] *n* embolia.

em·boss [ɪm'bɒs] *vt (metal)* lavorare a sbalzo; *(leather, paper)* imprimere in rilievo, goffrare.

em·brace [ɪm'breɪs] **1** *n* abbraccio. **2** *vt* **(a)** *(person, religion, cause etc)* abbracciare. **(b)** *(include)* comprendere. **3** *vi* abbracciarsi.

em·broi·der [ɪm'brɔɪdəʳ] *vt* ricamare; *(fig: truth, facts, story)* ricamare su.

em·broi·dery [ɪm'brɔɪdərɪ] **1** *n* ricamo. **2** *cpd (thread)* da ricamo.

em·broil [ɪm'brɔɪl] *vt:* **to ~ sb in sth** coinvolgere qn in qc; **to become ~ed (in sth)** restare invischiato (in qc).

em·bryo ['ɛmbrɪəʊ] *n* embrione *m;* **in ~** in embrione.

em·bry·on·ic [ˌɛmbrɪ'ɒnɪk] *adj (also fig)* embrionale.

emend [ɪ'mend] *vt (text)* correggere.

emen·da·tion [ˌiːmen'deɪʃən] *n* correzione *f.*

em·er·ald ['ɛmərəld] **1** *n (stone)* smeraldo; *(colour)* verde *m* smeraldo. **2** *adj (necklace, bracelet etc)* di smeraldi; *(also:* **~ green)** verde smeraldo *inv.*

emerge [ɪ'mɜːdʒ] *vi:* **to ~ (from)** spuntare (da); *(from water, fig: truth, facts, theory)* emergere (da); *(: problems, new nation)* sorgere (da); **it ~s that** risulta che.

emer·gence [ɪ'mɜːdʒəns] *n (of sun, theory etc)* apparizione *f; (of submarine)* emersione *f; (of nation)* nascita.

emer·gen·cy [ɪ'mɜːdʒənsɪ] **1** *n* emergenza; **in an ~**

in caso di emergenza; **prepared for any** ~ pronto ad ogni emergenza; **to declare a state of** ~ dichiarare lo stato di emergenza. **2** cpd (measures, powers) di sicurezza; (repair, landing) di fortuna; (Med: operation) d'urgenza; (rations, fund) di riserva; ~ **case** n caso urgente; ~ **exit** n uscita di sicurezza; ~ **service** n servizio di pronto intervento; ~ **stop** n (Aut) frenata improvvisa; ~ **ward** n reparto di pronto soccorso.

emer·gent [ɪ'mɜːdʒənt] adj emergente.

em·ery ['ɛmərɪ] **1** n smeriglio. **2** cpd: ~ **board** n limetta di carta; ~ **paper** n carta vetrata.

emet·ic [ɪ'mɛtɪk] n emetico.

emi·grant ['ɛmɪgrənt] n emigrante m/f.

emi·grate ['ɛmɪgreɪt] vi emigrare.

emi·gra·tion [ˌɛmɪ'greɪʃən] n emigrazione f.

émi·gré ['ɛmɪgreɪ] n emigrato/a.

emi·nence ['ɛmɪnəns] n **(a)** (fame) reputazione f; **to gain** or **win** ~ farsi un nome or una reputazione. **(b)** (frm: hill) altura. **(c)** (Rel): **His E~** Sua Eminenza.

emi·nent ['ɛmɪnənt] adj (person) insigne.

emi·nent·ly ['ɛmɪnəntlɪ] adv assolutamente, perfettamente.

emir [ɛ'mɪəʳ] n emiro.

emir·ate [ɛ'mɪərɪt] n emirato.

em·is·sary ['ɛmɪsərɪ] n emissario.

emis·sion [ɪ'mɪʃən] n (see emit) emissione f; esalazione f.

emit [ɪ'mɪt] vt (gen) emettere; (smell) esalare.

emolu·ment [ɪ'mɒljʊmənt] n (often pl: frm) emolumento.

emo·tion [ɪ'məʊʃən] n emozione f; (love, jealousy etc) sentimento.

emo·tion·al [ɪ'məʊʃənl] adj (person, nature) emotivo(a); (moment, experience, story) commovente; ~ **state** condizione f mentale; **to be in a very** ~ **state** essere in uno stato di estrema confusione mentale; **some films have a strong** ~ **appeal** certi film fanno presa sui sentimenti dello spettatore or coinvolgono emotivamente lo spettatore.

emo·tion·al·ism [ɪ'məʊʃnəlɪzəm] n (pej) sentimentalismo.

emo·tion·al·ly [ɪ'məʊʃnəlɪ] adv (behave, be involved) sentimentalmente; (speak) con emozione; **to be** ~ **deprived** soffrire di carenze affettive; **to be** ~ **disturbed** avere un equilibrio emotivo instabile.

emo·tive [ɪ'məʊtɪv] adj che fa presa sui sentimenti.

em·pa·thy ['ɛmpəθɪ] n immedesimazione f; **to feel** ~ **with sb** immedesimarsi con i sentimenti di qn.

em·per·or ['ɛmpərəʳ] n imperatore m.

em·pha·sis ['ɛmfəsɪs] n, pl **emphases** ['ɛmfəsiːz] (in word, phrase) accento; **to speak with** ~ parlare con enfasi; **to lay** or **place** ~ **on sth** (fig) mettere in risalto or in evidenza qc; **the** ~ **is on sport** si dà molta importanza allo sport.

em·pha·size ['ɛmfəsaɪz] vt (word, fact, point) sottolineare; (subj: garment etc) mettere in evidenza; **I must** ~ **that...** devo sottolineare il fatto che... .

em·phat·ic [ɪm'fætɪk] adj (tone, manner, person) energico(a); (speech) enfatico(a); (condemnation, denial) categorico(a).

em·phati·cal·ly [ɪm'fætɪkəlɪ] adv (speak) con enfasi; (deny, refuse) categoricamente.

em·pire ['ɛmpaɪəʳ] n impero.

em·piri·cal [ɛm'pɪrɪkəl] adj empirico(a).

em·piri·cism [ɛm'pɪrɪsɪzəm] n empirismo.

em·ploy [ɪm'plɔɪ] **1** n (frm): **in the** ~ **of sb** alle dipendenze di qn. **2** vt (give job to) dare lavoro a; (appoint) assumere; (make use of: thing, method,

person) servirsi di; (: time) impiegare; **he's** ~**ed in a bank** lavora in banca; **we** ~**ed a painter to decorate the house** ci siamo serviti di un imbianchino per pitturare la casa.

em·ployee [ˌɛmplɔɪ'iː] n dipendente m/f.

em·ploy·er [ɪm'plɔɪəʳ] n datore m di lavoro.

em·ploy·ment [ɪm'plɔɪmənt] **1** n occupazione f; (a job) lavoro; **to find** ~ trovare impiego or lavoro; **without** ~ disoccupato; **full** ~ la piena occupazione; **place of** ~ posto di lavoro. **2** cpd: ~ **agency** n agenzia di collocamento; ~ **exchange** n ufficio m collocamento inv.

em·pow·er [ɪm'paʊəʳ] vt: **to** ~ **sb to do sth** autorizzare qn a fare qc.

em·press ['ɛmprɪs] n imperatrice f.

emp·ti·ness ['ɛmptɪnɪs] n vuoto.

emp·ty ['ɛmptɪ] **1** adj (-ier, -iest) (gen) vuoto(a); (street, area) deserto(a); (post, job) vacante; (fig: threat, promise) vano(a); (words) vacuo(a), privo(a) di significato; **on an** ~ **stomach** a stomaco vuoto. **2:** **empties** npl vuoti mpl. **3** vt (contents, container) vuotare; (liquid) versare; **to** ~ **(out) one's pockets** vuotarsi le tasche; **to** ~ **a liquid from** or **out of sth into sth** travasare un liquido da qc in qc; **she emptied everything out of her bag onto the bed** ha rovesciato la borsa sul letto. **4** vi (room, container) vuotarsi; (water) scaricarsi; (river): **to** ~ **into** gettarsi in.

empty-handed [ˌɛmptɪ'hændɪd] adj a mani vuote; **to arrive/leave** ~ arrivare/andarsene a mani vuote.

empty-headed [ˌɛmptɪ'hɛdɪd] adj sciocco(a).

emu ['iːmjuː] n emù m inv.

emu·late ['ɛmjʊleɪt] vt emulare.

emul·si·fy [ɪ'mʌlsɪfaɪ] vt emulsionare.

emul·sion [ɪ'mʌlʃən] n (liquid) emulsione f; (also: ~ **paint**) pittura (lavabile).

en·able [ɪ'neɪbl] vt: **to** ~ **sb to do sth** consentire or permettere a qn di fare qc.

en·act [ɪn'ækt] vt **(a)** (law) emanare. **(b)** (play, scene) rappresentare.

enam·el [ɪ'næməl] **1** n smalto. **2** vt smaltare. **3** cpd smalto(a); ~ **paint** n vernice f a smalto.

en·camp·ment [ɪn'kæmpmənt] n accampamento.

en·case [ɪn'keɪs] vt: **to** ~ **in** (contain) racchiudere in; (cover) rivestire di.

en·chant [ɪn'tʃɑːnt] vt incantare.

en·chant·ing [ɪn'tʃɑːntɪŋ] adj incantevole.

en·chant·ment [ɪn'tʃɑːntmənt] n (charm, spell) incantesimo; (delight): **to fill with** ~ incantare.

en·chant·ress [ɪn'tʃɑːntrɪs] n incantatrice f.

en·cir·cle [ɪn'sɜːkl] vt circondare; (Mil) accerchiare; (waist, shoulders) stringere.

encl. abbr (= enclosed) all.

en·clave ['ɛnkleɪv] n enclave f.

en·close [ɪn'kləʊz] vt **(a)** (land, garden) recintare. **(b)** (with letter etc) allegare; **please find** ~**d a copy of...** qui acclusa è una copia di... .

en·closed [ɪn'kləʊzd] adj (garden, field) recintato(a); (space) chiuso(a); (in letter) allegato(a), accluso(a).

en·clo·sure [ɪn'kləʊʒəʳ] n (act) recinzione f; (place) recinto; (at racecourse) tondino; (in letter) allegato.

en·com·pass [ɪn'kʌmpəs] vt comprendere.

en·core [ɒŋ'kɔːʳ] **1** excl bis. **2** n bis m inv; **to give an** ~ concedere un bis.

en·coun·ter [ɪn'kaʊntəʳ] **1** n incontro. **2** vt (person) incontrare; (difficulty, danger, enemy etc) imbattersi in.

en·cour·age [ɪn'kʌrɪdʒ] vt (person): **to** ~ **sb (to do sth)** incoraggiare qn (a fare qc); (industry, growth etc) favorire.

en·cour·age·ment [ɪnˈkʌrɪdʒmənt] *n* incoraggiamento.

en·cour·ag·ing [ɪnˈkʌrɪdʒɪŋ] *adj* incoraggiante.

en·croach [ɪnˈkrəʊtʃ] *vi:* to ~ (up)on *(rights)* usurpare; *(land: of neighbour)* sconfinare in; *(land: by sea)* avanzare sopra; *(time)* portare via.

en·cum·ber [ɪnˈkʌmbər] *vt:* to ~ (with) *(person: with luggage)* caricare (di); *(: with debts)* gravare (di); *(room)* ingombrare (di).

en·cum·brance [ɪnˈkʌmbrəns] *n* peso; to be an ~ to sb essere di peso *or* di impaccio a qn.

en·cyc·li·cal [ɪnˈsɪklɪkəl] *n* enciclica.

en·cy·clo·p(a)edia [ɪn,saɪkləʊˈpiːdɪə] *n* enciclopedia.

en·cy·clo·p(a)edic [ɪn,saɪkləʊˈpiːdɪk] *adj* enciclopedico(a).

end [end] **1** *n* **(a)** *(of line, table, rope etc)* estremità *f inv; (of pointed object)* punta; *(of town)* parte *f;* **3rd from the** ~ il 3° da destra *(or* sinistra); **at the** ~ **of** in fondo a; **to place** ~ **to** ~ mettere uno contro l'altro; **from** ~ **to** ~ da un'estremità all'altra; **to stand sth on** ~ mettere qc in piedi; **his hair stood on** ~ gli si sono rizzati i capelli; **to change** ~**s** *(Sport)* cambiare campo; **it's the** ~ **of the road** *or* **line for us** *(fig)* non abbiamo futuro; **to make both** ~**s meet** *(fig)* far quadrare il bilancio, sbarcare il lunario; **to keep one's** ~ **up** *(fam)* conservare un contegno; **to get hold of the wrong** ~ **of the stick** *(fig)* capire fischi per fiaschi.

(b) *(conclusion)* fine *f;* **at the** ~ **of the day** *(fig)* in fin dei conti; **it's not the** ~ **of the world** *(fam)* non è poi la fine del mondo; **we'll never hear the** ~ **of it** *(fam)* non avremo più pace; **there's no** ~ **to it** *(fam)* non finisce mai; **that was the** ~ **of that!** e quella fu la fine!; **to the bitter** ~ fino all'ultimo sangue; **to come to a bad** ~ finire male; **in the** ~ alla fine, da ultimo; **to be at an** ~ essere finito; **to get to the** ~ **of** *(book, supplies, work etc)* finire; **to be at the** ~ **of** *(strength, patience)* essere al limite di; **to bring to an** ~ *(work, speech)* concludere; **to draw to an** ~ stare per finire; **to come to an** ~ finire; **to put an** ~ **to** *(argument, relationship, sb's tricks)* porre fine a; **for hours on** ~ per ore e ore; **no** ~ **of trouble** *(fam)* problemi a non finire; **no** ~ *(adv: fam)* enormemente; **without** ~ a non finire; **that's the** ~! *(fam)* è il colmo!; **he's the** ~! *(fam)* è impossibile!

(c) *(remnant: of loaf, meat)* avanzo; *(: of candle)* moccolo; **cigarette** ~ mozzicone *m.*

(d) *(aim)* fine *m;* **to achieve one's** ~ raggiungere i propri scopi; **it's an** ~ **in itself** è fine a se stesso; **to no** ~ invano; **to this** ~, **with this** ~ **in view** a questo fine; **the** ~ **justifies the means** il fine giustifica i mezzi.

2 *vt (gen)* porre fine a; *(speech, writing, broadcast):* **to** ~ **(with)** concludere (con); **to** ~ **one's life** mettere fine ai propri giorni; **to** ~ **it all** *(fam)* farla finita; **that was the meal to** ~ **all meals!** *(fam)* quel pranzo era imbattibile!

3 *vi* finire, terminare; *(road, period of time)* terminare; **to** ~ **by saying** concludere dicendo; **to** ~ **in** *(dispute, conflict)* sfociare in; *(subj: word)* finire per.

4 *cpd:* ~ **product** *n (Industry)* prodotto finale; *(fig)* risultato; ~ **result** *n* risultato finale.

♦ **end up** *vi + adv (finish)* finire; *(: road, path)* terminare.

en·dan·ger [ɪnˈdeɪndʒər] *vt* mettere in pericolo; **to** ~ **one's life** mettere a repentaglio la propria vita; **an** ~**ed species** *(of animal)* una specie in via di estinzione.

en·dear [ɪnˈdɪər] *vt:* **to** ~ **sb to** rendere qn caro(a) (a); **to** ~ **o.s. to sb** accattivarsi le simpatie di qn.

en·dear·ing [ɪnˈdɪərɪŋ] *adj (smile)* accattivante; *(characteristic, personality)* simpatico(a).

en·dear·ment [ɪnˈdɪəmənt] *n:* **to whisper** ~**s** sussurrare tenerezze; **term of** ~ vezzeggiativo, parola affettuosa.

en·deav·our [ɪnˈdevər] **1** *n (attempt)* sforzo, tentativo; **to make every** ~ **to do sth** fare tutto il possibile per fare qc. **2** *vt:* **to** ~ **to do** cercare di fare.

en·dem·ic [ɛnˈdɛmɪk] *adj* endemico(a).

end·ing [ˈendɪŋ] *n* fine *f;* *(Gram)* desinenza; **film with a happy** ~ film a lieto fine.

en·dive [ˈendaɪv] *n (curly)* indivia (riccia); *(smooth, flat)* indivia belga.

end·less [ˈendlɪs] *adj (gen)* senza fine; *(road, speech)* interminabile, senza fine; *(attempts)* innumerevole; *(arguments)* continuo(a); *(patience)* infinito(a): *(possibilities)* illimitato(a); *(resources)* inesauribile.

en·dorse [ɪnˈdɔːs] *vt (sign: cheque)* girare; *(approve: opinion, claim, plan)* approvare, appoggiare; *(Aut: licence)* registrare una contravvenzione su.

en·dorse·ment [ɪnˈdɔːsmənt] *n (signature)* girata; *(approval)* approvazione *f;* *(on licence)* contravvenzione *f* registrata sulla patente.

en·dow [ɪnˈdaʊ] *vt* **(a)** *(prize)* istituire; *(hospital)* fondare; *(institution):* **to** ~ **sth with sth** devolvere qc a favore di qc. **(b):** **to be** ~**ed with** *(fig)* essere dotato(a) di.

en·dow·ment [ɪnˈdaʊmənt] *n* **(a)** *(see vb)* istituzione *f;* fondazione *f.* **(b)** *(amount)* donazione *f.*

en·dur·ance [ɪnˈdjʊərəns] **1** *n* resistenza; **to come to the end of one's** ~ non farcela più; **past** *or* **beyond** ~ al di là di ogni sopportazione; **tried beyond** ~ messo a dura prova. **2** *cpd:* ~ **test** *n* prova di resistenza.

en·dure [ɪnˈdjʊər] **1** *vt* sopportare; **I can't** ~ **being teased** non sopporto di essere preso in giro. **2** *vi (friendship, memory, peace)* durare; *(book, building)* resistere.

en·dur·ing [ɪnˈdjʊərɪŋ] *adj* duraturo(a).

en·ema [ˈenɪmə] *n (Med)* clistere *m.*

en·emy [ˈenəmɪ] **1** *n (person)* nemico/a; *(Mil)* nemico; **to make an** ~ **of sb** inimicarsi qn; **he is his own worst** ~ è il peggior nemico di se stesso. **2** *cpd (territory, forces, aircraft)* nemico(a); *(morale, strategy)* del nemico.

en·er·get·ic [,enəˈdʒetɪk] *adj (person, protest etc)* energico(a); *(day)* attivo(a); **do you feel** ~ **enough to go for a walk?** sei abbastanza in forze per fare una passeggiata?

en·er·gy [ˈenədʒɪ] **1** *n* energia; **I haven't the** ~ non ho la forza; **to put all one's** ~ **into sth** dedicare tutte le proprie energie *or* forze a qc. **2** *cpd:* ~ **crisis** *n* crisi *f* energetica.

energy-saving [ˈenədʒɪ,seɪvɪŋ] **1** *adj (policy)* del risparmio energetico; *(device)* che risparmia energia. **2** *n* risparmio energetico.

en·er·vat·ing [ˈenəːveɪtɪŋ] *adj* snervante.

en·force [ɪnˈfɔːs] *vt (decision, policy)* attuare; *(law, regulation, obedience)* far rispettare; *(argument)* rafforzare.

en·fran·chise [ɪnˈfræntʃaɪz] *vt (give vote to)* concedere il diritto di voto a; *(set free)* affrancare.

en·gage [ɪnˈgeɪdʒ] **1** *vt (hire: servant, worker)* assumere; *(: actor)* ingaggiare; *(: lawyer)* incaricare; *(reserve: room)* prenotare; *(attract: attention)* attrarre; *(occupy: attention, interest)* assorbire; *(Mil: enemy)* attaccare; *(Tech):* **to** ~ **gear/the clutch** innestare la marcia/la frizione; **to** ~ **to do sth** impegnarsi a fare qc; **to** ~ **sb in conversation** attaccare conversazione con qn. **2**

vi (Tech) innestarsi; **to ~ in** *(discussion, politics)* impegnarsi in.

en·gaged [ɪn'geɪdʒd] *adj* **(a)** *(to be married)* fidanzato(a); **to get ~** fidanzarsi. **(b)** *(occupied)*: **to be ~ in doing sth** essere impegnato a fare qc; **to be ~ on sth** occuparsi di qc. **(c)** *(phone number, lavatory)* occupato(a).

en·gage·ment [ɪn'geɪdʒmənt] **1** *n* **(a)** *(to marry)* fidanzamento. **(b)** *(appointment, undertaking)* impegno; **I have a previous ~** ho già un impegno. **(c)** *(of worker, servant etc)* assunzione *f*; *(of actor)* ingaggio; *(of lawyer)* nomina. **(d)** *(Mil: battle)* scontro. **2** *cpd*: **~ ring** *n* anello di fidanzamento.

en·gag·ing [ɪn'geɪdʒɪŋ] *adj* attraente.

en·gine ['endʒɪn] **1** *n (motor: in car, ship, plane)* motore *m; (Rail)* locomotiva; **facing/with your back to the ~** nel senso della/in senso contrario alla marcia. **2** *cpd*: **~ driver** *n (of train)* macchinista *m; ~* **room** *n (Naut)* sala *f* macchine *inv*.

en·gi·neer [,endʒɪ'nɪəʳ] **1** *n (gen)* ingegnere *m; (tradesman)* meccanico; *(for domestic appliances)* tecnico; *(Naut, Am Rail)* macchinista *m;* **civil/ mechanical ~** ingegnere civile/meccanico; **the E~s** *(Mil)* il Genio. **2** *vt (contrive)* architettare, organizzare.

en·gi·neer·ing [,endʒɪ'nɪərɪŋ] **1** *n* ingegneria. **2** *cpd (works, factory, worker etc)* metalmeccanico(a).

Eng·land ['ɪŋglənd] *n* Inghilterra.

Eng·lish ['ɪŋglɪʃ] **1** *adj* inglese; **the ~ Channel** la Manica. **2** *n* **(a)**: **the ~** *(people)* gli Inglesi. **(b)** *(language)* inglese *m;* **in plain ~** ≃ in buon italiano.

English·man ['ɪŋglɪʃmən] *n, pl* **-men** inglese *m*.

English-speaker ['ɪŋglɪʃ,spiːkəʳ] *n* anglofono/a.

English-speaking ['ɪŋglɪʃ,spiːkɪŋ] *adj* di lingua inglese.

English·woman ['ɪŋglɪʃ,wʊmən] *n, pl* **-women** inglese *f*.

en·grave [ɪn'greɪv] *vt (Art, Typ etc)* incidere; *(: wood)* intagliare; *(fig)* imprimere.

en·grav·ing [ɪn'greɪvɪŋ] *n (picture)* incisione *f*.

en·grossed [ɪn'grəʊst] *adj*: **~ in** assorto(a) in, immerso(a) in.

en·gross·ing [ɪn'grəʊsɪŋ] *adj (study, play)* appassionante; *(book)* avvincente.

en·gulf [ɪn'gʌlf] *vt* inghiottire.

en·hance [ɪn'hɑːns] *vt (beauty, attraction)* valorizzare; *(position, reputation)* migliorare; *(chances, value)* aumentare.

enig·ma [ɪ'nɪgmə] *n* enigma *m*.

en·ig·mat·ic [,enɪg'mætɪk] *adj* enigmatico(a).

en·join [ɪn'dʒɔɪn] *vt (frm: obedience, silence, discretion)*: **to ~ (on)** imporre (a); **to ~ sb to sth/to do sth** ingiungere a qn qc/di fare qc.

en·joy [ɪn'dʒɔɪ] *vt* **(a)** *(take delight in)*: **did you ~ the film/wine/book?** ti è piaciuto il film/vino/libro?; **I ~ reading** mi piace leggere; **he ~s (going for) long walks** gli piace fare lunghe passeggiate; **to ~ life** godersi la vita; **to ~ o.s.** divertirsi; **~ yourself!** divertiti! **(b)** *(have benefit of: health)* godere (di); *(: income, advantage)* fruire di; *(: respect)* godere di.

en·joy·able [ɪn'dʒɔɪəbl] *adj* piacevole.

en·joy·ment [ɪn'dʒɔɪmənt] *n* piacere *m;* **to find ~ in sth/in doing sth** provare piacere in qc/nel fare qc.

en·large [ɪn'lɑːdʒ] **1** *vt (Phot)* ingrandire; *(house, circle of friends)* ampliare. **2** *vi*: **to ~ upon** entrare nei dettagli di.

en·larged [ɪn'lɑːdʒd] *adj (edition)* ampliato(a); *(Med: organ, gland)* ingrossato(a); *(: pores)* dilatato(a).

en·large·ment [ɪn'lɑːdʒmənt] *n (gen)* ampliamento; *(Med)* ingrossamento; *(Phot)* ingrandimento.

en·light·en [ɪn'laɪtn] *vt (inform)*: **to ~ sb (about or on sth)** fornire qualche chiarimento a qn (su qc).

en·light·ened [ɪn'laɪtnd] *adj* illuminato(a).

en·light·en·ing [ɪn'laɪtnɪŋ] *adj* istruttivo(a).

en·light·en·ment [ɪn'laɪtnmənt] *n (explanations)* chiarimenti *mpl;* **the (Age of) E~** l'Illuminismo.

en·list [ɪn'lɪst] **1** *vt (Mil: men)* arruolare. **2** *vi (Mil)*: **to ~ (in)** arruolarsi (in); **~ed man** *(Am Mil)* soldato semplice.

en·liv·en [ɪn'laɪvn] *vt (people)* rallegrare; *(events)* ravvivare.

en·mity ['enmɪtɪ] *n* inimicizia.

enor·mity [ɪ'nɔːmɪtɪ] *n (of crime, action)* atrocità *f inv*.

enor·mous [ɪ'nɔːməs] *adj (gen)* enorme; *(patience)* infinito(a); *(strength)* prodigioso(a); *(risk)* immenso(a); **an ~ number of** *(people, things)* una moltitudine di.

enor·mous·ly [ɪ'nɔːməslɪ] *adv* enormemente.

enough [ɪ'nʌf] **1** *adj, n* abbastanza; **~ people/ money** abbastanza gente/soldi; **have you had ~ to eat?** hai mangiato abbastanza?; **we earn ~ to live on** guadagniamo quel tanto che basta per vivere; **will £5 be ~?** bastano 5 sterline?; **that's ~ basta; more than ~ money** denaro più che sufficiente; **there's more than ~ for everyone** ce n'è più che a sufficienza per tutti; **~'s ~!** *(fam)* adesso basta!; **I've had ~!** non ne posso più!; **I've had ~ of (doing) this** ne ho avuto abbastanza di (fare) questo; **it's ~ to drive you mad** *(fam)* è quanto basta a tirarti scemo; **you can never have ~ of this scenery** non si è mai stanchi di questo paesaggio; **it was ~ to prove his innocence** è stato sufficiente a dimostrare la sua innocenza.

2 *adv* abbastanza; **he's old ~ to go alone** è abbastanza grande da poterci andare da solo; **she was fool ~ or ~ of a fool to listen to him** è stata così stupida da dargli retta; **he was kind ~ to lend me the money** è stato così gentile da prestarmi i soldi; **you know well ~ that...** sai bene che...; **oddly ~, ...** ma cosa strana, ...; **sure ~** come volevasi dimostrare; **fair ~!** *(fam)* d'accordo!

en·quire [ɪn'kwaɪəʳ] *etc* = **inquire** *etc*.

en·rage [ɪn'reɪdʒ] *vt* fare arrabbiare.

en·rich [ɪn'rɪtʃ] *vt* arricchire.

en·rich·ment [ɪn'rɪtʃmənt] *n* arricchimento.

en·rol, *(Am)* **en·roll** [ɪn'rəʊl] **1** *vt (gen)* iscrivere; *(Univ)* immatricolare. **2** *vi*: **to ~ (in)** iscriversi (a).

en·rol·ment, *(Am)* **en·roll·ment** [ɪn'rəʊlmənt] *n (see vb)* iscrizione *f;* immatricolazione *f*.

en route [ɒŋ'ruːt] *adv*: **~ for/from/to** in viaggio per/da/a; **it was stolen ~** è stato rubato durante il viaggio.

en·sconce [ɪn'skɒns] *vt*: **to ~ o.s.** sistemarsi bene.

en·sem·ble [ã:n'sãːmbl] *n* **(a)** *(Mus)* ensemble *m inv.* **(b)** *(Dress)* completo.

en·sign *n* **(a)** ['ensən] *(flag)* insegna. **(b)** ['ensaɪn] *(Am Naut)* guardiamarina *m inv*.

en·snare [ɪn'snɛəʳ] *vt* prendere in trappola; *(fig)* intrappolare.

en·sue [ɪn'sjuː] *vi (follow)* seguire; *(result)*: **to ~ (from)** risultare (da).

en·su·ing [ɪn'sjuːɪŋ] *adj (chaos, event)* che segue.

en·sure [ɪn'ʃʊəʳ] *vt* garantire; **to ~ that...** assicurarsi che... .

en·tail [ɪn'teɪl] *vt* comportare; **it ~ed buying a new car** comportava l'acquisto di una nuova macchina.

en·tan·gle [ɪn'tæŋgl] *vt (thread etc)* impigliare;

(fig): **to become ~d in sth** rimanere impegola-
to(a) in qc.

en·ter ['entə'] **1** *vt* **(a)** *(go into: house, vehicle etc)*
entrare in; *(road)* prendere; *(navy, army)* arruolarsi in; *(profession)* intraprendere; *(college,
school)* iscriversi a; *(debate, discussion, contest)*
partecipare a; **the thought never ~ed my head**
non mi è mai passato per la testa; **he ~ed the
church** si è fatto prete. **(b)** *(write down: name,
amount, order etc)* registrare; *(enrol: pupil, candidate, racehorse etc)*: **to ~ sb/sth for sth** iscrivere
qn/qc a qc. **2** *vi* entrare; *(Theatre)*: **~ Othello**
entra Otello; **to ~ for** *(competition, race)* iscriversi a.

♦ **enter into** *vi* + *prep* **(a)** *(gen)* entrare in; *(negotiations, argument)* prendere parte a; **to ~ into
conversation with sb** mettersi a parlare con qn.
(b) *(sb's plans, calculations)* rientrare in; **that
doesn't ~ into it** questo non c'entra. **(c)**: **to ~
into the spirit of things** entrare nello spirito
delle cose.

en·teri·tis [,entə'raɪtɪs] *n* enterite *f*.

en·ter·prise ['entəpraɪz] *n* **(a)** *(firm, undertaking)*
impresa. **(b)** *(initiative)* iniziativa.

en·ter·pris·ing ['entəpraɪzɪŋ] *adj (person)* intraprendente; *(venture)* audace.

en·ter·tain [,entə'teɪn] **1** *vt* **(a)** *(audience)* divertire; *(guest)* intrattenere; **to ~ sb to dinner** invitare qn a cena. **(b)** *(consider: idea, proposal)* prendere in considerazione; *(hopes, doubts)* nutrire. **2**
vi (have visitors) avere ospiti.

en·ter·tain·er [,entə'teɪnə'] *n* artista *m/f (di cabaret, radio, TV)*.

en·ter·tain·ing [,entə'teɪnɪŋ] **1** *adj* divertente. **2** *n*:
to do a lot of ~ avere molti ospiti.

en·ter·tain·ment [,entə'teɪnmənt] **1** *n* **(a)** *(of
audience)* divertimento; *(of guests)* trattenimento. **(b)** *(show)* spettacolo. **2** *cpd*: **~ allowance** *n*
spese *fpl* di rappresentanza; **the ~ world** il mondo dello spettacolo.

en·thral(l) [ɪn'θrɔːl] *vt* affascinare, avvincere.

en·thral·ling [ɪn'θrɔːlɪŋ] *adj* avvincente.

en·thuse [ɪn'θuːz] *vi*: **to ~** *(over or about)* entusiasmarsi (per).

en·thu·si·asm [ɪn'θuːzɪæzəm] *n* entusiasmo; **it
failed to arouse my ~** non mi ha entusiasmato.

en·thu·si·ast [ɪn'θuːzɪæst] *n* appassionato/a.

en·thu·si·as·tic [ɪn,θuːzɪ'æstɪk] *adj (person)* entusiasta; **to be ~ about sth/sb** essere appassionato
di qc/entusiasta di qn; **to become ~ about sth**
entusiasmarsi per qc.

en·tice [ɪn'taɪs] *vt* attirare; **to ~ sb away from
sb/sth** allontanare qn da qn/qc; **to ~ sb into doing
sth** indurre qn a fare qc; **to ~ sb with food/an
offer** *etc* allettare qn col cibo/con un'offerta *etc*.

en·tic·ing [ɪn'taɪsɪŋ] *adj* allettante.

en·tire [ɪn'taɪə'] *adj (whole)* intero(a), tutto(a);
(complete) completo(a), intero(a); *(unreserved)*
assoluto(a), pieno(a).

en·tire·ly [ɪn'taɪəlɪ] *adv* completamente; *(agree)*
assolutamente, pienamente.

en·tirety [ɪn'taɪərətɪ] *n*: **in its ~** nel suo complesso.

en·ti·tle [ɪn'taɪtl] *vt* **(a)** *(book etc)* intitolare. **(b)**
(give right) dare diritto a; **this ~s him to a free
ticket/to do it** questo gli dà diritto a un ingresso
gratuito/a farlo; **to be ~d to sth/to do sth** avere
diritto a qc/a fare qc; **you are quite ~d to do as
you wish** sei libero di fare ciò che vuoi.

en·tity ['entɪtɪ] *n* entità *f inv*.

ento·mol·ogy [,entə'mɒlədʒɪ] *n* entomologia.

en·tou·rage [,ɒntu'rɑːʒ] *n* entourage *m inv*.

en·trails ['entreɪlz] *npl* interiora *fpl*.

en·trance¹ ['entrəns] **1** *n* **(a)** *(way in)* entrata, in-

gresso. **(b)** *(act)* ingresso; *(right to enter)* ammissione *f*; **to make one's ~** *(Theatre)* fare il proprio
ingresso; **to gain ~** essere ammesso a. **2** *cpd*:
~ examination *n* *(to school)* esame *m* di ammissione; **~ fee** *n* *(for club etc)* quota di ammissione.

en·trance² [ɪn'trɑːns] *vt* mandare in estasi, incantare.

en·tranc·ing [ɪn'trɑːnsɪŋ] *adj* incantevole.

en·trant ['entrənt] *n* *(in race, competition)* concorrente *m/f*, partecipante *m/f*; *(in exam)* candidato/
a; **he's a new ~ to teaching** è nuovo all'insegnamento.

en·treat [ɪn'triːt] *vt*: **to ~ sb (to do sth)** implorare
qn (di fare qc).

en·treaty [ɪn'triːtɪ] *n* supplica; **a look of ~** uno
sguardo supplichevole.

en·trenched [ɪn'trentʃt] *adj (Mil)* trincerato(a);
(fig) radicato(a).

en·tre·pre·neur [,ɒntrəprə'nɜː'] *n* imprenditore
m.

en·trust [ɪn'trʌst] *vt*: **to ~ sth to sb, to ~ sb with sth**
affidare qc a qn.

en·try ['entrɪ] **1** *n* **(a)** *(place)* ingresso, entrata; **'no
~'** 'ingresso vietato'; *(Aut)* 'divieto d'accesso'.
(b) *(act)* ingresso. **(c)** *(Sport etc: total)* numero
degli iscritti; *(: thing, person entered in competition)* iscrizione *f*. **(d)** *(in reference book)* voce *f*; *(in
diary, ship's log)* annotazione *f*; *(in account book,
ledger, list)* registrazione *f*; **single/double ~
book-keeping** partita semplice/doppia. **2** *cpd*: **~
form** *n* modulo d'iscrizione; **~ permit** *n* visto
d'ingresso; **~ phone** *n* citofono.

en·twine [ɪn'twaɪn] *vt* intrecciare.

enu·mer·ate [ɪ'njuːməreɪt] *vt* enumerare.

enun·ci·ate [ɪ'nʌnsɪeɪt] *vt (words, sounds)* articolare; *(theory, idea)* enunciare.

enun·cia·tion [ɪ,nʌnsɪ'eɪʃən] *n* articolazione *f*.

en·vel·op [ɪn'veləp] *vt*: **to ~ (in)** avvolgere (in).

en·velope ['envələʊp] *n* busta.

en·vi·able ['envɪəbl] *adj* invidiabile.

en·vi·ous ['envɪəs] *adj*: **~ (of sb/sth)** invidioso(a)
(di qn/qc).

en·vi·ron·ment [ɪn'vaɪərənmənt] *n* ambiente *m*;
Department of the E~ ≃ Ministero dell'Ecologia.

en·vi·ron·men·tal [ɪn,vaɪərən'mentl] *adj* ambientale; **~ studies** *(in school etc)* ecologia.

en·vi·ron·men·tal·ist [ɪn,vaɪərən'mentəlɪst] *n*
studioso/a della protezione dell'ambiente.

en·vis·age [ɪn'vɪzɪdʒ] *vt (expect)* prevedere; *(imagine)* figurarsi.

en·voy ['envɔɪ] *n* *(gen)* inviato/a; *(diplomat)* ministro plenipotenziario.

envy ['envɪ] **1** *n* invidia; **her new car was the ~ of
all the neighbours** tutto il vicinato le invidiava la
macchina nuova. **2** *vt*: **to ~ (sb sth)** invidiare (qn
per qc).

en·zyme ['enzaɪm] *n* enzima *m*.

eon ['iːɒn] *n* = aeon.

ephem·er·al [ɪ'femərəl] *adj* effimero(a).

epic ['epɪk] **1** *adj* epico(a). **2** *n* poema *m* epico,
epopea; *(film)* epopea.

epi·cen·tre ['epɪsentə'] *n* epicentro.

epi·cure ['epɪkjʊə'] *n* buongustaio/a.

epi·dem·ic [,epɪ'demɪk] **1** *adj* epidemico(a). **2** *n*
epidemia.

epi·gram ['epɪgræm] *n* epigramma *m*.

epi·lep·sy ['epɪlepsɪ] *n* epilessia.

epi·lep·tic [,epɪ'leptɪk] *adj*, *n* epilettico(a)
(m/f).

epi·logue ['epɪlɒg] *n* epilogo.

Epipha·ny [ɪ'pɪfənɪ] *n* Epifania.

epis·co·pal [ɪ'pɪskəpəl] *adj* episcopale.

Epis·co·pa·lian [ɪ,pɪskə'peɪlɪən] *adj, n* episcopaliano(a) *(m/f)*.

epi·sode ['ɛpɪsəʊd] *n* episodio.

epis·tle [ɪ'pɪsl] *n* epistola.

epi·taph ['ɛpɪtɑːf] *n* epitaffio.

epi·thet ['ɛpɪθɛt] *n* epiteto.

epito·me [ɪ'pɪtəmɪ] *n (fig)*: **the ~ of kindness** *etc* la gentilezza *etc* in persona.

epito·mize [ɪ'pɪtəmaɪz] *vt (fig)* incarnare.

epoch ['iːpɒk] *n (period)* epoca, era.

epoch-making ['iːpɒk,meɪkɪŋ] *adj* che fa epoca.

eq·uable ['ɛkwəbl] *adj (climate)* costante; *(character)* equilibrato(a).

equal ['iːkwəl] **1** *adj*: **~ (to)** uguale (a); **an ~ amount of time** lo stesso tempo; **to be ~ in strength** avere la stessa forza; **all things being ~** se tutto va bene; **with ~ ease/indifference** con la stessa facilità/indifferenza; **on ~ terms** su un piano di parità; **to be/feel ~ to** *(task)* essere/sentirsi all'altezza di; **the ~(s) sign** *(Math)* segno d'uguaglianza; **the E~ Opportunities Commission** *(Brit)* ≈ la Commissione per la salvaguardia dei diritti civili. **2** *n (person, thing)* pari *m inv*, simile *m*; **without ~** senza pari. **3** *vt (Math)* fare; *(record, rival)* uguagliare.

equali·ty [ɪ'kwɒlɪtɪ] *n* uguaglianza; *(parity)* parità.

equal·ize ['iːkwəlaɪz] **1** *vt* livellare. **2** *vi (Sport)* pareggiare.

equal·iz·er ['iːkwəlaɪzə^r] *n (Sport)* pareggio.

equal·ly ['iːkwəlɪ] *adv* ugualmente; *(share)* in parti uguali; **they are ~ clever** sono intelligenti allo stesso modo; **she is ~ clever** è altrettanto intelligente; **~, you must remember...** allo stesso modo, ti devi ricordare... .

equa·nim·ity [,ɛkwə'nɪmɪtɪ] *n* serenità.

equate [ɪ'kweɪt] *vt* **(a)**: **to ~ (with)** mettere sullo stesso piano (con). **(b)** *(Math: make equal)* uguagliare.

equa·tion [ɪ'kweɪʒən] *n (Math)* equazione *f*.

equa·tor [ɪ'kweɪtə^r] *n* equatore *m*.

equa·to·rial [,ɛkwə'tɔːrɪəl] *adj* equatoriale.

eques·trian [ɪ'kwɛstrɪən] **1** *adj* equestre. **2** *n* cavaliere/amazzone.

equi·dis·tant [ɪːkwɪ'dɪstənt] *adj* equidistante.

equi·lib·rium [,iːkwɪ'lɪbrɪəm] *n* equilibrio.

equine ['ɛkwaɪn] *adj* equino(a).

equi·nox ['iːkwɪnɒks] *n* equinozio.

equip [ɪ'kwɪp] *vt*: **to ~ (with)** *(room etc)* equipaggiare (con), attrezzare (con); *(person)* preparare (a); **~ped with** *(machinery etc)* dotato di; *(supplies etc)* fornito di; **he is well ~ped for the job** ha i requisiti necessari per quel lavoro.

equip·ment [ɪ'kwɪpmənt] *n (no pl)* attrezzatura; *(: Tech, Elec)* apparecchiatura.

equi·table ['ɛkwɪtəbl] *adj* equo(a).

equi·ty ['ɛkwɪtɪ] *n* equità; *(Stock Exchange)*: **equities** azioni *fpl* ordinarie.

equiva·lent [ɪ'kwɪvələnt] **1** *adj* equivalente; **to be ~ to** equivalere a. **2** *n* equivalente *m*.

equivo·cal [ɪ'kwɪvəkəl] *adj* equivoco(a).

equivo·cate [ɪ'kwɪvəkeɪt] *vi* esprimersi in modo equivoco.

equivo·ca·tion [ɪ,kwɪvə'keɪʃən] *n* parole *fpl* equivoche.

era ['ɪərə] *n* era.

eradi·cate [ɪ'rædɪkeɪt] *vt* sradicare.

erase [ɪ'reɪz] *vt* cancellare.

eras·er [ɪ'reɪzə^r] *n (rubber)* gomma.

erect [ɪ'rɛkt] **1** *adj* dritto(a); **with head ~** a testa alta. **2** *vt (statue, temple)* erigere; *(flats, factory)* costruire; *(barricade, mast)* innalzare; *(machinery)* montare; *(theory, obstacles)* edificare.

erec·tion [ɪ'rɛkʃən] *n* **(a)** *(act: gen)* erezione *f*; *(of building)* costruzione *f*; *(of machinery)* montaggio. **(b)** *(Anat)* erezione *f*.

erode [ɪ'rəʊd] *vt (Geol)* erodere; *(metal, fig)* corrodere.

ero·sion [ɪ'rəʊʒən] *n (see vb)* erosione *f*; corrosione *f*.

erot·ic [ɪ'rɒtɪk] *adj* erotico(a).

eroti·cism [ɪ'rɒtɪsɪzəm] *n* erotismo.

err [ɜː^r] *vi (be mistaken)* sbagliare; *(sin)* peccare; **it is better to ~ on the side of caution** la prudenza non è mai troppa.

er·rand ['ɛrənd] **1** *n* commissione *f*; **to run ~s** fare commissioni; **~ of mercy** atto di carità. **2** *cpd*: **~ boy** *n* fattorino.

er·rat·ic [ɪ'rætɪk] *adj (person, conduct, opinions)* incostante; *(driving, results etc)* ineguale.

er·ro·neous [ɪ'rəʊnɪəs] *adj* erroneo(a).

er·ror ['ɛrə^r] *n* errore *m*; **typing/spelling ~** errore di battitura/di ortografia; **in ~** per errore; **to see the ~ of one's ways** riconoscere i propri errori.

eru·dite ['ɛrʊdaɪt] *adj* erudito(a).

erupt [ɪ'rʌpt] *vi (volcano)* entrare in eruzione *or* in attività; *(spots)* spuntare; *(anger)* esplodere; *(war, fighting, quarrel)* scoppiare; **he ~ed into the room** ha fatto irruzione nella stanza.

erup·tion [ɪ'rʌpʃən] *n (of volcano, spots)* eruzione *f*; *(of anger, violence)* esplosione *f*.

es·ca·late ['ɛskəleɪt] **1** *vi* **(a)** *(costs)* salire. **(b)** *(violence, fighting, bombing)* intensificarsi. **2** *vt* intensificare.

es·ca·la·tion [,ɛskə'leɪʃən] *n* escalation *f*.

es·ca·la·tor ['ɛskəleɪtə^r] *n* scala mobile.

es·ca·pade [,ɛskə'peɪd] *n (adventure)* avventura; *(misdeed)* scappatella.

es·cape [ɪs'keɪp] **1** *n (gen)* fuga; *(of prisoner)* fuga, evasione *f*; **to have a lucky ~** scamparla bella; **to make one's ~** evadere.

2 *vt (capture, pursuers, punishment)* sfuggire a; *(death)* scampare; *(danger)* scampare a; *(consequences)* sottrarsi a; **he narrowly ~d being killed** per poco non è rimasto ucciso; **his name ~s me** il suo nome mi sfugge; **to ~ notice** passare inosservato; **it had ~d his notice** era sfuggito alla sua attenzione; **nothing ~s her (attention)** non le sfugge nulla.

3 *vi (gen)* scappare; *(prisoner etc)* evadere; *(liquid, gas: leak)* fuoriuscire; **to ~ from** *(person)* sfuggire a; *(prison)* fuggire di; **to ~ to** *(another place)* fuggire in; *(freedom, safety)* fuggire verso; **he ~d with a few bruises** *(fig)* se l'è cavata con qualche livido; **an ~d prisoner** un evaso.

4 *cpd*: **~ clause** *n (fig: in agreement)* clausola scappatoia; **~ hatch** *n (in submarine, space rocket)* portello di sicurezza; **~ plan** *n* piano di fuga; **~ route** *n* percorso della fuga.

es·cap·ism [ɪs'keɪpɪzəm] *n* evasione *f*.

es·cap·ist [ɪs'keɪpɪst] **1** *adj* d'evasione. **2** *n* persona che cerca di evadere dalla realtà.

es·ca·polo·gist [,ɛskə'pɒlədʒɪst] *n* mago della fuga.

es·carp·ment [ɪs'kɑːpmənt] *n* scarpata.

es·cort ['ɛskɔːt] **1** *n (Mil, Naut etc)* scorta; *(lady's)* cavaliere *m*. **2** [ɪs'kɔːt] *vt* accompagnare; *(Mil, Naut)* scortare. **3** *cpd*: **~ agency** *n* agenzia di hostess; **~ duty** *n* servizio di scorta; **~ vessel** *n* battello di scorta.

Es·ki·mo ['ɛskɪməʊ] **1** *adj* eschimese. **2** *n (person)* eschimese *m/f*; *(language)* eschimese *m*.

esopha·gus [ɪ'sɒfəgəs] *n (Am)* = **oesophagus**.

eso·ter·ic [,ɛsəʊ'tɛrɪk] *adj* esoterico(a).

es·pe·cial [ɪs'pɛʃəl] *adj* particolare.

es·pe·cial·ly [ɪs'pɛʃəlɪ] *adv (particularly)* particolarmente; *(expressly)* appositamente; **it is ~ dif-**

ficult è particolarmente difficile; ~ **when it rains** soprattutto quando piove; **why me,** ~? perché proprio io?

es·pio·nage [ˌɛspɪəˈnɑːʒ] n spionaggio.

es·pla·nade [ˌɛspləˈneɪd] n lungomare m.

es·pouse [ɪsˈpaʊz] vt (fig frm) abbracciare.

Esq. abbr of **Esquire.**

es·quire [ɪsˈkwaɪəʳ] n: **Colin Smith E~** Egregio Signor Colin Smith.

es·say [ˈɛseɪ] n saggio.

es·say·ist [ˈɛseɪɪst] n saggista m/f.

es·sence [ˈɛsəns] n (gen, Culin) essenza; **in** ~ in sostanza; **speed is of the** ~ la velocità è di estrema importanza.

es·sen·tial [ɪˈsɛnʃəl] **1** adj (gen) essenziale; (important) indispensabile; **it is** ~ **that** è essenziale che + sub. **2** n (often pl) elemento essenziale.

es·sen·tial·ly [ɪˈsɛnʃəlɪ] adv fondamentalmente.

es·tab·lish [ɪsˈtæblɪʃ] vt **(a)** (set up: company) costituire; (: state) creare; (: committee) istituire; (: custom, precedent, relations) stabilire; (: power, authority, reputation) affermare; (: peace, order) ristabilire; **he** ~**ed his reputation as an architect** si è affermato come architetto. **(b)** (prove: fact, identity, sb's innocence) dimostrare.

es·tab·lished [ɪsˈtæblɪʃt] adj (person) affermato(a); (business) solido(a); (custom) radicato(a); (fact) stabilito(a); **the E~ Church** la religione di Stato; **a well-~ business** un'attività or una società ben avviata.

es·tab·lish·ment [ɪsˈtæblɪʃmənt] n **(a)** (of company) costituzione f; (of state) creazione f; (of committee) istituzione f; (of law) instaurazione f; (of reputation) affermazione f. **(b)** (business) azienda; (Admin, Mil, Naut: personnel) effettivo; **a teaching** ~ un istituto d'istruzione; **the E~** la classe dirigente, l'establishment; **the cultural E~** l'establishment culturale.

es·tate [ɪsˈteɪt] **1** n **(a)** (land) proprietà f inv, tenuta; **country** ~ tenuta; **housing** ~ complesso edilizio. **(b)** (Law: on death) patrimonio. **2** cpd: ~ **agency** n agenzia immobiliare; ~ **agent** n agente m immobiliare; ~ **car** n giardinetta, automobile f familiare.

es·teem [ɪsˈtiːm] **1** n stima; **I hold him in high** ~ gode di tutta la mia considerazione. **2** vt (think highly of) stimare; (consider) considerare; **I would** ~ **it an honour** sarebbe un onore per me.

es·thet·ic [iːsˈθɛtɪk] etc (Am) = **aesthetic** etc.

es·ti·mate [ˈɛstɪmɪt] **1** n (judgment) valutazione f; (Comm: for work to be done) preventivo; **to give sb an** ~ **of** fare a qn una valutazione approssimativa (or un preventivo) di; **at a rough** ~ approssimativamente. **2** [ˈɛstɪmeɪt] vt valutare; (Comm) preventivare; **we** ~ **the cost to be £150** preventiviamo un costo di circa 150 sterline. **3** [ˈɛstɪmeɪt] vi (Comm): **to** ~ **for** fare il preventivo per.

es·ti·ma·tion [ˌɛstɪˈmeɪʃən] n **(a)** (judgment) giudizio; **in my** ~ a mio giudizio, a mio avviso. **(b)** (esteem) stima; **she has gone up in my** ~ ho maggiore stima di lei.

es·tranged [ɪsˈtreɪndʒd] adj separato(a); **to become** ~**d** allontanarsi.

es·trange·ment [ɪsˈtreɪndʒmənt] n allontanamento.

es·tro·gen [ˈiːstrəʊdʒən] n (Am) = **oestrogen.**

es·tu·ary [ˈɛstjʊərɪ] n estuario.

etch [ɛtʃ] vt incidere all'acquaforte.

etch·ing [ˈɛtʃɪŋ] n (process) incisione f all'acquaforte; (print made from plate) acquaforte f.

eter·nal [ɪˈtɜːnl] adj eterno(a); (pej: complaints etc) continuo(a); **the** ~ **triangle** il classico triangolo.

eter·nity [ɪˈtɜːnɪtɪ] n eternità.

ether [ˈiːθəʳ] n etere m.

ethe·real [ɪˈθɪərɪəl] adj etereo(a).

eth·ic [ˈɛθɪk] n etica.

ethi·cal [ˈɛθɪkəl] adj etico(a), morale.

eth·ics [ˈɛθɪks] n (sg: study) etica; (pl: principles, system) morale f.

Ethio·pia [ˌiːθɪˈəʊpɪə] n Etiopia.

Ethio·pian [ˌiːθɪˈəʊpɪən] adj etiopico(a), etiope.

eth·nic [ˈɛθnɪk] adj etnico(a).

eth·nol·ogy [ɛθˈnɒlədʒɪ] n etnologia.

ethos [ˈiːθɒs] n (of culture, group) norma di vita.

eti·quette [ˈɛtɪkɛt] n etichetta; **court** ~ (royal) etichetta di corte; (Law) protocollo.

Etrus·can [ɪˈtrʌskən] adj etrusco(a).

ety·mo·logi·cal [ˌɛtɪməˈlɒdʒɪkəl] adj etimologico(a).

ety·mol·ogy [ˌɛtɪˈmɒlədʒɪ] n etimologia.

euca·lyp·tus [ˌjuːkəˈlɪptəs] n eucalipto.

Eucha·rist [ˈjuːkərɪst] n Eucaristia.

eulo·gize [ˈjuːlədʒaɪz] vt elogiare, encomiare.

eulogy [ˈjuːlədʒɪ] n elogio, encomio.

eunuch [ˈjuːnək] n eunuco.

eu·phe·mism [ˈjuːfəmɪzəm] n eufemismo.

euphemis·tic [ˌjuːfəˈmɪstɪk] adj eufemistico(a).

eupho·ria [juːˈfɔːrɪə] n euforia.

euphor·ic [juːˈfɒrɪk] adj euforico(a).

Eura·sia [jʊəˈreɪʃə] n Eurasia.

Eura·sian [jʊəˈreɪʃn] **1** adj eurasiatico(a). **2** n eurasiano/a.

Euro·crat [ˈjʊərəʊkræt] n eurocrate m/f.

Euro·dol·lar [ˈjʊərəʊdɒləʳ] n eurodollaro.

Europe [ˈjʊərəp] n Europa; **to go into** ~, **to join** ~ (Pol) entrare nel Mercato Comune.

Euro·pean [ˌjʊərəˈpiːən] **1** adj europeo(a); ~ **Economic Community** (abbr EEC) Comunità Economica Europea (abbr C.E.E. f). **2** n europeo/a.

eutha·na·sia [ˌjuːθəˈneɪzɪə] n eutanasia.

evacu·ate [ɪˈvækjʊeɪt] vt (people) sfollare; (building, area) evacuare.

evacu·ation [ɪˌvækjʊˈeɪʃən] n (see vb) sfollamento; evacuazione f.

evac·uee [ɪˌvækjʊˈiː] n sfollato/a.

evade [ɪˈveɪd] vt (capture, pursuers) sfuggire a; (punishment, blow) schivare; (question) eludere; (issue, truth, sb's gaze) evitare; (responsibility, obligation, military service) sottrarsi a; (taxation, customs duty) evadere.

evalu·ate [ɪˈvæljʊeɪt] vt valutare.

evalu·ation [ɪˌvæljʊˈeɪʃən] n valutazione f.

evan·geli·cal [ˌiːvænˈdʒɛlɪkəl] adj evangelico(a).

evan·gelist [ɪˈvændʒəlɪst] n (writer: also: E~) evangelista m; (preacher) predicatore m evangelista.

evapo·rate [ɪˈvæpəreɪt] **1** vt (liquid) far evaporare; ~**d milk** latte m concentrato. **2** vi (liquid) evaporare; (fig: hopes, fears, anger) svanire.

evapo·ra·tion [ɪˌvæpəˈreɪʃən] n evaporazione f.

eva·sion [ɪˈveɪʒən] n evasione f.

eva·sive [ɪˈveɪzɪv] adj (answer) evasivo(a); (person) sfuggente; **to take** ~ **action** (Mil) ritirarsi.

eve [iːv] n vigilia.

even [ˈiːvən] **1** adj **(a)** (level): ~ **(with)** allo stesso livello (di); (smooth) liscio(a). **(b)** (uniform: speed, breathing) regolare; (temperature etc) costante; (temper) calmo(a); (tone, voice, colour) uniforme. **(c)** (equal: quantities) uguale; (: score) pari inv; **to have an** ~ **chance (of doing sth)** avere una buona probabilità (di fare qc); **to get** ~ **with sb** vendicarsi di qn; **to break** ~ finire in pari or alla pari; **that makes us** ~ (in game, fig) siamo pari; **they are an** ~ **match** sono allo stesso livello. **(d)** (numbers) pari inv.

2 adv **(a)** perfino; **not** ~... nemmeno...; ~ **on**

Sundays perfino di domenica; **and he ~ sings** e sa anche *or* addirittura cantare; **~ though, ~ if** anche se; **if you ~ tried a bit harder** se solo ti sforzassi un po'; **~ as** proprio nel momento in cui; **~ now he can't do it** non lo può fare nemmeno ora; **without ~ reading it** senza neppure leggerlo; **he can't ~ read** non sa nemmeno leggere; **not ~ if/when** *etc* neppure se/quando *etc.* **(b)** *(+ comp adj or adv)* ancora; **~ faster** ancora più veloce.

♦ **even out 1** *vt + adv (smooth: also fig)* appianare; *(number, score)* pareggiare. **2** *vi + adv* pareggiarsi.

♦ **even up** *vt + adv* livellare; *(fig)* appianare.

eve·ning ['iːvnɪŋ] **1** *n* sera; *(length of time)* serata; **in the ~** di sera; **this ~** stasera, questa sera; **tomorrow/yesterday ~** domani/ieri sera; **on Sunday ~** domenica sera; **she spends her ~s knitting** trascorre le sue serate a fare la maglia; **good ~!** buona sera! **2** *cpd (paper, prayers, service)* della sera; *(performance)* serale; **~ class** *n* corso serale; **~ dress** *n (woman's)* abito da sera; **in ~ dress** *(man)* in abito scuro; *(woman)* in abito lungo.

even·ly ['iːvənlɪ] *adv (distribute, space, spread)* uniformemente; *(divide)* in parti uguali; *(breathe)* in modo regolare.

even·song ['iːvənsɒŋ] *n* ≃ vespro.

event [ɪ'vent] *n* avvenimento; *(Sport: in a programme)* gara; **at all ~s, in any ~** in ogni caso; **in either ~** in entrambi i casi; **in the ~ of/that...** in caso di/che + *sub...*; **in the ~** in realtà, di fatto; **in that ~** in quel caso; **in the normal course of ~s** secondo le regole; **in the course of ~s** nel corso degli eventi.

even-tempered [ˌiːvən'tempəd] *adj* equilibrato(a).

event·ful [ɪ'ventfʊl] *adj (life)* ricco(a) di avvenimenti; *(match, day)* movimentato(a).

even·tual [ɪ'ventʃʊəl] *adj* finale; *(probably resulting)* eventuale; **it resulted in the ~ loss of many lives** ha avuto come risultato finale la perdita di molte vite umane.

even·tu·al·ity [ɪˌventʃʊ'ælɪtɪ] *n* eventualità; **to be ready for any ~** essere pronto a ogni evenienza.

even·tu·al·ly [ɪ'ventʃʊəlɪ] *adv (at last)* alla fine, finalmente; *(given time):* **the species will become extinct** la specie finirà per estinguersi.

ever ['evəʳ] *adv* **(a)** *(always)* sempre; **~ ready** sempre pronto; **~ since I've known him** da quando lo conosco; **with ~ increasing frequency** con sempre maggior frequenza; **they lived happily ~ after** e da allora hanno vissuto felici e contenti; **as ~** come sempre; **for ~** per sempre; **they are for ~ fighting** litigano di continuo; **yours ~** *(in letters)* sempre tuo.
(b) *(at any time)* mai; **nothing ~ happens** non succede mai nulla; **if you ~ go there** se ti capita di andarci; **did you ~ meet him?** l'hai mai incontrato?; **have you ~ been there?** ci sei mai stato?; **we haven't ~ tried it** non l'abbiamo mai provato; **more beautiful than ~** più bello che mai; **now if ~ is the time** *or* **moment to...** ora o mai è il momento di...; **the best film ~** il miglior film che si sia mai visto; **he's a liar if ~ there was one** è il più grande bugiardo che io conosca.
(c) *(emphasizing):* **as soon as ~ you can** al più presto possibile; **why ~ did you do it?** perché mai l'hai fatto?; **why ~ not?** come mai?; **never ~** mai e poi mai; **he's ~ so strong** è fortissimo; **~ so slightly drunk** leggermente sbronzo; **we're ~ so grateful** siamo estremamente grati; **thank you ~ so much** grazie mille; **as if I ~ would!** non sia mai detto!

ever·green ['evəgriːn] *n* sempreverde *m or f.*

ever·lasting [ˌevə'lɑːstɪŋ] *adj* eterno(a); *(pej)* continuo(a).

every ['evrɪ] *adj (each)* ogni *inv; (all)* tutti(e); **~ one of them** ognuno di loro; **I gave you ~ assistance** ti ho dato tutta l'assistenza; **I have ~ confidence in him** ho piena fiducia in lui; **we wish you ~ success** ti auguriamo ogni successo; **~ day** ogni giorno, tutti i giorni; **~ three days, ~ third day** ogni tre giorni; **~ other month, ~ second month** ogni due mesi; **~ few days** ogni due o tre giorni; **~ so often, ~ now and then, ~ now and again** di tanto in tanto; **~ time** che ogni volta che; **~ single time** tutte le volte senza esclusione di una; **his ~ wish** ogni suo desiderio; **I enjoyed ~ minute of the party** mi è piaciuto ogni singolo istante della festa; **~ bit of the carpet** proprio tutto il tappeto; **~ bit as clever as** tanto intelligente quanto; **in ~ way** sotto tutti i profili; **~ man for himself** ognuno per sé.

every·body ['evrɪbɒdɪ] *pron* ognuno, ciascuno; *(all)* tutti; **~ knows about it** lo sanno tutti; **~ has his own view** ognuno *or* ciascuno la pensa come crede; **~ else** tutti gli altri.

every·day ['evrɪdeɪ] *adj (expression)* di uso corrente; *(use, occurrence, experience)* comune; *(shoes, clothes)* di tutti i giorni.

every·one ['evrɪwʌn] *pron* = **everybody.**

every·thing ['evrɪθɪŋ] *pron* tutto; **~ is ready** è tutto pronto; **you say is true** tutto ciò che dici è vero; **this shop sells ~** questo negozio vende di tutto; **he did ~ possible** ha fatto tutto il possibile.

every·where ['evrɪweəʳ] *adv* dappertutto; *(wherever)* ovunque; **~ you go you meet...** ovunque tu vada trovi... .

evict [ɪ'vɪkt] *vt* sfrattare.

evic·tion [ɪ'vɪkʃən] **1** *n* sfratto. **2** *cpd:* **~ notice** *n* avviso di sfratto.

evi·dence ['evɪdəns] *n (proof)* prove *fpl; (testimony)* testimonianza; *(sign)* indizio, traccia; **~ of a break-in** tracce di scasso; **to give ~** testimoniare; **to show ~ of** dimostrare; **to turn King's** *or* **Queen's** *or (Am)* **State's ~** testimoniare contro i propri complici; **to be in ~** essere visibile; **she was nowhere in ~** non la si vedeva da nessuna parte.

evi·dent ['evɪdənt] *adj* evidente, chiaro(a); **it is ~ from his speech** che risulta chiaro *or* evidente dal suo discorso che.

evi·dent·ly ['evɪdəntlɪ] *adv (clearly)* chiaramente; *(apparently)* evidentemente; **~ he cannot come** evidentemente non può venire.

evil ['iːvl] **1** *adj (person, deed, reputation)* cattivo(a); *(spirit, spell, influence etc)* malvagio(a); *(unhappy, hour, times)* infausto(a); **to put the ~ eye on sb** fare il malocchio a qn. **2** *n* male *m;* **the lesser of two ~s** il minore dei mali.

evil-doer ['iːvldu:əʳ] *n* malfattore *m.*

evil-minded [ˌiːvl'maɪndɪd] *adj* malvagio(a).

evince [ɪ'vɪns] *vt* manifestare.

evo·ca·tion [ˌevə'keɪʃən] *n* evocazione *f.*

evoca·tive [ɪ'vɒkətɪv] *adj:* **~ (of)** evocativo(a) (di).

evoke [ɪ'vəʊk] *vt (memories)* evocare; *(admiration)* suscitare.

evo·lu·tion [ˌiːvə'luːʃən] *n (development)* sviluppo; *(Bio)* evoluzione *f.*

evolve [ɪ'vɒlv] **1** *vt (system, theory, plan)* elaborare. **2** *vi (species)* evolversi; *(system, plan, science)* svilupparsi.

ewe [ju:] *n* pecora *(femmina).*

ex [eks] *pref* **(a)** *(former: husband, president etc)* ex; **~-serviceman** ex combattente *m.* **(b)** *(out of):* **the price ~ works** il prezzo franco fabbrica;

~-**directory (phone) number** numero non compreso nell'elenco telefonico.

ex·ac·er·bate [ɛksˈæsəbeɪt] *vt (pain)* aggravare; *(fig: relations, situation)* esacerbare, esasperare.

ex·act [ɪgˈzækt] **1** *adj (number, value, meaning, time)* esatto(a); *(instructions, description)* preciso(a); **it's an ~ copy of the original** è una copia perfetta dell'originale; **his ~ words were...** le sue precise parole erano...; **to be ~, there were 3 of us** per essere precisi eravamo in 3; **the ~ opposite (of)** l'esatto contrario (di). **2** *vt*: **to ~ (from)** esigere (da).

ex·act·ing [ɪgˈzæktɪŋ] *adj (task, profession, work)* impegnativo(a); *(person)* esigente.

ex·act·ly [ɪgˈzæktlɪ] *adv (describe, know, resemble)* esattamente; *(of time)* in punto; **~!** esatto!

ex·ag·ger·ate [ɪgˈzædʒəreɪt] **1** *vt (overstate)* esagerare; *(emphasize)* accentuare. **2** *vi* esagerare.

ex·ag·ger·at·ed [ɪgˈzædʒəreɪtɪd] *adj* esagerato(a); **to have an ~ opinion of o.s.** stimarsi troppo.

ex·ag·gera·tion [ɪgˌzædʒəˈreɪʃən] *n* esagerazione*f*.

ex·alt·ed [ɪgˈzɔːltɪd] *adj (high: position, person)* elevato(a); *(elated)* esaltato(a).

ex·ami·na·tion [ɪgˌzæmɪˈneɪʃən] *n (Scol: abbr:* **exam**) esame *m; (inspection: of machine, premises)* ispezione *f; (: of accounts, passport, at Customs)* controllo; *(of witness, suspect)* interrogatorio; *(Med)* visita; **to take** *or* **sit an ~** sostenere *or* dare un esame; **on ~** in seguito all'esame; **the matter is under ~** la questione è all'esame.

ex·am·ine [ɪgˈzæmɪn] *vt (test: pupil, candidate)*: **to ~ sb in** esaminare qn in; *(: orally)*: **to ~ sb on** interrogare qn in; *(inspect: machine, premises)* ispezionare; *(: luggage, passport)* controllare; *(witness, suspect)* interrogare; *(Med)* visitare.

ex·am·in·er [ɪgˈzæmɪnəʳ] *n* esaminatore/trice.

ex·am·ple [ɪgˈzɑːmpl] *n (gen)* esempio; *(person)* esempio, modello; *(copy)* esemplare *m; for* **~** per esempio; **to quote sth/sb as an ~** portare qc/qn ad esempio; **to set a good/bad ~** dare il buon/ cattivo esempio; **to make an ~ of sb** dare un esempio punendo qn; **to punish sb as an ~** punire qn per dare l'esempio.

ex·as·per·ate [ɪgˈzɑːspəreɪt] *vt* esasperare; **~d by, at, with** esasperato da; **to become ~d** esasperarsi.

ex·as·per·at·ing [ɪgˈzɑːspəreɪtɪŋ] *adj* esasperante.

ex·as·pera·tion [ɪgˌzɑːspəˈreɪʃən] *n* esasperazione *f*.

ex·ca·vate [ˈɛkskəveɪt] *vt (ground)* scavare; *(Archeol)* effettuare gli scavi di.

ex·ca·va·tion [ˌɛkskəˈveɪʃən] *n* scavo; *(Archeol)* scavi *mpl*.

ex·ca·va·tor [ˈɛkskəveɪtəʳ] *n (machine)* scavatrice *f*.

ex·ceed [ɪkˈsiːd] *vt (gen, speed limit)*: **to ~ (by)** superare (di); *(limit, bounds)* oltrepassare; *(powers, instructions, duty)* eccedere.

ex·ceed·ing·ly [ɪkˈsiːdɪŋlɪ] *adv* estremamente.

ex·cel [ɪkˈsɛl] **1** *vt* superare; **to ~ o.s.** superare se stesso. **2** *vi*: **to ~ at** *or* **in** eccellere in; **to ~ as** primeggiare come.

ex·cel·lence [ˈɛksələns] *n* superiorità.

Ex·cel·len·cy [ˈɛksələnsɪ] *n*: **His ~** Sua Eccellenza.

ex·cel·lent [ˈɛksələnt] *adj* ottimo(a), eccellente.

ex·cept [ɪkˈsɛpt] **1** *prep* eccetto, tranne; **~ that/if/ when** *etc* salvo che/quando *etc;* **there is nothing we can do ~ wait** non c'è nulla che possiamo fare se non aspettare; **~ for** se non fosse per; **~ for one old lady** se si fa eccezione per *or* tranne una vecchia signora. **2** *vt*: **to ~ (from)** escludere (da); **present company ~ed**

esclusi i presenti; **always ~ing the possibility...** sempre se si esclude la possibilità...; **not ~ing...** senza esclusione di... .

ex·cep·tion [ɪkˈsɛpʃən] *n* eccezione*f*; **with the ~ of** ad eccezione di; **without ~** senza eccezioni; **to make an ~** fare un'eccezione; **the ~ proves the rule** è l'eccezione che conferma la regola; **to take ~ to** fare obiezione a.

ex·cep·tion·al [ɪkˈsɛpʃənl] *adj* eccezionale; *(unusual)* insolito(a).

ex·cep·tion·al·ly [ɪkˈsɛpʃənəlɪ] *adv* eccezionalmente.

ex·cerpt [ˈɛksɜːpt] *n (from film)* spezzone *m; (from TV play)* estratto; *(from book, Mus)* brano.

ex·cess [ɪkˈsɛs] **1** *n* eccesso; **the ~ of losses over profits** l'eccedenza delle perdite sui guadagni; **in ~ of** al di sopra di; **to ~** all'eccesso; **to carry sth to ~** spingere qc all'eccesso. **2** *cpd (profit, weight, luggage)* in eccesso; **~ fare** *n* tariffa aggiuntiva, supplemento.

ex·ces·sive [ɪkˈsɛsɪv] *adj (drinking, spending, interest)* smodato(a); *(charges, rates)* eccessivo(a); *(fear)* esagerato(a).

ex·ces·sive·ly [ɪkˈsɛsɪvlɪ] *adv (see adj)* smodatamente; eccessivamente; esageratamente.

ex·change [ɪksˈtʃeɪndʒ] **1** *n* **(a)** scambio; **in ~ for** in cambio di; **an ~ of gunfire** uno scontro a fuoco. **(b)** *(Comm)*: **foreign ~** cambio. **(c)**: *(telephone)* **~** centralino. **2** *vt*: **to ~ sth for sth/ with sb** scambiare qc con qc/con qn; *(prisoners, stamps, greetings)* scambiarsi; **to ~ blows** venire alle mani. **3** *cpd*: **~ rate** *n* tasso di cambio.

ex·cheq·uer [ɪksˈtʃɛkəʳ] *n (treasury)* tesoro; **the E~** *(Brit Pol)* lo Scacchiere.

ex·cise [ˈɛksaɪz] *n (also:* **~ duty)** imposta indiretta.

ex·cit·able [ɪkˈsaɪtəbl] *adj* eccitabile.

ex·cite [ɪkˈsaɪt] *vt* **(a)** *(person)* far agitare; *(: pleasantly)* riempire di gioia *(or* interesse *etc); (: sexually)* eccitare; **to ~ sb to anger** provocare la rabbia di qn. **(b)** *(anger)* provocare; *(interest, enthusiasm)* suscitare.

ex·cit·ed [ɪkˈsaɪtɪd] *adj*: **~ (about)** eccitato(a) (per); **to get ~ (about sth)** agitarsi (per qc); **it's nothing to get ~ about** *(fig)* non è niente di particolare.

ex·cit·ed·ly [ɪkˈsaɪtɪdlɪ] *adv* con eccitazione.

ex·cite·ment [ɪkˈsaɪtmənt] *n* eccitazione*f*; **in the ~ of the departure/preparations** nell'eccitazione *or* agitazione della partenza/dei preparativi; **the book caused great ~** il libro ha fatto scalpore; **she enjoys ~** le piacciono le emozioni.

ex·cit·ing [ɪkˈsaɪtɪŋ] *adj (gen)* emozionante; *(idea, fashion, person)* entusiasmante.

ex·claim [ɪksˈkleɪm] **1** *vt* esclamare. **2** *vi*: **to ~ at sth** *(indignantly)* indignarsi per qc; *(admiringly)* esprimere meraviglia davanti a qc.

ex·cla·ma·tion [ˌɛkskləˈmeɪʃən] **1** *n* esclamazione *f*. **2** *cpd*: **~ mark** *n (Gram)* punto esclamativo.

ex·clude [ɪksˈkluːd] *vt (gen)* escludere; *(possibility of error etc)* scartare; **I'm ~d from taking part** non ho il diritto di partecipare.

ex·clud·ing [ɪksˈkluːdɪŋ] *prep*: **~ VAT** IVA esclusa; **~ the cleaners** escluse le donne delle pulizie.

ex·clu·sion [ɪksˈkluːʒən] *n* esclusione*f*; **to the ~ of** escludendo.

ex·clu·sive [ɪksˈkluːsɪv] *adj* **(a)** *(gen)* esclusivo(a); *(interest, attention)* totale; **an interview ~ to...** un'intervista in esclusiva a... . **(b)** *(not including)*: **~ of postage** spese postali escluse; **~ of service** servizio escluso; **from 1st to 15th March ~** dal 1° al 15 marzo esclusi.

ex·com·mu·ni·cate [ˌɛkskəˈmjuːnɪkeɪt] *vt* scomunicare.

ex·com·mu·ni·ca·tion [ˈɛkskəˌmjuːnɪˈkeɪʃən] n
scomunica.

ex·cre·ment [ˈɛkskrɪmənt] n escrementi mpl.

ex·cru·ci·at·ing [ɪksˈkruːʃɪeɪtɪŋ] adj (pain, suffering, fam: film etc) atroce; (noise) insopportabile.

ex·cur·sion [ɪksˈkɜːʃən] 1 n (journey) escursione f,
gita; (fig) digressione f. 2 cpd: ~ ticket n biglietto
a tariffa escursionistica; ~ train n treno speciale (per escursioni).

ex·cuse [ɪksˈkjuːs] 1 n scusa; there's no ~ for this
non ci sono scuse or scusanti per questo; on the
~ that... con la scusa or il pretesto che...; to
make ~s for sb trovare giustificazioni per qn. 2
[ɪksˈkjuːz] vt (a) (forgive) scusare; ~ me! mi scusi!; now, if you will ~ me... ora, mi scusi ma... .
(b) (justify) giustificare; to ~ o.s. (for (doing)
sth) giustificarsi (per (aver fatto) qc). (c)
(exempt): to ~ sb (from sth/from doing sth) esonerare or dispensare qn (da qc/dal fare qc); to ~
o.s. (from sth/from doing sth) farsi esonerare or
dispensare (da qc/dal fare qc); to ask to be ~d
chiedere di essere scusato.

ex·ecrable [ˈɛksɪkrəbl] adj (gen) pessimo(a); (manners) esecrabile.

ex·ecute [ˈɛksɪkjuːt] vt (a) (put to death) giustiziare. (b) (carry out) eseguire; (: scheme) attuare; (: will) rendere esecutivo(a).

ex·ecu·tion [ˌɛksɪˈkjuːʃən] n esecuzione f; in the ~
of one's duty nell'adempimento del proprio dovere.

ex·ecu·tion·er [ˌɛksɪˈkjuːʃnəʳ] n boia m inv.

ex·ecu·tive [ɪgˈzɛkjʊtɪv] 1 adj (powers, committee)
esecutivo(a); (position, job, duties) direttivo(a);
(secretary) di direzione; (offices, suite) della direzione; (car, plane) dirigenziale. 2 n (person)
dirigente m/f; (power, group of managers) esecutivo.

ex·ecu·tor [ɪgˈzɛkjʊtəʳ] n (of will) esecutore(trice)
testamentario(a).

ex·em·pla·ry [ɪgˈzɛmplərɪ] adj esemplare.

ex·em·pli·fy [ɪgˈzɛmplɪfaɪ] vt (illustrate) spiegare
con esempi; (be an example of) essere un esempio
di.

ex·empt [ɪgˈzɛmpt] 1 adj: ~ (from) (person: from
tax) esentato(a) (da); (: from military service etc)
esonerato(a) (da); (goods) esente (da). 2 vt: to ~
(from) (see adj) esentare (da); esonerare (da).

ex·emp·tion [ɪgˈzɛmpʃən] n (see adj) esenzione f;
esonero.

ex·er·cise [ˈɛksəsaɪz] 1 n (gen) esercizio m; (physical
activity) esercizio fisico; (Mil) esercitazione f; to
take ~ fare del movimento or moto. 2 vt (a) (use:
authority, right, influence) esercitare; (: patience,
restraint, tact) usare. (b) (mind, muscle, limb) tenere in esercizio; (dog) fare passeggiare. 3 vi
fare del movimento or moto. 4 cpd: ~ book n
quaderno.

ex·ert [ɪgˈzɜːt] vt (strength, force) impiegare; (influence, authority) esercitare; to ~ o.s. (physically) fare uno sforzo; don't ~ yourself! non fare
sforzi!; (hum) non sforzarti troppo!

ex·er·tion [ɪgˈzɜːʃən] n sforzo.

ex·eunt [ˈɛksɪʌnt] vi (Theatre) escono.

ex·hale [ɛksˈheɪl] vt, vi espirare.

ex·haust [ɪgˈzɔːst] 1 n (also: ~ pipe) tubo di scappamento. 2 vt (gen) esaurire; (tire out: person)
stremare; an ~ing journey/day un viaggio/una
giornata estenuante; to ~ o.s. sfiancarsi. 3 cpd:
~ fumes npl gas m di scarico; ~ system n scappamento.

ex·haus·tion [ɪgˈzɔːstʃən] n esaurimento.

ex·haus·tive [ɪgˈzɔːstɪv] adj (research, inquiry, inspection) approfondito(a), minuzioso(a); (ac-

count, description) esauriente; (list) completo(a).

ex·hib·it [ɪgˈzɪbɪt] 1 n (object: painting etc) oggetto
esposto; (Law) reperto. 2 vt (painting etc) esporre; (signs of emotion) mostrare; (courage) dar
prova di; (skill, ingenuity) dimostrare. 3 vi (painter etc) esporre.

ex·hi·bi·tion [ˌɛksɪˈbɪʃən] n (act) esposizione f,
dimostrazione f; (a public show) mostra; to be on
~ essere esposto; to make an ~ of o.s. dare
spettacolo di sé.

ex·hi·bi·tion·ist [ˌɛksɪˈbɪʃənɪst] n esibizionista m/f.

ex·hibi·tor [ɪgˈzɪbɪtəʳ] n espositore/trice.

ex·hila·rate [ɪgˈzɪləreɪt] vt (subj: sea, air) rinvigorire; (: good company, wine) rallegrare.

ex·hila·ra·tion [ɪgˌzɪləˈreɪʃən] n allegria.

ex·hort [ɪgˈzɔːt] vt: to ~ sb (to sth/to do sth) esortare qn (a qc/a fare qc).

ex·ile [ˈɛksaɪl] 1 n (state) esilio; (person) esule m/f;
in(to) ~ in esilio. 2 vt esiliare.

ex·ist [ɪgˈzɪst] vi (a) (live) vivere; to ~ on sth vivere
di qc. (b) (be in existence) esistere; (: doubt) sussistere; (occur) trovarsi.

ex·ist·ence [ɪgˈzɪstəns] n esistenza; to be in ~
esistere; to come into ~ essere creato; the only
one in ~ l'unico esistente.

ex·is·ten·tial [ˌɛgzɪsˈtɛnʃəl] adj esistenziale.

ex·is·ten·tial·ism [ˌɛgzɪsˈtɛnʃəlɪzəm] n esi-
stenzialismo.

exit [ˈɛksɪt] 1 n uscita; to make one's ~ andarsene.
2 vi (Theatre) uscire. 3 cpd: ~ visa n visto
d'uscita.

exo·dus [ˈɛksədəs] n (gen, Rel) esodo.

ex·on·er·ate [ɪgˈzɒnəreɪt] vt: to ~ sb (from sth)
discolpare qn (da qc).

ex·or·bi·tant [ɪgˈzɔːbɪtənt] adj (price) esorbitante;
(demands) spropositato(a).

ex·or·cise [ˈɛksɔːsaɪz] vt esorcizzare.

ex·or·cism [ˈɛksɔːsɪzəm] n esorcismo.

ex·ot·ic [ɪgˈzɒtɪk] adj esotico(a).

ex·pand [ɪksˈpænd] 1 vt (chest, muscles, economy
etc) sviluppare; (market, operations) espandere;
(business) ingrandire; (statement, notes) ampliare; (knowledge) approfondire; (horizons) allargare; (influence) estendere. 2 vi (see vt) svilupparsi; espandersi; ingrandirsi; (metal, lungs)
dilatarsi; to ~ on (notes, story etc) ampliare.

ex·panse [ɪksˈpæns] n distesa.

ex·pan·sion [ɪksˈpænʃən] n (gen) espansione f; (of
town, economy, idea) sviluppo; (of production)
aumento; (of knowledge) approfondimento; (of influence) estendersi m; (of gas, metal) dilatazione f.

ex·pan·sion·ism [ɪksˈpænʃənɪzəm] n espansionismo.

ex·pan·sion·ist [ɪksˈpænʃənɪst] adj espansioni-
stico(a).

ex·pan·sive [ɪksˈpænsɪv] adj (fig) espansivo(a).

ex·pat·ri·ate [ɛksˈpætrɪeɪt] adj, n espatriato(a)
(m/f).

ex·pect [ɪksˈpɛkt] 1 vt (a) (anticipate) aspettarsi;
(wait for: letter, guests, baby) aspettare; it's easier
than I ~ed è più facile del previsto; to ~ to do sth
pensare or contare di fare qc; I ~ed as much me
l'aspettavo; we'll ~ you for supper ti aspettiamo
per cena; that was (only) to be ~ed non potevamo che aspettarcelo; I did not know what to ~
non sapevo che cosa aspettarmi; as ~ed come
previsto; I'll ~ you when I see you (fam) non ti
aspetto per un'ora precisa.
(b) (suppose) pensare, supporre; I ~ so credo
di sì; yes, I ~ it is sì, è chiaro che lo è.
(c) (require): to ~ sth (from sb) esigere qc (da
qn); to ~ sb to do sth pretendere or esigere che
qn faccia qc; I ~ you to be punctual esigo che tu

sia puntuale; **you can't ~ too much from him** non puoi pretendere troppo da lui; **what do you ~ me to do about it?** cosa vuoi che ci faccia? **2** *vi:* **she's ~ing** è incinta.

ex·pec·tan·cy [ɪks'pɛktənsɪ] *n* attesa; **life ~** probabilità *fpl* di vita.

ex·pec·tant [ɪks'pɛktənt] *adj (person, crowd)* in attesa; *(look)* di attesa; **~ mother** gestante *f.*

ex·pect·ant·ly [ɪks'pɛktəntlɪ] *adv (look, listen)* con un'aria d'attesa; **the crowds waited ~** c'era un'aria di attesa tra la folla.

ex·pec·ta·tion [ˌɛkspɛk'teɪʃən] *n* attesa; **there is little ~ of sunshine today** ci sono poche speranze che venga fuori il sole oggi; **in ~ of** in previsione di; **against** *or* **contrary to all ~(s)** contro ogni aspettativa; **to come** *or* **live up to sb's ~s** rispondere alle attese di qn; **beyond (all) ~** al di là di ogni aspettativa.

ex·pe·di·ence [ɪks'piːdɪəns] *n*, **ex·pe·di·en·cy** [ɪk'piːdɪənsɪ] *n (advisability)* interesse *m; (pej)* interesse personale.

ex·pe·di·ent [ɪks'piːdɪənt] **1** *adj (convenient, politic)* opportuno(a). **2** *n* espediente *m.*

ex·pe·dite ['ɛkspɪdaɪt] *vt (speed up)* accelerare; *(: official matter, legal matter)* sollecitare; *(: task)* affrettare.

ex·pe·di·tion [ˌɛkspɪ'dɪʃən] *n* spedizione *f.*

ex·pe·di·tion·ary [ˌɛkspɪ'dɪʃənrɪ] *adj:* **~ force** corpo di spedizione.

ex·pel [ɪks'pɛl] *vt* espellere.

ex·pend [ɪks'pɛnd] *vt (money)* spendere; *(time, effort, energy)* consacrare.

ex·pend·able [ɪks'pɛndəbl] *adj* sacrificabile.

ex·pen·di·ture [ɪks'pɛndɪtʃəʳ] *n (of money etc)* spesa; *(of time, effort)* dispendio.

ex·pense [ɪks'pɛns] **1** *n (cost)* spesa; **at the ~ of** *(fig)* a spese di; **at the ~ of his life** a prezzo della vita; **at great ~** a gran prezzo; **at my ~** a mie spese; *(fig)* alle mie spalle; **to go to the ~ (of)** sobbarcarsi la spesa (di); **regardless of ~** senza badare a spese; **to put sb to the ~ of** fare affrontare a qn la spesa di; **to meet the ~ of** affrontare la spesa di; **it's on ~s** paga la ditta. **2** *cpd:* **~ account** *n* conto *m* spese *inv.*

ex·pen·sive [ɪks'pɛnsɪv] *adj* caro(a); *(costly)* costoso(a); *(fig: victory)* a caro prezzo; **she has ~ tastes** le piacciono le cose costose.

ex·pe·ri·ence [ɪks'pɪərɪəns] **1** *n (all senses)* esperienza; **to learn by ~** imparare per esperienza; **I know from bitter ~** so per amara esperienza, ho imparato a mie spese; **he has no ~ of** grief/being out of work non sa che cosa voglia dire il dolore/ restare senza lavoro; **he has plenty of ~** ha anni di esperienza; **have you any previous ~?** ha esperienza in questo campo?; **practical/teaching ~** esperienza pratica/d'insegnamento; **to have a pleasant/frightening ~** avere un'esperienza piacevole/terrificante; **it was quite an ~** *(also iro)* fu una bella esperienza. **2** *vt (feel: emotions, sensations)* provare; *(suffer: defeat, losses, hardship etc)* subire; **he has ~d some difficulty in walking** ha qualche difficoltà a camminare.

ex·pe·ri·enced [ɪks'pɪərɪənst] *adj:* **~ (in)** esperto(a) (di).

ex·pe·ri·ment [ɪks'pɛrɪmənt] **1** *n* esperimento; **to perform** *or* **carry out an ~** fare un esperimento; **as an ~** a titolo di esperimento. **2** [ɪks'pɛrɪment] *vi* fare un esperimento; **to ~ with a new vaccine** sperimentare un nuovo vaccino.

ex·peri·men·tal [ɪks,pɛrɪ'mentl] *adj* sperimentale; **the process is still at the ~ stage** il procedimento è ancora in via di sperimentazione.

ex·pert ['ɛkspɜːt] **1** *adj (gen)* esperto(a); *(touch,*

advice, opinion) da esperto; *(evidence)* di un esperto; **~ in** *or* **at doing sth** esperto nel fare qc; **~ witness** *(Law)* esperto/a. **2** *n* esperto/a; **an ~ on sth/in** *or* **at doing sth** un esperto di qc/nel fare qc.

ex·per·tise [ˌɛkspəˈtiːz] *n* competenza.

ex·pire [ɪks'paɪəʳ] *vi (document, time limit etc)* scadere; *(die)* spirare.

ex·pi·ry [ɪks'paɪərɪ] *n* scadenza.

ex·plain [ɪks'pleɪn] *vt (gen)* spiegare; *(mystery)* chiarire; **to ~ o.s.** spiegarsi.

♦ **explain away** *vt* + *adv* dar ragione di.

ex·pla·na·tion [ˌɛksplə'neɪʃən] *n* spiegazione *f;* **to find an ~ for sth** trovare la spiegazione di qc; **what have you to say in ~?** che cosa puoi dire a tua discolpa?

ex·plana·tory [ɪks'plænətərɪ] *adj (words)* di spiegazione; *(notes)* esplicativo(a).

ex·ple·tive [ɪks'pliːtɪv] *n (oath)* imprecazione *f.*

ex·plic·it [ɪks'plɪsɪt] *adj (instructions, intention, denial)* esplicito(a); *(details)* chiaro(a).

ex·plode [ɪks'pləud] **1** *vi* esplodere; **to ~ with laughter** scoppiare dalle risa. **2** *vt* far esplodere; *(fig: theory)* demolire; **to ~ a myth** distruggere un mito.

ex·ploit ['ɛksplɔɪt] **1** *n* impresa. **2** [ɪks'plɔɪt] *vt* sfruttare.

ex·ploi·ta·tion [ˌɛksplɔɪ'teɪʃən] *n* sfruttamento.

ex·plo·ra·tion [ˌɛksplɔː'reɪʃən] *n* esplorazione *f.*

ex·plora·tory [ɪks'plɒrətərɪ] *adj (expedition, Med)* d'esplorazione; *(step, discussion)* preliminare.

ex·plore [ɪks'plɔːʳ] *vt (gen, Med)* esplorare; *(fig: problems, subject)* sondare; **to ~ every avenue** sondare tutte le possibilità.

ex·plor·er [ɪks'plɔːrəʳ] *n* esploratore/trice.

ex·plo·sion [ɪks'pləuʒən] *n* esplosione *f.*

ex·plo·sive [ɪks'pləuzɪv] **1** *adj (also fig)* esplosivo(a). **2** *n* esplosivo.

ex·po·nent [ɪks'pəunənt] *n* esponente *m/f.*

ex·port ['ɛkspɔːt] **1** *n* esportazione *f.* **2** [ɪks'pɔːt] *vt* esportare. **3** *cpd (goods, permit, duty)* d'esportazione; **~ drive** *n* campagna a favore dell'esportazione; **~ manager** *n* direttore *m* delle esportazioni; **~ trade** *n* esportazioni *fpl.*

ex·port·er [ɪks'pɔːtəʳ] *n* esportatore/trice.

ex·pose [ɪks'pəuz] *vt (gen, also Phot)* esporre; *(uncover)* scoprire; *(sexual parts)* esibire; *(fig: reveal: plot)* rivelare; *(: criminal)* smascherare; *(one's ignorance)* mettere a nudo; **to be ~d to view** offrirsi alla vista; **to ~ sb/o.s. to ridicule** porre qn/porsi in ridicolo.

ex·posed [ɪks'pəuzd] *adj (land, house, town)* esposto(a); *(Elec: wire, Mil: country etc)* scoperto(a); *(pipe, beam)* a vista; **as a politician, he is in a very ~ position** come politico, è molto vulnerabile.

ex·po·si·tion [ˌɛkspə'zɪʃən] *n* esposizione *f.*

ex·pos·tu·late [ɪks'pɒstjuleɪt] *vi:* **to ~ with sb about sth** fare le proprie rimostranze a qn per qc.

ex·pos·tu·la·tion [ɪks,pɒstju'leɪʃən] *n* rimostranza.

ex·po·sure [ɪks'pəuʒəʳ] **1** *n (gen)* esposizione *f; (of plot etc)* smascheramento; *(Phot)* esposizione; *(: photo)* posa; *(Med)* assideramento; **to die of ~** morire assiderato; **to threaten sb with ~** minacciare di denunciare qn. **2** *cpd:* **~ meter** *n (Phot)* esposimetro.

ex·pound [ɪks'paund] *vt (theory, text)* spiegare; *(one's views)* esporre.

ex·press [ɪks'prɛs] **1** *adj (all senses)* espresso(a); **~ letter** espresso. **2** *adv:* **to send sth ~** spedire qc per espresso. **3** *n (train)* rapido. **4** *vt* **(a)** esprimere; **to ~ o.s.** esprimersi. **(b)** *(send: letter, parcel)* spedire per espresso.

ex·pres·sion [ɪksˈprɛʃən] n *(all senses)* espressione f; **set** ~ modo di dire.

ex·pres·sion·ism [ɪksˈprɛʃənɪzəm] n espressionismo.

ex·pres·sive [ɪksˈprɛsɪv] adj *(look, face, language)* espressivo(a); *(gesture)* eloquente.

ex·pro·pri·ate [ɛksˈprəuprɪeɪt] vt espropriare.

ex·pul·sion [ɪksˈpʌlʃən] n espulsione f.

ex·pur·gate [ˈɛkspɜːgeɪt] vt espurgare.

ex·quis·ite [ɪksˈkwɪzɪt] adj *(gen)* squisito(a); *(manners, sensibility, charm)* raffinato(a); *(sense of humour, pain)* acuto(a), sottile; *(joy, pleasure)* vivo(a).

ex·quis·ite·ly [ɪksˈkwɪzɪtlɪ] adv **(a)** *(paint, embroider)* meravigliosamente; *(dress, express o.s.)* in modo raffinato. **(b)** *(extremely)* estremamente.

ex·tant [ɛksˈtænt] adj esistente.

ex·tem·po·re [ɪksˈtɛmpərɪ] **1** adv senza preparazione. **2** adj improvvisato(a).

ex·tem·po·rize [ɪksˈtɛmpəraɪz] vi improvvisare.

ex·tend [ɪksˈtɛnd] **1** vt **(a)** *(stretch out: hand, arm)* tendere; *(offer: friendship, help, hospitality)* offrire; *(: thanks, condolences, welcome)* porgere; *(: invitation)* estendere; *(Fin: credit)* accordare. **(b)** *(prolong: road, line, deadline)* prolungare; *(: visit)* protrarre; *(enlarge: building, business, vocabulary)* ampliare; *(knowledge, research)* approfondire; *(powers)* estendere; *(frontiers)* allargare. **2** vi *(land, wall):* **to** ~ **to, as far as** estendersi fino a; *(term, meeting):* **to** ~ **to/for** protrarsi fino a/per; **the contract** ~**s to/for...** il contratto è valido fino a/per... .

ex·ten·sion [ɪksˈtɛnʃən] **1** n *(for table, electric flex)* prolunga; *(of road, term etc)* prolungamento; *(of contract, deadline)* proroga; *(Telec)* apparecchio supplementare; ~ **3718** interno 3718; **to have an** ~ **built onto one's house** far ingrandire la casa. **2** cpd: ~ **cable** n *(Elec)* prolunga; ~ **ladder** n scala allungabile.

ex·ten·sive [ɪksˈtɛnsɪv] adj *(grounds, forest)* vasto(a), esteso(a); *(damage)* esteso(a); *(knowledge, research)* approfondito(a); *(inquiries, reforms, investments)* su vasta scala; *(use)* largo(a); *(alterations)* radicale.

ex·ten·sive·ly [ɪksˈtɛnsɪvlɪ] adv *(altered, damaged etc)* radicalmente; *(study, investigate)* a fondo; *(use, travel)* molto.

ex·tent [ɪksˈtɛnt] n *(of land)* estensione f; *(of road)* lunghezza; *(of knowledge, activities, power)* portata; *(degree: of damage, loss)* proporzioni fpl; **to what** ~ in che misura; **to a certain/large** ~ in certa/larga misura; **to such an** ~ **that** a tal punto che; **to the** ~ **of** fino al punto di; **debts to the** ~ **of £5,000** debiti per 5.000 sterline.

ex·tenu·at·ing [ɪksˈtɛnjʊeɪtɪŋ] adj: ~ **circumstances** attenuanti fpl.

ex·te·ri·or [ɪksˈtɪərɪəʳ] **1** adj esterno(a). **2** n esterno; **on the** ~ all'esterno; *(fig)* in apparenza.

ex·ter·mi·nate [ɪksˈtɜːmɪneɪt] vt sterminare.

ex·ter·nal [ɛksˈtɜːnl] **1** adj *(walls etc)* esterno(a); *(appearance)* esteriore; ~ **affairs** affari mpl esteri; **for** ~ **use only** *(Med)* solo per uso esterno; ~ **examiner** esaminatore(trice) esterno(a). **2** n: **the** ~**s** le apparenze.

ex·tinct [ɪksˈtɪŋkt] adj *(volcano)* spento(a), inattivo(a); *(animal, race)* estinto(a).

ex·tin·guish [ɪksˈtɪŋgwɪʃ] vt *(gen)* spegnere; *(fig)* far crollare.

ex·tin·guish·er [ɪksˈtɪŋgwɪʃəʳ] n estintore m.

ex·tol [ɪksˈtəʊl] vt *(merits, virtues)* magnificare; *(person)* celebrare.

ex·tort [ɪksˈtɔːt] vt: **to** ~ **(from)** *(money, confession)*

estorcere (a); *(promise)* strappare (a).

ex·tor·tion [ɪksˈtɔːʃən] n estorsione f.

ex·tor·tion·ate [ɪksˈtɔːʃənɪt] adj esorbitante.

ex·tra [ˈɛkstrə] **1** adj in più; **she needs** ~ **help** ha bisogno di maggior aiuto; **an** ~ **charge** un supplemento; **wine is** ~ il vino è escluso; **take** ~ **care!** stai molto attento!; **for** ~ **safety** per maggior sicurezza; ~ **time** *(Ftbl)* tempi mpl supplementari; ~ **transport** corse fpl supplementari or straordinarie. **2** adv eccezionalmente; ~ **fine** extra fine; **wine will cost** ~ il vino è extra; ~ **large sizes** taglie fpl forti. **3** n extra m inv; *(Cine, Theatre; actor)* comparsa.

ex·tract [ˈɛkstrækt] **1** n *(from book)* brano; *(from film)* spezzone m; *(Culin, Chem)* estratto. **2** [ɪksˈtrækt] vt: **to** ~ **(from)** *(take out)* estrarre (da); *(obtain: confession, money)* estorcere (a); *(select: from book etc)* stralciare (da).

ex·trac·tion [ɪksˈtrækʃən] n estrazione f; **of German** ~ di origine tedesca.

extra·cur·ricu·lar [ˈɛkstrəkəˈrɪkjʊləʳ] adj *(Scol)* parascolastico(a).

extra·dite [ˈɛkstrədaɪt] vt: **to** ~ **sb (from/to)** estradare qn (da/in).

extra·di·tion [ˌɛkstrəˈdɪʃən] n estradizione f.

extra·mari·tal [ˈɛkstrəˈmærɪtl] adj extraconiugale.

extra·mu·ral [ˈɛkstrəˈmjʊərəl] adj *(Univ):* ~ **course** corso libero.

extra·neous [ɪksˈtreɪnɪəs] adj: ~ **(to)** estraneo(a) (a).

extraor·di·nary [ɪksˈtrɔːdnrɪ] adj *(gen)* straordinario(a); *(very strange)* strano(a); **the** ~ **thing is that...** la cosa strana è che... .

extra·sen·so·ry [ˈɛkstrəˈsɛnsərɪ] adj: ~ **perception** percezione f extrasensoriale.

extra·special [ˈɛkstrəˈspɛʃəl] adj *(care, person)* straordinario(a); *(occasion)* grande.

extra·strong [ˌɛkstrəˈstrɒŋ] adj molto forte.

ex·trava·gance [ɪksˈtrævəgəns] n *(excessive spending)* sperpero; *(wastefulness)* spreco; *(thing bought)* stravaganza.

ex·trava·gant [ɪksˈtrævəgənt] adj *(spending, claim, opinion)* eccessivo(a); *(lavish: person)* prodigo(a); *(: tastes)* dispendioso(a); *(exaggerated: praise)* esagerato(a); *(: prices)* esorbitante; **don't be** ~ **with the butter** non esagerare con il burro.

ex·treme [ɪksˈtriːm] **1** adj estremo(a); *(sorrow, anger)* profondo(a); **the** ~ **left/right** *(Pol)* l'estrema sinistra/destra; **the** ~ **end of sth** l'estremità di qc; **there's no need to be so** ~ non c'è bisogno di essere così drastico. **2** n estremo; ~**s of temperature** eccessivi sbalzi mpl di temperatura; **kind in the** ~ estremamente gentile; **to go/be driven to** ~**s** arrivare/essere portato agli estremi.

ex·treme·ly [ɪksˈtriːmlɪ] adv estremamente.

ex·trem·ist [ɪksˈtriːmɪst] adj, n estremista *(m/f)*.

ex·trem·ity [ɪksˈtrɛmɪtɪ] n *(gen)* estremità f inv; *(fig: of despair etc)* eccesso.

ex·tri·cate [ˈɛkstrɪkeɪt] vt *(object)* liberare; **to** ~ **sb/o.s. from trouble** togliere qn/togliersi d'impaccio.

extro·vert [ˈɛkstrəʊvɜːt] adj, n estroverso(a) *(m/f)*.

exu·ber·ance [ɪgˈzuːbərəns] n esuberanza.

exu·ber·ant [ɪgˈzuːbərənt] adj esuberante.

ex·ude [ɪgˈzjuːd] vt stillare; *(fig)* emanare.

ex·ult [ɪgˈzʌlt] vi: **to** ~ **in, over** esultare per.

ex·ult·ant [ɪgˈzʌltənt] adj *(person, smile)* esultante; *(shout, expression)* di giubilo.

ex·ul·ta·tion [ˌɛgzʌlˈteɪʃən] n giubilo; **in** ~ per la gioia.

eye [aɪ] **1** n occhio; *(of needle)* cruna; *(on dress etc)* occhiello; **he gave him a black** ~ gli ha fatto un occhio nero; **~s right/left!** attenti a destra/sinistra!; **as far as the ~ can see** a perdita d'occhio; **it happened before my very ~s** mi è successo proprio sotto gli occhi; **I saw it with my own ~s** l'ho visto con i miei occhi; **to be in the public ~** essere in vista; **in the ~s of** agli occhi di; **under the (watchful)** ~ **of** sotto gli occhi di; **to keep an ~ on sb/sth** dare un occhio a qn/qc; **to keep an ~ on things** (*fam*) tenere d'occhio la situazione; **keep your ~s on the road ahead!** guarda la strada!, stai attento a dove vai!; **to keep an ~ out for** *or* **one's ~s open for sth/sb** guardarsi intorno attentamente per trovare qc/qn; **I could hardly keep my ~s open** non riuscivo a tenere gli occhi aperti; **he didn't take his ~s off her** non le toglieva gli occhi di dosso; **to look at sth with** *or* **through the ~s of an expert** guardare qc con l'occhio dell'esperto; **with an ~ to sth** in vista di qc; **with an ~ to doing sth** con l'idea di fare qc; **with one's ~s (wide) open** (*fig*) perfettamente conscio di ciò che si fa; **to shut one's ~s to sth** (*fig: to the truth, dangers, evidence*) chiudere gli occhi di fronte a qc; (*: to sb's shortcomings*) chiudere un'occhio su qc; **to be up to one's ~s in work** essere pieno di lavoro fin sopra i capelli; **to catch sb's ~** attirare l'attenzione di qn; **to have an ~ for sth** avere occhio per qc; **there's more to this than meets the ~** non è così semplice come sembra; **to look sb (straight) in the ~** guardare qn (dritto) negli occhi; **I don't see ~ to ~ with him** non ci capiamo; **it's 5 years since I last set** *or* **laid ~s on him** sono 5 anni che non lo vedo; **use your ~s!** (*fam*) guarda un po' meglio!; **that's one in the ~ for him** (*fig fam*) gli sta bene; **to make (sheep's) ~s at sb** (*fam*) fare gli occhi dolci a qn; **he was all ~s** era tutt'occhi.

  2 *vt* (*look at carefully*) scrutare; (*ogle*) guardare con occhi pieni di desiderio.

eye·ball ['aɪbɔːl] *n* bulbo oculare.

eye·bath ['aɪbɑːθ] *n* occhino.

eye·brow ['aɪbraʊ] **1** *n* sopracciglio; **to raise one's ~s** inarcare le sopracciglia. **2** *cpd*: ~ **pencil** *n* matita per le sopracciglia.

eye-catching ['aɪ,kætʃɪŋ] *adj* che colpisce.

eye-drops ['aɪdrɒps] *n* gocce *fpl* per gli occhi, collirio.

eye·ful ['aɪfʊl] *n*: **he got an ~ of paint** gli è arrivato uno spruzzo di pittura negli occhi; **he got an ~ of her underwear** (*fam*) si è riempito gli occhi alla vista della sua biancheria.

eye·lash ['aɪlæʃ] *n* ciglio.

eye·let ['aɪlɪt] *n* occhiello.

eye·level ['aɪ,lɛvl] *adj* all'altezza degli occhi.

eye·lid ['aɪlɪd] *n* palpebra.

eye·liner ['aɪ,laɪnəʳ] *n* eye-liner *m inv*.

eye-opener ['aɪ,əʊpnəʳ] *n* rivelazione *f*.

eye·shadow ['aɪ,ʃædəʊ] *n* ombretto.

eye·sight ['aɪsaɪt] *n* vista.

eye·sore ['aɪsɔːʳ] *n* pugno in un occhio.

eye·strain ['aɪstreɪn] *n*: **to get ~** stancarsi gli occhi.

eye·tooth ['aɪtuːθ] *n*, *pl* -teeth canino superiore; **to give one's eye-teeth for sth/to do sth** (*fam fig*) dare non so che cosa per qc/per fare qc.

eye·witness ['aɪ,wɪtnɪs] *n* testimone *m/f* oculare.

ey·rie ['ɪərɪ] *n* nido (d'aquila).

F

F, f [εf] n **(a)** *(letter)* F, f *for m inv.* **(b)** *(Mus)* fa m.
F. *abbr of* **Fahrenheit.**
fa [fɑː] n *(Mus)* fa m.
fa·ble ['feɪbl] n favola.
fab·ric ['fæbrɪk] n *(cloth)* stoffa, tessuto; *(Archit)* struttura; *(fig):* **the ~ of society** la struttura della società.
fab·ri·cate ['fæbrɪkeɪt] vt fabbricare.
fab·ri·ca·tion [ˌfæbrɪ'keɪʃən] n fabbricazione f.
fabu·lous ['fæbjuləs] adj *(gen)* favoloso(a); *(fam:
wonderful)* meraviglioso(a), fantastico(a).
fa·cade [fə'sɑːd] n *(Archit)* facciata; *(fig)* apparenza.
face [feɪs] **1** n *(gen)* faccia; *(Anat)* faccia, viso; *(expression)* faccia, espressione f; *(of dial, watch)* quadrante m; *(surface: of the earth)* superficie f, faccia; *(of building)* facciata; *(of mountain, cliff)* parete f; **~ down(wards)/up(wards)** *(person)* a faccia in giù/in su; *(card)* coperto/scoperto; **in the ~ of** di fronte a; **to laugh in sb's ~** ridere in faccia a qn; **to look sb in the ~** guardare qn in faccia; **to say sth to sb's ~** dire qc in faccia a qn; **I told him to his ~** gliel'ho detto in faccia; **you can shout till you're black** *or* **blue in the ~**... puoi urlare fino a sgolarti...; **don't show your ~ here again!** non farti più vedere qui!; **it's vanished off the ~ of the earth** è sparito dalla faccia della terra; **the whole ~ of the town has changed** la città ha cambiato completamente faccia; **to have a good memory for ~s** essere un buon fisionomista; **to pull a long ~** fare la faccia lunga, fare il muso; **to keep a straight ~** rimanere serio; **to make** *or* **pull ~s (at sb)** fare le boccacce (a qn); **his ~ fell** *(fig)* il suo volto s'è fatto triste; **on the ~ of it** a prima vista; **to put a brave ~ on sth** affrontare qc con coraggio; **to lose ~** perdere la faccia; **to save ~** salvare la faccia.
  2 vt **(a)** *(be facing, be opposite)* essere di fronte a; *(overlook: road)* dare su; *(: sea)* guardare verso; **~ the wall!** girati verso il muro!; **to sit facing the engine** *(on train)* sedersi nella direzione della marcia; **the picture facing page 20** la figura di fronte a pagina 20; **the difficulties facing us** i problemi che ci aspettano.
  (b) *(confront: attacker, danger)* affrontare; **I can't ~ him** *(ashamed)* non ho il coraggio di guardarlo in faccia; *(fed up)* non ho nessuna voglia di vederlo; **I can't ~ doing it** non ho nessuna voglia di farlo; **to ~ the music** *(fig)* far fronte alla tempesta; **to ~ facts** affrontare la realtà; **to ~ the fact that...** riconoscere *or* ammettere che...; **we are ~d with serious problems** ci troviamo di fronte a gravi problemi; **let's ~ it!** *(fam)* diciamocelo chiaramente!
  (c) *(Tech)* rivestire, ricoprire; **a wall ~d with concrete** un muro rivestito di cemento.
  3 vi *(person):* **to ~ this way** girarsi da questa parte; **it ~s east/towards the east** è esposto a/ guarda verso est.
  4 cpd: **~ cloth** n guanto di spugna; **~ cream** n crema per il viso; **~ lift** n plastica facciale; **to have a ~ lift** *(person)* farsi la plastica facciale; *(building)* essere restaurato; **~ pack** n maschera di bellezza; **~ powder** n cipria; **~ value** n valore m nominale; **to take somebody** *(or* **something) at ~ value** *(fig)* lasciarsi ingannare dalle apparenze.
♦**face up to** vi + prep *(difficulty etc)* affrontare, far fronte a; **to ~ up to the fact that...** ammettere che... .
face·less ['feɪslɪs] adj anonimo(a).
face-saving ['feɪsˌseɪvɪŋ] adj che salva la faccia.
fac·et ['fæsɪt] n *(of gem)* sfaccettatura, faccetta; *(fig)* aspetto, lato.
fa·cetious [fə'siːʃəs] adj faceto(a); **don't be ~** non fare lo spiritoso.
face-to-face [ˌfeɪstə'feɪs] adv, adj a quattr'occhi.
fa·cial ['feɪʃəl] **1** adj del viso, facciale. **2** n trattamento del viso.
fac·ile ['fæsaɪl] adj *(gen pej: remark, answer)* superficiale; *(: victory)* facile.
fa·cili·tate [fə'sɪlɪteɪt] vt facilitare, agevolare.
fa·cil·ity [fə'sɪlɪtɪ] n *(easiness)* facilità; *(skill)* abilità; *(with languages)* predisposizione f; **facilities** *(gen)* servizi mpl; *(educational, leisure)* attrezzature fpl; *(transport)* mezzi mpl; **credit facilities** facilitazioni fpl di credito.
fac·ing ['feɪsɪŋ] n *(Constr)* rivestimento; *(Sewing)* paramontura.
fac·simi·le [fæk'sɪmɪlɪ] n facsimile m.
fact [fækt] n fatto; **it's a ~ that...** è un dato di fatto che...; **to know for a ~ that...** sapere per certo che...; **the ~s of life** *(sex)* i fatti riguardanti la vita sessuale; *(fig)* le realtà della vita; **~s and figures** dati e cifre; **~ and fiction** realtà e fantasia; **story founded on ~** storia basata sui fatti; **it has no basis in ~** non si basa su fatti realmente accaduti; **as a matter of ~, in point of ~** per la verità; **the ~ (of the matter) is that...** la verità è che...; **in ~** in realtà.
fact-finding ['fæktˌfaɪndɪŋ] adj: **a ~ tour/mission** un viaggio/una missione d'inchiesta.
fac·tion ['fækʃən] n fazione f.
fac·tor ['fæktə'] n **(a)** *(fact)* fattore m, elemento; **human ~** elemento umano; **safety ~** coefficiente m di sicurezza. **(b)** *(Math)* fattore m.
fac·to·ry ['fæktərɪ] **1** n fabbrica. **2** cpd *(inspector, work)* di fabbrica; **~ farming** n allevamento su scala industriale.
fac·tual ['fæktjuəl] adj *(report, description)* che si limita ai fatti; *(error)* che riguarda i fatti.
fac·ul·ty ['fækəltɪ] n facoltà f inv.
fad [fæd] n *(fashion)* pazzia.
fade [feɪd] vi **(a)** *(flower)* appassire; *(colour, fabric)* scolorirsi, sbiadirsi. **(b)** *(also:* **~ away:** *light)* affievolirsi, attenuarsi; *(: eyesight, hearing, memory)* indebolirsi; *(: hopes, smile)* svanire; *(: sounds)* affievolirsi, attutirsi; *(: person)* deperire; *(object):* **to ~ from sight** scomparire alla vista.
♦**fade in 1** vt + adv *(TV, Cine)* aprire in dissolvenza; *(Radio: sound)* aumentare gradualmente d'in-

tensità. **2** *vi* + *adv (TV, Cine)* aprirsi in dissolvenza; *(Radio)* aumentare gradualmente d'intensità.

♦ **fade out 1** *vt* + *adv (TV, Cine)* chiudere in dissolvenza; *(Radio)* diminuire gradualmente d'intensità. **2** *vi* + *adv (TV, Cine)* chiudere in dissolvenza; *(Radio)* diminuire gradualmente d'intensità.

fae·ces ['fiːsiːz] *npl* feci *fpl*.

fag [fæg] **1** *n (fam: effort, job)* faticata, sfacchinata; *(Brit fam: cigarette)* sigaretta, cicca; *(Brit Scol)* ≃ matricola; *(Am fam: homosexual)* frocio. **2** *vt (fam: also:* ~ **out)** stancare, affaticare. **3** *cpd:* ~ **end** *n* fine *f*, sgoccioli *mpl; (fam: of cigarette)* mozzicone *m*, cicca.

fag·got ['fægət] *n (for fire)* fascina; *(Brit fam)* bastardo/a; *(Am fam)* frocio.

Fahr·en·heit ['færənhaɪt] *adj* Fahrenheit *inv*.

fail [feɪl] **1** *vi* **(a)** *(gen)* fallire; *(in exam: candidate)* essere respinto(a) *or* bocciato(a); *(show, play)* essere un fiasco; **to** ~ **in one's duty** mancare al proprio dovere. **(b)** *(power, light)* mancare; *(crops)* andare perduto(a); *(health, sight, strength)* indebolirsi; *(engine)* fermarsi; *(brakes)* non funzionare. **2** *vt* **(a)** *(exam, subject)* non superare, essere bocciato(a) in; *(candidate)* respingere, bocciare. **(b)** *(subj: person, strength, memory)* abbandonare; **don't** ~ **me!** non abbandonarmi!; **his courage** ~**ed him** gli è mancato il coraggio; **words** ~ **me!** mi mancano le parole! **(c)** *(omit):* **to** ~ **to do sth** non fare qc, fare a meno di fare qc; **I** ~ **to see why/what** *etc* non vedo perché/che cosa *etc*. **3** *n:* **without** ~ senza fallo.

fail·ing ['feɪlɪŋ] **1** *prep* in mancanza di; ~ **that** se questo non è possibile. **2** *n* difetto.

fail·safe ['feɪlseɪf] *adj (device etc)* di sicurezza.

fail·ure ['feɪljəʳ] *n (gen)* fallimento; *(in exam)* insuccesso, bocciatura; *(of crops)* perdita; *(Tech)* guasto, avaria; *(person):* **he is a** ~ è un fallito; *(neglect):* **his** ~ **to come/answer** il fatto che non sia venuto/abbia risposto; **to end in** ~ fallire; **it was a complete** ~ è stato un vero fiasco; **heart** ~ collasso cardiaco.

faint [feɪnt] **1** *adj* **(-er, -est)** *(smell, breeze, trace)* leggero(a); *(outline)* indistinto(a); *(sound, voice)* fievole, debole; *(hope)* debole; *(idea, memory, resemblance)* vago(a); **to feel** ~ sentirsi svenire;. **I haven't the** ~**est idea** *(fam)* non ne ho la più pallida idea; ~ **with hunger** debole per la fame. **2** *n* svenimento. **3** *vi:* **to** ~ **(from)** svenire (da).

faint·hearted [,feɪnt'haːtɪd] *adj* timido(a), pusillanime.

faint·ly ['feɪntlɪ] *adv (gen)* leggermente; *(smiling, reminiscent)* vagamente.

fair¹ [feəʳ] **1** *adj* **(-er, -est) (a)** *(person, decision etc)* giusto(a), equo(a); *(hearing)* imparziale; *(sample)* rappresentativo(a); *(fight, competition, match)* leale; **it's not** ~! non è giusto!; **to be** ~ **(to her)...** per essere giusti (nei suoi confronti)...; **it's only** ~ **that...** è più che giusto che...; **it's** ~ **to say that...** bisogna riconoscere che...; ~ **enough!** d'accordo!, va bene!; **by** ~ **means or foul** con ogni mezzo; ~ **play** correttezza; **his** ~ **share of** la sua parte di.

(b) *(reasonable, average: work, result)* discreto(a); **he has a** ~ **chance** *or* **hope of success** ha buone probabilità di riuscire.

(c) *(quite large: sum)* discreto(a); *(: speed)* buono(a); **a** ~ **amount of** un bel po' di.

(d) *(light-coloured: hair, person)* biondo(a); *(: complexion, skin)* chiaro(a). **(e)** *(fine, good: weather)* buono(a), bello(a); *(copy)* bello(a); **the** ~ **sex** il gentil sesso; **through** ~ **and foul** con il buono o il cattivo tempo.

2 *adv:* **to play** ~ giocare correttamente; **to**

act/win ~ **and square** agire/vincere onestamente; **the ball hit me** ~ **and square in the face** la palla mi ha colpito in piena faccia.

fair² [feəʳ] *n (market)* fiera, mercato; *(trade* ~*)* fiera campionaria; *(fun~)* luna park *m inv*.

fair·ground ['feə,graʊnd] *n* spiazzo del luna park.

fair·haired [,feə'heəd] *adj (person)* biondo(a).

fair·ly ['feəlɪ] *adv* **(a)** *(justly)* in modo imparziale *or* equo; *(according to the rules)* lealmente, correttamente. **(b)** *(quite)* abbastanza, piuttosto; **I'm** ~ **sure** sono abbastanza sicuro; ~ **good** discreto. **(c)** *(fam: utterly)* completamente; **she was** ~ **raging** era completamente fuori di sé.

fair·minded ['feə'maɪndɪd] *adj* equo(a), imparziale.

fair·ness ['feənɪs] *n* **(a)** onestà, giustizia; *(of decision)* imparzialità; **in all** ~ per essere giusti, a dire il vero; **in (all)** ~ **to him** per essere giusti nei suoi confronti. **(b)** *(of hair, skin)* chiarezza.

fair·sized ['feə'saɪzd] *adj (crowd, audience)* numeroso(a); *(piece)* bello(a).

fairy ['feərɪ] **1** *n* fata; *(fam pej: homosexual)* finocchio. **2** *cpd:* ~ **godmother** *n* fata buona; ~ **lights** *npl* lanternine *fpl* colorate; ~ **queen** *n* regina delle fate; ~ **tale** *n* fiabɐ; *(lie)* frottola.

fairy·land ['feərɪlænd] *n* paese *m* delle fate.

fait ac·com·pli [,feɪtə'kɒmpliː] *n* fatto compiuto.

faith [feɪθ] **1** *n (Rel, doctrine)* fede *f; (trust)* fiducia; **to have** ~ **in sb/sth** avere fiducia in qn/qc; **to put one's** ~ **in sb/sth** fidarsi di qn/qc; **to keep/break** ~ **with sb** mantenere la parola/mancare alla parola con qn; **in (all) good** ~ in buona fede; **in bad** ~ in malafede. **2** *cpd:* ~ **healer** *n* guaritore/trice.

faith·ful ['feɪθfʊl] **1** *adj:* ~ **(to)** fedele (a). **2** *npl:* **the** ~ *(Rel)* i fedeli.

faith·ful·ly ['feɪθfəlɪ] *adv* fedelmente; **he promised** ~ **to come** ci ha dato la sua parola che sarebbe venuto; **yours** ~ *(in letters)* distinti saluti.

faith·less ['feɪθlɪs] *adj* infedele.

fake [feɪk] **1** *n (picture)* falso; *(thing)* imitazione *f; (person)* impostore/a. **2** *adj* fasullo(a). **3** *vt (accounts)* falsificare; *(illness)* fingere; *(painting)* contraffare. **4** *vi* fingere.

fal·con ['fɔːlkən] *n* falco.

fall [fɔːl] *(vb: pt* **fell,** *pp* **fallen) 1** *n* **(a)** *(gen)* caduta; *(decrease)* diminuzione *f*, calo; *(: in prices)* ribasso; *(: in temperature)* abbassamento; **he had a bad** ~ ha fatto una brutta caduta; **a** ~ **of earth** uno smottamento; **a** ~ **of snow** una nevicata; **a heavy/light** ~ **of rain** una pioggia forte/leggera.

(b): ~**s** *npl (waterfall)* cascate *fpl;* **the Niagara F**~**s** le cascate del Niagara.

(c) *(Am: autumn)* autunno.

2 *vi* **(a)** *(gen)* cadere; *(building)* crollare; *(decrease)* abbassarsi, diminuire; **night is** ~**ing** scende la notte; **darkness is** ~**ing** si fa buio; **to** ~ **to** *or* **on one's knees** cadere in ginocchio; **to** ~ **on one's feet** cadere in piedi; **to let sth** ~ lasciar cadere qc; **to let** ~ **that...** lasciar capire che...; **to** ~ **into bad habits** *or* **bad ways** prendere delle cattive abitudini; **to** ~ **into conversation with sb** mettérsi a parlare con qn; **his poems** ~ **into 3 categories** le sue poesie si dividono in 3 categorie; **to** ~ **from grace** *(Rel)* perdere la grazia di Dio; *(fig)* cadere in disgrazia; **he fell in my estimation** ha perso ai miei occhi; **it all began to** ~ **into place** *(fig)* ha cominciato a prendere forma; **the responsibility** ~**s on you** la responsabilità ricade su di te; **my birthday** ~**s on a Saturday** il mio compleanno cade di sabato; **he fell to wondering if...** si mise a pensare se...; **it** ~**s to**

me to say... tocca a me *or* è mio compito dire...; **to ~ short of** *(sb's expectations)* non corrispondere a; *(perfection)* non raggiungere; **the dart fell short of the board** la freccetta è caduta poco prima del bersaglio; **to ~ flat** *(on face)* cadere bocconi; *(subj: joke, party, plan)* essere un fiasco; **to ~ foul of** scontrarsi con.

(b) *(become)*: **to ~ asleep** addormentarsi; **to ~ due scadere; to ~ heir to sth** ereditare qc; **to ~ ill** ammalarsi; **to ~ in love (with sb/sth)** innamorarsi (di qn/qc); **to ~ silent** diventare silenzioso.

♦ **fall about** *vi + adv (fig fam)* torcersi dalle risa.

♦ **fall apart** *vi + adv* cadere a pezzi; *(fig)* crollare.

♦ **fall away** *vi + adv (slope steeply: ground)* scendere; *(crumble: plaster)* scrostarsi, sgretolarsi.

♦ **fall back** *vi + adv (retreat)* indietreggiare; *(Mil)* ritirarsi; **to ~ on sth** *(fig)* ripiegare su qc; **to have sth to ~ back on** avere qc di riserva.

♦ **fall behind** *vi + adv (in race etc)* rimanere indietro; *(fig: with payments)* essere in arretrato; *(:with work)* essere indietro.

♦ **fall down** *vi + adv (person)* cadere; *(building)* crollare; **but it ~s down on one aspect** *(fig)* ma ha un punto debole; **to ~ down on the job** *(fig)* non essere all'altezza del lavoro.

♦ **fall for** *vi + prep (fam: feel attracted to)* innamorarsi di; *(be deceived by)*: **to ~ for a trick** *(or a story etc)* cascarci.

♦ **fall in 1** *vi + adv* **(a)** *(person)* cadere dentro; *(roof, walls)* crollare; **to ~ in with sb** *(meet)* trovare qn; **to ~ in with sb's plans** *(person)* trovarsi d'accordo con i progetti di qn; *(event)* coincidere con i progetti di qn. **(b)** *(Mil)* allinearsi. **2** *vi + prep*: **to ~ in(to)** cadere in.

♦ **fall off 1** *vi + adv (person, leaf)* cadere; *(part)* staccarsi; *(diminish: demand, numbers, interest)* diminuire; *(: quality)* scadere. **2** *vi + prep* cadere da.

♦ **fall out** *vi + adv* **(a)** *(person, object)*: **to ~ out (of)** cadere (da). **(b)** *(Mil)* rompere le righe. **(c)** *(fig: quarrel)*: **to ~ out (with sb over sth)** litigare (con qn per qc). **(d)** *(happen)*: **it fell out that...** è andata a finire che...; **events fell out (just) as we had hoped** andò a finire proprio come avevamo sperato.

♦ **fall over 1** *vi + adv* cadere. **2** *vi + prep*: **he fell over the table** è inciampato nel tavolino ed è caduto; **he was ~ing over himself** *or* **over backwards to be polite** *(fam)* si faceva in quattro per essere gentile; **they were ~ing over each other to get it** *(fam)* lottavano per averlo.

♦ **fall through** *vi + adv (plans etc)* fallire.

♦ **fall (up)on** *vi + prep* scagliarsi su.

fal·la·cious [fə'leɪʃəs] *adj* fallace.

fal·la·cy ['fæləsɪ] *n* errore *m*.

fall·en ['fɔːlən] **1** *pp of* fall. **2** *adj* caduto(a); *(morally: woman, angel)* perduto(a). **3** *npl*: **the ~** *(Mil)* i caduti.

fal·lible ['fæləbl] *adj* fallibile.

fall·ing ['fɔːlɪŋ] *adj*: **~ star** stella cadente.

falling-off ['fɔːlɪŋ'ɒf] *n* calo.

fal·lo·pian [fə'ləʊpɪən] *adj*: **~ tube** *(Anat)* tuba di Falloppio.

fall·out ['fɔːlaʊt] **1** *n* pioggia radioattiva. **2** *cpd*: **~ shelter** *n* rifugio antiatomico.

fal·low ['fæləʊ] *adj* incolto(a), a maggese; **to lie ~** rimanere a maggese.

false [fɔːls] *adj (gen)* falso(a); **~ alarm** falso allarme; **~ start** falsa partenza; **under ~ pretences** con l'inganno; **~ tooth** dente finto; **~ teeth** dentiera; **with a ~ bottom** con doppio fondo.

false·hood ['fɔːlshʊd] *n (frm: lie)* menzogna.

false·ly ['fɔːlslɪ] *adv (accuse)* a torto; *(state)* falsamente.

fal·set·to [fɔːl'setəʊ] **1** *n* falsetto. **2** *adj* di falsetto.

fal·si·fy ['fɔːlsɪfaɪ] *vt* falsificare; *(figures)* alterare.

fal·ter ['fɔːltəʳ] *vi* vacillare; **his voice ~ed with emotion** la sua voce era rotta dall'emozione; **his steps ~ed** ha vacillato.

fame [feɪm] *n* fama, celebrità; **his ~ as a musician** la sua fama di musicista.

famed [feɪmd] *adj* famoso(a), celebre.

fa·mili·ar [fə'mɪljəʳ] *adj* **(a)** *(well-known: face, person, place)* conosciuto(a), familiare; *(common: experience, complaint, event)* comune; **her face looks ~** la sua faccia non mi è nuova. **(b)** *(well-acquainted)*: **to be ~ (with sb/sth)** conoscere bene (qn/qc); **to make o.s. ~ with** familiarizzarsi con; **to be on ~ ground** *(fig)* trovarsi sul proprio terreno. **(c)** *(language)* familiare; *(intimate: tone of voice)* di eccessiva confidenza; **to be on ~ terms with** essere in confidenza con; **to get too ~ with sb** *(pej)* prendersi troppa confidenza con qn.

fa·mili·ar·ity [fə,mɪlɪ'ærɪtɪ] *n (knowledge)*: **~ (with)** conoscenza (di); *(of tone etc)* confidenza, familiarità; **~ breeds contempt** l'eccessiva familiarità fa perdere il rispetto.

fa·mil·iar·ize [fə'mɪlɪəraɪz] *vt*: **to ~ o.s. with** familiarizzarsi con.

fami·ly ['fæmɪlɪ] **1** *n (gen)* famiglia; **it runs in the ~** è di famiglia; **she's one of the ~** fa parte della famiglia. **2** *cpd (jewels, name, life, business)* di famiglia; **~ allowance** *n* assegni *mpl* familiari; **~ butcher** *n* macellaio di famiglia; **~ doctor** *n* dottore *or* medico di famiglia; **~ man** *n* uomo amante della famiglia; **~ planning clinic** *n* consultorio familiare; **~ tree** *n* albero genealogico.

fam·ine ['fæmɪn] *n* carestia.

fam·ished ['fæmɪʃt] *adj* affamato(a); **I'm ~!** *(fam)* ho una fame da lupo!

fa·mous ['feɪməs] *adj* famoso(a), celebre; **~ last words!** *(fam hum)* le ultime parole famose!

fa·mous·ly ['feɪməslɪ] *adv* a meraviglia.

fan[1] [fæn] **1** *n* ventaglio; *(machine)* ventilatore *m*. **2** *vt (face, person)* fare aria a; **to ~ the flames** *(also fig)* soffiare sul fuoco. **3** *cpd*: **~ belt** *n (Aut)* cinghia della ventola; **~ heater** *n* stufa ad aria calda.

♦ **fan out** *vi + adv (troops etc)* aprirsi a ventaglio.

fan[2] [fæn] **1** *n (gen fam) m/f fan*, ammiratore/trice; *(Sport)* tifoso/a, fan; **he's a jazz ~** è un patito del jazz. **2** *cpd*: **~ club** *n* club *m inv* degli ammiratori; **~ mail** *n* lettere *fpl* degli ammiratori.

fa·nat·ic [fə'nætɪk] *n* fanatico/a.

fa·nat·ic(al) [fə'nætɪk(əl)] *adj* fanatico(a).

fa·nati·cism [fə'nætɪsɪzəm] *n* fanatismo.

fan·ci·ful ['fænsɪfʊl] *adj (explanation)* fantastico(a); *(person, idea, drawing)* fantasioso(a).

fan·cy ['fænsɪ] **1** *n* **(a)** *(whim)* voglia, capriccio; **a passing ~ (for sth)** una voglia passeggera (di qc); **when the ~ takes him** quando ne ha voglia; **to take a ~ to** *(person, thing)* affezionarsi a; **to catch** *or* **take sb's ~** conquistare qn. **(b)** *(imagination)* fantasia; **in the realm of ~** nel regno della fantasia; **I have a ~ that he'll be late** *(vague idea)* ho una mezza idea che arriverà tardi; **is it just my ~, or did I hear a knock at the door?** mi sbaglio o hanno bussato alla porta?

2 *adj (-ier, -iest) (ornamental)* elaborato(a); *(price)* esorbitante; *(idea)* stravagante; **a ~ design** un disegno fantasia; **nothing ~** niente di speciale; **~ cakes** pasticcini *mpl*; **~ goods** articoli *mpl* di ogni genere.

3 *vt* **(a)** *(imagine)* immaginare, credere; **he fancied himself to be in Spain** immaginava di essere in Spagna; **I rather ~ he's gone out** credo proprio che sia uscito; **~ that!** *(fam)* pensa un po'!, **ma guarda!; ~ meeting you here!** *(fam)* che combinazione incontrarti qui! **(b)** *(like, want)* avere voglia di; **do you ~ (going for) a stroll?** hai voglia *or* ti va di fare una passeggiatina?; **I don't ~ the idea** l'idea non mi attira; **I don't ~ his chances of winning** non credo che vincerà; **he fancies himself** *(fam)* ha un'alta opinione di sé; **he fancies himself as a footballer** *(fam)* crede di essere un gran calciatore; **she fancies him** *(fam)* le piace.

4 *cpd:* **~ dress** *n* costume *m;* **~ dress ball/ party** *n* ballo/festa in costume *or* in maschera.

fan·fare ['fænfɛə^r] *n* fanfara.

fang [fæŋ] *n* zanna; *(of snake)* dente *m.*

fan·light ['fænlaɪt] *n* lunetta (a ventaglio).

fan·ta·size ['fæntəzɪ] *vi* fantasticare, sognare.

fan·tas·tic [fæn'tæstɪk] *adj (gen)* fantastico(a); *(idea)* assurdo(a).

fan·ta·sy ['fæntəzɪ] *n (imagination)* fantasia; *(fanciful idea, wish)* sogno, idea fantastica; **in a world of ~** in un mondo fantastico.

far [fɑː^r] *comp* **farther** *or* **further,** *superl* **farthest** *or* **furthest 1** *adv* **(a)** lontano; **is it ~ (away)?** è lontano?; **is it ~ to London?** è lontana Londra?; **how ~ is it to the river?** quanto è lontano il fiume?; **it's not ~ (from here)** non è lontano (da qui); **as ~ as** fino a; **as ~ as the eye can see** a perdita d'occhio; **to go as ~ as Milan** andare fino a Milano; **to come from as ~ away as Milan** venire addirittura da Milano; **she swam as ~ as the others** ha nuotato tanto lontano quanto gli altri; **as ~ back as I can remember** per quanto *or* per quello che posso ricordare; **as ~ back as 1945** già nel 1945; **as** *or* **so ~ as I know** per quel che ne so, per quanto ne sappia; **as** *or* **so ~ as I am concerned** per quanto mi riguarda; **as ~ as possible** nei limiti del possibile; **I would go as** *or* **so ~ as to say that...** arriverei al punto di dire...; **from ~ and near** da ogni parte; **to come from ~ and wide** venire da ogni parte; **to travel ~ and wide** viaggiare in lungo e in largo; **~ away** *or* **off** lontano; **~ away** *or* **off in the distance** in lontananza; **not ~ away** *or* **off** non lontano; **~ away from one's family** lontano dalla famiglia; **Christmas is not ~ off** Natale non è lontano, non manca molto a Natale; **~ beyond** molto al di là di; **~ from** *(place)* lontano da; **~ from (doing sth)** invece di (fare qc); **we are ~ from having finished** siamo ben lungi dall'aver finito; **~ from it!** al contrario!; **he is ~ from well** non sta affatto *or* per niente bene; **~ be it from me to interfere, but...** non ho la minima intenzione di immischiarmi, ma...; **~ from easy** tutt'altro che facile; **~ into the night** fino a notte inoltrata; **~ out at sea** in alto mare; **our calculations are ~ out** i nostri calcoli sono completamente sbagliati; **to go ~** *(person)* andare lontano; **he'll go ~** farà molta strada; **it won't go ~** *(money, food)* non basterà; **how ~ are you going?** fin dove vai?; **how ~ have you got with your work?** dove sei arrivato con il tuo lavoro?; **he's gone too ~ this time** questa volta ha esagerato *or* oltrepassato i limiti; **he's gone too ~ to back out now** si è spinto troppo oltre per tirarsi indietro adesso; **the plans are too ~ advanced** i piani sono a uno stadio troppo avanzato; **he was ~ gone** *(fam: ill)* era molto malato; *(: drunk)* era ubriaco fradicio; **so ~** *(in distance)* fin qui; *(in time)* finora; **so ~ so good** fin qui tutto a posto; **so** *or* **thus ~ and no further** fin qui e non oltre.

(b) *(with comp: very much)* di gran lunga; **this car is ~ faster (than)** questa macchina è molto più veloce (di); **it's ~ and away the best, it's by ~ the best** è di gran lunga il migliore; **she's the prettier by ~** è di gran lunga la più carina; **it is ~ better not to go** è molto meglio non andare.

2 *adj:* **the F~ East** l'Estremo Oriente; **the F~ North** l'estremo Nord; **the ~ east** *etc* of the country l'estrema zona orientale *etc* del paese; **on the ~ side of** dall'altra parte di; **at the ~ end of** in fondo a; **the ~ left/right** *(Pol)* l'estrema sinistra/destra.

far·away ['fɑːrəweɪ] *adj (distant)* lontano(a); *(voice, look)* assente.

farce [fɑːs] *n (Theatre, fig)* farsa.

far·ci·cal ['fɑːsɪkəl] *adj* ridicolo(a); **the trial was ~** il processo fu una farsa.

fare [fɛə^r] **1** *n* **(a)** *(cost)* tariffa; **'~s please!'** *(conductor on bus)* 'biglietti, per favore!' **(b)** *(passenger in taxi)* passeggero, cliente *m/f.* **(c)** *(frm: food)* cibo; **bill of ~** *(menu)* lista, menu *m inv.* **2** *vi:* **how did you ~?** com'è andata?, come te la sei passata?; **I think they will ~ badly if...** penso che le cose si metteranno male per loro se.... **3** *cpd:* **~ stage** *n (for bus)* tronco.

fare·well [fɛə'wɛl] **1** *n, excl* addio; **to bid ~ (to sb)** salutare (qn), dire addio (a qn). **2** *cpd:* **~ dinner** *n* pranzo d'addio *or* di commiato; **~ party** *n* festa d'addio.

far·fetched [,fɑː'fɛtʃt] *adj (explanation)* stiracchiato(a), forzato(a); *(idea, scheme, story)* inverosimile.

farm [fɑːm] **1** *n* fattoria. **2** *vt* coltivare. **3** *vi (as profession)* fare l'agricoltore. **4** *cpd:* **~ labourer** *n,* **~ worker** *n* bracciante *m/f;* **~ produce** *n* prodotti *mpl* agricoli.

♦ **farm out** *vt + adv (work):* **to ~ out (to sb)** dare in consegna (a qn); *(hum: children):* **to ~ out (on)** rifilare (a).

farm·er ['fɑːmə^r] *n* agricoltore/trice, coltivatore/trice.

farm·hand ['fɑːmhænd] *n* bracciante *m/f.*

farm·house ['fɑːmhaʊs] *n* casa colonica, fattoria.

farm·ing ['fɑːmɪŋ] **1** *n* agricoltura; **sheep ~** allevamento di pecore. **2** *cpd:* **~ community** *n* comunità *f inv* agricola; **~ methods** *npl* metodi *mpl* di agricoltura.

farm·land ['fɑːmlænd] *n* terreno coltivabile.

farm·yard ['fɑːmjɑːd] *n* aia.

far·reaching ['fɑː,riːtʃɪŋ] *adj (effect)* di larga *or* vasta portata.

far·sighted [,fɑː'saɪtɪd] *adj (person)* previdente; *(plan, decision, measure)* lungimirante.

fart [fɑːt] *(fam)* **1** *n* scoreggia. **2** *vi* scoreggiare.

far·ther ['fɑːðə^r] *comp of* **far 1** *adv see* **further 1a. 2** *adj:* **on the ~ side of the street** dall'altra parte della strada.

far·thest ['fɑːðɪst] *adj, adv superl of* **far;** *see* **furthest.**

fas·ci·nate ['fæsɪneɪt] *vt* affascinare; **it ~s me how/why...** sono affascinato da come/perché....

fas·ci·nat·ing ['fæsɪneɪtɪŋ] *adj* affascinante.

fas·ci·na·tion [,fæsɪ'neɪʃən] *n* fascino.

fas·cism ['fæʃɪzəm] *n* fascismo.

fas·cist ['fæʃɪst] *adj, n* fascista *(m/f).*

fash·ion ['fæʃən] **1** *n* **(a)** *(manner)* modo, maniera; **after a ~** *(finish, manage etc)* così così; **in his usual ~** nel solito modo; **in the Greek ~** alla greca. **(b)** *(vogue: in clothing, speech etc)* moda; **to set a ~ for sth** lanciare la moda di qc; **to be in/out of ~** essere di/fuori moda; **to come into/go out of ~** diventare/passare di moda; **the latest ~** l'ultima moda; **the new Spring ~s** i nuovi modelli per la primavera; **it's no longer the ~** non va più

di moda; **women's/men's** ~s moda femminile/
maschile. **2** *vt (gen)* fabbricare; *(in clay)* modellare; *(clothes)* confezionare. **3** *cpd (editor, house
etc)* di moda; ~ **designer** *n* disegnatore/trice di
moda; ~ **model** *n* indossatore/trice; ~ **parade** *n*,
~ **show** *n* sfilata di moda.

fash·ion·able ['fæʃnəbl] *adj* alla moda; *(writer)* di
grido; **it is** ~ **to do...** è di moda fare... .

fash·ion·ably ['fæʃnəblɪ] *adv*: **to be** ~ **dressed**
essere vestito alla moda.

fast¹ [fɑːst] **1** *adj* (**-er, -est**) **(a)** *(speedy)* veloce,
rapido(a); *(Phot: film)* ad alta sensibilità; ~ **train**
rapido; **in the** ~ **lane** *(Aut)* ≃ nella corsia di
sorpasso; **he's a** ~ **worker** *(also fig)* non tira per le
lunghe; **to pull a** ~ **one on sb** *(fam)* giocare un
brutto tiro a qn. **(b)** *(clock)*: **to be** ~ andare
avanti; **my watch is 5 minutes** ~ il mio orologio
va avanti di 5 minuti. **(c)** *(dissipated: woman)*
dissoluto(a); *(: life)* dissipato(a). **(d)** *(firm: friend)*
devoto(a), fedele; *(: colour, dye)* resistente, che
non stinge; **to make a boat** ~ ormeggiare una
barca.

   2 *adv* **(a)** *(quickly)* in fretta, velocemente; **as**
~ **as I can** più in fretta possibile; **he ran off as** ~
as his legs would carry him è corso via come il
vento *or* a più non posso; **how** ~ **can you type?** a
che velocità scrivi a macchina?; **not so** ~! piano!; **the rain was falling** ~ pioveva forte, pioveva a dirotto. **(b)** *(firmly)* saldamente, bene; **tie it**
~ legalo bene; **it's stuck** ~ *(door)* è saldamente
bloccato; *(nail, screw)* è completamente incastrato; ~ **asleep** profondamente addormentato.

fast² [fɑːst] **1** *n* digiuno. **2** *vi* digiunare.

fas·ten ['fɑːsn] **1** *vt (with rope, string etc)* legare;
(with nail) inchiodare; *(secure: belt, dress, seat
belt)* allacciare; *(: door, box, window)* chiudere;
(attach) attaccare, fissare; **to** ~ **the blame/
responsibility (for sth) on sb** *(fig)* dare la colpa/
responsabilità (di qc) a qn. **2** *vi (door etc)* chiudersi; *(dress)* allacciarsi.

♦ **fasten down** *vt + adv (envelope)* incollare; *(blind
etc)* fissare bene.

♦ **fasten on** *vt + adv* fissare.

♦ **fasten up** *vt + adv (clothing)* allacciare; *(coat)*
abbottonare.

♦ **fasten (up)on** *vi + prep (idea)* cogliere al volo;
(excuse) ricorrere a.

fas·ten·er ['fɑːsnəʳ] *n* chiusura; *(zip* ~) chiusura
lampo.

fas·tidi·ous [fæs'tɪdɪəs] *adj (person: about cleanliness etc)* pignolo(a); *(in taste)* difficile.

fat [fæt] **1** *adj* (**-ter, -test**) *(person, meat)* grasso(a);
(face, cheeks) paffuto(a); *(limbs)* grassoccio(a);
(book) grosso(a); *(wallet, wage packet)* ben forni-
to(a); **to get** ~ diventare grasso, ingrassare; **he
grew** ~ **on the proceeds/profits** *(fig)* si è arricchito con i guadagni/gli incassi; **a** ~ **lot he knows
about it!** *(fam hum)* che vuoi che ne sappia lui!; **a**
~ **lot of good that is!** bella roba! **2** *n* grasso; **to fry
in deep** ~ friggere in molto olio; **to live off the** ~
of the land vivere nel lusso, avere ogni ben di
Dio; **the** ~**'s in the fire** *(fig)* adesso son guai.

fa·tal ['feɪtl] *adj (gen)* fatale; *(influence)* nefasto(a);
(fateful: words, decision) fatidico(a); **it was** ~ **to
mention that** è stato un grave errore parlarne.

fa·tal·ism ['feɪtəlɪzəm] *n* fatalismo.

fa·tal·ist ['feɪtəlɪst] *n* fatalista *m/f*.

fa·tal·is·tic [ˌfeɪtə'lɪstɪk] *adj* fatalistico(a).

fa·tal·ity [fə'tælɪtɪ] *n (death)* incidente *m* mortale,
morto.

fa·tal·ly ['feɪtəlɪ] *adv* mortalmente, a morte; ~ **ill**
condannato(a).

fate [feɪt] *n* **(a)** *(force)* destino, sorte *f*; **what has** ~

in store for us? cosa ci riserva il destino? **(b)**
(person's lot) sorte *f*; **to meet one's** ~ *(death)* trovare la morte; **to leave sb to his** ~ abbandonare
qn alla propria sorte.

fat·ed ['feɪtɪd] *adj (governed by fate)* destinato(a);
(person, project, friendship etc) destinato(a) a finire male; **it was** ~ **that...** era destino che... .

fate·ful ['feɪtfʊl] *adj (day, event)* fatale; *(words)*
fatidico(a).

fa·ther ['fɑːðəʳ] *n (gen)* padre *m*; **F~ Christmas**
Babbo Natale; **Our Father** *(Rel)* Padre Nostro;
from ~ **to son** di padre in figlio; **like** ~ **like son**
tale padre tale figlio; **Old F~ Time** il Tempo.

father-figure ['fɑːðə,fɪgəʳ] *n* figura paterna.

father·hood ['fɑːðəhʊd] *n* paternità.

father-in-law ['fɑːðərɪnlɔː] *n* suocero.

father·land ['fɑːðəlænd] *n* patria.

fa·ther·ly ['fɑːðəlɪ] *adj* paterno(a).

fath·om ['fæðəm] **1** *n (Naut)* braccio (= 1,83m). **2** *vt
(fig: also:* ~ **out)** capire; *(mystery)* penetrare; **I
can't** ~ **why** non riesco a capire perché; **I can't** ~
it out non ci capisco assolutamente niente.

fa·tigue [fə'tiːg] **1** *n* stanchezza, fatica; **to be on** ~
(Mil) essere in corvé; **metal** ~ fatica del metallo.
2 *vt (frm)* affaticare, stancare.

fat·ten ['fætn] *vt (animal: also:* ~ **up)** ingrassare;
chocolate is ~**ing** la cioccolata fa ingrassare.

fat·ty ['fætɪ] *adj (foods)* grasso(a); *(Anat: tissue)*
grasso(a), adiposo(a).

fatu·ous ['fætjʊəs] *adj* fatuo(a).

fau·cet ['fɔːsɪt] *n (Am)* rubinetto.

fault [fɔːlt] **1** *n (gen)* difetto; *(mistake)* errore *m*;
(Tennis) fault *m inv*; *(Geol)* faglia; **generous to a** ~
eccessivamente generoso; **to find** ~ **with sb/sth**
trovare da ridire su qn/qc; **to be at** ~ avere torto;
your memory is at ~ non ricordi bene; **it's all
your** ~ è tutta colpa tua; **whose** ~ **is it (if...)?** di
chi è la colpa (se...)? **2** *vt* trovare da ridire su.

fault·less ['fɔːltlɪs] *adj (person, behaviour)* irreprensibile; *(work, English)* impeccabile.

faulty ['fɔːltɪ] *adj* (**-ier, -iest**) difettoso(a).

fau·na ['fɔːnə] *n* fauna.

fa·vour, *(Am)* **fa·vor** ['feɪvəʳ] **1** *n* **(a)** *(kindness)*
favore *m*; **to do sb a** ~ fare un favore a qn; **to ask
a** ~ **of sb** chiedere un favore a qn; **as a** ~ **to me**
per farmi un favore; **do me a** ~ **and close the
window** fammi un favore, chiudi la finestra. **(b)**
(approval) favore *m*; **to be in** ~ **(with sb)** *(subj:
person)* essere entrato nelle grazie di qn; *(: style)*
piacere (a qn); **to be out of** ~ essere in disgrazia;
to find ~ **with sb** *(subj: person)* entrare nelle
buone grazie di qn; *(: suggestion)* avere l'approvazione di qn; **to gain sb's** ~, **to gain** ~ **with sb**
guadagnarsi la stima di qn. **(c)** *(support, advantage)* favore *m*; **to be in** ~ **of sth/of doing sth**
essere favorevole a qc/a fare qc; **that's a point in
his** ~ è un punto a suo favore; **to decide in** ~ **of
sb/sth** decidere in favore di qn/qc; **to decide in** ~
of doing sth decidere di fare qc; **to show** ~ **to sb**
mostrarsi parziale verso qn, favorire qn.

   2 *vt (approve: idea, scheme, view)* essere a
favore di; *(prefer: person, party)* preferire, favorire; *(: team)* essere per; **he eventually** ~**ed us
with a visit** finalmente ci ha fatto l'onore di una
visita.

fa·vour·able, *(Am)* **fa·vor·able** ['feɪvərəbl] *adj*: ~
(to sb/sth, for doing sth) favorevole (a qn/qc, a
fare qc).

fa·vour·ably, *(Am)* **fa·vor·ably** ['feɪvərəblɪ] *adv*
favorevolmente.

fa·voured, *(Am)* **fa·vored** ['feɪvəd] *adj* favori-
to(a); **the** ~ **few** i pochi privilegiati.

fa·vour·ite, *(Am)* **fa·vor·ite** ['feɪvərɪt] **1** *adj* favorito(a), preferito(a). **2** *n* favorito/a, preferito/a; *(Horse-racing)* favorito/a; **it's a ~ of mine** è uno dei miei preferiti, è tra i miei favoriti; **he sang some old ~s** ha cantato dei vecchi successi.

fa·vour·it·ism, *(Am)* **fa·vor·it·ism** ['feɪvərɪtɪzəm] *n* favoritismo.

fawn¹ [fɔːn] **1** *n* **(a)** *(Zool)* cerbiatto. **(b)** *(colour)* fulvo. **2** *adj* fulvo(a).

fawn² [fɔːn] *vi*: **to ~ (up)on sb** *(subj: animal)* fare festa a qn; *(: person: fig)* adulare servilmente qn.

FBI *Am abbr of Federal Bureau of Investigation.*

fear [fɪə'] **1** *n* paura; **there are ~s that...** si teme che...; **grave ~s have arisen for...** si nutrono seri timori per...; **for ~ of sb/of doing sth** per paura di qn/di fare qc; **for ~ that** per paura di *(or* che + *sub);* **to live in ~ of sb/sth/doing sth** vivere con la paura di qn/qc/fare qc; **to go in ~ of one's life/of being discovered** temere per la propria vita/di essere scoperto; **~ of heights** vertigini *fpl;* **~ of enclosed spaces** claustrofobia; **have no ~!** non temere!; **in ~ and trembling** tremante di paura; **to put the ~ of God into sb** *(fam)* far venire una paura del diavolo a qn; **without ~ nor favour** imparzialmente; **no ~!** *(fam)* neanche per sogno!; **there's no ~ of that!** neanche per sogno!; **there's not much ~ of his coming** non c'è pericolo che venga.

2 *vt* *(person, God, law)* temere, avere paura di; **to ~ the worst** temere il peggio; **to ~ that** avere paura di *(or* che + *sub),* temere di *(or* che + *sub);* **I ~ that I/he may be late** temo di essere in ritardo/ che sia in ritardo; **I ~ so/not** temo di sì/di no, ho paura di sì/di no.

3 *vi*: **to ~ for** temere per, essere in ansia per.

fear·ful ['fɪəful] *adj* **(a)** *(frightened)*: **to be ~ of** temere; **to be ~ that...** avere paura o temere che... . **(b)** *(frightening: accident)* pauroso(a), spaventoso(a); *(: sight, noise)* terrificante.

fear·ful·ly ['fɪəfəlɪ] *adv* *(timidly)* timorosamente; *(fam: very)* terribilmente, spaventosamente.

fear·less ['fɪəlɪs] *adj*: **~ (of)** senza paura (di).

fear·some ['fɪəsəm] *adj* *(opponent)* formidabile, terribile; *(sight)* terrificante.

fea·si·bil·ity [,fiːzə'bɪlɪtɪ] **1** *n* fattibilità, attuabilità. **2** *cpd*: **~ study** *n* studio della possibilità di realizzazione.

fea·sible ['fiːzəbl] *adj* *(practicable: plan, suggestion)* realizzabile, possibile; *(likely: story, theory)* verosimile, credibile.

feast [fiːst] **1** *n* *(meal)* pranzo; *(Rel, fig)* festa. **2** *vt*: **to ~ one's eyes on sth/sb** deliziarsi alla vista di qc/qn. **3** *vi* banchettare; **to ~ on sth** banchettare con qc. **4** *cpd*: **~ day** *n* *(Rel)* festa, festività *f inv.*

feat [fiːt] *n* impresa, prodezza; **a ~ of engineering** un trionfo dell'ingegneria.

feath·er ['fɛðə'] **1** *n* penna, piuma; **as light as a ~** leggero come una piuma; **that is a ~ in his cap** è un fiore all'occhiello per lui; **you could have knocked me down with a ~** *(fam)* avresti potuto farmi cadere con un soffio. **2** *vt*: **to ~ one's nest** *(fig)* arricchirsi. **3** *cpd* *(mattress, bed, pillow)* di piume; **~ duster** *n* piumino.

feather·brained ['fɛðəbreɪnd] *adj* sciocco(a), sventato(a).

feather·weight ['fɛðəweɪt] *(Boxing)* **1** *adj* dei pesi piuma. **2** *n* peso *m* piuma *inv.*

fea·ture ['fiːtʃə'] **1** *n* **(a)** *(gen, Comm, Tech)* caratteristica; *(of face)*: **~s** lineamenti *mpl,* fattezze *fpl.* **(b)** *(~ film)* film *m inv* (principale), lungometraggio. **(c)** *(Press)* articolo, servizio speciale; **a regular ~ in** *(newspapers)* un articolo che appare regolarmente in; **a (special) ~ on sth/sb** un servizio speciale su qc/qn. **2** *vt* *(person, name)*

avere come protagonista; *(event, news)* presentare, dare risalto a. **3** *vi* *(Cine)* apparire, essere protagonista; *(gen)*: **it ~d prominently in...** ha avuto un posto di prima importanza in... .

fea·ture·less ['fiːtʃəlɪs] *adj* privo(a) di carattere.

Feb·ru·ary ['fɛbruərɪ] *n* febbraio; *for usage see July.*

feck·less ['fɛklɪs] *adj* irresponsabile, incosciente.

fed [fɛd] *pt, pp of* **feed.**

fed·er·al ['fɛdərəl] *adj* federale.

fed·er·a·tion [,fɛdə'reɪʃən] *n* federazione *f.*

fed up ['fɛd'ʌp] *adj* *(fam)*: **to be ~ up (with)** essere stufo(a) (di); **to be ~ up doing sth** essere stufo di fare qc.

fee [fiː] *n* pagamento; *(professional)* onorario; *(entrance ~, membership ~)* quota d'iscrizione; **course** *or* **tuition ~s** *(Univ etc)* tasse *fpl* universitarie; **school ~s** tasse scolastiche; **for a small ~** per una somma modesta.

fee·ble ['fiːbl] *adj* **(-r, -st)** *(gen)* debole; *(joke)* pietoso(a); *(fam: person)* rammollito(a), debole.

feeble-minded [,fiːbl'maɪndɪd] *adj* sciocco(a), debole di mente.

feed [fiːd] *(vb: pt, pp* **fed) 1** *n* *(baby's)* pappa; *(fodder)* mangime *m,* foraggio; *(amount, portion)* razione *f; (fam: meal)*: **to have a good ~** fare una bella mangiata. **2** *vt* **(a)** *(gen)* nutrire; **to ~ sth to sb, ~ sb sth** dare qc da mangiare a qn. **(b)** *(fire, machine)* alimentare; *(information etc)* fornire; **to ~ sth into a machine** introdurre qc in una macchina; **to ~ information into a computer** introdurre dati in un computer. **3** *vi* *(baby, animal)* mangiare; **to ~ on sth** nutrirsi di qc.

♦ **feed back** *vt + adv* *(results)* riferire.

♦ **feed in** *vt + adv* *(wire, tape)* introdurre.

♦ **feed up** *vt + adv* *(person, animal)* ingrassare.

feed·back ['fiːdbæk] *n* *(from computer)* feed-back *m; (from person)* reazioni *fpl.*

feed·er ['fiːdə'] *n* *(bib)* bavaglino.

feed·ing ['fiːdɪŋ] **1** *n* alimentazione *f.* **2** *cpd*: **~ bottle** *n* poppatoio, biberon *m inv.*

feel [fiːl] *(vb: pt, pp* **felt) 1** *n* *(sense of touch)* tatto; *(sensation)* consistenza; **to be rough to the ~** essere ruvido al tatto; **to know sth by the ~ of it** riconoscere qc al tatto; **let me have a ~!** fammi toccare!; **to get the ~ of sth** *(fig)* abituarsi a qc.

2 *vt* **(a)** *(touch)* tastare; **to ~ sb's pulse** sentire *or* tastare il polso a qn; **to ~ one's way (towards)** avanzare a tastoni (verso); **I'm still ~ing my way** *(fig)* sto ancora tastando il terreno.

(b) *(be aware of)* sentire; *(experience: pity, anger, grief)* provare, sentire; **he doesn't ~ the cold** non sente il freddo; **she felt a hand on her shoulder** sentì una mano sulla spalla; **I felt something move** ho sentito qualcosa che si muoveva; **we are beginning to ~ the effects** cominciamo a sentire gli effetti; **I felt a great sense of relief** ho sentito un grande sollievo; **he ~s the loss of his father very deeply** sta risentendo molto della morte del padre.

(c) *(think, believe)* credere, pensare; **I ~ that you ought to do it** penso che dovresti farlo; **he felt it necessary to point out that...** ritenne necessario far notare che...; **since you ~ so strongly about it...** visto che ci tieni tanto...; **I ~ it in my bones that...** me lo sento nelle ossa che...; **what do you ~ about it?** cosa ne pensi?

3 *vi* **(a)** *(physically, mentally)* sentirsi; **to ~ cold/hungry/sleepy** avere freddo/fame/sonno; **to ~ ill** sentirsi male; **I ~ much better** mi sento molto meglio; **she's not ~ing quite herself** non si sente molto bene; **I felt (as if I was going to) faint** mi sono sentito svenire; **to ~ ashamed** avere vergogna; **I ~ sure that...** sono sicuro che...; **I ~ very cross/sorry** *etc* sono molto arrabbiato/ triste *etc*; **he ~s bad about leaving his wife alone** gli dispiace lasciare sola la moglie; **I ~ as if there is nothing we can do** ho la sensazione che non ci possiamo fare niente; **how do you ~ about him/about the idea?** che ne pensi di lui/dell'idea?; **what does it ~ like to do that?** che effetto ti fa fare ciò?; **to ~ like sth/doing sth** avere voglia di qc/di fare qc; **I don't ~ up to (doing)** it non me la sento (di farlo); **I felt (like) a fool** mi sono sentito uno stupido; **I ~ for you!** *(sympathize)* come ti capisco!

   (b) *(objects)*: **to ~ hard/cold/damp** *etc* **(to the touch)** essere duro(a)/freddo(a)/umido(a) *etc* al tatto; **the house ~s damp** la casa sembra umida; **it ~s like silk** sembra seta al tatto; **it ~s colder out here** sembra più freddo qui fuori; **it ~s like (it might) rain** sembra che voglia piovere; **it felt like being drunk, it felt as if I was drunk** mi sentivo come se fossi ubriaco.

   (c) *(grope: also:* **~ around)** cercare a tastoni; **to ~ around for sth in the dark** cercare a tastoni qc al buio; **to ~ in one's pockets for sth** frugarsi le tasche per cercare qc.

feel·er ['fiːlə^r] *n (of insect, snail)* antenna; *(of octopus)* tentacolo; **to put out ~s** *(fig)* tastare il terreno.

feel·ing ['fiːlɪŋ] *n* **(a)** *(physical)* senso, sensazione *f*; **a cold ~** una sensazione di freddo; **to have no ~ in one's arm, to have lost all ~ in one's arm** aver perso completamente la sensibilità in un braccio.

   (b) *(emotion)* sentimento, emozione *f*; *(sensitivity)* sensibilità; **bad** *or* **ill ~** ostilità, rancore *m*; **to speak/sing with ~** parlare/cantare con sentimento; **he shows no ~ for her** non mostra nessuna simpatia per lei; **a woman of great ~** una donna molto sensibile; **what are your ~s about the matter?** che cosa ne pensi?; **you can imagine my ~s** puoi immaginare quello che sento; **to hurt sb's ~s** offendere qn; **~s ran high about it** la cosa aveva provocato grande eccitazione; **no hard ~s!** senza rancore!

   (c) *(impression)* senso, impressione *f*; **a ~ of security/isolation** un senso di sicurezza/di isolamento; **I have a (funny) ~ that...** ho la (strana) sensazione che...; **I got the ~ that...** ho avuto l'impressione che...; **there was a general ~ that...** il sentimento generale era che... .

fee-paying ['fiːˌpeɪɪŋ] *adj (pupil)* che paga; **~ school** scuola privata.

feet [fiːt] *npl of* **foot**.

feign [feɪn] *vt* fingere, simulare.

feint [feɪnt] **1** *n* finta. **2** *vi* fare una finta.

fe·lic·i·ty [fɪ'lɪsɪtɪ] *n* felicità.

fe·line ['fiːlaɪn] *adj* felino(a).

fell[1] [fɛl] *pt of* **fall**.

fell[2] [fɛl] *vt (with a blow)* atterrare; *(tree)* abbattere.

fell[3] [fɛl] *adj*: **with one ~ blow** con un colpo terribile; **at one ~ swoop** in un colpo solo.

fell[4] [fɛl] *n (Brit: mountain)* monte *m*; *(: moorland)*: **the ~s** la brughiera.

fel·low ['fɛləʊ] **1** *n* **(a)** *(man, boy)* uomo, tipo; **poor ~!** povero diavolo!; **my dear ~** mio caro, caro mio. **(b)** *(comrade)* compagno; *(equal)* pari *m inv*. **(c)** *(of association, society etc)* membro; *(Univ)* ≈ docente *m/f*. **2** *cpd*: **~ citizen** *n* concittadino/a; **~ countryman/woman** *n* compatriota *m/f*; **one's ~ creatures** i propri simili; **~ doctor** *n* collega *m* (medico); **~ feeling** *n* simpatia; **~ men** *npl* simili *mpl*; **~ student** *n* compagno/a di studi; **~ traveller** *n* compagno/a di viaggio; *(Pol: with commun-*

ists) simpatizzante *m/f*; **~ worker** *n* compagno/a di lavoro.

fel·low·ship ['fɛləʊʃɪp] *n (companionship)* compagnia; *(club, society)* associazione *f*; *(Univ: paid research post)* posto di ricercatore/trice.

fel·on ['fɛlən] *n (Law)* criminale *m/f*.

felo·ny ['fɛlənɪ] *n* crimine *m*.

felt[1] [fɛlt] *pt, pp of* **feel**.

felt[2] [fɛlt] **1** *n* feltro. **2** *cpd*: **~ hat** *n* cappello di feltro.

felt-tip ['fɛlttɪp] *n (also:* **~ pen)** pennarello.

fe·male ['fiːmeɪl] **1** *adj (animal, plant)* femmina; *(subject, member, worker)* di sesso femminile; *(company, vote)* di donne; *(sex, quality, character)* femminile; **~ student/worker** *etc* studentessa/ operaia *etc*; **~ impersonator** *(Theatre)* attore comico che fa parti da donna. **2** *n (animal)* femmina; *(person: pej)* donna, femmina.

femi·nine ['fɛmɪnɪn] **1** *adj* femminile; **the ~ form** *(Gram)* il femminile. **2** *n (Gram)* femminile *m*; **in the ~** al femminile.

femi·nin·i·ty [ˌfɛmɪ'nɪnɪtɪ] *n* femminilità.

femi·nism ['fɛmɪnɪzəm] *n* femminismo.

femi·nist ['fɛmɪnɪst] *adj, n* femminista *(m/f)*.

fen [fɛn] *n (often pl)* zona paludosa.

fence [fɛns] **1** *n* **(a)** recinto, steccato; *(Racing)* ostacolo; **to sit on the ~** *(fig)* rimanere neutrale. **(b)** *(fam: receiver of stolen goods)* ricettatore/ trice. **2** *vi (Sport)* tirare di scherma.

♦ **fence in** *vt + adv (field)* recintare; *(bull)* rinchiudere in un recinto.

♦ **fence off** *vt + adv* separare con un recinto.

fenc·er ['fɛnsə^r] *n* schermitore/trice.

fenc·ing ['fɛnsɪŋ] **1** *n* **(a)** *(sport)* scherma. **(b)** *(material)* materiale *m* per recintare. **2** *cpd*: **~ match** *n* incontro di scherma.

fend [fɛnd] **1** *vt*: **to ~ off** *(attack, attacker)* respingere, difendersi da; *(blow)* parare; *(awkward question)* eludere. **2** *vi*: **to ~ for o.s.** arrangiarsi, badare a se stesso.

fend·er ['fɛndə^r] *n (round fire)* paracenere *m*; *(Am Aut: wing)* parafango; *(Am Rail)* paraurti *m inv*.

fen·nel ['fɛnl] *n* finocchio.

fer·ment 1 ['fɜːment] *n (excitement)* eccitazione *f*, fermento; **to be in a state of ~** essere in fermento *or* in uno stato di agitazione. **2** [fə'ment] *vt* far fermentare; *(fig)* fomentare. **3** [fə'ment] *vi* fermentare.

fer·men·ta·tion [ˌfɜːmen'teɪʃən] *n* fermentazione *f*.

fern [fɜːn] *n* felce *f*.

fe·ro·cious [fə'rəʊʃəs] *adj* feroce.

fe·roc·i·ty [fə'rɒsɪtɪ] *n* ferocia.

fer·ret ['fɛrɪt] **1** *n* furetto. **2** *vi* cacciare con il furetto.

♦ **ferret about, ferret around** *vi + adv* frugare.

♦ **ferret out** *vt + adv (person)* scovare, scoprire; *(secret, truth)* scoprire.

fer·ry ['fɛrɪ] **1** *n (~boat)* traghetto; *(large: for cars etc)* nave *f* traghetto *inv*. **2** *vt*: **to ~ sth/sb across** *or* **over** traghettare qc/qn da una parte all'altra; **to ~ sb to and fro** portare qn avanti e indietro.

ferry·man ['fɛrɪmən] *n, pl* **-men** traghettatore.

fer·tile ['fɜːtaɪl] *adj (gen)* fertile; *(creature, plant)* fertile, fecondo(a).

fer·til·i·ty [fə'tɪlɪtɪ] **1** *n (see adj)* fertilità; fecondità. **2** *cpd*: **~ drug** *n* farmaco fecondativo.

fer·ti·lize ['fɜːtɪlaɪz] *vt (egg)* fecondare; *(Agr: land, soil)* fertilizzare.

fer·ti·liz·er ['fɜːtɪlaɪzə^r] *n* fertilizzante *m*.

fer·vent ['fɜːvənt] *adj*, **fer·vid** ['fɜːvɪd] *adj (believer, supporter)* fervente; *(desire)* ardente.

fer·vour, *(Am)* **fer·vor** ['fɜːvəʳ] *n* fervore *m*, ardore *m*.

fes·ter ['fɛstəʳ] *vi (Med)* suppurare; *(anger, resentment)* covare.

fes·ti·val ['fɛstɪvəl] *n (Rel etc)* festa; *(Mus etc)* festival *m inv*.

fes·tive ['fɛstɪv] *adj* di festa; **the ~ season** il periodo delle feste natalizie; **in a ~ mood** di umore allegro.

fes·tiv·ity [fɛs'tɪvɪtɪ] *n* festa.

fes·toon [fɛs'tuːn] *vt:* **to ~ with** ornare di.

fetch [fɛtʃ] *vt* **(a)** *(bring)* portare; *(go and get)* andare a prendere; *(: doctor)* andare a chiamare; **~ it!** *(to dog)* prendilo! **(b)** *(sell for)* essere venduto(a) per; **how much did it ~?** a *or* per quanto lo hai venduto?

♦ **fetch in** *vt + adv (object)* portare dentro; *(person)* far venire.

♦ **fetch out** *vt + adv (person)* far uscire; *(object)* tirare fuori.

♦ **fetch up** *vi + adv* andare a finire.

fetch·ing ['fɛtʃɪŋ] *adj* attraente.

fête [feɪt] **1** *n* festa. **2** *vt* festeggiare.

fet·id ['fɛtɪd] *adj* fetido(a).

fet·ish ['fɛtɪʃ] *n (object of cult)* feticcio; *(fig: obsession)* fissazione *f*, mania.

fet·ish·ist ['fɛtɪʃɪst] *n* feticista *m/f*.

fet·ter ['fɛtəʳ] *vt (person)* incatenare; *(horse)* legare; *(fig)* ostacolare.

fet·ters ['fɛtəz] *npl* catene *fpl; (fig)* restrizioni *fpl*.

fet·tle ['fɛtl] *n:* **in fine ~** in gran forma.

fe·tus ['fiːtəs] *n (Am)* = **foetus.**

feud [fjuːd] **1** *n* faida; **a family ~** una lite in famiglia. **2** *vi:* **to ~ with sb** litigare *or* essere in lite con qn.

feu·dal ['fjuːdl] *adj* feudale.

feu·dal·ism ['fjuːdəlɪzəm] *n* feudalesimo.

fe·ver ['fiːvəʳ] *n* febbre *f*; **he has a ~** ha la febbre; **a bout of ~** un accesso di febbre; **a high/slight ~** una febbre alta/leggera; **the gambling ~** *(fig)* la smania del gioco; **in a ~ of excitement** in uno stato di eccitazione febbrile; **it reached ~ pitch** ha raggiunto il colmo dell'emozione.

fe·ver·ish ['fiːvərɪʃ] *adj (also fig)* febbrile; *(person)* febbricitante.

few [fjuː] *adj, pron* (**-er, -est) (a)** *(not many)* pochi(e); **~ books** pochi libri; **~ of them** pochi di loro; **~ (people) managed to do it** pochi riuscirono a farlo; **she is one of the ~ (people) who...** è una delle poche persone che...; **the ~ who... i** pochi che...; **in** *or* **over the past ~ days** negli ultimi giorni, in questi ultimi giorni; **in** *or* **over the next ~ days** nei prossimi giorni; **with ~ exceptions** con *or* salvo poche eccezioni; **every ~ weeks** a intervalli di qualche settimana; **they are ~ and far between** sono rari; **there are very ~ of us, we are very ~** siamo pochi; **the last** *or* **remaining ~ minutes** i pochi minuti che rimangono; **as ~ as 3 of them** solo 3 di loro; **too ~** troppo pochi; **there were 3 too ~** ne mancavano 3.

(b) *(some, several):* **a ~** alcuni(e), qualche; **a ~ books** alcuni libri, qualche libro; **a good ~, quite a ~** parecchi; **a good ~** *or* **quite a ~ books** parecchi libri, un bel po' di libri; **a good ~** *or* **quite a ~ (people) came** parecchie persone sono venute; **a ~ of them** alcuni di loro; **a ~ more days** qualche altro giorno; **in a ~ more days** fra qualche giorno.

few·er ['fjuːəʳ] *adj, pron, comp of* **few** meno; **~ than 10** meno di 10; **~ than you** meno di te; **no ~ than...** non meno di... .

few·est ['fjuːɪst] *adj, pron, superl of* **few** il minor

numero di; **we were ~ in number** eravamo i meno numerosi.

fi·an·cé(e) [fɪ'ɑ̃ːŋseɪ] *n* fidanzato/a.

fi·as·co [fɪ'æskəʊ] *n* fiasco.

fib [fɪb] **1** *n (fam)* bugia, frottola; **to tell a ~** dire una bugia. **2** *vi* dire bugie, raccontare storie.

fib·ber ['fɪbəʳ] *n (fam)* bugiardo/a.

fi·bre, *(Am)* **fi·ber** ['faɪbəʳ] *n* fibra.

fibre·board ['faɪbəbɔːd] *n* pannello di fibre.

fibre·glass ['faɪbəglɑːs] **1** *n* fibra di vetro. **2** *cpd* di fibra di vetro.

fi·bro·si·tis [,faɪbrə'saɪtɪs] *n* cellulite *f*.

fi·brous ['faɪbrəs] *adj* fibroso(a).

fick·le ['fɪkl] *adj* incostante, volubile.

fic·tion ['fɪkʃən] *n* **(a)** *(Literature)* narrativa; **a work of ~** un'opera di narrativa; **light ~** narrativa leggera. **(b)** *(sth made up)* finzione *f*.

fic·tion·al ['fɪkʃənl] *adj* immaginario(a).

fic·ti·tious [fɪk'tɪʃəs] *adj* **(a)** = **fictional. (b)** *(false)* falso(a), fittizio(a).

fid·dle ['fɪdl] **1** *n* **(a)** *(violin)* violino; **to play second ~ to sb** *(fig)* avere un ruolo di secondo piano rispetto a qn. **(b)** *(fam: cheat)* imbroglio, truffa; **it's a ~** un imbroglio; **tax ~** frode *f* fiscale; **to work a ~** fare un imbroglio; **to be on the ~** imbrogliare. **2** *vi (fidget)* giocherellare, gingillarsi; **do stop fiddling!** stai fermo!; **to ~ (about) with sth** giocherellare con qc. **3** *vt (fam: accounts, results etc)* falsificare, alterare.

♦ **fiddle about, fiddle around** *vi + adv* gingillarsi.

fid·dler ['fɪdləʳ] *n* **(a)** *(Mus)* violinista *m/f*. **(b)** *(fam: cheat)* imbroglione/a.

fiddle·sticks ['fɪdlstɪks] *excl* sciocchezze!

fid·dling ['fɪdlɪŋ] **1** *adj* insignificante; **~ little job** lavoretto. **2** *n (fam: cheating)* imbrogli *mpl*.

fid·dly ['fɪdlɪ] *adj* **(-ier, -iest)**: *(task)* da certosino; *(object)* complesso(a).

fi·del·ity [fɪ'dɛlɪtɪ] *n* fedeltà.

fidg·et ['fɪdʒɪt] **1** *n (person)* persona irrequieta; **to have the ~s** essere irrequieto *or* agitato. **2** *vi (also:* **~ about, ~ around)** agitarsi; **to ~ with sth** giocherellare con qc.

fidg·ety ['fɪdʒɪtɪ] *adj* agitato(a), irrequieto(a).

field [fiːld] **1** *n (gen)* campo; *(Geol)* giacimento; *(sphere of activity)* campo, settore *m*; **to give sth a year's trial in the ~** *(fig)* sperimentare qc sul mercato per un anno; **to study sth in the ~** osservare *or* studiare qc sul campo; **to die in the ~** *(Mil)* cadere sul campo di battaglia; **to take the ~** *(Sport)* scendere in campo; **to lead the ~** *(Sport, Comm)* essere in testa, essere al primo posto; **my particular ~** la mia specialità, il mio campo *or* settore; **~ of vision** campo visivo. **2** *vt (team)* far giocare, far scendere in campo; *(Cricket: catch: ball)* prendere. **3** *cpd:* **~ day** *n (Mil)* giorno di grandi manovre; **to have a ~ day** *(fig)* divertirsi, spassarsela; **~ events** *npl (Athletics)* atletica leggera; **~ glasses** *npl (binoculars)* binocolo; **~ hospital** *n* ospedale *m* da campo; **~ sports** *npl* sport *mpl* all'aria aperta *(caccia, pesca etc)*.

field-test ['fiːld,tɛst] **1** *n* prova pratica. **2** *vt* sperimentare sul mercato.

field·work ['fiːldwɜːk] *n (Sociol etc)* raccolta diretta di dati; *(Archeol, Geog)* lavoro sul campo.

fiend [fiːnd] *n* demonio; **you little ~!** *(fam)* piccolo delinquente!; **a tennis ~** un fanatico *or* patito del tennis.

fiend·ish ['fiːndɪʃ] *adj (cruelty, smile, plot)* diabolico(a); *(fam: difficult and unpleasant)* tremendo(a); **I had a ~ time trying to...** è stato un lavoraccio tentare di... .

fiend·ish·ly ['fiːndɪʃlɪ] *adv (see adj)*

diabolicamente; tremendamente.

fierce [fɪəs] *adj* (**-r, -st**) *(gen)* feroce; *(opponent)* accanito(a); *(look)* severo(a); *(wind, storm)* furioso(a); *(heat)* intenso(a).

fierce·ly ['fɪəslɪ] *adv (extremely)* intensamente; *(fight)* con accanimento; *(rage)* furiosamente.

fiery ['faɪərɪ] *adj* (**-ier, -iest**) *(gen)* infocato(a); *(red)* di fuoco; *(temperament, person)* focoso(a); *(liquor)* che brucia la gola.

fif·teen [fɪf'tiːn] **1** *adj* quindici *inv*; **about ~ people** una quindicina di persone. **2** *n* quindici *m inv*; *(Rugby)* squadra; *for usage see* **five**.

fif·teenth [fɪf'tiːnθ] **1** *adj* quindicesimo(a). **2** *n (in series)* quindicesimo/a; *(fraction)* quindicesimo; *for usage see* **fifth**.

fifth [fɪfθ] **1** *adj* quinto(a); **I was (the) ~ to arrive** sono stato il quinto ad arrivare; **he came ~ in the competition** è arrivato quinto al concorso; **si è piazzato al quinto posto; Henry the F~** Enrico Quinto; **the ~ of July, July the ~** il cinque luglio; **~ column** *(Pol)* quinta colonna; **~ form** *(Brit Scol)* ≈ terzo anno di scuola superiore. **2** *n (in series)* quinto/a; *(fraction)* quinto; *(Mus)* quinta; **I wrote to him on the ~** gli ho scritto il cinque.

fif·ti·eth ['fɪftɪɪθ] **1** *adj* cinquantesimo(a). **2** *n (in series)* cinquantesimo/a; *(fraction)* cinquantesimo; *for usage see* **fifth**.

fif·ty ['fɪftɪ] **1** *adj* cinquanta *inv*; **about ~ people/cars** una cinquantina di persone/di macchine; **he'll be ~ (years old)** next birthday **at** prossimo compleanno avrà cinquant'anni; **he's about ~** è sulla cinquantina. **2** *n* cinquanta *m inv*; **the fifties** *(1950s)* gli anni cinquanta; **to be in one's fifties** avere passato la cinquantina; **the temperature was in the fifties** la temperatura era al di sopra dei cinquanta gradi; **to do ~** *(Aut)* andare a 50 (all'ora).

fifty-fifty ['fɪftɪ'fɪftɪ] *adj, adv*: **to go ~ with sb** fare a metà con qn; **we have a ~ chance of success** abbiamo una probabilità su due di successo.

fig [fɪg] *n* fico.

fight [faɪt] *(vb: pt, pp* **fought**) **1** *n (Mil)* combattimento, lotta; *(Boxing)* incontro; *(between 2 persons)* lite *f*; *(struggle, campaign)*: **~ (for/against)** lotta (a favore di/contro); *(argument)*: **~ (over)** disputa (su); *(fighting spirit)* combattività; **to have a ~ with sb** *(quarrel, struggle)* avere una lite con qn, litigare con qn; **to put up a good ~** battersi *or* difendersi bene; **there was no ~ left in him** aveva perduto la sua combattività.

2 *vt (Mil: enemy, battle)* combattere; *(fire, disease, proposals, legislation)* lottare contro; *(Law: case)* difendere; **to ~ a duel** battersi in duello; **to ~ one's way through a crowd/across a room** farsi strada a fatica tra la folla/attraverso una stanza.

3 *vi (person)* azzuffarsi; *(animal)* battersi; *(troops, countries)*: **to ~ (against)** combattere (contro); *(quarrel)*: **to ~ (with sb)** litigare (con qn); *(fig)*: **to ~ (for/against)** lottare (per/contro); **to ~ for one's life** lottare per la (propria) vita.

♦ **fight back** *vi + adv* difendersi; *(Sport, after illness)* riprendersi. **2** *vt + adv (tears)* ricacciare; *(anger)* reprimere; *(despair, doubts)* scacciare.

♦ **fight down** *vt + adv (anger, anxiety)* vincere; *(urge)* reprimere.

♦ **fight off** *vt + adv (attack, attacker)* respingere; *(disease, sleep, urge)* lottare contro.

♦ **fight on** *vi + adv* continuare a combattere.

♦ **fight out** *vt + adv*: **to ~ it out** risolvere la questione a pugni.

fight·er ['faɪtə'] **1** *n* combattente *m/f*; *(plane)* caccia *m inv*; **he's a ~ for the cause of...** lotta per la

causa di.... **2** *cpd*: **~ pilot** *n* pilota *m* di caccia.

fighter-bomber ['faɪtə,bɒmə'] *n* cacciabombardiere *m*.

fight·ing ['faɪtɪŋ] **1** *n (Mil)* combattimento; *(in streets)* scontri *mpl*; *(in pub etc)* risse *fpl*, zuffe *fpl*. **2** *adj (forces, strength, troops)* da combattimento; **~ spirit** spirito combattivo; **a ~ chance** una buona probabilità.

fig·ment ['fɪgmənt] *n*: **~ of the imagination** frutto dell'immaginazione.

fig·ura·tive ['fɪgjʊrətɪv] *adj (meaning)* figurato(a); *(Art)* figurativo(a).

fig·ure ['fɪgə'] **1** *n* **(a)** *(shape)* figura; **he's a fine ~ of a man** è un bell'uomo; **he cuts a fine ~** ha molta classe; **to lose one's ~** perdere la linea. **(b)** *(person)* figura, personaggio; **public ~** personaggio pubblico. **(c)** *(drawing, Geom)* figura; *(diagram)* illustrazione *f*; **a ~ of eight** un otto. **(d)** *(Math: numeral)* cifra; **to be good at ~s** essere bravo a fare i conti; **a mistake in the ~s** un errore nei calcoli; **to reach double/three ~s** raggiungere le due/tre cifre. **(e)** *(Gram)*: **~ of speech** figura retorica; **it's just a ~ of speech** *(fig)* è solo un modo di dire. **2** *vi* **(a)** *(appear)* figurare. **(b)** *(esp Am: make sense)* essere logico(a); **that ~s!** *(fam)* è logico! **3** *vt (esp Am: think, calculate)* pensare, immaginare. **4** *cpd*: **~ skating** *n* pattinaggio artistico.

♦ **figure on** *vi + prep (Am)* contare su; **I ~d on him arriving by 6 o'clock** contavo sul fatto che sarebbe arrivato alle 6.

♦ **figure out** *vt + adv (understand)* capire; *(calculate: sum)* calcolare; **I just can't ~ it out!** non ci arrivo!

figure·head ['fɪgəhed] *n (Naut)* polena; *(fig)* figura rappresentativa.

fila·ment ['fɪləmənt] *n* filamento.

filch [fɪltʃ] *vt (fam: steal)* grattare.

file¹ [faɪl] **1** *n (tool)* lima; *(for nails)* limetta. **2** *vt* limare; **to ~ one's nails** limarsi le unghie.

file² [faɪl] **1** *n (folder)* cartella; *(ring binder)* raccoglitore *m*; *(dossier)* pratica, incartamento; *(in cabinet)* scheda; *(Computers)* archivio. **2** *vt* **(a)** *(also:* **~ away***: notes, information, work)* raccogliere; *(: under heading)* archiviare. **(b)** *(submit: claim, application, complaint)* presentare; *(Law)*: **to ~ a suit against sb** intentare causa contro qn.

file³ [faɪl] **1** *n (row)* fila; **in single ~** in fila indiana. **2** *vi*: **to ~ in/out** entrare/uscire in fila; **to ~ past (sth/sb)** sfilare davanti (a qc/qn).

fil·ial ['fɪlɪəl] *adj* filiale.

fili·bus·ter ['fɪlɪbʌstə'] **1** *n (esp Am Pol)* ostruzionista *m/f*. **2** *vi* fare ostruzionismo.

fili·gree ['fɪlɪgriː] **1** *n* filigrana. **2** *adj* a filigrana.

fil·ing cabi·net ['faɪlɪŋ,kæbɪnɪt] *n* schedario, casellario.

fil·ing clerk ['faɪlɪŋ,klɑːk] *n* archivista *m/f*.

fil·ings ['faɪlɪŋz] *npl* limatura.

fill [fɪl] **1** *vt (gen)*: **to ~ (with)** riempire (di); *(tooth)*: **to ~ (with)** otturare (con); *(subj: wind: sails)* gonfiare; *(supply: order, requirements, need)* soddisfare; **we've already ~ed that vacancy** abbiamo già assunto qualcuno per quel posto; **they asked her to ~ the vacancy** le hanno offerto il posto; **the position is already ~ed** il posto è già preso; **~ed with admiration (for)** pieno di ammirazione (per); **~ed with remorse/despair** in preda al rimorso/alla disperazione; **that ~s the bill** è quello che ci vuole. **2** *vi*: **to ~ (with)** riempirsi (di). **3** *n*: **to eat/drink one's ~** mangiare/bere a sazietà; **to have one's ~ of sth** *(fig)* averne le tasche piene di qc.

♦ **fill in 1** *vt + adv* **(a)** *(hole, gap, outline)* riempire.

(b) *(one's name)* mettere; *(form)* riempire; *(details, report)* completare; **to ~ sb in on sth** *(fam)* mettere qn al corrente di qc. **2** *vi + adv:* **to ~ in for sb** sostituire qn.

♦ **fill out 1** *vt + adv (form, receipt)* riempire, compilare. **2** *vi + adv (person, face)* ingrassarsi; *(sail)* gonfiarsi.

♦ **fill up 1** *vi + adv* **(a)***(Aut)* fare il pieno. **(b)** *(room etc)* riempirsi, gremirsi. **2** *vt + adv (container)* riempire; **~ it** *or* **her up!** *(fam: Aut)* faccia il pieno!

fill·er ['fɪlə^r] *n (for cracks: in wood, plaster)* stucco.

fil·let ['fɪlɪt] **1** *n* filetto. **2** *vt (meat)* disossare; *(fish)* tagliare a filetti.

fill·ing ['fɪlɪŋ] **1** *n (of tooth)* otturazione *f*; *(Culin)* ripieno, impasto. **2** *adj (food)* sostanzioso(a). **3** *cpd:* **~ station** *n* stazione *f* di rifornimento.

fil·ly ['fɪlɪ] *n* puledra.

film [fɪlm] **1** *n (gen)* strato sottile; *(Phot)* pellicola; *(for camera)* rullino; *(at cinema)* film *m inv.* **2** *vt* filmare. **3** *cpd:* **~ camera** *n* macchina da presa; **~ crew** *n* troupe *f inv* cinematografica; **~ library** *n* cineteca; **~ rights** *npl* diritti *mpl* di produzione; **~ script** *n* copione *m*; **~ star** *n* divo/a del cinema; **~ studio** *n* studio cinematografico.

film·strip ['fɪlmstrɪp] *n* filmina.

fil·ter ['fɪltə^r] **1** *n* filtro. **2** *vt* filtrare. **3** *vi:* **to ~ to the left** *(Aut)* imboccare la corsia di svolta continua. **4** *cpd:* **~ coffee** *n* caffè *m* da passare al filtro; **~ lane** *n (Aut)* corsia di svolta continua; **~ paper** *n* carta da filtro *or* filtrante.

♦ **filter back** *vi + adv (people)* ritornare a piccoli gruppi.

♦ **filter in, filter through** *vi + adv (news)* trapelare.

filter-tipped ['fɪltə,tɪpt] *adj* con filtro.

filth [fɪlθ] *n* sudiciume *m*; *(fig)* oscenità; **it's just sheer ~** non è che una porcheria.

filthy ['fɪlθɪ] *adj* **(-ier, -iest)** sudicio(a); *(language)* volgare; **what ~ weather!** che tempaccio!; **he's got a ~ mind** è uno sporcaccione.

fin [fɪn] *n (of fish etc)* pinna; *(of plane, bomb)* impennaggio.

fi·nal ['faɪnl] **1** *adj (last)* ultimo(a); *(conclusive)* finale, definitivo(a); *(victory)* conclusivo(a); *(exam)* finale; **the judge's decision is ~** la decisione del giudice è inappellabile; **and that's ~!** ho detto di no e basta! **2** *n (Sport)* finale *f*; **~s** *(Univ)* esami *mpl* dell'ultimo anno.

fi·na·le [fɪ'nɑ:lɪ] *n* finale *m*; **the grand ~** *(also fig)* il gran finale.

fi·nal·ist ['faɪnəlɪst] *n (Sport)* finalista *m/f*.

fi·nal·ity [faɪ'nælɪtɪ] *n* irrevocabilità; **with an air of ~** con risolutezza.

fi·nal·ize ['faɪnəlaɪz] *vt (preparations, arrangements, plans)* mettere a punto; *(agreement, decision, contract)* definire; *(report, text)* dare una stesura definitiva a; *(date)* fissare.

fi·nal·ly ['faɪnəlɪ] *adv (lastly)* alla fine; *(in conclusion)* in fine; *(eventually)* finalmente; *(once and for all)* definitivamente.

fi·nance [faɪ'næns] **1** *n* finanza; *(funds)* fondi *mpl*, capitale *m*; **Minister of F~** Ministro delle finanze. **2** *vt* finanziare. **3** *cpd (page, section, company)* finanziario(a).

fi·nan·cial [faɪ'nænʃəl] *adj* finanziario(a).

fi·nan·ci·er [faɪ'nænsɪə^r] *n* finanziatore/trice.

finch [fɪntʃ] *n* fringillide *m*.

find [faɪnd] *(vb: pt, pp* **found)** **1** *vt* **(a)** *(gen)* trovare; *(stn lost)* ritrovare; *(learn)* scoprire; **the book is nowhere to be found** il libro non si trova da nessuna parte; **this plant is found all over Europe** questa pianta si trova in tutta Europa; **it**

has been found that... è stato *or* si è scoperto che...; **if you can ~ the time** se riesci a trovare il tempo; **no cure has been found** non si è trovata nessuna cura; **I found it impossible to tell the difference** non riuscivo a distinguergli; **he ~s it easy/difficult to do...** non trova/trova difficoltà a *or* nel fare...; **to ~ (some) difficulty in doing sth** trovare delle difficoltà nel fare qc; **I ~ him very pleasant** lo trovo molto simpatico; **we found him in bed/reading** l'abbiamo trovato a letto/che stava leggendo; **I found myself at a loss** non sapevo cosa dire, non riuscivo a trovare le parole; **can you ~ your (own) way to the station?** sai come andare alla stazione?; **this found its way into my drawer** questo è andato a finire nel mio cassetto; **leave everything as you ~ it** lascia tutto come trovi; **to ~ fault with sb/sth** trovare da ridire sul conto di qn/su qc; **he was found guilty/innocent** *(Law)* fu dichiarato colpevole/innocente; **to ~ one's feet** *(fig)* ambientarsi.

(b) *(obtain)* trovare; **go and ~ me a pencil** vai a cercarmi una matita; **there are no more to be found** non ce ne sono più; **wages all found** stipendio più vitto e alloggio.

2 *vi (Law):* **to ~ for/against sb** emettere un verdetto a favore di/contro qn.

3 *n* scoperta.

♦ **find out 1** *vt + adv (information, answer)* scoprire; **to ~ out that...** scoprire che...; **to ~ sb out** smascherare qn. **2** *vi + adv:* **we found out about his death** abbiamo scoperto che era morto; **we found out all about...** abbiamo scoperto tutto su... .

find·ings ['faɪndɪŋz] *npl (of inquiry etc)* conclusioni *fpl.*

fine¹ [faɪn] **1** *adj* **(-r, -st) (a)** *(delicate, narrow, small)* fine; *(rain)* leggero(a); *(fig: distinction)* sottile; **not to put too ~ a point on it** per dirlo con schiettezza; **he's got it down to a ~ art** lo fa alla perfezione. **(b)** *(not coarse: metal)* fino(a); *(sense)* sottile; *(taste)* raffinato(a); *(feelings)* elevato(a). **(c)** *(good)* ottimo(a); *(beautiful, imposing)* bello(a); *(clothes)* elegante; **if the weather is ~** se il tempo è bello; **it's a ~ day today** è una bella giornata oggi; **~ workmanship** lavorazione raffinata *or* delicata; **he's a ~ man** è un'ottima persona; **~ art, the ~ arts** le belle arti; **that's ~** va benissimo; **he's ~** sta bene; **a ~ friend you are!** bell'amico sei!; **you're a ~ one to talk!** senti chi parla!; **a ~ thing!** bella roba!; **one ~ day** un bel giorno. **2** *adv* **(a)** *(well)* molto bene; **you're doing ~** te la cavi benissimo. **(b)** *(finely)* finemente; **to cut it ~** *(of time, money)* farcela per un pelo.

fine² [faɪn] **1** *n* multa; **to get a ~ for sth/doing sth** ricevere una multa per qc/per aver fatto qc. **2** *vt:* **to ~ sb (for sth/for doing sth)** multare qn *or* fare una multa a qn (per qc/per aver fatto qc).

fine·ly ['faɪnlɪ] *adv* **(a)** *(splendidly)* in modo stupendo. **(b)** *(chop)* finemente; *(adjust)* con precisione.

fin·ery [ˈfaɪnərɪ] *n* abiti *mpl* eleganti; **to be dressed in all one's ~** essere tutto in ghingheri.

fi·nesse [fɪ'nɛs] *n* finezza; *(Cards)* impasse *f*.

fin·ger [ˈfɪŋgə^r] **1** *n* dito; **his ~s are all thumbs, he is all ~s and thumbs** è molto maldestro; **keep your ~s crossed** fai gli scongiuri; **they never laid a ~ on her** non l'hanno nemmeno toccata; **he didn't lift a ~ to help** non ha mosso un dito per aiutare; **I can't quite put my ~ on what's wrong** non riesco a vedere cosa c'è di sbagliato; **to twist sb round one's little ~** fare quello che si vuole di qn; **to have a ~ in the** *or* **in every pie** avere le mani in pasta; **to pull one's ~ out** *(fig fam)* darsi una mossa. **2** *vt* toccare, tastare; *(keyboard)* far scorrere le dita su. **3** *cpd*: ~ **board** *n* manico.

finger·mark ['fɪŋgəmɑːk] *n* ditata.

finger·nail ['fɪŋgəneɪl] *n* unghia.

finger·print ['fɪŋgəprɪnt] **1** *n* impronta digitale. **2** *vt (person)* prendere le impronte digitali di.

finger·tip ['fɪŋgətɪp] *n* punta del dito; **to have sth at one's ~s** *(fig)* sapere qc sulla punta delle dita.

fin·icky ['fɪnɪkɪ] *adj* **(a)** *(person)*: ~ **(about)** pignolo(a) (su), difficile (per). **(b)** *(job)* che richiede pazienza.

fin·ish ['fɪnɪʃ] **1** *n* **(a)** *(end: esp Sport)* fine *f*; *(Sport: place)* traguardo; **to be in at the** ~ essere presente alla fine; **a fight to the** ~ un combattimento all'ultimo sangue. **(b)** *(appearance)* finitura. **2** *vt (gen)* finire, terminare; **to** ~ **doing sth** finire di fare qc; **that last mile nearly ~ed me** *(fam)* quell'ultimo miglio mi ha quasi distrutto. **3** *vi (film, meeting)* finire, terminare; *(book, game)* finire, concludersi; *(contract)* scadere; **the party was ~ing** la festa stava per finire; **she ~ed by saying that...** ha concluso dicendo che...; **to** ~ **first/ second** *(Sport)* arrivare primo/secondo; **I've ~ed with the paper** ho finito col giornale; **he's ~ed with politics** ha chiuso con la politica; **she's ~ed with him** ha chiuso con lui.

♦ **finish off** *vt* + *adv* finire.

♦ **finish up 1** *vi* + *adv* finire; **he ~ed up in Paris** è finito a Parigi; **it ~ed up as...** ha finito col diventare... . **2** *vt* + *adv (food etc)* finire.

fin·ished ['fɪnɪʃt] *adj (product)* finito(a); *(performance)* perfetto(a); *(fam: tired)* sfinito(a); *(: done for)* finito(a).

fin·ish·ing ['fɪnɪʃɪŋ] *adj*: ~ **line** *n (Sport)* traguardo; ~ **school** *n* scuola di perfezionamento; ~ **touches** *npl* ultimi ritocchi *mpl*; **to put the** ~ **touches to sth** dare gli ultimi ritocchi a qc.

fi·nite ['faɪnaɪt] *adj* **(a)** *(limited)* limitato(a). **(b)** *(Gram)* finito(a).

Fin·land ['fɪnlənd] *n* Finlandia.

Finn [fɪn] *n* finlandese *m/f*.

Finn·ish ['fɪnɪʃ] **1** *adj* finlandese. **2** *n (language)* finlandese *m*.

fiord [fjɔːd] *n* = **fjord**.

fir [fɜːʳ] **1** *n (also:* ~ **tree)** abete *m*. **2** *cpd*: ~ **cone** *n* pigna.

fire [faɪəʳ] **1** *n* **(a)** *(gen)* fuoco; *(house* ~ *etc)* incendio; **electric/gas** ~ stufa elettrica/a gas; **forest** ~ incendio boschivo; **to set** ~ **to sth, set sth on** ~ dar fuoco a qc, incendiare qc; **to catch** ~ prendere fuoco; **to be on** ~ essere in fiamme; **insured against** ~ assicurato contro gli incendi; **to play with** ~ *(fig)* scherzare col fuoco. **(b)** *(Mil)* fuoco; **to open** ~ **(on sb)** aprire il fuoco (contro *or* su qn); **to hold one's** ~ cessare il fuoco; **to be/come under** ~ **(from)** essere/finire sotto il fuoco *or* il tiro (di); **the government has come under** ~ **from the opposition** il governo è finito sotto il tiro dell'opposizione.

2 *vt* **(a)** *(gun, shot, salute)* sparare; *(rocket etc)* lanciare; **to** ~ **a gun at sb** fare fuoco contro qn; **to** ~ **questions at sb** bombardare qn di domande. **(b)** *(pottery etc: in kiln)* cuocere; *(fig: imagination etc)* accendere. **(c)** *(fam: dismiss)* licenziare; **you're ~d!** sei licenziato!

3 *vi (Mil etc)*: **to** ~ **(at)** sparare (a), far fuoco (contro); *(Aut: subj: engine)* accendersi; ~ **away** *or* **ahead!** *(fig fam)* spara!

4 *cpd*: ~ **alarm** *n* allarme *m* antincendio; ~ **brigade** *n*, *(Am)* ~ **department** *n* (corpo dei) pompieri *or* vigili del fuoco; ~ **drill** *n*, ~ **practice** *n* esercitazione *f* antincendio; ~ **engine** *n* autopompa antincendio; ~ **escape** *n* scala di sicurez-

za; ~ **exit** *n* uscita di sicurezza; ~ **extinguisher** *n* estintore *m*; ~ **hazard** *n*, ~ **risk** *n* rischio d'incendio; ~ **regulations** *npl* norme *fpl* antincendio; ~ **station** *n* caserma dei pompieri.

fire·arm ['faɪərɑːm] *n* arma da fuoco.

fire·guard ['faɪəgɑːd] *n* parafuoco.

fire·light ['faɪəlaɪt] *n* bagliore *m* del fuoco; **by** ~ alla luce del fuoco.

fire·man ['faɪəmən] *n*, *pl* **-men** vigile *m* del fuoco, pompiere *m*.

fire·place ['faɪəpleɪs] *n* caminetto, focolare *m*.

fire·proof ['faɪəpruːf] *adj (material)* resistente al fuoco; *(dish)* resistente al calore.

fire·side ['faɪəsaɪd] *n* angolo del focolare; **by the** ~ intorno al focolare.

fire·wood ['faɪəwʊd] *n* legna da ardere.

fire·works ['faɪəwɜːks] **1** *npl* fuochi *mpl* d'artificio. **2** *cpd*: ~ **display** *n* spettacolo pirotecnico.

fir·ing ['faɪərɪŋ] **1** *n* spari *mpl*. **2** *cpd*: ~ **line** *n* linea del fuoco; **to be in the** ~ **line** *(fig: liable to be criticized)* essere in prima linea; ~ **squad** *n* plotone *m* d'esecuzione.

firm[1] [fɜːm] *adj* **(-er, -est)** *(gen)* solido(a); *(steady)* saldo(a); *(belief)* fermo(a); *(steps, measures)* severo(a); *(look, voice)* risoluto(a); *(prices)* stabile; *(offer, decision)* definitivo(a); **as** ~ **as a rock** solido come una roccia; **to be a** ~ **believer in sth** credere fermamente in qc; **to be** ~ **with sb** essere deciso con qn; **they are** ~ **friends** sono molto amici; **to keep a** ~ **hold on** tenere saldamente; **to be on** ~ **ground** *(fig)* andare sul sicuro; **to stand** ~ *or* **take a** ~ **stand over sth** *(fig)* tener duro per quanto riguarda qc.

firm[2] [fɜːm] *n* azienda, ditta, impresa.

firm·ly ['fɜːmlɪ] *adv (fixed)* fermamente, solidamente; *(speak)* con fermezza; *(believe)* fermamente.

firm·ness ['fɜːmnɪs] *n (of voice, decision etc)* fermezza; *(of object)* solidità.

first [fɜːst] **1** *adj* primo(a); **the** ~ **of January** il primo (di) gennaio; **the** ~ **time** la prima volta; **Charles the F~** Carlo Primo; **to win** ~ **place** arrivare primo; **in the** ~ **place** per prima cosa, innanzi tutto; **in the** ~ **instance** prima di tutto, in primo luogo; ~ **thing in the morning** la mattina presto; **I'll do it** ~ **thing tomorrow** lo farò per prima cosa domani; ~ **things first!** prima le cose più importanti!; **I don't know the** ~ **thing about it** *(fam)* non ne so un bel niente.

2 *adv* **(a)** *(firstly)* prima; ~ **one, then another** prima uno, poi un altro; ~ **of all** prima di tutto; ~ **and foremost** prima di tutto, innanzi tutto; ~ **and last** *(above all)* prima di tutto; ~ **come,** ~ **served** chi tardi arriva, male alloggia; **ladies** ~! prima le signore!; **we arrived** ~ siamo arrivati per primi; **she came** ~ **in the race** è arrivata prima nella gara; **at** ~ sulle prime; **finish this work** ~ finisci questo lavoro prima; **head** ~ a capofitto. **(b)** *(for the first time)* per la prima volta; **I** ~ **met him in Paris** l'ho incontrato per la prima volta a Parigi. **(c)** *(rather)* piuttosto; **I'd die** ~! piuttosto morirei!

3 *n*: **the** ~ **to arrive** il primo ad arrivare; **from the (very)** ~ fin dall'inizio, fin dal primo momento; **from** ~ **to last** dall'inizio alla fine; **in** ~ **(gear)** *(Aut)* in prima (marcia); **he gained a** ~ **in French** *(Univ: class of degree)* si è laureato in francese col massimo dei voti.

4 *cpd*: ~ **aid** *n* pronto soccorso; ~ **cousin** *n* cugino di primo grado; ~ **edition** *n* prima edizione *f*; ~ **form** *or* **year** *n (Scol)* ≃ prima media; ~ **name** *n* nome *m*; ~ **night** *n (Theatre)* prima; ~

offender n (*Law*) incensurato/a; ~ **performance** n (*Theatre, Mus*) prima.

first-aid [ˈfɜːstˈeɪd] *adj* (*see also* **first 4**): ~ **classes** corso di pronto soccorso; ~ **kit/box** attrezzatura/cassetta di pronto soccorso; ~ **post** pronto soccorso.

first-class [ˌfɜːstˈklɑːs] **1** *adj* (**a**): ~ **ticket** (*Rail etc*) biglietto di prima classe; ~ **compartment** (*Rail*) scompartimento di prima classe; ~ **mail** ≃ espresso; ~ **honours degree** (*Univ*) ≃ laurea con centodieci e lode. (**b**) (*very good*) di prima qualità. **2** *adv*: **to travel** ~ viaggiare in prima classe; **to send a letter** ~ ≃ spedire una lettera per espresso.

first-degree [ˌfɜːstdɪˈgriː] *adj* di primo grado.

first-hand [ˌfɜːstˈhænd] **1** *adj* diretto(a). **2** *adv* direttamente.

first·ly [ˈfɜːstlɪ] *adv* prima, innanzi tutto.

first-rate [ˈfɜːstˈreɪt] *adj* di prim'ordine.

fis·cal [ˈfɪskəl] *adj* fiscale.

fish [fɪʃ] **1** *n, pl* ~ *or* ~**es** pesce *m*; ~ **and chips** pesce con patatine fritte; **to be like a** ~ **out of water** sentirsi come un pesce fuor d'acqua; **I've got other** ~ **to fry** (*fam*) ho altro da fare. **2** *vi* pescare; **to go** ~**ing** andare a pesca; **to go salmon** ~**ing** andare a pesca di salmoni; **to** ~ **for trout** pescare (le) trote; **to** ~ **for compliments/for information** (*fig*) andare a caccia di complimenti/ di informazioni; **to** ~ (**around**) **in one's pockets for sth** frugarsi le tasche in cerca di qc. **3** *vt* (*river, pond*) pescare in; (*trout, salmon*) pescare. **4** *cpd*: ~ **farm** *n* vivaio; ~ **knife** *n* coltello per il pesce; ~ **shop** *n* pescheria; ~ **slice** *n* posata per servire il pesce; ~ **tank** *n* acquario.

♦ **fish out** *vt* + *adv* (*from water*) ripescare; (*from box etc*) tirare fuori.

fish·bone [ˈfɪʃbəʊn] *n* lisca, spina.

fish·cake [ˈfɪʃkeɪk] *n* crocchetta di pesce.

fisher·man [ˈfɪʃəmən] *n, pl* -**men** pescatore *m*.

fish·ery [ˈfɪʃərɪ] *n* zona di pesca.

fish·finger [ˈfɪʃˈfɪŋgəʳ] *n* bastoncino di pesce.

fish·ing [ˈfɪʃɪŋ] **1** *n* pesca. **2** *cpd*: ~ **boat** *n* pescareccio; ~ **grounds** *npl* zona di pesca; ~ **industry** *n* industria della pesca; ~ **line** *n* lenza; ~ **net** *n* rete *f* da pesca; ~ **port** *n* porto di pesca; ~ **rod** *n* canna da pesca; ~ **tackle** *n* attrezzatura da pesca.

fish·monger [ˈfɪʃˌmʌŋgəʳ] *n* (*Brit*) pescivendolo; ~**'s** (**shop**) pescheria.

fishy [ˈfɪʃɪ] *adj* (-**ier, -iest**) (*smell, taste: usu pej*) di pesce; (*fam: suspect*) losco(a), sospetto(a).

fis·sion [ˈfɪʃən] *n* fissione *f*; **atomic/nuclear** ~ fissione atomica/nucleare.

fis·sure [ˈfɪʃəʳ] *n* fessura, fenditura.

fist [fɪst] *n* pugno; **to shake one's** ~ (**at sb**) minacciare (qn) con il pugno.

fist·ful [ˈfɪstfʊl] *n* manciata.

fit [fɪt] **1** *adj* (-**ter, -test**) (**a**) (*suitable*) adatto(a); **to be** ~ **for sth** andare bene per qc; **to be** ~ **for nothing** non essere buono a niente; **a meal** ~ **for a king** un pranzo da re; **he's not** ~ **for the job** non è la persona adatta per questo lavoro; ~ **for habitation** abitabile; **he is not** ~ **company for my daughter** non è la compagnia adatta per mia figlia; **he's not** ~ **to teach** non è adatto all'insegnamento; **he's not** ~ **to drive** non è in condizione di guidare; **you're not** ~ **to be seen** non sei presentabile; **it's not** ~ **to eat** *or* **to be eaten** non è mangiabile *or* commestibile; **I'm** ~ **to drop** (*fam*) sto per crollare; **do as you think** *or* **see** ~ fai come meglio credi.

(**b**) (*Med*) in forma; (*Sport*) in condizione, in forma; **to keep** ~ tenersi in forma; **to be** ~ **for**

work (*after illness*) essere in grado di riprendere il lavoro; **to be** (**as**) ~ **as a fiddle** essere sano come un pesce.

2 *n*: **to be a good** ~ (*shoes*) calzare bene; (*clothes*) andare bene; **it's a rather tight** ~ mi sta un po' stretto.

3 *vt* (**a**) (*subj: clothes*) andare bene a; (*: key etc*) adattarsi a; **it** ~**s you well** ti sta bene; **it** ~**s me like a glove** mi sta a pennello.

(**b**) (*match: facts etc*) concordare con; (*: description*) corrispondere a; **the punishment should** ~ **the crime** la punizione dovrebbe essere adeguata al reato.

(**c**) (*put in place*) mettere, fissare; **to** ~ **a key in the lock** mettere una chiave nella serratura; **to have a carpet** ~**ted** far mettere una moquette; **to** ~ **sth into place** sistemare qc; **to** ~ **sth on sth** mettere qc a *or* su qc.

(**d**) (*supply*) fornire, dotare; **a car** ~**ted with a radio** una macchina fornita di radio; **she has been** ~**ted with a new hearing aid** le hanno messo un nuovo apparecchio acustico; **to** ~ **a person/ship for an expedition** equipaggiare una persona/nave per una spedizione.

(**e**) (*make* ~) rendere adatto(a); **to** ~ **a dress (on sb)** provare un vestito (su qn); **her experience** ~**s her for the job** la sua esperienza la rende adatta a questo lavoro.

4 *vi* (**a**) (*subj: clothes*) andare bene; (*: key, part, object*) andare, entrare.

(**b**) (*match: facts*) quadrare; (*: story*) reggere; (*: description*) calzare; **it all** ~**s now!** tutto è chiaro adesso!

♦ **fit in 1** *vi* + *adv* (*fact, statement*): **to** ~ **in (with)** corrispondere (con), concordare (con); **he left because he didn't** ~ **in** se ne è andato perché non riusciva ad integrarsi; **to** ~ **in with sb's plans** adattarsi ai progetti di qn. **2** *vt* + *adv* (*object*) far entrare; (*fig: appointment, visitor*) trovare il tempo per; (*plan, activity*): **to** ~ **in (with)** conciliare (con).

♦ **fit out** *vt* + *adv* (*ship*) allestire; (*person*) fornire, equipaggiare.

fit² [fɪt] *n* (**a**) (*Med*) attacco; **to have** *or* **suffer a** ~ avere un attacco di convulsioni; ~ **of coughing** attacco di tosse. (**b**) (*outburst*) accesso; ~ **of anger/enthusiasm** accesso d'ira/d'entusiasmo; **to have a** ~ **of crying** scoppiare in un pianto dirotto; **to have** *or* **throw a** ~ (*fam*) andare su tutte le furie; **to be in** ~**s (of laughter)** scoppiare dalle risa; **by** *or* **in** ~**s and starts** a sbalzi.

fit·ful [ˈfɪtfʊl] *adj* (*breeze, showers*) intermittente; (*wind*) a raffiche; (*sleep*) agitato(a).

fit·ment [ˈfɪtmənt] *n* (**a**) (*accessory: of machine*) accessorio. (**b**) = **fitting 2b**.

fit·ness [ˈfɪtnɪs] *n* (**a**) (*suitability: for post etc*): ~ (**for**) idoneità (a); (*: of remark*) appropriatezza. (**b**) (*health*) forma, salute *f*.

fit·ted [ˈfɪtɪd] *adj* (*garment*) modellato(a); ~ **carpet** moquette *f*; ~ **cupboards** armadi *mpl* a muro; ~ **kitchen** cucina componibile.

fit·ter [ˈfɪtəʳ] *n* (*Tech*) installatore/trice; (*of garment*) sarto/a.

fit·ting [ˈfɪtɪŋ] **1** *adj* (*suitable*) adatto(a); **it is** ~ **that** (*frm*) è opportuno che. **2** *n* (**a**) (*of dress*) prova. (**b**): ~**s** *npl* (*of house*) accessori *mpl*; **bathroom** ~**s** accessori per il bagno. **3** *cpd*: ~ **room** *n* (*in shop*) camerino.

five [faɪv] **1** *adj* cinque *inv*; **she is** ~ (**years old**) ha cinque anni; **they live at number** ~/ **at** ~ **Green Street** vivono al numero cinque/al numero cinque di Green Street; **there are** ~ **of us** siamo in cinque; **all** ~ **of them came** sono venuti tutti e cinque; **it costs ~ pounds** costa cinque sterline; **~ and a quarter/half** cinque e un quarto/e mezzo; **it's ~ (o'clock)** sono le cinque. **2** *n* cinque *m inv;* **to divide sth into ~** dividere qc in cinque parti; **they are sold in ~s** sono venduti in gruppi di cinque. **3** *cpd:* **~ o'clock shadow** *n (scherz):* **you've got a ~ o'clock shadow** dovresti farti la barba.

five-day week [ˌfaɪvdeɪ'wiːk] *n* settimana di 5 giorni (lavorativi).

fiv·er ['faɪvəʳ] *n (fam)* biglietto da 5 sterline.

fix [fɪks] **1** *n* **(a)** *(Aer, Naut)* posizione *f.* **(b)** *(fam: of drug)* pera. **(c)** *(fam: predicament)* pasticcio, guaio; **to be in a ~** essere in un pasticcio, essere nei guai; **to get o.s. into a ~** cacciarsi nei guai. **(d): the fight was a ~** *(fam)* l'incontro è stato truccato. **2** *vt* **(a)** *(gen, Phot, fig)* fissare; *(with string etc)* legare, fissare; **to ~ one's gaze on** fermare lo sguardo su; **to ~ the blame on sb/sth** dare *or* attribuire la colpa a qn/qc; **to ~ sth in one's mind** imprimersi qc nella mente. **(b)** *(date, price)* fissare, stabilire; *(fight, race)* truccare; **I'll ~ everything** ci penso io, sistemo tutto io; **I'll ~ him!** *(fam)* lo sistemo io!, lo metto a posto io! **(c)** *(repair)* accomodare, riparare. **(d)** *(make ready: meal, drink)* preparare; **to ~ one's hair** darsi una pettinata.

♦ **fix on 1** *vt + adv (badge, lid)* fissare, attaccare. **2** *vi + prep (decide on)* fissare.

♦ **fix up** *vt + adv (arrange: date, meeting)* fissare, stabilire; **to ~ sb up with sth** procurare qc a qn.

fixa·tion [fɪk'seɪʃən] *n (Psych, fig)* fissazione *f*, ossessione *f.*

fixa·tive ['fɪksətɪv] *n* fissativo.

fixed [fɪkst] *adj* **(a)** *(gen)* fisso(a); **at a ~ time** ad un'ora stabilita; **~ price** prezzo fisso. **(b): how are you ~ for money?** *(fam)* a soldi come stai?; **how are you ~ for this evening?** cosa fai stasera?

fix·ed·ly ['fɪksɪdlɪ] *adv* fissamente.

fix·ings ['fɪksɪŋz] *npl (Am Culin)* guarnizioni *fpl.*

fix·ture ['fɪkstʃəʳ] *n* **(a)** *(of house etc):* **~s** impianti *mpl.* **(b)** *(Sport)* partita, incontro.

fizz [fɪz] **1** *n* effervescenza. **2** *vi* frizzare.

fiz·zle ['fɪzl] *vi (also: ~ out: fire, firework)* finire per spegnersi; *(: enthusiasm, interest)* smorzarsi, svanire; *(: plan)* fallire.

fizzy ['fɪzɪ] *adj* **(-ier, -iest)** *(drink)* frizzante, effervescente.

fjord [fjɔːd] *n* fiordo.

flab·ber·gast·ed ['flæbəgɑːstɪd] *adj* sbalordito(a).

flab·by ['flæbɪ] *adj* **(-ier, -iest)** flaccido(a), floscio(a).

flag¹ [flæg] *n (also: ~stone)* pietra per lastricare.

flag² [flæg] **1** *n (gen)* bandiera; *(for charity etc)* bandierina. **2** *vt (also: ~ down: taxi)* far cenno di fermarsi a. **3** *cpd:* **~ day** *n* giornata in cui si vendono bandierine *(per beneficenza).*

flag³ [flæg] *vi (strength)* indebolirsi; *(person)* stancarsi; *(enthusiasm etc)* affievolirsi; *(conversation)* languire.

flag·pole ['flægpəul] *n* pennone *m.*

fla·grant ['fleɪɡrənt] *adj* flagrante.

flag·ship ['flægʃɪp] *n* nave *f* ammiraglia.

flail [fleɪl] *vt (arms, legs)* agitare.

flair [flɛəʳ] *n:* **to have a ~ (for)** essere portato(a) per.

flake [fleɪk] **1** *n (of paint, soap etc)* scaglia; *(of skin)* squama; *(of snow)* fiocco. **2** *vi (also: ~ off: paint)* scrostarsi; *(: skin)* squamarsi.

flaky ['fleɪkɪ] *adj* **(-ier, -iest)** *(paintwork)* scrostato(a); *(skin)* squamoso(a); **~ pastry** *(Culin)* pasta sfoglia.

flam·boy·ant [flæm'bɔɪənt] *adj (character, speech)* stravagante; *(dress etc)* sgargiante, vistoso(a); *(style)* fiorito(a), ornato(a).

flame [fleɪm] **1** *n* fiamma; **to burst into ~s** divampare; **old ~** *(fam)* vecchia fiamma. **2** *vi (also: ~ up)* divampare; **her cheeks ~d with embarrassment** arrossì per l'imbarazzo.

flam·ing ['fleɪmɪŋ] *adj* **(a)** *(red, orange)* acceso(a). **(b)** *(Brit fam: furious)* furibondo(a), furioso(a).

fla·min·go [flə'mɪŋɡəu] *n* fenicottero.

flam·mable ['flæməbl] *adj* infiammabile.

flan [flæn] *n (Culin)* flan *m inv.*

flange [flændʒ] *n (Tech: on wheel)* flangia.

flank [flæŋk] **1** *n (gen, Mil)* fianco. **2** *vt (Mil etc)* fiancheggiare.

flan·nel ['flænl] *n (face ~)* pezzuola (per lavarsi); *(fabric)* flanella; **~s** *(trousers)* pantaloni *mpl* di flanella.

flan·nel·ette [ˌflænə'lɛt] *n* flanella di cotone.

flap [flæp] **1** *n* **(a)** *(of pocket)* patta; *(of envelope)* linguetta; *(of table)* ribalta; *(Aer)* flap *m inv.* **(b)** *(movement):* **to give sth a ~** sbattere qc; *(sound):* **they could hear the ~ of the sails** sentivano sbattere le vele; **to get into a ~** *(fam)* farsi prendere dal panico. **2** *vt (subj: bird: wings)* sbattere; *(shake: sheets, newspaper)* agitare, sbattere. **3** *vi* **(a)** *(wings, sails, flag etc)* sbattere. **(b)** *(fam: panic)* farsi prendere dal panico.

flap·jack ['flæpdʒæk] *n (Am: pancake)* frittella.

flare [flɛəʳ] **1** *n* **(a)** *(blaze)* chiarore *m; (signal)* segnale *m* luminoso; *(Mil: for target)* razzo illuminante. **(b)** *(Sewing)* svasatura. **2** *vi (match, torch)* accendersi con una fiammata.

♦ **flare up** *vi + adv (fire)* divampare; *(fig: person)* saltar su; *(: revolt, situation etc)* scoppiare.

flared ['flɛəd] *adj (skirt, trousers etc)* svasato(a).

flash [flæʃ] **1** *n* **(a)** *(of light)* sprazzo, lampo; *(Am: torch)* torcia elettrica, lampadina tascabile; **~ of lightning** lampo; **~ of inspiration** lampo di genio; **a ~ in the pan** *(fig)* un fuoco di paglia; **in a ~** in un baleno. **(b)** *(news ~)* flash *m inv.* **(c)** *(Phot)* flash *m inv.* **2** *vt (light, torch)* far lampeggiare; *(look)* lanciare; *(signal: message)* segnalare; **to ~ one's headlights** *(Aut)* far lampeggiare i fari; **to ~ sth about** *(fig fam: flaunt)* ostentare qc. **3** *vi* **(a)** *(light)* lampeggiare; *(lightning)* guizzare, balenare; *(jewels)* brillare, scintillare. **(b)** *(move quickly: person, vehicle):* **to ~ by** *or* **past** passare come un lampo.

flash·back ['flæʃbæk] *n (Cine)* flashback *m inv.*

flash·cube ['flæʃkjuːb] *n (Phot)* flash *m inv.*

flash·gun ['flæʃɡʌn] *n (Phot)* lampeggiatore *m.*

flash·light ['flæʃlaɪt] *n (Am: torch)* lampadina tascabile.

flashy ['flæʃɪ] *adj* **(-ier, -iest)** *(car, clothes)* vistoso(a); *(person)* appariscente.

flask [flɑːsk] *n (for brandy etc)* fiaschetta; *(vacuum ~)* thermos *m inv* ®; *(Chem)* beuta.

flat¹ [flæt] **1** *adj* **(-ter, -test)** **(a)** *(gen)* piatto(a); *(smooth)* liscio(a), piano(a); *(tyre)* sgonfio(a), a terra; **as ~ as a pancake** *(fam)* completamente piatto; *(: Aut: tyre)* completamente sgonfio *or* a terra; **to fall ~ on one's face** cadere a terra lungo disteso, finire faccia a terra; **~ race** corsa piana. **(b)** *(final: refusal, denial)* categorico(a), netto(a); **I'm not going, and that's ~!** *(fam)* non ci vado e basta! **(c)** *(Mus: voice)* stonato(a); *(: instrument)* scordato(a); **C ~** do *m* bemolle. **(d)** *(dull, lifeless: taste, style)* piatto(a); *(: joke)* che non fa ridere; *(drink)* svampito(a); *(battery)* scarico(a); *(colour)* scialbo(a); **to be feeling rather ~** sentirsi giù di corda *or* di morale. **(e)** *(fixed):* **~ rate of pay**

tariffa unica di pagamento; **at a ~ rate** a una tariffa unica.
2 *adv* **(a)** *(absolutely: refuse, tell etc)* seccamente, recisamente; **~ broke** *(fam)* al verde, in bolletta; **in ten minutes ~** in dieci minuti spaccati; **(to work) ~ out** (lavorare) a più non posso. **(b): to spread a map out ~ on the floor** stendere una cartina sul pavimento; **to be ~ out** *(lying)* essere disteso *or* sdraiato; *(asleep)* dormire della grossa. **(c)** *(Mus)* stonato(a).
3 *n (of hand)* palmo; *(of sword)* parte *f* piatta; *(Mus)* bemolle *m*; *(Aut)* gomma a terra.
flat² [flæt] *n (Brit)* appartamento.
flat·fish ['flætfɪʃ] *n* pesce *m* piatto.
flat·footed [,flæt'fʊtɪd] *adj* dai piedi piatti.
flat·let ['flætlɪt] *n (Brit)* appartamentino.
flat·ly ['flætlɪ] *adv (refuse etc)* categoricamente, nettamente.
flat·mate ['flætmeɪt] *n*: **he's my ~** divide l'appartamento con me.
flat·ten ['flætn] *vt (road, field)* spianare, appiattire; *(house, city)* abbattere, radere al suolo; *(map etc)* spiegare, aprire; **to ~ o.s. against sth** appiattirsi contro qc.
♦ **flatten out 1** *vi + adv (road, countryside)* appiattirsi. **2** *vt + adv (path, paper)* spianare.
flat·ter ['flætə'] *vt (praise)* adulare, lusingare; *(show to advantage)* donare a; **this photo ~s you** in questa foto sei venuto molto bene; **to ~ o.s. that one is...** illudersi di essere... .
flat·ter·ing ['flætərɪŋ] *adj (person, remark)* lusinghiero(a); *(clothes etc)* che dona, che abbellisce; **this photo of you is not very ~** questa foto non ti fa onore.
flat·tery ['flætərɪ] *n* adulazione *f*, lusinghe *fpl*.
flatu·lence ['flætjʊləns] *n* flatulenza.
flaunt [flɔːnt] *vt (pej)* sfoggiare, ostentare.
flau·tist ['flɔːtɪst] *n* flautista *m/f*.
fla·vour, *(Am)* **fla·vor** ['fleɪvə'] **1** *n* sapore *m*, gusto; *(of ice-cream etc)* gusto; *(flavouring)* aroma *m*; *(fig)* atmosfera. **2** *vt*: **to ~ (with)** *(Culin: cake etc)* aromatizzare (con); *(: soup etc)* condire (con).
fla·vour·ing, *(Am)* **fla·vor·ing** ['fleɪvərɪŋ] *n (for cake etc)* aroma *m*; *(for soup)* condimento; **vanilla ~** aroma di vaniglia.
flaw [flɔː] *n (gen)* difetto; *(crack: in china)* incrinatura.
flaw·less ['flɔːlɪs] *adj* perfetto(a).
flax [flæks] *n* lino.
flaxen-haired ['flæksən'heəd] *adj* dai capelli biondi.
flay [fleɪ] *vt (skin)* scorticare; *(criticize)* criticare aspramente, stroncare.
flea [fliː] **1** *n* pulce *f*. **2** *cpd*: **~ market** *n* mercato delle pulci.
fleck [flek] **1** *n (of mud, paint, colour)* macchiolina; *(of dust)* granello. **2** *vt (with blood, mud etc)* macchiettare; **brown ~ed with white** marrone screziato di bianco.
fled [fled] *pt, pp of* **flee.**
fledg·ling ['fledʒlɪŋ] *n* uccellino.
flee [fliː] *pt, pp* **fled 1** *vt (town, country)* fuggire da; *(danger, enemy)* sfuggire a. **2** *vi*: **to ~ (from)** fuggire (da *or* davanti a); **to ~ to sb/sth** correre da qn/verso qc; **to ~ to safety** mettersi in salvo.
fleece [fliːs] **1** *n* vello. **2** *vt (fig fam: rob)* pelare.
fleecy ['fliːsɪ] *adj (-ier, -iest) (blanket)* soffice; *(cloud)* come ovatta.
fleet¹ [fliːt] *n* flotta; *(of cars)* parco; **they were followed by a ~ of cars** erano seguiti da un corteo di macchine.
fleet² [fliːt] *adj (poet)*: **~(-footed)** svelto(a).
fleet·ing ['fliːtɪŋ] *adj (glimpse)* fuggevole; *(mo-*

ment, beauty etc) fugace, passeggero(a).
Flem·ish ['flemɪʃ] **1** *adj* fiammingo(a). **2** *n (language)* fiammingo; **the ~** *npl (people)* i Fiamminghi.
flesh [fleʃ] **1** *n (gen)* carne *f*; *(of fruit)* polpa; **in the ~** in carne ed ossa; **my own ~ and blood** la mia famiglia; **it's more than ~ and blood can stand** è più di quanto un essere umano possa sopportare. **2** *cpd*: **~ wound** *n* ferita superficiale.
fleshy ['fleʃɪ] *adj (-ier, -iest)* carnoso(a); *(Bot: fruit)* polposo(a).
flew [fluː] *pt of* **fly.**
flex [fleks] **1** *n (of lamp, telephone etc)* filo. **2** *vt (body, knees)* piegare; *(muscles)* stirare.
flex·ible ['fleksəbl] *adj* flessibile; **~ working hours** orario di lavoro flessibile.
flick [flɪk] **1** *n (gen)* colpetto. **2** *vt (with finger)* dare un colpetto a; **she ~ed her hair out of her eyes** buttò i capelli da una parte. **3** *vi*: **the snake's tongue ~ed in and out** la lingua del serpente guizzava. **4** *cpd*: **~ knife** *n* coltello a serramanico.
♦ **flick off** *vt + adv (dust, ash)* mandare via con un colpetto.
♦ **flick through** *vi + prep (book etc)* scartabellare.
flick·er ['flɪkə'] **1** *n (of light, flame)* tremolio; *(of eyelid)* battito; *(of hope)* barlume *m*. **2** *vi (light)* tremolare; *(flame)* guizzare.
flies [flaɪz] *npl of* **fly.**
flight¹ [flaɪt] **1** *n* **(a)** *(gen)* volo; *(of bullet)* traiettoria; **in ~** in volo; **how long does the ~ take?** quanto dura il volo?; **~s of fancy** *(fig)* voli di fantasia; **in the top ~** *(fig)* fra i migliori. **(b): ~ (of stairs)** rampa; **he lives two ~s up** abita due piani sopra. **2** *cpd*: **~ deck** *n (on aircraft carrier)* ponte *m* di decollo; *(of aeroplane)* cabina di pilotaggio; **~ recorder** *n* registratore *m* di volo.
flight² [flaɪt] *n (act of fleeing)* fuga; **to put to ~** mettere in fuga; **to take ~** darsi alla fuga.
flighty ['flaɪtɪ] *adj (-ier, -iest)* capriccioso(a), frivolo(a).
flim·sy ['flɪmzɪ] *adj (-ier, -iest) (thin: dress)* leggero(a); *(weak: building etc)* poco solido(a); *(: excuse, argument)* che non sta in piedi.
flinch [flɪntʃ] *vi*: **to ~ (from)** ritrarsi da; **without ~ing** senza fiatare.
fling [flɪŋ] *(vb: pt, pp* **flung) 1** *n*: **to have a last ~** fare un'ultima follia; **to have one's ~** godersela; **to have a ~ at doing sth** cercare *or* tentare di fare qc. **2** *vt (stone etc)* lanciare, scagliare; **to ~ one's arms round sb** gettare le braccia al collo di qn; **the door was flung open** la porta fu spalancata; **to ~ o.s into a chair** buttarsi su una poltrona; **to ~ o.s. into a job** gettarsi a capofitto in un lavoro; **to ~ on one's clothes** vestirsi in fretta e furia.
♦ **fling away** *vt + adv (waste)* gettare via, sperperare.
♦ **fling out** *vt + adv (unwanted object)* buttare via; *(person)* buttar fuori.
flint [flɪnt] *n (Geol)* silice *f*; *(of lighter)* pietrina.
flip [flɪp] **1** *n* colpetto. **2** *vt*: **to ~ a coin** lanciare una moneta in aria; **he ~ped the book open** ha aperto il libro con un rapido gesto della mano. **3** *cpd*: **~ side** *n (of record)* retro.
♦ **flip through** *vi + prep (book, records)* dare una scorsa a.
flip·pan·cy ['flɪpənsɪ] *n* irriverenza, frivolità.
flip·pant ['flɪpənt] *adj* irriverente, frivolo(a).
flip·per ['flɪpə'] *n* pinna.
flirt [flɜːt] **1** *n (woman)* civetta; *(man)*: **he's a terrible ~** è un gran donnaiolo. **2** *vi*: **to ~ (with)** flirtare (con); *(woman only)* civettare (con); **to ~ with an idea** trastullarsi con un'idea.

flir·ta·tion [flɜː'teɪʃən] n flirt m inv.

flit [flɪt] **1** vi (bats, butterflies) svolazzare; **to ~ in/out** (person) entrare/uscire svolazzando. **2** n (Brit): **to do a (moonlight) ~** squagliarsela (per non pagare l'affitto, il conto in albergo etc).

float [fləʊt] **1** n (gen) galleggiante m; (cork) sughero; (in procession) carro; (sum of money) somma. **2** vt (boat, logs) far galleggiare; (refloat) riportare a galla; (launch: company, loan) lanciare; (Fin: currency) far fluttuare. **3** vi (gen) galleggiare; (ship) stare a galla; (bather) fare il morto; (Fin: currency) fluttuare; **to ~ downstream** essere trascinato dalla corrente; **~ing vote** voto oscillante.

♦ **float away, float off** vi + adv (in water) andare alla deriva; (in air) volare via.

flock [flɒk] **1** n (of sheep, also Rel) gregge m; (of birds) stormo; (of people) stuolo, folla. **2** vi (crowd) affollarsi, ammassarsi; **to ~ around sb** affollarsi intorno a qn.

floe [fləʊ] n (ice ~) banchisa.

flog [flɒg] vt frustare; **to ~ a dead horse** (fig fam) perdere il proprio tempo; **to ~ o.s. to death** (fig fam) ammazzarsi di fatica.

flog·ging ['flɒgɪŋ] n fustigazione f.

flood [flʌd] **1** n inondazione f; **the river is in ~** il fiume è in piena; **the F~** (Rel) il diluvio universale; **a ~ of letters** una marea di lettere; **she was in ~s of tears** era in un mare di lacrime. **2** vt (town, fields, fig) inondare, allagare; (Aut: carburettor) ingolfare; **to ~ the market** (Comm) inondare il mercato. **3** vi (river) straripare; **the crowd ~ed into the streets** la folla si riversò nelle strade. **4** cpd: **~ tide** n alta marea, marea crescente.

♦ **flood in** vi + adv entrare in grande quantità; **the light ~ed in through the window** una gran luce entrava dalla finestra.

♦ **flood out** vt + adv (house) inondare; **they were ~ed out** l'inondazione li ha costretti ad abbandonare le loro case.

flood·light ['flʌdlaɪt] (vb: pt, pp **~ed** or **floodlit**) **1** n riflettore m. **2** vt illuminare a giorno.

flood·lit ['flʌdlɪt] **1** pt, pp of **floodlight**. **2** adj illuminato(a) a giorno.

floor [flɔːʳ] **1** n (a) (gen) suolo; (of room) pavimento; (of sea, valley) fondo; (dance ~) pista; **to take the ~** (dancer) mettersi a ballare; **to have the ~** (speaker) prendere la parola. **(b)** (storey) piano. **ground ~** (Brit) pianterreno; **on the first ~** (Brit) al primo piano; (Am) al pianterreno; **top ~** ultimo piano. **2** vt (a) (room): **to ~ (with)** pavimentare (con). **(b)** (fam: knock down: opponent) atterrare; (: baffle) confondere; (: silence) ridurre al silenzio. **3** cpd: **~ covering** n rivestimento (di pavimento); **~ show** n spettacolo (di cabaret etc).

floor·board ['flɔːbɔːd] n asse f di pavimento.

flop [flɒp] **1** n (fam: failure) fiasco. **2** vi (a) (person): **to ~ (into/on)** lasciarsi cadere (in/su). **(b)** (fam: play) far fiasco; (: scheme) fallire.

flop·py ['flɒpɪ] adj (-ier, -iest) floscio(a); **~ disc** floppy disk m inv.

flo·ra ['flɔːrə] n flora.

flo·ral ['flɔːrəl] adj floreale; (fabric, dress) a fiori.

flor·id ['flɒrɪd] adj (complexion) florido(a); (style) fiorito(a).

flo·rist ['flɒrɪst] n fioraio/a.

flot·sam ['flɒtsəm] n: **~ and jetsam** relitti mpl galleggianti.

flounce[1] [flaʊns] n (frill) balza.

flounce[2] [flaʊns] vi: **to ~ in/out** entrare/uscire stizzito(a).

floun·der[1] ['flaʊndəʳ] n (fish) passera.

floun·der[2] ['flaʊndəʳ] vi (also: **~ about**: in water,

mud etc) dibattersi, annaspare; (: in speech etc) impappinarsi, esitare.

flour ['flaʊəʳ] n farina.

flour·ish ['flʌrɪʃ] **1** n (movement) gran gesto; (under signature) svolazzo; (Mus: fanfare) fanfara; **to do sth with a ~** fare qc con ostentazione. **2** vt (weapon, stick etc) brandire. **3** vi (gen) fiorire; (person) essere in piena forma; (writer, artist) avere successo; (business etc) prosperare.

flour·ish·ing ['flʌrɪʃɪŋ] adj (plant) rigoglioso(a); (person) florido(a), in gran forma; (business) fiorente.

flout [flaʊt] vt (order) contravvenire; (advice) ignorare deliberatamente; (conventions, society) sfidare.

flow [fləʊ] **1** n (of river, also Elec) corrente f; (of tide) flusso; (of blood: from wound) uscita; (: in veins) circolazione f; (of words etc) fiume m; (of insults, orders) caterva; **the ~ of traffic** la circolazione. **2** vi (gen) fluire; (tide) salire; (blood in veins, traffic) circolare; (hair) ricadere (morbidamente); **~ing robes** abiti mpl di linea morbida; **money ~ed in** (fig) i soldi sono arrivati in grande quantità; **the river ~s into the sea** il fiume si getta nel mare; **to keep the conversation ~ing** mantenere la conversazione scorrevole. **3** cpd: **~ chart** n, **~ diagram** n organigramma m.

flow·er ['flaʊəʳ] **1** n fiore m; **in ~** in fiore. **2** vi fiorire. **3** cpd: **~ arrangement** n composizione f floreale; **~ shop** n negozio di fiori.

flower·bed ['flaʊəbed] n aiuola.

flower·pot ['flaʊəpɒt] n vaso da fiori.

flow·ery ['flaʊərɪ] adj (meadow) fiorito(a), in fiore; (dress, material) a fiori; (style, speech) fiorito(a).

flown [fləʊn] pt of **fly**.

flu [fluː] n (fam) influenza.

fluc·tu·ate ['flʌktjʊeɪt] vi (cost) fluttuare; (person): **he ~d between fear and excitement** passava da uno stato di paura a uno stato di eccitazione.

fluc·tu·a·tion [,flʌktjʊ'eɪʃən] n fluttuazione f, oscillazione f.

flue [fluː] n canna fumaria.

flu·en·cy ['fluːənsɪ] n facilità, scioltezza; **his ~ in English** la sua scioltezza nel parlare l'inglese.

flu·ent ['fluːənt] adj (style) fluido(a); (speaker) dalla parola facile; (French) corrente; **he is ~ in Italian** parla l'italiano correntemente.

fluff [flʌf] **1** n (from blankets etc) pelucchi mpl; (of chicks, kittens) lanugine f. **2** vt (a) (also: **~ out**) rendere soffice or vaporoso(a); (of feathers) arruffare; **to ~ up the pillows** sprimacciare i cuscini. **(b)** (fam: make mistake in) impaperarsi nel recitare.

fluffy ['flʌfɪ] adj (toy) di peluche; (bird) coperto(a) di lanugine; (pullover) morbido(a) e peloso(a).

flu·id ['fluːɪd] **1** adj (substance, movement) fluido(a); (plan, arrangements) flessibile, elastico(a). **2** n fluido, liquido; (in diet) liquido.

fluke [fluːk] n colpo di fortuna; **by a ~** per puro caso.

flung [flʌŋ] pt, pp of **fling**.

flunk [flʌŋk] vt (fam: course, esame) essere bocciato(a) or respinto(a) in or a.

fluo·res·cent [fluə'resnt] adj (lighting, tube) fluorescente.

fluo·ride ['fluəraɪd] **1** n fluoruro. **2** cpd: **~ toothpaste** n dentifricio al fluoro.

flur·ry ['flʌrɪ] n (of snow) turbine m; (of wind) folata; **a ~ of activity** uno scoppio di attività; **in a ~** in uno stato di agitazione or eccitazione.

flush [flʌʃ] **1** n (a) (lavatory ~) sciacquone m. **(b)** (blush) rossore m; (Med): **hot ~es** vampate fpl di calore. **(c)** (of beauty, health, youth) rigo-

glio, pieno vigore m; **in the first ~ of victory**
nell'ebbrezza della vittoria; **in a ~ of excitement**
in uno stato di eccitazione. **(d)** *(in poker)* colore
m. **2** *adj* **(a)** *(level)* : **~ (with)** a livello (di *or* con); **a**
door ~ with the wall una porta a livello con la
parete. **(b)** *(fam)*: **to be ~ (with money)** essere
pieno(a) di soldi. **3** *vi (person, face)*: **to ~ (with)**
arrossire (di). **4** *vt* **(a)** pulire con un getto d'acqua; **to ~ the lavatory** tirare l'acqua. **(b)** *(also:* **~**
out: *game, birds)* far alzare in volo; (*: fig: criminal*)
stanare.
♦ **flush away** *vt* + *adv*: **to ~ away** *(down lavatory)*
buttare nel gabinetto (e tirare l'acqua).
flus·ter ['flʌstə^r] **1** *n* stato di agitazione. **2** *vt (con-*
fuse, upset) mettere in agitazione, innervosire; **to**
get ~ed agitarsi.
flute [fluːt] *n* flauto.
flut·ter ['flʌtə^r] **1** *n (of wings, eyelashes)* battito; **to**
be in a ~ *(fig)* essere in uno stato di agitazione; **to**
have a ~ *(fam: gamble)* fare una scommessa. **2** *vt*
(wings) battere; **to ~ one's eyelashes at sb** fare
gli occhi dolci a qn. **3** *vi (bird etc)* svolazzare;
(flag) sventolare; *(heart)* palpitare.
flux [flʌks] *n*: **to be in a state of ~** essere in
continuo mutamento.
fly[1] [flaɪ] *n* mosca; **the ~ in the ointment** *(fig)* la
piccola pecca che sciupa tutto; **there are no**
flies on him *(fig)* è un tipo in gamba, la sa
lunga.
fly[2] [flaɪ] *pt* **flew**, *pp* **flown 1** *vi* **(a)** *(gen)* volare; *(air*
passengers) andare in aereo; *(flag)* sventolare;
the plane flew over London l'aereo ha sorvolato
Londra. **(b)** *(move quickly: time)* volare, passare
in fretta; **to ~ past sb** *(subj: car, person)* sfrecciare davanti a qn; **the door flew open** la porta si
è spalancata all'improvviso; **to knock** *or* **send**
sth/sb ~ing far volare qc/qn; **I must ~!** devo
scappare!; **to let ~ at sb** scagliarsi contro qn; **to**
~ into a rage infuriarsi. **(c)** *(flee)* fuggire, scappare; **to ~ for one's life** salvare la pelle scappan-
do. **2** *vt (aircraft)* pilotare; *(passenger, cargo)* trasportare in aereo; *(flag)* battere; **to ~ the**
Atlantic sorvolare l'Atlantico; **to ~ a kite** far
volare un aquilone. **3** *n (on trousers: also:* **flies)**
chiusura.
♦ **fly away** *vi* + *adv* volar via.
♦ **fly in 1** *vi* + *adv (person)* arrivare in aereo;
(plane) arrivare; **he flew in from Rome** è venuto
da Roma in aereo. **2** *vt* + *adv (supplies, troops)*
trasportare in aereo.
♦ **fly off** *vi* + *adv* volare via.
♦ **fly-fishing** ['flaɪˌfɪʃɪŋ] *n* pesca con la mosca.
fly·ing ['flaɪɪŋ] **1** *adj (gen)* volante; **to pass an exam**
with ~ colours superare un esame con brillanti
risultati; **~ saucer** disco volante; **~ start** partenza lanciata; **to get off to a ~ start** *(fig)* avere un
inizio brillante. **2** *n (action)* volo; *(activity)* aviazione *f*.
fly·leaf ['flaɪliːf] *n, pl* **-leaves** risguardo.
fly·over ['flaɪˌəʊvə^r] *n (Aut)* cavalcavia *m inv*.
fly·sheet ['flaɪʃiːt] *n (for tent)* sopratetto.
fly·weight ['flaɪweɪt] **1** *n* peso mosca. **2** *cpd (con-*
test) di pesi mosca.
fly·wheel ['flaɪwiːl] *n (Tech)* volano.
F.M. *abbr of* **frequency modulation.**
foal [fəʊl] *n* puledro.
foam [fəʊm] **1** *n (gen)* schiuma. **2** *vi (sea)* schiumeg-
giare; **to ~ at the mouth** avere la schiuma alla
bocca. **3** *cpd*: **~ rubber** *n* gommapiuma.
fob [fɒb] *vt*: **to ~ sb off (with sth)** rifiliare qc a qn;
to ~ sb off with promises tenere qn buono con
delle promesse.
f.o.b. *abbr of* **free on board.**

fo·cal ['fəʊkəl] *adj (Tech)* focale; **~ point** punto
focale; *(fig)* centro.
fo·c'sle ['fəʊksl] *n* castello di prua.
fo·cus ['fəʊkəs] **1** *n, pl* **~es** *or* **foci** ['fəʊkaɪ] *(gen)*
fuoco; *(of attention etc)* centro; **to be out of ~**
(Phot) essere sfocato. **2** *vt*: **to ~ (on)** *(camera,*
instrument) mettere a fuoco (su); *(attention, eyes*
etc) focalizzare (su). **3** *vi*: **to ~ (on)** *(light, heat*
rays) convergere (su); **to ~ on sth** *(eyes, person,*
also Phot) mettere a fuoco qc.
fod·der ['fɒdə^r] *n* foraggio.
foe [fəʊ] *n (poet)* nemico.
foe·tal, *(Am)* **fe·tal** ['fiːtl] *adj* fetale.
foe·tus, *(Am)* **fe·tus** ['fiːtəs] *n* feto.
fog [fɒg] **1** *n* nebbia. **2** *cpd*: **~ lamp** *n (Aut)* faro *m*
antinebbia *inv*.
fog·bound ['fɒgbaʊnd] *adj* fermo(a) a causa della
nebbia.
fo·gey ['fəʊgɪ] *n (fam)*: **old ~** matusa *m inv*.
fog·gy ['fɒgɪ] *adj* **(-ier, -iest)** nebbioso(a); **it's ~** c'è
nebbia; **I haven't the ~iest (idea)** *(fam)* non ne ho
la più pallida idea.
fog·horn ['fɒghɔːn] *n* corno da nebbia.
foi·ble ['fɔɪbl] *n* fissazione *f*, mania.
foil[1] [fɔɪl] *n* **(a)** *(also:* **tin~)** carta stagnola; **to act as**
a ~ to sb/sth *(fig)* far risaltare qn/qc. **(b)**
(Fencing) fioretto.
foil[2] [fɔɪl] *vt (thief)* fermare; *(attempt)* far fallire.
foist [fɔɪst] *vt*: **to ~ sth on sb** rifilare qc a qn.
fold[1] [fəʊld] *n (Agr)* ovile *m*.
fold[2] [fəʊld] **1** *n (also Geol)* piega. **2** *vt (gen)* piegare;
(wings) ripiegare; **she ~ed the paper in two** pie-
gò in due la carta; **to ~ one's arms** incrociare le
braccia. **3** *vi (chair, table)* piegarsi; *(fam: fail:*
business venture) crollare; *(: play)* chiudere.
♦ **fold away 1** *vi* + *adv (table, bed)* piegarsi, essere
pieghevole. **2** *vt* + *adv (clothes etc)* piegare, mettere a posto.
♦ **fold up 1** *vi* + *adv (fam: fail: business venture)*
fallire. **2** *vt* + *adv (paper etc)* piegare.
fold·er ['fəʊldə^r] *n (file)* cartella; *(binder)* raccoglitore *m*.
fold·ing ['fəʊldɪŋ] *adj (chair, doors)* pieghevole.
fo·li·age ['fəʊlɪdʒ] *n* fogliame *m*.
fo·lio ['fəʊlɪəʊ] *n (sheet)* foglio; *(book)* volume *m* in
folio.
folk [fəʊk] **1** *n (people)* gente *f*; **country/city ~**
gente di campagna/di città; **my ~s** *(fam)* i miei. **2**
cpd: **~ music** *n* musica folk; **~ singer** *n* cantante
m/f folk; **~ song** *n* canzone *f* folk.
folk·lore ['fəʊklɔː^r] *n* folclore *m*.
fol·low ['fɒləʊ] **1** *vt (gen)* seguire; *(football team)*
fare il tifo per; **the road ~s the coast** la strada
segue la costa; **we're being ~ed** qualcuno ci sta
seguendo; **to ~ sb's advice** seguire il consiglio di
qn; **he ~ed suit** ha fatto altrettanto; **I don't quite**
~ you non ti capisco *or* seguo affatto. **2** *vi* **(a)**
(gen) seguire; **as ~s** come segue; **to ~ in sb's**
footsteps seguire le orme di qn; **what is there to**
~? che c'è dopo?; **I don't ~** non capisco. **(b)**
(also: **~ on:** *deduction etc)* risultare; **it doesn't ~**
that... non vuol dire che...; **that doesn't ~** non
necessariamente.
♦ **follow on** *vi* + *adv* **(a)** *see* **follow 2b. (b)** *(con-*
tinue): **to ~ on from** seguire.
♦ **follow out** *vt* + *adv (implement: idea, plan)* eseguire, portare a termine.
♦ **follow through 1** *vt* + *adv* = **follow out. 2** *vi* +
adv (Sport) portare a termine l'azione.
♦ **follow up** *vt* + *adv (investigate: case, clue)*
esaminare. **(b)** *(take further action on: offer, sug-*
gestion) seguire. **(c)** *(reinforce: success, victory)*
rafforzare. **2** *vi* + *adv (Ftbl etc)*: **to ~ up with**

another goal segnare di nuovo.

fol·low·er ['fɒləʊə'] n (disciple) seguace m/f, discepolo/a; (of team) tifoso/a.

fol·low·ing ['fɒləʊɪŋ] **1** adj seguente; ~ **wind** vento in poppa; **the ~ day** il giorno seguente, l'indomani. **2** n **(a)** (Pol etc) seguito; (Sport) tifosi mpl. **(b): he said the ~** ha detto quanto segue; **see the ~** (in document etc) vedi quanto segue.

follow-up ['fɒləʊˌʌp] **1** n seguito. **2** cpd: ~ **letter** n sollecito; ~ **visit** n (Med) visita di controllo.

fol·ly ['fɒlɪ] n follia, pazzia.

fond [fɒnd] adj (-er, -est) (loving) affettuoso(a), tenero(a); (doting) che stravede; (fervent: hope, desire) grande; **to be ~ of sb** voler bene a qn; **she's ~ of swimming** le piace nuotare; **she's ~ of dogs** le piacciono i cani.

fon·dant ['fɒndənt] n fondente m.

fon·dle ['fɒndl] vt accarezzare.

fond·ly ['fɒndlɪ] adv (lovingly) affettuosamente; **he ~ believed that...** ha avuto l'ingenuità di credere che... .

fond·ness ['fɒndnɪs] n: ~ **(for sth)** predilezione f (per qc); ~ **(for sb)** affetto (per qn).

font [fɒnt] n (in church) fonte m battesimale.

food [fuːd] **1** n cibo; (for plants) fertilizzante m; **I've no ~ left in the house** non c'è più niente da mangiare in casa; **the ~ at the hotel is terrible** si mangia malissimo in albergo; **to be off one's ~** (fam) avere perso l'appetito; ~ **for thought** (fig) qualcosa su cui riflettere. **2** cpd: ~ **poisoning** n intossicazione f alimentare.

food·stuffs ['fuːdstʌfs] npl generi mpl alimentari.

fool [fuːl] **1** n sciocco/a, stupido/a; (jester) buffone m, giullare m; **you ~!** stupido!; **don't be a ~!** non fare lo stupido!; **I was a ~ not to** go sono stato stupido a non andarci; **some ~ of a civil servant** uno stupido di impiegato statale; **to play the ~** fare lo stupido; **to live in a ~'s paradise** (fig) vivere di illusioni; **he is nobody's ~** non gliela si dà a bere; **to make a ~ of sb** far fare a qn la figura dello scemo; **to make a ~ of o.s.** coprirsi di ridicolo. **2** adj (Am) sciocco(a). **3** vt (deceive) ingannare; **you can't ~ me** non mi inganni. **4** vi fare lo stupido; **I was only ~ing** stavo solo scherzando.

♦ **fool about, fool around** vi + adv **(a)** (waste time) perdere tempo. **(b)** (act the ~) fare lo stupido.

fool·hardy ['fuːlˌhɑːdɪ] adj (rash) temerario(a), imprudente.

fool·ish ['fuːlɪʃ] adj (senseless) sciocco(a), insensato(a); (ridiculous) ridicolo(a), assurdo(a); **that was very ~ of you** è stato molto sciocco da parte tua.

fool·ish·ly ['fuːlɪʃlɪ] adv stupidamente.

fool·ish·ness ['fuːlɪʃnɪs] n stupidità.

fool·proof ['fuːlpruːf] adj (method) infallibile; (machine) facile da usare.

fools·cap ['fuːlskæp] n carta protocollo.

foot [fʊt] **1** n, pl **feet** **(a)** (gen) piede m; (of animal) zampa; (of page, stairs etc) fondo; **on ~** a piedi; **to jump/rise to one's feet** balzare/mettersi in piedi; **to be on one's feet** essere in piedi; (after illness) essersi rimesso; **it's wet under ~** è bagnato per terra. **(b)** (fig phrases): **to find one's feet** ambientarsi; **to get cold feet** avere fifa; **to get under sb's feet** stare tra i piedi di qn; **to have one ~ in the grave** avere un piede nella fossa; **to put one's ~ down** (say no) imporsi; (Aut) schiacciare l'acceleratore; **to get a ~ in the door** essere già a metà strada; **to put one's ~ in it** fare una gaffe; **to put one's feet up** (fam) riposarsi; **I've never set ~ there** non ci ho mai messo piede; **to put one's**

best ~ forward (hurry) sbrigarsi; **to get off on the right/wrong ~** iniziare sul piede giusto/ sbagliato; **she didn't put a ~ wrong** non ha fatto neanche un errore. **(c)** (measure) piede m; **he's 6 ~ or feet tall** ≃ è alto 1 metro e 80. **2** vt: **to ~ the bill** (fam) pagare il conto.

foot-and-mouth (dis·ease) ['fʊtən'maʊθ(dɪˌziːz)] n afta epizootica.

foot·ball ['fʊtbɔːl] **1** n (Sport) calcio; (ball) pallone m. **2** cpd (ground, team, supporters) di calcio; ~ **league** n torneo di calcio; ~ **match** n partita di calcio.

foot·ball·er ['fʊtbɔːlə'] n calciatore m.

foot·bridge ['fʊtbrɪdʒ] n passerella.

-footed ['fʊtɪd] adj suf: **light~** dal passo leggero.

foot·hill ['fʊthɪl] n collina (bassa).

foot·hold ['fʊthəʊld] n punto d'appoggio; **to gain a ~** (fig) farsi una posizione.

foot·ing ['fʊtɪŋ] n (foothold) punto d'appoggio; (fig: basis) base f; **to lose one's ~** perdere l'equilibrio; **on an equal ~** (fig) su un piano di parità; **to be on a friendly ~ with sb** essere in rapporti d'amicizia con qn.

foot·lights ['fʊtlaɪts] npl (in theatre) luci fpl della ribalta.

foot·man ['fʊtmən] n, pl **-men** lacchè m inv.

foot·mark ['fʊtmɑːk] n orma.

foot·note ['fʊtnəʊt] n nota in fondo alla pagina.

foot·path ['fʊtpɑːθ] n (track) sentiero; (pavement) marciapiede m.

foot·print ['fʊtprɪnt] n orma, impronta.

foot·step ['fʊtstɛp] n passo.

foot·wear ['fʊtwɛə'] n calzatura.

foot·work ['fʊtwɜːk] n (Sport) lavoro di gambe.

for [fɔː'] **1** prep **(a)** (indicating destination, intention) per; **the train ~ London** il treno per Londra; **he left ~ Rome** è partito per Roma; **he swam ~ the shore** nuotava verso la riva; **is this ~ me?** è per me questo?; **here's a letter ~ you** ecco una lettera per te; **it's time ~ lunch** è ora di pranzo.

(b) (indicating purpose): **what ~?** perché?; **what's this button ~?** a cosa serve questo bottone?; **clothes ~ children** vestiti per bambini; **a cupboard ~ toys** un armadio per i giocattoli; **to pray ~ peace** pregare per la pace; **fit ~ nothing** buono a niente.

(c) (representing) per; **member ~ Hove** deputato che rappresenta Hove; **G ~ George** G come George; **I'll ask him ~ you** glielo chiederò a nome tuo; **I took him ~ his brother** l'ho scambiato or preso per suo fratello.

(d) (in exchange for) per; **to pay 50 pence ~ a ticket** pagare 50 penny per un biglietto; **I sold it ~ £5** l'ho venduto per 5 sterline.

(e) (with regard to) per; **as ~ him/that** quanto a lui/ciò; **a gift ~ languages** un dono per le lingue; **anxious ~ success** avido di successo; **it's cold ~ July** è freddo per luglio; **he's mature ~ his age** è maturo per la sua età; ~ **every one who voted yes, 50 voted no** per ogni voto a favore, ce n'erano 50 contro; **there's nothing ~ it but to jump** non c'è altro da fare che saltare.

(f) (in favour of) per, a favore di; **are you ~ or against us?** sei per noi o contro di noi?; **the campaign ~** la campagna a favore di or per; **I'm all ~ it** sono tutto a favore; **vote ~ me!** votate per me!

(g) (because of) per, a causa di; **if (it were) not ~ you** se non fosse per te; ~ **this reason** per questa ragione; **do it ~ my sake** fallo per me; **famous ~ its cathedral** famoso per la sua cattedrale; **to shout ~ joy** gridare di gioia; ~ **fear of being criticised** per paura di essere criticato.

(h) *(distance)* per; **there were roadworks** ~ **5 km** c'erano lavori in corso per 5 km; **we walked** ~ **miles** abbiamo camminato per chilometri.

(i) *(time)*: **he was away** ~ **2 years** è stato via per 2 anni; **it has not rained** ~ **3 weeks** non piove da 3 settimane; **I have known her** ~ **years** la conosco da anni; **I'll be away** ~ **3 weeks** starò via 3 settimane; **can you do it** ~ **tomorrow?** lo puoi fare per domani?; **he won't be back** ~ **a while** non tornerà per un po'.

(j) *(with infin clauses)*: ~ **this to be possible...** perché ciò sia possibile...; **it's not** ~ **me to decide** non sta a me decidere; **it would be best** ~ **you to go** sarebbe meglio che te ne andassi; **there is still time** ~ **you to do it** hai ancora tempo per farlo; **he brought it** ~ **us to see** l'ha portato per farcelo vedere.

(k) *(phrases)*: **oh** ~ **a cup of tea!** cosa non darei per una tazza di tè!; **you're** ~ **it!** *(fam)* vedrai adesso!

2 *conj* dal momento che, poiché.

for·age ['forɪdʒ] *vi*: **to** ~ **(for)** andare in cerca (di).

for·ay ['foreɪ] *n (esp Mil)* incursione *f*.

for·bad(e) [fə'bæd] *pt of* forbid.

for·bear·ance [fɔː'bɛərəns] *n* pazienza, tolleranza.

for·bid [fə'bɪd] *pt* forbad(e), *pp* forbidden *vt* proibire; **to** ~ **sb sth** proibire qc a qn; **to** ~ **sb to do sth** proibire a qn di fare qc; **'smoking** ~**den'** 'vietato fumare'.

for·bid·ding [fə'bɪdɪŋ] *adj* minaccioso(a).

force [fɔːs] **1** *n* **(a)** *(gen)* forza; **to resort to** ~ ricorrere alla violenza; ~ **of gravity** forza di gravità; **a** ~ **5 wind** un vento forza 5; **the** ~**s of evil** *(fig)* le forze del male; **by** ~ con la forza; **by** ~ **of habit** per abitudine; **by sheer** ~ **of character he...** grazie alla forza del suo carattere lui...; **to be in** ~ *(Law)* essere in vigore; **to turn out in** ~ manifestare in gran numero *or* in massa. **(b)** *(body of men)* gruppo; *(Mil)* forza; **the** ~ *(police* ~*)* la polizia, il corpo di polizia; **the** ~**s** *(Mil)* le forze armate; **the sales** ~ *(Comm)* l'effettivo dei rappresentanti; **to join** ~**s** unire le forze.

2 *vt* **(a)** *(compel: person)* forzare, costringere; **to** ~ **sb to do sth** costringere qn a fare qc. **(b)** *(impose)*: **to** ~ **sth on sb** imporre qc a qn; **to** ~ **o.s. on sb** imporsi a qn, imporre la propria presenza a qn. **(c)** *(push, squeeze)* schiacciare; **he** ~**d the clothes into the suitcase** ha fatto entrare a forza i vestiti nella valigia; **to** ~ **one's way into** entrare con la forza in; **to** ~ **one's way through** *(crowd)* farsi strada tra; *(hole)* attraversare *or* passare attraverso con la forza in. **(d)** *(break open: lock)* forzare; **to** ~ **an entry** entrare con la forza; **to** ~ **sb's hand** *(fig)* forzare la mano a qn. **(e)** *(produce with effort)*: **to** ~ **a smile/a reply** sforzarsi di sorridere/rispondere; **don't** ~ **the situation** non forzare le cose. **(f)** *(obtain by* ~*)*: **smile, confession)** strappare.

♦ **force back** *vt + adv (crowd, enemy)* respingere; *(tears)* ingoiare.

♦ **force down** *vt + adv (food)* sforzarsi di mangiare; *(aircraft)* forzare ad atterrare.

♦ **force out** *vt + adv (person)* costringere ad uscire; *(cork)* far uscire con la forza.

forced [fɔːst] *adj* forzato(a).

force-feed ['fɔːsfiːd] *pt, pp* force-fed ['fɔːsfed] *vt* sottoporre ad alimentazione forzata.

force·ful ['fɔːsfʊl] *adj (personality)* forte; *(argument)* valido(a).

force·meat ['fɔːsmiːt] *n (Culin)* ripieno.

for·ceps ['fɔːseps] *npl* forcipe *m*.

for·cible ['fɔːsəbl] *adj (done by force)* fatto(a) con

la forza; *(effective: argument, style)* convincente, efficace.

ford [fɔːd] **1** *n* guado. **2** *vt* guadare, passare a guado.

fore [fɔːʳ] **1** *adv (Naut)*: ~ **and aft** da prua a poppa. **2** *n*: **to come to the** ~ mettersi in luce.

fore·arm ['fɔːrɑːm] *n* avambraccio.

fore·bear ['fɔːbɛəʳ] *n* antenato.

fore·bod·ing [fɔː'bəʊdɪŋ] *n* presentimento.

fore·cast ['fɔːkɑːst] *(vb: pt, pp* ~ *or* ~**ed) 1** *n* previsione *f*; *(weather* ~*)* previsioni del tempo. **2** *vt (also Met)* prevedere.

fore·close [fɔː'kləʊz] *vt (Law: also:* ~ **on)** precludere il riscatto di.

fore·court ['fɔːkɔːt] *n (of garage)* spiazzo; *(of station)* piazzale *m*.

fore·fathers ['fɔːˌfɑːðəz] *npl* progenitori *mpl*.

fore·finger ['fɔːˌfɪŋgəʳ] *n* indice *m*.

fore·front ['fɔːfrʌnt] *n*: **to be in the** ~ **of** essere all'avanguardia di.

fore·going ['fɔːgəʊɪŋ] *adj* precedente.

fore·gone ['fɔːgɒn] *adj*: **it was a** ~ **conclusion** era un risultato scontato.

fore·ground ['fɔːgraʊnd] *n (Art)* primo piano; **in the** ~ *(fig)* in una posizione di primo piano.

fore·hand ['fɔːhænd] *n (Tennis)* diritto.

fore·head ['fɔrɪd] *n* fronte *f*.

for·eign ['fɒrən] *adj* **(a)** *(language, tourist)* straniero(a); *(policy, trade etc)* estero(a); **the F**~ **Office** *(Brit)* il Ministero degli Esteri; ~ **currency** valuta estera; ~ **exchange market** mercato dei cambi. **(b)** *(not natural)*: ~ **body** corpo estraneo; **deceit is** ~ **to his nature** ingannare non è nel suo carattere.

for·eign·er ['fɒrənəʳ] *n* straniero/a.

fore·leg ['fɔːleg] *n* zampa anteriore.

fore·man ['fɔːmən] *n, pl* -men *(of workers)* caporeparto; *(Law: of jury)* portavoce *m* della giuria.

fore·most ['fɔːməʊst] **1** *adj (outstanding: writer, politician)* più importante. **2** *adv*: **first and** ~ innanzitutto.

fore·name ['fɔːneɪm] *n* nome *m* di battesimo.

fore·noon ['fɔːnuːn] *n* mattina.

fo·ren·sic [fə'rensɪk] *adj (evidence, laboratory)* medico-legale; *(medicine)* legale; ~ **scientist** esperto della (polizia) scientifica.

fore·run·ner ['fɔːˌrʌnəʳ] *n* precursore *m*.

fore·see [fɔː'siː] *pt* foresaw [fɔː'sɔː], *pp* foreseen *vt* prevedere.

fore·see·able [fɔː'siːəbl] *adj (opportunity)* prevedibile; **in the** ~ **future** nell'immediato futuro.

fore·seen [fɔː'siːn] *pp of* foresee.

fore·shore ['fɔːʃɔːʳ] *n* litorale *m*.

fore·sight ['fɔːsaɪt] *n* previdenza.

fore·skin ['fɔːskɪn] *n (Anat)* prepuzio.

for·est ['fɒrɪst] *n* foresta.

fore·stall [fɔː'stɔːl] *vt (anticipate: event, accident)* prevenire; *(: rival, competitor)* anticipare.

for·est·ry ['fɒrɪstrɪ] *n* silvicoltura.

fore·tell [fɔː'tel] *pt, pp* foretold *vt* predire.

fore·thought ['fɔːθɔːt] *n* previdenza; **to act with** ~ essere previdente.

fore·told [fɔː'təʊld] *pt, pp of* foretell.

for·ever [fər'evəʳ] *adv (eternally)* per sempre, eternamente; *(fam: incessantly, repeatedly)* sempre, di continuo.

fore·warn [fɔː'wɔːn] *vt* avvisare in precedenza; ~**ed is forearmed** uomo avvisato è mezzo salvato.

fore·woman ['fɔːˌwʊmən] *n, pl* -women caporeparto *f inv*; *(of jury)* portavoce *f* della giuria.

fore·word ['fɔːwɜːd] *n* prefazione *f*.

for·feit ['fɔːfɪt] **1** *n (in game)* penitenza. **2** *vt (esp*

Law: one's right, status) perdere.

for·gave [fə'geɪv] *pt of* **forgive.**

forge [fɔːdʒ] **1** *n* (*furnace*) fornace *f*; (*of blacksmith*) fucina. **2** *vt* (**a**) (*metal*) forgiare; (*fig: friendship, plan, unity etc*) forgiare, formare. (**b**) (*falsify: document etc*) contraffare. **3** *vi:* **to ~ ahead** andare avanti con determinazione.

forged [fɔːdʒd] *adj* (*document*) falsificato(a), contraffatto(a); (*banknote, signature*) falso(a).

forg·er ['fɔːdʒəʳ] *n* falsario/a; contraffattore/trice.

for·gery ['fɔːdʒərɪ] *n* (*act*) falsificazione*f*, contraffazione *f*; (*thing*) falso/a.

for·get [fə'gɛt] *pt* **forgot,** *pp* **forgotten 1** *vt* dimenticare; **to ~ to do sth** dimenticare di fare qc; **to ~ how to do sth** dimenticare come si fa qc; **she never ~s a face** è fisionomista; **never to be forgotten** indimenticabile; **~ it!** (*fam*) lascia perdere!; **to ~ o.s.** (*lose self-control*) perdere la testa. **2** *vi* dimenticarsi, scordarsi; **I've forgotten all about it** me ne sono completamente dimenticato; **let's ~ about it!** non ne parliamo più!

for·get·ful [fə'gɛtfʊl] *adj* (*absent-minded*) distratto(a), di poca memoria; **it was very ~ of me not to...** è stata una grande dimenticanza quella di non... .

forget-me-not [fə'gɛtmɪnɒt] *n* nontiscordardimé *m inv.*

for·give [fə'gɪv] *pt* **forgave,** *pp* **forgiven** *vt* (*person, fault*) perdonare; **to ~ sb for sth/for doing sth** perdonare qc a qn/a qn di aver fatto qc.

for·give·ness [fə'gɪvnɪs] *n* (*pardon*) perdono; (*willingness to forgive*) clemenza, indulgenza.

for·giv·ing [fə'gɪvɪŋ] *adj* indulgente.

for·go [fɔː'gəʊ] *pt* **forwent,** *pp* **forgone** [fɔː'gɒn] *vt* (*do without*) rinunciare a, fare a meno di.

for·got [fə'gɒt] *pt of* **forget.**

for·got·ten [fə'gɒtən] *pp of* **forget.**

fork [fɔːk] **1** *n* (*at table*) forchetta; (*Agr*) forca, forcone *m*; (*in road*) biforcazione *f*, bivio. **2** *vi* (*road*) biforcarsi.

♦**fork out 1** *vt* + *adv* (*money, cash*) sborsare, tirare fuori. **2** *vi* + *adv* tirare fuori i soldi.

forked [fɔːkt] *adj* (*tail, branch*) biforcuto(a); (*lightning*) a zigzag.

fork-lift truck [,fɔːklɪft'trʌk] *n* carrello elevatore.

for·lorn [fə'lɔːn] *adj* (*person*) sconsolato(a); (*deserted: place*) abbandonato(a); (*desperate: attempt*) disperato(a); **a ~ hope** una speranza vana.

form [fɔːm] **1** *n* (**a**) (*gen*) forma; **in the ~ of** a forma di, sotto forma di; **the same thing in a new ~** la stessa cosa presentata in modo diverso; **a ~ of apology** una specie di scusa; **~ and content** contenuto e forma; **to take ~** prendere forma. (**b**) (*Sport, fig*): **to be in good ~** essere in forma; **true to ~** come sempre; **he was in great ~ last night** era in piena forma ieri sera. (**c**) (*document*) modulo. (**d**) (*frm: etiquette*) forma; **it's a matter of ~** è una questione di forma; **it's bad ~** è maleducato. (**e**) (*bench*) banco. (**f**) (*Brit Scol*) classe *f*; **in the first ~** ≃ in prima media.
2 *vt* (*gen*) formare; (*plan*) concepire; (*idea, opinion*) formarsi, farsi; (*habit*) prendere; **to ~ a circle/a queue** fare un cherchio/una coda; **he ~ed it out of a lump of clay** l'ha plasmato *or* modellato su un blocco di creta; **to ~ a government/group** formare un governo/gruppo; **those who ~ed the group** quelli che facevano parte del gruppo; **to ~ part of sth** far parte di qc.
3 *vi* formarsi.

for·mal ['fɔːməl] *adj* (*gen*) formale; (*official: visit, occasion, acceptance*) ufficiale; **~ garden** giar-

dino all'italiana; **there was no ~ agreement** non c'era un contratto formale; **~ dress** abito da cerimonia; (*evening dress*) abito da sera; **~ training** preparazione *f* specifica.

for·mal·ity [fɔː'mælɪtɪ] *n* formalità *f inv;* **it's a mere ~** è una semplice formalità.

for·mal·ize ['fɔːməlaɪz] *vt* rendere ufficiale.

for·mal·ly ['fɔːməlɪ] *adv* (*see adj*) in modo formale; ufficialmente; **to be ~ invited** ricevere un invito ufficiale.

for·mat ['fɔːmæt] *n* formato.

for·ma·tion [fɔː'meɪʃən] *n* formazione *f.*

forma·tive ['fɔːmətɪv] *adj* formativo(a).

for·mer ['fɔːməʳ] **1** *adj* (**a**) (*earlier, previous*) vecchio(a) (*before n*), precedente; (*: chairman, wife etc*) ex *inv* (*before n*); **in ~ days** nei tempi passati, in altri tempi; **the ~ president** l'ex presidente. (**b**) (*of two*) primo(a). **2** *pron:* **the ~** (*... the latter*) il primo (*... l'ultimo*).

for·mer·ly ['fɔːməlɪ] *adv* in passato, precedentemente.

For·mi·ca [fɔː'maɪkə] *n* ® Fòrmica ®.

for·mi·dable ['fɔːmɪdəbl] *adj* (*task, difficulties*) formidabile, terribile; (*person, appearance*) che incute rispetto.

for·mu·la ['fɔːmjʊlə] *n, pl* **formulae** ['fɔːmjʊliː] *or* **~s** (*Math, Chem etc*) formula; **F~ One** (*Aut*) formula uno.

for·mu·late ['fɔːmjʊleɪt] *vt* formulare.

for·ni·cate ['fɔːnɪkeɪt] *vi* fornicare.

for·sake [fə'seɪk] *pt* **forsook** [fə'sʊk], *pp* **forsaken** [fə'seɪkən] *vt* (*person*) abbandonare; (*place*) lasciare.

fort [fɔːt] *n* (*Mil*) forte *m;* **to hold the ~** (*fig*) prendere le redini (della situazione).

for·te ['fɔːtɪ] *n* forte *m.*

forth [fɔːθ] *adv* (**a**) in avanti; **to go back and ~** andare avanti e indietro; **to set ~** mettersi in cammino; **from this day ~** d'ora in poi. (**b**): **and so ~** e così via, e via dicendo.

forth·com·ing [fɔː'kʌmɪŋ] *adj* (*election, event*) prossimo(a); (*film*) che sta per uscire, imminente; (*book*) di prossima pubblicazione; **if help is ~** se c'è chi è disposto ad aiutare; **he wasn't very ~ about it** non sembrava molto disposto a parlarne.

forth·right ['fɔːθraɪt] *adj* (*person, answer etc*) franco(a), schietto(a).

forth·with ['fɔːθ'wɪθ] *adv* immediatamente, subito.

for·ti·eth ['fɔːtɪɪθ] **1** *adj* quarantesimo(a). **2** *n* (*in series*) quarantesimo/a; (*fraction*) quarantesimo; *for usage see* **fifth.**

for·ti·fi·ca·tion [fɔːtɪfɪ'keɪʃən] *n* fortificazione *f.*

for·ti·fy ['fɔːtɪfaɪ] *vt* (*Mil*) fortificare; (*fig: person*) armare; (*enrich: food*) arricchire; **fortified wine** vino ad alta gradazione alcolica.

for·ti·tude ['fɔːtɪtjuːd] *n* forza d'animo.

fort·night ['fɔːtnaɪt] *n* (*Brit*) quindici giorni, quindicina di giorni; **a ~ (from) today** oggi a quindici; **it's a ~ since...** sono due settimane da quando... .

fort·night·ly ['fɔːtnaɪtlɪ] (*esp Brit*) **1** *adj* quindicinale, bimensile. **2** *adv* ogni quindici giorni.

for·tress ['fɔːtrɪs] *n* fortezza.

for·tui·tous [fɔː'tjuːɪtəs] *adj* fortuito(a).

for·tu·nate ['fɔːtʃənɪt] *adj* (*coincidence, event, person*) fortunato(a); **he is ~ to have...** ha la fortuna di avere... .

for·tu·nate·ly ['fɔːtʃənɪtlɪ] *adv* fortunatamente.

for·tune ['fɔːtʃən] *n* (**a**) (*chance*) fortuna; **by good ~** per fortuna; **to tell sb's ~** predire l'avvenire a qn. (**b**) (*money*) fortuna; **to come into a ~** ereditare una fortuna; **to make a** ~ farsi una fortuna *or* un patrimonio; **a small** ~ *(fam)* un patrimonio.

fortune-hunter ['fɔːtʃən,hʌntəʳ] *n* cacciatore *m* di dote.

fortune-teller ['fɔːtʃən,telǝʳ] *n* indovino/a, chiromante *m/f*.

for-ty ['fɔːtɪ] *adj*, *n* quaranta *(m) inv*; **to have** ~ **winks** *(fam)* fare *or* schiacciare un pisolino; *for usage see* **fifty**.

fo-rum ['fɔːrəm] *n (History)* foro; *(fig)* luogo di pubblica discussione.

for-ward ['fɔːwəd] **1** *adj* **(a)** *(in position, movement)* in avanti; *(in time)* in anticipo; ~ **line** *(Sport)* linea d'attacco; *(Mil)* prima linea; ~ **planning** programmazione*f* in anticipo; ~ **thinking** dalle idee innovatrici. **(b)** *(precocious: child)* precoce; *(presumptuous: person, remark)* insolente, sfacciato(a). **2** *n (Sport)* attaccante *m*. **3** *vt (dispatch: goods)* spedire; *(send on: letter)* inoltrare; *(fig: sb's plans)* promuovere, appoggiare; **'please** ~**'** 'si prega di inoltrare'.

for-ward(s) ['fɔːwəd(z)] *adv (in place)* in avanti; *(in time)* avanti, innanzi; **to push o.s.** ~ farsi avanti, mettersi in evidenza; **to come** ~ farsi avanti; **from this time** ~ d'ora in poi, d'ora innanzi.

for-ward-ing ad-dress ['fɔːwədɪŋə'dres] *n:* **he didn't leave a** ~ non ha lasciato un nuovo indirizzo.

for-went [fɔː'went] *pt of* **forgo**.

fos-sil ['fɒsl] **1** *n* fossile *m*. **2** *adj* fossile; ~ **fuel** combustibile *m* fossile.

fos-ter ['fɒstəʳ] **1** *vt (child)* allevare; *(hope, ambition)* nutrire, accarezzare; *(encourage)* incoraggiare. **2** *adj (parent)* affidatario(a); *(child)* preso(a) in affido; ~ **brother** fratellastro.

fought [fɔːt] *pt*, *pp of* **fight**.

foul [faʊl] **1** *adj (putrid, disgusting: smell, breath, taste)* disgustoso(a); *(: water, air)* puzzolente, fetido(a); *(: nasty: weather)* brutto(a), orribile; *(: mood)* nero(a); *(obscene: language)* volgare; ~ **play** *(Sport)* gioco scorretto; **the police suspect** ~ **play** la polizia sospetta un atto criminale; **to fall** ~ **of sb/the law** entrare in contrasto con qn/con la giustizia. **2** *n (Sport)* fallo; *(Boxing)* colpo basso. **3** *vt* **(a)** *(pollute: air)* impestare; **the dog** ~**ed the pavement** il cane ha sporcato il marciapiede. **(b)** *(Sport: opponent)* commettere un fallo su. **(c)** *(entangle: anchor, propeller)* impigliarsi in.

found[1] [faʊnd] *pt*, *pp of* **find**.

found[2] [faʊnd] *vt (gen)* fondare; *(opinion, belief)* fondare, basare; **a statement** ~**ed on fact** una dichiarazione basata sulla realtà.

foun-da-tion [faʊn'deɪʃən] **1** *n (act, organization)* fondazione *f*; *(Archit)*: ~**s** *npl* fondamenta *fpl*; *(fig: basis)* fondamento, base *f*; **to lay the** ~**s** gettare le fondamenta; *(fig)* gettare le basi; **the story is without** ~ la storia è infondata. **2** *cpd*: ~ **cream** *n* fondo *m* tinta *inv*; ~ **stone** *n*: **to lay the** ~ **stone** posare la prima pietra.

found-er[1] ['faʊndəʳ] *n* fondatore/trice.

found-er[2] ['faʊndəʳ] *vi (Naut, also fig)* affondare, colare a picco.

found-ing ['faʊndɪŋ] *adj*: ~ **fathers** *(esp Am)* padri *mpl* fondatori; ~ **member** socio fondatore.

found-ry ['faʊndrɪ] *n* fonderia.

fount [faʊnt] *n* **(a)** *(poet: source)* fonte *f*, sorgente *f*. **(b)** *(in printing)* caratteri *mpl*.

foun-tain ['faʊntɪn] **1** *n (also fig)* fontana; *(drinking* ~*)* fontanella. **2** *cpd*: ~ **pen** *n* penna stilografica.

four [fɔːʳ] **1** *adj* quattro *inv*. **2** *n* quattro *m inv*; **on all** ~**s** (a) carponi; *for usage see* **five**.

four-footed [,fɔː'fʊtɪd] *adj* quadrupede.

four-letter word ['fɔː'letə'wəːd] *n* parolaccia.

four-poster ['fɔː'pəʊstəʳ] *n (also:* ~ **bed)** letto a quattro colonne.

four-score ['fɔː,skɔːʳ] *adj (old)* ottanta *inv*.

four-some ['fɔːsəm] *n (game)* partita a quattro; **we went in a** ~ siamo andati in quattro.

four-teen ['fɔː'tiːn] *adj*, *n* quattordici *(m) inv*; *for usage see* **five**.

four-teenth ['fɔː'tiːnθ] **1** *adj* quattordicesimo(a). **2** *n (in series)* quattordicesimo/a; *(fraction)* quattordicesimo; *for usage see* **fifth**.

fourth [fɔːθ] **1** *adj* quarto(a). **2** *n (in series)* quarto/a; *(fraction)* quarto; *(Aut: also:* ~ **gear)** quarta; *for usage see* **fifth**.

fowl [faʊl] *n* pollame *m*, volatile *m*.

fox [fɒks] **1** *n* volpe *f*. **2** *vt (deceive)* ingannare; *(puzzle)* lasciare perplesso(a). **3** *cpd*: ~ **fur** *n* volpe *f*, pelliccia di volpe.

fox-glove ['fɒksglʌv] *n (Bot)* digitale *f*.

fox-hunting ['fɒks,hʌntɪŋ] *n* caccia alla volpe.

fox-trot ['fɒkstrɒt] *n* fox-trot *m inv*.

foy-er ['fɔɪeɪ] *n* ridotto, foyer *m inv*.

fra-cas ['frækɑː] *n* rissa, lite *f*.

frac-tion ['frækʃən] *n (Math)* frazione *f*; **move it just a** ~ *(fig)* spostalo un pochino.

frac-tion-al-ly ['frækʃnəlɪ] *adv* un tantino, minimamente.

frac-tious ['frækʃəs] *adj (person, mood)* irritabile; **to be in a** ~ **mood** essere di cattivo umore *or* irritabile.

frac-ture ['fræktʃəʳ] **1** *n* frattura. **2** *vt* fratturare; **to** ~ **one's arm** fratturarsi un braccio. **3** *vi* fratturarsi.

frag-ile ['frædʒaɪl] *adj* fragile; **I'm feeling rather** ~ **this morning** *(hum: esp after drinking)* mi sento piuttosto debole stamattina.

frag-ment ['frægmənt] **1** *n* frammento. **2** [fræg'ment] *vi* frammentarsi.

frag-men-tary ['frægməntərɪ] *adj* frammentario(a).

fra-grance ['freɪgrəns] *n (of flowers etc)* fragranza; *(perfume, of toiletries)* profumo.

fra-grant ['freɪgrənt] *adj* fragrante.

frail [freɪl] *adj (-er, -est) (person, health, furniture)* fragile; *(fig: hope, relationship)* tenue, debole.

frail-ty ['freɪltɪ] *n (see adj)* fragilità; debolezza.

frame [freɪm] **1** *n (of person)* corporatura, ossatura; *(of ship, building, tent)* struttura; *(of spectacles)* montatura; *(of bicycle)* telaio; *(of picture)* cornice *f*; *(of window, door)* telaio, intelaiatura; *(Cine)* immagine *f*; ~ **of reference** sistema *m* di riferimento; ~ **of mind** stato d'animo, umore *m*; **in a happy** ~ **of mind** di buon umore. **2** *vt* **(a)** *(picture)* incorniciare. **(b)** *(formulate: plan etc)* ideare; *(: question)* formulare; *(: sentence)* costruire. **(c):** **to** ~ **sb** *(fam)* incastrare qn.

frame-work ['freɪmwɜːk] *n (also fig)* struttura.

franc [fræŋk] *n* franco.

France [frɑːns] *n* Francia.

fran-chise ['fræntʃaɪz] *n (Pol)* diritto di voto; *(Comm)* concessione *f*.

frank[1] [fræŋk] *adj (-er, -est)* franco(a).

frank[2] [fræŋk] *vt (letter)* affrancare.

frank-fur-ter ['fræŋk,fɜːtəʳ] *n* würstel *m inv*.

frank-in-cense ['fræŋkɪnsens] *n* incenso.

frank-ly ['fræŋklɪ] *adv* francamente.

frank-ness ['fræŋknɪs] *n* franchezza.

fran-tic ['fræntɪk] *adj (activity, pace)* frenetico(a); *(desperate: need, desire)* pazzo(a), sfrenato(a); *(: search)* affannoso(a); *(person)* fuori di sé; ~ **with worry** fuori di sé dalla preoccupazione; ~ **with joy** pazzo di gioia.

fra-ter-nal [frə'tɜːnl] *adj* fraterno(a).

fra-ter-nity [frə'tɜːnɪtɪ] *n* fraternità; *(Am Univ)* associazione f studentesca maschile.

frat·er·nize ['frætənaɪz] vi (esp Mil): **to ~ (with)** fraternizzare (con).

fraud [frɔːd] n (trickery, trick) truffa; (Law) frode f; (person) imbroglione/a, impostore/a.

fraudu·lent ['frɔːdjʊlənt] adj (behaviour) disonesto(a); (claims) fraudolento(a).

fraught [frɔːt] adj (tense) teso(a); **~ with danger** pieno di pericoli.

fray[1] [freɪ] n (old: fight) zuffa; **ready for the ~** (also fig) pronto a battersi.

fray[2] [freɪ] **1** vt (cloth, cuff, rope) consumare; **tempers were getting ~ed** (tutti) cominciavano a innervosirsi. **2** vi consumarsi.

freak [friːk] **1** n (abnormal: person) fenomeno da baraccone; (: animal, plant) mostro; (: event) avvenimento eccezionale; (fam: enthusiast) fanatico/a; **a ~ of nature** un capriccio della natura; **the result was a ~** il risultato è stato un caso eccezionale; **health ~** (fam) fanatico della salute. **2** adj (storm, conditions) anormale; (victory) inatteso(a).

♦ **freak out** vi + adv (fam: abandon convention) scatenarsi; (: on drugs) andare fuori di testa.

freak·ish ['friːkɪʃ] adj (result, appearance) strano(a), bizzarro(a); (moods) capriccioso(a); (weather) anormale.

freck·le ['frɛkl] n lentiggine f.

freck·led ['frɛkld] adj lentigginoso(a).

free [friː] **1** adj (-r, -st) **(a)** (at liberty) : **~ (from or of)** libero(a) (da); **~ from ties/cares** senza legami/preoccupazioni; **to be ~ of pain** non soffrire; **feel ~ (to help yourself)** fai pure; **to break ~ (of)** liberarsi (da); **to set ~** liberare; **~ and easy** rilassato; **he is not ~ to choose** non è libero di scegliere; **to give ~ rein to one's anger** etc dare libero sfogo alla propria rabbia etc; **to give sb a ~ hand** dare carta bianca a qn.

(b) (not occupied) libero(a); **is this seat ~?** è libero questo posto?; **are you ~ tomorrow?** sei libero domani?; **to have one's hands ~** avere le mani libere.

(c) (generous, open): **~ (with)** aperto(a) (con); (improper: behaviour, language) spinto(a); **to be ~ with one's money** non badare a quanto si spende; **he's too ~ with his remarks** è sempre pronto alla critica.

(d) (costing nothing: ticket, delivery) gratuito(a), gratis inv; **~ of charge** gratuito; **~ on board** (abbr f.o.b.) (Comm) franco bordo; **admission ~** entrata libera.

2 adv (without charge) gratuitamente, gratis; **I got in ~ or for ~** (fam) sono entrato gratis.

3 vt (gen) liberare; (untie: person, animal) sciogliere; **to ~ o.s. from** or of sth sbarazzarsi di qc.

4 cpd: **~ enterprise** n liberalismo economico; **~ gift** n regalo, omaggio; **~ kick** n (Ftbl) calcio di punizione; **~ love** n amore m libero; **~ sample** n campione m gratuito; **~ speech** n libertà di parola; **~ verse** n verso libero; **~ will** n libero arbitrio; **of his own ~ will** di sua propria volontà.

free·dom ['friːdəm] **1** n: **~ (from)** libertà (da); **to give sb the ~ of one's house** mettere la propria casa a disposizione di qn; **the ~ of the press** la libertà di stampa; **to give sb the ~ of the city** dare a qn la cittadinanza onoraria; **~ of speech** libertà di parola; **~ of movement** libertà di movimento. **2** cpd: **~ fighter** n combattente m/f per la libertà.

free-for-all ['friːfərˌɔːl] n parapiglia m generale.

free·hold ['friːhəʊld] n proprietà assoluta.

free·lance ['friːlɑːns] **1** adj: **~ contributor** colla-

borator·e/trice esterno(a); **~ work** collaborazione f esterna. **2** n collaboratore/trice esterno(a). **3** vi (journalist) essere un(a) giornalista indipendente.

free·ly ['friːlɪ] adv (confess, speak etc) liberamente, francamente; (generously) generosamente; **you may come and go ~** puoi andare e venire come vuoi.

free·mason ['friː,meɪsn] n massone m.

free·post ['friːpəʊst] n affrancatura a carica del destinatario.

free-range ['friː,reɪndʒ] adj (hen) ruspante; (eggs) di gallina ruspante.

free·sia ['friːzɪə] n fresia.

free·style ['friːstaɪl] n (in swimming) stile m libero.

free·way ['friːweɪ] n (Am) autostrada (senza pedaggio).

free·wheel [,friː'wiːl] vi (coast: on bicycle) andare a ruota libera; (: in car) andare in folle.

freeze [friːz] pt **froze**, pp **frozen** **1** vt (water) gelare; (food) congelare; (industrially) surgelare; (prices, wages, assets) bloccare, congelare. **2** vi (Met) gelare; (water, lake) ghiacciare; (food) congelarsi; (keep still) bloccarsi; **I'm freezing** mi sto congelando; **freezing fog** nebbia gelata; **to ~ to death** morire assiderato; **~!** non muoverti! **3** n (Met) gelata; (of prices, wages etc) blocco.

♦ **freeze over** vi + adv (lake, river) ghiacciarsi; (windows, windscreen) coprirsi di ghiaccio.

♦ **freeze up** vi + adv gelarsi.

freez·er ['friːzəʳ] n congelatore m; (in fridge) freezer m inv.

freez·ing ['friːzɪŋ] n (also: **~ point**): **5 degrees below ~** 5 gradi sotto zero.

freight [freɪt] n (goods transported) merce f, merci fpl; (charge) prezzo del trasporto. **2** vt (transport: goods) trasportare. **3** cpd (train, yard) merci inv.

French [frɛntʃ] **1** adj francese; (lesson, teacher etc) di francese. **2** n (language) francese m; **the ~** npl (people) i Francesi. **3** cpd: **~ bean** n fagiolino; **~ Canadian** adj, n francocanadese (m/f); **~ dressing** n (Culin) condimento per insalata; **~ fries** npl (Am) patatine fpl fritte; **~ windows** npl portafinestra.

French·man ['frɛntʃmən] n francese m.

French·woman ['frɛntʃˌwʊmən] n francese f.

fre·net·ic [frə'nɛtɪk] adj frenetico(a).

fren·zy ['frɛnzɪ] n frenesia; **he was in a ~ of anxiety** era quasi impazzito dall'ansia.

fre·quen·cy ['friːkwənsɪ] **1** n frequenza; **high/low ~** alta/bassa frequenza. **2** cpd: **~ modulation** n (abbr **F.M.**) modulazione f di frequenza (abbr **F.M.**).

fre·quent ['friːkwənt] **1** adj (gen) frequente; (visitor) abituale. **2** [frɪ'kwɛnt] vt frequentare.

fre·quent·ly ['friːkwəntlɪ] adv frequentemente, spesso.

fres·co ['frɛskəʊ] n affresco.

fresh [frɛʃ] **1** adj (-er, -est) **(a)** (gen: not stale) fresco(a); (new: sheet of paper, supplies, approach) nuovo(a); (: news) recente; **to put ~ courage into sb** infondere coraggio a qn; **to make a ~ start** cominciare da capo; **I need some ~ air** ho bisogno di aria fresca; **in the ~ air** all'aria aperta; **as ~ as a daisy** fresco come una rosa. **(b)** (not salt: water) dolce. **(c)** (fam: cheeky) sfacciato(a); **to get ~ with sb** prendersi delle libertà con qn. **(d)** (invigorating: breeze) fresco(a); **it's a bit ~** (Met) fa un po' freschino. **2** adv (baked, picked) fresco, da poco; **bread ~ from the oven** pane appena uscito dal forno; **to come ~ from New York** essere arrivato fresco fresco da New York.

fresh·en ['frɛʃn] vi (wind) rinforzarsi.
♦ **freshen up** vt + adv rinfrescara; **to** ~ **(o.s.) up** darsi una rinfrescata.
fresh·er ['frɛʃəʳ] n (Brit Univ fam) = **freshman.**
fresh·ly ['frɛʃlɪ] adv di recente, appena.
fresh·man ['frɛʃmən] n, pl **-men** (Univ) matricola.
fresh·ness ['frɛʃnɪs] n (see adj) freschezza (also of news); novità; impertinenza.
fresh·water ['frɛʃwɔ:təʳ] adj: ~ **fish** pesce m d'acqua dolce.
fret [frɛt] vi (worry) preoccuparsi; **don't** ~ non preoccuparti; **the baby is** ~**ting for its mother** il bambino piange perché vuole la madre.
fret·ful ['frɛtful] adj (child) irritabile.
fret·saw ['frɛtsɔ:] n sega da traforo.
fret·work ['frɛtwɜ:k] n lavoro di traforo.
Freud·ian ['frɔɪdɪən] adj freudiano(a); ~ **slip** lapsus m inv freudiano.
fri·ar ['fraɪəʳ] n frate m.
fric·as·see ['frɪkəsɪ] n (Culin) fricassea.
frica·tive ['frɪkətɪv] n fricativa.
fric·tion ['frɪkʃən] n frizione f, attrito.
Fri·day ['fraɪdɪ] n venerdì m inv; for usage see **Tuesday.**
fridge [frɪdʒ] n (Brit) frigorifero, frigo.
fried [fraɪd] adj (Culin) fritto(a); ~ **egg** uovo fritto.
friend [frɛnd] n amico/a; (at school etc) compagno/a; (at work) collega m/f; **a** ~ **of mine** un mio amico; **to make** ~**s with sb** fare amicizia con qn; **let's be** ~**s** facciamo pace; **we're just good** ~**s** siamo solo buoni amici; **Society of F**~**s** (Rel) Quaccheri mpl.
friend·li·ness ['frɛndlɪnɪs] n cordialità.
friend·ly ['frɛndlɪ] adj (-ier, -iest) cordiale, amichevole; **to be** ~ **to sb** essere cordiale con qn; **to be** ~ **with sb** essere amico di qn; **a** ~ **(match)** (Ftbl) una partita amichevole.
friend·ship ['frɛndʃɪp] n amicizia.
frieze [fri:z] n (Archit) fregio.
frig·ate ['frɪgɪt] n (Naut) fregata.
fright [fraɪt] n paura, spavento; **to get a** ~ spaventarsi; **what a** ~ **you gave me!** mi hai fatto paura!; **to take** ~ **(at)** spaventarsi (all'idea di); **she looked a** ~ (fam) era conciata da far paura.
fright·en ['fraɪtn] vt spaventare; **to** ~ **sb out of their wits** far morire qn dallo spavento; **to be** ~**ed of sth** avere paura di qc; **he was** ~**ed into doing it** l'ha fatto per paura; **I was** ~**ed to death** ero morto di paura.
♦ **frighten away, frighten off** vt + adv (birds, children etc) scacciare (facendogli paura).
fright·en·ing ['fraɪtnɪŋ] adj pauroso(a).
fright·ful ['fraɪtful] adj terribile, spaventoso(a).
fright·ful·ly ['fraɪtfəlɪ] adv (fam: late, cold) terribilmente, spaventosamente; **it was** ~ **good of her** è stato gentilissimo da parte sua; **I'm** ~ **sorry** mi dispiace moltissimo.
frig·id ['frɪdʒɪd] adj (atmosphere, look etc) glaciale; (Med) frigido(a).
frill [frɪl] n (on dress etc) fronzolo; **without** ~**s** (fig) senza fronzoli.
fringe [frɪndʒ] 1 n (on shawl, rug) frangia; (Brit: of hair) frangia, frangetta; (also: ~**s**: of forest) margine m; (: of city) periferia; **on the** ~ **of society** ai margini della società. 2 cpd: ~ **benefits** npl vantaggi mpl; ~ **theatre** n teatro d'avanguardia.
frisk [frɪsk] 1 vt (fam: suspect) perquisire. 2 vi (frolic) saltellare, sgambettare.
frisky ['frɪskɪ] adj (-ier, -iest) (person, horse) vispo(a).
frit·ter[1] ['frɪtəʳ] n (Culin) frittella.
frit·ter[2] ['frɪtəʳ] vt (also: ~ **away**) sprecare.
fri·vol·ity [frɪ'vɒlɪtɪ] n frivolezza.

frivo·lous ['frɪvələs] adj frivolo(a).
friz·zy ['frɪzɪ] adj (-ier, -iest) (hair) crespo(a); **to go** ~ incresparsi.
fro [frəu] adv: **to and** ~ avanti e indietro; **to go to and** ~ **between** fare la spola tra.
frock [frɒk] n (woman's) abito, vestito; (of monk) tonaca.
frog [frɒg] n rana; **to have a** ~ **in one's throat** avere la voce rauca.
frog·man ['frɒgmən] n, pl **-men** sommozzatore m, uomo rana.
frog·march ['frɒgmɑ:tʃ] vt: **to** ~ **sb in/out** portar qn dentro/fuori con la forza.
frol·ic ['frɒlɪk] pt, pp ~**ked** vi sgambettare.
from [frɒm] prep (a) (indicating starting place) da; **where is he** ~? da dove viene?, di dov'è?; **where has he come** ~? da dove arriva?; ~ **London to Glasgow** da Londra a Glasgow; ~ **house to house** di casa in casa; **to escape** ~ **sth/sb** fuggire da qc/qn.
(b) (indicating time) da; ~ **now on** d'ora in poi, d'ora innanzi; ~ **one o'clock to** or **until** or **till two** dall'una alle due; (as) ~ **Friday** da or a partire da venerdì; ~ **time to time** ogni tanto.
(c) (indicating distance) da; **the hotel is 1 km** ~ **the beach** l'albergo è a 1 km dalla spiaggia; **a long way** ~ **home** lontano da casa.
(d) (indicating origin etc) da; **a letter** ~ **my sister** una lettera da mia sorella; **a telephone call** ~ **Mr Smith** una telefonata dal Signor Smith; **tell him** ~ **me** diglielo da parte mia; **to drink** ~ **a stream/the bottle** bere a un ruscello/dalla bottiglia; **a quotation** ~ **Shakespeare** una citazione di Shakespeare; **to steal sth** ~ **sb** rubare qc a qn; **where did you get that** ~? dove l'hai trovato?; **take the gun** ~ **him!** levagli la pistola!; **painted** ~ **life** dipinto dal vero.
(e) (indicating price, number etc) da; **we have shirts** ~ **£8 (upwards)** abbiamo camicie da 8 sterline in su; **prices range** ~ **£10 to £50** i prezzi vanno dalle 10 alle 50 sterline; **there were** ~ **10 to 15 people there** c'erano da 10 a 15 persone.
(f) (indicating change): **things went** ~ **bad to worse** le cose andarono di male in peggio; **the interest rate increased** ~ **6% to 10%** il tasso d'interesse è aumentato dal 6% al 10%.
(g) (indicating difference): **to be different** ~ **sb** essere diverso da qn; **he can't tell red** ~ **green** non sa distinguere il rosso dal verde.
(h) (because of, on the basis of): **to act** ~ **conviction** agire per convinzione; **to die** ~ **exposure** morire assiderato; **weak** ~ **hunger** debole per la fame; ~ **what I can see** a quanto vedo; ~ **what I understood** da quanto ho capito; ~ **experience** per esperienza.
(i) (with prep): ~ **above** or **over sth** da sopra qc, dall'alto di qc; ~ **beneath** or **underneath sth** da sotto qc; ~ **inside/outside the house** dall'interno/esterno della casa; ~ **among the crowd** dalla folla.
frond [frɒnd] n fronda.
front [frʌnt] 1 adj (tooth) davanti inv; (garden) sul davanti; (wheel) anteriore; (row, page) primo(a); (carriage) di testa; (view) frontale.
2 n (a) (gen) davanti m inv; (of train) testa; **in** ~ davanti; **in** ~ **of** davanti a; (opposite) di fronte a; **at the** ~ **of the line** or **queue** in testa or all'inizio della fila; **to be in** ~ (Sport) essere in testa; **he sat at the** ~ **of the class** era seduto nei primi banchi (della classe); **to put on a bold** ~ (fig) mostrare coraggio; **to be a** ~ **for sth** (fam) servire da copertura per qc. (b) (Mil, Pol, Met) fronte m; **on all** ~**s** su tutti i fronti; **cold/warm** ~ (Met) fronte

freddo/caldo; **a united** ~ un fronte unito. **(c)** *(sea ~)* lungomare *m*.

3 *vi*: **to ~ onto sth** dare su qc, guardare verso qc.

4 *cpd*: ~ **bench** *n (Brit Pol)* banco dei ministri o dell'opposizione; ~ **door** *n* porta d'ingresso; ~ **line** *n (Mil)* prima linea; ~ **man** *n (fam)* prestanome *m*; ~ **page** *n (Press)* prima pagina; ~ **runner** *n (fig)* favorito/a.

front·age ['frʌntɪdʒ] *n* facciata.

front·al ['frʌntl] *adj* frontale.

fron·tier ['frʌntɪəʳ] *n* frontiera, confine *m*.

fron·tis·piece ['frʌntɪspiːs] *n* frontespizio.

frost [frɒst] **1** *n* gelo; *(hoar ~)* brina; *(on window)* ghiaccio; **an overnight ~** gelata notturna; **4 degrees of ~** 4 gradi sotto zero. **2** *vt (esp Am: ice: cakes)* glassare.

frost·bite ['frɒstbaɪt] *n* congelamento.

frost·bitten ['frɒstbɪtn] *adj* congelato(a).

frost·ed ['frɒstɪd] *adj (esp Am: cake)* glassato(a); ~ **glass** vetro smerigliato.

frost·ing ['frɒstɪŋ] *n (esp Am: icing)* glassa.

frosty ['frɒstɪ] *adj (-ier, -iest) (weather, also fig)* gelido(a); *(surface)* coperto(a) di ghiaccio *or* di brina; **it was ~ last night** ha gelato durante la notte.

froth [frɒθ] **1** *n* schiuma, spuma. **2** *vi* schiumare, spumare; **the dog was ~ing at the mouth** il cane aveva la schiuma alla bocca.

frown [fraʊn] **1** *n*: **he gave me a worried ~/a ~ of disapproval** mi ha guardato con un'espressione preoccupata/di disapprovazione. **2** *vi* aggrottare le sopracciglia; **to ~ at sth/sb** guardare qc/qn con cipiglio.

♦ **frown on** *vi + prep* disapprovare.

froze [frəʊz] *pt of* **freeze**.

fro·zen ['frəʊzn] **1** *pp of* **freeze**. **2** *adj (food)* congelato(a); *(deep ~)* surgelato(a); **I'm ~ stiff** sono gelato fino alle ossa.

fru·gal ['fruːgəl] *adj (person)* economo(a); *(meal)* frugale.

fruit [fruːt] **1** *n (Bot)* frutto; *(collectively)* frutta; **would you like some ~?** vuoi della frutta?; **to bear ~** dare frutti; *(fig)* dare frutto; **the ~s of one's labour** *(fig)* i frutti del proprio lavoro. **2** *cpd*: ~ **machine** *n (Brit)* slot-machine *f inv*; ~ **salad** *n* macedonia; ~ **tree** *n* albero da frutto.

fruit·er·er ['fruːtərəʳ] *n (esp Brit)* fruttivendolo.

fruit·ful ['fruːtfʊl] *adj (plant)* fruttifero(a); *(soil)* fertile; *(fig)* fruttuoso(a).

frui·tion [fruː'ɪʃən] *n*: **to come to ~** realizzarsi.

fruit·less ['fruːtlɪs] *adj (fig)* vano(a), inutile.

fruity ['fruːtɪ] *adj (-ier, -iest) (taste)* che sa di frutta.

frump [frʌmp] *n*: **to feel a ~** sentirsi infagottato(a).

frus·trate [frʌs'treɪt] *vt (plan, effort, hope)* rendere vano(a); *(person)* frustrare.

frus·trat·ed [frʌs'treɪtɪd] *adj (person)* frustrato(a); *(effort)* reso(a) vano(a); **he's a ~ artist** è un artista mancato; **I got more and more ~ with it** alla fine sono impazzito.

frus·trat·ing [frʌs'treɪtɪŋ] *adj (job)* frustrante; *(day)* disastroso(a); **how ~!** che seccatura!

frus·tra·tion [frʌs'treɪʃən] *n (condition)* frustrazione *f*; *(instance)* scocciatura.

fry¹ [fraɪ] *vt*, *vi* friggere.

fry² [fraɪ] *npl*: **small ~** pesci *mpl* piccoli.

fry·ing pan ['fraɪɪŋˌpæn] *n* padella; **to jump out of the ~ into the fire** cadere dalla padella nella brace.

ft. *abbr of* **foot**, **feet**.

fuch·sia ['fjuːʃə] *n* fucsia.

fuck [fʌk] *(fam!)* **1** *vt* **(a)** fottere. **(b)**: ~ **you!** va' a farti fottere! **2** *excl* cazzo.

♦ **fuck off** *vi + adv (fam!)*: ~ **off!** vaffanculo!*(!)*.

fud·dled ['fʌdld] *adj (muddled)* confuso(a); *(fam: tipsy)* brillo(a).

fudge [fʌdʒ] *n (Culin)* caramella fondente.

fuel [fjʊəl] **1** *n (gen)* combustibile *m*; *(for engine)* carburante *m*; **to add ~ to the flames** *(fig)* soffiare sul fuoco. **2** *vt (furnace etc)* alimentare; *(aircraft, ship etc)* rifornire di carburante. **3** *vi (aircraft, ship)* rifornirsi di carburante. **4** *cpd*: ~ **oil** *n* olio combustibile; ~ **pump** *n (Aut)* pompa del carburante; ~ **tank** *n* serbatoio del carburante.

fug [fʌg] *n* aria viziata.

fu·gi·tive ['fjuːdʒɪtɪv] **1** *adj* fuggitivo(a); *(fleeting)* fugace, fuggevole. **2** *n* fuggitivo/a; *(from prison)* evaso/a.

ful·fil, *(Am)* **ful·fill** [fʊl'fɪl] *vt (duty)* compiere; *(promise)* mantenere; *(ambition)* realizzare; *(wish, desire)* soddisfare, appagare; *(order)* eseguire; **to ~ o.s.** realizzarsi.

ful·filled [fʊl'fɪld] *adj (person)* realizzato(a), soddisfatto(a).

ful·fil·ment, *(Am)* **ful·fill·ment** [fʊl'fɪlmənt] *n (see vb)* compimento; mantenimento; realizzazione *f*; esecuzione *f*; soddisfazione; **sense of ~** soddisfazione.

full [fʊl] **1** *adj (-er, -est)* **(a)** *(gen)* pieno(a); *(vehicle etc)* completo(a); *(timetable)* denso(a); **to be ~ of...** essere pieno di...; ~ **of people** gremito di gente; **to be ~ of o.s.** essere pieno di sé; **we are ~ up for July** siamo al completo per luglio; **he's had a ~ life** ha avuto una vita piena *or* intensa; **I'm ~ (up)** *(fam)* sono pieno.

(b) *(complete)* completo(a); *(: employment)* pieno(a); *(: member)* effettivo(a); *(: price)* intero(a); **to pay ~ fare** pagare la tariffa intera; **to fall ~ length** cadere lungo disteso; **in ~ bloom** in piena fioritura; **in ~ colour** *(illustration)* a colori; **in ~ dress** in abito da cerimonia; **to be in ~ swing** essere in pieno fervore; **in the ~est sense of the word** nel pieno senso della parola; **at ~ speed** a tutta velocità; ~ **speed ahead** *(Naut)* avanti tutta; **the ~ particulars** tutti i particolari; **I waited a ~ hour** ho aspettato un'ora intera; ~ **moon** luna piena; ~ **name** nome *m* e cognome *m*; ~ **stop** punto; ~ **time** *(Ftbl)* fine *f* della partita.

(c) *(rounded: face)* pieno(a); *(: figure)* pienotto(a); *(: lips)* carnoso(a); *(: skirt, sleeves)* largo(a), ampio(a).

2 *adv*: ~ **well** benissimo; **it hit him ~ in the face** l'ha colpito in pieno viso.

3 *n*: **to write sth in ~** scrivere qc per intero; **to pay in ~** pagare tutto; **to the ~** fino in fondo, al massimo.

full·back ['fʊlbæk] *n (Ftbl)* terzino.

full·blooded [ˌfʊl'blʌdɪd] *adj (vigorous: attack)* energico(a); *(virile: male)* virile.

full·cream [ˌfʊl'kriːm] *adj*: ~ **milk** latte *m* intero.

full·grown [ˌfʊl'grəʊn] *adj* maturo(a).

full·length [ˌfʊl'leŋθ] *adj (portrait)* in piedi; *(dress)* lungo(a); *(film)* a lungometraggio.

full·ness ['fʊlnɪs] *n (of detail)* abbondanza; *(of figure, hips)* rotondità; *(of dress)* ampiezza; **in the ~ of time** *(eventually)* col tempo; *(at predestined time)* a tempo debito.

full·scale ['fʊlskeɪl] *adj (plan, model)* in grandezza naturale; *(search, retreat)* su vasta scala.

full·time [ˌfʊl'taɪm] *adj, adv* a tempo pieno.

ful·ly ['fʊlɪ] *adv (completely)* completamente; *(at*

least) almeno; ~ **dressed** completamente vestito.

ful·some ['fʊlsəm] *adj (pej: praise)* esagerato(a), eccessivo(a); *(: manner)* insincero(a).

fum·ble ['fʌmbl] **1** *vt*: **to ~ a catch** mancare una presa; **to ~ a ball** lasciarsi sfuggire di mano una palla. **2** *vi (also: ~ about)*: **to ~ in one's pockets** frugare *or* rovistare nelle tasche; **to ~ in the dark** andare a tastoni; **to ~ with sth** armeggiare con qc.

fume [fjuːm] **1** *npl*: ~**s** esalazioni *fpl*, vapori *mpl*. **2** *vi (chemicals etc)* emettere fumo; **to be fuming at** *or* **with sb** *(fig)* essere arrabbiatissimo *or* furioso con qn.

fu·mi·gate ['fjuːmɪgeɪt] *vt (room)* suffumicare.

fun [fʌn] *n (enjoyment)* divertimento; **for** *or* **in ~** per scherzo, per ridere; **it's great ~** è molto divertente; **don't spoil our ~** non fare il guastafeste; **there'll be ~ and games with that** *(fig iro)* ci sarà da divertirsi; **to do sth for the ~ of it** fare qc per ridere; **to have ~** divertirsi; **to make ~ of** *or* **poke ~ at sb** canzonare *or* prendere in giro qn.

func·tion ['fʌŋkʃən] **1** *n* **(a)** *(purpose)* funzione *f*. **(b)** *(reception)* ricevimento; *(official ceremony)* cerimonia, funzione *f*. **(c)** *(Math)* funzione *f*. **2** *vi (operate)* funzionare; **to ~ as** fungere da, funzionare da.

func·tion·al ['fʌŋkʃnəl] *adj* funzionale.

fund [fʌnd] **1** *n (reserve of money)* fondo; *(fig: stock)* provvista, riserva; ~**s** denaro, soldi *mpl*; **to raise** ~**s for** raccogliere fondi per; **to be a ~ of information** essere una miniera d'informazioni. **2** *vt (project)* finanziare.

fun·da·men·tal [ˌfʌndə'mɛntl] **1** *adj* fondamentale; **his ~ honesty** la sua innata onestà. **2** *npl*: ~**s** principi *mpl* fondamentali.

fun·da·men·tal·ly [ˌfʌndə'mɛntəlɪ] *adv* fondamentalmente.

fu·ner·al ['fjuːnərəl] *n* funerale *m*; *(procession)* corteo funebre; *(state ~)* funerali; **that's your** ~! *(fam)* è affar tuo!

fu·nereal [fjuː'nɪərɪəl] funereo(a), lugubre.

fun·fair ['fʌnfɛəʳ] *n (Brit)* luna park *m inv*.

fun·gus ['fʌŋgəs] *n, pl* **fungi** ['fʌŋgaɪ] fungo; *(mould)* muffa.

fu·nicu·lar [fjuː'nɪkjʊləʳ] *n (also: ~ railway)* funicolare *f*.

funk [fʌŋk] *n*: **to be in a (blue) ~** *(fam)* avere una gran fifa.

fun·nel ['fʌnl] *n (for pouring)* imbuto; *(Naut, of steam engine etc)* fumaiolo, ciminiera.

fun·ni·ly ['fʌnɪlɪ] *adv* **(a)** in modo divertente. **(b)** *(oddly)* stranamente; ~ **enough** strano a dirsi, per una strana coincidenza.

fun·ny ['fʌnɪ] *adj (-ier, -iest)* **(a)** divertente, buffo(a); **that's not ~** c'è poco da ridere; **to try to be ~** fare lo spiritoso. **(b)** *(odd)* strano(a); **this tastes ~** ha uno strano sapore; **a ~ feeling came over me** mi sono sentito strano; **the ~ thing about it is that...** la cosa strana è che...; **there's some ~ business going on here** *(fam)* c'è qualcosa di losco; ~ **bone** osso cubitale.

fur [fɜːʳ] **1** *n (of animal)* pelo, pelame *m*; *(single skin)* pelle *f*; *(as clothing)* pelliccia; *(in kettle)* incrostazione *f*. **2** *cpd*: ~ **coat** *n* pelliccia.

fu·ri·ous ['fjʊərɪəs] *adj (person)* furioso(a), infuriato(a); *(argument)* violento(a); *(effort etc)* accanito(a); **at a ~ speed** a velocità folle; **to be ~ with sb** essere furioso con qn; **to be ~ at sth/at having done sth** essere furioso per qc/per aver fatto qc.

fur·long ['fɜːlɒŋ] *n* duecentouno metri.

fur·nace ['fɜːnɪs] *n* fornace *f*.

fur·nish ['fɜːnɪʃ] *vt* **(a)** *(room, house)*: **to ~ (with)** arredare (con); ~**ing** fabric tessuto da arredamento; ~**ed flat** appartamento ammobiliato. **(b)** *(provide: excuse, information)* fornire, dare; **to ~ sb with sth** dare qc a qn.

fur·nish·ings ['fɜːnɪʃɪŋz] *npl* mobili *mpl*.

fur·ni·ture ['fɜːnɪtʃəʳ] *n* mobili *mpl*; **a piece of ~** un mobile; **to be part of the ~** *(fig fam)* confondersi con la tappezzeria.

fu·ro·re [fjʊə'rɔːrɪ] *n (protests)* scalpore *m*; *(enthusiasm)* entusiasmo.

fur·ri·er ['fʌrɪəʳ] *n* pellicciaio/a.

fur·row ['fʌrəʊ] **1** *n (Agr)* solco; *(on forehead)* solco, ruga. **2** *vt (forehead)* segnare di rughe.

fur·ry ['fɜːrɪ] *adj (animal)* peloso(a); *(toy)* di peluche.

fur·ther ['fɜːðəʳ] *comp of* **far 1** *adv* **(a)** *(in place, time)* oltre, più avanti; ~ **back** più indietro; ~ **on** *(also fig)* più avanti; **how much ~ is it?** quanto manca *or* dista?; **I got no ~ with him** *(fig)* non sono riuscito a cavare un ragno dal buco; **nothing is ~ from my thoughts** non ci penso neanche. **(b)** *(more)* di più; **and I ~ believe that...** e inoltre *or* per di più credo che...; ~ **to your letter of...** *(Comm)* con riferimento alla vostra lettera del...; **he heard nothing ~** non c'è stato alcun seguito. **2** *adj* **(a)** = **farther. (b)** *(additional)* ulteriore, supplementare; **until ~ notice** fino a nuovo avviso; **after ~ consideration** dopo un più attento esame; ~ **education** istruzione *f* superiore. **3** *vt (a cause)* appoggiare, favorire; **to ~ one's interests** fare i propri interessi.

further·more ['fɜːðəmɔːʳ] *adv* inoltre, per di più.

further·most ['fɜːðəməʊst] *adj* più lontano(a).

fur·thest ['fɜːðɪst] *superl of* **far 1** *adv*: **this is the ~ you can go** non puoi andare più lontano. **2** *adj* più lontano(a), più distante.

fur·tive ['fɜːtɪv] *adj (glance, action)* furtivo(a); *(person)* circospetto(a).

fury ['fjʊərɪ] *n (of storm, person)* furia; **she flew into a ~** andò su tutte le furie; **like ~** *(fam)* come un dannato.

fuse, *(Am)* **fuze** [fjuːz] **1** *n (Elec)* fusibile *m*; *(of bomb)* spoletta, miccia; **to blow a ~** far saltare una valvola; **a ~ has blown** è saltata una valvola. **2** *vt* **(a)** *(lights, television etc)* far saltare le valvole a. **(b)** *(metals)* fondere. **3** *vi* **(a)** *(Elec)*: **the lights have ~d** sono saltate le valvole. **(b)** *(metals)* fondersi. **4** *cpd*: ~ **box** *n* scatola dei fusibili; ~ **wire** *n* filo *(di fusibile)*.

fu·selage ['fjuːzəlɑːʒ] *n* fusoliera.

fu·sil·lade [ˌfjuːzɪ'leɪd] *n* scarica di fucileria; *(fig)* fuoco di fila, serie *f inv* incalzante.

fu·sion ['fjuːʒən] *n* fusione *f*.

fuss [fʌs] **1** *n (complaints, arguments)* storie *fpl*; *(anxious preparations etc)* agitazione *f*; **to make a ~ about sth** fare storie per qc; **don't make such a ~!** non fare tante storie!; **to make a ~ of sb** coprire qn di attenzioni; **he made a lot of ~ about nothing** ha fatto un sacco di storie per nulla. **2** *vi* agitarsi. **3** *vt (person)* infastidire, scocciare.

♦ **fuss over** *vi + prep (person)* circondare di premure.

fussy ['fʌsɪ] *adj (-ier, -iest) (person)* difficile, pignolo(a); *(clothes etc)* pieno(a) di fronzoli; **I'm not ~** *(fam)* per me è lo stesso.

fu·tile ['fjuːtaɪl] *adj* futile, vano(a).

fu·til·ity [fjuː'tɪlɪtɪ] *n* futilità.

fu·ture ['fjuːtʃəʳ] **1** *adj* futuro(a); **the ~ tense** il futuro; **at some ~ date** in futuro. **2** *n* futuro; **in the near ~** in un prossimo futuro; **there's no ~ in**

it non c'è futuro in questo campo; **in** ~ in futuro.

fu·tur·is·tic [ˌfjuːtʃəˈrɪstɪk] *adj* futurista.

fuze [fjuːz] *(Am)* = **fuse.**

fuzz [fʌz] *n (frizzy hair)* capelli *mpl* crespi; *(on chin)*
peluria; **the** ~ *(fam)* la polizia.

fuzzy [ˈfʌzɪ] *adj* (**-ier, -iest**) *(hair)* crespo(a);
(blurred: photo) sfocato(a), indistinto(a);
(: memory) confuso(a).

G

G, g [dʒiː] n **(a)** *(letter)* G, g *for* m *inv.* **(b)** *(Mus)* sol m.

g. *(abbr of* **gram(s), gramme(s))** g., gr.

gab [gæb] n *(fam):* **to have the gift of the** ~ avere lo scilinguagnolo sciolto.

gab·ar·dine ['gæbə,diːn] n = **gaberdine.**

gab·ble ['gæbl] **1** vt borbottare. **2** vi farfugliare; **they were gabbling away in French** chiacchieravano come macchinette in francese.

gab·er·dine [,gæbə'diːn] n gabardine m inv.

ga·ble ['geɪbl] n frontone m.

gad about ['gæd'baʊt] vi + adv *(fam)* svolazzare (qua e là).

gadg·et ['gædʒɪt] n aggeggio, arnese m.

Gael·ic ['geɪlɪk] **1** adj gaelico(a). **2** n *(language)* gaelico.

gaffe [gæf] n gaffe f inv.

gag [gæg] **1** n **(a)** *(over mouth)* bavaglio. **(b)** *(joke)* battuta, gag f inv. **2** vt *(silence)* imbavagliare. **3** vi *(retch)* avere conati di vomito.

gage [geɪdʒ] *(Am)* = **gauge.**

gag·gle ['gægl] n *(of geese)* branco.

gai·ety ['geɪtɪ] n allegria.

gai·ly ['geɪlɪ] adv *(sing etc)* allegramente, gaiamente; *(painted, decorated)* vivacemente; ~ **coloured** dai colori allegri.

gain [geɪn] **1** n *(increase):* ~ **(in)** aumento (di); *(advantage)* vantaggio, utile m; *(profit)* guadagno, profitto; **to do sth for** ~ fare qc per lucro; **his loss is our** ~ lui ci perde, noi ci guadagniamo; **the Conservatives made several** ~s i Conservatori hanno guadagnato diversi posti.

2 vt *(obtain, acquire: respect, approval)* ottenere; *(: reputation)* farsi; *(: experience, wealth, knowledge, territory)* acquistare; *(reach: summit, shore)* raggiungere, guadagnare; *(: aim)* raggiungere; *(increase: weight)* aumentare di; **to** ~ **3 kilos in weight** aumentare di 3 chili, prendere 3 chili; **what do I have to** ~ **by staying here?** che ci guadagno restando qui?; **to** ~ **strength** *(person)* riprendere le forze; *(theory)* avvalorarsi; **to** ~ **possession of** impadronirsi di, impossessarsi di; **to** ~ **ground** guadagnare terreno; **to** ~ **speed** prendere velocità; **my watch has** ~**ed 5 minutes** il mio orologio va 5 minuti avanti; **to** ~ **an advantage over sb** avvantaggiarsi rispetto a qn.

3 vi *(person)* guadagnare; *(watch)* andare avanti; **to** ~ **in weight** aumentare di peso; **to** ~ **in popularity** acquistare popolarità.

♦ **gain (up)on** vi + prep accorciare le distanze da, riprendere.

gain·ful ['geɪnfʊl] adj *(employment)* remunerativo(a).

gait [geɪt] n passo, andatura.

gal. [gæl] abbr of **gallon.**

gala ['gɑːlə] **1** n *(festive occasion)* festa; *(: important)* gran gala; **swimming** ~ manifestazione f di nuoto. **2** cpd: ~ **performance** n serata di gala.

gal·axy ['gæləksɪ] n galassia.

gale [geɪl] n bufera, vento forte; ~ **force 10** vento forza 10.

gall [gɔːl] **1** n *(Anat)* bile f; *(fig: impudence)* fegato, faccia. **2** vt urtare (i nervi a). **3** cpd: ~ **bladder** n cistifellea.

gal·lant ['gælənt] adj *(brave)* valoroso(a), prode; *(courteous)* galante.

gal·lant·ry ['gæləntrɪ] n *(see adj)* valore m militare, prodezza; galanteria.

gal·leon ['gælɪən] n galeone m.

gal·lery ['gælərɪ] n loggia; *(for spectators)* tribuna; *(in theatre)* loggione m, balconata; *(art ~: state owned)* museo; *(: private)* galleria; **to play to the** ~ fare l'istrione (per accattivarsi il pubblico).

gal·ley ['gælɪ] **1** n *(ship)* galea; *(ship's kitchen)* cambusa. **2** cpd: ~ **proof** n *(Typ)* bozza in colonna.

Gal·lic ['gælɪk] adj *(of Gaul)* gallico(a); *(French)* francese.

gal·lon ['gælən] n gallone m *(Brit = 4,55 litri; Am = 3,79 litri).*

gal·lop ['gæləp] **1** n *(pace)* galoppo; *(ride)* galoppata; **at a** ~ al galoppo. **2** vi *(horse, rider)* galoppare, andare al galoppo; **he** ~**ed through his home·work** *(fig)* ha fatto i compiti di volata.

gal·lows ['gæləʊz] npl forca, patibolo.

gall·stone ['gɔːlstəʊn] n calcolo biliare.

Gal·lup poll ['gæləp,pəʊl] n ® sondaggio d'opinione.

ga·lore [gə'lɔːʳ] adv a iosa, a profusione.

gal·va·nize ['gælvənaɪz] vt galvanizzare; *(fig):* **to** ~ **sb into action** galvanizzare qn, spronare qn all'azione.

gam·bit ['gæmbɪt] n *(Chess)* gambetto; *(fig)* mossa; **opening** ~ prima mossa.

gam·ble ['gæmbl] **1** n azzardo, rischio (calcolato); **to take a** ~ rischiare; **the** ~ **came off** è convenuto rischiare; **it's a** ~ è un salto nel buio. **2** vt *(money)* giocare. **3** vi giocare (d'azzardo); **to** ~ **on the Stock Exchange** giocare in Borsa; **to** ~ **on sth** puntare su qc, giocare su qc.

♦ **gamble away** vt + adv *(money etc)* giocarsi, perdere al gioco.

gam·bler ['gæmbləʳ] n giocatore/trice (d'azzardo).

gam·bling ['gæmblɪŋ] n gioco (d'azzardo). **2** cpd: ~ **debts** npl debiti mpl di gioco.

gam·bol ['gæmbəl] vi saltellare.

game [geɪm] n **(a)** *(gen)* gioco; *(match)* partita; ~**s** *(Scol)* attività fpl sportive; **that's 3** ~**s to you and 2 to me** siamo 3 a 2; **to have a** ~ **of cards/chess/tennis** fare una partita a carte/scacchi/tennis; **he plays a good** ~ **of football** gioca bene a football; ~ **of chance** gioco d'azzardo; ~**, set and match** *(Tennis)* game, set e partita; **he was off his** ~ non era nella sua forma migliore; **to play the** ~ *(also fig)* rispettare le regole del gioco; **to play sb's** ~ fare il gioco di qn; **come on lads, play the** ~ su ragazzi, siate sportivi; **to beat sb at his own** ~ battere qn con le sue stesse armi; **the** ~ **is up** è finita, è la fine; **I wonder what his** ~ **is?** mi chiedo a che gioco stia giocando; **two can play at that** ~ ti *(or lo etc)* ripagherò con la stessa moneta; **how long have you been in this** ~? *(fam)* da quant'è che fai questo mestiere?

(b) *(Culin, Hunting)* selvaggina; **fair** ~ *(fig)* legittimo bersaglio.
2 *adj (willing)*: **to be** ~ **starci**; ~ **for anything** pronto a tutto.
3 *cpd*: ~ **bird** *n* uccello selvatico; ~ **reserve** *n* riserva di caccia.
game·keep·er ['geɪm,kiːpəʳ] *n* guardacaccia *m inv.*
games·man·ship ['geɪmzmənʃɪp] *n*: **to be good at** ~ essere una vecchia volpe.
gam·mon ['gæmən] *n (ham)* prosciutto affumicato.
gam·ut ['gæmət] *n (Mus)* gamma; **to run the (whole)** ~ **of emotions** *(fig)* percorrere l'intera gamma dei sentimenti.
gan·der ['gændəʳ] *n (Zool)* (maschio dell')oca.
gang [gæŋ] *n (of thieves, youths)* banda; *(of friends)* truppa, comitiva; *(of workmen)* squadra.
♦ **gang up** *vi* + *adv*: **to** ~ **up (with)** mettersi insieme (a *or* con); **to** ~ **up on** *or* **against sb** far comunella contro qn.
gan·gling ['gæŋglɪŋ] *adj* allampanato(a).
gang·plank ['gæŋplæŋk] *n* passerella.
gan·grene ['gæŋgriːn] *n* cancrena.
gan·gre·nous ['gæŋgrɪnəs] *adj* cancrenoso(a).
gang·ster ['gæŋstəʳ] *n* gangster *m inv.*
gang·way ['gæŋweɪ] *n (Naut)* passerella; *(aisle: in theatre, cinema)* corsia; *(: in train)* corridoio; *(: in bus)* passaggio; ~**!** largo!
gan·try ['gæntrɪ] *n (for crane, railway signal)* cavalletto; *(for rocket)* torre *f* di lancio.
gaol [dʒeɪl] *n (Brit)* = **jail.**
gap [gæp] *n* **(a)** *(gen)* spazio vuoto; *(in line, traffic)* interruzione *f*; *(in trees, crowd, defences)* vuoto; *(in wall, fence)* apertura, buco; *(mountain pass)* passo, valico; *(between teeth)* spazio; *(between floorboards)* interstizio; *(fig: in knowledge etc)* lacuna; *(: in conversation)* pausa; *(of time)* intervallo; **he left a** ~ **which will be hard to fill** ha lasciato un vuoto difficile da colmare. **(b)** *(difference)*: ~ **(between)** divario (tra), divergenza (tra); **the** ~ **between them widened** la distanza tra di loro si fece più grande.
gape [geɪp] *vi* **(a)** *(mouth, hole)* essere spalancato(a). **(b)** *(person)*: **to** ~ **(at sb/sth)** guardare (qn/qc) a bocca aperta.
gap·ing ['geɪpɪŋ] *adj (wound)* aperto(a); *(hole)* grosso(a); ~ **seam** larga scucitura.
gar·age ['gæraːʒ] *n (of private house)* garage *m inv*; *(for car repairs)* garage, autorimessa.
garb [gaːb] *n* abiti *mpl*, veste *f.*
gar·bage ['gaːbɪdʒ] **1** *n (esp Am)* immondizie *fpl*, spazzatura, rifiuti *mpl*; *(fig: of film, book)* porcheria, robaccia; *(: nonsense)* fesserie *fpl*. **2** *cpd*: ~ **can** *n* bidone *m* della spazzatura; ~ **disposal unit** *n* tritarifiuti *m inv.*
gar·bled ['gaːbld] *adj (speech, account)* ingarbugliato(a); *(words)* incomprensibile.
gar·den ['gaːdn] **1** *n* giardino; **the G**~ **of Eden** il Paradiso Terrestre, l'Eden *m*; ~**s** *(public)* giardini pubblici; *(private)* parco. **2** *vi* fare (lavori di) giardinaggio. **3** *cpd*: ~ **centre** *n* vivaio; ~ **party** *n* festa all'aperto, garden-party *m*; ~ **path** *n*: **to lead sb up the** ~ **path** *(fig)* darla a bere a qn; ~ **shears** *npl* forbici *fpl* tosasiepi *inv.*
gar·den·er ['gaːdnəʳ] *n* giardiniere/a.
gar·den·ing ['gaːdnɪŋ] *n* giardinaggio.
gar·gle ['gaːgl] **1** *n (act)* gargarismo; *(liquid)* collutorio. **2** *vi* fare i gargarismi.
gar·goyle ['gaːgɔɪl] *n* gargolla.
gar·ish ['gɛərɪʃ] *adj* sgargiante, vistoso(a); *(light)* chiassoso(a).
gar·land ['gaːlənd] *n* ghirlanda.
gar·lic ['gaːlɪk] **1** *n* aglio. **2** *cpd*: ~ **sausage** *n* salamino all'aglio.

gar·ment ['gaːmənt] *n* articolo di vestiario, indumento.
gar·nish ['gaːnɪʃ] **1** *n (Culin)* decorazione *f.* **2** *vt*: **to** ~ **(with)** guarnire (con *or* di).
gar·ret ['gærət] *n* soffitta, mansarda.
gar·ri·son ['gærɪsən] **1** *n* guarnigione *f.* **2** *vt (town)* piazzare truppe in; *(: subj: troops)* presidiare. **3** *cpd*: ~ **town** *n* città *f inv* di guarnigione.
gar·ru·lous ['gærʊləs] *adj* loquace, ciarliero(a).
gar·ter ['gaːtəʳ] *n* giarrettiera.
gas [gæs] **1** *n* **(a)** *(gen)* gas *m inv*; *(as anaesthetic)* etere *m*; **Calor** ~ ® gas liquido *or* in bombole. **(b)** *(Am: petrol)* benzina. **2** *vt (person)* asfissiare (col gas); *(Mil)* uccidere col gas asfissiante; **to** ~ **o.s.** asfissiarsi. **3** *vi (fam: gab)* chiacchierare, cianciare. **4** *cpd (industry, cooker, pipe)* a gas; ~ **chamber** *n* camera a gas; ~ **lighter** *n* accendisigari *m inv* a gas; ~ **mask** *n* maschera *f* antigas *inv*; ~ **meter** *n* contatore *m* del gas; ~ **station** *n (Am)* distributore *m* di benzina; ~ **tank** *n (Am Aut)* serbatoio (di benzina).
gas·eous ['gæsɪəs] *adj* gassoso(a).
gash [gæʃ] **1** *n (in flesh)* taglio profondo, squarcio; *(in material)* spacco. **2** *vt (arm, head)* fare un brutto taglio in; *(seat etc)* squarciare.
gas·ket ['gæskɪt] *n (Tech)* guarnizione *f.*
gas·man ['gæsmæn] *n*, *pl* **-men** *(fam)*: **the** ~ l'uomo del gas.
gaso·line ['gæsəʊliːn] *n (Am)* benzina.
gas·om·eter [gæ'sɒmɪtəʳ] *n* gas(s)ometro.
gasp [gaːsp] **1** *n* respiro affannoso, ansito; **she gave a** ~ **of surprise** la sorpresa le mozzò il fiato; **to be at one's last** ~ **star** tirando l'ultimo respiro. **2** *vi* ansare, ansimare; *(in surprise)* restare senza fiato; **to** ~ **for breath** respirare a fatica.
gas·tric ['gæstrɪk] *adj* gastrico(a); ~ **flu** virus *m inv* intestinale.
gas·tri·tis ['gæs'traɪtɪs] *n* gastrite *f.*
gas·tro·en·teri·tis [,gæstrəʊ,ɛntə'raɪtɪs] *n* gastroenterite *f.*
gas·tro·nom·ic [,gæstrə'nɒmɪk] *adj* gastronomico(a).
gas·works ['gæswɜːks] *nsg or npl* impianto di produzione del gas.
gate [geɪt] *n (in garden, field)* cancello; *(of castle, town)* porta; *(at airport)* uscita; *(at level crossing)* barriera. **(b)** *(Sport: attendance)* (numero di) spettatori *mpl*, presenze *fpl*; *(: entrance money)* incassi *mpl.*
gâ·teau ['gætəʊ] *n*, *pl* **-x** ['gætəʊz] torta.
gate-crash ['geɪtkræʃ] *vt (fam: party)* intrufolarsi in.
gate-crasher ['geɪtkræʃəʳ] *n (at party)* intruso/a.
gate·post ['geɪtpəʊst] *n* pilastrino del cancello.
gate·way ['geɪtweɪ] *n* porta; **the** ~ **to success** la strada del successo.
gath·er ['gæðəʳ] **1** *vt* **(a)** *(also*: ~ **together)** *people)* radunare, riunire; *(: objects)* raccogliere, radunare; *(also*: ~ **up)** raccogliere; *(: flowers)* cogliere; *(also*: ~ **in)** *material)* riprendere, increspare; *(: taxes etc)* riscuotere; **to** ~ **the harvest** fare il raccolto; **to** ~ **dust** raccogliere la polvere; **to** ~ **one's thoughts/strength** raccogliere i propri pensieri/le proprie forze; **she** ~**ed her mink around her** si avvolse nel visone. **(b)** *(gain)*: **to** ~ **speed** prendere *or* acquistare velocità; **to** ~ **strength** *(wind, waves)* aumentare d'intensità. **(c)** *(understand)*: **to** ~ **(from/that)** comprendere (da/che), dedurre (da/che); **I** ~ **(that) you are leaving** ho saputo che parti; **as you will have** ~**ed** come avrai indovinato; **as far as I can** ~ da quel che ho potuto capire; **from what he says I** ~ **that...** da quel che dice mi pare di capire che... .

2 vi (people: also: ~ **together**) raccogliersi, radunarsi; (: crowd) assembrarsi; (dust) accumularsi; (clouds) addensarsi.
♦ **gather round** vi + adv radunarsi.
gath·er·ing ['gæðərɪŋ] n (assembly) raduno, riunione f; (crowd) gruppo.
gauche [gəʊʃ] adj goffo(a), maldestro(a).
gaudy ['gɔːdɪ] adj (-ier, -iest) vistoso(a), chiassoso(a).
gauge [geɪdʒ] 1 n (standard measure: of bullet etc) calibro; (: of pipe, wire) diametro; (: of railway track) scartamento; (instrument) indicatore m di livello; (fig) metro, criterio; **petrol** ~ indicatore or spia della benzina; **oil** ~ spia dell'olio; **pressure** ~ manometro. 2 vt (temperature, pressure) misurare; (fig: sb's capabilities, character) valutare, stimare; **to** ~ **the right moment** calcolare il momento giusto.
gaunt [gɔːnt] adj emaciato(a); (face) smunto(a).
gaunt·let ['gɔːntlɪt] n (of knight) guanto d'armatura, manopola; (of motorcyclist etc) guanto; **to run the** ~ **of** (fig) sottostare al fuoco di fila di; (: of angry crowd) affrontare l'ostilità di; **to throw down the** ~ gettare il guanto.
gauze [gɔːz] n garza.
gave [geɪv] pt of **give**.
gawky ['gɔːkɪ] adj (-ier, -iest) goffo(a), sgraziato(a).
gawp [gɔːp] vi = **gape** (b).
gay [geɪ] adj (-er, -est) **(a)** allegro(a), gaio(a). **(b)** (fam: homosexual) omosessuale, gay inv.
gaze [geɪz] 1 n sguardo (insistente). 2 vi: **to** ~ **at** guardare (con insistenza), fissare; **to** ~ **in wonderment at sb/sth** guardare rapito qn/qc.
ga·zelle [gə'zɛl] n gazzella.
ga·zette [gə'zɛt] n (newspaper) gazzetta; (official publication) gazzetta ufficiale.
gaz·et·teer [,gæzɪ'tɪər] n (book) dizionario di nomi geografici; (section of book) indice m dei nomi geografici.
ga·zump [gə'zʌmp] vi (Brit fam) mancare a un impegno di vendita di una casa accettando un prezzo più alto.
G.B. abbr of **Great Britain**.
G.C.E. n abbr of **General Certificate of Education**.
Gdns. abbr of **Gardens**.
gear [gɪər] 1 n **(a)** (Aut: mechanism) cambio; (: for speed) marcia; **the car is in** ~ la marcia è innestata; **out of** ~ in folle; **first** or **bottom** or **low** ~ prima; **to put the car into** ~ innestare or ingranare la marcia; **to change** ~ cambiare marcia; **she changed into second** ~ ha messo or ingranato la seconda. **(b)** (equipment) attrezzatura, equipaggiamento; (belongings) roba, cose fpl; (clothing) vestiti mpl; **dressed in the latest** ~ (fam) bardato all'ultima moda. **(c)** (Tech) dispositivo, congegno. 2 vt (fig: adapt) adattare; **the book is** ~**ed to adult students** il libro si rivolge a studenti di età adulta; **our service is** ~**ed to meet the needs of the disabled** la nostra organizzazione risponde espressamente alle esigenze degli handicappati. 3 cpd: ~ **lever** n, ~ **stick** n leva del cambio.
gear·box ['gɪəbɒks] n (Aut) scatola del cambio.
gear·shift ['gɪəʃɪft] n (Am) = **gear lever**.
gear·wheel ['gɪəwiːl] n ruota dentata.
geese [giːs] npl of **goose**.
Geiger count·er ['gaɪgə,kaʊntər] n geiger m inv.
gel [dʒɛl] n gel m inv.
gela·tin(e) ['dʒɛlətiːn] n gelatina.
gel·ig·nite ['dʒɛlɪgnaɪt] n gelatina esplosiva.
gem [dʒɛm] n gemma, pietra preziosa; (fig: person)

gioiello, perla; **I must read you this** ~ (fam) senti questa perla.
Gemi·ni ['dʒɛmɪniː] n Gemelli mpl; **to be** ~ essere dei Gemelli.
gen [dʒɛn] n (fam): **to give sb the** ~ **on sth** mettere qn al corrente di qc.
gen·der ['dʒɛndər] n (Gram) genere m.
gene [dʒiːn] n (Bio) gene m.
ge·neal·ogy [,dʒiːnɪ'ælədʒɪ] n genealogia.
gen·er·al ['dʒɛnərəl] 1 adj (gen) generale; (not detailed: plan, view) generale, complessivo(a); (: enquiry) generico(a); (not specialized: trader, store) di generi vari; **in** ~ **use** d'uso comune or corrente; **in** ~ **terms** in termini generici, in generale; **as a** ~ **rule** di norma, di regola; **the** ~ **idea is to...** l'idea base sarebbe di...; **the** ~ **public** il grande pubblico.
2 adv: **in** ~ (usually) generalmente; (as a whole) nel complesso.
3 n (Mil) generale m.
4 cpd: ~ **anaesthetic** n anestesia totale; ~ **election** n elezioni fpl legislative; ~ **headquarters** n (Mil) quartier m generale; ~ **hospital** n ospedale m generico, policlinico; ~ **knowledge** n cultura generale; **G**~ **Post Office** n (building) Posta Centrale; (Brit old: organization) Poste fpl e Telegrafi; ~ **practitioner** (abbr **G.P.**) n medico generico; (personal doctor) medico di famiglia.
gen·er·al·ity [,dʒɛnə'rælɪtɪ] n generalità f inv; **to talk in generalities** parlare in termini generici.
gen·er·ali·za·tion [,dʒɛnərəlaɪ'zeɪʃən] n generalizzazione f.
gen·er·al·ize ['dʒɛnərəlaɪz] vi: **to** ~ (about) generalizzare (per quel che riguarda); **to** ~ **from** generalizzare sulla base di.
gen·er·al·ly ['dʒɛnərəlɪ] adv (usually) in genere, di solito; (for the most part) nel complesso; **he's** ~ **disliked** è odiato da tutti; ~ **speaking** in genere.
gen·er·ate ['dʒɛnəreɪt] vt generare.
gen·era·tion [,dʒɛnə'reɪʃən] n **(a)** (of electricity etc) produzione f. **(b)** (people) generazione f; **the younger/older** ~ la nuova/vecchia generazione; **the** ~ **gap** il divario tra le generazioni.
gen·era·tor ['dʒɛnəreɪtər] n generatore m.
ge·ner·ic [dʒɪ'nɛrɪk] adj generico(a).
gen·er·os·ity [,dʒɛnə'rɒsɪtɪ] n generosità f.
gen·er·ous ['dʒɛnərəs] adj (gen) generoso(a); (plentiful: supply, quantity) abbondante; **to be** ~ **with sth** essere prodigo di qc.
gen·esis ['dʒɛnɪsɪs] n genesi f.
ge·net·ic [dʒɪ'nɛtɪk] adj genetico(a); ~ **engineering** selezione f genetica.
ge·net·ics [dʒɪ'nɛtɪks] nsg genetica.
Ge·neva [dʒɪ'niːvə] n Ginevra.
gen·ial ['dʒiːnɪəl] adj (manner, person) cordiale; (climate, weather) mite.
geni·tals ['dʒɛnɪtlz] npl genitali mpl.
geni·tive ['dʒɛnɪtɪv] n genitivo.
ge·ni·us ['dʒiːnɪəs] n genio; **to have a** ~ **for sth** essere tagliato per qc; **to have a** ~ **for doing sth** (also iro) essere bravissimo(a) a fare qc.
gent [dʒɛnt] n (abbr of **gentleman**) signore m; **the** ~**s** (fam: public toilet) toilette f inv (per uomini).
gen·teel [dʒɛn'tiːl] adj (excessively polite) affettato(a); (old use) distinto(a).
gen·tile ['dʒɛntaɪl] n gentile m.
gen·tle ['dʒɛntl] adj (-r, -st) (person, slope, voice) dolce; (touch) delicato(a); (hint, reminder) velato(a); (rebuke) discreto(a); (heat, exercise) moderato(a); (breeze, sound) leggero(a); **to be** ~ **with sb** trattare qn con delicatezza.
gentle·man ['dʒɛntlmən] n, pl **-men** signore m; (well-mannered, well-bred man) gentiluomo,

signore *m;* **gentlemen!** signori!; **(to be) a perfect ~** (dimostrarsi) un vero gentiluomo; **~'s agreement** impegno sulla parola.

gentle·man·ly ['dʒɛntlmənlı] *adv* da gentiluomo.

gen·tly ['dʒɛntlı] *adv (say, smile)* dolcemente; *(touch)* lievemente, con delicatezza; **~ does it!** piano!

gen·try ['dʒɛntrı] *npl* piccola nobiltà.

genu·flect ['dʒɛnjuflɛkt] *vi* genuflettersi.

genu·ine ['dʒɛnjʊɪn] *adj* **(a)** *(person, belief)* since-ro(a). **(b)** *(authentic: leather, silver)* vero(a); *(: painting, antique)* autentico(a).

ge·nus ['dʒɛnəs] *n, pl* **genera** ['dʒɛnərə] genere *m.*

ge·og·ra·pher [dʒɪ'ɒgrəfə'] *n* geografo/a.

geo·graph·ic(al) [dʒɪə'græfɪk(əl)] *adj* geografi-co(a).

ge·og·ra·phy [dʒɪ'ɒgrəfɪ] *n* geografia.

geo·logi·cal [dʒɪəʊ'lɒdʒɪkəl] *adj* geologico(a).

ge·olo·gist [dʒɪ'ɒlədʒɪst] *n* geologo/a.

ge·ol·ogy [dʒɪ'ɒlədʒɪ] *n* geologia.

geo·met·ric(al) [dʒɪəʊ'mɛtrɪk(əl)] *adj* geometri-co(a).

ge·om·etry [dʒɪ'ɒmɪtrɪ] *n* geometria.

Geor·gian ['dʒɔːdʒɪən] *adj* georgiano(a).

ge·ra·nium [dʒɪ'reɪnɪəm] *n* geranio.

geri·at·ric [,dʒɛrɪ'ætrɪk] *adj* geriatrico(a).

germ [dʒɜːm] **1** *n (Bio, also fig)* germe *m; (Med)* microbo. **2** *cpd:* **~ warfare** *n* guerra batteriolo-gica.

Ger·man ['dʒɜːmən] **1** *adj* tedesco(a); **~ measles** rosolia. **2** *n (person)* tedesco/a; *(language)* te-desco.

Ger·ma·ny ['dʒɜːmənı] *n* Germania; **East/West ~** Germania dell'Est/dell'Ovest.

ger·mi·nate ['dʒɜːmɪneɪt] *vi* germinare, germo-gliare.

ger·mi·na·tion [dʒɜːmɪ'neɪʃən] *n* germinazione *f.*

ger·und ['dʒɛrənd] *n* gerundio.

ges·ta·tion [dʒɛs'teɪʃən] *n (Bio)* gestazione *f.*

ges·ticu·late [dʒɛs'tɪkjʊleɪt] *vi* gesticolare.

ges·ture ['dʒɛstʃə'] **1** *n* gesto; **as a ~ of friendship** in segno d'amicizia. **2** *vi:* **he ~d towards the door** fece un gesto verso la porta; **to ~ to sb to do sth** far segno a qn di fare qc.

get [gɛt] *pt, pp* **got,** *(Am) pp* **gotten 1** *vt* **(a)** *(obtain by effort: money, visa)* ottenere, procurarsi; *(: re-sults, permission)* avere, ottenere; *(find: job, flat)* trovare; *(buy)* comprare, prendere; *(fetch: per-son, doctor)* chiamare; *(: object)* prendere; *(Telec: number)* avere; *(TV etc: station)* prendere; **to ~ sth for sb** prendere *or* procurare qc a qn; **I'll ~ it for you** vado a prendertelo io; **~ me Mr Jones, please** *(Telec)* mi passi il signor Jones, per favo-re; **I've been trying to ~ you (on the phone) all morning** ti ho cercato tutta la mattina al telefo-no; **I've still one to ~** me ne manca ancora uno; **to ~ breakfast** preparare la colazione; **can I ~ you a drink?** ti posso offrire da bere?

(b) *(receive: present, letter etc)* ricevere; *(ac-quire: reputation)* farsi; *(: prize)* ricevere, vince-re; **how much did you ~ for it?** quanto ti hanno dato?; **he ~s it from his father** in questo prende da suo padre; **I didn't ~ much from the film** quel film non mi è parso un gran che; **where did you ~ that idea from?** come ti sei fatto quest'idea?; **~ it into your head that...** mettiti bene in testa che...; **this room ~s very little sun** questa stanza è poco soleggiata; **he's in it for what he can ~** lo fa per interesse; **I'll ~ it!** *(phone)* rispondo io!; *(door)* vado io!; **he got 5 years for robbery** si è beccato 5 anni per rapina.

(c) *(catch)* prendere; *(hit: target etc)* colpire; **to ~ sb by the arm/throat** afferrare qn per un

braccio/alla gola; **got you!** *(fam)* preso!; **I'll ~ you for that!** *(fam)* ti faccio vedere io!; **you've got me there!** *(fam)* m'hai preso in castagna!; **the bullet got him in the leg** il proiettile l'ha colpito alla gamba.

(d) *(take, move)* portare; **to ~ sth to sb** far avere qc a qn; **I'll never ~ this upstairs** non riuscirò mai a portarlo di sopra; **we'll ~ you there somehow** in un modo o nell'altro ti ci por-tiamo; **to ~ sth past customs** riuscire a far pas-sare qc alla dogana; **where will that ~ us?** *(fam)* ma a che pro?; **crying won't ~ you anywhere** piangere non serve a niente; **the discussion got us nowhere** la discussione non è servita a nulla.

(e) *(understand)* afferrare; *(hear)* sentire; **sor-ry, I didn't ~ your name** scusi, non ho capito il suo nome; **I've got it!** ci sono arrivato!, ci sono!; **~ it?** *(fam)* capito?; **I don't ~ it** *(fam)* non capisco, non ci arrivo.

(f) *(fam: annoy)* dare ai nervi a.

(g) *(fam: thrill)* toccare.

(h) *(have, possess):* **to have got** avere; **how many have you got?** quanti ne hai?

(i): to ~ sth done *(do)* fare qc; *(have done)* far fare qc; **to ~ the washing/dishes done** fare il bucato/i piatti; **to ~ one's hair cut** farsi tagliare i capelli; **to ~ the car going** *or* **to go** mettere in moto *or* far partire la macchina; **I can't ~ the lock to turn** non riesco a far scattare la serratu-ra; **to ~ sb to do sth** far fare qc a qn; **to ~ sth/sb ready** preparare qc/qn; **to ~ one's hands dirty** sporcarsi le mani; **I wonder how he got his leg broken** mi chiedo come ha fatto a rompersi la gamba; **to ~ sb drunk** ubriacare qn.

2 *vi* **(a)** *(go):* **to ~ to/from** andare a/da; *(reach):* **to ~ to** arrivare a; **to ~ home** arrivare *or* tornare a casa; **he won't ~ far** non andrà lontano; **how did you ~ here?** come sei venuto?; **I've got as far as page 10** sono arrivato (fino) a pagina 10; **to ~ nowhere** *(fig)* non approdare a nulla; **to ~ somewhere** avere dei risultati.

(b) *(become, be)* diventare, farsi; **to ~ old/ tired** invecchiare/stancarsi; **to ~ (o.s.) dirty** sporcarsi; **I'm not ~ting any younger!** il tempo passa anche per me!; **to ~ killed** venire *or* rima-nere ucciso; **to ~ married** sposarsi; **to ~ used to sth** abituarsi a qc; **when do I ~ paid?** quando mi pagate?; **it's ~ting late** si sta facendo tardi; **how did it ~ like that?** *(fam)* com'è successo?

(c) *(begin)* mettersi a, cominciare a; **let's ~ going** *or* **started** muoviamoci!; **to ~ to know sb** incominciare a conoscere qn; **I'm ~ting to like him** incomincia a piacermi; **to ~ talking to sb** mettersi a parlare con *or* a qn.

(d) *modal aux vb:* **you've got to tell the police** devi dirlo alla polizia; **why have I got to do it?** perché devo farlo?

(e) *(be allowed to):* **I never ~ to go on holiday on my own** non riesco mai ad andare in vacanza da solo.

♦ **get about** *vi + prep (go out: socially, after illness)* uscire, muoversi; *(fig: news, rumour)* spargersi.

♦ **get across 1** *vt + adv* far capire. **2** *vi + adv* **(a)** *(cross road etc)* attraversare. **(b): to ~ across to** *(message, meaning)* comunicare a; *(subj: speaker)* comunicare con.

♦ **get ahead** *vi + adv* andare avanti, farsi strada; **to ~ ahead of sb** sorpassare *or* superare qn.

♦ **get along** *vi + adv* **(a)** *(leave)* scappare, andar-sene; **~ along with you!** vattene! **(b)** *(progress)* procedere; *(manage)* farcela, cavarsela; **how is your son ~ting along at school?** come va tuo figlio a scuola? **(c)** *(be on good terms)* andare d'accordo; **to ~ along well with sb** intendersela con qn.

♦ **get around** vt + adv (a) = get about. (b) = get round 2.

♦ **get at** vi + prep (a) (gain access to: object) arrivare a (prendere); (: place) raggiungere, arrivare a; (ascertain: facts, truth) accertare, scoprire; **just let me ~ at him!** (fam) lascia che mi capiti tra le mani! (b) (fam: criticize) stare or dare addosso a. (c) (fam: imply) avere in mente; **what are you ~ting at?** dove vuoi arrivare?

♦ **get away** vi (depart) partire; (go on holiday) andar via; **to ~ away (from)** (work, party) andarsene (da); (escape) liberarsi (da); **to ~ away from it all** andarsene lontano da tutto e da tutti; **there's no ~ting away from it** (fam) non c'è niente da fare.

♦ **get away with** vi + prep (a) (steal) dileguarsi con. (b) (fam: go unpunished) passarla liscia; (: to go undetected) farla franca; **he'll never ~ away with it!** non riuscirà a farla franca!; **that child ~s away with murder** (fig fam) a quel bambino gliele lasciano passare tutte.

♦ **get back 1** vt + adv (a) (recover: possessions) recuperare; (: sth borrowed) farsi restituire; (: strength) riprendere. (b) (return: object, person) riportare. **2** vi + adv (ri)tornare; **~ back!** indietro!; **to ~ back (home)** ritornare a casa, rincasare.

♦ **get back at** vi + prep (fam): **to ~ back at sb (for sth)** rendere pan per focaccia a qn.

♦ **get behind** vi + adv rimanere indietro.

♦ **get by** vi + adv (a) (pass) passare. (b) (: manage) cavarsela; (: be acceptable) essere passabile; **I can ~ by in Dutch** mi arrangio in olandese; **don't worry, he'll ~ by** non preoccuparti, se la caverà.

♦ **get down 1** vt + adv (a) (take down) tirar giù. (b) (swallow) mandar giù. (c) (note down) prender nota di. (d) (fam: depress) buttar giù; **don't let it ~ you down** non devi abbatterti per questo. **2** vi + adv (descend): **to ~ down (from** or **off)** scendere (da); **quick, ~ down!** giù presto!

♦ **get down to** vi + prep: **to ~ down to (doing) sth** mettersi a (fare) qc; **to ~ down to business** venire al dunque.

♦ **get in 1** vt + adv (a) (bring in: harvest) raccogliere; (: coal, shopping, supplies) fare provvista di. (b) (plant: bulbs etc) piantare. (c) (summon: expert etc) chiamare, far venire. (d) (insert: object) far entrare, infilare; (: comment, word) infilare. **2** vi + adv (a) (enter) entrare. (b) (arrive: train) arrivare; (reach home: person) rientrare. (c) (be admitted: to club) entrare; (be elected: party) andare al potere; (: M.P.) essere eletto(a); **he got in with a bad crowd** si è messo con una banda di cattivi soggetti.

♦ **get into** vi + prep (house, clothes) entrare in; (vehicle) salire in, montare in; (club) entrare in, essere ammesso(a) a; **to ~ into difficulties** trovarsi in difficoltà; **to ~ into trouble** ficcarsi nei guai; **to ~ into the habit of doing sth** prendere l'abitudine di fare qc; **to ~ into a rage** andare su tutte le furie.

♦ **get off 1** vt + adv (a) (remove: clothes, stain) levare, togliere. (b) (send off) spedire; **she got the baby off to sleep** ha fatto addormentare il bambino. (c) (save from punishment) far assolvere, tirar fuori. (d) (have as leave: day, time) prendersi. **2** vi + prep (vehicle etc) scendere da; (fam: escape: chore etc) riuscire a non fare, scansare. **3** vi + adv (a) (from vehicle) scendere; **to tell sb where to ~ off** (fam) dire a qn di andare a farsi benedire; **to ~ off to a good start** (fig) comincia-

re bene. (b) (depart: person) andare via. (c) (escape injury, punishment) cavarsela; **he got off with a fine** se l'è cavata con una multa. (d) (from work) staccare.

♦ **get off with** vi + prep (fam: start relationship with) mettersi con.

♦ **get on 1** vi + prep (vehicle): **to ~ on the bus/train** etc salire or montare sull'autobus/sul treno etc, salire or montare in autobus/in treno etc; **to ~ on a horse** montare a cavallo. **2** vi + adv (a) (mount) salire, montare. (b) (proceed): **to ~ on (with sth)** continuare a fare (qc); **~ on with it!** su, muoviti! (c) (progress) far progressi; (fare: in exam, etc): **how did you ~ on?** com'è andato?; **how are you ~ting on?** come va (la vita)?; **to be ~ting on** (person) essere avanti negli anni; **he's ~ting on for 70** va per i 70; **time is ~ting on** si sta facendo tardi. (d) (succeed) farsi strada. **(e** (be on good terms): **to ~ on (with sb)** andare d'accordo (con qn).

♦ **get on to** vt + prep (fam) (a) (contact: on phone etc) contattare, rintracciare. (b) (deal with) occuparsi di.

♦ **get out 1** vt + adv: **to ~ out (of)** (take out) tirare fuori (da); (money from bank etc) ritirare (da); (stain) levare (da), togliere (da); (book: from library) prendere in prestito (da); **~ those children out of here!** leva quei bambini di torno! **2** vi + adv (news etc) venirsi a sapere, spargersi; : **to ~ out (of)** (go out) uscire (da); (leave) andar via (da), uscire (da); (from vehicle) scendere (da); (escape) scappare (da).

♦ **get out of 1** vt + prep (extract: confession, words) tirare fuori di bocca a; (gain from: pleasure, benefit) trarre da; **to ~ sb out of bed** far alzare qn. **2** vi + prep (a) (see also get out 2) liberarsi da; (escape: duty, punishment) sottrarsi a. (b): **to ~ out of the habit of doing sth** perdere l'abitudine di fare qc.

♦ **get over 1** vi + adv (cross) attraversare. **2** vi + prep (a) (cross) attraversare. (b) (recover from: illness) riprendersi da, rimettersi da; (: disappointment) superare; (: surprise, shock) riaversi da; **I can't ~ over it!** non riesco a crederci!; **you'll ~ over it!** ti passerà! (c) (overcome: difficulty) superare; (: shyness) vincere. **3** vt + adv (a) (transport across) far passare. (b) (have done with) finire una buona volta; **let's ~ it over (with)** togliamoci il pensiero. (c) (communicate: idea etc) comunicare, passare.

♦ **get round 1** vi + prep (difficulty) aggirare, ovviare a; (: problem) superare; (law, regulation) eludere; **she knows how to ~ round him** sa come prenderlo. **2** vi + adv: **to ~ round to doing sth** trovare il tempo di fare qc; **I'll ~ round to it** prima o poi lo farò.

♦ **get through 1** vi + prep (a) (pass through: window etc) passare per or da; (: crowd) passare attraverso, farsi strada attraverso. (b) (finish: work) sbrigare; (: book) finire; (use up: food, money) far fuori, dar fondo a; **we got through a lot of work today** abbiamo sbrigato molto lavoro oggi. (c) (pass: exam) passare a. **2** vt + prep (cause to succeed: student) far passare; (: proposal, bill) far passare a, far approvare a. **3** vt + adv (succeed in sending: message, supplies) far arrivare or pervenire; (Pol: bill) far passare or approvare. **4** vi + adv (a) (pass through) passare; (news, supplies etc: arrive) raggiungere. (b) (pass, be accepted) passare; **they got through to the semifinal** sono entrati in semifinale. (c) (finish) finire, terminare. (d) (Telec) ottenere la comunicazione or la linea; **to ~ through to sb** mettersi in contatto con qn; *(fig: communicate with)* comunicare con qn.

♦ **get together 1** *vt + adv (people)* radunare; *(objects, thoughts, ideas)* raccogliere. **2** *vi + adv (group, club)* riunirsi; **to ~ together about sth** vedersi per discutere qc.

♦ **get up 1** *vi + adv* **(a)** *(rise: from chair, bed)* alzarsi; *(wind)* alzarsi, levarsi. **(b)** *(climb up)* salire. **2** *vt + adv* **(a)** *(person: from chair, floor)* sollevare, tirar su; *(: wake)* far alzare, svegliare. **(b)** *(gather: strength, speed)* prendere; **to ~ up enthusiasm for sth** entusiasmarsi per qc. **(c)** *(fam: organize: celebrations etc)* organizzare. **(d)** *(fam: dress up: person)*: **to ~ o.s. up in** farsi bello(a) con; **to ~ o.s. up as** travestirsi da. **3** *vi + prep (tree)* arrampicarsi su; *(ladder)* salire su per.

♦ **get up to** *vi + prep* **(a)** *(reach)* raggiungere, arrivare a; **I've got up to chapter 4** sono arrivato *or* sono al capitolo 4. **(b)**: **to ~ up to mischief** combinarne di tutti i colori; **what have you been ~ting up to?** cosa hai combinato?

get·away ['gɛtəweɪ] **1** *n*: **to make one's ~** darsi alla fuga. **2** *cpd*: **~ car** *n* macchina per la fuga.

get-togeth·er ['gɛttə,gɛðəʳ] *n (piccola) riunione f; (party)* festicciola.

get-up ['gɛtʌp] *n (fam: outfit)* tenuta.

get-well card [gɛt'wɛl,kɑːd] *n* cartolina di auguri di pronta guarigione.

gey·ser ['giːzəʳ] *n (Geog)* geyser *m inv; (water heater)* scaldabagno.

Gha·na ['gɑːnə] *n* Gana *m*.

ghast·ly ['gɑːstlɪ] *adj (horrible)* atroce, spaventoso(a); *(pale)* spettrale; *(fam: very bad: mistake etc)* pauroso(a); **we had a ~ time last night** è stata una serata orribile ieri sera.

gher·kin ['gɜːkɪn] *n* cetriolino.

ghet·to ['gɛtəʊ] *n* ghetto.

ghost [gəʊst] **1** *n* fantasma *m*, spettro; **Holy G~** *(Rel)* Spirito Santo; **he hasn't the ~ of a chance** *(fig)* non ha la più pallida *or* la minima possibilità. **2** *vt (book)* fare lo scrittore ombra per. **3** *cpd*: **~ story** *n* storia di fantasmi; **~ town** città fantasma *f inv*.

ghost·writ·er ['gəʊst,raɪtəʳ] *n* scrittore/trice ombra *inv*.

ghoul [guːl] *n vampiro che si nutre di cadaveri;* **she's a ~** *(fig)* ha proprio il gusto del macabro.

gi·ant ['dʒaɪənt] **1** *n* gigante *m*, colosso. **2** *cpd (strides)* da gigante; *(fern, panda)* gigante; **~ (size) packet** *n* confezione *f* gigante.

gib·ber ['dʒɪbəʳ] *vi (monkey)* squittire confusamente; *(idiot)* farfugliare; **to ~ with rage** non connettere più dalla rabbia.

gib·ber·ish ['dʒɪbərɪʃ] *n* parole *fpl* senza senso.

gib·bet ['dʒɪbɪt] *n* patibolo.

gib·bon ['gɪbən] *n* gibbone *m*.

gibe [dʒaɪb] **1** *n* frecciata, malignità *f inv*. **2** *vi*: **to ~ (at)** lanciare frecciate (a).

gib·lets ['dʒɪblɪts] *npl* frattaglie *fpl*.

Gi·bral·tar [dʒɪ'brɔːltəʳ] *n* Gibilterra.

gid·dy ['gɪdɪ] *adj (-ier, -iest) (dizzy)*: **to be ~** aver le vertigini; *(causing dizziness: height)* vertiginoso(a); *(: speed)* folle; **I feel ~** mi gira la testa.

gift [gɪft] *n* **(a)** *(present)* dono, regalo; *(Comm: also:* **free ~)** omaggio; **as a free ~** in omaggio, in dono; **it's a ~!** *(fam: easy)* è uno scherzo! **(b)** *(talent)*: **to have a ~ for sth** avere il dono di qc.

gift·ed ['gɪftɪd] *adj*: **~ (in)** dotato(a) (per).

gig [gɪg] *n (fam: of musician)* serata.

gi·gan·tic [dʒaɪ'gæntɪk] *adj* gigantesco(a).

gig·gle ['gɪgl] **1** *n* risolino (sciocco); **to get the ~s** farsi prendere dalla risarella. **2** *vi* ridacchiare (scioccamente), avere la risarella.

gild [gɪld] *vt (metal, frame)* dorare; *(fig)* indorare; **to**

~ the lily *(fig)* mettere i fronzoli alla bellezza.

gill¹ [gɪl] *n (of fish)* branchia.

gill² [dʒɪl] *n (measure)* = 0,142 l.

gilt [gɪlt] **1** *n* doratura. **2** *cpd* dorato(a).

gilt-edged ['gɪltedʒd] *adj* **(a)** *(Fin: stocks, securities)* della massima sicurezza. **(b)** *(book)* dal taglio dorato.

gim·let ['gɪmlɪt] *n (for wood)* succhiello.

gim·mick ['gɪmɪk] *n* trovata; **sales ~** trovata commerciale.

gin [dʒɪn] *n (drink)* gin *m inv*; **~ and tonic** gin tonic *m inv*.

gin·ger ['dʒɪndʒəʳ] **1** *n* zenzero. **2** *adj (hair)* rossiccio(a); **~ ale** *or* **beer** gazzosa allo zenzero.

ginger·bread ['dʒɪndʒəbred] *n* pan *m* pepato, pan di zenzero.

gin·ger·ly ['dʒɪndʒəlɪ] *adv* con circospezione.

ging·ham ['gɪŋəm] *n (material)* percalle *m*.

gip·sy ['dʒɪpsɪ] = **gypsy**.

gi·raffe [dʒɪ'rɑːf] *n* giraffa.

gird·er ['gɜːdəʳ] *n* trave *f*.

gir·dle ['gɜːdl] *n (corset)* busto.

girl [gɜːl] **1** *n (child)* bambina, ragazzina; *(young woman, fam: girlfriend)* ragazza; **factory ~** operaia; **shop ~** commessa; **the old ~** next door *(fam)* la vecchia qui accanto. **2** *cpd*: **G~ Guide** *(Brit)*, **G~ Scout** *(Am)* Giovane Esploratrice *f*.

girl·friend ['gɜːlfrend] *n (of girl)* amica, amichetta; *(of boy)* ragazza.

giro ['dʒaɪrəʊ] *n (bank ~)* versamento bancario; *(post office ~)* postagiro.

girth [gɜːθ] *n (for saddle)* sottopancia *m; (measure: of tree)* circonferenza; *(: of person's waist)* giro di vita.

gist [dʒɪst] *n (of speech, conversation etc)* succo, nocciolo.

give [gɪv] *(vb: pt* **gave**, *pp* **given) 1** *vt* **(a)** *(gen)* dare; *(as gift)* regalare, dare (in dono); *(description, promise, surprise)* fare; *(particulars)* dare, fornire; *(decision)* annunciare; *(title, honour)* conferire, dare; *(assign: job)* assegnare, dare; *(dedicate: life, time)* consacrare, dedicare; **to ~ sb sth** *or* **sth to sb** dare qc a qn; **how much did you ~ for it?** quanto (l')hai pagato?; **to ~ sb a kick/push** dare un calcio/una spinta a qn; **to ~ sb a cold** passare *or* attaccare il raffreddore a qn; **to ~ sb news of sth** dar notizie di qc a qn; **to ~ sb something to eat** dare (qualcosa) da mangiare a qn; **12 o'clock, ~ or take a few minutes** mezzogiorno, minuto più minuto meno; **to ~ as good as one gets** rendere pan per focaccia; **he gave it everything he'd got** *(fig)* ce l'ha messa tutta; **I'd ~ a lot/the world/anything to know...** *(fam)* darei moltissimo/tutto l'oro del mondo/non so che cosa per sapere...; **I can ~ you 10 minutes** posso darti 10 minuti; **~ them my regards** salutali da parte mia; **~ yourself an hour to get there** calcola un'ora per arrivare; **that ~s me an idea** mi fa venire un'idea; **he's honest, I'll ~ you that** è onesto, te lo concedo.

(b) *(produce)* dare, produrre; *(result, help, advice)* dare; **3 times 4 ~s 12** 3 per 4 fa 12; **to ~ the right/wrong answer** dare la risposta giusta/sbagliata.

(c) *(perform etc: jump, smile)* fare; *(deliver: speech, lecture)* fare, tenere; *(emit: cry)* lanciare; *(: sigh)* tirare, fare; **~ us a song** cantaci qualcosa; **he gave a good performance** *(musician)* è stata una buona esecuzione; *(actor)* ha recitato bene.

2 *vi* **(a)** *(give presents)* dare, donare; **to ~ to charity** fare la beneficenza.

(b) *(also: ~ way: collapse etc: roof, ground, door)* cedere; *(: knees)* piegarsi; **something's got**

to ~! *(fam)* non si può andare avanti così.
3 *n (of material)* elasticità; *(of bed)* morbidezza.

♦ **give away** *vt + adv* **(a)** *(money, goods)* dar via; *(bride)* condurre all'altare; *(present: prizes)* distribuire. **(b)** *(reveal: secret)* rivelare; *(betray: person)* tradire; **to ~ the game away** *(fig)* farsi scoprire.

♦ **give back** *vt + adv (return: sb's property)*: **to ~ back (to)** restituire (a), rendere (a), ridare (a).

♦ **give in 1** *vt + adv (hand in: form, essay)* consegnare; **to ~ in one's name** dare il proprio nome. **2** *vi + adv (yield)*: **to ~ in (to sb)** cedere (a qn); *(in guessing game etc)*: **I ~ in!** mi arrendo!

♦ **give off** *vt + adv (smell, smoke, heat)* emettere, sprigionare.

♦ **give out 1** *vt + adv* **(a)** *(distribute)* distribuire. **(b)** *(make known: news etc)* annunciare. **2** *vi + adv (be exhausted: supplies)* esaurirsi, venir meno; *(fail: engine)* fermarsi; *(: strength)* mancare; *(: legs)* non reggere più.

♦ **give up 1** *vt + adv* **(a)** *(surrender: place)* cedere; *(hand over: ticket)* consegnare; **to ~ o.s. up to the police** costituirsi alla polizia. **(b)** *(renounce: friend, boyfriend, job)* lasciare; *(: habit)* perdere; *(abandon: idea etc)* rinunciare a, abbandonare; *(abandon hope for: patient)* dare per spacciato(a); *(: expected visitor)* non aspettare più; **I gave it up as a bad job** *(fam)* ci ho rinunciato, ho abbandonato l'idea; **to ~ up drinking/smoking** smettere di bere/fumare. **(c)** *(devote: one's life, time)*: **to ~ up (to)** dedicare (a); *(sacrifice: one's life, career etc)*: **to ~ up (for)** dare (per), donare (per). **2** *vi + adv (stop trying)* rinunciar(ci), arrendersi; **I ~ up!** *(trying to guess)* mi arrendo!

♦ **give way** *vi + adv* **(a) = give 2b. (b)** *(yield)*: **to ~ way (to)** cedere (a); **to ~ way to despair** lasciarsi andare alla disperazione. **(c)** *(make room for)*: **to ~ way (to)** lasciare il posto (a). **(d)** *(Brit Aut)* dare la precedenza.

give-and-take [,gɪvən'teɪk] *n (fam)* elasticità (da ambo le parti), concessioni *fpl* reciproche.

give·away ['gɪvəweɪ] **1** *n (fam)*: **her expression was a dead ~** le si leggeva tutto in volto; **the exam was a ~!** l'esame è stato uno scherzo! **2** *cpd*: **~ prices** *npl* prezzi *mpl* irrisori.

giv·en ['gɪvn] **1** *pp of* **give. 2** *adj* **(a)** *(fixed: time, amount)* dato(a), determinato(a); **~ name** *(esp Am)* nome *m* di battesimo. **(b)**: **to be ~ to doing sth** essere incline *or* propenso(a) a fare qc. **3** *conj*: **~ (that)...** ammesso che..., supposto che...; **~ the circumstances...** date le circosanze...; **~ time, it would be possible** se ci fosse tempo, sarebbe possibile.

giv·er ['gɪvəʳ] *n* donatore/trice.

gla·cial ['gleɪsɪəl] *adj* glaciale.

glaci·er ['glæsɪəʳ] *n* ghiacciaio.

glad [glæd] *adj* **(-der, -dest)** *(pleased)* contento(a), compiaciuto; *(news, occasion)* lieto; **to be ~ about sth/that** essere contento *or* lieto di qc/che + *sub*; **I am ~ to hear it** mi fa molto piacere, ne sono felice; **I was ~ of his help** gli sono stato grato del suo aiuto; **he was only too ~ to do it** non chiedeva di meglio che farlo.

glad·den ['glædn] *vt* rallegrare.

glade [gleɪd] *n* radura.

gladia·tor ['glædɪeɪtəʳ] *n* gladiatore *m*.

glad·ly ['glædlɪ] *adv (joyfully)* lietamente; *(willingly)* con piacere.

glam·or·ous ['glæmərəs] *adj (gen)* favoloso(a); *(person)* affascinante; *(occasion)* brillante, elegante.

glam·our ['glæməʳ] *n* fascino.

glance [glɑːns] **1** *n* sguardo, occhiata; **to take** *or* **have a ~ at** dare un'occhiata a; **at a ~** a colpo d'occhio; **at first ~** a prima vista. **2** *vi* **(a)** *(look)*: **to ~ at** *(person)* lanciare uno sguardo *or* un'occhiata a; *(headlines)* dare uno sguardo *or* un'occhiata a; **to ~ away** distogliere lo sguardo; **to ~ through a report** dare una scorsa a un rapporto. **(b)**: **to ~ off sth** rimbalzare di striscio su qc.

glanc·ing ['glɑːnsɪŋ] *adj (blow)* di striscio.

gland [glænd] *n (Anat)* ghiandola.

glan·du·lar ['glændjʊləʳ] *adj* ghiandolare; **~ fever** mononucleosi *f*.

glare [glɛəʳ] **1** *n* **(a)** *(of light, sun)* luce *f or* bagliore *m* accecante; **the ~ of publicity** *(fig)* il chiasso della pubblicità. **(b)** *(look)* occhiata fulminante. **2** *vi* **(a)** *(light)* sfolgorare. **(b)** *(look)*: **to ~ at** fulminare con lo sguardo.

glar·ing ['glɛərɪŋ] *adj (dazzling: sun, light)* sfolgorante, accecante; *(: colour)* sgargiante; *(obvious: evidence)* lampante; *(: mistake)* palese.

glass [glɑːs] **1** *n* **(a)** *(material, pane of ~)* vetro; *(~ware)* cristalleria; *(drinking vessel, ~ful)* bicchiere *m*; *(barometer)* barometro; *(mirror)* specchio; **a wine ~** un bicchiere da vino, calice *m*. **(b)**: **~es** *npl (spectacles)* occhiali *mpl*. **2** *cpd (bottle, eye)* di vetro; *(industry)* del vetro; **~ case** *n* bacheca, vetrina; **~ fibre** *n* fibra di vetro; **~ wool** *n* lana di vetro.

glass-blowing ['glɑːs,bləʊɪŋ] *n* soffiatura del vetro.

glass·house ['glɑːshaʊs] *n (for plants)* serra.

glass·ware ['glɑːsweəʳ] *n* cristalleria, articoli *mpl* di vetro.

glassy ['glɑːsɪ] *adj (-ier, -iest) (sea, lake)* come uno specchio; *(eye, look)* vitreo(a).

glaze [gleɪz] **1** *n (on pottery)* smalto; *(Culin)* glassa. **2** *vt* **(a)** *(window)* mettere i vetri a. **(b)** *(pottery)* invetriare, smaltare (a vetro); *(Culin)* glassare. **3** *vi*: **his eyes ~d over** i suoi occhi si fecero vitrei.

gla·zi·er ['gleɪzɪəʳ] *n* vetraio.

gleam [gliːm] **1** *n (of light)* bagliore *m*; *(of moonlight)* chiarore *m*; *(of metal, water)* luccichio; **with a ~ in one's eye** con gli occhi scintillanti; *(mischievous)* con uno sguardo furbesco; **a ~ of hope** un barlume di speranza. **2** *vi (light, furniture)* brillare; *(metal, water)* luccicare; *(eyes)*: **to ~ (with)** brillare (di).

gleam·ing ['gliːmɪŋ] *adj* brillante, lucente; **the house was ~ing** la casa splendeva di pulizia.

glean [gliːn] *vt (gather: information)* racimolare.

glee [gliː] *n*: **with ~** *(gen)* con gioia; *(laugh)* di gusto.

glee·ful ['gliːfʊl] *adj (smile, laugh)* gioioso(a); *(: malicious)* malizioso(a).

glen [glɛn] *n* vallone *m*.

glib [glɪb] *adj (person)* dalla lingua sciolta; *(explanation, excuse)* facile, disinvolto(a).

glide [glaɪd] **1** *n (of dancer etc)* volteggio; *(Aer)* planata. **2** *vi (move smoothly)* scivolare silenziosamente; *(: dancer)* volteggiare; *(Aer)* planare.

glid·er ['glaɪdəʳ] *n (Aer)* aliante *m*.

glid·ing ['glaɪdɪŋ] *n (Aer)* volo con l'aliante.

glim·mer ['glɪməʳ] **1** *n (of light, also fig)* barlume *m*; *(of water)* luccichio. **2** *vi (light)* baluginare; *(water)* luccicare.

glimpse [glɪmps] **1** *n*: **to catch a ~ of** vedere di sfuggita. **2** *vt* intravedere.

glint [glɪnt] **1** *n (of metal etc)* scintillio; **he had a ~ in his eye** nei suoi occhi brillava una luce strana; **he had an angry ~ in his eye** aveva uno sguardo arrabbiato. **2** *vi* brillare.

glis·ten ['glɪsn] *vi (wet surface, water)* luccicare; *(eyes)*: **to ~ (with)** brillare (di).

glit·ter ['glɪtəʳ] **1** *n (of gold etc)* scintillio; *(on*

Christmas cards etc) polvere *f* d'oro. **2** *vi (gold etc)* luccicare; **all that ~s is not gold** non è tutt'oro quel che luccica.

gloat [gləʊt] *vi* gongolare; **to ~ over** *(money etc)* covare con gli occhi; *(victory, enemy's misfortune)* gongolare (di gioia) per, esultare per.

glob·al ['gləʊbl] *adj (world-wide)* mondiale; *(comprehensive)* globale.

globe [gləʊb] *n* globo; *(spherical map)* mappamondo, globo.

globe·trotter ['gləʊb,trɒtə'] *n* giramondo *m/f inv.*

glob·ule ['glɒbju:l] *n* gocciolina.

gloom [glu:m] *n* **(a)** *(darkness)* oscurità, buio; **in the ~** nell'oscurità, al buio. **(b)** *(sadness)* tristezza.

gloomy ['glu:mɪ] *adj (-ier, -iest) (place, character)* cupo(a); *(atmosphere, weather, day)* deprimente; *(outlook)* nero(a); **to feel ~** sentirsi giù *or* depresso; **to take a ~ view of things** vedere nero; **to feel ~ about sth** essere pessimista su qc.

glo·ri·fy ['glɔ:rɪfaɪ] *vt (exalt: God)* glorificare; *(: person)* onorare; *(pej: war, deeds)* magnificare, esaltare; **it was just a glorified...** non era altro che...

glo·ri·ous ['glɔ:rɪəs] *adj (deeds, victory)* glorioso(a); *(weather, view)* stupendo(a); *(colours)* festoso(a).

glo·ry ['glɔ:rɪ] **1** *n* gloria; *(splendour)* splendore *m*, magnificenza; **Rome at the height of its ~** Roma all'apogeo della gloria. **2** *vi:* **to ~ in sth** *(one's success etc)* gloriarsi di qc; *(another's misfortune)* gustare *or* assaporare qc. **3** *cpd:* **~ hole** *n (fam)* ripostiglio.

gloss [glɒs] **1** *n* **(a)** *(explanation)* glossa, nota esplicativa. **(b)** *(shine)* lucentezza, lustro; *(also:* **~ paint)** vernice *f* a olio. **2** *cpd:* **~ finish** *n:* **with a ~ finish** *(paint)* a olio; *(photo)* su carta lucida.

♦ **gloss over** *vt + adv (play down)* sorvolare su; *(hide)* coprire, mascherare.

glos·sa·ry ['glɒsərɪ] *n* glossario.

glossy ['glɒsɪ] *adj (-ier, -iest) (gen)* lucido(a); **~ magazine** rivista di lusso.

glove [glʌv] **1** *n* guanto. **2** *cpd:* **~ compartment** *n (Aut)* vano portaoggetti; **~ puppet** *n* burattino (di stoffa).

glow [gləʊ] **1** *n (of lamp, sunset etc)* luce *f* (diffusa); *(of cigarette, fire, city)* bagliore *m; (of bright colour)* luminosità; *(of cheeks)* colorito acceso; *(warm feeling: of pride etc)* vampata. **2** *vi (lamp, sunset etc)* ardere; *(fire)* sfavillare; *(colour, face)* risplendere; **to ~ with health** sprizzare salute (da tutti i pori).

glow·er ['glaʊə'] *vi:* **to ~ (at sb)** guardare (qn) con astio.

glow·ing ['gləʊɪŋ] *adj (light etc)* caldo(a); *(fire)* ardente; *(complexion)* luminoso(a); *(cheeks, colour)* acceso(a); *(person: with health)* fiorente; *(: with pleasure)* raggiante; *(fig: report, description etc)* entusiasta.

glow-worm ['gləʊwɜ:m] *n* lucciola.

glu·cose ['glu:kəʊs] *n* glucosio.

glue [glu:] **1** *n* colla. **2** *vt:* **to ~ (to)** incollare (a); **to ~ 2 things together** incollare 2 cose insieme; **she was ~d to the television** *(fig)* stava incollata alla televisione; **he was ~d to the spot** *(fig)* rimase di sasso.

glue-sniffing ['glu:,snɪfɪŋ] *n* sniffare *m* (colla).

glum [glʌm] *adj (-mer, -mest) (person)* giù *inv*; *(mood)* nero(a); *(expression)* cupo(a).

glut [glʌt] **1** *n* sovrabbondanza, surplus *m inv.* **2** *vt (market)* inondare, saturare.

glu·ti·nous ['glu:tɪnəs] *adj* colloso(a), appiccicoso(a).

glut·ton ['glʌtn] *n* goloso/a, ghiottone/a; **a ~ for**

work uno stacanovista; **a ~ for punishment** un masochista.

glut·tony ['glʌtənɪ] *n* ghiottoneria, golosità.

glyc·er·in(e) [,glɪsə'ri:n] *n* glicerina.

gm, gms *abbr of* **gram(s), gramme(s).**

gnarled [nɑ:ld] *adj* nodoso(a).

gnash [næʃ] *vt:* **to ~ one's teeth** digrignare i denti.

gnat [næt] *n* moscerino.

gnaw [nɔ:] **1** *vt (chew)* rosicchiare, rodere; *(fig: subj: remorse)* rodere; *(: hunger, pain)* tormentare. **2** *vi:* **to ~ through** rosicchiare da una parte all'altra; **to ~ at** rosicchiare; *(fig)* rodere.

gnome [nəʊm] *n* gnomo.

GNP *n abbr see* **gross.**

gnu [nu:] *n* gnu *m inv.*

go [gəʊ] *(vb: pt* **went,** *pp* **gone) 1** *vi* **(a)** *(gen)* andare; **to ~ to London** andare a Londra; **to ~ by car/on foot** andare in macchina/a piedi; **to ~ at 50 km/h** andare a 50 km l'ora *or* a 50 all'ora; **to ~ looking for sb/sth** andare in cerca di qn/qc; **to ~ swimming/shopping** *etc* andare a nuotare/a fare le spese *etc;* **to ~ for a walk/swim** andare a fare due passi/una nuotata; **to ~ to a party/to the dentist's** andare a una festa/dal dentista; **to ~ and see sb, to ~ to see sb** andare a trovare qn; **halt, who ~es there?** alt, chi va là?; **you ~ first** (vai) prima tu; **there he ~es!** eccolo (là)!; **he went that way** è andato di là; **there you ~ again!** *(fam)* ci risiamo!

(b) *(depart)* andar via, andarsene; *(train etc)* partire; *(disappear: person, object)* sparire; *(: money):* **to ~ (on)** andarsene (in); *(: time)* passare; *(be sold):* **to ~ (for)** essere venduto(a) (per); **my voice has gone** m'è andata via la voce; **the cake is all gone** il dolce è finito tutto; **that cupboard will have to ~** dobbiamo sbarazzarci di quell'armadio; **~!** *(Sport)* via!; **here ~es!** *(fam)* Dio me la mandi buona!; **gone are the days when...** sono finiti i tempi in cui...; **the day went slowly** la giornata non passava mai; **it's just gone 7** sono appena passate le 7; **only 2 days to ~** mancano solo 2 giorni; **~ing, ~ing, gone!** uno, due, tre, aggiudicato!; **it went for £10** è stato venduto per 10 sterline; **it's ~ing cheap** *(fam)* costa poco.

(c) *(extend)* arrivare; **the garden ~es down to the lake** il giardino arriva fino al lago; **money doesn't ~ far nowadays** non si fa molto coi soldi oggigiorno; **it's good as far as it ~es, but...** quello che c'è va bene, ma...; **as cooks ~, she's quite good** come cuoca non è male; **as package tours ~ it's quite cheap** per un viaggio organizzato è conveniente.

(d) *(function: machine etc)* andare; **I couldn't get the car to ~ at all** non sono riuscito a far partire la macchina; **to keep ~ing** *(person: also fig)* andare avanti; *(machine)* andare; **it ~es on petrol** *(Aut)* va a benzina; **to make sth ~, to get sth ~ing** far funzionare qc; *(engine, machine)* mettere in moto qc; **let's get ~ing** muoviamoci.

(e) *(progress, turn out)* andare; **the meeting went well** la riunione è andata bene; **how did the exam ~?** com'è andato l'esame?; **how's it ~ing?** *(fam)* come va (la vita)?; **we'll see how things ~** *(fam)* vediamo come vanno *or* come si mettono le cose; **he has a lot ~ing for him** molte cose giocano a suo favore; **how does that song ~?** come fa quella canzone?

(f): **to ~ (with)** *(match)* andare (con); *(coincide, co-occur)* accompagnarsi (a); **the curtains don't ~ with the carpet** le tende non vanno col tappeto.

(g) *(become)* diventare, farsi; **to ~ blind** perdere la vista; **to ~ hungry** fare la fame; **to ~**

without sth fare a meno di qc; **to ~ bad** *(food)* andare a male, guastarsi; **to ~ mad** impazzire; **to ~ to sleep** addormentarsi.

(h) *(fit, be contained)* andare, starci; **it won't ~ in the case** non ci sta nella valigia; **4 into 3 won't ~** il 4 nel 3 non ci sta.

(i) *(be acceptable)* andare, essere ammesso(a) *or* ammissibile; **anything ~es** *(fam)* tutto è permesso; **that ~es for me too** questo vale anche per me; **what he says ~es** la sua parola è legge.

(j) *(break etc: material)* consumarsi, logorarsi; *(: rope)* rompersi, cedere; *(: fuse, button)* saltare; *(: health, eyesight etc)* deteriorarsi; **this jumper has gone at the elbows** questo golf ha i gomiti bucati.

(k) *(be available)*: **there are several jobs ~ing** ci sono diversi posti disponibili; **is there any tea ~ing?** c'è un po' di tè?; **I'll take whatever is ~ing** prendo quello che c'è.

(l) *(prize, inheritance)*: **to ~ (to)** andare (a), toccare (a); **the money ~es to charity** il denaro va ad opere di beneficenza; **the money will ~ towards our holiday** questi soldi li mettiamo per la vacanza; **all his money ~es on drink** tutti i suoi soldi se ne vanno in alcool; **the qualities which ~ to make him a great writer** le qualità che fanno di lui un grande scrittore.

(m) *(make: sound or movement)* fare; *(doorbell, phone)* suonare; **~ like that (with your right hand)** fai così (con la destra).

(n) *(Am)*: ... **to ~** *(food)* ... da portar via.

2 *aux vb*: **I'm ~ing to do it** lo farò; *(intention)* ho intenzione di farlo; **I was ~ing to do it** stavo per farlo; *(intention)* volevo farlo; **it's ~ing to rain** sta per piovere; **there's ~ing to be trouble** saranno guai.

3 *vt (fam)*: **to ~ it alone** farlo da solo(a); **to ~ one better** *(action)* fare di meglio; *(story)* avere di meglio.

4 *n, pl* **~es (a)** *(fam: energy)* dinamismo; **he's always on the ~** non si ferma un minuto; **I've got two projects on the ~** ho due progetti per le mani; **it's all ~** non c'è un attimo di respiro.

(b) *(success)*: **to make a ~ of sth** riuscire in qc; *(scheme)* mandare in porto qc; **it's no ~** *(fam)* (non c'è) niente da fare.

(c) *(attempt)* tentativo; **to have a ~ (at doing sth)** provare (a fare qc); **at** *or* **in one ~** in un sol colpo; **it's your ~** tocca a te.

(d): **from the word ~** *(fam)* (fin) dal primo momento; **all systems (are) ~** tutto a posto.

◆ **go about 1** *vi + prep* **(a)** *(set to work on: task)* affrontare; **how does one ~ about getting the tickets?** come si fa a procurarsi i biglietti? **(b)** *(busy o.s. with)* continuare a fare; **to ~ about one's business** occuparsi delle proprie faccende. **2** *vi* *(also: ~* **around:** *wander about)* aggirarsi; *(circulate: flu etc)* esserci in giro.

◆ **go after** *vi + prep (pursue)* correr dietro a, rincorrere; *(criminal etc)* inseguire; *(job, record etc)* mirare a; *(girl)* star dietro a, fare la corte a.

◆ **go against** *vi + prep (be unfavourable to: result, events)* essere contro; *(be contrary to: principles, conscience, sb's wishes)* andare contro.

◆ **go ahead** *vi + adv (carry on)* tirare avanti; **he went ahead with his plan** mise in atto il suo piano; **~ (right) ahead!** fai pure!

◆ **go along** *vi + adv (proceed)* andare avanti; **check as you ~ along** verifichi man mano che procedi; **as we went along...** andando avanti...; **to ~ along with** *(accompany)* andare con, accompagnare; *(agree with: idea)* sottoscrivere, appoggiare; *(: person)* essere d'accordo con.

◆ **go around** *vi + adv see* **go about 2, go round a.**

◆ **go at** *vi + prep (fam: attack)* scagliarsi contro; *(tackle: job etc)* buttarsi in; **he really went at it** ci si è veramente buttato.

◆ **go away** *vi + adv (depart)* andarsene.

◆ **go back** *vi + adv* **(a): to ~ back (to)** *(return, revert)* ritornare (a), tornare (a); **there's no ~ing back now** non si può più tornare indietro. **(b)** *(date back)* risalire; **the controversy ~es back to 1929** la controversia risale al 1929. **(c)** *(extend: garden, cave)* estendersi.

◆ **go back on** *vi + prep (word, promise)* rimangiarsi, ritirare; *(decision)* tornare su.

◆ **go before** *vi + adv (happen before)* accadere prima, succedere prima.

◆ **go by 1** *vi + prep (be guided by: watch, compass)* seguire, basarsi su; **to ~ by appearances** giudicare dalle apparenze; **~ing by what he says...** stando a ciò che dice.... **(b): to ~ by the name of X** farsi chiamare X. **2** *vi + adv (pass by: person, car etc)* passare; *(opportunity)* scappare; **as time ~es** col passar del tempo.

◆ **go down** *vi + adv* **(a)** *(sun)* tramontare, calare; *(person: downstairs)* scendere, andar giù; *(sink: ship)* affondare; *(: person)* andar sotto; *(be defeated)* crollare; **that should ~ down well with him** dovrebbe incontrare la sua approvazione. **(b)** *(be written down)* venire registrato(a); **to ~ down in history/to posterity** passare alla storia/ai posteri. **(c)** *(decrease: prices, temperature etc)* scendere, calare; **he has gone down in my estimation** è sceso nella mia stima.

◆ **go for** *vi + prep* **(a)** *(attack)* lanciarsi contro *or* su, avventarsi su *or* contro; *(fig)* dare addosso a, attaccare. **(b)** *(fam: apply to)*: **that ~es for me too** questo vale anche per me. **(c)** *(fam: like, fancy)* andar matto(a) per; **I don't ~ for his films** i suoi film non mi dicono granché.

◆ **go forward** *vi + adv* **(a)** *(proceed: with plan etc)*: **to ~ forward (with)** procedere (con). **(b)** *(be put forward: suggestion)* essere avanzato(a), venire avanzato(a).

◆ **go in** *vi + adv* **(a)** *(enter)* entrare. **(b): the sun went in** il sole si è oscurato *or* nascosto. **(c)** *(fit)* entrarci, andarci.

◆ **go in for** *vi + prep* **(a)** *(enter for: race, competition)* prender parte a; *(: exam)* presentarsi a. **(b)** *(be interested in: hobby, sport)* essere appassionato(a) di; *(take as career)* scegliere; **she ~es in for all the latest styles** le piace vestirsi all'ultima moda.

◆ **go into** *vi + prep* **(a)** *(investigate, examine)* esaminare a fondo; *(explanation)* imbarcarsi in; **to ~ into details** entrare nei particolari; **let's not ~ into all that now** non parliamone per ora. **(b)** *(embark on: career)* darsi a. **(c)** *(trance, coma)* entrare in; **to ~ into fits of laughter** esser preso da un convulso di risa.

◆ **go off 1** *vi + adv* **(a)** *(leave)* andarsene, partire. **(b)** *(cease to operate: lights etc)* spegnersi. **(c)** *(bomb)* esplodere, scoppiare; *(alarm clock)* suonare; **the gun went off by accident** è partito un colpo accidentalmente. **(d)** *(go bad)* andare a male, guastarsi. **(e)** *(event)* andare; **the party went off well** la festa è andata *or* è riuscita bene. **2** *vi + prep (no longer like: thing)* perdere il gusto di; *(: person)* non poter più vedere; **I've gone off this dress** questo vestito non mi piace più.

◆ **go on 1** *vi + prep (be guided by: evidence etc)* basarsi su, fondarsi su; **there's nothing to ~ on** non abbiamo niente su cui basarci. **2** *vi + adv (a)* *(continue: war, talks)* continuare, protrarsi; *(: on journey)* proseguire; **to ~ on doing** continuare a fare; **he went on to say that...** ha aggiunto che..., **to ~ on about sth** *(fam)* non finirla più con qc; **what a way to ~ on!** *(pej)* bel modo di comportarsi! **(b)** *(lights)* accendersi; *(machine)* partire, mettersi in moto. **(c)** *(happen)* succedere, svolgersi; **what's ~ing on here?** che succede *or* che sta succedendo qui? **(d)** *(pass: time, years)* passare; **as time went on** con l'andar del tempo.

♦ **go on at** *vi + prep (nag)* assillare.

♦ **go on for** *vi + prep*: **it's ~ing on for 3 years now** sono 3 anni ormai; **he's ~ing on for 60** va per la sessantina; **it's ~ing on for 2 o'clock** sono quasi le 2.

♦ **go out** *vi + adv* **(a)** *(be extinguished: fire, light)* spegnersi. **(b)** *(leave)* uscire, andar fuori; *(socially)* uscire; *(in cards)* chiudere; *(ebb: tide)* calare; **to ~ out shopping/for a meal** andare a fare spese/a mangiar fuori; **to ~ out (of fashion)** passare (di moda); **to ~ out with sb** uscire con qn; **they've been ~ing out together for 2 years** sono 2 anni che stanno insieme.

♦ **go over 1** *vi + prep* **(a)** *(examine: report etc)* riguardare, controllare. **(b)** *(rehearse, review: speech, lesson etc)* ripassare; **to ~ over sth in one's mind** pensare bene a qc. **2** *vi + adv* **(a)**: **to ~ over (to)** *(cross over)* andare (a *or* in); *(fig: change habit, sides etc)* passare (a). **(b)** *(be received)* essere accolto(a); **his speech went over well** il suo discorso ha ricevuto una buona accoglienza.

♦ **go round** *vi + adv* **(a)** *(revolve)* girare; *(circulate: news, rumour)* circolare; **there is a rumour ~ing round that...** corre voce che.... **(b)** *(suffice)* bastare (per tutti); **is there enough food to ~ round?** c'è abbastanza da mangiare per tutti? **(c)** *(visit)*: **to ~ round (to sb's)** passare (da qn); **let's ~ round to John's place** facciamo un salto da John. **(d)** *(make a detour)*: **to ~ round (by)** passare (per).

♦ **go through 1** *vi + prep* **(a)** *(suffer)* passare. **(b)** *(examine: list, book)* leggere da capo a fondo; *(search through)* frugare in. **(c)** *(use up: money)* spendere, mangiarsi; *(consume, wear out)* consumare. **(d)** *(perform)* fare; *(: formalities)* sbrigare; **let's ~ through that scene again** rifacciamo quella scena (da capo). **2** *vi + adv* passare.

♦ **go through with** *vi + prep (plan, crime)* mettere in atto, eseguire; **I couldn't ~ through with it** non sono riuscito ad andare fino in fondo.

♦ **go together** *vi + adv (harmonize: people etc)* andar bene insieme; *(: colours)* intonarsi; *(coincide: events, conditions)* andare insieme.

♦ **go under** *vi + adv (sink: ship)* affondare, colare a picco; *(: person)* andare sotto; *(fig: business, firm)* fallire.

♦ **go up 1** *vi + adv* **(a)** *(rise: temperature, prices etc)* salire, aumentare; **to ~ up in price** aumentare (di prezzo). **(b)** *(ascend)* andare su. **(c)** *(be built: tower block etc)* venire costruito(a); *(: new district etc)* sorgere; *(: scaffolding)* venire eretto(a). **(d)** *(explode)* saltare in aria; **to ~ up in flames** andare in fiamme. **2** *vi + prep (ascend)* andare su per.

goad [gəʊd] *vt*: **to ~ sb into doing sth** *(fig)* pungolare qn perché faccia qc; **to ~ sb on** *(fig)* spronare qn, incitare qn.

go-ahead ['gəʊəhɛd] **1** *adj (firm, director)* intraprendente, pieno(a) d'iniziativa; *(policy, ideas)* avanzato(a). **2** *n*: **to give sb/sth the ~** dare l'okay a qn/qc.

goal [gəʊl] **1** *n* **(a)** *(Sport: score)* goal *m inv*; *(: net etc)* porta, rete *f*; **to play in ~** giocare in porta. **(b)** *(aim: in life)* scopo, obiettivo; *(: in journey)* meta. **2** *cpd*: **~ kick** *n (Ftbl)* rimessa (in gioco) dal fondo.

goal·keeper ['gəʊl,kiːpə^r] *n* portiere *m*.

goal·post ['gəʊlpəʊst] *n* palo (della porta).

goat [gəʊt] *n* capra; **to act the ~** *(fam)* fare lo stupido; **to get sb's ~** *(fam)* far uscire qn dai gangheri.

gob·ble ['gɒbl] *vt (also: ~ down, ~ up)* trangugiare, ingurgitare.

go-between ['gəʊbɪ,twiːn] *n* intermediario/a.

gob·let ['gɒblɪt] *n* calice *m*.

gob·lin ['gɒblɪn] *n* folletto.

god [gɒd] *n* dio; **G~** Dio; **the ~s** *(Theatre)* la piccionaia, il loggione; **(my) G~!** *(fam)* Dio (mio)!; **for G~'s sake!** per amor di Dio!; **G~ forbid!** per carità!; *(stronger)* Dio ce ne scampi e liberi!; **G~ (only) knows** Dio (solo) lo sa.

god·child ['gɒdtʃaɪld] *n, pl* **-children** figlioccio/a.

god·dess ['gɒdɪs] *n* dea.

god·father ['gɒd,faːðə^r] *n* padrino.

god·forsaken ['gɒdfə,seɪkən] *adj (fam: place)* abbandonato(a) da Dio e dagli uomini, sperduto(a).

god·less ['gɒdlɪs] *adj* empio(a).

god·ly ['gɒdlɪ] *adj (-ier, -iest)* pio(a).

god·mother ['gɒd,mʌðə^r] *n* madrina.

god·parents ['gɒd,pɛərənts] *npl*: **the ~** il padrino e la madrina.

god·send ['gɒdsɛnd] *n* dono del cielo; **it was a ~ to us** è stata una vera manna per noi.

goes [gəʊz] *3rd pers sg present of* **go.**

go-getter ['gəʊ,gɛtə^r] *n* arrivista *m/f.*

gog·gle ['gɒgl] *vi (look astonished)* sbarrare gli occhi, sgranare tanto d'occhi; *(stare)*: **to ~ (at)** stare con gli occhi incollati *or* appiccicati (a *or* addosso a).

gog·gles ['gɒglz] *npl (of skin-diver)* maschera; *(of skier)* occhiali *mpl* da sci; *(for workman)* occhiali (di protezione).

go·ing ['gəʊɪŋ] **1** *n* **(a)** *(pace)* andatura, ritmo; **it was slow ~** si andava a rilento. **(b)** *(state of road surface etc)* percorribilità; *(in horse-racing etc)* terreno; **let's cross while the ~ is good** attraversiamo finché c'è via libera; **it's heavy ~ talking to her** parlare con lei è una faticaccia. **2** *adj* **(a)** *(business, concern)* ben avviato(a). **(b)** *(current: price)* corrente, attuale; **the ~ rate** la tariffa in vigore.

goings-on ['gəʊɪŋz'ɒn] *npl (fam)* fatti *mpl* strani, cose *fpl* strane.

goi·tre, *(Am)* **goi·ter** ['gɔɪtə^r] *n* gozzo.

go-kart ['gəʊkaːt] *n* go-kart *m inv.*

gold [gəʊld] **1** *n* oro; **it's made of ~** è d'oro; **rolled ~** oro laminato. **2** *adj (bracelet, tooth, mine)* d'oro; *(reserves)* aureo(a); **~ leaf** lamina d'oro; **~ medal** *(Sport)* medaglia d'oro; **~ rush** *n* corsa all'oro; **~ standard** sistema *m* aureo.

gold·en ['gəʊldən] *adj (statue etc)* d'oro, in oro; *(hair etc)* biondo oro *inv; (age)* dell'oro; *(era)* d'oro; *(afternoon)* meraviglioso(a); **a ~ opportunity** un'occasione d'oro; **~ eagle** aquila reale; **~ handshake** gratifica di fine servizio; **~ jubilee** cinquantenario, giubileo; **~ rule** regola principale; **~ syrup** melassa (raffinata); **~ wedding (anniversary)** nozze *fpl* d'oro.

gold·fish ['gəʊldfɪʃ] *n* pesce *m* rosso.

gold·smith ['gəʊldsmɪθ] *n* orefice *m*, orafo.

golf [gɒlf] **1** *n* golf *m*; **to play ~** giocare a golf. **2** *cpd*: **~ club** *n (society)* circolo di golf; *(stick)* bastone *m* da golf; **~ course** *n* campo di golf.

golf·er ['gɒlfə^r] *n* giocatore/trice di golf.

gon·do·la ['gɒndələ] *n* gondola.

gon·do·lier [,gɒndə'lɪə^r] *n* gondoliere *m*.

gone [gɒn] *pp of* **go.**

gong [gɒŋ] *n* gong *m inv.*

gon·or·rhoea [,gɒnə'rɪə] *n* gonorrea.

goo [guː] *n (fam)* sostanza appiccicosa.

good [gʊd] **1** *adj (comp* **better,** *superl* **best) (a)** *(gen)* buono(a); ~ **manners** buona educazione *f,* buona creanza; **he has** ~ **judgment** sa giudicare; **be** ~! fai il bravo!; ~ **for you!** bravo!; **she's too** ~ **for him** lui non se la merita; **it's just not** ~ **enough!** è inaccettabile!; **the job is as** ~ **as done** il lavoro è praticamente finito; **as** ~ **as new** come nuovo; **she has been as** ~ **as gold** è stata un angelo, è stata d'oro; **(that's)** ~! bene!, ottimo!; **that's a** ~ **one!** questa sì che è bella!; **G**~ **Friday** *(Rel)* Venerdì Santo.

(b) *(pleasant: holiday, day, weather)* bello(a); *(: news)* buono(a), bello(a); **to feel** ~ sentirsi bene; **have a** ~ **journey!** buon viaggio!; **it's** ~ **to see you** che piacere vederti.

(c) *(handsome: looks, features)* bello(a); **you look** ~ **in that dress** quel vestito ti dona *or* ti sta bene; **she has a** ~ **figure** ha un bel personale.

(d) *(beneficial, advantageous, wholesome)* buono(a); ~ **to eat** buono da mangiare; **he's on to a** ~ **thing** ha trovato una miniera d'oro; **it's** ~ **for you** fa bene; **it's a** ~ **thing you were there** meno male che c'eri.

(e) *(competent: teacher, doctor)* bravo(a), buono(a); **he's** ~ **at English/telling jokes** è bravo in inglese/a raccontare barzellette; **she's** ~ **with children** (ci) sa fare coi bambini; **to be** ~ **for** andar bene per; **a ticket** ~ **for 3 months** un biglietto valido (per) 3 mesi; **he's** ~ **for £5** 5 sterline te le sgancia; **are you** ~ **for another kilometre?** ce la fai a fare un altro chilometro?

(f) *(kind)* gentile; **to be** ~ **to sb** essere gentile con *or* verso qn; **he's a** ~ **sort** *(fam)* è una brava persona; **would you be so** ~ **as to sign here?** avrebbe la gentilezza di firmare qui?; **that's very** ~ **of you** è molto gentile da parte sua; ~ **deeds** *or* **works** buone azioni *fpl,* opere *fpl* buone.

(g) *(considerable, not less than)* buono(a); **a** ~ **many/few people** parecchia/un bel po' di gente; **a** ~ **deal of money** un bel po' di soldi; **a** ~ **deal of work** parecchio lavoro; **a** ~ **3 hours** 3 ore buone; **it's a** ~ **distance from here** dista parecchio *or* un bel po' da qui.

(h) *(thorough)* bello(a); **to give sb a** ~ **scolding** fare una bella ramanzina a qn; **to have a** ~ **cry** farsi un bel pianto; **to take a** ~ **look (at sth)** guardare bene (qc).

(i) *(in greetings):* ~ **morning** buongiorno; ~ **afternoon** buongiorno; ~ **evening** buonasera; ~ **night** buonanotte.

2 *adv* **(a): a** ~ **strong stick** un bel bastone robusto; ~ **and strong** *(fam)* bello forte; **to hold** ~ **(for)** valere (per), reggere (in).

(b) *(esp Am fam: well)* bene.

3 *n* **(a)** *(what is morally right)* bene *m;* **to do** ~ fare del bene; ~ **and evil** il bene e il male; **he's up to no** ~ ne sta combinando qualcuna.

(b) *(pl: people of virtue):* **the** ~ i buoni.

(c) *(advantage, benefit)* bene *m,* interesse *m;* **for your own** ~ per il tuo bene; **for the common** ~ nell'interesse generale, per il bene comune; **to come to no** ~ andare a finire male; **what's the** ~ **of that?** a che pro?, a che serve?; **is this any** ~? *(will it do?)* va bene questo?; *(what's it like?)* com'è?; **that's no** ~ **to me** non mi va bene, non fa al caso mio; **that's all to the** ~! tanto meglio!, tanto di guadagnato!; **it's no** ~ **complaining** brontolare non serve a niente; **a (fat) lot of** ~ **that will do you** *(iro fam)* sai quanto ne ricavi.

(d) *(for ever):* **for** ~ **(and all)** per sempre, definitivamente.

good·bye [ˌgʊd'baɪ] **1** *excl* arrivederci. **2** *n* saluto;

addio; **to say** ~ **to** *(person)* salutare; *(fig: holiday, promotion etc)* dire addio a.

good-for-nothing [ˈgʊdfəˌnʌθɪŋ] **1** *adj* buono(a) a nulla. **2** *n* buono/a a nulla, vagabondo/a.

good-humoured [ˌgʊd'hjuːməd] *adj (person)* di buon umore; *(remark, joke)* bonario(a); *(discussion)* cordiale; **to be** ~ **about doing sth** fare qc di buon grado.

good-looking [ˌgʊd'lʊkɪŋ] *adj* bello(a), piacente.

good-natured [ˌgʊd'neɪtʃəd] *adj (person)* affabile; *(discussion)* amichevole, cordiale.

good·ness [ˈgʊdnɪs] **1** *n (virtue, kindness)* bontà *(d'animo); (good quality)* (buona) qualità. **2** *excl (fam)* **(my)** ~!, ~ **gracious!** santo cielo!, mamma mia!; **for** ~' **sake!** per amor del cielo!

goods [gʊdz] **1** *npl (Comm etc)* merci *fpl,* articoli *mpl;* **leather** ~ articoli di *or* in pelle; **canned** ~ scatolame *m;* **all my worldly** ~ *(frm)* tutti i miei beni *or* i miei averi; **all his** ~ **and chattels** tutti i suoi beni e effetti. **2** *cpd:* ~ **train** *n* treno *m* merci *inv.*

good-tempered [ˌgʊd'tempəd] *adj* buono(a).

good·will [ˌgʊd'wɪl] *n* buona volontà, buona fede *f; (Comm)* (valore *m* d')avviamento; **as a gesture of** ~ in segno di buona volÿntà.

goody-goody [ˈgʊdɪˌgʊdɪ] *n (pej)* santarellino/a.

goose [guːs] **1** *n, pl* **geese** oca. **2** *cpd:* ~ **step** *n (Mil)* passo dell'oca.

goose·berry [ˈgʊzbərɪ] *n* uva spina.

goose·flesh [ˈguːsfleʃ] *n,* **goose·pimples** [ˈguːspɪmplz] *npl* pelle *f* d'oca.

gore[1] [gɔːʳ] *n (of skirt)* spicchio.

gore[2] [gɔːʳ] *vt (subj: bull etc)* incornare.

gorge [gɔːdʒ] **1** *n (Geog)* gola. **2** *vt:* **to** ~ **o.s. (with** *or* **on)** rimpinzarsi (di), ingozzarsi (di).

gor·geous [ˈgɔːdʒəs] *adj (woman, dress)* stupendo(a); *(holiday, meal etc)* fantastico(a), formidabile.

go·ril·la [gəˈrɪlə] *n* gorilla *m inv.*

gorm·less [ˈgɔːmlɪs] *adj (fam)* tonto(a); *(: stronger)* deficiente.

gorse [gɔːs] *n* ginestrone *m.*

gory [ˈgɔːrɪ] *adj* **(-ier, -iest)** *(battle, death)* sanguinoso(a); **the** ~ **details** *(hum)* i dettagli più macabri.

gosh [gɒʃ] *excl (fam)* cribbio!, perdinci!

go-slow [ˌgəʊ'sləʊ] *n* ≈ sciopero bianco.

gos·pel [ˈgɒspəl] **1** *n (Rel)* vangelo; **the G**~ **according to St John** il Vangelo secondo (San) Giovanni; **you can take it as** ~ *(fam)* puoi giurarci su. **2** *cpd:* ~ **truth** *n:* **it's the** ~ **truth** è la verità sacrosanta, è vangelo.

gos·sa·mer [ˈgɒsəməʳ] *n (fabric)* garza, mussolina.

gos·sip [ˈgɒsɪp] **1** *n (talk)* chiacchiere *fpl; (scandal)* pettegolezzi *mpl; (person)* pettegolo/a, chiacchierone/a; **a piece of** ~ un pettegolezzo. **2** *vi (talk)* chiacchierare; *(talk scandal):* **to** ~ **(about)** fare pettegolezzi (su), chiacchierare (sul conto di). **3** *cpd:* ~ **column** *n* cronaca mondana.

got [gɒt] *pt, pp of* **get.**

Goth·ic [ˈgɒθɪk] *adj* gotico(a).

got·ten [ˈgɒtn] *(Am) pp of* **get.**

gouge [gaʊdʒ] *vt (also:* ~ **out:** *hole etc)* scavare; *(: initials)* scolpire; *(: sb's eyes)* cavare.

gou·lash [ˈguːlæʃ] *n* gulasch *m inv.*

gourd [gʊəd] *n* zucca.

gour·met [ˈgʊəmeɪ] *n* buongustaio/a.

gout [gaʊt] *n (Med)* gotta.

gov·ern [ˈgʌvən] *vt (rule: country)* governare; *(subj: king)* regnare; *(control: business)* dirigere; *(: city)* amministrare; *(: choice, decision)* regolare; *(: person)* guidare; *(: emotions)* dominare; *(Gram)* reggere.

gov·er·ness [ˈgʌvənɪs] n governante f, istitutrice f.

gov·ern·ing [ˈgʌvənɪŋ] adj (Pol) al potere, al governo; ~ **class** classe f dirigente; ~ **body** consiglio di amministrazione.

gov·ern·ment [ˈgʌvənmənt] 1 n governo; **local** ~ amministrazione f locale. 2 cpd: ~ **department** n dipartimento ministeriale; ~ **loan** n prestito statale; ~ **policy** n (gen) politica governativa; (of current government) politica del governo.

gov·er·nor [ˈgʌvənəʳ] n (of colony, state etc) governatore m; (director: of school) membro del consiglio di amministrazione; (: of prison) direttore/trice.

Govt abbr of **government**.

gown [gaʊn] n (dress) abito; (Law, Univ) toga.

G.P. n abbr see **general**.

grab [græb] 1 n (a) (snatch): **to make a** ~ **at** or **for sth** cercare di afferrare qc. (b) (Tech) benna. 2 vt (seize) afferrare, acchiappare; (: property) impossessarsi di; (greedily) agguantare; (fig: chance etc) cogliere al volo; **to** ~ **sth from sb** strappare qc di mano a qn. 3 vi: **to** ~ **at** tentare disperatamente di afferrare; (in falling) cercare di aggrapparsi a.

grace [greɪs] 1 n (Rel, elegance: of form, movement etc) grazia; (graciousness) garbo, cortesia; **he had the** ~ **to apologise** ha avuto la buonagrazia di scusarsi; **to do sth with good/bad** ~ fare qc volentieri/malvolentieri; **his sense of humour is his saving** ~ il suo senso dell'umorismo è quello che lo salva; **3 days'** ~ 3 giorni di proroga; **by the** ~ **of God** per grazia di Dio; **to say** ~ dire il benedicite; **His G**~ (duke, archbishop) Sua Eccellenza. 2 vt (adorn) adornare; (honour: occasion, event) onorare con la propria presenza; **he** ~**d the meeting with his presence** ci ha fatto l'onore di presenziare alla riunione.

grace·ful [ˈgreɪsfʊl] adj (gen) aggraziato(a), pieno(a) di grazia; (apology) garbato(a).

grace·ful·ly [ˈgreɪsfəlɪ] adv (see adj) con grazia; con garbo.

gra·cious [ˈgreɪʃəs] 1 adj (hostess, permission) cortese; (smile) benevolo(a); (mansion) di raffinata eleganza; (God) misericordioso(a); ~ **living** vita da gran signori. 2 excl: (good) ~! madonna (mia)!

grade [greɪd] 1 n (a) (on scale) categoria, livello; (in hierarchy, also Mil) grado; (Comm) qualità f inv; (size) misura, grandezza; **to make the** ~ (fig) farcela. (b) (Scol: mark) voto; (Am: school class) classe f, anno. (c) (Am: gradient) pendenza, gradiente m. 2 vt (a) (goods, eggs) classificare; (colours, exercises) graduare. (b) (Scol: mark) giudicare, dare un voto a. 3 cpd: ~ **crossing** n (Am Rail) passaggio a livello.

gra·di·ent [ˈgreɪdɪənt] n gradiente m, pendenza; **a** ~ **of 1 in 7** un gradiente del 7 per cento.

grad·ual [ˈgrædjʊəl] adj (change) graduale; (slope) dolce, lieve.

gradu·al·ly [ˈgrædjʊəlɪ] adv gradualmente, poco alla volta.

gradu·ate [ˈgrædjʊɪt] 1 n (Univ) laureato/a; (Am Scol) diplomato/a, licenziato/a; **he's a French** ~ or **a** ~ **in French** è laureato or ha la laurea in francese. 2 [ˈgrædjʊeɪt] vt (thermometer etc) graduare. 3 [ˈgrædjʊeɪt] vi (Univ) ≃ laurearsi; (Am Scol) ≃ dare gli esami di maturità; **to** ~ **from the University of Aberdeen** laurearsi all'università di Aberdeen.

gradua·tion [ˌgrædjʊˈeɪʃən] n (Univ: ceremony) consegna delle lauree; (Am Scol) consegna dei diplomi.

graf·fi·ti [grəˈfiːtɪ] npl graffiti mpl.

graft [grɑːft] 1 n (a) (Bot, Med) innesto. (b) (fam: corruption) corruzione f; (: hard work) duro lavoro. 2 vt innestare.

grain [greɪn] n (a) (no pl: cereals) cereali mpl; (Am: corn) grano. (b) (single seed: of wheat, rice etc) chicco, granello; (particle: of sand, salt, sense) grano, granello; **there's not a** ~ **of truth in it** non c'è un briciolo di verità. (c) (of wood, marble, leather, also Phot) grana; **it goes against the** ~ (fig) va contro la mia (or sua etc) natura.

gram(me) [græm] n grammo.

gram·mar [ˈgræmər] 1 n grammatica; **that's bad** ~ è sgrammaticato. 2 cpd: ~ **school** n (Brit) ≃ liceo.

gram·mati·cal [grəˈmætɪkəl] adj di grammatica; (sentence) grammaticale.

gramo·phone [ˈgræməfəʊn] n (Brit old) grammofono.

grana·ry [ˈgrænərɪ] n granaio.

grand [grænd] 1 adj (-er, -est) (splendid: occasion, person) splendido(a), magnifico(a); (person: important) altolocato(a); (style, house) sontuoso(a), grandioso(a); (fam: very pleasant) eccezionale, stupendo(a). 2 n (Am fam) mille dollari mpl. 3 cpd: ~ **finale** n gran finale m; ~ **jury** n (Am) giuria formata da 12 a 23 membri; ~ (**piano**) n pianoforte m a coda; **G**~ **Prix** n (Aut) Gran Premio, Grand Prix m inv; ~ **total** n somma complessiva.

grand·child [ˈgræntʃaɪld] n, pl -**children** nipote m/f, nipotino/a.

grand·(d)ad [ˈgrændæd] n (fam) nonno.

grand·daughter [ˈgræn,dɔːtəʳ] n nipotina, nipote f (di nonno).

gran·deur [ˈgrændjəʳ] n (of occasion, scenery etc) grandiosità, maestà; (of style, house) splendore m.

grand·father [ˈgrænd,fɑːðəʳ] 1 n nonno. 2 cpd: ~ **clock** n orologio a pendolo.

gran·di·ose [ˈgrændɪəʊz] adj grandioso(a).

grand·mother [ˈgræn,mʌðəʳ] n nonna.

grand·parent [ˈgræn,pɛərənt] n nonno/a.

grand·son [ˈgrænsʌn] n nipote m (di nonno), nipotino.

grand·stand [ˈgrændstænd] n (Sport) tribuna coperta.

gran·ite [ˈgrænɪt] n granito.

gran·ny, gran·nie [ˈgrænɪ] n (fam) nonna, nonnina.

grant [grɑːnt] 1 n (of money) sovvenzione f, sussidio; (Brit Univ) borsa (di studio). 2 vt (allow: extension, favour) accordare; (: pension) assegnare; (: request) accogliere; (admit): **to** ~ (**that**) ammettere (che); ~**ed** or ~**ing that...** ammesso che...; **I** ~ **him that** glielo concedo; **to take sth for** ~**ed** dare qc per scontato; **to take sb for** ~**ed** dare per scontata la presenza di qn.

granu·lat·ed [ˈgrænjʊleɪtɪd] adj: ~ **sugar** zucchero semolato.

gran·ule [ˈgrænjuːl] n granello.

grape [greɪp] n acino, chicco d'uva; **a bunch of** ~**s** un grappolo d'uva.

grape·fruit [ˈgreɪpfruːt] n pompelmo.

grape·vine [ˈgreɪpvaɪn] n vite f; **I heard it on the** ~ (fig) me l'ha detto l'uccellino.

graph [grɑːf] 1 n grafico, diagramma m. 2 cpd: ~ **paper** n carta millimetrata.

graph·ic [ˈgræfɪk] adj (gen) grafico(a); (vivid: description etc) di grande efficacia, vivido(a); **the** ~ **arts** le arti grafiche; ~ **designer** grafico/a.

graph·ics [ˈgræfɪks] n (art, process) grafica; (pl: drawings) illustrazioni fpl.

graph·ite [ˈgræfaɪt] n grafite f.

grap·ple [ˈgræpl] vi (wrestlers etc): **to** ~ (**with**) essere alle prese (con), lottare (con); **to** ~ **with a**

problem *(fig)* essere alle prese con un problema.

grap·pling iron ['græplɪŋ,aɪən] *n (Naut)* grappino.

grasp [grɑːsp] **1** *n (grip)* presa; **to lose one's ~ on reality** *(fig)* perdere il contatto con la realtà; **it is within everybody's ~** *(fig)* è alla portata di tutti; **it is beyond my ~** non ci arrivo; **to have a good ~ of** *(subject)* avere una buona padronanza di; **he has a good ~ of the difficulties** si rende perfettamente conto dei problemi. **2** *vt* **(a)** *(take hold of)* afferrare; *(hold firmly)* stringere; *(fig: chance, opportunity)* cogliere (al volo). **(b)** *(understand: meaning, hint)* afferrare.

♦ **grasp at** *vi + prep (rope etc)* afferrarsi a, aggrapparsi a; *(fig: opportunity)* non farsi sfuggire, approfittare di.

grasp·ing ['grɑːspɪŋ] *adj (fig)* avido(a).

grass [grɑːs] **1** *n (gen)* erba; *(pasture)* pascolo, prato; *(fam: informer)* informatore/trice; *(: exterrorist)* pentito/a; **'keep off the ~'** 'vietato calpestare l'erba'; **not to let the ~ grow under one's feet** *(fig)* non tirarla per le lunghe. **2** *cpd*: **~ roots** *npl (fig)* base *f*; **~ widow** *n* vedova bianca.

grass·hopper ['grɑːs,hɒpəʳ] *n* cavalletta.

grass·land ['grɑːslænd] *n* prateria.

grassy ['grɑːsɪ] *adj* (**-ier, -iest**) erboso(a).

grate[1] [greɪt] *n (in fireplace)* grata, griglia.

grate[2] [greɪt] **1** *vt* **(a)** *(cheese etc)* grattugiare, grattare. **(b)** *(scrape: metallic object, chalk etc)* far grattare; **to ~ one's teeth** digrignare i denti. **2** *vi (hinge)* cigolare; **to ~ (on or against)** *(chalk)* stridere (su); *(fig)*: **it really ~s (on me)** mi dà veramente ai or sui nervi.

grate·ful ['greɪtfʊl] *adj*: **~ (for)** grato(a) (per), riconoscente (per); **I am most ~ to you** ti sono veramente grato.

grat·er ['greɪtəʳ] *n* grattugia.

grati·fi·ca·tion [,grætɪfɪ'keɪʃən] *n* soddisfazione *f*.

grati·fy ['grætɪfaɪ] *vt (person)* far piacere a, dare soddisfazione a; *(desire, whim etc)* soddisfare, appagare.

grati·fy·ing ['grætɪfaɪɪŋ] *adj* gradito(a), soddisfacente.

grat·ing[1] ['greɪtɪŋ] *n (in wall, pavement)* grata.

grat·ing[2] ['greɪtɪŋ] *adj (sound)* stridulo(a), stridente.

gra·tis ['grætɪs] *adv* gratis.

grati·tude ['grætɪtjuːd] *n* gratitudine *f*, riconoscenza.

gra·tui·tous [grə'tjuːɪtəs] *adj* gratuito(a).

gra·tu·ity [grə'tjuːɪtɪ] *n (Mil)* indennità *f inv* di congedo; *(frm: tip)* mancia.

grave[1] [greɪv] *adj* (**-r, -st**) *(gen)* grave, serio(a).

grave[2] [greɪv] *n* tomba.

grave·dig·ger ['greɪv,dɪgəʳ] *n* becchino.

grav·el ['grævəl] **1** *n* ghiaia. **2** *cpd (path, pit)* di ghiaia.

grave·ly ['greɪvlɪ] *adj* gravemente, solennemente; **~ ill** in pericolo di vita.

grave·stone ['greɪvstəʊn] *n* pietra tombale, lapide *f*.

grave·yard ['greɪvjɑːd] *n* cimitero.

gravi·tate ['grævɪteɪt] *vi (fig)*: **to ~ (towards)** gravitare (verso).

gravi·ta·tion [,grævɪ'teɪʃən] *n* gravitazione *f*.

grav·ity ['grævɪtɪ] *n (all senses)* gravità.

gra·vy ['greɪvɪ] **1** *n (Culin)* sugo dell'arrosto, sughetto. **2** *cpd*: **~ boat** *n* salsiera; **the ~ train** *(esp Am fam)* l'albero della cuccagna.

gray [greɪ] = **grey**.

graze[1] [greɪz] **1** *vi* pascolare. **2** *vt (grass, field)* mettere or lasciare a pascolo; *(cattle)* far pascolare.

graze[2] [greɪz] **1** *n (injury)* scorticatura, escoriazione *f*. **2** *vt (touch lightly)* sfiorare, rasentare;

(scrape: skin) scorticare; **to ~ one's knees** sbucciarsi le ginocchia.

grease [griːs] **1** *n (gen)* grasso, unto; *(lubricant)* grasso, olio (di macchina). **2** *vt (baking tin)* ungere; *(Aut etc)* ingrassare, lubrificare.

grease·paint ['griːspeɪnt] *n* cerone *m*.

grease·proof ['griːspruːf] *adj*: **~ paper** carta oleata.

greasy ['griːsɪ] *adj* (**-ier, -iest**) *(substance etc)* grasso(a); *(hair)* untuoso(a), grasso(a); *(road, surface)* scivoloso(a); *(hands, clothes)* unto(a); *(stains)* d'unto.

great [greɪt] *adj* (**-er, -est**) **(a)** *(gen)* grande; *(pain, heat)* forte, intenso(a); *(care etc)* molto(a); *(age)* venerando(a); **they're ~ friends** sono grandi amici; **he was in ~ pain** soffriva molto; **it's of no ~ importance** non ha molta importanza; **he's a ~ reader** è un lettore accanito; **~ big** *(fam)* enorme; **G~ Britain** Gran Bretagna; **Alexander the G~** Alessandro Magno *or* il Grande; **the G~ War** la Grande Guerra; **you're a ~ one for arriving at the wrong moment!** *(fam)* sei speciale per arrivare al momento sbagliato!; **the ~ thing is that...** il bello è che.... **(b)** *(fam: excellent)* meraviglioso(a), favoloso(a); **it was ~!** è stato fantastico!; **he's ~ at football** nel calcio è una cannonata; **we had a ~ time** ci siamo divertiti un mondo.

great·er ['greɪtəʳ] *adj (comp of great)* più grande; **G~ London** Londra e sobborghi.

great·est ['greɪtɪst] *adj (superl of great)* il/la più grande; **he's the ~!** *(fam)* è grande!

great-grandchild [,greɪt'grænt∫aɪld] *n*, *pl* **-children** pronipote *m/f*.

great-grandparent [,greɪt'grænd,pɛərənt] *n* bisnonno/a.

great·ly ['greɪtlɪ] *adv (gen)* molto; **~ superior** di gran lunga superiore; **it is ~ to be regretted that...** *(frm)* ci rincresce infinitamente che....

great·ness ['greɪtnɪs] *n* grandezza.

Greece [griːs] *n* Grecia.

greed [griːd] *n*: **~ (for)** *(gen)* avidità (di), desiderio smodato (di); *(for food)* ingordigia (di), gola (per).

greedy ['griːdɪ] *adj* (**-ier, -iest**): **~ (for)** *(gen)* avido(a) (di); *(for food)* goloso(a) (di), ghiotto(a) (di).

Greek [griːk] **1** *adj* greco(a). **2** *n (person)* greco/a; *(language)* greco; **it's (all) ~ to me** *(fam)* per me è turco.

green [griːn] **1** *adj* (**-er, -est**) *(colour)* verde; *(unripe)* acerbo(a), verde; *(inexperienced)* alle prime armi; *(gullible)* ingenuo(a); **to have ~ fingers** *(fig)* avere il pollice verde; **to turn ~** *(fig: with nausea)* sbiancare; *(: with envy)* diventare verde; **~ beans** fagiolini *mpl* verdi; **~ pepper** peperone *m* verde; **~ salad** insalata verde. **2** *n (colour)* verde *m*; *(grassy area)* prato, spiazzo erboso; *(bowling ~)* campo da bocce; *(of golf course)* green *m inv*; **village ~** ≃ piazza del paese; **~s** *npl (Culin)* verdura.

green·ery ['griːnərɪ] *n* verde *m*.

green·fly ['griːnflaɪ] *n* afide *f*.

green·gage ['griːngeɪdʒ] *n* susina Regina Claudia.

green·grocer ['griːn,grəʊsəʳ] *n* fruttivendolo/a; **'~'s'** 'frutta e verdura'; **to go to the ~'s** andare dal fruttivendolo.

green·house ['griːnhaʊs] *n* serra.

Green·land ['griːnlənd] *n* Groenlandia.

greet [griːt] *vt* accogliere, salutare; **a strange sight ~ed his eyes** una strana scena si offrì ai suoi occhi; **the statement was ~ed with loud laughter** l'affermazione fu salutata da or con grasse risate.

greet·ing ['griːtɪŋ] *n* saluto; *(welcome)* accoglienza; **~s** saluti *mpl*; **Season's ~s** Buone Feste;

Christmas ~**s** auguri *mpl* di Natale; ~**s card** cartolina d'auguri.

gre·gari·ous [grɪ'gɛərɪəs] *adj (animal)* gregario(a); *(person)* socievole.

gre·nade [grɪ'neɪd] *n (also:* **hand** ~) granata.

grew [gruː] *pt of* **grow**.

grey [greɪ] **1** *adj* (**-er, -est**) grigio(a); *(complexion)* smorto(a); *(outlook, prospect)* poco roseo(a); **to go** ~ diventar grigio; **to go** ~ **with fear** *(person)* sbiancarsi in viso dalla paura; ~ **matter** *(fig fam)* materia grigia; **a** ~ **area** *(fig)* un punto oscuro. **2** *n (colour)* grigio.

grey-haired [,greɪ'hɛəd] *adj* dai capelli grigi.

grey·hound ['greɪhaʊnd] *n* levriero.

grid [grɪd] *n (grating)* grata, griglia; *(Elec, Gas: network)* rete *f*; *(on map)* reticolato; **the national** ~ la rete elettrica nazionale.

grid·dle ['grɪdl] *n (esp Am)* piastra.

grid·iron ['grɪd,aɪən] *n* graticola.

grief [griːf] *n (sorrow)* dolore *m*; *(cause of sorrow)* dolore, pena; **to come to** ~ *(plan)* naufragare; *(person)* finire male.

griev·ance ['griːvəns] *n (complaint)* lagnanza, rimostranza; *(cause for complaint)* motivo di risentimento.

grieve [griːv] **1** *vt* addolorare; **it** ~**s me to see...** mi rattrista vedere.... **2** *vi* addolorarsi, soffrire; **to** ~ **for sb** compiangere qn; *(dead person)* piangere qn.

griev·ous ['griːvəs] *adj:* ~ **bodily harm** *(Law)* aggressione *f*.

grill [grɪl] **1** *n* **(a)** *(Brit: on cooker)* griglia; *(gridiron also)* graticola; *(in restaurant)* grill-room *m inv;* **a mixed** ~ una grigliata mista. **(b)** *(also:* **grille:** *grating)* griglia; *(: at window)* grata. **2** *vt* **(a)** *(Culin)* cuocere ai ferri *or* alla griglia; ~**ed meat** carne *f* ai ferri *or* alla griglia. **(b)** *(fam: interrogate)* fare un interrogatorio di terzo grado a.

grim [grɪm] *adj* (**-mer, -mest**) *(hard, unpleasant: gen)* duro(a); *(: struggle)* accanito(a); *(: silence)* sinistro(a); *(: landscape)* desolato(a); *(: humour, tale)* macabro(a); *(determined: face)* risoluto(a), determinato(a); *(determination)* feroce; **to hold on (to sth) like** ~ **death** attaccarsi (a qc) con le unghie e coi denti.

gri·mace [grɪ'meɪs] **1** *n* smorfia. **2** *vi* fare smorfie.

grime [graɪm] *n* sporcizia, sudiciume *m*.

grin [grɪn] **1** *n (smile)* (gran) sorriso; *(cheeky)* sorrisetto. **2** *vi:* **to** ~ **(at)** fare un gran sorriso (a); **to** ~ **and bear it** stringere i denti e andare avanti.

grind [graɪnd] *(vb: pt, pp* **ground**) **1** *vt (coffee, corn)* macinare; *(sharpen: knife)* arrotare; *(polish: gem, lens)* molare; **to** ~ **one's teeth** digrignare i denti; **to** ~ **sth into the earth** schiacciare qc col piede. **2** *vi* stridere, cigolare; *(car gears)* grattare; **to** ~ **to a halt** *(vehicle)* arrestarsi con uno stridio di freni; *(fig: talks, scheme)* insabbiarsi; *(: work, production)* cessare del tutto. **3** *n:* **the daily** ~ *(fam)* il trantran quotidiano.

grind·er ['graɪndə'] *n (machine: for coffee)* macinino; *(: for sharpening)* affilacoltelli *m inv.*

grind·stone ['graɪndstəʊn] *n:* **to keep one's nose to the** ~ darci sotto.

grip [grɪp] **1** *n* **(a)** presa; **in the** ~ **of the recession** *(fig)* nel pieno della crisi; **to get to** ~**s with sb/sth** venire alle prese con qn/qc; **to have a firm** ~ **on sb/sth** tenere saldamente qn/qc; **to take a** ~ ~ **on** afferrarsi; **to lose one's** ~ perdere *or* allentare la presa; *(fig)* perdere la grinta; **to have a good** ~ **of a subject** avere una buona padronanza di una materia; **get a** ~ **on yourself!** *(fam)* controllati! **(b)** *(holdall)* sacca, borsone *m.* **2** *vt* **(a)** *(hold)* afferrare, stringere; **to** ~ **the road** *(tyres)* far

presa sulla strada; *(car)* tenere bene la strada. **(b)** *(fig: enthrall)* far presa su; *(: subj: fear)* prendere.

gripe [graɪp] **1** *n (Med)* colica; *(fam: complaint)* lagna. **2** *vi (fam: complain):* **to** ~ **(about)** lagnarsi (di).

grip·ping ['grɪpɪŋ] *adj (story, novel)* avvincente, appassionante.

gris·ly ['grɪzlɪ] *adj* (**-ier, -iest**) *(murder etc)* raccapricciante.

gris·tle ['grɪsl] *n* cartilagine *f.*

grit [grɪt] **1** *n (gravel)* sabbia, pietrisco; *(fig: courage)* fegato; **I've got a piece of** ~ **in my eye** ho un bruscolino nell'occhio. **2** *vt* **(a)** *(road)* buttare sabbia su. **(b): to** ~ **one's teeth** stringere i denti.

grits [grɪts] *npl (Am)* macinato grosso (di avena *etc).*

griz·zle ['grɪzl] *vi (cry)* piagnucolare.

griz·zled ['grɪzld] *adj (hair)* brizzolato(a).

griz·zly ['grɪzlɪ] *n (also:* ~ **bear)** orso grigio, grizzly *m inv.*

groan [grəʊn] **1** *n (of pain etc)* gemito. **2** *vi* gemere; *(tree, gate etc)* scricchiolare, cigolare.

gro·cer ['grəʊsə'] *n* negoziante *m/f* di alimentari; ~**'s (shop)** negozio di alimentari.

gro·ceries ['grəʊsərɪz] *npl* spesa.

gro·cery ['grəʊsərɪ] *n (shop)* (negozio di) alimentari.

grog [grɒg] *n* grog *m inv.*

grog·gy ['grɒgɪ] *adj* (**-ier, -iest**) stordito(a), intontito(a); *(shaky)* malfermo(a).

groin [grɔɪn] *n* inguine *m.*

groom [gruːm] **1** *n (in stable)* palafreniere *m*; *(bride~)* sposo. **2** *vt* **(a)** *(horse)* pulire; **well-~ed** *(person)* curato(a). **(b)** *(prepare: person):* **to** ~ **sb for** avviare qn alla carriera di.

groove [gruːv] *n (in wood, metal etc)* solco, scanalatura; *(of record)* solco.

grope [grəʊp] **1** *vi (also:* ~ **around,** ~ **about)** brancolare, andare a tentoni; **to** ~ **for sth** cercare qc a tentoni *or* a tastoni; *(fig: for words etc)* cercare (disperatamente). **2** *vt:* **to** ~ **one's way through** farsi strada a tentoni in *or* tra; **to** ~ **one's way towards** andare a tentoni verso; **to** ~ **sb** *(sexually)* mettere le mani addosso a qn.

gross [grəʊs] **1** *adj* (**-er, -est**) **(a)** *(fat: body)* obeso(a); *(vegetation)* lussureggiante; *(behaviour, language, error)* grossolano(a); *(impertinence)* sfacciato(a). **(b)** *(total: profit, income)* complessivo(a), totale; *(weight)* lordo(a); **£10,000** ~ 10.000 sterline lorde; ~ **national product** *(abbr* **GNP)** prodotto nazionale lordo. **2** *n, pl inv (twelve dozen)* grossa. **3** *vt (Comm)* incassare, avere un incasso lordo di.

gro·tesque [grəʊ'tɛsk] *adj* grottesco(a).

grot·to ['grɒtəʊ] *n* grotta.

grot·ty ['grɒtɪ] *adj* squallido(a); **I feel** ~ mi sento a terra.

grouch [graʊtʃ] *(fam)* **1** *vi* brontolare. **2** *n (person)* brontolone/a; *(complaint):* **she's always got a** ~ ha sempre da brontolare.

ground[1] [graʊnd] **1** *n* **(a)** *(soil)* terra, suolo, terreno.

(b) *(terrain)* terreno; **high** ~ altura; **hilly** ~ zona collinosa; **to gain/lose** ~ guadagnare/perdere terreno; **to be on dangerous** ~ muoversi su un terreno minato; **it suits me down to the** ~ per me va ottimamente, mi sta benissimo; **to cut the** ~ **from under sb's feet** tagliare le gambe a qn; **common** ~ terreno comune.

(c) *(surface)* terra; *(background)* terreno, sfondo; **on the** ~ per terra, a terra; **above** ~ in superficie; **below** ~ sottoterra; **to fall to the** ~

cadere a *or* per terra *or* al suolo; *(fig)* andare in fumo; **to get off the** ~ *(aircraft)* decollare; *(plans etc)* prendere il via; **to stand one's** ~ mantenere le proprie posizioni; **he covered a lot of** ~ **in his lecture** ha toccato molti argomenti nel corso della conferenza.

(**d**) *(pitch)*: **football** ~ campo di football *or* calcio; **parade** ~ piazza d'armi; **recreation** ~ parco giochi; ~**s** *(gardens)* giardini *mpl*, parco.

(**e**): ~**s** *npl (of coffee)* fondi *mpl* (di caffè).

(**f**) *(Am Elec)* (presa a) terra.

(**g**) *(reason: usu pl)* ragione *f*, motivo; **on medical** ~**s** per motivi di salute; ~**s for complaint** motivo *or* ragione di lamentarsi; **on the** ~(**s**) **that** per il motivo che.

2 *vt* (**a**) *(ship)* far incagliare; *(plane, pilot)* bloccare a terra. (**b**) *(Am Elec)* mettere la presa a terra a.

3 *vi (Naut)* incagliarsi.

4 *cpd*: ~ **control** *n (Aer, Space)* base *f* di controllo; ~ **floor** *n* pianterreno; ~ **frost** *n* brina; ~ **level** *n (of house)* piano terra; **at** ~ **level** *(Aer, Geog)* a bassa quota; ~ **plan** *n* pianta; ~ **staff** *n (Aer)* personale *m* di terra.

ground[2] *(grund)* **1** *pt, pp of* **grind. 2** *adj (coffee etc)* macinato(a); ~ **glass** vetro smerigliato.

ground·ing ['graundɪŋ] *n* fondamento, basi *fpl*; **he has a good** ~ **in French** ha delle buone basi in francese.

ground·less ['graundlɪs] *adj* infondato(a).

ground·nut ['graundnʌt] *n* arachide *f*.

ground·sheet ['graundʃiːt] *n (in tent)* telone *m* impermeabile.

grounds·man ['graundzmən] *n, pl* -**men** *(Sport)* custode *m* (di campo sportivo).

ground·work ['graundwɜːk] *n* lavoro preparatorio.

group [gruːp] **1** *n (gen)* gruppo; *(set, clique: of people)* circolo, gruppo; *(Mus: pop* ~*)* complesso, gruppo; **blood** ~ *(Med)* gruppo sanguigno. **2** *vt (also:* ~ **together)** raggruppare. **3** *vi (see vt)* raggrupparsi. **4** *cpd (discussion, photo, therapy)* di gruppo, collettivo(a); ~ **captain** *n (Aer)* comandante *m* di gruppo; ~ **practice** *n (Med)* ambulatorio medico con più dottori.

grouse[1] [graus] *n, pl inv* gallo cedrone, urogallo.

grouse[2] [graus] *(fam)* **1** *n (complaint)* mugugno. **2** *vi:* **to** ~ (**about**) brontolare (su).

grove [grəuv] *n* boschetto.

grov·el ['grɒvl] *vi:* **to** ~ **to** *or* **before sb** strisciare di fronte a qn.

grow [grəu] *pt* **grew,** *pp* **grown 1** *vt (Agr)* coltivare; *(beard etc)* farsi crescere. **2** *vi* (**a**) *(plant, person, hair)* crescere; *(increase: in numbers etc)* aumentare, salire; *(: in membership etc)* ingrandirsi; *(develop: friendship, love)* rafforzarsi; *(: custom etc)* affermarsi, diffondersi; **to** ~ **in stature/popularity** veder aumentare il proprio prestigio/la propria popolarità; **that painting is** ~**ing on me** quel quadro più lo guardo più mi piace. (**b**) *(become)* farsi, diventare; **to** ~ **dark** farsi buio; **to** ~ **rich** arricchirsi; **to** ~ **tired of waiting** stancarsi di aspettare; **to** ~ **to like sb** imparare ad apprezzare qn.

♦ **grow apart** *vi* + *adv (fig)* estraniarsi.

♦ **grow away from** *vi* + *prep (fig)* allontanarsi da, staccarsi da.

♦ **grow into** *vi* + *prep* (**a**) *(clothes)*: **he'll** ~ **into them** quando crescerà gli andranno bene. (**b**) *(become)* farsi, diventare; **she has** ~**n into a beautiful woman** si è fatta una gran bella donna.

♦ **grow out of** *vi* + *prep* (**a**) *(clothes)* non entrare più in; *(habit)* perdere (col tempo). (**b**) *(arise*

from) nascere da, essere la conseguenza di.

♦ **grow up** *vi* + *adv* (**a**) *(become adult)* diventar grande; **I grew up in the country** sono cresciuto in campagna; ~ **up!** *(fam)* non fare il bambino! (**b**) *(develop: friendship etc)* nascere.

grow·er ['grəuə'] *n (Agr)* coltivatore/trice.

grow·ing ['grəuɪŋ] *adj*: ~ **pains** *(also fig)* problemi *mpl* di crescita.

growl [graul] **1** *n (of animal)* ringhio; *(of thunder)* brontolio; **the dog gave a** ~ il cane ringhiò. **2** *vi* ringhiare; *(person, thunder)* brontolare.

grown [grəun] **1** *pp of* **grow. 2** *adj (also:* **fully** ~*)* adulto(a), grande.

grown-up [,grəun'ʌp] **1** *adj* da grande. **2** *n* grande *m/f*, adulto/a.

growth [grəuθ] *n* (**a**) *(increase)* crescita, aumento; *(development)* sviluppo; **he has 5 days'** ~ (**of beard**) ha una barba di 5 giorni; **to reach full** ~ raggiungere il pieno sviluppo. (**b**) *(Med)* tumore *m*.

groyne [grɔɪn] *n* frangiflutti *m inv*.

grub [grʌb] *n* (**a**) *(larva)* bruco, larva. (**b**) *(fam: food)* qualcosa da mettere sotto i denti; ~('**s**) **up!** si mangia!, a tavola!.

grub·by ['grʌbɪ] *adj (-ier, -iest)* sudicio(a).

grudge [grʌdʒ] **1** *n*: ~ (**against**) risentimento (verso), rancore *m* (verso); **to bear a** ~ **against sb** portare *or* serbare rancore a qn. **2** *vt*: **to** ~ **sb sth** *(money etc)* dare qc a qn a malincuore; **I don't** ~ **you your success** non t'invidio il tuo successo; **to** ~ **doing sth** non fare qc volentieri.

grudg·ing ['grʌdʒɪŋ] *adj (praise etc)* tirato(a) coi denti; **she gave him her** ~ **support** gli ha dato di malavoglia il suo appoggio.

gru·el·ling, (*Am*) **gru·el·ing** ['gruəlɪŋ] *adj* estenuante.

grue·some ['gruːsəm] *adj* orrendo(a), agghiacciante.

gruff [grʌf] *adj (-er, -est)* burbero(a).

grum·ble ['grʌmbl] **1** *n (complaint)* lamentela; *(noise)* brontolio; *(: of guns)* rombo. **2** *vi (complain):* **to** ~ (**about**) brontolare (su); *(thunder etc)* brontolare; **a grumbling appendix** un'appendice infiammata.

grumpy ['grʌmpɪ] *adj (-ier, -iest)* scorbutico(a).

grunt [grʌnt] **1** *n* grugnito. **2** *vi* grugnire.

G-string ['dʒiːstrɪŋ] *n* tanga *m inv*.

guar·an·tee [,gærən'tiː] **1** *n* garanzia; *(guarantor)* garante *m/f*, mallevadore *m*. **2** *vt (gen)* garantire; **he can't** ~ (**that**) **he'll come** non può garantire che verrà.

guar·an·tor [,gærən'tɔː'] *n* garante *m/f*, mallevadore *m*.

guard [gɑːd] **1** *n* (**a**) *(gen, also Mil, Sport)* guardia; *(security* ~*)* guardia giurata; *(esp Am: prison* ~*)* secondino; *(Brit Rail)* ≃ capotreno; *(also:* ~ **duty: watch)** (turno di) guardia; *(fig: watchfulness)* vigilanza; ~'**s van** *(Brit Rail)* vagone *m* di servizio; **to change** ~ *(Mil)* cambiare la guardia; **to be on** ~ *(Mil etc)* essere di guardia; **to be on one's** ~ *(fig)* stare in guardia; **to keep sb under** ~ tenere qn sotto vigilanza; **to catch sb off his** ~ cogliere *or* prendere qn alla sprovvista; **to keep** ~ **over sb/sth** *(Mil, fig)* fare la guardia a qn/qc. (**b**) *(safety device: on machine)* schermo protettivo; *(protection)* riparo, protezione *f*; *(fire* ~*)* parafuoco; *(mud* ~*)* parurti *m inv*.

2 *vt (prisoner, treasure)* fare la guardia a, stare a guardia di; *(secret)* custodire; *(protect):* **to** ~ (**against** *or* **from**) proteggere (da), salvaguardare (da).

3 *cpd*: ~ **dog** *n* cane *m* da guardia.

♦ **guard against** *vi* + *prep* (take care to avoid:

illness) guardarsi da; *(: suspicion, accidents)* premunirsi contro *or* da; **to ~ against doing sth** guardarsi dal fare qc.

guard·ed ['gɑːdɪd] *adj (reply, tone)* guardingo(a), circospetto(a).

guard·ian ['gɑːdɪən] **1** *n* tutore/trice. **2** *cpd:* ~ **angel** *n* angelo custode.

guer·ril·la [gə'rɪlə] **1** *n* guerrigliero/a. **2** *cpd:* ~ **warfare** *n* guerriglia.

guess [gɛs] **1** *n* supposizione *f*, congettura; **to make** *or* **have a ~** provare a indovinare; **at a (rough) ~** a occhio e croce; **my ~ is that...** suppongo che...; **it's anybody's ~** Dio solo (lo) sa; **your ~ is as good as mine** ne so quanto te. **2** *vt* **(a)** *(gen)* indovinare; **~ what?** sai l'ultima?; **I ~ed as much** me lo immaginavo. **(b)** *(esp Am: suppose)* supporre, credere; **I ~ so** direi di sì; **I ~ you're right** mi sa che hai ragione. **3** *vi* **(a)** indovinare; **to ~ at sth** provare a indovinare qc; **to ~ correctly** azzeccarci; **he's just ~ing** sta tirando a indovinare; **to keep sb ~ing** tenere qn in sospeso *or* sulla corda. **(b)** *(esp Am: suppose)* supporre, credere; **he's happy, I ~** è felice, immagino.

guess·work ['gɛswɜːk] *n:* **I got the answer by ~** ho azzeccato la risposta.

guest [gɛst] **1** *n (in house, on TV programme)* ospite *m/f; (at party)* invitato/a; *(at hotel)* cliente *m/f; (in boarding house)* pensionante *m/f;* ~ **of honour** ospite d'onore; **be my ~** *(fam)* fai come (se fossi) a casa tua. **2** *cpd:* ~ **room** *n* stanza *or* camera degli ospiti.

guest·house ['gɛsthaʊs] *n* pensione *f* familiare.

guf·faw [gʌ'fɔː] **1** *n* risata fragorosa. **2** *vi* ridere fragorosamente.

guid·ance ['gaɪdəns] *n (counselling)* consigli *mpl,* guida; *(leadership)* guida, direzione *f;* **marriage/ vocational ~** consulenza matrimoniale/per l'avviamento professionale.

guide [gaɪd] **1** *n (gen)* guida; *(manual)* guida, manuale *m; (fig: indication, model)* indicazione *f;* **let conscience be your ~** lasciati guidare dalla coscienza. **2** *vt* guidare; **to be ~d by sb/sth** farsi *or* lasciarsi guidare da qn/qc. **3** *cpd:* ~ **dog** *n* cane *m* per ciechi.

guide·book ['gaɪdbʊk] *n* guida.

guid·ed ['gaɪdɪd] *adj (missile)* (tele)guidato(a); *(tour)* guidato(a).

guide·lines ['gaɪdlaɪnz] *npl* direttive *fpl.*

guild [gɪld] *n (History)* corporazione *f,* arte *f; (club)* associazione *f.*

guild·hall ['gɪldhɔːl] *n (town hall)* palazzo del municipio.

guile [gaɪl] *n* astuzia.

guil·lo·tine [gɪlə'tiːn] *n* ghigliottina; *(for paper)* taglierina.

guilt [gɪlt] *n (being guilty)* colpevolezza; *(feeling guilty)* colpa, senso di colpa.

guilty ['gɪltɪ] *adj (-ier, -iest) (Law, gen)* colpevole; *(conscience)* sporco(a); ~ **of sth** colpevole di qc; **the ~ person** *or* **party** il/la responsabile; **to feel ~ (about)** sentirsi in colpa (per); **to find sb ~** riconoscere qn colpevole; **to plead ~/not ~** dichiararsi colpevole/innocente.

guinea ['gɪnɪ] *n (Brit old)* ghinea.

guinea pig ['gɪnɪ,pɪg] *n* porcellino d'India, cavia; *(fig)* cavia.

gui·tar [gɪ'tɑːʳ] *n* chitarra.

gui·tar·ist [gɪ'tɑːrɪst] *n* chitarrista *m/f.*

gulch [gʌltʃ] *n (Am)* burrone *m.*

gulf [gʌlf] **1** *n (bay)* golfo; *(chasm: also fig)* abisso; **the (Persian) G~** il Golfo Persico. **2** *cpd:* **the G~ States** i paesi del Golfo Persico; **the G~ Stream** la corrente del Golfo.

gull [gʌl] *n* gabbiano.

gul·let ['gʌlɪt] *n* gola.

gul·lible ['gʌlɪbl] *adj* credulone(a).

gul·ly ['gʌlɪ] *n (ravine)* burrone *m,* gola; *(channel)* canale *m* di scolo.

gulp [gʌlp] **1** *n (of liquid)* sorso; *(of food)* boccone *m;* **in** *or* **at one ~** in un sorso, d'un fiato. **2** *vt (also:* ~ **down)** tranguagiare, inghiottire. **3** *vi (while drinking)* deglutire; *(through fear etc)* sentirsi serrare la gola.

gum¹ [gʌm] *n (Anat)* gengiva.

gum² [gʌm] **1** *n (glue)* colla, gomma arabica; *(~ tree)* albero della gomma; *(chewing ~)* gomma americana; *(sweet)* caramella gommosa. **2** *vt (stick together)* incollare, ingommare; *(also:* ~ **down:** *label)* attaccare; *(: envelope)* incollare.

♦ **gum up** *vt + adv:* **to ~ up the works** *(fam)* mettere il bastone tra le ruote.

gum·boots ['gʌmbuːts] *npl* stivali *mpl* di gomma.

gump·tion ['gʌmpʃən] *n (fam: initiative)* spirito d'iniziativa, buonsenso.

gun [gʌn] **1** *n (pistol)* pistola, rivoltella; *(rifle)* fucile *m; (cannon)* cannone *m;* **to draw a ~ on sb** spianare la pistola contro qn; **to stick to one's ~s** *(fig)* tener duro. **2** *vt (also:* ~ **down)** abbattere a colpi di pistola *or* fucile. **3** *cpd:* ~ **barrel** *n* canna di fucile; ~ **dog** *n* cane *m* da caccia.

♦ **gun for** *vi + prep (fig)* avercela a morte con.

gun·boat ['gʌnbəʊt] *n* cannoniera.

gun·fire ['gʌnfaɪəʳ] *n* colpi *mpl* d'arma da fuoco.

gunge [gʌndʒ] *n (fam)* pappa schifosa.

gun·man ['gʌnmən] *n, pl* **-men** uomo armato, bandito; *(hired)* sicario.

gun·ner ['gʌnəʳ] *n* artigliere *m.*

gun·point ['gʌnpɔɪnt] *n:* **at ~** sotto la minaccia delle armi.

gun·powder ['gʌn,paʊdəʳ] *n* polvere *f* da sparo.

gun·running ['gʌn,rʌnɪŋ] *n* contrabbando d'armi.

gun·shot ['gʌnʃɒt] **1** *n (noise)* sparo. **2** *cpd:* ~ **wound** *n* ferita da arma da fuoco.

gun·smith ['gʌnsmɪθ] *n* armaiolo.

gur·gle ['gɜːgl] **1** *n (in all senses)* gorgoglio. **2** *vi* gorgogliare, ciangottare.

guru ['gʊruː] *n* guru *m inv.*

gush [gʌʃ] **1** *n (of liquid)* getto; *(of blood)* fiotto; *(of feeling)* ondata. **2** *vi* **(a)** *(also:* ~ **out:** *water, blood):* **to ~ (from)** sgorgare (da). **(b)** *(fam: enthuse):* **to ~ (about** *or* **over)** andare in brodo di giuggiole (di fronte a).

gus·set ['gʌsɪt] *n (in tights, pants)* rinforzo; *(in skirt etc)* gherone *m.*

gust [gʌst] *n (of wind)* folata; *(: stronger, of rain)* raffica; *(of smoke)* vampata; *(of laughter)* scoppio.

gus·to ['gʌstəʊ] *n:* **with ~** di *or* con gran gusto.

gut [gʌt] **1** *n* **(a)** *(Anat)* intestino; *(for violin, racket)* minugia, budello. **(b):** ~**s** *npl (fam: innards)* budella *fpl; (: of animals)* interiora *fpl; (fig: courage)* fegato; **to hate sb's ~s** odiare qn a morte. **2** *vt* **(a)** *(poultry, fish)* levare le interiora a, sventrare. **(b)** *(building):* **the blaze ~ted the entire building** le fiamme hanno completamente divorato l'interno dell'edificio. **3** *cpd:* ~ **reaction** *n* reazione *f* istintiva.

gut·ter ['gʌtəʳ] **1** *n (in street)* cunetta, scolo; *(on roof)* grondaia; **to rise from the ~** *(fig)* venire dai bassifondi *or* dalla strada. **2** *cpd:* ~ **press** *n* stampa scandalistica.

gut·tur·al ['gʌtərəl] *adj* gutturale.

guy¹ [gaɪ] *n (fam: man)* tizio, tipo; *(effigy)* pupazzo; **a wise ~** un dritto; **a tough ~** un duro; **he's a nice ~** è simpatico.

guy² [gaɪ] *n (also:* ~**-rope)** *n (for tent etc)* tirante *m,* cavo.

guz·zle [ˈgʌzl] **1** *vt (food)* ingozzare; *(drink)* tracannare; *(hum: petrol)* bere. **2** *vi* gozzovigliare.

gym [dʒɪm] *n (fam: gymnasium)* palestra; *(: gymnastics)* ginnastica.

gym·kha·na [dʒɪmˈkɑːnə] *n* gimkana.

gym·na·sium [dʒɪmˈneɪzɪəm] *n* palestra.

gym·nast [ˈdʒɪmnæst] *n* ginnasta *m/f.*

gym·nas·tics [dʒɪmˈnæstɪks] *nsg* ginnastica.

gy·nae·colo·gist, *(Am)* **gy·ne·colo·gist** [ˌgaɪnɪˈkɒlədʒɪst] *n* ginecologo/a.

gy·nae·col·ogy, *(Am)* **gy·ne·col·ogy** [ˌgaɪnɪˈkɒlədʒɪ] *n* ginecologia.

gyp·sy [ˈdʒɪpsɪ] **1** *n* zingaro/a. **2** *adj (life)* da zingaro, zingaresco(a); *(caravan)* degli zingari; *(music)* zigano(a).

gy·rate [ˌdʒaɪəˈreɪt] *vi (spin)* roteare, girare (su se stesso); *(dance)* volteggiare.

gy·ro·scope [ˈdʒaɪərəskəʊp] *n* giroscopio.

H

H, h |eɪtʃ| n (letter) H, h f or m inv.
hab·er·dash·ery [ˌhæbə'dæʃərɪ] n merceria; (Am) camiceria.
hab·it ['hæbɪt] n (a) (customary behaviour, individual ~) abitudine f; **a bad** ~ una brutta or cattiva abitudine; **to be in the** ~ **of doing sth** avere l'abitudine di fare qc; **to fall into bad** ~**s** prendere delle cattive abitudini; **to get out of/into the** ~ **of doing sth** perdere/prendere l'abitudine di fare qc; **to get sb into the** ~ **of doing** abituare qn a fare; **out of sheer** ~ per (forza di) abitudine; **don't make a** ~ **of it!** che non diventi un'abitudine! **(b)** (dress: of monk, nun) tonaca; (: of priest) abito talare; (: riding ~) completo da amazzone.
hab·it·able ['hæbɪtəbl] adj abitabile.
habi·tat ['hæbɪtæt] n habitat m inv.
habi·ta·tion [ˌhæbɪ'teɪʃən] n abitazione f; **fit for human** ~ abitabile.
ha·bitu·al [hə'bɪtjʊəl] adj abituale, consueto(a); (drunkard, smoker etc) incallito(a); (liar) inveterato(a).
hack¹ [hæk] **1** n (of sword, axe) colpo; (of sabre) fendente m. **2** vt (cut) tagliare; **to** ~ **one's way through** aprirsi un varco (a colpi d'ascia etc) tra; **to** ~ **sth to pieces** tagliare a pezzi qc.
♦ **hack down** vt + adv (tree etc) abbattere (a colpi d'ascia etc).
hack² [hæk] **1** n (a) (old horse) ronzino; (ride) passeggiata a cavallo. **(b)** (writer) scribacchino/a. **2** vi: **to go** ~**ing** (andare a) fare una passeggiata a cavallo.
hack·ing ['hækɪŋ] adj **(a)**: ~ **jacket** giacca da equitazione. **(b)**: **a** ~ **cough** una brutta tosse.
hack·les ['hæklz] npl: **to make sb's** ~ **rise** (fig) rendere qn furioso(a).
hack·ney car·riage ['hæknɪˌkærɪdʒ] n (frm) autopubblica.
hack·neyed ['hæknɪd] adj (saying etc) trito(a); (tune) sentito(a) e risentito(a); ~ **expression** luogo comune.
hack·saw ['hæksɔː] n seghetto per metalli.
had [hæd] pt, pp of **have**.
had·dock ['hædək] n eglefino (tipo di merluzzo).
hadn't ['hædnt] = **had not**.
haema·tol·ogy, (Am) **hema·tol·ogy** [ˌhiːmə'tɒlədʒɪ] n ematologia.
haemo·glo·bin, (Am) **hemo·glo·bin** [ˌhiːməʊ'gləʊbɪn] n emoglobina.
haemo·philia, (Am) **hemo·philia** [ˌhiːməʊ'fɪlɪə] n emofilia.
haem·or·rhage, (Am) **hem·or·rhage** ['hɛmərɪdʒ] **1** n emorragia. **2** vi avere un'emorragia.
haem·or·rhoids, (Am) **hem·or·rhoids** ['hɛmərɔɪdz] npl emorroidi fpl.
hag [hæg] n (ugly) befana; (nasty) megera; (witch) strega.
hag·gard ['hægəd] adj (face) tirato(a).
hag·gis ['hægɪs] n (Scot) insaccato a base di frattaglie di pecora e avena.

hag·gle ['hægl] vi: **to** ~ **(over)** (bargain) contrattare (su); (argue) discutere (su).
Hague [heɪg] n: **the** ~ l'Aia.
hail¹ [heɪl] (Met) **1** n grandine f; (fig: of bullets) pioggia; (: of abuse) valanga. **2** vi grandinare.
hail² [heɪl] **1** n (greeting, call) grido di saluto; **within** ~ a portata d'orecchio. **2** excl (old, poet): ~, **Caesar!** ave, Cesare!; **the H**~ **Mary** l'Ave Maria f. **3** vt (acclaim): **to** ~ **(as)** acclamare (come); (greet) salutare; (signal: taxi) fermare. **4** vi: **where does that ship** ~ **from?** qual'è il porto di provenienza di quella nave?; **he** ~**s from Scotland** viene dalla Scozia.
hail·stone ['heɪlstəʊn] n chicco di grandine.
hail·storm ['heɪlstɔːm] n grandinata.
hair [hɛəʳ] **1** n (a) (collective: of person) capelli mpl; (: on body) peli mpl; (: of animal) pelo; **to comb one's** ~ pettinarsi; **to put one's** ~ **up** raccogliersi i capelli; **to have one's** ~ **done** andare dal parrucchiere; **to get one's** ~ **cut** farsi tagliare i capelli; **to remove unwanted** ~ (from legs etc) depilarsi; **to make sb's** ~ **stand on end** far rizzare i capelli (in testa) a qn; **to let one's** ~ **down** (fig) svagarsi. **(b)** (single ~: of person) capello; (: of body, animal) pelo; **to split** ~**s** (fig) cercare il pelo nell'uovo; **he didn't turn a** ~ non ha battuto ciglio; **try a** ~ **of the dog (that bit you)** (fam) prendi un bicchierino per farti passare la sbornia.
  2 cpd **(a)** (mattress etc) di crine. **(b)** (lacquer etc) per capelli; ~ **oil** brillantina; ~ **piece** n toupet m inv; ~ **remover** n crema depilatoria.
hair·brush ['hɛəbrʌʃ] n spazzola per capelli.
hair·cut ['hɛəkʌt] n taglio (di capelli); **to have or get a** ~ farsi tagliare i capelli.
hair·do ['hɛəduː] n (fam) pettinatura.
hair·dresser ['hɛəˌdrɛsəʳ] n parrucchiere/a; **at the** ~**'s** dal parrucchiere.
hair·dryer ['hɛəˌdraɪəʳ] n asciugacapelli m inv, föhn m inv.
-haired [hɛəd] adj suf: **fair/long**~ dai capelli biondi/lunghi.
hair·line ['hɛəlaɪn] **1** n attaccatura dei capelli. **2** cpd: ~ **crack** n incrinatura, sottilissima crepa; ~ **fracture** n incrinatura.
hair·pin ['hɛəpɪn] **1** n forcina. **2** cpd: ~ **bend** n tornante m.
hair·raising ['hɛəˌreɪzɪŋ] adj (story, adventure) da far rizzare i capelli, terrificante.
hair's-breadth ['hɛəzbrɛtθ] n: **by a** ~ per un pelo.
hair·style ['hɛəstaɪl] n pettinatura, acconciatura.
hairy ['hɛərɪ] adj (-ier, -iest) **(a)** peloso(a). **(b)** (fam: frightening) da far rizzare i capelli.
hake [heɪk] n nasello.
hal·cy·on ['hælsɪən] adj sereno(a).
hale [heɪl] adj: ~ **and hearty** che scoppia di salute.
half [hɑːf] pl **halves 1** n (a) metà f inv; **one** ~ **of the apple** la or una metà della mela; ~ **an orange** mezza arancia; ~ **a dozen** mezza dozzina; **3 and a** ~ **hours** tre ore e mezza; ~ **an hour** mezz'ora; ~ **of my friends** la metà dei miei amici; **to cut in** ~/**into halves** tagliare a or in metà/in due; **his** (or

her) better ~ *(fam hum)* la sua (dolce) metà; **he doesn't do things by halves** non fa mai le cose a metà; **to go halves (with sb)** fare a metà (con qn); **bigger by** ~ una volta e mezzo più grande; **he's too clever by** ~ *(fam)* è troppo furbo per i miei gusti. **(b)** *(Sport: of match)* tempo; *(: of ground)* metà campo; *(player)* mediano. **(c)** *(of beer)* mezza pinta. **(d)** *(child's ticket)* (ridotto per) bambino.

  2 *adj (bottle, quantity, fare, pay)* mezzo(a), metà *inv;* ~ **a glass, a** ~ **glass** un mezzo bicchiere; ~ **measures** mezze misure; ~ **term** *(Brit Scol)* vacanza a *or* di metà trimestre.

  3 *adv* **(a)** (a) metà; ~ **empty/closed** mezzo vuoto/chiuso, semivuoto/semichiuso; ~ **asleep** mezzo addormentato; ~ **as big (as)** la metà (di); ~ **as big again** una volta e mezzo più grande; **I was** ~ **afraid that...** avevo un po' paura che... + *sub;* **not** ~**!** *(fam)* altroché!, eccome!; **it isn't** ~ **hot** *(fam)* scotta da pazzi. **(b)** *(time):* ~ **past 3** le 3 e mezza; ~ **past 12** le 12 e mezza.

half·back [ˈhɑːfˌbæk] *n (Ftbl)* mediano.

half-baked [ˌhɑːfˈbeɪkt] *n (fig fam: idea, scheme)* mal combinato(a), che non sta in piedi.

half-brother [ˈhɑːfˌbrʌðəʳ] *n* fratellastro.

half-caste [ˈhɑːfkɑːst] *n* meticcio/a.

half-hearted [ˌhɑːfˈhɑːtɪd] *adj (effort)* poco convinto(a), svogliato(a); **he made a** ~ **attempt** ha fatto un mezzo tentativo.

half-hour [ˌhɑːfˈaʊəʳ] *n* mezz'ora.

half-mast [ˌhɑːfˈmɑːst] *n:* **at** ~ **a** mezz'asta.

half-moons [ˌhɑːfˈmuːnz] *npl (spectacles)* mezze lunette *fpl.*

half·penny [ˈheɪpnɪ] *n, pl* **-pennies** *or* **-pence** [ˈheɪpəns] *(Brit)* mezzo penny *m inv.*

half-price [ˌhɑːfˈpraɪs] *adv, adj* a metà prezzo.

half-time [ˌhɑːfˈtaɪm] **1** *n (Sport)* intervallo; *(Industry)* mezza giornata. **2** *adj, adv (see n)* all'intervallo, a mezza giornata.

half-truth [ˈhɑːftruːθ] *n* mezza verità *f inv.*

half-way [ˈhɑːfˈweɪ] **1** *adv* **a** metà strada; ~ **up** (*or* **down**) **the stairs** a metà delle scale; **to meet sb** ~ *(fig)* arrivare a un compromesso con qn; ~ **through sth** a metà di qc; **we are** ~ **through the work** abbiamo fatto metà del lavoro. **2** *adj (mark etc)* di mezzo.

half-witted [ˌhɑːfˈwɪtɪd] *adj (reply, action)* da idiota; **a** ~ **person** un(a) idiota.

half-yearly [ˌhɑːfˈjɪəlɪ] **1** *adv* semestralmente, ogni sei mesi. **2** *adj* semestrale.

hali·but [ˈhælɪbət] *n* ippoglosso.

hali·to·sis [ˌhælɪˈtəʊsɪs] *n* alitosi *f.*

hall [hɔːl] **1** *n* **(a)** *(entrance* ~*)* ingresso, entrata; *(Am: passage)* corridoio. **(b)** *(large room)* salone *m,* sala; **church** ~ sala dell'oratorio. **(c)** *(mansion)* palazzo; *(Brit Univ: also:* ~ **of residence)** casa dello studente. **2** *cpd:* ~ **stand** *n* attaccapanni *m inv.*

hal·le·lu·jah [ˌhælɪˈluːjə] *n, excl* alleluia *m inv.*

hall·mark [ˈhɔːlmɑːk] *n (also fig)* marchio.

hal·lo [həˈləʊ] *excl* = **hullo.**

Hal·low·e'en [ˌhæləʊˈiːn] *n* vigilia d'Ognissanti.

hal·lu·ci·na·tion [həˌluːsɪˈneɪʃən] *n* allucinazione *f.*

hall·way [ˈhɔːlweɪ] *n* corridoio; *(entrance)* ingresso.

halo [ˈheɪləʊ] *n (Rel)* aureola; *(Astron)* alone *m.*

halt [hɔːlt] **1** *n* sosta, fermata; *(train stop)* fermata; **to come to a** ~ fermarsi, arrestarsi; **to call a** ~ **(to sth)** *(fig)* mettere *or* porre fine (a qc). **2** *vt (vehicle, production etc)* fermare, arrestare. **3** *vi* fermarsi, arrestarsi; ~**!** alt! **4** *cpd:* ~ **sign** *n* segnale *m* d'arresto.

hal·ter [ˈhɔːltəʳ] *n (for horse)* cavezza.

halter·neck [ˈhɔːltənɛk] *adj* allacciato(a) dietro il collo.

halt·ing [ˈhɔːltɪŋ] *adj* esitante.

halve [hɑːv] *vt (divide):* **to** ~ **(between)** dividere a metà *or* in due (tra); *(reduce by half)* dimezzare, ridurre della metà.

halves [hɑːvz] *npl* of **half.**

ham [hæm] *n* **(a)** *(Culin)* prosciutto; ~ **and eggs** uova *fpl* al prosciutto. **(b)** *(fam: radio* ~*)* radioamatore/trice; *(:* ~ *actor)* attore/trice senza talento.

♦ **ham up** *vt + adv:* **to** ~ **it up** *(fam)* fare l'esagerato/a.

ham·burg·er [ˈhæmˌbɜːgəʳ] *n* hamburger *m inv.*

ham-fisted [ˌhæmˈfɪstɪd] *adj* maldestro(a).

ham·let [ˈhæmlɪt] *n* paesetto, paesino.

ham·mer [ˈhæməʳ] **1** *n (tool)* martello; **the** ~ **and sickle** la falce e il martello; **to go at it** ~ **and tongs** *(fam: work)* darci dentro; *(: argue)* azzuffarsi. **2** *vt* martellare; *(fig fam: defeat)* stracciare; *(: thrash)* picchiare; **to** ~ **nails into wood** piantare chiodi nel legno; **to** ~ **sth into shape** *(metal)* dare una forma a qc col martello; *(fig: team etc)* mettere a punto qc; **to** ~ **a point home to sb** cacciare un'idea in testa a qn. **3** *vi* dare colpi di martello; **to** ~ **on** *or* **at the door** picchiare alla porta.

♦ **hammer down** *vt + adv (lid etc)* fissare con colpi di martello; *(nail)* piantare (a martellate).

♦ **hammer out** *vt + adv (metal)* spianare (a martellate); *(fig: solution, agreement)* mettere a punto.

ham·mock [ˈhæmək] *n* amaca.

ham·per[1] [ˈhæmpəʳ] *n (basket)* cesto, cestino.

ham·per[2] [ˈhæmpəʳ] *vt (hinder)* impedire, ostacolare.

ham·ster [ˈhæmstəʳ] *n* criceto.

hand [hænd] **1** *n* **(a)** *(of person)* mano *f;* *(of instrument, clock)* lancetta; **to have in one's** ~ *(knife, victory)* avere in mano *or* in pugno; *(book, money)* avere in mano; **to take sb by the** ~ prendere per mano qn; **on (one's)** ~**s and knees** carponi, a quattro zampe; ~**s up!** *(during hold-up)* mani in alto!; *(to pupils)* alzate la mano!; ~ **s off!** *(fam)* giù le mani!; **to be clever** *or* **good with one's** ~ avere le mani d'oro; **made/delivered by** ~ fatto/consegnato a mano; **to live from** ~ **to mouth** vivere alla giornata; **they gave him a big** ~ *(fig)* gli hanno fatto un bell'applauso.

  (b) *(worker: in factory)* operaio/a, manovale *m;* *(: farm~)* bracciante *m;* *(: deck~)* marinaio; **all** ~**s on deck!** *(Naut)* tutti in coperta!; **to be an old** ~ essere vecchio del mestiere.

  (c) *(~ writing)* scrittura, mano *f;* **in one's own** ~ di proprio pugno, di propria mano.

  (d) *(Cards)* mano *f;* **a** ~ **of bridge/poker** una partita a bridge/poker.

  (e) *(measurement: of horse)* ≃ dieci centimetri.

  (f) *(phrases with verb):* **to be** ~ **in glove with sb** essere in combutta con qn; **to change** ~**s** cambiare (di) mano; **to force sb's** ~ forzare la mano a qn; **to give** *or* **lend sb a hand** dare una mano a qn; **to keep one's** ~ **in** tenersi in esercizio, non perdere la mano; **he can turn his** ~ **to anything** sa fare un po' di tutto; **he asked for her** ~ *(in marriage)* ha chiesto la sua mano; **to wait on sb** ~ **and foot** essere a totale disposizione di qn; **to have one's** ~**s full (with sb/sth)** essere troppo preso (con qn/qc); **to win** ~**s down** vincere senza difficoltà; **to be making/losing money** ~ **over fist** fare/perdere un sacco di soldi; **to have a free** ~ avere carta bianca; **to have the upper** ~ avere la meglio *or* il sopravvento; **to have a** ~ **in sth** essere immischiato in qc.

(g) *(phrases with prep before n)*: **at** ~ a portata di mano; **to be near** *or* **close at** ~ essere a due passi; **at first** ~ di prima mano; ~ **in** ~ mano nella mano; **to be in sb's** ~**s** essere nelle mani di qn; **to have £50 in** ~ avere ancora 50 sterline a disposizione; **we have the matter in** ~ ci stiamo occupando della cosa; **to take sb in** ~ controllare qn; **to play into sb's** ~**s** fare il gioco di qn; **to fall into the** ~**s of the enemy** cadere in mano al nemico; **on** ~ *(person)* disponibile; *(object)* sottomano, a portata di mano; **on the right/left** ~ sulla destra/sinistra; **(on the one** ~)... **on the other** ~ (da una parte) ... d'altra parte; **to have sth left on one's** ~**s** ritrovarsi con qc, rimanere con qc; **to take sth off sb's** ~**s** togliere qc di torno a qn; **to condemn sb out of** ~ condannare qn a priori; **to get out of** ~ diventare incontrollabile; **to** ~ a portata di mano.

2 *vt (pass)*: **to** ~ **sb sth**, ~ **sth to sb** passare qc a qn; **you've got to** ~ **it to him** *(fam)* questo glielo devi riconoscere; **it was** ~**ed to him on a plate** *(fam)* glielo hanno dato su un piatto d'argento.

3 *cpd (cream etc)* per le mani; ~ **luggage** *n* bagaglio a mano.

♦ **hand back** *vt + adv* restituire.

♦ **hand down** *vt + adv (suitcase etc)* passare (giù); *(heirloom)* lasciare in eredità; *(tradition)* tramandare.

♦ **hand in** *vt + adv (form etc)* consegnare; *(resignation)* rassegnare, dare.

♦ **hand out** *vt + adv (leaflets)* distribuire; *(advice)* elargire.

♦ **hand over** *vt + adv (pass over)* consegnare; *(powers, property, business)* cedere.

♦ **hand round** *vt + adv (information, papers)* far passare; *(distribute: chocolates etc)* far girare; *(subj: hostess)* offrire.

hand·bag ['hændbæg] *n* borsa, borsetta.

hand·ball ['hændbɔːl] *n* pallamano.

hand·bill ['hændbɪl] *n* volantino.

hand·book ['hændbʊk] *n (manual)* manuale *m*, libretto di istruzioni; *(for tourists)* guida (turistica).

hand·brake ['hændbreɪk] *n* freno a mano.

hand·cuffs ['hændkʌfs] *npl* manette *fpl*.

hand·ful ['hændfʊl] *n (quantity)* manciata; **a** ~ **of people** uno sparuto gruppo di persone; **that child's a real** ~ *(fam)* quel bambino è proprio un terremoto.

handi·cap ['hændɪkæp] **1** *n* menomazione *f*; *(Sport)* handicap *m inv.* **2** *vt* handicappare, menomare; **to be physically** ~**ped** essere handicappato; **to be mentally** ~**ped** essere un handicappato mentale.

handi·craft ['hændɪkrɑːft] *n (art)* lavoro artigianale; *(product)* prodotto di artigianato.

handi·work ['hændɪwɜːk] *n* lavorazione *f* a mano; **this looks like his** ~ *(pej)* qui c'è il suo zampino.

hand·ker·chief ['hæŋkətʃɪf] *n* fazzoletto.

han·dle ['hændl] **1** *n (gen)* manico; *(of knife)* manico, impugnatura; *(of door, drawer etc)* maniglia; *(of wheelbarrow)* stanga; *(of pump)* braccio; *(for winding)* manovella; **to fly off the** ~ *(fig)* perdere le staffe, uscire dai gangheri.

2 *vt* **(a)** *(touch)* toccare; *(use)* maneggiare; *(Ftbl: ball)* toccare con la mano; '~ **with care'** 'fragile'; **the police** ~**d him roughly** è stato malmenato dalla polizia. **(b)** *(deal with: theme)* trattare; *(: situation)* far fronte a; *(: resources)* amministrare; *(cope with: people)* trattare con; *(: animals)* occuparsi di; *(Comm: goods)* trattare, occuparsi di; *(ship, car)* manovrare; *(use: gun,*

machine, money) maneggiare; **I'll** ~ **this** me ne occupo io, ci penso io; **she knows how to** ~ **her son** sa come prendere suo figlio; **we** ~ **2000 travellers a day** abbiamo un traffico di 2000 passeggeri al giorno.

3 *vi (ship, plane, car)* rispondere ai comandi.

handle·bars ['hændlbɑːz] *npl (on bicycle)* manubrio.

hand·made [,hænd'meɪd] *adj (clothes etc)* fatto(a) a mano; *(biscuits etc)* fatto(a) in casa.

hand·me·down ['hændmɪ,daʊn] *n* vestito smesso.

hand·out ['hændaʊt] *n (leaflet)* volantino; *(press* ~) comunicato stampa; *(at lecture)* ciclostile *m*; *(fam: money)* elemosina.

hand·picked [,hænd'pɪkt] *adj (produce)* scelto(a), selezionato(a); *(staff etc)* scelto(a).

hand·rail ['hændreɪl] *n (on staircase etc)* corrimano.

hand·shake ['hændʃeɪk] *n* stretta di mano.

hand·some ['hænsəm] *adj* (-**r**, -**st**) *(gen)* bello(a); *(salary)* buono(a); *(considerable: fortune, profit)* considerevole, grosso(a).

hand·stand ['hændstænd] *n* verticale *f (ginnastica)*.

hand-to-mouth [,hændtə'maʊθ] *adj (existence)* precario(a).

hand·writing ['hænd,raɪtɪŋ] *n* scrittura.

handy ['hændɪ] *adj* (-**ier**, -**iest**) **(a)** *(close at hand)* a portata di mano, sottomano. **(b)** *(convenient)* comodo(a); *(useful: machine etc)* pratico(a), utile; **to come in** ~ servire; **that would come in very** ~ farebbe proprio molto comodo. **(c)** *(skilful)* bravo(a); **he's** ~ **with a paintbrush** è proprio bravo come imbianchino.

handy·man ['hændɪmæn] *n, pl* -**men** tuttofare *m inv.*

hang [hæŋ] *pt, pp* **hung 1** *vt* **(a)** *(gen)* appendere; *(washing)* stendere; *(door)* montare (sui cardini); *(wallpaper)* mettere, incollare; *(coat etc)*: **to** ~ **(on)** appendere (a); **the walls were hung with tapestries** i muri erano coperti di arazzi; **the Christmas tree was hung with lights** l'albero di Natale era decorato di *or* con luci colorate. **(b)** *(pt, pp* **hanged**: *criminal)* impiccare; ~ **(it)!** *(fam)* accidenti!, porca miseria! **to** ~ **one's head** abbassare la testa (per la vergogna). **2** *vi* **(a)** *(rope, dangling object etc)*: **to** ~ **(from)** penzolare (da), pendere (da); *(garment)* cadere; *(criminal)* essere impiccato(a); **that dress** ~**s well** quel vestito cade bene. **(b)**: **to** ~ **over** *(smoke, fog)* sovrastare; *(threat)* incombere su; *(hawk)* essere sospeso(a) su. **3** *n*: **he couldn't get the** ~ **of the game** *(fam)* non riusciva ad afferrare il senso del gioco; **you'll soon get the** ~ **of this** *(fam)* ti farai presto la mano a questo.

♦ **hang about 1** *vi + adv (also:* ~ **around**: *loiter)* gironzolare; *(: wait)* rimanere ad aspettare; **to keep sb** ~**ing about** far aspettare qn; **don't** ~ **about, there is work to do** non perder tempo, c'è un sacco di lavoro da fare. **2** *vi + prep (the streets etc)* aggirarsi per, bighellonare per.

♦ **hang back** *vi + adv (hesitate)*: **to** ~ **back (from doing)** essere riluttante (dal fare).

♦ **hang on 1** *vi + prep (depend on: decision etc)* dipendere da. **(b)** *(listen eagerly)* bersi le parole di; **she hung on his every word** pendeva dalle sue labbra. **2** *vi + adv* **(a)** *(keep hold)*: **to** ~ **on (to)** aggrapparsi a, attaccarsi a; *(keep)*: **to** ~ **on to** tenere. **(b)** *(fam: wait)* aspettare; ~ **on a minute!** aspetta un momento!

♦ **hang out 1** *vt + adv (washing)* stendere (fuori); *(flags)* metter fuori. **2** *vi + adv* **(a)**: **to** ~ **out of sth** penzolare fuori da qc, pendere fuori da qc; **his shirt was** ~**ing out** la camicia gli usciva dai pantaloni. (b) *(fam: live)* stare; **he ~s out in the local bars** bazzica nei bar locali. (c): **to ~ out for more money** *(fam)* continuare a chiedere più soldi.

♦ **hang together** *vi + adv (fam: people)* stare insieme; *(cohere: argument etc)* stare in piedi.

♦ **hang up 1** *vt + adv (coat)* appendere; *(picture)* attaccare, appendere. **2** *vi + adv (Telec)* riattaccare, riagganciare; **to ~ up on sb** metter giù il ricevitore a qn.

hang·ar ['hæŋəʳ] *n* hangar *m inv,* aviorimessa.

hang·dog ['hæŋdɒg] *adj (guilty: look, expression)* da cane bastonato.

hang·er ['hæŋəʳ] *n (for clothes)* ometto, gruccia.

hanger-on [,hæŋəʳ'rɒn] *n,* *pl* **hangers-on** *(fam)* parassita *m/f inv.*

hang-gliding ['hæŋglaɪdɪŋ] *n* deltaplano.

hang·ing ['hæŋɪŋ] **1** *n* (a) *(execution)* impiccagione *f.* (b) *(curtains etc):* **~s** *pl* tende *fpl,* tendaggi *mpl.* **2** *adj (bridge)* sospeso(a); *(offence, matter)* da punire con l'impiccagione *or* la forca; **~ lamp** lampadario.

hang·man ['hæŋmən] *n,* *pl* **-men** boia *m,* carnefice *m.*

hang·out ['hæŋaʊt] *n (fam)* ritrovo.

hang·over ['hæŋ,əʊvəʳ] *n* (a) *(after drinking)* postumi *mpl* di una sbornia; **I've got an awful ~** ho un terribile cerchio alla testa. (b) *(sth left over)* residuato.

hang-up ['hæŋʌp] *n (fam)* complesso, ossessione *f.*

hank [hæŋk] *n (of wool)* matassa; *(of hair)* ciocca.

hank·er ['hæŋkəʳ] *vi:* **to ~ after** *or* **for** *(fame, power)* essere assetato(a) di; *(sympathy)* avere molto desiderio di.

hank·er·ing ['hæŋkərɪŋ] *n:* **~ (for)** voglia matta (di).

hanky ['hæŋkɪ] *n (fam)* fazzoletto.

hanky-panky ['hæŋkɪ'pæŋkɪ] *n (fam):* **there's some ~ going on here** qui c'è del losco; **you can drive me home, but no ~!** puoi portarmi a casa se tieni le mani a posto!

hap·haz·ard [,hæp'hæzəd] *adj (fatto(a)* a caso *or* a casaccio; *(arrangement)* casuale, fortuito(a).

hap·pen ['hæpən] *vi* (a) *succedere, accadere, capitare;* **what's ~ing?** cosa succede?, cosa sta succedendo?; **these things will ~** sono cose che capitano *or* succedono; **don't let it ~ again** che non si ripeta *or* succeda mai più; **as if nothing had ~ed** come se niente fosse; **what has ~ed to him?** *(befallen)* cosa gli è successo?; *(become of)* che fine ha fatto?; **if anything should ~ to him...** se gli dovesse accadere qc... . (b) *(chance):* **it ~ed that...** si dava il caso che... + *sub;* **do you ~ to know if...** sai per caso se...; **if anyone should ~ to see John** se a qualcuno capita di vedere John; **I ~ to know that...** si dà il caso che io sappia che...; **as it ~s** *(per)* combinazione; **it so ~ed that...** guarda caso... .

♦ **happen (up)on** *vi + prep* capitare su.

hap·pen·ing ['hæpnɪŋ] *n (event)* avvenimento, evento; *(in theatre)* happening *m inv.*

hap·pi·ly ['hæpɪlɪ] *adv (contentedly: play, work)* tranquillamente; *(cheerfully: say)* con gioia; *(: laugh)* con allegria; *(fortunately)* per fortuna, fortunatamente; **and they lived ~ ever after** e vissero per sempre felici e contenti.

hap·pi·ness ['hæpɪnɪs] *n* felicità, gioia.

hap·py ['hæpɪ] *adj* (-ier, -iest) (a) *(pleased, content)* contento(a), felice; *(cheerful)* allegro(a); *(at ease, unworried)* tranquillo(a); **we are not entirely ~ about the plan** non siamo del tutto contenti del progetto; **we're very ~ for you** ci rallegriamo per te, siamo molto felici per te; **yes, I'd be ~ to**

(certo,) con piacere, (ben) volentieri; **I am ~ to tell you that...** sono felice *or* ho il piacere di informarti che...; **a ~ event/ending** un lieto evento/fine; **to be as ~ as a lark** essere felice *or* contento come una pasqua; **~ birthday!** buon compleanno!; **~ Christmas/New Year!** buon natale/anno!

(b) *(well-chosen: phrase, idea)* felice, indovinato(a); *(lucky: position)* fortunato(a), favorevole; **by a ~ chance** per fortuna; **a ~ medium** una giusta via di mezzo.

happy-go-lucky ['hæpɪgəʊ,lʌkɪ] *adj* spensierato(a).

ha·rangue [hə'ræŋ] **1** *n* tirata, arringa. **2** *vt* arringare.

har·ass ['hærəs] *vt (also Mil)* assillare.

har·assed ['hærəst] *adj* assillato(a); **you look ~** hai una faccia sconvolta.

har·ass·ment ['hærəsmənt] *n* persecuzione *f.*

har·bour, *(Am)* **har·bor** ['hɑːbəʳ] **1** *n* porto. **2** *vt (retain: grudge etc)* covare, nutrire; *(shelter: criminal, spy)* dar rifugio a, tener nascosto(a). **3** *cpd:* **~ master** *n* capitano di porto.

hard [hɑːd] **1** *adj* (-er, -est) (a) *(substance)* duro(a); *(mud)* indurito(a); **to grow ~** indurirsi; **~ cash** *(fam)* denaro contante *or* sonante; **~ court** *(Tennis)* campo in terra battuta; **~ shoulder** *(Aut)* corsia d'emergenza.

(b) *(severe, tough: gen)* duro(a); *(: climate, weather, winter)* rigido(a); *(: frost, drink)* forte; *(: drug)* pesante; **to take a long ~ look at sth** esaminare qc attentamente; **the ~ fact is that...** la verità nuda e cruda è che...; **~ luck!, ~ lines!** *(Brit fam)* peccato!, scalogna!; **a ~ luck story** una storia pietosa; **he's as ~ as nails** *(physically)* è forte come un toro *or* una quercia; *(in temperament)* è duro; **to take a ~ line over sth** adottare una linea dura in merito a qc; **to be ~ on sb** essere severo con qn; **to be a ~ worker** essere un (gran) lavoratore; **10 years ~ labour** 10 anni di lavori forzati.

(c) *(difficult: gen)* arduo(a), difficile; **I find it ~ to believe that...** stento *or* faccio fatica a credere che... + *sub;* **to be ~ to please** essere esigente, essere difficile da accontentare; **~ of hearing** duro d'orecchio.

2 *adv* (-er, -est) *(push)* forte; *(work)* sodo; *(think)* bene; *(hit)* forte, duramente; **to freeze ~** gelare; **it's snowing/raining ~** sta nevicando/piovendo forte; **he was breathing ~** respirava affannosamente; **to be ~ hit** *(fig)* essere duramente colpito; **to be ~ done by** *(fam)* essere trattato molto male; **to be ~ at it** *(fam)* darci dentro; **to be ~ put (to it)** non riuscire molto bene (a); **to try one's ~est to do sth** fare di tutto per fare qc; **to take sth ~** prendere (molto) male qc; **to be ~ up** *(fam)* essere al verde; **to be ~ up for sth** essere a corto di qc.

hard-and-fast [,hɑːdən'fɑːst] *adj* ferreo(a).

hard·back ['hɑːdbæk] **1** *n (book)* libro con copertina rigida *or* in edizione rilegata. **2** *adj (edition)* rilegato(a).

hard·board ['hɑːdbɔːd] *n* faesite *f.*

hard-boiled [,hɑːd'bɔɪld] *adj (egg)* sodo(a); *(fig: tough, cynical)* duro(a).

hard-core [,hɑːd'kɔːʳ] *adj* (a) *(pornography)* hardcore *inv.* (b) *(supporters)* irriducibile.

hard·en ['hɑːdn] **1** *vt (gen)* indurire; *(steel)* temprare; *(fig: determination)* rafforzare; **to ~ one's heart** non lasciarsi commuovere. **2** *vi (substance)* indurirsi.

hard·ened ['hɑːdnd] *adj (criminal)* incallito(a); **to be ~ to sth** essere (diventato) insensibile a qc.

hard-headed [ˌhɑːdˈhɛdɪd] *adj* pratico(a).
hard-hearted [ˌhɑːdˈhɑːtɪd] *adj* che non si lascia commuovere, dal cuore duro.

hard·ly [ˈhɑːdlɪ] *adv (scarcely)* appena, a mala pena; **she can ~ read** riesce a malapena a leggere; **that can ~ be true** non può essere vero; **I ~ know him** lo conosco appena; **it's ~ the case** non è proprio il caso; **I can ~ believe it** stento a crederci; **I need ~ point out that...** non c'è bisogno che io faccia notare che...; **this is ~ the time** non è di sicuro il momento; **~ anyone/anything** quasi nessuno/niente; **~ ever** quasi mai; **~!** figuriamoci!, neanche per idea!

hard·ness [ˈhɑːdnɪs] *n (gen)* durezza.
hard·ship [ˈhɑːdʃɪp] *n* privazioni *fpl*; *(suffering)* sofferenze *fpl.*
hard·ware [ˈhɑːdwɛəʳ] **1** *n (for domestic use)* ferramenta *fpl*; *(Mil)* armamenti *mpl*; *(Computers)* hardware *m.* **2** *cpd*: **~ shop** *or* **store** *n* (negozio di) ferramenta.
hard-wearing [ˌhɑːdˈwɛərɪŋ] *adj (gen)* resistente; *(shoes)* robusto(a).
hard-working [ˌhɑːdˈwɜːkɪŋ] *adj* lavoratore (trice).
har·dy [ˈhɑːdɪ] *adj* (**-ier, -iest**) forte, robusto(a); *(Bot)* resistente al gelo.
hare [hɛəʳ] *n* lepre *f.*
hare-brained [ˈhɛəˌbreɪnd] *adj* insensato(a).
hare-lip [ˌhɛəˈlɪp] *n* labbro leporino.
har·em [hɑːˈriːm] *n* harem *m inv.*
hari·cot [ˈhærɪkəʊ] *n (also: ~ bean)* fagiolo bianco.
hark [hɑːk] *vi*: **~!** *(poet)* udite!; **~ at him!** *(fam)* ma sentilo!
♦ **hark back** *vi + adv*: **to ~ back to** *(former days)* rievocare; *(earlier occasion)* ritornare a *or* su.
harm [hɑːm] **1** *n (gen)* male *m*; **to do sb ~** far del male a qn; **to do ~ to** *(reputation, interests etc)* danneggiare; **out of ~'s way** al sicuro; **to keep out of ~'s way** tenersi alla larga; **there's no ~ in trying** tentar non nuoce; **it does more ~ than good** fa più male che bene; **you will come to no ~** non ti succederà nulla; **he means no ~** non ha nessuna cattiva intenzione; **he meant no ~ by what he said** non l'ha detto con cattiveria. **2** *vt (person)* far male a; *(reputation, interests, health)* danneggiare, nuocere a; *(object, crops etc)* danneggiare.
harm·ful [ˈhɑːmfʊl] *adj*: **~ (to)** dannoso(a) (per), nocivo(a) (per).
harm·less [ˈhɑːmlɪs] *adj (gen)* innocuo(a); *(innocent: conversation, joke)* innocente.
har·moni·ca [hɑːˈmɒnɪkə] *n* armonica a bocca.
har·mo·ni·ous [hɑːˈməʊnɪəs] *adj* armonioso(a).
har·mo·nium [hɑːˈməʊnɪəm] *n* armonium *m inv.*
har·mo·nize [ˈhɑːmənaɪz] **1** *vt (Mus)* armonizzare; *(colours)* intonare, armonizzare. **2** *vi (Mus)* armonizzare; **to ~ (with)** *(colours)* armonizzarsi (a), intonarsi (a).
har·mo·ny [ˈhɑːmənɪ] *n* armonia.
har·ness [ˈhɑːnɪs] **1** *n (for horse)* bardatura, finimenti *mpl*; *(for baby)* briglie *fpl*; *(safety ~)* imbracatura; **to die in ~** *(fig)* morire sul lavoro *or* sulla breccia. **2** *vt (horse)* bardare, mettere i finimenti a; *(: to carriage)* attaccare a; *(resources etc)* sfruttare.
harp [hɑːp] *n* arpa.
♦ **harp on** *vi + adv (fam)*: **to ~ on (about)** continuare a menarla (con).
har·poon [hɑːˈpuːn] **1** *n* arpione *m.* **2** *vt* arpionare.
harp·si·chord [ˈhɑːpsɪkɔːd] *n* clavicembalo, cembalo.
har·row [ˈhærəʊ] *(Agr)* **1** *n* erpice *m.* **2** *vt* erpicare.

har·row·ing [ˈhærəʊɪŋ] *adj (experience, story)* straziante, sconvolgente.
har·ry [ˈhærɪ] *vt (Mil)* attaccare ripetutamente; *(person)* assillare.
harsh [hɑːʃ] *adj* (**-er, -est**) **(a)** *(punishment, person etc)* severo(a), duro(a); *(words)* duro(a); *(weather)* rigido(a); *(taste, cloth)* pungente. **(b)** *(discordant: voice)* sgradevole; *(: colour)* chiasso so(a), squillante; *(light)* troppo forte; *(contrast)* brusco(a).
har·vest [ˈhɑːvɪst] **1** *n (of crop)* raccolto; *(grapes)* vendemmia. **2** *vt (grain)* fare il raccolto di; *(grain)* mietere; *(grapes)* vendemmiare. **3** *cpd*: **~ festival** *n* festa del raccolto; **~ moon** *n* plenilunio *(più vicino all'equinozio d'autunno).*
har·vest·er [ˈhɑːvɪstəʳ] *n (person)* mietitore/trice; *(machine)* mietitrice *f*; *(combine ~)* mietitrebbia *f.*
has [hæz] *3rd pers sg* of **have.**
has-been [ˈhæzbiːn] *n (fam: person)* uomo/donna superato(a); *(: thing)* anticaglia.
hash [hæʃ] *n* **(a)** *(Culin)* spezzatino fatto con avanzi di carne cotta. **(b)** *(fam)*: **to make a ~ of sth** fare un bel pasticcio di qc. **(c)** *(fam: hashish)* hascisc *m.*
hash·ish [ˈhæʃɪʃ] *n* hascisc *m.*
hasn't [ˈhæznt] = **has not.**
has·sle [ˈhæsl] *n (fam)* sacco di problemi.
has·sock [ˈhæsək] *n (Rel)* cuscino usato come inginocchiatoio.
haste [heɪst] *n* fretta, premura; **to make ~** sbrigarsi, affrettarsi; **more ~ less speed** *(Proverb)* presto e bene raro avviene.
has·ten [ˈheɪsn] **1** *vt (growth)* accelerare; *(steps)* affrettare, accelerare; **to ~ sb's departure** affrettare la partenza di qn. **2** *vi*: **to ~ (to do sth)** affrettarsi (a fare qc); **I ~ to add that...** mi preme di aggiungere che... .
hasti·ly [ˈheɪstɪlɪ] *adv (hurriedly)* in (gran) fretta, in fretta e furia; *(without thinking)* troppo in fretta, senza riflettere; **he ~ suggested that...** s'è affrettato a proporre che... .
has·ty [ˈheɪstɪ] *adj* (**-ier, -iest**) *(hurried)* frettoloso(a); *(rash)* affrettato(a), precipitoso(a).
hat [hæt] *n* cappello; **to pass the ~ round** *(fig)* fare la colletta; **I take my ~ off to him** *(fig)* gli faccio tanto di cappello; **to keep sth under one's ~** *(fig)* tenere qc per sé; **keep it under your ~!** acqua in bocca!; **to talk through one's ~** *(fam)* dire delle stupidaggini; **that's old ~!** *(fam)* sono storie vecchie! **2** *cpd*: **~ stand** *n* attaccapanni *m*; **~ trick** *n*: **to get a ~ trick** segnare tre punti consecutivi (*or* vincere per tre volte consecutive).
hatch¹ [hætʃ] *n (Naut: ~way)* boccaporto; *(service ~)* sportello passavivande.
hatch² [hætʃ] **1** *vt (chick)* fare; *(eggs)* fare schiudere; *(fig: scheme, plot)* elaborare, mettere a punto. **2** *vi (chick)* uscire dal *or* rompere il guscio; *(egg)* schiudersi.
hatch·back [ˈhætʃbæk] *n (car)* macchina a tre (*or* cinque) porte.
hatch·et [ˈhætʃɪt] *n* accetta, ascia.
hate [heɪt] **1** *n* odio. **2** *vt (person)* odiare, *(weaker)* detestare; *(thing)* detestare; **I ~ having to do it** detesto doverlo fare; **I ~ to trouble you, but...** mi dispiace disturbarla, ma...; **he ~s to be** *or* **he ~s being corrected** non sopporta le critiche *or* le osservazioni.
hate·ful [ˈheɪtfʊl] *adj* odioso(a), detestabile.
hat·pin [ˈhætpɪn] *n* spillone *m.*
ha·tred [ˈheɪtrɪd] *n*: **~ (of)** *(of person)* odio (per); *(of thing)* avversione *f* (per).
hat·ter [ˈhætəʳ] *n* cappellaio; **as mad as a ~** matto da legare.

haugh·ty [ˈhɔːtɪ] *adj* (**-ier, -iest**) altezzoso(a).
haul [hɔːl] **1** *n* (**a**) (*distance*) tragitto, viaggio; **it's a long ~** è una lunga tirata. (**b**) (*amount taken: of fish*) retata; (*fig: from robbery etc*) bottino. **2** *vt* (*drag: heavy object*) tirare, trascinare; **to ~ sb over the coals** (*fig*) dare una strigliata a qn.
♦ **haul down** *vt + adv* (*gen*) tirare giù; (*flag, sail*) ammainare.
haul·age [ˈhɔːlɪdʒ] **1** *n* (*road transport*) trasporto, autotrasporto; (*cost*) costo del trasporto. **2** *cpd*: **~ contractor** *n* (*firm*) impresa di trasporti; (*person*) autotrasportatore *m*.
haul·ier [ˈhɔːlɪəʳ] *n* (*Brit*) autotrasportatore *m*.
haunch [hɔːntʃ] *n* (*of person, animal*) anca; (*Culin*) coscia; **to sit on one's ~es** (*person*) accocolarsi; (*animal*) sedersi (sulle zampe posteriori).
haunt [hɔːnt] **1** *n* (*of criminals*) covo; **it's one of his favourite ~s** è un dei suoi posticini favoriti. **2** *vt* (*subj: ghost*) abitare; (*fig: memory etc*) perseguitare; **he ~s the local bars** frequenta assiduamente i bar della zona.
haunt·ed [ˈhɔːntɪd] *adj* (*castle etc*) abitato(a) dai fantasmi *or* dagli spiriti; (*look*) ossessionato(a), tormentato(a).
haunt·ing [ˈhɔːntɪŋ] *adj* (*sight, music*) che non si riesce a togliere dalla mente, che perseguita.
have [hæv] *3rd pers sg present* **has**, *pt, pp* **had 1** *aux vb* (**a**) (*gen*) avere; (*with many intransitive verbs*) essere; **he has been kind/promoted** è stato gentile/promosso; **to ~ arrived** essere arrivato(a); **to ~ eaten** aver mangiato; **has/hasn't he told you?** te l'ha/non te l'ha detto?; **having finished** *or* **when he had finished**, he left dopo aver finito se n'è andato.
(**b**) (*in tag questions*): **you've done it, ~n't you?** l'hai fatto, (non è) vero?; **he hasn't done it, has he?** non l'ha fatto, vero?
(**c**) (*in short answers and questions*): **you've made a mistake — no I ~n't/so I ~** hai fatto uno sbaglio — ma no, niente affatto/eh sì, è vero; **we ~n't paid — yes we ~**! non abbiamo pagato — sì che abbiamo pagato!; **I've been there before, ~ you?** ci sono già stato, e tu?
2 *modal aux vb* (*be obliged*): **to ~ (got) to do sth** dover fare qc; **I ~ (got) to finish this work** devo finire questo lavoro; **you ~n't to tell her** non glielo devi dire; **I ~n't got to** *or* **I don't ~ to wear glasses** non ho bisogno di portare gli occhiali; **it will ~ to wait till tomorrow** bisogna rimandarlo a domani; **this has to be a mistake** dev'essere un errore, deve trattarsi di un errore.
3 *vt* (**a**) (*possess*) avere; **he has (got) blue eyes** ha gli occhi azzurri; **I ~n't got blue eyes, I don't ~ blue eyes** non ho gli occhi azzurri; **~ you (got)** *or* **do you ~ a pen?** hai una penna?; **I've (got) somebody staying next week** ho un ospite la settimana prossima; **I ~ (got) no Spanish** non so una parola di spagnolo; **I ~ (got) an idea** ho un'idea, mi è venuta un'idea.
(**b**) (*meals etc*) fare, prendere; **to ~ breakfast** far colazione; **to ~ lunch** pranzare; **to ~ dinner** cenare; **what will you ~?** — **I'll ~ a coffee** cosa bevi *or* prendi? — prendo un caffè; **he had a cigarette** fumò una sigaretta; **will you ~ some more?** ne vuoi ancora?; **I must ~ a drink** devo bere qualcosa.
(**c**) (*receive, obtain etc*) avere, ricevere; **let me ~ your address** dammi il tuo indirizzo; **you can ~ it for £5** te lo lascio per 5 sterline; **there was no bread to be had** non avevano più *or* non c'era più pane; **I ~ it on good authority that...** so da fonte sicura che...; **I must ~ it by tomorrow** mi occorre per domani; **to ~ a child** avere un figlio.

(**d**) (*hold*) avere, tenere; **he had him by the throat** lo teneva per la gola; **I ~ (got) him where I want him** ce l'ho in mano *or* in pugno.
(**e**) (*maintain, allow*): **he will ~ it that he is right** sostiene *or* asserisce di aver ragione; **rumour has it (that)...** si dice *or* corre voce che...; **she won't ~ it said that...** non permette che si dica che...; **I won't ~ this nonsense** non tollero queste assurdità.
(**f**) (*causative*): **to ~ sth done** far fare qc; **to ~ one's hair cut** farsi tagliare i capelli; **to ~ one's luggage brought up** farsi portar su le valigie; **to ~ sb do sth** far fare qc a qn; **he had them all dancing** è riuscito a farli ballare tutti; **I'd ~ you know that...** voglio che tu sappia che...; **what would you ~ me do?** cosa vuoi che faccia?
(**g**) (*experience, suffer*): **she had her bag stolen** le hanno rubato la borsa; **he had his arm broken** gli hanno rotto il braccio; **to ~ an operation** avere *or* subire un'operazione.
(**h**) (+ *n* = *vb identical with n*): **to ~ a swim/walk** fare una nuotata/passeggiata; **let's ~ a look** diamo un'occhiata; **let me ~ a try** fammi *or* lasciami provare.
(**i**) (*phrases*): **to ~ a good time** divertirsi; **to ~ a pleasant evening** passare una piacevole serata; **to ~ a party** dare una festa; **thank you for having me** grazie dell'ospitalità; **let him ~ it!** (*fam*) dagliele!, picchialo!; **you've had it!** (*fam*) sei fritto!, sei fregato!; **you ~ me there!** mi hai colto in fallo!; **you've been had!** (*fam*) ci sei cascato!
♦ **have in** *vt + adv* (**a**) (*visitor*) avere (in casa); (*candidate*) far passare *or* entrare; (*doctor*) chiamare. (**b**): **to ~ it in for sb** (*fam*) avercela con qn.
♦ **have on 1** *vt + adv* (**a**) (*garment*) avere addosso. (**b**) (*be busy with*) avere da fare, avere in programma; **~ you anything on tomorrow?** hai qualcosa in programma per domani? **2** *vt + prep* (*money*): **I don't ~ any money on me** non ho soldi addosso.
♦ **have out** *vt + adv* (**a**) (*tooth, tonsils etc*) farsi togliere *or* levare. (**b**): **to ~ sth out with sb** chiarire qc *or* mettere qc in chiaro con qn.
♦ **have up** *vt*: **to be had up** (*fam: to court*) esser portato(a) in tribunale.
ha·ven [ˈheɪvn] *n* (*fig*) rifugio, riparo.
have-nots [ˈhævnɒts] *npl see* **haves**.
haven't [ˈhævnt] = **have not**.
hav·er·sack [ˈhævəsæk] *n* zaino.
haves [hævz] *npl* (*fam*): **the ~ and the have-nots** gli abbienti e i non abbienti.
hav·oc [ˈhævək] *n* danni *mpl*; **to wreak ~ in** devastare; **to play ~ with** (*fig*) mettere sottosopra.
Ha·waii [həˈwaɪiː] *n* le Hawai.
hawk[1] [hɔːk] *n* (*also fig*) falco.
hawk[2] [hɔːk] *vt* (*goods for sale*) vendere per strada.
hawk-eyed [ˈhɔːkaɪd] *adj* dagli occhi di falco.
haw·thorn [ˈhɔːθɔːn] *n* biancospino.
hay [heɪ] **1** *n* fieno; **to make ~ while the sun shines** (*Proverb*) approfittare dell'occasione. **2** *cpd*: **~ fever** *n* febbre *f or* raffreddore *m* da fieno.
hay·stack [ˈheɪstæk] *n* pagliaio.
hay·wire [ˈheɪwaɪəʳ] *adj* (*fam*): **to go ~** (*person*) mettersi a dare i numeri; (*machine*) impazzire; (*scheme etc*) andare a catafascio.
haz·ard [ˈhæzəd] **1** *n* rischio; (*more serious*) pericolo; **to be a health/fire ~** essere pericoloso per la salute/in caso d'incendio. **2** *vt* (*one's life*) rischiare, mettere a repentaglio; (*remark*) azzardare; **to ~ a guess** tirare a indovinare.

haz·ard·ous ['hæzədəs] *adj* rischioso(a), pericoloso(a).

haze [heɪz] *n (mist)* foschia; *(of smoke etc)* velo.

ha·zel ['heɪzl] **1** *n (tree)* nocciolo. **2** *adj (eyes)* (color) nocciola *inv*.

ha·zel·nut ['heɪzlnʌt] *n* nocciola.

hazy ['heɪzɪ] *adj* **(-ier, -iest)** *(day)* di foschia; *(weather)* caliginoso(a); *(view)* indistinto(a); *(photograph)* leggermente sfocato(a); *(fig: uncertain)* confuso(a).

H-bomb ['eɪtʃbɒm] *n* bomba H.

he [hiː] **1** *pers pron* lui, egli; ~ **has gone out** è uscito; **there ~ is** eccolo; **HE didn't do it** non è stato lui a farlo; ~ **who hesitates is lost** chi dubita è perduto. **2** *n*: **it's a** ~ *(animal, fam: baby)* è un maschio.

head [hɛd] **1** *n* **(a)** *(Anat)* testa, capo; ~ **of hair** capigliatura; ~ **down** a testa bassa; ~ **first** a capofitto, di testa; **my** ~ **aches** mi fa male la testa, ho mal di testa; **to fall** ~ **over heels in love with sb** innamorarsi perdutamente *or* follemente di qn; **from** ~ **to foot** dalla testa ai piedi; **his** ~**'s in the clouds** ha la testa fra le nuvole; **to keep one's** ~ **above water** *(fig)* mantenersi a galla; **the horse won by a** ~ il cavallo ha vinto per una testa; **on your** ~ **be it** la responsabilità è tua; **I could do it standing on my** ~ *(fam)* potrei farlo a occhi chiusi; **they went over my** ~ **to the manager** mi hanno scavalcato e sono andati direttamente dal direttore; **wine goes to my** ~ il vino mi dà *or* va alla testa; **success has gone to his** ~ il successo gli ha dato alla testa; **to shout one's** ~ **off** *(fam)* sgolarsi.

(b) *(intellect, mind)* cervello, testa; **two ~s are better than one** *(Proverb)* due occhi vedono meglio di uno; **it never entered my** ~ non mi è mai passato per la testa; **to have a** ~ **for business** essere tagliato per gli affari; **to have no** ~ **for heights** soffrire di vertigini; **to lose/to keep one's** ~ perdere/non perdere la testa; **let's put our ~s together** pensiamoci insieme; **it was above** *or* **over their ~s** non erano all'altezza di capirlo; **to do a sum in one's** ~ fare un calcolo a mente; **I couldn't tell you off the top of my** ~ *(fam)* non te lo saprei dire con esattezza; **to get sth into one's** ~ ficcarsi in testa qc; **to be off one's** ~ *(fam)* essere matto.

(c) *(leader: of family, business)* capo; *(: of school)* direttore/trice, preside *m/f*; ~ **of state** *(Pol)* capo di Stato.

(d) *(on coin)* testa; **~s or tails?** testa o croce?; **I couldn't make** ~ **nor tail of it** non riuscivo a capirci niente *or* un'acca.

(e) *(no pl: unit)*: **20** ~ **of cattle** 20 capi *mpl* di bestiame; **£10 a** *or* **per** ~ 10 sterline a testa.

(f) *(of hammer, bed, flower)* testa; *(of nail etc)* capocchia; *(of arrow)* punta; *(of lettuce)* cespo; *(of river)* sorgente *f*; *(of stairs, page)* cima; *(on beer)* schiuma; *(on tape recorder)* testina; **at the** ~ **of** *(organization etc)* a capo di; *(train, procession)* in testa a, alla testa di; *(queue)* all'inizio di; **to sit at the** ~ **of the table** sedersi a capotavola; **to come to a** ~ *(abscess etc)* maturarsi; *(fig: situation etc)* precipitare.

2 *vt* **(a)** *(parade, list, poll)* essere in testa a; *(company)* essere a capo di.

(b) *(Ftbl)*: **to** ~ **a ball** colpire di testa una palla.

(c) *(chapter etc)* intitolare.

3 *vi* dirigersi; **to** ~ **for** dirigersi *or* andare verso; **to** ~ **home** andare a casa; **he was ~ing up the stairs** stava salendo le scale; **he is ~ing for trouble** sta andando incontro a dei guai.

4 *cpd* **(a)** *(clerk, typist etc)* capo *inv*; ~ **office** *n*

sede *f* centrale; ~ **waiter** *n* capocameriere *m*.

(b): ~ **cold** *n* raffreddore *m* di testa; ~ **start** *n*: **to have a** ~ **start** *(Sport, fig)* partire avvantaggiato(a).

head·ache ['hɛdeɪk] *n (pain)* mal *m* di testa; *(fig)* grattacapo; **to have a** ~ aver mal di testa.

head·band ['hɛdbænd] *n* fascia per i capelli.

head·dress ['hɛddrɛs] *n (of Indian etc)* copricapo; *(of bride)* acconciatura.

head·er ['hɛdə'] *n (fam: Ftbl)* colpo di testa; *(: fall)* caduta di testa.

head·gear ['hɛdgɪə'] *n (hat etc)* copricapo.

head·ing ['hɛdɪŋ] *n (title)* titolo; *(section)* sezione *f*.

head·lamp ['hɛdlæmp] *n (Aut)* faro, fanale *m*.

head·land ['hɛdlənd] *n* capo, punta.

head·light ['hɛdlaɪt] *n* = **headlamp**.

head·line ['hɛdlaɪn] *n (in newspaper)* titolo; *(TV, Radio)*: ~ **s** sommario; **to hit the ~s** far titolo.

head·long ['hɛdlɒŋ] **1** *adj (fall, dive)* a capofitto, a testa in giù; *(rush etc)* a tutta velocità. **2** *adv* a capofitto; a tutta velocità.

head·master [ˌhɛd'mɑːstə'] *n (of primary school)* direttore *m*; *(of secondary school)* preside *m*.

head·mistress [ˌhɛd'mɪstrɪs] *n (of primary school)* direttrice *f*; *(of secondary school)* preside *f*.

head-on [ˌhɛd'ɒn] **1** *adj (collision)* frontale; *(confrontation)* diretto(a), faccia a faccia. **2** *adv (collide)* frontalmente.

head·phones ['hɛdfəunz] *npl* cuffia.

head·quarters [ˌhɛd'kwɔːtəz] *npl (Mil)* quartier *m* generale; *(of party, organization)* sede *f* centrale; *(Police)* centrale *f*.

head·rest ['hɛdrɛst] *n* poggiatesta *m inv*.

head·room ['hɛdrum] *n (under ceiling)* spazio (per la testa); *(under bridge etc)* altezza libera di passaggio.

head·scarf ['hɛdskɑːf] *n* foulard *m inv*, fazzoletto da testa.

head·set ['hɛdsɛt] *n* cuffia.

head·square ['hɛdskwɛə'] *n* = **headscarf**.

head·stone ['hɛdstəun] *n (on grave)* lapide *f*, pietra tombale.

head·strong ['hɛdstrɒŋ] *adj* testardo(a), cocciuto(a).

head·way ['hɛdweɪ] *n*: **to make** ~ *(Naut)* avanzare; *(fig)* fare progressi *or* passi avanti.

head·wind ['hɛdwɪnd] *n* vento di prua.

heady ['hɛdɪ] *adj* **(-ier, -iest)** *(wine, scent, success)* inebriante; *(atmosphere)* euforico(a).

heal [hiːl] **1** *vt (wound)* guarire, cicatrizzare; *(person)* guarire; *(fig: differences)* appianare. **2** *vi (also:* ~ **up)** cicatrizzarsi.

health [hɛlθ] **1** *n (gen)* salute *f*; **Ministry of H**~ Ministero della Sanità; **to be in good/bad** ~ essere in buona/cattiva salute; **to drink sb's** ~ bere alla salute di qn; **your ~!** (alla tua) salute! **2** *cpd*: ~ **centre** *n* poliambulatorio; ~ **food(s)** *n(pl)* alimenti *mpl* integrali.

healthy ['hɛlθɪ] *adj* **(-ier, -iest)** *(person)* sano(a), in buona salute; *(skin, diet)* sano(a); *(air, place etc)* salubre; *(appetite)* buono(a); *(exercise, fig: respect)* salutare; *(: interest)* vivace; *(: economy)* florido(a); *(: bank balance)* solido(a).

heap [hiːp] **1** *n (pile)* mucchio, cumulo; *(fam: old car)* macinino; *(: lots)*: ~ **s (of)** un sacco (di), un mucchio (di); **we have ~s of time** abbiamo un mucchio *or* sacco di tempo; **I was struck** *or* **knocked all of a** ~ *(fam)* sono rimasto di stucco. **2** *vt*: **to** ~ **sth onto sth** ammucchiare qc su qc; **the waitress ~ed potatoes onto my plate** la cameriera mi ha dato una montagna *or* un mucchio di patate; **to** ~ **sth with sth** colmare qc di qc; **to** ~ **favours/praise/gifts** *etc* **on sb** ricolmare qn di favori/lodi/regali *etc*; ~ed spoonful *(Culin)* cucchiaio colmo.

♦ **heap up** *vt* + *adv* accumulare, ammucchiare.

hear [hɪəʳ] *pt, pp* **heard** [hɜːd] **1** *vt (gen)* sentire; *(be informed of: piece of news)* apprendere, sentire; *(Law: case)* esaminare; **I can't ~ you** non ti sento; **I could hardly make myself heard** facevo fatica a farmi sentire; **I ~ you've lost your watch** ho saputo che hai perso l'orologio; **to ~ him speak you'd think…** a sentirlo parlare si direbbe che… . **2** *vi (gen)* sentire; *(get news)* aver notizie; **I heard about her from her mother** ho avuto sue notizie tramite sua madre; **I've never heard of that book** non ho mai sentito parlare di quel libro; **I've never heard of** non ho mai sentito parlare; **I won't ~ of it** *(allow)* non ne voglio proprio sapere; **I won't ~ of you paying for this** non è proprio il caso che tu paghi; **~! ~!** *(bravo)* bravo!, bene!

♦ **hear out** *vt* + *adv* ascoltare senza interrompere; **~ me out!** fammi finire!

hear·ing [ˈhɪərɪŋ] **1** *n* **(a)** *(sense of ~)* udito; **to be within/out of ~** *(distance)* essere/non essere a portata di voce; **in my ~** in mia presenza. **(b)** *(Law)* udienza; **to give sb a ~** dare ascolto a qn. **2** *cpd*: **~ aid** *n* apparecchio acustico.

hear·say [ˈhɪəseɪ] *n* diceria, chiacchiere *fpl*.

hearse [hɜːs] *n* carro funebre.

heart [hɑːt] **1** *n* **(a)** *(also fig)* cuore *m*; **to have a weak ~** avere il cuore debole; **he's a man after my own ~** è proprio il tipo che mi piace; **he's a good boy at ~** in fondo è un buon ragazzo; **to have sb's interests at ~** avere a cuore gli interessi di qn; **from the (bottom of one's) ~** dal profondo del cuore, con tutto il cuore; **in his ~ of ~s** nel suo intimo; **~ and soul** anima e corpo; **his ~ was in his boots** *(terrified)* aveva il cuore in gola; *(dejected)* aveva la morte nel cuore; **to wear one's ~ on one's sleeve** non fare mistero dei propri sentimenti; **my ~ sank** mi sono sentito mancare; **to learn/know/recite by ~** imparare/sapere/ripetere a memoria; **to one's ~'s content** a volontà; **his ~ is in the right place** in fondo è buono; **to cry one's ~ out** piangere disperatamente *or* a calde lacrime; **have a ~!** *(fam)* sii buono!; **he has a ~ of gold** ha un cuore d'oro; **to take sth to ~** prendersi a cuore qc; **his ~ was not in it** gli mancava l'entusiasmo; **to set one's ~ on sth/on doing sth** tenere molto a qc/a fare qc; **with all one's ~** con tutto il cuore; **to break sb's ~** spezzare il cuore a qn; **to be in good ~** essere su di morale; **I did not have the ~ to tell her** non ho avuto cuore *or* il coraggio di dirglielo; **to have one's ~ in one's mouth** avere il cuore in gola; **to lose ~** perdersi di coraggio *or* d'animo, scoraggiarsi; **to take ~** farsi coraggio *or* animo; **in the ~ of the country** in mezzo alla campagna; **the ~ of the matter** il nocciolo della questione.
(b) *(Cards)*: **~s** *pl* cuori *mpl*.
2 *cpd*: **~ attack** *n* *(Med)* infarto, attacco cardiaco; **~ failure** *n* *(Med)* arresto cardiaco; **~ surgeon** *n* cardiochirurgo; **~ transplant** *n* trapianto del cuore.

heart·ache [ˈhɑːteɪk] *n* dolore *m*, pena.

heart·beat [ˈhɑːtbiːt] *n* *(single)* battito del cuore; *(rate)* battiti *mpl* del cuore.

heart·break [ˈhɑːtbreɪk] *n* immenso dolore *m*.

heart·broken [ˈhɑːt,brəʊkən] *adj* affranto(a); **to be ~** avere il cuore spezzato.

heart·burn [ˈhɑːtbɜːn] *n* *(Med)* bruciore *m or* bruciori *mpl* di stomaco.

-hearted [ˈhɑːtɪd] *adj suf* dal cuore…; **a kind~ person** una persona molto gentile.

heart·en·ing [ˈhɑːtnɪŋ] *adj* incoraggiante.

heart·felt [ˈhɑːtfɛlt] *adj* profondo(a), sincero(a).

hearth [hɑːθ] **1** *n* *(for fire)* focolare *m*. **2** *cpd*: **~ rug** *n* tappeto *(che si mette davanti al camino)*.

heart·i·ly [ˈhɑːtɪlɪ] *adv (agree)* in pieno, completamente; *(laugh)* di cuore, di gusto; *(eat)* di buon appetito, di gusto; *(thank, welcome)* calorosamente; **to be ~ sick of** essere veramente stufo di, essere arcistufo di.

heart·less [ˈhɑːtlɪs] *adj* spietato(a), crudele.

heart·rend·ing [ˈhɑːt,rɛndɪŋ] *adj* straziante.

heart-to-heart [ˌhɑːttəˈhɑːt] *adj, adv* a cuore aperto.

heart-warm·ing [ˈhɑːt,wɔːmɪŋ] *adj* che fa piacere, che dà gioia.

hearty [ˈhɑːtɪ] *adj (person)* gioviale; *(support)* caloroso(a); *(dislike)* vivo(a); *(laugh)* di cuore, di gusto; *(appetite)* robusto(a); *(meal)* abbondante; *(welcome, thanks)* cordiale, caloroso(a); **a ~ eater** una buona forchetta.

heat [hiːt] **1** *n* **(a)** *(gen)* calore *m*; **I can't stand the ~** non sopporto il caldo; **at low ~** *(Culin: on stove)* a fuoco basso; *(: in oven)* a calore moderato; **in the ~ of the moment** *(fig)* nella foga del momento; **in the ~ of the battle** nella furia della battaglia; **to put the ~ on sb** fare pressione a *or* su qn; **he replied with some ~** rispose piuttosto irritato. **(b)** *(Sport)* batteria, prova eliminatoria. **(c)** *(Zool)*: **in** *or* **on ~** in calore. **2** *vt (far)* scaldare. **3** *vi* scaldarsi.

♦ **heat up 1** *vi* + *adv* scaldarsi. **2** *vt* + *adv* scaldare.

heat·ed [ˈhiːtɪd] *adj* riscaldato(a); *(fig: discussion etc)* acceso(a), animato(a); **~ words** parole *fpl* di fuoco; **to grow ~** *(discussion etc)* accendersi.

heat·er [ˈhiːtəʳ] *n* calorifero, termosifone *m*; *(stove)* stufa.

heath [hiːθ] *n* *(moor)* landa, brughiera; *(plant)* erica, brugo.

hea·then [ˈhiːðən] *adj, n* pagano(a) *(m/f)*.

heath·er [ˈhɛðəʳ] *n* erica.

heat·ing [ˈhiːtɪŋ] *n* riscaldamento.

heat-resistant [ˈhiːtrɪ,zɪstənt] *adj* termoresistente.

heat·stroke [ˈhiːtstrəʊk] *n* *(Med)* colpo di calore.

heat·wave [ˈhiːtweɪv] *n* ondata di caldo.

heave [hiːv] **1** *n* sforzo; *(of waves)* movimento. **2** *vt (pull)* tirare con forza; *(drag)* trascinare a fatica; *(lift)* sollevare a fatica; *(throw)* scagliare; **to ~ a sigh** emettere *or* mandare un sospiro; **to ~ a sigh of relief** tirare un sospiro di sollievo; **to ~ anchor** *(Naut)* salpare l'ancora. **3** *vi* **(a)** *(sea, chest, stomach)* alzarsi ed abbassarsi; *(pull)*: **to ~ at, to ~ on** tirare con forza; **he ~d with all his might** ha tirato con tutta la sua forza. **(b)** *(feel sick)* avere i conati di vomito; **her stomach ~d** le si rivoltò lo stomaco. **(c)** *(Naut: pt, pp* **hove**): **to ~ in(to) sight** comparire all'orizzonte.

♦ **heave to** *pt, pp* **hove** *vi* + *adv* *(Naut)* mettersi in cappa.

heav·en [ˈhɛvn] *n* *(Rel)* cielo, paradiso; *(fig)* paradiso; **to go to ~** andare in paradiso; **(good) ~s!** santo cielo!; **thank ~!** grazie al cielo!; **for ~'s sake!** *(pleading)* per amor del cielo!, per carità!; *(protesting)* santo cielo!, in nome del cielo!; **this is ~!** *(fam)* che meraviglia!; **to move ~ and earth to do sth** muovere mari e monti *or* fare il possibile e l'impossibile per fare qc; **in seventh ~** al settimo cielo; **the ~s opened** si è messo a diluviare.

heav·en·ly [ˈhɛvnlɪ] *adj (Rel)* celeste, divino(a); *(fam)* divino(a); **~ body** *(Astron)* corpo celeste.

heavi·ly [ˈhɛvɪlɪ] *adv (gen)* pesantemente; *(rain, snow, gamble)* forte; *(breathe, sigh, sleep)* profondamente; *(rely, drink, smoke)* eccessivamente; **it**

weighs ~ **on him** questo gli pesa molto.

heavily-built [ˌhevɪlɪˈbɪlt] adj di corporatura robusta, massiccio(a).

heavy [ˈhevɪ] adj (-ier, -iest) (gen, fig) pesante; (sigh, sleep) profondo(a), pesante; (blow, rain, taxation) forte; (sea) grosso(a) (after n); (expense, casualties) ingente; (traffic) intenso(a); (atmosphere) opprimente; (crop) abbondante; (Mil: fighting) accanito(a); (: fire) nutrito(a), fitto(a); (loss) grave; **how ~ are you?** quanto pesi?; **to have a ~ cold** avere un forte raffreddore; **it's a ~ burden for her to bear** è un peso troppo grande per lei; **with a ~ heart** col cuore gonfio; **the air was ~ with scent** nell'aria c'era un forte profumo; **to be a ~ drinker/smoker** essere un forte bevitore/fumatore; **my car is ~ on petrol** la mia macchina consuma troppo; **to be a ~ sleeper** avere il sonno duro or pesante; **it's ~ going** è una gran fatica; **~ goods vehicle** (abbr HGV) veicolo per trasporti pesanti.

heavy-duty [ˌhevɪˈdjuːtɪ] adj molto resistente.

heavy-handed [ˌhevɪˈhændɪd] adj (clumsy, tactless) pesante; (harsh: person) che ha la mano pesante, severo(a).

heavy-weight [ˈhevɪweɪt] n (Boxing) (peso) massimo; (fig: important or influential person) autorità f inv, pezzo grosso.

He·brew [ˈhiːbruː] **1** adj (language) ebraico(a); (person, nation) ebreo(a). **2** n (person) ebreo/a; (language) ebraico.

heck·le [ˈhekl] vt, vi: **to ~ (sb)** fare azione di disturbo (contro qn) (interrompendo continuamente).

heck·ler [ˈheklə'] n agitatore/trice.

heck·ling [ˈheklɪŋ] n azione f di disturbo.

hec·tare [ˈhektɑː'] n ettaro.

hec·tic [ˈhektɪk] adj (busy) frenetico(a); (eventful) movimentato(a).

hec·tor [ˈhektə'] vt usare le maniere forti con.

he'd [hiːd] = **he would; he had**.

hedge [hedʒ] **1** n siepe f; (fig) difesa; **as a ~ against inflation** per cautelarsi contro l'inflazione. **2** vt (Agr) recintare con una siepe; **to be ~d (about) with** (fig) essere irto di; **to ~ one's bets** (fig) mettersi al sicuro, premunirsi. **3** vi tergiversare.

hedge·hog [ˈhedʒhɒg] n riccio.

hedge·hop [ˈhedʒhɒp] vi volare raso terra.

hedge·row [ˈhedʒrəʊ] n siepe f.

he·don·ism [ˈhiːdənɪzəm] n edonismo.

heed [hiːd] **1** n: **to pay (no) ~ to, to take (no) ~ of** (non) ascoltare, (non) tener conto di. **2** vt fare attenzione a.

heed·less [ˈhiːdlɪs] adj (not thinking) avventato(a); (not caring) noncurante; **to be ~ of** essere insensibile or sordo a.

heel [hiːl] **1** n **(a)** tallone m, calcagno; (of shoe) tacco; **~, boy!** (to dog) vieni qua!; **to be at sb's ~s** stare alle calcagna di qn; **to take to one's ~s** (fam) darsela a gambe, alzare i tacchi; **to turn on one's ~** girare i tacchi. **(b)** (fam: person) carogna. **2** vt (shoe) fare i tacchi a; (ball) colpire di tacco; **to be well-~ed** (fam) esser pieno di soldi.

hefty [ˈheftɪ] adj (gen) pesante; (person) robusto(a); (load) grosso(a) (before n); (price) alto(a), bello(a) (before n).

heif·er [ˈhefə'] n (Zool) giovenca.

height [haɪt] n **(a)** (measurement) altezza; (of person) altezza, statura; (altitude) altezza, altitudine f; (high ground) altura; **what ~ are you?** quanto sei alto?; **of average ~** di statura media; **to be 20 metres in ~** essere alto 20 metri; **~ above sea level** altezza sopra il livello del mare; **to be**

afraid of ~s soffrire di vertigini. **(b)** (fig: of career, success) apice m; (: of rudeness, stupidity) colmo; **at the ~ of** (storm, battle etc) al punto culminante di; **it's the ~ of fashion** è l'ultimo grido della moda; **in the ~ of summer** nel pieno dell'estate.

height·en [ˈhaɪtn] vt (raise) alzare; (increase) far aumentare; (enhance) mettere in risalto.

hei·nous [ˈheɪnəs] adj nefando(a), atroce.

heir [ɛə'] n erede m/f.

heir·ess [ˈɛərɛs] n erede f; (rich) ereditiera.

heir·loom [ˈɛəluːm] n: **a family ~** un gioiello, quadro etc di famiglia.

heist [haɪst] n (fam: hold-up) rapina.

held [held] pt, pp of **hold**.

heli·cop·ter [ˈhelɪkɒptə'] n (Aer) elicottero.

heli·port [ˈhelɪpɔːt] n (Aer) eliporto.

he·lium [ˈhiːlɪəm] n elio.

hell [hel] n inferno; **in ~** all'inferno; **to go ~ for leather** andare or correre come un demonio; **all ~ was let loose** è successo il or un finimondo; **a ~ of a noise** (fam) un casino infernale, un fracasso del diavolo; **a ~ of a lot of** (fam) un sacco or mucchio or casino di; **we had a ~ of a time** (fam: good) ci siamo divertiti da pazzi; (: bad) è stato terribile; **to have a ~ of a time doing sth** (fam) diventar matto a fare qc; **to make sb's life ~** (fam) rendere la vita un inferno a qn; **to give sb ~** (fam) dirne di tutti i colori a qn; **to run like ~** (fam) correre come un matto; **what the ~ do you want?** (fam) che diavolo vuoi?; **just for the ~ of it** (fam) per il gusto di farlo; **go to ~!** (fam) va' all'inferno!, va' al diavolo!; **to ~ with it!** (fam) al diavolo!; **oh ~!** (fam) porca miseria!, accidenti!

he'll [hiːl] = **he will; he shall**.

hell·ish [ˈhelɪʃ] adj (fam) infernale, bestiale.

hel·lo [həˈləʊ] = **hullo**.

helm [helm] n (Naut) timone m; **to be at the ~** (fig) essere al comando.

hel·met [ˈhelmɪt] n (gen) casco; (Mil, of miner) elmetto; (of knight) elmo.

help [help] **1** n **(a)** aiuto; **with the ~ of** con l'aiuto di; **without the ~ of sb/sth** senza l'aiuto di qn/qc; **to be of ~ to sb** essere di aiuto or essere utile a qn; **to call for ~** chiedere or gridare aiuto; **he gave me no ~** non mi ha dato nessun aiuto; **he is beyond ~** è senza speranza; **there's no ~ for it** non c'è altro or nient'altro da fare; **~!** aiuto!

(b) (employee) aiutante m/f; (domestic) domestico/a; (daily) donna di servizio.

2 vt **(a)** (aid, assist) aiutare; (scheme etc) contribuire a; (progress) favorire; (pain) far passare, alleviare; **to ~ sb (to) do sth** aiutare qn a far qc; **to ~ sb with sth** aiutare qn con qc; **I ~ed him with his luggage** l'ho aiutato a portare i bagagli; **I got my sister to ~ me** mi sono fatta aiutare da mia sorella; **that won't ~ much** non servirà a gran che; **can I ~ you?** (in shop) desidera?; **to ~ sb on/off with his coat** aiutare qn a mettersi/togliersi il cappotto; **to ~ sb across/up/down** aiutare qn ad attraversare/a salire/a scendere.

(b) (at table): **to ~ sb to soup** servire la minestra a qn; **to ~ o.s.** (to food) servirsi, prendere; (to other things: steal) prendersi, arraffare.

(c): **he can't ~ coughing** non riesce a or non può trattenere la tosse; **she can't ~ being ugly** cosa può fare se è brutta?; **I couldn't ~ thinking...** non potevo fare a meno di pensare...; **it can't be ~ed** non ci si può fare (più) niente, non c'è niente da fare; **he won't do it if I can ~ it** se appena posso glielo impedirò; **he can't ~ himself** non può farne a meno.

♦ **help out 1** vi + adv aiutare, dare una mano. **2** vt

+ *adv* aiutare, dare una mano a.

help·er ['hɛlpə'] *n* aiutante *m/f*, assistente *m/f*.

help·ful ['hɛlpfʊl] *adj (person: willing)* che si rende utile; *(: useful)* di grande aiuto; *(object, advice etc)* utile.

help·ful·ly ['hɛlpfʌlɪ] *adv* gentilmente.

help·ing ['hɛlpɪŋ] *n* porzione *f*; **you've had two ~s of dessert already** ti sei già servito due volte di dolce.

help·less ['hɛlplɪs] *adj (gen)* incapace; *(baby)* indifeso(a); **a ~ invalid** un infermo; **a ~ old lady** una povera vecchietta; **~ with laughter** morto dalle risate.

helter-skelter ['hɛltə'skɛltə'] **1** *adv* in fretta e furia. **2** *n (in funfair)* scivolo (a spirale).

hem [hɛm] **1** *n (hemline)* orlo. **2** *vt* fare l'orlo a.

♦ **hem in** *vt* + *adv* circondare; **to feel ~med in** *(fig)* sentirsi soffocare.

he-man ['hiːmæn] *n, pl* -**men** *(fam)* fusto.

hemi·sphere ['hɛmɪsfɪə'] *n* emisfero; **northern/ southern ~** emisfero settentrionale *or* boreale/ meridionale *or* australe.

hem·lock ['hɛmlɒk] *n* cicuta.

hema·tol·ogy [,hiːmə'tɒlədʒɪ] *etc (Am) see* **haematology** *etc.*

hemp [hɛmp] *n* canapa; *(drug)* canapa indiana, hascisc *m inv.*

hen [hɛn] **1** *n (fowl)* gallina; *(with chicks)* chioccia; *(female bird)* femmina. **2** *cpd:* **~ party** *n (fam)* festa di sole donne; **~ pheasant** *n* fagiana.

hence [hɛns] *adv* **(a)** *(therefore)* per cui. **(b)** *(old: place)* da qui, di qui; *(time: frm):* **5 years ~** da qui a 5 anni.

hence·forth [,hɛns'fɔːθ] *adv (frm)* d'ora innanzi *or* in poi.

hench·man ['hɛntʃmən] *n, pl* -**men** accolito *(peg)*.

hen·na ['hɛnə] *n* henna.

hen-pecked ['hɛnpɛkt] *adj (fam):* **to be ~** essere succube (della moglie).

hepa·ti·tis [,hɛpə'taɪtɪs] *n* epatite *f*.

her [hɑː'] **1** *pers pron* **(a)** *(direct: unstressed)* la, l' + *vowel*; *(: stressed)* lei; **I hear ~** la sento; **I heard ~** l'ho sentita; **I've never seen her** lei, non l'ho mai vista. **(b)** *(indirect)* le; **I gave ~ the book** le ho dato il libro; **I spoke to ~** le ho parlato. **(c)** *(after prep, in comparisons etc)* lei; **without ~** senza di lei; **I was thinking of ~** pensavo a lei; **she had a case with ~** aveva con sé una valigia; **if I were ~** se fossi in lei; **it's ~** è lei; **I'm older than ~** sono più vecchio di lei. **2** *poss adj* il(la) suo(a), *pl* i(le) suoi(sue); **this is ~ house** questa è la sua casa; **~ brother** suo fratello.

her·ald ['hɛrəld] **1** *n* araldo; *(fig)* messaggero. **2** *vt (fig)* preannunciare.

he·ral·dic [hɛ'rældɪk] *adj* araldico(a).

her·ald·ry ['hɛrəldrɪ] *n* araldica.

herb [hɜːb] *n (Med)* erba medicinale; *(Culin)* erba aromatica.

her·ba·ceous [hɜː'beɪʃəs] *adj* erbaceo(a).

herb·al ['hɜːbəl] *adj* di erbe.

herd [hɜːd] **1** *n (of cattle, horses)* mandria; *(of wild animals, swine)* branco; *(of people):* **the (common) ~** il gregge. **2** *vt (drive, gather: animals)* guidare; *(: people)* radunare. **3** *cpd:* **~ instinct** *n* istinto gregario.

♦ **herd together 1** *vi* + *adv* stringersi uno vicino all'altro. **2** *vt* + *adv* radunare.

here [hɪə'] *adv (place)* qui, qua; *(at this point)* qui, a questo punto; **come ~!** vieni qui!; **~!** *(at roll call)* presente!; **over ~** da questa parte, di qua; **~ I am** eccomi qua; **~ are the books** ecco (qua) i libri; **~ you are!** *(giving sb sth)* ecco qui!; **~ she comes** eccola (che viene); **~ and there** qua e là;

~, there and everywhere dappertutto; **winter is ~** l'inverno è arrivato; **my friend ~ will do it** il mio amico qui lo farà; **that's neither ~ nor there** non ha molta importanza; **~'s to John!** alla salute di John!

here·abouts ['hɪərə,baʊts] *adv* da queste parti.

here·after [,hɪər'ɑːftə'] **1** *adv (frm)* d'ora in poi, da qui in avanti. **2** *n:* **the ~** l'al di là *m*.

here·by [,hɪə'baɪ] *adv (frm)* con questo.

he·redi·tary [hɪ'rɛdɪtərɪ] *adj* ereditario(a).

he·red·ity [hɪ'rɛdɪtɪ] *n* eredità.

her·esy ['hɛrəsɪ] *n* eresia.

her·etic ['hɛrətɪk] *n* eretico/a.

he·reti·cal [hɪ'rɛtɪkəl] *adj* eretico(a).

here·upon [,hɪərə'pɒn] *adv* e con ciò.

here·with [,hɪə'wɪθ] *adv (Comm)* con la presente.

her·it·age ['hɛrɪtɪdʒ] *n* eredità; *(fig)* retaggio; **our national ~** il nostro patrimonio nazionale.

her·met·ic [hɜː'mɛtɪk] *adj* ermetico(a).

her·meti·cal·ly [hɜː'mɛtɪkəlɪ] *adv* ermeticamente; **~ sealed** ermeticamente chiuso.

her·mit ['hɜːmɪt] *n* eremita *m*.

her·nia ['hɜːnɪə] *n* ernia.

hero ['hɪərəʊ] **1** *n, pl* -**es** eroe *m*. **2** *cpd:* **~ worship** *n* divismo.

he·ro·ic [hɪ'rəʊɪk] *adj* eroico(a).

hero·in ['hɛrəʊɪn] **1** *n* eroina. **2** *cpd:* **~ addict** *n* eroinomane *m/f*.

hero·ine ['hɛrəʊɪn] *n* eroina.

hero·ism ['hɛrəʊɪzəm] *n* eroismo.

her·on ['hɛrən] *n* airone *m*.

her·ring ['hɛrɪŋ] *n* aringa.

hers [hɜːz] *poss pron* il(la) suo(a), *pl* i(le) suoi(sue); **a friend of ~** un suo amico; **~ is red, mine is green** il suo è rosso, il mio è verde; **this is ~** questo è (il) suo.

her·self [hɜː'sɛlf] *pers pron (reflexive)* si; *(emphatic)* lei stessa; *(after preposition)* sé, se stessa; **she's not ~ today** ha qualcosa che non va oggi; **she did it (all) by ~** l'ha fatto (tutto) da sola; *see also* oneself.

he's [hiːz] = **he is; he has.**

hesi·tant ['hɛzɪtənt] *adj* esitante, titubante; **to be ~ about doing sth** esitare a fare qc.

hesi·tate ['hɛzɪteɪt] *vi* esitare; **to ~ to do sth** esitare a fare qc; **to ~ about** *or* **over sth** esitare in qc; **don't ~ to ask (me)** non aver timore *or* paura di chiedermelo.

hesi·ta·tion [,hɛzɪ'teɪʃən] *n* esitazione *f*; **I have no ~ in saying (that)...** non esito a dire che... .

hes·sian ['hɛsɪən] *n* tela di canapa.

hetero·geneous ['hɛtərəʊ'dʒiːnɪəs] *adj* eterogeneo(a).

hetero·sex·ual ['hɛtərəʊ'sɛksjʊəl] *adj, n* eterosessuale *(m/f)*.

hew [hjuː] *pt* ~**ed**, *pp* ~**ed** *or* **hewn** [hjuːn] *vt (wood)* tagliare; *(stone, coal)* scavare; *(statue etc)* scolpire.

hex [hɛks] *(Am)* **1** *n* stregoneria. **2** *vt* stregare.

hexa·gon ['hɛksəgən] *n* esagono.

hex·ago·nal [hɛk'sægənəl] *adj* esagonale.

hey [heɪ] *excl* ehi!

hey·day ['heɪdeɪ] *n* età *or* tempi *mpl* d'oro; **in his ~** quand'era in auge, ai bei tempi.

hi [haɪ] *excl* ciao!, salve!

hia·tus [haɪ'eɪtəs] *n* vuoto; *(Gram)* iato.

hi·ber·nate ['haɪbəneɪt] *vi* cadere in letargo, ibernare.

hi·ber·na·tion [,haɪbə'neɪʃən] *n* letargo, ibernazione *f*.

hic·cough, hic·cup ['hɪkʌp] **1** *n* singhiozzo; **to have ~s** avere il singhiozzo. **2** *vi* avere il singhiozzo, singhiozzare.

hick [hɪk] n (Am fam) bifolco/a.
hid [hɪd] pt of **hide**.
hid·den ['hɪdn] **1** pp of **hide**. **2** adj (gen) nascosto(a); (meaning) recondito(a); **there are no ~ extras** è veramente tutto compreso nel prezzo.
hide[1] [haɪd] pt **hid**, pp **hidden 1** vt (gen) nascondere; (feelings, truth) dissimulare; **the clouds hid the sun** le nuvole hanno nascosto or coperto il sole; **to ~ sth from sb** nascondere qc a qn. **2** vi nascondersi; **he's hiding behind his illness** si trincera dietro la sua malattia.
♦ **hide away 1** vi + adv nascondersi, rifugiarsi. **2** vt + adv nascondere.
♦ **hide out** vi + adv nascondersi.
hide[2] [haɪd] n (skin) pelle f; (leather) cuoio.
hide-and-seek [,haɪdən'siːk] n nascondino.
hide·away ['haɪdə,weɪ] n nascondiglio; (secluded spot) rifugio.
hid·eous ['hɪdɪəs] adj (sight, person) orribile, orrendo(a); (crime) atroce.
hide-out ['haɪdaʊt] n nascondiglio.
hid·ing[1] ['haɪdɪŋ] **1** n: **to be in ~** tenersi nascosto(a); **to go into ~** darsi alla macchia. **2** cpd: **~ place** n nascondiglio.
hid·ing[2] ['haɪdɪŋ] n botte fpl; **to give sb a good ~** suonarle a qn.
hi·er·ar·chy ['haɪərɑːkɪ] n gerarchia.
hi·ero·glyph·ic [,haɪərə'glɪfɪk] **1** adj geroglifico(a). **2: ~s** npl geroglifici mpl.
hi-fi ['haɪ'faɪ] (abbr of **high fidelity**) **1** n stereo. **2** adj ad alta fedeltà, hi-fi inv.
higgledy-piggledy ['hɪgldɪ'pɪgldɪ] adv alla rinfusa.
high [haɪ] **1** adj (-er, -est) (a) (gen) alto(a); **a building 60 metres ~** un palazzo alto 60 metri; **how ~ is Ben Nevis?** quanto è alto il Ben Nevis?; **since she was so ~** (fam) fin da quando era grande or alta così; **at ~ tide** or **water** quando c'è l'alta marea; **to leave sb ~ and dry** (fig) piantare in asso qn; **to be on one's ~ horse** (fig) montare or salire in cattedra; **to be** or **act ~ and mighty** darsi delle arie.
(b) (frequency, pressure, temperature, salary, price) alto(a); (speed, wind) forte; (: character, ideals) nobile; (value, respect) grande; **the ~est common factor** (Math) il massimo comun divisore; **to pay a ~ price for sth** pagare (molto) caro qc; **his colour is very ~** è molto rosso in viso; **to have a ~ old time** (fam) spassarsela; **it's ~ time you were in bed** (fam) dovresti essere già a letto da un pezzo.
(c) (Mus: note) alto(a); (sound, voice) acuto(a).
(d) (fam: on drugs) fatto(a); (: on drink) su di giri.
(e) (Culin: meat, game) frollato(a); (spoilt) andato a male.
2 adv (fly, aim, climb etc) in alto; **the doves flew ~ in the sky** le colombe volavano alte nel cielo; **~ up** molto in alto; **~ above the clouds** in alto sopra le nuvole; **~er and ~er** sempre più alto; **the bidding went as ~ as £50** le offerte sono arrivate fino a 50 sterline; **to hunt ~ and low** cercare per mare e per terra; **feelings were running ~** c'era molta tensione.
3 n (a): **on ~** (in heaven) nell'alto dei cieli; **orders from on ~** (also hum) ordini dall'alto.
(b): **exports have reached a new ~** le esportazioni hanno toccato un nuovo record.
(c) (Met) anticiclone m, area di alta pressione.
4 cpd: ~ **altar** n altar m maggiore; ~ **command** n (Mil) stato maggiore; ~ **commissioner** n alto commissario; ~ **court** n (Law) corte f suprema; (: in Italy) corte di Cassazione; ~ **explo**-

sive n esplosivo ad alto potenziale; ~ **fidelity** adj ad alta fedeltà; ~ **finance** n alta finanza; **to have ~ jinks** (fam) darsi alla pazza gioia; ~ **jump** n (Sport) salto in alto; **you'll be for the ~ jump when Dad finds out** papà ti ammazza quando lo viene a sapere; ~ **life** n vita dell'alta società or del bel mondo; **H~ Mass** n messa solenne or cantata; ~ **noon** n mezzogiorno; ~ **priest** n gran sacerdote m; ~ **school** n scuola secondaria; **on the ~ seas** in altomare; ~ **society** n alta società; ~ **spirits** npl buonumore m, euforia; ~ **spot** n clou m inv; ~ **street** n strada principale; ~ **summer** n piena estate f; ~ **tea** n (Brit) tè servito con panini o una pietanza e consumato verso le sei di sera al posto della cena; ~ **treason** n alto tradimento.
high·ball ['haɪbɔːl] n (Am: drink) whisky (or brandy) e soda con ghiaccio.
high·brow ['haɪbraʊ] **1** n intellettualoide m/f. **2** adj (book etc) intellettualoide.
high·chair ['haɪtʃɛəʳ] n seggiolone m.
high-class ['haɪklɑːs] adj (neighbourhood) elegante; (hotel) di prim'ordine; (person) di gran classe; (food) raffinato(a).
high·er ['haɪəʳ] **1** adj (form of life, study etc) superiore. **2** adv più in alto, più in su.
high-flier [,haɪ'flaɪəʳ] n uno/a che ha delle mire ambiziose.
high-handed [,haɪ'hændɪd] adj autoritario(a), dispotico(a).
high-heeled [,haɪ'hiːld] adj con il tacco alto.
high·lands ['haɪləndz] npl zona montuosa; **the H~** le Highlands scozzesi.
high-level ['haɪ,lɛvl] adj (talks etc) ad alto livello.
high·light ['haɪlaɪt] **1** n (Art) luce f; (in hair) riflesso; (fig: evening etc) clou m inv. **2** vt (fig) mettere in evidenza; (in painting, drawing etc) lumeggiare.
high·ly ['haɪlɪ] adv estremamente, molto; ~ **paid** pagato molto bene; ~ **spiced dishes** piatti molto piccanti; ~ **specialized** altamente specializzato; ~ **strung** ipersensibile; **to think ~ of sb** avere molta stima di qn; **to speak ~ of** parlare molto bene di.
high·ness ['haɪnɪs] n: **Your H~** Vostra Altezza.
high-pitched [,haɪ'pɪtʃt] adj acuto(a).
high-powered [,haɪ'paʊəd] adj (engine) molto potente, ad alta potenza; (fig: person) di prestigio.
high-pressure [,haɪ'prɛʃəʳ] adj ad alta pressione; (fig) aggressivo(a).
high-rise ['haɪraɪz] adj: ~ **block** grattacielo.
high·road ['haɪrəʊd] n strada principale or maestra.
high·way ['haɪweɪ] **1** n strada principale or maestra. **2** cpd: **H~ Code** n codice m della strada.
highway·man ['haɪweɪmən] n, pl **-men** ≈ bandito.
hi·jack ['haɪdʒæk] **1** n dirottamento; (also: ~**ing**) pirateria aerea. **2** vt (aircraft) dirottare; (lorry etc) impadronirsi di.
hi·jack·er ['haɪdʒækəʳ] n (of aircraft) dirottatore/trice.
hike [haɪk] **1** n escursione f a piedi. **2** vi fare un'escursione or una gita a piedi; **to go hiking** fare escursioni a piedi.
hik·er ['haɪkəʳ] n escursionista m/f.
hi·lari·ous [hɪ'lɛərɪəs] adj spassosissimo(a).
hi·lar·ity [hɪ'lærɪtɪ] n ilarità.
hill [hɪl] n collina, (lower) colle m; (slope) pendio, costa; **up ~ and down dale** per monti e per valli; **to be over the ~** (fig fam) essere sul viale del tramonto; **as old as the ~s** vecchio come Matusalemme.

hill·bil·ly ['hɪl,bɪlɪ] n (Am) montanaro dal sud degli Stati Uniti; (pej) zotico/a.

hill·ock ['hɪlək] n collinetta, poggio.

hill·side ['hɪlsaɪd] n pendio.

hilly ['hɪlɪ] adj (-ier, -iest) collinoso(a), montagnoso(a); **this road is very** ~ questa strada è un continuo saliscendi.

hilt [hɪlt] n (of sword) elsa, impugnatura; **to back sb to the** ~ dare il proprio appoggio incondizionato a qn; **to be in debt up to the** ~ essere nei debiti fino al collo; **to mortgage sth up to the** ~ ipotecare completamente qc.

him [hɪm] pers pron (a) (direct: unstressed) lo, l' + vowel; (: stressed) lui; **I hear** ~ lo sento; **I heard** ~ l'ho sentito; **I've never seen** HIM lui, non l'ho mai visto. (b) (indirect) gli; **I gave** ~ **the book** gli ho dato il libro; **I spoke to** ~ gli ho parlato. (c) (after prep, in comparatives etc) lui; **without** ~ senza di lui; **I was thinking of** ~ pensavo a lui; **he had a case with** ~ aveva con sé una valigia; **if I were** ~ se io fossi in lui; **it's** ~ è lui; **I'm older than** ~ sono più vecchio di lui.

him·self [hɪm'sɛlf] pers pron (reflexive) si; (emphatic) lui stesso; (after preposition) sé, se stesso; **(all) by** ~ (tutto) da solo or da sé; **he's not** ~ **today** ha qualcosa che non va oggi; see also **oneself**.

hind[1] [haɪnd] adj (leg etc) posteriore.

hind[2] [haɪnd] n (Zool) cerva.

hin·der ['hɪndə'] vt (prevent): **to** ~ **sb (from doing sth)** impedire a qn (di fare qc); (delay) ritardare; (oppose) ostacolare, intralciare.

Hin·di ['hɪndiː] n (language) hindi m.

hind·quarters ['haɪnd,kwɔːtəz] npl (Zool) posteriore m.

hin·drance ['hɪndrəns] n intralcio, ostacolo; **to be a** ~ intralciare, ostacolare.

hind·sight ['haɪndsaɪt] n senno di poi; **with the benefit of** ~ con il senno di poi.

Hin·du ['hɪn'duː] adj, n indù (m/f) inv.

Hin·du·ism ['hɪnduˌɪzəm] n (Rel) induismo.

hinge [hɪndʒ] 1 n (of door, gate) cardine m; (of box) cerniera. 2 vi: **to** ~ **on** (fig) dipendere da.

hinged [hɪndʒd] adj (door) provvisto(a) di cardini; (box, lid) incernierato(a).

hint [hɪnt] 1 n (suggestion) allusione f; ~**s on do-it-yourself** consigli pratici per il fai-da-te; **a gentle** ~ una velata allusione; **to give sb a broad** ~ far capire chiaramente a qn; **to drop a** ~ lasciar capire; **to take the** ~ capire l'antifona; **with a** ~ **of irony/sadness** con una punta d'ironia/tristezza; **give me a** ~ dammi almeno un'idea, dammi un'indicazione. 2 vt alludere a; **to** ~ **(to sb) that...** lasciar capire (a qn) che... .

♦ **hint at** vi + prep accennare a, alludere a, fare allusione a.

hip[1] [hɪp] 1 n (Anat) anca; (side) fianco; **to put one's hands on one's** ~**s** mettere le mani sui fianchi. 2 cpd: ~ **bath** n semicupio; ~ **flask** n fiaschetta da liquore tascabile; ~ **joint** n articolazione f dell'anca; ~ **pocket** n tasca posteriore dei calzoni.

hip[2] [hɪp] n (Bot) frutto della rosa canina.

hip·pie, hip·py ['hɪpɪ] n hippy m/f inv.

hippo·pota·mus [ˌhɪpə'pɒtəməs] n, pl ~**es** or **hippo·pota·mi** [ˌhɪpə'pɒtəmaɪ] ippopotamo.

hire ['haɪə'] 1 n noleggio; (cost) nolo; **'for** ~**'** 'a nolo', 'noleggiasi'; (of taxi) 'libero'; **on** ~ a nolo. 2 vt (car etc) noleggiare; (employee) assumere; ~**d hand** bracciante m; ~**d car** macchina a nolo; ~**d assassin** sicario.

♦ **hire out** vt + adv noleggiare, dare a nolo or noleggio, affittare.

hire-purchase [ˌhaɪə'pɜːtʃɪs] n (Brit: abbr **H.P.**)

acquisto a rate; **to buy sth on** ~ comprare qc a rate.

his [hɪz] poss adj, pron il(la) suo(a), pl i(le) suoi(sue); ~ **house** la sua casa; ~ **brother** suo fratello; **a friend of** ~ un suo amico; ~ **is red, mine is green** il suo è rosso, il mio è verde; **this is** ~ questo è (il) suo.

hiss [hɪs] 1 n (of snake) sibilo; (of kettle, protest etc) fischio; (of cat) soffio. 2 vi (see n) sibilare; fischiare; soffiare. 3 vt fischiare.

his·to·rian [hɪs'tɔːrɪən] n storico/a.

his·tor·ic [hɪs'tɒrɪk] adj storico(a).

his·tori·cal [hɪs'tɒrɪkəl] adj storico(a).

his·to·ry ['hɪstərɪ] n storia; **a** ~ **book** un libro di storia; **to make** ~ fare storia; **to go down in** ~ passare alla storia; **there's a long** ~ **of that illness in his family** ci sono molti precedenti (della malattia) nella sua famiglia.

hit [hɪt] 1 n (a) (blow) colpo; (Sport) tiro, colpo; **she made 3** ~**s and 2 misses** ha messo a segno 3 colpi e ne ha mancati 2; **to score a direct** ~ colpire in pieno.

(b) (Mus, Theatre etc) successo; **to be a** ~ essere un (gran) successo; **the song is a big** ~ è una canzone di successo; **she's a** ~ **with everyone** (fam) ha successo con tutti, fa colpo su tutti.

2 vt (a) (strike: gen) colpire; (thrash: person) picchiare; (knock against) sbattere; (collide with) urtare, sbattere contro; (affect adversely: person) colpire; **to** ~ **sb a blow** dare un colpo a qn; **to** ~ **a man when he's down** (fig) infierire su un uomo morto; **to** ~ **the mark** (fig) colpire nel segno, raggiungere lo scopo; **to** ~ **one's head against a wall** (fig) battere or picchiare la testa contro il muro; **then it** ~ **me** (of realization: fam) solo allora me ne sono reso conto; **the news** ~ **him hard** la notizia è stata un brutto colpo per lui.

(b) (reach: target, musical note) raggiungere; (: road) trovare, capitare su; (: speed) toccare; (: difficulty) incontrare, imbattersi in; (fam: arrive at: town) sbarcare a; **to** ~ **the papers** finire sui giornali; **to** ~ **the headlines** far titolo; **to** ~ **the front page** apparire in prima pagina; **to** ~ **the bottle** (fam) darsi al bere; **to** ~ **the ceiling** (fig fam) dare in escandescenze; **to** ~ **the road** or **the trail** (fam) levare le tende; **to** ~ **the hay** or **the sack** (fam) andare a letto.

3 vi: **to** ~ **against** sbattere contro.

4 cpd (song, film) di successo; ~ **parade** n hit-parade f.

♦ **hit back** 1 vi + adv: **to** ~ **back at sb** restituire il colpo a qn; (fig) reagire contro qn. 2 vt + adv restituire il colpo a.

♦ **hit off** vt + adv: **to** ~ **it off with sb** intendersela bene or andare d'accordo con qn.

♦ **hit out at** vi + prep sferrare dei colpi contro; (fig) attaccare.

♦ **hit (up)on** vi + prep (answer) imbroccare, azzeccare; (solution) trovare (per caso).

hit-and-run ['hɪtænd,rʌn] adj: ~ **driver** pirata m della strada.

hitch [hɪtʃ] 1 n (impediment, obstacle) intoppo, contrattempo; **technical** ~ difficoltà tecnica; **without a** ~ senza intoppi, a gonfie vele. 2 vt (a) (fasten) attaccare; (: to post) legare; **to get** ~**ed** (fam) sposarsi. (b) (fam): **to** ~ **a lift** fare l'autostop. 3 vi (fam) = **hitchhike**.

♦ **hitch up** vt + adv (trousers etc) tirarsi su; (horse, cart) attaccare.

hitch·hike ['hɪtʃhaɪk] vi fare l'autostop; **we** ~**d through Europe** abbiamo girato tutta l'Europa in autostop.

hitch·hiker [ˈhɪtʃhaɪkəʳ] *n* autostoppista *m/f*.

hitch·hiking [ˈhɪtʃhaɪkɪŋ] *n* autostop *m*.

hith·er [ˈhɪðəʳ] *adv (old)* qui, qua; ~ **and thither** *(not old)* qua e là.

hit-or-miss [ˌhɪtəˈmɪs] *adj (attitude)* disinvolto(a); *(work)* così cosà; **it's ~ whether...** è in dubbio se... .

hive [haɪv] *n* alveare *m; (bees collectively)* sciame *m;* **the shop was a ~ of activity** *(fig)* c'era una grande attività nel negozio.

♦ **hive off** *(fam)* **1** *vi + adv:* **to ~ off (from)** staccarsi (da). **2** *vt + adv* separare.

H.M.S. *abbr of His (Her) Majesty's Ship.*

hoard [hɔːd] **1** *n (of food)* provviste *fpl,* scorta; *(of money)* gruzzolo; ~**s of money** *(fam)* un mucchio di soldi. **2** *vt (also: ~* **up***: provisions)* fare incetta *or* provvista di; *(: money)* ammonticchiare; *(: old newspapers etc)* accumulare.

hoard·ing [ˈhɔːdɪŋ] *n* staccionata, palizzata; *(for advertisements)* tabellone *m or* riquadro per affissioni.

hoar·frost [ˈhɔːˈfrɒst] *n* brina.

hoarse [hɔːs] *adj* (**-r, -st**) rauco(a); **they shouted themselves ~** si sono sgolati a forza di urlare.

hoax [həʊks] **1** *n* scherzo; *(of bomb scare etc)* falso allarme *m*. **2** *vt* prendere in giro; **he ~ed me into believing that...** mi ha fatto credere che... .

hob·ble [ˈhɒbl] *vi* zoppicare.

hob·by [ˈhɒbɪ] *n* hobby *m inv*, passatempo (preferito).

hobby-horse [ˈhɒbɪhɔːs] *n (fig)* chiodo fisso.

hob·nob [ˈhɒbnɒb] *vi:* **to ~ (with)** mescolarsi (con).

hobo [ˈhəʊbəʊ] *n (Am)* vagabondo.

hock¹ [hɒk] *n (of animal, Culin)* garretto.

hock² [hɒk] *n* vino bianco del Reno.

hock·ey [ˈhɒkɪ] **1** *n* hockey *m* (su prato); **ice ~** hockey su ghiaccio. **2** *cpd:* ~ **stick** *n* bastone *m* da hockey.

hocus-pocus [ˈhəʊkəsˈpəʊkəs] *n (trickery)* trucco; *(words: of magician)* abracadabra; *(talk)* ciance *fpl.*

hoe [həʊ] **1** *n* zappa. **2** *vt (ground)* zappare; *(weeds)* togliere con la zappa.

hog [hɒg] **1** *n* porco, maiale *m;* **to go the whole ~** *(fig)* fare le cose fino in fondo. **2** *vt (fam)* accaparrarsi; **to ~ the road** guidare nel mezzo della strada.

hoi pol·loi [ˌhɔɪpəˈlɔɪ] *n (pej)* gentaglia.

hoist [hɔɪst] **1** *vt* issare. **2** *n* paranco; *(goods lift)* montacarichi *m inv.*

hold [həʊld] *(vb: pt, pp* **held**) **1** *n* **(a)** presa; **to seize** *or* **grab ~ of sth/sb** afferrare qc/qn; **to catch** *or* **get (a) hold of** afferrare, attaccarsi a; **to get ~ of sb** *(fig: contact)* mettersi in contatto con qn; **where can I get ~ of some red paint?** dove posso trovare della vernice rossa?; **to get (a) ~ of o.s.** *(fig)* trattenersi; **no ~s barred** *(fig)* senza esclusione di colpi; **to have a ~ over sb** *(fig)* avere un forte ascendente *or* molta influenza su qn.
  (b) *(Mountaineering)* appiglio.
  (c) *(Naut, Aer)* stiva.
  2 *vt* **(a)** *(gen)* tenere; *(contain)* contenere; *(fig: audience)* mantenere viva l'attenzione di; *(: attention, interest)* mantenere; *(: belief, opinion)* avere; **to ~ hands** tenersi per mano; **to ~ a baby** tenere in braccio un bambino; **the hall ~s 500 people** nella sala c'è posto per 500 persone; **the chair won't ~ you** la sedia non sopporterà il tuo peso; **to ~ o.s. upright/ready** tenersi dritto/pronto; **to ~ one's head high** andare a testa alta; **to ~ sb to a promise** far mantenere una promessa a qn; **to ~ one's own** sapersi difendere, difendersi bene; **he ~s the view that...** è del parere che...; **to**

~ **the line** *(Telec)* rimanere *or* restare in linea; **this car ~s the road well** questa macchina tiene bene la strada; **what does the future ~?** cosa ci riserva il futuro?
  (b) *(restrain: person)* trattenere; **to ~ sb prisoner** tenere prigioniero qn; **there's no ~ing him** non lo ferma più nessuno; **to ~ one's breath** trattenere il respiro; **I held my breath in amazement** sono rimasto a bocca aperta per lo stupore; **to ~ one's tongue** *(fig)* tacere, star zitto; ~ **it!** *(fam)* alt!, fermati!
  (c) *(position, title, passport)* avere; *(shares: Fin)* possedere, avere; *(record: Sport)* detenere; *(position: Mil)* tenere, mantenere; **to ~ office** *(Pol)* essere in carica.
  (d) *(meeting, election)* tenere, indire; *(conversation)* tenere, sostenere; *(Rel: service)* celebrare.
  (e) *(consider):* **to ~ (that)** ritenere (che), sostenere (che); **to ~ sb in high esteem** avere molta stima di qn; **to ~ sth/sb dear** tenere molto a qc/qn; **to ~ sb responsible for sth** considerare *or* ritenere qn responsabile di qc.
  3 *vi (rope, nail etc)* tenere; *(continue)* mantenersi, durare; *(be valid)* essere valido(a); **to ~ firm** *or* **fast** resistere bene, tenere.

♦ **hold against** *vt + prep:* **to ~ sth against sb** *(fig)* rinfacciare qc a qn.

♦ **hold back 1** *vi + adv:* **to ~ back from sth** tirarsi indietro da qc; **to ~ back from doing sth** trattenersi dal fare qc; **he always ~s back when introduced to new people** quando viene presentato a nuova gente è poco espansivo. **2** *vt + adv* **(a)** *(restrain: crowd, river)* trattenere, contenere; *(: emotions)* trattenere, frenare; **to ~ sb back from doing sth** impedire a qn di fare qc. **(b)** *(information, name)* nascondere, non dare; **he's ~ing something back** non sta dicendo tutta la verità.

♦ **hold down** *vt + adv* **(a)** *(keep low, on ground)* tener giù; *(keep in place)* tener fermo(a). **(b)** *(job)* conservare.

♦ **hold forth** *vi + adv* fare *or* tenere una concione.

♦ **hold in** *vt + adv (stomach)* tirare *or* tenere in dentro; **to ~ o.s. in** *(fig)* frenarsi, trattenersi.

♦ **hold off 1** *vt + adv (enemy)* tenere a distanza; *(attack)* sventare; *(visitor etc: fig)* far aspettare. **2** *vi + adv (rain):* **if the rain ~s off** se continua a non piovere.

♦ **hold on 1** *vi + adv (endure)* resistere; *(wait)* aspettare; *(Telec)* attendere, restare in linea. **2** *vt + adv* tenere a posto.

♦ **hold on to** *vi + prep (grasp)* tenersi (attaccato(a)) a; *(keep)* tenere; *(fig: retain: hope)* rimanere aggrappato(a) a.

♦ **hold out 1** *vi + adv* **(a)** *(supplies)* durare. **(b)** *(stand firm)* tener duro; **to ~ out (against)** resistere (a). **2** *vt + adv:* **to ~ out (sth to sb)** allungare (qc a qn); *(one's arms, hand)* tendere; *(fig: offer)* presentare; *(: hope)* nutrire.

♦ **hold out on** *vi + prep:* **you've been ~ing out on me!** *(fam)* mi hai tenuto nascosto qualcosa!

♦ **hold over** *vt + adv (meeting etc)* rimandare, rinviare.

♦ **hold up 1** *vi + adv (survive, last)* resistere; **how are your shoes ~ing up?** in che stato sono le tue scarpe? **2** *vt + adv* **(a)** *(raise)* sollevare, alzare; ~ **up your hand** alza la mano; **to ~ sth up to the light** alzare qc verso la luce. **(b)** *(support: roof etc)* sostenere. **(c)** *(delay: person)* trattenere; *(: traffic)* rallentare; *(stop)* bloccare. **(d)** *(rob: bank)* assaltare; *(: person)* assalire.

hold·all [ˈhəʊldɔːl] *n* sacca *or* borsa da viaggio.

hold·er [ˈhəʊldə^r] n (a) (of ticket) possessore/posseditrice; (owner: of property) proprietario/a; (tenant) affittuario/a; (of bonds, shares) titolare m/f, intestatario/a; (of title) chi ha or possiede; (of passport, office, post) titolare; (of record) detentore/trice. (b) (container) contenitore m; pencil ~ portamatite m inv.

hold·ing [ˈhəʊldɪŋ] 1 n (land) podere m, tenuta; ~s terre fpl, proprietà fpl terriere; ~s (Comm) azioni fpl, titoli mpl. 2 cpd: ~ company n (Comm) holding f inv.

hold-up [ˈhəʊldʌp] n (robbery) rapina; (stoppage, delay) intoppo; (of traffic) ingorgo.

hole [həʊl] 1 n (a) (in ground, road, also Golf) buca; (in wall, fence, clothes) buco; (in dam, ship) falla; (in defences) breccia; (in rabbit, fox) tana; **to wear a ~ in sth** usare qc tanto da farci un buco; **to make a ~ in** (fig: argument) dimostrare che fa acqua; **it made a ~ in my savings** ha mangiato gran parte dei miei risparmi; **to pick ~s in** (fig) trovare da ridire su; **~ in the heart** (Med) morbo blu. (b) (fig fam: difficulty): **to be in a ~** essere nei guai; **he got me out of a ~** mi ha tirato fuori dai pasticci or dai guai. (c) (fam: place) buco. 2 vt bucare; (Golf: ball) mandare in buca; **the boat was ~d when it hit the rocks** quando la barca ha urtato gli scogli si è aperta una falla nello scafo.

♦ **hole up** vi + adv nascondersi, rifugiarsi.

hole-and-corner [ˌhəʊləndˈkɔːnə^r] adj clandestino(a), sottobanco inv.

holi·day [ˈhɒlɪdeɪ] 1 n (vacation) vacanza; (from work) ferie fpl; (day off) giorno di vacanza; **the school ~s** le vacanze scolastiche; **~ with pay** ferie pagate or retribuite; **public ~** festa (nazionale); **to be on ~** essere in vacanza. 2 cpd (town) di villeggiatura; ~ **camp** n = villaggio (di vacanze); (for children) colonia (di villeggiatura); ~ **season** n stagione f delle vacanze.

holiday-maker [ˈhɒlɪdeɪˌmeɪkə^r] n villeggiante m/f.

ho·li·ness [ˈhəʊlɪnɪs] n santità; **His H~** Sua Santità.

Hol·land [ˈhɒlənd] n Olanda.

hol·ler [ˈhɒlə^r] vt, vi (fam) urlare, gridare.

hol·low [ˈhɒləʊ] 1 adj (-er, -est) cavo(a), vuoto(a); (eyes, cheeks) infossato(a); (sound, voice) cupo(a); (sympathy, promises) falso(a), vano(a); **a ~ victory** una vittoria di Pirro; **to give a ~ laugh** ridere a denti stretti. 2 adv: **to beat sb ~** (fam) stracciare qn. 3 n (of back) incavo; (of hand) cavo; (in ground) cavità f inv, affossamento; (small valley) conca.

♦ **hollow out** vt + adv scavare, incavare.

hol·ly [ˈhɒlɪ] n (also: ~ tree) agrifoglio.

hol·ly·hock [ˈhɒlɪhɒk] n malvone m.

holo·caust [ˈhɒləkɔːst] n olocausto.

hol·ster [ˈhəʊlstə^r] n fondina.

holy [ˈhəʊlɪ] adj (-ier, -iest) (gen) santo(a); (ground) consacrato(a); (person) pio(a); (vow) religioso(a); **the H~ Bible** la Sacra Bibbia; **H~ Communion** la Santa Comunione; **the H~ Father** il Santo Padre; **the H~ Ghost** lo Spirito Santo; **the H~ Land** la Terra Santa; **the H~ Trinity** la Santissima Trinità; **~ orders** ordini mpl (sacri); **a ~ terror** (fam) un demonio.

hom·age [ˈhɒmɪdʒ] n omaggio; **to pay ~ to** rendere omaggio a.

home [həʊm] 1 n (a) (residence, house) casa; (country, area) patria, paese m natale, paese natio; (Bot, Zool) habitat m inv; **to have a ~ of one's own** avere una casa propria; **it's near my ~** è vicino a casa mia; **it's a ~ from ~** è come essere a casa propria; **there's no place like ~** non si sta mai bene come a casa propria; **he comes from a good ~** viene da una buona famiglia; **he comes from a broken ~** i suoi sono divisi; **to give sb/sth a ~** prendersi in casa qn/qc; **he made his ~ in Italy** si è stabilito in Italia; **Scotland is the ~ of the haggis** la Scozia è la patria dell'haggis; **at ~** a casa; **Celtic is playing at ~ on Saturday** il Celtic gioca in casa sabato; **make yourself at ~** fai come se fossi a casa tua; **to make sb feel at ~** far sentire qn a proprio agio; **he is at ~ with the topic** conosce la materia benissimo; **I'm not at ~ to anyone** (fig) non ci sono per nessuno.

(b) (institution) istituto; **children's ~** orfanotrofio; **old people's ~** casa di riposo.

2 adv (a) a casa; **to go ~** andare a casa; **to come ~** tornare (a casa); **to stay ~** stare a or restare in casa; **I got ~ at 10 o'clock** sono rientrato alle 10; **on the way ~** sulla via di casa; **can I see you ~?** posso accompagnarti a casa?; **we're ~ and dry** (fig) siamo salvi.

(b) (right in) a fondo; **to drive a nail ~** conficcare un chiodo; **to bring sth ~ to sb** (fig) aprire gli occhi a qn su qc; **that remark hit ~** ciò che ha detto ha colpito nel segno.

3 vi (pigeons) tornare alla base.

4 cpd (life) familiare; (cooking) casalingo(a); (improvements) alla casa; (comforts) di casa; (native: town) natale, natio(a); (Comm: trade, market) nazionale, interno(a); (: product, industries) nazionale; (news) dall'interno; (Sport: team) di casa; (: match, win) in casa; ~ **address** n indirizzo di casa or privato; **H~ Counties** npl contee fpl intorno a Londra; ~ **economics** n economia domestica; ~ **front** n fronte m interno; ~ **help** n colf f inv; **H~ Office/Secretary** n (Brit) ministero/ministro degli Interni or dell'Interno; ~ **rule** n autogoverno, autonomia; ~ **straight** n (Sport) dirittura d'arrivo; **in the ~ straight** (fig) quasi arrivato; ~ **truths** npl: **to tell sb a few ~ truths** dire a qn quello che si merita.

♦ **home in on** vi + prep (missiles) dirigersi (automaticamente) verso.

home-brew [həʊmˈbruː] n birra or vino fatto(a) in casa.

home·coming [ˈhəʊmˌkʌmɪŋ] n ritorno.

home-grown [ˌhəʊmˈɡrəʊn] adj nostrano(a), di produzione locale.

home·land [ˈhəʊmlænd] n patria.

home·less [ˈhəʊmlɪs] 1 adj senza tetto. 2: **the ~** npl i senzatetto.

home·ly [ˈhəʊmlɪ] adj (-ier, -iest) (food, person) semplice, alla buona; (atmosphere) familiare, accogliente; (advice) pratico(a); (plain: person, features) insignificante.

home-made [ˌhəʊmˈmeɪd] adj fatto(a) in casa.

home·sick [ˈhəʊmsɪk] adj: **to be ~** avere la nostalgia, sentire la mancanza di casa.

home·stead [ˈhəʊmsted] n casa colonica.

home·ward [ˈhəʊmwəd] adj (journey) di ritorno.

home·ward(s) [ˈhəʊmwəd(z)] adv verso casa.

home·work [ˈhəʊmwɜːk] n compiti mpl.

homi·ci·dal [ˌhɒmɪˈsaɪdl] adj omicida.

homi·cide [ˈhɒmɪsaɪd] n omicidio.

hom·ing [ˈhəʊmɪŋ] adj (device, missile) autocercante; ~ **pigeon** piccione m viaggiatore.

homoeo·path, (Am) **homeo·path** [ˈhəʊmɪəʊpæθ] n omeopatico.

homoeo·path·ic, (Am) **homeo·path·ic** [ˌhəʊmɪəʊˈpæθɪk] adj omeopatico(a).

homoeopa·thy, (Am) **homeop·a·thy** [ˌhəʊmɪˈɒpəθɪ] n omeopatia.

homo·genei·ty [ˌhɒməʊdʒəˈniːɪtɪ] n omogeneità.

homo·geneous [ˌhɒməˈdʒiːnɪəs] adj omogeneo(a).

ho·mog·enize [həˈmɒdʒənaɪz] vt omogeneizzare.

homo·nym [ˈhɒmənɪm] n omonimo.

homo·sex·ual [ˈhɒməʊˈsɛksjʊəl] adj, n omosessuale (m/f).

hon·est [ˈɒnɪst] adj (person, face, actions) onesto(a); (answer) franco(a), schietto(a); (means, method) onesto(a), lecito(a); (wages, profit) decente, ragionevole; (opinion) sincero(a); **to be quite ~ with you...** se devo dirti la verità...; **please be ~ with me** ti prego di essere sincero con me.

hon·est·ly [ˈɒnɪstlɪ] adv onestamente; (truly) sinceramente, francamente; **I didn't do it, ~!** non l'ho fatto, sul serio!; **~?** davvero?; **~!** (exasperated) (ma) veramente!

hon·es·ty [ˈɒnɪstɪ] n onestà; **in all ~** a voler essere or per essere proprio sincero.

hon·ey [ˈhʌnɪ] n miele m; (Am fam) tesoro, amore m.

honey·comb [ˈhʌnɪkəʊm] **1** n favo; (fig) disegno (or struttura etc) a nido d'ape. **2** vt (fig) sforacchiare, perforare.

honey·moon [ˈhʌnɪmuːn] **1** n luna di miele, viaggio di nozze. **2** vi fare la luna di miele, andare in viaggio di nozze.

honey·suckle [ˈhʌnɪˌsʌkl] n caprifoglio.

honk [hɒŋk] vi (car) suonare il clacson; (goose) schiamazzare.

hon·or·ary [ˈɒnərərɪ] adj (person) onorario(a); (duty, title) onorifico(a); **an ~ degree** una laurea honoris causa or ad honorem.

hon·our, (Am) **hon·or** [ˈɒnəʳ] **1** n **(a)** (gen) onore m; (esteem, respect) stima, rispetto; **in ~ of** in onore di; **on my ~!** sul mio onore!; **to be on one's ~ to do sth** aver dato la propria parola (d'onore) di fare qc; **to do ~ to sb, to do sb ~** (to show courtesy to) presentare i propri rispetti a qn; (to bring respect to) fare onore a qn; **to be an ~ to one's profession** fare onore alla propria professione; **it's a great ~ to be invited** (frm) è un grande onore essere invitati; **I had the ~ of meeting him** (frm) ho avuto l'onore d'incontrarlo; **(in) ~ bound** moralmente obbligato.

(b): **~s** pl (distinction, award) onorificenze fpl; (Univ): **he got first-class ~s in French** ≈ si è laureato in francese con la lode; **to be buried with full ~s** essere sepolto con grandi onori; **to do the ~s** (fam) fare gli onori di casa.

(c) (title): **Your H~** (judge) Vostro Onore; (Am: mayor) signor sindaco.

2 vt (dignify): **to ~ sb (with)** onorare qn (con); **to ~ sb with a title** conferire a qn un titolo.

hon·our·able, (Am) **hon·or·able** [ˈɒnərəbl] adj (gen) onorevole; (person) d'onore; **~ mention** menzione f onorevole, attestato di merito.

hood [hʊd] n (of cloak, raincoat) cappuccio; (on pram, Aut) capote f inv; (Am Aut) cofano; (on cooker, chimney pot) cappa; (Am fam) malvivente m/f.

hood·ed [ˈhʊdɪd] adj incappucciato(a); (robber) mascherato(a).

hood·lum [ˈhuːdləm] n (fam) teppista m/f.

hood·wink [ˈhʊdwɪŋk] vt gabbare, imbrogliare.

hoof [huːf] n, pl **~s** or **hooves** zoccolo.

hook [hʊk] **1** n (gen, also Boxing) gancio; (Fishing) amo; (on dress) gancetto; **~s and eyes** gancetti; **to leave the phone off the ~** lasciare staccato il ricevitore; **by ~ or by crook** in un modo o nell'altro, di rotta o di raffa; **to get sb off the ~** salvare qn; **he fell for it ~, line and sinker** (fig) l'ha bevuta tutta. **2** vt (fasten) agganciare, attaccare; (Fishing) prendere all'amo; **to ~ one's arms/legs around sth** aggrapparsi a qc con le braccia/le gambe; **she finally ~ed him** (fam) è finalmente riuscita a incastrarlo; **to be ~ed on** (fam) essere

fanatico di; **he's ~ed on heroin** (or cocaine etc) (fam) è un eroinomane (or cocainomane etc). **3** vi (fasten) agganciarsi.

♦ **hook on 1** vi + prep: **to ~ on(to)** agganciarsi (a), attaccarsi (a). **2** vt + prep: **to ~ on(to)** agganciare (a).

♦ **hook up** vt + adv (dress) agganciare; (Radio, TV etc) allacciare, collegare.

hoo·li·gan [ˈhuːlɪgən] n teppista m/f.

hoo·li·gan·ism [ˈhuːlɪgənɪzəm] n teppismo.

hoop [huːp] n (gen) cerchio; (for skirt) guardinfante m, crinolina; (croquet ~) archetto; **to put sb through the ~s** (fig) mettere qn sotto il torchio.

hoot [huːt] **1** n (of owl) verso; (of horn) colpo di clacson; (of siren) ululato; (of whistle) fischio; **a ~ of derision** una risata di scherno; **I don't care a ~** (fam) non me ne importa un accidente, me ne infischio; **it was a ~** (fam) è stato divertentissimo or uno spasso. **2** vi (owl) gufare; (person: in scorn) farsi una risata (di scherno); (Aut: person) strombazzare; (ship, train, factory hooter) fischiare; **to ~ with laughter** farsi una gran risata.

hoot·er [ˈhuːtəʳ] n (Brit: of ship, factory) sirena; (Aut) clacson m inv, tromba (d'automobile); (Brit fam: nose) nasone m.

hoo·ver [ˈhuːvəʳ] ® **1** n aspirapolvere m inv. **2** vt passare or pulire con l'aspirapolvere.

hooves [huːvz] npl of **hoof**.

hop¹ [hɒp] **1** n (jump) saltello; (dance: fam) ballo; (Aer): **it's a short ~ from Paris to London** è un salto da Parigi a Londra in aereo; **to catch sb on the ~** (fam) prendere qn alla sprovvista. **2** vi (person, bird, animal) saltellare; (make short journey) fare un salto or balzo; **he ~ped over the wall** è balzato al di là del muro; **to ~ out of bed** saltare giù or fuori dal letto; **~ in!** salta dentro! or su!, monta su!; **~ it!** (fam) sparisci!, smamma!

hop² [hɒp] n (Bot) luppolo.

hope [həʊp] **1** n speranza; **he is past** or **beyond all ~** per lui non c'è più nessuna speranza; **to live in ~** vivere sperando or nella speranza; **in the ~ of doing sth** nella speranza di fare qc; **in the ~ of sth** nella speranza di avere or ottenere qc; **there is no ~ of that** non c'è da farci nessun conto; **with high ~s** con grandi speranze; **to raise sb's ~s** incoraggiare le speranze di qn; **to lose ~** disperarsi; **what a ~!** (fam), **some ~(s)!** (fam) figurati! **2** vt: **to ~ that/to do** sperare che/di fare. **3** vi sperare, augurarsi; **to ~ for the best** sperare in bene or per il meglio; **I ~ so/not** spero di sì/no; **let's ~ for success** speriamo di riuscire; **to ~ against ~** sperare malgrado tutto.

hope·ful [ˈhəʊpfʊl] **1** adj (person) ottimista m/f, fiducioso(a); (future, situation, youngster) promettente; (sign, response) incoraggiante, buono(a) (before n); **I'm ~ that she'll manage to come** ho buone speranze che venga. **2** n: **a young ~** una giovane promessa or speranza.

hope·ful·ly [ˈhəʊpfʌlɪ] adv (speak) con ottimismo; **to look ~ at sb** guardare speranzoso qn; **~ he will recover** speriamo che si riprenda.

hope·less [ˈhəʊplɪs] adj (impossible, useless: situation) impossibile; (: outlook, case) disperato(a); (drunkard etc) incorreggibile, inguaribile; (bad: work: fam) disastroso(a); **I'm ~ at it** (fam) sono completamente negato per questo; **it's ~ trying to convince her** è perfettamente inutile or è fiato sprecato cercare di convincerla.

hope·less·ly [ˈhəʊplɪslɪ] adv (live etc) senza speranza; (involved, complicated) spaventosamente; (late) disperatamente, irrimediabilmente; **I'm ~ confused/lost** sono completamente confuso/perso; **~ in love** perdutamente innamorato.

hop·per ['hɒpə'] n (chute) tramoggia.

hop·scotch ['hɒpskɒtʃ] n (gioco del) mondo.

horde [hɔːd] n orda; **they came in their ~s** sono venuti a frotte.

ho·ri·zon [hə'raɪzn] n (also fig) orizzonte m.

hori·zon·tal [ˌhɒrɪ'zɒntl] **1** adj orizzontale; **the shelf is ~ to the floor** la mensola è parallela al pavimento. **2** n linea or piano orizzontale.

hori·zon·tal·ly [ˌhɒrɪ'zɒntəlɪ] adv orizzontalmente.

hor·mone ['hɔːməʊn] n ormone m.

horn [hɔːn] n (gen, Mus) corno; (of snail, insect) antenna; (Aut) clacson m inv; **to draw in one's ~s** (fig: back down) cedere; (: spend less) ridurre le spese.

hor·net ['hɔːnɪt] n calabrone m.

horn-rimmed ['hɔːn'rɪmd] adj (spectacles) con la montatura di corno.

horny ['hɔːnɪ] adj (-ier, -iest) incallito(a), calloso(a); (fam: randy) arrapato(a).

horo·scope ['hɒrəskəʊp] n oroscopo.

hor·ri·ble ['hɒrɪbl] adj (gen) orribile, orrendo(a); (accident) spaventoso(a).

hor·ri·bly ['hɒrɪblɪ] adv (see adj) in modo orribile or orrendo; spaventosamente.

hor·rid ['hɒrɪd] adj (unpleasant: person) odioso(a); (: thing, weather) orribile, orrendo(a); (: meal) schifoso(a); (unkind) cattivo(a).

hor·rif·ic [hə'rɪfɪk] adj (accident) spaventoso(a); (film) orripilante.

hor·ri·fy ['hɒrɪfaɪ] vt lasciare inorridito(a).

hor·ri·fy·ing ['hɒrɪfaɪɪŋ] adj terrificante.

hor·ror ['hɒrə'] **1** n (terror, dread) spavento, terrore m; (loathing, hatred) orrore m; (fam) peste f; **he ran away in ~** è scappato terrorizzato; **to have a ~ of** avere il terrore di; **that gives me the ~s** (fam) quello mi fa venire i brividi. **2** cpd: **~ film** n film m inv dell'orrore.

horror-struck ['hɒrəstrʌk] adj, **horror-stricken** ['hɒrəˌstrɪkən] adj inorridito(a).

hors d'oeu·vres [ɔː'dɜːvr] npl (course) antipasto; (single items) antipasti mpl.

horse [hɔːs] **1** n cavallo; **it's straight from the ~'s mouth** (fam) è di fonte sicura; **never look a gift ~ in the mouth** (Proverb) a caval donato non si guarda in bocca. **2** cpd (race) di cavalli; (meat) di cavallo; **~ chestnut** n (tree) ippocastano; (nut) castagna d'India or matta; **~ show** n, **~ trials** npl concorso ippico, gare fpl ippiche.

♦ **horse about, horse around** vi + adv (fam) fare lo sciocco.

horse·back ['hɔːsbæk]: **on ~** adv a cavallo.

horse·box ['hɔːsbɒks] n carro or furgone m per il trasporto dei cavalli.

horse·fly ['hɔːsflaɪ] n tafano, mosca cavallina.

horse·hair ['hɔːsheə'] n crine m (di cavallo).

horse·man ['hɔːsmən] n, pl **-men** cavaliere m.

horse·man·ship ['hɔːsmənˌʃɪp] n equitazione f.

horse·play ['hɔːspleɪ] n giochi mpl scatenati.

horse·power ['hɔːsˌpaʊə'] n (abbr **H.P.**) cavallo (vapore) (abbr c.v.).

horse-racing ['hɔːsreɪsɪŋ] n (sport) ippica; (events) corse fpl dei cavalli.

horse-radish ['hɔːsˌrædɪʃ] n rafano.

horse-shoe ['hɔːsʃuː] **1** n ferro di cavallo. **2** cpd a ferro di cavallo.

horse-trader ['hɔːsˌtreɪdə'] n commerciante m/f di cavalli; (fig) vecchia volpe f.

horse·whip ['hɔːswɪp] vt frustare.

horse·woman ['hɔːsˌwʊmən] n amazzone f.

horsey ['hɔːsɪ] adj (-ier, -iest) (fam: person) che adora i cavalli; (appearance) cavallino(a), da cavallo.

hor·ti·cul·tur·al [ˌhɔːtɪ'kʌltʃərəl] adj di orticoltura.

hor·ti·cul·ture ['hɔːtɪkʌltʃə'] n orticoltura.

hor·ti·cul·tur·ist [ˌhɔːtɪ'kʌltʃərɪst] n orticoltore/trice.

hose [həʊz] n **(a)** (hosepipe) tubo di gomma. **(b)** (pl: stockings, socks) calze fpl, calzini mpl; (: old) calzamaglia.

♦ **hose down** vt + adv lavare con un getto d'acqua.

ho·siery ['həʊʒərɪ] n maglieria.

hos·pice ['hɒspɪs] n ricovero, ospizio.

hos·pi·table ['hɒsˌpɪtəbl] adj ospitale.

hos·pi·tal ['hɒspɪtl] **1** n ospedale m. **2** cpd (staff, treatment) ospedaliero(a); (bed) di or dell'ospedale.

hos·pi·tal·ity [ˌhɒspɪ'tælɪtɪ] n ospitalità.

hos·pi·tal·ize ['hɒspɪtəlaɪz] vt ricoverare (in or all'ospedale).

host[1] [həʊst] **1** n ospite m/f; (TV, Radio) presentatore/trice. **2** vt (TV programme, games) presentare.

host[2] [həʊst] n (crowd) moltitudine f; **for a whole ~ of reasons** per tutta una serie di ragioni.

host[3] [həʊst] n (Rel) ostia.

hos·tage ['hɒstɪdʒ] n ostaggio; **to take sb ~** prendere qn in ostaggio.

hos·tel ['hɒstəl] n (for students, nurses etc) pensionato; (for homeless people) ospizio, ricovero; (youth ~) ostello della gioventù.

hos·tel·ling ['hɒstəlɪŋ] n: **to go (youth) ~** passare le vacanze negli ostelli della gioventù.

host·ess ['həʊstes] n ospite f; (Aer) hostess f inv; (in nightclub) entraineuse f inv.

hos·tile ['hɒstaɪl] adj: **~ (to)** ostile (a).

hos·til·ity [hɒs'tɪlɪtɪ] n ostilità f inv.

hot [hɒt] **1** adj (-ter, -test) **(a)** caldo(a); **to be ~** (person) aver caldo; (thing) essere caldo(a); (Met) far caldo; **to get ~** (person) incominciare ad aver caldo; (thing) scaldarsi; (Met) incominciare a far caldo; **this room is ~** fa caldo in questa stanza; **I don't like ~ weather** non sopporto il caldo; **to get ~ under the collar** (fam) scaldarsi; **to be all ~ and bothered** essere tutto accaldato; (flustered) essere tutto agitato; **to be/get into ~ water** essere/cacciarsi nei guai; **you're getting ~!** (fig: when guessing) fuoco!

(b) (curry) piccante; (news) fresco(a); (temperament) focoso(a); **she's got a ~ temper** è un tipo collerico; **~ favourite** grande favorito; **I've got a ~ tip for the Derby** (fam) ho un cavallo sicuro per il Derby; **I'll make things ~ for you** (fam) ti rendo la vita difficile; **to be in the ~ seat** avere un posto che scotta; **to be in ~ pursuit of sb** stare alle calcagna di qn; **he's pretty ~ at maths** (fam) se la cava bene in matematica; **those goods are ~** (fam: stolen) è roba che scotta.

2 adv: **to be ~ on sb's trail** essere sulle tracce di qn; **to be ~ on the heels of sb** essere alle calcagna di qn.

3 cpd: **~ air** n (fam) ciance fpl; **~ dog** n (Culin) hot dog m inv; **~ line** n (Pol) telefono rosso; **~ potato** n (fam) questione f che scotta; **~ rod** n (Aut: fam) macchina truccata; **~ spot** n zona calda; **~ spring** n sorgente f termale; **to be ~ stuff** (fam) essere eccezionale.

♦ **hot up** (fam) **1** vi + adv (situation) farsi più teso(a); (party) scaldarsi. **2** vt + adv (pace) affrettare; (engine) truccare.

hot-air bal·loon [ˌhɒtˌeəbə'luːn] n (Aer) mongolfiera.

hot·bed ['hɒtbed] n (fig) focolaio.

hot-blooded [ˌhɒt'blʌdɪd] adj dal sangue caldo, appassionato(a).

hotch·potch ['hɒtʃpɒtʃ] n pot-pourri m.

ho·tel [həʊ'tel] **1** n albergo, hotel m inv. **2** cpd: ~ **industry** n industria alberghiera; ~ **room** n camera d'albergo.

ho·tel·ier [həʊ'telɪə^r] n albergatore/trice.

hot·foot ['hɒt,fʊt] adv di gran carriera.

hot·head ['hɒthed] n testa calda.

hot-headed [,hɒt'hedɪd] adj impetuoso(a).

hot·house ['hɒthaʊs] n serra.

hot·ly ['hɒtlɪ] adv accanitamente, con accanimento; **he was ~ pursued by the policeman** il poliziotto lo rincorreva senza dargli tregua.

hot·plate ['hɒtpleɪt] n (on cooker) piastra (riscaldante); (for keeping food warm) scaldavivande m inv.

hot·pot ['hɒtpɒt] n (Brit Culin) stufato.

hot-tempered [,hɒt'tempəd] adj irascibile.

hound [haʊnd] **1** n segugio; **the ~s** la muta; **to follow the ~s, to ride to ~s** fare la caccia alla volpe. **2** vt (fig) perseguitare.

♦ **hound down** vt + adv riuscire a stanare.

♦ **hound out** vt + adv: **to ~ out of** cacciare da.

hour ['aʊə^r] **1** n ora; **at 30 miles an ~** a 30 miglia all'ora; ~ **by ~** ora per ora; **on the ~** ad ogni ora precisa; **in the early or small ~s** alle ore piccole; **at all ~s (of the day and night)** a tutte le ore (del giorno e della notte); **lunch ~** intervallo di pranzo; **visiting ~s** orario delle visite; **at this late ~** all'ultimo momento; **he thought his (last) ~ had come** pensò che fosse giunta la sua ora; **in the ~ of danger** nel momento del pericolo; **to pay sb by the ~** pagare qn a ore; **to wait (for) ~s** aspettare per (delle) ore; **~s and ~s** ore e ore; **to keep regular ~s** fare una vita regolare; **out of ~s** fuori orario; **after ~s** (at office) dopo le ore d'ufficio; (at shop, pub) dopo l'ora di chiusura. **2** cpd: ~ **hand** n lancetta delle ore.

hour·glass ['aʊəglɑːs] n clessidra.

hour·ly ['aʊəlɪ] **1** adj (intervals) di un'ora; (bus service) (ad) ogni ora; (rate) orario(a). **2** adv ogni ora; ~ **paid workers** operai pagati a ore; **we expected him ~** lo aspettavamo da un momento all'altro.

house [haʊs] n, pl **houses** ['haʊzɪz] **1** n **(a)** casa; **at** (or **to**) **my ~** a casa mia; **to keep ~** mandare avanti la casa; **to set up ~** metter su casa; **to put or set one's ~ in order** (fig) sistemare i propri affari; **to get on like a ~ on fire** (2 persons: fam) andare d'amore e d'accordo. **(b)** (Pol) camera; **the H~ of Commons/Lords** (Brit) la Camera dei Comuni/Lords; **the H~ of Representatives** (Am) la Camera dei Rappresentanti; **H~s of Parliament** (Brit) palazzo del Parlamento. **(c)** (Theatre etc): **full ~** il tutto esaurito; '~ **full**' 'biglietti esauriti'; **in the front of the ~** tra gli spettatori, in sala; **to bring the ~ down** (fig) scatenare un uragano di applausi; **the second ~** il secondo spettacolo. **(d)** (Comm) ditta, casa; **it's on the ~** (paid by company) paga la ditta; (free) è offerto dalla casa. **(e)** (family, line) casa, casato.

2 [haʊz] vt sistemare; **this building ~s 6 families** in quest'edificio abitano 6 famiglie.

3 cpd: ~ **arrest** n arresto domiciliare; ~ **doctor** n ≃ interno; ~ **plant** n pianta da appartamento.

house·boat ['haʊsbəʊt] n house boat f inv.

house·bound ['haʊsbaʊnd] adj confinato(a) in casa.

house·break·er ['haʊs,breɪkə^r] n svaligiatore/trice, scassinatore/trice.

house·coat ['haʊskəʊt] n vestaglia.

house·hold ['haʊshəʊld] **1** n casa, famiglia. **2** cpd (accounts, expenses, equipment) della casa, domestico(a); **H~ Cavalry** n (Mil) cavalleria della guardia reale; ~ **word** n: **it's a ~ word** (fig) è un nome conosciuto da tutti.

house·holder ['haʊs,həʊldə^r] n padrone/a di casa; (head of house) capofamiglia m/f.

house·hunting ['haʊs,hʌntɪŋ] n: **to go ~** mettersi a cercar casa.

house·keeper ['haʊs,kiːpə^r] n governante f.

house·keeping ['haʊs,kiːpɪŋ] n (work) andamento della casa; (also: ~ **money**) soldi mpl per le spese di casa.

house·maid ['haʊsmeɪd] n cameriera, domestica.

house·man ['haʊsmən] n, pl **-men** (Med) ≃ interno.

house-proud ['haʊspraʊd] adj che è maniaco(a) della pulizia.

house·room ['haʊsrʊm] n: **I wouldn't give it ~** (fam) non lo vorrei avere in casa mia neanche se me lo regalassero.

house-to-house [,haʊstə'haʊs] adj (collection) di porta in porta; (search) casa per casa.

house-trained ['haʊstreɪnd] adj (Brit: animal) che non sporca in casa.

house-warming ['haʊs,wɔːmɪŋ] n festa per inaugurare la casa.

house·wife ['haʊswaɪf] n, pl **-wives** massaia, casalinga.

house·wife·ly ['haʊswaɪflɪ] adj della massaia, della casalinga.

house·work ['haʊswɜːk] n faccende fpl or lavori mpl di casa, lavori domestici.

hous·ing ['haʊzɪŋ] **1** n **(a)** alloggiamento. **(b)** (houses) alloggi mpl, case fpl. **2** cpd (problem, shortage) degli alloggi; ~ **association** n cooperativa edilizia; ~ **conditions** npl condizioni fpl di abitazione; ~ **estate** n quartiere m or zona residenziale.

hove [həʊv] pt, pp of **heave** (Naut).

hov·el ['hɒvəl] n tugurio.

hov·er ['hɒvə^r] vi (bird) librarsi; (helicopter) volare a punto fisso; **a smile ~ed on her lips** un sorriso indugiava sulle sue labbra; **to ~ on the brink of disaster** essere sull'orlo del disastro.

♦ **hover about, hover around** vi + adv stare or girare intorno.

hover·craft ['hɒvə,krɑːft] n hovercraft m inv.

hover·port ['hɒvə,pɔːt] n porto per hovercraft.

how [haʊ] adv **(a)** (gen) come; ~ **did you do it?** come hai fatto?, come l'hai fatto?; **I know ~ you did it** so come hai fatto; **to know ~ to do sth** sapere come fare qc; ~ **is school?** come va la scuola?; ~ **was the film?** com'era il film?; ~ **is it that...?** com'è che...?; ~ **are you?** come stai?, come va?; ~ **do you do?** piacere!, molto lieto!; ~ **come?** (fam) come mai?; ~ **come he's leaving?** (fam) come mai se ne va?; ~ **about going for a drink?** che ne diresti di andare a bere qualcosa?; **and ~!** (fam) eccome!

(b) (to what degree) quanto(a); ~ **much is it?** quanto costa?; ~ **long have you been here?** da quanto tempo stai qui?; ~ **many people?** quante persone?; ~ **much milk?** quanto latte?; ~ **often do you go?** quanto spesso ci vai?; ~ **lovely!** bello!; ~ **kind of you!** è molto gentile da parte sua!

(c) (that) che, di come; **she told me ~ she'd found the money in an old suitcase** mi ha raccontato di come aveva trovato il denaro in una vecchia valigia.

how·ever [haʊ'evə^r] **1** conj (still, nevertheless) però, comunque, tuttavia. **2** adv: ~ **I do it** in qualunque modo lo faccia; ~ **cold it is** per quanto freddo faccia; ~ **much I try** per quanto ci possa provare; ~ **did you do it?** (fam) come diavolo hai fatto?; ~ **that may be** comunque sia.

how·itz·er ['haʊɪtsəʳ] *n (Mil)* obice *m*.

howl [haʊl] **1** *n (of animal)* ululato; **a** ~ **of pain** un urlo di dolore; **a** ~ **of protest** un grido di protesta; ~**s of laughter** scrosci *mpl* di risate. **2** *vi (person)* gridare, urlare; *(animal, wind)* ululare; *(weep)* piangere; **to** ~ **with laughter** rotolarsi dalle risate. **3** *vt* urlare.

♦ **howl down** *vt + adv* zittire a forza di urla.

howl·er ['haʊləʳ] *n (fam)* abbaglio; (: *in homework)* perla.

H.P., h.p. *abbr of* hire-purchase; horse power.

HQ *abbr of* **headquarters.**

hr(s) *abbr (= hour(s))* h.

hub [hʌb] *n* mozzo; *(fig)* centro, fulcro.

hub·bub ['hʌbʌb] *n* baccano.

hub·cap ['hʌbkæp] *n (Aut)* coprimozzo.

hud·dle ['hʌdl] **1** *n* gruppetto, capannello; **to go into a** ~ *(fam)* fare capannello. **2** *vi* raggomitolarsi, rannicchiarsi.

♦ **huddle together** *vi + adv* stringersi l'uno(a) vicino all'altro(a).

♦ **huddle up** *vi + adv* rannicchiarsi, raggomitolarsi.

hue¹ [hjuː] *n (colour)* colore *m*, tinta.

hue² [hjuː] *n*: ~ **and cry** clamorosa protesta.

huff [hʌf] *n*: **in a** ~ *(fam)* imbronciato(a).

hug [hʌg] **1** *n* abbraccio, stretta; **to give sb a** ~ abbracciare qn. **2** *vt* abbracciare, tener stretto(a) a sé; *(subj: bear etc)* stringere; *(keep close to: kerb)* tenersi vicino a; **to** ~ **the coast** tenersi sotto costa.

huge [hjuːdʒ] *adj (gen)* enorme; *(appetite, helping)* smisurato(a); *(success)* strepitoso(a).

hulk [hʌlk] *n (abandoned ship)* nave *f* in disarmo; *(building etc)* mastodonte *m*; **a great** ~ **of a man** *(fam)* un bestione.

hulk·ing ['hʌlkɪŋ] *adj (fam)* mastodontico(a).

hull [hʌl] *n* scafo.

hul·la·ba·loo [ˌhʌləbə'luː] *n (fam: noise)* fracasso.

hul·lo [hʌ'ləʊ] *excl (on meeting sb)* ciao!; *(Telec)* pronto!; *(to attract attention)* ehi!; *(in surprise)* eh!

hum [hʌm] **1** *n (also Elec)* ronzio; *(of traffic, machines)* rumore *m*; *(of voices etc)* mormorio, brusio. **2** *vt (tune)* canticchiare. **3** *vi (insect)* ronzare; *(person)* canticchiare a labbra chiuse; *(engine, machine)* fare rumore; *(wireless)* mandare un brusio; *(fig fam: be busy)* animarsi; **to** ~ **with activity** pullulare di attività; **to** ~ **and haw** essere incerto sul da farsi.

hu·man ['hjuːmən] **1** *adj* umano(a); ~ **being** essere *m* umano. **2** *n* essere *m* umano.

hu·mane [hjuː'meɪn] *adj* umanitario(a).

hu·man·ism ['hjuːmənɪzəm] *n* umanesimo.

hu·man·ist ['hjuːmənɪst] *n* umanista *m/f*.

hu·mani·tar·ian [hjuːˌmænɪ'tɛərɪən] *adj* umanitario(a).

hu·man·ity [hjuː'mænɪtɪ] *n* umanità; **the human-ities** gli studi letterari, le lettere.

hu·man·ly ['hjuːmənlɪ] *adv* umanamente.

hu·man·oid ['hjuːmənɔɪd] **1** *adj* che sembra umano(a). **2** *n* umanoide *m/f*.

hum·ble ['hʌmbl] **1** *adj* (**-r, -st**) umile; *(opinion, occupation)* modesto(a); **to eat** ~ **pie** rimangiarsi tutto. **2** *vt* umiliare; **to** ~ **o.s.** abbassarsi, umiliarsi.

hum·bly ['hʌmblɪ] *adv* umilmente.

hum·bug ['hʌmbʌg] *n (person)* ipocrita *m/f*, impostore *m*; *(nonsense)* sciocchezze *fpl*, stupidaggini *fpl*; *(Brit: sweet)* caramella alla menta.

hum·drum ['hʌmdrʌm] *adj* monotono(a), banale.

hu·mid ['hjuːmɪd] *adj* umido(a).

hu·midi·fi·er [hjuː'mɪdɪfaɪəʳ] *n* umidificatore *m*.

hu·mid·ity [hjuː'mɪdɪtɪ] *n* umidità.

hu·mili·ate [hjuː'mɪlɪeɪt] *vt* umiliare.

hu·mili·at·ing [hjuː'mɪlɪeɪtɪŋ] *adj* umiliante.

hu·milia·tion [hjuːˌmɪlɪ'eɪʃən] *n* umiliazione *f*.

hu·mil·ity [hjuː'mɪlɪtɪ] *n* umiltà.

humming·bird ['hʌmɪŋˌbɜːd] *n* colibrì *m inv*.

hu·mor·ist ['hjuːmərɪst] *n* umorista *m/f*.

hu·mor·ous ['hjuːmərəs] *adj (person)* spiritoso(a); *(book, story, situation)* divertente; *(tone)* scherzoso(a).

hu·mour, (*Am*) **hu·mor** ['hjuːməʳ] **1** *n* **(a)** *(sense of fun)* umorismo; *(of situation)* lato divertente *or* umoristico; **sense of** ~ senso dell'umorismo. **(b)** *(mood)* umore *m*; **to be in a good/bad** ~ essere di buon/cattivo umore. **2** *vt (person)* accontentare; *(whims)* assecondare.

hu·mour·less, (*Am*) **hu·mor·less** ['hjuːməlɪs] *adj* privo(a) di umorismo.

hump [hʌmp] **1** *n (Anat)* gobba; **it gives me the** ~ *(Brit fam)* mi mette di mal umore; **we're over the** ~ *(fig)* il peggio è passato, il più è fatto. **2** *vt (a)* *(arch: back)* inarcare. **(b)** *(fam: carry)* portare.

hump·backed ['hʌmpˌbækt] *adj (person)* gobbo(a); *(bridge)* a schiena d'asino.

hu·mus ['hjuːməs] *n (Bio)* humus *m*.

hunch [hʌntʃ] **1** *n (fam: idea)* impressione *f*; **I have a** ~ **that** ho la vaga impressione che; **he's acting on a** ~ sta andando a naso. **2** *vt (also:* ~ **up)** incurvare. **3** *vi* star curvo(a); **to sit** ~**ed up** star seduto curvo.

hunch·back ['hʌntʃˌbæk] *n* gobbo/a.

hun·dred ['hʌndrɪd] **1** *adj* cento *inv*; **about a** ~ **people** un centinaio di persone; **a** ~ **and one** centouno; ~ **and first** centounesimo(a); **I'm a** ~ **per cent sure** sono sicuro al cento per cento. **2** *n* cento *m inv*; **to live to be a** ~ vivere fino all'età di cent'anni; *(less exactly)* diventare centenario(a); ~**s of people** centinaia *fpl* di persone; **they came in their** ~**s** sono arrivati a centinaia.

hun·dredth ['hʌndrɪdθ] **1** *adj* centesimo(a). **2** *n (in series)* centesimo/a; *(fraction)* centesimo.

hundred·weight ['hʌndrɪdˌweɪt] *n (Brit)* = 50,7 kg, *(Am)* = 45, 3 kg.

hung [hʌŋ] *pt, pp of* hang.

Hun·gar·ian [hʌŋ'gɛərɪən] **1** *adj* ungherese. **2** *n (person)* ungherese *m/f*; *(language)* ungherese *m*.

Hun·ga·ry ['hʌŋgərɪ] *n* Ungheria.

hun·ger ['hʌŋgəʳ] **1** *n* fame *f*; *(also fig)*: ~ **(for)** sete *f* (di). **2** *cpd*: ~ **strike** *n* sciopero della fame.

♦ **hunger after, hunger for** *vi + prep* desiderare moltissimo, morire dalla voglia di.

hun·gri·ly ['hʌŋgrɪlɪ] *adv* avidamente.

hun·gry ['hʌŋgrɪ] *adj*: **to be** ~ aver fame; **to make sb** ~ far venire fame a qn; **to go** ~ *(starve)* patire la fame; *(skip a meal)* fare a meno di mangiare; ~ **for** *(fig)* assetato di.

hunk [hʌŋk] *n* bel pezzo.

hunt [hʌnt] **1** *n* caccia; *(search)*: ~ **(for)** ricerca (di); *(huntsmen)* cacciatori *mpl*; **tiger** ~ caccia alla tigre; **I've had a** ~ **for the book** ho cercato il libro dappertutto. **2** *vt (animal)* andare a caccia di; *(search)* cercare; **to** ~ **sb from** *or* **off** scacciare di; **I've** ~**ed the house for it** ho messo la casa sottosopra per trovarlo. **3** *vi (Sport)* cacciare; **to go** ~**ing** andare a caccia; **to** ~ **for** *(animal)* cacciare; *(object, information)* cercare dappertutto; **she** ~**ed in her bag for the keys** ha rovistato nella borsa per trovare le chiavi.

♦ **hunt down** *vt + adv* scovare.

♦ **hunt up** *vt + adv* scovare.

hunt·er ['hʌntəʳ] *n* cacciatore/trice; *(horse)* cavallo da caccia.

hunt·ing ['hʌntɪŋ] 1 n (Sport) caccia. 2 cpd: ~ **lodge** n casino di caccia.

hunts·man ['hʌntsmən] n, pl -men cacciatore m.

hur·dle ['hɜːdl] n (for fence) graticcio; (Sport, fig) ostacolo; **the 100 metre** ~s (race) i cento metri a ostacoli.

hurl [hɜːl] vt (throw) scagliare, scaraventare; **to** ~ **abuse** or **insults at sb** scagliare or lanciare degli insulti a qn.

hur·rah [huˈrɑː] excl, **hur·ray** [huˈreɪ] excl urrà!, evviva!; ~ **for Mr Jones!** viva Mr Jones!

hur·ri·cane ['hʌrɪkən] n uragano.

hur·ried ['hʌrɪd] adj (gen) affrettato(a); (steps) frettoloso(a).

hur·ried·ly ['hʌrɪdlɪ] adv in fretta (e furia).

hur·ry ['hʌrɪ] 1 n fretta, premura; **to be in a** ~ **(to do)** avere una gran fretta (di fare); **done in a** ~ fatto in fretta; **are you in a** ~ **for this?** ti serve subito?; **what's the** ~? che fretta c'è?; **there's no** ~ non c'è fretta or premura; **he won't do that again in a** ~ (fam) non lo rifarà tanto facilmente.
2 vt (person) far fretta a; (work etc) fare in fretta; **to** ~ **to do sth** affrettarsi a fare qc; **he won't be hurried** non gli si può far fretta; **she hurried him into the car** l'ha spinto in macchina; **he was hurried to the hospital** è stato portato d'urgenza all'ospedale; **he hurried his lunch** ha mangiato il pranzo alla svelta; **troops were hurried to the spot** le truppe furono spedite in fretta sul posto.
3 vi fare in fretta; **to** ~ **back/home** affrettarsi a tornare indietro/a casa; **to** ~ **after sb** precipitarsi dietro a qn; **to** ~ **over sth** (meal) trangugiare; (work) fare in fretta; **to** ~ **in/out** entrare/uscire in fretta.

♦ **hurry along** 1 vi + adv camminare in fretta. 2 vt + adv = **hurry up** 2.

♦ **hurry away**, **hurry off** 1 vi + adv andarsene in fretta. 2 vt + adv spedire fuori in fretta; **to be hurried off to** essere spedito in fretta a.

♦ **hurry on** 1 vi + adv; **to** ~ **on to** passare in fretta a. 2 vt + adv far fretta a.

♦ **hurry up** 1 vi + adv sbrigarsi. 2 vt + adv (person) far fretta a; (work) fare in fretta; ~ **him up will you!** digli di fare in fretta!

hurt [hɜːt] (vb: pt, pp **hurt**) 1 vt (a) (injure) ferire; (cause pain to, harm) far male a; **I** ~ **my arm** mi sono fatto male al braccio; (b) (business, interests etc) colpire, danneggiare. 2 vi far male; **my arm** ~s a male il braccio; **where does it** ~? dove ti fa male? 3 n male m, ferita. 4 adj (foot etc) ferito(a); (feelings, look, tone) offeso(a).

hurt·ful ['hɜːtful] adj (harmful) dannoso(a), nocivo(a); (remark etc) che fa male.

hurt·le ['hɜːtl] vi sfrecciare; **he** ~**d down the stairs** si è precipitato giù per le scale.

hus·band ['hʌzbənd] 1 n marito. 2 vt dosare.

hush [hʌʃ] 1 n silenzio, pace f; ~! silenzio! 2 vt quietare, calmare. 3: **to pay sb** ~ **money** (fam) comprare il silenzio di qn.

♦ **hush up** vt + adv (fact) cercare di far passare sotto silenzio; (scandal) mettere a tacere; (person) far star zitto(a).

hushed [hʌʃt] adj sommesso(a).

hush-hush ['hʌʃhʌʃ] adj (fam) segretissimo(a).

husk [hʌsk] n (of wheat, rice) pula; (of nuts) pellicina.

husky[1] ['hʌskɪ] adj -ier, -iest) (throat) rauco(a); (voice) roco(a); (tough: person) ben piantato(a).

husky[2] ['hʌskɪ] n, pl -ies cane m eschimese.

hus·tings ['hʌstɪŋz] npl (Pol) comizi mpl elettorali.

hus·tle ['hʌsl] 1 n: ~ **and bustle** trambusto, via vai

m. 2 vt (push: person): **to** ~ **in/out** etc far entrare/uscire etc in fretta; **we'll have to** ~ **things along** dobbiamo fare più in fretta. 3 vi: **to** ~ **in/out** etc entrare/uscire etc in fretta.

hut [hʌt] n capanna; (in mountains) baita; (Mil) baracca.

hutch [hʌtʃ] n gabbia (per conigli).

hya·cinth ['haɪəsɪnθ] n giacinto.

hy·brid ['haɪbrɪd] 1 n ibrido. 2 adj ibrido(a).

hy·dran·gea [haɪˈdreɪndʒə] n ortensia.

hy·drant ['haɪdrənt] n (also: **fire** ~) idrante m.

hy·drau·lic [haɪˈdrɒlɪk] adj idraulico(a).

hy·drau·lics [haɪˈdrɒlɪks] nsg idraulica.

hydro... ['haɪdrəʊ] pref idro...; ~**chloric acid** acido cloridrico.

hydro·dy·nam·ics ['haɪdrəʊdaɪˈnæmɪks] n idrodinamica.

hydro·elec·tric ['haɪdrəʊɪˈlɛktrɪk] adj idroelettrico(a).

hydro·foil ['haɪdrəfɔɪl] n aliscafo.

hydro·gen ['haɪdrɪdʒən] 1 n idrogeno. 2 cpd: ~ **bomb** n bomba all'idrogeno; ~ **peroxide** n acqua ossigenata.

hydro·pho·bia [,haɪdrəˈfəʊbɪə] n idrofobia.

hydro·plane ['haɪdrəʊpleɪn] n idrovolante m.

hy·ena [haɪˈiːnə] n iena.

hy·giene ['haɪdʒiːn] n igiene f.

hy·gien·ic [haɪˈdʒiːnɪk] adj igienico(a).

hymn [hɪm] 1 n inno (sacro). 2 cpd: ~ **book** n libro dei canti.

hym·nal ['hɪmnəl] n libro dei canti.

hyper... ['haɪpə'] pref iper... .

hyper·ac·tive [,haɪpər'æktɪv] adj iperattivo(a).

hyper·bo·le [haɪˈpɜːbəlɪ] n iperbole f.

hyper·criti·cal ['haɪpə'krɪtɪkəl] adj ipercritico(a).

hyper·mar·ket ['haɪpəmɑːkɪt] n ipermercato.

hyper·sen·si·tive ['haɪpə'sɛnsɪtɪv] adj ipersensibile.

hyper·ten·sion ['haɪpə'tɛnʃən] n (Med) ipertensione f.

hy·phen ['haɪfən] n trattino, lineetta.

hy·phen·ate ['haɪfəneɪt] vt unire con un trattino.

hyp·no·sis [hɪp'nəʊsɪs] n ipnosi f.

hyp·not·ic [hɪp'nɒtɪk] adj ipnotico(a).

hyp·no·tism ['hɪpnətɪzəm] n ipnotismo.

hyp·no·tist ['hɪpnətɪst] n ipnotizzatore/trice.

hyp·no·tize ['hɪpnətaɪz] vt ipnotizzare.

hypo·chon·dria [,haɪpəʊ'kɒndrɪə] n ipocondria.

hypo·chon·dri·ac [,haɪpəʊ'kɒndrɪæk] n ipocondriaco(a).

hy·poc·ri·sy [hɪ'pɒkrɪsɪ] n ipocrisia.

hypo·crite ['hɪpəkrɪt] n ipocrita m/f.

hypo·criti·cal [,hɪpə'krɪtɪkəl] adj ipocrita.

hypo·der·mic [,haɪpə'dɜːmɪk] 1 adj ipodermico(a). 2 n (syringe) siringa ipodermica.

hy·pot·enuse [haɪ'pɒtɪnjuːz] n (Math) ipotenusa.

hy·po·ther·mia [,haɪpəʊ'θɜːmɪə] n ipotermia.

hy·poth·esis [haɪ'pɒθɪsɪs] n, pl **hypotheses** [haɪ'pɒθɪsiːz] ipotesi f inv.

hypo·theti·cal [,haɪpəʊ'θɛtɪkəl] adj ipotetico(a).

hypo·theti·cal·ly [,haɪpəʊ'θɛtɪkəlɪ] adv ipoteticamente, per ipotesi.

hys·ter·ec·to·my [,hɪstə'rɛktəmɪ] n isterectomia.

hys·te·ria [hɪs'tɪərɪə] n (Psych) isteria; (gen) isterismo.

hys·teri·cal [hɪs'tɛrɪkəl] adj isterico(a).

hys·teri·cal·ly [hɪs'tɛrɪkəlɪ] adv istericamente; **it was** ~ **funny** era buffo da morire.

hys·ter·ics [hɪs'tɛrɪks] npl crisi f inv isterica; **to have** ~ avere una crisi isterica; (fam: laugh) crepar dal ridere.

I

I¹, i [aɪ] *n (letter)* I, i *f or m inv.*

I² [aɪ] *pers pron* io; **I'LL do it** lo faccio io.

Iberian [aɪˈbɪərɪən] *adj* iberico(a); **the ~ Peninsula** la Penisola iberica.

ice [aɪs] **1** *n* **(a)** ghiaccio; **as cold as ~** freddo come il ghiaccio; **to break the ~** *(fig)* rompere il ghiaccio; **it cuts no ~ with me** con me non attacca; **to keep sth on ~** *(fig: plan, project)* mettere da parte (per il momento), accantonare; **to skate on thin ~** *(fig)* essere sul filo del rasoio, dover fare degli equilibrismi. **(b)** *(ice cream)* gelato. **2** *vt (cake)* glassare. **3** *cpd:* **I~ Age** *n* era glaciale; **~ axe** *n* piccozza; **~ bucket** *n* secchiello del ghiaccio; **~ cream** *n* gelato; **~ cube** *n* cubetto di ghiaccio; **~ floe** *n* banco di ghiaccio; **~ hockey** *n* hockey *m* su ghiaccio; **~ lolly** *n* ghiacciolo; **~ rink** *n* pista di pattinaggio (su ghiaccio); **~ skate** *n* pattino da ghiaccio.

♦ **ice over, ice up** *vi + adv (river)* gelarsi, ghiacciarsi; *(windscreen, wings of plane)* ricoprirsi di ghiaccio, incrostarsi di ghiaccio.

ice·berg [ˈaɪsbɜːg] *n* iceberg *m inv;* **tip of the ~** *(also fig)* punta dell'iceberg.

ice·bound [ˈaɪsbaʊnd] *adj* bloccato(a) dal ghiaccio.

ice·box [ˈaɪsbɒks] *n (Am: refrigerator)* frigorifero; *(Brit: part of refrigerator)* freezer *m inv.*

ice·breaker [ˈaɪsˌbreɪkəʳ] *n* rompighiaccio *m inv.*

ice·cap [ˈaɪskæp] *n* calotta polare.

ice·cold [ˈaɪsˈkəʊld] *adj* ghiacciato(a).

ice-cream soda [ˈaɪskriːmˈsəʊdə] *n* (gelato) affogato al seltz.

iced [aɪst] *adj (drink)* ghiacciato(a); *(coffee, tea)* freddo(a); *(cake)* glassato(a).

Ice·land [ˈaɪslənd] *n* Islanda.

Icelander [ˈaɪsləndəʳ] *n* islandese *m/f.*

Ice·land·ic [aɪsˈlændɪk] **1** *adj* islandese. **2** *n (language)* islandese *m.*

ice-skate [ˈaɪsˌskeɪt] *vi* pattinare sul ghiaccio.

ice-skating [ˈaɪsˌskeɪtɪŋ] *n* pattinaggio sul ghiaccio.

ici·cle [ˈaɪsɪkl] *n* ghiacciolo.

ici·ly [ˈaɪsɪlɪ] *adv* gelidamente.

ic·ing [ˈaɪsɪŋ] **1** *n (on cake)* glassa. **2** *cpd:* **~ sugar** *n* zucchero a velo.

icon [ˈaɪkɒn] *n* icona.

icono·clas·tic [aɪˌkɒnəˈklæstɪk] *adj (opinions)* iconoclastico(a); *(person)* iconoclasta.

icy [ˈaɪsɪ] *adj (-ier, -iest) (road, hand)* ghiacciato(a); *(weather, stare)* gelido(a); **it's ~ cold** si gela.

id [ɪd] *n (Psych)* Id *m*, Es *m.*

I'd [aɪd] = **I would; I had.**

idea [aɪˈdɪə] *n* idea; **good ~!** buon'idea!; **that was a brilliant ~** è stata un'idea splendida; **he had no ~ of the answer** non aveva nessuna idea della risposta; **to have an ~ that...** aver l'impressione che...; **I haven't the least** *or* **slightest** *or* **foggiest ~** non ne ho la minima *or* la più pallida idea; **it would not be a bad ~ to paint it** non sarebbe forse una cattiva idea verniciarlo; **to put ~s into sb's head** mettere delle (strane) idee in testa a qn; **it wasn't my ~** non è stata un'idea mia, non

sono io che ho avuto l'idea; **if that's your ~ of a joke...** se credi di essere spiritoso...; **I've got the general ~** mi sono fatto un'idea; **that's the ~** ecco, proprio così; **what's the big ~?** *(fam)* cosa credi di fare?; **the ~ is to sell it** l'idea è di venderlo.

ideal [aɪˈdɪəl] *adj, n* ideale *(m).*

ideal·ism [aɪˈdɪəlɪzəm] *n* idealismo.

ideal·ist [aɪˈdɪəlɪst] *n* idealista *m/f.*

ideal·ly [aɪˈdɪəlɪ] *adv* perfettamente, assolutamente; **it is ~ situated** si trova in un posto ideale; **they are an ~ matched couple** sono una coppia ideale; **~ the book should have...** l'ideale sarebbe che il libro avesse... .

iden·ti·cal [aɪˈdɛntɪkəl] *adj* identico(a); **~ twins** gemelli monovulari.

iden·ti·fi·ca·tion [aɪˌdɛntɪfɪˈkeɪʃən] *n* identificazione *f; (document)* documento (di riconoscimento *or* di identità).

iden·ti·fy [aɪˈdɛntɪfaɪ] **1** *vt* identificare; **to ~ o.s.** dimostrare la propria identità; **to ~ o.s. with** identificarsi con. **2** *vi:* **to ~ with** identificarsi con.

iden·ti·kit [aɪˈdɛntɪkɪt] *n:* **~ (picture)** identikit *m inv.*

iden·tity [aɪˈdɛntɪtɪ] **1** *n* identità *f inv;* **a case of mistaken ~** uno scambio di persona. **2** *cpd:* **~ card** *n* carta d'identità; **~ disc** *n* piastrina; **~ parade** *n* confronto all'americana.

ideo·logi·cal [ˌaɪdɪəˈlɒdʒɪkəl] *adj* ideologico(a).

ideol·ogy [ˌaɪdɪˈɒlədʒɪ] *n* ideologia.

idi·om [ˈɪdɪəm] *n (phrase)* frase *f* idiomatica; *(style of expression)* linguaggio.

idio·mat·ic [ˌɪdɪəˈmætɪk] *adj* idiomatico(a).

idio·syn·cra·sy [ˌɪdɪəˈsɪŋkrəsɪ] *n* originalità *f inv*, peculiarità *f inv.*

idi·ot [ˈɪdɪət] *n* idiota *m/f*, imbecille *m/f;* **you stupid ~** brutto cretino.

idi·ot·ic [ˌɪdɪˈɒtɪk] *adj* stupido(a); *(price)* assurdo(a), folle.

idi·oti·cal·ly [ˌɪdɪˈɒtɪkəlɪ] *adv (stare)* con aria inebetita; *(behave)* stupidamente, come un cretino.

idle [ˈaɪdl] **1** *adj* **(a)** *(lazy: student)* pigro(a), indolente; *(inactive: machine, factory, workers)* inattivo(a); **the ~ rich** i ricchi fannulloni; **in my ~ moments** nei miei momenti liberi; **an ~ life** una vita d'ozio; **to stand ~** *(factory, machine)* rimaner fermo *or* inattivo. **(b)** *(fear, speculation)* infondato(a); *(gossip)* ozioso(a), futile; *(threat)* campato(a) in aria. **2** *vi (engine)* girare al minimo.

♦ **idle away** *vt + adv (time)* sprecare, buttar via.

idle·ness [ˈaɪdlnɪs] *n* pigrizia, ozio.

idly [ˈaɪdlɪ] *adv* pigramente; **he stood ~ by watching the others working** è restato lì senza far niente a guardare gli altri che lavoravano.

idol [ˈaɪdl] *n* idolo.

idol·ize [ˈaɪdəlaɪz] *vt* idolatrare.

idyll [ˈɪdɪl] *n* idillio.

idyl·lic [ɪˈdɪlɪk] *adj* idillico(a), idilliaco(a).

i.e. *abbr (= that is)* cioè.

if [ɪf] **1** *conj* **(a)** se; **~ anyone comes in** se viene *or* venisse qualcuno; **I'll go** ~ **you come with me** ci vado (solo) se vieni anche tu; **I'd be pleased** ~ **you could do it** sarei molto contento se potessi farlo; ~ **necessary** se (è) necessario; ~ **I were you** se fossi in te, io al tuo posto; ~ **you ask me...** se vuoi proprio saperlo.... .

(b) *(whenever)* tutte le volte che, ogni volta che, quando; ~ **we are in Scotland, we always go to see her** quando siamo in Scozia, andiamo sempre a trovarla.

(c) *(although)*: **(even)** ~ anche se; **I am determined to do it (even)** ~ **it takes all week** sono deciso a farlo, dovessi impiegarci una settimana.

(d) *(whether)* se; **I don't know** ~ **he is here** non so se c'è *or* ci sia.

(e) *(in phrases)*: ~ **so** se è così; ~ **not** se no; ~ **only** se solo *or* soltanto; **I would like to see her** ~ **only for a few minutes** vorrei vederla magari *or* anche solo per pochi minuti; ~ **only I could** se soltanto potessi, magari (potessi); **as** ~ come se; **as** ~ **by chance** come per caso; *see* **as, even** *etc.*

2 *n*: **there are a lot of** ~**s and buts** ci sono molti se e ma; **that's** *or* **it's a big** ~ è un grosso punto interrogativo.

ig·loo ['ɪgluː] *n* igloo *m inv*.

ig·nite [ɪg'naɪt] **1** *vt (fire, match)* accendere; *(wood)* dar fuoco a. **2** *vi* accendersi.

ig·ni·tion [ɪg'nɪʃən] **1** *n (Chem)* ignizione *f*; *(Aut)* accensione *f*; **to switch on the** ~ girare la chiavetta dell'accensione. **2** *cpd*: ~ **key** *n* chiave *f* dell'accensione; ~ **switch** *n* interruttore *m* dell'accensione.

ig·no·ble [ɪg'nəʊbl] *adj* ignobile.

ig·no·mini·ous [ɪgnə'mɪnɪəs] *adj* vergognoso(a), ignominioso(a).

ig·no·miny ['ɪgnəmɪnɪ] *n* ignominia.

ig·no·ra·mus [ɪgnə'reɪməs] *n* ignorante *m/f*.

ig·no·rance ['ɪgnərəns] *n*: ~ **(of)** ignoranza (di); **to keep sb in** ~ **of sth** tenere qn all'oscuro di qc; **to show one's** ~ dimostrare la propria ignoranza.

ig·no·rant ['ɪgnərənt] *adj (lacking education)* ignorante; **to be** ~ **of** *(subject)* essere ignorante in; *(events)* essere ignaro(a) di.

ig·nore [ɪg'nɔːʳ] *vt (person, problem)* ignorare; *(remark)* non far caso a; *(advice, letter)* non tener in nessun conto; *(danger)* non curarsi di; *(sb's behaviour)* chiudere un occhio su.

ill [ɪl] **1** *adj* **(a)** *(Med)* ammalato(a), malato(a); **to fall** *or* **be taken** ~ ammalarsi; **to feel** ~ **(with)** star male (per *or* a causa di); **to be in** ~ **health** essere indisposto. **(b)** *(comp* **worse,** *superl* **worst)** *(bad)* cattivo(a); **to be** ~ **at ease** essere a disagio; ~ **will** rancore *m*; ~ **fortune,** ~ **luck** sfortuna; **no** ~ **feelings** nessun rancore; ~ **effects** brutte conseguenze *fpl*; **it's an** ~ **wind that blows nobody any good** *(Proverb)* non tutto il male viene per nuocere. **2** *adv* male; **we can** ~ **afford to lose him/to buy it** non possiamo certo permetterci di perderlo/di comprarlo; **to speak/think** ~ **of sb** parlar/pensar male di qn. **3**: ~**s** *npl (fig)* mali *mpl*, malanni *mpl*.

I'll [aɪl] = **I will, I shall.**

ill-advised [ɪləd'vaɪzd] *adj (plan, remark)* sconsiderato(a), avventato(a); *see also* **advise.**

ill-bred [ɪl'brɛd] *adj* maleducato(a).

ill-considered [ɪlkən'sɪdəd] *adj (plan)* avventato(a).

ill-disposed [ɪldɪs'pəʊzd] *adj*: **to be** ~ **towards sb/sth** essere maldisposto(a) verso qn/qc *or* nei riguardi di qn/qc.

il·legal [ɪ'liːgəl] *adj* illegale.

il·legal·ity [ɪliː'gælɪtɪ] *n* illegalità.

il·leg·ible [ɪ'lɛdʒəbl] *adj* illeggibile, indecifrabile.

il·legiti·mate [ɪlɪ'dʒɪtɪmɪt] *adj* illegittimo(a).

ill-fated [ɪl'feɪtɪd] *adj (person)* sventurato(a); *(event, occurrence)* infausto(a).

ill-favoured [ɪl'feɪvəd] *adj* sgraziato(a), brutto(a).

il·lic·it [ɪ'lɪsɪt] *adj* illecito(a).

ill-informed [ɪlɪn'fɔːmd] *adj (judgement, speech)* pieno(a) di inesattezze; *(person)* male informato(a).

il·lit·er·ate [ɪ'lɪtərɪt] **1** *adj (person)* analfabeta, illetterato(a); *(letter)* sgrammaticato(a). **2** *n* analfabeta *m/f*, illetterato/a.

ill-mannered [ɪl'mænəd] *adj* maleducato(a).

ill·ness ['ɪlnɪs] *n* malattia.

il·logi·cal [ɪ'lɒdʒɪkəl] *adj* illogico(a).

ill-suited [ɪl'suːtɪd] *adj (couple)* mal assortito(a); **he is** ~ **to the job** è inadatto a quel lavoro.

ill-timed [ɪl'taɪmd] *adj* intempestivo(a), inopportuno(a).

ill-treat [ɪl'triːt] *vt* maltrattare.

ill-treatment [ɪl'triːtmənt] *n* maltrattamenti *mpl*.

il·lu·mi·nate [ɪ'luːmɪneɪt] *vt (light up)* illuminare; *(fig: problem, question)* far luce su, chiarire; ~**d sign** insegna luminosa; ~**d manuscript** manoscritto *or* codice *m* miniato.

il·lu·mi·nat·ing [ɪ'luːmɪneɪtɪŋ] *adj* chiarificatore (trice).

il·lu·mi·na·tion [ɪluːmɪ'neɪʃən] *n* illuminazione *f*; ~**s** luminarie *fpl*.

il·lu·sion [ɪ'luːʒən] *n* illusione *f*; **optical** ~ illusione ottica; **to be under an** ~ illudersi, ingannarsi; **to be under the** ~ **that** avere l'impressione che.

il·lu·sive [ɪ'luːsɪv] *adj*, **il·lu·sory** [ɪ'luːsərɪ] *adj* illusorio(a).

il·lus·trate ['ɪləstreɪt] *vt* illustrare.

il·lus·tra·tion [ɪləs'treɪʃən] *n* illustrazione *f*; *(example)* esemplificazione *f*; **by way of** ~ a titolo d'esempio.

il·lus·tra·tive ['ɪləstrətɪv] *adj* illustrativo(a).

il·lus·tra·tor ['ɪləstreɪtəʳ] *n* illustratore/trice.

il·lus·tri·ous [ɪ'lʌstrɪəs] *adj* illustre.

I'm [aɪm] = **I am.**

im·age ['ɪmɪdʒ] *n (gen)* immagine *f*; **to be the very** *or* **the spitting** ~ **of sb** essere il ritratto sputato di qn; **mirror** ~ immagine speculare.

im·age·ry ['ɪmɪdʒərɪ] *n* linguaggio figurato.

im·agi·nable [ɪ'mædʒɪnəbl] *adj* immaginabile, che si possa immaginare.

im·agi·nary [ɪ'mædʒɪnərɪ] *adj* immaginario(a).

im·agi·na·tion [ɪmædʒɪ'neɪʃən] *n* immaginazione *f*; *(inventiveness)* immaginazione, fantasia; **it's all** ~**! sono tutte fantasie!; **it's all in your** ~ è tutto frutto della tua immaginazione; **to have a vivid** ~ avere una fervida fantasia *or* una viva immaginazione; **she lets her** ~ **run away with her** si lascia trasportare dalla fantasia; **use your** ~**! su, un po' di fantasia!

im·agi·na·tive [ɪ'mædʒɪnətɪv] *adj* ricco(a) di fantasia *or* di immaginazione.

im·agi·na·tive·ly [ɪ'mædʒɪnətɪvlɪ] *adv* con molta fantasia *or* immaginazione.

im·ag·ine [ɪ'mædʒɪn] *vt* **(a)** *(visualize)* immaginar(si); **just** ~**! pensa un po'!; **you can** ~ **how I felt** puoi (ben) immaginare *or* immaginarti cosa ho provato; **you are just imagining things** che idee!, è tutto frutto della tua immaginazione. **(b)** *(suppose, think)* pensare, credere; **I never** ~**d that he would be there** non avrei mai immaginato che lui sarebbe stato lì.

im·bal·ance [ɪm'bæləns] *n* squilibrio.

im·becile ['ɪmbəsiːl] *n* idiota, imbecille.

im·bibe [ɪm'baɪb] vt (old: drink) bere; (fig: absorb) assorbire, assimilare.

imi·tate ['ɪmɪteɪt] vt imitare.

imi·ta·tion [,ɪmɪ'teɪʃən] **1** n imitazione f. **2** cpd finto(a); ~ **jewels** npl gioielli mpl falsi.

imi·ta·tive ['ɪmɪtətɪv] adj imitativo(a).

imi·ta·tor ['ɪmɪteɪtəʳ] n imitatore/trice.

im·macu·late [ɪ'mækjʊlɪt] adj (gen) impeccabile; **the I~ Conception** (Rel) l'Immacolata Concezione f.

im·macu·late·ly [ɪ'mækjʊlɪtlɪ] adv in maniera impeccabile, impeccabilmente.

im·ma·terial [,ɪmə'tɪərɪəl] adj irrilevante, insignificante; **it is ~ whether** poco importa se or che + sub.

im·ma·ture [,ɪmə'tjʊəʳ] adj immaturo(a).

im·ma·tu·rity [,ɪmə'tjʊərɪtɪ] n immaturità, mancanza di maturità.

im·meas·ur·able [ɪ'mɛʒərəbl] adj incommensurabile.

im·media·cy [ɪ'miːdɪəsɪ] n immediatezza.

im·medi·ate [ɪ'miːdɪət] adj (decision, answer, reaction) immediato(a); (need, problem) più urgente, immediato(a); (area) che si trova nelle immediate vicinanze; (neighbour) della casa accanto; **in the ~ future** nell'immediato futuro; **to take ~ action** prendere immediati provvedimenti.

im·medi·ate·ly [ɪ'miːdɪətlɪ] **1** adv **(a)** (at once: reply, come, agree) immediatamente, subito; (directly: affect, concern) direttamente; ~ **in front of sb/sth** proprio davanti a qn/qc. **2** conj (non) appena.

im·mense [ɪ'mɛns] adj (distance) smisurato(a); (size) enorme; (fig: difference, enjoyment) immenso(a), enorme.

im·mense·ly [ɪ'mɛnslɪ] adv (differ) enormemente; (difficult, rich) estremamente, straordinariamente; (like, enjoy) tantissimo.

im·merse [ɪ'mɜːs] vt: **to ~ sth in water** immergere qc nell'acqua; ~**d in sth** (fig) immerso in qc; **to ~ o.s. in sth** (fig) tuffarsi or buttarsi a capofitto in qc.

im·mer·sion [ɪ'mɜːʃən] **1** n immersione f. **2** cpd: ~ **heater** n scaldaacqua m inv a immersione.

im·mi·grant ['ɪmɪgrənt] adj, n (newly arrived) immigrante (m/f); (established) immigrato(a) (m/f).

im·mi·gra·tion [,ɪmɪ'greɪʃən] **1** n immigrazione f. **2** cpd: ~ **authorities** npl ufficio stranieri; ~ **laws** npl leggi fpl relative all'immigrazione.

im·mi·nent ['ɪmɪnənt] adj imminente.

im·mo·bile [ɪ'məʊbaɪl] adj immobile.

im·mo·bi·lize [ɪ'məʊbɪlaɪz] vt immobilizzare.

im·mo·der·ate [ɪ'mɒdərɪt] adj (person) smodato(a), sregolato(a); (opinion, reaction, demand) eccessivo(a).

im·mod·est [ɪ'mɒdɪst] adj (indecent) indecente, impudico(a); (boasting) presuntuoso(a).

im·mod·es·ty [ɪ'mɒdɪstɪ] n (see adj) indecenza, impudicizia; presunzione f.

im·mor·al [ɪ'mɒrəl] adj immorale.

im·mo·ral·ity [,ɪmə'rælɪtɪ] n immoralità.

im·mor·tal [ɪ'mɔːtl] adj immortale.

im·mor·tal·ity [,ɪmɔː'tælɪtɪ] n immortalità.

im·mov·able [ɪ'muːvəbl] adj (object) non movibile; (person) irremovibile.

im·mune [ɪ'mjuːn] adj: ~ **(to, from, against)** (naturally) immune (da); (after injection etc) reso(a) immune (a), immunizzato(a) (contro); (fig): ~ **(to)** immune (a).

im·mu·nity [ɪ'mjuːnɪtɪ] n (also fig: of diplomat) immunità.

im·mu·ni·za·tion [,ɪmjʊnaɪ'zeɪʃən] n immunizzazione f.

im·mu·nize ['ɪmjʊnaɪz] vt immunizzare.

imp [ɪmp] n (small devil) folletto, diavoletto; (child) diavoletto.

im·pact ['ɪmpækt] n (force of collision) impatto, urto; (fig: effect) effetto; **on** ~ nell'urto, nell'impatto; **the book made a great ~ on me/the public** il libro ha prodotto una forte impressione su di me/sul pubblico.

im·pair [ɪm'pɛəʳ] vt (health) danneggiare; (sight, hearing) deteriorare, indebolire; (visibility) ridurre; (relations) deteriorare, danneggiare.

im·part [ɪm'pɑːt] vt **(a)** (make known) comunicare. **(b)** (bestow) impartire.

im·par·tial [ɪm'pɑːʃəl] adj imparziale, equo(a).

im·par·ti·al·ity [ɪm,pɑːʃɪ'ælɪtɪ] n imparzialità.

im·pass·able [ɪm'pɑːsəbl] adj (road) intransitabile; (mountain pass) impraticabile; (barrier) invalicabile; (river) non attraversabile.

im·pas·sioned [ɪm'pæʃnd] adj appassionato(a).

im·pas·sive [ɪm'pæsɪv] adj impassibile.

im·pa·tience [ɪm'peɪʃəns] n: ~**(with sb/to do sth)** impazienza (con or nei confronti di qn/di fare qc).

im·pa·tient [ɪm'peɪʃənt] adj (eager): ~ **(to do sth)** impaziente (di fare qc); (irascible) insofferente; **to get ~ (with sb/over sth)** perdere la pazienza (con qn/per qc).

im·pa·tient·ly [ɪm'peɪʃəntlɪ] adv con impazienza.

im·peach [ɪm'piːtʃ] vt **(a)** (doubt: character, motive) mettere in dubbio; **that accusation ~ed his character** quell'accusa metteva in discussione la sua figura. **(b)** (try: public official etc) mettere sotto accusa.

im·pec·cable [ɪm'pɛkəbl] adj impeccabile.

im·pede [ɪm'piːd] vt ostacolare.

im·pedi·ment [ɪm'ɛdɪmənt] n **(a)** (Law) impedimento. **(b)** (Med: also: speech ~) difetto di pronuncia.

im·pel [ɪm'pɛl] vt (force): **to ~ sb (to do sth)** costringere or obbligare qn (a fare qc); (drive) spingere.

im·pend·ing [ɪm'pɛndɪŋ] adj (birth, storm, retirement) imminente; (doom, disaster) incombente.

im·pen·etrable [ɪm'pɛnɪtrəbl] adj (jungle, fortress) impenetrabile; (fig) incomprensibile.

im·pera·tive [ɪm'pɛrətɪv] **1** adj (essential) essenziale; (authoritative: manner) imperioso(a); (command) tassativo(a); (Gram) imperativo(a); **it is ~ that he comes** è indispensabile che lui venga. **2** n (Gram) imperativo; **in the ~** all'imperativo, nel modo imperativo.

im·per·cep·tible [,ɪmpə'sɛptəbl] adj impercettibile.

im·per·fect [ɪm'pɜːfɪkt] **1** adj **(a)** (car, machine, product) difettoso(a); (vision, hearing) difettoso(a), imperfetto(a). **(b)** (Gram) imperfetto(a). **2** n (Gram) imperfetto; **in the ~** all'imperfetto.

im·per·fec·tion [,ɪmpə'fɛkʃən] n imperfezione f; (flaw) difetto.

im·perial [ɪm'pɪərɪəl] adj (gen) imperiale; (imperious) imperioso(a); (Brit: weights, measures) legale.

im·peri·al·ism [ɪm'pɪərɪəlɪzəm] n imperialismo.

im·peri·ous [ɪm'pɪərɪəs] adj imperioso(a).

im·per·son·al [ɪm'pɜːsnl] adj **(a)** (manner, treatment etc) impersonale, distaccato(a). **(b)** (Gram) impersonale.

im·per·son·al·ly [ɪm'pɜːsnəlɪ] adv impersonalmente.

im·per·son·ate [ɪm'pɜːsəneɪt] vt fingersi; (Theatre) imitare.

im·per·sona·tion [ɪm‚pɜːsə'neɪʃən] n (gen, Theatre) imitazione f.

im·per·sona·tor [ɪm'pɜːsəneɪtə'] n (gen, Theatre) imitatore/trice.

im·per·ti·nence [ɪm'pɜːtɪnəns] n impertinenza.

im·per·ti·nent [ɪm'pɜːtɪnənt] adj: ~ (to) impertinente (con or nei confronti di).

im·per·turb·able [‚ɪmpə'tɜːbəbl] adj imperturbabile.

im·per·vi·ous [ɪm'pɜːvɪəs] adj: ~ (to) impermeabile (a); (fig) indifferente (a).

im·petu·os·ity [ɪm‚petʊ'ɒsɪtɪ] n impetuosità.

im·petu·ous [ɪm'petjʊəs] adj impetuoso(a).

im·petus ['ɪmpɪtəs] n (force) spinta; (fig) impulso.

im·pinge [ɪm'pɪndʒ] vi: to ~ on (person) urtare; (sb's life) influire su; (rights) ledere.

imp·ish ['ɪmpɪʃ] adj malizioso(a), birichino(a).

im·plac·able [ɪm'plækəbl] adj implacabile.

im·plant [ɪm'plɑːnt] vt (Med) innestare; (fig: idea, principle) inculcare.

im·plau·sible [ɪm'plɔːzəbl] adj non plausibile.

im·ple·ment ['ɪmplɪmənt] **1** n utensile m. **2** ['ɪmplɪment] vt (decision, plan, idea) attuare; (law) applicare.

im·pli·cate ['ɪmplɪkeɪt] vt: to ~ sb in sth implicare qn in qc.

im·pli·ca·tion [‚ɪmplɪ'keɪʃən] n (in crime etc; hint) implicazione f; the ~ of your remark is that... la tua osservazione implica che...; by ~ implicitamente.

im·plic·it [ɪm'plɪsɪt] adj (a) (implied: threat, agreement) implicito(a). (b) (unquestioning: faith, belief) assoluto(a).

im·plore [ɪm'plɔː'] vt: to ~ sb (to do sth) implorare qn (di fare qc), supplicare qn (di fare qc); to ~ sb's forgiveness implorare il perdono di qn.

im·plor·ing [ɪm'plɔːrɪŋ] adj implorante, supplichevole.

im·plor·ing·ly [ɪm'plɔːrɪŋlɪ] adv in modo implorante.

im·ply [ɪm'plaɪ] vt (hint, suggest) insinuare; (indicate) implicare, significare; it implies a lot of work implica or significa una grande quantità di lavoro.

im·po·lite [‚ɪmpə'laɪt] adj (person) scortese, sgarbato(a); (remark) maleducato(a).

im·po·lite·ly [‚ɪmpə'laɪtlɪ] adv in modo scortese, maleducatamente.

im·po·lite·ness [‚ɪmpə'laɪtnɪs] n (of person) scortesia; (of remark) villania.

im·pon·der·able [ɪm'pɒndərəbl] adj imponderabile.

im·port ['ɪmpɔːt] **1** n (Comm: article) articolo importato; (: importation) importazione f. **2** [ɪm'pɔːt] vt importare. **3** cpd (duty, licence etc) d'importazione.

im·por·tance [ɪm'pɔːtəns] n importanza; to attach great ~ to sth dare or attribuire molta importanza a qc; to be of great/little ~ importare molto/poco, essere molto/poco importante.

im·por·tant [ɪm'pɔːtənt] adj important; it's not ~ non ha importanza; it is ~ that è importante che + sub; to try to look ~ (pej) darsi arie d'importanza.

im·por·tant·ly [ɪm'pɔːtəntlɪ] adv (pej) con (un'aria d')importanza; but, more ~, ... ma, quel che più conta or importa, ...

im·port·er [ɪm'pɔːtə'] n importatore/trice.

im·pose [ɪm'pəʊz] vt (conditions, fine, tax): to ~ (on sb/sth) imporre (a qn/su qc).

♦ **impose (up)on** vi + prep approfittare di, abusare di.

im·pos·ing [ɪm'pəʊzɪŋ] adj imponente.

im·po·si·tion [‚ɪmpə'zɪʃən] n (of tax, fine etc) imposizione f; it's a bit of an ~ è proprio pretendere un po' tanto.

im·pos·sibil·ity [ɪm‚pɒsə'bɪlɪtɪ] n: ~ (of sth/of doing sth) impossibilità (di qc/di fare qc).

im·pos·sible [ɪm'pɒsəbl] adj impossibile; it is ~ for me to leave now mi è impossibile venir via adesso; it is ~/not ~ for her to do that le è impossibile/non le è impossibile farlo; to make it ~ for sb to do sth mettere qn nell'impossibilità di fare qc; to do the ~ fare l'impossibile.

im·pos·sibly [ɪm'pɒsəblɪ] adv (badly: behave, act) in un modo impossibile; (extremely: late, early) incredibilmente, spaventosamente; (: difficult) eccessivamente.

im·pos·tor [ɪm'pɒstə'] n impostore/a.

im·po·tence ['ɪmpətəns] n impotenza.

im·po·tent ['ɪmpətənt] adj impotente.

im·pound [ɪm'paʊnd] vt (gen) sequestrare, confiscare; (stray animal) rinchiudere.

im·pov·er·ished [ɪm'pɒvərɪʃt] adj impoverito(a).

im·prac·ti·cable [ɪm'præktɪkəbl] adj inattuabile.

im·prac·ti·cal [ɪm'præktɪkəl] adj (person) privo(a) di senso pratico; (plan) poco realistico(a), poco pratico(a).

im·pre·cise [‚ɪmprɪ'saɪs] adj impreciso(a).

im·pre·ci·sion [‚ɪmprɪ'sɪʒən] n imprecisione f.

im·preg·nable [ɪm'pregnəbl] adj (Mil) inespugnabile; (fig: position) inattaccabile.

im·preg·nate ['ɪmpregneɪt] vt (fertilize) fecondare; (saturate): to ~ (with) impregnare (di).

im·pre·sa·rio [‚ɪmpre'sɑːrɪəʊ] n impresario.

im·press [ɪm'pres] vt (a) (make good impression on) fare una buon'impressione a o su, colpire (favorevolmente); how did she ~ you? che impressione ti ha dato or fatto?; he ~ed me quite favourably mi ha fatto or dato un'ottima impressione. (b) (mark, stamp) imprimere; to ~ sth on sb (fig) far comprendere qc a qn.

im·pres·sion [ɪm'preʃən] n (a) (most senses) impressione f; to be under or have the ~ that avere l'impressione che; he gives the ~ of knowing a lot dà l'impressione di saperne molto; to make a good/bad ~ on sb fare una buona/cattiva impressione a or su qn; my words made no ~ on him le mie parole non hanno avuto nessun effetto su di lui. (b) (imitation) imitazione f; to do ~s fare delle imitazioni.

im·pres·sion·able [ɪm'preʃnəbl] adj (person) impressionabile; to be at an ~ age essere in un'età in cui ci si impressiona facilmente.

im·pres·sion·ism [ɪm'preʃənɪzəm] n impressionismo.

im·pres·sion·ist [ɪm'preʃənɪst] adj, n impressionista (m/f).

im·pres·sive [ɪm'presɪv] adj (person, achievement) notevole; (occasion) spettacolare; (building) imponente, che fa colpo.

im·print ['ɪmprɪnt] **1** n (Publishing) sigla editoriale. **2** [ɪm'prɪnt] vt imprimere.

im·pris·on [ɪm'prɪzn] vt imprigionare, incarcerare; after being ~ed for 3 weeks dopo 3 settimane di or in carcere.

im·pris·on·ment [ɪm'prɪznmənt] n reclusione f; during his ~ mentre era in carcere; life ~ l'ergastolo.

im·prob·abil·ity [ɪm‚prɒbə'bɪlɪtɪ] n (see adj) improbabilità; inverosimiglianza.

im·prob·able [ɪm'prɒbəbl] adj (event) improbabile, poco probabile; (excuse, story) inverosimile.

im·promp·tu [ɪm'prɒmptjuː] **1** adj improvvisato(a), estemporaneo(a). **2** adv improvvisando, così su due piedi.

im·prop·er [ɪm'prɒpəʳ] *adj (unseemly, indecent)* sconveniente; *(wrong)* improprio(a).

im·pro·pri·ety [ˌɪmprə'praɪətɪ] *n (unseemliness)* scorrettezza; *(indecency)* indecenza.

im·prove [ɪm'pruːv] **1** *vt (gen)* migliorare; *(property, land)* apportare dei miglioramenti a; *(production, yield, salary)* aumentare, accrescere; **to ~ one's Italian** perfezionare il proprio italiano; **to ~ one's chances of success** aumentare le proprie probabilità di successo; **to ~ one's mind** coltivare la propria mente. **2** *vi (gen)* migliorare; *(person: in skill etc)* fare dei progressi; **to ~ in sth** migliorare *or* fare dei progressi in qc; **to ~ with age/use** migliorare con gli anni/con l'uso.

♦ **improve (up)on** *vi + prep (offer)* aumentare; *(work)* ottenere dei miglioramenti *or* dei risultati migliori rispetto a; *(method, quality)* apportare dei miglioramenti a, migliorare; **I can't ~ (up)on my offer to you** non posso farti un'offerta migliore.

im·prove·ment [ɪm'pruːvmənt] *n:* ~ **(in)** *(gen)* miglioramento (in); *(in production, salary)* aumento (di *or* in), miglioramento (di *or* in); **it's an ~ on the old one** è meglio di quello vecchio; **there is room for ~** si può migliorare *or* far meglio; **to make ~s to** migliorare, apportare dei miglioramenti a; *(property)* apportare dei miglioramenti a; *(method)* migliorare, perfezionare.

im·prov·ing [ɪm'pruːvɪŋ] *adj (book etc)* edificante.

im·provi·sa·tion [ˌɪmprəvaɪ'zeɪʃən] *n* improvvisazione *f*.

im·pro·vise ['ɪmprəvaɪz] *vt, vi* improvvisare.

im·pru·dent [ɪm'pruːdənt] *adj* imprudente.

im·pu·dence ['ɪmpjʊdəns] *n* impudenza.

im·pu·dent ['ɪmpjʊdənt] *adj* impertinente, impudente.

im·pulse ['ɪmpʌls] **1** *n* impulso; **to act on ~** agire d'impulso *or* impulsivamente. **2** *cpd:* ~ **buying** *n* tendenza ad acquistare sull'impulso del momento *(cose che non sarebbero necessarie)*.

im·pul·sive [ɪm'pʌlsɪv] *adj* impulsivo(a).

im·pu·nity [ɪm'pjuːnɪtɪ] *n:* **with ~** impunemente.

im·pure [ɪm'pjʊəʳ] *adj (Chem, morally)* impuro(a); *(air)* inquinato(a).

im·pu·rity [ɪm'pjʊərɪtɪ] *n* impurità *f inv*.

in [ɪn] **1** *prep* **(a)** *(place, position)* in; **~ the house/ garden** in casa/giardino; **~ my hand** in mano; **~ the town/country** in città/campagna; **~ school** a scuola; **~ the school** nella scuola; **~ here/there** qui/lì dentro.

(b) *(with place names: of town)* a; *(: of region, country)* in; **~ London** a Londra; **~ England** in Inghilterra; **~ the United States** negli Stati Uniti; **~ Yorkshire** nello Yorkshire; **~ Sicily** in Sicilia.

(c) *(time: during)* in; **~ 1986** nel 1986; **~ May** in maggio, nel mese di maggio; **~ the eighties** negli anni ottanta; **~ the 20th century** nel ventesimo secolo; **~ spring/autumn** in primavera/ autunno; **~ summer/winter** in estate/inverno, d'estate/d'inverno; **~ the morning** di *or* alla mattina, la mattina, nella mattinata; **~ the mornings** di *or* alla mattina, la mattina; **~ the daytime** di *or* durante il giorno, durante la giornata; **at 4 o'clock ~ the afternoon** alle 4 del pomeriggio; **~ those days** a quei tempi, allora; **~ the past** nel *or* in passato; **she has not been here ~ years** non è stata qui da molti anni, sono anni che non viene qui.

(d) *(time: in the space of)* in; **I did it ~ 3 hours/days** l'ho fatto in 3 ore/giorni; **she will**

return the money ~ a month restituirà i soldi tra un mese.

(e) *(manner etc):* **~ a loud/soft voice** a voce alta/bassa; **~ a whisper** sussurrando; **~ Italian/ English** in italiano/inglese; **~ ink** in inchiostro; **~ pencil** a matita; **~ writing** per iscritto; **~ watercolour** ad acquerello; **~ person** di persona; **~ large/small quantities** in grosse/piccole quantità; **to pay ~ dollars** pagare in dollari; **~ alphabetical order** in ordine alfabetico; **~ part** in parte; **painted ~ red** dipinto di rosso; **dressed ~ green/a skirt/trousers** vestito di verde/con una gonna/con i calzoni; **the man ~ the hat** l'uomo con il cappello; **a statue carved ~ wood** una statua intagliata nel legno.

(f) *(circumstance):* **~ the sun** al sole; **~ the rain** sotto la pioggia; **~ the shade** all'ombra; **~ (the) daylight** alla *or* con la luce del giorno; **~ (the) dark(ness)** al buio, nell'oscurità; **~ the moonlight** al chiaro di luna; **~ all weathers** con qualsiasi tempo, qualsiasi tempo faccia; **to be 10 metres ~ height/length** *etc* essere alto/lungo *etc* 10 metri; **a change ~ policy** un cambiamento di politica; **a rise ~ prices** un aumento dei prezzi.

(g) *(mood, state):* **~ tears** in lacrime; **~ anger** per la rabbia, in collera; **to be ~ a rage** essere su tutte le furie; **lame ~ the left leg** zoppo dalla gamba sinistra; **~ despair** disperato; **~ good condition** *or* **repair** in buono stato, in buone condizioni; **to live ~ luxury** vivere nel lusso; **~ private** in privato; **~ secret** in segreto.

(h) *(ratio, number):* **one person/car ~ ten** una persona/macchina su dieci; **20 pence ~ the pound** 20 pence per sterlina; **once ~ a hundred years** una volta ogni cento anni; **~ twos** a due a due.

(i) *(people, works)* in; **~ (the works of) Shakespeare** in Shakespeare; **this is common ~ children/cats** questo è normale nei *or* per i bambini/gatti; **she has it ~ her to succeed** ha in sé la capacità di riuscire; **they have a good leader ~ him** hanno in lui un ottimo capo.

(j) *(in profession etc):* **to be ~ teaching** fare l'insegnante, insegnare; **to be ~ publishing** essere nell'editoria; **to be ~ the motor trade** lavorare nel settore automobilistico; **to be ~ the army** essere nell'esercito.

(k) *(after superlative)* di; **the biggest/smallest ~ Europe** il più grande/più piccolo d'Europa.

(l) *(with prp):* **~ saying this** dicendo questo, nel dir questo.

(m): **~ that** dal momento che, visto che; **~ all** in tutto.

2 *adv:* **to be ~** *(person)* esserci; *(train, ship, plane)* essere arrivato(a); *(crops, harvest)* essere raccolto(a); *(in season)* essere di stagione; *(in fashion)* essere di moda; *(in power)* essere al potere; **we're ~ for a snow storm** (ci) si prepara una tormenta; **he is ~ for trouble** lo aspettano dei guai; **he's ~ for it** *(fam)* avrà quello che si merita; **to have it ~ for sb** avercela contro qn; **to be ~ on a plan/secret** essere al corrente *or* a conoscenza di un progetto/segreto; **to ask sb ~** invitare qn a entrare; **day ~, day out** un giorno dopo l'altro; **to be ~ and out of work** non durare mai molto in un impiego; **to be ~ and out of hospital/prison** essere sempre dentro e fuori dall'ospedale/di prigione; **my luck is ~** la fortuna è dalla mia (parte).

3 *n:* **the ~s and outs of the problem** tutti i particolari del problema.

in., ins *abbr of* **inch, inches.**

in·abil·ity [ˌɪnə'bɪlɪtɪ] *n (physical, mental)* incapacità, inabilità; ~ **to do sth** incapacità di fare qc; ~ **to pay** impossibilità di pagare.

in·ac·ces·sibil·ity ['ɪnæk,sɛsə'bɪlɪtɪ] *n* inaccessibilità.

in·ac·ces·sible [,ɪnæk'sɛsəbl] *adj*: ~ **(to)** inaccessibile (a), irraggiungibile (per *or* da).

in·ac·cu·ra·cy [ɪn'ækjʊrəsɪ] *n (see adj)* inaccuratezza; inesattezza; imprecisione *f; (usu pl: mistake)* errore *m*, sbaglio.

in·ac·cu·rate [ɪn'ækjʊrɪt] *adj (statement, report, story)* inaccurato(a); *(figures)* inesatto(a); *(translation)* impreciso(a).

in·ac·tion [ɪn'ækʃən] *n* inazione *f.*

in·ac·tive [ɪn'æktɪv] *adj* inattivo(a).

in·ac·tiv·ity [,ɪnæk'tɪvɪtɪ] *n* inattività.

in·ad·equate [ɪn'ædɪkwɪt] *adj (insufficient)* inadeguato(a), insufficiente; *(person)* inadeguato(a), inadatto(a); **he felt quite** ~ non si sentiva assolutamente all'altezza.

in·ad·mis·si·ble [,ɪnəd'mɪsəbl] *adj* inammissibile.

in·ad·vert·ent [,ɪnəd'vɜːtənt] *adj* involontario(a).

in·ad·vert·ent·ly [,ɪnəd'vɜːtəntlɪ] *adv* inavvertitamente, senza volerlo.

in·ad·vis·able [,ɪnəd'vaɪzəbl] *adj* sconsigliabile.

in·ane [ɪ'neɪn] *adj (remark)* sciocco(a), stupido(a).

in·ani·mate [ɪn'ænɪmɪt] *adj* inanimato(a).

in·an·ity [ɪ'nænɪtɪ] *n* stupidità *f inv.*

in·ap·pli·cable [ɪn'æplɪkəbl] *adj* inapplicabile.

in·ap·pro·pri·ate [,ɪnə'prəʊprɪɪt] *adj (action, punishment, treatment)* inadeguato(a), non appropriato(a); *(word, phrase)* non appropriato(a), inadatto(a); *(behaviour)* fuori luogo, sconveniente.

in·ar·ticu·late [,ɪnɑː'tɪkjʊlɪt] *adj (person)* che non sa esprimersi, che si esprime male; *(speech)* inarticolato(a), confuso(a).

in·at·ten·tion [,ɪnə'tɛnʃən] *n*: ~ **(to)** mancanza di attenzione (per *or* nei confronti di), disattenzione *f* (per *or* nei confronti di).

in·at·ten·tive [,ɪnə'tɛntɪv] *adj* disattento(a), distratto(a).

in·audible [ɪn'ɔːdəbl] *adj* che non si riesce a sentire.

in·augu·ral [ɪ'nɔːgjʊrəl] *adj* inaugurale.

in·augu·rate [ɪ'nɔːgjʊreɪt] *vt (president, official)* insediare; *(start: new age etc)* inaugurare.

in·aus·pi·cious [,ɪnɔːs'pɪʃəs] *adj* poco propizio(a).

in·between [ɪnbɪ'twiːn] *adj* intermedio(a).

in·born ['ɪnbɔːn] *adj* innato(a).

in·bred ['ɪnbrɛd] *adj (tendency)* congenito(a); **an** ~ **family** una famiglia in cui vi è un alto indice di incroci fra consanguinei.

Inc. *abbr of* **incorporated.**

in·cal·cu·lable [ɪn'kælkjʊləbl] *adj* incalcolabile.

in·can·ta·tion [,ɪnkæn'teɪʃən] *n* incantesimo.

in·ca·pable [ɪn'keɪpəbl] *adj*: ~ **(of doing sth)** incapace (di fare qc); **a question** ~ **of solution** un problema che non può essere risolto *or* che non ha una soluzione.

in·ca·paci·tate [,ɪnkə'pæsɪteɪt] *vt (person)* rendere inabile; **physically** ~**d** menomato fisicamente.

in·ca·pac·ity [,ɪnkə'pæsɪtɪ] *n* incapacità.

in·car·cer·ate [ɪn'kɑːsəreɪt] *vt* imprigionare.

in·car·nate [ɪn'kɑːnɪt] *adj (Rel)* incarnato(a); **the devil** ~ il diavolo personificato *or* in persona.

in·car·na·tion [,ɪnkɑː'neɪʃən] *n (Rel)* incarnazione *f.*

in·cen·di·ary [ɪn'sɛndɪərɪ] **1** *adj* incendiario(a). **2** *n (bomb)* bomba incendiaria.

in·cense ['ɪnsɛns] **1** *n* incenso. **2** [ɪn'sɛns] *vt* fare infuriare.

in·censed [ɪn'sɛnst] *adj* furente, furibondo(a).

in·cen·tive [ɪn'sɛntɪv] **1** *n* incentivo. **2** *cpd*: ~

bonus *n* premio d'incentivazione.

in·cep·tion [ɪn'sɛpʃən] *n* inizio, principio.

in·ces·sant [ɪn'sɛsnt] *adj* incessante.

in·cest ['ɪnsɛst] *n* incesto.

in·ces·tu·ous [ɪn'sɛstjʊəs] *adj* incestuoso(a).

inch [ɪntʃ] **1** *n* pollice *m (= cm 2,54);* **a few** ~**es** ≈ qualche centimetro; **the car missed me by** ~**es** c'è mancato un pelo che la macchina mi investisse; **to lose a few** ~**es** *(fam)* perdere un po' di ciccia; ~ **by** ~ a poco a poco; **every** ~ **of it was used** è stato utilizzato tutto fino all'ultimo millimetro *or* centimetro; **he's every** ~ **a soldier** è un soldato dalla testa ai piedi; **to be within an** ~ **of death/disaster** essere a un passo dalla morte/dalla rovina; **he didn't give** *or* **budge an** ~ *(fig)* non ha ceduto di un millimetro.

♦ **inch forward** *vi* + *adv* avanzare pian piano.

♦ **inch up** *vi* + *adv* salire a poco a poco.

in·ci·dence ['ɪnsɪdəns] *n (extent: of disease, crime)* incidenza; **the angle of** ~ *(Phys)* l'angolo d'incidenza.

in·ci·dent ['ɪnsɪdənt] *n (gen)* caso, evento, avvenimento; *(diplomatic, military etc)* incidente *m; (in book)* episodio; *(in play)* scena; **without** ~ senza incidenti (di rilievo).

in·ci·den·tal [,ɪnsɪ'dɛntl] **1** *adj (secondary)* di secondaria importanza, di secondo piano; ~ **expenses** spese *fpl* accessorie; ~ **music** sottofondo (musicale), musica di sottofondo. **2:** ~**s** *npl* spese *fpl* accessorie.

in·ci·den·tal·ly [,ɪnsɪ'dɛntəlɪ] *adv (by the way)* fra parentesi, a proposito.

in·cin·er·ate [ɪn'sɪnəreɪt] *vt* incenerire.

in·cin·era·tor [ɪn'sɪnəreɪtə'] *n* inceneritore *m.*

in·cipi·ent [ɪn'sɪpɪənt] *adj (disease)* incipiente; *(revolt)* che è agli inizi.

in·ci·sion [ɪn'sɪʒən] *n* incisione *f.*

in·ci·sive [ɪn'saɪsɪv] *adj (mind, remark)* acuto(a); *(criticism)* tagliente, incisivo(a).

in·ci·sor [ɪn'saɪzə'] *n* incisivo.

in·cite [ɪn'saɪt] *vt*: **to** ~ **sb (to sth/to do sth)** incitare qn a qc/a fare qc; istigare qn (a qc/a fare qc).

in·cite·ment [ɪn'saɪtmənt] *n* incitamento, istigazione *f.*

in·ci·vil·ity [,ɪnsɪ'vɪlɪtɪ] *n* inciviltà.

in·clem·ent [ɪn'klɛmənt] *adj* inclemente.

in·cli·na·tion [,ɪnklɪ'neɪʃən] *n* **(a)** *(wish)* tendenza, inclinazione *f;* **he felt no** ~ **to join in the fun** non aveva nessuna voglia di unirsi alla gazzarra; **her** ~ **was to ignore him** era incline ad ignorarlo, avrebbe voluto ignorarlo; **against my** ~ controvoglia; **to follow one's** ~ seguire le proprie tendenze. **(b)** *(slope)* pendio, china. **(c)** *(bow)* cenno.

in·cline ['ɪnklaɪn] **1** *n* pendenza, pendio. **2** [ɪn'klaɪn] *vt* **(a)** *(bend: head, body)* chinare, piegare, inclinare. **(b)** *(tend to):* **to be** ~**d to do sth** essere incline a fare qc; *(out of habit)* tendere a fare qc; *(from preference)* essere propenso(a) a fare qc; **it is** ~**d to break** ha la tendenza a rompersi; **if you feel so** ~**d** se lo desideri, se ne hai voglia. **3** [ɪn'klaɪn] *vi* **(a)** *(slope)* declinare. **(b)** *(tend to):* **to** ~ **to(wards)** tendere a; **I** ~ **to the belief/opinion that...** sono propenso *or* tendo a credere che.... .

in·clude [ɪn'kluːd] *vt* comprendere, includere; **your name is not** ~**d** in the list il tuo nome non è compreso nella lista; **he sold everything, books** ~**d** ha venduto tutto, compresi i libri; **the tip is/is not** ~**d** la mancia è compresa/esclusa.

in·clud·ing [ɪn'kluːdɪŋ] *prep* compreso(a), incluso(a); ~ **tip** mancia compresa, compresa la mancia; **seven books** ~ **this one** sette libri con *or*

in·clu·sive [ɪn'kluːsɪv] **1** *adj* (*sum, price*) tutto compreso *inv*; ~ **of** incluso(a); **$50,** ~ **of all surcharges** 50 dollari, incluse tutte le soprattasse. **2** *adv*: **from the 10th to the 15th** ~ dal 10 al 15 incluso.

in·cog·ni·to [ɪn'kɒgnɪtəʊ] *adv* (*travel*) in incognito; **to remain** ~ mantenere l'incognito.

in·co·her·ent [ˌɪnkəʊ'hɪərənt] *adj* (*person*) incoerente; **he was** ~ **with rage** sragionava dalla rabbia.

in·come ['ɪnkʌm] **1** *n* (*gen*) reddito; (*from receipts*) incasso; **gross/net** ~ reddito lordo/netto; **private** ~ rendita; **to live within/beyond one's** ~ vivere secondo i propri mezzi/al di sopra dei propri mezzi. **2** *cpd*: ~**s policy** *n* politica dei redditi; ~ **tax** *n* imposta sul reddito; ~ **tax return** *n* dichiarazione *f* dei redditi.

in·com·ing ['ɪn,kʌmɪŋ] *adj* (*passengers*) in arrivo; (*tide*) montante; (*government, tenant*) subentrante.

in·com·mu·ni·ca·do [,ɪn,kəmjʊnɪ'kɑːdəʊ] *adj*: **to hold sb** ~ tenere qn in segregazione.

in·com·pa·rable [ɪn'kɒmpərəbl] *adj* incomparabile.

in·com·pat·ible [,ɪnkəm'pætəbl] *adj* incompatibile.

in·com·pe·tence [ɪn'kɒmpɪtəns] *n* incompetenza, incapacità.

in·com·pe·tent [ɪn'kɒmpɪtənt] *adj* (*person*): ~ **(at)** incompetente (in fatto di), incapace (di); (*work*) da incompetenti.

in·com·plete [,ɪnkəm'pliːt] *adj* (*partial*) incompleto(a); (*unfinished: work*) non finito(a); (: *book, painting*) incompiuto(a).

in·com·pre·hen·sible [ɪn,kɒmprɪ'hɛnsəbl] *adj* incomprensibile.

in·con·ceiv·able [,ɪnkən'siːvəbl] *adj* inimmaginabile.

in·con·clu·sive [,ɪnkən'kluːsɪv] *adj* (*not decisive*) non risolutivo(a), inconcludente; (*not convincing*) inconcludente.

in·con·gru·ous [ɪn'kɒŋgrʊəs] *adj* (*appearance, behaviour*) stonato(a), assurdo(a), incongruo(a).

in·con·se·quen·tial [ɪn,kɒnsɪ'kwɛnʃəl] *adj* (*conversation*) senza importanza.

in·con·sid·er·able [,ɪnkən'sɪdərəbl] *adj* trascurabile, irrilevante, da poco.

in·con·sid·er·ate [,ɪnkən'sɪdərɪt] *adj* (*person*) privo(a) di riguardo; (*reply, behaviour*) sconsiderato(a), avventato(a), inconsiderato(a); **you were very** ~ **to her** le hai mancato di riguardo, non l'hai trattata con il riguardo che si merita.

in·con·sist·en·cy [,ɪnkən'sɪstənsɪ] *n* **(a)** (*of actions etc*) incongruenza; (*of work*) irregolarità. **(b)** (*of statement etc*) contraddizione *f*.

in·con·sist·ent [,ɪnkən'sɪstənt] *adj* (*contradictory: action*) contraddittorio(a); (*uneven: work*) irregolare, ad alti e bassi, non costante; **his actions were** ~ **with his principles** le sue azioni non erano coerenti con i suoi principi; **that is** ~ **with what you told me earlier** questo è in contraddizione con quanto mi avevi riferito prima.

in·con·sol·able [,ɪnkən'səʊləbl] *adj* inconsolabile.

in·con·spic·u·ous [,ɪnkən'spɪkjʊəs] *adj* (*place*) che non dà nell'occhio, poco in vista; (*colour*) poco appariscente; (*person*) dimesso(a); **to make o.s.** ~ cercare di passare inosservato(a).

in·con·stant [ɪn'kɒnstənt] *adj* incostante, volubile.

in·con·ti·nence [ɪn'kɒntɪnəns] *n* incontinenza.

in·con·ti·nent [ɪn'kɒntɪnənt] *adj* incontinente.

in·con·tro·vert·ible [ɪn,kɒntrə'vɜːtəbl] *adj* incontrovertibile.

in·con·ven·ience [,ɪnkən'viːnɪəns] **1** *n* (*see adj*) scomodità *f inv*; scarsa funzionalità; inopportunità; **not having a car was a great** ~ non aver la macchina era una gran scomodità *or* seccatura; **to put sb to great** ~ creare degli inconvenienti a qn. **2** *vt* recare disturbo *or* incomodo a, incomodare; **don't** ~ **yourself** non si disturbi.

in·con·ven·ient [,ɪnkən'viːnɪənt] *adj* (*time, appointment, location*) scomodo(a); (*house, design*) poco funzionale; (*arrival*) inopportuno(a); **that time is very** ~ **for me** quell'ora mi è molto scomoda, non è un'ora adatta per me.

in·con·vert·ible [,ɪnkən'vɜːtəbl] *adj* inconvertibile.

in·cor·po·rate [ɪn'kɔːpəreɪt] *vt* (*include*) includere, comprendere; (*integrate*) incorporare.

in·cor·po·rat·ed [ɪn'kɔːpəreɪtɪd] *adj* (*Am Comm*): ~ **company** società registrata.

in·cor·rect [,ɪnkə'rɛkt] *adj* (*statement, fact*) inesatto(a); (*conclusion*) errato(a); (*behaviour*) scorretto(a), sconveniente; (*dress*) sconveniente; **that is** ~ questo è inesatto.

in·cor·ri·gible [ɪn'kɒrɪdʒəbl] *adj* incorreggibile.

in·crease [ɪn'kriːs] **1** *vi* aumentare; (*population, demand, supply, sales*) aumentare, crescere; (*prices*) aumentare, salire; (*salaries*) aumentare, venire aumentato(a); (*joy*) farsi più intenso(a); (*rain, wind*) intensificarsi, crescere; **to** ~ **in number/size** crescere di numero/di dimensioni; **to** ~ **in volume/weight** aumentare di volume/di peso; **to** ~ **in value** aumentare di valore, acquistare valore; **to** ~ **by 100** aumentare di 100; **the stain is increasing in size** la macchia si sta allargando. **2** *vt* (*see vi*) aumentare; accrescere; intensificare; **to** ~ **speed** aumentare la velocità, accelerare; **to** ~ **one's efforts** aumentare or intensificare i propri sforzi. **3** ['ɪnkriːs] *n* (*see vi*) aumento; accrescimento; intensificazione *f*; **an** ~ **in size/volume** un aumento delle dimensioni/ di volume; **an** ~ **of £5/10%** un aumento di 5 sterline/del 10%; **to be on the** ~ essere in aumento; (*prices*) essere in aumento *or* in rialzo; (*sales, trade*) essere in aumento *or* in fase di espansione.

in·creas·ing [ɪn'kriːsɪŋ] *adj* crescente, in aumento.

in·creas·ing·ly [ɪn'kriːsɪŋlɪ] *adv* sempre più.

in·cred·ible [ɪn'krɛdəbl] *adj* incredibile.

in·cred·ibly [ɪn'krɛdəblɪ] *adv* incredibilmente.

in·credu·lous [ɪn'krɛdjʊləs] *adj* incredulo(a).

in·cre·ment ['ɪnkrɪmənt] *n* incremento.

in·crimi·nate [ɪn'krɪmɪneɪt] *vt* incriminare.

in·crimi·na·ting [ɪn'krɪmɪneɪtɪŋ] *adj* incriminante.

in·cu·bate ['ɪnkjubeɪt] **1** *vt* (*eggs*) covare. **2** *vi* (*egg*) essere in incubazione; (*disease*) avere un'incubazione.

in·cu·ba·tion [,ɪnkju'beɪʃən] **1** *n* incubazione *f*. **2** *cpd*: ~ **period** *n* incubazione *f*.

in·cu·ba·tor ['ɪnkjubeɪtəʳ] *n* (*for eggs, baby*) incubatrice *f*; (*for bacteria*) stufa batteriologica.

in·cul·cate ['ɪnkʌlkeɪt] *vt*: **to** ~ **sth in sb** inculcare qc a qn, instillare qc a qn.

in·cur [ɪn'kɜːʳ] *vt* (*anger*) attirarsi; (*debt, obligation*) contrarre; (*expenditure*) andare incontro a; (*loss*) subire.

in·cur·able [ɪn'kjʊərəbl] *adj* (*disease*) incurabile, inguaribile; (*habit*) incorreggibile; (*fig: optimist*) inguaribile.

in·cur·ably [ɪn'kjʊərəblɪ] *adv*: **the** ~ **ill** i malati incurabili; **to be** ~ **optimistic** essere un inguaribile ottimista.

in·cur·sion [ɪn'kɜːʃən] *n* incursione *f*.

in·debt·ed [ɪn'dɛtɪd] *adj (fig):* **to be ~ to sb (for sth)** essere molto obbligato(a) a qn (per *or* di qc).

in·de·cen·cy [ɪn'diːsnsɪ] *n* indecenza.

in·de·cent [ɪn'diːsnt] *adj (dress, behaviour)* indecente; **~ assault** *(Law)* aggressione *f* a scopo di violenza sessuale; **~ exposure** *(Law)* atti *mpl* osceni in luogo pubblico.

in·de·ci·pher·able [,ɪndɪ'saɪfərəbl] *adj* indecifrabile.

in·de·ci·sion [,ɪndɪ'sɪʒən] *n* indecisione *f.*

in·de·ci·sive [,ɪndɪ'saɪsɪv] *adj (person)* indeciso(a), esitante; *(result)* non decisivo(a).

in·deed [ɪn'diːd] *adv* **(a)** veramente, infatti, in effetti; **I feel, ~ I know he is wrong** ho l'impressione, anzi sono addirittura certo che si sbaglia; **there are ~ mistakes, but...** certo, ci sono degli errori, però..., ci sono certamente degli errori, però...; **thank you very much ~** grazie infinite; **that is praise ~** questa è decisamente una lode; **it is ~ difficult** è proprio difficile. **(b)** *(in answer to question)* **yes ~** certo; **isn't that right? — ~ it is** non è vero? — altroché; **are you coming? — ~ I am** vieni? — certo; **may I come in? — ~ you may not** posso entrare? — no di certo.

in·de·fati·gable [,ɪndɪ'fætɪgəbl] *adj* infaticabile, instancabile.

in·de·fen·sible [,ɪndɪ'fɛnsəbl] *adj (town)* che non si può difendere, indifendibile; *(conduct)* ingiustificabile.

in·de·fin·able [,ɪndɪ'faɪnəbl] *adj* indefinibile.

in·defi·nite [ɪn'dɛfɪnɪt] *adj (answer, plans)* vago(a); *(time, period)* indeterminato(a), indefinito(a); *(Gram)* indefinito(a).

in·defi·nite·ly [ɪn'dɛfɪnɪtlɪ] *adv (postpone)* a tempo indeterminato; *(wait)* indefinitamente, all'infinito.

in·del·ible [ɪn'dɛlɪbl] *adj* indelebile; *(fig)* incancellabile, indelebile.

in·deli·cate [ɪn'dɛlɪkɪt] *adj (tactless)* indelicato(a), privo(a) di tatto; *(not polite)* sconveniente.

in·dem·ni·fy [ɪn'dɛmnɪfaɪ] *vt (compensate):* **to ~ sb for sth** indennizzare qn di qc, risarcire qn di qc; *(safeguard):* **to ~ sb against sth** assicurare qn contro qc.

in·dem·nity [ɪn'dɛmnɪtɪ] *n (see vb)* indennizzo, risarcimento, indennità *f inv;* assicurazione *f.*

in·dent [ɪn'dɛnt] **1** *vt (Typ: word, line)* rientrare dal margine. **2** *vi (Comm):* **to ~ for sth** ordinare *or* commissionare qc.

in·den·ta·tion [,ɪndɛn'teɪʃən] *n (dent)* tacca; *(Typ)* rientranza; *(notch: in cloth etc)* dentellatura.

in·dent·ed [ɪn'dɛntɪd] *adj (Typ)* rientrante; *(surface)* intaccato(a); *(coastline)* frastagliato(a).

in·de·pend·ence [,ɪndɪ'pɛndəns] **1** *n* indipendenza. **2** *cpd:* **I~ Day** *n (Am)* anniversario dell'indipendenza americana *(il 4 luglio).*

in·de·pend·ent [,ɪndɪ'pɛndənt] *adj* indipendente; **of ~ means** finanziariamente indipendente; **to ask for an ~ opinion** chiedere il parere di un terzo.

in·de·pend·ent·ly [,ɪndɪ'pɛndəntlɪ] *adv (move, decide)* indipendentemente; *(arrive)* separatamente.

in·de·scrib·able [,ɪndɪs'kraɪbəbl] *adj* indescrivibile.

in·de·scrib·ably [,ɪndɪs'kraɪbəblɪ] *adv:* **~ horrible/beautiful** di una bruttezza/bellezza indescrivibile.

in·de·struct·ible [,ɪndɪs'trʌktəbl] *adj* indistruttibile.

in·dex ['ɪndɛks] **1** *n* **(a)** *(pl ~es: in book)* indice *m;* **the I~** *(Rel)* l'Indice. **(b)** *(pl indices: pointer)* indicazione *f,* indizio; *(: Math)* indice *m.* **2** *cpd:* **~**

card *n* scheda; **~ finger** *n* (dito) indice *m.*

index-link [,ɪndɛks'lɪŋk] *vt* indicizzare al costo della vita.

In·dia ['ɪndɪə] *n* India.

In·dian ['ɪndɪən] **1** *adj* **(a)** *(from India)* indiano(a). **(b)** *(American ~)* indiano(a) (d'America), amerindio(a). **2** *n* **(a)** *(from India)* Indiano/a. **(b)** *(American ~)* indiano/a (d'America), amerindio/a. **3** *cpd:* **~ elephant** *n* elefante *m* indiano; **~ ink** *n* inchiostro di china; **~ Ocean** *n* Oceano Indiano; **~ summer** *n (fig)* estate *f* di San Martino.

india-rubber [,ɪndɪə'rʌbə'] *n (rubber)* cauciù *m; (eraser)* gomma *(per cancellare).*

in·di·cate ['ɪndɪkeɪt] **1** *vt* **(a)** *(point out: place)* indicare; *(: with finger)* additare, indicare; *(register: temperature, speed)* segnare, indicare. **(b)** *(show: feelings)* denotare; *(suggest)* indicare, lasciar intendere. **2** *vi (Aut)* segnalare (il cambiamento di direzione), mettere la freccia; **to ~ left/right** mettere la freccia a sinistra/a destra.

in·di·ca·tion [,ɪndɪ'keɪʃən] *n* indicazione *f;* **there is no ~ that** non c'è niente che faccia pensare che; **this is some ~ that** questo fa pensare *or* sembra indicare che.

in·dica·tive [ɪn'dɪkətɪv] **1** *adj* **(a):** **to be ~ of sth** essere indicativo(a) *or* un indice di qc. **(b)** *(Gram)* indicativo(a). **2** *n (Gram)* indicativo; **in the ~** all'indicativo.

in·di·ca·tor ['ɪndɪkeɪtə'] *n (sign)* segno *m; (: fig)* indice *m; (in station, airport etc)* tabellone *m; (Aut)* indicatore *m or* luce *f* di direzione, freccia; *(Chem)* rivelatore *m.*

in·di·ces ['ɪndɪsiːz] *npl of* **index 1b.**

in·dict [ɪn'daɪt] *vt:* **to ~ sb for** accusare *or* imputare qn di.

in·dict·able [ɪn'daɪtəbl] *adj:* **~ offence** atto che costituisce reato.

in·dict·ment [ɪn'daɪtmənt] *n (charge)* accusa, imputazione *f;* **to bring an ~ against sb** accusare *or* imputare qn di qc.

in·dif·fer·ence [ɪn'dɪfrəns] *n (see adj)* indifferenza; mediocrità.

in·dif·fer·ent [ɪn'dɪfrənt] *adj (apathetic):* **~ (to)** indifferente (a); *(mediocre)* mediocre.

in·dig·enous [ɪn'dɪdʒɪnəs] *adj* indigeno(a).

in·di·ges·tion [,ɪndɪ'dʒɛstʃən] *n* cattiva digestione *f; (chronic)* dispepsia.

in·dig·nant [ɪn'dɪgnənt] *adj* indignato(a); **to be ~ at *or* about sth/with sb** essere indignato per qc/ contro qn.

in·dig·na·tion [,ɪndɪg'neɪʃən] *n* indignazione *f,* sdegno.

in·dig·nity [ɪn'dɪgnɪtɪ] *n* umiliazione *f.*

in·di·go ['ɪndɪgəʊ] **1** *n* indaco. **2** *adj* (color) indaco *inv.*

in·di·rect [,ɪndɪ'rɛkt] *adj (road, route)* meno diretto(a); *(answer, question)* indiretto(a), tortuoso(a), involuto(a); *(tax)* indiretto(a).

in·dis·creet [,ɪndɪs'kriːt] *adj* indiscreto(a).

in·dis·cre·tion [,ɪndɪs'krɛʃən] *n* indiscrezione *f.*

in·dis·crimi·nate [,ɪndɪs'krɪmɪnɪt] *adj* indiscriminato(a).

in·dis·pen·sable [,ɪndɪs'pɛnsəbl] *adj* indispensabile.

in·dis·posed [,ɪndɪs'pəʊzd] *adj (ill)* indisposto(a).

in·dis·put·able [,ɪndɪs'pjuːtəbl] *adj (evidence)* indiscutibile, incontrovertibile; *(winner)* incontestabile.

in·dis·tinct [,ɪndɪs'tɪŋkt] *adj* indistinto(a).

in·dis·tin·guish·able [,ɪndɪs'tɪŋgwɪʃəbl] *adj* indistinguibile.

in·di·vid·ual [,ɪndɪ'vɪdjʊəl] **1** *adj* **(a)** *(separate: member, case)* (ogni) singolo(a). **(b)** *(own: taste,* *style*) personale, individuale; *(for one person: portion)* individuale. **2** *n* individuo.

in·di·vidu·al·ist [ˌɪndɪ'vɪdjʊəlɪst] *n* individualista *m/f*.

in·di·vidu·al·ity [ˌɪndɪˌvɪdjʊ'ælɪtɪ] *n* individualità *f* *inv*.

in·di·vid·ual·ly [ˌɪndɪ'vɪdjʊəlɪ] *adv* singolarmente, uno(a) per uno(a).

in·di·vis·ible [ˌɪndɪ'vɪzəbl] *adj* indivisibile.

Indo- ['ɪndəʊ] *pref* indo... .

Indo·china [ˌɪndəʊ'tʃaɪnə] *n* Indocina.

in·doc·tri·nate [ɪn'dɒktrɪneɪt] *vt* indottrinare.

in·doc·tri·na·tion [ɪnˌdɒktrɪ'neɪʃən] *n* indottrinamento.

in·do·lent ['ɪndələnt] *adj* indolente.

In·do·nesia [ˌɪndəʊ'niːzɪə] *n* Indonesia.

In·do·nesian [ˌɪndəʊ'niːzɪən] *adj*, *n* indonesiano(a) *(m/f)*.

in·door ['ɪndɔːʳ] *adj (shoes)* da casa; *(plant)* da appartamento; *(sport)* praticato(a) al coperto; *(tennis court)* al coperto; *(swimming pool)* coperto(a); *(photography)* di interni; *(hobby)* di casa, casalingo(a), domestico(a); **~aerial** antenna interna.

in·doors [ɪn'dɔːz] *adv (in building)* all'interno; *(at home)* in casa; *(under cover)* al coperto; **to go ~** rientrare, andar dentro.

in·duce [ɪn'djuːs] *vt (persuade)*: **to ~ sb to do sth** persuadere qn a fare qc; *(cause: sleep, birth etc)* provocare.

in·duce·ment [ɪn'djuːsmənt] *n* incentivo.

in·duc·tion [ɪn'dʌkʃən] **1** *n (Elec, Philosophy)* induzione *f*. **2** *cpd*: **~ course** *n* corso preparatorio.

in·duc·tive [ɪn'dʌktɪv] *adj* induttivo(a).

in·dulge [ɪn'dʌldʒ] *vt (give into: desire, appetite)* soddisfare, appagare; *(: person)* assecondare (i desideri di), accontentare; *(spoil: child)* viziare; **why not ~ yourself and have a cigarette?** va' là, concediti una sigaretta.

♦ **indulge in** *vi* + *prep (activity, emotion)* lasciarsi andare a, darsi a; *(cigarette etc)* concedersi.

in·dul·gence [ɪn'dʌldʒəns] *n (also Rel)* indulgenza; *(bad habit)* vizio.

in·dul·gent [ɪn'dʌldʒənt] *adj*: **~ (to or towards sb)** indulgente (con or verso qn).

in·dus·trial [ɪn'dʌstrɪəl] *adj (area, town, processes)* industriale; *(worker)* dell'industria; *(accident)* sul lavoro; *(disease)* del lavoro; **~ action** azione *f* rivendicativa; **~ estate**, *(Am)* **~ park** zona industriale; **~ unrest** agitazione *f* (sindacale).

in·dus·tri·al·ist [ɪn'dʌstrɪəlɪst] *n* industriale *m/f*.

in·dus·tri·al·ize [ɪn'dʌstrɪəlaɪz] *vt* industrializzare.

in·dus·tri·ous [ɪn'dʌstrɪəs] *adj* diligente.

in·dus·try ['ɪndəstrɪ] *n* **(a)** l'industria; **the tourist ~** l'industria turistica. **(b)** *(industriousness)* operosità.

in·ebri·at·ed [ɪ'niːbrɪeɪtɪd] *adj* ubriaco(a).

in·ed·ible [ɪn'edɪbl] *adj (not to be eaten)* non commestibile; *(not fit to be eaten)* immangiabile.

in·ef·fec·tive [ˌɪnɪ'fektɪv] *adj*, **in·ef·fec·tual** [ˌɪnɪ'fektjʊəl] *adj (remedy)* inefficace; *(person)* incapace.

in·ef·fi·cien·cy [ˌɪnɪ'fɪʃənsɪ] *n* inefficienza.

in·ef·fi·cient [ˌɪnɪ'fɪʃənt] *adj* inefficiente.

in·el·egant [ɪn'elɪgənt] *adj* poco elegante.

in·eli·gible [ɪn'elɪdʒəbl] *adj* ineleggibile; **to be ~ for sth/to do sth** non avere diritto a qc/a fare qc.

in·ept [ɪ'nept] *adj (person)* inetto(a), incapace; *(remark, behaviour)* stupido(a).

in·epti·tude [ɪ'neptɪtjuːd] *n* inettitudine *f*, stupidità.

in·equal·ity [ˌɪnɪ'kwɒlɪtɪ] *n* ineguaglianza, disuguaglianza.

in·equi·table [ɪn'ekwɪtəbl] *adj* iniquo(a).

in·ert [ɪ'nɜːt] *adj* inerte.

in·er·tia [ɪ'nɜːʃə] *n* inerzia.

inertia reel seat belt [ɪ,nɜːʃə,riːl'siːt,belt] *n* cintura di sicurezza con arrotolatore.

in·evi·tabil·ity [ɪn,evɪtə'bɪlɪtɪ] *n* inevitabilità.

in·evi·table [ɪn'evɪtəbl] *adj* inevitabile, scontato(a).

in·evi·tably [ɪn'evɪtəblɪ] *adv* inevitabilmente; **as ~ happens...** come immancabilmente succede... .

in·ex·act [ˌɪnɪg'zækt] *adj* inesatto(a), impreciso(a).

in·ex·cus·able [ˌɪnɪks'kjuːzəbl] *adj* imperdonabile.

in·ex·haust·ible [ˌɪnɪg'zɔːstəbl] *adj* inesauribile.

in·ex·pen·sive [ˌɪnɪks'pensɪv] *adj* a buon mercato, economico(a).

in·ex·pe·ri·ence [ˌɪnɪks'pɪərɪəns] *n* inesperienza.

in·ex·pe·ri·enced [ˌɪnɪks'pɪərɪənst] *adj* inesperto(a); **to be ~ in sth** essere poco pratico di qc.

in·ex·pli·cable [ˌɪnɪks'plɪkəbl] *adj* inspiegabile.

in·ex·press·ible [ˌɪnɪks'presəbl] *adj* inesprimibile.

in·ex·pres·sive [ˌɪnɪks'presɪv] *adj (style)* piatto(a), inespressivo(a); *(look, face)* senza espressione.

in·fal·libil·ity [ɪn,fælə'bɪlɪtɪ] *n* infallibilità.

in·fal·lible [ɪn'fæləbl] *adj* infallibile.

in·fa·mous ['ɪnfəməs] *adj (person)* famigerato(a), infame; *(crime)* infame.

in·fa·my ['ɪnfəmɪ] *n* infamia.

in·fan·cy ['ɪnfənsɪ] *n (childhood)* prima infanzia; *(Law)* minore età; **in its ~** *(fig: early stage)* ai primi passi.

in·fant ['ɪnfənt] **1** *n* bambino/a; *(Law)* minorenne *m/f*; minore *m/f*. **2** *cpd*: **~ mortality** *n* mortalità infantile; **~ school** *n (Brit)* ≃ prima e seconda elementare.

in·fan·tile ['ɪnfəntaɪl] *adj* infantile.

in·fan·try ['ɪnfəntrɪ] *n* fanteria.

in·fantry·man ['ɪnfəntrɪmən] *n*, *pl* **-men** fante *m*.

in·fatu·at·ed [ɪn'fætjʊeɪtɪd] *adj*: **~ (with sb)** infatuato(a) (di qn); **to become ~ (with sb)** infatuarsi (di qn).

in·fatu·a·tion [ɪn,fætjʊ'eɪʃən] *n* infatuazione *f*.

in·fect [ɪn'fekt] *vt (Med)* infettare; *(fig: person)* contagiare; **to ~ sb with a disease** contagiare qn di una malattia; **to become ~ed** *(wound)* infettarsi; **~ed with measles** affetto da morbillo; **he's ~ed everybody with his enthusiasm** ha comunicato il suo entusiasmo a tutti, ha contagiato tutti col suo entusiasmo.

in·fect·ed [ɪn'fektɪd] *adj (wound)* infetto(a); *(person)* contagiato(a).

in·fec·tion [ɪn'fekʃən] *n* infezione *f*.

in·fec·tious [ɪn'fekʃəs] *adj (disease)* infettivo(a), contagioso(a); *(person, laughter)* contagioso(a).

in·fer [ɪn'fɜːʳ] *vt*: **to ~ (from)** dedurre (da), concludere (da).

in·fer·ence ['ɪnfərəns] *n* deduzione *f*, illazione *f*.

in·fe·ri·or [ɪn'fɪərɪəʳ] *adj (in quality, rank)*: **~ (to)** inferiore a; *(work, goods)* scadente; **to feel ~** sentirsi inferiore.

in·fe·ri·or·ity [ɪn,fɪərɪ'ɒrɪtɪ] **1** *n* inferiorità. **2** *cpd*: **~ complex** *n* complesso di inferiorità.

in·fer·no [ɪn'fɜːnəʊ] *n* inferno, rogo.

in·fer·tile [ɪn'fɜːtaɪl] *adj* sterile.

in·fer·til·ity [ɪnfɜː'tɪlɪtɪ] *n* sterilità.

in·fest [ɪn'fest] *vt* infestare; **to be ~ed with sth** essere infestato da qc.

in·fi·del·ity [ɪnfɪ'delɪtɪ] *n* infedeltà *f inv*.

in·fighting ['ɪnfaɪtɪŋ] *n (fam)* lotte *fpl* interne.

in·fil·trate ['ɪnfɪltreɪt] **1** *vt* infiltrarsi in. **2** *vi*: **to ~ (into)** infiltrarsi (in).

in·fil·tra·tion [ˌɪnfɪl'treɪʃən] n infiltrazione f.

in·fi·nite ['ɪnfɪnɪt] adj infinito(a); **an ~ amount of time/money** un'illimitata quantità di tempo/denaro.

in·fi·nite·ly ['ɪnfɪnɪtlɪ] adv infinitamente.

in·fini·tesi·mal [ˌɪnfɪnɪ'tɛsɪməl] adj infinitesimale.

in·fini·tive [ɪn'fɪnɪtɪv] 1 adj (Gram) infinitivo(a). 2 n infinito; **in the ~** all'infinito.

in·fin·ity [ɪn'fɪnɪtɪ] n (infiniteness) infinità; (in time, space, Math) infinito.

in·firm [ɪn'fɜːm] adj infermo(a).

in·fir·ma·ry [ɪn'fɜːmərɪ] n (hospital) ospedale m; (in school, prison, barracks) infermeria.

in·flame [ɪn'fleɪm] vt **(a)** (Med: wound etc) infiammare; **to become ~d** infiammarsi. **(b)** (fig: feelings) irritare; (: person) provocare l'ira di.

in·flam·mable [ɪn'flæməbl] adj (substance, fabric) infiammabile; (fig) esplosivo(a).

in·flam·ma·tion [ˌɪnflə'meɪʃən] n infiammazione f.

in·flam·ma·tory [ɪn'flæmətərɪ] adj (speech) incendiario(a).

in·flat·able [ɪn'fleɪtɪbl] adj gonfiabile.

in·flate [ɪn'fleɪt] vt (tyre, boat) gonfiare; (fig: prices) inflazionare.

in·flat·ed [ɪn'fleɪtɪd] adj (tyre) gonfiato(a); (fig: price, pride) esagerato(a).

in·fla·tion [ɪn'fleɪʃən] n (Econ) inflazione f.

in·fla·tion·ary [ɪn'fleɪʃnərɪ] adj inflazionistico(a).

in·flect [ɪn'flɛkt] vt (voice) modulare; (Gram) flettere.

in·flex·ibil·ity [ɪnˌflɛksɪ'bɪlɪtɪ] n (see adj) rigidità; inflessibilità.

in·flex·ible [ɪn'flɛksəbl] adj (object) rigido(a); (fig: person, ideas) inflessibile, rigido(a).

in·flict [ɪn'flɪkt] vt: **to ~ (on)** (penalty) infliggere (a); (tax) imporre (a); (suffering, damage) procurare (a); **to ~ a blow/wound on sb** assestare un colpo a/ferire qn; **to ~ o.s. on sb** imporre la propria compagnia a qn.

in·flight ['ɪnflaɪt] adj a bordo.

in·flu·ence ['ɪnfluəns] 1 n influenza; **to have an ~ on sb/sth** (subj: person) avere un'influenza su qn/qc; (: event) influenzare qn/qc; (: weather) influire su qn/qc; **to have ~ with sb** avere un ascendente su qn; **to be a good/bad ~ on sb** avere or esercitare una buona/cattiva influenza su qn; **under the ~ of drink/drugs** sotto l'influenza or l'effetto dell'alcool/della droga; **he was under the ~** (fam) era un po' sbronzo or bevuto. 2 vt (person) influenzare; (action, decision) influire su, influenzare; **to be easily ~d** essere facilmente influenzabile.

in·flu·en·tial [ˌɪnflu'ɛnʃəl] adj influente.

in·flu·en·za [ˌɪnflu'ɛnzə] n influenza.

in·flux ['ɪnflʌks] n (of people, objects) afflusso, affluenza; (of ideas) flusso.

in·form [ɪn'fɔːm] vt informare, avvertire; **to ~ sb about sth** informare or avvertire qn di qc; **I am happy to ~ you that** sono lieto di comunicarle che; **keep me ~ed** tienimi informato; **a well-~ed person** una persona ben informata.

in·for·mal [ɪn'fɔːməl] adj (person) semplice, informale, che non fa inutili cerimonie; (manner, tone) senza tante formalità; (: of letter) poco formale; (language, style) colloquiale; (dinner, party) fra amici; (meeting, arrangement, visit) non ufficiale; **'dress ~'** è richiesto l'abito scuro'.

in·for·mal·ity [ˌɪnfɔː'mælɪtɪ] n (of person, manner, tone) semplicità, mancanza di formalità; (of language, style) tono colloquiale; (of occasion) tono familiare; (of meeting, negotiations, announcement) carattere m non ufficiale.

in·for·mal·ly [ɪn'fɔːməlɪ] adv senza cerimonie; (invite) in modo non ufficiale; **the Queen visited the hospital ~** la regina ha visitato l'ospedale in forma privata; **I have been ~ told that...** mi è stato comunicato ufficiosamente che... .

in·form·ant [ɪn'fɔːmənt] n informatore/trice.

in·for·ma·tion [ˌɪnfə'meɪʃən] 1 n: **~ (about or on)** informazioni fpl (riguardo a or su); **a piece of ~** un'informazione; **to give sb ~ about or on sb/sth** dare a qn informazioni su qn/i particolari di qc; **for your ~** a titolo d'informazione, per sua informazione. 2 cpd: **~ bureau** n ufficio m informazioni inv; **~ processing** n elaborazione f delle informazioni; **~ science** n scienza dell'informazione; **~ technology** n informatica.

in·forma·tive [ɪn'fɔːmətɪv] adj (speech, book) informativo(a), istruttivo(a); **she wasn't very ~ about it** non ha detto gran che.

in·formed [ɪn'fɔːmd] adj (observer) (ben) informato(a); **an ~ guess** un'ipotesi fondata.

in·form·er [ɪn'fɔːmə^r] n informatore/trice; **to turn ~** (Police) denunciare i complici.

infra·red ['ɪnfrə'rɛd] adj infrarosso(a).

infra·struc·ture ['ɪnfrəˌstrʌktʃə^r] n infrastruttura.

in·fre·quent [ɪn'friːkwənt] adj infrequente, raro(a).

in·fringe [ɪn'frɪndʒ] vt (law, copyright) infrangere, violare; (rights) violare, ledere.

♦ **infringe (up)on** vi + prep (rights) ledere; (privacy) violare.

in·fringe·ment [ɪn'frɪndʒmənt] n (of law, rule, etc) violazione f; (of rights) lesione f, violazione f.

in·furi·ate [ɪn'fjuərɪeɪt] vt far infuriare, rendere furioso(a); **to become ~d** infuriarsi, andare in bestia.

in·furi·at·ing [ɪn'fjuərɪeɪtɪŋ] adj esasperante, molto irritante.

in·fuse [ɪn'fjuːz] vt **(a)** (with courage, enthusiasm): **to ~ sb with sth** infondere qc a qn, riempire qn di qc; **to ~ courage into sb** infondere coraggio a qn. **(b)** (Culin: herbs, tea) lasciare in infusione.

in·fu·sion [ɪn'fjuːʒən] (tea etc) infuso, infusione f.

in·gen·ious [ɪn'dʒiːnɪəs] adj ingegnoso(a).

in·genu·ity [ˌɪndʒɪ'njuːɪtɪ] n ingegnosità.

in·genu·ous [ɪn'dʒɛnjuəs] adj ingenuo(a).

in·got ['ɪŋgət] n lingotto.

in·grained ['ɪn'greɪnd] adj (dirt) incancrenito(a); (fig: ideas, tradition) inveterato(a), radicato(a).

in·gra·ti·ate [ɪn'greɪʃɪeɪt] vt: **to ~ o.s. with sb** ingraziarsi qn, cattivarsi qn.

in·gra·ti·at·ing [ɪn'greɪʃɪeɪtɪŋ] adj (smile, speech) suadente, cattivante; (person) compiacente.

in·grati·tude [ɪn'grætɪtjuːd] n ingratitudine f.

in·gre·di·ent [ɪn'griːdɪənt] n (Culin) ingrediente m; (fig) componente f, elemento.

in·grow·ing ['ɪngrəuɪŋ] adj: **~ (toe)nail** unghia incarnita.

in·hab·it [ɪn'hæbɪt] vt (house) abitare (in); (town, country) vivere in.

in·hab·it·able [ɪn'hæbɪtəbl] adj abitabile.

in·hab·it·ant [ɪn'hæbɪtənt] n abitante m/f.

in·hale [ɪn'heɪl] 1 vt (gas, smoke) respirare; (Med) inalare. 2 vi (smoker) aspirare; (Med) respirare.

in·her·ent [ɪn'hɪərənt] adj: **~ (in)** intrinseco(a) (a); (kindness, cruelty) innato(a).

in·her·ent·ly [ɪn'hɪərəntlɪ] adv (easy, difficult) di per sé (stesso(a)); **~ lazy** pigro di natura.

in·her·it [ɪn'hɛrɪt] vt ereditare.

in·her·it·ance [ɪn'hɛrɪtəns] n eredità; (fig) retaggio.

in·hib·it [ɪn'hɪbɪt] vt inibire; **to ~ sb from doing sth** impedire a qn di fare qc.

in·hib·it·ed [ɪnˈhɪbɪtɪd] *adj (person)* inibito(a).
in·hi·bi·tion [ˌɪnhɪˈbɪʃən] *n* inibizione *f*.
in·hos·pi·table [ˌɪnhɒsˈpɪtəbl] *adj* inospitale.
in·hu·man [ɪnˈhjuːmən] *adj (cruelty, etc)* inumano(a), disumano(a).
in·hu·mane [ˌɪnhjuˈ(ː)meɪn] *adj* inumano(a), disumano(a).
in·hu·man·ity [ˌɪnhjuːˈmænɪtɪ] *n* inumanità *f inv*, disumanità *f inv*.
in·imi·table [ɪˈnɪmɪtəbl] *adj* inimitabile.
ini·tial [ɪˈnɪʃəl] **1** *adj* iniziale. **2** *n* iniziale *f*; **to sign sth with one's** ~s siglare qc. **3** *vt* siglare.
ini·tial·ly [ɪˈnɪʃəlɪ] *adv* all'inizio.
ini·ti·ate [ɪˈnɪʃɪeɪt] *vt* (a) *(begin)* iniziare; *(: talks)* iniziare, avviare; *(: reform)* promuovere, introdurre; **to** ~ **proceedings against sb** *(Law)* intentare causa a *or* contro qn. (b) *(admit)*: **to** ~ **sb (into sth)** iniziare qn (a qc).
ini·tia·tion [ɪˌnɪʃɪˈeɪʃən] **1** *n* iniziazione *f*. **2** *cpd*: ~ **ceremony** *n* rito d'iniziazione.
ini·tia·tive [ɪˈnɪʃətɪv] *n* iniziativa; **on one's own** ~ di propria iniziativa, da sé; **to take the** ~ prendere l'iniziativa.
in·ject [ɪnˈdʒɛkt] *vt (Med: drug)* iniettare; *(: person)* fare un'iniezione a; *(fig: money)*: **to** ~ **into** immettere in; **to** ~ **enthusiasm into sth/sb** dare una carica di entusiasmo a qc/qn.
in·jec·tion [ɪnˈdʒɛkʃən] *n* iniezione *f; (Med)* iniezione, puntura; **to give sb an** ~ fare un'iniezione *or* una puntura a qn; **to have an** ~ farsi fare un'iniezione *or* una puntura.
in·ju·di·cious [ˌɪndʒuˈdɪʃəs] *adj* poco saggio(a).
in·junc·tion [ɪnˈdʒʌŋkʃən] *n (Law)* ingiunzione *f*, intimazione *f*.
in·jure [ˈɪndʒəʳ] *vt* (a) *(physically)* ferire; **he** ~**d his arm** si è fatto male a *or* si è ferito a un braccio; **to** ~ **o.s.** farsi male. (b) *(fig: reputation, trade etc)* nuocere a; *(: feelings)* offendere.
in·jured [ˈɪndʒəd] **1** *adj (person, leg etc)* ferito(a); *(tone, feelings)* offeso(a); ~ **party** *(Law)* parte *f* lesa. **2** *npl*: **the** ~ i feriti.
in·ju·ri·ous [ɪnˈdʒʊərɪəs] *adj*: ~ **(to)** nocivo(a) (a), pregiudizievole (per).
in·ju·ry [ˈɪndʒərɪ] **1** *n (physical)* ferita, lesione *f; (fig: to reputation)* danno; *(: to feelings)* offesa; **to escape without** ~ rimanere illeso. **2** *cpd*: ~ **time** *n (Sport)* tempo supplementare.
in·jus·tice [ɪnˈdʒʌstɪs] *n* ingiustizia; **you do me an** ~ mi fai un torto, sei ingiusto verso di me.
ink [ɪŋk] *n* inchiostro; **in** ~ a penna.
ink·ling [ˈɪŋklɪŋ] *n (hint)* indizio; *(suspicion, vague idea)* mezza idea; **to give sb an** ~ **that** lasciar capire *or* intuire a qn che; **I had no** ~ **that** non avevo la minima idea che.
ink·pad [ˈɪŋkpæd] *n* tampone *m*, cuscinetto per timbri.
ink·well [ˈɪŋkwɛl] *n* calamaio.
inky [ˈɪŋkɪ] *adj (-ier, -iest)* macchiato(a) d'inchiostro, sporco(a) d'inchiostro; *(fig: darkness)* nero(a) come l'inchiostro.
in·laid [ˈɪnˈleɪd] *adj (gen)*: ~ **(with)** incrostato(a) (di); *(table, box)* intarsiato(a).
in·land [ˈɪnlænd] **1** *adj (town)* dell'interno; *(sea, waterway)* interno(a); *(trade, mail)* nazionale, interno(a). **2** *adv* nell'entroterra. **3** *cpd*: **I**~ **Revenue** *n (Brit)* Fisco.
in·laws [ˈɪnˌlɔːz] *npl (fam)* (parents-in-law) suoceri *mpl; (others)* famiglia del marito (*or* della moglie).
in·let [ˈɪnlɛt] *n* (a) *(Geog)* insenatura; *(of sea)* braccio di mare. (b) *(Tech)* apertura di ammissione.
in·mate [ˈɪnmeɪt] *n (of prison)* detenuto/a; *(of asylum)* internato/a.

in·most [ˈɪnməʊst] *adj* più profondo(a), più intimo(a).
inn [ɪn] *n* locanda.
in·nards [ˈɪnədz] *npl (fam)* interiora *fpl*, budella *fpl*.
in·nate [ɪˈneɪt] *adj* innato(a).
in·ner [ˈɪnəʳ] *adj (place)* interno(a); *(thoughts, emotions)* interiore, intimo(a); ~ **city** centro di una zona urbana; ~ **sole** *(in shoe)* soletta; ~ **tube** *(in tyre)* camera d'aria.
inner·most [ˈɪnəməʊst] *adj* = **inmost**.
in·nings [ˈɪnɪŋz] *nsg (in cricket)* turno di battuta.
inn·keeper [ˈɪnkiːpəʳ] *n* padrone/a della locanda, locandiere/a.
in·no·cence [ˈɪnəsns] *n* innocenza.
in·no·cent [ˈɪnəsnt] *adj* innocente.
in·nocu·ous [ɪˈnɒkjuəs] *adj* innocuo(a).
in·no·vate [ˈɪnəʊveɪt] *vi* fare delle innovazioni.
in·no·va·tion [ˌɪnəʊˈveɪʃən] *n* innovazione *f*.
in·nu·en·do [ˌɪnjuˈɛndəʊ] *n* insinuazione *f*, allusione *f* (maligna).
in·nu·mer·able [ɪˈnjuːmərəbl] *adj* innumerevole.
in·ocu·late [ɪˈnɒkjuleɪt] *vt*: **to** ~ **sb with sth/against sth** inoculare qc a qn/qn contro qc.
in·ocu·la·tion [ɪˌnɒkjuˈleɪʃən] *n* inoculazione *f*.
in·of·fen·sive [ˌɪnəˈfɛnsɪv] *adj* inoffensivo(a), innocuo(a).
in·op·por·tune [ɪnˈɒpətjuːn] *adj* inopportuno(a).
in·or·di·nate [ɪˈnɔːdɪnɪt] *adj* eccessivo(a).
in·or·di·nate·ly [ɪˈnɔːdɪnɪtlɪ] *adv*: **an** ~ **large sum of money/amount of food** una quantità esorbitante di soldi/cibo; **an** ~ **long time** un'infinità di tempo.
in·or·gan·ic [ˌɪnɔːˈɡænɪk] *adj* inorganico(a).
in·pa·tient [ˈɪnˌpeɪʃənt] *n* degente *m/f*, ricoverato/a.
in·put [ˈɪnpʊt] *n (Elec)* alimentazione *f; (in amplifiers)* ingresso; *(in computers)* dati *mpl*, input *m; (fig)* immissione *f*.
in·quest [ˈɪnkwɛst] *n (Law)* inchiesta giudiziaria.
in·quire [ɪnˈkwaɪəʳ] **1** *vt*: **to** ~ **sth of sb** informarsi su qc presso qn; **to** ~ **when/where/whether** informarsi di quando/su dove/se. **2** *vi*: **to** ~ **(about sth)** informarsi (di *or* su qc), chiedere informazioni (su qc); **to** ~ **into sth** indagare su qc, fare delle indagini *or* ricerche su qc; **to** ~ **for/after sb** chiedere di qn; **to** ~ **after sb's health** informarsi della salute di qn.
in·quir·ing [ɪnˈkwaɪərɪŋ] *adj (mind)* pieno(a) di curiosità, indagatore(trice); *(look)* interrogativo(a).
in·quiry [ɪnˈkwaɪrɪ] **1** *n* (a) *(question)* domanda, richiesta di informazioni; **'Inquiries'** *(on sign etc)* 'Informazioni'; **on** ~ **he found that...** essendosi informato trovò che...; **to make inquiries (about sth)** informarsi (di *or* su qc). (b) *(Admin, Law)* inchiesta; **committee of** ~ commissione *f* d'inchiesta; **to hold an** ~ **into sth** fare un'inchiesta su qc; **the police are making inquiries** la polizia sta indagando. **2** *cpd*: ~ **desk** *n* banco delle informazioni; ~ **office** *n* ufficio *m* informazioni *inv*.
in·qui·si·tion [ˌɪnkwɪˈzɪʃən] *n* inquisizione *f*, inchiesta; **the Spanish I**~ l'Inquisizione spagnola.
in·quisi·tive [ɪnˈkwɪzɪtɪv] *adj* (troppo) curioso(a).
in·road [ˈɪnrəʊd] *n (Mil)* incursione *f*; **to make** ~s **into** *(time)* portar via un bel po' di; *(savings, supplies)* intaccare (seriamente).
in·sane [ɪnˈseɪn] **1** *adj (person)* pazzo(a), matto(a); *(Med)* alienato(a); *(act etc)* folle, insensato(a); **to drive sb** ~ *(fig)* far impazzire *or* far diventar matto qn. **2** *npl*: **the** ~ gli alienati; **an asylum for the** ~ un manicomio.
in·sani·tary [ɪnˈsænɪtərɪ] *adj* malsano(a).

in·san·ity [ɪnˈsænɪtɪ] n (Med) infermità mentale; (gen) pazzia, follia.

in·sa·tiable [ɪnˈseɪʃəbl] adj insaziabile.

in·scribe [ɪnˈskraɪb] vt (engrave) incidere; (write) scrivere.

in·scrip·tion [ɪnˈskrɪpʃən] n (on stone) iscrizione f; (in book) dedica.

in·scru·table [ɪnˈskruːtəbl] adj (person) imperscrutabile; (face, eyes, gaze) impenetrabile.

in·sect [ˈɪnsekt] 1 n insetto. 2 cpd: ~ bite n puntura or morsicatura di insetto; ~ powder n polvere f insetticida; ~ repellent n insettifugo.

in·sec·ti·cide [ɪnˈsektɪsaɪd] n insetticida m.

in·secure [ˌɪnsɪˈkjʊəʳ] adj (structure, lock, door etc) malsicuro(a); (Psych: person) insicuro(a).

in·secu·rity [ˌɪnsɪˈkjʊərɪtɪ] n (of foundations etc) instabilità; (of lock etc) scarsa sicurezza; (of person) insicurezza.

in·sen·sible [ɪnˈsensəbl] adj (unconscious) privo(a) di sensi or di conoscenza; (unaware): ~ of ignaro(a) di, inconsapevole di.

in·sen·si·tive [ɪnˈsensɪtɪv] adj (person): ~ (to) insensibile (a); (action, behaviour) privo(a) di sensibilità.

in·sen·si·tiv·ity [ɪnˌsensɪˈtɪvɪtɪ] n mancanza di sensibilità.

in·sepa·rable [ɪnˈsepərəbl] adj inseparabile.

in·sert [ˈɪnsɜːt] 1 n inserto. 2 [ɪnˈsɜːt] vt inserire; (needle) introdurre.

in·ser·tion [ɪnˈsɜːʃən] n inserzione f.

in·shore [ˈɪnˈʃɔːʳ] 1 adv (fish) sotto costa; (sail) verso riva; (blow) dal mare. 2 adj (fishing) costiero(a); (wind) dal mare.

in·side [ˈɪnˈsaɪd] 1 n (a) interno; (of road: Brit) sinistra; (: Am, in Europe etc) destra; to overtake on the ~ (Brit) sorpassare a sinistra; (Am, Europe etc) sorpassare a destra; to know sth from the ~ conoscere qc per esperienza diretta. (b): to be ~ out essere alla rovescia; to turn sth ~ out rivoltare qc; to know sth ~ out conoscere qc a fondo; (place) conoscere qc come le proprie tasche. (c) (fam: stomach): ~(s) pancia.

2 adv dentro, all'interno; to be ~ (fam: in prison) essere dentro.

3 prep (a) (of place) dentro; come ~ the house vieni dentro casa. (b) (of time) in meno di; he is ~ the record sta battendo il record.

4 cpd all'interno; ~ forward n mezzala, interno; ~ left/right n interno sinistro/destro, mezzala sinistra/destra; ~ information n informazioni fpl riservate; ~ job n (fam: crime) colpo organizzato dal di dentro or dall'interno; ~ leg measurement n lunghezza interna; ~ story n storia segreta.

in·sid·er [ɪnˈsaɪdəʳ] n uno(a) che ha le mani in pasta.

in·sidi·ous [ɪnˈsɪdɪəs] adj insidioso(a), subdolo(a).

in·sight [ˈɪnsaɪt] n (perception) perspicacia; to gain or get an ~ into sth potersi render conto di qc.

in·sig·nia [ɪnˈsɪgnɪə] npl insegne fpl.

in·sig·nifi·cance [ˌɪnsɪgˈnɪfɪkəns] n scarsa importanza, irrilevanza.

in·sig·nifi·cant [ˌɪnsɪgˈnɪfɪkənt] adj insignificante.

in·sin·cere [ˌɪnsɪnˈsɪəʳ] adj (person) falso(a), insincero(a); (behaviour, smile) ipocrita.

in·sin·cer·ity [ˌɪnsɪnˈserɪtɪ] n falsità, insincerità.

in·sinu·ate [ɪnˈsɪnjʊeɪt] vt insinuare; to ~ o.s. into sb's favour insinuarsi nelle grazie di qn.

in·sinu·ation [ɪnˌsɪnjʊˈeɪʃən] n insinuazione f.

in·sip·id [ɪnˈsɪpɪd] adj insipido(a); (fig) insulso(a), insipido(a).

in·sist [ɪnˈsɪst] 1 vi: to ~ (on sth/on doing sth)

insistere (su qc/a fare qc); she ~s on leaving tomorrow insiste che vuole partire domani. 2 vt: to ~ that (order) insistere che + sub; (maintain) insistere nel dire che; he ~s that he is innocent insiste nel dire che è innocente; I must ~ that you let me pay insisto che tu mi lasci pagare.

in·sist·ence [ɪnˈsɪstəns] n insistenza; at her ~ perché lei ha insistito (molto), dietro sua insistenza.

in·sist·ent [ɪnˈsɪstənt] adj insistente.

in·sole [ˈɪnˌsəʊl] n soletta.

in·so·lence [ˈɪnsələns] n insolenza.

in·so·lent [ˈɪnsələnt] adj insolente.

in·sol·uble [ɪnˈsɒljubl] adj insolubile.

in·sol·ven·cy [ɪnˈsɒlvənsɪ] n insolvenza.

in·sol·vent [ɪnˈsɒlvənt] adj insolvente.

in·som·nia [ɪnˈsɒmnɪə] n insonnia.

in·som·ni·ac [ɪnˈsɒmnɪæk] n chi soffre di insonnia.

in·spect [ɪnˈspekt] vt (a) (examine) controllare; to ~ sth for faults sottoporre qc a controllo or verifica. (b) (Mil: troops) passare in rassegna.

in·spec·tion [ɪnˈspekʃən] n (of goods) controllo, ispezione f; (of ticket, document) controllo; (Mil, of school) ispezione; on ~ it was found that ad un controllo si scoprì che.

in·spec·tor [ɪnˈspektəʳ] n (police ~, schools ~) ispettore/trice; (on bus, train) controllore m; ~ of taxes ispettore m del fisco.

in·spi·ra·tion [ˌɪnspəˈreɪʃən] n ispirazione f; to have a sudden ~ avere un lampo di genio.

in·spire [ɪnˈspaɪəʳ] vt: to ~ sth in sb, to ~ sb with sth ispirare qc a qn; to ~ sb (to do sth) ispirare qn (a fare qc).

in·spired [ɪnˈspaɪəd] adj (writer, book etc) ispirato(a); in an ~ moment in un momento d'ispirazione.

in·spir·ing [ɪnˈspaɪərɪŋ] adj ispiratore(trice).

inst. abbr (= of the present month) c.m.

in·stabil·ity [ˌɪnstəˈbɪlɪtɪ] n instabilità.

in·stall [ɪnˈstɔːl] vt (machine, equipment, telephone) installare; (mayor, official etc) insediare.

in·stal·la·tion [ˌɪnstəˈleɪʃən] n (see vb) installazione f; insediamento.

in·stal·ment, (Am) **in·stall·ment** [ɪnˈstɔːlmənt] n (a) (Comm: part payment) rata, pagamento rateale; to pay in ~s pagare a rate. (b) (of serial, story) puntata, episodio; (of publication) dispensa.

in·stance [ˈɪnstəns] n (example) esempio, caso; for ~ per esempio; in that ~ in quel caso; in the first ~ in primo luogo.

in·stant [ˈɪnstənt] 1 adj (reply, reaction, success) immediato(a); (coffee) solubile; ~ potatoes fiocchi mpl di patate. 2 n istante m, attimo; come here this ~ vieni immediatamente or subito qui; in an ~ in un attimo.

in·stan·ta·neous [ˌɪnstənˈteɪnɪəs] adj istantaneo(a).

in·stant·ly [ˈɪnstəntlɪ] adv immediatamente.

in·stead [ɪnˈsted] 1 adv invece; don't take Tom, take Fred ~ non prendere Tom, prendi piuttosto Fred; I have no coffee, will cocoa do ~? non ho caffè, va bene lo stesso il cacao?; if you're not going I shall go ~ se non vai tu andrò io al posto tuo. 2 prep: ~ of invece di, al posto di; ~ of doing sth invece di fare qc.

in·step [ˈɪnstep] n (of foot) collo del piede; (of shoe) collo della scarpa.

in·sti·gate [ˈɪnstɪgeɪt] vt (rebellion, strike, crime) istigare a; (new ideas etc) promuovere.

in·sti·ga·tion [ˌɪnstɪˈgeɪʃən] n: at sb's ~ per or in seguito al suggerimento di qn.

in·stil [ɪnˈstɪl] vt: to ~ sth into sb instillare qc a qn.

in·stinct [ˈɪnstɪŋkt] n istinto; **by** ~ per istinto, istintivamente.

in·stinc·tive [ɪnˈstɪŋktɪv] adj istintivo(a).

in·sti·tute [ˈɪnstɪtjuːt] **1** n istituto. **2** vt (start: reform) introdurre; (: inquiry, investigation) istituire, aprire; (: legal proceedings) intentare.

in·sti·tu·tion [ˌɪnstɪˈtjuːʃən] n **(a)** (organization) istituzione f; (charitable ~, mental ~) istituto. **(b)** (custom etc) istituzione f.

in·struct [ɪnˈstrʌkt] vt **(a)** (teach) istruire. **(b)** (order): **to** ~ **sb to do sth** ordinare a qn di fare qc.

in·struc·tion [ɪnˈstrʌkʃən] **1** n **(a)** (teaching) istruzione f. **(b)**: ~**s** (orders, directions) istruzioni fpl; **to give sb** ~**s (to do sth)** dare istruzioni a qn (di fare qc); ~**s for use** istruzioni per l'uso. **2** cpd: ~ **book** n libretto di istruzioni.

in·struc·tive [ɪnˈstrʌktɪv] adj istruttivo(a).

in·struc·tor [ɪnˈstrʌktəʳ] n (gen) istruttore/trice; (Ski) maestro/a.

in·stru·ment [ˈɪnstrʊmənt] **1** n (also Mus) strumento; **to fly on** ~**s** (Aer) fare il volo strumentale. **2** cpd: ~ **panel** n (Aer) quadro degli strumenti.

in·stru·men·tal [ˌɪnstrʊˈmentl] adj **(a)**: **to be** ~ **in sth/in doing sth** avere un ruolo importante in qc/nel fare qc. **(b)** (music etc) strumentale.

in·stru·men·tal·ist [ˌɪnstrʊˈmentəlɪst] n strumentalista m/f.

in·sub·or·di·nate [ˌɪnsəˈbɔːdənɪt] adj insubordinato(a).

in·sub·or·di·na·tion [ˈɪnsəˌbɔːdɪˈneɪʃən] n insubordinazione f.

in·suf·fer·able [ɪnˈsʌfərəbl] adj insopportabile.

in·suf·fi·cient [ˌɪnsəˈfɪʃənt] adj insufficiente.

in·su·lar [ˈɪnsjələʳ] adj (climate) insulare; (fig: person) di mentalità ristretta; ~ **attitude** chiusura mentale, ristrettezza di idee.

in·su·late [ˈɪnsjʊleɪt] vt (against cold) isolare termicamente; (against noise) isolare acusticamente; (Elec: wire) isolare; (fig: person): **to** ~ **sb (from)** tener qn lontano (da).

in·su·lat·ing tape [ˈɪnsjʊleɪtɪŋˌteɪp] n nastro isolante.

in·su·la·tion [ˌɪnsjʊˈleɪʃən] n (see vb) isolamento termico; isolamento acustico; isolamento (elettrico); (material) (materiale m) isolante.

in·su·lin [ˈɪnsjʊlɪn] n insulina.

in·sult [ˈɪnsʌlt] **1** n insulto. **2** [ɪnˈsʌlt] vt insultare.

in·sult·ing [ɪnˈsʌltɪŋ] adj insolente, insultante.

in·su·per·able [ɪnˈsuːpərəbl] adj insuperabile.

in·sur·ance [ɪnˈʃʊərəns] **1** n assicurazione f; **life** ~ assicurazione sulla vita; **to take out** ~ **(against)** fare un'assicurazione (contro), assicurarsi (contro). **2** cpd (agent, broker) di assicurazioni; (certificate, company, policy) di assicurazione.

in·sure [ɪnˈʃʊəʳ] vt (house, car, parcel): **to** ~ **(against)** assicurare (contro); **to** ~ **o.s.** or **one's life** assicurarsi (sulla vita); **to** ~ **sb** or **sb's life** assicurare qn sulla vita; **to be** ~**d for £5000** essere assicurato per 5000 sterline.

in·sured [ɪnˈʃʊəd] n: **the** ~ l'assicurato/a.

in·sur·er [ɪnˈʃʊərəʳ] n assicuratore/trice.

in·sur·gent [ɪnˈsɜːdʒənt] **1** adj ribelle. **2** n insorto/a, rivoltoso/a.

in·sur·mount·able [ˌɪnsəˈmaʊntəbl] adj insormontabile.

in·sur·rec·tion [ˌɪnsəˈrekʃən] n insurrezione f.

in·tact [ɪnˈtækt] adj intatto(a).

in·take [ˈɪnteɪk] n **(a)** (Tech: of air, water, gas etc) immissione f. **(b)** (quantity: of students) afflusso; (: of workers) assunzioni fpl; (: of food) consumo.

in·tan·gible [ɪnˈtændʒəbl] adj **(a)** (fears, hopes) indefinibile. **(b)** (Comm: asset) immateriale.

in·te·gral [ˈɪntɪɡrəl] adj **(a)** (essential: part) integrante. **(b)** (Math): ~ **calculus** calcolo integrale.

in·te·grate [ˈɪntɪɡreɪt] vt (gen, Math) integrare; (Am: school, community) operare un'integrazione razziale all'interno di.

in·te·grat·ed [ˈɪntɪɡreɪtɪd] adj (population, school) in cui si è operata un'integrazione razziale; (personality) equilibrato(a).

in·te·gra·tion [ˌɪntɪˈɡreɪʃən] n integrazione f; **ra·cial** ~ integrazione razziale.

in·teg·rity [ɪnˈtɛɡrɪtɪ] n integrità.

in·tel·lect [ˈɪntɪlekt] n intelletto.

in·tel·lec·tual [ˌɪntɪˈlektjʊəl] **1** adj (person) intellettuale; (interests) culturale. **2** n intellettuale m/f.

in·tel·li·gence [ɪnˈtelɪdʒəns] **1** n (cleverness) intelligenza; (information) informazioni fpl; **I** ~ **(Service)** (Mil, Pol) servizio segreto. **2** cpd: ~ **quotient** n (abbr **IQ**) quoziente m d'intelligenza; ~ **test** n test m inv d'intelligenza.

in·tel·li·gent [ɪnˈtelɪdʒənt] adj intelligente.

in·tel·li·gi·ble [ɪnˈtelɪdʒəbl] adj intelligibile.

in·tem·per·ate [ɪnˈtempərɪt] adj (climate) rigido(a); (person, habits) smoderato(a).

in·tend [ɪnˈtend] vt (mean): **to** ~ **to do sth** avere (l')intenzione di fare qc, intendere fare qc; (remark, gift): **to** ~ **sth for sb/sth** destinare qc a qn/qc; **I** ~ **him to come too** voglio che venga anche lui; **it was** ~**ed as a compliment** voleva essere un complimento; **I** ~**ed no harm** non intendevo fare del male; **did you** ~ **that?** è questo che intendevi?

in·tense [ɪnˈtens] adj (heat, cold, expression) intenso(a); (interest, enthusiasm) vivo(a), profondo(a); (person) di forti sentimenti.

in·tense·ly [ɪnˈtenslɪ] adv (difficult, hot, cold) estremamente; (moved) profondamente.

in·ten·si·fy [ɪnˈtensɪfaɪ] **1** vt intensificare. **2** vi intensificarsi.

in·ten·si·ty [ɪnˈtensɪtɪ] n intensità f inv.

in·ten·sive [ɪnˈtensɪv] adj (study) intenso(a); (course) intensivo(a); (bombing) a tappeto; ~ **care unit** centro di rianimazione; **to be in** ~ **care** essere ricoverato al centro di rianimazione.

in·tent [ɪnˈtent] **1** adj **(a)** (absorbed) assorto(a); **to be** ~ **on sth** essere intento(a) a qc. **(b)** (determined): **to be** ~ **on doing sth** essere deciso(a) a fare qc. **2** n intenzione f, intento; **with** ~ **to kill** con l'intento di uccidere; **to all** ~**s and purposes** praticamente.

in·ten·tion [ɪnˈtenʃən] n intenzione f; **I have no** ~ **of going** non ho nessuna intenzione di andare; **I have every** ~ **of going** ho tutte le intenzioni di andare; **with the best of** ~**s** con le migliori intenzioni del mondo.

in·ten·tion·al [ɪnˈtenʃənl] adj intenzionale; **it wasn't** ~ non l'ho (or l'hai etc) fatto apposta.

in·ten·tion·al·ly [ɪnˈtenʃnəlɪ] adv deliberatamente.

inter... [ˈɪntəʳ] pref inter... .

inter·act [ˌɪntərˈækt] vi interagire.

inter·ac·tion [ˌɪntərˈækʃən] n interazione f.

inter·cede [ˌɪntəˈsiːd] vi: **to** ~ **with sb/on behalf of sb** intercedere presso qn/a favore di qn.

inter·cept [ˌɪntəˈsept] vt intercettare.

inter·cep·tion [ˌɪntəˈsepʃən] n intercettazione f, intercettamento.

inter·change [ˈɪntəˌtʃeɪndʒ] **1** n **(a)** (of views, ideas) scambio. **(b)** (on motorway etc) incrocio pluridirezionale. **2** [ˌɪntəˈtʃeɪndʒ] vt (views) scambiarsi.

inter·change·able [ˌɪntəˈtʃeɪndʒəbl] adj intercambiabile.

inter·city [ˌɪntəˈsɪtɪ] adj: ~ **(train)** ≈ (treno) rapido.

inter·com [ˈɪntəkɒm] n (fam) interfono.

inter·con·ti·nen·tal ['ɪntə,kɒntɪ'nentl] adj intercontinentale.

inter·course ['ɪntəkɔːs] n rapporti mpl, relazioni fpl; (sexual ~) rapporti sessuali.

inter·de·pend·ent [,ɪntədɪ'pendənt] adj interdipendente.

inter·dict ['ɪntədɪkt] n interdizione f.

in·ter·est ['ɪntrɪst] 1 n (a) interesse m; to have or take an ~ in sth interessarsi di or a qc; to have or take no ~ in sth non interessarsi di qc; to be of ~ to sb interessare qn; to lose ~ in sth perdere l'interesse per qc; I have lost ~ in motor racing le corse automobilistiche non mi interessano più.

(b) (profit, advantage) interesse m; in one's own ~(s) nel proprio interesse; to act in sb's ~(s) agire nell'interesse di qn; to have a vested ~ in sth essere direttamente interessato in or a qc; in the public ~ nel pubblico interesse.

(c) (Comm: share, concern) interessi mpl; business ~s attività fpl commerciali; British ~s in the Middle East gli interessi (commerciali) britannici nel Medio Oriente.

(d) (Comm: on loan, shares etc) interesse m; compound/simple ~ interesse composto/ semplice; at an ~ of 5% all'interesse del 5%; to bear ~ at 5% fruttare il 5% (di interesse); to lend at ~ prestare denaro a interesse.

2 vt interessare; to be ~ed in sth interessarsi di qc; he's ~ed in buying a car è interessato all'acquisto di una macchina; to ~ o.s. in sth interessarsi a qc.

3 cpd: ~ rate n tasso di interesse.

in·ter·est·ed ['ɪntrɪstɪd] adj (expression) interessato(a), pieno(a) di interesse; (person) che s'interessa; ~ party parte f interessata.

interest-free ['ɪntrɪst'friː] adj senza interesse.

in·ter·est·ing ['ɪntrɪstɪŋ] adj interessante.

inter·fere [,ɪntə'fɪər] vi: to ~ (in sth) interferire (in qc), intromettersi (in qc); to ~ with sth (hinder) intralciare qc, interferire con qc; (Radio, TV) causare delle interferenze in qc; he is always interfering si intromette sempre in tutto; stop interfering! non essere invadente!

inter·fer·ence [,ɪntə'fɪərəns] n interferenza, intromissione f; (Radio, TV) interferenza.

inter·fer·ing [,ɪntə'fɪərɪŋ] adj invadente.

in·ter·im ['ɪntərɪm] 1 n: in the ~ nel frattempo. 2 adj (report) provvisorio(a); (government) ad interim; ~ dividend acconto di dividendo.

in·te·ri·or [ɪn'tɪərɪər] 1 adj interno(a). 2 n interno; Department of the I~ Ministero degli Interni or dell'Interno. 3 cpd: ~ decorator n decoratore/ trice (d'interni).

inter·jec·tion [,ɪntə'dʒekʃən] n interiezione f.

inter·lop·er ['ɪntələupər] n intruso/a.

inter·lude ['ɪntəluːd] n parentesi f inv, intervallo; (Theatre) intermezzo; musical ~ interludio.

inter·mar·ry ['ɪntə'mærɪ] vi fare un matrimonio misto.

inter·medi·ary [,ɪntə'miːdɪərɪ] n mediatore/trice, intermediario/a.

inter·medi·ate [,ɪntə'miːdɪət] adj intermedio(a); (student) che frequenta un corso intermedio.

in·ter·mi·nable [ɪn'tɜːmɪnəbl] adj interminabile.

inter·mis·sion [,ɪntə'mɪʃən] n (pause) interruzione f, sosta, pausa; (Theatre) intervallo

inter·mit·tent [,ɪntə'mɪtənt] adj intermittente.

in·tern [ɪn'tɜːn] 1 vt internare. 2 ['ɪntɜːn] n (Am: doctor) (medico) interno.

in·ter·nal [ɪn'tɜːnl] adj interno(a); ~ injuries lesioni fpl interne; I~ Revenue Service (Am) Fisco; ~ combustion engine motore m a combustione interna or a scoppio.

in·ter·nal·ly [ɪn'tɜːnəlɪ] adv internamente; to bleed ~ avere un'emorragia interna; 'not to be taken ~' 'per uso esterno'.

inter·na·tion·al [,ɪntə'næʃnəl] 1 adj internazionale; ~ date line linea del cambiamento di data; I~ Monetary Fund Fondo monetario internazionale. 2 n (Sport: game) incontro internazionale; (: player) giocatore/trice della squadra nazionale.

in·ternee [,ɪntɜː'niː] n internato/a.

in·tern·ment [ɪn'tɜːnmənt] n internamento.

inter·play ['ɪntəpleɪ] n interazione f.

Inter·pol ['ɪntə,pɒl] n Interpol f.

in·ter·pret [ɪn'tɜːprɪt] 1 vt (a) (translate orally): to ~ sth (into) fare l'interpretazione di qc (verso). (b) (explain, understand) interpretare. 2 vi fare da interprete.

in·ter·pre·ta·tion [ɪn,tɜːprɪ'teɪʃən] n interpretazione f.

in·ter·pret·er [ɪn'tɜːprɪtər] n interprete m/f.

inter·re·lat·ed [,ɪntərɪ'leɪtɪd] adj correlato(a), in relazione (l'uno(a) con l'altro(a)).

in·ter·ro·gate [ɪn'terəgeɪt] vt interrogare.

in·ter·ro·ga·tion [ɪn,terə'geɪʃən] n interrogatorio.

in·ter·rog·ative [,ɪntə'rɒgətɪv] adj interrogativo(a).

in·ter·ro·ga·tor [ɪn'terəgeɪtər] n interrogatore/ trice.

in·ter·rupt [,ɪntə'rʌpt] vt, vi interrompere.

in·ter·rup·tion [,ɪntə'rʌpʃən] n interruzione f.

inter·sect [,ɪntə'sekt] 1 vt (Math) intersecare. 2 vi (Math) intersecarsi; (roads) incrociarsi, intersecarsi.

inter·sec·tion [,ɪntə'sekʃən] n (Math) intersezione f; (crossroads) incrocio.

inter·sperse [,ɪntə'spɜːs] vt: to ~ sth with sth inframmezzare qc con qc.

in·ter·val ['ɪntəvəl] n intervallo; at ~s di tanto in tanto, a tratti; at regular ~s a intervalli regolari; sunny ~s (Met) schiarite fpl.

inter·vene [,ɪntə'viːn] vi (event, circumstances) sopraggiungere; (person): to ~ (in) intervenire (in); in the intervening years negli anni che sono intercorsi.

inter·ven·tion [,ɪntə'venʃən] n intervento.

inter·view ['ɪntəvjuː] 1 n (for job) colloquio; (on radio, in paper etc) intervista; to have an ~ with the director avere un colloquio con il direttore. 2 vt (see n) sottoporre a colloquio; intervistare.

inter·view·er ['ɪntəvjuːər] n (on radio etc) intervistatore/trice.

in·tes·tate [ɪn'testɪt] adj (Law): to die ~ morire intestato(a).

in·tes·ti·nal [ɪn'testɪnl] adj intestinale.

in·tes·tine [ɪn'testɪn] n intestino.

in·ti·ma·cy ['ɪntɪməsɪ] n (friendship) intimità; (sexual ~) rapporti mpl intimi.

in·ti·mate ['ɪntɪmɪt] 1 adj intimo(a); (knowledge) profondo(a); to be/become ~ with sb (friendly) essere/diventare amico intimo di qn; (sexually) avere rapporti intimi con qn. 2 ['ɪntɪmeɪt] vt: to ~ (that) far or lasciar capire (che).

in·ti·ma·tion [,ɪntɪ'meɪʃən] n (hint) accenno.

in·timi·date [ɪn'tɪmɪdeɪt] vt intimidire; (witness) sottoporre ad intimidazione.

in·timi·da·tion [ɪn,tɪmɪ'deɪʃən] n intimidazione f.

into ['ɪntʊ] prep (a) (of place) in, dentro; put it ~ the box mettilo nella or dentro la scatola; to go ~ the wood entrare nel bosco; to go ~ town/the country andare in città/in campagna; to get ~ the plane/car salire sull'aereo/in macchina. (b) (change in condition etc) in; to translate sth ~

Italian tradurre qc in italiano; **to burst ~ tears** scoppiare in lacrime; **to change pounds ~ dollars** cambiare delle sterline in dollari; **he is really ~ jazz** *(fam)* è un appassionato *or* ha la passione del jazz. **(c)** *(Math)*: **2 ~ 6 goes 3 times** il 2 nel 6 sta 3 volte; **to divide 3 ~ 12** dividere 12 per 3.

in·tol·er·able [ɪn'tɒlərəbl] *adj* insopportabile, intollerabile.

in·tol·er·ance [ɪn'tɒlərəns] *n* intolleranza.

in·tol·er·ant [ɪn'tɒlərənt] *adj:* **~ (of)** intollerante (di).

in·to·na·tion [ˌɪntəʊ'neɪʃən] *n (Linguistics)* intonazione *f.*

in·toxi·cate [ɪn'tɒksɪkeɪt] *vt (subj: alcohol)* ubriacare, dare alla testa a; *(: success)* inebriare.

in·toxi·cat·ed [ɪn'tɒksɪkeɪtɪd] *adj* ubriaco(a); **~ (with)** *(fig)* inebriato(a) (di); **to become ~** ubriacarsi.

in·toxi·ca·tion [ɪnˌtɒksɪ'keɪʃən] *n (see adj)* ubriacatura, ebbrezza, esaltazione *f.*

in·trac·table [ɪn'træktəbl] *adj (person, mood)* intrattabile; *(illness)* difficile da curare; *(problem)* insolubile.

in·tran·si·gence [ɪn'trænsɪdʒəns] *n* intransigenza.

in·tran·si·gent [ɪn'trænsɪdʒənt] *adj* intransigente.

in·tran·si·tive [ɪn'trænsɪtɪv] *adj (Gram)* intransitivo(a).

intra·venous [ˌɪntrə'viːnəs] *adj* endovenoso(a).

in·trep·id [ɪn'trepɪd] *adj* intrepido(a), audace.

in·tri·cate ['ɪntrɪkɪt] *adj (pattern, plot, problem)* intricato(a), complicato(a); *(machinery, mechanism)* complicato(a), complesso(a).

in·trigue [ɪn'triːg] **1** *n (plot)* intrigo; *(amorous)* tresca. **2** *vt* incuriosire; *(fascinate)* incantare. **3** *vi* complottare, tramare.

in·tri·guing [ɪn'triːgɪŋ] **1** *adj* affascinante. **2** *n* intrighi *mpl.*

in·trin·sic [ɪn'trɪnsɪk] *adj* intrinseco(a).

intro·duce [ˌɪntrə'djuːs] *vt* **(a)** *(bring in: reform, new fashion, idea)* introdurre; *(: Pol: bill; TV, Radio: programme)* presentare; **to ~ sb into a firm** far entrare qn in una ditta. **(b)** *(make acquainted)*: **to ~ sb to sb** presentare qn a qn; **to ~ sb to sth** far conoscere qc a qn; **she ~d us to the delights of Indian cookery** ci ha iniziato ai piaceri della cucina indiana; **may I ~...?** permette che le presenti...?

intro·duc·tion [ˌɪntrə'dʌkʃən] *n (vedi vb)* introduzione *f;* presentazione *f;* **my ~ to maths** il mio primo contatto con la matematica; **a letter of ~** una lettera di presentazione.

intro·duc·tory [ˌɪntrə'dʌktərɪ] *adj* introduttivo(a); **~ remarks** osservazioni preliminari; **an ~ offer** un'offerta di lancio.

intro·spec·tion [ˌɪntrəʊ'spekʃən] *n* introspezione *f.*

intro·spec·tive [ˌɪntrəʊ'spektɪv] *adj* introspettivo(a).

intro·vert ['ɪntrəʊvɜːt] *n* introverso/a.

in·trude [ɪn'truːd] *vi* intromettersi; **to ~ on** *(person)* importunare; *(conversation)* intromettersi in; **I hope I'm not intruding** spero di non intromettermi.

in·trud·er [ɪn'truːdə'] *n* intruso/a.

in·tru·sion [ɪn'truːʒən] *n* intrusione *f.*

in·tru·sive [ɪn'truːsɪv] *adj* importuno(a).

in·tui·tion [ˌɪntjuː'ɪʃən] *n (no pl: power)* intuito, intuizione *f;* *(feeling)* intuito.

in·tui·tive [ɪn'tjuːɪtɪv] *adj* intuitivo(a).

in·un·date ['ɪnʌndeɪt] *vt:* **to ~ (with)** inondare (di); *(fig)* sommergere (di).

in·ure [ɪn'jʊə'] *vt:* **to ~ (to)** assuefare (a).

in·vade [ɪn'veɪd] *vt (Mil, gen, fig)* invadere; *(privacy)*

intromettersi in; *(sb's rights)* violare.

in·vad·er [ɪn'veɪdə'] *n* invasore *m.*

in·va·lid[1] ['ɪnvəlɪd] **1** *n (sick person)* infermo/a, malato/a; *(disabled)* invalido/a. **2** *adj (see n)* infermo(a), malato(a); invalido(a); **~ chair** sedia a rotelle.

in·val·id[2] [ɪn'vælɪd] *adj (document, cheque)* non valido(a), nullo(a); *(excuse, argument)* non valido(a); *(marriage)* nullo(a).

in·vali·date [ɪn'vælɪdeɪt] *vt (passport, contract)* annullare, rendere nullo(a); *(argument)* smentire; **the will was ~d** il testamento è stato invalidato.

in·valu·able [ɪn'væljʊəbl] *adj* prezioso(a); inestimabile.

in·vari·able [ɪn'vɛərɪəbl] *adj* costante, invariabile.

in·vari·ably [ɪn'vɛərɪəblɪ] *adv* invariabilmente; **she is ~ late** è immancabilmente in ritardo.

in·va·sion [ɪn'veɪʒən] *n* invasione *f;* **an ~ of sb's privacy** una violazione della privacy di qn.

in·vec·tive [ɪn'vektɪv] *n* invettiva.

in·vei·gle [ɪn'viːgl] *vt:* **to ~ sb into (doing) sth** circuire qn per (fargli fare) qc.

in·vent [ɪn'vent] *vt* inventare.

in·ven·tion [ɪn'venʃən] *n* invenzione *f.*

in·ven·tive [ɪn'ventɪv] *adj (genius)* inventivo(a); *(mind)* ricco(a) d'inventiva.

in·ven·tor [ɪn'ventə'] *n* inventore/trice.

in·ven·tory ['ɪnventrɪ] *n* inventario; **to draw up/take an ~** fare l'inventario.

in·verse ['ɪnvɜːs] *adj* inverso(a); **in ~ proportion (to)** in modo inversamente proporzionale (a); **to be in ~ proportion** essere inversamente proporzionale.

in·vert [ɪn'vɜːt] *vt (object)* capovolgere; *(elements, words)* invertire; **in ~ed commas** tra virgolette.

in·ver·tebrate [ɪn'vɜːtɪbrɪt] *n* invertebrato(a).

in·vest [ɪn'vest] **1** *vt* **(a)** *(money, capital)* investire; *(fig: time, effort)* impiegare. **(b): to ~ sb with sth** investire qn di qc. **2** *vi:* **to ~ in** *(company etc)* investire in, fare (degli) investimenti in; *(hum: buy)* comprarsi.

in·ves·ti·gate [ɪn'vestɪgeɪt] *vt (crime, motive)* indagare su; *(possibilities)* studiare, esaminare.

in·ves·ti·ga·tion [ɪnˌvestɪ'geɪʃən] *n* indagine *f;* **police ~s** le investigazioni *or* le indagini della polizia.

in·ves·ti·gative [ɪn'vestɪgətɪv] *adj:* **~ journalism** giornalismo investigativo.

in·ves·ti·ga·tor [ɪn'vestɪgeɪtə'] *n* investigatore/trice; **a private ~** un investigatore privato, un detective.

in·vest·ment [ɪn'vestmənt] *n (Comm)* investimento.

in·ves·tor [ɪn'vestə'] *n (gen)* investitore/trice; *(shareholder)* azionista *m/f.*

in·vidi·ous [ɪn'vɪdɪəs] *adj (distinction, comparison)* ingiusto(a); *(task)* poco invidiabile.

in·vigi·late [ɪn'vɪdʒɪleɪt] *vt, vi (in exam)* sorvegliare.

in·vigi·la·tor [ɪn'vɪdʒɪleɪtə'] *n* chi sorveglia agli esami.

in·vig·or·at·ing [ɪn'vɪgəreɪtɪŋ] *adj (thought, speech, sight)* rincuorante; *(exercise, walk)* tonificante; *(air, breeze)* vivificante.

in·vin·cible [ɪn'vɪnsəbl] *adj* invincibile.

in·vis·ible [ɪn'vɪzəbl] *adj* invisibile.

in·vi·ta·tion [ˌɪnvɪ'teɪʃən] *n* invito; **by ~ only** esclusivamente su *or* per invito; **at sb's ~** dietro invito di qn.

in·vite [ɪn'vaɪt] *vt (person):* **to ~ sb (to do)** invitare qn (a fare); *(subscriptions, applications)* sollecitare, richiedere (cortesemente); *(opinions)* chiedere; *(discussion)* invitare a; *(ridicule)* provocare, suscitare; *(trouble etc)* cercare; **to ~ sb to dinner** invitare qn a cena; **to ~ sb in/up** *etc* invitare qn a entrare/salire *etc*.

♦ **invite out** *vt + adv* invitare fuori; **he ~d us out to dinner** ci ha invitato a cena fuori.

♦ **invite over** *vt + adv* invitare (a casa).

in·vit·ing [ɪn'vaɪtɪŋ] *adj (prospect, goods)* invitante, allettante; *(smile)* invitante; *(food, smell)* invitante, appetitoso(a).

in·voice ['ɪnvɔɪs] **1** *n* fattura. **2** *vt (goods)* fatturare; **to ~ sb for goods** inviare a qn la fattura per le *or* delle merci.

in·voke [ɪn'vəʊk] *vt* invocare.

in·vol·un·tary [ɪn'vɒləntərɪ] *adj* involontario(a).

in·volve [ɪn'vɒlv] *vt* **(a)** *(associate)* coinvolgere; *(implicate)* implicare, coinvolgere; **to be/become ~d in sth** essere/rimanere coinvolto in qc; **to involve o.s./sb in sth** *(politics etc)* impegnarsi/impegnare qn in qc; **don't ~ me in your quarrels!** non tiratemi in mezzo alle vostre beghe!; **don't ~ yourself in unnecessary expense** non metterti a fare spese inutili; **how did he come to be ~d?** come ha fatto a trovarcisi in mezzo?; **the factors ~d** i fattori in causa *or* in gioco; **the persons ~d** le persone in questione *or* coinvolte; **I feel personally ~d** mi sento personalmente coinvolto; **to become** *or* **get ~d with sb** *(socially)* legarsi a qn, mettersi con qn; *(emotionally)* legarsi sentimentalmente a qn.

(b) *(entail)* implicare, comportare; **it ~s a lot of expense/trouble** comporta un mucchio di spese/difficoltà.

in·volved [ɪn'vɒlvd] *adj* complicato(a), complesso(a).

in·volve·ment [ɪn'vɒlvmənt] *n* **(a)** *(being involved)* impegno, partecipazione *f; (emotional)* legame *m*, relazione *f*; **we don't know the extent of his ~** non sappiamo fino a che punto sia coinvolto; **financial ~s** impegni *mpl* finanziari. **(b)** *(complexity)* complessità.

in·vul·ner·able [ɪn'vʌlnərəbl] *adj* invulnerabile; *(argument)* inattaccabile.

in·ward ['ɪnwəd] *adj (peace, happiness)* interiore; *(thought)* intimo(a).

in·ward·ly ['ɪnwədlɪ] *adv* nel proprio intimo, dentro di sé; *(direction)* verso l'interno.

in·ward(s) ['ɪnwəd(z)] *adv* verso l'interno.

iodine ['aɪədiːn] *n* iodio.

ion ['aɪən] *n* ione *m*.

Ion·ic [aɪ'ɒnɪk] *adj* ionico(a).

iota [aɪ'əʊtə] *n (letter)* iota; *(of truth, commonsense)* briciolo.

IOU [,aɪəʊ'juː] *abbr (= I owe you)* pagherò *m inv*.

IQ *abbr of* **intelligence quotient.**

I.R.A. *n (abbr of Irish Republican Army)* I.R.A.

Iran [ɪ'rɑːn] *n* Iran *m*.

Ira·nian [ɪ'reɪnɪən] **1** *adj* iraniano(a). **2** *n (person)* iraniano/a; *(language)* iranico.

Iraq [ɪ'rɑːk] *n* Iraq *m*.

Ira·qi [ɪ'rɑːkɪ] *adj, n* iracheno(a) *(m/f)*.

iras·cible [ɪ'ræsɪbl] *adj* irascibile.

irate [aɪ'reɪt] *adj* irato(a), infuriato(a).

Ire·land ['aɪələnd] *n* Irlanda; **Northern ~** Irlanda del Nord; **Republic of I~** Repubblica d'Irlanda, Eire *f*.

iris ['aɪərɪs] *n* **(a)** *(Anat)* iride *f*. **(b)** *(Bot)* iris *f inv*, giaggiolo.

Irish ['aɪərɪʃ] **1** *adj* irlandese; **the ~ Sea** il Mar d'Irlanda. **2** *n* **(a):** **the ~** *npl* gli irlandesi. **(b)** *(language)* irlandese.

Irish·man ['aɪərɪʃmən] *n, pl* **-men** irlandese *m*.

Irish·woman ['aɪərɪʃ,wʊmən] *n, pl* **-women** irlandese *f*.

irk·some ['ɜːksəm] *adj* noioso(a), seccante.

iron ['aɪən] **1** *n (also fig)* ferro; *(Golf)* mazza da golf di ferro; *(for ironing clothes)* ferro (da stiro); **a will of ~** una volontà ferrea *or* di ferro; **he rules his children with a rod of ~** comanda a bacchetta i figli; **to strike while the ~ is hot** *(fig)* battere finché il ferro è caldo; **to have a lot of/too many ~s in the fire** *(fig)* avere molta/troppa carne al fuoco. **2** *vt (clothes)* stirare. **3** *vi* stirare; **this dress ~s well** questo vestito è facile da stirare. **4** *cpd (bridge, bar, tool etc)* di ferro; *(fig: will, determination)* ferreo(a), di ferro; **the I~ Age** l'età del ferro; **~ constitution** *n (fig)* costituzione *f* robusta; **I~ Curtain** *n (fig, Pol)* cortina di ferro; **I~ Curtain countries, countries behind the I~ Curtain** gli stati d'oltrecortina; **~ foundry** *n* fonderia; **~ lung** *n (Med)* polmone *m* d'acciaio; **~ ore** *n* minerale *m* di ferro; **the ~ and steel industry** l'industria siderurgica.

♦ **iron out** *vt + adv (creases)* stirare; *(fig: problems, disagreements)* appianare.

iron·ic(al) [aɪ'rɒnɪk(əl)] *adj* ironico(a); **it's ~ that...** è un'ironia (della sorte) che... .

ironi·cal·ly [aɪ'rɒnɪkəlɪ] *adv* ironicamente.

iron·ing ['aɪənɪŋ] **1** *n (act)* stirare *m; (clothes)* roba da stirare; **mother is doing the ~** la mamma sta stirando. **2** *cpd:* **~ board** *n* asse *f* da stiro.

iron·monger ['aɪən,mʌŋɡə⁻] *n (Brit):* **~'s (shop)** negozio di ferramenta.

iro·ny ['aɪərənɪ] *n* ironia; **the ~ of it is that...** l'ironia maggiore è che...; **it's one of life's ironies** è un'ironia della sorte *or* del destino.

ir·ra·tion·al [ɪ'ræʃənl] *adj* irragionevole; **an ~ fear** una paura irrazionale.

ir·rec·on·cil·able [ɪ,rekən'saɪləbl] *adj (persons)* irreconciliabile; *(belief)* inconciliabile.

ir·re·deem·able [,ɪrɪ'diːməbl] *adj* irreparabile.

ir·re·fut·able [,ɪrɪ'fjuːtəbl] *adj* irrefutabile.

ir·regu·lar [ɪ'reɡjʊlə⁻] *adj* irregolare.

ir·regu·lar·ity [ɪ,reɡjʊ'lærɪtɪ] *n* irregolarità *f inv*.

ir·rel·evance [ɪ'reləvəns] *n* non pertinenza.

ir·rel·evant [ɪ'reləvənt] *adj* non pertinente; **if he has the qualifications, his age is ~** se ha i titoli, la sua età non ha importanza.

ir·re·li·gious [,ɪrɪ'lɪdʒəs] *adj* irreligiosa(a).

ir·repa·rable [ɪ'repərəbl] *adj* irrimediabile, irreparabile.

ir·re·place·able [,ɪrɪ'pleɪsəbl] *adj* insostituibile.

ir·re·press·ible [,ɪrɪ'presəbl] *adj* irrefrenabile.

ir·re·proach·able [,ɪrɪ'prəʊtʃəbl] *adj (conduct)* irreprensibile.

ir·re·sist·ible [,ɪrɪ'zɪstəbl] *adj* irresistibile.

ir·reso·lute [ɪ'rezəluːt] *adj (person, character)* irresoluto(a), indeciso(a).

ir·re·spec·tive [,ɪrɪ'spektɪv] **: ~ of** *prep* a prescindere da, qualunque + *sub;* **~ of the weather** qualunque tempo faccia.

ir·re·spon·sible [,ɪrɪs'pɒnsəbl] *adj (person, behaviour)* irresponsabile.

ir·re·triev·able [,ɪrɪ'triːvəbl] *adj (object)* irrecuperabile; *(loss, damage)* irreparabile.

ir·rev·er·ent [ɪ'revərənt] *adj* irriverente.

ir·revo·cable [ɪ'revəkəbl] *adj* irrevocabile.

ir·ri·gate ['ɪrɪɡeɪt] *vt* irrigare.

ir·ri·ga·tion [,ɪrɪ'ɡeɪʃən] *n* irrigazione *f*.

ir·ri·table ['ɪrɪtəbl] *adj* irritabile.

ir·ri·tant ['ɪrɪtənt] *n* sostanza irritante.

ir·ri·tate ['ɪrɪteɪt] *vt* irritare.

ir·ri·tat·ing ['ɪrɪteɪtɪŋ] *adj* irritante.

ir·ri·ta·tion [,ɪrɪ'teɪʃən] *n (gen, Med)* irritazione *f; (fig: irritating thing)* seccatura.

is [ɪz] *3rd pers sg present of* **be.**

Is·lam ['ɪzlɑːm] *n* Islam *m inv*.

Is·lam·ic [ɪzˈlæmɪk] *adj* islamico(a).

is·land [ˈaɪlənd] **1** *n* isola. **2** *cpd*: ~ **people** *npl* isolani *mpl*.

is·land·er [ˈaɪləndəʳ] *n* isolano/a.

isle [aɪl] *n (poet)* isola.

isn't [ˈɪznt] = **is not**.

iso·late [ˈaɪsəʊleɪt] *vt (gen, Med)*: **to ~ (from)** isolare (da); *(pinpoint: cause etc)* individuare, isolare.

iso·lat·ed [ˈaɪsəʊleɪtɪd] *adj* isolato(a).

iso·la·tion [ˌaɪsəʊˈleɪʃən] **1** *n* isolamento. **2** *cpd*: ~ **ward** *n* reparto isolamento.

iso·tope [ˈaɪsəʊtəʊp] *n* isotopo.

Is·ra·el [ˈɪzreɪl] *n* Israele *m*.

Is·rae·li [ɪzˈreɪlɪ] **1** *adj* israeliano(a), d'Israele. **2** *n* israeliano/a.

is·sue [ˈɪʃuː] **1** *n* **(a)** *(matter, question)* questione *f*, problema *m*; **a political** ~ una questione politica; **the (real/main)** ~ **is whether...** la questione (reale/fondamentale) è quella di sapere se...; **to confuse** *or* **obscure the** ~ confondere le cose; **to avoid the** ~ evitare la discussione; **to face the** ~ affrontare la questione; **to make an** ~ **of sth** fare un problema di qc; **the point/matter at** ~ il punto in discussione; **to take** ~ **with sb (over sth)** prendere posizione contro qn (riguardo a qc); **I must take** ~ **with you over your last remark** mi dispiace, ma non sono affatto d'accordo sulla tua ultima osservazione; **he took** ~ **with his son over his late arrival home** se l'è presa con suo figlio perché era tornato a casa tardi.

(b) *(of stamps, banknotes, shares)* emissione *f*; *(of passports, driving licences)* rilascio; *(of rations)* distribuzione *f*; **these coins are a new** ~ queste sono le nuove monete.

(c) *(copy: of magazine etc)* numero, fascicolo; **back** ~ vecchio numero.

(d) *(outcome: frm)* risultato, esito.

(e) *(Law: offspring)* prole *f*, discendenti *mpl*; **to die without** ~ morire senza lasciare discendenti.

2 *vt (book)* pubblicare; *(stamps, cheques, banknotes, shares)* emettere; *(passports, documents)* rilasciare; *(rations, goods)* distribuire; *(tickets for performance)* mettere in vendita; *(order)* dare, impartire; *(statement)* diramare; *(warrant, writ, summons)* spiccare, emettere; **to ~ sth to sb, ~ sb with sth** consegnare qc a qn; **the police ~d a warning to people to remain indoors** la polizia ha raccomandato alla popolazione di rimanere in casa.

3 *vi*: **to ~ (from)** uscire (da), venir fuori (da).

isth·mus [ˈɪsməs] *n* istmo.

it [ɪt] *pron* **(a)** *(specific: subj)* esso(a) *(often not translated)*; *(: direct object)* lo(la), l' *(before vowel)*; *(: indirect object)* gli(le); **where's my book?** — ~'**s on the table** dov'è il mio libro? — è sul tavolo; **have you seen my pen/book?** — **I can't find** ~ **anywhere** hai visto la mia penna/il mio libro? — non la/lo trovo da nessuna parte; **here's the book** — **give** ~ **to me** ecco il libro — dammelo; **of** ~, **from** ~, **about** ~, **out of** ~ *etc* ne; **in** ~, **to** ~, **at** ~ *etc* ci; **I spoke to him about** ~ gliene ho parlato; **she asked him about** ~ **yesterday** glielo ha chiesto ieri; **I'm afraid of** ~ ne ho paura; **I'm proud of** ~ ne sono fiero; **I doubt** ~ ne dubito; **did you go to** ~? ci sei andato?; **in front of/behind** ~ lì

davanti/dietro; **above** ~, **over** ~ **(al)** di sopra; **below** ~, **under** ~ **(al)** di sotto.

(b) *(impersonal)*: ~'**s raining** sta piovendo, piove; ~'**s cold today** oggi fa freddo; ~'**s Friday tomorrow** domani è venerdì; ~'**s the 10th of October** è il 10 ottobre; ~'**s 6 o'clock** sono le 6; **how far is** ~? — ~'**s 10 miles** quant'è lontano? — (sono) 10 miglia; ~'**s 2 hours on the train** sono *or* ci vogliono 2 ore di treno; **I like** ~ **here**, ~'**s quiet** qui mi piace, è tranquillo; ~ **was kind of you** è stato gentile da parte tua; ~'**s no use worrying** preoccuparsi è inutile; ~'**s easy to talk** parlare è facile; **who is** ~? chi è?; ~'**s me** sono io; ~ **was Peter who phoned** è Peter che ha telefonato; **what is** ~? cosa c'è?; **that's** ~! *(approval, agreement)* ecco!, è proprio così!; *(disapproval)* basta!; *(finishing)* (questo) è tutto; **I'm against/(all) for** ~ sono contro/pro.

Ital·ian [ɪˈtæljən] **1** *adj* italiano(a); *(lesson, teacher, dictionary)* d'italiano; *(king)* d'Italia. **2** *n (person)* italiano/a; *(language)* italiano; **the I~s** gli Italiani.

ital·ic [ɪˈtælɪk] **1** *adj (Typ)* corsivo(a). **2**: ~**s** *npl* (carattere *m*) corsivo; **in** ~**s** in corsivo.

Ita·ly [ˈɪtəlɪ] *n* Italia.

itch [ɪtʃ] **1** *n* prurito; **to have an** ~ **to do sth** *(fig)* avere la smania di fare qc. **2** *vi* avere il prurito; **my leg** ~**es** mi prude la gamba; **to be** ~**ing for sth/to do sth** *(fig fam)* aver una gran voglia di qc/di fare qc.

itchy [ˈɪtʃɪ] *adj* (**-ier, -iest**) *(feeling)* di prurito; **my leg is** ~ mi prude la gamba; **I've got** ~ **feet** *(fig)* mi scotta la terra sotto i piedi; **to have** ~ **fingers** *(fig)* aver le mani lunghe.

it'd [ˈɪtd] = **it would, it had**.

item [ˈaɪtəm] *n (in list, catalogue, newspaper)* articolo; *(in bill, account)* voce *f*; *(on agenda)* argomento *or* questione *f* all'ordine del giorno; *(in programme)* numero; ~**s of clothing** capi *mpl* di abbigliamento; **the main** ~ **of news** la notizia più importante.

item·ize [ˈaɪtəmaɪz] *vt* specificare (uno(a) per uno(a)).

itin·er·ant [ɪˈtɪnərənt] *adj (actors)* girovago(a), ambulante; *(preacher)* itinerante.

itin·er·ary [aɪˈtɪnərərɪ] *n* itinerario.

it'll [ˈɪtl] = **it will, it shall**.

its [ɪts] *poss adj* il(la) suo(a), *pl* i(le) suoi(sue); **the dog hurt** ~ **paw** il cane si è fatto male alla zampa; **this doll has lost** ~ **leg** questa bambola ha perso una gamba.

it's [ɪts] = **it is, it has**.

it·self [ɪtˈsɛlf] *pron* **(a)** *(reflexive)* si; **the dog injured** ~ il cane si è fatto male; **the cat is washing** ~ il gatto si pulisce; **the door closed by** ~ la porta si è chiusa da sé. **(b)** *(emphatic)*: **the theatre** ~ il teatro stesso; **Barra,** ~ **a beautiful island...** Barra, di per sé un'isola bellissima...; **she is kindness** ~ è la bontà fatta persona.

ITV *n abbr of Independent Television*.

I.U.D. *n abbr of intra-uterine device*.

I've [aɪv] = **I have**.

ivo·ry [ˈaɪvərɪ] **1** *n* avorio. **2** *adj (colour)* avorio *inv*; *(object)* d'avorio; ~ **tower** *(fig)* torre *f* d'avorio.

ivy [ˈaɪvɪ] **1** *n (Bot)* edera. **2** *cpd*: **I~ League** *n (Am)* insieme delle grandi università del Nord-Est degli Stati Uniti.

J

J, j [dʒeɪ] *n (letter)* J, j *f* or *m inv.*
jab [dʒæb] **1** *n (poke)* colpo (di punta); *(Boxing)*
diretto; *(Med fam)* iniezione *f*. **2** *vt*: to ~ **sth into**
conficcare qc in; **to** ~ **a finger at sb** puntare un
dito contro qn. **3** *vi*: **to** ~ **at** dare colpi a.
jab·ber ['dʒæbə^r] **1** *n (of person)* chiacchierio; *(of
monkey)* schiamazzo. **2** *vt* farfugliare, borbotta-
re. **3** *vi (see n)* ciarlare, chiacchierare; schiamazzare; **they were** ~**ing away in Russian** parlavano
fitto fitto in russo.
jack [dʒæk] *n (Tech, Aut)* cric *m inv*, martinetto;
(Bowls) boccino, pallino; *(Cards)* fante *m*.
♦ **jack in** *vt + adv (fam)* mollare; **let's** ~ **it in** è ora
di smettere.
♦ **jack up** *vt + adv* **(a)** *(Tech)* sollevare con il cric.
(b) *(raise: prices etc)* alzare.
jack·al ['dʒækɔːl] *n* sciacallo.
jack·ass ['dʒækæs] *n (also fig)* asino, somaro.
jack·daw ['dʒækdɔː] *n* taccola.
jack·et ['dʒækɪt] **1** *n (garment)* giacca; *(of boiler etc)*
rivestimento; *(of book)* foderina, copertina. **2**
cpd: ~ **potatoes** *npl* patate *fpl* al cartoccio.
jack-in-the-box ['dʒækɪnðəbɒks] *n* scatola a sorpresa (con pupazzo a molla).
jack-knife ['dʒæknaɪf] **1** *n* coltello a serramanico.
2 *vi*: **the lorry** ~**d** il rimorchio del camion si è
messo di traverso.
jack-of-all-trades [,dʒækəv'ɔːltreɪdz] *n* uno che fa
un po' di tutto.
jack·pot ['dʒækpɒt] *n* primo premio (in denaro); **to
hit the** ~ vincere il primo premio; *(fig)* fare
centro.
ja·cuz·zi [dʒə'kuːzi] *n* jacuzzi *m inv*.
jade [dʒeɪd] **1** *n* giada. **2** *adj (statue, carving, necklace)* di giada; *(also:* ~**-green)** verde giada *inv*.
jad·ed ['dʒeɪdɪd] *adj (person)* sfibrato(a); **to have a**
~ **appetite** non avere più appetito.
jag·ged ['dʒæɡɪd] *adj (edge)* dentellato(a), seghet-
tato(a); *(rock)* frastagliato(a).
jagu·ar ['dʒæɡjuə^r] *n* giaguaro.
jail [dʒeɪl] **1** *n* prigione *f*, carcere *m*; **in** ~ **in** prigione; **to send sb to** ~ mandare qn in prigione. **2**
vt mandare qn in prigione; **he was** ~**ed for 10
years** è stato condannato a 10 anni di prigione.
jail·bird ['dʒeɪlbɜːd] *n* avanzo di galera.
jail·break ['dʒeɪlbreɪk] *n* evasione *f*.
jail·er ['dʒeɪlə^r] *n* carceriere *m*.
ja·lopy [dʒə'lɒpɪ] *n (fam)* macinino.
jam[1] [dʒæm] **1** *n (food)* marmellata; **you want** ~ **on
it!** *(fig fam)* vuoi troppo!, sei incontentabile!;
that's money for ~! *(fig fam)* ti *(or* lo *etc)* pagano
per far niente! **2** *cpd (tart)* alla marmellata; ~ **jar**
n barattolo *or* vasetto per marmellata.
jam[2] [dʒæm] **1** *n* **(a)** *(of people)* folla, calca; *(traffic
~)* ingorgo. **(b)** *(fig fam)*: **to be in/get into a** ~
essere/ficcarsi nei pasticci; **to get sb out of a** ~
tirare qn fuori dai pasticci.
   2 *vt* **(a)** *(block: mechanism, drawer etc)* bloccare; *(: machine)* far inceppare; *(subj: people,
cars: passage, exit)* bloccare, ostruire; *(Radio:
station, broadcast)* creare interferenze in; **to** ~ **a**

door open *(or shut)* bloccare una porta; **streets**
~**med with people** strade molto affollate;
streets ~**med with cars** strade congestionate;
the telephone lines are ~**med** le linee sono so-
vraccariche; **to** ~ **one's brakes on** fare una brusca frenata. **(b)** *(cram)*: **to** ~ **sth into sth** *(drawer,
suitcase etc)* ficcare *or* far entrare qc a forza in
qc; *(room, vehicle)* far entrare qc in qc; **he** ~**med
his hat on his head** si è ficcato il cappello in testa;
I ~**med my finger in the door** mi sono schiacciato il dito nella porta.
   3 *vi (mechanism)* bloccarsi, incepparsi.
   4 *cpd*: ~ **session** *n* improvvisazione *f* jazzi-
stica.
Ja·mai·ca [dʒə'meɪkə] *n* Giamaica.
jamb [dʒæm] *n* stipite *m*.
jam-packed [,dʒæm'pækt] *adj*: ~ **(with)** pieno(a)
zeppo(a) (di), strapieno(a) (di).
jan·gle ['dʒæŋɡl] **1** *n (of bells)* suono stonato; *(of
coins, chains)* rumore *m* metallico. **2** *vt* far risuonare. **3** *vi (see n)* suonare in modo stonato;
produrre un rumore metallico.
jani·tor ['dʒænɪtə^r] *n (doorkeeper)* portiere *m*, portinaio; *(caretaker)* custode *m*; *(: Scol)* bidello.
Janu·ary ['dʒænjuərɪ] *n* gennaio; *for usage see* **July.**
Ja·pan [dʒə'pæn] *n* Giappone *m*.
Japa·nese [,dʒæpə'niːz] **1** *adj* giapponese. **2** *n (person: pl inv)* giapponese *m/f*; *(language)* giapponese
m.
jar[1] [dʒɑː^r] *n (container)* vasetto; *(: of glass)* barattolo; *(: of earthenware)* vaso.
jar[2] [dʒɑː^r] **1** *n (jolt)* scossa, scossone *m*; *(fig)* colpo,
scossa. **2** *vt (also fig)* scuotere; *(elbow)* urtare. **3** *vi
(clash: sounds)* stonare; *(: colours)*: **to** ~ **(with)**
stonare (con); *(: opinions)*: **to** ~ **(with)** discordare
(con); **to** ~ **on sb's nerves** urtare i nervi a qn; **to**
~ **on sb's ears** fare male alle orecchie di qn.
jar·gon ['dʒɑːɡən] *n* gergo.
jar·ring ['dʒɑːrɪŋ] *adj (sound, colour)* stonato(a); **to
strike a** ~ **note (in, at)** *(fig)* portare una nota
stonata (a).
jas·mine ['dʒæzmɪn] *n* gelsomino.
jaun·dice ['dʒɔːndɪs] *n* itterizia.
jaun·diced ['dʒɔːndɪst] *adj (Med)* itterico(a); *(fig:
embittered)* amareggiato(a); **with a** ~ **eye** con
occhio ostile.
jaunt [dʒɔːnt] *n* gita; **to go for a** ~ fare una gita.
jaun·ty ['dʒɔːntɪ] *adj* spigliato(a), disinvolto(a); **at
a** ~ **angle** *(hat)* sulle ventitré.
jave·lin ['dʒævlɪn] *n* giavellotto; **to throw the** ~
(Sport) lanciare il giavellotto.
jaw [dʒɔː] *n (Anat)* mascella; ~**s** *(Tech: of vice etc)*
morsa.
jaw·bone ['dʒɔːbəun] *n* mandibola.
jay [dʒeɪ] *n* ghiandaia.
jay·walk·er ['dʒeɪ,wɔːkə^r] *n* pedone *m* indisciplina-
nato.
jazz [dʒæz] **1** *n (Mus)* jazz *m*; **... and all that** ~ *(fam)*
... e chi più ne ha più ne mette. **2** *cpd*: ~ **band** *n*
banda *f* jazz *inv*.
♦ **jazz up** *vt + adv* **(a)** *(Mus: play)* suonare a ritmo

di jazz; *(: arrange)* adattare a ritmo di jazz. **(b)** *(party etc)* rendere più vivace.

jeal·ous ['dʒɛləs] *adj:* ~ **(of)** geloso(a) (di); **to make sb** ~ **far** ingelosire qn.

jeal·ous·ly ['dʒɛləslı] *adv (enviously)* con gelosia; *(watchfully)* gelosamente.

jeal·ousy ['dʒɛləsı] *n* gelosia.

jeans [dʒi:nz] *npl* jeans *mpl*.

jeep [dʒi:p] *n* jeep *f inv*.

jeer [dʒıə⁺] **1** *n (from crowd):* ~(**s**) fischi *mpl; (from individual)* parola di scherno. **2** *vi:* **to** ~ **(at sb)** *(crowd)* fischiare (qn); *(individual)* farsi beffe (di qn).

jeer·ing ['dʒıərıŋ] **1** *adj (crowd)* che urla e fischia; *(remark, laughter)* di scherno. **2** *n (see vb)* fischi *mpl;* parole *fpl* di scherno.

jell [dʒɛl] *vi* = **gel.**

jel·ly ['dʒɛlı] *n* gelatina.

jelly·fish ['dʒɛlıfıʃ] *n* medusa.

jeop·ard·ize ['dʒɛpədaız] *vt* mettere in pericolo, mettere a repentaglio.

jeop·ardy ['dʒɛpədı] *n* rischio, pericolo; **to place** *or* **put in** ~ mettere a repentaglio.

jerk [dʒɜ:k] **1** *n* **(a)** *(movement)* sobbalzo, scossa; *(Med)* sussulto; **he sat up with a** ~ si sollevò di scatto. **(b)** *(Am fam)* tonto, povero scemo. **2** *vt (pull)* tirare con uno strattone; **he** ~**ed it away from me** me l'ha strappato di mano. **3** *vi* muoversi a scatti; **to** ~ **along** procedere a sbalzi; **the bus** ~**ed to a halt** l'autobus si fermò con un sobbalzo.

jer·kin ['dʒɜ:kın] *n* panciotto.

jerky ['dʒɜ:kı] *adj (-ier, -iest) (motion)* traballante, convulso(a); *(ride)* pieno(a) di scossoni; *(speech)* a scatti.

jerry-built ['dʒɛrıbılt] *adj* fatto(a) di cartapesta.

jer·ry can ['dʒɛrı,kæn] *n* tanica.

Jer·sey ['dʒɜ:zı] *n* Jersey *f.*

jer·sey ['dʒɜ:zı] *n (garment)* maglia; *(fabric)* jersey *m.*

Je·ru·sa·lem [dʒə'ru:sələm] *n* Gerusalemme.

jest [dʒɛst] **1** *n* scherzo, facezia; **in** ~ per scherzo. **2** *vi* scherzare.

jest·er ['dʒɛstə⁺] *n* buffone *m.*

Jesu·it ['dʒɛzjuıt] *adj, n* gesuita (*m*).

Jesus ['dʒi:zəs] *n* Gesù *m;* ~ **Christ** Gesù Cristo.

jet¹ [dʒɛt] **1** *n* giaietto. **2** *cpd:* ~ **black** *adj* nero(a) intenso(a); *(hair)* corvino(a).

jet² [dʒɛt] **1** *n* **(a)** *(of liquid, steam, gas)* getto; *(nozzle: of gas burner etc)* becco, beccuccio. **(b)** (~ *plane)* aereo a reazione, jet *m inv.* **2** *cpd (aircraft, engine, propulsion)* a reazione; ~ **lag** *n* (problemi *mpl* dovuti allo) sbalzo dei fusi orari; **the** ~ **set** *n* il jet-set.

jet-propelled [,dʒɛtprə'pɛld] *adj* a reazione.

jet·ti·son ['dʒɛtısn] *vt (burden)* alleggerirsi di; *(Naut)* gettare in mare; *(fig)* abbandonare.

jet·ty ['dʒɛtı] *n (breakwater)* molo, banchina; *(landing pier)* imbarcadero.

Jew [dʒu:] *n* ebreo.

jew·el ['dʒu:əl] *n (stone)* pietra preziosa; *(ornament)* gioiello; *(of watch)* rubino; *(fig)* gioiello, perla.

jew·elled, *(Am)* **jew·eled** ['dʒu:əld] *adj* ornato(a) di pietre preziose.

jew·el·ler, *(Am)* **jew·el·er** ['dʒu:ələ⁺] *n* gioielliere *m;* ~**'s (shop)** gioielleria.

jew·el·lery, *(Am)* **jew·el·ry** ['dʒu:əlrı] *n* gioielli *mpl,* gioie *fpl;* **a piece of** ~ un gioiello.

Jew·ess ['dʒu:ıs] *n* ebrea.

Jew·ish ['dʒu:ıʃ] *adj* ebreo(a), ebraico(a).

jib¹ [dʒıb] *n (Naut)* fiocco; *(of crane)* braccio.

jib² [dʒıb] *vi (horse)* impennarsi; *(person)* impun-

tarsi, recalcitrare; **to** ~ **at doing sth** essere restio a fare qc.

jibe [dʒaıb] = **gibe.**

jif·fy ['dʒıfı] *n (fam):* **in a** ~ in un baleno, in un batter d'occhio; **wait a** ~ aspetta un momento.

jig [dʒıg] *n (dance, tune)* giga.

jig·saw ['dʒıgsɔ:] *n* **(a)** *(also:* ~ **puzzle)** puzzle *m inv.* **(b)** *(tool)* sega da traforo.

jilt [dʒılt] *vt* piantare *(fidanzato/a).*

jin·gle ['dʒıŋgl] **1** *n (of bells, keys, coins etc)* tintinnio; *(advertising* ~) canzonetta pubblicitaria. **2** *vt* far tintinnare. **3** *vi* tintinnare.

jin·go·ism ['dʒıŋgəuızəm] *n* sciovinismo.

jinx [dʒıŋks] *n (person)* iettatore/trice; *(thing)* cosa che porta sfortuna; **there's a** ~ **on him** è scalognato.

jit·ters ['dʒıtəz] *npl (fam)* fifa; **to have the** ~ avere fifa.

jit·tery ['dʒıtərı] *adj (fam)* nervoso(a), agitato(a).

jiu·jit·su [dʒu:'dʒıtsu:] *n* = **jujitsu.**

job [dʒɒb] **1** *n* **(a)** *(employment)* lavoro, posto, impiego; **to look for a** ~ cercare lavoro; **to be out of a** ~ essere senza lavoro *or* disoccupato; **a part-time/full-time** ~ un lavoro a mezza giornata/a tempo pieno; **this is a case of** ~**s for the boys** *(fam pej)* questo è il modo di sistemare amici e parenti.

(b) *(piece of work)* lavoro; *(task)* compito; **on the** ~ sul lavoro; **to make a good/bad** ~ **of sth** fare bene/male qc; **he's done a good** ~ **of work** ha fatto un buon lavoro; **that's not my** ~ non è compito mio; **to know one's** ~ essere pratico del proprio mestiere; **he's only doing his** ~ non fa che il suo dovere; **I had the** ~ **of telling him** è stato compito mio dirglielo; **that car is a nice little** ~ *(fam)* quella macchina è un gioiello.

(c): **that's just the** ~! è proprio quello che ci vuole!; **to give sth up as a bad** ~ lasciar perdere qc; **it's a good job that...** meno male che...; **a good** ~ **too!** ci mancherebbe altro!; **we had quite a** ~ **getting here** *or* **to get here** è stata un'impresa arrivare qui; **he was caught doing a bank** ~ *(fam)* l'hanno preso mentre faceva un colpo alla banca.

2 *cpd* **(a)** *(Industry):* ~ **centre** *n* ufficio di collocamento; ~ **creation scheme** *n* progetto per la creazione di nuovi posti di lavoro; ~ **description** *n* caratteristiche *fpl (di un lavoro)*; ~ **hunting** *n:* **to go** ~ **hunting** cercare lavoro; ~ **satisfaction** *n* soddisfazione *f* nel lavoro.

(b): ~ **lot** *n* partita di articoli disparati.

job·ber ['dʒɒbə⁺] *n (Stock Exchange)* intermediario tra agenti di cambio.

job·bing ['dʒɒbıŋ] *adj (gardener, carpenter etc)* a ore, a giornata.

job·less ['dʒɒblıs] *adj* disoccupato(a).

jock·ey ['dʒɒkı] **1** *n* fantino. **2** *vt:* **to** ~ **sb into doing sth** indurre qn a fare qc (con manovre). **3** *vi:* **to** ~ **for position** *(fig)* manovrare per mettersi in una posizione vantaggiosa.

jocu·lar ['dʒɒkjulə⁺] *adj* gioviale; *(joking)* scherzoso(a).

jog [dʒɒg] **1** *n* **(a)** *(push etc)* spinta, colpetto. **(b)** *(pace: also:* ~ **trot)** andatura lenta; *(: of horse)* piccolo trotto; *(run):* **to go for a** ~ andare a fare footing *or* jogging. **2** *vt (push etc)* urtare; *(sb's memory)* rinfrescare; **to** ~ **sb into doing sth** *(fig)* spingere qn a fare qc. **3** *vi (Sport)* fare footing, fare jogging.

♦ **jog along** *vi + adv (vehicle)* procedere con leggeri scossoni; *(fig):* **we're** ~**ging along** si tira avanti; **the work is** ~**ging along nicely** il lavoro procede senza scosse.

jog·ger ['dʒɒgəʳ] n persona che fa footing or jogging.

jog·ging ['dʒɒgɪŋ] n (Sport) footing m, jogging m.

jog·gle ['dʒɒgl] vt (fam) scuotere leggermente.

join [dʒɔɪn] **1** n (in wood, crockery etc) giuntura; (Sewing) cucitura.

2 vt **(a)** (fasten): **to ~ (together)** unire, attaccare; (link) collegare; (: fig) unire; **to ~ hands** prendersi per mano; **to ~ battle (with)** attaccare battaglia (con); **to ~ A and B, to ~ A to B** unire A e B, unire A a B; **to ~ forces (with)** allearsi (con or a); (fig) mettersi insieme (a).

(b) (procession) unirsi a; (club) divenire socio di; (firm, university, religious order) entrare in or a; (Pol: party) iscriversi a; (army, navy) entrare in; **to ~ a queue** mettersi in fila; **to ~ one's ship** imbarcarsi; **to ~ one's regiment** raggiungere il proprio reggimento.

(c) (person) unirsi a; **may I ~ you?** posso?, permette?; **will you ~ us?** (come with us) viene con noi?; (in restaurant etc) vuole sedersi con noi?; **will you ~ us for dinner?** viene a cena con noi?; **will you ~ me in a drink?** posso offrirle qualcosa da bere?; **I'll ~ you later** vi raggiungo più tardi; **they ~ed us in protesting** si sono uniti a noi nel protestare.

(d) (river) confluire in, gettarsi in; (road) immettersi in.

3 vi **(a):** **to ~ (together)** (parts, people) unirsi; (lines) incontrarsi; (roads) congiungersi; (rivers) confluire, congiungersi.

(b) (member of club) divenire socio, farsi socio.

♦ **join in** **1** vi + prep (game, discussion, protest) unirsi a, prendere parte a, partecipare a; **they all ~ed in the chorus** tutti cantavano il ritornello. **2** vi + adv partecipare; (in singing etc): **~ in!** unitevi a noi!

♦ **join on** **1** vt + adv fissare, attaccare. **2** vi + adv (in queue) mettersi in coda; (part) unirsi.

♦ **join up** **1** vi + adv (Mil) arruolarsi. **2** vt + adv (wires etc) unire, collegare.

join·er ['dʒɔɪnəʳ] n falegname m.

join·ery ['dʒɔɪnərɪ] n falegnameria.

joint [dʒɔɪnt] **1** adj (action, effort, work etc) comune; (responsibility) collettivo(a); (committee) misto(a); **to make a ~ declaration on sth** dichiararsi di comune accordo su or a proposito di qc; **~ ownership** comproprietà; **~ account** conto in partecipazione, conto comune. **2** n **(a)** (of chair etc) giuntura. **(b)** (of meat) pezzo di carne; (: cooked) arrosto. **(c)** (Anat) articolazione f; **out of ~** slogato; **to put sb's nose out of ~** (fig fam) far indispettire qn. **(d)** (fam: place: esp Am) buco. **(e)** (Drugs slang: reefer) spinello. **3** vt (Culin) tagliare a pezzi.

joint·ly ['dʒɔɪntlɪ] adv in comune, di comune accordo.

joint-stock com·pa·ny ['dʒɔɪntstɒk,kʌmpənɪ] n società f inv per azioni.

joist [dʒɔɪst] n trave f.

joke [dʒəʊk] **1** n (verbal) battuta; (practical ~) scherzo; **to tell a ~** raccontare una barzelletta; **to make a ~ about sth** fare una battuta su qc; **for a ~** per scherzo; **what a ~!** (ma) scherzi!, bello scherzo!; **it's no ~** non è uno scherzo; **the ~ is that...** la cosa buffa è che...; **the ~ is on you** chi ci perde, comunque, sei tu; **it's (gone) beyond a ~** non è più uno scherzo; **to play a ~ on sb** fare uno scherzo a qn; **I don't see the ~** non mi fa ridere; **he can't take a ~** non sa stare allo scherzo. **2** vi scherzare; **I was only joking** scherzavo; **you're**

joking!, you must be joking! scherzi!, stai scherzando!

jok·er ['dʒəʊkəʳ] n **(a)** burlone/a; (fam) buffone/a. **(b)** (Cards) jolly m inv, matta.

jok·ing ['dʒəʊkɪŋ] **1** adj scherzoso(a). **2** n scherzi mpl.

jol·ly ['dʒɒlɪ] **1** adj (ier, -iest) (person) allegro(a), gioviale; (laugh) allegro(a), gioioso(a); (party etc) piacevole. **2** adv (Brit fam): **he's ~ lucky!** è fortunatissimo!; **you've ~ well got to** devi assolutamente or proprio farlo; **it ~ well serves you right** te lo meriti proprio; **~ good!** benissimo! **3** vt: **to ~ sb along** cercare di tenere qn su (di morale).

jolt [dʒəʊlt] **1** n (jerk) scossa, sobbalzo; (fig) colpo. **2** vt (gen) urtare; (fig) scuotere; **to ~ sb into doing sth** spingere qn a fare qc. **3** vi (vehicle) sobbalzare; **to ~ along** avanzare a sbalzi.

Jor·dan ['dʒɔːdn] n (country) Giordania; (river) Giordano.

joss stick ['dʒɒsstɪk] n bastoncino d'incenso.

jos·tle ['dʒɒsl] **1** vt sballottare. **2** vi darsi gomitate; **to ~ against sb** urtare qn; **to ~ for a place** farsi largo a gomitate.

jot [dʒɒt] **1** n briciolo; **there's not a ~ of evidence** non c'è la ben che minima prova. **2** vt (also: ~ **down**: ideas, notes) buttare giù; (: address, number) prendere.

jot·ter ['dʒɒtəʳ] n blocchetto.

jot·tings ['dʒɒtɪŋz] npl appunti mpl.

jour·nal ['dʒɜːnl] n (diary) diario; (periodical) rivista, periodico; (newspaper) giornale m.

jour·nal·ese [ˌdʒɜːnəˈliːz] n (pej) gergo giornalistico.

jour·nal·ism ['dʒɜːnəlɪzəm] n giornalismo.

jour·nal·ist ['dʒɜːnəlɪst] n giornalista m/f.

jour·ney ['dʒɜːnɪ] **1** n (trip) viaggio; (distance) tragitto; **a 5-hour ~** un viaggio or un tragitto di 5 ore; **to reach one's ~'s end** arrivare a destinazione; **the outward/return ~** il viaggio di andata/di ritorno; **the ~ there and back** il viaggio di andata e ritorno. **2** vi viaggiare.

jo·vial ['dʒəʊvɪəl] adj gioviale, allegro(a).

jowl [dʒaʊl] n (cheek) guancia; (jaw) mandibola; **a man with heavy ~s** un uomo con le guance cascanti.

joy [dʒɔɪ] **1** n gioia; **to jump for ~** fare salti di gioia; **I wish you ~ of it!** (iro) buon pro ti faccia!; **the ~s of camping** (also hum) i piaceri del campeggio; **it's a ~ to hear him** è un piacere ascoltarlo; **no ~!** (fam) niente da fare!; **did you have any ~?** ci sei riuscito? **2** cpd: **~ ride** n: **to go for a ~ ride** farsi un giro in automobile (spesso rubata).

joy·ful ['dʒɔɪfʊl] adj lieto(a), felice.

joy·ous ['dʒɔɪəs] adj (poet) = joyful.

joy·stick ['dʒɔɪstɪk] n (Aer) barra di comando.

J.P. abbr see **justice**.

Jr abbr = **junior**.

ju·bi·lant ['dʒuːbɪlənt] adj esultante.

ju·bi·lee ['dʒuːbɪliː] n giubileo; **silver ~** venticinquesimo anniversario.

judge [dʒʌdʒ] **1** n giudice m; **to be a good/bad ~ of sth** sapere/non sapere giudicare qc; **I'm no ~ of wines** non sono un intenditore di vini; **he's no ~ of character** capire le persone non è il suo forte. **2** vt (Law, gen) giudicare; (estimate: weight, size etc) calcolare, valutare; (consider) ritenere; **he ~d the moment well** ha saputo scegliere il momento giusto; **I ~d it necessary to inform him** ho ritenuto necessario informarlo; **I ~d it to be right** l'ho ritenuto giusto. **3** vi (act as judge) fare da giudice; **judging or to ~ by his expression** a giudicare dalla sua espressione; **to ~ for o.s.**

giudicare da sé; **as far as I can** ~ a mio giudizio.

judg(e)·ment ['dʒʌdʒmənt] **1** n giudizio; **error of** ~ errore m di valutazione; **to pass** ~ **(on)** (Law) pronunciare un giudizio (su); (fig) dare giudizi affrettati (su); **in my** ~ a mio giudizio; **against my better** ~ nonostante non ne fossi convinto. **2** cpd: **J**~ **Day** n giorno del giudizio.

ju·di·cial [dʒuː'dɪʃəl] adj **(a)** (enquiry, decision) giudiziario(a); **to bring** ~ **proceedings against sb** procedere per vie legali contro qn. **(b)** (mind, faculty) critico(a).

ju·di·ci·ary [dʒuː'dɪʃərɪ] n magistratura.

ju·di·cious [dʒuː'dɪʃəs] adj giudizioso(a).

judo ['dʒuːdəʊ] n judo.

jug [dʒʌg] n **(a)** (container) brocca; (for milk) lattiera. **(b)** (fam: prison) gattabuia.

jugged hare [,dʒʌgd'hɛəʳ] n lepre f in salmì.

jug·ger·naut ['dʒʌgənɔːt] n (lorry) autotreno.

jug·gle ['dʒʌgl] **1** vi fare giochi di destrezza. **2** vt fare giochi di destrezza con; (fig) manipolare.

jug·gler ['dʒʌgləʳ] n giocoliere m.

Ju·go·sla·via ['juːgəʊ'slɑːvɪə] etc = Yugoslavia etc.

jugu·lar ['dʒʌgjʊləʳ] adj: ~ **vein** vena giugulare.

juice [dʒuːs] n (of fruit) succo; (of meat) sugo; (Anat): ~**s** succhi mpl; **we've run out of** ~ (fam: petrol) siamo rimasti a secco; (: electricity) siamo al buio.

juicy ['dʒuːsɪ] adj (-ier, -iest) (fruit) succoso(a); (meat) sugoso(a); (story) piccante.

ju·jit·su [,dʒuː'dʒɪtsuː] n jujitsu m.

juke·box ['dʒuːkbɒks] n juke-box m inv.

July [dʒuː'laɪ] n luglio; **the first of** ~ il primo luglio; **(on) the eleventh of** ~ l'undici luglio; **in the month of** ~ nel mese di luglio; **at the beginning/end of** ~ all'inizio/alla fine di luglio; **in the middle of** ~ a metà luglio; **during** ~ durante (il mese di) luglio; **in** ~ **of next year** a luglio dell'anno prossimo; **each or every** ~ ogni anno a luglio; ~ **was wet this year** ha piovuto molto a luglio quest'anno.

jum·ble ['dʒʌmbl] **1** n (also fig) miscuglio, accozzaglia. **2** vt (also: ~ **together**, ~ **up**) mettere alla rinfusa. **3** cpd: ~ **sale** n (Brit) vendita (di beneficenza) di roba usata.

jum·bo ['dʒʌmbəʊ] adj (fam): ~ **(jet)** jumbo m inv.

jump [dʒʌmp] **1** n **(a)** (gen, Sport) salto; **to give a** ~ (also fig: nervously) fare un salto; **in or at one** ~ in un salto; **a** ~ **in prices** un rapido aumento dei prezzi; **my heart gave a** ~ ho provato un tuffo al cuore; **to be one** ~ **ahead of sb** (fig) essere un passo avanti a qn. **(b)** (Showjumping) salto; (: fence) ostacolo.

2 vt (ditch etc) saltare; (horse) far saltare; **to** ~ **the rails** (train) deragliare; **to** ~ **bail** (Law) scappare quando si è in libertà provvisoria sotto cauzione; **don't** ~ **the gun!** (fig fam) non correre troppo!; **to** ~ **the lights** (Aut) passare col (semaforo) rosso; **to** ~ **ship** lasciare la nave senza permesso; **to** ~ **sb** (fam) assalire qn.

3 vi (leap: also Sport) saltare; (nervously) fare un salto, trasalire; (prices) aumentare di colpo; **to** ~ **over sth** saltare qc; **to** ~ **in/out** saltare dentro/fuori; **to** ~ **off/on(to)** sth saltare giù da/su qc; **he** ~ed **into a taxi** è saltato su un tassì; **to** ~ **up and down** saltellare; **there's no need to** ~ **down my throat!** non è il caso di darmi addosso!; **he** ~ed **to his feet** si alzò di scatto, balzò in piedi; **I almost** ~ed **out of my skin!** (fam) mi è venuto un collasso!; ~ **to it!** (fam) sbrigati!; **to** ~ **to conclusions** arrivare a conclusioni affrettate.

♦ **jump about** vi + adv fare salti, saltellare.
♦ **jump at** vi + prep (fig) cogliere or afferrare al

volo; **he** ~ed **at the offer** si affrettò ad accettare l'offerta.

♦ **jump down** vi + adv saltare giù.
♦ **jump up** vi + adv saltare in piedi.

jumped-up ['dʒʌmpt'ʌp] adj (pej) presuntuoso(a).

jump·er ['dʒʌmpəʳ] n (Sport) saltatore/trice; (Brit: sweater) maglione m, pullover m inv; (Am: pinafore dress) scamiciato.

jumpy ['dʒʌmpɪ] adj (-ier, -iest) nervoso(a).

Jun. abbr of **junior.**

junc·tion ['dʒʌŋkʃən] n (of roads) bivio, incrocio; (Rail) nodo (ferroviario).

junc·ture ['dʒʌŋktʃəʳ] n (fig: point) congiuntura; **at this** ~ in questo frangente.

June [dʒuːn] n giugno; for usage see **July.**

jun·gle ['dʒʌŋgl] **1** n giungla. **2** cpd della giungla.

jun·ior ['dʒuːnɪəʳ] **1** adj (in age) più giovane; (on staff, in rank) subalterno(a); (section: in competition etc) per ragazzi; ~ **executive** giovane dirigente m; **Roy Smith, J**~ Roy Smith junior. **2** n persona più giovane; **3 years my** ~, **my** ~ **by 3 years** più giovane di me di 3 anni. **3** cpd: ~ **high school** n (Am) scuola media (da 12 a 15 anni); ~ **minister** n (Pol) ministro che non fa parte del Cabinet; ~ **(miss)** size n misura per giovanette; ~ **school** n (Brit) scuola elementare (da 7 a 11 anni).

ju·ni·per ['dʒuːnɪpəʳ] n ginepro.

junk [dʒʌŋk] **1** n (Chinese boat) giunca; (rubbish) cianfrusaglie fpl; (fam: goods of poor quality) robaccia. **2** cpd: ~ **dealer** n rigattiere m; ~ **foods** npl porcherie fpl.

jun·ket ['dʒʌŋkɪt] n **(a)** (Culin) giuncata. **(b)** (fam: also: ~**ing**): **to go on a** ~, **go** ~**ing** fare bisboccia.

junkie ['dʒʌŋkɪ] n (fam) drogato/a.

junk·shop ['dʒʌŋkʃɒp] n (fam) negozio di anticaglie.

Junr abbr of **junior.**

jun·ta ['dʒʌntə] n giunta.

Ju·pi·ter ['dʒuːpɪtəʳ] n (Mythology, Astron) Giove m.

ju·ris·dic·tion [,dʒʊərɪs'dɪkʃən] n giurisdizione f; **it falls or comes within/outside our** ~ è/non è di nostra competenza.

ju·ror ['dʒʊərəʳ] n (Law) giurato/a; (for contest) membro della giuria.

jury ['dʒʊərɪ] **1** n (Law, for contest) giuria; **to serve on a** ~ far parte di una giuria. **2** cpd: ~ **box** n banco della giuria.

just¹ [dʒʌst] adj (fair) giusto(a).

just² [dʒʌst] adv **(a)** (exactly) proprio, esattamente; ~ **here/there** proprio qui/là; ~ **behind/in front of/near** etc proprio dietro a/davanti a/ vicino a etc; ~ **when it was going well...** proprio quando tutto andava a gonfie vele...; ~ **then**, ~ **at that moment** proprio in quel momento; **it's** ~ **(on) 10 o'clock** sono le 10 in punto; **it costs** ~ **(on) £20** non costa più di 20 sterline; **it's** ~ **what I wanted** è proprio quello che volevo; ~ **what did he say?** cosa ha detto esattamente?; **come** ~ **as you are** vieni così come sei; **leave it** ~ **as it is** lascialo esattamente come è; **they are** ~ **like brothers** sono proprio come fratelli; **that's** ~ **it!**, **that's** ~ **the point!** precisamente!, proprio così!, per l'appunto!; **that's** ~ **(like) him,** always late è proprio da lui arrivare sempre in ritardo; ~ **as I thought!** proprio come pensavo!; ~ **as I arrived** proprio mentre arrivavo; ~ **as you wish** come vuoi; **he likes everything** ~ **so** (fam) gli piace che tutto sia a puntino.

(b) (recently, soon) appena, or ora; **I've** ~ **seen him** l'ho appena visto; ~ **this minute** proprio adesso; **the book is** ~ **out** il libro è appena stato pubblicato; **we were** ~ **going** stavamo uscendo; **I**

was ~ **about to phone** stavo proprio per telefonare.

(c) *(only)* soltanto, solo; ~ **the two of us** soltanto noi due; **it's** ~ **3 o'clock** sono soltanto *or* appena le 3; ~ **yesterday/this morning** soltanto ieri/questa mattina; ~ **for a laugh** tanto per ridere; **it's** ~ **around the corner** è appena dietro l'angolo; ~ **a minute!,** ~ **one moment!** un attimo!

(d) *(simply)* semplicemente, soltanto; **I** ~ **told him to go away** gli ho semplicemente detto di andarsene; ~ **ask someone the way** basta che tu chieda la strada a qualcuno; **I** ~ **wanted to say that...** volevo solo dire che...; **I** ~ **can't imagine** non riesco proprio a immaginare; **it's** ~ **that I don't like it** semplicemente non mi piace; **it's** ~ **one of those things** *(fam)* così è la vita.

(e) *(slightly)* poco; ~ **over/under 2 kilos** un po' più/meno di 2 chili; ~ **before 5 o'clock** poco prima delle 5; ~ **after 5 o'clock** poco dopo le 5; ~ **after I arrived** subito dopo il mio arrivo; **it's** ~ **after 10 (o'clock)** sono le 10 appena suonate; **it's** ~ **to the left/right** è proprio a sinistra/destra.

(f) *(barely)* appena; *(almost not)* per un pelo; ~ **in time** appena in tempo; **I had** ~ **enough money** avevo giusto i soldi che mi servivano; ~ **enough money for sth/to do sth** soldi appena sufficienti per qc/per fare qc; **he (only)** ~ **caught/missed it, he caught/missed it, but only** ~ l'ha preso/perso proprio per un pelo.

(g) *(in comparison)*: **it's** ~ **as good** è altrettanto buono; **it's** ~ **as good as...** è proprio buono come...; **he speaks Italian** ~ **as well as I do** il suo italiano è buono almeno quanto il mio.

(h) *(with imperatives)* un po'; ~ **imagine!** pensa un po'!; ~ **look at this mess!** guarda un po' che disordine!; ~ **wait a minute!** un momento!; ~ **let me get my hands on him!** *(fam)* se lo prendo!

(i) *(emphatic)* veramente, proprio; **that's** ~ **fine!** va proprio bene!; **did he like it? — I should** ~ **say he did!** gli è piaciuto? — eccome!; **do you**

like **ice cream? — don't I** ~! ti piace il gelato? — eccome!

(j) *(phrases)*: **I've** ~ **about had enough of this noise!** *(fam)* ne ho proprio avuto abbastanza di questo rumore!; **it's** ~ **as well you didn't go** per fortuna non ci sei andato; **it would be** ~ **as well if you didn't mention it** faresti bene a non parlarne; **not** ~ **yet** non ancora; ~ **now** proprio adesso; **not** ~ **now** non proprio adesso; **I'm busy** ~ **now** in questo momento sono occupato; ~ **in case** non si sa mai; ~ **in case I don't see you** caso mai non ti vedessi; ~ **the same, I'd rather...** ciononostante, preferirei...; **I'd** ~ **as soon not go** preferirei non andarci.

jus·tice ['dʒʌstɪs] *n* **(a)** *(Law)* giustizia; **to bring sb to** ~ consegnare qn alla giustizia. **(b)** *(fairness)*: **in** ~ **to her, she...** per essere giusti, lei...; **she never does herself** ~ non mostra mai quel che vale; **this biography doesn't do him** ~ questa biografia non gli rende giustizia; **this photo doesn't do you** ~ questa foto non ti fa giustizia; **to do** ~ **to a meal** fare onore a un pranzo. **(c)** *(person)* giudice *m*; **J**~ **of the Peace** *(abbr* **J.P.**) *(Brit)* giudice conciliatore.

jus·ti·fi·able [,dʒʌstɪ'faɪəbl] *adj* giustificabile.

jus·ti·fi·ably [,dʒʌstɪ'faɪəblɪ] *adv* legittimamente, con ragione.

jus·ti·fi·ca·tion [,dʒʌstɪfɪ'keɪʃən] *n* giustificazione *f*; **in** ~ **of** *or* **for a** giustificazione di.

jus·ti·fy ['dʒʌstɪfaɪ] *vt* giustificare; **to be justified in doing sth** avere ragione di fare qc; **am I justified in thinking that...** mi sbaglio o... .

jut [dʒʌt] *vi* *(also:* ~ **out)** sporgere.

jute [dʒuːt] *n* iuta.

ju·ve·nile ['dʒuːvənaɪl] **1** *adj* *(books, sports etc)* per ragazzi; *(pej)* puerile, infantile; *(Law: court)* minorile. **2** *n* minorenne *m/f*. **3** *cpd:* ~ **delinquency** *n* delinquenza minorile; ~ **delinquent** *n* delinquente *m/f* minorenne.

jux·ta·po·si·tion [,dʒʌkstəpə'zɪʃən] *n* giustapposizione *f*.

K

K, k [keɪ] n (letter) K, k f or m inv.

kaf·tan ['kæftæn] n caffettano.

kale [keɪl] n cavolo verde.

ka·lei·do·scope [kə'laɪdəskəup] n caleidoscopio.

kan·ga·roo [,kæŋgə'ruː] n canguro.

ka·put [kə'pʊt] adj (fam) kaputt inv.

ka·ra·te [kə'rɑːtɪ] n karatè m.

ke·bab [kə'bæb] n spiedino.

keel [kiːl] n (Naut) chiglia; **on an even ~** (Naut) di pescaggio uniforme; **to keep things on an even ~** (fig) far filar tutto dritto.

♦ **keel over** vi + adv (Naut) capovolgersi; (person) crollare.

keen [kiːn] adj (-er, -est) (a) (edge, blade) affilato(a), tagliente; (wind, air) tagliente; (hearing) fine; (appetite) buono(a); (intelligence, eyesight, observation) acuto(a); (desire, delight, sense) intenso(a), forte; (interest) vivo(a), forte; (price, rate) competitivo(a); (competition, match, struggle) duro(a), spietato(a). (b) (Brit: person) entusiasta; **to be ~ on sth** (opera, theatre etc) essere un appassionato di qc; (plan, idea etc) essere entusiasta di qc; **to be ~ on sb** avere un debole per qn; **she's very ~ on pop music** va matta per la musica pop; **I'm not ~ on going** non mi va di andare; **I'm not ~ on his going** non mi piace l'idea che vada; **I'm not ~ to do it** non ci tengo a farlo.

keen·ly ['kiːnlɪ] adv (a) (acutely) intensamente, profondamente; **to feel sth ~** sentire qc profondamente; **he looked at her ~** la rivolse uno sguardo penetrante. (b) (enthusiastically) con entusiasmo.

keen·ness ['kiːnnɪs] n entusiasmo.

keep [kiːp] (vb: pt, pp kept) 1 n (a) vitto e alloggio; **to earn one's ~** guadagnarsi la vita.

(b): **for ~s** (fam) per sempre.

(c) (Archit) torrione m, maschio.

2 vt (a) (gen) tenere; **~ the change** tenga il resto; **he ~s himself to himself** si tiene in disparte, se ne sta per conto suo; **to ~ sth clean** tenere qc pulito; **she ~s herself fit** si tiene or si mantiene in forma; **the garden is well kept** il giardino è tenuto bene; **he has kept his looks** è ancora un bell'uomo; **to ~ sb waiting** far aspettare qn; **~ him at it!** fallo continuare!; **to ~ the engine running** tenere il motore acceso; **I'll ~ you to your promise** ti farò mantenere la promessa; **to ~ sth from sb** (fig) tenere qc nascosto a qn; **to ~ it to yourself, ~ it under your hat** (fam) non lo dire a nessuno, tienilo per te.

(b) (put aside) tenere da parte, mettere da parte; (store) tenere, conservare; **~ it in a safe place, ~ it somewhere safe** mettilo in un posto sicuro; **'~ in a cool place'** 'conservare al freddo'.

(c) (detain, restrain) trattenere; **to ~ sb in prison** tenere qn in prigione; **I mustn't ~ you, don't let me ~ you** non voglio trattenerti; **what kept you?** si può sapere cosa ti ha trattenuto?; **to ~ sb from doing sth** impedire a qn di fare qc; **to ~ o.s. from doing sth** trattenersi dal fare qc;

you're **~ing me from my work** mi stai impedendo di lavorare; **~ him from school** non mandarlo a scuola.

(d) (fulfil, observe: promise, vow) mantenere; (: law, rule, Lent) osservare; (: treaty, agreement) rispettare; (: Christmas, Easter) celebrare; **to ~ an appointment** andare ad un appuntamento.

(e) (own, have, also Comm: stock) avere; (Agr: animals) allevare.

(f) (support: family) mantenere; **he earns enough to ~ himself** guadagna abbastanza per mantenersi; **to ~ sb in food and clothing** nutrire e vestire qn.

(g) (accounts, diary) tenere; **to ~ a record** or **note of sth** prendere nota di qc; **~ a note of how much you spend** tieni il conto di quanto spendi.

3 vi (a) (continue) continuare; (remain) stare; **to ~ (to the) left/right** tenere la sinistra/la destra; **to ~ straight on** continuare dritto; **to ~ to** (promise) mantenere; (subject, text) attenersi a; **to ~ doing sth** continuare a fare qc; **to ~ fit/in good health** tenersi or mantenersi in forma/in buona salute; **~ going!** forza!; **to ~ at sb** (fam: pester) stare dietro a qn, non dare pace a qn; **to ~ at sth** (fam: continue) continuare a fare qc; **~ at it!** (fam) continua, dai!; **to ~ still/quiet** stare or rimanere fermo/zitto; **to ~ together** tenersi insieme; **to ~ from doing sth** trattenersi or frenarsi dal fare qc; **to ~ to one's room/bed** rimanere in camera/a letto; **they ~ to themselves** si tengono in disparte, stanno per conto loro.

(b) (in health): **how are you ~ing?** come stai?; **he's not ~ing very well** non si sente molto bene; **she's ~ing better** si sente meglio.

(c) (food) mantenersi, conservarsi; (fig: wait): **this business can ~** quest'affare può aspettare.

♦ **keep away** 1 vt + adv: **to ~ sth/sb away from sb** tenere qc/qn lontano da qn; **they kept him away from school** non l'hanno mandato a scuola. 2 vi + adv: **to ~ away (from)** stare lontano (da).

♦ **keep back** 1 vt + adv (a) (crowds, tears, money) trattenere; **I don't want to ~ you back** (make late) non voglio trattenerti. (b) (conceal: information): **to ~ sth back from sb** nascondere qc a qn. 2 vi tenersi indietro; **please ~ back!** indietro per favore!

♦ **keep down** 1 vt + adv (a) (control: prices, spending) contenere, ridurre; (: anger) controllare, contenere; (: dog) controllare; (rebellion) soffocare, reprimere; **you can't ~ a good man down** è uno che non si dà per vinto. (b) (retain: food) trattenere, ritenere. (c) (Scol): **he was kept down a year** gli hanno fatto ripetere l'anno. 2 vi tenersi giù, stare giù.

♦ **keep in** 1 vt + adv (invalid, child) tenere a casa; (Scol) trattenere a scuola; (stomach) tenere dentro; (elbows) tenere giù. 2 vi (fam): **to ~ in with sb** tenersi buono qn.

♦ **keep off** 1 vt + adv: **~ your hands off!** non toccare!, giù le mani! 2 vt + prep (dog, person) tenere lontano da; **~ your hands off that cake** non toccare quella torta. **3** *vi* + *prep* stare alla larga da; '~ **off the grass**' 'non calpestare l'erba'. **4** *vi* + *adv*: **if the rain** ~**s off** se non piove.

♦ **keep on 1** *vt* + *adv (hat, house, employee)* tenere; *(light)* tenere acceso(a). **2** *vi* + *adv (continue)* continuare; ~ **on along this road until...** continui per questa strada finché...; **to** ~ **on doing sth** continuare a fare qc; **to** ~ **on at sb about sth** *(pester)* non dare pace a qn per qc; **don't** ~ **on so!**, **don't** ~ **on about it!** basta!, smettila!

♦ **keep out 1** *vt* + *adv (exclude: person, dog)* tenere fuori; **this coat** ~**s out the cold** questo cappotto protegge dal freddo; **to** ~ **sb out of trouble** tenere qn lontano dai pasticci. **2** *vi* + *adv (not enter)* restare fuori; '~ **out**' 'vietato l'ingresso'; **to** ~ **out of trouble** tenersi fuori dai guai; **to** ~ **out of a quarrel** non immischiarsi in una lite; **you** ~ **out of this!** non immischiarti!

♦ **keep up 1** *vt* + *adv* **(a)** *(hold up: shelf etc)* tenere su, sorreggere; **to** ~ **up one's spirits** *(fig)* tenersi su di spirito, non perdersi d'anima; **the noise kept me up all night** il rumore m'ha tenuto sveglio tutta la notte. **(b)** *(continue: tradition, study)* mantenere, continuare; *(correspondence, subscription)* mantenere; *(foreign language)* mantenersi in esercizio con; ~ **up the good work!** bravo, continua così!; ~ **it up!** continua così!; **he'll never** ~ **it up!** non ce la farà! **(c)** *(maintain: property)* mantenere.

2 *vi* + *adv* **(a)** *(weather)* continuare; *(prices)* mantenersi allo stesso livello. **(b): to** ~ **up with sb** *(in race etc)* mantenersi al passo con qn; *(fig: in comprehension)* seguire qn; *(: by correspondence)* mantenere i rapporti con qn; **to** ~ **up with the times** mantenersi al passo coi tempi; **to** ~ **up with the Joneses** *(fig)* non essere da meno dei vicini.

keep·er ['kiːpə^r] *n (in park, zoo etc)* guardiano; *(in museum)* custode *m*; *(game~)* guardacaccia *m inv; (goal~)* portiere *m*.

keep-fit [,kiːp'fɪt] **1** *n* ginnastica. **2** *cpd*: ~ **class** *n* corso di ginnastica; ~ **exercises** *npl* esercizi *mpl* di ginnastica.

keep·ing ['kiːpɪŋ] *n* **(a):** **in/out of** ~ **(with)** in armonia/disaccordo (con); **that modern building is out of** ~ **with the houses round about** quella costruzione moderna stona con le case intorno. **(b): in the** ~ **of** in custodia di; **in safe** ~ al sicuro.

keep·sake ['kiːpseɪk] *n* ricordo.

keg [keg] *n* barile *m*.

ken·nel ['kenl] *n* canile *m;* **to put a dog in** ~**s** mettere un cane al canile.

Ken·ya ['kenjə] *n* Kenia *m*.

kept [kept] *pt, pp* of **keep**.

kerb [kɜːb] *n (Brit)* bordo del marciapiede.

ker·nel ['kɜːnl] *n (of nut)* gheriglio; *(of fruit stone)* seme *m*.

kero·sene ['kerəsiːn] *n* cherosene *m*.

kes·trel ['kestrəl] *n* gheppio.

ketch·up ['ketʃəp] *n* ketchup *m*.

ket·tle ['ketl] *n* bollitore *m;* **that's a different** ~ **of fish** *(fig)* questo è un altro paio di maniche.

key [kiː] **1** *n* **(a)** *(also fig)* chiave *f; (for winding clock, toy)* chiave, chiavetta; *(can opener)* chiavetta; *(on map)* leggenda; **the** ~ **to success** la chiave del successo. **(b)** *(of typewriter, piano)* tasto; *(of wind instrument)* chiave *f*. **(c)** *(Mus)* chiave *f;* **in the** ~ **of C/F** in chiave di do/fa; **major/minor** ~ tonalità maggiore/minore; **to change** ~ cambiare tonalità; **to be in/off** ~ essere in/fuori chiave. **2** *cpd (vital: position, industry etc)* chiave *inv;* ~ **man** *n* uomo chiave; ~ **ring** *n* anello *m* portachiavi *inv*.

key·board ['kiːbɔːd] *n* tastiera.

keyed up ['kiːd'ʌp] *adj*: **to be (all)** ~ essere (tutto(a)) agitato(a).

key·hole ['kiːhəʊl] *n* buco della serratura.

key·note ['kiːnəʊt] *n (Mus)* nota di chiave; *(fig)* nota dominante.

kha·ki ['kɑːkɪ] *n (cloth)* tela cachi; *(colour)* cachi *m*.

kib·butz [kɪ'bʊts] *n, pl* ~**im** kibbutz *m inv*.

kick [kɪk] **1** *n (gen)* calcio; *(of firearm)* rinculo; **to take a** ~ **at sth/sb** tirare un calcio a qc/qn; **to give sth/sb a** ~ dare un calcio a qc/qn; **this cocktail's got a** ~ **in it** è forte questo cocktail; **it was a** ~ **in the teeth for him** *(fig fam)* è stato un duro colpo per lui; **he gets a** ~ **out of it** *(fam)* ci prova un gusto matto; **to do something for** ~**s** *(fam)* fare qc per divertimento; **he needs a** ~ **in the pants** *(fig fam)* ha bisogno di una buona spinta.

2 *vt (person, ball etc)* dare un calcio a; *(subj: animal)* tirare un calcio a; **to** ~ **sb downstairs** scaraventare qn per le scale; **to** ~ **sth out of the way** spostare qc con un calcio; **to** ~ **the bucket** *(fig fam)* tirare le cuoia; **I could have** ~**ed myself** *(fig fam)* mi sarei preso a calci; **to** ~ **a habit** *(fig fam)* liberarsi da un vizio.

3 *vi* dare calci, tirare calci; *(baby)* scalciare; **to** ~ **at sth** dare or tirare un calcio a qc.

♦ **kick about, kick around 1** *vt* + *adv*: **to** ~ **a ball about** giocare a pallone. **2** *vi (fam: object, person)* essere in giro.

♦ **kick back 1** *vi* + *adv (gun)* rinculare. **2** *vt* + *adv (ball)* rimandare, rinviare.

♦ **kick down** *vt* + *adv* abbattere a calci.

♦ **kick in** *vt* + *adv* abbattere, sfasciare; **to** ~ **sb's teeth in** *(fam)* spaccare la faccia a qn.

♦ **kick off** *vi* + *adv (Ftbl)* dare il calcio d'inizio; *(fig fam: meeting etc)* cominciare.

♦ **kick out 1** *vi* + *adv*: **to** ~ **out (at)** tirare calci (a). **2** *vt* + *adv (fig fam)*: **to** ~ **sb out (of)** cacciare qn via (da), buttare qn fuori (da).

♦ **kick up** *vt* + *adv (fig fam)*: **to** ~ **up a row** *or* **a din** fare un putiferio; **to** ~ **up a fuss about** *or* **over sth** fare storie su or per qc.

kick-off ['kɪk,ɒf] *n (Ftbl, fig)* calcio d'inizio.

kick-start ['kɪk,stɑːt] *n (also:* ~**er)** pedale *m* d'avviamento.

kid [kɪd] **1** *n (goat, leather)* capretto; *(fam: child)* ragazzino/a, bambino/a. **2** *vt (fam)*: **to** ~ **sb (on) that...** dar da bere a qn che...; **to** ~ **sb (on) about sth** prendere in giro qn per qc; **don't** ~ **yourself!** non illuderti! **3** *vi (fam: also:* ~ **on)** scherzare; **I'm only** ~**ding** sto solo scherzando; **no** ~**ding!** sul serio! **4** *cpd (gloves, leather)* di capretto; **to handle sth/sb with** ~ **gloves** trattare qc/qn con i guanti. **(b)** *(fam: brother, sister)* più giovane.

kid·nap ['kɪdnæp] *vt* rapire, sequestrare.

kid·nap·per ['kɪdnæpə^r] *n* rapitore/trice.

kid·nap·ping ['kɪdnæpɪŋ] *n* sequestro (di persona).

kid·ney ['kɪdnɪ] **1** *n (Anat)* rene *m; (Culin)* rognone *m*. **2** *cpd (disease, failure, transplant)* renale, dei reni; ~ **bean** *n* fagiolo borlotto; ~ **machine** *n* rene *m* artificiale.

kill [kɪl] **1** *vt* **(a)** uccidere, ammazzare; **to be** ~**ed in action** morire or cadere in battaglia; **to** ~ **two birds with one stone** *(fig)* prendere due piccioni con una fava; **he certainly doesn't** ~ **himself!** *(fig hum)* non si affatica proprio!; **this heat is** ~**ing me** *(fig fam)* questo caldo mi uccide; **my feet are** ~**ing me** *(fig fam)* i piedi mi fanno male da morire; **he was** ~**ing himself laughing** *(fig fam)* moriva dal ridere or dalle risate. **(b)** *(fig: story, paragraph)* sopprimere; *(: rumour)* mettere fine a; *(: feeling, hope)* distruggere; *(: flavour, smell)* soffocare; *(: sound)* attutire, smorzare;

(: *engine, motor*) fermare, spegnere; **to ~ time** ammazzare il tempo. **2** *n (Hunting, at bullfight)* uccisione *f;* **to be in at the ~** partecipare *or* assistere all'uccisione.

♦ **kill off** *vt + adv* sterminare; *(fig)* eliminare, soffocare.

kill·er ['kɪlə^r] **1** *n (murderer)* assassino; **flu can be a ~** l'influenza può essere una malattia mortale. **2** *cpd:* **~ disease** *n* malattia mortale; **~ instinct** *n (fig):* **he has the ~ instinct** sa essere spietato; **~ shark** *n* squalo; **~ whale** *n* orca.

kill·ing ['kɪlɪŋ] **1** *adj (blow)* mortale; *(fig: work)* estenuante; *(fam: funny)* divertentissimo(a). **2** *n (murder)* uccisione *f;* **to make a ~** *(Fin)* fare un bel colpo.

kill·joy ['kɪldʒɔɪ] *n* guastafeste *m/f inv.*

kiln [kɪln] *n* fornace *f.*

kilo ['kiːləʊ] *n* chilo.

kilo·gram(me), *(Am)* **kilo·gram** ['kɪləʊgræm] *n* chilogrammo.

kilo·metre, *(Am)* **kilo·meter** ['kɪləʊˌmiːtə^r, kɪ'lɒmɪtə^r] *n* chilometro.

kilo·watt ['kɪləʊwɒt] *n* chilowatt *m inv.*

kilt [kɪlt] *n* kilt *m inv.*

kin [kɪn] *n* parenti *mpl*, familiari *mpl;* **next of ~** parente più stretto.

kind [kaɪnd] **1** *adj (-er, -est)* gentile; **to be ~ to sb** essere gentile con qn; **would you be ~ enough to...?, would you be so ~ as to...?** sarebbe così gentile da...?; **it's very ~ of you (to do)** è molto gentile da parte sua (di fare); **thank you for the ~ loan of your car** grazie per avermi gentilmente prestato la macchina.

2 *n* tipo, genere *m;* **all ~s of things** ogni genere di cose; **some ~ of animal** una specie di animale; **he's not the ~ of person to...** non è il tipo da...; **what ~ of an answer is that?, what ~ of an answer do you call that?** che razza di risposta è questa?; **what ~ of person do you take me for?** per chi mi prendi?; **I had a ~ of feeling that would happen** avevo una vaga idea che *or* me lo sentivo che sarebbe successo; **you know the ~ of thing I mean** sai cosa intendo *or* voglio dire; **something of the ~** o qualcosa del genere; **nothing of the ~!** niente affatto!; **it's not his ~ of film** non è il tipo *or* genere di film che piace a lui, non è il suo genere di film; **they're two of a ~** sono molto simili; **it's the only one of its ~** è l'unico nel suo genere; **it was tea of a ~** *(pej)* era una sottospecie di tè; **I ~ of thought this would happen** *(fam)* quasi mi l'aspettavo; **she looked ~ of worried** *(fam)* sembrava una po' preoccupata; **payment in ~** pagamento in natura; **to repay sb in ~** *(after good deed)* ricambiare la cortesia a qn; *(after bad deed)* ripagare qn con la stessa moneta.

kin·der·gar·ten ['kɪndəˌgɑːtn] *n* asilo (infantile).

kind-hearted [ˌkaɪnd'hɑːtɪd] *adj* buono(a), gentile.

kin·dle ['kɪndl] *vt (wood etc)* far accendere, fare prendere fuoco a; *(fire, interest)* accendere; *(emotion)* far nascere.

kin·dling ['kɪndlɪŋ] *n* frasche *fpl*, ramoscelli *mpl.*

kind·ly ['kaɪndlɪ] **1** *adj (-ier, -iest) (gen)* gentile; *(person, smile, tone)* gentile, benigno(a). **2** *adv (speak, act)* con gentilezza, gentilmente; **~ wait a moment** abbia la cortesia *or* gentilezza di aspettare un momento; **he doesn't take ~ to being kept waiting** non gli piace affatto dover aspettare.

kind·ness ['kaɪndnɪs] *n (towards sb)* gentilezza, bontà; *(act)* gentilezza; **out of the ~ of her heart** per bontà d'animo; **to do sb a ~** fare una cortesia *or* una gentilezza a qn.

kin·dred ['kɪndrɪd] **1** *adj (tribes, peoples)* imparen-

tato(a); *(language)* affine; **~ spirits** anime *fpl* gemelle; **to have a ~ feeling for sb** sentirsi molto vicino a qn. **2** *n (relations)* familiari *mpl*, parenti *mpl.*

ki·net·ic [kɪ'nɛtɪk] **1** *adj* cinetico(a). **2: ~s** *nsg* cinetica.

king [kɪŋ] *n (also fig, Chess, Cards)* re *m inv; (Draughts)* dama.

king·dom ['kɪŋdəm] *n* regno; **the K~ of Heaven** il Regno dei Cieli; **till ~ come** *(fam)* fino al giorno del giudizio.

king·fisher ['kɪŋˌfɪʃə^r] *n* martin *m inv* pescatore.

king·pin ['kɪŋpɪn] *n (Tech, fig)* perno.

king-size(d) ['kɪŋˌsaɪz(d)] *adj (gen: object)* più grande del normale; *(packet)* gigante; *(cigarette)* extra lungo(a).

kink [kɪŋk] **1** *n (in rope etc)* attorcigliamento; *(in hair)* ondina; *(fig: emotional, psychological, sexual)* aberrazione *f.* **2** *vi* attorcigliarsi.

kinky ['kɪŋkɪ] *adj (-ier, -iest) (fam: hair)* crespo(a); *(: pej: person, idea, fashion)* bizzarro(a), eccentrico(a); *(: sexually)* dai gusti particolari.

kin·ship ['kɪnʃɪp] *n* parentela.

kins·man ['kɪnzmən] *n, pl* **-men** parente *m.*

kins·woman ['kɪnzˌwʊmən] *n, pl* **-women** parente *f.*

ki·osk ['kiːɒsk] *n (gen)* chiosco; **telephone ~** *(Brit)* cabina (telefonica); **newspaper ~** edicola.

kip·per ['kɪpə^r] *n* aringa affumicata.

kiss [kɪs] **1** *n* bacio; **~ of life** *(artificial respiration)* respirazione *f* bocca a bocca; **~ of death** *(fig)* colpo di grazia. **2** *vt* baciare, dare un bacio a; **to ~ sb goodbye** congedarsi da qn con un bacio; **to ~ sb goodnight** dare a qn il bacio della buonanotte. **3** *vi* baciarsi.

kit [kɪt] *n* **(a)** *(equipment: gen)* equipaggiamento, attrezzatura; *(Mil)* equipaggiamento; *(Sport, outfit)* tenuta; *(: gear)* attrezzi *mpl; (tools)* arnesi *mpl;* **tool ~** cassetta *or* borsa degli attrezzi; **first-aid ~** cassetta di pronto soccorso. **(b)** *(parts for assembly):* **kitchen units in ~ form** mobili *mpl* per cucina da montare; **toy aircraft ~** una scatola di montaggio per aeromodello.

♦ **kit out** *vt + adv* attrezzare, equipaggiare.

kit·bag ['kɪtbæg] *n (Mil)* sacco militare; *(Sport)* borsa sportiva.

kitch·en ['kɪtʃɪn] **1** *n* cucina. **2** *cpd (cupboard, equipment etc)* da cucina; **~ sink** *n* lavello, acquaio; **to take everything but the ~ sink** *(fam hum)* portarsi dietro un arsenale; **~ sink drama** *n (fam)* teatro raffigurante la vita della classe operaia spesso in modo sordido; **~ unit** *n* elemento da cucina.

kitch·en·ette [ˌkɪtʃɪ'nɛt] *n* cucinino.

kite [kaɪt] *n (bird)* nibbio; *(toy)* aquilone *m.*

kith [kɪθ] *n:* **~ and kin** amici e parenti *mpl.*

kit·ten ['kɪtn] *n* gattino/a; **I had ~s when...** *(fig fam)* mi è venuto un colpo quando... .

kit·ty ['kɪtɪ] *n* **(a)** *(funds)* fondo comune; *(Cards)* posta. **(b)** *(fam: cat)* micio, micino.

klep·to·ma·nia [ˌklɛptəʊ'meɪnɪə] *n* cleptomania.

klep·to·ma·ni·ac [ˌklɛptəʊ'meɪnɪæk] *n* cleptomane *m/f.*

knack [næk] *n* abilità, capacità; **to have the ~ of doing sth** avere l'abilità di fare qc; **to learn the ~ of doing sth** imparare la tecnica per fare qc; **there's a ~ to doing this** c'è un trucco per fare questo.

knap·sack ['næpsæk] *n* zaino.

knave [neɪv] *n* furfante *m; (Cards)* fante *m.*

knead [niːd] *vt (dough, clay)* impastare, lavorare; *(muscle)* massaggiare.

knee [niː] *n (Anat, of garment)* ginocchio; **on one's ~s** in ginocchio; **on one's hands and ~s** carponi;

to go down on one's ~s (to sb) inginocchiarsi (davanti a qn).

knee·cap ['niːkæp] n (Anat) rotula.

knee-deep ['niː'diːp] adj: **the water was ~** l'acqua ci arrivava alle ginocchia.

knee-high ['niːhaɪ] adj che arriva al ginocchio.

kneel [niːl] pt, pp **knelt** [nɛlt] vi (also: **~ down**) inginocchiarsi.

knee·pad ['niːˌpæd] n ginocchiera.

knew [njuː] pt of **know**.

knick·ers ['nɪkəz] npl mutande fpl.

knick-knack ['nɪknæk] n ninnolo.

knife [naɪf] **1** n, pl **knives** (gen) coltello; (pocket ~) temperino; **~, fork and spoon** coperto; **to get one's ~ into sb** (fam) avercela a morte con qn; **to be on a ~ edge** (fig: person) essere sui carboni ardenti; (: result) essere legato a un filo. **2** vt (stab) accoltellare; **to ~ sb to death** uccidere qn a colpi di coltello.

knife-sharpener ['naɪfˌʃɑːpnəʳ] n (tool) affilacoltelli m inv.

knight [naɪt] **1** n cavaliere m; (Chess) cavallo. **2** vt fare cavaliere.

knight·hood ['naɪthʊd] n titolo di cavaliere.

knit [nɪt] **1** vt (garment) fare a maglia or ai ferri; **to ~ one's brows** aggrottare le sopracciglia. **2** vi lavorare a maglia; (bone: also: **~ together**) saldarsi.

knit·ted ['nɪtɪd] adj lavorato(a) a maglia.

knit·ting ['nɪtɪŋ] **1** n (activity) (lavorare m a) maglia; (product) lavoro a maglia. **2** cpd: **~ machine** n macchina per maglieria; **~ needle** n ferro (da calza); **~ pattern** n modello (per maglia).

knit·wear ['nɪtwɛəʳ] n maglieria.

knives [naɪvz] npl of **knife**.

knob [nɒb] n pomo; (on radio, TV) manopola; **a ~ of butter** una noce di burro.

knob·b(l)y ['nɒb(l)ɪ] adj (-ier, -iest) (wood, surface) nodoso(a); (knee) ossuto(a).

knock [nɒk] **1** n (a) (blow) colpo; (in collision) botta; **there was a ~ at the door** hanno bussato alla porta; **I heard a ~** ho sentito bussare; **his pride took a ~** il suo orgoglio ha subito un duro colpo. **(b)** (in engine) rumore m.

2 vt (a) (strike) colpire; **to ~ a nail into sth** conficcare un chiodo in qc; **to ~ sb on the head** colpire qn in or alla testa; **to ~ one's head on/ against sth** batter or sbattere la testa su/contro qc; **to ~ sb unconscious** or **out** or **cold** stordire qn; **to ~ the bottom out of sth** (box) sfondare qc; (fig: argument) demolire qc; **he ~ed the knife out of her hand** le ha fatto cadere il coltello di mano; **to ~ spots off sb/sth** (fig fam) dare dei punti a qn/qc; **to ~ sb sideways** (fig fam) stordire qn; **to ~ some sense into sb** (fam) far venire un po' di buon senso a qn. **(b)** (fam: criticize) criticare.

3 vi (a) (strike) bussare; **he ~ed at the door** ha bussato alla porta; **his knees were ~ing** gli tremavano le ginocchia. **(b)** (bump): **to ~ into sb/ against sb/sth** sbattere or urtare contro qn/qc. **(c)** (engine) battere.

♦ **knock about, knock around 1** vt + adv (person, object) maltrattare. **2** vi + adv (fam: person) vagabondare; (: thing) **it's ~ing around here somewhere** sta in giro da qualche parte.

♦ **knock back** vt + adv (fam) **(a)** (drink) scolare, tracannare. **(b)** (cost): **it ~ed me back £10** mi ha alleggerito di 10 sterline.

♦ **knock down** vt + adv **(a)** (building) demolire; (person) buttare a terra, gettare a terra; (pedestrian) investire; (tree) abbattere; (door) buttare giù; **you could have ~ed me down with a feather!** sono rimasto di stucco! **(b)** (price)

abbassare; (object at auction) aggiudicare.

♦ **knock in** vt + adv (nail) conficcare.

♦ **knock off 1** vt + adv **(a)** (strike off) far cadere; (fig: from price, record): **to ~ off £10, to ~ £10 off the price** fare uno sconto di 10 sterline, abbassare il prezzo di 10 sterline. **(b)** (fam: steal) sgraffignare, grattare. **(c)** (fam: do quickly) buttare giù. **(d)** (fam: stop): **~ it off!** piantala!, basta! **2** vi + adv (fam: stop work) staccare.

♦ **knock out** vt + adv **(a)** (stun) stordire; (Boxing) mettere fuori combattimento or knock out. **(b)** (nails) far uscire, levare; (pipe) vuotare; (in fight etc: teeth) spaccare. **(c)** (in competition) eliminare.

♦ **knock over** vt + adv (object) far cadere; (pedestrian) investire.

♦ **knock together** vt + adv **(a)** (two objects) battere uno contro l'altro. **(b)** (make hastily) mettere insieme alla svelta.

♦ **knock up** vt + adv **(a)** (lever etc) tirare in alto. **(b)** (Brit: waken) svegliare (bussando alla porta). **(c)** (make hastily) fare alla svelta.

knock·down ['nɒkdaʊn] adj (price) imbattibile.

knock·er ['nɒkəʳ] n (on door) battente m.

knock·ing ['nɒkɪŋ] n colpi mpl.

knock-kneed [ˌnɒk'niːd] adj che ha le gambe a X.

knock·out ['nɒkaʊt] **1** n (a) (Boxing etc: abbr **K.O.**) knock out m inv (abbr K.O.). **(b)** (fam: stunner) schianto, cannonata. **2** cpd (competition etc) a eliminazione; **~ drops** npl (fam) sonnifero.

knock-up ['nɒkʌp] n (Tennis) palleggio.

knot [nɒt] **1** n (in rope, wood, also Naut: speed) nodo; (group: of people) capannello; **to tie a ~** fare un nodo; **to tie o.s. up in ~s** (fig) ingarbugliarsi. **2** vt fare un nodo a; **to ~ together** annodare.

knot·ty ['nɒtɪ] adj (-ier, -iest) (wood) nodoso(a); (fig: problem) complesso(a).

know [nəʊ] pt **knew**, pp **known 1** vt (a) (facts, dates etc) sapere; **to get to ~ sth** venire a sapere qc; **to ~ how to do sth** saper fare qc; **he ~s all the answers** sa rispondere a tutte le domande; (pej) sa sempre tutto; **he ~s what he's talking about** sa quello che dice, parla con cognizione di causa; **to ~ one's (own) mind** sapere ciò che si vuole; **I ~ nothing about it** non ne so niente; **there's no ~ing what may happen** chissà cosa succederà; **it soon became ~n that...** si è presto venuto a sapere che...; **to make sth ~n to sb** far sapere qc a qn; **he is ~n to have been there** si sa che c'è stato; **it's worth ~ing what/how etc...** vale la pena sapere che cosa/come etc...; **to ~ sth backwards** conoscere qc a menadito; **let me ~ how you get on** fammi sapere come va; **you ~ how it is** sai com'è; **I knew it!** lo sapevo!

(b) (be acquainted with: person, place, subject) conoscere; **to ~ sb by sight/by name** conoscere qn di vista/di nome; **to get to ~ sb** fare la conoscenza di qn; **I don't ~ him to speak to** non lo conosco abbastanza bene da rivolgergli la parola; **to make o.s. ~n to sb** presentarsi a qn; **he is ~n as X** è conosciuto con or sotto il nome di X.

(c) (recognize) riconoscere; **I knew him by his voice** l'ho riconosciuto dalla voce; **she ~s a good painting when she sees one** sa riconoscere un buon dipinto; **to ~ the difference between...** saper distinguere fra...; **to ~ right from wrong** distinguere il bene dal male.

2 vi sapere; **as far as I ~...** che io sappia..., per quanto io ne sappia...; **we'll let you ~** ti faremo sapere; **how should I ~?** come vuoi che lo sappia?; **no, not that I ~ of** no, che io sappia; **there's no (way of) ~ing** non si può sapere, non c'è modo di saperlo; **it's not easy, you ~** non è facile, sai;

yes, I ~ sì, lo so; **I don't** ~ non lo so; **you ought to** ~ **better (than to...)** dovresti saperlo da solo (che non è il caso di...); **she says she didn't do it, but I** ~ **better** ha detto che non è stata lei a farlo, ma io la so più lunga; **he doesn't** ~ **any better** non può saperlo; **you** ~ **best** nessuno può saperlo meglio di te; **(well,) what do you** ~! *(fam)* (ma) pensa un po'!; **to** ~ **about** *or* **of sth/sb** conoscere qc/qn; **to get to** ~ **about sth** venire a sapere qc; **how many 'don't** ~s' **are there?** quanti sono gli incerti?
    3 *n:* **to be in the** ~ *(fam)* essere al corrente.
know-all ['nəʊɔːl] *n (pej)* sapientone/a.
know-how ['nəʊhaʊ] *n* abilità, conoscenza tecnica.
know·ing ['nəʊɪŋ] *adj (shrewd)* scaltro(a); *(look, smile)* d'intesa.
know·ing·ly ['nəʊɪŋlɪ] *adv (intentionally)* deliberatamente; *(smile, look etc)* con un'aria d'intesa.
know-it-all ['nəʊɪtɔːl] *n (Am)* = **know-all.**
knowl·edge ['nɒlɪdʒ] *n* **(a)** *(information, awareness, understanding)* conoscenza; **to have no** ~ **of** ignorare, non sapere; **not to my** ~ che io sappia, no; **without my** ~ a mia insaputa; **to (the best of) my** ~ che io sappia, per quanto io ne sappia; **it is**

common ~ **that...** è risaputo che...; **it has come to my** ~ **that...** sono venuto a sapere che... . **(b)** *(learning)* scienza, sapere *m;* **to have a working** ~ **of Italian** avere una conoscenza pratica dell'italiano; **to have a thorough** ~ **of sth** conoscere qc a fondo.
knowl·edge·able ['nɒlɪdʒəbl] *adj (person)* ben informato(a); *(remark, report, thesis etc)* ben documentato(a).
known [nəʊn] **1** *pp of* **know. 2** *adj (thief, facts)* noto(a); *(expert)* riconosciuto(a).
knuck·le ['nʌkl] *n (Anat)* nocca.
♦ **knuckle under** *vi + adv* cedere.
knuckle·duster ['nʌkl,dʌstəʳ] *n* tirapugni *m inv.*
K.O. ['keɪ'əʊ] *abbr of* knockout.
koa·la [kəʊ'ɑːlə] *n (also:* ~ **bear)** koala *m inv.*
Ko·ran [kɒ'rɑːn] *n* Corano.
Ko·rea [kə'rɪə] *n* Corea.
ko·sher ['kəʊʃəʳ] *adj* kasher *inv.*
kow·tow ['kaʊ'taʊ] *vi:* **to** ~ **to sb** mostrarsi ossequioso(a) verso qn.
ku·dos ['kjuːdɒs] *n* gloria, fama.
kw *abbr (= kilowatt(s))* KW.

L

L, l [ɛl] n (letter) L, l f or m inv.
l. abbr of **left; litre.**
lab [læb] n fam abbr of **laboratory.**
la·bel ['leɪbl] **1** n etichetta; **he records on the E.M.I.** ~ incide per la E.M.I. **2** vt **(a)** (goods) mettere l'etichetta su, marcare; **a bottle** ~**led poison** una bottiglia con l'etichetta veleno. **(b)** (fig) classificare, etichettare.
la·bora·tory [ləˈbɒrətərɪ] **1** n laboratorio. **2** cpd di laboratorio.
la·bo·ri·ous [ləˈbɔːrɪəs] adj faticoso(a), laborioso(a).
la·bour, (Am) **la·bor** ['leɪbər] **1** n **(a)** (toil) lavoro; **hard** ~ (Law) lavori forzati; ~ **of love** lavoro fatto per il puro piacere di farlo. **(b)** (workforce) manodopera. **(c)** (Pol): L~ partito laburista; **he votes** L~ vota (per il partito) laburista. **(d)** (Med) doglie fpl; **to be in** ~ avere le doglie.
2 vt (point) insistere su.
3 vi (with effort): **to** ~ **at** lavorare sodo a; (with difficulty): **to** ~ **at** faticare a fare; (engine, motor) essere sotto sforzo; **to** ~ **under a delusion/ misapprehension** essere vittima di un'illusione/ di un malinteso; **to** ~ **up a hill** arrancare su per una collina.
4 cpd **(a)** (relations) di lavoro; ~ **dispute** n conflitto tra lavoratori e datori di lavoro; ~ **force** n manodopera; L~ **Exchange** n (Brit) ufficio di collocamento; ~ **union** n (Am) sindacato; L~ **Day** n (Am) festa del lavoro. **(b)** (Pol): L~ laburista; L~ **party** n partito laburista. **(c)** (Med): ~ **pains** npl doglie fpl.
la·boured, (Am) **la·bored** ['leɪbəd] adj (breathing) affaticato(a), affannoso(a); (style) elaborato(a), pesante.
la·bour·er, (Am) **la·bor·er** ['leɪbərər] n (on roads etc) manovale m; (farm ~) bracciante m.
labour-intensive, (Am) **labor-intensive** ['leɪbərɪnˌtɛnsɪv] adj che assorbe molta manodopera.
labour-saving, (Am) **labor-saving** ['leɪbəˌseɪvɪŋ] adj che fa risparmiare fatica or lavoro.
laby·rinth ['læbɪrɪnθ] n labirinto.
lace [leɪs] **1** n **(a)** (open fabric) pizzo, merletto. **(b)** (of shoe, corset) laccio. **2** adj di pizzo. **3** vt **(a)** (also: ~ **up:** shoes etc) allacciare. **(b)** (drink: fortify with spirits) correggere.
lace·making ['leɪsˌmeɪkɪŋ] n fabbricazione f dei pizzi or dei merletti.
lac·er·ate ['læsəreɪt] vt (Med) lacerare.
lac·era·tion [ˌlæsəˈreɪʃən] n lacerazione f.
lace-up ['leɪsʌp] adj (shoes etc) con i lacci, con le stringhe.
lack [læk] **1** n mancanza, scarsità; **for** or **through** ~ **of** per mancanza or scarsità di; **there is no** ~ **of money** i soldi non mancano. **2** vt: **we** ~ **(the) time to do it** ci manca il tempo di or per farlo; **he** ~**s confidence** non è sicuro di sé. **3** vi: **to be** ~**ing** mancare, non esserci; **he is** ~**ing in confidence** non è sicuro di sé; **he** ~**s for nothing** non gli manca niente.

lacka·dai·si·cal [ˌlækəˈdeɪzɪkəl] adj disinteressato(a), svogliato(a).
lack·ey ['lækɪ] n (also fig) lacchè m inv.
lack·lustre, (Am) **lack·luster** ['lækˌlʌstər] adj (surface) opaco(a); (style) scialbo(a); (eyes) spento(a).
la·con·ic [ləˈkɒnɪk] adj laconico(a).
lac·quer ['lækər] **1** n lacca; **hair** ~ lacca per (i) capelli. **2** vt (wood) laccare; (hair) mettere la lacca su.
la·crosse [ləˈkrɒs] n (sport) lacrosse m.
lacy ['leɪsɪ] adj (-ier, -iest) (like lace) che sembra un pizzo.
lad [læd] n ragazzo; (in stable etc) mozzo or garzone m di stalla; **when I was a** ~ quand'ero ragazzo or giovane; **come on,** ~**s!** forza, or dai, ragazzi!; **a drink with the** ~**s** una bevuta con gli amici; **he's a bit of a** ~ (fam) è uno a cui piace far bisboccia.
lad·der ['lædər] **1** n scala a pioli; (step~) scala a libretto; (in tights) smagliatura; **rope** ~ scala di corda; **social** ~ scala sociale; **it's a first step up the** ~ **of success** è il primo passo sulla via del successo. **2** vt (tights) smagliare. **3** vi (tights) smagliarsi.
lad·en ['leɪdn] adj: ~ **(with)** carico(a) (di); **fully** ~ (truck, ship) a pieno carico.
la-di-da ['lɑːdɪˈdɑː] adj (fam: person) affettato(a) e pretenzioso(a); (: voice) affettato(a).
la·dle ['leɪdl] **1** n (Culin) mestolo. **2** vt (also: ~ **out:** soup) servire con il mestolo; (: fig: advice) elargire, distribuire; (: money) tirar fuori.
lady ['leɪdɪ] **1** n signora; **the** ~ **of the house** la padrona di casa; **Ladies and Gentlemen!** signore e signori!; **young** ~ (married) signora; (unmarried) signorina; **ladies' hairdresser** parrucchiere per signora; **he's a ladies' man** è un donnaiolo; **Our L**~ (Rel) la Madonna; 'Ladies' (lavatory) 'signore'; **ladies' room** toilette f inv; **where is the Ladies?** dov'è la toilette?; L~ **Jane Grey** lady Jane Grey. **2** cpd: ~ **doctor** n dottoressa; ~ **friend** n amica; L~ **Mayoress** n moglie f (or figlia) del Lord Mayor.
lady·bird ['leɪdɪbɜːd] n, (Am) **lady·bug** ['leɪdɪbʌg] n coccinella.
lady·killer ['leɪdɪˌkɪlər] n dongiovanni m inv.
lady·like ['leɪdɪlaɪk] adj (person) ben educato(a), distinto(a); (manners) distinto(a).
la·dy·ship ['leɪdɪʃɪp] n: **Her L**~ **the Countess** etc la signora contessa etc; **Your L**~ signora contessa etc.
lag¹ [læg] **1** n (also: time-~) lasso or intervallo di tempo. **2** vi (also: ~ **behind**) restare indietro; **we** ~ **behind in space exploration** siamo in ritardo or ancora indietro nel campo dell'esplorazione spaziale.
lag² [læg] vt (boiler, pipes) rivestire con materiale isolante.
lag³ [læg] n (fam): **old** ~ vecchia conoscenza (della polizia).
la·ger ['lɑːgər] n birra bionda, birra chiara.

226

lag·ging ['lægɪŋ] n (Tech) rivestimento termo-isolante.

la·goon [lə'guːn] n laguna.

laid [leɪd] pt, pp of lay³.

lain [leɪn] pp of lie².

lair [lɛəʳ] n (of animal) tana; (of thieves) covo.

la·ity ['leɪɪtɪ] collective n: the ~ (as opposed to cler-gy) i laici, il laicato; (as opposed to lawyers etc) i profani.

lake [leɪk] n (Geog) lago.

lamb [læm] 1 n (animal, meat) agnello; **my poor ~!** oh, povero tesoro! 2 vi figliare, partorire. 3 cpd: ~ **chop** n cotoletta d'agnello.

lambs·wool ['læmzwʊl] n lamb's wool m.

lame [leɪm] 1 adj (-r, -st) zoppo(a); (also fig: argu-ment, excuse) zoppicante; **to be ~** zoppicare, es-sere zoppo(a); **to be ~ in one foot** esser zoppo da un piede; ~ **duck** (fig: person) persona inetta; (: firm) azienda traballante. 2 vt (person) rendere zoppo(a); (horse) azzoppare.

lamé ['lɑːmeɪ] n lamé m inv.

lame·ly ['leɪmlɪ] adv (fig) in modo poco convin-cente.

la·ment [lə'mɛnt] 1 n (poet) lamento. 2 vt lamen-tare, piangere; **to ~ sb** piangere la morte di qn. 3 vi: **to ~ over sth** lamentarsi di qc; **to ~ for sb** affliggersi per qn.

lam·en·table ['læməntəbl] adj (performance) pe-noso(a); (disregard, waste) deplorevole.

lami·na·ted ['læmɪneɪtɪd] adj laminato(a).

lamp [læmp] n (for table etc) lampada; (in street) lampione m; (Aut) faro, luce f; (Rail) lanterna; (bulb) lampadina.

lamp·light ['læmplaɪt] n: **by ~** a lume della lam-pada.

lam·poon [læm'puːn] n satira.

lamp·post ['læmppəʊst] n lampione m.

lamp·shade ['læmpʃeɪd] n paralume m.

lance [lɑːns] 1 n lancia. 2 vt (Med) incidere.

lan·cet ['lɑːnsɪt] n (Med) bisturi m inv.

land [lænd] 1 n (a) terra; (soil, ground) terreno; (estate) terreni mpl, terre fpl; **to go/travel by ~** andare/viaggiare per via di terra; (dry) ~ ter-raferma; **to work on the ~** lavorare la terra; **to live off the ~** vivere dei prodotti della terra; **to own ~** possedere dei terreni, avere delle pro-prietà (terriere); **to see how the ~ lies** (fig) ta-stare il terreno. (b) (nation, country) paese m; **throughout the ~** in tutto il paese; **to be in the ~ of the living** essere nel mondo dei vivi.

2 vt (a) (cargo, passengers: from ship) (far) sbarcare, scaricare; (plane) far atterrare; (catch: fish) tirare in secco; (fig: job, contract) accaparrarsi. (b) (fam: place): **to ~ a blow on sb** assestare or piazzare un colpo a qn; **it ~ed him in jail** gli è costato la galera; **to ~ sb in debt/in trouble** cacciare qn nei debiti/nei guai; **I got ~ed with the job** è toccato a me fare il lavoro; **I got ~ed with him** mi è toccato restare con lui, me lo sono dovuto sorbire io.

3 vi (a) (plane, bird, passenger) atterrare; (from boat) sbarcare. (b) (after fall, jump) atter-rare; **the hat ~ed in my lap** il cappello è venuto a finire sulle mie ginocchia; **the bomb ~ed on the building** la bomba è caduta sul palazzo; **to ~ on one's feet** cadere in piedi; (fig: to be lucky) cascar bene.

4 cpd: ~ **defences** npl difese fpl terrestri; ~ **forces** npl forze fpl terrestri; ~ **reform** n riforma fondiaria.

♦ **land up** vi + adv (fig fam) andare a finire.

land·ed ['lændɪd] adj (gentry, property) terriero(a).

land·ing ['lændɪŋ] 1 n (a) (of aircraft) atterraggio;

(of troops) sbarco. (b) (in house) pianerottolo. 2 cpd: ~ **card** n carta di sbarco; ~ **craft** n mezzo da sbarco; ~ **stage/party** n (Naut) pontile m/reparto da sbarco; ~ **strip/gear** n (Aer) pista/carrello d'atterraggio.

land·lady ['læn,leɪdɪ] n (of flat etc) padrona di casa; (of pub) proprietaria.

land·locked ['lændlɒkt] adj senza sbocco sul mare.

land·lord ['lænlɔːd] n (landowner etc) proprietario (di beni immobili); (of flat) padrone m di casa; (of pub) proprietario.

land·mark ['lænmɑːk] n punto di riferimento; **a ~ in history** una pietra miliare nella storia.

land·owner ['lænd,əʊnəʳ] n proprietario(a) ter-riero(a).

land·scape ['lænskeɪp] 1 n paesaggio. 2 vt siste-mare con criteri architettonici. 3 cpd: ~ **gar-dening** n, ~ **architecture** n architettura del pae-saggio; ~ **painting** n (Art) paesaggistica; ~ **painter** n (Art) paesaggista m/f, paesista m/f.

land·slide ['lændslaɪd] 1 n frana; (Pol) valanga di voti. 2 cpd: ~ **victory** n (Pol) vittoria schiac-ciante.

lane [leɪn] n (in country) stradina; (in town) stradi-na, viuzza; (Sport, Aut) corsia; **shipping ~** rotta (marittima).

lan·guage ['læŋgwɪdʒ] 1 n (faculty, style of speech) linguaggio; (national tongue, also fig) lingua; **the Italian ~** la lingua italiana; **legal/scientific ~** linguaggio legale/scientifico; **we don't speak the same ~** (fig) non parliamo la stessa lingua; **to use bad ~** dire parolacce; **watch your ~!** attento a come parli! 2 cpd: ~ **degree** n laurea in lingue; ~ **laboratory** n laboratorio linguistico; ~ **studies** npl studi mpl linguistici.

lan·guid ['læŋgwɪd] adj languido(a), debole.

lan·guish ['læŋgwɪʃ] vi: **to ~ for love/over sb/in prison** languire d'amore/per qn/in prigione.

lan·guor ['læŋgəʳ] n languore m.

lan·guor·ous ['læŋgərəs] adj languido(a).

lank [læŋk] adj (hair) pesante e opaco(a).

lanky ['læŋkɪ] adj (-ier, -iest) (person) spilungo-ne(a).

lano·lin(e) ['lænəʊlɪn] n lanolina.

lan·tern ['læntən] n lanterna.

lap¹ [læp] n (Anat) grembo, ginocchia fpl; **to sit on sb's ~** sedersi in grembo a or sulle ginocchia di qn; **to live in the ~ of luxury** vivere nel lusso; **in the ~ of the gods** (fig) nelle mani di Dio.

lap² [læp] n (Sport) giro; **we're on the last ~ now** (fig) siamo quasi arrivati in porto.

lap³ [læp] 1 vt (milk etc) leccare. 2 vi (waves) sciabordare; **to ~ against** lambire.

♦ **lap up** vt + adv leccare; (fig: compliments, atten-tion) bearsi di.

la·pel [lə'pɛl] n risvolto.

Lap·land ['læplænd] n Lapponia.

lapse [læps] 1 n (a) (fault) mancanza; (in behaviour) scorrettezza; **a ~ of memory** un vuoto di me-moria; **a ~ into bad habits** un ritorno alle cattive abitudini. (b) (of time) intervallo. 2 vi (a) (err) sgarrare; **to ~ in one's duty** mancare al proprio dovere. (b) (fall slowly): **to ~ into bad habits** prendere delle cattive abitudini; **to ~ into one's old ways** ritornare alle solite; **to let one's atten-tion ~** distrarsi; **to ~ into silence** tacere; **he ~d into unconsciousness** perse conoscenza. (c) (law) cadere, andare in prescrizione; (member-ship, passport etc) scadere.

lar·ceny ['lɑːsənɪ] n (Law) furto.

larch [lɑːtʃ] n larice m.

lard [lɑːd] n lardo, strutto.

lar·der ['lɑːdəʳ] n dispensa.

large [lɑːdʒ] **1** adj (-**r**, -**st**) (gen) grande; (garden, room) grande, ampio(a); (person, animal) grosso(a); (sum, loss) grosso(a), ingente; (family, population) numeroso(a); **to grow** ~(**r**) ingrandirsi; **to make** ~(**r**) ingrandire; **we had a** ~ **meal** abbiamo mangiato tanto; **a** ~ **number of people** molta gente; **on a** ~ **scale** su vasta scala; **as** ~ **as life** in carne e ossa. **2** n: **at** ~ in libertà; (generally) in generale, nell'insieme; **the world at** ~ il mondo intero. **3** adv: **by and** ~ generalmente.

large·ly [ˈlɑːdʒlɪ] adv in gran parte, per la maggior parte.

large·ness [ˈlɑːdʒnɪs] n grandezza.

large-scale [ˌlɑːdʒˈskeɪl] adj (map, drawing etc) in grande scala; (reforms, business activities) su vasta scala.

lark[1] [lɑːk] n (bird) allodola.

lark[2] [lɑːk] n (joke etc) scherzo; **for a** ~ per scherzo.

♦ **lark about, lark around** vi + adv: **to** ~ **about** (**with**) fare lo stupido (con).

lar·va [ˈlɑːvə] n, pl **larvae** [ˈlɑːviː] larva.

lar·yn·gi·tis [ˌlærɪnˈdʒaɪtɪs] n laringite f.

lar·ynx [ˈlærɪŋks] n laringe f.

las·civ·i·ous [ləˈsɪvɪəs] adj lascivo(a), libidinoso(a).

la·ser [ˈleɪzəʳ] **1** n laser m inv. **2** cpd: ~ **beam** n raggio m laser inv.

lash [læʃ] **1** n (**a**) (eye~) ciglio. (**b**) (thong) laccio (di cuoio); (stroke) frustata, colpo di frusta; (of tail) colpo. **2** vt (**a**) (beat etc) frustare; (subj: rain, waves: also: ~ **against**) picchiare (contro), sbattere (contro); **the wind** ~**ed the sea into a fury** il vento ha trasformato il mare in una furia. (**b**) (esp Naut: tie) legare.

♦ **lash down 1** vt + adv assicurare (con corde). **2** vi + adv (rain) scrosciare.

♦ **lash out** vi + adv (**a**): **to** ~ **out** (**at** or **against sb/sth**) menare colpi (contro qn/a qc); (verbally) inveire (contro qn/qc). (**b**) (fam: spend): **to** ~ **out** (**on sth**) spendere un sacco di soldi (per qc).

lash·ing [ˈlæʃɪŋ] n (**a**) (beating) frustata, sferzata. (**b**): ~**s of** (fam) un mucchio di, una montagna di.

lass [læs] n (esp Scot) ragazza.

las·so [læˈsuː] **1** n lasso, lazo. **2** vt prendere al lasso.

last[1] [lɑːst] **1** adj (**a**) (most recent) ultimo(a); (week, month, year) scorso(a), passato(a); ~ **Monday** lunedì scorso; ~ **night** ieri sera or notte; **during the** ~ **week** nel corso della settimana scorsa; **during the** ~ **2 years** negli ultimi 2 anni; **the night before** ~ l'altro ieri sera or notte; ~ **time** l'ultima volta; ~ **thing** come ultima cosa. (**b**) (final: in series) ultimo(a); **the** ~ **page** l'ultima pagina; **the** ~ **slice of cake** l'ultima fetta di torta; **that was the** ~ **thing I expected** era l'ultima cosa che mi sarei aspettato; **you're the** ~ **person I'd trust with it** sei l'ultima persona al mondo di cui mi fiderei per questo; ~ **but one, second** ~ penultimo(a).

2 n: **the** ~ **of the wine/bread** quello che resta del vino/del pane; **they were the** ~ **to arrive** erano gli ultimi arrivati; **the** ~ **in the series** l'ultimo della serie; **each one better than the** ~ uno meglio dell'altro; **I shall be glad to see the** ~ **of this** sarò contento di vederne la fine; **we shall never hear the** ~ **of it** chissà per quanto ci toccherà sentirne parlare; **at (long)** ~ finalmente; **to the** ~ fino all'ultimo.

3 adv (**a**) (per) ultimo; **to do/come/arrive** ~ (**of all**) fare come/venire per/arrivare ultimo; ~ **but not least**... come ultimo, ma non per questo meno importante...; **when I** ~ **saw them** l'ultima volta che li ho visti.

last[2] [lɑːst] **1** vi (rain, film, pain etc) durare; (also: ~

out: person) resistere; (: money, resources) durare, bastare; **it** ~**s (for) 2 hours** dura 2 ore; **this material will** ~ (**for**) **years** questa stoffa durerà degli anni; **he didn't** ~ **long in the job** non ha resistito a lungo in quell'impiego; **it's too good to** ~, **it can't** ~ è troppo bello per durare. **2** vt durare; **he won't** ~ **the winter** non sopravviverà all'inverno; **it will** ~ **you a lifetime** ti durerà una vita.

last-ditch [ˈlɑːstˌdɪtʃ] adj ultimo(a).

last·ing [ˈlɑːstɪŋ] adj duraturo(a), durevole; **to his** ~ **shame** con sua profonda vergogna.

last·ly [ˈlɑːstlɪ] adv infine, per finire, per ultimo.

last-minute [ˈlɑːstˌmɪnɪt] adj dell'ultimo momento.

latch [lætʃ] n chiavistello; **the door is on the** ~ la porta non è chiusa a chiave.

♦ **latch on to** vi + prep (**a**) (cling to: person) attaccarsi a, appiccicarsi a. (**b**) (idea) afferrare, capire.

latch·key [ˈlætʃkiː] n chiave f (della porta d'ingresso).

late [leɪt] (-**r**, -**st**) **1** adj (**a**) (not on time) in ritardo; **to be (10 minutes)** ~ essere in ritardo (di 10 minuti); **to be** ~ **in arriving** arrivare tardi or in ritardo; **to make sb** ~ far far tardi a qn; **to be** ~ **with one's work** essere in ritardo con il proprio lavoro; **the** ~ **arrival of the flight** il ritardo del volo; ~ **delivery** consegna ritardata.

(**b**) (towards end of period) tardi, tardivo(a); (edition, concerto) ultimo(a); **to be/be getting** ~ essere/farsi tardi; **to keep** ~ **hours** andare a letto tardi, stare alzato fino a tardi; **at this** ~ **hour** a un'ora così tarda, a quest'ora; **at this** ~ **stage** a questo punto delle cose; **in (the)** ~ **spring** nella tarda primavera, a fine primavera; **she's in her** ~ **sixties** è vicina ai settanta.

(**c**) (dead) defunto(a); (former) ex inv; **the** ~ **Mrs Smith** la defunta signora Smith; **our** ~ **prime minister** il nostro ex primo ministro; **my** ~-**lamented husband** il mio povero marito.

2 adv (**a**) (not on time) in ritardo, tardi; **to arrive/leave 10 minutes** ~ arrivare/partire con 10 minuti di ritardo; **to arrive/leave too** ~ arrivare/partire troppo tardi; **better** ~ **than never** meglio tardi che mai.

(**b**) (towards end of period) tardi; **to work** ~ lavorare fino a tardi; ~ **at night** a tarda notte; **into the night** fino a tarda notte, fino a notte fonda; ~ **in life** in età avanzata; ~ **in 1978** verso la fine del 1978.

(**c**) (recently): **as** ~ **as 1981** ancora nel 1981; **of** ~ negli ultimi tempi, recentemente.

late·comer [ˈleɪtkʌməʳ] n ritardatario/a.

late·ly [ˈleɪtlɪ] adv ultimamente, di recente; **till** ~ fino a poco or non molto tempo fa.

late·ness [ˈleɪtnɪs] n (of person, vehicle) ritardo.

la·tent [ˈleɪtənt] adj latente.

lat·er [ˈleɪtəʳ] **1** adj comp of **late** (meeting, train) successivo(a); (edition) più recente, successivo(a); **he was** ~ **than usual** è arrivato più tardi del solito; **Easter is** ~ **this year** Pasqua è più tardi quest'anno; **at a** ~ **stage** or **date** in un secondo momento; **his** ~ **symphonies** le sue ultime sinfonie; **this version is** ~ **than that one** questa versione è posteriore a or più recente di quella. **2** adv comp of **late** (**a**) (not on time) più tardi. (**b**) (after) dopo, più tardi; **a few years** ~ pochi anni dopo or più tardi. (**c**): ~ **on** più avanti; ~ **on today** oggi più tardi.

lat·er·al [ˈlætərəl] adj laterale.

lat·est [ˈleɪtɪst] **1** adj superl of **late** (gen) ultimo(a); **her** ~ **exhibition** la sua ultima mostra; **the** ~

news le ultime notizie. **2** *n* **(a)** *(fam: most recent)* ultima novità; **the** ~ **in cars** l'ultima novità in fatto di auto; **have you heard the** ~? *(news)* hai sentito le ultimissime *or* l'ultima? **(b): at the** ~ **al più tardi; the** ~ **it will arrive will be tomorrow** arriverà al più tardi domani.
la·tex ['leɪtɛks] *n* latice *m*.
lath [lɑːθ] *n*, *pl* ~**s** [lɑːðz] listello.
lathe [leɪð] *n* tornio.
lath·er ['lɑːðəʳ] **1** *n* schiuma (di sapone); *(of sweat)* sudata; **the horse was in a** ~ il cavallo schiumava; **in a** ~ *(fig)* tutto affannato *or* scalmanato. **2** *vt (one's face)* insaponarsi. **3** *vi (soap)* far schiuma.
Lat·in ['lætɪn] **1** *adj (language, temperament)* latino(a); *(textbook, scholar, lessons)* di latino. **2** *n (language)* latino.
Lat·in Ameri·ca ['lætɪnə'mɛrɪkə] *n* America Latina, Sudamerica *m*.
Lat·in-Ameri·can ['lætɪnə'mɛrɪkən] *adj* dell'America Latina, sudamericano(a).
lati·tude ['lætɪtjuːd] *n* **(a)** *(Geog)* latitudine *f*. **(b)** *(fig: freedom)* libertà d'azione.
la·trine [lə'triːn] *n* latrina.
lat·ter ['lætəʳ] **1** *adj* **(a)** *(later)* ultimo(a); **the** ~ **years of his life** gli ultimi anni della sua vita. **(b)** *(of two):* **the** ~ **part of the story** la seconda *or* l'ultima parte della storia. **2** *n:* **of the two, the** ~ **is better** fra i due è meglio il secondo.
lat·ter·ly ['lætəlɪ] *adv* negli ultimi tempi.
lat·tice ['lætɪs] **1** *n (gen)* reticolato; *(for plants)* graticcio, traliccio. **2** *cpd:* ~ **window** *n* finestra con vetrata a losanghe.
laud·able ['lɔːdəbl] *adj* lodevole, degno(a) di lode.
laugh [lɑːf] **1** *n* risata; **to get** *or* **raise a** ~ **(from sb)** far ridere (qn); **to have a good** ~ **at sth** farsi una bella risata su *or* sopra qc; **do you want a** ~? vuoi ridere?; **to do sth for a** ~ *(fam)* fare qc per scherzo *or* per ridere; **what a** ~! che ridere!; **good for a** ~ divertente; **we'll see who has the last** ~ *(fig)* ride bene chi ride ultimo.
2 *vi* ridere; **to** ~ **at** *or* **over** *or* **about sth** ridere di *or* per qc; **we all** ~**ed about it later** più tardi ci abbiamo riso sopra; **to** ~ **at sb** ridere di qn; **it's nothing to** ~ **about** non c'è niente da ridere; **to** ~ **to o.s.** ridere dentro di sé *or* fra sé e sé; **I** ~**ed till I cried** ho riso fino alle lacrime; **to** ~ **in sb's face** ridere in faccia a qn; **then we'll be** ~**ing** poi saremo tranquilli; **to** ~ **up one's sleeve** ridere sotto i baffi.
3 *vt:* **to** ~ **sb out of sth** far dimenticare qc a qn facendolo ridere; **to** ~ **sb to scorn** ridere dietro a qn.
♦ **laugh off** *vt + adv (pain, accusation)* ridere sopra, prendere sottogamba; **to** ~ **one's head off** *(fam)* sbellicarsi dalle risate.
laugh·able ['lɑːfəbl] *adj* ridicolo(a).
laugh·ing ['lɑːfɪŋ] **1** *adj* ridente, che ride. **2** *cpd:* ~ **gas** *n* gas *m* esilarante; ~ **matter** *n:* **this is no** ~ **matter** non è una cosa da ridere; ~ **stock** *n* zimbello.
laugh·ter ['lɑːftəʳ] *n* risata; **he roared with** ~ si è fatto una fragorosa risata.
launch [lɔːntʃ] **1** *n* **(a)** *(gen)* lancio; *(of boat)* varo. **(b)** *(also:* **motor** ~) motolancia; *(pleasure boat)* battello. **2** *vt (gen, also fig)* lanciare; *(new vessel)* varare; *(shore lifeboat)* far uscire; *(ship's boat)* calare (in mare). **3** *vi:* **to** ~ **into sth** lanciarsi in qc.
♦ **launch forth, launch out** *vi + adv (fig):* **to** ~ **forth (into)** lanciarsi (in).
launch·ing ['lɔːntʃɪŋ] **1** *n (of ship)* varo; *(of shore lifeboat)* uscita; *(of ship's boat)* calo, calata (in mare). **2** *cpd:* ~ **pad** *n* rampa di lancio.

laun·der ['lɔːndəʳ] *vt* lavare (e stirare).
laun·der·ette [,lɔːndə'rɛt] *n* lavanderia (automatica).
laun·dry ['lɔːndrɪ] *n (establishment)* lavanderia; *(clothes)* biancheria; **to do the** ~ fare il bucato, lavare la biancheria.
lau·rel ['lɒrəl] *n* alloro; **to rest on one's** ~**s** riposare *or* dormire sugli allori.
lava ['lɑːvə] *n* lava.
lava·tory ['lævətrɪ] **1** *n (room)* gabinetto, toilette *f inv; (appliance)* water *m inv*, gabinetto. **2** *cpd:* ~ **paper** *n* carta igienica.
lav·en·der ['lævɪndəʳ] *n* lavanda.
lav·ish ['lævɪʃ] **1** *adj (helping, meal)* generoso(a), abbondante; *(surroundings, apartment)* sontuoso(a), lussuoso(a); *(expenditure)* considerevole; ~ **with** prodigo(a) di; **to be** ~ **with one's gifts** non badare a spese in fatto di regali. **2** *vt:* **to** ~ **sth on sb** colmare qn di qc.
lav·ish·ly ['lævɪʃlɪ] *adv (give, spend)* generosamente; *(furnished)* sontuosamente, lussuosamente.
law [lɔː] **1** *n* legge *f;* **against the** ~ contro la legge; **by** ~ a norma di *or* per legge; **by British** ~ secondo la legge britannica; **civil/criminal** ~ diritto civile/penale; **to study** ~ studiare diritto; **Faculty of L**~ facoltà di Legge; ~ **and order** l'ordine pubblico *or* costituito; **court of** ~ corte *f* di giustizia, tribunale *m;* **to go to** ~ ricorrere alle vie legali; **to have the** ~ **on one's side** avere la legge dalla propria (parte); **to be above the** ~ essere al di sopra delle leggi; **to be a** ~ **unto o.s.** non conoscere altra legge che la propria; **there's no** ~ **against it** non c'è nessuna legge che lo impedisca *or* vieti; **to take the** ~ **into one's own hands** farsi giustizia da sé; **his word is** ~ la sua parola è legge.
2 *cpd:* ~ **court** *n* (aula del) tribunale *m;* ~ **school** *n (Am)* facoltà *f inv* di legge; ~ **student** *n* studente/essa in legge.
law-abiding ['lɔːə,baɪdɪŋ] *adj* rispettoso(a) delle leggi.
law·breaker ['lɔː,breɪkəʳ] *n* trasgressore *m*.
law·ful ['lɔːfʊl] *adj* legale.
law·less ['lɔːlɪs] *adj* che non conosce nessuna legge.
lawn [lɔːn] **1** *n* prato all'inglese. **2** *cpd:* ~ **mower** *n* tagliaerba *m inv;* ~ **tennis** *n* tennis *m* su prato.
law·suit ['lɔːsuːt] *n* causa, processo; **to bring a** ~ **against** intentare causa a.
law·yer ['lɔːjəʳ] *n* avvocato, legale *m*.
lax [læks] *adj* **(-er, -est)** *(conduct)* rilassato(a); *(person: careless)* negligente; *(: on discipline)* permissivo(a); **to be** ~ **about** *or* **on punctuality** non tenere *or* badare alla puntualità.
laxa·tive ['læksətɪv] *n* lassativo.
lax·ity ['læksɪtɪ] *n*, **lax·ness** ['læksnɪs] *n (see adj)* rilassatezza; negligenza; permissività.
lay[1] [leɪ] *adj (Rel)* laico(a); *(: brother, sister)* laico(a), converso(a); *(fig: non-specialist)* profano(a).
lay[2] [leɪ] *pt of* lie[2].
lay[3] [leɪ] *pt, pp* laid **1** *vt* **(a)** *(put, set)* mettere, posare; *(carpet)* stendere; *(bricks)* posare; *(cable, pipe)* installare, fare la posa di; *(subj: bird: egg)* deporre, fare; **to** ~ **sth over sth** stendere qc su qc; **to** ~ **sth on sth** coprire qc con qc; **to** ~ **the facts/one's proposals before sb** presentare i fatti/delle proposte a qn; **to be laid low with flu** essere costretto a letto con l'influenza; **to be laid to rest** *(euph: buried)* essere sepolto; **I don't know where to** ~ **my hands on it** non saprei dove trovarlo; **to** ~ **o.s. open to attack/criticism** esporsi agli attacchi/alle critiche; **to** ~ **the**

blame (for sth) on sb dar la colpa (di qc) a qn; to ~ claim to sth reclamare qc; to lay odds *or* a bet on sth scommettere su qc. (b) *(prepare: fire)* preparare; *(: trap, snare)* tendere; *(: mine)* posare, piantare; *(: table)* apparecchiare. (c) *(suppress: ghost)* placare, esorcizzare; *(: doubts, fears)* eliminare, dissipare.

2 vi *(bird)* fare le uova, deporre le uova.

♦ **lay aside, lay by** *vt + adv* mettere da parte.

♦ **lay down** *vt + adv* (a) *(put down: luggage)* posare, metter giù; *(: arms)* deporre, posare; *(: wine)* mettere in cantina; to ~ down one's life for sb/sth sacrificare la propria vita per qn/qc. (b) *(dictate: condition)* stabilire, fissare; *(: principle, rule, policy)* formulare, fissare; to ~ down the law *(fig)* dettar legge.

♦ **lay in** *vt + adv* fare una scorta di.

♦ **lay into** *vi + prep (fam: attack, scold)* aggredire.

♦ **lay off 1** *vt + adv (workers)* licenziare; *(temporarily)* ≈ mettere in cassa integrazione. 2 *vi + adv (fam)* smettere. 3 *vi + prep (fam):* ~ off it! piantala!; ~ off him! non rompergli le scatole!, lascialo in pace!

♦ **lay on** *vt + adv (provide: water, electricity)* provvedere di; to ~ on (for) *(meal, entertainment)* offrire (a); *(facilities, transport)* mettere a disposizione (di); to ~ it on thick *(fam: flatter)* fare degli elogi eccessivi; *(: exaggerate)* metterla giù dura.

♦ **lay out** *vt + adv* (a) *(plan: garden, house, town)* pianificare, progettare; *(: page, letter)* impostare; **the way the house is laid out** la disposizione della casa. (b) *(prepare: clothes)* preparare; *(: goods for sale)* sistemare, disporre; *(: body for burial)* preparare, comporre. (c) *(spend)* sborsare. (d) *(knock out)* stendere.

♦ **lay up** *vt + adv* (a) *(store: provisions)* far scorta or provvista di; to ~ up trouble for o.s. crearsi dei guai. (b) *(put out of service: vessel)* ritirare in cantiere; **to be laid up with flu** essere costretto a letto con l'influenza.

lay·about ['leɪəˌbaʊt] *n (fam)* fannullone/a.

lay-by ['leɪbaɪ] *n (Aut)* piazzola di sosta.

lay·er ['leɪə^r] *n* strato.

lay·ette [leɪ'ɛt] *n* corredino (per neonato).

lay·man ['leɪmən] *n, pl* **-men** *(Rel)* laico; *(fig: non-professional)* profano.

lay-off ['leɪɒf] *n* sospensione *f*, licenziamento.

lay·out ['leɪaʊt] *n (of town)* piano urbanistico; *(of house, garden)* disposizione *f*; *(Typing)* impostazione *f*.

laze [leɪz] *vi (also:* ~ **around,** ~ **about)** oziare.

la·zi·ness ['leɪzɪnɪs] *n* pigrizia.

lazy ['leɪzɪ] *adj (-ier, -iest)* pigro(a).

lazy·bones ['leɪzɪˌbəʊnz] *n (fam)* poltrone/a, fannullone/a.

lb. *abbr of* **pound.**

lead¹ [lɛd] **1** *n (metal)* piombo; *(in pencil)* mina; *(for sounding)* scandaglio. **2** *adj (pipes)* di piombo; *(paint)* a base di piombo; ~ **pencil** matita con la mina di grafite; ~ **poisoning** saturnismo; ~ **weight** piombino, piombo.

lead² [liːd] *(vb: pt, pp* **led)** **1** *n* **(a): to be in the** ~ *(Sport)* essere in testa; *(fig)* essere all'avanguardia; **to be in the** ~ **by 5 points to 4** condurre *or* essere in testa per 5 a 4; **to take the** ~ *(Sport)* passare in testa; *(fig)* prendere l'iniziativa; **to have a 3-second** ~ avere un vantaggio di 3 secondi; **to follow sb's** ~ seguire l'esempio di qn; **it's your** ~ *(Cards)* sei tu di mano. (b) *(clue)* indizio, pista. (c) *(Theatre)* parte *f or* ruolo principale; **male/female** ~ protagonista *m/f* maschile/

femminile. (d) *(leash)* guinzaglio. (e) *(Elec)* filo (elettrico).

2 *vt* **(a)** *(conduct)* condurre; *(street)* portare, condurre; **he is easily led** si lascia facilmente convincere *or* influenzare; **to** ~ **the way** fare strada. **(b)** *(be the leader of: government)* essere a capo di; *(: party)* essere alla guida *or* a capo di; *(: expedition, movement)* guidare; *(: revolution)* capeggiare; *(: team)* capitanare; *(: league, procession)* essere in testa a; *(: orchestra: Brit)* essere il primo violino di; *(: Am)* dirigere; **to** ~ **the field** essere in testa; *(fig)* essere all'avanguardia nel campo. **(c)** *(life, existence)* condurre. **(d)** *(influence)* portare; **to** ~ **sb to do sth** portare qn a fare qc; **to** ~ **sb to believe that...** far credere a qn che...; **it led me to the conclusion that...** mi ha fatto concludere che..., mi ha portato alla conclusione che... .

3 *vi* **(a)** *(go in front)* andare avanti; *(Cards)* essere di mano. **(b)** *(in match, race)* essere in testa; **to** ~ **by 3 goals** avere 3 gol di vantaggio. **(c)** *(street, corridor)* portare; **where does this door** ~? cosa c'è oltre questa porta? **(d)** *(result in):* **to** ~ **to** portare a; **one thing led to another...** una cosa tira l'altra... .

♦ **lead away** *vt + adv* portar via.

♦ **lead back** *vt + adv* riportare, ricondurre.

♦ **lead off 1** *vt + adv* **(a)** portare; **he led us off on a visit of the museum** ci ha portato a visitare il museo. **(b)** *(fig: begin)* dare inizio a, cominciare. **2** *vi + prep* partire da; **a street** ~**ing off the main road** una trasversale della strada principale.

♦ **lead on** *vt + adv* **(a)** *(tease)* prendere in giro. **(b)** *(incite):* **to** ~ **sb on (to do sth)** spingere *or* trascinare qn (a fare qc).

♦ **lead up** *vi + adv:* **to** ~ **up (to)** portare (a); **what's all this** ~**ing up to?** dove si vuole arrivare con questo?

lead·ed ['lɛdɪd] *adj:* ~ **windows** vetrate *fpl* (artistiche).

lead·en ['lɛdn] *adj (colour, sky)* plumbeo(a); *(fig: atmosphere)* teso(a); *(: silence)* opprimente; **with a** ~ **heart** con la morte nel cuore.

lead·er ['liːdə^r] *n* **(a)** *(of group, expedition)* capo; *(of party, union)* capo, leader *m inv; (Mus: of orchestra: Brit)* primo violino; *(: Am)* direttore *m* d'orchestra; *(guide)* guida; **he's a born** ~ è nato per comandare. **(b)** *(Sport: in race)* chi è in testa; **the** ~**s of the First Division** le squadre in testa alla classifica di serie A; **they are** ~**s in their field** *(fig)* sono all'avanguardia nel loro campo. **(c)** *(Brit Press)* articolo di fondo, editoriale *m*.

lead·er·ship ['liːdəʃɪp] *n* **(a)** direzione *f*; **under the** ~ **of...** sotto la direzione *or* guida di...; **qualities of** ~ qualità *fpl* di un capo. **(b)** *(leaders)* dirigenti *mpl*.

lead-free ['lɛd'friː] *adj* che non contiene piombo.

lead·ing ['liːdɪŋ] *adj (horse, car: in race)* (che è) in testa, di testa; *(: in procession)* che apre la sfilata; *(chief: member etc)* principale, preminente; *(: Theatre etc: role, character)* principale, di primo piano; ~ **man/lady** *(Cine, Theatre etc)* attore/trice principale; ~ **light** *(fig)* personaggio di primo piano; **one of the** ~ **figures of this century** una delle più importanti figure di questo secolo; **a** ~ **question** una domanda tendenziosa.

leaf [liːf] *n, pl* **leaves** **(a)** *(of plant)* foglia. **(b)** *(of book)* foglio, pagina; **to turn over a new** ~ *(fig)* cambiar vita; **to take a** ~ **out of sb's book** *(fig)* prendere esempio da qn. **(c)** *(of table: fold-down)* ribalta; *(: extending)* asse *f* estraibile.

♦ **leaf through** *vi + prep (book)* sfogliare.

leaf·let ['li:flɪt] *n* (*gen*) dépliant *m inv*; (*handout*) volantino.

leafy ['li:fɪ] *adj* (**-ier, -iest**) ricco(a) di foglie.

league [li:g] *n* (**a**) (*alliance*) associazione *f*, lega; **in ~ with** in associazione con; (*pej*) in combutta con, in lega con. (**b**) (*Ftbl, Rugby*) campionato; **they're not in the same ~** (*fig fam*) non c'è paragone.

leak [li:k] 1 *n* (*in pipe*) perdita, fuoriuscita; (*in boat*) falla; (*in roof*) buco; (*of gas*) fuga, perdita, fuoriuscita; (*fig: of information*) fuga di notizie. 2 *vi* (**a**) (*roof, bucket*) perdere; (*shoes*) lasciar passare l'acqua. (**b**) (*also: ~ out: liquid*) uscire (fuori); (*: gas*) esalare, uscire; (*fig: news*) trapelare; **water was ~ing into the cellar** l'acqua si stava infiltrando nella cantina. 3 *vt* (*liquid*) gocciolare, perdere; (*fig: information*) divulgare.

leak·age ['li:kɪdʒ] *n* (*of water, gas etc*) perdita.

leaky ['li:kɪ] *adj* (**-ier, -iest**) (*pipe, bucket, roof*) che perde; (*shoe*) che lascia passare l'acqua; (*boat*) che fa acqua.

lean[1] [li:n] *adj* (**-er, -est**) magro(a); **the ~ years** i tempi di magra.

lean[2] [li:n] *pt, pp* **leaned** *or* **leant** 1 *vi* (**a**) (*gatepost, wall etc*) essere inclinato(a), pendere; **to ~ to(wards) the left/right** (*Pol*) avere tendenze di sinistra/di destra. (**b**) (*for support: person*): **to ~ on, ~ against** appoggiarsi a; (*: ladder etc*): **to be ~ing against** essere appoggiato(a) a *or* contro; **to ~ on sb** (*also fig: for support*) appoggiarsi a qn; (*fig: put pressure on*) far pressione su qn. 2 *vt* (*ladder, bicycle*): **to ~ sth against sth** appoggiare qc a *or* contro qc; **to ~ one's head on sth** appoggiare la testa su qc.

♦ **lean back** *vi* + *adv* appoggiarsi all'indietro; **she ~ed back against the pillows** si è adagiata sui cuscini.

♦ **lean forward** *vi* + *adv* piegarsi in avanti.

♦ **lean out** *vi* + *adv*: **to ~ out (of)** sporgersi (da).

♦ **lean over** 1 *vi* + *adv* chinarsi, piegarsi; **to ~ over backwards to help sb** (*fig fam*) farsi in quattro per aiutare qn. 2 *vi* + *prep* (*balcony, gate*) sporgersi da, affacciarsi a; (*desk*) piegarsi su, chinarsi su.

lean·ing ['li:nɪŋ] 1 *n*: **~ (towards)** tendenza (a). 2 *adj* inclinato(a), pendente; **the ~ Tower of Pisa** la torre (pendente) di Pisa.

leant [lɛnt] *pt, pp of* **lean**[2].

lean-to ['li:ntu:] *n* (*roof*) tettoia; (*building*) edificio con tetto appoggiato ad altro edificio.

leap [li:p] (*vb: pp, pt* **leaped** *or* **leapt**) 1 *n* salto, balzo; **a ~ in the dark** (*fig*) un salto nel buio; **by ~s and bounds** a passi da gigante. 2 *vi* saltare, balzare; **he leapt into/out of the train** saltò sul/ giù dal treno; **to ~ to one's feet** scattare in piedi; **to ~ about** saltellare qua e là; **to ~ out** saltare fuori; **to ~ out at sb** saltare addosso a qn; **to ~ over sth** saltare qc d'un balzo; **to ~ for joy** far salti *or* balzi di gioia; **my heart leapt** ho avuto un tuffo al cuore; **to ~ at an offer** afferrare al volo una proposta. 3 *vt* (*fence, ditch*) saltare. 4 *cpd*: **~ year** *n* anno bisestile.

♦ **leap up** *vi* + *adv* (*person*) alzarsi d'un balzo, balzare su; (*flames*) divampare.

leap·frog ['li:pfrɒg] 1 *n* cavallina. 2 *vi*: **to ~ over sb/sth** saltare (alla cavallina) qn/qc.

leapt [lɛpt] *pt, pp of* **leap**.

learn [lɜ:n] *pt, pp* **learned** *or* **learnt** 1 *vt* imparare; **to ~ (how) to do sth** imparare a fare qc; **to ~ that...** apprendere che...; **we were sorry to ~ that it was closing down** la notizia della chiusura ci ha fatto dispiacere; **I think he's ~t his lesson** (*fig*) penso che gli sia servito di lezione. 2 *vi*: **to ~ about sth** (*Scol*) studiare qc, imparare qc; (*hear*) sentire qc, apprendere qc; **I've ~t from experience not to trust him** l'esperienza mi ha insegnato a non fidarmi di lui; **you ~ from your mistakes** sbagliando s'impara.

learn·ed ['lɜ:nɪd] *adj* (*person*) colto(a), dotto(a); (*book, profession*) dotto(a).

learn·er ['lɜ:nə^r] *n* principiante *m/f*; **she's a fast ~** è una che impara subito *or* con facilità; **slow ~** (*Scol*) ragazzo/a che ha difficoltà di apprendimento; **he's a ~ (driver)** sta imparando a guidare.

learn·ing ['lɜ:nɪŋ] *n* cultura.

lease [li:s] 1 *n* contratto di affitto; **on ~** in affitto; **to give sb a new ~ of life** (*fig*) ridare nuova vita a qn. 2 *vt* (*take*) affittare, prendere in affitto; (*give: also: ~ out*) affittare, dare in affitto.

lease·hold ['li:shəʊld] 1 *n* (*contract*) contratto di affitto (*a lungo termine con responsabilità simili a quelle di un proprietario*). 2 *adj* in affitto.

leash [li:ʃ] *n* guinzaglio.

least [li:st] *superl of* **little**[2] 1 *adj* minimo(a), più piccolo(a); **she wasn't in the ~ bit interested** non era minimamente interessata; **she always orders whatever costs the ~ money** ordina sempre quello che costa di meno; **that's the ~ of my worries** è la cosa che mi preoccupa di meno *or* che meno mi preoccupa.

2 *n* minimo; **it's the ~ one can do** è il minimo che si possa fare; **to say the ~** a dir poco; **the ~ said about the meeting, the better** meno parliamo della riunione e meglio è; **at ~** almeno; **I can at ~ try** posso sempre provarci; **at the very ~** come minimo; **not in the ~** niente affatto, per niente.

3 *adv* meno; **the ~ expensive car** l'auto meno cara; **she is ~ able to afford it** è quella che se lo può permettere meno di tutti; **~ of all me** e men che meno io; **for a number of reasons, not ~...** per molte ragioni, e non ultimo il fatto che... .

leath·er ['lɛðə^r] 1 *n* (*hide: soft*) pelle *f*; (*: hard*) cuoio; (*wash~*) pelle di daino. 2 *adj* (*see n*) di *or* in pelle; di cuoio; **~ goods** pelletteria, pelletterie *fpl*.

leave [li:v] (*vb: pt, pp* **left**) 1 *n* (**a**) (*permission*) permesso, autorizzazione *f*; **without so much as a 'by your ~'** senza nemmeno chiedere il permesso.

(**b**) (*permission to be absent*) permesso; (*: of public employee*) congedo; (*: Mil*) licenza; **on ~ of absence** in permesso; in congedo; in licenza.

(**c**): **to take (one's) ~ of sb** accomiatarsi da qn; **have you taken ~ of your senses?** ma sei impazzito?

2 *vt* (**a**) (*go away from: town*) lasciare, andarsene da; (*: room*) lasciare, uscire da; (*: station*) partire da; (*: hospital*) uscire da; (*: person*) lasciare; **to ~ school** finire la scuola; **to ~ home** uscire di casa; (*permanently*) andarsene di casa; **they have left this address** se ne sono andati da qui; **may I ~ the room?** (*euph: to go to the lavatory*) posso uscire?; **to ~ the table** alzarsi da tavola; **the car left the road** la macchina è uscita di strada; **the train is leaving in 10 minutes** il treno parte fra 10 minuti.

(**b**) (*forget*) lasciare, dimenticare; (*give: in will, as tip*) lasciare.

(**c**): (*allow to remain*) lasciare; **to ~ the window open** lasciare la finestra aperta; **let's ~ it at that** per ora basta (così); **~ it to me!** ci penso io!, lascia fare a me!; **I'll ~ it to you to decide** decidi tu, lo lascio decidere a te; ~ **it with me** lascia che me ne occupi io; **she left him to it** lo ha lasciato alle sue occupazioni; **he ~s a wife and a child** lascia la moglie e un figlio; **to ~ sb alone** lasciare qn (da) solo; ~ **me alone** or **in peace!** lasciami in pace!; **don't ~ anything to chance** non lasciar niente al caso; **it ~s much to be desired** lascia molto a desiderare; **take it or ~ it!** prendere o lasciare!; **3 from 10 ~s 7** 10 meno 3 fa 7.

(d) (remaining): **to be left (over)** rimanere, restare, avanzare; **all the money I have left (over)** tutti i soldi che mi restano or che mi sono avanzati; **how many are (there) left?** quanti ne restano?, quanti ce ne sono ancora?; **nothing was left for me (to do)** but to sell it non mi rimaneva or restava altro (da fare) che venderlo.

3 vi (plane, train etc) partire; (person) uscire, andarsene; **he's already left for the airport** è già uscito per andare all'aeroporto.

♦ **leave about, leave around** vt + adv lasciare in giro.

♦ **leave behind** vt + adv (also fig) lasciare indietro; (forget) dimenticare; **she ~s everybody else behind** è superiore a tutti gli altri; **you'll be left behind** by the rest rimarrai indietro rispetto agli altri.

♦ **leave in** vt + adv lasciare, non togliere.

♦ **leave off** vt + adv (a) (cover, lid) non mettere; (heating, light) non accendere. (b) (fam: stop): **to ~ off doing sth** smetterla or piantarla di fare qc. **2** vi + adv (fam: stop) smetterla.

♦ **leave on** vt + adv (coat, lid) lasciare su; (light, fire, cooker) lasciare acceso(a).

♦ **leave out** vt + adv (a) (omit) tralasciare; (: in reading etc) saltare; **he feels left out** si sente escluso or lasciato in disparte. (b) (not put back) lasciare fuori.

♦ **leave over** vt + adv (postpone) rimandare.

leaves [liːvz] npl of **leaf**.·

leave·taking ['liːvˌteɪkɪŋ] n commiato, addio.

leav·ings ['liːvɪŋz] npl avanzi mpl, rimasugli mpl.

Leba·non ['lebənən] n: **the ~** il Libano.

lech·er·ous ['letʃərəs] adj (person) lascivo(a), libidinoso(a); (grin) voglioso(a).

lec·ture ['lektʃəʳ] **1** n (a) (Univ) lezione f; (by visitor) conferenza; **to deliver** or **give a ~ on** tenere una conferenza su. (b) (reproof) paternale f, sermone m. **2** vi: **to ~ (in sth)** essere professore incaricato (di qc); **to ~ (to sb on sth)** (Univ) fare lezione (a qn di qc); (: visiting lecturer) tenere una conferenza (a qn su qc). **3** vt (reprove) rimproverare, fare una ramanzina a. **4** cpd: ~ **hall** n, ~ **theatre** n aula magna; ~ **notes** npl appunti mpl (del corso or delle lezioni).

lec·tur·er ['lektʃərəʳ] n (visitor) conferenziere/a; (Univ) docente m universitario.

led [led] pt, pp of **lead**².

ledge [ledʒ] n (on wall) sporgenza; (of window) davanzale m; (on mountain) cengia.

ledg·er ['ledʒəʳ] n libro mastro.

lee [liː] **1** n parte f sottovento; **in the ~ of** a ridosso di, al riparo di. **2** adj sottovento inv.

leech [liːtʃ] n sanguisuga.

leek [liːk] n porro.

leer [lɪəʳ] **1** n (lustful) espressione f libidinosa; (evil) espressione f malvagia. **2** vi: **to ~ at sb** (lustfully) guardare qn con occhi vogliosi; (cruelly) guardare qn con malvagità.

lee·ward ['liːwəd] (Naut) **1** adj sottovento inv. **2** n lato sottovento; **to ~** sottovento.

lee·way ['liːweɪ] n (Naut) deriva; (fig) margine m; **they gave him a great deal of ~** gli hanno lasciato ampia libertà di azione.

left¹ [left] pt, pp of **leave**.

left² [left] **1** adj sinistro(a). **2** adv a sinistra. **3** n (also Pol) sinistra; **on my ~, to my ~** alla mia sinistra; **on the ~, to the ~** a sinistra; **he has always been on the L~** ha sempre avuto idee di sinistra.

left-hand ['lefthænd] adj: ~ **drive** guida a sinistra; ~ **page** pagina a or di sinistra; ~ **side** (parte f) sinistra; **on the ~ side** a sinistra.

left-handed [ˌleft'hændɪd] adj mancino(a); (fig: compliment) ambiguo(a); ~ **scissors** forbici per mancini.

leftie ['leftɪ] n (fam) sinistroide m/f.

left-ist ['leftɪst] adj (Pol) di sinistra.

left-luggage [ˌleft'lʌgɪdʒ] n: ~ **office** deposito bagagli.

left-overs ['leftəuvəz] npl avanzi mpl.

left-wing [ˌleft'wɪŋ] adj (Pol) di sinistra.

left-winger [ˌleft'wɪŋəʳ] n (Pol) uno/a di sinistra; (Sport) ala sinistra.

leg [leg] n (gen) gamba; (of animal, bird) zampa; (Culin: of chicken, turkey, frog) coscia; (: of lamb, pork) cosciotto; (stage: of journey etc) tappa; **to be on one's last ~s** (person, animal) stare in piedi per miracolo; (machine, car) funzionare per miracolo; **he hasn't got a ~ to stand on** (fig) non ha una scusa che regga or una ragione che tenga; **to pull someone's ~** (fig) prendere in giro qn; **to stretch one's ~s** sgranchirsi le gambe.

lega·cy ['legəsɪ] n eredità f inv; (fig) retaggio.

le·gal ['liːgəl] adj (a) (lawful) legale; (: requirement) di legge; **these coins are no longer ~ currency** or **tender** queste monete sono fuori corso. (b) (relating to the law: gen) legale; (: error) giudiziario(a); **as a member of the ~ profession** come legale; **to take ~ action** or **proceedings against sb** intentare un'azione legale contro qn, far causa a qn; ~ **adviser** consulente m/f legale; ~ **department** (of a firm) ufficio legale, contenzioso; ~ **aid** assistenza legale gratuita.

le·gal·ity [lɪ'gælɪtɪ] n legalità.

le·gal·ize ['liːgəlaɪz] vt legalizzare, rendere legale.

le·gal·ly ['liːgəlɪ] adv legalmente.

le·ga·tion [lɪ'geɪʃən] n legazione f.

leg·end ['ledʒənd] n leggenda.

leg·end·ary ['ledʒəndərɪ] adj leggendario(a).

-leg·ged ['legɪd] adj ending in cpds: **four~** (animal) quadrupede; (stool) a quattro gambe; **cross~** a gambe incrociate.

leg·gy ['legɪ] adj dalle gambe lunghe.

leg·ibil·ity [ˌledʒɪ'bɪlɪtɪ] n leggibilità.

leg·ible ['ledʒəbl] adj leggibile.

le·gion ['liːdʒən] n legione f; (fig) schiera, stuolo.

le·gion·naire [ˌliːdʒə'nɛəʳ] n legionario.

leg·is·late ['ledʒɪsleɪt] vi legiferare, promulgare delle leggi.

leg·is·la·tion [ˌledʒɪs'leɪʃən] n legislazione f; **a piece of ~** una legge.

leg·is·la·tive ['ledʒɪslətɪv] adj legislativo(a).

leg·is·la·ture ['ledʒɪslətʃəʳ] n organi mpl legislativi, corpo legislativo.

le·giti·mate [lɪ'dʒɪtɪmɪt] adj (lawful) legittimo(a); (argument, cause, excuse) buono(a), valido(a); (complaint) legittimo(a); (conclusion) logico(a).

le·giti·mize [lɪ'dʒɪtɪmaɪz] vt (gen) legalizzare, rendere legale; (child) legittimare.

leg-room ['legrom] n spazio per le gambe.

lei·sure ['leʒəʳ] **1** n svago, tempo libero; **a life of ~** una vita comoda; **to be a lady of ~** (hum) fare la bella vita; **do it at your ~** fallo con comodo. **2** cpd (activities) del tempo libero; **in one's ~ time** durante il proprio tempo libero.

lei·sure·ly ['leʒəlɪ] adj (day, stroll, trip) tranquillo(a); **in a ~ way** con comodo.

lem·on ['lemən] **1** *n (fruit)* limone *m*. **2** *adj (colour)* giallo limone *inv*. **3** *cpd*: ~ **cheese** *n*, ~ **curd** *n* crema di limone *(che si spalma sul pane etc)*; ~ **juice** *n* succo di limone; ~ **sole** *n* limanda; ~ **tea** *n* tè *m inv* al limone; ~ **tree** *n* albero di limone.

lem·on·ade [,lemə'neɪd] *n* limonata.

lend [lend] *pt, pp* **lent** *vt (gen)* prestare; *(fig: impart: importance, mystery, authority)* conferire; **to** ~ **out** prestare, dare in prestito; **to** ~ **a hand** dare una mano; **to** ~ **an ear to sb/sth** prestare ascolto a qn/qc; **it does not** ~ **itself to being filmed** non si presta ad essere filmato.

length [leŋθ] *n* **(a)** *(size, extent)* lunghezza; *(duration)* durata; **it is 2 metres in** ~ è lungo 2 metri; **what is its** ~?, **what** ~ **is it?** quant'è lungo?; **throughout the** ~ **and breadth of Italy** in tutta Italia; **to fall full** ~ cadere lungo disteso; **for what** ~ **of time?** per quanto tempo?; **1000 words in** ~ di 1000 parole; **a concert 2 hours in** ~ un concerto della durata di *or* che dura 2 ore; **their team won the boat race by 2** ~**s** la loro squadra ha vinto la gara di canottaggio per 2 lunghezze; **at length** *(finally)* alla fine, finalmente; **to speak at** ~ dilungarsi, parlare a lungo; **I even went to the** ~ **of telephoning** sono perfino arrivato al punto di telefonare; **to go to any** ~ **to do sth** fare qualsiasi cosa pur di *or* per fare qc.

(b) *(piece: gen)* pezzo; *(: material)* taglio, altezza; **a dress/skirt** ~ un taglio per vestito/gonna.

length·en ['leŋθən] **1** *vt* allungare; *(holiday, visit etc)* prolungare. **2** *vi* allungarsi.

length·ways ['leŋθweɪz] *adv*, **length·wise** ['leŋθwaɪz] *adv* per la lunghezza.

lengthy ['leŋθɪ] *adj* (-**ier**, -**iest**) lungo(a); *(tedious)* interminabile.

le·ni·ence ['liːnɪəns] *n*, **le·ni·en·cy** ['liːnɪənsɪ] *n* clemenza, mitezza.

le·ni·ent ['liːnɪənt] *adj (person)* indulgente; *(sentence, punishment)* leggero(a).

lens [lenz] *n (Anat)* cristallino; *(of spectacles)* lente *f*; *(of camera etc)* obiettivo.

Lent [lent] *n* quaresima.

lent [lent] *pt, pp of* **lend**.

len·til ['lentɪl] *n* lenticchia.

Leo ['liːəʊ] *n (Astron, Astrology)* Leone *m*; **to be** ~ essere del Leone.

leop·ard ['lepəd] *n* leopardo.

leo·tard ['liːətɑːd] *n* body *m inv*.

lep·er ['lepə'] **1** *n* lebbroso/a. **2** *cpd*: ~ **colony** *n* lebbrosario.

lep·ro·sy ['leprəsɪ] *n* lebbra.

les·bian ['lezbɪən] **1** *adj* lesbico(a). **2** *n* lesbica.

le·sion ['liːʒən] *n (Med)* lesione *f*.

less [les] *comp of* **little**[2] **1** *adj* meno; **now we eat** ~ **bread** ora mangiamo meno pane; **she has** ~ **time to spare** ha meno tempo a disposizione; **of** ~ **importance** di minor importanza.

2 *pron* meno; **we see** ~ **of them now** li vediamo di meno adesso; **the** ~ **you read the** ~ **you learn** meno leggi meno impari; **can't you let me have it for** ~? mi potrebbe fare un piccolo sconto?; **the** ~ **said about it the better** meno se ne parla e meglio è; ~ **than £1/a kilo/3 metres** meno di una sterlina/un chilo/3 metri; ~ **than you think** meno di quanto tu creda; **the holiday was** ~ **than perfect** la vacanza non è stata proprio stupenda; **it's nothing** ~ **than a disaster** è un disastro bell'e buono; **a tip of £10, no** ~! *(fam)* nientemeno che 10 sterline di mancia!

3 *adv* meno, di meno; **to go out** ~ **(often)** uscire di meno (spesso); ~ **and** ~ sempre meno; **still** ~ ancora meno; **none the** ~... ugualmente..., lo stesso... .

4 *prep* meno; ~ **5%** meno il 5%.

...less *suf* senza; **breath**~ senza fiato; **meaning**~ privo di significato.

les·see [le'siː] *n* affittuario/a, locatario/a.

less·en ['lesn] **1** *vt (gen)* diminuire; *(pain)* alleviare; *(cost, tension)* ridurre; *(shock)* attutire, attenuare. **2** *vi (gen)* diminuire; *(shock)* attenuarsi.

less·en·ing ['lesnɪŋ] *n* diminuzione *f*.

less·er ['lesə'] *adj* minore, più piccolo(a); **to a** ~ **extent** *or* **degree** in grado *or* misura minore; **the** ~ **of 2 evils** il minore dei 2 mali.

les·son ['lesn] *n* lezione *f*; **to give** ~**s in** dare *or* impartire lezioni di; **a French** ~ una lezione di francese; **to teach sb a** ~ *(fig)* dare una lezione a qn; **it taught him a** ~ *(fig)* gli è servito di lezione.

les·sor [le'sɔː'] *n* locatore/trice.

lest [lest] *conj (frm)* nel timore che + *sub*; ~ **we forget** affinché non *or* in modo che non ce ne dimentichiamo.

let [let] *pt, pp* **let** *vt* **(a)** *(permit)* lasciare, permettere; **to** ~ **sb past** lasciar *or* far passare qn; **to** ~ **sb do sth** lasciar fare qc a qn, lasciare che qn faccia qc; ~ **me have a look** fammi vedere; **to** ~ **sb have sth** dare qc a qn; **to** ~ **sb get away with sth** *(fam)* lasciarla correre a qn; **I'll** ~ **you have it back tomorrow** te lo ridò *or* restituisco domani; **don't** ~ **me catch** *or* **see you copying again!** che non ti peschi *or* sorprenda mai più a copiare!; ~ **him alone** *or* **be** lascialo stare *or* in pace; **to** ~ **sb/sth go**, ~ **go of sb/sth** lasciar andare *or* mollare qn/qc.

(b) *(in verb forms)*: ~**'s** *or* ~ **us go!** andiamo!; ~**'s see, what was I saying?** dunque, cosa stavo dicendo?; ~ **them wait** che aspettino (pure); ~ **that be a warning to you!** che questo ti serva di lezione!; ~ **x = 1 and y = 2** sia x = 1 e y = 2.

(c) *(rent out)* affittare, dare in affitto; **'To L~'** 'Affittasi'.

♦ **let down** *vt* + *adv* **(a)** *(dress)* allungare; *(hem)* allungare, lasciar giù; *(tyre)* sgonfiare; *(one's hair)* sciogliersi; *(on rope)* calare (giù). **(b)** *(fail)* deludere; **that car/watch always** ~**s me down** quella macchina/quell'orologio mi fa sempre degli strani scherzi.

♦ **let in** *vt* + *adv (roof, shoes etc)* lasciar passare l'acqua. **2** *vt* + *adv* far entrare, far passare; **to** ~ **sb in** far *or* lasciar entrare qn; **shoes which** ~ **the water in** scarpe che lasciano passare l'acqua; **to** ~ **sb in for a lot of trouble** procurare *or* dare un mucchio di fastidi a qn; **what have you** ~ **yourself in for?** in che guai *or* pasticci sei andato a cacciarti?; **to** ~ **sb in on a secret** rivelare *or* confidare un segreto a qn.

♦ **let off** *vt* + *adv* **(a)** *(explode)* far esplodere; *(fireworks)* accendere; **to** ~ **off steam** *(fig fam)* sfogarsi, scaricarsi. **(b)** *(allow to go)* lasciar andare *or* uscire; *(not punish)* far passar liscia a; **to** ~ **sb off lightly** non calcare la mano nel punire qn; **to** ~ **sb off with a warning** limitarsi ad ammonire qn. **(c)** *(subj: taxi driver, bus driver)* far scendere.

♦ **let on** *vi* + *adv (fam)* dire, lasciar capire; **to** ~ **on to sb about sth** far capire qc a qn; **to** ~ **on (that...)** dare a intendere (che...).

♦ **let out** *vt* + *adv* **(a)** *(gen)* far uscire; *(secret)* spifferare; *(news)* divulgare; **don't get up, I'll** ~ **myself out** non occorre che mi accompagni alla porta; **to** ~ **out a cry/sigh** emettere un grido/un sospiro; **to** ~ **the air out of a tyre** sgonfiare una gomma; **that** ~**s him out** questo lo esclude. **(b)** *(dress, seam)* allargare. **(c)** *(rent out)* affittare, dare in affitto.

♦ **let up 1** *vi* + *adv (bad weather)* diminuire; *(talker,* *worker)* smettere, fermarsi. **2** *vt + adv* far alzare.

let-down ['lɛtdaʊn] *n (disappointment)* delusione *f.*

le·thal ['liːθəl] *adj (gen)* letale; *(wound, blow)* mortale; **this coffee's ~!** *(fig fam)* ma questo non è caffè, è veleno!

le·thar·gic [lɛ'θɑːdʒɪk] *adj* letargico(a).

let·ter ['lɛtə^r] *n* **(a)** *(of alphabet)* lettera; **the ~ G** la (lettera) G; **small/capital ~** lettera minuscola/ maiuscola; **she's got a lot of ~s after her name** ha un mucchio di titoli; **the ~ of the law** *(fig)* la lettera della legge; **to follow instructions to the ~** seguire alla lettera le istruzioni. **(b)** *(missive)* lettera; **covering ~** lettera *or* nota esplicativa; **~ of credit** lettera di credito; **~ of introduction/ application/protest** lettera di presentazione/di domanda/di protesta; **by ~** per lettera. **(c)** *(learning):* **man of ~s** uomo di lettere.

letter-bomb ['lɛtə͵bɒm] *n* lettera contenente una bomba.

letter-box ['lɛtəbɒks] *n* cassetta delle lettere.

letter·head ['lɛtəhɛd] *n* intestazione *f.*

let·ter·ing ['lɛtərɪŋ] *n (engraving)* iscrizione *f; (letters)* caratteri *mpl.*

letter-opener ['lɛtər͵əʊpnə^r] *n* tagliacarte *m inv.*

letter·press ['lɛtəprɛs] *n (method)* rilievografia; *(printed page)* testo.

let·tuce ['lɛtɪs] *n* lattuga.

let-up ['lɛtʌp] *n (fam)* interruzione *f;* **without (a) ~** ininterrottamente, senza smettere.

leu·kae·mia, *(Am)* **leu·ke·mia** [luːˈkiːmɪə] *n* leucemia.

lev·el ['lɛvl] **1** *adj* **(a)** *(flat: ground, surface)* piano(a), piatto(a); *(: shelf)* diritto(a); **I'll do my ~ best** *(fam)* farò del mio meglio, farò tutto il possibile; **a ~ spoonful** *(Culin)* un cucchiaio raso; **~ crossing** *(Rail)* passaggio a livello. **(b)** *(steady: voice, tone)* normale; *(: gaze)* diretto(a), sicuro(a); **to keep a ~ head** mantenere il sangue freddo *or* la calma. **(c)** *(equal)* alla pari; **to be ~ with sb** *(in race, league, studies)* essere alla pari di qn; *(in rank)* avere lo stesso grado di qn; **to draw ~ with** *(team)* mettersi alla pari di; *(runner, car)* affiancarsi a.

2 *n* **(a)** livello; **to find one's own ~** trovare la giusta dimensione; **above/at/below sea ~** sul/al/ sotto il livello del mare; **talks at ministerial ~** colloqui a livello ministeriale; **to be on a ~ with** essere al livello di; *(fig)* essere allo stesso livello di; **to come down to sb's ~** *(fig)* scendere *or* abbassarsi al livello di qn; **he's on the ~** *(fig fam)* è a posto. **(b)** *(spirit ~)* livella (a bolla d'aria). **(c)** *(Brit Scol):* **A ~s =** esami *mpl* di maturità; **O ~s** *esami fatti in Inghilterra all'età di 16 anni.*

3 *vt* **(a)** *(make ~: ground, site)* livellare, spianare; *(raze: building)* radere al suolo; *(fig)* livellare. **(b)** *(aim):* **to ~ (at)** *(blow)* tirare (a), allungare (a); *(gun)* puntare (verso); *(accusation):* **to ~ (against)** lanciare (a *or* contro).

♦ **level off, level out** *vi + adv (ground)* diventare pianeggiante; *(prices, curve on graph)* stabilizzarsi; *(aircraft)* volare in quota.

♦ **level with** *vi + prep (fam):* **to ~ with sb** esser franco(a) con qn.

level-headed [͵lɛvl'hɛdɪd] *adj* equilibrato(a), con la testa a posto *or* sulle spalle.

lev·el·ling ['lɛvəlɪŋ] *adj (process, effect)* di livellamento.

lev·er ['liːvə^r] **1** *n (also fig)* leva. **2** *vt:* **to ~ sth up/off** sollevare/togliere qc (con una leva).

lev·er·age ['liːvərɪdʒ] *n:* **~ (on)** forza (su); *(fig)* ascendente *m* (su); **to exert ~ on sb/sth** far leva su qn/qc.

lev·ity ['lɛvɪtɪ] *n* leggerezza, frivolezza.

levy ['lɛvɪ] **1** *n (amount)* imposta, tassa; *(collection)* riscossione *f.* **2** *vt (tax, contributions)* imporre; *(fine)* dare; *(army)* formare.

lewd [luːd] *adj (-er, -est)* osceno(a).

lexi·cal ['lɛksɪkəl] *adj* lessicale.

lexi·cog·ra·phy [͵lɛksɪ'kɒɡrəfɪ] *n* lessicografia.

lia·bil·ity [͵laɪə'bɪlɪtɪ] *n (responsibility)* responsabilità; *(burden)* peso; *(person)* peso morto; **liabilities** *(Comm)* passivo, passività.

lia·ble ['laɪəbl] *adj* **(a)** *(responsible):* **to be ~ for** essere responsabile di. **(b)** *(subject):* **to be ~ for military service** essere tenuto a svolgere il servizio militare; **to be ~ to a fine** essere passibile di multa; **he's ~ to colds** prende facilmente il raffreddore. **(c)** *(likely):* **she's ~ to get cross** è probabile che si arrabbi; **it's ~ to break** è probabile che si rompa; **we are ~ to get shot at here** qui c'è il rischio che ci sparino.

li·aise [liː'eɪz] *vi:* **to ~ (with)** mantenere i contatti (con).

liai·son [liː'eɪzɒn] **1** *n (coordination)* coordinamento, collegamento. **2** *cpd:* **~ committee** *n* comitato di coordinamento; **~ officer** *n* ufficiale *m* di collegamento.

liar ['laɪə^r] *n* bugiardo/a.

li·bel ['laɪbəl] **1** *n (Law)* diffamazione *f,* libello. **2** *vt* diffamare.

li·bel·lous, *(Am)* **li·bel·ous** ['laɪbələs] *adj* diffamatorio(a).

lib·er·al ['lɪbərəl] **1** *adj (gen)* liberale, generoso(a); *(views)* liberale. **2** *n (Pol):* **L~** liberale *m/f.*

lib·er·al·ism ['lɪbərəlɪzəm] *n* liberalismo.

lib·er·al·ity [͵lɪbə'rælɪtɪ] *n (generosity)* generosità, liberalità.

lib·er·al·ize ['lɪbərəlaɪz] *vt* liberalizzare.

lib·er·al·ly ['lɪbərəlɪ] *adv* generosamente.

liberal-minded [͵lɪbərəl'maɪndɪd] *adj* tollerante.

lib·er·ate ['lɪbəreɪt] *vt* liberare; **a ~d woman** una donna emancipata.

lib·era·tion [͵lɪbə'reɪʃən] *n* liberazione *f.*

lib·era·tor ['lɪbəreɪtə^r] *n* liberatore/trice.

lib·er·ty ['lɪbətɪ] *n* libertà; **~ of conscience** libertà di coscienza; **at ~** *(not detained)* in libertà; **to be at ~ to do sth** essere libero di fare qc; **to take the ~ of doing sth** prendersi la libertà di fare qc; **to take liberties** prendersi delle libertà; **what a ~!** *(fam)* come ti permetti? *(or* si permette? *etc).*

li·bi·do [lɪ'biːdəʊ] *n* libido *f inv.*

Li·bra ['liːbrə] *n (Astron, Astrology)* Bilancia; **to be ~** essere della Bilancia.

li·brar·ian [laɪ'brɛərɪən] *n* bibliotecario/a.

li·brary ['laɪbrərɪ] **1** *n* biblioteca. **2** *cpd:* **~ book** *n* libro della biblioteca; **~ ticket** *n* tesserino della biblioteca.

li·bret·to [lɪ'brɛtəʊ] *n* libretto.

Libya ['lɪbɪə] *n* Libia.

Liby·an ['lɪbɪən] *adj, n* libico(a) *(m/f).*

lice [laɪs] *npl of* **louse.**

li·cence, *(Am)* **li·cense**[1] ['laɪsəns] **1** *n* **(a)** *(permit)* autorizzazione *f,* permesso; *(for car)* bollo, tassa di circolazione; *(TV, Radio)* abbonamento; *(: amount paid)* canone *m,* abbonamento; *(for manufacturing, trading)* licenza; *(for dog)* tassa; **married by special ~** sposato con dispensa; **driving ~** patente *f* di guida; **provisional driving ~ ≈** foglio rosa; **pilot's ~** brevetto; **import ~** licenza di importazione; **produced under ~** prodotto su licenza. **(b)** *(excessive freedom)* libertà; **poetic ~** licenza poetica. **2** *cpd:* **~ number** *n (Aut)* numero di targa; **~ plate** *n (Aut)* targa (automobilistica).

li·cense[2] ['laɪsəns] *vt* **(a)** *(person):* **to ~ sb to do** autorizzare qn a fare. **(b)** *(car)* pagare la tassa di circolazione *or* il bollo di; **are you ~ed to drive a bus?** hai la patente per guidare gli autobus?; **~d premises** *locali che sono autorizzati alla vendita di bevande alcoliche.*

li·cen·see [ˌlaɪsənˈsiː] *n (in pub)* detentore/trice di autorizzazione alla vendita di bevande alcoliche.

li·cen·tious [laɪˈsɛnʃəs] *adj* licenzioso(a).

lick [lɪk] **1** *n* **(a)** leccata; **a ~ of paint** una passata di pittura; **a ~ and a promise** *(fig fam)* una pulitina sommaria. **(b)** *(fam: speed):* **at full ~** a tutta birra. **2** *vt* **(a)** *(with tongue)* leccare; *(subj: flames)* lambire; **to ~ one's plate clean** pulire il piatto con la lingua; **to ~ one's lips** leccarsi le labbra; *(hungrily)* leccarsi i baffi; **to ~ one's wounds** *(also fig)* leccarsi le ferite; **to ~ sb's boots** *(fig fam)* leccare i piedi a qn; **to ~ sth into shape** *(fig fam)* mettere a punto qc. **(b)** *(fam: defeat)* suonarle a, stracciare.

lico·rice [ˈlɪkərɪs] *n* = **liquorice.**

lid [lɪd] *n* coperchio; **to take the ~ off sth** *(fig)* smascherare qc.

lido [ˈliːdəʊ] *n (swimming pool)* piscina (all'aperto); *(part of the beach)* lido, stabilimento balneare.

lie¹ [laɪ] **1** *n* bugia, menzogna; **to tell ~s** raccontare *or* dir bugie; **to give the ~ to** smentire. **2** *vi (prp* **lying)** mentire. **3** *cpd:* **~ detector** *n* macchina della verità.

lie² [laɪ] *pt* **lay,** *pp* **lain,** *prp* **lying** *vi* **(a)** *(also: ~ down)* sdraiarsi, distendersi; *(be lying)* essere sdraiato(a) *or* disteso(a); *(dead body)* giacere; **he lay where he had fallen** era disteso *(or* giaceva) a terra nel punto in cui era caduto; **to ~ still** rimanere immobile; **she lay in bed until 10 o'clock** è rimasta a letto fino alle 10; **to ~ low** *(fig)* tenersi nell'ombra; *(: hide)* nascondersi.

(b) *(be situated)* trovarsi, essere; *(remain)* rimanere; **the book lay on the table** il libro giaceva sul tavolo; **the snow lay half a metre deep** la neve formava una coltre di mezzo metro; **the town lies in a valley** la città è situata *or* si trova in una valle; **the plain lay before us** la pianura si stendeva dinanzi a noi; **in spite of the obstacles lying in his way** nonostante gli ostacoli che aveva di fronte; **where does the difficulty/difference ~?** dov'è *or* qual'è la difficoltà/differenza?; **the fault ~s with you** l'errore è tuo; **the best remedy lies in...** il miglior rimedio consiste nel... .

♦ **lie about, lie around** *vi + adv (things)* essere in giro; *(person)* bighellonare; **it must be lying about somewhere** dev'essere in giro da qualche parte.

♦ **lie back** *vi + adv* stendersi.

♦ **lie down** *vi + adv* stendersi, sdraiarsi; *(to dog):* **~ down!** cuccia!; **to take sth lying down** *(fig)* accettare supinamente qc.

♦ **lie in** *vi + adv (stay in bed)* rimanere a letto.

♦ **lie up** *vi + adv (hide)* nascondersi.

lie-down [ˈlaɪdaʊn] *n:* **to have a ~** sdraiarsi, distendersi.

lie-in [ˈlaɪɪn] *n:* **to have a ~** starsene a letto.

lieu [luː] *n:* **in ~ of** invece di, al posto di.

lieu·ten·ant [lɛfˈtɛnənt, *(Am)* luːˈtɛnənt] *n (Mil)* tenente *m; (Naut)* tenente *m* di vascello; **~ colonel** tenente colonnello; **~ general** tenente generale.

life [laɪf] **1** *n, pl* **lives (a)** *(animate state)* vita; **~ on earth** vita terrestre *or* sulla terra; **bird ~** gli uccelli; **a matter of ~ and death** una questione di vita o di morte; **to bring sb back to ~** riportare in vita qn; **to come to ~** rianimarsi, riprendere vita.

(b) *(existence)* vita; *(of battery etc)* durata; **to spend one's ~ as sth/doing sth** passare tutta la propria vita come qc/a fare qc; **during the ~ of this government** durante questo governo, nel corso di questa amministrazione; **to begin ~ as** cominciare come; **to be sent to prison for ~** essere condannato all'ergastolo; **in early ~** in gioventù; **in later ~** con gli anni; **a quiet/hard ~** una vita tranquilla/dura; **country/city ~** vita di campagna/di città; **how's ~?** *(fam)* come va (la vita)?; **that's ~** così è (la vita); **to lose one's ~** perdere la vita; **3 lives were lost** 3 persone sono morte *or* hanno perso la vita; **a danger to ~ and limb** un pericolo mortale; **to risk ~ and limb** rischiare l'osso del collo; **to take one's own ~** *(euph: commit suicide)* togliersi la vita; **you'll be taking your ~ in your hands if you climb up there** *(fam)* rischi la pelle se ti arrampichi lassù; **his ~ won't be worth living** rimpiangerà di esser nato; **not on your ~!** *(fam)* neanche morto!, fossi matto!; **to see ~** vedere il mondo; **to run for one's ~** correre per mettersi in salvo; **I can't for the ~ of me imagine...** *(fam)* non riesco assolutamente a immaginare...; **true to ~** fedele alla realtà; **to paint from ~** dipingere dal vero.

(c) *(liveliness) (in village)* vita, animazione *f; (in person)* vita, vivacità, **the ~ and soul of the party** l'anima della festa; **to put** *or* **breathe new ~ into** *(person)* ridare entusiasmo a; *(project, area etc)* ridare nuova vita a.

2 *cpd:* **~ assurance** *n,* **~ insurance** *n* assicurazione *f* sulla vita; **~ belt** *n,* **~ buoy** *n* salvagente *m;* **~ cycle** *n* ciclo vitale; **~ expectancy** *n* durata media della vita; **~ imprisonment** *n* ergastolo; **~ jacket** *n* giubbotto di salvataggio.

life-and-death [ˈlaɪfənˌdɛθ] *adj:* **~ struggle** lotta all'ultimo sangue.

life·blood [ˈlaɪfblʌd] *n (fig)* linfa vitale.

life·boat [ˈlaɪfbəʊt] *n (from shore)* lancia di salvataggio; *(from ship)* scialuppa di salvataggio.

life·guard [ˈlaɪfɡɑːd] *n (on beach)* bagnino/a.

life·less [ˈlaɪflɪs] *adj (body)* privo(a) di vita, inanimato(a); *(fig: person)* privo(a) di energia; *(: style)* piatto(a); *(: hair)* senza corpo.

life·like [ˈlaɪflaɪk] *adj* che sembra vero(a).

life·line [ˈlaɪflaɪn] *n (on ship)* sagola di salvataggio; *(for diver)* cavo di recupero; **it was his ~** *(fig)* era vitale per lui.

life·long [ˈlaɪflɒŋ] *adj (ambition etc)* di tutta la propria vita; *(friend)* di sempre.

life-size(d) [ˈlaɪfsaɪz(d)] *adj* in grandezza naturale.

life·time [ˈlaɪftaɪm] *n* vita; **a ~'s work, the work of a ~** il lavoro di tutta una vita; **in my ~** nel corso della mia vita; **the chance of a ~** un'occasione unica *or* che capita una sola volta nella vita; **it seemed a ~** sembrò (che fosse passato) un'eternità.

lift [lɪft] **1** *n* **(a)** *(Brit: elevator)* ascensore *m; (for goods)* montacarichi *m.* **(b)** *(esp Brit: in car)* passaggio; **to give sb a ~** dare un passaggio a qn. **(c)** *(Aer)* spinta; *(fig):* **it gave him a tremendous ~** lo ha tirato incredibilmente su di morale. **2** *vt* **(a)** *(thing, person)* sollevare, alzare; **to ~ sb over sth** far passare qn sopra qc; **to ~ one's head** alzare *or* sollevare la testa; **she never ~s a finger to help** non alza *or* muove mai neanche un dito per aiutare. **(b)** *(fig: restrictions, ban)* revocare. **(c)** *(fam: steal: idea, quotation)* prendere di sana pianta. **3** *vi* sollevarsi, alzarsi; *(fog)* alzarsi. **4** *cpd:* **~ attendant** *n* ascensorista *m/f;* **~ shaft** *n* tromba dell'ascensore.

♦ **lift down** *vt + adv* tirar giù.

♦ **lift off 1** *vt + adv* togliere. **2** *vi + adv (rocket)* partire; *(helicopter)* decollare.

♦ **lift out** vt + adv tirar fuori; (troops, evacuees etc) far evacuare per mezzo di elicotteri (or aerei).

♦ **lift up** vt + adv sollevare, alzare.

lift-off ['lɪftɒf] n (of rocket) partenza.

liga·ment ['lɪɡəmənt] n legamento.

light[1] [laɪt] (vb: pt, pp lit or lighted) **1** n (a) (in general) luce f; **electric** ~ illuminazione f or luce elettrica; **at first** ~ alle prime luci dell'alba; **by the** ~ **of the moon** alla luce della luna; **in the cold** ~ **of day** (also fig) alla luce del giorno; **you're (standing) in my** ~ mi fai ombra; **to hold sth up to** or **against the** ~ tenere qc controluce.

(**b**) (fig): **in the** ~ **of** alla luce di; **to bring to** ~ portare alla luce; **to come to** ~ venire in luce, emergere; **to cast** or **shed** or **throw** ~ **on** gettare luce su; **I was hoping that you could shed some** ~ **on it (for me)** speravo che tu potessi darmi degli schiarimenti su questo; **to see the** ~ (Rel) convertirsi; (fig) ravvedersi; **to reveal sb/sth in a new** ~ rivelare qn/qc sotto una luce diversa; **according to one's** ~s secondo le proprie capacità intellettive.

(**c**) (single ~) luce f; (Aut) faro; **to turn the** ~ **on/off** accendere/spegnere la luce; **rear** ~s luci or fari posteriori; **the (traffic)** ~s **were at red** il semaforo era rosso.

(**d**) (flame) fiamma; **pilot** ~ (on stove) fiammella di sicurezza; **have you a** ~? (for cigarette) hai da accendere?; **to put a** ~ **to sth** dar fuoco a qc.

2 adj (-er, -est) (**a**) (bright) chiaro(a); **to get** ~**er** rischiararsi, schiarirsi.

(**b**) (colour, skin) chiaro(a); (hair) biondo(a); ~ **yellow** giallo chiaro.

3 vt (**a**) (illuminate) illuminare, rischiarare; **to** ~ **sb's way** far luce a qn.

(**b**) (cigarette, fire etc) accendere.

4 vi (ignite) accendersi.

5 cpd: ~ **bulb** n lampadina; ~ **meter** n (Phot) esposimetro.

♦ **light up 1** vi + adv (**a**) (lamp) accendersi; (face, eyes) illuminarsi. (**b**) (fam: smoke) accendersi una sigaretta (or la pipa etc). **2** vt + adv illuminare, rischiarare.

light[2] [laɪt] **1** adj (-er, -est) (gen) leggero(a); ~ **ale** birra chiara; ~ **opera** operetta; **some** ~ **reading** qualcosa di leggero da leggere; **she is a** ~ **sleeper** ha il sonno leggero; **as a feather** leggero come una piuma; **to be** ~ **on one's feet** avere il passo leggero; **with a** ~ **heart** a cuor leggero; **to make** ~ **work of sth** fare qc con molta facilità; **to make** ~ **of sth** (fig) prendere alla leggera qc, non dar peso a qc. **2** adv (travel) con poco bagaglio.

light·en[1] ['laɪtn] **1** vt (darkness) rischiarare; (hair, colour) schiarire. **2** vi schiararsi; (room) rischiararsi.

light·en[2] ['laɪtn] vt (load) alleggerire; (fig: make cheerful: heart, atmosphere) sollevare.

light·er ['laɪtə'] n (for cigarettes) accendino, accendisigari m inv.

light-fingered ['laɪt,fɪŋɡəd] adj lesto(a) di mano.

light-haired [,laɪt'hɛəd] adj dai capelli biondi.

light-headed [,laɪt'hɛdɪd] adj (by temperament) senza testa; (dizzy) intontito(a); (with fever) vaneggiante; (with excitement) eccitato(a); **it made him feel** ~ gli ha fatto girare la testa.

light-hearted ['laɪt'hɑːtɪd] adj (person, laugh) spensierato(a), gaio(a); (discussion) non impegnato(a).

light·house ['laɪthaʊs] n faro.

light·ing ['laɪtɪŋ] n (system) illuminazione f; (in theatre) luci fpl.

lighting-up [,laɪtɪŋ'ʌp] adj: ~ **time** (Aut) ora in cui bisogna accendere i fari.

light·ly ['laɪtlɪ] adv leggermente; **to get off** ~ cavarsela a buon mercato; **to sleep** ~ avere il sonno leggero.

light·ness ['laɪtnɪs] n (**a**) (brightness) chiarezza. (**b**) (in weight etc) leggerezza.

light·ning ['laɪtnɪŋ] **1** n fulmine m, lampo; **a lot of** ~ molti lampi; **a flash of** ~ un lampo, un fulmine; **as quick as** ~, **like (greased)** ~ (fam) (veloce) come un fulmine, in un lampo. **2** cpd: ~ **attack** n incursione f lampo; ~ **conductor** n, ~ **rod** n parafulmine m; ~ **strike** n sciopero m lampo inv.

light·weight ['laɪtweɪt] **1** adj (also fig) leggero(a); (Boxing) di pesi leggeri. **2** n (Boxing) peso leggero.

light-year ['laɪtjɪə'] n anno m luce inv.

like[1] [laɪk] **1** adj simile; **in** ~ **cases** in casi simili or analoghi; **rabbits, mice and** ~ **creatures** conigli, topi e animali simili; **to be as** ~ **as two peas (in a pod)** essere come due gocce d'acqua.

2 prep (**a**) (similar to) come, uguale a; (in comparisons) come; **to be** ~ **sb/sth** essere come qn/qc; **they are very** ~ **each other** si somigliano molto; **a house** ~ **mine** una casa come la mia; **people** ~ **that** tipi del genere; **what's he** ~? che tipo è?, com'è?; **what's the weather** ~? che tempo fa?; **this portrait is not** ~ **him** questo ritratto non gli somiglia affatto; **he thinks** ~ **us** la pensa come noi; **she behaved** ~ **an idiot** si è comportata come una or da cretina; **it's not** ~ **him to do that** non è tipo da fare cose del genere; **I never saw anything** ~ **it** non ho mai visto una cosa simile; **that's more** ~ **it** (fam) così va meglio; **that's nothing** ~ **it** non ha niente a che vedere con quello; **something** ~ **that** qualcosa del genere; **don't talk** ~ **that** non parlare così; **there's nothing** ~ **a holiday** non c'è niente di meglio di or niente come una vacanza; **it happened** ~ **this...** è andata così...; ~ **father** ~ **son** tale padre tale figlio; **we ran** ~ **mad** (fam) abbiamo fatto una corsa pazzesca; **it rained** ~ **mad** (fam) ha piovuto a dirotto; **I feel** ~ **a drink** avrei voglia di bere qualcosa; **it looks** ~ **a diamond** sembra un diamante.

(**b**) (such as) come.

3 adv: **it's nothing** ~ **as hot as it was** non fa più così caldo come faceva prima; **as** ~ **as not** (molto) probabilmente.

4 conj (as) come; ~ **we used to (do)** come facevamo una volta.

5 n: **did you ever see the** ~ **(of it)?** hai mai visto niente del genere?; **the** ~ **of which I never saw** come non ne avevo mai visti; **sparrows, blackbirds and the** ~ ~ passeri, merli e altri uccelli simili; **the** ~s **of him** (fam pej) quelli come lui.

like[2] [laɪk] **1** vt (**a**): **I** ~ **swimming/that book** mi piace nuotare/quel libro; **I** ~ **hats** mi piacciono i cappelli; **I** ~ **her** mi piace; **which do you** ~ **best?** quale preferisci?; **well, I** ~ **that!** (fam hum) questa sì che è bella! (**b**) (want) desiderare, volere; **I should** ~ **more time** vorrei or mi piacerebbe avere più tempo; **I should** ~ **to know why** vorrei or mi piacerebbe sapere perché; **would you** ~ **me to wait outside?** vuoi or desideri che aspetti fuori?; **I didn't** ~ **to (do it)** non volevo (farlo); **as you** ~ come vuoi; **if you** ~ se vuoi; **whenever you** ~ quando vuoi. **2**: ~s npl gusti mpl, preferenze fpl; **my** ~s **and dislikes** ciò che mi piace e non mi piace.

like·able ['laɪkəbl] adj simpatico(a).

like·li·hood ['laɪklɪhʊd] n probabilità; **in all** ~ con ogni probabilità, molto probabilmente; **there is**

no ~ of that è da escludersi; **there is little ~ that he'll come** è difficile che venga.

like·ly ['laɪklɪ] **1** adj (-ier, -iest) (outcome, winner) probabile; (place) adatto(a), buono(a); **a ~ explanation** una spiegazione attendibile or possibile; **a ~ story!** (iro) bella questa storia!; **when is the likeliest time to find you at home?** quando è più probabile trovarti a casa?; **it's ~ that I'll be late** è probabile che sarò in ritardo; **an incident ~ to cause trouble** un incidente che probabilmente causerà dei problemi; **it's not ~ that he'll come, he is not ~ to come** è difficile che venga. **2** adv probabilmente; **most** or **very ~ they've lost it** con molta probabilità or molto probabilmente l'hanno perso; **not ~!** (fam) neanche per sogno!

like-minded [,laɪk'maɪndɪd] adj che la pensa allo stesso modo.

lik·en ['laɪkən] vt paragonare.

like·ness ['laɪknɪs] n **(a)** (similarity) somiglianza; **there is a family ~** ci sono tratti caratteristici della famiglia; **that's a good ~ of you** ti rassomiglia molto. **(b)** (form): **in the ~ of** sotto le apparenze or l'aspetto di.

like·wise ['laɪkwaɪz] adv (similarly) allo stesso modo; (also) anche; (moreover) inoltre, per di più; **to do ~** fare altrettanto.

lik·ing ['laɪkɪŋ] n (for person) simpatia; (for thing) predilezione f; **to have a ~ for sb/sth** avere un debole per qn/qc; **to be to sb's ~** essere di gusto or gradimento di qn; **to take a ~ to sb** prendere qn in simpatia; **to take a ~ to sth/to doing sth** scoprire il piacere di qc/di fare qc.

li·lac ['laɪlək] **1** n lilla m inv. **2** adj (colour) lilla inv.

lilt [lɪlt] n cadenza.

lily ['lɪlɪ] n giglio; **~ of the valley** mughetto.

limb [lɪm] n (Anat) arto; (of tree) (grosso) ramo; **to be out on a ~** (fig) sentirsi spaesato or tagliato fuori; **to go out on a ~** (fig) esporsi.

lim·ber up [,lɪmbər'ʌp] vi + adv scaldarsi (i muscoli).

lim·bo ['lɪmbəʊ] n (Rel) limbo; **to be in ~** (fig) essere lasciato nel dimenticatoio.

lime¹ [laɪm] n (Chem) calce f.

lime² [laɪm] n (Bot: linden) tiglio.

lime³ [laɪm] n (Bot: citrus fruit) limetta.

lime·light ['laɪmlaɪt] n: **to be in the ~** essere alla ribalta.

lim·er·ick ['lɪmərɪk] n poemetto umoristico a 5 versi.

lime·stone ['laɪmstəʊn] n calcare m, roccia calcarea.

lim·it ['lɪmɪt] **1** n limite m; **weight/speed ~** limite di peso/di velocità; **there's a ~ to my patience** la mia pazienza ha un limite; **within ~s** entro certi limiti; **there is a ~ to what one can do** c'è un limite a quello che si può fare; **he's the ~!** (fam) lui passa tutti i limiti!; **well, that's the ~!** (fam) questo è il massimo or il colmo! **2** vt limitare; **to ~ o.s. to a few remarks** limitarsi ad alcune osservazioni; **I ~ myself to 10 cigarettes a day** mi limito a (fumare) 10 sigarette al giorno.

limi·ta·tion [,lɪmɪ'teɪʃən] n limitazione f, restrizione f; **he has/knows his ~s** ha/conosce i suoi limiti.

lim·it·ed ['lɪmɪtɪd] adj limitato(a); (means, income) scarso(a); **to a ~ extent** entro certi limiti, fino a un certo punto; **~ edition** edizione f a bassa tiratura; **~ company** (abbr **Ltd**) società f inv per azioni (abbr SpA).

lim·it·less ['lɪmɪtlɪs] adj illimitato(a).

lim·ou·sine ['lɪməzi:n] n limousine f inv.

limp¹ [lɪmp] **1** n: **to have** or **walk with a ~** zoppicare. **2** vi zoppicare; **to ~ in/out** entrare/uscire

zoppicando; **the ship ~ed home** la nave è tornata faticosamente in porto.

limp² [lɪmp] adj (gen) molle; (dress) floscio(a); (person) fiacco(a); **she went ~** si afflosciò; **let your arm go ~** rilassa completamente il braccio.

lim·pet ['lɪmpɪt] n patella.

lim·pid ['lɪmpɪd] adj (poet) limpido(a).

linch·pin ['lɪntʃpɪn] n acciarino, bietta; (fig) perno.

lin·den ['lɪndən] n = **lime²**.

line¹ [laɪn] **1** n **(a)** (gen) linea; (pen stroke) tratto; (wrinkle) ruga; **to draw a ~ under sth** sottolineare qc; **to draw a ~ through sth** tirare una riga sopra qc; **to draw the ~ at (doing) sth** (fig) rifiutarsi di fare qc; **to know where to draw the ~** (fig) saper rispettare i limiti; **in ~ to the throne** nella linea di successione al trono; **she comes from a long ~ of teachers** i suoi sono insegnanti da generazioni.

(b) (rope) corda, fune f; (fishing ~) lenza; (wire) filo; (Elec, Telec) linea; **the ~ went dead** (Telec) è caduta la linea; **hold the ~ please** (Telec) resti in linea per cortesia; **Mr Smith is on the ~** (Telec) il signor Smith è in linea; **clothes ~** filo or corda del bucato.

(c) (row) fila; (queue) fila, coda; **to stand in ~** mettersi in fila; **to be in ~ for sth** (fig) essere in lista per qc; **to bring sth into ~ with sth** mettere qc al passo con qc; **to fall into ~ with sb/sth** adeguarsi a qn/qc; **to step out of ~** (fig) sgarrare.

(d) (direction, course) linea, direzione f; **~ of vision** visuale f; **~ of inquiry** pista; **in the ~ of fire** (Mil) sulla linea di tiro; **~ of attack** (Mil) piano d'attacco; (fig) piano d'azione; **to follow** or **take the ~ of least resistance** seguire la via più facile; **in the ~ of duty** nell'esercizio delle proprie funzioni; **~ of argument** filo del ragionamento; **~ of research/business** settore m or ramo di ricerca/d'attività; **~ of interest** sfera di interesse; **it's not my ~** (fam: speciality) non sono un esperto in materia; **to take a strong** or **firm ~ on sth** essere deciso per quanto riguarda qc; **to take the ~ that...** essere del parere che...; **to toe** or **follow the party ~** attenersi alla or seguire la linea politica del partito; **in ~ with** in linea con; **along the same ~s** dello stesso tipo or genere; **we are thinking along the same ~s** la pensiamo più o meno allo stesso modo; **on the right ~s** sulla buona strada.

(e) (of print) riga; (of verse) verso; **to learn one's ~s** (Theatre) imparare la propria parte; **to read between the ~s** (fig) leggere fra le righe; **drop me a ~** mandami due righe.

(f) (Rail: route) linea; (shipping company) compagnia di navigazione; **all along the ~** (fig) fin da principio; **to reach** or **come to the end of the ~** (fig: relationship) arrivare a un punto di rottura.

(g) (Comm) linea; **a new ~ in cosmetics** una nuova linea di cosmetici.

2 cpd: **~ drawing** n disegno (a tratteggio).

♦ **line up 1** vt + adv (people, objects) allineare, mettere in fila; **have you got anyone ~d up for the job?** hai già in mente qualcuno per quel posto?; **to have sth ~d up** avere qc in programma. **2** vi + adv (in queue) mettersi in fila; (in row) allinearsi.

line² [laɪn] vt: **to ~ (with)** (clothes) foderare (di); (box) rivestire (di), foderare (di); **the streets were ~d with people/trees** c'erano file di persone/di alberi ai bordi delle strade.

lin·ear ['lɪnɪər] adj lineare.

lined¹ [laɪnd] adj (paper) a righe, rigato(a); (face) rugoso(a).

lined² [laɪnd] adj (clothes) foderato(a).

lin·en ['lɪnɪn] **1** *n* (*cloth*) (tela di) lino; (*sheets, tablecloth etc*) biancheria; **to wash one's dirty ~ in public** (*fig*) lavare i panni sporchi in pubblico. **2** *adj* di lino. **3** *cpd* (*basket, cupboard*) della biancheria.

lin·er ['laɪnə^r] *n* **(a)** (*ship*) nave *f* di linea, transatlantico. **(b):** **dustbin ~** sacchetto per la pattumiera.

lines·man ['laɪnzmən] *n, pl* **-men** (*Sport*) guardalinee *m inv*, segnalinee *m inv*; (*Rail*) guardalinee *m inv*; (*Telec*) guardafili *m inv*.

line-up ['laɪnʌp] *n* (*row*) fila, allineamento; (*Ftbl etc*) formazione *f* della squadra.

lin·ger ['lɪŋgə^r] *vi* (*person: dawdle*) indugiare; (*: wait*) attardarsi; (*: be on the point of death*) trascinarsi; (*smell, memory, tradition*) persistere; **to ~ over a meal** attardarsi a tavola; **to ~ on a subject** dilungarsi su un argomento.

lin·gerie ['lænʒəriː] *n* biancheria intima (femminile).

lin·ger·ing ['lɪŋgərɪŋ] *adj* (*smell, doubt*) persistente; (*look*) insistente; (*death*) lento(a).

lin·go ['lɪŋgəʊ] *n* (*fam pej*) lingua del posto; (*: jargon*) gergo.

lin·guist ['lɪŋgwɪst] *n* linguista *m/f*; **I'm no ~** sono negato per le lingue.

lin·guis·tic [lɪŋ'gwɪstɪk] *adj* linguistico(a).

lin·guis·tics [lɪŋ'gwɪstɪks] *nsg* linguistica.

lin·ing ['laɪnɪŋ] *n* (*of clothes etc*) fodera; (*Tech*) rivestimento (interno); (*of brake*) guarnizione *f*.

link [lɪŋk] **1** *n* (*of chain*) anello; (*fig: connection*) legame *m*, rapporto; **cultural ~s** rapporti culturali; **rail ~** collegamento ferroviario. **2** *vt* (*also fig*) collegare; **to ~ arms with sb** prendere sottobraccio qn.

♦ **link up** *vi + adv* (*people: meet*) ritrovarsi; (*: join*) unirsi; (*spaceships etc*) agganciarsi; (*railway lines, roads*) congiungersi.

links [lɪŋks] *npl* (*Golf ~s*) terreno *or* campo di golf.

link-up ['lɪŋkʌp] *n* legame *m*; (*of roads*) nodo; (*of spaceships*) aggancio; (*Radio, TV*) collegamento.

lino ['laɪnəʊ] *n*, **li·no·leum** [lɪ'nəʊlɪəm] *n* linoleum *m*.

lin·seed ['lɪnsiːd] *n*: **~ oil** olio di semi di lino.

lint [lɪnt] *n* (*Med*) garza.

lin·tel ['lɪntl] *n* architrave *f*.

lion ['laɪən] *n* leone *m*; (*fig: person*) celebrità *f inv*; **to get *or* take the ~'s share** farsi la parte del leone.

li·on·ess ['laɪənɪs] *n* leonessa.

lip [lɪp] **1** *n* (*Anat*) labbro; (*of jug*) beccuccio; (*of glass etc*) orlo; (*fam: insolence*) sfacciataggine *f*. **2** *cpd*: **~ service** *n*: **he pays ~ service to communism but...** si professa comunista ma...; **that was just ~ service on her part** l'ha detto solo pro forma.

lip-read ['lɪp,riːd] *vt, vi* capire dal movimento delle labbra.

lip·stick ['lɪpstɪk] *n* rossetto.

liq·ue·fy ['lɪkwɪfaɪ] **1** *vt* liquefare. **2** *vi* liquefarsi.

li·queur [lɪ'kjʊə^r] *n* liquore *m*.

liq·uid ['lɪkwɪd] **1** *adj* (*gen*) liquido(a); **~ assets** (*Fin*) attività *fpl* liquide, crediti *mpl* liquidi. **2** *n* liquido.

liq·ui·date ['lɪkwɪdeɪt] *vt* liquidare.

liq·ui·da·tion [,lɪkwɪ'deɪʃən] *n* liquidazione *f*; **to go into ~** andare in liquidazione.

li·quid·ity [lɪ'kwɪdɪtɪ] *n* (*Fin*) liquidità.

liq·uid·ize ['lɪkwɪdaɪz] *vt* (*Culin*) passare al frullatore.

liq·uid·iz·er ['lɪkwɪdaɪzə^r] *n* (*Culin*) frullatore *m* (a brocca).

liq·uor ['lɪkə^r] *n* bevande *fpl* alcoliche.

liquo·rice ['lɪkərɪs] *n* liquirizia.

lisp [lɪsp] **1** *n* pronuncia blesa della 's'; **with a ~** con la lisca (*fam*). **2** *vi* avere una pronuncia blesa della 's', parlare con la lisca (*fam*).

lis·som ['lɪsəm] *adj* leggiadro(a).

list[1] [lɪst] **1** *n* lista, elenco; (*Comm*) listino; **shopping ~** lista *or* nota della spesa. **2** *vt* (*include in ~*) fare una lista di; (*: expenses etc*) fare la nota di; (*enumerate*) elencare; **it is not ~ed** non è *or* non figura nell'elenco; **~ed building** (*Archit*) edificio sotto la protezione delle Belle Arti. **3** *cpd*: **~ price** *n* prezzo di listino.

list[2] [lɪst] *vi* (*Naut*) inclinarsi, sbandare.

lis·ten ['lɪsn] *vi* ascoltare; **to ~ to sb/sth** ascoltare qn/qc; **~!** ascolta!, senti!; **he wouldn't ~ to me** non mi ha voluto dar retta *or* ascolto; **he wouldn't ~ to reason** non ha voluto sentire ragione; **~ (out) for the car** senti se arriva la macchina; **~ (out) for your name** aspetta che ti chiamino; **to ~ in on a conversation** origliare qc; **to ~ in to sth on the radio** ascoltare qc per radio.

lis·ten·er ['lɪsnə^r] *n* ascoltatore/trice; **to be a good ~** saper ascoltare.

list·less ['lɪstlɪs] *adj* (*gen*) fiacco(a), svogliato(a); (*uninterested*) apatico(a).

lists [lɪsts] *npl* (*History*) lizza; **to enter the ~ (against sb/sth)** (*fig*) entrare in lizza (contro qn/qc).

lit [lɪt] *pt, pp of* **light**[1].

lita·ny ['lɪtənɪ] *n* litania.

lit·era·cy ['lɪtərəsɪ] **1** *n* il saper leggere e scrivere. **2** *cpd*: **~ campaign** *n* lotta contro l'analfabetismo.

lit·er·al ['lɪtərəl] **1** *adj* (*meaning, translation*) letterale; (*account*) testuale; (*person*) prosaico(a). **2** *n* (*in text*) refuso.

lit·er·al·ly ['lɪtərəlɪ] *adv* (*gen*) letteralmente; (*interpret*) alla lettera; **it was ~ impossible to work** there era letteralmente impossibile lavorarci.

lit·er·ary ['lɪtərərɪ] *adj* letterario(a); **a ~ man** un letterato.

lit·er·ate ['lɪtərɪt] *adj* che sa leggere e scrivere; **highly ~** molto colto, molto istruito.

lit·era·ture ['lɪtərɪtʃə^r] *n* (*writings*) letteratura; (*brochures etc*) opuscoli *mpl*; (*written information*) materiale *m*.

lithe [laɪð] *adj* agile.

li·thog·ra·phy [lɪ'θɒgrəfɪ] *n* litografia.

liti·ga·tion [,lɪtɪ'geɪʃən] *n* causa (giudiziaria).

lit·mus ['lɪtməs] *n*: **~ paper** cartina di tornasole.

li·tre, (*Am*) **li·ter** ['liːtə^r] *n* litro.

lit·ter ['lɪtə^r] **1** *n* **(a)** (*rubbish*) rifiuti *mpl*; (*papers*) cartacce *fpl*. **(b)** (*Zool*) nidiata; (*: of dogs*) cucciolata. **2** *vt* (*subj: person*) lasciare rifiuti in; (*subj: books, rubbish*) coprire; **the room was ~ed with books** nella stanza c'erano libri dappertutto; **a pavement ~ed with papers** un marciapiede pieno di cartacce. **3** *cpd*: **~ basket** *n*, **~ bin** *n* cestino dei rifiuti; **~ lout** *n* persona che butta per *terra le cartacce o i rifiuti*.

litter·bug ['lɪtə,bʌg] *n* (*Am*) = litter lout.

lit·tle[1] ['lɪtl] *adj* (*small: gen*) piccolo(a); **a ~ chair** una seggiolina; **a ~ cup** una tazzina; **my ~ brother** il mio fratellino; **a ~ girl** una bambina; **~ finger** mignolo; **poor ~ thing!** poverino! **(b)** (*short*) breve; **we went for a ~ ride/walk** siamo andati a fare un giretto/una passeggiatina; **it's only a ~ way to the station** la stazione non è lontana; **a ~ holiday** una breve vacanza.

lit·tle[2] ['lɪtl] *comp* **less**, *superl* **least 1** *adj, pron* (*not much*) un poco (di), un po' (di); **a ~ wine** un po' di vino; **~ money** pochi soldi; **with ~ difficulty** senza fatica *or* difficoltà; **to see/do ~** non vedere/fare molto, vedere/fare molto poco; **we did**

what ~ we could abbiamo fatto quel poco che abbiamo potuto; ~ or nothing poco o nulla; that has ~ to do with it! questo c'entra ben poco!; as ~ as £5 soltanto 5 sterline; to make ~ of sth (fail to understand) capire poco di qc; (belittle) tenere qc in poco conto; ~ by ~ poco a poco; for a ~ while per un po'.

2 adv (a): a ~ un po'; a ~ big un po' grande; a ~ longer un po' più a lungo; we were a ~ surprised eravamo un po' sorpresi; a ~ more milk un po' più di latte; a ~ more ancora un po'. (b) (not much): a ~-known fact un fatto poco noto; it's ~ better non è certo meglio; as ~ as possible il meno possibile; ~ more than a month ago appena più di un mese fa; I like it as ~ as you do non mi piace più di quanto piace a te; ~ does he know that... non si rende ben conto che... .

lit·ur·gy ['lɪtədʒɪ] n liturgia.

live[1] [lɪv] 1 vi (a) (exist, survive) vivere; to ~ to be 100 vivere fino all'età di 100 anni; he hasn't long to ~ non gli resta molto da vivere; as long as I ~ finché vivo or campo; to ~ through an experience sopravvivere a un'esperienza; he ~d through 2 wars ha visto 2 guerre; to ~ like a lord vivere da signori or da re; she ~s for her family vive solo per i propri figli; I'm living for the day when... vivo solo nell'attesa del giorno in cui...; the doctors have given her 3 months to ~ i medici le hanno dato 3 mesi di vita; you'll ~! (iro) vedrai che non morirai!; to ~ with a memory essere perseguitato da un ricordo; I can't ~ with that pink door any more non sopporto più quella porta rosa; I'll learn to ~ with it mi ci abituerò; he's not easy to ~ with non è facile vivere con lui; you ~ and learn c'è sempre qualcosa da imparare; ~ and let ~ vivi e lascia vivere; to ~ by .../by doing... guadagnarsi da vivere con .../facendo...; long ~ the King! viva il re!

(b) (reside) abitare, vivere; to ~ in London abitare a Londra; to ~ with sb vivere con qn; to ~ together vivere insieme, convivere.

2 vt: to ~ a happy life/a life of hardship avere una vita felice/dura; to ~ life to the full godersi la vita; to ~ a life of luxury vivere nel lusso; to ~ the part (Theatre, fig) immedesimarsi nella parte.

♦ **live down** vt + adv (disgrace) far dimenticare (alla gente).

♦ **live in** vi + adv (students, nurses) essere interno(a); (servants) avere vitto e alloggio.

♦ **live off** vi + prep (land, fish etc) vivere di; (pej: parents etc) vivere alle spalle or a spese di.

♦ **live on 1** vi + prep (fruit, salary etc) vivere di; to ~ on £50 a week vivere con 50 sterline la settimana; enough to ~ on abbastanza da vivere. 2 vi + adv continuare a vivere.

♦ **live out 1** vi + adv (students) essere esterno(a); (housekeeper) essere a mezzo servizio. 2 vt + adv: to ~ out one's days or life trascorrere gli ultimi anni.

♦ **live up** vt + adv: to ~ it up (fam) fare la bella vita.

♦ **live up to** vi + prep (principles) tenere fede a; (reputation) essere all'altezza di; the film didn't ~ up to our expectations il film ci ha deluso.

live[2] [laɪv] adj (a) (animal) vivo(a); (issue) scottante, d'attualità; (Radio, TV: broadcast) in diretta; a real ~ crocodile un coccodrillo in carne e ossa. (b) (shell, ammunition: not blank) carico(a); (: unexploded) inesploso(a); (Elec: rail) sotto tensione; (: wire) ad alta tensione; (still burning: coal) ardente; he's a ~ wire (fig fam) è una persona piena di vitalità.

live·li·hood ['laɪvlɪhʊd] n mezzi mpl di sostentamento; to earn one's ~ guadagnarsi da vivere.

live·li·ness ['laɪvlɪnɪs] n vivacità, brio.

live·ly ['laɪvlɪ] adj (-ier, -iest) (gen) vivace; (imagination) fervido(a); (conversation, argument) animato(a); (interest) vivo(a); (party, scene etc) movimentato(a); (pace) sostenuto(a); things are getting ~ l'ambiente or l'atmosfera comincia a scaldarsi.

liv·en up [,laɪvən'ʌp] 1 vt + adv (room etc) ravvivare; (discussion, evening) animare. 2 vi + adv animarsi.

liv·er ['lɪvə'] 1 n (Anat, Culin) fegato. 2 cpd di fegato.

liv·er·ish ['lɪvərɪʃ] adj: to be ~, feel ~ sentirsi il fegato ingrossato.

liv·ery ['lɪvərɪ] 1 n livrea. 2 cpd: ~ stable n scuderia (di cavalli da nolo).

lives [laɪvz] npl of life.

live·stock ['laɪvstɒk] n bestiame m.

liv·id ['lɪvɪd] adj (a) (angry) furioso(a), furibondo(a). (b) (in colour: complexion etc) livido(a); (: sky) plumbeo(a); (: bruise) bluastro(a).

liv·ing ['lɪvɪŋ] 1 adj (alive: gen) vivo(a); (: person) vivente, in vita; within ~ memory a memoria d'uomo; the greatest ~ pianist il più grande pianista vivente. 2 n vita; cost of ~ costo della vita, carovita m; standard of ~ tenore m di vita; what do you do for a ~? come ti guadagni da vivere?; to earn or make a ~ guadagnarsi da vivere; the ~ (people) i vivi. 3 cpd: ~ conditions npl condizioni fpl di vita; ~ expenses npl spese fpl di mantenimento; ~ room n soggiorno; ~ standards npl tenore m or livello di vita; a ~ wage uno stipendio che permette di vivere decentemente.

liz·ard ['lɪzəd] n lucertola.

lo [ləʊ] excl: ~ and behold... quand'ecco che... .

load [ləʊd] 1 n (a) (gen) carico; (: weight) peso; (Elec) carica. (b) (fig): that's (taken) a ~ off my mind questo mi ha tolto un peso; ~s of, a ~ of (fam) un sacco or un mucchio di; it's a ~ of old rubbish (fam) sono un mucchio di sciocchezze. 2 vt (also: ~ up): to ~ (with) caricare (di); (gun, camera): to ~ (with) caricare (con); he's ~ed (down) with debts/worries è carico di debiti/preoccupazioni.

load·ed ['ləʊdɪd] adj (a): a ~ question una domanda a doppio taglio. (b) (dice) truccato(a); the dice are ~ against him (fig) ha tutto contro di lui. (c): to be ~ (fam: rich) essere pieno(a) di soldi.

load·ing bay ['ləʊdɪŋ,beɪ] n piazzola di carico.

loaf[1] [ləʊf] n, pl loaves pagnotta, pane m.

loaf[2] [ləʊf] vi (also: ~ about, ~ around) oziare.

loam [ləʊm] n terriccio (fertile).

loan [ləʊn] 1 n prestito; to give sb the ~ of sth prestare or dare in prestito qc a qn; to ask for the ~ of chiedere in prestito qc; on ~ (book, painting) in prestito; (employee) distaccato; to raise a ~ (money) ottenere un prestito or un mutuo. 2 vt prestare, dare in prestito.

loath [ləʊθ] adj: to be ~ to do sth essere riluttante or restio(a) a fare qc.

loathe [ləʊð] vt (thing, person) detestare; I ~ doing it detesto farlo; to ~ sb's doing sth detestare che qn faccia qc.

loath·ing ['ləʊðɪŋ] n ribrezzo, disgusto; it fills me with ~ mi riempie di disgusto, mi fa ribrezzo.

loath·some ['ləʊðsəm] adj (gen) ripugnante; (person) detestabile, odioso(a).

loaves [ləʊvz] npl of loaf.

lob [lɒb] vt (ball) lanciare; to ~ sth over to sb lanciare qc a qn.

lob·by ['lɒbɪ] **1** n **(a)** atrio, ingresso. **(b)** (Parliament: pressure group) gruppo di pressione. **2** vt (Pol) far pressione su. **3** vi fare pressioni; **to ~ for a reform** fare pressioni per ottenere una riforma.

lobe [ləʊb] n lobo.

lob·ster ['lɒbstə'] **1** n aragosta. **2** cpd: **~ pot** n nassa per aragoste.

lo·cal ['ləʊkəl] **1** adj (gen) locale; (resident, shop) del posto; (Telec: call) urbano(a); **~ doctor** dottore m della zona; **~ education/health authority** ≃ direzione f regionale della pubblica istruzione/della sanità; **~ government** amministrazione f locale; **~ anaesthetic** (Med) anestesia locale. **2** n (fam) **(a)**: **he's a ~** è uno del posto; **the ~s** la gente del posto. **(b)** (Brit: pub) ≃ bar m all'angolo.

lo·cal·ity [ləʊ'kælɪtɪ] n (place) località f inv; (neighbourhood) vicinanze fpl.

lo·cal·ize ['ləʊkəlaɪz] vt localizzare.

lo·cal·ly ['ləʊkəlɪ] adv (nearby) nei paraggi, nelle vicinanze; (in the locality) sul posto, in loco; **showers ~** tempo localmente piovoso, locali rovesci.

lo·cate [ləʊ'keɪt] vt (place) situare, collocare; (find) trovare; (cause) individuare, trovare.

lo·ca·tion [ləʊ'keɪʃən] n **(a)** (place) posto; (placing) posizione f, ubicazione f. **(b)** (Cine): **to be on ~ in Mexico** girare gli esterni in Messico; **film shot on ~** film girato in esterni.

loch [lɒx] n (Scot) lago.

lock¹ [lɒk] n (of hair) ciocca; **~s** (poet) chioma.

lock² [lɒk] **1** n **(a)** (on door, box etc) serratura; (Aut): **steering ~** bloccasterzo; **under ~ and key** sotto chiave; **~ stock and barrel** (fig) in blocco; **he moved out, ~ stock and barrel** se n'è andato con armi e bagagli. **(b)** (of canal) chiusa. **(c)** (Aut: turning) sterzo; **on full ~** a tutto sterzo. **2** vt (door etc) chiudere a chiave; (Tech) bloccare; **she ~ed the steering mechanism** ha messo il bloccasterzo; **to ~ sb/sth in a place** chiudere qn/qc in un posto; **they were ~ed in each other's arms** erano abbracciati stretti; **to be ~ed in combat** lottare corpo a corpo. **3** vi (door etc) chiudersi; (wheel etc) bloccarsi.

♦ **lock away** vt + adv (valuables) tenere (rinchiuso(a)) al sicuro; (criminal) mettere dentro; (mental patient) rinchiudere.

♦ **lock in** vt + adv chiudere dentro (a chiave).

♦ **lock out** vt + adv chiudere fuori; (Industry): **to ~ workers out** fare una serrata.

♦ **lock up 1** vt + adv (object) mettere al sicuro, chiudere (a chiave); (criminal) mettere dentro; (mental patient) rinchiudere; (funds) vincolare, immobilizzare; **she checked that the house was properly ~ed up** ha controllato che tutto fosse ben chiuso. **2** vi + adv chiudere tutto (a chiave).

lock·er ['lɒkə'] n armadietto.

lock·et ['lɒkɪt] n medaglione m (portaritratti).

lock·jaw ['lɒkdʒɔː] n tetano.

lock·out ['lɒkaʊt] n (Industry) serrata.

lock·smith ['lɒksmɪθ] n magnano.

lock·up ['lɒkʌp] n (prison) prigione f; (cell) guardina; (~ garage) box m inv.

lo·co·mo·tion [ˌləʊkə'məʊʃən] n locomozione f.

lo·co·mo·tive [ˌləʊkə'məʊtɪv] n (Rail) locomotiva.

lo·cust ['ləʊkəst] n locusta, cavalletta.

lodge [lɒdʒ] **1** n (house) casetta del guardiano; (porter's ~) portineria, guardiola; (Freemasonry) loggia. **2** vt (person: give lodging) dare alloggio a; (: find lodging) trovare alloggio per; (money) depositare; (complaint) sporgere, presentare; (statement) rilasciare; **to ~ an appeal** ricorrere in corte d'appello. **3** vi **(a)** (person): **to ~** (with)

(friends) alloggiare (con); (landlady) essere a pensione (presso). **(b)** (bullet) conficcarsi.

lodg·er ['lɒdʒə'] n (with meals) pensionante m/f; (room only) persona che ha una camera in affitto; **she takes in ~s** fa l'affittacamere.

lodg·ing ['lɒdʒɪŋ] **1** n (accommodation) alloggio; **~s** (room) camera ammobiliata; (small flat) appartamentino; **to look for ~s** cercarsi una camera ammobiliata (or un appartamentino). **2** cpd: **~ house** n casa con camere in affitto.

loft [lɒft] n solaio, soffitta; **hay~** fienile m.

lofty ['lɒftɪ] adj (-ier, -iest) (sentiments, aims) nobile; (haughty: manner) di superiorità, altezzoso(a); (poet: mountain) alto(a).

log [lɒg] **1** n **(a)** (tree trunk) tronco; (for fire) ceppo. **(b)** = logbook. **2** vt **(a)** (Naut, Aer) annotare or registrare sul giornale di bordo. **(b)** (Aut: also: **~ up:** speed, distance) fare; **to ~ 50 mph** ≃ fare 80 km/h. **3** cpd: **~ cabin** n capanna di tronchi; **~ fire** n fuoco di legna.

loga·rithm ['lɒgərɪθəm] n logaritmo.

log·book ['lɒgbʊk] n (Naut, Aer) giornale m di bordo; (Aut: of lorry driver etc) diario di bordo; (: of car) libretto di circolazione.

log·ger·heads ['lɒgəhedz] npl: **at ~** (with sb) in violento contrasto (con qn).

log·ic ['lɒdʒɪk] n logica.

logi·cal ['lɒdʒɪkəl] adj logico(a).

logi·cal·ly ['lɒdʒɪkəlɪ] adv logicamente; **~, we should...** a rigor di logica, dovremmo....

lo·gis·tics [lə'dʒɪstɪks] nsg logistica.

loin [lɔɪn] **1** n (of meat) lombata; **~s** (frm) fianchi mpl. **2** cpd: **~ chop** n (Culin) lombatina, bistecca di lombo; **~ cloth** n perizoma m.

loi·ter ['lɔɪtə'] vi (idle) bighellonare; (lag behind) fermarsi (ad ogni momento); **to ~** (with intent) (Law) aggirarsi (con intenzioni sospette).

loll [lɒl] vi (head, tongue) ciondolare; **to ~ about** or **around** starsene pigramente sdraiato; **to ~ against sth, ~ back on sth** appoggiarsi pigramente a qc.

lol·li·pop ['lɒlɪpɒp] n lecca lecca m inv.

lol·ly ['lɒlɪ] n **(a)** = lollipop. **(b)** (fam: money) grana, quattrini mpl.

Lon·don ['lʌndən] n Londra.

Lon·don·er ['lʌndənə'] n londinese m/f.

lone [ləʊn] adj (person) solitario(a), solo(a); (house) isolato(a); **~ wolf** (fig) tipo solitario.

lone·li·ness ['ləʊnlɪnɪs] n solitudine f.

lone·ly ['ləʊnlɪ] adj (-ier, -iest) (gen) solitario(a); (place etc: isolated) isolato(a); (: deserted) deserto(a); **to feel ~** sentirsi solo(a); **~ hearts' club** club m inv dei cuori solitari.

lon·er ['ləʊnə'] n tipo(a) solitario(a).

lone·some ['ləʊnsəm] adj solo(a).

long¹ [lɒŋ] **1** adj (-er, -est) **(a)** (in size) lungo(a); **how ~ is it?** quant'è lungo?; **it is 6 metres ~** è lungo 6 metri; **to get ~er** allungarsi; **to pull a ~ face** fare il muso lungo; **it's a ~ shot** (fam) le probabilità sono minime; **~ jump** (Sport) salto in lungo. **(b)** (in time) lungo(a); **(for) a ~ time** (per) molto tempo; **how ~ is the film?** quanto è lunga or dura il film?; **2 hours ~** che dura 2 ore; **a ~ walk/holiday** una lunga camminata/vacanza; **a ~ job** un lavoro lungo; **to have a ~ memory** avere buona memoria; **a ~ drink** un long drink; **it's been a ~ day** (fig) è stata una giornata lunga; **to take a ~ look at sth** esaminare ben bene qc; **at ~ last** finalmente.

2 adv a lungo, per molto tempo; **I shan't be ~** non ne avrò per molto; **he won't be ~ in finishing** non ci metterà molto a finire; **we didn't stay (for) ~** non ci siamo fermati a lungo; **I have ~**

believed that... è da molto tempo che credo che...; ~ **before** molto tempo prima; ~ **before now** molto prima; ~ **before you came** molto prima che tu arrivassi; **before** ~ (+ *future*) presto, fra poco; (+ *past*) poco tempo dopo; **he's** ~ **since departed** se n'è andato molto tempo fa; **how** ~ **is it since you saw them?** da quant'è che non li vedi?; ~ **ago** molto tempo fa; **how** ~ **ago?** quanto tempo fa?; ~ **ago as 1960** nientemeno che nel 1960; **he no** ~**er comes** non viene più; **all day** ~ tutto il giorno; **so** ~ **as, as** ~ **as** (*while*) finché; (*provided that*) sempre che + *sub*; **so** ~! (*fam, esp Am*) ciao!; **don't be** ~! fai presto!; **it won't take** ~ è questione di poco.

3 *n*: **the** ~ **and the short of it is that...** (*fig*) a farla breve... .

long² [lɒŋ] *vi*: **to** ~ **for sth/sb** desiderare molto qc/qn; **to** ~ **to do sth** morire dalla voglia di fare qc; **to** ~ **for sb to do sth** desiderare tanto che qn faccia qc.

long-awaited [ˌlɒŋəˈweɪtɪd] *adj* tanto atteso(a), sospirato(a).

long-distance [ˌlɒŋˈdɪstəns] *adj* (*Telec: call*) interurbano(a); (*race*) di fondo; ~ **runner** fondista *m/f*.

long-drawn-out [ˌlɒŋdrɔːnˈaʊt] *adj* che va per le lunghe, interminabile.

long-haired [lɒŋˈhɛəd] *adj* (*person*) dai capelli lunghi; (*animal*) dal pelo lungo.

long·hand [ˈlɒŋhænd] *n* scrittura (normale).

long·ing [ˈlɒŋɪŋ] **1** *n* desiderio; (*for food*) voglia; (*nostalgia*) nostalgia. **2** *adj* (*look*) pieno(a) di desiderio.

long·ing·ly [ˈlɒŋɪŋlɪ] *adv* con desiderio (*or* nostalgia).

lon·gi·tude [ˈlɒŋgɪtjuːd] *n* longitudine *f*.

long-legged [ˈlɒŋˌlɛgd] *adj* (*person*) dalle gambe lunghe; (*animal*) con le zampe lunghe.

long-lost [ˈlɒŋˌlɒst] *adj* perduto(a) da tempo.

long-playing [ˈlɒŋˌpleɪɪŋ] *adj*: ~ **record** (*abbr* **L.P.**) (disco) 33 giri *m inv*.

long-range [ˌlɒŋˈreɪndʒ] *adj* (*gun, missile*) a lunga portata; (*aircraft*) a lungo raggio d'azione; (*weather forecast*) a lungo termine.

long-sighted [ˌlɒŋˈsaɪtɪd] *adj* presbite; (*fig*) lungimirante.

long-sleeved [ˈlɒŋsliːvd] *adj* a maniche lunghe.

long-standing [ˈlɒŋˌstændɪŋ] *adj* di vecchia data.

long-suffer·ing [ˌlɒŋˈsʌfərɪŋ] *adj* molto paziente.

long-term [ˈlɒŋtɜːm] *adj* (*plans, effects*) a lungo termine; **to take a** ~ **view of sth** proiettare qc nel futuro.

long-winded [ˌlɒŋˈwɪndɪd] *adj* prolisso(a).

loo [luː] *n* (*fam: toilet*) gabinetto.

look [lʊk] **1** *n* (**a**) (*glance*) occhiata; (*expression*) sguardo, aria; **she gave me a dirty** ~ mi ha dato un'occhiataccia; **with a** ~ **of despair** con un'aria *or* un'espressione disperata; **to have a** ~ **at sth** dare un'occhiata a qc; **let me have a** ~ fammi vedere; **to take a good** ~ **at sb/sth** guardare (per) bene qn/qc; **to have a** ~ **for sth** cercare qc; **shall we have a** ~ **round the town?** andiamo a visitare la città?

(**b**) (*air, appearance*) aspetto, aria; **he has a** ~ **of his mother about him** ha qualcosa di sua madre; **good** ~**s** bellezza; **she has kept her (good)** ~**s** è rimasta bella; **there's a mischievous** ~ **about that child** quel bambino ha un'aria birichina; **by the** ~ **of things it's going to rain** ha tutta l'aria di (voler) piovere; **by the** ~ **of him** a vederlo; **I don't like the** ~ **of him** non mi piace per niente; **you can't go by** ~**s** non si può giudi-

care dalle apparenze; **leather** ~ (*Fashion*) moda del cuoio.

2 *vi* (**a**) (*see, glance*) guardare; **to** ~ **at** (*person, object*) guardare; (*problem, situation*) considerare; **it isn't much to** ~ **at** non è niente di speciale; **could you** ~ at **the engine for me?** puoi dare un'occhiata al motore?; **I wouldn't even** ~ **at the job** non penserei nemmeno di chiedere per quel lavoro; **to** ~ **for sb/sth** cercare qn/qc; **I'm just** ~**ing** (*in shop*) sto solo dando un'occhiata; **to** ~ **into** (*matter, possibility*) esaminare; **I'll** ~ **and see** vado a vedere; ~ **who's here!** (ma) guarda chi si vede!; **to** ~ **the other way** guardare dall'altra parte; (*fig*) far finta di non vedere; **to** ~ **ahead** guardare avanti; (*fig*) cominciare a pensare al futuro; **my room** ~**s onto the garden** la mia camera si affaccia sul *or* dà sul giardino; ~ **before you leap** (*fig*) non buttarti alla cieca.

(**b**) (*seem, appear*) sembrare, aver l'aria; **he** ~**s (as if he's) happy** sembra *or* ha l'aria felice; **she** ~**ed prettier than ever** era più graziosa che mai; **he** ~**s about 60 (years old)** dimostra una sessantina d'anni; **it** ~**s about 4 metres long** sarà lungo un 4 metri; **you don't** ~ **yourself** non mi sembri in forma; **you** ~ *or* **you're** ~**ing well** ti trovo bene; **it** ~**s good on you** ti sta bene, ti dona; **it makes you** ~ **younger** ti ringiovanisce, ti fa sembrare più giovane; **it** ~**s all right to me** a me pare che vada bene.

(**c**): **he** ~**s like his brother** assomiglia a suo fratello; **this photo doesn't** ~ **like him** in questa foto non sembra lui; **it** ~**s like cheese to me** mi sembra formaggio; **it certainly** ~**s like it** ne ha tutta l'aria; **the party** ~**s like being fun** la festa promette bene; **it** ~**s like rain** mi sa che sta per piovere; **it** ~**s as if** *or* **as though the train will be late** mi sa tanto che il treno sarà in ritardo.

3 *vt* guardare; **to** ~ **sb (straight) in the eye** *or* (**full**) **in the face** guardare qn (dritto) negli occhi *or* in faccia; **to** ~ **sb up and down** squadrare qn da capo a piedi; ~ **where you're going!** guarda dove vai!; **to** ~ **one's best** essere in piena forma; **to** ~ **one's age** dimostrare la propria età.

♦ **look after** *vi* + *prep* (*gen*) occuparsi di; (*possessions*) prendersi cura di; **to** ~ **after sth for sb** dare un'occhiata a qc per qn; **he doesn't** ~ **after himself** si trascura; **she's old enough to** ~ **after herself** è abbastanza grande per badare a se stessa.

♦ **look around** *vi* + *adv* guardarsi intorno; **to** ~ **around for sb/sth** cercare qn/qc.

♦ **look away** *vi* + *adv* distogliere lo sguardo.

♦ **look back** *vi* + *adv* girarsi indietro, voltarsi indietro; (*remember*) ripensare al passato; **to** ~ **back at sth/sb** voltarsi a guardare qc/qn; **he's never** ~**ed back** (*fig*) non ha fatto che migliorare; **to** ~ **back on** (*event, period*) ripensare a.

♦ **look down** *vi* + *adv* abbassare gli occhi *or* lo sguardo; (*from height*) guardare giù; **to** ~ **down at sb/sth** guardare giù verso qn/qc; **to** ~ **down on sb/sth** guardare giù verso qn/qc; (*fig*) guardare qn/qc dall'alto al basso.

♦ **look forward to** *vi* + *prep*: **to** ~ **forward to doing sth** non vedere l'ora di fare qc; **I'm** ~**ing forward to his visit/the film** non vedo l'ora che venga/di vedere il film; **I'm not** ~**ing forward to it** non ne ho nessuna voglia; ~**ing forward to hearing from you** (*in letter*) aspettando tue notizie.

♦ **look in** *vi* + *adv* guardar dentro; **to** ~ **in on sb** (*visit*) fare un salto da qn.

♦ **look on 1** *vi* + *adv* rimanere a guardare. **2** *vi* + *prep* considerare.

♦ **look out 1** *vi* + *adv* **(a)** *(watch)* guardar fuori; **to ~ out for sb/sth** *(seek)* cercare qn/qc; *(watch for)* guardare se arriva qn/qc. **(b)** *(take care)*: **to ~ out (for)** stare attento(a) (a); **~ out!** attento! **2** *vt* + *adv* *(find)* tirar fuori.

♦ **look over** *vt* + *adv* *(essay)* dare un'occhiata a, riguardare; *(town, building)* vedere; *(person)* esaminare.

♦ **look round 1** *vi* + *adv* *(turn)* girarsi, voltarsi; *(in shop)* dare un'occhiata; **to ~ round for sth** guardarsi intorno cercando qc. **2** *vi* + *prep* *(museum, factory)* visitare; *(shops)* dare un'occhiata a.

♦ **look through** *vi* + *prep* **(a)** *(papers, book)* esaminare; *(: briefly)* scorrere; *(: revise)* rivedere. **(b)** *(telescope)* guardare attraverso.

♦ **look to** *vi* + *prep* *(turn to)* rivolgersi a; *(look after)* badare a.

♦ **look up 1** *vi* + *adv* **(a)** *(glance)* alzare gli occhi; **to ~ up to sb** *(fig: respect)* avere rispetto per qn. **(b)** *(improve: prospects)* migliorare; *(: business)* riprendersi; *(: sales)* aumentare; *(: shares)* essere in rialzo; *(: weather)* mettersi al bello; **things are ~ing up** le cose stanno migliorando. **2** *vt* + *adv* **(a)** *(information)* cercare. **(b)** *(visit: person)* andare a trovare. **3** *vi* + *prep* *(dictionary etc)* consultare, cercare su.

looker-on [ˌlʊkər'ɒn] *n*, *pl* **lookers-on** astante *m/f*.

look-in ['lʊkɪn] *n (fam)*: **not to get a ~** non avere la minima possibilità di (partecipare, vincere *etc*).

look·ing-glass ['lʊkɪŋglɑːs] *n* specchio.

look-out ['lʊkaʊt] **1** *n* **(a)**: **to keep a ~** fare la guardia; **keep a ~ for a post box** guarda se vedi una buca per le lettere; **to be on the ~ for sth** cercare qc. **(b)** *(viewpoint)* posto di vedetta; *(person: thief)* palo; *(: Mil)* sentinella; *(: Naut)* vedetta. **(c)** *(prospect)* prospettiva; **it's a grim** *or* **poor ~** è una prospettiva poco allegra; **that's his ~!** questo è affar suo! **2** *cpd*: **~ post** *n* posto di vedetta.

loom[1] [luːm] *n (weaving ~)* telaio.

loom[2] [luːm] *vi (also: ~ up: building, mountain)* apparire indistintamente; **the ship ~ed (up) out of the mist** nella nebbia apparve la nave; **to ~ large** *(fig)* essere imminente.

loony ['luːnɪ] *adj*, *n (fam)* pazzo(a) *(m/f)*.

loop [luːp] **1** *n (in string etc)* cappio; *(fastening)* asola; *(for belt)* passante *m*; *(bend: in river)* ansa. **2** *vt*: **to ~ a rope round a post** passare una corda intorno a un palo; **to ~ the loop** *(Aer)* fare il giro della morte.

loop·hole ['luːphəʊl] *n (fig)* scappatoia, via d'uscita.

loose [luːs] **1** *adj* **(a)** *(not firm, attached: plaster, button)* che si stacca; *(: knot, shoelace, screw)* allentato(a); *(: hair)* sciolto(a); *(: tooth)* che dondola; *(: page)* staccato(a); *(: sheet of paper)* volante; **to come** *or* **work ~** allentarsi; **to turn** *or* **let ~** *(animal)* lasciare in libertà; **to get ~** *(animal)* scappare; **to tie up ~ ends** *(fig)* avere ancora qualcosa da sistemare; **to be at a ~ end** *(fig)* non saper cosa fare; **~ chippings** *(Aut)* ghiaino; **~ connection** *(Elec)* filo che fa contatto; **~ covers** *(on settee, chair)* fodere *fpl*. **(b)** *(not tight: clothing)* ampio(a); **~ weave** tessuto a trama larga. **(c)** *(not packed: fruit, cheese)* non confezionato(a); **~ change** spiccioli *mpl*, moneta. **(d)** *(fig: translation)* libero(a); *(: style)* prolisso(a); *(: discipline)* rilassato(a); *(: associations, links, thinking)* vago(a); *(: life, morals)* dissoluto(a).

2 *n (fam)*: **to be on the ~** *(criminal, animal etc)* essere in libertà.

3 *vt (free)* liberare; *(untie)* sciogliere; *(slacken)* allentare; *(also: ~ off: arrow)* scoccare; **to ~ one's gun (off)** at sparare a *or* contro; **to ~ the**

dogs on *or* **at sb** sguinzagliare i cani contro qn.

loose-fitting ['luːs,fɪtɪŋ] *adj* ampio(a).

loose-leaf ['luːsliːf] *adj*: **~ binder** *or* **folder** raccoglitore *m*.

loose-limbed ['luːslɪmd] *adj* snodato(a), agile.

loose·ly ['luːslɪ] *adv (hold, tie)* senza stringere; *(associate)* vagamente; *(translate)* liberamente; *(use word)* in modo improprio.

loos·en ['luːsn] **1** *vt (slacken: screw, belt, knot)* allentare; *(: rope, grip)* mollare; *(: clothing)* slacciare; *(untie)* disfare; *(fig: tongue)* sciogliere. **2** *vi (all senses)* allentarsi.

♦ **loosen up** *vi* + *adv (before game)* sciogliere i muscoli, scaldarsi; *(fam: relax)* rilassarsi.

loot [luːt] **1** *n* bottino. **2** *vt* saccheggiare, depredare. **3** *vi*: **to go ~ing** darsi al saccheggio.

loot·er ['luːtəʳ] *n* saccheggiatore/trice.

lop [lɒp] *vt (also: ~ off: also fig)* tagliar (via).

lope [ləʊp] *vi*: **to ~ along/off** *etc* procedere/partire *etc* a grandi balzi.

lop-sided ['lɒp'saɪdɪd] *adj (building)* sbilenco(a); *(fig: view)* distorto(a).

lo·qua·cious [lə'kweɪʃəs] *adj (frm)* loquace.

lord [lɔːd] **1** *n* signore *m*; **~ of the manor** signore del castello; **~ and master** signore e maestro; **L~ Smith** Lord Smith; **the (House of) L~s** Camera dei Lord; **Our L~** *(Rel)* Nostro Signore; **the L~'s prayer** il padrenostro; **my L~** *(to bishop, noble)* Eccellenza; *(to judge)* signor giudice; **good L~!** Dio mio! **2** *vt*: **to ~ it over sb** *(fam)* darsi arie da gran signore con qn.

lord·ship ['lɔːdʃɪp] *n*: **his ~ the Count** *etc* Sua Eccellenza il conte *etc*; **Your L~** Sua Eccellenza.

lore [lɔːʳ] *n* tradizioni *fpl*; **plant/weather ~** cognizioni *fpl* sulle piante/sul tempo.

lor·ry ['lɒrɪ] **1** *n* camion *m inv*. **2** *cpd*: **~ driver** *n* camionista *m/f*; **~ load** *n* carico.

lose [luːz] *pt, pp* **lost 1** *vt* **(a)** *(gen)* perdere; **to get lost** *(object)* andare perso *or* perduto; *(person)* perdersi, smarrirsi; **get lost!** *(fam)* vattene!, sparisci!; **to ~ one's life** perdere la vita; **many lives were lost** molti sono morti; **there were no lives lost** non ci sono stati morti; **lost at sea** perito in mare; **he's lost his licence** *(Aut)* gli è stata ritirata la patente; **you've got nothing to ~** non hai niente da perdere; **to ~ one's way** perdere la strada; **to ~ interest/one's appetite** perdere interesse/l'appetito; **to ~ weight** dimagrire; **to ~ patience** spazientirsi; **to ~ no time (in doing sth)** non perdere tempo (a fare qc); **there's no time to ~** non c'è tempo da perdere; **he managed to ~ his pursuers** è riuscito a seminare i suoi inseguitori.

(b): **that mistake lost us the game** quell'errore ci ha fatto perdere il gioco.

(c): **this watch ~s 5 minutes every day** quest'orologio resta indietro di 5 minuti al giorno.

2 *vi* perdere; **they lost (by) 3 goals to 2** hanno perso (per) 3 a 2; **to ~ to sb** perdere contro qn; **to ~ (out) on sth** *(deal)* rimetterci in qc; *(trip)* perdersi qc; **the clock is losing** l'orologio resta indietro.

los·er ['luːzəʳ] *n* perdente *m/f*; **he's a born ~** è un perdente nato; **to be a bad ~** non saper perdere.

los·ing ['luːzɪŋ] *adj* perdente; **to fight a ~ battle** *(fig)* combattere una battaglia perduta.

loss [lɒs] **1** *n* **(a)** *(gen)* perdita; **heavy ~es** *(Mil)* gravi perdite; **without ~ of life** senza perdita di vite umane; **to cut one's ~es** rimetterci il meno possibile; **it's your ~!** quello che ci rimette sei tu!; **he's a dead ~** *(fam)* è un disastro; **he's no great ~** *(fam)* nessuno lo rimpiange di certo; **to sell sth at a ~** vendere qc in perdita. **(b)**: **to be at a ~ to**

explain sth non saper come fare a spiegare qc; **to be at a ~ for words** essere senza parole. **2** cpd: ~ **leader** n (Comm) articolo a prezzo ridottissimo per attirare la clientela.

lost [lɒst] **1** pt, pp of **lose**. **2** adj (gen, fig) perso(a); (bewildered) smarrito(a); **the ~ sheep** la pecorella smarrita; **some ~ children** dei bambini che si erano smarriti; **~ in thought** immerso or perso nei propri pensieri; **to feel a bit ~** sentirsi smarrito; **the remark/joke was ~ on him** non ha capito l'osservazione/la barzelletta; **my advice was ~ on her** non ha ascoltato il mio consiglio; **I feel ~ without my car/him** mi sento perso senza la mia macchina/di lui; **to make up for ~ time** recuperare il tempo perduto; **to give sth up for ~** dare qc per perso; **~ cause** causa persa; **~ property,** (Am) **~ and found property** oggetti mpl smarriti; **~ property office** or **department,** (Am) **~ and found** ufficio oggetti smarriti.

lot [lɒt] n **(a)** (destiny) sorte f, destino; **the common ~** il destino comune; **it fell to my ~ to do it** è toccato a me farlo; **to throw in one's ~ with sb** unirsi a qn.

(b) (random selection) sorte f; **to draw ~s (for sth)** tirare a sorte (per qc).

(c) (at auction) lotto, partita; **he's a bad ~** (fig) è un pessimo soggetto.

(d) (plot of land) lotto di terreno; **parking ~** parcheggio.

(e) (fam): **the ~** (all, everything) tutto (quanto); **he took the ~** ha preso tutto (quanto); **that's the ~** (questo) è tutto; **the (whole) ~ of them** tutti quanti.

(f) (large amount) molto; **a ~ of money, ~s of money** un sacco di soldi, molti soldi; **a ~ of people, ~s of people** molta gente, molti; **quite a ~ of noise** parecchio rumore; **such a ~ of people** talmente tanta gente; **there was not a ~** we could say/do c'era ben poco da dire/da fare; **I'd give a ~ to know...** darei non so cosa per sapere...; **I read a ~** leggo molto; **he feels a ~** or **~s better** si sente molto meglio; **thanks a ~!** (also iro) grazie tante!

lo·tion [ˈləʊʃən] n lozione f.

lot·tery [ˈlɒtəri] n lotteria.

loud [laʊd] **1** adj (-er, -est) (gen) forte; (laugh, applause, thunder) fragoroso(a), forte; (noisy: behaviour, party, protests) rumoroso(a); (pej: striking: colour, clothes) chiassoso(a); **the radio's too ~** il volume della radio è troppo alto. **2** adv (speak etc) forte; **out ~** ad alta voce; **~ and clear** molto chiaramente.

loud·hailer [ˌlaʊdˈheɪləʳ] n megafono.

loud·ly [ˈlaʊdlɪ] adv (gen) forte; (laugh, applaud) fragorosamente; (protest) rumorosamente; (proclaim: out loud) ad alta voce; (: on banner etc) a lettere cubitali.

loud·mouthed [ˌlaʊdˈmaʊθd] adj (person) che sbraita; (protests) rumoroso(a).

loud·speaker [ˌlaʊdˈspiːkəʳ] n altoparlante m inv.

lounge [laʊndʒ] **1** n soggiorno, salotto; (of hotel) salone m; (of airport) sala d'attesa. **2** vi (also: ~ about) oziare, poltrire. **3** cpd: **~ bar** n bar m inv con servizio a tavolino; **~ suit** n completo da uomo.

louse [laʊs] n, pl **lice** pidocchio; (pej fam: person) verme m.

♦ **louse up** vt + adv (fam) rovinare.

lousy [ˈlaʊzɪ] adj (Med) pidocchioso(a); (fam: very bad) schifoso(a); (: headache, cough) orrendo(a); **to feel ~** stare da cani; **she's a ~ cook** fa schifo come cuoca; **a ~ trick** uno sporco trucco.

lout [laʊt] n zotico.

lov·able [ˈlʌvəbl] adj adorabile.

love [lʌv] **1** n **(a)**: ~ **(of, for)** amore m (di, per); (of hobby, object) passione f (per); **it was ~ at first sight** è stato un amore a prima vista or un colpo di fulmine; **he studies history for the ~ of it** studia storia per il puro piacere di farlo; **to be in ~ (with sb)** essere innamorato (di qn); **to fall in ~ (with sb)** innamorarsi (di qn); **to make ~** (euph: to have sex) fare l'amore or all'amore; **to make ~ to sb** (woo) fare la corte a qn; **there is no ~ lost between them** non si possono soffrire; **~ from Anne** (in letter) con affetto, Anne; **to send one's ~ to sb** mandare i propri saluti a qn. **(b)**: **(my) ~** amore m (mio), tesoro (mio). **(c)** (Tennis etc): **~ all** zero a zero; **30 ~** 30 a zero.

2 vt (person etc) amare, voler bene a; (food, activity, place): **he ~s tennis/Florence** gli piace (molto) il tennis/Firenze; **he ~s swimming, he ~s to swim** gli piace (molto) nuotare; **I'd ~ to come** mi piacerebbe molto venire.

3 cpd: **~ affair** n relazione f; **~ letter** n lettera d'amore; **~ life** n vita sentimentale; **~ song** n canzone f d'amore; **~ story** n storia d'amore.

love·ly [ˈlʌvlɪ] adj (-ier, -iest) (beautiful: gen) bello(a); (delightful: meal, voice) delizioso(a); (: evening, party) bellissimo(a); (: holiday, weather, idea) bello(a); (delicious: smell, food) buono(a); **it's ~ and warm** fa un bel calduccio; **it's been ~ seeing you** è stato un piacere vederti; **we had a ~ time** ci siamo divertiti molto.

love·making [ˈlʌvˌmeɪkɪŋ] n il fare l'amore or all'amore.

lov·er [ˈlʌvəʳ] n **(a)** (sexually) amante m/f; (romantically) innamorato/a. **(b)**: ~ **(of)** (hobby) appassionato/a (di); ~ **of good food** buongustaio/a.

love·sick [ˈlʌvsɪk] adj malato(a) d'amore.

lov·ing [ˈlʌvɪŋ] adj affettuoso(a).

lov·ing·ly [ˈlʌvɪŋlɪ] adv affettuosamente; (stronger) amorosamente.

low¹ [ləʊ] **1** adj (-er, -est) (gen) basso(a); (bow) profondo(a); (murmur) sommesso(a); (intelligence) scarso(a); (quality) scadente; (Bio, Zool: form of life) primitivo(a); (pej: opinion, taste) cattivo(a); (: character) pessimo(a); (: behaviour) ignobile; (: café, place) malfamato(a); **a ~ trick** un tiro mancino, uno scherzo ignobile; **to feel ~** sentirsi (un po') giù; **supplies are ~** le scorte si stanno esaurendo; **we are ~ on flour** non c'è rimasta molta farina; **in a ~ voice** a bassa voce; **in ~ gear** (Aut) con una marcia bassa; **on ~ ground** in pianura; **~er down** più in basso; **at ~ tide** quando c'è la bassa marea; **~er deck/floor** ponte/piano inferiore; **~er case** (Typ) minuscole fpl; **the ~er classes** le classi inferiori.

2 adv (aim) in basso; (sing) a bassa voce; (fly) a bassa quota, basso; (bow) profondamente; **to sink ~er** affondare sempre di più; **to fall** or **sink ~** (fig) cadere in basso; **to turn sth down ~** (gas, radio etc) abbassare qc; **supplies are running** or **getting ~** le scorte stanno per finire.

3 n **(a)** (Met) depressione f, zona di bassa pressione. **(b)** (fig: low point): **to reach a new** or **an all-time ~** toccare il livello più basso or il minimo.

low² [ləʊ] vi muggire.

low·brow [ˈləʊbraʊ] **1** adj (person) senza pretese intellettuali; (interests) non impegnato(a). **2** n persona senza pretese intellettuali.

low-calorie [ˈləʊˌkælərɪ] adj a basse calorie.

low-cut [ˈləʊkʌt] adj scollato(a).

low-down [ˈləʊdaʊn] **1** n (fam): **he gave me the ~ on it** mi ha messo al corrente dei fatti. **2** adj (mean) ignobile.

low·er[1] ['ləʊəʳ] **1** adj comp of **low**[1]. **2** adv comp of **low**[1]. **3** vt (gen) calare; (flag, sail) ammainare; (reduce: price) abbassare, ridurre; (resistance) indebolire; **to ~ sb's morale** demoralizzare qn; **to ~ one's guard** (Boxing) abbassare la guardia; (fig) allentare la sorveglianza; **to ~ one's voice** abbassare la voce; **to ~ o.s. to do sth** (fig) abbassarsi a fare qc.

low·er[2] ['laʊəʳ] vi (person): **to ~ (at sb)** dare un'occhiataccia (a qn); (sky) minacciare.

low-flying ['ləʊ,flaɪɪŋ] adj che vola a bassa quota.

low-key [,ləʊ'kiː] adj moderato(a); (operation) condotto(a) con discrezione.

low·land ['ləʊlənd] n bassopiano, pianura; **the L~s of Scotland** i bassopiani scozzesi.

low-level ['ləʊ,levl] adj a basso livello; (flying) a bassa quota.

low·ly ['ləʊlɪ] adj modesto(a), umile.

low-lying [,ləʊ'laɪɪŋ] adj a basso livello.

low-paid [,ləʊ'peɪd] adj mal pagato(a).

low-spirit·ed [,ləʊ'spɪrɪtɪd] adj abbacchiato(a), giù (di morale).

loy·al ['lɔɪəl] adj (-er, -est) leale, fedele.

loy·al·ist ['lɔɪəlɪst] n lealista m/f.

loy·al·ly ['lɔɪəlɪ] adv con lealtà, lealmente.

loy·al·ty ['lɔɪəltɪ] n lealtà f inv, fedeltà f inv.

loz·enge ['lɒzɪndʒ] n (Med) pastiglia; (Geom) losanga.

L.P. abbr of **long-playing record**.

L-plates ['el,pleɪts] npl cartelli obbligatori sul veicolo di chi sta imparando a guidare.

Ltd abbr see **limited**.

lub·ri·cant ['luːbrɪkənt] n lubrificante m.

lu·bri·cate ['luːbrɪkeɪt] vt lubrificare; **lubricating oil** lubrificante m.

lu·bri·ca·tion [,luːbrɪ'keɪʃən] n lubrificazione f.

lu·cid ['luːsɪd] adj (person) lucido(a); (instructions) chiaro(a); (moments) di lucidità.

luck [lʌk] n fortuna; **good ~** (buona) fortuna; **bad ~** sfortuna; **good ~!** buona fortuna!; **bad ~!** che sfortuna!; **it's good/bad ~ to do...** porta fortuna/sfortuna fare...; **no such ~!** magari!, purtroppo no!; **with any ~** con un po' di fortuna; **to be in ~** essere fortunato; **to be out of ~** essere sfortunato; **to be down on one's ~** essere scalognato; **I had the ~ to** ho avuto la fortuna di; **better ~ next time!** andrà meglio la prossima volta!; **he's got the ~ of the devil!** (fam) ha una fortuna sfacciata!; **to trust to ~** affidarsi al caso; **as ~ would have it** come volle il caso; **it's the ~ of the draw** (fig) è una questione di fortuna.

lucki·ly ['lʌkɪlɪ] adv per fortuna, fortunatamente.

lucky ['lʌkɪ] adj (-ier, -iest) (gen) fortunato(a); (horseshoe, number) portafortuna inv; **~ charm** portafortuna m inv; **it was a ~ guess** è stata tutta fortuna; **he's ~ to be alive** è vivo per miracolo; **~ you!**, **you ~ thing!** beato te!; **it was very ~ for you (that...)** per fortuna (che...); **~ dip** (at fair etc) pesca.

luc·ra·tive ['luːkrətɪv] adj lucrativo(a).

lu·di·crous ['luːdɪkrəs] adj ridicolo(a).

lug [lʌg] vt (fam) trascinare.

lug·gage ['lʌgɪdʒ] **1** n bagagli mpl, bagaglio. **2** cpd: **~ rack** n (on train etc) reticella (per i bagagli); (Aut) portabagagli m inv; **~ van** n bagagliaio.

lu·gu·bri·ous [luː'guːbrɪəs] adj lugubre.

luke·warm ['luːkwɔːm] adj (also fig: support etc) tiepido(a); (: person) poco entusiasta.

lull [lʌl] **1** n (gen) momento di calma; (in business) periodo di stasi; (in conversation) pausa; (in fighting) tregua. **2** vt (fears) calmare; **to ~ a baby to sleep** cullare un bambino finché si addormenta; **to be ~ed into a false sense of security**

illudersi che tutto vada bene.

lulla·by ['lʌləbaɪ] n ninnananna.

lum·ba·go [lʌm'beɪgəʊ] n lombaggine f.

lum·ber[1] ['lʌmbəʳ] **1** n (wood: esp Am) legname m inv; (junk: esp Brit) roba vecchia. **2** vt (Brit fam): **to ~ sb with sth/sb** affibbiare or rifilare qc/qn a qn; **he got ~ed with the job** è toccato a lui fare quel lavoro; **I got ~ed with him for the evening** me lo sono dovuto sorbire per tutta la serata. **3** cpd: **~ room** n ripostiglio; **~ yard** n segheria.

lum·ber[2] ['lʌmbəʳ] vi (also: **~ about, ~ along**: gen) muoversi pesantemente; **to ~ past** (vehicle) passare facendo fracasso.

lumber·jack ['lʌmbədʒæk] n taglialegna m inv.

lu·mi·nous ['luːmɪnəs] adj luminoso(a).

lump [lʌmp] **1** n (in geo) pezzo; (of earth) zolla; (of sugar) zolletta; (in sauce) grumo; (hard swelling) nodulo; (bump) bernoccolo; (person: fam pej) bestione m; **with a ~ in one's throat** (fig) con un nodo alla gola. **2** vt (fam: endure): **if he doesn't like it he can ~ it** dovrà mandarla giù, che gli piaccia o no. **3** cpd: **~ sugar** n zucchero in zollette; **~ sum** n somma globale; (payment) pagamento unico.

♦ **lump together** vt + adv mettere insieme.

lumpy ['lʌmpɪ] adj (-ier, -iest) (flour, sauce) grumoso(a); (mattress) bitorzoluto(a).

lu·na·cy ['luːnəsɪ] n (also fig) pazzia; **it's sheer ~!** ma è una vera pazzia!

lu·nar ['luːnəʳ] adj lunare.

lu·na·tic ['luːnətɪk] **1** n (old) matto/a; (fig) pazzo/a. **2** adj (person) pazzo(a); (idea: crazy) pazzo(a), pazzesco(a); (: stupid) idiota; (driving) da pazzi; **~ asylum** (old) manicomio; **the ~ fringe** la frangia estremista.

lunch [lʌntʃ] **1** n pranzo, (seconda) colazione f; **to invite sb to or for ~** invitare qn a pranzo; **to have ~** pranzare, fare colazione. **2** cpd: **~ break** n, **~ hour** n intervallo del pranzo.

lunch·eon ['lʌntʃən] **1** n (frm) pranzo. **2** cpd: **~ meat** n ≈ mortadella; **~ voucher** n buono pasto.

lunch·time ['lʌntʃtaɪm] n ora di pranzo.

lung [lʌŋ] **1** n polmone m; **to shout at the top of one's ~s** gridare a squarciagola. **2** cpd: **~ disease** n malattia polmonare or dei polmoni; **~ cancer** n cancro del polmone.

lunge [lʌndʒ] **1** n balzo (in avanti); (Fencing) affondo. **2** vi (also: **~ forward**) fare un balzo in avanti; **to ~ at sb** balzare su qn; **to ~ out with one's fists/feet** tirare dei pugni/calci.

lurch[1] [lɜːtʃ] **1** n sobbalzo; (of ship, plane) rollata. **2** vi (person) barcollare; (car) sobbalzare; (ship, plane) rollare; **to ~ along** (person) procedere barcollando; (car) procedere a balzi.

lurch[2] [lɜːtʃ] n: **to leave sb in the ~** piantare in asso qn.

lure [ljʊəʳ] **1** n (decoy, bait) richiamo, esca; (fig: charm) attrazione f. **2** vt attirare (con l'inganno); **to ~ sb into a trap** attirare qn in una trappola; **~ out** etc far uscire etc con l'inganno.

lu·rid ['ljʊərɪd] adj **(a)** (details, description: gruesome) impressionante, sconvolgente; (: sensational) sensazionale, scandalistico(a). **(b)** (colour) vistoso(a); (sunset) fiammeggiante.

lurk [lɜːk] vi (person: hide) stare in agguato, appostarsi; (: creep about) girare furtivamente; (danger) stare in agguato; (doubt) persistere.

lus·cious ['lʌʃəs] adj appetitoso(a).

lush [lʌʃ] adj rigoglioso(a), lussureggiante.

lust [lʌst] **1** n (greed) sete f; (sexual) libidine f. **2** vi: **to ~ for** or **after** (woman) desiderare; (power, wealth etc) aver sete di.

lus·tre, (Am) **lus·ter** ['lʌstəʳ] n lucentezza, lustro.

lus·trous ['lʌstrəs] *adj* lucente, splendente.

lusty ['lʌstɪ] *adj* (**-ier, -iest**) *(person)* vigoroso(a); *(cry etc)* forte.

lute [luːt] *n* liuto.

Lux·em·bourg ['lʌksəmbɜːg] *n* Lussemburgo.

luxu·ri·ant [lʌg'zjʊərɪənt] *adj (growth, jungle)* lussureggiante; *(beard)* folto(a); *(fig: imagination)* ricco(a), fervido(a).

luxu·ri·ous [lʌg'zjʊərɪəs] *adj (gen)* lussuoso(a); *(food)* sontuoso(a).

luxu·ry ['lʌkʃərɪ] **1** *n (gen)* lusso; *(article)* (oggetto di) lusso. **2** *cpd (goods, apartment)* di lusso.

ly·ing ['laɪɪŋ] **1** *adj (statement, story)* falso(a); *(person)* bugiardo(a). **2** *n* bugie *fpl*, menzogne *fpl*.

lynch [lɪntʃ] *vt* linciare.

lynch·ing ['lɪntʃɪŋ] *n* linciaggio.

lynx [lɪŋks] *n* lince *f*.

lyre ['laɪə'] *n* lira.

lyr·ic ['lɪrɪk] **1** *adj* lirico(a). **2** *n (poem)* lirica; ~**s** *(words of song)* parole *fpl*.

lyri·cal ['lɪrɪkəl] *adj* lirico(a); *(fig)* entusiasta; **to wax** *or* **become** ~ **about sth** infervorarsi a parlare di qc.

M

M, m [ɛm] *n* **(a)** *(letter)* M, m *f or m inv.* **(b)** *(abbr of motorway)*: M8 ≃ A8.
m. *abbr of* **metre; mile; million.**
M.A. *abbr see* **master.**
ma [mɑː] *n (fam)* mamma.
mac [mæk] *n Brit fam abbr of* **mackintosh.**
ma·ca·bre [məˈkɑːbrə] *adj* macabro(a).
maca·ro·ni [ˌmækəˈrəʊnɪ] **1** *n* maccheroni *mpl.* **2** *cpd*: ~ **cheese** *n* pasta al forno *or* al gratin.
maca·roon [ˌmækəˈruːn] *n* amaretto *(biscotto).*
mace[1] [meɪs] *n (weapon, ceremonial)* mazza.
mace[2] [meɪs] *n (spice)* macis *m or f.*
ma·chete [məˈtʃeɪtɪ] *n* machete *m inv.*
Machia·vel·lian [ˌmækɪəˈvɛlɪən] *adj* machiavellico(a).
machi·na·tion [ˌmækɪˈneɪʃən] *n* macchinazione *f*, intrigo.
ma·chine [məˈʃiːn] **1** *n (gen)* macchina; *(Pol etc)* apparato, macchina. **2** *vt (Tech)* lavorare (a macchina); *(Sewing)* cucire a macchina. **3** *cpd*: ~ **gun** *n* mitragliatrice *f*; ~ **shop** *n* officina meccanica; ~ **tool** *n* macchina utensile; ~ **washable** *adj* lavabile in lavatrice.
ma·chin·ery [məˈʃiːnərɪ] *n (machines)* macchine *fpl*, macchinari *mpl*; *(mechanism)* meccanismo; *(fig)* macchina, apparato; **a piece of** ~ un macchinario.
ma·chin·ist [məˈʃiːnɪst] *n (Tech)* meccanico; *(Sewing)* operaio(a) addetto(a) alla macchina da cucire.
macke·rel [ˈmækrəl] *n*, *pl inv* sgombro.
mack·in·tosh [ˈmækɪntɒʃ] *n* impermeabile *m.*
macro... [ˈmækrəʊ] *pref* macro... .
mad [mæd] *adj* **(-der, -dest)** *(person)* pazzo(a), matto(a); *(bull)* furioso(a); *(dog)* rabbioso(a); *(rash: person, idea, plan)* folle; *(fam: angry)*: ~ **(at or with sb)** furibondo(a) (con qn); **to go** ~ impazzire, diventar matto; **to drive sb** ~ far diventar matto qn, far impazzire qn; **as** ~ **as a hatter** *or* **a March hare** matto da legare; **are you** ~? sei matto?, sei impazzito?; ~ **with grief** pazzo di dolore; **he's hopping** ~ è furibondo; **I'm in a** ~ **rush** vado di gran fretta; **like** ~ *(adv phrase: fam)* come un pazzo *(or* una pazza); ~ **(keen) about** *or* **on sb** pazzo di qn; **to be** ~ **(keen) about** *or* **on sth** andar pazzo *or* matto per qc.
mad·am [ˈmædəm] *n* **(a)** signora; **can I help you** ~? (la signora) desidera?; **M**~ **Chairman** Signora Presidentessa. **(b): a little** ~ un tipetto a cui piace comandare. **(c)** *(of brothel)* tenutaria.
mad·den [ˈmædn] *vt (infuriate)* far impazzire, esasperare.
mad·den·ing [ˈmædnɪŋ] *adj* esasperante.
made [meɪd] *pt, pp of* **make.**
Ma·dei·ra [məˈdɪərə] *n (Geog)* Madera; *(wine)* madera *m.*
made-to-measure [ˌmeɪdtəˈmɛʒəʳ] *adj* su misura.
mad·ly [ˈmædlɪ] *adv (behave)* come un pazzo *(or* una pazza); *(love)* alla follia; **to be** ~ **in love with sb** essere follemente innamorato di qn; **I'm not** ~ **keen on the idea** l'idea non mi entusiasma.

mad·man [ˈmædmən] *n*, *pl* **-men** pazzo, folle *m.*
mad·ness [ˈmædnɪs] *n* pazzia, follia.
mad·woman [ˈmædwʊmən] *n*, *pl* **-women** pazza, folle *f.*
maes·tro [ˈmaɪstrəʊ] *n* maestro.
maga·zine [ˌmægəˈziːn] *n* **(a)** *(journal)* rivista. **(b)** *(in rifle)* caricatore *m*; *(Mil: store)* deposito di esplosivi.
mag·got [ˈmægət] *n* verme *m*, baco.
mag·ic [ˈmædʒɪk] **1** *adj* magico(a); *(beauty)* straordinario(a), soprannaturale; **to say the** ~ **word** pronunciare la formula magica. **2** *n* magia; *(conjuring tricks)* giochi *mpl* di prestigio; **like** ~ come per incanto. **3** *cpd*: ~ **carpet** *n* tappeto volante *or* magico; ~ **lantern** *n* lanterna magica; ~ **wand** *n* bacchetta magica.
magi·cal [ˈmædʒɪkəl] *adj* magico(a).
ma·gi·cian [məˈdʒɪʃən] *n* mago/a; *(conjuror)* illusionista *m/f*, mago/a.
mag·is·trate [ˈmædʒɪstreɪt] *n* magistrato.
mag·nani·mous [mægˈnænɪməs] *adj* magnanimo(a).
mag·nate [ˈmægneɪt] *n* magnate *m.*
mag·ne·sia [mægˈniːʃə] *n* magnesia.
mag·ne·sium [mægˈniːzɪəm] *n* magnesio.
mag·net [ˈmægnɪt] *n* calamita, magnete *m.*
mag·net·ic [mægˈnɛtɪk] *adj* magnetico(a).
mag·net·ism [ˈmægnɪtɪzəm] *n* magnetismo.
mag·net·ize [ˈmægnɪtaɪz] *vt* magnetizzare, calamitare.
mag·nifi·ca·tion [ˌmægnɪfɪˈkeɪʃən] *n* ingrandimento.
mag·nifi·cence [mægˈnɪfɪsəns] *n* magnificenza.
mag·nifi·cent [mægˈnɪfɪsənt] *adj* magnifico(a).
mag·ni·fy [ˈmægnɪfaɪ] *vt* **(a)** *(gen)* ingrandire; *(sound)* amplificare; ~**ing glass** lente *f* d'ingrandimento. **(b)** *(exaggerate)* esagerare.
mag·ni·tude [ˈmægnɪtjuːd] *n (gen)* vastità, ampiezza; *(importance)* importanza; *(Astron)* magnitudine *f.*
mag·pie [ˈmægpaɪ] *n* gazza.
ma·hoga·ny [məˈhɒgənɪ] *n* mogano.
maid [meɪd] *n* **(a)** *(servant)* cameriera. **(b)** *(old, poet: young girl)* ragazza, fanciulla; ~ **of honour** damigella d'onore.
maid·en [ˈmeɪdn] **1** *n (old, poet)* fanciulla, ragazza. **2** *cpd* **(a)** *(flight, voyage)* inaugurale; ~ **speech** *n* primo discorso *(in Parlamento etc).* **(b):** ~ **aunt** *n* zia nubile, *(pej)* zia zitella; ~ **name** *n* nome *m* da ragazza *or* da nubile.
maiden·hair [ˈmeɪdnˌhɛəʳ] *n (also:* ~ **fern)** capelvenere *m.*
mail [meɪl] **1** *n* posta; **by** ~ per posta. **2** *vt* spedire (per posta), inviare (per posta); ~**ing list** elenco di indirizzi, indirizzario *(per l'invio di materiale pubblicitario etc).* **3** *cpd*: ~ **train** *n* treno postale; ~ **van** *n (Aut)* furgone *m* postale; *(Rail)* vagone *m* postale.
mail·box [ˈmeɪlbɒks] *n (Am)* cassetta delle lettere.
mail·man [ˈmeɪlmæn] *n*, *pl* **-men** *(Am)* portalettere *m inv*, postino.

mail-order [ˈmeɪlˌɔːdəʳ] adj: ~ **firm** or **house** ditta di vendita per corrispondenza.
mail·shot [ˈmeɪlʃɒt] n campagna promozionale a mezzo posta.
maim [meɪm] vt storpiare, mutilare.
main [meɪn] **1** adj (gen) principale; **the ~ body of an army** il grosso di un esercito; **the ~ thing is to...** l'essenziale è...; **the ~ thing to remember is...** bisogna soprattutto non dimenticare che.... **2** n (a) (pipe: for water, gas etc) conduttura or tubatura principale; (Elec) linea principale; ~ **(sewer)** collettore m; **water from the ~s** acqua delle condutture; **it works by battery or from the ~s** funziona a pile o a corrente; **to turn sth off at the ~s** (water) chiudere le condutture; (electricity, gas) chiudere il contatore. **(b): in the ~** nel complesso. **3** cpd: ~ **course** n (Culin) piatto principale, piatto forte; ~ **deck** n (of ship) ponte m principale; (: Mil) ponte di batteria; ~ **line** n linea principale; ~ **road** n strada principale.
main·land [ˈmeɪnlənd] n continente m, terraferma; **the Greek ~** la Grecia continentale.
main·ly [ˈmeɪnlɪ] adv principalmente, soprattutto.
main·spring [ˈmeɪnsprɪŋ] n (of clock, watch) molla principale; (fig) molla.
main·stay [ˈmeɪnsteɪ] n (fig) sostegno, pilastro.
main·stream [ˈmeɪnstriːm] n (fig) corrente f principale.
main·tain [meɪnˈteɪn] vt (a) (keep up: gen) mantenere; (: attack) continuare; (: lead in race) mantenere, conservare; **if the improvement is ~ed** se il miglioramento continua. **(b)** (support: family, army) mantenere. **(c)** (keep in good condition) mantenere in buono stato. **(d)** (claim): **to ~ that...** sostenere che....
main·te·nance [ˈmeɪntɪnəns] **1** n (gen) mantenimento; (of car etc) manutenzione f; (after divorce) alimenti mpl. **2** cpd: ~ **contract** n contratto di manutenzione; ~ **costs** npl spese fpl di manutenzione; ~ **order** n (Dir) obbligo degli alimenti.
mai·son·ette [ˌmeɪzəˈnet] n appartamentino su due piani (indipendente).
maize [meɪz] n granturco, mais m.
ma·jes·tic [məˈdʒestɪk] adj maestoso(a).
maj·es·ty [ˈmædʒɪstɪ] n maestà f inv; **His M~** Sua Maestà.
ma·jor [ˈmeɪdʒəʳ] **1** adj (also Math, Mus) maggiore; (repairs) grosso(a), sostanziale; (disaster, loss) grave; (interest, artist, success) grande; **a ~ operation** una grossa operazione; ~ **road** strada con diritto di precedenza. **2** n (a) (Mil) maggiore m. **(b)** (Law) maggiorenne m/f. **(c)** (Am Univ) materia di specializzazione. **3** vi (Am Univ): **to ~ (in)** specializzarsi (in). **4** cpd: ~ **general** n (Mil) generale m di divisione.
ma·jor·ity [məˈdʒɒrɪtɪ] **1** n (a) maggioranza; **the ~ of people** la maggior parte della gente. **(b)** (Law): **the age of ~** la maggiore età. **2** cpd (verdict) maggioritario(a); (government) di maggioranza; ~ **holding** n (Fin): **to have a ~ holding** essere maggiore azionista.
make [meɪk] pt, pp **made 1** vt (a) (gen) fare; (Comm) produrre, fabbricare; (building) costruire; (points, score) fare, segnare; **God made the world** Dio creò il mondo; **she made the material into a dress** con la stoffa ha fatto un vestito; **made of silver** (fatto) d'argento; **made in Italy** fabbricato in Italia; (on label) made in Italy; **to show what one is made of** far vedere di che tempra or che stoffa si è fatti; **they were made for each other** erano fatti l'uno per l'altra.
(b) (cause to be or become) fare; (+ adj) rendere; **to ~ sb happy** rendere or far felice qn; **to ~**

sb angry far arrabbiare qn; **to ~ sth difficult** render difficile qc; **to ~ sth into sth else** fare di qc qualcos'altro; **to ~ sb a judge** nominare qn giudice; **let's ~ it 6 o'clock** facciamo alle 6; **to ~ o.s. heard** farsi sentire; ~ **yourself comfortable** si accomodi; **you'll ~ yourself ill!** starai male!
(c) (cause to do) fare; (: stronger) costringere; **to ~ sb do sth** far fare qc a qn, costringere qn a fare qc; **to ~ sb wait** far aspettare qn; **to ~ o.s. do sth** sforzarsi a fare qc; **if you don't want to I can't ~ you** se non vuoi non posso costringerti; **this made him leave** questo lo ha fatto partire or ha fatto sì che partisse; **what made you say that?** perché hai detto questo?; **what ~s you think that?** cosa te lo fa pensare?; **to ~ sth do, to ~ do with sth** arrangiarsi con qc.
(d) (earn) guadagnare; **to ~ money** far soldi; **to ~ a profit of £500** ricavare un profitto di 500 sterline; **to ~ a loss of £500** subire una perdita di 500 sterline; **he made a profit/loss** ci ha rimesso/ guadagnato; **he made £500 on the deal** l'affare gli ha fruttato 500 sterline.
(e) (reach: destination) arrivare a; (catch: bus, train etc) prendere; **they made (it to) the finals** sono entrati in finale; **to ~ it** (arrive) arrivare; (achieve sth) farcela; **to ~ it in life** riuscire nella vita; **can you ~ it for 4 o'clock?** ce la fai per le 4?; **to ~ port** raggiungere il porto.
(f) (cause to succeed): **he's made for life** il suo avvenire è assicurato, è a posto per sempre; **this film made her** questo film l'ha resa celebre; **that's made my day!** questo ha trasformato la mia giornata!; **to ~ or break sb** essere il successo o la rovina di qn.
(g) (equal, constitute) fare; **2 and 2 ~ 4** 2 più 2 fa 4; **that ~s 20** questo fa 20; **does that book ~ good reading?** è un libro interessante?; **these records ~ a set** questi dischi formano un set; **he made a good husband** è stato un buon marito.
(h) (estimate): **how far do you ~ it to the village?** quanto pensi che ci sia da qui al paese?; **I ~ it 6 o'clock** io faccio le 6; **what do you ~ of this?** cosa pensi che voglia dire questo?; **what do you ~ of him?** che te ne pare di lui?
2 vi (a) (go) andare, dirigersi; **to ~ towards the door** dirigersi verso la porta; **to ~ after sb** inseguire qn.
(b): to ~ as if to do fare (come) per fare.
3 n (a) (brand) marca; **it's our own ~** è di nostra produzione.
(b): to be on the ~ (fam) essere a caccia di successo.

♦ **make away** vi + adv = **make off**.
♦ **make away with** vi + prep (kill) far fuori, togliere di mezzo.
♦ **make for** vi + prep (a) (place) essere diretto(a) a; (subj: ship) far rotta verso. **(b)** (fig: result in) produrre; (: contribute to) contribuire a.
♦ **make off** vi + adv svignarsela; **to ~ off with sth** svignarsela con qc.
♦ **make out 1** vt + adv (a) (write out: cheque, receipt, list) fare; (: document) redigere; (: form) riempire, compilare; **to ~ out a case for sth** presentare delle valide ragioni in favore di qc. **(b)** (see, discern) riuscire a vedere, distinguere; (decipher) decifrare; (understand) (riuscire a) capire; **how do you ~ that out?** che cosa te lo fa pensare? **(c)** (claim, imply): **to ~ out (that)** voler far credere (che), darla a intendere (che); **to ~ sb out to be stupid** far passare qn per stupido. **2** vi + adv (fam: get on) cavarsela.
♦ **make over** vt + adv (assign): **to ~ over (to)** passare (a), trasferire (a).

◆ **make up 1** *vt + adv* **(a)** *(invent: story)* inventare. **(b)** *(put together, prepare: list, parcel, bed)* fare; *(food, medicine)* preparare; **she made the books up into a parcel** ha impacchettato i libri. **(c)** *(settle: dispute)* mettere fine a; **to ~ it up with sb** far la pace con qn. **(d)** *(complete: total, quantity)* completare; *(loss, deficit, lost time)* recuperare; **I need £5 to ~ up the sum we require** mi occorrono 5 sterline per raggiungere la somma stabilita; **to ~ it up to sb (for sth)** compensare qn (per qc). **(e)** *(constitute)* comporre, formare; **to be made up of** essere composto di *or* formato da. **(f)** *(apply cosmetics to)* truccare. **2** *vi + adv* **(a)** *(after quarrelling)* fare la pace, riconciliarsi. **(b)** *(apply cosmetics)* truccarsi. **(c)** *(catch up)*: **to ~ up on sb** riprendere qn.

◆ **make up for** *vi + prep (lost time)* recuperare, riguadagnare; *(trouble caused)* farsi perdonare; *(mistake)* rimediare a; *(loss, injury)* compensare.

◆ **make up to** *vi + prep (fam: curry favour with)* cercare di entrare nelle simpatie di, lisciare.

make-believe ['meɪkbɪ,liːv] *n*: **the land of ~** il mondo dei sogni; **it's just ~** *(activity)* è solo per finta; *(story)* sono frottole.

mak·er ['meɪkəʳ] *n (manufacturer)* fabbricante *m*; *(Rel)*: **our M~** il Creatore.

make·shift ['meɪkʃɪft] *adj* di fortuna, improvvisato(a).

make-up ['meɪkʌp] **1** *n* **(a)** *(nature: of object, group)* composizione *f*; *(: of football team)* formazione *f*; *(: of person)* carattere *m*. **(b)** *(cosmetics)* trucco. **2** *cpd*: **~ bag** *n* borsa del trucco.

mak·ing ['meɪkɪŋ] *n (a) (Comm, gen)* fabbricazione *f*; *(of dress, food)* confezione *f*; **it's still in the ~** non è ancora finito; **it's history in the ~** è un momento storico; **it was the ~ of him** ha fatto di lui un uomo. **(b)**: **he has the ~s of an actor** ha la stoffa dell'attore; **the ~s of a good film** quello che ci vuole per fare un buon film.

mal·ad·just·ed [,mælə'dʒʌstɪd] *adj (Psych)* disadattato(a).

mala·droit [,mælə'drɔɪt] *adj* maldestro(a).

ma·laise [mæ'leɪz] *n* malessere *m*.

ma·laria [mə'lɛərɪə] *n* malaria.

male [meɪl] **1** *adj (gen, sex)* maschile; *(animal)* maschio *inv*; **~ nurse** infermiere *m*; **~ chauvinist pig** *(fam)* sporco maschilista *m*. **2** *n* maschio.

ma·levo·lent [mə'lɛvələnt] *adj* malevolo(a).

mal·func·tion [,mæl'fʌŋkʃən] *n* cattivo funzionamento.

mal·ice ['mælɪs] *n* cattiveria, malizia; **I bear him no ~** non gli serbo nessun rancore; **~ aforethought** *(Law)* premeditazione *f*.

ma·li·cious [mə'lɪʃəs] *adj* cattivo(a); *(Law)* doloso(a); **~ gossip** malignità *fpl*.

ma·lign [mə'laɪn] **1** *adj* malefico(a), nocivo(a). **2** *vt* diffamare, calunniare.

ma·lig·nant [mə'lɪgnənt] *adj* maligno(a), malevolo(a); *(Med: tumour)* maligno(a).

ma·lin·ger·er [mə'lɪŋgərəʳ] *n* uno(a) che si finge malato(a) *(per non lavorare)*.

mal·le·able ['mælɪəbl] *adj* malleabile.

mal·let ['mælɪt] *n (tool)* mazzuolo; *(in croquet)* maglio; *(in polo)* mazza.

mal·nu·tri·tion [,mælnjʊ'trɪʃən] *n* denutrizione *f*.

mal·prac·tice [,mæl'præktɪs] *n (by doctor)* negligenza (colposa); *(by minister, lawyer)* prevaricazione *f*.

malt [mɔːlt] **1** *n* malto. **2** *cpd (vinegar, whisky)* di malto; **~ bread** *n* pane *m* al malto.

Mal·ta ['mɔːltə] *n* Malta.

malt·ed ['mɔːltɪd] *adj*: **~ milk** latte *m* al malto.

mal·treat [,mæl'triːt] *vt* maltrattare.

mam(m)a [mə'mɑː] *n (fam)* mamma.

mam·mal ['mæməl] *n* mammifero.

mam·moth ['mæməθ] **1** *n* mammut *m inv*. **2** *adj* colossale, mostruoso(a).

man [mæn] **1** *n, pl* **men** *(gen, Mil, Sport)* uomo; *(in office, shop etc)* impiegato; *(Chess)* pezzo; *(Draughts)* pedina; *(humanity)*: **M~** l'uomo, l'umanità; **an old ~** un vecchio; **a blind ~** un cieco; **~ and wife** marito e moglie; **her ~ is in the army** il suo uomo è nell'esercito; **the ~ in the street** l'uomo della strada; **he was ~ enough to apologize** ha avuto il coraggio di scusarsi; **he's a ~ about town** è un uomo di mondo; **a ~ of the world** un uomo di mondo *or* di grande esperienza; **men say that...** si dice che...; **no ~** nessuno; **any ~** chiunque; **that ~ Jones** quel Jones; **as one ~** come un sol uomo; **they agreed to a ~** hanno approvato all'unanimità; **he's not the ~ for the job** non è l'uomo adatto per questo lavoro; **I'm not a drinking ~** non sono un bevitore; **he's a family ~** è un uomo tutto casa e famiglia; **he's a Glasgow ~** è di Glasgow; **the ice-cream ~** il gelataio; **come on, ~!** dai, forza!; **good ~!** bravo! **2** *vt (ship, fortress etc)* fornire di uomini; *(fleet)* armare; **the ship is ~ned by Americans** l'equipaggio della nave è americano; **the telephone is ~ned all day** c'è sempre una persona che risponde al telefono; **~ the guns!** uomini ai cannoni!

mana·cle ['mænəkl] *n* manetta.

man·age ['mænɪdʒ] **1** *vt* **(a)** *(direct: company, organization, hotel)* dirigere; *(: shop, restaurant)* gestire; *(: household, property, affairs)* amministrare; *(: football team, pop star)* essere il manager di; **the election was ~d** *(pej)* le elezioni erano truccate. **(b)** *(handle, control: tool)* maneggiare; *(: ship, vehicle)* manovrare; *(: person, child)* saper prendere *or* trattare; **I can ~ him** so come trattarlo *or* prenderlo. **(c)**: **to ~ to do sth** riuscire a far qc; **he ~d not to get his feet wet** è riuscito a non bagnarsi i piedi; **£5 is the most I can ~** posso metterci 5 sterline ma non di più; **I shall ~ it** ce la farò; **can you ~ the cases?** ce la fai a portare le valigie?; **can you ~ 8 o'clock?** alle 8 ti va bene? **2** *vi* farcela; **can you ~?** ce la fai?; **how do you ~?** come riesci a farcela?; **I have to ~ on £20** mi devo arrangiare con 20 sterline; **to ~ without sth/sb** fare a meno di qc/qn.

man·age·able ['mænɪdʒəbl] *adj (car, boat, size, proportions)* maneggevole; *(person)* trattabile, arrendevole; **~ hair** capelli docili al pettine.

man·age·ment ['mænɪdʒmənt] *n (a) (act: see vb 1a)* direzione *f*; gestione *f*; amministrazione *f*. **(b)** *(persons: of business, firm)* dirigenti *mpl*; *(: of hotel, shop, theatre)* direzione *f*; **'under new ~'** 'sotto nuova gestione'; **~ and workers** i dirigenti e i lavoratori.

man·ag·er ['mænɪdʒəʳ] *n (gen)* direttore *m*; *(of shop, restaurant)* gestore *m*, gerente *m*; *(of football team, pop star)* manager *m inv*; *(of estate)* amministratore *m*; **sales ~** direttore *m* delle vendite.

man·ag·er·ess [,mænɪdʒə'rɛs] *n (gen)* direttrice *f*; *(of shop, restaurant)* gerente *f*.

mana·gerial [,mænə'dʒɪərɪəl] *adj (class)* dirigente, manageriale; *(ability, post)* direttivo(a).

man·ag·ing di·rec·tor ['mænɪdʒɪŋ,dɪ'rɛktəʳ] *n* amministratore *m* delegato.

man·da·rin ['mændərɪn] *n* **(a)** *(person)* mandarino. **(b)** *(also: ~ orange)* mandarino.

man·date ['mændeɪt] *n* mandato.

man·da·tory ['mændətərɪ] *adj* obbligatorio(a).

man·do·lin(e) ['mændəlɪn] *n* mandolino.

mane [meɪn] *n* criniera.

ma·neu·ver [mə'nu:vəʳ] *(Am)* = **manoeuvre**.

man·ful ['mænfʊl] *adj* coraggioso(a), valoroso(a).

man·ga·nese [,mæŋgə'ni:z] *n* manganese *m*.

man·gle¹ ['mæŋgl] *n* strizzatoio.

man·gle² ['mæŋgl] *vt (mutilate: body)* straziare, maciullare; *(: object)* stritolare.

man·go ['mæŋgəʊ] *n* mango.

man·handle ['mæn,hændl] *vt (treat roughly)* malmenare; *(move by hand: goods)* spostare a mano.

man·hole ['mænhəʊl] **1** *n* botola stradale. **2** *cpd:* ~ **cover** *n* tombino, chiusino.

man·hood ['mænhʊd] *n* **(a)** *(state)* età virile. **(b)** *(manliness)* virilità. **(c)** *(men)* uomini *mpl*.

man·hour ['mænaʊəʳ] *n (Industry)* ora di lavoro.

man·hunt ['mænhʌnt] *n* caccia all'uomo.

ma·nia ['meɪnɪə] *n* mania; **to have a** ~ **for (doing) sth** avere la mania di (fare) qc.

ma·ni·ac ['meɪnɪæk] *n* maniaco/a; **sports** ~ *(fig fam)* maniaco dello sport; **he drives like a** ~! guida come un pazzo!

manic-depres·sive [,mænɪkdɪ'presɪv] *(Psych)* **1** *adj* maniaco-depressivo(a). **2** *n* persona affetta da mania depressiva.

mani·cure ['mænɪ,kjʊəʳ] **1** *n* manicure *f inv*. **2** *vt:* **to** ~ **one's hands** *(or* one's nails) fare manicure; **well-~d hands** mani ben curate.

mani·fest ['mænɪfest] **1** *adj* evidente, palese. **2** *vt* manifestare.

mani·fes·ta·tion [,mænɪfes'teɪʃən] *n* manifestazione *f*.

mani·fes·to [,mænɪ'festəʊ] *n, pl* ~**es** manifesto.

mani·fold ['mænɪfəʊld] **1** *adj* molteplice. **2** *n (Aut etc):* **exhaust** ~ collettore *m* di scarico.

ma·nipu·late [mə'nɪpjʊleɪt] *vt (tool)* maneggiare; *(controls)* azionare; *(limb)* manipolare; *(facts, figures etc)* manipolare, alterare; *(public opinion, person etc)* manipolare.

ma·nipu·la·tion [mə,nɪpjʊ'leɪʃən] *n (see vb)* maneggiare *m*; capacità di azionare; manipolazione *f*.

man·kind [mæn'kaɪnd] *n* l'umanità, il genere umano.

man·li·ness ['mænlɪnɪs] *n* virilità.

man·ly ['mænlɪ] *adj* **(-ier, -iest)** virile.

man-made ['mæn,meɪd] *adj* artificiale.

man·na ['mænə] *n* manna.

man·ne·quin ['mænɪkɪn] *n (dummy)* manichino; *(fashion model)* indossatrice *f*.

man·ner ['mænəʳ] *n* **(a)** *(mode)* modo, maniera; **in this** ~ in questo modo, così; **in such a** ~ **that** in modo tale che + *indic (actual result) or* + *sub (intended result);* **he spoke in such a** ~ **as to offend them** ha parlato in modo tale da offenderli *or* che li ha offesi; **after** *or* **in the** ~ **of X** alla maniera di X, nello stile di X; **in a** ~ **of speaking** per così dire; **(as) to the** ~ **born** come se ce l'avesse nel sangue.
  (b) *(behaviour)* comportamento; *(attitude)* atteggiamento; **I don't like his** ~ ha un modo di fare che non mi piace.
  (c): (good) ~**s** buona educazione *f*, buone maniere *fpl*; **bad** ~**s** maleducazione *f*; **it's bad** ~**s to talk with your mouth full** è da maleducati parlare con la bocca piena; **she has no** ~**s** non conosce le buone maniere; **to teach sb** ~**s** insegnare l'educazione a qn; **a novel of** ~**s** un romanzo di costume.
  (d) *(class, type):* **all** ~ **of** ogni sorta di.

man·ner·ism ['mænərɪzəm] *n* **(a)** *(habit)* particolare modo di fare *(or* muoversi *etc)*. **(b)** *(Art etc)* manierismo.

man·ner·ly ['mænəlɪ] *adj* educato(a), civile.

ma·noeu·vrable [mə'nu:vrəbl] *adj* facile da

manovrare; *(car)* maneggevole; *(ship, plane)* manovriero(a).

ma·noeu·vre [mə'nu:vəʳ] **1** *n* manovra; **the soldiers were out on** ~**s** i soldati stavano facendo le manovre *or* le esercitazioni. **2** *vt (Mil)* manovrare; **I couldn't** ~ **the settee through the door** non sono riuscito a far passare il divano attraverso la porta; **he** ~**d himself into a job** è riuscito a ottenere un posto con abili manovre; **to** ~ **sb into doing sth** costringere abilmente qn a fare qc. **3** *vi (Mil, fig)* manovrare; *(Aut)* far manovra.

man·or ['mænəʳ] *n* maniero.

man·power ['mæn,paʊəʳ] *n (gen, Industry)* manodopera; *(Mil)* effettivi *mpl*.

man·sion ['mænʃən] *n (in town)* palazzo (signorile); *(in country)* villa, maniero.

man·slaughter ['mæn,slɔːtəʳ] *n* omicidio colposo.

mantel·piece ['mæntl,piːs] *n* mensola del caminetto.

man·tle ['mæntl] *n (old: garment)* mantello, manto; *(gas* ~*)* reticella; **a** ~ **of snow** un manto di neve.

man-to-man [,mæntə'mæn] *adj, adv* da uomo a uomo.

manu·al ['mænjʊəl] **1** *adj* manuale; ~ **worker** *n* manovale *m*; ~ **workers** manovalanza. **2** *n (book)* manuale *m*.

manu·fac·ture [,mænjʊ'fæktʃəʳ] **1** *n (act)* fabbricazione *f*, manifattura; *(of clothes)* confezione *f*; *(sth* ~*d)* manufatto. **2** *vt* fabbricare; *(clothes)* confezionare; *(fig: excuse, lie)* architettare, inventare; ~**d goods** manufatti *mpl*; **manufacturing industries** industrie *fpl* manifatturiere.

manu·fac·tur·er [,mænjʊ'fæktʃərəʳ] *n* fabbricante *m*.

ma·nure [mə'njʊəʳ] **1** *n* concime *m*; *(organic)* letame *m*. **2** *vt* concimare.

manu·script ['mænjʊskrɪpt] *n* manoscritto.

many ['menɪ] *adj, pron* molti(e), tanti(e); **too** ~ **difficulties** troppe difficoltà; **so** ~ **books** (così) tanti libri; ~ **people** molta *or* tanta gente, molte persone; **there were as** ~ **as 100 at the meeting** alla riunione c'erano ben 100 persone; ~ **a man** più d'uno, molti; ~ **a time** più volte; **he has as** ~ **as I have** ne ha tanti quanti ne ho io; **there's one too** ~ ce n'è uno in più; **he's had one too** ~ ha bevuto un bicchiere di troppo; **as** ~ **again** altrettanti; **twice as** ~ due volte tanto; **a good** ~ **houses, a great** ~ **houses** moltissime case, un gran numero di case; **how** ~**?** quanti(e)?; **how** ~ **people?** quanta gente?, quante persone?; **there are too** ~ **of you** siete (in) troppi; **however** ~ there may be per quanti ce ne siano; ~ **of them** came molti di loro sono venuti.

many-coloured [,menɪ'kʌləd] *adj* multicolore.

map [mæp] **1** *n (gen)* carta (geografica); *(of town)* pianta; **treasure** ~ mappa del tesoro; **this will put Eastdean on the** ~ *(fig)* questo darà notorietà a *or* farà conoscere Eastdean; **off the** ~ *(fig)* in capo al mondo. **2** *vt* tracciare una carta *(or* una pianta *or* una mappa) di.

♦ **map out** *vt* + *adv* tracciare una carta *(or* una pianta *or* una mappa) di; *(fig: career, holiday, essay)* pianificare.

ma·ple ['meɪpl] *n* acero.

mar [mɑːʳ] *vt* sciupare, guastare.

mara·thon ['mærəθən] **1** *n* maratona. **2** *adj (debate)* lunghissimo; ~ **runner** maratoneta *m/f*; **a** ~ **session** una seduta fiume.

ma·raud·er [mə'rɔːdəʳ] *n* predone *m*, saccheggiatore/trice.

ma·raud·ing [mə'rɔːdɪŋ] *adj* che si dà al saccheggio.

mar·ble ['mɑːbl] **1** *n* **(a)** *(material, sculpture etc)* marmo. **(b)** *(toy)* biglia; **to play ~s** giocare alle biglie. **2** *adj* di marmo.

March [mɑːtʃ] *n* marzo; *for usage see* **July**.

march [mɑːtʃ] **1** *n (all senses)* marcia; **on the ~** in marcia; **a day's ~** una giornata di marcia. **2** *vt (Mil)* far marciare; **to ~ sb off to prison/to bed** spedire qn in prigione/a letto. **3** *vi (Mil)* marciare; **quick ~!** avanti, marsc!; **to ~ into a room** entrare a passo deciso in una stanza; **to ~ past** sfilare; **to ~ past sb** sfilare davanti a qn; **to ~ up to sb** andare risolutamente da qn.

march·ing ['mɑːtʃɪŋ] *n:* **~ orders** *(Mil)* ordini *mpl* di partenza; **to give sb his ~ orders** *(fig)* dare il benservito a qn.

mar·chion·ess ['mɑːʃənɪs] *n* marchesa.

march-past ['mɑːtʃ,pɑːst] *n (Mil)* sfilata.

mare [mɛəʳ] *n* giumenta, cavalla.

mar·ga·rine [,mɑːdʒəˈriːn] *n*, **marge** [mɑːdʒ] *n (fam)* margarina.

mar·gin ['mɑːdʒɪn] *n (gen, fig)* margine *m*; **to win by a wide/narrow ~** vincere con largo margine/di stretta misura.

mar·gin·al ['mɑːdʒɪnl] *adj* marginale; **~ seat** *(Pol)* seggio elettorale ottenuto con una stretta maggioranza.

mar·gin·al·ly ['mɑːdʒɪnəlɪ] *adv (bigger, better)* lievemente, di poco; *(different)* un po'.

mari·gold ['mærɪɡəʊld] *n* calendula.

ma·ri·jua·na [,mærɪˈhwɑːnə] *n* marijuana.

ma·ri·na [məˈriːnə] *n* marina.

mari·nade [,mærɪˈneɪd] *n* marinata.

mari·nate ['mærɪneɪt] *vt* marinare.

ma·rine [məˈriːn] **1** *adj (animal, plant)* marino(a); *(products)* del mare; *(vegetation, forces, insurance)* marittimo(a); *(engineering)* navale. **2** *n* **(a): merchant** *or* **mercantile ~** marina mercantile. **(b)** *(Mil)* fante *m* di marina; *(Am)* marine *m inv*; **tell that to the ~s!** *(fam)* va' a raccontarla a un altro!

mari·ner ['mærɪnəʳ] *n* marinaio.

mari·on·ette [,mærɪəˈnet] *n* marionetta.

mari·tal ['mærɪtl] *adj* coniugale.

mar·jo·ram ['mɑːdʒərəm] *n* maggiorana.

mark[1] [mɑːk] **1** *n* **(a)** *(gen)* segno; *(of shoes, fingers: in mud etc)* impronta; **to leave a ~ on sth** lasciare un segno su qc; **there wasn't a ~ on him** *or* **on his body** non aveva nemmeno un graffio; **it's the ~ of a gentleman** è da gentiluomo; **it bears the ~ of genius** ha l'impronta del genio; **to make one's ~ (as)** *(fig)* farsi un nome (come); **to leave one's ~ on sth** *(fig)* lasciare un segno (in qc); **as a ~ of my gratitude** come segno della mia gratitudine; **punctuation ~s** segni di punteggiatura; **finger ~** impronta del dito.

(b) *(instead of signature)* croce *f (al posto della firma)*; **to make one's ~** fare una croce.

(c) *(Scol)* voto; **good/bad ~** buon *or* bel/brutto voto; **he failed by 2 ~s** l'hanno bocciato per 2 punti; **full ~s** pieni voti; **full ~s for trying!** un bravo per aver tentato!; **there are no ~s for guessing where I've been!** non ci vuole un genio per sapere dove sono stato!

(d) *(Tech)*: **M~** serie *f inv*; **M~ 1** prima serie.

(e) *(Sport etc: target)* bersaglio; **to hit the ~** far centro; *(fig)* azzeccare in pieno; **to be wide of the ~** essere lontano dal bersaglio; *(fig)* essere lontano dal vero.

(f) *(Sport: starting line)* linea di partenza; **on your ~s! get set! go!** ai vostri posti! pronti! attenti! via!; **to be quick off the ~** *(in doing)* *(fig)* non perdere tempo (per fare); **up to the ~** *(in health)* in forma; *(in efficiency)* all'altezza.

2 *vt* **(a)** *(make a ~ on)* segnare; *(stain)* macchiare, lasciare dei segni su.

(b) *(indicate: score)* segnare; *(: price)* mettere; *(: place)* indicare, segnare; *(: change, improvement)* indicare; **this ~s the frontier** questo segna la frontiera; **the qualities which ~ a good swimmer** le qualità che contraddistinguono un buon nuotatore.

(c) *(heed):* **~ my words** fa' attenzione a quello che ti dico.

(d) *(exam)* correggere; **to ~ sth wrong** segnare qc come errore.

(e) *(Sport: player)* marcare.

(f): to ~ time *(Mil, fig)* segnare il passo. **3** *vi* macchiarsi.

♦ **mark down** *vt + adv* **(a)** *(note down)* prendere nota di. **(b)** *(reduce: prices, goods)* ribassare, ridurre.

♦ **mark off** *vt + adv* **(a)** *(separate)* dividere, separare. **(b)** *(tick off)* spuntare, cancellare.

♦ **mark out** *vt + adv* **(a)** *(zone, road)* delimitare. **(b)** *(single out: for promotion etc)* designare; *(characterize)* distinguere.

♦ **mark up** *vt + adv* **(a)** *(write up)* segnare. **(b)** *(increase: goods)* aumentare il prezzo di *(: price)* aumentare.

mark[2] [mɑːk] *n (currency)* marco.

marked [mɑːkt] *adj (accent, contrast, bias)* marcato(a); *(improvement, increase)* sensibile; **he's a ~ed man** è sotto tiro.

mark·ed·ly ['mɑːkɪdlɪ] *adv* visibilmente, notevolmente.

mark·er ['mɑːkəʳ] *n (stake)* paletto; *(pen)* marcatore *m*; *(in book)* segnalibro; *(person: in exams)* persona addetta a correggere le prove d'esame; *(scorekeeper in games)* segnapunti *m inv*.

mar·ket ['mɑːkɪt] **1** *n* mercato; *(stock ~)* mercato azionario *or* dei titoli; **to go to ~** andare al mercato; **open ~** mercato libero; **there is a good ~ for videos** c'è una grossa richiesta di video; **is there a ~ for that?** c'è uno sbocco sul mercato per quello?; **it appeals to the Italian ~** è richiesto sul mercato italiano; **to be in the ~ for sth** avere intenzione di comprare qc; **to be on the ~** essere (messo) in vendita *or* in commercio; **to come on(to) the ~** essere introdotto sul mercato; **to play the ~** giocare *or* speculare in borsa.

2 *vt (sell)* vendere; *(promote)* lanciare sul mercato.

3 *cpd:* **~ garden** *n* orto (industriale); **~ leader** *n* leader *m inv* del mercato; **~ place** *n* (piazza del) mercato; *(world of trade)* piazza, mercato; **~ price** *n* prezzo di mercato; **~ research** *n* indagine *f or* ricerca di mercato; **~ trend** *n* tendenza del mercato.

mar·ket·ing ['mɑːkɪtɪŋ] *n* marketing *m*.

mark·ing ['mɑːkɪŋ] **1** *n* **(a)** *(on animal)* marcatura di colore; *(on road)* segnaletica orizzontale. **(b)** *(Scol)* correzione *f* (dei compiti). **2** *cpd:* **~ ink** *n* inchiostro indelebile.

marks·man ['mɑːksmən] *n, pl* **-men** tiratore *m* scelto.

mark-up ['mɑːkʌp] *n (Comm: margin)* margine *m* di vendita; *(: increase)* aumento.

mar·ma·lade ['mɑːməleɪd] *n* marmellata d'arance.

ma·roon[1] [məˈruːn] *adj, n (colour)* bordeaux *(m) inv*.

ma·roon[2] [məˈruːn] *vt:* **~ed** *(on island)* abbandonato(a); *(by sea, traffic, snow)* bloccato(a).

mar·quee [mɑːˈkiː] *n* grande tenda.

mar·quess, mar·quis ['mɑːkwɪs] *n* marchese *m*.

mar·riage ['mærɪdʒ] **1** *n* matrimonio; **he's my uncle by ~** è uno zio acquisito. **2** *cpd (vows)* di matrimonio; *(bed)* coniugale; **~ guidance** *n* consulenza matrimoniale; **~ licence** *n* licenza matrimoniale; ~ **lines** npl, ~ **certificate** n certificato di matrimonio.

mar·riage·able ['mærɪdʒəbl] adj: **of** ~ **age** (woman) da marito; (man) da prendere moglie.

mar·ried ['mærɪd] adj (person) sposato(a); (life, love) coniugale; (name) da sposata.

mar·row ['mærəʊ] n (a) (Anat) midollo; **to be frozen to the** ~ sentirsi il gelo or il freddo nelle ossa. (b) (vegetable) zucca; **baby** ~ zucchino.

marrow·bone ['mærəʊbəʊn] n ossobuco, osso con il midollo.

mar·ry ['mærɪ] **1** vt sposare. **2** vi (also: **to get married**) sposarsi; **to** ~ **again** risposarsi; **to** ~ **into a rich family** imparentarsi con una famiglia ricca.

Mars [mɑːz] n (Astron, Mythology) Marte m.

Mar·seilles [mɑːˈseɪlz] n Marsiglia.

marsh [mɑːʃ] n palude f.

mar·shal ['mɑːʃəl] **1** n (Mil etc) maresciallo; (for demonstration, meeting) membro del servizio d'ordine. **2** vt (soldiers, procession) schierare, adunare; (fig: facts etc) ordinare.

mar·shal·ling ['mɑːʃəlɪŋ] n: ~ **yard** scalo smistamento.

marsh·mal·low ['mɑːʃˌmæləʊ] n (Bot) altea; (sweet) caramella soffice e gommosa.

marshy ['mɑːʃɪ] adj (-ier, -iest) paludoso(a).

mar·su·pial [mɑːˈsuːpɪəl] adj, n marsupiale (m).

mar·tial ['mɑːʃəl] adj marziale.

mar·tin ['mɑːtɪn] n (house ~) balestruccio.

mar·tyr ['mɑːtəʳ] n martire m; **to be a** ~ **to arthritis** essere una vittima dell'artrite.

mar·tyr·dom ['mɑːtədəm] n martirio.

mar·vel ['mɑːvəl] **1** n (of nature) meraviglia; (of science, skill) prodigio; **if he gets there it will be a** ~ (fam) se ci arriva è un miracolo; **it's a** ~ **to me how she does it** (fam) non so proprio come riesca a farlo; **you're a** ~! (fam) sei un fenomeno! **2** vi: **to** ~ **(at)** (awestruck) rimanere incantato(a) (davanti a); (surprised) stupirsi (di fronte a).

mar·vel·lous, (Am) **mar·vel·ous** ['mɑːvələs] adj meraviglioso(a).

Marx·ism ['mɑːksɪzəm] n marxismo.

Marx·ist ['mɑːksɪst] adj, n marxista (m/f).

mar·zi·pan [ˌmɑːzɪˈpæn] n marzapane m.

mas·cara [mæsˈkɑːrə] n mascara m inv.

mas·cot ['mæskət] n mascotte f inv, portafortuna m inv.

mas·cu·line ['mæskjʊlɪn] **1** adj (also Gram) maschile; (woman) mascolino(a). **2** n (Gram) maschile m.

mash [mæʃ] **1** n (for animals) pastone m; (also: ~ed potatoes) puré m (di patate). **2** vt (Culin) passare, schiacciare.

mask [mɑːsk] **1** n maschera. **2** vt mascherare.

maso·chism ['mæsəʊkɪzəm] n masochismo.

maso·chist ['mæsəʊkɪst] n masochista m/f.

maso·chis·tic [ˌmæsəʊˈkɪstɪk] adj masochistico(a).

ma·son ['meɪsn] n (a) (builder) muratore m. (b) (free~) massone m.

ma·son·ic [məˈsɒnɪk] adj massonico(a).

ma·son·ry ['meɪsnrɪ] n (a) muratura; (skill) arte f muratoria. (b) (free~) massoneria.

mas·quer·ade [ˌmæskəˈreɪd] **1** n (pretence) mascherata. **2** vi: **to** ~ **as** farsi passare per.

mass¹ [mæs] n (Rel) la messa; **to say** ~ dir messa; **to go to** ~ andare a or alla messa.

mass² [mæs] **1** n massa; **he's a** ~ **of bruises** è coperto di lividi; **in the** ~ nella gran maggioranza; **the** ~es le masse; **~es (of)** (fam) un sacco (di), un mucchio (di). **2** vt adunare. **3** vi (Mil) adunarsi, concentrarsi; (crowd) radunarsi; (clouds) addensarsi. **4** cpd (culture, demonstra-

tion) di massa; (education) delle masse; (hysteria) collettivo(a); (murders) in massa; ~ **media** n mass media mpl; ~ **meeting** n (of everyone concerned) riunione f generale; (huge) adunata popolare; ~ **production** n produzione f in serie.

mas·sa·cre ['mæsəkəʳ] **1** n massacro. **2** vt massacrare.

mas·sage ['mæsɑːʒ] **1** n massaggio. **2** vt massaggiare.

mas·seur [mæˈsɜːʳ] n massaggiatore m.

mas·seuse [mæˈsɜːz] n massaggiatrice f.

mas·sive ['mæsɪv] adj massiccio(a).

mass-produce ['mæsprəˌdjuːs] vt produrre in serie.

mast [mɑːst] n (Naut) albero; (flagpole) asta; (Radio, TV) pilone m (a traliccio).

mas·ter ['mɑːstəʳ] **1** n (a) (of servant, house, dog) padrone m; **the** ~ **of the house** il padron di casa; **to be one's own** ~ non aver padroni; **I am (the)** ~ **now** ora comando io; **to be** ~ **of the situation** essere padrone della situazione. (b) (Naut: of ship) capitano. (c) (musician, painter etc) maestro. (d) (teacher) insegnante m; **fencing** ~ maestro di scherma. (e): **M~ Paul Moran** il signorino Paul Moran; (on letters) il signor Paul Moran.

2 vt (a) (animal) domare; (person) dominare; (one's emotions) controllare. (b) (theory: understand) capire a fondo; (subject, skill) avere la padronanza di.

3 cpd: **M~ of Arts/Science** n detentore di titolo accademico in lettere/scienze superiore alla laurea; ~ **builder** n capomastro; ~ **of ceremonies** n maestro di cerimonie; ~**'s degree** n titolo accademico superiore alla laurea; ~ **key** n passepartout m inv; ~ **plan** n piano generale, progetto di massima; ~ **race** n razza superiore.

mas·ter·ful ['mɑːstəfʊl] adj autoritario(a), imperioso(a).

mas·ter·ly ['mɑːstəlɪ] adj magistrale, da maestro.

master·mind ['mɑːstəmaɪnd] **1** n (genius) mente f superiore; (in crime etc) cervello. **2** vt ideare e dirigere.

master·piece ['mɑːstəpiːs] n capolavoro.

master·stroke ['mɑːstəstrəʊk] n colpo magistrale or da maestro.

mas·tery ['mɑːstərɪ] n (of subject, musical instrument): ~ **(of)** padronanza (di); (skill): ~ **(at)** virtuosità (a), maestria (a); (of the seas etc): ~ **(of)** dominio (su), supremazia (su); (over competitors etc): ~ **(over)** superiorità (su).

mas·tiff ['mæstɪf] n mastino inglese.

mas·tur·bate ['mæstəbeɪt] vi masturbarsi.

mas·tur·ba·tion [ˌmæstəˈbeɪʃən] n masturbazione f.

mat¹ [mæt] n (on floor) tappetino; (: of straw etc) stuoia; (at door) zerbino; (on table) sottopiatto.

mat² [mæt] adj = **matt**.

match¹ [mætʃ] n fiammifero; **to put a** ~ **to sth** dar fuoco a qc.

match² [mætʃ] **1** n (a) (of colours etc): **to be a good** ~ **(for)** intonarsi (a); **Paul and Jane make a good** ~ Paul e Jane fanno una bella coppia. (b) (equal) uguale m/f, pari m/f inv; **to be a** ~/**no** ~ **for sb** riuscire/non riuscire a tenere testa a qn; **to meet one's** ~ trovare il pane per i propri denti. (c) (marriage) partito. (d) (Sport) incontro; (: Ftbl, Rugby) partita, incontro.

2 vt (a) (find similar to: also: ~ **up**): **can you** ~ **this wool for me?** mi trova della lana che vada bene con questa?; **to** ~ **sb against sb** opporre qn a qn; **they are well** ~**ed** (opponents) son ben assortiti; (friends, husband and wife) fanno una bella coppia. **(b)** *(equal)* uguagliare; **the results did not ~ our hopes** i risultati non hanno corrisposto alle nostre speranze; **I can't ~ that** per me è troppo. **(c)** *(subj: clothes, colours)* intonare; **his tie ~es his socks** la sua cravatta s'intona ai calzini.

3 *vi (colours, materials)* intonarsi; **with a skirt to ~, with a ~ing skirt** con una gonna adatta *or* intonata.

match·box ['mætʃbɒks] *n* scatola per fiammiferi.

match·make ['mætʃmɛɪk] *vi:* **she's always matchmaking** cerca sempre di combinare matrimoni.

mate¹ [mɛɪt] *n (Chess)* scaccomatto.

mate² [mɛɪt] **1** *n* **(a)** *(at work)* compagno/a *(di lavoro); (fam: friend)* amico/a; **look here, ~** ehi tu, senti. **(b)** *(assistant)* aiutante *m/f*. **(c)** *(Zool)* compagno/a, maschio/femmina. **(d)** *(Merchant Navy)* secondo. **2** *vt (Zool)* accoppiare. **3** *vi (Zool)* accoppiarsi.

ma·te·ri·al [mə'tɪərɪəl] **1** *adj* **(a)** *(things, needs, success)* materiale. **(b)** *(important)* sostanziale; *(relevant):* **~ to** pertinente a; *(Law: evidence)* determinante; **a ~ witness** un testimone chiave. **2** *n* **(a)** *(substance)* materiale *m; (cloth)* stoffa, tessuto; **he is university ~** è adatto agli studi universitari; **he is officer ~** ha la stoffa dell'ufficiale. **(b)** *(equipment etc):* **~s** *npl* occorrente *m;* **building ~s** materiali *mpl* da costruzione; **raw ~s materie** *fpl* prime; **have you any writing ~s?** hai l'occorrente per scrivere? **(c)** *(for novel, report etc)* materiale *m,* documentazione *f.*

ma·teri·al·ism [mə'tɪərɪəlɪzəm] *n* materialismo.

ma·teri·al·ize [mə'tɪərɪəlaɪz] *vi* materializzarsi; *(idea, hope etc)* avverarsi, realizzarsi; **so far he hasn't ~d** *(fam)* per ora non si è visto.

ma·teri·al·ly [mə'tɪərɪəlɪ] *adv (see adj)* dal punto di vista materiale; sostanzialmente.

ma·ter·nal [mə'tɜːnl] *adj* materno(a).

ma·ter·nity [mə'tɜːnɪtɪ] **1** *n* maternità. **2** *cpd:* **~ benefit** *n* sussidio di maternità; **~ dress** *n* vestito *m* pre-maman *inv;* **~ home** *n,* **~ hospital** *n* maternità *f inv;* **~ ward** *n* reparto *m* maternità *inv.*

math [mæθ] *n Am fam abbr of* **mathematics.**

math·emati·cal [,mæθə'mætɪkəl] *adj* matematico(a).

math·ema·ti·cian [,mæθəmə'tɪʃən] *n* matematico/a.

math·emat·ics [,mæθə'mætɪks] *nsg* matematica.

maths [mæθs] *n fam abbr of* **mathematics.**

mati·née ['mætɪneɪ] *n* matinée *f inv.*

mat·ing ['mɛɪtɪŋ] **1** *n* accoppiamento. **2** *adj* dell'accoppiamento.

ma·tri·arch ['mɛɪtrɪɑːk] *n* capo di un matriarcato.

ma·tri·ces ['mɛɪtrɪsiːz] *npl of* **matrix.**

ma·tricu·late [mə'trɪkjʊlɛɪt] *vi* immatricolarsi.

mat·ri·mo·nial [,mætrɪ'məʊnɪəl] *adj (vows)* di matrimonio; *(state, troubles)* coniugale.

mat·ri·mo·ny ['mætrɪmənɪ] *n* matrimonio.

ma·trix ['mɛɪtrɪks] *n, pl* **matrices** *or* **-es** matrice *f.*

ma·tron ['mɛɪtrən] *n (in hospital)* capoinfermiera; *(in school)* infermiera; *(old use)* matrona.

ma·tron·ly ['mɛɪtrənlɪ] *adj (figure, behaviour)* da matrona.

matt [mæt] *adj* opaco(a), matto(a).

mat·ted ['mætɪd] *adj (hair)* ingarbugliato(a), arruffato(a); *(sweater)* infeltrito(a).

mat·ter ['mætə'] **1** *n* **(a)** *(substance: gen, Phys etc)* materia; **colouring ~** colorante *m;* **foreign ~** sostanza estranea; **advertising ~** pubblicità; **printed ~** stampe *fpl;* **reading ~** qualcosa da leggere.

(b) *(Med: pus)* pus *m.*

(c) *(content)* contenuto.

(d) *(question, affair)* questione *f,* faccenda; **money ~s** questioni finanziarie; **the ~ in hand** l'argomento *or* la faccenda in questione; **there's the ~ of my wages** ci sarebbe la questione del mio stipendio; **and to make ~s worse...** e come se non bastasse...; **that will only make ~s worse** questo servirà solo a peggiorare la situazione; **it's a ~ of great concern to us** è una cosa che ci preoccupa molto; **it's no laughing ~** è una cosa *or* faccenda seria; **it will be a ~ of a few weeks** ci vorrà qualche settimana; **it's a ~ of a few pounds** si tratta di poche sterline; **in the ~ of** in fatto di, per quanto riguarda; **for that ~** peraltro; **as a ~ of course** di conseguenza, come cosa naturale; **as a ~ of fact** per (dire) la verità; **it's a ~ of opinion** è una questione di punti di vista.

(e) *(importance):* **no ~!** non importa!; **do it, no ~ how** non importa come, basta che tu lo faccia; **no ~ how you do it** comunque tu lo faccia; **no ~ what he says** qualsiasi *or* qualunque cosa dica; **no ~ how big it is** per quanto grande sia; **no ~ when** in qualsiasi momento; **no ~ who** chiunque.

(f) *(difficulty, problem etc):* **what's the ~?** cosa c'è (che non va)?; **what's the ~ with you?** cos'hai?; **what's the ~ with my hair?** cos'hanno i miei capelli che non va?; **there's something the ~ with my arm** c'è qualcosa che non va al braccio; **as if nothing was the ~** come se niente fosse; **something's the ~ with the lights** le luci hanno qualcosa che non va; **nothing's the ~** non è successo niente; **nothing's the ~ with me** non ho niente.

2 *vi* importare; **it doesn't ~** non importa, non fa niente; **what does it ~?** cosa importa?, che importanza ha?; **what does it ~ to you?** ma a te che te ne importa?; **why should it ~ to me?** e perché dovrebbe importarmi?

matter-of-fact [,mætərəv'fækt] *adj (person, attitude)* pratico(a); *(tone, voice)* neutro(a); *(account)* che si limita ai fatti.

mat·tress ['mætrɪs] *n* materasso.

ma·ture [mə'tjʊə'] **1** *adj (-r, -st) (gen)* maturo(a); *(cheese)* stagionato(a); **he's much more ~** è molto più maturo. **2** *vi (gen)* maturarsi, maturare; *(cheese)* stagionarsi.

ma·tur·ity [mə'tjʊərɪtɪ] *n* maturità.

maud·lin ['mɔːdlɪn] *adj* piagnucoloso(a).

maul [mɔːl] *vt (subj: tiger etc)* dilaniare, sbranare; **~ed to death** morto sbranato.

mau·so·leum [,mɔːsə'lɪəm] *n* mausoleo.

mauve [məʊv] *adj (color)* malva *inv.*

mav·er·ick ['mævərɪk] *n (fig)* chi sta fuori del branco.

mawk·ish ['mɔːkɪʃ] *adj* svenevole.

max. *abbr (= maximum)* max.

max·im ['mæksɪm] *n* massima.

maxi·ma ['mæksɪmə] *npl of* **maximum.**

max·im·ize ['mæksɪmaɪz] *vt (profits etc)* massimizzare; *(chances)* aumentare al massimo.

maxi·mum ['mæksɪməm] **1** *n, pl* **maxima** *or* **~s** massimo. **2** *adj* massimo(a).

May [meɪ] **1** *n* maggio; *for usage see* **July. 2** *cpd:* **~ Day** *n* il primo maggio *(festa dei lavoratori).*

may [meɪ] *pt* **might** *modal aux vb* **(a)** *(possibility):* **he ~ come** può darsi che venga, può venire; **he might come** potrebbe venire, può anche darsi che venga; **he ~ not be hungry** potrebbe non aver fame, può darsi che non abbia fame; **they ~ well be connected** può darsi benissimo che ci sia un legame; **that's as ~ be** può anche darsi; **be that as it ~** comunque sia, sia come sia; **you ~ well ask!** è quello che mi chiedo anch'io!

(b) *(of permission)*: ~ **I have a cigarette? - yes, you ~** potrei avere una sigaretta? - sì, prego; ~ **I sit here?** le dispiace se mi sieda qua?; **if I ~ say** so se mi è concesso dirlo; ~ **I?** permette?; **might I suggest that...?** con il suo permesso suggerirei che...; **he said I might leave** mi ha detto che potevo andare.

(c): I hope he ~ succeed spero che ci riesca; **I hoped he might succeed this time** speravo che stavolta ci sarebbe riuscito; **we ~ or might as well go** tanto vale che ci andiamo; **he might have offered to help** avrebbe potuto offrirsi di aiutare; **as you might expect** come c'era da aspettarsi.

(d) *(in wishes)*: ~ **you have a happy life together** possiate vivere insieme felici; ~ **God bless you!** (che) Dio la benedica!

may·be ['meɪbi:] *adv* forse, può darsi; ~ **not** forse no, può darsi di no; ~ **tomorrow** forse *or* magari domani; ~ **he'll come** può darsi che venga, magari *or* forse verrà.

may·day ['meɪdeɪ] *n* (Aer, Naut) S.O.S. *m inv.*

may·on·naise [,meɪə'neɪz] *n* maionese *f*.

mayor [mɛəʳ] *n* sindaco; **Lord M~** titolo del sindaco nelle grandi città.

mayor·ess ['mɛərɛs] *n* moglie *f* del sindaco.

may·pole ['meɪpəʊl] *n* palo ornato di fiori attorno a cui si danza durante la festa di maggio.

maze [meɪz] *n* dedalo, labirinto.

M.C. *abbr of* **Master of Ceremonies.**

M.D. *abbr of* **Doctor of Medicine.**

me [mi:] *pers pron* **(a)** *(direct: unstressed)* mi, m' + *vowel or silent 'h'; (: stressed)* me; **he can hear ~** mi sente; **he heard ~** mi ha *or* m'ha sentito; **he heard me!** ha sentito me! **(b)** *(indirect)* mi, m' + *vowel or silent 'h';* **he gave ~ the money, he gave the money to ~** mi ha *or* m'ha dato i soldi; **he gave them to ~** me li ha dati; **give them to ~** dammeli. **(c)** *(after prep etc)* me; **it's for ~** è per me; **without ~** senza (di) me; **it's ~** sono io.

mead·ow ['mɛdəʊ] *n* prato, pascolo.

mea·gre, *(Am)* **mea·ger** ['mi:gəʳ] *adj* magro(a), misero(a).

meal[1] [mi:l] *n (flour etc)* farina.

meal[2] [mi:l] **1** *n* pasto; **to have a ~** mangiare; **to have a good ~** mangiar bene; **to go out for a ~** mangiare fuori; **what a lovely ~** che pranzo delizioso (*or* cena deliziosa); **to make a ~ of sth** *(fam)* fare di qc un affare di stato. **2** *cpd:* ~ **ticket** *n (Am)* buono *m* pasto *inv; (fig fam: job)* che dà di che vivere; **he's her ~ ticket** la mantiene.

meal·time ['mi:ltaɪm] *n* ora di mangiare.

mealy-mouthed ['mi:lɪmaʊðd] *adj* che parla per eufemismi.

mean[1] [mi:n] *adj* **(-er, -est) (a)** *(with money)* avaro(a), spilorcio(a); ~ **with** avaro con. **(b)** *(unkind, spiteful)* meschino(a); **a ~ trick** uno scherzo ignobile; **you ~ thing!** *(fam)* che meschino!; **it made me feel ~** mi ha fatto sentire un verme. **(c)** *(Am: vicious: animal)* cattivo(a); *(: person)* perfido(a). **(d)** *(poor: appearance, district)* misero(a); **she's no ~ cook** è una cuoca tutt'altro che disprezzabile.

mean[2] [mi:n] **1** *n* **(a)** *(middle term)* mezzo; *(Math)* media; **the golden** *or* **happy ~** il giusto mezzo.

(b): ~**s** *(method or way of doing)* mezzo, modo; **to find the ~s to do** *or* **of doing sth** trovare il mezzo di fare qc; **to find a ~s of doing sth** trovare il modo per fare qc; **a ~s to an end** un modo *or* mezzo per raggiungere i propri fini; **there is no ~s of doing it** non c'è mezzo *or* modo di farlo; **by ~s of** per mezzo di; **by this ~s** in questo modo, così; **by some ~s or other** in un modo o nell'altro;

by all ~s! ma certamente!; **by no ~s, not by any** ~s per niente, niente affatto; **by all manner of** ~s in tutti i modi. **(c):** ~**s** *npl (Fin)* mezzi *mpl;* **private** ~**s** rendite *fpl;* **to live within/beyond one's** ~**s** vivere secondo i/al di sopra dei propri mezzi.

2 *adj* medio(a).

3 *cpd:* ~**s test** *n* accertamento dei redditi *(per una persona che ha chiesto un aiuto finanziario).*

mean[3] [mi:n] *pt, pp* **meant** *vt* **(a)** significare, voler dire; **what does that word ~?** che significa quella parola?; **what do you ~ by that?** cosa vuoi dire con questo?; **you don't ~ that, do you?** non parli sul serio, vero?; **I ~ what I say** parlo sul serio; **it** ~**s a lot of expense for us** per noi questo vuol dire una grossa spesa; **the play didn't ~ a thing to me** la commedia non mi ha detto niente; **your friendship** ~**s much to me** la tua amicizia è molto importante per me; **his name** ~**s nothing to me** il suo nome non mi dice niente; **she** ~**s nothing to me** non conta niente per me.

(b) *(intend)* intendere; **to ~ to do sth** intendere fare qc; **I meant it for her** era destinato a lei; **I meant it as a joke** volevo solo scherzare; **what do you ~ to do?** cosa intendi fare?; **cosa pensi di fare?; he didn't ~ to do it** non intendeva *or* non era sua intenzione farlo; **do you ~ me?** *(are you speaking to me?)* dici a me?; *(about me)* ti riferisci a me?; **was the remark meant for me?** l'osservazione era diretta a me?; **Roberta is meant to do it** è Roberta che lo deve fare; **I ~ to be obeyed** intendo essere ubbidito; **he ~s well** ha delle buone intenzioni; **he said it as if he meant it** l'ha detto senza scherzare; **do you really ~ it?** dici sul serio?

me·ander [mɪ'ændəʳ] *vi (river)* fare dei meandri; *(person etc)* girovagare; *(: fig)* divagare.

mean·ing ['mi:nɪŋ] *n* significato; **a look full of ~** uno sguardo eloquente; **do you get my ~?** capisci cosa voglio dire?; **what's the ~ of this?** *(as reprimand)* e questo cosa significa?

mean·ing·ful ['mi:nɪŋfʊl] *adj (word, look)* significativo(a), eloquente; *(relationship)* valido(a).

mean·ing·less ['mi:nɪŋlɪs] *adj* senza senso; **your remarks are quite ~** i tuoi commenti non vogliono dire niente.

mean·ness ['mi:nnɪs] *n (see adj)* avarizia, spilorceria; meschinità; cattiveria; perfidia.

meant [mɛnt] *pt, pp of* **mean.**

mean·time ['mi:ntaɪm] *adv,* **mean·while** ['mi:nwaɪl] *adv (also:* **in the ~)** nel frattempo, e intanto.

mea·sles ['mi:zlz] *n* morbillo.

mea·sly ['mi:zlɪ] *adj* **(-ier, -iest)** *(fam)* misero(a), miserabile.

meas·ure ['mɛʒəʳ] **1** *n* **(a)** *(gen)* misura; *(tape ~)* metro; **a litre ~** una misura da un litro; **to give full ~** dare il peso giusto (*or* la quantità giusta); **for good ~** *(fig)* in più, in aggiunta; **her happiness was beyond ~** era felice oltre ogni limite; **in some/large ~** in parte/gran parte; **some ~ of success** un certo successo; **I've got her ~** *(fig)* so quanto vale. **(b)** *(step)* misura, provvedimento; **to take ~s to do sth** prendere provvedimenti per fare qc. **2** *vt* misurare; *(take sb's measurements)* prendere le misure di; **to ~ one's length** *(fig: fall)* cadere lungo disteso.

♦ **measure off** *vt + adv* misurare.

♦ **measure out** *vt + adv* calcolare.

♦ **measure up** *vi + adv:* **to ~ up (to)** dimostrarsi *or* essere all'altezza (di).

meas·ured ['mɛʒəd] *adj* misurato(a).

meas·ure·ment ['mɛʒəmənt] *n (act)* misurazione *f; (measure)* misura; **to take sb's ~s** prendere le misure di qn.

meat [miːt] n carne f; **cold** ~s affettati mpl; **crab** ~ polpa di granchio; ~ **and drink** da mangiare e da bere; **this is** ~ **and drink to them** (fig) questo per loro è una delizia.

meat·ball ['miːtbɔːl] n polpetta di carne.

meaty ['miːtɪ] adj (-ier, -iest) (flavour) di carne; (fig: book, talk) sostanzioso(a).

me·chan·ic [mɪ'kænɪk] n meccanico; **motor** ~ motorista m.

me·chani·cal [mɪ'kænɪkəl] adj (also fig) meccanico(a); ~ **engineer** ingegnere m meccanico; ~ **engineering** (science) ingegneria meccanica; (industry) costruzioni fpl meccaniche.

me·chan·ics [mɪ'kænɪks] n (a) (sg: science) meccanica. (b) (pl: of car etc) meccanismo, meccanica; (: fig: of legal system etc) meccanismo; (: of novel writing etc) tecnica.

mecha·nism ['mekənɪzəm] n meccanismo.

mecha·nize ['mekənaɪz] vt (process, industry) meccanizzare; (troops etc) motorizzare.

med·al ['medl] n medaglia.

me·dal·lion [mɪ'dæljən] n medaglione m.

med·al·list, (Am) **med·al·ist** ['medəlɪst] n: to be a gold/silver ~ essere medaglia d'oro/d'argento.

med·dle ['medl] vi (interfere): to ~ (in) immischiarsi (in); (tamper): to ~ with sth toccare qc; **stop meddling!** smettila di impicciarti!

med·dler ['medlər] n (busybody) impiccione/a; (touching things) uno/a che tocca tutto.

med·dle·some ['medlsəm] adj, **med·dling** ['medlɪŋ] adj (interfering) che mette il naso dappertutto; (touching things) che tocca tutto.

me·dia ['miːdɪə] npl (a) pl of medium. (b) (Press, Radio, TV): the ~ i mass media; all the ~ were there tutta la stampa e la televisione erano sul posto.

me·di·aeval [,medɪ'iːvəl] adj = medieval.

me·di·ate ['miːdɪeɪt] 1 vi fare da mediatore (or mediatrice). 2 vt (settlement) mediare.

me·dia·tion [,miːdɪ'eɪʃən] n mediazione f.

me·dia·tor ['miːdɪeɪtər] n mediatore/trice.

medi·cal ['medɪkəl] 1 adj (school, student, ward) di medicina; (test, treatment) medico(a); ~ **board** commissione f sanitaria; ~ **certificate** certificato medico; ~ **examination** visita medica; ~ **jurisprudence** medicina legale. 2 n visita medica.

Medi·care ['medɪkeər] n (Am) assistenza medica agli anziani.

medi·ca·ted ['medɪkeɪtɪd] adj medicato(a).

medi·ca·tion [,medɪ'keɪʃən] n (drugs etc) medicinali mpl, farmaci mpl.

me·dici·nal [me'dɪsɪnl] adj medicinale, medicamentoso(a).

medi·cine ['medsɪn, 'medɪsɪn] 1 n (a) (drug) medicina; **to give sb a taste of his own** ~ (fig) rendere pan per focaccia. (b) (science) medicina. 2 cpd: ~ **cabinet** or **chest** n armadietto delle medicine; ~ **man** n stregone m.

me·di·eval [,medɪ'iːvəl] adj medievale, del medio evo.

me·dio·cre [,miːdɪ'əʊkər] adj mediocre.

me·di·oc·rity [,miːdɪ'ɒkrɪtɪ] n mediocrità.

medi·tate ['medɪteɪt] 1 vi: to ~ (on or about) meditare (su). 2 vt meditare.

medi·ta·tion [,medɪ'teɪʃən] n meditazione f.

Medi·ter·ra·nean [,medɪtə'reɪnɪən] adj mediterraneo(a); the ~ (Sea) il (mar) Mediterraneo.

me·dium ['miːdɪəm] 1 adj medio(a); ~ **wave** (Radio) onde fpl medie. 2 n, pl media or ~s (a) (gen, Phys) mezzo; (environment) ambiente m, habitat m inv; **through the** ~ **of the press** per mezzo della stampa; **an advertising** ~ un organo di pubblici-

tà; **the artist's** ~ i mezzi espressivi dell'artista. (b) (midpoint): **happy** ~ giusta misura. (c) (spiritualist) medium m/f inv.

medium-sized ['miːdjəm,saɪzd] adj (tin etc) di grandezza media; (clothes) di taglia media.

med·ley ['medlɪ] n miscuglio, accozzaglia; (Mus) pot-pourri m inv.

meek [miːk] adj dolce, mite; ~ **and mild** mite come un agnello.

meet [miːt] pt, pp met 1 vt (a) (gen) incontrare; (coming in opposite direction) incrociare; (by arrangement) dare appuntamento a; **to arrange to** ~ **sb** dare appuntamento a qn; **she ran out to** ~ **us** ci è corsa incontro; **to** ~ **sb off the train** (andare a) aspettare or andare a prendere qn al treno; **the car will** ~ **the train** ci sarà una macchina all'arrivo del treno; **to** ~ **sb's eye** or gaze guardar qn dritto negli occhi; **a terrible sight met him** or **his eyes** gli si presentò un orrendo spettacolo; **there's more to this than** ~s **the eye** è molto più complicato di quanto possa sembrare a prima vista.

(b) (get to know, be introduced to) fare la conoscenza di, essere presentato(a) a; ~ **my brother** le presento mio fratello; **pleased to** ~ **you!** lieto di conoscerla!, piacere!

(c) (encounter: team, difficulty) incontrare; (face: enemy, danger, death) affrontare; **to** ~ **one's death** trovare la morte.

(d) (give satisfaction on: requirement, demand, need) soddisfare, andare incontro a; (: criticism, objection) ribattere a; (: bill, expenses) far fronte a; **we agree to** ~ **your expenses** siamo d'accordo a pagarle le spese.

2 vi (a) (gen) incontrarsi; (by arrangement) darsi appuntamento, trovarsi; (committee, society) riunirsi; **until we** ~ **again!** arrivederci (alla prossima volta)!; **haven't we met before?** non ci conosciamo già?

(b) (join: rivers, teams, armies) incontrarsi.

3 n (Hunting) raduno (dei partecipanti alla caccia alla volpe); (Am Sport) raduno (sportivo).

♦ **meet up** vi + adv incontrarsi, vedersi; **to** ~ **up with sb** incontrare qn.

♦ **meet with** vi + prep (a) (success, difficulties, praise etc) incontrare; (welcome) ricevere; **they met with an accident** hanno avuto un incidente. (b) (have meeting with) incontrarsi con.

meet·ing ['miːtɪŋ] 1 n (a) (between individuals) incontro; (arranged) appuntamento; (formal) colloquio; **the minister had a** ~ **with the ambassador** il ministro ha avuto un colloquio con or si è incontrato con l'ambasciatore. (b) (of club, committee, council) riunione f; (of members, citizens, employees) assemblea; **to call a** ~ convocare una riunione; **Mr Stark is in a** ~ il signor Stark è in riunione. (c) (Sport: rally) raduno. 2 cpd: ~ **place** n luogo d'incontro.

mega·lo·ma·ni·ac [,megələʊ'meɪnɪæk] n megalomane m/f.

mega·phone ['megəfəʊn] n megafono.

mel·an·choly ['melənkəlɪ] 1 adj (person) malinconico(a); (duty, subject) triste. 2 n malinconia.

mel·low ['meləʊ] 1 adj (-er, -est) (fruit) ben maturo(a); (wine) maturo(a) e pastoso(a); (colour, light) caldo(a) e morbido(a); (person, character) addolcito(a) dall'età. 2 vi (fruit, wine) maturare, maturarsi; (colour, sound) attenuarsi, smorzarsi; (person, character) addolcirsi. 3 vt: **old age has** ~**ed him** con l'età si è addolcito.

me·lo·dious [mɪ'ləʊdɪəs] adj melodioso(a).

melo·dra·ma ['melaʊ,drɑːmə] n melodramma m.

melo·dra·mat·ic [ˌmɛləʊdrə'mætɪk] adj melo-drammatico(a).

melo·dy ['mɛlədɪ] n melodia.

mel·on ['mɛlən] n melone m.

melt [mɛlt] **1** vt **(a)** (gen) sciogliere; (metal) fondere; ~ed butter burro fuso. **(b)** (fig: heart) intenerire; (: anger) far svanire. **2** vi **(a)** sciogliersi; it ~s in the mouth si scioglie in bocca. **(b)** (fig: anger, determination) svanire; (: heart) intenerirsi; he ~ed into the crowd si confuse tra la folla.
♦ **melt away** vi + adv (snow, ice) sciogliersi completamente; (fog) dileguarsi; (anger, anxiety, opposition) svanire; (savings) andare in fumo; (crowd) disperdersi; he ~ed away into the crowd svanì tra la folla.
♦ **melt down** vt + adv fondere.

melt·ing ['mɛltɪŋ] **1** adj (snow) che si scioglie (or scioglieva etc); (voice, look) tenero(a). **2** cpd: ~ point n punto di fusione; ~ pot n (fig) crogiolo; to be in the ~ pot essere ancora in discussione.

mem·ber ['mɛmbə'] **1** n (gen) membro; (of club) socio/a, iscritto/a; (of political party) iscritto/a; she's like a ~ of the family è come una di famiglia; '~s only' 'riservato ai soci'; ~ of staff (Scol, Univ) insegnante m/f; a ~ of the staff (gen) un dipendente; ~ of parliament ≈ deputato (al parlamento); ~ of the public privato cittadino. **2** cpd: ~ countries npl paesi mpl membri.

mem·ber·ship ['mɛmbəʃɪp] **1** n: ~ (of) iscrizione f (a); the club has a ~ of 950 il club ha 950 iscritti. **2** cpd: ~ card n tessera (di iscrizione).

mem·brane ['mɛmbreɪn] n membrana.

me·men·to [mə'mɛntəʊ] n ricordo, souvenir m inv.

memo ['mɛməʊ] **1** n (abbr of memorandum) promemoria m inv; (: to staff) comunicazione f interna. **2** cpd: ~ pad n blocchetto per appunti.

mem·oir ['mɛmwɑː'] n (essay) saggio monografico; (biography) nota biografica; ~s (autobiographical) memorie fpl.

memo·rable ['mɛmərəbl] adj (day) memorabile; (beauty) notevole.

memo·ran·dum [ˌmɛmə'rændəm] n, pl memoranda (gen) memorandum m inv; (within company) comunicazione f interna.

me·mo·rial [mɪ'mɔːrɪəl] **1** adj commemorativo(a). **2** n monumento; as a ~ to in commemorazione di; War M~ monumento ai caduti.

memo·rize ['mɛməraɪz] vt imparare a memoria.

memo·ry ['mɛmərɪ] n **(a)** (faculty, of computer) memoria; to have a good/bad ~ aver buona/cattiva memoria; loss of ~ amnesia; I have a bad ~ for faces non sono fisionomista; he recited the poem from ~ ha recitato la poesia a memoria. **(b)** (recollection) ricordo; I have no ~ of it non me lo ricordo affatto. **(c)**: in ~ of in memoria di; to the ~ of alla memoria di.

men [mɛn] npl of **man**.

men·ace ['mɛnɪs] **1** n minaccia; (fam: nuisance) peste f; a public ~ un pericolo pubblico. **2** vt minacciare.

men·ac·ing ['mɛnɪsɪŋ] adj minaccioso(a).

mend [mɛnd] **1** n: to be on the ~ star migliorando. **2** vt (repair: fence, car, clothes) aggiustare; (improve): to ~ one's ways correggersi; to ~ matters risolvere le cose. **3** vi (broken bone) rimettersi a posto.

men·folk ['mɛnfəʊk] npl uomini mpl.

me·nial ['miːnɪəl] adj (position) subalterno(a); (work, task) umile, servile.

men·in·gi·tis [ˌmɛnɪn'dʒaɪtɪs] n meningite f.

meno·pause ['mɛnəʊpɔːz] n menopausa.

men·stru·ate ['mɛnstrʊeɪt] vi avere le mestruazioni.

men·stru·a·tion [ˌmɛnstrʊ'eɪʃən] n mestruazione f.

men·tal ['mɛntl] adj **(a)** (gen) mentale, della mente; (ability, powers) intellettuale; (treatment) psichiatrico(a); to make a ~ note of sth prendere mentalmente nota di qc; ~ arithmetic calcolo mentale; ~ defective ritardato mentale; ~ home or hospital or institution ospedale m per malattie mentali; ~ illness malattia mentale. **(b)** (fam: mad) pazzo(a).

men·tal·ity [mɛn'tælɪtɪ] n mentalità f inv.

men·tal·ly ['mɛntəlɪ] adv (calculate) mentalmente, a mente; to be ~ handicapped/defective essere minorato psichico/ritardato mentale; she is ~ ill è malata di mente.

men·thol ['mɛnθɒl] **1** n mentolo. **2** adj al mentolo.

men·tion ['mɛnʃən] **1** n menzione f, accenno; it's hardly worth a ~ non è neanche il caso di parlarne. **2** vt (gen) accennare a; (name, person) fare il nome di, menzionare; I ~ed it to him glielo ho accennato; just ~ my name basta che tu faccia il mio nome; all those people, too numerous to ~, who... tutti coloro che qui sarebbe troppo lungo elencare, i quali...; I need hardly ~ that... inutile dire che...; not to ~, without ~ing per non parlare di, senza contare; don't ~ it! non c'è di che!

menu ['mɛnjuː] n menù m inv.

mer·ce·nary ['mɜːsɪnərɪ] **1** adj (person) mercenario(a); (motive) venale. **2** n mercenario.

mer·chan·dise ['mɜːtʃəndaɪz] **1** n merce f. **2** vt commercializzare.

mer·chant ['mɜːtʃənt] **1** n (trader) commerciante m; (shopkeeper) negoziante m. **2** cpd: ~ bank n istituto di sconto; ~ navy n marina mercantile; ~ seaman n marinaio (di nave mercantile).

mer·ci·ful ['mɜːsɪfʊl] adj (Rel) misericordioso(a); (person) compassionevole; it was a ~ release è stata una vera liberazione.

mer·ci·ful·ly ['mɜːsɪfəlɪ] adv con clemenza; (fortunately) per fortuna.

mer·ci·less ['mɜːsɪlɪs] adj spietato(a).

Mer·cu·ry ['mɜːkjʊrɪ] n (Astron, Mythology) Mercurio.

mer·cu·ry ['mɜːkjʊrɪ] n (Chim) mercurio.

mer·cy ['mɜːsɪ] **1** n pietà, clemenza; (Rel) misericordia; to be at the ~ of sb/sth essere alla mercè or in balia di qn/qc; to have ~ on sb avere pietà di qn; to be left to the tender mercies of sb essere lasciato alle buone cure di qn (iro); it's a ~ that è una fortuna che + sub. **2** cpd: ~ killing n eutanasia.

mere [mɪə'] adj (formality) semplice, puro(a) (before n); (thought etc) solo(a) (before n); (chance, coincidence, spite) puro(a) (before n); she's a ~ child non è che una bambina; the ~ sight of him irritates her solo a vederlo s'arrabbia; she's a ~ secretary è una semplice segretaria.

mere·ly ['mɪəlɪ] adv soltanto, semplicemente.

merge [mɜːdʒ] **1** vt (Comm) fondere. **2** vi (colours, sounds, shapes etc): to ~ (into, with) fondersi (con), confondersi (con); (roads): to ~ (with) unirsi (a); (river): to ~ (with) confluire (in). **(b)** (Comm) fondersi.

mer·ger ['mɜːdʒə'] n (Comm) fusione f.

me·ringue [mə'ræŋ] n meringa.

mer·it ['mɛrɪt] **1** n merito; to look or inquire into the ~s of sth valutare or pesare il pro e il contro di qc; to treat a case on its ~s trattare un caso con obiettività. **2** vt meritare.

meri·toc·ra·cy [ˌmɛrɪ'tɒkrəsɪ] n meritocrazia.

mer·maid ['mɜːmeɪd] n sirena.

mer·ri·ment ['mɛrɪmənt] n allegria; (laughter) ilarità.

mer·ry ['mɛrɪ] adj (-ier, -iest) (cheerful) allegro(a),

festoso(a); *(fam: tipsy)* brillo(a); **M~ Christmas!** Buon Natale!

merry-go-round ['mɛrɪgəʊ,raʊnd] *n* giostra.

mesh [mɛʃ] *n* **(a)** *(in net etc)* maglia; **a 6-cm ~ net** una rete con maglie di 6 cm. **(b)** *(network, net)* rete *f;* **wire ~** rete metallica. **(c)** *(gears etc)*: **in ~** ingranato(a).

mes·mer·ize ['mɛzmǝraɪz] *vt* ipnotizzare; **she was ~d** *(fig)* non poteva distogliere lo sguardo.

mess [mɛs] *n* **(a)** *(confusion of objects)* disordine *m,* confusione *f; (dirt)* sporcizia; *(awkward predicament)* pasticcio; **you look a ~!** guarda in che stato sei!; **to be (in) a ~** *(house, room)* essere in disordine *(or* molto sporco*); (fig: marriage, life etc)* essere un caos; **to make a ~** fare un gran disordine *(or* sporcare*)* dappertutto; **the dog has made a ~** il cane ha sporcato; **to make a ~ of** *(dirty)* sporcare; *(tear)* strappare; *(wreck)* sfasciare; **to make a ~ of one's life/career** rovinarsi la vita/la carriera; **I made a ~ of the exam** ho fatto un pasticcio all'esame; **to be/get (o.s.) in a ~** essere/cacciarsi in un pasticcio. **(b)** *(Mil etc)* mensa.

♦**mess about, mess around** *(fam)* **1** *vt + adv (person)* prendere in giro; *(plans)* scombinare. **2** *vi + adv (play the fool)* far confusione; *(waste time)* perdere tempo; *(in water, mud)* pasticciare; **to ~ about** *or* **around with sth** armeggiare *or* trafficare con qc; **to ~ about** *or* **around with sb** divertirsi con qn; **what are you doing? — just ~ing about** cosa fai? — niente di speciale.

♦**mess up** *vt + adv (room etc)* mettere sottosopra; *(dress)* sporcare; *(hair)* scompigliare; *(fig: plan, marriage, situation)* mandare a monte.

mes·sage ['mɛsɪdʒ] *n* messaggio; **to get the ~** *(fig fam)* capire l'antifona.

mes·sen·ger ['mɛsɪndʒǝʳ] **1** *n* messaggero/a; *(in office)* messo. **2** *cpd:* **~ boy** *n* fattorino.

Mes·si·ah [mɪ'saɪǝ] *n* Messia *m.*

Messrs ['mɛsǝz] *abbr (on letters)* Spett.

messy ['mɛsɪ] *adj* (**-ier, -iest**) *(dirty: clothes etc)* sporco(a); *(: job)* che insudicia; *(untidy)* disordinato(a); *(confused: situation etc)* ingarbugliato(a).

met [mɛt] *pt, pp of* **meet.**

met·al ['mɛtl] **1** *n* metallo; **road ~** pietrisco. **2** *adj* in metallo; **~ polish** lucido per metalli.

me·tal·lic [mɪ'tælɪk] *adj* metallico(a).

met·al·lur·gy [mɛ'tælǝdʒɪ] *n* metallurgia.

metal·work ['mɛtlwɜːk] *n (craft)* lavorazione *f* del metallo.

meta·mor·pho·sis [,mɛtǝ'mɔːfǝsɪs] *n, pl* **metamorphoses** [,mɛtǝ'mɔːfǝsiːz] metamorfosi *f inv.*

meta·phor ['mɛtǝfǝʳ] *n* metafora.

meta·phor·ic(al) [,mɛtǝ'fɒrɪk(ǝl)] *adj* metaforico(a).

meta·physi·cal [,mɛtǝ'fɪzɪkǝl] *adj* metafisico(a).

meta·phys·ics [,mɛtǝ'fɪzɪks] *nsg* metafisica.

mete [miːt] *vi:* **to ~ out** *(punishment)* ripartire.

me·teor ['miːtɪǝʳ] *n* meteora.

me·teor·ic [,miːtɪ'ɒrɪk] *adj* meteorico(a); *(fig)* fulmineo(a).

me·teor·ite ['miːtɪǝraɪt] *n* meteorite *m.*

me·teoro·logi·cal [,miːtɪǝrǝ'lɒdʒɪkǝl] *adj* meteorologico(a).

me·teor·ol·ogy [,miːtɪǝ'rɒlǝdʒɪ] *n* meteorologia.

me·ter[1] ['miːtǝʳ] *n (gen)* contatore *m; (parking ~)* parchimetro; **electricity/gas ~** contatore della luce/del gas.

me·ter[2] ['miːtǝʳ] *n (Am)* = **metre.**

me·thane ['miːθeɪn] *n* metano.

meth·od ['mɛθǝd] *n* **(a)** metodo; **there's ~ in his madness** la sua follia non è priva di logica. **(b)** *(manner, way)* metodo, sistema *m;* **my ~ of**

working il mio metodo di lavoro; **~ of payment** modo *or* modalità *f inv* di pagamento.

me·thodi·cal [mɪ'θɒdɪkǝl] *adj* metodico(a).

meth·od·ol·ogy [,mɛθǝ'dɒlǝdʒɪ] *n* metodologia.

meths [mɛθs] *n abbr of* **methylated spirit(s).**

meth·yl·at·ed spir·it(s) ['mɛθɪleɪtɪd'spɪrɪt(s)] *n(pl)* alcool *m inv* denaturato.

me·ticu·lous [mɪ'tɪkjʊlǝs] *adj* meticoloso(a).

me·tre, *(Am)* **me·ter** ['miːtǝʳ] *n (all senses)* metro.

met·ric ['mɛtrɪk] *adj* metrico(a); **to go ~** adottare il sistema metrico decimale.

met·ri·ca·tion [,mɛtrɪ'keɪʃǝn] *n* conversione *f* al sistema metrico decimale.

me·tropo·lis [mɪ'trɒpǝlɪs] *n* metropoli *f inv.*

met·ro·poli·tan [,mɛtrǝ'pɒlɪtǝn] *adj* metropolitano(a).

met·tle ['mɛtl] *n:* **to be on one's ~** essere pronto(a) a dare il meglio di se stesso(a).

mew [mjuː] **1** *n* miagolio. **2** *vi* miagolare.

mews [mjuːz] *n (Brit):* **~ flat** appartamentino ricavato da una vecchia scuderia.

Mexi·can ['mɛksɪkǝn] *adj, n* messicano(a) *(m/f).*

Mexi·co ['mɛksɪkǝʊ] *n* Messico.

mezzo-soprano [,mɛtsǝʊsǝ'prɑːnǝʊ] *n (voice, singer)* mezzosoprano.

mi·aow [miː'aʊ] **1** *n* miao. **2** *vi* miagolare.

mica ['maɪkǝ] *n* mica.

mice [maɪs] *npl of* **mouse.**

mick·ey ['mɪkɪ] *n (fam):* **to take the ~ out of sb** prendere qn per i fondelli *or* in giro.

micro... ['maɪkrǝʊ] *pref* micro... .

mi·crobe ['maɪkrǝʊb] *n* microbo.

micro·bi·ol·ogy [,maɪkrǝʊbaɪ'ɒlǝdʒɪ] *n* microbiologia.

micro·chip ['maɪkrǝʊtʃɪp] *n (Elec)* microcircuito integrato, chip *m inv.*

micro·com·put·er [,maɪkrǝʊkǝm'pjuːtǝʳ] *n* microcomputer *m inv.*

micro·cosm ['maɪkrǝʊkɒzǝm] *n* microcosmo.

micro·film ['maɪkrǝʊfɪlm] *n* microfilm *m inv.*

micro·phone ['maɪkrǝfǝʊn] *n* microfono.

micro·scope ['maɪkrǝskǝʊp] *n* microscopio; **under the ~** al microscopio.

micro·scop·ic(al) [,maɪkrǝ'skɒpɪk(ǝl)] *adj* microscopico(a).

mid [mɪd] *adj:* **in ~ morning** a metà (della) mattina; **in ~ journey** a metà del viaggio; **in ~ June** a metà giugno; **in ~ air** a mezz'aria; *(fig: abandon sth etc)* in sospeso; **in ~ Atlantic** in mezzo all'Atlantico; **he's in his ~ thirties** ha passato la trentina.

mid·day [mɪd'deɪ] **1** *n* mezzogiorno; **at ~** a mezzogiorno. **2** *cpd* di mezzogiorno.

mid·dle ['mɪdl] **1** *adj (of place)* di mezzo, centrale; *(in quality, size etc)* medio(a); **the ~ chair in the row** la sedia nel centro della fila. **2** *n (centre)* mezzo, centro; *(fam: waist)* vita, cintura; **in the ~ of the field** in mezzo al campo; **a village in the ~ of nowhere** un paese sperduto; **in the ~ of summer** in piena estate; **I'm in the ~ of reading it** sto proprio leggendolo ora. **3** *cpd:* **~ age** *n* mezza età; **the M~ Ages** *npl* il Medio Evo; **~ C** *n (Mus)* do sotto il rigo; **the ~ class(es)** *n(pl)* il ceto medio, la borghesia; **M~ East** *n* Medio Oriente *m;* **~ finger** *n* medio; **~ management** *n* quadri *mpl* intermedi; **~ name** *n* secondo nome *m.*

middle-aged [,mɪdl'eɪdʒd] *adj* di mezza età.

middle-class [,mɪdl'klɑːs] *adj* borghese, della borghesia.

middle·man ['mɪdlmæn] *n, pl* **-men** *(gen)* intermediario; *(Comm)* rivenditore *m.*

middle-of-the-road [,mɪdlǝvðǝ'rǝʊd] *adj* moderato(a).

midge [mɪdʒ] *n* moscerino; *(biting)* pappataci *m inv*.

midg·et ['mɪdʒɪt] *n* nano/a.

Mid·lands ['mɪdləndz] *npl* regione *f* centrale dell'Inghilterra.

mid·night ['mɪdnaɪt] **1** *n* mezzanotte *f;* **at** ~ a mezzanotte. **2** *cpd (gen)* di mezzanotte; *(attack)* a mezzanotte; **to burn the** ~ **oil** lavorare fino a tarda notte.

mid·riff ['mɪdrɪf] *n (diaphragm)* diaframma *m; (stomach)* stomaco.

midst [mɪdst] *n*: **in the** ~ **of** in mezzo a; *(during)* durante.

mid·sum·mer ['mɪd,sʌmə^r] *n* piena estate *f;* **M~('s) Day** festa di San Giovanni *(24 giugno)*.

mid·way [,mɪd'weɪ] *adv, adj* a metà strada.

mid·week [,mɪd'wi:k] *adv, adj* a metà settimana.

mid·wife ['mɪdwaɪf] *n, pl* -**wives** levatrice *f*, ostetrica.

mid·win·ter [,mɪd'wɪntə^r] *n* pieno inverno.

might[1] [maɪt] *pt of* **may**.

might[2] [maɪt] *n* forza, forze *fpl;* **with all one's** ~ con tutte le proprie forze.

mighty ['maɪtɪ] **1** *adj* (**-ier, -iest**) *(ruler, nation, warrior)* possente; *(ocean)* vasto(a). **2** *adv (fam)* molto.

mi·graine ['mi:greɪn] *n* emicrania.

mi·grant ['maɪgrənt] **1** *adj (bird)* migratore(trice); *(worker)* emigrante. **2** *n (see adj)* migratore/trice; emigrante *m/f*.

mi·grate [maɪ'greɪt] *vi (bird)* migrare; *(worker)* emigrare.

mi·gra·tion [maɪ'greɪʃən] *n (see vb)* migrazione *f;* emigrazione *f*.

mike [maɪk] *n (fam)* microfono.

mild [maɪld] *adj* (**-er, -est**) *(climate, punishment, weather)* mite; *(character, person, cheese)* dolce; *(taste, curry)* non piccante; *(illness, sedative, beer, cigar)* leggero(a); *(effect)* blando(a); **it's** ~ **today** non fa freddo oggi.

mil·dew ['mɪldju:] *n* muffa.

mild·ly ['maɪldlɪ] *adv (gently)* gentilmente, dolcemente; *(slightly)* vagamente; **to put it** ~ *(fam)* per usare un eufemismo, a dir poco.

mile [maɪl] *n* miglio *(=* 1609,33 *m);* **to do 20** ~**s per gallon** = usare 14 litri per cento chilometri; ~**s and** ~**s** ≃ chilometri e chilometri; **they live** ~**s away** abitano lontanissimo; **it stands** *or* **sticks out a** ~ si capisce *(or* si vede) lontano un miglio.

mile·age ['maɪlɪdʒ] *n* ≃ chilometraggio; **what** ~ **does your car do?** = quanti chilometri al litro fa la tua macchina?

mile·om·eter [maɪ'lɒmɪtə^r] *n* = contachilometri *m inv*.

mile·stone ['maɪlstəʊn] *n (also fig)* pietra miliare.

mi·lieu ['mi:ljɜː] *n* ambiente *m* sociale.

mili·tant ['mɪlɪtənt] *adj, n* militante *(m/f)*.

mili·ta·rism ['mɪlɪtərɪzəm] *n* militarismo.

mili·ta·ris·tic [,mɪlɪtə'rɪstɪk] *adj* militaristico(a).

mili·tary ['mɪlɪtərɪ] **1** *adj* militare. **2** *npl:* **the** ~ i militari, l'esercito.

mili·tate ['mɪlɪteɪt] *vi:* **to** ~ **against** pregiudicare, essere di ostacolo a.

mi·li·tia [mɪ'lɪʃə] *n* milizie *fpl*.

milk [mɪlk] **1** *n* latte *m;* ~ **of magnesia** latte di magnesia; **it's no good crying over spilt** ~ *(Proverb)* è inutile piangere sul latte versato. **2** *vt* mungere; *(fig: person)* spillare quattrini a; *(: situation)* sfruttare fino in fondo. **3** *cpd:* ~ **chocolate** *n* cioccolato al latte; ~ **float** *n* furgone *m* del lattaio; ~ **shake** *n* frappé *m inv,* frullato; ~ **tooth** *n* dente *m* di latte.

milk·ing ma·chine ['mɪlkɪŋmə,ʃi:n] *n* mungitrice *f*.

milk·man ['mɪlkmən] *n, pl* -**men** lattaio.

milky ['mɪlkɪ] *adj* (**-ier, -iest**) *(substance)* lattiginoso(a); *(complexion)* latteo(a); *(coffee)* con tanto latte; **M~ Way** Via Lattea.

mill [mɪl] **1** *n* **(a)** *(gen)* mulino; *(Industry: for grain)* macina; *(wind~)* mulino a vento; **pepper** ~ macinapepe *m inv;* **coffee** ~ macinino da caffè; **to put sb through the** ~ *(fig)* mettere qn sotto torchio. **(b)** *(factory)* fabbrica, stabilimento; **cotton** ~ cotonificio; **paper** ~ cartiera; **steel** ~ acciaieria. **2** *vt (coffee, pepper, flour)* macinare; *(metal)* laminare; *(coin)* zigrinare. **3** *cpd:* ~ **worker** *n* operaio/a di cotonificio.

♦ **mill about, mill around** *vi* + *adv (crowd)* brulicare.

mil·len·nium [mɪ'lenɪəm] *n (period)* millennio; *(anniversary)* millenario; **the** ~ periodo (futuro) di pace e felicità.

mil·ler ['mɪlə^r] *n* mugnaio.

mil·let ['mɪlɪt] *n* miglio.

mil·li·gram(me) ['mɪlɪgræm] *n* milligrammo.

mil·li·li·tre, *(Am)* **mil·li·li·ter** ['mɪlɪ,li:tə^r] *n* millilitro.

mil·li·metre, *(Am)* **mil·li·meter** ['mɪlɪ,mi:tə^r] *n* millimetro.

mil·li·ner ['mɪlɪnə^r] *n* modista.

mil·lion ['mɪljən] *n* milione *m;* **a** ~ **women** un milione di donne; **thanks a** ~! *(fam)* grazie mille!; **she's one in a** ~ *(fam)* come lei ce ne sono poche; ~**s of** *(fam)* migliaia di, miliardi di; **you look like a** ~ **dollars** *(fam)* sei in forma smagliante.

mil·lion·aire [,mɪljə'nɛə^r] *n* milionario/a, ≃ miliardario/a.

mil·li·pede ['mɪlɪpi:d] *n* millepiedi *m inv*.

mill·pond ['mɪlpɒnd] *n*: **the sea is like a** ~ il mare è liscio come l'olio.

mill·stone ['mɪlstəʊn] *n* macina, mola; **it's a** ~ **round his neck** è un grosso peso per lui.

mime [maɪm] **1** *n (play)* mimo; *(skill, gestures)* mimica; *(actor)* mimo/a. **2** *vt, vi* mimare.

mim·ic ['mɪmɪk] **1** *n* imitatore/trice. **2** *vt (subj: comedian)* imitare; *(: animal, person)* scimmiottare.

mim·ic·ry ['mɪmɪkrɪ] *n* imitazioni *fpl; (Zool)* mimetismo.

min. *abbr (=* **minute(s); minimum**) min.

mince [mɪns] **1** *n (Culin)* carne *f* tritata *or* macinata. **2** *vt* tritare, macinare; **not to** ~ **one's words** non aver peli sulla lingua. **3** *vi (in walking)* camminare a passettini; *(in talking)* parlare con affettazione.

mince·meat ['mɪnsmi:t] *n* composto di frutta secca tritata e spezie; **to make** ~ **of** *(fig: person)* ridurre in polpette; *(: argument)* demolire.

minc·er ['mɪnsə^r] *n* tritacarne *m inv,* tritatutto *m inv*.

mind [maɪnd] **1** *n* **(a)** *(gen)* mente *f; (intellect)* intelletto; **a case of** ~ **over matter** una vittoria dello spirito sulla materia; **one of Britain's finest** ~**s** uno dei più grandi cervelli della Gran Bretagna; **I am not clear in my** ~ **about the idea** non ho delle idee chiare in proposito; **to be uneasy in one's** ~ avere dei dubbi, essere un po' preoccupato; **what's on your** ~? cosa c'è che ti preoccupa?; **I can't get it out of my** ~ non riesco a togliermelo dalla mente; **to put** *or* **set** *or* **give one's** ~ **to sth** concentrarsi su qc, applicarsi a qc; **that will take your** ~ **off it** questo ti aiuterà a non pensarci (più); **to bear** *or* **keep sth in** ~ *(take account of)* tener presente qc; *(remember)* non dimenticare qc, ricordare qc; **it went right out of my** ~ mi è completamente passato di mente, me ne sono completamente dimenticato; **to bring** *or* **call sth to** ~ riportare *or* richiamare qc alla mente.

(b) *(inclination, intention)* mente *f,* intenzione *f,* idea; **to have sb/sth in** ~ avere in mente qn/qc; **to have in** ~ **to do sth** avere intenzione *or* in mente di fare qc; **I have a good** ~ **to do it** avrei molta voglia di farlo; **I have half a** ~ **to do it** ho una mezza idea di farlo; **nothing was further from my** ~ non mi era nemmeno passato per l'anticamera del cervello; **to change one's** ~ cambiare idea.

(c) *(opinion)*: **to make up one's** ~ decidersi; **to be in two** ~**s about sth** essere incerto su qc; **to be in two** ~**s about doing sth** non sapersi decidere se fare qc o no; **of one** ~ della stessa idea; **I am still of the same** ~ sono ancora dello stesso parere; **to have a** ~ **of one's own** *(person: think for o.s.)* saper pensare con la propria testa; *(: not conform)* avere delle idee (tutte) proprie; **my car has a** ~ **of its own** la mia macchina fa un po' quello che vuole lei; **to my** ~ a mio parere, secondo me.

(d) *(sanity)* cervello, mente *f*, testa; **to go out of** *or* **lose one's** ~ impazzire; **to be out of one's** ~ essere pazzo, essere fuori di sé.

2 *vt* **(a)** *(pay attention to, be careful of)* fare attenzione a; **never** ~ *(don't worry)* non preoccuparti; *(it makes no odds)* non importa, non fa niente; **'please** ~ **the step'** 'attenti al gradino'; ~ **you don't fall** attento a non cadere; ~ **your language!** controlla le tue parole!; ~ **you, ...** *(fam)* sì, però va detto che...; ~ **your own business!** pensa ai fatti tuoi!; **never** ~ **him** non badargli, non fargli caso; **never** ~ **the expense** se costa caro, pazienza!; **don't** ~ **me!** *(iro)* per carità, non fare caso a me!

(b) *(oversee: shop, machine, children)* occuparsi di, badare a.

(c) *(be put out by, object to)*: **I don't** ~ **what he does** non m'importa cosa fa; **which? — I don't** ~ **quale? —** è indifferente; **I don't** ~ **the cold** il freddo non mi dà noia *or* fastidio; **would you** ~ **opening the door?** le dispiace aprire la porta?; **do you** ~ **if I open the window? — I don't** ~ le dispiace se apro la finestra? — faccia pure!; **I wouldn't** ~ **a cup of tea** prenderei volentieri una tazza di tè.

-minded ['maɪndɪd] *adj suf*: **fair**~ imparziale; **an industrially**~ **nation** una nazione orientata verso l'industria.

mind·ful ['maɪndfʊl] *adj*: ~ **of** conscio(a) di, consapevole di.

mind·less ['maɪndlɪs] *adj* *(violence, crime)* insensato(a); *(task)* che non richiede nessuna intelligenza, idiota.

mine[1] [maɪn] *poss pron* il(la) mio(a), pl i(le) miei(mie); **a friend of** ~ un mio amico; **his is red,** ~ **is green** il suo è rosso, il mio è verde; **this is** ~ questo è (il) mio.

mine[2] [maɪn] **1** *n* **(a)** *(Mineralogy)* miniera; **coal** ~ miniera di carbone; **to work down the** ~**s** lavorare in miniera; **a** ~ **of information** *(fig)* una miniera di informazioni. **(b)** *(Mil, Naut etc)* mina; **to lay** ~**s** posare delle mine. **2** *vt* **(a)** *(coal, metal)* estrarre. **(b)** *(Mil, Naut)* minare. **3** *vi* fare degli scavi minerari; **to** ~ **for sth** estrarre qc. **4** *cpd*: ~ **detector** *n* rivelatore *m* di mine.

mine·field ['maɪnfiːld] *n (also fig)* campo minato.

min·er ['maɪnəʳ] *n* minatore *m*.

min·er·al ['mɪnərəl] **1** *adj (substance, kingdom)* minerale; *(wealth, deposits, ore)* minerario(a); ~ **water** acqua minerale; *(soft drink)* bevanda gasata. **2** *n* minerale *m*; *(soft drink)*: ~**s** bevande *fpl* gasate.

mine·sweeper ['maɪn,swiːpəʳ] *n* dragamine *m inv*.

min·gle ['mɪŋgl] **1** *vt*: **to** ~ **(with)** mescolare (a). **2**

vi: **to** ~ **(with)** *(sounds etc)* mescolarsi (a); **to** ~ **with one's guests** mescolarsi agli ospiti.

mini ['mɪnɪ] *n* (~**skirt**) mini *f inv*.

minia·ture ['mɪnɪtʃəʳ] **1** *n* miniatura; **in** ~ in miniatura. **2** *cpd (gen)* in miniatura; *(poodle)* nano(a).

mini·bus ['mɪnɪbʌs] *n* minibus *m inv*, pulmino.

mini·mal ['mɪnɪml] *adj* minimo(a).

mini·mize ['mɪnɪmaɪz] *vt* minimizzare.

mini·mum ['mɪnɪməm] **1** *n* minima; **he does the** ~ **of work** lavora il meno possibile *or* il minimo indispensabile; **to reduce to a** ~ ridurre al minimo. **2** *adj* minimo(a); **the** ~ **temperature** la (temperatura) minima; ~ **wage** salario minimo garantito.

min·ing ['maɪnɪŋ] **1** *n* **(a)** estrazione *f* mineraria. **(b)** *(Mil, Naut)* posa di mine. **2** *cpd (industry, engineer, area)* minerario(a); *(community, family)* di minatori.

mini·skirt ['mɪnɪskɜːt] *n* minigonna.

min·is·ter ['mɪnɪstəʳ] *n (Pol)* ministro; *(Rel)* pastore *m*; **M**~ **for Defence** Ministro della Difesa.

min·is·terial [,mɪnɪs'tɪərɪəl] *adj (Pol)* ministeriale.

min·is·try ['mɪnɪstrɪ] *n* **(a)** *(Pol)* ministero; **M**~ **of Defence** Ministero della Difesa. **(b)** *(Rel)*: **the** ~ il ministero sacerdotale.

mink [mɪŋk] **1** *n* visone *m*. **2** *cpd*: ~ **coat** *n* pelliccia di visone.

mi·nor ['maɪnəʳ] **1** *adj (also Math, Mus)* minore; *(detail, role, importance)* secondario(a); *(repairs, operation, expense)* piccolo(a). **2** *n* **(a)** *(Law)* minore *m/f*, minorenne *m/f*. **(b)** *(Am Univ)* materia complementare.

mi·nor·ity [maɪ'nɒrɪtɪ] **1** *n* minoranza; **to be in a** ~ essere in minoranza. **2** *cpd (verdict)* minoritario(a); *(government)* di minoranza.

min·strel ['mɪnstrəl] *n* menestrello.

mint[1] [mɪnt] **1** *n* zecca; **to be worth a** ~ **(of money)** valere un patrimonio. **2** *adj*: **in** ~ **condition** in perfette condizioni, che sembra nuovo(a) di zecca. **3** *vt* coniare.

mint[2] [mɪnt] **1** *n* *(Bot)* menta; *(sweet)* mentina, pasticca di menta. **2** *cpd* alla menta; ~ **sauce** *n* salsa alla menta.

minu·et [,mɪnjʊ'et] *n* minuetto.

mi·nus ['maɪnəs] **1** *prep (Math etc)* meno; *(fam: without)* senza. **2** *adj*: ~ **quantity** *(Math)* quantità negativa; ~ **(sign)** (segno) meno *inv*.

min·ute[1] ['mɪnɪt] **1** *n* **(a)** *(of time)* minuto, (minuto) primo; *(of degree)* minuto, primo; **it is 5** ~**s past 3** sono le 3 e 5 (minuti); **I'll come in a** ~ vengo subito *or* tra un attimo; **wait a** ~! (aspetta) un momento!; **come here this** ~! vieni subito!; **I won't be a** ~ vengo *(or* torno) subito; *(I've nearly finished)* faccio subito; **at that** ~ **the phone rang** in quel (preciso) istante suonò il telefono; **tell me the** ~ **he arrives** (non) appena arriva dimmelo; **up to the** ~ *(fashions, news)* ultimissimo; *(equipment)* modernissimo. **(b)** *(official note)* nota ufficiale; ~**s** *(of meeting)* verbale *m*. **2** *cpd*: ~ **hand** *n* lancetta dei minuti.

min·ute[2] [maɪ'njuːt] *adj (small)* minuscolo(a); *(: change, improvement)* piccolissimo(a); *(detailed, exact)* minuzioso(a); **in** ~ **detail** minuziosamente.

mi·nute·ly [maɪ'njuːtlɪ] *adv (by a small amount)* di poco; *(in detail)* minuziosamente.

mira·cle ['mɪrəkl] *n (also fig)* miracolo; **it's a** ~ **that** è un miracolo che + *sub*; **by some** ~ per qualche miracolo; **to work** ~**s** *(also fig)* far miracoli.

mi·racu·lous [mɪ'rækjʊləs] *adj* miracoloso(a).

mi·rage ['mɪrɑːʒ] *n* miraggio.

mir·ror ['mɪrəʳ] **1** *n* specchio; *(Aut)* specchietto (retrovisore); **to look at o.s. in the** ~ guardarsi allo specchio. **2** *vt* riflettere. **3** *cpd:* ~ **image** *n* immagine *f* speculare.

mirth [mɜ:θ] *n* ilarità.

mis·ad·ven·ture [ˌmɪsəd'vɛntʃəʳ] *n* sfortuna, disavventura; **death by** ~ *(Law)* morte *f* accidentale.

mis·an·thro·pist [mɪ'zænθrəpɪst] *n* misantropo/a.

mis·ap·ply [ˌmɪsə'plaɪ] *vt* impiegare male.

mis·ap·pre·hen·sion ['mɪsˌæprɪ'hɛnʃən] *n* equivoco, malinteso; **to be (labouring) under a** ~ sbagliarsi.

mis·ap·pro·pri·ate [ˌmɪsə'prəʊprɪeɪt] *vt* appropriarsi indebitamente di.

mis·ap·pro·pria·tion ['mɪsəˌprəʊprɪ'eɪʃən] *n* appropriazione *f* indebita.

mis·be·have [ˌmɪsbɪ'heɪv] *vi* comportarsi male.

misc. *abbr of* **miscellaneous**.

mis·cal·cu·late [ˌmɪs'kælkjʊleɪt] *vt*, *vi* calcolare male.

mis·cal·cu·la·tion ['mɪsˌkælkjʊ'leɪʃən] *n* errore *m* di calcolo.

mis·car·riage [ˌmɪs'kærɪdʒ] *n* **(a)** *(Med)* aborto (spontaneo). **(b):** ~ **of justice** errore *m* giudiziario.

mis·car·ry [ˌmɪs'kærɪ] *vi* **(a)** *(Med)* abortire. **(b)** *(fail: plans)* andare a monte, fallire.

mis·cel·la·neous [ˌmɪsɪ'leɪnɪəs] *adj (objects)* vario(a), diverso(a); *(collection)* eterogeneo(a); ~ **expenses** spese varie.

mis·cel·la·ny [mɪ'sɛlənɪ] *n* misto(a); *(Literature)* miscellanea; *(Radio, TV)* selezione *f*.

mis·chance [ˌmɪs'tʃɑ:ns] *n*: **by (some)** ~ per sfortuna.

mis·chief ['mɪstʃɪf] *n (roguishness)* furberia; *(naughtiness)* birichinate *fpl; (maliciousness)* cattiveria; **he's always getting into** ~ ne combina sempre una; **to keep sb out of** ~ tenere qn occupato così che non può combinare guai; **full of** ~ birichino; **to do o.s. a** ~ farsi male.

mis·chie·vous ['mɪstʃɪvəs] *adj (roguish)* malizioso(a); *(: child)* birichino(a); *(troublemaking):* ~ **rumours** malignità *fpl*.

mis·con·cep·tion [ˌmɪskən'sɛpʃən] *n (false idea/ opinion)* idea/convinzione *f* sbagliata; *(misunderstanding)* malinteso.

mis·con·duct [ˌmɪs'kɒndʌkt] *n* cattiva condotta; *(sexual)* adulterio.

mis·con·strue [ˌmɪskən'stru:] *vt* interpretare male.

mis·deed [ˌmɪs'di:d] *n (old)* misfatto.

mis·de·mean·our, *(Am)* **mis·de·mean·or** [ˌmɪsdɪ'mi:nəʳ] *n* trasgressione *f*.

mi·ser ['maɪzəʳ] *n* avaro/a.

mis·er·able ['mɪzərəbl] *adj* **(a)** *(unhappy)* infelice; *(deplorable: sight, failure)* penoso(a); **to feel** ~ sentirsi avvilito *or* giù di morale; *(physically)* sentirsi a terra; **don't look so** ~! non fare quella faccia da funerale! **(b)** *(filthy, wretched)* miserabile; *(unpleasant: weather)* deprimente. **(c)** *(contemptible)* miserabile; **a** ~ **£2** 2 miserabili sterline.

mis·er·ably ['mɪzrəblɪ] *adv (smile, answer)* tristemente; *(fail, live, pay)* miseramente.

mi·ser·ly ['maɪzəlɪ] *adj* taccagno(a), avaro(a).

mis·ery ['mɪzərɪ] *n (sadness)* tristezza; *(suffering)* tormento, dolore *m; (fam: person)* lagna; **to put an animal out of its** ~ uccidere un animale (per non farlo soffrire più); **to put sb out of his** ~ *(fig)* non far soffrire più qn; **to make sb's life a** ~ rovinare la vita a qn.

mis·fire [ˌmɪs'faɪəʳ] *vi (gun, plan, joke)* far cilecca; *(engine)* perdere colpi.

mis·fit ['mɪsfɪt] *n (person)* disadattato/a.

mis·for·tune [mɪs'fɔ:tʃən] *n* disgrazia, sventura.

mis·giv·ing [mɪs'gɪvɪŋ] *n* apprensione *f*, diffidenza; **to have** ~**s about sth** essere diffidente *or* avere dei dubbi per quanto riguarda qc.

mis·guid·ed [ˌmɪs'gaɪdɪd] *adj* malaccorto(a).

mis·han·dle [ˌmɪs'hændl] *vt (object)* maneggiare senza precauzioni; *(person)* non prendere per il verso giusto; *(affair)* condurre male; **he** ~**d the whole situation** ha sbagliato tutto.

mis·hap ['mɪshæp] *n* incidente *m;* **without** ~ senza incidenti.

mis·hear ['mɪs'hɪəʳ] *pt, pp* **misheard** ['mɪs'hɜ:d] *vt, vi* capire male.

mish·mash ['mɪʃmæʃ] *n (fam)* minestrone *m*, guazzabuglio.

mis·in·ter·pret [ˌmɪsɪn'tɜ:prɪt] *vt* interpretare male.

mis·judge [ˌmɪs'dʒʌdʒ] *vt* calcolare male; *(person)* giudicare male.

mis·lay [ˌmɪs'leɪ] *pt, pp* **mislaid** [ˌmɪs'leɪd] *vt* non trovare più.

mis·lead [ˌmɪs'li:d] *pt, pp* **misled** *vt* trarre in inganno; **to** ~ **sb into thinking that...** far credere a qn che... .

mis·lead·ing [ˌmɪs'li:dɪŋ] *adj* che trae in inganno.

mis·led ['mɪs'lɛd] *pt, pp of* **mislead**.

mis·man·age [ˌmɪs'mænɪdʒ] *vt* amministrare male.

mis·no·mer [ˌmɪs'nəʊməʳ] *n:* **to call her a cook is a** ~ non si può certo definirla una cuoca.

mi·sogy·nist [mɪ'sɒdʒɪnɪst] *n* misogino.

mis·place [ˌmɪs'pleɪs] *vt* **(a)** *(mislay)* non trovare più. **(b): to be** ~**d** *(trust etc)* essere malriposto(a).

mis·print ['mɪsprɪnt] *n* errore *m* di stampa, refuso.

mis·pro·nounce [ˌmɪsprə'naʊns] *vt* pronunciare male.

mis·quote [ˌmɪs'kwəʊt] *vt* citare erroneamente.

mis·read ['mɪs'ri:d] *pt, pp* **misread** [ˌmɪs'rɛd] *vt* leggere male; *(misinterpret)* interpretare male.

mis·rep·re·sent ['mɪsˌrɛprɪ'zɛnt] *vt (facts)* travisare; *(person)* dare un'impressione sbagliata di.

miss[1] [mɪs] **1** *n (shot)* colpo mancato *or* a vuoto; **it was a near** ~ c'è mancato un pelo; **to give sth a** ~ *(fam)* lasciar perdere qc.

2 *vt* **(a)** *(gen: train, opportunity, film etc)* perdere; *(appointment, class)* mancare a; *(target)* mancare; *(remark: not hear)* non sentire; *(: not understand)* non capire; *(omit: meal, page etc)* saltare; **you haven't** ~**ed much!** non hai perso molto!; **I** ~**ed you at the station** non ti ho visto alla stazione; **to** ~ **the boat** *or* **bus** *(fig)* lasciarsi sfuggire (di mano) l'occasione; **we must have** ~**ed the sign for London** ci dev'essere sfuggito il cartello per Londra; **you can't** ~ **our house, it's...** non puoi sbagliarti: la nostra casa è...; **don't** ~ **this film** non perderti questo film; **I** ~**ed what you said** mi è sfuggito quello che hai detto; **you're** ~**ing the point** non capisci.

(b) *(escape or avoid: accident, bad weather)* evitare; **the bus just** ~**ed the wall** l'autobus per un pelo non è andato a finire contro il muro; **he narrowly** ~**ed being run over** per poco non è stato investito.

(c) *(notice loss of: money etc)* accorgersi di non avere più; **then I** ~**ed my wallet** allora mi sono accorto che mi mancava *or* che non avevo più il portafoglio.

(d) *(long for: person etc):* **I** ~ **you so** mi manchi tanto; **do you** ~ **Trieste?** senti la mancanza di *or* ti manca Trieste?

3 *vi (person, shot)* mancare il bersaglio; **you can't** ~! non puoi fallire!

♦ **miss out** *vt* + *adv* saltare.

♦ **miss out on** *vi* + *prep* (*fun, party*) perdersi; (*chance, bargain*) lasciarsi sfuggire; **I feel I've been** ~**ing out on life** sento di non aver goduto la vita come avrei potuto.

miss² [mɪs] *n* signorina; **M**~ **Smith** la signorina Smith, Sig.na Smith; (*in letter*): **Dear M**~ **Smith** Cara Signorina, (*more frm*) Gentile Signorina; **M**~ **World 1985** Miss Mondo 1985.

mis·sal ['mɪsəl] *n* messale *m*.

mis·sile ['mɪsaɪl] **1** *n* (*Mil*) missile *m*; (*frm: any object thrown as weapon*) proiettile *m*. **2** *cpd*: ~ **base** *n* base *f* missilistica; ~ **launcher** *n* lanciamissili *m inv*.

mis·sing ['mɪsɪŋ] *adj* (*not able to be found*) smarrito(a); (*not there*) mancante; (*person: also Mil*) disperso(a); **to be** ~ mancare; **there are several books** ~ mancano diversi libri; **the** ~ **link** l'anello mancante; ~ **person** scomparso/a, disperso/a.

mis·sion ['mɪʃən] *n* (*all senses*) missione *f*; **on a** ~ **to sb** in missione da qn; **it's her** ~ **in life** è la sua missione nella vita.

mis·sion·ary ['mɪʃənrɪ] *n* (*Rel*) missionario/a.

mis·spell [ˌmɪs'spɛl] *pt, pp* **misspelled** *or* **misspelt** [ˌmɪs'spɛlt] *vt* sbagliare l'ortografia di.

mis·spent ['mɪsspɛnt] *adj*: **a** ~ **youth** una gioventù sprecata.

mist [mɪst] **1** *n* foschia, nebbiolina; (*on glass etc*) appannamento; (*of perfume*) nuvola; **through a** ~ **of tears** attraverso un velo di lacrime; **lost in the** ~**s of time** perduto nella notte dei tempi. **2** *vi* (*also*: ~ **over**, ~ **up**: *scene, landscape*) annebbiarsi, offuscarsi; (: *mirror, window*) appannarsi; (*eyes: also*: ~ **over**) velarsi.

mis·take [mɪs'teɪk] (*vb: pt* **mistook**, *pp* **mistaken**) **1** *n* errore *m*, sbaglio; **to make a** ~ (*in writing, calculating etc*) fare uno sbaglio *or* un errore; **to make a** ~ (**about sb/sth**) sbagliarsi (sul conto di qn/su qc); **my** ~! è colpa mia!; **you're making a big** ~ commetti un grosso *or* grave errore; **I made the** ~ **of trusting him** ho fatto l'errore di fidarmi di lui; **by** ~ per sbaglio; **he took my hat in** ~ **for his** ha preso il mio cappello credendo fosse il suo; **there must be some** ~ ci dev'essere un errore; **make no** ~ (**about it**) non aver paura, sta' tranquillo; **she's pretty and no** ~ (*fam*) è proprio una bella ragazza.

2 *vt* (*meaning, remark etc*) capir male, fraintendere; (*road etc*) sbagliare; (*time*) sbagliarsi su; **to** ~ **A for B** prendere *or* scambiare A per B; **to be** ~**n** sbagliarsi; **if I'm not** ~**n** se non sbaglio.

mis·tak·en [mɪs'teɪkən] **1** *pp* of **mistake**. **2** *adj* (*wrong: idea, conclusion*) sbagliato(a), errato(a); (*misplaced: loyalty, generosity*) malriposto(a).

mis·tle·toe ['mɪsltəʊ] *n* vischio.

mis·took [mɪs'tʊk] *pt* of **mistake**.

mis·trans·la·tion [ˌmɪstrænz'leɪʃən] *n* errore *m* di traduzione.

mis·treat [ˌmɪs'triːt] *vt* maltrattare, trattare male.

mis·tress ['mɪstrɪs] *n* (*of servant etc*) padrona. (**b**) (*lover*) amante *f*. (**c**) (*teacher*) insegnante *f*.

mis·trust [ˌmɪs'trʌst] **1** *n*: ~ (**of**) diffidenza (nei confronti di). **2** *vt* (*person, motives*) diffidare di; (*one's own abilities*) dubitare di.

mis·trust·ful [mɪs'trʌstfʊl] *adj*: ~ (**of**) diffidente (nei confronti di).

misty ['mɪstɪ] *adj* (**-ier, -iest**) (*day, morning*) brumoso(a), di foschia; (*mirror, window*) appannato(a); **it's** ~ **today** c'è foschia oggi.

mis·under·stand [ˌmɪsʌndə'stænd] *pt, pp* **misunderstood** *vt* fraintendere.

mis·under·stand·ing [ˌmɪsʌndə'stændɪŋ] *n* malinteso.

mis·under·stood [ˌmɪsʌndə'stʊd] **1** *pt, pp* of **misunderstand**. **2** *adj* incompreso(a).

mis·use [ˌmɪs'juːs] **1** *n* (*of power, authority*) abuso; (*of word, tool*) uso improprio; (*of resources, time, energies*) cattivo uso. **2** [ˌmɪs'juːz] *vt* (*see n*) abusare di; usare impropriamente; fare cattivo uso di.

mite [maɪt] *n* (**a**) (*small quantity*) briciolo; **the widow's** ~ (*Bible*) l'obolo della vedova. (**b**) (*small child*): **poor** ~! povera creaturina!

miti·gate ['mɪtɪgeɪt] *vt* (*punishment*) mitigare; (*suffering*) alleviare; **mitigating circumstances** circostanze *fpl* attenuanti.

miti·ga·tion [ˌmɪtɪ'geɪʃən] *n* (*see vb*) mitigazione *f*; alleviamento.

mi·tre, (*Am*) **mi·ter** ['maɪtə'] *n* (**a**) (*Rel*) mitra. (**b**) (*Tech: also*: ~ **joint**) giunto ad angolo retto.

mitt [mɪt] *n* (**a**) (*also*: **mitten**: *with cut-off fingers*) mezzo guanto; (: *no separate fingers*) muffola, manopola. (**b**) (*baseball glove*) guantone *m*.

mix [mɪks] **1** *n* mescolanza; **cake** ~ preparato per torta; **the school has a good social** ~ gli studenti di questa scuola provengono da diverse classi sociali. **2** *vt* (**a**) mescolare; (*cocktail, sauce*) preparare (mescolando); ~ **to a smooth paste** mescolare fino ad ottenere una pasta omogenea; **to** ~ **sth with sth** mischiare qc a qc; **to** ~ **business with pleasure** unire l'utile al dilettevole. **3** *vi* mescolarsi; **he doesn't** ~ **well** non riesce a legare; **he** ~**es with all sorts of people** ha a che fare con persone di ogni tipo; **they just don't** ~ (*people*) non legano fra di loro; (*patterns*) non stanno bene insieme.

♦ **mix in** *vt* + *adv* (*eggs etc*) incorporare.

♦ **mix up** *vt* + *adv* (**a**) (*prepare: drink, medicine*) preparare. (**b**) (*get in a muddle: documents etc*) confondere, mescolare; (*confuse*): **to** ~ **sb/sth up** (**with**) scambiare qn/qc (per). (**c**) (*involve*): **to** ~ **sb up in sth** coinvolgere *or* immischiare qn in qc; **to be** ~**ed up in sth** essere coinvolto in qc; **she got herself** ~**ed up with some shady characters** ha avuto a che fare con dei tipi loschi.

mixed [mɪkst] *adj* (*biscuits, nuts*) assortito(a); (*school, marriage, economy*) misto(a); **we had** ~ **weather** il tempo è stato un po' bello e un po' brutto; **it's a** ~ **blessing** è una cosa buona che ha il suo risvolto negativo; **I have** ~ **feelings** sono combattuto; **the announcement got a** ~ **reception** non tutti hanno accolto favorevolmente l'annuncio; **it's a** ~ **bag** (*fig fam*) c'è un po' di tutto; ~ **doubles** (*Sport*) doppio misto; ~ **grill** grigliata mista; ~ **metaphor** metafora che non sta in piedi.

mixed-up [ˌmɪkst'ʌp] *adj* (*person, ideas*) confuso(a); (*papers*) mescolato(a), in disordine; **I'm all** ~ sono disorientato.

mix·er ['mɪksə'] *n* (**a**) (*Culin: electric*) frullatore *m*; (: *hand*) frullino; (*cement* ~) betoniera. (**b**): **he's a good** ~ è molto socievole.

mix·ture ['mɪkstʃə'] *n* mistura, miscuglio; (*Med*) preparato; **cough** ~ sciroppo per la tosse.

mix-up ['mɪksʌp] *n* confusione *f*.

moan [məʊn] **1** *n* (*gen*) gemito; (*complaint*) lamentela, lagna. **2** *vi* (*gen*) gemere; **to** ~ (**about**) lamentarsi (di).

moat [məʊt] *n* fossato.

mob [mɒb] **1** *n* (*of people*) folla, massa; (*rioting, violent*) folla inferocita; (*fam: criminal gang*) cricca, banda; **the** ~ (*pej*) la plebaglia. **2** *vt* (*person*) assalire; (*place*) prendere d'assalto.

mo·bile ['məʊbaɪl] *adj* (*gen*) mobile; **the old man is no longer** ~ il vecchio non può più muoversi; **are you** ~ **today?** hai un mezzo oggi?; **applicants**

must be ~ i candidati devono essere disposti a viaggiare; ~ **home** casa viaggiante *or* su ruote; ~ **library** biblioteca ambulante; ~ **unit** unità mobile.

mo·bil·ity [məʊ'bɪlɪtɪ] *n* mobilità; *(of applicant)* disponibilità a viaggiare.

moc·ca·sin ['mɒkəsɪn] *n* mocassino.

mock [mɒk] **1** *adj (gen)* finto(a); *(battle, exams)* simulato(a); ~ **Tudor** in stile Tudor; ~ **turtle soup** zuppa di testina di vitello. **2** *vt (ridicule: person)* canzonare, farsi beffe di; *(: plan, efforts)* ridicolizzare; *(mimic)* scimmiottare. **3** *vi*: **to ~ at** farsi beffe di.

mock·ery ['mɒkərɪ] *n (derision)* scherno; **it was a ~ of a trial** il processo è stato tutto una farsa; **to make a ~ of** rendere ridicolo.

mock·ing ['mɒkɪŋ] *adj (gen)* beffardo(a); *(tone)* di scherno.

mocking·bird ['mɒkɪŋbɜːd] *n* mimo *(uccello)*.

mock-up ['mɒkʌp] *n* modello.

mod cons [,mɒd'kɒnz] *npl fam abbr of* **modern conveniences.**

mode [məʊd] *n* **(a)** *(gen)* modo, maniera; *(of transport)* mezzo. **(b)** *(fashion)* moda.

mod·el ['mɒdl] **1** *n (gen, fig, Archit etc)* modello; *(small-scale)* modellino; *(fashion ~)* indossatore/trice; *(artist's ~)* modello/a; **male ~** indossatore. **2** *vt* **(a): to ~ sb/sth on** prendere a modello qn/qc per; **to ~ o.s. on sb** prendere a modello qn. **(b)** *(make a ~: in clay)* modellare, plasmare; *(: in wood)* scolpire. **(c)** *(clothes)* indossare. **3** *vi (Art, Phot)* fare da modello *(or* modella), posare; *(fashion)* fare l'indossatore *(or* l'indossatrice). **4** *cpd* **(a)** *(small-scale: railway, village)* in miniatura; ~ **car** n modellino di auto. **(b)** *(prison, school, husband)* modello *inv.*

mod·er·ate ['mɒdərɪt] **1** *adj (gen)* moderato(a); *(climate)* temperato(a); *(size, income)* medio(a); *(demands, price)* modico(a), ragionevole; *(language, terms)* misurato(a); *(quality, ability)* mediocre, modesto(a). **2** *n (Pol)* moderato/a. **3** ['mɒdəreɪt] *vt* moderare. **4** ['mɒdəreɪt] *vi (pain, wind, anger)* calmarsi, attenuarsi.

mod·er·ate·ly ['mɒdərɪtlɪ] *adv* con moderazione; *(expensive, difficult)* non troppo; *(pleased, happy)* abbastanza, discretamente; **it was ~ successful** ha avuto un discreto successo.

mod·era·tion [,mɒdə'reɪʃən] *n* moderazione *f*; **in ~** *(eat, drink)* in quantità moderata, con moderazione.

mod·ern ['mɒdən] *adj* moderno(a); **all ~ conveniences** *(abbr* **mod cons)** tutti i comfort; ~ **languages** lingue *fpl* moderne.

mo·der·nity [mɒ'dɜːnɪtɪ] *n* modernità.

mod·erni·za·tion [,mɒdənaɪ'zeɪʃən] *n* rimodernamento, modernizzazione *f*.

mod·ern·ize ['mɒdənaɪz] *vt* modernizzare.

mod·est ['mɒdɪst] *adj (all senses)* modesto(a); **to be ~ about sth** non vantarsi di qc.

mod·es·ty ['mɒdɪstɪ] *n* modestia; **in all ~** in tutta modestia.

modi·cum ['mɒdɪkəm] *n*: **a ~ of** un minimo di.

modi·fi·ca·tion [,mɒdɪfɪ'keɪʃən] *n*: ~ **(to, in)** modifica (a); **to make ~s** fare *or* apportare delle modifiche.

modi·fy ['mɒdɪfaɪ] *vt (change: also Gram)* modificare; *(moderate: demands)* moderare.

modu·late ['mɒdjʊleɪt] *vt* modulare.

modu·la·tion [,mɒdjʊ'leɪʃən] *n* modulazione *f*.

mod·ule ['mɒdjuːl] *n* modulo.

mo·hair ['məʊhɛər] *n* mohair *m*.

Mohammed [məʊ'hæmɪd] *n* Maometto.

Mo·ham·med·an [məʊ'hæmɪdən] *adj, n* maomettano(a) *(m/f)*.

moist [mɔɪst] *adj (-er, -est) (gen)* umido(a); *(cake)* morbido(a); **eyes ~ with tears** occhi umidi di lacrime.

mois·ten ['mɔɪsn] *vt* inumidire; **to ~ one's lips** umettarsi le labbra.

mois·ture ['mɔɪstʃər] *n (gen)* umidità; *(on glass)* vapore *m* condensato.

mois·tur·ize ['mɔɪstʃəraɪz] *vt (skin)* idratare.

mois·tur·iz·er ['mɔɪstʃəraɪzər] *n (prodotto)* idratante *m*.

mo·lar ['məʊlər] *adj, n* molare *(m)*.

mo·las·ses [məʊ'læsɪz] *n* melassa.

mold [məʊld] *etc (Am)* = **mould** *etc.*

mole[1] [məʊl] *n (on skin)* neo.

mole[2] [məʊl] *n (Zool, fig)* talpa.

mol·ecule ['mɒlɪkjuːl] *n* molecola.

mo·lest [məʊ'lɛst] *vt (trouble)* importunare; *(harm)* molestare; *(Law: sexually)* attentare al pudore di.

mol·lusc, *(Am)* **mol·lusk** ['mɒləsk] *n* mollusco.

molly·coddle ['mɒlɪkɒdl] *vt* coccolare.

mol·ten ['məʊltən] *adj (metal)* fuso(a); *(lava)* allo stato liquido.

mo·ment ['məʊmənt] *n* **(a)** momento, istante *m*; **(at) any ~, any ~ now** da un momento all'altro; **at the (present) ~, at this ~** in time al momento, in questo momento; **at the last ~** all'ultimo momento; **for a** *or* **one ~** per un momento; **for the ~** per il momento, per ora; **not for a** *or* **one ~** neanche per un istante; **in a ~** *(very soon)* tra un momento; *(quickly)* in un attimo; **one ~!, wait a ~!** (aspetta) un momento!; **I shan't be a ~** vengo subito; **it won't take a ~** è solo questione di un attimo; **I've just this ~ heard about it** l'ho saputo in questo (preciso) istante; **the ~ he arrives** (non) appena arriva; **from the ~ I saw him** dal primo momento in cui l'ho visto; **the man of the ~** l'uomo del momento; **the ~ of truth** il momento della verità. **(b)** *(Phys)* momento. **(c)** *(importance)* importanza, rilievo.

mo·men·tari·ly ['məʊməntərɪlɪ] *adv* per un momento; *(Am: very soon)* da un momento all'altro.

mo·men·tary ['məʊməntərɪ] *adj* momentaneo(a).

mo·men·tous [məʊ'mɛntəs] *adj (molto)* importante.

mo·men·tum [məʊ'mɛntəm] *n (Phys)* momento; *(fig)* slancio, impeto; **to gather** *or* **gain ~** *(vehicle, person)* acquistare *or* prendere velocità; *(fig)* prendere *or* guadagnare terreno.

mon·arch ['mɒnək] *n* monarca *m*.

mon·ar·chism ['mɒnəkɪzəm] *n* monarchia.

mon·ar·chist ['mɒnəkɪst] *adj, n* monarchico(a) *(m/f)*.

mon·ar·chy ['mɒnəkɪ] *n* monarchia.

mon·as·tery ['mɒnəstərɪ] *n* monastero.

mo·nas·tic [mə'næstɪk] *adj* monastico(a).

Mon·day ['mʌndɪ] *n* lunedì *m inv; for usage see* **Tuesday.**

mon·etary ['mʌnɪtərɪ] *adj* monetario(a).

mon·ey ['mʌnɪ] **1** *n* denaro, soldi *mpl*; **paper ~** banconote *fpl*; **Italian ~** moneta italiana; **there's ~ in it** c'è da farci i soldi; **I've got no ~** left non ho più neanche una lira; **to make ~** *(person)* fare (i) soldi; *(business)* rendere; **we didn't make any ~ on that deal** in quell'affare non ci abbiamo guadagnato niente; **that's the one for my ~!** è quello su cui sono pronto a scommettere!; **it's ~ for jam** *or* **old rope** *(fam)* son soldi guadagnati senza fatica; **to be in the ~** nuotare nell'oro, essere pieno di soldi; **to get one's ~'s worth** spender bene i propri soldi; **to earn good ~** guadagnar bene; ~ **doesn't grow on trees!** non me li tirano mica dietro i soldi!; **I'm not made of** ~ non nuoto nell'oro. **2** cpd: ~ **market** n mercato monetario; ~ **order** n vaglia m inv postale.

mon·eyed ['mʌnɪd] adj danaroso(a); **the ~ classes** le classi più abbienti.

money-grubbing ['mʌnɪ,grʌbɪŋ] adj avido(a) di denaro.

money·lender ['mʌnɪ,lendə'] n chi presta soldi; (pej) usuraio/a.

money·maker ['mʌnɪ,meɪkə'] n affare m lucrativo.

money·making ['mʌnɪ,meɪkɪŋ] adj che rende (bene or molto), lucrativo(a).

mon·gol ['mɒŋgəl] n (Med) mongoloide m/f.

mon·goose ['mɒŋguːs] n mangusta.

mon·grel ['mʌŋgrəl] n (also: ~ **dog**) (cane m) bastardo.

moni·tor ['mɒnɪtə'] **1** n (a) (Scol) ≈ capoclasse m/f. **(b)** (TV, Tech: screen) monitor m inv; (Radio: person) addetto/a all'ascolto delle trasmissioni estere. **2** vt (foreign station) ascoltare le trasmissioni di; (machine, progress) controllare; (discussion) dirigere.

monk [mʌŋk] n frate m, monaco.

mon·key ['mʌŋkɪ] **1** n scimmia; (fig: child) birbante m/f. **2** cpd: ~ **business** n, ~ **tricks** npl (fam) scherzi mpl; ~ **nut** n nocciolina americana; ~ **wrench** n chiave f inglese a rullino.

♦**monkey about, monkey around** vi + adv (fam) far lo scemo (or la scema); **to ~ about with sth** armeggiare con qc.

mono ['mɒnəʊ] **1** adj mono inv; (broadcast) in mono. **2** n: **in ~** in mono.

mono... ['mɒnəʊ] pref mono... .

mono·chrome ['mɒnəkrəʊm] adj (painting, print) monocromatico(a), monocromo(a); (television) in bianco e nero.

mono·cle ['mɒnəkl] n monocolo.

mono·gram ['mɒnəgræm] n monogramma m.

mono·lith ['mɒnəʊlɪθ] n monolito.

mono·logue ['mɒnəlɒg] n monologo.

mono·plane ['mɒnəʊpleɪn] n monoplano.

mo·nopo·lize [mə'nɒpəlaɪz] vt monopolizzare.

mo·nopo·ly [mə'nɒpəlɪ] n monopolio.

mono·rail ['mɒnəʊreɪl] n monorotaia.

mono·syl·lab·ic [,mɒnəʊsɪ'læbɪk] adj monosillabico(a).

mono·syl·la·ble ['mɒnə,sɪləbl] n monosillabo; **to speak/answer in ~s** parlare/rispondere a monosillabi.

mono·tone ['mɒnətəʊn] n: **in a ~** con voce monotona.

mo·noto·nous [mə'nɒtənəs] adj monotono(a).

mo·noto·ny [mə'nɒtənɪ] n monotonia.

mon·ox·ide [mɒ'nɒksaɪd] n monossido; **carbon ~** ossido di carbonio.

mon·soon [mɒn'suːn] n monsone m.

mon·ster ['mɒnstə'] **1** adj (enormous) gigantesco(a). **2** n mostro.

mon·stros·ity [mɒns'trɒsɪtɪ] n mostruosità f inv.

mon·strous ['mɒnstrəs] adj (huge) colossale, enorme; (dreadful) mostruoso(a); **it is ~ that...** è scandaloso or pazzesco che... + sub.

month [mʌnθ] n mese m; **in the ~ of May** nel mese di maggio, in maggio; **300 dollars a ~** 300 dollari al mese; **which day of the ~ is it?** quanti ne abbiamo (oggi)?; **every ~** (happen) tutti i mesi; (pay) mensilmente, ogni mese.

month·ly ['mʌnθlɪ] **1** adj (gen) mensile; (ticket) valevole per un mese. **2** adv mensilmente, ogni mese; **twice ~** due volte al mese. **3** n (Press) mensile m.

monu·ment ['mɒnjʊmənt] n monumento.

monu·men·tal [,mɒnjʊ'mentl] adj monumentale.

moo [muː] **1** n muggito. **2** vi muggire.

mooch [muːtʃ] vi (fam): **to ~ about** or **around** bighellonare.

mood¹ [muːd] n (Gram) modo.

mood² [muːd] n umore m; **what kind of ~ are you in?** di che umore sei?; **to be in a good/bad ~** essere di buonumore/cattivo umore; **to be in a generous ~** sentirsi generoso; **she's in one of her ~s** ha la luna; **to be in the ~ for sth/to do sth** sentirsi in vena or aver voglia di qc/di fare qc; **I'm not in the ~** non mi sento in vena; **I'm in no ~ to argue** non ho voglia di discutere.

moody ['muːdɪ] adj (-ier, -iest) (variable) lunatico(a); (bad-tempered) imbronciato(a).

moon [muːn] **1** n luna; **full/new ~** luna piena/nuova; **by the light of the ~** al chiaro di luna; **once in a blue ~** a ogni morte di papa; **to be over the ~** (fam) essere al settimo cielo. **2** cpd: ~ **landing** n allunaggio.

♦**moon about, moon around** vi + adv aggirarsi con aria trasognata.

moon·beam ['muːnbiːm] n raggio di luna.

moon·light ['muːnlaɪt] **1** n chiaro di luna; **in the ~** al chiaro di luna. **2** vi (fam) fare del lavoro nero. **3** cpd (walk) al chiaro di luna; **to do a ~ flit** (fam) andarsene alla chetichella senza pagare l'affitto.

moon·lit ['muːnlɪt] adj illuminato(a) dalla luna.

moon·shine ['muːnʃaɪn] n (fam: nonsense) frottole fpl.

moon·shot ['muːn,ʃɒt] n lancio sulla luna.

moon·struck ['muːnstrʌk] adj lunatico(a).

moor¹ [mʊə'] n brughiera.

moor² [mʊə'] **1** vt ormeggiare. **2** vi ormeggiarsi, attraccare.

moor·ing ['mʊərɪŋ] n (place) ormeggio; ~**s** (ropes, fixtures) ormeggi mpl.

moose [muːs] n, pl inv alce m.

moot [muːt] **1** adj: **it's a ~ point** è un punto controverso. **2** vt: **it has been ~ed whether...** è stata sollevata la questione se... .

mop [mɒp] **1** n (for floor) lavapavimenti m inv; (for dishes) spazzolino per i piatti; (fam: hair) zazzera. **2** vt (floor) lavare; **to ~ one's face** asciugarsi il viso.

♦**mop up** vt + adv (a) asciugare con uno straccio. **(b)** (Mil) eliminare.

mope [məʊp] vi essere avvilito(a).

♦**mope about, mope around** vi + adv trascinarsi or aggirarsi con aria avvilita.

mo·ped ['məʊped] n ciclomotore m.

mor·al ['mɒrəl] **1** adj (gen) morale; (person) di saldi principi morali; **to lower ~ standards** rilassare i costumi. **2** n (a) (lesson) morale f. **(b)**: ~**s** npl principi mpl morali.

mo·rale [mɒ'rɑːl] n morale m; **to raise sb's ~** risollevare il morale di qn.

mo·ral·ity [mə'rælɪtɪ] n moralità.

mor·al·ize ['mɒrəlaɪz] vi: **to ~ (about)** fare il (or la) moralista (riguardo), moraleggiare (riguardo).

mor·al·ly ['mɒrəlɪ] adv (act) in base a dei principi morali; ~ **wrong** moralmente sbagliato.

mo·rass [mə'ræs] n pantano.

mor·bid ['mɔːbɪd] adj morboso(a).

more [mɔː'] comp of **many**, **much 1** adj (greater in number etc) più inv; (in addition) ancora inv; **I have ~ wine/money than you** ho più vino/soldi di te; **I have ~ wine than beer** ho più vino che birra; **there was ~ snow this winter than last** c'è stato più neve quest'inverno che l'inverno scorso; ~ **letters than we expected** più lettere di quante ne aspettavamo; **many ~ people** molta più gente; **I have no ~ pennies** non ho più pennies; **a few ~ weeks** ancora qualche settimana; **do you want some ~ tea?** vuoi ancora un po' di tè?; **is there any ~ wine?** c'è ancora del vino?; **the ~ fool you for giving her the money** sei ancora più stupido tu che le hai dato i soldi.

2 *pron* **(a)** *(greater amount)* più *inv; (further or additional amount)* ancora; **~ than 10** più di 10; **~ than ever** più che mai; **4/a few ~** ancora 4/qualcuno; **a little ~** ancora un po'; **many/much ~** molti/molto di più; **is there any ~?** ce n'è ancora?; **there's no ~** non ce n'è più; **it cost ~ than we had expected** è costato (di) più di quanto pensavamo; **let's say no ~ about it** non parliamone più; **you couldn't ask for ~** non potresti chiedere di più; **and what's ~...** e per di più...; **(b): (all) the ~ (molto) di più; the ~ you give him the ~ he wants** più gliene dai e più ne vuole; **the ~ the merrier** più gente c'è, meglio è.

3 *adv* (di) più; **~ easily** più facilmente; **~ difficult** più difficile; **~ and ~** sempre di più; **it's ~ and ~ difficult to...** è sempre più difficile...; **~ or less** più o meno; **(all) the ~ so as...** anche perché...; **it will ~ than meet the demand** supererà ampiamente la richiesta; **he was ~ surprised than angry** era più sorpreso che arrabbiato; **once ~** ancora (una volta), un'altra volta; **no ~, not any ~** non ... più; **I don't want to go any ~** non ci voglio più andare.

more·over [mɔːˈrəʊvəˈ] *adv* per di più, inoltre.
morgue [mɔːg] *n* obitorio.
mori·bund [ˈmɒrɪbʌnd] *adj* moribondo(a).
morn·ing [ˈmɔːnɪŋ] **1** *n (part of day)* mattina, mattino; *(expressing duration)* mattinata; **this ~** stamattina; **yesterday ~** ieri mattina; **tomorrow ~** domani mattina, domattina; **on Monday ~** lunedì mattina; **a ~'s work** il lavoro di una mattinata; **in the ~** di mattina; *(tomorrow)* domattina; **I work in the ~s** lavoro la mattina; **at 7 o'clock in the ~** alle 7 del mattino; **on the ~ of September 19th** la mattina del 19 settembre. **2** *cpd (walk)* mattutino(a); *(papers)* del mattino; **~ dress** *n* frac *m inv;* **~ sickness** *n (Med)* nausee *fpl* mattutine.
Mo·roc·co [məˈrɒkəʊ] *n* Marocco.
mor·on [ˈmɔːrɒn] *n* idiota *m/f*.
mo·rose [məˈrəʊs] *adj* cupo(a), imbronciato(a).
mor·phia [ˈmɔːfɪə] *n,* **mor·phine** [ˈmɔːfiːn] *n* morfina.
Morse [mɔːs] *n (also:* **~ code)** alfabeto Morse.
mor·sel [ˈmɔːsl] *n (of food)* boccone *m; (fig)* briciolo.
mor·tal [ˈmɔːtl] *adj, n* mortale *(m/f)*.
mor·tal·ity [mɔːˈtælɪtɪ] *n* mortalità.
mor·tal·ly [ˈmɔːtəlɪ] *adv* mortalmente.
mor·tar [ˈmɔːtəˈ] *n* **(a)** *(cannon, bowl)* mortaio. **(b)** *(cement)* malta.
mort·gage [ˈmɔːgɪdʒ] **1** *n (in house buying)* mutuo ipotecario; *(second loan)* ipoteca; **to take out a ~** contrarre un mutuo *(or* un'ipoteca); **to pay off a ~** pagare un mutuo *(or* un'ipoteca). **2** *vt* ipotecare.
mor·tice [ˈmɔːtɪs] *n* = **mortise**.
mor·ti·cian [mɔːˈtɪʃən] *n (Am)* impresario di pompe funebri.
mor·ti·fi·ca·tion [ˌmɔːtɪfɪˈkeɪʃən] *n* mortificazione *f,* umiliazione *f.*
mor·ti·fy [ˈmɔːtɪfaɪ] *vt* mortificare.
mor·tise [ˈmɔːtɪs] **1** *n* mortasa. **2** *cpd:* **~ lock** *n* serratura incastrata.
mor·tu·ary [ˈmɔːtjʊərɪ] *n* obitorio.
mo·sa·ic [məʊˈzeɪɪk] *n* mosaico.
Mos·cow [ˈmɒskəʊ] *n* Mosca.
Mos·lem [ˈmɒzləm] *adj, n* musulmano(a) *(m/f)*.

mosque [mɒsk] *n* moschea.
mos·qui·to [mɒsˈkiːtəʊ] **1** *n, pl* **~es** zanzara. **2** *cpd:* **~ net** *n* zanzariera.
moss [mɒs] *n (Bot)* muschio.
mossy [ˈmɒsɪ] *adj* muscoso(a).
most [məʊst] *superl of* **many, much 1** *adj* **(a)** più (di tutti); **the ~ pleasure** il piacere più grande; **who has (the) ~ money?** chi ha più soldi (di tutti)?; **for the ~ part** in gran parte. **(b)** *(the majority of):* **~ men** la maggior parte *or* la grande maggioranza degli uomini.

2 *pron:* **~ of it/them** quasi tutto/tutti; **~ of the money/her friends/the time** la maggior parte dei soldi/dei suoi amici/del tempo; **do the ~ you can** fai più che puoi; **at (the) ~, at the very ~** al massimo; **to make the ~ of sth** sfruttare al massimo qc; **make the ~ of it!** approfittane!

3 *adv* **(a)** *(spend, eat)* di più; **the ~ attractive/difficult/comfortable** il(la) più attraente/difficile/confortevole; **which one did it ~ easily?** chi ha avuto più facilità a farlo? **(b)** *(intensive):* **~ likely** molto probabilmente; **a ~ interesting book** un libro estremamente interessante.

most·ly [ˈməʊstlɪ] *adv (chiefly)* per lo più; *(usually)* in genere.
M.O.T. *abbr (= Ministry of Transport Test):* **to have an ~** = fare una revisione alla Motorizzazione.
mo·tel [məʊˈtel] *n* motel *m inv.*
moth [mɒθ] *n* falena, farfalla notturna; *(clothes* **~)** tarma.
moth·ball [ˈmɒθbɔːl] *n* pallina di naftalina.
moth·eaten [ˈmɒθˌiːtn] *adj* tarmato(a).
moth·er [ˈmʌðəˈ] **1** *n* madre *f;* **M~'s Day** la festa della mamma; **~'s help** bambinaia. **2** *vt (care for)* fare da madre a; *(spoil)* essere troppo chioccia con. **3** *cpd:* **~ country** *n* patria; **~ tongue** *n* lingua materna, madrelingua.
moth·er·hood [ˈmʌðəhʊd] *n* maternità.
mother-in-law [ˈmʌðərɪnlɔː] *n, pl* **mothers-in-law** suocera.
moth·er·ly [ˈmʌðəlɪ] *adj* materno(a).
mother-of-pearl [ˌmʌðərəvˈpɜːl] *n* madreperla.
mother-to-be [ˌmʌðətəˈbiː] *n, pl* **mothers-to-be** futura mamma.
moth·proof [ˈmɒθpruːf] *adj* trattato(a) con antitarmico.
mo·tif [məʊˈtiːf] *n* motivo.
mo·tion [ˈməʊʃən] **1** *n* **(a)** *(movement)* moto, movimento; **to be in ~** *(vehicle)* essere in moto; *(machine)* essere in funzione; **to set in ~** avviare; **to go through the ~s of doing sth** *(fig)* essere troppo qc pro forma. **(b)** *(gesture)* cenno, gesto; *(proposal)* mozione *f.* **(c)** *(bowel* **~)** evacuazione *f* (intestinale). **2** *vt, vi:* **to ~ (to) sb to do sth** far cenno *or* segno a qn di fare qc. **3** *cpd:* **~ picture** *n* film *m inv;* **the ~-picture industry** l'industria cinematografica.
mo·tion·less [ˈməʊʃənlɪs] *adj* immobile.
mo·ti·vate [ˈməʊtɪveɪt] *vt (act, decision)* dare origine a, motivare; *(person)* spingere.
mo·ti·va·tion [ˌməʊtɪˈveɪʃən] *n* motivazione *f.*
mo·tive [ˈməʊtɪv] *n (gen)* motivo, ragione *f; (for crime)* movente *m; from the best* **~s** con le migliori intenzioni.
mot·ley [ˈmɒtlɪ] *adj (many-coloured)* variopinto(a); *(mixed)* eterogeneo(a).
mo·tor [ˈməʊtəˈ] **1** *n* **(a)** *(engine)* motore *m.* **(b)** *(fam: car)* macchina. **2** *vi* andare in automobile. **3** *cpd:* **~ racing** *n (Sport)* corse *fpl* automobilistiche; **~ scooter** *n* scooter *m inv;* **~ show** *n* salone *m* dell'automobile.
motor·bike [ˈməʊtəbaɪk] *n (fam)* moto *f inv.*
motor·boat [ˈməʊtəbəʊt] *n* motoscafo.
motor·car [ˈməʊtəkɑːˈ] *n* automobile *f.*

motor·coach ['məʊtəkəʊtʃ] *n* pullman *m inv*.

motor·cycle ['məʊtə,saɪkl] *n* motocicletta.

motor·cyclist ['məʊtə,saɪklɪst] *n* motociclista *m/f*.

mo·tor·ing ['məʊtərɪŋ] **1** *adj (accident)* d'auto, automobilistico(a); *(holiday)* in auto; *(offence)* di guida; the ~ **public** gli automobilisti. **2** *n*: **the hazards of** ~ i rischi dell'andare in macchina.

mo·tor·ist ['məʊtərɪst] *n* automobilista *m/f*.

mo·tor·ize ['məʊtəraɪz] *vt* motorizzare.

motor·way ['məʊtəweɪ] *n (Brit)* autostrada.

mot·tled ['mɒtld] *adj (leaves, bird)* variopinto(a); *(marble)* variegato(a); *(animal)* pezzato(a); *(complexion)* a chiazze.

mot·to ['mɒtəʊ] *n, pl* ~**es** motto.

mould[1], *(Am)* **mold** [məʊld] *n (fungus)* muffa.

mould[2], *(Am)* **mold** [məʊld] **1** *n (Art, Culin, Tech etc)* stampo. **2** *vt (clay, figure)* plasmare, modellare; *(fig: character)* plasmare.

mould·er, *(Am)* **mold·er** ['məʊldə'] *vi (cheese)* ammuffire; *(building)* sgretolarsi, andare in rovina.

mould·ing, *(Am)* **mold·ing** ['məʊldɪŋ] *n (Archit)* modanatura.

mouldy, *(Am)* **moldy** ['məʊldɪ] *adj* **(-ier, -iest)** ammuffito(a); **to smell** ~ avere odore di muffa; **to go** ~ ammuffire.

moult, *(Am)* **molt** [məʊlt] *vi (bird)* fare la muta *or* muda; *(mammal)* fare la muta, perdere il pelo.

mound [maʊnd] *n* **(a)** *(pile)* mucchio. **(b)** *(hillock)* collinetta; *(burial* ~) tumulo; *(earthwork)* terrapieno.

mount[1] [maʊnt] *n (poet)* monte *m*, montagna; M~ **Everest** il monte Everest.

mount[2] [maʊnt] **1** *n* **(a)** *(horse etc)* cavalcatura. **(b)** *(support, base)* piedestallo; *(of machine)* incastellatura di sostegno; *(of jewel, photo)* montatura; *(of slide)* telaietto. **2** *vt* **(a)** *(horse)* montare a; *(platform etc)* salire su; *(stairs)* salire. **(b)** *(exhibition)* organizzare; *(play)* montare; *(attack)* sferrare, condurre. **(c)** *(picture, stamp)* sistemare; *(jewel)* montare. **(d):** **to** ~ **guard (on or over)** fare la guardia (a); *(Mil)* montare la guardia (a). **3** *vi* **(a)** *(get on horse)* montare a cavallo. **(b)** *(quantity, price etc: also:* ~ **up)** aumentare, salire.

moun·tain ['maʊntɪn] **1** *n (also fig)* montagna; **in the** ~**s** sulle montagne; **to have a holiday in the** ~**s** fare una vacanza in montagna; **to make a** ~ **out of a molehill** fare di una mosca un elefante. **2** *cpd (people)* montanaro(a); *(shoes)* da montagna; *(animal, plant, path)* di montagna; ~ **cat** *or* **lion** *n* puma *m inv*; ~ **range** *n* catena montuosa *or* di montagne.

moun·tain·eer [,maʊntɪ'nɪə'] *n* alpinista *m/f*.

moun·tain·eer·ing [,maʊntɪ'nɪərɪŋ] *n* alpinismo.

moun·tain·ous ['maʊntɪnəs] *adj (country)* montagnoso(a), montuoso(a); *(fig)* gigantesco(a).

moun·tain·side ['maʊntɪnsaɪd] *n* fianco della montagna.

mount·ed ['maʊntɪd] *adj* a cavallo.

mourn [mɔːn] **1** *vt* piangere, lamentare. **2** *vi* piangere; **to** ~ **for sb** piangere la morte di qn.

mourn·er ['mɔːnə'] *n* parente *m/f (or* amico/a) del defunto.

mourn·ful ['mɔːnfʊl] *adj (person)* triste, malinconico(a); *(tone, sound)* lugubre.

mourn·ing ['mɔːnɪŋ] *n* lutto; **to be in** ~ essere in lutto; **to wear** ~ portare il lutto.

mouse [maʊs] *n, pl* **mice** topo.

mouse·trap ['maʊstræp] *n* trappola per i topi.

mousse [muːs] *n* mousse *f inv*.

mous·tache, *(Am)* **mus·tache** [məs'tɑːʃ] *n* baffi *mpl*.

mous(e)y ['maʊsɪ] *adj* **(-ier, -iest)** *(person)* timi-

do(a), schivo(a); ~ **hair** capelli né chiari né scuri.

mouth [maʊθ] **1** *n, pl* **mouths** [maʊðz] *(gen)* bocca; *(of cave etc)* imboccatura, imbocco; *(of river)* foce *f*; **to keep one's** ~ **shut** *(fig)* tener la bocca chiusa; **shut your** ~! ma sta' un po' zitto! **2** [maʊð] *vt (insincerely)* blaterare; *(soundlessly)* esprimere col semplice movimento delle labbra. **3** *cpd:* ~ **organ** *n* armonica (a bocca).

mouth·ful ['maʊθfʊl] *n (of food)* boccone *m*, boccata; *(of drink)* (grosso) sorso.

mouth·piece ['maʊθpiːs] *n (Mus)* imboccatura, bocchino; *(of breathing apparatus)* boccaglio; *(of telephone)* microfono; *(fig: person)* portavoce *m/f inv*.

mouth-to-mouth ['maʊθtə'maʊθ] *adj:* ~ **resuscitation** respirazione *f* bocca a bocca.

mouth·wash ['maʊθwɒʃ] *n* collutorio.

mouth·water·ing ['maʊθ,wɔːtərɪŋ] *adj* che fa venire l'acquolina in bocca.

mov·able ['muːvəbl] *adj* mobile, movibile.

move [muːv] **1** *n* **(a)** *(movement)* mossa, movimento; **to be on the** ~ *(travelling)* spostarsi; *(active, busy)* essere indaffarato; *(fig: developments etc)* essere in continuo progresso; **get a** ~ **on (with that)!** *(fam)* sbrigati (con quello)!; **to make a** ~ *(start to leave, go etc)* andarsene; *(begin to take action)* muoversi; **he made a** ~ **towards her** fece come per andare verso di lei. **(b)** *(in game)* mossa; *(fig: step, action)* passo; **it's my** ~ tocca a me; **a good/bad** ~ una mossa buona/sbagliata; **what's the next** ~? è adesso cosa facciamo?; **to make the first** ~ *(fig)* fare il primo passo; **his first** ~ **after his victory** la prima cosa che ha fatto dopo la sua vittoria; **there was a** ~ **to oust him from the party** ci fu un tentativo di buttarlo fuori dal partito. **(c)** *(to different house)* trasloco; *(to different job)* trasferimento.

2 *vt* **(a)** *(change place of)* spostare; *(: limbs, chesspiece etc)* muovere; *(transport)* trasportare; *(transfer: employee, troops)* trasferire; ~ **those children off the grass!** fate andar via i bambini dal prato!; **to** ~ **house** traslocare, cambiar casa; **we asked a (removal) firm to** ~ **us** abbiamo chiesto a una ditta (traslochi) di farci il trasloco. **(b)** *(fig: sway):* **to** ~ **sb from an opinion** smuovere qn da un'idea; **to** ~ **sb to do sth** spingere qn a far qc; **he will not be easily** ~**d** non cambierà facilmente idea. **(c)** *(cause emotion in)* commuovere; **to be** ~**d** essere commosso(a); **to** ~ **sb to tears** commuovere qn fino alle lacrime; **to** ~ **sb to anger/pity** far arrabbiare/impietosire qn. **(d)** *(frm: propose):* **to** ~ **a resolution** avanzare una proposta; **to** ~ **that...** proporre che... + *sub*.

3 *vi* **(a)** *(gen)* muoversi; *(traffic)* circolare; *(from a place)* spostarsi; ~! muoviti! **let's** ~! andiamo! **she** ~**s beautifully** si muove con molta grazia; **I'll not** ~ **from here** di qui non mi muovo; **to** ~ **freely** *(piece of machinery)* aver gioco; *(person)* circolare liberamente; *(traffic)* scorrere; **the policeman kept the traffic moving** il vigile ha fatto circolare il traffico; **things are moving at last** finalmente qualcosa si è mosso; **to** ~ **in high society** frequentare l'alta società. **(b)** *(~ house)* traslocare; **the family** ~**d to a new house** la famiglia è andata ad abitare in una nuova casa. **(c)** *(in games)* muovere; **it's you to** ~ tocca a te. **(d)** *(take steps)* intervenire.

♦ **move about, move around 1** *vt + adv (furniture)* spostare; *(person)* far spostare. **2** *vi + adv (fidget)* agitarsi; *(walk about)* muoversi; *(travel)* spostarsi.

♦ **move along 1** *vt + adv (crowd)* far circolare;

(car) spostare. **2** *vi + adv* spostarsi.

♦ **move away 1** *vt + adv (demonstrators)* allontanare; *(employee)* trasferire; *(object)* spostare. **2** *vi + adv (move aside)* spostarsi; *(leave)* allontanarsi; *(move house)* traslocare.

♦ **move back 1** *vt + adv* **(a)** *(to former place: person)* far tornare; *(: object)* rimettere dov'era. **(b)** *(to rear: crowd)* sospingere indietro; *(: car)* spostare indietro; *(: troops)* far indietreggiare. **2** *vi + adv* **(a)** *(return)* ritornare. **(b)** indietreggiare.

♦ **move down 1** *vt + adv (person)* far scendere; *(object)* spostare in basso; *(demote)* far retrocedere. **2** *vi + adv* scendere; *(be demoted)* retrocedere.

♦ **move forward 1** *vt + adv (object)* spostare in avanti; *(troops, chesspiece)* far avanzare; *(fig: date)* anticipare. **2** *vi + adv* avanzare.

♦ **move in 1** *vt + adv (police etc)* far intervenire; *(take inside)* portar dentro; **we haven't ~d the furniture in yet** non ci abbiamo ancora messo i mobili. **2** *vi + adv* **(a)** *(to house)* traslocare. **(b)** *(police etc)* intervenire; *(fig fam: try to control)* cercare di intromettersi.

♦ **move off 1** *vt + adv (object)* togliere. **2** *vi + adv* **(a)** *(go away)* allontanarsi. **(b)** *(start moving)* partire.

♦ **move on 1** *vt + adv (crowd)* far circolare; *(hands of clock)* spostare in avanti. **2** *vi + adv* ripartire; **the policeman asked them to ~ on** il vigile ha chiesto loro di circolare; **to ~ on to** *(fig: point etc)* passare a.

♦ **move out 1** *vt + adv (gen)* portar fuori; *(person)* mandare fuori; *(troops)* far ritirare; **~ the chair out of the corner** togli la sedia dall'angolo. **2** *vi + adv (leave accommodation)* trasferirsi; *(withdraw: troops)* ritirarsi.

♦ **move over 1** *vt + adv* spostare. **2** *vi + adv* spostarsi.

♦ **move up 1** *vt + adv (person)* portare su; *(object)* spostare in alto; *(promote: employee)* promuovere. **2** *vi + adv* **(a)** *(move along)* andare avanti. **(b)** *(fig: shares)* salire; *(: rates)* aumentare; *(be promoted)* passare di grado.

move·ment ['muːvmənt] *n (gen)* movimento; *(of stars, water, physical)* moto; **~ (of the bowels)** *(Med)* evacuazione *f;* **the police questioned him about his ~s** la polizia lo ha interrogato circa i suoi spostamenti.

movie ['muːvɪ] **1** *n (esp Am)* film *m inv;* **to go to the ~s** andare al cinema. **2** *cpd:* **~ camera** *n* cinepresa.

movie·goer ['muːvɪˌgəʊəʳ] *n (Am)* frequentatore/trice di cinema.

mov·ing ['muːvɪŋ] *adj* **(a)** *(parts, staircase)* mobile; *(vehicle)* in moto, in corsa. **(b)** *(fig: instigating)* animatore(trice). **(c)** *(causing emotion)* commovente.

mow [məʊ] *pt* **mowed,** *pp* **mown** [məʊn] *or* **mowed** *vt (corn)* falciare; *(grass)* tagliare; **to ~ sb down** falciare qn.

M.P. *n abbr* (= *Member of Parliament)* deputato; *(on envelope etc):* **Paul Smith, ~ On.** Paul Smith.

m.p.g. *abbr* (= *miles per gallon)* ≃ km/l.

m.p.h. *abbr* (= *miles per hour)* ≃ km/h.

Mr ['mɪstəʳ] *n* signore *m;* **~ Smith** il signor Smith, Sig. Smith; *(direct address)* signor Smith.

Mrs ['mɪsɪz] *n* signora; **~ Black** la signora Black, Sig.ra Black; *(direct address)* signora Black.

Ms *abbr* (= *Miss or Mrs)* Sig.a.

much [mʌtʃ] *comp* **more,** *superl* **most 1** *adj, pron* **(a)** molto(a); **how ~ money?** quanti soldi?; **how ~ is it?** quanto costa?; **~ of this is true** molto di questo è vero; **there's not ~ to do** non c'è molto

da fare; **he/it isn't up to ~** *(fam)* (lui/esso) non vale granché; **I'm not ~ of a cook/singer** non sono un granché come cuoco/cantante; **that wasn't ~ of a party** la festa non è stata un granché; **we don't see ~ of each other** non ci vediamo molto spesso.

(b): three times as ~ tea tre volte tanto tè; **as ~ again** altrettanto(a); **as ~ as you want** quanto vuoi; **he spends as ~ as he earns** spende tanto quanto guadagna; **he has (just) as ~ money as you** ha tanti soldi quanto te; **he drinks as ~ beer as I do** beve tanta birra quanto me; **I thought as ~** c'era da aspettarselo; **it's as ~ as he can do to stand up** stare in piedi è il massimo che riesce a fare; **so ~** talmente tanto(a); **the problem is not so ~ one of money as time** non è tanto una questione di soldi quanto di tempo; **at so ~ a pound** (a) un tot alla libbra; **so ~ for that!** pazienza!; **too ~** troppo; **that's too ~!, that's a bit (too) ~!** *(fam)* questo è (un po') troppo!; **the job is too ~ for her** quel lavoro è al di sopra delle sue capacità.

(c): to make ~ of sb *(treat as important)* coprire qn di attenzioni; **to make ~ of** *(success, failure)* fare un sacco di storie per; *(item of news, scandal)* dare rilievo a; **I couldn't make ~ of that** *(fam)* non ci ho capito molto.

2 *adv* **(a)** molto; **how ~?** quanto?; **he was ~ embarrassed** era molto imbarazzato; **so ~** così (tanto); **too ~** troppo; **I like it very/so ~** mi piace moltissimo/così tanto; **thank you very ~** molte grazie; **it doesn't ~ matter** non ha molta importanza; **however ~ he tries** per quanto ci provi; **~ to my surprise** con mia grande sorpresa; **~ as I would like to go I can't** anche se ho una gran voglia di andarci, non posso; **I hardly know her, ~ less her mother** conosco appena lei e ancora meno sua madre.

(b) *(by far)* di gran lunga; **~ the biggest** di gran lunga il più grande; **I would ~ rather stay** preferirei di molto restare.

(c) *(almost)* pressappoco, quasi; **they're ~ the same** sono praticamente uguali.

muck [mʌk] *n* **(a)** *(dirt)* sporcizia, sudiciume *m; (mud)* fango; *(manure)* letame *m.* **(b)** *(fig)* porcherie *fpl.*

♦ **muck about, muck around** *(fam)* **1** *vt + adv:* **to ~ sb about** complicare la vita a qn. **2** *vi + adv* **(a)** *(lark about)* fare lo(la) stupido(a); *(do nothing in particular)* non fare niente di speciale. **(b)** *(tinker)* armeggiare.

♦ **muck in** *vi + adv (fam)* mettersi insieme.

♦ **muck out** *vt + adv (stable)* pulire.

♦ **muck up** *vt + adv (fam)* **(a)** *(dirty)* sporcare. **(b)** *(spoil)* rovinare.

muck·rak·ing ['mʌkˌreɪkɪŋ] *n (fig fam)* caccia agli scandali.

mucky ['mʌkɪ] *adj* **(-ier, -iest)** *(muddy)* fangoso(a); *(filthy)* sudicio(a).

mu·cus ['mjuːkəs] *n* muco.

mud [mʌd] **1** *n* **(a)** fango. **(b)** *(fig):* **his name is ~** non è molto ben visto; **to sling ~ at sb** gettar fango addosso a qn. **2** *cpd:* **~ bath** *n:* **to have a ~ bath** fare i fanghi; **~ flat** *n* distesa fangosa.

mud·dle ['mʌdl] **1** *n (perplexity)* confusione *f; (disorder)* disordine *m;* **to get into a ~** *(person)* fare confusione; *(things)* finire sottosopra; **in a ~** *(room, books)* in disordine; *(person)* molto confuso; *(plan, arrangements)* per aria; **there's been a ~ over the seats** è successo un pasticcio per quel che riguarda i posti. **2** *vt (also:* **~ up) (a)** *(papers etc)* mettere sottosopra; **you've ~d up A and B**

hai confuso A con B. **(b)** *(person, story, details)* confondere.

◆ **muddle along, muddle on** *vi + adv* andare avanti a casaccio.

◆ **muddle through** *vi + adv* cavarsela alla meno peggio.

muddle-headed ['mʌdl,hɛdɪd] *adj (person)* confusionario(a); *(ideas)* confuso(a).

mud·dy ['mʌdɪ] *adj* **(-ier, -iest)** *(road, ground etc)* fangoso(a); *(hands)* coperto(a) di fango; *(clothes)* infangato(a); *(shoes)* fangoso(a), infangato(a); *(liquid)* torbido(a); *(complexion)* smorto(a), terreo(a).

mud·guard ['mʌdgɑːd] *n* parafango.

mud·pack ['mʌdpæk] *n* maschera di fango.

muff[1] [mʌf] *n* manicotto.

muff[2] [mʌf] *vt (shot, catch etc)* mancare, sbagliare; **to ~ it** sbagliare tutto; **to ~ one's lines** *(actor)* impappinarsi.

muf·fle ['mʌfl] *vt* **(a)** *(wrap warmly: also: ~ up)* imbacuccare. **(b)** *(deaden)* smorzare, attutire; *(: screams)* soffocare.

muf·fled ['mʌfld] *adj (sound etc)* attutito(a).

muf·fler ['mʌflər] *n (scarf)* sciarpa (pesante); *(Am Aut)* marmitta; *(on motorbike)* silenziatore *m*.

muf·ti ['mʌftɪ] *n*: **in ~** in borghese.

mug [mʌg] **1** *n* **(a)** *(cup)* tazzone *m*; *(for beer)* boccale *m*. **(b)** *(fam: dupe)* salame *m*; **it's a ~'s game** è proprio (una cosa) da fessi. **(c)** *(fam: face)* muso. **2** *vt (attack and rob)* aggredire.

◆ **mug up** *vt + adv (fam: also: ~ up on)* studiare bene.

mug·ger ['mʌgər] *n* rapinatore/trice.

mug·ging ['mʌgɪŋ] *n* aggressione *f* (a scopo di rapina).

mug·gins ['mʌgɪnz] *n (Brit fam)* fesso/a.

mug·gy ['mʌgɪ] *adj* **(-ier, -iest)** *(weather)* afoso(a).

mu·lat·to [mjuː'lætəʊ] *n, pl* **~es** mulatto/a.

mul·berry ['mʌlbərɪ] *n (fruit)* mora (di gelso); *(tree)* gelso, moro.

mule [mjuːl] *n* mulo/a; **(as) stubborn as a ~** testardo come un mulo.

mull [mʌl] *vt (wine)* scaldare con aromi e zucchero; **~ed wine** vin brûlé *m inv*.

◆ **mull over** *vt + adv* rimuginare.

◆ **multi...** ['mʌltɪ] *pref* multi... .

multi·col·oured, *(Am)* **multi·col·ored** ['mʌltɪ,kʌləd] *adj* multicolore, variopinto(a).

multi·fari·ous [,mʌltɪ'fɛərɪəs] *adj* molteplice, svariato(a).

multi·lat·er·al [,mʌltɪ'lætərəl] *adj (Pol)* multilaterale.

multi·mil·lion·aire ['mʌltɪ,mɪljə,nɛər] *n* multimiliardario/a.

multi·na·tion·al [,mʌltɪ'næʃənl] **1** *n* multinazionale *f*. **2** *adj* multinazionale.

multi·ple ['mʌltɪpl] **1** *adj* **(a)** *(with sg n)* multiplo(a); **a ~ crash** una serie di incidenti a catena. **(b)** *(with pl n: many)* molteplici. **2** *n* **(a)** *(Math)* multiplo. **(b)** *(Brit: also: ~ store)* grande magazzino che fa parte di una catena. **3** *cpd*: **~ choice** *n* esercizi *mpl* a scelta multipla; **~ sclerosis** *n* sclerosi *f* a placche.

multi·pli·ca·tion [,mʌltɪplɪ'keɪʃən] **1** *n* moltiplicazione *f*. **2** *cpd*: **~ table** *n* tavola pitagorica.

multi·plic·ity [,mʌltɪ'plɪsɪtɪ] *n* molteplicità; **for a ~ of reasons** per svariati motivi.

multi·ply ['mʌltɪplaɪ] **1** *vt (Math)* moltiplicare. **2** *vi* **(a)** *(Math)* moltiplicare; **she can't ~** non sa fare le moltiplicazioni. **(b)** *(increase)* moltiplicarsi.

multi·racial ['mʌltɪ,reɪʃəl] *adj* multirazziale.

multi·tude ['mʌltɪtjuːd] *n* moltitudine *f*.

mum[1] [mʌm] *adj*: **to keep ~ (about sth)** non fare

parola (di qc); **~'s the word!** acqua in bocca!

mum[2] [mʌm] *n (Brit fam: mother)* mamma.

mum·ble ['mʌmbl] *vt, vi* borbottare.

mum·bo jum·bo [,mʌmbəʊ 'dʒʌmbəʊ] *n* sfilza di paroloni.

mum·mi·fy ['mʌmɪfaɪ] *vt* mummificare.

mum·my[1] ['mʌmɪ] *n (corpse)* mummia.

mum·my[2] ['mʌmɪ] *n (Brit fam: mother)* mamma.

mumps [mʌmps] *n* orecchioni *mpl*.

munch [mʌntʃ] *vt, vi* sgranocchiare.

mun·dane [,mʌn'deɪn] *adj (worldly)* di questo mondo; *(pej: humdrum)* banale.

mu·nici·pal [mjuː'nɪsɪpəl] *adj* municipale, comunale.

mu·nici·pal·ity [mjuː,nɪsɪ'pælɪtɪ] *n (place)* comune *m*.

mu·nifi·cence [mjuː'nɪfɪsns] *n (frm)* munificenza.

mu·ni·tions [mjuː'nɪʃənz] *npl* munizioni *fpl*.

mu·ral ['mjʊərəl] **1** *adj* murale. **2** *n* pittura murale.

mur·der ['mɜːdər] **1** *n* **(a)** omicidio, assassinio; **to commit ~** commettere un omicidio. **(b)** *(fam)*: **it was ~!** è stato pazzesco!; **to scream blue ~** strepitare; **she gets away with ~** se la cava sempre. **2** *vt (person)* assassinare; *(fig: song etc)* massacrare. **3** *cpd*: **~ case** *n* caso di omicidio; **~ weapon** *n* arma del delitto.

mur·der·er ['mɜːdərər] *n* assassino/a, omicida *m/f*.

mur·der·ous ['mɜːdərəs] *adj (intentions)* omicida; *(look)* assassino(a).

murky ['mɜːkɪ] *adj* **(-ier, -iest)** *(gen)* oscuro(a), cupo(a); *(thick)* fitto(a); *(: smoke)* denso(a); *(fig)* torbido(a).

mur·mur ['mɜːmər] **1** *n (soft speech)* mormorio; *(of traffic, voices)* brusio; *(of bees)* ronzio; *(of leaves)* fruscio; **heart ~** soffio al cuore; **there were ~s of disagreement** c'era un mormorio di disapprovazione; **without a ~** senza fiatare. **2** *vt* mormorare. **3** *vi* borbottare.

mus·cle ['mʌsl] **1** *n* muscolo; *(fig)* energia, forza; **he never moved a ~** rimase fermo immobile. **2** *vi*: **to ~ in (on sth)** *(fam)* far di tutto per intromettersi (in qc).

mus·cu·lar ['mʌskjʊlər] *adj (tissue etc)* muscolare; *(person)* muscoloso(a).

muse[1] [mjuːz] *n* musa.

muse[2] [mjuːz] *vi*: **to ~ on** *or* **about sth** rimuginare su qc.

mu·seum [mjuː'zɪəm] *n* museo.

mush [mʌʃ] *n* pappa.

mush·room ['mʌʃrʊm] **1** *n (Bot)* fungo. **2** *adj (soup, omelette)* ai *or* coi funghi; *(flavour)* di funghi; *(colour)* color beige rosato *inv*. **3** *vi (town)* svilupparsi rapidamente; *(houses)* spuntare come funghi; **the cloud of smoke went ~ing up** la nuvola di fumo si alzò prendendo la forma di fungo. **4** *cpd*: **~ cloud** *n* fungo di un'esplosione nucleare.

mushy ['mʌʃɪ] *adj* **(-ier, -iest)** *(over ripe)* come pappa; *(fig)* sdolcinato(a); **~ peas** puré *m inv* di piselli.

mu·sic ['mjuːzɪk] **1** *n* musica; **to set to ~** mettere in musica *or* musicare. **2** *cpd (teacher, lesson)* di musica; **~ box** *n* carillon *m inv*; **~ critic** *n* critico musicale; **~ hall** *n* teatro di varietà; **~ lover** *n* appassionato/a di *or* amante *m/f* della musica; **~ stand** *n* leggio.

mu·si·cal ['mjuːzɪkəl] **1** *adj (gen)* musicale; **~ box** carillon *m inv*; **he's very ~** *(fond of)* è amante della musica; *(skilled)* è portato per la musica; **he comes from a ~ family** viene da una famiglia di musicisti. **2** *n (Cine, Theatre)* musical *m inv*.

mu·si·cian [mjuː'zɪʃən] *n* musicista *m/f*.

mu·si·colo·gist [,mjuːzɪ'kɒlədʒɪst] *n* musicologo/a.

musk [mʌsk] **1** *n* muschio. **2** *cpd*: **~ rose** *n (Bot)* rosa muschiata.

mus·ket ['mʌskɪt] n moschetto.
musk·rat ['mʌskræt] n topo muschiato; (fur) rat musqué m inv.
musky ['mʌskɪ] adj (-ier, -iest) muschiato(a).
Mus·lim ['mʊslɪm] = **Moslem.**
mus·lin ['mʌzlɪn] 1 n mussola (di cotone). 2 cpd di mussola.
mus·quash ['mʌskwɒʃ] n (fur) rat musqué m inv.
muss [mʌs] vt (also: ~ **up**: hair) scompigliare; (: dress) spiegazzare.
mus·sel ['mʌsl] n cozza.
must¹ [mʌst] n = **mustiness.**
must² [mʌst] modal aux vb 1 (a) (obligation) dovere; I ~ do it devo farlo; if you ~ se proprio devi; one ~ not be too hopeful non bisogna sperare troppo; there ~ be a reason ci deve (pur) essere un motivo; I ~ say francamente. (b) (probability): he ~ be back by now a quest'ora dovrebbe essere tornato; it ~ be cold up there dev'essere freddo lassù. 2 n (fam): this programme/trip is a ~ è un programma/viaggio da non perdersi.
mus·tache ['mʌstæʃ] n (Am) = **moustache.**
mus·tard ['mʌstəd] 1 n senape f. 2 cpd: ~ gas n (Chem) iprite f.
mus·ter ['mʌstəʳ] 1 n (gathering) adunata; (roll-call) appello; to pass ~ (fig) essere (considerato) accettabile. 2 vt (men, helpers) radunare, mettere insieme; (money, sum) mettere insieme; (also: ~ up: strength, courage) fare appello a; I can't ~ up any enthusiasm non riesco ad entusiasmarmi. 3 vi radunarsi.
musti·ness ['mʌstɪnɪs] n odor di muffa or di stantio.
mustn't ['mʌsnt] = **must not.**
mus·ty ['mʌstɪ] adj (-ier, -iest) (smell) di stantio, di muffa; (ideas) ammuffito(a), stantio(a); to smell ~ aver odore di stantio.
mu·tant ['mjuːtənt] adj, n mutante (m).
mu·tate [mjuː'teɪt] vi subire una mutazione.
mu·ta·tion [mjuː'teɪʃən] n mutazione f.
mute [mjuːt] 1 adj (-r, -st) muto(a). 2 n (person) muto/a; (Mus) sordina.
mut·ed ['mjuːtɪd] adj (noise) attutito(a), smorzato(a); (criticism) attenuato(a).
mu·ti·late ['mjuːtɪleɪt] vt mutilare.
mu·ti·la·tion [ˌmjuːtɪ'leɪʃən] n mutilazione f.

mu·ti·nous ['mjuːtɪnəs] adj (sailor) ammutinato(a); (attitude) ribelle.
mu·ti·ny ['mjuːtɪnɪ] 1 n ammutinamento. 2 vi ammutinarsi.
mut·ter ['mʌtəʳ] 1 n borbottio. 2 vt borbottare, bofonchiare. 3 vi borbottare; (thunder) brontolare.
mut·ton ['mʌtn] n montone m; a leg of ~ un cosciotto di montone; ~ dressed as lamb (fig) una vecchia che vuol sembrare una giovincella.
mu·tu·al ['mjuːtjʊəl] adj (affection, suspicion etc) reciproco(a); (friend, cousin, interests) comune; to our (or your etc) ~ satisfaction che possa soddisfare entrambi.
mu·tu·al·ly ['mjuːtjʊəlɪ] adv reciprocamente.
muz·zle ['mʌzl] 1 n (snout) muso; (gun) bocca (da fuoco); (for dog) museruola. 2 vt (dog) mettere la museruola a; (fig: person) costringere a tacere.
muz·zy ['mʌzɪ] adj (-ier, -iest) (outline, ideas etc) confuso(a); (person) intontito(a).
my [maɪ] poss adj il(la) mio(a); pl i(le) miei(mie); this is ~ house questa è la mia casa; ~ brother mio fratello.
my·op·ic [maɪ'ɒpɪk] adj miope.
my·self [maɪ'sɛlf] pers p͡on (reflexive) mi; (emphatic) io stesso(a); (after preposition) me, me stesso(a); I did it (all) by ~ l'ho fatto (tutto) da solo; I'm not ~ today non mi sento del tutto apposto oggi; see also **oneself.**
mys·teri·ous [mɪs'tɪərɪəs] adj misterioso(a).
mys·teri·ous·ly [mɪs'tɪərɪəslɪ] adv misteriosamente.
mys·tery ['mɪstərɪ] n mistero; it's a ~ to me where it can have gone dove sia finito (per me) è un mistero.
mys·tic ['mɪstɪk] adj, n mistico(a) (m/f).
mys·ti·cal ['mɪstɪkəl] adj mistico(a).
mys·ti·cism ['mɪstɪsɪzəm] n misticismo.
mys·ti·fy ['mɪstɪfaɪ] vt (bewilder) lasciare perplesso(a).
mys·tique [mɪs'tiːk] n fascino.
myth [mɪθ] n mito.
mythi·cal ['mɪθɪkəl] adj mitico(a).
mytho·logi·cal [ˌmɪθə'lɒdʒɪkəl] adj mitologico(a).
my·thol·ogy [mɪ'θɒlədʒɪ] n mitologia.
myxo·ma·to·sis [ˌmɪksəʊmə'təʊsɪs] n mixomatosi f.

N

N¹, n [ɛn] n (letter) N, n f or m inv.

N² abbr (= north) N.

nab [næb] vt (fam: thief etc) acciuffare; (: person to speak to) acchiappare, bloccare.

na·dir ['neɪdɪə'] n (Astron) nadir m; (fig) punto più basso.

nag¹ [næg] n (horse) ronzino.

nag² [næg] **1** vt (also: ~ at) assillare, tormentare; **the children ~ged (at) their parents to take them to the fair** i bambini hanno tormentato i genitori per farsi portare alle giostre; **the family ~ged me into buying a new car** a forza di insistere in famiglia mi hanno fatto comprare una macchina nuova. **2** vi lagnarsi, brontolare in continuazione. **3** n brontolone/a.

nag·ging ['nægɪŋ] **1** adj (person) brontolone(a); (pain) insistente, molesto(a); (doubt, fear etc) tormentoso(a), angoscioso(a). **2** n brontolii mpl, osservazioni fpl continue.

nail [neɪl] **1** n (a) (Anat) unghia; **to bite one's ~s** mangiarsi le unghie. **(b)** (metal) chiodo; **to hit the ~ on the head** (fig) cogliere or colpire nel segno; **to pay cash on the ~** pagare a tamburo battente. **2** vt (also fig) inchiodare; (wrongdoer) cogliere sul fatto; **to ~ the lid on a box** inchiodare il coperchio di una cassa. **3** cpd: ~ **polish** n, ~ **varnish** n smalto per unghie; ~ **polish** or **varnish remover** n acetone m, solvente m; ~ **scissors** npl forbicine fpl per unghie.

♦ **nail down** vt + adv inchiodare, fissare con chiodi; (fig): **to ~ sb down to a promise/a price** ottenere una promessa/un prezzo preciso da qn.

nail·brush ['neɪl,brʌʃ] n spazzolino da unghie.

nail·file ['neɪl,faɪl] n lima or limetta per le unghie.

na·ive [naɪ'iːv] adj ingenuo(a).

na·ive·té [,naːiːv'teɪ] n, **na·ive·ty** [naɪ'iːvtɪ] n ingenuità f inv.

na·ked ['neɪkɪd] adj (person) nudo(a); (hillside, trees) spoglio(a), nudo(a); **the ~ truth** la verità nuda e cruda; **to the ~ eye, with the ~ eye** a occhio nudo.

name [neɪm] **1** n nome m; (of book etc) titolo; (reputation) (buon) nome, fama, reputazione f; **what's your ~?** come ti chiami?; **my ~ is Peter** mi chiamo Peter; **by the ~ of Jones** di nome Jones; **to go by or under the ~ of** farsi chiamare; **she knows them all by ~** li conosce tutti per nome; **I know him only by ~** lo conosco solo di nome; **in the ~ of the law/of God** in nome della legge/di Dio; **in the ~ of all those present** a nome di tutti i presenti; **in ~ only** solo di nome; **to take sb's ~ and address** prendere nome e indirizzo di qn; (Police etc) prendere le generalità di qn; **to put one's ~ down for** (car, ticket) mettersi in lista per avere; (school, course) iscriversi a; **to call sb ~s** insultare qn; **he's a big ~ in show business** è una personalità or un grosso nome nel mondo dello spettacolo; **he has a ~ for being honest** è noto per la sua onestà; **to protect one's (good) name** salvaguardare il proprio buon nome; **to make a ~ for o.s.** farsi un nome; **the firm has a good ~** l'azienda ha una buona reputazione; **to get (o.s.) a bad ~** farsi una cattiva fama or una brutta reputazione.

2 vt **(a)** chiamare, dare un nome a; (ship) battezzare; **a man ~d Jones** un uomo di nome Jones; **he was ~d after his father** gli è stato dato il nome del padre. **(b)** (give name of) nominare, fare il nome di; (identify) dire il nome di, indicare; (: accomplice) fare il nome di, rivelare il nome di; **to ~ sb for a post** proporre qn per or proporre la candidatura di qn a una carica; **you ~ it, we've got it** abbiamo di tutto. **(c)** (date, price etc) stabilire, fissare; **have you ~d the day yet?** (for wedding) a quando i confetti?

name-dropping ['neɪm,drɒpɪŋ] n: **there was a lot of ~ in his speech** il suo discorso era farcito di nomi altisonanti; **he's always ~** si dà tante arie vantando amicizie importanti.

name·less ['neɪmlɪs] adj (unknown) senza nome; (anonymous) ignoto(a), anonimo(a); (indefinable: fears, crimes) indescrivibile, innominabile; **a certain person who shall be ~** una persona che resterà sconosciuta.

name·ly ['neɪmlɪ] adv vale a dire, cioè.

name·plate ['neɪm,pleɪt] n (on door etc) targa.

name·sake ['neɪm,seɪk] n omonimo/a.

nan·ny ['nænɪ] **1** n (children's) bambinaia, tata (fam). **2** cpd: ~ **goat** n capra.

nap¹ [næp] n sonnellino, pisolino; **to have or take a ~** fare or farsi un sonnellino, schiacciare un pisolino.

nap² [næp] n (on cloth) pelo; **against the ~** contropelo.

na·palm ['neɪpɑːm] n napalm m.

nape [neɪp] n: ~ **of the neck** nuca.

nap·kin ['næpkɪn] **1** n (table ~) tovagliolo, salvietta; (Brit: also: **nappy**) pannolino. **2** cpd: ~ **ring** n portatovagliolo.

Na·ples ['neɪplz] n Napoli f.

nar·cis·sus [nɑː'sɪsəs] n, pl narcissi [nɑː'sɪsaɪ] narciso.

nar·cot·ic [nɑː'kɒtɪk] **1** adj narcotico(a). **2** n narcotico, stupefacente m.

narked [nɑːkt] adj (Brit fam) scocciato(a).

nar·rate [nə'reɪt] vt narrare, raccontare.

nar·ra·tion [nə'reɪʃən] n narrazione f.

nar·ra·tive ['nærətɪv] **1** adj narrativo(a). **2** n narrazione f; (art) narrativa.

nar·ra·tor [nə'reɪtə'] n narratore/trice.

nar·row ['nærəʊ] **1** adj (-er, -est) (gen) stretto(a); (advantage, majority) scarso(a), minimo(a); (outlook, mind) ristretto(a), limitato(a); (interpretation) limitato(a); (resources, means) limitato(a), modesto(a); **to live in ~ circumstances** vivere nelle ristrettezze; **to have a ~ escape** cavarsela per un pelo, scamparla bella.

2 vt **(a)** (also: ~ **down**: road) restringere, fare più stretto(a); (: investigations) restringere; (: choice) restringere, limitare, ridurre; **we have ~ed the field (down) to 3 candidates** abbiamo ristretto il campo a 3 candidati.

(b) *(eyes)* socchiudere.

3 *vi (road)* stringersi, restringersi; *(majority)* ridursi, scendere; *(eyes)* socchiudersi; **so the question ~s down to this...** dunque la questione si riduce a questo... .

nar·row·ly ['nærəulɪ] *adv* **(a)** *(miss, escape etc)*: **Maria ~ escaped drowning** per un pelo Maria non è affogata; **he ~ missed hitting the cyclist** per poco non ha investito il ciclista. **(b)** *(interpret: rules etc)* rigorosamente.

narrow-minded [,nærəu'maɪndɪd] *adj (pej: person)* di idee ristrette; *(: views, outlook etc)* ristretto(a).

na·sal ['neɪzəl] *adj* nasale.

na·sal·ize ['neɪzəlaɪz] *vt* nasalizzare.

nas·ti·ly ['nɑːstɪlɪ] *adv (unpleasantly)* sgradevolmente; *(spitefully)* malignamente.

nas·ti·ness ['nɑːstɪnɪs] *n (of person, remark)* cattiveria; *(: spitefulness)* malignità.

na·stur·tium [nəs'tɜːʃəm] *n* cappuccina, nasturzio (indiano).

nas·ty ['nɑːstɪ] *adj* **(-ier, -iest)** *(smell, taste)* cattivo(a), sgradevole; *(moment, experience)* brutto(a), spiacevole; *(accident, wound, corner, trick)* brutto(a); *(person)* antipatico(a), villano(a); *(: spiteful: also: remark, mind)* maligno(a); *(temper, nature)* brutto(a); *(weather)* brutto(a), cattivo(a); *(book, film etc: obscene)* sconcio(a), osceno(a); **to smell ~** aver cattivo odore, puzzare; **to turn ~** *(situation)* mettersi male; *(weather)* guastarsi; *(person)* incattivirsi; **he's a ~ piece of work** *(fam)* è una canaglia; **what a ~ mind you have!** quanto sei maligno!; **he had a ~ time of it** l'ha passata brutta; **she gave me a ~ look** mi ha guardato storto.

na·tion ['neɪʃən] *n* nazione *f*.

na·tion·al ['næʃənl] **1** *adj* nazionale. **2** *n* cittadino/a. **3** *cpd*: **~ anthem** *n* inno nazionale; **~ debt** *n* debito pubblico; N**~ Health Service** *n (Brit: abbr* **N.H.S.)** ≃ S.A.U.B. *f*; **I got it on the N~ Health** l'ho avuto con la mutua; N**~ Insurance** *n (Brit)* ≃ Previdenza Sociale; **~ news** *n* notizie *fpl* dall'interno; **~ service** *n (Mil)* servizio militare; N**~ Trust** *n (Brit)* ≃ Italia Nostra.

na·tion·al·ism ['næʃnəlɪzəm] *n* nazionalismo.

na·tion·al·ist ['næʃnəlɪst] **1** *adj* nazionalista; *(sympathies)* nazionalistico(a). **2** *n* nazionalista *m/f*.

na·tion·al·ity [,næʃə'nælɪtɪ] *n* nazionalità *f inv*; *(citizenship)* cittadinanza, nazionalità.

na·tion·al·i·za·tion [,næʃnəlaɪ'zeɪʃən] *n* nazionalizzazione *f*.

na·tion·al·ize ['næʃnəlaɪz] *vt* nazionalizzare.

na·tion·al·ly ['næʃnəlɪ] *adv (consider)* da un punto di vista nazionale; *(broadcast)* in tutto il paese; *(apply etc)* a livello nazionale.

nation-wide ['neɪʃən,waɪd] *adj, adv* su scala nazionale.

na·tive ['neɪtɪv] **1** *adj* **(a)** *(country, town)* natale, natio(a), nativo(a); *(dialect)* nativo(a); **he's a ~ Italian speaker** è di madrelingua italiana; **~ language** lingua materna, madrelingua; **~ land** paese *m* natio, patria. **(b)** *(innate: ability)* innato(a), naturale. **(c)** *(indigenous: animal, plant)* indigeno(a); *(: product, resources)* del luogo, del paese; **~ to** originario di; **Britain's ~ red squirrel** lo scoiattolo rosso originario dell'Inghilterra. **(d)** *(of the natives: customs, costume, rites etc)* del luogo, del paese; *(: quarter, labour)* indigeno(a).

2 *n* **(a)** *(of birth, nationality)* abitante *m/f* del luogo; **he's a ~ of Japan** è giapponese di nascita; **he speaks Italian like a ~** parla l'italiano come uno del luogo. **(b)** *(esp of colony)* indigeno/a.

Na·tiv·ity [nə'tɪvɪtɪ] *n* Natività.

NATO ['neɪtəu] *n abbr (* = *North Atlantic Treaty Organisation)* N.A.T.O. *f*.

nat·ter ['nætə'] *(fam)* **1** *n*: **to have a ~** fare quattro chiacchiere. **2** *vi* chiacchierare.

natu·ral ['nætʃrəl] **1** *adj (gen)* naturale; **death from ~ causes** *(Law)* morte per cause naturali; **he died a ~ death** è morto di morte naturale; **in its ~ state** allo stato naturale; **he never knew his ~ parents** non ha mai conosciuto i suoi veri genitori; **it's ~ to be tired after a long journey** è naturale essere stanchi dopo un lungo viaggio; **it seemed the ~ thing to do** è sembrata la cosa più ovvia *or* più naturale da farsi; **it is ~ that...** è naturale che...+ *sub*; **he's a ~ painter** è un pittore nato; **C ~** *(Mus)* do naturale. **2** *n* **(a)** *(Mus: sign)* bequadro. **(b): she's a ~!** ci è nata! **3** *cpd*: **~ childbirth** *n* parto indolore; **~ gas** *n* gas *m* naturale.

natu·ral·ist ['nætʃrəlɪst] *n* naturalista *m/f*.

natu·rali·za·tion [,nætʃrəlaɪ'zeɪʃən] *n (see vb)* naturalizzazione *f*; acclimatazione *f*.

natu·ral·ize ['nætʃrəlaɪz] *vt*: **to be ~d** *(person)* naturalizzarsi; **to become ~d** *(plant, animal)* acclimatarsi.

natu·ral·ly ['nætʃrəlɪ] *adv* **(a)** *(by nature)* naturalmente, per natura; **he is ~ lazy** è pigro per natura; **my hair is ~ curly** i miei capelli sono ricci per natura; **a ~ optimistic person** un ottimista per natura; **it comes ~ to him to do...** gli viene spontaneo fare... . **(b)** *(unaffectedly: behave, speak)* con naturalezza, in modo naturale. **(c)** *(of course)* naturalmente, certo.

na·ture ['neɪtʃə'] **1** *n* **(a)** natura; **a law of ~** una legge di natura; **the laws of ~** le leggi naturali *or* della natura; **to draw/paint from ~** disegnare/dipingere dal vero. **(b)** *(character: of person)* natura, indole *f*; *(: of thing)* natura; **by ~** per natura; **it is not in his ~ to say** that non è nella sua natura *or* nel suo carattere parlare così; **it's second ~ to him to do that** per lui è istintivo farlo. **(c)** *(kind, type)* natura; **things of this ~** cose *fpl* di questo genere; **documents of a confidential ~** documenti *mpl* di natura privata; **something in the ~ of an apology** una specie di scusa. **2** *cpd*: **~ lover** *n* amante *m/f* della natura; **~ reserve** *n* parco naturale; **~ trail** *n* percorso tracciato in parchi nazionali etc con scopi educativi.

-natured ['neɪtʃəd] *adj ending in cpds*: **ill~** maldisposto(a); **jealous~** geloso(a) di natura, di temperamento geloso.

na·tur·ism ['neɪtʃərɪzəm] *n* naturismo, nudismo.

na·tur·ist ['neɪtʃərɪst] *n* naturista *m/f*, nudista *m/f*.

naught [nɔːt] *n* **(a)** *(Math)* = **nought**. **(b)** *(old, poet: nothing)* niente *m*, nulla *m*; **to come to ~** finire in nulla.

naugh·ti·ly ['nɔːtɪlɪ] *adv (behave)* male, con cattiveria; *(say)* maliziosamente.

naugh·ti·ness ['nɔːtɪnɪs] *n* cattiveria.

naugh·ty ['nɔːtɪ] *adj* **(-ier, -iest)** **(a)** *(child)* cattivo(a), birichino(a); **that was a ~ thing to do** non si fanno queste cose. **(b)** *(joke, song etc)* spinto(a).

nau·sea ['nɔːsɪə] *n* nausea.

nau·se·ate ['nɔːsɪeɪt] *vt (Med, fig)* nauseare.

nau·se·at·ing ['nɔːsɪeɪtɪŋ] *adj* nauseante; *(fig)* disgustoso(a).

nau·se·ous ['nɔːsɪəs] *adj (Med, fig)* nauseabondo(a).

nau·ti·cal ['nɔːtɪkəl] *adj* nautico(a); **~ mile** miglio nautico *or* marino.

na·val ['neɪvəl] *adj (battle, strength, base, academy)* navale; *(affairs, barracks)* della marina; **~ forces** forze *fpl* navali, marina da guerra; **~ officer** ufficiale *m* di marina.

nave [neɪv] n (of church) navata.
na·vel ['neɪvəl] n ombelico.
navi·gable ['nævɪgəbl] adj (river etc) navigabile; (ship etc): **in a ~ condition** in condizione di navigare.
navi·gate ['nævɪgeɪt] **1** vt (ship, plane) pilotare, governare; (seas, river) navigare. **2** vi navigare; (Aut) fare da navigatore.
navi·ga·tion [,nævɪ'geɪʃən] n navigazione f.
navi·ga·tor ['nævɪgeɪtə'] n (Naut, Aer) ufficiale m di rotta; (explorer) navigatore m; (Aut) secondo pilota m, copilota m.
nav·vy ['nævɪ] n (Brit) sterratore m, manovale m.
navy ['neɪvɪ] n marina (militare or da guerra); **to join the ~** arruolarsi in marina.
navy(-blue) ['neɪvɪ('bluː)] adj blu marino inv.
nay [neɪ] adv (old: no) no.
Nazi ['nɑːtsɪ] adj, n nazista (m/f).
N.B. abbr (= nota bene) N.B.
N.C.O. n abbr of **non-commissioned officer.**
Nea·poli·tan [nɪə'pɒlɪtən] adj, n napoletano(a) (m/f).
near [nɪə'] **1** adv vicino; **I like to know that you are ~** mi piace sapere che tu sei (qui) vicino or accanto; **~ at hand** a portata di mano; (event) imminente, alle porte; **to come** or **draw ~** (person, event) avvicinarsi; **come ~er** vieni più vicino, avvicinati; **to bring sth ~er (to)** portare qc più vicino (a); **he came ~ to being drowned** per poco non è annegato; **~ to tears** sul punto di piangere; **that's ~ enough** va bene così; **there were 100 people there, ~ enough** c'erano pressappoco 100 persone; **nowhere ~ full** ben lontano dall'essere pieno.
2 prep (also: **~ to**) (of place) vicino a; (in time) circa, quasi; **~ here/there** qui/lì vicino; **he was standing ~ the door** era in piedi vicino alla porta; **it was somewhere ~ midnight** era circa mezzanotte; **it's somewhere ~ here** dev'essere da queste parti; **the passage is ~ the end of the book** il brano è verso la fine del libro; **his views are very ~ my own** le di vedute molto simili alle mie; **nobody comes anywhere ~ her at cooking** nessuno può competere con lei in cucina.
3 adj (**-er**, **-est**) (a) (in space, time) vicino(a); **in the ~ distance** a breve distanza; **the ~est way** la via or strada più breve; **£25000 or ~est offer** 25000 sterline trattabili; **in the ~ future** in un prossimo futuro. **(b)** (relation) stretto(a), prossimo(a); (friend) intimo(a). **(c)** (race, contest) combattuto(a); (result) quasi pari; **it was a ~ finish** hanno finito quasi pari; **that was a ~ miss** (also fig) c'è mancato poco; **he had a ~ miss with that car** per un pelo non ha investito quella macchina; **that was a ~ thing** c'è mancato poco.
4 vt (place, event) avvicinarsi a; **the building is ~ing completion** il palazzo è quasi terminato or ultimato.
near·by [nɪə'baɪ] **1** adv (qui or lì) vicino. **2** adj vicino(a).
near·ly ['nɪəlɪ] adv (a) (gen) quasi; **did you win? – very ~!** ha vinto? — c'è mancato poco!; **not ~ very ~!** ha vinto? — c'è mancato poco!; **not ~** non ... affatto; **it's not ~ ready** non è pronto nemmeno a pensarci, non è pronto affatto; **that's not ~ enough** non basta davvero. **(b)** (with vb): **I ~ lost it** per poco non lo perdevo; **she was ~ crying** era lì lì per piangere; **he very ~ died** ha rischiato di morire.
near·ness ['nɪənɪs] n prossimità, vicinanza.
near·side ['nɪəsaɪd] **1** n (Aut: in Britain) lato sinistro; (: in Italy etc) lato destro. **2** adj (see n) sinistro(a); destro(a).
near-sighted [,nɪə'saɪtɪd] adj miope.

neat [niːt] adj (**-er**, **-est**) **(a)** (tidy: person, handwriting) ordinato(a); (: room, house, desk) ordinato(a), in ordine; (well-dressed) curato(a) nel vestire; (skilful: work) accurato(a), ben fatto(a); (: solution, plan) indovinato(a); (Am: fam: excellent) delizioso(a), favoloso(a); **she is a ~ worker** è molto accurata nel lavoro; **he has made a ~ job of the bathroom** ha fatto un buon lavoro or un lavoro accurato nel bagno; **she has a ~ figure** è ben proporzionata; **a ~ little car** una macchinetta deliziosa. **(b)** (undiluted: spirits) liscio(a).
neat·ly ['niːtlɪ] adv **(a)** (tidily: fold, wrap, dress) accuratamente, con cura; (: write) bene, in bella calligrafia. **(b)** (skilfully) abilmente; **~ put** ben detto.
neat·ness ['niːtnɪs] n **(a)** (tidiness) ordine m. **(b)** (skilfulness) abilità.
nebu·lous ['nɛbjʊləs] adj (also fig) nebuloso(a).
nec·es·sari·ly ['nɛsɪsərɪlɪ] adv necessariamente, per forza; (lead to, give rise to) inevitabilmente; **not ~** non è detto, non necessariamente.
nec·es·sary ['nɛsɪsərɪ] **1** adj (gen) necessario(a); (result, effect) inevitabile; **a ~ evil** un male necessario; **is it ~ to make so much noise?** è proprio necessario or indispensabile far tanto rumore?; **it is ~ for you to go** or **that you go** è necessario che or bisogna che tu vada; **don't do more than is ~** non fare più del necessario; **if ~** se necessario; **the ~ qualifications (for)** i requisiti necessari (per); **~ to health** necessario alla salute. **2** n (fam: what is needed): **to do the ~** fare il necessario; (: money): **the ~** i quattrini.
ne·ces·si·tate [nɪ'sɛsɪteɪt] vt rendere necessario(a).
ne·ces·sity [nɪ'sɛsɪtɪ] n **(a)** necessità; **there is no ~ for you to do that** non è necessario che or non c'è bisogno che tu lo faccia; **the ~ of doing sth** la necessità di fare qc; **is there any ~?** è proprio necessario?, c'è proprio bisogno?; **of ~** di necessità, necessariamente; **from** or **out of ~** per necessità or bisogno; **in case of ~** in caso di necessità. **(b)** (necessary thing) cosa indispensabile, necessità f inv; **the bare necessities** lo stretto necessario, il minimo indispensabile.
neck [nɛk] **1** n (Anat, of bottle) collo; (of garment) collo, colletto; (: Dressmaking) scollo; **to break one's ~** rompersi il collo; (fig) affannarsi; **to have a stiff ~** avere il torcicollo; **the favourite won by a ~** (Horseracing) il favorito ha vinto per un'incollatura; **~ and ~** testa a testa; **to be up to one's ~ in work** (fam) essere immerso nel lavoro fino al collo; **he is in it up to his ~** (fam) c'è dentro fino al collo; **to risk one's ~** rischiare l'osso del collo, rischiare la pelle; **to save one's ~** salvare la pelle; **to stick one's ~ out** (fam) rischiare (forte); **in this ~ of the woods** (fam) in questi paraggi, da queste parti; **dress with a low ~, low-~ed dress** vestito scollato.
2 vi (fam) pomiciare, sbaciucchiarsi.
neck·lace ['nɛklɪs] n collana; **pearl ~** collana di perle.
neck·line ['nɛklaɪn] n scollatura.
neck·tie ['nɛktaɪ] n cravatta.
nec·tar ['nɛktə'] n nettare m.
nec·tar·ine ['nɛktərɪn] n nocepesca.
née [neɪ] adj nata; **Mary Green ~ Smith** Mary Green nata Smith, Mary Smith in Green.
need [niːd] **1** n **(a)** (necessity, obligation) bisogno, necessità; **if ~(s) be** se necessario; **in case of ~** in caso di bisogno or necessità; **there's no ~ to worry** non c'è da or non c'è bisogno di preoccuparsi; **there's no ~ for you to come too** non c'è bisogno or non occorre che venga anche tu; **what**

~ **is there to buy it?** che bisogno c'è di comprarlo?
(b) *(want, lack)* bisogno; *(poverty)* povertà, bisogno; **to be in ~ of, have ~ of** aver bisogno di; **there's a great ~ for a book on this subject** c'è molto bisogno di un libro su questo argomento; **she felt in ~ of a friend** sentiva il bisogno di un amico; **in times of ~** nei momenti difficili; **to be in ~** essere bisognoso(a).
(c) *(thing needed)* bisogno, necessità *f inv;* **£10 will meet my immediate ~s** 10 sterline mi basteranno per le necessità più urgenti; **his ~s are few** ha poche esigenze; **the ~s of industry** le esigenze dell'industria.
2 *vt* aver bisogno di; **he ~s money** ha bisogno di soldi, gli occorrono soldi; **I ~ it** ne ho bisogno, mi serve; **it's just what I ~** è proprio quel che mi ci vuole; **a signature is ~ed** occorre *or* ci vuole una firma; **a much ~ed holiday** una meritata vacanza; **all that you ~** tutto ciò che occorre; **he doesn't ~ me to tell him what to do** non c'è bisogno che sia io a dirgli cosa deve fare; **he ~s watching** *or* **to be watched** va tenuto d'occhio; **this book ~s careful reading** questo libro richiede un'attenta lettura; **the report ~s no comment** il rapporto non ha bisogno di commenti; **he ~s to have everything explained to him** bisogna spiegargli sempre tutto; **he doesn't ~ to be told all the details** non c'è bisogno di *or* non occorre dirgli tutti i particolari; **you only ~ed to ask** bastava che lo chiedessi; **it ~ed a war to alter things** c'è voluta una guerra per cambiare le cose.
3 *(modal aux vb)*: **~ I go?** devo (proprio) andarci?; **I ~ hardly tell you that...** non c'è bisogno che io le dica *or* di dirle che...; **I ~ to do it** lo devo fare, bisogna che io lo faccia; **you ~n't wait** non c'è bisogno che *or* non è necessario che aspetti; **you ~n't have bothered to come** non era necessario che tu venissi; **it ~ not be done now** non c'è bisogno di farlo ora; **it ~ not follow that...** non ne consegue necessariamente che... + *sub.*

nee·dle ['niːdl] **1** *n* ago; *(on record player)* puntina; **knitting ~** ferro da calza; **it's like looking for a ~ in a haystack** è come cercare un ago in un pagliaio; **he gives me the ~** *(fam: annoy)* mi dà ai nervi. **2** *vt (fam: annoy)* irritare, dare ai nervi a; *(: tease, provoke)* pungere, punzecchiare; **she was ~d into replying** punzecchiata, alla fine ha risposto.
need·less ['niːdlɪs] *adj* inutile; **~ to say he didn't keep his promise** inutile dire che non ha mantenuto la promessa.
need·less·ly ['niːdlɪslɪ] *adv* inutilmente.
needle·work ['niːdlwɜːk] *n* cucito (e ricamo).
needy ['niːdɪ] *adj* **(-ier, -iest)** bisognoso(a).
ne·ga·tion [nɪˈgeɪʃən] *n* negazione *f.*
nega·tive ['negətɪv] **1** *adj* negativo(a). **2** *n* **(a)** *(answer)*: **his answer was a firm ~** ha risposto con un fermo no *or* con un fermo diniego; **an answer in the ~** una risposta negativa; **to answer in the ~** rispondere negativamente *or* di no. **(b)** *(Gram)* negazione *f;* **to put a sentence into the ~** mettere una frase in forma negativa. **(c)** *(Phot)* negativa, negativo. **(d)** *(Elec)* polo negativo.
ne·glect [nɪˈglɛkt] **1** *n* trascuratezza; *(of rule etc)* mancata osservanza; **~ of one's appearance** trascuratezza nel vestire; **his ~ of his friends...** l'aver trascurato gli amici...; **the fire started through ~** l'incendio è scoppiato per incuria *or* per negligenza; **in a state of ~** *(house, garden)* in stato di

abbandono. **2** *vt (friends, children, garden etc)* trascurare; *(opportunity)* lasciarsi sfuggire; *(obligations)* mancare a; **to ~ to do sth** trascurare *or* tralasciare di fare qc.
ne·glect·ed [nɪˈglɛktɪd] *adj* trascurato(a).
ne·glect·ful [nɪˈglɛktful] *adj (gen)* negligente; **to be ~ of sb/sth** trascurare qn/qc.
neg·li·gee ['nɛglɪʒeɪ] *n* négligé *m inv.*
neg·li·gence ['nɛglɪdʒəns] *n* negligenza; **through ~** per negligenza; **criminal ~** reato d'omissione.
neg·li·gent ['nɛglɪdʒənt] *adj* **(a)** *(careless)* negligente; **she has become ~ in her work** è diventata trascurata nel lavoro. **(b)** *(offhand: gesture, manner)* noncurante, disinvolto(a).
neg·li·gible ['nɛglɪdʒəbl] *adj* trascurabile.
ne·go·tiable [nɪˈgəʊʃɪəbl] *adj* **(a)** *(Comm etc)* negoziabile; **not ~** *(cheque)* non trasferibile. **(b)** *(road etc)* transitabile, percorribile; *(river)* navigabile; *(hill)* valicabile.
ne·go·ti·ate [nɪˈgəʊʃɪeɪt] **1** *vt* **(a)** *(treaty, loan, sale)* negoziare, trattare. **(b)** *(obstacle, hill, river)* superare, passare; *(bend in road)* prendere; *(difficulty)* superare. **2** *vi* trattare, condurre (le) trattative; **to ~ with sb for sth** trattare con qn per ottenere qc.
ne·go·tia·tion [nɪˌgəʊʃɪˈeɪʃən] *n* trattativa; *(Pol)* negoziato; **to enter into ~s with sb** entrare in trattative *(or* intavolare i negoziati) con qn.
ne·go·tia·tor [nɪˈgəʊʃɪeɪtəʳ] *n* negoziatore/trice.
Ne·gress ['niːgres] *n* negra.
Ne·gro ['niːgrəʊ] **1** *adj* negro(a). **2** *n, pl* **~es** negro.
neigh [neɪ] **1** *vi* nitrire. **2** *n* nitrito.
neigh·bour, *(Am)* **neigh·bor** ['neɪbəʳ] *n* vicino/a; *(Bible etc)* prossimo/a.
neigh·bour·hood, *(Am)* **neigh·bor·hood** ['neɪbəhʊd] *n (district)* quartiere *m*, vicinato; *(surrounding area)* vicinanze *fpl;* **the whole ~ knows her** tutto il vicinato *or* il quartiere la conosce; **in the ~ of the station** nelle vicinanze *or* nei paraggi della stazione; **(something) in the ~ of £80** qualcosa come 80 sterline.
neigh·bour·ing, *(Am)* **neigh·bor·ing** ['neɪbərɪŋ] *adj* vicino(a), confinante, limitrofo(a).
neigh·bour·ly, *(Am)* **neigh·bor·ly** ['neɪbəlɪ] *adj (person, feelings)* cordiale, amichevole; *(action)* da buon vicino; **people here aren't very ~** la gente qua non ha il senso del vicinato.
nei·ther ['naɪðəʳ] **1** *adv* né; **~ he nor I can go** né io né lui possiamo andare; **he ~ smokes nor drinks** non fuma né beve; **he likes ~ the house nor the people** non gli piace né la casa né la gente; **that's ~ here nor there** *(fig)* questo non c'entra. **2** *conj:* **if you aren't going, ~ am I** se tu non ci vai, non ci vado neanch'io *or* nemmeno io; **I don't like it — ~ do I** non mi piace — nemmeno a me. **3** *adj:* **on ~ side** né da una parte né dall'altra; **~ story is true** nessuna delle due storie è vera. **4** *pron* né l'uno(a) né l'altro(a), nessuno(a) dei(delle) due; **~ of them has any money** né l'uno né l'altro *or* nessuno dei due ha soldi, non hanno soldi né l'uno né l'altro.
neo... ['niːəʊ] *prefix* neo...; **~classical** *adj* neoclassico(a); **~fascist** *adj, n* neofascista *(m/f).*
neo·lith·ic [ˌniːəʊˈlɪθɪk] *adj* neolitico(a).
ne·olo·gism [nɪˈɒlədʒɪzəm] *n* neologismo.
neon ['niːɒn] **1** *n* neon *m.* **2** *cpd* al neon; **~ sign** *n* insegna al neon.
neph·ew ['nɛvjuː] *n* nipote *m (di zii).*
nepo·tism ['nɛpətɪzəm] *n* nepotismo.
nerve [nɜːv] **1** *n* **(a)** *(Anat)* nervo; *(Bot)* nervatura; **she suffers from ~s** soffre di nervi; **my ~s are on edge** ho i nervi tesi; **a fit of ~s** una crisi di nervi; **it/he gets on my ~s** mi dà ai nervi, mi fa

venire i nervi; **war of**~**s** guerra psicologica. **(b)** *(courage)* coraggio; *(calm)* sangue *m* freddo; *(self-confidence)* fiducia in se stesso; *(fam: cheek)* sfacciataggine *f*, faccia tosta; **a man of** ~ un uomo di fegato; **to lose one's** ~ *(self-confidence)* perdere fiducia in se stesso; **I lost my** ~ *(courage)* mi è mancato il coraggio; **I hadn't the** ~ **to do it** non ho avuto il coraggio di farlo; *(cheek)* non ho avuto la faccia tosta di farlo; **he's got a** ~! ha una bella faccia tosta!

2 *vt*: **to** ~ **o.s. to do sth** farsi coraggio *or* animo per fare qc, armarsi di coraggio per fare qc.

3 *cpd*: ~ **cell** *n* cellula nervosa; ~ **centre** *n (Anat)* centro nervoso; *(fig)* cervello, centro vitale; ~ **gas** *n* gas *m* nervino.

nerve-racking ['nɜːv,rækɪŋ] *adj* snervante.

nerv·ous ['nɜːvəs] *adj (Anat, Med)* nervoso(a); *(edgy)* nervoso(a), agitato(a); *(apprehensive)* apprensivo(a), ansioso(a); ~ **breakdown** esaurimento nervoso; **he's full of** ~ **energy** è tutto nervi; **he is making me** ~ mi innervosisce; **I was** ~ **about speaking to her** *(apprehensive)* l'idea di parlarle mi agitava; *(excited)* ero emozionato all'idea di parlarle; **I'm** ~ **about flying** ho paura di andare in aereo; **he's a** ~ **wreck** ha i nervi a pezzi.

nerv·ous·ly ['nɜːvəslɪ] *adv* nervosamente; *(apprehensively)* con ansia.

nervy ['nɜːvɪ] *adj* (**-ier, -iest**) *(Brit fam: tense)* teso(a), nervoso(a); *(: Am: cheeky)* sfacciato(a).

nest [nɛst] **1** *n* nido. **2** *vi* fare il nido, nidificare. **3** *cpd*: ~ **egg** *n (fig)* gruzzolo; ~ **of tables** tavolini *mpl* cicogna *inv*.

nes·tle ['nɛsl] *vi* accoccolarsi; **to** ~ **up to** *or* **against sb** stringersi a qn, rannicchiarsi accanto a qn; **to** ~ **down in bed** sistemarsi ben bene nel letto; **a village nestling among hills** un paesetto annidato tra le colline.

nest·ling ['nɛslɪŋ] *n* uccellino di nido, nidiaceo.

net¹ [nɛt] **1** *n (gen, fig)* rete *f*; *(fabric)* tulle *m*; **hair**~ retina (per capelli). **2** *vt (fish, game)* prendere con la rete. **3** *cpd*: ~ **curtains** *npl* tende *fpl* di tulle.

net² [nɛt] **1** *adj (weight, price, salary)* netto(a); ~ **of tax** netto, al netto di tasse; **he earns £10,000** ~ **per year** guadagna 10.000 sterline nette all'anno. **2** *vt (subj: person)* ricavare un utile netto di; *(: deal, sale)* dare un utile netto di.

net·ball ['nɛtbɔːl] *n* sport simile alla pallacanestro.

Neth·er·lands ['nɛðələndz] *npl*: **the** ~ i Paesi Bassi.

net·ting ['nɛtɪŋ] *n (nets)* reti *fpl*; *(mesh)* rete; *(wire* ~*)* rete metallica, reticolato; *(fabric)* tulle *m*.

net·tle ['nɛtl] **1** *n* ortica. **2** *vt* esasperare; **he is easily** ~**d** è una persona facilmente irritabile.

net·work ['nɛtwɜːk] *n (Elec, TV, fig)* rete *f*; ~ **of roads** rete stradale; **spy** ~ rete spionistica *or* di spie.

neu·ral·gia [njʊə'rældʒə] *n* nevralgia.

neu·ro·sis [njʊə'rəʊsɪs] *n, pl* **neuroses** [njʊə'rəʊsiːz] nevrosi *f inv.*

neu·rot·ic [njʊə'rɒtɪk] **1** *adj (person, disease)* nevrotico(a); **she's getting quite** ~ **about it** *(fig)* se ne sta facendo un'ossessione. **2** *n* nevrotico/a.

neu·ter ['njuːtə'] **1** *adj* neutro(a). **2** *n (Gram)* neutro. **3** *vt (cat etc)* castrare.

neu·tral ['njuːtrəl] **1** *adj* **(a)** *(person, country, opinion)* neutrale. **(b)** *(Chem, colour)* neutro(a). **2** *n (Aut)* folle *f*; **in** ~ in folle.

neu·tral·ity [njuː'trælɪtɪ] *n* neutralità.

neu·tral·ize ['njuːtrəlaɪz] *vt* neutralizzare.

neu·tron ['njuːtrɒn] **1** *n* neutrone *m*. **2** *cpd*: ~ **bomb** *n* bomba al neutrone.

nev·er ['nɛvə'] *adv* **(a)** non ... mai; **they** ~ **go out** non escono mai; **I have** ~ **read it** non l'ho mai letto; **have you been to Rome?** — ~ è mai stato a Roma? — mai; ~ **before had he been so bored** non si era mai annoiato tanto; **she's** ~ **been here before** non ci è mai venuta prima; ~ **again!** mai più! **(b)** *(emphatic negative)*: **I** ~ **slept a wink all night** non ho chiuso occhio tutta la notte; **he** ~ **so much as smiled** non ha nemmeno accennato un sorriso; **I told the boss what I thought of him** — ~! *or* **you** ~ **did!** ho detto al capo quel che pensavo di lui — no, non mi dire! *or* non ci credo!; **well I** ~! chi l'avrebbe (mai) detto!, ma guarda un po'!; ~ **mind** non fa niente.

never-ending [,nɛvər'ɛndɪŋ] *adj* interminabile.

never-never [,nɛvə'nɛvə'] *n*: **to buy sth on the** ~ *(Brit fam)* comprare qc a rate.

never-the-less [,nɛvəðə'lɛs] *adv* tuttavia, ciò nonostante, nondimeno.

new [njuː] **1** *adj* **(-er, -est)** nuovo(a); *(different)* nuovo(a), altro(a); *(bread)* fresco(a); **he buys a** ~ **car every year** *(brand-new)* si compra una macchina nuova ogni anno; *(different)* si compra una nuova macchina *or* una macchina diversa ogni anno; **bring me a** ~ **glass** portami un altro bicchiere; ~ **potatoes** patate *fpl* novelle; **the** ~ **moon** la luna nuova; **as good as** ~ come nuovo; **that's nothing** ~ non è una novità; **what's** ~? ci sono novità?; **are you** ~ **here?** sei nuovo di qui? **I'm** ~ **to this job** sono nuovo del mestiere; **the idea was quite** ~ **to him** l'idea gli riusciva nuova.

2 *cpd*: ~ **boy/girl** *n (Scol)* nuovo(a) scolaro(a); **N**~ **Testament** *n* Nuovo Testamento; **the N**~ **World** il Nuovo Mondo; **N**~ **Year** **1** *n* anno nuovo, nuovo anno; **to bring in the N**~ **Year** brindare all'anno nuovo; **Happy N**~ **Year!** Buon Anno!; **to wish sb a happy N**~ **Year** augurare Buon Anno a qn; **N**~ **Year's Day** Capodanno; **N**~ **Year's Eve** la notte di San Silvestro, la vigilia di Capodanno; **2** *cpd (party etc)* di Capodanno; *(resolution)* per l'anno nuovo; **N**~ **Zealand** **1** *n* Nuova Zelanda; **2** *adj* neozelandese; **N**~ **Zealander** *n* neozelandese *m/f*.

new·born ['njuː,bɔːn] *adj* neonato(a); ~ **baby** neonato.

new·comer ['njuː,kʌmə'] *n* nuovo(a) venuto(a).

new-fangled ['njuː,fæŋgld] *adj (pej)* stramoderno(a).

new-laid ['njuː'leɪd] *adj (egg)* fresco(a).

new·ly ['njuːlɪ] *adv (recently)* appena, da poco, di recente; *(in a new way)* in modo nuovo; ~ **made** appena fatto(a).

newly-weds ['njuːlɪwɛdz] *npl* sposini *mpl*, sposi *mpl* novelli.

new·ness ['njuːnɪs] *n* novità.

news [njuːz] **1** *nsg (gen, Press)* notizie *fpl*; *(report: on radio)* notiziario, giornale *m* radio; *(: on TV)* notiziario, telegiornale *m*; **a piece of** *or* **an item of** ~ una notizia; *(in newspaper)* articolo; **have you heard the** ~? hai saputo la notizia?; **have you heard the** ~ **about Maria?** hai saputo di Maria?; **have you any** ~ **of Maria/of her?** hai notizie di Maria/sue notizie?; **what's your** ~? (ci sono) novità?; **what's the latest** ~ **about the earthquake?** si sa qualcosa di nuovo sul terremoto?; **is there any** ~? ci sono notizie?; **good/bad** ~ buone/cattive notizie; **I've got** ~ **for you!** non sai l'ultima!; **this is** ~ **to me** questo mi giunge nuovo; **they're in the** ~ ne parlano i giornali; **home/foreign** ~ notizie dall'interno/dall'estero; **financial** ~ *(Press)* pagina economica e finanziaria; *(Radio, TV)* notiziario economico.

2 *cpd*: ~ **agency** *n* agenzia stampa *or* di informazioni; ~ **bulletin** *n (Radio, TV)* notiziario; ~

flash *n* (notizia *f*) flash *m inv*; ~ **headlines** *npl* titoli *mpl* delle principali notizie.

news·agent ['njuːz,eɪdʒənt] *n* (*Brit*) giornalaio/a.

news·cast ['njuːz,kɑːst] *n* (*esp Am Radio, TV*) notiziario.

news·caster ['njuːz,kɑːstəʳ] *n* (*Radio*) annunciatore/trice; (*TV*) presentatore/trice.

news·dealer ['njuːz,diːləʳ] *n* (*Am*) giornalaio/a.

news·flash ['njuːz,flæʃ] *n* (notizia *f*) flash *m inv*.

news·letter ['njuːz,letəʳ] *n* bollettino (*di ditta, associazione*).

news·paper ['njuːs,peɪpəʳ] *n* giornale *m; daily* ~ quotidiano; **weekly** ~ settimanale *m*.

news·paper·man ['njuːspeɪpə,mæn] *m* giornalista *m*.

news·print ['njuːzprɪnt] *n* carta da giornale.

news·reader ['njuːz,riːdəʳ] *n* = **newscaster**.

news·reel ['njuːzriːl] *n* cinegiornale *m*.

news·room ['njuːz,rʊm] *n* (*Press*) redazione *f*; (*Radio, TV*) studio.

news·stand ['njuːz,stænd] *n* edicola.

news·worthy ['njuːz,wɜːðɪ] *adj* che fa notizia.

newsy ['njuːzɪ] *adj* (*fam*) ricco(a) di notizie.

newt [njuːt] *n* tritone *m*.

next [nekst] **1** *adj* (a) (*immediately adjoining: house, street, room*) vicino(a), accanto *inv*; (*immediately following: bus stop, turning: in future*) prossimo(a); (*: in past*) successivo(a), (subito) dopo; **'turn to the ~ page'** 'vedi pagina seguente'; the ~ **size (up)** la misura più grande; **get off at the ~ stop** scendi alla prossima fermata; **he got off at the ~ stop** è sceso alla fermata successiva; **I arrived at 3 and Mary was ~ to arrive** io sono arrivato alle 3 e dopo di me è arrivata Mary; **it's the ~ door but one on the right** è la seconda porta a destra; **who's ~?** a chi tocca?; **you're ~** tocca a lei.

(b) (*in time: day, week etc*): ~ **month** il mese prossimo; **the ~ month** il mese dopo *or* successivo; **the week after** ~ fra due settimane; **(the)** ~ **time you come** quando vieni la prossima volta, la prossima volta che vieni; **this time** ~ **year** in questo periodo fra un anno; **the ~ day** il giorno dopo, l'indomani; **the ~ morning** l'indomani mattina, la mattina dopo *or* seguente.

2 *adv* (a) dopo, poi; **first he opened his letters and** ~ **he read the paper** prima ha aperto la corrispondenza e dopo *or* poi ha letto il giornale; **what will you do ~?** e adesso che farai?; **when you ~ see him** quando lo vedi la prossima volta, la prossima volta che lo vedi; **when ~ I saw him** quando l'ho visto la volta dopo *or* una seconda volta; **what comes ~?** che cosa viene dopo?; **what ~?** e poi?; (*expressing surprise etc*) che altro mai?; **the ~ best thing would be...** la migliore alternativa sarebbe...; **the ~ to last** il penultimo.

(b): ~ **to** (*beside*) di fianco a, accanto a; (*nearly*) quasi, pressoché; **his room is** ~ **to mine** la sua stanza è accanto alla mia; **I don't like wearing synthetics** ~ **to the skin** non mi piacciono le fibre sintetiche a contatto della pelle; **to nothing** quasi niente; **we got it for** ~ **to nothing** non ci è costato quasi niente, l'abbiamo comprato per una sciocchezza; **there is** ~ **to no news** non si sa quasi niente.

3 *n* prossimo/a; ~ **please!** (avanti) il prossimo!; **the** ~ **to speak is Carla** Carla sarà la prossima a parlare, ora tocca a Carla parlare.

next door ['neks'dɔːʳ] **1** *adv* accanto; ~ **to us** accanto a noi, nella casa accanto; **the girl** ~ la ragazza della porta accanto. **2** *n* la casa accanto; **from** ~ della casa accanto. **3 next-door** *adj*: ~

house casa accanto; ~ **neighbour** vicino/a di casa.

N.H.S. *abbr of* **National Health Service**.

nib [nɪb] *n* (*of pen*) pennino.

nib·ble ['nɪbl] **1** *vt* (*also:* ~ **at**) (a) (*subj: mouse*) rosicchiare; (*: fish*) mordicchiare; (*: person: biscuits, nuts*) sgranocchiare; (*: bread, cheese*) sbocconcellare. (b) (*fig: offer*) mostrarsi tentato(a) da. **2** *vi* (*person*) mangiucchiare.

nice [naɪs] *adj* (**-r, -st**) (a) (*gen: pleasant*) bello(a), piacevole; (*: person*) simpatico(a), piacevole, gentile; (*: taste, smell, meal*) buono(a); (*attractive, pretty*) carino(a), bello(a); **he's a** ~ **man** è una brava persona, è un uomo simpatico; **he was very** ~ **about it** è stato molto gentile; **be** ~ **to him** sii gentile con lui; **how** ~ **you look!** come stai bene!; **did you have a** ~ **time?** ti sei divertito?; **it's** ~ **here** si sta bene qua.

(b) (*iro*) bello(a); **that's a** ~ **thing to say!** belle cose da dirsi!, son cose da dirsi, queste!; **you've got us into a** ~ **mess!** ci hai messo in un bel pasticcio!

(c) (*refined, polite*) gentile, garbato(a); **he has** ~ **manners** ha modi gentili *or* garbati; ~ **girls don't go out at night on their own** le ragazze per bene non escono da sole la sera; **that's not** ~ non sta bene.

(d) (*intensifier: fam*) bello(a) + *adj*; **he gets** ~ **long holidays** le sue vacanze sono belle lunghe; **it's** ~ **and warm here** è bello caldo qui, c'è un bel calduccio qui; ~ **and early** di buon'ora.

(e) (*subtle: distinction*) sottile, fine.

nice-looking ['naɪs,lʊkɪŋ] *adj* bello(a).

nice·ly ['naɪslɪ] *adv* bene; (*kindly*) gentilmente; **that will do** ~ andrà benissimo; **he's getting on** ~ **in his new job** se la cava bene nel nuovo lavoro.

ni·cety ['naɪsɪtɪ] *n* (a) (*of judgment*) accuratezza; **a question of some** ~ una questione piuttosto delicata; **to a** ~ alla perfezione. (b): **niceties** particolari *mpl*, finezze *fpl*.

niche [niːʃ] *n* (*Archit*) nicchia; (*fig*): **to find a** ~ **for o.s.** trovare la propria strada.

nick [nɪk] **1** *n* (a) (*in wood, blade*) tacca; (*on skin*) taglietto; (*in plate*) scheggiatura; **in the** ~ **of time** appena in tempo. (b) (*fam*): **in good** ~ decente, in buono stato. (c) (*Brit fam: prison*) galera; (*: police station*) centrale *f* (di polizia); **in the** ~ in galera. **2** *vt* (a) (*see n*) intaccare; tagliare; (*surface*) scalfire. (b) (*fam: steal*) fregare. (c) (*fam: arrest*) beccare; **to get** ~**ed** farsi beccare.

nick·el ['nɪkl] *n* (*metal*) nichel *m*; (*Am: coin*) (moneta da) cinque centesimi *mpl*.

nick·name ['nɪkneɪm] **1** *n* soprannome *m*; (*humorous, malicious*) nomignolo. **2** *vt*: **to** ~ **sb sth** soprannominare qn qc.

nico·tine ['nɪkətiːn] *n* nicotina.

niece [niːs] *n* nipote *f* (*di zii*).

nif·ty ['nɪftɪ] *adj* (**-ier, -iest**) (*fam: car, jacket*) chic *inv*; (*: gadget, tool*) ingegnoso(a); **that was a** ~ **piece of work** è stato un bel lavoretto.

Ni·geria [naɪ'dʒɪərɪə] *n* Nigeria.

nig·gard·ly ['nɪgədlɪ] *adj* (*person*) tirchio(a), spilorcio(a); (*allowance, amount*) misero(a).

nig·ger ['nɪgəʳ] *n* (*fam!*) negro/a.

nig·gle ['nɪgl] **1** *vi* fare il(la) pignolo(a). **2** *vt* assillare.

nig·gling ['nɪglɪŋ] *adj* (*detail*) insignificante; (*doubt, pain*) persistente; (*person*) pignolo(a).

night [naɪt] **1** *n* notte *f*; (*evening*) sera; **good** ~! buona notte!; **at** ~ di notte, la notte; **in the** ~, **during the** ~ durante la notte; **by** ~ di notte; **last** ~ la notte scorsa, stanotte, ieri notte; **Tuesday** ~ martedì notte, la notte di martedì, la notte fra martedì e mercoledì; *(evening)* martedì sera, la sera di martedì; **the ~ before** la notte prima; *(evening)* la sera prima; **the ~ before last** l'altro ieri notte; *(evening)* l'altro ieri sera; **11 o'clock at ~** le 11 di sera; **the last 3 ~s of** *(Theatre etc)* le 3 ultime serate *or* rappresentazioni di; **to have a ~ out** uscire la sera; **we had a lovely ~ out** abbiamo passato una bellissima serata fuori; **to spend the ~** passare la notte; **I spent the ~ studying** ho passato la notte a studiare; **to have a good/bad ~** dormire bene/male; **to have a late ~** andare a letto tardi; **he's working ~s** è di notte, fa il turno di notte.

2 *cpd (porter, work, nurse, train etc)* di notte; **~ clothes** *npl* pigiama *m*; **~ flight** *n* volo notturno *or* di notte; **~ life** *n* vita notturna; **~ safe** *n* cassa continua; **~ school** *n* scuola serale; **~ watchman** *n* guardiano notturno.

night·bird ['naɪt,bɜːd] *n* uccello notturno; *(fig)* nottambulo/a.

night·cap ['naɪtkæp] *n* papalina, berretto da notte; *(drink)* bicchierino prima di andare a letto.

night·club ['naɪtklʌb] *n* locale *m* notturno, night(-club) *m inv.*

night·dress ['naɪtdres] *n* camicia da notte.

night·fall ['naɪtfɔːl] *n*: **at ~** al calar della notte.

night·gown ['naɪtgaʊn] *n*, **nightie** ['naɪtɪ] *n* camicia da notte.

night·in·gale ['naɪtɪŋgeɪl] *n* usignolo.

night·ly ['naɪtlɪ] 1 *adv* ogni notte, tutte le notti; *(evening)* ogni sera, tutte le sere. 2 *adj* di ogni notte, di tutte le notti; di ogni sera, di tutte le sere.

night·mare ['naɪtmɛəʳ] *n* incubo.

night·shade ['naɪtʃeɪd] *n*: **deadly ~** *(Bot)* belladonna.

night·shift ['naɪtʃɪft] *n* turno di notte; **to be on ~** fare il turno di notte, essere di notte.

night-time ['naɪt,taɪm] *n* notte *f*; **at ~** di notte, la notte.

ni·hil·ism ['naɪɪlɪzəm] *n* nichilismo.

nil [nɪl] *n* nulla *m*; *(Sport)* zero.

nim·ble ['nɪmbl] *adj* (**-r**, **-st**) *(in moving)* agile; *(mentally)* vivace, sveglio(a).

nim·bly ['nɪmblɪ] *adv* agilmente.

nine [naɪn] *adj*, *n* nove *(m inv)*; **~ times out of ten** *(fig)* nove volte su dieci; **they were dressed up to the ~s** si erano messi in pompa magna; *for usage see* **five**.

nine·teen [naɪn'tiːn] *adj*, *n* diciannove *(m inv)*; **to talk ~ to the dozen** *(fam)* parlare come una mitragliatrice; *for usage see* **five**.

nine·teenth ['naɪn'tiːnθ] 1 *adj* diciannovesimo(a). 2 *n (in series)* diciannovesimo/a; *(fraction)* diciannovesimo; *for usage see* **fifth**.

nine·ti·eth ['naɪntɪɪθ] 1 *adj* novantesimo(a). 2 *n (in series)* novantesimo/a; *(fraction)* novantesimo; *for usage see* **fifth**.

nine·ty ['naɪntɪ] *adj*, *n* novanta *(m inv)*; *for usage see* **fifty**.

ninth [naɪnθ] 1 *adj* nono(a). 2 *n (in series)* nono/a; *(fraction)* nono; *for usage see* **fifth**.

nip¹ [nɪp] 1 *n (pinch)* pizzico; *(bite)* morso; **there's a ~ in the air** l'aria è pungente. 2 *vt (pinch)* pizzicare; *(bite)* morsicare; *(prune: bud, shoot)* spuntare; *(subj: cold: plant)* assiderare; *(: face)* pungere; **to ~ sth in the bud** *(fig)* stroncare qc sul nascere. 3 *vi (Brit fam)*: **to ~ inside** andar dentro un attimo; **to ~ out/down/up** fare un salto fuori/giù/di sopra; **where has she ~ped off to?** dov'è sparita?; **I ~ped round to the shop** ho fatto un salto al negozio.

nip² [nɪp] *n (drink)* goccio, bicchierino.

nip·ple ['nɪpl] *n (Anat)* capezzolo.

nip·py ['nɪpɪ] *adj* (**-ier**, **-iest**) *(fam)* **(a)** *(person, car)* svelto(a); **be ~ about it!** sbrigati!, fa' alla svelta! **(b)** *(wind, weather)* pungente; **it's ~** l'aria è pungente.

nit [nɪt] *n* **(a)** *(of louse)* lendine *m*. **(b)** *(fam: idiot)* cretino/a, scemo/a.

nit-pick ['nɪtpɪk] *vi (fam)* cercare il pelo nell'uovo.

ni·tro·gen ['naɪtrədʒən] *n* azoto.

ni·tro·glyc·er·in(e) ['naɪtrəʊ'glɪsəriːn] *n* nitroglicerina.

nitty-gritty ['nɪtɪ'grɪtɪ] *n (fam)*: **to get down to the ~** venire al sodo.

nit·wit ['nɪtwɪt] *n (fam)* imbecille *m/f*, scemo/a.

no [nəʊ] 1 *adv* **(a)** *(opposite of 'yes')* no.

(b) *(emphatic)*: **it is ~ easy task** non è un'impresa facile; **it is ~ small matter** non è una cosa da poco; **in ~ uncertain terms** in termini tutt'altro che ambigui; **there is ~ such thing** una cosa simile non esiste.

(c) *(in comparatives)*: **I am ~ taller than you** non sono più alto di te; **there were ~ fewer** *or* **~ less than 100 people** c'erano non meno di 100 persone; **I can stand it ~ longer** non ne posso più; **he wants to become prime minister, ~ less!** vuole diventare nientemeno che primo ministro!

2 *adj* **(a)** *(not any)* nessuno(a); **she has ~ furniture** non ha mobili, non ha nessun mobile; **I have ~ money** non ho soldi; **there is ~ more coffee** non c'è più caffè; **~ other man** nessun altro; **~ two houses are alike** le case sono tutte diverse l'una dall'altra; **~ two men think alike** non ci sono due persone che la pensino allo stesso modo; **it's ~ trouble** non ci sono problemi; **it is of ~ interest to us** non siamo interessati; **'~ smoking'** 'vietato fumare'; **'~ parking'** 'divieto di sosta'; **there's ~ denying it** non si può negarlo.

(b) *(quite other than)*: **he's ~ friend of mine** non è affatto un mio amico; **he's ~ fool** è tutt'altro che stupido, non è affatto (uno) stupido; **she's ~ beauty** non è certo una bellezza.

3 *n*, *pl* **~es** no *m inv*; **I won't take ~ for an answer** non accetterò un rifiuto.

No., Nos. *abbr* (= *number(s)*) n., nn.

nob·ble ['nɒbl] *vt (Brit fam)* **(a)** *(bribe: person)* comprare. **(b)** *(catch: thief)* beccare; *(: person to speak to)* bloccare. **(c)** *(Racing: horse, dog)* drogare *(per impedirgli di vincere)*.

Nobel prize ['nəʊbel'praɪz] *n* premio Nobel.

no·bil·ity [nəʊ'bɪlɪtɪ] *n* nobiltà.

no·ble ['nəʊbl] 1 *adj* (**-r**, **-st**) nobile; *(also iro)* generoso(a); **of ~ birth** di nobili natali. 2 *n* nobile *m*.

noble·man ['nəʊblmən] *n*, *pl* **-men** nobile *m*, nobiluomo.

noble·woman ['nəʊblwʊmən] *n*, *pl* **-women** nobile *f*, nobildonna.

no·bly ['nəʊblɪ] *adv (selflessly)* generosamente.

no·body ['nəʊbədɪ] 1 *pron* nessuno; **I saw ~** non ho visto nessuno; **~ spoke** nessuno ha parlato, non ha parlato nessuno; **~ else** nessun altro. 2 *n*: **she's a ~** è una nullità.

noc·tur·nal [nɒk'tɜːnl] *adj* notturno(a).

noc·turne ['nɒktɜːn] *n (Mus)* notturno.

nod [nɒd] 1 *n* cenno del capo; **to give sb a ~** fare un cenno col capo a qn; *(answering yes)* accennare di sì a qn, fare di sì col capo a qn. 2 *vt*: **to ~ one's head** fare di sì col capo; **he ~ded a greeting** accennò un saluto col capo; **they ~ded their agreement** accennarono di sì (col capo). 3 *vi* **(a)** fare un cenno col capo; *(say yes)* far segno di sì col capo, annuire; **he ~ded to me in a friendly way** mi ha salutato amichevolmente con un cenno del capo; **we have a ~ding acquaintance** ci conosciamo solo di vista. **(b)** *(doze)* ciondolare il capo (per il sonno).

♦ **nod off** *vi* + *adv* appisolarsi, assopirsi.

node [nəʊd] *n* nodo.

noise [nɔɪz] *n (sound)* rumore *m; (din)* fracasso; *(Telec, Radio, TV)* disturbo, interferenza; **to make a ~** fare un rumore; **stop making a ~!** smettila di far rumore!; **my wife's making ~s about starting a family** mia moglie mi ha fatto capire che vuole avere un bambino; **a big ~** *(fam: person)* un pezzo grosso.

noise·less [ˈnɔɪzlɪs] *adj* silenzioso(a).

noisi·ly [ˈnɔɪzɪlɪ] *adv* rumorosamente.

noisy [ˈnɔɪzɪ] *adj* (**-ier, iest**) rumoroso(a); *(child, party)* rumoroso(a), chiassoso(a); **stop being ~!** smettila di far rumore!

no·mad [ˈnəʊmæd] *n* nomade *m/f.*

no·mad·ic [nəʊˈmædɪk] *adj* nomade.

no-man's-land [ˈnəʊmænzlænd] *n* terra di nessuno.

nom de plume [ˈnɒmdəˈpluːm] *n (Literature)* pseudonimo.

no·men·cla·ture [nəʊˈmenklətʃəʳ] *n* nomenclatura.

nomi·nal [ˈnɒmɪnl] *adj (Gram, rent etc)* nominale; *(rule)* di nome.

nomi·nal·ly [ˈnɒmɪnəlɪ] *adv* nominalmente.

nomi·nate [ˈnɒmɪneɪt] *vt:* **to ~ sb (for sth)** *(propose)* proporre qn come candidato (a qc); *(appoint)* nominare *or* designare qn (a qc).

nomi·na·tion [ˌnɒmɪˈneɪʃən] *n (see vb)* candidatura; nomina.

nomi·na·tive [ˈnɒmɪnətɪv] *(Gram)* **1** *adj* nominativo(a). **2** *n* nominativo.

nomi·nee [ˌnɒmɪˈniː] *n* candidato/a.

non... [nɒn] *pref* non...; **~aggression** *n* non aggressione *f;* **~alcoholic** *adj* analcolico(a); **~aligned** *adj* non allineato(a); **~arrival** *n* mancato arrivo; **~believer** *n* non credente *m/f.*

non·cha·lance [ˈnɒnʃələns] *n* indifferenza, disinvoltura.

non·cha·lant [ˈnɒnʃələnt] *adj* indifferente, disinvolto(a).

non·com·bat·ant [ˌnɒnˈkɒmbətənt] *n* militare *m* non combattente.

non-com·mis·sioned [ˌnɒnkəˈmɪʃnd] *adj:* **~ officer** sottufficiale *m.*

non·com·mit·tal [ˈnɒnkəˈmɪtl] *adj (statement)* non impegnativo(a), evasivo(a); *(person)* che non si compromette, evasivo(a).

non·con·form·ist [ˈnɒnkənˈfɔːmɪst] **1** *adj* anticonformista. **2** *n* anticonformista *m/f;* (*Brit Rel)* dissidente *m/f.*

non·co·op·era·tion [ˈnɒnkəʊˌɒpəˈreɪʃən] *n* non cooperazione *f*, non collaborazione *f.*

non·de·script [ˈnɒndɪskrɪpt] *adj (person, clothes)* qualunque *inv; (colour)* indefinito(a).

none [nʌn] **1** *pron* nessuno(a), nemmeno uno(a), neanche uno(a); **~ of them wants to go** nessuno di loro vuole andarci; **~ of the machines are working** nessuna delle macchine funziona, non c'è neanche una macchina che funzioni; **I have ~ of the books, I have ~** non ho nessuno dei libri, non ne ho nemmeno uno; **~ of this is yours** niente di questo è tuo; **~ of this money** neanche un centesimo di questi soldi; **~ of this wine** neanche una goccia di questo vino; **any news? — ~** ci sono novità? — niente *or* nessuna; **there's ~ left** non ce n'è più; **~ of that!** basta!; **he would have ~ of it** non ne ha voluto sapere; **~ at all** proprio niente; *(not one)* nemmeno uno; **our host was ~ other than the president** il nostro ospite

era nientemeno che il presidente.

2 *adv:* **I was ~ too comfortable** non ero per niente a mio agio; **it's ~ too warm** non fa molto caldo; **and ~ too soon!** ed era ora!; **I like him ~ the worse for it** non per questo mi piace di meno; **he is ~ the worse for his experience** non sembra aver risentito di quell'esperienza; **he is ~ the worse for having stayed up all night** non sembra essere così stanco pur essendo stato su tutta la notte.

non·en·tity [nɒˈnentɪtɪ] *n* persona insignificante, nullità *f inv.*

non·es·sen·tial [ˈnɒnɪˈsenʃəl] **1** *adj* non essenziale. **2:** **~s** *npl* superfluo *sg*, cose *fpl* superflue.

none·the·less [ˌnʌnðəˈles] *adv* nondimeno.

non-event [ˈnɒnɪˈvent] *n* delusione *f;* **the party turned out to be a ~** la festa è stata deludente *or* una delusione.

non·ex·ist·ence [ˌnɒnɪɡˈzɪstəns] *n* inesistenza.

non·ex·ist·ent [ˌnɒnɪɡˈzɪstənt] *adj* inesistente.

non-fic·tion [ˈnɒnˈfɪkʃən] *n* opere non narrative.

non-flam·mable [ˈnɒnˈflæməbl] *adj* ininfiammabile.

non-inter·ven·tion [ˈnɒnˌɪntəˈvenʃən] *n* non intervento.

non-iron [ˈnɒnˈaɪən] *adj* che non si stira.

non-mem·ber [ˈnɒnˈmembəʳ] *n* non socio/a.

non-party [ˈnɒnˈpɑːtɪ] *adj (decision, vote)* indipendente.

non-pay·ment [ˈnɒnˈpeɪmənt] *n* mancato pagamento.

non·plus [ˈnɒnˈplʌs] *pt, pp* **non·plussed** *vt* sconcertare.

non-profit-making [ˈnɒnˈprɒfɪtˌmeɪkɪŋ] *adj,* (*Am*) **non-profit** [ˈnɒnˈprɒfɪt] *adj* senza scopo di lucro.

non-resi·dent [ˈnɒnˈrezɪdənt] *n* non residente *m/f; (in hotel)* ospite *m/f* di passaggio.

non·sense [ˈnɒnsəns] *n* sciocchezze *fpl*, assurdità *fpl;* **(what) ~!** che sciocchezze!, che assurdità!; **it is ~ to say that...** è un'assurdità *or* non ha senso dire che...; **to talk ~** dire sciocchezze *or* assurdità; **that's a piece of ~!** è una sciocchezza!; **to make (a) ~ of sth** rendere assurdo qc; **to stand no ~ (from sb)** non lasciarsi mettere sotto ai piedi (di qn).

non·sen·si·cal [nɒnˈsensɪkəl] *adj* assurdo(a), sciocco(a).

non-shrink [ˈnɒnˈʃrɪŋk] *adj* irrestringibile.

non-skid [ˈnɒnskɪd] *adj* antisdrucciolo(a).

non-smok·er [ˈnɒnˈsməʊkəʳ] *n* **(a)** *(person)* non fumatore/trice; **I'm a ~** non fumo. **(b)** *(Rail)* scompartimento per non fumatori.

non-smok·ing [ˈnɒnˈsməʊkɪŋ] *adj (person)* che non fuma; *(Rail)* per non fumatori.

non-stick [ˈnɒnˈstɪk] *adj (saucepan)* con rivestimento antiaderente.

non-stop [ˈnɒnˈstɒp] **1** *adj* continuo(a), senza sosta; *(train)* diretto(a); *(flight)* diretto(a), senza scalo; **~ entertainment** spettacolo continuo. **2** *adv* ininterrottamente, senza sosta; *(Rail)* diretto; **I flew ~ to New York** ho preso un volo diretto per New York.

non-vio·lent [ˈnɒnˈvaɪələnt] *adj* non violento(a).

non-white [ˈnɒnˈwaɪt] **1** *adj* di colore. **2** *n* persona di colore.

noo·dles [ˈnuːdlz] *npl* pastina.

nook [nʊk] *n* angolino; **we searched every ~ and cranny** abbiamo frugato dappertutto *or* in ogni angolo.

noon [nuːn] *n* mezzogiorno; **at ~** a mezzogiorno.

no-one [ˈnəʊwʌn] *pron* = **nobody.**

noose [nuːs] *n (loop)* nodo scorsoio, cappio; *(for animal trapping)* laccio; *(of hangman)* cappio; **to**

put one's head in the ~ (fig) farsi mettere in trappola.

nope [nəʊp] adv (fam) no.

nor [nɔːʳ] **1** conj = **neither. 2** adv see **neither.**

norm [nɔːm] n norma.

nor·mal ['nɔːməl] **1** adj normale; **it was quite ~ for him to object** era perfettamente normale che obiettasse; **it is perfectly ~ to be left-handed** è perfettamente normale or naturale essere mancini. **2** n: **to return to ~** tornare alla normalità; **above/below ~** al disopra/al disotto della norma.

nor·mal·ity [nɔː'mælɪtɪ] n normalità.

nor·mal·ize ['nɔːməlaɪz] vt normalizzare.

nor·mal·ly ['nɔːməlɪ] adv normalmente.

north [nɔːθ] **1** n nord m, settentrione m; **(to the) ~ of** a nord di; **in the ~** nel nord di; **the wind is from the ~** il vento soffia da nord; **to veer to the ~ (wind)** girare verso nord. **2** adj (gen) nord inv; (wind) del nord; (coast) settentrionale. **3** adv verso nord; **to sail ~** navigare verso nord; **the town lies ~ of the border** la città si trova a nord del confine; **a house facing ~** una casa esposta a nord. **4** cpd: N~ **Africa** n Africa del Nord; N~ **African** adj, n nordafricano(a) (m/f); N~ **America** n America del Nord; N~ **American** adj, n nordamericano(a) (m/f); N~ **Pole** n polo nord; N~ **Sea** n mare m del Nord; N~ **Sea oil** n petrolio del mare del Nord; N~ **Star** n stella polare.

north·bound ['nɔːθbaʊnd] adj (traffic) diretto(a) a nord; (carriageway) nord inv.

north-east [,nɔːθ'iːst] **1** n nordest m. **2** adj di nordest. **3** adv verso nordest.

north-easter·ly [,nɔːθ'iːstəlɪ] adj (wind) che viene dal nordest; (direction) verso nordest.

north-eastern [,nɔːθ'iːstən] adj del nordest.

nor·ther·ly ['nɔːðəlɪ] adj (wind) del nord; (direction) verso nord; **house with a ~ aspect** casa esposta a nord.

north·ern ['nɔːðən] adj (region) del nord, settentrionale; (wall) (esposto(a) a) nord inv; (coast) settentrionale; **in ~ Spain** nel nord della Spagna, nella Spagna settentrionale; N~ **Ireland** Irlanda del Nord; ~ **lights** aurora boreale.

north·ern·er ['nɔːðənəʳ] n settentrionale m/f, abitante m/f del nord.

north·ern·most ['nɔːðənməʊst] adj (il or la) più a nord; **the ~ town in Europe** la città più a nord dell'Europa.

north·ward(s) ['nɔːθwəd(z)] adv verso nord.

north-west [,nɔːθ'wɛst] **1** n nordovest m. **2** adj di nordovest. **3** adv verso nordovest.

north-wester·ly [,nɔːθ'wɛstəlɪ] adj (wind) che viene dal nordovest; (direction) verso nordovest.

north-western [,nɔːθ'wɛstən] adj del nordovest.

Nor·way ['nɔːweɪ] n Norvegia.

Nor·we·gian [nɔː'wiːdʒən] **1** adj norvegese. **2** n (person) norvegese m/f; (language) norvegese m.

nose [nəʊz] **1** n naso; (of animal, plane) muso; **to speak through one's ~** parlare col naso; **to blow one's ~** soffiarsi il naso; **my ~ is bleeding** perdo sangue dal naso; **right under my ~** (fig) proprio sotto il naso; **to follow one's ~** andare a naso; **to pay through the ~ (for sth)** (fam) pagare (qc) un occhio della testa; **to poke or stick one's ~ into sth** (fam) ficcare or cacciare il naso in qc; **to turn up one's ~ (at sth)** arricciare il naso (di fronte a qc); **to look down one's ~ at** disprezzare; (person) guardare dall'alto in basso; **to have a (good) ~ for** aver buon fiuto or buon naso per.

2 vi (also: ~ **one's way**) avanzare cautamente; **the car ~d (its way) into the stream of traffic** l'auto si è infilata poco a poco nella corrente del traffico.

3 cpd: ~ **drops** npl gocce fpl per il naso.

♦ **nose about, nose around** vi + adv aggirarsi.

♦ **nose out** vt + adv (subj: dog; fig) fiutare.

nose·bag ['nəʊzbæg] n sacchetto per il foraggio.

nose·bleed ['nəʊzbliːd] n emorragia nasale.

-nosed [nəʊzd] adj ending in cpds dal naso...; **red~** dal naso rosso.

nose-dive ['nəʊz,daɪv] **1** n (Aer) picchiata; (fig) calo vertiginoso. **2** vi (see n) scendere in picchiata; calare vertiginosamente.

nos(e)y ['nəʊzɪ] adj (-ier, -iest) (fam) curioso(a); **don't be so ~** non fare il ficcanaso; **she's a ~ girl** è una ficcanaso; ~ **parker** (Brit fam) ficcanaso m/f.

nosh [nɒʃ] n (Brit fam) cibo.

nosh-up ['nɒʃʌp] n (Brit fam) mangiata, abbuffata.

nos·tal·gia [nɒs'tældʒɪə] n nostalgia.

nos·tal·gic [nɒs'tældʒɪk] adj nostalgico(a).

nos·tril ['nɒstrəl] n narice f; (of horse) frogia.

nosy ['nəʊzɪ] adj = **nosey.**

not [nɒt] adv non; **he is ~ here** non è qui, non c'è; **I haven't seen anybody** non ho visto nessuno; **it's too late, is it ~ or isn't it?** è troppo tardi, vero? or no?; **she will ~ or won't go** non ci andrà; **he asked me ~ to do it** mi ha chiesto di non farlo; **whether you go or ~** che tu ci vada o no; ~ **that I don't like him** non che (lui) non mi piaccia; **big, ~ to say enormous** grosso, per non dire enorme; **why ~?** perché no?; **I hope ~** spero di no; ~ **at all** niente affatto, per niente; (after thanks) prego, s'immagini; ~ **one book** neanche un libro; ~ **me/you** etc io/tu etc no; ~ **yet** non ancora; see **even, much, only** etc.

no·table ['nəʊtəbl] adj (person) notevole, eminente; (events) notevole, degno(a) di nota.

no·tably ['nəʊtəblɪ] adv (noticeably) notevolmente; (in particular) in particolare.

no·ta·ry ['nəʊtərɪ] n (also: ~ **public**) notaio.

no·ta·tion [nəʊ'teɪʃən] n notazione f.

notch [nɒtʃ] **1** n (in wood, blade) tacca; (in wheel, saw) dente m; (in belt) buco. **2** vt (stick, blade) intagliare, fare tacche in.

♦ **notch up** vt + adv (score, victory) marcare, segnare.

note [nəʊt] **1** n **(a)** (gen, Diplomacy) nota; **to take** or **make ~s** prendere appunti; **Italian lecture ~s** appunti mpl di italiano; **to take** or **make a ~ of sth** prendere nota di qc; **I must make a ~ to buy some more** devo ricordarmi di comprarne di più; **to compare ~s** (fig) scambiarsi le impressioni.

(b) (informal letter) biglietto, due righe; **just a quick ~ to let you know...** ti scrivo solo due righe per informarti... .

(c) (Mus, of bird, fig) nota; **to play** (or sing) **a false ~** prendere una stecca; **to strike the right/wrong ~ (at)** (fig) intonarsi (a)/stonarsi (con); **with a ~ of anxiety in his voice** con una nota di ansia nella voce.

(d) (Comm) nota; (bank~) banconota, biglietto; **delivery ~** bolletta di consegna; **five-pound ~** biglietto da cinque sterline.

(e) (of person): **of ~** eminente, importante.

(f) (notice): **worthy of ~** degno(a) di nota; **to take ~ of** prendere nota di.

2 vt (observe) notare, osservare; (take ~ of) prendere nota di, prendere atto di; (also: ~ **down**) annotare, prendere nota di.

note·book ['nəʊtbʊk] n taccuino; (Scol) blocco per appunti; (for shorthand) bloc-notes m inv.

not·ed ['nəʊtɪd] adj: ~ **(for)** famoso(a) (per).

note·paper ['nəʊt,peɪpəʳ] n carta da lettere.

note·worthy ['nəʊt,wɜːðɪ] *adj* degno(a) di nota, importante.

noth·ing ['nʌθɪŋ] **1** *n* **(a)** niente *m*, nulla *m*; *(Math, Sport)* zero; ~ **happened** non è successo niente *or* nulla; **I've eaten** ~ non ho mangiato niente *or* nulla; **there is** ~ **to eat** non c'è niente *or* nulla da mangiare.

(b) *(in phrases)*: **as if** ~ **had happened** come se niente fosse; ~ **at all** proprio niente; ~ **else** nient'altro; ~ **much/new** *etc* niente di speciale/ nuovo *etc*; ~ **but** nient'altro che; **she does** ~ **but sleep** non fa altro che dormire; **there is** ~ **for it but to go** non c'è altra scelta che andare; **there is** ~ **in it** *(not true)* non c'è niente di vero; *(not interesting)* non è per niente interessante; *(nearly the same)* non c'è una grande differenza; **there's** ~ **in it for us** non ci guadagniamo niente; **there's** ~ **to it!** *(it's easy)* è una cosa da niente!; **to have** ~ **on** *(naked)* non aver niente addosso; *(not busy)* non aver niente in programma; **for** ~ *(free, unpaid)* per niente, gratis; *(in vain)* per niente, inutilmente; *(for no reason)* senza ragione; **he is** ~ **if not careful** è soprattutto attento; **I can do** ~ **about it** non posso farci nulla; **to come to** ~ finire in nulla; **to say** ~ **of...** per non parlare di...; **to think** ~ **of doing sth** non trovare niente di strano nel fare qc; **think** ~ **of it!** s'immagini!, si figuri!; **I can make** ~ **of it** non ci capisco niente; **a mere** ~ una cosa da nulla *or* da niente; **to whisper sweet** ~**s to sb** sussurrare tenerezze a qn; ~ **doing!** *(fam)* niente da fare!

2 *adv* per niente, niente affatto; **it was** ~ **like as expensive as we thought** era molto meno caro di quanto credessimo.

noth·ing·ness ['nʌθɪŋnɪs] *n (non-existence)* nulla *m; (worthlessness, insignificance)* nullità.

no·tice ['nəʊtɪs] **1** *n* **(a)** *(intimation, warning)* avviso; *(period)* preavviso; **without** ~ senza preavviso; **advance** *or* **previous** ~ preavviso; **to give** ~ *(tenant)* dare la disdetta a; *(landlord)* dare il preavviso a; **to give sb** ~ *(Admin: inform)* notificare qn; *(: sack)* licenziare qn; **to give** ~, **hand in one's** ~ *(subj: employee)* licenziarsi; **a week's** ~ una settimana di preavviso; **to give** ~ **of sth** annunciare qc; **to give sb** ~ **of sth** avvisare qn di qc; **at short** ~ con un breve preavviso; **at a moment's** ~ immediatamente, all'istante; **until further** ~ fino a nuovo avviso.

(b) *(announcement)* avviso; *(Press)* annuncio; *(sign)* cartello; *(poster)* manifesto, cartellone *m;* **to put a** ~ **in the paper** mettere un annuncio sul giornale.

(c) *(review: of play etc)* critica, recensione *f.*

(d) *(attention)*: **to bring sth to sb's** ~ far notare qc a qn; **to take** ~ **of sb/sth** notare qn/qc, accorgersi di qn/qc; **to take no** ~ **of sb/sth** non prestare attenzione a qn/qc; **he keeps waving at me — take no** ~**!** continua a farmi dei cenni — ignoralo! *or* fai finta di niente!; **it has come to my** ~ **that...** sono venuto a sapere che...; **to escape** *or* **avoid** ~ passare inosservato; **it escaped my** ~ **that...** non ho notato che...

2 *vt* accorgersi di, notare; **he pretended not to** ~ **us** ha fatto finta di non vederci; **I** ~ **you have a new car** vedo che ha una macchina nuova.

3 *cpd:* ~ **board** *n* tabellone *m (per affissi).*

no·tice·able ['nəʊtɪsəbl] *adj (perceptible)* percettibile; *(obvious)* evidente; *(considerable)* notevole; **the scar is hardly** ~ la cicatrice si vede appena; **there has been a** ~ **increase in prices** c'è stato un notevole aumento dei prezzi.

no·ti·fi·ca·tion [,nəʊtɪfɪ'keɪʃən] *n (see vb)* notifica; denuncia; *(announcement)* annuncio.

no·ti·fy ['nəʊtɪfaɪ] *vt:* **to** ~ **sb of sth** informare qn di qc; **to** ~ **sth to sb** notificare qc a qn; **you should** ~ **the police that your car has been stolen** deve denunciare il furto della macchina alla polizia.

no·tion ['nəʊʃən] *n* idea; **to have no** ~ **of time** non avere la nozione del tempo; **I haven't the slightest** *or* **foggiest** ~ non ho la più pallida idea; **I have no** ~ **of what you mean** non ho la più vaga idea di cosa tu voglia dire.

no·to·ri·ety [,nəʊtə'raɪətɪ] *n* notorietà.

no·to·ri·ous [nəʊ'tɔːrɪəs] *adj (thief, criminal, prison etc)* famigerato(a); *(liar)* ben noto(a); *(place, crime)* tristemente famoso(a); **a town** ~ **for its fog** una città purtroppo famosa per la nebbia.

no·to·ri·ous·ly [nəʊ'tɔːrɪəslɪ] *adv* notoriamente.

not·with·stand·ing [,nɒtwɪθ'stændɪŋ] **1** *prep* nonostante, malgrado. **2** *adv* ciononostante, nondimeno. **3** *conj:* ~ **that** benché + *sub.*

nou·gat ['nuːgɑː] *n* torrone *m.*

nought [nɔːt] *n (Math)* zero; ~**s and crosses** *(Brit)* gioco in cui si segnano 'o' e 'x' in un quadrato di 9 caselle.

noun [naʊn] *n* sostantivo, nome *m.*

nour·ish ['nʌrɪʃ] *vt* nutrire.

nour·ish·ing ['nʌrɪʃɪŋ] *adj* nutriente.

nour·ish·ment ['nʌrɪʃmənt] *n* nutrimento.

nou·veau riche [,nuːvəʊ'riːʃ] *n, pl* **nouveaux riches** nuovo(a) ricco(a) *m/f*, arricchito/a.

nov·el ['nɒvəl] **1** *adj* originale, nuovo(a) *after n.* **2** *n (Literature)* romanzo.

nov·el·ist ['nɒvəlɪst] *n* romanziere/a.

nov·el·ty ['nɒvəltɪ] *n* **(a)** *(no pl)* novità. **(b)** *(Comm)* articolo *m* novità *inv.*

No·vem·ber [nəʊ'vembəʳ] *n* novembre *m; for usage see* July.

nov·ice ['nɒvɪs] *n* principiante *m/f; (Rel)* novizio/a.

now [naʊ] **1** *adv* **(a)** *(at present, these days)* adesso, ora; *(at that time)* allora, ora; **right** ~ subito, immediatamente; ~ **is the time to do it** questo è il momento per farlo; **they won't be long** ~ ormai non tarderanno; **it happened just** ~ è successo proprio ora; **(every)** ~ **and again, (every)** ~ **and then** ogni tanto, di tanto in tanto; **it's** ~ **or never** ora o mai più.

(b) *(with prep):* **between** ~ **and Monday** da qui a lunedì, entro lunedì; **I couldn't do it before** ~ non potevo farlo prima; **long before** ~ molto tempo fa; **by** ~ ormai; **the train should have arrived by** ~ il treno dovrebbe essere già arrivato; **in 3 days from** ~ fra 3 giorni; **from** ~ **on** d'ora in poi; **from** ~ **until then** da adesso fino a quel momento; **that's all for** ~ per ora basta; **until** ~, **up to** ~ fino ad ora.

(c) *(without temporal force):* ~ **(then)!** dunque!, allora!; ~ **then, no more quarrelling** ora *or* adesso basta con i litigi; **well** ~ vediamo, dunque; **well** ~, **look who it is!** ma guarda un po' chi si vede!; **be careful** ~**!** ma sta' attento!

2 *conj:* ~ **(that)** adesso che, ora che.

now·a·days ['naʊədeɪz] *adv* al giorno d'oggi, oggi, oggigiorno; ~ **I haven't got time to watch television** in questo periodo non ho il tempo per guardare la televisione.

no·where ['nəʊwɛəʳ] *adv* in nessun posto, da nessuna parte; **I went** ~ non sono andato in nessun posto *or* da nessuna parte; ~ **in Italy** in nessuna parte d'Italia, da nessuna parte in Italia; ~ **else** in nessun altro posto; **it/he is** ~ **to be found** non si riesce a trovarlo da nessuna parte; **we're getting** ~ non stiamo concludendo niente; **that will get you** ~ ciò non le servirà a nulla; **he appeared from** ~ è saltato fuori da chissà dove; **Paul is** ~ **near as tall as John** Paul non è neanche lontanamente alto come John; **it's ~ near as good** non vale neanche la metà; **~ near enough** ben lontano dall'essere sufficiente.

nox·ious ['nɒkʃəs] *adj* nocivo(a).

noz·zle ['nɒzl] *n (of hose, vacuum cleaner, syringe)* bocchetta; *(of fire extinguisher)* lancia.

nth [ɛnθ] *adj (Math):* **to the ~ power** *or* **degree** all'ennesima potenza; **for the ~ time** *(fam)* per l'ennesima volta.

nu·ance ['njuːɑ̃ːns] *n* sfumatura.

nu·bile ['njuːbaɪl] *adj* nubile.

nu·clear ['njuːklɪəʳ] *adj* nucleare; *(warfare)* atomico(a); **~ disarmament** disarmo nucleare.

nu·cleus ['njuːklɪəs] *n*, *pl* **nuclei** ['njuːklɪaɪ] nucleo.

nude [njuːd] **1** *adj* (**-r**, **-st**) nudo(a). **2** *n (Art)* nudo; **in the ~** nudo(a).

nudge [nʌdʒ] **1** *n* gomitata. **2** *vt* dare un colpetto col gomito a; **he ~d me out of the way** mi ha spinto via con una gomitata.

nud·ist ['njuːdɪst] **1** *adj* nudista; **~ colony** colonia di nudisti. **2** *n* nudista *m/f*.

nu·dity ['njuːdɪtɪ] *n* nudità.

nug·get ['nʌgɪt] *n* pepita.

nui·sance ['njuːsns] *n (state of affairs, thing)* fastidio, seccatura; *(person)* peste *f*; **what a ~!** che seccatura!; **it's a ~ having to shave** doversi radere è una (gran) seccatura; **to make a ~ of o.s.** rendersi insopportabile.

null [nʌl] *adj:* **~ and void** *(Law)* nullo(a).

nul·li·fy ['nʌlɪfaɪ] *vt* annullare.

numb [nʌm] **1** *adj* **(a)** *(fingers etc)* intorpidito(a); **~ with cold** intirizzito (dal freddo); **my leg has gone ~** mi si è intorpidita una gamba. **(b)** *(fig):* **~ with** *(fear)* paralizzato(a) da, impietrito(a) da; *(grief)* impietrito(a) da. **2** *vt* **(a)** intorpidire; **the cold ~s you as soon as you step outside** appena si esce si resta paralizzati dal freddo. **(b)** *(fig)* rendere insensibile; **she drinks to ~ her grief** beve per attenuare il dolore.

num·ber ['nʌmbəʳ] **1** *n* **(a)** *(Math)* numero; *(figure)* cifra, numero; **in round ~s** in cifra tonda; **even/odd ~** numero pari/dispari.

(b) *(quantity)* numero, quantità *f inv*; **a ~ of people** un certo numero di persone, diversa gente; **a fair ~ of** *(reasons, mistakes, people)* una buona quantità di; **on a ~ of occasions** diverse volte, in diverse occasioni; **any ~ of** una gran quantità di, moltissimi; **they were 15 in ~** erano in tutto 15; **times without ~** tantissime volte; **one of their ~** uno di loro.

(c) *(of house etc)* numero; **at ~ 15** al (numero) 15; **reference ~** numero di riferimento; **telephone ~** numero di telefono; **wrong ~** *(Telec)* numero sbagliato; **N~ Ten** *(Brit Pol)* residenza del Primo Ministro del Regno Unito; **opposite ~** *(person)* controparte *f*; **his ~'s up!** *(fam)* è venuta la sua ora!

(d) *(issue: of newspaper etc)* numero.

(e) *(song, act etc)* numero; *(piece of music)* pezzo.

2 *vt* **(a)** *(count, include)* contare; **to ~ sb among one's friends** considerare qn un amico.

(b) *(amount to)* ammontare a; **they ~ed 10 in all** erano 10 in tutto.

(c) *(assign ~ to)* numerare; **his days are ~ed** *(fig)* ha i giorni contati.

3 *cpd:* **~ plate** *n (Brit Aut)* targa.

num·ber·less ['nʌmbəlɪs] *adj* innumerevole, senza numero.

numb·ness ['nʌmnɪs] *n* intorpidimento; *(due to cold)* intirizzimento.

nu·mera·cy ['njuːmərəsɪ] *n* nozioni *fpl* di calcolo.

nu·mer·al ['njuːmərəl] *n* numerale *m*.

nu·mer·ate ['njuːmərɪt] *adj:* **to be ~** saper far di conto.

nu·meri·cal [njuː'mɛrɪkəl] *adj* numerico(a); **in ~ order** in ordine numerico.

nu·mer·ous ['njuːmərəs] *adj* numeroso(a).

nun [nʌn] *n* suora, monaca.

nup·tial ['nʌpʃəl] *adj* nuziale.

nurse [nɜːs] **1** *n* **(a)** *(in hospital etc)* infermiere/a; **student ~** allievo(a) infermiere(a); **male ~** infermiere *m*. **(b)** *(children's)* bambinaia. **2** *vt* **(a)** *(patient)* curare, assistere; **she ~d him back to health** è guarito grazie alle sue cure; **to ~ a cold** curarsi un raffreddore. **(b)** *(baby: suckle)* allattare, dare il latte a. **(c)** *(cradle)* cullare; *(fig: hope)* nutrire, cullare; *(anger, grudge)* covare.

nurse·maid ['nɜːs,meɪd] *n* bambinaia.

nurse·ry ['nɜːsərɪ] **1** *n* **(a)** *(room)* camera dei bambini. **(b)** *(Agr)* vivaio. **2** *cpd:* **~ rhyme** *n* filastrocca; **~ school** *n* asilo infantile, scuola materna.

nurs·ing ['nɜːsɪŋ] **1** *adj* **(a)** *(mother)* che allatta. **(b)** *(of hospital):* **the ~ staff** gli infermieri, il personale infermieristico; **~ auxiliary** infermiere(a) non diplomato(a); **~ home** clinica. **2** *n (care of invalids)* assistenza; *(profession)* professione *f* di infermiera; **she's going in for ~** ha deciso di fare l'infermiera.

nut [nʌt] **1** *n* **(a)** *(Bot)* termine generico per frutti che hanno un guscio *(no generic term in Italian)*; **a bag of mixed ~s** un sacchetto di noci, nocciole, noccioline, mandorle *etc*. **(b)** *(Tech)* dado. **(c)** *(fam: head)* zucca; **he is off his ~** *(fam)* gli manca una rotella, è svitato. **(d)** *(fam: person)* pazzo/a, matto/a. **(e):** **~s!** *(fam: nonsense)* col cavolo! **2** *adj (chocolate etc)* alla nocciola *etc*.

nut·case ['nʌt,keɪs] *n (fam)* matto/a, pazzo/a.

nut·crackers ['nʌt,krækəz] *npl* schiaccianoci *m inv*.

nut·house ['nʌt,haʊs] *n (fam)* manicomio.

nut·meg ['nʌtmɛg] *n* noce *f* moscata.

nu·tri·ent ['njuːtrɪənt] **1** *adj* nutriente. **2** *n* sostanza nutritiva.

nu·tri·tion [njuː'trɪʃən] *n* nutrizione *f*, alimentazione *f*.

nu·tri·tious [njuː'trɪʃəs] *adj*, **nu·tri·tive** ['njuːtrɪtɪv] *adj* nutriente, nutritivo(a).

nuts [nʌts] *adj (fam)* matto(a), pazzo(a); **to be ~ about sb** essere pazzo di qn; **to be ~ about sth** andare matto per qc; **to go ~s** impazzire, dare i numeri.

nut·shell ['nʌtʃɛl] *n* guscio di noce *(or* nocciola *etc)*; **in a ~** in poche parole; **to put it in a ~** per farla breve.

nut·ty ['nʌtɪ] *adj* (**-ier**, **-iest**) **(a)** *(cake)* con le noci; *(chocolate)* alla nocciola *etc*; *(flavour)* che ha sapore di noce *etc*. **(b)** *(fam)* pazzo(a), matto(a).

nuz·zle ['nʌzl] *vi:* **to ~ up to** strofinare il muso contro.

ny·lon ['naɪlɒn] **1** *n* nailon *m*; **~s** calze *fpl* di nailon. **2** *adj* di nailon.

nymph [nɪmf] *n* ninfa.

nym·pho·ma·nia [,nɪmfəʊ'meɪnɪə] *n* ninfomania.

nym·pho·ma·ni·ac [,nɪmfəʊ'meɪnɪæk] *adj*, *n* ninfomane *(f)*.

O

O, o [əʊ] **1** *n (letter)* O, o *f* or *m inv*; *(number: Telec etc)* zero. **2** *excl (poet)* oh!

oaf [əʊf] *n* zoticone/a.

oaf·ish ['əʊfɪʃ] *adj (behaviour)* da zoticone; **an ~ person** uno zoticone.

oak [əʊk] **1** *n* quercia. **2** *cpd* di quercia; **~ apple** *n* cecidio di quercia.

O.A.P. *abbr of* **old-age pensioner.**

oar [ɔːʳ] *n* remo; **to put** *or* **shove one's ~ in** *(fig fam)* intromettersi.

oars·man ['ɔːzmən] *n, pl* **-men** rematore *m*; *(Sport)* vogatore *m*.

oasis [əʊ'eɪsɪs] *n, pl* **oases** [əʊ'eɪsiːz] oasi *f inv*.

oat·cake ['əʊtkeɪk] *n* focaccia di farina d'avena.

oath [əʊθ] *n* **(a)** *(solemn promise etc)* giuramento; **under ~, on ~** sotto giuramento; **to put sb on** *or* **under ~ to do sth** far giurare qn di fare qc; **to take the ~** giurare; **to swear on ~** *or* **on one's ~** giurare solennemente. **(b)** *(curse)* bestemmia.

oat·meal ['əʊtmiːl] **1** *n* farina d'avena. **2** *adj (colour)* beige *inv*.

oats ['əʊts] *npl* avena.

ob·du·rate ['ɒbdjʊrɪt] *adj (stubborn)* testardo(a); *(sinner)* incallito(a); *(unyielding)* ostinato(a), irremovibile.

obedi·ence [ə'biːdɪəns] *n* ubbidienza; **in ~ to your orders** *(frm)* secondo i vostri ordini.

obedi·ent [ə'biːdɪənt] *adj* ubbidiente; **to be ~ to sb/sth** ubbidire a qn/qc.

obedi·ent·ly [ə'biːdɪəntlɪ] *adv* docilmente.

ob·elisk ['ɒbɪlɪsk] *n* obelisco.

obese [əʊ'biːs] *adj* obeso(a).

obesity [əʊ'biːsɪtɪ] *n* obesità.

obey [ə'beɪ] **1** *vt (person)* ubbidire a; *(instructions)* seguire; *(regulations)* osservare; **to ~ one's conscience** seguire i dettami della coscienza. **2** *vi* ubbidire.

obi·tu·ary [ə'bɪtjʊərɪ] **1** *n* necrologio. **2** *cpd:* **~ column** *n* colonna degli annunci mortuari; **~ notice** *n* necrologio.

ob·ject ['ɒbdʒɪkt] **1** *n* **(a)** *(gen)* oggetto; **she was an ~ of ridicule** era oggetto di scherno. **(b)** *(aim)* scopo, obiettivo; **with this ~ in view** *or* **in mind** in vista di questo scopo; **with the ~ of doing** al fine di fare; **what's the ~ of doing that?** a che serve farlo?; **expense is no ~** non si bada a spese. **(c)** *(Gram)* complemento; **direct/indirect ~** complemento oggetto/indiretto.

2 [əb'dʒɛkt] *vt:* **to ~ that** obiettare che.

3 [əb'dʒɛkt] *vi* sollevare obiezione a; **if you don't ~** se te va bene, se sei d'accordo; **to ~ to sb doing sth** disapprovare che qn faccia qc; **she ~s to my behaviour** disapprova il mio comportamento; **do you ~ to my smoking?** ti disturba se fumo?; **I ~!** *(frm)* mi oppongo!

4 *cpd:* **~ lesson** *n (fig):* **~ lesson (in)** dimostrazione *f* (di).

ob·jec·tion [əb'dʒɛkʃən] *n* obiezione *f*; **to make** *or* **raise an ~** sollevare un'obiezione; **there is no ~ to your going** non c'è niente in contrario alla tua partenza; **are there any ~s?** ci sono obiezioni?;

have you any ~ to my smoking? ti disturba se fumo?

ob·jec·tion·able [əb'dʒɛkʃnəbl] *adj (person)* antipatico(a); *(smell)* sgradevole; *(conduct)* spiacevole; *(language)* riprovevole.

ob·jec·tive [əb'dʒɛktɪv] **1** *adj* **(a)** *(impartial)* obiettivo(a). **(b)** *(Gram, Philosophy)* oggettivo(a). **2** *n (aim)* obiettivo.

ob·jec·tive·ly [əb'dʒɛktɪvlɪ] *adv (all senses)* oggettivamente.

ob·jec·tiv·ity [,ɒbdʒɛk'tɪvɪtɪ] *n (see adj)* obiettività; oggettività.

ob·jec·tor [əb'dʒɛktəʳ] *n* oppositore/trice; **a conscientious ~** un obiettore di coscienza.

ob·li·ga·tion [,ɒblɪ'geɪʃən] *n* obbligo; **'without ~'** 'senza impegno'; **to be under an ~ to sb/to do sth** essere in dovere verso qn/di fare qc; **I'm under no ~ to do it** non sono tenuto a farlo; **to meet one's ~s** mantenere i propri impegni; **to fail to meet one's ~s** venire meno ai propri impegni.

ob·liga·tory [ɒ'blɪgətərɪ] *adj* obbligatorio(a); **to make it ~ for sb to do sth** obbligare qn a fare qc.

oblige [ə'blaɪdʒ] *vt* **(a)** *(compel)* obbligare, costringere; **to ~ sb to do sth** costringere qn a fare qc; **to be ~d to do sth** essere in dovere di fare qc. **(b)** *(gratify)* fare una cortesia a; **anything to ~!** *(fam)* questo e altro!; **to be ~d to sb for sth** essere grato a qn per qc; **much ~d!** molto grato!, obbligato!; **I am ~d to you for your help** ti sono grato per il tuo aiuto.

oblig·ing [ə'blaɪdʒɪŋ] *adj* gentile; **it was very ~ of them** è stato molto gentile da parte loro.

oblique [ə'bliːk] **1** *adj (angle etc)* obliquo(a); *(fig)* indiretto(a). **2** *n (Typ)* barra.

oblique·ly [ə'bliːklɪ] *adv* obliquamente; *(fig)* indirettamente.

oblit·erate [ə'blɪtəreɪt] *vt* cancellare.

oblivi·on [ə'blɪvɪən] *n* oblio; **to fall** *or* **sink into ~** essere dimenticato, cadere nell'oblio.

oblivi·ous [ə'blɪvɪəs] *adj:* **~ of, ~ to** ignaro(a) di.

ob·long ['ɒblɒŋ] **1** *adj* oblungo(a). **2** *n* rettangolo.

ob·nox·ious [əb'nɒkʃəs] *adj (person, behaviour)* detestabile; *(fumes etc)* pestifero(a).

oboe ['əʊbəʊ] *n* oboe *m*.

ob·scene [əb'siːn] *adj* osceno(a).

ob·scen·ity [əb'sɛnɪtɪ] *n* oscenità *f inv*.

ob·scure [əb'skjʊəʳ] **1** *adj* **(-r, -st)** *(gen)* oscuro(a); *(feeling, memory)* vago(a). **2** *vt (darken)* oscurare; *(hide: sun)* coprire; *(issue, idea)* confondere.

ob·scu·rity [əb'skjʊərɪtɪ] *n (obscure point)* punto oscuro; *(lack of fame)* anonimato.

ob·se·qui·ous [əb'siːkwɪəs] *adj* ossequioso(a).

ob·ser·vance [əb'zɜːvəns] *n* osservanza; **religious ~s** pratiche *fpl* religiose.

ob·ser·vant [əb'zɜːvənt] *adj (watchful)* attento(a); *(Rel, Law):* **~ (of)** osservante (di).

ob·ser·va·tion [,ɒbzə'veɪʃən] **1** *n* **(a)** *(gen)* osservazione *f*; *(of the law)* osservanza; **the police are keeping him under ~** la polizia lo tiene sotto sorveglianza; **he is under ~ in hospital** è in ospedale sotto osservazione; **powers of ~** capa-

---

279

città d'osservazione; **to escape** ~ sfuggire alla sorveglianza. (**b**) *(remark)* osservazione *f*, commento. **2** *cpd*: ~ **post** *n (Mil)* osservatorio; ~ **tower** *n* torre *f* di osservazione.

ob·ser·va·tory [əb'zɜːvətrɪ] *n* osservatorio.

ob·serve [əb'zɜːv] *vt* osservare.

ob·serv·er [əb'zɜːvəˈ] *n* osservatore/trice.

ob·sess [əb'sɛs] *vt* ossessionare; **to be ~ed by** *or* **with sb/sth** essere ossessionato da qn/qc.

ob·ses·sion [əb'sɛʃən] *n* ossessione *f*; **football is an** ~ **with him** è maniaco del football; **his** ~ **with her** la sua fissazione per lei; **his** ~ **about cleanliness** la sua mania della pulizia.

ob·ses·sive [əb'sɛsɪv] *adj* ossessivo(a).

ob·so·les·cence [ˌɒbsə'lɛsns] *n* obsolescenza.

ob·so·les·cent [ˌɒbsə'lɛsnt] *adj* obsolescente.

ob·so·lete ['ɒbsəliːt] *adj* obsoleto(a), in disuso.

ob·sta·cle ['ɒbstəkl] **1** *n* ostacolo; **to be an** ~ **to sb/sth** essere di ostacolo a qn/qc; **to put an** ~ **in the way of sb** ostacolare qn; **that is no** ~ **to our doing it** questo non ci impedisce affatto di farlo. **2** *cpd*: ~ **race** *n (Sport)* corsa ad ostacoli.

ob·ste·tri·cian [ˌɒbstə'trɪʃən] *n* ostetrico/a.

ob·stet·rics [ɒb'stɛtrɪks] *nsg* ostetricia.

ob·sti·na·cy ['ɒbstɪnəsɪ] *n* ostinazione *f*.

ob·sti·nate ['ɒbstɪnɪt] *adj (gen)* ostinato(a); *(resistance)* strenuo(a); *(illness)* persistente; **as** ~ **as a mule** testardo come un mulo.

ob·sti·nate·ly ['ɒbstɪnɪtlɪ] *adv* ostinatamente.

ob·strep·er·ous [əb'strɛpərəs] *adj* turbolento(a).

ob·struct [əb'strʌkt] *vt (block: pipe, artery)* ostruire; *(: traffic, road, Sport)* bloccare; *(hinder)* ostacolare; **you're** ~**ing my view** mi impedisci di vedere.

ob·struc·tion [əb'strʌkʃən] *n (sth which obstructs)* ostacolo; *(in pipe, artery)* ostruzione *f*; **to cause an** ~ *(in road)* bloccare la strada.

ob·struc·tive [əb'strʌktɪv] *adj* che crea impedimenti; **stop being** ~! non fare l'ostruzionista!

ob·tain [əb'teɪn] *vt (gen)* ottenere; *(goods)*: **to** ~ **sth (for o.s.)** procurarsi qc; **to** ~ **sth for sb** procurare qc a qn.

ob·tain·able [əb'teɪnəbl] *adj*: **where is that** ~? dove si può trovare?

ob·trude [əb'truːd] **1** *vi* imporsi. **2** *vt* imporre.

ob·tru·sive [əb'truːsɪv] *adj (person)* invadente; *(opinions)* ostentato(a); *(smell)* pungente; *(building)* che disturba la visuale.

ob·tuse [əb'tjuːs] *adj (gen, Math)* ottuso(a); *(remark)* stupido(a).

ob·vi·ate ['ɒbvɪeɪt] *vt (gen)* ovviare a; *(danger, objection)* prevenire.

ob·vi·ous ['ɒbvɪəs] *adj (clear, perceptible)* ovvio(a), evidente; *(unsubtle)* scontato(a), banale; **it's** ~ **that...** è ovvio che...; **he's the** ~ **man for the job** è chiaramente la persona che ci vuole per quel lavoro; **the** ~ **thing to do is to leave** la cosa più logica da fare è andarsene; **try not to make it** ~ **that you're bored** cerca di non mostrarti annoiato.

ob·vi·ous·ly ['ɒbvɪəslɪ] *adv* ovviamente, evidentemente; **he was** ~ **not drunk** si vedeva che non era ubriaco; **he was not** ~ **drunk** non si vedeva che era ubriaco; ~! certo!; ~ **not!** certo che no!

oc·ca·sion [ə'keɪʒən] **1** *n* (**a**) *(point in time)* occasione *f*; **on** ~ di tanto in tanto; **on several** ~s **in** varie occasioni; **on that** ~ in quell'occasione, quella volta. (**b**) *(special* ~) occasione *f*, avvenimento; **it was quite an** ~ è stato un avvenimento importante; **music written for the** ~ musica scritta per l'occasione; **on the** ~ **of** in occasione di; **to rise to the** ~ mostrarsi all'altezza della situazione. (**c**) *(reason)* motivo, ragione *f*; **there**

was no ~ **for it** non ce n'era motivo; **to have** ~ **to do sth** avere l'occasione di fare qc; **if you ever have** ~ **to be in London** se ti capita di essere a Londra. **2** *vt (frm)* causare; *(: remark)* dare origine a.

oc·ca·sion·al [ə'keɪʒənl] **1** *adj (gen)* occasionale; *(showers)* sporadico(a); **I like an** ~ **cigarette** ogni tanto apprezzo una sigaretta. **2** *cpd*: ~ **table** *n* tavolino.

oc·ca·sion·al·ly [ə'keɪʒnəlɪ] *adv* ogni tanto; **very** ~ molto raramente.

oc·cult [ɒ'kʌlt] **1** *adj* occulto(a). **2** *n*: **the** ~ l'occulto.

oc·cu·pant ['ɒkjʊpənt] *n (of house)* inquilino/a; *(of boat, car etc)* persona a bordo; *(of job, post)* titolare *m/f*.

oc·cu·pa·tion [ˌɒkjʊ'peɪʃən] *n* (**a**) *(employment)* mestiere *m*, professione *f*; *(pastime)* occupazione *f*; **he's a joiner by** ~ è falegname di mestiere. (**b**) *(gen, Mil)* occupazione *f*; **army of** ~ esercito d'occupazione; **the** ~ **of Paris** l'occupazione di Parigi; **the house is ready for** ~ la casa è pronta per essere abitata.

oc·cu·pa·tion·al [ˌɒkjʊ'peɪʃənl] *adj (disease)* professionale; *(hazard)* del mestiere; ~ **therapy** ergoterapia.

oc·cu·pi·er ['ɒkjʊpaɪəˈ] *n (of house)* inquilino/a; *(of post)* titolare *m/f*.

oc·cu·py ['ɒkjʊpaɪ] *vt* occupare; **this job occupies all my time** questo lavoro occupa *or* prende tutto il mio tempo; **to be occupied with sth/in doing sth** essere preso da qc/occupato a fare qc; **she occupies herself by knitting** lei passa il tempo lavorando a maglia; **to keep one's mind occupied** tenere la mente occupata.

oc·cur [ə'kɜːˈ] *vi* (**a**) *(event)* accadere; *(difficulty, opportunity)* presentarsi; *(phenomenon)* aver luogo; *(error, word, plant)* trovarsi; **to** ~ **again** ripetersi. (**b**) *(come to mind)*: **to** ~ **to sb** venire in mente a qn; **such an idea would never have** ~**red to her** una tale idea non le sarebbe mai venuta in mente.

oc·cur·rence [ə'kʌrəns] *n* evento; **an everyday** ~ un fatto quotidiano.

ocean ['əʊʃən] **1** *n* oceano; ~s **of** *(fam)* un sacco di. **2** *cpd*: ~ **bed** *n* fondale *m* oceanico; ~ **cruise** *n* crociera nell'oceano; ~ **liner** *n* transatlantico.

ocean-going ['əʊʃən,ɡəʊɪŋ] *adj* d'alto mare.

ocean·ic [ˌəʊʃɪ'ænɪk] *adj* oceanico(a).

ocean·og·ra·phy [ˌəʊʃə'nɒɡrəfɪ] *n* oceanografia.

ochre, *(Am)* **ocher** ['əʊkəˈ] *n* ocra.

o'clock [ə'klɒk] *adv*: **it is one** ~ è l'una; **at 9** ~ alle 9; **at twelve** ~ *(midday)* a mezzogiorno; *(midnight)* a mezzanotte.

oc·ta·gon ['ɒktəɡən] *n* ottagono.

oc·tago·nal [ɒk'tæɡənl] *adj* ottagonale.

oc·tane ['ɒkteɪn] *n* ottano; **high-**~ **petrol** benzina ad alto numero di ottani.

oc·tave ['ɒktɪv] *n* ottava.

oc·tet [ɒk'tɛt] *n* ottetto.

Oc·to·ber [ɒk'təʊbəˈ] *n* ottobre *m*; *for usage see* **July.**

oc·to·genar·ian [ˌɒktəʊdʒɪ'nɛərɪən] *n* ottuagenario/a.

oc·to·pus ['ɒktəpəs] *n* piovra.

ocu·list ['ɒkjʊlɪst] *n* oculista *m/f*.

odd [ɒd] *adj* (**-er, -est**) (**a**) *(strange)* strano(a); **how** ~! che strano!; **he says some** ~ **things** dice cose strane. (**b**) *(Math)* dispari *inv*. (**c**) *(extra, left over)* avanzato(a); *(unpaired: sock etc)* spaiato(a); **if you have the** ~ **minute** se hai un momento libero; **the** ~ **man out, the** ~ **one out** l'eccezione *f*. (**d**) *(occasional)* occasionale; **at** ~ **moments** in certi momenti; **he has written the ~ article** ha scritto qualche articolo; **~ jobs** lavori *mpl* occasionali. **(e)** *(and more)*: **30 ~ 30** e rotti, poco più di 30.

odd·ball ['ɒdbɔːl] *n (fam)* eccentrico/a.

odd·ity ['ɒdɪtɪ] *n* **(a)** *(also:* **oddness)** stranezza, bizzarria. **(b)** *(person)* originale *m/f.*

odd-job man [ɒd'dʒɒb'mæn] *n* tuttofare *m inv.*

odd·ly ['ɒdlɪ] *adv* stranamente; **they are ~ similar** tra di loro c'è una strana somiglianza; **~ enough you are right** stranamente hai ragione.

odd·ments ['ɒdmənts] *npl (Comm)* rimanenze *fpl,* fondi *mpl* di magazzino.

odd·ness ['ɒdnɪs] *n* = **oddity (a).**

odds [ɒdz] *npl* **(a)** *(Betting)* probabilità *fpl;* **the ~ on the horse are 5 to 1** danno il cavallo 5 a 1; **short/long ~** alta/bassa probabilità; **the ~ are in his favour** i pronostici sono a suo favore; **to fight against overwhelming ~** lottare contro enormi difficoltà; **to succeed against all the ~** riuscire contro ogni aspettativa; **the ~ are that...** è facile *or* probabile che...; **~-on favourite** gran favorito/grande favorita; **it's ~-on that...** è quasi certo che.... **(b)** *(difference)*: **what's the ~?** *(fam)* che differenza fa?, cosa cambia?; **it makes no ~** non fa differenza. **(c)** *(variance, strife)*: **to be at ~ with sb over sth** essere in disaccordo con qn su qc. **(d):** **~ and ends** avanzi *mpl.*

ode [əʊd] *n* ode *f.*

odi·ous ['əʊdɪəs] *adj* odioso/a).

odour, *(Am)* **odor** ['əʊdə'] *n* odore *m;* **to be in bad ~ with sb** *(fig)* essere disapprovato da qn.

odour·less, *(Am)* **odorless** ['əʊdəlɪs] *adj* inodore.

od·ys·sey ['ɒdɪsɪ] *n* odissea.

Oedipus ['iːdɪpəs] *n:* **~ complex** *(Psych)* complesso di Edipo.

oesopha·gus [iːˈsɒfəgəs] *n* esofago.

oes·tro·gen ['iːstrəʊdʒən] *n* estrogeno.

of [ɒv, əv] *prep* **(a)** *(gen)* di; **the house ~ my uncle** la casa di mio zio; **the love ~ God** l'amore di Dio; **a friend ~ mine** un mio amico; **that was very kind ~ you** è stato molto carino da parte tua; **free ~ charge** gratis; **loss ~ appetite** perdita dell'appetito; **south ~ Glasgow** a sud di Glasgow; **a quarter ~ 4** *(Am)* le 4 meno un quarto; **the City ~ New York** la Città di New York; **a boy ~ 8** un ragazzo di 8 anni; **a man ~ great ability** un uomo di grande abilità; **that idiot ~ a minister** quell'idiota di ministro.

(b) *(cause)* di, per; **~ necessity** necessariamente, per necessità; **to die ~ pneumonia** morire di polmonite.

(c) *(material)* di, in; **made ~ steel** fatto di *or* in acciaio.

(d) *(concerning)* di; **what do you think ~ him?** cosa pensi di lui?; **what ~ it?** e allora?

(e) *(partitive etc)* di; **how much ~ this do you need?** quanto te ne serve?; **there were 4 ~ us** eravamo in 4; **4 ~ us went** 4 di noi sono andati; **there were 4 ~ them** *(people)* erano in 4; *(things)* ce n'erano 4; **a kilo ~ flour** un chilo di farina.

off [ɒf] **1** *adv* **(a)** *(distance, time)*: **a place 2 miles ~** un posto distante 2 miglia; **it's a long way ~** è molto lontano; **the game was/is 3 days ~** la gara era dopo/è tra 3 giorni. **(b)** *(departure)*: **he's ~ to Paris tonight** parte per Parigi stasera; **I must be ~** devo andare; **he's gone ~ to see the boss** è andato a parlare col capo; **~ we go** via, partiamo. **(c)** *(removal)*: **with his hat ~** senza cappello; **the lid was ~** non c'era il coperchio; **a button came ~** è venuto via un bottone; **5% ~** *(Comm)* ridotto del 5%; **~ with those wet clothes!** togliti quei vestiti bagnati! **(d)** *(not at work)*: **he's ~ sick** è in malattia; **I'm ~ on Fridays** il venerdì non lavoro;

to take a day ~ prendersi una giornata di vacanza. **(e)** *(in phrases)*: **~ and on, on and ~** di tanto in tanto; **right** *or* **straight ~** immediatamente.

2 *adj* **(a)** *(inoperative)*: **to be ~** *(machine, light, engine etc)* essere spento(a); *(water, gas, tap)* essere chiuso(a). **(b)** *(cancelled)* sospeso(a); *(not available: in restaurant)* finito(a); **I'm afraid the chicken is ~** purtroppo il pollo è finito; **the wedding is ~** il matrimonio non si fa più; **the play is ~** la commedia è sospesa. **(c)** *(not fresh)* andato(a) a male; **this cheese is ~** questo formaggio è andato a male; **that's a bit ~, isn't it?** *(fig fam)* non è molto carino, vero? **(d):** **to be well/badly ~** essere/non essere benestante; **the less well ~** i meno abbienti; **you'd be better ~ staying where you are** faresti meglio a rimanere dove sei; **how are you ~ for cash?** come stai a soldi? **(e):** **to have an ~ day** *(fam)* avere una giornata no.

3 *prep* **(a)** *(indicating motion, removal etc)* da; **to fall ~ a cliff** cadere da una scogliera; **she took the picture ~ the wall** tolse il quadro dalla parete; **we dined ~ turkey** facemmo una cena a base di tacchino; **there are two buttons ~ my coat** al mio cappotto mancano due bottoni; **he was ~ work for three weeks** è stato in malattia per tre settimane; **he knocked £2 ~ the price** *(fam)* ha fatto uno sconto di 2 sterline. **(b)** *(distant from)*: **a street ~ the square** una strada che parte dalla piazza; **height ~ the ground** altezza dal suolo; **it's just ~ the M1** è appena fuori della M1; **his flat is somewhere ~ Baker Street** il suo appartamento è dalle parti di Baker Street. **(c):** **I'm ~ fried food** non mangio più cibi fritti; **I've gone ~ fried food** ho smesso di mangiare i fritti.

of·fal ['ɒfəl] *n* frattaglie *fpl.*

off·beat [ˌɒf'biːt] *adj (fig)* originale.

off-centre, *(Am)* **off-center** [ˌɒf'sɛntə'] *adj* storto(a), fuori centro.

off-chance ['ɒftʃɑːns] *n:* **on the ~ of seeing him** nella vaga speranza di incontrarlo.

off-colour, *(Am)* **off-color** [ˌɒf'kʌlə'] *adj (ill)* malato(a); **to feel ~** sentirsi poco bene.

of·fence, *(Am)* **of·fense** [ə'fɛns] *n* **(a)** *(crime)* infrazione *f;* *(: more serious)* reato; *(moral)* offesa; **first ~** primo reato; **to commit an ~** commettere un reato; **it is an ~ to...** è vietato... . **(b):** **to give ~ (to sb)** offendere (qn); **to take ~ (at sth)** offendersi (per qc).

of·fend [ə'fɛnd] **1** *vt (person)* offendere; *(ears, eyes)* ferire; **it ~s my sense of justice** offende il mio senso di giustizia; **to be ~ed (at)** offendersi (per). **2** *vi:* **to ~ against** *(law, rule)* trasgredire; *(God)* disubbidire a; *(common sense)* andare contro; *(good taste)* offendere.

of·fend·er [ə'fɛndə'] *n (criminal)* criminale *m/f;* *(against traffic regulations etc)* trasgressore *m.*

of·fen·sive [ə'fɛnsɪv] **1** *adj* **(a)** *(causing offence, unpleasant: behaviour, remark)* offensivo(a); *(: person)* antipatico(a); *(: smell, sight)* sgradevole; **to be ~ to sb** offendere qn. **(b)** *(attacking)* offensivo(a). **2** *n (Mil, Sport)* offensiva; **to go over to the ~, take the ~** passare all'offensiva.

of·fen·sive·ly [ə'fɛnsɪvlɪ] *adv (unpleasantly etc)* in modo offensivo.

of·fer ['ɒfə'] **1** *n (gen)* offerta; **~ of marriage** proposta di matrimonio; **to make an ~ for sth** fare un'offerta per qc; **~s over £25** offerte dalle 25 sterline in su; **to be on ~** *(Comm)* essere in offerta (speciale). **2** *vt (gen)* offrire; *(apology)* presentare; *(comment, opinion)* dare; **to ~ sth to sb, ~ sb sth** offrire qc a qn; **to ~ to do sth** offrirsi di fare qc; **to ~ resistance** opporre resistenza.

of·fer·ing ['ɒfərɪŋ] n offerta.
of·fer·tory ['ɒfətərɪ] n (Rel: part of service) offertorio; (: collection) questua.
off·hand ['ɒf'hænd] **1** adj (casual) disinvolto(a); (curt) brusco(a). **2** adv: **I can't tell you ~** non posso dirtelo sui due piedi.
off·handed·ly ['ɒf'hændɪdlɪ] adv (see adj) con disinvoltura; bruscamente.
of·fice ['ɒfɪs] **1** n **(a)** (place) ufficio; (: of lawyer, doctor) studio; **ticket ~** biglietteria; **head ~** sede f centrale. **(b)** (public position) ufficio, carica; (duty, function) incarico, compito; **to be in ~, to hold ~** (person) essere in carica; (political party) essere al potere; **to come into ~, to take ~** (person) assumere la carica; (political party) prendere il potere. **(c): through his good ~s** con il suo prezioso aiuto; **through the ~s of** grazie all'aiuto di. **(d)** (Rel) ufficio, funzione f. **2** cpd (job, staff) d'ufficio; (furniture) da ufficio; (supplies) per ufficio; **~ bearer** n (of club etc) membro dell'amministrazione; **~ block** n palazzo per uffici; **~ boy** n fattorino; **~ hours** npl orario d'ufficio; **~ worker** n impiegato/a.
of·fic·er ['ɒfɪsəʳ] n **(a)** (Mil, Naut, Aer) ufficiale m; **~s' mess** mensa degli ufficiali. **(b)** (official) funzionario; **police ~** ufficiale m di polizia; **excuse me, ~** mi scusi, agente.
of·fi·cial [ə'fɪʃəl] **1** adj ufficiale; (formal) ufficiale, formale. **2** n (in local government) funzionario; (of club, organization) dirigente m/f.
of·fi·cial·dom [ə'fɪʃəldəm] n (pej) burocrazia.
of·fi·cial·ese [ə,fɪʃə'liːz] n (pej) linguaggio burocratico.
of·fi·cial·ly [ə'fɪʃəlɪ] adv ufficialmente.
of·fi·ci·ate [ə'fɪʃɪeɪt] vi (Rel) ufficiare; **to ~ as Mayor** esplicare le funzioni di sindaco; **to ~ at a marriage** celebrare un matrimonio.
of·fi·cious [ə'fɪʃəs] adj invadente.
of·fing ['ɒfɪŋ] n: **in the ~** in vista.
off·key [,ɒf'kiː] **1** adj stonato(a). **2** adv fuori tono.
off·licence ['ɒf,laɪsns] n (Brit) negozio di alcolici (da non consumare sul luogo).
off·limits [,ɒf'lɪmɪts] adj (Am Mil) vietato(a) (al personale militare).
off·load ['ɒf,ləʊd] vt scaricare.
off·peak ['ɒf'piːk] adj (time) non di punta; (ticket, heating) a tariffa ridotta; (tariff) ridotto(a).
off·putting ['ɒf,pʊtɪŋ] adj (person, manner) un po' scostante; (welcome) poco caloroso(a).
off·season ['ɒf,siːzn] n bassa stagione f.
off·set ['ɒfset] (vb: pt, pp offset) **1** n (Typ) offset m inv. **2** vt bilanciare, compensare. **3** cpd: **~ printing** n stampa in offset.
off·shoot ['ɒfʃuːt] n (Bot) germoglio; (fig) diramazione f.
off·shore ['ɒf'ʃɔːʳ] adj (breeze) di terra; (island etc) vicino(a) alla costa; (fishing) costiero(a).
off·side ['ɒf'saɪd] **1** adj **(a)** (Sport) in fuorigioco. **(b)** (Aut: in Britain) destro(a); (: in Italy etc) sinistro(a). **2** adv (Aut: see adj) destra; sinistra.
off·spring ['ɒfsprɪŋ] n, pl inv (of person) rampollo; (: with pl sense) prole f; (of animal) piccolo/a.
off·stage ['ɒf'steɪdʒ] adj, adv dietro le quinte.
off·white ['ɒf,waɪt] adj bianco sporco inv.
of·ten ['ɒfən] adv spesso; **as ~ as not** il più delle volte; **more ~ than not** quasi sempre; **every so ~** (of time) una volta ogni tanto; (of distance, spacing) regolarmente, a intervalli regolari; **how ~ do you see him?** ogni quanto lo vedi?; **his behaviour is ~ disappointing** il suo comportamento è spesso deludente; **it's not ~ that I ask you to help me** non succede tutti i giorni che io ti

chieda di aiutarmi.
ogle ['əʊgl] vt mangiarsi con gli occhi.
ogre ['əʊgəʳ] n orco.
oh [əʊ] excl oh!
O.H.M.S. abbr of **On Her** (or **His**) **Majesty's Service**.
oil [ɔɪl] **1** n **(a)** (Art, Aut, Culin etc) olio; **fried in ~** fritto nell'olio. **(b)** (petroleum) petrolio; **to pour ~ on troubled waters** placare le acque. **2** vt oliare, lubrificare; **to ~ the wheels** (fig) appianare le difficoltà. **3** cpd (lamp, stove) a olio; (refinery) di petrolio; (industry) petroliero(a); **~ colours** npl colori mpl a olio; **~ gauge** n indicatore m del livello dell'olio; **~ painting** n dipinto a olio; **she's no ~ painting** (fam) non è una bellezza; **~ slick** n macchia d'olio sull'acqua; **~ tanker** n petroliera; **~ well** n pozzo petrolifero.
oil·can ['ɔɪlkæn] n oliatore m.
oil·field ['ɔɪlfiːld] n giacimento petrolifero.
oil·fired ['ɔɪlfaɪəd] adj a nafta.
oil·skin ['ɔɪlskɪn] n tela cerata; **~s** cerata.
oily ['ɔɪlɪ] adj (-ier, -iest) (liquid, consistency) oleoso(a); (hands) unto(a); (fig pej) untuoso(a).
oint·ment ['ɔɪntmənt] n unguento.
O.K., okay ['əʊ'keɪ] (fam) **1** excl OK!, va bene! **2** adj: **the film was ~** il film non era male; **are you ~ for money?** sei a posto coi soldi?; **it's ~ with** or **by me** per me va bene; **is it ~ with you if...?** ti va bene se...?; **did you hurt yourself? — no, I'm ~** ti sei fatto male? — no, sto bene; **is the car ~?** è a posto la macchina?; **that may have been ~ last year** questo poteva forse andar bene l'anno scorso. **3** n: **to give sth one's ~** approvare qc. **4** vt (pt, pp **O.K.'d, okayed**) approvare.
old [əʊld] **1** adj **(a)** (gen) vecchio(a); **an ~ man** un vecchio; **~ people, ~ folk(s)** i vecchi; **to grow ~(er), get ~(er)** invecchiare; **he's ~ for his years** è maturo per la sua età; **the ~ country** la madrepatria; **as ~ as the hills** vecchio come Matusalemme; **the ~ part of Glasgow** la parte vecchia di Glasgow; **an ~ friend of mine** un mio vecchio amico; **here's ~ Peter coming!** ecco che arriva il vecchio Peter!; **she's a funny ~ thing** è un tipetto buffo; **we had a high ~ time** (fam) ci siamo divertiti un sacco; **any ~ thing** will do va bene qualsiasi cosa; **I say, ~ man** or **~ boy!** (fam) carissimo!
(b): **how ~ are you?** quanti anni hai?; **he is 8 years ~** ha 8 anni; **an 8-year-~ boy** un bambino di 8 anni; **she is 2 years ~er than you** ha 2 anni più di te; **my ~er brother** mio fratello maggiore; **the ~er generation** la generazione precedente; **he's ~ enough to look after himself** è grande abbastanza per sbrigarsela da solo; **to be ~ enough to vote** avere l'età per votare; **you're ~ enough to know better!** alla tua età dovresti avere più senno!; **when you're ~er** (to child) quando sarai grande; **if I were 20 years ~er** se avessi 20 anni di più.
(c) (former) precedente; **my ~ school** la mia vecchia scuola; **in the ~ days** una volta; **it's not as good as our ~ one** non è buono come quello vecchio.
2 n **(a): the ~** pl i vecchi.
(b): of ~ da tempo; **in days of ~** nei tempi passati.
3 cpd: **~ age** n vecchiaia; **in one's ~ age** nella vecchiaia; **~-age pension** n pensione f di anzianità; **~-age pensioner** (abbr **O.A.P.**) n pensionato/a; **~ boy** n (Scol) ex alunno; **O~ English** n l'inglese m antico; **~ maid** n zitella; **~ master** n grande pittore europeo del periodo compreso tra il 16° e il 18° secolo; **~ people's home** n ricovero per anziani; **O~ Testament** n Vecchio Testamento;

~ **wives' tale** *n* vecchia superstizione *f;* **O~ World** *n* Vecchio Mondo.

old·en ['əʊldən] *adj:* **in ~ times** *or* **days** nei tempi antichi, nei giorni passati.

old·es·tab·lished ['əʊldɪs'tæblɪʃt] *adj* antico(a).

old-fashioned ['əʊld'fæʃnd] *adj* antiquato(a).

old-time ['əʊldtaɪm] *adj* di una volta.

old-timer [,əʊld'taɪmə^r] *n* veterano/a.

old-world ['əʊld'wɜːld] *adj* di vecchio stile, di vecchio stampo.

olean·der [,əʊlɪ'ændə^r] *n* oleandro.

oli·gar·chy ['ɒlɪgɑːkɪ] *n* oligarchia.

ol·ive ['ɒlɪv] **1** *n (fruit)* oliva; *(also:* ~ **tree)** ulivo. **2** *adj (skin)* olivastro(a); *(also:* ~**-green)** verde oliva *inv.* **3** *cpd:* ~ **branch** *n* ramoscello d'ulivo; ~ **oil** *n* olio d'oliva.

Olym·pic [ə'lɪmpɪk] **1** *adj* olimpico(a); **the ~ Games** i giochi olimpici. **2** *n:* **the ~s** *pl* le Olimpiadi.

om·buds·man ['ɒmbʊdzmən] *n, pl* **-men** *funzionario incaricato della protezione dei diritti dei cittadini.*

ome·let(te) ['ɒmlɪt] *n* frittata, omelette *f inv.*

omen ['əʊmən] *n* segno, auspicio.

omi·nous ['ɒmɪnəs] *adj* minaccioso(a), infausto(a).

omi·nous·ly ['ɒmɪnəslɪ] *adv* minacciosamente.

omis·sion [ə'mɪʃən] *n* omissione *f.*

omit [ə'mɪt] *vt* omettere; **to ~ to do sth** tralasciare *or* trascurare di fare qc.

om·ni·bus ['ɒmnɪbəs] *n (old: bus)* autobus *m inv; (book)* raccolta.

om·nipo·tent [ɒm'nɪpətənt] *adj* onnipotente.

om·nis·ci·ent [ɒm'nɪsɪənt] *adj* onnisciente.

om·niv·or·ous [ɒm'nɪvərəs] *adj* onnivoro(a).

on [ɒn] **1** *prep* **(a)** *(position)* su; ~ **the table** sul tavolo; **hanging ~ the wall** appeso al muro; ~ **page 2** a pagina 2; **with her hat ~ her head** col cappello in testa; ~ **the right** sulla *or* a destra; ~ **the Continent** nell'Europa continentale; **the house is ~ the main road** la casa è sulla strada principale; **I haven't any money ~ me** non ho soldi con me.

(b) *(fig):* **an attack ~ the government** un attacco al governo; ~ **foot** a piedi; ~ **the train/ plane** in treno/aereo; ~ **the telephone** al telefono; ~ **the radio/television** alla radio/televisione; ~ **Channel 4** sul Canale 4; **he played it ~ the violin/piano** l'ha suonato col violino/al pianoforte; **he is ~ the committee** fa parte della commissione; ~ **his authority** con la sua autorizzazione; **we're ~ irregular verbs** stiamo facendo i verbi irregolari; **she lives ~ cheese** vive di formaggio; **he's ~ £6000 a year** guadagna 6000 sterline all'anno; **he's ~ heroin** si droga di eroina; **to be ~ holiday** essere in vacanza; **he's away ~ business** è via per affari; **prices are up ~ last year('s)** i prezzi sono rincarati rispetto all'anno scorso; **based ~ fact** basato sui fatti; **the march ~ Rome** la marcia su Roma; **have it ~ me** offro io; **this round's ~ me** questo giro lo offro io.

(c) *(of time):* ~ **Friday** venerdì; ~ **Fridays** il *or* di venerdì; ~ **May 14th** il 14 maggio; ~ **a day like this** in una giornata come questa; **a week ~ Friday** venerdì a otto; ~ **my arrival** al mio arrivo; ~ **seeing him** nel vederlo, vedendolo.

(d) *(about, concerning)* su, di; **a book ~ physics** un libro di *or* sulla fisica; **he lectured ~ Keats** tenne un corso su Keats; **have you read Purnell ~ Churchill?** hai letto cosa scrive Purnell su Churchill?; **while we're ~ the subject** visto che siamo in argomento.

2 *adv* **(a)** *(covering):* **she put her boots ~** si mise gli stivali; **to have one's coat ~** avere indosso il cappotto; **what's she got ~?** cosa indossa?;

screw the lid ~ tightly avvita il coperchio ben stretto; ~ **with your coat!** mettiti il cappotto!

(b) *(forward):* **from that day ~** da quel giorno in poi; **it's getting ~ for ten o'clock** si avvicinano le dieci; **it was well ~ in the evening** era sera inoltrata; **it was well ~ in May** era maggio avanzato; **they talked well ~ into the night** continuarono a parlare fino a notte inoltrata.

(c) *(continuation):* **to go ~, walk ~** *etc* continuare, proseguire; **to read ~** continuare a leggere, proseguire nella lettura; **he rambled ~ and ~** continuava a divagare; **and so ~** e così via.

(d) *(in phrases):* **my father's always ~ at me to get a job** *(fam)* mio padre mi sta sempre addosso perché trovi un lavoro; **what are you ~ about?** cosa vai dicendo?

3 *adj* **(a)** *(functioning, in operation: radio, light etc)* acceso(a); *(: tap)* aperto(a); *(: brake etc)* inserito(a); **the meeting is still ~** la riunione è ancora in corso; **is the meeting still ~ tonight?** è confermato l'incontro di stasera?; **the programme is ~ in a minute** il programma inizierà tra un minuto; **there's a good film ~ at the cinema** danno un buon film al cinema; **sorry, I've got something ~ tonight** mi spiace, stasera sono impegnato.

(b): **you're ~!** d'accordo!; **that's not ~** *(fam)* non se ne parla neanche.

once [wʌns] **1** *adv* **(a)** *(on one occasion)* una volta; **I've only met him ~ before** prima d'ora l'ho incontrato una volta sola; ~ **only** solo una volta; ~ **or twice** un paio di volte; ~ **again,** ~ **more** ancora una volta; **(every) ~ in a while** (una volta) ogni tanto; ~ **a week** una volta alla settimana; ~ **and for all** una volta per tutte; **just this ~** solo (per) questa volta; **for ~** una volta tanto; **it never ~ occurred to me** non mi è mai venuto in mente. **(b)** *(formerly)* un tempo; **I knew him ~** un tempo *or* in passato lo conoscevo; ~ **upon a time there was** c'era una volta. **(c):** **at ~** *(immediately)* subito, immediatamente; *(simultaneously)* contemporaneamente; **all at ~** *(suddenly)* tutt'a un tratto, improvvisamente; *(in one go)* tutto in una volta.

2 *conj* una volta che, non appena; ~ **he had finished he left** una volta che *or* non appena ebbe finito andò via.

once-over ['wʌns,əʊvə^r] *n (fam):* **to give sb/sth the ~** dare un'occhiata a qn/qc.

on·coming ['ɒnkʌmɪŋ] *adj* che si avvicina in senso contrario.

one [wʌn] **1** *adj* **(a)** uno(a); ~ **hundred and fifty** centocinquanta; **twenty-~ years ago** ventuno anni fa; ~ **or two people** una o due persone, alcune persone; **the baby is ~ (year old)** il bambino ha un anno; **it's ~ (o'clock)** è l'una; **for ~ reason or another** per un motivo o per l'altro; **that's ~ way of doing it** questo è uno dei modi per farlo; ~ **day** un giorno; ~ **cold winter's day** una fredda giornata d'inverno.

(b) *(sole)* unico(a); ~ **and only** unico e solo; **the ~ and only Charlie Chaplin** l'inimitabile Charlie Chaplin; **his ~ worry** la sua unica *or* sola preoccupazione; **the ~ man who** il solo *or* l'unico che; **no ~ man could do it** nessuno potrebbe farlo da solo.

(c) *(same)* stesso(a); **in the ~ car** nella stessa macchina; **they are ~ and the same person** sono la stessa persona; **it is ~ and the same thing** è la stessa cosa.

2 *n* uno(a); ~ **hundred and ~** cento uno; **twenty-~** ventuno; **in ~s and twos** poco alla volta; **I for ~ am not going** per quanto mi riguarda non vengo; ~ **and all** tutti; ~ **after the other** uno dopo l'altro; ~ **by** ~ a uno a uno; **to be** ~ **up on sb** essere avvantaggiato rispetto a qn; **to go** ~ **better than sb** fare meglio di qn; **to be at** ~ (**with sb**) andare d'accordo (con qn); **she's cook and housekeeper in** ~ è contemporaneamente cuoca e governante; **I belted him** ~ (*fam*) gli ho mollato un cazzotto; **to have** ~ **for the road** farsi l'ultimo bicchiere.

3 *pron* (**a**): **this** ~ questo(a); **that** ~ quello(a); ~ **or two** uno o due; ~ **or two of the books were damaged** c'erano un paio di libri rovinati; **which** ~ **do you want?** quale vuoi?; **the** ~ **on the floor** quello sul pavimento; **the** ~ **who** (*or that or which*) quello che; **the** ~**s who** (*or that or which*) quelli che; **I'll have the grey** ~ prenderò quello grigio; **what about this little** ~? cosa ne dici di questo piccolino?; **our dear** ~s i nostri cari; **that's a difficult** ~ quello è un osso duro; **the little** ~s i bambini, i piccoli; **you're a fine** ~! (*fam*) sei un bel tipo!; **he's a great** ~ **for chess** va matto per gli scacchi; **he is not** ~ **to protest** non è il tipo che protesta; **have you got** ~? ne hai uno?; ~ **of them** uno di loro; **I lost** ~ **of them** ne ho perso uno; **any** ~ **of us** chiunque *or* uno qualsiasi di noi.

(**b**): ~ **another** l'un l'altro; **they all kissed** ~ **another** si baciarono tutti a vicenda; **do you see** ~ **another much?** vi vedete spesso?

(**c**) (*impersonal*): ~ **never knows** non si sa mai; ~ **must eat** bisogna mangiare; **to cut** ~**'s finger** tagliarsi un dito.

one-armed [ˌwʌn'ɑːmd] *adj* con un braccio solo, monco(a) (di un braccio); ~ **bandit** (*fam*) slot-machine *f inv*.

one-eyed [ˌwʌn'aɪd] *adj* con un occhio solo.

one-legged [ˌwʌn'legɪd] *adj* con una gamba sola.

one-man ['wʌn'mæn] *adj* (*business*) gestito(a) da una sola persona; (*art exhibition*) personale; (*boat*) a un posto; ~ **woman** donna fedele; ~ **band** (*Mus: person*) suonatore di più strumenti contemporaneamente; **it's a** ~ **band** (*fig fam*) c'è solo una persona a mandare avanti la baracca.

one-night ['wʌn,naɪt] *adj*: ~ **stand** (*Theatre*) spettacolo unico.

one-off [ˌwʌn'ɒf] 1 *n* (*Brit fam*) fatto eccezionale. 2 *cpd* eccezionale.

one-piece ['wʌn,piːs] *adj* (*bathing suit*) intero(a).

on·er·ous ['ɒnərəs] *adj* (*task, duty*) gravoso(a); (*responsibility*) pesante.

one·self [wʌn'self] *pers pron* (*reflexive*) si; (*after prep*) se stesso(a), sé; (*emphatic*) da sé; **to hurt** ~ farsi male; **to be by** ~ stare da solo, stare per conto proprio; **to do sth by** ~ fare qc da solo *or* sé; **to keep sth for** ~ tenere qc per sé; **to see for** ~ vedere con i propri occhi; **to say to** ~ dire a se stesso; **to talk to** ~ parlare da solo.

one-shot [ˌwʌn'ʃɒt] *n* (*Am*) = **one-off.**

one-sided [ˌwʌn'saɪdɪd] *adj* (*decision, view*) unilaterale; (*judgment, account*) parziale; (*game, contest*) impari *inv*.

one-time ['wʌn,taɪm] *adj* ex.

one-to-one [ˌwʌntə'wʌn] *adj* (*correlation*) univoco(a); **teaching is on a** ~ **basis** l'insegnamento è organizzato in lezioni individuali.

one-track ['wʌn,træk] *adj*: **to have a** ~ **mind** essere fissato(a).

one-upmanship [ˌwʌn'ʌpmənʃɪp] *n*: **the art of** ~ l'arte di primeggiare.

one-way ['wʌn,weɪ] *adj* (*traffic, street*) a senso unico; (*ticket*) di sola andata.

on·going ['ɒngəʊɪŋ] *adj* (*in progress*) in corso, attuale; (*continuing*) che si sviluppa.

on·ion ['ʌnjən] 1 *n* cipolla. 2 *cpd* di cipolla; ~ **rings** *npl* fettine *fpl* di cipolla; ~ **soup** *n* zuppa di cipolle.

on·look·er ['ɒn,lʊkə'] *n* spettatore/trice.

only ['əʊnlɪ] 1 *adj* solo(a), unico(a); **it's the** ~ **one left** è l'unico rimasto; **your** ~ **hope is to hide** la tua unica possibilità di salvezza sta nel nasconderti; **you are the** ~ **one who can help us** sei l'unico che possa *or* che può aiutarci; **you are not the** ~ **one** non sei l'unico; **an** ~ **child** un figlio unico; **the** ~ **thing I don't like about it is...** l'unica cosa che non mi va è... .

2 *adv* solo, soltanto, solamente; **we have** ~ **5** ne abbiamo solo 5; ~ **one choice** una sola possibilità, un'unica scelta; ~ **time will tell** chi vivrà vedrà; **I'm** ~ **the porter** io sono solo il portinaio; **I** ~ **touched it** l'ho soltanto toccato; ~ **when I...** solo quando io...; **not** ~ **A but also B** non solo A ma anche B; **I saw her** ~ **yesterday** l'ho vista appena ieri; **we can** ~ **hope** non possiamo far altro che sperare; **I'd be** ~ **too pleased to help** sarei proprio felice di essere d'aiuto; **it's** ~ **too true** è proprio vero.

3 *conj* solo che, ma (purtroppo); **I would come,** ~ **I'm very busy** verrei volentieri, solo che sono molto occupato.

ono·mato·poeia [ˌɒnəʊmætəʊ'piːə] *n* onomatopea.

on·rush ['ɒnrʌʃ] *n* afflusso.

on·set ['ɒnset] *n* (*of season*) arrivo; (*illness, old age*) inizio, insorgenza.

on·slaught ['ɒnslɔːt] *n* (*Mil, fig*) attacco.

onto ['ɒntʊ] *prep* su, sopra; **to be** ~ **sb** (*suspect*) scoprire qn; **I'm** ~ **something** sono su una buona pista; **to be** ~ **a good thing** (*fam*) trovare l'America; **I'll get** ~ **him about it** gliene parlerò io.

onus ['əʊnəs] *n* (*no pl*): **the** ~ **is upon him to prove it** sta a lui dimostrarlo; **to shift the** ~ **for sth onto sb** addossare la colpa di qc a qn; **the** ~ **of proof is on the prosecution** l'onere della prova spetta all'accusa.

on·ward ['ɒnwəd] 1 *adj* in avanti. 2 *adv* (*also*: ~s) in avanti; **from the 12th century** ~(s) dal XII secolo in poi.

onyx ['ɒnɪks] *n* onice *f*.

ooze [uːz] 1 *n* melma. 2 *vi* (*water*) filtrare; (*gum, resin*) trasudare; (*pus*) uscire. 3 *vt*: **the wound** ~d **blood** la ferita stillava sangue; **he simply** ~s **confidence** (*pej*) trabocca di sicurezza.

opal ['əʊpəl] *n* opale *m or f*.

opaque [əʊ'peɪk] *adj* opaco(a).

OPEC ['əʊpek] *n abbr* O.P.E.C. *f*.

open ['əʊpən] 1 *adj* (**a**) (*gen*) aperto(a); (*flower*) aperto(a), dischiuso(a); **wide** ~ (*door etc*) spalancato(a); **half** ~, **slightly** ~ socchiuso(a); ~ **at the neck** col collo aperto; **to welcome with** ~ **arms** accogliere a braccia aperte; **to cut a sack** ~ aprire un sacco con un taglio; **to keep** ~ **house** (*fig*) aprire la propria casa a tutti; ~ **to the public on Mondays** aperto al pubblico di lunedì; ~ **day** (*Brit*) giornata di apertura al pubblico.

(**b**) (*fig: letter*) aperto(a); (: *river*) navigabile; (: *road*) transitabile; (: *cheque*) non sbarrato(a); **in the** ~ **air** all'aria aperta; **road** ~ **to traffic** strada aperta al traffico; ~ **to the elements/to attack** esposto alle intemperie/all'attacco; ~ **sandwich** canapè *m inv*, tartina; ~ **country** aperta campagna; ~ **ground** (*among trees*) radura; (*waste ground*) terreno non edificato; **to lay o.s.** ~ **to criticism** esporsi alle critiche; ~ **to persuasion** disposto a farsi convincere; **it is** ~ **to doubt whether...** è in dubbio se... .

(**c**) (*competition, scholarship*) aperto(a) a tutti; (*meeting*) pubblico(a); (*trial*) a porte aperte; **what**

choices are ~ **to me?** che strade mi si aprono?; **the post is still** ~ il posto è sempre libero; **in** ~ **court** (*Law*) a porte aperte.

(**d**) (*person, face*) aperto(a); (*hatred, admiration*) evidente, palese; (*enemy*) dichiarato(a); **it's an** ~ **secret that...** è il segreto di Pulcinella che...; **in** ~ **revolt** in aperta rivolta; **to be** ~ **with sb** essere franco con qn.

(**e**) (*undecided: question*) aperto(a); **the race was still wide** ~ il risultato della gara era ancora molto incerto; ~ **verdict** verdetto del '*coroner*' in cui non vengono specificate le cause del decesso; ~ **ticket** biglietto open; **to have an** ~ **mind** (**on sth**) non avere ancora deciso (su qc); **to leave the matter** ~ lasciare la faccenda in sospeso.

2 *n*: **out in the** ~ (*out of doors*) fuori, all'aperto; (*in the country*) in campagna, all'aperto; **their true feelings came into the** ~ vennero a galla i loro veri sentimenti.

3 *vt* (*gen*) aprire; (*legs*) divaricare; **to** ~ **sth wide** spalancare qc; **to** ~ **a road to traffic** aprire al traffico una strada; **to** ~ **a road through a forest** tagliare *or* aprire una strada nella foresta; **to** ~ **Parliament** aprire il Parlamento; **to** ~ **a bank account** aprire un conto in banca; **to** ~ **fire** (*Mil*) aprire il fuoco; **I didn't** ~ **my mouth** non ho aperto bocca; **to** ~ **one's heart to sb** confidarsi con qn; **to** ~ **one's mind to sth** aprirsi a qc.

4 *vi* (**a**) (*gen*) aprirsi; (*shops, museum etc*) aprire; **the shops** ~ **at 9** i negozi aprono alle 9; **to** ~ **onto** *or* **into** dare su.

(**b**) (*begin*) cominciare; (*Cards, Chess*) aprire; **the play** ~**s next Monday** la prima della commedia è lunedì prossimo; **the book** ~**s with a long description** il libro si apre *or* comincia con una lunga descrizione.

♦ **open out 1** *vi* + *adv* aprirsi, dischiudersi. **2** *vt* + *adv* (*unfold*) aprire, spiegare.

♦ **open up 1** *vi* + *adv* (**a**) (*flower, shop*) aprirsi. (**b**) (*start shooting*) aprire il fuoco. **2** *vt* + *adv* aprire; **to** ~ **up a country for trade** aprire il mercato di un paese.

open-air [ˌəʊpnˈɛəʳ] *adj* all'aperto.

open-and-shut [ˌəʊpənənˈʃʌt] *adj*: ~ **case** caso indubbio.

open-cast [ˈəʊpnkɑːst] *adj*: ~ **mining** estrazione *f* a cielo aperto.

open-ended [ˌəʊpnˈɛndɪd] *adj* (*fig*) aperto(a), senza limiti.

open-er [ˈəʊpnəʳ] *n*: **bottle-**~ apribottiglie *m inv*; **can** ~ apriscatole *m inv*.

open-handed [ˌəʊpnˈhændɪd] *adj* generoso(a).

open-heart [ˌəʊpnˈhɑːt] *adj*: ~ **surgery** chirurgia a cuore aperto.

open-ing [ˈəʊpnɪŋ] **1** *adj* (*gen*) d'apertura; (*ceremony, speech*) d'apertura, inaugurale. **2** *n* (**a**) (*gap*) apertura; (: *in wall*) breccia. (**b**) (*beginning*) inizio; (*official* ~: *of factory etc*) inaugurazione *f*; (*first performance: of film, play*) prima (rappresentazione *f*). (**c**) (*chance*) apertura, possibilità *f inv*; (*post*) posto vacante; **to give one's opponent an** ~ offrire il fianco all'avversario. **3** *cpd*: ~ **night** *n* prima; ~ **time** *n* (*Brit*) ora d'apertura (*dei pub*).

open-ly [ˈəʊpənlɪ] *adv* apertamente.

open-minded [ˌəʊpnˈmaɪndɪd] *adj* aperto(a), dalla mentalità aperta.

open-mouthed [ˌəʊpnˈmaʊðd] *adj* a bocca aperta.

open-necked [ˈəʊpnˌnɛkt] *adj* col collo slacciato.

open-ness [ˈəʊpnnɪs] *n* (*frankness*) franchezza, sincerità.

open-plan [ˈəʊpənˌplæn] *adj* senza pareti divisorie.

op-era [ˈɒpərə] **1** *n* (*work*) opera (lirica); (*genre*) opera, lirica. **2** *cpd*: ~ **glasses** *npl* binocolo da teatro; ~ **house** *n* teatro lirico; ~ **singer** *n* cantante *m/f* d'opera *or* lirico(a).

op-er-able [ˈɒpərəbl] *adj* (*Med*) operabile.

op-er-ate [ˈɒpəreɪt] **1** *vt* (**a**) (*machine, switchboard, brakes etc*) azionare, far funzionare; **a machine** ~**d by electricity** una macchina funzionante a corrente; **can you** ~ **this tool?** sai usare questo strumento? (**b**) (*company etc*) dirigere, gestire; (*system, law etc*) applicare. **2** *vi* (**a**) (*function: machine etc*) funzionare, andare; (: *mind*) funzionare. (**b**) (*drug, propaganda*) agire. (**c**) (*company, firm*) operare; (*bus, airport*) essere in funzione; (*person*) agire. (**d**) (*Med*) operare; **to be** ~**d on** subire un'operazione; **she was** ~**d on for appendicitis** fu operata di appendicite.

op-er-at-ic [ˌɒpəˈrætɪk] *adj* operistico(a), lirico(a).

op-er-at-ing [ˈɒpəreɪtɪŋ] *adj* (**a**) (*Comm: costs*) di gestione. (**b**) (*Med*) operatorio(a); (: *nurse*) di sala operatoria; ~ **theatre** sala operatoria.

op-era-tion [ˌɒpəˈreɪʃən] *n* (**a**) (*gen, Med, Mil*) operazione *f*; **to have an** ~ **for appendicitis** essere operato di appendicite; **to undergo an** ~ subire un'operazione; **the company's** ~**s during the year** le operazioni della compagnia durante l'anno. (**b**): **to be in** ~ (*machine*) essere in funzione; (*plan, system*) essere in azione; (*law*) essere in vigore; **to come into** ~ entrare in funzione (*or* in azione *etc*); **to bring** *or* **put into** ~ mettere in funzione (*or* in azione); (*law*) far entrare in vigore.

op-era-tion-al [ˌɒpəˈreɪʃənl] *adj* (*relating to operations*) operativo(a); (*Comm*) di gestione, d'esercizio; (*ready for use or action*) in attività, in funzione; **when the service is fully** ~ quando il servizio sarà completamente in funzione.

op-era-tive [ˈɒpərətɪv] **1** *adj* (**a**) (*law, measure*) in vigore, operante; **the** ~ **word** la parola chiave. (**b**) (*Med*) operatorio(a). **2** *n* operaio/a.

op-era-tor [ˈɒpəreɪtəʳ] *n* (*of machine etc*) operatore/trice; (*Telec*) centralinista *m/f*; **a smooth** ~ (*fam*) un dritto.

oph-thal-mic [ɒfˈθælmɪk] *adj* oftalmico(a).

opi-ate [ˈəʊpɪɪt] *n* oppiato.

opin-ion [əˈpɪnjən] **1** *n* (*belief, view*) opinione *f*; **public** ~ opinione pubblica; **in my** ~ secondo me, a mio avviso; **in the** ~ **of those who know** secondo gli esperti; **it's a matter of** ~ è discutibile *or* opinabile; **what is your** ~ **of him?** tu che cosa pensi di lui?; **to be of the** ~ **that...** essere dell'opinione che..., ritenere che...; **to ask sb's** ~ chiedere il parere di qn, consultare qn; **to give one's** ~ dare il proprio parere; **to form an** ~ **of sb/sth** formarsi un'opinione di qn/qc; **to have a high/poor** ~ **of sb** avere/non avere un'alta opinione di qn, stimare molto/poco qn; **to have a high** ~ **of o.s.** avere un'alta opinione di sé, credersi chissà chi; **to seek a second** ~ consultarsi con un altro medico. **2** *cpd*: ~ **poll** *n* sondaggio di opinioni.

opin-ion-at-ed [əˈpɪnjənˌeɪtɪd] *adj* dogmatico(a).

opium [ˈəʊpɪəm] *n* oppio.

op-po-nent [əˈpəʊnənt] *n* avversario/a; (*in debate, discussion*) oppositore/trice.

op-por-tune [ˈɒpətjuːn] *adj* opportuno(a); **to be** ~ capitare a proposito.

op-por-tune-ly [ˈɒpətjuːnlɪ] *adv* opportunamente.

op-por-tun-ism [ˌɒpəˈtjuːnɪzəm] *n* opportunismo.

op-por-tun-ist [ˌɒpəˈtjuːnɪst] *n* opportunista *m/f*.

op-por-tu-nity [ˌɒpəˈtjuːnɪtɪ] *n* opportunità *f inv*, occasione *f*; **to have the** ~ **to do** *or* **of doing** avere l'opportunità di fare; **to take the** ~ **to do** *or* **of doing** cogliere l'occasione per fare; **at the ear-**

liest ~ appena possibile, alla prima occasione; **when I** (*or* **you etc**) **get the** ~ quando capita l'occasione; **to miss one's** ~ perdere l'occasione; **opportunities for promotion** possibilità di carriera.

op·pose [ə'pəʊz] *vt* (*gen*) opporsi a; **she** ~**s my leaving** è contraria alla mia partenza.

op·posed [ə'pəʊzd] *adj:* **to be** ~ **to** essere contrario(a) a; **as** ~ **to** a differenza di.

op·pos·ing [ə'pəʊzɪŋ] *adj* avversario(a).

op·po·site ['ɒpəzɪt] **1** *adv* di fronte; **they live directly** ~ vivono proprio di fronte. **2** *prep* di fronte a; ~ **one another** l'uno di fronte all'altro; **a house** ~ **the school** una casa di fronte alla scuola; **to play** ~ **sb** (*Theatre*) essere il (*or* la) partner di qn. **3** *adj* (*house*) di fronte; (*end, direction, side*) opposto(a); (*point of view*) opposto(a), contrario(a); **on the** ~ **side of the road** dall'altro lato della strada; **on the** ~ **page** sulla pagina a fronte; **the** ~ **sex** l'altro sesso. **4** *n* contrario; **quite the** ~! al contrario!; **she said just the** ~ lei ha detto esattamente il contrario.

op·po·si·tion [,ɒpə'zɪʃən] *n* (**a**) (*resistance*) opposizione *f*, resistenza; (*people opposing*) avversari *mpl*; **in** ~ **to** in contrasto con. (**b**) (*Brit Pol*): **the O**~ l'Opposizione *f*; **leader of the O**~ leader *m inv* dell'Opposizione; **to be in** ~ essere all'opposizione.

op·press [ə'prɛs] *vt* opprimere.

op·pres·sion [ə'prɛʃən] *n* oppressione *f*.

op·pres·sive [ə'prɛsɪv] *adj* (*regime etc*) oppressivo(a); (*fig: heat, thought*) opprimente.

op·pres·sive·ly [ə'prɛsɪvlɪ] *adv* (*see adj*) in modo oppressivo; in modo opprimente.

op·pres·sor [ə'prɛsə'] *n* oppressore *m*.

opt [ɒpt] *vi*: **to** ~ **for sth** optare per qc; **to** ~ **to do sth** scegliere di fare qc, optare per fare qc.

♦ **opt out** *vi* + *adv* ritirarsi; **I think I'll** ~ **out of going** credo che deciderò di non andare.

op·tic ['ɒptɪk] *adj* ottico(a).

op·ti·cal ['ɒptɪkəl] *adj* ottico(a); ~ **illusion** illusione *f* ottica.

op·ti·cian [ɒp'tɪʃən] *n* ottico.

op·tics ['ɒptɪks] *nsg* ottica.

op·ti·mism ['ɒptɪmɪzəm] *n* ottimismo.

op·ti·mist ['ɒptɪmɪst] *n* ottimista *m/f*.

op·ti·mis·tic [,ɒptɪ'mɪstɪk] *adj* (*attitude*) ottimistico(a); (*person*) ottimista.

op·ti·mis·ti·cal·ly [,ɒptɪ'mɪstɪklɪ] *adv* ottimisticamente, in modo ottimistico.

op·ti·mum ['ɒptɪməm] *adj* ottimale.

op·tion ['ɒpʃən] *n* (**a**) (*choice*) scelta; **I have no** ~ non ho scelta; **she had no** ~ **but to leave** non poteva far altro che partire; **to keep one's** ~**s open** tenersi aperte tutte le possibilità; **imprisonment without the** ~ **of bail** (*Law*) carcerazione senza possibilità di libertà provvisoria. (**b**) (*Comm*) opzione *f*; **with the** ~ **to buy** con opzione per l'acquisto. (**c**) (*Scol, Univ*) materia facoltativa.

op·tion·al ['ɒpʃənl] *adj* (*course, part, fitting etc*) facoltativo(a); ~ **extras** optional *m inv*.

opu·lence ['ɒpjʊləns] *n* opulenza.

opu·lent ['ɒpjʊlənt] *adj* opulento(a).

opus ['əʊpəs] *n*, *pl* **opera** ['ɒprə] (*Mus*) opera.

or [ɔː'] *conj* (*gen*) o; (~ *else*) oppure; ~ **rather** o meglio; ~ **else** oppure, altrimenti; **do it** ~ **else!** (*fam*) fallo, altrimenti!; **20** ~ **so** circa 20, più o meno 20; **let me go** ~ **I'll scream!** lasciami andare o griderò!; **without relatives** ~ **friends** senza (né) parenti né amici; **he can't read** ~ **write** non sa né leggere né scrivere.

ora·cle ['ɒrəkl] *n* oracolo.

oral ['ɔːrəl] **1** *adj* orale. **2** *n* (*esame m*) orale.

oral·ly ['ɔːrəlɪ] *adv* oralmente; (*medicine*) per via orale.

or·ange ['ɒrɪndʒ] **1** *n* (*fruit*) arancia; (*tree*) arancio; (*colour*) arancio, arancione *m*. **2** *adj* (*in colour*) arancio(a), arancione. **3** *cpd* (*juice, jelly*) d'arancia; (*marmalade*) di arance; (*cake*) all'arancia; ~ **blossom** *n* fiore *m* d'arancio; ~ **squash** *n* aranciata; ~ **stick** *n* scalzapelli *m inv*.

or·ange·ade [,ɒrɪndʒ'eɪd] *n* aranciata.

Orange·man ['ɒrɪndʒmən] *n*, *pl* **-men** orangista *m*.

orang·utan [ɔː,ræŋu'tæn] *n* orango, orang-utan *m inv*.

ora·tion [ɔː'reɪʃən] *n* orazione *f*; **funeral** ~ orazione funebre.

ora·tor ['ɒrətə'] *n* oratore/trice.

ora·to·rio [,ɒrə'tɔːrɪəʊ] *n* (*Mus*) oratorio.

ora·tory[1] ['ɒrətərɪ] *n* (*art*) oratoria.

ora·tory[2] ['ɒrətərɪ] *n* (*Rel*) oratorio.

or·bit ['ɔːbɪt] **1** *n* orbita; **to be in/go into** ~ (**round**) essere/entrare in orbita (attorno a); **it's outside my** ~ (*fig*) non rientra nel mio campo. **2** *vi* (*satellite, astronaut*) orbitare. **3** *vt* (*earth, moon*) orbitare attorno a.

or·chard ['ɔːtʃəd] *n* frutteto; **apple** ~ meleto.

or·ches·tra ['ɔːkɪstrə] *n* orchestra.

or·ches·tral [ɔː'kɛstrəl] *adj* orchestrale.

or·ches·trate ['ɔːkɪstreɪt] *vt* (*Mus, fig*) orchestrare.

or·ches·tra·tion [,ɔːkɪs'treɪʃən] *n* orchestrazione *f*.

or·chid ['ɔːkɪd] *n* orchidea.

or·dain [ɔː'deɪn] *vt* (**a**) (*order*) ordinare, decretare; **it was** ~**ed that...** (*fig*) era predestinato che.... (**b**) (*Rel*) ordinare.

or·deal [ɔː'diːl] *n* prova (terrible).

or·der ['ɔːdə'] **1** *n* (**a**) (*sequence*) ordine *m*; **in alphabetical** ~ in ordine alfabetico; **in** ~ **of merit** in ordine di merito; **put these in the right** ~ mettili nell'ordine giusto; **to be in the wrong** ~ *or* **out of** ~ non essere in ordine; **she had no** ~ **in her life** aveva una vita disordinata; **in the** ~ **of things** nell'ordine delle cose.

(**b**) (*good* ~) ordine *m*; **in** ~ (*room, documents*) in ordine, a posto; **a machine in working** ~ una macchina che funziona bene; **to be out of** ~ (*machine, toilets*) essere guasto(a); (*telephone*) essere fuori servizio.

(**c**) (*peace, control*) ordine *m*; **to keep** ~ mantenere l'ordine; **to keep children in** ~ tenere i bambini sotto controllo.

(**d**) (*command*) ordine *m*, comando; (*of court etc*) ingiunzione *f*, ordine; **by** ~ **of** per ordine di; **on the** ~**s of** agli ordini di; **to be under** ~**s to do sth** avere l'ordine di fare qc; **to give sb** ~**s to do sth** ordinare a qn di fare qc; **to take** ~**s from sb** prendere ordini da qn; **to obey** ~**s** ubbidire agli ordini; ~ **of the day** ordine del giorno; **violence is the** ~ **of the day** (*fig*) la violenza è all'ordine del giorno.

(**e**) (*correct procedure: at meeting, Parliament etc*) procedura; ~ (~)! all'ordine!; **to call sb to** ~ richiamare qn all'ordine; **a point of** ~ una questione di procedura; **is it in** ~ **for me to go to Rome?** mi è permesso andare a Roma?

(**f**) (*Comm*) ordinazione *f*; **to be on** ~ essere stato ordinato; **to ask for a repeat** ~ chiedere che venga rinnovata un'ordinazione; **rush** ~ ordinazione urgente; **made to** ~ fatto su commissione; (*clothes*) fatto su misura; **to place an** ~ **for sth with sb** ordinare qc a qn; **to the** ~ **of** (*Banking*) all'ordine di.

(**g**): **in** ~ **to do sth** per fare qc; **in** ~ **that** perché + *sub*, affinché + *sub*; **he cancelled his** holiday in ~ that he might stay at home cancellò la vacanza così da poter restare a casa.

(**h**) *(of society etc, also Bio)* ordine *m;* **the lower ~s** i ceti bassi; **his income is of the ~ of £4,000 per year** il suo reddito annuale è nell'ordine di 4.000 sterline; **Benedictine O~** Ordine Benedettino; **holy ~s** ordini (sacri); **to be in/take ~s** aver ricevuto/prendere gli ordini.

2 *vt* (**a**) *(command)* ordinare; **to ~ sb to do sth** ordinare a qn di fare qc; **the referee ~ed the player off the field** l'arbitro espulse il giocatore dal campo.

(**b**) *(put in ~)* ordinare, fare ordine in.

(**c**) *(goods, meal)* ordinare; *(taxi)* chiamare.

3 *vi* ordinare.

4 *cpd:* **~ form** *n* ordine *m,* modulo di ordinazione; **~ number** *n* numero di ordinazione.

♦ **order about, order around** *vt + adv* comandare, dare ordini a.

or·der·ly ['ɔːdəlɪ] **1** *adj (methodical, tidy, well-behaved)* ordinato(a). **2** *n (Mil)* attendente *m; (Med)* inserviente *m.*

or·di·nal ['ɔːdɪnl] **1** *adj* ordinale. **2** *n* (numero) ordinale *m.*

or·di·nance ['ɔːdɪnəns] *n* ordinanza.

or·di·nari·ly ['ɔːdnrɪlɪ] *adv* normalmente, di solito.

or·di·nary ['ɔːdnrɪ] **1** *adj* (**a**) *(usual)* abituale, solito(a); **in the ~ way** normalmente, di norma; **in ~ use** usato normalmente. (**b**) *(average)* comune, normale; *(pej)* mediocre, ordinario(a); **the ~ Italian** l'italiano comune; **the meal was very ~** il pranzo non era niente di speciale. (**c**) *(Fin: shares)* ordinario(a). **2** *n:* **out of the ~** diverso dal solito, fuori dell'ordinario.

or·di·na·tion [ˌɔːdɪˈneɪʃən] *n (Rel)* ordinazione *f.*

ord·nance ['ɔːdnəns] *(Mil)* **1** *n (guns)* artiglieria; *(supplies)* materiale *m* militare. **2** *cpd:* **O~ Survey map** *n (Brit) carta topografica ufficiale della Gran Bretagna.*

ore [ɔːʳ] *n* minerale *m* grezzo; **copper ~** minerale grezzo di rame.

orega·no [ˌɒrɪˈɡɑːnəʊ] *n* origano.

or·gan ['ɔːɡən] *n (all senses)* organo.

organ-grinder ['ɔːɡənˌɡraɪndəʳ] *n* suonatore/trice di organetto.

or·gan·ic [ɔːˈɡænɪk] *adj (also fig)* organico(a).

or·gan·ism ['ɔːɡənɪzəm] *n (Bio)* organismo.

or·gan·ist ['ɔːɡənɪst] *n* organista *m/f.*

or·gani·za·tion [ˌɔːɡənaɪˈzeɪʃən] *n* organizzazione *f.*

or·gan·ize ['ɔːɡənaɪz] *vt* organizzare; **to get ~d** organizzarsi.

or·gan·ized ['ɔːɡənaɪzd] *adj* organizzato(a).

or·gan·iz·er ['ɔːɡənaɪzəʳ] *n* organizzatore/trice.

or·gasm ['ɔːɡæzəm] *n* orgasmo.

orgy ['ɔːdʒɪ] *n (also fig)* orgia.

ori·ent ['ɔːrɪənt] *n (also:* **O~**) Oriente *m.*

ori·en·tal [ˌɔːrɪˈentəl] **1** *adj* orientale. **2** *n:* **O~** orientale *m/f.*

ori·en·tate ['ɔːrɪənteɪt] *vt* orientare.

ori·en·ta·tion [ˌɔːrɪənˈteɪʃən] *n* orientamento.

ori·en·teer·ing [ˌɔːrɪənˈtɪərɪŋ] *n (sport)* azimut *m.*

ori·fice ['ɒrɪfɪs] *n* orifizio.

ori·ga·mi [ˌɒrɪˈɡɑːmɪ] *n* origami *m.*

ori·gin ['ɒrɪdʒɪn] *n* origine *f;* **country of ~** paese *m* d'origine; **to be of humble ~, to have humble ~s** essere di umili origini *or* di bassi natali.

origi·nal [əˈrɪdʒɪnl] **1** *adj (gen)* originale; *(inhabitant)* originario(a), primitivo(a); *(previous: splendour)* originario(a). **2** *n (manuscript, painting etc)* originale *m; (garment)* capo firmato; *(person)*

originale *m/f;* **he reads Homer in the ~** legge Omero nell'originale.

origi·nal·ity [əˌrɪdʒɪˈnælɪtɪ] *n* originalità.

origi·nal·ly [əˈrɪdʒənəlɪ] *adv (at first)* originariamente, all'inizio; *(in an original way)* in modo originale.

origi·nate [əˈrɪdʒɪneɪt] **1** *vt* dare origine a. **2** *vi:* **to ~ (from)** *(gen)* avere origine (da); *(suggestion, idea)* derivare (da); *(goods)* provenire (da); **to ~ in** *(river)* nascere (in); *(custom)* avere origine (in).

origi·na·tor [əˈrɪdʒɪneɪtəʳ] *n* iniziatore/trice.

Ork·neys ['ɔːknɪz] *npl* Orcadi *fpl.*

or·lon ['ɔːlɒn] *n* ® orlon *m inv* ®.

or·na·ment ['ɔːnəmənt] **1** *n (gen)* ornamento; *(vase etc)* soprammobile *m.* **2** ['ɔːnəment] *vt* ornare, decorare.

or·na·men·tal [ˌɔːnəˈmentl] *adj* ornamentale.

or·na·men·ta·tion [ˌɔːnəmenˈteɪʃən] *n (act)* ornamentazione *f; (ornaments)* decorazione *f.*

or·nate [ɔːˈneɪt] *adj (decor)* ricco(a); *(style in writing etc)* ornato(a).

or·ni·tholo·gist [ˌɔːnɪˈθɒlədʒɪst] *n* ornitologo/a.

or·ni·thol·ogy [ˌɔːnɪˈθɒlədʒɪ] *n* ornitologia.

or·phan ['ɔːfən] **1** *adj, n* orfano(a) *(m/f).* **2** *vt:* **to be ~ed** restare orfano(a).

or·phan·age ['ɔːfənɪdʒ] *n* orfanatrofio.

ortho·dox ['ɔːθədɒks] *adj* ortodosso(a).

ortho·doxy ['ɔːθədɒksɪ] *n* ortodossia.

or·thog·ra·phy [ɔːˈθɒɡrəfɪ] *n* ortografia.

ortho·paedic, *(Am)* **ortho·pedic** [ˌɔːθəʊˈpiːdɪk] *adj* ortopedico(a).

ortho·paedics, *(Am)* **ortho·pedics** [ˌɔːθəʊˈpiːdɪks] *nsg* ortopedia.

ortho·paedist, *(Am)* **ortho·pedist** [ˌɔːθəʊˈpiːdɪst] *n* ortopedico/a.

os·cil·late ['ɒsɪleɪt] *vi* oscillare.

os·cil·la·tion [ˌɒsɪˈleɪʃən] *n* oscillazione *f.*

os·prey ['ɒspreɪ] *n* falco pescatore.

os·si·fy ['ɒsɪfaɪ] *vi* ossificarsi.

os·ten·sible [ɒsˈtensəbl] *adj* apparente.

os·ten·sibly [ɒsˈtensəblɪ] *adv* apparentemente.

os·ten·ta·tion [ˌɒstenˈteɪʃən] *n* ostentazione *f.*

os·ten·ta·tious [ˌɒstenˈteɪʃəs] *adj (lifestyle)* pretenzioso(a); *(gesture, wealth)* ostentato(a); **to be ~ about sth** ostentare qc.

os·ten·ta·tious·ly [ˌɒstenˈteɪʃəslɪ] *adv* in modo ostentato, con ostentazione.

os·teo·ar·thri·tis [ˌɒstɪəʊɑːˈθraɪtɪs] *n* osteoartrite *f.*

os·teo·path ['ɒstɪəpæθ] *n* specialista *m/f* di osteopatia.

os·teopa·thy [ˌɒstɪˈɒpəθɪ] *n* osteopatia.

os·tra·cism ['ɒstrəsɪzəm] *n* ostracismo.

os·tra·cize ['ɒstrəsaɪz] *vt* ostracizzare, dare l'ostracismo a.

os·trich ['ɒstrɪtʃ] *n* struzzo.

oth·er ['ʌðəʳ] **1** *adj* altro(a); **the ~ one** l'altro(a); **~ people** altri, altre persone; **some ~ people have still to arrive** (alcuni) altri devono ancora arrivare; **the ~ day** l'altro giorno; **some ~ time** un'altra volta, in un altro momento; **if there are no ~ questions...** se non ci sono altre domande...; **some actor or ~** un certo attore; **~ people's property** la proprietà altrui.

2 *pron:* **the ~** l'altro(a); **the ~s** gli altri; **one after the ~** uno dopo l'altro; **are there any ~s?** ce ne sono altri?; **one or ~ of them** will come qualcuno di loro verrà; **somebody or ~** qualcuno; **no ~** nessun altro; **no ~ than** non altri che; **the car was none ~ than Roberta's** la macchina era proprio di Roberta.

3 *adv:* **~ (than)** diversamente (da); **nothing ~**

than nient'altro che; **he could not act ~ than as he did** non poteva agire diversamente (da come fece); **somewhere or ~** da qualche parte.

other·wise ['ʌðəwaɪz] **1** adv **(a)** (in another way) diversamente; **it cannot be ~** non può essere diversamente or altrimenti; **she was ~ engaged** era già impegnata (altrimenti); **except where ~ stated** salvo indicazione contraria. **(b)** (in other respects) altrimenti, a parte questo; **an ~ good piece of work** un lavoro comunque buono. **2** conj (if not) altrimenti, se no.

other-worldly [,ʌðə'wɜːldlɪ] adj (person) disinteressato(a) alle cose materiali.

ot·ter ['ɒtəʳ] n lontra.

ouch [aʊtʃ] excl ohi!, ahi!

ought¹ [ɔːt] n = **aught**.

ought² [ɔːt] pt **ought** modal aux vb **(a)** (moral obligation): **I ~ to do it** dovrei farlo; **one ~ not to do it** non lo si dovrebbe fare. **(b)** (vague desirability): **you ~ to go and see it** dovresti andare a vederlo, faresti bene ad andarlo a vedere. **(c)** (probability): **that ~ to be enough** quello dovrebbe bastare; **he ~ to have arrived by now** dovrebbe essere già arrivato.

ounce [aʊns] n oncia (= 28, 35 grams).

our ['aʊəʳ] poss adj il(la) nostro(a), pl i(le) nostri(e); **this is ~ house** questa è la nostra casa; **at ~ house** a casa nostra; **~ brother** nostro fratello.

ours ['aʊəz] poss pron il(la) nostro(a), pl i(le) nostri(e); **a friend of ~** un nostro amico; **theirs is red, ~ is green** il loro è rosso, il nostro è verde; **this is ~** questo è (il) nostro.

our·selves [,aʊə'sɛlvz] pers pron (reflexive) ci; (emphatic, after preposition) noi stessi(e); **we did it (all) by ~** l'abbiamo fatto (tutto) da soli; see also **oneself**.

oust [aʊst] vt cacciare, soppiantare.

out [aʊt] **1** adv prep **(a)** (gen) fuori; **they're ~ in the garden** sono fuori in giardino; **Mr Green is ~** il signor Green è fuori; **to be ~ and about again** essere di nuovo in piedi; **to have a night ~** passare una serata fuori; **it's cold ~ here** fa freddo qui fuori; **the journey ~** l'andata; **the ball is ~** (Sport) la palla è fuori; **~!** (Tennis) fuori!; **speak ~ (loud)!** parla forte!; **~ with it!** vuota il sacco!, sputa l'osso!

(b) (indicating distance): **she's ~ in Kuwait** è via in Kuwait; **the boat was 10 km ~** la barca era a 10 km dalla costa; **three days ~ from Plymouth** (Naut) a tre giorni di navigazione da Plymouth; **it carried us ~ to sea** ci portò in alto mare.

(c) (fig): **to be ~** (person: unconscious) essere privo(a) dei sensi; (: on strike) essere in sciopero; (: out of game etc) essere eliminato(a); (out of fashion) essere démodé inv or passato(a) di moda; (have appeared: sun, moon) splendere; (: tulips etc) essere in fiore; (: news, secret) essere svelato(a); (: book) uscire; (extinguished: fire, light, gas) essere spento(a); **the tide is ~** c'è bassa marea; **before the week was ~** entro la fine della settimana; **he was ~ in his reckoning (by 5%)** si sbagliava nei suoi calcoli (del 5%); **I was not far ~** non mi sbagliavo di tanto; **I'm only ~ for a good time** voglio solo divertirmi; **he's ~ for all he can get** sta cercando di trarne il massimo profitto; **he's ~ to make money** è deciso a fare soldi; **they're ~ to get me** sono decisi a farmi la pelle; **it's the biggest swindle ~** è la truffa più grossa che ci sia; **she is ~ and away the best** è di gran lunga la migliore.

2: **~ of** prep **(a)** (outside, beyond) fuori; **to go ~ of the house** uscire di casa, andare fuori casa; **to look ~ of the window** guardare fuori dalla fine-

stra; **to be ~ of danger** essere fuori pericolo; **to disappear ~ of sight** sparire alla vista; **to be ~ of sight** non essere visibile; **we're well ~ of it** (fam) per fortuna che ne siamo fuori; **to feel ~ of it** (fam) sentirsi escluso.

(b) (cause, motive) per; **~ of curiosity** per curiosità.

(c) (origin) da; **to drink sth ~ of a cup** bere qc da una tazza; **to take sth ~ of a drawer** prendere qc da un cassetto; **to copy sth ~ of a book** copiare qc da un libro; **a box made ~ of wood** una scatola in legno; **it was like something ~ of a nightmare** era come se fosse un incubo; **Blue Ribbon, by Black Rum ~ of Grenada** (esp Horsebreeding) Blue Ribbon, figlio di Black Rum e Grenada.

(d) (from among) tra; **1 ~ of every 3 smokers** 1 fumatore su 3.

(e) (without) senza; **to be ~ of sth** essere rimasto senza qc; **to be ~ of breath** essere senza fiato; **it's ~ of stock** (Comm) non è disponibile.

3 n: see in **3**.

out-and-out [,aʊtnd'aʊt] adj vero(a) e proprio(a).

out·back ['aʊtbæk] n (in Australia) interno, entroterra.

out·bid [,aʊt'bɪd] pt, pp **outbid** vt fare un'offerta più alta di.

out·board ['aʊtbɔːd] adj, n: **~ (motor)** fuoribordo.

out·break ['aʊtbreɪk] n (of war, disease, crime etc) scoppio; **at the ~ of war** allo scoppio della guerra.

out·building ['aʊtbɪldɪŋ] n costruzione f annessa.

out·burst ['aʊtbɜːst] n scoppio; (of applause) scroscio.

out·cast ['aʊtkɑːst] n reietto/a; (socially) emarginato/a.

out·class [,aʊt'klɑːs] vt surclassare.

out·come ['aʊtkʌm] n esito, risultato.

out·crop ['aʊtkrɒp] n affioramento.

out·cry ['aʊtkraɪ] n protesta; **to raise an ~ about sth** lanciare una protesta contro qc.

out·dat·ed [,aʊt'deɪtɪd] adj antiquato(a), sorpassato(a).

out·did [aʊt'dɪd] pt of **outdo**.

out·distance [,aʊt'dɪstəns] vt distanziare.

out·do [aʊt'duː] pt **outdid**, pp **outdone** [aʊt'dʌn] vt: **to ~ sb (in)** superare or battere qn (in); **he was not to be outdone** non voleva essere da meno.

out·door [aʊt'dɔːʳ] adj (activity, life) all'aperto, all'aria aperta; (swimming pool) scoperto(a); (clothes) pesante (e impermeabile).

out·doors [aʊt'dɔːz] **1** adv (go) fuori; (live, sleep) all'aria aperta. **2** nsg: **the great ~** l'aria aperta.

out·er ['aʊtəʳ] adj esterno(a); **~ space** spazio cosmico.

out·fit ['aʊtfɪt] n **(a)** (clothes) completo; (for sports) tenuta; (for dressing up) costume m. **(b)** (equipment) attrezzatura. **(c)** (fam: organization) organizzazione f.

out·fit·ter ['aʊtfɪtəʳ] n: **gentleman's ~'s** negozio di abbigliamento maschile; **sports ~'s** negozio di articoli sportivi.

out·go·ing ['aʊt,gəʊɪŋ] adj **(a)** (president, tenant) uscente; (means of transport) in partenza. **(b)** (character) socievole.

out·go·ings ['aʊt,gəʊɪŋz] npl spese fpl, uscite fpl.

out·grow [aʊt'grəʊ] pt **outgrew** [aʊt'gruː], pp **outgrown** [aʊt'grəʊn] vt (clothes) diventare troppo grande per; (habit etc) superare (col tempo).

out·house ['aʊthaʊs] n = **outbuilding**.

out·ing ['aʊtɪŋ] n gita, escursione f.

out·land·ish [aʊt'lændɪʃ] adj (dress, person) esotico(a).

out·last [,aʊt'lɑːst] vt sopravvivere a.

out·law ['aʊtlɔ:] **1** *n* fuorilegge *m*, bandito. **2** *vt* bandire.

out·lay ['aʊtleɪ] *n* spesa.

out·let ['aʊtlɛt] **1** *n (for water etc)* scarico; *(of river)* foce *f; (Comm)* mercato; *(: also:* retail ~*)* punto di vendita; *(Am Elec)* presa di corrente; *(fig: for emotion, talents etc)* sfogo. **2** *cpd (Tech)* di scarico.

out·line ['aʊtlaɪn] **1** *n (of object)* contorno; *(of face, building)* profilo; *(summary)* traccia, riassunto; *(general idea: also:* ~s*)* caratteristiche *fpl* principali; **give me the broad** ~(s) spiegamelo a grandi linee. **2** *vt (theory, plan, idea)* abbozzare; *(book, event)* riassumere; *(facts, details)* descrivere a grandi linee; **to be** ~d **against sth** stagliarsi contro qc.

out·live [aʊt'lɪv] *vt* sopravvivere a.

out·look ['aʊtlʊk] *n (view)* vista, veduta; *(prospects)* prospettive *fpl; (opinion)* visione *f*, concezione *f*; **the** ~ **for next Saturday is sunny** si prevede bel tempo per sabato prossimo.

out·ly·ing ['aʊt,laɪɪŋ] *adj (distant)* fuori mano; *(outside town boundary)* periferico(a).

out·ma·noeu·vre, *(Am)* **out·ma·neu·ver** [,aʊtmə'nu:vəʳ] *vt (Mil, fig)* superare in strategia.

out·mod·ed [,aʊt'məʊdɪd] *adj* = **outdated.**

out·num·ber [,aʊt'nʌmbəʳ] *vt* superare numericamente.

out-of-date [,aʊtəv'deɪt] *adj (passport, ticket)* scaduto(a); *(theory, idea)* sorpassato(a), superato(a); *(custom)* antiquato(a); *(clothes)* fuori moda.

out-of-doors [,aʊtəv'dɔ:z] *adv* = **outdoors.**

out-of-the-way [,aʊtəvðə'weɪ] *adj (remote)* fuori mano; *(unusual)* originale, insolito(a).

out·pa·tient ['aʊt,peɪʃənt] *n* paziente *m/f* esterno(a); ~s' **department** ambulatorio *(all'interno di un ospedale).*

out·post ['aʊtpəʊst] *n (Mil, fig)* avamposto.

out·put ['aʊtpʊt] *n (of machine, factory)* produzione *f; (of person)* rendimento; *(of computer)* output *m inv; (Elec)* erogazione *f*.

out·rage ['aʊtreɪdʒ] **1** *n (wicked, violent deed)* atrocità *f inv; (emotion)* sdegno; **bomb** ~ attentato dinamitardo; **it's a public** ~ suscita lo sdegno dell'opinione pubblica; **an** ~ **against good taste** un oltraggio al buon gusto; **an** ~ **against humanity** un crimine contro l'umanità; **it's an** ~! è una vergogna! **2** *vt* offendere; **to be** ~d **by sth** essere scandalizzato da qc.

out·ra·geous [aʊt'reɪdʒəs] *adj (language, joke: offensive)* scioccante; *(price)* esorbitante; *(clothes)* stravagante; *(crime)* atroce; **it's** ~ **that...** è scandaloso che... .

out·ra·geous·ly [aʊt'reɪdʒəslɪ] *adv (see adj)* in modo scioccante; in modo stravagante; in modo atroce; *(expensive)* terribilmente.

out·ran [,aʊt'ræn] *pt of* **outrun.**

out·rid·er ['aʊt,raɪdəʳ] *n* battistrada *m inv.*

out·right [aʊt'raɪt] **1** *adv (kill)* sul colpo; *(win)* di netto, nettamente; *(own)* completamente; *(buy)* in contanti; *(refuse, reject)* categoricamente. **2** ['aʊtraɪt] *adj (winner, refusal)* netto(a); *(liar, selfishness)* bell'e buono(a).

out·run [,aʊt'rʌn] *pt* **outran,** *pp* **outrun** *vt* superare *(nella corsa); (fig)* superare.

out·set ['aʊtsɛt] *n* inizio.

out·shine [,aʊt'ʃaɪn] *pt, pp* **outshone** [,aʊt'ʃɒn] *vt (fig)* eclissare.

out·side ['aʊt'saɪd] **1** *adv* fuori; **to be/go** ~ stare/andare fuori; **seen from** ~ visto dall'esterno *or* da fuori.

2 *prep* **(a)** fuori di; **the car** ~ **the house** la macchina fuori della casa; **he waited** ~ **the door** aspettò fuori della porta; ~ **the city** fuori (della)

città; **don't go** ~ **the garden** non andare fuori del *or* oltre il giardino. **(b)** *(not included in)* al di fuori di; **he has no interests** ~ **his job** non ha altri interessi al di là del lavoro; **it's** ~ **my experience** è al di fuori della mia esperienza.

3 *adj* **(a)** *(exterior)* esterno(a); **an** ~ **broadcast** *(Radio, TV)* una trasmissione in esterno; **the** ~ **lane** *(Aut)* ≃ la corsia di sorpasso; **an** ~ **seat** un posto di corridoio; ~ **contractor** appaltatore *m* esterno; **to get an** ~ **opinion** chiedere un parere esterno. **(b)** *(maximum: price etc)* massimo(a), massimale. **(c)** *(remote, unlikely):* **an** ~ **chance** una vaga possibilità.

4 *n* esterno; **to overtake on the** ~ *(Aut)* ≃ sorpassare sulla sinistra; **judging from the** ~ *(fig)* a giudicare dalle apparenze, a quanto sembra; **at the (very)** ~ al massimo.

5 *cpd:* ~ **left/right** *n (Sport)* ala sinistra/destra.

out·sid·er ['aʊt'saɪdəʳ] *n (stranger)* estraneo/a; *(in racing etc)* outsider *m/f inv.*

out·size ['aʊtsaɪz] *adj (gen)* gigante; *(clothes)* di taglia forte; ~ **department** reparto taglie forti.

out·skirts ['aʊtskɜ:ts] *npl (of town)* sobborghi *mpl,* periferia; *(of wood)* margine *m,* confine *m.*

out·spo·ken [aʊt'spəʊkən] *adj* franco(a).

out·spread ['aʊtsprɛd] *adj (gen)* aperto(a); *(wings)* aperto(a), spiegato(a).

out·stand·ing [aʊt'stændɪŋ] *adj* **(a)** *(exceptional)* eccezionale; *(: feature)* saliente. **(b)** *(not settled: bill)* in sospeso, in pendenza; *(: problem)* irrisolto(a); **the work is still** ~ il lavoro non è ancora stato finito.

out·stand·ing·ly [aʊt'stændɪŋlɪ] *adv* eccezionalmente, notevolmente.

out·stay [,aʊt'steɪ] *vt:* **to** ~ **sb** trattenersi più a lungo di qn; **to** ~ **one's welcome** abusare dell'ospitalità di qn.

out·stretched [,aʊt'strɛtʃt] *adj (body, legs)* disteso(a), steso(a); **with** ~ **arms** a braccia aperte.

out·strip [,aʊt'strɪp] *vt (also fig)* superare.

out·vote [aʊt'vəʊt] *vt:* **it was** ~d **(by...)** fu respinto (con una maggioranza di...); **I wanted to go dancing but I was** ~d volevo andare a ballare ma gli altri non hanno voluto.

out·ward ['aʊtwəd] *adj* **(a)** *(movement)* verso l'esterno; **on the** ~ **journey** durante il viaggio di andata. **(b)** *(appearance etc)* esterno(a), apparente; **with an** ~ **show of interest** mostrando un apparente interesse.

out·ward(s) ['aʊtwəd(z)] *adv* verso l'esterno; **outward bound** in partenza.

out·ward·ly ['aʊtwədlɪ] *adv* esteriormente; *(apparently)* apparentemente.

out·weigh [,aʊt'weɪ] *vt* superare.

out·wit [,aʊt'wɪt] *vt* superare in astuzia, essere più furbo(a) di.

out·worn ['aʊt'wɔ:n] *adj (idea, expression)* trito(a); *(custom)* superato(a).

oval ['əʊvəl] *adj, n* ovale *(m).*

ova·ry ['əʊvərɪ] *n (Anat)* ovaia; *(Bot)* ovario.

ova·tion [əʊ'veɪʃən] *n* ovazione *f.*

oven ['ʌvn] **1** *n* forno; **it's like an** ~ **in there** è un forno lì dentro. **2** *cpd:* ~ **glove** *n* guanto da forno.

oven·proof ['ʌvn,pru:f] *adj* che si può mettere in forno.

oven-ready [,ʌvn'rɛdɪ] *adj* pronto(a) da infornare.

oven·ware ['ʌvn,wɛəʳ] *n* vasellame *m* da mettere in forno.

over ['əʊvəʳ] **1** *adv* **(a)** *(across):* ~ **here** qui; ~ **there** laggiù; ~ **in France** in Francia; **he's** ~ **from France for a few days** è venuto dalla Francia per alcuni giorni; ~ **against the wall** (lì *or* là) contro il muro; **the baby went** ~ **to its mother** il bambino andò da sua madre; **to drive ~ to the other side of town** andare (in macchina) dall'altra parte della città; **can you come ~ tonight?** puoi venire da me (or noi) stasera?; **~ to you!** (Telec etc) a te la parola!; **now ~ to our Paris correspondent** diamo ora la linea al nostro corrispondente da Parigi; **to go ~ to the enemy** passare al nemico.

(b): **the world ~** in tutto il mondo; **I ache all ~** mi fa male dappertutto; **I looked all ~ for you** ti ho cercato dappertutto; **that's him all ~** è veramente da lui.

(c) (indicating movement from one side to another, from upright position): **she hit me and ~ I went** mi ha colpito e sono caduto; **to turn sth ~ (and ~)** girare (e rigirare) qc.

(d) (finished) finito(a); **the rain is ~** la pioggia è cessata; **the danger was soon ~** il pericolo cessò presto; **it's all ~ between us** tra me e te tutto è finito.

(e) (again): **to tell ~ and ~** dire mille volte; **to start (all) ~ again** ricominciare da capo; **several times ~** diverse volte.

(f) (excessively) molto, troppo; **she's not ~ intelligent** non è troppo intelligente.

(g) (remaining) rimasto(a); **there are 3 ~** ne sono rimasti 3; **is there any cake (left) ~?** è rimasta la torta?

(h) (more): **persons of 21 and ~** persone dai 21 anni in su.

(i) (esp in signalling and radio): **~ and out** passo e chiudo.

2 prep **(a)** (on top of, above) su; **to spread a sheet ~ sth** mettere un lenzuolo su qc; **~ my head** sopra la mia testa; **his speech went ~ my head** il suo discorso era troppo complicato per me; **he's ~ me** è il mio capo; **to have an advantage ~ sb** avere un vantaggio su qn.

(b) (across): **the pub ~ the road** il pub di fronte; **it's ~ the river** è al di là del fiume; **the bridge ~ the river** il ponte sul fiume; **the ball went ~ the wall** la palla andò al di là del muro; **~ the page** alla pagina seguente.

(c) (everywhere in): **all ~ the world** in tutto il mondo; **you've got mud all ~ your shoes** hai le scarpe tutte infangate.

(d) (in excess of): **~ 200** più di 200; **he must be ~ 60** deve aver superato i 60; **~ and above normal requirements** oltre ai soliti requisiti; **an increase of 5% ~ last year's total** un aumento del 5% rispetto al totale dell'anno scorso.

(e) (during) durante, nel corso di; **~ the last few years** negli ultimi anni; **~ the winter** durante l'inverno; **let's discuss it ~ dinner** discutiamolo durante la cena; **how long will you be ~ it?** quanto tempo ti prenderà?

(f) (means): **I heard it ~ the radio** l'ho sentito alla radio.

(g) (about, concerning): **they fell out ~ money** litigarono per una questione di denaro.

over... pref e.g.: **~abundance** n sovrabbondanza; **~anxious** adj troppo ansioso(a); **~heat** vi surriscaldare.

over·abun·dant [ˌəʊvərəˈbʌndənt] adj sovrabbondante.

over·act [ˌəʊvərˈækt] vi recitare con troppa enfasi.

over·ac·tive [ˌəʊvərˈæktɪv] adj troppo attivo(a).

over·all [ˌəʊvərˈɔːl] **1** adj (improvement) generale; (width, length, majority) totale; **~ dimensions** (Aut) ingombro. **2** adv nel complesso, complessivamente.

over·alls [ˈəʊvərɔːlz] npl tuta.

over·anx·ious [ˌəʊvərˈæŋkʃəs] adj troppo ansioso(a).

over·ate [ˌəʊvərˈeɪt] pt of **overeat**.

over·awe [ˌəʊvərˈɔː] vt intimidire.

over·bal·ance [ˌəʊvəˈbæləns] **1** vi sbilanciarsi. **2** vt sbilanciare.

over·bear·ing [ˌəʊvəˈbeərɪŋ] adj autoritario(a), prepotente.

over·board [ˈəʊvəbɔːd] adv (Naut) fuori bordo; **to fall ~** cadere in mare; **man ~!** uomo in mare!; **to go ~ for sth** (fig) impazzire per qc.

over·bur·den [ˌəʊvəˈbɜːdn] vt sovraccaricare.

over·came [ˌəʊvəˈkeɪm] pt of **overcome**.

over·cast [ˈəʊvəkɑːst] adj nuvoloso(a), coperto(a).

over·cau·tious [ˌəʊvəˈkɔːʃəs] adj troppo cauto(a).

over·charge [ˌəʊvəˈtʃɑːdʒ] vt **(a)**: **to ~** far pagare troppo qc a qn. **(b)** (Elec) sovraccaricare.

over·coat [ˈəʊvəkəʊt] n (light) soprabito; (heavy) cappotto.

over·come [ˌəʊvəˈkʌm] pt **overcame**, pp **overcome** vt (enemies) sopraffare; (obstacle, difficulty) superare; (rage, temptation) vincere; (sb's doubts) dissolvere; **to be ~ by the heat** essere sopraffatto dall'afa; **to be ~ by remorse** essere preso dal rimorso; **she was quite ~ by the occasion** era estremamente colpita dall'occasione.

over·con·fi·dent [ˌəʊvəˈkɒnfɪdənt] adj troppo sicuro(a) (di sé), presuntuoso(a).

over·crowd·ed [ˌəʊvəˈkraʊdɪd] adj sovraffollato(a).

over·crowd·ing [ˌəʊvəˈkraʊdɪŋ] n sovraffollamento.

over·do [ˌəʊvəˈduː] pt **overdid** [ˌəʊvəˈdɪd], pp **overdone** vt **(a)** (exaggerate) esagerare; **don't ~ the smoking** non esagerare con le sigarette; **to ~ it, to ~ things** (work too hard) lavorare troppo; (convalescent) forzare le cose. **(b)** (cook too long) cuocere troppo.

over·done [ˌəʊvəˈdʌn] **1** pp of **overdo**. **2** adj (exaggerated) esagerato(a); (overcooked) troppo cotto(a).

over·dose [ˈəʊvədəʊs] n overdose f inv.

over·draft [ˈəʊvədrɑːft] n (Fin) conto scoperto; **to have an ~ at the bank** avere il conto scoperto in banca.

over·draw [ˌəʊvəˈdrɔː] pt **overdrew** [ˌəʊvəˈdruː], pp **overdrawn** [ˌəʊvəˈdrɔːn] vi avere il conto scoperto.

over·drive [ˈəʊvədraɪv] n (Aut) overdrive m inv.

over·due [ˌəʊvəˈdjuː] adj (bill) insoluto(a); (library book) col prestito scaduto; (train etc) in ritardo; **this work is 2 days ~** questo lavoro andava consegnato 2 giorni fa; **that change was long ~** quel cambiamento ci voleva da tempo.

over·eat [ˌəʊvərˈiːt] pt **overate**, pp **overeaten** [ˌəʊvərˈiːtn] vi mangiare troppo.

over·es·ti·mate [ˌəʊvərˈestɪmeɪt] vt esagerare nel calcolare; (fig) sopravvalutare.

over·ex·cit·ed [ˌəʊvərɪkˈsaɪtɪd] adj sovraeccitato(a).

over·ex·er·tion [ˌəʊvərɪgˈzɜːʃən] n fatica eccessiva, sforzo.

over·ex·pose [ˌəʊvərɪksˈpəʊz] vt (Phot) sovraesporre.

over·feed [ˌəʊvəˈfiːd] pt, pp **overfed** [ˌəʊvəˈfed] vt dar troppo da mangiare a.

over·flow [ˈəʊvəfləʊ] **1** n (pipe etc) troppopieno; (fig: people): **the ~ filled the courtyard** quelli che non riuscirono ad entrare si accalcarono nel cortile. **2** [ˌəʊvəˈfləʊ] vi (gen) traboccare; (river) straripare; (people) riversarsi; **the theatre was ~ing with people** il teatro traboccava di gente.

over·fly [ˌəʊvə'flaɪ] pt **overflew** [ˌəʊvə'fluː]. pp **overflown** [ˌəʊvə'fləʊn] vt sorvolare.

over·full [ˌəʊvə'fʊl] adj troppo pieno(a).

over·gen·er·ous [ˌəʊvə'dʒɛnərəs] adj troppo generoso(a).

over·grown ['əʊvə'grəʊn] adj (garden): ~ **with weeds/ivy** coperto(a) di erbacce/edera; **he's just an ~ schoolboy** è proprio un bambinone.

over·hang ['əʊvə'hæŋ] pt, pp **overhung 1** vt sporgere da. **2** vi sporgere.

over·hang·ing ['əʊvə'hæŋɪŋ] adj sporgente.

over·haul ['əʊvəhɔːl] **1** n revisione f. **2** [ˌəʊvə'hɔːl] vt (service: machine) revisionare; (revise: plans etc) rivedere.

over·head [ˌəʊvə'hɛd] **1** adv in alto, in cielo. **2** ['əʊvəhɛd] adj (railway) sopraelevato(a); (cable) aereo(a). **3**: ~**s** npl costi mpl di gestione.

over·hear [ˌəʊvə'hɪər] pt, pp **overheard** [ˌəʊvə'hɜːd] vt sentire (per caso); **she was overheard complaining** la sentirono lamentarsi.

over·heat [ˌəʊvə'hiːt] vi (engine) surriscaldare.

over·hung ['əʊvə'hʌŋ] pt, pp of **overhang**.

over·joyed [ˌəʊvə'dʒɔɪd] adj: ~ **(at)** pazzo(a) di gioia (per).

over·kill ['əʊvəkɪl] n (Mil) potenziale m nucleare superiore al necessario; (fig) strafare m.

over·land ['əʊvəlænd] adv, adj per via di terra.

over·lap ['əʊvəlæp] **1** n sovrapposizione f; (fig) coincidenza. **2** [ˌəʊvə'læp] vi sovrapporsi; (fig) coincidere.

over·lay [ˌəʊvə'leɪ] pt, pp **overlaid** [ˌəʊvə'leɪd] vt ricoprire.

over·leaf [ˌəʊvə'liːf] adv a tergo.

over·load [ˌəʊvə'ləʊd] vt sovraccaricare.

over·look [ˌəʊvə'lʊk] vt **(a)** (subj: building) dare su; **our garden is not** ~**ed** nel nostro giardino nessuno ci può vedere. **(b)** (not notice) lasciarsi scappare; (tolerate) chiudere un occhio su.

over·man·ning [ˌəʊvə'mænɪŋ] n eccedenza di manodopera.

over·much [ˌəʊvə'mʌtʃ] adv troppo.

over·night ['əʊvə'naɪt] **1** adv (rain) durante la notte; (travel) di notte; (fig: quickly) da un giorno all'altro; **to stay ~** fermarsi a dormire; **we can't solve this one ~** non possiamo risolvere questo da un giorno all'altro. **2** adj (stay) di una notte; (journey) di notte; (fig: success) istantaneo(a).

over·paid [ˌəʊvə'peɪd] pt, pp of **overpay**.

over·par·ticu·lar [ˌəʊvəpə'tɪkjʊlər] adj (on rules) pignolo(a); **not to be ~ about sth** non badare molto or troppo a qc.

over·pass ['əʊvəpɑːs] n (Am) cavalcavia m inv.

over·pay [ˌəʊvə'peɪ] pt, pp **overpaid** vt strapagare; **to ~ sb by £50** pagare 50 sterline in più a qn.

over·popu·lated [ˌəʊvə'pɒpjʊleɪtɪd] adj sovrappopolato(a).

over·pow·er [ˌəʊvə'paʊər] vt sopraffare.

over·pow·er·ing [ˌəʊvə'paʊərɪŋ] adj (smell, heat) soffocante; (desire) irrefrenabile.

over·rate [ˌəʊvə'reɪt] vt sopravvalutare.

over·reach [ˌəʊvə'riːtʃ] vt: **to ~ o.s.** volere strafare.

over·react [ˌəʊvəri:'ækt] vi avere una reazione eccessiva.

over·ride [ˌəʊvə'raɪd] pt **overrode** [ˌəʊvə'rəʊd]. pp **overridden** [ˌəʊvə'rɪdn] vt (law) calpestare; (person) scavalcare; (sb's wishes, orders etc) non tener conto di; (Tech: cancel) annullare.

over·rid·ing [ˌəʊvə'raɪdɪŋ] adj (factor) preponderante; (importance) essenziale, assoluto(a).

over·ripe [ˌəʊvə'raɪp] adj troppo maturo(a).

over·rule [ˌəʊvə'ruːl] vt (person) prevalere su; (request etc) respingere.

over·run [ˌəʊvə'rʌn] pt **overran** [ˌəʊvə'ræn]. pp **overrun 1** vt (Mil: country etc) invadere; (time limit etc) superare, andare al di là di; **the town is ~ with tourists** la città è invasa dai turisti. **2** vi protrarsi.

over·seas ['əʊvə'siːz] **1** adv (abroad) all'estero; **visitors from ~** visitatori stranieri. **2** adj (countries) d'oltremare; (foreign) straniero(a); (trade, market) estero(a).

over·see [ˌəʊvə'siː] pt **oversaw** [ˌəʊvə'sɔː]. pp **overseen** [ˌəʊvə'siːn] vt sorvegliare.

over·seer ['əʊvə,sɪər] n sorvegliante m/f; (foreman) caposquadra m.

over·shad·ow [ˌəʊvə'ʃædəʊ] vt (fig) eclissare.

over·shoot [ˌəʊvə'ʃuːt] pt, pp **overshot** [ˌəʊvə'ʃɒt] vt andare oltre.

over·sight ['əʊvəsaɪt] n (omission) dimenticanza, svista; **due to an ~** per una svista.

over·sim·pli·fy [ˌəʊvə'sɪmplɪfaɪ] vt semplificare troppo.

over·sleep [ˌəʊvə'sliːp] pt, pp **overslept** [ˌəʊvə'slɛpt] vi dormire troppo, non svegliarsi (in tempo).

over·spend [ˌəʊvə'spɛnd] pt, pp **overspent** [ˌəʊvə'spɛnt] vi spendere troppo; **we have overspent by 5 dollars** abbiamo speso 5 dollari di troppo.

over·spill ['əʊvəspɪl] n (population) eccedenza di popolazione; **an ~ town** una città satellite.

over·staffed [ˌəʊvə'stɑːft] adj: **to be ~** avere troppo personale.

over·staffing [ˌəʊvə'stɑːfɪŋ] n eccedenza di personale.

over·state [ˌəʊvə'steɪt] vt: **to ~ one's case** esagerare nel presentare le proprie ragioni.

over·state·ment [ˌəʊvə'steɪtmənt] n esagerazione f.

over·step [ˌəʊvə'stɛp] vt: **to ~ the mark** superare ogni limite.

overt [əʊ'vɜːt] adj evidente, aperto(a).

over·take [ˌəʊvə'teɪk] pt **overtook** [ˌəʊvə'tʊk]. pp **overtaken** [ˌəʊvə'teɪkən] **1** vt (catch up) raggiungere; (pass) superare; **events have ~n us** gli eventi ci hanno colto di sorpresa. **2** vi sorpassare; **'no overtaking'** 'divieto di sorpasso'.

over·tax [ˌəʊvə'tæks] vt (Fin) imporre tasse eccessive a, tassare eccessivamente; (fig: strength, patience) mettere alla prova, abusare di; **to ~ o.s.** chiedere troppo alle proprie forze.

over·throw ['əʊvəθrəʊ] (vb: pt **overthrew** [ˌəʊvə'θruː]. pp **overthrown** [ˌəʊvə'θrəʊn]) **1** n (of government etc) rovesciamento. **2** vt [ˌəʊvə'θrəʊ] (king, system etc) rovesciare.

over·time ['əʊvətaɪm] n straordinario; **to do or work ~** fare lo straordinario; **your imagination has been working ~!** corri un po' troppo con la fantasia!

over·tired [ˌəʊvə'taɪəd] adj stanchissimo(a), sovraffaticato(a).

over·tone ['əʊvətəʊn] n (fig) sfumatura.

over·ture ['əʊvətjʊər] n **(a)** (Mus) ouverture f inv. **(b)**: **to make ~s to sb** mostrarsi conciliante verso qn; (sexually) fare approcci a qn.

over·turn [ˌəʊvə'tɜːn] **1** vt (car, boat, saucepan etc) capovolgere; (government etc) rovesciare. **2** vi (car, boat etc) rovesciarsi.

over·use [ˌəʊvə'juːz] vt abusare di.

over·value [ˌəʊvə'væljuː] vt sopravvalutare.

over·weight [ˌəʊvə'weɪt] adj: **to be ~** (person) essere troppo grasso(a); (suitcase) superare il peso consentito; **the parcel is a kilo ~** il pacco pesa un chilo di troppo.

over·whelm [ˌəʊvə'wɛlm] vt (opponent, team etc) schiacciare; (with questions, requests, work etc) sommergere; **sorrow** ~**ed him** il dolore lo sopraffece; ~**ed by her kindness** confuso dalla sua gentilezza; **to be** ~**ed** *(touched, impressed)* rimanere colpito; **we have been** ~**ed with offers of help** siamo stati sommersi da offerte di aiuto.

over·whelm·ing [‚əʊvə'wɛlmɪŋ] *adj (defeat, victory, majority)* schiacciante; *(pressure, heat, desire, emotion)* intenso(a); **one's** ~ **impression is of heat** l'impressione dominante è quella di caldo.

over·whelm·ing·ly [‚əʊvə'wɛlmɪŋlɪ] *adv (defeat, win)* in modo schiacciante; *(vote)* in massa.

over·work [‚əʊvə'wɜːk] **1** *n* lavoro eccessivo. **2** *vi* lavorare troppo.

over·wrought [‚əʊvə'rɔːt] *adj* sovreccitato(a).

over·zeal·ous [əʊvə'zɛləs] *adj* troppo zelante.

ovu·late ['ɒvjʊleɪt] *vi* ovulare.

ovu·la·tion [‚ɒvjʊ'leɪʃən] *n* ovulazione *f*.

owe [əʊ] *vt (gen)*: **to** ~ **sth (to)** dovere qc (a); **to what do I** ~ **the honour of your visit?** a che devo l'onore della visita?; **you** ~ **it to yourself to come** è per te (stesso) che devi venire.

ow·ing ['əʊɪŋ] **1** *adj* da pagare; **how much is** ~ **to you now?** quanto ti devono adesso? **2**: ~ **to** *prep (due to)* a causa di; ~ **to the bad weather** a causa del maltempo.

owl [aʊl] *n (small)* civetta; *(big)* gufo.

own [əʊn] **1** *adj* proprio(a); **I made it with my** ~ **hands** l'ho fatto con le mie proprie mani; **it's all my** ~ **money** sono tutti soldi miei; **the house has its** ~ **garage** la casa ha il suo garage.

2 *pron*: **the house is her (very)** ~ la casa è di sua proprietà; **can I have it for my (very)** ~**?** posso averlo tutto per me?; **he has a style all his** ~ ha uno stile tutto suo; **she has money of her** ~ ha dei soldi suoi personali; **I'll give you a copy of your** ~ ti darò una copia tutta per te; **a place of one's** ~ un posto tutto per sé; **to come into one's** ~ mostrare le proprie qualità; **to be on one's** ~ stare per conto proprio; **if I can get him on his** ~ se riesco a beccarlo da solo; **to do sth on one's** ~

(unaided) fare qualcosa da solo; **I am so busy I can scarcely call my time my** ~ sono così occupato che non dispongo del mio tempo; **without a chair to call my** ~ senza una sedia che possa chiamare mia; **to get one's** ~ **back** rendere pan per focaccia.

3 *vt* **(a)** *(possess)* possedere, essere proprietario(a) di; **does anybody** ~ **this pen?** è di qualcuno questa penna?; **he acts as if he** ~**s the place** si comporta come se fosse il padrone; **you don't** ~ **me!** non sei il mio padrone! **(b)** *(admit)* ammettere.

4 *vi*: **to** ~ **to sth** ammettere qc; **to** ~ **to having done sth** ammettere di aver fatto qc.

♦ **own up** *vi + adv*: **to** ~ **up (to sth)** confessare (qc), ammettere (qc); **to** ~ **up to having done sth** ammettere di aver fatto qc.

own·er ['əʊnə^r] *n* proprietario/a.

owner-occupier [‚əʊnər'ɒkjʊpaɪə^r] *n* proprietario/a della casa in cui abita.

own·er·ship ['əʊnəʃɪp] *n* proprietà, possesso; **it's under new** ~ ha un nuovo proprietario; **under his** ~ **the business flourished** in suo possesso la ditta prosperava.

ox [ɒks] *n, pl* ~**en** ['ɒksən] bue *m*.

oxi·da·tion [‚ɒksɪ'deɪʃən] *n* ossidazione *f*.

ox·ide ['ɒksaɪd] *n* ossido.

oxi·dize ['ɒksɪdaɪz] *vt* ossidare.

Oxon *abbr of Oxfordshire; Oxford university.*

ox·tail ['ɒksteɪl] *n*: ~ **soup** zuppa di coda di bue.

oxy·acety·lene [‚ɒksɪə'sɛtɪliːn] *adj* ossiacetilenico(a); ~ **burner,** ~ **torch** cannello ossiacetilenico.

oxy·gen ['ɒksɪdʒən] **1** *n* ossigeno. **2** *cpd*: ~ **mask** *n* maschera per ossigeno; ~ **tent** *n* tenda ad ossigeno.

oys·ter ['ɔɪstə^r] *n* ostrica.

oz. *abbr of* **ounce(s).**

ozone ['əʊzəʊn] *n* ozono.

P

P, p[1] |piː| n (letter) P, p for m inv; **mind your p's and q's!** bada a come parli!

p[2] abbr of **penny, pence.**

P.A. abbr of **personal assistant; public address system.**

p.a. abbr of **per annum.**

pace |peɪs| **1** n **(a)** (step) passo; **30 ~s away** a 30 passi di distanza; **to put sb through his ~s** (fig) mettere qn alla prova. **(b)** (speed) passo, andatura; **at a good ~** (walk) di buon passo; (work) ad un buon ritmo; **at a slow ~** lentamente; **the ~ of life** il ritmo di vita; **to keep ~ with** (person) andare di pari passo con; (fig: technology) procedere di pari passo con; (: events) tenersi al corrente di; **to set the ~** (running) fare l'andatura; (fig) dare il la or il tono. **2** vt (room) andare su e giù per; **to ~ sth off** or **out** misurare a passi qc. **3** vi: **to ~ up and down** camminare su e giù or avanti e indietro.

pace·maker |'peɪs,meɪkə[r]| n (Med) pace-maker m inv, stimolatore m cardiaco; (Sport) chi fa l'andatura.

pace·setter |'peɪs,sɛtə[r]| n (Am) = **pacemaker** (Sport).

Pa·cif·ic |pə'sɪfɪk| adj del Pacifico; **the ~ (Ocean)** l'Oceano Pacifico, il Pacifico.

paci·fi·er |'pæsɪfaɪə[r]| n (Am: dummy) succhiotto, ciuccio (fam).

paci·fism |'pæsɪfɪzəm| n pacifismo.

paci·fist |'pæsɪfɪst| n pacifista m/f.

paci·fy |'pæsɪfaɪ| vt (person) calmare; (country) riportare la calma in; (fears) placare; (creditors) ammansire.

pack |pæk| **1** n **(a)** (packet) pacco; (Comm) confezione f; (Am: of cigarettes) pacchetto; (rucksack, Mil) zaino; (of cards) mazzo; (Rugby) pacchetto; **a ~ of lies** un mucchio or sacco di bugie. **(b)** (of hounds) muta; (of wolves) branco; (of thieves) banda; (of fools) massa.

2 vt **(a)** (objects, goods) imballare; **~ed in dozens** (Comm) in confezioni da dodici; **to ~ one's bags** fare le valigie or i bagagli; (fig) far fagotto; **I still have a few things to ~** ho ancora qualcosa da mettere in valigia; **~ed lunch** (for walker) pranzo al sacco; (for traveller) cestino da viaggio; **I always take a ~ed lunch to work** mi porto sempre qualcosa da casa sul lavoro. **(b)** (cram full): **to ~ (with)** (container) riempire di; (room, car) stipare di; **the place was ~ed** il posto era affollato; **can you ~ two more into your car?** riesci a infilarci ancora due nella tua macchina? **(c)** (make firm: soil etc) comprimere, pressare.

3 vi **(a)** (do one's luggage) fare le valigie or i bagagli; **to send sb ~ing** (fam) spedire via qn. **(b)** (people): **to ~ (into)** accalcarsi (in), pigiarsi (in); **~ed like sardines** pigiati come sardine.

4 cpd (animal, horse) da soma; **~ ice** n banchisa.

♦ **pack in 1** vi + adv (break down: watch, car) guastarsi. **2** vt + adv (fam) mollare, piantare; **~ it in!** piantala!

♦ **pack off** vt + adv: **to ~ sb off to school/bed** spedire qn a scuola/letto.

♦ **pack up 1** vi + adv (fam: machine) guastarsi; (: person) far fagotto. **2** vt + adv **(a)** (belongings, clothes) mettere in una valigia; (goods, presents) imballare. **(b)** = **pack in 2.**

pack·age |'pækɪdʒ| **1** n (parcel) pacco; (smaller) pacchetto; (fig: terms of agreement) pacchetto. **2** vt (Comm: goods) confezionare. **3** cpd: **~ deal** n insieme m di proposte; **~ holiday** n vacanza organizzata.

pack·ag·ing |'pækɪdʒɪŋ| n confezione f, imballo.

pack·er |'pækə[r]| n (person) imballatore/trice; (machine) imballatrice f.

pack·et |'pækɪt| n (gen) pacchetto; (of sweets, crisps) sacchetto; (of needles, seeds) bustina; **to make a ~** (fam) fare un mucchio or un sacco di soldi; **that must have cost a ~** (fam) dev'essere costato un sacco di soldi.

pack·ing |'pækɪŋ| **1** n **(a)** (of luggage): **to do one's ~** fare le valigie or i bagagli. **(b)** (material) materiale m da imballaggio. **2** cpd: **~ case** n cassa da imballaggio.

pact |pækt| n patto.

pad |pæd| n **(a)** (to prevent friction etc) cuscinetto; (Ftbl) parastinco; (Hockey) gambiera; (brake ~) pastiglia; (for ink) tampone m. **(b)** (writing ~) blocco di carta da lettere; (note~) bloc-notes m inv, blocchetto. **(c)** (launch ~) rampa di lancio. **(d)** (of animal's foot) cuscinetto. **(e)** (fam: flat) appartamentino. **2** vt (cushion, shoulders etc) imbottire. **3** vi: **to ~ about/in** etc camminare/entrare etc a passi felpati.

♦ **pad out** vt + adv (speech etc) farcire.

pad·ded |'pædɪd| adj imbottito(a).

pad·ding |'pædɪŋ| n (material) imbottitura; (fig: in speech etc) riempitivo.

pad·dle |'pædl| **1** n **(a)** (oar) pagaia; (blade of wheel) pala. **(b)**: **to have a ~** camminare nell'acqua bassa. **2** vt (boat) fare andare a colpi di pagaia. **3** vi **(a)** (boat) vogare con la pagaia. **(b)** (walk in water) sguazzare. **4** cpd: **~ boat** n, **~ steamer** n battello a ruote.

pad·dling |'pædlɪŋ| adj: **~ pool** piscina per bambini.

pad·dock |'pædək| n (field) recinto; (of racecourse) paddock m inv.

pad·dy |'pædɪ| **~ field** n risaia.

pad·lock |'pædlɒk| **1** n lucchetto. **2** vt chiudere con il lucchetto.

pae·di·at·ric |,piːdɪ'ætrɪk| etc = **pediatric** etc.

pa·gan |'peɪgən| adj, n pagano(a) (m/f).

page[1] |peɪdʒ| n (servant) fattorino; (at wedding) paggio. **2** vt: **to ~ sb** (far) chiamare qn.

page[2] |peɪdʒ| n (of book etc) pagina; **on ~ 2** a pagina 2; **on both sides of the ~** su tutt'e due le facciate (del foglio).

pag·eant |'pædʒənt| n (show) spettacolo di rievocazione storica; (procession) corteo in costume.

pag·eant·ry |'pædʒəntrɪ| n sfarzo.

page·boy ['peɪdʒbɔɪ] n (servant) paggio; (hairstyle) pettinatura alla paggio.

pa·go·da [pə'gəʊdə] n pagoda.

paid [peɪd] **1** pt, pp of **pay. 2: to put ~ to** sth metter fine a qc.

paid-up ['peɪdʌp] adj, (Am) **paid-in** ['peɪdɪn] adj (member) che ha pagato la sua quota; (share) interamente pagato(a); **~ capital** capitale m interamente versato.

pail [peɪl] n secchio.

pain [peɪn] **1** n **(a)** dolore m; **to cause ~ to** (physical) provocare dolori a; (mental) far soffrire; **to be in ~** soffrire; **I have a ~ in my leg** ho male or un dolore a una gamba; **he's a real ~ (in the neck)** (fam) è un gran rompiscatole. **(b): ~s** pl (efforts) sforzi mpl; **and all I got for my ~s was...** e come ringraziamento ho avuto...; **to take ~s over** sth mettercela tutta in qc; **to be at (great) ~s to do** sth fare di tutto per fare qc. **(c)** (penalty): **on ~ of death** sotto pena di morte. **2** vt (mentally) addolorare, affliggere.

pained [peɪnd] adj addolorato(a), afflitto(a).

pain·ful ['peɪnfʊl] adj (wound) doloroso(a); (leg) che fa male; (task, sight, also fam) penoso(a); **it is my ~ duty to tell you that...** purtroppo ho il dovere di informarla che...; **it was ~ to watch** (fam) era penoso (a vedersi).

pain·ful·ly ['peɪnfəlɪ] adv (walk, breathe) a fatica; (thin) penosamente; **the cut throbbed ~** la ferita pulsava e faceva male; **it was ~ clear that...** era fin troppo chiaro che... .

pain·killer ['peɪnˌkɪləʳ] n antidolorifico.

pain·less ['peɪnlɪs] adj (gen) indolore; (fig: exam) non troppo difficile; (: interview) non spiacevole.

pains·taking ['peɪnzˌteɪkɪŋ] adj (person) coscienzioso(a), diligente; (work) accurato(a); (accuracy) minuzioso(a).

paint [peɪnt] **1** n (Art) colore m; (for house etc) tinta, vernice f; **a tin of ~** un barattolo di tinta or vernice; **a box of ~s** una scatola di colori. **2** vt (Art, house) dipingere; (door) verniciare; **to ~** sth **blue/red** dipingere (or verniciare) qc di blu/rosso; **to ~ the town red** (fig) far baldoria; **he's not as black as he's ~ed** è molto meno cattivo di quanto si dica in giro. **3** vi dipingere.

paint·box ['peɪntbɒks] n scatola di colori.

paint·brush ['peɪntbrʌʃ] n pennello.

paint·er ['peɪntəʳ] n (Art) pittore/trice; (decorator) imbianchino.

paint·ing ['peɪntɪŋ] n (Art: picture) dipinto, quadro; (: activity) pittura; (decorating: of doors etc) verniciatura; (: of walls) imbiancatura.

paint-stripper ['peɪntˌstrɪpəʳ] n (tool) raschietto; (chemical) sverniciante m.

paint·work ['peɪntwɜːk] n (gen) tinta; (of car) vernice f.

pair [pɛəʳ] **1** n (of gloves, shoes etc) paio; (of people) coppia; **a ~ of scissors/trousers** un paio di forbici/pantaloni; **arranged in ~s** disposti a due a due. **2** vt accoppiare, appaiare.

♦ **pair off 1** vt + adv trovar marito (or moglie) a. **2** vi + adv: **to ~ off (with** sb) fare coppia (con qn).

pais·ley ['peɪzlɪ] adj: **~ pattern** disegno cachemire.

pa·jam·as [pə'dʒɑːməz] npl (Am) = **pyjamas.**

Pa·ki·stan [ˌpɑːkɪ'stɑːn] n Pakistan m.

Pa·ki·stani [ˌpɑːkɪs'tɑːnɪ] adj, n pakistano(a) (m/f).

pal [pæl] n (fam) amico/a.

pal·ace ['pælɪs] n palazzo.

pal·at·able ['pælətəbl] adj (frm: tasty) gradevole (al palato); (fig) piacevole, gradevole.

pala·tal ['pælətl] adj palatale.

pal·ate ['pælɪt] n (Anat, fig) palato.

pa·la·tial [pə'leɪʃəl] adj sontuoso(a), sfarzoso(a).

pa·la·ver [pə'lɑːvəʳ] n (fam: fuss) storie fpl; (: talk) tiritera.

pale[1] [peɪl] **1** adj **(-r, -st)** (gen) pallido(a); (colour) chiaro(a), pallido(a); **to grow ~, to turn ~** diventare pallido, impallidire. **2** vi impallidire; **to ~ into insignificance (beside)** perdere d'importanza (nei confronti di).

pale[2] [peɪl] n: **to be beyond the ~** aver oltrepassato ogni limite.

pale·ness ['peɪlnɪs] n pallore m.

Pal·es·tine ['pælɪstaɪn] n Palestina.

Pal·es·tin·ian [ˌpælɪs'tɪnɪən] adj, n palestinese (m/f).

pal·ette ['pælɪt] n tavolozza.

pall[1] [pɔːl] n (on coffin) drappo funebre; (of smoke) coltre f, cappa.

pall[2] [pɔːl] vi: **to ~ (on)** perdere il proprio fascino (per), diventare noioso(a) (per).

pall·bearer ['pɔːlˌbɛərəʳ] n persona che porta la bara.

pal·let ['pælɪt] n (for goods) paletta.

pal·lia·tive ['pælɪətɪv] n palliativo.

pal·lid ['pælɪd] adj pallido(a), smorto(a).

pal·lor ['pæləʳ] n pallore m.

pal·ly ['pælɪ] adj (-ier, -iest) (fam): **to be ~ with** sb essere molto amico (or amica) di qn.

palm[1] [pɑːm] **1** n (Bot: also: **~ tree**) palma. **2** cpd: **~ oil** n olio di palma; **P~ Sunday** n Domenica delle Palme.

palm[2] [pɑːm] n (Anat) palma, palmo; **to read** sb's **~** leggere la mano a qn; **to grease** sb's **~** (fig) dare una bustarella a qn; **to have** sb **in the ~ of one's hand** avere or tenere in pugno qn.

♦ **palm off** vt + adv: **to ~** sth **off on** sb rifilare qc a qn.

palm·ist ['pɑːmɪst] n chiromante m/f.

pal·pable ['pælpəbl] adj (lie, mistake) palese, evidente.

pal·pably ['pælpəblɪ] adv palesemente, evidentemente.

pal·pi·tate ['pælpɪteɪt] vi palpitare.

pal·pi·ta·tion [ˌpælpɪ'teɪʃən] n: **to have ~s** avere le palpitazioni.

pal·try ['pɔːltrɪ] adj irrisorio(a); **for a ~ £5** per la somma irrisoria di 5 sterline.

pam·pas ['pæmpəs] npl pampe fpl.

pam·per ['pæmpəʳ] vt viziare, coccolare.

pam·phlet ['pæmflɪt] n (informative, brochure) opuscolo, dépliant m inv; (political, handed out in street) volantino, manifestino.

pan [pæn] **1** n (Culin) pentola; (milk ~) pentolino; (of scales) piatto; (of lavatory) tazza. **2** vt **(a)** (gold etc) passare al vaglio. **(b)** (fam: play) stroncare. **3** vi **(a): to ~ for gold** (lavare le sabbie aurifere per) cercare l'oro. **(b)** (Cine) fare una panoramica.

♦ **pan out** vi + adv andare; (turn out well) riuscire.

pan- [pæn] pref pan...; **~African** adj panafricano(a).

pana·cea [ˌpænə'sɪə] n panacea.

pa·nache [pə'næʃ] n stile m.

Pana·ma ['pænəˌmɑː] **1** n Panama m. **2** cpd: **~ Canal** n Canale m di Panama.

pana·ma ['pænəˌmɑː] n (also: **~ hat**) (cappello di) panama m inv.

pan·cake ['pænkeɪk] **1** n frittella, crêpe f inv. **2** cpd: **P~ Day** n martedì m grasso.

pan·cre·as ['pæŋkrɪəs] n pancreas m inv.

pan·da ['pændə] **1** n panda m inv. **2** cpd: **~ car** n (Brit) auto della polizia.

pan·de·mo·nium [ˌpændɪ'məʊnɪəm] n pandemonio.

pan·der ['pændə'] *vi*: to ~ to *(person, whims)* assecondare; **to ~ to sb's tastes** piegarsi ai gusti di qn.

pane [peɪn] *n* vetro.

pan·el ['pænl] **1** *n* **(a)** *(gen)* pannello; *(of triptych)* tavola; *(of ceiling)* cassettone *m*; *(of instruments, switches)* quadro. **(b)** *(of judges)* giuria; *(of experts, researchers etc)* gruppo. **2** *vt (wall, door)* rivestire di *or* con pannelli. **3** *cpd*: ~ **beater** *n* carrozziere *m*; ~ **discussion** *n* tavola rotonda; ~ **game** *n* quiz *m inv* a squadre.

pan·elled, *(Am)* **pan·eled** ['pænəld] *adj (door etc)* a pannelli.

pan·el·ling, *(Am)* **pan·el·ing** ['pænəlɪŋ] *n* rivestimento di *or* a pannelli.

pan·el·list, *(Am)* **pan·el·ist** ['pænlɪst] *n* partecipante *m/f (al quiz, alla tavola rotonda etc).*

pang [pæŋ] *n*: **a ~ of guilt/sadness** un senso di colpa/tristezza; **without a ~** senza rimpianti; **the ~s of hunger** i morsi della fame.

pan·ic ['pænɪk] **1** *n* panico; **to get into a ~ about sth** farsi prendere dal panico per qc; **to throw into a ~** *(crowd)* seminare il panico tra; *(person)* buttare in uno stato di agitazione. **2** *vi* lasciarsi prendere dal panico; **don't ~!** non agitarti! **3** *cpd*: **to be at ~ stations** essere in preda al panico.

pan·icky ['pænɪkɪ] *adj (person)* che si lascia prendere dal panico; *(newspaper, report)* allarmista; *(decision)* dettato(a) dal panico.

panic-stricken ['pænɪk,strɪkən] *adj (person)* preso(a) dal panico, in preda al panico; *(look)* terrorizzato(a).

pan·ni·er ['pænɪə'] *n (gen)* paniere *m*; *(on bicycle)* borsa.

pano·ra·ma [,pænə'rɑːmə] *n* panorama *m*.

pano·ram·ic [,pænə'ræmɪk] *adj* panoramico(a).

pan·sy ['pænzɪ] *n (Bot)* viola del pensiero, pensée *f inv*; *(fam pej)* checca.

pant [pænt] *vi* ansimare, avere il fiatone; **he was ~ing for a drink** moriva dalla voglia di bere.

pan·tech·ni·con [pæn'tɛknɪkən] *n* grosso furgone *m* per traslochi.

pan·ther ['pænθə'] *n* pantera.

panties ['pæntɪz] *npl* mutandine *fpl.*

pan·to·mime ['pæntəmaɪm] *n (Brit: at Christmas)* spettacolo natalizio *(sulla falsariga delle favole per bambini); (mime)* pantomima.

pan·try ['pæntrɪ] *n* dispensa.

pants [pænts] *npl (Brit: underwear)* mutande *fpl*, slip *m inv; (Am: trousers)* pantaloni *mpl*, calzoni *mpl*; **to catch sb with his ~ down** *(fam)* prendere qn alla sprovvista.

pa·pa·cy ['peɪpəsɪ] *n* papato.

pa·pal ['peɪpəl] *adj* papale, pontificio(a).

pa·per ['peɪpə'] **1** *n* **(a)** *(material)* carta; *(wall~)* carta da parati, tappezzeria; **a piece of ~** *(odd bit)* un pezzo di carta; *(sheet)* un foglio (di carta); **on ~** sulla carta; **to put sth down on ~** mettere qc per iscritto. **(b)**: **~s** *pl (writings, documents)* carte *fpl; (identity ~s)* documenti *mpl* (di riconoscimento); **old ~s** scartoffie *fpl*; **Churchill's private ~s** gli scritti *or* i documenti privati di Churchill. **(c)** *(exam questions)* prova scritta, scritto; *(lecture)* relazione *f*. **(d)** *(newspaper)* giornale *m*; **the ~s** i giornali; **it was in the ~s** è stato sui giornali; **to write to the ~s about sth** scrivere una lettera aperta *or* ai giornali su qc.

   2 *vt (wall, room)* tappezzare.

   3 *vi*: **to ~ over the cracks** *(fig)* appianare le divergenze.

   4 *cpd (towel, handkerchief, cup)* di carta; *(industry)* cartario(a), della carta; ~ **bag** *n* sacchetto di carta; ~ **clip** *n* graffetta, clip *f inv*; ~ **knife** *n*

tagliacarte *m inv;* ~ **mill** *n* cartiera; ~ **money** *n* cartamoneta, moneta cartacea; ~ **shop** *n* giornalaio.

paper·back ['peɪpəbæk] *n* tascabile *m*.

paper·boy ['peɪpəbɔɪ] *n (selling)* strillone *m; (delivering)* ragazzo che recapita i giornali.

paper·weight ['peɪpəweɪt] *n* fermacarte *m inv*.

paper·work ['peɪpəwɜːk] *n* lavoro d'ufficio.

papier-mâché [,pæpjeɪ'mæʃeɪ] *n* cartapesta.

pa·pist ['peɪpɪst] *n* papista *m/f.*

pap·ri·ka ['pæprɪkə] *n (spice)* paprica; *(vegetable)* peperone *m* rosso.

par [pɑː'] *n*: **to be below ~** *(person: ill)* non essere in forma; **to be on a ~ with sb/sth** essere allo stesso livello di qn/qc; **that's ~ for the course** *(fig)* è normale; **to be above/below ~** essere al di sopra/al di sotto della norma.

para·ble ['pærəbl] *n* parabola.

para·chute ['pærəʃuːt] **1** *n* paracadute *m inv*. **2** *vt* paracadutare. **3** *vi (also:* ~ **down)** paracadutarsi.

para·chut·ist ['pærəʃuːtɪst] *n* paracadutista *m/f.*

pa·rade [pə'reɪd] **1** *n (procession)* sfilata; *(: Mil)* parata; *(Mil: ceremony, inspection)* rivista; **to be on ~** *(Mil: marching)* sfilare; *(: for inspection)* essere schierato; **a fashion ~** una sfilata di moda. **2** *vt (troops: in ceremonial order)* schierare in parata; *(: for a march)* far sfilare; *(placard etc)* portare in giro *or* in corteo; *(show off: learning, wealth, new clothes)* fare sfoggio di, sfoggiare, ostentare. **3** *vi (Mil: march)* sfilare; *(: in ceremonial order)* schierarsi in parata; *(boy scouts, demonstrators)* marciare in corteo; **to ~ about** *or* **around** *(fam)* pavoneggiarsi; **the strikers ~d through the town** gli scioperanti hanno attraversato la città in corteo. **4** *cpd*: ~ **ground** *n* piazza d'armi.

para·digm ['pærədaɪm] *n* paradigma *m*.

para·dise ['pærədaɪs] *n* paradiso.

para·dox ['pærədɒks] *n* paradosso.

para·doxi·cal [,pærə'dɒksɪkəl] *adj* paradossale.

par·af·fin ['pærəfɪn] **1** *n (Chem)* paraffina; *(fuel)* cherosene *m*; **liquid ~** olio di paraffina. **2** *cpd*: ~ **heater** *n* stufa al cherosene; ~ **lamp** *n* lampada al cherosene; ~ **wax** *n* paraffina solida.

para·gon ['pærəgən] *n* modello di perfezione *or* di virtù.

para·graph ['pærəgrɑːf] *n (gen)* paragrafo; *(in newspaper)* trafiletto; **to begin a new ~** andare a capo.

para·keet ['pærəkiːt] *n (Zool)* parrocchetto.

par·al·lel ['pærəlɛl] **1** *adj*: ~ **(with, to)** parallelo(a) (a); **the road runs ~ to the railway** la strada corre parallela alla ferrovia; ~ **bars** parallele *fpl*. **2** *n (Geom)* parallela; *(Geog)* parallelo; *(fig)* confronto, paragone *m*; **to draw a ~ between** *(fig)* fare un parallelo fra. **3** *vt (fig: equal)* uguagliare; *(: be similar to)* essere analogo(a) *or* parallelo(a) a.

par·al·lelo·gram [,pærə'lɛləʊgræm] *n* parallelogramma *m*.

pa·raly·sis [pə'ræləsɪs] *n* paralisi *f.*

para·lyt·ic [,pærə'lɪtɪk] *adj (Med: person)* paralitico(a); *(: stroke)* di paralisi; *(fam: drunk)* ubriaco(a) fradicio(a).

para·lyze ['pærəlaɪz] *vt (Med, fig)* paralizzare; ~d **with fear** paralizzato dalla paura.

para·mili·tary [,pærə'mɪlɪtərɪ] *adj* paramilitare.

para·mount ['pærəmaʊnt] *adj*: **of ~ importance** di capitale importanza.

para·noia [,pærə'nɔɪə] *n* paranoia.

para·noid [,pærənɔɪd] *adj* paranoico(a); *(fig)*: ~ **(about)** ossessionato(a) (da).

para·nor·mal [,pærə'nɔːməl] *n*: **the ~** i fenomeni paranormali.

para·pet |'pærəpɪt| n parapetto.

para·pher·na·lia |,pærəfə'neɪlɪə| n armamentario.

para·phrase |'pærəfreɪz| **1** n parafrasi f inv. **2** vt parafrasare.

para·plegia |,pærə'pli:dʒə| n paraplegia.

para·plegic |,pærə'pli:dʒɪk| adj, n paraplegico(a) (m/f).

para·site |'pærəsaɪt| n parassita m.

para·sit·ic(al) |,pærə'sɪtɪk(əl)| adj (gen) parassita; (disease) parassitario(a).

para·sol |,pærə'sɒl| n parasole m.

para·trooper |'pærətru:pə'| n (Mil) paracadutista m, parà m inv.

para·troops |'pærətru:ps| npl paracadutisti mpl.

par·boil |'pɑ:bɔɪl| vt sbollentare.

par·cel |'pɑ:sl| **1** n (gen) pacchetto; (larger) pacco; (of land) appezzamento; (fig: of fools etc) branco; (: of lies) mucchio; **to be part and ~ of** essere parte integrante di. **2** cpd: **~ bomb** n pacchetto esplosivo; **~ post** n servizio pacchi.

◆ **parcel up** vt + adv impacchettare, fare un pacco di.

parched |pɑ:tʃt| adj (land, garden) disseccato(a), riarso(a); **I'm ~!** (fam) muoio di sete!

parch·ment |'pɑ:tʃmənt| n pergamena.

par·don |'pɑ:dn| **1** n perdono, scusa; (Rel) indulgenza; (Law) condono della pena, grazia; **general ~** amnistia. **2** vt (forgive) perdonare; (Law) graziare; **to ~ sb for sth/doing sth** perdonare qc a qn/qn per aver fatto qc. **3** excl (apologizing) mi scusi!; (not hearing) scusi?, come?, prego?

pare |pɛə'| vt (nails) tagliarsi; (fruit etc) sbucciare, pelare.

◆ **pare down** vt + adv (costs etc) ridurre, limitare.

par·ent |'pɛərənt| **1** n padre m (or madre f); **his ~s i** suoi genitori. **2** cpd: **~ company** n società madre f inv.

par·ent·age |'pɛərəntɪdʒ| n natali mpl; **of unknown ~** di genitori sconosciuti.

pa·ren·tal |pə'rɛntl| adj dei genitori.

pa·ren·thesis |pə'rɛnθɪsɪs| n, pl **parentheses** |pə'rɛnθɪsi:z| parentesi f inv; **in parentheses** fra parentesi.

par·en·theti·cal |,pærən'θɛtɪkəl| adj (clause) parentetico(a); (statement) fra parentesi.

par·ent·hood |'pɛərənthʊd| n paternità (or maternità).

parent-teacher |,pɛərənt'ti:tʃə'| adj attr: **~ association** comitato scolastico.

par ex·cel·lence |,pɑ:r'ɛksəlɑ̃:ns| adv per eccellenza.

Par·is |'pærɪs| n Parigi f.

par·ish |'pærɪʃ| **1** n (Rel) parrocchia; (civil) ≈ comune m. **2** cpd (church, hall) parrocchiale; **~ council** n consiglio comunale; **~ priest** n parroco.

pa·rish·ion·er |pə'rɪʃənə'| n parrocchiano/a.

Pa·ris·ian |pə'rɪzɪən| adj, n parigino(a) (m/f).

par·ity |'pærɪtɪ| n parità.

park |pɑ:k| **1** n (gen) parco; (public) giardino pubblico. **2** vt (Aut) parcheggiare. **3** vi (Aut) parcheggiare, parcheggiarsi.

par·ka |'pɑ:kə| n eskimo.

park·ing |'pɑ:kɪŋ| **1** n (~ space) parcheggio; (act) parcheggiare m; **'no ~'** 'sosta vietata'. **2** cpd (fine) per divieto di sosta; (place, space) di parcheggio; **~ lights** npl luci fpl di posizione; **~ lot** n (Am) posteggio, parcheggio; **~ offence** n infrazione f al divieto di sosta; **~ meter** n parchimetro; **~ ticket** n multa per sosta vietata.

park·land |'pɑ:klænd| n parco.

park·way |'pɑ:kweɪ| n (Am) viale m.

parky |'pɑ:kɪ| adj (-ier, -iest) (fam) freddino(a).

par·lance |'pɑ:ləns| n: **in common/modern ~** nel gergo or linguaggio comune/moderno.

par·ley |'pɑ:lɪ| vi conferire, parlamentare.

par·lia·ment |'pɑ:ləmənt| n parlamento; **to get into ~** essere eletto (deputato) al parlamento.

par·lia·men·tar·ian |,pɑ:ləmən'tɛərɪən| n parlamentare m/f.

par·lia·men·ta·ry |,pɑ:lə'mɛntərɪ| adj parlamentare.

par·lour, (Am) **par·lor** |'pɑ:lə'| n (in house) salotto; **beauty ~** istituto di bellezza; **ice-cream ~** gelateria.

Par·me·san |,pɑ:mɪ'zæn| n (also: **~ cheese**) parmigiano.

pa·ro·chial |pə'rəʊkɪəl| adj (of parish) parrocchiale; (fig pej) provinciale, ristretto(a).

paro·dy |'pærədɪ| **1** n parodia. **2** vt parodiare.

pa·role |pə'rəʊl| n (Law) libertà per buona condotta; **on ~** in libertà per buona condotta; **to break (one's) ~** commettere un atto che ha per conseguenza la revoca della libertà per buona condotta.

par·ox·ysm |'pærəksɪzəm| n (Med) parossismo; (of anger, laughter, coughing) convulso; (of grief) attacco.

par·quet |'pɑ:keɪ| n (also: **~ floor**) parquet m inv.

par·rot |'pærət| n pappagallo.

parrot-fashion |'pærət,fæʃən| adv a pappagallo.

par·ry |'pærɪ| vt (blow) parare; (fig: question) eludere.

par·si·mo·ni·ous |,pɑ:sɪ'məʊnɪəs| adj parsimonioso(a).

pars·ley |'pɑ:slɪ| n prezzemolo.

pars·nip |'pɑ:snɪp| n pastinaca.

par·son |'pɑ:sn| n (gen) pastore m; (Church of England) parroco.

par·son·age |'pɑ:sənɪdʒ| n canonica, casa parrocchiale.

part |pɑ:t| **1** n **(a)** (portion, fragment) parte f; (of serial) episodio; **in ~** in parte; **it was funny in ~s** è stato divertente a tratti; **for the most ~** nell'insieme, per lo più; **the greater ~ of it is done** il più è fatto; **for the better ~ of the day** per la maggior parte della giornata; **two ~s of sand to one of cement** due parti di sabbia e una (parte) di cemento.

(b) (Tech: component) pezzo or parte f (di ricambio); (Mus) parte; **moving ~** parte meccanica; **~ of speech** (Gram) parte del discorso; **the principal ~s of the verb** i tempi principali del verbo; **soprano ~** la parte del soprano; **2-~ song** canto a 2 voci.

(c) (role: also Theatre) parte f, ruolo; **to take ~ in sth** prendere parte or partecipare a qc; **to have no ~ in sth** non aver nulla a che fare con qc; **to play a ~ in sth/doing sth** avere una certa parte in qc/nel fare qc; **to look the ~** essere (fisicamente) perfetto nella parte.

(d) (region) parte f; **in these ~s** da queste parti; **a lovely ~ of the country** una bella regione.

(e) (behalf, side) parte f; **to take sb's ~** parteggiare per or prendere le parti di qn; **for my ~** da parte mia, per quanto mi riguarda; **a mistake on the ~ of my brother** un errore da parte di mio fratello; **to take sth in good/bad ~** prendere bene/male qc.

2 adv (partly) in parte; **a ~ eaten apple** una mela mezzo mangiata.

3 vt (curtains, branches) scostare; (boxers) separare; (lovers) dividere, separare; **to ~ one's hair** farsi la riga or la scriminatura (nei capelli).

4 vi (curtains etc) aprirsi; (boxers) separarsi; (rope: break) spezzarsi, rompersi; (friends, lovers) lasciarsi; **to ~ (from sb)** separarsi (da qn); **they ~ed friends** si sono lasciati da buoni amici; **to ~ with** (possessions) separarsi da, disfarsi di; (money) sborsare; **I hate ~ing with it** mi dispiace disfarmene.

5 cpd: **~ exchange** n: **we will take your car in ~ exchange for a new one** detrarremo il valore della sua vecchia auto da quello della nuova; **~ owner** n comproprietario/a; **~ payment** n acconto.

par·take |paː'teɪk| pt **partook**, pp **partaken** |paː'teɪkən| vi (frm) **(a):** **to ~ of sth** consumare qc, prendere qc. **(b): to ~ in an activity** partecipare or prender parte ad una attività.

par·tial |'paːʃəl| adj (gen) parziale; **to be in ~ agreement** essere parzialmente or in parte d'accordo; **to be ~ to sth** (like) avere un debole per qc.

par·tial·ity |ˌpaːʃɪ'ælɪtɪ| n (bias): **~ (towards)** parzialità (verso); (liking): **~ (for, to)** predilezione f (per), debole m (per).

par·tial·ly |'paːʃəlɪ| adv (partly) parzialmente, in parte.

par·tici·pant |paː'tɪsɪpənt| n: **~ (in)** partecipante m/f (a).

par·tici·pate |paː'tɪsɪpeɪt| vi: **to ~ (in)** partecipare (a), prendere parte (a).

par·tici·pa·tion |paːˌtɪsɪ'peɪʃən| n: **~ (in)** partecipazione f (a).

par·ti·ci·ple |'paːtɪsɪpl| n participio.

par·ti·cle |'paːtɪkl| n (Gram, Phys) particella; (of dust) granello; (of food) pezzettino; (fig: of truth, sense) briciolo.

par·ticu·lar |pə'tɪkjʊləʳ| **1** adj **(a)** (specific, special) particolare; **that ~ house/train** quella casa/quel treno in particolare; **to pay ~ attention to,** **to take ~ care over** fare molta attenzione a; **in this ~ case** in questo caso particolare; **for no ~ reason** senza una ragione precisa or particolare; **she's a ~ friend of mine** è una mia carissima amica. **(b)** (fastidious, fussy) pignolo(a); **to be very ~ about** essere molto pignolo su; **he's ~ about his food** è molto difficile nel mangiare; **I'm not ~** per me va bene tutto. **2** n **(a)** (detail) particolare m; **~s** (information) particolari mpl, dettagli mpl; (personal details) dati mpl; **full ~s** informazioni fpl complete. **(b): in ~** in particolare, particolarmente; **nothing in ~** nulla in or di particolare.

par·ticu·lar·ize |pə'tɪkjʊləraɪz| vt, vi particolareggiare.

par·ticu·lar·ly |pə'tɪkjʊləlɪ| adv (especially) particolarmente; **I ~ wanted it for tomorrow** lo volevo proprio per domani; **~ since...** soprattutto perché... .

part·ing |'paːtɪŋ| **1** adj (kiss etc) d'addio; **his ~ words** le sue ultime parole; **~ shot** (fig) battuta finale; **and with this ~ shot he left** e detto ciò se ne andò. **2** n **(a)** separazione f; **we have reached the ~ of the ways** (fig) a questo punto le nostre strade si dividono. **(b)** (in hair) scriminatura, riga.

par·ti·san |ˌpaːtɪ'zæn| **1** adj (gen) fazioso(a); (fighter) partigiano(a); **~ spirit** spirito di parte. **2** n (fighter) partigiano/a.

par·ti·tion |paː'tɪʃən| **1** n **(a)** (wall) parete f divisoria, tramezzo. **(b)** (Pol) suddivisione f, divisione f. **2** vt (country etc) suddividere, dividere.

♦ **partition off** vt + adv ricavare per mezzo di una parete divisoria.

part·ly |'paːtlɪ| adv parzialmente, in parte.

part·ner |'paːtnəʳ| **1** n (gen) partner m/f inv; (Comm) socio/a; (in crime) complice m/f. **2** vt (Sport) essere in coppia con; (at dance) accompagnare; (in individual dance) ballare con.

part·ner·ship |'paːtnəʃɪp| n (gen) associazione f; (Comm) società; **to take sb into ~** prendere qn come socio; **to go into ~ (with), form a ~ (with)** mettersi in società (con), associarsi (a).

par·took |paː'tʊk| pt of **partake**.

par·tridge |'paːtrɪdʒ| n pernice f.

part-time |'paːt'taɪm| adv, adj part time (inv).

par·ty |'paːtɪ| **1** n **(a)** (Pol) partito. **(b)** (group) gruppo; (Mil) squadra; **a ~ of travellers** una comitiva. **(c)** (celebration) festa; **to have** or **give** or **throw a ~** dare una festa or un party; **birthday ~** festa di compleanno; **dinner ~** cena. **(d)** (Law etc) parte f (in causa); **the parties to a dispute** le parti in causa; **to be a ~ to a crime** essere coinvolto in un reato. **2** cpd (politics, leader) del partito, di partito; (dress, finery) della festa; **~ line** n (Pol) linea del partito; (Telec) duplex m inv; **~ political broadcast** n trasmissione riservata a un partito politico; **~ wall** n muro di confine or divisorio.

pass¹ |paːs| n (Geog) passo, valico.

pass² |paːs| **1** n **(a)** (permit) lasciapassare m inv; (for bus, train etc) tesserino; (Mil etc) permesso.

(b) (Sport) passaggio.

(c) (in exams) sufficienza; **to get a ~ in German** prendere la sufficienza in tedesco.

(d): things have come to a pretty ~ ecco a cosa siamo arrivati.

(e): to make a ~ at sb (fam) fare delle proposte or delle avances a qn.

2 vt **(a)** (move past) passare, oltrepassare; (in opposite direction) incrociare; (Aut: overtake) sorpassare; **they ~ed each other on the way** si sono incrociati per strada.

(b) (hand, reach) (far) passare; (Sport: ball) passare; **he ~ed his hand over his forehead** si passò la mano sulla fronte; **to ~ a thread through a hole** far passare un filo attraverso un buco; **to ~ sb sth** or **sth to sb** passare qc a qn.

(c) (Scol etc: exam) superare; (: candidate) promuovere.

(d) (approve: motion, plan etc) approvare, votare.

(e) (spend: time) passare, trascorrere; **we ~ed the weekend pleasantly** abbiamo trascorso or passato piacevolmente il fine settimana; **it ~es the time** fa passare il tempo.

(f) (express: remark) fare; (: opinion) esprimere; **to ~ the time of day with sb** scambiarsi i (soliti) convenevoli.

3 vi **(a)** (come, go): **to ~ (through)** passare (per); (Aut: overtake) sorpassare; **he ~ed by the cinema** è passato davanti al cinema; **to ~ out of sight** scomparire dalla vista; **to ~ into oblivion** cadere nell'oblio; **to ~ into history** passare alla storia.

(b) (be accepted: behaviour) essere accettabile; (: plan) essere approvato(a); **she could ~ for twenty-five** potrebbe passare per una venticinquenne; **what ~es for art these days** quel che si definisce arte oggigiorno; **is this okay? — oh, it'll ~** questo va bene? — sì, può andare; **I decided to let it ~** ho deciso di lasciar passare.

(c) (time, day) passare; **how time ~es!** come vola il tempo!

(d) (pain, opportunity) passare; (memory) dileguarsi.

(e) (in exam) essere promosso(a).

(f) (happen) accadere; **all that ~ed between them** tutto quello che c'è stato fra loro; **should it come to ~ that...** (frm) dovesse accadere che... .

(g) *(Cards)* passare.

♦ **pass away** *vi +˙adv (die)* spegnersi, mancare.

♦ **pass by 1** *vi + adv* passare (di qui or lì). **2** *vt + adv (ignore)* ignorare, passar sopra a; **life has ~ed her by** non ha davvero vissuto.

♦ **pass down** *vt + adv (customs, inheritance)* tramandare, trasmettere.

♦ **pass off 1** *vi + adv (happen)* svolgersi, andare; *(wear off: faintness etc)* passare. **2** *vt + adv:* **to ~ sb/sth off as far** passare qn/qc per.

♦ **pass on 1** *vi + adv (die)* spegnersi, mancare; *(proceed):* **to ~ on (to)** passare (a). **2** *vt + adv (hand on):* **to ~ on (to)** *(news, information, object)* passare (a); *(cold, illness)* attaccare (a); *(benefits)* trasmettere (a); *(price rises)* riversare (su).

♦ **pass out** *vi + adv (become unconscious)* svenire; *(Mil)* uscire dall'accademia.

♦ **pass over 1** *vi + adv (die)* spirare. **2** *vt + adv* lasciare da parte.

♦ **pass through 1** *vi + adv* essere di passaggio. **2** *vt + adv (country, city)* passare per; *(hardships)* attraversare.

♦ **pass up** *vt + adv (opportunity)* lasciarsi sfuggire, perdere.

pass·able ['pɑːsəbl] *adj* **(a)** *(tolerable)* passabile. **(b)** *(road)* transitabile; *(river)* attraversabile.

pas·sage ['pæsɪdʒ] *n* **(a)** *(way through)* passaggio; *(corridor)* corridoio. **(b)** *(Naut: voyage)* traversata; **to grant sb safe ~** garantire a qn di passare incolume. **(c)** *(passing)* passare *m*; *(: of bill through parliament)* iter *m inv*; **with the ~ of time** col passar del tempo. **(d)** *(section: of book, music)* brano.

passage·way ['pæsɪdʒweɪ] *n* passaggio.

pass·book ['pɑːsbʊk] *n* libretto di risparmio.

pas·sen·ger ['pæsɪndʒəʳ] **1** *n (in boat, plane, car)* passeggero/a; *(on train)* viaggiatore/trice. **2** *cpd (aircraft, liner)* di linea, passeggeri *inv*; *(train)* viaggiatori *inv*; **~ list** lista dei passeggeri.

passer·by ['pɑːsə'baɪ] *n, pl* **passers-by** passante *m/f*.

pass·ing ['pɑːsɪŋ] *adj (fleeting: fancy, thought)* passeggero(a); *(glance, remark)* di sfuggita; *(car, person)* di passaggio. **2** *n (of customs, euph: death)* scomparsa; **with the ~ of the years** col passar degli anni; **to mention sth in ~** accennare a qc di sfuggita.

pas·sion ['pæʃən] *n* passione *f;* **the P~** *(Rel)* la Passione; **his ~ for seafood** la sua passione per i frutti di mare; **his ~ for accuracy** il suo amore per la precisione; **to get into a ~ (about sth)** andare su tutte le furie (per qc).

pas·sion·ate ['pæʃənɪt] *adj (embrace, speech)* appassionato(a); *(temperament, person)* passionale; *(believer)* convinto(a); *(desire)* ardente.

pas·sion·ate·ly ['pæʃənɪtlɪ] *adv (embrace, speak)* appassionatamente; *(believe, desire)* ardentemente.

passion·flower ['pæʃən,flaʊəʳ] *n* passiflora, fiore *m* della passione.

passion·fruit ['pæʃənfruːt] *n* frutto della passione, frutto della passiflora.

pas·sive ['pæsɪv] **1** *adj (gen, Gram)* passivo(a). **2** *n* passivo; **in the ~** al passivo.

pass·key ['pɑːskiː] *n* passe-partout *m inv.*

Pass·over ['pɑːsəʊvəʳ] *n* Pasqua ebraica.

pass·port ['pɑːspɔːt] *n* passaporto; *(fig):* **~ (to)** chiave *f* (di).

pass·word ['pɑːswɜːd] *n* parola d'ordine.

past [pɑːst] **1** *adv:* **to walk ~, go ~** passare; **to run** *or* **dash ~** passare di corsa; **the days flew ~** i giorni sono volati (via).

2 *prep* **(a)** *(in place: in front of)* davanti a;

(: beyond) oltre, dopo; **I go ~ the school every day** passo davanti alla scuola ogni giorno; **it's just ~ the church** è appena oltre la chiesa. **(b)** *(in time)* passato(a); **quarter/half ~ four** le quattro e un quarto/e mezzo; **at twenty ~ four** alle quattro e venti. **(c)** *(beyond the limits of)* al di là di, oltre; **it's ~ belief** è assolutamente incredibile; **I'm ~ caring** non me ne importa più nulla; **she's ~ forty** ha passato i quaranta; **it's ~ it** *(fam: person)* essere finito; *(: object)* essere da buttar via; **I wouldn't put it ~ her to do it** *(fam)* non me ne meraviglierei affatto se lo facesse.

3 *adj (gen, Gram)* passato(a); *(president etc)* ex *inv;* **for some time ~** da qualche tempo; **in ~ years** negli anni passati; **those days are ~ now** è passato quel tempo.

4 *n* passato; **in the ~** in *or* nel passato; *(Gram)* al passato; **it's a thing of the ~** è una cosa del passato.

5 *cpd:* **~ master** *n:* **to be a ~ master at** essere molto esperto in; **~ participle** *n* participio passato.

pas·ta ['pæstə] *n (Culin)* pasta.

paste [peɪst] **1** *n* **(a)** *(substance, consistency)* impasto; *(glue)* colla; **tomato ~** concentrato di pomodoro; **almond ~** pasta di mandorle; **fish ~** pâté *m inv* di pesce. **(b)** *(gems)* strass *m.* **2** *adj (diamonds etc)* di strass. **3** *vt (put glue on)* spalmare di colla; *(fasten with glue)* incollare; **to ~ sth to the wall** appiccicare qc al muro.

paste·board ['peɪstbɔːd] *n* cartone *m.*

pas·tel ['pæstəl] **1** *n (crayon, drawing)* pastello; *(colour)* colore *m* pastello *inv.* **2** *adj (colour)* pastello *inv; (drawing)* a pastello.

pas·teur·ized ['pæstəraɪzd] *adj* pastorizzato(a).

pas·tille ['pæstɪl] *n* pastiglia.

pas·time ['pɑːstaɪm] *n* passatempo.

pas·tor ['pɑːstəʳ] *n* pastore *m.*

pas·to·ral ['pɑːstərəl] *adj (land)* da pascolo; *(scene, poetry; also Rel)* pastorale.

pas·try ['peɪstrɪ] *n (dough)* pasta *(per rustici, dolci); (cake)* pasta, pasticcino.

pas·ture ['pɑːstʃəʳ] **1** *n* pascolo; **to put animals out to ~** condurre gli animali al pascolo; **to move on to ~s new** *(fig)* cambiare aria. **2** *cpd:* **~ land** *n* pascolo.

pasty[1] ['pæstɪ] *n (pie)* sfogliatina salata ripiena di carne e patate.

pasty[2] ['peɪstɪ] *adj (complexion)* smorto(a).

pat[1] [pæt] **1** *n* **(a)** *(with hand)* colpetto (affettuoso); *(to animal)* carezza; **to give sb/o.s. a ~ on the back** *(fig)* congratularsi *or* compiacersi con qn/se stesso. **(b)** *(of butter)* noce *f.* **2** *vt (hair, face etc)* dare dei colpetti leggeri a; *(dog)* accarezzare; *(sb's shoulder etc)* dare un colpetto (affettuoso) su.

pat[2] [pæt] *adj, adv:* **he knows it (off) ~** lo conosce *or* sa a menadito; **the answer came** *or* **was too ~** la risposta è stata troppo pronta.

patch [pætʃ] **1** *n (piece of cloth etc)* toppa, pezza; *(on tyre)* toppa; *(eye ~)* benda; *(area of colour)* macchia; *(piece of land)* appezzamento, pezzo; **a ~ of blue sky** un pezzetto di cielo azzurro; **a vegetable ~** un orticello; **the team is going through a bad ~** la squadra sta attraversando un brutto periodo; **it's not a ~ on the one** *(fam)* non vale neanche la metà dell'altro. **2** *vt (garment, hole)* rattoppare, mettere una pezza a.

♦ **patch up** *vt + adv (clothes)* rattoppare; *(car, machine)* riparare alla meglio; *(quarrel)* appianare; *(marriage)* rimettere in sesto.

patch·work ['pætʃwɜːk] **1** *n* patchwork *m inv;* **a ~**

of fields *(fig)* un mosaico di campi. **2** *cpd (quilt etc)* patchwork *inv.*

patchy ['pætʃɪ] *adj (-ier, -iest) (performance etc)* pieno(a) di alti e bassi; *(knowledge)* incompleto(a); *(fog)* a banchi.

pâté ['pæteɪ] *n* pâté *m inv.*

pa·tent ['peɪtənt] **1** *adj* **(a)** *(obvious)* evidente, palese. **(b)** *(~ed: invention)* brevettato(a); **~ medicine** specialità *f inv* medicinale. **2** *n* brevetto. **3** *vt* brevettare.

pa·tent leath·er ['peɪtənt'lɛðə^r] *n* vernice *f,* pelle *f* lucida.

pa·tent·ly ['peɪtəntlɪ] *adv* palesemente.

pa·ter·nal [pə'tɜːnl] *adj* paterno(a).

pa·ter·nal·ist(ic) [pə'tɜːnəlɪst, pə'tɜːnə'lɪstɪk] *adj* paternalistico(a).

pa·ter·nity [pə'tɜːnɪtɪ] **1** *n* paternità. **2** *cpd:* **~ suit** *n (Law)* causa di riconoscimento della paternità.

path [pɑːθ] *n, pl* **paths** [pɑːðz] **(a)** *(gen)* sentiero; *(in garden)* vialetto; *(fig)* strada. **(b)** *(of river)* corso; *(of sun, missile)* traiettoria.

pa·thet·ic [pə'θetɪk] *adj* **(a)** *(piteous)* patetico(a), toccante. **(b)** *(very bad)* penoso(a), pietoso(a).

pa·theti·cal·ly [pə'θetɪklɪ] *adv* da far pena, da far pietà; **~ thin/weak** spaventosamente magro/debole; **a ~ inadequate answer** una risposta da far cascar le braccia.

patho·logi·cal [ˌpæθə'lɒdʒɪkəl] *adj (also fig)* patologico(a).

pa·tholo·gist [pə'θɒlədʒɪst] *n* patologo/a.

pa·thol·ogy [pə'θɒlədʒɪ] *n* patologia.

pa·thos ['peɪθɒs] *n* pathos *m.*

path·way ['pɑːθweɪ] *n* sentiero.

pa·tience ['peɪʃəns] *n* **(a)** pazienza; **to lose one's ~** spazientirsi; **to lose one's ~ with sb/sth** perdere la pazienza con qn/qc; **he has no ~ with children** non ha pazienza con i bambini. **(b)** *(Brit Cards)* solitario; **to play ~** fare un solitario.

pa·tient ['peɪʃənt] **1** *adj* paziente; **to be ~ with sb** essere paziente *or* aver pazienza con qn. **2** *n (Med)* paziente *m/f,* malato/a.

pa·tient·ly ['peɪʃəntlɪ] *adv* pazientemente.

pa·tio ['pætɪəʊ] *n* terrazza.

pa·tri·arch ['peɪtrɪɑːk] *n (Rel)* patriarca *m.*

pa·tri·ot ['peɪtrɪət] *n* patriota *m/f.*

pat·ri·ot·ic [ˌpætrɪ'ɒtɪk] *adj* patriottico(a).

pat·ri·ot·ism ['pætrɪətɪzəm] *n* patriottismo.

pa·trol [pə'trəʊl] **1** *n* **(a)** *(gen)* ronda, giro d'ispezione; *(by plane)* ricognizione *f; (by boat)* perlustrazione *f;* **to be on ~** fare la ronda; essere in ricognizione; essere in perlustrazione. **(b)** *(~ unit)* pattuglia. **2** *vt* pattugliare. **3** *vi* fare la ronda; **to ~ up and down** andare avanti e indietro. **4** *cpd:* **~ car** *n* autoradio *f inv* della polizia; **~ wagon** *n (Am)* (furgone *m)* cellulare *m.*

patrol·man [pə'trəʊlmən] *n, pl* **-men (a)** *(Am)* agente *m* della polizia. **(b)** *(Aut)* membro del personale del soccorso stradale.

pa·tron ['peɪtrən] *n (of artist)* mecenate *m/f; (of charity)* benefattore/trice; *(of society)* patrono/essa; *(of shop, hotel etc)* cliente *m/f* abituale; *(~ saint)* patrono/a.

pat·ron·age ['pætrɪnɪdʒ] *n (gen)* patrocinio, *(of shop etc)* clientela; **under the ~ of** sotto l'alto patrocinio di.

pat·ron·ize ['pætrənaɪz] *vt* **(a)** *(treat condescendingly)* trattare con condiscendenza. **(b)** *(shop)* essere cliente abituale di; *(cinema)* frequentare.

pat·ron·iz·ing ['pætrənaɪzɪŋ] *adj* condiscendente.

pat·ter¹ ['pætə^r] *n (fam: talk)* parlantina.

pat·ter² ['pætə^r] **1** *n (of feet)* rumore *m; (of rain)* picchiettio. **2** *vi (person)* trotterellare; *(rain)* picchiettare.

pat·tern ['pætən] **1** *n* **(a)** *(design)* motivo, disegno. **(b)** *(Sewing etc)* modello (di carta), cartamodello; *(fig)* modello; **~ of events** schema *m* degli eventi; **behaviour ~s** tipi *mpl* di comportamento. **(c)** *(sample)* campione *m.* **2** *vt (model):* **to ~ a dress on** fare un vestito sul modello di; **to ~ o.s. on sb/sth** prendere a modello qn/qc. **3** *cpd:* **~ book** *n* album *m inv* di modelli.

pat·terned ['pætənd] *adj* a disegni, a motivi; *(material)* fantasia *inv.*

paunch [pɔːntʃ] *n* pancia.

pau·per ['pɔːpə^r] *n* indigente *m/f.*

pause [pɔːz] **1** *n* pausa; *(Mus)* pausa; *(: sign)* corona; **there was a ~ while...** ci fu un momento di attesa mentre... . **2** *vi (gen)* fermarsi un momento; *(in speech)* fare una pausa; **to ~ for breath** fermarsi un attimo per riprender fiato.

pave [peɪv] *vt (gen)* lastricare; *(road)* pavimentare, lastricare; **to ~ the way for sb/sth** *(fig)* spianare la strada a qn/qc.

pave·ment ['peɪvmənt] *n (Brit)* marciapiede *m; (Am)* pavimentazione *f* stradale.

pa·vil·ion [pə'vɪlɪən] *n (gen)* padiglione *m; (Sport)* edificio annesso ad un campo sportivo.

pav·ing ['peɪvɪŋ] **1** *n* pavimentazione *f.* **2** *cpd:* **~ stone** *n* lastra di pavimentazione.

paw [pɔː] **1** *n (of animal, also fam: hand)* zampa. **2** *vt* **(a)** *(subj: animal)* dare una zampata a; **to ~ the ground** *(also fig)* scalpitare. **(b)** *(pej: sexually)* palpare, mettere le mani addosso a.

pawn¹ [pɔːn] *n (Chess)* pedone *m; (fig)* pedina; **to be sb's ~** lasciarsi manovrare da qn.

pawn² [pɔːn] **1** *n:* **in ~** impegnato(a) al monte di pietà; **to leave** *or* **put sth in ~** impegnare qc. **2** *vt* impegnare.

pawn·broker ['pɔːnˌbrəʊkə^r] *n* prestatore/trice su pegno.

pawn·shop ['pɔːnʃɒp] *n* monte *m* di pietà.

pay [peɪ] *(vb: pt, pp* **paid) 1** *n (gen)* paga; **to be in sb's ~** essere pagato da *or* essere al servizio di qn.

2 *vt* **(a)** *(gen)* pagare; *(debt, account)* saldare, pagare; **he paid him £10** gli ha pagato 10 sterline; **I paid £5 for that record** quel disco l'ho pagato 5 sterline; **how much did you ~ for it?** quanto l'hai pagato?; **to be** *or* **get paid on Fridays** prendere *or* riscuotere la paga il venerdì; **a badly paid worker** un lavoratore mal pagato; **that's what you're paid for** sei pagato per questo; **to ~ one's way** *(to contribute one's share)* pagare la propria parte; *(to remain solvent: company)* coprire le spese; **to put paid to** *(plan, person)* rovinare; *(trip)* impedire; **to ~ the penalty** *(fig)* pagare le conseguenze; **to ~ dividends** *(Fin)* pagare dividendi; *(fig)* dare buoni frutti. **(b)** *(be profitable: also fig)* convenire a; **it won't ~ you to do that** non ti conviene farlo. **(c)** *(attention)* fare, prestare; *(homage)* rendere; *(respects)* porgere; *see* **visit.**

3 *vi* **(a)** pagare; **to ~ in advance** pagare in anticipo; **don't worry, I'll ~** non preoccuparti, pagherò io; **they paid for her to go to Italy** le hanno pagato il viaggio in Italia. **(b)** *(be profitable)* rendere, convenire; **the business doesn't ~** l'attività non rende *or* non è redditizia; **it ~s to be courteous** ci si guadagna sempre ad essere gentile; **it ~s to advertise** far pubblicità conviene sempre; **crime doesn't ~** il delitto non rende. **(c)** *(fig: to suffer)* pagare; **she paid for it with her life** le è costato la vita, ha pagato con la vita; **I'll make you ~ for this!** te la farò pagare!

4 *cpd:* **~ packet** *n, (Am)* **~ envelope** *n* busta *f* paga *inv;* **~ phone** *n, (Am)* **~ station** *n* cabina telefonica; **~ slip** *n* foglio *m* paga *inv.*

♦ **pay back** *vt + adv* **(a)** restituire; **to ~ sb back** rimborsare qn. **(b)** *(in revenge)* farla pagare a qn; **to ~ sb back for doing sth** farla pagare a qn per aver fatto qc.

♦ **pay in** *vt + adv* versare, depositare.

♦ **pay off 1** *vt + adv* **(a)** *(debts)* saldare; *(creditor)* pagare; *(mortgage)* estinguere; **to ~ sth off in instalments** pagare qc a rate. **(b)** *(discharge)* licenziare. **2** *vi + adv (scheme, ruse)* funzionare; *(patience, decision)* dare dei frutti.

♦ **pay out** *vt + adv* **(a)** *(money)* sborsare, tirar fuori; *(subj: cashier)* pagare. **(b)** *(rope)* far allentare.

♦ **pay up** *vt + adv, vi + adv* saldare, pagare.

pay·able [ˈpeɪəbl] *adj* pagabile; **to make a cheque ~ to sb** intestare un assegno a (nome di) qn.

pay·day [ˈpeɪdeɪ] *n* giorno di paga.

P.A.Y.E. *Brit abbr (= pay as you earn) sistema di pagamento delle imposte mediante trattenute sulle retribuzioni.*

payee [peɪˈiː] *n* beneficiario/a.

pay·ing [ˈpeɪɪŋ] *adj (business, scheme)* redditizio(a); **~ guest** ospite *m/f* pagante, pensionante *m/f.*

pay·master [ˈpeɪˌmɑːstə'] *n (Mil)* ufficiale *m* pagatore.

pay·ment [ˈpeɪmənt] *n (gen)* pagamento; *(of debt, account, interest)* saldo, pagamento; *(fig: reward)* ricompensa; **advance ~** *(part sum)* anticipo, acconto; *(total sum)* pagamento anticipato; **deferred ~, ~ by instalments** pagamento dilazionato *or* a rate; **as ~ for, in ~ for** *(goods, sum owed)* in pagamento di; *(help, efforts, kindness)* in cambio di, come ricompensa per; **on ~ of £5** dietro pagamento di 5 sterline.

pay·off [ˈpeɪɒf] *n (fam: payment)* saldo; *(: reward)* ricompensa; *(: retribution)* resa dei conti; *(of joke)* finale *m.*

pay·roll [ˈpeɪrəʊl] *n (list)* lista del personale; *(money)* paga (di tutto il personale); *(employees)* personale *m*; **to be on a firm's ~** far parte del personale di una ditta.

p.c. *abbr of* **postcard; per cent.**

pea [piː] **1** *n* pisello; **green ~s** pisellini *mpl.* **2** *cpd:* **~ soup** *n* passato *or* crema di piselli.

peace [piːs] **1** *n (gen)* pace *f*; **to be at ~ with sb/sth** essere in pace con qn/qc; **he is at ~** *(euph: dead)* riposa in pace; **to make ~ between** rappacificare; **to make one's ~ with** fare la pace con; **~ of mind** tranquillità di spirito; **~ and quiet** pace e tranquillità; **to keep the ~** *(subj: policeman)* mantenere l'ordine pubblico; *(: citizen)* rispettare l'ordine pubblico; *(fig)* calmare le acque. **2** *cpd:* **~ conference** *n* conferenza per la pace; **~ offering** *n (fig)* dono in segno di riconciliazione; **~ treaty** *n* trattato di pace.

peace·able [ˈpiːsəbl] *adj* pacifico(a).

peace·ful [ˈpiːsfʊl] *adj (person, coexistence)* pacifico(a); *(demonstration)* non violento(a); *(period)* di pace; *(place, life, sleep)* tranquillo(a).

peace·ful·ly [ˈpiːsfəlɪ] *adv (coexist, reign)* in pace; *(demonstrate)* senza violenza; *(sleep, work, live)* tranquillamente.

peace·keeping [ˈpiːsˌkiːpɪŋ] *adj (operation)* di pacificazione; *(force)* per la tutela *or* il mantenimento della pace.

peace·loving [ˈpiːsˌlʌvɪŋ] *adj* pacifico(a).

peace·maker [ˈpiːsˌmeɪkə'] *n (between nations)* mediatore/trice della pace; *(between individuals)* paciere *m/f.*

peace·time [ˈpiːstaɪm] *n:* **in ~** in tempo di pace.

peach [piːtʃ] **1** *n* **(a)** *(fruit)* pesca; *(tree)* pesco. **(b)** *(fam:)* **she's a ~** è un amore. **2** *adj (blossom)* di pesco; *(colour)* color pesca *inv.*

pea·cock [ˈpiːkɒk] **1** *n* pavone *m.* **2** *cpd:* **~ blue** *adj, n* azzurro pavone *(m) inv.*

peak [piːk] **1** *n (of mountain)* vetta, cima; *(mountain itself)* picco; *(of roof etc)* cima; *(of cap)* visiera; *(on graph)* vertice *m*; *(fig: of power, career)* apice *m*, vertice; **to be at its ~** *(fame, career, empire)* essere all'apice; *(business)* essere nella fase culminante; *(traffic, demand)* aver raggiunto il livello massimo; **he was at the ~ of his fitness** era in perfetta forma. **2** *cpd (period)* di punta; *(demand, production)* massimo(a); **~ hour** *adj (traffic etc)* delle ore di punta; **~ hours** *npl* ore *fpl* di punta.

peaky [ˈpiːkɪ] *adj (-ier, -iest) (fam)* sbattuto(a); **I'm feeling a bit ~** mi sento un po' giù.

peal [piːl] **1** *n (sound of bells)* scampanio; **~ of thunder** fragore *m* di tuono; **~s of laughter** scoppi *mpl* di risa. **2** *vt* suonare (a distesa). **3** *vi (also:* **~ out***: bell)* suonare (a distesa); *(: thunder)* rimbombare.

pea·nut [ˈpiːnʌt] **1** *n* arachide *f*; **it's just ~s** *(fam)* è una bazzecola. **2** *cpd:* **~ butter** *n* burro di arachidi.

pear [pɛə'] *n (fruit)* pera; *(tree)* pero.

pearl [pɜːl] **1** *n* perla; *(mother-of-pearl)* madreperla; **~ of wisdom** *(fig)* perla di saggezza; **to cast ~s before swine** *(fig)* gettare le perle ai porci. **2** *cpd (necklace, brooch)* di perle; *(buttons)* di perla; **~ barley** *n* orzo perlato; **~ diver** *n* pescatore *m* di perle; **~ oyster** *n* ostrica perlifera.

pearly [ˈpɜːlɪ] *adj (-ier, -iest) (teeth)* come perle; *(buttons)* a perla; **~ white** bianco perla *inv*; **the P~ Gates** *(hum)* le porte del paradiso.

pear-shaped [ˈpɛəʃeɪpt] *adj* a forma di pera.

peas·ant [ˈpɛznt] **1** *n* contadino/a. **2** *cpd (life)* dei contadini; *(societies)* contadino(a); *(dress)* da contadino(a); **~ farmer** *n* contadino.

pea·shooter [ˈpiːˌʃuːtə'] *n* cerbottana.

peat [piːt] *n* torba.

peaty [ˈpiːtɪ] *adj (-ier, -iest)* torboso(a).

peb·ble [ˈpɛbl] **1** *n* ciottolo; **you're not the only ~ on the beach** *(fam)* non ci sei mica solo tu. **2** *cpd:* **~ dash** *n* intonaco a pinocchino.

peb·bly [ˈpɛblɪ] *adj* pieno(a) di ciottoli.

peck [pɛk] **1** *n (of bird etc)* beccata; *(fam: kiss)* bacetto; **to take a ~ at** beccare. **2** *vt (subj: bird: grain)* beccare; *(: person)* dare una beccata a; *(hole)* fare a furia di beccate. **3** *vi:* **to ~ at** *(subj: bird)* beccare; **he ~ed at his food** sbocconcellò il suo cibo.

peck·ing [ˈpɛkɪŋ] *n:* **~ order** *(fig)* ordine *m* gerarchico.

peck·ish [ˈpɛkɪʃ] *adj (fam):* **to feel a bit ~** avere un languorino.

pe·cu·li·ar [pɪˈkjuːlɪə'] *adj* **(a)** *(strange: idea, smell)* strano(a), curioso(a). **(b)** *(particular: importance, qualities)* particolare; **~ to** tipico di, caratteristico di; **it is a phrase ~ to him** è un modo di dire tutto suo.

pe·cu·li·ar·ity [pɪˌkjɔlɪˈærɪtɪ] *n* peculiarità *f inv.*

pe·cu·liar·ly [pɪˈkjuːlɪəlɪ] *adv* **(a)** *(exceptionally)* particolarmente. **(b)** *(strangely)* in un modo strano, in un modo curioso.

pe·cu·ni·ary [pɪˈkjuːnɪərɪ] *adj* pecuniario(a).

peda·gog·ic(al) [ˌpɛdəˈgɒdʒɪk(əl)] *adj* pedagogico(a).

ped·al [ˈpɛdl] **1** *n* pedale *m.* **2** *vi:* **to ~ up/down** *etc* pedalare su per/giù per *etc.* **3** *vt:* **she ~led her bicycle up the hill** salì la collina in bicicletta. **4** *cpd:* **~ bin** *n* pattumiera a pedale; **~ car** *n* automobilina a pedali.

ped·ant [ˈpɛdənt] *n* pedante *m/f.*

pe·dan·tic [pɪˈdæntɪk] *adj* pedante.

ped·ant·ry ['pɛdəntrɪ] n pedanteria.

ped·dle ['pɛdl] vt (goods) andare in giro a vendere; (drugs) spacciare; (gossip) mettere in giro.

ped·dler ['pɛdlə'] n (Am) = **pedlar**.

ped·er·ast ['pɛdəræst] n pederasta m.

ped·es·tal ['pɛdɪstl] n piedistallo; **to put sb on a ~** (fig) mettere qn su un piedistallo.

pe·des·trian [pɪ'dɛstrɪən] 1 n pedone m. 2 adj (dull, commonplace) mediocre. 3 cpd: ~ **crossing** n passaggio pedonale; ~ **precinct** n zona pedonale.

pe·di·at·ric [ˌpiːdɪ'ætrɪk] adj pediatrico(a).

pe·dia·tri·cian [ˌpiːdɪə'trɪʃən] n pediatra m/f.

pe·di·at·rics [ˌpiːdɪ'ætrɪks] nsg pediatria.

pedi·cure ['pɛdɪkjuə'] n pedicure f inv.

pedi·gree ['pɛdɪɡriː] 1 n (of person) discendenza; (of animal) pedigree m inv. 2 cpd di (pura) razza.

ped·lar ['pɛdlə'] n venditore/trice ambulante; (of drugs) spacciatore/trice.

pe·dom·eter [pɪ'dɒmɪtə'] n pedometro, contapassi m inv.

pee [piː] (fam) = **piss**.

peek [piːk] 1 n sbirciatina; **to take** or **have a ~ at** dare una sbirciatina a. 2 vi sbirciare.

peel [piːl] 1 n (gen) buccia; (of orange, lemon etc) scorza, buccia. 2 vt (fruit etc) sbucciare; (shrimps etc) sgusciare. 3 vi (wallpaper) staccarsi; (paint etc) scrostarsi; (skin) squamarsi; (person) spellarsi.

♦ **peel away** 1 vi + adv (skin) squamarsi; (paint) scrostarsi; (wallpaper) staccarsi. 2 vt + adv (gen) staccare; (paint) scrostare; (wrapper) togliere.

♦ **peel back** vt + adv togliere, levare.

♦ **peel off** 1 vt + adv (a) = **peel away** 2. (b) (clothes) togliersi, sfilarsi. 2 vi + adv = **peel away** 1.

peel·er ['piːlə'] n: potato ~ (tool) sbucciapatate m inv; (machine) sbucciapatate f inv.

peel·ings ['piːlɪŋz] npl bucce fpl.

peep[1] [piːp] 1 n (of bird etc) squittio; (of whistle) trillo; **we haven't heard a ~ out of them** (fam) non hanno aperto bocca. 2 vi (mouse, bird) squittire; (whistle) trillare.

peep[2] [piːp] 1 n sbirciata; **to take** or **have a ~ (at sth)** dare una sbirciata (a qc). 2 vi: **to ~ at sth** sbirciare qc; **the sun ~ed out from behind the clouds** il sole fece capolino da dietro le nuvole.

peep·hole ['piːphəʊl] n spioncino.

peep·ing ['piːpɪŋ]: **P~ Tom** n guardone m, voyeur m inv.

peer[1] [pɪə'] n pari m inv.

peer[2] [pɪə'] vi: **to ~ at sth** aguzzare gli occhi per vedere qc; **to ~ into a room** guardare in una stanza.

peer·age ['pɪərɪdʒ] n dignità di pari; **he was given a ~** gli è stato conferito il titolo di pari.

peer·less ['pɪəlɪs] adj impareggiabile, senza pari.

peeved [piːvd] adj (fam) seccato(a), stizzito(a).

peev·ish ['piːvɪʃ] adj scontroso(a), stizzoso(a).

pee·wit ['piːwɪt] n pavoncella.

peg [pɛɡ] 1 n (tent ~) picchetto; (clothes ~) molletta; (for coat, hat) attaccapanni m inv; **off the ~** di confezione; **to take sb down a ~ (or two)** far abbassare la cresta a qn; **a ~ on which to hang a theory** un pretesto per presentare una teoria. 2 vt (clothes) appendere con le mollette; (groundsheet) fissare con i picchetti; (fig: prices, wages) fissare, stabilizzare.

♦ **peg out** vi + adv (fam: die) crepare, tirare le cuoia.

pe·jo·ra·tive [pɪ'dʒɒrɪtɪv] adj peggiorativo(a).

pe·kin·ese [ˌpiːkɪ'niːz] n pechinese m (cane).

peli·can ['pɛlɪkən] n pellicano.

pel·let ['pɛlɪt] n (of paper, bread) pallina; (for gun) pallino; (Med) pillola.

pell-mell ['pɛl'mɛl] adv disordinatamente, alla rinfusa.

pel·met ['pɛlmɪt] n (wooden) cassonetto; (cloth) mantovana.

pelt[1] [pɛlt] 1 vt: **to ~ sb with sth** tirare qc addosso a qn; **to ~ sth with sth** colpire qc con qc; **they ~ed him with questions** lo hanno tempestato di domande. 2 vi (a): **the rain is ~ing (down)** (fam) piove a dirotto. (b) (fam: go fast): **she ~ed across the road** ha attraversato sparata la strada.

pelt[2] [pɛlt] n (of animal) pelliccia.

pel·vis ['pɛlvɪs] n bacino, pelvi f inv.

pen[1] [pɛn] 1 n (for animals) recinto, chiuso; (play~) box m inv; (Am fam: prison) galera. 2 vt (also: ~ in, ~ up) rinchiudere.

pen[2] [pɛn] 1 n (gen) penna; (felt-tip ~) pennarello; **to put ~ to paper** prendere la penna in mano. 2 vt scrivere. 3 cpd: ~ **name** n pseudonimo.

pe·nal ['piːnl] adj (gen) penale; (offence) punibile, passibile di pena; ~ **servitude** lavori mpl forzati.

pe·nal·ize ['piːnəlaɪz] vt (a) (punish) punire. (b) (Sport) penalizzare. (c) (handicap) andicappare.

pen·al·ty ['pɛnəltɪ] 1 n (a) (punishment) pena; (fig: disadvantage) svantaggio; **those who break the rules do so on ~ of dismissal** coloro che infrangono il regolamento verranno puniti con il licenziamento; **the ~ for not doing this is...** se non si fa questo la punizione sarà.... (b) (Sport) calcio di rigore. 2 cpd (a) (Law, Comm): ~ **clause** n penale f. (b) (Ftbl): ~ **area** n area di rigore; ~ **goal** n goal m inv su calcio di rigore; ~ **kick** n calcio di rigore.

pen·ance ['pɛnəns] n penitenza; **to do ~ for** fare la penitenza per.

pence [pɛns] npl of **penny**.

pen·chant ['pɑ̃ːŋʃɑ̃ːŋ] n debole m.

pen·cil ['pɛnsl] 1 n matita. 2 vt (also: ~ **in**) scrivere a matita. 3 cpd (drawing, line) a matita; ~ **case** n astuccio per matite; ~ **sharpener** n temperamatite m inv.

pen·dant ['pɛndənt] n pendaglio.

pend·ing ['pɛndɪŋ] 1 adj in sospeso. 2 prep in attesa di; ~ **the arrival of** in attesa dell'arrivo di.

pen·du·lum ['pɛndjʊləm] n pendolo.

pen·etrate ['pɛnɪtreɪt] 1 vt (gen, Mil) penetrare in; (infiltrate) infiltrarsi in; (understand: meaning, mystery) penetrare; (: truth) afferrare. 2 vi (go right through) penetrare; **the significance of what he was saying finally ~d** il significato delle sue parole fu finalmente chiaro.

pen·etrat·ing ['pɛnɪtreɪtɪŋ] adj (eyesight, sound) penetrante, acuto(a); (question etc) acuto(a); (person, mind etc) perspicace.

pen·etra·tion [ˌpɛnɪ'treɪʃən] n penetrazione f.

pen·friend ['pɛn,frɛnd] n corrispondente m/f.

pen·guin ['pɛŋɡwɪn] n pinguino.

peni·cil·lin [ˌpɛnɪ'sɪlɪn] n penicillina.

pen·in·su·la [pɪ'nɪnsjʊlə] n penisola.

pe·nis ['piːnɪs] n pene m.

peni·tence ['pɛnɪtəns] n penitenza.

peni·tent ['pɛnɪtənt] 1 adj pentito(a). 2 n penitente m/f.

peni·ten·tia·ry [ˌpɛnɪ'tɛnʃərɪ] n (esp Am: prison) penitenziario.

pen·knife ['pɛnnaɪf] n, pl **-knives** ['pɛnnaɪvz] temperino.

pen·nies ['pɛnɪz] npl of **penny**.

pen·ni·less ['pɛnɪlɪs] adj senza un soldo or una lira.

pen·ny ['pɛnɪ] n, pl **pennies** or **pence** (Brit) penny m; (Am) centesimo; **in for a ~, in for a pound** ho (or hai etc) fatto trenta, faccio (or fai etc) trentuno; **I'm not a ~ the wiser** continuo a capirci quanto prima; **he hasn't a ~ to his name** non ha un soldo bucato; **he turns up like a bad ~** te lo ritrovi sempre tra i piedi; **a ~ for your thoughts** a che pensi?; **and then the ~ dropped!** improvvisamente ci sono arrivato!

pen·pusher ['pɛn,puʃə'] n (pej) scribacchino.

pen·sion ['pɛnʃən] **1** n pensione f. **2** cpd: **~ fund** n fondo pensioni; **~ scheme** n sistema m di pensionamento.

♦ **pension off** vt + adv mandare in pensione.

pen·sion·er ['pɛnʃənə'] n pensionato/a.

pen·sive ['pɛnsɪv] adj pensoso(a).

pen·ta·gon ['pɛntəgən] n pentagono; **the P~** (Am Pol) il Pentagono.

pen·tath·lon [pɛn'tæθlən] n pentathlon m.

Pen·tecost ['pɛntɪkɒst] n (Rel) Pentecoste f.

pent·house ['pɛnthaʊs] n attico.

pent-up ['pɛnt'ʌp] adj (emotions) represso(a); (person) teso(a).

pe·nul·ti·mate [pɪ'nʌltɪmɪt] adj penultimo(a).

penu·ry ['pɛnjʊrɪ] n indigenza.

peo·ny ['pɪənɪ] n peonia.

peo·ple ['piːpl] **1** n **(a)** (pl: persons) persone fpl, gente f; **old ~** i vecchi; **young ~** i giovani; **some ~** alcuni mpl, certa gente; **what do you ~ think?** e voi (altri) cosa ne pensate?; **some ~ are born lucky** c'è chi nasce con la camicia; **you of all ~ should...** se c'è uno che dovrebbe ... quello sei tu. **(b)** (pl: in general) gente f; **many ~ think that...** molti pensano che..., molta gente pensa che...; **~ say that...** si dice or la gente dice che.... **(c)** (pl: inhabitants) abitanti mpl; **the ~ of London** i Londinesi; **country ~** la gente di campagna; **town ~** la gente di città. **(d)** (pl: Pol etc: citizens) popolo; (: general public) pubblico; **the ~** il popolo; **~ at large** il grande pubblico; **a man of the ~** un uomo del popolo. **(e)** (pl: family) famiglia. **(f)** (sg: nation etc) popolo, nazione f.
2 vt: **to ~ (with)** popolare (con); **to be ~d with** essere popolato di.

pep [pɛp] (fam) **1** n dinamismo, vitalità. **2** cpd: **~ pill** n stimolante m; **~ talk** n discorso d'incoraggiamento.

♦ **pep up** vt + adv (person) tirar su; (party) animare; (drink) correggere.

pep·per ['pɛpə'] **1** n (spice) pepe m; (vegetable) peperone m. **2** vt pepare; **to ~ a work with quotations** (fig) infarcire un lavoro di citazioni.

pepper·corn ['pɛpəkɔːn] n grano di pepe.

pepper·mint ['pɛpəmɪnt] n (Bot) menta peperita; (sweet) caramella alla menta.

pepper·pot ['pɛpəpɒt] n pepaiola.

pep·pery ['pɛpərɪ] adj pepato(a); (fig) irascibile.

pep·tic ['pɛptɪk] adj: **~ ulcer** ulcera peptica.

per [pɜː'] prep per, a; **~ annum** all'anno; **£7 ~ week/dozen** 7 sterline la or alla settimana/dozzina; **~ capita** pro capite; **~ person** a testa, a or per persona; **as ~ your instructions** secondo le vostre istruzioni.

per·ceive [pə'siːv] vt (sound, meaning, change) percepire; (person, object) notare; (realize) accorgersi di.

per cent [pə'sɛnt] n per cento; **a 20 ~ discount** uno sconto del 20 per cento.

per·cent·age [pə'sɛntɪdʒ] n percentuale f; **as a ~ in** percentuale; **to get a ~ on all sales** avere una percentuale sulle vendite; **on a ~ basis** a percentuale.

per·cep·tible [pə'sɛptəbl] adj percettibile.

per·cep·tibly [pə'sɛptɪblɪ] adv visibilmente.

per·cep·tion [pə'sɛpʃən] n (gen) percezione f; **one's**

~ of a situation il proprio modo di vedere una situazione.

per·cep·tive [pə'sɛptɪv] adj (gen) perspicace; (analysis) acuto(a).

perch¹ [pɜːtʃ] n (fish) pesce m persico.

perch² [pɜːtʃ] **1** n (of bird) pertica, posatoio; (in tree) ramo; (fig: for person etc) posto di vedetta. **2** vt poggiare. **3** vi (bird, person) appollaiarsi.

per·co·late ['pɜːkəleɪt] **1** vt filtrare; **~d coffee** caffè filtrato. **2** vi passare, filtrare; (fig: news) filtrare.

per·co·la·tor ['pɜːkəleɪtə'] n caffettiera a filtro.

per·cus·sion [pə'kʌʃən] **1** n **(a)** percussione f. **(b)** (Mus) strumenti mpl a percussione. **2** cpd: **~ instrument** n strumento a percussione.

per·egrine ['pɛrɪgrɪn]: **~ falcon** n falco pellegrino.

per·emp·tory [pə'rɛmptərɪ] adj perentorio(a).

per·en·nial [pə'rɛnɪəl] **1** adj perenne. **2** n (Bot) pianta perenne.

per·fect ['pɜːfɪkt] **1** adj (gen) perfetto(a); **it's a ~ day for skiing** è una giornata ideale per sciare; **he's a ~ stranger to me** mi è completamente sconosciuto; **~ tense** (Gram) perfetto; **~ pitch** (Mus) intonazione f giusta. **2** n (Gram): **present ~** passato prossimo; **future ~** futuro anteriore. **3** [pə'fɛkt] vt perfezionare.

per·fec·tion [pə'fɛkʃən] n perfezione f; **to ~** a or alla perfezione.

per·fec·tion·ist [pə'fɛkʃənɪst] n perfezionista m/f.

per·fect·ly ['pɜːfɪktlɪ] adv (gen) perfettamente, alla perfezione; **she's ~ lovely** è una bellezza; **I'm ~ happy with the situation** sono completamente soddisfatta della situazione; **you know ~ well** sai benissimo.

per·fidi·ous [pɜː'fɪdɪəs] adj perfido(a).

per·fo·rate ['pɜːfəreɪt] vt perforare; **~d line** linea punteggiata; **~d ulcer** (Med) ulcera perforata.

per·fo·ra·tion [,pɜːfə'reɪʃən] n (act) perforazione f; (in stamps) dentellatura; (hole) foro.

per·form [pə'fɔːm] **1** vt **(a)** (function, task) svolgere; (duty) adempiere a; (miracles, experiments) fare, compiere; (ceremony) celebrare; **to ~ an operation** (Med) operare. **(b)** (play, ballet, opera) rappresentare; (duet, symphony) eseguire; (acrobatics) fare. **2** vi **(a)** (company) dare una rappresentazione; (person) esibirsi; **a ~ing seal** una foca ammaestrata. **(b)** (vehicle, machine, also fig: student) comportarsi; **if you want a car that ~s really well...** se volete una macchina che dia ottime prestazioni... .

per·for·mance [pə'fɔːməns] n **(a)** (see vt a) svolgimento; adempimento; celebrazione f; **in the ~ of his duties** nell'adempimento dei suoi doveri. **(b)** (presentation: of play, opera) rappresentazione f; (: of film, ballet) spettacolo; (by actor, of a part) interpretazione f; **he gave a splendid ~** la sua interpretazione è stata magnifica; **a fine ~ of the Ninth Symphony** un'ottima esecuzione della nona sinfonia. **(c)** (effectiveness: of machine etc) prestazioni fpl; (: of company) rendimento; (: of racehorse, athlete) performance f inv; **the team put up a good ~** la squadra ha giocato una bella partita; **what a ~!** (fam) quale scene or storie!

per·form·er [pə'fɔːmə'] n artista m/f.

per·fume ['pɜːfjuːm] **1** n profumo. **2** [pə'fjuːm] vt profumare.

per·fum·ery [pə'fjuːmərɪ] n profumeria.

per·func·to·ri·ly [pə'fʌŋktərɪlɪ] adv (agree, answer) tanto per fare; (greet, smile) meccanicamente.

per·func·tory [pə'fʌŋktərɪ] adj (inspection, inquiry) superficiale, proforma inv; (nod) meccanico(a).

per·haps [pə'hæps. præps] *adv* forse; ~ **so/not** forse sì/no, può darsi di sì/di no; ~ **he'll come** magari *or* forse verrà, può darsi che venga.

per·il ['perɪl] *n* pericolo; **at your** ~ a tuo rischio e pericolo.

peri·lous ['perɪləs] *adj* pericoloso(a).

peri·lous·ly ['perɪləslɪ] *adv* pericolosamente; **they came** ~ **close to being caught** sono stati a un pelo dall'esser presi.

pe·rim·eter [pə'rɪmɪtəʳ] **1** *n* perimetro. **2** *cpd:* ~ **wall** *n* muro di cinta.

pe·ri·od ['pɪərɪəd] **1** *n* **(a)** *(length of time)* periodo; *(stage: in career, development etc)* periodo, momento; *(Am Ftbl)* tempo; **for a** ~ **of three weeks** per un periodo di *or* per la durata di tre settimane; **at that** ~ *(of my life)* in quel periodo *(della mia vita)*; **the holiday** ~ il periodo delle vacanze; **the Victorian** ~ l'epoca *or* l'età vittoriana; **a painting of his early** ~ un dipinto del suo primo periodo. **(b)** *(Scol)* ora. **(c)** *(full stop)* punto. **(d)** *(menstruation)* mestruazioni *fpl.* **2** *cpd:* ~ **dress** *n* costume *m* dell'epoca *or* del tempo; ~ **furniture** *n (genuine)* mobili *mpl* d'epoca; *(copy)* mobili in stile; ~ **pains** *npl* dolori *mpl* mestruali; ~ **piece** *n* bell'esemplare *m* dell'epoca.

pe·ri·od·ic [,pɪərɪ'ɒdɪk] *adj* periodico(a); ~ **table** *(Chem)* sistema *m* periodico.

pe·ri·odi·cal [,pɪərɪ'ɒdɪkəl] **1** *adj* periodico(a). **2** *n* periodico.

pe·ri·odi·cal·ly [,pɪərɪ'ɒdɪkəlɪ] *adv* periodicamente.

peri·pa·tet·ic [,perɪpə'tetɪk] *adj (salesman)* ambulante; *(teacher)* peripatetico(a).

pe·riph·er·al [pə'rɪfərəl] *adj (gen)* periferico(a); *(interest)* marginale.

pe·riph·ery [pə'rɪfərɪ] *n* periferia.

peri·scope ['perɪskəup] *n* periscopio.

per·ish ['perɪʃ] *vi (person etc)* perire, morire; *(material)* deteriorarsi.

per·ish·able ['perɪʃəbl] **1** *adj* deperibile. **2:** ~**s** *npl* merci *fpl* deperibili.

per·ish·ing ['perɪʃɪŋ] *adj (fam):* **it's** ~ **(cold)** fa un freddo da morire.

peri·to·ni·tis [,perɪtə'naɪtɪs] *n* peritonite *f.*

peri·win·kle ['perɪ,wɪŋkl] *n (Bot)* pervinca; *(Zool)* littorina.

per·jure ['pɜːdʒəʳ] *vt:* **to** ~ **o.s.** spergiurare; *(Law)* giurare il falso.

per·jury ['pɜːdʒərɪ] *n* spergiuro; *(Law)* falso giuramento; **to commit** ~ spergiurare; *(Law)* giurare il falso.

perk [pɜːk] *n (fam)* vantaggio.

perk up ['pɜːk'ʌp] **1** *vt + adv* **(a)** *(fig: cheer up)* tirar su. **(b): he** ~**ed up his ears** drizzò le orecchie. **2** *vi + adv (cheer up)* rianimarsi; *(show interest)* animarsi.

perky ['pɜːkɪ] *adj (-ier, -iest) (cheerful)* allegro(a); *(bright)* vivace; *(cheeky)* impertinente.

perm [pɜːm] **1** *n (abbr of* **permanent wave)** permanente *f.* **2** *vt:* **to** ~ **sb's hair** fare la permanente a qn; **to have one's hair** ~**ed** farsi fare la permanente.

per·ma·nence ['pɜːmənəns] *n* permanenza.

per·ma·nen·cy ['pɜːmənənsɪ] *n* **(a)** permanenza. **(b)** *(job)* occupazione *f* fissa, lavoro fisso.

per·ma·nent ['pɜːmənənt] *adj (state, building, agreement)* permanente; *(job, position)* fisso(a); *(dye, ink)* indelebile; **I'm not** ~ **here** non sono fisso qui; ~ **address** residenza fissa; ~ **wave** permanente *f.*

per·ma·nent·ly ['pɜːmənəntlɪ] *adv* definitivamente; **he is** ~ **drunk** è perennemente ubriaco.

per·man·ga·nate [pɜː'mæŋgənɪt] *n* permanganato.

per·me·ate ['pɜːmɪeɪt] **1** *vt (gen)* filtrare attraverso; *(Tech)* permeare; *(subj: smell)* pervadere; *(:fig: ideas etc)* diffondersi in. **2** *vi* filtrare; *(fig)* diffondersi.

per·mis·sible [pə'mɪsɪbl] *adj (action)* permesso(a); *(behaviour)* accettabile; *(attitude)* ammissibile; **it is not** ~ **to do that** non è permesso farlo.

per·mis·sion [pə'mɪʃən] *n* permesso; *(official)* autorizzazione *f;* **with your** ~ se mi permette, con il suo permesso; **to give sb** ~ **to do sth** dare a qn il permesso di fare qc.

per·mis·sive [pə'mɪsɪv] *adj (parents, society)* permissivo(a); **teenagers are more** ~ **nowadays** c'è più permissività tra i giovani oggigiorno.

per·mit ['pɜːmɪt] *n (gen)* autorizzazione *f* (scritta); *(for specific activity)* permesso; *(entrance pass)* lasciapassare *m;* **fishing** ~ licenza di pesca; **building/export** ~ permesso *or* licenza di costruzione/di esportazione. **2** [pə'mɪt] *vt* permettere; **to** ~ **sb to do sth** permettere a qn di fare qc; **to** ~ **sth to take place** permettere che qc avvenga. **3** [pə'mɪt] *vi* permettere; **to** ~ **of** *(frm)* ammettere, consentire; **weather** ~**ting** tempo permettendo.

per·mu·ta·tion [,pɜːmju'teɪʃən] *n* permutazione *f.*

per·ni·cious [pɜː'nɪʃəs] *adj* nocivo(a), dannoso(a); *(Med)* pernicioso(a).

per·nick·ety [pə'nɪkətɪ] *adj (fam: person)* pignolo(a); *(: job)* da certosino.

per·pen·dicu·lar [,pɜːpən'dɪkjʊləʳ] **1** *adj (gen, Math)* perpendicolare; *(cliff)* a picco. **2** *n* perpendicolare *f.*

per·pe·trate ['pɜːpɪtreɪt] *vt* perpetrare, commettere.

per·pe·tra·tor ['pɜːpɪtreɪtəʳ] *n (of crime)* autore/trice.

per·pet·ual [pə'petjʊəl] *adj (gen, motion)* perpetuo(a); *(ice, snow)* perenne; *(continuous: noise, complaining)* incessante, continuo(a).

per·petu·ate [pə'petjʊeɪt] *vt* perpetuare.

per·pe·tu·ity [,pɜːpɪ'tjuːɪtɪ] *n:* **in** ~ in perpetuo.

per·plex [pə'pleks] *vt* lasciare perplesso(a); **I was** ~**ed by his behaviour** il suo comportamento mi ha lasciato perplesso.

per·plexed [pə'plekst] *adj* perplesso(a).

per·plex·ing [pə'pleksɪŋ] *adj* che lascia perplesso(a).

per·plex·ity [pə'pleksɪtɪ] *n* imbarazzo, perplessità.

per·secute ['pɜːsɪkjuːt] *vt* perseguitare.

per·secu·tion [,pɜːsɪ'kjuːʃən] **1** *n* persecuzione *f.* **2** *cpd:* ~ **complex** *n (Psych)* mania di persecuzione.

per·sever·ance [,pɜːsɪ'vɪərəns] *n* perseveranza.

per·severe [,pɜːsɪ'vɪəʳ] *vi* perseverare.

per·sever·ing [,pɜːsɪ'vɪərɪŋ] *adj* perseverante.

Per·sia ['pɜːʃə] *n* Persia.

Per·sian ['pɜːʃən] **1** *adj* persiano(a). **2** *cpd:* ~ **carpet** *n* tappeto persiano; ~ **cat** *n* (gatto) persiano; ~ **Gulf** *n* Golfo Persico; ~ **lamb** *n (animal)* karakul *m inv; (skin)* persiano.

per·sim·mon [pɜː'sɪmən] *n* cachi *m inv.*

per·sist [pə'sɪst] *vi (person)* persistere, ostinarsi; *(custom, rain)* persistere, durare; **to** ~ **in sth/in doing sth** ostinarsi in qc/a fare qc, persistere in qc/nel *or* a fare qc.

per·sis·tence [pə'sɪstəns] *n (tenacity)* perseveranza; *(obstinacy)* ostinazione *f; (continuing to exist)* persistere *m.*

per·sis·tent [pə'sɪstənt] *adj (person, attempt, questions)* insistente; *(cough, pain, smell)* persistente; *(lateness, rain)* continuo(a); ~

offender *(Law)* delinquente *m/f* abituale.

per·sis·tent·ly [pə'sɪstəntlɪ] *adv* con insistenza; *(continuously)* continuamente.

per·son ['pɜ:sn] *n* **(a)** *(pl* **people** *or (frm)*: ~s) persona; **a** ~ **to** ~ **call** *(Telec)* una comunicazione con preavviso. **(b)** *(pl* ~s: *Gram, Law)* persona. **(c)** *(body, physical presence)* figura, personale *m; (appearance)* aspetto; **in** ~ di *or* in persona, personalmente; **in the** ~ **of my uncle** nella persona di mio zio; **on** *or* **about one's** ~ *(weapon)* su di sé; *(money)* con sé.

per·son·able ['pɜ:snəbl] *adj* di bell'aspetto, prestante.

per·son·age ['pɜ:snɪdʒ] *n* personaggio.

per·son·al ['pɜ:snl] *adj (gen, Gram)* personale; *(application)* di persona; ~ **belongings** oggetti d'uso personale; **a** ~ **question** una domanda indiscreta; **a** ~ **interview** un incontro privato; **for** ~ **reasons** per motivi personali; **to make a** ~ **appearance** apparire di persona; **to have** ~ **knowledge of sth** conoscere qc per esperienza personale; **don't get** ~! non entriamo nel personale!; **one's** ~ **habits** le proprie piccole manie; '~' *(on letter)* 'riservata', 'personale'. **2** *cpd:* ~ **assistant** *n (abbr* **P.A.**) segretaria personale; ~ **call** *n (Brit Telec: person to person)* chiamata con preavviso; *(: private)* telefonata personale; ~ **column** *n ≃* messaggi *mpl* personali.

per·son·al·ity [,pɜ:sə'nælɪtɪ] **1** *n (nature)* personalità *f inv; (famous person)* personalità, personaggio; **let's not indulge in personalities** lasciamo da parte i commenti personali. **2** *cpd:* ~ **cult** *n* culto della personalità.

per·son·al·ly ['pɜ:snəlɪ] *adv (for my part)* personalmente; ~ **I think that...** personalmente penso che...; **don't take it too** ~ non prenderla come un'offesa *or* una critica personale. **(b)** *(in person)* personalmente, di persona; **to hand sth over** ~ consegnare qc di persona.

per·soni·fi·ca·tion [pɜ:,sɒnɪfɪ'keɪʃən] *n* personificazione *f.*

per·soni·fy [pɜ:'sɒnɪfaɪ] *vt* personificare.

per·son·nel [,pɜ:sə'nel] **1** *n* personale *m inv.* **2** *cpd:* ~ **department** *n* ufficio del personale; ~ **manager** *n* direttore/trice del personale; ~ **officer** *n* addetto/a all'ufficio del personale.

per·spec·tive [pə'spektɪv] *n* prospettiva; *(fig)*: **to see** *or* **look at sth in** ~ vedere qc nella giusta prospettiva; **to get sth into** ~ ridimensionare qc.

per·spex ['pɜ:speks] *n ⓡ* plexiglas *m ⓡ.*

per·spi·ca·cious [,pɜ:spɪ'keɪʃəs] *adj* perspicace.

per·spi·ra·tion [,pɜ:spə'reɪʃən] *n* traspirazione *f.*

per·spire [pə'spaɪə^r] *vi* traspirare.

per·suade [pə'sweɪd] *vt* persuadere; **to** ~ **sb of sth/that** persuadere qn di qc/che; **to** ~ **sb to do sth** persuadere qn a fare qc; **but they** ~**d me not to** ma mi hanno persuaso a non farlo; **she is easily** ~**d** si lascia facilmente persuadere *or* convincere; **I am** ~**d that...** sono persuaso *or* convinto che... + *sub.*

per·sua·sion [pə'sweɪʒən] *n* **(a)** *(persuading)* persuasione *f.* **(b)** *(creed)* convinzione *f,* credo.

per·sua·sive [pə'sweɪsɪv] *adj (person)* convincente; *(argument)* persuasivo(a), convincente.

per·sua·sive·ly [pə'sweɪsɪvlɪ] *adv* in modo persuasivo.

pert [pɜ:t] *adj (-er, -est) (girl, answer)* impertinente; *(hat)* spiritoso(a).

per·tain [pɜ:'teɪn] *vi (frm)*: **to** ~ **to** *(concern)* riferirsi a, riguardare; *(belong to)* appartenere a; **documents** ~**ing to the case** documenti relativi al caso.

per·ti·nence ['pɜ:tɪnəns] *n* pertinenza.

per·ti·nent ['pɜ:tɪnənt] *adj* pertinente.

per·turb [pə'tɜ:b] *vt* turbare, agitare.

per·turb·ing [pə'tɜ:bɪŋ] *adj* inquietante.

Peru [pə'ru:] *n* Perù *m.*

pe·rus·al [pə'ru:zəl] *n* lettura.

pe·ruse [pə'ru:z] *vt* leggere.

per·vade [pɜ:'veɪd] *vt (subj: smell, feeling, atmosphere)* pervadere; *(: influence, ideas)* insinuarsi in, diffondersi in.

per·va·sive [pɜ:'veɪsɪv] *adj (smell)* penetrante; *(influence)* dilagante; *(gloom, feelings, ideas)* diffuso(a).

per·verse [pə'vɜ:s] *adj (contrary: behaviour)* da bastian contrario; *(wicked)* cattivo(a); *(desires)* perverso(a); *(circumstances)* avverso(a); **to be** ~ *(person)* essere un bastian contrario.

per·ver·sion [pə'vɜ:ʃən] *n (Med, Psych)* perversione *f; (of justice, truth)* travisamento.

per·ver·sity [pə'vɜ:sɪtɪ] *n (wickedness)* perversità, malvagità; *(contrariness)* spirito di contraddizione.

per·vert [pə'vɜ:t] **1** *vt (mind)* pervertire; *(speech, truth etc)* travisare; **to** ~ **the course of justice** deviare il corso della giustizia. **2** ['pɜ:vɜ:t] *n* pervertito/a.

pes·si·mism ['pesɪmɪzəm] *n* pessimismo.

pes·si·mist ['pesɪmɪst] *n* pessimista *m/f.*

pes·si·mis·tic [,pesɪ'mɪstɪk] *adj (attitude, forecast)* pessimistico(a); *(person)* pessimista.

pest [pest] **1** *n* **(a)** *(Zool)* insetto *(or* animale *m)* nocivo. **(b)** *(fig: person)* peste *f; (: thing)* rottura. **2** *cpd:* ~ **control** *n* disinfestazione *f.*

pes·ter ['pestə^r] *vt* tormentare.

pes·ti·cide ['pestɪsaɪd] *n* pesticida *m.*

pes·ti·lent ['pestɪlənt] *adj,* **pes·ti·len·tial** [,pestɪ'lenʃəl] *adj (fam: exasperating)* pestifero(a).

pes·tle ['pesl] *n* pestello.

pet [pet] **1** *n* **(a)** *(animal)* animale *m* domestico; **my dad won't let me have any** ~**s** il mio papà non mi lascia tenere *(in casa)* nessun animale. **(b)** *(favourite)* preferito/a, beniamino/a; **teacher's** ~ beniamino dell'insegnante; **come here** ~ *(fam)* vieni qua tesoro. **2** *vt (indulge)* coccolare; *(fondle)* accarezzare. **3** *vi (sexually)* pomiciare, fare il petting. **4** *cpd* **(a)** *(monkey)* addomesticato(a); *(food)* per animali domestici; **we have a** ~ **dog** abbiamo un cane; ~ **shop** *n* negozio di animali domestici. **(b)** *(favourite: pupil, subject etc)* preferito(a); **my** ~ **aversion** la cosa che detesto di più; ~ **name** *n* nomignolo.

pet·al ['petl] *n* petalo.

pe·ter ['pi:tə^r] *vi*: **to** ~ **out** *(supply)* esaurirsi; *(stream)* perdersi; *(plan)* andare in fumo; *(interest, excitement)* svanire; *(fire, conversation)* spegnersi; *(song, noise)* cessare.

pe·tite [pə'ti:t] *adj (woman)* minuta e graziosa.

pe·ti·tion [pə'tɪʃən] **1** *n (list of names)* petizione *f; (frm: request)* richiesta, istanza. **2** *vt (person)* presentare una petizione a. **3** *vi* richiedere; **to** ~ **for divorce** presentare un'istanza di divorzio.

pet·ri·fy ['petrɪfaɪ] *vt* **(a)** pietrificare. **(b)** *(fig)* terrorizzare; **to be petrified (with fear)** rimanere impietrito *(dallo spavento).*

pet·ro·chemi·cal [,petrəʊ'kemɪkl] *adj* petrolchimico(a).

pet·rol ['petrəl] *(Brit)* **1** *n* benzina. **2** *cpd (can, gauge, tank etc)* di *or* della benzina; ~ **pump** *n (at garage, in car)* pompa della benzina; ~ **station** *n* stazione *f* di servizio.

pe·tro·leum [pɪ'trəʊlɪəm] **1** *n* petrolio. **2** *cpd:* ~ **jelly** *n* vaselina.

pet·ti·coat ['petɪkəʊt] *n (full-length)* sottoveste *f; (waist)* sottogonna.

pet·ti·fog·ging |'pɛtɪfɒgɪŋ] adj (details) insignificante; (objections) cavilloso(a).

pet·ty |'pɛtɪ] 1 adj (-ier, -iest) (a) (trivial: detail, complaint) insignificante, di poca importanza. (b) (minor: official) piccolo(a). (c) (small-minded, spiteful) meschino(a). 2 cpd: ~ cash n fondo per le piccole spese; ~ officer n sottufficiale m di marina.

petu·lance |'pɛtjʊləns] n irritabilità.

petu·lant |'pɛtjʊlənt] adj irritabile.

pew |pjuː] n (in church) banco; take a ~! (fig fam) accomodati!, siediti!

pew·ter |'pjuːtəʳ] n peltro.

phal·lic |'fælɪk] adj fallico(a).

phan·tom |'fæntəm] 1 adj fantasma inv. 2 n fantasma m.

Phar·aoh |'fɛərəʊ] n faraone m.

phar·ma·ceu·ti·cal |,fɑːmə'sjuːtɪkəl] adj farmaceutico(a).

phar·ma·cist |'fɑːməsɪst] n farmacista m/f.

phar·ma·col·ogy |,fɑːmə'kɒlədʒɪ n farmacologia.

phar·ma·cy |'fɑːməsɪ] n farmacia.

phase [feɪz] 1 n fase f; to be out of ~ (Tech, Elec) essere fuori fase or sfasato; she's just going through a ~ sta attraversando un periodo difficile, le passerà. 2 vt (introduce gradually) introdurre gradualmente; (coordinate) sincronizzare; ~d withdrawal ritirata progressiva.

♦ **phase in** vt + adv introdurre gradualmente.

♦ **phase out** vt + adv eliminare gradualmente.

Ph.D. abbr of Doctor of Philosophy.

pheas·ant |'fɛznt] n fagiano.

phe·no·bar·bi·tone |,fiːnəʊ'bɑːbɪtəʊn] n fenilbarbiturico, luminal m®.

phe·nom·enal |fɪ'nɒmɪnl] adj fenomenale.

phe·nom·enon |fɪ'nɒmɪnən] n, pl **phenomena** |fɪ'nɒmɪnə] fenomeno.

phew |fjuː] excl (heat, tiredness) uff!; (relief, surprise) uh!

phi·lan·der·er |fɪ'lændərəʳ] n donnaiolo.

phil·an·throp·ic |,fɪlən'θrɒpɪk] adj filantropico(a).

phi·lan·thro·pist |fɪ'lænθrəpɪst] n filantropo/a.

phi·lan·thro·py |fɪ'lænθrəpɪ] n filantropia.

phi·lat·ely |fɪ'lætəlɪ] n filatelia.

phil·har·mon·ic |,fɪlɑː'mɒnɪk] adj filarmonico(a).

phi·lol·ogy |fɪ'lɒlədʒɪ] n filologia.

phi·loso·pher |fɪ'lɒsəfəʳ] n filosofo/a.

philo·soph·i·cal |,fɪlə'sɒfɪkəl] adj filosofico(a); (fig: resigned) filosofico(a), rassegnato(a); he's been very ~ about it l'ha presa con molta filosofia.

phi·loso·phize |fɪ'lɒsəfaɪz] vi: to ~ (about or on) fiulosofare (su).

phi·loso·phy |fɪ'lɒsəfɪ] n fiulosofiua; her ~ of life la sua massima or fiulosofiua; **Doctor of P~** (Univ) ≈ dottorato di ricerca (in qualsiasi disciplina eccetto legge, medicina e teologia).

phlegm |flɛm] n flemma.

phleg·mat·ic |flɛg'mætɪk] adj flemmatico(a).

pho·bia |'fəʊbɪə] n fobia; to have a ~ about sth avere la fobia di qc.

phoe·nix |'fiːnɪks] n fenice f.

phone |fəʊn] n, vt, vi abbr of **telephone**.

phone-in |'fəʊnɪn] n trasmissione radiofonica o televisiva con intervento telefonico degli ascoltatori.

pho·neme |'fəʊniːm] n fonema m.

pho·net·ic |fəʊ'nɛtɪk] adj fonetico(a).

pho·net·ics |fəʊ'nɛtɪks] nsg fonetica.

pho·ney |'fəʊnɪ] (fam) 1 adj (gen) falso(a); (accent) fasullo(a). 2 n (person) venditore/trice di fumo, ciarlatano.

pho·no·graph |'fəʊnəgrɑːf] n (old) fonografo; (Am) giradischi m inv.

pho·nol·ogy |fəʊ'nɒlədʒɪ] n fonologia.

pho·ny |'fəʊnɪ] (Am) = **phoney**.

phos·phate |'fɒsfeɪt] n fosfato.

phos·pho·res·cent |,fɒsfə'rɛsnt] adj fosforescente.

phos·pho·rus |'fɒsfərəs] n fosforo.

pho·to |'fəʊtəʊ] 1 n (abbr of **photograph**) foto f inv. 2 cpd: ~ finish n fotofinish m inv.

photo·copi·er |'fəʊtəʊ,kɒpɪəʳ] n fotocopiatrice f.

photo·copy |'fəʊtəʊ,kɒpɪ] 1 n fotocopia. 2 vt fotocopiare.

photo·elec·tric |,fəʊtəʊɪ'lɛktrɪk] adj: ~ cell cellula fotoelettrica.

photo·gen·ic |,fəʊtəʊ'dʒɛnɪk] adj fotogenico(a).

photo·graph |'fəʊtəgræf] 1 n fotografia; to take a ~ of sb fare una fotografia a or fotografare qn; to take a ~ of sth fotografare qc. 2 vt fotografare. 3 cpd: ~ album n album m inv per (or delle) fotografie.

pho·tog·ra·pher |fə'tɒgrəfəʳ] n fotografo/a.

photo·graph·ic |,fəʊtə'græfɪk] adj fotografico(a).

pho·tog·ra·phy |fə'tɒgrəfɪ] n fotografia.

photo·stat |'fəʊtəʊstæt] ® = **photocopy**.

photo·syn·the·sis |,fəʊtəʊ'sɪnθəsɪs] n fotosintesi f.

phrase [freɪz] 1 n (a) (Gram) locuzione f; (saying) espressione f; noun ~ sintagma m nominale. (b) (Mus) frase f. 2 vt (a) (thought) esprimere; (letter) redigere. (b) (Mus) dividere in frasi.

phrase·book |'freɪzbʊk] n vocabolarietto.

phra·seol·ogy |,freɪzɪ'ɒlədʒɪ] n fraseologia.

physi·cal |'fɪzɪkəl] adj (a) (of the body) fisico(a); ~ examination visita medica; ~ exercises, ~ jerks (fam) ginnastica; ~ education educazione f fisica. (b) (world, object) materiale; (of physics) fisico(a); it's a ~ impossibility è un'impossibilità materiale.

physi·cal·ly |'fɪzɪkəlɪ] adv fisicamente; it's ~ impossible è materialmente impossibile.

phy·si·cian |fɪ'zɪʃən] n medico.

physi·cist |'fɪzɪsɪst] n fisico.

phys·ics |'fɪzɪks] nsg fisica.

physio·logi·cal |,fɪzɪə'lɒdʒɪkəl] adj fisiologico(a).

physi·ol·ogy |,fɪzɪ'ɒlədʒɪ] n fisiologia.

physio·thera·pist |,fɪzɪə'θɛrəpɪst] n fisioterapista m/f.

physio·thera·py |,fɪzɪə'θɛrəpɪ] n fisioterapia.

phy·sique |fɪ'ziːk] n fisico.

pia·nist |'pɪənɪst] n pianista m/f.

pia·no |'pjɑːnəʊ] 1 n piano(forte) m. 2 cpd (lesson, teacher) di piano(forte); (concerto, stool) per piano(forte); ~ accordion n fisarmonica (a tastiera).

pic·co·lo |'pɪkələʊ] n (Mus) ottavino.

pick |pɪk] 1 n (a) (also: ~axe) piccone m. (b) (choice, right to choose) scelta; take your ~! scegli quello che vuoi!, prendi quello che ti pare!; it's the ~ of the bunch è il migliore di tutti.

2 vt (a) (choose) scegliere; to ~ a winner puntare sul vincente; (fig) fare un ottimo affare, imbroccarla giusta; to ~ one's way through attraversare stando ben attento a dove mettere i piedi; to ~ a fight/quarrel with sb attaccar rissa/briga con qn. (b) (flowers) cogliere; (fruit) raccogliere. (c) (scab, spot) grattarsi; to ~ one's nose mettersi le dita nel naso; to ~ one's teeth pulirsi i denti con uno stuzzicadenti; to ~ a lock far scattare una serratura; to ~ a bone spolpare un osso; to ~ holes in sth (fig) trovare i punti deboli in qc; to ~ sb's pocket alleggerire qn del portafoglio; to ~ sb's brains farsi dare dei suggerimenti da qn.

3 vi: to ~ and choose scegliere con cura; to ~ at one's food piluccare; to ~ at a scab grattarsi una crosta.

♦ **pick off** vt + adv **(a)** (remove: fluff) togliere; (: flower, leaf) cogliere. **(b)** (shoot) abbattere (uno dopo l'altro).

♦ **pick on** vi + prep **(a)** (fam: harass) avercela con, prendersela con. **(b)** (single out) beccare; **they always ~ on him to do it** lo fanno sempre fare a lui.

♦ **pick out** vt + adv **(a)** (choose) scegliere. **(b)** (place: on map) trovare; (person: in crowd, photo) individuare; (: in identification parade) identificare. **(c)** (Mus): **to ~ out a tune on the piano** trovare gli accordi di un motivo al piano.

♦ **pick up** 1 vt + adv **(a)** (lift: sth dropped) raccogliere, raccattare; (: sb fallen) tirar su; **to ~ o.s. up** rialzarsi; **to ~ up a child** prendere in braccio un bambino; **to ~ up the phone** alzare il ricevitore; **to ~ up the bill** (fig) pagare (il conto); **the car ~ed up speed** la macchina ha accelerato velocità or ha accelerato; **to ~ sb up for having made a mistake** riprendere qn per aver fatto uno sbaglio.

(b) (collect: goods, person) passare a prendere; (subj: bus etc) far salire, caricare; (rescue) raccogliere; (: from sea) ripescare; (arrest) arrestare.

(c) (acquire: sale bargain) trovare; (: information, points in exam, germ) prendere; (learn: habit, ideas) prendere; (: skill, language, tricks) imparare; **can you ~ up some information while you're there?** puoi prendere delle informazioni mentre sei lì?; **he ~ed up a girl at the disco** (fam) ha rimorchiato una ragazza in discoteca.

(d) (Radio, TV, Telec) captare.

2 vi + adv **(a)** (improve: gen) migliorare; (: wages) aumentare; (: invalid, business) riprendersi; (: weather) rimettersi.

(b) (continue) continuare, riprendere; **to ~ up where one left off** riprendere dal punto in cui ci si era fermati.

picka·back ['pɪkəbæk] adv: **to carry sb ~** portare qn in groppa.

pick·axe, (Am) **pick·ax** ['pɪkæks] n piccone m.

pick·et ['pɪkɪt] 1 n **(a)** (stake) picchetto. **(b)** (band of strikers) picchetto; (Mil: sentry) sentinella; (: group) picchetto. 2 vt picchettare. 3 vi picchettare. 4 cpd: **~ duty** n: **to be on ~ duty** (Mil, Industry) essere di picchetto; **~ fence** n steccato, palizzata; **~ line** n cordone m degli scioperanti.

pick·ings ['pɪkɪŋz] npl (pilferings): **there are good ~ to be had here** qui ci sono buone possibilità di intascare qualcosa sottobanco.

pick·le ['pɪkl] 1 n (food): **~s** sottaceti mpl; **mixed ~s** giardiniera; **to be in a ~** (fig fam) essere in un guaio or pasticcio. 2 vt mettere sottaceto; **~d onions** cipolline fpl sottaceto.

pick-me-up ['pɪkmiːʌp] n (drink) goccetto; (Med) tonico.

pick·pocket ['pɪk.pɒkɪt] n borsaiolo, borseggiatore/trice.

pick-up ['pɪkʌp] n **(a)** (on record player: also: **~ arm**) pick-up m inv. **(b)** (also: **~ truck**) camioncino.

pic·nic ['pɪknɪk] (vb: pt, pp **picnicked**) 1 n picnic m inv; **to go on a ~** andare a fare un picnic; **it was no ~** (fig fam) non è stato un divertimento or uno scherzo. 2 vi fare un picnic. 3 cpd: **~ basket** n cestino per il picnic.

pic·nick·er ['pɪknɪkə'] n chi partecipa a un picnic.

pic·to·rial [pɪk'tɔːrɪəl] adj (magazine) illustrato(a); (description) pittoresco(a); (masterpiece) di pittura; **a ~ record of one's travels** una serie di immagini in ricordo dei propri viaggi.

pic·ture ['pɪktʃə'] 1 n **(a)** (Art: painting) quadro,

dipinto; (: drawing) disegno; (: portrait) ritratto; (photo) fotografia; (in book) illustrazione f; **to take a ~ of sb/sth** fare una foto a qn/di qc; **he looked the ~ of health** sembrava il ritratto della salute; **you're the ~ of your mother** sei (proprio) il ritratto di tua madre; **the garden is a ~ in June** il giardino in giugno è uno spettacolo; **his face was a ~!** avresti dovuto vedere la sua faccia! **(b)** (TV) immagine f; **we get a good ~ here** la ricezione qui è buona. **(c)** (Cine) film m inv; **to go to the ~s** andare al cinema. **(d)** (mental image) immagine f, idea; **the other side of the ~** il rovescio della medaglia; **he painted a black ~ of the future** ha dipinto il futuro a tinte fosche; **the overall ~** il quadro generale; **to put sb in the ~** mettere qn al corrente.

2 vt (imagine) immaginare; (remember) ricordare.

3 cpd: **~ book** n libro illustrato; **~ frame** n cornice f; **~ gallery** n (public) pinacoteca; (private) galleria (d'arte); **~ postcard** n cartolina illustrata; **~ window** n finestra panoramica.

pic·tur·esque [.pɪktʃə'rɛsk] adj pittoresco(a).

pie [paɪ] n (of fruit) torta; (of fish, meat) pasticcio in crosta; **as easy as ~** (facile) come bere un bicchier d'acqua; **~ in the sky** castelli in aria.

piece [piːs] 1 n **(a)** (gen, also Chess) pezzo; (smaller) pezzetto; (of land) appezzamento; (fragment) frammento; (Draughts etc) pedina; (item): **a ~ of furniture/clothing/advice** un mobile/indumento/consiglio; **a ~ of news/poetry** una notizia/poesia; **a ~ of luck** un colpo di fortuna; **a 10p ~** una moneta da 10 pence; **a six-~ band** un complesso di sei strumenti; **a 21-~ tea set** ≃ un servizio da tè per 6 persone; **a piano ~** un pezzo or componimento per piano; **it is made all in one ~** è fatto in un pezzo solo; **in one ~** (object) intatto; **to get back all in one ~** (person) tornare a casa incolume or sano e salvo; **~ by ~** poco alla volta; **to be in ~s** (taken apart) essere smontato; (broken) essere a pezzi; **to take sth to ~s** smontare qc; **to come** or **fall to ~s** sfasciarsi; **to smash sth to ~s** mandare in frantumi or in mille pezzi qc; **to go to ~s** (fig) crollare; **to say one's ~** dire la propria; **to give sb a ~ of one's mind** dire a qn il fatto suo.

(b) (fam: woman) pezzo di ragazza.

2 cpd (rate, worker) a cottimo; **~ work** n lavoro a cottimo.

♦ **piece together** vt + adv (also fig) ricostruire.

piece·meal ['piːsmiːl] 1 adv a spizzichi, poco alla volta. 2 adj (essay) frammentario(a); (argument) che manca di rigore.

pier [pɪə'] n pontile m; (landing stage) imbarcadero, pontile.

pierce [pɪəs] vt (gen) bucare, forare; (subj: cold, wind) penetrare; (: shriek, light) squarciare; **to have one's ears ~d** farsi fare i buchi per gli orecchini.

pierc·ing ['pɪəsɪŋ] adj (gen) penetrante; (cry) lacerante; (wind, sarcasm) pungente.

pi·ety ['paɪətɪ] n pietà.

pig [pɪg] 1 n **(a)** maiale m, porco; **to buy a ~ in a poke** (fig) fare un acquisto alla cieca or a scatola chiusa. **(b)** (fam: person: nasty) stronzo; (: greedy, dirty) porco, maiale m; **to make a ~ of o.s.** mangiare (e bere) come un porco. 2 cpd: **~ iron** n ghisa.

pi·geon ['pɪdʒən] n piccione m; **that's your ~** (fig) sono affari tuoi.

pigeon·hole ['pɪdʒənhəʊl] 1 n casella. 2 vt classificare.

pigeon-toed |'pɪdʒən'təʊd| adj: **to be ~** camminare con i piedi in dentro.

pig·gery |'pɪgərɪ| n allevamento di maiali.

piggy·back |'pɪgɪbæk| adv = **pickaback.**

pig·gy bank |'pɪgɪbæŋk| n salvadanaio.

pig-headed |pɪg'hɛdɪd| adj testardo(a), cocciuto(a).

pig·let |'pɪglɪt| n maialino, porcellino.

pig·ment |'pɪgmənt| n pigmento.

pig·men·ta·tion |,pɪgmən'teɪʃən| n pigmentazione f.

pig·my |'pɪgmɪ| n = **pygmy.**

pig·skin |'pɪgskɪn| n cinghiale m.

pig·sty |'pɪgstaɪ| n (also fig) porcile m.

pig·tail |'pɪgteɪl| n treccina.

pike |paɪk| n (fish) luccio.

pil·chard |'pɪltʃəd| n sardina.

pile[1] |paɪl| **1** n **(a)** (heap: of books, records) pila; (less tidy) mucchio, cumulo; **he put his things in a ~** ha ammucchiato le sue cose; **in a ~** ammucchiato. **(b)** (fam: large amount) mucchio, sacco; **~s of** un mucchio di; **a ~ of** una montagna di. **(c)** (fam: fortune) fortuna. **2** vt (stack) impilare; (heap) ammucchiare; **a table ~d high with books** un tavolo coperto da pile di libri. **3** vi (fam): **~ in!** salta su!; **to ~ into a car** stiparsi or ammucchiarsi in una macchina; **to ~ on/off a bus** far ressa per salire sull'autobus/scendere dall'autobus.

♦ **pile on** vt + adv: **to ~ on the pressure** (fam) fare pressione; **to ~ it on** (fam) esagerare, drammatizzare; **to ~ work on sb** caricare qn di lavoro.

♦ **pile up** vi + adv (also fig) accumularsi. **2** vt + adv ammucchiare, accumulare.

pile[2] |paɪl| n (of carpet, cloth) pelo.

pile[3] |paɪl| n (Constr) palo.

piles |paɪlz| npl (Med) emorroidi fpl.

pile-up |'paɪlʌp| n (Aut fam) tamponamento a catena.

pil·fer |'pɪlfə'| **1** vt rubacchiare. **2** vi fare dei furtarelli.

pil·grim |'pɪlgrɪm| n pellegrino/a.

pil·grim·age |'pɪlgrɪmɪdʒ| n pellegrinaggio.

pill |pɪl| n pillola; **to be on the ~** prendere la pillola.

pil·lage |'pɪlɪdʒ| **1** vt saccheggiare. **2** vi darsi al saccheggio.

pil·lar |'pɪlə'| **1** n (round) colonna; (square) pilastro; **a ~ of smoke** una colonna di fumo; **a ~ of the church** (fig) uno dei pilastri della chiesa; **to be driven from ~ to post** essere sballottato a destra e a manca. **2** cpd: **~ box** n (Brit) cassetta delle lettere (a colonnina); **~-box red** n rosso fiammante.

pil·lion |'pɪljən| **1** n sellino posteriore (di moto). **2** adv: **to ride ~** viaggiare dietro. **3** cpd: **~ passenger** n passeggero/a (che viaggia sul sellino posteriore).

pil·low |'pɪləʊ| n cuscino, guanciale m.

pillow·case |'pɪləʊkeɪs| n, **pillow·slip** |'pɪləʊslɪp| n federa.

pi·lot |'paɪlət| **1** n (Aer, Naut) pilota m/f. **2** vt (Aer, Naut) pilotare; (fig: guide) guidare, dirigere. **3** cpd (scheme etc) pilota inv; **~ boat** n pilotina; **~ light** n (on cooker etc) fiammella di sicurezza.

pi·men·to |pɪ'mɛntəʊ| n peperoncino.

pimp |pɪmp| n ruffiano.

pim·ple |'pɪmpl| n foruncolo.

pim·ply |'pɪmplɪ| adj (-ier, -iest) foruncoloso(a).

pin |pɪn| **1** n (gen, as ornament) spillo; (safety ~) spillo di sicurezza; (drawing ~) puntina da disegno; (Tech) perno; (in grenade) spoletta; (Med) chiodo; (Elec: of plug) spinotto; (Bowling) birillo; **~s and needles** formicolio; **as neat as a (new) ~** (room) come nuovo; (person) impeccabile; **you**

could have heard a **~** drop non si sentiva una mosca volare; **for two ~s I'd have hit him!** (fam) per poco non l'avrei picchiato!

2 vt **(a)** (with drawing pin) attaccare con una puntina; (sewing) attaccare con gli spilli. **(b)** (fig): **to ~ sb against a wall** mettere qn con le spalle al muro; **to ~ sb's arms to his sides** immobilizzare le braccia di qn contro i fianchi; **to ~ one's hopes on sth** riporre le proprie speranze in qc; **to ~ a crime on sb** (fam) addossare la colpa di un delitto addosso a qn.

3 cpd: **~ money** n denaro per le piccole spese.

♦ **pin down** vt + adv **(a)** (fasten or hold down) immobilizzare. **(b)** (fig): **to ~ sb down to a date** far fissare una data a qn; **to ~ sb down to a promise** costringere qn a mantenere una promessa; **to ~ sb down about his beliefs** far dire a qn quello che pensa; **there's something strange here but I can't quite ~ it down** c'è qualcosa di strano qua ma non riesco a capire cos'è.

♦ **pin up** vt + adv (notice) attaccare (al muro) con una puntina; (hair) appuntare con le forcine; (hem) appuntare con gli spilli.

pina·fore |'pɪnəfɔː'| **1** n (overall, apron) grembiule m. **2** cpd: **~ dress** n scamiciato.

pin·ball |'pɪnbɔːl| n (also: **~ machine**) flipper m inv.

pin·cers |'pɪnsəz| npl (of crab etc) pinze fpl, chele fpl; (tool) tenaglie fpl.

pinch |pɪntʃ| **1** n **(a)** (with fingers) pizzicotto; **to feel the ~** (fig) trovarsi nelle ristrettezze; **at a ~** (fig) all'occorrenza, se è (proprio) necessario; **if it comes to the ~** se le cose si mettono male. **(b)** (small quantity) pizzico, presa; **to take sth with a ~ of salt** (fig) prendere qc con un grano di sale. **2** vt **(a)** (with fingers) pizzicare; **my shoes are ~ing me** le scarpe mi vanno strette. **(b)** (fam: steal) fregare, grattare; (: idea) rubare. **(c)** (fam: arrest) pizzicare. **3** vi (shoe) essere (troppo) stretto(a); **to ~ and scrape** fare economia (su tutto).

pinched |'pɪntʃt| adj **(a)** (drawn) dai lineamenti tirati; **~ with cold** raggrinzito dal freddo; **~ with hunger** scavato dalla fame. **(b)** (short): **~ for money/space** a corto di soldi/di spazio.

pin·cushion |'pɪn,kʊʃn| n puntaspilli m inv.

pine[1] |paɪn| **1** n pino. **2** cpd: **~ cone** n pigna; **~ needle** n ago di pino; **~ nut** n, **~ kernel** n pinolo.

pine[2] |paɪn| vi: **to ~ for sb/sth** desiderare ardentemente qn/qc; **to ~ away** languire, deperire.

pine·apple |'paɪn,æpl| n ananas m inv.

ping |pɪŋ| **1** n suono metallico; (of bell) tintinnio. **2** vi (see n) produrre un suono metallico; tintinnare.

ping-pong |'pɪŋpɒŋ| n ping-pong m.

pin·ion |'pɪnjən| n (Tech) pignone m.

pink[1] |pɪŋk| **1** n **(a)** (colour) rosa m inv. **(b)** (Bot) garofano a piumino rosa. **(c):** **to be in the ~** (of health) essere in perfetta salute. **2** adj **(a)** (colour) rosa inv; **to turn ~** (flush) arrossire. **(b)** (Pol fam) con tendenze di sinistra.

pink[2] |pɪŋk| vt (Sewing) dentellare.

pinkie |'pɪŋkɪ| n (Scot fam, Am fam) mignolo.

pink·ing shears |'pɪŋkɪŋʃɪəz| npl forbici fpl a zigzag.

pin·na·cle |'pɪnəkl| n (Archit) pinnacolo; (of rock) guglia; (top of mountain) vetta, cima; (fig) apice m, vertice m.

pin·point |'pɪnpɔɪnt| vt (on map) localizzare con esattezza; (problem) mettere a fuoco, individuare con esattezza.

pin·prick |'pɪnprɪk| n puntura di spillo.

pin·stripe |'pɪnstraɪp| adj: **~ suit** gessato.

pint |paɪnt| n (measure) pinta (Brit = 0,568 litri; Am

= *0,4732 litri)*; *(Brit fam: of beer)* ≃ mezza birra.
pin·ta [ˈpaɪntə] *n (Brit fam)* pinta di latte.
pin·up (girl) [ˈpɪnʌp(ˌgɜːl)] *n* pin-up girl *f inv*.
pio·neer [ˌpaɪəˈnɪəʳ] **1** *n* pioniere/a. **2** *vt* essere un pioniere in.
pi·ous [ˈpaɪəs] *adj* pio(a); *(pej)* bigotto(a); **a ~ hope** una vana speranza.
pip[1] [pɪp] *n:* **to give sb the ~** *(Brit fam)* far venire le paturnie a qn.
pip[2] [pɪp] *n (Bot)* seme *m*; *(on card, dice)* punto; *(Brit Mil fam: on uniform)* stelletta; *(on radar screen)* segnale *m*; **the ~s** *(Telec)* il segnale acustico; *(Radio)* il segnale orario.
pip[3] [pɪp] *vt (Brit fam):* **to be ~ped at the post** essere battuto sul traguardo.
pipe [paɪp] **1** *n* **(a)** *(tube)* tubo; **~s** *(piping)* tubazione *f*, conduttura. **(b)** *(Mus: of organ)* canna; *(: wind instrument)* piffero; **(bag)~s** cornamusa. **(c)** *(smoker's)* pipa; **to smoke a ~** fumare la pipa; **put that in your ~ and smoke it!** *(fam)* che ti piaccia o no, è così! **2** *vt* **(a)** *(water, oil etc)* portare per mezzo di tubature; **~d music** musica di sottofondo. **(b)** *(Mus)* suonare (col piffero *or* con la cornamusa); *(speak or sing in high voice)* dire *(or* cantare) con un tono di voce acuto; **to ~ sb aboard** *(Naut)* salutare a bordo qn (con i tradizionali colpi di fischietto). **(c)** *(Culin):* **to ~ icing on a cake** decorare un dolce con la glassa. **3** *cpd:* **~ cleaner** *n* scovolino; **~ dream** *n* sogno impossibile.
♦ **pipe down** *vi + adv (fam)* calmarsi, star zitto(a).
♦ **pipe up** *vi + adv (fam)* farsi sentire.
pipe·line [ˈpaɪplaɪn] *n (gen)* conduttura; *(for oil)* oleodotto; *(for natural gas)* metanodotto; **it is in the ~** *(fig)* è in arrivo.
pip·er [ˈpaɪpəʳ] *n (on bagpipes)* suonatore/trice di cornamusa.
pip·ing [ˈpaɪpɪŋ] **1** *n (tubing)* tubature *fpl*; *(Sewing)* cordoncino. **2** *adv:* **~ hot** bollente.
pip·pin [ˈpɪpɪn] *n* renetta.
pi·quan·cy [ˈpiːkənsɪ] *n (of food)* gusto piccante; *(of conversation)* arguzia.
pi·quant [ˈpiːkənt] *adj (sauce)* piccante; *(conversation)* stimolante; **her face has a ~ charm** ha un volto avvincente.
pique [piːk] **1** *n* ripicca, dispetto. **2** *vt* indispettire.
pi·ra·cy [ˈpaɪərəsɪ] *n* pirateria.
pi·rate [ˈpaɪərɪt] **1** *n (also fig)* pirata *m*. **2** *vt (product)* contraffare; *(idea)* impossessarsi di; *(record, video, book)* riprodurre abusivamente. **3** *cpd:* **~ radio** *n* radio *f inv* pirata.
pi·rated [ˈpaɪərɪtɪd] *adj (book, record etc)* riprodotto(a) abusivamente.
pirou·ette [ˌpɪruˈɛt] **1** *n* piroetta. **2** *vi* piroettare.
Pi·sces [ˈpaɪsiːz] *n* Pesci *mpl*; **to be ~** essere dei Pesci.
plss [pɪs] *vi (fam)* pisciare.
pissed [pɪst] *adj (fam: drunk)* ubriaco(a) fradicio(a).
pis·ta·chio [pɪsˈtɑːʃɪəʊ] *n* pistacchio.
pis·tol [ˈpɪstl] **1** *n* pistola. **2** *cpd:* **~ shot** *n* colpo di pistola.
pis·ton [ˈpɪstən] **1** *n (gen)* stantuffo; *(Aut)* pistone *m*. **2** *cpd:* **~ engine** *n* motore *m* a pistoni; **~ rod** *n* biella.
pit[1] [pɪt] **1** *n* **(a)** *(hole in ground)* buca, fossa; *(on moon)* cratere *m*; *(coalmine)* miniera di carbone; *(quarry)* cava; *(to trap animals)* buca; **in the ~ of one's stomach** alla bocca dello stomaco; **he works down the ~(s)** lavora in miniera. **(b)** *(Aut: in garage)* fossa; *(: Motor racing)* box *m inv*. **(c)** *(Brit Theatre)* platea; **orchestra ~** fossa dell'orchestra. **2** *vt* **(a)** *(subj: chickenpox)* butterare;

(: rust) corrodere in più punti; **~ted with** *(chickenpox)* butterato da; *(potholes)* pieno di. **(b):** **to ~ A against B** mettere A a confronto con B; **to ~ one's wits against sb** misurarsi contro qn. **3** *cpd:* **~ worker** *n* minatore *m* di carbone.
pit[2] [pɪt] *n (in fruit)* nocciolo, seme *m*.
pita·pat [ˈpɪtəˈpæt] *adv:* **to go ~** *(heart)* palpitare, battere forte; *(rain)* picchiettare.
pitch[1] [pɪtʃ] *n (tar)* pece *f*.
pitch[2] [pɪtʃ] **1** *n* **(a)** *(chiefly Brit Sport)* campo. **(b)** *(angle, slope: of roof)* inclinazione *f*. **(c)** *(Naut, Aer)* beccheggio. **(d)** *(of note, voice, instrument)* intonazione *f*; *(fig: degree)* grado, punto; **I can't keep working at this ~** non posso continuare a lavorare a questo ritmo; **at its (highest) ~** al massimo, al colmo; **his anger reached such a ~ that...** la sua furia raggiunse un punto tale che... .
2 *vt* **(a)** *(throw: ball, object)* lanciare; *(: hay)* sollevare col forcone; **he was ~ed off his horse** fu sbalzato da cavallo *or* disarcionato. **(b)** *(Mus: song)* intonare; *(: note)* dare; **she can't ~ a note properly** non riesce a prendere una nota giusta; **to ~ one's aspirations too high** mirare troppo in alto; **to ~ it too strong** *(fam)* esagerare, calcare troppo la mano. **(d)** *(set up: tent)* piantare.
3 *vi* **(a)** *(fall)* cascare, cadere; **to ~ forward** essere catapultato in avanti. **(b)** *(Naut, Aer)* beccheggiare.
4 *cpd:* **~ pine** *n* pitch pine *m*.
♦ **pitch in** *vi + adv (fam)* darci dentro *or* sotto.
♦ **pitch into** *vi + prep (attack)* saltare addosso a; *(start: work, food)* attaccare, buttarsi su.
pitch-black [ˌpɪtʃˈblæk] *adj (also:* **pitch-dark**): **the room was ~** nella stanza c'era un buio pesto.
pitched [pɪtʃt] *adj:* **~ battle** *(Mil, also fig)* battaglia campale.
pitch·er[1] [ˈpɪtʃəʳ] *n (jar)* brocca.
pitch·er[2] [ˈpɪtʃəʳ] *n (Baseball)* lanciatore *m*.
pitch·fork [ˈpɪtʃfɔːk] **1** *n* forcone *m*. **2** *vt:* **to ~ sb into a job** *(fig)* costringere qn ad accettare un posto di punto in bianco.
pit·eous [ˈpɪtɪəs] *adj* pietoso(a).
pit·fall [ˈpɪtfɔːl] *n (fig)* tranello.
pith [pɪθ] *n (Bot)* midollo; *(of oranges, lemons etc)* parte *f* bianca della scorza; *(fig: core: of argument)* nocciolo, succo.
pit·head [ˈpɪthed] *n* imbocco della miniera.
pithy [ˈpɪθɪ] *adj* **(-ier, -iest)** *(fig: argument)* vigoroso(a); *(: remarks)* arguto(a); *(: account)* preciso(a).
piti·able [ˈpɪtɪəbl] *adj* pietoso(a).
piti·ful [ˈpɪtɪful] *adj* **(a)** *(sight, story)* pietoso(a); *(person)* che fa pietà *or* compassione. **(b)** *(pej: attempt)* pietoso(a); *(: cowardice)* deplorevole; *(: sum)* miserabile.
piti·ful·ly [ˈpɪtɪfəlɪ] *adv (gen)* pietosamente; *(thin etc)* da far pietà; **it's ~ obvious** è penosamente chiaro.
piti·less [ˈpɪtɪlɪs] *adj* spietato(a).
pit·tance [ˈpɪtəns] *n* miseria, somma miserabile.
pitter-patter [ˌpɪtəˈpætəʳ] = **patter**[2].
pity [ˈpɪtɪ] **1** *n* **(a)** compassione *f*, pietà *f*; **to feel ~ for sb** provare compassione per qn; **for ~'s sake!** per amor del cielo!; *(pleading)* per pietà!; **to have *or* take ~ on sb** aver pietà di qn. **(b)** *(cause of regret)* peccato; **what a ~!** che peccato!; **more's the ~** purtroppo; **it is a ~ that you can't come** è un peccato che tu non possa venire. **2** *vt* compatire, commiserare.
pity·ing [ˈpɪtɪɪŋ] *adj* compassionevole; *(with contempt)* di commiserazione.
piv·ot [ˈpɪvət] **1** *n (Mil, Tech, fig)* perno. **2** *vt* imperniare. **3** *vi* imperniarsi, essere imperniato(a).

pixie ['pɪksɪ] *n* folletto.

plac·ard ['plækɑːd] *n* cartello.

pla·cate [plə'keɪt] *vt* placare, calmare.

place [pleɪs] **1** *n* **(a)** *(in general)* posto; *(more formally)* luogo; **to take ~** *(incident)* succedere, accadere; *(meeting)* aver luogo; **we came to a ~ where...** siamo arrivati in un posto dove...; **from ~ to ~** da un posto all'altro; **this is no ~ for you** questo non è un posto per te; **~ of business** posto di lavoro; **~ of worship/birth** luogo di culto/nascita; **all over the ~** dappertutto; **to go ~s** *(travel)* andare in giro (per il mondo); **he's going ~s** *(fig fam)* si sta facendo strada; **we're going ~s at last** *(fig fam)* finalmente abbiamo sfondato; **it's only a small ~** *(town)* è solo un paesino; *(house)* è piccolina; **his ~ in the country** la sua casa in campagna; **come to our ~** venite da noi *or* a casa nostra; **to put sth back in its ~** rimettere qc al suo posto; **that remark was quite out of ~** quell'osservazione era proprio fuori luogo; **I feel rather out of ~ here** qui mi sento un po' fuori posto; **this isn't the ~ to discuss politics!** questo non è il posto giusto per discutere di politica!; **to change ~s with sb** scambiare il posto con qn; **to take the ~ of sb/sth** sostituire qn/qc, prendere il posto di qn/qc; **in ~ of** al posto di, invece di.

(b) *(in street names)* via; **market ~** piazza del mercato.

(c) *(in book)*: **to find one's ~** trovare la pagina giusta; **to lose one's ~** perdere il segno.

(d) *(seat)* posto (a sedere); *(: at table)* posto (a tavola); *(: in restaurant)* coperto; **to lay an extra ~ for sb** aggiungere un posto a tavola per qn.

(e) *(job, vacancy in team, school etc)* posto; **he found a ~ for his nephew in the firm** ha trovato un posto a suo nipote nella ditta.

(f) *(social position etc)* posizione *f*, rango; **friends in high ~s** amici altolocati *or* nelle alte sfere; **to know one's ~** *(fig)* sapere stare al proprio posto; **it is not my ~ to do it** non sta a me farlo; **to put sb in his ~** *(fig)* mettere a posto qn, mettere qn al suo posto.

(g) *(in series, rank etc)*: **in the first/second ~** in primo/secondo luogo; **she took second ~ in the race** si è piazzata *or* è arrivata seconda nella gara; **she took second ~ in the exam** ha preso il secondo miglior voto nell'esame; **A won with B in second ~** A ha vinto e B è finito secondo.

2 *vt* **(a)** *(put: gen)* posare, mettere; **~ it on the table** mettilo *or* posalo sul tavolo; **we should ~ no trust in that** non dovremmo farci nessun affidamento.

(b) *(town)* situare; *(picture)* mettere; *(person)* piazzare; **we are better ~d than a month ago** siamo in una situazione migliore *or* siamo messi meglio di un mese fa; **awkwardly ~d** *(shop)* piazzato male; *(fig: person)* messo male; *(: in embarrassing situation)* in una posizione delicata.

(c) *(contract, bet)* fare; *(goods)* piazzare; **to ~ an order with sb (for)** fare un'ordinazione a qn (di); **to ~ a book with a publisher** trovare un editore per un libro; **to ~ sth in sb's hands** mettere qc nelle mani di qn; **we could ~ 200 men** possiamo procurare lavoro a 200 uomini.

(d) *(in exam, race etc)* classificare; **to be ~d second** classificarsi *or* piazzarsi al secondo posto.

(e) *(recall, identify: person)* ricordarsi di; *(: face, accent)* riconoscere; **I can't ~ him** non riesco a ricordarmi dove l'ho visto.

3 *cpd*: **~ card** *n* segnaposto; **~ mat** *n (in wood etc)* sottopiatto; *(in linen etc)* tovaglietta; **~ name** *n* toponimo.

pla·cebo [plə'siːbəʊ] *n* placebo *m inv.*

pla·cen·ta [plə'sentə] *n* placenta.

plac·id ['plæsɪd] *adj* placido(a).

pla·gia·rism ['pleɪdʒərɪzəm] *n* plagio.

pla·gia·rize ['pleɪdʒəraɪz] *vt* plagiare.

plague [pleɪg] **1** *n (disease, also fig)* peste *f*; *(of rats, locusts)* invasione *f*; **to avoid sb/sth like the ~** evitare qn/qc come la peste. **2** *vt (fig)* tormentare; **to ~ sb with questions** assillare qn di domande.

plaice [pleɪs] *n* passera di mare.

plaid [plæd] *n (cloth)* tessuto scozzese.

plain [pleɪn] **1** *adj* **(-er, -est) (a)** *(clear, obvious)* chiaro(a), evidente; *(path, track)* ben segnato(a); **it's as ~ as a pikestaff** *or* **as the nose on your face** *(fam)* è chiaro come il sole; **you have made your feelings ~ to sb** ti sei spiegato benissimo; **to make sth ~ to sb** far capire chiaramente qc a qn; **do I make myself ~?** mi sono spiegato?

(b) *(outspoken, honest)* franco(a), schietto(a); **~ dealing** sincerità, franchezza; **in ~ language** *or* **English** in parole povere; **I shall be ~ with you** sarò franco con te.

(c) *(simple, with nothing added)* semplice; *(paper: unlined)* non rigato(a); *(fabric: in one colour)* in tinta unita; **the ~ truth** la pura verità; **he's a ~ man** è un uomo semplice; **~ stitch** *(Knitting)* maglia a diritto; **it's just ~ commonsense** *(fam)* è una questione di semplice buon senso; **to send sth under ~ cover** spedire qc in busta riservata.

(d) *(not pretty)* bruttino(a).

2 *adv* **(a)** *(fam: simply, completely)* semplicemente, veramente.

(b): **I can't put it ~er than that** non posso esprimermi più chiaramente.

3 *n* **(a)** *(Geog)* pianura.

(b) *(Knitting)* (maglia a) diritto.

4 *cpd*: **~ chocolate** *n* cioccolato fondente; **~ clothes** *npl*: **in ~ clothes** in borghese; **~ flour** *n* farina; **~ sailing** *n (fam)*: **it'll be ~ sailing from now on** d'ora in poi andrà tutto liscio.

plain·ly ['pleɪnlɪ] *adv (clearly)* chiaramente; *(speak)* con franchezza; *(dress)* con semplicità, sobriamente.

plain·ness ['pleɪnnɪs] *n (simplicity)* semplicità; *(lack of beauty)* insignificanza.

plain-spoken [,pleɪn'spəʊkən] *adj (person)* franco(a), schietto(a); *(criticism)* senza mezze parole.

plain·tiff ['pleɪntɪf] *n* attore/trice.

plain·tive ['pleɪntɪv] *adj (voice, song)* lamentoso(a); *(look)* struggente; **~ cry** lamento.

plait [plæt] **1** *n* treccia. **2** *vt (raffia)* intrecciare; **to ~ one's hair** farsi una treccia (or le trecce).

plan [plæn] **1** *n* **(a)** *(scheme)* piano, progetto; *(Pol, Econ etc)* piano; **~ of campaign** *(Mil)* piano di battaglia; **development ~** piano *or* progetto di sviluppo; **to draw up a ~** fare *or* elaborare un programma; **if everything goes according to ~** se tutto va secondo le previsioni *or* il previsto; **to make ~s** far programmi *or* progetti; **the best ~ would be to...** la cosa migliore sarebbe...; **have you got any ~s for today?** che programmi hai per oggi? **(b)** *(diagram, map: of building, town)* pianta; *(: for novel, speech)* schema *m*.

2 *vt* **(a)** *(arrange: robbery, holiday, campaign)* organizzare; *(economy, research)* pianificare; *(essay)* fare lo schema di; **to ~ one's family** praticare il controllo delle nascite. **(b)** *(intend)* avere in progetto; **to ~ to do** avere l'intenzione di fare; **how long do you ~ to stay?** quanto conti di restare? **(c)** *(design)* progettare; **a well-~ned town** una città che ha un buon piano urbanistico.

3 *vi*: **to ~ (for)** far progetti (per); **one has to ~ months ahead** bisogna cominciare a pensarci diversi mesi prima; **to ~ on sth/on doing sth** contare su qc/di fare qc.

plane[1] [pleɪn] *n (Bot)* platano.

plane[2] [pleɪn] **1** *adj (Geom)* piano(a). **2** *n* **(a)** *(Art, Math etc)* piano. **(b)** *(fig)* piano, livello. **(c)** *(tool)* pialla. **3** *vt* piallare; **to ~ sth smooth** levigare qc con la pialla. **4** *vi (bird, glider, boat)* planare.

plane[3] [pleɪn] *n (abbr of* **aeroplane, airplane)** aereo.

plan·et ['plænɪt] *n* pianeta *m*.

plan·etar·ium [,plænɪ'tɛərɪəm] *n* planetario.

plank [plæŋk] *n (of wood)* tavola.

plank·ton ['plæŋktən] *n* plancton *m inv*.

plan·ner ['plænə'] *n* pianificatore/trice, progettista *m/f*; **town ~** urbanista *m/f*.

plan·ning ['plænɪŋ] **1** *n (Pol, Econ)* pianificazione *f; (Industry)* progettazione *f*. **2** *cpd:* **~ committee** *n (in local government)* commissione *f* urbanistica; **~ permission** *n* permesso di costruzione.

plant [plɑːnt] **1** *n* **(a)** *(Bot)* pianta; **(b)** *(no pl: machinery etc)* impianto; *(factory)* stabilimento. **2** *vt* **(a)** *(trees, seeds, flowers)* piantare; **to ~ a field with corn** piantare *or* coltivare un terreno a grano. **(b)** *(stick: pole etc)* piantare, conficcare; *(bomb)* mettere; *(kiss)* stampare; **to ~ an idea in sb's mind** ficcare *or* cacciare in testa un'idea a qn; **he ~ed himself right in her path** le si è piantato di fronte; **to ~ sth on sb** *(fam)* nascondere qc su qn per incriminarlo. **3** *cpd:* **~ life** *n* flora; **~ pot** *n* vaso (di fiori).

plan·ta·tion [plæn'teɪʃən] *n* piantagione *f*.

plant·er ['plɑːntə'] *n (person)* piantatore/trice; *(machine)* piantatrice *f*.

plaque [plæk] *n (on building etc)* placca, targa; *(on teeth)* placca batterica.

plas·ma ['plæzmə] *n* plasma *m*.

plas·ter ['plɑːstə'] **1** *n* **(a)** *(Constr)* intonaco. **(b)** *(Med: for broken leg etc)* gesso; **with his leg in ~** con la gamba ingessata. **(c)** *(Brit: sticking ~)* cerotto. **2** *vt* **(a)** *(Constr)* intonacare. **(b)** *(fam: cover)* impiastricciare; **to be ~ed with** *(mud)* essere impiastricciato di; **to ~ a wall with posters** tappezzare un muro di manifesti. **3** *cpd:* **~ cast** *n (Med)* ingessatura, gesso; *(model, statue)* modello in gesso; **~ of Paris** *n* gesso.

plaster·board ['plɑːstə'bɔːd] *n* lastra di cartone ingessato.

plas·tered ['plɑːstəd] *adj (fam: drunk)* ubriaco(a) fradicio(a).

plas·ter·er ['plɑːstərə'] *n* intonacatore *m*.

plas·tic ['plæstɪk] **1** *n* plastica, materia plastica; **~s** materie plastiche. **2** *adj* **(a)** *(made of ~)* di plastica. **(b)** *(flexible)* plastico(a); **the ~ arts** le arti plastiche. **3** *cpd:* **~ bag** *n* sacchetto di plastica; **~ explosive** *n* plastico; **~s industry** *n* industria delle materie plastiche; **~ surgery** *n* chirurgia plastica.

plas·ti·cine ['plæstɪsiːn] *n*® plastilina®.

plate [pleɪt] **1** *n* **(a)** *(flat dish, ~ful)* piatto; *(for church collection)* piatto delle elemosine; **to hand sb sth on a ~** *(fig fam)* offrire qc a qn su un piatto d'argento; **to have a lot on one's ~** *(fig fam)* avere un sacco di cose da fare. **(b):** **gold/silver ~** vasellame *m* d'oro/d'argento; *(electroplated)* metallo placcato in oro/in argento. **(c)** *(Phot)* lastra; *(Tech)* placca; *(on door)* targa, targhetta; *(Aut: number ~)* targa; *(on cooker: hot ~)* piastra. **(d)** *(dental ~)* dentiera. **(e)** *(book illustration)* tavola fuori testo. **2** *vt (gen)* placcare; *(with gold)* dorare; *(with silver)* argentare; **chromium ~d**

cromato. **3** *cpd:* **~ glass** *n* vetro piano; **~ rack** *n* scolapiatti *m inv*.

plat·eau ['plætəʊ] *n, pl* **~s** *or* **~x** *(Geog)* altopiano.

plat·form ['plætfɔːm] **1** *n (on bus)* piattaforma; *(at meeting, for band)* palco; *(Pol)* piattaforma, programma *m* (di base); *(Rail)* marciapiede *m*, banchina; **the train leaves from ~ 7** il treno parte dal binario 7. **2** *cpd:* **~ shoe** *n* scarpa a suola alta; **~ ticket** *n* biglietto d'ingresso ai binari.

plat·ing ['pleɪtɪŋ] *n (gold/silver ~)* placcatura; *(chrome ~)* cromatura.

plati·num ['plætɪnəm] *n* platino; **a ~ blonde** una bionda platinata.

plati·tude ['plætɪtjuːd] *n* luogo comune, banalità *f inv*.

pla·ton·ic [plə'tɒnɪk] *adj* platonico(a).

pla·toon [plə'tuːn] *n (Mil)* plotone *m*.

plat·ter ['plætə'] *n* piatto da portata.

plau·sible ['plɔːzəbl] *adj (argument, story)* plausibile, credibile; *(person)* convincente.

plau·sibly ['plɔːzəblɪ] *adv* in modo convincente.

play [pleɪ] **1** *n* **(a)** *(recreation)* gioco; **the children were at ~** i bambini giocavano; **to do/say sth in ~** fare/dire qc per scherzo; **a ~ on words** un gioco di parole.

(b) *(Sport)* gioco; **~ began at 3 o'clock** la partita è cominciata alle 3; **there was some good ~ in the first half** ci sono state delle belle azioni nel primo tempo; **to be in/out of ~** *(ball)* essere in/fuori gioco.

(c) *(Theatre)* commedia; **radio/television ~** commedia radiofonica/per la televisione.

(d) *(Tech etc)* gioco; **there's not enough ~ in the rope** la fune non ha abbastanza gioco.

(e) *(fig phrases):* **to bring** *or* **call into ~** *(plan)* mettere in azione; *(emotions)* esprimere; **to give full ~ to one's imagination** dare libero sfogo alla propria fantasia; **to make great ~ of sth** giocare molto su qc; **to make a ~ for sb** fare il filo a qn; **to make a ~ for sth** darsi da fare per ottenere qc; **the ~ of light on the water** i giochi di luce sull'acqua.

2 *vt* **(a)** *(game, card)* giocare; *(cards, chess, tennis etc)* giocare a; *(opponent)* giocare contro; *(chesspiece)* muovere; **to ~ a game of tennis** giocare una partita a tennis; **to ~ sb at chess** giocare contro qn a scacchi; **they ~ed him in goal** l'hanno fatto giocare in porta; **don't ~ games with me** non prendermi in giro; **to ~ a trick on sb** fare uno scherzo a qn; **my eyes must be ~ing tricks on me** devo avere le traveggole; **to ~ the field** *(fig)* cercare di farsi strada in varie attività; **to ~ a fish** *(Angling)* stancare un pesce.

(b) *(perform: role)* interpretare; *(: play)* rappresentare, dare; *(perform in: town)* esibirsi a, dare uno spettacolo *(or* una serie di spettacoli) a; **to ~ sth for laughs** interpretare qc in chiave comica.

(c) *(Mus etc)* suonare; *(record)* mettere; *(radio)* ascoltare.

(d) *(direct: light, hose)* puntare, dirigere.

3 *vi* **(a)** *(gen)* giocare; **to ~ at tennis** giocare a tennis; **to go out to ~** andar fuori a giocare; **to ~ with a stick** giocherellare con un bastone; **they're ~ing at soldiers** stanno giocando ai soldati; **to ~ with fire** *(fig)* scherzare col fuoco; **to ~ for money** giocare a soldi; **to ~ for time** *(fig)* cercare di guadagnar tempo; **to ~ into sb's hands** *(fig)* fare il gioco di qn; **to ~ safe** giocare sul sicuro; **to ~ for high ~** il prezioso; **what are you ~ing at?** *(fam)* cosa cavolo stai facendo?; **he's just ~ing at it** non lo sta prendendo sul serio.

(b) *(move about, form patterns)*: we watched the fountains ~ing guardavamo i giochi d'acqua delle fontane; **the sun was ~ing on the water** il sole creava giochi di luce sull'acqua; **a smile** ~ed on his lips un sorriso gli sfiorò le labbra.

(c) *(Mus)* suonare; *(radio)* essere acceso(a); **the radio is ~ing too loudly** il volume della radio è troppo alto; **to ~ on the piano** suonare il piano.

(d) *(Theatre, Cine)* recitare (una parte); **to ~ dead** *(fig)* fare il morto.

♦ **play about, play around** *vi + adv (person)* divertirsi; **to ~ about** *or* **around with** *(fiddle with)* giocherellare con; *(idea)* accarezzare.

♦ **play along 1** *vi + adv*: **to ~ along with** *(fig: person)* stare al gioco di; *(: plan, idea)* fingere di assecondare. **2** *vt + adv*: **to ~ sb along** *(fig)* tenere qn in sospeso.

♦ **play back** *vt + adv* riascoltare, risentire.

♦ **play down** *vt + adv* minimizzare.

♦ **play off 1** *vt + adv*: **to ~ X off against Y** mettere X e Y l'uno(a) contro l'altro(a). **2** *vi + adv (Sport)* giocare lo spareggio.

♦ **play on 1** *vi + adv (Sport)* continuare a giocare. *(Mus)* continuare a suonare. **2** *vi + prep (sb's feelings, credulity)* giocare su; **to ~ on sb's nerves** dare sui nervi a qn.

♦ **play out** *vt + adv*: **to be ~ed out** *(vein in mine)* essere esaurito(a); *(joke, argument)* essere (ormai) sfruttato(a).

♦ **play through** *vt + adv* suonare.

♦ **play up 1** *vi + adv* **(a)** *(Brit fam: cause trouble: child, engine)* fare dei capricci; *(: leg, ulcer)* farsi sentire. **(b)** *(fam: flatter)*: **to ~ up to sb** arruffianarsi qn. **2** *vt + adv (fam)* **(a)** *(cause trouble to)*: **to ~ sb up** *(subj: child)* combinarne di tutti i colori a qn; *(: leg)* fare male a qn. **(b)** *(exaggerate)* esagerare, gonfiare.

play·act ['pleɪækt] *vi (fig)* fare la commedia.

play·bill ['pleɪbɪl] *n* manifesto (di teatro), locandina.

play·boy ['pleɪbɔɪ] *n* playboy *m inv*.

play·er ['pleɪə'] *n (Sport)* giocatore/trice; *(Mus)* suonatore/trice; *(Theatre)* attore/trice.

play·ful ['pleɪfʊl] *adj (child, puppy)* giocherellone(a); *(mood, smile, remark)* scherzoso(a).

play·ground ['pleɪgraʊnd] *n (in school)* cortile *m* per la ricreazione; *(in park)* parco *m* giochi inv.

play·group ['pleɪgruːp] *n* kindergarten *m inv*, giardino d'infanzia.

play·house ['pleɪhaʊs] *n (theatre)* teatro; *(for children)* casetta per i giochi.

play·ing ['pleɪɪŋ] **1** *adj*: **~ card** carta da gioco; **~ field** campo da gioco. **2** *n*: **some fine ~** *(Sport)* delle belle azioni.

play·mate ['pleɪmeɪt] *n* compagno/a di gioco.

play·off ['pleɪɒf] *n (Sport)* (partita di) spareggio.

play·pen ['pleɪpɛn] *n* box *m inv (per bimbi)*.

play·room ['pleɪrʊm] *n* stanza dei giochi.

play·thing ['pleɪθɪŋ] *n (also fig)* giocattolo.

play·time ['pleɪtaɪm] *n (Scol)* ricreazione *f*.

play·wright ['pleɪraɪt] *n* commediografo/a, drammaturgo/a.

plea [pliː] *n* **(a)** *(entreaty: for donations)* appello; *(: for leniency)* supplica; *(excuse)* scusa, pretesto; **on the ~ of** con la scusa di. **(b)** *(Law)*: **to enter a ~ of guilty** dichiararsi colpevole; **to put forward a ~ of self-defence** invocare la legittima difesa.

plead [pliːd] *pt, pp* **~ed** *or (esp Am)* **pled 1** *vt* **(a)** *(argue)* difendere; **to ~ sb's case** *(Law)*, **to ~ sb's cause** *(fig)* perorare la causa di qn. **(b)** *(as excuse: ignorance)* addurre come pretesto; *(Law)*: **to ~ insanity** dichiararsi infermo mentale. **2** *vi* **(a)** *(beg)*: **to ~ with sb (to do sth)** supplicare *or* im-

plorare qn (di fare qc); **to ~ for sth** *(beg for)* implorare qc; *(make speech in favour of)* parlare in favore di qc. **(b)** *(Law: lawyer)*: **to ~ for/against** perorare in favore di/contro; **to ~ guilty/not guilty** *(defendant)* dichiararsi colpevole/innocente.

plead·ing ['pliːdɪŋ] **1** *n (entreaties)* suppliche *fpl*. **2** *adj* supplichevole.

pleas·ant ['plɛznt] *adj (gen)* piacevole; *(surprise, news)* bello(a); *(smell)* gradevole, buono(a); *(people, smile)* simpatico(a); *(weather)* bello(a); **we had a ~ time** ci siamo divertiti.

pleas·ant·ly ['plɛzntlɪ] *adv (behave, smile, greet)* cordialmente; **I am ~ surprised** sono piacevolmente sorpreso.

pleas·ant·ness ['plɛzntnɪs] *n (of person)* amabilità; *(of place)* amenità.

pleas·ant·ry ['plɛzntrɪ] *n (joke)* battuta di spirito, spiritosaggine *f*; *(polite remark)*: **to exchange pleasantries** scambiarsi i convenevoli.

please [pliːz] **1** *excl* per piacere, per favore; (yes,) **~** sì, grazie; **come in, ~** entrate, prego; **~ pass the salt, pass the salt ~** per piacere *or* per favore, mi passi il sale?; **~ don't cry!** ti prego, non piangere! **2** *vi* **(a)**: **if you ~** *(frm: in request)* per piacere, per favore; **he wanted 10, if you ~!** ne voleva 10, figurati!; **he does as he ~s** fa' come gli pare. **(b)** *(cause satisfaction)* far piacere, piacere; **anxious** *or* **eager to ~** desideroso di piacere; **a gift that is sure to ~** un dono sicuramente gradito. **3** *vt (give pleasure to)* far piacere a; *(satisfy)* accontentare; **I did it just to ~ you** l'ho fatto per farti piacere; **there's no pleasing him** non c'è verso di accontentarlo; **to ~ o.s.** far come si vuole; **~ yourself!** come vuoi!, come ti pare!

pleased [pliːzd] *adj (happy)* felice, lieto(a); *(satisfied)* contento(a), soddisfatto(a); **to be ~ (about sth)** essere contento (di qc); **~ to meet you!** *(fam)* piacere!; **I am not ~ at your decision** la tua decisione non mi ha fatto piacere; **to be ~ with sb/sth** essere contento *or* soddisfatto di qn/qc; **to be ~ with o.s.** compiacersi, essere compiaciuto di sé; **we are ~ to inform you that...** abbiamo il piacere di informarla che...

pleas·ing ['pliːzɪŋ] *adj (person)* simpatico(a); *(news, sight)* piacevole, che fa piacere.

pleas·ur·able ['plɛʒərəbl] *adj (molto)* piacevole.

pleas·ure ['plɛʒə'] **1** *n* **(a)** *(satisfaction, happiness)* piacere *m*; **with ~** con piacere, volentieri; **my ~!, the ~ is mine!** *(frm: returning thanks)* prego!, il piacere è (tutto) mio!; **I have much ~ in informing you that...** sono lieto di informarla che...; **may I have the ~?** *(frm: at dance)* mi concede l'onore di questo ballo?; **Mr and Mrs Smith request the ~ of your company** *(frm)* i Signori Smith gradirebbero averla come ospite.

(b) *(source of ~)* piacere *m*; **all the ~s of London** tutti i divertimenti di Londra; **is this trip for business or ~?** è un viaggio d'affari o di piacere?

(c) *(frm: will)* desiderio, volontà; **at sb's ~** secondo i desideri di qn; **we await your ~** *(Comm)* siamo a vostra disposizione; **to be detained during her Majesty's ~** *(Law)* = essere trattenuto secondo le disposizioni delle autorità competenti.

2 *cpd (cruise)* di piacere; **~ boat** *n* battello da diporto.

pleasure-loving ['plɛʒə,lʌvɪŋ] *adj*: **she's a ~ person** è amante dei piaceri.

pleat [pliːt] **1** *n* piega. **2** *vt* pieghettare.

ple·beian [plɪ'biːən] *adj, n* plebeo(a) *(m/f)*.

pled [plɛd] *(esp Am) pt, pp of* **plead**.

pledge |plɛdʒ| 1 n (security, token) pegno; (promise) promessa solenne; **to be under a ~ of secrecy** aver promesso di mantenere il segreto; **as a ~ of** come pegno or testimonianza di; **to sign** or **take the ~** (hum fam) promettere solennemente di non toccare alcool. 2 vt (a) (promise): **to ~ sth/to do sth** promettere qc/di fare qc; **to ~ sb to secrecy** far promettere a qn di mantenere il segreto; **to ~ support for sb** impegnarsi a sostenere qn. (b) (pawn) impegnare.

ple·na·ry |'pliːnərı| adj plenario(a); **in ~ session** in seduta plenaria.

pleni·po·ten·ti·ary |ˌplɛnıpə'tɛnʃərı| 1 n plenipotenziario. 2 adj plenipotenziario(a).

plen·ti·ful |'plɛntıfʊl| adj abbondante; **to be in ~ supply** abbondare, esserci in gran quantità.

plen·ty |'plɛntı| n (a) abbondanza; **in ~** (in large quantities) in abbondanza; **land of ~** paese m di Cuccagna. (b): **~ of** (lots of) molto(a), tanto(a); (enough) abbastanza; **he has ~ of friends** ha tanti amici; **I've got ~** ne ho abbastanza; **there's ~ to go on** (information) ci sono indizi più che sufficienti; **we've got ~ of time to get there** abbiamo abbastanza tempo per arrivarci.

pleu·ri·sy |'plʊərısı| n pleurite f.

pli·able |'plaıəbl| adj (substance) pieghevole, flessibile; (of: person) malleabile.

pli·ers |'plaıəz| npl (also: **pair of ~**) pinze fpl.

plight |plaıt| n situazione f (critica); **the country's economic ~** le gravi condizioni economiche del paese.

plim·soll |'plımsəl| n (Brit) scarpa da tennis.

plinth |plınθ| n plinto.

plod |plɒd| vi: **to ~ up/down** etc trascinarsi su per/giù per etc; **to ~ away at sth** (fig) sgobbare su qc; **we must ~ on** (fig) dobbiamo farci forza e tirare avanti.

plod·der |'plɒdə'| n sgobbone/a.

plonk[1] |plɒŋk| n (Brit fam: wine) vino ordinario.

plonk[2] |plɒŋk| 1 n (sound) tonfo. 2 adv: **~ in the middle** nel bel mezzo. 3 vt (fam: also: **~ down**) appoggiare pesantemente; **to ~ o.s. down** lasciarsi cadere di peso; **there's ~ to yourself down** siediti.

plop |plɒp| 1 n plop m inv. 2 vi (stone) fare plop.

plot[1] |plɒt| n (of land) appezzamento; **a vegetable ~** un orticello.

plot[2] |plɒt| n (a) (conspiracy) complotto, congiura. (b) (Literature, Theatre) intreccio, trama. 2 vt (a) (course, graph etc) tracciare; **to ~ one's position** (Naut) fare il punto. (b) (conspire) complottare, tramare. 3 vi complottare.

plough, (Am) **plow** |plaʊ| 1 n aratro; **the P~** (Astron) l'Orsa Maggiore, il Gran Carro. 2 vt (field) arare; (furrow) scavare; **to ~ one's way through a book** (fig) leggere con fatica un libro. 3 vi (fig) arare; **the car ~ed into the wall** l'auto ha sfondato il muro; **to ~ through the mud** avanzare a fatica nel fango.

♦ **plough back** vt + adv (profits) reinvestire.

♦ **plough up** vt + adv (field) arare, dissodare.

plough·man, (Am) **plow·man** |'plaʊmən| n, pl **-men** aratore m; **~'s lunch** semplice pasto a base di pane, formaggio e birra.

plow |plaʊ| (Am) = **plough**.

ploy |plɔı| n stratagemma m, manovra.

pluck |plʌk| 1 n (courage) coraggio, fegato. 2 vt (fruit, flower) cogliere; (also: **~ out**) strappare; (Mus: strings) pizzicare; (: guitar) pizzicare le corde di; (Culin) spennare; **to ~ one's eyebrows** depilarsi le sopracciglia; **to ~ up (one's) courage** farsi coraggio, armarsi di coraggio. 3 vi: **to ~ at sb's sleeve** tirare qn per la manica.

plucky |'plʌkı| adj (**-ier, -iest**) coraggioso(a).

plug |plʌg| 1 n (a) (of bath, basin, barrel, volcano) tappo; (for stopping a leak) tampone m. (b) (Elec) spina; (Aut: spark ~) candela. (c) (fam: piece of publicity) pubblicità f inv, réclame f inv; **to give sb/sth a ~** fare pubblicità a qn/qc. 2 vt (a) (also: **~ up**) tappare; (tooth) otturare. (b) (insert) infilare, cacciare; **to ~ a lead into a socket** mettere un filo in una presa di corrente. (c) (fam: publicize) fare pubblicità a; (: push, put forward) fare propaganda a.

♦ **plug away** vi + adv (fam): **to ~ away (at sth)** sgobbare (su qc).

♦ **plug in** (Elec) 1 vi + adv inserire la spina; **the TV ~s in behind the table** la presa per la TV è dietro il tavolo. 2 vt + adv attaccare a una presa.

plug·hole |'plʌghəʊl| n scarico.

plum |plʌm| 1 n (fruit) prugna, susina; (also: **~ tree**) prugno, susino; **a real ~** (of a job) (fig fam) un lavoro favoloso. 2 cpd (a) (tart, tree) di prugne; (**~-coloured**) color prugna inv. (b) (fig fam: job) favoloso(a).

plum·age |'pluːmıdʒ| n piume fpl, piumaggio.

plumb |plʌm| 1 n piombo. 2 adv (fam): **~ in the middle** esattamente nel centro; **he's ~ stupid** (Am) è proprio stupido. 3 vt scandagliare; (sb's mind) sondare; **to ~ the depths** scandagliare gli abissi; (fig) toccare il fondo. 4 cpd: **~ bob** n piombino; **~ line** n filo a piombo; (Naut) scandaglio.

♦ **plumb in** vt + adv (washing machine) collegare all'impianto idraulico.

plumb·er |'plʌmə'| n idraulico.

plumb·ing |'plʌmıŋ| n (craft) lavoro or mestiere m di idraulico; (piping) impianto idraulico.

plume |pluːm| n piuma, penna; (on hat, helmet) penna, pennacchio; **a ~ of smoke** un pennacchio di fumo.

plum·met |'plʌmıt| vi (bird) calare a piombo; (plane) precipitare; (temperature, price, sales) calare bruscamente; (spirits, morale) calare a zero.

plump |plʌmp| adj (**-er, -est**) (person, arms, chicken) bene in carne; (cheeks, face) paffuto(a); (wallet, cushion) (bello(a)) gonfio(a).

♦ **plump down** 1 vt + adv lasciar cadere di peso. 2 vi + adv lasciarsi cadere di peso or di schianto.

♦ **plump for** vi + prep decidersi per.

♦ **plump up** vt + adv sprimacciare.

plun·der |'plʌndə'| 1 n (act) saccheggio; (loot) bottino. 2 vt (gen) saccheggiare; (villagers) depredare; (objects) far man bassa di.

plunge |plʌndʒ| 1 n (dive) tuffo; (fig: into debt, of currency etc) caduta; (rash investment) speculazione f azzardata; **to take the ~** (fig) buttarsi, fare il gran passo.

2 vt (a) (immerse) immergere, tuffare; (thrust: knife) conficcare; (: hand) ficcare, tuffare; **he was ~d forwards when the bus braked suddenly** quando l'autobus frenò bruscamente fu sbalzato in avanti; **to ~ a dagger into sb's chest** conficcare un pugnale nel petto di qn. (b) (fig): **to ~ a room into darkness** far piombare una stanza nel buio; **we were ~d into gloom by the news** la notizia ci ha gettato nella costernazione; **to ~ sb into debt** precipitare qn nei debiti.

3 vi (a) (dive) tuffarsi. (b) (fall) precipitare; **he ~d to his death** ha fatto una caduta mortale. (c) (share prices, currency etc) calare precipitosamente; **to ~ into debt** riempirsi di debiti. (d) (fig: rush): **to ~ into one's work** buttarsi a capofitto nel proprio lavoro; **to ~ heedlessly into danger** buttarsi allo sbaraglio.

plung·er ['plʌndʒər] n (for clearing drain) sturala-
vandini m inv.

plung·ing ['plʌndʒɪŋ] adj (neckline) profondo(a);
(back of dress) profondamente scollato(a).

plu·per·fect [,plu:'pɜ:fɪkt] n (Gram) piuccheperfetto.

plu·ral ['plʊərəl] **1** adj (Gram: form) plurale, del
plurale; (noun, verb) plurale, al plurale. **2** n
(Gram) plurale m; **in the** ~ al plurale.

plus [plʌs] **1** prep più. **2** adj (Math, Elec) positivo(a);
twenty ~ più di venti; **you must be 20** ~ devi
avere vent'anni compiuti; **a** ~ **factor** (fig) un
vantaggio. **3** n (Math: ~ sign) più m inv; (fig:
advantage) vantaggio.

plush [plʌʃ] n felpa. **2** adj (also: **plushy**: fam)
sontuoso(a), lussuoso(a).

Pluto ['plu:təʊ] n (Astron, Mythology) Plutone m.

plu·toc·ra·cy [,plu:'tɒkrəsɪ] n plutocrazia.

plu·to·crat ['plu:təʊkræt] n plutocrate m/f.

plu·to·nium [plu:'təʊnɪəm] n plutonio.

ply¹ [plaɪ] n: **three-~ wood** compensato a tre strati;
three-~ wool lana a tre capi.

ply² [plaɪ] **1** vt (knitting needle, tool etc) maneggiare; (sea, river, route) viaggiare regolarmente su;
to ~ **one's trade** esercitare il proprio mestiere;
to ~ **sb with questions** continuare a far domande
a qn; **to** ~ **sb with drink** continuare a offrir da
bere a qn. **2** vi: **to** ~ **between** far la spola fra, fare
servizio regolare fra; **to** ~ **for hire** andare avanti
e indietro in attesa di clienti.

ply·wood ['plaɪwʊd] n (legno) compensato.

P.M. abbr of **Prime Minister**.

p.m. abbr (= post meridiem) del pomeriggio.

pneu·mat·ic [nju:'mætɪk] adj pneumatico(a); ~
drill martello pneumatico.

pneu·mo·nia [nju:'məʊnɪə] n polmonite f.

P.O. abbr (= Post Office) P.T.

poach¹ [pəʊtʃ] vt (Culin: fish) cuocere in bianco;
~**ed egg** uovo affogato or in camicia.

poach² [pəʊtʃ] **1** vt (hunt: game) cacciare di frodo;
(fish) pescare di frodo; (fig fam: steal) soffiare,
portar via. **2** vi cacciare (or pescare) di frodo; **to**
~ **on sb's preserves** (fig) invadere il campo di qn.

poach·er ['pəʊtʃər] n (of game) bracconiere m.

poach·ing ['pəʊtʃɪŋ] n bracconaggio.

pock·et ['pɒkɪt] **1** n (in garment etc) tasca; **breast** ~
taschino; **with his hands in his** ~s con le mani in
tasca; **to have sb in one's** ~ (fig) tenere in pugno
qn; **to have sth in one's** ~ (fig) avere qc (già) in
tasca, tenere in pugno qc; **to be in** ~ guadagnarci; **to be out of** ~ rimetterci; **to be £5 in/out of** ~
trovarsi con 5 sterline in più/in meno; **to line
one's** ~s arricchirsi, fare i soldi; **to put one's
hand in one's** ~ (fig) metter mano al portafoglio;
to go through sb's ~s frugare le tasche di qn; **to
live in each other's** ~s rimanere or essere sempre appiccicati; ~ **of resistance/warm air** sacca
di resistenza/di aria calda; **air** ~ vuoto d'aria.

2 vt (fig: gain, steal) intascare; **to** ~ **one's pride**
(fig) metter da parte l'orgoglio.

3 cpd (edition, calculator) tascabile; ~ **hand·
kerchief** n fazzoletto; ~ **money** n (of child) stipendio (settimanale).

pocket·book ['pɒkɪtbʊk] n (wallet) portafoglio;
(notebook) taccuino; (Am: handbag) busta;
(: paperback) tascabile m.

pocket·knife ['pɒkɪtnaɪf] n, pl -**knives** temperino.

pocket·size(d) ['pɒkɪtsaɪz(d)] adj (book) tascabile;
(garden) piccolissimo(a).

pock·marked ['pɒkmɑ:kt] adj (face) butterato(a);
(surface) bucherellato(a).

pod [pɒd] n baccello.

podgy ['pɒdʒɪ] adj (-ier, -iest) grassottello(a).

po·dia·trist [pɒ'di:ətrɪst] n (Am) callista m/f, pedicure m/f.

po·dia·try [pɒ'di:ətrɪ] n (Am) mestiere m di callista.

po·dium ['pəʊdɪəm] n podio.

poem ['pəʊɪm] n poesia.

poet ['pəʊɪt] n poeta/essa.

po·et·ic [pəʊ'etɪk] adj poetico(a); ~ **justice** giustizia ideale; ~ **licence** licenza poetica.

po·et·ry ['pəʊɪtrɪ] **1** n poesia; **to write** ~ scrivere
delle poesie. **2** cpd: ~ **reading** n lettura di poesie.

poign·an·cy ['pɔɪnjənsɪ] n (of grief) intensità; **the** ~
of his speech il suo discorso commovente.

poign·ant ['pɔɪnjənt] adj struggente.

point [pɔɪnt] **1** n **(a)** (dot, punctuation mark, Geom)
punto; (decimal ~) virgola; **2** ~ **6 (2.6)** 2 virgola 6
(2,6).

(b) (on scale, compass etc) punto; **boiling/
freezing** ~ punto di ebollizione/congelamento;
from all ~s **of the compass** da tutte le parti del
mondo; **up to a** ~ (fig) fino a un certo punto.

(c) (of needle, pencil, knife etc) punta; **on** ~s
(Ballet) sulle punte; **at the** ~ **of a gun/sword** sotto
la minaccia di un fucile/una spada; **not to put too
fine a** ~ **on it** (fig) parlando chiaro.

(d) (place) punto; **the train stops at Carlisle
and all** ~s **south** il treno ferma a Carlisle e in
tutte le stazioni a sud di Carlisle; ~ **of departure**
(also fig) punto di partenza; **to reach the** ~ **of no
return** (also fig) arrivare a un punto da cui non è
più possibile tornare indietro; ~ **of sale** (Comm)
punto di vendita; ~ **of view** punto di vista; **at this**
~ (spatially) in questo punto; (in time) a questo
punto; **from that** ~ **on** (in time) da quel momento
in poi; (in space) da quel punto in poi; **to be on the**
~ **of doing sth** essere sul punto di or stare (proprio) per fare qc; **when it comes to the** ~ quando
si arriva a dunque; **when it came to the** ~ **of
leaving** quando giunse il momento di partire;
abrupt to the ~ **of rudeness** brusco al punto di
essere villano.

(e) (counting unit: Sport, in test, Stock
Exchange) punto; **to win on** ~s vincere ai punti;
the index is down 3 ~s l'indice è sceso di 3 punti.

(f) (purpose) scopo, motivo; (matter) questione f, argomento; (main idea, important part: of
joke, argument) nocciolo; **there's no** ~ **in staying**
è inutile or non ha senso restare; **I don't see** or **get
the** ~ (of joke) mi sfugge; **I don't see the** ~ **of** or **in
doing that** non vedo il motivo di farlo; **the** ~ **is
that...** il fatto è che...; **that's the whole** ~! precisamente!, sta tutto lì!; **the** ~ **at issue** l'argomento in discussione or questione; **a 5-~ plan** un
piano articolato in 5 punti; **in** ~ **of fact** a dire il
vero; **to be beside the** ~ non entrarci; **to get off
the** ~ divagare; **to come** or **get to the** ~ venire al
punto or al fatto; **to keep** or **stick to the** ~ restare
in argomento; **to make a** ~ **of doing sth** non
mancare di fare qc; **to make a** ~ fare un'osservazione; **to make one's** ~ dimostrare la propria
tesi; **to stretch a** ~ fare uno strappo (alla regola)
or un'eccezione; **his remarks were to the** ~ le
sue osservazioni erano pertinenti or a proposito;
you've got a ~ **there!** giusto!, hai ragione!; **I
missed the** ~ **of that joke** non ho afferrato quella
battuta; **you've missed the whole** ~! non hai
capito niente!; **a** ~ **of principle** una questione di
principio.

(g) (characteristic) caratteristica, qualità f
inv; **good/bad** ~s lati positivi/negativi; **tact isn't
one of his strong** ~s il tatto non è il suo forte;
what ~s **should I look for?** a cosa devo stare
attento?

(h) *(Brit Rail):* ~s *pl* scambio.
(i) *(Aut):* ~s *pl* puntine *fpl.*
(j) *(Brit Elec: also:* **power** ~) presa (di corrente).
2 *vt* **(a)** *(aim, direct: gun, hosepipe etc):* **to** ~ **sth (at sb/sth)** puntare qc (contro *or* su qn/qc); he ~**ed the car at the gap** diresse la macchina verso l'apertura; **to** ~ **one's finger at sb** indicare qn con il dito; **to** ~ **one's toes** stendere il piede.
(b) *(indicate, show)* indicare, mostrare; *(fig: stress)* sottolineare; **to** ~ **the way** *(also fig)* indicare la strada *or* la direzione da seguire.
(c) *(Constr)* riempire gli interstizi di.
3 *vi* **(a)** indicare (con il dito); **to** ~ **at** *or* **to** *or* **towards sth/sb** indicare qc/qn.
(b) *(indicate: signpost, hand)* indicare, segnare; **everything** ~**s to him being guilty** tutti gli indizi fanno pensare che sia colpevole; **it** ~**s (to the) north** *(compass needle)* segna *or* indica il nord; **this** ~**s to the fact that...** questo fa pensare che... .
4 *cpd:* ~ **duty** *n* servizio di controllo del traffico.
♦ **point out** *vt + adv* **(a)** *(show)* additare, indicare.
(b) *(mention)* far notare.
♦ **point up** *vt + adv* sottolineare, mettere in evidenza.
point-blank [,pɔɪnt'blæŋk] **1** *adj (shot, answer)* a bruciapelo; *(refusal)* categorico(a), secco(a); **at** ~ **range** a bruciapelo. **2** *adv (fire)* a bruciapelo; *(refuse)* categoricamente.
point-ed ['pɔɪntɪd] *adj* **(a)** *(sharp: stick, chin)* appuntito(a); *(beard)* a punta; *(roof)* aguzzo(a); *(arch)* a sesto acuto. **(b)** *(obvious in intention: remark, question)* pregno(a) di significati; **in a** ~ **manner** in modo significativo.
point-ed-ly ['pɔɪntɪdlɪ] *adv (reply)* in modo significativo; *(say)* in un tono pieno di sottintesi.
point-er ['pɔɪntə'] *n* **(a)** *(indicator)* lancetta; *(stick)* bacchetta. **(b)** *(dog)* pointer *m inv.* **(c)** *(clue)* indizio; *(advice)* consiglio; **to give sb some** ~**s on...** consigliare qn su...; **this is a** ~ **to the guilty man** questo è un indizio che ci aiuta ad identificare il colpevole.
point-less ['pɔɪntlɪs] *adj (suffering, existence, journey)* inutile; *(crime)* senza senso; *(remark)* superfluo(a); *(story, joke)* senza capo né coda.
poise [pɔɪz] **1** *n (carriage of head, body)* portamento; *(balance)* equilibrio; *(composure, dignity of manner)* padronanza di sé. **2** *vt (balance)* mettere in equilibrio; *(hold balanced)* tenere in equilibrio; **to be** ~**d** *(balanced, positioned)* essere (immobile) in posizione; **her pen was** ~**d over the paper** era pronta a scrivere; **they are** ~**d to attack** *or* **for the attack** sono *or* si tengono pronti ad attaccare.
poi-son ['pɔɪzn] **1** *n (also fig)* veleno; **they hate each other like** ~ si odiano a morte; **what's your** ~? *(fam)* cosa bevi? **2** *vt* **(a)** *(person, food)* avvelenare; *(atmosphere)* inquinare. **(b)** *(fig):* **to** ~ **sb's mind** corrompere qn; **to** ~ **sb's mind against sb/sth** sobillare qn contro qn/qc. **3** *cpd:* ~ **gas** *n* gas tossico; ~ **ivy** *n* edera del Canada.
poi-son-ing ['pɔɪznɪŋ] *n (also fig)* avvelenamento; **arsenic** ~ avvelenamento da arsenico; **to die of** ~ morire avvelenato.
poi-son-ous ['pɔɪznəs] *adj* **(a)** *(snake, plant)* velenoso(a); *(fumes)* venefico(a), tossico(a). **(b)** *(fig) (tongue)* velenoso(a); *(propaganda)* venefico(a); *(ideas, literature)* pernicioso(a); *(rumours, individual)* perfido(a); *(fam: coffee etc)* schifoso(a).
poke [pəʊk] **1** *n (jab)* colpetto; *(with elbow)* gomitata; **to give the fire a** ~ attizzare il fuoco. **2** *vt*

(a) *(jab with stick, finger etc)* dare un colpetto a; **to** ~ **sb with one's umbrella** dare un colpetto con l'ombrello a qn; **you** ~**d me in the eye** mi hai messo un dito nell'occhio; **to** ~ **the fire** attizzare il fuoco. **(b)** *(Am fam: punch)* dare un pugno a. **(c)** *(thrust)* cacciare, ficcare; **to** ~ **one's head out of the window** mettere la testa fuori dalla finestra. **(d)** *(make by poking):* **to** ~ **a hole in sth** fare un buco in qc *(con il dito, un bastone etc).* **3** *vi:* **to** ~ **at** dare dei colpetti a.
♦ **poke about, poke around** *vi + adv (fam: in drawers, attic etc)* frugare, rovistare; *(: round shops)* curiosare.
♦ **poke out 1** *vi + adv* spuntar fuori, sporger fuori.
2 *vt + adv:* **to** ~ **sb's eye out** cavare un occhio a qn.
pok-er[1] ['pəʊkə'] *n (for fire)* attizzatoio.
pok-er[2] ['pəʊkə'] *n (Cards)* poker *m.*
poker-faced [,pəʊkə'feɪst] *adj* dalla faccia impassibile.
pok(e)y ['pəʊkɪ] *adj (-ier, -iest) (pej)* angusto(a).
Po-land ['pəʊlənd] *n* Polonia.
po-lar ['pəʊlə'] *adj (Elec, Geog)* polare; ~ **bear** orso bianco.
po-lar-ity [pəʊ'lærɪtɪ] *n* polarità.
po-lari-za-tion [,pəʊləraɪ'zeɪʃən] *n* polarizzazione *f.*
po-lar-ize ['pəʊləraɪz] *(also fig)* **1** *vt* polarizzare. **2** *vi* polarizzarsi.
Pole [pəʊl] *n* polacco/a.
pole[1] [pəʊl] **1** *n (gen)* palo; *(flag~, for vaulting)* asta; *(of tent, fence)* paletto; *(for punting)* pertica; *(curtain* ~) bastone *m.* **2** *cpd:* ~ **vault** *n* salto con l'asta.
pole[2] [pəʊl] **1** *n (Elec, Geog, Astron)* polo; **North/ South P**~ polo nord/sud; ~**s apart** *(fig)* agli antipodi. **2** *cpd:* **P**~ **Star** *n* stella polare.
pole-cat ['pəʊlkæt] *n (Brit)* puzzola; *(Am)* moffetta.
po-lem-ic [pɒ'lemɪk] *n* polemica.
po-lice [pə'liːs] **1** *npl (organization)* polizia; *(policemen)* poliziotti *mpl;* **the** ~ **have caught him** è stato preso dalla polizia; **extra** ~ **were brought in for the occasion** sono state fatte intervenire forze di polizia supplementari; **to join the** ~ arruolarsi nella polizia. **2** *vt (streets, city, frontier)* presidiare; *(fig: agreements, prices)* controllare; **to** ~ **a football match** presidiare lo stadio durante un incontro di calcio. **3** *cpd (escort, protection)* di agenti di polizia; *(state)* poliziesco(a); *(car)* della polizia; ~ **constable** *n (Brit),* ~ **officer** *n* agente *m* di polizia; ~ **dog** *n* cane *m* poliziotto *inv;* ~ **force** *n* corpo di polizia, polizia; ~ **inspector** *n* ispettore *m* di polizia; ~ **record** *n:* **to have a** ~ **record** avere precedenti penali; ~ **station** *n* commissariato di Pubblica Sicurezza; ~ **superintendent** *n* commissario di Pubblica Sicurezza.
police-man [pə'liːsmən] *n, pl* **-men** poliziotto, agente *m* di polizia.
police-woman [pə'liːswʊmən] *n, pl* **-women** donna *f* poliziotto *inv.*
poli-cy[1] ['pɒlɪsɪ] **1** *n (gen)* politica; *(of newspaper, company)* linea di condotta, prassi *f inv;* **it is our** ~ **to do that** fa parte della nostra prassi *or* politica fare questo; **foreign** ~ politica estera; **it's a matter of** ~ è una questione di principio; **it would be good/bad** ~ **to do that** sarebbe una buona/cattiva politica fare questo. **2** *cpd (discussion, statement)* sulla linea di condotta.
poli-cy[2] ['pɒlɪsɪ] **1** *n (also: insurance* ~) polizza; **to take out a** ~ fare *or* stipulare un'assicurazione. **2** *cpd:* ~ **holder** *n* assicurato/a.
po-lio ['pəʊlɪəʊ] *n* polio *f.*

Po·lish ['pəʊlɪʃ] **1** *adj* polacco(a). **2** *n* *(language)* polacco.

pol·ish ['pɒlɪʃ] **1** *n* **(a)** *(for shoes, car)* lucido; *(for furniture, floor)* cera; *(nail* ~*)* smalto per le unghie. **(b)** *(act)* lucidata; **to give sth a** ~ dare una lucidata *or* lustrata a qc. **(c)** *(shine)* lucido, lucentezza; **it has a very high** ~ è molto lucido; **to put a** ~ **on sth** far brillare qc. **(d)** *(fig: of person)* raffinatezza; *(: of style, performance)* eleganza. **2** *vt* *(also:* ~ **up)** **(a)** *(gen)* lucidare, lustrare; *(stones, glass)* levigare. **(b)** *(fig: improve)* perfezionare.
♦ **polish off** *vt + adv* *(food, drink)* far fuori; *(work, correspondence)* sbrigare.

pol·ished ['pɒlɪʃt] *adj* *(surface)* lucidato(a); *(stone)* levigato(a); *(fig: person, manner, performer)* raffinato(a); *(: performance)* elegante.

po·lite [pə'laɪt] *adj* (**-r**, **-st**) educato(a), garbato(a); **it's not** ~ **to do that** non è educato *or* buona educazione fare questo; **to be** ~ **to sb/about sth** essere cortese con qn/riguardo a qc; **in** ~ **society** nella buona società.

po·lite·ness [pə'laɪtnɪs] *n* educazione *f*, cortesia.

poli·tic ['pɒlɪtɪk] *adj* accorto(a).

po·liti·cal [pə'lɪtɪkəl] *adj* politico(a); **I'm not at all** ~ non mi interesso di politica; ~ **asylum** asilo politico.

poli·ti·cian [,pɒlɪ'tɪʃən] *n* politico.

poli·tics ['pɒlɪtɪks] *n* *(sg: career)* politica; *(: subject)* scienze *fpl* politiche; *(pl: views, policies)* tendenze *fpl or* idee *fpl* politiche; **to talk** ~ parlare di politica; **to go into** ~ darsi alla politica.

pol·ka ['pɒlkə] **1** *n* *(dance)* polca. **2** *cpd:* ~ **dot** *n* pois *m inv.*

poll [pəʊl] **1** *n* **(a)** *(voting)* votazione *f*, votazioni *fpl*; *(election)* votazione; **to take a** ~ **(on sth)** mettere (qc) ai voti; **they got 65% of the** ~ hanno ottenuto 65% dei voti; **there was a** ~ **of 84%** la percentuale dei votanti è stata dell'84%; **to go to the** ~**s** *(voters)* andare alle urne; *(government)* indire le elezioni; **a defeat at the** ~**s** una sconfitta alle elezioni. **(b)** *(opinion* ~*)* sondaggio; **to take a** ~ fare un sondaggio. **2** *vt* **(a)** *(votes)* ottenere. **(b)** *(in opinion poll)* sondare l'opinione di.

pol·len ['pɒlən] **1** *n* polline *m.* **2** *cpd:* ~ **count** *n* indice ufficiale della quantità di polline nell'aria.

pol·li·nate ['pɒlɪneɪt] *vt* impollinare.

pol·li·na·tion [pɒlɪ'neɪʃən] *n* impollinazione *f.*

pol·ling ['pəʊlɪŋ] **1** *n* votazione *f*, votazioni *fpl*; ~ **has been heavy** c'è stata un'alta percentuale di votanti. **2** *cpd:* ~ **booth** *n* cabina elettorale; ~ **day** *n* giorno delle elezioni; ~ **station** *n* seggio elettorale.

pol·lute [pə'luːt] *vt* inquinare; *(fig)* inquinare, corrompere.

pol·lu·tion [pə'luːʃən] *n* *(see vb)* inquinamento; corruzione *f.*

polo ['pəʊləʊ] **1** *n* *(sport)* polo. **2** *cpd:* ~ **neck** **(sweater)** *n* maglione *m* a collo alto.

pol·ter·geist ['pɒltəgaɪst] *n* spirito che si manifesta con colpi o rumori.

poly ['pɒlɪ] *n* Brit abbr of **polytechnic**.

poly... ['pɒlɪ] *pref* poli... .

poly·an·dry ['pɒlɪændrɪ] *n* poliandria.

poly·es·ter [,pɒlɪ'ɛstəʳ] *n* poliestere *m.*

po·lyga·my [pɒ'lɪgəmɪ] *n* poligamia.

poly·glot ['pɒlɪglɒt] *adj*, *n* poliglotta *(m/f).*

poly·gon ['pɒlɪgən] *n* poligono.

poly·mer ['pɒlɪməʳ] *n* *(Chem)* polimero.

Poly·nesia [,pɒlɪ'niːzɪə] *n* Polinesia.

pol·yp ['pɒlɪp] *n* *(Med)* polipo.

poly·phon·ic [,pɒlɪ'fɒnɪk] *adj* *(Mus)* polifonico(a).

po·lypho·ny [pə'lɪfənɪ] *n* polifonia.

poly·sty·rene [,pɒlɪ'staɪriːn] *n* polistirolo.

poly·tech·nic [,pɒlɪ'tɛknɪk] *n* *(Brit)* istituto a livello universitario specializzato nell'insegnamento di materie tecniche.

poly·thene ['pɒlɪθiːn] **1** *n* *(Brit)* polietilene *m*, politene *m.* **2** *cpd:* ~ **bag** *n* sacchetto di plastica.

poly·urethane [,pɒlɪ'jʊərɪθeɪn] *n* poliuretano.

pom·egran·ate ['pɒmə,grænɪt] *n* melagrana.

pom·mel ['pʌml] *n* pomo.

pom·my ['pɒmɪ] *adj*, *n* *(Australian fam, pej)* inglese *(m/f).*

pomp [pɒmp] *n* pompa, fasto; ~ **and circumstance** grande *or* magnifico apparato.

pom·pon ['pɒmpɒn] *n*, **pom·pom** ['pɒmpɒm] *n* *(on hat etc)* pompon *m inv.*

pom·pos·ity [pɒm'pɒsɪtɪ] *n* pomposità.

pomp·ous ['pɒmpəs] *adj* *(pej: speech, attitude)* pomposo(a); *(: person)* pieno(a) di boria.

pon·cho ['pɒntʃəʊ] *n* poncho *m inv.*

pond [pɒnd] *n* stagno; *(in park)* laghetto.

pon·der ['pɒndəʳ] **1** *vt* ponderare. **2** *vi:* **to** ~ **(on** *or* **over)** riflettere (su), meditare (su).

pon·der·ous ['pɒndərəs] *adj* pesante.

pong [pɒŋ] *(Brit fam)* **1** *n* puzzo. **2** *vi* puzzare.

pon·tiff ['pɒntɪf] *n* pontefice *m.*

pon·tifi·cate [pɒn'tɪfɪkeɪt] *vi:* **to** ~ **about** *or* **on** pontificare su.

pon·toon¹ [pɒn'tuːn] *n* pontone *m.*

pon·toon² [pɒn'tuːn] *n* *(Cards)* ventuno.

pony ['pəʊnɪ] **1** *n* pony *m inv.* **2** *cpd:* ~ **trekking** *n* escursione *f* a cavallo.

pony·tail ['pəʊnɪteɪl] *n* *(hairstyle)* coda di cavallo.

poo·dle ['puːdl] *n* barboncino, barbone *m.*

poof [pʊf] *n* *(fam)* finocchio.

pooh [puː] *excl* puah!

pooh-pooh [puː'puː] *vt* *(fam)* farsi beffe di.

pool¹ [puːl] *n* *(of water, rain, blood)* pozza; *(of light)* cerchio; *(pond)* stagno; *(: artificial)* vasca; *(swimming* ~*)* piscina; *(in river)* tonfano.

pool² [puːl] **1** *n* **(a)** *(common fund)* cassa comune; *(at poker)* piatto. **(b)** *(supply, source: of money, goods, workers)* riserva; *(: of experience, ideas)* fonte *f*; *(: of experts)* equipe *f inv*; *(of cars)* parco; **typing** ~ servizio comune di dattilografia. **(c):** **to do the (football)** ~**s** = fare la schedina, giocare al totocalcio. **(d)** *(Am: billiards)* biliardo. **(e)** *(Comm: consortium)* pool *m inv*; *(Am: monopoly trust)* trust *m inv.* **2** *vt* *(money, resources)* mettere insieme, mettere in un fondo comune; *(efforts, knowledge)* mettere insieme.

poor [pʊəʳ] **1** *adj* (**-er**, **-est**) *(gen)* povero(a); *(crop, light, visibility)* scarso(a); *(effort, excuse)* misero(a); *(memory, health, quality)* cattivo(a); **he's a** ~ **loser** non sa perdere; **it has a** ~ **chance of success** ha scarse possibilità di successo; **it's a** ~ **thing when...** è deplorevole che... + *sub*; **to be** ~ **at maths** essere debole in matematica; **as** ~ **as a church mouse** povero in canna; **I'm a** ~ **traveller** sopporto male i viaggi; **you** ~ **thing!** poverino!; **you** ~ **fool!** povero scemo! **2: the** ~ *npl* i poveri. **3** *cpd:* ~ **box** *n* cassetta per i poveri.

poor·ly ['pʊəlɪ] **1** *adv* **(a)** *(badly)* male; **a** ~ **paid job** un lavoro mal retribuito; **a** ~ **furnished room** una stanza arredata squallidamente. **(b)** *(financially)* poveramente; **to be** ~ **off** non avere molti soldi. **2** *adj* *(ill)* indisposto(a); **I'm a bit** ~ **today** oggi mi sento poco bene.

pop¹ [pɒp] **1** *n* **(a)** *(sound)* schiocco; **to go** ~ schioccare. **(b)** *(fam: drink)* bevanda gasata. **2** *vt* **(a)** *(balloon)* far scoppiare; *(cork)* far saltare. **(b)** *(put)* mettere; **I'll just** ~ **my coat on** m'infilo il cappotto; **she** ~**ped her head out** *(of the window)* sporse fuori la testa; *(from under the blankets)* fece capolino; **to** ~ **the question** *(fig)* fare la proposta di matrimonio. **3** vi **(a)** (balloon) scoppiare; (cork, buttons) saltare; (ears) sbloccarsi; (corn) scoppiettare; **his eyes nearly ~ped out of his head** sgranò tanto d'occhi. **(b)** (go quickly or suddenly): **to ~ out to the shops** fare un salto ai negozi; **she's just ~ped upstairs** è andata di sopra un attimo; **let's ~ round to Joe's** facciamo un salto da Joe.

♦ **pop in** vi + adv fare un salto, entrare un attimo.

♦ **pop off** vi + adv **(a)** (fam: die) tirar le cuoia. **(b)** (leave) andarsene.

♦ **pop up** vi + adv apparire, sorgere.

pop² [pɒp] (abbr of **popular**) **1** adj pop inv. **2** n (~ music) musica pop.

pop³ [pɒp] n (fam: dad) papà m inv, babbo.

pop·corn ['pɒpkɔːn] n pop-corn m inv.

pope [pəʊp] n papa m.

pop·gun ['pɒpɡʌn] n fucile m or pistola giocattolo inv (che spara tappi di sughero etc).

pop·lar ['pɒpləʳ] n pioppo.

pop·lin ['pɒplɪn] n popeline f.

pop·per ['pɒpəʳ] n bottone m automatico, bottone a pressione.

pop·pet ['pɒpɪt] n (fam) tesoro, amore m.

pop·py ['pɒpɪ] **1** n papavero. **2** cpd: **P~ Day** n (Brit) giorno della commemorazione dei caduti delle due guerre mondiali; **~ seed** n seme m di papavero.

poppy·cock ['pɒpɪkɒk] n (fam) scempiaggini fpl.

popu·lace ['pɒpjʊlɪs] n popolo, popolino.

popu·lar ['pɒpjʊləʳ] adj **(a)** (well-liked): **to be ~ (with)** (person) essere benvoluto(a) or ben visto(a) (da); (decision) essere gradito(a) (a); (product) essere molto richiesto(a) (da); **a ~ song** una canzone di successo; **a ~ colour** un colore che va di moda. **(b)** (for the layman) popolare. **(c)** (widespread: theory, fallacy) comune; (: support) popolare; **by ~ request** a richiesta generale.

popu·lar·ity [,pɒpjʊ'lærɪtɪ] n popolarità.

popu·lar·ize ['pɒpjʊləraɪz] vt **(a)** (make well-liked: person) rendere popolare; (make fashionable: product, fashion) diffondere. **(b)** (make available to laymen) rendere accessibile ai più.

popu·lar·ly ['pɒpjʊləlɪ] adv comunemente.

popu·late ['pɒpjʊleɪt] vt popolare.

popu·la·tion [,pɒpjʊ'leɪʃən] **1** n popolazione f. **2** cpd: **~ explosion** n forte espansione f demografica.

popu·lous ['pɒpjʊləs] adj popoloso(a), densamente popolato(a).

por·age ['pɒrɪdʒ] n = **porridge**.

porce·lain ['pɔːsəlɪn] n porcellana; **a piece of ~** una porcellana.

porch [pɔːtʃ] n veranda; (of church) sagrato.

por·cu·pine ['pɔːkjʊpaɪn] n porcospino.

pore¹ [pɔːʳ] n (Anat) poro.

pore² [pɔːʳ] vi: **to ~ over** (map, problem) studiare attentamente; (book) essere immerso(a) in.

pork [pɔːk] **1** n (carne f di) maiale m. **2** cpd: **~ butcher** n ≃ salumiere m; **~ chop** n braciola or costoletta di maiale; **~ pie** n pasticcio di maiale in crosta.

porn [pɔːn] n, (esp Am) **por·no** ['pɔːnəʊ] n (fam) porno.

por·no·graph·ic [,pɔːnə'ɡræfɪk] adj pornografico(a).

por·no·ra·phy [pɔː'nɒɡrəfɪ] n pornografia.

po·rous ['pɔːrəs] adj poroso(a).

por·poise ['pɔːpəs] n focena.

por·ridge ['pɒrɪdʒ] **1** n porridge m. **2** cpd: **~ oats** npl fiocchi mpl d'avena.

port¹ [pɔːt] **1** n (harbour) porto; (town) città f inv portuale; **~ of call** (porto di) scalo; **to come into ~** entrare in porto; **any ~ in a storm** (fig) neces-

sità fa legge. **2** cpd: **~ authorities** npl capitaneria di porto.

port² [pɔːt] (Naut, Aer: left side) **1** n babordo. **2** adj (cabin) di sinistra; **on the ~ side** a babordo.

port³ [pɔːt] n (wine) porto.

port·able ['pɔːtəbl] adj portatile.

por·tal ['pɔːtl] n portale m.

por·ter ['pɔːtəʳ] n (of office etc) portinaio/a, portiere/a; (of hotel) portiere/a; (Rail, Aer) facchino; (Am Rail) addetto ai vagoni letto.

port·fo·lio [,pɔːt'fəʊlɪəʊ] n (case) cartella; (Pol: office; Fin) portafoglio; (of artist, designer etc) raccolta dei propri lavori; **~ of shares** portafoglio titoli.

port·hole ['pɔːthəʊl] n oblò m inv.

por·tion ['pɔːʃən] n (part, piece) parte f; (of food) porzione f.

port·ly ['pɔːtlɪ] adj (-ier, -iest) corpulento(a).

port·man·teau [,pɔːt'mæntəʊ] **1** n baule m portabiti. **2** cpd: **~ word** n parola coniata dalla fusione di due parole.

por·trait ['pɔːtrɪt] **1** n ritratto. **2** cpd: **~ painter** n ritrattista m/f.

por·tray [pɔː'treɪ] vt (painter, writer, novel) ritrarre; (painting) raffigurare; (actor) interpretare.

Por·tu·gal ['pɔːtjʊɡəl] n Portogallo.

Por·tu·guese [,pɔːtjʊ'ɡiːz] **1** adj portoghese; **~ man-of-war** (jellyfish) medusa. **2** n (person: pl inv) portoghese m/f; (language) portoghese m.

pose [pəʊz] **1** n posa; **to strike a ~** mettersi in posa; **it's only a ~** (fig) è tutta una posa. **2** vt **(a)** (person) mettere in posa. **(b)** (problem, difficulty) porre, creare; (question) fare. **3** vi (for artist etc, also fig: attitudinize) posare; **to ~ as a policeman** farsi passare per un poliziotto.

pos·er ['pəʊzəʳ] n (fam) domanda difficile.

po·seur [pəʊ'zɜːʳ] n persona affettata.

posh [pɒʃ] (fam) **1** adj (-er, -est) (people, neighbourhood) per bene; (car, hotel, clothes) elegante. **2** adv: **to talk ~** parlare in modo snob.

po·si·tion [pə'zɪʃən] **1** n **(a)** (gen) posizione f; (of furniture etc) disposizione f; (in class, league etc) posizione, posto; **to be in/out of ~** essere al proprio posto/non essere al proprio posto; **in an uncomfortable ~** (also fig) in una posizione scomoda; **in a reclining ~** (of chair) reclinato; (of person) semisdraiato; **what ~ do you play?** (Sport) in che posizione giochi?; **he's lying in second ~** si trova al secondo posto or in seconda posizione.

(b) (post) posto, impiego; **to have a good ~ in a bank** avere un buon posto in banca; **a ~ of trust** un posto di fiducia.

(c) (fig: situation, standing) posizione f; **a man in his ~** un uomo nella sua posizione; **to be in a ~ to do sth** essere nella posizione di fare qc; **he's in no ~ to criticize** non sta proprio a lui criticare; **put yourself in my ~** si metta al mio posto.

(d) (fig: point of view, attitude) posizione f; **to take up a ~ on sth** prendere posizione su qc; **what's your ~ on this?** qual'è la tua posizione riguardo a questo?

2 vt (place in ~: chairs, lamp) sistemare; (: model) mettere in posa; (: soldiers) disporre; **I ~ed myself to get the best view** mi sono piazzato in modo da poter vedere bene.

posi·tive ['pɒzɪtɪv] adj **(a)** (gen, also Elec, Math, Phot) positivo(a); (constructive: advice, help, criticism) costruttivo(a); **we look forward to a ~ reply** (Comm) in attesa di una risposta favorevole. **(b)** (definite: gen) positivo(a); (: improvement, increase) deciso(a); (: proof) inconfutabile; **are you sure? — yes, ~** sei sicuro? — decisamente; **to make a ~ contribution to sth** dare un contributo effettivo a qc; **he's a ~ nuisance** è un vero rompiscatole.

posi·tive·ly ['pɒzɪtɪvlɪ] adv (gen) positivamente; (decisively) decisamente; (effectively) concretamente; (fam: really, absolutely) assolutamente; **to think ~** pensare in modo costruttivo.

pos·se ['pɒsɪ] n (Am) gruppo armato di volontari.

pos·sess [pə'zɛs] vt possedere; **like one ~ed** come un ossesso; **to be ~ed by an idea** essere ossessionato da un'idea; **whatever can have ~ed you?** cosa ti ha preso?

pos·ses·sion [pə'zɛʃən] n (a) possesso; **in ~ of** in possesso di; **to have sth in one's ~** avere qc in proprio possesso; **to get ~ of** entrare in possesso di; **to take ~ of sth** impossessarsi or impadronirsi di qc; **to take ~ of a house** prendere possesso di una casa; **to get/have ~ of the ball** (Sport) impossessarsi/essere in possesso della palla. **(b)** (thing possessed) bene m, avere m.

pos·ses·sive [pə'zɛsɪv] **1** adj (gen, also Gram) possessivo(a); **to be ~ about sth/towards sb** essere possessivo nei confronti di qc/qn. **2** n (Gram) possessivo.

pos·ses·sor [pə'zɛsəʳ] n possessore m, proprietario/a; **to be the proud ~ of sth** essere orgoglioso di possedere qc.

pos·sibil·ity [,pɒsə'bɪlɪtɪ] n possibilità f inv; **it's a distinct ~** è molto probabile; **there is no ~ of his agreeing to it** non c'è la minima possibilità or probabilità che accetti; **he's a ~ for the part** è uno dei candidati per la parte; **to foresee all the possibilities** prevedere tutte le eventualità; **to have possibilities** (person) avere delle (buone) possibilità; **your idea has possibilities** la tua idea ha delle buone possibilità di successo; **this job has possibilities** questo lavoro offre molte possibilità.

pos·sible ['pɒsəbl] **1** adj possibile; **it is ~ that he'll come** può darsi che or è possibile che venga; **it is ~ to do it** è possibile farlo; **it will be ~ for you to leave early** potrai uscire prima; **as soon as ~** appena possibile; **as far as ~** nei limiti del possibile; **if (at all) ~** se (appena è) possibile; **the best ~ result** il miglior risultato possibile; **to make sth ~ for sb** rendere qc possibile a qn; **what ~ excuse can you give for your behaviour?** quale possibile scusa puoi trovare per il tuo comportamento?; **a ~ candidate** un possibile candidato. **2** n: **a list of ~s for the job** una lista dei possibili candidati al posto; **he's a ~ for Saturday's match** è uno dei possibili giocatori per la partita di sabato.

pos·sibly ['pɒsəblɪ] adv **(a): he did all he ~ could** ha fatto tutto il possibile; **as often as I ~ can** quanto più spesso posso; **how can I ~?** come posso?; **I cannot ~ do it** non posso assolutamente farlo; **could you ~...?** potresti...? **(b)** (perhaps) forse.

post¹ [pəʊst] **1** n palo; **starting/finishing ~** (Sport) palo di partenza/arrivo; **to be left at the ~** rimanere indietro alla partenza. **2** vt **(a)** (also: **~ up**: notice, list) affiggere. **(b)** (announce) annunciare; **to ~ sb/sth (as) missing** (Mil) dare qn/qc per disperso.

post² [pəʊst] **1** n (mail) posta; **by ~** per posta; **by return of ~** a giro di posta; **to catch/miss the ~** arrivare/non arrivare in tempo per la levata; **it's in the ~** è stato spedito; **to take sth to the ~** andare a spedire qc. **2** vt **(a)** (send) spedire per posta, mandare per posta; (put in mailbox) impostare, imbucare. **(b)** (inform): **to keep sb ~ed** tenere qn al corrente. **3** cpd: **~ office** n (place)

ufficio postale, posta; **the P~ Office** (institution) ≃ le Poste e Telecomunicazioni; **P~ Office Box** (abbr **P.O. Box**) n casella postale (abbr C.P.); **P~ Office Savings Bank** n cassa di risparmio (presso gli uffici postali); **~ office worker** n impiegato postale or delle poste; **~ paid** adj già affrancato(a).

post³ [pəʊst] **1** n **(a)** (job) posto; **to take up one's ~** assumere la propria carica. **(b)** (Mil) posto; **at one's ~** al proprio posto; **last ~** (bugle call) silenzio. **(c)** (trading ~) stazione f commerciale. **2** vt **(a)** (position: sentry) piazzare. **(b)** (send, assign) inviare; (: Mil) assegnare.

post... [pəʊst] pref post...; **~-1950** dopo il 1950.

post·age ['pəʊstɪdʒ] **1** n affrancatura. **2** cpd: **~ stamp** n francobollo.

post·al ['pəʊstəl] adj (service, charges) postale; (vote) per posta; **~ order** vaglia m inv postale.

post·bag ['pəʊstbæg] n (Brit) sacco postale, sacco della posta.

post·box ['pəʊstbɒks] n (Brit) buca delle lettere, cassetta delle lettere.

post·card ['pəʊstkɑːd] n cartolina (postale).

post·code ['pəʊstkəʊd] n (Brit) codice m (di avviamento) postale.

post·date [,pəʊst'deɪt] vt postdatare.

post·er ['pəʊstəʳ] **1** n (for advertising) manifesto; (for decoration) poster m inv. **2** cpd: **~ paint** n tempera.

poste res·tante [,pəʊst'rɛstɑːnt] n fermo posta m.

pos·teri·or [pɒs'tɪərɪəʳ] n (hum) deretano, didietro.

pos·ter·ity [pɒs'tɛrɪtɪ] n posterità.

post-free [,pəʊst'friː] adj, adv franco di porto.

post·gradu·ate ['pəʊst'grædjʊɪt] **1** adj (studies, course) successivo(a) alla laurea. **2** n laureato/a che continua gli studi.

post·haste [,pəʊst'heɪst] adv in gran fretta.

post·hu·mous ['pɒstjʊməs] adj postumo(a).

post·hu·mous·ly ['pɒstjʊməslɪ] adv dopo la sua (loro etc) morte.

post·man ['pəʊstmən] n, pl **-men** postino.

post·mark ['pəʊstmɑːk] **1** n timbro postale. **2** vt timbrare; **it was ~ed Rome** il timbro postale era di Roma.

post·master ['pəʊst,mɑːstəʳ] **1** n direttore m di un ufficio postale. **2** cpd: **P~ General** n ≃ ministro delle Poste.

post·mistress ['pəʊst,mɪstrɪs] n direttrice f di un ufficio postale.

post-mortem [,pəʊst'mɔːtəm] n (also: **~ exami-nation**) autopsia; (fig) analisi f inv a posteriori.

post·na·tal ['pəʊst'neɪtl] adj post-parto inv.

post·pone [,pəʊst'pəʊn] vt: **to ~ sth for a month/ until Monday** rimandare or rinviare or posticipare qc di un mese/fino a lunedì.

post·pone·ment [pəʊst'pəʊnmənt] n rinvio.

post·script ['pəʊsskrɪpt] n poscritto.

pos·tu·late ['pɒstjʊleɪt] vt postulare.

pos·ture ['pɒstʃəʳ] **1** n posizione f; (carriage) portamento. **2** vi (pej) mettersi in posa, posare.

post·war [,pəʊst'wɔːʳ] adj del dopoguerra.

posy ['pəʊzɪ] n mazzolino (di fiori).

pot [pɒt] **1** n **(a)** (for cooking) pentola, casseruola; (tea~) teiera; (coffee~) caffettiera; (for jam) vasetto; (piece of pottery) ceramica; **~s and pans** pentole; **to go to ~** (fam: plans, business) andare in malora; (: person) lasciarsi andare. **(b)** (pot-ful): **a ~ of jam** un vasetto di marmellata; **a ~ of tea for two, please** tè per due, per piacere. **(c): ~s of** (fam) un sacco di; **to have ~s of money** avere quattrini a palate. **(d)** (fam: marijuana) erba. **2** vt **(a)** (plant) mettere in un vaso; (jam) mettere nei vasetti. **(b)** (shoot: pheasant etc) ammazzare. **(c)** *(Billiards)* mandare in buca *or* biglia. **3** *cpd:* ~ **plant** *n* pianta in vaso; ~ **roast** *n* brasato; ~ **shot** *n*: **to take a** ~ **shot at sth** sparare a casaccio contro qc.

pot·ash ['pɒtæʃ] *n* potassa.

po·tas·sium [pə'tæsɪəm] *n* potassio.

po·ta·to [pə'teɪtəʊ] **1** *n, pl* ~**es** patata. **2** *cpd:* ~ **chips** *npl (Am)*, ~ **crisps** *npl (Brit)* patatine *fpl.*

pot·bel·lied ['pɒt,belɪd] *adj (from overeating)* panciuto(a); *(from malnutrition)* dal ventre gonfio.

pot·bound ['pɒtbaʊnd] *adj*: **this plant is** ~ il vaso è ormai troppo piccolo per questa pianta.

po·ten·cy ['pəʊtənsɪ] *n (see adj)* potenza; validità.

po·tent ['pəʊtənt] *adj (gen)* potente; *(fig: argument, reason)* validissimo(a).

po·ten·tate ['pəʊtənteɪt] *n* potentato.

po·ten·tial [pəʊ'tenʃəl] **1** *adj* potenziale. **2** *n* **(a)** *(possibilities)* potenziale *m*; **to realize one's full** ~ realizzarsi; **sales** ~ potenziale di vendita; **to show** ~ promettere bene; **to have** ~ essere promettente. **(b)** *(Elec, Math, Phys)* potenziale *m*.

po·ten·tial·ly [pəʊ'tenʃəlɪ] *adv* potenzialmente.

pot·hole ['pɒthəʊl] *n (in road)* buca; *(Geol)* marmitta.

pot·holer ['pɒthəʊlə'] *n* speleologo/a.

pot·hol·ing ['pɒthəʊlɪŋ] *n* esplorazione *f* speleologica.

po·tion ['pəʊʃən] *n* pozione *f*, filtro.

pot·luck [,pɒt'lʌk] *n*: **to take** ~ *(for food)* mangiare quel che passa il convento; *(for other things)* tentare la sorte.

pot·pour·ri [,pəʊ'pʊriː] *n* **(a)** *(flowers)* miscuglio di petali essiccati per profumare un ambiente. **(b)** *(of music, writing)* pot-pourri *m inv.*

pot·ted ['pɒtɪd] *adj* **(a)** *(fish, meat)* conservato(a) in vaso; *(plant)* in vaso. **(b)** *(fig: shortened)* condensato(a).

pot·ter[1] ['pɒtə'] *n* vasaio/a; ~**'s wheel** tornio (da vasaio).

pot·ter[2] ['pɒtə'] *vi, (Am)* **put·ter** ['pʌtə'] *vi*: **to** ~ **round the shops** fare un tranquillo giretto per i negozi; **to** ~ **round the house** sbrigare con calma le faccende di casa; **he likes** ~**ing about in the garden** gli piace fare qualche lavoretto in giardino.

pot·tery ['pɒtərɪ] **1** *n (workshop)* fabbrica *or* laboratorio di ceramiche; *(craft)* ceramica; *(pots)* ceramiche; **a piece of** ~ una ceramica. **2** *cpd (dish, jug)* di ceramica.

pot·ty[1] ['pɒtɪ] *n (fam)* vasino.

pot·ty[2] ['pɒtɪ] *adj* (**-ier, -iest**) *(Brit fam: mad)* matto(a); *(: idea)* balordo(a); **you drive me** ~! mi fai diventare matto!

potty-trained ['pɒtɪ,treɪnd] *adj* che ha imparato a farla nel vasino.

pouch [paʊtʃ] *n (Anat, for tobacco)* borsa; *(for money)* borsellino; *(Zool)* marsupio.

pouf(fe) [puːf] *n* **(a)** *(seat)* pouf *m inv*. **(b)** *(Brit fam)* = **poof.**

poul·ter·er ['pəʊltərə'] *n (Brit)* pollivendolo/a.

poul·tice ['pəʊltɪs] *n* impiastro, cataplasma *m*.

poul·try ['pəʊltrɪ] **1** *n* pollame *m*. **2** *cpd:* ~ **farm** *n* azienda avicola; ~ **farmer** *n* pollicoltore/trice.

pounce [paʊns] **1** *n* balzo. **2** *vi (cat, tiger)* balzare (sulla preda); *(bird)* piombare (sulla preda); **to** ~ **on sb/sth** *(animal)* balzare su qn/qc; *(bird)* piombare su qn/qc; *(person)* piombare *or* balzare su qn/qc; **he** ~**d on my offer of help** ha colto al volo la mia offerta di aiuto; **he** ~**d on my suggestion that...** *(attack)* è saltato su quando ho suggerito che... .

pound[1] [paʊnd] *n* **(a)** *(weight)* libbra; **sold by the** ~ venduto alla libbra; **half a** ~ mezza libbra. **(b)**

(money) (lira) sterlina; **one** ~ **sterling** una sterlina; **a one-**~ **note** una banconota da una sterlina.

pound[2] [paʊnd] **1** *vt (hammer, strike: door, table, person)* picchiare; *(: piano)* pestare i tasti di; *(: typewriter)* battere sui tasti di; *(subj: sea, waves)* sbattere contro; *(: guns, bombs)* martellare; *(pulverize: drug, spices, meat)* pestare; *(: dough)* lavorare; **to** ~ **sth to pieces** fare qc a pezzi; **to** ~ **sth to a pulp** ridurre qc in poltiglia. **2** *vi* **(a)** *(heart)* battere forte; *(drums)* rullare; *(sea)* sbattere; *(person)*: **to** ~ **at** *or* **on** dare dei gran colpi a *or* su; *(piano)* pestare i tasti di. **(b)** *(run, walk heavily)*: **to** ~ **in/out** *etc* entrare/uscire *etc* a passi pesanti.

pound[3] [paʊnd] *n (enclosure: for dogs)* canile *m* municipale; *(: for cars)* deposito *m* auto *inv (per auto sottoposte a rimozione forzata).*

pound·ing ['paʊndɪŋ] *n*: **to take a** ~ *(team)* prendere una batosta; *(ship)* essere sbattuto(a) violentemente dalle onde; *(town: in war)* venire duramente colpito(a).

pour [pɔː'] **1** *vt* versare; **to** ~ **sth away** *or* **off** buttar via qc, versar fuori qc; **let me** ~ **you a drink** lascia che ti versi da bere; **to** ~ **money into a project** investire molti soldi in un progetto. **2** *vi* **(a)**: **to come** ~**ing in** *(water)* entrare a fiotti; *(letters)* arrivare a valanghe; *(cars, people)* affluire in gran quantità; **the sunshine** ~**ed into the room** la luce del sole inondava la stanza; **the sweat is** ~**ing off you!** sei grondante di sudore!; **tourists are** ~**ing in** i turisti stanno arrivando in massa. **(b)**: **it's** ~**ing (with rain)** sta piovendo a dirotto.

♦ **pour out** *vt + adv (drink)* versare; *(dirty water)* buttar via; *(fig: feelings)* sfogare; *(: troubles)* sfogarsi parlando di; *(: story)* raccontare tutto d'un fiato; **she** ~**ed out her complaints** si lamentò apertamente.

pour·ing ['pɔːrɪŋ] *adj (custard)* da versare; *(rain)* torrenziale; **a** ~ **wet day** una giornata molto piovosa.

pout [paʊt] **1** *n* broncio. **2** *vi* fare il broncio, mettere il muso.

pov·er·ty ['pɒvətɪ] **1** *n* miseria, povertà; ~ **of resources** mancanza di risorse; **to live in** ~ vivere in miseria. **2** *cpd:* ~ **trap** *n* circolo vizioso della povertà.

poverty-stricken ['pɒvətɪ,strɪkən] *adj (gen)* poverissimo(a); *(hum: hard up)* al verde.

pow·der ['paʊdə'] **1** *n (gen)* polvere *f*; *(face* ~*)* cipria; *(medicine)* polverina. **2** *vt (reduce to* ~*)* ridurre in polvere; ~**ed milk** latte in polvere; ~**ed sugar** *(Am)* zucchero a velo. **(b)** *(apply* ~ *to: face)* incipriarsi; **to** ~ **one's body** mettersi il talco; **to** ~ **one's nose** incipriarsi il naso; *(euph)* andare alla toilette. **3** *cpd:* ~ **compact** *n* portacipria *m inv*; ~ **puff** *n* piumino della cipria; ~ **room** *n* toilette *f inv (per signore).*

pow·dery ['paʊdərɪ] *adj (substance)* come polvere; *(surface)* impolverato(a); *(snow)* farinoso(a).

pow·er ['paʊə'] **1** *n* **(a)** *(physical strength, also fig)* forza; *(energy)* energia; *(force: of engine, blow, explosion etc)* potenza; *(: of sun)* intensità; **to cut off the** ~ *(Elec)* togliere la corrente; **the ship returned under its own** ~ la nave è tornata con i propri mezzi; **more** ~ **to your elbow!** *(fam)* dacci dentro!

(b) *(ability, capacity)* capacità *f inv*, potere *m*; *(faculty)* facoltà *f inv*; **mental** ~**s** capacità mentali; **it is beyond his** ~ **to save her** non può far nulla per salvarla; **to do all in one's** ~ **to help sb** fare tutto quello che si può per aiutare qn; **the** ~ **of speech** la facoltà *or* l'uso della parola; ~**s of**

persuasion/imagination forza di persuasione/ immaginazione.

(c) *(Pol etc: authority)* potere *m*, autorità *f inv*; **the ~ of the Church** l'autorità della Chiesa; **that is beyond my ~(s)** questo è al di là dei miei poteri; **to have ~ over sb** aver potere su qn; **to have sb in one's ~** avere qn in proprio potere; **to be in sb's ~** essere in potere di qn; **to be in ~** essere al potere; **to come to ~** salire al potere; **~ of attorney** *(Law)* procura; **the ~ behind the throne** l'eminenza grigia; **the world ~s** le grandi potenze; **the ~s that be** le autorità costituite; **the ~s of darkness** *or* **evil** le forze del male.

(d) *(Math)* potenza; **7 to the ~ (of)** 3 7 al cubo *or* alla terza.

(e) *(fam: a lot of)*: **it did me a ~ of good** mi ha fatto un bene enorme.

2 *vt* azionare; **nuclear-~ed submarine** sottomarino a propulsione atomica; **plane ~ed by 4 jets** aereo azionato da 4 motori a reazione.

3 *cpd* *(saw, drill, also Elec: cable, pack, line)* elettrico(a); *(supply, consumption)* di energia elettrica; **~ cut** *n* interruzione *f or* mancanza di corrente; **~ point** *n (Elec)* presa di corrente; **~ politics** *npl* politica della forza; **~ station** *n* centrale *f* elettrica; **~ steering** *n (Aut: also:* **~-assisted steering)** servosterzo; **~ structure** *n* gerarchia di poteri.

power·boat [ˈpauəbəut] *n* motobarca, imbarcazione *f* a motore.

power-driven [ˈpauə‚drɪvn] *adj* a motore; *(Elec)* elettrico(a).

pow·er·ful [ˈpauəful] *adj (gen)* potente; *(person: physically)* possente; *(film, actor, speech)* formidabile.

pow·er·ful·ly [ˈpauəfəlɪ] *adv*: **to be ~ built** essere di costituzione robusta.

power·house [ˈpauəhaus] *n (fig: person)* persona molto dinamica; **a ~ of ideas** una miniera di idee.

pow·er·less [ˈpauəlɪs] *adj* impotente.

p.p. *abbr (= by proxy)* p.p.

P.R. *abbr* **(a)** *(= public relations)* R.P., P.R. **(b)** *abbr of* **proportional representation.**

prac·ti·cabil·ity [‚præktɪkəˈbɪlɪtɪ] *n* praticabilità.

prac·ti·cable [ˈpræktɪkəbl] *adj* praticabile.

prac·ti·cal [ˈpræktɪkəl] *adj (gen)* pratico(a); **for all ~ purposes** in pratica, agli effetti pratici; **he's very ~** è un tipo molto pratico; **~ joke** scherzo.

prac·ti·cal·ity [‚præktɪˈkælɪtɪ] *n (of person)* senso pratico; *(of scheme etc)* fattibilità; **practicalities** dettagli *mpl* pratici.

prac·ti·cal·ly [ˈpræktɪklɪ] *adv (almost)* praticamente, quasi.

prac·tice [ˈpræktɪs] **1** *n* **(a)** *(habit)* abitudine *f*, consuetudine *f*; **it's common ~** è d'uso; **it is not our ~ to do that** generalmente non lo facciamo.

(b) *(exercise)* esercizio; *(training)* allenamento; *(rehearsal)* prove *fpl*; **target ~** pratica di tiro; **piano ~** esercizi *mpl* al piano; **football ~** allenamento di calcio; **to be out of ~** esser fuori esercizio *(or* allenamento); **~ makes perfect** le cose si imparano a forza di pratica.

(c) *(not theory)* pratica; **in ~** in pratica; **to put sth into ~** mettere qc in pratica.

(d) *(of doctor, lawyer)*: **to be in ~** esercitare la professione; **he has a small ~** *(doctor)* ha un numero ristretto di pazienti; *(lawyer)* ha un numero ristretto di clienti; **his ~ is in Trieste** il suo studio è a Trieste; **to set up in ~ as** cominciare ad esercitare la professione di.

2 *vt, vi (Am)* = **practise.**

prac·tise, *(Am)* prac·tice [ˈpræktɪs] **1** *vt* **(a)**: **to ~ patience/self-control** cercare di avere-pazienza/

di controllarsi; **to ~ charity** essere caritatevole; **to ~ what one preaches** mettere in pratica ciò che si predica. **(b)** *(train o.s. at: piano etc)* esercitarsi a; *(: song)* esercitarsi per imparare; **to ~ a shot** esercitarsi in un tiro; **to ~ doing sth** esercitarsi a fare qc; **I ~d my Italian on her** ho fatto pratica d'italiano con lei. **(c)** *(follow, exercise: profession)* esercitare; *(: religion)* praticare; *(: method)* seguire. **2** *vi* **(a)** *(in order to acquire skill: gen, Mus)* esercitarsi; *(: Sport)* allenarsi. **(b)** *(lawyer, doctor)* esercitare.

prac·tised, *(Am)* prac·ticed [ˈpræktɪst] *adj (person)* esperto(a); *(performance)* da virtuoso(a); *(liar)* matricolato(a); **with a ~ eye** con un occhio esperto.

prac·tis·ing, *(Am)* prac·tic·ing [ˈpræktɪsɪŋ] *adj (lawyer)* che esercita (la professione); *(Jew, Catholic etc)* praticante; *(homosexual)* attivo(a).

prac·ti·tion·er [prækˈtɪʃənəʳ] *n (of an art)* professionista *m/f*; *(Med)* medico.

prag·mat·ic [prægˈmætɪk] *adj* pragmatico(a).

prag·ma·tism [ˈprægmətɪzəm] *n* pragmatismo.

prai·rie [ˈprɛərɪ] *n* prateria; **the ~s** le grandi praterie.

praise [preɪz] **1** *n* elogio, lode *f*; **he spoke in ~ of their achievements** ha elogiato i loro risultati; **I have nothing but ~ for her** non posso che lodarla; **~ be to God!** sia lode a Dio!; **~ be!** *(fam)* sia ringraziato il cielo! **2** *vt* lodare, elogiare; *(God)* render lode a; **to ~ sb for sth/for doing sth** lodare *or* elogiare qn per qc/per aver fatto qc.

praise·worthy [ˈpreɪz‚wɜːðɪ] *adj* lodevole, degno(a) di lode.

pram [præm] *n (Brit)* carrozzina.

prance [prɑːns] *vi (horse)* caracollare; *(person: proudly)* pavoneggiarsi; *(: gaily)* saltellare; **to ~ in/out** entrare/uscire pavoneggiandosi *(or* saltellando).

prank [præŋk] *n* scherzetto, burla; **a student ~** uno scherzo da studente.

prat·tle [ˈprætl] *vi* chiacchierare, cianciare.

prawn [prɔːn] **1** *n* gambero. **2** *cpd*: **~ cocktail** *n* cocktail *m inv* di gamberetti.

pray [preɪ] *vi (say prayers)* pregare; **to ~ to God** pregare Dio; **to ~ for sb/sth** pregare per qn/qc; **to ~ for forgiveness** implorare il perdono; **we are ~ing for good weather** preghiamo Dio che faccia bello.

prayer [prɛəʳ] **1** *n* preghiera; **to say one's ~s** dire *or* recitare le preghiere. **2** *cpd*: **~ book** *n* libro di preghiere; **~ mat** *n* tappeto da preghiera; **~ meeting** *n* incontro di preghiera.

pre... [priː] *pref* pre...; **pre-1970** prima del 1970.

preach [priːtʃ] **1** *vt (gen)* predicare; *(sermon)* fare. **2** *vi* predicare; **to ~ at sb** far la predica a qn; **to ~ to the converted** *(fig)* cercare di convincere chi è già convinto.

preach·er [ˈpriːtʃəʳ] *n (of sermon)* predicatore *m*; *(Am: minister)* pastore *m*.

pre·am·ble [priːˈæmbl] *n* preambolo.

pre·ar·range [‚priːəˈreɪndʒ] *vt* prestabilire.

pre·cari·ous [prɪˈkɛərɪəs] *adj* precario(a).

pre·cau·tion [prɪˈkɔːʃən] *n* precauzione *f*; **as a ~** per precauzione; **to take ~s** prendere precauzioni; **to take the ~ of doing** prendere la precauzione di fare.

pre·cau·tion·ary [prɪˈkɔːʃənərɪ] *adj (measure)* precauzionale.

pre·cede [prɪˈsiːd] *vt (in space, time)* precedere; *(in rank)* avere la precedenza su.

prec·edence [ˈpresɪdəns] *n (in rank)* precedenza; *(in importance)* priorità; **to take ~ over sb/sth** avere la precedenza su qn/qc.

prec·e·dent ['prɛsɪdənt] n (also Law) precedente m; **without** ~ senza precedenti; **to establish** or **set a** ~ creare un precedente.

pre·ced·ing [prɪ'siːdɪŋ] adj precedente.

pre·cept ['priːsɛpt] n precetto.

pre·cinct ['priːsɪŋkt] n (a): ~s pl (environs) dintorni mpl; (of cathedral etc) recinto; **pedestrian** ~ isola pedonale. (b) (Am: district) circoscrizione f.

pre·cious ['prɛʃəs] 1 adj prezioso(a); ~ **stone** pietra preziosa; **your** ~ **dog** (iro) il tuo amatissimo cane. 2 adv (fam): ~ **little/few** ben poco/pochi.

preci·pice ['prɛsɪpɪs] n precipizio.

pre·cipi·tate [prɪ'sɪpɪteɪt] 1 adj precipitoso(a), affrettato(a). 2 vt (a) (bring on: crisis) accelerare. (b) (Chem) precipitare; (Met) far condensare.

pre·cipi·tous [prɪ'sɪpɪtəs] adj (slope, path) a precipizio; (decision, action) precipitoso(a).

pré·cis ['preɪsiː] n riassunto.

pre·cise [prɪ'saɪs] adj (gen) preciso(a); (pej: over ~) pignolo(a), pedante; **there were 5, to be** ~ ce n'erano 5, per essere precisi; **at that** ~ **moment** in quel preciso istante; **he's very** ~ **in everything he does** è sempre molto preciso in quello che fa; **a** ~ **old lady** una vecchietta meticolosa.

pre·cise·ly [prɪ'saɪslɪ] adv con precisione; **at 4 o'clock** ~, **at** ~ **4 o'clock** alle 4 precise or in punto; ~! precisamente!, proprio così!

pre·ci·sion [prɪ'sɪʒən] 1 n precisione f. 2 cpd: ~ **instrument** n strumento di precisione.

pre·clude [prɪ'kluːd] vt (possibility) precludere; (misunderstanding, doubt) non lasciar adito a; **we are** ~d **from doing that** siamo impossibilitati a farlo.

pre·co·cious [prɪ'kəʊʃəs] adj precoce.

pre·co·cious·ness [prɪ'kəʊʃəsnɪs] n, **pre·coc·ity** [prɪ'kɒsɪtɪ] n precocità.

pre·con·ceived [ˌpriːkən'siːvd] adj preconcetto(a).

pre·con·cep·tion [ˌpriːkən'sɛpʃən] n preconcetto.

pre·con·di·tion [ˌpriːkən'dɪʃən] n condizione f indispensabile.

pre·cur·sor [ˌpriːˈkɜːsəʳ] n precursore m.

pre·date [ˌpriːˈdeɪt] vt (put earlier date on) retrodatare; (precede) precedere.

preda·tor ['prɛdətəʳ] n predatore/trice.

pre·de·cease ['priːdɪ'siːs] vt morire prima di.

pre·de·ces·sor ['priːdɪsɛsəʳ] n predecessore/a.

pre·des·ti·na·tion [priːˌdɛstɪ'neɪʃən] n predestinazione f.

pre·des·tine [ˌpriːˈdɛstɪn] vt predestinare.

pre·de·ter·mine [ˌpriːdɪ'tɜːmɪn] vt predeterminare, determinare in anticipo.

pre·dica·ment [prɪ'dɪkəmənt] n situazione f difficile (or imbarazzante).

predi·cate ['prɛdɪkɪt] n (Gram) predicato.

pre·dict [prɪ'dɪkt] vt predire.

pre·dict·able [prɪ'dɪktəbl] adj prevedibile.

pre·dict·ably [prɪ'dɪktəblɪ] adv (behave, react) in modo prevedibile; ~ **she didn't arrive** come era da prevedere, non è arrivata.

pre·dic·tion [prɪ'dɪkʃən] n predizione f.

pre·di·lec·tion [ˌpriːdɪ'lɛkʃən] n predilezione f.

pre·dis·pose ['priːdɪs'pəʊz] vt predisporre.

pre·domi·nance [prɪ'dɒmɪnəns] n predominanza.

pre·domi·nant [prɪ'dɒmɪnənt] adj predominante.

pre·domi·nant·ly [prɪ'dɒmɪnəntlɪ] adv prevalentemente, per lo più.

pre·domi·nate [prɪ'dɒmɪneɪt] vi predominare.

pre·eminent [ˌpriː'ɛmɪnənt] adj eccezionale.

pre·eminent·ly [ˌpriː'ɛmɪnəntlɪ] adv soprattutto, preminentemente.

preen [priːn] vt (subj: bird) lisciare (con il becco); **to** ~ **itself** (bird) lisciarsi le penne (con il becco);

to ~ **o.s.** (person) agghindarsi; (: fig) inorgoglirsi, gongolare.

pre·fab ['priːfæb] n (fam) casetta prefabbricata.

pre·fab·ri·ca·ted [ˌpriː'fæbrɪkeɪtɪd] adj prefabbricato(a).

pref·ace ['prɛfɪs] n prefazione f; (to speech) introduzione f.

pre·fect ['priːfɛkt] n (Brit Scol) studente anziano con funzioni disciplinari; (French etc Admin) prefetto.

pre·fer [prɪ'fɜːʳ] vt (a) preferire; **to** ~ **coffee to tea** preferire il caffè al tè; **I** ~ **walking to going by car** preferisco camminare piuttosto che andare in macchina; **I** ~ **to stay home** preferisco restare a casa. (b) (Law: charges, complaint) sporgere; (: action) intentare.

pref·er·able ['prɛfərəbl] adj preferibile.

pref·er·ably ['prɛfərəblɪ] adv di preferenza.

pref·er·ence ['prɛfərəns] 1 n preferenza; **my** ~ **is for...**, **I have a** ~ **for...** preferisco...; **in** ~ **to sth** piuttosto che qc; **to give** ~ **to sb/sth** dare la preferenza a qn/qc. 2 cpd: ~ **shares** npl azioni fpl privilegiate.

pref·er·en·tial [ˌprɛfə'rɛnʃəl] adj preferenziale.

pre·fix ['priːfɪks] n (Gram) prefisso.

preg·nan·cy ['prɛgnənsɪ] 1 n gravidanza. 2 cpd: ~ **test** n analisi f inv di gravidanza.

preg·nant ['prɛgnənt] adj (woman) incinta; (animal) gravido(a); (fig: remark, pause) significativo(a); **3 months** ~ incinta di 3 mesi; ~ **with meaning** pregno di significato.

pre·his·tor·ic [ˌpriːhɪ'stɒrɪk] adj preistorico(a).

pre·his·to·ry [ˌpriːˈhɪstərɪ] n preistoria.

pre·judge [ˌpriːˈdʒʌdʒ] vt farsi a priori un giudizio di.

preju·dice ['prɛdʒʊdɪs] 1 n (a) (biased opinion) pregiudizio; (collective n) pregiudizi mpl; **his** ~ **against sb/sth** i suoi pregiudizi nei riguardi di qn/qc. (b) (Law: injury, detriment) pregiudizio; **without** ~ **to** senza pregiudicare. 2 vt (a) (bias): **to** ~ **sb in favour of/against** disporre bene/male qn verso. (b) (injure) pregiudicare, compromettere.

preju·diced ['prɛdʒʊdɪst] adj (person) pieno(a) di pregiudizi, prevenuto(a); (view, opinion) preconcetto(a); **to be** ~ **against sb/sth** essere prevenuto contro qn/qc; **to be** ~ **in favour of sb/sth** essere ben disposto verso qn/qc.

preju·di·cial [ˌprɛdʒʊ'dɪʃəl] adj: ~ (**to**) pregiudizievole (per or a).

prel·ate ['prɛlɪt] n prelato.

pre·limi·nary [prɪ'lɪmɪnərɪ] 1 adj preliminare. 2 prep: ~ **to sth/doing sth** prima di qc/fare qc. 3: **preliminaries** npl preliminari mpl.

prel·ude ['prɛljuːd] n preludio.

pre·mari·tal [ˌpriːˈmærɪtl] adj prematrimoniale.

prema·ture ['prɛmə,tjʊəʳ] adj (baby, birth, decision) prematuro(a); (arrival) (molto) anticipato(a); **you are being a little** ~ sei un po' troppo precipitoso.

prema·ture·ly ['prɛmə,tjʊəlɪ] adv prematuramente, prima del tempo.

pre·medi·tate [ˌpriːˈmɛdɪteɪt] vt premeditare.

pre·men·stru·al [ˌpriːˈmɛnstrʊəl] adj: ~ **tension** (Med) tensione f premestruale.

prem·ier ['prɛmɪəʳ] n (Pol) premier m inv.

premi·ère ['prɛmɪeəʳ] n prima.

prem·ise ['prɛmɪs] n (a) (hypothesis) premessa. (b): ~s pl (property) locali mpl; **business** ~s locali commerciali; **on the** ~s nel locale; **he was asked to leave the** ~s l'hanno invitato ad abbandonare il locale.

pre·mium ['priːmɪəm] 1 n (gen) premio; (additional charge) maggiorazione f; **to sell at a** ~ (shares) vendere sopra la pari; **to be at a** ~ *(fig)* essere ricercatissimo. **2** *cpd*: ~ **bond** *n (Brit)* obbligazione emessa dal governo, che non frutta interessi, ma che dà al titolare il diritto di partecipare ad una lotteria mensile; ~ **deal** *n (Comm)* offerta speciale.

premo·ni·tion [ˌpriːməˈnɪʃən] *n* presentimento, premonizione *f*.

pre·oc·cu·pa·tion [priːˌɒkjuˈpeɪʃən] *n* preoccupazione *f*; **his** ~ **with death** la sua ossessione della morte.

pre·oc·cu·py [ˌpriːˈɒkjupaɪ] *vt (gen)* preoccupare; *(mind, thoughts)* occupare.

prep [prep] *(Scol) fam abbr of* **preparation, preparatory.**

pre·paid [ˌpriːˈpeɪd] *adj* pagato(a) in anticipo; *(envelope)* affrancato(a).

prepa·ra·tion [ˌprepəˈreɪʃən] *n* **(a)** *(preparing)* preparazione *f*; **in** ~ **for sth** in vista di qc; **to be in** ~ essere in (corso di) preparazione. **(b)** *(preparatory measure)*: ~s preparativi *mpl*; **to make** ~s fare i preparativi. **(c)** *(Brit Scol)* compiti *mpl*.

pre·para·tory [prɪˈpærətərɪ] *adj (work)* preparatorio(a); *(measure)* preliminare; ~ **to sth/to doing sth** prima di qc/di fare qc; ~ **school** *(Brit)* scuola elementare privata; *(Am)* liceo privato.

pre·pare [prɪˈpɛəʳ] **1** *vt* preparare; ~ **yourself for a shock** preparati a uno shock; **to** ~ **the way for sth** preparare il terreno per qc; **to** ~ **to do sth** prepararsi a fare qc. **2** *vi*: **to** ~ **for** *(journey, party, sb's arrival)* fare dei preparativi per; *(exam, future)* prepararsi per; **to** ~ **for war** prepararsi alla guerra.

pre·pared [prɪˈpɛəd] *adj* **(a)** *(speech, answer)* preparato(a) in anticipo; *(food)* pronto(a). **(b)** *(in state of readiness)* pronto(a); **to be** ~ **for anything** essere pronto a tutto; **we were not** ~ **for this** questo ci ha colto alla sprovvista *or* non ce lo aspettavamo. **(c)** *(willing)*: **to be** ~ **to help sb** essere disposto *or* pronto ad aiutare qn.

pre·pon·der·ance [prɪˈpɒndərəns] *n* preponderanza.

pre·pon·der·ant [prɪˈpɒndərənt] *adj* preponderante.

prepo·si·tion [ˌprepəˈzɪʃən] *n* preposizione *f*.

pre·pos·sess·ing [ˌpriːpəˈzesɪŋ] *adj* simpatico(a), attraente.

pre·pos·ter·ous [prɪˈpɒstərəs] *adj* ridicolo(a), assurdo(a).

pre·re·cord [ˌpriːrɪˈkɔːd] *vt* registrare in anticipo; ~**ed broadcast** trasmissione *f* registrata; ~**ed cassette** (musi)cassetta.

pre·requi·site [ˌpriːˈrekwɪzɪt] *n* presupposto necessario.

pre·roga·tive [prɪˈrɒgətɪv] *n* prerogativa.

Pres·by·ter·ian [ˌprezbɪˈtɪərɪən] *adj, n* presbiteriano(a) *(m/f).*

pre·school [ˈpriːˌskuːl] *adj (child)* in età prescolastica; *(age)* prescolastico(a).

pre·scribe [prɪsˈkraɪb] *vt (gen, Med)* prescrivere; *(fig)* consigliare; ~**d books** *(Scol, Univ)* testi *mpl* in programma.

pre·scrip·tion [prɪsˈkrɪpʃən] **1** *n (Med)* ricetta (medica); **to make up** *or* **fill** *(Am)* **a** ~ preparare *or* fare una ricetta; **only available on** ~ ottenibile solo dietro presentazione di ricetta medica. **2** *cpd*: ~ **charges** *npl (Brit)* ticket *m inv.*

pres·ence [ˈprezns] *n* presenza; ~ **of mind** presenza di spirito; **in the** ~ **of** in presenza di, davanti a; **to make one's** ~ **felt** far sentire la propria presenza.

pres·ent [ˈpreznt] **1** *adj* **(a)** *(in attendance)* presente; **to be** ~ **at** *(gen)* essere presente a; *(officially)* presenziare a; **those** ~ i presenti. **(b)** *(of the moment)* attuale; **in the** ~ **circumstances** date le circostanze attuali; **at the** ~ **moment** al momento attuale; **its** ~ **value** il suo valore attuale. **(c)** *(Gram)* presente.

2 *n* **(a)** *(~ time)* presente *m*; *(Gram)* (tempo) presente *m*; **at** ~ al momento; **for the** ~ per il momento, per adesso, per ora; **up to the** ~ fino a questo momento, finora. **(b)** *(gift)* regalo; **I got this watch as a** ~ questo orologio mi è stato regalato; **to make sb a** ~ **of sth** regalare qc a qn.

3 [prɪˈzent] *vt* **(a)** *(hand over: gen)* presentare; *(: prize, certificate)* consegnare; *(give as gift)* offrire (in omaggio); *(proof, evidence)* fornire; *(Dir etc: case)* esporre; **to** ~ **sb with sth,** ~ **sth to sb** fare dono di qc a qn; *(prize)* consegnare qc a qn; **to** ~ **arms** *(Mil)* presentare le armi; **to** ~ **o.s. for an interview** presentarsi per un colloquio. **(b)** *(offer: difficulty, problem, opportunity)* presentare; *(: features)* offrire. **(c)** *(put on: play, concert, film)* dare; *(TV, Radio: act as presenter of)* presentare; **to** ~ **the news** *(TV, Radio)* leggere le notizie; ~**ing Jack Nicholson as...** con Jack Nicholson nella parte di.... **(d)** *(introduce)*: **to** ~ **sb to sb** presentare qn a qn; **may I** ~ **Miss Clark?** permette che le presenti la signorina Clark?

pre·sent·able [prɪˈzentəbl] *adj* presentabile; **to make o.s.** ~ rendersi presentabile, mettersi in ordine.

pres·en·ta·tion [ˌprezənˈteɪʃən] *n* **(a)** *(act of presenting)* presentazione *f*; *(Law: of case)* esposizione *f*; **on** ~ **of the voucher** dietro presentazione del buono. **(b)** *(Radio, TV, Theatre)* rappresentazione *f*. **(c)** *(of prizes etc)* consegna ufficiale; *(gift)* regalo; **to make the** ~ fare la consegna ufficiale.

present-day [ˈprezntˌdeɪ] *adj* attuale, di oggi.

pre·sent·er [prɪˈzentəʳ] *n (Radio, TV)* presentatore/trice.

pre·sen·ti·ment [prɪˈzentɪmənt] *n* presentimento.

pres·ent·ly [ˈprezntlɪ] *adv (shortly)* tra poco, a momenti; *(Am: now)* adesso, ora.

pres·er·va·tion [ˌprezəˈveɪʃən] **1** *n* conservazione *f*; *(of peace, one's dignity)* mantenimento. **2** *cpd*: ~ **order** *n (on monument etc)* ordine *m* per la salvaguardia.

pre·serva·tive [prɪˈzɜːvətɪv] *n (Culin)* conservante *m.*

pre·serve [prɪˈzɜːv] **1** *vt* **(a)** *(maintain: traditions)* conservare, mantenere; *(: dignity, peace)* mantenere; *(keep intact: buildings, memory)* conservare. **(b)** *(keep from decay)* preservare; **well** ~**d** ben conservato; **he is well** ~**d** *(hum)* si conserva bene. **(c)** *(Culin)* conservare, mettere in conserva. **(d)** *(keep from harm, save)* proteggere; ~ **me from that!** *(che)* Dio mi scampi! **2** *n* **(a)** *(Culin)* conserva. **(b)** *(Hunting)* riserva.

pre·shrunk [ˌpriːˈʃrʌŋk] *adj* irrestringibile.

pre·side [prɪˈzaɪd] *vi*: **to** ~ **(at** *or* **over)** presiedere (a).

presi·den·cy [ˈprezɪdənsɪ] *n (Pol etc)* presidenza; *(Am: of company)* direzione *f.*

presi·dent [ˈprezɪdənt] *n (Pol etc)* presidente *m*; *(Am: of company)* direttore/trice generale.

presi·den·tial [ˌprezɪˈdenʃəl] *adj (Pol)* presidenziale.

press [pres] **1** *n* **(a)** *(apparatus, machine: gen)* pressa; *(: for wine)* torchio; **trouser** ~ stiracalzoni *m inv.*

(b) *(printing press)* torchio da stampa; *(: place)* tipografia; **to go to** ~ *(newspaper)* andare in macchina; **to be in the** ~ *(being printed)* essere in (corso di) stampa; *(in the newspapers)* essere sui giornali; **the** ~ *(newspapers)* la stampa, i giornali; **to get a good/bad ~** avere una buona/cattiva stampa.

2 *vt* **(a)** *(push: button)* premere, schiacciare; *(: doorbell)* suonare; *(: trigger)* premere; *(squeeze: lemon, grapes)* spremere; *(: flowers)* pressare; *(: hand)* stringere; **to ~ sb/sth to one's heart** stringersi qn/qc al petto *or* al cuore.

(b) *(iron)* stirare.

(c) *(urge, entreat)*: **to ~ sb to do** *or* **into doing sth** fare pressione su qn affinché faccia qc; *(force)*: **to ~ sth on sb** *(food, gift)* insistere perché qn accetti qc; *(one's opinions)* voler imporre qc su qn; *(insist on: attack)* rendere più pressante; *(: claim, demands)* insistere su *or* in; **to ~ sb for an answer** insistere perché qn risponda; **to be hard ~ed** essere alle strette; **to ~ one's opponent** incalzare l'avversario; **to ~ home an advantage** sfruttare al massimo un vantaggio; **to ~ the point** insistere sul punto; **to be ~ed for time** aver poco tempo; **to be ~ed for money** essere a corto di soldi; **to ~ sb into service** metter qn sotto a lavorare; **to ~ sth into service** far uso di qc; **to ~ charges against sb** *(Law)* sporgere una denuncia contro qn.

3 *vi* **(a)** *(in physical sense)* spingere, premere; **the people ~ed round him** la gente gli si è accalcata intorno; **the crowd ~ed towards the exit** la folla si accalcava all'uscita; **to ~ ahead** *or* **forward (with sth)** *(fig)* proseguire (in qc).

(b) *(urge, agitate)*: **to ~ for sth** fare pressioni per ottenere qc; **time ~es** il tempo stringe.

4 *cpd (agency, campaign, cutting)* di stampa; **~ agent** *n* agente *m* pubblicitario; **~ conference** *n* conferenza *f* stampa *inv*; **~ gallery** *n* tribuna della stampa; **~ photographer** *n* fotoreporter *m/f inv*; **~ stud** *n* (bottone *m*) automatico.

♦ **press on** *vi + adv*: **to ~ on with sth** continuare (a fare) qc.

press-gang ['prɛsɡæŋ] *vt*: **to ~ sb into doing sth** costringere qn a viva forza a fare qc.

press·ing ['prɛsɪŋ] *adj (matter, problem)* urgente, pressante; *(request, invitation)* insistente, pressante; **he was very ~** era molto insistente.

press·man ['prɛsmæn] *n, pl* **-men** giornalista *m*, cronista *m*.

pres·sure ['prɛʃəʳ] **1** *n* **(a)** *(Phys, Tech, Met)* pressione *f*; **high/low ~** alta/bassa pressione; **at full ~** *(Tech)* al livello massimo di pressione.

(b) *(compulsion, influence)* pressione *f*, pressioni *fpl*; **he's under ~ from his wife to give up smoking** sua moglie fa pressione perché lui smetta di fumare; **to put ~ on sb** fare pressione su qn; **they are really putting the ~ on** ci *(or* vi *etc)* stanno assillando; **to use ~ to obtain sth** far pressione per ottenere qc; **to work under ~** lavorare sotto pressione; **he's under a lot of ~** è sotto pressione; **the ~ of these events** la tensione creata da questi avvenimenti; **~ of work prevented her from going** non ha potuto andare per via del troppo lavoro.

2 *vt* = **pressurize b.**

3 *cpd*: **~ cooker** *n* pentola a pressione; **~ gauge** *n* manometro; **~ group** *n* gruppo di pressione.

pres·sur·ize ['prɛʃəraɪz] *vt* **(a)** pressurizzare. **(b)** *(fig)*: **to ~ sb (into doing sth)** fare delle pressioni su qn (per costringerlo a fare qc).

pres·tige [prɛsˈtiːʒ] *n* prestigio.

pres·tig·ious [prɛsˈtɪdʒəs] *adj* prestigioso(a), di grande prestigio.

pre·sum·ably [prɪˈzjuːməblɪ] *adv*: **~ he did it** penso *or* presumo che l'abbia fatto.

pre·sume [prɪˈzjuːm] **1** *vt* **(a)** *(suppose)*: **to ~ (that)**

supporre (che); **I ~ he'll come** suppongo che verrà; **I ~ he did it** suppongo che l'abbia fatto. **(b)** *(venture)*: **to ~ to do sth** permettersi di fare qc. **2** *vi (take liberties)* prendersi troppe libertà; **to ~ on sb's friendship** approfittarsi dell'amicizia di qn.

pre·sump·tion [prɪˈzʌmpʃən] *n* **(a)** *(arrogance)* presunzione *f*. **(b)** *(thing presumed)* supposizione *f*; **there is a strong ~ that...** tutto fa supporre *or* presumere che.... .

pre·sump·tu·ous [prɪˈzʌmptjʊəs] *adj* presuntuoso(a).

pre·sup·pose [ˌpriːsəˈpəʊz] *vt* presupporre.

pre·tence, *(Am)* **pre·tense** [prɪˈtɛns] *n* **(a)**: **his ~ of innocence/sympathy** la sua finta *or* falsa innocenza/comprensione; **she is devoid of all ~** non si nasconde dietro false apparenze; **to make a ~ of doing sth** far finta di fare qc; **it's all (a) ~** è tutta una finta, è tutta scena. **(b)** *(claim)* pretesa. **(c)** *(pretext)* pretesto, scusa; **on** *or* **under the ~ of doing sth** con il pretesto *or* la scusa di fare qc.

pre·tend [prɪˈtɛnd] **1** *vt* **(a)** *(feign)*: **to ~ illness/ignorance** fingersi malato(a)/ignorante, far finta di essere malato(a)/ignorante; **to ~ to do sth** far finta *or* fingere di fare qc; **he's ~ing he can't hear us** fa finta di non sentirci; **he was ~ing to be a lawyer** si spacciava per avvocato. **(b)** *(claim)*: **to ~ to do/that** pretendere di fare/che + *sub*. **2** *vi (feign)* far finta, fingere; **she is only ~ing** sta solo facendo finta. **3** *adj (fam: gun, money)* finto(a).

pre·tense [prɪˈtɛns] *n (Am)* = **pretence.**

pre·ten·sion [prɪˈtɛnʃən] *n (claim)* pretesa; **to have no ~s to sth/to being sth** non avere la pretesa di avere qc/di essere qc.

pre·ten·tious [prɪˈtɛnʃəs] *adj* pretenzioso(a).

pret·er·ite ['prɛtərɪt] *n* (tempo) passato.

pre·text ['priːtɛkst] *n* pretesto; **on** *or* **under the ~ of doing sth** col pretesto di fare qc.

pret·ty ['prɪtɪ] **1** *adj* **(-ier, -iest)** grazioso(a), carino(a); **he wasn't a ~ sight** non era bello da vedere; **it'll cost you a ~ penny!** ti costerà una bella sommetta! **2** *adv (rather)* piuttosto; *(very)* molto; **~ well** *(not badly)* piuttosto bene; *(also: ~ nearly, almost)* quasi, praticamente; **it's ~ much the same** *(fam)* è praticamente uguale.

pret·zel ['prɛtsl] *n* taralluccio.

pre·vail [prɪˈveɪl] *vi* **(a)** *(gain mastery)*: **to ~ (against, over)** prevalere (su). **(b)** *(be current; fashion, belief etc)* essere diffuso(a); **the conditions that ~** le condizioni attuali. **(c)** *(persuade)*: **to ~ (up)on sb to do sth** convincere qn a fare qc.

pre·vail·ing [prɪˈveɪlɪŋ] *adj (conditions)* attuale; *(belief, customs, attitude)* predominante; *(wind)* dominante.

preva·lence ['prɛvələns] *n (of crime, customs, attitude)* larga diffusione *f*; *(of conditions)* prevalere *m*.

preva·lent ['prɛvələnt] *adj (belief, disease, fashion etc)* diffuso(a); **the conditions which are ~ in...** le condizioni esistenti in... .

pre·vari·cate [prɪˈværɪkeɪt] *vi* tergiversare.

pre·vari·ca·tion [prɪˌværɪˈkeɪʃən] *n* tergiversazione *f*.

pre·vent [prɪˈvɛnt] *vt (crime, accidents, fire)* prevenire; **to ~ sb/sth (from doing sth)** impedire a qn/qc (di fare qc); **to ~ sb's doing sth** impedire che qn faccia qc, impedire a qn di fare qc.

pre·ven·ta·tive [prɪˈvɛntətɪv] *adj* preventivo(a).

pre·ven·tion [prɪˈvɛnʃən] *n* prevenzione *f*; **Society for the P~ of Cruelty to Children/Animals** Società per la protezione dei fanciulli/degli animali.

pre·ven·tive |prɪ'vɛntɪv| *adj* preventivo(a).

pre·view |'priːvjuː| *n* (*of film etc*) anteprima; **to give sb a ~ of sth** (*fig*) dare a qn un'idea di qc.

pre·vi·ous |'priːvɪəs| *adj* precedente; **the ~ day** il giorno prima *or* precedente; **~ experience** precedente esperienza; **he has no ~ experience in that field** non ha esperienza in quel campo; **I have a ~ engagement** ho già (preso) un impegno; **on a ~ occasion** in un'altra occasione; **in a ~ life** in un'altra vita; **to have no ~ convictions** (*Law*) non aver precedenti penali; **to have 5 ~ convictions** essere già stato condannato 5 volte.

pre·vi·ous·ly |'priːvɪəslɪ| *adv* (*before*) prima; (*in the past*) in precedenza; (*already*) già.

pre·war |ˌpriː'wɔː'| *adj* dell'anteguerra.

prey |preɪ| **1** *n* (*also fig*) preda; **beast/bird of ~** animale *m*/uccello da preda; **to be a ~ to** (*fig*) essere in preda a. **2** *vi* **: to ~ on** (*subj: animals*) predare; (*: person*) depredare; (*: doubts, anxiety*): **to ~ on sb's mind** ossessionare qn.

price |praɪs| **1** *n* **(a)** (*also fig*) prezzo; **to go up** *or* **rise in ~** salire *or* aumentare di prezzo; **to go down** *or* **fall in ~** scendere *or* calare di prezzo; **I got a good ~ for it** me lo hanno pagato bene; **what is the ~ of that painting?** quanto costa quel quadro?; **at a reduced ~** a prezzo ribassato; **we pay top ~s for silver** offriamo ottimi prezzi per l'argento; **every man has his ~** ogni uomo ha il suo prezzo; **the ~ of fame** il prezzo del successo; **it's a small ~ to pay for it** (*fig*) non è che un piccolo sacrificio; **to pay a high ~ for sth** (*also fig*) pagare qc caro; **what ~ his promises now?** a che valgono ora le sue promesse?; **peace at any ~** pace ad ogni costo *or* costi quello che costi; **not at any ~** per nessuna cosa al mondo; **he regained his freedom, but at a ~** ha riconquistato la sua libertà, ma a caro prezzo.

(b) (*value, valuation*) valore *m*; **to put a ~ on sth** valutare *or* stimare qc; **to put a ~ on sb's head** mettere una taglia sulla testa di qn; **you can't put a ~ on it** (*fig: friendship, loyalty etc*) è inestimabile.

(c) (*Betting: odds*) quotazione *f*.

2 *vt* (*fix ~ of*) fissare il prezzo di; (*put ~ label on*) prezzare, mettere il prezzo su; (*ask ~ of*) chiedere il prezzo di; **it was ~d at £20** il prezzo era di 20 sterline; **it was ~d too high/low** aveva un prezzo troppo alto/basso; **to be ~d out of the market** (*article*) essere così caro da diventare invendibile; (*producer, nation*) non poter sostenere la concorrenza.

3 *cpd* (*control, index, war*) dei prezzi; **~ fixing** *n* (*also pej*) controllo dei prezzi; **~ limit** *n* limite *m* di prezzo; **~ list** *n* listino (dei) prezzi; **~ range** *n* gamma di prezzi; **it's within my ~ range** rientra nelle mie possibilità; **~ tag** *n* cartellino del prezzo.

price·less |'praɪslɪs| *adj* (*jewels, necklace*) di valore inestimabile; (*fam: amusing*) impagabile, spassosissimo(a); **friendship is ~** l'amicizia è un bene inestimabile.

pricey |'praɪsɪ| *adj* (*Brit fam*) caruccio(a).

prick |prɪk| **1** *n* (*act, sensation*) puntura; (*mark*) buco; **~s of conscience** rimorsi *mpl*. **2** *vt* (*puncture: balloon, blister*) bucare; (*subj: plant, needle*) pungere; (*: conscience*) rimordere; **to ~ a hole in sth** fare un buco in qc; **to ~ one's finger (with/on sth)** pungersi un dito (con/su qc).

♦ **prick up** *vt + adv*: **to ~ up one's ears** (*also fig*) drizzare le orecchie.

prick·le |'prɪkl| *n* **(a)** (*on plant, animal etc*) spina. **(b)** (*sensation*) sensazione *f* di prurito; (*: of fear*) brivido.

prick·ly |'prɪklɪ| **1** *adj* (*-ier, -iest*) **(a)** (*plant*) spinoso(a); (*animal*) pieno(a) di spine; (*beard*) ispido(a); (*wool*) che dà prurito. **(b)** (*fig: person*) irritabile; (*: subject*) spinoso(a). **2** *cpd*: **~ heat** *n* (*Med*) sudamina; **~ pear** *n* (*plant, fruit*) fico d'India.

pride |praɪd| **1** *n* **(a)** (*arrogance*) superbia, orgoglio; (*self-respect*) orgoglio, amor proprio; (*satisfaction*) fierezza; **false ~** vanità; **to take (a) ~ in** (*appearance, punctuality*) tenere molto a; (*children, achievements*) essere orgoglioso di; **she takes (a) ~ in arriving on time** va molto orgogliosa del fatto che è sempre puntuale; **his ~ was hurt** fu ferito nell'orgoglio; **he is a (great) source of ~ to her** lei è (molto) fiera *or* orgogliosa di lui; **her ~ and joy** tutto il suo orgoglio; **false ~** orgoglio ingiustificato; **to have ~ of place** essere al primo posto. **(b)** (*of lions*) branco. **2** *vt*: **to ~ o.s. on sth** vantarsi per qc.

priest |priːst| *n* prete *m*, sacerdote *m*.

priest·ess |'priːstɪs| *n* sacerdotessa.

priest·hood |'priːsthʊd| *n*: **to enter the ~** farsi prete.

priest·ly |'priːstlɪ| *adj* sacerdotale.

prig |prɪg| *n*: **don't be such a ~!** non fare il(la) moralista!; **what a ~ she is!** ma chi si crede di essere!

prim |prɪm| *adj* (*-mer, -mest*) (*demure: person, dress*) per benino; (*: house, garden*) in cui nulla è fuori posto; (*manner, smile*) da persona per benino; (*prudish: also*: **~ and proper**) per benino.

pri·ma fa·cie |ˌpraɪmə'feɪʃɪ| **1** *adv* a prima vista. **2** *adj* (*a prima vista*) legittimo(a); **to have a ~ case** (*Law*) presentare una causa in apparenza fondata.

pri·mari·ly |'praɪmərɪlɪ| *adv* (*chiefly*) principalmente, essenzialmente.

pri·ma·ry |'praɪmərɪ| **1** *adj* (*chief, main: gen*) principale, primario(a); **of ~ importance** di primaria *or* fondamentale importanza. **2** *n* (*Am: election*) primarie *fpl*. **3** *cpd*: **~ colour** *n* colore *m* fondamentale; **~ education** *n* istruzione *f* elementare *or* primaria; **~ school** *n* scuola elementare *or* primaria; **~ teacher** *n* insegnante *m/f* di scuola elementare, maestro/a.

pri·mate |'praɪmeɪt| *n* **(a)** (*Zool*) primate *m*. **(b)** |'praɪmɪt| (*Rel*) primate *m*.

prime |praɪm| **1** *adj* **(a)** (*chief, major: gen*) principale, fondamentale; (*: cause, reason*) primo(a), fondamentale; **of ~ importance** della massima importanza. **(b)** (*excellent: example*) superbo(a); (*: meat*) di prima scelta; **of ~ quality** di prima scelta; **in ~ condition** (*car, athlete*) in perfette condizioni; (*fruit etc*) in condizioni perfette. **2** *n*: **in the ~ of life, in one's ~** nel fiore degli anni; **to be past one's ~** non essere più quello di una volta. **3** *vt* (*gun*) innescare; (*pump*) adescare; (*surface etc*) preparare; (*fig: instruct*) istruire; **he arrived well ~d** è arrivato ben preparato. **4** *cpd*: **P~ Minister** (*abbr* **P.M.**) *n* Primo Ministro; **~ number** *n* (*Math*) numero primo.

prim·er |'praɪmə'| *n* **(a)** (*textbook*) testo elementare; (*paint*) mano *f* preparatoria.

pri·meval |praɪ'miːvəl| *adj* primordiale; **~ forests** foreste originarie.

primi·tive |'prɪmɪtɪv| *adj, n* primitivo(a) (*m/f*).

prim·rose |'prɪmrəʊz| **1** *n* (*Bot*) primula (gialla). **2** *adj* (*also*: **~ yellow**) giallo pulcino *inv*.

primu·la |'prɪmjʊlə| *n* (*Bot*) primula.

Pri·mus (stove) |'praɪməs(ˌstəʊv)| *n*® fornello a petrolio.

prince |prɪns| **1** *n* principe *m*. **2** *cpd*: **~ charming** *n* principe *m* azzurro; **~ consort/regent** *n* principe *m* consorte/reggente.

prince·ly ['prɪnslɪ] *adj (also fig)* principesco(a).

prin·cess [prɪn'ses] *n* principessa.

prin·ci·pal ['prɪnsɪpəl] **1** *adj* principale; **the ~ violin** il primo violino. **2** *n* **(a)** *(of school, college etc)* preside *m/f; (in play)* protagonista *m/f; (in orchestra)* primo(a) strumentista *m/f*. **(b)** *(Fin)* capitale *m*.

prin·ci·pal·ity [,prɪnsɪ'pælɪtɪ] *n* principato.

prin·ci·pal·ly ['prɪnsɪpəlɪ] *adv* principalmente.

prin·ci·ple ['prɪnsəpl] *n* principio; **in ~** in linea di principio; **on ~** per principio; **it's a matter of ~**, **it's the ~ of the thing** è una questione di principio; **a man of ~(s)** un uomo di saldi principi; **it's against my ~s** è contrario ai miei principi.

print [prɪnt] **1** *n* **(a)** *(mark, imprint: of foot, tyre etc)* impronta. **(b)** *(typeface, characters)* caratteri *mpl; (printed matter)* stampa; **that book is in/out of ~** quel libro è disponibile/esaurito; **to see o.s. in ~** vedere il proprio nome stampato; **in small/large ~** stampato a caratteri piccoli/grandi. **(c)** *(fabric)* stampato. **(d)** *(Art)* stampa; *(Phot)* fotografia. **2** *vt* **(a)** *(Typ, Textiles, Phot)* stampare; *(fig: on memory)* imprimere. **(b)** *(publish)* pubblicare, stampare. **(c)** *(write in block letters)* scrivere in stampatello.

♦ **print out** *vt + adv (Computers)* stampare.

print·ed ['prɪntɪd] *adj* stampato(a); **~ matter** *or* **papers** stampe *fpl*; **the power of the ~ word** il potere di tutto ciò che è stampato.

print·er ['prɪntə^r] *n (person)* tipografo/a; *(machine)* stampante *m*; **at the ~'s** *(book)* in tipografia; **~'s ink** inchiostro tipografico.

print·ing ['prɪntɪŋ] **1** *n* **(a)** *(process, also Phot)* stampa. **(b)** *(block writing)* stampatello; *(characters)* caratteri *mpl; (print)* stampa. **(c)** *(quantity printed)* tiratura. **2** *cpd:* **~ press** *n* pressa tipografica; **~ works** *n* tipografia, stamperia.

print·out ['prɪntaut] *n (Computers)* tabulato.

pri·or[1] ['praɪə^r] *adj* **(a)** *precedente;* **without ~ notice** senza preavviso; **to have a ~ claim to sth** avere un diritto di precedenza su qc. **(b):** **~ to sth/to doing sth** prima di qc/di fare qc.

pri·or[2] ['praɪə^r] *n (Rel)* priore *m*.

pri·or·ity [praɪ'ɒrɪtɪ] *n* priorità, precedenza; **to have** *or* **take ~ over sth** avere la precedenza su qc; **we must get our priorities right** dobbiamo decidere quali sono le cose più importanti per noi; **to treat sth as a ~** dare la precedenza a qc.

prise, *(Am)* **prize** [praɪz] *vt:* **to ~ sth open** aprire qc (forzando il coperchio *etc*); **to ~ a lid up/off** aprire/togliere un coperchio facendo leva.

prism ['prɪzəm] *n (Geom, Tech etc)* prisma *m*.

pris·mat·ic [prɪz'mætɪk] *adj* prismatico(a).

pris·on ['prɪzn] **1** *n* prigione *f*, carcere *m*; **to be in ~** essere in prigione; **to go to ~ for 5 years** essere condannato a 5 anni di carcere *or* di reclusione; **to send sb to ~ for 2 years** condannare qn a 2 anni di reclusione. **2** *cpd (system)* carcerario(a); *(conditions, food)* nelle *or* delle prigioni; **~ camp** *n* campo di prigionia; **~ life** *n* vita carceraria.

pris·on·er ['prɪznə^r] **1** *n (under arrest)* arrestato/a; *(convicted)* detenuto/a; *(Mil, fig)* prigioniero/a; **the ~ at the bar** l'accusato, l'imputato; **to take sb ~** far prigioniero qn. **2** *cpd:* **~ of war** *n* prigioniero/a di guerra; **~ of war camp** *n* campo di prigionia.

pris·tine ['prɪstaɪn] *adj (unspoiled)* immacolato(a).

pri·va·cy ['prɪvəsɪ] *n* privacy *f*; **his desire for ~** il suo desiderio di stare da solo; *(actor, popstar)* il suo desiderio di privacy; **in the ~ of one's own home** nell'intimità della propria casa; **in the strictest ~** nella massima segretezza.

pri·vate ['praɪvɪt] **1** *adj* **(a)** *(not public: conversa-*

tion, meeting, land etc) privato(a); *(: funeral, wedding)* intimo(a); *(: showing)* per pochi invitati; *(confidential: letter)* personale; *(: agreement, information)* confidenziale; **'~'** *(on door)* 'privato'; *(on envelope)* 'riservata'; **this information must be kept ~** quest'informazione deve rimanere strettamente confidenziale; **he is a very ~ person** è una persona molto riservata; **in (his) ~ life** nella vita privata; **~ place** posto segreto; **~ hearing** *(Law)* udienza a porte chiuse.

(b) *(for one person: car, house, secretary etc)* privato(a), personale; *(: lessons)* privato(a); *(personal: bank account, reasons etc)* personale; **a man of ~ means** un uomo che vive di rendita.

(c) *(not state-owned etc: company, army, nursing home)* privato(a); *(: doctor, nursing home)* non convenzionato(a), privato(a); **the ~ sector** il settore privato.

2 *n* **(a)** *(Mil)* soldato semplice.

(b): **in ~ = privately a, b.**

3 *cpd:* **~ citizen** *n* privato (cittadino); **~ detective** *n*, **~ investigator** *n*, **~ eye** *n (fam)* investigatore/trice *or* detective *m/f inv* privato(a); **~ enterprise** *n* iniziativa privata; **~ member** *n (Parliament)* semplice deputato; **~ member's bill** *n (Parliament)* progetto di legge ad iniziativa personale; **~ parts** *npl (Anat)* parti *fpl* intime; **~ (medical) practice** *n* studio *or* ambulatorio (medico) privato; **to be in ~ practice** essere medico non convenzionato (con la mutua); **~ school** *n* scuola privata; **~ view** *n (Art)* vernissage *m inv*.

pri·vate·ly ['praɪvɪtlɪ] *adv* **(a)** *(not publicly)* privatamente, in privato. **(b)** *(secretly)* in privato; *(personally)* personalmente. **(c)** *(unofficially)* a titolo personale.

pri·va·tion [praɪ'veɪʃən] *n* **(a)** *(state)* privazione *f*. **(b)** *(hardship)* privazioni *fpl*, stenti *mpl*.

pri·va·tize ['praɪvɪtaɪz] *vt* privatizzare.

priv·et ['prɪvɪt] *n* ligustro.

privi·lege ['prɪvɪlɪdʒ] **1** *n* privilegio; *(Parliament)* prerogativa; **I had the ~ of meeting her** ho avuto il privilegio *or* l'onore di incontrarla. **2** *vt:* **to be ~d to do sth** avere il privilegio *or* l'onore di fare qc.

privi·leged ['prɪvɪlɪdʒd] *adj* privilegiato(a); **a ~ few** pochi privilegiati; **the ~ few** i pochi privilegiati.

privy ['prɪvɪ] **1** *adj* **(a):** **to be ~ to sth** essere a conoscenza di qc. **(b):** **P~ Council/Councillor** *(Brit)* Consiglio/Consigliere *m* della Corona. **2** *n (toilet)* gabinetto.

prize[1] [praɪz] **1** *n (gen)* premio; **to win first ~** *(in game, race, lottery)* vincere il primo premio; *(Scol etc)* ottenere il primo premio. **2** *adj* **(a)** *(awarded a ~)* premiato(a); *(worthy of a ~)* eccellente; **a ~ idiot** *(fam)* un cretino patentato. **(b)** *(awarded as a ~: cup, medal)* premio *inv (after n)*. **(c)** *(offering a ~: draw)* a premio, a premi. **3** *vt (honesty, friendship)* stimare, valutare; **he ~s his medals** è molto orgoglioso delle sue medaglie; **her most ~d possession** il suo avere più prezioso. **4** *cpd:* **~ draw** *n* estrazione *f* a premi *or* a premio; **~ fight** *n (Boxing)* incontro di pugilato fra professionisti; **~ money** *n* soldi *mpl* del premio.

prize[2] [praɪz] *vt (Am)* = **prise.**

prize-giving ['praɪz,gɪvɪŋ] *n* premiazione *f*.

prize-winner ['praɪz,wɪnə^r] *n (in competition, lottery)* vincitore/trice; *(Scol, in flower show)* premiato/a.

prize-winning ['praɪz,wɪnɪŋ] *adj (gen)* vincente; *(novel, essay etc)* premiato(a).

pro[1] [prəʊ] *n:* **the ~s and cons** i pro e i contro.

pro² [prəʊ] n (fam) professionista m/f.
pro- [prəʊ] pref (in favour of) filo...; ~**Soviet** filoso-vietico(a).
prob·abil·ity [ˌprɒbə'bɪlɪtɪ] n probabilità; **in all** ~ con ogni probabilità.
prob·able ['prɒbəbl] adj probabile; **it is** ~/**hardly** ~ **that**... è probabile/poco probabile che... + sub.
prob·ably ['prɒbəblɪ] adv probabilmente.
pro·bate ['prəʊbɪt] n (Law) omologazione f (di un testamento).
pro·ba·tion [prə'beɪʃən] **1** n: **to be on** ~ (Law) essere in libertà condizionale; (gen: in employment etc) essere in prova, fare un periodo di prova; **to put sb on** ~ (Law) dare a qn la libertà condizionale. **2** cpd: ~ **officer** n (Law) funzionario incaricato della sorveglianza dei condannati in libertà condizionale.
probe [prəʊb] **1** n (a) (Med, Space) sonda. (b) (inquiry) indagine f. **2** vt (hole, crack) tastare; (Med) esplorare, sondare; (Space) esplorare; (also: ~ **into**) indagare su; **the policeman kept probing me** il poliziotto continuò a farmi domande.
prob·ing ['prəʊbɪŋ] adj (look) penetrante; (question) sottile; (interrogation, study) approfondito(a).
pro·bity ['prəʊbɪtɪ] n probità, rettitudine f.
prob·lem ['prɒbləm] **1** n (also Math) problema m; **to have** ~**s with the car** avere dei problemi con la macchina; **my son is a** ~ mio figlio è un problema; **the housing** ~ la crisi degli alloggi; **to have a drinking** ~ avere il vizio del bere; **I had no** ~ **in finding her** non mi è stato difficile trovarla; **what's the** ~? che cosa c'è?; **no** ~! ma certamente!, non c'è problema! **2** cpd (child, family) difficile; ~ **page** n posta del cuore.
prob·lem·at·ic(al) [ˌprɒblɪ'mætɪk(l)] adj problematico(a), dubbio(a); **it is** ~ **whether...** è in dubbio se... .
pro·cedure [prə'siːdʒə'] n procedura; **the usual** ~ **is to...** la procedura normale or prassi è di...; **cashing a cheque is a simple** ~ riscuotere un assegno è un'operazione semplice.
pro·ceed [prə'siːd] **1** vi (a) (move forward) procedere; (continue) proseguire; **let us** ~ **with caution** procediamo con cautela; **let us** ~ **to the next item** passiamo al prossimo punto; **things are** ~**ing according to plan** tutto procede or si svolge secondo i piani; **I am not sure how to** ~ non so bene come fare. (b) (originate): **to** ~ **from** (sound) provenire da; (fear) derivare da. (c): **to** ~ **against sb** (Law) procedere contro qn. **2** vt: **to** ~ **to do sth** cominciare or mettersi a fare qc.
pro·ceed·ing [prə'siːdɪŋ] n (a) (action, course of action) modo d'agire. (b): ~**s** pl (function) cerimonia; (meeting) seduta; (discussions) dibattito. (c): ~**s** pl (esp Law: measures) provvedimenti mpl; **to take** ~**s (in order to do sth)** prendere i provvedimenti necessari (per fare qc); **to take** ~**s (against sb)** (Law) promuovere un'azione legale (contro qn). (d): ~**s** pl (record: of learned society) atti mpl.
pro·ceeds ['prəʊsiːdz] npl proventi mpl, ricavato.
pro·cess¹ ['prəʊses] **1** n (a) processo; **the whole** ~ l'intera operazione; **in the** ~ **of restoring the picture he discovered...** stava restaurando il quadro quando ha scoperto...; **in** ~ **of construction** in (corso di) costruzione; **we are in the** ~ **of moving to...** stiamo per trasferirci a... . (b) (specific method) procedimento, metodo; **the Bessemer** ~ il processo Bessemer. (c) (Law: action) processo; (: summons) mandato di comparizione, citazione f in giudizio. **2** vt (Tech) trat-

tare; (Phot) sviluppare e stampare; (Admin: application etc) sbrigare; (Computers) elaborare; ~**ed cheese**, (Am) ~ **cheese** formaggio fuso.
pro·cess² [prə'ses] vi (frm: go in procession) sfilare, procedere in corteo.
pro·cess·ing ['prəʊsesɪŋ] n (of data) elaborazione f; (of food) trattamento; (of film) sviluppo e stampa; (of application) disbrigo.
pro·ces·sion [prə'seʃən] n (of people, cars etc) processione f, corteo; (Rel) processione.
pro·claim [prə'kleɪm] vt (a) (gen) proclamare; (peace, public holiday) dichiarare; **to** ~ **sb king/that** proclamare qn re/che. (b) (fig: reveal) dimostrare, rivelare.
proc·la·ma·tion [ˌprɒklə'meɪʃən] n proclama m.
pro·cliv·ity [prə'klɪvɪtɪ] n tendenza, propensione f.
pro·cras·ti·nate [prəʊ'kræstɪneɪt] vi procrastinare.
pro·cras·ti·na·tion [prəʊˌkræstɪ'neɪʃən] n procrastinazione f.
pro·crea·tion [ˌprəʊkrɪ'eɪʃən] n procreazione f.
pro·cure [prə'kjʊə'] vt (a) procurare, ottenere; **to** ~ **sb sth, to** ~ **sth for sb** procurare qc a qn, ottenere qc per qn; **I managed to** ~ **a copy for myself** sono riuscito a procurarmene una copia. (b) (for prostitution) procurare.
prod [prɒd] **1** n (push, jab) colpetto; (with elbow) gomitata. **2** vt (jab: with stick, finger etc) dare un colpetto a; **he** ~**ded the page with his finger** ha puntato il dito sulla pagina; **he has to be** ~**ded along** (fig) ha bisogno di essere pungolato. **3** vi: **he** ~**ded at the picture with a finger** ha puntato il dito sul quadro.
prod·i·gal ['prɒdɪgəl] adj prodigo(a).
pro·di·gious [prə'dɪdʒəs] adj prodigioso(a), straordinario(a).
prod·i·gy ['prɒdɪdʒɪ] n prodigio; **child** ~, **infant** ~ bambino/a prodigio inv.
pro·duce ['prɒdjuːs] **1** n (Agr) prodotto; (collective n) prodotti mpl. **2** [prə'djuːs] vt (a) (manufacture: gen) produrre; (create: book, essay) scrivere; (: work of art) fare; (: meal) preparare; (: ideas, profit) dare; (: interest) suscitare; (give birth to) partorire. (b) (bring, show: gen) tirar fuori; (: tickets) esibire, mostrare; (: proof of identity) produrre, fornire; **I can't suddenly** ~ **£50!** da dove te lo tiro fuori 50 sterline? **(c)** (play, film etc) produrre. (d) (cause: gen) causare, provocare; (: results) produrre; (: interest) suscitare; **this** ~**d a stir** ha fatto sensazione.
pro·duc·er [prə'djuːsə'] n (Agr, Cine, TV) produttore/trice; (Theatre) regista m/f.
prod·uct ['prɒdʌkt] n (also Math) prodotto; (fig) frutto.
pro·duc·tion [prə'dʌkʃən] **1** n (a) (manufacture) produzione f; **to put into** ~ mettere in produzione; **to take out of** ~ togliere dalla produzione; **the country's steel** ~ la produzione siderurgica del paese. (b) (showing) presentazione f; (: of documents) produzione f; **on** ~ **of this ticket** dietro presentazione di questo biglietto. (c) (of play, film etc) produzione f; (work produced) realizzazione f teatrale (or cinematografica). **2** cpd (Industry): ~ **line** n catena di montaggio; ~ **manager** n direttore m di produzione.
pro·duc·tive [prə'dʌktɪv] adj (gen) produttivo(a); (meeting, discussion) fruttuoso(a); (shop, business) che rende; (writer) prolifico(a); (land, imagination) fertile; **he had a very** ~ **day** ha avuto una giornata molto soddisfacente.
prod·uc·tiv·ity [ˌprɒdʌk'tɪvɪtɪ] **1** n produttività. **2** cpd: ~ **agreement** n accordo sui tempi di produzione; ~ **bonus** n premio di produzione.

pro·fane [prəˈfeɪn] **1** *adj* (a) *(secular)* profano(a). **(b)** *(irreverent)* irriverente; *(: language)* blasfemo(a). **2** *vt* profanare.

pro·fan·ity [prəˈfænɪtɪ] *n (oath)* bestemmia.

pro·fess [prəˈfes] *vt* **(a)** *(faith, belief etc)* professare. **(b)** *(claim)* dichiarare; **he ~es extreme regret** si dichiara molto dispiaciuto; **I do not ~ to be an expert** non pretendo di essere un esperto.

pro·fessed [prəˈfest] *adj (Rel)* professo(a); *(self-declared)* dichiarato(a).

pro·fes·sion [prəˈfeʃən] *n* **(a)** *(gen)* professione *f;* **the ~s** le professioni liberali; **by ~** di professione; **the medical ~** *(calling)* la professione medica; *(doctors collectively)* i medici. **(b)** *(declaration)* dichiarazione *f;* **~ of faith** professione *f* di fede.

pro·fes·sion·al [prəˈfeʃənl] **1** *adj* **(a)** *(capacity)* professionale; *(diplomat, soldier)* di carriera; **a ~ man** un professionista; **to take ~ advice** consultare un esperto; **to be a ~ singer** essere un cantante professionista *or* di professione; **to turn** *or* **go ~** *(Sport)* passare al professionismo. **(b)** *(competent, skilled: worker)* esperto(a); *(: piece of work, approach)* da professionista; *(: attitude)* professionale; **it's not up to ~ standards** non è da professionista. **2** *n* professionista *m/f.*

pro·fes·sion·al·ism [prəˈfeʃnəlɪzəm] *n* professionismo.

pro·fes·sion·al·ly [prəˈfeʃnəlɪ] *adv (play)* come professionista; *(sing)* per professione; **I only know him ~** lo conosco solo per lavoro; **to be ~ qualified** essere abilitato alla professione.

pro·fes·sor [prəˈfesəʳ] *n (Univ: Brit, Am)* professore *m* titolare (di cattedra); *(Am: teacher)* professore/essa.

prof·fer [ˈprɒfəʳ] *vt (remark)* profferire; *(hand)* porgere; *(apologies)* porgere, presentare; *(advice)* fornire.

pro·fi·cien·cy [prəˈfɪʃənsɪ] *n* competenza.

pro·fi·cient [prəˈfɪʃənt] *adj* provetto(a), competente.

pro·file [ˈprəʊfaɪl] *n* profilo; **in ~** di profilo; **to keep a low ~** *(fig)* cercare di passare inosservato *or* di non farsi notare troppo.

prof·it [ˈprɒfɪt] **1** *n (Comm)* profitto, utile *m,* guadagno; *(fig)* profitto, vantaggio; **~ and loss account** conto perdite e profitti; **to make a ~ out of** *or* **on sth** guadagnarci sopra qc; **to sell sth at a ~** vendere qc con un utile. **2** *vi:* **to ~ by** *or* **from sth** approfittare di qc. **3** *cpd:* **~ margin** *n* margine *m* di profitto.

prof·it·abil·ity [ˌprɒfɪtəˈbɪlɪtɪ] *n* redditività.

prof·it·able [ˈprɒfɪtəbl] *adj (Comm)* remunerativo(a), redditizio(a); *(fig: beneficial: scheme)* vantaggioso(a); *(: meeting, visit)* fruttuoso(a).

prof·it·ably [ˈprɒfɪtəblɪ] *adv (Comm)* con profitto; *(fig)* vantaggiosamente; *(: spend time)* utilmente.

profi·teer [ˌprɒfɪˈtɪəʳ] **1** *vi* speculare. **2** *n* profittatore/trice, speculatore/trice.

profi·teer·ing [prɒfɪˈtɪərɪŋ] *n (pej)* affarismo.

profit-making [ˈprɒfɪtˌmeɪkɪŋ] *adj* a scopo di lucro.

profit-sharing [ˈprɒfɪtˌʃeərɪŋ] *n* compartecipazione *f* agli utili.

prof·li·gate [ˈprɒflɪgɪt] *adj (dissolute: behaviour, act)* dissipato(a); *(: person)* debosciato(a); *(extravagant):* **he's very ~ with his money** è uno che sperpera i suoi soldi.

pro for·ma [ˈprəʊˈfɔːmə] *adv:* **~ invoice** fattura proforma.

pro·found [prəˈfaʊnd] *adj* profondo(a).

pro·fun·dity [prəˈfʌndɪtɪ] *n* profondità.

pro·fuse [prəˈfjuːs] *adj (tears, bleeding, vegetation)* copioso(a), abbondante; *(thanks, praise, apologies)* infinito(a); **she was ~ in her thanks** si è profusa in ringraziamenti.

pro·fuse·ly [prəˈfjuːslɪ] *adv (sweat, bleed)* abbondantemente; *(praise)* a profusione; *(grow)* rigogliosamente; **he apologized ~** si è profuso in scuse.

pro·fu·sion [prəˈfjuːʒən] *n* profusione *f;* **in ~** a profusione.

prog·eny [ˈprɒdʒɪnɪ] *n* progenie *f.*

prog·no·sis [prɒgˈnəʊsɪs] *n, pl* **prognoses** [prɒgˈnəʊsiːz] *(Med)* prognosi *f inv.*

pro·gramme, *(Am)* **pro·gram** [ˈprəʊgræm] **1** *n (gen, Pol, Computers)* programma *m; (Radio, TV: broadcast)* programma, trasmissione *f; (: station)* canale *m;* **what's the ~ for today?** che cosa facciamo oggi? **2** *vt (arrange)* programmare, stabilire; *(computer, machine)* programmare.

pro·gram·mer [ˈprəʊgræməʳ] *n* programmatore/trice.

pro·gram·ming, *(Am)* **pro·gram·ing** [ˈprəʊgræmɪŋ] *n* programmazione *f.*

pro·gress [ˈprəʊgres] **1** *n (gen)* progresso, progressi *mpl;* **to make ~** *(gen)* fare progressi; *(walk forward etc)* avanzare; **the pupil is making good ~** l'allievo fa dei buoni progressi; **the work is making little ~** il lavoro procede lentamente; **the ~ of events** il corso degli avvenimenti; **in ~** *(meeting, work etc)* in corso. **2** [prəʊˈgres] *vi* **(a)** *(go forward)* avanzare, procedere. **(b)** *(in time)* procedere; **as the match ~ed** man mano che la partita procedeva. **(c)** *(improve, make ~: person)* far progressi; *(: investigation, studies)* progredire. **3** *cpd:* **~ report** *n (Med)* bollettino medico; *(Admin)* rendiconto dei lavori; *(Scol)* pagella.

pro·gres·sion [prəˈgreʃən] *n* progresso; *(Math)* progressione *f.*

pro·gres·sive [prəˈgresɪv] *adj* **(a)** *(increasing: disease, taxation)* progressivo(a). **(b)** *(favouring progress: idea, party)* progressista.

pro·gres·sive·ly [prəˈgresɪvlɪ] *adv* progressivamente, gradualmente.

pro·hib·it [prəˈhɪbɪt] *vt* **(a)** *(forbid)* proibire, vietare; **to ~ sb from doing sth** vietare *or* proibire a qn di fare qc; **'smoking ~ed'** 'vietato fumare'. **(b)** *(prevent):* **to ~ sb from doing sth** impedire a qn di fare qc.

pro·hi·bi·tion [ˌprəʊɪˈbɪʃən] *n* proibizione *f,* divieto; **P~** *(Am)* proibizionismo.

pro·hibi·tive [prəˈhɪbɪtɪv] *adj* proibitivo(a).

proj·ect [ˈprɒdʒekt] **1** *n (scheme, plan)* progetto, piano; *(study)* progetto, lavoro di ricerca; *(: Scol, Univ)* ricerca. **2** [prəˈdʒekt] *vt (film)* proiettare; *(voice)* spiegare; *(one's personality)* mettere in luce; *(visit)* progettare. **3** [prəˈdʒekt] *vi (jut out)* sporgere in fuori.

pro·jec·tile [prəˈdʒektaɪl] *n* proiettile *m.*

pro·jec·tion [prəˈdʒekʃən] *n* **(a)** *(of films, figures)* proiezione *f.* **(b)** *(forecast: of cost)* preventivo. **(c)** *(overhang, protrusion etc)* sporgenza, prominenza. **2** *cpd:* **~ room** *n (Cine)* cabina *or* sala di proiezione.

pro·jec·tion·ist [prəˈdʒekʃənɪst] *n (Cine)* proiezionista *m/f.*

pro·jec·tor [prəˈdʒektəʳ] *n (Cine)* proiettore *m.*

pro·lapse [ˈprəʊlæps] *n (Med)* prolasso.

pro·letar·ian [ˌprəʊləˈtɛərɪən] *adj, n* proletario(a) *(m/f).*

pro·letari·at [ˌprəʊləˈtɛərɪət] *n* proletariato.

pro·lif·er·ate [prəˈlɪfəreɪt] *vi (Bio, fig)* proliferare; *(animals)* prolificare.

pro·lif·era·tion [prəˌlɪfəˈreɪʃən] *n (see vb)* proliferazione *f;* prolificazione *f.*

pro·lif·ic [prə'lɪfɪk] *adj (rabbit)* prolifico(a); *(crop)* che dà molti frutti; *(writer)* fecondo(a).

pro·logue, *(Am)* **pro·log** ['prəʊlɒg] *n* prologo.

pro·long [prə'lɒŋ] *vt* prolungare.

pro·lon·ga·tion [ˌprəʊlɒŋ'geɪʃən] *n* prolungamento.

prom [prɒm] *n abbr* **(a)** *(Brit fam)* = **promenade;** **promenade concert. (b)** *(Am)* ballo studentesco.

prom·enade [ˌprɒmɪ'nɑːd] **1** *n (at seaside)* lungomare *m.* **2** *vi (stroll)* passeggiare. **3** *cpd:* **~ concert** *n* concerto di musica classica *(con posti in piedi);* **~ deck** *n* ponte *m* di passeggiata.

promi·nence ['prɒmɪnəns] *n (of ridge)* prominenza; *(conspicuousness)* imponenza; *(of role)* importanza; **to come into ~** *(fig)* venire alla ribalta.

promi·nent ['prɒmɪnənt] *adj* **(a)** *(projecting: ridge)* prominente; *(: teeth)* sporgente; *(: cheekbones)* marcato(a). **(b)** *(conspicuous)* che spicca; **put it in a ~ position** mettilo ben in vista. **(c)** *(leading: role, feature)* di rilievo. **(d)** *(well-known: personality)* molto in vista; **he is ~ in the field of...** è un'autorità nel campo di... .

promi·nent·ly ['prɒmɪnəntlɪ] *adv (display, set)* ben in vista; **he figured ~ in the case** ha avuto una parte di primo piano nella faccenda.

promis·cu·ity [ˌprɒmɪs'kjuːɪtɪ] *n (sexual)* promiscuità.

pro·mis·cu·ous [prə'mɪskjʊəs] *adj (sexually: person)* di facili costumi; *(: habits)* licenzioso(a).

prom·ise ['prɒmɪs] **1** *n* promessa; **to make sb a ~** fare una promessa a qn; **to keep one's ~** mantenere la propria promessa; **a young man of ~** un giovane promettente; **to show ~** promettere bene. **2** *vt* promettere; **to ~ (sb) to do sth** promettere (a qn) di fare qc; **to ~ sb sth, to ~ sth to sb** promettere qc a qn; **to ~ sb the earth** *or* **the moon** *(fig)* promettere a qn mari e monti; **to ~ o.s. sth** promettere a se stesso qc. **3** *vi:* **I can't ~, but...** non te *(or* ve *etc)* lo prometto, ma...; **to ~ well** promettere bene.

prom·is·ing ['prɒmɪsɪŋ] *adj* promettente; **it doesn't look ~** non sembra promettente.

prom·is·sory ['prɒmɪsərɪ] **~ note** *n* pagherò *m inv.*

prom·on·tory ['prɒməntrɪ] *n* promontorio.

pro·mote [prə'məʊt] *vt* **(a)** *(in rank):* **to ~ sb (from sth) to sth** promuovere qn (da qc) a qc; **the team was ~d to the second division** *(Ftbl)* la squadra è stata promossa in serie B. **(b)** *(encourage: trade, plan, concert)* promuovere; *(: firm, campaign)* lanciare; *(: product)* lanciare, reclamizzare.

pro·mot·er [prə'məʊtə'] *n (gen)* promotore/trice; *(of company, business)* fondatore/trice.

pro·mo·tion [prə'məʊʃən] *n (gen)* promozione *f;* **to get ~** ottenere la promozione.

prompt [prɒmpt] **1** *adj* **(-er, -est)** *(action)* tempestivo(a); *(delivery)* immediato(a); *(payment)* pronto(a), immediato(a); **to be ~ to do sth** essere sollecito nel fare qc; **they're very ~** *(punctual)* sono molto puntuali. **2** *adv:* **at 6 o'clock ~** alle 6 in punto. **3** *vt* **(a): to ~ sb to do sth** spingere qn a fare qc; **it ~s the thought that...** questo fa pensare che... . **(b)** *(Theatre)* suggerire a.

prompt·er ['prɒmptə'] *n (Theatre)* suggeritore/trice.

prompt·ly ['prɒmptlɪ] *adv (speedily)* prontamente; *(punctually)* puntualmente.

prone [prəʊn] *adj* **(a)** *(face down)* a faccia in giù. **(b)** *(liable):* **~ to** incline a; **to be ~ to illness** essere *or* andare soggetto a malattie; **she is ~ to burst into tears if...** può facilmente scoppiare in lacrime se... .

prong [prɒŋ] *n (of fork)* rebbio, dente *m;* **three-~ed**

(fork) **a tre rebbi** *or* denti; *(attack)* su tre fronti, triplice.

pro·noun ['prəʊnaʊn] *n* pronome *m.*

pro·nounce [prə'naʊns] **1** *vt* **(a)** *(letter, word)* pronunciare. **(b)** *(declare)* dichiarare; **they ~d him unfit to drive** lo hanno dichiarato inabile alla guida; **to ~ o.s. for/against sth** dichiararsi in favore di/contro qc; **to ~ sentence** *(Law)* emettere la sentenza. **2** *vi:* **to ~ in favour of/against sth** pronunciarsi in favore di/contro qc; **to ~ on sth** pronunciarsi su qc.

pro·nounced [prə'naʊnst] *adj (marked: improvement)* netto(a); *(: ideas)* preciso(a); **he has a ~ limp** zoppica in modo molto pronunciato.

pro·nounce·ment [prə'naʊnsmənt] *n* dichiarazione *f.*

pron·to ['prɒntəʊ] *adv (fam)* subito, immediatamente.

pro·nun·cia·tion [prəˌnʌnsɪ'eɪʃən] *n* pronuncia.

proof [pruːf] **1** *n (a) (evidence)* prova; **~ of identity** documento d'identità; **I have ~ that he did it** ho prove che è stato lui a farlo; **as** *or* **in ~ of** come prova *or* testimonianza di; **to give** *or* **show ~ of** dar prova di. **(b)** *(test, trial):* **to put sth to the ~** mettere alla prova qc. **(c)** *(Typ)* bozza, prova di stampa; *(Phot)* provino. **(d)** *(of alcohol):* **70° ~** ≃ 40° in volume. **2** *adj:* **to be ~ against** essere a prova di. **3** *vt (tent, anorak)* impermeabilizzare.

proof·reader ['pruːfˌriːdə'] *n* correttore/trice di bozze.

prop[1] [prɒp] **1** *n* sostegno, puntello; *(fig)* sostegno. **2** *vt (also:* **~ up) (a)** *(rest, lean: ladder etc)* appoggiare. **(b)** *(support)* sostenere, puntellare; *(fig)* tenere su, tenere in piedi.

prop[2] [prɒp] *n abbr fam of* **property 1c.**

propa·gan·da [ˌprɒpə'gændə] **1** *n* propaganda. **2** *cpd (campaign, leaflets)* propagandistico(a).

propa·gate ['prɒpəgeɪt] **1** *vt* propagare. **2** *vi (plants, theories)* propagarsi; *(birds)* riprodursi.

propa·ga·tion [ˌprɒpə'geɪʃən] *n (see vb)* propagazione *f;* riproduzione *f.*

pro·pel [prə'pɛl] *vt* spingere.

pro·pel·ler [prə'pɛlə'] *n* elica.

pro·pel·ling pen·cil [prəˌpɛlɪŋ'pɛnsl] *n* portamina *m inv.*

pro·pen·sity [prə'pɛnsɪtɪ] *n:* **~ (for)** propensione *f* (per).

prop·er ['prɒpə'] **1** *adj* **(a)** *(suitable, appropriate: clothes, tools)* adatto(a), appropriato(a); *(correct, right: order, way, method)* giusto(a); *(seemly: behaviour, person)* decente, perbene; **the ~ time** il momento adatto *or* giusto; **in the ~ way** come si deve; **to go through the ~ channels** *(Admin)* seguire la regolare procedura; **~ noun** *(Gram)* nome *m* proprio; **do as you think ~** fa' come ritieni opportuno; **it isn't ~ to do that** non sta bene fare così; **to do the ~ thing by sb** agire bene verso qn; **to ~ to** *(Chem, Philosophy etc)* proprio di.

   (b) *(actual, authentic)* vero(a) e proprio(a); **physics ~** la fisica propriamente detta; **he isn't a ~ doctor** non è un medico come si deve; **in the ~ sense of the word** nel vero senso della parola; **in the city ~** nella città vera e propria.

   (c) *(fam: real: lady etc)* vero(a), autentico(a); *(: thorough: mess etc)* vero(a), bello(a); **it's a ~ nuisance** è proprio una bella scocciatura.

   2 *adv (Brit fam: very)* proprio; **to talk ~** parlare bene.

prop·er·ly ['prɒpəlɪ] *adv* **(a)** *(correctly: speak, write)* bene, come si deve; *(: use)* in modo giusto; **she very ~ refused** ha giustamente rifiutato; **~ speaking** propriamente parlando. **(b)** *(in seemly fashion)* correttamente; **not ~ dressed** vestito in maniera sconveniente. **(c)** *(fam: really, thoroughly)* veramente.

prop·er·ty |'prɒpətɪ| **1** *n* **(a)** *(quality)* proprietà *f inv*, caratteristica. **(b)** *(possessions)* beni *mpl; (land, building)* proprietà *f inv*; **he owns ~ in Spain** ha delle proprietà in Spagna; **personal ~** beni *mpl* mobili; **a man of ~** un possidente; **is this your ~?** è di tua proprietà?; **lost ~** oggetti *mpl* smarriti. **(c)** *(Theatre)* (elemento del) materiale *m* di scena. **2** *cpd:* **~ developer** *n* costruttore *m* edile; **~ man** *n*, **~ manager** *n (Theatre)* trovarobe *m inv*; **~ owner** *n* proprietario/a.

proph·ecy |'prɒfɪsɪ| *n* profezia.

proph·esy |'prɒfɪsaɪ| *vt* predire, profetizzare.

proph·et |'prɒfɪt| *n* profeta *m*.

proph·et·ess |'prɒfɪtɪs| *n* profetessa.

pro·phet·ic |prə'fetɪk| *adj* profetico(a).

pro·pi·ti·ate |prə'pɪʃɪeɪt| *vt* propiziarsi.

pro·pi·tious |prə'pɪʃəs| *adj* propizio(a).

pro·por·tion |prə'pɔːʃən| **1** *n* **(a)** *(ratio)* proporzione *f;* **the ~ of blacks to whites** la proporzione dei negri rispetto ai bianchi; **to be in/out of ~ (to one another)** essere proporzionati/sproporzionati (tra di loro); **to be in/out of ~ to** *or* **with sth** essere in proporzione/sproporzione rispetto a qc; **to see sth in ~** *(fig)* dare il giusto peso a qc; **sense of ~** *(fig)* senso della misura. **(b)** *(part, amount)* parte *f.* **(c):** **~s** *pl (size)* proporzioni *fpl.* **2** *vt* proporzionare; **well-~ed** ben proporzionato.

pro·por·tion·al |prə'pɔːʃənl| *adj:* **~ (to)** proporzionale (a); **~ representation** *(Pol)* rappresentanza proporzionale.

pro·por·tion·al·ly |prə'pɔːʃnəlɪ| *adv* proporzionalmente.

pro·por·tion·ate |prə'pɔːʃnɪt| *adj:* **~ (to)** proporzionato(a) (a).

pro·po·sal |prə'pəʊzl| *n (offer)* offerta, proposta; *(: of marriage)* proposta di matrimonio; *(suggestion):* **~ (for sth/to do sth)** proposta (di qc/di fare qc); *(plan)* proposta, proposta.

pro·pose |prə'pəʊz| **1** *vt* **(a)** proporre; **to ~ doing sth** proporre di fare qc; **to ~ that sth should be done** proporre che sia fatto qc; **I ~ that we go by bus** propongo di andare con l'autobus; **to ~ marriage to sb** fare una proposta di matrimonio a qn; **to ~ sb for a job/as treasurer** proporre qn per un posto/come tesoriere; **to ~ a toast to sb** proporre un brindisi a qn. **(b)** *(have in mind):* **to ~ sth/to do** *or* **doing sth** proporsi qc/di fare qc. **2** *vi (offer marriage)* fare una proposta di matrimonio.

pro·pos·er |prə'pəʊzə'| *n (of motion)* proponente *m/f.*

propo·si·tion |,prɒpə'zɪʃən| *n* **(a)** *(statement, Math, Logic etc)* proposizione *f.* **(b)** *(proposal)* proposta; **to make sb a ~** proporre qc a qn. **(c)** *(person or thing to be dealt with):* **he's a tough ~** è un osso duro; **that's a tough ~** è un'impresa.

pro·pound |prə'paʊnd| *vt (idea, scheme, theory)* proporre; *(problem, question)* porre.

pro·pri·etary |prə'praɪətərɪ| *adj (Comm):* **~ article** prodotto con marchio depositato; **~ brand** marchio di fabbrica; **~ medicine** specialità farmaceutica; **~ name** nome depositato *or* registrato.

pro·pri·etor |prə'praɪətə'| *n* proprietario/a.

pro·pri·ety |prə'praɪətɪ| *n (seemliness)* decoro, rispetto delle convenienze sociali; *(appropriateness)* convenienza; **the proprieties** le convenzioni sociali.

pro·pul·sion |prə'pʌlʃən| *n:* **jet ~** propulsione *f* a getto.

pro·sa·ic |prəʊ'zeɪɪk| *adj (dull)* prosaico(a), banale.

pro·scribe |prəʊs'kraɪb| *vt* proscrivere.

prose |prəʊz| *n* prosa; *(Scol: translation)* traduzione *f* dalla lingua madre.

pros·ecute |'prɒsɪkjuːt| *vt* **(a)** *(Law)* intentare azione contro; **'trespassers will be ~d'** 'i trasgressori saranno perseguiti a norma di legge'. **(b)** *(frm: carry on inquiry etc)* proseguire.

pros·ecu·tion |,prɒsɪ'kjuːʃən| *n (Law: act, proceedings)* azione *f* giudiziaria; **witness for the ~** testimone per l'accusa; **the ~** ≃ il pubblico ministero.

pros·ecu·tor |'prɒsɪkjuːtə'| *n (Law):* **public ~** ≃ procuratore *m* della Repubblica.

pros·pect |'prɒspekt| **1** *n (outlook)* vista; *(fig)* prospettiva; *(: hope, chance)* speranza, probabilità *f inv;* **future ~s** *(of person, country etc)* prospettive; **it's a grim ~** è una prospettiva poco allegra; **we are faced with the ~ of leaving** rischiamo di dovercene andare; **there's little ~ of its happening** ci sono poche probabilità che accada; **what have you got in ~?** cos'hai in vista?; **there is every ~ of an early victory** tutto lascia prevedere una rapida vittoria; **what are his ~s?** che prospettiva ha?; **a job with no ~s** un lavoro che non offre nessuna prospettiva; **he is a good ~ for the team** è una speranza per la squadra; **to seem a good ~** sembrare promettente. **2** |prə'spekt| *vt* esplorare. **3** |prə'spekt| *vi:* **to ~ for gold** cercare l'oro.

pro·spec·tive |prəs'pektɪv| *adj (buyer)* probabile; *(legislation, son-in-law)* futuro(a).

pro·spec·tor |prəs'pektə'| *n* prospettore/trice; **gold ~** cercatore *m* d'oro.

pro·spec·tus |prəs'pektəs| *n* prospetto.

pros·per |'prɒspə'| *vi (person)* raggiungere il benessere (economico); *(business, trade)* prosperare.

pros·per·ity |prɒs'perɪtɪ| *n* benessere *m*, prosperità.

pros·per·ous |'prɒspərəs| *adj (industry)* prospero(a), fiorente; *(businessman)* di successo.

pros·tate |'prɒsteɪt| *n (also:* **~ gland)** prostata, ghiandola prostatica.

pros·ti·tute |'prɒstɪtjuːt| **1** *n* prostituta; **male ~** uomo che si prostituisce. **2** *vt* prostituire.

pros·ti·tu·tion |,prɒstɪ'tjuːʃən| *n* prostituzione *f.*

pros·trate |'prɒstreɪt| **1** *adj* bocconi *inv; (in respect, submission)* prosternato(a), prostrato(a); *(exhausted):* **~ (with)** prostrato(a) (da). **2** |prɒ'streɪt| *vt:* **to ~ o.s.** *(before sb)* prostrarsi, prosternarsi; *(on the floor)* stendersi bocconi; *(fig)* abbattersi.

pro·tago·nist |prəʊ'tægənɪst| *n* protagonista *m/f.*

pro·tect |prə'tekt| *vt (gen)* proteggere; *(from cold etc)* riparare; *(interests, rights)* salvaguardare.

pro·tec·tion |prə'tekʃən| **1** *n* **(a)** protezione *f; (against cold, wind)* riparo; **to be under sb's ~** essere sotto la protezione di qn. **(b)** *(also:* **~ money)** tangente *f.* **2** *cpd:* **~ racket** *n* racket *m inv.*

pro·tec·tive |prə'tektɪv| *adj (gen)* protettivo(a); **~ custody** *(Police)* protezione *f.*

pro·tec·tor |prə'tektə'| *n* protettore/trice.

pro·té·gé(e) |'prəʊtɪʒeɪ| *n* protetto/a.

pro·tein |'prəʊtiːn| *n* proteina.

pro·test |'prəʊtest| **1** *n* protesta; **to do sth under ~** fare qc protestando. **2** |prə'test| *vt* protestare. **3** |prə'test| *vi:* **to ~ against/about** protestare contro/per; **to ~ to sb** fare le proprie rimostranze a qn. **4** *cpd:* **~ march** *n* marcia di protesta.

Prot·es·tant |'prɒtɪstənt| *adj, n* protestante *(m/f).*

Prot·es·tant·ism |'prɒtɪstəntɪzəm| *n* protestantesimo.

pro·tes·ta·tion |,prɒtes'teɪʃən| *n* protesta.

pro·test·er |prə'testə'| *n* contestatore/trice; *(in*

demonstration) dimostrante _m/f._

proto·col ['prəʊtəkɒl] _n_ protocollo.

proto·type ['prəʊtəʊtaɪp] _n_ prototipo.

pro·tract·ed [prə'træktɪd] _adj_ protratto(a), prolungato(a).

pro·trude [prə'truːd] _vi_ sporgere.

pro·trud·ing [prə'truːdɪŋ] _adj_ sporgente.

pro·tu·ber·ant [prə'tjuːbərənt] _adj (eyes)_ sporgente.

proud [praʊd] **1** _adj_ **(a)** _(person)_ orgoglioso(a), fiero(a); (_: arrogant_) superbo(a); **to be ~ to do sth** essere onorato di fare qc; **he was as ~ as a peacock** si è gonfiato come un tacchino; **that's nothing to be ~ of!** non mi pare che sia il caso di vantarsene! **(b)** _(splendid: ship)_ superbo(a), splendido(a). **2** _adv_: **to do sb ~** non far mancare nulla a qn; **to do o.s. ~** trattarsi bene.

proud·ly ['praʊdlɪ] _adv (see adj)_ orgogliosamente, con fierezza; superbamente.

prove [pruːv] _pt_ ~**d**, _pp_ ~**d** _or_ **proven** ['pruːvən] **1** _vt_ **(a)** _(verify)_ provare, dimostrare; **to ~ sb innocent** provare _or_ dimostrare che qn è innocente; **to ~ o.s.** dar prova di sé; **he was ~d right in the end** alla fine i fatti gli hanno dato ragione. **(b)** _(put to the test: courage, usefulness etc)_ dimostrare, mettere alla prova. **(c)** _(turn out)_: **to ~ (to be) useful** rivelarsi utile; **if it ~s (to be) otherwise** dovesse rivelarsi altrimenti. **2** _vi_ = _vt_ c.

prov·erb ['prɒvɜːb] _n_ proverbio.

pro·ver·bial [prə'vɜːbɪəl] _adj_ proverbiale.

pro·vide [prə'vaɪd] **1** _vt_ **(a)** _(supply)_ fornire; **it ~s plenty of scope for development** offre molte possibilità di sviluppo; **to ~ sb with sth, ~ sth for sb** fornire qc a qn; **to be ~d with** essere dotato _or_ munito di. **(b)** _(legislation etc)_ prevedere. **2** _vi_: **the Lord will ~** Dio provvederà.

♦ **provide for** _vi_ + _prep_ **(a)** _(financially)_ provvedere a; (_: in the future)_ provvedere al futuro di. **(b)**: **the treaty does not ~ for that** il trattato non prevede questo; **we have ~d for that** vi abbiamo provveduto.

pro·vid·ed [prə'vaɪdɪd] _conj_: ~ **(that)** sempre che + _sub_, a patto che + _sub._

provi·dence ['prɒvɪdəns] _n_ provvidenza.

provi·den·tial [ˌprɒvɪ'dɛnʃəl] _adj_ provvidenziale.

pro·vid·ing [prə'vaɪdɪŋ] _conj_: ~ **(that)** _see_ **provided.**

prov·ince ['prɒvɪns] _n_ provincia; **they live in the ~s** vivono in provincia; **it's not within my ~** questo non rientra nel mio campo.

pro·vin·cial [prə'vɪnʃəl] **1** _adj (gen)_ di provincia; _(pej)_ provinciale. **2** _n (usu pej)_ provincialotto/a.

pro·vi·sion [prə'vɪʒən] _n_ **(a)** _(supplying: of power, water)_ fornitura; _(: of food)_ approvvigionamento; _(: of hospitals, housing)_ costruzione _f._ **(b)** _(supply)_ provvista, rifornimento, scorta; ~**s** _(food)_ provviste, scorte; **to lay in a ~ of** fare provvista di; **to get** _or_ **lay in** ~**s** fare provviste. **(c)** _(preparation)_: **to make ~ for** _(one's family, future)_ pensare a; _(journey)_ fare i preparativi per. **(d)** _(stipulation etc)_ disposizione _f_, clausola; **with the ~ that a** condizione che; **there's no ~ for this in the contract** il contratto non lo prevede.

pro·vi·sion·al [prə'vɪʒənl] _adj_ provvisorio(a); ~ **licence** _(Aut)_ ≃ foglio _m_ rosa _inv._

pro·vi·sion·al·ly [prə'vɪʒnəlɪ] _adv (accept)_ provvisoriamente; _(appoint)_ a titolo provvisorio.

pro·vi·so [prə'vaɪzəʊ] _n_: **with the ~ that** a condizione che + _sub_, a patto che + _sub._

provo·ca·tion [ˌprɒvə'keɪʃən] _n_ provocazione _f_; **she acted under ~** ha agito così perché è stata provocata.

pro·voca·tive [prə'vɒkətɪv] _adj (causing anger)_

provocatorio(a); _(seductive)_ provocante; _(thought-provoking)_ stimolante.

pro·voke [prə'vəʊk] _vt (gen)_ provocare; **to ~ sb to sth/to do** _or_ **into doing sth** spingere qn a qc/a fare qc.

pro·vok·ing [prə'vəʊkɪŋ] _adj_ irritante, esasperante.

prov·ost ['prɒvəst] _n (Univ)_ rettore _m_; _(Scot)_ sindaco.

prow [praʊ] _n_ prua.

prow·ess ['praʊɪs] _n (skill)_: **his ~ as a footballer** le sue capacità di calciatore; _(courage)_ prodezza, ardimento.

prowl [praʊl] _vi (also:_ ~ **about** _or_ **around)** aggirarsi.

prowl·er ['praʊləʳ] _n_: **there was a ~ downstairs** c'era qualcuno che si aggirava furtivamente di sotto.

prox·im·ity [prɒk'sɪmɪtɪ] _n_ vicinanza; **in the ~ of** in prossimità di.

proxy ['prɒksɪ] _n (power)_ procura, delega; _(person)_ mandatario/a; **by ~** per procura.

prude [pruːd] _n_ puritano/a.

pru·dence ['pruːdəns] _n_ prudenza.

pru·dent ['pruːdənt] _adj_ prudente.

prud·ish ['pruːdɪʃ] _adj_ puritano(a), che si scandalizza facilmente.

prune[1] [pruːn] _n (fruit)_ prugna (secca).

prune[2] [pruːn] _vt (tree)_ potare.

pru·ri·ent ['prʊərɪənt] _adj_ libidinoso(a).

pry[1] [praɪ] _vi_ essere troppo curioso(a); **to ~ into sb's affairs** cacciare il naso negli affari di qn.

pry[2] [praɪ] _vt (Am)_ = **prise.**

P.S. _abbr (= postscript)_ P.S.

psalm [sɑːm] _n_ salmo.

pseud ['sjuːd] _n (fam: intellectually)_ intellettualoide _m/f_; _(: socially)_ snob _m/f inv._

pseu·do ['sjuːdəʊ] _adj (pej)_ fasullo(a), finto(a).

pseudo... ['sjuːdəʊ] _pref_ pseudo... .

pseudo·nym ['sjuːdənɪm] _n_ pseudonimo.

psyche ['saɪkɪ] _n (Psych)_ psiche _f._

psychedel·ic [ˌsaɪkɪ'dɛlɪk] _adj_ psichedelico(a).

psy·chi·at·ric [ˌsaɪkɪ'ætrɪk] _adj (treatment, hospital)_ psichiatrico(a); _(disease, illness)_ mentale.

psy·chia·trist [saɪ'kaɪətrɪst] _n_ psichiatra _m/f._

psy·chia·try [saɪ'kaɪətrɪ] _n_ psichiatria.

psy·chic ['saɪkɪk] _adj_ **(a)** _(supernatural)_ metapsichico(a), paranormale; _(telepathic)_ che ha dei poteri telepatici; **you must be ~!** _(fam)_ devi essere un indovino! **(b)** _(Psych)_ psichico(a), della psiche.

psy·cho ['saɪkəʊ] _n (Am fam)_ psicopatico/a.

psycho·ana·lyse, _(Am)_ **psycho·ana·lyze** [ˌsaɪkəʊ'ænəlaɪz] _vt_ psicanalizzare.

psy·cho·analy·sis [ˌsaɪkəʊə'nælɪsɪs] _n_ psicanalisi _f._

psycho·ana·lyst [ˌsaɪkəʊ'ænəlɪst] _n_ psicanalista _m/f._

psycho·logi·cal [ˌsaɪkə'lɒdʒɪkəl] _adj_ psicologico(a).

psy·cholo·gist [saɪ'kɒlədʒɪst] _n_ psicologo/a.

psy·chol·ogy [saɪ'kɒlədʒɪ] _n_ psicologia.

psycho·path ['saɪkəʊpæθ] _n_ psicopatico/a.

psy·cho·sis [saɪ'kəʊsɪs] _n, pl_ **psychoses** [saɪ'kəʊsiːz] psicosi _f inv._

psycho·so·mat·ic [ˌsaɪkəʊsəʊ'mætɪk] _adj_ psicosomatico(a).

psycho·thera·py [ˌsaɪkəʊ'θerəpɪ] _n_ psicoterapia.

psy·chot·ic [saɪ'kɒtɪk] _adj, n_ psicotico(a) _(m/f)._

PTO _abbr (= please turn over)_ v.r.

pub [pʌb] _n (Brit)_ pub _m inv._

pub-crawl ['pʌbkrɔːl] _n (fam)_: **to go on a ~** fare il giro dei pub.

pu·ber·ty ['pju:bətɪ] n pubertà.

pu·bic ['pju:bɪk] adj pubico(a), del pube.

pub·lic ['pʌblɪk] **1** adj (gen) pubblico(a); (Comm: industry) statale; **in the ~ interest** nel pubblico interesse; **to be ~ knowledge** essere di dominio pubblico; **he's a ~ figure, he's in ~ life** è un personaggio della vita pubblica; **this place is too ~ to discuss it** c'è troppa gente qui per poterne discutere; **to make sth ~** render noto or di pubblico dominio qc; **to be in the ~ eye** essere una persona molto in vista; **her ~ support of** il suo aperto appoggio a; **to create more ~ awareness (of)** focalizzare l'attenzione del pubblico (su); **to go ~** (Comm) immettere le azioni sul mercato.

2 n: **the ~** il pubblico; **in ~** in pubblico; **the sporting/reading ~** il pubblico sportivo/dei lettori.

3 cpd: **~ convenience** n gabinetti mpl pubblici; **~ holiday** n giorno festivo, festa nazionale; **~ house** n (Brit) pub m inv; **~ opinion** n opinione f pubblica; **~ opinion poll** n sondaggio dell'opinione pubblica; **~ ownership** n: **to be taken into ~ ownership** essere statalizzato; **~ relations** npl relazioni fpl pubbliche; **~ relations officer** n addetto/a alle relazioni pubbliche; **~ school** n (Brit) scuola superiore privata; (Am) scuola statale; **~ sector** n settore m pubblico; **~ service** n (Civil Service) amministrazione f pubblica; **~ speaking** n arte f oratoria; **~ transport** n mezzi mpl pubblici.

public-address [ˌpʌblɪkə'drɛs]: **~ system** n impianto di amplificazione.

pub·li·can ['pʌblɪkən] n (Brit) gestore m (or proprietario) di un pub.

pub·li·ca·tion [ˌpʌblɪ'keɪʃən] n pubblicazione f.

pub·lic·ity [pʌb'lɪsɪtɪ] **1** n (a) pubblicità. (b) (Comm: advertising, advertisements) pubblicità, réclame f. **2** cpd (campaign, material, budget) pubblicitario(a); (manager) della pubblicità.

pub·li·cize ['pʌblɪsaɪz] vt (a) (make public) far sapere in giro. (b) (advertise) fare (della) pubblicità a, reclamizzare.

public-spirit·ed [ˌpʌblɪk'spɪrɪtɪd] adj (attitude) che denota senso civico; (act) di civismo; (person) che ha senso civico.

pub·lish ['pʌblɪʃ] vt pubblicare; **who ~es Moravia?** chi è l'editore di Moravia?; **'~ed weekly'** 'edito settimanalmente', 'pubblicato settimanalmente'.

pub·lish·er ['pʌblɪʃəʳ] n (person) editore/trice; (firm) casa editrice.

pub·lish·ing ['pʌblɪʃɪŋ] **1** n (trade) editoria, industria editoriale; (of book etc) pubblicazione f. **2** cpd: **~ company** n casa or società editrice.

puce [pjuːs] adj marroncino rosato inv.

puck·er ['pʌkəʳ] vt (also: **~ up**: lips) increspare; (: brow) aggrottare, corrugare; (: Sewing) increspare.

pud·ding ['pʊdɪŋ] **1** n (dessert) dolce m, dessert m inv; (steamed ~) dolce cotto a bagnomaria a base di uova, burro, farina e latte; **black ~** sanguinaccio; **rice ~** budino di riso. **2** cpd: **~ basin** n terrina.

pud·dle ['pʌdl] n pozzanghera.

pu·er·ile ['pjʊəraɪl] adj puerile, infantile.

puff [pʌf] **1** n (a) (of breathing) soffio; (of engine) sbuffare m; (of air, wind) folata, soffio; (of smoke) sbuffo; (on cigarette etc) tiro, boccata; **I'm out of ~** (fam) sono senza fiato. (b) (powder ~) piumino della cipria. (c) (Culin): **cream ~** sfogliatina alla panna.

2 vt (a): **to ~ (out) smoke** etc mandar fuori fumo etc. (b) (also: **~ out**: sails, cheeks) gonfiare; **his face was all ~ed up** la sua faccia era tutta

gonfia. (c): **I'm ~ed (out)** (fam) sono senza fiato.

3 vi (breathe heavily) ansimare; (blow) soffiare; **the train ~ed into the station** il treno entrò sbuffando in stazione; **to ~ (away) at** or **on one's pipe** tirare boccate di fumo dalla pipa.

4 cpd: **~ pastry** n, (Am) **~ paste** n pasta sfoglia.

puf·fin ['pʌfɪn] n pulcinella m di mare.

puffy ['pʌfɪ] adj (-ier, -iest) gonfio(a).

pug [pʌg] n (also: **~ dog**) carlino.

pug·na·cious [pʌg'neɪʃəs] adj bellicoso(a), battagliero(a).

pug-nosed ['pʌgnəʊzd] adj dal naso rincagnato.

puke [pjuːk] vi (fam) vomitare.

pull [pʊl] **1** n (a) (tug) strattone m, tirata, strappo; (of moon, magnet, the sea etc) attrazione f; (fig: attraction: of personality) forza di attrazione; (: of family ties) forza; **I felt a ~ at my sleeve** ho sentito qualcuno che mi tirava per la manica; **he has some ~ with the manager** (fam: influence) ha dell'influenza sul direttore.

(b) (at pipe) boccata, tirata; (at beer) sorsata; **he took a ~ at the bottle** ha bevuto un sorso dalla bottiglia.

(c) (handle of drawer etc) maniglia, pomolo; (of bell) cordone m.

2 vt (a) (draw: cart) tirare, trascinare; (: curtains) tirare; (: fig: crowd) attirare; **to ~ a door shut/open** chiudere/aprire la porta tirandola.

(b) (tug: handle, rope etc) tirare; (: trigger) premere; **to ~ sb's hair** tirare i capelli a qn; **to ~ to pieces** or **to bits** (toy) fare a pezzi; (argument) demolire; (person, play) stroncare; **she didn't ~ any punches** non ha risparmiato nessun colpo; **to ~ sb's leg** prendere qn in giro; **to ~ strings (for sb)** muovere qualche pedina (per qn); **to ~ one's weight** fare la propria parte di lavoro.

(c) (extract, draw out: gen) togliere; (: gun, knife) tirar fuori; (: weeds) strappare; (: onions etc) raccogliere; (: beer) spillare; **to ~ a gun on sb** estrarre una pistola e puntarla contro qn.

(d) (strain: muscle, tendon) farsi uno strappo a; (tear: thread) tirare.

(e) (fam: carry out, do: robbery etc) fare; **to ~ a fast one on sb** combinarla a qn.

3 vi (a) (tug) tirare; **to ~ at sb's sleeve** tirare qn per la manica; **the car is ~ing to the right** lo sterzo or la macchina tira a destra; **to ~ at** or **on one's pipe** tirare boccate dalla pipa.

(b) (move): **to ~ for the shore** remare verso la riva; **the train ~ed into/out of the station** il treno è entrato in/è partito dalla stazione; **he ~ed alongside the kerb** ha accostato al marciapiede; **we ~ed clear of the traffic** ci siamo lasciati il traffico alle spalle.

♦ **pull about** vt + adv (handle roughly: object) strapazzare; (person) malmenare.

♦ **pull apart** vt + adv (a) (pull to pieces) smontare; (break) fare a pezzi, sfasciare; (separate) separare. (b) (fig fam: search thoroughly) frugare dappertutto in; (: criticize: novel, theory) demolire.

♦ **pull away 1** vt + adv strappare via. **2** vi + adv (move off: vehicle) muoversi, partire; **to ~ away from** (kerb) allontanarsi da; (quay) staccarsi da; (platform) muoversi da; (subj: runner: competitors) distanziare.

♦ **pull back 1** vt + adv (person, lever) tirare indietro; (curtains) aprire. **2** vi + adv tirarsi indietro; (Mil) ritirarsi.

♦ **pull down** vt + adv (a) (gen) tirar giù; (opponent) stendere a terra. (b) (demolish: buildings) demolire, buttar giù.

♦ **pull in 1** vt + adv (a) (rope, fishing line) tirare su;

(person: into car, room) tirare dentro; *(stomach)* tirare in dentro. **(b)** *(rein in: horse)* trattenere. **(c)** *(attract: crowds)* attirare. **(d)** *(fam: take into custody)* mettere dentro. **2** *vi + adv (Aut etc: arrive)* arrivare; *(: stop)* fermarsi.

♦ **pull off** *vt + adv* **(a)** *(remove: wrapping paper)* strappare; *(: clothes, shoes, gloves)* levarsi, togliersi. **(b)** *(fam: succeed in: plan, attack etc)* portare a termine; **he didn't ~ it off** non gli è riuscito il colpo.

♦ **pull on** *vt + adv (clothes)* mettersi.

♦ **pull out 1** *vt + adv* **(a)** *(take out: tooth, splinter)* togliere; *(: gun, knife, person)* tirare fuori. **(b)** *(withdraw: troops, police)* (far) ritirare. **2** *vi + adv* **(a)** *(withdraw)* ritirarsi. **(b)** *(leave: train, car etc)* uscire; **he ~ed out to overtake** si è spostato per sorpassare.

♦ **pull over 1** *vt + adv* **(a)** *(box etc)*: ~ **it over here/there** tiralo in qua/in là; ~ **it over to the window** tiralo vicino alla finestra. **(b)** *(topple)* far cascare, tirar giù. **2** *vi + adv* accostare.

♦ **pull through 1** *vt + adv* **(a)** tirare dall'altra parte. **(b)** *(fig)* aiutare a venirne fuori. **2** *vi + adv (fig)* cavarsela.

♦ **pull together 1** *vt + adv (fig)*: **to ~ o.s. together** ricomporsi. **2** *vi + adv (make common effort)* cooperare, mettersi insieme.

♦ **pull up 1** *vt + adv* **(a)** *(raise by pulling)* tirar su. **(b)** *(uproot: weeds etc)* sradicare. **(c)** *(stop: horse, car)* fermare. **(d)** *(scold)* riprendere. **2** *vi + adv (stop)* fermarsi.

pul·ley ['pulɪ] *n* puleggia.

Pull·man ['pulmən] *n (also:* ~ **car)** pullman *m inv.*

pull-out ['pulaut] **1** *n* inserto. **2** *cpd* staccabile.

pull·over ['puləuvə'] *n* pullover *m inv.*

pulp [pʌlp] **1** *n* **(a)** *(for paper)* pasta (di legno *or* stracci *etc)*; **to reduce sth to** ~ spappolare qc. **(b)** *(of fruit, vegetable)* polpa. **(c)** *(magazines, books)* stampa di qualità e di tono scadenti. **2** *vt (fruit, vegetables)* spappolare; *(paper, book)* mandare al macero.

pul·pit ['pulpɪt] *n* pulpito.

pul·sate [pʌl'seɪt] *vi (heart, blood)* pulsare; *(music)* vibrare.

pulse[1] [pʌls] *n (Anat)* polso; *(Phys)* impulso; *(fig: of drums, music)* vibrazione *f*; **to feel** *or* **take sb's** ~ sentire *or* tastare il polso a qn.

pulse[2] [pʌls] *n (Culin)* legumi *mpl.*

puma ['pju:mə] *n* puma *m inv.*

pum·ice (stone) ['pʌmɪs(stəun)] *n* (pietra) pomice *f.*

pum·mel ['pʌml] *vt* prendere a pugni.

pump [pʌmp] **1** *n* pompa; **petrol** ~ distributore *m* (di benzina). **2** *vt* **(a)** pompare; **to** ~ **sth dry** prosciugare qc con una pompa; **to** ~ **air into a tyre** gonfiare uno pneumatico; **to** ~ **money into a project** immettere capitali in un progetto; **to** ~ **sb for information** cercare di strappare delle informazioni a qn. **(b)** *(handle etc)* alzare e abbassare vigorosamente; **to** ~ **sb's hand up and down** dare una vigorosa stretta di mano a qn.

♦ **pump in** *vt + adv (water)* far passare (con una pompa); *(foam into walls etc)* iniettare; *(fig: money etc)* immettere.

♦ **pump out** *vt + adv* pompare fuori; **to** ~ **out sb's stomach** fare la lavanda gastrica a qn.

♦ **pump up** *vt + adv (tyre)* gonfiare.

pump·kin ['pʌmpkɪn] *n* zucca.

pun [pʌn] *n* gioco di parole.

Punch [pʌntʃ] *n* Pulcinella *m*; ~ **and Judy show** spettacolo di burattini.

punch[1] [pʌntʃ] **1** *n* **(a)** *(for making holes: in metal, leather)* punzonatrice *f*; *(: in paper)* perforatore

m; (: for tickets) pinza per forare; *(for stamping metal)* punzone *m.* **(b)** *(blow)* pugno; *(fig: vigour)* mordente *m.* **2** *vt* **(a)** *(with tool: gen)* punzonare; *(: ticket)* forare; **to** ~ **a hole in sth** forare qc. **(b)** *(with fist)*: **to** ~ **sb** dare un pugno a qn; **to** ~ **a ball** colpire una palla con un pugno; **to** ~ **sb's nose** dare un pugno sul naso a qn. **3** *cpd*: ~**(ed) card** *n* scheda perforata; ~ **line** *n (of joke)* battuta finale; *(of story)* finale *m.*

punch[2] [pʌntʃ] *n (drink)* punch *m inv.*

punch·ball ['pʌntʃbɔːl] *n* punching-ball *m inv.*

punch·bowl ['pʌntʃbəul] *n* grande coppa da punch.

punch-drunk ['pʌntʃ,drʌŋk] *adj* stordito(a).

punch·ing bag ['pʌntʃɪŋbæg] *n (Am)* = **punchball.**

punch-up ['pʌntʃʌp] *n (Brit fam)* scazzottata, rissa.

punc·tili·ous [pʌŋk'tɪlɪəs] *adj* scrupoloso(a).

punc·tu·al ['pʌŋktjuəl] *adj (person)* puntuale; *(train)* in orario.

punc·tu·al·ity [,pʌŋktjʊ'ælɪtɪ] *n* puntualità.

punc·tu·al·ly ['pʌŋktjuəlɪ] *adv (see adj)* puntualmente; in orario; **it will start** ~ **at 6** comincerà alle 6 precise *or* in punto.

punc·tu·ate ['pʌŋktjueɪt] *vt (Gram)* mettere la punteggiatura a *or* in; **his speech was** ~**d by bursts of applause** il suo discorso fu ripetutamente interrotto da scrosci di applausi.

punc·tua·tion [,pʌŋktjʊ'eɪʃən] **1** *n (Gram)* punteggiatura. **2** *cpd*: ~ **mark** *n* segno d'interpunzione.

punc·ture ['pʌŋktʃə'] **1** *n (in balloon)* foratura, bucatura; *(in skin)* puntura; *(in tyre)* foratura; **I have a** ~ *(Aut)* ho forato (una gomma). **2** *vt* bucare, forare. **3** *vi* bucarsi, forarsi.

pun·dit ['pʌndɪt] *n (iro)* esperto/a.

pun·gen·cy ['pʌndʒənsɪ] *n (see adj)* asprezza; acredine *f*; sapore *m* piccante; causticità.

pun·gent ['pʌndʒənt] *adj (smell, taste)* pungente, aspro(a); *(smoke)* acre; *(sauce)* piccante; *(remark, satire)* caustico(a).

pun·ish ['pʌnɪʃ] *vt* **(a)**: **to** ~ **sb for sth/for doing sth** punire qn per qc/per aver fatto qc. **(b)** *(fig fam: car)* mettere a dura prova; *(: horse)* sfiancare; *(: opposition)* dare una bella batosta a; *(: meal, bottle of whisky)* far fuori.

pun·ish·able ['pʌnɪʃəbl] *adj* punibile.

pun·ish·ing ['pʌnɪʃɪŋ] **1** *adj (fig: exhausting)* sfiancante. **2** *n* punizione *f.*

pun·ish·ment ['pʌnɪʃmənt] *n* **(a)** *(punishing)* punizione *f*, castigo; *(penalty)* pena; **to take one's** ~ subire il castigo. **(b)** *(fig fam)*: **to take a lot of** ~ *(boxer)* incassare parecchi colpi; *(car)* essere messo(a) a dura prova; *(furniture)* essere maltrattato(a).

punk [pʌŋk] *n* **(a)** *(person: also:* ~ **rocker)** punk *m/f inv; (music: also:* ~ **rock)** musica punk, punk rock *m.* **(b)** *(Am fam: hoodlum)* teppista *m.*

punt[1] [pʌnt] **1** *n (boat)* barchino. **2** *vt (boat)* spingere con la pertica; *(ball)* calciare al volo. **3** *vi*: **to go** ~**ing** andare in barchino.

punt[2] [pʌnt] *vi (bet)* scommettere.

punt·er ['pʌntə'] *n (gambler)* scommettitore/trice.

puny ['pju:nɪ] *adj (-ier, -iest) (person)* gracile, striminzito(a); *(effort)* penoso(a).

pup [pʌp] *n* cucciolo, cagnolino.

pu·pil[1] ['pju:pl] *n (Scol etc)* allievo/a, scolaro/a.

pu·pil[2] ['pju:pl] *n (Anat)* pupilla.

pup·pet ['pʌpɪt] **1** *n (glove* ~) burattino; *(string* ~) marionetta; *(fig)* burattino, fantoccio. **2** *cpd*: ~ **government** *n* governo fantoccio; ~ **show** *n* spettacolo di burattini *(or* di marionette).

pup·py ['pʌpɪ] **1** *n* cucciolo, cagnolino. **2** *cpd*: ~ **fat** *n* pinguedine *f* infantile; ~ **love** *n* infatuazione *f* giovanile.

pur·chase ['pɜːtʃɪs] **1** *n* **(a)** *(act)* acquisto; *(thing purchased)* acquisto, compera. **(b)** *(grip)* presa; **to get a ~ on** trovare un appoggio su. **2** *vt (frm)* acquistare, comprare; **purchasing power** potere *m* d'acquisto. **3** *cpd:* ~ **order** *n* ordine *m* d'acquisto, ordinazione *f;* ~ **price** *n* prezzo d'acquisto; ~ **tax** *n (Brit)* tassa d'acquisto.

pur·chas·er ['pɜːtʃɪsəʳ] *n* acquirente *m/f,* compratore/trice.

pure [pjʊəʳ] *adj* (**-r, -st**) puro(a); **the ~ in heart** i puri di cuore; **as ~ as the driven snow** innocente come un bambino; **a ~ wool jumper** un golf di pura lana; ~ **mathematics** matematica pura; **it's laziness ~ and simple** è pura pigrizia; **by ~ chance** per puro caso.

pure·bred ['pjʊəbred] *adj* di razza pura.

pure·ly [,pjʊəlɪ] *adv* puramente.

pur·ga·tive ['pɜːɡətɪv] **1** *n (Med)* purgante *m.* **2** *adj* purgativo(a).

pur·ga·tory ['pɜːɡətərɪ] *n (Rel, fig)* purgatorio.

purge [pɜːdʒ] **1** *n (gen, Med, Pol)* purga. **2** *vt* **(a)** *(Med)* purgare; *(Pol):* **to ~ (of)** epurare (da); **to ~ one's sins** espiare i propri peccati; **to ~ o.s. of sth** liberarsi da qc. **(b)** *(Law: offence, crime)* espiare.

pu·ri·fi·ca·tion [,pjʊərɪfɪ'keɪʃən] *n (see vb)* depurazione *f;* purificazione *f.*

pu·ri·fy ['pjʊərɪfaɪ] *vt (water, air)* depurare; *(person)* purificare.

pur·ist ['pjʊərɪst] *n* purista *m/f.*

pu·ri·tan ['pjʊərɪtən] *adj, n* puritano(a) *(m/f).*

pu·ri·tani·cal [,pjʊərɪ'tænɪkəl] *adj* puritano(a).

pu·rity ['pjʊərɪtɪ] *n* purezza.

purl [pɜːl] **1** *n* (maglia *or* punto a) rovescio. **2** *vt* lavorare a rovescio.

pur·ple ['pɜːpl] **1** *adj* viola *inv;* **to go ~ (in the face)** diventare paonazzo; ~ **passage** *(fig)* brano d'effetto. **2** *n (colour)* viola *m inv; (Rel):* **the ~** la porpora.

pur·port ['pɜːpət] **1** *n* significato, senso generale. **2** [pɜː'pɔːt] *vt:* **to ~ to be** voler sembrare.

pur·pose ['pɜːpəs] *n* **(a)** *(intention)* scopo, intenzione *f; (use)* uso; **she has a ~ in life** ha uno scopo nella vita; **for our ~s** per i nostri scopi; **for teaching ~s** per l'insegnamento; **for the ~s of this meeting** agli effetti di questa riunione; **for all practical ~s** a tutti gli effetti pratici, in pratica; **on ~** di proposito, apposta; **to the ~** a proposito, pertinente; **with the ~ of** con il proposito di; **to some ~** con qualche risultato; **to no ~** senza nessun risultato, inutilmente; **to good ~** con buoni risultati. **(b)** *(resolution, determination):* **sense of ~** risolutezza.

purpose-built ['pɜːpəs,bɪlt] *adj* costruito(a) allo scopo.

pur·pose·ful ['pɜːpəsfʊl] *adj* deciso(a), risoluto(a).

pur·pose·ly ['pɜːpəslɪ] *adv* di proposito, apposta.

purr [pɜːʳ] **1** *n (of cat)* le fusa. **2** *vi* far le fusa.

purse [pɜːs] **1** *n (for money)* borsellino, portamonete *m inv; (Am: handbag)* borsetta, borsa; *(esp Sport: prize)* premio in denaro. **2** *vt:* **to ~ one's lips** increspare le labbra. **3** *cpd:* **to hold the ~ strings** *(fig)* tenere i cordoni della borsa.

purs·er ['pɜːsəʳ] *n (Naut)* commissario di bordo.

pur·sue [pə'sjuː] *vt* **(a)** *(chase)* inseguire; *(: pleasures)* essere alla ricerca di; *(subj: bad luck etc)* perseguitare. **(b)** *(carry on: studies)* proseguire (in); *(: career)* intraprendere; *(: inquiry, matter)* approfondire; *(: plan)* andare avanti con.

pur·su·er [pə'sjuːəʳ] *n* inseguitore/trice.

pur·suit [pə'sjuːt] *n* **(a)** *(chase)* inseguimento; *(fig: of pleasure, happiness, knowledge)* ricerca; **in (the) ~ of sb** all'inseguimento di qn; **in (the) ~ of sth** alla ricerca di qc; **with two policemen in hot**

~ con due poliziotti alle calcagna. **(b)** *(occupation)* attività *f inv,* occupazione *f; (pastime)* svago, passatempo.

pur·vey·or [pɜː'veɪəʳ] *n (frm)* fornitore/trice.

pus [pʌs] *n* pus *m.*

push [pʊʃ] **1** *n* **(a)** *(shove)* spinta, spintone *m;* **to give sb a push** ~ dare una spinta a qn/qc; **to give sb the** ~ *(Brit fam)* dare il benservito a qn.

(b) *(drive, aggression)* iniziativa.

(c) *(effort)* grosso sforzo; *(Mil: offensive)* offensiva.

(d) *(fam):* **at a** ~ in caso di necessità; **if or when it comes to the** ~ al momento critico.

2 *vt* **(a)** *(shove, move by ~ing)* spingere; *(press: button)* schiacciare, premere; **to ~ a door open/shut** aprire/chiudere una porta con una spinta *or* spingendola; **he ~ed it into my hands** me lo ha cacciato nelle mani; **the accident ~ed everything else out of my mind** l'incidente mi ha fatto dimenticare tutto il resto.

(b) *(fig: press, advance: views)* imporre; *(: claim)* far valere; *(: product)* spingere le vendite di; *(: candidate)* appoggiare; **to ~ home an advantage** sfruttare a fondo un vantaggio; **to ~ home an attack** portare a conclusione un attacco; **to ~ drugs** spacciare droga; **don't ~ your luck!** *(fam)* non sfidare la fortuna!; **she is ~ing 50** *(fam)* va per i 50.

(c) *(fig: put pressure on):* **to ~ sb into doing sth** costringere qn a fare qc; **to ~ sb to do sth** spingere qn a fare qc; **don't ~ her too far** non esigere troppo da lei; **that's ~ing it a bit** *(fam)* è un po' troppo; **to be ~ed for time/money** essere a corto di tempo/soldi; **I'm really ~ed today** oggi non ho un minuto di tempo.

3 *vi* spingere; **to ~ for** *(better pay, conditions)* fare pressione per ottenere; **to ~ past sb** spingere qn per passare; **to ~ into a room** entrare in una stanza facendosi largo; **to ~ through a crowd** farsi largo *or* aprirsi un varco tra la folla; '**~**' *(on door)* 'spingere'; *(on bell)* 'suonare'.

♦ **push about, push around** *vt + adv (fig fam: bully)* fare il prepotente con.

♦ **push aside** *vt + adv* spingere da parte; *(fig: suggestions)* scartare; *(: problems)* accantonare.

♦ **push away** *vt + adv* respingere.

♦ **push back** *vt + adv (blankets)* spingere via, buttare all'indietro; *(curtains)* aprire; *(lock of hair)* ricacciare all'indietro; *(enemy forces)* respingere.

♦ **push down 1** *vi + adv:* **to ~ down on** schiacciare, premere. **2** *vt + adv (switch, knob)* abbassare, tirare giù; *(knock over: fence, person)* buttare giù.

♦ **push forward 1** *vi + adv (Mil)* avanzare. **2** *vt + adv* spingere in avanti; **he tends to ~ himself forward** *(fig)* cerca sempre di mettersi in mostra.

♦ **push in 1** *vt + adv* **(a)** *(person)* spingere dentro; *(stick, rag: into hole)* ficcare dentro, cacciare dentro; **to ~ sb into the water** spingere qn nell'acqua; **she ~ed her way in** è entrata facendosi largo. **(b)** *(break: door etc)* sfondare. **2** *vi + adv* introdursi a forza.

♦ **push off 1** *vt + adv (gen)* buttare giù; *(lid, top)* spingere via; **he ~ed me off the wall** mi ha buttato giù dal muro. **2** *vi + adv* **(a)** *(in boat)* prendere il largo. **(b)** *(fam: leave)* filare, smammare.

♦ **push on 1** *vi + adv (with journey)* continuare; *(with job)* perseverare. **2** *vt + adv (fig: incite, urge on)* spronare, spingere.

♦ **push out** *vt + adv (car, person)* spingere fuori; *(cork)* far uscire.

♦ **push over** vt + adv **(a)** (over cliff etc) spingere giù; **to ~ sth over the edge** spingere qc oltre il bordo. **(b)** (knock over) far cadere.

♦ **push through 1** vt + adv **(a)** (gen) spingere dall'altra parte; **to ~ one's way through** farsi largo. **(b)** (force acceptance of: decision) far accettare; (: Parliament: bill) riuscire a far votare. **2** vi + adv farsi strada, farsi largo; (troops) aprirsi un varco.

♦ **push up** vt + adv **(a)** spingere in su. **(b)** (fig: raise, increase) far salire.

push-bike ['puʃbaɪk] n (Brit) bicicletta.

push-button ['puʃ,bʌtn] adj a pulsante; **~ warfare** guerra dei bottoni.

push-chair ['puʃtʃɛə'] n (Brit) passeggino.

push·er ['puʃə'] n (fam) **(a)** (of drugs) spacciatore/trice. **(b)** (ambitious person) arrivista m/f.

push·over ['puʃəuvə'] n (fam): **it's a ~** è una cosa da bambini; **she's a ~** si lascia convincere facilmente.

pushy ['puʃɪ] adj (-ier, -iest) (fam) troppo intraprendente.

pu·sil·lani·mous [,pjuːsɪ'lænɪməs] adj pusillanime.

puss [pus] n (fam), **pussy** ['pusɪ] n (fam) micio/a.

pussy wil·low ['pusɪ,wɪləu] n salicone m.

put [put] pt, pp **put 1** vt **(a)** (place) mettere; (~ down) posare, metter giù; **we ~ the children to bed** abbiamo messo a letto i bambini; **my brother ~ me on the train** mio fratello mi ha messo sul treno; **to ~ the ball in the net** mandare la palla in rete; **to ~ sth to one's ear** avvicinarsi qc all'orecchio; **she ~ her head on my shoulder** appoggiò la testa sulla mia spalla; **to ~ one's signature to sth** apporre la propria firma a qc; **to ~ a lot of time into sth** dedicare molto tempo a qc; **she has ~ a lot into her marriage** ha fatto molto per la riuscita del suo matrimonio; **to ~ money into a company** investire or mettere dei capitali in un'azienda; **to ~ money on a horse** scommettere su un cavallo. **(b)** (thrust; direct) cacciare; **he ~ his finger right in my eye** mi ha cacciato un dito nell'occhio; **I ~ my fist through the window** sfondai la finestra con il pugno; **to ~ one's pen through sth** cancellare qc con un frego; **he ~ his head round the door** fece capolino alla porta; **to ~ the shot** (Sport) lanciare il peso. **(c)** (cause to be): **to ~ sb in a good/bad mood** mettere qn di buon/cattivo umore; **to ~ sb in charge of sth** incaricare qn di qc; **to ~ sb to a lot of trouble** scomodare qn; **I ~ her to answering the phone** le ho dato l'incarico di rispondere al telefono; **he ~ her to work immediately** l'ha messa subito al lavoro. **(d)** (express) esprimere, dire; **let me ~ it another way** te lo spiego in un altro modo; **how shall I ~ it?** come dire?; **let me ~ it this way** diciamo così; **as Dante ~s it** come dice Dante; **to ~ it bluntly** per parlar chiaro; **~ it to him gently** diglielo senza spaventarlo; **to ~ sth into French** tradurre qc in francese; **to ~ the words to music** mettere in musica or musicare le parole. **(e)** (expound: case, problem) esporre; (: proposal) presentare; **I ~ it to you that...** io sostengo che...; **to ~ a question to sb** rivolgere una domanda a qn. **(f)** (estimate) valutare, stimare; **what would you ~ it at?** quanto pensi che valga?; **I'd ~ his age at 40** direi che ha 40 anni.

2 vi (Naut): **to ~ to sea** prendere il mare; **to ~ into port** entrare in porto.

3 adv: **to stay ~** non muoversi.

♦ **put about 1** vt + adv (circulate: news, rumour) mettere in giro. **2** vi + adv (Naut) virare di bordo, invertire la rotta.

♦ **put across** vt + adv **(a)** (communicate: ideas etc) comunicare, far capire; (: new product) propagandare; **she can't put herself across** non sa far valere le sue doti. **(b)** (fam: play trick): **to ~ it** or **one across on sb** darla a bere a qn.

♦ **put aside** vt + adv **(a)** (lay down: book etc) mettere da una parte, posare. **(b)** (save) mettere da parte; (in shop) tenere da parte. **(c)** (fig: forget, abandon: idea, hope, doubt) mettere da parte; (: anger, grief) dimenticare.

♦ **put away** vt + adv **(a)** (clothes, toys etc) mettere via. **(b)** = **put aside** b. **(c)** (fam: consume: food, drink) far fuori. **(d)** (fam: lock up in prison) mettere dentro; (: in mental hospital) rinchiudere.

♦ **put back 1** vt + adv **(a)** (replace) rimettere (a posto). **(b)** (postpone) rimandare, rinviare; (retard: production etc) rallentare; (set back: watch, clock) mettere indietro; **this will ~ us back 10 years** questo ci farà tornare indietro di 10 anni; **you can't ~ the clock back** (fig) non si può tornare indietro. **2** vi + adv (Naut) rientrare (in porto).

♦ **put by** vt + adv = **put aside** a, b.

♦ **put down 1** vt + adv **(a)** (set down) mettere giù, posare; (passenger) far scendere; **I couldn't ~ that book down** (fig) non potevo smettere di leggere quel libro. **(b)** (lower: umbrella) chiudere; (: car roof) abbassare. **(c)** (crush: revolt) reprimere; (: gambling, prostitution) abolire; (: rumour) mettere a tacere; (humiliate) mortificare. **(d)** (pay: deposit) versare. **(e)** (destroy: pet) abbattere. **(f)** (write down) scrivere; **to ~ sth down in writing** mettere qc per iscritto; **~ it down on my account** (Comm) me lo addebiti or metta in conto; **~ me down for £15** segnami or mettimi in lista per 15 sterline; **he's ~ his son down for Harrow** ha iscritto suo figlio sulla lista d'attesa per Harrow. **(g)** (classify) considerare; **I'd ~ her down as about forty** le darei una quarantina d'anni; **I ~ him down as a troublemaker** io lo considero un elemento disturbatore. **(h)** (attribute): **to ~ sth down to sth** attribuire qc a qc. **2** vi + adv (Aer) atterrare.

♦ **put forward** vt + adv **(a)** (propose: gen) proporre; (: theory) avanzare; (: opinion) esprimere. **(b)** (advance: date, meeting, function) anticipare; (: clock) mettere avanti.

♦ **put in 1** vt + adv **(a)** (place inside: drawer, bag etc) mettere dentro. **(b)** (insert: in book, speech etc) aggiungere, inserire. **(c)** (interpose: remark) fare; **she ~ in her piece** ha detto la sua. **(d)** (enter: claim, application) presentare; **to ~ in a plea of not guilty** (Law) dichiararsi innocente; **to ~ one's name in for sth** iscriversi a qc; **to ~ sb in for an exam** presentare qn a un esame; **to ~ sb in for an award** proporre qn per un premio. **(e)** (install: central heating) mettere, installare. **(f)** (Pol: elect) eleggere. **(g)** (devote, expend: time) passare, dedicare; **to ~ in a few extra hours** fare qualche ora in più; **to ~ in a good day's work** fare una bella giornata di lavoro. **2** vi + adv (Naut) fare scalo.

♦ **put in for** vi + prep (job) far domanda per; (promotion) far domanda di.

♦ **put off** vt + adv **(a)** (set down: passenger) far scendere. **(b)** (postpone, delay: match, decision) rinviare, rimandare; (: *guest*) chiedere di rimandare; **to ~ off doing sth** rimandare qc a più tardi; **to ~ sb off with an excuse** liberarsi di qn con una scusa. **(c)** (*discourage*) far passar la voglia a; **to ~ sb off their food** far passare a qn la voglia di mangiare. **(d)** (*repel: smell*) disgustare. **(e)** (*switch off*) spegnere.

♦ **put on** *vt + adv* **(a)** (*shoes, clothes*) mettere, mettersi.

(b) (*assume: accent, manner*) affettare; (: *airs*) darsi; (*fam: kid, have on: esp Am*) prendere in giro; **to ~ on an innocent expression** assumere un'aria innocente; **she's just ~ting it on** sta solo facendo finta.

(c) (*add, increase: speed, pressure*) aumentare; **to ~ on weight** ingrassare, aumentare di peso.

(d) (*concert, exhibition etc*) allestire, organizzare; (*extra bus, train etc*) mettere in servizio.

(e) (*on telephone*): **~ me on to Mr Strong please** mi passi il signor Strong per favore.

(f) (*switch on etc*) accendere; (*kettle, meal*) metter su; **to ~ the brakes on** frenare.

(g) (*inform, indicate*): **to ~ sb on to sb/sth** indicare qn/qc a qn; **she ~ us on to you** è lei che ci ha detto di rivolgerci a te; **who ~ the police on to him?** chi lo ha segnalato alla polizia?; **what ~ you on to it?** cosa te lo ha fatto capire?

♦ **put out 1** *vt + adv* **(a)** (*place outside*) mettere (di) fuori; **to ~ clothes out to dry** stendere la biancheria; **to be ~ out** (*asked to leave*) essere buttato fuori; **she couldn't ~** him out of her head non riusciva a toglierselo dalla testa.

(b) (*stretch out: arm, foot, leg*) allungare; (: *tongue*) tirar fuori; (*push out: leaves etc*) spuntare; **to ~ one's head out of a window** metter fuori *or* sporgere la testa da una finestra.

(c) (*lay out in order*) disporre.

(d) (*circulate: propaganda*) fare; (: *news*) annunciare; (: *rumour*) mettere in giro; (*bring out: new book*) pubblicare; (: *regulations*) emettere.

(e) (*extinguish: fire, cigarette, light*) spegnere.

(f) (*discontent, vex*) contrariare, seccare; **to be ~ out by sth/sb** essere contrariato da qc/qn.

(g) (*inconvenience*): **to ~ o.s. out (for sb)** scomodarsi *or* disturbarsi per qn.

(h) (*dislocate: shoulder, knee*) lussarsi; (: *back*) farsi uno strappo a.

(i) (*subcontract*) dare (da eseguire) fuori.

2 *vi + adv* (*Naut*): **to ~ out to sea** prendere il largo; **to ~ out from Plymouth** partire da Plymouth.

♦ **put over** *vt + adv* = **put across**.

♦ **put through** *vt + adv* **(a)** (*complete: business, deal*) concludere; (*have accepted: reform, bill*) far approvare, far passare. **(b)** (*Telec: connect: person*) mettere in comunicazione; (: *call*) passare; **~ me through to Miss Blair** mi passi la signorina Blair.

♦ **put together** *vt + adv* **(a)** mettere insieme, riunire; **she's worth more than all the others ~ together** vale più lei da sola che tutte le altre messe insieme. **(b)** (*assemble: furniture*) montare; (: *model*) fare; (: *essay*) comporre; (: *meal*) improvvisare; (: *evidence*) raccogliere; (: *team*) mettere insieme, formare.

♦ **put up 1** *vt + adv* **(a)** (*raise, lift up: hand*) alzare; (: *umbrella*) aprire; (: *collar*) rialzare; (*hoist: flag, sail*) issare; **~ 'em up!** (*fam: hands: in surrender*) arrenditi!; (: *in robbery*) mani in alto!; (: *fists: to fight*) forza, difenditi! **(b)** (*fasten up*): **to ~ up (on)** attaccare (su), appendere (su); (*notice*) affiggere (su). **(c)** (*erect: building, barrier, fence*) erigere, costruire; (: *tent*) montare. **(d)** (*send up: space probe, missile*) lanciare, mettere in orbita. **(e)** (*increase*) aumentare. **(f)** = **put forward a**. **(g)** (*offer*): **to ~ sth up for sale** mettere in vendita qc; **they ~ up a struggle** hanno opposto resistenza. **(h)** (*give accommodation to*) ospitare. **(i)** (*provide: money, funds*) fornire; (: *reward*) offrire. **(j)** (*incite*): **to ~ sb up to doing sth** istigare qn a fare qc.

2 *vi + adv* **(a)**: **to ~ up (at)** (*at hotel*) alloggiare (in); (: *for the night*) pernottare (in). **(b)** (*offer o.s.*): **to ~ up (for)** presentarsi come candidato (a).

♦ **put upon** *vi + prep*: **to be ~ upon** (*imposed on*) farsi mettere sotto i piedi.

♦ **put up with** *vi + prep* sopportare; **she has a lot to ~ up with** ha un sacco di problemi.

pu·tre·fy ['pjuːtrɪfaɪ] *vi* putrefarsi.

pu·trid ['pjuːtrɪd] *adj* putrido(a); **to turn ~** putrefarsi.

putsch [pʊtʃ] *n* putsch *m inv*, colpo di Stato.

putt [pʌt] *n* (*Golf*) putting *m*.

putt·ing ['pʌtɪŋ]: **~ green** *n* green *m inv*.

put·ty ['pʌtɪ] *n* (*for windows*) stucco, mastice *m* da vetrai; **to be ~ in sb's hands** (*fig*) essere come la creta nelle mani di qn.

put-up ['pʊtʌp] *adj*: **~ job** (*fam*) montatura.

puz·zle ['pʌzl] **1** *n* **(a)** (*game*) rompicapo; (*word game*) rebus *m inv*; (*crossword*) parole *fpl* incrociate, cruciverba *m inv*; (*riddle*) indovinello; (*jigsaw*) puzzle *m inv*. **(b)** (*mystery*) enigma *m*, mistero; **it's a ~ to me how it happened** non so come sia successo, per me resta un enigma. **2** *vt* lasciar perplesso(a); **to be ~d about sth** domandarsi il perché di qc. **3** *vi*: **to ~ about** *or* **over** (*sb's actions*) cercare di capire; (*mystery, problem*) cercare di risolvere.

♦ **puzzle out** *vt + adv* (*problem*) risolvere; (*mystery, person, attitude*) capire; (*writing, instructions*) decifrare; (*answer, solution*) trovare.

puz·zled ['pʌzld] *adj* perplesso(a).

puz·zle·ment ['pʌzlmənt] *n* perplessità.

puz·zling ['pʌzlɪŋ] *adj* (*question*) poco chiaro(a); (*attitude, set of instructions*) incomprensibile.

PVC *n abbr* (= *polyvinyl chloride*) P.V.C.

pyg·my ['pɪgmɪ] *n* pigmeo/a.

py·ja·mas, (*Am*) **pa·ja·mas** [pə'dʒɑːməz] *npl* pigiama *m*; **a pair of ~** un pigiama.

py·lon ['paɪlən] *n* pilone *m*.

pyra·mid ['pɪrəmɪd] *n* piramide *f*.

pyre ['paɪə'] *n* pira.

Py·rex ['paɪreks] **1** *n* ® Pirex *m inv*®. **2** *cpd*: **casserole** *n* pirofila.

pyro·ma·ni·ac [ˌpaɪrəʊ'meɪnɪæk] *n* piromane *m/f*.

pyro·tech·nics [ˌpaɪrəʊ'tekniks] *n* **(a)** (*sg: Phys*) pirotecnica. **(b)** (*pl: fireworks display*) spettacolo pirotecnico.

py·thon ['paɪθən] *n* pitone *m*.

Q

Q, q [kjuː] *n (letter)* Q, q *f or m inv.*
quack[1] [kwæk] **1** *n* qua qua *m inv.* **2** *vi* fare qua qua.
quack[2] [kwæk] *n (pej)* ciarlatano/a; *(fam: doctor)* dottore/essa.
quad [kwɒd] *n* **(a)** *abbr of* **quadrangle b. (b)** *abbr of* **quadruplet.**
quad·ran·gle ['kwɒdræŋgl] *n* **(a)** *(Math)* quadrangolo, quadrilatero. **(b)** *(courtyard)* cortile *m (di collegio etc).*
quad·rat·ic [kwɒ'drætɪk] *adj (equation)* di secondo grado, quadratico(a).
quad·ri·lat·er·al [ˌkwɒdrɪ'lætərəl] *adj* quadrilatero(a).
quad·ru·ped ['kwɒdrʊpɛd] *n* quadrupede *m.*
quad·ru·ple ['kwɒdrʊpl] **1** *adj* quadruplo(a), quadruplice. **2** *vt* quadruplicare. **3** *vi* quadruplicarsi.
quad·ru·plet [kwɒ'druːplɪt] *n* uno/a di quattro gemelli.
quag·mire ['kwægmaɪər] *n* pantano.
quail[1] [kweɪl] *n (bird)* quaglia.
quail[2] [kweɪl] *vi (flinch):* **to ~ (at)** perdersi d'animo (davanti a).
quaint [kweɪnt] *adj* (**-er, -est**) *(odd)* strano(a), bizzarro(a); *(picturesque)* pittoresco(a).
quaint·ly ['kweɪntlɪ] *adv (see adj)* in modo strano, in modo bizzarro; pittorescamente.
quake [kweɪk] **1** *vi:* **to ~ (with)** tremare (di). **2** *n (earth~)* terremoto.
Quak·er ['kweɪkər] *n* quacchero/a.
quali·fi·ca·tion [ˌkwɒlɪfɪ'keɪʃən] *n* **(a):** **~s** *(gen)* qualifiche *fpl,* requisiti *mpl; (paper ~s)* titoli *mpl* di studio; **what are your ~s?** quali sono le sue qualifiche?; *(paper ~s)* quali sono i suoi titoli di studio?; **I've got a teaching ~** sono abilitato *or* ho l'abilitazione all'insegnamento. **(b)** *(reservation)* riserva.
quali·fied ['kwɒlɪfaɪd] *adj* **(a)** *(gen):* **~ for/to do** qualificato(a) per/fare; *(engineer, doctor, teacher etc)* abilitato(a); *(nurse)* diplomato(a); **he's not ~ for the job** non ha i requisiti necessari per questo lavoro. **(b)** *(support)* condizionato(a); *(acceptance)* con riserva; **it was a ~ success** è stato un successo parziale; **the film has received ~ praise** il film è stato accolto piuttosta favorevolmente.
quali·fy ['kwɒlɪfaɪ] **1** *vt* **(a)** *(make competent)* qualificare; **his experience in South Africa qualifies him to speak on apartheid** la sua esperienza nel Sudafrica lo autorizza a parlare sull'apartheid. **(b)** *(modify)* modificare; *(: support, approval)* porre delle condizioni a. **(c)** *(Gram)* qualificare. **2** *vi (gen)* avere i requisiti necessari; *(professionally)* abilitarsi, essere abilitato(a); *(Sport)* qualificarsi; **to ~ as an engineer** diventare un perito tecnico; *(with degree)* laurearsi in ingegneria; **to ~ for a job** avere i requisiti necessari per un lavoro; **he hardly qualifies as a major dramatist** non si può certamente definirlo un grande drammaturgo.
quali·fy·ing ['kwɒlɪfaɪɪŋ] *adj (Gram)* qualificati-

vo(a); *(exam)* di ammissione; *(round)* eliminatorio(a).
quali·ta·tive ['kwɒlɪtətɪv] *adj* qualitativo(a).
qual·ity ['kwɒlɪtɪ] **1** *n* qualità *f inv;* **of good ~** di buona qualità; **of poor ~** scadente. **2** *cpd* di qualità.
qualm [kwɑːm] *n (often pl: fear)* apprensione *f;* *(: scruple)* scrupolo, esitazione *f;* **to have ~s about sth** avere degli scrupoli per qc.
quan·da·ry ['kwɒndərɪ] *n:* **to be in a ~ (about sth)** essere molto incerto(a) (su qc).
quan·ti·ta·tive ['kwɒntɪtətɪv] *adj* quantitativo(a).
quan·tity ['kwɒntɪtɪ] **1** *n* quantità *f inv; (Comm)* quantità, quantitativo; **in ~** in grande quantità. **2** *cpd:* **~ surveyor** *n* geometra *m (che valuta il costo del materiale e della manodopera necessari per una costruzione.*
quan·tum ['kwɒntəm] **1** *n* quanto. **2** *cpd (number)* quantico(a); *(mechanics)* quantistico(a); **~ theory** teoria quantistica *or* dei quanti.
quar·an·tine ['kwɒrəntiːn] *n* quarantena.
quar·rel ['kwɒrəl] **1** *n (argument)* litigio, lite *f;* **to have a ~ with sb** litigare con qn; **to pick a ~ (with sb)** cercare dei pretesti per litigare (con qn); **I've no ~ with him** non ho niente contro di lui. **2** *vi:* **to ~ (with sb about sth)** litigare (con qn per qc); **they ~led about** *or* **over money** hanno litigato per i soldi; **I can't ~ with that** non ho niente da ridire su questo.
quar·rel·ling, *(Am)* **quar·rel·ing** ['kwɒrəlɪŋ] *n* litigi *mpl.*
quar·rel·some ['kwɒrəlsəm] *adj* litigioso(a).
quar·ry[1] ['kwɒrɪ] *n (Hunting, fig)* preda.
quar·ry[2] ['kwɒrɪ] **1** *n (mine)* cava. **2** *vt* cavare.
quart [kwɔːt] *n* quarto di gallone *(Brit = 1,136 litri; Am = 0,964 litri).*
quar·ter ['kwɔːtər] **1** *n* **(a)** *(fourth part)* quarto; *(of year)* trimestre *m;* **a ~ (of a pound) of tea** ≃ un etto di tè; **a ~ of a century** un quarto di secolo; **to divide sth into ~s** dividere qc in quattro (parti); **to pay by the ~** pagare trimestralmente. **(b)** *(Am, Canada: 25 cents)* quarto di dollaro, 25 centesimi. **(c)** *(time):* **a ~ of an hour** un quarto d'ora; **an hour and a ~** un'ora e un quarto; **it's a ~ to 3,** *(Am)* **it's a ~ of 3** sono le 3 meno un quarto, manca un quarto alle 3; **it's a ~ past 3,** *(Am)* **it's a ~ after 3** sono le 3 e un quarto. **(d)** *(district)* quartiere *m.* **(e)** *(direction):* **from all ~s** da tutte le parti *or* direzioni; **at close ~s** a distanza ravvicinata; **you won't get any help from that ~** non otterrai nessun aiuto da quella parte. **(f):** **~s** *pl (accommodation)* alloggio; *(Mil)* quartiere *m;* *(: temporary)* alloggiamento. **(g):** **to give sb no ~** essere implacabile verso qn.
2 *vt* **(a)** *(divide into 4)* dividere in quattro (parti). **(b)** *(Mil)* alloggiare.
quarter-deck ['kwɔːtədɛk] *n* cassero.
quarter-final ['kwɔːtə,faɪnl] *n* quarti *mpl* di finale.
quar·ter·ly ['kwɔːtəlɪ] **1** *adj* trimestrale. **2** *n* periodico trimestrale. **3** *adv* trimestralmente.
quarter·master ['kwɔːtə,mɑːstər] *n (Mil)* furiere

335

m; (Naut) timoniere m.

quar·tet [kwɔːˈtɛt] n quartetto.

quar·to [ˈkwɔːtəu] adj, n in quarto (m) inv.

quartz [kwɔːts] 1 n quarzo. 2 cpd di quarzo; (clock) al quarzo.

quash [kwɒʃ] vt (a) (destroy: enemies) stroncare. (b) (reject) respingere; (: Law: sentence, conviction) revocare, annullare.

quasi- [ˈkwaːzɪ] pref semi...; (pej) pseudo...; ~official adj semiufficiale; ~religious adj quasi religioso(a); ~revolutionary adj, n pseudorivoluzionario(a) (m/f).

qua·ver [ˈkweɪvəʳ] 1 n (when speaking) tremolio; (Mus: note) croma. 2 vi (voice) tremare, tremolare.

quay [kiː] n molo.

quay·side [ˈkiːsaɪd] n banchina.

quea·sy [ˈkwiːzɪ] adj (-ier, -iest) (stomach) nauseato(a); to feel ~ avere la nausea, provare un senso di nausea.

queen [kwiːn] 1 n regina; (Cards, Chess) regina, donna; Q~ Elizabeth la regina Elisabetta. 2 cpd: ~ bee n ape f regina inv; ~ mother n regina madre.

queer [kwɪəʳ] 1 adj (-er, -est) (a) (odd) strano(a), singolare. (b) (ill) strano(a), non giusto(a); to feel ~ avere un po' di malessere, sentirsi poco bene. (c) (fam: homosexual) omosessuale. 2 n (fam: male homosexual) finocchio. 3 vt: to ~ sb's pitch rovinare tutto a qn, rompere le uova nel paniere a qn.

quell [kwɛl] vt (passion etc) reprimere; (rebellion) soffocare;(attempt) sventare.

quench [kwɛntʃ] vt (thirst) togliere, levare.

queru·lous [ˈkwɛrʊləs] adj querulo(a).

que·ry [ˈkwɪərɪ] 1 n (question) domanda; (question mark) punto interrogativo; (fig: doubt) interrogativo. 2 vt (a) (ask): to ~ sb about sth rivolgere delle domande a qn riguardo a qc. (b) (doubt) mettere in dubbio; (disagree with, dispute) sollevare (dei) dubbi su, contestare.

quest [kwɛst] 1 n ricerca; in ~ of alla ricerca di, in cerca di.

ques·tion [ˈkwɛstʃən] 1 n (a) (interrogative) domanda; to ask sb a ~, put a ~ to sb fare una domanda a qn.

(b) (matter, issue) questione f, argomento; it is an open ~ whether... resta da vedere se..., è una questione aperta se...; the ~ is... il problema è...; it is a ~ of whether... si tratta di sapere se...; that is not the ~ non è questo il problema; there is no ~ of outside help non c'è nessuna possibilità di aiuto esterno; there can be no ~ of your resigning che lei dia le dimissioni non è nemmeno da prendersi in considerazione; it's out of the ~ è fuori discussione.

(c) (doubt etc): beyond ~, past ~ fuori discussione or questione; in ~ in discussione, in dubbio; there is no ~ about it su questo non c'è (assolutamente) nessun dubbio; to bring or call sth into ~ mettere in dubbio qc.

2 vt (a) (interrogate: person) interrogare.

(b) (doubt) mettere in dubbio, dubitare di; I ~ whether it is worthwhile mi domando se ne vale or valga la pena.

3 cpd: ~ mark n punto interrogativo.

ques·tion·able [ˈkwɛstʃənəbl] adj discutibile.

ques·tion·er [ˈkwɛstʃənəʳ] n interrogante m/f.

ques·tion·ing [ˈkwɛstʃənɪŋ] 1 adj (mind) inquisitore(trice), indagatore(trice). 2 n interrogatorio.

ques·tion·naire [ˌkwɛstʃəˈnɛəʳ] n questionario.

queue [kjuː] 1 n coda, fila; to form a ~ mettersi in

fila or in coda; to stand in a ~ essere in fila or in coda, fare la fila or la coda; to jump the ~ passare davanti agli altri (in una coda). 2 vi (also: ~ up) fare la fila, fare la coda.

quib·ble [ˈkwɪbl] 1 n cavillo, sottigliezza. 2 vi cavillare, sottilizzare.

quick [kwɪk] 1 adj (-er, -est) (fast: in motion) veloce; (: in time) svelto(a), veloce; (agile: reflexes) pronto(a); (: in mind) svelto(a); a ~ temper un temperamento irascibile; the ~est method il metodo più rapido; a ~ reply una risposta pronta; be ~ about it! fa' presto!, sbrigati!; she was ~ to see that... ha visto subito che...; to be ~ to act agire prontamente; to be ~ to take offence essere permaloso, offendersi subito; do you fancy a ~ one? (fam: drink) andiamo a bere qualcosa? 2 adv in fretta; come ~! vieni subito!; as ~ as a flash or as lightning rapido come il fulmine. 3 n: to cut sb to the ~ pungere qn sul vivo.

quick·en [ˈkwɪkən] 1 vt affrettare, accelerare; (fig: feelings) stimolare; to ~ one's pace affrettare or allungare il passo. 2 vi: the pace ~ed il ritmo divenne più veloce.

quickie [ˈkwɪkɪ] n (fam) cosa fatta velocemente; (question) domanda veloce; do you fancy a ~? (drink) andiamo a bere qualcosa?

quick·lime [ˈkwɪklaɪm] n calce f viva.

quick·ly [ˈkwɪklɪ] adv in fretta, rapidamente; he talks too ~ parla troppo velocemente; we must act ~ dobbiamo agire tempestivamente.

quick·ness [ˈkwɪknɪs] n velocità, rapidità; (of mind) prontezza.

quick·sand [ˈkwɪksænd] n sabbie fpl mobili.

quick·silver [ˈkwɪkˌsɪlvəʳ] n argento vivo, mercurio.

quick·step [ˈkwɪkstɛp] n (dance) quick step m inv.

quick-tempered [ˌkwɪkˈtɛmpəd] adj che si arrabbia facilmente.

quick-witted [ˌkwɪkˈwɪtɪd] adj sveglio(a).

quid [kwɪd] n (Brit fam: pl inv) sterlina.

qui·et [ˈkwaɪət] 1 adj (-er, -est) (a) (person: silent) silenzioso(a), tranquillo(a); (: reserved) quieto(a), taciturno(a); (: calm) tranquillo(a), calmo(a); be ~!, keep ~! silenzio!, sta' zitto!; (when moving about) non far rumore!, fa' piano!; to keep sb ~ tener tranquillo or quieto qn; they paid him £100 to keep him ~ gli hanno dato 100 sterline perché stesse zitto.

(b) (not noisy: engine) silenzioso(a); (: music, voice, laugh) sommesso(a); (: sound) basso(a), leggero(a).

(c) not busy: day) calmo(a), tranquillo(a); (: place) tranquillo(a); the shops/trains are always ~ on a Monday i negozi/treni non sono mai affollati al lunedì; business is ~ at this time of year questa è la stagione morta.

(d) (discreet: manner) dolce, garbato(a); (: colours) tenue, smorzato(a); (: humour) garbato(a); (private, intimate) intimo(a); I'll have a ~ word with him gli dirò due parole in privato; to lead a ~ life fare una vita tranquilla; he managed to keep the whole thing ~ è riuscito a tener segreta tutta la faccenda; we had a ~ wedding abbiamo avuto un matrimonio semplice.

2 n (silence) silenzio; (calm) pace f, tranquillità; on the ~ (fam: act) di nascosto; (: tell) in confidenza.

3 vt = quieten 1.

qui·et·en [ˈkwaɪətən] 1 vt (also: ~ down) calmare, placare. 2 vi (also: ~ down) calmarsi.

qui·et·ly [ˈkwaɪətlɪ] adv (softly, silently) silenziosamente, senza far rumore; (not loudly: speak, sing) in modo sommesso; (calmly) tranquillamente, con calma; **to be** ~ **dressed** essere vestito in modo sobrio; ~ **situated** *(house)* in un posto tranquillo; **let's get married** ~ sposiamoci con una cerimonia semplice; **he slipped off** ~ **to avoid being noticed** se n'è andato alla chetichella per non essere notato.

qui·et·ness ['kwaɪətnɪs] *n (silence)* silenzio; *(peacefulness)* tranquillità, quiete *f; (softness: of voice, music)* dolcezza.

quill [kwɪl] *n (feather)* penna; *(pen)* penna d'oca; *(of porcupine)* aculeo.

quilt [kwɪlt] **1** *n* trapunta; **continental** ~ piumino. **2** *vt* trapuntare.

quilt·ed ['kwɪltɪd] *adj* trapuntato(a).

quin [kwɪn] *n abbr of* **quintuplet.**

quince [kwɪns] **1** *n (fruit)* (mela) cotogna; *(tree)* cotogno. **2** *cpd:* ~ **jelly** *n* cotognata.

qui·nine [kwɪ'niːn] *n* chinino.

quin·tes·sence [kwɪn'tɛsns] *n* quintessenza.

quin·tet [kwɪn'tɛt] *n* quintetto.

quin·tu·plet [kwɪn'tjuːplɪt] *n* uno/a di cinque gemelli.

quip [kwɪp] *n* battuta di spirito.

quirk [kwɜːk] *n (oddity)* stranezza, bizzarria; **by some** ~ **of fate** per un capriccio della sorte.

quirky ['kwɜːkɪ] *adj* (-**ier**, -**iest**) stravagante, capriccioso(a).

quit [kwɪt] *pt, pp* **quit** *or* **quitted 1** *vt (a) (cease: work)* lasciare, piantare; **to** ~ **doing sth** smettere di fare qc; ~ **stalling!** *(Am fam)* non tirarla per le lunghe! **(b)** *(leave: place)* lasciare. **2** *vi (resign)* dare le dimissioni, dimettersi; *(give up: in game etc)* abbandonare; *(accept defeat)* darsi per vinto. **3** *adj:* ~ **of** sbarazzato(a) di, liberato(a) di.

quite [kwaɪt] *adv* **(a)** *(completely)* proprio, perfettamente; ~ **new** proprio nuovo; ~ **(so)!** appunto!, proprio (così)!, precisamente!; **that's** ~

enough è più che abbastanza, basta così; **I can** ~ **believe that...** non faccio fatica a credere che...; **not** ~ **as many as last time** non proprio così tanti come l'ultima volta; **I** ~ **understand** capisco perfettamente; **that's not** ~ **right** non è proprio esatto. **(b)** *(rather)* abbastanza, piuttosto; **I** ~ **like that idea** è un'idea che non mi dispiace; ~ **a few people** un bel po' di gente; **she's** ~ **pretty** è piuttosto carina; **he's** ~ **a good writer** è uno scrittore abbastanza bravo.

quits [kwɪts] *adv:* **to be** ~ **(with sb)** essere pari (con qn); **let's call it** ~ adesso siamo pari.

quiv·er[1] ['kwɪvə'] *n (for arrows)* faretra, turcasso.

quiv·er[2] ['kwɪvə'] *vi (person, voice):* **to** ~ **(with)** tremare (per *or* da); *(eyelids)* sbattere.

quix·ot·ic [kwɪk'sɒtɪk] *adj* donchisciottesco(a).

quiz [kwɪz] **1** *n* quiz *m inv.* **2** *vt:* **to** ~ **sb about** interrogare qn su.

quiz·zi·cal ['kwɪzɪkəl] *adj (glance)* interrogativo(a) (e beffardo(a)).

quoit [kwɔɪt] *n* anello *(per il gioco degli anelli).*

quor·um ['kwɔːrəm] *n* quorum *m inv.*

quo·ta ['kwəʊtə] *n* quota.

quo·ta·tion [kwəʊ'teɪʃən] **1** *n* **(a)** *(words)* citazione *f.* **(b)** *(Comm: estimate)* preventivo. **2** *cpd:* ~ **marks** *npl* virgolette *fpl.*

quote [kwəʊt] **1** *vt* **(a)** *(words, author)* citare; **can you** ~ **me an example?** puoi citarmi *or* farmi un esempio? **(b)** *(Comm: sum, figure)* indicare; **the figure** ~**d for the repairs** il preventivo per le riparazioni. **2** *vi* citare; **and I** ~ *(from text)* cito testualmente; *(sb's words)* riferisco *or* ripeto testualmente; ~ **... unquote** *(in dictation)* aprire le virgolette ... chiudere le virgolette; *(in lecture, report)* cito ... fine della citazione. **3** *n* **(a)** = **quotation 1. (b):** ~**s** *pl (inverted commas)* virgolette *fpl;* **in** ~**s** tra virgolette.

quo·tient ['kwəʊʃənt] *n* quoziente *m.*

R

R, r |ɑ:ʳ| *n (letter)* R, r *f or m inv;* **the three R's** leggere, scrivere e far di conto.
rab·bi [ˈræbaɪ] *n* rabbino.
rab·bit [ˈræbɪt] **1** *n* coniglio. **2** *cpd:* ~ **hole** *n* tana di coniglio; ~ **hutch** *n* conigliera.
rab·ble [ˈræbl] *n* confusione *f* di gente; **the** ~ *(pej)* il popolino.
rab·id [ˈræbɪd] *adj (dog)* idrofobo(a), rabbioso(a); *(fig: furious)* arrabbiato(a); *(: fanatical)* fanatico(a).
ra·bies [ˈreɪbiːz] *n* rabbia, idrofobia.
RAC *n abbr of Royal Automobile Club.*
rac·coon [rəˈkuːn] *n* procione *m.*
race[1] [reɪs] **1** *n (Sport etc)* corsa; **the 100 metres** ~ la corsa sui 100 metri, i 100 metri; **a** ~ **against time** una corsa contro il tempo; **the arms** ~ la corsa agli armamenti. **2** *vt* **(a)** *(horse)* far gareggiare. **(b)** *(person)* correre contro, gareggiare contro; **I'll** ~ **you around the block** ti sfido a una corsa intorno all'isolato. **3** *vi* **(a): to** ~ *(against sb)* correre (contro qn). **(b)** *(rush)* correre; **to** ~ **in/out** *etc* precipitarsi dentro/fuori *etc;* **he** ~**d across the road** ha attraversato la strada di corsa. **(c)** *(pulse)* battere precipitosamente; *(engine)* imballarsi.
race[2] [reɪs] **1** *n* razza; **the human** ~ la razza umana. **2** *cpd (hatred, riot)* razziale; ~ **relations** *npl* rapporti *mpl* razziali.
race·course [ˈreɪskɔːs] *n* ippodromo, campo di corse.
race·horse [ˈreɪshɔːs] *n* cavallo da corsa.
race·track [ˈreɪstræk] *n (for horses, Aut etc)* pista.
ra·cial [ˈreɪʃəl] *adj (discrimination, tension)* razziale; *(harmony, equality)* fra le razze.
ra·cial·ism [ˈreɪʃəlɪzəm] *n* razzismo.
ra·cial·ist [ˈreɪʃəlɪst] *adj, n* razzista *(m/f).*
rac·ing [ˈreɪsɪŋ] **1** *n* corsa; *(horse-*~) corse *fpl.* **2** *cpd (car, cycle)* da corsa; ~ **driver** *n* corridore *m* automobilista; ~ **stables** *npl* scuderia di cavalli da corsa; ~ **yacht** *n* yacht *m inv* da competizone.
rac·ism [ˈreɪsɪzəm] *n* razzismo.
rack[1] [ræk] **1** *n* **(a)** *(storage framework)* rastrelliera; *(for luggage)* rete *f;* *(for hats, coats)* appendiabiti *m inv;* *(in shops)* scaffale *m.* **(b)** *(for torture)* cavalletto, ruota. **2** *vt (subj: pain, cough)* torturare; **to** ~ **one's brains** scervellarsi.
rack[2] [ræk] *n:* **to go to** ~ **and ruin** *(building)* andare in rovina; *(business)* andare in malora *or* a catafascio; *(country)* andare a catafascio; *(person)* lasciarsi andare completamente.
rack-and-pinion [ˌrækənˈpɪnjən] *n (Tech)* rocchetto-cremagliera *m.*
rack·et[1] [ˈrækɪt] *n* racchetta.
rack·et[2] [ˈrækɪt] *n* **(a)** *(din)* baccano, fracasso. **(b)** *(organised fraud)* traffico, racket *m inv;* *(swindle)* imbroglio, truffa.
rack·et·eer [ˌrækɪˈtɪəʳ] *n (esp Am)* trafficante *m/f.*
rac·on·teur [ˌrækɒnˈtɜːʳ] *n* raccontatore/trice.
ra·coon [rəˈkuːn] *n* = **raccoon.**
rac·quet [ˈrækɪt] *n* = **racket**[1].

racy [ˈreɪsɪ] *adj (-ier, -iest) (style, speech, humour)* spigliato(a), brioso(a).
ra·dar [ˈreɪdɑːʳ] **1** *n* radar *m.* **2** *cpd (station, screen)* radar *inv;* ~ **operator** *n* radarista *m/f;* ~ **trap** *n* multanova *m* ®.
ra·dial [ˈreɪdɪəl] *adj (tyre)* radiale.
ra·di·ance [ˈreɪdɪəns] *n (brilliance)* splendore *m,* fulgore *m; (fig)* radiosità.
ra·di·ant [ˈreɪdɪənt] *adj (heat)* radiante; *(light)* sfolgorante; *(fig):* ~ **(with)** raggiante (di).
ra·di·ate [ˈreɪdɪeɪt] **1** *vt (heat)* irraggiare, irradiare; *(fig: happiness)* irraggiare. **2** *vi:* **to** ~ **from** irraggiarsi da, irradiarsi da.
ra·dia·tion [ˌreɪdɪˈeɪʃən] **1** *n (nuclear etc)* radiazione *f; (of heat etc)* irradiamento. **2** *cpd:* ~ **sickness** *n* malattia da radiazioni.
ra·dia·tor [ˈreɪdɪeɪtəʳ] **1** *n* radiatore *m.* **2** *cpd:* ~ **grill** *n* mascherina, calandra.
radi·cal [ˈrædɪkəl] *adj, n* radicale *(m/f).*
radi·cal·ly [ˈrædɪkəlɪ] *adv* radicalmente.
ra·dio [ˈreɪdɪəʊ] **1** *n (Telec)* radio *f; (*~ **set)** radio *f inv,* apparecchio *m* radio *inv;* **by** ~ per radio; **on the** ~ alla radio. **2** *vi:* **to** ~ **to sb** comunicare via radio con qn. **3** *vt (information)* trasmettere per radio; *(one's position)* comunicare via radio; *(person)* chiamare via radio. **4** *cpd (programme)* radiofonico(a); *(station, frequency, wave)* radio *inv;* ~ **announcer** *n* annunciatore/trice della radio; ~ **beacon** *n* radiofaro; ~ **taxi** *n* radiotaxi *m inv.*
radio·ac·tive [ˌreɪdɪəʊˈæktɪv] *adj* radioattivo(a).
radio·ac·tiv·ity [ˌreɪdɪəʊækˈtɪvɪtɪ] *n* radioattività.
radio-controlled [ˌreɪdɪəʊkənˈtrəʊld] *adj* radiocomandato(a), radioguidato(a).
radio·gram [ˈreɪdɪəʊgræm] *n* **(a)** *(combined radio and gramophone)* radiogrammofono. **(b)** *(Med)* radiografia, radiogramma *m.*
ra·di·og·ra·pher [ˌreɪdɪˈɒgrəfəʳ] *n* radiologo/a.
ra·di·og·ra·phy [ˌreɪdɪˈɒgrəfɪ] *n* radiografia.
ra·di·ol·ogy [ˌreɪdɪˈɒlədʒɪ] *n* radiologia.
radio·tele·phone [ˌreɪdɪəʊˈtelɪfəʊn] *n* radiotelefono.
rad·ish [ˈrædɪʃ] *n* ravanello.
ra·dium [ˈreɪdɪəm] *n* radio *m.*
ra·dius [ˈreɪdɪəs] *n, pl* **radii** [ˈreɪdɪaɪ] raggio; **within a** ~ **of 50 miles** in un raggio di 50 miglia.
RAF *n abbr of Royal Air Force.*
raf·fia [ˈræfɪə] *n* rafia.
raf·fle [ˈræfl] **1** *n* riffa, lotteria. **2** *vt (object)* mettere in palio.
raft [rɑːft] *n* zattera.
raft·er [ˈrɑːftəʳ] *n* puntone *m (Archit),* trave *f* (del tetto).
rag[1] [ræg] **1** *n* **(a)** *(piece of cloth)* straccio, cencio; ~**s** *(old clothes)* stracci *mpl;* **in** ~**s** stracciato; **dressed in** ~**s** vestito di stracci; **to feel like a wet** ~ *(fam)* sentirsi (come) uno straccio. **(b)** *(fam: newspaper)* giornaletto. **2** *cpd:* ~ **doll** *n* bambola di pezza; **the** ~ **trade** *(fam)* l'abbigliamento.
rag[2] [ræg] **1** *n (practical joke)* scherzo; *(Univ: parade)* festa studentesca a scopo benefico. **2** *vt (tease)* prendere in giro.

rag-and-bone man [ˌrægənd'bəʊn,mæn] *n, pl* **-men** straccivendolo.

rag·bag ['rægbæg] *n (fig: mixture)* guazzabuglio, accozzaglia.

rage [reɪdʒ] **1** *n* **(a)** *(anger)* collera, furia; **to fly into a ~** andare *or* montare su tutte le furie; **to be in a ~** essere furioso *or* su tutte le furie. **(b)** *(fashion, trend)* mania; **it's all the ~** fa furore. **2** *vi (person)* essere furioso(a), infuriarsi; *(sea, fire, plague, wind)* infuriare.

rag·ged ['rægɪd] *adj (dress)* stracciato(a); *(person)* lacero(a), cencioso(a); *(edge)* irregolare.

rag·ing ['reɪdʒɪŋ] *adj (all senses)* furioso(a); **in a ~ temper** su tutte le furie.

raid [reɪd] **1** *n (Mil)* incursione *f*; *(by police)* irruzione *f*; *(by bandits)* razzia; *(by criminals)* rapina. **2** *vt (see n)* fare un'incursione in; fare irruzione in; fare razzia in; rapinare; **the boys ~ed the orchard** i ragazzi hanno saccheggiato il frutteto.

raid·er ['reɪdə^r] *n (bandit)* bandito; *(bank ~ etc)* rapinatore/trice.

rail [reɪl] *n* **(a)** *(bar)* sbarra, traversa; *(of balcony, terrace)* davanzale *m*; *(banister)* corrimano; *(towel ~)* portasciugamani *m inv*; **bath ~** maniglia del bagno. **(b)** *(for train)* rotaia; **to go off the ~s** *(train)* deragliare, uscire dal binario; *(fig: become confused)* andare fuori strada; *(: err)* sviarsi; **by ~** in treno, per ferrovia.

rail·ings ['reɪlɪŋz] *npl* cancellata.

rail·road ['reɪlrəʊd] **1** *n (Am)* = **railway**. **2** *vt (fig)*: **to ~ sb into doing sth** costringere qn a fare qc in fretta e furia.

rail·way ['reɪlweɪ] **1** *n (system)* ferrovia; *(track)* strada ferrata. **2** *cpd (bridge, timetable, network)* ferroviario(a); **~ engine** *n* locomotiva; **~ line** *n* linea ferroviaria; **~ station** *n* stazione *f* (ferroviaria).

rail·way·man ['reɪlweɪmən] *n, pl* **-men** ferroviere *m*.

rain [reɪn] **1** *n* pioggia; **in the ~** sotto la pioggia; **come ~ or shine** qualunque tempo faccia; *(fig)* qualunque cosa succeda. **2** *vi* piovere; **it is ~ing** piove; **it's ~ing cats and dogs** piove a catinelle; **it never ~s but it pours** *(Proverb)* piove sul bagnato; **to ~ down (on sb)** *(blows etc)* piovere (addosso a qn).

rain·bow ['reɪnbəʊ] *n* arcobaleno.

rain·check ['reɪntʃɛk] *n*: **I'll take a ~** *(fam)* sarà per un'altra volta.

rain·coat ['reɪnkəʊt] *n* impermeabile *m*.

rain·drop ['reɪndrɒp] *n* goccia di pioggia.

rain·fall ['reɪnfɔːl] *n* piovosità, precipitazioni *fpl*.

rain·water ['reɪn,wɔːtə^r] *n* acqua piovana.

rainy ['reɪnɪ] *adj* **(-ier, -iest)** *(climate)* piovoso(a); *(season)* delle piogge; **~ day** giorno piovoso; **to put sth away for a ~ day** *(fig)* mettere qc da parte.

raise [reɪz] **1** *vt* **(a)** *(lift: gen)* sollevare, alzare; *(: shipwreck)* riportare alla superficie; *(: flag)* alzare, issare; *(: dust)* sollevare; *(fig: spirits, morale)* risollevare, tirar su; *(: to power, in rank)* elevare; *(Math)*: **to ~ to the third power** elevare alla terza potenza; **to ~ o.s. up on one's elbows** sollevarsi sui gomiti; **he ~d his hat to me** si è tolto il cappello in segno di saluto; **to ~ one's glass to sb/sth** brindare a qn/qc; **to ~ one's voice** alzare la voce; **he didn't ~ an eyebrow** non ha battuto ciglio; **to ~ sb's hopes** accendere le speranze di qn; **to ~ from the dead** risuscitare dai morti.

(b) *(erect: building, statue)* erigere.

(c) *(increase: salary, production)* aumentare; *(: price)* aumentare, alzare.

(d) *(bring up, breed: family, livestock)* allevare;

(e) *(produce: question, objection)* sollevare; *(: problem)* porre; *(: doubts, suspicions)* far sorgere, far nascere; **to ~ a laugh/a smile** far ridere/sorridere; **to ~ hell** *or* **the roof** *(fam)* fare il diavolo a quattro.

(f) *(get together: funds, army)* raccogliere; *(: taxes)* imporre; *(: money)* procurarsi; **to ~ a loan** chiedere un prestito.

(g) *(end: siege, embargo)* togliere. **2** *n (payrise)* aumento.

rai·sin ['reɪzən] *n* uvetta.

rai·son d'être [ˌreɪzɔ̃:n'deɪtrə] *n* ragione *f* di vita.

rake¹ [reɪk] **1** *n* rastrello. **2** *vt (sand, leaves, soil)* rastrellare; *(strafe: ship, row of men)* spazzare; **they ~d in a profit of £100** ci hanno fatto un guadagno di 100 sterline.

♦ **rake up** *vt* + *adv (subject, memories)* rivangare, riesumare.

rake² [reɪk] *n (old use: dissolute man)* libertino.

rak·ish ['reɪkɪʃ] *adj* **(a)** *(person)* libertino(a), dissoluto(a). **(b): at a ~ angle** *(hat)* sulle ventitré.

ral·ly ['rælɪ] **1** *n (of troops, people: also Pol)* raduno, riunione *f*; *(Aut)* rally *m inv*; *(Tennis)* lungo scambio di colpi. **2** *vt (troops, supporters)* riunire, radunare. **3** *vi (troops, supporters)* riunirsi; *(revive, recover: patient, strength, share prices)* riprendersi.

♦ **rally round** *vi* + *adv (fig)* accorrere in aiuto.

ral·ly·ing point ['rælɪŋ, pɔɪnt] *n (Pol, Mil)* punto di riunione, punto di raduno.

ram [ræm] *n* **1** *(Zool)* montone *m*, ariete *m*; *(Astrology, Mil)* ariete. **2** *vt* **(a): to ~ (into)** *(pack tightly)* calcare (in), pigiare (in); *(push down)* ficcare (in); **to ~ one's hat down on one's head** calcarsi il cappello in testa; **they ~med their ideas down my throat** mi hanno imbottito la testa con le loro idee. **(b)** *(collide with: Naut)* speronare; **the car ~med the lamppost** la macchina è andata a sbattere con il muso contro il lampione.

ram·ble ['ræmbl] **1** *n (lunga) passeggiata; (hike)* escursione *f*. **2** *vi* **(a)** *(walk)* gironzolare, vagare; *(hike)* fare escursioni. **(b)** *(fig: in speech)* divagare, dilungarsi; **his mind has started to ~** è un po' svanito.

ram·bler ['ræmblə^r] *n (hiker)* escursionista *m/f*.

ram·bling ['ræmblɪŋ] *adj (plant)* rampicante; *(speech, book)* sconnesso(a), slegato(a); *(house)* tutto(a) nicchie e corridoi.

rami·fi·ca·tion [ˌræmɪfɪ'keɪʃən] *n* ramificazione *f*.

rami·fy ['ræmɪfaɪ] *vi (tree, problem)* ramificare; *(system)* ramificarsi.

ramp [ræmp] *n (on road etc)* rampa; *(in garage)* ponte *m* idraulico; *(Aer)* scala d'imbarco; '**~**' *(Aut)* 'fondo stradale in rifacimento'.

ram·page [ræm'peɪdʒ] **1** *n*: **to go on the ~** scatenarsi. **2** *vi* scatenarsi.

ram·pant ['ræmpənt] *adj* **(a)** *(fig)*: **to be ~** imperversare. **(b)** *(Heraldry)* rampante.

ram·part ['ræmpɑːt] *n* terrapieno, bastione *m*.

ram·shack·le ['ræm,ʃækl] *adj (house)* cadente, malandato(a); *(car, table)* sgangherato(a).

ran [ræn] *pt of* **run**.

ranch [rɑːntʃ] *n* ranch *m inv*.

ran·cid ['rænsɪd] *adj* rancido(a).

ran·cour, (Am) ran·cor ['ræŋkə^r] *n* rancore *m*.

ran·dom ['rændəm] **1** *adj (arrangement)* casuale, fortuito(a); *(sample)* a caso; *(bullet)* a casaccio; **~ access** *(Computers)* accesso casuale. **2** *n*: **at ~ a caso**, come capita.

randy ['rændɪ] *adj* **(-ier, -iest)** *(Brit fam)* in fregola.

rang [ræŋ] *pt of* **ring²**.

range [reɪndʒ] **1** *n* **(a)** *(distance attainable, scope: of gun)* portata, gittata; *(: of ship, plane)* autonomia;

within (firing) ~ a portata di tiro; out of (firing) ~ fuori portata di tiro; at short/long ~ a breve/lunga distanza; ~ of vision campo visivo.

(b) *(extent between limits: of temperature)* variazioni *fpl;* (: *of salaries, prices)* scala; *(: Mus: of instruments, voice)* gamma, estensione *f;* *(selection: of colours, feelings, speeds)* gamma; *(: of goods)* assortimento, gamma; *(domain, sphere)* raggio, sfera; **the ~ of sb's mind** le capacità mentali di qn; **she has a wide ~ of interests** ha interessi molto vari; **do you have anything else in this price ~?** ha nient'altro su *or* di questo prezzo?

(c) *(row)* serie *f inv,* fila; *(of mountains)* catena.

(d) *(Am Agr)* prateria.

(e) *(shooting ~: in open)* campo di tiro, poligono di tiro; *(: at fair)* tiro a segno.

(f) *(kitchen ~)* cucina economica.

2 *vt (arrange)* disporre, allineare.

3 *vi* **(a)** *(mountains, discussion, search)* estendersi; *(numbers, opinions, results)* andare; *(temperatures)* variare; **the discussion ~d over a wide number of topics** la discussione ha toccato vari argomenti.

(b) *(roam):* **to ~ over** percorrere.

range·finder [ˈreɪndʒˈfaɪndəʳ] *n* telemetro.

rang·er [ˈreɪndʒəʳ] *n (forest ~)* guardia forestale; *(Am: mounted policeman)* poliziotto a cavallo.

rank[1] [ræŋk] **1** *n* **(a)** *(row)* fila; **taxi ~** posteggio.

(b) *(status: also Mil)* grado; **people of all ~s** gente di tutti i ceti. **(c)** *(Mil):* **the ~s** la truppa; **he rose from the ~s** è venuto dalla gavetta; **to close ~s** *(Mil)* serrare le righe; *(fig)* serrare i ranghi; **to break ~s** rompere le righe; **I've joined the ~s of the unemployed** mi sono aggiunto alla massa dei disoccupati; **the ~ and file** *(of political party etc)* la base. **2** *vt* considerare, ritenere; **I ~ him 6th** gli dò il sesto posto, lo metto al sesto posto. **3** *vi:* **to ~ 4th** essere quarto(a), essere al quarto posto; **to ~ above sb** essere superiore a qn; *(Mil)* essere superiore in grado a qn; **he ~s among the best** è uno dei migliori.

rank[2] [ræŋk] *adj* **(a)** *(plants)* troppo rigoglioso(a).

(b) *(smell)* puzzolente, fetido(a); *(fats)* rancido(a). **(c)** *(hypocrisy, injustice etc)* bello(a) e buono(a); *(traitor)* sporco(a).

ran·kle [ˈræŋkl] *vi:* **to ~ (with sb)** bruciare (a qn).

ran·sack [ˈrænsæk] *vt (town)* saccheggiare; *(drawer, room)* frugare, rovistare.

ran·som [ˈrænsəm] **1** *n* riscatto; **to hold sb to ~** tenere in ostaggio qn *(per denaro).* **2** *vt* riscattare. **3** *cpd:* **~ demand** *n* richiesta di riscatto.

rant [rænt] *vi:* **to ~ (at sb)** tuonare (contro qn).

rap [ræp] **1** *n (noise)* colpetti *mpl; (at the door)* bussata; **to take the ~** *(fam)* pagare di persona. **2** *vt (window)* dare dei colpetti su; *(door)* bussare a; **to ~ sb's knuckles** dare un colpo secco sulle nocche di qn; *(fig)* dare una tirata d'orecchi a qn. **3** *vi:* **to ~ (at)** *(see vt)* dare dei colpetti (su); bussare (a).

♦ **rap out** *vt + adv (order)* dire bruscamente.

ra·pa·cious [rəˈpeɪʃəs] *adj* rapace.

rape [reɪp] **1** *n* stupro, violenza carnale. **2** *vt* violentare, stuprare.

rap·id [ˈræpɪd] *adj* rapido(a).

ra·pid·ity [rəˈpɪdɪti] *n* rapidità.

rap·ids [ˈræpɪdz] *npl (in river)* rapida.

ra·pi·er [ˈreɪpɪəʳ] *n* spadino.

rap·ist [ˈreɪpɪst] *n* violentatore *m,* stupratore *m.*

rap·port [ræˈpɔːʳ] *n* rapporto.

rapt [ræpt] *adj (attention)* rapito(a), profondo(a); **to be ~ in contemplation** essere in estatica contemplazione.

rap·ture [ˈræptʃəʳ] *n* estasi *f;* **to be in ~s over sth/sb** essere estasiato di fronte a qc/qn.

rap·tur·ous [ˈræptʃərəs] *adj (smile)* estasiato(a); *(welcome, praise)* entusiastico(a); *(applause)* delirante.

rare [rɛəʳ] *adj* **(-r, -st) (a)** raro(a); **in a moment of ~ generosity** in un momento di insolita generosità; **it is ~ to find that...** capita di rado *or* raramente che... + *sub.* **(b)** *(air)* rarefatto(a). **(c)** *(meat)* al sangue, poco cotto(a).

rare·bit [ˈrɛəbɪt] *n:* **Welsh ~** toast *m* al formaggio fuso.

rar·efied [ˈrɛərɪfaɪd] *adj (atmosphere, air)* rarefatto(a); *(fig)* raffinato(a).

rare·ly [ˈrɛəlɪ] *adv* di rado, raramente.

rar·ity [ˈrɛərɪti] *n* **(a)** *(also:* **rareness)** rarità. **(b)** *(rare thing)* rarità *f inv.*

ras·cal [ˈrɑːskəl] *n (scoundrel)* mascalzone *m; (child)* birbante *m.*

rash[1] [ræʃ] *n (Med: gen)* eruzione *f,* sfogo; *(: from food)* orticaria; **to come out in a ~** *(gen)* avere uno sfogo; **strawberries bring me out in a ~** le fragole mi fanno venire l'orticaria.

rash[2] [ræʃ] *adj* imprudente, avventato(a).

rash·er [ˈræʃəʳ] *n:* **a ~ of bacon** una fettina di pancetta.

rasp [rɑːsp] **1** *n (tool)* raspa; *(sound)* stridio, suono stridulo. **2** *vt (file)* raspare, raschiare; *(speak: also:* **~ out)** gracchiare.

rasp·berry [ˈrɑːzbərɪ] **1** *n (fruit)* lampone *m;* **to blow a ~** *(fam)* fare una pernacchia. **2** *adj (jam)* di lamponi; *(ice cream, syrup)* di lampone.

rasp·ing [ˈrɑːspɪŋ] *adj* stridulo(a), stridente.

rat [ræt] **1** *n* ratto; **you dirty ~!** *(fam)* brutta carogna!; **to smell a ~** *(fig)* subodorare qualcosa. **2** *vi:* **to ~ on sb** *(fam)* fare una spiata *or* una soffiata su qn; **to ~ on a deal** *(fam)* rimangiarsi la parola. **3** *cpd:* **~ race** *n* carrierismo, corsa al successo.

ratch·et [ˈrætʃɪt] **1** *n* arpionismo. **2** *cpd:* **~ wheel** *n* ruota dentata.

rate [reɪt] **1** *n* **(a)** *(ratio)* tasso; *(speed)* velocità *f inv;* **at a ~ of 60 kph** alla velocità di 60 km all'ora; **at a great ~, at a ~ of knots** *(fam)* a tutta velocità; **~ of growth** tasso di crescita; **at a steady ~** a un ritmo costante; **birth/death ~** tasso *or* indice *m* di natalità/di mortalità; **failure ~** percentuale *f* dei bocciati; **~ of flow/consumption** flusso/consumo medio; **pulse ~** frequenza delle pulsazioni; **at this ~** di questo passo, con questo ritmo; **at any ~** in *or* ad ogni modo, comunque.

(b) *(price, charge)* tariffa; *(Comm, Fin)* tasso; **at a ~ of 5% per annum** al tasso (annuo) del 5%; **postage ~s** tariffe postali; **insurance ~s** premi *mpl* assicurativi; **~ of exchange** tasso di cambio; **~ of pay** compenso medio; **bank ~** tasso d'interesse bancario.

(c): **~s** *pl (Brit: local tax)* imposta (immobiliare) comunale.

2 *vt* **(a)** *(evaluate, appraise)* valutare; **to ~ sb/sth highly** stimare molto qn/qc; **how do you ~ that film?** cosa pensi di quel film?; **I ~ it as one of the best** lo considero uno fra i migliori.

(b) *(Brit):* **the house is ~d at £84 per annum** la casa ha un valore imponibile (agli effetti delle imposte comunali) di 84 sterline all'anno.

3 *vi:* **it ~s as one of the worst** è fra i peggiori; **how does it ~ among the critics?** che cosa ne hanno detto i critici?

rate·able [ˈreɪtəbl] *adj:* **~ value** valore *m* imponibile (agli effetti delle imposte comunali).

rate·payer [ˈreɪtpeɪəʳ] *n (Brit)* contribuente *m/f (di imposte comunali).*

ra·ther [ˈrɑːðəʳ] **1** *adv* **(a)** *(preference)* piuttosto; **~**

than wait, she... piuttosto che aspettare, lei...;
I'd ~ have this one than that preferirei avere
questo piuttosto che quello; **would you ~ stay
here?** preferisci rimanere qui?; **I'd ~ you didn't
come** preferirei che tu non venissi; **I'd ~ not**
preferirei di no; **I'd ~ not come** preferirei non
venire.
   (b) *(to a considerable degree)* piuttosto;
(somewhat) abbastanza; *(to some extent)* un po'; **a
~ difficult task** un compito piuttosto difficile; **I
feel ~ more happy today** oggi mi sento molto più
contento; **that is ~ too dear** è un po' troppo caro;
I ~ think he won't come credo proprio che non
verrà; **it's ~ a pity** è proprio *or* davvero un
peccato.
   (c): or ~ *(more accurately)* anzi, per essere
(più) precisi.
   2 *excl* eccome!
rati·fy ['rætɪfaɪ] *vt* ratificare.
rat·ing ['reɪtɪŋ] *n* **(a)** *(assessment)* valutazione *f.*
(b) *(Naut)* marinaio semplice.
ra·tio ['reɪʃɪəʊ] *n* rapporto, proporzione *f*; **in the ~
of 2 to 1** in rapporto di 2 a 1.
ra·tion ['ræʃən] **1** *n* razione *f*; **to be on ~** *(food)*
essere razionato; **to be on short ~s** *(person)* essere a razioni ridotte. **2** *vt* *(also:* **~ out**: *thing)*
razionare; **to ~ sb to sth** imporre a qn un limite
di qc.
ra·tion·al ['ræʃənl] *adj* *(being)* ragionevole; *(Med:
lucid)* lucido(a); *(faculty, action, argument)* razionale; *(solution, explanation)* logico(a), razionale.
ra·tion·ale [ræʃə'nɑ:l] *n* fondamento logico.
ra·tion·ali·za·tion [ˌræʃnəlaɪ'zeɪʃən] *n* *(see vb)* logica; razionalizzazione *f.*
ra·tion·al·ize ['ræʃnəlaɪz] *vt* *(ideas etc)* dare una
spiegazione *or* giustificazione logica a; *(reorganize: industry etc)* razionalizzare.
ra·tion·ing ['ræʃnɪŋ] *n* razionamento.
rat-tat-tat ['ræt'tæt] *n* *(on door)* toc-toc *m*; *(of machine gun)* ta-ta-ta *m.*
rat·tle ['rætl] **1** *n* **(a)** *(of train, car)* rumore *m* di
ferraglia; *(of stone in tin, of windows etc)* tintinnio;
(of typewriter) ticchettio; *(of hail, rain, bullets)*
crepitio; **a ~ of bottles/chains** un rumore di
bottiglie/catene; **death ~** rantolo. **(b)** *(instrument: used by football fan)* raganella; *(: child's)*
sonaglio. **2** *vt* **(a)** *(shake)* agitare; *(: moneybox)*
far tintinnare. **(b)** *(fam: person)* innervosire; **to
get ~d** innervosirsi. **3** *vi* *(box, objects in box,
machinery)* far rumore; *(bullets, hailstones)* crepitare; *(window)* vibrare; **the train ~d over the
crossing** il treno passò sferragliando al passaggio a livello.
♦ **rattle off** *vt + adv* *(poem)* snocciolare.
♦ **rattle on** *vi + adv* blaterare.
rattle·snake ['rætlsneɪk] *n* crotalo, serpente *m* a
sonagli.
rat·ty ['rætɪ] *adj* (**-ier, iest**) *(fam)* incavolato(a); **to
get ~** incavolarsi.
rau·cous ['rɔːkəs] *adj* rauco(a), gracchiante.
rav·age ['rævɪdʒ] **1** *n* devastazione *f*; **the ~s of time**
i danni del tempo. **2** *vt* devastare.
rave [reɪv] **1** *vi* *(be delirious)* delirare; *(talk wildly)*
farneticare; *(talk furiously)* fare una sfuriata;
(talk enthusiastically): **to ~ (about)** andare in
estasi (per). **2** *cpd*: **~ review** *n* *(fam)* critica
entusiastica.
ra·ven ['reɪvn] *n* corvo (imperiale).
rav·en·ous ['rævənəs] *adj* *(person)* affamato(a);
(appetite, animal) famelico(a), vorace.
ra·vine [rə'viːn] *n* burrone *m.*
rav·ing ['reɪvɪŋ] *adj*: **a ~ lunatic** un pazzo furioso;
you must be ~ mad! sei matto da legare!

rav·ings ['reɪvɪŋz] *npl* vaneggiamenti *mpl.*
rav·ish·ing ['rævɪʃɪŋ] *adj* *(sight)* incantevole;
(beauty) affascinante.
raw [rɔː] **1** *adj* **(a)** *(food)* crudo(a); *(spirit)* puro(a);
(silk, leather, cotton, ore etc) greggio(a); *(sugar)*
non raffinato(a); **~ materials** materie *fpl* prime;
~ deal *(fam: bad bargain)* bidonata; *(: harsh
treatment)* trattamento ingiusto. **(b)** *(wind,
weather)* gelido(a). **(c)** *(wound: open)* aperto(a);
(skin) screpolato(a). **(d)** *(person: inexperienced)*
inesperto(a); **he's still ~** è ancora un pivello *or*
un novellino. **2** *n*: **it got him on the ~** *(fig)* lo ha
punto sul vivo; **life in the ~** la vita così com'è.
ray[1] [reɪ] *n* raggio; *(of hope etc)* barlume *m*, raggio.
ray[2] [reɪ] *n* *(fish)* razza.
ray·on ['reɪɒn] *n* raion *m.*
raze [reɪz] *vt* *(also:* **~ to the ground**) radere al
suolo.
ra·zor ['reɪzəʳ] **1** *n* rasoio. **2** *cpd*: **~ blade** *n* lametta
(da barba).
razor-sharp ['reɪzə'ʃɑːp] *adj* *(edge)* tagliente come
un rasoio; *(mind)* molto acuto(a); *(wit)* tagliente.
R.C. *abbr of* **Roman Catholic.**
Rd *abbr of* **road.**
re [riː] *prep* *(Comm)* oggetto.
re... [riː] *pref* ri..., re... .
reach [riːtʃ] **1** *n* **(a)** *(easy; within (easy) ~* a
portata di mano; **it's within easy ~ by bus** lo si
raggiunge facilmente in autobus; **out of ~** fuori
portata. **(b)** *(of river)* tratto; **the upper ~es of the
Thames** l'alto corso del Tamigi.
   2 *vt* *(arrive at, attain)* arrivare a; *(: goal, limit,
person)* raggiungere; **to ~ a conclusion** trarre
una conclusione; **when the news ~ed my ears**
quando mi è arrivata all'orecchio la notizia; **to ~
a compromise** arrivare a *or* raggiungere un compromesso; **can I ~ you at your hotel?** posso
trovarla al suo albergo?; **to ~ sb by phone** contattare qn per telefono.
   3 *vi* *(stretch out hand: also:* **~ down, ~
over, ~ across** *etc)* allungare una mano; **he ~ed
(over) for the book** si è allungato per prendere il
libro. **(b)** *(stretch: land etc)* estendersi; *(: wire,
rope)* arrivare; *(voice, sound)* giungere.
re·act [riː'ækt] *vi*: **to ~ (against/to)** reagire
(contro/a).
re·ac·tion [riː'ækʃən] *n* reazione *f.*
re·ac·tion·ary [riː'ækʃənrɪ] *adj, n* reazionario(a)
(m/f).
re·ac·tor [riː'æktəʳ] *n* reattore *m.*
read [riːd] *(vb: pt, pp* **read** [rɛd]*)* **1** *vt* **(a)** *(gen)*
leggere; **to ~ o.s. to sleep** leggere per addor-
mentarsi; **to take sth as read** *(fig)* dare qc per
scontato; **to take the minutes as read** *(Admin)*
passare subito all'ordine del giorno; **do you ~
me?** *(Telec)* mi ricevete? **(b)** *(Univ: study)* studiare; **to ~ Chemistry** fare *or* studiare chimica.
(c) *(interpret: dream)* interpretare; *(: hand)* leggere; **she can ~ me like a book** mi legge nel
cuore, per lei sono come un libro aperto; **to ~
sb's thoughts** leggere nel pensiero di qn; **to ~
between the lines** leggere tra le righe; **to ~ too
much into sth** dare troppa importanza a qc.
   2 *vi* **(a)** leggere; **I read about him in the paper**
ho letto qualcosa su di lui sul giornale; **I read
about it in the paper** l'ho letto sul giornale; **to ~
to sb** leggere qualcosa a qn; **the book ~s well** è
un libro che si legge bene. **(b)** *(indicate: meter,
clock)* segnare; **the inscription ~s 'To my son'** la
dedica dice 'A mio figlio'.
   3 *n*: **to have a quiet ~** leggersi qualcosa in
santa pace; **that book's a good ~** quel libro è una
buona lettura.

♦ **read back** vt + adv rileggere.
♦ **read on** vi + adv continuare a leggere.
♦ **read out** vt + adv leggere (ad alta voce).
♦ **read over** vt + adv rileggere attentamente.
♦ **read through** vt + adv (quickly) dare una scorsa a; (thoroughly) leggere da cima a fondo.
♦ **read up** vt + adv, **read up on** vi + prep studiare bene.

read·able ['riːdəbl] adj (writing) leggibile; (book etc) che si legge volentieri.

read·er ['riːdəʳ] n (a) lettore/trice. (b) (Brit Univ) ≈ professore m incaricato. (c) (book) libro di lettura; (: anthology) antologia.

read·er·ship ['riːdəʃɪp] n (numero di) lettori mpl.

read·ily ['redɪlɪ] adv (quickly, willingly) prontamente; (easily) con facilità.

readi·ness ['redɪnɪs] n prontezza; **to be in ~ for** essere pronto per.

read·ing ['riːdɪŋ] 1 n (a) (gen) lettura; (of proofs) correzione f; **I like ~** mi piace leggere. (b) (interpretation) interpretazione f; (of original text, manuscript) lezione f. (c) (of thermometer etc) lettura; **to take a ~** prendere or fare una lettura. (d) (recital: of play, poem) lettura; **to give a poetry ~** leggere poesie. 2 cpd: **~ matter** n qualcosa da leggere; **~ room** n sala di lettura.

re·adjust ['riːə'dʒʌst] 1 vt regolare (di nuovo). 2 vi riadattarsi.

ready ['redɪ] 1 adj (-ier, -iest) pronto(a); **are you ~?** sei pronto?; **~ for use** pronto per l'uso; **~ for anything** pronto a tutto; **~ money** denaro contante, contanti mpl; **to be ~ to do sth** essere pronto a fare qc; **to get ~ to do** prepararsi a fare; **~ to serve** (food) già pronto; **to get sth ~** preparare qc; **~, steady, go!** pronti, attenti, via!; **I'm ~ for him!** lo sto aspettando!; **we were ~ to give up there and then** eravamo sul punto di piantare lì tutto. 2 n: **at the ~** (Mil) pronto(a) (a far fuoco); (fig) pronto(a). 3 cpd: **~ reckoner** n prontuario di calcolo.

ready-made [,redɪ'meɪd] adj (clothes) confezionato(a); (excuses, solution) pronto(a); (ideas) preconcetto(a).

ready-to-wear [,redɪtə'wɛəʳ] adj prêt-à-porter inv.

real [rɪəl] 1 adj (gen) vero(a); (reason, motive) reale, vero(a); (Philosophy) reale; **in ~ life** nella realtà; **he's a ~ villain** è un vero mascalzone; **she has no ~ authority** in pratica non ha alcun'autorità; **once you've tasted the ~ thing...** una volta provato l'originale.... 2 adv (fam) veramente, proprio. 3 n: **for ~** (fam) per davvero, sul serio.

re·al·ism ['rɪəlɪzəm] n realismo.

re·al·ist ['rɪəlɪst] n realista m/f.

re·al·is·tic [rɪə'lɪstɪk] adj (thing) realistico(a); (person) realista.

re·al·ity [riː'ælɪtɪ] n realtà f inv; **in ~** in realtà.

re·ali·za·tion [,rɪəlaɪ'zeɪʃən] n (of hopes, plans, assets) realizzazione f; (awareness) presa di coscienza.

re·al·ize ['rɪə,laɪz] vt (a) (become aware of) rendersi conto di, accorgersi di; (understand) capire; **I ~ that...** mi rendo conto or capisco che...; **without realizing it** senza rendersene conto, senza accorgersene; **he ~d how/why** ha capito come/perché. (b) (hopes, ambitions, assets) realizzare; (plan) attuare, realizzare.

re·al·ly ['rɪəlɪ] adv davvero, veramente; **I don't ~ know** a dire la verità non lo so; **he doesn't ~ speak Chinese, does he?** non parla cinese sul serio, vero?

realm [relm] n regno.

re·al·tor ['rɪəltɔːʳ] n (Am) agente m immobiliare.

ream [riːm] n risma; **~s** (fig fam) pagine e pagine fpl.

reap [riːp] vt mietere; (fig: profit) raccogliere.

re·appear ['riːə'pɪəʳ] vi ricomparire, riapparire.

re·appear·ance ['riːə'pɪərəns] n ricomparsa, riapparizione f.

re·apprais·al ['riːə'preɪzəl] n riesame m.

rear[1] [rɪəʳ] 1 adj (gen) di dietro, posteriore; (Aut: door, window etc) posteriore. 2 n (back part) didietro, parte f posteriore; (Anat fam: buttocks) didietro, sedere m; (Mil) retroguardia; **in or at the ~ (of)** dietro (a), didietro (a); **to bring up the ~** venire per ultimo; (Mil) formare la retroguardia.

rear[2] [rɪəʳ] 1 vt (a) (raise: cattle, family) allevare; (crops) coltivare. (b) (one's head) drizzare. 2 vi (esp horse) impennarsi.

re·arm [,riː'ɑːm] 1 vt riarmare. 2 vi riarmarsi.

re·arma·ment [,riː'ɑːməmənt] n riarmo.

re·arrange ['riːə'reɪndʒ] vt ridisporre, riordinare.

rear-view mir·ror ['rɪəvjuː'mɪrəʳ] n (Aut) retrovisore m.

rea·son ['riːzn] 1 n (a) (motive) ragione f, motivo; **the ~ for/why** la ragione or il motivo di/per cui; **the ~ (why) I'm late is...** sono in ritardo perché..., la ragione del mio ritardo è...; **don't ask the ~ why** non chiedere il perché; **for no ~** senza ragione; **she claims with good ~ that she's underpaid** ritiene di essere malpagata e ha tutte le ragioni (del mondo); **all the more ~ why you should not sell** it ragione di più per non venderlo; **we have ~ to believe that...** abbiamo motivo di ritenere che...; **by ~ of** a causa di.

(b) (faculty, good sense) ragione f; **to lose one's ~** perdere la ragione; **to listen to ~** ascoltare (la voce della) ragione; **it stands to ~** è logico; **within ~** entro limiti ragionevoli, entro certi limiti.

2 vt: **to ~ that** concludere che, fare il ragionamento che.

3 vi: **to ~ (with sb)** ragionare (con qn).

rea·son·able ['riːznəbl] adj ragionevole; **a perfectly ~ thing to do** una cosa accettabilissima; **it is ~ to conclude that...** si può concludere che... .

rea·son·ably ['riːznəblɪ] adv in modo ragionevole; **a ~ accurate report** una relazione abbastanza accurata; **one can ~ suppose that...** uno può facilmente supporre che... .

rea·soned ['riːznd] adj argomentato(a); **a well ~ argument** una forte argomentazione.

rea·son·ing ['riːznɪŋ] n ragionamento.

re·assur·ance [,riːə'ʃʊərəns] n rassicurazione f.

re·assure [,riːə'ʃʊəʳ] vt rassicurare.

re·assur·ing [,riːə'ʃʊərɪŋ] adj rassicurante.

re·bate ['riːbeɪt] n rimborso.

re·bel ['rebl] 1 adj, n ribelle (m/f). 2 [rɪ'bel] vi: **to ~ (against sb/sth)** ribellarsi (a qn/contro qc).

re·bel·lion [rɪ'beljən] n ribellione f.

re·bel·lious [rɪ'beljəs] adj ribelle.

re·birth ['riː'bɜːθ] n rinascita.

re·bound ['riːbaʊnd] 1 n: **on the ~** di rimbalzo. 2 [rɪ'baʊnd] vi rimbalzare.

♦ **rebound on** vi + prep ricadere su, ritorcersi contro.

re·buff [rɪ'bʌf] 1 n secco rifiuto. 2 vt rifiutare, respingere.

re·buke [rɪ'bjuːk] 1 n rimprovero. 2 vt rimproverare.

re·but [rɪ'bʌt] vt confutare.

re·but·tal [rɪ'bʌtl] n confutazione f.

re·cal·ci·trant [rɪ'kælsɪtrənt] adj recalcitrante.

re·call [rɪ'kɔːl] 1 n richiamo; **those days are gone beyond ~** quei tempi sono passati per sempre. 2

vt **(a)** *(call back: gen)* richiamare; *(: parliament)* riconvocare; *(: past)* far rivivere. **(b)** *(remember)* ricordare, ricordarsi di.

re·cant [rɪ'kænt] *vi* abiurare.

re·cap ['riːkæp] *(fam)* **1** *n* riepilogo, ricapitolazione *f*. **2** *vt*, *vi* riepilogare, ricapitolare.

re·ca·pitu·late [ˌriːkə'pɪtjʊleɪt] *vt*, *vi* riepilogare, ricapitolare.

re·cap·ture ['riː'kæptʃər] *vt* (*prisoner etc*) catturare (di nuovo); *(town)* riconquistare, riprendere; *(memory, scene)* ritrovare.

re·cede [rɪ'siːd] *vi* (*tide, flood*) ritirarsi, abbassarsi; *(view)* allontanarsi; *(danger etc)* diminuire, ridursi; **your hair is receding** ti sei (un po') stempiato; **receding chin** mento sfuggente.

re·ceipt [rɪ'siːt] *n* **(a)** *(document)* ricevuta. **(b)** *(esp Comm)* ricevimento; **to acknowledge ~ of** accusare ricevuta di; **we are in ~ of...** abbiamo ricevuto.... **(c)** *(money taken):* **~s** *pl* incassi *mpl*, introiti *mpl*.

re·ceive [rɪ'siːv] *vt* (*gen, Radio, TV*) ricevere; *(stolen goods)* ricettare; **'~d with thanks'** *(Comm)* 'per quietanza'; **to ~ sb into one's home** ricevere qn in casa; **the book was not well ~d** il libro non ha avuto *or* ricevuto un'accoglienza favorevole.

re·ceiv·er [rɪ'siːvər] *n* **(a)** *(gen)* persona che riceve qualcosa; *(of letter)* destinatario/a; *(of stolen goods)* ricettatore/trice; *(liquidator):* **(official) ~** curatore/trice fallimentare. **(b)** *(Radio)* apparecchio ricevente; *(Telec)* ricevitore *m*.

re·cent ['riːsnt] *adj* recente; **in ~ memory** in tempi recenti; **in ~ years** negli ultimi anni.

re·cent·ly ['riːsntlɪ] *adv* di recente, recentemente, ultimamente; **as ~ as 1970** soltanto nel 1970; **until ~** fino a poco tempo fa.

re·cep·ta·cle [rɪ'sɛptəkl] *n* *(frm)* recipiente *m*.

re·cep·tion [rɪ'sɛpʃən] **1** *n* *(gen)* ricevimento; *(Radio, TV)* ricezione *f*; *(also:* **~ desk:** *in hotel)* **reception** *f inv*; *(: in hospital, at doctor's)* accettazione *f*; *(: in large building, offices)* portineria; **to get a warm ~** avere *or* ricevere un'accoglienza calorosa. **2** *cpd:* **~ centre** *n* centro di raccolta.

re·cep·tion·ist [rɪ'sɛpʃənɪst] *n* *(in hotel, offices)* receptionist *m/f inv*; *(at doctor's)* segretaria.

re·cep·tive [rɪ'sɛptɪv] *adj* ricettivo(a).

re·cess [rɪ'sɛs] *n* **(a)** *(Law, Parliament: cessation of business)* ferie *fpl*, vacanza; *(Am Law: short break)* sospensione *f*; *(Scol: esp Am)* intervallo. **(b)** *(for bed)* rientranza; *(for statue)* nicchia; *(fig: of mind etc)* recesso.

re·ces·sion [rɪ'sɛʃən] *n* *(Econ)* recessione *f*.

re·charge ['riː'tʃɑːdʒ] *vt* *(battery)* ricaricare.

re·cher·ché [rə'ʃɛəʃeɪ] *adj* ricercato(a).

re·cidi·vist [rɪ'sɪdɪvɪst] *n* recidivo/a.

reci·pe ['rɛsɪpɪ] *n* *(also fig)* ricetta.

re·cipi·ent [rɪ'sɪpɪənt] *n* *(of letter)* destinatario/a; *(of cheque)* beneficiario/a; *(of award)* assegnatario/a.

re·cip·ro·cal [rɪ'sɪprəkəl] *adj* reciproco(a).

re·cip·ro·cate [rɪ'sɪprəkeɪt] *vt*, *vi* ricambiare, contraccambiare.

re·cit·al [rɪ'saɪtl] *n* *(Mus)* concerto *(di solista)*; *(of poetry)* recita; *(: event)* recital *m inv*; *(account)* resoconto.

reci·ta·tion [ˌrɛsɪ'teɪʃən] *n* recitazione *f*; **to give ~s from Shakespeare** recitare brani da Shakespeare.

re·cite [rɪ'saɪt] **1** *vt* *(poem)* recitare; *(facts, details)* fare l'elenco di, enumerare. **2** *vi* recitare.

reck·less ['rɛklɪs] *adj* *(gen)* imprudente, *(stronger)* incosciente; *(driver, driving)* spericolato(a).

reck·on ['rɛkən] **1** *vt* *(calculate)* calcolare; *(believe)* pensare, credere; *(judge)* considerare; **I ~ him to be one of the best** lo considero uno dei migliori, per me è uno dei migliori; **I ~ (that) we'll be late** prevedo che saremo in ritardo. **2** *vi* contare, calcolare; **to ~ on sth** prevedere qc; **to ~ on doing sth** far conto di fare qc; **to ~ with sb** fare i conti con qn; **he is somebody to be ~ed with** è uno da non sottovalutare; **to ~ without sb/sth** non tener conto di qn/qc; **to ~ without doing sth** non calcolare di fare qc.

reck·on·ing ['rɛknɪŋ] *n* calcoli *mpl*, conti *mpl*; **to be out in one's ~** aver sbagliato *or* fatto male i propri conti; **day of ~** *(fig)* momento della resa dei conti.

re·claim [rɪ'kleɪm] *vt* *(gen)* ricuperare; *(land)* bonificare.

rec·la·ma·tion [ˌrɛklə'meɪʃən] *n* *(see vb)* ricupero; bonifica.

re·cline [rɪ'klaɪn] *vi* *(person)* essere sdraiato(a).

re·clin·ing [rɪ'klaɪnɪŋ] *adj* *(seat)* ribaltabile.

re·cluse [rɪ'kluːs] *n* recluso/a.

rec·og·ni·tion [ˌrɛkəg'nɪʃən] *n* riconoscimento; **in ~ of** in *or* come segno di riconoscimento per; **to change/change sth beyond ~** diventare/rendere qc irriconoscibile.

rec·og·niz·able ['rɛkəgnaɪzəbl] *adj* riconoscibile.

rec·og·nize ['rɛkəgnaɪz] *vt* *(all senses)* riconoscere.

rec·og·nized ['rɛkəgnaɪzd] *adj* riconosciuto(a).

re·coil [rɪ'kɔɪl] *vi* *(person):* **to ~ (from)** indietreggiare (di fronte a); *(gun)* rinculare; **to ~ from doing sth** rifuggire dal fare qc.

rec·ol·lect [ˌrɛkə'lɛkt] *vt* rammentare.

rec·ol·lec·tion [ˌrɛkə'lɛkʃən] *n* memoria, ricordo; **to the best of my ~** per quello che mi ricordo.

rec·om·mend [ˌrɛkə'mɛnd] *vt* *(course of action, product, doctor)* consigliare; *(person: for job)* raccomandare; **I ~ that he sees a doctor** gli consiglierei di vedere un medico; **to ~ sb for sth** raccomandare qn per qc; **she has a lot to ~ her** ha molti elementi a suo favore.

rec·om·men·da·tion [ˌrɛkəmɛn'deɪʃən] *n* raccomandazione *f*; **to do sth on sb's ~** fare qc su *or* dietro consiglio di qn.

rec·om·pense ['rɛkəmpɛns] **1** *n* ricompensa; *(Law: for damage)* risarcimento. **2** *vt* ricompensare; *(Law):* **to ~ sb (for sth)** risarcire qn (di qc).

rec·on·cile ['rɛkənsaɪl] *vt* *(persons)* riconciliare; *(theories etc)* conciliare; **to become ~d** *(people)* riconciliarsi; **to ~ o.s. to sth** rassegnarsi a qc.

rec·on·cilia·tion [ˌrɛkənsɪlɪ'eɪʃən] *n* riconciliazione *f*.

re·con·di·tion ['riːkən'dɪʃən] *vt* rimettere a nuovo.

re·con·nais·sance [rɪ'kɒnɪsəns] **1** *n* ricognizione *f*. **2** *cpd:* **~ flight** *n* volo di ricognizione.

rec·on·noi·tre, *(Am)* **rec·on·noi·ter** [ˌrɛkə'nɔɪtər] *(Mil)* **1** *vt* fare una ricognizione di. **2** *vi* fare una ricognizione.

re·con·sid·er ['riːkən'sɪdər] *vt* riconsiderare.

re·con·struct ['riːkən'strʌkt] *vt* ricostruire.

re·con·struc·tion ['riːkən'strʌkʃən] *n* ricostruzione *f*.

rec·ord ['rɛkɔːd] **1** *n* **(a)** *(report)* rapporto; *(minutes: of meeting)* verbale *m*; *(Law)* registro; *(historical report)* documento; *(of attendance)* registro delle presenze; **public ~s** archivi *mpl*; **there is no ~ of it** non c'è niente che lo possa comprovare; **to keep a ~ of sth** tener nota di qc; **he is on ~ as saying that...** ha dichiarato pubblicamente che...; **it is on ~ that...** è stato registrato che...; **to place** *or* **put sth on ~** mettere qc agli atti; **he told me off the ~** *(fam)* me l'ha detto ufficiosamente; **to set the ~ straight** mettere le cose in chiaro. **(b)** *(person's past in general)* precedenti *mpl*;

(as dossier) resoconto; *(also:* **criminal** ~) precedenti *mpl* penali; **he has a clean** ~ ha la fedina penale pulita; **police** ~s schedario della polizia; **Italy's excellent** ~ i brillanti successi italiani; **the school has a poor** ~ **of exam passes** in quella scuola si registra una bassa percentuale di promozioni.

(c) *(Sport etc)* record *m inv*, primato; **to beat** *or* **break a** ~ battere un record *or* un primato; **to hold the** ~ **(for sth)** detenere il primato (di qc).

(d) *(Mus)* disco.

2 *adj attr* record *inv*; **in** ~ **time** a tempo di record *or* di primato.

3 [rɪ'kɔːd] *vt* (a) *(set down)* annotare, riportare; **to** ~ **one's vote** votare; ~**ed-delivery letter** *(Post)* lettera raccomandata.

(b) *(Mus etc)* registrare.

4 *cpd:* ~ **holder** *n* primatista *m/f;* ~ **library** *n* discoteca; ~ **player** *n* giradischi *m inv;* ~ **token** *n buono per l'acquisto di dischi.*

record-breaking ['rɛkɔːd,breɪkɪŋ] *adj* che batte tutti i record.

re·cord·er [rɪ'kɔːdə*ʳ*] *n* (a) *(tape* ~) registratore *m.* (b) *(Mus)* flauto diritto.

re·cord·ing [rɪ'kɔːdɪŋ] **1** *n (of programme, song)* registrazione *f.* **2** *cpd:* ~ **studio** *n* studio di registrazione.

re·count [rɪ'kaʊnt] *vt* raccontare.

re-count ['riːkaʊnt] **1** *n (of votes)* nuovo conteggio. **2** [,riː'kaʊnt] *vt* ricontare, rifare il conteggio di.

re·coup [rɪ'kuːp] *vt* ricuperare.

re·course [rɪ'kɔːs] *n:* **to have** ~ **to** ricorrere a, far ricorso a.

re·cov·er [rɪ'kʌvə*ʳ*] **1** *vt (belongings, goods, wreck, lost time)* ricuperare; *(reclaim: money)* ottenere il rimborso di; *(Law: damages)* ottenere il risarcimento di; *(balance, appetite, health etc)* ritrovare, ricuperare; **to** ~ **one's senses** riprendere i sensi; *(fig)* ritornare in sé. **2** *vi (all senses)* riprendersi.

re-cover [,riː'kʌvə*ʳ*] *vt* ricoprire.

re·cov·ery [rɪ'kʌvərɪ] *n* (a) *(see recover vt)* ricupero; rimborso; risarcimento. (b) *(see recover vi)* ripresa; **to make a** ~ *(Med)* avere *or* fare un miglioramento; *(Sport, Fin)* avere una ripresa.

rec·rea·tion [,rɛkrɪ'eɪʃən] *n* ricreazione *f.*

rec·rea·tion·al [,rɛkrɪ'eɪʃənəl] *adj* ricreativo(a).

re·crimi·na·tion [rɪ,krɪmɪ'neɪʃən] *n* recriminazione *f.*

re·cruit [rɪ'kruːt] **1** *n (Mil)* recluta; *(gen: to club)* nuovo(a) iscritto(a); *(: to staff)* nuovo(a) assunto(a). **2** *vt (gen, Mil)* reclutare.

re·cruit·ment [rɪ'kruːtmənt] *n* reclutamento.

rec·tan·gle ['rɛk,tæŋgl] *n* rettangolo.

rec·tan·gu·lar [rɛk'tæŋgjʊlə*ʳ*] *adj* rettangolare.

rec·ti·fy ['rɛktɪfaɪ] *vt* rettificare.

rec·ti·tude ['rɛktɪtjuːd] *n* rettitudine *f.*

rec·tor ['rɛktə*ʳ*] *n (Rel)* parroco *(anglicano); (Univ)* rettore/trice; *(of school)* preside *m/f.*

rec·tum ['rɛktəm] *n (Anat)* retto.

re·cu·per·ate [rɪ'kuːpəreɪt] **1** *vi (Med)* ristabilirsi. **2** *vt (losses)* ricuperare.

re·cu·pera·tion [rɪ,kuːpə'reɪʃən] *n (after illness)* convalescenza; *(of losses)* ricupero.

re·cu·pera·tive [rɪ'kuːpərətɪv] *adj (powers)* di ricupero.

re·cur [rɪ'kɜː*ʳ*] *vi (pain, event, mistake)* ripetersi; *(idea, theme)* ricorrere, riapparire; *(difficulty, opportunity)* ripresentarsi, ripetersi.

re·cur·rence [rɪ'kʌrəns] *n (see vb)* ripetersi *m;* ricorrenza.

re·cur·rent [rɪ'kʌrənt] *adj* ricorrente.

re·cur·ring [rɪ'kɜːrɪŋ] *adj (Math)* periodico(a).

red [rɛd] **1** *adj* (**-der, -dest**) *(all senses)* rosso(a); **to be** ~ **in the face** *(from physical effort)* essere tutto rosso, avere il viso rosso; *(embarrassed)* essere rosso (in viso); **it's like a** ~ **rag to a bull with him** è una cosa che gli fa vedere rosso. **2** *n (colour)* rosso; *(Pol)* rosso/a; **in the** ~ *(Fin: account, firm)* nel rosso; **to see** ~ *(fig)* vederci rosso. **3** *cpd:* **R~ Cross** *n* Croce Rossa; ~ **deer** *n* cervo; ~ **herring** *n* falsa pista; **R~ Indian** *n* pellerossa *m/f;* ~ **light** *n (Aut)* (semaforo) rosso; **to go through a** ~ **light** passare col rosso; ~ **light district** *n* quartiere *m* del vizio *or* dei casini; **R~ Sea** *n* Mar *m* Rosso; ~ **tape** *n* scartoffie *fpl*, complicazioni *fpl* burocratiche.

red-blooded ['rɛd'blʌdɪd] *adj* virile.

red·breast ['rɛdbrɛst] *n (bird)* pettirosso.

red·brick ['rɛd,brɪk] *adj:* ~ **university** *(Brit)* università *f inv* istituita alla fine del secolo scorso.

red·den ['rɛdn] **1** *vt* arrossare, tingere di rosso. **2** *vi (sky, leaves)* diventar rosso, tingersi di rosso; *(person)* arrossire.

red·dish ['rɛdɪʃ] *adj* rossiccio(a), rossastro(a); *(hair)* rossiccio(a).

re·deem [rɪ'diːm] *vt (Rel: sinner)* redimere; *(buy back: pawned goods)* disimpegnare; *(Fin: debt, mortgage)* estinguere, ammortare; *(fulfil: promise)* mantenere; *(: obligation)* adempiere a; *(compensate for: fault)* compensare; **to** ~ **o.s.** farsi perdonare.

Re·deem·er [rɪ'diːmə*ʳ*] *n* Redentore *m.*

re·deem·ing [rɪ'diːmɪŋ] *adj:* ~ **feature** unico aspetto positivo.

re·demp·tion [rɪ'dɛmpʃən] *n (Rel)* redenzione *f.*

red-faced [,rɛd'feɪst] *adj (also fig)* rosso(a) in viso.

red-haired [,rɛd'hɛəd] *adj* con i *or* dai capelli rossi.

red-handed [,rɛd'hændɪd] *adj:* **to catch sb** ~ prendere qn con le mani nel sacco, cogliere qn in flagrante.

red·head ['rɛd,hɛd] *n* rosso/a.

red-hot [,rɛd'hɒt] *adj* arroventato(a), rovente.

re·di·rect [,riːdaɪ'rɛkt] *vt (letter)* rispedire *(a un nuovo indirizzo).*

red-letter [,rɛd'lɛtə*ʳ*] *adj:* ~ **day** giorno memorabile.

red·ness ['rɛdnɪs] *n (of skin)* rossore *m; (of hair, colour)* rosso.

redo·lent ['rɛdəʊlənt] *adj:* ~ **of** che sa di, profumato(a) di.

re·dou·ble [riː'dʌbl] *vt* raddoppiare.

re·doubt·able [rɪ'daʊtəbl] *adj* formidabile, temibile.

re·dound [rɪ'daʊnd] *vi:* **to** ~ **upon sb** riversarsi su qn; **to** ~ **to sb's credit** tornare a credito di qn.

re·dress [rɪ'drɛs] **1** *n* riparazione *f.* **2** *vt* riparare; **to** ~ **the balance** ristabilire l'equilibrio.

red-skin ['rɛdskɪn] *n* pellerossa *m/f.*

re·duce [rɪ'djuːs] **1** *vt* (a) *(gen)* ridurre; *(prices, expenses, taxes)* abbassare, ridurre, diminuire; *(speed, voltage, Med: swelling)* ridurre, diminuire; *(temperature)* far diminuire, far scendere; **to** ~ **sth by/to** ridurre qc di/a; **to** ~ **sth to ashes** ridurre qc in cenere; **to** ~ **sb to silence/despair/tears** ridurre qn al silenzio/alla disperazione/in lacrime; **we were** ~**d to begging** eravamo ridotti all'elemosina; ~**d to nothing** ridotto a zero. (b) *(Mil):* **to** ~ **sb to the ranks** degradare qn a soldato semplice. **2** *vi (slim)* dimagrire.

re·duced [rɪ'djuːst] *adj (decreased)* ridotto(a); **at a** ~ **price** a prezzo ribassato *or* ridotto; **'greatly** ~ **prices'** 'grandi ribassi'; **in** ~ **circumstances** nelle ristrettezze.

re·duc·tion [rɪ'dʌkʃən] *n (see vt* a) riduzione *f;*

diminuzione *f*; ~ **for cash** sconto per (il pagamento in) contanti.

re·dun·dan·cy [rɪ'dʌndənsɪ] **1** *n* superfluità; *(Literature)* ridondanza; *(Industry)* licenziamento (per eccesso di personale). **2** *cpd*: ~ **payment** *n* indennità *f* inv di licenziamento.

re·dun·dant [rɪ'dʌndənt] *adj (superfluous)* superfluo(a); *(Literature)* ridondante; *(worker)* licenziato(a) (per eccesso di personale); **to be made** ~ *(worker)* essere licenziato (per eccesso di personale).

red·wood ['rɛdwʊd] *n* sequoia.

reed [riːd] *n (Bot)* canna; *(Mus: in mouthpiece)* ancia.

reedy ['riːdɪ] *adj* (-ier, -iest) *(voice, instrument)* acuto(a).

reef[1] [riːf] *n (Geog)* scogliera, banco di scogli; **coral** ~ barriera corallina.

reef[2] [riːf] **1** *n (sail)* terzarolo. **2** *cpd*: ~ **knot** *n* nodo piano.

reek [riːk] *vi*: **to** ~ **of sth** puzzare di qc.

reel [riːl] **1** *n* **(a)** *(in fishing etc)* mulinello; *(cotton* ~) rocchetto, spoletta, bobina; *(for tape recorder etc)* bobina; *(Phot: for small camera)* rotolino, rullino; (: *of cine film)* bobina, pizza. **(b)** *(Mus: dance)* danza scozzese molto vivace. **2** *vi (person)* vacillare, barcollare; **my head is** ~**ing** mi gira la testa.

♦ **reel in** *vt + adv (fish)* tirare su.

♦ **reel off** *vt + adv (poem, list)* sciorinare.

re-enact ['riːɪ'nækt] *vt (crime, scene)* ricostruire.

re-entry [,riː'ɛntrɪ] *n* rientro.

ref [rɛf] *n (Sport fam: abbr of referee)* arbitro.

re·fec·tory [rɪ'fɛktərɪ] *n* refettorio.

re·fer [rɪ'fɜː] **1** *vt (gen)*: **to** ~ **sth to sb** *(matter, decision)* sottoporre qc a qn; **to** ~ **sb to sth** richiamare l'attenzione di qn su qc; **he** ~**red me to the manager** mi ha detto di rivolgermi al direttore. **2** *vi*: **to** ~ **to (a)** *(relate to)* riferirsi a; **does that** ~ **to me?** vale anche per me? **(b)** *(allude to: directly)* fare riferimento a; (: *indirectly)* fare allusione a; **we will not** ~ **to it again** non ne riparleremo più. **(c)** *(turn attention to, consult)* consultare; **please** ~ **to section 3** vedi sezione 3.

ref·eree [,rɛfə'riː] *n (in dispute, Sport etc)* arbitro; *(for application, post)* referenza.

ref·er·ence ['rɛfrəns] **1** *n* **(a)** *(allusion: direct)* riferimento; (: *indirect)* allusione *f*; *(relation, connection)* rapporto; **with** ~ **to** con riferimento a; **without** ~ **to any particular case** senza nessun riferimento specifico. **(b)** *(in book)* rimando; *(on letter)* numero di riferimento; *(on map)* coordinate *fpl*. **(c)** *(testimonial)*: ~(**s**) referenze *fpl*; **may I give you as a** ~? posso dare il suo nome per referenze? **2** *cpd (book, library)* di consultazione; *(number, point)* di riferimento.

ref·er·en·dum [,rɛfə'rɛndəm] *n*, *pl* ~**s** *or* **referenda** [,rɛfə'rɛndə] referendum *m* inv.

re·fill ['riːfɪl] **1** *n* ricambio. **2** [,riː'fɪl] *vt (gen)* riempire (di nuovo); *(pen, lighter)* ricaricare.

re·fine [rɪ'faɪn] *vt (sugar, oil, tastes, style)* raffinare; *(design, technique, machine)* perfezionare.

♦ **refine (up)on** *vi + prep* perfezionare, migliorare.

re·fined [rɪ'faɪnd] *adj* raffinato(a).

re·fine·ment [rɪ'faɪnmənt] *n (of person, language)* raffinatezza, finezza; *(in machine etc)* miglioramento.

re·fin·ery [rɪ'faɪnərɪ] *n* raffineria.

re·fit ['riːfɪt] **1** *n (Naut)* raddobbo. **2** [,riː'fɪt] *vt (ship)* raddobbare.

re·flate [,riː'fleɪt] *vt (economy)* rilanciare.

re·fla·tion [riː'fleɪʃən] *n* rilancio.

re·fla·tion·ary [riː'fleɪʃənərɪ] *adj* nuovamente inflazionario(a).

re·flect [rɪ'flɛkt] **1** *vt* **(a)** *(light, image, heat etc)* riflettere; *(fig)* rispecchiare; **to** ~ **credit on sb** fare onore a qn. **(b)** *(think)*: **to** ~ **that** fare la riflessione che, riflettere sul fatto che. **2** *vi* **(a)** *(think, meditate)*: **to** ~ **(on sth)** riflettere (su qc). **(b)** *(discredit)*: **to** ~ **(up)on sb/sth** ripercuotersi su qn/qc.

re·flec·tion [rɪ'flɛkʃən] *n* **(a)** *(act)* riflessione *f*; (*in mirror etc)* riflesso. **(b)** *(thought)* riflessione *f*; **on** ~ dopo aver riflettuto, pensandoci sopra. **(c)** *(aspersion, doubt)* dubbio; **this is no** ~ **on your honesty** questa non è un'insinuazione sulla tua onestà.

re·flec·tor [rɪ'flɛktər] *n (Aut: also: **rear** ~)* catarifrangente *m*.

re·flex ['riːflɛks] **1** *adj* riflesso(a); ~ **camera** reflex *m* inv. **2** *n* riflesso.

re·flex·ive [rɪ'flɛksɪv] *adj* riflessivo(a).

re·form [rɪ'fɔːm] **1** *n* riforma. **2** *vt (society, morals)* riformare; *(criminal, person's character)* correggere, emendare. **3** *vi (person)* emendarsi.

Ref·or·ma·tion [,rɛfə'meɪʃən] *n (Rel)* Riforma.

re·form·er [rɪ'fɔːmə[r]] *n* riformatore/trice.

re·frac·tion [rɪ'frækʃən] *n* rifrazione *f*.

re·frac·tory [rɪ'fræktərɪ] *adj* refrattario(a).

re·frain[1] [rɪ'freɪn] *n (Mus etc)* ritornello, refrain *m* inv.

re·frain[2] [rɪ'freɪn] *vi*: **to** ~ **from sth/from doing sth** astenersi da qc/dal fare qc.

re·fresh [rɪ'frɛʃ] *vt (subj: drink)* rinfrescare; (: *sleep, bath)* ristorare; *(fig: memory)* rinfrescare.

re·fresh·ing [rɪ'frɛʃɪŋ] *adj (drink)* rinfrescante; *(sleep)* riposante, ristoratore(trice); *(change etc)* piacevole; *(idea, point of view)* originale.

re·fresh·ment [rɪ'frɛʃmənt] *n*: ~**s** rinfreschi *mpl*.

re·frig·er·ate [rɪ'frɪdʒəreɪt] *vt* refrigerare.

re·frig·era·tion [rɪ,frɪdʒə'reɪʃən] *n* refrigerazione *f*.

re·frig·era·tor [rɪ'frɪdʒəreɪtə[r]] *n* frigorifero.

re·fu·el ['riː'fjʊəl] **1** *vi* rifornirsi di carburante. **2** *vt* rifornire di carburante.

ref·uge ['rɛfjuːdʒ] *n (shelter)* riparo; *(for climbers, fig)* rifugio; **place of** ~ rifugio; **to take** ~ **in** *(also fig)* rifugiarsi in.

refu·gee [,rɛfjʊ'dʒiː] **1** *n* rifugiato/a, profugo/a. **2** *cpd*: ~ **camp** *n* campo (di) profughi.

re·fund ['riːfʌnd] **1** *n* rimborso. **2** [rɪ'fʌnd] *vt* rimborsare.

re·fur·bish [,riː'fɜːbɪʃ] *vt* rimettere a nuovo.

re·fus·al [rɪ'fjuːzəl] *n*: ~ **(to do)** rifiuto (di *or* a fare); **to have first** ~ **on sth** avere il diritto d'opzione su qc.

ref·use[1] ['rɛfjuːs] **1** *n* rifiuti *mpl*. **2** *cpd*: ~ **disposal** *n* sistema *m* di scarico dei rifiuti; ~ **dump** *n* discarica di rifiuti.

re·fuse[2] [rɪ'fjuːz] **1** *vt (all senses)* rifiutare; **to** ~ **sb sth** rifiutare qc a qn; **to** ~ **to do sth** rifiutare *or* rifiutarsi di fare qc. **2** *vi* rifiutarsi; *(horse)* rifiutare (l'ostacolo).

re·fute [rɪ'fjuːt] *vt* confutare.

re·gain [rɪ'geɪn] *vt (gen)* riguadagnare; *(balance, consciousness)* riprendere; *(confidence)* riacquistare; *(health)* ricuperare; **to** ~ **possession of sth** rientrare in possesso di qc.

re·gal ['riːgəl] *adj (bearing, manners)* regale; *(person)* dal portamento regale.

re·gale [rɪ'geɪl] *vt* deliziare, intrattenere.

re·ga·lia [rɪ'geɪlɪə] *n (royal trappings)* insegne *fpl* reali; *(gen: insignia)* abiti *mpl* da cerimonia.

re·gard [rɪ'gɑːd] **1** *n* **(a)** *(relation)*: **in** *or* **with** ~ **to**

per quanto riguarda, riguardo a; **in this** ~ **a** questo riguardo *or* proposito. **(b)** *(esteem, concern)* riguardo; **out of** ~ **for** per riguardo a; **to have a high** ~ **for sb, hold sb in high** ~ aver molta stima per qn, tenere qn in grande considerazione; **he shows little** ~ **for their feelings** non tiene molto conto dei loro sentimenti. **(c)** *(in messages):* ~**s to Maria, please give my** ~**s to Maria** salutami Maria, fai i miei saluti a Maria; *(as letter-ending):* **(kind)** ~**s** cordiali saluti. **2** *vt* **(a)** *(consider)* considerare; **we don't** ~ **it as necessary** non lo riteniamo necessario. **(b)** *(concern)* riguardare; **as** ~**s...** per quel che riguarda... .

re·gard·ing [rɪ'gɑːdɪŋ] *prep* riguardo a, per quanto riguarda.

re·gard·less [rɪ'gɑːdlɪs] **1** *adj:* ~ **of** senza preoccuparsi di; ~ **of rank** senza distinzioni; ~ **of race** senza distinzioni di razza. **2** *adv (fam):* **she did it** ~ l'ha fatto lo stesso.

re·gat·ta [rɪ'gætə] *n* regata.

re·gen·er·ate [rɪ'dʒɛnəreɪt] *vt (Bio, fig: society)* rigenerare; *(: feelings, enthusiasm)* far rinascere.

re·gen·er·a·tion [rɪ,dʒɛnə'reɪʃən] *n* rigenerazione *f; (of feelings, enthusiasm)* rinnovamento.

re·gent ['riːdʒənt] *n* reggente *m/f.*

reg·gae ['regeɪ] *n (Mus)* reggae *m.*

ré·gime [reɪ'ʒiːm] *n* regime *m.*

regi·ment ['redʒɪmənt] **1** *n (Mil)* reggimento. **2** ['redʒɪ,ment] *vt (fig)* irreggimentare.

regi·men·tal [,redʒɪ'mentl] *adj* reggimentale.

regi·men·ta·tion [,redʒɪmen'teɪʃən] *n (pej)* irreggimentazione *f.*

re·gion ['riːdʒən] *n (all senses)* regione *f; (fig):* **in the** ~ **of 40** circa 40, intorno a 40.

re·gion·al ['riːdʒənl] *adj* regionale; ~ **development** *(Brit Admin)* sviluppo economico delle regioni.

reg·is·ter ['redʒɪstə'] **1** *n (gen)* registro; *(of members)* elenco; **electoral** ~ lista elettorale; **the** ~ **of births, marriages and deaths** l'anagrafe *f.* **2** *vt* **(a)** *(fact, birth, death)* registrare; *(car)* immatricolare; *(trademark)* depositare; *(complaint)* sporgere; **to** ~ **a protest** fare un esposto. **(b)** *(Post: letter)* assicurare; *(Rail: luggage)* spedire assicurato(a). **(c)** *(indicate: speed, temperature etc)* registrare, segnare; *(: emotion)* dar segno di, mostrare. **3** *vi* **(a)** *(gen)* iscriversi; *(at hotel)* firmare il registro; **to** ~ **with a doctor** mettersi nella lista di un medico come paziente; **to** ~ **for a course** iscriversi a un corso. **(b)** *(have impact, become clear):* **it didn't** ~ **(with me)** non me ne sono reso conto.

reg·is·tered ['redʒɪstəd] *adj* **(a)** *(student, voter)* iscritto(a); *(car)* immatricolato(a); *(Comm: design, trademark)* registrato(a), depositato(a); *(charity)* riconosciuto(a); ~ **nurse** *(Am)* infermiere(a) diplomato(a). **(b)** *(letter, luggage)* assicurato(a).

reg·is·trar [,redʒɪs'trɑː'] *n (of births etc)* ufficiale *m* di stato civile; *(Univ)* segretario/a; *(Med)* medico ospedaliero superiore ad un interno.

reg·is·tra·tion [,redʒɪs'treɪʃən] **1** *n (gen)* registrazione *f; (of vehicle)* immatricolazione *f; (of voters, members)* iscrizione *f; during* ~ *(Scol)* durante l'appello; **a B**—**'s car** lettera della targa che indica l'anno di fabbricazione. **2** *cpd:* ~ **number** *n (Aut)* (numero di) targa.

reg·is·try ['redʒɪstrɪ] *n (also:* ~ **office)** anagrafe *f;* **we got married in a** ~ **office** ci siamo sposati in municipio.

re·gress [rɪ'gres] *vi* regredire.

re·gres·sion [rɪ'greʃən] *n* regresso.

re·gret [rɪ'gret] **1** *n* **(a)** rimpianto, rammarico; **much to my** ~, **to my great** ~ con mio grande dispiacere; **I have no** ~**s** non ho rimpianti. **(b):** ~**s** *pl (excuses)* scuse *fpl.* **2** *vt (news, death)* essere dispiaciuto(a) per, essere desolato(a) per; **I** ~ **that I cannot come to your party** *(frm)* mi dispiace *or* rincresce di non poter venire alla vostra festa; **we** ~ **to inform you that...** siamo spiacenti di informarla che... .

re·gret·ful·ly [rɪ'gretfəlɪ] *adv (sadly)* con molto rimpianto; *(unwillingly)* a malincuore.

re·gret·table [rɪ'gretəbl] *adj (deplorable)* deplorevole; *(unfortunate):* **her absence is** ~ ci rincresce che non ci sia.

re·gret·tably [rɪ'gretəblɪ] *adv* purtroppo, sfortunatamente.

re·group [,riː'gruːp] *vi* raggrupparsi (di nuovo).

regu·lar ['regjʊlə'] **1** *adj* **(a)** *(gen: shape, pulse, employment, army, verb)* regolare; **as** ~ **as clockwork** *(person, event)* puntuale come un orologio; *(visits)* molto regolare; **at** ~ **intervals** a intervalli regolari. **(b)** *(habitual: visitor, client)* fisso(a); *(: listener, reader)* fedele; *(Comm: price, size)* normale; **what is your** ~ **time for getting up?** a che ora ti alzi di solito? **(c)** *(permissible: action, procedure)* corretto(a). **(d)** *(fam: intensive):* **it's a** ~ **nuisance** è una solenne scocciatura. **2** *n (customer etc)* habitué *m/f inv,* assiduo(a) cliente *m/f; (Mil)* soldato regolare.

regu·lar·ity [,regjʊ'lærɪtɪ] *n* regolarità.

regu·lar·ize ['regjʊləraɪz] *vt* regolarizzare.

regu·lar·ly ['regjʊləlɪ] *adv* regolarmente.

regu·late ['regjʊleɪt] *vt* regolare.

regu·la·tion [,regjʊ'leɪʃən] **1** *n* regolamento. **2** *cpd (Mil)* di ordinanza.

regu·la·tor ['regjʊleɪtə'] *n (Tech)* regolatore *m.*

re·ha·bili·tate [,riːə'bɪlɪteɪt] *vt (disabled, refugees, demobilized troops)* reintegrare; *(disgraced person)* riabilitare.

re·ha·bili·ta·tion ['riːə,bɪlɪ'teɪʃən] **1** *n (see vb)* reintegrazione *f;* riabilitazione *f.* **2** *cpd:* ~ **centre** *n* istituto per la rieducazione.

re·hash [,riː'hæʃ] **1** *n* rimaneggiamento, rifacimento. **2** *vt* rimaneggiare.

re·hears·al [rɪ'hɜːsəl] *n* prova; **dress** ~ prova generale.

re·hearse [rɪ'hɜːs] *vt (Mus, Theatre)* provare; *(: one's part)* ripassare; *(what one is going to say)* ripetere.

re·house [,riː'haʊz] *vt* rialloggiare.

reign [reɪn] **1** *n* regno; **in the** ~ **of** sotto *or* durante il regno di; ~ **of terror** regno del terrore. **2** *vi (also fig)* regnare; **the** ~**ing champion** il campione in carica.

re·im·burse [,riːɪm'bɜːs] *vt:* **to** ~ **sb for sth** rimborsare qc a qn.

rein [reɪn] *n* redine *f,* briglia; **to keep a tight** ~ **on sb** *(fig)* tenere a freno qn; **to give sb free** ~ *(fig)* lasciare completa libertà a qn.

♦ **rein in** *vt + adv* trattenere (tirando le briglie).

re·incar·na·tion ['riːɪnkɑː'neɪʃən] *n* reincarnazione *f.*

rein·deer ['reɪndɪə'] *n, pl inv* renna.

re·inforce [,riːɪn'fɔːs] *vt (army, material, structure)* rinforzare; *(fig: theory, belief)* rafforzare. **2** *cpd:* ~**d concrete** *n* cemento armato.

re·inforce·ment [,riːɪn'fɔːsmənt] *n* **(a)** *(action)* rinforzo, rafforzamento; *(thing)* rinforzo. **(b)** *(Mil):* ~**s** *pl* rinforzi *mpl.*

re·instate [,riːɪn'steɪt] *vt* reintegrare.

re·issue [,riː'ɪʃjuː] *vt (book)* fare una ristampa di; *(record, film)* rimettere in circolazione.

re·it·er·ate [riː'ɪtəreɪt] *vt* ripetere, reiterare.

re·ject ['riːdʒɛkt] **1** n (person, thing: also Comm) scarto. **2** [rɪ'dʒɛkt] vt (offer etc) rifiutare, respingere; (applicant etc) scartare, respingere; (subj: body: food) rifiutare; **the patient's body** ~**ed the new organ** il malato ha avuto una crisi di rigetto; **to feel** ~**ed** sentirsi respinto.

re·jec·tion [rɪ'dʒɛkʃən] n (of offer, applicant) rifiuto; (of new organ) rigetto.

re·joice [rɪ'dʒɔɪs] vi rallegrarsi; **to** ~ **in sth** godere di qc.

re·joic·ings [rɪ'dʒɔɪsɪŋz] npl festeggiamenti mpl.

re·join[1] [ˌriː'dʒɔɪn] vt (Mil: ship, regiment) raggiungere; (club, library) iscriversi di nuovo a.

re·join[2] [rɪ'dʒɔɪn] vi (retort) replicare.

re·join·der [rɪ'dʒɔɪndəʳ] n (retort) replica.

re·ju·venate [rɪ'dʒuːvɪneɪt] vt (far) ringiovanire.

re·kindle [ˌriː'kɪndl] vt (also fig) riaccendere.

re·lapse [rɪ'læps] **1** n ricaduta; **to have a** ~ una ricaduta. **2** vi (gen): **to** ~ (**into**) ricadere (in); (Med) avere una ricaduta.

re·late [rɪ'leɪt] **1** vt **(a)** (tell: story) raccontare, riferire. **(b)** (establish relation between) collegare. **2** vi: **to** ~ **to (a)** (connect) riferirsi a. **(b)** (get on with) stabilire un rapporto con.

re·lat·ed [rɪ'leɪtɪd] adj **(a)** (connected: subject) connesso(a); (: substances, languages) affine. **(b)** (attached by family: person) imparentato(a); **we are distantly** ~ siamo parenti alla lontana.

re·lat·ing [rɪ'leɪtɪŋ] : ~ **to** prep relativo(a) a, riguardo a.

re·la·tion [rɪ'leɪʃən] n **(a)** (relationship) rapporto, relazione f; **to bear a** ~ **to** corrispondere a; **in** ~ **to** con riferimento a; **to have good** ~**s with sb** essere in or avere buoni rapporti con qn; **diplomatic/international** ~**s** rapporti diplomatici/internazionali; **sexual** ~**s** rapporti sessuali. **(b)** (family: relative) parente m/f; (: kinship) parentela; **what** ~ **is she to you?** che legami di parentela ha con te?

re·la·tion·ship [rɪ'leɪʃənʃɪp] n **(a)** (family ties) legami mpl di parentela. **(b)** (connection: between two things) rapporto, nesso; (: with sb) rapporti; **to see a** ~ **between** vedere un nesso fra; **to have a** ~ **with sb** (sexual) avere una relazione con qn; **they have a good** ~ vanno molto d'accordo.

rela·tive ['rɛlətɪv] **1** adj (comparative, Gram) relativo(a); (connected): ~ **to** legato(a) a; **the** ~ **merits of X and Y** i meriti rispettivi di X e Y. **2** n parente m/f.

rela·tive·ly ['rɛlətɪvlɪ] adv relativamente; (fairly, rather) abbastanza.

rela·tiv·ity [ˌrɛlə'tɪvɪtɪ] n relatività.

re·lax [rɪ'læks] **1** vt (muscles, person) rilassare; (restrictions) diminuire; (discipline) allentare; **to** ~ **one's hold on sth** allentare la presa di qc. **2** vi (sb's grip) allentarsi; (rest) rilassarsi; (amuse oneself) svagarsi; (calm down): ~! calma!; **his face** ~**ed into a smile** il suo viso si distese in un sorriso.

re·laxa·tion [ˌriːlæk'seɪʃən] n (rest) relax m; **he plays the piano for** ~ suona il piano per rilassarsi.

re·laxed [rɪ'lækst] adj (muscles) rilassato(a), rilasciato(a); (person, mood) disteso(a), rilassato(a).

re·lax·ing [rɪ'læksɪŋ] adj rilassante.

re·lay ['riːleɪ] **1** n **(a)** (of workmen, horses) ricambio; **to work in** ~**s** lavorare a squadre (dandosi il cambio). **(b)** (Radio, TV) ripetitore m; (Elec) relè m inv; (Sport: also: ~ **race**) corsa a staffetta. **2** vt (Radio, TV) ripetere, ritrasmettere; (pass on: message) passare.

re·lease [rɪ'liːs] **1** n **(a)** (gen) rilascio; (from army) congedo; (from suffering) liberazione f. **(b)** (of gas) emissione f; (of film, record) uscita; (of book) pubblicazione f. **(c)** (record, film etc): **new** ~ nuovo disco (or film etc); **his latest** ~ il suo ultimo disco (or film etc). **2** vt **(a)** (let go) lasciare andare, mollare; (: bomb) sganciare; (: fig: tension) allentare. **(b)** (set free) rilasciare; (: Dir) rimettere in libertà; (: from wreckage) liberare; (: from promise, vow) sciogliere. **(c)** (issue: gas) emettere; (: book, record) mettere in circolazione; (: film) distribuire; (: statement) rilasciare. **(d)** (Tech: catch, clasp) liberare; (Phot: shutter) far scattare; (handbrake) togliere.

rel·egate ['rɛlɪgeɪt] vt (demote) relegare; (Sport) (far) retrocedere.

rel·ega·tion [ˌrɛlɪ'geɪʃən] n (see vb) relegazione f; retrocessione f.

re·lent [rɪ'lɛnt] vi cedere.

re·lent·less [rɪ'lɛntlɪs] adj implacabile.

rel·evance ['rɛləvəns] n pertinenza.

rel·evant ['rɛləvənt] adj: ~ (**to**) (remark, fact) pertinente (a); (information, papers) relativo(a) (a); (course of action) adeguato(a) (a).

re·li·abil·ity [rɪˌlaɪə'bɪlɪtɪ] n (see adj) attendibilità; affidabilità; (of person) serietà.

re·li·able [rɪ'laɪəbl] adj (report, source) attendibile; (machine etc) affidabile; (person: trustworthy) fidato(a); (: capable) capace.

re·li·ably [rɪ'laɪəblɪ] adv: **I am** ~ **informed that...** so da fonti sicure che....

re·li·ance [rɪ'laɪəns] n: ~ (**on**) dipendenza (da).

re·li·ant [rɪ'laɪənt] adj: **to be** ~ **on sth/sb** dipendere da qc/qn.

rel·ic ['rɛlɪk] n (Rel) reliquia; (fig: of the past) avanzo.

re·lief [rɪ'liːf] **1** n **(a)** (from pain, anxiety): ~ (**from**) sollievo (a); **by way of light** ~ come diversivo; **that's a** ~! che sollievo! **(b)** (Mil: of town) soccorso. **(c)** (tax) ~ sgravio. **(d)** (Art, Geog) rilievo; **to throw sth into** ~ (fig) mettere qc in evidenza or in risalto. **2** cpd (bus, typist) supplementare; (work, organization, troops) di soccorso; ~ **map** n carta in rilievo; ~ **road** n circonvallazione f.

re·lieve [rɪ'liːv] vt **(a)** (pain, anxiety, boredom) alleviare; (person) sollevare; **I am** ~**d to hear you are better** sono sollevato dalla notizia che stai meglio; **to** ~ **sb of sth** (load) alleggerire qn di qc; (anxiety) sollevare qn da qc; (duty) esonerare qn da qc; **to** ~ **sb of his command** (Mil) esonerare qn dal comando; **to** ~ **one's anger** sfogare la propria rabbia; **to** ~ **congestion in sth** (Med) decongestionare qc; **to** ~ **o.s.** (go to lavatory) fare i propri bisogni. **(b)** (replace: also Mil) dare il cambio a; (Mil: town) liberare.

re·li·gion [rɪ'lɪdʒən] n religione f.

re·li·gious [rɪ'lɪdʒəs] adj (gen) religioso(a); (conscientious) scrupoloso(a).

re·lin·quish [rɪ'lɪŋkwɪʃ] vt (right, control, responsibility) rinunciare a; (post) lasciare, abbandonare; **to** ~ **one's hold on sth** lasciare andare qc.

rel·ish ['rɛlɪʃ] **1** n **(a)**: ~ (**for**) gusto (per); **to do sth with** ~ fare qc di gusto. **(b)** (sauce) condimento, salsa. **2** vt (food, wine) gustare; (fig: like): **I don't** ~ **the idea** non mi piace or mi attira l'idea; **I** ~ **doing that** mi piace da matti farlo.

re·luc·tance [rɪ'lʌktəns] n riluttanza.

re·luc·tant [rɪ'lʌktənt] adj (person) riluttante, restio(a); (praise, consent) concesso(a) a malincuore; **to be** ~ **to do sth** essere restio a fare qc.

re·luc·tant·ly [rɪ'lʌktəntlɪ] adv a malincuore.

rely [rɪ'laɪ] vi: **to** ~ **on sb/sth** contare su qn/qc; **you can't** ~ **on my discretion** puoi fidarti della mia discrezione; **you can't** ~ **on the trains** non si può fare affidamento sui treni; **she relies on him for**

financial support dipende da lui finanziariamente.

re·main [rɪ'meɪn] *vi* rimanere, restare; **it ~s to be
seen whether...** resta da vedere se...; **it will ~ in
my memory** resterà sempre impresso nel mio
ricordo; **the fact ~s that...** resta il fatto che...; **to
~ faithful to sb** rimanere *or* mantenersi fedele a
qn; **to ~ silent** restare in silenzio; **to ~ behind**
fermarsi; **I ~, yours faithfully** *(in letters)* distinti
saluti.

re·main·der [rɪ'meɪndə'] *n (also Math)* resto, avanzo; *(people)* altri/e *m/fpl;* **~s** *(Comm: books)* remainder *mpl,* copie *fpl* invendute a prezzo ridotto; *(: other goods)* giacenze *fpl* di magazzino.

re·main·ing [rɪ'meɪnɪŋ] *adj* restante, rimasto(a);
the 3 ~ possibilities le 3 possibilità che restano
or che rimangono.

re·mains [rɪ'meɪnz] *npl (gen)* resti *mpl; (of food)*
avanzi *mpl;* **the ~ of his fortune** ciò che restava
del suo patrimonio.

re·make ['ri:meɪk] *n (Cine)* rifacimento.

re·mand [rɪ'mɑ:nd] *(Law)* **1** *n:* **on ~ in** detenzione
preventiva. **2** *vt* rinviare; **to ~ sb in custody**
mettere qn in detenzione preventiva. **3** *cpd:* **~
home** *n* riformatorio, casa di correzione.

re·mark [rɪ'mɑ:k] **1** *n* osservazione *f,* commento;
worthy of ~ degno di nota. **2** *vt (say, notice)*
osservare, notare. **3** *vi:* **to ~ on sth** fare dei
commenti su qc.

re·mark·able [rɪ'mɑ:kəbl] *adj* notevole.

re·mark·ably [rɪ'mɑ:kəblɪ] *adv* eccezionalmente,
notevolmente.

re·marry ['ri:'mærɪ] *vi* risposarsi.

re·medial [rɪ'mi:dɪəl] *adj (Med)* correttivo(a); *(action)* atto(a) a porre rimedio; *(school, teaching)*
speciale; *(class)* di ricupero.

rem·edy ['rɛmədɪ] **1** *n:* **~ (for)** rimedio (contro). **2**
vt (illness) curare; *(situation)* rimediare a; *(loss)*
porre riparo a.

re·mem·ber [rɪ'mɛmbə'] *vt* ricordare, ricordarsi
di; **I ~ seeing it, I ~ having seen it** (mi) ricordo
di averlo visto; **she ~ed to do it** si è ricordata di
farlo; **give me sth to ~ you by** lasciami un tuo
ricordo; **to ~ sb in one's prayers** ricordare qn
nelle proprie preghiere; **~ me to your wife and
children!** saluta tua moglie e i bambini da parte
mia!; **that's worth ~ing** buono a sapersi.

re·mem·brance [rɪ'mɛmbrəns] **1** *n* ricordo, memoria; **in ~ of** in memoria di. **2** *cpd:* **R~ Day**
giorno della commemorazione dei caduti.

re·mind [rɪ'maɪnd] *vt* ricordare, rammentare; **to ~
sb of sth/to do sth** ricordare *or* rammentare a qn
qc/di fare qc; **she ~s me of Anne** mi ricorda
Anne; **that ~s me!** a proposito!

re·mind·er [rɪ'maɪndə'] *n* **(a)** *(note)* promemoria;
(Comm: letter etc) (lettera di) sollecito; **as a ~
that** per ricordarsi che. **(b)** *(memento)* ricordo.

remi·nisce [,rɛmɪ'nɪs] *vi* abbandonarsi ai ricordi.

remi·nis·cence [,rɛmɪ'nɪsəns] *n* reminiscenza.

remi·nis·cent [,rɛmɪ'nɪsənt] *adj:* **~ of** che ricorda,
che fa venire in mente.

re·miss [rɪ'mɪs] *adj* negligente; **it was ~ of me** è
stata una negligenza da parte mia.

re·mis·sion [rɪ'mɪʃən] *n (gen, Rel, Med)* remissione
f; (Law, of debts) condono.

re·mit [rɪ'mɪt] *vt* **(a)** *(send: amount due)* rimettere.
(b) *(refer: decision)* rimettere. **(c)** *(Rel: sins)* rimettere, perdonare; *(fee, penalty)* condonare,
rimettere.

re·mit·tance [rɪ'mɪtəns] *n* rimessa (di pagamento).

rem·nant ['rɛmnənt] *n (remainder)* resto, *(: of food)*
avanzo, resto, *(: of cloth)* scampolo.

re·mon·strance [rɪ'mɒnstrəns] *n (complaint)* rimostranza, protesta.

re·mon·strate ['rɛmənstreɪt] *vi* protestare; **to ~
with sb about sth** fare le proprie rimostranze a
qn circa qc.

re·morse [rɪ'mɔ:s] *n* rimorso; **without ~** senza
pietà.

re·morse·ful [rɪ'mɔ:sfʊl] *adj* pieno(a) di rimorsi.

re·morse·less [rɪ'mɔ:slɪs] *adj* senza rimorsi; *(fig)*
spietato(a), implacabile.

re·mote [rɪ'məʊt] **1** *adj* (**-r, -st**) **(a)** *(place, period)*
remoto(a); *(ancestor)* lontano(a); *(in concept:
idea)* lontano(a); *(aloof: person)* distante; **~ from
the matter in hand** non pertinente alla questione.
(b) *(slight: possibility, resemblance)* vago(a); **not
the ~st idea/hope** neanche la più vaga idea/
speranza; **there is a ~ possibility that...** c'è una
vaga possibilità che... **+** *sub.* **2** *cpd:* **~ control** *n*
telecomando.

remote-controlled [rɪ'məʊtkən'trəʊld] *adj* tele-
comandato(a).

re·mote·ly [rɪ'məʊtlɪ] *adv* **(a)** *(distantly)* lontanamente, alla lontana; **~ situated** in una posizione
isolata. **(b)** *(slightly)* vagamente.

re·mov·able [rɪ'mu:vəbl] *adj (detachable)* che si
può togliere, amovibile.

re·mov·al [rɪ'mu:vəl] **1** *n* **(a)** *(of person)* allontanamento; *(: from post)* rimozione *f; (of problem)*
allontanamento; *(of doubt, fear, obstacle, stain)*
eliminazione *f; (Med)* asportazione *f.* **(b)** *(move
from house)* trasloco. **2** *cpd:* **~ van** *n* camion *m inv*
per *or* dei traslochi.

re·move [rɪ'mu:v] **1** *vt (gen):* **to ~ (from)** togliere
(da), levare (da); *(person)* allontanare; *(: from
post)* rimuovere; *(stain)* togliere, eliminare;
(problem) allontanare; *(doubt, fear)* eliminare,
dissipare; *(obstacle)* rimuovere, eliminare;
(Med: appendix etc) asportare; **to ~ one's make-
up** struccarsi; **first cousin once ~d** cugino di
secondo grado; **far ~d from** *(fig)* ben lontano da.
2 *vi* traslocare; **to ~ from London to the country**
trasferirsi da Londra in campagna.

re·mov·er [rɪ'mu:və'] *n* **(a)** *(removal man)* addetto
ai traslochi; **~s** *(firm)* ditta *or* impresa di traslochi. **(b)** *(of stains)* smacchiatore *m; (of nail varnish)* solvente *m;* **make-up ~** struccatore *m.*

re·mu·nera·tion [rɪ,mju:nə'reɪʃən] *n* rimunerazione *f,* ricompensa.

Re·nais·sance [rɪ'neɪsɑ:ns] **1** *n* Rinascimento. **2**
cpd (style) (del) Rinascimento; *(palace, art)* rinascimentale, del Rinascimento.

re·nal ['ri:nl] *adj* renale.

ren·der ['rɛndə'] *vt* **(a)** *(thanks, honour, service)*
rendere; *(account)* presentare. **(b)** *(make)* rendere; **this ~s it impossible for me to leave** questo rende impossibile la mia partenza. **(c)** *(interpret: sonata, role, play)* interpretare; *(translate:
text)* tradurre.

ren·der·ing ['rɛndərɪŋ] *n (translation)* traduzione *f;
(of song, role)* interpretazione *f.*

ren·dez·vous ['rɒndɪvu:] **1** *n (meeting)* appuntamento; *(meeting place)* punto *or* luogo di
ritrovo. **2** *vi* ritrovarsi; *(spaceship)* effettuare un
rendez-vous.

ren·di·tion [rɛn'dɪʃən] *n (Mus)* interpretazione *f.*

ren·egade ['rɛnɪgeɪd] *n* rinnegato/a.

re·new [rɪ'nju:] *vt (gen)* rinnovare; *(negotiations,
discussion, strength)* riprendere; **to ~ one's acquaintance with sb** riprendere contatto con qn.

re·new·al [rɪ'nju:əl] *n (see vb)* rinnovo; ripresa.

re·nounce [rɪ'naʊns] *vt (gen)* rinunciare a; **to ~
one's faith** abiurare.

reno·vate ['rɛnəʊveɪt] *vt (house)* rinnovare, rimet-

tere a nuovo; *(furniture, building)* restaurare.
reno·va·tion [rɛnəʊ'veɪʃən] *n (see vb)* rimessa a nuovo; restauro.

re·nown [rɪ'naʊn] *n* rinomanza, fama.

re·nowned [rɪ'naʊnd] *adj* famoso(a), rinomatò(a).

rent [rɛnt] **1** *n* (canone *m* di) affitto, pigione *f*. **2** *vt* **(a)** *(take for rent: house)* affittare, prendere in affitto; *(: car, TV)* noleggiare, prendere a noleggio. **(b)** *(also:* ~ **out**: *house)* affittare, dare in affitto; *(: car, TV)* noleggiare, dare a noleggio.

rent·al ['rɛntl] *n (cost: on TV, telephone)* abbonamento; *(: on car)* nolo, noleggio.

re·nun·cia·tion [rɪ,nʌnsɪ'eɪʃən] *n (see* **renounce)** rinuncia; abiura.

re·open [,riː'əʊpən] **1** *vt (gen)* riaprire; *(discussion, hostilities)* riaprire, riprendere. **2** *vi* riaprirsi.

re·or·gani·za·tion ['riː,ɔːgənaɪ'zeɪʃən] *n* riorganizzazione *f*.

re·or·gan·ize ['riː'ɔːgənaɪz] *vt* riorganizzare.

rep [rɛp] *n* **(a)** *(Comm) abbr of* **representative. (b)** *(Theatre) abbr of* **repertory.**

re·paid [riː'peɪd] *pt, pp of* **repay.**

re·pair [rɪ'pɛəʳ] **1** *n* riparazione *f;* **under** ~ in riparazione; **in good** ~**, in a good state of** ~ in buono stato; **it is damaged beyond** ~ è irrimediabilmente rovinato; **closed for** ~**s** chiuso per lavori. **2** *vt (car, shoes etc)* aggiustare, riparare; *(fig: wrong)* rimediare a.

repa·rable ['rɛpərəbl] *adj (damage)* riparabile; *(loss, mistake)* rimediabile.

repa·ra·tion [,rɛpə'reɪʃən] *n* riparazione *f;* **to make** ~ **for sth** riparare a qc.

rep·ar·tee [,rɛpɑː'tiː] *n* risposta pronta, battuta.

re·pat·ri·ate [riː'pætrɪeɪt] *vt* rimpatriare.

re·pat·ria·tion [riː,pætrɪ'eɪʃən] *n* rimpatrio.

re·pay [riː'peɪ] *pt, pp* **repaid** *vt (money)* restituire; *(debt)* pagare; *(lender)* rimborsare, restituire i soldi a; *(sb's kindness etc)* ricambiare; **how can I ever** ~ **you?** come potrò ricompensarti?

re·pay·able [riː'peɪəbl] *adj* rimborsabile.

re·pay·ment [riː'peɪmənt] *n (of money)* pagamento; *(of expenses)* rimborso.

re·peal [rɪ'piːl] **1** *vt (law)* abrogare; *(sentence)* revocare. **2** *n (see vb)* abrogazione *f;* revoca.

re·peat [rɪ'piːt] **1** *vt (gen, Scol)* ripetere; **don't** ~ **it to anybody** non riferirlo a nessuno; **this offer cannot be** ~**ed** offerta irripetibile; **to** ~ **an order** *(Comm)* rinnovare un'ordinazione; **in spite of** ~**ed reminders** malgrado diversi *or* ripetuti solleciti. **3** *n* replica; *(TV)* replica, ripresa. **3** *cpd:* ~ **order** *n (Comm):* **to place a** ~ **order (for)** rinnovare l'ordinazione (di); ~ **performance** *n (fig):* **I don't want a** ~ **performance** of that non vorrei che questo si ripeta.

re·peat·ed·ly [rɪ'piːtɪdlɪ] *adv* ripetutamente, più e più volte.

re·pel [rɪ'pɛl] *vt (force back)* respingere; *(disgust)* ripugnare a.

re·pel·lent [rɪ'pɛlənt] *adj (disgusting)* ripugnante, repellente.

re·pent [rɪ'pɛnt] *vi:* **to** ~ **(of)** pentirsi (di).

re·pent·ance [rɪ'pɛntəns] *n* pentimento.

re·pent·ant [rɪ'pɛntənt] *adj* pentito(a).

re·per·cus·sions [,riːpə'kʌʃnz] *npl* ripercussioni *fpl*.

rep·er·toire ['rɛpətwɑːʳ] *n* repertorio.

rep·er·tory ['rɛpətərɪ] **1** *n (Theatre, fig: of jokes etc)* repertorio. **2** *cpd:* ~ **company** *n* compagnia di repertorio; ~ **theatre** *n* teatro di repertorio.

rep·eti·tion [,rɛpɪ'tɪʃən] *n* ripetizione *f*.

rep·eti·tious [,rɛpɪ'tɪʃəs] *adj,* **re·peti·tive** [rɪ'pɛtɪtɪv] *adj (work)* ripetitivo(a), monotono(a); *(speech)* pieno(a) di ripetizioni.

re·place [rɪ'pleɪs] *vt* **(a)** *(put back)* rimettere (a posto); *(: Telec: receiver)* riattaccare. **(b)** *(get replacement for, take the place of):* **to** ~ **(by, with)** rimpiazzare (con), sostituire (con).

re·place·ment [rɪ'pleɪsmənt] *n (substitute: thing)* pezzo *or* parte *f* di ricambio; *(: person)* sostituto/a.

re·play [,riː'pleɪ] *(Sport)* **1** *vt (match)* ripetere. **2** *vi* ripetere l'incontro. **3** ['riːpleɪ] *n (of match)* partita ripetuta; *(TV: playback)* replay *m inv;* **to hold a** ~ ripetere l'incontro.

re·plen·ish [rɪ'plɛnɪʃ] *vt (tank etc)* riempire (di nuovo); *(one's wardrobe)* rifare; **to** ~ **one's supplies of** sth rifornirsi di qc.

re·plete [rɪ'pliːt] *adj:* ~ **(with)** sazio(a) (di).

rep·li·ca ['rɛplɪkə] *n* replica.

re·ply [rɪ'plaɪ] **1** *n* risposta; **in** ~ in risposta; **what did you say in** ~? cos'hai risposto?; **there's no** ~ *(Telec)* non risponde (nessuno). **2** *vt, vi* rispondere.

re·port [rɪ'pɔːt] **1** *n* **(a)** *(account: written)* rapporto, relazione *f; (: spoken)* resoconto; *(Press, Radio, TV)* reportage *m inv,* servizio; *(Scol)* pagella (scolastica); **annual** ~ *(Comm)* relazione annuale; **weather** ~ bollettino meteorologico; **to give a** ~ **on** sth fare una relazione *or* un rapporto su qc; fare un resoconto di qc; **I have heard a** ~ **that...** ho sentito (dire) che.... **(b)** *(bang)* detonazione *f; (shot)* sparo.

2 *vt (gen, Press, TV)* riportare; *(notify: accident, culprit)* denunciare; **it is** ~**ed from Berlin that...** ci è stato riferito da Berlino che...; **what have you to** ~? che cos'ha da riferire?; **to** ~ **progress** riferire sugli sviluppi della situazione; **to** ~ **one's findings** riferire sulle proprie conclusioni; ~**ed speech** *(Gram)* discorso indiretto.

3 *vi* **(a):** **to** ~ **(on)** fare un rapporto (su); *(Press, Radio, TV)* fare un reportage (su). **(b)** *(present oneself):* **to** ~ **(to)** presentarsi (a); **to** ~ **for duty** presentarsi al lavoro; **to** ~ **sick** darsi malato.

♦ **report back** *vi + adv* **(a)** *(come back)* ritornare. **(b)** *(make report)* tornare a riferire.

re·port·er [rɪ'pɔːtəʳ] *n (Press)* cronista *m/f,* reporter *m/f inv; (Radio)* radiocronista *m/f; (TV)* telecronista *m/f*.

re·pose [rɪ'pəʊz] *(frm)* **1** *n* riposo; **in** ~ in riposo. **2** *vi* riposare.

rep·re·hen·sible [,rɛprɪ'hɛnsɪbl] *adj* riprovevole.

rep·re·sent [,rɛprɪ'zɛnt] *vt (all senses)* rappresentare.

rep·re·sen·ta·tion [,rɛprɪzɛn'teɪʃən] *n* rappresentazione *f; (Pol)* rappresentanza; **to make** ~**s to sb** *(protest)* fare delle rimostranze a qn.

rep·re·senta·tive [,rɛprɪ'zɛntətɪv] **1** *adj:* ~ **(of)** rappresentativo(a) (di). **2** *n (gen)* rappresentante *m/f,* delegato/a; *(Comm)* rappresentante (di commercio); *(Am Pol):* **R**~ deputato/essa.

re·press [rɪ'prɛs] *vt* reprimere.

re·pressed [rɪ'prɛst] *adj* represso(a).

re·pres·sion [rɪ'prɛʃən] *n* repressione *f*.

re·pres·sive [rɪ'prɛsɪv] *adj* repressivo(a).

re·prieve [rɪ'priːv] **1** *n (Law)* commutazione *f* della pena capitale; *(delay: also gen)* proroga. **2** *vt (Law)* rinviare l'esecuzione di; *(grant a delay)* concedere una proroga a; *(: fig)* dare tregua a.

rep·ri·mand ['rɛprɪmɑːnd] **1** *n* rimprovero. **2** *vt* redarguire, rimproverare.

re·print ['riːprɪnt] **1** *n* ristampa. **2** [riː'prɪnt] *vt* ristampare.

re·pris·al [rɪ'praɪzəl] *n:* ~**s** rappresaglie *fpl;* **to take** ~**s** fare delle rappresaglie; **as a** ~ **for** come rappresaglia a.

re·proach [rɪ'prəʊtʃ] **1** *n* rimprovero; **above** *or*

beyond ~ irreprensibile. **2** vt: **to** ~ **sb for sth/for doing sth** rimproverare qn di qc/di aver fatto qc; **don't** ~ **yourself for what happened** non devi sentirti in colpa per quello che è successo.

re·proach·ful [rɪ'prəʊtʃfʊl] adj (look etc) di rimprovero.

rep·ro·bate ['rɛprəʊbeɪt] n (hum) canaglia.

re·pro·duce [ˌriːprə'djuːs] **1** vt riprodurre. **2** vi riprodursi.

re·pro·duc·tion [ˌriːprə'dʌkʃən] **1** n (all senses) riproduzione f. **2** cpd: ~ **furniture** n riproduzioni fpl di mobili antichi.

re·proof [rɪ'pruːf] n riprovazione f.

re·proof ['riː'pruːf] vt (garment) impermeabilizzare di nuovo.

re·prove [rɪ'pruːv] vt: **to** ~ **(for)** rimproverare (di or per).

rep·tile ['rɛptaɪl] n rettile m.

re·pub·lic [rɪ'pʌblɪk] n repubblica.

re·pub·li·can [rɪ'pʌblɪkən] adj, n repubblicano(a) (m/f).

re·pu·di·ate [rɪ'pjuːdɪeɪt] vt (charge, offer of friendship) respingere; (debt, treaty) disconoscere, rifiutarsi di onorare; (one's wife) ripudiare.

re·pug·nance [rɪ'pʌgnəns] n ripugnanza.

re·pug·nant [rɪ'pʌgnənt] adj ripugnante; **to be** ~ **to sb** ripugnare a qn.

re·pulse [rɪ'pʌls] vt respingere.

re·pul·sion [rɪ'pʌlʃən] n ripulsione f, ribrezzo.

re·pul·sive [rɪ'pʌlsɪv] adj ripugnante, ributtante.

repu·table ['rɛpjʊtəbl] adj (firm etc) degno(a) di fiducia, serio(a).

repu·ta·tion [ˌrɛpjʊ'teɪʃən] n reputazione f; **he has a** ~ **for being awkward** ha la fama di essere un tipo difficile; **to live up to one's** ~ non smentirsi, non smentire la propria reputazione.

re·pute [rɪ'pjuːt] **1** n reputazione f; **of (good)** ~ (person) che ha una buona reputazione; (place) che ha un buon nome; **by** ~ di fama. **2** vt: **to be** ~**d to be rich/intelligent** etc essere ritenuto(a) ricco(a)/intelligente etc.

re·put·ed·ly [rɪ'pjuːtɪdlɪ] adv (stando) a quel che si dice.

re·quest [rɪ'kwɛst] **1** n richiesta, domanda; **to make a** ~ **for sth** fare richiesta di qc; **at the** ~ **of** su richiesta di; **on** or **by** ~ a or su richiesta; **by popular** ~ a grande richiesta. **2** vt: **to** ~ **sth from sb/sb to do sth** richiedere qc a qn/a qn di fare qc; **'you are** ~**d not to smoke'** 'si prega di non fumare'. **3** cpd: ~ **(bus) stop** n fermata facoltativa or a richiesta.

requi·em ['rɛkwɪɛm] n requiem m inv.

re·quire [rɪ'kwaɪə'] vt **(a)** (subj: person) aver bisogno di; (: thing, action) richiedere; **it** ~**s careful thought** richiede un attento esame; **what qualifications are** ~**d?** che requisiti ci vogliono?; **if** ~**d** se necessario; **when** ~**d** quando è necessario. **(b)** (demand, order): **to** ~ **sb to do sth/sth of sb** esigere che qn faccia qc/qc da qn; **to** ~ **that sth be done** esigere che qc sia fatto; **passengers are** ~**d to show their tickets** i passeggeri devono esibire i biglietti; ~**d by law** prescritto dalla legge.

re·quired [rɪ'kwaɪəd] adj (qualifications, exams) richiesto(a); (amount) voluto(a); **in the** ~ **time** nel tempo prescritto.

re·quire·ment [rɪ'kwaɪəmənt] n (need) esigenza; (condition) requisito, condizione f (richiesta); **to meet sb's** ~**s** soddisfare le esigenze di qn; **she meets all the** ~**s for the job** risponde a tutti i requisiti.

requi·site ['rɛkwɪzɪt] n occorrente m, necessario; **toilet** ~**s** articoli mpl da bagno.

requi·si·tion [ˌrɛkwɪ'zɪʃən] **1** n requisizione f. **2** vt requisire.

re·scind [rɪ'sɪnd] vt (Law) abrogare; (contract, order etc) rescindere.

res·cue ['rɛskjuː] **1** n (saving) salvataggio; (help) soccorso; **to come/go to sb's** ~ venire/andare in aiuto a or di qn. **2** vt salvare. **3** cpd: ~ **team** n squadra di soccorso or di salvataggio.

res·cu·er ['rɛskjʊə'] n soccorritore/trice.

re·search [rɪ'sɜːtʃ] **1** n ricerca; **a piece of** ~ un lavoro di ricerca; **to do** ~ fare ricerca. **2** vi: **to** ~ **(into sth)** fare ricerca (su qc). **3** vt documentarsi su; **a well** ~**ed book** un libro ben documentato. **4** cpd (centre, laboratory) di ricerca; ~ **work** n lavoro di ricerca; ~ **worker** n ricercatore/trice.

re·search·er [rɪ'sɜːtʃə'] n ricercatore/trice.

re·sem·blance [rɪ'zɛmbləns] n somiglianza; **to bear a strong** ~ **to** somigliare moltissimo a.

re·sem·ble [rɪ'zɛmbl] vt somigliare, assomigliare.

re·sent [rɪ'zɛnt] vt risentirsi per; **I** ~ **your remarks** le tue osservazioni mi irritano; **he** ~**s my being here** è contrariato dalla mia presenza.

re·sent·ful [rɪ'zɛntfʊl] adj (person) pieno(a) di risentimento; (tone) risentito(a); **to be** or **feel** ~ **of sb** provare del risentimento per qn.

re·sent·ment [rɪ'zɛntmənt] n risentimento.

res·er·va·tion [ˌrɛzə'veɪʃən] n **(a)** (booking) prenotazione f; **to make a** ~ prenotare, fare una prenotazione. **(b)** (doubt) riserva; **without** ~ senza riserve; **with** ~**s** con le dovute riserve. **(c)** (area of land) riserva.

re·serve [rɪ'zɜːv] **1** n (most senses) riserva; (hiding one's feelings) riserbo; **in** ~ in riserva; **without** ~ senza riserve. **2** vt **(a)** (table, seat etc) prenotare, riservare; (set aside) riservare; **to** ~ **one's strength** risparmiarsi le forze. **(b)**: **to** ~ **judgment (on)** (fig) riservarsi di decidere in merito (a); **to** ~ **the right to do** riservarsi il diritto di fare. **3** cpd: ~ **team** n (Sport) seconda squadra.

re·served [rɪ'zɜːvd] adj (booked: table etc) prenotato(a), riservato(a); (fig: person) riservato(a).

res·er·voir ['rɛzəvwɑː'] n (artificial lake) bacino idrico; (tank etc) serbatoio.

re·shuf·fle [ˌriː'ʃʌfl] n: **Cabinet** ~ rimpasto ministeriale.

re·side [rɪ'zaɪd] vi (frm) risiedere; (: fig: power etc): **to** ~ **in** or **with** essere nelle mani di.

resi·dence ['rɛzɪdəns] **1** n (gen) residenza; (stay) permanenza, soggiorno; **'desirable** ~ **for sale'** 'abitazione signorile vendesi'; **to take up** ~ prendere residenza; **in** ~ (queen etc) in sede; (doctor) fisso. **2** cpd: ~ **permit** n permesso di soggiorno.

resi·dent ['rɛzɪdənt] **1** adj (doctor, tutor etc) fisso(a); (population etc) stabile; **to be** ~ **in a town/in London** risiedere in una città/a Londra. **2** n abitante m/f; (of hotel) cliente m/f; **local** ~**s** abitanti della zona.

resi·den·tial [ˌrɛzɪ'dɛnʃəl] adj (area) di abitazione; ~ **nurse** infermiera interna.

re·sid·ual [rɪ'zɪdjʊəl] adj residuo(a).

resi·due ['rɛzɪdjuː] n residuo, residui mpl.

re·sign [rɪ'zaɪn] **1** vt (office, leadership) lasciare; (claim, task etc) rinunciare a; **to** ~ **o.s. to (doing) sth** rassegnarsi a (fare) qc. **2** vi: **to** ~ **(from)** dimettersi (da), dare le dimissioni (da).

res·ig·na·tion [ˌrɛzɪg'neɪʃən] n **(a)** (from job) dimissioni fpl; **to tender one's** ~ dare le dimissioni. **(b)** (mental state) rassegnazione f.

re·signed [rɪ'zaɪnd] adj rassegnato(a).

re·sili·ence [rɪ'zɪlɪəns] n (see adj) elasticità; capacità di ricupero.

re·sili·ent [rɪ'zɪlɪənt] adj (substance) elastico(a);

(fig) che ha buone capacità di ripresa.

res·in [ˈrezɪn] n resina.

re·sist [rɪˈzɪst] **1** vt (gen) resistere a; (change) opporsi a; **he couldn't ~ laughing** non è riuscito a trattenersi dal ridere. **2** vi resistere.

re·sist·ance [rɪˈzɪstəns] **1** n (all senses) resistenza; **to offer ~ (to)** opporre resistenza (a); **to take the line of least ~** scegliere la strada più facile. **2** cpd (fighter, movement) della resistenza.

re·sist·ant [rɪˈzɪstənt] adj: **~ (to)** resistente (a).

reso·lute [ˈrezəluːt] adj risoluto(a).

reso·lu·tion [ˌrezəˈluːʃən] n **(a)** (determination) risolutezza; (resolve) fermo proposito; **to make a ~** fare un proposito. **(b)** (of problem, Chem) soluzione f. **(c)** (Pol etc: motion) risoluzione f.

re·solve [rɪˈzɒlv] **1** n (resoluteness) risolutezza; **to make a ~ to do sth** risolversi a fare qc. **2** vt **(a)** (sort out) risolvere. **(b)** (decide): **to ~ to do sth/ that** decidere di fare qc/che; **the committee ~d against appointing him** il comitato ha deliberato contro la sua nomina.

reso·nance [ˈrezənəns] n (see adj) risonanza; sonorità.

reso·nant [ˈrezənənt] adj (sound) risonante; (voice) sonoro(a), risonante.

re·sort [rɪˈzɔːt] **1** n **(a)** (recourse) ricorso; (thing resorted to) risorsa; **without ~ to force** senza ricorrere or far ricorso alla forza; **as a last ~, in the last ~** come ultima risorsa. **(b)** (place) località f inv; **holiday ~** località di villeggiatura; **seaside/winter sports ~** stazione f balneare/di sport invernali. **2** vi: **to ~ to** (violence, treachery) far ricorso a; **to ~ to drink/stealing etc** mettersi or ridursi a bere/rubare etc.

re·sound [rɪˈzaʊnd] vi risonare.

re·sound·ing [rɪˈzaʊndɪŋ] adj (noise) fragoroso(a); (victory, defeat) clamoroso(a).

re·source [rɪˈsɔːs] n risorsa; **as a last ~** come ultima risorsa; **to leave sb to his (or her) own ~s** (fig) lasciare che qn si arrangi (per conto suo); **natural ~s** risorse naturali.

re·source·ful [rɪˈsɔːsfʊl] adj (person) pieno(a) di risorse; (scheme) ingegnoso(a).

re·spect [rɪsˈpekt] **1** n **(a)** (gen) rispetto; **to have or show ~ for** aver rispetto per; **out of ~ for** per rispetto or riguardo a; **with due ~ (for)** con tutto il rispetto (per); **with due ~ I still think you're wrong** con rispetto parlando continuo a pensare che ti sbagli; **to pay one's ~s to sb** (frm) fare i propri ossequi a qn. **(b)** (point, detail): **in some ~s** sotto certi aspetti; **I like the town except in one ~** la città mi piace salvo che per una cosa. **(c)** (reference, regard): **in ~ of** quanto a; **with ~ to** per quanto riguarda. **2** vt rispettare.

re·spect·abil·ity [rɪsˌpektəˈbɪlɪtɪ] n rispettabilità.

re·spect·able [rɪsˈpektəbl] adj **(a)** (decent) rispettabile; **for perfectly ~ reasons** per motivi più che leciti; **in ~ society** nella società bene. **(b)** (quite big: amount etc) considerevole; (quite good: player, result etc) niente male inv.

re·spect·ably [rɪsˈpektəblɪ] adv (dress, behave) perbene; (quite well: perform, sing) (piuttosto) bene.

re·spect·ful [rɪsˈpektfʊl] adj rispettoso(a).

re·spect·ing [rɪsˈpektɪŋ] prep riguardante, concernente.

re·spec·tive [rɪsˈpektɪv] adj rispettivo(a).

res·pi·ra·tion [ˌrespɪˈreɪʃən] n respirazione f.

res·pira·tory [rɪsˈpaɪərətərɪ] adj respiratorio(a).

res·pite [ˈrespaɪt] n tregua; **without ~** senza tregua; **they gave us no ~** non ci hanno dato (un attimo di) pace or respiro.

re·splend·ent [rɪsˈplendənt] adj risplendente.

re·spond [rɪsˈpɒnd] vi rispondere; **to ~ to treatment** (Med) reagire (bene) alla cura.

re·sponse [rɪsˈpɒns] n (answer) risposta; (reaction) reazione f; **in ~ to** in risposta a.

re·spon·sibil·ity [rɪsˌpɒnsəˈbɪlɪtɪ] n responsabilità f inv; **to place the ~ for sth on sb** ritenere qn responsabile di qc; **on one's own ~** di propria iniziativa; **to take ~ for sth/sb** assumersi or prendersi la responsabilità di qc/per qn; **that's his ~** è compito suo.

re·spon·sible [rɪsˈpɒnsəbl] adj responsabile; **to be ~ to sb (for sth)** dover rispondere a qn (di qc); **to be ~ for sth** essere responsabile di qc; **to hold sb ~ for** ritenere qn responsabile di; **it's a ~ job** è un posto di responsabilità.

re·spon·sive [rɪsˈpɒnsɪv] adj (audience, class, pupil) che reagisce bene; (to affection) affettuoso(a); **he has a very ~ nature** è un tipo molto aperto.

rest¹ [rest] **1** n **(a)** (repose) riposo; (pause) pausa; (: in walking etc) sosta; **to come to ~** (object) fermarsi; **to have a good night's ~** farsi una buona or bella dormita; **at ~** (not moving) fermo; (euph: dead) in pace; **to set sb's mind at ~** tranquillizzare qn. **(b)** (Mus) pausa. **(c)** (support) appoggio, supporto.

2 vt **(a)** (far) riposare; **God ~ his soul!** pace all'anima sua!; **to ~ one's eyes** or **gaze on** posare lo sguardo su. **(b)** (support: ladder, bicycle, head) appoggiare.

3 vi **(a)** (repose) riposarsi, riposare; **may he ~ in peace** riposi in pace; **we shall never ~ until it is settled** non avremo pace finché la cosa non sarà sistemata. **(b)** (remain) stare; **it ~s with him to decide** sta a lui decidere; **it doesn't ~ with me** non dipende da me; **~ assured that...** stai tranquillo che...; **let the argument ~ there** lascia le cose come stanno. **(c)**: **to ~ on** (perch) posarsi su; (be supported) poggiare su; (Dir: case) basarsi su; **her head ~ed on my shoulder** il suo capo era appoggiato alla mia spalla; **a heavy responsibility ~s on her** ha una grossa responsabilità sulle spalle.

4 cpd: **~ cure** n cura del riposo; **~ day** n giorno di riposo; **~ home** n casa di riposo; **~ room** n (Am) toilette f inv.

rest² [rest] n (remainder): **the ~** (of money, substance) il resto; (of people, things) gli(le) altri(e); **the ~ of us will see you later** noialtri vi vediamo più tardi.

res·tau·rant [ˈrestərɔ̃ːŋ] **1** n ristorante m. **2** cpd: **~ car** n (Rail) vagone m ristorante inv; **~ owner** n proprietario/a di ristorante.

rest·ful [ˈrestfʊl] adj riposante.

res·ti·tu·tion [ˌrestɪˈtjuːʃən] n restituzione f.

res·tive [ˈrestɪv] adj irrequieto(a), nervoso(a).

rest·less [ˈrestlɪs] adj (gen) irrequieto(a); (crowd etc) inquieto(a); **to get ~** spazientirsi; **I had a ~ night** ho passato una notte agitata; **if you're ~ why not read for a while?** se non riesci a dormire perché non leggi per un po'?

res·to·ra·tion [ˌrestəˈreɪʃən] n (see vb) restauro; restituzione f; ripristino; (History): **the R~** la Restaurazione.

re·store [rɪsˈtɔːʳ] vt **(a)** (repair: building etc) restaurare. **(b)** (give back: gen) restituire; (introduce again: confidence, custom, law and order) ripristinare; **~d to health** ristabilito.

re·stor·er [rɪsˈtɔːrəʳ] n (Art etc) restauratore/trice.

re·strain [rɪsˈtreɪn] vt (gen): **to ~ sb (from doing sth)** trattenere qn (dal fare qc); (dog etc) tenere sotto controllo; **to ~ o.s.** controllarsi, trattenersi.

re·strained [rɪs'treɪnd] *adj (person, style etc)* contenuto(a).

re·straint [rɪs'treɪnt] *n* **(a)** *(check, control)* limitazioni *fpl*, restrizioni *fpl*; **wage** ~ restrizioni salariali. **(b)** *(constraint: of manner)* ritegno, riservatezza; *(self-control)* autocontrollo; **without** ~ senza reticenze, liberamente.

re·strict [rɪs'trɪkt] *vt* limitare.

re·strict·ed [rɪs'trɪktɪd] 1 *adj (gen)* limitato(a); *(by law)* soggetto(a) a restrizioni; **he has rather a** ~ **outlook** *(fig)* ha una visione piuttosto limitata delle cose. 2 *cpd:* ~ **area** *n (Brit Aut)* zona con limitazione di velocità; ~ **zone** *n (Mil)* zona militare.

re·stric·tion [rɪs'trɪkʃən] *n* limitazione *f*, restrizione *f*; **to place** ~s **on sth** imporre delle restrizioni su qc.

re·stric·tive [rɪs'trɪktɪv] *adj* restrittivo(a); ~ **practices** *(Industry)* pratiche restrittive di produzione.

re·sult [rɪ'zʌlt] 1 *n* risultato; **as a** ~ **(of)** in *or* di conseguenza (a), in seguito (a); **as a** ~ **of the strike...** in seguito allo sciopero...; **to get** ~s *(fam: person)* rendere; *(: action)* dare dei risultati. 2 *vi:* **to** ~ **(from)** essere una conseguenza (di), essere causato(a) (da); **to** ~ **in** avere come conseguenza; **if the police leave, disorder will** ~ se la polizia se ne andrà, ne risulteranno dei disordini; **the inquiry** ~**ed in several dismissals** l'inchiesta si è conclusa con diversi licenziamenti.

re·sult·ant [rɪ'zʌltənt] *adj* risultante, conseguente.

re·sume [rɪ'zjuːm] 1 *vt* **(a)** *(start again)* riprendere; **to** ~ **one's seat** rimettersi a sedere. **(b)** *(sum up)* riassumere. 2 *vi (class, meeting)* riprendere.

ré·su·mé ['reɪzjuːmeɪ] *n* riassunto.

re·sump·tion [rɪ'zʌmpʃən] *n* ripresa.

res·ur·rec·tion [ˌrezə'rekʃən] *n (Rel)* risurrezione *f*.

re·sus·ci·tate [rɪ'sʌsɪteɪt] *vt* risuscitare.

re·tail ['riːteɪl] 1 *adj (price, trade)* al dettaglio, al minuto; ~ **outlet** punto di vendita al dettaglio. 2 *adv* al dettaglio, al minuto. 3 *vt (Comm)* vendere al minuto; *(gossip)* riferire. 4 *vi (Comm):* **to** ~ **at** essere in vendita al pubblico al prezzo di.

re·tail·er ['riːteɪlər] *n* dettagliante *m/f*.

re·tain [rɪ'teɪn] *vt (hold)* tenere; *(keep)* conservare; *(remember)* tenere a mente *or* a memoria; *(sign up: lawyer)* impegnare *(pagando una parte dell'onorario in anticipo)*.

re·tain·er [rɪ'teɪnər] *n (fee)* onorario *(versato in anticipo)*.

re·tali·ate [rɪ'tælɪeɪt] *vi:* **to** ~ **(against sb/sth)** vendicarsi *(contro qn/di qc)*.

re·talia·tion [rɪˌtælɪ'eɪʃən] *n* rappresaglie *fpl*; **by way of** ~, **in** ~ per rappresaglia; **in** ~ **for** per vendicarsi di.

re·talia·tory [rɪ'tælɪətərɪ] *adj* di rappresaglia, di ritorsione.

re·tard·ed [rɪ'tɑːdɪd] *adj (Med)* ritardato(a).

retch [retʃ] *vi* avere dei conati di vomito.

re·ten·tive [rɪ'tentɪv] *adj* ritentivo(a).

reti·cence ['retɪsəns] *n* reticenza.

reti·cent ['retɪsənt] *adj* reticente, riservato(a).

reti·na ['retɪnə] *n* retina.

reti·nue ['retɪnjuː] *n* seguito, scorta.

re·tire [rɪ'taɪər] 1 *vt* mandare in pensione. 2 *vi* **(a)** *(withdraw, go to bed, Sport)* ritirarsi. **(b)** *(at age limit)* andare in pensione; *(from business)* ritirarsi.

re·tired [rɪ'taɪəd] *adj* **(a)** *(no longer working)* in pensione, pensionato(a). **(b)** *(quiet, secluded)* ritirato(a), appartato(a).

re·tire·ment [rɪ'taɪəmənt] *n:* **to look forward to**

one's ~ non vedere l'ora di andare in pensione; **on his** ~ **he hopes to...** quando va in pensione spera di...; **early** ~ prepensionamento.

re·tir·ing [rɪ'taɪərɪŋ] *adj* **(a)** *(shy)* riservato(a). **(b)** *(departing: chairman)* uscente; *(age)* pensionabile.

re·tort [rɪ'tɔːt] 1 *n* **(a)** *(answer)* risposta *(per le rime)*. **(b)** *(Chem)* storta. 2 *vt (answer)* ribattere.

re·trace [rɪ'treɪs] *vt* ripercorrere; **to** ~ **one's steps** ritornare sui propri passi.

re·tract [rɪ'trækt] 1 *vt (statement)* ritrattare; *(draw in: claws)* ritrarre; *(: wheels of plane)* far rientrare. 2 *vi (see vt)* ritrattarsi; ritrarsi; rientrare.

re·tread ['riːtred] *n* gomma rigenerata.

re·treat [rɪ'triːt] 1 *n* **(a)** *(place)* rifugio; *(Rel)* ritiro *(spirituale)*; **a country** ~ una tranquilla casa in campagna. **(b)** *(Mil)* ritirata; **to beat a hasty** ~ *(fig)* battersela. 2 *vi (Mil)* ritirarsi, battere in ritirata; *(move back)* ritrarsi.

re·trench [rɪ'trentʃ] 1 *vt* ridurre. 2 *vi* fare delle economie.

re·tri·al ['riː'traɪəl] *n (Law)* nuovo processo.

ret·ri·bu·tion [ˌretrɪ'bjuːʃən] *n* retribuzione *f*.

re·triev·al [rɪ'triːvəl] *n (see vb)* ricupero; riconquista; rimedio; richiamo.

re·trieve [rɪ'triːv] *vt* **(a)** *(get back: object, money)* ricuperare; *(: honour, position)* riconquistare; *(set to rights: error, loss, situation)* rimediare a. **(b)** *(Computers)* richiamare.

re·triev·er [rɪ'triːvər] *n* cane *m* da riporto.

retro·ac·tive [ˌretrəʊ'æktɪv] *adj* retroattivo(a).

retro·grade ['retrəʊgreɪd] *adj* retrogrado(a).

retro·rock·et ['retrəʊ'rɒkɪt] *n* retrorazzo.

retro·spect ['retrəʊspekt] *n:* **in** ~ ripensandoci.

retro·spec·tive [ˌretrəʊ'spektɪv] *adj (gen)* retrospettivo(a); *(pay rise)* retroattivo(a).

re·turn [rɪ'tɜːn] 1 *n* **(a)** *(going, coming back)* ritorno; *(sending back)* rinvio; *(reappearance: of illness etc)* ricomparsa; **on my** ~ al mio ritorno; **by** ~ **of post** a stretto giro di posta; **many happy** ~s **(of the day)!** cento di questi giorni! **(b)** *(of thing borrowed, lost)* restituzione *f*; *(of money)* rimborso; *(Comm: of merchandise)* resa. **(c)** *(Comm: profit)* profitto, guadagno; **to bring in a good** ~ *or* **good** ~s fruttare *or* dare un buon guadagno. **(d)** *(reward):* **in** ~ **(for)** in cambio (di). **(e):** **tax** ~ dichiarazione *f* dei redditi; **census/election** ~s risultati *mpl* del censimento/delle elezioni. **(f)** *(~ ticket)* (biglietto di) andata e ritorno.

2 *vt* **(a)** *(give back)* restituire; *(bring back)* riportare; *(put back)* rimettere; *(send back)* rinviare; *(: buy back)* rispedire; *(Mil: gunfire)* rispondere a; *(favour, love, sb's visit)* ricambiare; '~ **to sender**' 'restituire al mittente'. **(b)** *(Law):* **to** ~ **a verdict of guilty/not guilty** pronunciare un verdetto di colpevolezza/di innocenza. **(c)** *(Pol: elect)* eleggere; ~**ing officer** ≈ presidente *m* del seggio elettorale.

3 *vi (go, come back)* (ri)tornare; *(illness, symptoms etc)* ricomparire; **to** ~ **home** (ri)tornare a casa; **to** ~ **to** *(room, office)* (ri)tornare in; *(school, work)* (ri)tornare a; *(subject, argument)* (ri)tornare su.

4 *cpd (ticket, fare)* di andata e ritorno; ~ **journey** *n* viaggio di ritorno; ~ **match** *n (Sport)* partita di ritorno.

re·turn·able [rɪ'tɜːnəbl] *adj:* ~ **bottle** vuoto a rendere.

re·union [rɪ'juːnjən] *n* riunione *f*.

re·unite ['riːjuː'naɪt] 1 *vt* riunire. 2 *vi* riunirsi.

rev [rev] 1 *n (Aut: abbr of* **revolution***)* giro; **to keep the** ~s **up** tenere il motore su di giri. 2 *vt (engine)* mandare su di giri. 3 *vi (also:* ~ **up:** *car)* andar su di giri, imballarsi; *(: driver)* imballare il motore, tenere il motore su di giri.

Rev. *abbr of* **Reverend.**

re·value ['riː'væljuː] *vt* rivalutare.

re·vamp ['riː'væmp] *vt (methods etc)* modernizzare; *(play etc)* rendere di nuovo attuale.

re·veal [rɪ'viːl] *vt* rivelare; *(uncover: hidden object)* scoprire.

re·veal·ing [rɪ'viːlɪŋ] *adj (remarks, attitude)* rivelatore(trice); *(dress)* scollato(a).

re·veil·le [rɪ'vælɪ] *n (Mil)* sveglia.

rev·el ['rɛvl] *vi* far baldoria; **to ~ in sth/in doing sth** godere di qc/nel fare qc.

rev·ela·tion [,rɛvə'leɪʃən] *n* rivelazione *f*.

rev·el·ry ['rɛvlrɪ] *n* baldoria.

re·venge [rɪ'vɛndʒ] **1** *n* vendetta; **to get one's ~ (for sth)** vendicarsi (di qc); **to take ~ on sb (for sth)** vendicarsi su qn (per qc). **2** *vt* vendicare; **to be ~d (on sb)** vendicarsi (su qn).

rev·enue ['rɛvənjuː] *n* entrate *fpl*, reddito.

re·ver·ber·ate [rɪ'vɜːbəreɪt] *vi* rimbombare; *(fig)* ripercuotersi.

re·ver·bera·tion [rɪ,vɜːbə'reɪʃən] *n (see vb)* rimbombo; ripercussione *f*.

re·vere [rɪ'vɪəʳ] *vt* venerare.

rev·er·ence ['rɛvərəns] **1** *n* venerazione *f*. **2** *vt* venerare.

Rev·er·end ['rɛvərənd] *adj (in titles)* reverendo(a).

rev·er·ent ['rɛvərənt] *adj* reverente.

rev·erie ['rɛvərɪ] *n* fantasticheria, sogno ad occhi aperti.

re·ver·sal [rɪ'vɜːsəl] *n (gen)* inversione *f*; *(turning upside down)* capovolgimento; *(of decision etc)* revoca.

re·verse [rɪ'vɜːs] **1** *adj (order)* inverso(a); *(direction)* opposto(a); *(side)* altro(a); **in ~ order** in ordine inverso; **~ (gear)** *(Aut)* marcia indietro. **2** *n* **(a)** *(opposite)*: **the ~** il contrario, l'opposto. **(b)** *(face: of coin, paper etc)* rovescio. **(c)** *(Aut)* retromarcia, marcia indietro; **to go into ~** fare marcia indietro. **3** *vt (gen, fig)* invertire; *(movement)* invertire la direzione di; *(garment)* mettere alla rovescia; *(Law)* revocare; **to ~ the charges** *(Telec)* fare una telefonata a carico del destinatario; **to ~ one's car** fare marcia indietro. **4** *vi (Aut)* fare marcia indietro; **I ~d into the car behind** facendo retromarcia ho urtato la macchina di dietro.

re·vers·ible [rɪ'vɜːsəbl] *adj (garment)* double-face *inv*; *(procedure)* reversibile.

re·vert [rɪ'vɜːt] *vi (gen)*: **to ~ (to)** ritornare (a); **to ~ to type** *(Bio)* ritornare allo stato primitivo; *(fig)* tornare alla propria natura.

re·view [rɪ'vjuː] **1** *n* **(a)** *(survey, taking stock)* revisione *f*; *(Mil: of troops)* rivista; *(critique)* critica, recensione *f*; **to come under ~** essere preso in esame; **the play got good ~s** lo spettacolo ha ricevuto critiche favorevoli. **(b)** *(journal)* rivista, periodico. **2** *vt (take stock of)* fare una revisione di; *(situation)* fare il punto di; *(Mil: troops)* passare in rivista; *(book, play, film)* fare la recensione di.

re·vile [rɪ'vaɪl] *vt* insultare.

re·vise [rɪ'vaɪz] **1** *vt* **(a)** *(look over: subject, notes)* ripassare. **(b)** *(alter: text, decision, opinion)* rivedere; **~d edition** edizione riveduta. **2** *vi (for exams)* ripassare.

re·vi·sion [rɪ'vɪʒən] *n* **(a)** *(see vb)* ripasso; revisione *f*. **(b)** *(revised version)* versione *f* riveduta e corretta.

re·viv·al [rɪ'vaɪvəl] *n (of person, business, play)* ripresa; *(of custom, usage: bringing back)* ripristino; *(: coming back)* rinascita.

re·vive [rɪ'vaɪv] **1** *vt (person)* rianimare; *(: from faint)* far riprendere i sensi a; *(fig: spirits)* risollevare; *(old customs)* far tornare di moda; *(hopes)* riaccendere; *(suspicions)* risvegliare, ridestare; *(Theatre: play)* riprendere. **2** *vi (person, business, trade)* riprendersi; *(hope, emotions)* riaccendersi, rinascere.

re·voke [rɪ'vəʊk] *vt (law)* abrogare; *(order, decision)* revocare.

re·volt [rɪ'vəʊlt] **1** *n* rivolta; **to be in open ~** essere in aperta rivolta. **2** *vt (far)* rivoltare. **3** *vi* **(a)** *(rebel)*: **to ~ (against sb/sth)** ribellarsi (a qn/qc). **(b)** *(feel disgust)*: **to ~ at** *or* **against** rivoltarsi (a *or* di fronte a).

re·volt·ing [rɪ'vəʊltɪŋ] *adj* rivoltante, ripugnante.

revo·lu·tion [,rɛvə'luːʃən] *n (gen, fig)* rivoluzione *f*; *(of record, engine)* giro.

revo·lu·tion·ary [,rɛvə'luːʃnərɪ] *adj, n* rivoluzionario(a) *(m/f)*.

revo·lu·tion·ize [,rɛvə'luːʃənaɪz] *vt* rivoluzionare.

re·volve [rɪ'vɒlv] **1** *vt (far)* girare. **2** *vi* girare; **to ~ around sth** girare *or* ruotare intorno a qc; **the Earth ~s on its own axis** la Terra ruota intorno al proprio asse; **he thinks everything ~s round him** si crede il centro dell'universo.

re·volv·er [rɪ'vɒlvəʳ] *n* rivoltella.

re·volv·ing [rɪ'vɒlvɪŋ] *adj* girevole.

re·vue [rɪ'vjuː] *n (Theatre)* rivista.

re·vul·sion [rɪ'vʌlʃən] *n* ripugnanza.

re·ward [rɪ'wɔːd] **1** *n* ricompensa, premio; **as a ~ for (doing) sth** in premio *or* come ricompensa per (aver fatto) qc. **2** *vt* premiare, ricompensare.

re·ward·ing [rɪ'wɔːdɪŋ] *adj (activity)* di grande soddisfazione, gratificante; *(book)* che vale la pena di leggere; *(financially)* ~ conveniente dal punto di vista economico.

re·wire ['riː'waɪəʳ] *vt (house)* rifare l'impianto elettrico di.

rhap·so·dy ['ræpsədɪ] *n (Mus)* rapsodia; **to go into a ~ over sth** *(fig)* andare in estasi per qc.

rhe·sus ['riːsəs] **1** *n (also: ~ monkey)* reso. **2** *cpd:* **~ factor** *(Med)* fattore *m* Rh.

rheto·ric ['rɛtərɪk] *n* retorica.

rhe·tori·cal [rɪ'tɒrɪkəl] *adj* retorico(a).

rheu·mat·ic [ruː'mætɪk] *adj* reumatico(a).

rheu·mat·ics [ruː'mætɪks] *n* reumatismi *mpl*.

rheu·ma·tism ['ruːmətɪzəm] *n* reumatismo *m*.

rheu·ma·toid ar·thri·tis ['ruːmətɔɪdɑː'θraɪtɪs] *n* artrite *f* reumatoide.

Rhine [raɪn] *n*: **the ~** il Reno.

rhi·no ['raɪnəʊ] *n abbr of* **rhinoceros.**

rhi·noc·er·os [raɪ'nɒsərəs] *n* rinoceronte *m*.

Rhodes [rəʊdz] *n* Rodi *f*.

rho·do·den·dron [,rəʊdə'dɛndrən] *n* rododendro.

Rhone [rəʊn] *n*: **the R~** il Rodano.

rhu·barb ['ruːbɑːb] **1** *n* rabarbaro. **2** *cpd (jam, pie, tart)* di rabarbaro.

rhyme [raɪm] **1** *n* rima; **without ~ or reason** senza capo né coda. **2** *vi*: **to ~ (with)** fare rima (con).

rhym·ing ['raɪmɪŋ] *adj* rimato(a), in rima.

rhythm ['rɪðəm] *n* ritmo.

rhyth·mic(al) ['rɪðmɪk(əl)] *adj* ritmico(a).

rib [rɪb] **1** *n (Anat)* costola; *(Culin)* costata; *(of umbrella)* stecca; *(of leaf)* nervatura; *(Knitting)* costa. **2** *vt (tease)* punzecchiare.

rib·ald ['rɪbəld] *adj* sguaiato(a).

rib·bon ['rɪbən] **1** *n (gen, of typewriter)* nastro; *(Mil etc)* nastrino; **to tear sth to ~s** ridurre qc a brandelli; *(fig)* demolire qc. **2** *cpd:* **~ development** *n* sviluppo urbano lineare sul bordo delle strade periferiche.

rice [raɪs] **1** *n* riso. **2** *cpd:* **~ pudding** *n* budino di riso.

rich [rɪtʃ] *adj* (**-er**, **-est**) *(gen)* ricco(a); *(food)* so- stanzioso(a); *(colour)* intenso(a); **that's ~**! *(fam iro)* questa sì che è bella!; **the ~** i ricchi; **to be ~ in sth** essere ricco di qc; **to become** *or* **get** *or* **grow ~(er)** arricchirsi, diventar ricco.

riches ['rɪtʃɪz] *npl* ricchezze *fpl.*

rich·ly ['rɪtʃlɪ] *adv* riccamente; *(dressed)* sontuo- samente; *(deserved)* pienamente.

rich·ness ['rɪtʃnɪs] *n* (*see adj*) ricchezza; so- stanziosità; intensità.

rick·ets ['rɪkɪts] *nsg* rachitismo.

rick·ety ['rɪkɪtɪ] *adj* (*furniture*) traballante.

rick·shaw ['rɪkʃɔː] *n* risciò *m inv.*

rico·chet ['rɪkəʃeɪ] **1** *n* rimbalzo. **2** *vi:* **to ~ (off)** rimbalzare (contro).

rid [rɪd] *pt*, *pp* **rid** *or* **ridded** *vt:* **to ~ sb/sth of** sbarazzare qn/qc di, liberare qn/qc da; **to get ~ of sb/sth, ~ o.s. of sb/sth** sbarazzarsi *or* liberarsi di qn/qc.

rid·dance ['rɪdəns] *n:* **good ~**! *(fam)* finalmente fuori dai piedi!

rid·den ['rɪdn] *pp of* **ride.**

rid·dle¹ ['rɪdl] *n* indovinello; **to speak in ~s** parla- re per enigmi.

rid·dle² ['rɪdl] **1** *n* (*sieve*) setaccio, vaglio. **2** *vt* (*soil, coal etc*) setacciare, vagliare; *(fig):* **to ~ with** (*bullets etc*) crivellare di.

ride [raɪd] (*vb: pt* **rode**, *pp* **ridden**) **1** *n* (*on horse*) cavalcata; (*in car, on bike etc*) giro; **to go for a ~** andare a fare una cavalcata; andare a fare un giro; **it was a rough ~** è stato un viaggio scomo- do; **it's a 10-minute ~ on the bus** ci vogliono 10 minuti in autobus; **he gave me a ~ into town** (*in car*) mi ha dato un passaggio in città; **to take sb for a ~** (*in car*) portare qn a fare un giro in macchina; (*fig: make fool of, swindle*) prendere in giro qn.

2 *vt:* **to ~ a horse** andare a cavallo; (*subj: jockey*) montare un cavallo; **to ~ a donkey/camel** cavalcare un asino/cammello; **to ~ a bicycle** andare in bicicletta; **he rode his horse into town** è venuto in città a cavallo; **can you ~ a bike?** sai andare in bicicletta?; **we rode 10 km yesterday** ieri abbiamo fatto 10 km a cavallo (*or* in bici- cletta *etc*); **to ~ a good race** fare un'ottima gara.

3 *vi* (*~ a horse*) andare a cavallo; (*go by car/ bicycle etc*) andare in macchina/in bicicletta *etc*; **to ~ along/through** *etc* passare/attraversare *etc* a cavallo (*or* in macchina *etc*); **can you ~?** (*~ a horse*) sai andare a cavallo?, sai cavalcare?; **he's riding high at the moment** in questo momento è sulla cresta dell'onda; **to ~ at anchor** (*ship*) es- sere all'ancora; **to let things ~** lasciare che le cose seguano il loro corso.

♦ **ride out** *vt + adv* (*Naut: storm*) sostenere; (*fig: difficult period*) superare; **to ~ out the storm** (*fig*) mantenersi a galla.

♦ **ride up** *vi + adv* (*skirt, dress*) salire.

rid·er ['raɪdəʳ] *n* (**a**) (*horse ~*) uomo/donna a caval- lo; (*: skilled*) cavallerizzo/a; (*cyclist*) ciclista *m/f*; (*motorcyclist*) motociclista *m/f.* (**b**) (*addition*) clausola addizionale.

ridge [rɪdʒ] *n* (*of mountain*) cresta; (*of chain of mountains*) crinale *m*; (*of nose*) dorso; (*of roof*) colmo; (*in ploughed field*) porca; (*Met*): **~ of high pressure** fascia di alta pressione.

ridge·pole ['rɪdʒpəʊl] *n* (*on tent*) asta di colmo.

ridi·cule ['rɪdɪkjuːl] **1** *n* ridicolo; **to hold sb/sth up to ~** mettere in ridicolo qn/qc. **2** *vt* mettere in ridicolo.

ri·dicu·lous [rɪ'dɪkjʊləs] *adj* ridicolo(a); **to make o.s. (look) ~** rendersi ridicolo.

ri·dicu·lous·ly [rɪ'dɪkjʊləslɪ] *adv* (*stupidly*) in modo

ridicolo; (*disproportionately*) incredibilmente; **a ~ large/small amount** una quantità assurda/ irrisoria.

rid·ing ['raɪdɪŋ] **1** *n* (*horse-~*) equitazione *f*. **2** *cpd:* **~ breeches** *npl* pantaloni *mpl* da cavallerizzo; **~ crop** *or* **whip** *n* frustino; **~ school** *n* scuola di equitazione.

rife [raɪf] *adj:* **to be ~** dilagare, imperversare.

riff·raff ['rɪfræf] *n* gentaglia.

ri·fle¹ ['raɪfl] *vt* (*house, till etc*) ripulire, svuotare.

♦ **rifle through** *vi + prep* frugare.

ri·fle² ['raɪfl] **1** *n* fucile *m*, carabina. **2** *cpd:* **~ range** *n* (*Mil*) poligono di tiro; (*at fair*) tiro a segno.

rift [rɪft] *n* (*gen*) spaccatura; (*in clouds*) squarcio; (*Pol: in party*) dissensi *mpl.*

rig [rɪg] **1** *n* (*oil ~*) impianto di trivellazione (per il petrolio); (*: offshore*) piattaforma di trivellazio- ne. **2** *vt* (*election, competition*) truccare; (*prices*) manipolare.

♦ **rig out** *vt + adv:* **to ~ out (as/in)** vestire (da/di).

♦ **rig up** *vt + adv* mettere in piedi; (*fig: arrange*) organizzare.

rig·ging ['rɪgɪŋ] *n* (*Naut*) attrezzatura.

right [raɪt] **1** *adj* (**a**) (*morally good*) retto(a), one- sto(a); (*just*) giusto(a); **it's not ~ to steal** non è buona cosa rubare; **it's not ~**! non è giusto!; **it is only ~ that…** è più che giusto che…; **to do what is ~** fare ciò che si crede giusto; **I thought it ~ to warn him** mi è sembrato giusto avvertirlo.

(**b**) (*suitable: person, clothes, time*) adatto(a); **to choose the ~ moment for sth/to do sth** sce- gliere il momento giusto *or* adatto per qc/per fare qc; **that's the ~ attitude!** così va bene!, questo è l'atteggiamento giusto!; **to say the ~ thing** dire la cosa giusta; **you did the ~ thing** hai fatto bene; **what's the ~ thing to do?** qual'è la cosa migliore da farsi?; **to know the ~ people** conoscere la gente giusta.

(**c**) (*correct: answer, solution etc*) giusto(a), esatto(a), corretto(a); (*: size*) giusto(a); **~ first time!** hai azzeccato al primo colpo!; **to get sth ~** far giusto qc; **I got every question ~** ho risposto giusto a tutte le domande; **let's get it ~ this time!** cerchiamo di farlo bene stavolta!; **to get one's facts ~** sapere di che cosa si parla; **(yes,) that's ~** sì, esatto; **the ~ road** la strada buona; **the ~ time** l'ora esatta; **to get on the ~ side of sb** (*fig*) entrare nelle grazie di qn; **to put a clock ~** rimettere (all'ora esatta) un orologio; **to put a mistake ~** correggere un errore; **~ you are!**, **~-oh!** (*fam*) va bene!, d'accordo!

(**d**): **to be ~** (*person*) aver ragione; **you're quite ~**, (*fam*) **you're dead ~** hai proprio *or* per- fettamente ragione; **you were ~ to come to me** hai fatto bene a venire da me.

(**e**) (*well, in order*): **to be/feel as ~ as rain** essere/sentirsi completamente ristabilito; **he is not quite ~ in the head** *or* **in the mind** gli manca una rotella; **I don't feel quite ~** non mi sento del tutto a posto; **all's ~ with the world** tutto va bene; **the stereo still isn't ~** lo stereo ha ancora qualcosa che non va.

(**f**) (*not left*) destro(a); **I'd give my ~ arm to know…** darei un occhio per sapere… .

(**g**) (*Math: angle*) retto(a); **at ~ angles (to)** ad angolo retto (con).

(**h**) (*fam: intensive*): **a ~ idiot** un perfetto idiota.

2 *adv* (**a**) (*directly, exactly*): **~ now** in questo momento, proprio adesso; (*immediately*) subito; **~ away** subito; **~ off** subito; (*at the first attempt*) al primo colpo; **~ here** proprio qui; **he (just) went ~ on talking** ha continuato a parlare lo stesso; ~ **behind/in front of** proprio dietro/ davanti a; ~ **before/after** subito prima/dopo; ~ **in the middle** proprio nel bel mezzo; *(of target)* in pieno centro; ~ **round sth** tutt'intorno a qc; ~ **at the end** proprio alla fine.

(b) *(completely)* completamente; **to go ~ back to the beginning of sth** ricominciare qc da capo; **to go ~ to the end of sth** andare fino in fondo a qc; **to push sth ~ in** spingere qc fino in fondo; **to read a book ~ through** leggere un libro dall'inizio alla fine.

(c) *(correctly)* giusto, bene; *(well)* bene; **if I remember ~** se mi ricordo bene; **if everything goes ~** se tutto va bene.

(d) *(properly, fairly)* giustamente, con giustizia; **to treat sb ~** trattare qn in modo giusto; **you did ~ not to go** hai fatto bene a non andarci.

(e) *(not left)* a destra; ~, **left and centre** *(fig)* da tutte le parti.

(f): ~, **who's next?** bene, chi è il prossimo?; ~ **then, let's begin!** (va) bene allora, cominciamo!

(g): all ~! va bene!, d'accordo!; *(that's enough)* va bene!; **it's all ~** *(don't worry)* va (tutto) bene; **it's all ~ for you!** già, per te va benissimo!; **is it all ~ for me to go at 4?** va bene se esco alle 4?; **I'm/I feel all ~ now** adesso sto/mi sento bene.

3 *n* **(a):** ~ **and wrong** il bene e il male; **to be in the ~** aver ragione, essere nel giusto; **to know ~ from wrong** distinguere il bene dal male; **I want to know the ~s and wrongs of it** voglio sapere chi ha ragione e chi ha torto; **two wrongs don't make a ~** la miglior vendetta è il perdono.

(b) *(claim, authority)* diritto; **film ~s** diritti di riproduzione cinematografica; **to have a ~ to sth** aver diritto a qc; **you have a ~ to your own opinions** è tuo diritto pensarla come vuoi; **the ~ to be/say/do sth** il diritto di essere/dire/fare qc; **what ~ have you got to...?** che diritto hai di...?; **by ~s** di diritto; **to be within one's ~s** avere tutti i diritti; **to own sth in one's own ~** possedere qc per conto proprio; **she's a good actress in her own ~** è una brava attrice anche per conto suo; ~ **of way** *(across property)* diritto di accesso; *(Aut etc: precedence)* precedenza.

(c) *(not left)* destra; *(Pol):* **the R~** la destra; *(Boxing: punch)* destro; **to the ~ (of)** sul lato destro (di), a destra (di); **on the ~ (of)** a destra (di), sulla destra (di).

(d): to set *or* **put to ~s** mettere a posto.

4 *vt (correct: mistake)* correggere; *(: wrong, injustice)* riparare a; *(vehicle)* raddrizzare; **to ~ itself** *(vehicle)* raddrizzarsi; *(situation)* risolversi da solo *or* da sé.

5 *cpd:* ~ **wing** *n* (Pol) destra; *(Sport: position, person)* ala destra.

right-angled ['raɪt,æŋgld] *adj* ad angolo retto; *(triangle)* rettangolo(a).

right-eous ['raɪtʃəs] *adj (person)* virtuoso(a); *(indignation etc)* giustificato(a).

right-ful ['raɪtful] *adj* legittimo(a).

right-hand ['raɪthænd] *adj (side)* destro(a); ~ **drive** *(Aut)* guida a destra; ~ **man** *(fig: personal aide)* braccio destro.

right-handed [,raɪt'hændɪd] *adj (person)* che usa la mano destra.

right-ly ['raɪtlɪ] *adv* giustamente; **I don't ~ know** non so di preciso; **if I remember ~** se mi ricordo bene; ~ **or wrongly** a torto o a ragione.

right-minded [,raɪt'maɪndɪd] *adj* di buon senso, sensato(a).

right-wing [,raɪt'wɪŋ] *adj* (Pol) di destra.

right-winger [,raɪt'wɪŋəʳ] *n* (Pol) uno/a di destra; *(Sport)* ala destra.

rig-id ['rɪdʒɪd] *adj (material)* rigido(a); *(discipline, specifications)* rigoroso(a); *(rules)* severo(a); *(person, ideas)* inflessibile; ~ **with fear** impietrito dalla paura.

rig-id-ly ['rɪdʒɪdlɪ] *adv (strictly)* rigorosamente; *(inflexibly)* inflessibilmente; **to stand ~ to attention** stare impalato sull'attenti.

rig-ma-role ['rɪgmərəʊl] *n (pej: speech)* storia; *(: complicated procedure)* trafila.

rig-or-ous ['rɪgərəs] *adj (discipline)* rigoroso(a); *(hardships)* grave; *(study)* intenso(a).

rig-our, *(Am)* **rig-or** ['rɪgəʳ] *n* rigore *m*.

rim [rɪm] *n (of cup etc)* orlo; *(of wheel)* cerchione *m*; *(of spectacles)* montatura.

rim-less ['rɪmlɪs] *adj (spectacles)* non cerchiati.

rind [raɪnd] *n (of fruit)* buccia; *(of lemon etc)* scorza; *(of cheese)* crosta; *(of bacon)* cotenna.

ring¹ [rɪŋ] **1** *n* **(a)** *(gen)* anello; *(for napkin)* portatovagliolo; **wedding ~** fede *f;* **to run ~s round sb** *(fig)* surclassare qn. **(b)** *(of people)* cerchio; *(gang)* cricca, banda; *(of spies)* rete *f;* **they were sitting in a ~** erano seduti in circolo *or* in cerchio. **(c)** *(arena etc: Boxing)* ring *m inv,* quadrato; *(: at circus)* pista. **2** *vt (surround)* circondare, accerchiare; *(mark with ring)* fare un circoletto intorno a. **3** *cpd:* ~ **binder** *n* classificatore *m* a anelli; ~ **finger** *n* anulare *m;* ~ **road** *n* circonvallazione *f.*

ring² [rɪŋ] *(vb: pt* **rang,** *pp* **rung)** **1** *n* **(a)** *(of bell)* scampanellata; *(of telephone)* squillo; *(tone of voice)* tono; **that has the ~ of truth about it** questo ha l'aria d'essere vero. **(b)** *(Brit Telec):* **to give sb a ~** dare un colpo di telefono a qn.

2 *vt* **(a)** *(bell, doorbell)* suonare; **to ~ the changes** *(fig)* variare; **the name doesn't ~ a bell (with me)** questo nome non mi dice niente. **(b)** *(Brit Telec):* **to ~ sb (up)** telefonare a qn, dare un colpo di telefono a qn.

3 *vi* **(a)** *(bell, telephone etc)* suonare; **to ~ for sb/sth** (suonare il campanello per) chiamare qn/ chiedere qc. **(b)** *(telephone)* telefonare. **(c)** *(words, voice)* risuonare; *(blast)* rimbombare; *(ears)* fischiare; **their laughter rang through the room** le loro risate risuonavano nella stanza; **my ears are still ~ing from the blast** mi fischiano ancora le orecchie per via dell'esplosione; **to ~ true/false** *(fig)* suonare vero/falso.

♦ **ring back** *vt + adv (Brit Telec)* richiamare.

♦ **ring off** *vi + adv (Brit Telec)* mettere giù, riattaccare.

♦ **ring out** *vi + adv* suonare, riecheggiare.

♦ **ring up** *vt + adv* = **ring 2b.**

ring·ing ['rɪŋɪŋ] **1** *adj (voice, tone)* sonoro(a); *(Telec):* ~ **tone** segnale *m* di libero. **2** *n (of bell)* scampanio; *(: louder)* scampanellata; *(of telephone)* squillo; *(in ears)* fischio, ronzio.

ring-leader ['rɪŋ,li:dəʳ] *n* capobanda *m.*

ring-let ['rɪŋlɪt] *n* boccolo.

ring-master ['rɪŋ,mɑ:stəʳ] *n* direttore *m* del circo.

rink [rɪŋk] *n (for ice-skating)* pista di pattinaggio (su ghiaccio); *(for roller-skating)* pista di pattinaggio (a rotelle).

rinse [rɪns] **1** *n* (ri)sciacquatura, (ri)sciacquata; *(hair-colouring)* cachet *m inv.* **2** *vt* (ri)sciacquare.

♦ **rinse out** *vt + adv* sciacquare; **to ~ out one's mouth** sciacquarsi la bocca.

riot ['raɪət] **1** *n* disordini *mpl;* **a ~ of colour** un'orgia di colori; **to put down a ~** sopprimere i disordini; **to read sb the riot act** *(fam)* dare una lavata di capo a qn; **to run ~** *(out of control)* scatenarsi. **2** *vi* tumultuare, manifestare violentemente. **3** *cpd:* ~ **police** *n* ≈ la Celere.

ri·ot·er ['raɪətə'] *n* dimostrante *m/f (durante dei disordini)*.

ri·ot·ous ['raɪətəs] *adj (person, mob, party)* scatenato(a); *(living)* sfrenato(a); *(very funny)* divertente da pazzi.

ri·ot·ous·ly ['raɪətəslɪ] *adv* sfrenatamente; ~ **funny** divertente da pazzi.

rip [rɪp] **1** *n* strappo. **2** *vt* strappare; **to** ~ **sth to pieces** stracciare in mille pezzi qc; **to** ~ **open** strappare (per aprire). **3** *vi* strapparsi; **to let** ~ *(fig)* scatenarsi; **to let** ~ **at sb** dirne di tutti di colori a qn.
♦ **rip off** *vt + adv* **(a)** strappare. **(b)** *(fam: overcharge)* pelare; *(: cheat)* fregare.
♦ **rip up** *vt + adv* stracciare.
rip·cord ['rɪpkɔːd] *n (Aer)* cavo di spiegamento.
ripe [raɪp] *adj (gen)* maturo(a); *(cheese)* stagionato(a); **to be** ~ **for sth** *(fig)* essere pronto per qc; **to live to a** ~ **old age** vivere fino a una bella età.
rip·en ['raɪpən] **1** *vt* maturare. **2** *vi* maturarsi.
rip-off ['rɪpɒf] *n (fam)*: **it's a** ~! è un furto!
ri·poste [rɪ'pɒst] *n* risposta per le rime.
rip·ple ['rɪpl] **1** *n (small wave)* increspatura; *(noise: of voices)* mormorio; *(: of laughter)* fremito. **2** *vt* incrspare. **3** *vi* incresparsi.
rip-roaring ['rɪp'rɔːrɪŋ] *adj (party, success)* travolgente.
rise [raɪz] *(vb: pt* **rose,** *pp* **risen** [rɪzn]) **1** *n* **(a)** *(of sun)* sorgere *m; (of theatre curtain)* alzarsi *m; (fig: ascendancy)* ascesa; ~ **to power** ascesa al potere; **to take a** ~ **out of sb** *(fam)* stuzzicare qn.
(b) *(increase: in prices, wages etc)*: ~ **(in)** aumento (di).
(c) *(upward slope)* salita; *(small hill)* altura.
(d) *(origin: of river)* sorgente *f;* **to give** ~ **to** *(fig)* sollevare, far nascere.
2 *vi* **(a)** *(get up)* alzarsi; *(fig: building)* sorgere; **to** ~ **to one's feet** alzarsi in piedi; **the House rose** *(Parliament)* la seduta della Camera è stata tolta; **to** ~ **to the occasion** dimostrarsi all'altezza della situazione.
(b) *(go higher: sun)* sorgere; *(: smoke)* alzarsi, levarsi; *(: dough, cake etc)* crescere (di volume), lievitare; *(: ground)* salire; *(fig: spirits)* sollevarsi; **the plane rose to 4000 metres** l'aereo si è alzato a 4000 metri; **to** ~ **from the ranks** *(Mil)* venir su dalla gavetta; **to** ~ **from nothing** venir su dal niente; **he rose to be President** ascese alla carica di Presidente; **to** ~ **to the surface** *(also fig)* venire a galla, affiorare; **to** ~ **above sth** *(fig)* essere al di sopra di qc; **to** ~ **to a higher sum** offrire di più, fare un'offerta più alta.
(c) *(increase: prices)* aumentare, rincarare; *(temperature, shares, numbers)* salire; *(wind, sea)* alzarsi; **his voice rose in anger** alzò la voce per la rabbia.
(d) *(river)* nascere.
♦ **rise up** *vi + adv (rebel)* sollevarsi.
ris·er ['raɪzə'] *n*: **to be an early/late** ~ alzarsi sempre presto/tardi.
ris·ing ['raɪzɪŋ] **1** *adj* **(a)** *(increasing: number)* sempre crescente; *(: prices)* in aumento; *(: tide)* montante; *(: anger, alarm, doubt etc)* crescente. **(b)** *(getting higher: sun, moon)* nascente, che sorge; *(: ground)* in salita; *(fig: promising)* promettente. **2** *n (uprising)* sommossa. **3** *cpd*: ~ **damp** *n* infiltrazioni *fpl* d'umidità.
risk [rɪsk] **1** *n* rischio; **fire/health/security** ~ rischio d'incendio/per la salute/per la sicurezza; **there's not much** ~ **of rain** non c'è pericolo che piova; **to take a** ~ rischiare, correre un rischio; **to run the** ~ **of sth** correre il rischio di qc; **it's not**

worth the ~ non vale la pena di correre il rischio; **at** ~ in pericolo; **to put sth at** ~ mettere a repentaglio qc; **he put his job at** ~ ha rischiato di giocarsi il posto; **at one's own** ~ a proprio rischio e pericolo; **at the** ~ **of seeming stupid** a costo di sembrare stupido.
2 *vt (life, health, money)* rischiare, arrischiare; *(criticism, anger, defeat)* rischiare; **I'll** ~ **it** ci proverò lo stesso; **to** ~ **losing/being caught** *etc* rischiare di perdere/di esser preso *etc;* **to** ~ **one's neck** rischiare la pelle.
risky ['rɪskɪ] *adj* (**-ier, -iest**) rischioso(a).
ris·qué ['riːskeɪ] *adj* audace, spinto(a).
ris·sole ['rɪsəʊl] *n (Culin)* polpetta.
rite [raɪt] *n* rito; *(Rel)*: **last** ~**s** l'estrema unzione.
ritu·al ['rɪtjʊəl] *adj, n* rituale *(m)*.
ri·val ['raɪvəl] **1** *adj (team)* rivale; *(firm)* concorrente; *(claim, attraction)* in concorrenza. **2** *n (see adj)* rivale *m/f;* concorrente *m/f.* **3** *vt* rivaleggiare con.
ri·val·ry ['raɪvəlrɪ] *n* rivalità.
riv·er ['rɪvə'] *n* fiume *m;* **up/down** ~ a monte/valle; **the R**~ **Thames** il Tamigi.
river·bank ['rɪvəbæŋk] *n* sponda (del fiume).
river·bed ['rɪvəbed] *n* letto del fiume.
river·side ['rɪvəsaɪd] *n* riva (del fiume); **by the** ~ in riva al fiume; **along the** ~ lungo il fiume.
riv·et ['rɪvɪt] **1** *n* ribattino, rivetto. **2** *vt* rivettare.
riv·et·ing ['rɪvɪtɪŋ] *adj (fig)* avvincente.
Rivi·era [‚rɪvɪ'eərə] *n*: **the Italian** ~ la Riviera; **the French** ~ la Costa Azzurra.
RN *abbr of* **Royal Navy**.
road [rəʊd] **1** *n (route, fig)* strada, via; *(residential* R~) via; **main** ~ strada principale; **'A'-/'B'-**~ ≈ strada statale/secondaria; **country** ~ strada di campagna; **it takes 4 hours by** ~ sono 4 ore di macchina *(or* in camion); **just across the** ~ **(from)** proprio di fronte (a); **to be off the** ~ *(car: for repairs)* essere in riparazione; *(: laid up)* essere fuori uso; **he shouldn't be allowed on the** ~ dovrebbero togliergli la patente; **that car shouldn't be allowed on the** ~ non dovrebbero lasciar circolare quella macchina; **to hold the** ~ *(Aut)* tenere la strada; **'**~ **up'** 'attenzione: lavori in corso'; **to be on the** ~ *(pop group etc)* essere in tournée; *(salesman)* viaggiare; **on the** ~ **to success** sulla via del successo; **to take to the** ~ *(tramp)* darsi al vagabondaggio; **to have one for the** ~ *(fam)* bere il bicchiere della staffa; **somewhere along the** ~ *(fig)* a un certo punto.
2 *cpd (accident, sign)* stradale; ~ **haulage** *or* **transport** *n* autotrasporti *mpl;* ~ **safety** *n* sicurezza sulle strade; ~ **works** *npl* lavori *mpl* stradali.
road·block ['rəʊdblɒk] *n* blocco stradale.
road·hog ['rəʊdhɒg] *n* pirata *m* della strada.
road·map ['rəʊdmæp] *n* carta stradale, carta automobilistica.
road·roller ['rəʊd‚rəʊlə'] *n* rullo compressore.
road·side ['rəʊdsaɪd] *n* ciglio della strada; **by the** ~ a lato della strada.
road·sweeper ['rəʊd‚swiːpə'] *n (person)* spazzino; *(vehicle)* autospazzatrice *f.*
road·way ['rəʊdweɪ] *n* carreggiata.
road·worthy ['rəʊd‚wɜːðɪ] *adj* (meccanicamente) in ordine.
roam [rəʊm] **1** *vt (streets etc)* vagabondare per, gironzolare per. **2** *vi (person)* vagabondare, gironzolare; *(thoughts)* vagare.
roar [rɔː'] **1** *n (of lion)* ruggito; *(of bull)* mugghio; *(of crowd)* urlo; *(of waves)* fragore *m;* **with great** ~**s of laughter** con fragorose risate. **2** *vi (lion)* ruggire; *(bull)* mugghiare; *(crowd, audience)* urlare; *(thunder)* rimbombare; *(guns)* tuonare; **to** ~ **with**

laughter ridere fragorosamente; **the lorry ~ed past** il camion passò rombando.
roar·ing ['rɔ:rɪŋ] *adj (lion)* ruggente; *(bull)* mugghiante; *(crowd)* urlante; *(sea, thunder)* fragoroso(a); **a ~ fire** un bel fuoco, una bella fiammata; **a ~ success** un successo strepitoso; **to do a ~ trade** fare affari d'oro.
roast [rəʊst] **1** *n* arrosto. **2** *adj* arrosto *inv.* **3** *vt (meat)* arrostire; *(coffee)* tostare, torrefare. **4** *vi* arrostire; **I'm ~ing!** *(fam)* sto crepando dal caldo!
rob [rɒb] *vt (gen)* derubare; *(with weapon)* rapinare; *(till, bank)* svaligiare; **to ~ sb of sth** *(money etc)* derubare qn di qc; *(fig: happiness etc)* privare qn di qc.
rob·ber ['rɒbəʳ] *n* ladro; *(armed)* rapinatore *m.*
rob·bery ['rɒbərɪ] *n* furto; *(armed ~)* rapina; **it's daylight ~!** *(fam)* (ma) è una rapina!
robe [rəʊb] *n (garment)* tunica; *(bath~)* accappatoio; *(also: ~s)* abiti *mpl* da cerimonia; *(lawyer's, Univ)* toga.
rob·in ['rɒbɪn] *n* pettirosso.
ro·bot ['rəʊbɒt] *n* robot *m inv,* automa *m.*
ro·bust [rəʊ'bʌst] *adj* robusto(a).
rock [rɒk] **1** *n* **(a)** *(gen)* roccia; *(large stone, boulder)* roccia, masso; *(in sea)* scoglio; **on the ~s** *(ship)* sugli scogli; *(drink)* con ghiaccio; **their marriage is on the ~s** il loro matrimonio sta naufragando. **(b):** **stick of ~** *(sweet)* bastoncino di zucchero candito. **(c)** *(Mus)* rock *m.* **2** *vt (gently: cradle, boat)* far dondolare; *(: baby)* cullare; *(violently: boat)* sballottare; *(subj: earthquake)* squassare; *(fig: shake, startle)* sconvolgere; **to ~ the boat** *(fig fam)* piantare grane. **3** *vi (gently)* dondolare; *(violently)* oscillare. **4** *cpd:* **~ climber** *n* rocciatore/ trice, scalatore/trice; **~ climbing** *n (Sport)* roccia; **~ face** *n* parete *f* di roccia; **~ plant** *n* pianta rupestre; **~ salt** *n* salgemma *m.*
rock-bottom ['rɒk'bɒtəm] *n (fig):* **to reach** *or* **touch ~** *(price)* raggiungere il livello più basso; *(person)* toccare il fondo.
rock·er ['rɒkəʳ] *n (chair)* sedia a dondolo; **to be off one's ~** *(fam)* essere pazzo.
rock·ery ['rɒkərɪ] *n* rocciato.
rock·et ['rɒkɪt] **1** *n* razzo; **to give sb a ~** *(fig fam)* fare un cicchetto a qn. **2** *vi (prices)* salire alle stelle. **3** *cpd:* **~ launcher** *n* lanciarazzi *m inv.*
rock·ing chair ['rɒkɪŋ,tʃɛəʳ] *n* sedia a dondolo.
rock·ing horse ['rɒkɪŋ,hɔ:s] *n* cavallo a dondolo.
rocky¹ ['rɒkɪ] *adj (-ier, -iest)* roccioso(a); **the R~ Mountains** le Montagne Rocciose.
rocky² ['rɒkɪ] *adj (-ier, -iest) (shaky, unsteady)* malfermo(a), traballante; *(fig: situation)* instabile; *(: government etc)* vacillante.
ro·co·co [rəʊ'kəʊkəʊ] *adj, n* rococò *(m) inv.*
rod [rɒd] *n (wooden, plastic)* bacchetta; *(metallic, Tech)* asta, sbarra; *(fishing ~)* canna da pesca; *(curtain ~)* bastone *m;* **to rule with a ~ of iron** comandare a bacchetta.
rode [rəʊd] *pt of* **ride.**
ro·dent ['rəʊdənt] *n* roditore *m.*
ro·deo ['rəʊdɪəʊ] *n* rodeo.
roe [rəʊ] *n (of fish):* **hard ~** uova *fpl* di pesce; **soft ~** latte *m* di pesce.
roe·buck ['rəʊbʌk] *n* capriolo maschio.
roe deer ['rəʊ,dɪəʳ] *n (species)* capriolo; *(female deer: pl inv)* capriolo femmina.
rogue [rəʊg] **1** *n* mascalzone *m;* **~s' gallery** foto *fpl* di pregiudicati. **2** *cpd (elephant)* solitario(a).
ro·guish ['rəʊgɪʃ] *adj (look, smile etc)* malizioso(a); *(child)* birichino(a).
role [rəʊl] *n* ruolo.
roll [rəʊl] **1** *n* **(a)** *(gen)* rotolo; *(of film)* rotolino,

rullino; *(of cloth)* pezza, rotolo; *(of fat, flesh)* cuscinetto. **(b)** *(of bread)* panino; **cheese ~** panino al formaggio. **(c)** *(list)* lista; **to have 500 pupils on the ~** avere 500 iscritti (alla scuola). **(d)** *(sound: of thunder)* brontolio; *(of drums)* rullio. **(e)** *(movement: of ship, plane)* rollio.
2 *vt (ball)* far rotolare; *(road, lawn, pitch)* cilindrare, rullare; *(pastry)* spianare; *(metal)* laminare; **to ~ a cigarette** farsi una sigaretta; **~ the meatballs in breadcrumbs** passare le polpette nel pangrattato; **to ~ one's eyes** roteare gli occhi; **to ~ one's r's** pronunciare bene la erre; **~ed gold** *(n)* oro laminato; *(adj)* laminato oro.
3 *vi* **(a)** *(gen)* rotolare; *(dog, horse)* rotolarsi; *(in pain)* contorcersi; **it ~ed under the chair** è rotolato sotto la seggiola; **tears ~ed down her cheeks** le lacrime le scendevano sulle guance; **they're ~ing in money, they're ~ing in it** *(fam)* sono pieni di soldi. **(b)** *(sound: thunder)* brontolare; *(: drum)* rullare. **(c)** *(ship)* rollare.
4 *cpd:* **~ call** *n* appello.
♦ **roll about** *vi + adv (ball, coin etc)* rotolare qua e là; *(person, dog)* rotolarsi; *(: in pain)* contorcersi.
♦ **roll away** *vi + adv (ball)* rotolare (via); *(clouds, vehicle)* allontanarsi.
♦ **roll back** *vt + adv* arrotolare, togliere arrotolando.
♦ **roll by** *vi + adv (vehicle, years)* passare.
♦ **roll in** *vi + adv (money, letters)* continuare ad arrivare; *(fam: person)* arrivare.
♦ **roll on** *vi + adv (time)* passare; **~ on the holidays!** speriamo che vengano presto le vacanze!
♦ **roll out** *vt + adv (pastry)* spianare; *(carpet, map)* srotolare, spiegare.
♦ **roll over** *vi + adv (object)* rotolare; *(person, animal)* (ri)girarsi, (ri)voltarsi.
♦ **roll up 1** *vi + adv* **(a)** *(animal):* **to ~ up into a ball** appallottolarsi. **(b)** *(arrive)* arrivare; **~ up!** venite, venite! **2** *vt + adv (cloth, map)* arrotolare; *(sleeves)* rimboccare; **to ~ o.s. up into a ball** raggomitolarsi.
roll·er ['rəʊləʳ] **1** *n* **(a)** *(gen)* rullo, cilindro; *(in metallurgy)* laminatoio; *(road~)* rullo compressore; *(castor)* rotella; *(for hair)* bigodino. **(b)** *(wave)* cavallone *m.* **2** *cpd:* **~ blind** *n (Brit)* avvolgibile *m;* **~ coaster** *n* montagne *fpl* russe; **~ skate** *n* pattino a rotelle; **~ skating** *n* pattinaggio a rotelle.
roll·ing ['rəʊlɪŋ] **1** *adj (waves, sea)* ondeggiante; *(countryside)* ondulato(a). **2** *cpd:* **~ mill** *n* fabbrica di laminati; **~ pin** *n* matterello; **~ stock** *n* materiale *m* rotabile.
Ro·man ['rəʊmən] **1** *adj* romano(a); **~ numerals** numeri romani. **2** *n (person)* Romano/a; *(Typ):* **r~** *(carattere m)* romano. **3** *cpd:* **~ Catholic** *adj, n* cattolico(a) *(m/f).*
ro·mance [rəʊ'mæns] **1** *n* **(a)** *(love affair)* storia d'amore. **(b)** *(romantic character)* fascino, romanticismo. **(c)** *(love story)* romanzo *m* rosa *inv;* *(film)* film *m inv* d'amore; *(medieval)* romanzo *(cavalleresco);* *(Mus)* romanza. **2** *adj (language):* **R~** romanzo/a.
Ro·man·esque [,rəʊmə'nɛsk] *adj (Archit)* romanico(a).
ro·man·tic [rəʊ'mæntɪk] *adj, n* romantico(a) *(m/f).*
ro·man·ti·cism [rəʊ'mæntɪsɪzəm] *n* romanticismo.
ro·man·ti·cize [rəʊ'mæntɪsaɪz] *vt* romanzare, romanticizzare.
Roma·ny ['rɒmənɪ] **1** *adj* zingaresco(a). **2** *n (person)* zingaro/a; *(language)* lingua degli zingari.
Rome [rəʊm] *n* Roma *f;* **when in ~ (do as the Romans do)** paese che vai usanze che trovi.
romp [rɒmp] **1** *n* gioco chiassoso. **2** *vi (children,*

puppies) giocare chiassosamente; **she ~ed through the examination** *(fig)* ha passato l'esame a occhi chiusi; **to ~ home** *(horse)* vincere senza difficoltà, stravincere.

romp·ers ['rɒmpəz] *npl* tutina, pagliaccetto.

roof [ru:f] **1** *n* tetto; **~ of the mouth** palato; **to have a ~ over one's head** avere un tetto sopra la testa. **2** *vt (also:* **~ in, ~ over)** mettere *or* fare il tetto a. **3** *cpd:* **~ rack** *n (Aut)* portapacchi *m inv.*

rook[1] [rʊk] **1** *n (bird)* corvo (comune). **2** *vt (fam: swindle)* imbrogliare.

rook[2] [rʊk] *n (Chess)* torre *f.*

rookie ['rʊkɪ] *n (Mil fam)* burba.

room [rʊm] **1** *n* **(a)** *(in house)* stanza, locale *m; (bed~, in hotel)* camera; *(large, public)* sala; **a 5-~ed house** una casa di 5 locali; **they've always lived in ~s** hanno sempre abitato in camere ammobiliate. **(b)** *(space)* spazio, posto; **is there ~ for this?** c'è spazio per questo?, ci sta anche questo?; **is there ~ for me?** c'è posto per me?, ci sto anch'io?; **to make ~ for sb** far posto a qn; **standing ~ only** solo posti in piedi; **there is no ~ for doubt** non c'è nessuna possibilità di dubbio; **there is ~ for improvement** si potrebbe migliorare. **2** *cpd:* **~ service** *n* servizio in camera; **~ temperature** *n* temperatura ambiente.

rooming-house ['rʊmɪŋ͵haʊs] *n (Am)* casa con camere ammobiliate.

room·mate ['rʊm͵meɪt] *n* compagno/a di camera.

roomy ['rʊmɪ] *adj* **(-ier, -iest)** *(flat, cupboard etc)* spazioso(a); *(garment)* ampio(a).

roost [ru:st] **1** *n* posatoio; **to rule the ~** dettar legge. **2** *vi* appollaiarsi; **it will all come home to ~!** chi la fa l'aspetti!

roost·er ['ru:stə'] *n* gallo.

root [ru:t] **1** *n (gen, Math)* radice *f;* **to pull up by the ~s** sradicare; **to take ~** *(plant)* attecchire, prendere; *(idea)* far presa; **the ~ of the problem is that…** il problema deriva dal fatto che…; **to put down ~s in a country** mettere radici in un paese. **2** *vt (plant)* far fare le radici a, far radicare; **to be ~ed to the spot** *(fig)* rimanere inchiodato sul posto. **3** *vi (Bot)* attecchire, mettere radici.

♦ **root for** *vi + prep (Am fam)* fare il tifo per.

♦ **root out** *vt + adv (find)* scovare, pescare; *(remove)* eradicare.

rope [rəʊp] **1** *n* fune *f*, corda; *(Naut)* cavo; **to give sb more ~** *(fig)* allentare le redini a qn; **to know/learn the ~s** *(fig)* conoscere/imparare i segreti del mestiere; **a ~ of pearls** una lunga collana di perle. **2** *vt* legare (con una fune *or* una corda). **3** *cpd:* **~ ladder** *n* scala di corda.

♦ **rope in** *vt + adv (fam)* accalappiare, tirar dentro.

♦ **rope off** *vt + adv* isolare con dei cordoni.

ropy ['rəʊpɪ] *adj* **(-ier, -iest)** *(fam)* scadente.

ro·sary ['rəʊzərɪ] *n (Rel)* rosario.

rose[1] [rəʊz] **1** *n* **(a)** *(flower, colour)* rosa; *(bush)* rosaio; **my life isn't all ~s** *(fam)* la mia vita non è tutta rose e fiori. **(b)** *(on shower, watering can)* bulbo (forato); *(on ceiling)* rosone *m (motivo).* **2** *adj (~-coloured)* rosa *inv.* **3** *cpd:* **~ garden** *n* roseto; **~ window** *n* rosone *m (vetrata).*

rose[2] [rəʊz] *pt of* **rise.**

rose·bed ['rəʊzbed] *n* rosaio, roseto.

rose-coloured ['rəʊz͵kʌləd] *adj* color rosa *inv;* **to see sth through ~ spectacles** *(fig)* vedere qc tutto rosa.

rose·mary ['rəʊzmərɪ] *n* rosmarino.

rose-red ['rəʊz'red] *adj* vermiglio(a).

ro·sette [rəʊ'zet] *n (emblem, as prize)* coccarda; *(Archit)* rosone *m.*

rose·wood ['rəʊzwʊd] *n* palissandro.

ros·ter ['rɒstə'] *n* = **rota.**

ros·trum ['rɒstrəm] *n* podio.

rosy ['rəʊzɪ] *adj* **(-ier, -iest)** roseo(a).

rot [rɒt] **1** *n* putrefazione *f*, marciume *m; (fam: nonsense)* fesserie *fpl*, stupidaggini *fpl*; **the ~ has set in** *(fig)* le cose si sono guastate; **to stop the ~** *(fig)* salvare la situazione; **dry/wet ~** funghi parassiti del legno. **2** *vt* far marcire. **3** *vi:* **to ~ (away)** marcire.

rota ['rəʊtə] *n* tabella dei turni.

ro·ta·ry ['rəʊtərɪ] *adj (movement)* rotatorio(a); *(blades)* rotante.

ro·tate [rəʊ'teɪt] **1** *vt (revolve)* far girare; *(change round: crops, staff)* avvicendare, fare la rotazione di. **2** *vi (wheel, Earth)* rotare; *(staff etc)* alternarsi, avvicendarsi.

ro·ta·tion [rəʊ'teɪʃən] *n* rotazione *f;* **in ~** a turno, in rotazione.

ro·tor ['rəʊtə'] *n* rotore *m.*

rot·ten ['rɒtn] *adj* **(a)** *(meat)* andato(a) a male: *(fruit, eggs etc)* marcio(a); *(tooth)* cariato(a); *(wood)* marcio(a), marcito(a); *(fig: morally)* corrotto(a), marcio(a); **~ to the core** completamente marcio. **(b)** *(fam: bad)* schifoso(a); **what ~ luck!** che scalogna!; **what a ~ thing to do!** che vigliaccata!, che carognata!; **I feel ~ (ill)** mi sento da cani; *(mean)* mi sento un verme.

ro·tund [rəʊ'tʌnd] *adj (person)* grassoccio(a).

rou·ble, *(Am)* **ru·ble** ['ru:bl] *n* rublo.

rouge [ru:ʒ] *n* belletto.

rough [rʌf] **1** *adj* **(-er, -est) (a)** *(uneven: ground, road, path, edge)* accidentato(a); *(not smooth: skin, cloth, surface, hands)* ruvido(a).

(b) *(voice)* rauco(a); *(taste, wine)* aspro(a); *(coarse, unrefined: person, manners, life)* rozzo(a); *(harsh ie: person, game)* violento(a); *(neighbourhood)* poco raccomandabile; *(sea crossing, weather)* brutto(a); **the sea is ~ today** c'è mare grosso oggi; **I don't want any ~ stuff!** *(fam)* niente risse!; **a ~ customer** *(fam)* un duro; **to have a ~ time (of it)** passare un periodaccio; **to give sb a ~ time (of it)** rendere la vita dura a qn; **it's ~ on him** che sfortuna per lui; **to feel ~** *(fam)* sentirsi male.

(c) *(calculation, figures)* approssimativo(a), approssimato(a); *(plan, sketch)* sommario(a), approssimativo(a); **~ work, ~ draft, ~ copy** brutta copia; **~ sketch** schizzo; **~ justice** giustizia sommaria; **~ estimate** approssimazione *f;* **at a ~ guess** *or* **estimate** ad occhio e croce; **he's a ~ diamond** sotto quei modi un po' grezzi si nascondeun cuore d'oro.

2 *adv:* **to play ~** *(Sport)* fare un gioco pesante; *(children)* fare dei giochi violenti; **to sleep ~** dormire all'addiaccio; **to live ~** vivere alla giornata.

3 *n* **(a)** *(fam: person)* duro. **(b):** **to take the ~ with the smooth** prendere le cose come vengono. **(c)** *(Golf)* erba alta. **4** *vt:* **to ~ it** *(fam)* far vita dura.

♦ **rough out** *vt + adv (plan etc)* fare un abbozzo di, abbozzare.

rough·age ['rʌfɪdʒ] *n* alimenti *mpl* ricchi di cellulosa.

rough-and-ready [͵rʌfən'redɪ] *adj* rudimentale.

rough-and-tumble [͵rʌfən'tʌmbl] *n* zuffa.

rough·en ['rʌfn] *vt* rendere ruvido(a), irruvidire.

rough·ly ['rʌflɪ] *adv* **(a)** *(not gently: push, play)* brutalmente; *(: speak, order)* bruscamente; **to treat sb/sth ~** maltrattare qn/qc. **(b)** *(not finely: make, sew)* grossolanamente; **to sketch sth ~** fare uno schizzo di qc. **(c)** *(approximately)* grosso modo, pressappoco; ~ **speaking** grosso modo, ad occhio e croce; **there were** ~ **50 people** c'erano pressappoco 50 persone.

rough·neck ['rʌf,nɛk] n (Am fam) duro, bestione m.

rough·ness ['rʌfnɪs] n (of hands, surface) ruvidità, ruvidezza; (of person: abruptness) modi mpl bruschi; (: harshness) durezza; (of sea) violenza; (of road) cattive condizioni fpl.

rough·shod ['rʌfʃɒd] adv: **to ride** ~ **over** (person) mettere sotto i piedi; (objection) passare sopra a.

rou·lette [ruːˈlɛt] n roulette f.

round [raʊnd] **1** adj rotondo(a); (arms, body) grassoccio(a); (cheeks) paffuto(a); **in** ~ **figures** in cifra tonda; **a** ~ **dozen** una dozzina completa; **the** ~ **trip** il viaggio di andata e ritorno.

2 adv: **all** ~, **right** ~ tutt'intorno, tutt'in giro; **the wheels go** ~ le ruote girano; **all year** ~ (durante) tutto l'anno; **to ask sb** ~ invitare qn (a casa propria); **we were** ~ **at my sister's** eravamo da mia sorella; **I'll be** ~ **at 6 o'clock** ci sarò alle 6; **to take the long way** ~ fare il giro più lungo.

3 prep intorno a, attorno a; ~ **the table** intorno alla tavola; **all** ~ **the house** (inside) dappertutto in casa; (outside) tutt'intorno alla casa; **she arrived** ~ (about) **noon** è arrivata intorno a mezzogiorno; **it's just** ~ **the corner** è appena girato l'angolo; **to look** ~ **a house/a town** visitare una casa/una città; **I've been** ~ **all the shops** ho fatto il giro di tutti i negozi; ~ **the clock** ininterrottamente; **wrap a blanket** ~ **him** avvolgilo in una coperta.

4 n (a) (circle) cerchio; (slice: of bread, meat) fetta; **a** ~ (of sandwiches) due tramezzini. (b): **the daily** ~ (fig) la routine quotidiana. (c) (of watchman, postman) giro; **I've got a paper** ~ porto i giornali in giro; **the doctor's on his** ~**s** il dottore sta facendo il suo giro di visite; **the story went the** ~**s** la storia è passata di bocca in bocca. (d) (Boxing) round m inv; (Golf) partita; (Showjumping) percorso; (in tournament, competition) incontro; **a** ~ **of talks** una serie di incontri; **in the first** ~ **of the elections** nella prima votazione; **a** ~ **of drinks** un giro di bevute; **it's my** ~ tocca a me offrire; **a** ~ **of ammunition** un colpo; **a** ~ **of applause** un applauso.

5 vt (a) (make ~: lips) arrotondare; (: edges etc) smussare. (b) (go ~: corner) girare, voltare; (: bend) superare; (: Naut) doppiare.

♦ **round off** vt + adv chiudere in bellezza.

♦ **round on** vi + prep assalire.

♦ **round up** vt + adv (a) (cattle) radunare; (friends etc) riunire; (criminals) fare una retata di. (b) (figures) arrotondare.

round·about ['raʊndəbaʊt] **1** adj (route) indiretto(a); **I heard the news in a** ~ **way** ho saputo la notizia per vie traverse; **to speak in a** ~ **way about sth** accennare indirettamente a qc. **2** n (Brit: at fair) giostra; (: Aut) rotatoria.

round·ly ['raʊndlɪ] adv (say, tell) chiaro e tondo; **I cursed him** ~ gliene ho dette di tutti i colori.

round-shouldered [,raʊnd'ʃəʊldəd] adj con le spalle curve.

round·up ['raʊndʌp] n (of cattle, people) raduno; (of suspects etc) retata; **a** ~ **of the latest news** un sommario or riepilogo delle ultime notizie.

rouse [raʊz] vt (person: from sleep) svegliare; (: from apathy) scuotere; (interest, suspicion, admiration) suscitare, destare; **to** ~ **sb to action** spronare qn ad agire; **to** ~ **sb to fury** far infuriare qn.

rous·ing ['raʊzɪŋ] adj (cheer) entusiasmante; (welcome, applause) entusiastico(a); (speech, song) trascinante.

rout[1] [raʊt] **1** n (defeat) disfatta, rotta. **2** vt mettere in rotta, sbaragliare.

rout[2] [raʊt] vi (search): **to** ~ **about** frugare, rovistare.

♦ **rout out** vt + adv (find) scovare; (force out) (far) sloggiare.

route [ruːt] n (gen) itinerario; **shipping/air** ~**s** rotte fpl marittime/aeree; **bus** ~ percorso dell'autobus; **we're on the main bus** ~ abitiamo vicino alla linea dell'autobus; **the best** ~ **to London** la strada migliore per andare a Londra; **en** ~ **for** strada; **en** ~ **from ... to** viaggiando da ... a; **en** ~ **for** in viaggio verso.

rou·tine [ruːˈtiːn] **1** n (normal procedure) ordinaria amministrazione f; (study ~, work ~) ritmo di lavoro; **daily** ~ routine f, tran tran m. **2** adj (duties, work) abituale; (inspection, medical examination) comune; (questions) di prammatica; ~ **procedure** prassi f.

rov·ing ['rəʊvɪŋ] adj vagabondo(a); **he has a** ~ **eye** gli piace adocchiare le donne.

row[1] [rəʊ] n (line) fila; (: of plants) fila, filare m; (Knitting) ferro; **in a** ~ in fila; **in the front** ~ in prima fila; **for 5 days in a** ~ per 5 giorni di fila.

row[2] [rəʊ] **1** vt (boat) remare; **to** ~ **sb across a river** trasportare qn dall'altra parte di un fiume su una barca a remi. **2** vi remare; (Sport) vogare; **to go** ~**ing** andare a fare una remata.

row[3] [raʊ] **1** n (noise) baccano, fracasso; (quarrel) lite f, litigio; (scolding) sgridata; **to make a** ~ far baccano; **to have a** ~ litigare; **to get (into) a** ~ prendersi una sgridata; **to give sb a** ~ sgridare qn. **2** vi litigare.

ro·wan ['raʊən] n (also: ~ tree) sorbo.

row·boat ['rəʊbəʊt] n (Am) = **rowing boat**.

row·dy ['raʊdɪ] **1** adj (-ier, -iest) (noisy) chiassoso(a); (rough) turbolento(a). **2** n teppista m/f.

row·er ['rəʊər] n rematore/trice; (Sport) vogatore/trice.

row·ing ['rəʊɪŋ] **1** n remare m; (Sport) canottaggio. **2** cpd: ~ **boat** n barca a remi.

roy·al ['rɔɪəl] adj reale; ~ **blue** blu reale inv; **they gave us a** ~ **welcome** ci hanno fatto un'accoglienza principesca; **R**~ **Air Force** (Brit: abbr: **RAF**) ≃ Aeronautica Militare (abbr A.M.); **R**~ **Navy** (Brit: abbr: **RN**) ≃ Marina Militare (abbr M.M.).

roy·al·ist ['rɔɪəlɪst] adj, n realista (m/f).

roy·al·ty ['rɔɪəltɪ] n (a) (persons) reali mpl. (b) (payment: also: **royalties**) diritti mpl d'autore; (from oil well, to inventor) royalty n inv.

r.p.m. abbr (= revs per minute): 33⅓/45 ~ 33⅓/45 giri.

RSVP abbr (= répondez s'il vous plaît) si prega di dare gentile conferma.

Rt Hon. abbr (= Right Honourable) On.

rub [rʌb] **1** n: **to give sth a** ~ strofinare qc; (sore place) massaggiare qc; **there's the** ~! (fig) qui casca l'asino! **2** vt sfregare, strofinare; **to** ~ **one's hands together/one's nose** sfregarsi le mani/il naso; **to** ~ **sth dry** asciugare qc sfregando; **to** ~ **a hole in sth** fare un buco in qc strofinando. **3** vi: **to** ~ **against sth,** ~ **on sth** strofinarsi contro or su qc.

♦ **rub along** vi + adv (fam: two people) andare bene o male d'accordo.

♦ **rub down** vt + adv (a) (body) strofinare, frizionare; (horse) strigliare. (b) (door, wall etc) levigare.

♦ **rub in** vt + adv (ointment) far penetrare (massaggiando or frizionando); (cream, polish: into leather etc) far penetrare (strofinando); **don't** ~ **it in!** (fam) non rivoltare il coltello nella piaga!

♦ **rub off 1** *vi* + *adv* venire (*or* andare) via; **to ~ off onto sth** restare attaccato a qc; **his opinions have ~bed off on me** ho finito col pensarla come lui. **2** *vt* + *prep* (*writing*) cancellare; (*dirt etc*) togliere (strofinando), levare (strofinando).

♦ **rub out 1** *vt* + *adv* cancellare. **2** *vi* + *adv* cancellarsi.

♦ **rub up** *vt* + *adv* (*silver, vase*) lucidare; **to ~ sb up the wrong way** (*fig*) prendere qn per il verso sbagliato.

rub·ber[1] [ˈrʌbəʳ] **1** *n* (*material*) gomma, cauccìu *m*; (*eraser*) gomma (da cancellare). **2** *cpd* (*ball, dinghy, gloves*) di gomma; ~ **band** *n* elastico; ~ **industry** *n* industria della gomma; ~ **plant** *n* ficus *m inv*; ~ **ring** *n* (*for swimming*) ciambella; ~ **stamp** *n* timbro.

rub·ber[2] [ˈrʌbəʳ] *n* (*Bridge*) rubber *m inv*.

rub·bery [ˈrʌbərɪ] *adj* gommoso(a).

rub·bish [ˈrʌbɪʃ] **1** *n* (*waste material*) detriti *mpl*; (*household* ~) spazzatura, immondizie *fpl*; (*nonsense*) sciocchezze *fpl*, stupidaggini *fpl*; **children today eat a lot of** ~ oggigiorno i bambini mangiano un sacco di porcherie; **the film was** ~ il film non valeva niente; **what you've just said is** ~ quello che hai appena detto è una sciocchezza; ~! (*fam*) sciocchezze!, stupidaggini! **2** *cpd*: ~ **dump** *n* discarica delle immondizie.

rub·bishy [ˈrʌbɪʃɪ] *adj* scadente, che non vale niente.

rub·ble [ˈrʌbl] *n* detriti *mpl*; (*of building*) macerie *fpl*.

ruby [ˈruːbɪ] **1** *n* rubino. **2** *adj* (*colour*) (color) rubino *inv*; (*lips*) rosso(a); (*made of rubies: necklace, ring*) di rubini.

ruck·sack [ˈrʌksæk] *n* zaino.

ruc·tions [ˈrʌkʃənz] *npl* putiferio, finimondo; **there will be** ~ if la succederà il finimondo se.

rud·der [ˈrʌdəʳ] *n* timone *m*.

rud·dy[1] [ˈrʌdɪ] *adj* (-ier, -iest) (*complexion*) rubicondo(a); (*sky etc*) rossastro(a).

rud·dy[2] [ˈrʌdɪ] *adj* (-ier, -iest) (*Brit fam*) dannato(a).

rude [ruːd] *adj* (-r, -st) (a) (*impolite*) villano(a), maleducato(a); (*indecent*) indecente; **to be** ~ **to sb** essere maleducato con qn; **it's** ~ **to talk with your mouth full** è cattiva educazione parlare con la bocca piena; **a** ~ **word** una parolaccia. (b): **a** ~ **awakening** un brusco risveglio; (*fig*) una doccia fredda; **to be in** ~ **health** essere in ottima salute. (c) (*primitive*) rozzo(a).

rude·ness [ˈruːdnɪs] *n* (*impoliteness*) maleducazione *f*, insolenza.

ru·di·men·ta·ry [ˌruːdɪˈmɛntərɪ] *adj* rudimentale.

ru·di·ments [ˈruːdɪmənts] *npl* (primi) rudimenti *mpl*.

rue·ful [ˈruːfʊl] *adj* mesto(a).

ruff [rʌf] *n* (*Dress*) gorgiera; (*Zool*) collare *m*.

ruf·fian [ˈrʌfɪən] *n* manigoldo.

ruf·fle [ˈrʌfl] *vt* (*surface*) (far) increspare; (*hair, feathers*) arruffare; (*person*) (far) agitare, (far) innervosire; **nothing ~s him** non si scompone mai.

rug [rʌg] *n* (*floor mat*) tappeto; (*bedside* ~) scendiletto; (*travelling* ~) coperta (da viaggio); (*in tartan*) plaid *m inv*.

rug·by [ˈrʌgbɪ] **1** *n* rugby *m*. **2** *cpd* (*team, player*) di rugby; ~ **league** *n* il rugby a tredici.

rug·ged [ˈrʌgɪd] *adj* (*terrain*) accidentato(a); (*coastline, mountains*) frastagliato(a); (*character*) rude; (*features*) marcato(a).

rug·ger [ˈrʌgəʳ] *n* (*fam*) = **rugby**.

ruin [ˈruːɪn] **1** *n* (a) rudere *m*; ~**s** rovine *fpl*; **in** ~**s**

in rovina; **to fall into** ~ cadere in rovina. (b) (*fig*) rovina. **2** *vt* rovinare.

ru·in·ous [ˈruːɪnəs] *adj* disastroso(a).

rule [ruːl] **1** *n* (a) (*gen*) regola; (*regulation*) regola, regolamento; **the ~s of the road** le norme della circolazione; ~**s and regulations** norme e regolamenti; **it's against the** ~**s** è contro le regole *or* il regolamento; **as a** ~ normalmente, di regola; **to make it a** ~ **to do sth** essersi imposto la regola di fare qc; **by** ~ **of thumb** a lume di naso. (b) (*dominion etc*): **under British** ~ sotto la sovranità britannica; **majority** ~ (*Pol*) governo di maggioranza; **the** ~ **of law** l'autorità della legge. (c) (*for measuring*) riga; **slide** ~ regolo (calcolatore).

2 *vt* (a) (*govern: also:* ~ **over:** *country*) governare; **he's ~d by his wife** è sua moglie che comanda. (b) (*subj: umpire, judge*): **to** ~ (**that**) decretare (che), decidere (che). (c) (*paper, page*): ~**d paper** carta a righe.

3 *vi* (a) (*monarch*) regnare. (b) (*Law*): **to** ~ **against/in favour of/on** pronunciarsi a sfavore di/in favore di/su.

♦ **rule out** *vt* + *adv* escludere; **murder cannot be** ~**d out** non si esclude che si tratti di omicidio.

rul·er [ˈruːləʳ] *n* (a) (*sovereign*) sovrano/a; (*in a republic etc*) capo. (b) (*for measuring*) righello.

rul·ing [ˈruːlɪŋ] **1** *adj* (*factor*) principale, decisivo(a); (*passion*) grande, dominante; (*party*) al potere; **the** ~ **classes** la classe dirigente. **2** *n* decisione *f*.

rum[1] [rʌm] *n* (*drink*) rum *m inv*.

rum[2] [rʌm] *adj* (*fam*) strambo(a).

Ru·ma·nia [ruːˈmeɪnɪə] *n* Romania.

rum·ble[1] [ˈrʌmbl] **1** *n* (*of traffic, thunder etc*) rombo. **2** *vi* (*thunder, cannon etc*) rimbombare; (*stomach*) brontolare; (*pipe*) gorgogliare; **the train ~d past** il treno passò sferragliando.

rum·ble[2] [ˈrʌmbl] *vt* (*Brit fam*) scoprire.

rum·bus·tious [rʌmˈbʌstʃəs] *adj* (*person*): **to be** ~ essere un terremoto.

ru·mi·nate [ˈruːmɪneɪt] *vi* ruminare.

rum·mage [ˈrʌmɪdʒ] *vi*: **to** ~ (**about** *or* **around**) rovistare, frugare; **to** ~ **about in sth/for sth** rovistare *or* frugare in qc/per trovare qc.

ru·mour, (*Am*) **ru·mor** [ˈruːməʳ] **1** *n* voce *f*; ~ **has it that...** corre voce che... . **2** *vt*: **it is ~ed that...** si dice in giro che... .

rump [rʌmp] *n* (*of horse etc*) groppa (posteriore), culatta; (*Culin*) scamone *m*.

rum·ple [ˈrʌmpl] *vt* (*clothes*) spiegazzare, sgualcire; (*hair*) arruffare, scompigliare.

rump·steak [ˌrʌmpˈsteɪk] *n* scamone *m*.

rum·pus [ˈrʌmpəs] *n* (*fam*) putiferio, casino; **to kick up a** ~ fare un putiferio.

run [rʌn] (*vb: pt* **ran,** *pp* **run**) **1** *n* (a) (*act of running*) corsa; **to go for a** ~ andare a correre; **at a** ~ di corsa; **to break into a** ~ mettersi a correre; **a prisoner on the** ~ un evaso; **he's on the** ~ **from the police** è ricercato dalla polizia; **to keep the enemy on the** ~ premere il nemico in fuga; **we've got them on the** ~ now adesso li abbiamo messi in fuga; **he's on the** ~ **from his creditors** cerca di sfuggire ai creditori; **to make a** ~ **for it** scappare, tagliare la corda; **to give sb a** ~ **for his money** non darla vinta a qn prima del tempo; **she's had a good** ~ (*on death, retirement*) ha avuto il suo; **to have the** ~ **of sb's house** essere libero di andare e venire in casa di qn.

(b) (*outing*) giro; **to go for a** ~ **in the car** fare un giro in macchina; **do you want a** ~ **into town?** vuoi che ti accompagni in città?

(c) (*Rail etc*) viaggio, tragitto; **it's a 10-minute bus** ~ è un tragitto di 10 minuti in autobus; **boats** on the Calais ~ navi che fanno il servizio per Calais.

(d) *(sequence)* serie *f inv; (Cards)* scala; a ~ of luck un periodo di fortuna; he's different from the common ~ of men è diverso dai soliti uomini; it stands out from the general ~ of books è un libro fuori dal comune; the play had a long ~ lo spettacolo ha tenuto a lungo il cartellone; in the long ~ alla fin fine; in the short ~ sulle prime.

(e) *(Comm etc)*: there's been a ~ on... c'è stata una forte richiesta di... .

(f) *(for animals)* recinto.

(g) *(for skiing, bobsleighing)* pista.

(h) *(in stocking, tights)* smagliatura.

2 vt (a) correre; *(race)* partecipare a; she ran a good race ha fatto una buona gara; the race is ~ over 4 km la gara si svolge su un percorso di 4 km; to let things ~ their course lasciare che le cose seguano il loro corso; to ~ a horse far correre un cavallo.

(b) *(move)*: to ~ sb into town accompagnare *or* portare qn in città; to ~ the car into a lamppost andare a sbattere con la macchina contro un lampione; to ~ errands andare a fare commissioni.

(c) *(organize etc: business)* dirigere; *(: hotel etc)* gestire; *(: country)* governare; *(: campaign)* organizzare; are they ~ning any trains today? ci sono treni oggi?; they ran an extra train hanno messo un treno straordinario; she ~s everything è lei che manda avanti tutto; I want to ~ my own life voglio essere io a gestire la mia vita.

(d) *(operate: machine)* usare; we ~ 2 cars abbiamo 2 macchine; it's very cheap to ~ comporta poche spese.

(e): to be ~ off one's feet doversi fare in quattro; to ~ it close *or* fine ridursi all'ultimo momento; to ~ a (high) temperature avere la febbre (alta); to ~ a risk correre un rischio.

(f) *(with adv or prep)*: to ~ one's eye over a letter dare una scorsa a una lettera; to ~ a fence round a field costruire un recinto intorno a un campo; to ~ a pipe through a wall far passare un tubo attraverso un muro; to ~ one's fingers through sb's hair passare le dita fra i capelli di qn; to ~ a comb through one's hair darsi una pettinata; to ~ water into the bath far correre l'acqua nella vasca; to ~ a bath for sb preparare un bagno a qn.

3 vi (a) correre; *(flee)* scappare; ~ and see corri a vedere; to ~ in/out/etc entrare/uscire/etc di corsa; to ~ for the bus fare una corsa per prendere l'autobus; to ~ to help sb accorrere in aiuto di qn, correre ad aiutare qn; don't come ~ning to me when you've got problems non correre da me quando avrai dei problemi; we shall have to ~ for it ci toccherà tagliar la corda; he's ~ning for the Presidency si è presentato come candidato per la presidenza; a rumour ran through the town that... si è sparsa la voce in città che...; that tune keeps ~ning through my head continua a venirmi in mente quel motivo; it ~s in the family è un tratto di famiglia.

(b): the train ~s between Gatwick and Victoria il treno fa servizio fra Gatwick e la stazione di Victoria; the bus ~s every 20 minutes c'è un autobus ogni 20 minuti.

(c) *(function)* funzionare, andare; leave the engine ~ning lascia il motore acceso; to ~ on petrol/on diesel/off batteries andare a benzina/a diesel/a batterie; things did not ~ smoothly for them *(fig)* le cose non gli sono andate molto bene.

(d) *(extend: contract etc)* essere valido(a); it has another 5 years to ~ scade fra altri 5 anni; the play ran for 2 years lo spettacolo ha tenuto il cartellone per 2 anni; the cost ran to hundreds of pounds alla fine la spesa è stata di centinaia di sterline; my salary won't ~ to a car col mio stipendio non posso permettermi una macchina.

(e) *(river, tears, curtains, drawer)* scorrere; *(nose, tap)* colare; *(eyes)* lacrimare; *(pen)* perdere; *(sore, abscess)* spurgare; *(melt: butter, icing)* fondere; *(colour, ink)* sbavare; *(colour: in washing)* stingere; the tears ran down her cheeks le lacrime le scorrevano sulle guance; you left the tap ~ning hai lasciato il rubinetto aperto; the river ~s into the sea il fiume sfocia nel mare; the road ~s into the square la strada sbocca nella piazza; the milk ran all over the floor il latte si è sparso sul pavimento; to ~ high *(river, sea)* ingrossarsi; *(feelings)* inasprirsi; his face was ~ning with sweat il sudore colava sul suo viso; his blood ran cold gli si è gelato il sangue.

(f) *(with adv or prep)*: to ~ across the road attraversare di corsa la strada; the road ~s along the river la strada corre lungo il fiume; the road ~s by our house la strada passa davanti a casa nostra; the path ~s from our house to the station il sentiero va da casa nostra fino alla stazione; the car ran into the lamppost la macchina è andata a sbattere contro il lampione; he ran up to me mi corse incontro; he ran up the stairs salì su per le scale di corsa; the ivy ~s up the wall l'edera si arrampica sul muro.

♦ run about vi + adv correre (di) qua e (di) là.

♦ run across vi + prep *(meet, find)* incontrare per caso, imbattersi in.

♦ run along vi + adv correre, andare; ~ along and play su, vai a giocare.

♦ run away vi + adv (a) scappare di corsa; to ~ away from home scappare di casa. (b) *(water)* scolare.

♦ run away with vi + prep scappare con; *(fig)*: he let his imagination ~ away with him si lasciò trasportare dalla fantasia; don't ~ away with the idea that... non credere che... .

♦ run down 1 vt + adv (a) *(Aut)* investire, mettere sotto. (b) *(reduce: production)* ridurre gradualmente; *(: factory, shop)* rallentare l'attività di. (c) *(disparage)* parlar male di, denigrare. 2 vi + adv: to be ~ down *(battery)* essere scarico(a); *(person)* essere giù (di corda).

♦ run in vt + adv (a) *(car)* rodare, fare il rodaggio di. (b) *(fam: arrest)* mettere dentro.

♦ run into vi + prep *(meet: person)* incontrare per caso; *(difficulties, troubles etc)* incontrare, trovare; to ~ into debt trovarsi nei debiti.

♦ run off 1 vi + adv = run away. 2 vt + adv *(copies)* fare.

♦ run off with vi + prep = run away with.

♦ run on vi + adv (a) *(fam: person, talk, meeting)* andare avanti. (b) *(Typ)* continuare senza andare a capo.

♦ run out vi + adv *(contract, lease)* scadere; *(food, money etc)* finire, esaurirsi; time is ~ning out ormai c'è poco tempo.

♦ run out of vi + prep esaurire, non avere più; I've ~ out of petrol sono rimasto senza benzina.

♦ run out on vi + prep *(abandon)* piantare.

♦ run over 1 vi + adv *(overflow)* traboccare. 2 vi + prep *(reread)* rileggere; *(recapitulate)* ricapitolare. 3 vt + adv *(Aut)* investire, mettere sotto.

♦ run through vi + prep (a) *(use up: fortune)* far fuori, dilapidare. (b) *(read quickly: notes etc)* dare un'occhiata a. (c) *(rehearse: play)* riprovare, ripetere; *(recapitulate)* ricapitolare.

◆ **run up** vt + adv (a) (debt etc) accumulare. (b) (dress etc) mettere insieme.

◆ **run up against** vi + prep (person, problem) imbattersi in.

run·away ['rʌnəwcɪ] adj (gen) in fuga; (child) scappato(a) di casa; (horse) imbizzarrito(a); (success, victory etc) trascinante; ~ **inflation** inflazione galoppante.

run·down ['rʌndaʊn] n (a) (of industry etc) riduzione f graduale dell'attività di. (b): **to give sb a ~ on sth** mettere qn al corrente di qc.

rung[1] [rʌŋ] n (of ladder) piolo; (of chair) traversa.

rung[2] [rʌŋ] pp of **ring**.

run·ner ['rʌnər] **1** n (a) (athlete) corridore m; (horse) partente m. (b) (of sledge, aircraft) pattino; (of skate) lama; (of drawer) guida. **2** cpd: ~ **bean** n fagiolino.

runner-up ['rʌnər'ʌp] n secondo(a) arrivato(a).

run·ning ['rʌnɪŋ] **1** adj (water) corrente; (tap) che corre; (sore) che spurga; ~ **costs** (of business) costi mpl d'esercizio; (of car) spese fpl di mantenimento; ~ **battle** lotta continua; ~ **commentary** (Radio, fig) radiocronaca; (TV) telecronaca; ~ **mate** (Am Pol) candidato alla vicepresidenza; **for the sixth time** ~ per la sesta volta di fila or di seguito. **2** n (of business etc) gestione f; (of machine) funzionamento; **to be in/out of the ~ for sth** essere/non essere più in lizza per qc.

run·ny ['rʌnɪ] adj (-ier, -iest) (butter) sciolto(a); (sauce) troppo liquido(a); (nose) che cola, che gocciola.

run-of-the-mill [,rʌnəvðə'mɪl] adj banale.

run-up ['rʌnʌp] n: ~ **to sth** periodo che precede qc.

run·way ['rʌnwcɪ] n (Aer) pista.

rup·ture ['rʌptʃər] **1** n rottura; (Med: hernia) ernia. **2** vt (blood vessel etc) farsi scoppiare; **to ~ o.s.** farsi venire un'ernia.

ru·ral ['rʊərəl] adj (gen) rurale; (scene) campestre; (life) di campagna.

ruse [ruːz] n stratagemma m, astuzia.

rush[1] [rʌʃ] **1** n giunco. **2** cpd: ~ **matting** n stuoia.

rush[2] [rʌʃ] **1** n (a) (of people) affollamento, ressa; **the Christmas** ~ la ressa di Natale; **gold** ~ corsa all'oro; **there was a** ~ **to** or **for the door** tutti si precipitarono verso la porta; **we've had a** ~ **of orders** abbiamo avuto una valanga di ordinazioni. (b) (hurry) fretta, premura; **I'm in a** ~ (**to do**) ho fretta or premura (di fare); **it was all done in a** ~ è stato fatto tutto in gran fretta; **it got lost in the** ~ nella fretta è andato perso; **what's all the** ~ **about?** cos'è tutta questa fretta?; **is there any** ~ **for this?** è urgente?; **we had a** ~ **to get it ready in time** abbiamo dovuto affrettarci per prepararlo in tempo. (c) (current): **a** ~ **of air** una corrente d'aria; **a** ~ **of water** un flusso d'acqua.

2 vt (a) (person) far fretta or premura a; (work,

order) fare in fretta; **to** ~ **sth off** spedire con urgenza qc; **I hate being** ~ed non mi piace che mi si faccia premura; **we were** ~ed off our feet abbiamo dovuto correre come i matti; **he was** ~ed (off) to hospital lo hanno portato d'urgenza all'ospedale. (b) (attack: town) prendere d'assalto; (: person) precipitarsi contro; **the crowd** ~ed the barriers la folla ha dato l'assalto ai cancelli.

3 vi (person: run) precipitarsi; (: be in a hurry) essere di corsa; (car) andare veloce; **don't** ~ **at it**, take it slowly non farlo in fretta, prenditela con comodo; **to** ~ **up/down** etc precipitarsi su/giù etc; **I** ~ed **to her side** sono corso subito da lei; **I was** ~ing **to finish it** mi affrettavo a finirlo.

4 cpd: ~ **hour** n ora di punta; ~ **hour traffic** il traffico delle ore di punta; ~ **job** n (urgent) lavoro urgente; (botched, hurried) lavoro fatto in fretta.

◆ **rush about, rush around** vi + adv correre su e giù.

◆ **rush over** vi + adv: **to** ~ **over** (**to sb/to do sth**) precipitarsi (da qn/a fare qc).

◆ **rush through 1** vi + prep (meal) mangiare in fretta; (book) dare una scorsa frettolosa a; (work) sbrigare frettolosamente; (town) attraversare in fretta. **2** vt + adv (Comm: order) eseguire d'urgenza; (supplies) mandare d'urgenza.

◆ **rush up** vi + adv = **rush over**.

rusk [rʌsk] n fetta biscottata.

rus·set ['rʌsɪt] adj (colour) marrone rossiccio inv.

Rus·sia ['rʌʃə] n Russia.

Rus·sian ['rʌʃən] **1** adj russo(a). **2** n (person) russo/ a; (language) russo.

rust [rʌst] **1** n ruggine f. **2** vi arrugginire, arrugginirsi. **3** vt (far) arrugginire.

rust-coloured ['rʌst,kʌləd] adj (color) ruggine inv.

rus·tic ['rʌstɪk] adj (gen) rustico(a); (scene) campestre.

rus·tle[1] ['rʌsl] **1** n fruscio. **2** vt far frusciare. **3** vi frusciare.

rus·tle[2] ['rʌsl] vt (cattle) rubare.

◆ **rustle up** vt + adv (fam: find) ripescare; (: money) racimolare; (: make) rimediare, mettere insieme.

rus·tler ['rʌslər] n ladro di bestiame.

rust·proof ['rʌst,pruːf] adj, **rust-re·sist·ant** ['rʌstrɪ,zɪstənt] adj inattaccabile dalla ruggine.

rusty ['rʌstɪ] adj (-ier, -iest) rugginoso(a), arrugginito(a); **my Greek is pretty** ~ (fig) il mio greco è molto arrugginito.

rut [rʌt] n solco; **to get into a** ~ (fig) adagiarsi troppo.

ruth·less ['ruːθlɪs] adj spietato(a).

rye [raɪ] **1** n segale f; (Am: whisky) whisky m inv di segale. **2** cpd: ~ **bread** n pane m di segale.

S

S¹, s [ɛs] *n (letter)* S, s *f or m inv*.
S² *abbr (= south)* S.
Sab·bath ['sæbəθ] *n (Jewish)* sabato; *(Christian)* domenica.
sab·bati·cal [sə'bætɪkəl] *adj* sabbatico(a).
sa·ble ['seɪbl] *n* zibellino.
sabo·tage ['sæbətɑːʒ] **1** *n* sabotaggio. **2** *vt* sabotare.
sabo·teur [ˌsæbə'tɜːʳ] *n* sabotatore/trice.
sa·bre, *(Am)* **sa·ber** ['seɪbəʳ] *n* sciabola.
sac·cha·rin(e) ['sækərɪn] *n* saccarina.
sa·chet ['sæʃeɪ] *n* bustina.
sack¹ [sæk] **1** *n* **(a)** *(bag)* sacco; ~ **of coal** sacco per il carbone; ~ **of coal** sacco di carbone. **(b)** *(fam)*: **to get the** ~ essere licenziato(a); **to give sb the** ~ licenziare qn, mandare qn a spasso. **2** *vt (fam)* licenziare, mandare a spasso. **3** *cpd*: ~ **dress** *n* vestito a sacco; ~ **race** *n* corsa nei sacchi.
sack² [sæk] **1** *n (plundering)* saccheggio; **the** ~ **of Rome** il sacco di Roma. **2** *vt* saccheggiare.
sack·ing ['sækɪŋ] *n* **(a)** *(cloth)* tela di sacco. **(b)** *(fam: dismissal)* licenziamento.
sac·ra·ment ['sækrəmənt] *n* sacramento; **the Blessed S~** l'Eucaristia.
sa·cred ['seɪkrɪd] *adj (holy)* sacro(a); **the S~ Heart** il Sacro Cuore; **a** ~ **promise** *(fig)* una promessa solenne; **is nothing** ~? non c'è più religione!; ~ **cow** *(fam)* persona *(or idea etc)* intoccabile.
sac·ri·fice ['sækrɪfaɪs] **1** *n* sacrificio; **to make** ~**s (for sb)** fare (dei) sacrifici (per qn). **2** *vt* sacrificare.
sac·ri·fi·cial [ˌsækrɪ'fɪʃəl] *adj (act, altar)* sacrificale; *(lamb)* destinato(a) al sacrificio.
sac·ri·lege ['sækrɪlɪdʒ] *n* sacrilegio.
sac·ri·legious [ˌsækrɪ'lɪdʒəs] *adj* sacrilego(a).
sac·ris·ty ['sækrɪstɪ] *n* sagrestia.
sac·ro·sanct ['sækrəʊsæŋkt] *adj* sacrosanto(a).
sad [sæd] *adj (-der, -dest)* **(a)** *(sorrowful, depressing)* triste; **to make sb** ~ rattristare qn; **how** ~! che tristezza!; ~**der but wiser** maturato dall'esperienza. **(b)** *(deplorable)* deplorevole; **it's a** ~ **state of affairs when...** è deplorevole quando... .
sad·den ['sædn] *vt* rattristare.
sad·dle ['sædl] **1** *n (of horse, also Culin)* sella; *(of bicycle)* sellino, sella. **2** *vt (horse: also:* ~ **up)** sellare; **to** ~ **sb with sth** *(fam: task, bill, name)* appioppare qc a qn; *(: responsibility)* accollare qc a qn; **I got** ~**d with him again** me lo sono dovuto sorbire di nuovo.
saddle·bag ['sædlbæg] *n* bisaccia; *(on bicycle)* borsa.
sad·ism ['seɪdɪzəm] *n* sadismo.
sad·ist ['seɪdɪst] *n* sadico/a.
sa·dis·tic [sə'dɪstɪk] *adj* sadico(a).
sad·ly ['sædlɪ] *adv (unhappily)* tristemente; *(regrettably)* sfortunatamente; ~ **lacking in...** penosamente privo di... .
sad·ness ['sædnɪs] *n* tristezza, malinconia.
sa·fa·ri [sə'fɑːrɪ] **1** *n* safari *m inv*; **to be on** ~ fare un safari. **2** *cpd*: ~ **park** *n* zoosafari *m inv*.

safe [seɪf] **1** *adj* **(-r, -st) (a)** *(not in danger: person)* salvo(a), fuori pericolo; *(: money, jewel, secret)* al sicuro; ~ **and sound** sano(a) e salvo(a); **he didn't feel very** ~ **up there** non si sentiva molto (al) sicuro lassù; **to be** ~ **from** essere al sicuro da; **you'll be** ~ **here** qui sarai al sicuro. **(b)** *(not dangerous: toy, beach, animal)* non pericoloso(a); *(: ladder)* sicuro(a); *(secure: hiding place, investment)* sicuro(a); *(prudent: choice)* prudente; ~ **journey!** buon viaggio!; **in** ~ **hands** in buone mani; **the** ~ **period** *(Med)* il periodo sicuro; **just to be on the** ~ **side** per andare sul sicuro; **better** ~ **than sorry!** meglio essere prudenti!; **it's a** ~ **bet** ci puoi scommettere; **it is** ~ **to say that...** si può affermare con sicurezza che... .
2 *n (for money etc)* cassaforte *f*.
safe-breaker ['seɪfˌbreɪkəʳ] *n* scassinatore *m*.
safe-conduct [ˌseɪf'kɒndʌkt] *n* salvacondotto.
safe-deposit ['seɪfdɪˌpɒzɪt] *n (vault)* caveau *m inv*; *(box)* cassetta di sicurezza.
safe·guard ['seɪfgɑːd] **1** *n* salvaguardia. **2** *vt* salvaguardare.
safe-keeping ['seɪf'kiːpɪŋ] *n*: **in** ~, **for** ~ in custodia.
safe·ly ['seɪflɪ] *adv (without danger)* senza (correre) rischi, tranquillamente; *(without accident)*: **to arrive** ~ arrivare sano(a) e salvo(a); *(securely)* al sicuro; **I can** ~ **say...** posso tranquillamente asserire... .
safe·ty ['seɪftɪ] **1** *n* sicurezza; **to reach** ~ riuscire a mettersi in salvo; **in a place of** ~ al sicuro; **road** ~ sicurezza sulle strade; **there's** ~ **in numbers** l'unione fa la forza; ~ **first!** la prudenza innanzitutto!; **for** ~'s **sake** per (maggior) sicurezza. **2** *cpd (device, measure, margin etc)* di sicurezza; ~ **belt** *n* cintura di sicurezza; ~ **catch** *n* sicura; ~ **curtain** *n (Theatre)* telone *m*; ~ **match** *n* fiammifero di sicurezza, svedese *m*; ~ **net** *n* rete *f* di protezione; ~ **pin** *n* spilla da balia *or* di sicurezza; ~ **valve** *n* valvola di sicurezza.
saf·fron ['sæfrən] **1** *n* zafferano. **2** *adj (colour)* color zafferano *inv*.
sag [sæg] *vi (sink, curve)* incurvarsi; *(slacken: rope)* allentarsi; *(fig: spirits)* deprimersi; **his knees** ~**ged** gli hanno ceduto le ginocchia.
saga ['sɑːgə] *n* saga; *(fig)* odissea.
sa·ga·cious [sə'geɪʃəs] *adj* sagace.
sage¹ [seɪdʒ] *adj, n* saggio(a) *(m/f)*.
sage² [seɪdʒ] **1** *n (herb)* salvia. **2** *cpd*: ~ **green** *adj, n* verde salvia *(m) inv*.
Sag·it·ta·rius [ˌsædʒɪ'tɛərɪəs] *n (Astron, Astrology)* Sagittario; **to be** ~ essere del Sagittario.
sago ['seɪgəʊ] *n* sagù *m*.
said [sɛd] **1** *pt, pp of* **say. 2** *adj* detto(a).
sail [seɪl] **1** *n (of boat)* vela; *(of windmill)* pala; **to set** ~ salpare; **under** ~ a vela; **to go for a** ~ andare a fare un giro in barca a vela. **2** *vt* **(a)** *(ship)* condurre. **(b)**: **to** ~ **the Atlantic** attraversare l'Atlantico; **to** ~ **the seas** solcare i mari. **3** *vi* **(a)** *(boat)*: **to** ~ **into harbour** entrare in porto; **the ship sails at 5 o'clock** la nave salpa alle 5; **the**

ship ~ed into Naples la nave è arrivata a Napoli; to ~ round the Cape doppiare il Capo; to ~ round the world fare il giro del mondo. (b) *(person)* andare in barca a vela; we ~ed into Genoa siamo entrati nel porto di Genova; he ~ed round the world ha fatto il giro del mondo in barca; to ~ close to the wind *(fig)* tirare troppo la corda. (c) *(fig: clouds)* attraversare; *(: swan)* scivolare maestoso(a); she ~ed into the room fece il suo ingresso solenne nella stanza; the plate ~ed over my head il piatto è volato al di sopra della mia testa.

♦ **sail through** 1 *vi + adv (fig)* farcela tranquillamente. 2 *vt + adv (fig)* passare tranquillamente; *(: pass: exam, driving test)* passare con scioltezza.

sail·boat ['seɪlbəʊt] *n (Am)* = sailing boat.

sail·ing ['seɪlɪŋ] 1 *n (sport)* vela; *(departure)* partenza; now it's all plain ~ il resto è liscio come l'olio. 2 *cpd:* ~ boat *n* barca a vela; ~ ship *n* veliero.

sail·or ['seɪlə'] *n* marinaio; to be a bad ~ soffrire il mal di mare.

saint [seɪnt] *n (also fig)* santo/a; All S~s' Day Ognissanti *m inv;* S~ John San Giovanni; S~ Stephen's Day il giorno di Santo Stefano; S~ Mark's (Church) (la chiesa di) San Marco.

saint·ly ['seɪntlɪ] *adj* (-ier, -iest) *(expression)* da santo(a); *(life)* santo(a); a ~ person un santo.

sake [seɪk] *n:* for the ~ of sb/sth per amor di qn/qc; for my ~ per amor mio, per me; for God's/for heaven's ~! per amor di Dio!/del cielo!; art for art's ~ l'arte per l'arte; for your own ~ per te (stesso), per il tuo bene; for pity's ~ per pietà; for old times' ~ in ricordo del passato; for argument's ~, for the ~ of argument tanto per fare un esempio.

sal·ad ['sæləd] 1 *n* insalata; ~ insalata di pomodori; ham ~ prosciutto e insalata. 2 *cpd:* ~ bowl *n* insalatiera; ~ cream *n* ≃ maionese *f (in bottiglia);* ~ dressing *n* condimento per l'insalata.

sa·la·mi [sə'lɑːmɪ] *n* salame *m.*

sala·ried ['sælərɪd] *adj* stipendiato(a).

sala·ry ['sælərɪ] 1 *n* stipendio. 2 *cpd:* ~ earner *n* stipendiato/a; ~ range *n* fascia salariale; ~ scale *n* scala dei salari.

sale [seɪl] 1 *n (a) (of article)* vendita; 'for ~' 'vendesi', 'vendonsi'; to put a house up for ~ mettere in vendita una casa; to be on ~ essere in vendita; sold on a ~ or return basis *venduto con possibilità di resa;* ~ auction ~ vendita all'asta. (b) *(Comm: also:* ~s) svendita, saldi *mpl;* in the ~(s) in svendita; the January ~s ≃ i saldi di fine anno; a closing-down ~ una liquidazione. 2 *cpd:* ~s clerk *n (Am)* commesso/a; ~s force *n* personale *m* addetto alle vendite; ~s manager *n* direttore *m* commerciale; ~ price *n* prezzo di liquidazione.

sale·able ['seɪləbl] *adj* vendibile.

sale·room ['seɪlruːm] *n* sala di vendite all'asta.

sales·man ['seɪlzmən] *n, pl* -men *(in shop)* commesso; *(representative)* rappresentante *m* (di commercio).

sales·man·ship ['seɪlzmənʃɪp] *n* arte *f* del vendere.

sales·woman ['seɪlzwʊmən] *n, pl* -women commessa.

sa·li·ent ['seɪlɪənt] *adj (fig)* saliente.

sa·line ['seɪlaɪn] *adj* salino(a).

sa·li·va [sə'laɪvə] *n* saliva.

sali·vate ['sælɪveɪt] *vi* salivare.

sal·low ['sæləʊ] *adj* giallastro(a).

sal·ly forth [,sælɪ'fɔːθ] *vi,* **sal·ly out** [,sælɪ'aʊt] *vi* uscire di gran carriera.

salm·on ['sæmən] 1 *n* salmone *m.* 2 *cpd:* ~ pink *adj, n* rosa salmone *(m) inv,* color salmone *(m) inv;* ~ steak *n* trancio di salmone.

sa·lon ['sælɔ̃ːŋ] *n* salone *m.*

sa·loon [sə'luːn] *n (a) (Naut)* sala, salone *m.* (b) *(Brit: car)* berlina. (c) *(Am: bar)* saloon *m inv,* bar *m inv; (Brit: also:* ~ bar) saletta (di pub).

sal·si·fy ['sælsɪfɪ] *n (Bot)* sassefrica.

salt [sɔːlt] 1 *n* sale *m;* to rub ~ into the wound *(fig)* mettere il dito sulla piaga; he's the ~ of the earth è eccezionale; an old ~ un lupo di mare. 2 *vt (flavour)* salare; *(preserve)* mettere sotto sale. 3 *cpd (water etc)* salato(a); *(beef, meat)* salato(a), sotto sale; *(mine)* di sale; *(spoon)* per il sale; ~ flats *npl* saline *fpl.*

♦ **salt away** *vt + adv (fig)* mettere via.

salt·cellar ['sɔːlt,selə'] *n* saliera.

salt·water ['sɔːlt,wɔːtə'] *adj attr (fish etc)* di mare.

salty ['sɔːltɪ] *adj (taste)* salato(a).

sa·lu·bri·ous [sə'luːbrɪəs] *adj* salubre; *(fig: district etc)* raccomandabile.

salu·tary ['sæljʊtərɪ] *adj* salutare.

sa·lute [sə'luːt] 1 *n (Mil: with hand)* saluto; *(: with guns)* salva; to take the ~ passare in rassegna le truppe. 2 *vt (Mil, fig)* salutare.

sal·vage ['sælvɪdʒ] 1 *n (a) (rescue: of ship etc)* salvataggio; *(: for re-use)* ricupero. (b) *(things rescued)* oggetti *mpl* salvati *or* ricuperati; *(for re-use)* materiale *m* di ricupero. 2 *vt (boat, things)* ricuperare; *(fig: sth from a theory, policy etc)* salvare. 3 *cpd (operation, vessel)* di salvataggio.

sal·va·tion [sæl'veɪʃən] *n* salvezza.

Sal·va·tion Army [sæl,veɪʃən'ɑːmɪ] *n* l'Esercito della Salvezza.

salve [sælv] *vt:* to ~ his conscience per sentirsi a posto con la coscienza.

Sa·mari·tan [sə'mærɪtən] *n:* the Good ~ il buon Samaritano; the ~s *(organization)* ≃ telefono amico.

same [seɪm] 1 *adj* stesso(a); the same car as... la stessa macchina che...; on the ~ day lo stesso giorno; the *or* that ~ day il *or* quel giorno stesso; in the ~ way allo stesso modo; the ~ table as usual la solita tavola; it comes to the ~ thing è la stessa cosa; at the ~ time allo stesso tempo; to go the ~ way as sb *(fig pej)* mettersi sulla stessa strada di qn.

2 *pron:* the ~ lo(la) stesso(a), gli(le) stessi(e); it's all the ~ to me per me fa lo stesso; just the ~ as usual come al solito; the ~ again *(in bar etc)* un altro; all *or* just the ~ lo stesso; they're one and the ~ *(person)* sono la stessa persona; *(thing)* sono la stessa cosa; I'll do the ~ for you farò altrettanto per te; I would do the ~ again farei di nuovo lo stesso; do the ~ as your father fa' come tuo padre; and the ~ to you! altrettanto a te!; I don't feel the ~ about it non la vedo allo stesso modo; I still feel the ~ about you provo sempre lo stesso sentimento nei tuoi confronti; ~ here! anch'io!

same·ness ['seɪmnɪs] *n (monotony)* monotonia.

sam·ple ['sɑːmpl] 1 *n (gen)* campione *m; (fig)* saggio; to take a ~ prelevare un campione; to take a blood ~ fare un prelievo di sangue; free ~ campione omaggio. 2 *vt (food, wine)* assaggiare.

sana·to·rium [,sænə'tɔːrɪəm] *n, pl* sanatoria (a) convalescenziario; *(for tuberculosis)* sanatorio. (b) *(Scol)* infermeria.

sanc·ti·fy ['sæŋktɪfaɪ] *vt* santificare.

sanc·ti·mo·ni·ous [,sæŋktɪ'məʊnɪəs] *adj (person)* che fa la morale; *(tone)* moraleggiante.

sanc·tion ['sæŋkʃən] **1** n (gen) sanzione f; **to impose economic** ~s **on** or **against** adottare sanzioni economiche contro. **2** vt sancire, sanzionare.

sanc·tity ['sæŋktɪtɪ] n (of person, marriage) santità; (of oath, place) carattere m sacro.

sanc·tu·ary ['sæŋktjʊərɪ] n (Rel) santuario; (fig, Pol: refuge) asilo; (for wildlife, birds) riserva.

sand [sænd] **1** n sabbia; (beach): ~s spiaggia. **2** vt (a) (road) cospargere di sabbia. (b) (also: ~ **down**: wood etc) cartavetrare. **3** cpd: ~ **dune** n duna.

san·dal ['sændl] n sandalo.

sand·bag ['sændbæg] n sacco di sabbia.

sand·bank ['sændbæŋk] n banco di sabbia.

sand·blast ['sændblɑːst] vt sabbiare.

sand·castle ['sændkɑːsl] n castello di sabbia.

sand·paper ['sænd,peɪpə'] **1** n carta vetrata. **2** vt trattare con la carta vetrata.

sand·pit ['sændpɪt] n cava di sabbia; (for children) buca di sabbia.

sand·shoes ['sændʃuːz] npl scarpe fpl di tela.

sand·stone ['sændstəʊn] n arenaria.

sand·storm ['sændstɔːm] n tempesta di sabbia.

sand·wich ['sænwɪdʒ] **1** n tramezzino, sandwich m inv; **a ham** ~ un sandwich al prosciutto. **2** vt (also: ~ **in**: person, appointment etc) infilare; **to be** ~**ed between** essere incastrato fra. **3** cpd: ~ **course** n ≃ corso di formazione professionale; ~ **man** n uomo sandwich.

sandy ['sændɪ] adj (-ier, -iest) (gen) sabbioso(a); (colour) color sabbia inv; (hair) biondo sabbia inv.

sane [seɪn] adj (-r, -st) (person) sano(a) di mente; (judgment etc) sensato(a), assennato(a).

sang [sæŋ] pt of **sing**.

sang·froid [,sɑ̃ːŋ'frwɑː] n sangue m freddo.

san·guine ['sæŋgwɪn] adj (fig) ottimista.

sani·ta·rium [,sænɪ'tɛərɪəm] n (Am) = **sanatorium**.

sani·tary ['sænɪtərɪ] adj (clean) igienico(a); (for health protection) sanitario(a). **2** cpd: ~ **towel** n, (Am) ~ **napkin** n assorbente m (igienico).

sani·ta·tion [,sænɪ'teɪʃən] n (plumbing: in house) impianti mpl igienici; (: in town) fognature fpl.

san·ity ['sænɪtɪ] n (of person) sanità mentale; (of judgment) buonsenso.

sank [sæŋk] pt of **sink**[1].

Santa Claus [,sæntə'klɔːz] n Babbo Natale.

sap[1] [sæp] n (Bot) linfa.

sap[2] [sæp] vt (strength) fiaccare; (confidence) far perdere.

sap·ling ['sæplɪŋ] n alberello.

sap·phire ['sæfaɪə'] **1** n zaffiro. **2** cpd (necklace) di zaffiri; ~ **ring** n anello di zaffiri (or con uno zaffiro).

sar·casm ['sɑːkæzəm] n sarcasmo.

sar·cas·tic [sɑː'kæstɪk] adj sarcastico(a); **to be** ~ fare del sarcasmo.

sar·dine [sɑː'diːn] n sardina.

Sar·dinia [sɑː'dɪnɪə] n Sardegna.

sar·don·ic [sɑː'dɒnɪk] adj sardonico(a).

sash[1] [sæʃ] n (of dress etc) fusciacca; (on uniform) fascia.

sash[2] [sæʃ] **1** n (window ~) telaio. **2** cpd: ~ **window** n finestra a saliscendi.

sat [sæt] pt, pp of **sit**.

Satan ['seɪtn] n Satana m.

sa·tan·ic [sə'tænɪk] adj satanico(a).

satch·el ['sætʃəl] n cartella.

sat·el·lite ['sætəlaɪt] **1** n (all senses) satellite m. **2** cpd: ~ **town** n città f inv satellite.

sa·ti·ate ['seɪʃɪeɪt] vt saziare.

sat·in ['sætɪn] **1** n raso. **2** adj (dress, blouse etc) di raso; (paper) satinato(a); **with a** ~ **finish** satinato.

sat·ire ['sætaɪə'] n: ~ (**on**) satira (di, su).

sa·tiri·cal [sə'tɪrɪkəl] adj satirico(a).

sati·rist ['sætərɪst] n (writer etc) scrittore(trice) etc satirico(a); (cartoonist) caricaturista m/f.

sat·is·fac·tion [,sætɪs'fækʃən] n (gen) soddisfazione f; (of ambitions, hopes) realizzazione f; **has it been done to your** ~? ne è rimasto soddisfatto?; **it gives me great** ~ **to learn that...** è con mio grande piacere che apprendo che... .

sat·is·fac·tory [,sætɪs'fæktərɪ] adj soddisfacente; (Scol) sufficiente.

sat·is·fy ['sætɪsfaɪ] vt (a) (make content) soddisfare, contentare. (b) (need, condition, creditor) soddisfare; (hunger) calmare; **to** ~ **the requirements** rispondere ai requisiti. (c) (convince): **to** ~ **sb** (**that**) convincere qn (che), persuadere qn (che); **to** ~ **o.s. of sth** accertarsi di qc.

sat·is·fy·ing ['sætɪsfaɪɪŋ] adj (gen) soddisfacente; (food, meal) sostanzioso(a).

satu·rate ['sætʃəreɪt] vt: **to** ~ (**with**) inzuppare (di); (Chem) saturare (di).

satu·ra·tion [,sætʃə'reɪʃən] **1** n saturazione f. **2** cpd: **to reach** ~ **point** (Chem) raggiungere il punto di saturazione; (fig) arrivare a saturazione.

Sat·ur·day ['sætədɪ] n sabato; for usage see **Tuesday**.

sa·tyr ['sætə'] n satiro.

sauce [sɔːs] n (a) salsa. (b) (fam: impudence) faccia tosta.

sauce·pan ['sɔːspən] n pentola, casseruola.

sau·cer ['sɔːsə'] n piattino.

saucy ['sɔːsɪ] adj (-ier, -iest) (impertinent) sfacciato(a); (look) provocante.

Sau·di Ara·bia ['saʊdɪə'reɪbɪə] n Arabia Saudita.

sau·na ['sɔːnə] n sauna.

saun·ter ['sɔːntə'] vi: **to** ~ **in/out** entrare/uscire con disinvoltura; **to** ~ **up and down** passeggiare su e giù.

sau·sage ['sɒsɪdʒ] **1** n (to be cooked) salsiccia; (salami etc) salame m. **2** cpd: ~ **meat** n carne macinata per salsicce; ~ **roll** n involtino di pasta sfoglia ripieno di salsiccia.

sau·té ['saʊteɪ] **1** adj (Culin: potatoes) saltato(a); (: onions) soffritto(a). **2** vt (see adj) far saltare; far soffriggere.

sav·age ['sævɪdʒ] **1** adj (a) (gen) violento(a); (animal) feroce; (murderer) selvaggio(a). (b) (primitive: custom, tribe) selvaggio(a). **2** n selvaggio/a. **3** vt (subj: dog etc) sbranare; (fig) fare a pezzi.

sa·van·nah [sə'vænə] n savana.

save[1] [seɪv] **1** vt (a) (rescue: also Rel): **to** ~ (**from**) salvare (da); **to** ~ **sb from falling** impedire a qn di cadere; **to** ~ **sb's life** salvare la vita a qn; **I couldn't do it to** ~ **my life** (fig fam) non lo farei manco morto; **to** ~ **the situation** or **the day** salvare la situazione; **to** ~ **one's (own) skin** (fam) salvare la (propria) pelle; **to** ~ **face** salvare la faccia; **to** ~ **a goal** (Ftbl) parare un goal; **God** ~ **the Queen!** Dio salvi la Regina!

(b) (put aside: money: also: ~ **up**) risparmiare, mettere da parte; (: food, newspapers) conservare, tenere (da parte); (collect: stamps) raccogliere; **I** ~**d you a piece of cake** ti ho messo or tenuto da parte una fetta di dolce; ~ **me a seat** tienimi il posto; **to** ~ **sth till last** tenere qc per ultimo.

(c) (avoid using: money, effort etc) risparmiare; **it** ~**d us a lot of trouble/another journey** ci ha evitato or risparmiato una bella seccatura/un altro viaggio; **it will** ~ **me an hour** mi farà risparmiare un'ora; ~ **time...** per risparmiare or guadagnare tempo...; ~ **your breath** risparmia il fiato.

2 *vi* (a) *(also:* ~ **up**): to ~ **(for)** mettere i soldi da parte (per).

(b): to ~ on **time/energy** *etc* risparmiare tempo/energia *etc;* to ~ on **food/transport** risparmiare *or* economizzare sul vitto/trasporto. 3 *n (Sport)* parata.

save[2] [seɪv] *prep (poet, old)* salvo, a eccezione di.

sav·eloy ['sævələɪ] *n* cervellata.

sav·ing ['seɪvɪŋ] 1 *n (of time, money):* ~ **(of, in)** risparmio (di); **life** ~s i risparmi di tutta una vita; to **make** ~s fare economia; to **live on** *or* **off one's** ~s vivere dei propri risparmi. 2 *cpd:* ~ **grace** *n:* her kindness is her ~ grace si salva grazie alla sua gentilezza; ~s **account** *n* libretto di risparmio; ~s **bank** *n* cassa di risparmio.

sav·iour, *(Am)* **sav·ior** ['seɪvjə[r]] *n* salvatore/trice.

sa·vour, *(Am)* **sa·vor** ['seɪvə[r]] 1 *n* sapore *m,* gusto. 2 *vt (also fig)* assaporare, gustare. 3 *vi:* to ~ **of** sth sapere di qc.

sa·voury, *(Am)* **sa·vory** ['seɪvərɪ] 1 *adj (appetizing)* appetitoso(a), saporito(a); *(not sweet)* salato(a); **not very** ~ *(fig: district)* poco raccomandabile; *(: subject)* poco appetitoso(a). 2 *n (Culin)* piatto salato; *(: on toast)* crostino.

saw[1] [sɔː] *(vb: pt* sawed, *pp* sawed *or* sawn) 1 *n* sega. 2 *vt* segare; to ~ sth **up** fare a pezzi qc con la sega; to ~ sth **off** segare via qc. 3 *vi:* to ~ **through** segare.

saw[2] [sɔː] *pt of* see.

saw·dust ['sɔːdʌst] *n* segatura.

saw·mill ['sɔːmɪl] *n* segheria.

sawn [sɔːn] *pp of* saw[1].

sawn-off ['sɔːn,ɒf] *adj:* ~ **shotgun** fucile *m* a canne mozze.

saxo·phone ['sæksəfəʊn] *n* sassofono.

say [seɪ] *(vb: pt, pp* said) 1 *vt, vi* (a) *(gen)* dire; *(subj: dial, gauge)* indicare; he **said (that)** he'd do it ha detto che l'avrebbe fatto; she **said (that)** I was to give you this ha detto di darti questo; my **watch** ~s 3 **o'clock** il mio orologio fa le 3; the **rules** ~ that... il regolamento dice che...; to ~ **mass/a prayer** dire messa/una preghiera; to ~ **yes/no** dire sì/di no; to ~ **yes/no to a proposal** accettare/rifiutare una proposta; I **wouldn't** ~ **no** *(Brit fam)* non mi dispiacerebbe; to ~ **goodbye/goodnight to sb** dire arrivederci/buonanotte a qn; to ~ **sth again** ripetere qc; ~ **after me...** ripetete con me...; **I've nothing more to** ~ non ho altro da dire; **I'll** ~ **more about it later** ne riparlerò più tardi; let's ~ **no more about it** non ne parliamo più; **I'd rather not** ~ preferisco non pronunciarmi; I **should** ~ **it's worth about £100** direi che vale sulle 100 sterline; (let's) ~ **it's worth £20** diciamo *or* ammettiamo che valga 20 sterline; **shall we** ~ **Tuesday?** facciamo martedì?; will **you take an offer of,** ~, **£50?** accetti un'offerta di, diciamo, 50 sterline?

(b) *(in phrases):* **that is to** ~ vale a dire, cioè; to ~ **nothing of** per non parlare di; to ~ **the least** a dir poco; she **hasn't much** *or* has **nothing to** ~ **for herself** *(by way of excuse)* non ha una scusa decente; *(by way of conversation)* non sa dire due parole; **that doesn't** ~ **much for him** non torna a suo credito; **it goes without** ~ing **(that)** va da sé (che); **there's no** ~ing **what he'll do** Dio solo sa cosa farà; **it's not for me to** ~ non sta a me dire; **what do** *or* **would you** ~ **to a walk?** che ne dici *or* diresti di una passeggiata?; **when all is said and done** in fin dei conti; **it is said that...**, they ~ **that...** si dice che... + *sub,* dicono che... + *sub;* **there is something** *or* **a lot to be said for it** ha i suoi lati positivi; **it must be said that...** bisogna ammettere che...; **he is said to have...** si dice che

abbia...; **it is easier** *or* **sooner said than done** è facile a dirsi; ~! *(Am),* I ~! *(Brit) (calling attention)* senta!, scusi!; *(in surprise, appreciation)* accipicchia!; **I'll** ~! *(fam)* e come!; **I should** ~ **it is** *or* so!, **you can** ~ **THAT again!** *(fam)* altro che!; **you don't** ~! *(fam: often hum)* ma va'!, ma che dici!; **you've said it!** *(fam: emphatic)* l'hai detto!; ~ **no more!** basta così!

2 *n:* to **have one's** ~ dire la propria; to **have a** ~/**no** ~ **in the matter** avere/non avere voce in capitolo.

say·ing ['seɪɪŋ] *n* detto; **as the** ~ **goes** come dice il proverbio.

say-so ['seɪsəʊ] *n (fam: authority):* to **do sth on sb's** ~ fare qc col permesso di qn; **why should I believe it just on your** ~? perché dovrei crederci, solo perché lo dici tu?

scab [skæb] *n* (a) *(Med)* crosta. (b) *(fam pej: blackleg)* crumiro/a.

scaf·fold ['skæfəld] *n (Constr: also:* ~ing) impalcatura, ponteggio; *(for execution)* patibolo.

scald [skɔːld] 1 *n* scottatura. 2 *vt (gen)* scottare; *(Culin: tomatoes etc)* sbollentare; *(sterilize)* sterilizzare.

scald·ing ['skɔːldɪŋ] *adj (also:* ~ **hot)** bollente.

scale[1] [skeɪl] 1 *n (of fish, reptile etc)* scaglia, squama; *(flake: of rust, chalk)* scaglia; *(: of skin)* squama. 2 *vt (fish)* squamare; *(kettle)* scrostare.

scale[2] [skeɪl] 1 *n* (a) *(on ruler, thermometer)* scala graduata; *(of model, map)* scala; **pay** ~ scala dei salari; ~ **of charges** tariffa; **on a** ~ **of 1 cm to 5 km** in scala di 1 a 500.000; **on a large** ~ su vasta scala; **on a small** ~ su scala ridotta; to **draw sth to** ~ disegnare qc in scala. (b) *(Mus)* scala. 2 *vt (wall, mountain)* scalare. 3 *cpd:* ~ **drawing** *n* disegno in scala; ~ **model** *n* modellino.

♦ **scale down** *vt* + *adv* ridurre (proporzionalmente).

scales [skeɪlz] *npl:* **(pair** *or* **set of)** ~ bilancia; **tips the** ~ **at 70 kilos** pesa 70 chili; to **turn** *or* **tip the** ~ **in sb's/sth's favour** far pendere la bilancia dalla parte di qn/qc; to **turn** *or* **tip the** ~ **against sb** giocare a sfavore di qn.

scal·lop ['skɒləp] *n* (a) *(Zool)* pettine *m.* (b) *(Sewing)* smerlo.

scalp [skælp] 1 *n* cuoio capelluto; *(as trophy)* scalpo. 2 *vt* scotennare.

scal·pel ['skælpəl] *n* bisturi *m inv.*

scamp [skæmp] *n (fam: child)* peste *f.*

scamp·er ['skæmpə[r]] *vi* + *adv (child):* to ~ **about** sgambettare; to ~ **in/out** *etc* entrare/uscire *etc* sgambettando.

scan [skæn] 1 *vt* (a) *(inspect closely: horizon, sb's face)* scrutare; *(: crowd)* scrutare tra; *(: newspaper)* scorrere attentamente. (b) *(glance at)* dare un'occhiata a. (c) *(Radar: sea bed)* scandagliare; *(: sky)* esplorare. 2 *vi (Poetry)* scandire. 3 *n (Med)* ecografia.

scan·dal ['skændl] *n* (a) *(public furore, disgrace)* scandalo; **it's a** ~ **that...** è uno scandalo *or* è scandaloso che... + *sub.* (b) *(gossip)* chiacchiere *fpl;* **have you heard the latest** ~ **about...?** hai sentito l'ultima su...?

scan·dal·ize ['skændəlaɪz] *vt* scandalizzare.

scandal·monger ['skændl,mʌŋgə[r]] *n* malalingua.

scan·dal·ous ['skændələs] *adj* scandaloso(a).

Scan·di·na·via [,skændɪ'neɪvɪə] *n* Scandinavia.

Scan·di·na·vian [,skændɪ'neɪvɪən] *adj, n* scandinavo(a) *(m/f).*

scan·ner ['skænə[r]] *n (Radar, Med)* scanner *m inv.*

scant [skænt] *adj* (-er, -est) scarso(a); **with** ~ **courtesy** poco cortesemente; to **pay** ~ **attention to** prestare poca attenzione a.

scanti·ly ['skæntɪlɪ] *adv*: ~ **clad** *or* **dressed** succintamente vestito(a).

scanty ['skæntɪ] *adj* (**-ier, -iest**) *(meal etc)* scarso(a); *(clothing)* succinto(a).

scape·goat ['skeɪpgəʊt] *n* capro espiatorio.

scar [skɑːʳ] **1** *n (Med)* cicatrice *f; (on face)* sfregio, cicatrice; *(fig: on building, landscape etc)* segno, marchio; **it left a deep** ~ **on his mind** gli ha lasciato il segno. **2** *vt (gen)* lasciare delle cicatrici su; *(face)* sfregiare; *(fig)* segnare, lasciare il segno su; ~**red by smallpox** butterato dal vaiolo. **3** *vi (also:* ~ **over:** *heal)* cicatrizzarsi.

scarce [skeəs] *adj* (**-r, -st**) *(money, food, resources)* scarso(a); **to be** ~ scarseggiare; **to grow** *or* **become** ~ diventare raro(a); **to make o.s.** ~ *(fig fam)* squagliarsela, tagliare la corda.

scarce·ly ['skeəslɪ] *adv (barely)* appena; ~ **anybody** quasi nessuno; ~ **ever** quasi mai; **I** ~ **know what to say** non so proprio che dire; **I can** ~ **believe it** faccio fatica a crederci; **I've** ~ **seen him** l'ho visto raramente.

scar·city ['skeəsɪtɪ] *n*, **scarce·ness** ['skeəsnɪs] *n* scarsità.

scare ['skeəʳ] **1** *n* spavento, paura; **to cause a** ~ *(amongst)* creare il panico (in *or* tra); **to give sb a** ~ far prendere uno spavento a qn, mettere paura a qn; **there was a bomb** ~ **at Harrods** hanno evacuato Harrods per paura di un attentato dinamitardo. **2** *vt* spaventare, impaurire; **to** ~ **sb to death,** ~ **sb stiff** *(fam)* far prendere un colpo a qn, spaventare qn a morte; **to be** ~**d to death, be** ~**d stiff** avere una paura folle, morire dalla paura; **to be** ~**d out of one's wits** *(fam)* non capire più niente dalla paura.

♦ **scare away, scare off** *vt + adv (subj: dog)* mettere in fuga; *(: price etc)* far scappare.

scare·crow ['skeəkrəʊ] *n* spaventapasseri *m inv*.

scared [skeəd] *adj (see also* **scare 2**): **to be** ~ **(of)** aver paura (di).

scare·monger ['skeə,mʌŋgəʳ] *n* allarmista *m/f*.

scarf [skɑːf] *n, pl* **scarves** *(woollen)* sciarpa; *(head*~*)* foulard *m inv*.

scar·let ['skɑːlɪt] **1** *n* scarlatto. **2** *adj* scarlatto(a); ~ **fever** scarlattina.

scarves [skɑːvz] *npl of* **scarf.**

scary ['skeərɪ] *adj* (**-ier, -iest**) *(fam)* che fa paura.

scath·ing ['skeɪðɪŋ] *adj (remark, criticism)* aspro(a); *(look)* sprezzante; **to be** ~ **about sth** essere molto critico rispetto a qc.

scat·ter ['skætəʳ] **1** *vt* **(a)** *(gen)* spargere; *(papers)* sparpagliare. **(b)** *(disperse: crowd, clouds)* disperdere; *(: enemy)* mettere in fuga; **her relatives are** ~**ed about the world** la sua famiglia è sparsa per il mondo. **2** *vi (crowd)* disperdersi, sbandarsi.

scatter·brain ['skætəbreɪn] *n (fam)* scervellato/a.

scatter·brained ['skætəbreɪnd] *adj (fam: also:* **scatty)** sventato(a), scervellato(a).

scav·enge ['skævɪndʒ] *vi (person)*: **to** ~ **(for)** frugare tra i rifiuti (alla ricerca di); *(hyenas etc)* nutrirsi di carogne.

scav·en·ger ['skævɪndʒəʳ] *n (Zool)* insetto *(or* animale *m)* necrofago; *(person)* accattone/a.

sce·nario [sɪ'nɑːrɪəʊ] *n (Theatre, Cine)* copione *m; (fig)* situazione *f*.

scene [siːn] *n* **(a)** *(gen, Theatre, Cine, TV)* scena; **indoor/outdoor** ~**s** interni/esterni *mpl*; **the** ~ **is set in a castle** la scena si svolge in un castello; **to set the** ~ *(fig)* creare l'atmosfera; **behind the** ~**s** *(also fig)* dietro le quinte; **the political** ~ **in Italy** il quadro politico in Italia; **the Punk** ~ il mondo dei Punk; ~**s of violence** scene di violenza; **to make a** ~ *(fam: fuss)* fare una scenata. **(b)** *(place)*

luogo, scena; **at the** ~ **of the crime** sul luogo *or* sulla scena del delitto; **she needs a change of** ~ ha bisogno di cambiare aria *or* ambiente; **to appear** *or* **come on the** ~ *(also fig)* entrare in scena; **it's not my** ~ *(fam)* non è il mio genere. **(c)** *(sight)* scena, spettacolo; *(view)* vista, spettacolo; **a** ~ **of utter destruction** una scena di totale distruzione.

scen·ery ['siːnərɪ] *n (landscape)* paesaggio; *(Theatre)* scenario, scenari *mpl*.

sce·nic ['siːnɪk] *adj (postcard, view)* pittoresco(a); *(road, railway)* panoramico(a).

scent [sɛnt] **1** *n* **(a)** *(smell, perfume)* profumo. **(b)** *(Hunting etc)* tracce *fpl*, pista; **to follow/lose the** ~ seguire/perdere le tracce *or* la pista; **to pick up the** ~ fiutare le tracce; **to put** *or* **throw sb off the** ~ *(fig)* far perdere le tracce a qn, sviare qn. **2** *vt* **(a)** *(make sth smell nice)*: **to** ~ **(with)** profumare (di *or* con). **(b)** *(smell)* fiutare.

scep·tic, *(Am)* **skep·tic** ['skeptɪk] *n* scettico/a.

scep·ti·cal, *(Am)* **skep·ti·cal** ['skeptɪkəl] *adj*: ~ **(of** *or* **about)** scettico(a) (su *or* in fatto di).

scep·ti·cism, *(Am)* **skep·ti·cism** ['skeptɪsɪzəm] *n* scetticismo.

scep·tre, *(Am)* **scep·ter** [ˈsɛptəʳ] *n* scettro.

sched·ule ['ʃedjuːl. *(Am)* 'skedjuːl] *n* **(a)** *(timetable: of work, visits, events)* programma *m; (: of trains)* orario; **the work is behind/ahead of** ~ il lavoro è in ritardo/in anticipo sul previsto; **on** ~ in orario; **we are working to a very tight** ~ il nostro programma di lavoro è molto intenso; **everything went according to** ~ tutto è andato secondo i piani *or* secondo il previsto. **(b)** *(list: of contents, goods)* lista; *(Customs, Tax etc)* tabella.

sched·uled ['ʃedjuːld. *(Am)* 'skedjuːld] *adj (date, time)* fissato(a); *(visit, event)* programmato(a); *(train, bus, stop)* previsto(a) (sull'orario); ~ **flight** volo di linea; **the meeting is** ~ **for 7.00** *or* **to begin at 7.00** la riunione è fissata per le 7; **this building is** ~ **for demolition** questo edificio è destinato alla demolizione.

sche·mat·ic [skɪ'mætɪk] *adj* schematico(a).

scheme [skiːm] **1** *n* **(a)** *(plan)* piano, progetto; **a** ~ **to rebuild** *or* **for rebuilding sth** un piano per la ricostruzione di qc; **a** ~ **of work** un piano di lavoro; **colour** ~ combinazione *f* di colori; **it's some crazy** ~ **of his** è una delle sue idee balzane. **(b)** *(plot)*: ~ **(to do** *or* **for doing sth/for sth)** piano (per fare qc/per qc). **2** *vi*: **to** ~ **(to do)** tramare (per fare), complottare (per fare).

schem·ing ['skiːmɪŋ] **1** *adj* intrigante. **2** *n* intrighi *mpl*.

schism ['sɪzəm] *n* scisma *m*.

schizo·phre·nia [ˌskɪtsəʊ'friːnjə] *n* schizofrenia.

schizo·phren·ic [ˌskɪtsəʊ'frenɪk] *adj, n* schizofrenico(a) *(m/f)*.

schol·ar ['skɒləʳ] *n (learned person)* studioso/a; **a famous Dickens** ~ un noto studioso di Dickens; **he's never been much of a** ~ non è mai stato uno studioso.

schol·ar·ly ['skɒləlɪ] *adj* dotto(a), erudito(a).

schol·ar·ship ['skɒləʃɪp] *n (learning)* erudizione *f*, cultura; *(award)* borsa (di studio).

scho·las·tic [skə'læstɪk] *adj* scolastico(a).

school [skuːl] **1** *n* **(a)** *(gen)* scuola; **to be at/go to** ~ frequentare la/andare a scuola; **to leave** ~ lasciare la scuola; ~ **of motoring** scuola guida, autoscuola; **the Dutch** ~ la scuola olandese; ~ **of thought** corrente *f* di pensiero; **of the old** ~ *(fig)* della vecchia scuola. **(b)** *(Univ)* facoltà *f inv*; **medical/law** ~ facoltà di medicina/legge; **art** ~ accademia delle Belle Arti; **she's at law** ~ studia legge; **S**~ **of Interpreters** Scuola Interpreti. **2** *vt* *(animal)* addestrare; *(reaction, voice etc)* controllare; **he ~ed himself in patience** *or* **to be patient** si è abituato ad essere paziente. **3** *cpd (year, fees, report etc)* scolastico(a); **~ age** *n* età scolare; **~ bus** *n* scuolabus *m inv;* **during ~ hours, in ~ time** nelle ore di scuola.

school² [sku:l] *n (of fish)* banco.

school·book ['sku:lbʊk] *n* libro scolastico, libro di scuola.

school·boy ['sku:lbɔɪ] **1** *n* scolaro. **2** *cpd:* **~ slang** *n* gergo studentesco.

school·child ['sku:ltʃaɪld] *n, pl* **-children** scolaro/a.

school·days ['sku:ldeɪz] *npl* tempi *mpl* della scuola.

school·girl ['sku:lgɜ:l] *n* scolara.

school·ing ['sku:lɪŋ] *n* istruzione *f;* **compulsory ~** istruzione *f* obbligatoria, scuola dell'obbligo.

school-leaver ['sku:l,li:vəʳ] *n* chi lascia la scuola.

school-leaving age [,sku:l'li:vɪŋ,eɪdʒ] *n* limite *m* d'età della scuola dell'obbligo.

school·master ['sku:l,mɑ:stəʳ] *n (in primary school)* maestro; *(in secondary school)* insegnante *m,* professore *m.*

school·mistress ['sku:l,mɪstrɪs] *n (in primary school)* maestra; *(in secondary school)* insegnante *f,* professoressa.

school·teacher ['sku:l,ti:tʃəʳ] *n (in primary school)* maestro/a; *(in secondary school)* insegnante *m/f.*

schoon·er ['sku:nəʳ] *n (Naut)* schooner *m inv.*

sci·ati·ca [saɪ'ætɪkə] *n (Med)* sciatica.

sci·ence ['saɪəns] **1** *n* scienza; **the natural/social ~s** le scienze naturali/sociali; **the ~s** le scienze; *(Scol)* le materie scientifiche. **2** *cpd (teacher, exam)* di scienze; *(subject, equipment, laboratory)* scientifico(a); **S~ Faculty** *n (Univ)* Facoltà di Scienze; **~ fiction** *n* fantascienza.

sci·en·tif·ic [,saɪən'tɪfɪk] *adj* scientifico(a).

sci·en·tist ['saɪəntɪst] *n* scienziato/a.

Scil·ly Isles ['sɪlɪaɪlz] *npl* isole *fpl* Scilly.

scin·til·lat·ing ['sɪntɪleɪtɪŋ] *adj (jewels, chandelier)* scintillante; *(wit, conversation, company)* brillante.

scis·sors ['sɪzəz] *npl* forbici *fpl.*

scle·ro·sis [sklɪ'rəʊsɪs] *n (Med)* sclerosi *f.*

scoff [skɒf] **1** *vi:* **to ~ (at sb/sth)** ridere (di qn/qc). **2** *vt (fam: eat)* papparsi; **he ~ed the lot** si è pappato tutto.

scold [skəʊld] *vt:* **to ~ sb (for doing sth)** sgridare qn (per aver fatto qc).

scold·ing ['skəʊldɪŋ] *n* lavata di capo, sgridata.

scol·lop ['skɒləp] *n* = **scallop.**

scone [skɒn] *n* tipo di focaccina da tè.

scoop [sku:p] **1** *n* **(a)** *(for flour etc)* paletta; *(for ice cream)* misurino; *(for water)* mestolo, ramaiolo. **(b)** *(by newspaper)* colpo (giornalistico); *(Comm)* (grosso) colpo, affarone *m.* **2** *vt (Comm: market)* accaparrarsi; *(: profit)* intascare; *(Comm, Press: competitors)* battere sul tempo; *(Press):* **to ~ an exclusive (about)** accaparrarsi l'esclusiva (su).

♦ scoop out *vt + adv (flour, water etc)* prendere con la paletta *(of il misurino) etc; (hole)* scavare.

♦ scoop up *vt + adv (child)* prendere (in braccio); *(books)* prendere su.

scoot·er ['sku:təʳ] *n (child's)* monopattino; *(adult's)* scooter *m inv.*

scope [skəʊp] *n (opportunity: for action etc)* possibilità *fpl; (range: of law, activity)* ambito; *(capacity: of person)* capacità *fpl;* **it's beyond the ~ of a child's mind** è al di sopra delle capacità di un bambino; **it's well within his ~ to...** è perfettamente in grado di...; **there is plenty of ~ for improvement** ci sono notevoli possibilità di miglioramento; **it is within/beyond the ~ of this**

book rientra/non rientra nei limiti di questo libro.

scorch [skɔ:tʃ] **1** *n (also:* **~ mark)** bruciacchiatura. **2** *vt (fabric etc)* bruciacchiare, strinare; *(subj: sun, fire: grass)* bruciare.

scorch·er ['skɔ:tʃəʳ] *n (fam: hot day)* giornata da crepare di caldo.

scorch·ing ['skɔ:tʃɪŋ] *adj (also:* **~ hot)** rovente; *(: day)* torrido(a); *(: sun)* che spacca le pietre; *(: sand)* bollente; **it's ~** fa un caldo pazzesco.

score [skɔ:ʳ] **1** *n* **(a)** *(Sport, Cards)* punteggio; **to keep (the) ~** segnare i punti; **there's no ~ yet** *(Sport)* finora nessuno ha segnato (un punto); **there was no ~ in the match** *(Sport)* hanno finito zero a zero; **what's the ~?** *(fig fam)* a che punto siamo?; **to know the ~** *(fig fam)* sapere come stanno le cose; **to have an old ~ to settle with sb** *(fig)* avere un vecchio conto da saldare con qn. **(b)** *(account)* motivo, titolo; **on that ~** per questo (motivo). **(c)** *(cut, mark: on wood)* scalfittura; *(: on leather, card)* incisione *f.* **(d)** *(Mus: of opera)* partitura, spartito; *(: of film)* colonna sonora. **(e)** *(twenty):* **a ~** venti; **a ~ of people** una ventina di persone; **~s of people** *(fig)* un sacco di gente.

2 *vt* **(a)** *(goal, point, runs)* segnare, fare; **to ~ 75% in an exam** prendere 75 su 100 a *or* in un esame; **to ~ a hit** *(Fencing)* fare una stoccata; *(Shooting)* prendere il bersaglio; **to ~ a hit with sth** *(fig)* far centro con qc; **to ~ a hit with sb** *(fig)* far colpo su qn. **(b)** *(cut: leather, wood, card)* incidere. **(c)** *(music: for piano etc)* scrivere; *(: for film)* scrivere la colonna sonora per.

3 *vi (Sport: goal)* segnare; *(: points)* fare punti; *(: keep ~)* segnare i punti; **to ~ over sb** *(fig)* dare dei punti a qn.

♦ score off *vt + adv* **(a)** *(name, item on list)* cancellare. **(b)** *(fig: in argument):* **to ~ points off sb** avere la meglio su qn.

score·board ['skɔ:bɔ:d] *n* tabellone *m* (segnapunti).

scor·er ['skɔ:rəʳ] *n (keeping score)* segnapunti *m/f inv; (player)* marcatore/trice.

scorn ['skɔ:n] **1** *n* disprezzo, scherno; **to pour ~ on sb/sth** deridere qn/qc. **2** *vt (gen)* disprezzare; *(advice, offer, attempt)* accogliere con disprezzo; **to ~ to tell a lie** rifiutarsi di dire una bugia.

scorn·ful ['skɔ:nfʊl] *adj* sprezzante; **to be ~ about** sth parlare con disprezzo di qc.

Scor·pio ['skɔ:pɪəʊ] *n (Astron, Astrology)* Scorpione *m;* **to be ~** essere dello Scorpione.

scor·pi·on ['skɔ:pɪən] *n* scorpione *m.*

Scot [skɒt] *n* scozzese *m/f.*

Scotch [skɒtʃ] **1** *adj:* **~ egg** uovo sodo ricoperto di salsiccia; **~ tape** *n* ® scotch *m.* **2** *n (whisky)* scotch *m inv.*

scotch [skɒtʃ] *vt (attempt, plan)* bloccare; *(revolt, uprising)* stroncare; *(rumour, claim)* mettere a tacere.

scot-free [,skɒt'fri:] *adj:* **to get off ~** *(unpunished)* farla franca; *(unhurt)* uscire illeso(a).

Scot·land ['skɒtlənd] *n* Scozia.

Scots [skɒts] *adj* scozzese.

Scots·man ['skɒtsmən] *n, pl* **-men** scozzese *m.*

Scots·woman ['skɒtswʊmən] *n, pl* **-women** scozzese *f.*

Scot·tish ['skɒtɪʃ] *adj* scozzese.

scoun·drel ['skaʊndrəl] *n* farabutto, furfante *m/f.*

scour ['skaʊəʳ] *vt* **(a)** *(pan, floor etc)* sfregare. **(b)** *(search: area, countryside)* setacciare, battere palmo a palmo.

scour·er ['skaʊərəʳ] *n (pad)* paglietta; *(powder)* (detersivo) abrasivo.

scourge [skɜ:dʒ] *n* flagello.

scout [skaʊt] **1** *n (person: Mil)* ricognitore *m; (boy)* boy-scout *m inv.* **2** *vi:* **to ~ around for** andare alla ricerca di.

scout·master ['skaʊt,mɑːstəʳ] *n* capogruppo dei boy-scout.

scowl [skaʊl] **1** *n* sguardo torvo; **with a ~** con io sguardo torvo. **2** *vi* accigliarsi; **to ~ at sb** guardare qn in malo modo.

scrab·ble ['skræbl] **1** *vi:* **to ~ about** *or* **around for sth** cercare affannosamente qc. **2** *n (game):* **S~** ® Scarabeo ®.

scrag·gy ['skrægɪ] *adj* **(-ier, -iest)** *(neck, limb)* scheletrico(a); *(animal)* pelle e ossa *inv.*

scram [skræm] *vi (fam)* filare, filarsela.

scram·ble ['skræmbl] **1** *vi* **(a): to ~ down/along** *etc* scendere/avanzare *etc* a fatica; **to ~ for** *(coins, seats, job)* azzuffarsi per (prendere); **he ~d up (the hill)** si è inerpicato su (per la collina). **(b)** *(Sport):* **to go scrambling** fare il motocross. **2** *vt* **(a)** *(Culin)* strapazzare; **~d eggs** uova strapazzate. **(b)** *(Telec: message)* ingarbugliare. **3** *n* **(a)** *(rush)* corsa. **(b)** *(Sport: motorcycle meeting)* gara di motocross.

scram·bler ['skræmbləʳ] *n (Telec)* dispositivo che neutralizza le intercettazioni telefoniche.

scrap[1] [skræp] **1** *n* **(a)** *(small piece)* pezzo, pezzetto; *(fig: of truth)* briciolo, ombra; **a ~ of conversation** un frammento di conversazione; **there's not a ~ of proof** non c'è la benché minima prova; **it's not a ~ of use** non serve a un bel niente. **(b): ~s** *pl (left-overs)* avanzi *mpl.* **(c)** *(~ metal)* rottami *mpl* di ferro, ferraglia; **to sell sth for ~** vendere qc come ferro vecchio. **2** *vt (gen)* buttar via; *(ship)* demolire; *(plan etc)* scartare. **3** *cpd:* **~ dealer** *n,* **~ merchant** *n* commerciante *m* di ferraglia; **~ heap** *n* mucchio di rottami; **to throw sth on the ~ heap** *(fig)* mettere qc nel dimenticatoio; **~ metal** *n* ferraglia; **~ paper** *n* cartastraccia. **~ yard** *n* deposito di rottami; *(for cars)* cimitero delle macchine.

scrap[2] [skræp] *(fam)* **1** *n (fight)* baruffa. **2** *vi:* **to ~ (with sb)** fare a botte (con qn).

scrap·book ['skræpbʊk] *n* album *m inv* (di ritagli).

scrape [skreɪp] **1** *n* **(a)** *(act)* raschiatura; *(sound)* stridio; *(mark)* graffio; *(on leg, elbow)* scorticatura, sbucciatura. **(b)** *(fig)* pasticcio, guaio; **to get into/out of a ~** mettersi nei/tirarsi fuori dai pasticci *or* dai guai. **2** *vt (knee etc)* scorticare, sbucciare; *(clean: vegetables)* raschiare, grattare; *(: walls, woodwork)* raschiare; **the lorry ~d the wall** il camion ha strisciato il muro; **to ~ a living** sbarcare il lunario; **we managed to ~ enough money together** siamo riusciti a racimolare abbastanza soldi; **to ~ the bottom of the barrel** *(fig)* esser ridotto proprio male. **3** *vi (make sound)* grattare; *(rub):* **to ~ (against)** strusciare (contro).

♦ **scrape along** *vi + adv (fam: manage)* cavarsela; *(: live)* tirare avanti.

♦ **scrape off 1** *vt + adv (also: ~ away)* grattare via, raschiare via. **2** *vt + prep* grattare via.

♦ **scrape through 1** *vi + adv (succeed)* farcela per un pelo, cavarsela. **2** *vi + prep (exam)* passare per miracolo, passare per il rotto della cuffia.

scrap·er ['skreɪpəʳ] *n* raschietto.

scrap·py ['skræpɪ] *adj* **(-ier, -iest)** *(essay etc)* che non ha né capo né coda; *(knowledge, education)* frammentario(a); *(meal)* arrangiato(a).

scratch [skrætʃ] **1** *n* **(a)** *(mark)* graffio, graffiatura; **it's just a ~** è solo un graffio; **without a ~** *(unharmed)* illeso(a). **(b)** *(noise):* **I heard a ~ at the door** ho sentito grattare alla porta. **(c): to start from ~** *(fig)* cominciare da zero; **his work**

wasn't *or* **didn't come up to ~** il suo lavoro non ha raggiunto il livello desiderato; **to keep sth up to ~** mantenere qc in condizioni decenti.

2 *vt* **(a)** *(gen)* graffiare; *(one's name)* incidere; **we've barely ~ed the surface** *(fig: of problem, topic etc)* l'abbiamo appena sfiorato. **(b)** *(to relieve itch)* grattare; **he ~ed his head** si è grattato la testa; **you ~ my back and I'll ~ yours** *(fig)* una mano lava l'altra. **(c)** *(cancel: meeting, game)* cancellare; *(cross off list: horse, competitor)* eliminare.

3 *vi (person, dog etc)* grattarsi; *(hens)* razzolare, raspare; *(pen)* grattare, raschiare; *(clothing)* pungere; **the dog ~ed at the door** il cane raspava alla porta.

4 *cpd:* **~ meal** *n* pranzo arrangiato; **~ team** *n* squadra messa insieme a casaccio.

♦ **scratch out** *vt + adv (from list)* cancellare; **to ~ sb's eyes out** cavare gli occhi a qn.

scratch·pad ['skrætʃpæd] *n (Am)* notes *m inv,* blocchetto.

scratchy ['skrætʃɪ] *adj* **(-ier, -iest)** *(fabric)* ruvido(a); *(pen)* che gratta.

scrawl [skrɔːl] **1** *n (handwriting)* grafia illeggibile; *(brief note)* due righe *fpl.* **2** *vt* scribacchiare.

scrawny ['skrɔːnɪ] *adj* **(-ier, -iest)** *(neck, limb)* scheletrico(a); *(animal, person)* (tutto(a)) pelle e ossa.

scream [skriːm] **1** *n (of pain, fear)* grido, urlo, strillo; **~s of laughter** grasse risate; **he let out a ~** cacciò un urlo; **it was a ~** *(fig fam)* era da crepar dal ridere; **he's a ~** *(fig fam)* è una sagoma, è uno spasso. **2** *vt (subj: person: abuse etc)* gridare, urlare; *(subj: poster, headlines)* strombazzare. **3** *vi* gridare, urlare; **to ~ at sb (to do sth)** gridare a qn (di fare qc); **to ~ (out) with pain** gridare di *or* dal dolore; **to ~ for help** gridare aiuto; **to ~ with laughter** sbellicarsi dalle risa.

scree [skriː] *n* ghiaione *m.*

screech [skriːtʃ] **1** *n (of brakes, tyres)* stridio, stridore *m; (of owl)* strido; *(of person)* strillo, grido (acuto). **2** *vi (person)* strillare, mandare un grido acuto; *(owl, brakes)* stridere.

screeds [skriːdz] *npl (fam):* **to write ~** scrivere un romanzo *(iro).*

screen [skriːn] **1** *n* **(a)** *(in room)* paravento; *(for fire)* parafuoco; *(fig: of trees etc)* barriera; *(: of smoke)* cortina. **(b)** *(Cine, TV, Radar etc)* schermo; **stars of the big/small ~** divi dello schermo/del piccolo schermo. **2** *vt* **(a): to ~ (from)** *(hide: from view, sight)* nascondere (da); *(protect)* riparare (da); **he ~ed his eyes (from the sun) with his hand** si proteggeva gli occhi (dal sole) con la mano. **(b)** *(show: film)* proiettare. **(c)** *(sieve: coal)* vagliare; *(fig: person: for security)* passare al vaglio; *(: for illness)* sottoporre a controlli medici. **3** *cpd:* **~ test** *n* provino *(cinematografico).*

screen·ing ['skriːnɪŋ] *n* **(a)** *(of film)* proiezione *f.* **(b)** *(medical ~)* serie di controlli; *(for security)* controlli *mpl* di sicurezza.

screen·play ['skriːnpleɪ] *n* sceneggiatura.

screw [skruː] **1** *n* **(a)** *(Brit: of sweets)* cartoccio; **he's got a ~ loose** *(fig fam)* gli manca qualche rotella, è un po' svitato; **to put the ~s on sb** *(fig fam)* far pressione su qn. **(b)** *(propeller)* elica. **(c)** *(fam: prison officer)* secondino. **(d)** *(Brit fam: income)* paga. **2** *vt* avvitare; **to ~ sth to the wall** fissare qc al muro con viti; **to ~ sth (up) tight** avvitare bene qc; **to ~ money out of sb** *(fam)* far scucire soldi a qn; **to ~ one's head round** storcere la testa; **to have one's head ~ed on** avere la testa sulle spalle.

♦ **screw together 1** *vi + adv* avvitarsi. **2** *vt + adv* *(kit)* montare con viti; *(two pieces)* avvitare.

♦ **screw up** *vt + adv (paper, material)* spiegazzare; **to ~ up one's eyes** strizzare gli occhi; **to ~ up one's face** fare una smorfia; **to ~ up one's courage** *(fig)* armarsi di coraggio; **he really ~ed it up this time!** *(fig fam)* stavolta ha fatto davvero un macello!

screw·ball ['skruːbɔːl] *n (fam: esp Am)* testa matta.

screw·driver ['skruːˌdraɪvəʳ] *n* cacciavite *m inv*.

screwy ['skruːɪ] *adj* (**-ier**, **-iest**) *(fam: mad)* strambo(a).

scrib·ble ['skrɪbl] **1** *n* scarabocchio. **2** *vt* scribacchiare, scarabocchiare; **to ~ sth down** scribacchiare qc. **3** *vi* scarabocchiare.

scribe [skraɪb] *n* scriba *m*.

scrim·mage ['skrɪmɪdʒ] *n* tafferuglio, zuffa.

scrimp [skrɪmp] *vi*: **to ~ and save** risparmiare fino all'ultimo centesimo.

script [skrɪpt] *n* **(a)** *(Cine, Theatre etc)* copione *m;* *(in exam)* elaborato. **(b)** *(writing)* scrittura.

script·ed ['skrɪptɪd] *adj (Radio, TV)* preparato(a).

Scrip·ture ['skrɪptʃəʳ] *n (also:* **Holy ~**) Sacre Scritture *fpl*.

script·writer ['skrɪptˌraɪtəʳ] *n* soggettista *m/f*.

scroll [skrəʊl] *n (roll of parchment)* rotolo (di pergamena); *(ancient manuscript)* papiro, pergamena; *(Archit)* voluta.

scro·tum ['skrəʊtəm] *n* scroto.

scrounge [skraʊndʒ] *(fam)* **1** *n*: **to be on the ~ (for sth)** scroccare (qc); **here he comes, on the ~ again** eccolo il solito scroccone. **2** *vt (gen)* scroccare. **3** *vi*: **to ~ on** *or* **off sb** vivere alle spalle di qn.

scroung·er ['skraʊndʒəʳ] *n (fam)* scroccone/a; *(on society)* parassita *m/f*.

scrub¹ [skrʌb] *n (brushwood)* boscaglia.

scrub² [skrʌb] **1** *n* strofinata. **2** *vt* **(a)** *(clean)* strofinare (con lo spazzolone); *(hands etc)* pulire con lo spazzolino; **to ~ sth clean** pulire qc strofinandolo. **(b)** *(fam: cancel)* cancellare; *(: holiday, plan)* far(ci) una croce sopra.

♦ **scrub down** *vt + adv (room, wall)* pulire a fondo (con lo spazzolone).

♦ **scrub off** *vt + adv (mark, stain)* togliere (strofinando).

♦ **scrub up** *vi + adv (doctor etc)* lavarsi le mani.

scrubbing-brush ['skrʌbɪŋˌbrʌʃ] *n* spazzolone *m*.

scruff [skrʌf] *n* **(a)**: **by the ~ of the neck** per la collottola. **(b)** *(fam: untidy person)* straccione/a.

scruffy ['skrʌfɪ] *adj* (**-ier**, **-iest**) *(person, clothes, appearance)* trasandato(a); *(building)* squallido(a); *(paintwork)* malandato(a).

scrum [skrʌm] *(Rugby)* **1** *n* mischia. **2** *cpd*: **~ half** *n* mediano di mischia.

scrump·tious ['skrʌmpʃəs] *adj (fam: food, smell)* delizioso(a).

scru·ple ['skruːpl] *n* scrupolo; **to have no ~s about doing sth** non avere scrupoli a fare qc.

scru·pu·lous ['skruːpjʊləs] *adj* scrupoloso(a).

scru·pu·lous·ly ['skruːpjʊləslɪ] *adv* scrupolosamente; **he tries to be ~ fair/honest** cerca di essere più imparziale/onesto che può.

scru·ti·nize ['skruːtɪnaɪz] *vt (work etc)* esaminare attentamente; *(person's face)* scrutare; *(votes)* fare lo scrutinio di, scrutinare.

scru·ti·ny ['skruːtɪnɪ] *n* esame *m* scrupoloso; *(Pol: of votes)* scrutinio; **under the ~ of sb** sotto la sorveglianza di qn; **it does not stand up to ~** non regge a un esame accurato.

scu·ba ['skuːbə] **1** *n* autorespiratore *m*. **2**: **~ diving** *n* attività *fpl* subacquee.

scuff [skʌf] *vt (shoes)* scorticare; *(floor)* segnare; *(feet)* strascicare.

scuf·fle ['skʌfl] **1** *n* tafferuglio. **2** *vi*: **to ~ (with sb)** venire alle mani (con qn), azzuffarsi (con qn).

scul·lery ['skʌlərɪ] *n* retrocucina *m inv*.

sculpt [skʌlpt] *vt, vi* scolpire.

sculp·tor ['skʌlptəʳ] *n* scultore *m*.

sculp·tress ['skʌlptrɪs] *n* scultrice *f*.

sculp·ture ['skʌlptʃəʳ] **1** *n* scultura. **2** *vt, vi* scolpire.

scum [skʌm] *n (on liquid)* schiuma; *(fig)* feccia; **the ~ of the earth** la feccia della società.

scup·per ['skʌpəʳ] *vt (Naut)* autoaffondare; *(fig: plan)* far naufragare.

scur·ril·ous ['skʌrɪləs] *adj (remark)* scurrile; *(attack)* di bassa lega.

scur·ry ['skʌrɪ] *vi*: **to ~ along/away** *etc* procedere/ andarsene *etc* a tutta velocità.

scur·vy ['skɜːvɪ] *n* scorbuto.

scut·tle¹ ['skʌtl] *vt (ship)* autoaffondare.

scut·tle² ['skʌtl] *vi*: **to ~ away** *or* **off** sgattaiolare via; **to ~ in** entrare precipitosamente.

scythe [saɪð] **1** *n* falce *f*. **2** *vt* falciare.

sea [siː] **1** *n* mare *m; by* or *beside the ~ (holiday)* al mare; *(village)* sul mare; **on the ~** *(boat)* sul mare, in mare; *(village)* sul mare; **to go by ~** andare per mare; **to go to ~** *(person)* diventare marinaio; **to put to ~** *(sailor)* uscire in mare; *(boat)* salpare; **to spend 3 years at ~** passare 3 anni in mare; **(out) at ~** al largo; **to look out to ~** guardare il mare; **heavy** *or* **rough ~(s)** mare grosso *or* agitato; **to be all at ~ (about** *or* **with sth)** *(fig)* non capirci niente (di qc); **a ~ of faces** *(fig)* una marea di gente.

   2 *cpd (breeze)* marino(a), di mare; *(bird, fish, air, water)* di mare; *(route, transport)* marittimo(a); *(battle, power)* navale; **~ anemone** *n* anemone *m* di mare; **~ bathing** *n* bagni *mpl* di mare; **~ bed** *n* fondo marino; **~ front** *n* lungomare *m;* **~ legs** *npl*: **to find one's ~ legs** abituarsi al mare; **~ level** *n* livello del mare; **~ lion** *n* leone *m* marino; **~ urchin** *n* riccio (di mare); **~ wall** *n* diga marittima.

sea·board ['siːbɔːd] *n* litorale *m*.

sea·faring ['siːˌfɛərɪŋ] *adj (community)* marinaro(a); *(life)* da marinaio.

sea·food ['siːfuːd] *n* frutti *mpl* di mare.

sea·going ['siːˌɡəʊɪŋ] *adj (nation)* marinaro(a); *(ship)* che solca i mari.

sea·gull ['siːɡʌl] *n* gabbiano.

seal¹ [siːl] *n (Zool)* foca.

seal² [siːl] **1** *n (gen)* sigillo; *(on parcel)* piombino; *(of door, lid)* chiusura ermetica; **to set one's ~ to sth, to give the ~** *or* **one's ~ of approval to sth** dare il proprio beneplacito a qc; **to set the ~ on sth** *(fig)* concludere qc. **2** *vt* **(a)** *(put ~ on: document)* sigillare; *(close: envelope)* chiudere, incollare; *(: jar, tin)* chiudere ermeticamente; *(Culin: meat)* rosolare; **my lips are ~ed** tengo la bocca chiusa. **(b)** *(decide: sb's fate)* segnare; *(: bargain)* concludere.

♦ **seal off** *vt + adv (close up: building, room)* sigillare; *(forbid entry to: area)* bloccare l'accesso a.

♦ **seal up** *vt + adv (parcel)* sigillare, chiudere bene; *(jar, door)* chiudere ermeticamente.

seal·ing wax ['siːlɪŋwæks] *n* ceralacca.

seal·skin ['siːlskɪn] *n* pelle *f* di foca.

seam [siːm] *n* **(a)** *(Sewing)* cucitura; *(Welding)* saldatura; **to come apart at the ~s** scucirsi; **my dress is bursting at the ~s** scoppio dentro questo vestito; **the hall was bursting at the ~s** l'aula era piena zeppa. **(b)** *(Geol)* filone *m*, vena.

sea·man ['siːmən] *n, pl* **-men** marinaio.

sea·man·ship ['siːmənʃɪp] *n* tecnica di navigazione.

seam·stress ['sɛmstrɪs] *n* sarta.

seamy ['siːmɪ] *adj* (**-ier, -iest**) *(fam: district)* malfamato(a); **the ~ side of life** l'aspetto più squallido della vita.

sé·ance ['seɪɑ̃ːns] *n* seduta (spiritica).

sea·plane ['siːpleɪn] *n* idrovolante *m*.

sea·port ['siːpɔːt] *n* porto di mare.

search [sɜːtʃ] **1** *n* (**a**) *(for sth lost)* ricerca; **in ~ of** alla ricerca di; **to make a ~ for sb/sth** fare delle ricerche per trovare qn/qc. (**b**) *(of person, building etc)* perquisizione *f*; **to make a ~ of sth** *(subj: police, customs official)* fare *or* eseguire una perquisizione di qc; *(: thief)* frugare in qc.

2 *vt* (**a**): **to ~ (for)** *(subj: police etc)* perquisire (alla ricerca di); *(: thief)* frugare (alla ricerca di); *(area, woods etc)* perlustrare *or* setacciare (alla ricerca di); **the police ~ed him for drugs** la polizia l'ha perquisito alla ricerca di droga; **~ me!** *(fig fam)* e che ne so io? (**b**) *(scan: records, documents, photograph)* esaminare; *(: noticeboard, newspaper)* leggere attentamente; *(: one's conscience)* interrogare; *(: one's memory)* frugare in; **he ~ed her face for some sign of affection** scrutava il suo viso in cerca di un segno di affetto.

3 *vi* cercare; **to ~ after** *or* **for sb/sth** cercare qn/qc; **to ~ through** *or* **in sth for sth** frugare *or* rovistare qc alla ricerca di qc.

4 *cpd:* **~ party** *n* squadra di soccorso; **~ warrant** *n* mandato di perquisizione.

search·er ['sɜːtʃə'] *n* chi cerca.

search·ing ['sɜːtʃɪŋ] *adj (look)* indagatore(trice); *(examination)* minuzioso(a); *(question)* pressante.

search·light ['sɜːtʃlaɪt] *n* riflettore *m*.

sear·ing ['sɪərɪŋ] *adj (heat)* rovente; *(pain)* acuto(a).

sea·scape ['siːskeɪp] *n (Art)* paesaggio marino.

sea·shell ['siːʃɛl] *n* conchiglia.

sea·shore ['siːʃɔː'] *n* riva (del mare), spiaggia; **by the ~** in riva al mare; **on the ~** sulla riva del mare.

sea·sick ['siːsɪk] *adj:* **to be ~** avere il mal di mare.

sea·sick·ness ['siːsɪknɪs] *n* mal *m* di mare.

sea·side ['siːsaɪd] **1** *n* spiaggia, litorale *m*; **to go to the ~** andare al mare; **at the ~** al mare. **2** *cpd (town)* di mare; *(holiday)* al mare; **~ resort** *n* centro *or* stazione *f* balneare.

sea·son ['siːzn] **1** *n (gen)* stagione *f*; **to be in/out of ~** essere di/fuori stagione; **the Christmas ~** il periodo natalizio; **'S~'s Greetings'** 'Buone Feste'; **the busy ~** *(for shops)* il periodo di punta; *(for hotels etc)* l'alta stagione; **football/fishing ~** stagione calcistica/della pesca; **the open ~** *(Hunting)* la stagione della caccia; **it's against the law to hunt during the closed ~** è contro la legge cacciare quando la stagione della caccia è chiusa; **in ~** *(Zool)* in calore. **2** *vt* (**a**) *(wood)* stagionare. (**b**) *(Culin)* aggiungere sale, pepe e spezie a. **3** *cpd:* **~ ticket** *n (Theatre, Rail etc)* abbonamento.

sea·son·able ['siːznəbl] *adj (weather)* di stagione.

sea·son·al ['siːzənl] *adj* stagionale.

sea·soned ['siːznd] *adj (wood)* stagionato(a); *(fig: worker, actor, troops)* con esperienza; **a ~ campaigner** un veterano.

sea·son·ing ['siːznɪŋ] *n* condimento.

seat [siːt] **1** *n* (**a**) *(chair)* sedia; *(in theatre etc)* posto; *(in bus, train, car etc)* posto, sedile *m*; *(on cycle)* sella, sellino; **are there any ~s left?** ci sono posti?; **to take one's ~** prendere posto; **do take a ~** si accomodi prego. (**b**) *(Pol)* seggio; **to keep/lose one's ~** essere/non essere rieletto; **to win 4 ~s from the nationalists** strappare 4 seggi ai nazionalisti; **to take one's ~ in the (House of)**

Commons ≃ occupare il proprio posto in Parlamento. (**c**) *(of chair)* sedile *m*; *(of trousers)* fondo. (**d**) *(centre: of government etc, of infection)* sede *f*; *(: of learning)* centro; *(: of trouble)* fonte *f*.

2 *vt* (**a**) *(person etc)* far sedere; **to be ~ed** essere seduto; **please remain ~ed** rimanete ai vostri posti per cortesia. (**b**) *(subj: hall, cinema etc)* avere posti (a sedere) per.

3 *cpd:* **~ belt** *n* cintura di sicurezza.

seat·ing ['siːtɪŋ] **1** *n* posti *mpl* a sedere. **2** *cpd:* **~ arrangements** *npl* sistemazione *f or* disposizione *f* dei posti; **~ capacity** *n* posti *mpl* a sedere.

sea·way ['siːweɪ] *n* rotta marittima.

sea·weed ['siːwiːd] *n* alghe *fpl*; **a strand of ~** un'alga.

sea·worthy ['siːˌwɜːðɪ] *adj* in condizione di navigare.

sec. [sɛk] *abbr of* **second(s).**

seca·teurs [ˌsɛkə'tɜːz] *npl* forbici *fpl* per potare.

se·ces·sion [sɪ'sɛʃən] *n:* **~ (from)** secessione *f* (da).

se·clud·ed [sɪ'kluːdɪd] *adj (house)* appartato(a), isolato(a); *(life)* ritirato(a).

se·clu·sion [sɪ'kluːʒən] *n* isolamento.

sec·ond[1] ['sɛkənd] **1** *adj* secondo(a); **he's a ~ Beethoven** è un nuovo Beethoven; **give him a ~ chance** dagli un'altra opportunità; **~ floor** *(Brit)* secondo piano; *(Am)* primo piano; **in ~ gear** *(Aut)* in seconda; **to ask for a ~ opinion** *(Med)* chiedere un altro *or* ulteriore parere; **~ cousin** cugino di secondo grado; **~ person** *(Gram)* seconda persona; **Charles the S~** Carlo Secondo; **every ~ day/week** ogni due giorni/settimane; **to be ~ to none** non essere secondo a nessuno; **to have ~ sight** essere chiaroveggente; **to have ~ thoughts (about doing sth)** avere dei ripensamenti (quanto a fare qc); **we had ~ thoughts about it** ci abbiamo ripensato; **on ~ thoughts...** a ripensarci... .

2 *adv* (**a**) *(in race, competition etc)* al secondo posto; **to come ~** arrivare *or* piazzarsi secondo(a); **it's the ~ largest fish I've ever caught** ho preso soltanto un pesce più grosso di questo finora. (**b**) *(~ly)* in secondo luogo, secondo.

3 *n* (**a**) *(Boxing, in duel)* secondo. (**b**): **in ~** *(Aut)* in seconda. (**c**): **he came a good ~** *(in race)* è arrivato secondo con un buon tempo; *(in exam etc)* ha ottenuto un secondo posto con un buon punteggio; **he came a poor ~** è arrivato secondo ma con notevole scarto. (**d**): **~s** *pl (Comm)* scarti *mpl* di fabbricazione.

4 *vt* (**a**) *(motion, statement)* appoggiare, dichiararsi a favore di; **I'll ~ that** *(fig)* approvo, d'accordo. (**b**) [sɪ'kɒnd] *(employee)* distaccare.

sec·ond[2] ['sɛkənd] **1** *n (in time, Geog, Math)* secondo, minuto secondo; **at that very ~** (proprio) in quell'istante; **just a ~!** un attimo!; **it won't take a ~** ci vuole un attimo. **2** *cpd:* **~ hand** *n* lancetta dei secondi.

sec·ond·ary ['sɛkəndərɪ] *adj* secondario(a); **~ school** scuola secondaria.

sec·ond-best [ˌsɛkənd'bɛst] **1** *n* ripiego. **2** *adv:* **to come off ~** avere la peggio.

second-class [ˌsɛkənd'klɑːs] **1** *adj* (**a**) *(mail)* ordinario(a); *(ticket, carriage)* di seconda classe. (**b**) *(pej: goods, quality)* scadente; **~ citizen** cittadino di second'ordine. **2** *adv:* **to send sth ~** spedire qc per posta ordinaria; **to travel ~** viaggiare in seconda (classe).

second·hand [ˌsɛkənd'hænd] **1** *adj* di seconda mano. **2** *adv:* **to buy sth ~** comprare qc di seconda mano; **to hear sth ~** venire a sapere qc da terze persone.

second-in-command [ˌsɛkəndɪnkəˈmɑːnd] n (Mil) comandante m in seconda; (Admin) aggiunto.

sec·ond·ly [ˈsɛkəndlɪ] adv secondo, in secondo luogo, secondariamente.

se·cond·ment [sɪˈkɒndmənt] n distaccamento.

second-rate [ˌsɛkəndˈreɪt] adj di second'ordine, scadente.

se·cre·cy [ˈsiːkrəsɪ] n segretezza; **there's no ~ about...** non ci sono segreti circa...; **in ~** in segreto, in tutta segretezza.

se·cret [ˈsiːkrɪt] 1 adj segreto(a); **to keep sth ~ (from sb)** tenere qc segreto (a qn), tenere qc nascosto (a qn); **~ agent** agente segreto; **~ police** polizia segreta. 2 n segreto; **to keep a ~** mantenere il segreto; **to let sb into a ~** mettere qn a parte di un segreto, confidare un segreto a qn; **to make no ~ of sth** non far mistero di qc; **to do sth in ~** fare qc in segreto.

sec·re·tar·ial [ˌsɛkrəˈtɛərɪəl] adj (work) da segretario/a; (college, course) di segretariato.

sec·re·tari·at [ˌsɛkrəˈtɛərɪət] n segretariato.

sec·re·tary [ˈsɛkrətrɪ] n segretario/a; **S~ of State** (Brit) ministro; (Am) segretario di Stato, ≈ Ministro degli Esteri; **S~ of State for Education** (Brit) Ministro della Pubblica Istruzione.

sec·retary-general [ˌsɛkrətrɪˈdʒɛnərəl] n segretario generale.

se·crete [sɪˈkriːt] vt (a) (Med, Anat, Bio) secernere. (b) (hide) nascondere.

se·cre·tion [sɪˈkriːʃən] n secrezione f.

se·cre·tive [ˈsiːkrətɪv] adj riservato(a); **to be ~ about sth** essere riservato a proposito di qc.

se·cret·ly [ˈsiːkrətlɪ] adv in segreto, segretamente.

sect [sɛkt] n setta.

sec·tar·ian [sɛkˈtɛərɪən] adj settario(a).

sec·tion [ˈsɛkʃən] n (a) (part: gen) sezione f, parte f; (of community, population) settore m, fascia; (: of town) quartiere m; (of document, law etc) articolo; (of pipeline, road etc) tratto; (of machine, furniture) pezzo; **the business ~** (Press) la pagina economica. (b) (department) sezione f. (c) (cut) sezione f; **vertical ~** sezione verticale, spaccato.

sec·tion·al [ˈsɛkʃənl] adj (a) (bookcase etc) scomponibile, smontabile. (b) (interests) settoriale. (c) (drawing etc) in sezione.

sec·tor [ˈsɛktəʳ] n settore m.

secu·lar [ˈsɛkjʊləʳ] adj (authority, school) laico(a); (writings, music) profano(a); (clergy) secolare.

se·cure [sɪˈkjʊəʳ] 1 adj (-r, -st) (a) (firm: knot) saldo(a), sicuro(a); (: nail) ben piantato(a); (: rope) ben fissato(a); (: door) ben chiuso(a); (: ladder, chair) stabile; (: hold) fermo(a); **to make sth ~** fissare bene qc. (b) (safe: place, container) sicuro(a); (certain: career, success) assicurato(a); (victory) certo(a); **~ from** or **against sth** al sicuro da qc. (c) (unworried) sicuro(a), tranquillo(a); **to rest ~ in the knowledge that...** stare tranquillo sapendo che... .

2 vt (a) (fix: rope) assicurare; (: door, window) fermare bene, chiudere bene; (tie up: person, animal) legare. (b) (make safe): **to ~ (from** or **against)** proteggere (da). (c) (frm: obtain: job, staff etc) assicurarsi; **to ~ sth for sb** procurare qc per or a qn. (d) (Fin: loan) garantire.

se·cu·rity [sɪˈkjʊərɪtɪ] 1 n (a) (safety, stability) sicurezza; **job ~** sicurezza dell'impiego. (b) (against theft etc) (misure fpl di) sicurezza; **to increase/tighten ~** aumentare/intensificare la sorveglianza. (c) (Fin: on loan) garanzia; **to lend money on ~** prestare denaro su or dietro garanzia. (d) (Fin): **securities** titoli mpl. 2 cpd: **~ forces** npl forze fpl dell'ordine; **~ guard** n guardia giurata; **~ leak** n fuga di notizie; **~ police** npl

servizi mpl di sicurezza; **~ risk** n minaccia alla sicurezza dello stato.

se·date [sɪˈdeɪt] 1 adj posato(a), pacato(a). 2 vt (Med) somministrare sedativi a.

se·da·tion [sɪˈdeɪʃən] n (Med): **to be under ~** essere sotto l'azione di sedativi.

seda·tive [ˈsɛdətɪv] 1 adj calmante, sedativo(a). 2 n sedativo, calmante m.

sed·en·tary [ˈsɛdntrɪ] adj sedentario(a).

sedi·ment [ˈsɛdɪmənt] n (in liquids, boiler) deposito, fondo; (Geol) sedimento.

se·di·tious [səˈdɪʃəs] adj sedizioso(a).

se·duce [sɪˈdjuːs] vt sedurre.

se·duc·tion [sɪˈdʌkʃən] n seduzione f.

se·duc·tive [sɪˈdʌktɪv] adj (gen) seducente; (dress) sexy inv; (offer) allettante.

see[1] [siː] pt **saw**, pp **seen** vt, vi (a) (gen) vedere; **I can't ~ him** non lo vedo; **I saw him writing the letter** l'ho visto scrivere or mentre scriveva la lettera; **I saw him write the letter** l'ho visto scrivere la lettera; **there was nobody to be ~n** non c'era anima viva; **I can't ~ to read** non ci vedo a leggere; **let me ~** (show me) fammi vedere; (let me think) vediamo (un po'); **can you ~ your way to helping us?** (fig) puoi trovare il modo di aiutarci?; **to go and ~ sb** andare a trovare qn; **~ you soon/later/tomorrow!** a presto/più tardi/domani!; **now ~ here!** (in anger) ma insomma!; **so I ~** sì, vedo; **~ for yourself** vai a vedere con i tuoi occhi; **as you can ~** come vedi; **I must be ~ing things** (fam) devo avere le allucinazioni; **I ~ in the paper that...** vedo che sul giornale è scritto che...; **I ~ nothing wrong in it** non ci trovo niente di male; **I don't know what she ~s in him** non so che cosa ci trova in lui; (go and) **~ who it is** vai a vedere chi è, vedi chi è; **this car has ~n better days** questa macchina ha conosciuto tempi migliori; **I never thought I'd ~ the day when...** non avrei mai creduto che un giorno... .

(b) (understand, perceive) vedere, capire; (: joke) afferrare; **to ~ the funny side of sth** vedere il lato comico di qc; **I ~!** capisco!; **I don't** or **can't ~ how/why** etc... non vedo come/perché etc...; **as far as I can ~** da quanto posso vedere; **the way I ~ it** a parer mio, a mio giudizio.

(c) (accompany) accompagnare; **to ~ sb to the door/home** accompagnare qn alla porta/a casa.

(d) (ensure, check) vedere, guardare; **to ~ if/that...** vedere se + indic/che... + sub; **~ that he has all he needs** vedi che non gli manchi nulla; **I'll ~ that he gets it** farò in modo che lo riceva.

(e) (imagine) vedere; **I can just ~ him as a teacher** lo vedo benissimo nei panni dell'insegnante; **I can't ~ myself as...** non mi vedo come...; **I can't ~ him winning** ho l'impressione che non vincerà lui.

♦ **see about** vi + prep (a) (deal with) occuparsi di. (b) (consider): **I'll ~ about it** devo vedere un attimino; **we'll ~ about it** si vedrà.

♦ **see in** vt + adv: **to ~ the New Year in** festeggiare l'Anno Nuovo.

♦ **see off** vt + adv salutare alla partenza.

♦ **see out** vt + adv (person) accompagnare alla porta; **I'll ~ myself out** (fam) non c'è bisogno che mi (si) accompagni; **she won't ~ the week out** non arriva alla fine di questa settimana.

♦ **see over** vi + prep (visit) visitare.

♦ **see through** 1 vi + prep (promises, behaviour) non lasciarsi ingannare da; (person): **I finally saw through him** sono finalmente riuscito a capire il tipo. 2 vt + adv (project, deal) portare a termine; **we'll ~ him through** lo aiuteremo noi. 3 vt + prep: **£10 will ~ him through the week** 10 sterline gli basteranno fino alla fine della settimana.

♦ **see to** vi + prep (deal with) occuparsi di; (: workload) sbrigare; (mend) mettere a posto; **please ~ to it that you lock all doors** si assicuri di aver chiuso tutte le porte.

see² [si:] n (Rel) sede f vescovile; **the Holy S~** la Santa Sede.

seed [si:d] **1** n **(a)** (Bot, fig) seme m; (for sowing) semi mpl, semenza; **to go to ~, run to ~** (plant) fare seme; (fig: person) ridursi male. **(b)** (Tennis: player) testa di serie. **2** vt **(a)** (lawn etc) seminare. **(b)** (remove the seed: raisins, grapes) togliere i semi a. **(c)** (Tennis): **he was ~ed fifth** è stato classificato quinta testa di serie. **3** vi fare seme. **4** cpd (potato, corn) da semina; **~ merchant** n commerciante m/f di semenze; **~ pearls** npl semenza.

seed·less ['si:dlɪs] adj senza semi.

seed·ling ['si:dlɪŋ] n piantime m.

seedy ['si:dɪ] adj (-ier, -iest) (fam: sordid, shabby) squallido(a); **I feel decidedly ~ today** non mi sento affatto bene oggi.

see·ing ['si:ɪŋ] conj: **~ (that)** visto che.

seek [si:k] pt, pp sought **1** vt (gen): **to ~ (sth/to do sth)** cercare (qc/di fare qc); **to ~ shelter (from)** cercar riparo (da); **to ~ one's fortune** cercar fortuna; **to ~ advice/help from sb** chiedere consiglio/aiuto a qn. **2** vi: **to ~ after, ~ for** cercare.

♦ **seek out** vt + adv (person) andare a cercare.

seem [si:m] vi sembrare, parere; **he ~s capable** sembra (essere) in gamba; **he ~ed to be in difficulty** sembrava (trovarsi) in difficoltà; **she ~s to know you** sembra or pare che lei ti conosca; **she ~s not to want to leave** non dà segni di voler andar via; **I ~ed to be sinking** mi sembrava di affondare; **I ~ to have heard that before** questa mi pare di averla già sentita; **I can't ~ to do it** a quanto pare non ci riesco; **how did he ~ to you?** come ti è parso?; **it ~s (that)...** sembra or pare che... **+ sub; so it ~s** pare proprio di sì; **it ~s not** pare di no; **it ~s you're right** pare che tu abbia ragione; **it ~s ages since...** mi sembra una vita da quando...; **what ~s to be the trouble?** cosa c'è che non va?; **there ~s to be a mistake** ci dev'essere un errore; **she died yesterday, it ~s** pare che sia morta ieri; **I did what ~ed best** ho fatto quello che mi sembrava la cosa migliore da fare.

seem·ing ['si:mɪŋ] adj apparente.

seem·ing·ly ['si:mɪŋlɪ] adv (evidently) a quanto pare; (from appearances) in apparenza, apparentemente.

seem·ly ['si:mlɪ] adj (-ier, -iest) (frm: behaviour, language, dress) decoroso(a).

seen [si:n] pp of **see¹**.

seep [si:p] vi: **to ~ (through/from/into)** filtrare (attraverso/da/in or dentro); **to ~ away** scolar via (a poco a poco).

see·saw ['si:sɔ:] **1** n altalena (a bilico). **2** vi (fig) oscillare.

seethe [si:ð] vi (liquid) gorgogliare; (street): **to ~ (with)** brulicare (di); **to ~ or be seething with anger** bollire or fremere di rabbia.

see-through ['si:,θru:] adj trasparente.

seg·ment ['segmənt] n (section) parte f; (of orange) spicchio; (Math) segmento.

seg·re·gate ['segrɪgeɪt] vt: **to ~ (from)** segregare (da).

seg·re·ga·tion [,segrɪ'geɪʃən] n segregazione f.

seize [si:z] vt (clutch) afferrare; (Mil, Law: person, territory) prendere; (: articles) sequestrare; (opportunity) cogliere (al volo); **to ~ hold of sth/sb** afferrare qc/qn; **he was ~d with a bout of** coughing gli è venuto un accesso di tosse; **he was ~d with fear/rage** è stato preso dalla paura/rabbia; **I was ~d by the desire to laugh** mi è venuta la voglia di ridere.

♦ **seize (up)on** vi + prep (chance, mistake) non lasciarsi sfuggire; (idea) sfruttare prontamente.

♦ **seize up** vi + adv (machine) grippare.

sei·zure ['si:ʒəʳ] n **(a)** (of goods) sequestro, confisca; (of land, city, ship) presa. **(b)** (Med) attacco.

sel·dom ['seldəm] adv di rado, raramente.

se·lect [sɪ'lekt] **1** vt (team, candidate) scegliere, selezionare; (book, gift etc) scegliere; **~ed works** opere fpl scelte. **2** adj (hotel, restaurant) chic inv; (club) esclusivo(a); (group) ristretto(a); (audience) scelto(a); **a ~ few** pochi eletti mpl.

se·lec·tion [sɪ'lekʃən] **1** n (gen) scelta; (of goods etc) scelta, selezione f; **~s from** (Mus, Literature) brani scelti da. **2** cpd: **~ committee** n comitato di selezione.

se·lec·tive [sɪ'lektɪv] adj (gen) selettivo(a).

se·lec·tor [sɪ'lektəʳ] n (person) selezionatore/trice; (Tech) selettore m.

self [self] n, pl **selves**: **the ~** l'io inv; **my better ~** la parte migliore di me stesso; **his true ~** il suo vero io; **he's quite his old ~ again** è tornato quello di una volta.

self- [self] pref: **self-addressed** adj: **self-addressed envelope** busta col proprio nome e indirizzo; **self-adhesive** adj autoadesivo(a); **self-adjusting** adj che si regola da sé; **self-assured** adj sicuro(a) di sé; **self-catering** adj in cui ci si cucina da sé; **self-catering apartment** appartamento (per le vacanze); **self-centred, (Am) self-centered** adj egocentrico(a); **self-cleaning** adj autopulente; **self-confessed** adj (alcoholic) dichiarato(a); **he's a self-confessed thief/liar** ha ammesso di essere un ladro/bugiardo; **self-confidence** n sicurezza (di sé); **self-conscious** adj impacciato(a); **self-contained** adj indipendente; **self-control** n (also: **self-restraint**) autocontrollo m, autocontrollo; **self-defeating** adj futile; **self-defence** n autodifesa; **to act in self-defence** agire per legittima difesa; **self-discipline** n autodisciplina; **self-employed** adj che lavora in proprio; **self-esteem** n amor proprio m; **self-evident** adj lampante; **self-explanatory** adj che non ha bisogno di spiegazioni; **self-governing** adj autonomo(a); **self-help** n iniziativa individuale; **self-importance** n sufficienza; **self-indulgent** adj indulgente con se stesso; **self-interest** n interesse m personale.

self·ish ['selfɪʃ] adj egoista.

self·ish·ness ['selfɪʃnɪs] n egoismo.

self·less ['selflɪs] adj dimentico(a) di sé, altruista.

self-made [,self'meɪd] adj: **~ man** self-made man m inv, uomo che si è fatto da sé.

self-pity [,self'pɪtɪ] n autocommiserazione f.

self-portrait [,self'pɔ:trɪt] n autoritratto.

self-possessed [,selfpə'zest] adj padrone(a) di sé, composto(a).

self-preser·va·tion ['self,prezə'veɪʃən] n istinto di conservazione.

self-raising [,self'reɪzɪŋ] adj, (Am) **self-rising** [,self'raɪzɪŋ] adj: **~ flour** miscela di farina e lievito.

self-respect [,selfrɪs'pekt] n rispetto di sé.

self-righteous [,self'raɪtʃəs] adj compiaciuto(a).

self-sacrifice [,self'sækrɪfaɪs] n abnegazione f.

self-same ['selfseɪm] adj stesso(a).

self-satisfied [,self'sætɪsfaɪd] adj soddisfatto(a) di sé.

self-service [,self'sɜ:vɪs] adj self-service inv.

self-styled [,self'staɪld] adj sedicente.

self-sufficien·cy [,selfsə'fɪʃənsɪ] n autosufficienza.

self-support·ing [ˌsɛlfsə'pɔːtɪŋ] *adj* economicamente indipendente.

self-taught [ˌsɛlf'tɔːt] *adj* autodidatta.

sell [sɛl] *pt, pp* **sold 1** *vt* vendere; **to ~ sth for £1/at £1 per dozen** vendere qc per 1 sterlina/a 1 sterlina la dozzina; **to ~ sth to sb** vendere qc a qn; **I was sold this in London** mi hanno venduto questo a Londra; **to ~ sb down the river** vendere qn; **to ~ sb an idea** *(fig)* far accettare un'idea a qn; **to ~ sb a pup** *(fig)* imbrogliare qn; **to be sold on sb/sth** *(fam)* essere entusiasta di qn/qc; **he doesn't ~ himself very well** non riesce a valorizzare le proprie capacità. **2** *vi* vendersi; **they ~ at 15p each** sono in vendita a 15p l'uno.

♦ **sell off** *vt + adv (stocks and shares, goods)* svendere, liquidare.

♦ **sell out 1** *vi + adv*: **to ~ out (to sb/sth)** *(Comm)* vendere (tutto) (a qn/qc); **to ~ out to the enemy** *(fig)* passare al nemico. **2** *vt + adv* esaurire; **the tickets are all sold out** i biglietti sono esauriti; **we're sold out of bread** non c'è più pane.

♦ **sell up 1** *vi + adv* vendere (tutto). **2** *vt + adv* vendere.

sell·er ['sɛlə'] *n* venditore/trice; **~'s market** mercato favorevole alle vendite.

sell·ing ['sɛlɪŋ] *adj*: **~ price** prezzo di vendita.

sell·lo·tape ['sɛləʊteɪp] ® **1** *n* scotch *m inv*. **2** *vt* attaccare con lo scotch.

sell·out ['sɛlaʊt] *n* **(a)** *(Theatre)*: **it was a ~** registrò il tutto esaurito. **(b)** *(betrayal: to enemy)* capitolazione *f*.

sel·vage, sel·vedge ['sɛlvɪdʒ] *n (Sewing)* cimosa.

selves [sɛlvz] *pl of* **self**.

se·man·tics [sɪ'mæntɪks] *nsg* semantica.

sema·phore ['sɛməfɔː'] *n* **(a)** *(system)* segnalazioni *fpl* con bandierine. **(b)** *(Rail: signal post)* semaforo (ferroviario).

sem·blance ['sɛmbləns] *n* parvenza, apparenza.

se·men ['siːmən] *n* seme *m*, sperma *m*.

se·mes·ter [sɪ'mestə'] *n (Am)* semestre *m*.

semi... ['sɛmɪ] *pref* semi...

semi·breve ['sɛmɪbriːv] *n (Brit Mus)* semibreve *f*.

semi·cir·cle ['sɛmɪsɜːkl] *n* semicerchio.

semi·cir·cu·lar [ˌsɛmɪ'sɜːkjʊlə'] *adj* semicircolare.

semi·co·lon [ˌsɛmɪ'kəʊlən] *n* punto e virgola.

semi·con·duc·tor [ˌsɛmɪkən'dʌktə'] *n* semiconduttore *m*.

semi·con·scious [ˌsɛmɪ'kɒnʃəs] *adj* parzialmente cosciente.

semi·de·tached [ˌsɛmɪdɪ'tætʃt] *adj*: **~ house** casa con un muro divisorio in comune con un'altra.

semi·fi·nal [ˌsɛmɪ'faɪnl] *n* semifinale *f*.

semi·fi·nal·ist [ˌsɛmɪ'faɪnəlɪst] *n* semifinalista *m/f*.

semi·nal ['sɛmɪnl] *adj (fig)* fondamentale.

semi·nar ['sɛmɪnɑː'] *n* seminario.

semi·nary ['sɛmɪnərɪ] *n (Rel)* seminario.

semi·precious ['sɛmɪˌprɛʃəs] *adj* semiprezioso(a).

semi·qua·ver ['sɛmɪˌkweɪvə'] *n (Brit Mus)* semicroma.

semi·skilled [ˌsɛmɪ'skɪld] *adj (worker)* parzialmente qualificato(a); *(work)* che richiede una specializzazione parziale.

semo·li·na [ˌsɛmə'liːnə] *n* semolino.

sen·ate ['sɛnɪt] *n (Pol)* senato; *(Univ)* senato accademico.

sena·tor ['sɛnɪtə'] *n (Pol)* senatore/trice.

send [sɛnd] *pt, pp* **sent** *vt* **(a)** *(gen)* mandare; *(letter, telegram)* mandare, spedire; *(arrow, rocket, ball)* lanciare; **to ~ by post** spedire per posta; **to ~ by telex** mandare per telex; **to ~ word that...** mandare a dire che...; **she ~s (you) her love** ti saluta affettuosamente; **to ~ sb for sth** mandare qn a prendere qc; **to ~ sb to do sth** mandare qn a fare qc; **to ~ sb home** mandare qn a casa; *(from abroad)* rimpatriare qn; **to ~ sb to prison/bed/school** mandare qn in prigione/a letto/a scuola; **to ~ sb to sleep/into fits of laughter** far addormentare/scoppiare dal ridere qn; **the explosion sent a cloud of dust into the air** l'esplosione ha sollevato una nuvola di polvere; **to ~ a shiver down sb's spine** far venire i brividi a qn; **to ~ sb flying** mandare qn a gambe per aria; **to ~ sth flying** far volare via qc. **(b)** *(cause to become)*: **to ~ sb mad** far impazzire qn; **that really ~s me** *(fam)* mi manda in visibilio.

♦ **send away 1** *vi + adv*: **to ~ away for sth** ordinare qc per posta. **2** *vt + adv (person)* mandare; *(: get rid of)* mandare via.

♦ **send back** *vt + adv* rimandare.

♦ **send down** *vt + adv (person, prices)* far scendere; *(pupil)* cacciare, mandar via.

♦ **send for** *vi + prep* **(a)** *(doctor, police etc)* (mandare a) chiamare, far venire. **(b)** *(by post)* ordinare per posta.

♦ **send in** *vt + adv (person)* far entrare; *(troops)* inviare; *(report, application, resignation)* presentare.

♦ **send off 1** *vi + adv* = **send away 1**. **2** *vt + adv (person)* mandare; *(letter, goods)* spedire; *(Ftbl: player)* espellere; **to ~ sb off to do sth** mandare qn a fare qc.

♦ **send on** *vt + adv (letter)* inoltrare; *(luggage etc: in advance)* spedire in anticipo; *(: afterwards)* mandare, spedire.

♦ **send out 1** *vi + adv*: **to ~ out for sth** mandare a prendere qc. **2** *vt + adv* **(a)** *(person)* mandar fuori; *(troops)* inviare. **(b)** *(post: invitations)* mandare, spedire. **(c)** *(emit: light, heat)* mandare, emanare; *(: signals)* emettere.

♦ **send round** *vt + adv (letter, document etc)* far circolare; *(person)*: **to ~ sb round (to sb)** mandare qn (da qn); **I'll ~ it round later** te lo farò pervenire più tardi.

♦ **send up** *vt + adv* **(a)** *(person, luggage)* mandar su; *(balloon, rocket, flare)* lanciare; *(smoke, dust)* sollevare; *(prices)* far salire. **(b)** *(fam: make fun of: person, book etc)* fare la parodia di.

send·er ['sɛndə'] *n* mittente *m/f*.

send-off ['sɛndɒf] *n*: **to give sb a ~** festeggiare la partenza di qn.

send-up ['sɛndʌp] *n (fam)* parodia.

se·nile ['siːnaɪl] *adj* senile; **I'm not ~ yet!** non sono ancora rimbambito!

sen·ior ['siːnɪə'] **1** *adj* **(a)** *(in age)* maggiore, più anziano(a); **she is 10 years ~ to me** ha 10 anni più di me; **P. Jones ~** P. Jones senior, P. Jones padre; **~ citizens** anziani *mpl*; **~ high school** *(Am)* liceo; **~ year** *(Am Univ, Scol)* ultimo anno di studi. **(b)** *(of higher rank: employee, officer)* di grado superiore; *(: partner)* più anziano(a); **he holds a ~ position in the company** ha un posto importante nella ditta; **he's ~ to me in the firm** sta sopra di me nella ditta. **2** *n* **(a)** *(in age)* persona più anziana; **he is my ~ by 2 years** ha 2 anni più di me. **(b)** *(Am Univ)* studente/essa dell'ultimo anno.

sen·ior·ity [ˌsiːnɪ'ɒrɪtɪ] *n (in age, years of service)* anzianità; *(in rank)* superiorità.

sen·sa·tion [sɛn'seɪʃən] *n (a)* *(physical feeling; impression)* sensazione *f*; **he is completely without ~ in that leg** ha perso completamente la sensibilità alla gamba. **(b)** *(excitement)* sensazione *f*, scalpore *m*; **to be** *or* **cause a ~** fare sensazione, destare scalpore.

sen·sa·tion·al [sɛn'seɪʃənl] *adj (gen, also fam: marvellous)* sensazionale; *(newspaper, novel etc)* a sensazione; *(account, description)* a tinte forti.

sense [sɛns] **1** *n* **(a)** *(faculty)* senso; **a keen ~ of smell/hearing** un olfatto/udito fine; **to come to one's ~s** *(regain consciousness)* riprendere i sensi; **sixth ~** sesto senso; **~ of direction** senso di orientamento; **to lose all ~ of time** perdere la nozione del tempo; **~ of humour** (senso dell')umorismo.
(b) *(feeling)* senso, sensazione *f;* **~ of duty/guilt** senso del dovere/di colpa; **a ~ of well-being** una sensazione di benessere.
(c) *(common ~)* buonsenso, senso comune; **he should have had more ~ than to do it** avrebbe dovuto avere il buonsenso di non farlo; **there is no ~ in (doing) that** non ha senso (farlo); **he had the ~ to call the doctor** ha avuto il buonsenso di chiamare il medico; **to make sb see ~** far ragionare qn, far intendere ragione a qn.
(d) *(sanity)*: **~s pl** ragione *f,* senno; **to come to one's ~s** *(become reasonable)* tornare in sé; **to bring sb to his ~s** riportare qn alla ragione, far rinsavire qn; **to take leave of one's ~s** perdere il lume *or* l'uso della ragione.
(e) *(meaning)* senso; **it doesn't make ~** non ha senso; **I can't make (any) ~ of this** non ci capisco niente; **in one** *or* **a ~** in (un) certo senso; **in every ~ (of the word)** in tutti i sensi.
2 *vt (presence, interest)* avvertire, intuire; *(danger)* fiutare, avere sentore di; **to ~ that all is not well** sentire che c'è qualcosa che non va.
sense·less ['sɛnslɪs] *adj* **(a)** *(stupid)* insensato(a); *(: idea)* assurdo(a). **(b)** *(unconscious)* privo(a) di sensi, senza conoscenza.
sen·sibil·ities [ˌsɛnsɪ'bɪlɪtɪz] *npl* suscettibilità *fsg.*
sen·sible ['sɛnsəbl] *adj* **(a)** *(having good sense: person)* assennato(a), di buon senso; **(b)** *(act, decision, choice)* sensato(a), ragionevole; *(clothing etc)* pratico(a); **it would be more ~ (to do)** avrebbe più senso (fare). **(c)** *(noticeable)* sensibile, rilevante.
sen·si·tive ['sɛnsɪtɪv] *adj (person, tooth, instrument, film)*: **~ (to)** sensibile (a); *(delicate: skin, question)* delicato(a); *(easily offended)* suscettibile; **he is very ~ about it** è un tasto che è meglio non toccare con lui.
sen·si·tiv·ity [ˌsɛnsɪ'tɪvɪtɪ] *n (see adj)* sensibilità; delicatezza; suscettibilità.
sen·si·tized ['sɛnsɪtaɪzd] *adj* sensibilizzato(a).
sen·sual ['sɛnsjʊəl] *adj (gen)* sensuale; *(pleasures)* dei sensi.
sen·su·al·ity [ˌsɛnsjʊ'ælɪtɪ] *n* sensualità.
sen·su·ous ['sɛnsjʊəs] *adj* voluttuoso(a).
sent [sɛnt] *pt, pp of* **send**.
sen·tence ['sɛntəns] **1** *n* **(a)** *(Gram)* proposizione *f; (: complex ~)* periodo. **(b)** *(Law: verdict)* sentenza; *(: punishment)* condanna; **to pass ~ on sb** condannare qn; *(fig)* giudicare qn; **~ of death** condanna a morte; **under ~ of death** condannato a morte; **the judge gave him a 6-month ~** il giudice lo ha condannato a 6 mesi di prigione. **2** *vt*: **to ~ sb to death/to 5 years (in prison)** condannare qn a morte/a 5 anni (di prigione).
sen·ti·ment ['sɛntɪmənt] *n* **(a)** *(feeling)* sentimento; *(opinion)* opinione *f.* **(b)** *(sentimentality)* sentimentalismo.
sen·ti·ment·al [ˌsɛntɪ'mɛntl] *adj* sentimentale; **I have a ~ attachment to this pen** sono attaccato a questa penna per motivi sentimentali.
sen·ti·men·tal·ity [ˌsɛntɪmɛn'tælɪtɪ] *n* sentimentalità, sentimentalismo.
sen·try ['sɛntrɪ] **1** *n* sentinella. **2** *cpd:* **~ box** *n* garitta; **~ duty** *n*: **to be on ~ duty** essere di sentinella.

sepa·rable ['sɛpərəbl] *adj* separabile.
sepa·rate ['sɛprɪt] **1** *adj (gen)* separato(a); *(organization, career)* indipendente; *(occasion, issue)* diverso(a); **they went their ~ ways** *(also fig)* sono andati ognuno per la propria strada; **we sat at ~ tables** ci siamo seduti a tavoli diversi; **it was discussed at a ~ meeting** è stato discusso a un'altra riunione; **~ from** separato da; **under ~ cover** *(Comm)* in plico a parte. **2** *n (clothes)*: **~s** *pl* coordinati *mpl.* **3** ['sɛpəreɪt] *vt* separare, dividere; *(divide up)*: **to ~ into** dividere in; **to ~ sth from sth** separare qc da qc; **he is ~d from his wife, but not divorced** è separato dalla moglie ma non divorziato. **4** ['sɛpəreɪt] *vi* separarsi; *(married couple, boxers)* separarsi, dividersi; *(unmarried couple)* lasciarsi.
sepa·rate·ly ['sɛprɪtlɪ] *adv* separatamente.
sepa·ra·tion [ˌsɛpə'reɪʃən] *n* separazione *f.*
sepa·ra·tist ['sɛpərətɪst] *adj, n* separatista *(m/f).*
se·pia ['siːpjə] *n* nero di seppia.
Sep·tem·ber [sɛp'tɛmbəʳ] *n* settembre *m; for usage see* **July**.
sep·tic ['sɛptɪk] *adj* settico(a); *(wound)* infetto(a); **to go ~** infettarsi; **~ tank** fossa settica.
sep·ti·cae·mia, *(Am)* **sep·ti·cemia** [ˌsɛptɪ'siːmɪə] *n* setticemia.
sep·ul·chre, *(Am)* **sep·ul·cher** ['sɛpəlkəʳ] *n* sepolcro.
se·quel ['siːkwəl] *n (of film, book)*: **~ (to)** seguito (di); *(of event)* conseguenza, strascico.
se·quence ['siːkwəns] *n* **(a)** *(order)* successione *f,* ordine *m;* **in ~** in ordine, di seguito; **~ of tenses** *(Gram)* concordanza dei tempi. **(b)** *(series)* serie *f; (Mus, Cards, film ~)* sequenza.
se·quin ['siːkwɪn] *n* paillette *f inv,* lustrino.
ser·enade [ˌsɛrə'neɪd] **1** *n* serenata. **2** *vt* fare la serenata a.
se·rene [sə'riːn] *adj (person, sky)* sereno(a); *(sea)* calmo(a).
se·ren·ity [sɪ'rɛnɪtɪ] *n* serenità.
serge [sɜːdʒ] *n* serge *f.*
ser·geant ['sɑːdʒənt] **1** *n (Mil)* sergente *m; (Police)* brigadiere *m.* **2** *cpd:* **~ major** *n* maresciallo.
se·rial ['sɪərɪəl] **1** *n (in magazine)* romanzo a puntate; *(TV/Radio)* teleromanzo/commedia radiofonica a puntate. **2** *cpd:* **~ number** *n (of goods, machinery, banknotes etc)* numero di serie.
se·rial·ize ['sɪərɪəlaɪz] *vt (Press)* pubblicare a puntate; *(TV/Radio)* fare l'adattamento televisivo/radiofonico di.
se·ries ['sɪərɪz] *n, pl inv (gen)* serie *f inv; (set of books)* collana.
se·ri·ous ['sɪərɪəs] *adj* **(a)** *(earnest)* serio(a); **to give ~ thought to sth** considerare seriamente qc; **he's a ~ student of jazz** s'interessa seriamente di jazz; **she's getting ~ about him** si sta innamorando sul serio di lui; **are you ~ (about it)?** parli sul serio?; **you can't be ~!** stai scherzando! **(b)** *(causing concern)* serio(a), grave; **the patient's condition is ~** il paziente versa in gravi condizioni.
se·ri·ous·ly ['sɪərɪəslɪ] *adv* **(a)** *(in earnest)* seriamente; **to take sth/sb ~** prendere qc/qn sul serio; **~ though...** scherzi a parte..., sul serio.... **(b)** *(wounded)* gravemente; *(worried)* seriamente.
se·ri·ous·ness ['sɪərɪəsnɪs] *n (gen)* serietà, gravità; *(of error)* gravità; **in all ~** in tutta sincerità.
ser·mon ['sɜːmən] *n* sermone *m.*
ser·pent ['sɜːpənt] *n (poet)* serpente *m.*
ser·rat·ed [sɪ'reɪtɪd] *adj* seghettato(a).
se·rum ['sɪərəm] *n* siero.
serv·ant ['sɜːvənt] *n (domestic)* domestico/a, persona di servizio; *(fig)* servo/a, servitore *m.*

serve [sɜːv] 1 vt (a) (work for: employer, God, one's country) servire.

(b) (be used for or useful as): to ~ (as) servire (da); that ~s to explain... così si spiega...; it ~s a variety of purposes ha svariati usi; it ~s my purpose fa al caso mio, serve al mio scopo; it ~s its purpose serve allo scopo; it ~s no useful purpose non serve a niente; it ~s you right ti sta bene; his knowledge ~d him well le sue conoscenze gli sono tornate utili.

(c) (in shop, restaurant): to ~ sb (with) sth servire qc a qn; (food, meal) servire; (Tennis) servire; are you being ~d? la stanno servendo?; this dish should be ~d hot è un piatto che va servito caldo; the power station ~s the entire region la centrale rifornisce l'intera regione; the railway line ~s 5 cities la ferrovia collega 5 città.

(d) (complete): to ~ an apprenticeship fare tirocinio; to ~ a prison sentence scontare una condanna; he has ~ed time (in prison) è stato in prigione; he has ~ed his time (prisoner) ha scontato la sua condanna; (apprentice) ha finito il periodo di prova.

(e) (Law: summons, writ): to ~ sth on sb notificare qc a qn; to ~ a summons on sb notificare a qn una citazione; (Criminal law) spiccare un mandato di comparizione contro qn.

2 vi (a) (servant, soldier etc) prestare servizio; (shop assistant, waiter) servire; (Tennis) servire, battere; to ~ on a committee/jury far parte di un comitato/una giuria; she ~d for 2 years as chairwoman è stata presidentessa per 2 anni.

(b) (be useful): to ~ for or as servire da.

3 n (Tennis etc) servizio.

♦ **serve out** vt + adv (meal) servire (in tavola).
♦ **serve up** vt + adv (meal) servire (in tavola).

serv·er ['sɜːvəʳ] n (a) (Rel) chierichetto; (Tennis) battitore/trice. (b) (piece of cutlery) posata di servizio; (tray) vassoio, piatto da portata.

ser·vice ['sɜːvɪs] 1 n (a) (gen, also Mil) servizio; to see ~ (Mil) prestare servizio; military ~ servizio militare; at your ~ al suo (or vostro) servizio; to be of ~ (to sb) essere utile (a qn); to do sb a ~ fare un (gran) favore a qn; this old chair has seen a lot of ~ questa vecchia sedia ne ha viste tante; in ~ (domestic) a servizio; On Her (or His) Majesty's Service (abbr O.H.M.S.) al servizio di Sua Maestà; in the ~ of one's country al servizio della patria.

(b) (department, system) servizio; medical/social ~s servizi sanitari/sociali; the essential ~s i servizi primari; the S~s (Mil) le Forze Armate; the train ~ to London il servizio di treni per Londra; the number 13 bus ~ la linea del 13.

(c) (Rel) funzione f; funeral ~ rito funebre; to hold a ~ celebrare una funzione.

(d) (maintenance work) revisione f (periodica); to put the car in for a ~ portare a far revisionare la macchina.

(e) (set of crockery) servizio; a tea/coffee/dinner ~ un servizio da tè/da caffè/di piatti.

(f) (Tennis etc) servizio, battuta.

2 vt (car, washing machine etc) revisionare.

3 cpd: ~ area n (on motorway) area di servizio; ~ charge n servizio; ~ industries npl settore m terziario; ~ station n (Aut) stazione f di servizio.

ser·vice·able ['sɜːvɪsəbl] adj (practical: clothes etc) pratico(a), comodo(a); (usable, working) usabile.

ser·vice·man ['sɜːvɪsmən] n, pl -men militare m.

ser·vi·ette [ˌsɜːvɪ'et] n tovagliolo, salvietta.

ser·vile ['sɜːvaɪl] adj servile.

ses·sion ['seʃən] n (a) (sitting) seduta; (meeting)

riunione f; to be in ~ (parliament, court) essere in seduta; the court is now in ~ la seduta è aperta; I had a long ~ with her (talk) ho avuto un lungo colloquio con lei; (work) ho avuto una lunga riunione di lavoro con lei. (b) (Scol, Univ: year) anno; the new parliamentary ~ begins in October il parlamento si riapre a ottobre.

set [set] (vb: pt, pp set) 1 n (a) (gen) serie f inv; (of kitchen tools, saucepans) batteria; (of books) raccolta; (of dishes) servizio; a ~ of false teeth una dentiera; he still has a full ~ of teeth ha ancora tutti i denti; a ~ of dining-room furniture una camera da pranzo; a chess/draughts ~ un gioco di scacchi/dama; a painting ~ una scatola di colori; a writing ~ un servizio da scrittoio; these articles are sold in ~s questi articoli si vendono in serie complete.

(b) (Tennis) set m inv; (Math) insieme m.

(c) (Elec) apparecchio; television ~ televisore m.

(d) (Cine) set m inv; (Theatre) scena.

(e) (Hairdressing) messa in piega.

(f) (group: often pej) banda; the smart ~ il bel mondo.

2 adj (a) (unchanging: gen) fisso(a); (smile) artificiale; (purpose) definito(a), preciso(a); (lunch) a prezzo fisso; (speech, talk) preparato(a); (date, time) preciso(a), stabilito(a); (Scol: subjects) obbligatorio(a); (: books) in programma (per l'esame); ~ in one's ways abitudinario; ~ in one's opinions rigido nelle proprie convinzioni; a ~ phrase una frase fatta; at a ~ time a un'ora stabilita.

(b) (determined) deciso(a); (ready) pronto(a); he is (dead) ~ on doing it si è ficcato in testa di farlo; he is (dead) ~ on a new car si è ficcato in testa di comprare una nuova macchina; to be (dead) ~ against (doing) sth essere assolutamente contrario a (fare) qc; to be all ~ to do sth essere pronto fare qc; the scene was ~ for... (fig) tutto era pronto per....

3 vt (a) (place, put) mettere, porre; a novel ~ in Rome un romanzo ambientato a Roma; to ~ a higher value on happiness than on wealth dar più valore alla felicità che alla ricchezza; to ~ the value of a ring at £500 valutare un anello 500 sterline; to ~ fire to sth dare or appiccare fuoco a qc; to ~ a dog on sb aizzare un cane contro qn.

(b) (arrange, adjust: clock, mechanism) regolare; (: alarm clock, trap) mettere; (: hair) mettere in piega; (: broken arm, leg: in plaster) ingessare; (: with splint) mettere una stecca a; (: type) comporre; to ~ a poem to music mettere in musica una poesia; see sail, table etc.

(c) (fix, establish: date, limit) fissare, stabilire; (: record) stabilire; (: fashion) lanciare; (dye, colour) fissare; to ~ course for (Naut) far rotta per.

(d) (gem) montare.

(e) (assign: task, homework) dare, assegnare; to ~ sb a problem porre un problema a qn; to ~ sb an exam in Italian far fare un esame d'italiano a qn; to ~ an exam in Italian preparare il testo or le domande di un esame d'italiano.

(f) (start, cause to start): to ~ sth going mettere in moto qc; it ~ me thinking mi ha fatto pensare; to ~ sb to work mettere qn al lavoro; to ~ to work mettersi al lavoro.

4 vi (a) (sun, moon) tramontare.

(b) (broken bone, limb) saldarsi; (jelly, jam) rapprendersi, coagularsi; (concrete, glue) indurirsi, rassodarsi; (fig: face) fissarsi.

♦ **set about** vi + prep (a) (task): to ~ about doing sth mettersi a fare qc; I don't know how to ~

about it non so da che parte cominciare. **(b)** *(attack)* assalire.

♦ **set against** *vt + prep* **(a)**: **to ~ sb against sb/sth** mettere qn contro qn/qc. **(b)** *(balance against)*: **to ~ sth against sth** contrapporre qc a qc.

♦ **set aside** *vt + adv* **(a)** *(book, work)* mettere via; *(money, time)* mettere da parte; *(differences, quarrels)* accantonare. **(b)** *(reject: objection)* respingere; *(: will, judgment)* invalidare, annullare.

♦ **set back** *vt + adv* **(a)** *(clock)* mettere indietro; *(progress)* ritardare; **the strike has set us back 6 months** lo sciopero ci ha fatto perdere 6 mesi. **(b)**: **a house ~ back from the road** una casa a una certa distanza dalla strada. **(c)** *(fam: cost)*: **it ~ me back £900** mi è costato la bellezza di 900 sterline.

♦ **set down** *vt + adv* **(a)** *(put down: object)* posare; *(: passenger)* lasciar, far scendere. **(b)** *(record)* prendere nota di; **to ~ sth down in writing** *or* **on paper** mettere qc per scritto *or* sulla carta.

♦ **set in** *vi + adv* *(infection)* svilupparsi; *(complications)* intervenire; **the rain has ~ in for the day** ormai pioverà tutto il giorno; **before the rot ~s in** prima che la situazione degeneri.

♦ **set off 1** *vi + adv* *(leave)* avviarsi, mettersi in cammino; **to ~ off on a journey (to)** mettersi in viaggio (per). **2** *vt + adv* **(a)** *(bomb)* far esplodere; *(mechanism, burglar alarm)* azionare. **(b)** *(enhance)* mettere in risalto, far risaltare.

♦ **set out 1** *vi + adv*: **to ~ out (for)** avviarsi (verso, a); **to ~ out (from)** partire (da); **to ~ out in search of sb/sth** mettersi alla ricerca di qn/qc; **to ~ out to do sth** intendere fare qc. **2** *vt + adv* *(goods etc; fig: reasons, ideas)* esporre; *(chess pieces)* schierare, disporre.

♦ **set to** *vi + adv*: **to ~ to (and do sth)** mettersi all'opera (e fare qc).

♦ **set up 1** *vi + adv*: **to ~ up (in business) as a baker/lawyer** aprire una panetteria/uno studio legale; **when did you ~ up in business?** quand'è che ti sei messo in affari? **2** *vt + adv* **(a)** *(place in position: chairs, stalls, road blocks)* disporre; *(tent)* rizzare, piantare. **(b)** *(start: firm, business etc)* avviare, impiantare; *(: school)* fondare; *(: fund)* costituire; *(: inquiry)* aprire; *(: committee)* nominare, istituire; *(: infection)* provocare; **to ~ up house** mettere su casa; **to ~ up camp** accamparsi; **to ~ up shop** *(Comm)* mettersi in commercio; **to ~ sb up in business** avviare qn negli affari; **to ~ o.s. up as sth** *(fig)* pretendere di essere qc.

♦ **set upon** *vi + prep* *(attack)* assalire.

set·back ['sɛtbæk] *n* contrattempo; *(more serious)* momento di crisi; *(in health)* ricaduta.

set·square ['sɛtskwɛəʳ] *n* squadra.

set·tee [sɛ'tiː] *n* divano.

set·ter ['sɛtəʳ] *n* *(dog)* setter *m inv*.

set·ting ['sɛtɪŋ] **1** *n* **(a)** *(of novel etc)* ambiente *m*, ambientazione *f*; *(scenery)* sfondo; *(of jewels)* montatura; **a house in a beautiful ~** una casa in una posizione meravigliosa. **(b)** *(Mus)* adattamento *(musicale)*. **(c)** *(of controls)* posizione *f*. **2** *cpd*: **~ lotion** *n* fissatore *m*.

set·tle ['sɛtl] **1** *vt* **(a)** *(place carefully)* sistemare; **to ~ o.s., get ~d** sistemarsi, mettersi comodo(a).
(b) *(decide, finalize: details, date etc)* definire, fissare, stabilire; *(pay: bill, account)* regolare, saldare; *(solve: problem)* risolvere; *(: difficulty)* appianare; *(: dispute)* comporre; **to ~ a case** *or* **claim out of court** definire una causa in via amichevole; **that's ~d then** allora è deciso; **that ~s it!** *(no more problem)* così il problema è risolto!; *(I've decided)* ecco, ho deciso!
(c) *(calm down: nerves)* distendere; *(: doubts)*

dissipare; **to ~ one's stomach** calmare il mal di stomaco.
(d) *(colonize: land)* colonizzare.
(e) *(Law)*: **to ~ sth on sb** assegnare qc a qn.

2 *vi* **(a)** *(bird, insect)* posarsi; *(sediment, dust, snow)* depositarsi; *(building)* assestarsi; *(conditions, situation)* stabilizzarsi; *(weather)* mettersi al bello; *(emotions)* calmarsi; *(nerves)* distendersi; **to ~ into** *(armchair)* accomodarsi (ben bene) in, sistemarsi in; *(new job, way of life)* abituarsi a; *(habit)* prendere; **I couldn't ~ to anything** non riuscivo a concentrarmi.
(b) *(go to live: in town, country)* stabilirsi; *(: in new house)* sistemarsi; *(: as colonist)* insediarsi; **to feel ~d** *(in a place)* sentirsi a casa.
(c): **to ~ with sb for the cost of sth** concordare il prezzo di qc con qn; **can I ~ with you later?** posso darti i soldi più tardi?; **he ~d for £100** ha accettato 100 sterline; **to ~ out of court** *(Law)* giungere a un accordo in via amichevole; **to ~ on sth** *(choose)* decidere *or* optare per qc.

♦ **settle down** *vi + adv* *(person: in house, armchair etc)* sistemarsi; *(: become calmer)* calmarsi; *(: after wild youth)* mettere la testa a posto; *(situation)* sistemarsi, tornare alla normalità; **to ~ down to work** mettersi a lavorare; **has he ~d down in his new job?** si è adattato bene al nuovo lavoro?; **to get married and ~ down** (mettere su famiglia e) sistemarsi.

♦ **settle in** *vi + adv* *(in new house)* sistemarsi; *(in new job, neighbourhood)* ambientarsi.

♦ **settle up** *vi + adv*: **to ~ up (with sb)** saldare *or* regolare il conto (con qn).

set·tle·ment ['sɛtlmənt] *n* **(a)** *(of bill, debt)* regolamento; *(of question)* soluzione *f*; *(of dispute)* composizione *f*; **in ~ of our account** *(Comm)* a saldo del nostro conto. **(b)** *(agreement)* accordo. **(c)** *(village)* insediamento, comunità *f inv*; *(colony)* colonia.

set·tler ['sɛtləʳ] *n* colono/a.

set-to ['sɛt'tuː] *n* *(fam: fight)* zuffa; *(: quarrel)* baruffa.

set·up ['sɛtʌp] *n* *(fam: situation)* situazione *f*.

sev·en ['sɛvn] *adj, n* sette *(m) inv; for usage see* **five**.

sev·en·teen [,sɛvn'tiːn] *adj, n* diciassette *(m) inv; for usage see* **five**.

sev·en·teenth [,sɛvn'tiːnθ] **1** *adj* diciassettesimo(a). **2** *n* *(in series)* diciassettesimo/a; *(fraction)* diciassettesimo; *for usage see* **fifth**.

sev·enth ['sɛvnθ] **1** *adj* settimo(a). **2** *n* *(in series)* settimo/a; *(fraction)* settimo; *for usage see* **fifth**.

sev·en·ti·eth ['sɛvntɪɪθ] **1** *adj* settantesimo(a). **2** *n* *(in series)* settantesimo/a; *(fraction)* settantesimo; *for usage see* **fifth**.

sev·en·ty ['sɛvntɪ] *adj, n* settanta *(m) inv; for usage see* **fifty**.

sev·er ['sɛvəʳ] *vt* *(rope)* tagliare; *(limb)* staccare; *(fig: relations)* troncare, rompere; *(: communications)* interrompere.

sev·er·al ['sɛvrəl] **1** *adj* parecchi(ie), diversi(e); **~ times** diverse volte. **2** *pron* parecchi(ie); **~ of us** parecchi di noi.

sev·er·ance ['sɛvərəns] **1** *n* *(of relations)* rottura. **2** *cpd*: **~ pay** *n* *(Industry)* indennità di licenziamento.

se·vere [sɪ'vɪəʳ] *adj* *(-r, -st)* *(person)*: **~ (with** *or* **on** *or* **towards sb)** severo(a) (con *or* verso qn); *(climate, winter, cold)* rigido(a); *(frost)* violento(a); *(flooding, defeat, injuries)* grave; *(examination)* rigoroso(a), severo(a); *(damage)* ingente; *(pain)* forte, acuto(a); **a ~ cold** un forte raffreddore.

se·vere·ly [sɪ'vɪəlɪ] *adv* *(gen)* severamente; *(wounded, ill)* gravemente.

se·ver·ity [sɪ'verɪtɪ] n (gen) severità; (of climate etc) rigore m; (of flooding, defeat, injuries) gravità; (of damage) ingenza; (of pain) acutezza.

sew [səʊ] pt **sewed**, pp **sewn** or **sewed** vt, vi cucire; **to ~ a button on sth** attaccare un bottone a qc.

♦ **sew up** vt + adv (tear) rammendare; (wound) ricucire; (hem) cucire; (seam) fare; **it's all ~n up** (fig fam) è tutto apposto.

sew·age ['sjuːɪdʒ] **1** n acque fpl di rifiuto or di fogna. **2** cpd: ~ **farm** n impianto per il riciclaggio delle acque di rifiuto.

sew·er ['sjʊəʳ] n fogna.

sew·ing ['səʊɪŋ] **1** n cucito. **2** cpd: ~ **machine** n macchina da cucire.

sewn [səʊn] pp of **sew**.

sex [seks] **1** n (gender) sesso; (sexual intercourse) rapporti mpl sessuali; **to have ~ with sb** avere rapporti sessuali con qn; **the opposite ~** l'altro sesso. **2** cpd (discrimination, education) sessuale; ~ **appeal** n sex appeal m; ~ **maniac** n maniaco sessuale; ~ **shop** n sex-shop m inv.

sex·ism ['seksɪzəm] n sessismo.

sex·ist ['seksɪst] adj sessista.

sex·tet [seks'tet] n sestetto.

sex·ton ['sekstən] n sagrestano.

sex·ual ['seksjʊəl] adj sessuale; ~ **intercourse** rapporti mpl sessuali; ~ **assault** violenza carnale.

sexu·al·ity [ˌseksjʊ'ælɪtɪ] n sessualità.

sexy ['seksɪ] adj (-ier, -iest) sexy inv.

shab·bi·ness ['ʃæbɪnɪs] n (of dress, person) trasandatezza; (of building) squallore m; (of treatment) meschinità.

shab·by ['ʃæbɪ] adj (-ier, -iest) (building) malandato(a), squallido(a); (clothes) sciatto(a); (person: also: ~**looking**) trasandato(a); (behaviour) meschino(a); **a ~ trick** un tiro mancino.

shack [ʃæk] **1** n capanno; (in slum) baracca. **2** vi: **to ~ up with sb** (fam) vivere con qn.

shade [ʃeɪd] **1** n **(a)** ombra; **in the ~** all'ombra; **to put in the ~** (fig) mettere in ombra, oscurare. **(b)** (lamp~) paralume m; (eye~) visiera; (Am: window ~) veneziana; ~**s** (Am: sunglasses) occhiali mpl da sole. **(c)** (of colour) tonalità f inv, sfumatura; (fig: of meaning, opinion) sfumatura; **several ~s darker/lighter** di una tonalità parecchio più scura/chiara; **this lipstick comes in several ~s** questo rossetto è disponibile in diverse gradazioni. **(d)** (small quantity): **just a ~ more** un tantino di più; **a ~ bigger** un tantino più grande. **2** vt (from sun, light) riparare; **to ~ one's eyes from the sun** ripararsi gli occhi dal sole.

♦ **shade in** vt + adv ombreggiare.

shad·ow ['ʃædəʊ] **1** n ombra; **in ~** in ombra, all'ombra; **in the ~ (of)** all'ombra (di); **without** or **beyond a ~ of doubt** senz'ombra di dubbio; **to cast a ~ over** proiettare ombra su or sopra, far ombra su; (fig) offuscare; **he's only a ~ of his former self** è diventato l'ombra di se stesso; **to have ~s under one's eyes** avere le occhiaie or gli occhi cerchiati. **2** vt (follow) pedinare. **3** cpd: ~ **boxing** n allenamento contro l'ombra; ~ **cabinet** n (Pol) gabinetto m ombra inv; **the ~ Foreign Secretary** il portavoce dell'opposizione per gli Affari Esteri.

shad·owy ['ʃædəʊɪ] adj (form, figure) indistinto(a), vago(a).

shady ['ʃeɪdɪ] adj (-ier, -iest) (place) ombroso(a), ombreggiato(a); (tree) ombroso(a); (fig: person, deal) losco(a), equivoco(a).

shaft [ʃɑːft] n **(a)** (of arrow, spear) asta; (of tool) manico; (of cart etc) stanga; (Aut, Tech) albero; ~ **of light/sunlight** raggio di luce/sole. **(b)** (of mine,

lift etc) pozzo; **ventilator ~** condotto di ventilazione.

shag·gy ['ʃægɪ] adj (-ier, -iest) (mane, hair) ispido(a), arruffato(a); (dog) a pelo lungo e arruffato; ~ **dog story** (fig) barzelletta interminabile.

shake [ʃeɪk] (vb: pt **shook**, pp **shaken**) **1** n scossa, scrollata; **with a ~ of her head...** scuotendo la testa..., scrollando il capo...; **to give a rug a good ~** dare una bella sbattuta a un tappeto; **he's no great ~s at swimming** (fam) nel nuoto non è che brilli; **in two ~s** (fam) in quattro e quattr'otto.

2 vt **(a)** (person, object) scuotere; (building, windows) far tremare; (bottle, dice) agitare; **to ~ one's fist at sb** minacciare qn col pugno; **to ~ hands (with sb)** dare or stringere la mano (a qn); **to ~ one's head** (in refusal, dismay) scuotere la testa. **(b)** (harm: confidence, belief, opinion) scuotere; (: reputation) minare; (: amaze, disturb) scuotere, sconvolgere; **nothing will ~ our resolve** niente ci smuoverà; **the firm's reputation has been badly ~n** la reputazione dell'azienda ha subito una forte scossa; **he needs to be ~n out of his apathy** bisogna scuoterlo or scrollarlo dalla sua apatia.

3 vi (person, building, voice etc) tremare; **to ~ with fear/cold** tremare di paura/freddo; **to ~ with laughter** torcersi dal ridere; **the walls shook at the sound** il colpo fece tremare la casa.

♦ **shake off** vt + adv (raindrops, snow) scrollarsi di dosso; (dust) scuotersi di dosso; (fig: cold, cough) sbarazzarsi di; (: habit) togliersi; (: pursuer) seminare.

♦ **shake out** vt + adv (sail) sciogliere; (blanket etc) scuotere; (bag) svuotare scuotendo.

♦ **shake up** vt + adv **(a)** (bottle) agitare; (pillow) sprimacciare. **(b)** (disturb: person) sconvolgere, scuotere. **(c)** (rouse, stir: person, company etc) scuotere, dare una scossa salutare a.

shak·en ['ʃeɪkən] pp of **shake**.

shake-up ['ʃeɪkʌp] n (fig) rimpasto generale.

shaki·ly ['ʃeɪkɪlɪ] adv (reply) con voce tremante; (walk) con passo malfermo; (write) con mano tremante.

shaky ['ʃeɪkɪ] adj (-ier, -iest) (table, building) traballante; (trembling: voice) tremulo(a); (: hands) tremante; (: handwriting) tremolante; (fig: health) vacillante, malfermo(a); (: memory) labile; (: knowledge) incerto(a); **I feel a bit ~** mi gira un po' la testa; **my Spanish is rather ~** il mio spagnolo lascia un po' a desiderare.

shale [ʃeɪl] n scisto.

shall [ʃæl] aux vb **(a)** (used to form 1st person in future tense and questions): **I ~** or **I'll go tomorrow** ci andrò domani, ci vado domani; ~ **I open the door or will you?** devo aprire io la porta o lo fai tu?; ~ **we hear from you soon?** ci manderai presto tue notizie?; **I'll get some,** ~ **I?** ne prendo un po', va bene?; **let's go out,** ~ **we?** usciamo, vuoi? **(b)** (in commands, emphatic): **you ~ pay for this!** me la pagherai!; **it ~ be done this way** dev'essere fatto così; **but I wanted to see him — and so you ~** ma volevo vederlo! — lo vedrai!

shal·lot [ʃə'lɒt] n scalogno.

shal·low ['ʃæləʊ] **1** adj (-er, -est) (water etc) basso(a), poco profondo(a); (dish etc) poco profondo(a); (breathing) leggero(a); (fig: person) superficiale, leggero(a); (: conversation) futile, frivolo(a). **2:** ~**s** npl secche fpl.

shalt [ʃælt] (old) 2nd pers sg of **shall**.

sham [ʃæm] **1** adj (piety) falso(a); (politeness) finto(a); (elections) fasullo(a); (battle, illness) simulato(a). **2** n **(a)** (imposture) messinscena, finta.

(b) *(person)* ciarlatano/a, impostore *m*. **3** *vt* fingere, simulare; **to ~ illness** far finta di essere malato. **4** *vi* fingere, far finta; **he's just ~ming** fa solo finta.

sham·bles [ˈʃæmblz] *nsg (scene of confusion)* macello; **the area was (in) a ~ after the earthquake** la zona era nella distruzione più totale dopo il terremoto; **the economy is (in) a complete ~** l'economia è nel caos più totale; **the place was (in) a ~** c'era un macello; **the game was a ~** la partita è stata un disastro.

shame [ʃeɪm] **1** *n* **(a)** *(feeling)* vergogna, pudore *m*; *(humiliation)* vergogna; **~ on you!** vergognati!; **to put sb/sth to ~** *(fig)* far sfigurare qn/qc. **(b)** *(pity)*: **it's a ~** *(that/to do)* è un peccato (che + *sub*/fare); **what a ~!** che peccato! **2** *vt (make ashamed)* far vergognare; *(bring disgrace on)* disonorare; **to ~ sb into doing sth** convincere qn a fare qc facendolo vergognare.

shame·faced [ˈʃeɪmfeɪst] *adj (ashamed)* tutto(a) vergognoso(a); *(confused)* confuso(a).

shame·ful [ˈʃeɪmfʊl] *adj* vergognoso(a).

shame·less [ˈʃeɪmlɪs] *adj* svergognato(a), spudorato(a).

sham·my [ˈʃæmɪ] *n (also: ~ leather)* pelle *f* di camoscio.

sham·poo [ʃæmˈpuː] **1** *n* shampoo *m inv*; **~ and set** shampoo e messa in piega. **2** *vt (hair)* fare lo shampoo a; *(carpet)* lavare con lo shampoo; **to ~ one's hair** farsi lo shampoo.

sham·rock [ˈʃæmrɒk] *n* trifoglio.

shan·dy [ˈʃændɪ] *n (Brit) miscela di birra e gassosa.*

shan't [ʃɑːnt] **= shall not.**

shan·ty[1] [ˈʃæntɪ] *n (also:* **sea ~**) canzone *f* marinaresca.

shan·ty[2] [ˈʃæntɪ] *n* baracca.

shanty·town [ˈʃæntɪtaʊn] *n* bidonville *f inv.*

shape [ʃeɪp] **1** *n* forma; **what ~ is it?** di che forma è?, che forma ha?; **in the ~ of a heart** a forma di cuore; **it is rectangular in ~** è di forma rettangolare; **his ears are a funny ~** le sue orecchie hanno una forma buffa; **in all ~s and sizes** d'ogni forma e dimensione; **I can't bear gardening in any ~ or form** detesto il giardinaggio d'ogni genere e specie; **to take the ~ of** prendere la forma di; **the news reached him in the ~ of a telegram** ha ricevuto la notizia sotto forma di telegramma; **the ~ of things to come** il volto del futuro; **to take ~** prendere forma; **to lose its ~** *(sweater etc)* perdere la forma, sformarsi; **to be in good/poor ~** *(person)* essere in (buona) forma/ giù di forma; *(object)* essere in buone/cattive condizioni; **to knock** *or* **hammer sth into ~** dar forma a qc a colpi di martello; **to knock** *or* **lick into ~** *(fig: business etc)* rimettere in sesto; *(: plan, team)* mettere a punto; *(: athlete)* rimettere in forma; **to get o.s. into ~** rimettersi in forma; **a ~ loomed up out of the fog** una forma indistinta emerse dalla nebbia.

2 *vt (clay, stone)* dar forma a; *(fig: ideas, character)* formare; *(: course of events)* determinare, condizionare; **heart-~d** a forma di cuore.

3 *vi (fig)*: **things are shaping (up) well** le cose si mettono bene; **he's shaping (up) nicely** sta facendo dei progressi.

shape·less [ˈʃeɪplɪs] *adj* informe, senza forma.

shape·ly [ˈʃeɪplɪ] *adj (-ier, -iest) (woman)* ben fatto(a).

share [ʃɛəʳ] **1** *n* **(a)** parte *f*; **to have a ~ in the profits** partecipare agli utili; **to have a ~ in sth** aver parte in qc; **he has a 50% ~ in a new business venture** è socio al 50% in una nuova iniziativa; **he had a ~ in it** *(fig)* c'è entrato anche lui; **to take a ~ in sth** partecipare a qc; **fair ~s for all** parti giuste *or* uguali (per tutti); **she's had more than her (fair) ~ of suffering** ha sofferto più del giusto; **the minister came in for his ~ of criticism** il ministro ha avuto la sua parte di critiche; **to do one's (fair) ~** fare la propria parte. **(b)** *(Fin)*: **~ (in)** azione *f* (di), titolo (di).

2 *vt* **(a)** *(also:* **~ out**): **to ~ (among, between)** dividere (tra); **the thieves ~d (out) the money** i ladri si sono spartiti i soldi. **(b)** *(have a share in)*: **to ~ (with)** dividere (con); **shall we ~ the last bottle of wine?** ci beviamo insieme l'ultima bottiglia di vino?; **~d line** *(Telec)* duplex *m inv.* **(c)** *(fig: have in common)* condividere; **she ~s his love of gardening** hanno in comune la passione del giardinaggio.

3 *vi*: **children must learn to ~** i bambini devono imparare a dividere ciò che hanno; **~ and ~ alike** un po' per uno non fa male a nessuno; **to ~ in** *(gen)* partecipare a; *(blame)* prendersi la propria parte di.

4 *cpd*: **~ capital** *n (Fin)* capitale *m* azionario; **~ index** *n (Fin)* listino di Borsa; **~ price** *n (Fin)* valore *m* azionario.

share·holder [ˈʃɛəˌhəʊldəʳ] *n* azionista *m/f.*

share-out [ˈʃɛəraʊt] *n* spartizione *f*, ripartizione *f.*

shark [ʃɑːk] *n (fish)* squalo, pescecane *m*; *(fam: swindler)* pirata *m*; *(: a successful and rich one)* pescecane *m.*

sharp [ʃɑːp] **1** *adj* **(-er, -est)** **(a)** *(edge, razor, knife)* tagliente, affilato(a); *(point)* acuminato(a); *(pencil)* appuntito(a); *(needle, stone)* aguzzo(a); *(angle)* acuto(a); *(curve, bend)* stretto(a), accentuato(a); *(features)* angoloso(a), affilato(a).

(b) *(abrupt: change, halt)* brusco(a); *(: descent)* ripido(a); *(: rise, fall)* improvviso(a), forte.

(c) *(well-defined: outline)* nitido(a), netto(a); *(: contrast)* spiccato(a), marcato(a); *(TV: picture)* chiaro(a).

(d) *(harsh: smell, taste)* acuto(a), aspro(a); *(: pain, cry)* acuto(a); *(: blow)* violento(a); *(: tone, voice)* secco(a), aspro(a); *(: wind, frost)* penetrante, pungente; *(: rebuke)* aspro(a); *(: retort, tongue)* tagliente; *(: words)* duro(a), pungente; **to be ~ with sb** rimproverare qn.

(e) *(acute: eyesight, hearing, sense of smell)* acuto(a), fine; *(: mind, intelligence)* acuto(a), penetrante; *(: person)* sveglio(a), svelto(a); **~ practice** *(pej)* pratiche *fpl* poco oneste.

(f) *(Mus)*: **C ~** do diesis.

2 *adv* **(a)** *(Mus)* in diesis.

(b): **at 5 o'clock ~** alle 5 in punto; **turn ~ left** gira tutto a sinistra; **to stop ~** fare una fermata brusca.

3 *n (Mus)* diesis *m inv.*

sharp·en [ˈʃɑːpən] *vt* **(a)** *(tool, blade etc)* affilare; *(pencil)* temperare. **(b)** *(outline)* mettere in risalto, far spiccare; *(contrast, difference)* sottolineare, evidenziare; *(TV picture)* mettere a fuoco; *(conflict)* intensificare; *(desire, pain)* acuire; *(appetite)* aguzzare; **to ~ one's wits** aguzzare l'ingegno.

sharp·en·er [ˈʃɑːpnəʳ] *n (for pencils)* temperamatite *m inv; (for knives)* affilacoltelli *m inv.*

sharp-eyed [ˌʃɑːpˈaɪd] *adj*, **sharp-sighted** [ˌʃɑːpˈsaɪtɪd] *adj* dalla vista acuta.

sharp-faced [ˌʃɑːpˈfeɪst] *adj*, **sharp-featured** [ˌʃɑːpˈfiːtʃəd] *adj* dal volto affilato.

sharp·ly [ˈʃɑːplɪ] *adv* **(a)** *(abruptly: turn, rise, stop)* bruscamente. **(b)** *(clearly: stand out, contrast)* nettamente. **(c)** *(harshly: criticize, retort)* duramente, aspramente.

sharp-shooter [ˈʃɑːpˌʃuːtəʳ] *n* tiratore *m* scelto.

sharp-tempered [,ʃɑːp'tɛmpəd] *adj* irascibile.

shat·ter ['ʃætəʳ] **1** *vt (glass, window)* frantumare, mandare in frantumi; *(door)* fracassare; *(health)* rovinare; *(career)* compromettere definitivamente; *(nerves)* mandare in pezzi; *(self-confidence, hope)* distruggere. **2** *vi* frantumarsi, andare in frantumi; **it ~ed into a thousand pieces** è andato in mille pezzi.

shat·tered ['ʃætəd] *adj (grief-stricken)* sconvolto(a); *(fam: amazed)* strabiliato(a), senza parole; *(: exhausted)* a pezzi, distrutto(a).

shat·ter·ing ['ʃætərɪŋ] *adj (attack)* schiacciante; *(defeat, news)* disastroso(a); *(experience)* traumatico(a); **it was a ~ blow to his hopes** è stato un colpo disastroso per le sue speranze.

shatter·proof ['ʃætəpruːf] *adj* infrangibile.

shave [ʃeɪv] **1** *n*: **to have a ~** farsi la barba, radersi, rasarsi; **to have a close ~** *(fig)* cavarsela per un pelo. **2** *vt (person, face)* radere, rasare, sbarbare; *(wood)* piallare; *(fig: graze)* sfiorare, rasentare; **to ~ off one's beard** tagliarsi la barba. **3** *vi (person)* farsi la barba, radersi, rasarsi.

shav·en ['ʃeɪvn] *adj (person)* rasato(a), sbarbato(a); *(head)* raso(a).

shav·er ['ʃeɪvəʳ] *n (electric ~)* rasoio elettrico.

shav·ing ['ʃeɪvɪŋ] **1** *n (of wood etc)* truciolo. **2** *cpd (brush, cream)* da barba.

shawl [ʃɔːl] *n* scialle *m*.

she [ʃiː] **1** *pers pron* ella, lei; **~ has gone out** è uscita; **there ~ is** eccola; **SHE didn't do it** non è stata lei a farlo. **2** *n*: **it's a ~** *(animal, fam: baby)* è una femmina.

she-bear ['ʃiːbɛəʳ] *n* orsa.

sheaf [ʃiːf] *n, pl* **sheaves** *(Agr)* covone *m*; *(of papers)* fascio.

shear [ʃɪəʳ] *pt* **sheared**, *pp* **sheared** *or* **shorn** *vt (sheep)* tosare.

♦ **shear off** *vi + adv (break off)* spezzarsi.

shears [ʃɪəz] *npl (for sheep)* forbici *fpl* da tosatore; *(for gardening, dressmaking)* cesoie *fpl*.

sheath [ʃiːθ] **1** *n (gen)* guaina; *(for sword)* guaina, fodero; *(contraceptive)* preservativo. **2** *cpd*: **~ knife** *n* coltello con fodero).

sheaves [ʃiːvz] *pl of* **sheaf**.

shed[1] [ʃɛd] *pt, pp* **shed** *vt* **(a)** *(get rid of: gen)* perdere; *(: clothes)* togliersi; *(: employees)* liberarsi di. **(b)** *(tears, blood)* versare. **(c)** *(send out: light, warmth)* emanare; **to ~ light on** *(problem, mystery)* far luce su.

shed[2] [ʃɛd] *n (in garden)* capanno; *(for bicycles)* rimessa; *(Industry, Rail)* capannone *m*; *(for cattle)* stalla.

sheen [ʃiːn] *n* lucentezza.

sheep [ʃiːp] **1** *n, pl inv* pecora; **to make ~'s eyes at sb** *(fig)* far gli occhi dolci a qn. **2** *cpd*: **~ farm** *n* fattoria con allevamento di pecore *or* ovini; **~ farmer** *n* allevatore *m* di pecore.

sheep·dog ['ʃiːpdɒg] *n* cane *m* (da) pastore.

sheep·ish ['ʃiːpɪʃ] *adj (look, smile)* confuso(a), imbarazzato(a).

sheep·skin ['ʃiːpskɪn] **1** *n* pelle *f* di pecora *or* di montone. **2** *cpd (gloves)* di montone; **~ jacket** *n* (giacca di) montone *m*.

sheer [ʃɪəʳ] *adj (-er, -est)* **(a)** *(utter: madness, greed)* puro(a); *(: waste of time)* totale; *(: necessity)* assoluto(a); **that's ~ robbery!** è un furto bello e buono!; **the ~ impossibility of...** l'assoluta impossibilità di...; **by ~ chance, by a ~ accident** per puro caso, per pura combinazione. **(b)** *(transparent)* trasparente. **(c)** *(precipitous)* a picco; **a ~ drop** uno strapiombo.

sheet [ʃiːt] **1** *n (on bed)* lenzuolo; *(dust ~)* telo; *(of paper, plastic)* foglio; *(of metal, glass, ice)* lastra;

(of water) distesa; *(of flame)* muro. **2** *cpd*: **~ lightning** *n* lampeggio diffuso; **~ metal** *n* lamiera; **~ music** *n* fogli *mpl* di musica.

sheik(h) [ʃeɪk] *n* sceicco.

shelf [ʃɛlf] **1** *n, pl* **shelves** **(a)** *(in cupboard, oven)* ripiano; *(fixed to wall)* scaffale *m*, mensola; **to be on the ~** *(fig fam: woman)* essere votata allo zitellaggio. **(b)** *(in rock face, underwater)* piattaforma. **2** *cpd*: **~ life** *n (Comm)* durata di conservazione; **~ mark** *n (in libraries)* collocazione *f*.

shell [ʃɛl] **1** *n* **(a)** *(of egg, nut, tortoise etc)* guscio; *(of oyster, mussel)* conchiglia; *(of lobster)* corazza, guscio; **to come out of one's ~** *(fig)* uscire dal (proprio) guscio. **(b)** *(of building)* struttura; *(of ship)* ossatura. **(c)** *(Mil)* granata. **2** *vt* **(a)** *(nuts, shellfish)* sgusciare; *(peas, beans)* sgranare. **(b)** *(Mil)* bombardare.

♦ **shell out** *(fam)* **1** *vi + adv*: **to ~ out (for)** sganciare soldi (per). **2** *vt + adv (money)*: **to ~ out (for)** sganciare (per).

shell·fish ['ʃɛlfɪʃ] *n, pl inv (crab etc)* crostaceo; *(mollusc)* mollusco; *(pl:* Culin*)* frutti *mpl* di mare.

shell·ing ['ʃɛlɪŋ] *n* bombardamento.

shell·proof ['ʃɛlpruːf] *adj* a prova di bomba.

shel·ter ['ʃɛltəʳ] **1** *n* **(a)** *(protection)* riparo; **under the ~ of** al riparo di; **to seek ~ (from)** cercare riparo (da, contro), ripararsi (da); **to take ~ (from)** mettersi al riparo (da). **(b)** *(construction: on mountain etc)* rifugio; **bus ~** pensilina; **air-raid ~** rifugio antiaereo. **2** *vt* **(a)** *(protect)*: **to ~ (from)** riparare (da); *(from blame etc)* proteggere (da). **(b)** *(give lodging to: homeless, criminal etc)* dare asilo a. **3** *vi* ripararsi, mettersi al riparo; **to ~ from the rain** ripararsi dalla pioggia; **to ~ under a tree** rifugiarsi sotto un albero.

shel·tered ['ʃɛltəd] *adj (place)* riparato(a); *(childhood)* tranquillo(a); *(environment)* protetto(a); **she has led a very ~ life** è vissuta nella bambagia.

shelve [ʃɛlv] *vt (fig: postpone)* accantonare.

shelves [ʃɛlvz] *npl of* **shelf**.

shelv·ing ['ʃɛlvɪŋ] *n* scaffalature *fpl*.

shep·herd ['ʃɛpəd] **1** *n* pastore *m*; **~'s pie** *(Culin)* timballo di carne macinata e purè di patate. **2** *vt*: **to ~ sb in/out** *etc* accompagnare qn dentro/fuori *etc*; **he ~ed the children across the road** ha aiutato i bambini ad attraversare la strada.

sher·bet ['ʃɜːbət] *n (Brit: powder)* polvere effervescente al gusto di frutta; *(Am: water ice)* sorbetto.

sher·iff ['ʃɛrɪf] *n* sceriffo.

sher·ry ['ʃɛrɪ] *n* sherry *m inv*.

she's [ʃiːz] = **she is**; **she has**.

Shet·land ['ʃɛtlənd] **1** *n (also:* **the ~ Isles, the ~s)** le isole Shetland, le Shetland. **2** *cpd (wool)* shetland *inv*; **~ pony** *n* pony *m inv* delle Shetland.

shield [ʃiːld] **1** *n (armour)* scudo; *(on machine etc)* schermo (di protezione). **2** *vt*: **to ~ sb from sth** riparare qn da qc; **to ~ sb with one's body** fare scudo a qn con il proprio corpo.

shift [ʃɪft] **1** *n* **(a)** *(change: in wind, opinion etc)* cambiamento; *(movement: of load)* spostamento. **(b)** *(period of work, group of workers)* turno; **to work in ~s** fare i turni (di lavoro); **to work on night/day ~** fare il turno di notte/di giorno. **(c)** *(expedient)* espediente *m*; **to make ~ with/without sth** arrangiarsi con/senza qc. **(d)** *(Am Aut: gear ~)* cambio.

2 *vt (gen)* spostare; *(sth stuck)* smuovere; *(employee)* trasferire; *(change: position etc)* cambiare; **to ~ scenery** *(Theatre)* cambiare le scene; **to ~ the blame on to sb** scaricare la colpa su qualcun altro.

3 *vi* **(a)** *(gen)* spostarsi; *(opinions)* mutare;

(change one's mind) cambiare idea; **the wind has ~ed to the south** il vento si è girato e soffia da sud; **he ~ed over to the door** si è avvicinato alla porta; **~ off the sofa** togliti dal divano; **~ up** *or* **over** *or* **along** spostati; **that car's certainly ~ing** *(fam)* quella macchina va molto forte; **to ~ into second gear** *(Aut)* mettere la seconda. **(b): to ~ for o.s.** arrangiarsi da sé, cavarsela da solo(a).

4 *cpd:* **~ key** *n (on typewriter)* tasto delle maiuscole; **~ work** *n:* **to do ~ work** fare i turni.

shift·less [ˈʃɪftlɪs] *adj:* **a ~ person** un fannullone.

shifty [ˈʃɪftɪ] *adj* (**-ier, -iest**) *(person)* losco(a), equivoco(a); *(behaviour)* equivoco(a); *(eyes)* sfuggente.

shil·ling [ˈʃɪlɪŋ] *n* scellino.

shilly-shally [ˈʃɪlɪˌʃælɪ] *vi* esitare; **don't ~!, stop ~ing!** deciditi una buona volta!

shim·mer [ˈʃɪməʳ] *vi (gen)* luccicare, scintillare; *(heat haze)* tremolare.

shim·mer·ing [ˈʃɪmərɪŋ] *adj (gen)* luccicante, scintillante; *(haze)* tremolante; *(satin etc)* cangiante.

shin [ʃɪn] **1** *n* stinco. **2** *vi:* **to ~ up/down a tree** arrampicarsi in cima a/scivolare giù da un albero; **to ~ over** scavalcare.

shin·bone [ˈʃɪnbəʊn] *n* tibia.

shin·dy [ˈʃɪndɪ] *n (fam: noise)* gazzarra; *(: brawl)* rissa; **to kick up a ~** fare un gran baccano.

shine [ʃaɪn] *(vb: pt, pp* **shone**) **1** *n (of sun, metal)* lucentezza; **to give sth a ~** dare una lucidata a qc; **those shoes have got a good ~** quelle scarpe luccicano; **to take the ~ off sth** far perdere il lucido a qc; *(fig)* offuscare qc; **to take a ~ to sb** *(fig)* prendere qn in simpatia; **come rain or ~...** che il tempo sia brutto o bello.... .

2 *vt* **(a)** *(polish: pt, pp* **shone** *or* **~d**) lucidare, lustrare. **(b): ~ the light** *or* **your torch over here** fai luce in questa direzione (con la pila).

3 *vi* splendere, brillare; **the light was shining in his eyes** aveva la luce negli occhi; **the light was shining under the door** si vedeva la luce sotto la porta; **the metal shone in the sun** il metallo brillava al sole; **her face shone with happiness** il suo viso splendeva di felicità; **her eyes shone with joy** i suoi occhi brillavano di gioia; **to ~ at maths** *(fig)* brillare in matematica.

shin·gle [ˈʃɪŋgl] *n* **(a)** *(on beach)* ciottoli *mpl.* **(b)** *(on roof)* assicella (di rivestimento). **(c)** *(Am: signboard)* insegna.

shin·gles [ˈʃɪŋglz] *nsg (Med)* herpes zoster *m.*

shin·ing [ˈʃaɪnɪŋ] *adj (surface, hair)* lucente; *(light)* brillante; *(eyes)* splendente; **a ~ example** *(fig)* un fulgido esempio.

shiny [ˈʃaɪnɪ] *adj* (**-ier, -iest**) lucido(a).

ship [ʃɪp] **1** *n* nave *f,* bastimento; **Her** *(or* **His) Majesty's S~** *(abbr* **H.M.S.)** **Ark Royal** l'Ark Royal; **on board ~** a bordo; **~'s company** equipaggio; **~'s papers** carte *fpl* di bordo. **2** *vt* **(a)** *(take on board: goods, water)* imbarcare; *(: oars)* tirare in barca. **(b)** *(transport: usu by ship)* spedire; **a new engine had to be ~ped out to them** hanno dovuto spedire loro un motore nuovo.

ship·builder [ˈʃɪpˌbɪldəʳ] *n* costruttore *m* navale.

ship·building [ˈʃɪpˌbɪldɪŋ] *n* costruzione *f* di navi.

ship·load [ˈʃɪpləʊd] *n* carico; *(fig fam)* marea.

ship·mate [ˈʃɪpmeɪt] *n* compagno di bordo.

ship·ment [ˈʃɪpmənt] *n (act)* spedizione *f; (quantity)* carico.

ship·owner [ˈʃɪpˌəʊnəʳ] *n* armatore *m.*

ship·per [ˈʃɪpəʳ] *n* spedizioniere *m* (marittimo).

ship·ping [ˈʃɪpɪŋ] **1** *n (ships)* imbarcazioni *fpl; (traffic)* navigazione *f;* **a danger to ~** un pericolo per la navigazione. **2** *cpd:* **~ agent** *n* agente *m* marit-

timo; **~ company** *n,* **~ line** *n* compagnia di navigazione; **~ lane** *n* rotta (di navigazione).

ship·shape [ˈʃɪpʃeɪp] *adj* in perfetto ordine.

ship·wreck [ˈʃɪprɛk] **1** *n (ship)* relitto; *(event)* naufragio. **2** *vt:* **to be ~ed** naufragare, fare naufragio.

ship·yard [ˈʃɪpjɑːd] *n* cantiere *m* navale.

shire [ˈʃaɪəʳ] *n (old)* contea.

shirk [ʃɜːk] **1** *vt (duty)* sottrarsi a, sfuggire a; *(issue)* ignorare; *(work)* scansare; **to ~ doing sth** evitare di fare qc. **2** *vi* fare lo scansafatiche.

shirk·er [ˈʃɜːkəʳ] *n* scansafatiche *m/f,* lavativo/a.

shirt [ʃɜːt] *n (man's)* camicia; *(woman's)* camicetta; **in one's ~ sleeves** in maniche di camicia; **to put one's ~ on sth** *(fig: Betting)* giocarsi anche la camicia su qc; **keep your ~ on!** *(fig fam)* non agitarti!

shirty [ˈʃɜːtɪ] *adj* (**-ier, -iest**) *(fam):* **he was pretty ~ about it** si è abbastanza incavolato per questa storia qui.

shiv·er [ˈʃɪvəʳ] **1** *n* brivido; **it sends ~s down my spine, it gives me the ~s** mi fa venire i brividi. **2** *vi:* **to ~ (with)** *(cold, fear)* rabbrividire (da).

shiv·ery [ˈʃɪvərɪ] *adj (from cold)* che ha i brividi; *(from emotion)* tremante; **I feel ~** ho i brividi.

shoal [ʃəʊl] *n* banco.

shock [ʃɒk] **1** *n* **(a)** *(Elec, of earthquake)* scossa; *(of explosion)* scossone *m; (of collision)* urto; **to get a ~** *(Elec)* prendere la scossa. **(b)** *(emotional)* shock *m inv,* colpo; **the ~ was too much for him** non ha sopportato il colpo *or* lo shock; **it came as a ~ to hear that...** è stata una grossa sorpresa sentire che...; **it may come as a ~ to you, but...** per quanto possa sorprenderti...; **to give sb a ~** far venire un colpo a qn. **(c)** *(Med)* shock *m,* collasso; **to be suffering from ~** essere in stato di shock.

2 *vt (startle)* far venire un colpo a; *(affect emotionally, scandalize)* scioccare; **he is easily ~ed** si scandalizza facilmente; **to ~ sb out of his complacency** far perdere a qn un po' della propria boria.

3 *vi* far scandalo, destare scalpore.

4 *cpd:* **~ absorber** *n (Aut)* ammortizzatore *m;* **~ reaction** *n (fam)* grande scalpore *m;* **~ tactics** *n (Mil etc)* tattica d'urto; **~ treatment** *n,* **~ therapy** *n (Med etc)* shockterapia; **~ wave** *n* onda d'urto.

shock·ing [ˈʃɒkɪŋ] *adj (appalling: news)* traumatizzante; *(: sight, crime)* agghiacciante; *(scandalizing: behaviour, film)* scandaloso(a); *(: price)* sbalorditivo(a); *(: waste)* vergognoso(a); *(very bad: weather, handwriting)* orribile; *(: results)* disastroso(a).

shod [ʃɒd] *pt, pp of* **shoe.**

shod·dy [ˈʃɒdɪ] *adj* (**-ier, -iest**) scadente.

shoe [ʃuː] *(vb: pt, pp* **shod**) **1** *n* scarpa; *(horse~)* ferro di cavallo; *(brake~)* ganascia (del freno); **I wouldn't like to be in his ~s** non vorrei trovarmi nei suoi panni. **3** *vt (horse)* ferrare. **3** *cpd:* **~ polish** *n* lucido da scarpe; **~ repairs** *npl* riparazioni *fpl* di scarpe.

shoe·brush [ˈʃuːbrʌʃ] *n* spazzola per le scarpe.

shoe·horn [ˈʃuːhɔːn] *n* calzante *m.*

shoe·lace [ˈʃuːleɪs] *n* laccio (delle scarpe), stringa.

shoe·maker [ˈʃuːˌmeɪkəʳ] *n* calzolaio *m.*

shoe·shop [ˈʃuːʃɒp] *n* calzoleria.

shoe·string [ˈʃuːstrɪŋ] *n* stringa (delle scarpe); **on a ~** *(fig: do sth)* con quattro soldi; *(: live)* contando il centesimo.

shoe·tree [ˈʃuːtriː] *n* forma per scarpe.

shone [ʃɒn] *pt, pp of* **shine.**

shoo [ʃuː] **1** *excl* sciò!, via! **2** *vt (also:* ~ **away,** ~ **off)** cacciare (via).

shook [ʃʊk] *pt of* **shake.**

shoot [ʃuːt] *(vb: pt, pp* **shot) 1** *n* **(a)** *(Bot)* germoglio.
(b) *(shooting party)* partita di caccia; *(competition)* gara di tiro; *(preserve)* riserva di caccia.
2 *vt* **(a)** *(hit)* colpire, sparare a; *(hunt)* cacciare, andare a caccia di; *(execute)* fucilare; *(kill)* uccidere; **he was shot in the arm** è stato colpito al braccio; **you'll get shot if you do that!** *(fig fam)* puoi rimetterci le penne! **(b)** *(fire: bullet, missile)* sparare; *(: arrow)* tirare; **to** ~ **one's way out** aprirsi un varco a colpi di pistola; **to** ~ **an arrow at sb** tirare una freccia contro qn; **to** ~ **dice** giocare a dadi. **(c)** *(direct: look, smile)* lanciare; **to** ~ **a question at sb** sparare una domanda a qn. **(d)** *(Cine: film, scene)* girare; *(: person, object)* riprendere. **(e)** *(pass quickly: rapids)* scendere.
3 *vi* **(a): to** ~ **(at sb/sth)** *(with gun)* sparare a qn/qc); *(with bow)* tirare (su *or* contro qn/qc); **to** ~ **on sight** sparare a vista; **to** ~ **back** rispondere al fuoco; **to** ~ **at goal** *(Ftbl etc)* tirare in porta, sparare in rete. **(b)** *(rush):* **to** ~ **in/out** entrare/uscire come una freccia; **to** ~ **past sb** passare vicino a qn come un fulmine; **the pain shot up his leg** sentì una fitta lancinante nella gamba; **the bullet shot past his head** il colpo gli ha sfiorato la testa.

♦ **shoot down** *vt + adv (aeroplane)* abbattere; *(person)* uccidere; *(fig: person)* distruggere; *(: argument)* demolire.

♦ **shoot out 1** *vt + adv:* **he shot out his arm and saved me** mi ha afferrato prontamente e mi ha salvato; **to** ~ **it out** decidere la questione a colpi di pistola. **2** *vi + adv (water)* sprizzare, uscire con violenza; *(flames)* divampare.

♦ **shoot up** *vi + adv* **(a)** *(flames, rocket)* alzarsi; *(water)* scaturire con forza; *(price)* salire alle stelle. **(b): he's** ~**ing up** sta crescendo a vista d'occhio; **he has shot up** è cresciuto molto.

shoot·ing [ˈʃuːtɪŋ] **1** *n* **(a)** *(shots)* spari *mpl*, colpi *mpl* d'arma da fuoco; *(continuous* ~*)* sparatoria. **(b)** *(act: murder)* uccisione *f* (a colpi d'arma da fuoco); *(: wounding)* ferimento. **(c)** *(Cine)* riprese *fpl*. **(d)** *(Hunting)* caccia. **2** *adj (pain)* lancinante. **3** *cpd:* ~ **brake** *n (old: Aut)* giardinetta; ~ **gallery** *n* tiro a segno; ~ **match** *n:* **the whole** ~ **match** *(fig fam)* l'intera faccenda, tutta questa storia; ~ **star** *n* stella cadente *or* filante; ~ **stick** *n* bastone da passeggio trasformabile in sgabello.

shop [ʃɒp] **1** *n* **(a)** *(Comm)* negozio; **to shut up** ~ chiudere; *(fig)* chiudere bottega; **to talk** ~ *(fig)* parlare di lavoro; **all over the** ~ *(fig fam)* dappertutto. **(b)** *(Industry: work*~*)* officina; **repair** ~ officina di riparazione. **2** *vi (gen)* fare acquisti, fare compere; *(for food)* fare la spesa; **to go** ~**ping** andare a fare acquisti; andare a fare la spesa; **I was** ~**ping for a dress** cercavo un vestito. **3** *vt (fam: betray)* tradire. **4** *cpd:* ~ **assistant** *n* commesso/a; ~ **floor** *n (Industry):* **he works on the** ~ **floor** è un operaio; **the** ~ **floor (workers)** gli operai; ~ **steward** *n (Industry)* rappresentante *m/f* sindacale; ~ **window** *n* vetrina.

♦ **shop around** *vi + adv* fare il giro dei negozi.

shop·keeper [ˈʃɒpˌkiːpəʳ] *n* negoziante *m/f*.

shop·lift [ˈʃɒplɪft] *vi* taccheggiare.

shop·lifter [ˈʃɒplɪftəʳ] *n* taccheggiatore/trice.

shop·lifting [ˈʃɒplɪftɪŋ] *n* taccheggio.

shop·per [ˈʃɒpəʳ] *n* **(a)** *(person)* persona che fa spese *or* compere. **(b)** *(bag)* borsa per la spesa.

shop·ping [ˈʃɒpɪŋ] **1** *n (goods)* acquisti *mpl*; *(: food)* spesa. **2** *cpd:* ~ **bag** *n* borsa per la spesa; ~

basket *n* cestino della spesa, sporta; ~ **centre** *n* centro commerciale.

shop·soiled [ˈʃɒpsɔɪld] *adj* deteriorato(a) (da lunga esposizione in vetrina).

shore[1] [ʃɔːʳ] **1** *n (of sea, lake)* riva, sponda; *(beach)* spiaggia; *(coast)* costa; **on** ~ **a terra; to go on** ~ sbarcare; **the ship hugged the** ~ la nave navigava sotto costa. **2** *cpd:* ~ **leave** *n (Naut)* franchigia.

shore[2] [ʃɔːʳ] *vt:* **to** ~ **up** *(tunnel)* puntellare; *(fig)* consolidare; *(: prices)* mantenere.

shorn [ʃɔːn] *pp of* **shear.**

short [ʃɔːt] **1** *adj (-er, -est)* **(a)** *(in length, distance)* corto(a); *(in time)* breve; *(person)* basso(a); **the days are getting** ~**er** le giornate si stanno accorciando; **to be** ~ **in the leg** *(person)* avere le gambe corte; *(trousers)* essere corti; **to win by a** ~ **head** *(Racing)* vincere di mezza incollatura; **a** ~ **time ago** poco tempo fa; **time is getting** ~ il tempo stringe; **that was** ~ **and sweet** è stato sbrigativo; **to make** ~ **work of sb** *(fig)* sistemare qn; **to make** ~ **work of sth** *(job)* sbrigare qc; *(cake etc)* far fuori qc.
(b) *(insufficient):* **I'm £3** ~ mi mancano 3 sterline; **to give** ~ **weight** *or* ~ **measure to sb** imbrogliare qn sul peso *or* sulla misura; **to be in** ~ **supply** scarseggiare; **to be** ~ **of sth** *(money)* essere a corto di qc; **I'm** ~ **of time** ho poco tempo; ~ **of breath** senza fiato, col fiato grosso; **it's little** ~ **of madness** è pazzia bella e buona; **3 miles** ~ **of home** a 3 miglia da casa.
(c) *(concise)* breve; ~ **and to the point** breve e conciso; **'Pat' is** ~ **for 'Patricia'** 'Pat' è il diminutivo di 'Patricia'; **in** ~ in breve, a farla breve.
(d) *(reply, manner)* secco(a), brusco(a); **to have a** ~ **temper** essere un tipo irascibile; **to be** ~ **with sb** essere brusco con qn.
2 *adv* **(a)** *(suddenly, abruptly):* **to stop** ~ fermarsi di colpo; **I'd stop** ~ **of stealing** non arriverei mai a rubare; **he wouldn't stop** ~ **of murder** arriverebbe al punto di uccidere; **to pull up** ~ frenare bruscamente.
(b) *(insufficiently):* **to run** ~ **of sth** rimanere senza qc; **we never went** ~ **(of anything) as children** da bambini non ci è mancato mai nulla; **to come** *or* **fall** ~ **of** *(expectations)* venire meno a; *(needs)* non soddisfare; **to sell sb** ~ *(fig)* sminuire qn, buttar giù qn; **to be taken** ~ *(fam)* dover andare urgentemente in bagno.
(c) *(except):* ~ **of selling the house, what can we do?** non vedo cos'altro potremo fare, a parte vendere la casa; **I'll do anything** ~ **of...** farò tutto tranne che...; **nothing** ~ **of a miracle can save him** niente può salvarlo tranne un miracolo.
3 *n* **(a)** *(Elec)* = **short circuit.**
(b) *(fam: drink)* alcolico.
4 *vt, vi (Elec)* = **short-circuit.**
5 *cpd:* ~ **circuit** *n (Elec)* cortocircuito; ~**(crust) pastry** *n* pasta frolla; ~ **cut** *n* scorciatoia; ~ **list** *n* graduatoria finale; ~ **story** *n* racconto, novella; ~ **term** *n:* **in the** ~ **term** nell'immediato futuro; ~ **time** *n:* **to work** ~ **time, be on** ~ **time** *(Industry)* essere *or* lavorare a orario ridotto; ~ **wave** *n (Radio)* onde *fpl* corte.

short·age [ˈʃɔːtɪdʒ] *n* carenza, scarsità; **the housing** ~ la crisi degli alloggi.

short·bread [ˈʃɔːtbred] *n* biscotto di pasta frolla.

short·cake [ˈʃɔːtkeɪk] *n (Am)* torta farcita di frutta e panna; *(Brit)* biscotto di pasta frolla.

short-change [ˌʃɔːrˈtʃeɪndʒ] *vt:* **to** ~ **sb** imbrogliare qn sul resto.

short-circuit [ˌʃɔːtˈsɜːkɪt] **1** *vt (Elec)* mettere in cortocircuito. **2** *vi (Elec)* fare cortocircuito.

short·coming [ˌʃɔːtˈkʌmɪŋ] n difetto.
short·en [ˈʃɔːtn] **1** vt (gen) accorciare. **2** vi accorciarsi.
short·hand [ˈʃɔːthænd] **1** n stenografia; **to take sth down in** ~ stenografare qc. **2** cpd: ~ **typist** n stenodattilografo/a.
short-list [ˈʃɔːt,lɪst] vt includere nella graduatoria finale.
short-lived [ˈʃɔːtˈlɪvd] adj (fig) di breve durata.
short·ly [ˈʃɔːtlɪ] adv **(a)** (soon) tra poco, tra breve; ~ **before/after** poco prima/dopo. **(b)** (curtly) seccamente, bruscamente.
shorts [ʃɔːts] npl shorts mpl, calzoncini mpl.
short-sighted [ˌʃɔːtˈsaɪtɪd] adj miope; (fig: policy etc) poco avveduto(a).
short-staffed [ˌʃɔːtˈstɑːft] adj a corto di personale.
short-tempered [ˌʃɔːtˈtempəd] adj (in general) irascibile; (in a bad mood) di cattivo umore.
short-term [ˈʃɔːttɜːm] adj a breve scadenza.
short-wave [ˈʃɔːtweɪv] adj (radio) a onde corte.
shot [ʃɒt] **1** n **(a)** (from gun, also sound) sparo, colpo (d'arma da fuoco); (shotgun pellets) pallottole fpl; **to fire a** ~ **at sb/sth** sparare un colpo a qn/qc; **a warning** ~ un colpo di avvertimento; **good** ~**!** bel colpo!; **he was off like a** ~ (fig) è partito come un razzo; **it was a** ~ **in the dark** (fig) è stata un'ipotesi azzardata. **(b)** (person) tiratore/trice; **he's a good/bad** ~ è un buon/pessimo tiratore; **a big** ~ (fam) un pezzo grosso, un papavero. **(c)** (Ftbl, Golf, Tennis etc) tiro; (throw) lancio; **to put the** ~ lanciare il peso; **a** ~ **at goal** un tiro in porta; **good shot!** bel tiro!; bel lancio! **(d)** (attempt) prova; (turn to play) turno; **to have a** ~ **at sth/doing sth** provarci con qc/a fare qc. **(e)** (injection) puntura, iniezione f; (of alcohol) bicchierino; **the economy needs a** ~ **in the arm** l'economia ha bisogno di una sferzata. **(f)** (Phot) foto f inv; (Cine) inquadratura.
  2 pt, pp of **shoot**; **to get** ~ **of sb/sth** (fam) sbarazzarsi di qn/qc.
shot·gun [ˈʃɒtgʌn] **1** n fucile m da caccia. **2** cpd: ~ **wedding** n (fam) matrimonio riparatore.
should [ʃʊd] aux vb **(a)** (cond tense): **I** ~ **go, I'd go** andrei, ci andrei; **I** ~ **have liked to** mi sarebbe piaciuto, avrei voluto; **I** ~ **think so!** mi pare!, direi!; **who** ~ **I see but Maria!** e chi dovevo vedere se non Maria!; ~ **he phone...** se telefonasse.... **(b)** (future in the past): **I told you I** ~ **be late** ti ho detto che avrei fatto tardi. **(c)** (duty, advisability, desirability): **all cars have seat belts** tutte le macchine dovrebbero essere fornite di cinture di sicurezza; **I** ~ **have been a doctor** avrei dovuto fare il medico; **you** ~**n't do that** non dovresti farlo; **I** ~**n't if I were you** se fossi in te non lo farei; **how** ~ **I know?** e che ne so io? **(d)** (probability): **he** ~ **pass his exams** dovrebbe superare gli esami; **they** ~ **have arrived by now** a quest'ora dovrebbero essere già arrivati; **this** ~ **be good** dovrebbe essere bello.
shoul·der [ˈʃəʊldəʳ] **1** n (gen) spalla; **to carry sth over one's** ~ portare qc a spalla; **to cry on sb's** ~ piangere sulla spalla di qn; **to look over one's** ~ guardarsi alle spalle; **to look over sb's** ~ guardare da dietro le spalle di qn; (fig) stare addosso a qn; ~ **to** ~ spalla a spalla; **to have broad** ~**s** avere le spalle larghe; (fig) avere buone spalle; **to put one's** ~ **to the wheel** (fig) mettersi all'opera; **to rub** ~**s with sb** (fig) essere a contatto con qn; **to give sb the cold** ~ (fig) trattare qn con freddezza; **he stands head and** ~**s above every-**

body else è di gran lunga superiore a tutti gli altri.
  2 vt (fig: responsibilities etc) accollarsi, addossarsi; **to** ~ **sb aside** spingere qn da parte a spallate; **to** ~ **one's way through the crowd** farsi largo a spallate tra la folla.
  3 cpd: ~ **bag** n borsa a tracolla; ~ **blade** n scapola; ~ **strap** n spallina, bretella.
shoulder-length [ˈʃəʊldə,leŋθ] adj (lungo(a)) fino alle spalle.
shouldn't [ˈʃʊdnt] = **should not**.
shout [ʃaʊt] **1** n (gen) urlo, grido; **a** ~ **of laughter** una risata fragorosa; **to give sb a** ~ dare una voce a qn. **2** vt (order, name) gridare, urlare. **3** vi gridare, urlare; **to** ~ **to sb to do sth** gridare a qn di fare qc; **to** ~ **with pain** urlare per il or di dolore; **to** ~ **for help** gridare aiuto; **to** ~ **with laughter** scoppiare a ridere.
♦ **shout at** vi + prep gridare a, urlare a; (angrily): **to** ~ **at sb** sgridare qn.
♦ **shout down** vt + adv zittire.
♦ **shout out 1** vi + adv emettere un grido. **2** vt + adv gridare.
shout·ing [ˈʃaʊtɪŋ] n grida fpl; **it's all over bar the** ~ (fig) è fatta.
shove [ʃʌv] **1** n spintone m; **to give sb a** ~ dare uno spintone a qn; **to give sth a** ~ dare una spinta a qc. **2** vt (gen) spingere; (thrust) cacciare, ficcare; **he** ~**d me out of the way** mi ha spinto da parte; **to** ~ **in/out** etc spingere dentro/fuori etc; **he** ~**d his fist/stick into my face** mi ha minacciato con il pugno/bastone. **3** vi spingere; **he** ~**d (his way) through the crowd** si è fatto largo tra la folla a spintoni; **to** ~ **past sb** passare davanti a qn con uno spintone.
♦ **shove off** vi + adv (fam) sloggiare, smammare.
♦ **shove over, shove up** vi + adv (fam) farsi più in là.
shov·el [ˈʃʌvl] **1** n pala. **2** vt (coal) prendere con la pala; (snow) spalare; (sth spilt) raccogliere con una paletta; **he was** ~**ling food into his mouth** mangiava a quattro ganasce.
show [ʃəʊ] (vb: pt **showed**, pp **shown**) **1** n **(a)** (of feeling, emotion) manifestazione f; (of strength, goodwill) dimostrazione f, prova; (ostentation) mostra; **to ask for a** ~ **of hands** chiedere che si voti per alzata di mano.
  (b) (exhibition: Art) mostra, esposizione f; (: Comm, Tech) salone m, fiera; (: Agr) fiera; **to be on** ~ essere esposto; **the garden is a splendid** ~ il giardino è uno spettacolo.
  (c) (Theatre etc) spettacolo; (variety ~) varietà m; **to go to a** ~ andare a vedere uno spettacolo; **on with the** ~**!** (fig) andiamo avanti!; **good** ~**!** (fam) complimenti!, bravo!; **the last** ~ (Theatre) l'ultima rappresentazione; (Cine) l'ultimo spettacolo; **she stole the** ~ aveva tutti gli occhi puntati su di sé; **to put up a good** ~ (fam) difendersi bene; **to put up a poor** ~ essere una delusione; **it's a poor** ~ **when...** (fam) siamo proprio ridotti male se....
  (d) (outward appearance) mostra, figura; **it's just for** ~ è solo per far scena; **to make a** ~ **of doing sth** far finta di fare qc; **to make a** ~ **of anger** far finta di essere arrabbiato; **to make a** ~ **of resistance** accennare una qualche resistenza.
  (e) (organization) baracca; **who's running the** ~ **here?** chi è il padrone qui?; **this is my** ~ qui comando io.
  2 vt **(a)** (gen) mostrare; (film, slides) proiettare; (goods for sale, pictures) esporre; (animals) presentare; **he** ~**ed me his new car** mi ha mostrato la sua macchina nuova; **to** ~ **a film at**

Cannes presentare un film a Cannes; **what's ~ing at the Odeon?** cosa danno all'Odeon?; **white shoes soon ~ the dirt** le scarpe bianche si sporcano in fretta; **don't ~ your face here again!** non farti vedere più qui!; **to ~ one's hand** or **one's cards** scoprire le carte; (fig) mettere le carte in tavola; **I have nothing to ~ for it** non ho niente in cambio; **I'll ~ him!** (fam) gli faccio vedere io!

(b) (indicate) indicare, segnare; **as ~n in the illustration** come da illustrazione; **the motorways are ~n in black** le autostrade sono segnate in nero; **to ~ a profit/loss** (Comm) registrare un utile/una perdita.

(c) (reveal: interest, surprise etc) dimostrare, mostrare; **her action ~ed intelligence** la sua azione ha rivelato molta intelligenza or ha dato prova di intelligenza; **her face ~ed her happiness/fear** le si leggeva la felicità/paura in viso; **the choice of dishes ~s excellent taste** la scelta dei piatti rivela un ottimo gusto; **this ~s him to be a coward** questo dimostra la sua vigliaccheria; **it just goes to ~ that...** il che sta a dimostrare che... .

(d) (direct, conduct: person) condurre, accompagnare; **to ~ sb the way** indicare la strada a qn; **to ~ sb into a room** far entrare qn in una stanza; **to ~ sb to his seat/to the door** accompagnare qn al suo posto/alla porta; **to ~ sb the door** (fig) mettere qn alla porta; **to ~ sb round** or **over a house** far visitare or vedere la casa a qn; **to ~ sb in/out/up** far entrare/uscire/salire qn.

3 vi (stain, emotion, underskirt etc) vedersi; **it doesn't ~** non si vede; **don't worry, it won't ~** sta' tranquillo che non si vedrà.

4 cpd: **~ business** n, **~ biz** n (fam) industria dello spettacolo, mondo dello spettacolo; **~ stopper** n (fam) cosa eccezionale.

♦ **show off 1** vi + adv darsi delle arie. **2** vt + adv (ability, one's figure) mostrare; (knowledge) ostentare; (subj: colour, dress) mettere in risalto, valorizzare.

♦ **show up 1** vi + adv **(a)** (be visible: gen) risaltare; (: mistake) saltare all'occhio. **(b)** (fam: arrive) farsi vivo(a), farsi vedere. **2** vt + adv **(a)** (reveal: thief, fraud) smascherare; (: deception) mettere a nudo; **he was ~n up as an impostor** è stato rivelato che era un impostore; **the bright lighting ~ed up her scars** la forte luce metteva in evidenza le sue cicatrici. **(b)** (embarrass) far fare una figuraccia a.

show·case ['ʃəʊkeɪs] n vetrina.

show·down ['ʃəʊdaʊn] n prova di forza.

show·er ['ʃaʊə^r] **1** n **(a)** (of rain) acquazzone m; **a ~ of hail** una grandinata; **a snow ~** una nevicata. **(b)** (fig: of arrows, stones) pioggia; (: of blows) gragnuola, scarica; (: of bullets) scarica. **(c)** (Am: party) festa (di fidanzamento etc) in cui si fanno regali alla persona festeggiata. **(d)** (~ bath) doccia; **to have** or **take a ~** fare la doccia. **2** vt (fig): **to ~ sb with** (gifts, abuse) coprire qn di; (blows) riempire qn di; **he was ~ed with invitations** è stato inondato di inviti. **3** vi (take a ~) fare la doccia. **4** cpd: **~ cap** n cuffia da doccia.

shower·proof ['ʃaʊəpruːf] adj impermeabile.

show·ery ['ʃaʊərɪ] adj con piogge intermittenti.

show·girl ['ʃəʊgɜːl] n girl f inv.

show·ground ['ʃəʊgraʊnd] n area di esposizione.

show·ing ['ʃəʊɪŋ] n (of film) proiezione f; (cinema session) spettacolo.

show·jumping ['ʃəʊ,dʒʌmpɪŋ] n concorso ippico (su percorso a ostacoli).

show·man ['ʃəʊmən] n, pl **-men** (at fair, circus) impresario; (fig) attore m.

shown [ʃəʊn] pp of **show**.

show-off ['ʃəʊɒf] n (fam) esibizionista m/f.

show·piece ['ʃəʊpiːs] n (of exhibition) pezzo forte; **that hospital is a ~** quell'ospedale è un ospedale modello.

show·place ['ʃəʊpleɪs] n (tourist attraction) centro d'attrazione turistica.

show·room ['ʃəʊrʊm] n (Comm) show-room m inv; (Art) sala d'esposizione.

showy ['ʃəʊɪ] adj (-ier, -iest) vistoso(a), appariscente.

shrank [ʃræŋk] pt of **shrink**.

shrap·nel ['ʃræpnl] n shrapnel m.

shred [ʃred] **1** n (of cloth) brandello; (of paper) strisciolina; (fig: of truth, evidence) briciolo; **you haven't got a ~ of evidence** non ne hai la benché minima prova; **in ~s** a brandelli; **to tear to ~s** fare a brandelli; (fig: argument) demolire. **2** vt (paper) stracciare, strappare; (mechanically) trinciare; (food: with grater) grattugiare; (: with knife) tagliare a fette sottili.

shred·der ['ʃredə^r] n (for documents, papers) distruttore m di documenti.

shrew [ʃruː] n (Zool) toporagno; (fig pej: woman) strega.

shrewd [ʃruːd] adj (-er, -est) (person, assessment) acuto(a), accorto(a); (lawyer, businessman) accorto(a), avveduto(a); (plan, look) astuto(a); (guess) perspicace; **I have a ~ idea that...** mi sa tanto che... .

shrewd·ly ['ʃruːdlɪ] adv (act) con accortezza; (reason) con perspicacia; **to look at sb ~** lanciare uno sguardo astuto a qn.

shrewd·ness ['ʃruːdnɪs] n (see adj) acume m; accortezza; astuzia; perspicacia.

shriek [ʃriːk] **1** n strillo, grido acuto; **a ~ of pain** un grido di dolore; **~s of laughter** risate fpl fragorose. **2** vi strillare; **to ~ at sb** strillare a qn; **to ~ with laughter** sbellicarsi dalle risa.

shrift [ʃrɪft] n (fig): **to give sb short ~** mandare qn a spasso; **to get short ~ from sb** essere trattato in modo sbrigativo da qn.

shrill [ʃrɪl] adj (-er, -est) (bell, sound) acuto(a), penetrante; (laugh, voice) stridulo(a).

shrimp [ʃrɪmp] n (Zool) gamberetto; (fig pej) scricciolo.

shrine [ʃraɪn] n (tomb) sepolcro; (place) santuario; (reliquary) reliquiario.

shrink [ʃrɪŋk] pt **shrank**, pp **shrunk 1** vt far restringere. **2** vi **(a)** (clothes) restringersi, ritirarsi; (metal) contrarsi; (gums) ritirarsi; (piece of meat) ridursi; (area, person) rimpicciolirsi; **to ~ in the wash** restringersi con il lavaggio. **(b)** (also: ~ away, ~ back) ritrarsi, tirarsi indietro; **to ~ from doing sth** rifuggire dal fare qc; **he didn't ~ from telling her the truth** non ha esitato a dirle la verità.

shrink·age ['ʃrɪŋkɪdʒ] n (of clothes) restringimento; (Comm: in shops) diminuzione f.

shriv·el ['ʃrɪvl] (also: ~ up) **1** vt (plant etc) far rinsecchire; (skin) far raggrinzire. **2** vi (see vi) rinsecchirsi; raggrinzirsi.

shroud [ʃraʊd] **1** n (round corpse) sudario. **2** vt (fig): **~ed in** avvolto in, avviluppato in.

Shrove Tues·day [,ʃrəʊv'tjuːzdɪ] n martedì m inv grasso.

shrub [ʃrʌb] n cespuglio.

shrub·bery ['ʃrʌbərɪ] n gruppo di cespugli.

shrug [ʃrʌg] **1** n alzata di spalle; **a ~ of indifference** un gesto d'indifferenza. **2** vt: **to ~ (one's shoulders)** alzare le spalle, fare spallucce.

♦ **shrug off** vt + adv (danger) prendere sottogamba; (insult) ignorare; (troubles) minimizzare;

(cold, illness) sbarazzarsi di.
shrunk [ʃrʌŋk] *pp of* **shrink**.
shrunk·en [ˈʃrʌŋkən] *adj (body)* rinsecchito(a).
shud·der [ˈʃʌdəʳ] **1** *vi (person)*: **to ~ (with)** rab-brividire (per, da); *(machinery)* vibrare; **the car ~ed to a halt** dopo vari sussulti la macchina si fermò; **I ~ to think!** rabbrividisco al solo pensiero! **2** *n (of person)* brivido; *(of machinery)* vibrazione *f;* **to give a ~** *(person)* rabbrividire; *(car)* avere un sussulto, sussultare.
shuf·fle [ˈʃʌfl] **1** *n* **(a)** passo strascicato. **(b)** *(Cards)* mescolata; **to give the cards a ~** dare una mescolata alle carte. **2** *vt* **(a)** *(feet)* strascicare. **(b)** *(mix up: cards)* mescolare, mischiare; *(: papers)* sfogliare. **3** *vi (walk)* strascicare i piedi; **to ~ in/out** *etc* entrare/uscire *etc* con passo strascicato.
shun [ʃʌn] *vt (person, work, publicity)* evitare, sfuggire; *(obligation)* sottrarsi a.
shunt [ʃʌnt] *vt (Rail: direct)* smistare; *(: divert)* deviare; *(fig: from one place to another)* spostare.
shunt·ing yard [ˈʃʌntɪŋ,jɑːd] *n* fascio di smistamento.
shush [ʃʊʃ] **1** *excl* zitto(a)! **2** *vt (fam)* zittire.
shut [ʃʌt] *pt, pp* **shut 1** *vt (gen)* chiudere; **to ~ the door in sb's face** sbattere la porta in faccia a qn; **to ~ one's finger in the door** chiudersi un dito nella porta; **to ~ sb in a room** rinchiudere qn in una stanza; **~ your mouth!** *(fam)* chiudi il becco! **2** *vi (door, window)* chiudersi; *(shop, bank etc)* chiudersi, chiudere.
♦ **shut away** *vt + adv (person, animal)* rinchiudere, chiudere; *(valuables)* mettere al sicuro.
♦ **shut down 1** *vi + adv (factory, shop)* chiudere (definitivamente), chiudere i battenti. **2** *vt + adv (factory, shop)* chiudere; *(machine)* fermare.
♦ **shut in** *vt + adv* rinchiudere.
♦ **shut off** *vt + adv* **(a)** *(stop: power)* staccare; *(: water)* chiudere; *(: engine)* spegnere. **(b)** *(isolate)*: **to ~ off (from)** tagliar fuori (da), isolare (da).
♦ **shut out** *vt + adv (person, noise, cold)* non far entrare; *(block: view)* impedire, bloccare; *(: memory)* scacciare; **to be ~ out of the house** rimanere chiuso fuori casa.
♦ **shut up 1** *vi + adv (fam: be quiet)* star zitto(a); **~ up!** zitto! **2** *vt + adv* **(a)** *(factory, business, house)* chiudere. **(b)** *(person, animal)* rinchiudere, chiudere; *(valuables)* mettere al sicuro. **(c)** *(fam: silence)* far stare zitto(a).
shut·down [ˈʃʌtdaʊn] *n* chiusura.
shut-in [ˌʃʌtˈɪn] *adj (feeling)* di soffocamento.
shut·ter [ˈʃʌtəʳ] *n (on window)* imposta; *(for shop)* battente *m; (Phot)* otturatore *m.*
shut·tered [ˈʃʌtəd] *adj* con le imposte.
shut·tle [ˈʃʌtl] **1** *n (of loom)* spola, navetta; *(of sewing machine)* spoletta; *(fig: plane etc)* navetta. **2** *vi (subj: vehicle, person)* fare la spola. **3** *vt (to and fro: passengers)* portare (avanti e indietro); **I was/the papers were ~d from one department to another** sono stato sballottato/la pratica è stata mandata da un ufficio all'altro. **4** *cpd*: **~ service** *n* servizio di navetta.
shuttle·cock [ˈʃʌtlkɒk] *n (Badminton)* volano.
shy [ʃaɪ] **1** *adj* **(-er, -est)** timido(a); *(unsociable)* scontroso(a); **to be ~ of doing sth** essere restio a fare qc; **don't be ~ of asking for...** non esitare a chiedere...; **to fight ~ of sth** tenersi alla larga da qc; **to fight ~ of doing sth** cercare in tutti i modi di evitare qc. **2** *vi (horse)*: **to ~ (at)** fare uno scarto (davanti a); **the horse shied at the noise** il cavallo ha fatto uno scarto quando ha sentito il rumore; **to ~ away from sth** tenersi alla larga da

qc; **to ~ away from doing sth** *(fig)* rifuggire dal fare qc.
shy·ly [ˈʃaɪlɪ] *adv* timidamente.
shy·ness [ˈʃaɪnɪs] *n* timidezza.
shy·ster [ˈʃaɪstəʳ] *n (Am fam)* lestofante *m; (: lawyer)* azzeccagarbugli *m inv.*
Sia·mese [ˌsaɪəˈmiːz] *adj* siamese; **~ cat** gatto siamese; **~ twins** fratelli *mpl (or* sorelle *fpl)* siamesi.
sibi·lant [ˈsɪbɪlənt] **1** *adj* sibilante. **2** *n* sibilante *f.*
sib·ling [ˈsɪblɪŋ] *n (frm)* fratello/sorella.
Si·cil·ian [sɪˈsɪlɪən] *adj, n* siciliano(a) *(m/f).*
Sici·ly [ˈsɪsɪlɪ] *n* Sicilia.
sick [sɪk] **1** *adj* **(-er, -est) (a)** *(ill)* malato(a), ammalato(a); **a ~ person** un malato; **to fall** *or* **take ~** ammalarsi; **to be (off) ~** essere assente perché malato; **to go** *or* **report ~** marcare visita; **to be ~** *(vomiting)* vomitare, rimettere, dare di stomaco; **to feel ~** avere la nausea. **(b)** *(fig: mind, imagination)* malato(a); *(: humour)* macabro(a); *(: joke)* di gusto macabro; **to be ~ (and tired) of sth/sb, to be ~ to death of sth/sb** averne fin sopra i capelli di qc/qn; **~ at heart** desolato; **to be ~ of the sight of sb/sth** non poterne più di qn/qc; **you make me ~!** mi fai schifo! **2** *npl*: **the ~** i malati, gli ammalati. **3** *cpd*: **~ benefit** *n =* **sickness benefit**; **~ leave** *n*: **on ~ leave** in congedo per motivi di salute *or* per malattia; **~ list** *n*: **on the ~ list** sulla lista dei malati; **~ pay** *n* quotaparte *f* dello stipendio *(versata in caso di malattia).*
♦ **sick up** *vt + adv (fam)* vomitare, rimettere.
sick·bay [ˈsɪkbeɪ] *n* infermeria.
sick·bed [ˈsɪkbɛd] *n* letto di ammalato.
sick·en [ˈsɪkn] **1** *vt* nauseare, stomacare; *(fig)* far star male. **2** *vi* sentirsi male, ammalarsi; **to ~ of** sth stufarsi di qc; **to be ~ing for sth** *(cold, flu etc)* covare qc.
sick·en·ing [ˈsɪknɪŋ] *adj (smell, sight)* nauseante; *(fig: crime, waste, behaviour)* disgustoso(a); *(: crash)* pauroso(a); *(fam: annoying)* esasperante.
sick·le [ˈsɪkl] *n* falce *f.*
sick·ly [ˈsɪklɪ] *adj* **(-ier, -iest)** *(person)* malaticcio(a); *(plant, animal)* malato(a); *(smile)* stentato(a); *(complexion)* giallastro(a); *(climate)* malsano(a); *(taste, smell)* stomachevole; *(cake)* stucchevole.
sick·ness [ˈsɪknɪs] **1** *n* malattia; **there's a lot of ~ about** c'è molta gente malata; **wave of ~** ondata di malessere; **bouts of ~** vomito. **2** *cpd*: **~ benefit** *n* indennità di malattia.
sick·room [ˈsɪkrʊm] *n* stanza di malato.
side [saɪd] **1** *n* **(a)** *(of person, body)* fianco; **~ of beef** quarto di bue; **at** *or* **by sb's ~** al fianco di qn, accanto a qn; **~ by ~** *(people)* fianco a fianco; *(objects)* uno accanto all'altro.
(b) *(edge: of box, square etc)* lato; *(: of building)* fianco, lato; *(: of boat, vehicle)* fiancata; *(: of hill)* fianco; *(: of lake)* riva; *(: of road)* bordo, ciglio.
(c) *(face, surface: gen)* faccia; *(: of paper)* facciata; *(: of slice of bread)* lato; *(fig: aspect)* aspetto, lato; **the right/wrong ~** il dritto/rovescio; **the other ~ of the coin** *(fig)* il rovescio della medaglia; **to hear both ~s of the question** ascoltare ambedue le parti in causa.
(d) *(part)* parte *f,* lato; **from all ~s, from every ~** da tutte le parti, da ogni parte; **from ~ to ~** da una parte all'altra; **to move to one ~** scostarsi, farsi *or* tirarsi da (una) parte; **to take sb on one ~** prendere qn da parte *or* in disparte; **to put sth to** *or* **on one ~ (for sb)** mettere qc da parte (per qn); **on the mother's ~** per parte di

madre; **to be on the wrong/right** ~ **of 30** aver/non aver superato la trentina; **he's on the wrong** ~ **of 40 to begin a new career** ha superato la quarantina ed è troppo vecchio per cominciare una nuova carriera; **to get on the wrong/right** ~ **of sb** prendere qn dalla parte sbagliata/giusta; **on this** ~ **of town** da questa parte della città; **it's a bit on the large** ~ è un po' abbondante; **to make a bit (of money) on the** ~ *(fam)* farsi un po' di soldi in più.

(e) *(team: Sport)* squadra; *(: Pol etc)* parte *f;* **the other** ~ la parte opposta; **God is on our** ~ Dio è con noi; **to be on sb's** ~ essere dalla parte di or con qn; **to be on the** ~ **of moderation** essere per la moderazione; **to have age/justice** *etc* **on one's** ~ avere l'età/la giustizia *etc* dalla propria; **to pick** *or* **choose** ~**s** formare le squadre; **to take** ~**s** prendere partito; **to take** ~**s with sb** schierarsi con qn; **to take the** ~ **down** *(Sport, fig)* piantare tutto.

2 *vi:* **to** ~ **with sb** prendere le parti di qn, parteggiare per qn.

3 *cpd (door, entrance)* laterale; *(road)* secondario(a); ~ **dish** *n* contorno; ~ **effect** *n* effetto collaterale; ~ **plate** *n* piattino; ~ **street** *n* traversa; ~ **view** *n* inquadratura di profilo.

side·board ['saɪdbɔːd] *n* credenza.

side·boards ['saɪdbɔːdz] *npl, (Am)* **side·burns** ['saɪdbɜːnz] *npl* basette *fpl.*

side·car ['saɪdkɑːʳ] *n* sidecar *m inv.*

-sided ['saɪdɪd] *adj ending in cpds:* **a 6-~ figure** una figura a 6 lati; **a many-~ problem** un problema complesso.

side·kick ['saɪdkɪk] *n (fam: esp Am: assistant)* accolito; *(: friend)* compagno/a.

side·light ['saɪdlaɪt] *n (Aut)* luce *f* di posizione.

side·line ['saɪdlaɪn] *n* **(a)** *(Ftbl etc)* linea laterale. **(b)** *(Comm)* attività collaterale.

side·long ['saɪdlɒŋ] *adj:* **to give a** ~ **glance at sth** guardare qc con la coda dell'occhio.

side·saddle ['saɪd,sædl] *adv* all'amazzone.

side·show ['saɪdʃəʊ] *n* attrazione *f* (secondaria).

side·splitting ['saɪd,splɪtɪŋ] *adj (fam)* da crepar dal ridere.

side·step ['saɪdstep] **1** *vt (question)* eludere; *(problem)* scavalcare. **2** *vi (Boxing etc)* spostarsi di lato.

side·track ['saɪdtræk] *vt (person)* sviare, mettere fuori strada; **I got** ~**ed** mi hanno distratto.

side·walk ['saɪdwɔːk] *n (Am: pavement)* marciapiede *m.*

side·ways ['saɪdweɪz] **1** *adj* laterale; **to give a** ~ **glance at sth** guardare qc con la coda dell'occhio. **2** *adv (move)* di lato, di fianco; *(look)* con la coda dell'occhio.

sid·ing ['saɪdɪŋ] *n (Rail)* binario di raccordo.

si·dle ['saɪdl] *vi:* **to** ~ **up to sb** avvicinarsi (furtivamente) a qn; **to** ~ **out/past** *etc* uscire/passare *etc* furtivamente.

siege [siːdʒ] *n* assedio; **in a state of** ~ in stato d'assedio; **to lay** ~ **to** porre l'assedio a.

si·en·na [sɪ'enə] *n* terra di Siena.

si·es·ta [sɪ'estə] *n* siesta; **to have a** ~ fare la siesta.

sieve [sɪv] **1** *n (for flour)* setaccio; *(for liquid)* colino; *(for coal etc)* crivello; **to have a memory like a** ~ *(fam)* avere una memoria che fa acqua. **2** *vt (soil, flour etc)* setacciare, passare al setaccio; *(coal etc)* passare al crivello; *(liquid)* colare.

sift [sɪft] **1** *vt (flour, sand etc)* setacciare; *(coal etc)* passare al crivello; *(fig: evidence)* passare al setaccio; **to** ~ **out** *(truth etc)* separare. **2** *vi (fig):* **to** ~ **through** esaminare minuziosamente; *(statement, evidence)* vagliare accuratamente.

sigh [saɪ] **1** *n (of person)* sospiro; *(of wind)* sussurro;

to heave a ~ tirare un sospiro. **2** *vi:* **to** ~ **(with)** sospirare (di); **to** ~ **over** *(sth lost)* piangere su; **to** ~ **after a fur coat** sospirare una pelliccia.

sigh·ing ['saɪɪŋ] *n* sospiri *mpl; (of wind)* sussurrio.

sight [saɪt] **1** *n* **(a)** *(faculty, act of seeing)* vista; **to have good/poor (eye)**~ avere la vista buona/cattiva; **at first** ~ a prima vista; **to shoot on** ~ sparare a vista; **I know her by** ~ la conosco di vista; **to be within** ~ **of** *(sea)* essere in vista di; *(victory)* essere vicino a; **the bus was still in** ~ l'autobus si vedeva ancora; **the end is in** ~ si può intravvedere la fine; **a solution is in** ~ una soluzione è in vista; **to come into** ~ *(thing)* profilarsi all'orizzonte; **Carla came into** ~ abbiamo scorto Carla; **to catch** ~ **of sth/sb** scorgere qc/qn; **keep out of my** ~! stai lontano da me!; **don't let it out of your** ~ non perderlo di vista; **when it's out of** ~ quando non si vede più; **out of** ~ **out of mind** *(Proverb)* lontano dagli occhi lontano dal cuore; **to lose** ~ **of sb/sth** perdere di vista qn/qc; **to hate the** ~ **of sb/sth** non sopportare la vista di qn/qc.

(b) *(spectacle)* spettacolo; **to see** *or* **visit the** ~**s of Rome** vedere *or* visitare le attrazioni turistiche di Roma; **it's not a pretty** ~ non è uno spettacolo edificante; **you're a** ~ **for sore eyes!** al solo vederti mi si allarga il cuore!; **you look a** ~! *(fam)* come sei conciato!; **it's a** ~ **to be seen** è uno spettacolo da non perdere.

(c) *(on gun: often pl)* mirino; **in one's** ~**s** sotto mira; **to set one's** ~**s on sth/on doing sth** mirare a qc/a fare qc; **to set one's** ~**s too high** *(fig)* mirare troppo in alto.

(d) *(fam: a great deal)* molto; **a** ~ **more** molto di più; **it isn't finished by a long** ~ è ben lungi dall'essere finito; **a** ~ **too clever** fin troppo furbo.

2 *vt (rare animal, land)* avvistare; *(person)* scorgere.

sight·ed ['saɪtɪd] *adj* che ha il dono della vista; **partially** ~ parzialmente cieco; ~ **people** i vedenti.

sight·ing ['saɪtɪŋ] *n:* **several** ~**s have been reported** si dice che è stato visto più volte.

sight·read ['saɪtriːd] *vt, vi (Mus)* suonare *(or* cantare) a prima vista.

sight·see·ing ['saɪt,siːɪŋ] *n* turismo; **to go** ~, **do some** ~ *(gen)* fare un giro turistico; *(in town)* visitare la città.

sight·seer ['saɪt,siːəʳ] *n* turista *m/f.*

sign [saɪn] **1** *n* **(a)** *(with hand etc)* segno, gesto; **to communicate by** ~**s** comunicare a gesti; **to make a** ~ **to sb (to do sth)** far segno a qn (di fare qc); **to make the** ~ **of the Cross** far(si) il segno della croce, segnarsi.

(b) *(indication)* segno, indizio; **as a** ~ **of** in segno di; **it's a** ~ **of the times** è sintomo dei tempi che corrono; **it's a good/bad** ~ è buon/brutto segno; **all the** ~**s are that...** tutto fa prevedere che...; **at the first** *or* **slightest** ~ **of** al primo *or* al minimo segno di; **to show** ~**s/no** ~ **of doing sth** accennare/non accennare a fare qc; **there was no** ~ **of him anywhere** non c'era traccia di lui da nessuna parte; **there was no** ~ **of life in the village** il paesetto non dava segno di vita.

(c) *(road* ~) segnale *m; (shop* ~) insegna *f; (notice)* cartello, avviso.

(d) *(written symbol)* segno; **plus/minus** ~ segno del più/meno.

2 *vt (letter, contract)* firmare; **to** ~ **one's name** firmare, apporre la propria firma; **she** ~**s herself B. Smith** si firma B. Smith.

(b) *(Ftbl: player)* ingaggiare.

3 *vi* **(a)** *(with signature)* firmare; *(Ftbl)* firmare un contratto.
(b) *(signal)*: **to ~ to sb to do sth** far segno a qn di fare qc.
4 *cpd*: **~ language** *n* linguaggio dei muti.
♦ **sign away** *vt + adv (rights etc)* cedere *(con una firma)*.
♦ **sign in** *vi + adv (in hotel)* firmare il registro; *(in factory)* timbrare il cartellino.
♦ **sign off** *vi + adv (Radio, TV)* chiudere le trasmissioni.
♦ **sign on 1** *vi + adv (Mil etc: enlist)* arruolarsi; *(as unemployed)* iscriversi sulla lista (dell'ufficio di collocamento); *(as worker)* prendere servizio; *(enrol)*: **to ~ on for a course** iscriversi a un corso. **2** *vt + adv (employees)* assumere; *(Mil: enlisted man)* arruolare.
♦ **sign out** *vi + adv* firmare il registro (delle uscite).
♦ **sign over** *vt + adv (rights etc)*: **to ~ over (to)** cedere con scrittura legale (a).
♦ **sign up 1** *vi + adv (Mil: enlist)* arruolarsi; *(enrol: for course)* iscriversi. **2** *vt + adv (employee)* assumere; *(Mil)* arruolare.
sig·nal ['sɪgnl] **1** *n*: **~ (for)** segnale *m* (di); **at a prearranged ~** a un segnale convenuto; **distress ~** segnale di soccorso; **traffic ~s** semafori *mpl*; **railway ~s** segnali *mpl* ferroviari; **the engaged ~** *(Telec)* il segnale di occupato; **the ~ is very weak** *(TV)* l'audio *(or* l'immagine*)* è molto debole.
2 *vt* **(a)** *(message)* comunicare per mezzo di segnali; **to ~ a left/right turn** *(Aut)* segnalare un cambiamento di direzione a sinistra/destra; **to ~ sb on/through** far segno a qn di avanzare/passare. **(b)** *(signify)* segnare. **3** *vi (gen)* segnalare; *(for help)* fare segnalazioni; **to ~ to sb (to do sth)** far segno a qn (di fare qc). **4** *cpd*: **~ box** *n (Rail)* cabina di manovra.
signal·man ['sɪgnlmən] *n, pl* **-men** *(Rail)* deviatore *m*.
sig·na·tory ['sɪgnətərɪ] *n* firmatario/a.
sig·na·ture ['sɪgnətʃəʳ] **1** *n* **(a)** *(of person)* firma; **to put one's ~ to sth** firmare qc, mettere la propria firma a qc. **(b)** *(Mus)*: **key ~** segnatura in chiave; **time ~** indicazione *f* del tempo. **2** *cpd*: **~ tune** *n* sigla (musicale).
sig·nifi·cance [sɪg'nɪfɪkəns] *n (of remark)* significato; *(of event, speech)* importanza; **that is of no ~** ciò non ha importanza.
sig·nifi·cant [sɪg'nɪfɪkənt] *adj (discovery, change)* importante; *(increase, improvement, amount)* notevole; *(evidence, look, smile)* significativo(a); **it is ~ that...** è significativo che... .
sig·nifi·cant·ly [sɪg'nɪfɪkəntlɪ] *adv (smile)* in modo significativo; *(improve, increase)* considerevolmente, decisamente; **and, ~, ...** e, fatto significativo, ...
sig·ni·fy ['sɪgnɪfaɪ] **1** *vt (mean)* significare; *(indicate)* segnare; *(make known)* manifestare, esprimere. **2** *vi* avere importanza.
sign·post ['saɪnpəʊst] **1** *n* indicazione *f* stradale, cartello stradale. **2** *vt (roads, town)* indicare.
si·lage ['saɪlɪdʒ] *n* insilato.
si·lence ['saɪləns] **1** *n* silenzio; **~!** silenzio!; **in (dead *or* complete) ~** in (totale) silenzio; **there was ~ on *or* about the subject** non si è parlato dell'argomento; **to pass over sth in ~** passare qc sotto silenzio. **2** *vt (person, critics)* ridurre al silenzio, far tacere; *(conscience)* mettere a tacere.
si·lenc·er ['saɪlənsəʳ] *n (Aut)* marmitta; *(on motorbike, gun)* silenziatore *m*.
si·lent ['saɪlənt] *adj (person)* silenzioso(a); *(film,*

prayer etc) muto(a); **silent 'h'** 'h' muta; **to fall ~** zittirsi, tacere; **to keep *or* remain ~** tacere, stare zitto.
si·lent·ly ['saɪləntlɪ] *adv* silenziosamente, in silenzio.
sil·hou·ette [ˌsɪluː'et] **1** *n (gen)* sagoma; *(drawing)* silhouette *f inv.* **2** *vt*: **to be ~d against** stagliarsi contro.
sili·con ['sɪlɪkən] **1** *n* silicio. **2** *cpd*: **~ chip** *n* chip *m inv.*
sili·cone ['sɪlɪkəʊn] *n* silicone *m.*
sili·co·sis [ˌsɪlɪ'kəʊsɪs] *n* silicosi *f.*
silk [sɪlk] **1** *n* seta. **2** *cpd (blouse, stockings)* di seta; *(industry)* della seta, serico(a); **~ factory** *n* setificio.
silk-screen ['sɪlkskriːn] *n*: **~ printing** serigrafia.
silk·worm ['sɪlkwɜːm] *n* baco da seta.
silky ['sɪlkɪ] *adj (-ier, -iest) (hair, skin)* di seta, come la seta; *(voice)* vellutato(a).
sill [sɪl] *n (window~)* davanzale *m*; *(Aut)* predellino.
sil·ly ['sɪlɪ] *adj (-ier, -iest) (stupid)* sciocco(a), stupido(a); *(ridiculous)* ridicolo(a); **don't be ~** non fare lo sciocco; **to do something ~** fare una sciocchezza.
silo ['saɪləʊ] *n* silo.
silt [sɪlt] *n* limo.
♦ **silt up 1** *vi + adv* insabbiarsi. **2** *vt + adv* ostruire.
sil·ver ['sɪlvəʳ] **1** *n (metal)* argento; *(~ware, cutlery)* argenteria, argento; *(money)* monete *fpl* da 5, 10 *o* 50 pence. **2** *adj (ring, coin)* d'argento. **3** *cpd*: **~ birch** *n* betulla d'argento; **~ foil** *n* stagnola; **~ jubilee** *n* venticinquesimo anniversario; **~ paper** *n* carta argentata; **~ plate** *n (material)* argentatura; *(objects)* oggetti *mpl* placcati in argento; **~ wedding** *n* nozze *fpl* d'argento.
silver-plated [ˌsɪlvə'pleɪtɪd] *adj* placcato(a) in argento.
silver·smith ['sɪlvəsmɪθ] *n* argentiere *m.*
silver·ware ['sɪlvəweəʳ] *n* argenteria, argento.
sil·very ['sɪlvərɪ] *adj (colour)* argenteo(a); *(hair)* argentato(a); *(sound)* argentino(a).
simi·lar ['sɪmɪləʳ] *adj*: **~ (to)** simile (a), dello stesso tipo (di); **~ in size** *(objects)* della stessa misura; *(people)* della stessa altezza; **...and ~ products** ...e simili.
simi·lar·ity [ˌsɪmɪ'lærɪtɪ] *n* somiglianza, similarità *f inv.*
simi·lar·ly ['sɪmɪləlɪ] *adv (in a similar way)* allo stesso modo; *(as is similar)* così pure; **and ~, ...** e allo stesso modo, ...
simi·le ['sɪmɪlɪ] *n* similitudine *f*, paragone *m.*
sim·mer ['sɪməʳ] **1** *vt (far)* cuocere a fuoco lento. **2** *vi (water)* sobbollire; *(food)* cuocere a fuoco lento; *(fig: revolt)* covare; **to ~ with rage** ribollire dalla rabbia.
♦ **simmer down** *vi + adv (fig fam)* calmarsi.
sim·per ['sɪmpəʳ] **1** *n* sorrisetto sciocco. **2** *vi* fare lo(la) smorfioso(a).
sim·per·ing ['sɪmpərɪŋ] *adj* lezioso(a), smorfioso(a).
sim·ple ['sɪmpl] *adj (-r, -st) (gen)* semplice; *(foolish)* sempliciotto(a), ingenuo(a); **to make ~(r)** semplificare; **it's as ~ as ABC** è come bere un bicchier d'acqua; **to make it ~ for you...** per semplificarti le cose...; **the ~ truth** la pura verità; **in ~ terms, in ~ English** in parole povere; **for the ~ reason that** per il semplice motivo che; **~ interest** *(Fin)* interesse *m*; **~ equation** *(Mat)* equazione *f* di primo grado.
simple-minded [ˌsɪmpl'maɪndɪd] *adj* sempliciotto(a).
sim·ple·ton ['sɪmpltən] *n* semplicione/a, sempliciotto/a.

sim·plic·ity [sɪm'plɪsɪtɪ] *n* semplicità.

sim·pli·fi·ca·tion [ˌsɪmplɪfɪ'keɪʃən] *n* semplificazione *f*.

sim·pli·fy ['sɪmplɪfaɪ] *vt* semplificare.

simp·ly ['sɪmplɪ] *adv* (*gen*) semplicemente; **I ~ said that...** ho semplicemente detto che...; **you ~ MUST come!** devi assolutamente venire!; **a ~ furnished room** una stanza arredata con semplicità.

simu·late ['sɪmjʊleɪt] *vt* simulare.

simu·la·tion [ˌsɪmjʊ'leɪʃən] *n* simulazione *f*.

simu·lat·or ['sɪmjʊleɪtə'] *n* simulatore *m*.

sim·ul·ta·neous [ˌsɪməl'teɪnɪəs] *adj* simultaneo(a); **~ equations** (*Math*) sistema *m* di equazioni.

sim·ul·ta·neous·ly [ˌsɪməl'teɪnɪəslɪ] *adv* simultaneamente, contemporaneamente; **~ with** contemporaneamente a.

sin [sɪn] **1** *n* peccato; **mortal ~** peccato mortale; **it would be a ~ to do that** (*Rel*) sarebbe peccato farlo; (*fig*) sarebbe un peccato farlo. **2** *vi* peccare.

since [sɪns] **1** *adv* da allora; **ever ~** da allora (in poi); **not long ~** non molto tempo fa. **2** *prep* da; **~ Monday** da lunedì; **(ever) ~ then/that...** da allora...; **~ leaving** da quando sono (*or* è etc) partito; **how long is it ~ his last visit?** da quanto tempo non viene? **3** *conj* **(a)** (*time*) da quando; **(ever) ~ I arrived** (fin) da quando sono arrivato; **how long is it ~ you last saw him?** da quando non lo vedi? **(b)** (*because*) siccome, dato che.

sin·cere [sɪn'sɪə'] *adj* sincero(a).

sin·cere·ly [sɪn'sɪəlɪ] *adv* sinceramente; **Yours ~** (*at end of letter*) distinti saluti.

sin·cer·ity [sɪn'sɛrɪtɪ] *n* sincerità.

sine [saɪn] *n* (*Math*) seno.

si·necure ['saɪnɪkjʊə'] *n* sinecura.

sin·ew ['sɪnjuː] *n* (*tendon*) tendine *m*; **~s** (*muscles*) muscoli *mpl*; (*fig: strength*) forza.

sin·ewy ['sɪnjʊɪ] *adj* (*person*) muscoloso(a); (*meat*) pieno(a) di nervi.

sin·ful ['sɪnfʊl] *adj* (*Rel*) peccaminoso(a); (*waste, act*) vergognoso(a).

sing [sɪŋ] *pt* **sang**, *pp* **sung 1** *vt* cantare; **to ~ the tenor part** cantare come tenore; **to ~ sb's praises** (*fig*) cantare le lodi di qn; **to ~ a child to sleep** cantare la ninna nanna a un bambino; **to ~ like a lark** cantare come un usignolo. **2** *vi* (*person, bird*) cantare; (*ears, kettle, bullet*) fischiare.

♦ **sing out** *vi* + *adv* (*fam: call*) chiamare.

singe [sɪndʒ] *vt* bruciacchiare.

sing·er ['sɪŋə'] *n* cantante *m/f*.

sing·ing ['sɪŋɪŋ] **1** *n* (*of person, bird*) canto; (*of kettle, bullet, in ears*) fischio. **2** *cpd* (*lessons, teacher*) di canto.

sin·gle ['sɪŋgl] **1** *adj* **(a)** (*only one*) solo(a) (*before n*); **a ~ tree in a garden** un solo albero in un giardino; **only on one ~ occasion** in una sola occasione; **he gave her a ~ rose** le ha dato una rosa; **I haven't a ~ moment to spare** non ho neanche un attimo da perdere; **not a ~ one was left** non ne è rimasto nemmeno uno; **he didn't see a ~ person** *or* **soul** non ha visto anima viva; **every ~ day** tutti i santi giorni; **~ parent: the problems of ~-parent families** i problemi delle famiglie con un solo genitore. **(b)** (*not double etc*) unico(a); (*: flower*) semplice; (*: ticket*) di (sola) andata; **~ bed** letto a una piazza; **~ room** camera singola; **in ~ file** in fila indiana; **~ spacing** (*Typ*) interlinea uno. **(c)** (*not married: man*) celibe; (*: woman*) nubile.

   2 *n* **(a):** **~s** (*Tennis*) singolo. **(b)** (*Rail etc*) biglietto di andata. **(c)** (*record*): **a ~** un 45 giri.

♦ **single out** *vt* + *adv* (*choose*) scegliere; (*distinguish*) distinguere.

single-breasted ['sɪŋgl,brɛstɪd] *adj* monopetto *inv*.

single-decker [ˌsɪŋgl'dɛkə'] *n* autobus *m inv* a un piano solo.

single-handed [ˌsɪŋgl'hændɪd] **1** *adj* (*voyage*) solitario(a); (*achievement*) fatto(a) da solo. **2** *adv* da solo(a).

single-minded [ˌsɪŋgl'maɪndɪd] *adj* (*person*) deciso(a), risoluto(a); (*ambition, attempt*) ostinato(a); **to be ~ about sth** concentrare tutte le proprie forze in qc.

sin·gle·ness ['sɪŋglnɪs] *n*: **~ of purpose** tenacia.

single-seater [ˌsɪŋgl'siːtə'] *adj*: **~ aeroplane** aeroplano monoposto.

sin·glet ['sɪŋglɪt] *n* canottiera.

single-track ['sɪŋgl,træk] *adj* (*Rail*) a un solo binario.

sin·gly ['sɪŋglɪ] *adv* singolarmente, uno(a) a uno(a).

sing·song ['sɪŋsɒŋ] **1** *adj* (*tone*) cantilenante. **2** *n* (*songs*): **to have a ~** farsi una cantata.

sin·gu·lar ['sɪŋgjʊlə'] **1** *adj* **(a)** (*Gram*) singolare. **(b)** (*extraordinary*) strano(a), singolare. **2** *n* (*Gram*) singolare *m*; **in the ~** al singolare; **in the feminine ~** al femminile singolare.

sin·gu·lar·ity [ˌsɪŋgjʊ'lærɪtɪ] *n* singolarità.

sin·gu·lar·ly ['sɪŋgjʊləlɪ] *adv* stranamente.

sin·is·ter ['sɪnɪstə'] *adj* sinistro(a).

sink¹ [sɪŋk] *pt* **sank**, *pp* **sunk 1** *vt* **(a)** (*ship, object*) far affondare; (*fig: project*) far naufragare; (*: person*) distruggere; **to be sunk** (*fam*) essere nei guai; **I'm sunk without it** sono perso senza; **to be sunk in thought** essere immerso nei pensieri; **to be sunk in despair** essere assolutamente disperato; **let's ~ our differences** accantoniamo le divergenze. **(b)** (*mineshaft, well*) scavare; (*foundations*) gettare; (*stake*) piantare, conficcare; (*pipe etc*) interrare; **to ~ the ball** (*Golf*) fare buca; **to ~ money into an enterprise** investire denaro in un'impresa.

   2 *vi* (*in water*) affondare; (*level of water, sun*) calare; (*ground*) cedere; (*temperature, value, voice*) abbassarsi; (*sales*) diminuire; **to ~ to the bottom** (*ship*) colare a picco; **to ~ to one's knees** cadere in ginocchio; **he sank into a chair/the mud** sprofondò in una poltrona/nel fango; **the water sank slowly into the ground** l'acqua è penetrata lentamente nel terreno; **he's ~ing fast** (*dying*) deperisce rapidamente; **he has sunk in my estimation** è scaduto ai miei occhi; **he was left to ~ or swim** (*fig*) fu lasciato a cavarsela da solo; **to ~ like a stone** andar giù come un sasso; **to ~ out of sight** scomparire alla vista; **the shares** *or* **share prices have sunk to 3 dollars** le azioni sono scese a 3 dollari; **my heart sank** mi sentii venir meno.

♦ **sink in** *vi* + *adv* (*person, car*) sprofondare; (*liquid: into ground, carpet*) penetrare; (*remark, explanation*) essere capito(a); **it hasn't sunk in yet** (*fig*) non mi rendo (*or* si rende *etc*) ancora conto; **it took a long time to ~ in** ci ho (*or* ha *etc*) messo molto a capirlo.

sink² [sɪŋk] **1** *n* (*bathroom* **~**) lavandino; (*kitchen* **~**) acquaio, lavello. **2** *cpd*: **~ unit** *n* blocco lavello.

sink·ing ['sɪŋkɪŋ] **1** *n* (*shipwreck*) naufragio. **2** *adj*: **a ~ feeling** una stretta allo stomaco; **I have a ~ feeling that things have gone wrong** ho la strana sensazione che le cose siano andate male; **with ~ heart** con il cuore in gola.

sin·ner ['sɪnə'] *n* peccatore/trice.

sinu·ous ['sɪnjʊəs] *adj* (*course, route*) sinuoso(a),

tortuoso(a); *(dance, movement)* flessuoso(a).

si·nus ['sainəs] *n (Anat)* seno.

sip [sip] **1** *n* sorso. **2** *vt* sorseggiare, centellinare.

si·phon ['saifən] **1** *n* sifone *m*. **2** *vt (also:* ~ **off,** ~ **out***: liquid)* travasare; *(fig: traffic)* deviare; *(: funds)* trasferire.

sir [sɜːʳ] *n* signore *m*; **yes,** ~ sì signore; *(Mil)* sissignore; **Dear S~** *(in letter)* Egregio signor *(followed by name)*; **Dear S~s** Spettabile ditta; **S~ Winston Churchill** Sir Winston Churchill.

si·ren ['saiərən] *n* sirena.

sir·loin ['sɜːlɔin] *n* controfiletto; ~ **steak** bistecca di controfiletto.

si·sal ['saisəl] *n* sisal *f inv*.

sis·sy ['sisi] *n (fam)* femminuccia.

sis·ter ['sistəʳ] **1** *n (a) (relation)* sorella. **(b)** *(Med)* (infermiera) caposala. **(c)** *(Rel)* suora; **S~ Mary** Suor Maria. **2** *cpd:* ~ **nations** *npl* nazioni *fpl* sorelle; ~ **organization** *n* organizzazione *f* affine; ~ **ship** *n* nave *f* gemella.

sister-in-law ['sistərin,lɔː] *n* cognata.

sis·ter·ly ['sistəli] *adj* fraterno(a), da sorella.

sit [sit] *pt, pp* **sat 1** *vi (a) (also:* ~ **down)** sedersi; **to be** ~**ting down** essere seduto(a); ~**!** *(to dog)* a cuccia!, seduto!; ~ **beside me** siediti accanto a me; **he just** ~**s at home all day** sta a casa tutto il giorno senza far nulla; **this unit** ~**s on top of that one** questo pezzo poggia su quello; **to** ~ **still/ straight** stare seduto fermo/dritto; **to** ~ **tight** non fare nulla; **to be** ~**ting pretty** *(fig fam)* passarsela bene; **to** ~ **on a committee** far parte di una commissione; **to** ~ **for** *(a constituency)* avere il seggio di; **to** ~ **for a painter/portrait** posare per un pittore/ritratto; **to** ~ **for an examination** dare *or* sostenere un esame; **to** ~ **through** *(a film, play)* resistere fino alla fine di; **to** ~ **over one's work** *or* **books** stare con la testa sui libri. **(b)** *(assembly, committee)* riunirsi; **the committee is** ~**ting now** il comitato è in riunione; **Parliament** ~**s from November till June** il Parlamento inizia i lavori a novembre e li chiude di giugno. **(c)** *(bird, insect)* posarsi; *(on eggs)* covare. **(d)** *(dress etc)* cadere; **that jacket** ~**s well** quella giacca cade bene.

2 *vt* **(a)** *(guest, child etc)* far sedere. **(b)** *(exam)* dare, sostenere.

♦ **sit about, sit around** *vi + adv* star seduto(a) (senza far nulla).

♦ **sit back** *vi + adv (in seat)* appoggiarsi allo schienale; *(doing nothing)* stare con le mani in mano.

♦ **sit down 1** *vi + adv* sedersi; **please,** ~ **down** prego, si accomodi; **to be** ~**ting down** essere seduto. **2** *vt + adv* far sedere, far accomodare.

♦ **sit in** *vi + adv* **(a): to** ~ **in on a discussion** assistere ad una discussione. **(b)** *(demonstrate)*: **to** ~ **in a building** occupare un edificio.

♦ **sit on** *vi + prep (fig fam)* **(a)** *(keep secret: news, information)* tenere segreto(a); *(delay taking action on: document, application)* tenere in un cassetto. **(b)** *(person: silence)* far tacere.

♦ **sit out** *vt + adv (dance etc)* non partecipare a, saltare; *(lecture, play)* restare fino alla fine di.

♦ **sit up 1** *vi + adv* **(a)** *(upright)* stare seduto(a) diritto(a); *(in bed)* tirarsi su a sedere; **to make sb** ~ **up (and take notice)** *(fig)* far drizzare le orecchie a qn. **(b)** *(stay up late)* restare alzato(a); **to** ~ **up with** *(invalid)* fare la notte al capezzale di; **to** ~ **up for sb** aspettare qn alzato. **2** *vt + adv (baby, doll)* mettere a sedere, mettere seduto(a).

sit·com ['sitkɒm] *n (fam: Radio, TV)* commedia di situazione.

sit-down ['sitdaʊn] *adj:* **a** ~ **strike** un sit-in; **a** ~ **meal** un pranzo.

site [sait] **1** *n (of town, building)* ubicazione *f*; *(Archeol)* località *f inv*; *(Constr)* cantiere *m*; *(camp* ~*)* campeggio; **the** ~ **of the accident** il luogo dell'incidente; **the** ~ **of the battle** il campo di battaglia. **2** *vt* collocare; **a badly** ~**d building** un edificio in una brutta posizione.

sit-in ['sitin] *n* sit-in *m inv*; **to hold a** ~ fare un sit-in.

sit·ter ['sitəʳ] *n (Art)* modello/a; *(baby~)* babysitter *m/f inv*.

sit·ting ['sitiŋ] **1** *n (Pol etc)* seduta; *(in canteen)* turno; *(for portrait)* seduta (di posa). **2** *cpd:* ~ **duck** *n (fig)* facile bersaglio; ~ **member** *n (Pol)* deputato/a in carica; ~ **room** *n* salotto; ~ **tenant** *n* attuale affittuario.

situ·ate ['sitjʊeit] *vt* collocare.

situ·ated ['sitjʊeitid] *adj* situato(a); **well** ~ *(house)* in una bella posizione; **how are you** ~ **for money?** *(fig)* come stai a soldi?

situa·tion [,sitjʊ'eiʃən] **1** *n (position)* posizione *f*; *(fig)* situazione *f*; *(job)* lavoro, impiego; '~**s vacant**' 'offerte *fpl* di impiego'. **2** *cpd:* ~ **comedy** *n (TV, Radio)* commedia di situazione.

six [siks] **1** *adj* sei *inv*. **2** *n* sei *m inv*; **to be (all) at** ~**es and sevens** *(fig: person, things)* essere sottosopra; **it's** ~ **of one and half a dozen of the other** *(fig)* è più o meno lo stesso, siamo lì; *for usage see* **five.**

six-footer [,siks'fʊtəʳ] *n*: **he's a** ~ ≃ è alto un metro e ottanta.

six-shooter ['siks,ʃuːtəʳ] *n* rivoltella (a sei colpi).

six·teen [,siks'tiːn] **1** *adj* sedici *inv*. **2** *n* sedici *m inv; for usage see* **five.**

six·teenth [,siks'tiːnθ] **1** *adj* sedicesimo(a). **2** *n (in series)* sedicesimo/a; *(fraction)* sedicesimo; *for usage see* **fifth.**

sixth [siksθ] **1** *adj* sesto(a). **2** *n (in series)* sesto/a; *(fraction)* sesto; **the upper/lower** ~ *(Scol)* l'ultimo/il penultimo anno di scuola superiore; *for usage see* **fifth.**

six·ti·eth ['sikstiiθ] **1** *adj* sessantesimo(a). **2** *n (in series)* sessantesimo/a; *(fraction)* sessantesimo; *for usage see* **fifth.**

six·ty ['siksti] **1** *adj* sessanta *inv*. **2** *n* sessanta *m inv; for usage see* **fifty.**

sixty-four ['siksti'fɔːʳ] *adj*: **that's the** ~ **(thousand) dollar question** *(fam)* questa è la domanda del giorno.

size[1] [saiz] *n (gen)* dimensioni *fpl*; *(fig: of problem, operation etc)* proporzioni *fpl*; *(of garments)* taglia, misura; *(of shoes)* numero, misura; *(of hat)* misura; **I take** ~ **5 shoes** ≃ porto il 38 di scarpe; **I take** ~ **14 in a dress** ≃ porto la 44 di vestiti; **what** ~ **(of) collar?** che misura di colletto?; **what** ~ **are you?, what** ~ **do you take?** che misura porti?; **he's about your** ~ sarà più o meno come te; **it's the** ~ **of a brick/nut** sarà grande come un mattone/una noce; **I'd like the small/large** ~ *(of soap powder etc)* vorrei la confezione piccola/grande; *(of clothes)* vorrei la misura piccola/grande; **to cut sth to** ~ tagliare qc nella misura desiderata *or* voluta; **to cut sb down to** ~ *(fig fam)* ridimensionare qn; **that's about the** ~ **of it** *(fig)* le cose stanno più o meno così.

♦ **size up** *vt + adv (person, problem etc)* farsi un'idea di, valutare.

size[2] [saiz] **1** *n (for fabric)* bozzima; *(for walls)* colla. **2** *vt (fabric)* imbozzimare; *(wall)* dare una mano di colla a.

size·able ['saizəbl] *adj (house, diamond)* abbastanza grande; *(sum, problem)* considerevole, notevole.

siz·zle ['sizl] *vi* sfrigolare.

skate[1] [skeɪt] *n (fish)* razza.

skate[2] [skeɪt] **1** *n* pattino; **to get one's ~s on** *(fig: hurry up)* affrettarsi, sbrigarsi. **2** *vi* pattinare; **to go skating** andare a pattinare; **it went skating across the room** *(fig)* è scivolato lungo la stanza; **to ~ across/down** *etc* attraversare/scendere *etc* pattinando.

♦ **skate over, skate around** *vi + prep (problem, issue)* prendere alla leggera, prendere sottogamba.

skate·board ['skeɪtbɔːd] *n* skate-board *m inv.*

skat·ing ['skeɪtɪŋ] **1** *n* pattinaggio; **figure ~** pattinaggio artistico. **2** *cpd:* **~ rink** *n* pista di pattinaggio.

skein [skeɪn] *n (of wool)* matassa.

skel·eton ['skelɪtn] **1** *n (of person)* scheletro; *(of building etc)* struttura, ossatura; *(of novel, report)* schema *m*; **a walking ~** *(fig)* uno scheletro ambulante; **the ~ at the feast** *(fig)* il *(or* la) guastafeste; **~ in the cupboard** *(fig)* scheletro nell'armadio. **2** *cpd (staff, service)* ridotto(a) (all'essenziale); **~ key** *n* passe-partout *m inv.*

skep·tic ['skeptɪk] *(Am)* = **sceptic.**

sketch [sketʃ] **1** *n* **(a)** *(drawing)* schizzo, abbozzo; *(fig: rough draft: of ideas, plan)* abbozzo, schema *m*; *(: description)* schizzo. **(b)** *(Theatre)* sketch *m inv.* **2** *vt (draw)* schizzare, abbozzare; *(fig: ideas, plan)* abbozzare; **to ~ a map for sb** fare una piantina per qn.

♦ **sketch in** *vt + adv (details)* inserire, aggiungere.

sketch·book ['sketʃbʊk] *n*, **sketch·pad** ['sketʃpæd] *n* album *m inv* per schizzi.

sketchy ['sketʃɪ] *adj* **(-ier, -iest)** *(drawing, plan)* approssimato(a); *(plans, knowledge)* vago(a).

skew·er ['skjʊəʳ] **1** *n (for roasts)* spiedo; *(for kebabs)* spiedino. **2** *vt* infilzare in uno spiedo.

skew-whiff ['skjuːwɪf] *adj (fam)* storto(a).

ski [skiː] **1** *n* sci *m inv.* **2** *vi* sciare; **to ~ down a slope** fare una discesa con gli sci; **to go ~ing** andare a sciare. **3** *cpd:* **~ boot** *n* scarpone *m* da sci; **~ instructor** *n* maestro/a di sci; **~ jump** *n (slope)* trampolino; **~ jumping** *n* salto con gli sci; **~ lift** *n* ski-lift *m inv*, sciovia; **~ pants** *npl*, **~ trousers** *npl* pantaloni *mpl* da sci; **~ resort** *n* località *f inv* sciistica; **~ run** *n* pista (da sci); **~ stick** *n* racchetta (da sci).

skid [skɪd] **1** *n (Aut)* slittamento; *(: sideways slip)* sbandamento; **to go into a ~** slittare; sbandare; **to get out of a ~, correct a ~** riprendere controllo della macchina *(or* camion *etc).* **2** *vi (Aut)* slittare; *(: slip sideways)* sbandare; *(person, object)* scivolare; **to ~ into sth** *(car)* slittare e sbattere contro qc; *(person, object)* scivolare contro qc. **3** *cpd:* **~ mark** *n* segno della frenata.

ski·er ['skiːəʳ] *n* sciatore/trice.

skiff [skɪf] *n* skiff *m inv.*

ski·ing ['skiːɪŋ] **1** *n* sci *m (sport).* **2** *cpd (holiday etc)* sciistico(a).

skil·ful, *(Am)* **skill·ful** ['skɪlfʊl] *adj* abile.

skil·ful·ly, *(Am)* **skill·ful·ly** ['skɪlfəlɪ] *adv* abilmente.

skill [skɪl] *n* **(a)** *(gen)* capacità *f inv*, abilità *f inv*; *(talent)* talento; **her ~ in dealing with people** la sua abilità nel trattare con le persone; **his ~ as a mechanic** la sua abilità come meccanico; **a writer of great ~** uno scrittore di grande talento; **to make use of sb's ~s** sfruttare le capacità di qn. **(b)** *(technique)* tecnica; **there's a certain ~ to doing it** ci vuole una certa tecnica *or* arte nel farlo.

skilled [skɪld] *adj* **(a)** *(gen)* abile, esperto(a). **(b)** *(job, work, worker)* specializzato(a).

skil·let ['skɪlɪt] *n* padella.

skim [skɪm] **1** *vt* **(a)** *(soup)* schiumare; *(milk)* scremare; **to ~ the fat off the soup** schiumare il brodo; **to ~ the cream off the milk** scremare il latte; **~med milk** latte *m* scremato. **(b)** *(stone)* far rimbalzare; *(subj: bird, plane):* **to ~ the water/ground** sfiorare *or* rasentare l'acqua/il suolo. **2** *vi:* **to ~ across** *or* **along** sfiorare; **the stone ~med across the surface of the lake** il sasso rimbalzò sulla superficie del lago; **to ~ through a book** *(fig)* scorrere *or* dare una scorsa a un libro.

skimp [skɪmp] *vi:* **to ~ on**, *vt (material etc)* risparmiare; *(work)* raffazzonare; *(praise)* essere avaro(a) di.

skimpy ['skɪmpɪ] *adj* **(-ier, -iest)** *(skirt etc)* striminzito(a); *(hem)* piccolo(a); *(allowance)* modico(a); *(meal)* frugale.

skin [skɪn] **1** *n (gen)* pelle *f*; *(of fruit, vegetable)* buccia; *(of boat, aircraft)* rivestimento; *(for duplicating)* matrice *f* per duplicatori; *(crust: on paint, milk pudding: thin)* pellicola; *(: thick)* crosta; **next to the ~** a contatto con la pelle; **to have a thick/thin ~** *(fig)* non essere/essere suscettibile; **by the ~ of one's teeth** *(fig)* per un pelo; **wet** *or* **soaked to the ~** bagnato fino al midollo; **to be ~ and bone** *(fig)* essere pelle e ossa; **to get under sb's ~** *(fig)* irritare qn, dare sui nervi a qn; **I've got you under my ~** mi hai colpito profondamente; **it's no ~ off my nose** *(fig fam: does not concern me)* non sono affari miei; *(: does not hurt me)* non mi costa niente.

2 *vt (animal)* spellare, scoiare; *(fruit etc)* sbucciare; **to ~ one's knee/elbow** sbucciarsi un ginocchio/gomito; **I'll ~ him alive!** *(fig)* gli faccio la pelle!; **keep your eyes ~ned for a garage** tieni gli occhi bene aperti per un distributore.

3 *cpd:* **~ colour** *n* colore *m* della pelle; **~ disease** *n* malattia della pelle; **~ diver** *n* subacqueo; **~ diving** *n* immersione *f* con autorespiratore; **~ graft** *n* innesto epidermico; **~ test** *n* prova di reazione cutanea.

skin-deep [ˌskɪn'diːp] *adj (also fig)* superficiale.

skin·flint ['skɪnflɪnt] *n* taccagno/a, tirchio/a.

skin·ful ['skɪnfʊl] *n (fam):* **to have (had) a ~** prendere una sbornia.

skin·head ['skɪnhed] *n* testa rapata; *(thug)* teppista *m.*

skin·ny ['skɪnɪ] *adj* **(-ier, -iest)** *(person)* magro(a), gracile, mingherlino(a); *(jumper)* striminzito(a).

skin·tight ['skɪnˌtaɪt] *adj* aderente.

skint [skɪnt] *adj (fam):* **to be ~** essere in bolletta, essere al verde.

skip[1] [skɪp] **1** *n* saltello. **2** *vi* saltellare, salterellare; *(with rope)* saltare la corda; **to ~ in/out** *etc* entrare/uscire saltellando; **to ~ off** *(fig)* tagliare la corda; **to ~ over sth** *(fig)* sorvolare qc; **to ~ from one subject to another** passare da un argomento a un altro. **3** *vt (fig: meal, lesson, page)* saltare; *(: school)* marinare, bigiare; **let's ~ it!** *(fam)* lasciamo perdere!

skip[2] [skɪp] *n* benna.

skip·per ['skɪpəʳ] *n (Sport, Naut)* capitano.

skip·ping ['skɪpɪŋ] **1** *n* salto della corda. **2** *cpd:* **~ rope** *n* corda per saltare.

skir·mish ['skɜːmɪʃ] *n* scaramuccia.

skirt [skɜːt] **1** *n* gonna. **2** *vt (also:* **~ around:** *town, table)* girare intorno a; *(: obstacle, difficulty)* aggirare; *(: argument, subject)* schivare.

skirt·ing (board) ['skɜːtɪŋ(ˌbɔːd)] *n* zoccolo, battiscopa *m inv.*

skit [skɪt] *n (Theatre)* sketch *m inv* satirico.

skit·tish ['skɪtɪʃ] *adj (horse)* ombroso(a).

skit·tle ['skɪtl] *n* birillo; **to play ~s** giocare a birilli.

skive [skaɪv] *vi (fam)* fare il lavativo; **to ~ off** svignarsela, filarsela.

skiv·vy ['skɪvɪ] *n (fam pej)* sguattera.

skulk [skʌlk] *vi (also: ~ about)* aggirarsi furtivamente; **to ~ into/out of** entrare/uscire furtivamente.

skull [skʌl] *n (of live person)* cranio; *(of dead person)* teschio; **~ and crossbones** teschio; *(flag)* bandiera dei pirati.

skull·cap ['skʌlkæp] *n (worn by Jews)* zucchetto; *(worn by Pope)* papalina.

skunk [skʌŋk] *n (Zool)* moffetta; *(fam)*: **you ~!** farabutto!, mascalzone!

sky [skaɪ] *n* cielo; **to sleep under the open ~** dormire sotto le stelle *or* all'aperto; **to praise sb to the skies** portare alle stelle qn; **the ~'s the limit** *(fig fam)* non ci sono limiti.

sky·blue ['skaɪ'bluː] **1** *n* azzurro (cielo), celeste *m*. **2** *adj* azzurro(a), celeste.

sky·high [,skaɪ'haɪ] *adv (throw)* molto in alto; **to blow sth ~** far saltare in aria qc; **to blow a theory ~** confutare una teoria; **prices have gone ~** i prezzi sono saliti alle stelle.

sky·lab ['skaɪlæb] *n* laboratorio spaziale.

sky·lark ['skaɪlɑːk] **1** *n (bird)* allodola. **2** *vi (fig fam)* scatenarsi.

sky·light ['skaɪlaɪt] *n* lucernario.

sky·line ['skaɪlaɪn] *n (horizon)* orizzonte *m*; *(of city)* profilo.

sky·scraper ['skaɪ,skreɪpəʳ] *n* grattacielo.

sky·writing ['skaɪ,raɪtɪŋ] *n* pubblicità aerea.

slab [slæb] *n (of stone, metal)* lastra; *(of wood)* tavola; *(in mortuary)* tavolo mortuario; *(of chocolate)* tavoletta; *(of meat, cheese)* pezzo.

slack [slæk] **1** *adj (-er, -est)* **(a)** *(not tight: rope, knot)* lento(a); *(: grip)* debole. **(b)** *(lax: work)* trascurato(a); *(: student, worker)* negligente; *(lazy)* pigro(a), fiacco(a); **to be ~ about one's work** essere negligente nel proprio lavoro. **(c)** *(Comm: market)* stagnante; *(: demand)* scarso(a); *(period)* morto(a); **business is ~** l'attività commerciale è scarsa. **2** *n* **(a)** *(part of rope etc)*: **to take up the ~ in a rope** tendere una corda. **(b)** *(Mineralogy)* polvere *f* di carbone. **3** *vi (fam)* fare il lavativo.

slack·en ['slækn] *(also: ~ off)* **1** *vt (rope, grip, reins, nut)* allentare; *(pressure)* diminuire; **to ~ speed** ridurre la velocità; **to ~ one's pace** rallentare il passo. **2** *vi (gen)* allentarsi; *(pressure, speed, activity)* diminuire; *(gale)* placarsi; *(trade)* calare, ridursi.

slack·er ['slækəʳ] *n (fam)* scansafatiche *m/f*, lavativo/a.

slack·ness ['slæknɪs] *n (of rope, cable)* mancanza di tensione; *(of person)* negligenza; *(of trade)* ristagno.

slacks [slæks] *npl* pantaloni *mpl*.

slag [slæg] **1** *n (Metallurgy)* scorie *fpl*. **2** *cpd*: **~ heap** *n* cumulo di scorie.

slain [sleɪn] **1** *pp of* slay. **2** *npl*: **the ~** i caduti.

slake [sleɪk] *vt (one's thirst)* spegnere.

slam [slæm] **1** *n* **(a)** *(of door)* colpo. **(b)** *(Bridge)* slam *m inv*. **2** *vt* **(a)** *(door, lid)* sbattere; **to ~ sth shut** chiudere qc sbattendolo; **to ~ sth (down) on the table** sbattere qc sul tavolo; **to ~ on the brakes** frenare di colpo. **(b)** *(criticize)* stroncare. **3** *vi (door, lid)* sbattere.

slan·der ['slɑːndəʳ] **1** *n* calunnia; *(Law)* diffamazione *f*. **2** *vt* calunniare; *(Law)* diffamare.

slan·der·ous ['slɑːndərəs] *adj* calunnioso(a); *(Law)* diffamatorio(a).

slang [slæŋ] **1** *n (gen)* slang *m*, gergo; **to talk ~** parlare in gergo. **2** *adj (word)* gergale. **3** *vt (fam: insult, criticize)* lanciare ingiurie a *or* contro; **a**

~ing match uno scambio di insulti.

slangy ['slæŋɪ] *adj (-ier, -iest)* *(fam)* gergale.

slant [slɑːnt] **1** *n* pendenza, inclinazione *f*; *(fig: point of view)* punto di vista; **to be on a ~** essere inclinato; **to give a new ~ on sth** offrire un nuovo punto di vista su qc; **to get a new ~ on sth** vedere qc da un altro punto di vista. **2** *vt (roof etc)* inclinare; **to ~ a report** *(fig)* dare una versione dei fatti distorta. **3** *vi* essere inclinato(a), pendere.

slant·ing ['slɑːntɪŋ] *adj (handwriting)* inclinato(a); *(roof)* spiovente; *(line)* obliquo(a); *(rain)* che cade di traverso.

slant·wise ['slɑːntwaɪz] *adj* di traverso.

slap [slæp] **1** *n* schiaffo, ceffone *m*; **a ~ in the face** uno schiaffo in faccia; *(fig)* uno schiaffo morale; **a ~ on the back** una pacca sulla spalla. **2** *adv (fam)*: **to run ~ into** *(tree, lamppost)* andare a finire dritto contro; *(person)* imbattersi in; **it fell ~ in the middle** cadde proprio nel mezzo. **3** *vt* **(a)** dare uno schiaffo a; **to ~ a child's bottom** sculacciare un bambino; **to ~ sb on the back** dare una pacca sulla spalla a qn; **to ~ sb down** *(fig: child)* zittire; *(: opposition)* stroncare. **(b)**: **he ~ped the book on the table** sbattè il libro sul tavolo; **~ a coat of paint on it** dagli una mano di vernice.

slap·bang [,slæp'bæŋ] *adv (fam)*: **he ran ~ into the door** andò a sbattere dritto contro la porta; **it fell ~ in the middle** cadde proprio nel mezzo.

slap·dash ['slæpdæʃ] *adj*, **slap·happy** ['slæp,hæpɪ] *adj (person)* negligente; *(work)* raffazzonato(a).

slap·stick ['slæpstɪk] *n (also: ~ comedy)* farsa grossolana.

slap·up ['slæpʌp] *adj (fam)*: **~ meal** pranzo coi fiocchi.

slash [slæʃ] **1** *n* colpo. **2** *vt (with knife: gen)* tagliare; *(: face, painting)* sfregiare; *(with whip, stick)* sferzare; *(fig: price)* ridurre fortemente.

slat [slæt] *n (of wood)* stecca; *(of plastic)* lamina.

slate [sleɪt] **1** *n* ardesia; **to wipe the ~ clean** *(fig)* mettere una pietra sopra; **to mark sth on sb's ~** mettere qc sul conto di qn. **2** *vt* **(a)** *(roof)* ricoprire d'ardesia. **(b)** *(fam: criticize)* criticare, stroncare. **3** *cpd* di ardesia.

slate·blue [,sleɪt'bluː] *adj* (blu) ardesia *inv*.

slate·grey [,sleɪt'greɪ] *adj* (grigio(a)) ardesia *inv*; *(sky, storm clouds)* plumbeo(a).

slaugh·ter ['slɔːtəʳ] **1** *n (of animals)* macellazione *f*; *(of persons)* strage *f*, massacro. **2** *vt (animals)* macellare; *(person)* trucidare; *(people)* massacrare, fare strage di; *(fig)* distruggere, massacrare.

slaughter·house ['slɔːtəhaʊs] *n* macello, mattatoio.

Slav [slɑːv] *adj*, *n* slavo(a) *(m/f)*.

slave [sleɪv] **1** *n* schiavo/a; **to be a ~ to sth** *(fig)* essere schiavo di qc. **2** *vi*: **to ~ (away) at sth/at doing sth** ammazzarsi di fatica *or* sgobbare per qc/per fare qc. **3** *cpd*: **~ driver** *n* sorvegliante *m* di schiavi; *(fig)* aguzzino/a; **~ labour** *n* lavoro degli schiavi; *(fig)* lavoro da schiavi; **we're just ~ labour here** siamo solamente sfruttati qui dentro; **~ trade** *n* tratta degli schiavi.

slav·er ['slævəʳ] *vi (dribble)* sbavare.

slav·ery ['sleɪvərɪ] *n (condition)* schiavitù *f*; *(system)* schiavismo.

slav·ish ['sleɪvɪʃ] *adj (devotion)* servile; *(imitation)* pedissequo(a).

slav·ish·ly ['sleɪvɪʃlɪ] *adv (see adj)* servilmente; pedissequamente.

slay [sleɪ] *pt* slew, *pp* slain *vt (poet: kill)* uccidere.

slea·zy ['sliːzɪ] *adj (-ier, -iest)* squallido(a).

sledge [sledʒ] **1** *n (also: sled)* slitta. **2** *vi*: **to go sledging** andare in slitta; **to ~ down a hill**

scendere in slitta giù per una collina.

sledge·hammer ['sledʒ,hæməʳ] *n* martello da fabbro.

sleek [sliːk] **1** *adj* (**-er, -est**) *(shiny: hair, coat)* liscio(a) e lucente; *(cat)* sano(a) e bello(a); *(person: in appearance)* azzimato(a); *(: in manner)* untuoso(a). **2** *vt*: **to ~ one's hair down** lisciarsi i capelli.

sleep [sliːp] *(vb: pt, pp* **slept***)* **1** *n* sonno; **deep ~, sound ~** sonno profondo; **to have a good night's ~** farsi una bella dormita; **to drop off to ~, to go to ~** addormentarsi; **to go to ~** *(limb)* intorpidirsi; **to put to sleep** *(patient)* far addormentare; *(animal: euph: kill)* abbattere; **to talk in one's ~** parlare nel sonno; **to walk in one's ~** camminare nel sonno; **to send sb to ~** *(bore)* far addormentare qn; **I shan't lose any ~ over it** *(fig)* non starò a perderci il sonno.

2 *vt*: **we can ~ 4** abbiamo 4 posti letto, possiamo alloggiare 4 persone.

3 *vi* dormire; **to ~ like a log** *or* **top** dormire della grossa *or* come un ghiro; **he was ~ing soundly** *or* **deeply** era profondamente addormentato; **to ~ lightly** avere il sonno leggero; **let's ~ on it** *(fig)* la notte porta consiglio, dormiamoci sopra; **~ tight!** sogni d'oro!; **I slept through the storm/alarm clock** non ho sentito il temporale/la sveglia; **he slept at his mother's** ha dormito dalla mamma; **to ~ with sb** *(euph: have sex)* andare a letto con qn.

♦ **sleep around** *vi + adv (fam)* andare a letto con tutti.

♦ **sleep in** *vi + adv (lie late)* dormire fino a tardi; *(oversleep)* non svegliarsi.

♦ **sleep off** *vt + adv*: **to ~ sth off** smaltire qc dormendo.

sleep·er ['sliːpəʳ] *n* (**a**) *(person)*: **to be a heavy/light ~** avere il sonno pesante/leggero. (**b**) *(Rail: track)* traversina; *(: berth)* cuccetta; *(: coach)* vagone *m* letto *inv*. (**c**) *(earring)* orecchino.

sleepi·ly ['sliːpɪlɪ] *adv* con aria assonnata.

sleep·ing ['sliːpɪŋ] **1** *adj* addormentato(a); **the S~ Beauty** la Bella Addormentata nel bosco; **let ~ dogs lie** *(Proverb)* non toccare il can che dorme. **2** *cpd*: **~ bag** *n* sacco a pelo; **~ car** *n (Rail)* vagone *m* letto *inv*; **~ partner** *n (Comm)* socio inattivo; **~ pill** *n* sonnifero; **~ quarters** *npl* dormitorio; **~ sickness** *n* malattia del sonno.

sleep·less ['sliːplɪs] *adj (person)* insonne; *(night)* insonne, in bianco.

sleep·walk·er ['sliːp,wɔːkəʳ] *n* sonnambulo/a.

sleepy ['sliːpɪ] *adj* (**-ier, -iest**) *(person, voice, look)* assonnato(a), sonnolento(a); *(village)* addormentato(a); **to be** *or* **feel ~** avere sonno.

sleet [sliːt] **1** *n* nevischio. **2** *vi*: **it was ~ing** cadeva nevischio.

sleeve [sliːv] *n (of garment)* manica; *(of record)* copertina; **to have sth up one's ~** *(fig)* avere in serbo qc.

sleeve·less ['sliːvlɪs] *adj* senza maniche.

sleigh [sleɪ] *n* slitta.

sleight [slaɪt] *n*: **~ of hand** destrezza di mano.

slen·der ['slendəʳ] *adj (person)* sottile, snello(a); *(waist, neck, hand)* sottile; *(fig: resources, majority)* scarso(a), esiguo(a); *(: hope, chance)* piccolo(a), scarso(a).

slept [slept] *pt, pp* of **sleep**.

sleuth [sluːθ] *n (hum)* segugio.

slew [sluː] *pt* of **slay**.

slice [slaɪs] **1** *n* (**a**) *(of meat etc)* fetta; *(of lemon, cucumber)* fettina; **a ~ of the profits** *(fig)* una fetta dei profitti; **a ~ of life** *(fig)* uno scorcio della vita. (**b**) *(tool)* paletta. **2** *vt (meat etc)* affettare; *(rope etc)* tagliare di netto; *(Sport: ball)* col-

pire di taglio; **to ~ sth thickly/thinly** affettare *or* tagliare qc grosso/sottile; **~d loaf** pane *m* a cassetta.

♦ **slice off** *vt + adv* tagliare.

♦ **slice through** *vi + prep* tagliare di netto; *(fig: the air, waves)* fendere.

♦ **slice up** *vt + adv* affettare.

slic·er ['slaɪsəʳ] *n* affettatrice *f*.

slick [slɪk] **1** *adj* (**-er, -est**) *(pej: answer, excuse)* troppo pronto(a); *(: person: glib)* che ha la parlantina; *(: cunning)* furbo(a); **a ~ character** un furbacchione. **2** *n*: **oil ~** macchia d'olio. **3** *vt (also: ~ down: hair: with comb)* lisciare; *(: with haircream)* impomatare.

slide [slaɪd] *(vb: pt, pp* **slid***)* **1** *n (action: on ice, mud etc)* scivolone *m*; *(in playground, swimming pool)* scivolo; *(land ~)* frana; *(hair ~)* fermacapelli *m inv*; *(microscope ~)* vetrino; *(Phot)* diapositiva; **the ~ in share prices** la caduta del prezzo delle azioni. **2** *vi* scivolare; **these drawers ~ in and out easily** questi cassetti scorrono bene; **to ~ down the banisters** scivolare giù per il corrimano; **to let things ~** *(fig)* lasciare andare tutto, trascurare tutto. **3** *vt (box, case)* far scivolare; *(bolt)* far scorrere; **he slid the gun from its holster** ha tirato la pistola fuori dalla custodia. **4** *cpd*: **~ projector** *n (Phot)* proiettore *m* per diapositive; **~ rule** *n (Math)* regolo calcolatore; **~ show** *n (Phot)* proiezione *f* di diapositive.

slid·ing ['slaɪdɪŋ] *adj (part, seat)* mobile; *(door)* scorrevole; **~ roof** *n (Aut)* capotte *f inv*; **~ scale** *(Admin etc)* scala mobile.

slight [slaɪt] **1** *adj* (**-er, -est**) (**a**) *(person: slim)* minuto(a); *(: frail)* gracile, delicato(a). (**b**) *(trivial: cold)* leggero(a); *(: error)* piccolo(a); **a ~ pain in the arm** un leggero dolore al braccio. (**c**) *(small)* piccolo(a), leggero(a); **a ~ improvement** un piccolo miglioramento; **there's not the ~est possibility** non c'è la minima possibilità; **there's not the ~est danger** non c'è il minimo pericolo; **not in the ~est** per nulla, niente affatto. **2** *n* offesa, affronto. **3** *vt (person)* snobbare.

slight·ing ['slaɪtɪŋ] *adj* offensivo(a).

slight·ly ['slaɪtlɪ] *adv* (**a**) *(better, nervous)* leggermente; **I know her ~** la conosco appena. (**b**): **~ built** esile.

slim [slɪm] **1** *adj* (**-mer, -mest**) (**a**) *(figure, person)* magro(a), snello(a); *(ankle, wrist, book)* sottile. (**b**) *(fig: resources)* scarso(a), magro(a); *(: evidence)* insufficiente; *(: excuse)* povero(a); *(: hope)* poco(a); **his chances are pretty ~** le sue possibilità sono molto scarse. **2** *vi* dimagrire.

slime [slaɪm] *n (mud)* melma, limo; *(sticky substance)* sostanza viscida; *(of snail)* bava.

slim·ming ['slɪmɪŋ] *adj (diet, pills)* dimagrante; *(food)* ipocalorico(a).

slimy ['slaɪmɪ] *adj* (**-ier, -iest**) *(also fig: person)* viscido(a); *(covered with mud)* melmoso(a).

sling [slɪŋ] *(vb: pt, pp* **slung***)* **1** *n (weapon)* fionda; *(catapult)* catapulta; *(Med)* fascia; **to have one's arm in a ~** avere un braccio al collo. **2** *vt (throw)* scagliare; *(hang: hammock)* appendere; **to ~ over** *or* **across one's shoulder** *(rifle, load)* mettere in spalla; *(coat, shawl)* buttarsi sulle spalle.

♦ **sling out** *vt + adv (fam: object)* buttare via; *(: person)* buttare fuori, mettere alla porta.

slink [slɪŋk] *pt, pp* **slunk** *vi*: **to ~ away, to ~ off** svignarsela.

slinky ['slɪŋkɪ] *adj* (**-ier, -iest**) *(fam: dress)* aderente; *(: movement)* sinuoso(a).

slip [slɪp] **1** *n* (**a**) *(slide)* scivolone *m*; *(trip)* caduta, scivolone *m*; *(land~)* smottamento; **to give sb the ~** seminare qn, sfuggire a qn. (**b**) *(mistake)* errore *m*, sbaglio; *(moral)* sbaglio; **a ~ of the tongue** un lapsus linguae; **a ~ of the pen** un errore involontario nello scrivere; **a Freudian ~** un lapsus freudiano. **(c)** *(undergarment)* sottoveste *f*; *(pillow~)* federa. **(d)** *(paper)* bigliettino, talloncino; **a ~ of paper** un foglietto; **wages ~** foglio *m* paga *inv*; **a ~ of a girl** *(fig)* una ragazzina.

  2 *vi* **(a)** *(slide)* scivolare; **I ~ped** sono scivolato; **my foot ~ped** mi è scivolato un piede; **it ~ped from her hand** le sfuggì di mano; **to ~ into bad habits** prendere delle cattive abitudini; **it ~ped out that...** è saltato fuori che...; **he let (it) ~ that...** si è lasciato sfuggire che...; **to let a chance ~ by** lasciarsi scappare un'occasione; **you're ~ping** *(fig fam)* perdi colpi. **(b)** *(move quickly)*: **to ~ into/out of** spattoiolare dentro/fuori da; **to ~ away** *or* **off** filarsela, svignarsela; **to ~ out to the shops** fare una scappatina per la spesa; **to ~ into a dress** infilarsi un vestito; **the months/years have ~ped by** i mesi/gli anni sono passati.

  3 *vt* **(a)** *(slide)* far scivolare; **to ~ a coin into a slot** infilare una moneta in una fessura; **to ~ sb a fiver** allungare 5 sterline a qn; **to ~ an arm round sb's waist** mettere il braccio attorno alla vita di qn; **to ~ on a jumper** infilarsi un maglione; **to ~ sth in** inserire qc inaspettatamente; **a ~ped disc** *(Med)* un'ernia al disco. **(b)** *(escape)* sfuggire a; **the dog ~ped its collar** il cane si liberò dal collare; **it ~ped my memory** *or* **attention** mi è sfuggito.

  4 *cpd*: **~ road** *n* *(on motorway)* rampa di accesso.

♦ **slip up** *vi* *(fam)* sbagliarsi.

slip·knot [ˈslɪpnɒt] *n* nodo scorsoio.

slip-on [ˈslɪpɒn] *adj* *(gen)* comodo(a) da mettere; *(shoes)* senza allacciatura.

slip·per [ˈslɪpəʳ] *n* pantofola.

slip·pery [ˈslɪpərɪ] *adj* sdrucciolevole, scivoloso(a); *(fig pej: person)* viscido(a); **it's ~ underfoot** si scivola fuori; **he's as ~ as they come** *or* **as an eel** è un tipo viscido.

slips [slɪps] *npl*: **in the ~** *(Theatre)* tra le quinte; *(Naut)* sullo scalo.

slip·shod [ˈslɪpʃɒd] *adj* sciatto(a), trascurato(a).

slip·stream [ˈslɪpstriːm] *n* *(Aer)* risucchio.

slip-up [ˈslɪpʌp] *n* *(fam: mistake)* errore *m*.

slip·way [ˈslɪpweɪ] *n* *(Naut)* scalo.

slit [slɪt] *(vb: pt, pp* **slit**) **1** *n* *(opening)* fessura; *(cut)* taglio; *(tear)* strappo; *(in skirt)* spacco. **2** *vt* tagliare; **to ~ open** *(letter)* aprire; *(sack)* aprire con un taglio; **to ~ sb's throat** tagliare la gola a qn.

slith·er [ˈslɪðəʳ] *vi* *(person)* scivolare; *(snake)* strisciare; **he was ~ing about on the ice** avanzava slittando sul ghiaccio.

sliv·er [ˈslɪvəʳ] *n* *(of glass, wood)* scheggia; *(of cheese, sausage)* fettina.

slob [slɒb] *n* *(fam)* sciattone/a.

slob·ber [ˈslɒbəʳ] *vi* *(pej)* sbavare.

slog [slɒg] **1** *n* faticata; **it's a hard ~ to the top** è una faticaccia arrivare in cima. **2** *vi* **(a)** *(work)* faticare, sudare, sgobbare; **to ~ away at sth** sgobbare su qc. **(b)** *(walk etc)*: **to ~ along** avanzare a fatica; **we ~ged on for 8 kilometres** ci trascinammo per 8 chilometri. **3** *vt* *(ball, opponent)* colpire con forza.

slo·gan [ˈsləʊgən] *n* slogan *m inv*.

slog·ger [ˈslɒgəʳ] *n* *(hard worker)* sgobbone/a.

slop [slɒp] **1** *vi* *(also: ~ over)* traboccare, versarsi; **the water was ~ping about in the bucket** l'acqua quasi traboccava dal secchio. **2** *vt* versare, rovesciare.

slope [sləʊp] **1** *n* *(gen, of hill)* pendio; *(side of hill)* versante *m*; *(of roof)* pendenza; *(of floor)* inclina-

zione *f*; *(ski ~)* pista; **the car got stuck on a ~** la macchina si è bloccata su una salita. **2** *vi* *(path, roof, handwriting)* essere inclinato(a); **the garden ~s down to the stream** il giardino digrada verso il ruscello.

♦ **slope off** *vi + adv* *(fam)* filarsela, tagliare la corda.

slop·ing [ˈsləʊpɪŋ] *adj* inclinato(a).

slop·pi·ly [ˈslɒpɪlɪ] *adv* **(a)** *(carelessly)* con trascuratezza; **to dress ~** essere sciatto nel vestire. **(b)** *(sentimentally)* in modo sdolcinato.

slop·py [ˈslɒpɪ] *adj* (**-ier, -iest**) *(food)* brodoso(a); *(work etc)* trascurato(a); *(appearance, dress)* trasandato(a), sciatto(a); *(sentimental)* sdolcinato(a), svenevole.

slops [slɒps] *npl* *(for invalids)* pappetta; *(dirty water)* acqua sporca; *(: in teapot)* rimasugli *mpl*.

slosh [slɒʃ] *(fam)* **1** *vt* **(a)** *(liquid)* spargere; **to ~ some water over sth** gettare dell'acqua su qc. **(b)** *(hit: person)* colpire. **2** *vi*: **to ~ about in the puddles** sguazzare nelle pozzanghere.

sloshed [slɒʃt] *adj* *(fam)* ubriaco(a), sbronzo(a); **to get ~** prendere una sbornia *or* sbronza.

slot [slɒt] **1** *n* *(in machine etc)* fessura; *(groove)* scanalatura; *(fig: in time∧able, Radio, TV)* spazio. **2** *vt* *(object)* infilare; *(fig: activity, speech)* inserire. **3** *vi*: **to ~ (into)** inserirsi (in). **4** *cpd*: **~ machine** *n* *(for selling)* distributore *m* automatico; *(for amusement)* slot-machine *f inv*; **~ meter** *n* contatore a gettoni.

sloth [sləʊθ] *n* **(a)** *(vice)* pigrizia, accidia. **(b)** *(Zool)* bradipo.

sloth·ful [ˈsləʊθfʊl] *adj* pigro(a), indolente.

slouch [slaʊtʃ] *vi* *(when walking)* camminare dinoccolato(a); **don't ~!** raddrizza la schiena!, non stare con la schiena curva!; **to ~ in/out** trascinarsi dentro/fuori; **she was ~ing in a chair** era sprofondata in una poltrona.

slov·en·ly [ˈslʌvnlɪ] *adj* *(person)* trascurato(a), sciatto(a); *(work)* poco accurato(a).

slow [sləʊ] **1** *adj* (**-er, -est**) **(a)** *(gen)* lento(a); **at a ~ speed** a bassa velocità; **he's a ~ worker** lavora lentamente; **this car is ~er than my old one** questa macchina va più piano di quella che avevo; **to be ~ to act/decide** essere lento ad agire/a decidere; **to be ~ to anger** non arrabbiarsi facilmente.

  (b) *(of clock)*: **to be ~** essere *or* andare indietro; **my watch is 20 minutes ~** il mio orologio è indietro di 20 minuti.

  (c) *(person: stupid)* lento(a), tardo(a); **~ to understand/notice** tardo a capire/notare; **he's a bit ~ at maths** fa un po' di fatica in matematica.

  (d) *(boring, dull: film, play)* lento(a); *(: party)* poco movimentato(a); **life here is ~** qui la vita scorre lenta; **the game is very ~** il gioco è molto lento; **business is ~** *(Comm)* gli affari procedono a rilento.

  (e) *(slowing down movement: track, surface)* pesante; **the ~ lane** la corsia per il traffico lento; **bake for two hours in a ~ oven** cuocere per due ore a forno moderato; **in ~ motion** *(Cine)* al rallentatore.

  2 *adv* (**-er, -est**) lentamente; **to go ~** *(driver)* andare piano; *(in industrial dispute)* fare uno sciopero bianco; *(be cautious)* andare con i piedi di piombo; **'(go) ~'** 'rallentare'.

  3 *vt* *(also: ~ down, ~ up: progress, machine)* rallentare; *(: person)* far rallentare; *(: pace of novel etc)* rendere più lento(a); **the interruptions have ~ed us down** le interruzioni ci hanno fatto perdere tempo; **that car ~s up the traffic** quella macchina fa rallentare il traffico.

4 vi (also: ~ **down**, ~ **up**) rallentare; **production has ~ed to almost nothing** la produzione si è ridotta a livelli minimi.

slow-acting ['sləu,æktɪŋ] adj che agisce lentamente, ad azione lenta.

slow-coach ['sləukəutʃ] n (fam: dawdler) lumaca; (: dullard) testone/a.

slow·ly ['sləulɪ] adv lentamente; **to drive** ~ andare piano; ~ **but surely** lentamente ma sicuramente; **work is proceeding** ~ **but surely** il lavoro procede piano ma bene; **to go more** ~ rallentare.

slow·ness ['sləunɪs] n lentezza.

slow-witted [,sləu'wɪtɪd] adj tardo(a), ottuso(a).

slow·worm ['sləuwɜ:m] n orbettino.

sludge [slʌdʒ] n (mud, sediment) melma; (sewage) deposito di fognatura.

slug [slʌg] **1** n (Zool) lumaca, limaccia; (bullet) pallottola; (fam: blow) colpo; **a ~ of whisky** (fam) un goccio di whisky. **2** vt (fam: hit) colpire.

slug·gish ['slʌgɪʃ] adj (indolent) pigro(a), indolente; (slow-moving: river, engine, car, liver) lento(a); (: business, market, sales) stagnante, fiacco(a).

sluice [slu:s] **1** n (~gate) chiusa; (~way) canale m di chiusa. **2** vt: **to ~ down** or **out** lavare (con abbondante acqua).

slum [slʌm] **1** n (house) catapecchia, tugurio; **to live in the ~s** vivere nei quartieri bassi. **2** cpd: ~ **clearance (programme)** n risanamento edilizio.

slum·ber ['slʌmbə^r] **1** n (also: ~s) sonno. **2** vi dormire (tranquillamente).

slump [slʌmp] **1** n (gen) caduta, crollo; (in production, sales) calo, crollo; (economic) crisi f inv, depressione f; **the ~ in the price of copper** la caduta del prezzo del rame. **2** vi **(a)** (price etc) cadere, crollare; (production, sales) calare, diminuire; (fig: morale etc) abbassarsi. **(b)**: **to ~ into a chair** lasciarsi cadere su una sedia; **he was ~ed over the wheel** era curvo sul volante.

slung [slʌŋ] pt, pp of **sling**.

slunk [slʌŋk] pt, pp of **slink**.

slur [slɜ:^r] **1** n **(a)** (stigma) macchia; (insult) affronto; **to cast a ~ on sb** calunniare qn; **it's no ~ on him to say...** non è calunniarlo dire.... **(b)** (Mus) legatura. **2** vt (word etc) pronunciare in modo inarticolato; (Mus) legare; **his speech was ~red** si mangiava le parole.

slurp [slɜ:p] vt, vi (fam) bere rumorosamente.

slurred [slɜ:d] adj (pronunciation) inarticolato(a), disarticolato(a).

slush [slʌʃ] **1** n (melting snow, mud) poltiglia, fanghiglia; (fam: literature etc) letteratura etc sdolcinata. **2** cpd: ~ **fund** n fondi mpl neri.

slushy ['slʌʃɪ] adj (-ier, -iest) (snow) che si scioglie; (fam: poetry etc) sdolcinato(a).

slut [slʌt] n (immoral) puttana, sgualdrina; (dirty, untidy) sciattona.

sly [slaɪ] **1** adj (-ier, -iest) (wily) astuto(a), scaltro(a); (secretive) furtivo(a); (mischievous: trick) cattivello(a); (: smile) sornione(a), malizioso(a). **2** n: **on the** ~ di nascosto, di soppiatto.

sly·ly ['slaɪlɪ] adv (see adj) astutamente, scaltramente; furtivamente; (smile, wink) maliziosamente.

smack¹ [smæk] vi: **to ~ of** (fig: intrigue etc) puzzare di, sapere di.

smack² [smæk] **1** n (slap: on back) pacca; (: on face) schiaffo, ceffone m; (sound) colpo secco; (: of lips, whip) schiocco; **it was a ~ in the eye for them** è stato uno smacco per loro; **to give a child a ~** sculacciare un bambino; **to have a ~ at doing sth** (fig) provare a fare qc. **2** vt (child) sculacciare; (face) schiaffeggiare; **she ~ed the child's bot-** tom sculacciò il bambino; **to ~ one's lips** schioccare le labbra. **3** adv: **it fell ~ in the middle** (fam) cadde giusto nel mezzo; **she ran ~ into the door** andò a sbattere dritto contro la porta.

smack³ [smæk] n (also: fishing ~) barca da pesca.

small [smɔ:l] **1** adj (-er, -est) (gen: in size, number) piccolo(a); (: in height) basso(a); (stock, supply, population) scarso(a); (waist) sottile; (meal) leggero(a); (letter) minuscolo(a); (minor, unimportant) da poco, insignificante; (: increase, improvement) piccolo(a), leggero(a); **when we were** ~ quando eravamo piccoli; **there was only a** ~ **audience** c'era poco pubblico; **this house makes the other one look** ~ questa casa fa sembrare piccola l'altra; **the ~est possible number of books** il minor numero di libri possibile; **the ~est details** i minimi dettagli; **to have a ~ appetite** avere poco or scarso appetito; **in a ~ voice** con un filo di voce; **to feel** ~ (fig) sentirsi umiliato or sminuito; **to get** or **grow ~er** (stain, town) rimpicciolire; (debt, organization, numbers) ridursi; **to make ~er** (amount, income) ridurre; (garden, object, garment) rimpicciolire; **to have ~ hope of success** avere scarse speranze di successo; **to have ~ cause** or **reason to do sth** non avere molti motivi per fare qc; **to start in a ~ way** cominciare da poco; **a ~ shopkeeper** un piccolo negoziante.

2 n: ~ **of the back** reni fpl; ~**s** (fam: underwear) biancheria intima.

3 adv: **to cut sth up** ~ tagliare finemente qc.

4 cpd: ~ **ad** n piccolo annuncio; ~ **arms** npl armi fpl portatili or leggere; ~ **change** n moneta, spiccioli mpl; ~ **hours** npl ore fpl piccole; ~ **print** n caratteri mpl piccoli; (in contract etc) parte f scritta in piccolo; **the ~ screen** (TV) il piccolo schermo; ~ **talk** n conversazione f mondana.

small·holding ['smɔ:l,həuldɪŋ] n piccola tenuta.

small·ish ['smɔ:lɪʃ] adj piccolino(a).

small·minded [,smɔ:l'maɪndɪd] adj meschino(a).

small·ness ['smɔ:lnɪs] n (gen) piccolezza; (of person) bassa statura; (of income, sum) scarsità.

small·pox ['smɔ:lpɒks] n (Med) vaiolo.

small-scale ['smɔ:lskeɪl] adj (map, model) in scala ridotta; (business, farming) modesto(a).

small-time ['smɔ:ltaɪm] adj (fam) da poco; **a** ~ **criminal** un piccolo delinquente; **a** ~ **thief** un ladro di polli.

small-town ['smɔ:ltaun] adj (pej) provinciale.

smarmy ['smɑ:mɪ] adj (-ier, -iest) (fam) untuoso(a), servile.

smart [smɑ:t] **1** adj (-er, -est) **(a)** (elegant) elegante, chic inv; (fashionable) di moda; **the ~ set** il bel mondo; **to look** ~ essere elegante; **that's a ~ car** è una bella macchina. **(b)** (bright) intelligente, brillante; (quick-witted) sveglio(a), furbo(a); **that was pretty ~ of you!** che furbo!; ~ **work by the police led to...** una brillante operazione della polizia ha portato a.... **(c)** (quick: pace, action) svelto(a), rapido(a); **look ~ about it!** sbrigati!, spicciati! **2** vi **(a)** (cut, graze etc) bruciare; **my eyes are ~ing** mi bruciano gli occhi. **(b)** (fig): **she's still ~ing from his remarks** le bruciano ancora le sue osservazioni; **to ~ under an insult/ a reproof** soffrire per un insulto/un rimprovero.

smart aleck ['smɑ:t,ælɪk] n (fam) sapientone/a.

smart·en ['smɑ:tn] **1** vt (also: ~ up: room, house etc) abbellire, ravvivare; (: child) far bello(a); (: o.s.) farsi bello(a); **to ~ up one's ideas** darsi una mossa. **2** vi (also: ~ up) abbellirsi.

smart·ly ['smɑ:tlɪ] adv (elegantly) elegantemente; (cleverly) con arguzia or intelligenza; (quickly: walk) velocemente; (: answer) con prontezza.

smart·ness ['smɑ:tnɪs] *n (see adv)* eleganza; intelligenza; velocità; prontezza.

smash [smæʃ] **1** *n (sound)* fracasso; *(collision)* scontro; *(Tennis etc)* schiacciata, smash *m inv; (powerful blow)* pugno; *(Fin)* crollo; **he died in a car ~** morì in un incidente automobilistico; **the ~ of plates** il rumore di piatti rotti.

2 *vt (break)* rompere; *(shatter)* infrangere, frantumare; *(defeat: enemy, opponent)* schiacciare; *(: record)* polverizzare; *(wreck, also fig)* distruggere; *(Tennis etc)* schiacciare; **he ~ed it against the wall** lo scagliò contro la parete; **we will ~ this crime ring** distruggeremo quest'organizzazione criminale; **he ~ed his way out of the building** uscì dall'edificio abbattendo gli ostacoli.

3 *vi (break)* rompersi, andare in frantumi; **the car ~ed into the wall** la macchina andò a sbattere contro il muro.

♦ **smash down** *vt + adv (door)* abbattere.

♦ **smash in** *vt + adv (door, window)* abbattere; **to ~ one's way in** entrare di forza; **to ~ sb's face in** *(fam)* spaccare la faccia a qn.

♦ **smash up** *vt + adv (car)* sfasciare; *(room)* distruggere.

smash·er ['smæʃəʳ] *n:* **she's a ~** *(in appearance)* è una bomba; *(in character)* è fantastica.

smash-hit [,smæʃ'hɪt] *n* successone *m.*

smash·ing ['smæʃɪŋ] *adj (fam)* meraviglioso(a), bellissimo(a); **we had a ~ time** ci siamo divertiti come pazzi.

smat·ter·ing ['smætərɪŋ] *n:* **to have a ~ of** avere un'infarinatura di.

smear [smɪəʳ] **1** *n* traccia; *(dirty mark, also fig)* macchia; *(insult)* calunnia; *(Med)* striscio. **2** *vt* **(a)** *(butter etc)* spalmare; **to ~ cream on one's hands, to ~ one's hands with cream** spalmarsi le mani di crema. **(b)** *(make dirty)* sporcare; *(smudge: ink, paint)* sbavare; **the page was ~ed** c'erano delle sbavature sulla pagina; **his hands were ~ed with oil/ink** aveva le mani sporche di olio/inchiostro. **(c)** *(fig: libel)* calunniare, diffamare. **3** *vi (paint, ink etc)* sbavare. **4** *cpd:* **~ campaign** *n* campagna diffamatoria; **~ test** *n (Med)* Pap-test *m inv.*

smell [smɛl] *(vb: pt, pp* **smelled** *or* **smelt) 1** *n* **(a)** *(sense of ~)* olfatto, odorato; *(animal, fig)* fiuto; **to have a keen sense of ~** avere l'olfatto sviluppato; *(animal)* avere un fiuto finissimo. **(b)** *(odour)* odore *m; (: pleasant)* profumo; *(stench)* puzzo; **it has a nice ~** ha un buon odore; **there's a strong ~ of gas here** c'è un forte puzzo di gas qui.

2 *vt (gas, cooking)* sentire odore di; *(rose, milk)* annusare; **to ~ something burning** sentire odore di bruciato; **to ~ danger** *(fig)* fiutare un pericolo; **I ~ a rat** *(fig)* qui gatta ci cova.

3 *vi (pleasantly)* sapere, odorare; *(unpleasantly)* puzzare; **my fingers ~ of garlic** ho le dita che puzzano di aglio; **it ~s like chicken** odora di pollo; **it ~s good** ha un buon odore; **it ~s damp in here** c'è un odore di umidità qui dentro; **his breath ~s** gli puzza l'alito.

♦ **smell out** *vt + adv* **(a)** *(animal, also fig)* fiutare. **(b): your feet ~ the room out!** i tuoi piedi appestano la stanza!

smell·ing ['smɛlɪŋ] *adj:* **~ salts** sali *mpl.*

smelly ['smɛlɪ] *adj (-ier, -iest) (fam)* puzzolente; **it's ~ in here** qui c'è puzza.

smelt¹ [smɛlt] *pt, pp of* **smell.**

smelt² [smɛlt] *vt (ore)* fondere.

smile [smaɪl] **1** *n* sorriso; **she said with a ~** disse sorridendo; **with a ~ on one's lips** col sorriso sulle labbra; **to be all ~s** essere raggiante, avere il volto ridente; **to give sb a ~** sorridere a qn; **I'll**

soon wipe the ~ off your face! ti faccio io passare la voglia di ridere! **2** *vi* sorridere; **to ~ at sb/sth** sorridere a qn/qc; **to keep smiling** continuare a sorridere; *(fig)* conservare l'allegria; **fortune ~d on him** la fortuna gli arrise. **3** *vt:* **he ~d his appreciation** sorrise in segno di apprezzamento.

smil·ing ['smaɪlɪŋ] *adj* sorridente.

smirk [smɜ:k] **1** *n (affected)* sorriso affettato; *(self-satisfied)* sorriso compiaciuto; *(knowing)* sorriso furbo. **2** *vi (see n)* sorridere in modo affettato; sorridere compiaciuto(a); fare un sorriso furbo.

smite [smaɪt] *pt* **smote,** *pp* **smitten** *vt (old: strike)* colpire; *(: punish)* punire.

smith [smɪθ] *n* fabbro.

smith·er·eens [,smɪðə'ri:nz] *npl:* **to be smashed to ~** andare in (mille) frantumi.

smithy ['smɪðɪ] *n* fucina.

smit·ten ['smɪtn] **1** *pp of* **smite. 2** *adj pred:* **to be ~ with** *(remorse, desire, fear)* essere preso(a) da; *(idea)* entusiasmarsi per; **to be ~ (with sb)** avere una cotta (per qn); **to be ~ with flu** essere colpito dall'influenza.

smock [smɒk] *n (blouse)* blusa; *(to protect clothing)* grembiule *m.*

smock·ing ['smɒkɪŋ] *n* ricamo a nido d'ape.

smog [smɒg] *n* smog *m inv.*

smoke [sməʊk] **1** *n* **(a)** fumo; **there's no ~ without fire** non c'è fumo senza fuoco; **to go up in ~** *(house etc)* bruciare, andare distrutto dalle fiamme; *(fig)* andare in fumo. **(b)** *(cigarette etc):* **to have a ~** fare una fumatina. **2** *vt* **(a)** *(tobacco)* fumare. **(b)** *(bacon, fish, cheese)* affumicare. **3** *vi (gen)* fumare; *(chimney)* fare fumo; **do you ~?** fumi? **4** *cpd:* **~ bomb** *n* bomba fumogena; **~ ring** *n:* **to blow ~ rings** fare anelli di fumo; **~ screen** *n (Mil)* cortina fumogena *or* di fumo; *(fig)* copertura; **~ signal** *n* segnale *m* di fumo.

♦ **smoke out** *vt + adv (insects etc)* snidare col fumo.

smoked [sməʊkt] *adj (bacon, fish, etc)* affumicato(a); **~ glass** vetro fumé *or* affumicato.

smoke·less ['sməʊklɪs] *adj:* **~ fuel** carburante *m* che non dà fumo; **~ zone** zona dove sono vietati gli scarichi di fumo.

smok·er ['sməʊkəʳ] *n (person)* fumatore/trice; *(railway carriage)* carrozza (per) fumatori; **~'s cough** tosse *f* da fumo.

smok·ing ['sməʊkɪŋ] **1** *adj* fumante. **2** *n* fumo; **'no ~'** 'vietato fumare'; **he's given up ~** ha smesso di fumare; **~ can damage your health** il fumo può danneggiare la salute. **3** *cpd:* **~ compartment** *n, (Am)* **~ car** *n* carrozza (per) fumatori; **~ jacket** *n* giacca da casa.

smoky ['sməʊkɪ] *adj (-ier, -iest) (chimney, fire)* fumoso(a), che fa fumo; *(room, atmosphere)* fumoso(a), pieno(a) di fumo; *(flavour, surface etc)* affumicato(a).

smol·der ['sməʊldəʳ] *vi (Am)* = **smoulder.**

smooch [smu:tʃ] *vi (fam)* sbaciucchiarsi, pomiciare.

smooth [smu:ð] **1** *adj (-er, -est)* **(a)** *(surface, skin)* liscio(a); *(chin: hairless)* imberbe; *(sea)* liscio(a), calmo(a). **(b)** *(in consistency: paste etc)* omogeneo(a). **(c)** *(movement, breathing, pulse)* regolare; *(landing, take-off, flight)* senza scosse; *(crossing, trip, life)* tranquillo(a). **(d)** *(not harsh: cigarette)* leggero(a); *(: drink)* dal gusto morbido; *(: voice, sound)* dolce. **(e)** *(pej: person)* mellifluo(a); **he's a ~ operator** ci sa fare; **he's a ~ talker** è un parlatore astuto. **2** *vt* **(a)** *(also: ~* **down:** *hair etc)* lisciare; **to ~ the way for sb** *(fig)* spianare la strada a qn. **(b)** *(stone, wood)* levigare; **to ~ away**

wrinkles far sparire le rughe. **(c):** to ~ **cream into one's face** massaggiarsi la crema sul viso.
♦ **smooth out** *vt + adv (fabric, creases)* lisciare, spianare; *(fig: difficulty)* appianare.
♦ **smooth over** *vt + adv:* to ~ **things over** *(fig)* sistemare le cose.

smooth·ly ['smuːðlɪ] *adv (easily)* liscio; *(gently)* dolcemente; *(move)* senza scosse; *(talk)* in modo mellifluo; **the car is running** ~ la macchina cammina bene; **everything went** ~ tutto andò liscio.

smooth·ness ['smuːðnɪs] *n (of stone, wood)* levigatezza; *(of skin)* morbidezza; *(of sauce)* omogeneità; *(of sea)* calma; *(of trip, life)* tranquillità; *(of manner)* mellifluità.

smote [sməʊt] *pt of* smite.

smoth·er ['smʌðəʳ] *vt* **(a)** *(stifle)* soffocare. **(b)** *(cover)* coprire; **fruit** ~ed **in cream** frutta ricoperta di panna.

smoul·der, *(Am)* **smol·der** ['sməʊldəʳ] *vi (fire)* covare sotto la cenere; *(fig: passion etc)* covare.

smudge [smʌdʒ] **1** *n* sbavatura. **2** *vt* sporcare. **3** *vi* sbavare.

smug [smʌg] *adj* (**-ger**, **-gest**) compiaciuto(a).

smug·gle ['smʌgl] *vt (tobacco, drugs)* portare di contrabbando; **to** ~ **in/out** *(goods etc)* far entrare/ uscire di contrabbando; *(fig: person, letter etc)* far entrare/uscire di nascosto; **to** ~ **sth past** *or* **through Customs** passare la dogana con qc senza dichiararlo.

smug·gler ['smʌgləʳ] *n* contrabbandiere/a.

smug·gling ['smʌglɪŋ] *n* contrabbando.

smug·ly ['smʌglɪ] *adv* con sufficienza, con compiacimento.

smut [smʌt] *n (grain of soot)* granello di fuliggine; *(mark)* segno nero; *(in conversation etc)* sconcezze *fpl*.

smut·ty ['smʌtɪ] *adj* (**-ier**, **-iest**) *(dirty)* sporco(a), sudicio(a); *(crude)* osceno(a), sconcio(a).

snack [snæk] **1** *n* spuntino; **to have a** ~ fare uno spuntino. **2** *cpd:* ~ **bar** *n* snack-bar *m inv*, tavola calda.

sna·fu [snæ'fuː] *adj (Am fam)* confuso(a).

snag [snæg] *n (pulled thread)* filo tirato; *(difficulty)* intralcio, intoppo; **the** ~ **is that...** il guaio è che...; **what's the** ~? qual è il problema?; **to run into** *or* **hit a** ~ incontrare una difficoltà, trovare un intoppo.

snail [sneɪl] *n* chiocciola; **at a** ~**'s pace** a passo di lumaca.

snake [sneɪk] *n* serpente *m;* ~ **in the grass** *(fig)* traditore/trice. **2** *cpd:* ~ **charmer** *n* incantatore *m* di serpenti; ~s **and ladders** *n* ≃ gioco dell'oca.

snake·bite ['sneɪkbaɪt] *n* morso di serpente.

snake·skin ['sneɪkskɪn] **1** *n* serpente *m.* **2** *cpd (bag, shoes)* di serpente.

snap [snæp] **1** *n* **(a)** *(sound: of sth breaking, closing)* colpo secco; *(: of fingers)* schiocco; *(also:* ~ **fastener)** automatico; **a cold** ~ *(fam)* un'improvvisa ondata di freddo; **the dog made a** ~ **at the biscuit** il cane ha cercato di afferrare il biscotto. **(b)** *(*~*shot)* istantanea. **(c)** *(Cards)* rubamazzo.

2 *adj attr (sudden: strike)* improvviso(a); *(: decision, answer, judgment)* su due piedi.

3 *vt* **(a)** *(break)* rompere (con un colpo secco). **(b)** *(fingers)* schioccare; **to** ~ **one's fingers at sb/sth** *(fig)* infischiarsi di qn/qc; **to** ~ **a box shut** chiudere una scatola di colpo. **(c):** 'be quiet!', she ~ped 'sta' zitto!', disse bruscamente. **(d)** *(Phot)* fotografare, scattare un'istantanea di.

4 *vi* **(a)** *(break: elastic)* rompersi. **(b)** *(whip)* schioccare; **it** ~ped **shut** si chiuse con un colpo secco; **to** ~ **back into place** scattare di nuovo a

posto; **everything** ~ped **into place** *(fig)* tutto fu chiaro. **(c):** to ~ **at sb** *(dog)* cercare di mordere qn; *(person)* rivolgersi a qn con tono brusco.
♦ **snap off** *vt + adv* rompere (con un colpo secco); **to** ~ **sb's head off** *(fig)* rispondere male a qn.
♦ **snap out 1** *vi + adv:* ~ **out of it!** *(fam)* datti una scrollata! **2** *vt + adv (order etc)* dare bruscamente.
♦ **snap up** *vt + adv:* **to** ~ **up a bargain** *(fig)* prendere un affare al volo.

snap·dragon ['snæp,drægən] *n (Bot)* antirrino.

snap·pish ['snæpɪʃ] *adj* irritabile, bisbetico(a).

snap·py ['snæpɪ] *adj* (**-ier**, **-iest**) *(fam: slogan, answer)* d'effetto; *(: conversation)* vivace; *(: smart)* elegante; **he's a** ~ **dresser** è molto elegante nel vestire; **make it** ~! sbrigati!, svelto!

snap·shot ['snæpʃɒt] *n (Phot)* istantanea.

snare [snɛəʳ] **1** *n* trappola. **2** *vt* prendere in trappola, intrappolare.

snarl[1] [snɑːl] **1** *n* ringhio. **2** *vi:* to ~ **(at sb)** ringhiare (a qn).

snarl[2] [snɑːl] **1** *n (in wool etc)* garbuglio. **2** *vt:* **to get** ~ed **up** *(wool, plans)* ingarbugliarsi; *(traffic)* intasarsi.

snarl-up ['snɑːlʌp] *n (of traffic)* intasamento.

snatch [snætʃ] **1** *n* **(a)** *(act of* ~*ing):* **to make a** ~ **at sth** cercare di afferrare qc. **(b)** *(fam: theft)* furto; *(: kidnapping)* rapimento; **there was a wages** ~ dei ladri hanno rubato le paghe. **(c)** *(snippet)* pezzo; ~es **of conversation** frammenti *mpl* di conversazione; **to sleep in** ~es dormire a intervalli. **2** *vt (grab: object)* afferrare; *(: opportunity)* cogliere; *(: few days, short break)* prendersi; *(steal, also fig: kiss)* rubare; *(kidnap)* rapire, portar via; **to** ~ **a sandwich** mangiarsi in fretta un panino; **to** ~ **some sleep** riuscire a dormire un po'; **to** ~ **a knife out of sb's hand** strappare di mano un coltello a qn. **3** *vi:* **don't** ~! non strappare le cose di mano!; **to** ~ **at** *(object)* cercare di afferrare; *(opportunity)* cogliere (al volo).
♦ **snatch away** *vt + adv:* **to** ~ **sth away from sb** strappare qc a qn.
♦ **snatch up** *vt + adv* raccogliere in fretta, afferrare.

sneak [sniːk] **1** *vt:* **to** ~ **sth out of a place** portare fuori qc di nascosto da un luogo; **to** ~ **a look at sth** guardare di soppiatto qc; **to** ~ **a quick cigarette** fumarsi una sigaretta di nascosto. **2** *vi* **(a):** **to** ~ **in/out** entrare/uscire di nascosto *or* di soppiatto; **to** ~ **away** *or* **off** allontanarsi di nascosto *or* di soppiatto; **to** ~ **off with sth** portare via di soppiatto qc. **(b):** **to** ~ **on sb** *(fam)* fare la spia a qn. **3** *n (fam: tale-teller)* spione/a. **4** *cpd:* ~ **thief** *n* ladruncolo/a.

sneak·ers ['sniːkəz] *npl (Am)* scarpe *fpl* da ginnastica.

sneak·ing ['sniːkɪŋ] *adj (dislike, preference)* segreto(a); **to have a** ~ **dislike of sb** provare una segreta antipatia per qn; **to have a** ~ **feeling/ suspicion that...** avere la vaga impressione/il vago sospetto che... .

sneaky ['sniːkɪ] *adj* (**-ier**, **-iest**) *(fam)* vile.

sneer [snɪəʳ] **1** *n (expression)* sogghigno; *(remark)* commento sarcastico. **2** *vi* sogghignare; **to** ~ **at sb/sth** farsi beffe di qn/qc.

sneeze [sniːz] **1** *n* starnuto. **2** *vi* starnutire; **an offer not to be** ~d **at** *(fig)* un'offerta da non trascurare.

snide [snaɪd] *adj (fam)* maligno(a).

sniff [snɪf] **1** *n:* **to have a** ~ **of sth** annusare qc; **one** ~ **of this is enough to kill you** se uno annusa questo è morto; **he gave a** ~ **of contempt** ha arricciato il naso con disprezzo. **2** *vt (gen)* annusare; *(glue, drug)* sniffare; *(inhalant)* fare

inalazioni di. 3 *vi (person)* tirare su col naso; *(: disdainfully)* arricciare il naso.

♦ **sniff at** *vi + prep* annusare; **it's not to be ~ed at** non è da disprezzare.

♦ **sniff out** *vt + adv* fiutare; *(fig)* fiutare, subodorare.

snif·fle ['snɪfl] = **snuffle**.

snif·ter ['snɪftər] *n (fam: of whisky etc)* goccio, goccetto.

snig·ger ['snɪgər] **1** *n* risolino. **2** *vi* ridacchiare, ridere sotto i baffi; **to ~ at** ridere sotto i baffi per.

snip [snɪp] **1** *n (cut)* taglio; *(small piece)* ritaglio; *(fam: bargain)* affare *m*, occasione *f*; **with a ~ of the scissors** con un colpo di forbici. **2** *vt* tagliare; **to ~ sth off** tagliare via qc.

snipe [snaɪp] **1** *n, pl inv (bird)* beccaccino. **2** *vt*: **to ~ at sb** sparare a qn da un nascondiglio; *(fig)* lanciare frecciatine a qn.

snip·er ['snaɪpər] *n* franco tiratore *m*, cecchino.

snip·pet ['snɪpɪt] *n (of cloth, paper)* ritaglio; *(of information, conversation etc)* frammento.

snitch [snɪtʃ] *vi*: **to ~ on sb** *(fam)* fare la spia a qn.

sniv·el ['snɪvl] *vi* piagnucolare, frignare.

sniv·el·ling ['snɪvlɪŋ] *adj* piagnucoloso(a).

snob [snɒb] *n* snob *m/f inv*; **he's an intellectual ~** è uno snob in fatto di cultura.

snob·bery ['snɒbərɪ] *n* snobismo.

snob·bish ['snɒbɪʃ] *adj* snob *inv*.

snook [snuːk] *n (fam)*: **to cock a ~ at sb** *(fig)* prendere in giro qn.

snook·er ['snuːkər] **1** *n* ≈ bigliardo *(con palle colorate)*. **2** *vt*: **to be properly ~ed** *(fig fam)* essere in un bel pasticcio.

snoop [snuːp] **1** *n (act)*: **to have a ~ round** curiosare. **2** *vi (also: ~ about, ~ around)* curiosare; **to ~ into sb's affairs** ficcare il naso negli affari di qn; **to ~ on sb** spiare qn.

snoop·er ['snuːpər] *n* ficcanaso *m/f*.

snooty ['snuːtɪ] *adj (-ier, -iest) (fam)* altezzoso(a).

snooze [snuːz] **1** *n* sonnellino, pisolino; **to have a ~** fare un sonnellino, schiacciare un pisolino. **2** *vi* sonnecchiare.

snore [snɔːr] **1** *n*: **to give a loud ~** russare sonoramente. **2** *vi* russare.

snor·kel ['snɔːkl] *n (of submarine)* presa d'aria; *(of swimmer)* respiratore *m* a tubo.

snort [snɔːt] **1** *n* sbuffata, sbuffo. **2** *vi (horse, person)* sbuffare; **to ~ with laughter** soffocare dalle risate.

snort·er ['snɔːtər] *n (fam)* **(a): a real ~ of a problem** un bel rompicapo. **(b)** *(drink)* bicchierino, goccio.

snot [snɒt] *n (fam)* moccio.

snot·ty ['snɒtɪ] *adj (-ier, -iest) (fam)* moccioso(a); *(: fig: snooty)* sprezzante.

snout [snaʊt] *n (of animal)* muso; *(: of pig)* grugno.

snow [snəʊ] **1** *n* **(a)** neve *f*; *(~fall)* nevicata; *(fam: cocaine)* coca. **(b)** *(on TV screen)* puntini *mpl*. **2** *vt*: **to be ~ed in** *or* **up** essere isolato(a) a causa della neve; **to be ~ed under with work** essere sommerso di lavoro. **3** *vi* nevicare. **4** *cpd*: **~ blindness** *n (Med)* amblíopía da riflesso della neve; **~ report** *n (Met)* bollettino della neve.

snow·ball ['snəʊbɔːl] **1** *n* palla di neve. **2** *vi (fig: scheme, appeal)* crescere a vista d'occhio.

snow·bound ['snəʊbaʊnd] *adj (village)* isolato(a) dalla neve; *(person, road)* bloccato(a) dalla neve; *(countryside)* coperto(a) dalla neve.

snow-capped ['snəʊkæpt] *adj (mountain)* con la cima coperta di neve; *(peak)* coperto(a) di neve.

snow-covered ['snəʊ,kʌvəd] *adj* coperto(a) di neve.

snow·drift ['snəʊdrɪft] *n* cumulo di neve.

snow·drop ['snəʊdrɒp] *n* bucaneve *m inv*.

snow·fall ['snəʊfɔːl] *n (fall of snow)* nevicata; *(amount that falls)* neve *f* caduta.

snow·flake ['snəʊfleɪk] *n* fiocco di neve.

snow·man ['snəʊmæn] *n, pl* **-men** pupazzo di neve; **the abominable ~** l'abominevole uomo delle nevi.

snow·plough, **(Am)** **snow·plow** ['snəʊplaʊ] *n* spazzaneve *m inv*.

snow·shoe ['snəʊʃuː] *n* racchetta da neve.

snow·storm ['snəʊstɔːm] *n* tormenta, tempesta di neve.

snow-white [,snəʊ'waɪt] *adj* candido(a).

snowy ['snəʊɪ] *adj (-ier, -iest) (climate, region, day etc)* nevoso(a); *(hills, roof)* innevato(a); *(white as snow)* candido(a), niveo(a); **it's been very ~ recently** ha nevicato molto di recente.

snub [snʌb] **1** *n* affronto, offesa. **2** *vt (person)* snobbare.

snub-nosed [,snʌb'nəʊzd] *adj* camuso(a).

snuff [snʌf] *n* tabacco da fiuto; **to take ~** fiutare tabacco. **2** *vt (also: ~ out: candle)* spegnere; **to ~ it** *(fam)* tirare le cuoia.

snuff·box ['snʌfbɒks] *n* tabacchiera.

snuf·fle ['snʌfl] **1** *n*: **I've got a ~** mi cola il naso; **I've got the ~s** ho il raffreddore. **2** *vi* tirare su col naso.

snug [snʌg] *adj (-ger, -gest) (cosy: room)* accogliente; *(safe: harbour)* sicuro(a); *(fitting closely)* attillato(a); **warm and ~ by the fire** accoccolato vicino al fuoco; **to be ~ in bed** essere al calduccio nel letto.

snug·gle ['snʌgl] *vi*: **to ~ down in bed** accovacciarsi nel letto; **to ~ up to sb** stringersi a qn.

snug·ly ['snʌglɪ] *adv* comodamente; **it fits ~** *(object in pocket etc)* entra giusto giusto; *(garment)* sta ben attillato.

so [səʊ] **1** *adv* **(a)** *(in comparisons: before adj and adv)* così; **~ quickly** *(early)* così presto; *(fast)* così forte; **it is ~ big that...** è così grosso che...; **it was ~ much more difficult than I expected** era tanto più difficile di quanto pensassi; **she's not ~ clever as him** lei non è intelligente come lui; **he's not ~ foolish as I thought** non è così scemo come pensavo; **I wish you weren't ~ clumsy** vorrei che tu non fossi così maldestro.

(b) *(very)* così; **~ much** tanto; **~ many** tanti; **I love you ~ (much)** ti amo tanto; **I'm ~ worried** sono così preoccupato; **I'm ~ glad to see you again** sono così felice di rivederti; **I've got ~ much to do** ho tanto da fare; **I've got ~ much to do that...** ho così tanto da fare che...; **thank you ~ much** grazie infinite *or* mille.

(c) *(thus, in this way, likewise)* così, in questo modo; **the article is ~ written as to...** l'articolo è scritto in modo da...; **if ~** se è così, quand'è così; **he likes things just ~** gli piacciono le cose fatte a puntino; **you did ~!** sì che l'hai fatto!; **~ do I** anch'io; **he's wrong and ~ are you** lui si sbaglia e tu pure; **and ~ forth, and ~ on** e così via; **~ it is!, ~ it does!** davvero!; **it ~ happens that...** si dà il caso che... **+ sub**; **while she was ~ doing** mentre lo stava facendo; **you should do it ~** dovresti farlo così; **I hope ~** lo spero; **I think ~** penso di sì; **~ he says** così dice; **~ to speak** per così dire; **don't worry ~** non preoccuparti così tanto; **I told you ~** te l'avevo detto; **~ saying he walked away** così dicendo se ne andò; **do ~** fallo.

(d) *(phrases)*: **she didn't ~ much as send me a birthday card** non mi ha neanche mandato un biglietto di auguri per il compleanno; **I haven't ~ much as a penny** non ho neanche una lira; **~**

much for her promises! a fidarsi delle sue promesse!; **at ~ much per week** a un tot alla settimana; **ten or ~** circa dieci; **just ~!, quite ~!** esattamente!; **even ~** comunque; **~ long!** *(fam)* ciao!, ci vediamo!

2 *conj* **(a)** *(expressing purpose):* **~ as to do sth** in modo *or* così da fare qc; **we hurried ~ as not to be late** ci affrettammo per non fare tardi; **~ (that)** affinché + *sub*, perché + *sub*; **I bought it ~ that you should see it** l'ho comperato perché tu lo vedessi; **~ as to prevent cheating** così da evitare imbrogli.

(b) *(expressing result):* **it was raining and ~ we could not go out** pioveva e così non potemmo uscire; **as her French improved ~ did her confidence** man mano che il suo francese è migliorato ha acquistato più sicurezza; **~ you see...** così vedi... .

(c) *(in questions, exclamations):* **~ you're Spanish?** e così sei spagnolo?; **~ that's the reason!** allora è questo il motivo!, ecco perché!; **~ there you are!** ah eccoti qua!; **~ there!** ben ti sta!; **~ (what)?** *(fam)* e allora?, e con questo?

soak [səuk] **1** *vt* **(a)** *(bread etc)* inzuppare; *(clothes)* mettere a mollo; **to get ~ed (to the skin)** inzupparsi *or* bagnarsi (fino alle ossa); **to be ~ed through** essere bagnato fradicio. **(b)** *(fam):* **to ~ the rich** mungere i ricchi. **2** *vi* *(clothes)* essere a mollo; **to leave sth to ~** lasciare qc in ammollo. **3** *n (fam: drunkard)* ubriacone/a.

♦ **soak in** *vi + adv* penetrare; **it took a long time to ~ in** *(fig)* ci è voluto tanto prima che mi *(or* gli *etc)* entrasse in testa.

♦ **soak up** *vt + adv (liquid)* assorbire; *(information)* raccogliere.

soak·ing (wet) ['səukɪŋ('wɛt)] *adj* fradicio(a).

so-and-so ['səuənsəu] *n (somebody)* un tale; **Mr/ Mrs ~** *(fam)* signor/signora tal dei tali; **he's a ~!** *(fam)* che tipo odioso che è!

soap [səup] **1** *n* sapone *m; (cake of ~)* saponetta; **soft ~** *(fam)* lusinghe *fpl*. **2** *vt* insaponare. **3** *cpd:* **~ opera** *n* telenovella; **~ powder** *n* detersivo (in polvere).

soap·box ['səupbɒks] *n* palco improvvisato.

soap·flakes ['səupfleɪks] *npl* sapone *m* in scaglie.

soap·suds ['səupsʌdz] *npl* saponata.

soapy ['səupɪ] *adj* **(-ier, -iest)** *(covered in soap: person)* insaponato(a); *(: water)* saponato(a); *(like soap)* saponoso(a); **to taste ~** sapere di sapone.

soar [sɔːʳ] *vi* **(a)** *(rise: bird)* librarsi, *(: plane, ball)* volare. **(b)** *(fig: tower etc)* elevarsi, ergersi; *(: price, morale, spirits)* salire alle stelle; *(: ambitions, hopes)* aumentare notevolmente.

soar·ing ['sɔːrɪŋ] *adj (flight)* altissimo(a); *(building)* slanciato(a); *(prices)* salito(a) alle stelle; *(hopes, imagination)* ardito(a); **~ inflation** inflazione *f* galoppante.

sob [sɒb] **1** *n* singhiozzo. **2** *vi* singhiozzare. **3** *vt:* **to ~ one's heart out** piangere disperatamente. **4** *cpd:* **~ story** *n (fam)* storia lacrimosa.

so·ber ['səubəʳ] **1** *adj* **(a)** *(not drunk)* sobrio(a); **to be far from ~** non essere affatto sobrio; **to be as ~ as a judge, to be stone-cold ~** essere perfettamente sobrio. **(b)** *(rational, sedate: life, person, colour)* sobrio(a); *(: opinion, statement, estimate)* ponderato(a); *(: occasion)* solenne; **the ~ truth** la verità pura e semplice; **in a ~ mood** serio. **2** *vt* *(also: ~ up)* far passare la sbornia a; *(fig)* calmare. **3** *vi* *(also: ~ up)* smaltire la sbornia; *(fig)* calmarsi; **her mother's rebuke had a ~ing effect on her** il rimprovero di sua madre la fece pensare.

so·ber·ly ['səubəlɪ] *adv* in modo sobrio, sobriamente.

so·bri·ety [səu'braɪətɪ] *n* **(a)** *(not being drunk)* sobrietà. **(b)** *(seriousness, sedateness)* sobrietà, pacatezza.

Soc. *abbr* (= *society)* Soc.

so-called [,səu'kɔːld] *adj* cosiddetto(a).

soc·cer ['sɒkəʳ] **1** *n* calcio, football *m.* **2** *cpd (club, season, match)* calcistico(a), di calcio; **~ pitch** *n* campo di calcio; **~ player** *n* calciatore *m.*

so·cia·ble ['səuʃəbl] *adj (person)* socievole; *(evening, gathering)* amichevole; **I don't feel very ~** non ho molta voglia di vedere gente; **I'll have one drink, just to be ~** berrò qualcosa tanto per gradire.

so·cial ['səuʃəl] **1** *adj (all senses)* sociale; **man is a ~ animal** l'uomo è un animale socievole. **2** *n* festicciola. **3** *cpd:* **~ class** *n* classe *f* sociale; **~ climber** *n* arrampicatore/trice sociale, arrivista *m/f;* **~ club** *n* circolo; **~ column** *n (Press)* cronaca mondana; **S~ Democrat** *n* socialdemocratico/a; **S~ Democratic** *adj* socialdemocratico(a); **~ disease** *n* malattia venerea; **~ insurance** *n (Am)* assicurazione *f* sociale; **~ life** *n:* **to have a good ~ life** avere un'intensa vita sociale; **~ outcast** *n* emarginato/a; **~ science** *n* scienze *fpl* sociali; **~ security** *n* previdenza sociale; **to be on ~ security** *(fam)* ricevere sussidi dalla previdenza sociale; **the ~ services** *npl* i servizi sociali; **~ welfare** *n* assistenza *f* sociale; **~ work** *n* assistenza sociale; **~ worker** *n* assistente *m/f* sociale.

so·cial·ism ['səuʃəlɪzəm] *n* socialismo.

so·cial·ist ['səuʃəlɪst] *adj, n* socialista *(m/f).*

so·cial·ite ['səuʃəlaɪt] *n* persona in vista nel bel mondo.

so·cial·ize ['səuʃəlaɪz] **1** *vi (be with people)* frequentare la gente; *(make friends)* farsi degli amici; *(chat)* chiacchierare; **he has to ~ a lot because he's a salesman** deve mantenere molti contatti a causa del suo lavoro di rappresentante. **2** *vt (Pol, Psych)* socializzare.

so·cial·ly ['səuʃəlɪ] *adv (gen)* socialmente; **I know him ~** lo incontro in società.

so·ci·ety [sə'saɪətɪ] **1** *n* **(a)** *(social community)* società *f inv;* **he was a danger to ~** era un pericolo pubblico. **(b)** *(company)* compagnia; **in the ~ of** in compagnia di; **I enjoyed his ~** ho gradito la sua compagnia. **(c)** *(high ~)* alta società; **polite ~** società bene. **(d)** *(club, organization)* società *f inv,* associazione *f;* **S~ of Jesus** Compagnia di Gesù; **film ~** cineclub *m inv;* **learned ~** circolo culturale. **2** *cpd (party, column)* mondano(a); **~ wedding** *n* matrimonio nell'alta società.

so·cio·eco·nom·ic [,səusɪəu,iːkə'nɒmɪk] *adj* socioeconomico(a).

so·cio·logi·cal [,səusɪə'lɒdʒɪkəl] *adj* sociologico(a).

so·ci·olo·gist [,səusɪ'ɒlədʒɪst] *n* sociologo/a.

so·ci·ol·ogy [,səusɪ'ɒlədʒɪ] *n* sociologia.

sock[1] [sɒk] *n (short)* calzino; *(long)* calzettone *m;* **to pull one's ~s up** *(fig)* darsi una regolata.

sock[2] [sɒk] *(fam)* **1** *n (blow)* colpo, pugno; **to give sb a ~ on the jaw** dare un pugno sul muso a qn. **2** *vt* colpire, picchiare; **come on, ~ him one!** su, dagliele!

sock·et ['sɒkɪt] *n (of eye)* orbita; *(of joint)* cavità *f inv;* *(Elec: for plug)* presa (di corrente); *(: for lightbulb)* portalampada *m inv.*

sod[1] [sɒd] *n (of earth)* zolla.

sod[2] [sɒd] *n (Brit fam)* bastardo; **you lazy ~!** lazzarone!, sfaticato!

soda ['səudə] **1** *n* **(a)** *(Chem)* soda. **(b)** *(drink)* seltz *m inv;* **gin and** ~ gin *m inv* e soda. **(c)** *(Am: pop)* gassosa. **2** *cpd:* ~ **fountain** *n (Am)* chiosco delle bibite; ~ **siphon** *n* sifone *m* del seltz; ~ **water** *n* acqua di seltz.

sod·den ['sɒdn] *adj* fradicio(a).

so·dium ['səʊdɪəm] **1** *n* sodio. **2** *cpd:* ~ **chloride** *n* cloruro di sodio; ~ **lamp** *n* lampada al sodio.

sodo·my ['sɒdəmɪ] *n* sodomia.

sofa ['səʊfə] *n* sofà *m inv*, divano.

soft [sɒft] **1** *adj* (-**er**, -**est**) **(a)** *(not hard, rough etc: gen)* morbido(a); *(: snow, ground)* soffice; *(: wood, metal, stone)* dolce; *(: cheese)* a pasta molle; *(: pej: muscles)* flaccido(a); ~ **soap** *(fam)* adulazioni *fpl;* ~ **drugs** droghe *fpl* leggere.

(b) *(gentle, not harsh: breeze, rain, pressure)* leggero(a); *(: colour, light)* tenue; *(: look, smile, answer, landing)* dolce; *(: heart)* tenero(a); *(: life, option)* facile; *(: job)* non pesante; *(: teacher, parent)* indulgente; **you're too** ~ **with him** sei troppo indulgente con lui; **to have a** ~ **spot for sb** avere un debole per qn; **he has a** ~ **time of it** lui se la passa bene; **to be a** ~ **touch** *(fam)* lasciarsi mungere facilmente.

(c) *(not loud: sound, laugh, voice)* dolce, sommesso(a); *(: steps, whisper)* leggero(a); **the music is too** ~ il volume della musica è troppo basso.

(d) *(fam: person: no stamina)* smidollato(a); *(stupid):* **to be** ~ **(in the head)** essere un po' tocco; **to be** ~ **on sb** essere innamorato cotto di qn.

(e) *(Linguistics: consonant)* dolce.

2 *cpd:* ~ **currency** *n* moneta debole; ~ **drink** *n* analcolico; ~ **fruit** *n* = frutta rossa; ~ **furnishings** *npl* tessuti *mpl* d'arredo, tappezzerie *fpl;* ~ **goods** *n (Comm)* tessili *mpl;* ~ **palate** *n* palato molle; ~ **pedal** *n (on piano)* sordina; ~ **sell** *n* persuasione *f* all'acquisto; ~ **shoulder** *n (Aut)* banchina non transitabile; ~ **toy** *n* giocattolo di peluche; ~ **verge** *n* = ~ **shoulder;** ~ **water** *n* acqua non calcarea.

soft-boiled ['sɒft‚bɔɪld] *adj (egg)* alla coque.

sof·ten ['sɒfn] **1** *vt (gen)* ammorbidire; *(light)* attenuare; *(sound, impression)* attutire; *(colour, anger)* smorzare; *(resistance)* fiaccare; *(person: weaken)* addolcire; **he became** ~**ed by luxurious living** vivendo nel lusso si è rammollito; **to** ~ **the blow** *(fig)* attutire il colpo. **2** *vi (see vt)* ammorbidirsi; attenuarsi; attutirsi; smorzarsi; *(resistance)* affievolirsi; *(person, character)* addolcirsi; **her heart** ~**ed** si intenerì.

sof·ten·er ['sɒfnəʳ] *n* ammorbidente *m.*

soft-hearted [‚sɒft'hɑːtɪd] *adj* dal cuore tenero.

soft·ly ['sɒftlɪ] *adv (gen)* dolcemente; *(walk)* silenziosamente; *(gently: knock)* lievemente.

soft·ness ['sɒftnɪs] *n (of skin, bed, snow, leather etc)* morbidezza; *(of voice, manner, glance)* dolcezza; *(indulgence)* indulgenza.

soft-pedal [‚sɒft'pɛdl] *vt (fig)* minimizzare.

soft-spoken ['sɒft‚spəʊkən] *adj* dalla voce dolce.

soft·ware ['sɒftweəʳ] *n* software *m.*

softy, softie ['sɒftɪ] *n (fam: weak)* rammollito/a; *(: tender-hearted)* persona dal cuore tenero.

sog·gy ['sɒgɪ] *adj* (-**ier**, -**iest**) bagnato(a), fradicio(a); *(bread, cake)* molle.

soil [sɔɪl] **1** *n* terreno, terra; **chalky/poor** ~ terreno calcareo/povero; **cover it with** ~ copri lo di terra; **on British** ~ sul suolo britannico; **the** ~ *(fig: farmland)* la terra. **2** *vt (dirty)* sporcare; *(fig: reputation, honour etc)* infangare.

soiled [sɔɪld] *adj* sporco(a), sudicio(a).

so·lar ['səʊləʳ] *adj* solare; ~ **plexus** *(Anat)* plesso solare.

so·lar·ium [səʊ'lɛərɪəm] *n, pl* **solaria** [səʊ'lɛərɪə] solarium *m inv.*

sold [səʊld] *pt, pp of* **sell.**

sol·der ['səʊldəʳ] **1** *n* lega per saldatura. **2** *vt* saldare; ~**ing iron** saldatore *m.*

sol·dier ['səʊldʒəʳ] **1** *n* soldato; **a girl** ~ una soldatessa; **toy** ~ soldatino; **an old** ~ *(also fig)* un veterano; **to play at** ~**s** giocare alla guerra. **2** *vi* fare il soldato; **to** ~ **on** perseverare.

sole¹ [səʊl] **1** *n (Anat)* pianta (del piede); *(of shoe)* suola. **2** *vt* risolare.

sole² [səʊl] *n (fish)* sogliola.

sole³ [səʊl] *adj* **(a)** *(only)* unico(a), solo(a); **the** ~ **reason** la sola *or* l'unica ragione. **(b)** *(exclusive)* esclusivo(a).

sol·ecism ['sɒlɪsɪzəm] *n (Gram)* solecismo; *(in behaviour etc)* scorrettezza.

sole·ly ['səʊllɪ] *adv* solamente, unicamente; **I will hold you** ~ **responsible** ti considererò il solo responsabile.

sol·emn ['sɒləm] *adj* solenne.

so·lem·nity [sə'lɛmnɪtɪ] *n* solennità *f inv.*

sol·em·nize ['sɒləmnaɪz] *vt* solennizzare.

sol·emn·ly ['sɒləmlɪ] *adv* solennemente.

sol-fa ['sɒl'fɑː] *n (Mus)* solfeggio.

so·lic·it [sə'lɪsɪt] **1** *vt (request)* richiedere, sollecitare. **2** *vi (prostitute)* adescare i passanti.

so·lic·itor [sə'lɪsɪtəʳ] *n (Brit)* ≈ avvocato/essa; *(Am)* rappresentante *m* legale *(di una città o di un ministero).*

so·lic·itous [sə'lɪsɪtəs] *adj (anxious):* ~ **(about** *or* **for)** ansioso(a) (per); ~ **to please** desideroso di piacere.

so·lic·itude [sə'lɪsɪtjuːd] *n* sollecitudine *f.*

sol·id ['sɒlɪd] **1** *adj (gen)* solido(a); *(not hollow)* pieno(a); *(gold, wood)* massiccio(a); *(crowd, row)* compatto(a); *(line)* ininterrotto(a); *(vote)* unanime; **to become** ~ solidificarsi; **cut out of** ~ **rock** scolpito nella roccia viva; **as** ~ **as a rock** solido come una roccia; **to be frozen** ~ essere completamente ghiacciato; **we waited 2** ~ **hours** abbiamo aspettato due ore buone; **a man of** ~ **build** un uomo robusto; **the street was packed** ~ **with people** la strada era affollatissima; **a** ~ **mass of colour** una massa uniforme di colore; **he's a good** ~ **worker** è un gran lavoratore; **a** ~ **argument** un argomento fondato *or* valido; **common sense** solido buon senso; **Burnley is** ~ **for Labour** Burnley è in gran maggioranza laburista.

2 *n (gen)* solido.

3 *cpd:* ~ **fuel** *n* combustibile *m* solido; ~ **geometry** *n* geometria solida; ~ **ground** *n:* **to be on** ~ **ground** essere su terraferma; *(fig)* muoversi su terreno sicuro.

soli·dar·ity [‚sɒlɪ'dærɪtɪ] *n* solidarietà.

so·lidi·fy [sə'lɪdɪfaɪ] **1** *vt* solidificare. **2** *vi* solidificarsi.

sol·id·ly ['sɒlɪdlɪ] *adv (gen)* solidamente; **to vote** ~ **for sb** votare all'unanimità per qn; **a** ~**-built house** una casa costruita solidamente; **to work** ~ lavorare sodo.

solid-state [‚sɒlɪd‚steɪt] *adj (Elec)* a transistor; ~ **physics** fisica dei solidi.

so·lilo·quy [sə'lɪləkwɪ] *n* soliloquio.

soli·taire [‚sɒlɪ'teəʳ] *n (game, gem)* solitario.

soli·tary ['sɒlɪtərɪ] *adj (alone, secluded)* solitario(a); *(solo: example, case)* solo(a); **not a** ~ **one** neanche uno; **to be in** ~ **confinement** *(Law)* essere in cella d'isolamento.

soli·tude ['sɒlɪtjuːd] *n* solitudine *f.*

solo ['səʊləʊ] **1** *n, pl* ~**s** *(Mus)* assolo; **a tenor** ~ un assolo di tenore. **2** *adj:* ~ **flight** volo da solo; **passage for** ~ **violin** brano per violino solista. **3** *adv (Mus):* **to play** *(o sing)* ~ fare un assolo;

to fly ~ volare da solo.

so·lo·ist ['səʊləʊɪst] n solista m/f.

sol·stice ['sɒlstɪs] n solstizio.

sol·uble ['sɒljʊbl] adj solubile.

so·lu·tion [sə'lu:ʃən] n soluzione f.

solve [sɒlv] vt risolvere.

sol·ven·cy ['sɒlvənsɪ] n (Fin) solvenza, solvibilità.

sol·vent ['sɒlvənt] 1 adj (Chem, Fin) solvente. 2 n (Chem) solvente m. 3 cpd: ~ abuse n abuso di solventi.

som·bre, (Am) **som·ber** ['sɒmbə'] adj (mood, person) triste, tetro(a); (colour) scuro(a); a ~ prospect una triste prospettiva.

some [sʌm] 1 adj (a) (a certain amount or number of): ~ tea/water/biscuits/girls del tè/dell'acqua/dei biscotti/delle ragazze; if you have ~ queries se hai delle domande; have ~ more crisps prendi ancora delle patatine; all I have left is ~ chocolate mi è rimasto solo del cioccolato; he asked me ~ questions about the accident mi ha fatto qualche domanda or alcune domande or delle domande sull'incidente; there were ~ people outside c'era della gente fuori.

(**b**) (certain: in contrast) certo(a); ~ people hate fish certa gente odia il pesce; ~ people say that... certa gente dice che...; in ~ ways per certi versi, in un certo senso.

(**c**) (vague, indeterminate) un(a) certo(a), qualche; at ~ place in Sweden da qualche parte in Svezia; in ~ form or other in una forma o nell'altra; ~ politician or other un certo politico; ~ man was asking for you un tale chiedeva di te; ~ other time! sarà per un'altra volta!; ~ day un giorno; ~ day next week un giorno della prossima settimana.

(**d**) (considerable amount of): ~ distance away abbastanza lontano; ~ days ago parecchi giorni fa; it took ~ courage to do that ci è voluto un bel po' di coraggio per farlo; after ~ time dopo un po'; at ~ length a lungo.

(**e**) (emphatic: a few, a little): there's still SOME petrol in the tank c'è ancora un po' di benzina nel serbatoio; that's SOME consolation! questo è già qualcosa!

(**f**) (fam: intensive): that's ~ fish! questo sì che è un pesce!; it was ~ party è stata una grande festa; you're ~ help! (iro) hai dato un bell'aiuto!

2 pron (**a**) (a certain number) alcuni(e) m(f)pl, certi(e) m(f)pl; ~ went this way and ~ that alcuni andarono di qua e altri or alcuni di là; ~ of them are crazy alcuni di loro sono pazzi; I've got ~ (books etc) ne ho alcuni; ~ (of them) have been sold alcuni sono stati venduti; do take ~ prendine un po'; would you like ~? ne vorresti qualcuno?

(**b**) (a certain amount) un po'; could I have ~ of that cheese? potrei avere un po' di quel formaggio?; have ~ more cake prendi ancora un po' di torta; have ~! prendine un po'!; I've got ~ (milk, money) ne ho un po'; I've read ~ of the book ho letto parte del libro; ~ of what he said was true parte di ciò che disse era vero.

3 adv: ~ 20 people circa 20 persone.

...some [səm] n ending in cpds: three~ gruppo di tre.

some·body ['sʌmbədɪ] 1 pron qualcuno; there's ~ coming sta arrivando qualcuno; ~ knocked at the door hanno bussato alla porta; ~ else qualcun altro; ~ Italian un italiano; ~ told me so me l'ha detto qualcuno; ~ or other qualcuno. 2 n: to be ~ essere qualcuno; she thinks she's ~ si crede importante.

some·how ['sʌmhaʊ] adv (**a**) (in some way) in qualche modo; it must be done ~ or other bene o male va fatto. (**b**) (for some reason) per un motivo o per l'altro; it seems odd ~ non so perché, ma mi sembra strano.

some·one ['sʌmwʌn] pron = somebody.

some·place ['sʌmpleɪs] adv (Am) = somewhere.

som·er·sault ['sʌməsɔːlt] 1 n (by person) capriola; (in air) salto mortale; (by car etc) ribaltamento, cappottamento. 2 vi (see n: also: turn a ~) fare una capriola; fare un salto mortale; cappottare, ribaltare.

some·thing ['sʌmθɪŋ] 1 pron qualche cosa, qualcosa; ~ nice qualcosa di bello; ~ to do qualcosa da fare; ~ else altro, qualcos'altro; ~ has happened è successo qualcosa; ~ of the kind qualcosa del genere; she said ~ or other about it mi ha detto qualcosa a proposito; he's a lecturer in ~ or other è professore di non so che; he's a doctor or ~ è un dottore o qualcosa del genere; there's ~ the matter c'è qualcosa che non va; to have ~ to live for avere uno scopo nella vita; there's ~ in what you say c'è del vero in quello che dici; will you have ~ to drink? vuoi qualcosa da bere?; he's called John ~ si chiama John vattelappesca; give her ~ for herself dalle qualcosa; here's ~ for your trouble eccoti qualcosa per il disturbo; I hope to see ~ of you spero di vederti qualche volta; I think you may have ~ there penso che tu abbia ragione; (good idea) mi sembra una buon'idea, la tua; there's ~ about him that... c'è qualcosa in lui che...; she has a certain ~ ha un certo non so che; that's really ~! mica male!

2 adv (**a**): ~ over/under 200 un po' più/meno di 200; ~ like 200 circa 200; he's ~ like me mi assomiglia un po'; now that's ~ like a rose! questa sì che è una rosa!

(**b**): it's ~ of a problem è un bel problema; he is ~ of a liar è piuttosto bugiardo; he's ~ of a musician è un musicista abbastanza bravo.

(**c**) (fam): the weather was ~ shocking faceva un tempo da cani.

some·time ['sʌmtaɪm] 1 adv un giorno, uno di questi giorni; ~ before tomorrow prima di domani; ~ next year (nel corso del)l'anno prossimo; ~ soon presto, uno di questi giorni; I'll finish it ~ lo finirò prima o poi; ~ or (an)other it will have to be done bisognerà farlo prima o poi. 2 adj (former) ex, vecchio(a) (before n).

some·times ['sʌmtaɪmz] adv qualche volta, a volte.

some·what ['sʌmwɒt] adv piuttosto, alquanto.

some·where ['sʌmwɛə'] adv (**a**) (in space) da qualche parte, in qualche posto; ~ else da qualche altra parte; I lost it ~ l'ho perso da qualche parte; ~ in Wales da qualche parte nel Galles; ~ or other in Scotland da qualche parte in Scozia. (**b**) (approximately) circa, all'incirca, più o meno; he paid ~ about £12 l'ha pagato circa 12 sterline; he's ~ in his fifties ha passato la cinquantina.

som·nam·bu·list [sɒm'næmbjʊlɪst] n sonnambulo/a.

som·no·lent ['sɒmnələnt] adj sonnolento(a).

son [sʌn] n figlio; come here ~ (fam) vieni qui figliolo.

so·nar ['səʊnɑː'] n sonar m.

so·na·ta [sə'nɑːtə] n sonata.

song [sɒŋ] 1 n (ballad etc) canzone f; (of birds) canto; give us a ~! cantaci una canzone!; to make a great ~ and dance about sth (fig) fare un sacco di storie per qc; I got it for a ~ (fig) l'ho avuto per quattro soldi. **2** *cpd:* ~ **book** *n* canzoniere *m;* ~ **cycle** *n* ciclo di canzoni.

song·bird ['sɒŋbɜːd] *n* uccello canoro.

song·writer ['sɒŋˌraɪtəʳ] *n* compositore/trice di canzoni.

son·ic ['sɒnɪk] *adj (boom)* sonico(a); ~ **depth finder** scandaglio acustico.

son-in-law ['sʌnɪnlɔː] *n* genero.

son·net ['sɒnɪt] *n* sonetto.

son·ny ['sʌnɪ] *n (fam)* figlio mio, ragazzo mio.

so·nor·ity [sə'nɒrɪtɪ] *n* sonorità.

so·no·rous ['sɒnərəs] *adj* sonoro(a).

soon [suːn] *adv* **(a)** *(before long)* presto, fra poco; **come back** ~! torna presto!; ~ **afterwards** poco dopo; **it will** ~ **be summer** presto *or* fra poco sarà estate; **you would** ~ **get lost** ti perderesti subito; **see you** ~! a presto!; **very/quite** ~ molto/abbastanza presto; **he** ~ **changed his mind** ha presto cambiato idea.

(b) *(early)* presto; **how** ~ **can you be ready?** fra quanto tempo sarai pronto?; **Friday is too** ~ venerdì è troppo presto; **it's too** ~ **to tell it** è troppo presto per dirlo; **all too** ~ fin troppo presto; **we were none too** ~ siamo arrivati appena in tempo; **an hour too** ~ con un'ora di anticipo.

(c) *(with* as*):* **as** ~ **as possible** appena possibile, il più presto possibile; **I'll do it as** ~ **as I can** lo farò appena posso; **as** ~ **as it was finished** appena finito.

(d) *(expressing preference):* **I would as** ~ **not go** preferirei non andarci; **I would as** ~ **he didn't know** preferirei che non lo sapesse.

soon·er ['suːnəʳ] *adv* **(a)** *(of time)* prima; ~ **or later** prima o poi; **when are you leaving? — the** ~ **the better** quando parti? — prima parto meglio è; **no** ~ **had we left than...** eravamo appena partiti, quando...; **no** ~ **said than done** detto fatto. **(b)** *(of preference):* **I had** ~ **not do it, I would** ~ **not do it** preferirei non farlo; **I'd** ~ **die!** *(fam)* piuttosto morirei!

soot [sʊt] *n* fuliggine *f.*

soothe [suːð] *vt (gen)* calmare; *(pain, anxieties)* alleviare.

sooth·ing ['suːðɪŋ] *adj (ointment etc)* calmante; *(tone, words etc)* rassicurante; *(bath)* rilassante.

sooty ['sʊtɪ] *adj* **(-ier, -iest)** fuligginoso(a).

sop [sɒp] *n (food):* ~s pappette *fpl;* *(fig):* **to give sb a** ~ dare il contentino a qn; **as a** ~ **to his pride** per lusingare il suo amor proprio.

so·phis·ti·cat·ed [sə'fɪstɪkeɪtɪd] *adj (method, machine)* sofisticato(a); *(person)* raffinato(a), sofisticato(a); *(clothes, room)* raffinato(a); *(mind, discussion, film)* sottile.

so·phis·ti·ca·tion [sə,fɪstɪ'keɪʃən] *n (of method, machine)* complessità; *(of person, clothes etc)* raffinatezza; *(of argument etc)* sottigliezza.

sopo·rif·ic [,sɒpə'rɪfɪk] *adj* soporifero(a).

sop·ping ['sɒpɪŋ] *adj:* ~ **(wet)** fradicio(a).

sop·py ['sɒpɪ] *adj* **(-ier, -iest)** *(fam: sentimental)* sdolcinato(a); *(: silly)* sciocco(a).

so·pra·no [sə'prɑːnəʊ] **1** *n, pl* ~s *(Mus)* soprano *m/f.* **2** *adj* di soprano.

sor·bet ['sɔːbɪt] *n* sorbetto.

sor·cer·er ['sɔːsərəʳ] *n* stregone *m.*

sor·cery ['sɔːsərɪ] *n* stregoneria.

sor·did ['sɔːdɪd] *adj (place, room etc)* sordido(a); *(deal, motive etc)* meschino(a), sordido(a).

sore [sɔːʳ] **1** *adj* **(-r, -st) (a): I feel** ~ **all over** sono tutto indolenzito; **that's** ~! mi fa male!; ~ **throat** mal *m* di gola; **my eyes are** ~, **I have** ~ **eyes** mi fanno male gli occhi; **he's like a bear with a** ~ **head** *(fig)* è molto irascibile. **(b)** *(fig):* **it's a** ~ **point** è un punto delicato; **to touch on a** ~ **point**

mettere il dito sulla piaga; **to feel** ~ **about sth** *(fam)* essere molto seccato per qc; **don't get** ~! *(fam)* non te la prendere! **2** *n (Med)* piaga; **to open old** ~s *(fig)* riaprire una piaga.

sore·ly ['sɔːlɪ] *adv (tempted)* fortemente; *(regretted)* amaramente; **it is** ~ **needed** ce n'è un estremo bisogno; **she is** ~ **missed by her family** la sua famiglia sente molto la sua mancanza; **he has been** ~ **tried** è stato duramente provato.

sor·rel ['sɒrəl] *n* **(a)** *(Bot)* acetosa. **(b)** *(horse)* sauro.

sor·row ['sɒrəʊ] *n* dolore *m;* **her** ~ **at the death of her son** il suo dolore per la morte del figlio; **more in** ~ **than in anger** più con dolore che con rabbia.

sor·row·ful ['sɒrəʊfʊl] *adj* addolorato(a), triste.

sor·ry ['sɒrɪ] *adj* **-ier, -iest) (a)** *(regretful, sad)* triste, addolorato(a); **I'm** ~ **to hear that...** mi dispiace (sentire) che...; **I'm** ~ **to tell you that...** mi dispiace dirti che...; **it was a failure, I'm** ~ **to say** purtroppo è stato un fiasco; **I can't say I'm** ~ non posso dire che mi dispiaccia.

(b) *(in apologizing, repentant):* ~! scusa!, mi scusi! *(polite form);* **awfully** ~!, **so** ~!, **very** ~! scusa tanto!, scusi tanto! *(polite form);* **to be** ~ essere spiacente; **to say** ~ **(to sb for sth)** chiedere scusa (a qn per qc); **to be** ~ **about sth** essere dispiaciuto *or* spiacente di qc; **I'm** ~ **about what happened last night** scusa per quello che è successo ieri sera; **I'm** ~, **but you're wrong** mi dispiace, ma hai torto; **to be** ~ **to have to do sth** essere spiacente di dover fare qc.

(c) *(pitying):* **to be** *or* **feel** ~ **for sb** dispiacer'si per qn; **to be** *or* **feel** ~ **for o.s.** compiangersi; **you'll be** ~ **for this!** te ne pentirai!

(d) *(condition, tale)* pietoso(a); *(sight, failure)* triste; *(excuse)* che non regge; **in a** ~ **state** in uno stato pietoso.

sort [sɔːt] **1** *n* **(a)** *(gen)* specie *f inv,* genere *m,* tipo; *(make: of coffee, car etc)* tipo; **what** ~ **do you want?** che tipo vuole?; **I know his** ~ conosco il suo tipo; **books of all** ~s libri di ogni genere; **he's a painter of a** ~, **he's a painter of** ~s è, per così dire, un pittore; **of the worst** ~ della peggior specie; **something of the** ~ qualcosa del genere; **it's tea of a** ~ è una specie di tè; **I shall do nothing of the** ~! nemmeno per sogno!; **behaviour of that** ~ comportamento del genere; **it takes all** ~s **(to make a world)** il mondo è bello perché è vario.

(b): ~ **of: what** ~ **of car?** che tipo di macchina?; **what** ~ **of man is he?** che tipo di uomo è?; **it's my** ~ **of film** è il tipo di film che piace a me; **he's not the** ~ **of man to say that** non è il tipo da dire cose del genere; **all** ~s **of dogs** cani di ogni tipo; **he's some** ~ **of painter** è una specie di pittore; **it's a** ~ **of dance** è una specie di danza; **and all that** ~ **of thing** e così via; **what** ~ **of an answer is that?** che razza di risposta è quella?; **that's the** ~ **of person I am** io sono fatto così; **you know the** ~ **of thing I mean** sai cosa intendo; **it's** ~ **of awkward** *(fam)* è piuttosto difficile; **it's** ~ **of yellow** *(fam)* è una specie di giallo; **aren't you pleased?** — ~ **of** *(fam)* non sei contento? — insomma; **I** ~ **of thought that would happen** *(fam)* me lo sentivo che sarebbe successo.

(c) *(person):* **he's a good** ~ è una brava persona; **he's not my** ~ non è il mio tipo; **he's an odd** ~ è un tipo strano.

(d): to be out of ~s *(in a bad temper)* aver la luna; *(unwell)* non essere in forma.

2 *vt (classify: documents, stamps)* classificare; *(put in order: papers, clothes)* mettere in ordine;

(: *letters*) smistare; (*separate*) separare, dividere.

♦ **sort out** *vt* + *adv* (**a**) = **sort 2.** (**b**) (*straighten out: room*) mettere in ordine; (: *papers, one's ideas*) fare ordine fra; (*solve: problem etc*) risolvere; **have you managed to** ~ **out what's happening?** sei riuscito a sapere cosa succede?; **things will** ~ **themselves out** le cose andranno a posto da sole; **we've got it** ~**ed out now** la faccenda è risolta. (**c**): **I'll** ~ **him out!** (*fam*) lo sistemo io!

sor·tie ['sɔːtɪ] *n* (*Aer, Mil*) sortita.

sort·ing of·fice ['sɔːtɪŋ,ɒfɪs] *n* (*Post*) ufficio di smistamento.

SOS [,ɛsəʊ'ɛs] *n* S.O.S. *m.*

so-so ['səʊsəʊ] *adv* così così.

souf·flé ['suːfleɪ] *n* soufflé *m inv*; **cheese** ~ soufflé di formaggio; ~ **dish** stampo per soufflé.

sought [sɔːt] *pt, pp of* seek.

sought-after ['sɔːtɑːftəʳ] *adj* richiesto(a).

soul [səʊl] **1** *n* (**a**) anima; **with all one's** ~ con tutta l'anima; **All S**~**'s Day** il giorno dei morti; **God rest his** ~ pace all'anima sua; **he's the** ~ **of discretion** è la discrezione in persona. (**b**) (*person*) anima; **the ship sank with all** ~**s** la nave affondò con tutti a bordo; **I didn't see a** ~ non ho visto anima viva; **the poor** ~ **had nowhere to sleep** il poveraccio non aveva dove dormire. (**c**) (*also:* ~ **music**) musica soul. **2** *cpd*: ~ **mate** *n* anima gemella.

soul-destroy·ing ['səʊldɪ'strɔɪɪŋ] *adj* (*fig: boring*) che abbrutisce; (: *depressing*) demoralizzante.

soul·ful ['səʊlfʊl] *adj* (*gen*) commovente; (*eyes*) espressivi.

soul-searching ['səʊl,sɜːtʃɪŋ] *n*: **after much** ~ dopo un profondo esame di coscienza.

sound[1] [saʊnd] **1** *adj* (**-er, -est**) (**a**) (*in good condition, healthy*) sano(a); (: *structure, organization, investment*) solido(a); **to be of** ~ **mind** essere sano di mente; **as** ~ **as a bell** (*person*) sano come un pesce; (*thing*) in perfette condizioni. (**b**) (*valid: argument, policy, claim*) valido(a); (: *move*) sensato(a); (*dependable: person*) affidabile; **a** ~ **conservative** un conservatore convinto; **he's** ~ **on government policy** conosce molto bene la politica del governo. (**c**) (*thorough*): **to give sb a** ~ **beating** picchiare qn di santa ragione. (**d**) (*sleep: deep; untroubled*) profondo(a); **he's a** ~ **sleeper** è uno che dorme sodo.

2 *adv*: **to be** ~ **asleep** dormire sodo, dormire profondamente.

sound[2] [saʊnd] **1** *n* (*gen*) suono *m*; (*of sea, breaking glass etc*) rumore *m*; (*volume*) volume *m*; **the speed of** ~ la velocità del suono; **to the** ~ **of the national anthem** al suono dell'inno nazionale; **not a** ~ **was to be heard** non si sentiva volare una mosca; **a language with many consonant** ~**s** una lingua piena di consonanti; **I don't like the** ~ **of it** (*fig: of film etc*) non mi dice niente; (: *of news*) è preoccupante.

2 *vt* (**a**) (*alarm, bell, horn*) suonare; **to** ~ **the retreat** (*Mil*) suonare la ritirata; **to** ~ **a note of warning** (*fig*) dare un segnale d'allarme. (**b**): **your 'r's more** pronuncia la r più chiaramente. (**c**) (*Med*): **to** ~ **sb's chest** auscultare il torace di qn.

3 *vi* (**a**) (*trumpet, bell, alarm*) suonare; (*voice, siren*) risuonare; **a cannon** ~**ed a long way off** si sentì un colpo di cannone in lontananza. (**b**): **it** ~**s hollow** suona vuoto; **he** ~**s Italian to me** da come parla mi sembra italiano; **it** ~**s like French** somiglia al francese; **it** ~**s better like that** suona meglio così; **that** ~**s like them arriving now** mi sembra di sentirli arrivare; **you** ~ **like your**

mother mi sembra di sentire parlare tua madre; **he** ~**ed angry** mi sembrava arrabbiato. (**c**) (*seem*): **that** ~**s very odd** sembra molto strano; **how does it** ~ **to you?** che ne pensi?; **that** ~**s like a good idea** sembra una buona idea; **she** ~**s like a nice girl** sembra una brava ragazza; **it** ~**s as if she won't be coming** ho l'impressione che non verrà.

4 *cpd*: ~ **barrier** *n* barriera del suono; ~ **effect** *n* effetto sonoro; ~ **engineer** *n* tecnico del suono; ~ **wave** *n* (*Phys*) onda sonora.

♦ **sound off** *vi* + *adv* (*fam*): **to** ~ **off (about)** (*give one's opinions*) fare dei grandi discorsi (su); (*boast*) vantarsi (di); (*grumble*) brontolare (per).

sound[3] [saʊnd] *vt* (*Naut*) scandagliare, sondare; **to** ~ **sb out about sth** sondare le opinioni di qn su qc.

sound[4] [saʊnd] *n* (*Geog*) stretto.

sound·ing ['saʊndɪŋ] **1** *n* (*Naut*) scandaglio. **2** *cpd*: ~ **board** *n* (*Mus*) tavola armonica; (*fig*) banco di prova.

sound·ly ['saʊndlɪ] *adv* (*build*) solidamente; (*argue*) giudiziosamente; (*invest*) saggiamente; **to beat sb** ~ (*thrash*) picchiare duramente qn; (*defeat*) battere duramente qn; **to sleep** ~ dormire profondamente.

sound·ness ['saʊndnɪs] *n* (*of body, mind*) sanità *f*; (*of argument, judgment*) validità; (*of business, building*) solidità; (*solvency*) solvibilità.

sound·proof ['saʊndpruːf] **1** *adj* isolato(a) acusticamente. **2** *vt* isolare acusticamente.

sound·track ['saʊndtræk] *n* colonna sonora, sonoro.

soup [suːp] **1** *n* minestra; (*thick* ~) zuppa; (*clear* ~) brodo; **vegetable** ~ minestra di verdura; **to be in the** ~ (*fam*) essere or trovarsi nei pasticci. **2** *cpd*: ~ **kitchen** *n* mensa per i poveri; ~ **plate** *n* piatto fondo; ~ **spoon** *n* cucchiaio da minestra.

soup·çon ['suːpsɔ̃ː] *n* (*Culin*) ombra.

souped-up ['suːptʌp] *adj* (*fam*) truccato(a).

sour ['saʊəʳ] *adj* (**-er, -est**) (*gen*) aspro(a); (*milk, fig: person, remark*) acido(a); (*smell*) acre; **whisky** ~ cocktail di whisky al limone; **to go or turn** ~ (*milk, wine*) inacidirsi; (*fig: relationship, plans*) guastarsi; **it was** ~ **grapes on his part** (*fig*) è stata solo invidia da parte sua; **to be in a** ~ **mood** (*fig*) essere di umore nero.

source [sɔːs] *n* (*of river*) sorgente *f*; (*fig: of problem, epidemic*) causa, origine *f*; **oranges are a** ~ **of vitamin C** le arance sono ricche di vitamina C; **I have it from a reliable** ~ **that...** ho saputo da fonte sicura che... .

sour·ness ['saʊənɪs] *n* (*see adj*) asprezza; acidità; acredine *f*.

souse [saʊs] *vt* (*Culin: pickle*) mettere in salamoia; (*plunge*) immergere nell'acqua; (*soak*) mettere a mollo; **to** ~ **sth with water** inzuppare qc d'acqua.

south [saʊθ] **1** *n* sud *m*, meridione *m*; (**to the**) ~ **of a** sud di; **in the** ~ **of** nel sud di; **the wind is from the** ~ il vento soffia da sud; **to veer to the** ~ (*wind*) girare verso sud; **the S**~ **of France** il sud della Francia. **2** *adj* (*gen*) sud *inv*; (*coast*) meridionale; (*wind*) del sud. **3** *adv* verso sud; ~ **of the border** a sud del confine; **to travel** ~ viaggiare verso sud; **this house faces** ~ questa casa è esposta a sud *or* a mezzogiorno. **4** *cpd*: S~ **Africa** *n* Sudafrica; S~ **African** *adj, n* sudafricano(a) (*m/f*); S~ **America** *n* Sudamerica, America del sud; S~ **American** *adj, n* sudamericano(a) (*m/f*); S~ **Pole** *n* Polo sud; S~ **Sea Islands** *npl* isole *fpl* dei Mari del Sud; **the** S~ **Seas** i Mari del Sud.

south·bound ['saʊθbaʊnd] *adj* (*gen*) diretto(a) a sud; (*carriageway*) sud *inv.*

south-east [ˌsaʊθ'iːst] **1** *n* sudest *m*. **2** *adj (wind)* di sudest; *(counties etc)* sudorientale; S~ **Asia** Asia sudorientale. **3** *adv* verso sudest.

south-easter·ly [ˌsaʊθ'iːstəlɪ] *adj (wind)* che viene dal sudest; *(direction)* verso sudest.

south-eastern [ˌsaʊθ'iːstən] *adj* del sudest, sudorientale.

south·er·ly ['sʌðəlɪ] *adj (wind)* del sud; *(direction)* verso sud; **house with a ~ aspect** casa esposta a sud.

south·ern ['sʌðən] *adj (region)* del sud, meridionale; *(coast)* meridionale; *(wall)* (esposto(a) a) sud; **the ~ hemisphere** l'emisfero australe; S~ **Europe** l'Europa del sud *or* meridionale; **in ~ Spain** nel sud della Spagna, nella Spagna meridionale.

south·ern·er ['sʌðənəᵊ] *n* abitante *m/f* del sud.

south·ward(s) ['saʊθwəd(z)] *adv* verso sud.

south·west [ˌsaʊθ'wɛst] **1** *n* sudovest *m*. **2** *adj* di sudovest. **3** *adv* verso sudovest.

south·west·er·ly [ˌsaʊθ'wɛstəlɪ] *adj (wind)* che viene dal sudovest; *(direction)* verso sudovest.

south·western [ˌsaʊθ'wɛstən] *adj* del sudovest.

sou·venir [ˌsuːvəˈnɪəᵊ] *n* souvenir *m inv*, ricordo.

sou'·west·er [saʊˈwɛstəᵊ] *n* cappello di cerata.

sov·er·eign ['sɒvrɪn] **1** *adj (gen)* sovrano(a); **with ~ contempt** *(fig)* con sommo disprezzo; **a ~ remedy** un rimedio sovrano. **2** *n (monarch)* sovrano/a; *(coin)* sovrana.

sov·er·eign·ty ['sɒvrəntɪ] *n* sovranità.

so·vi·et ['səʊvɪət] **1** *n* soviet *m inv*. **2** *adj* sovietico(a); **the S~ Union** l'Unione *f* Sovietica.

sow[1] [səʊ] *pt* sowed, *pp* sown *vt* seminare; **to ~ (the seeds of) doubt in sb's mind** far sorgere dei dubbi a qn; **to ~ (the seeds of) discord** seminare zizzania.

sow[2] [saʊ] *n* scrofa.

sow·ing ['səʊɪŋ] *n* semina.

sown [səʊn] *pp of* sow.

soya ['sɔɪə], *(Am)* **soy** [sɔɪ] **1** *n* soia. **2** *cpd:* ~ **bean** *n* seme *m* di soia; ~ **sauce** *n* salsa di soia.

soz·zled ['sɒzld] *adj (fam)* sbronzo(a); **to get ~** sbronzarsi.

spa [spɑː] *n* stazione *f* termale.

space [speɪs] *n (all senses)* spazio; **to stare into ~** guardare nel vuoto; **to clear a ~ for sth** fare posto per qc; **to take up a lot of ~** occupare molto spazio; **to buy ~ in a newspaper** comprare spazio pubblicitario su un giornale; **blank ~** spazio in bianco; **answer in the ~ provided** rispondere negli appositi spazi; **in a confined ~** in un luogo chiuso; **I couldn't find a ~ for my car** non sono riuscito a trovare un posto per la macchina; **in a short ~ of time** in breve tempo; **(with)in the ~ of an hour/three generations** nell'arco di un'ora/di tre generazioni; **for the ~ of a fortnight** per un periodo di due settimane; **after a ~ of two hours** dopo un intervallo di due ore.

　2 *vt (also:* ~ **out:** *gen)* distanziare; *(: payments)* scaglionare; *(: type)* spaziare.

　3 *cpd (research, capsule, probe etc)* spaziale; ~ **bar** *n (on typewriter)* barra spaziatrice; ~ **shuttle** *n* shuttle *m inv*.

space-craft ['speɪskrɑːft] *n* veicolo spaziale.

space·man ['speɪsmən] *n, pl* **-men** astronauta *m*, cosmonauta *m*.

space·ship ['speɪʃʃɪp] *n* astronave *f*, navicella spaziale.

space·suit ['speɪssuːt] *n* tuta spaziale.

space·walk ['speɪswɔːk] *n* passeggiata spaziale.

spa·cious ['speɪʃəs] *adj* spazioso(a).

spade [speɪd] *n* **(a)** *(tool)* vanga; *(child's)* paletta; **to call a ~ a ~** *(fig)* dire pane al pane (e vino al

vino). **(b)** *(Cards):* ~**s** *pl* picche *fpl;* **the three of** ~**s** il tre di picche; **to play** ~**s** giocare picche; **to play a** ~ giocare una carta di picche.

spade·work ['speɪdwɜːk] *n (fig)* grosso dei preparativi.

spa·ghet·ti [spəˈgɛtɪ] *n* spaghetti *mpl*.

Spain [speɪn] *n* Spagna.

span[1] [spæn] **1** *n (of hand)* spanna; *(of bridge, arch, roof)* luce *f; (of time)* periodo; **a short attention ~** una limitata capacità di concentrazione; **the average ~ of life** la durata media della vita. **2** *vt (subj: bridge etc)* attraversare; **to ~ 3 decades** abbracciare un periodo di 30 anni; **his memory ~ned 50 years** riusciva a ricordare tutto quello che era accaduto nell'arco di 50 anni.

span[2] [spæn] *pt of* spin.

Span·iard ['spænjəd] *n* spagnolo/a.

span·iel ['spænjəl] *n* spaniel *m inv*.

Span·ish ['spænɪʃ] **1** *adj (gen)* spagnolo(a); *(teacher, lesson, book)* di spagnolo; ~ **onion** cipollone *m;* ~ **omelette** frittata di cipolle, pomodori e peperoni. **2** *n (language)* spagnolo; **the ~** *pl (people)* gli Spagnoli.

spank [spæŋk] *vt* sculacciare.

span·ner ['spænəᵊ] *n* chiave *f* fissa; **to throw a ~ in the works** *(fig)* mettere il bastone tra le ruote.

spar[1] [spɑːᵊ] *n (Naut)* asta, palo.

spar[2] [spɑːᵊ] *vi:* **to ~ (with sb)** *(Boxing)* allenarsi (con qn); *(argue)* discutere (con qn); ~**ring partner** compagno di allenamento.

spare [spɛəᵊ] **1** *adj* **(a)** *(surplus)* in più; *(reserve)* di riserva; **I haven't enough ~ cash to go on holiday** non mi avanzano soldi per andare in vacanza; **is there any string ~?** c'è rimasto un po' di spago?; **there are 2 going ~** ce ne sono 2 in più; **to go ~** *(fam)* andare su tutte le furie.

　(b) *(of build etc)* asciutto(a); **she's tall and ~** è alta e asciutta.

　2 *n* pezzo di ricambio.

　3 *vt* **(a)** *(be grudging with):* **she ~d no effort** *or* **pains in helping me** ha fatto tutto il possibile per aiutarmi; **to ~ no expense** non badare a spese.

　(b) *(do without)* fare a meno di; **can you ~ this for a moment?** puoi prestarmelo per un attimo?; **if you can ~ it** se puoi farne a meno; **can you ~ the time?** hai tempo?; **to ~ a thought for** pensare a; **can you ~ (me) £10?** puoi prestarmi 10 sterline?; **there is none to ~** ce n'è appena a sufficienza; **I've a few minutes to ~** ho un attimino di tempo; **I got to the station with 3 minutes to ~** sono arrivato alla stazione a 3 minuti dalla partenza; **I had £1 to ~** mi avanzava 1 sterlina; **there is no time to ~** non c'è tempo da perdere.

　(c) *(show mercy to)* risparmiare; **to ~ sb's feelings** avere riguardo per i sentimenti di qn; **she doesn't ~ herself** non si risparmia.

　(d) *(save from need or trouble):* **to ~ sb the trouble of doing sth** risparmiare a qn la fatica di fare qc; ~ **me the details** risparmiami i particolari.

　4 *cpd:* ~ **part** *n* pezzo di ricambio; ~ **room** *n* stanza degli ospiti; ~ **time** *n* tempo libero; ~ **tyre** *n (Aut)* gomma di scorta; ~ **wheel** *n (Aut)* ruota di scorta.

spar·ing ['spɛərɪŋ] *adj (amount, use)* moderato(a); **to be ~ of praise** essere avaro di lodi.

spar·ing·ly ['spɛərɪŋlɪ] *adv (eat, live)* frugalmente; *(praise, drink)* con moderazione.

spark [spɑːk] **1** *n (from fire)* scintilla; *(fig):* **there wasn't a ~ of life in the battery** la batteria non dava segni di vita; **he didn't show a ~ of interest** non ha mostrato il benché minimo interesse; **bright ~** *(fam)* genio. **2** *vt (also:* ~ **off:** *debate,* *quarrel, revolt)* provocare; *(: interest)* suscitare. **3** *cpd:* ~**(ing) plug** *n (Aut)* candela.

spar·kle ['spɑːkl] **1** *n (gen)* scintillio; *(fig: of person, conversation)* brio. **2** *vi (flash, shine)* scintillare, luccicare; *(: eyes)* scintillare, brillare; *(: person, conversation)* brillare; *(: wine)* frizzare.

spar·kling ['spɑːklɪŋ] *adj (gen)* scintillante; *(person, conversation)* brillante, frizzante; *(wine)* frizzante.

spar·row ['spærəʊ] *n* passero.

sparse [spɑːs] *adj* (**-r, -st**) *(vegetation)* rado(a); *(population)* scarso(a).

sparse·ly ['spɑːslɪ] *adv* poco, scarsamente.

spar·tan ['spɑːtən] *adj (fig)* spartano(a).

spasm ['spæzəm] *n (Med)* spasmo; *(of coughing)* attacco; *(fig)* accesso; **there was a brief ~ of activity** c'è stato un momento di attività spasmodica.

spas·mod·ic [spæz'mɒdɪk] *adj (Med)* spasmodico(a); *(fig: growth)* irregolare; **he made ~ attempts at giving up smoking** ha tentato più volte di smettere di fumare.

spas·tic ['spæstɪk] *adj, n* spastico(a) *(m/f).*

spat [spæt] *pt, pp of* spit.

spate [speɪt] *n (fig: of letters, orders)* valanga; *(: of words, abuse)* torrente *m; (: of accidents)* gran numero; **to be in ~** *(river)* essere in piena.

spa·tial ['speɪʃəl] *adj* spaziale.

spat·ter ['spætər] *vt:* **to ~ (with)** schizzare (di); **~ed with mud** inzaccherato.

spatu·la ['spætjʊlə] *n* spatola.

spawn [spɔːn] **1** *n (of fish, frogs)* uova *fpl.* **2** *vi* deporre le uova. **3** *vt (pej)* produrre.

speak [spiːk] *pt* **spoke**, *pp* **spoken 1** *vt (words, lines)* dire; *(language)* parlare; **he ~s Italian** parla italiano; **to ~ the truth** dire la verità; **to ~ one's mind** dire quello che si pensa.

2 *vi* **(a)** *(gen)* parlare; **to ~ to sb** parlare a qn; *(converse with)* parlare con qn; **to ~ about** *(or* **on** *or* **of) sth** parlare di qc; **to ~ in a whisper** bisbigliare; **since they quarrelled they don't ~ to each other** da quando hanno litigato non si rivolgono la parola; **I'll ~ to him about it** *(problem, idea)* gliene parlerò; *(his lateness etc)* glielo farò presente; **to ~ at a conference/in a debate** partecipare ad una conferenza/ad un dibattito; **he's very well spoken of** tutti ne parlano bene; **I don't know him to ~ to** so chi è ma non gli ho mai parlato; **so to ~** per così dire; **it's nothing to ~ of** non è niente di speciale; **he has no money to ~ of** non si può dire che sia proprio ricco; **~ing of holidays** a proposito di vacanze; **roughly ~ing** grosso modo; **~ing for myself** per quel che mi riguarda; **~ing as a student myself, I…** parlando da studente, io… .

(b) *(Telec)* **~ing!** sono io!; **this is Peter ~ing** sono Peter; **who is that ~ing?** chi parla?

♦ **speak for** *vi + prep:* **to ~ for sb** parlare a nome di qn; **~ for yourself!** *(fam)* parla per te!; **let her ~ for herself** lascia che dica la sua opinione; **it ~s for itself** parla da sé; **that picture is already spoken for** *(in shop)* quel quadro è già stato venduto.

♦ **speak out, speak up** *vi + adv* **(a)** *(raise voice)* parlare a voce alta. **(b)** *(fig)* parlare apertamente; **to ~ out against sth** dichiararsi contrario a qc; **to ~ up for sb** parlare a favore di qn.

speak·er ['spiːkər] *n* **(a)** *(gen)* chi parla; *(in discussion)* interlocutore/trice; *(in public)* oratore/trice; **he's a good/poor ~** parla bene/male. **(b)** *(of language)* **are you a Welsh ~?** parla gallese? **(c)** *(loud~)* altoparlante *m.* **(d)** *(Brit Parliament)* **the S~** ≈ il Presidente della Camera dei deputati.

speak·ing ['spiːkɪŋ] **1** *adj* parlante; **Italian-~ people** persone che parlano italiano; **I am not on ~ terms with her** la conosco solo di vista; **they are not on ~ terms** *(after quarrel)* non si parlano. **2** *n (skill)* arte *f* del parlare.

spear [spɪər] *n* lancia.

spear·head ['spɪəhɛd] **1** *n* punta di lancia; *(Mil)* reparto d'assalto; *(fig)* capi *mpl.* **2** *vt (attack etc)* condurre.

spear·mint ['spɪəmɪnt] *n (Bot etc)* menta verde.

spec [spɛk] *n (fam):* **to buy sth on ~** comprare qc sperando di fare un affare; **I went to the theatre on ~** sono andato al teatro nella speranza di trovare un biglietto.

spe·cial ['spɛʃəl] **1** *adj* **(a)** *(specific)* particolare, speciale; **have you any ~ date in mind?** hai in mente una data particolare?; **I've no-one ~ in mind** non penso a nessuno in particolare.

(b) *(exceptional: price, favour, legislation)* speciale; *(: powers)* straordinario(a); *(particular: care, situation, attention)* particolare; **to make a ~ effort** fare del proprio meglio; **this is a ~ day for me** è una giornata speciale per me; **you're extra ~** *(fam)* sei veramente speciale; **to expect ~ treatment** aspettarsi un trattamento speciale; **nothing ~** niente di speciale; **what's so ~ about her?** che cosa ha di tanto speciale?

2 *n (train)* treno supplementare; *(newspaper)* edizione *f* straordinaria; **the chef's ~** la specialità dello chef.

3 *cpd:* **~ agent** *n* agente *m* segreto; **~ correspondent** *n* inviato speciale; **~ delivery** *n (Post):* **by ~ delivery** per espresso; **~ feature** *n (Press)* servizio speciale; **~ offer** *n (Comm)* offerta speciale.

spe·cial·ist ['spɛʃəlɪst] **1** *n* specialista *m/f;* **a heart ~** *(Med)* un cardiologo. **2** *adj (dictionary)* specializzato(a); *(knowlege, work)* da specialista.

spe·ci·al·ity [ˌspɛʃɪ'ælɪtɪ], *(Am)* **spe·cial·ty** ['spɛʃəltɪ] *n* specialità *f inv;* **to make a ~ of sth** specializzarsi in qc.

spe·ciali·za·tion [ˌspɛʃəlaɪ'zeɪʃən] *n* specializzazione *f.*

spe·cial·ize ['spɛʃəlaɪz] *vi:* **to ~ (in)** specializzarsi (in).

spe·cial·ly ['spɛʃəlɪ] *adv (specifically)* specialmente; *(on purpose)* apposta; *(particularly)* particolarmente.

spe·cies ['spiːʃiːz] *n, pl inv* specie *f inv.*

spe·cif·ic [spə'sɪfɪk] *adj* **(a)** *(example, order etc)* preciso(a); *(meaning)* specifico(a); **he was very ~ about that** è stato molto chiaro in proposito. **(b)** *(Bio, Phys, Chem, Med)* specifico(a); **~ gravity** peso specifico.

spe·cif·ical·ly [spə'sɪfɪkəlɪ] *adv (explicitly: state, warn)* chiaramente, esplicitamente; *(especially: design, intend)* appositamente.

speci·fi·ca·tion [ˌspɛsɪfɪ'keɪʃən] *n (gen)* specificazione *f;* **~s** *(of car, machine)* dati *mpl* caratteristici; *(for building)* dettagli *mpl.*

speci·fy ['spɛsɪfaɪ] **1** *vt* specificare. **2** *vi* precisare, specificare; **unless otherwise specified** salvo indicazioni contrarie.

speci·men ['spɛsɪmɪn] **1** *n (sample: gen)* campione *m; (: of rock, species)* esemplare *m.* **2** *cpd:* **~ copy** *n* campione *m;* **~ signature** *n* firma depositata.

spe·cious ['spiːʃəs] *adj* specioso(a).

speck [spɛk] *n (of dust, dirt)* granello; *(of ink, paint etc)* macciolina; **it was just a ~ on the horizon** era solo un puntino all'orizzonte.

speck·led ['spɛkld] *adj* screziato(a).

specs [spɛks] *npl (fam)* occhiali *mpl.*

spec·ta·cle ['spɛktəkl] **1** *n* **(a)** spettacolo; **to make**

a ~ of o.s. *(fig)* coprirsi di ridicolo. **(b):** ~s
occhiali *mpl*. **2 cpd:** ~ **case** *n* fodero per gli
occhiali.

spec·tacu·lar [spɛk'tækjʊlə^r] **1** *adj (gen)* spettacolare; *(view)* favoloso(a). **2** *n (Cine,TV)* kolossal *m*.

spec·ta·tor [spɛk'teɪtə^r] *n* spettatore/trice.

spec·tre, *(Am)* **spec·ter** ['spɛktə^r] *n* spettro, fantasma *m*.

spec·trum ['spɛktrəm] *n, pl* **spectra** *(Phys)* spettro;
(fig) gamma.

specu·late ['spɛkjʊleɪt] *vi (Fin)* fare speculazioni,
speculare; *(wonder):* **to ~ (about** *or* **on sth/
whether)** chiedersi (qc/se); **I can only ~** posso
solo fare congetture.

specu·la·tion [,spɛkjʊ'leɪʃən] *n (guessing)* congetture *fpl; (Fin)* speculazione *f*.

specu·la·tive ['spɛkjʊlətɪv] *adj (Philosophy, Fin)*
speculativo(a); *(expression)* indagatore(trice).

specu·la·tor ['spɛkjʊleɪtə^r] *n* speculatore/trice.

sped [spɛd] *pt, pp of* **speed.**

speech [spiːtʃ] **1** *n* **(a)** *(faculty)* parola; *(manner of
speaking)* parlata, modo di parlare; **to lose the
power of ~** perdere l'uso della parola; **freedom
of ~** libertà di parola. **(b)** *(language)* linguaggio;
children's ~ il linguaggio dei bambini. **(c)** *(oration)* discorso; **to make a ~** fare un discorso. **(d)**
(Brit Gram): **direct/indirect ~** discorso diretto/
indiretto. **2 cpd:** ~ **day** *n (Brit)* giorno della premiazione; ~ **impediment** *n* difetto di pronuncia;
~ **therapy** *n* logoterapia.

speech·less ['spiːtʃlɪs] *adj* senza parola, ammuto-
lito(a).

speed [spiːd] **1** *n* **(a)** *(rate of movement)* velocità *f
inv; (rapidity, haste)* rapidità; **at ~** velocemente;
at full ~, at top ~ alla massima velocità; **at a ~
of 70 km/h** a una velocità di 70 km l'ora; **the ~ of
light/sound** la velocità della luce/del suono; **what
~ were you doing?** *(Aut)* a che velocità andavi?;
to pick up *or* **gather ~** *(car)* acquistare velocità;
(project, work) procedere più speditamente; **the
~ of his reactions** la sua prontezza di riflessi;
shorthand/typing ~s numero di parole al minuto
in stenografia/dattilografia. **(b)** *(Aut, Tech: gear)*
marcia; **a five-~ gearbox** un cambio a cinque
marce. **(c)** *(Phot: of film)* rapidità; *(: of shutter)*
tempo di apertura.
  2 *vi* **(a)** *(pt, pp* **sped):** **to ~ along** *(car, work)*
procedere velocemente; **to ~ away** *or* **off** *(car,
person)* sfrecciare via; **the years sped by** gli anni
sono volati. **(b)** *(pt, pp* **speeded)** *(Aut: exceed ~
limit)* andare a velocità eccessiva.
  3 cpd: ~ **cop** *n (fam)* agente *m* della stradale;
~ **limit** *n* limite *m* di velocità; ~ **trap** *n (Aut)* tratto
di strada sul quale la polizia controlla la velocità dei
veicoli.

♦ **speed up** *pt, pp* **speeded up 1** *vi + adv (gen)*
andare più veloce; *(Aut)* accelerare; *(walker/
worker/train etc)* camminare/lavorare/viaggiare
più veloce; *(engine, machine)* girare più veloce;
(production) accelerarsi. **2** *vt + adv* accelerare.

speed·boat ['spiːdbəʊt] *n* motoscafo.

speed·ing ['spiːdɪŋ] *n (Aut)* eccesso di velocità.

speed·om·eter [spɪ'dɒmɪtə^r] *n* tachimetro.

speed·way ['spiːdweɪ] *n:* ~ **racing** corsa motoci-
clistica (su pista).

speedy ['spiːdɪ] *adj* **(-ier, -iest)** *(gen)* veloce, rapi-
do(a); *(reply)* pronto(a).

spell¹ [spɛl] *n* incantesimo; *(words)* formula magica; **an evil ~** una stregoneria; **to cast** *or* **put a ~
on sb** fare un incantesimo a qn; *(fig)* stregare
qn; **to fall under sb's ~** *(fig)* subire il fascino di
qn; **to break the ~** *(also fig)* rompere l'incantesimo.

spell² [spɛl] *pt, pp* **spelled** *or* **spelt** *vt:* **how do you ~
your name?** come si scrive il tuo nome?; **can you
~ it for me?** me lo puoi dettare lettera per
lettera?; **c-a-t ~s 'cat'** c-a-t formano la parola
'cat'; **I can't spell** faccio errori di ortografia; **it
~s disaster for us** *(fig)* significa la nostra rovina.

♦ **spell out** *vt + adv (fig):* **to ~ sth out for sb**
spiegare qc a qn per filo e per segno.

spell³ [spɛl] *n (period)* periodo; **cold ~** periodo di
freddo; **to do a ~ of duty** fare un turno; **they're
going through a bad ~** stanno attraversando un
brutto periodo.

spell·bound ['spɛlbaʊnd] *adj* incantato(a); **to hold
sb ~** affascinare qn.

spell·ing ['spɛlɪŋ] **1** *n* ortografia. **2 cpd:** ~ **mistake**
n errore *m* di ortografia.

spelt [spɛlt] *pt, pp of* **spell².**

spend [spɛnd] *pt, pp* **spent** *vt* **(a)** *(money)* spendere;
to ~ money on sb/sth spendere soldi per qn/qc;
without ~ing a penny senza spendere una lira;
to ~ a penny *(Brit fam)* fare pipì. **(b)** *(pass)* passare, trascorrere; **he ~s his time sleeping** passa
il tempo dormendo. **(c)** *(devote):* **to ~ time/
money/effort on sth** dedicare tempo/soldi/ener-
gie a qc; **I spent 2 hours writing that letter** ho
passato 2 ore a scrivere quella lettera.

spend·ing ['spɛndɪŋ] **1** *n* spesa; **government ~**
spesa pubblica. **2 cpd:** ~ **money** *n* denaro per le
piccole spese; ~ **power** *n* potere *m* d'acquisto.

spend·thrift ['spɛndθrɪft] **1** *adj* che spende e span-
de. **2** *n* spendaccione/a.

spent [spɛnt] **1** *pt, pp of* **spend. 2** *adj (cartridge,
bullets, match)* usato(a); *(supplies)* esaurito(a);
he's a ~ force è un uomo finito.

sperm [spɜːm] **1** *n (Bio)* sperma *m*. **2 cpd:** ~ **whale** *n*
capodoglio.

sphere [sfɪə^r] *n (gen)* sfera; **his ~ of interest** la sua
sfera d'interessi; **his ~ of activity** il suo campo
di attività; **within a limited ~** in un ambito molto
ristretto; **that's outside my ~** non rientra nelle
mie competenze.

spheri·cal ['sfɛrɪkəl] *adj* sferico(a).

sphinx [sfɪŋks] *n* sfinge *f*.

spice [spaɪs] **1** *n (Culin)* droga; *(fig)* sapore *m;*
mixed ~(s) spezie *fpl* miste; **variety is the ~ of
life** la varietà dà sapore alla vita. **2** *vt (Culin)*
condire (con spezie); **a highly ~d account** un
racconto molto gustoso.

spick-and-span [,spɪkən'spæn] *adj* lindo(a) e pu-
lito(a).

spicy ['spaɪsɪ] *adj* **(-ier, -iest)** *(Culin, fig)* piccante.

spi·der ['spaɪdə^r] *n* ragno; ~'s **web** ragnatela.

spiel [spiːl] *n (fam)* tiritera.

spike [spaɪk] **1** *n (point)* punta; *(on shoe)* chiodo; ~s
(Sport) scarpe *fpl* chiodate. **2** *vt (fig):* **to ~ sb's
guns** rompere le uova nel paniere a qn; **a ~d
drink** *(fam)* una bevanda corretta.

spiky ['spaɪkɪ] *adj* **(-ier, -iest)** *(bush, branch)* spi-
noso(a); *(animal)* ricoperto(a) di aculei.

spill [spɪl] *pt, pp* **spilled** *or* **spilt** [spɪlt] **1** *vt (gen)*
rovesciare, versare; *(blood)* spargere; **to ~ the
beans** *(fam)* spiattellare tutto. **2** *vi* rovesciarsi,
versarsi.

♦ **spill out** *vi + adv* uscire fuori; *(fall out)* cadere
fuori; **the audience spilt out of the cinema** gli
spettatori si riversarono fuori dal cinema. **2** *vt +
adv (contents etc)* rovesciare; *(fig: story)* rivelare.

♦ **spill over** *vi + adv:* **to ~ over (into)** *(liquid)*
versarsi (in); *(crowd)* riversarsi (in).

spin [spɪn] *(vb: pt* **spun** *or* **span,** *pp* **spun) 1** *n* **(a)**
(revolution) giro; **to give a wheel a ~** far girare
una ruota; **to give sth a long/short ~** *(in washing
machine)* tenere qc a lungo/poco tempo nella

centrifuga; **to be in a flat** ~ *(fam)* essere in preda al panico; **to go into a flat** ~ lasciarsi prendere dal panico. **(b)** *(on ball)* effetto; **to put a** ~ **on a ball** imprimere l'effetto a una palla. **(c)** *(Aer)*: **to go into a** ~ discendere in vite; *(Aut)* fare testacoda. **(d)** *(ride)*: **to go for a** ~ fare un giretto.

   2 *vt* **(a)** *(cotton, wool etc)* filare; *(subj: spider)* tessere. **(b)** *(turn: wheel etc)* far girare; *(clothes)* mettere nella centrifuga; *(ball)* imprimere l'effetto a; **to** ~ **a coin** lanciare in aria una moneta.

   3 *vi* **(a)** filare. **(b)** *(revolve: person)* girarsi; *(: ball)* ruotare; *(: wheel)* girare; **to** ~ **round and round** girare su se stesso; **the car spun out of control** la macchina ha sbandato e ha girato su se stessa; **to send sb** ~**ning** mandare qn a gambe all'aria; **it makes my head** ~ mi fa girare la testa.

♦ **spin out** *vt + adv (fam: visit, holiday)* prolungare; *(: speech, food)* far durare.

spin·ach ['spɪnɪdʒ] *n* spinaci *mpl*.

spi·nal ['spaɪnl] *adj* spinale; ~ **column** colonna vertebrale, spina dorsale; ~ **cord** midollo spinale; ~ **injury** lesione *f* alla spina dorsale.

spin·dle ['spɪndl] *n (for spinning)* fuso; *(Tech)* perno, asse *m*.

spin·dly ['spɪndlɪ] *adj* (**-ier, -iest**) *(gen)* lungo(a) e sottile; *(person)* smilzo(a).

spin-dry [,spɪn'draɪ] *vt* asciugare con la centrifuga.

spin-dryer [,spɪn'draɪə^r] *n* centrifuga.

spine [spaɪn] *n (Anat)* spina dorsale; *(Zool)* aculeo; *(Bot)* spina; *(of book)* dorso; *(of mountain range)* cresta.

spine-chiller ['spaɪn'tʃɪlə^r] *n (film, book etc)* film *m* (*or* libro *etc*) dell'orrore.

spine-chilling ['spaɪn,tʃɪlɪŋ] *adj* agghiacciante.

spine·less ['spaɪnlɪs] *adj (fig)* smidollato(a).

spin·ner ['spɪnə^r] *n (of cloth etc)* tessitore/trice; *(Fishing)* cucchiaino; *(fam: spin-dryer)* centrifuga.

spin·ney ['spɪnɪ] *n* boschetto.

spin·ning ['spɪnɪŋ] **1** *n* filatura. **2** *cpd:* ~ **top** *n* trottola; ~ **wheel** *n* filatoio.

spin-off ['spɪnɒf] *n* applicazione *f* secondaria; *(product)* prodotto secondario.

spin·ster ['spɪnstə^r] *n* zitella.

spi·ral ['spaɪərəl] **1** *adj* a spirale; ~ **staircase** scala a chiocciola. **2** *n* spirale *f*; **the inflationary** ~ la spirale dell'inflazione. **3** *vi (prices)* salire verticalmente; **to** ~ **up/down** *(also Aer)* salire/scendere a spirale.

spire ['spaɪə^r] *n* guglia.

spir·it ['spɪrɪt] **1** *n* **(a)** *(soul)* spirito; **I'll be with you in** ~ ti sarò vicino in spirito; **one of the greatest** ~**s of the age** uno dei più grandi personaggi dell'epoca; **one of the leading** ~**s in the party** uno dei principali animatori del partito.

   (b) *(ghost, supernatural being)* spirito; **Holy S**~ Spirito Santo.

   (c) *(courage)* coraggio; *(energy)* energia; *(vitality)* brio, vitalità.

   (d) *(attitude etc)* spirito; **community** ~, **public** ~ senso civico; **in a** ~ **of optimism** con un atteggiamento ottimista; **to enter into the** ~ **of sth** entrare nello spirito di qc; **that's the** ~! *(fam)* bravo!, così va bene!; **the** ~ **of the law** lo spirito della legge; **to take sth in the right/wrong** ~ prendere qc bene/male.

   (e): ~**s** *pl (state of mind)*: **high** ~**s** vivacità; **to be in low** ~**s** essere giù di morale; **we kept our** ~**s up by singing** ci siamo tenuti su di morale cantando; **my** ~**s rose somewhat** mi sono tirato un po' su.

   (f): ~**s** *pl (alcohol)* liquori *mpl*; **raw** ~**s** alcool *m* puro.

   (g) *(Chem)* spirito, alcool *m inv*.

   2 *cpd:* ~ **lamp** *n* lampada a spirito; ~ **level** *n* livella a bolla d'aria.

♦ **spirit away, spirit off** *vt + adv* far sparire misteriosamente.

spir·it·ed ['spɪrɪtɪd] *adj (horse)* focoso(a); *(conversation)* animato(a); *(person, attack etc)* energico(a); *(description)* vivace; **he gave a** ~ **performance** *(Mus, Theatre)* ha fornito una brillante interpretazione.

spir·itu·al ['spɪrɪtjʊəl] **1** *adj* spirituale. **2** *n (Mus)* canto religioso, spiritual *m inv*.

spir·itu·al·ism ['spɪrɪtjʊəlɪzəm] *n (occult)* spiritismo.

spir·itu·al·ist ['spɪrɪtjʊəlɪst] *n (occult)* spiritista *m/f*.

spir·itu·al·ity [,spɪrɪtjʊ'ælɪtɪ] *n* spiritualità.

spit[1] [spɪt] *n (Culin)* spiedo; *(of land)* lingua di terra.

spit[2] [spɪt] *(vb: pt, pp* **spat**) **1** *n (spittle)* sputo; *(saliva)* saliva; **a bit of** ~ **and polish** *(fam)* una bella lucidata; **to be the dead** ~ **of sb** *(fam)* essere il ritratto sputato di qn. **2** *vt* sputare. **3** *vi:* **to** ~ **(at)** sputare (addosso a); *(cat)* soffiare (contro); **to** ~ **on the ground** sputare per terra; **it is** ~**ting with rain** sta piovigginando.

♦ **spit out** *vt + adv (sparks)* sprigionare; *(fat)* schizzare; ~ **it out!** *(fam: say it)* sputa fuori!

spite [spaɪt] **1** *n* **(a)** *(ill will)* dispetto; **to do sth out of** *(or* **from)** ~ fare qc per dispetto; **to have a** ~ **against sb** *(fam)* serbare rancore a qn. **(b): in** ~ **of** *(despite)* nonostante, malgrado; **in** ~ **of the fact that** malgrado *or* nonostante (il fatto che) + *sub;* **she laughed in** ~ **of herself** ha riso nonostante tutto. **2** *vt* far dispetto a.

spite·ful ['spaɪtfʊl] *adj (person, behaviour)* dispettoso(a); *(tongue, remark)* maligno(a), velenoso(a).

spit·fire ['spɪt,faɪə^r] *n:* **she's a real** ~ è una persona molto irascibile.

spit·ting ['spɪtɪŋ] **1** *n:* '~ **prohibited**' 'vietato sputare'. **2** *adj:* **to be the** ~ **image of sb** essere il ritratto vivente *or* sputato di qn.

spit·tle ['spɪtl] *n (ejected)* sputo; *(dribbled)* saliva; *(of animal)* bava.

splash [splæʃ] **1** *n* (~**ing noise)** tonfo; *(series of* ~**es)** sciabordio; *(mark)* spruzzo, macchia; *(fig: of colour, light)* chiazza, macchia; **to make a** ~ *(fig)* far furore. **2** *vt* schizzare; **to** ~ **sb with water** schizzare qn d'acqua; **to** ~ **sth over sb** schizzare qc addosso a qn; **to** ~ **one's face with water** spruzzarsi acqua sul viso; **to** ~ **paint on the floor** schizzare il pavimento di vernice; **the story was** ~**ed across the front page** *(fam)* la notizia è stata sbattuta in prima pagina. **3** *vi (liquid, mud etc)* schizzare; *(person, animal in water: also:* ~ **about)** sguazzare; **to** ~ **across a stream** attraversare un ruscello a guado; **to** ~ **into the water** *(stone)* cadere nell'acqua con un tonfo.

♦ **splash down** *vi + adv* ammarare.

♦ **splash out** *vi + adv (fam)* fare spese folli.

splash·down ['splæʃdaʊn] *n* ammaraggio.

spleen [spliːn] *n (Anat)* milza; **to vent one's** ~ *(fig)* sfogarsi.

splen·did ['splendɪd] *adj (ceremony, clothes)* splendido(a), magnifico(a); *(idea, example)* eccellente, ottimo(a); **that's** ~! magnifico!, fantastico!

splen·did·ly ['splendɪdlɪ] *adv* splendidamente, magnificamente.

splen·dour, *(Am)* **splen·dor** ['splendə^r] *n* splendore *m*, magnificenza.

splice [splaɪs] *vt (rope, film)* giuntare.

splint [splɪnt] n (Med) stecca; **to put sb's arm in ~s** steccare il braccio di qn.

splin·ter ['splɪntə'] **1** n scheggia. **2** vi (wood, glass) scheggiarsi; (fig: party) staccarsi, separarsi. **3** vt (wood, glass) scheggiare; (fig: party) dividere. **4** cpd: **~ group** n gruppo dissidente.

split [splɪt] (vb: pt, pp split) **1** n **(a)** (in ground, wall, rock) fessura, crepa; (in wood) spacco; (in garment, fabric) strappo. **(b)** (fig: division, quarrel) scissione f, rottura; **there are fears of a ~ in the party** si teme una scissione nel partito. **(c):** **to do the ~s** fare la spaccata. **(d)** (cake etc): **jam ~** focaccina ripiena di marmellata; **banana ~** banana-split f inv.

2 vt **(a)** (cleave) spaccare; (tear) strappare; **to ~ the atom** scindere l'atomo; **to ~ sth open** aprire qc spaccandola; **he ~ his head open** si è spaccato la testa; **to ~ sth down the middle** (also fig) spaccare qc a metà; **to ~ hairs** (fig) spaccare un capello in quattro; **to ~ one's sides laughing** (fig) ridere a crepapelle. **(b)** (divide: also fig) dividere; **to ~ sth into three parts** dividere qc in tre; **to ~ the profit five ways** dividere il guadagno in cinque parti; **to ~ the difference** dividersi la differenza.

3 vi **(a)** (wood, stone) spaccarsi; (cloth) strapparsi; (fig: party, church) dividersi; **to ~ open** spaccarsi; **my head is ~ting** mi scoppia la testa. **(b)** (fam: tell tales): **don't you ~ on me to the police!** non denunciarmi alla polizia!

4 cpd: **~ infinitive** n infinito dove un avverbio divide il 'to' dal verbo; **~ peas** npl piselli mpl secchi spaccati; **~ personality** n doppia personalità; **~ second** n frazione f di secondo.

♦ **split off 1** vi + adv (also fig) staccarsi, separarsi. **2** vt + adv (also fig) staccare, separare.

♦ **split up 1** vi + adv (stone etc) spaccarsi; (ship on rocks) schiantarsi; (meeting, crowd) disperdersi; (: into groups) dividersi; (partners) separarsi; (friends) rompere. **2** vt + adv (stone etc) spaccare; (movement, party, money, work) dividere; (crowd) disperdere; (partners) separare.

split-level ['splɪt,levl] adj (house) a piani sfalsati.

split·ting ['splɪtɪŋ] adj: **a ~ headache** un mal di testa terribile.

splodge [splɒdʒ] n, **splotch** [splɒtʃ] n macchia.

splut·ter ['splʌtə'] vi (person: spit) sputacchiare; (: stutter) farfugliare; (fire) crepitare; (fat) schizzare; (engine) scoppiettare.

spoil [spɔɪl] (vb: pt, pp spoiled or spoilt) **1** n (also: ~s: booty) bottino. **2** vt **(a)** (ruin, detract from) rovinare; (ballot paper) rendere nullo(a), invalidare; **don't ~ our fun** non fare il guastafeste; **to ~ one's appetite** guastarsi l'appetito. **(b)** (pamper) viziare. **3** vi **(a)** (food) guastarsi, andare a male; **(: while cooking)** rovinarsi; **to be ~ing for a fight** morire dalla voglia di litigare.

spoil·sport ['spɔɪlspɔːt] n (fam) guastafeste m/f.

spoilt [spɔɪlt] **1** pt, pp of **spoil**. **2** adj (child) viziato(a); (meal) rovinato(a); (ballot paper) nullo(a).

spoke¹ [spəʊk] n raggio; **to put a ~ in sb's wheel** mettere i bastoni fra le ruote a qn.

spoke² [spəʊk] pt of **speak**.

spo·ken ['spəʊkən] pp of **speak**.

spokes·man ['spəʊksmən] n, pl **-men** portavoce m inv.

spokes·woman ['spəʊkswʊmən] n, pl **-women** portavoce f inv.

sponge [spʌndʒ] **1** n spugna; (Culin: also: **~ cake**) pan m di Spagna; **to throw in the ~** (fig) gettare la spugna. **2** vt (wash) lavare con una spugna; **to ~ a stain off** pulire una macchia con una spugna. **3** vi (fam: scrounge) scroccare; **to ~ off or on sb** vive-

re alle spalle di qn. **4** cpd: **~ bag** n nécessaire m inv.

♦ **sponge down** vt + adv lavare con una spugna.

spong·er ['spʌndʒə'] n (fam) scroccone/a.

spon·gy ['spʌndʒɪ] adj (-ier, -iest) spugnoso(a).

spon·sor ['spɒnsə'] **1** n (of enterprise, bill, for fund raising) promotore/trice; (for loan) garante m/f; (of member) socio garante; (Radio, TV, Sport etc) sponsor m/f inv; (godparent) padrino/madrina. **2** vt (enterprise etc) promuovere; (borrower, member of club) garantire; (Parliamentary bill) presentare; (Radio, TV, Sport etc) sponsorizzare; (as godparents) tenere a battesimo; **I ~ed him at 3p a mile** (in fund-raising race) mi sono impegnato a pagare 3 penny per ogni miglio che fa.

spon·sor·ship ['spɒnsəʃɪp] n (see sponsor n) promozione f; garanzia; sponsorizzazione f.

spon·ta·neity [,spɒntə'neɪɪtɪ] n spontaneità.

spon·ta·neous [spɒn'teɪnɪəs] adj spontaneo(a); **~ combustion** autocombustione f.

spon·ta·neous·ly [spɒn'teɪnɪəslɪ] adv spontaneamente.

spoof [spuːf] n (fam) presa in giro.

spook [spuːk] n (fam) fantasma m, spettro.

spooky ['spuːkɪ] adj (-ier, -iest) (fam) sinistro(a).

spool [spuːl] n (Phot, on sewing machine, on fishing line) bobina; (~ of thread) rocchetto.

spoon [spuːn] **1** n cucchiaio; **to be born with a silver ~ in one's mouth** essere nato con la camicia. **2** vt: **to ~ out** (sauce, cream) servire con il cucchiaio; **to ~ sth into a plate** versare qc in un piatto con il cucchiaio.

spoon·er·ism ['spuːnərɪzəm] n papera consistente nello scambio delle iniziali di due parole.

spoon-feed ['spuːnfiːd] pt, pp **spoon-fed** ['spuːnfed] vt imboccare, nutrire con il cucchiaio; (fig) scodellare la pappa a.

spoon·ful ['spuːnfʊl] n cucchiaiata.

spoor [spʊə'] n traccia, pista.

spo·rad·ic [spə'rædɪk] adj (attempts, gunfire) sporadico(a); (flow of work) discontinuo(a).

spore [spɔː'] n spora.

sport [spɔːt] **1** n **(a)** sport m inv; **indoor/outdoor ~s** sport pl al chiuso/all'aria aperta; **to be good at ~** riuscire bene nello sport; **~s** (meeting) gare fpl. **(b)** (amusement) divertimento; **to say sth in ~** dire qc per scherzo. **(c)** (fam: person) persona di spirito; **be a ~!** sii buono! **2** vt sfoggiare. **3** cpd: **~s car** n automobile f sportiva; **~s ground** n campo sportivo; **~s jacket** n giacca sportiva.

sport·ing ['spɔːtɪŋ] adj sportivo(a); **there's a ~ chance that** c'è una buona probabilità che + sub.

sports·man ['spɔːtsmən] n, pl **-men** sportivo.

sports·man·ship ['spɔːtsmənʃɪp] n spirito sportivo.

sports·wear ['spɔːtsweə'] n abbigliamento sportivo.

sports·woman ['spɔːts,wʊmən] n, pl **-women** sportiva.

sporty ['spɔːtɪ] adj (-ier, -iest) (fam) sportivo(a).

spot [spɒt] **1** n **(a)** (dot) puntino; (on dress) pois m inv, pallino; (stain, also fig) macchia; **a cloth with blue ~s** una stoffa a pallini or pois blu; **to knock ~s off sb** (fig fam) dare dei punti a qn; **to have ~s before one's eyes** vedere dei puntini.

(b) (Med etc) foruncolo; **to break or come out in ~s** coprirsi di foruncoli.

(c) (place) posto; **a pleasant ~** un bel posto; **to have a tender ~ on the arm** avere un punto nel braccio che fa male; **the reporter was on the ~** il reporter era sul posto; **the firemen were on the ~ in 3 minutes** i pompieri sono arrivati sul posto in 3 minuti; **an on-the-~ broadcast** una trasmissione in diretta; **to do sth on the ~** fare qc immediatamente *or* lì per lì; **to be in a (tight) ~** *(fig)* essere nei guai *or* nei pasticci; **to put sb in a ~** *or* **on the ~** *(fig)* mettere in difficoltà qn; **that's my weak ~** *(fig)* è il mio punto debole.

(d) *(Brit fam: small quantity)*: **a ~ of** un po' di; *(: of milk, wine etc)* un goccio di; **just a ~, thanks** pochissimo, grazie; **we had a ~ of rain yesterday** ha fatto qualche goccia di pioggia ieri; **would you like a ~ of lunch?** vuoi mangiare un boccone?; **to have a ~ of bother** avere noie.

(e) *(Radio, Theatre, TV: in show)* numero; *(Radio, TV: advertisement)* spazio, spot *m inv*.

(f) *(fam: spotlight)* riflettore *m*.

2 *vt* **(a)** *(speckle)*: **to ~ (with)** macchiare (di).

(b) *(notice, see: mistake, person in a crowd)* notare; *(: car, person in the distance)* scorgere; *(recognize: winner)* indovinare; *(: talent, sb's ability)* scoprire; *(: bargain)* riconoscere.

3 *cpd*: **~ check** *n* controllo casuale; **~ remover** *n* smacchiatore *m*.

spot·less ['spɒtlɪs] *adj* pulitissimo(a); *(fig: reputation)* senza macchia; *(: character)* retto(a).

spot·less·ly ['spɒtlɪslɪ] *adv*: **~ clean** pulitissimo(a).

spot·light ['spɒtlaɪt] *n (lamp)* spot *m inv*; *(beam)* fascio luminoso; *(Aut)* faro *m* battistrada *inv*; **in the ~** sotto la luce dei riflettori; *(fig)* al centro dell'attenzione; **to turn the ~ on sb/sth** *(fig)* mettere in risalto qn/qc, richiamare l'attenzione su qn/qc.

spot-on ['spɒt'ɒn] *adj* esatto(a).

spot·ted ['spɒtɪd] *adj (material)* a pois, a pallini; *(animal)* macchiato(a).

spot·ty ['spɒtɪ] *adj* **(-ier, -iest)** *(fam)* pieno(a) di foruncoli.

spouse [spauz] *n* sposo/a.

spout [spaut] **1** *n (of teapot etc)* becco, beccuccio; *(of guttering)* scarico; *(for tap)* frangigetto; *(column of water)* getto; **my holiday's up the ~** *(fam)* la mia vacanza è andata in fumo. **2** *vt (water)* gettare; *(lava)* eruttare; *(smoke)* emettere; *(fam: poetry etc)* declamare.

sprain [spreɪn] **1** *n* slogatura; *(of muscle)* strappo muscolare. **2** *vt (muscle)* stirarsi; **to ~ one's wrist/ankle** slogarsi un polso/una caviglia.

sprang [spræŋ] *pt of* **spring**.

sprawl [sprɔːl] **1** *vi (person: sit, lie)* stare sdraiato(a); *(: fall)* cadere; *(town)* estendersi (disordinatamente); *(plant)* allungarsi; **her handwriting ~ed all over the page** la sua scrittura copriva tutta la pagina; **to send sb ~ing** mandare qn a gambe all'aria. **2** *n*: **urban ~** sviluppo urbanistico incontrollato; **a ~ of buildings lay below them** un gruppo di edifici si estendeva disordinatamente dinanzi ai loro occhi.

sprawl·ing ['sprɔːlɪŋ] *adj (person)* sdraiato(a); *(: in armchair)* sprofondato(a); *(handwriting)* disordinato(a); *(city)* disordinatamente esteso(a).

spray[1] [spreɪ] **1** *n* **(a)** *(from hosepipe)* getto; *(from wet road)* schizzi *mpl*; *(of sea, fountain)* spruzzi *mpl*; *(from atomizer, aerosol)* spruzzo. **(b)** *(aerosol, atomizer)* spray *m inv*, bomboletta; *(: of perfume)* vaporizzatore *m*; *(: for paint, garden)* spruzzatore *m*; *(Med)* spray. **2** *vt (gen)* spruzzare; **to ~ sth/sb with water** spruzzare qc/qn d'acqua; **to ~ sth/sb with bullets** sparare una scarica di proiettili contro qc/qn. **3** *cpd (deodorant)* spray *inv*; *(gun, paint)* a spruzzo.

spray[2] [spreɪ] *n (of greenery)* ramoscello; *(of flowers)* mazzolino; *(brooch)* spilla a forma di ramoscello.

spray·er ['spreɪə[r]] *n* = **spray 1b**.

spread [spred] *(vb: pt, pp spread)* **1** *n* **(a)** *(of fire, infection)* propagazione *f*; *(of idea, knowledge)* diffusione *f*; *(of crime)* dilagare *m*; **the ~ of nuclear weapons** la proliferazione delle armi nucleari. **(b)** *(extent: of bridge)* ampiezza; *(: of wings, arch)* apertura; *(: of prices, of figures, marks etc)* gamma; **middle-age ~** pancetta. **(c)** *(fam: of food etc)* banchetto. **(d)** *(bed~)* copriletto. **(e)** *(for bread)*: **anchovy ~ =** pasta d'acciughe; **cheese ~** formaggio da spalmare. **(f)** *(Press, Typ: two pages)* doppia pagina; *(: across columns)* articolo a più colonne.

2 *vt* **(a)** *(open or lay out: also: ~ out: wings, sails etc)* spiegare; *(: fingers)* distendere; *(: arms)* allargare; **to ~ a map out on the table** spiegare una cartina sul tavolo; **to ~ one's wings** *(fig)* esprimere a pieno le proprie capacità. **(b)** *(butter, cream etc)* spalmare; **to ~ cream on one's face** spalmarsi la crema sul viso. **(c)** *(distribute: also: ~ out: sand, fertilizer)*: **to ~ sth on sth** cospargere qc di qc; *(: goods, objects)* disporre; *(: cards, toys)* spargere; *(: soldiers, payments)* scaglionare; *(: resources)* distribuire; **repayments will be ~ over 18 months** i versamenti saranno scaglionati lungo un periodo di 18 mesi. **(d)** *(disseminate: germs, disease)* propagare; *(: knowledge, panic etc)* diffondere; *(: news)* spargere.

3 *vi (news, rumour etc)* diffondersi, spargersi; *(pain, fire, flood etc)* estendersi; *(milk etc)* spargersi; *(disease, weeds)* propagarsi; **to ~ into sth** estendersi fino a qc; **margarine ~s better than butter** la margarina si spalma meglio del burro.

♦ **spread out 1** *vi + adv (view, valley)* stendersi; *(soldiers, police)* disporsi. **2** *vt + adv* = **spread 2a** *and c*.

spread-eagled [,spred'iːgld] *adj*: **to be** *or* **lie ~** essere disteso/a a gambe e braccia aperte.

spree [spriː] *n (fam)*: **to go on a spending ~** fare spese folli; **to go on a ~** darsi alla pazza gioia, fare baldoria.

sprig [sprɪg] *n* ramoscello.

spright·ly ['spraɪtlɪ] *adj* **(-ier, -iest)** vivace; **a ~ old man** un vecchietto arzillo.

spring [sprɪŋ] *(vb: pt* **sprang**, *pp* **sprung)** **1** *n* **(a)** *(of water)* sorgente *f*; **hot ~** sorgente termale. **(b)** *(season)* primavera; **in ~, in the ~** in primavera; **~ is in the air** c'è aria di primavera. **(c)** *(leap)* salto; **in one ~** in un salto. **(d)** *(bounciness)* elasticità; **to walk with a ~ in one's step** camminare con passo elastico. **(e)** *(gen, also Tech)* molla; **~s** *(Aut)* sospensione *f*, balestre *fpl*.

2 *vt (trap, lock etc)* far scattare; **to ~ a leak** *(pipe etc)* cominciare a perdere; **the boat has sprung a leak** s'è aperta una falla nella barca; **he sprang a question on me** *(fig)* mi ha fatto una domanda a bruciapelo; **to ~ a surprise on sb** fare una sorpresa a qn; **he sprang the news on me** mi ha sorpreso con quella notizia; **he sprang it on me** mi ha preso alla sprovvista.

3 *vi* **(a)** *(leap)* saltare; **to ~ aside/forward** balzare da una parte/in avanti; **to ~ back** saltare *or* scattare all'indietro; **the door sprang open** la porta si aprì di scatto; **where on earth did you ~ from?** *(fam)* da dove spunti?; **to ~ into the air** fare un balzo in aria; **to ~ into action** entrare (rapidamente) in azione; **to ~ to one's feet** scattare in piedi; **to ~ to mind** venire in mente. **(b)** *(originate: gen)* sorgere; *(: tears)* sgorgare; *(: rumours)* saltar fuori; *(: wind)* alzarsi.

4 *cpd* **(a)** *(of season)* di primavera, primaverile; **~ onion** *n* cipollina. **(b)** *(with ~s: mattress)* a molle; **~ binder** *n (file)* raccoglitore *m* a molla.

◆ **spring up** vi + adv (person) saltar su; (plant, weeds, building) spuntare, venire su; (problem, obstacle) presentarsi; (wind, storm) alzarsi, levarsi; (doubt, friendship, rumour) nascere.

spring·board ['sprɪŋbɔːd] n trampolino.

spring·cleaning [,sprɪŋ'kliːnɪŋ] n pulizie fpl di primavera or di Pasqua.

spring·time ['sprɪŋtaɪm] n primavera.

springy ['sprɪŋɪ] adj (-ier, -iest) (gen) elastico(a); (carpet, turf) morbido(a); (mattress) molleggiato(a).

sprin·kle ['sprɪŋkl] vt: to ~ with (gen) cospargere di; (water) spruzzare di; **they are ~d about here and there** sono sparsi un po' dovunque.

sprin·kler ['sprɪŋklə^r] n (for lawn etc) irrigatore m; (for fire-fighting) sprinkler m inv.

sprin·kling ['sprɪŋklɪŋ] n (of water) qualche goccia; (of salt, sugar) pizzico; (of snow) spruzzatina; **there was a ~ of young people** c'era qualche giovane.

sprint [sprɪnt] 1 n (in race) sprint m inv, scatto; (dash) corsa; **the 200-metres ~** i 200 metri piani. 2 vi (in race) scattare; (dash: for bus etc) fare una corsa.

sprint·er ['sprɪntə^r] n (Sport) velocista m/f.

sprout [spraʊt] 1 n (from bulb, seeds) germoglio; **(Brussels) ~s** cavoletti mpl di Bruxelles. 2 vt (leaves, shoots) mettere, produrre; **to ~ a moustache** farsi crescere i baffi. 3 vi germogliare; (child) crescere in fretta; **skyscrapers are ~ing up everywhere** i grattacieli spuntano dappertutto.

spruce[1] [spruːs] n (Bot) abete m.

spruce[2] [spruːs] adj (outfit) elegante; (lawn) ben curato(a); (person) azzimato(a).

◆ **spruce up** vt + adv (tidy) mettere in ordine; (smarten up: room etc) abbellire; **to ~ o.s. up** farsi bello; **all ~d up** tutto azzimato or agghindato.

sprung [sprʌŋ] 1 pp of **spring**. 2 adj (seat, mattress) a molle; **interior-~ mattress** materasso a molle.

spry [spraɪ] adj vivace, arzillo(a).

spud [spʌd] n (fam: potato) patata.

spun [spʌn] pt, pp of **spin**.

spunk [spʌŋk] n (fam): **she's got ~** ha fegato.

spur [spɜː^r] 1 n (also Geog) sperone m; (fig) sprone m, stimolo; **on the ~ of the moment** su due piedi. 2 vt (also: ~ on: horse, fig) spronare; **to ~ sb on to do sth** spronare qn a fare qc.

spu·ri·ous ['spjʊərɪəs] adj (gen) falso(a); (affection, interest) falso(a), simulato(a).

spurn [spɜːn] vt respingere.

spurt [spɜːt] 1 n (of water, steam etc) getto; (of speed, energy, anger) scatto; **to put in** or **on a ~** (runner) fare uno scatto; (fig: in work etc) affrettarsi, sbrigarsi. 2 vi (gush: also: ~ out) sgorgare.

sput·nik ['spʊtnɪk] n sputnik m inv.

spy [spaɪ] 1 n spia; (police ~) informatore/trice (della polizia). 2 vt (catch sight of) scorgere. 3 vi spiare, fare la spia; **to ~ on sb** spiare qn. 4 cpd (film, story) di spionaggio.

◆ **spy out** vt + adv: **to ~ out the land** esplorare il terreno.

spy·glass ['spaɪglɑːs] n cannocchiale m.

spy·ing ['spaɪɪŋ] n spionaggio.

Sq abbr (= Square: in address) Pzza.

sq (Math) abbr of **square**.

squab·ble ['skwɒbl] 1 n battibecco. 2 vi: **to ~ (over** or **about)** bisticciarsi (per).

squad [skwɒd] 1 n (Mil) drappello, plotone m; (of police, workmen etc) squadra; **flying ~** (Police) volante f; **the Ireland ~** (Ftbl) la (squadra) nazionale irlandese. 2 cpd: **~ car** n (Police) automobile f della polizia.

squad·ron ['skwɒdrən] n (Mil) squadrone m; (Aer, Naut) squadriglia.

squal·id ['skwɒlɪd] adj squallido(a).

squall [skwɔːl] 1 n (Met) bufera, burrasca. 2 vi (baby) strillare, urlare.

squal·or ['skwɒlə^r] n squallore m.

squan·der ['skwɒndə^r] vt (money) sperperare; (time, opportunity) sprecare, perdere.

square [skwɛə^r] 1 n (a) (gen) quadrato; (check on material) quadro; **with red and blue ~s** a quadri rossi e blu; **to cut into ~s** tagliare in (pezzi) quadrati; **we're back to ~ one** (fig) siamo al punto di partenza.

    (b) (in town) piazza; (Am: block of houses) blocco, isolato; **the town ~** la piazza principale.

    (c) (Math) quadrato; **16 is the ~ of 4** 16 è il quadrato di 4.

    (d) (fam: old-fashioned person) matusa m inv; **he's a real ~** è proprio un matusa.

    2 adj **(a)** (in shape) quadrato(a); **~ bracket** (Typ) parentesi f inv quadra; **he's like a ~ peg in a round hole in that job** è un lavoro che non fa per lui.

    (b) (Math) quadrato(a); **a ~ kilometre** un chilometro quadrato; **a kilometre ~** un quadrato di un chilometro (per lato).

    (c): **a ~ meal** un buon pasto, un pasto sostanzioso.

    (d) (fair, honest) onesto(a), retto(a); **to give sb a ~ deal** trattare qn onestamente; **I'll be ~ with you** sarò franco con te.

    (e) (even: accounts, figures) in ordine; **to get one's accounts ~** mettere in ordine i propri conti; **to get ~ with sb** (also fig) regolare i conti con qn; **now we're all ~** (fig, Sport) adesso siamo pari.

    (f) (fam: old-fashioned: person) di vecchio stampo, all'antica; (: idea) sorpassato(a); (: style) fuori moda.

    3 adv: **~ in the middle** esattamente or proprio nel centro; **to look sb ~ in the face** guardare qn (diritto) negli occhi or in faccia.

    4 vt **(a)** (make ~: stone, timber) squadrare; (: shape) rendere quadrato(a); **to ~ one's shoulders** raddrizzare le spalle.

    (b) (settle etc: accounts, books) mettere in ordine; (: debts) saldare; (reconcile): **can you ~ it with your conscience?** puoi conciliarlo con la tua coscienza?; **I'll ~ it with him** (fam) sistemo io le cose con lui.

    (c) (Math) elevare al quadrato; **2 ~d is 4** 2 al quadrato è 4.

    5 vi: **to ~ (with)** quadrare (con).

    6 cpd: **~ dance** n quadriglia; **~ root** n radice f quadrata.

◆ **square off** vt + adv (wood, edges) squadrare.

◆ **square up** vi + adv (a): **to ~ up (to)** (boxer, fighter) mettersi in guardia (contro); (fig: difficulties) far fronte (a). **(b)** (settle) saldare, pagare; **to ~ up with sb** regolare i conti con qn.

square·ly ['skwɛəlɪ] adv **(a)** (directly) direttamente; **to place sth ~ in the middle of the table** mettere qc proprio in mezzo al tavolo; **to face sth ~** affrontare qc con coraggio. **(b)** (honestly, fairly) onestamente; **to deal ~ with sb** trattare qn onestamente.

squash[1] [skwɒʃ] 1 n **(a)** (drink): **orange/lemon ~** ≃ sciroppo di arancia/limone. **(b)** (crowd) ressa, calca. 2 vt **(a)** (flatten) schiacciare; **can you ~ 2 more in the car?** puoi farne entrare altri due (in macchina)?; **to be ~ed together** essere schiacciati l'uno contro l'altro. **(b)** (fig: argument) soffocare, reprimere; (: person) umiliare.

3 *vi*: **to ~ in** riuscire a entrare; **to ~ up to make room for sb** stringersi per fare posto a qn.

squash² [skwɒʃ] *n (vegetable)* zucca.

squash³ [skwɒʃ] *n (Sport)* squash *m*.

squat [skwɒt] **1** *adj* (**-ter, -test**) *(person)* tarchiato(a), tozzo(a); *(building, shape etc)* tozzo(a). **2** *vi* **(a)** *(also:* **~ down**) accovacciarsi, acquattarsi. **(b)** *(on property)* occupare abusivamente. **3** *n (fam: house)* casa occupata.

squat·ter ['skwɒtəʳ] *n* occupatore(trice) abusivo(a).

squaw [skwɔː] *n* squaw *f inv.*

squawk [skwɔːk] **1** *n* strido rauco. **2** *vi (parrot, baby, person)* strillare; *(fam: complain)* lamentarsi.

squeak [skwiːk] **1** *n (of hinge, wheel etc)* cigolio; *(of shoes)* scricchiolio; *(of mouse etc)* squittio; **a ~ of surprise** un gridolino di sorpresa; **I don't want to hear a ~ out of you!** non voglio sentire una parola! **2** *vi (see noun)* cigolare; scricchiolare; squittire; emettere un gridolino.

squeaky ['skwiːkɪ] *adj* (**-ier, -iest**) *(hinge, wheel)* cigolante; *(shoes)* scricchiolante.

squeal [skwiːl] **1** *n (gen)* strillo; *(of tyres, brakes)* stridore *m*; **a ~ of laughter** una risatina. **2** *vi (see n)* strillare; stridere; *(fam: inform)*: **to ~ (on sb)** fare la spia (a qn).

squeam·ish ['skwiːmɪʃ] *adj (queasy)* nauseato(a); *(fig)* facilmente impressionabile; **to feel ~** avere la nausea.

squeeze [skwiːz] **1** *n (pressure)* pressione *f*; *(of hand)* stretta; *(crush, crowd)* ressa, calca; *(credit ~)* restrizione *f* creditizia; **to give sb's hand a ~** dare una lieve stretta di mano a qn; **it was a tight ~ to get through** c'era appena il posto per passare; **we're in a tight ~** *(fig fam)* ci troviamo in difficoltà; **a ~ of lemon** una spruzzata di limone; **give me a ~ of toothpaste** dammi un po' di dentrifricio; **to put the ~ on sb** far pressione su qn.

2 *vt (gen)* premere; *(sponge)* strizzare; *(lemon etc)* spremere; *(hand, arm)* stringere; **to ~ the juice out of a lemon** spremere un limone; **to ~ toothpaste out of a tube** spremere il dentifricio da un tubetto; **to ~ clothes into a case** pigiare i vestiti in una valigia; **to ~ information out of sb** cavare delle informazioni da qn; **can you ~ 2 more in?** riesci a farcene entrare altri due?

3 *vi*: **to ~ past/under sth** passare vicino/sotto a qc con difficoltà; **to ~ in** infilarsi; **to ~ through a hole** passare a forza attraverso un buco; **to ~ through the crowd** riuscire ad aprirsi un varco tra la folla.

squelch [skwɛltʃ] *vi*: **to ~ in/out** *etc* entrare/uscire sguazzando.

squib [skwɪb] *n* petardo.

squid [skwɪd] *n* calamaro.

squint [skwɪnt] **1** *n (Med)* strabismo; *(sidelong look)* occhiata, sbirciata; **to have a ~** *(Med)* essere strabico(a); **let's have a ~** *(fam)* diamo un'occhiata. **2** *vi (Med)* essere strabico(a); **to ~ at sth** guardare qc di traverso; *(quickly)* dare un'occhiata a qc; **he ~ed in the sunlight** la luce del sole gli faceva strizzare gli occhi.

squire ['skwaɪəʳ] *n (old: landowner)* possidente *m* (terriero).

squirm [skwɜːm] *vi* contorcersi; *(with embarrassment)* sentirsi a disagio.

squir·rel ['skwɪrəl] *n* scoiattolo.

squirt [skwɜːt] **1** *n (of water)* schizzo; *(of detergent, perfume)* spruzzo. **2** *vt* spruzzare. **3** *vi* schizzare.

Sr *n abbr of* **senior.**

St *abbr of* **saint; street.**

stab [stæb] **1** *n* **(a)** *(with knife)* coltellata; *(with dagger)* pugnalata; *(of pain)* fitta; **a ~ in the back** *(also fig)* una pugnalata alla schiena; **he felt a ~ of remorse** gli rimordeva la coscienza. **(b)**: **to have a ~ at sth** provare a fare qc. **2** *vt (with dagger)* pugnalare; *(with knife)* accoltellare; **to ~ sb to death** uccidere qn a coltellate; **to ~ sb in the back** *(also fig)* pugnalare qn alla schiena; **he was ~bed through the heart** fu pugnalato al cuore.

stab·bing ['stæbɪŋ] **1** *n*: **there's been a ~** qualcuno è stato pugnalato. **2** *adj (pain, ache)* lancinante.

sta·bil·ity [stə'bɪlɪtɪ] *n (see* **stable¹**) stabilità; solidità; equilibrio.

sta·bi·lize ['steɪbəlaɪz] **1** *vt* stabilizzare. **2** *vi* stabilizzarsi.

sta·bi·li·zer ['steɪbəlaɪzəʳ] *n (Aer, Naut)* stabilizzatore *m*.

sta·ble¹ ['steɪbl] *adj* (**-r, -st**) *(ladder, government, economy)* stabile; *(relationship)* solido(a); *(person: emotionally, mentally)* equilibrato(a); **the patient is ~** *(Med)* le condizioni del paziente sono stazionarie.

sta·ble² ['steɪbl] **1** *n (building)* stalla; *(establishment)* scuderia; **riding ~s** maneggio. **2** *vt (keep in ~)* tenere in una stalla.

stack [stæk] **1** *n* **(a)** *(pile)* pila, mucchio; *(fam)* mucchio, sacco; **there's ~s of time to finish it** abbiamo un sacco di tempo per finirlo. **(b)** *(chimney ~)* comignolo; *(: of factory)* ciminiera. **2** *vt (books, boxes)* fare una pila di; *(chairs)* mettere l'uno sopra l'altro; *(aircraft)* tenere a quote assegnate in attesa dell'atterraggio; **the cards are ~ed against us** *(fig)* tutto è contro di noi.

sta·dium ['steɪdɪəm] *n* stadio.

staff [stɑːf] **1** *n* **(a)** *(personnel: gen)* personale *m*; *(: servants)* domestici *mpl*; *(Mil)* Stato Maggiore; **the administrative ~** il personale amministrativo; **the teaching ~** il corpo insegnante; **to be on the ~** far parte del personale; **a ~ of 15** un personale di 15 persone; **to join the ~** entrare a far parte del personale. **(b)** *(old: stick)* bastone *m*; *(Rel)* bastone pastorale; *(of flag)* asta. **(c)** *(Mus: pl* **staves**) pentagramma *m*.

2 *vt* fornire di personale; **to be ~ed by Asians/ women** avere un personale asiatico/costituito da donne; **to be well ~ed** essere ben fornito di personale.

3 *cpd*: **~ meeting** *n* riunione *f* del personale; *(Scol)* riunione dei professori; **~ officer** *n* ufficiale *m* di Stato Maggiore; **~ room** *n* sala dei professori.

stag [stæg] **1** *n (Zool)* cervo. **2** *cpd*: **~ night** *n* festa di addio al celibato.

stage [steɪdʒ] **1** *n* **(a)** *(platform)* palco, piattaforma; *(: in theatre)* palcoscenico; **the ~** *(profession)* il teatro; **to go on the ~** entrare in scena; *(fig)* fare del teatro. **(b)** *(period, section: of process, development)* fase *f*, stadio; *(: of journey)* tappa; *(: of pipeline)* sezione *f*; *(: of rocket)* stadio; **in ~s** *(travel, work etc)* a tappe; **in or by easy ~s** a piccole tappe; **in the early/final ~s** negli stadi iniziali/finali; **at this ~ in the negotiations** in questa fase dei negoziati; **to go through a difficult ~** attraversare un periodo difficile.

2 *vt (play)* mettere in scena, rappresentare; *(arrange: welcome, demonstration)* organizzare; *(fake: accident)* simulare; **to ~ a scene** allestire una scena; *(fig)* fare una scenata; **to ~ a quick recovery** riprendersi subito; **to ~ a comeback** fare ritorno.

3 *cpd*: **~ door** *n* ingresso degli artisti; **~ fright** *n* panico prima di andare in scena; **to get ~**

fright essere assalito dal panico prima di andare in scena; ~ **manager** *n* direttore/trice di scena; ~ **whisper** *n* (*fig*) sussurro perfettamente udibile.

stage·coach ['steɪdʒkəʊtʃ] *n* diligenza.

stage·hand ['steɪdʒhænd] *n* macchinista *m*.

stage-manage ['steɪdʒˌmænɪdʒ] *vt* (*play, production*) allestire le scene per; (*fig: event, confrontation*) montare.

stage-struck ['steɪdʒstrʌk] *adj*: **to be** ~ morire dalla voglia di fare l'attore (*or* l'attrice) (di teatro).

stag·ger ['stægəʳ] **1** *vt* (**a**) (*amaze*) sbalordire. (**b**) (*holidays, payments*) scaglionare; (*objects*) disporre a intervalli. **2** *vi* barcollare; **to** ~ **along/in/out** avanzare/entrare/uscire barcollando; **he** ~**ed to the door** andò verso la porta barcollando.

stag·gered ['stægəd] *adj* (**a**) (*amazed*) sbalordito(a), stupefatto(a). (**b**) (*hours, holidays etc*) scaglionato(a).

stag·ger·ing ['stægərɪŋ] *adj* sbalorditivo(a), incredibile.

stag·nant ['stægnənt] *adj* stagnante.

stag·nate [stæg'neɪt] *vi* (*water*) stagnare; (*fig: economy*) ristagnare; (*: person*) vegetare; (*: mind*) intorpidirsi.

stag·na·tion [stæg'neɪʃən] *n* (*of water, economy*) ristagno; (*of mind*) intorpidimento.

staid [steɪd] *adj* (*-er, -est*) troppo serio(a).

stain [steɪn] **1** *n* (**a**) (*also fig*) macchia; **grease** ~ macchia di grasso. (**b**) (*dye*) colorante *m*. **2** *vt* (**a**) (*also fig*) macchiare; **to** ~ **with** macchiare di. (**b**) (*wood*) tingere; (*: glass*) colorare. **3** *vi* macchiarsi.

stained [steɪnd]: ~ **glass** *n* vetro colorato; ~**-glass window** *n* vetrata.

stain·less ['steɪnlɪs] *adj* (*steel*) inossidabile.

stair [stɛəʳ] *n* (*single step*) scalino, gradino; (*whole flight: usu:* ~**s**) scale *fpl*; **he fell down the** ~**s** è caduto (giù) per le scale; **on the** ~**s** per le *or* sulle scale.

stair·case ['stɛəkeɪs] *n*, **stair·way** ['stɛəweɪ] *n* scala.

stair·well ['stɛəwɛl] *n* tromba delle scale.

stake [steɪk] **1** *n* (**a**) (*gen*) palo; (*for plant*) bastoncino. (**b**) (*for execution*): **to be burnt at the** ~ essere bruciato sul rogo. (**c**) (*bet*) puntata; (*stake*) interesse *m*; **to be at** ~ essere in gioco; **to have a** ~ **in sth** avere un interesse in qc. **2** *vt* (**a**) (*also:* ~ **out:** *area*) delimitare con paletti; (*also:* ~ **up:** *plant*) legare a un bastoncino; **to** ~ **a claim (to sth)** rivendicare (qc). (**b**) (*bet*): **to** ~ **(on)** scommettere (su); **I'd** ~ **my reputation on it** ci giocherei la reputazione.

stal·ac·tite ['stæləktaɪt] *n* stalattite *f*.

stal·ag·mite ['stæləgmaɪt] *n* stalagmite *f*.

stale [steɪl] *adj* (*-r, -st*) (*food: gen*) stantio(a), vecchio(a); (*: bread*) raffermo(a); (*air*) viziato(a); (*news, joke*) vecchio(a) come il cucco, trito(a); **I'm getting** ~ non rendo più.

stale·mate ['steɪlmeɪt] *n* (*Chess*) stallo; (*fig*) punto morto; **to reach a** ~ (*fig*) arrivare a un punto morto.

stalk[1] [stɔːk] **1** *vt* (*animal, person*) inseguire. **2** *vi*: **to** ~ **in/out** *etc* entrare/uscire *etc* impettito(a); **she** ~**ed out of the room angrily** uscì furiosa dalla stanza.

stalk[2] [stɔːk] *n* (*Bot*) gambo, stelo; (*of cabbage*) torsolo; (*of fruit*) picciolo.

stall [stɔːl] **1** *n* (**a**) (*Agr: stable*) stalla; (*in market*) bancarella, banco; (*at exhibition, fair*) stand *m inv*; **a newspaper/flower** ~ chiosco del giornalaio/del fioraio. (**b**) (*Theatre*): **the** ~**s** la platea. **2** *vt* (*plane*) far andare in stallo; **he** ~**ed the car** gli si è bloccata la macchina. **3** *vi* (**a**) (*car, engine*) bloccarsi; (*plane*) andare in stallo. (**b**) (*fig: delay*): **to** ~ **for time** prendere tempo; **stop** ~**ing!** smettila di menare il can per l'aia!

stall·holder ['stɔːlˌhəʊldəʳ] *n* bancarellista *m/f*.

stal·lion ['stæljən] *n* stallone *m*.

stal·wart ['stɔːlwət] **1** *adj* (*person: in spirit*) prode, coraggioso(a); (*party member*) fidato(a); (*supporter, opponent*) risoluto(a), deciso(a). **2** *n* prode *m*, persona coraggiosa.

sta·men ['steɪmen] *n* stame *m*.

stami·na ['stæmɪnə] *n* resistenza.

stam·mer ['stæməʳ] **1** *n* balbuzie *f*. **2** *vi, vt* balbettare.

stamp [stæmp] **1** *n* (**a**) (*postage* ~) francobollo; (*trading* ~) bollo premio; **National Insurance S**~ ≈ marchetta. (**b**) (*rubber* ~) timbro; (*mark*) bollo; **it bears the** ~ **of genius** porta l'impronta del genio. (**c**): **with an angry** ~ **of her foot** battendo il piede per terra per la rabbia.

2 *vt* (**a**): **to** ~ **one's feet** battere i piedi; (*in anger*) pestare i piedi; **to** ~ **the ground** (*person*) pestare i piedi per terra; (*horse*) scalpitare. (**b**) (*letter*) affrancare; ~**ed addressed envelope** (*abbr* **s.a.e.**) busta affrancata per la risposta. (**c**) (*mark with rubber* ~) timbrare, bollare; (*emboss*) imprimere su; **they** ~**ed my passport at the frontier** mi hanno timbrato il passaporto al confine.

3 *vi* (*single movement*) battere il piede per terra; **to** ~ **in/out** entrare/uscire infuriato; **ouch, you** ~**ed on my foot!** ahi, mi hai pestato un piede!

4 *cpd* : ~ **album** *n* album *m inv* per francobolli; ~ **collecting** *n* filatelia; ~ **machine** *n* distributore *m* automatico di francobolli.

♦ **stamp out** *vt* + *adv* (*fire*) estinguere; (*crime*) eliminare; (*opposition*) soffocare.

stam·pede [stæm'piːd] **1** *n* (*of cattle*) fuga precipitosa; (*of people*) fuggifuggi *m inv*; **there was a sudden** ~ **for the door** ci fu un fuggifuggi verso la porta. **2** *vt* (*cattle*) far scappare; **to** ~ **sb into doing sth** spingere qn a fare qc senza dargli il tempo di riflettere. **3** *vi* (*cattle*) fuggire precipitosamente; (*fig*) precipitarsi.

stance [stæns] *n* posizione *f*.

stand [stænd] (*vb: pt, pp* **stood**) **1** *n* (**a**) (*stance: also fig*) posizione *f*; (*resistance*) resistenza; **to take (up) one's** ~ **at the door** prendere il proprio posto vicino alla porta; **to take a** ~ **on an issue** prendere posizione su un problema; **to make a** ~ **against sth** (*Mil, fig*) opporre resistenza contro qc.

(**b**) (*also:* **taxi** ~) posteggio di taxi.

(**c**) (*market stall*) banco, bancarella; (*at exhibition, fair*) stand *m inv*; (*raised area: band*~) palco; (*: Sport*) tribuna; (*: Am Law: witness* ~) banco; **a music** ~ un leggio; **he kicked the ball into the** ~**s** con un calcio ha tirato la palla in tribuna.

2 *vt* (**a**) (*place*) mettere; **to** ~ **sth against a wall** appoggiare qc a un muro; **to** ~ **sth on end** mettere qc in piedi; **it made my hair** ~ **on end** mi ha fatto rizzare i capelli.

(**b**) (*withstand, bear: weight*) reggere a, sopportare; **it won't** ~ **serious examination** non reggerà ad un esame accurato; **the troops stood heavy bombardment** le truppe hanno sopportato pesanti bombardimenti; **the company will have to** ~ **the loss** la ditta dovrà sostenere la perdita.

(**c**) (*tolerate*) sopportare; **I can't** ~ **him** non lo sopporto; **I can't** ~ **the sight of him** non lo posso vedere; **I can't** ~ **it any longer!** non ce lo faccio più!; **I can't ~ waiting for people** non sopporto aspettare la gente.

(**d**) *(fam: treat)*: **to ~ sb a drink/meal** offrire da bere/un pranzo a qn; **to ~ the cost of** provvedere alle spese di.

(**e**) *(phrases)*: **to ~ guard** *or* **watch** *(Mil)* essere di guardia; **to ~ guard over** *(Mil, fig)* fare la guardia a.

3 *vi* (**a**) *(be upright)* stare in piedi; *(stay ~ing)* restare in piedi; *(get up)* alzarsi; **I had to ~** sono dovuto restare in piedi; **he could hardly ~** si reggeva a stento; **the woman ~ing over there** la donna in piedi laggiù; **don't just ~ there — help me!** non stare lì impalato — aiutami!; **the house is still ~ing** la casa è ancora in piedi; **they stood talking for hours** restarono a parlare per delle ore; **they kept us ~ing about** *or* **around for ages** ci hanno fatto aspettare in piedi per ore; **to ~ on sb's foot** pestare il piede a qn; **to ~ in sb's way** intralciare il passaggio a qn; **I won't ~ in your way** *(fig)* non ti sarò d'ostacolo; **nothing ~s in our way** la via è libera; **that was all that stood between him and...** era tutto ciò che si frapponeva fra lui e...; **nothing ~s between us** non c'è niente che ci separa; **to be left ~ing** *(building)* essere rimasto in piedi; *(fig: competitor)* essere bruciato in partenza; **to ~ still** stare fermo (in piedi); **to ~ fast** tener duro; **to ~ on one's own two feet** *(fig)* cavarsela da solo; **to ~ on one's head/hands** fare la verticale in appoggio/la verticale; **to ~ on the brakes** *(Aut)* frenare di colpo; **to ~ on one's dignity** stare sulle sue.

(**b**): **he ~s over 6 feet** è alto più di 1,80m; **the tower ~s 50m high** la torre è alta 50m.

(**c**) *(be situated: building, tree)* trovarsi, stare; **the car ~s outside all year round** la macchina sta fuori tutto l'anno.

(**d**) *(remain undisturbed: tea)* lasciare in infusione; *(: dough)* riposare; **my objection still ~s** la mia obiezione è ancora valida; **to let sth ~ as it is** lasciare qc così com'è; **the theory ~s or falls on this** è questo il presupposto su cui si basa la teoria.

(**e**) *(fig: be placed)* stare; **to ~ accused of** essere accusato di; **how do things ~?** come stanno le cose?; **as things ~** stando così le cose; **to ~ at** *(thermometer, clock)* indicare, segnare; *(offer, price, sales)* ammontare a; *(score)* essere.

(**f**) *(Pol)*: **to ~ as a candidate** presentarsi come candidato; **to ~ in an election** presentarsi ad un'elezione; **to ~ for Parliament** presentarsi come candidato al Parlamento.

(**g**) *(Naut)*: **to ~ out to sea** stare al largo.

♦ **stand aside** *vi* + *adv* farsi da parte, scostarsi; **to ~ aside in favour of** *(fig)* farsi da parte in favore di.

♦ **stand back** *vi* + *adv* tirarsi indietro; *(building: be placed further back)*: **to ~ back from** essere lontano(a) *or* distante da.

♦ **stand by 1** *vi* + *adv* *(be onlooker)* stare là (a non far niente); *(be ready)* tenersi pronto(a); **~ by for further news** tenetevi pronti a ricevere altre notizie. **2** *vi* + *prep* *(person)* rimanere vicino(a) a qn; *(promise)* tenere fede a.

♦ **stand down** *vi* + *adv* *(withdraw)* ritirarsi; *(Mil)* smontare di guardia; *(Law)* lasciare il banco dei testimoni.

♦ **stand for** *vi* + *prep* (**a**) *(represent: principle, honesty)* rappresentare; *(: subj: initials)* indicare. (**b**) *(tolerate)* tollerare, sopportare; **I won't ~ for that** non tollero una cosa del genere. (**c**) *(Pol)* see **stand 3f**.

♦ **stand in** *vi* + *adv*: **to ~ in for sb** sostituire qn.

♦ **stand out** *vi* + *adv* (**a**) *(be noticeable: veins etc)* sporgere; *(: colours)* risaltare; *(: person)* distinguersi; *(mountains)* stagliarsi; **that ~s out a mile!** si vede lontano un miglio! (**b**) *(be firm, hold out)* resistere, tener duro; **to ~ out against sth** opporsi fermamente a qc; **to ~ out for sth** rivendicare qc, insistere su qc.

♦ **stand over 1** *vi* + *adv* *(items for discussion)* rimanere in sospeso. **2** *vt* + *prep* *(person)* stare adosso a.

♦ **stand up 1** *vi* + *adv* *(rise)* alzarsi; *(be standing)* stare in piedi; *(fig: argument)* reggersi; **to ~ up for sb/sth** difendere qn/qc; **to ~ up for o.s.** difendersi; **to ~ up to sb** tenere testa a qn, affrontare qn con coraggio; **it ~s up to hard wear** è resistente (all'uso). **2** *vt* + *adv* *(fam: girlfriend, boyfriend)*: **she stood me up** non si è fatta viva.

stand·ard ['stændəd] **1** *n* (**a**) *(flag)* insegna; *(Mil)* stendardo. (**b**) *(norm)* standard *m inv*; *(intellectual ~)* livello; **the gold ~** *(Fin)* il tallone aureo; **to be** *or* **come up to ~** rispondere ai requisiti; **to set a high ~** essere molto esigente; **~ of living** tenore *m or* standard di vita; **at first-year university ~** a livello di un primo anno d'università; **of** (**a**) **high/low ~** di un livello alto/basso; **below** *or* **not up to ~** *(work)* mediocre. (**c**) *(moral ~: usu pl)* scala di valori; **moral ~s** valori *mpl* morali; **to accept sb's ~s** accettare la scala di valori di qn; **to apply a double ~** usare metri diversi (nel giudicare *or* fare etc).

2 *adj* *(gen)* standard *inv*; *(reference book)* classico(a).

3 *cpd*: **~ English** *n* inglese *m* standard *or* corrente; **~ lamp** *n* lampada a stelo; **~ model** *n* modello di serie; **~ practice** *n* procedura normale; **it's ~ practice to do so** è d'ordinaria amministrazione fare così; **to become ~ practice** diventare normale; **~ time** *n* ora ufficiale.

stand·ard·ize ['stændədaɪz] *vt* standardizzare.

stand-by ['stændbaɪ] **1** *n*: **do you have a ~ should that fail?** hai qualcosa che ti rimpiazzi nel caso che non funzioni?; **to be on ~** *(gen)* tenersi pronto; *(doctor)* essere di guardia. **2** *cpd*: **~ generator** *n* generatore *m* d'emergenza; **~ passenger** *n* *(Aer)* passeggero/a sulla lista d'attesa.

stand-in ['stændɪn] *n* sostituto/a; *(Cine)* controfigura.

stand·ing ['stændɪŋ] **1** *adj* (**a**) *(passenger)* in piedi; *(upright: corn)* non mietuto(a); **~ room** posto in piedi; **he was given a ~ ovation** tutti si alzarono per applaudirlo; **~ stone** menhir *m inv*. (**b**) *(permanent: committee)* permanente; *(: rule)* fisso(a); *(: army)* regolare; *(grievance)* continuo(a); **it's a ~ joke** è diventato proverbiale; **~ order** *(Fin)* ordine *m* di pagamento (permanente).

2 *n* (**a**) *(social position)* rango, posizione *f*; *(repute)* reputazione *f*; **financial ~ standing** *m*; **a man of some ~** un uomo di una certa importanza; **what is his ~ locally?** che reputazione ha da queste parti? (**b**) *(duration)*: **of 6 months' ~** che dura da 6 mesi; **of long ~** di lunga data.

stand-offish [ˌstænd'ɒfɪʃ] *adj* scostante, freddo(a).

stand·pipe ['stændpaɪp] *n* fontanella.

stand·point ['stændpɔɪnt] *n* punto di vista.

stand·still ['stændstɪl] *n*: **to bring a car to a ~** fermare una macchina; **to be at a ~** *(vehicle)* essere fermo; *(industry etc)* ristagnare, essere paralizzato; **to come to a ~** *(vehicle)* fermarsi; *(industry etc)* rimanere paralizzato; *(production)* arrestarsi; *(talks, negotiations)* giungere a un punto morto.

stand-up ['stændʌp] *adj* *(fight)* accanito(a); *(meal)* in piedi; ~ **collar** colletto rigido (e alto).

stank [stæŋk] *pt of* **stink.**

stan·za ['stænzə] *n* stanza *(poesia).*

sta·ple[1] ['steɪpl] **1** *n (for papers)* punto metallico, graffetta. **2** *vt (also:* ~ **together)** unire con un punto metallico *or* una graffetta.

sta·ple[2] ['steɪpl] **1** *adj (diet, food, products)* base *inv; (crop, industry)* principale. **2** *n (chief product)* prodotto principale.

sta·pler ['steɪplə[r]] *n,* **sta·pling ma·chine** ['steɪplɪŋmə,ʃiːn] *n* cucitrice *f.*

star [stɑː[r]] **1** *n* **(a)** *(gen)* stella; *(Mil)* stelletta; *(Typ etc)* asterisco; **the S~s and Stripes** la bandiera stellata; **four-~ hotel** ≃ albergo di prima categoria; **4-~ petrol** super *f;* **born under a lucky ~** nato sotto una buona stella; **the ~s** *(horoscope)* le stelle; **you can thank your lucky ~s that...** puoi ringraziare la tua buona stella che... +*sub;* **to see ~s** *(fig)* vedere le stelle. **(b)** *(person)* divo/a; *(actress only)* stella. **2** *vt (Cine etc)* essere interpretato(a) da; **a film ~ring Greta Garbo** un film con Greta Garbo. **3** *vi (Cine etc):* **to ~ in a film** essere il *(or* la) protagonista di un film; **he ~red as Othello** ha interpretato il ruolo di Otello. **4** *cpd:* ~ **attraction** *n* numero principale; ~ **player** *n* giocatore *m* di prima grandezza; ~ **turn** *n* attrazione *f* principale.

star·board ['stɑːbəd] *n* tribordo; **on the ~ side** a dritta, a tribordo.

starch [stɑːtʃ] **1** *n* amido. **2** *vt* inamidare.

starchy ['stɑːtʃɪ] *adj* **(-ier, -iest)** *(food)* ricco(a) di amido.

star·dom ['stɑːdəm] *n* celebrità.

stare [stɛə[r]] **1** *n* sguardo (fisso); **a vacant ~** uno sguardo assente. **2** *vt:* **it's staring you in the face** *(obvious)* salta agli occhi; *(very near)* ce l'hai sotto il naso. **3** *vi:* **to ~ at sb/sth** fissare qn/qc, guardare fissamente qn/qc; **to ~ into space** fissare il vuoto; **to ~ at sb in surprise** fissare qn sorpreso; **it's rude to ~** non sta bene fissare la gente.

star·fish ['stɑːfɪʃ] *n* stella di mare.

star·gaz·ing ['stɑː,geɪzɪŋ] *n (fig):* **to be ~** avere la testa nelle nuvole.

stark [stɑːk] **1** *adj* **(-er, -est)** *(outline)* aspro(a); *(landscape)* desolato(a); *(simplicity, colour)* austero(a); *(contrast)* forte; *(reality, poverty, truth)* crudo(a). **2** *adv:* ~ **(staring) mad** matto(a) da legare; ~ **naked** *(also:* **starkers)** completamente nudo(a).

star·let ['stɑːlɪt] *n (Cine)* stellina.

star·light ['stɑːlaɪt] *n:* **in the ~** alla luce delle stelle.

star·ling ['stɑːlɪŋ] *n* storno.

star·lit ['stɑːlɪt] *adj* stellato(a).

star·ry ['stɑːrɪ] *adj* **(-ier, -iest)** stellato(a).

starry-eyed [,stɑːrɪ'aɪd] *adj (idealistic, gullible)* ingenuo(a); *(from wonder)* meravigliato(a); *(from love)* perdutamente innamorato(a).

star-studded ['stɑː,stʌdɪd] *adj:* **a ~ cast** un cast di attori famosi.

start [stɑːt] **1** *n* **(a)** *(fright etc)* sussulto, sobbalzo; **to give a ~** trasalire; **to give sb a ~** far trasalire qn; **to wake with a ~** svegliarsi di soprassalto.

(b) *(beginning)* inizio; *(in race)* partenza; *(: starting line)* linea di partenza; **at the ~** all'inizio; **the ~ of the school year** l'inizio dell'anno scolastico; **from the ~** dall'inizio; **for a ~** tanto per cominciare; **to get off to a good** *or* **flying ~** cominciare bene; **to make an early ~** partire di buon'ora; **to make a fresh** *(or* **new) ~ in life** ricominciare daccapo or da zero.

(c) *(advantage)* vantaggio; **the thieves had 3 hours' ~** i ladri avevano 3 ore di vantaggio; **to**

give sb a 5-minute ~ dare un vantaggio di 5 minuti a qn.

2 *vt* **(a)** *(begin: gen)* cominciare, incominciare; *(: bottle)* aprire; *(: habit)* prendere; **to ~ doing sth** *or* **to do sth** cominciare a fare qc; **to ~ negotiations** avviare i negoziati; **he ~ed life as a labourer** ha cominciato (nella vita) come operaio.

(b) *(cause to begin or happen: conversation, discussion)* iniziare; *(: quarrel)* cominciare, provocare; *(: rumour)* mettere in giro; *(: series of events, policy)* dare l'avvio a; *(: reform)* avviare; *(: fashion)* lanciare; *(found: business, newspaper)* fondare, creare; *(car, engine)* mettere in moto, avviare; **to ~ a fire** provocare un incendio; **to ~ a race** dare il via a una gara; **you ~ed it!** hai cominciato tu!; **don't ~ anything!** non cominciare!; **don't ~ him on that!** non toccare quest'argomento in sua presenza!

3 *vi* **(a)** *(in fright):* **to ~ (at)** trasalire (a), sobbalzare (a); **his eyes were ~ing out of his head** aveva gli occhi fuori dalle orbite.

(b) *(begin: gen)* cominciare; *(: rumour)* nascere; *(on journey)* partire; *(car, engine)* mettersi in moto, avviarsi, partire; ~ **ing from Tuesday** a partire da martedì; **to ~ on a task** cominciare un lavoro; **to ~ at the beginning** cominciare dall'inizio; **it ~ed (off) well/badly** è cominciato bene/male; **she ~ed (off) down the street** s'incamminò giù per la strada; **what shall we ~ (off) with?** con che cosa cominciamo?; **she ~ed (off) as a nanny** ha cominciato come bambinaia; **to ~ (off) with...** *(firstly)* per prima cosa...; *(at the beginning)* all'inizio...; **he ~ed (off) by saying (that)...** cominciò col dire che... .

◆ **start off 1** *vi + adv (leave)* partire; *see also* **start 3b. 2** *vt + adv* causare, far nascere; **to ~ sb off** *(on complaints, story etc)* far cominciare qn; *(give initial help)* aiutare qn a cominciare; **that was enough to ~ him off** è bastato questo a farlo cominciare.

◆ **start out** *vi + adv (begin journey)* partire; *(fig):* **to ~ out as** cominciare come; **to ~ out to do sth** cominciare con l'intenzione di fare qc.

◆ **start over** *vi + adv (Am)* ricominciare.

◆ **start up 1** *vi + adv (engine)* mettersi in moto; *(driver)* mettere in moto; *(music)* cominciare. **2** *vt + adv (car, engine)* mettere in moto, avviare.

start·er ['stɑːtə[r]] *n* **(a)** *(person: judge)* starter *m inv; (: competitor)* concorrente *m/f;* **he was a late ~** *(child)* ha cominciato a leggere e a scrivere tardi. **(b)** *(Aut etc: motor)* motorino d'avviamento; *(on machine)* bottone *m* d'accensione. **(c)** *(Culin):* **as a ~** come *or* per antipasto; **for ~s** *(fig)* per cominciare.

start·ing ['stɑːtɪŋ] *adj:* ~ **point** punto di partenza; ~ **post** palo di partenza; ~ **price** prezzo *m* base *inv.*

star·tle ['stɑːtl] *vt* far trasalire, spaventare.

star·tling ['stɑːtlɪŋ] *adj (surprising)* sorprendente; *(alarming)* impressionante.

star·va·tion [stɑː'veɪʃən] **1** *n* inedia; **it might be fuel ~** *(Tech)* probabilmente la benzina non arriva al motore. **2** *cpd:* ~ **diet** *n* dieta da fame; ~ **wages** *npl* salario da fame.

starve [stɑːv] **1** *vt* far patire la fame a; **to ~ sb to death** far morire qn di fame; **to ~ o.s.** soffrire la fame; **to ~ sb into submission** prendere qn per fame; **to be ~d of affection** soffrire per mancanza di affetto. **2** *vi (lack food)* soffrire la fame; **to ~ (to death)** morire di fame; **I'm starving!** *(fam)* muoio di fame!

starv·ing ['stɑːvɪŋ] *adj* affamato(a).

stash [stæʃ] *vt (fam)*: **to ~ sth away** nascondere qc da qualche parte.

state [steɪt] **1** *n* **(a)** *(condition)* stato, condizione *f*; **~ of emergency** stato di emergenza; **~ of mind** stato d'animo; **~ of war** stato di guerra; **to be in a bad/good ~** essere in cattivo/buono stato; **he's not in a (fit) ~ to do it** non è in condizioni di farlo; **he arrived home in a shocking ~** è arrivato a casa ridotto proprio male; **the ~ of the art** il livello di tecnologia *(or* cultura *etc)*. **(b)** *(anxiety)* agitazione *f*; **now don't get into a ~** non metterti in agitazione. **(c)** *(pomp)*: **in ~** in pompa; **to lie in ~** essere esposto solennemente. **(d)** *(Pol)*: **the S~** lo Stato; **the S~s** *(USA)* gli Stati Uniti.

2 *vt (gen)* dichiarare, affermare; *(time, place)* decidere, fissare; *(conditions)* indicare; *(case, problem, theory, facts)* esporre; **as ~d above** come indicato sopra; **~ your name and address** fornisca il suo nome e l'indirizzo; **cheques must ~ the amount clearly** gli assegni debbono indicare chiaramente la somma.

3 *cpd (business, control, security)* di Stato; *(security)* dello Stato; **~ banquet** *n* banchetto ufficiale; **S~ Department** *n (Am)* Dipartimento di Stato, ≃ Ministero degli Esteri; **~ education** *n (Brit)* istruzione *f* pubblica *or* statale; **~ school** *n (Brit)* scuola statale; **to pay a ~ visit to a country** andare in visita ufficiale in un paese.

stat·ed ['steɪtɪd] *adj* stabilito(a); **within ~ limits** entro i limiti stabiliti.

state·less ['steɪtlɪs] *adj* apolide.

state·ly ['steɪtlɪ] *adj* **(-ier, -iest)** maestoso(a); **~ home** *(Brit)* residenza nobiliare.

state·ment ['steɪtmənt] *n (gen)* dichiarazione *f*; *(of views, facts)* esposizione *f*; *(Law)* deposizione *f*; *(Fin)* rendiconto; **~ of account, bank ~** estratto conto; **official ~** comunicato ufficiale; **to make a ~** fare una dichiarazione; *(Law)* fare una deposizione.

state-owned ['steɪt'əʊnd] *adj* statalizzato(a).

state·room ['steɪtrʊm] *n (in palace)* salone *m* per i ricevimenti; *(on ship)* cabina di lusso.

states·man ['steɪtsmən] *n*, *pl* **-men** statista *m*, uomo di stato.

states·man·ship ['steɪtsmənʃɪp] *n* abilità politica.

stat·ic ['stætɪk] **1** *adj* statico(a). **2** *n (noise)* disturbo.

sta·tion ['steɪʃən] **1** *n* **(a)** *(gen, Rail)* stazione *f*; *(fire ~)* caserma; *(police ~)* commissariato *(di* Pubblica Sicurezza*)*; *(esp Mil: post)* base *f*; **action ~s** posti *mpl* di combattimento. **(b)** *(Radio)* stazione *f*. **(c)** *(social position)* condizione *f* sociale, rango; **to have ideas above one's ~** montarsi la testa. **2** *vt (Mil: troops, sentry)* stanziare; *(fig)* piazzare; **to be ~ed in** *(Mil)* essere di stanza in; **to ~ o.s. by the door** piazzarsi sulla porta. **3** *cpd (Rail: staff, bookstall)* della stazione; **~ master** *n (Rail)* capostazione *m*; **~ wagon** *n (Aut)* giardinetta.

sta·tion·ary ['steɪʃənərɪ] *adj (gen)* fermo, immobile; *(vehicle)* in sosta; *(temperature)* stazionario(a); *(not movable)* fisso(a); **to remain ~** rimanere fermo.

sta·tion·er ['steɪʃənəʳ] *n* cartolaio.

sta·tion·ery ['steɪʃənərɪ] *n* articoli *mpl* di cancelleria; *(writing paper)* carta da lettere.

sta·tis·ti·cal [stə'tɪstɪkəl] *adj* statistico(a).

stat·is·ti·cian [,stætɪs'tɪʃən] *n* esperto di statistica.

sta·tis·tics [stə'tɪstɪks] *n (sg: subject)* statistica; *(pl: numbers)* statistiche *fpl*.

statue ['stætjuː] *n* statua.

statu·esque [,stætjʊ'esk] *adj* statuario(a).

statu·ette [,stætjʊ'et] *n* statuetta.

stat·ure ['stætʃəʳ] *n* **(a)** *(build)* statura; **to be of short ~** essere basso *or* di bassa statura. **(b)** *(fig)* levatura.

sta·tus ['steɪtəs] **1** *n (of person: legal, marital)* stato; *(: economic, official etc)* posizione *f*; *(of agreement etc)* validità; **social ~** status *m*. **2** *cpd*: **~ quo** *n* statu(s) quo *m*; **~ symbol** *n* status symbol *m inv*.

stat·ute ['stætjuːt] **1** *n* statuto. **2** *cpd*: **~ book** *n* codice *m*.

statu·tory ['stætjʊtərɪ] *adj (right, wage, control etc)* stabilito(a) dalla legge; *(offence)* legalmente punibile.

staunch¹ [stɔːntʃ] *adj* **(-er, -est)** *(supporter, friend)* fedele; *(believer, Christian)* convinto(a).

staunch² [stɔːntʃ] *vt (flow)* arrestare; *(blood)* arrestare il flusso di.

stave [steɪv] *n (Mus)* = **staff 1c.**

♦ **stave in** *vt* + *adv (pt, pp* **stove in)** sfondare.

♦ **stave off** *vt* + *adv (pt, pp* **staved off)** *(crisis, illness)* evitare; *(attack)* respingere; *(: temporarily)* allontanare.

staves [steɪvz] *npl of* **staff 1c.**

stay [steɪ] **1** *n* **(a)** soggiorno; *(in hospital)* degenza; **a ~ of 10 days** un soggiorno di 10 giorni. **(b)** *(Law)*: **~ of execution** sospensione *f* dell'esecuzione.

2 *vi* **(a)** *(remain in a place or situation)* rimanere, restare; *(reside, visit: in hotel)* alloggiare, stare; *(: with friends)* stare; **you ~ right there** stai fermo dove sei, stai là; **to ~ to dinner** rimanere a pranzo; **how long can you ~?** quanto tempo puoi fermarti?; **to ~ with friends** stare con degli amici; **to ~ overnight with friends** passare la notte da amici; **video recorders are here to ~** i videoregistratori non sono un fenomeno temporaneo. **(b)** *(continue, remain: with adj)* rimanere; **if it ~s fine** se il tempo si mantiene bello. **3** *vt* **(a)** *(last out)*: **to ~ the course** *(also fig)* resistere fino alla fine. **(b)** *(punishment)* sospendere; *(spread of disease, flow)* fermare; **to ~ sb's hand** fermare la mano a qn.

♦ **stay away** *vi* + *adv*: **to ~ away from** *(person)* stare lontano da; *(school, party etc)* non andare a; **to ~ away for** *(period of time)* stare via per.

♦ **stay behind** *vi* + *adv (after school, work etc)* fermarsi; *(not to go)* non andare.

♦ **stay in** *vi* + *adv (person)* rimanere a casa, non uscire; *(screw etc)* tenere.

♦ **stay on** *vi* + *adv* rimanere, restare; **he ~ed on as manager** è rimasto con la carica di direttore.

♦ **stay out** *vi* + *adv (overnight, outside)* rimanere fuori, restare fuori; *(strikers)* continuare lo sciopero; **to ~ out late** stare fuori fino a tardi; **to ~ out of trouble** non mettersi nei pasticci; **you ~ out of this!** non ti immischiare!

♦ **stay over** *vi* + *adv* fermarsi.

♦ **stay up** *vi* + *adv (trousers, tent)* tenersi su; *(person: wait up)* rimanere alzato(a) *or* in piedi; **to ~ up late** rimanere alzato fino a tardi.

stay-at-home ['steɪrəthəʊm] *n* tipo casalingo.

stay·er ['steɪəʳ] *n (in race)* persona *(or* cavallo *etc)* che ha resistenza; *(fig)* chi tiene duro, chi non si dà per vinto.

stay·ing pow·er ['steɪŋpaʊəʳ] *n* capacità di resistenza.

STD *abbr of* **subscriber trunk dialling.**

stead [sted] *n*: **to stand sb in good ~** essere utile a qn; **in sb's ~** al posto di qn.

stead·fast ['stedfəst] *adj* costante, risoluto(a).

stead·fast·ly ['stedfəstlɪ] *adv* fermamente.

steadi·ly ['stedɪlɪ] *adv (walk)* con passo fermo; *(speak)* con tono risoluto; *(hold, grasp)* saldamente; *(improve, decrease)* gradualmente; *(rain)* di continuo; **it gets ~ worse** continua a peggiorare;

to gaze ~ at sb guardare dritto in faccia a qn; to work ~ lavorare senza interruzione or costantemente.

steady ['stɛdɪ] **1** adj (-ier, -iest) (not wobbling: gen) fermo(a); (: voice, gaze) sicuro(a); (: nerves) saldo(a); (not fluctuating: prices, sales) stabile; (regular: temperature, demand, improvement) costante; (reliable: person, character) serio(a); (boyfriend etc) fisso(a); a ~ job un lavoro fisso or sicuro; a ~ hand una mano ferma; we were going at a ~ 70 km/h andavamo a una velocità costante di 70 km l'ora.
2 adv: ~! calma!, piano!; they are going ~ (fam) fanno coppia fissa, filano.
3 n (fam) ragazzo(a) fisso(a).
4 vt (wobbling object) tenere fermo(a); (nervous person) calmare; to ~ o.s. tenersi fermo, reggersi; she smokes to ~ her nerves fuma per calmarsi; to have a ~ing influence on sb rendere più calmo qn.

steak [steɪk] n (beef) carne f di manzo; (piece of beef, pork etc) bistecca; a cod ~ un trancio or una fetta di merluzzo.

steal [stiːl] pt stole, pp stolen **1** vt (also fig) rubare; to ~ money/an idea from sb rubare denaro/un'idea a qn; to ~ a glance at sb dare un'occhiata furtiva a qn; to ~ a march on sb battere qn sul tempo. **2** vi **(a)** (thieve) rubare. **(b)** (move quietly): to ~ in/out etc entrare/uscire etc furtivamente; to ~ away or off svignarsela, andarsene alla chetichella; to ~ up on sb avvicinarsi furtivamente a qn.

stealth [stɛlθ] n: by ~ furtivamente, di nascosto.

stealthy ['stɛlθɪ] adj (-ier, -iest) furtivo(a).

steam [stiːm] **1** n vapore m; to get up ~ (train, ship) aumentare la pressione; (worker, project) mettersi in moto; to let off ~ (fig) sfogarsi; under one's own ~ (fig) da solo, con i propri mezzi; to run out of ~ (fig: person) non farcela più; (: project, movement) perdere vigore. **2** vt (Culin) cuocere a vapore; to ~ open an envelope aprire una busta con il vapore. **3** vi **(a)** (give off ~: liquid, food etc) fumare. **(b)**: the ship ~ed into harbour la nave entrò nel porto; to ~ away (ship, train) partire; (fig: person, car) partire a tutto gas. **4** cpd: ~ engine n locomotiva a vapore; ~ iron n ferro a vapore.
♦ **steam up** vi + adv (window) appannarsi; to get ~ed up about sth (fig) andare in bestia per qc.

steam·boat ['stiːmbəʊt] n nave f a vapore; (small) vaporetto.

steam·er ['stiːmə'] n (steamship) nave f a vapore, piroscafo.

steam·roller ['stiːm.rəʊlə'] n rullo compressore.

steam·ship ['stiːmʃɪp] n piroscafo, nave f a vapore.

steamy ['stiːmɪ] adj (-ier, -iest) (room etc) pieno(a) di vapore; (window) appannato(a); (atmosphere, heat) umido(a).

steed [stiːd] n (poet) corsiero, destriero.

steel [stiːl] **1** n acciaio; nerves of ~ nervi di acciaio. **2** vt: to ~ one's heart against costruirsi un muro di insensibilità nei confronti di; to ~ o.s. for sth/to do sth farsi forza per affrontare qc/per fare qc. **3** cpd (knife, tool) d'acciaio; ~ band n banda di strumenti a percussione (tipica dei Caribi); ~ industry n industria dell'acciaio; ~ mill n acciaieria; ~ wool n lana d'acciaio, paglietta.

steel·works ['stiːlwɜːks] n, pl inv acciaieria.

steely ['stiːlɪ] adj (-ier, -iest) (determination) inflessibile; (gaze) duro(a); (eyes) freddo(a) come l'acciaio; ~ grey color piombo inv.

steel·yard ['stiːljɑːd] n stadera.

steep[1] [stiːp] adj (-er, -est) (gen) ripido(a); (cliff)

scosceso(a); (increase, drop) drastico(a); (fig fam: price) alto(a); (: demands) eccessivo(a); (: story) inverosimile; it's a bit ~! (fig fam) è un po' troppo!

steep[2] [stiːp] vt (washing, Culin): to ~ (in) mettere a bagno (in); (fig): a town ~ed in history una città impregnata di storia; ~ed in prejudice pieno di pregiudizi.

stee·ple ['stiːpl] n campanile m.

steeple·chase ['stiːpltʃeɪs] n corsa ad ostacoli, steeplechase m inv.

steeple·jack ['stiːpldʒæk] n chi ripara campanili e ciminiere.

steer[1] [stɪə'] **1** vt **(a)** (car, fig: conversation, person) guidare; (ship, boat) dirigere. **(b)** (handle controls of: ship) governare; (: boat) sterzare; (on ship) dirigere; to ~ towards or for sth dirigersi verso qc; to ~ clear of sb/sth (fig) tenersi alla larga da qn/qc.

steer[2] [stɪə'] n (animal) manzo.

steer·ing ['stɪərɪŋ] adj: ~ column (Aut) piantone m dello sterzo; ~ committee (Amm) comitato direttivo; ~ wheel (Aut) volante m.

stem [stɛm] **1** n (of plant) gambo, stelo; (of fruit, leaf) gambo, picciolo; (of glass) stelo; (of word) radice f. **2** vt (check, stop) frenare, arrestare; (river) arginare; (disease) contenere; to ~ the tide of events arrestare il corso degli eventi. **3** vi: to ~ from derivare da.

stench [stɛntʃ] n puzzo.

sten·cil ['stɛnsl] n (for lettering etc) stampino; (in typing) matrice f.

ste·nog·ra·pher [stɛ'nɒgrəfə'] n stenografo/a.

ste·nog·ra·phy [stɛ'nɒgrəfɪ] n stenografia.

step [stɛp] **1** n **(a)** (gen) passo; to take a ~ back/forward fare un passo indietro/avanti; ~ by ~ un passo dietro l'altro; (fig) poco a poco; to be in/out of ~ with (also fig) stare/non stare al passo con; to keep in ~ (with) (also fig) mantenersi al passo (con); to watch one's ~ fare attenzione or guardare dove si mettono i piedi; (fig) fare attenzione.
(b) (fig: move) mossa, passo; (measure) misura; it's a great ~ forward è un gran passo avanti; a ~ in the right direction un passo nella direzione giusta; to take ~s to solve a problem prendere le misure necessarie per risolvere un problema.
(c) (stair) gradino, scalino; (of ladder) piolo; (of vehicle) predellino; (fig: in scale) gradino; ~s (stairs) scala; (: outside building) scalinata; (: ladder) scala a pioli; folding ~s, pair of ~s scala a libretto; a ~ up in his career (fig) un passo avanti nella carriera.
2 vi fare un passo, andare; to ~ aside farsi da parte, scansarsi; to ~ inside entrare; she ~ped into the car salì in macchina; to ~ back tirarsi indietro; ~ this way, please! da questa parte, per favore!; to ~ over sth scavalcare qc; to ~ off the pavement scendere dal marciapiede; to ~ on sth calpestare qc; ~ on it! (fam) muoviti!; to ~ out of line (fig) sgarrare.
♦ **step down** vi + adv scendere; (fig: resign): to ~ down (in favour of sb) dimettersi or dare le dimissioni (a favore di qn).
♦ **step forward** vi + adv fare un passo avanti; (fig: volunteer) farsi avanti.
♦ **step in** vi + adv entrare; (fig) intromettersi.
♦ **step up** vt + adv (production) aumentare; (efforts, campaign) intensificare; to ~ up work on sth accelerare i lavori per qc.

step·brother ['stɛp'brʌðə'] n fratellastro.

step·child ['stɛptʃaɪld] n, pl -children figliastro/a.

step·daughter ['stɛp,dɔːtə^r] *n* figliastra.
step·father ['stɛp,fɑːðə^r] *n* patrigno.
step·ladder ['stɛp,lædə^r] *n* scala a pioli.
step·mother ['stɛp,mʌðə^r] *n* matrigna.
steppe [stɛp] *n* steppa.
step·ping stone ['stɛpɪŋstəʊn] *n* pietra di un guado; *(fig)*: ~ **(to)** trampolino di lancio (verso).
step·sister ['stɛp,sɪstə^r] *n* sorellastra.
step·son ['stɛpsʌn] *n* figliastro.
ste·reo ['stɛrɪəʊ] **1** *n (hi-fi equipment)* stereo *m inv*; *(sound)* stereofonia; **in** ~ **in** stereofonia. **2** *cpd* stereofonico(a), stereo *inv.*
ste·reo·phon·ic [,stɛrɪə'fɒnɪk] *adj* stereofonico(a).
ste·reo·type ['stɛrɪətaɪp] *n* stereotipo.
ster·ile ['stɛraɪl] *adj* sterile.
ste·ril·ity [stɛ'rɪlɪtɪ] *n* sterilità.
steri·li·za·tion [,stɛrɪlaɪ'zeɪʃən] *n* sterilizzazione *f.*
steri·lize ['stɛrɪlaɪz] *vt* sterilizzare.
ster·ling ['stɜːlɪŋ] **1** *n (Econ)* sterlina. **2** *adj* **(a)** *(silver)* al titolo di 925/1000; *(Econ)*: **pound** ~ lira sterlina; ~ **area** area della sterlina. **(b)** *(fig)*: of ~ **qualities** di gran pregio; **he is of** ~ **character** è una persona fidata.
stern[1] [stɜːn] *adj* (**-er**, **-est**) *(discipline)* rigido(a); *(person, warning)* severo(a).
stern[2] [stɜːn] *n (Naut)* poppa.
ster·num ['stɜːnəm] *n* sterno.
ster·oid ['stɛrɔɪd] *n* steroide *m.*
stetho·scope ['stɛθəskəʊp] *n* stetoscopio.
ste·vedore ['stiːvɪdɔː^r] *n* scaricatore *m* di porto.
stew [stjuː] **1** *n* **(a)** *(Culin)* stufato. **(b)** *(fig)*: **to be in a** ~ **(about sth)** essere agitato (per qc); **to get into a** ~ **(about sth)** mettersi in agitazione (per qc). **2** *vt (meat)* stufare, cuocere in umido; ~**ed fruit** frutta cotta. **3** *vi (tea)* diventare troppo forte; **to let sb** ~ **in his own juice** *(fig)* lasciar cuocere qn nel suo brodo.
stew·ard ['stjuːəd] *n (on estate etc)* fattore *m*; *(butler)* maggiordomo; *(Aer, Naut)* steward *m inv*; *(shop* ~*)* rappresentante *m/f* sindacale.
stew·ard·ess ['stjʊədɛs] *n (Aer, Naut)* hostess *f inv.*
stew·ing ['stjuːɪŋ] *adj*: ~ **steak** carne *f* (di manzo) per stufato.
stick [stɪk] *(vb: pt, pp* **stuck**) **1** *n (gen)* bastone *m*; *(twig)* ramoscello; *(support for plants)* asticella, bastoncino; *(of celery, rhubarb)* gambo; *(of shaving soap)* bastoncino; *(of dynamite)* candelotto; **to wield the big** ~ *(fig)* fare il prepotente or l'autoritario; **to get hold of the wrong end of the** ~ *(fig)* capire male; **a few** ~**s of furniture** pochi mobili sgangherati; **to live in the** ~**s** *(fam)* abitare a casa del diavolo; **to give sb** ~ *(fig)* sgridare qn.
  2 *vt* **(a)** *(with glue etc)* incollare; **to** ~ **two things together** incollare due cose; **he was** ~**ing stamps into his album** attaccava i francobolli nell'album; **she stuck the envelope down** incollò la busta.
  (b) *(thrust, poke: hand etc)* ficcare; *(sth pointed: pin, needle)* conficcare; **he stuck his hand in his pocket** ficcò una mano in tasca; **to** ~ **a knife into sb** accoltellare qn.
  (c) *(fam: place, put)* mettere; ~ **it in your case** mettilo *or* ficcalo nella borsa.
  (d) *(fam: tolerate)* sopportare.
  (e): **to be stuck** *(door, window)* essere bloccato(a); *(knife, screw)* essere incastrato(a); **it's stuck in my throat** mi si è conficcato in gola; **to be stuck with sb/sth** *(fam)* doversi sorbire qn/qc; **I'm stuck** *(fam: with crossword, puzzle)* non riesco ad andare avanti; **I'm stuck in bed** sono inchiodato a letto; **I'm stuck at home all day** sono bloccato a casa tutto il giorno; **to be stuck for an answer** non sapere cosa rispondere; **he's never**

stuck for an answer ha sempre la risposta pronta.
  3 *vi (glue, sticky object etc)* attaccarsi, appiccicarsi; *(food, sauce)* attaccarsi; *(get jammed: door, lift)* bloccarsi; *(: lock)* incepparsi; *(in mud etc)* impantanarsi; *(sth pointed)* conficcarsi; **it stuck to the wall** è rimasto attaccato al muro; **the name seems to have stuck** *(fam)* sembra che il nome gli *(or* le *etc)* sia rimasto; **to** ~ **to** *(one's word, promise)* mantenere; *(principles)* tener fede a; *(text)* rimanere fedele a; *(facts)* attenersi a; **decide what you're going to do, then** ~ **to it** decidi quello che vuoi fare e poi fallo; **it stuck in my mind** mi è rimasto in mente; **we'll all stick by you** *(support you)* siamo tutti con te; *(stay with you)* resteremo tutti con te; **I'll** ~ **with the job for another few months** continuerò a fare questo lavoro per qualche altro mese; **she will** ~ **at nothing to get what she wants** è capace di tutto per ottenere quello che vuole; **just** ~ **at it and I'm sure you'll manage it** persevera e sono sicuro che riuscirai a farlo.
♦ **stick around** *vi* + *adv (fam)* restare, fermarsi.
♦ **stick on** *vt* + *adv (stamp, label)* incollare.
♦ **stick out 1** *vi* + *adv* **(a)** *(protrude)* sporgere; *(be noticeable)* spiccare; **his teeth** ~ **out** ha i denti sporgenti; **his ears** ~ **out** ha le orecchie a sventola; **to** ~ **out like a sore thumb** essere un pugno nell'occhio. **(b)**: **to** ~ **out for sth** battersi per qc. **2** *vt* + *adv (tongue)* tirar fuori; *(arm)* allungare; *(head)* mettere fuori; **to** ~ **it out** *(fam)* tener duro.
♦ **stick together** *vi* + *adv (people)* restare uniti; *(things)* attaccarsi.
♦ **stick up 1** *vi* + *adv (protrude)* rimanere diritto(a); **to** ~ **up out of the water** uscire dall'acqua; **to** ~ **up for sb/sth** *(fam)* difendere qn/qc, battersi per qn/qc. **2** *vt* + *adv* **(a)** *(fam: raise: hand)* alzare; *(: rob)* rapinare; ~ **'em up!** mani in alto! **(b)** *(notice)* affiggere.
stick·er ['stɪkə^r] *n (label)* etichetta; *(on car etc)* adesivo.
stick·ing plas·ter ['stɪkɪŋ,plɑːstə^r] *n* cerotto adesivo.
stick-in-the-mud ['stɪkɪnðəmʌd] *n (fam)* matusa *m/f inv.*
stickle·back ['stɪklbæk] *n* spinarello.
stick·ler ['stɪklə^r] *n*: **to be a** ~ **for** essere estremamente esigente in fatto di.
stick-on ['stɪkɒn] *adj (label)* adesivo(a).
sticky ['stɪkɪ] *adj* (**-ier**, **-iest**) appiccicoso(a); *(fam: situation)* difficile, imbarazzante; *(: person)*: **he was a bit** ~ **about lending me the money** ha fatto un sacco di storie prima di prestarmi i soldi; **to come to a** ~ **end** *(fam)* fare una brutta fine.
stiff [stɪf] *adj* (**-er**, **-est**) **(a)** *(gen)* rigido(a); *(starched: shirt)* inamidato(a); *(brush)* duro(a); *(dough)* compatto(a), denso(a); *(arm, joint)* rigido(a), indolenzito(a); **to have a** ~ **neck/back** avere il torcicollo/mal di schiena; **the door's** ~ la porta si apre *(or* si chiude) con difficoltà; **as** ~ **as a ramrod** *or* **a poker** dritto come un palo; **to keep a** ~ **upper lip** *(fig)* restare impassibile. **(b)** *(fig: climb, examination, test)* duro(a), difficile; *(: competition, breeze, drink)* forte; *(: resistance)* tenace; *(punishment, fine)* severo(a); *(price)* salato(a); *(: manner, smile, reception)* piuttosto freddo(a); **that's a bit** ~ **!** *(fam)* è un po' troppo!; **it was a** ~ **price to pay** *(fig)* l'hanno pagato un po' troppo caro; **bored** ~ annoiato a morte.
stiff·en ['stɪfn] **1** *vt (legs etc)* irrigidire, indolenzire; *(with starch)* inamidare; *(fig: resistance etc)* rafforzare. **2** *vi (person, manner)* irrigidirsi; *(determination)* rafforzarsi; *(morale)* rinvigorirsi.

stiff·ly ['stɪflɪ] *adv (walk, move)* rigidamente; *(smile, bow)* freddamente.

stiff·ness ['stɪfnɪs] *n (gen)* rigidità; *(of punishment)* durezza; *(of climb)* difficoltà; *(of back etc)* indolenzimento; *(of manner)* freddezza; *(of resolution)* fermezza.

sti·fle ['staɪfl] **1** *vt (yawn, sob, anger)* soffocare; *(desire, smile)* reprimere; *(revolt, opposition)* stroncare. **2** *vi* soffocare.

sti·fling ['staɪflɪŋ] *adj* soffocante; **it's ~ in here** qui non si respira.

stig·ma ['stɪgmə] *n* stigma *m*.

stig·ma·ta [stɪg'mɑːtə] *npl (Rel)* stigmate *fpl*.

stig·ma·tize ['stɪgmətaɪz] *vt* stigmatizzare.

stile [staɪl] *n* scaletta *(per scavalcare una siepe)*.

sti·let·to [stɪ'letəʊ] **1** *n (knife)* stiletto. **2** *cpd:* **~ heel** *n* tacco a spillo.

still[1] [stɪl] *adv* **(a)** *(up to now)* ancora; **she's ~ in bed** è ancora *or* sempre a letto; **he ~ hasn't arrived** non è ancora arrivato; **she ~ doesn't believe me** ancora non mi crede. **(b)** *(with comp: even)* ancora; **~ better, better ~** meglio ancora. **(c)** *(nevertheless)* tuttavia, nonostante ciò; **~, it was worth it però**, ne valeva la pena; **she's ~ your sister** è sempre tua sorella.

still[2] [stɪl] **1** *adj* **(-er, -est)** *(motionless)* fermo(a), immobile; *(quiet)* tranquillo(a), silenzioso(a); *(orange juice etc)* non gassato(a); **keep ~!** stai fermo!; **~ waters run deep** *(Proverb)* le acque chete rovinano i ponti. **2** *n* **(a): in the ~ of the night** nel silenzio della notte. **(b)** *(Cine)* fotogramma *m*. **3** *adv:* **to stand ~, sit ~** stare fermo(a); **to hold ~** tenersi fermo(a). **4** *cpd:* **~ life** *n (Art)* natura morta.

still[3] [stɪl] *n (for alcohol)* alambicco; *(: place)* distilleria.

still·birth ['stɪlbɜːθ] *n* bambino(a) nato(a) morto(a).

still·born ['stɪlbɔːn] *adj* nato(a) morto(a).

still·ness ['stɪlnɪs] *n* immobilità; *(quietness)* silenzio, tranquillità.

stilt [stɪlt] *n* trampolo; **to walk on ~s** camminare sui trampoli.

stilt·ed ['stɪltɪd] *adj (style)* artificioso(a); *(way of speaking)* formale; *(translation)* che non suona bene.

stimu·lant ['stɪmjʊlənt] *n* stimolante *m*.

stimu·late ['stɪmjʊleɪt] *vt* stimolare; **to ~ sb to do sth** stimolare qn a fare qc.

stimu·lat·ing ['stɪmjʊleɪtɪŋ] *adj* stimolante.

stimu·la·tion [ˌstɪmjʊ'leɪʃən] *n* stimolazione *f*.

stimu·lus ['stɪmjʊləs] *n, pl* **stimuli** ['stɪmjʊlaɪ] stimolo; **it gave trade a new ~** ha dato un nuovo impulso al commercio; **under the ~ of** stimolato da.

sting [stɪŋ] *(vb: pt, pp* **stung) 1** *n (Zool)* pungiglione *m; (Bot)* pelo urticante; *(pain, mark)* puntura; *(of iodine, antiseptic)* bruciore *m;* **to take the ~ out of sth** *(fig)* rendere qc meno pungente. **2** *vt* **(a)** *(subj: insect, nettle)* pungere; *(: jellyfish)* pizzicare; *(: iodine, cold wind)* bruciare; *(fig: remark, criticism)* pungere sul vivo; **he was stung into action** fu spronato all'azione; **she was stung by remorse** fu presa dal rimorso. **(b)** *(fam):* **they stung me for £4** mi hanno scucito 4 sterline. **3** *vi (iodine etc)* bruciare; *(remark, criticism)* far male; **my eyes are ~ing** mi bruciano gli occhi.

stin·gy ['stɪndʒɪ] *adj (-ier, -iest) (person)* avaro(a), spilorcio(a); *(gift etc)* misero(a); **to be ~ with** *(one's praise, money)* essere avaro di; *(food)* razionare.

stink [stɪŋk] *(vb: pt* **stank,** *pp* **stunk) 1** *n* puzzo, puzza; **to raise** *or* **kick up a ~** *(fig fam)* fare un

putiferio. **2** *vi:* **to ~ (of)** puzzare (di); **it ~s in here c'è puzza qui; it ~s to high heaven** puzza tremendamente; **the whole thing ~s** *(fig fam)* quest'affare puzza. **3** *vt (also:* **~ out:** *room)* appestare. **4** *cpd:* **~ bomb** *n* bomba puzzolente.

stink·er ['stɪŋkə[r]] *n (fam: person)* carogna, fetente *m/f;* **this problem is a ~** questo problema è una brutta gatta da pelare; **he wrote her a real ~** gliene ha scritte di tutti i colori.

stink·ing ['stɪŋkɪŋ] **1** *adj:* **a ~ cold** un terribile raffreddore; **what ~ weather!** che tempaccio! **2** *adv:* **~ rich** ricco da far paura.

stint [stɪnt] **1** *n:* **to do one's ~ (at sth)** fare la propria parte (di qc); **I do a ~ in the pool every day** faccio una nuotata in piscina ogni giorno; **to do a ~ at the wheel** *(Aut)* fare il proprio turno al volante. **2** *vt, vi:* **he did not ~ his praises** *or* **on praise** non è stato avaro di complimenti; **don't ~ yourself!** *(iro)* non farti mancare niente!

sti·pend ['staɪpend] *n* stipendio.

stipu·late ['stɪpjʊleɪt] *vt:* **to ~ (that)** stabilire (che).

stipu·la·tion [ˌstɪpjʊ'leɪʃən] *n* stipulazione *f;* **on the ~ that** a condizione che + *sub.*

stir [stɜː[r]] **1** *n* **(a): to give sth a ~** mescolare qc. **(b)** *(fig)* agitazione *f,* scalpore *m;* **to cause a ~** fare scalpore. **2** *vt* **(a)** *(liquid etc)* mescolare; *(fire)* attizzare. **(b)** *(move)* muovere, agitare; **she didn't ~ a finger** non ha mosso un dito; **the breeze ~red the leaves** la brezza muoveva le foglie. **(c)** *(fig: emotions, interest)* risvegliare; *(: person)* commuovere; *(: imagination, curiosity)* eccitare, stimolare; **to ~ sb to do sth** incitare qn a fare qc; **come on, ~ yourself!** forza, muoviti! **3** *vi (move)* muoversi; **he never ~red from the spot** non si è mosso.

♦ **stir up** *vt* + *adv (memories)* risvegliare; *(hatred)* fomentare, *(trouble)* provocare; *(revolt)* fomentare; **he's always trying to ~ things up** cerca sempre di creare problemi.

stir·ring ['stɜːrɪŋ] *adj (exciting)* entusiasmante; *(moving)* commovente.

stir·rup ['stɪrəp] *n* staffa.

stitch [stɪtʃ] **1** *n (Sewing, Med)* punto; *(Knitting)* maglia; *(pain in side)* fitta al fianco; **to put a few ~es in sth** dare un punto a qc; **a ~ in time saves 9** *(Proverb)* un punto in tempo ne salva 100; **to put ~es in a wound** cucire una ferita; **she hadn't a ~ on** era completamente nuda; **we were in ~es** *(fam)* ridevamo a crepapelle. **2** *vt (Sewing)* cucire; *(Med)* suturare, cucire; **to ~ up a hem/wound** cucire un orlo/una ferita.

stoat [stəʊt] *n* ermellino.

stock[1] [stɒk] **1** *n* **(a)** *(supply, store)* provvista, scorta; *(in bank: of money)* riserva; *(Comm)* stock *m inv;* **out of ~** esaurito; **to have sth in ~** avere qc in magazzino; **to take ~** *(Comm)* fare l'inventario; **to take ~** *(of the situation)* fare il punto della situazione; **to lay in a ~ of** fare una scorta di.
   (b) *(Agr: live~)* bestiame *m*.
   (c) *(Culin)* brodo.
   (d) *(Rail: rolling ~)* materiale *m* rotabile.
   (e) *(Fin: company's capital)* capitale *m* azionario; *(: investor's shares)* titoli *mpl,* azioni *fpl;* **~s and shares** valori *mpl* di borsa; **government ~** titoli di Stato.
   (f) *(descent, origin)* stirpe *f*.
   (g): to be on the ~s *(ship)* essere in cantiere; *(fig: piece of work)* essere in lavorazione; **the ~s** *npl (History: for punishment)* la gogna.
   2 *vt (Comm: goods)* tenere, vendere; *(supply: shop, library, freezer, cupboard)* rifornire; *(: lake, river)* ripopolare; *(: farm)* fornire di bestiame;

(: *shelves*) riempire; **a well-~ed shop/library** un negozio/una biblioteca ben fornito(a).

3 *cpd* (*Comm: goods, size*) standard *inv*; (*fig: response, arguments, excuse*) solito(a); (: *greeting*) usuale; **~ car** *n* (*Sport*) stock-car *m inv*; **~ cube** *n* (*Culin*) dado; **S~ Exchange** *n* (*Fin*) Borsa valori; **~ market** *n* (*Fin*) mercato azionario; **~ phrase** *n* frase *f* fatta.

♦ **stock up** *vi* + *adv*: **to ~ up (on)** rifornirsi (di), fare provvista (di).

stock² [stɒk] *n* (*Bot*) violacciocca.

stock·ade [stɒˈkeɪd] *n* palizzata.

stock·broker [ˈstɒkˌbrəʊkəʳ] *n* agente *m* di cambio.

stock·holder [ˈstɒkˌhəʊldəʳ] *n* azionista *m/f*.

stock·ing [ˈstɒkɪŋ] *n* calza.

stock-in-trade [ˌstɒkɪnˈtreɪd] *n* (*tools etc*) strumenti *mpl* di lavoro; (*fig*) ferri *mpl* del mestiere.

stock·ist [ˈstɒkɪst] *n* fornitore *m*.

stock·pile [ˈstɒkpaɪl] **1** *n* riserva, scorta. **2** *vt* fare riserve di.

stock·room [ˈstɒkrʊm] *n* magazzino.

stock-still [ˌstɒkˈstɪl] *adv*: **to be** *or* **stand ~** stare immobile; (*from shock, horror*) restare impietrito.

stock·taking [ˈstɒkˌteɪkɪŋ] *n* inventario.

stocky [ˈstɒkɪ] *adj* (**-ier, -iest**) tarchiato(a), tozzo(a).

stodge [stɒdʒ] *n* (*fam*) cibo pesante.

stodgy [ˈstɒdʒɪ] *adj* (**-ier, -iest**) (*food, book*) pesante, indigesto(a); (: *person*) pesante.

sto·ic [ˈstəʊɪk] *n* stoico/a.

stoi·cal [ˈstəʊɪkəl] *adj* stoico(a).

stoi·cism [ˈstəʊɪsɪzəm] *n* stoicismo.

stoke [stəʊk] *vt* (*also: ~ up: fire*) attizzare; (: *furnace*) alimentare.

stok·er [ˈstəʊkəʳ] *n* fochista *m*.

stole¹ [stəʊl] *n* stola.

stole² [stəʊl] *pt of* **steal**.

stol·en [ˈstəʊlən] *pp of* **steal**.

stol·id [ˈstɒlɪd] *adj* impassibile, imperturbabile.

stom·ach [ˈstʌmək] **1** *n* (*gen*) stomaco; (*abdomen*) ventre *m*; **it turns my ~** mi rivolta lo stomaco; **they have no ~ for the fight** (*fig*) non hanno nessuna voglia di lottare. **2** *vt* (*fig fam*) sopportare, digerire. **3** *cpd*: **~ ache** *n* mal *m* di stomaco; **~ pump** *n* pompa gastrica; **~ trouble** *n* disturbi *mpl* gastrici; **~ ulcer** *n* ulcera allo stomaco.

stomp [stɒmp] *vi*: **to ~ in/out** *etc* entrare/uscire *etc* con passo pesante.

stone [stəʊn] **1** *n* **(a)** (*material*) pietra; (*single pebble, rock*) sasso; (*gem~*) pietra preziosa, gemma; (*of fruit*) nocciolo; (*Med*) calcolo; (*grave~*) lastra tombale, lapide *f*; **to turn to ~** (*vt*) pietrificare; (*vi*) rimanere pietrificato; **within a ~'s throw of the station** a due passi dalla stazione; **to leave no ~ unturned** non lasciare nulla d'intentato. **(b)** (*Brit: weight: pl gen inv*) ≃ 6,348 kg. **2** *adj* (*wall*) di pietra; **the S~ Age** l'età della pietra. **3** *vt* **(a)** (*person*) lapidare. **(b)** (*fruit*) snocciolare.

stoned [stəʊnd] *adj pred* (*fam: drunk*) sbronzo(a); (: *on drugs*) fuori *inv*.

stone-dead [ˌstəʊnˈdɛd] *adj* morto(a) stecchito(a).

stone-deaf [ˌstəʊnˈdɛf] *adj* sordo(a) come una campana.

stone·mason [ˈstəʊnˌmeɪsn] *n* scalpellino.

stone·wall [ˌstəʊnˈwɔːl] *vi* (*fig*) tergiversare.

stone·ware [ˈstəʊnwɛəʳ] *n* gres *m*.

stone·work [ˈstəʊnwɜːk] *n* lavoro in pietra.

stony [ˈstəʊnɪ] *adj* (**-ier, -iest**) (*ground*) sassoso(a); (*beach*) pieno(a) di ciottoli; (*fig: glance, silence*) freddo(a); **a ~ heart** un cuore di pietra.

stony-broke [ˈstəʊnɪˈbrəʊk] *adj* (*fam*): **to be ~**

essere al verde, essere in bolletta.

stood [stʊd] *pt, pp of* **stand**.

stooge [stuːdʒ] *n* (*Theatre*) spalla; (*pej*) lacchè *m inv*, tirapiedi *m/f inv*.

stool [stuːl] **1** *n* (*seat*) sgabello; **to fall between two ~s** (*fig*) rimanere a bocca asciutta (*lasciandosi sfuggire due occasioni*). **2** *cpd*: **~ pigeon** *n* (*fam*) informatore/trice.

stoop [stuːp] **1** *n*: **to have a ~** avere la schiena curva; **to walk with a ~** camminare curvo(a). **2** *vi* **(a)** (*bend: also: ~ down*) chinarsi, abbassarsi; (*have a ~*) avere la schiena curva. **(b)** (*fig*): **to ~ to sth/doing sth** abbassarsi a qc/a fare qc; **I wouldn't ~ so low!** non mi abbasserei a tanto!

stop [stɒp] **1** *n* **(a)** (*halt*) arresto; (*break, pause*) pausa; (: *overnight*) sosta; **a 20 minute ~ for coffee** una pausa di 20 minuti per il caffè; **without a ~** senza fermarsi; **to come to a ~** (*traffic, production*) arrestarsi; (*work*) fermarsi; **to bring to a ~** (*traffic, production*) arrestare; (*work*) fermare; **to make a ~** (*bus*) fare una fermata; (*train*) fermarsi; (*plane, ship*) fare scalo; **to put a ~ to sth** mettere fine a qc.

  (b) (*~ping place: for bus etc*) fermata.

  (c) (*Typ: also:* **full ~**) punto; (*in telegrams*) stop *m inv*.

  (d) (*Mus: on organ*) registro; (: *on trombone etc*) chiave *f*; **to pull out all the ~s** (*fig*) mettercela tutta.

  2 *vt* **(a)** (*block: hole: also: ~ up*) bloccare, otturare; (: *leak, flow of blood*) arrestare, fermare; **to ~ one's ears** tapparsi *or* turarsi le orecchie.

  (b) (*arrest movement of: runaway, engine, car*) fermare, bloccare; (: *blow, punch*) parare; **~, thief!** al ladro!

  (c) (*put an end to: gen*) mettere fine a; (: *noise*) far cessare; (: *pain*) far passare; (: *production: permanently*) arrestare; (: *temporarily*) interrompere, sospendere; **she drew the curtains to ~ the light coming in** ha tirato le tende per impedire che la luce entrasse; **rain ~ped play** la partita è stata sospesa per mal tempo.

  (d) (*prevent*) impedire; **to ~ sb (from) doing sth** impedire a qn di fare qc; **to ~ sth (from) happening** impedire che qc succeda; **can't you ~ him?** non puoi fermarlo?; **to ~ o.s. (from doing sth)** trattenersi (dal fare qc); **I managed to ~ myself in time** sono riuscito a fermarmi in tempo.

  (e) (*cease*) smettere; **to ~ doing sth** smettere di fare qc; **I'm trying to ~ smoking** sto cercando di smettere di fumare; **~ it!** smettila!, basta!; **I just can't ~ it** (*help it*) proprio non riesco a smetterla.

  (f) (*suspend: payments, wages*) sospendere; (: *subscription*) cancellare; (: *leave*) revocare; (: *cheque*) bloccare; **to ~ a pound from sb's wages** trattenere una sterlina dallo stipendio di qn.

  3 *vi* **(a)** (*stop moving, pause: gen*) fermarsi; (*cease: engine*) cessare; (*machine, production*) arrestarsi; (*play, concert, speaker*) finire; **~! fermo!**; **without ~ping** senza fermarsi; **to ~ in one's tracks** fermarsi di colpo; **to ~ at nothing (to do sth)** non fermarsi davanti a niente (pur di fare qc); **to know where to ~** (*fig*) avere il senso della misura.

  (b) (*fam: stay*): **to ~ (at/with)** fermarsi (a/da); **I'm not ~ping** non mi fermo.

♦ **stop away** *vi* + *adv* (*fam*) stare via.

♦ **stop by** *vi* + *adv* passare, fare un salto.

♦ **stop in** *vi* + *adv* rimanere a casa.

♦ **stop off** *vi* + *adv* fermarsi.

♦ **stop over** *vi + adv*: **to** ~ **over (in)** fermarsi (a), fare una sosta (a); *(Aer)* fare scalo (a).

♦ **stop up** *vt + adv see* **stop 2a.**

stop·cock ['stɒpkɒk] *n* rubinetto di arresto.

stop·gap ['stɒpgæp] **1** *n (person)* tappabuchi *m/f inv; (measure)* ripiego. **2** *cpd (measures, solution)* di fortuna.

stop·over ['stɒpəʊvəʳ] *n* (breve) sosta; *(Aer)* scalo intermedio.

stop·page ['stɒpɪdʒ] *n (in pipe etc)* ostruzione *f; (of work)* interruzione *f; (strike)* sciopero; *(of leave, payment, wages)* sospensione *f; (from wages)* detrazione *f,* trattenuta.

stop·per ['stɒpəʳ] *n* tappo.

stop·press ['stɒppres] *n* notizie *fpl* dell'ultima ora.

stop·watch ['stɒpwɒtʃ] *n* cronometro.

stor·age ['stɔːrɪdʒ] **1** *n (of goods, fuel, Computers)* immagazzinamento; *(of heat, electricity)* accumulazione *f; (of documents)* conservazione *f;* **to put sth into** ~ immagazzinare qc; **the cupboards provide ample** ~ gli armadi offrono ampio spazio per tenere la roba. **2** *cpd:* ~ **capacity** *n* capienza di magazzino; ~ **charges** *npl* magazzinaggio; ~ **heater** *n* radiatore *m* elettrico che accumula calore; ~ **space** *n*: **we don't have much** ~ **space** non abbiamo molto spazio per riporre la roba.

store [stɔːʳ] **1** *n* **(a)** *(stock)* provvista, scorta, riserva; *(fig: of knowledge etc)* bagaglio, miniera; ~ **s** *(food)* rifornimenti *mpl,* scorte *fpl;* **to lay in a** ~ **of sth** fare provvista di qc; **in** ~ di riserva, come provvista; **who knows what is in** ~ **for us** chissà cosa ci riserva il futuro; **to set great/little** ~ **by sth** dare molta/poca importanza a qc. **(b)** *(~house, ~room)* deposito; **to put one's furniture in(to)** ~ mettere i mobili in un deposito. **(c)** *(shop)* negozio; *(department ~)* grande magazzino. **2** *vt* **(a)** *(also:* ~ **up:** *food, fuel, goods)* fare provvista di; *(: heat, electricity)* accumulare; *(: documents)* conservare. **(b)** *(also:* ~ **away:** *food, fuel)* mettere da parte; *(: grain, goods)* immagazzinare; *(: information: in memory)* immagazzinare; *(: in filing system)* schedare.

store·house ['stɔːhaʊs] *n* magazzino, deposito.

store·keeper ['stɔːˌkiːpəʳ] *n (shopkeeper)* negoziante *m/f.*

store·room ['stɔːrʊm] *n* deposito.

sto·rey ['stɔːrɪ] *n* piano; **a 9-**~ **building** un edificio a 9 piani.

stork [stɔːk] *n* cicogna.

storm [stɔːm] **1** *n* **(a)** *(Met)* tempesta; *(: at sea)* burrasca, tempesta; *(: thunder~)* temporale *m; (fig: of applause)* scroscio; *(: of abuse)* torrente *m; (: of protests)* uragano; *(: of weeping, tears)* mare *m; (: uproar)* scompiglio; **it caused a** ~ *(fig)* ha creato scompiglio; **a** ~ **in a teacup** *(fig)* tanto rumore per niente. **(b)** *(Mil):* **to take a town by** ~ prendere d'assalto una città; **the play took Paris by** ~ *(fig)* la commedia ha trionfato a Parigi.

2 *vt (Mil)* prendere d'assalto.

3 *vi (wind, rain)* infuriare; *(person):* **to** ~ **in/out** entrare/uscire come una furia; **she** ~**ed up the stairs** si è precipitata di sopra furiosa; **'get out!' she** ~**ed** 'fuori!' urlò.

4 *cpd (signal, warning)* di burrasca; ~ **cloud** *n* nube *f* temporalesca; **there are** ~ **clouds on the horizon** *(fig)* c'è aria di burrasca; ~ **door** *n* controporta; ~ **troops** *npl (Mil)* truppe *fpl* d'assalto; ~ **window** *n* controfinestra.

stormy ['stɔːmɪ] *adj* **(-ier, -iest)** *(also fig)* burrascoso(a).

story¹ ['stɔːrɪ] *n* **(a)** *(account, lie)* storia; *(of book, film)* trama; *(tale, Literature)* racconto; **short** ~

(Literature) novella; **that's not the whole** ~ non è tutto; **it's the same old** ~ è sempre la solita storia; **to cut a long** ~ **short** per farla breve; **but that's another** ~ ma questa è un'altra storia; **that's the** ~ **of my life!** *(fam)* per me va sempre a finire così!; **to tell stories** *(fam: lies)* raccontare storie. **(b)** *(Press)* articolo; **he covered the** ~ **of the earthquake** ha fatto il servizio sul terremoto.

story² ['stɔːrɪ] *n (Am)* = **storey.**

story·book ['stɔːrɪbʊk] *n* libro di racconti.

stout [staʊt] **1** *adj* **(-er, -est)** *(sturdy: stick, shoes etc)* robusto(a); *(fat: person)* corpulento(a); *(determined: supporter, resistance)* tenace; *(: refusal)* deciso(a); **with** ~ **hearts** coraggiosamente, valorosamente; **a** ~ **fellow** *(fig)* un tipo in gamba. **2** *n (beer)* birra scura.

stout-hearted [ˌstaʊt'hɑːtɪd] *adj* coraggioso(a), valoroso(a).

stove¹ [stəʊv] *n* **(a)** *(for heating)* stufa. **(b)** *(for cooking)* cucina; **gas/electric** ~ cucina a gas/elettrica.

stove² [stəʊv]: ~ **in** *pt, pp of* **stave in.**

stow [stəʊ] *vt (Naut: cargo)* stivare; *(also:* ~ **away:** *put away)* mettere via.

♦ **stow away 1** *vt + adv* mettere via. **2** *vi + adv* imbarcarsi clandestinamente.

stow·away ['stəʊəweɪ] *n* passeggero(a) clandestino(a).

strad·dle ['strædl] *vt (subj: person: stream)* stare a gambe divaricate su; *(: chair)* stare a cavalcioni di; *(: horse)* stare in groppa a; *(subj: bridge: stream)* essere appoggiato(a) sopra; *(subj: town: border)* essere a cavallo di.

strafe [strɑːf] *vt* mitragliare.

strag·gle ['strægl] *vi (lag behind)* rimanere indietro; *(spread untidily)* estendersi disordinatamente; **to** ~ **in/out** entrare/uscire a piccoli gruppi.

strag·gler ['stræɡləʳ] *n* chi rimane indietro.

strag·gling ['stræɡlɪŋ] *adj (village)* sparso(a); *(hair)* in disordine; *(line)* irregolare; *(plant)* che cresce in modo disordinato.

straight [streɪt] **1** *adj* **(-er, -est)** **(a)** *(gen)* diritto(a), dritto(a); *(hair)* liscio(a); *(Geom)* retto(a); *(posture)* eretto(a); **the picture isn't** ~ il quadro non è diritto; **to be (all)** ~ *(tidy)* essere a posto, essere sistemato; *(clarified)* essere chiaro; **let's get this** ~ mettiamo le cose in chiaro; **to put** ~ *(picture)* raddrizzare; *(hat, tie)* aggiustare; *(house, room, accounts)* mettere in ordine; **to put things or matters** ~ chiarire le cose; **he soon put me** ~ mi ha corretto immediatamente; **I couldn't keep a** ~ **face** *or* **keep my face** ~ non riuscivo a stare serio.

(b) *(continuous, direct)* diritto; **ten** ~ **wins** dieci vittorie di fila.

(c) *(honest: person)* onesto(a); *(: answer)* franco(a); *(: denial)* netto(a); ~ **speaking,** ~ **talking** franchezza; **I'll be** ~ **with you** sarò franco con te.

(d) *(plain, uncomplicated)* semplice; *(drink)* liscio(a); *(Theatre: part, play)* serio(a); *(person: conventional)* serio(a); *(: heterosexual)* eterosessuale.

2 *adv* **(a)** *(in a* ~ *line: gen)* diritto; **to go** ~ **up/down** andare dritto su/giù; **it's** ~ **across the road from us** è proprio di fronte a noi; ~ **ahead** avanti dritto; **to go** ~ **on** andare dritto; **to go** ~ *(fig)* rigare dritto.

(b) *(directly, without diversion)* direttamente, diritto; **I went** ~ **home** sono andato direttamente a casa; **to come** ~ **to the point** venire al sodo.

(c) *(immediately)* subito, immediatamente; ~ **away,** ~ **off** subito.

(d) *(frankly)* chiaramente, francamente; ~ out chiaro e tondo.

3 *n (on racecourse)* dirittura d'arrivo; **to cut sth on the** ~ tagliare qc in drittofilo; **to keep to the** ~ **and narrow** *(fig)* seguire la retta via.

straight·en ['streɪtn] **1** *vt (sth bent: also:* ~ **out)** raddrizzare; *(: hair)* stirare; *(tablecloth, tie)* aggiustare; *(tidy: also:* ~ **up)** mettere in ordine; *(fig: problem: also:* ~ **out)** spianare, risolvere; **to** ~ **things out** mettere le cose a posto. **2** *vi (person: also:* ~ **(o.s.) up)** raddrizzarsi.

straight-faced [ˌstreɪt'feɪst] **1** *adj* impassibile, imperturbabile. **2** *adv* con il viso serio.

straight·forward [ˌstreɪt'fɔːwəd] *adj (honest)* franco(a), schietto(a); *(simple)* semplice.

strain¹ [streɪn] **1** *n* **(a)** *(Tech: on rope)* tensione *f*; *(: on beam)* sollecitazione *f*; *(on person: physical)* sforzo; *(: mental)* tensione *f* nervosa; *(: tiredness)* fatica; **to take the** ~ **off sth** ridurre la tensione di *(or* la sollecitazione su) qc; **the bridge is showing signs of** ~ il ponte mostra segni di deformazione; **the rope broke under the** ~ la corda si è spezzata a causa della tensione; **she's under a lot of** ~ è molto tesa, è sotto pressione; **I can't stand the** ~ non resisto, non ce la faccio più; **the** ~**s of modern life** il logorio della vita moderna; **to put a great** ~ **on** *(marriage, friendship)* mettere a dura prova; *(person, savings, budget)* pesare molto su. **(b)** *(Med: sprain)* strappo. **(c): to the** ~**s of** *(Mus)* sulle note di; **he continued in that** ~ *(fig)* e continuò su questo tono.

2 *vt* **(a)** *(stretch)* tendere, tirare. **(b)** *(put* ~ *on)* sottoporre a sforzo; *(: fig: friendship etc)* mettere a dura prova; *(: resources etc)* gravare su, pesare su; *(: meaning)* forzare; *(Med: shoulder, muscle etc)* slogare; *(: eyes, heart)* affaticare; **don't** ~ **yourself!** *(also iro)* non affaticarti troppo!; **to** ~ **the truth** deformare la verità; **to** ~ **every nerve to do sth** fare ogni sforzo per fare qc; **to** ~ **one's voice** sforzare la voce; **to** ~ **one's ears** aguzzare le orecchie; **to** ~ **to see sth** aguzzare la vista per vedere qc. **(c)** *(soup)* passare; *(vegetables, pasta)* scolare.

3 *vi:* **to** ~ **at sth** *(push/pull)* spingere/tirare qc con tutte le forze; **to** ~ **against** *(ropes, bars)* far forza contro.

strain² [streɪn] *n (breed)* razza; *(lineage)* stirpe *f*; *(of virus)* tipo.

strained [streɪnd] *adj (muscle)* stirato(a); *(arm, ankle)* slogato(a); *(heart, eyes)* affaticato(a); *(laugh, smile etc)* forzato(a); *(relations)* teso(a); *(liquid)* filtrato(a); *(solid food)* passato(a).

strain·er ['streɪnəʳ] *n (Culin)* passino, colino.

strait [streɪt] *n (Geog)* stretto; **the S~s of Dover** lo stretto di Dover; **to be in dire** ~**s** *(fig)* essere nei guai.

strait·ened ['streɪtnd] *adj:* **to be in** ~ **circumstances** *(frm)* vivere nelle ristrettezze.

strait·jacket ['streɪtˌdʒækɪt] *n* camicia di forza.

strait-laced [ˌstreɪt'leɪst] *adj* puritano(a).

strand [strænd] *n (of thread, pearls)* filo; *(of hair)* ciocca.

strand·ed ['strændɪd] *adj:* **to be (left)** ~ *(ship, fish)* essere arenato(a); *(person: without transport)* essere lasciato(a) a piedi; *(: without money etc)* trovarsi nei guai; **to leave sb** ~ lasciare qn nei guai.

strange [streɪndʒ] *adj* **(-r, -st) (a)** *(unknown, unfamiliar)* sconosciuto(a); **I felt rather** ~ **at first** all'inizio mi sentivo spaesato; **to wake up in a** ~ **bed** svegliarsi in un letto che non è il proprio; **the work is** ~ **to him** non è pratico di questo lavoro. **(b)** *(odd)* strano(a); **it is** ~ **that...** è strano che...;

~ **as it may seem...** per quanto possa sembrare strano...; **I felt rather** ~ mi sono sentito strano.

strange·ly ['streɪndʒlɪ] *adv* stranamente; ~ **(enough), I've never met him** stranamente, non l'ho mai incontrato.

stran·ger ['streɪndʒəʳ] *n (unknown person)* sconosciuto/a; *(from another place)* forestiero/a; **I'm a** ~ **here** non sono del posto; **he's a complete** ~ **to me** non lo conosco affatto, per me è un perfetto sconosciuto; **I'm no** ~ **to Rome** conosco Roma.

stran·gle ['stræŋgl] *vt* strangolare, strozzare.

strangle·hold ['stræŋglhəʊld] *n (Sport)* presa di gola; **to have a** ~ **on sb/sth** *(fig)* tenere qn/qc in pugno.

stran·gler ['stræŋgləʳ] *n* strozzatore/trice.

stran·gling ['stræŋglɪŋ] *n* strangolamento.

stran·gu·la·tion [ˌstræŋgjʊ'leɪʃən] *n* strangolamento.

strap [stræp] **1** *n (of watch, shoes)* cinturino; *(for suitcase)* cinghia; *(in bus etc)* sostegno (a pendaglio); *(shoulder* ~: *of bra)* bretella, spallina; *(: of bag)* tracolla; *(safety* ~*)* fascia, striscia; **to give sb the** ~ punire qn con la cinghia. **2** *vt* **(a)** *(fasten):* **to** ~ **down,** ~ **in,** ~ **on,** ~ **up** legare; **to** ~ **sb in** *(in car, plane)* allacciare la cintura di sicurezza a qn. **(b)** *(Med: also:* ~ **up)** fasciare.

strap·hanging ['stræpˌhæŋɪŋ] *n* viaggiare *m* in piedi *(su mezzi pubblici reggendosi a un sostegno)*.

strap·less ['stræplɪs] *adj (bra, dress)* senza spalline.

strap·ping ['stræpɪŋ] *adj (person)* robusto(a), ben piantato(a).

stra·ta ['strɑːtə] *npl of* **stratum**.

strata·gem ['strætɪdʒəm] *n* stratagemma *m*.

stra·tegic [strə'tiːdʒɪk] *adj (also fig)* strategico(a).

strat·egy ['strætɪdʒɪ] *n (also fig)* strategia.

strato·sphere ['strætəʊsfɪəʳ] *n* stratosfera.

stra·tum ['strɑːtəm] *n, pl* **strata** *(also fig)* strato.

straw [strɔː] **1** *n* paglia; *(drinking* ~*)* cannuccia; **it's the last** ~! è il colmo!, questa è la goccia che fa traboccare il vaso! **2** *cpd:* ~ **hat** *n* cappello di paglia, paglietta.

straw·berry ['strɔːbərɪ] **1** *n* fragola. **2** *cpd (jam, tart)* di fragole; *(ice cream)* alla fragola; ~ **mark** *n* voglia di fragola.

straw-coloured ['strɔːˌkʌləd] *adj* color paglia *inv*.

stray [streɪ] **1** *adj (dog, cat)* randagio(a); *(person, cow, sheep)* smarrito(a); **he was killed by a** ~ **bullet** fu ucciso per sbaglio in una sparatoria; **a few** ~ **cars** qualche rara macchina. **2** *n (animal)* animale *m* randagio. **3** *vi (animal: get lost)* smarrirsi, perdersi; *(wander: person)* allontanarsi, staccarsi (dal gruppo); *(: speaker)* divagare; *(: thoughts)* vagare; **a few cows** ~**ed into the garden** delle mucche sono entrate in giardino.

streak [striːk] **1** *n (line)* striscia, riga; *(of mineral)* filone *m*, vena; **he had** ~**s of grey in his hair** aveva delle ciocche di capelli grigi; **to have** ~**s in one's hair** avere le mèches nei capelli; **like a** ~ **of lightning** come un fulmine; **to have a** ~ **of madness** avere una vena di pazzia; **he had a cruel** ~ **(in him)** aveva una tendenza ad essere crudele; ~ **of luck** periodo di fortuna; **a winning/losing** ~ un periodo fortunato/sfortunato. **2** *vt* rigare, striare, ~**ed with** *(tears)* rigato di; *(subj: sky)* striato di; *(: clothes)* macchiato di. **3** *vi (move quickly):* **to** ~ **in/out/past** entrare/uscire/passare come un fulmine; *(run naked)* fare lo streaking.

streak·er ['striːkəʳ] *n* chi fa lo streaking.

streaky ['striːkɪ] *adj:* ~ **bacon** pancetta.

stream [striːm] **1** *n (brook)* ruscello; *(current)* corrente *f*; *(flow: of liquid, people, words)* fiume *m*; *(: of cars)* colonna; *(: of air)* soffio; *(: of light)* fascio; **against the** ~ controcorrente; **an unbroken**

~ **of cars** un fiume ininterrotto di macchine; **divided into 3** ~**s** *(Scol)* diviso in 3 gruppi di diverso livello; **the B** ~ *(Scol)* il gruppo B; **to come on** ~ *(oilwell, production line)* entrare in funzione. **2** *vt* **(a)** *(water etc)* scendere a fiumi; **his face** ~**ed blood** il suo viso grondava sangue. **(b)** *(Scol)* dividere in gruppi di diverso livello.

3 *vi (liquid)* scorrere, uscire a fiotti; *(cars, people)* riversarsi; **her eyes were** ~**ing** *(because of smoke)* le lacrimavano gli occhi; **her cheeks were** ~**ing with tears** fiumi di lacrime le rigavano il volto; **cars kept** ~**ing past me** fiumi di macchine continuavano a passarmi davanti; **to** ~ **in/out** *etc* entrare/uscire *etc* a fiotti.

stream·er ['striːməʳ] *n (of paper, at parties etc)* stella filante.

stream·line ['striːmlaɪn] *vt* dare una linea aerodinamica a; *(fig)* razionalizzare.

stream·lined ['striːmlaɪnd] *adj (see vb)* aerodinamico(a); razionalizzato(a).

street [striːt] **1** *n* strada; **the back** ~**s** le strade secondarie; **to be on the** ~**s** *(homeless)* essere senza tetto; *(as prostitutes)* battere il marciapiede; **it's right up my** ~ *(fig: job)* è proprio quello che fa per me; **to be** ~**s ahead of sb** *(fam)* essere di gran lunga superiore a qn. **2** *cpd:* ~ **cleaner** *n*, ~ **sweeper** *n* spazzino; ~ **lamp** *n* lampione *m*; ~ **lighting** *n* illuminazione *f* stradale; ~ **market** *n* mercato all'aperto; ~ **musician** *n* suonatore/trice ambulante; ~ **plan** *n* pianta (di una città); ~ **theatre** *n* teatro di piazza.

street·car ['striːtkɑːʳ] *n (Am)* tram *m inv*.

street·walker ['striːt‚wɔːkəʳ] *n* prostituta.

strength [streŋθ] *n* **(a)** *(gen, fig)* forza; *(of wall, nail, wood etc)* solidità; *(of rope)* resistenza; *(of chemical solution)* concentrazione *f*; *(of wine)* gradazione *f* alcolica; **you'll soon get your** ~ **back** presto ti rimetterai in forze; **his** ~ **failed him** gli sono mancate le forze; ~ **of character/mind** forza di carattere/d'animo; ~ **of purpose** risolutezza; **on the** ~ **of** sulla base di, in virtù di; **to go from** ~ **to** ~ andare di bene in meglio. **(b)** *(Mil etc)* effettivo; **at full/below** ~ con gli effettivi al completo/ridotti; **to come in** ~ *(fig)* venire in gran numero.

strength·en ['streŋθən] **1** *vt (person, muscles)* irrobustire; *(wall, building)* rinforzare; *(economy, currency)* consolidare; *(desire, determination)* rafforzare. **2** *vi (economy, currency)* consolidarsi; *(wind)* aumentare di intensità; *(desire, determination)* rafforzarsi.

strenu·ous ['strenjʊəs] *adj (person, denial, attempt)* energico(a); *(game, match, day)* faticoso(a); *(opposition, efforts, resistance)* accanito(a).

stress [stres] **1** *n* **(a)** *(Tech)* sforzo; *(psychological etc: strain)* tensione *f*, stress *m*; **to be under** ~ essere sotto tensione; *(fig)* essere sotto pressione; **in times of** ~ in momenti di grande tensione; **the** ~**es and strains of modern life** il logorio della vita moderna. **(b)** *(emphasis)* enfasi *f*; *(Linguistics, Poetry)* accento; **to lay great** ~ **on sth** dare grande importanza a qc. **2** *vt (emphasize)* sottolineare, mettere in rilievo.

stressed [strest] *adj (syllable)* accentato(a).

stress·ful ['stresful] *adj (job)* difficile, stressante.

stretch [stretʃ] **1** *n* **(a)** *(elasticity)* elasticità; **to have a** ~ *(person)* stiracchiarsi; **to be at full** ~ lavorare a tutta forza; **by no** ~ **of the imagination** in nessun modo. **(b)** *(distance)* tratto; *(expanse)* distesa; *(of time)* periodo; **for a long** ~ **it runs between...** per un lungo *or* bel tratto passa fra...; **for 3 days at a** ~ per tre giorni di seguito *or*

di fila; **he's done a 5-year** ~ *(fam: in prison)* è stato dentro 5 anni.

2 *vt* **(a)** *(pull out: elastic)* tendere, tirare; *(: rope etc)*: **to** ~ **(between)** tendere (fra); *(make larger: pullover, shoes)* allargare; *(spread on ground etc)* stendere; **to** ~ **one's legs** sgranchirsi le gambe; **to** ~ **o.s.** *(after sleep etc)* stiracchiarsi. **(b)** *(money, resources, meal)* far bastare. **(c)** *(meaning)* forzare; *(truth)* esagerare; **to** ~ **a point** fare uno strappo alla regola. **(d)** *(athlete, student etc)* far sforzare al massimo; **to be fully** ~**ed** essere impegnato a fondo; **to** ~ **o.s.** mettercela tutta, impegnarsi a fondo.

3 *vi* **(a)** *(~ one's limbs)* stirarsi, stiracchiarsi; **I** ~**ed across for the book** mi sono allungato per prendere il libro. **(b)** *(be elastic)* essere elastico(a); *(become larger: clothes, shoes)* allargarsi. **(c)** *(reach, extend: area of land)*: **to** ~ **(to)** estendersi (fino a); *(: meeting)*: **to** ~ **(into)** prolungarsi (fino a); *(reach: rope, power, influence)*: **to** ~ **(to)** andare (fino a); *(be enough: money, food)*: **to** ~ **(to)** bastare (per).

4 *cpd (fabric, trousers)* elasticizzato(a); ~ **marks** *npl* smagliature *fpl*.

♦ **stretch out 1** *vt + adv (arm, leg)* allungare; *(rope)* tendere; *(net, blanket)* stendere. **2** *vi + adv (person)* allungarsi; *(: lie down)* stendersi; *(countryside etc)* estendersi, stendersi; **a life of poverty** ~**ed out before him** lo aspettava una vita di miseria.

stretch·er ['stretʃəʳ] *n (Med)* barella.

stretcher-bearer ['stretʃə‚bɛərəʳ] *n* barelliere *m*.

strew [struː] *pt* **strewed**, *pp* **strewed** *or* **strewn** [struːn] *vt (scatter: sand, straw, wreckage)* spargere; *(cover)*: **to** ~ **(with)** ricoprire (di); **to** ~ **one's belongings about the room** disseminare la roba in giro per la stanza.

strick·en ['strɪkən] **1** *(old) pp* **of strike. 2** *adj (distressed, upset)* colpito(a); *(wounded)* ferito(a); *(damaged: ship etc)* in avaria; *(: city)* colpito(a); **grief** ~ affranto; **she was** ~ **with remorse** fu presa dal rimorso.

strict [strɪkt] *adj* **(-er, -est) (a)** *(stern, severe: person, principles, views)* severo(a), rigido(a); *(: order, rule)* rigoroso(a); *(: supervision)* stretto(a); *(: discipline, ban)* rigido(a). **(b)** *(precise: meaning, accuracy)* preciso(a); *(absolute: secrecy, truth)* assoluto(a); *(: time limit)* stretto(a); **in the** ~ **sense of the word** nel senso stretto della parola; **in** ~ **confidence** in assoluta confidenza.

strict·ly ['strɪktlɪ] *adv (see adj)* severamente; rigidamente; rigorosamente; strettamente; precisamente; assolutamente; **she was** ~ **brought up** ha ricevuto un'educazione rigida; ~ **confidential** strettamente confidenziale; **it is** ~ **forbidden** è severamente proibito; ~ **speaking** a rigor di termini; ~ **between ourselves...** detto fra noi... .

strict·ness ['strɪktnɪs] *n (of person)* severità, rigidezza.

stric·ture ['strɪktʃəʳ] *n (usu pl: criticism)* critica.

stride [straɪd] *(vb: pt* **strode**, *pp* **stridden** ['strɪdn]) **1** *n* passo; **to get into one's** ~ *(fig)* trovare il ritmo giusto; **to take in one's** ~ *(fig: changes etc)* prendere con tranquillità; *(: exam)* sostenere senza grossi problemi; **to make great** ~**s** *(fig)* fare grandi passi avanti. **2** *vi:* **to** ~ **in/out** *etc* entrare/uscire a grandi passi; **to** ~ **along** camminare a grandi passi; **to** ~ **up and down** camminare avanti e indietro.

stri·dent ['straɪdənt] *adj (sound)* stridente, stridulo(a); *(voice)* stridulo(a); *(protest)* energico(a).

strife [straɪf] *n* conflitto.

strike [straɪk] (vb: pt, pp **struck**) **1** n **(a)** (by workers) sciopero; **to go on** or **come out on** ~ mettersi in sciopero; **to call a** ~ organizzare uno sciopero.
(b) (discovery: of oil, gold) scoperta; **to make a** ~ scoprire un giacimento.
(c) (Baseball, Bowling) strike m inv.
(d) (Mil: air ~) attacco.
2 vt **(a)** (hit: gen) colpire; **to** ~ **a blow at sb** sferrare un colpo a qn; **who struck the first blow?** chi ha colpito per primo?; **to** ~ **a blow for freedom** spezzare una lancia in favore della libertà; **to** ~ **a man when he's down** (fig) uccidere un uomo morto; **the president was struck by two bullets** il presidente è stato colpito da due pallottole; **the clock struck nine o'clock** l'orologio ha suonato le nove; **to be struck by lightning** essere colpito da un fulmine; **to** ~ **sth out of sb's hand** far cadere qc di mano a qn.
(b) (collide with, meet) urtare, sbattere contro; (: rocks etc) sbattere contro; (: difficulty, obstacle) incontrare; **she struck her head against the wall** ha battuto la testa contro il muro; **a ghastly sight struck our eyes** una scena orribile si presentò ai nostri occhi; **disaster struck us** ci è successo un disastro.
(c) (produce, make: coin, medal) coniare; (: agreement, deal) concludere; (: a light, match) accendere; (: sparks) far sprizzare; **to** ~ **an attitude** assumere un atteggiamento; **to** ~ **a balance** (fig) trovare il giusto mezzo; **to be struck dumb** ammutolire; **to** ~ **terror into sb's heart** terrorizzare qn.
(d) (occur to) colpire; **the thought** or **it** ~**s me that...** mi viene in mente che...; **it** ~**s me as being most unlikely** mi sembra molto improbabile; **how does it** ~ **you?** che te ne pare?, che ne pensi?; **I'm not much struck with him** non mi ha fatto una buona impressione.
(e) (find: gold, oil) trovare, scoprire; **he struck it rich** (fig) ha fatto fortuna, ha trovato l'America.
(f) (pp also: **stricken**: remove, cross out): **to** ~ **(from)** cancellare (da).
3 vi **(a)** (attack: Mil etc) attaccare, sferrare un attacco; (: tiger) saltare sulla preda; (: snake) mordere; (: disease, disaster) colpire, abbattersi; **panic struck** tutti furono presi dal panico; **now is the time to** ~ questo è il momento di agire; **it** ~**s at our very existence** minaccia di distruggerci; **to** ~ **at** (person, evil) colpire; **to** ~ **at the root of a problem** intervenire alla radice di un problema.
(b) (clock) rintoccare, suonare.
(c) (workers) scioperare; **to** ~ **for higher wages** scioperare per un aumento dei salari.
(d): to ~ **on an idea** avere un'idea.
4 cpd (pay, committee) di sciopero.
♦ **strike back** vi + adv (Mil) fare rappresaglie; (fig) reagire.
♦ **strike down** vt + adv (subj: illness etc: incapacitate) colpire, abbattere; (: kill) uccidere; **he was struck down in his prime** è morto nel fiore degli anni.
♦ **strike off 1** vt + adv **(a)** (from list) cancellare; (: doctor etc) radiare. **(b): he struck off across the fields** ha tagliato per i campi. **2** vt + prep (name off list) cancellare da.
♦ **strike out 1** vt + adv (cross out) cancellare. **2** vi + adv **(a)** (hit out): **to** ~ **out (at)** tirare colpi (a), dare botte (a). **(b)** (set out): **to** ~ **out (for)** dirigersi (verso); **to** ~ **out across country** tagliare per la campagna; **to** ~ **out on one's own** (fig: in business) mettersi in proprio.
♦ **strike up 1** vt + adv **(a)** (friendship) fare; **to** ~ **up**

a conversation attaccare discorso. **(b)** (tune) attaccare. **2** vi + adv (band) attaccare.
strike·breaker [ˈstraɪkˌbreɪkəʳ] n crumiro/a.
strik·er [ˈstraɪkəʳ] n (in industry) scioperante m/f; (Sport) attaccante m.
strik·ing [ˈstraɪkɪŋ] adj (arresting: picture, dress, colour) che colpisce; (: person) che fa colpo; (obvious: contrast, resemblance) evidente, lampante; (shocking: change, sight) impressionante; **to be within** ~ **distance of sth** (Mil, fig) essere a un tiro di schioppo da qc.
strik·ing·ly [ˈstraɪkɪŋlɪ] adv straordinariamente.
string [strɪŋ] (vb: pt, pp **strung**) **1** n **(a)** (cord) spago; (of puppet) filo; (row: of onions) treccia; (: of beads) filo; (of vehicles, people) fila; (: of excuses) sfilza, serie f inv; **to pull** ~**s for sb** raccomandare qn; **to get a job by pulling** ~**s** ottenere un lavoro a forza di raccomandazioni; **with no** ~**s attached** (fig) senza vincoli, senza obblighi. **(b)** (on musical instrument, racket) corda; **the** ~**s** gli archi; **to have more than one** ~ **to one's bow** (fig) essere pieno di risorse. **2** vt (pearls) infilare; (lights, decorations) appendere; (rope): **to** ~ **across/between** tendere attraverso/tra; (violin, bow) incordare; (tennis racket) mettere le corde a; **he can't even** ~ **two sentences together** non sa neanche mettere due frasi insieme. **3** cpd: ~ **bean** n fagiolino; ~ **quartet** n quartetto d'archi; ~ **vest** n canottiera a rete.
♦ **string along** vt + adv (fam) menare per il naso.
♦ **string out** vt + adv: **to be strung out behind sb/along sth** formare una fila dietro a qn/lungo qc.
stringed [strɪŋd] adj (instrument) a corda.
strin·gent [ˈstrɪndʒənt] adj (measures, economies, tests) rigoroso(a); (reasons, arguments) stringente; ~ **rules** regolamento stretto.
strip [strɪp] **1** n **(a)** (gen) striscia; (of metal) nastro; (Aer) pista; **comic** ~ fumetto; **to tear a** ~ **off sb** (fig fam) dare una lavata di capo a qn. **(b)** (Sport: clothes) divisa. **2** vt **(a)** (person, plants, bushes) spogliare; (bed) disfare; (house) vuotare, svuotare; (wallpaper): **to** ~ **(from)** staccare (da); (paint) togliere; (furniture) sverniciare; **to** ~ **sb/sth of sth** spogliare qn/qc di qc; **he was** ~**ped of his rank** (Mil) è stato degradato. **(b)** (Tech: also: ~ **down:** engine) smontare. **3** vi (undress) spogliarsi, svestirsi; (do striptease) fare lo spogliarello; **to** ~ **to the waist** spogliarsi fino alla cintola. **4** cpd: ~ **cartoon** n fumetto; ~ **lighting** n illuminazione f al neon; ~ **poker** n strip-poker m; ~ **show** n spettacolo di spogliarello.
♦ **strip off** vi + adv spogliarsi.
stripe [straɪp] n **(a)** riga, striscia; **white with green** ~**s** bianco a strisce verdi. **(b)** (Mil) gallone m.
striped [straɪpt] adj a strisce, a righe.
strip·per [ˈstrɪpəʳ] n (paint ~) sverniciatore m; (striptease) spogliarellista.
strip·tease [ˈstrɪptiːz] n spogliarello.
strive [straɪv] pt **strove**, pp **striven** [ˈstrɪvn] vi sforzarsi; ~ **as he might** per quanto si sforzasse; **to** ~ **after** or **for sth** lottare per ottenere qc; **to** ~ **to do sth** sforzarsi di fare qc, fare ogni sforzo per fare qc.
strode [strəʊd] pt of **stride**.
stroke [strəʊk] **1** n **(a)** (blow) colpo; **at a** ~, **at one** ~ d'un solo colpo. **(b)** (caress) carezza. **(c)** (Cricket, Golf) colpo; (Rowing) vogata, remata; (Swimming: single movement) bracciata; (: style) nuoto; **butterfly** ~ nuoto a farfalla; **he hasn't done a** ~ (of work) non ha fatto un bel niente; **a** ~ **of genius** un lampo di genio; **a** ~ **of luck** un colpo di fortuna; **to put sb off his** ~ (Sport) far perdere il

ritmo a qn; *(fig)* far perdere la concentrazione a qn. **(d)** *(of bell, clock)* rintocco; **on the ~ of** 12 allo scoccare delle 12. **(e)** *(of piston)* corsa; **two-~ engine** motore a due tempi. **(f)** *(Med)* colpo. **(g)** *(of pen)* tratto; *(of brush)* pennellata. *2 vt (cat, sb's hair)* accarezzare.

stroll [strəul] 1 *n* passeggiatina, giretto; **to go for a ~, have** *or* **take a ~** andare a fare un giretto *or* due passi. 2 *vi*: **to ~ around** *or* **through** gironzolare per; **to ~ in/out** *etc* entrare/uscire *etc* tranquillamente.

stroll·er ['strəulə'] *n (Am: pushchair)* passeggino.

strong [strɒŋ] 1 *adj* (-**er**, -**est**) *(gen)* forte; *(sturdy: table, shoes, fabric)* solido(a), resistente; *(candidate)* che ha buone possibilità; *(protest, letter, measures)* energico(a); *(concentrated, intense: bleach, acid)* concentrato(a); *(marked, pronounced: characteristic)* marcato(a); *(: accent)* marcato(a), forte; **as ~ as a horse** *or* **an ox** *(powerful)* forte come un toro; *(healthy)* sano come un pesce; **he's never been very ~** è sempre stato di salute cagionevole; **there's a ~ possibility that...** ci sono buone possibilità che...; **there are ~ indications that...** tutto sembra indicare che...; **to have a ~ stomach** avere uno stomaco di ferro; **I have ~ feelings on the matter** ho molto a cuore quel problema; **to be a ~ believer in** credere fermamente a *or* in; **~ language** *(swearing)* linguaggio volgare; *(frank and critical)* linguaggio incisivo; **he's not very ~ on grammar** non è molto forte in grammatica; **geography was never my ~ point** la geografia non è mai stata il mio forte; **they are 20 ~** sono in 20.

2 *adv*: **to be going ~** *(company)* andare a gonfie vele; *(song, singer)* andare forte, avere successo; *(person)* essere attivo(a).

3 *cpd*: **~ drink** *n* alcolici *mpl*; **~ verb** *n* verbo forte.

strong-arm ['strɒŋɑːm] *adj (tactics, methods)* energico(a).

strong·box ['strɒŋbɒks] *n* cassaforte *f*.

strong·hold ['strɒŋhəuld] *n* fortezza; *(fig)*: **the last ~ of...** l'ultimo bastione di... .

strong·ly ['strɒŋlɪ] *adv (made, built)* solidamente; *(tempted, influenced)* fortemente; *(remind)* tantissimo; *(protest, support, argue)* energicamente; *(believe)* fermamente; *(feel)* profondamente, intensamente; **to feel ~ about sth** avere molto a cuore qc; **she ~ resembles her mother** somiglia molto a sua madre; **it smells ~ of garlic** ha un forte odore di aglio; **a ~-worded letter** una lettera dura.

strong·room ['strɒŋrum] *n* camera blindata.

strong-willed ['strɒŋ'wɪld] *adj* risoluto(a), deciso(a).

stron·tium ['strɒntɪəm] *n* stronzio.

strove [strəuv] *pt of* **strive**.

struck [strʌk] *pt, pp of* **strike**.

struc·tur·al ['strʌktʃərəl] *adj* strutturale.

struc·ture ['strʌktʃə'] 1 *n (gen, Chem, of building)* struttura; *(building itself)* costruzione *f*, fabbricato. 2 *vt (essay, argument)* strutturare.

strug·gle ['strʌgl] 1 *n (fight)* lotta; *(effort)* sforzo; **he lost his glasses in the ~** ha perso gli occhiali nella zuffa; **a power ~** una lotta per il potere; **the ~ for survival** la lotta per la sopravvivenza; **without a ~** *(surrender)* senza opporre resistenza; *(without difficulty)* senza problemi; **to have a ~ to do sth** avere dei problemi per fare qc. 2 *vi (physically)* lottare; **to ~ with sth/sb** lottare con qc/qn; **to ~ to one's feet** alzarsi con uno sforzo; **to ~ through the crowd** avanzare a fatica tra la folla. 3 *vt*: **to ~ to do sth** lottare per fare qc; **to ~**

to make ends meet *(fig)* riuscire a malapena a sbarcare il lunario.

strum [strʌm] *vt (guitar etc)* strimpellare.

strung [strʌŋ] *pt, pp of* **string**; *see also* **highly**.

strut[1] [strʌt] *vi*: **to ~ about** *or* **around** pavoneggiarsi; **he ~ted past** mi passò davanti impettito; **to ~ into a room** entrare impettito in una stanza.

strut[2] [strʌt] *n (beam)* supporto.

strych·nine ['strɪkniːn] *n* stricnina.

stub [stʌb] 1 *n (of cigarette, pencil)* mozzicone *m*; *(of candle)* moccolo; *(of cheque, receipt)* matrice *f*. 2 *vt*: **to ~ one's toe (on sth)** urtare *or* sbattere il dito del piede (contro qc); **to ~ out a cigarette** spegnere una sigaretta.

stub·ble ['stʌbl] *n* stoppia; *(on chin)* barba corta.

stub·born ['stʌbən] *adj (gen)* ostinato(a); *(person)* cocciuto(a), testardo(a); *(stain)* persistente.

stub·born·ness ['stʌbənnɪs] *n* testardaggine *f*, ostinazione *f*.

stub·by ['stʌbɪ] *adj* tozzo(a).

stuc·co ['stʌkəu] *n* stucco.

stuck [stʌk] *pt, pp of* **stick**.

stuck-up [ˌstʌk'ʌp] *adj (fam)* presuntuoso(a).

stud[1] [stʌd] 1 *n (in road)* chiodo; *(of football boots)* tacchetto; *(decorative)* borchia; *(collar ~, shirt ~)* bottoncino. 2 *vt*: **~ded with** *(fig)* ornato(a) di, tempestato(a) di.

stud[2] [stʌd] *n (~ farm)* scuderia di allevamento; *(~ horse)* stallone *m*.

stu·dent ['stjuːdənt] 1 *n (Scol, Univ)* studente/essa; *(of human nature etc)* studioso/a; **a law/medical ~** uno studente di legge/di medicina. 2 *cpd (life, unrest)* studentesco(a); *(attitudes, opinions)* degli studenti; *(canteen)* universitario(a); **~ hall of residence** *n* casa dello studente; **~ teacher** *n* studente che fa il tirocinio di insegnamento; **~s' union** *n (association)* circolo universitario; *(building)* sede *f* del circolo universitario.

stud·ied ['stʌdɪd] *adj (calm, simplicity)* studiato(a); *(insult)* premeditato(a), intenzionale; *(pose, style)* affettato(a).

stu·dio ['stjuːdɪəu] 1 *n* studio. 2 *cpd*: **~ flat** *n*, **~ apartment** *n* appartamento monolocale; **~ portrait** *n (Phot)* fotoritratto.

stu·di·ous ['stjuːdɪəs] *adj (person)* studioso(a); *(attention to detail)* accurato(a); *(politeness, avoidance)* studiato(a).

study ['stʌdɪ] 1 *n (activity, room)* studio; **to make a ~ of sth** fare uno studio su qc; **his face was a ~!** *(fig)* ha fatto una faccia!; **it repays closer ~** vale la pena di studiarlo a fondo. 2 *vt (gen)* studiare; *(examine: evidence, painting)* esaminare, studiare. 3 *vi* studiare; **she's ~ing to be a doctor** studia medicina; **to ~ under sb** *(Univ)* essere uno degli studenti di qn; *(subj: artist, composer)* essere allievo di qn; **to ~ for an exam** prepararsi a un esame.

stuff [stʌf] 1 *n* **(a)** *(substance)* roba; **there is some good ~ in that book** ci sono delle buone cose in quel libro; **it's dangerous ~** è roba pericolosa; **do you call this ~ beer?** chiami questa robaccia birra?; **I can't read his ~** non riesco a leggere quello che scrive; **he's the ~ that heroes are made of** ha la stoffa dell'eroe. **(b)** *(possessions, equipment etc)* cose *fpl*, roba; **he leaves his ~ scattered about** lascia la sua roba sparsa in giro. **(c)** *(fam: nonsense)*: **all that ~ about her leaving** tutte quelle storie sulla sua partenza; **~ and nonsense!** sciocchezze! **(d)** *(fam)*: **to do one's ~** fare la propria parte; **go on, do your ~!** forza, fai quello che devi fare!; **he certainly knows his ~** sa il fatto suo.

2 *vt (fill)*: **to ~ (with)** *(container)* riempire (di);

(cushion, toy) imbottire (di); *(stow: contents)*: to ~ **(into)** ficcare (in); *(Culin)* farcire; *(animal: for exhibition)* impagliare; **he** ~**ed it into his pocket** se lo ficcò in tasca; **my nose is** ~**ed up** ho il naso chiuso; **get** ~**ed!** *(fam)* va' a quel paese!; ~**ed shirt** *(fam)* tipo pomposo; ~**ed toy** giocattolo di peluche; **to** ~ **o.s. (with food)** rimpinzarsi.

stuff·ing ['stʌfɪŋ] *n (in cushion etc)* imbottitura; *(Culin)* ripieno.

stuffy ['stʌfɪ] *adj (-ier, -iest)* **(a)** *(room)* mal ventilato(a), senz'aria; **it's terribly** ~ **in here** qui non si respira; **it smells** ~ c'è odore di chiuso. **(b)** *(ideas)* antiquato(a); *(person)* all'antica.

stul·ti·fy ['stʌltɪfaɪ] *vt* istupidire.

stum·ble ['stʌmbl] *vi* inciampare; *(in speech)* incespicare; **to** ~ **against sth** inciampare contro qc; **to** ~ **in/out** entrare/uscire barcollando; **to** ~ **on** *or* **across sth** *(fig: secret)* scoprire qc per caso; *(: photo etc)* trovare qc per caso.

stum·bling ['stʌmblɪŋ] *adj*: ~ **block** *(fig)* ostacolo, scoglio.

stump [stʌmp] **1** *n (of limb)* moncone *m; (of pencil, tail)* mozzicone *m; (of tree)* troncone *m; (of tooth)* pezzo; *(Cricket)* paletto *(della porta)*. **2** *vt (perplex)* sconcertare, lasciare perplesso(a); **to be** ~**ed for an answer** essere incapace di rispondere. **3** *vi*: **to** ~ **in/out** *etc* entrare/uscire *etc* con passo pesante.

♦ **stump up 1** *vt adv (fam)* tirar fuori, sborsare. **2** *vi + adv (fam)* sborsare i soldi, tirar fuori i soldi.

stun [stʌn] *vt (subj: blow)* stordire, tramortire; *(fig: amaze)* sbalordire, stupefare; **the news** ~**ned everybody** la notizia sbalordì tutti.

stung [stʌŋ] *pt, pp of* **sting**.

stunk [stʌŋk] *pp of* **stink**.

stun·ning ['stʌnɪŋ] *adj (news etc)* sbalorditivo(a), stupefacente; *(dress, girl etc)* fantastico(a), splendido(a).

stunt[1] [stʌnt] *vt (tree, person)* arrestare la crescita or lo sviluppo di; *(growth)* arrestare.

stunt[2] [stʌnt] *n (for film etc)* acrobazia; *(Comm)* montatura pubblicitaria, trovata pubblicitaria; **it's just a** ~ **to get your money** è tutto un trucco per farti tirar fuori i soldi.

stunt·ed ['stʌntɪd] *adj (tree)* striminzito(a); *(person)* rachitico(a).

stunt·man ['stʌntmæn] *n, pl* **-men** stunt-man *m inv.*

stu·pefac·tion [ˌstjuːpɪˈfækʃən] *n* stupefazione *f,* stupore *m.*

stu·pefy ['stjuːpɪfaɪ] *vt (subj: tiredness, alcohol)* intontire, istupidire; *(fig: astound)* stupire, sbalordire.

stu·pefy·ing ['stjuːpɪfaɪɪŋ] *adj* sbalorditivo(a), stupefacente.

stu·pen·dous [stjuːˈpendəs] *adj (fam: film, holiday etc)* stupendo(a), fantastico(a); *(: price, mistake)* enorme.

stu·pid ['stjuːpɪd] *adj (gen)* stupido(a); *(person)* stupido(a), sciocco(a); *(: from sleep, drink)* intontito(a), istupidito(a); **that was** ~ **of you, that was a** ~ **thing to do** hai fatto una stupidaggine; **he drank himself** ~ **last night** era ubriaco fradicio ieri sera.

stu·pid·ity [stjuːˈpɪdɪtɪ] *n* stupidità.

stu·por ['stjuːpəʳ] *n (from heat, alcohol)* intontimento, stordimento.

stur·di·ness ['stɜːdɪnɪs] *n (see adj)* robustezza; solidità; risolutezza.

stur·dy ['stɜːdɪ] *adj (-ier, -iest)* *(person, tree)* robusto(a), forte; *(boat, material)* resistente, solido(a); *(fig: supporter, refusal)* risoluto(a).

stur·geon ['stɜːdʒən] *n* storione *m.*

stut·ter ['stʌtəʳ] **1** *n* balbuzie *f;* **he has a bad** ~ **ha**

una balbuzie pronunciata. **2** *vi, vt* balbettare.

stut·ter·er ['stʌtərəʳ] *n* balbuziente *m/f.*

sty [staɪ] *n (for pigs)* porcile *m.*

sty(e) [staɪ] *n (Med)* orzaiolo.

style [staɪl] *n* **(a)** *(gen)* stile *m;* **in the Renaissance** ~ in stile rinascimentale; **that's the** ~**!** così va bene! **(b)** *(of dress etc)* modello, linea; *(hair* ~*)* pettinatura; *(: more elaborate)* acconciatura; **in the latest** ~ all'ultima moda; **something in this** ~ qualcosa di questo tipo. **(c)** *(elegance: of person, car, film)* classe *f,* stile *m;* **to dress with** ~ vestirsi con un certo stile; **she has** ~ ha classe *or* stile; **to live in** ~ avere un elevato tenore di vita; **to do things in** ~ fare le cose in grande stile.

sty·li ['staɪlaɪ] *npl of* **stylus**.

styl·ish ['staɪlɪʃ] *adj (person)* che ha classe; *(car, district, furniture)* elegante; *(film)* raffinato(a).

styl·ist ['staɪlɪst] *n*: **hair** ~ parrucchiere/a.

sty·lis·tic [staɪˈlɪstɪk] *adj* stilistico(a).

sty·lis·tics [staɪˈlɪstɪks] *nsg* stilistica.

styl·ized ['staɪlaɪzd] *adj* stilizzato(a).

sty·lus ['staɪləs] *n, pl* **styli** *(pen)* stilo; *(of gramophone)* puntina.

styp·tic ['stɪptɪk] *adj* emostatico(a); ~ **pencil** matita emostatica.

suave [swɑːv] *adj* suadente.

sub [sʌb] *n abbr of* **submarine; subscription**.

sub... [sʌb] *pref* sub..., sotto... .

sub·al·tern ['sʌbltən] *n (Mil)* subalterno.

sub·com·mit·tee ['sʌbkəˌmɪtɪ] *n* sottocomitato.

sub·con·scious [ˌsʌbˈkɒnʃəs] **1** *adj* subcosciente. **2** *n*: **the** ~ il subcosciente, il subconscio.

sub·con·scious·ly [ˌsʌbˈkɒnʃəslɪ] *adv* inconsciamente.

sub·con·ti·nent [ˌsʌbˈkɒntɪnənt] *n*: **the (Indian)** ~ il subcontinente (indiano).

sub·con·tract [sʌbˈkɒntrækt] **1** *n* subappalto. **2** [ˌsʌbkənˈtrækt] *vt* subappaltare.

sub·con·trac·tor [ˌsʌbkənˈtræktəʳ] *n* subappaltatore/trice.

sub·di·vide [ˌsʌbdɪˈvaɪd] *vt* suddividere.

sub·due [səbˈdjuː] *vt (enemy)* sottomettere; *(children)* far star buono(a); *(high spirits)* calmare; *(passions etc)* controllare.

sub·dued [səbˈdjuːd] *adj (gen)* pacato(a), calmo(a); *(colours)* tenue; *(lighting)* soffuso(a); **he's rather** ~ **these days** è un po' troppo tranquillo ultimamente.

sub·edi·tor [ˌsʌbˈɛdɪtəʳ] *n* redattore(trice) aggiunto(a).

sub·hu·man [ˌsʌbˈhjuːmən] *adj* subumano(a).

sub·ject ['sʌbdʒɪkt] **1** *n* **(a)** *(Pol: of country)* cittadino/a; *(: of sovereign)* suddito/a. **(b)** *(Gram)* soggetto. **(c)** *(topic: gen)* argomento, soggetto; *(Scol)* materia; **let's keep to the** ~ non divaghiamo; **let's drop the** ~ lasciamo perdere; **(while we're) on the** ~ **of money...** a proposito di soldi...; **to change the** ~ cambiare discorso.

2 *adj* **(a)** *(people, nation)* assoggettato(a), sottomesso(a). **(b)**: ~ **to** *(liable to: law, tax, disease, delays)* soggetto(a) a; *(conditional upon)*: ~ **to doing that** a condizione di fare ciò, a condizione che si faccia ciò; ~ **to confirmation in writing** a condizione di ricevere conferma scritta; **these prices are** ~ **to change without notice** questi prezzi sono soggetti a modifiche senza preavviso.

3 [səbˈdʒɛkt] *vt*: **to** ~ **sb to sth** sottoporre qn a qc; **to** ~ **o.s. to ridicule/criticism** esporsi al ridicolo/a critiche; **she was** ~**ed to severe criticism** è stata severamente criticata.

4 *cpd*: ~ **matter** *n* argomento.

sub·jec·tion [səbˈdʒɛkʃən] *n (state)*: ~ **(to)**

sottomissione *f* (a), soggezione *f* (a); **to hold a people in** ~ tenere un popolo in servitù.
sub·jec·tive [səb'dʒɛktɪv] *adj* soggettivo(a).
sub·jec·tive·ly [səb'dʒɛktɪvlɪ] *adv* soggettivamente.
sub·ju·di·ce [ˌsʌb'juːdɪsɪ] *adj pred* sub iudice.
sub·ju·gate ['sʌbdʒʊgeɪt] *vt* sottomettere, soggiogare.
sub·junc·tive [səb'dʒʌŋktɪv] **1** *adj* congiuntivo(a). **2** *n* congiuntivo; **in the** ~ al congiuntivo.
sub·let [ˌsʌb'lɛt] *pt, pp* **sublet** *vt, vi* subaffittare.
sub·lieu·ten·ant [ˌsʌblɛf'tɛnənt] *n* (*Naut*) sottotenente *m* di vascello; (*Mil*) sottotenente.
sub·li·mate ['sʌblɪmeɪt] *vt* (*Psych*) sublimare.
sub·lime [sə'blaɪm] *adj* (*beauty, emotion, achievement*) sublime; (*indifference, contempt*) supremo(a).
sub·limi·nal [ˌsʌb'lɪmɪnl] *adj* subliminale.
sub·machine gun [ˌsʌbmə'ʃiːngʌn] *n* mitragliatore *m*, mitra *m inv*.
sub·ma·rine ['sʌbməriːn] *n* sottomarino, sommergibile *m*.
sub·merge [səb'mɜːdʒ] **1** *vt* (*plunge*): **to** ~ **(in)** immergere (in); (*flood*) sommergere. **2** *vi* (*submarine*) immergersi.
sub·mer·sion [səb'mɜːʃən] *n* (*see vt*) immersione *f*; sommersione *f*.
sub·mis·sion [səb'mɪʃən] *n* sottomissione *f*; (*to committee etc*) richiesta, domanda.
sub·mis·sive [səb'mɪsɪv] *adj* sottomesso(a), remissivo(a).
sub·mit [səb'mɪt] **1** *vt* (*proposal, claim*) presentare; **I** ~ **that...** propongo che..., suggerisco che.... **2** *vi* (*give in*): **to** ~ **to** (*pressure, threats*) cedere a; (*sb's will*) sottomettersi a.
sub·nor·mal [ˌsʌb'nɔːməl] *adj* subnormale.
sub·or·di·nate [sə'bɔːdnɪt] **1** *adj* (*rank, officer*) subalterno(a); (*Gram*): ~ **clause** proposizione *f* subordinata. **2** *n* subalterno/a, subordinato/a. **3** [sə'bɔːdɪneɪt] *vt*: **to** ~ **(to)** subordinare (a); **subordinating conjunction** (*Gram*) congiunzione *f* subordinativa.
sub·orn [sʌ'bɔːn] *vt* (*witness*) subornare.
sub·poe·na [səb'piːnə] (*Law*) **1** *n* citazione *f*, mandato di comparizione. **2** *vt* citare in giudizio.
sub·scribe [səb'skraɪb] **1** *vi*: **to** ~ **to** (*magazine etc*) abbonarsi a; (*fund*) sottoscrivere a; (*opinion*) trovarsi d'accordo con, approvare. **2** *vt* (*money*) devolvere.
sub·scrib·er [səb'skraɪbəʳ] *n* (*to magazine, telephone etc*): ~ **(to)** abbonato/a (a).
sub·scrip·tion [səb'skrɪpʃən] *n* (*to magazine etc*) abbonamento; (*membership fee*) quota d'iscrizione; **to take out a** ~ **to** abbonarsi a.
sub·se·quent ['sʌbsɪkwənt] *adj* (*later*) successivo(a); (*further*) ulteriore; ~ **to** in seguito a.
sub·se·quent·ly ['sʌbsɪkwəntlɪ] *adv* successivamente, in seguito.
sub·ser·vi·ent [səb'sɜːvɪənt] *adj*: ~ **(to)** remissivo(a) (a), sottomesso(a) (a).
sub·side [səb'saɪd] *vi* (*floods*) calare, decrescere; (*road, land*) cedere, avvallarsi; (*wind, anger etc*) calmarsi, placarsi.
sub·sid·ence [səb'saɪdəns] *n* (*of land etc*) cedimento, avvallamento; (*of waters etc*) abbassamento.
sub·sidi·ary [səb'sɪdɪərɪ] **1** *adj* (*company*) sussidiario(a); (*role etc*) secondario(a); (*Univ: subject*) complementare. **2** *n* (*Univ*) materia complementare; (*Comm*) filiale *f*.
sub·si·dize ['sʌbsɪdaɪz] *vt* sovvenzionare.
sub·si·dy ['sʌbsɪdɪ] *n* sovvenzione *f*, sussidio.
sub·sist [səb'sɪst] *vi*: **to** ~ **on sth** vivere di qc.
sub·sist·ence [səb'sɪstəns] **1** *n* sopravvivenza;

means of ~ mezzi di sussistenza. **2** *cpd*: ~ **allowance** *n* indennità *f inv* di trasferta; ~ **level** *n* livello minimo di vita; ~ **wage** *n* paga appena sufficiente per vivere.
sub·stance ['sʌbstəns] *n* (*gen*) sostanza; **to lack** ~ (*argument*) essere debole; (*accusation*) essere privo di fondamento; (*film, book*) non essere un gran che in quanto a contenuto; **a man of** ~ un uomo benestante; **in** ~ sostanzialmente, fondamentalmente.
sub·stand·ard [ˌsʌb'stændəd] *adj* (*goods*) scadente; (*housing*) di qualità scadente.
sub·stan·tial [səb'stænʃəl] *adj* (**a**) (*solid: building, table*) solido(a); (*: meal*) sostanzioso(a); (*considerable: improvement, increase, profits*) notevole, considerevole; (*: majority, proportion*) largo(a), grande; (*: difference*) sostanziale; (*wealthy: landowner, businessman*) ricco(a). (**b**) (*frm: real*) reale.
sub·stan·tial·ly [səb'stænʃəlɪ] *adv* (**a**) (*considerably*) notevolmente; ~ **bigger** molto più grande; ~ **different** molto diverso. (**b**) (*in essence*) sostanzialmente. (**c**) (*solidly: built*) solidamente.
sub·stan·ti·ate [səb'stænʃɪeɪt] *vt* dimostrare la fondatezza di.
sub·stan·tive ['sʌbstəntɪv] (*Gram*) **1** *adj* sostantivo(a). **2** *n* sostantivo.
sub·sti·tute ['sʌbstɪtjuːt] **1** *n* (*person*) sostituto/a; (*teacher*) supplente *m/f*; (*thing*) prodotto sostitutivo; **coffee** ~ surrogato di caffè; **there's no** ~ **for butter** non c'è niente di meglio del burro. **2** *vt*: **to** ~ **sb/sth (for)** sostituire qn/qc (con). **3** *vi*: ~ **for sb** sostituire qn.
sub·sti·tu·tion [ˌsʌbstɪ'tjuːʃən] *n* (*gen*) sostituzione *f*; (*in school*) supplenza.
sub·ter·fuge ['sʌbtəfjuːdʒ] *n* sotterfugio.
sub·ter·ra·nean [ˌsʌbtə'reɪnɪən] *adj* sotterraneo(a).
sub·ti·tle ['sʌbˌtaɪtl] *n* (*Cine*) sottotitolo.
sub·tle ['sʌtl] *adj* (*gen*) sottile; (*flavour, perfume*) delicato(a).
sub·tle·ty ['sʌtltɪ] *n* (*see adj*) sottigliezza; delicatezza.
sub·tly ['sʌtlɪ] *adv* (*see adj*) sottilmente; delicatamente.
sub·to·tal [ˌsʌb'təʊtl] *n* somma parziale.
sub·tract [səb'trækt] *vt* sottrarre.
sub·trac·tion [səb'trækʃən] *n* sottrazione *f*.
sub·urb ['sʌbɜːb] *n* sobborgo; **to live in the** ~s vivere in periferia.
sub·ur·ban [sə'bɜːbən] *adj* suburbano(a), della periferia.
sub·ur·bia [sə'bɜːbɪə] *n* periferia, sobborghi *mpl*.
sub·ver·sion [səb'vɜːʃən] *n* sovversione *f*.
sub·ver·sive [səb'vɜːsɪv] *adj, n* sovversivo(a) (*m/f*).
sub·way ['sʌbweɪ] *n* (*underpass*) sottopassaggio; (*railway: esp Am*) metropolitana.
sub·zero [ˌsʌb'zɪərəʊ] *adj*: ~ **temperatures** temperature *fpl* sotto zero.
suc·ceed [sək'siːd] **1** *vi* (**a**) (*be successful: gen*) riuscire, avere successo; **to** ~ **in life/business** avere successo nella vita/negli affari; **to** ~ **in doing sth** riuscire a fare qc. (**b**) (*follow*): **to** ~ **(to)** succedere (a). **2** *vt* (*monarch*) succedere a; **to** ~ **sb in a post** succedere a qn in un posto.
suc·ceed·ing [sək'siːdɪŋ] *adj* (*following: in past*) successivo(a), seguente; (*: in future*) futuro(a); ~ **generations** generazioni future; **on 3** ~ **Mondays** per 3 lunedì consecutivi; **each** ~ **year brought...** ogni anno che passava recava...; **each** ~ **year will bring further wealth** con ogni anno che passa aumenterà la ricchezza.
suc·cess [sək'sɛs] *n* (*gen*) successo, riuscita; **he**

was a great ~ ha avuto un grande successo; **without** ~ senza successo *or* risultato; **to make a** ~ **of sth** riuscire bene in qc; **to meet with** ~ avere successo.

suc·cess·ful [sək'sɛsful] *adj (person: in attempt)* che ha successo; *(: in life)* affermato(a), arrivato(a); *(attempt, plan)* riuscito(a), coronato(a) da successo; *(play, film)* di successo; *(business)* prospero(a); **to be** ~ **in doing sth** riuscire a fare qc.

suc·ces·sion [sək'sɛʃən] *n* **(a)** *(series)* serie *f;* **in** ~ di seguito; **in quick** ~ in rapida successione, velocemente. **(b)** *(to post etc)* successione *f.*

suc·ces·sive [sək'sɛsɪv] *adj (days, months)* consecutivo(a); *(generations)* successivo(a); **on 3** ~ **days** per 3 giorni consecutivi *or* di seguito; **each** ~ **failure** ogni nuovo fiasco.

suc·ces·sor [sək'sɛsəʳ] *n (in office)* successore *m; (heir)* erede *m/f.*

suc·cinct [sək'sɪŋkt] *adj* succinto(a).

suc·cu·lent ['sʌkjʊlənt] **1** *adj (tasty)* succulento(a). **2** *n (Bot):* ~**s** piante *fpl* grasse.

suc·cumb [sə'kʌm] *vi:* **to** ~ **to** *(temptation, illness)* soccombere a; *(entreaties, charms)* cedere a.

such [sʌtʃ] **1** *adj* tale, del genere; ~ **a book** un tale libro, un libro del genere; ~ **books** tali libri, libri del genere; **books** ~ **as these** libri come questi; ~ **books as I have** quei pochi libri che ho; **did you ever hear of** ~ **a thing?** hai mai sentito una cosa del genere?; **there's no** ~ **thing** non esiste; **there's no** ~ **thing as a unicorn** gli unicorni non esistono; **there's no** ~ **place in Italy** questo posto in Italia non esiste; **I said no** ~ **thing** non ho detto niente del genere; ~ **a man as you, a man** ~ **as you** un uomo come te; ~ **writers as Updike, writers** ~ **as Updike** scrittori come Updike; **I was in** ~ **a hurry** avevo una tale fretta; **I was in** ~ **a hurry that...** avevo così fretta che...; **it was** ~ **as to/that** era tale da/che; **have you got** ~ **a thing as a torch?** hai una pila o qualcosa del genere?; **in** ~ **cases** in casi del genere; **we had** ~ **a case last year** si è avuto un caso del genere l'anno scorso; **but** ~ **is not the case** ma non è questo caso; **some** ~ **idea** un'idea del genere; **he's not** ~ **a fool as you think** non è così scemo come pensi; ~ **was his answer** questa è stata la sua risposta; ~ **is life** così è la vita; ~ **as?** per esempio?; **I had** ~ **a fright** ho preso un tale spavento; **this is my car** ~ **as it is** questa è la mia macchina se così si può chiamare.

2 *adv* **(a)** *(so very)* talmente, così; ~ **good food** cibo così buono; ~ **a clever girl** una ragazza così intelligente; **it's** ~ **a long time since we saw each other** è da tanto tempo che non ci vediamo; ~ **a long time ago** tanto tempo fa. **(b)** *(in comparisons)* **I haven't had** ~ **good tea for ages** erano secoli che non bevevo un tè così buono.

3 *(pron):* ~ **as wish to go** chi desidera andare; **and as** ~ **he was promoted** e come tale fu promosso; **doctors as** ~ **are...** i medici in quanto tali sono...; **the work as** ~ **is poorly paid** il lavoro di per sé non è pagato bene; **there's no garden as** ~ non c'è un vero e proprio giardino; **and** ~ **(like)** e così via.

such-and-such ['sʌtʃənsʌtʃ] **1** *adj:* **they live in** ~ **a street** abitano nella tale strada. **2** *n:* **Mr** ~ il signor tal dei tali.

such·like ['sʌtʃlaɪk] *(fam)* **1** *adj* simile, di tal genere; **sheep and** ~ **animals** pecore e animali del genere. **2** *pron:* **and** ~ e così via.

suck [sʌk] **1** *vt (gen)* succhiare; *(subj: baby)* poppare, succhiare; *(: pump, machine)* aspirare; **to** ~ **one's thumb** succhiarsi il dito; **to** ~ **sth through a straw** bere qc con la cannuccia; **to** ~ **an orange**

dry succhiarsi tutta un'arancia; **to** ~ **dry** *(fig: person: of money)* ripulire dei soldi; *(: of energy)* spossare, sfiancare. **2** *vi (baby)* succhiare, poppare; **to** ~ **at sth** succhiare qc.

♦ **suck down** *vt* + *adv (subj: current, mud)* inghiottire, risucchiare.

♦ **suck in** *vt* + *adv (subj: machine: dust, air etc)* aspirare; **to** ~ **one's cheeks in** succhiarsi le guance.

♦ **suck up 1** *vt* + *adv (dust, liquid etc)* aspirare. **2** *vi* + *adv (fam):* **to** ~ **up to sb** leccare i piedi a qn.

suck·er ['sʌkəʳ] *n (Zool, Tech)* ventosa; *(Bot)* pollone *m; (Am: lollipop)* lecca lecca; *(fam: person)* babbeo/a, citrullo/a; **he's a** ~ **for a pretty girl** *(fam)* ha un debole per le belle ragazze.

suck·le ['sʌkl] *vt* allattare.

su·crose ['suːkrəʊz] *n* saccarosio.

suc·tion ['sʌkʃən] **1** *n* aspirazione *f.* **2** *cpd:* ~ **pump** *n* pompa aspirante.

sud·den ['sʌdn] *adj* improvviso(a); **this is so** ~! non me l'aspettavo!; **all of a** ~ all'improvviso, improvvisamente. ·

sud·den·ly ['sʌdnlɪ] *adv* improvvisamente, all'improvviso, di colpo.

sud·den·ness ['sʌdnnɪs] *n:* **the** ~ **of his death/ departure** la sua morte/partenza improvvisa.

suds [sʌdz] *npl (lather)* schiuma; *(soapy water)* saponata.

sue [suː] **1** *vt:* **to** ~ **sb for libel/damages** *etc* citare qn per diffamazione/danni *etc.* **2** *vi:* **to** ~ **(for)** intentare causa (per); **to** ~ **for divorce** intentare causa di divorzio.

suede [sweɪd] **1** *n* pelle *f* scamosciata. **2** *cpd* di pelle scamosciata.

suet ['sʊɪt] *n* grasso di rognone.

Suez ['suːɪz] *n:* ~ **Canal** canale *m* di Suez.

suf·fer ['sʌfəʳ] **1** *vt* **(a)** *(hardship, hunger)* soffrire; *(pain)* provare; *(undergo: loss, setback)* subire; **to** ~ **pangs of hunger** provare i morsi della fame. **(b)** *(tolerate: opposition, rudeness)* sopportare, tollerare; **she doesn't** ~ **fools gladly** proprio non sopporta gli stupidi.

2 *vi (physically)* soffrire; *(be adversely affected: town)* subire danni; *(: regiment)* subire perdite; **to** ~ **from** *(rheumatism, headaches, deafness)* soffrire di; *(malnutrition, the cold)* soffrire; *(a cold, influenza, bad memory)* avere; **she** ~**s from a limp** è zoppa, zoppica; **she was** ~**ing from shock** era sotto shock; **to** ~ **from the effects of alcohol/a fall** risentire degli effetti dell'alcool/di una caduta; **the house is** ~**ing from neglect** la casa è in uno stato di abbandono; **your health will** ~ la tua salute ne risentirà; **to** ~ **for one's sins** scontare i propri peccati; **you'll** ~ **for it!** la pagherai!

suf·fer·ance ['sʌfərəns] *n:* **he was only there on** ~ era più che altro sopportato lì.

suf·fer·er ['sʌfərəʳ] *n (Med):* ~ **(from)** malato/a (di).

suf·fer·ing ['sʌfərɪŋ] *n (pain, grief)* sofferenza; *(hardship, deprivation)* privazione *f.*

suf·fice [sə'faɪs] *(frm)* **1** *vi* bastare. **2** *vt:* ~ **it to say...** basti dire che... .

suf·fi·cient [sə'fɪʃənt] *adj:* ~ **(for)** sufficiente (per); **that's** ~ basta così; **do you have** ~ **money?** hai abbastanza denaro or soldi a sufficienza?

suf·fi·cient·ly [sə'fɪʃəntlɪ] *adv* sufficientemente, abbastanza; ~ **large** *(quantity)* sufficiente; *(number)* abbastanza grande; **she is** ~ **intelligent to understand** è abbastanza *or* sufficientemente intelligente per capire.

suf·fix ['sʌfɪks] *n* suffisso.

suf·fo·cate ['sʌfəkeɪt] *vt, vi* soffocare.

suf·fo·cat·ing ['sʌfəkeɪtɪŋ] *adj (heat, atmosphere)* soffocante, opprimente.

suf·fo·ca·tion [ˌsʌfə'keɪʃən] *n* soffocazione *f*; *(Med)* asfissia; **to die from** ~ morire per asfissia.

suf·frage ['sʌfrɪdʒ] *n* suffragio.

suf·fra·gette [ˌsʌfrə'dʒɛt] *n* suffragetta.

suf·fuse [sə'fjuːz] *vt:* **to** ~ **(with)** *(colour)* tingere (di); **her face was** ~**d with joy** la gioia si dipingeva sul suo volto; **the room was** ~**d with light** nella stanza c'era una luce soffusa.

sug·ar ['ʃʊgə'] **1** *n* zucchero. **2** *vt (tea etc)* zuccherare; **to** ~ **the pill** *(fig)* indorare la pillola. **3** *cpd:* ~ **basin** *n* ~ **bowl** *n* zuccheriera; ~ **beet** *n* barbabietola da zucchero; ~ **cane** *n* canna da zucchero; ~ **daddy** *n (fam)* vecchio amante *m* danaroso; ~ **lump** *n* zolletta di zucchero; ~ **plantation** *n* piantagione *f* di canne da zucchero; ~ **refinery** *n* raffineria di zucchero; ~ **tongs** *npl* mollette *fpl* da zucchero.

sugar-coated ['ʃʊgə,kəʊtɪd] *adj* ricoperto(a) di zucchero.

sug·ared ['ʃʊgəd] *adj:* ~ **almonds** confetti *mpl* alla mandorla.

sug·ary ['ʃʊgərɪ] *adj (food etc)* zuccherato(a), zuccheroso(a); *(fig: sentimental)* sdolcinato(a), stucchevole.

sug·gest [sə'dʒɛst] *vt (gen)* suggerire; *(evoke)* evocare, far pensare a; **to** ~ **doing sth** proporre or suggerire di fare qc; **he** ~**ed (that) they should come too** ha proposto or suggerito che venissero anche loro; **this** ~**s that...** questo fa pensare or indica che...; **what are you trying to** ~**?** cosa stai cercando di insinuare?; **nothing** ~**s itself** non mi viene in mente niente; **what do you** ~ **I do?** cosa mi suggerisci di fare?

sug·ges·tion [sə'dʒɛstʃən] *n* **(a)** suggerimento; **if I may make** or **offer a** ~ se mi è concesso fare un suggerimento; **it was your** ~ **to come** è stata una tua idea quella di venire; **my** ~ **is that...** propongo or suggerisco che...; **at sb's** ~ su suggerimento di qn; **there's no** ~ **of** non c'è niente che indichi or che faccia pensare a. **(b)** *(trace: of garlic)* punta; *(: of liquid)* goccia.

sug·ges·tive [sə'dʒɛstɪv] *adj* **(a)** *(evocative):* **to be** ~ **of** far pensare a, evocare. **(b)** *(indecent)* spinto(a), indecente.

sui·cid·al [ˌsʊɪ'saɪdl] *adj* suicida *inv; (fig)* fatale, disastroso(a).

sui·cide ['sʊɪsaɪd] **1** *n* **(a)** *(also fig)* suicidio; **to attempt** ~ tentare il suicidio; **to commit** ~ suicidarsi. **(b)** *(person)* suicida *m/f.* **2** *cpd:* ~ **attempt** *n,* ~ **bid** *n* tentato suicidio.

suit [suːt] **1** *n* **(a)** *(for man)* completo; *(for woman)* tailleur *m inv,* completo; *(for bathing)* costume *m; (driver's, astronaut's)* tuta; **a** ~ **of armour** un'armatura. **(b)** *(law~)* causa; **to bring a** ~ **against sb** intentare causa a qn. **(c)** *(Cards)* colore *m,* seme *m;* **to follow** ~ *(fig)* fare altrettanto.

2 *vt* **(a)** *(adapt):* **to** ~ **(to)** adattare (a); **to** ~ **one's language to one's audience** usare un linguaggio adatto a chi ascolta; **to** ~ **the action to the word** mettere in pratica le proprie parole; **to be** ~**ed to sth** *(suitable for)* essere adatto a qc; **they are well** ~**ed (to each other)** sono fatti l'uno per l'altro. **(b)** *(be acceptable: time, day)* andare bene a; *(: food, climate)* fare per; *(: clothes, colour)* stare bene a; **that** ~**s me (down to the ground)** per me va benissimo; **it doesn't** ~ **me to leave now** non mi va di partire ora; **the post** ~**ed her perfectly** il posto faceva proprio per lei. **(c)** *(please)* contentare; ~ **yourself whether you do it or not** se vuoi farlo fallo, se no lascia perdere; ~ **yourself!** fa' come ti pare!

suit·abil·ity [ˌsuːtə'bɪlɪtɪ] *n (for job)* idoneità; **I doubt the** ~ **of this book for children** dubito che sia un libro adatto ai bambini.

suit·able ['suːtəbl] *adj (gen)* adatto(a); **I haven't anything** ~ **to wear** non ho niente di adatto da mettermi; **the most** ~ **man for the job** l'uomo più adatto a questo lavoro; **the film is not** ~ **for children** non è un film adatto ai bambini.

suit·ably ['suːtəblɪ] *adv (dress)* in modo adatto; *(thank)* adeguatamente; **he was** ~ **impressed** ha ricevuto un'impressione favorevole; **to reply** ~ dare una risposta adeguata.

suit·case ['suːtˌkeɪs] *n* valigia.

suite [swiːt] *n (of rooms)* appartamento; *(Mus)* suite *f inv;* **a bathroom** ~ un bagno; **a bedroom** ~ una camera da letto; **a three-piece** ~ un divano e due poltrone.

suit·or ['suːtə'] *n* corteggiatore *m,* spasimante *m.*

sulk [sʌlk] **1** *vi* tenere il broncio, tenere il muso. **2** *n:* **to have the** ~**s** tenere il muso, tenere il broncio.

sulky ['sʌlkɪ] *adj* **(-ier, -iest)** imbronciato(a).

sul·len ['sʌlən] *adj (person)* scontroso(a); *(answer)* brusco(a); *(sky)* cupo(a); **to have a** ~ **face** avere il viso imbronciato.

sul·ly ['sʌlɪ] *vt (poet)* macchiare.

sul·phate ['sʌlfeɪt] *n* solfato; **copper** ~ solfato di rame.

sul·phide ['sʌlfaɪd] *n* solfuro.

sul·phur ['sʌlfə'] *n* zolfo.

sul·phu·ric [sʌl'fjʊərɪk] *adj:* ~ **acid** acido solforico.

sul·tan ['sʌltən] *n* sultano.

sul·tana [sʌl'tɑːnə] *n (fruit)* uva sultanina.

sul·try ['sʌltrɪ] *adj (weather)* afoso(a), pesante, opprimente; *(woman, character)* passionale.

sum [sʌm] *n (piece of arithmetic)* somma, addizione *f; (amount of money)* somma; **the** ~ **of 6 and 4 is 10** 6 più 4 fa 10; **that is the** ~ **(total) of his achievements** questo è tutto quello che ha fatto.

♦ **sum up 1** *vt + adv (review)* riassumere, ricapitolare; *(evaluate rapidly)* valutare, giudicare; **to** ~ **up an argument** riassumere una discussione; **she quickly** ~**med him up** capì subito che tipo era; **he** ~**med up the situation quickly** valutò subito la situazione. **2** *vi + adv* riassumere; **to** ~ **up...** per riassumere..., riassumendo....

sum·ma·rize ['sʌməraɪz] *vt* riassumere.

sum·mary ['sʌmərɪ] **1** *n* riassunto. **2** *adj (dismissal, treatment)* sommario(a); *(perusal)* sbrigativo(a).

sum·mer ['sʌmə'] **1** *n* estate *f;* **in (the) summer** d'estate; **in the** ~ **of 1985** nell'estate del 1985; **last/next** ~ l'estate scorsa/prossima. **2** *cpd (gen)* estivo(a); ~ **camp** *n* colonia (estiva); ~ **school** *n* corsi *mpl* estivi; ~ **time** *n (Brit: daylight saving time)* ora legale.

summer·house ['sʌməhaʊs] *n (in garden)* padiglione *m.*

summer·time ['sʌmətaɪm] *n (season)* stagione *f* estiva.

sum·mery ['sʌmərɪ] *adj* estivo(a).

summing-up [ˌsʌmɪŋ'ʌp] *n (Law)* ricapitolazione *f* del processo.

sum·mit ['sʌmɪt] *n* cima, vetta, sommità; *(fig)* culmine *m; (Pol: also:* ~ **conference)** (conferenza al) vertice *m.*

sum·mon ['sʌmən] *vt (meeting)* convocare; *(aid, doctor, servant etc)* chiamare; *(Law):* **to** ~ **a witness** citare un testimone.

♦ **summon up** *vt + adv (courage, interest)* trovare; **to** ~ **up all one's courage** farsi coraggio, armarsi di coraggio; **to** ~ **up all one's strength** fare appello a tutte le proprie forze; **I couldn't** ~ **up the** courage to tell him non ho trovato il coraggio di dirglielo.

sum·mons ['sʌmənz] **1** n (Law) citazione f, mandato di comparizione; **to serve a ~ on sb** notificare una citazione a qn. **2** vt citare (in giudizio).

sump [sʌmp] n (Aut) coppa dell'olio, carter m inv.

sump·tu·ous ['sʌmptjuəs] adj sontuoso(a).

sun [sʌn] **1** n sole m; **to get up with the ~** alzarsi allo spuntar del sole; **the ~ is in my eyes** ho il sole negli occhi; **in the ~** al sole; **a place in the ~** (also fig) un posto al sole; **they have everything under the ~** hanno tutto ciò che possono desiderare; **there's nothing new under the ~** non c'è niente di nuovo sotto il sole. **2** vt: **to ~ o.s.** godersi il sole. **3** cpd: **~ cream** n crema solare; **~ umbrella** n ombrellone m.

sun·bathe ['sʌnbeɪð] vi prendere il sole.

sun·beam ['sʌnbiːm] n raggio di sole.

sun·bed ['sʌnbɛd] n lettino solare.

sun·blind ['sʌnblaɪnd] n tenda da sole.

sun·burn ['sʌnbɜːn] n (tan) abbronzatura; (painful) scottatura.

sun·burnt ['sʌnbɜːnt] adj (tanned) abbronzato(a); (painfully) scottato(a).

sun·dae ['sʌndeɪ] n coppa di gelato guarnita.

Sun·day ['sʌndɪ] **1** n domenica; **he'll never succeed in a month of ~s** non riuscirà mai e poi mai. **2** cpd: **~ best** n abito della domenica; **~ school** n ≃ scuola di catechismo; for usage see **Tuesday.**

sun·deck ['sʌndɛk] n ponte m scoperto.

sun·dial ['sʌndaɪəl] n meridiana.

sun·down ['sʌndaʊn] n tramonto.

sun·drenched ['sʌndrɛntʃt] adj inondato(a) dal sole.

sun·dry ['sʌndrɪ] **1** adj vari(e), diversi(e); **all and ~** tutti quanti. **2: sundries** npl (Comm) articoli mpl vari.

sun·flower ['sʌnflaʊəʳ] n girasole m.

sung [sʌŋ] pp of **sing.**

sun·glasses ['sʌnglɑːsɪz] npl occhiali mpl da sole.

sunk [sʌŋk] pp of **sink.**

sunk·en ['sʌŋkən] adj (ship) affondato(a); (eyes, cheeks) infossato(a); (bath) incassato(a).

sun·lamp ['sʌnlæmp] n lampada a raggi ultravioletti.

sun·less ['sʌnlɪs] adj senza sole.

sun·light ['sʌnlaɪt] n (luce f del) sole m; **in the ~** alla luce del sole.

sun·lit ['sʌnlɪt] adj assolato(a), soleggiato(a).

sun·ny ['sʌnɪ] adj (-ier, -iest) **(a)** (place, room etc) assolato(a), soleggiato(a); (day) di sole; **it is ~** c'è il sole; **the outlook is ~** (Met) si prevede il sole. **(b)** (fig: person, disposition) allegro(a); (: smile) radioso(a), luminoso(a); **she always sees the ~ side of things** vede sempre il lato buono delle cose.

sun·rise ['sʌnraɪz] n alba, aurora; **at ~** allo spuntar del sole.

sun·roof ['sʌnruːf] n (on building) tetto a terrazzo; (Aut) tetto apribile.

sun·set ['sʌnsɛt] n tramonto.

sun·shade ['sʌnʃeɪd] n (portable) parasole m; (for eyes) visiera; (in car) aletta parasole; (awning) tenda da sole.

sun·shine ['sʌnʃaɪn] **1** n (luce f del) sole m; **hours of ~** (Met) ore fpl di sole; **she's a little ray of ~** (iro) è una dolce creatura. **2** cpd: **~ roof** n (Aut) tetto apribile.

sun·spot ['sʌnspɒt] n (Astron) macchia solare.

sun·stroke ['sʌnstrəʊk] n colpo di sole, insolazione f.

sun·tan ['sʌntæn] **1** n abbronzatura, tintarella. **2** cpd: **~ cream/oil** n crema/olio solare.

sun·tanned ['sʌntænd] adj abbronzato(a).

sun·trap ['sʌntræp] n luogo molto assolato.

su·per ['suːpəʳ] adj (fam) fantastico(a), splendido(a); **we had a ~ time** ci siamo divertiti da morire.

super... ['suːpəʳ] pref super..., sovra..., iper...; **~critical** ipercritico(a); **~sensitive** ipersensibile.

supera·bun·dance ['suːpərə,bʌndəns] n sovrabbondanza.

super·an·nua·tion [,suːpə,rænjʊ'eɪʃən] n (pension) pensione f; (contribution) contributi mpl pensionistici.

su·perb [suː'pɜːb] adj superbo(a).

super·charged ['suːpətʃɑːdʒd] adj (Aut) sovralimentato(a).

super·char·ger ['suːpə,tʃɑːdʒəʳ] n compressore m.

super·cili·ous [,suːpə'sɪlɪəs] adj altezzoso(a), sprezzante.

super·fi·cial [,suːpə'fɪʃəl] adj superficiale.

super·fi·ci·al·ity ['suːpə,fɪʃɪ'ælɪtɪ] n superficialità.

super·fi·cial·ly [,suːpə'fɪʃəlɪ] adv superficialmente.

super·flu·ous [suː'pɜːfluəs] adj superfluo(a); **he felt rather ~** si sentì di troppo.

super·hu·man [,suːpə'hjuːmən] adj sovrumano(a).

super·im·pose [,suːpərɪm'pəʊz] vt: **to ~ (on)** sovrapporre (a).

super·in·ten·dent [,suːpərɪn'tɛndənt] n soprintendente m/f; (Police) commissario di Pubblica Sicurezza.

su·peri·or [suː'pɪərɪəʳ] **1** adj (gen): **~ (to)** superiore (a); (Comm: goods, quality) di prim'ordine, superiore; (smug: person) che fa il superiore; (: smile, air) di superiorità; (: remark) altezzoso(a); **~ number** (Typ) esponente m; **he felt rather ~** si sentì importante. **2** n (in rank) superiore m/f; **Mother S~** (Rel) Madre f Superiora, Superiora.

su·peri·or·ity [suː,pɪərɪ'ɒrɪtɪ] n superiorità.

super·la·tive [suː'pɜːlətɪv] **1** adj (superb: quality, achievement) eccellente; (: indifference) sommo(a); (Gram) superlativo(a). **2** n (Gram) superlativo; **to talk in ~s** fare largo uso di superlativi nel parlare.

super·man ['suːpəmæn] n, pl **-men** superuomo.

super·mar·ket ['suːpə,mɑːkɪt] n supermercato.

super·natu·ral [,suːpə'nætʃərəl] adj, n soprannaturale (m).

super·pow·er ['suːpə,paʊəʳ] n (Pol) superpotenza.

super·sede [,suːpə'siːd] vt sostituire, soppiantare; **a ~d method** un metodo sorpassato.

super·son·ic [,suːpə'sɒnɪk] adj supersonico(a).

super·star ['suːpəstɑːʳ] n superstar m/f inv.

super·sti·tion [,suːpə'stɪʃən] n superstizione f.

super·sti·tious [,suːpə'stɪʃəs] adj superstizioso(a).

super·struc·ture ['suːpə,strʌktʃəʳ] n sovrastruttura.

super·tank·er ['suːpə,tæŋkəʳ] n superpetroliera.

super·tax ['suːpə,tæks] n soprattassa, imposta supplementare.

super·vise ['suːpəvaɪz] vt (person) sorvegliare; (work, research) soprintendere a.

super·vi·sion [,suːpə'vɪʒən] n supervisione f, sorveglianza.

super·vi·sor ['suːpəvaɪzəʳ] n sorvegliante m/f, supervisore m; (Univ) relatore/trice; (Comm) capocommesso/a.

super·vi·sory ['suːpəvaɪzərɪ] adj di sorveglianza.

sup·per ['sʌpəʳ] n (evening meal) cena; (late-night snack) spuntino; **to have ~** cenare.

sup·plant [sə'plɑːnt] vt soppiantare.

sup·ple ['sʌpl] *adj* (**-r, -st**) flessibile; *(person)* agile.

sup·plement ['sʌplɪmənt] **1** *n* supplemento. **2** [,sʌplɪ'ment] *vt* *(diet etc)* integrare; *(income)* arrotondare; *(information)* completare.

sup·plemen·ta·ry [,sʌplɪ'mentərɪ] *adj* supplementare; ~ **benefit** *forma di indennità assistenziale.*

sup·pli·ca·tion [,sʌplɪ'keɪʃən] *n* supplica.

sup·pli·er [sə'plaɪə'] *n (Comm)* fornitore/trice.

sup·ply [sə'plaɪ] **1** *n (delivery)* fornitura; *(stock)* provvista; **the electricity/water/gas** ~ l'erogazione di corrente/d'acqua/di gas; **to cut off the water** ~ togliere l'acqua; **the** ~ **of fuel to the engine** l'afflusso di carburante al motore; ~ **and demand** domanda e offerta; **to be in short** ~ scarseggiare, essere scarso(a); **supplies** *pl (food)* viveri *mpl;* *(Mil)* approvvigionamenti *mpl,* rifornimenti *mpl;* **medical supplies** materiale *m* sanitario; **office supplies** forniture *fpl* per ufficio.

2 *vt (goods, materials, information etc)* fornire; *(fill: need, want)* soddisfare; **to** ~ **sb (with sth)** *(with goods)* fornire qc a qn, rifornire qn di qc; *(Mil)* approvvigionare qn (di qc); **she supplied us with the necessary evidence** ci ha fornito le prove necessarie; **the car comes supplied with a radio** l'auto viene fornita completa di radio; **who will** ~ **their needs?** chi farà fronte ai *or* soddisferà i loro bisogni?

3 *cpd (ship, train)* di rifornimento; ~ **teacher** *n* supplente *m/f.*

sup·port [sə'pɔːt] **1** *n (gen)* sostegno; *(object)* sostegno, supporto; **she was a great** ~ **to me** mi è stata di grande conforto; **moral** ~ sostegno morale; **he has no visible means of** ~ non è ben chiaro come si mantenga; **to speak in** ~ **of a candidate** parlare a favore di un candidato; **to lean on sb for** ~ *(also fig)* appoggiarsi a qn; **they stopped work in** ~ **(of)** hanno smesso di lavorare per solidarietà (con); **our** ~ **comes from the workers** abbiamo l'appoggio degli operai; **there's a great deal of** ~ **for his views** le sue opinioni sono ampiamente condivise.

2 *vt (gen)* sostenere, sorreggere; *(fig: person: emotionally)* sostenere; *(: financially)* mantenere; *(: proposal, project)* appoggiare; *(: Sport: team)* fare il tifo per; *(: corroborate: evidence)* confermare, convalidare; **to** ~ **o.s.** *(financially)* mantenersi; **all that is necessary to** ~ **life** tutto ciò che rende possibile l'esistenza di una forma di vita.

sup·port·er [sə'pɔːtə'] *n (of proposal, project)* sostenitore/trice; *(Pol etc)* sostenitore/trice, fautore/trice; *(Sport)* tifoso/a.

sup·port·ing [sə'pɔːtɪŋ] *adj (Theatre: role)* secondario(a), di secondo piano; *(: actor)* che ha un ruolo secondario.

sup·pose [sə'pəuz] *vt* **(a)** *(assume as hypothesis)* supporre + *sub,* mettere + *sub;* **let us** ~ **that...** supponiamo che..., mettiamo che...; **but just** ~ **he's right** ma supponi *or* metti che abbia ragione; **even supposing (that)** it were true anche nel caso che fosse vero; **always supposing (that) he comes** ammesso *or* non concesso che venga; ~ *or* **supposing it rains, what shall we do?** metti che piova, cosa facciamo?

(b) *(assume, believe):* **I** ~ **she'll come** suppongo che verrà; **I don't** ~ **she'll come** non credo che venga; **I** ~ **she won't come** penso che non verrà; ~ **she doesn't come?** e se non venisse?; **I** ~ **so/not** credo di sì/di no; **I don't** ~ **so** non credo; **you'll accept, I** ~? accetti, immagino?; **I don't** ~ **you could lend me a pound?,** **I** ~ **you couldn't lend me a pound?** non potresti per caso prestarmi una

sterlina?; **he's** ~**d to be an expert** dicono che sia un esperto, passa per un esperto.

(c) *(in passive: ought):* **to be** ~**d to do sth** essere tenuto(a) a fare qc; **you're not** ~**d to do that** non dovresti farlo.

(d) *(in imperative: I suggest):* ~ **you do it now?** e se lo facessi adesso?; ~ **we change the subject?** e se parlassimo d'altro?

(e) *(presuppose)* presupporre.

sup·posed [sə'pəuzd] *adj (presumed)* presunto(a); *(so-called)* cosiddetto(a).

sup·pos·ed·ly [sə'pəuzɪdlɪ] *adv (presumably)* presumibilmente; *(seemingly)* apparentemente.

sup·po·si·tion [,sʌpə'zɪʃən] *n* supposizione *f;* **on the** ~ **that...** partendo dal presupposto che... + *sub.*

sup·pos·i·tory [sə'pɒzɪtərɪ] *n* supposta, suppositorio.

sup·press [sə'pres] *vt (emotion, revolt)* reprimere, soffocare; *(scandal)* soffocare; *(yawn, smile)* trattenere; *(publication)* sopprimere; *(news, the truth)* occultare.

sup·pres·sion [sə'preʃən] *n (of emotions etc)* repressione *f;* *(of scandal)* soffocamento; *(of truth)* occultamento.

sup·pu·rate ['sʌpjuəreɪt] *vi* suppurare.

supra·na·tion·al [,suːprə'næʃənl] *adj* sopranazionale.

su·prema·cy [su'preməsɪ] *n* supremazia.

su·preme [su'priːm] *adj (in authority)* supremo(a); *(very great)* sommo(a), massimo(a); **with** ~ **indifference** con somma indifferenza; **the** ~ **sacrifice** il sacrificio supremo; ~ **court** corte *f* suprema; **to reign** ~ *(fig)* dominare.

su·preme·ly [su'priːmlɪ] *adv* estremamente, sommamente.

sur·charge ['sɜːtʃɑːdʒ] *n (gen)* supplemento, sovrapprezzo; *(tax)* soprattassa.

sure [ʃuə'] **1** *adj* (**-r, -st**) *(gen)* sicuro(a); *(definite, convinced)* sicuro(a), certo(a); **it's** ~ **to rain** pioverà di sicuro; **I'm** ~ **it's going to rain** sono sicuro che pioverà; **I'm not** ~ **how/why/when** non so bene come/perché/quando + *sub;* **be** ~ **to tell me if you see him** mi raccomando, dimmi se lo vedi; **to be** ~ **of sth** essere sicuro di qc; **to be** ~ **of o.s.** essere sicuro di sé; **to be** ~ **of one's facts** essere sicuro dei fatti; **you can be** ~ **of a good time there** puoi essere sicuro che ti divertirai; **to make** ~ **of sth** assicurarsi di qc; **be** *or* **make** ~ **you do it right** bada di farlo bene; **I'll find out for** ~ vedrò di accertarmene; **I think I locked up, but I'll just make** ~ credo di aver chiuso a chiave, ma voglio assicurarmene; **just to make** ~ per sicurezza; **do you know for** ~? ne sei proprio sicuro?; **he'll leave, for** ~ senza dubbio partirà; **I'm** ~ **I don't know, I don't know, I'm** ~ che vuoi che ne sappia io?; **he's a** ~ **thing for president** ha la presidenza assicurata.

2 *adv:* **is that O.K.?** — ~! va bene? — certo! *or* sicuro!; **that** ~ **is pretty, that's** ~ **pretty** *(Am)* è veramente *or* davvero carino; ~ **enough!** *(of course)* sicuro!; ~ **enough** *(predictably)* infatti; **as** ~ **as fate** ovviamente; **as** ~ **as eggs is eggs, as** ~ **as I'm standing here** e com'è vero Dio.

sure-fire ['ʃuə,faɪə'] *adj (fam)* infallibile, sicuro(a).

sure-footed [,ʃuə'futɪd] *adj* dal passo sicuro.

sure·ly ['ʃuəlɪ] *adv (certainly)* certamente, sicuramente; ~ **we've met before?** ma non ci siamo già incontrati?; ~ **you don't mean that!** non parlerai sul serio!; ~ **not!** ma non è possibile!

sure·ness ['ʃuənɪs] *n (of aim, footing)* sicurezza; *(positiveness)* certezza.

sure·ty ['ʃʊərətɪ] *n* caparra; **to go** *or* **stand ~ for sb** farsi garante per qn.

surf [sɜːf] *n* (*waves*) cavalloni *mpl*; (*foam*) spuma.

sur·face ['sɜːfɪs] **1** *n* (*gen*) superficie *f*; (*of road*) piano stradale; **on the ~ it seems that…** (*fig*) superficialmente sembra che…; **we've only scratched the ~** (*fig: of argument, work*) abbiamo appena iniziato. **2** *vt* (*road*) asfaltare. **3** *vi* (*submarine etc*) risalire in superficie; (*fig: person: after absence*) farsi vivo(a); (*: from bed*) emergere; **he ~s in London occasionally** ogni tanto si fa vedere a Londra. **4** *cpd* (Mil, Naut) di superficie; **~-to-air missile** *n* missile *m* terra aria; **~ area** *n* superficie *f*; **~ mail** *n* posta ordinaria.

surf·board ['sɜːfbɔːd] *n* tavola per surfing.

sur·feit ['sɜːfɪt] *n* sovrabbondanza.

surf·er ['sɜːfəʳ] *n* chi pratica il surfing.

surf·ing ['sɜːfɪŋ] *n*, **surf·riding** ['sɜːfraɪdɪŋ] *n* surfing *m*.

surge [sɜːdʒ] **1** *n* (*of sea*) impeto; (*of people, sympathy etc*) ondata; **a ~ of anger** un impeto di rabbia. **2** *vi* (*water, people*) riversarsi; (*waves*) sollevarsi; **to ~ into/over sth** riversarsi in/su qc; **to ~ forward** buttarsi avanti; **to ~ round sb/sth** accalcarsi intorno a qn/qc; **the blood ~d to her cheeks** il sangue le affluì al viso.

sur·geon ['sɜːdʒən] *n* chirurgo.

sur·gery ['sɜːdʒərɪ] **1** *n* (*art*) chirurgia; (*operation*) intervento chirurgico; (*consulting room*) gabinetto medico, ambulatorio. **2** *cpd*: **~ hours** *npl* orario delle visite *or* di consultazione.

sur·gi·cal ['sɜːdʒɪkəl] *adj* chirurgico(a); **~ spirit** alcool *m* denaturato; **~ cotton** cotone *m* idrofilo.

sur·ly ['sɜːlɪ] *adj* (**-ier, -iest**) burbero(a).

sur·mise ['sɜːmaɪz] **1** *n* congettura. **2** [sɜː'maɪz] *vt* supporre, congetturare; **I ~d as much** me lo immaginavo.

sur·mount [sɜː'maʊnt] *vt* (*difficulty*) sormontare.

sur·mount·able [sɜː'maʊntəbl] *adj* sormontabile.

sur·name ['sɜːneɪm] *n* cognome *m*.

sur·pass [sɜː'pɑːs] *vt* (*expectations, person*) superare; **it ~ed all his hopes** è andata meglio di quanto lui stesso sperasse.

sur·plice ['sɜːpləs] *n* (Rel) cotta.

sur·plus ['sɜːpləs] **1** *n* (Fin, Comm) surplus *m inv*; **to have a ~ of sth** avere qc in eccedenza; **labour ~** eccedenza di manodopera. **2** *adj* che avanza; (Fin, Comm) di sovrappiù, in eccedenza; **~ stock** merce *f* in sovrappiù; **it is ~ to our requirements** eccede i nostri bisogni.

sur·prise [sə'praɪz] **1** *n* (*gen*) sorpresa; (*astonishment*) stupore *m*, sorpresa; **it came as quite a ~ to me** fu una grande sorpresa per me; **a look of ~** uno sguardo di sorpresa; **much to my ~, to my great ~** con mia grande sorpresa; **to take by ~** (*person*) cogliere di sorpresa; (Mil: *town, fort*) attaccare di sorpresa; **to give sb a ~** fare una sorpresa a qn.
2 *vt* (*astonish*) sorprendere, stupire; (*catch unawares*) sorprendere, cogliere di sorpresa; **he was ~d to learn that…** fu sorpreso di sapere che…; **I'm ~d at you!** mi meraviglio di te!; **he ~d me into accepting** ho accettato perché colto alla sprovvista; **I should not be ~d if he accepts** non mi sorprenderebbe se accettasse; **don't be ~d if he comes** non ti meravigliare se viene.
3 *cpd* (*present, visit*) inaspettato(a); (*attack*) di sorpresa.

sur·pris·ing [sə'praɪzɪŋ] *adj* sorprendente.

sur·pris·ing·ly [sə'praɪzɪŋlɪ] *adv* (*good, bad*) straordinariamente; (**somewhat**) **~**, **he agreed** cosa (alquanto) sorprendente, ha accettato; **not**

~ he refused come c'era da aspettarsi ha rifiutato.

sur·re·al·ism [sə'rɪəlɪzəm] *n* surrealismo.

sur·re·al·ist [sə'rɪəlɪst] *adj*, *n* surrealista (*m/f*).

sur·re·al·is·tic [sə,rɪə'lɪstɪk] *adj* surreale; (Art) surrealistico(a).

sur·ren·der [sə'rendəʳ] **1** *n* resa; **no ~!** non ci arrendiamo! **2** *vt* (*gen, Mil*): **to ~ (to)** consegnare (a); (*lease*) cedere; (*claim, right*) rinunciare a; (*hope*) abbandonare; (*insurance policy*) riscattare. **3** *vi*: **to ~ (to)** arrendersi (a).

sur·rep·ti·tious [,sʌrəp'tɪʃəs] *adj* furtivo(a).

sur·round [sə'raʊnd] **1** *vt* circondare; **a town ~ed by hills** una città circondata da colline. **2** *n* bordo.

sur·round·ing [sə'raʊndɪŋ] *adj* circostante; **the ~ hills** le colline circostanti.

sur·round·ings [sə'raʊndɪŋz] *npl* (*of place*) dintorni *mpl*; (*environment*) ambiente *m*; **in beautiful ~** (*house, hotel*) in una bella posizione.

sur·tax ['sɜːtæks] *n* soprattassa.

sur·veil·lance [sɜː'veɪləns] *n*: **under ~** sotto sorveglianza.

sur·vey ['sɜːveɪ] **1** *n* (*a*) (*comprehensive view: of situation, developments*) quadro generale. (**b**) (*inquiry, study*) indagine *f*, studio; **a ~ of public opinion** un sondaggio d'opinione; **to carry out a ~ of** fare un'indagine di. (**c**) (*Surveying: of building*) perizia; (*of land*) rilevamento; (*of country*) rilevamento topografico. **2** [sɜː'veɪ] *vt* (**a**) (*look at*) guardare; (*: prospects, trends*) passare in rassegna. (**b**) (*examine*) studiare, esaminare; **the book ~s events up to 1972** il libro esamina gli eventi fino al 1972. (**c**) (*Surveying: building*) fare una perizia di; (*: land*) fare il rilevamento di; (*: country*) fare il rilevamento topografico di.

sur·vey·ing [sə'veɪɪŋ] *n* (*of land*) agrimensura.

sur·vey·or [sə'veɪəʳ] *n* (*of building*) perito; (*of land*) agrimensore *m*.

sur·viv·al [sə'vaɪvəl] **1** *n* (*act*) sopravvivenza; (*relic*) retaggio. **2** *cpd*: **~ course** *n* corso di sopravvivenza; **~ kit** *n* equipaggiamento di prima necessità.

sur·vive [sə'vaɪv] **1** *vi* (*gen*) sopravvivere; (*fig: in job etc*) durare. **2** *vt* sopravvivere a.

sur·vi·vor [sə'vaɪvəʳ] *n* superstite *m/f*, sopravvissuto/a.

sus·cep·ti·bil·ity [sə,septə'bɪlɪtɪ] *n* suscettibilità; (Med) predisposizione *f*.

sus·cep·ti·ble [sə'septəbl] *adj* (*to attack, illness etc*): **~ to** predisposto(a) a, soggetto(a) a; (*to persuasion, flattery etc*): **~ to** sensibile a; (*touchy*) permaloso(a); **~ of change** (*frm*) suscettibile di cambiamenti.

sus·pect ['sʌspekt] **1** *adj* sospetto(a). **2** *n* persona sospetta. **3** [sə'spekt] *vt* (*person*): **to ~ (of)** sospettare (di); (*think likely*): **to ~ that** avere il sospetto che + *sub*, supporre che + *sub*; (*doubt: motives*) dubitare di; **to ~ sb of a crime** sospettare qn di un delitto; **I ~ that he is the author** immagino che sia lui l'autore; **he ~s nothing** non sospetta niente.

sus·pend [sə'spend] *vt* (*gen*) sospendere; **a ~ed sentence** (Law) una condanna con la condizionale; **it was ~ed from the ceiling/between two posts** era appeso al soffitto/sospeso tra due pali.

sus·pend·er [sə'spendəʳ] **1** *n* (*for stocking*) gancio (di reggicalze); **~s** (*Am: braces*) bretelle *fpl*. **2** *cpd*: **~ belt** *n* reggicalze *m inv*.

sus·pense [sə'spens] *n* incertezza, apprensione *f*; (*in film, book*) suspense *m*; **we waited in ~** attendevamo ansiosamente; **the ~ is killing me!**

muoio dalla curiosità!; **to keep sb in** ~ tenere qn in sospeso.

sus·pen·sion [sə'spenʃən] **1** *n (gen, Aut)* sospensione *f.* **2** *cpd:* ~ **bridge** *n* ponte *m* sospeso.

sus·pi·cion [sə'spɪʃən] *n* **(a)** *(suspicious belief)* sospetto; *(lack of trust)* diffidenza; **I had no** ~ **that...** non avevo il benché minimo sospetto che...; **my** ~ **is that...** ho il sospetto che... + *sub;* **arrested on** ~ **of murder** arrestato come presunto omicida; **to be under** ~ essere sospettato; **above** ~ al di sopra di ogni sospetto; **I had my** ~**s about him** non mi ha mai convinto troppo. **(b)** *(trace: of garlic etc)* traccia, punta.

sus·pi·cious [sə'spɪʃəs] *adj (feeling suspicion):* ~ **(of)** sospettoso(a); diffidente (di); *(causing suspicion)* sospetto(a); **to be** ~ **of** *or* **about sb/sth** nutrire sospetti nei riguardi di qn/qc; **that made him** ~ questo lo ha insospettito; **a** ~ **character** un tipo sospetto.

sus·pi·cious·ly [sə'spɪʃəslɪ] *adv (look etc)* con sospetto; *(behave etc)* in modo sospetto; **it looks** ~ **like measles** ha tutta l'aria di essere morbillo.

sus·tain [sə'steɪn] *vt* **(a)** *(weight)* sostenere, sopportare; *(body, life)* mantenere; *(Mus: note)* tenere; *(effort, role, pretence)* sostenere; **objection** ~**ed** *(Am Law)* obiezione accolta. **(b)** *(receive: damage, loss etc)* subire, soffrire.

sus·tained [sə'steɪnd] *adj (effort etc)* prolungato(a).

sus·te·nance ['sʌstɪnəns] *n (food)* nutrimento; *(livelihood)* mezzi *mpl* di sussistenza; **there's not much** ~ **in it** non è molto nutriente.

su·ture ['suːtʃəʳ] *n* sutura.

swab [swɒb] **1** *n (Med: for cleaning wound)* tampone *m; (: for specimen)* campione *m* (prelevato per esame). **2** *vt (Naut: also:* ~ **down)** radazzare.

swag [swæg] *n (fam)* malloppo.

swag·ger ['swægəʳ] **1** *n* andatura spavalda. **2** *vi* pavoneggiarsi; **to** ~ **in** entrare pavoneggiandosi.

swal·low[1] ['swɒləʊ] **1** *n (act)* deglutizione *f; (of food)* boccone *m; (of drink)* sorso. **2** *vt (food, drink)* inghiottire, mandar giù, ingoiare; *(fig: suppress: anger etc)* inghiottire; *(: believe: story etc)* bersi; **to** ~ **one's pride** mettere il proprio orgoglio sotto i piedi; **that's hard to** ~ è difficile da ingoiare; **they** ~**ed it whole!** *(story)* se la sono bevuta in pieno!; **to** ~ **the bait** *(fig)* abboccare all'amo. **3** *vi* inghiottire; *(fig):* **he** ~**ed hard and said...** con l'emozione che gli serrava la gola ha detto... .

♦ **swallow up** *vt + adv (fig)* inghiottire; **they were soon** ~**ed up in the darkness** furono presto inghiottiti dalle tenebre; **I wished the ground would open and** ~ **me up** avrei voluto sprofondare.

swal·low[2] ['swɒləʊ] *n (bird)* rondine *f.*

swam [swæm] *pt of* **swim**.

swamp [swɒmp] **1** *n* palude *f*, pantano. **2** *vt (flood)* inondare, allagare; *(: boat etc)* sommergere; *(fig):* **to** ~ **(with)** sommergere (di).

swampy ['swɒmpɪ] *adj* paludoso(a), pantanoso(a).

swan [swɒn] **1** *n* cigno. **2** *vi (fam):* **to** ~ **around** fare la bella vita; **he** ~**ned off to New York** se n'è andato bellamente a New York. **3** *cpd:* ~ **song** *n* canto del cigno.

swank [swæŋk] *(fam)* **1** *n* **(a)** *(vanity, boastfulness)* ostentazione *f;* **he does it for** ~ lo fa per mettersi in mostra. **(b)** *(person)* spaccone/a. **2** *vi* mettersi in mostra; **to** ~ **about sth** vantarsi di qc.

swanky ['swæŋkɪ] *adj* **(-ier, -iest)** *(fam: person)* pieno(a) di sé; *(: car etc)* vistoso(a).

swap [swɒp] **1** *n (exchange)* scambio. **2** *vt (cars, stamps etc)* scambiare; **to** ~ **sth for sth else** scambiare qc con qualcos'altro; **to** ~ **places with**

sb cambiare di posto con qn. **3** *vi* fare uno scambio.

swarm[1] [swɔːm] **1** *n (of bees, flying insects)* sciame *m; (of crawling insects)* brulichio; *(fig: of tourists etc)* sciame, frotta; ~ **of ants** formicaio; **in** ~**s** *(fig)* a frotte. **2** *vi (bees)* sciamare; **to** ~ **about** *(crawling insects, people)* brulicare; **to** ~ **in/out** *etc* entrare/uscire *etc* a frotte; **to** ~ **with** *(people, insects)* brulicare di.

swarm[2] [swɔːm] *vi:* **to** ~ **up a tree/rope** arrampicarsi su un albero/su per una corda.

swarthy ['swɔːðɪ] *adj* **(-ier, -iest)** di colorito scuro.

swash·buck·ling ['swɒʃˌbʌklɪŋ] *adj* spericolato(a).

swas·ti·ka ['swɒstɪkə] *n* svastica.

swat [swɒt] **1** *vt (fly)* schiacciare. **2** *n (also:* **fly** ~**)** ammazzamosche *m inv.*

swath [swɔːθ] *n, pl* **swaths** [swɔːðz] = **swathe**[1].

swathe[1] [sweɪð] *n (of grass etc)* falciata.

swathe[2] [sweɪð] *vt:* **to** ~ **in** *(bandages, blankets)* avvolgere in.

sway [sweɪ] **1** *n* **(a)** *(movement: gen)* ondeggiamento; *(of boat)* dondolio. **(b)** *(rule, power):* ~ **(over)** influenza (su); **to hold** ~ **over sb** dominare qn. **2** *vi (gen)* ondeggiare; *(bridge, train)* oscillare; *(person)* barcollare; **the train** ~**ed from side to side** il treno oscillava violentemente. **3** *vt* **(a)** *(move)* far oscillare; **to** ~ **one's hips** ancheggiare. **(b)** *(influence)* influenzare; **these factors finally** ~**ed me** questi fattori hanno finito per influenzarmi.

swear [swɛəʳ] *pt* **swore**, *pp* **sworn 1** *vt (gen)* giurare; **to** ~ **a oath** prestare giuramento; **I** ~ **it!** lo giuro!; **I** ~ **(that) I did not steal it** giuro che non l'ho rubato, giuro di non averlo rubato; **to** ~ **to do sth** giurare di fare qc; **I could have sworn that was Louise** avrei giurato che era *or* che fosse Louise; **to** ~ **sb to secrecy** far giurare a qn di mantenere il segreto. **2** *vi* **(a)** *(solemnly)* giurare; **to** ~ **on the Bible** giurare sulla Bibbia; **to** ~ **to the truth of sth** giurare che qc è vero; **I can't** ~ **to it** non posso giurarlo. **(b)** *(use swearwords):* **to** ~ **(at sb)** bestemmiare *or* imprecare (contro qn); **to** ~ **like a trooper** bestemmiare come uno scaricatore di porto.

♦ **swear by** *vi + prep (fam):* **my mother** ~**s by hot baths for backache** mia madre giurerebbe che un bagno caldo è il rimedio migliore contro il mal di schiena.

♦ **swear in** *vt + adv* far prestare giuramento a.

swear·word ['swɛəˌwɜːd] *n* parolaccia; *(curse)* bestemmia.

sweat [swɛt] **1** *n* sudore *m*; **by the** ~ **of one's brow** con il sudore della fronte; **to get in** *or* **into a** ~ **about sth** *(fam)* farsi prendere dal panico per qc; **to be in a cold** ~ *(also fig)* avere i sudori freddi; **it was a real** ~**!** è stata una faticaccia!; **no** ~**!** *(fam)* non ci sono problemi! **2** *vi (person)* sudare; *(walls)* trasudare; *(fam: hard work):* **to** ~ **(over sth)** sudare (su qc); **to** ~ **like a pig** essere in un bagno di sudore. **3** *vt:* **to** ~ **blood** *(fig: work hard)* sudare sangue, sudare sette camicie; *(: be anxious)* sudare freddo; **to** ~ **it out** *(fig fam)* armarsi di pazienza.

sweat·band ['swɛt'bænd] *n (Sport)* fascia elastica *(per assorbire il sudore).*

sweat·er ['swɛtəʳ] *n* maglione *m.*

sweat·shirt ['swɛtʃɜːt] *n* maglione *m* in cotone felpato.

sweat·shop ['swɛtʃɒp] *n* azienda o fabbrica dove i dipendenti sono sfruttati.

sweaty ['swɛtɪ] *adj* **(-ier, -iest)** *(gen)* sudaticcio(a); *(smell)* di sudore.

Swede [swiːd] n svedese m/f.
swede [swiːd] n (vegetable) rapa svedese.
Swe·den ['swiːdn] n Svezia.
Swe·dish ['swiːdɪʃ] **1** adj svedese. **2** n (language) svedese m.

sweep [swiːp] **1** n (**a**) (of room) scopata; (of chimney) pulita. (**b**) (chimney ~) spazzacamino. (**c**) (movement: of arm) ampio gesto; (: of scythe, sword) colpo; (: of beam, searchlight) fascio luminoso; (curve: of road, hills etc) curva; (expanse: of countryside) distesa; **a wide ~ of country** una vasta distesa di campi.

2 vt (**a**) (stairs, floor) scopare, spazzare; (chimney) pulire; (dust, snow) spazzare; **to ~ (out) a room** scopare una stanza; **to ~ a problem under the carpet** (fig) accantonare un problema. (**b**) (move over: subj: searchlight, waves, wind) spazzare; (: disease) propagarsi in; (: fashion, craze) invadere; **the sea for mines** dragare il mare; **to ~ the horizon** (with eyes, binoculars) percorrere l'orizzonte; **to ~ the board** (fig) stravincere. (**c**) (remove with ~ing movement) spazzar via; **to be swept overboard** essere spazzato fuori bordo; **the crowd swept him along** fu trascinato dalla folla; **he swept her off her feet** (fig) l'ha conquistata.

3 vi (**a**) (with broom) scopare, spazzare. (**b**) (move): **to ~ in/out/along** entrare/uscire/procedere maestosamente; **the hurricane swept through the city** l'uragano infuriava su tutta la città; **panic swept through the crowd** il panico ha assalito la folla; **he swept past in a sports car** è passato sfrecciando alla guida di un'auto sportiva; **the mountains ~ down to the coast** le montagne digradano maestose fino al mare.

♦ **sweep aside** vt + adv spingere di lato; (fig: objections) scartare.
♦ **sweep away** vt + adv (dust, rubbish) spazzar via; (subj: crowd, current) trascinare via.
♦ **sweep up 1** vi + adv pulire con la scopa. **2** vt + adv (leaves, rubbish) raccogliere; (pick up: books etc) acchiappare.

sweep·er ['swiːpə'] n (cleaner) spazzino; (machine) scopatappeti m inv; (Ftbl) libero.
sweep·ing ['swiːpɪŋ] adj (gesture) ampio(a); (statement etc) generico(a); (changes) radicale.
sweep·stake ['swiːpsteɪk] n lotteria (spesso abbinata alle corse dei cavalli).

sweet [swiːt] **1** adj (-er, -est) (**a**) (taste) dolce; **this coffee is too ~** questo caffè è troppo dolce; **to have a ~ tooth** essere ghiotto di dolci; **I'm very fond of ~ things** mi piacciono molto i dolci. (**b**) (fresh, pleasant: smell, perfume, sound) dolce; (: breath) fresco(a); (fig: revenge, success) allettante; **the ~ smell of success** la gioia del successo; **it was ~ to his ear** era musica per le sue orecchie. (**c**) (charming: person) carino(a), dolce; (: smile, character) dolce; (: appearance, village, kitten) grazioso(a), carino(a); **that's very ~ of you** è molto gentile da parte tua; **what a ~ little dress!** che vestitino grazioso!; **he carried on in his own ~ way** (iro) ha continuato (a fare) come gli pareva.

2 adv: **to smell/taste ~** avere un odore/sapore dolce.

3 n (Brit: toffee etc) caramella; (: dessert) dolce m.

4 cpd: **~ and sour** adj agrodolce; **~ chestnut** n (Bot) castagno; **~ corn** n granturco dolce; **~ pea** n (Bot) pisello odoroso; **~ potato** n patata americana, patata dolce.

sweet·breads ['swiːtbredz] npl animelle fpl.
sweet·en ['swiːtn] vt (tea etc) zuccherare; (air)

profumare; (fig: temper) addolcire; (: task) rendere più piacevole; (also: ~ **up**: person) ingraziarsi; (: child) tenere buono(a).
sweet·en·er ['swiːtnə'] n (Culin) dolcificante m; (fam: bribe) contentino.
sweet·heart ['swiːthɑːt] n innamorato/a; **yes, ~** sì, tesoro.
sweet·ness ['swiːtnɪs] n (gen) dolcezza; (of taste) sapore m dolce; (of breath) freschezza; **now all is ~ and light** adesso tutti sono felici e contenti.
sweet·shop ['swiːtʃɒp] n (Brit) ≃ pasticceria.
sweet·smelling ['swiːt,smelɪŋ] adj profumato(a).
swell [swel] (vb: pt **swelled**, pp **swollen**) **1** n (of sea) mare m lungo, mare morto. **2** adj (Am: fine, good) eccezionale; **that's just ~** perfetto. **3** vi (ankle, eye etc: also: ~ **up**) gonfiarsi; (sails: also: ~ **out**) prendere il vento; (in size, number) aumentare; (sound, music) diventare più forte; (river etc) ingrossarsi; **to ~ with pride** gonfiarsi d'orgoglio; **the cheers ~ed to a roar** gli applausi si tramutarono in un boato. **4** vt (numbers, sales etc) far aumentare; (sails) gonfiare; (river) ingrossare.
swell-headed [,swel'hedɪd] adj (fam) borioso(a), pieno(a) di sé.
swell·ing ['swelɪŋ] n (Med) gonfiore m.
swel·ter·ing ['sweltərɪŋ] adj soffocante, afoso(a); **I'm ~** sto soffocando.
swept [swept] pt, pp of **sweep**.
swerve [swɜːv] **1** n deviazione f brusca; (in car) sterzata. **2** vi deviare bruscamente; (in car, ship) sterzare; **nothing will make him ~ from his aims** niente lo distoglierà dai suoi propositi.
swift [swɪft] **1** adj (-er, -est) (movement) rapido(a); (runner) veloce; (reply, reaction) pronto(a). **2** n (bird) rondone m.
swift·ly ['swɪftlɪ] adv (see adj) rapidamente; velocemente; prontamente.
swift·ness ['swɪftnɪs] n (see adj) rapidità; velocità; prontezza.
swig [swɪg] (fam) **1** n sorsata; **he took a ~ at his bottle** ha bevuto un lungo sorso dalla bottiglia. **2** vt tracannare.
swill [swɪl] **1** n (also pej) brodaglia. **2** vt (**a**) (clean: also: ~ **out**) risciacquare. (**b**) (fam: drink: beer etc) tracannare.
swim [swɪm] (vb: pt **swam**, pp **swum**) **1** n (**a**) nuotata; **it's a long ~ back to the shore** è una bella nuotata fino alla spiaggia; **to go for a ~** andare a fare una nuotata; **to have a ~** fare una nuotata. (**b**) (fam): **to be in the ~** essere al corrente. **2** vt (river etc) attraversare a nuoto; (distance) nuotare per; **to ~ the crawl** nuotare a crawl; **to ~ a length** fare una vasca (a nuoto); **she can't ~ a stroke** non sa nuotare. **3** vi (gen) nuotare; (as sport) fare del nuoto; **to go ~ming** andare a nuotare; **to ~ across a river** attraversare un fiume a nuoto; **my head is ~ming** (fig) mi gira la testa; **the meat was ~ming in gravy** la carne galleggiava nel sugo; **eyes ~ming with tears** occhi inondati di lacrime.
swim·mer ['swɪmə'] n nuotatore/trice.
swim·ming ['swɪmɪŋ] **1** n nuoto. **2** cpd (gear, trunks) da bagno; **~ baths** npl piscina pubblica; **~ costume** n costume m da bagno; **~ pool** n piscina; **~ trunks** npl costume m da bagno (per uomo).
swim·suit ['swɪmsuːt] n costume m da bagno.
swin·dle ['swɪndl] **1** n truffa. **2** vt imbrogliare, truffare; **to ~ sb out of sth** estorcere qc a qn con l'inganno.
swin·dler ['swɪndlə'] n imbroglione/a.
swine [swaɪn] n (**a**) pl (pigs) suini mpl. (**b**) (fig fam: person) porco; **you ~!** brutto porco!

swing [swɪŋ] (*vb: pt, pp* **swung**) **1** *n* **(a)** *(of pendulum, needle)* oscillazione *f; (distance)* arco; **to take a ~ at sb** mollare un pugno a qn. **(b)** *(Pol: in votes etc)*: **there has been a ~ towards/away from Labour** c'è stato un aumento/una diminuzione di voti per i Laburisti; **a sudden ~ in public opinion** un improvviso cambiamento dell'opinione pubblica; **a ~ to the left** una svolta a sinistra. **(c)** *(seat for ~ing)* altalena; **to have a ~** andare sull'altalena; **it's ~s and roundabouts** *(fig)* a conti fatti il risultato non cambia. **(d)** *(Boxing, Golf)* swing *m inv.* **(e)** *(rhythm)* ritmo; **to get into the ~ of things** entrare nel pieno delle cose; **to be in full ~** essere in pieno corso; **the party went with a ~** la festa è stata una bomba. **(f)** *(also: ~* **music)** swing *m.*

2 *vt* **(a)** *(pendulum)* far oscillare; *(person on swing, in hammock)* far dondolare; *(arms, legs)* dondolare; **to ~ the door open** spalancare la porta. **(b)** *(wield: axe, sword)* brandire; **he swung the case up onto his shoulder** si è messo la valigia sulla spalla; **he swung himself over the wall** si è lanciato al di là del muro; **she swung the car round** girò di colpo la macchina. **(c)** *(influence: opinion, decision)* influenzare; **she managed to ~** it so that we could all go *(fam)* è riuscita a fare in modo che ci potessimo andare tutti; **what swung it for me was...** ciò che mi ha fatto decidere è stato.... .

3 *vi* dondolare; *(on swing, hammock)* dondolarsi; *(arms, legs)* penzolare; **to ~ to and fro** dondolare; **the door swung open** la porta si spalancò; **the door swung shut** la porta si chiuse sbattendo; **he'll ~ for it** *(fam)* lo impiccheranno; **the road ~s south** la strada prende la direzione sud; **he swung round** si girò bruscamente; **the car swung into the square** la macchina svoltò bruscamente nella piazza; **to ~ to the right** *(fig Pol)* prendere una svolta a destra; **to ~ into action** entrare in azione.

4 *cpd:* **~ bridge** *n* ponte *m* girevole; **~ door** *n* porta a vento.

swinge·ing ['swɪndʒɪŋ] *adj (cuts)* drastico(a); *(attack, blow)* violento(a); *(defeat, majority)* schiacciante; *(taxation)* forte.

swipe [swaɪp] **1** *n:* **to take a ~ at sb** dare una schiaffo a qn. **2** *vt* **(a)** *(hit: ball, person)* colpire. **(b)** *(fam: steal)* fregare, grattare. **3** *vi:* **to ~ at sb/sth** tentare di colpire qn/qc.

swirl [swɜːl] **1** *n (movement)* turbinio; *(of cream etc)* ricciolo. **2** *vi* turbinare.

swish [swɪʃ] **1** *n (sound: of whip)* sibilo; *(: of skirts, grass)* fruscio. **2** *adj (fam: smart)* all'ultimo grido. **3** *vt (whip)* far schioccare; *(skirt)* far frusciare; *(tail)* agitare. **4** *vi (whip)* schioccare, sibilare; *(skirts, grass)* frusciare.

Swiss [swɪs] **1** *adj* svizzero(a). **2** *n, pl inv* svizzero/a.

switch [swɪtʃ] **1** *n* **(a)** *(Elec etc)* interruttore *m.* **(b)** *(Rail: points)* scambio. **(c)** *(stick)* bacchetta; **riding ~** frustino. **(d)** *(change)* cambiamento, mutamento; *(exchange)* scambio; **a rapid ~ of plan** un improvviso cambiamento di programma.

2 *vt* **(a)** *(change: plans, jobs)* cambiare; *(: allegiance):* **to ~ (to)** spostare (a); *(: conversation):* **to ~ (to)** spostare (su). **(b)** *(exchange)* scambiarsi; *(transpose: also: ~* **round, ~ over)** scambiare; *(: 2 objects)* invertire; **I ~ed hats with him, we ~ed hats** ci siamo scambiati i cappelli. **(c)** *(TV, Radio: programme)* cambiare; **to ~ the TV/radio to another programme** cambiare programma *or* canale/programma *or* stazione; **to ~ the heater to high** regolare la stufa al massimo. **(d)** *(Rail)* deviare.

3 *vi (also: ~* over) passare; **he ~ed to another topic** è passato a un altro argomento; **he has ~ed (over) to Labour** è passato al partito laburista.

♦ **switch off 1** *vt + adv (Elec, TV etc)* spegnere; *(Aut: ignition)* staccare. **2** *vi + adv (Elec, TV)* spegnere; *(fig fam: not listen)* tapparsi le orecchie.

♦ **switch on 1** *vt + adv (Elec, TV etc)* accendere; *(water supply)* aprire; *(machine)* mettere in moto, avviare; *(Aut: ignition)* inserire. **2** *vi + adv* **(a)** *(heater, oven)* accendersi. **(b)** *(Radio/TV)* accendere la radio/televisione.

switch·back ['swɪtʃbæk] *n (roller coaster)* montagne *fpl* russe.

switch·board ['swɪtʃbɔːd] **1** *n* centralino. **2** *cpd:* **~ operator** *n* centralinista *m/f.*

Swit·zer·land ['swɪtsələnd] *n* Svizzera.

swiv·el ['swɪvl] **1** *n* perno. **2** *vi (also: ~* **round)** girarsi.

swol·len ['swəʊlən] **1** *pp of* swell. **2** *adj (ankle, finger, stomach)* gonfio(a); *(river)* in piena; **her eyes were ~ with tears** aveva gli occhi gonfi di pianto; **you'll give him a ~ head** *(fig)* si monterà la testa.

swoon [swuːn] *(old)* **1** *n* svenimento. **2** *vi* svenire; **to ~ over sb** *(fig)* morire dietro a qn.

swoop [swuːp] **1** *n (of bird etc)* picchiata; *(by police):* **~ (on)** incursione *f* (in). **2** *vi (bird: also: ~* **down)** scendere in picchiata; *(police):* **to ~ (on)** fare un'incursione (in); **the plane ~ed low over the village** l'aereo è sceso in picchiata sul villaggio.

swop [swɒp] = **swap.**

sword [sɔːd] *n* spada.

sword·fish ['sɔːdfɪʃ] *n* pesce *m* spada *inv.*

swords·man ['sɔːdzmən] *n* spadaccino.

swore [swɔːʳ] *pt of* swear.

sworn [swɔːn] **1** *pp of* swear. **2** *adj (enemy)* giurato(a); *(friend)* per la pelle; *(ally)* fedele; *(testimony)* giurato(a), dato(a) sotto giuramento.

swot [swɒt] *vt, vi (fam):* **to ~ up (on) one's maths** ripassare tutta la matematica; **to ~ for an exam** sgobbare per un esame.

swum [swʌm] *pp of* swim.

swung [swʌŋ] *pt, pp of* swing.

syca·more ['sɪkəmɔːʳ] *n* sicomoro.

syco·phant ['sɪkəfənt] *n* adulatore/trice, leccapiedi *m/f.*

syl·la·ble ['sɪləbl] *n* sillaba.

syl·la·bus ['sɪləbəs] *n (Scol, Univ)* programma *m;* **on the ~** in programma d'esame.

syl·lo·gism ['sɪlədʒɪzəm] *n* sillogismo.

sylph [sɪlf] *n* silfo.

sylph·like ['sɪlflaɪk] *adj (woman)* snella; *(figure)* da silfide.

sym·bol ['sɪmbəl] *n* simbolo.

sym·bol·ic [sɪm'bɒlɪk] *adj* simbolico(a); **to be ~ of sth** simboleggiare qc.

sym·bol·ism ['sɪmbəlɪzəm] *n* simbolismo.

sym·bol·ize ['sɪmbəlaɪz] *vt* simboleggiare.

sym·met·ri·cal [sɪ'mɛtrɪkəl] *adj* simmetrico(a).

sym·me·try ['sɪmɪtrɪ] *n* simmetria.

sym·pa·thet·ic [,sɪmpə'θɛtɪk] *adj (showing pity)* compassionevole; *(kind, understanding)* comprensivo(a); **they were ~ but could not help** sono stati molto comprensivi ma non hanno potuto aiutare; **to be ~ to a cause** *(well-disposed)* simpatizzare per una causa; **to be ~ towards** *(person)* essere comprensivo con *or* nei confronti di.

sym·pa·theti·cal·ly [,sɪmpə'θɛtɪkəlɪ] *adv (see adj)* in modo compassionevole; con comprensione.

sym·pa·thize ['sɪmpəθaɪz] *vi:* **to ~ (with sb)** *(feel pity)* compatire (qn); *(understand)* capire (qn); **I**

~ **with you in your grief** ti sono molto vicino nel dolore; **I** ~ **with what you say, but... capisco quello che vuoi dire, ma...** .

sym·pa·thiz·er ['sɪmpəθaɪzəʳ] *n (fig: esp Pol):* ~ **(with)** simpatizzante *m/f* (di).

sym·pa·thy ['sɪmpəθɪ] *n* **(a)** *(pity, compassion)* comprensione *f;* **you have my deepest** ~ *or* **sympathies** hai tutta la mia comprensione; **you won't get any** ~ **from me!** non venire a piangere da me!; **a letter of** ~ una lettera di cordoglio. **(b)** *(understanding)* comprensione *f; (fellow-feeling, agreement)* solidarietà; **I am in** ~ **with your suggestions** mi trovo d'accordo con i tuoi suggerimenti; **to strike in** ~ **with sb** fare uno sciopero di solidarietà con qn.

sym·phon·ic [sɪm'fɒnɪk] *adj* sinfonico(a).

sym·pho·ny ['sɪmfənɪ] *n* sinfonia.

sym·po·sium [sɪm'pəʊzɪəm] *n, pl* **symposia** simposio.

symp·tom ['sɪmptəm] *n* sintomo.

symp·to·mat·ic [ˌsɪmptə'mætɪk] *adj:* ~ **(of)** sintomatico(a) (di).

syna·gogue ['sɪnəgɒg] *n* sinagoga.

syn·chro·mesh [ˌsɪŋkrəʊ'mɛʃ] *n* cambio sincronizzato.

syn·chro·nize ['sɪŋkrənaɪz] *vt* sincronizzare.

syn·di·cate ['sɪndɪkɪt] **1** *n (Comm etc)* sindacato; *(Press)* agenzia di stampa. **2** ['sɪndɪkeɪt] *vt (Press)* vendere tramite un'agenzia di stampa.

syn·drome ['sɪndrəʊm] *n* sindrome *f.*

syn·od ['sɪnəd] *n* sinodo.

syno·nym ['sɪnənɪm] *n* sinonimo.

syn·ony·mous [sɪ'nɒnɪməs] *adj:* ~ **(with)** sinonimo(a) (di).

syn·op·sis [sɪ'nɒpsɪs] *n, pl* **synopses** [sɪ'nɒpsiːz] sinossi *f inv.*

syn·tax ['sɪntæks] *n* sintassi *f.*

syn·the·sis ['sɪnθəsɪs] *n, pl* **syntheses** ['sɪnθəsiːz] sintesi *f inv.*

syn·the·size ['sɪnθəsaɪz] *vt* sintetizzare.

syn·the·siz·er ['sɪnθəˌsaɪzəʳ] *n (Mus)* sintetizzatore *m.*

syn·thet·ic [sɪn'θetɪk] **1** *adj (fabric etc)* sintetico(a). **2** *n* prodotto sintetico; *(Textiles)* fibra sintetica.

syphi·lis ['sɪfɪlɪs] *n* sifilide *f.*

sy·phon ['saɪfən] = **siphon.**

Syria ['sɪrɪə] *n* Siria.

Syr·ian ['sɪrɪən] *adj, n* siriano(a).

sy·ringe [sɪ'rɪndʒ] **1** *n* siringa. **2** *vt (Med)* siringare.

syr·up ['sɪrəp] *n* sciroppo; **golden** ~ *(Brit)* melassa raffinata.

sys·tem ['sɪstəm] *n (method)* sistema *m; (network)* rete *f; (digestive* ~, *respiratory* ~ *etc)* apparato; **it was quite a shock to his** ~ è stato uno shock per il suo organismo; **to get sth out of one's** ~ *(fig)* riuscire a liberarsi di qc; ~**s analyst** *(Computers)* analista *m* sistemi *inv.*

sys·tem·at·ic [ˌsɪstə'mætɪk] *adj* sistematico(a).

sys·tem·ati·cal·ly [ˌsɪstə'mætɪkəlɪ] *adv* sistematicamente.

T

T, t [tiː] *n (letter)* T, t *f* or *m inv*; **it fits you to a T** ti sta a pennello; **that's him to a T** è proprio lui.

ta [tɑː] *excl (fam)* grazie!

tab [tæb] **1** *n abbr of* **tabulator**. **2** *n (label)* etichetta; *(loop on garment)* appendino; *(Am fam: café check)* conto; **to keep ~s on sb/sth** *(fam)* tenere d'occhio qn/qc; **to pick up the ~** *(Am fam)* pagare il conto.

tab·by [tæbɪ] *n (also:* ~ **cat)** soriano/a; *(female cat)* gatta.

tab·er·nac·le [ˈtæbənækl] *n* tabernacolo.

ta·ble [ˈteɪbl] **1** *n* **(a)** tavolo; *(coffee ~ etc)* tavolino; *(for meals)* tavola; **card ~** tavolino da gioco; **to lay** *or* **set the ~** apparecchiare la tavola; **to clear the ~** sparecchiare; **at ~** a tavola; **the entire ~ was in fits of laughter** l'intera tavolata moriva dalle risate; **to drink sb under the ~** battere qn nel bere; **to turn the ~s on sb** *(fig)* rovesciare la situazione a danno di qn. **(b)** *(Math, Chem, illustration)* tavola; *(chart)* tabella; **multiplication ~s** tabelline *fpl*; **league ~** *(Ftbl, Rugby)* classifica. **2** *vt (bill, motion: Brit: propose)* presentare; *(: Am: postpone)* rinviare. **3** *cpd:* ~ **lamp** *n* lampada da tavolo; ~ **manners** *npl* maniere *fpl* a tavola; ~ **talk** *n* conversazione *f* a tavola; ~ **tennis** *n* ping-pong *m;* ~ **wine** *n* vino da tavola.

tab·leau [ˈtæbləʊ] *n, pl* ~**x** *(Theatre)* quadro vivente.

table·cloth [ˈteɪblklɒθ] *n* tovaglia.

table d'hôte [ˌtɑːblˈdəʊt] *n* pasto a prezzo fisso.

table·land [ˈteɪblænd] *n* tavolato, altopiano.

table·spoon [ˈteɪblspuːn] *n* cucchiaio da portata; *(also:* ~**ful)** cucchiaiata.

tab·let [ˈtæblɪt] *n (inscribed stone)* lapide *f; (Med)* compressa; *(: for sucking)* pastiglia; *(of chocolate)* tavoletta; ~ **of soap** saponetta.

tab·loid [ˈtæblɔɪd] *n (newspaper)* tabloid *m inv (giornale illustrato di formato ridotto).*

ta·boo [təˈbuː] *adj,* n tabù *(m) inv.*

tabu·late [ˈtæbjʊleɪt] *vt* mettere in colonna.

tabu·la·tor [ˈtæbjʊleɪtəʳ] *n* tabulatore *m.*

ta·chom·eter [tæˈkɒmɪtəʳ] *n* tachimetro.

tac·it [ˈtæsɪt] *adj* tacito(a).

taci·turn [ˈtæsɪtɜːn] *adj* taciturno(a).

tack [tæk] **1** *n* **(a)** *(nail)* chiodo corto; *(: for upholstery)* borchia; **to get down to brass ~s** venire al sodo. **(b)** *(Naut: course)* bordo; **to be on the port/ starboard ~** avere le mura a sinistra/dritta; **to change ~** *(fig)* cambiare linea di condotta; **to be on the right ~** *(fig)* essere sulla buona strada; **to try a different ~** *(fig)* prendere le cose per un altro verso. **(c)** *(Sewing)* punto d'imbastitura. **2** *vt* **(a)** *(nail)* fissare con chiodi. **(b)** *(Sewing)* imbastire; **to ~ sth on to (the end of) sth** *(of letter, book)* aggiungere qc alla fine di qc. **3** *vi (Naut)* virare di bordo in prua.

tack·le [ˈtækl] **1** *n* **(a)** *(lifting gear)* paranco. **(b)** *(equipment: esp for sport)* attrezzatura. **(c)** *(Ftbl)* contrasto; *(Rugby)* placcaggio. **2** *vt (Ftbl)* contrastare; *(Rugby)* placcare; *(thief, intruder)* agguantare; *(fig: person, problem, job)* affrontare;

I'll ~ him about it at once affronterò subito la cosa con lui.

tacky [ˈtækɪ] *adj* (**-ier, -iest**) *(sticky)* appiccicoso(a); *(Am: shabby)* scadente.

tact [tækt] *n* tatto.

tact·ful [ˈtæktfʊl] *adj (person)* pieno(a) di tatto; *(remark etc)* discreto(a); **to be ~** avere tatto.

tac·tic [ˈtæktɪk] *n* tattica; ~**s** la tattica; **strong-arm ~s** le maniere forti.

tac·ti·cal [ˈtæktɪkəl] *adj* tattico(a).

tac·tile [ˈtæktaɪl] *adj* tattile.

tact·less [ˈtæktlɪs] *adj (person)* privo(a) di tatto; *(remark)* indelicato(a).

tad·pole [ˈtædpəʊl] *n* girino.

taf·fe·ta [ˈtæfɪtə] *n* taffettà *m.*

taf·fy [ˈtæfɪ] *n (Am)* caramella *f* mou *inv.*

tag [tæg] **1** *n* **(a)** *(label)* etichetta; *(loop on garment)* appendino; **price/name ~** etichetta del prezzo/ con il nome. **(b)** *(game)* chiapparello. **2** *vi:* **to ~ along behind sb** stare sempre appresso a qn; **do you mind if I ~ along?** ti dispiace se vengo anch'io?

tail [teɪl] **1** *n (gen)* coda; *(of shirt)* estremità *f inv* inferiore; ~**s** *(Dress)* frac *m;* **heads or ~s** testa o croce; **to put a ~ on sb** *(fig fam)* far pedinare qn; **he was right on my ~** mi stava alle calcagna; **to turn ~** voltare la schiena; **he went off with his ~ between his legs** *(fig)* se ne è andato con la coda fra le gambe. **2** *vt (follow: suspect etc)* pedinare. **3** *cpd:* ~ **end** *n (of queue, party, storm etc)* fine *f; (of procession)* coda; **to be at the ~ end of the queue/ procession** essere in fondo alla coda/in coda alla processione; ~ **light** *n (Aut)* fanalino di coda; *(Rail)* luce *f* di coda.

♦ **tail away, tail off** *vi + adv* diminuire d'intensità.

tail·back [ˈteɪlbæk] *n (Aut)* coda.

tail·gate [ˈteɪlgeɪt] *n (Aut)* portellone *m* posteriore.

tai·lor [ˈteɪləʳ] **1** *n* sarto; ~**'s dummy** manichino (da sarto); ~**'s (shop)** sartoria (da uomo). **2** *vt (suit)* confezionare; *(fig):* **to ~ sth (to)** adattare qc (alle esigenze di).

tailor-made [ˈteɪləˈmeɪd] *adj* **(a)** fatto(a) su misura, *di* sartoria. **(b)** *(fig):* **it's ~ for you** è fatto apposta per te.

tail·plane [ˈteɪlpleɪn] *n (Aer)* stabilizzatore *m.*

tail·spin [ˈteɪlspɪn] *n (Aer)* vite *f* di coda.

tail·wind [ˈteɪlwɪnd] *n* vento in coda.

taint [teɪnt] **1** *n (fig)* macchia; **the ~ of madness** il marchio della pazzia. **2** *vt (meat, food)* far avariare; *(fig: reputation)* infangare.

Tai·wan [ˌtaɪˈwɑːn] *n* Repubblica di Taiwan.

take [teɪk] *(vb: pt* **took**, *pp* **taken) 1** *vt* **(a)** *(gen)* prendere; *(remove, steal)* portar via; **let me ~ your coat** posso prenderti il cappotto?; **to ~ sb's hand** prendere qn per mano; **to ~ sb's arm** poggiarsi al braccio di qn; **to ~ sb by the throat** afferrare qn alla gola; **he must be ~n alive** deve essere preso vivo; **to ~ the train** prendere il treno; ~ **the first on the left** prendi la prima a sinistra; **he hasn't ~n any food for 4 days** non mangia nulla da 4 giorni; **how much alcohol has he ~n?** quanto ha bevuto?; **to ~ notes** prendere appunti; **~ 6 from 9** *(Math)* 9 meno 6; **he took £5 off the price** ha fatto uno sconto di 5 sterline; **to ~ a trick** *(Cards)* fare una presa; **'to be ~n 3 times a day'** *(Med)* 'da prendersi tre volte al dì'; **to ~ cold/fright** prendere freddo/paura; **to be ~n ill** avere un malore.

(b) *(carry, lead)* portare; **I took the children with me** ho portato i bambini con me.

(c) *(require)* volerci; *(Gram)* prendere; **it took me 2 hours to do it, I took 2 hours to do it** mi ci sono volute due ore per farlo; **it won't ~ long** non ci vorrà molto tempo; **she's got what it ~s to do the job** ha i requisiti necessari per quel lavoro; **it ~s a brave man to do that** ci vuole del coraggio per farlo; **that will ~ some explaining** ci toccherà dare delle spiegazioni; **it ~s some believing** bisogna mettercela tutta per crederci.

(d) *(accept, receive)* accettare; *(obtain, win: prize)* vincere; *(: 1st place)* conquistare; *(Comm: money)* incassare; **he didn't ~ my advice** non mi ha ascoltato; **how did he ~ the news?** come ha preso la notizia? **please ~ a seat** prego, si sieda; **is this seat ~n?** è occupato?; **it's worth taking a chance** vale la pena di correre il rischio; **it's £50, ~ it or leave it** sono 50 sterline, prendere o lasciare; **can you ~ it from here?** *(handing over task etc)* puoi prendere avanti tu?; **you must ~ us as you find us** devi prenderci per quel che siamo.

(e) *(have room or capacity for)* contenere; *(support: subj: bridge)* avere una portata di; *(: chair etc)* sopportare; **the hall will ~ 200 people** nel salone c'è posto per 200 persone; **the bus ~s 60 passengers** l'autobus porta 60 persone; **it will ~ at least 5 litres** contiene almeno 5 litri.

(f) *(conduct: meeting)* condurre; *(: church service)* officiare; *(teach, study: course, exam, test)* fare; **the professor is taking the French course himself** sarà il professore stesso a fare *or* tenere il corso di francese; **I only took Russian for one year** ho fatto russo solo per un anno; **I took the driving test** ho fatto l'esame di guida.

(g) *(understand, assume)* pensare; *(consider: case, example)* prendere; **how old do you ~ him to be?** quanti anni pensi che abbia?; **I took him for a doctor** l'ho preso per un dottore; **I took him to be foreign** l'ho preso per uno straniero; **may I ~ it that...?** allora posso star certo che...?; **~ it from me!** credimi!; **~ D.H. Lawrence, for example** prendete D.H. Lawrence, per esempio.

. **(h)** *(put up with, endure: climate, alcohol)* sopportare; **she can't ~ the heat** non sopporta il caldo; **I can't ~ any more!** non ce la faccio più!; **I won't ~ no for an answer** non accetterò una risposta negativa *or* un rifiuto.

(i) *(negotiate: bend)* prendere *(: fence)* saltare.

(j): to be ~n with sb/sth *(attracted)* essere tutto preso da qn/qc; **I'm quite ~n with the idea** l'idea non mi dispiace per niente.

(k) *(as function verb: see other element)*: **to ~ a photograph** fare una fotografia; **to ~ a bath/ shower** fare un bagno/una doccia; **~ your time!** calma!; **it took me by surprise** mi ha colto di sorpresa.

2 *vi (dye, fire etc)* prendere; *(injection)* fare effetto; *(plant)* attecchire.

3 *n (Cine)* ripresa.

♦ **take after** *vi + prep* assomigliare a.
♦ **take along** *vt + adv* portare.
♦ **take apart** *vt + adv (clock, machine etc)* smontare; *(fig fam: criticize)* demolire.
♦ **take aside** *vt + adv* prendere in disparte.

♦ **take away 1** *vi + adv*: **to ~ away from sth** danneggiare qc; **his bad temper took away from the pleasure of our party** ci ha un po' guastato la festa con il suo cattivo umore. **2** *vt + adv* **(a)** *(subtract)*: **to ~ away (from)** sottrarre (da). **(b)** *(remove: person, thing, privilege)* togliere; *(carry away, lead away)* portar via; **we took him away on holiday** l'abbiamo portato in vacanza; **pizzas to ~ away** pizze da portar via.

♦ **take back** *vt + adv* **(a)** *(get back, reclaim)* riprendere; *(retract: statement, promise)* ritirare. **(b)** *(return: book, goods, person)* riportare; **can you ~ him back home?** puoi riaccompagnarlo a casa?; **to ~ sb back to his childhood** *(fig)* riportare qn indietro alla propria infanzia.

♦ **take down** *vt + adv* **(a)** *(curtains, picture, vase from shelf)* tirare giù. **(b)** *(dismantle: scaffolding)* smontare; *(: building)* demolire. **(c)** *(write down: notes, address)* prendere; *(: letter)* scrivere.

♦ **take in** *vt + adv* **(a)** *(bring in: object, harvest)* portare dentro; *(: person)* far entrare; *(: lodgers)* prendere; *(: orphan)* accogliere; *(: stray dog)* raccogliere. **(b)** *(receive: money)* incassare; *(: laundry, sewing)* prendere a domicilio. **(c)** *(Sewing)* stringere. **(d)** *(include, cover)* coprire; *(prices)* includere; **we took in Florence on the way** abbiamo visitato anche Firenze durante il viaggio. **(e)** *(grasp, understand: meaning, complex subject)* capire; *(: situation)* rendersi conto di; *(: impressions, sights etc)* assorbire; *(: visually: surroundings, people, area)* prendere nota con uno sguardo; **he took the situation in at a glance** ha afferrato la situazione all'istante. **(f)** *(deceive, cheat)* abbindolare; **to be ~n in by appearances** farsi ingannare dalle apparenze.

♦ **take off 1** *vi + adv (plane, passengers)* decollare; *(high jumper)* spiccare il salto. **2** *vt + adv* **(a)** *(remove: clothes)* togliersi; *(: price tag, lid, item from menu)* togliere; *(: train)* sopprimere; *(: leg, limb)* amputare. **(b)** *(deduct: from bill, price)*: **she took 50p off** ha fatto 50 penny di sconto. **(c)** *(lead away etc: person, object)* portare; **she was ~n off to hospital** è stata portata all'ospedale; **to ~ o.s. off** andarsene. **(d)** *(imitate)* imitare. **3** *vt + prep* **(a)** *(remove: clothes, price tag, lid)* togliere da; *(: train, item from menu)* eliminare da; **to ~ sb off sth** *(remove from duty, job)* allontanare qn da qc; **they took him off the Financial Page** gli hanno tolto la pagina dell'economia. **(b)** *(deduct: from bill, price)*: **he took 5% off the price for me** mi ha fatto uno sconto del 5% sul prezzo.

♦ **take on 1** *vi + adv* **(a)** *(fam: become upset)* prendersela. **(b)** *(song, fashion etc)* fare presa. **2** *vt + adv* **(a)** *(work)* prendersi; *(responsibility)* addossarsi; *(bet, challenger)* sfidare. **(b)** *(worker, fig: qualities, form)* assumere; *(cargo, passengers)* caricare; **her face took on a wistful expression** sul suo volto si era dipinta un'espressione di malinconia.

♦ **take out** *vt + adv* **(a)** *(bring, carry out)* portare fuori; **he took the dog out for a walk** ha portato il cane a passeggio; **can I ~ you out to lunch?** posso invitarti a pranzo fuori? **(b)** *(pull out: from pocket, drawer etc)*: **to ~ sth out of sth** tirare fuori qc da qc; *(extract: appendix, tooth; remove: stain etc)* togliere. **(c)** *(insurance, patent, licence)* procurarsi. **(d)**: **to ~ sb out of himself** far distrarre qn; **redecorating a house ~s it out of you** è spossante ridipingere una casa; **don't ~ it out on me!** non prendertela con me!

♦ **take over 1** *vi + adv (dictator, political party)* prendere il potere; **to ~ over (from sb)** continuare il lavoro (di qn). **2** *vt + adv (debts, business)* rilevare; *(company)* assumere il controllo di; **to ~ over sb's job** subentrare a qn nel lavoro, prendere il lavoro di qn; **the tourists have ~n over Florence** *(fig)* i turisti hanno preso d'assalto Firenze.

♦ **take to** *vi + prep* **(a)** *(form liking for: person)* prendere in simpatia; *(: game, surroundings, action etc)* prendere gusto a; **I just can't ~ to my friend's husband** il marito della mia amica non riesce proprio a piacermi; **she didn't ~ kindly to the idea** l'idea non le è piaciuta per niente. **(b)** *(form habit of)*: **to ~ to sth** darsi a qc; **to ~ to doing sth** prendere *or* cominciare a fare qc. **(c)** *(escape to)* fuggire verso; **to ~ to one's bed** mettersi a letto.

♦ **take up 1** *vi + adv*: **to ~ up with sb** fare amicizia con qn; **she took up with bad company** si è messa a frequentare cattive compagnie.

  2 *vt + adv* **(a)** *(raise, lift)* raccogliere; *(: subj: bus)* prendere; *(: carpet, floorboards)* sollevare; *(: road)* spaccare; *(: dress, hem)* accorciare.

  (b) *(lead, carry upstairs etc)* portare su.

  (c) *(continue)* riprendere.

  (d) *(occupy: time, attention)* assorbire; *(: space)* occupare; **it will ~ up the whole of our Sunday** ci porterà via tutta la domenica; **he's very ~n up with his work** è molto preso dal suo lavoro; **he's very ~n up with her** non fa che pensare a lei.

  (e) *(absorb: liquids)* assorbire.

  (f) *(raise question of: matter, point)* affrontare.

  (g) *(start: hobby, sport)*: **to ~ up painting/golf/photography** cominciare a dipingere/giocare a golf/fare fotografie; *(: job, duties)* cominciare; **to ~ up a career as** intraprendere la carriera di.

  (h) *(accept: offer, challenge)* accettare; **I'll ~ you up on your offer** accetto la tua offerta.

  (i) *(adopt: cause, case, person)* appoggiare.

♦ **take upon** *vt + prep*: **to ~ sth upon o.s.** prendersi la responsabilità di qc; **to ~ it upon o.s. to do sth** prendersi la responsabilità di fare qc.

take-away ['teɪkəwəɪ] **1** *n* ≈ rosticceria. **2** *cpd* *(food)* da portar via.

take-home pay ['teɪkhəum,peɪ] *n* paga netta.

tak·en ['teɪkən] *pp* of **take**.

take-off ['teɪkɒf] *n* **(a)** *(Aer)* decollo. **(b)** *(imitation)* imitazione *f*.

take-over ['teɪk,əuvə⁽ʳ⁾] **1** *n* assorbimento. **2** *cpd*: **~ bid** *n* offerta di assorbimento.

tak·ing ['teɪkɪŋ] *adj (attractive)* accattivante.

tak·ings ['teɪkɪŋz] *npl (Fin)* introiti *mpl*, entrate *fpl*; *(at show etc)* incasso.

talc [tælk] *n*, **tal·cum** (**pow·der**) ['tælkəm(,paudə⁽ʳ⁾)] *n* talco.

tale [teɪl] *n (gen)* storia; *(story)* racconto; *(legend)* leggenda; **to tell ~s** fare la spia.

tal·ent ['tælənt] **1** *n (skill)* talento; **there isn't much musical ~ in this town** non ci sono molti grandi talenti musicali in questa città; **there's no ~ here tonight** *(fam: opposite sex)* non c'è niente di buono qui stasera. **2** *cpd*: **~ scout** *n* talent scout *m/f inv*.

tal·ent·ed ['tæləntɪd] *adj* di talento.

tal·is·man ['tælɪzmən] *n* talismano.

talk [tɔːk] **1** *n* **(a)** *(conversation)* conversazione *f*; *(chat)* chiacchierata; **~s** *(Pol etc)* colloqui *mpl*; **I must have a ~ with you** devo parlarti. **(b)** *(lecture)* conferenza; **to give a ~** tenere una conferenza; **he will give us a ~ on...** ci parlerà di...; **to give a ~ on the radio** parlare alla radio. **(c)** *(gossip)* dicerie *fpl*; **the ~ was all about the wedding** non si faceva che parlare del matrimonio; **there has been a lot of ~ about him** si è

molto parlato di lui; **she's the ~ of the town** è sulla bocca di tutti; **it's just ~** sono solo chiacchiere.

  2 *vi (gen)* parlare; *(discuss)* discutere; **to ~ to/with sb about** *or* **of sth** parlare a/con qn di qc; **to ~ to o.s** parlare da solo; **try to keep him ~ing** cerca di farlo parlare; **to get o.s. ~ed about** far parlare di sé; **it's all right for you to ~!** parli bene tu!; **look who's ~ing!** parli proprio tu!; **now you're ~ing!** questo sì che è parlare!; **he ~s too much** parla troppo; *(indiscreet)* non sa tenere la bocca chiusa; **they are ~ing of going to Sicily** pensano di andare in Sicilia; **who were you ~ing to?** con chi stavi parlando?; **he knows what he's ~ing about** lui sì che se ne intende; **~ing of films, have you seen...?** a proposito di film, hai visto...?

  3 *vt (a language, slang)* parlare; **they were ~ing Arabic** parlavano arabo; **to ~ business** parlare di affari; **to ~ nonsense** dire stupidaggini; **to ~ sb into doing sth** persuadere qn a fare qc; **to ~ sb out of doing sth** dissuadere qn dal fare qc.

♦ **talk down 1** *vi + adv*: **to ~ down to sb** parlare a qn con condiscendenza. **2** *vt + adv*: **to ~ a plane** *(or* **pilot) down** guidare l'atterraggio dalla torre di controllo.

♦ **talk over** *vt + adv* discutere.

talka·tive ['tɔːkətɪv] *adj* loquace.

talked-of ['tɔːktɒv] *adj*: **a much ~ event** un avvenimento di cui si parla molto.

talk·er ['tɔːkə⁽ʳ⁾] *n* parlatore/trice; *(pej)* chiacchierone/a.

talk·ing ['tɔːkɪŋ] **1** *adj (doll, bird)* parlante. **2** *n* parlare *m*; **I'll do the ~** parlo io; **she does all the ~** è lei che tiene in piedi la conversazione. **3** *cpd*: **~ point** *n* argomento di conversazione.

talking-to ['tɔːkɪŋ,tuː] *n*: **to give sb a good ~** fare una bella paternale a qn.

tall [tɔːl] *adj* (**-er, -est**) alto(a); **how ~ are you?** quanto sei alto?; **I'm 6 feet ~** sono alto 1 metro 80; **that's a ~ order!** è una bella pretesa!; **a ~ story** *(fig)* una storia incredibile.

tall·boy ['tɔːlbɔɪ] *n* cassettone *m*.

tal·low ['tæləu] *n* sego.

tal·ly ['tælɪ] **1** *n (running total)* totale *m*; *(score)* punteggio; **to keep a ~ of sth** tener il conto di qc. **2** *vi*: **to ~ (with)** corrispondere (a).

tal·on ['tælən] *n* artiglio.

tam·bou·rine [,tæmbə'riːn] *n* tamburino.

tame [teɪm] **1** *adj* (**-r, -st**) *(animal)* addomesticato(a); *(fig: person)* docile; *(: book, performance)* banale. **2** *vt (animal)* addomesticare; *(lion, tiger, passion etc)* domare.

tam·per ['tæmpə⁽ʳ⁾] *vi*: **to ~ with** manomettere; **don't ~ with that** non continuare a toccarlo.

tam·pon ['tæmpən] *n* tampone *m*.

tan [tæn] **1** *n (suntan)* abbronzatura; *(colour)* color *m* marrone chiaro; **to get a ~** abbronzarsi. **2** *adj* marrone chiaro *inv*. **3** *vi* abbronzarsi. **4** *vt (person, skin)* abbronzare; *(leather)* conciare; **to ~ sb's hide** *(fam)* darle a qn.

tan·dem ['tændəm] **1** *n (bicycle)* tandem *m inv*. **2**: **in ~** *adv* in tandem.

tang [tæŋ] *n (taste)* sapore *m* forte; *(smell)* odore *m* penetrante.

tan·gent ['tændʒənt] *n (Geom)* tangente *f*; **to go off at a ~** *(fig)* partire per la tangente.

tan·ge·rine [,tændʒə'riːn] *n* specie di mandarino.

tan·gible ['tændʒəbl] *adj (proof, results)* tangibile; *(difference)* sostanziale; **~ assets** patrimonio reale.

tan·gle ['tæŋgl] **1** *n (of wool etc)* groviglio; *(fig: mud-*

dle) confusione *f;* **to get into a ~** *(gen)* aggrovigliarsi; *(hair)* arruffarsi; *(person)* combinare un pasticcio. **2** *vt (also:* **~ up)** aggrovigliare; *(: hair)* arruffare. **3** *vi* aggrovigliarsi; *(hair)* ingarbugliarsi; **to ~ with sb** *(fig fam)* azzuffarsi con qn.

tan·go ['tæŋgəʊ] *n* tango.

tank [tæŋk] *n* **(a)** *(container: for gas, petrol etc)* serbatoio; *(: for rainwater)* cisterna; *(fish ~)* acquario. **(b)** *(Mil)* carro armato.

tank·ard ['tæŋkəd] *n* boccale *m* (con coperchio).

tanked-up [,tæŋkt'ʌp] *adj (fam):* **to be ~** essere pieno(a) (di vino *etc).*

tank·er ['tæŋkə'] *n (ship: for water etc)* nave *f* cisterna; *(: for oil)* petroliera; *(aircraft)* aereocisterna; *(lorry)* autocisterna.

tanned [tænd] *adj* abbronzato(a).

tan·nin ['tænɪn] *n* tannino.

tan·noy ['tænɔɪ] *n*®*:* **over the ~** per altoparlante.

tan·ta·lize ['tæntəlaɪz] *vt* tormentare.

tan·ta·liz·ing ['tæntəlaɪzɪŋ] *adj (food)* stuzzicante; *(idea, offer)* allettante.

tan·ta·mount ['tæntəmaʊnt] *adj:* **to be ~ to** equivalere a.

tan·trum ['tæntrəm] *n:* **to throw a ~** fare le bizze.

tap[1] [tæp] **1** *n (Brit)* rubinetto; **beer on ~** birra alla spina; **on ~** *(fig: resources)* a disposizione. **2** *vt (barrel)* spillare; *(telephone)* mettere sotto controllo; *(telephone conversation)* intercettare; *(resources)* sfruttare.

tap[2] [tæp] **1** *n* colpetto; **there was a ~ on the door** hanno bussato leggermente alla porta. **2** *vt (pat, knock)* picchiare leggermente su; **I ~ped him on the shoulder** gli ho dato un colpetto sulla spalla; **to ~ one's foot** *(impatiently)* battere il piede; *(in time to music)* segnare il tempo con il piede. **3** *vi (knock)* bussare; *(rain)* picchiettare. **4** *cpd:* **~ dancing** *n* tip tap *m.*

tape [teɪp] **1** *n (gen, Sport, for recording)* nastro; *(Sewing)* fettuccia; **on ~** *(song etc)* su nastro; **to break the ~** *(Sport)* tagliare la linea del traguardo. **2** *vt (record)* registrare; *(also:* **~ up)** legare con un nastro; **I've got him** *(or* it) **~d** *(fam)* adesso l'ho capito. **3** *cpd:* **~ deck** *n* piastra di registrazione; **~ measure** *n* metro a nastro; **~ recorder** *n* registratore *m;* **~ recording** *n* registrazione *f.*

ta·per ['teɪpə'] **1** *n* cerino. **2** *vi (also:* **~ off)** assottigliarsi; *(: trousers)* restringersi.

tape-record ['teɪprɪ,kɔːd] *vt* registrare (su nastro).

ta·per·ing ['teɪpərɪŋ] *adj* affusolato(a).

tap·es·try ['tæpɪstrɪ] *n (object)* arazzo; *(art)* mezzo punto.

tape·worm ['teɪpwɜːm] *n* tenia, verme *m* solitario.

tapio·ca [,tæpɪ'əʊkə] *n* tapioca.

tap·pet ['tæpɪt] *n* punteria.

tar [tɑː'] **1** *n* catrame *m; low-/middle-~* **cigarettes** sigarette a basso/medio contenuto di nicotina. **2** *vt (road etc)* incatramare; **he's ~red with the same brush** *(fig)* è della stessa razza.

ta·ran·tu·la [tə'ræntjʊlə] *n* tarantola.

tare [tɛə'] *n (Comm)* tara.

tar·get ['tɑːgɪt] *n (gen)* obiettivo; *(Mil, in archery, fig)* bersaglio; **she has been the ~ of criticism** è stata fatta oggetto *or* bersaglio di critiche; **the ~s for production in 1980** gli obiettivi della produzione per il 1980; **to be on ~** *(project)* essere nei tempi (di lavorazione).

tar·iff ['tærɪf] *n* tariffa.

tar·mac ['tɑːmæk] *n (substance)* macadam *m* al catrame; *(runway)* pista d'atterraggio.

tar·nish ['tɑːnɪʃ] **1** *vt* ossidare; *(fig)* infangare. **2** *vi* ossidarsi.

ta·rot ['tærəʊ] **1** *n* tarocco. **2** *cpd:* **~ cards** *npl* tarocchi *mpl.*

tar·pau·lin [tɑː'pɔːlɪn] *n* telone *m* incerato.

tar·ra·gon ['tærəgən] *n* dragoncello.

tart[1] [tɑːt] *adj (fruit, flavour)* aspro(a); *(fig: remark etc)* caustico(a).

tart[2] [tɑːt] *n* **(a)** *(Culin: large)* crostata; *(: individual)* crostatina. **(b)** *(pej: prostitute)* sgualdrina.

♦ **tart up** *vt + adv (fam)* agghindare; **to ~ o.s. up, get ~ed up** agghindarsi.

tar·tan ['tɑːtən] *n* tartan *m inv,* tessuto scozzese.

Tar·tar ['tɑːtə'] *n (fig)* despota *m.*

tar·tar ['tɑːtə'] **1** *n ~* (in *Chem etc)* tartaro. **2** *cpd:* **~ sauce** *n* salsa tartara.

task [tɑːsk] **1** *n* compito; **to take sb to ~ (for sth)** richiamare qn all'ordine (per qc). **2** *cpd:* **~ force** *n* reparto operativo.

task·master ['tɑːsk,mɑːstə'] *n:* **he's a hard ~** è un vero tiranno.

tas·sel ['tæsəl] *n* nappa.

taste [teɪst] **1** *n (gen)* gusto; *(flavour)* sapore *m;* **the soup had an odd ~** la minestra aveva un sapore un po' strano; **may I have a ~?** posso assaggiare?; **have a ~ of everything** assaggia un po' di tutto; **he acquired a ~ for sports cars** gli è preso il gusto delle macchine sportive; **it's not to my ~** non è di mio gusto; **to be in bad** *or* **poor ~** essere di cattivo gusto; **'sweeten to ~'** *(Culin)* 'zucchero a volontà'. **2** *vt* **(a)** *(sample)* assaggiare; **just ~ this** assaggiane un pochino. **(b)** *(notice flavour of)* sentire il sapore di. **(c)** *(fig: experience)* assaporare; **once he had ~d power** una volta assaporato il gusto del potere. **3** *vi:* **to ~ of sth** sapere di qc; **it ~s good/bad** ha un buon/cattivo sapore. **4** *cpd:* **~ bud** *n* papilla gustativa.

taste·ful ['teɪstful] *adj* di (buon) gusto.

taste·less ['teɪstlɪs] *adj (food)* insipido(a); *(decor, joke)* di cattivo gusto.

tasty ['teɪstɪ] *adj* **(-ier, -iest)** *(food)* saporito(a); *(dish, meal)* succulento(a).

tat·tered ['tætəd] *adj* sbrindellato(a).

tat·ters ['tætəz] *npl* stracci *mpl;* **to be in ~** essere sbrindellato.

tat·too[1] [tə'tuː] *n (Mil: signal)* ritirata; *(: show)* parata militare.

tat·too[2] [tə'tuː] **1** *n (on arm etc)* tatuaggio. **2** *vt* tatuare.

tat·ty ['tætɪ] *adj* **(-ier, -iest)** *(fam: shabby)* malridotto(a); *(: paint)* scrostato(a).

taught [tɔːt] *pt, pp* of **teach.**

taunt [tɔːnt] **1** *n* presa in giro. **2** *vt:* **to ~ sb (with)** prendere qn in giro (per).

Tau·rus ['tɔːrəs] *n (Astron, Astrology)* Toro; **to be ~** essere del Toro.

taut [tɔːt] *adj* **(-er, -est)** *(also fig)* teso(a).

tau·to·logi·cal [,tɔːtə'lɒdʒɪkəl] *adj* tautologico(a).

tau·tol·ogy [tɔː'tɒlədʒɪ] *n* tautologia.

tav·ern ['tævən] *n (old)* taverna.

taw·dry ['tɔːdrɪ] *adj* **(-ier, -iest)** pacchiano(a).

taw·ny ['tɔːnɪ] *adj* **(-ier, -iest)** fulvo(a).

tax [tæks] **1** *n* tassa, imposta; **before/after ~** al lordo/netto delle tasse; **a third of my wages goes in ~** un terzo del mio stipendio se ne va in tasse; **how much ~ do you pay?** quanto paghi di tasse?; **to put a ~ on sth** mettere una tassa su qc; **free of ~** esentasse, esente da imposte.

2 *vt* **(a)** *(Fin: people, salary, goods)* tassare; **tobacco and petrol are heavily ~ed** le tasse sul tabacco e sulla benzina sono altissime. **(b)** *(fig: resources etc)* gravare su; **to ~ sb's patience** mettere alla prova la pazienza di qn. **(c)** *(fig: accuse):* **to ~ sb with sth/with doing sth** accusare qn di qc/di aver fatto qc.

3 cpd: ~ **avoidance** n evitare legalmente il pagamento di imposte; ~ **collector** n esattore m delle imposte; ~ **evasion** n evasione f fiscale; ~ **haven** n paradiso fiscale; ~ **inspector** n ispettore m delle tasse; ~ **rebate** n rimborso (delle tasse); ~ **return** n dichiarazione f dei redditi; ~ **system** n sistema m fiscale.

tax·able ['tæksəbl] adj imponibile.

taxa·tion [tæk'seɪʃən] n (act) tassazione f; (taxes) tasse fpl, imposte fpl; **system of** ~ sistema m fiscale.

taxi ['tæksɪ] **1** n taxi m inv. **2** vi (Aer) rullare. **3** cpd: ~ **driver** n tassista m/f; ~ **rank** n posteggio di taxi.

taxi·der·mist ['tæksɪdɜ:mɪst] n tassidermista m/f.

taxi·meter ['tæksɪ,miːtər] n tassametro.

tax·payer ['tæks,peɪər] n contribuente m/f.

TB n (abbr of **tuberculosis**) TBC f.

T-bone (steak) ['ti:bəʊn('steɪk)] n bistecca alla fiorentina.

tea [ti:] **1** n (a) (beverage) tè m inv; **I made a pot of** ~ ho fatto un po' di tè; ~ **with lemon** tè al limone; **it's just my cup of** ~! (fig) è proprio quello che fa per me! (b) (meal) tè m inv; (for children) ≃ merenda; **we're invited to** ~ **at the Browns'** siamo stati invitati per il tè dai Brown. **2** cpd: ~ **bag** n bustina di tè; ~ **break** n intervallo per il tè; ~ **caddy** n barattolo per il tè; ~ **cart** n (Am) = ~ **trolley**; ~ **chest** n cassa per il tè; ~ **cloth** n (for dishes) strofinaccio; (for trolley, tray) tovaglietta da tè; ~ **cosy** n copriteiera; ~ **leaf** n foglia di tè; ~ **party** n tè m inv (ricevimento); ~ **pot** n teiera; ~ **service** n, ~ **set** n servizio da tè; ~ **strainer** n colino per il tè; ~ **towel** n strofinaccio; ~ **tray** n vassoio da tè; ~ **trolley** n carrello da tè.

tea·cake ['ti:keɪk] n panino dolce all'uva.

teach [ti:tʃ] pt, pp **taught 1** vt insegnare; **I** ~ **English** insegno inglese; **to** ~ **sb** insegnare qc a qn; **to** ~ **sb (how) to do sth** insegnare a qn come si fa qc; **I taught him (how) to write** gli ho insegnato a scrivere; **it taught him a lesson** (fig) gli è servito da lezione; **I'll** ~ **you to leave the gas on!** ti faccio vedere io cosa ti succede quando lasci il gas aperto! **2** vi insegnare; **his wife** ~**es in our school** sua moglie insegna nella nostra scuola.

teach·er ['ti:tʃər] **1** n (gen) insegnante m/f; (in primary school) maestro/a; (in secondary school) professore/essa; **French** ~ insegnante di francese. **2** cpd: ~ **training college** n (for primary schools) ≃ istituto magistrale; (for secondary schools) scuola universitaria per l'abilitazione all'insegnamento nelle medie superiori.

teach·ing ['ti:tʃɪŋ] **1** n (gen) insegnamento; **she went into** ~ **10 years ago** ha incominciato a insegnare 10 anni fa. **2** cpd: ~ **aids** npl materiali mpl per l'insegnamento; ~ **hospital** n (Brit) clinica universitaria; ~ **staff** n corpo insegnante.

tea·cup ['ti:kʌp] n tazza da tè.

teak [ti:k] n tek m.

team [ti:m] **1** n (of people) équipe f inv; (: Sport) squadra; (of horses) tiro; **home** ~ squadra di casa. **2** vi: **to** ~ **up (with)** mettersi insieme (a). **3** cpd: ~ **game** n gioco a squadre; ~ **spirit** n spirito di squadra.

team·work ['ti:mwɜ:k] n lavoro d'équipe.

tear¹ [teər] (vb: pt **tore,** pp **torn**) **1** n (rip, hole) strappo; **your shirt has a** ~ **in it** hai uno strappo nella camicia, hai la camicia strappata. **2** vt (gen) strappare; **torn by remorse** tormentato dal rimorso; **torn by war** (fig) devastato dalla guerra; **torn by his emotions** combattuto; **he was torn between going and staying** era combattuto tra

andare e restare; **to** ~ **to pieces** or **to bits** or **to shreds** (also fig) fare a pezzi or a brandelli; **to** ~ **a muscle** strapparsi un muscolo; **to** ~ **a hole in** (shirt) fare un buco in; (argument) dimostrare che fa acqua; **to** ~ **a letter** or **an envelope open** aprire una busta strappandola; **that's torn it!** (fam) sono fregato! (or siamo fregati! etc). **3** vi (a) (be ripped) strapparsi; (subj: person, animal): **to** ~ **at sth** strappare qc. (b) (go quickly): **to** ~ **along/out** etc correre per/fuori etc.

♦ **tear apart** vt + adv (also fig) distruggere.

♦ **tear away** vt + adv strappar via; **to** ~ **o.s. away (from sth)** (fig) staccarsi (da qc).

♦ **tear down** vt + adv (flag, hangings etc) tirare giù; (building) demolire.

♦ **tear off 1** vt + adv (wrapping) strappare; (perforated section) staccare; (roof) portare via. **2** vt + prep (piece of material) strappare da.

♦ **tear out** vt + adv (sheet of paper, cheque) staccare; **to** ~ **one's hair out** strapparsi i capelli.

♦ **tear up** vt + adv (a) (also fig) strappare; (agreement) annullare. (b) (plant, stake) sradicare.

tear² [tɪər] **1** n lacrima; **to be close to** ~**s** stare per piangere; **to burst into** ~**s** scoppiare in lacrime; **to bring** ~**s to sb's eyes** far venire le lacrime agli occhi di qn. **2** cpd: ~ **gas** n gas m lacrimogeno.

tear·away ['teərəweɪ] n (fam) teppista m/f.

tear·drop ['tɪədrɒp] n lacrima.

tear·ful ['tɪəful] adj (face) coperto(a) di lacrime; (person) in lacrime; **she looked a bit** ~ sembrava che stesse per piangere.

tear-jerker ['tɪə,dʒɜ:kər] n (fam): **the film/story is a real** ~ è veramente un film/una storia strappalacrime.

tea·room ['ti:rum] n sala da tè.

tease [ti:z] **1** n (person) burlone/a. **2** vt (playfully) stuzzicare; (: make fun of) prendere in giro; (cruelly) tormentare.

♦ **tease out** vt + adv (tangles) sciogliere; (fig: information etc) carpire.

teas·er ['ti:zər] n (fam: problem) rompicapo.

tea·spoon ['ti:spu:n] n cucchiaino.

teat [ti:t] n (of bottle) tettarella; (of animal) capezzolo.

tea·time ['ti:taɪm] n ora del tè.

tech·ni·cal ['teknɪkəl] adj (process, word) tecnico(a); **this book is too** ~ **for me** questo libro è troppo tecnico or specifico per me; ~ **college** ≃ istituto tecnico; ~ **expert** tecnico specializzato; ~ **offence** (Law) infrazione f.

tech·ni·cal·ity [,teknɪ'kælɪtɪ] n tecnicità; (detail) dettaglio tecnico; **on a legal** ~ grazie a un cavillo legale; **I don't understand all the technicalities** non riesco a capire tutti i dettagli tecnici.

tech·ni·cal·ly ['teknɪkəlɪ] adv (from the point of view tecnico; (in theory) tecnicamente, in teoria.

tech·ni·cian [tek'nɪʃən] n tecnico/a.

tech·nique [tek'ni:k] n tecnica.

tech·no·logi·cal [,teknə'lɒdʒɪkəl] adj tecnologico(a).

tech·nol·ogy [tek'nɒlədʒɪ] n tecnologia.

ted·dy (bear) ['tedɪ(,beər)] n orsacchiotto.

te·di·ous ['ti:dɪəs] adj noioso(a).

te·di·ous·ness ['ti:dɪəsnɪs] n, **te·dium** ['ti:dɪəm] n tedio.

tee [ti:] n (Golf) tee m inv.

♦ **tee off** vi + adv (Golf) cominciare la partita.

teem [ti:m] vi (a): **to** ~ **(with)** (insects, fish) brulicare (di). (b): **it's** ~**ing (with rain)** piove a dirotto.

teen·age ['ti:neɪdʒ] adj (problems) da adolescente; (rebelliousness) adolescenziale; (fashion) da teenager; ~ **girl/boy** adolescente m/f.

teen·ager ['tiːn,eɪdʒəʳ] n adolescente m/f, teenager m/f inv.

teens [tiːnz] npl: **he is still in his ~** è ancora un adolescente.

tee-shirt ['tiːʃɜːt] n = T-shirt.

tee·ter ['tiːtəʳ] vi camminare barcollando; **to ~ on the edge** or **brink of** vacillare sull'orlo di.

teeth [tiːθ] npl of tooth.

teethe [tiːð] vi mettere i denti.

teeth·ing ['tiːðɪŋ] 1 n dentizione f. 2 cpd: **~ troubles** npl disturbi mpl della dentizione; (fig) difficoltà fpl iniziali.

tee·to·tal ['tiːˈtəʊtl] adj astemio(a).

tee·to·tal·ler, (Am) **tee·to·tal·er** ['tiːˈtəʊtləʳ] n (person) astemio/a.

Tef·lon ['teflɒn] n ℗ Teflon m ℗.

tele·com·mu·ni·ca·tions ['telɪkə,mjuːnɪˈkeɪʃnz] npl telecomunicazioni fpl.

tele·gram ['telɪɡræm] n telegramma m.

tele·graph ['telɪɡrɑːf] 1 n (apparatus) telegrafo; (message) telegramma m; **by ~** via telegrafo. 2 vt trasmettere per telegrafo. 3 cpd: **~ pole** n, **~ post** n palo del telegrafo; **~ wire** n filo del telegrafo.

tele·path·ic [,telɪˈpæθɪk] adj telepatico(a).

te·lepa·thy [tɪˈlepəθɪ] n telepatia.

tele·phone ['telɪfəʊn] 1 n telefono; **to be on the ~** (subscriber) avere il telefono; (be speaking) essere al telefono; **I've just been on the ~ to my mother** ho appena parlato al telefono con mia madre. 2 vi telefonare. 3 vt telefonare a. 4 cpd: **~ box** n, **~ booth** n cabina telefonica; **~ call** n telefonata; **~ directory** guida del telefono, elenco telefonico; **~ exchange** n centralino; **~ kiosk** n = **~ box**; **~ number** n numero di telefono.

te·lepho·nist [tɪˈlefənɪst] n telefonista m/f.

tele·photo ['telɪ,fəʊtəʊ] adj: **~ lens** teleobiettivo.

tele·print·er ['telɪ,prɪntəʳ] n telescrivente f.

tele·prompt·er ['telɪ,prɒmptəʳ] n ℗ gobbo.

tele·scope ['telɪskəʊp] 1 n telescopio. 2 vi chiudersi a telescopio; (fig: vehicles) accartocciarsi.

tele·scop·ic [,telɪsˈkɒpɪk] adj telescopico(a); (umbrella) pieghevole.

tele·vise ['telɪvaɪz] vt trasmettere per televisione.

tele·vi·sion ['telɪ,vɪʒən] 1 n (broadcasts, broadcasting industry) televisione f; (also: **~ set**) televisione, televisore m; **to watch ~** guardare la televisione; **on ~** alla televisione. 2 cpd televisivo(a); **~ licence** n abbonamento alla televisione.

tel·ex ['teleks] 1 n telex m inv. 2 vt, vi trasmettere per telex.

tell [tel] pt, pp told 1 vt (a) (gen) dire; (story, adventure) raccontare; (secret) svelare; **to ~ sb sth/sb to do sth** dire qc a qn/a qn di fare qc; **to ~ sb about sth** dire a qn di qc; raccontare qc a qn; **I have been told that...** mi è stato detto che...; **I am glad to ~ you that...** (frm) ho il piacere di comunicarle che...; **I cannot ~ you how pleased I am** non so come esprimere la mia felicità; **so much happened that I can't begin to ~ you** sono successe tante cose che non saprei da dove incominciare a raccontarti; **(I) ~ you what...** so io che cosa fare...; **I told you so!, didn't I ~ you so?** te l'avevo (pur) detto!; **I was furious, I can ~ you** ti dirò che ero furioso; **let me ~ you** credimi; **you're ~ing me!** (fam) a me lo dici!, lo vieni a dire a me!; **don't ~ me you can't do it!** non starmi a raccontare che non sei capace!; **~ me another!** (fam) raccontala giusta!; **to ~ the time** leggere l'ora; **can you ~ me the time?** puoi dirmi l'ora?; **to ~ the future/sb's fortune** predire il futuro/il futuro a qn; **do as you are told!** fai come ti si dice!; **he won't be told** non dà ascolto.

(b) (indicate: subj: sign, dial): **to ~ sb sth** indicare qc a qn; **there was a sign ~ing us which way to go** c'era un cartello che ci indicava la strada.

(c) (distinguish) distinguere; (know, be sure of) sapere; **to ~ right from wrong** distinguere il bene dal male; **I couldn't ~ them apart** non riuscivo a distinguerli; **how can you ~ what he'll do?** come fai a prevedere cosa farà?; **there's no ~ing what may happen** non si può prevedere cosa succederà; **you can ~ he's unhappy** si vede che è infelice.

(d): 400 all told 400 in tutto.

2 vi (a) (talk): **to ~ (of)** parlare (di); (fam: sneak, tell secrets) fare la spia; **more than words can ~** più di quanto non riescano ad esprimere le parole; **that would be ~ing!** non te lo dico!

(b) (know, be certain) sapere; **I can't ~** non saprei dire; **who can ~?** chi lo può dire?; **there is no ~ing** non si sa; **you never can ~** non si può mai dire.

(c) (have effect) farsi sentire; **to ~ against sb** ritorcersi contro qn; **the strain is beginning to ~** la fatica incomincia a farsi sentire; **their lack of fitness began to ~** incominciavano a risentire della mancanza di forma.

♦ **tell off** vt + adv: **to ~ sb off (for sth/for doing sth)** sgridare qn (per qc/per aver fatto qc).

tell·er ['teləʳ] n (a) (of story) narratore/trice. (b) (person: in bank) cassiere/a; (: at election) scrutatore/trice.

tell·ing ['telɪŋ] adj (effective: blow) efficace; (significant: figures, remark) rivelatore(trice).

telling-off ['telɪŋɒf] n (fam): **to give sb a ~** dare a qn una lavata di testa.

tell·tale ['telteɪl] 1 adj (sign) rivelatore(trice). 2 n (person) spione/a.

tel·ly ['telɪ] n (Brit fam) tele f inv.

te·mer·ity [tɪˈmerɪtɪ] n audacia.

temp [temp] 1 n (abbr of temporary) segretaria temporanea. 2 vi lavorare come segretaria temporanea.

tem·per ['tempəʳ] 1 n (nature) temperamento, indole f; (mood) umore m; **she has a sweet ~** è dolce per temperamento or di indole; **to be in a ~** essere in collera; **to be in a good/bad ~** essere di buon/cattivo umore; **to keep one's ~** restare calmo; **to lose one's ~** perdere le staffe; **in a fit of ~** in un accesso d'ira; **to fly into a ~** andare su tutte le furie; **mind your ~!, ~, ~!** cerca di controllarti!, calma, calma! 2 vt (moderate) moderare; (soften: metal) temprare.

tem·pera·ment ['tempərəmənt] n (nature) temperamento; (moodiness) umore m.

tem·pera·men·tal [,tempərəˈmentl] adj **(a)** (moody) capriccioso(a). **(b)** (caused by one's nature) innato(a).

tem·per·ance ['tempərəns] 1 n (teetotalism) astinenza dall'alcool. 2 cpd: **~ society** n lega antialcolica; **~ hotel** n albergo dove non si vendono alcolici.

tem·per·ate ['tempərɪt] adj (climate, zone) temperato(a).

tem·pera·ture ['temprɪtʃəʳ] n temperatura; **to have** or **run a ~** avere la febbre.

tem·pest ['tempɪst] n (poet) tempesta.

tem·pes·tu·ous [temˈpestjʊəs] adj (relationship, meeting) burrascoso(a).

tem·plate, (Am) **tem·plet** ['templɪt] n sagoma.

tem·ple ['templ] n **(a)** (Rel) tempio. **(b)** (Anat) tempia.

tem·po ['tempəʊ] n, pl tempi ['tempiː] (Mus) tempo; (fig): **the busy ~ of city life** il ritmo caotico della vita di città.

tem·po·ral ['tɛmpərəl] *adj* temporale.
tem·po·rari·ly ['tɛmpərərılı] *adv* temporaneamente.
tem·po·rary ['tɛmpərərı] *adj (gen)* provvisorio(a); *(powers, relief, improvement)* temporaneo(a); **a ~ teacher** un/una supplente; **a ~ illness** una malattia passeggera.
tempt [tɛmpt] *vt (person)* tentare; *(fig: fate, providence)* sfidare; **to be ~ed to do sth** essere tentato di fare qc; **can I ~ you with another cake?** posso tentarti con un altro dolce?
temp·ta·tion [tɛmp'teıʃən] *n* tentazione *f*; **there is always a ~ to...** si ha sempre la tentazione di...; **I couldn't resist the ~** non sono riuscito a resistere alla tentazione.
tempt·ing ['tɛmptıŋ] *adj (offer etc)* allettante; *(food)* appetitoso(a).
ten [tɛn] **1** *adj* dieci *inv*. **2** *n* dieci *m inv*; **~s of thousands** decine di migliaia; **~ to one he'll be late** *(fam)* dieci a uno che arriva tardi; **they're ~ a penny** *(fam)* ce ne sono a bizzeffe; *for usage see* **five**.
ten·able ['tɛnəbl] *adj* sostenibile.
te·na·cious [tı'neıʃəs] *adj* tenace.
te·nac·ity [tı'næsıtı] *n* tenacia.
ten·an·cy ['tɛnənsı] *n* contratto d'affitto; **during his ~** durante il periodo in cui abitava lì.
ten·ant ['tɛnənt] *n* inquilino/a.
tend[1] [tɛnd] *vi* tendere; **to ~ to do sth** tendere a fare qc; **that ~s to be the case with young people** questa è la tendenza tra i giovani; **to ~ towards sth** propendere per qc.
tend[2] [tɛnd] *vt (sick etc)* prendersi cura di; *(cattle, machine)* sorvegliare.
ten·den·cy ['tɛndənsı] *n* tendenza; **to have a ~ to do** avere la tendenza a fare.
ten·den·tious [tɛn'dɛnʃəs] *adj* tendenzioso(a).
ten·der[1] ['tɛndəʳ] *n (Rail, Naut)* tender *m inv*.
ten·der[2] ['tɛndəʳ] **1** *n* **(a)** *(Comm)* offerta; **to make a ~ (for)**, **put in a ~ (for)** fare un'offerta (per); **to put work out to ~** dare lavoro in appalto. **(b):** **to be legal ~** essere in corso legale. **2** *vt* presentare. **3** *vi (Comm):* **to ~ (for)** fare un'offerta (per), concorrere a un appalto (per).
ten·der[3] ['tɛndəʳ] *adj* **(a)** tenero(a); **to bid sb a ~ farewell** salutare qn con tenerezza. **(b)** *(sore: part of body)* sensibile; *(fig: subject)* delicato(a); **~ to the touch** sensibile al tatto.
tender-hearted [,tɛndə'hɑːtıd] *adj* dal cuore tenero, sensibile.
ten·der·ly ['tɛndəlı] *adv (affectionately)* teneramente.
ten·der·ness ['tɛndənıs] *n (see adj)* tenerezza; sensibilità.
ten·don ['tɛndən] *n* tendine *m*.
ten·dril ['tɛndrıl] *n* viticcio.
ten·ement ['tɛnımənt] **1** *n* casamento. **2** *cpd:* **~ block** *n* isolato.
ten·et ['tɛnət] *n* principio.
ten·ner ['tɛnəʳ] *n (banconota da)* dieci sterline *fpl*.
ten·nis ['tɛnıs] **1** *n* tennis *m*. **2** *cpd:* **~ ball** *n* palla da tennis; **~ club** *n* tennis club *m inv*; **~ court** *n* campo da tennis; **~ elbow** *n (Med)* gomito del tennista; **~ match** *n* partita di tennis; **~ player** *n* tennista *m/f*; **~ racket** *n* racchetta da tennis.
ten·or ['tɛnəʳ] **1** *adj (voice)* tenorile; *(part)* del tenore; *(instrument)* tenore *inv*. **2** *n* tenore *m*.
ten-pin bowl·ing [,tɛnpın'bəʊlıŋ] *n* bowling *m*.
tense[1] [tɛns] *n (Gram)* tempo.
tense[2] [tɛns] **1** *adj (-r, -st)* teso(a). **2** *vt (tighten: muscles)* tendere.
tense·ly ['tɛnslı] *adv* nervosamente.
ten·sion ['tɛnʃən] *n* tensione *f*.

tent [tɛnt] **1** *n* tenda. **2** *cpd:* **~ peg** *n* picchetto (da tenda).
ten·ta·cle ['tɛntəkl] *n* tentacolo.
ten·ta·tive ['tɛntətıv] *adj (hesitant: person)* esitante; *(provisional: arrangement)* provvisorio(a).
tenter·hooks ['tɛntəhʊks] *npl:* **to be on ~** essere sulle spine; **to keep sb on ~** tenere qn sulle spine.
tenth [tɛnθ] **1** *adj* decimo(a). **2** *n (in series)* decimo/a; *(fraction)* decimo *m; for usage see* **fifth**.
tenu·ous ['tɛnjʊəs] *adj (thread)* tenue; *(argument)* debole.
ten·ure ['tɛnjʊəʳ] *n (of land)* possesso; *(of office)* incarico; *(guaranteed employment):* **to have ~** essere di ruolo.
tep·id ['tɛpıd] *adj (also fig)* tiepido(a).
term [tɜːm] **1** *n* **(a)** *(limit)* termine *m*; *(period)* periodo; **in the short ~** a breve scadenza; **in the long ~** a lungo andare; **during his ~ of office** durante il suo incarico; **~ of imprisonment** periodo di detenzione; **to serve a 3-year ~ of imprisonment** scontare 3 anni di carcere.
(b). *(in school)* trimestre *m;* **the autumn/spring/summer ~** il primo/secondo/terzo trimestre.
(c). *(word, expression)* termine *m;* **to tell sb sth in no uncertain ~s** dire qc a qn molto chiaramente; **in ~s of...** in termini di... .
(d): **~s** *pl (conditions)* condizioni *fpl;* **~s of employment** condizioni di impiego; **~s of reference** termini *mpl* (stabiliti); **on one's own ~s** a modo proprio; **to come to ~s with** arrivare a un accordo con qn; **to come to ~s with a situation** accettare una situazione; **reduced ~s for pensioners** agevolazioni *fpl* per i pensionati; **not on any ~s** a nessuna condizione.
(e): **~s** *pl (relations):* **to be on good ~s with** avere buoni rapporti con; **not to be on speaking ~s with** non rivolgere la parola a.
2 *vt (name)* chiamare.
ter·mi·nal ['tɜːmınl] **1** *adj (patient)* incurabile; *(disease)* nello stadio finale; *(stages)* finale, conclusivo(a). **2** *n* **(a)** *(Elec, Computers)* terminale *m*. **(b)** *(of bus)* capolinea *m; (of train)* stazione *f* finale; *(building: also Aer)* terminal *m inv*.
ter·mi·nate ['tɜːmıneıt] **1** *vt* terminare; *(contract)* rescindere. **2** *vi (contract)* terminare, concludersi; *(train, bus)* finire.
ter·mi·na·tion [,tɜːmı'neıʃən] *n* fine *f; (of contract)* rescissione *f;* **~ of pregnancy** interruzione *f* della gravidanza.
ter·mi·nol·ogy [,tɜːmı'nɒlədʒı] *n* terminologia.
ter·mi·nus ['tɜːmınəs] *n, pl* **termini** ['tɜːmınaı] *(of bus)* capolinea *m; (of train)* ultima fermata; *(building: Rail)* stazione *f* di testa.
ter·mite ['tɜːmaıt] *n* termite *f*.
term-time ['tɜːmtaım] *n:* **in ~** durante il trimestre.
ter·race ['tɛrəs] *n* **(a)** *(patio, verandah)* terrazza, terrazzo. **(b)** *(of houses)* fila di case a schiera. **(c):** **the ~s** *(Sport)* la gradinata.
ter·raced ['tɛrıst] *adj (layered: hillside, garden)* terrazzato(a); *(in a row: house, cottage etc)* a schiera.
ter·ra·cot·ta [,tɛrə'kɒtə] *n* terracotta.
ter·rain [tɛ'reın] *n* terreno.
ter·res·trial [tı'rɛstrıəl] *adj* terrestre.
ter·ri·ble ['tɛrəbl] *adj (gen)* terribile, tremendo(a); *(play, film)* orrendo(a); *(performance, report)* pessimo(a); **to be ~ at sth** essere un disastro in qc.
ter·ri·bly ['tɛrəblı] *adv (very)* tremendamente, terribilmente; *(very badly: play, sing)* malissimo.
ter·ri·er ['tɛrıəʳ] *n* terrier *m inv*.
ter·rif·ic [tə'rıfık] *adj (very good: performance, book, news)* fantastico(a), stupendo(a); *(terrifying)* terrificante; *(extreme: heat, speed, noise,*

anxiety) spaventoso(a); (: *amount, scare*) enorme.
ter·ri·fy ['tɛrɪfaɪ] *vt* terrificare; **to be terrified** essere atterrito; **to be terrified of** avere il terrore folle di.
ter·ri·fy·ing ['tɛrɪfaɪɪŋ] *adj* terrificante.
ter·ri·to·rial [,tɛrɪ'tɔːrɪəl] *adj* territoriale; **T~ Army** Milizia Territoriale; **~ waters** acque *fpl* territoriali.
ter·ri·tory ['tɛrɪtərɪ] *n* territorio.
ter·ror ['tɛrəʳ] *n* terrore *m*; *(fam: child)* peste *f*; **to live in ~ of sth** vivere nel terrore di qc; **she's a ~ on the roads** al volante è un pericolo pubblico; **you little ~!** piccola peste!
ter·ror·ism ['tɛrərɪzəm] *n* terrorismo.
ter·ror·ist ['tɛrərɪst] *adj, n* terrorista *(m/f).*
ter·ror·ize ['tɛrəraɪz] *vt* terrorizzare.
terror-stricken ['tɛrə,strɪkən] *adj* terrorizzato(a), atterrito(a).
terse [tɜːs] *adj* **(-r, -st)** *(style)* conciso(a); *(reply)* laconico(a).
ter·tiary ['tɜːʃərɪ] *adj (gen)* terziario(a); **~ education** educazione *f* superiore post-scolastica.
Tery·lene ['tɛrəliːn] *n* Ⓡ terital *m* Ⓡ, terilene *m* Ⓡ.
test [tɛst] **1** *n (gen)* prova; *(of goods)* controllo; *(of machinery)* collaudo; *(Med, Chem)* analisi *f inv; (Psych)* test *m inv; (Scol: written)* ≃ compito in classe; *(: oral)* interrogazione *f; (driving ~)* esame *m* di guida; **a weekly Italian ~** un compito in classe di italiano alla settimana; **to do ~s on sth** fare delle prove su qc; **to put sth to the ~** mettere qc alla prova; **it has stood the ~ of time** ha resistito alla prova del tempo.
2 *vt (gen)* controllare; *(try, ascertain the worth of)* mettere alla prova; *(machine)* collaudare; *(Chem)* analizzare; *(blood, urine)* fare le analisi di; *(new drug)* sperimentare; *(Psych)* fare un test psicologico a; **to have one's eyes** *etc* **~ed** farsi controllare la vista *etc;* **to ~ sb's patience** mettere alla prova la pazienza di qn; **to ~ sb in mathematics** esaminare *or* interrogare qn in matematica; **to ~ sb for sth** fare delle analisi a qn per qc; **to ~ sth for sth** analizzare qc alla ricerca di qc.
3 *vi:* **to ~ (for)** fare ricerche (per trovare); **~ing, ~ing...** *(Telec etc)* prova, prova... .
4 *cpd:* **(nuclear) ~ ban** *n* divieto di sperimenti nucleari; **~ card** *n (TV)* monoscopio; **~ case** *n (Law)* causa che costituisce un precedente; **~ flight** *n (Aer)* volo di collaudo; **~ match** *n (Cricket)* ≃ partita internazionale; **~ paper** *n (Chem)* carta reattiva; **~ pilot** *n* pilota *m* collaudatore; **~ tube** *n (Chem)* provetta.
tes·ta·ment ['tɛstəmənt] *n* testamento; **the Old/New T~** *(Rel)* il Vecchio/Nuovo Testamento.
tes·ti·cle ['tɛstɪkl] *n* testicolo.
tes·ti·fy ['tɛstɪfaɪ] *vi (Law)* testimoniare; **to ~ in favour of/against sb** testimoniare a favore di/contro qn; **to ~ to sth** *(Law)* testimoniare qc; *(gen)* comprovare *or* dimostrare qc; *(: be sign of)* essere una prova di qc.
tes·ti·mo·nial [,tɛstɪ'məʊnɪəl] *n* **(a)** *(reference about person)* referenze *fpl.* **(b)** *(gift)* regalo di addio.
tes·ti·mo·ny ['tɛstɪmənɪ] *n* testimonianza.
test·ing ['tɛstɪŋ] *adj (difficult: time)* duro(a).
test·ing ground ['tɛstɪŋ,ɡraʊnd] *n* terreno di prova.
test-tube ['tɛst,tjuːb] *adj:* **~ baby** bambino(a) nato(a) in provetta.
tes·ty ['tɛstɪ] *adj* **(-ier, -iest)** *(impatient: person)* irritabile; *(: remark)* stizzoso(a).
teta·nus ['tɛtənəs] *n* tetano.
tetchy ['tɛtʃɪ] *adj* **(-ier, -iest)** irritabile.
tête-à-tête ['teɪtɑː'teɪt] *n* tête-à-tête *m inv.*
teth·er ['tɛðəʳ] **1** *n* laccio; **to be at the end of one's ~**

(fig) essere al limite (delle proprie forze). **2** *vt (animal)* legare.
text [tɛkst] *n* testo.
text·book ['tɛkstbʊk] *n* libro di testo.
tex·tile ['tɛkstaɪl] **1** *adj* tessile. **2: ~s** *npl* tessuti *mpl.*
tex·tu·al ['tɛkstjʊəl] *adj (error, differences)* di testo; *(criticism)* testuale, basato(a) sul testo.
tex·ture ['tɛkstʃəʳ] *n* consistenza; **the material has a rough ~** la stoffa è ruvida al tatto; **he admired the smooth ~ of her skin** ha ammirato la sua pelle liscia.
Thai [taɪ] *adj, n* tailandese *(m/f).*
Thai·land ['taɪlænd] *n* Tailandia.
tha·lido·mide [θə'lɪdəʊmaɪd] *n* Ⓡ talidomide *m* Ⓡ.
Thames [tɛmz] *n:* **the ~** il Tamigi.
than [ðæn, *weak form* ðən] *conj* che; *(with numerals, pronouns, proper names)* di; **you have more ~ me/Maria/ten** ne hai più di me/Maria/dieci; **more ~ ever** più che mai; **she is older ~ you think** è più vecchia di quanto tu (non) creda; **it was a better play ~ we expected** la commedia è stata migliore di quanto (non) pensassimo; **they have more money ~ we have** hanno più soldi di noi; **it is better to phone ~ to write** è meglio telefonare che scrivere; **more/less than 90** più/meno di 90; **more ~ once** più di una volta; **more often ~ not** il più delle volte; **I'd die rather ~ admit I'm wrong** piuttosto che ammettere di aver torto morirei; **no sooner did he leave ~ the phone rang** non appena uscì il telefono suonò.
thank [θæŋk] **1** *vt:* **to ~ sb (for sth/for doing sth)** ringraziare qn (per qc/per aver fatto qc); **~ you (very much)** grazie (mille); **no ~ you** no grazie; **to have only o.s. to ~ for sth** dovere ringraziare se stesso per qc; **I have John to ~ for getting me the job** devo ringraziare John per avermi trovato il lavoro; **I know who to ~!** *(iro)* so io chi devo ringraziare!; **~ heavens/God!** grazie al cielo/a Dio! **2: ~s** *npl* grazie *fpl;* **(very) many ~s** mille grazie; **that's all the ~s I get!** bel ringraziamento!; **~s to you...** *(also iro)* grazie a te...; **it's all ~s to** *(also iro)* è tutto merito di; **it's small** *or* **no ~s to you that...** non è di sicuro merito tuo se...; **~s be to God** rendiamo grazie a Dio.
thank·ful ['θæŋkfʊl] *adj:* **~ (to sb for sth)** grato(a) (a qn per qc), riconoscente (a qn per qc); **let us be ~ that it's over** ringraziamo il cielo che è tutto finito.
thank·ful·ly ['θæŋkfəlɪ] *adv (gratefully)* con riconoscenza; *(with relief)* con sollievo; **~ there were few victims** grazie al cielo ci sono state poche vittime.
thank·less ['θæŋklɪs] *adj (unrewarding: task)* ingrato(a).
thanks·giving ['θæŋks,ɡɪvɪŋ] **1** *n* ringraziamento. **2** *cpd:* **T~ Day** *n (Am)* giorno del ringraziamento.
that [ðæt, *weak form* ðət] **1** *dem adj (pl* those*)* quel (quell', quello) *m;* quella(quell') *f; (as opposed to* 'this'*)* quello(a) là; **~ man/woman/book** quell'uomo/quella donna/quel libro; **~ one over there** quello là; **it's not this picture but ~ one** I like non mi piace questo quadro ma quello là; **I only met her ~ once** l'ho incontrata solo quella volta; **what about ~ cheque?** e quel famoso assegno?; **~ wretched dog!** quel cagnaccio!; **~ crazy son of yours** quel pazzo di tuo figlio.
2 *dem pron (pl* those*)* ciò; *(as opposed to* 'this'*)* quello(a); **who/what is ~?** chi è/che cos'è quello? **~'s Joe** quello è Joe; **~'s my house** quella è la mia casa; **I prefer this to ~** preferisco questo a quello; **£5? — it must have cost more than ~ 5** sterline? — dev'essere costato di più; **~'s true** è proprio vero; **~ is (to say), ... cioè...; ~'s ~!**

punto e basta!; **you can't go and ~'s ~**! non puoi andare e basta!; **~'s odd!** che strano!; **after ~** dopo; **and after ~** he left dopodiché uscì; **at** or **with ~, she...** con ciò lei...; **and they were late at ~** e per di più erano in ritardo; **do it like ~** fallo così; **if it comes to ~** se è per quello; **how do you like ~?** *(iro)* niente male, ti pare?

3 *dem adv* così; **cheer up, it isn't ~ bad** coraggio, non va poi così male; **I didn't know he was ~ ill** non sapevo che fosse così malato; **~ much/ many** così tanto/tanti; **this one isn't ~ much more difficult** questo non è poi tanto più difficile; **he was ~ angry** *(fam)* tanto era arrabbiato.

4 *rel pron* **(a)** che; *(indirect)* cui; **the book (~) I read** il libro che ho letto; **the man (~) I saw** l'uomo che ho visto; **all (~) I have** tutto ciò che ho; **the box (~) I put it in** la scatola in cui l'ho messo; **the house (~) we're speaking of** la casa di cui stiamo parlando; **the people (~) I spoke to** le persone con cui or con le quali ho parlato; **the man (~) I gave it to** l'uomo (a) cui l'ho dato; **not ~ I know of** non che io sappia. **(b)** *(of time: when)* in cui; **the evening/winter ~** la sera/l'inverno in cui.

5 *conj* che; **he said ~...** disse che...; **I believe ~ he exists** credo che esista; **~ he should behave like this!** che si sia comportato così!; **~ he should behave like this is incredible** è incredibile che si sia comportato così; **oh ~ I could...** oh se potessi...; **not ~ I want to**, of course non che lo voglia, naturalmente; **so ~, in order ~** affinché + *sub*, perché + *sub*.

thatch [θætʃ] **1** *n* *(on roof)* copertura di paglia *(or* frasche *etc)*. **2** *vt* coprire con paglia *(or* frasche *etc)*.

thatched [θætʃt] *adj* *(roof)* di paglia *(or* frasche *etc)*; *(cottage)* con il tetto di paglia *(or* frasche *etc)*.

thaw [θɔː] **1** *n* disgelo; *(fig: easing up)* distensione *f.* **2** *vt* *(also:* **~ out**) *(fare)* scongelare. **3** *vi* *(Met)* sgelare; *(ice)* sciogliersi; *(also:* **~ out**: *frozen food, cold toes)* scongelarsi; *(fig: person)* aprirsi; *(: relations)* distendersi; **it is ~ing** sta sgelando.

the [ðiː, *weak form* ðə] **1** *def art* **(a)** il(lo, l') *m*; la(l') *f*; i(gli) *mpl*; le *fpl*; **I haven't ~ time/money** non ho il tempo/i soldi; **do you know ~ Smiths?** conosci gli Smith?; **to play ~ piano/~ violin** suonare il piano/il violino; **it was ~ year of the student riots** quello era l'anno delle manifestazioni studentesche.

(b): **~ rich and ~ poor** i ricchi e i poveri; **she was ~ elder** era la maggiore delle due; **if it is within the realms of ~ possible** se è umanamente possibile; **in this age of ~ computer...** in quest'era di computer... .

(c) *(distributive)*: **this car does 30 miles to ~ gallon** ≃ questa macchina fa 11 chilometri con un litro; **700 lire to ~ dollar** 700 lire per un dollaro; **eggs are usually sold by ~ dozen** di solito le uova si vendono alla dozzina; **paid by ~ hour** pagato a ore.

(d) *(emphatic)*: **he's THE man for the job** è proprio l'uomo adatto al lavoro.

(e) *(in titles)*: **Richard ~ Second** Riccardo secondo; **Ivan ~ Terrible** Ivan il terribile.

2 *adv*: **~ more he works ~ more he earns** più lavora più guadagna; **she looks all ~ better for it** adesso ha un aspetto molto più sano; **(all) ~ more so because...** soprattutto perché...; **~ sooner ~ better** prima è, meglio è.

thea·tre, *(Am)* **thea·ter** [ˈθɪətəʳ] *n* teatro.

theatre·goer, *(Am)* **theater·goer** [ˈθɪətə,gəʊəʳ] *n* habitué *m/f inv* del teatro.

the·at·ri·cal [θɪˈætrɪkəl] *adj* *(also fig)* teatrale.

thee [ðiː] *pron* *(old, poet)* ti.

theft [θeft] *n* furto.

their [ðɛəʳ] *poss adj* il(la) loro, *pl* i(le) loro.

theirs [ðɛəz] *poss pron* il(la) loro, *pl* i(le) loro; **a friend of ~** un loro amico; **this car is ~** questa macchina è loro.

them [ðɛm, *weak form* ðəm] *pers pron pl* **(a)** *(direct: unstressed)* li(le); *(: stressed: people)* loro; *(: things)* essi(e); **I watched ~** li(or le) ho guardati(e); **he knows THEM** conosce LORO; **if I were ~** se io fossi in loro; **it's ~!** eccoli! **(b)** *(indirect: people)* loro, gli *(fam)*; *(: things)* essi(e); **she gave ~ the money** ha dato loro i soldi, gli ha dato i soldi *(fam)*. **(c)** *(after prep: people)* loro; *(: things)* essi(e); **I'm thinking of ~** penso a loro; **as for ~** quanto a loro *(or* a questi)*; **both of ~** tutt'e due; **several of ~** molti (di loro or di essi); **give me a few of ~** dammene un po' or qualcuno; **I don't like either of ~** non mi piace nessuno dei due; **none of ~ would do it** nessuno (di loro) lo voleva fare; **that was very good of ~** è stato molto gentile da parte loro.

theme [θiːm] **1** *n* *(of speech, argument etc)* tema *m*, argomento; *(Mus)* tema. **2** *cpd:* **~ tune** *n* tema *m* musicale; **~ song** *n* motivo conduttore.

them·selves [ðəmˈselvz] *pers pron pl* *(reflexive)* si; *(after prep)* se stessi(e); *(emphatic)* loro stessi(e); **they did it (all) by ~** hanno fatto tutto da soli; *see also* **oneself**.

then [ðen] **1** *adv* **(a)** *(at that time)* allora; **it was ~ that...** fu allora che...; **before/since ~** prima di/da allora; **until ~** fino ad allora; **from ~ on** da allora in poi; **by ~** allora; **~ and there** all'istante. **(b)** *(afterwards, next)* poi; **what happened ~?** e poi cos'è successo?; **and ~ what?** e poi?, e allora? **(c)** *(in that case)* allora, dunque; **what do you want me to do ~?** allora cosa vuoi che faccia?; **well ~** dunque; **and** or **but ~ again** ma del resto; **I like it, but ~ I'm biased** mi piace, ma del resto non sono del tutto imparziale; **it would be awkward at work, and ~ there's the family** sarebbe difficile al lavoro, e poi c'è la famiglia. **2** *adj:* **the ~ king** l'allora re.

theo·lo·gian [θɪəˈləʊdʒɪən] *n* teologo/a.

theo·logi·cal [θɪəˈlɒdʒɪkəl] *adj* teologico(a).

the·ol·ogy [θɪˈɒlədʒɪ] *n* teologia.

theo·rem [ˈθɪərəm] *n* *(Math)* teorema *m*.

theo·ret·ic(al) [θɪəˈretɪk(əl)] *adj* *(Science etc)* teorico(a); *(possibility)* teorico(a).

theo·reti·cal·ly [θɪəˈretɪkəlɪ] *adv* in linea teorica; **~ possible** teoricamente possibile.

theo·rize [ˈθɪəraɪz] *vi*: **to ~ (about)** teorizzare (su).

theo·ry [ˈθɪərɪ] *n* *(statement, hypothesis)* teoria; **in ~** in teoria.

thera·peu·tic [ˌθerəˈpjuːtɪk] *adj* terapeutico(a).

thera·pist [ˈθerəpɪst] *n* terapista *m/f.*

thera·py [ˈθerəpɪ] *n* terapia.

there [ðɛəʳ] **1** *adv* **(a)** *(at that place)* là, lì; **put it ~** mettilo là or lì; **we left ~** siamo partiti di là; **we shall be ~ at 8** saremo lì alle 8; **we shall be ~ for sure** ci saremo di sicuro; **to go ~ and back** andarci e ritornare; **back ~** là dietro; **down ~** laggiù; **over ~** là; **in ~** là dentro; **through ~** di là; **he's not all ~** *(fam)* gli manca un venerdì. **(b)** *(for drawing attention to sb, sth)*: **mind out ~!** attenzione!; **that man ~** quell'uomo là; **you ~!** ehilà!; **~'s the bus** ecco l'autobus; **~ he is!** eccolo (là)!; **~ we differ** su questo non siamo d'accordo; **~ you are wrong** in questo hai torto; **~ you go again** eccoti di nuovo; **~ you are!** eccoti!; *(I told you so)* visto! **(c):** **~ is** c'è; **~ are** ci sono; **~ were 10 of them** erano in 10; **~ will be 8 people for dinner tonight**

ci saranno 8 persone a cena stasera; ~ **was laughter at this** al che ci fu uno scoppio di risa; ~ **is no wine left** non c'è più vino; ~ **might be time/room** *etc* forse c'è tempo/posto *etc*; ~ **has been**... c'è stato... .

2 *excl*: ~, ~, **don't cry** su, su, non piangere.

there·abouts ['ðeərə,baʊts] *adv (place)* nei pressi, nei dintorni, da quelle parti; *(amount)* giù di lì, all'incirca.

there·after [,ðeər'ɑːftəʳ] *adv (past)* da allora in poi; *(future)* in seguito.

there·by [,ðeə'baɪ] *adv* con ciò.

there·fore ['ðeəfɔːʳ] *adv* perciò, quindi; **it isn't ~ any better** per questo non è meglio.

there's [ðeəz] = **there is; there has.**

there·upon [,ðeərʌ'pɒn] *adv (at that point)* a quel punto; *(frm: on that subject)* in merito.

ther·mal ['θɜːməl] *adj (currents, spring)* termale; *(underwear)* termico(a).

ther·mo·dy·nam·ics [,θɜːməʊdaɪ'næmɪks] *nsg* termodinamica.

ther·mom·eter [θə'mɒmɪtəʳ] *n* termometro.

ther·mo·nu·clear [,θɜːməʊ'njuːklɪəʳ] *adj* termonucleare.

Ther·mos ['θɜːməs] *n* ® *(also: ~ flask or bottle)* thermos *m inv* ®.

ther·mo·stat ['θɜːməstæt] *n* termostato.

the·sau·rus [θɪ'sɔːrəs] *n* dizionario dei sinonimi.

these [ðiːz] *(pl of* **this)** **1** *dem adj* questi(e); *(as opposed to 'those')* questi(e) (qui); ~ **ones over here** questi qui; **how are you getting on ~ days?** come ti va di questi tempi? **2** *dem pron* questi(e).

the·sis ['θiːsɪs] *n, pl* **theses** ['θiːsiːz] tesi *f inv*.

they [ðeɪ] *pers pron pl* **(a)** *(gen)* essi(e); *(people only)* loro; ~ **have gone** sono partiti *(or* partite); **there ~ are** eccoli *(or* eccole) là; THEY **know nothing about it** LORO non ne sanno nulla. **(b)** *(people in general)* si; ~ **say that**... si dice che... .

they'd [ðeɪd] = **they would; they had.**

they'll [ðeɪl] = **they will, they shall.**

they're [ðeəʳ] = **they are.**

they've [ðeɪv] = **they have.**

thick [θɪk] **1** *adj* **(-er, -est)** **(a)** *(gen)* grosso(a); *(wall, layer, line etc)* spesso(a); *(hair)* folto(a); *(soup, paint, smoke etc)* denso(a); *(fog, vegetation etc)* fitto(a); *(strong: accent)* marcato(a); **a wall 2 metres ~** una parete di due metri di spessore; **the furniture was ~ with dust** sui mobili c'era la polvere di mesi; **the air was ~ with petrol fumes** l'aria era satura di gas di scarico; **the leaves were ~ on the ground** sul terreno c'era una spessa coltre di foglie; **they're ~ as thieves** *(fig)* sono amici per la pelle. **(b)** *(fam: stupid)* ottuso(a); **he's as ~ as two short planks** *(fam)* è proprio duro di comprendonio.

2 *adv*: **to spread sth ~** spalmare uno spesso strato di qc; **to cut sth ~** tagliare qc a fette grosse; ~ **and fast** senza tregua; **to lay it on (a bit) ~** *(fig)* spararla grossa.

3 *n*: **in the ~ of battle** nel folto della battaglia; **he likes to be in the ~ of things** gli piace stare in mezzo alla gente; **through ~ and thin** nella buona e nella cattiva sorte.

thick·en ['θɪkən] **1** *vt (gen)* ispessire. **2** *vi (gen)* ispessirsi; *(grow denser: wood, jungle)* infittirsi; **the plot ~s** *(fig)* il mistero s'infittisce.

thick·et ['θɪkɪt] *n* boscaglia.

thick·headed [,θɪk'hedɪd] *adj (fam)* ottuso(a), tonto(a).

thick·ly ['θɪklɪ] *adv (spread)* a strati spessi; *(cut)* a fette grosse; *(populated)* densamente; **the snow fell ~** la neve cadeva fitta fitta; **a ~-wooded slope** un pendio molto boscoso.

thick·ness ['θɪknɪs] *n (gen)* spessore *m; (of fog)* densità; *(of hair)* abbondanza.

thick·set [,θɪk'set] *adj (person)* tarchiato(a); *(features)* grossolano(a).

thick·skinned [,θɪk'skɪnd] *adj (fig: insensitive)* insensibile, coriaceo(a).

thief [θiːf] *n, pl* **thieves** [θiːvz] ladro/a.

thieve [θiːv] *vi* rubare.

thiev·ing ['θiːvɪŋ] **1** *adj* ladro(a); **you ~ scoundrel!** brutto ladruncolo! **2** *n* furti *mpl*.

thigh [θaɪ] *n* coscia.

thim·ble ['θɪmbl] *n* ditale *m*.

thin [θɪn] **1** *adj* **(-ner, -nest)** *(gen)* sottile; *(hair, paper, glass)* fine; *(blanket, parcel, coat)* leggero(a); *(soup, paint, honey etc)* poco denso(a); *(vegetation, beard, fur)* rado(a); *(crowd)* sparso(a); *(population)* scarso(a); *(person)* snello(a), esile, magro(a); *(crop, excuse, argument)* magro(a); **at 20,000 metres the air is ~** a 20.000 metri l'aria è molto rarefatta; **he's as ~ as a rake** è magro come un chiodo; **to vanish into ~ air** volatilizzarsi; **doctors are ~ on the ground at the moment** i dottori scarseggiano in questo periodo.

2 *adv*: **to spread sth ~** spalmare uno strato sottile di qc; **to cut sth ~** tagliare qc a fette sottili.

3 *vt (also: ~ down: paint, sauce)* diluire; *(also: ~ out: trees, plants)* sfoltire.

4 *vi (fog)* diradarsi; *(as: ~ out: crowd)* disperdersi; **his hair is ~ning** sta perdendo i capelli.

thine [ðaɪn] *poss pron (old, poet)* il tuo(la tua).

thing [θɪŋ] *n* **(a)** cosa; **a ~ of beauty** una bella cosa, un bell'oggetto; **~s of value** oggetti di valore; **what's that ~?** cos'è quell'affare?; **the main ~ is to**... la cosa più importante è di...; **the first/only ~ to do is**... la prima/l'unica cosa da fare è...; **for one ~** in primo luogo; **what with one ~ and another** tra una cosa e l'altra; **if it's not one ~ it's the other** se non è una è l'altra; **it's neither one ~ nor the other** non è né carne né pesce; **first ~ (in the morning)** come *or* per prima cosa (di mattina); **last ~ (at night)** come *or* per ultima cosa (di sera); **it's a good ~ that he left** è stato un bene che se ne sia andato; **it was a close ~,** it was a **near ~** ce l'ha fatto per un pelo; **it's the very ~,** it's just the **~** è proprio quello che ci vuole; **the ~ is**... il fatto è che...; **it's just one of those ~s** sono cose che capitano; **what a ~ to say!** cosa dici mai!; **how are ~s with you?** come ti va?; **~s are going badly** le cose vanno male; **~s aren't what they used to be** non è più come una volta; **not a ~ to say/to wear** niente da dire/da mettersi; **I haven't done a ~ about it yet** non ho ancora fatto niente; **he knows a ~ or two** la sa lunga; **to make a mess of ~s** farla grossa, combinare un casino *(fam)*; **you did the right ~** hai fatto la cosa migliore; **to make a (big) ~ out of sth** *(fam)* fare una tragedia di qc.

(b): **~s** *pl (belongings, clothes, equipment)* roba; **take your wet ~s off** togliti quella roba bagnata di dosso; **the tea ~s** la roba per il tè; **take your ~s and go!** prendi la tua roba e vattene!

(c): **to do one's own ~** *(fam)* fare quello che si vuole; **she's got a ~ about mice** è terrorizzata dai topi; **he's got a ~ about brunettes** ha un debole per le brune; **the latest ~ in hats** l'ultimo grido in fatto di cappelli.

(d) *(creature)*: **poor ~** poveretto/a; **what a sweet little ~!** che carino!

thingu·ma·bob ['θɪŋəmɪbɒb] *n (fam),* **thinga·ma·jig** ['θɪŋəmɪ,dʒɪg] *n (fam),* **thingum·my** ['θɪŋəmɪ] *n (fam)* coso, cosa.

think [θɪŋk] (vb: pt, pp thought) 1 vi (gen): to ~ of or about sth/doing sth pensare a qc/di fare qc; (more carefully): to ~ about or of sth riflettere su qc; to act without ~ing agire senza riflettere or pensare; ~ before you reply rifletti or pensa prima di rispondere; ~ carefully pensaci bene; ~ again! rifletti!, pensaci su!; just ~! ma pensa un po'!; let me ~ fammi pensare; let's ~ pensiamoci un attimo; to ~ twice before doing sth pensare due volte prima di fare qc; to ~ straight concentrarsi; to ~ aloud pensare ad alta voce; to ~ for o.s. pensare con la propria testa.

2 vt (a) (use one's brain, have ideas) pensare; (imagine) pensare, immaginare; I can't ~ what he can want non riesco ad immaginare che cosa possa volere; did you ~ to bring a corkscrew? hai pensato a portare un cavatappi?; I thought I might go swimming ho pensato che potrei andare a nuotare; ~ what you've done pensa a ciò che hai fatto; ~ what we could do pensa che cosa potremmo fare; to ~ evil thoughts avere cattivi pensieri.

(b) (believe, consider): to ~ (that) pensare (che), credere (che); we all thought him a fool pensavamo tutti che fosse un cretino; I don't ~ it likely penso che sia improbabile; who'd have thought it possible? chi l'avrebbe mai pensato?; I don't ~ it can be done non penso che si possa fare; I ~ (that) you're wrong penso che tu abbia torto; I thought as much lo sapevo io; I ~ so penso or credo di sì; I should ~ so too! lo credo bene!; what do you ~? che cosa ne pensi?; who do you ~ you are? ma chi credi di essere?; what do you ~ I should do? cosa pensi che dovrei fare?; what do you ~ you're doing? ma cosa stai facendo?; anyone would have thought she was dying sembrava che stesse per morire.

3 n: to have a ~ about sth riflettere su qc; I'd like to have a ~ about it vorrei pensarci su; you've got another ~ coming! (fam) ti sbagli!, hai capito male!

♦ **think about** vi + prep (remember) pensare a; (consider) pensare di; I'll ~ about it ci penserò; what are you ~ing about? a cosa stai pensando?; what were you ~ing about! che cosa ti è saltato in mente!

♦ **think of** vi + prep (a) (remember: names etc) ricordare; you can't ~ of everything non ci si può ricordare di tutto, non si può pensare a tutto; I'll be ~ing of you ti penserò.

(b) (consider, esteem) pensare di, pensare a; I thought of going to Spain pensavo di andare in Spagna; he never ~s of other people's feelings non si cura mai dei sentimenti degli altri; ~ of the expense pensa a quanto costa; to ~ highly of sb stimare qn; what do you ~ of him? che cosa pensi di lui?; what do you ~ of it? che cosa ne pensi?; I didn't ~ much of it non mi è piaciuto molto, non mi ha convinto; I told him what I thought of him gli ho detto ciò che pensavo di lui; I wouldn't ~ of such a thing! non mi sognerei mai di fare una cosa simile!

(c) (devise: plan) escogitare; (: solution) trovare; what will he ~ of next? una ne fa e cento ne pensa!

♦ **think out** vt + adv (plan) elaborare; (solution) trovare; this needs ~ing out bisogna pensarci su.

♦ **think over** vt + adv (offer, suggestion) riflettere su; I'd like to ~ things over vorrei pensarci su.

♦ **think through** vt + adv riflettere a fondo su.

♦ **think up** vt + adv (idea, solution) escogitare, ideare.

think·able ['θɪŋkəbl] adj: it isn't ~ that... è impensabile che... + sub.

think·er ['θɪŋkə'] n pensatore/trice.

think·ing ['θɪŋkɪŋ] 1 adj: to any ~ person a ogni persona ragionevole; to put on one's ~ cap chiudersi nel pensatoio. 2 n pensiero; to my (way of) ~ a mio parere; I've done some ~ about it ci ho pensato sopra un po'.

thin·ly ['θɪnlɪ] adv (spread) in uno strato sottile; (cut) a fette sottili; (scantily: dressed) scarsamente; (disguised) malamente.

thin-skinned ['θɪn'skɪnd] adj (fig: person) permaloso(a).

third [θɜːd] 1 adj terzo(a); ~ time lucky! questa è la volta buona! 2 n (in series) terzo/a; (fraction) terzo. 3 cpd: ~ party n (Law) terzo; ~-party insurance assicurazione f contro terzi; T~ World 1 n terzo mondo; 2: ~-world adj del terzo mondo; for usage see fifth.

third-class ['θɜːd'klɑːs] adj di terza classe.

third-degree ['θɜːddɪ'griː] adj (burns) di terzo grado.

third·ly ['θɜːdlɪ] adv in terzo luogo, terzo.

third-rate [,θɜːd'reɪt] adj scadente, di terz'ordine.

thirst [θɜːst] 1 n sete f; ~ for knowledge sete di conoscenza. 2 vi: to ~ for (fig) essere assetato(a) di.

thirsty ['θɜːstɪ] adj (-ier, -iest) assetato(a); (hum: work) che fa venire sete; to be ~ aver sete.

thir·teen [θɜː'tiːn] adj, n tredici (m) inv; for usage see five.

thir·teenth ['θɜːtiːnθ] 1 adj tredicesimo(a). 2 n (in series) tredicesimo/a; (fraction) tredicesimo; for usage see fifth.

thir·ti·eth ['θɜːtɪɪθ] 1 adj trentesimo(a). 2 n (in series) trentesimo/a; (fraction) trentesimo; for usage see fifth.

thir·ty ['θɜːtɪ] adj, n trenta (m) inv; for usage see fifty.

this [ðɪs] 1 dem adj (pl these) questo(a); (as opposed to 'that') questo(a) (qui); ~ man/woman/book quest'uomo/questa donna/questo libro; ~ one here questo qui; it's not that picture but ~ one I like non è quel quadro che mi piace ma questo qui; ~ time questa volta; ~ time next week a quest'ora la settimana prossima; ~ time last year l'anno scorso in questo periodo; ~ way da questa parte.

2 dem pron (pl these) questo(a); (as opposed to 'that') questo(a) (qui); who/what is ~? chi è/che cos'è questo?; ~ is Mr Brown (in introductions, in photo) questo è il signor Brown; (on telephone) sono il signor Brown; I prefer ~ to that preferisco questo a quello; ~ is April/Friday etc è aprile/venerdì etc; where did you find ~? dove l'hai trovato?; ~ is where I live io abito qui; do it like ~ fallo così; it was like ~ è successo or è andata così; what's all ~ I hear about you leaving? mi hanno detto che te ne vai, è vero?; and with ~ he left e con ciò se ne andò; what with ~ and that I was busy all week tra una cosa e l'altra non ho avuto un momento libero questa settimana; they were talking of ~ and that stavano parlando del più e del meno.

3 dem adv: ~ far fino qui; ~ high alto così.

this·tle ['θɪsl] n cardo.

thong [θɒŋ] n laccio di cuoio.

thor·ax ['θɔːræks] n torace m.

thorn [θɔːn] n spina; you're a ~ in my side or flesh (fig) sei la mia croce or spina.

thorny ['θɔːnɪ] adj (-ier, -iest) irto(a) di spine; (fig: tricky) spinoso(a), scabroso(a).

thor·ough ['θʌrə] adj (work, worker) preciso(a), accurato(a); (search) minuzioso(a); (examination) approfondito(a); *(complete: attr only: idiot, scoundrel)* vero(a); **he has a ~ knowledge of the subject** ha una profonda conoscenza in materia; **he's a ~ rascal** è un delinquente matricolato, è un vero delinquente.

thorough·bred [ˈθʌrəbred] **1** *adj (horse)* purosangue *inv*. **2** *n* purosangue *m/f inv*.

thorough·fare [ˈθʌrəfɛəʳ] *n* strada transitabile; **'no ~'** 'divieto di transito'.

thorough·going [ˈθʌrəˌgəʊɪŋ] *adj (examination, search)* accurato(a), minuzioso(a); **he's a ~ idiot** è un perfetto idiota.

thor·ough·ly [ˈθʌrəlɪ] *adv* **(a)** *(with vb: agree)* completamente; *(: understand)* perfettamente; *(: search, clean)* a fondo. **(b)** *(with adj: very)* assolutamente; **~ clean** completamente pulito; **a ~ unpleasant person** una persona assolutamente antipatica.

thor·ough·ness [ˈθʌrənɪs] *n* precisione *f*.

those [ðəʊz] *(pl of* **that**) **1** *dem adj* quei(quegli) *mpl*, quelle *fpl*; *(as opposed to 'these')* quelli(e) (là). **2** *dem pron* quelli(e); *(as opposed to 'these')* quelli(e) (là); **~ of you who were here yesterday** quelli di voi che erano qua ieri; **~ of us who fought in the war** noi che abbiamo combattuto la guerra.

thou [ðaʊ] *pron (old, poet)* tu.

though [ðəʊ] **1** *conj* benché + *sub*, sebbene + *sub*; **~ it was raining** benché piovesse; **even ~** anche se; **strange ~ it may appear** per quanto strano possa sembrare. **2** *adv* tuttavia, comunque; **it's not so easy, ~** tuttavia non è così facile.

thought [θɔːt] **1** *pt, pp of* **think**. **2** *n (reflection, mental activity)* pensiero; *(idea)* idea; **to be lost** *or* **deep in ~** essere assorto *or* perso nei propri pensieri; **after much ~** dopo molti ripensamenti; **I've just had a ~** mi è appena venuta un'idea; **that's a ~!** che bell'idea!; **I shudder at the very ~ of it** rabbrividisco solo al pensiero; **to collect one's ~s** raccogliere le proprie idee; **my ~s were elsewhere** avevo la testa altrove; **with no ~ for o.s.** senza pensare a se stesso; **to give sth some ~** prendere qc in considerazione, riflettere su qc; **it's the ~ that counts** è il pensiero che conta.

thought·ful [ˈθɔːtfʊl] *adj* **(a)** *(pensive)* pensieroso(a), pensoso(a); *(serious: book)* ragionato(a). **(b)** *(kind)* gentile; **how ~ of you!** che pensiero gentile!

thought·ful·ly [ˈθɔːtfəlɪ] *adv* **(a)** *(pensively)* con aria pensierosa; **he looked at me ~** mi ha guardato pensieroso. **(b)** *(considerately)* gentilmente.

thought·less [ˈθɔːtlɪs] *adj (person, remark, words)* sconsiderato(a); *(behaviour)* scortese; **~ of the consequences** senza pensare alle conseguenze.

thought·less·ly [ˈθɔːtlɪslɪ] *adv (see adj)* sconsideratamente; scortesemente.

thou·sand [ˈθaʊzənd] **1** *adj* mille. **2** *n* mille *m*; **one/two/five ~** mille/duemila/cinquemila; **a ~ and one/two** mille e uno/due; **about a ~** circa un migliaio; **in their ~s, by the ~** a migliaia; **~s of** migliaia di.

thou·sandth [ˈθaʊzəntθ] **1** *adj* millesimo(a). **2** *n (in classification)* millesimo/a; *(fraction)* millesimo.

thrash [θræʃ] **1** *vt (gen)* percuotere; *(with whip)* frustare; *(with stick)* bastonare; *(Sport fam: defeat)* dare una batosta a. **2** *vi (also:* **~ about, ~ around)** agitarsi.

♦ **thrash out** *vt + adv (problem, difficulty: discuss)* dibattere; *(: solve)* risolvere; *(plan)* mettere a punto con difficoltà.

thrash·ing [ˈθræʃɪŋ] *n*: **to give sb a ~** *(beat)* picchiare qn di santa ragione; *(Sport: defeat)* dare una batosta a qn.

thread [θred] **1** *n* **(a)** filo; **cotton/nylon ~** filo di

cotone/nailon; **to hang by a ~** *(fig)* essere appeso a un filo; **to lose the ~ (of what one is saying)** perdere il filo; **to pick up the ~ again** *(fig)* riprendere il filo. **(b)** *(of screw)* filettatura. **2** *vt (needle, beads etc)* infilare; **to ~ one's way through a crowd** infilarsi *or* farsi largo tra una folla.

thread·bare [ˈθredbɛəʳ] *adj (coat, blanket etc)* logoro(a), consumato(a); *(fig: argument)* trito(a).

threat [θret] *n* minaccia; **to be a ~ to sb/sth** costituire una minaccia per qn/qc; **to be under ~ of** *(closure, extinction)* rischiare di; *(exposure)* essere minacciato di.

threat·en [ˈθretn] *vt* minacciare; **to ~ sb with sth** minacciare qn di qc; **to ~ to do sth** minacciare di fare qc.

threat·en·ing [ˈθretnɪŋ] *adj* minaccioso(a).

three [θriː] **1** *adj* tre *inv*. **2** *n* tre *m inv*; **the best of ~** *(Sport)* partita, rivincita e bella; *for usage see* **five**.

three-D [ˌθriːˈdiː] *(also:* **3-D)** **1** *adj (also:* **three-dimensional)** tridimensionale. **2** *n*: **to be in ~** essere tridimensionale.

three-legged [ˌθriːˈlegɪd] *adj (table)* a tre gambe; **~ race** corsa a coppie *(con due gambe legate insieme).*

three-piece [ˈθriːpiːs] *adj*: **~ suite** salotto comprendente un divano e due poltrone; **a ~ suit** un tre pezzi.

three-ply [ˌθriːˈplaɪ] *adj (wood)* a tre strati; *(wool)* a tre capi.

three-point turn [ˌθriːpɔɪntˈtɜːn] *n (Aut)* inversione a U eseguita in tre manovre.

three-quarters [ˌθriːˈkwɔːtəz] *npl* tre quarti *mpl*; **~ full** pieno per tre quarti.

three·some [ˈθriːsəm] *n (people)* terzetto.

three-wheeler [ˌθriːˈwiːləʳ] *n (car)* veicolo a tre ruote; *(tricycle)* triciclo.

thresh [θreʃ] *vt (corn)* trebbiare.

thresh·ing ma·chine [ˈθreʃɪŋməˌʃiːn] *n* trebbiatrice *f*, trebbia.

thresh·old [ˈθreʃhəʊld] *n (also fig)* soglia; **to be on the ~ of** *(fig)* essere sulla soglia di.

threw [θruː] *pt of* **throw**.

thrift [θrɪft] *n*, **thrifti·ness** [ˈθrɪftɪnɪs] *n* parsimonia.

thrifty [ˈθrɪftɪ] *adj* parsimonioso(a).

thrill [θrɪl] **1** *n (of fear)* brivido; *(of pleasure, joy)* fremito; **it gave me a great ~** è stata un'esperienza emozionante. **2** *vt (with fear)* far rabbrividire; *(with pleasure)* entusiasmare; **I was ~ed to get your letter** la tua lettera mi ha fatto veramente piacere. **3** *vi*: **to ~ at** *or* **to sth** fremere (di gioia) a qc.

thrill·er [ˈθrɪləʳ] *n* thriller *m inv*.

thrill·ing [ˈθrɪlɪŋ] *adj (book, play etc)* pieno(a) di suspense; *(news, discovery)* entusiasmante.

thrive [θraɪv] *vi (be healthy: person, animal)* crescere robusto(a); *(: plant)* crescere rigoglioso(a); *(fig)* prosperare; **children ~ on milk** il latte è ottimo per i bambini; **she ~s on hard work** il lavoro le fa bene; **business is thriving** il commercio prospera.

thriv·ing [ˈθraɪvɪŋ] *adj (industry etc)* fiorente.

throat [θrəʊt] *n* gola; **to clear one's ~** schiarirsi la gola; **to have a sore ~** avere il mal di gola.

throaty [ˈθrəʊtɪ] *adj (-ier, -iest) (voice)* roco(a).

throb [θrɒb] **1** *n (of heart etc)* palpito, battito; *(of pain)* fitta; *(of music)* battito; *(of machine)* vibrazione *f*; *(of drum)* rullio. **2** *vi (heart)* palpitare, battere forte; *(wound)* pulsare; *(machine)* vibrare; **my head is ~bing** mi martellano le tempie; **~bing with life** *(fig: town etc)* pullulante di vita.

throes [θrəʊz] *npl*: **in the ~ of death** in agonia; **in the ~ of war** dilaniato dalla guerra; **to be in the ~ of doing sth** *(fig)* essere alle prese con qc.

throm·bo·sis [θrɒm'bəusɪs] n trombosi f; **coronary** ~ trombosi coronarica.

throne [θrəun] n trono; **to ascend to the** ~ salire al trono; **the heir to the** ~ l'erede al trono.

throng [θrɒŋ] **1** n moltitudine f. **2** vt affollare. **3** vi affollarsi.

throt·tle ['θrɒtl] **1** n (on motorboats etc) (leva del) gas; (motorcycle) (manopola del) gas; (valve) valvola a farfalla; **to give an engine full** ~ andare a tutto gas. **2** vt (strangle) strangolare, strozzare. **3** vi: **to** ~ **back** or **down** togliere il gas.

through [θruː] **1** prep **(a)** (place) attraverso; **to look** ~ **a telescope** guardare attraverso un telescopio; **to look** ~ **the window** (look out) guardare dalla finestra; (look in) guardare dentro; **to walk** ~ **the woods** camminare per or attraversare i boschi; **he shot her** ~ **the head** le ha sparato in testa; **to go** ~ (house, garden, wood) attraversare; **to go** ~ **one's pockets** frugarsi le tasche; **to go** ~ **sb's papers** scartabellare le carte di qn.
  (b) (time, process) per; **all** or **right** ~ **the night** per tutta la notte; **he won't live** ~ **the night** non supererà la notte; **(from)** Monday ~ Friday (Am) da lunedì a venerdì; **to go** ~ **a bad/good period** attraversare un brutto momento/periodo felice; **I am halfway** ~ **the book** sono a metà libro.
  (c) (by, because of) per; (thanks to) grazie a; ~ **lack of resources** per mancanza di mezzi; ~ **the post** per posta; **he got the job** ~ **them** ha avuto quel posto grazie a loro; **it was** ~ **you that we were late** è colpa tua se siamo arrivati tardi; **I heard it** ~ **my sister** l'ho saputo da mia sorella.
  2 adv **(a)** (place): **the soldiers didn't let us** ~ i soldati non ci hanno lasciato passare; **please go** ~ **into the dining room** prego, entrate in sala da pranzo; **does this train go** ~ **to London?** va direttamente a Londra questo treno?; **the nail went right** ~ il chiodo è passato da parte a parte; **I am wet** ~ sono bagnato fino al midollo; **my coat is wet** ~ ho il cappotto inzuppato; **he is** ~ **to the finals** ce l'ha fatta a entrare in finale; **the wood has rotted** ~ il legno è completamente marcio; **to put sb** ~ (Telec) passare la linea a qn; **you're** ~! (Telec) è in linea!
  (b) (time, process): **the party lasted right** ~ **until morning** la festa è andata avanti fino al mattino; **I read the book right** ~ ho letto il libro da cima a fondo.
  (c): ~ **and** ~ fino in fondo.
  3 adj **(a)** (attr: traffic) di passaggio; **'no** ~ **road'** (sign) 'strada senza uscita'.
  (b) (pred: finished) finito(a); **we'll be** ~ **at 7** avremo finito per le sette; **I'm** ~ **with my girlfriend** ho chiuso con la mia ragazza; **I'm not** ~ **with you** yet con te non ho ancora finito; **you're** ~! sei finito!

through·out [θruː'aut] **1** prep **(a)** (place) in tutto(a); ~ **Italy** in tutta l'Italia. **(b)** (time, process) per tutto(a); ~ **last summer** per tutta l'estate scorsa. **2** adv **(a)** (everywhere) dappertutto; **the house is carpeted** ~ c'è la moquette dappertutto in casa. **(b)** (the whole time) dal principio alla fine.

through·put ['θruput] n (of goods, materials) materiale m in lavorazione; (Computers) volume m di dati immessi.

throw [θrəu] (vb: pt **threw**, pp **thrown**) **1** n lancio; (in judo, wrestling) atterramento.
  2 vt (gen, fig) lanciare, gettare; (ball, javelin, hammer) lanciare; (dice) gettare; (horserider) disarcionare, gettare a terra; (judo opponent) atterrare, mettere al tappeto; (pottery) tornire; (fig fam: disconcert) sconcertare; **to** ~ **a ball 200 metres** lanciare una palla a duecento metri; **to** ~

a coat round one's shoulders buttarsi un cappotto sulle spalle; **to** ~ **a switch** (Elec) azionare una leva; **he was** ~**n from his horse** fu disarcionato; **to** ~ **a party** dare una festa; **to** ~ **open** (doors, windows) spalancare; (house, gardens etc) aprire al pubblico; (competition, race) aprire a tutti; **to** ~ **o.s. off a cliff/into a river** gettarsi da una scogliera/in un fiume; **to** ~ **o.s. at sb** (rush at) gettarsi or scagliarsi su qn; (fig) buttarsi su qn; **to** ~ **o.s. into one's work** buttarsi a capofitto nel lavoro; **to** ~ **o.s. at sb's feet** gettarsi ai piedi di qn; **to** ~ **o.s. on sb's mercy** rimettersi alla pietà di qn.

♦**throw about, throw around** vt + adv (litter etc) spargere; **to** ~ **money about** sperperare il denaro; **to** ~ **one's weight about** far pesare la propria presenza.

♦**throw away** vt + adv (rubbish etc) buttar via; (chance, money, time) sprecare.

♦**throw back** vt + adv **(a)** (return: ball) rinviare. **(b)** (head, hair) buttare all'indietro; (shoulders) raddrizzare; **she was** ~**n back on her own resources** (fig) se l'è dovuta cavare da sola.

♦**throw in** vt + adv (Sport: ball) rimettere in gioco; (sth extra) aggiungere; (say casually: remark) buttar lì.

♦**throw off** vt + adv (get rid of) liberarsi di; (escape: pursuers, dogs) sbarazzarsi di, seminare; **to** ~ **sb off the trail** mettere qn fuori pista.

♦**throw out** vt + adv **(a)** (rubbish, person) buttar fuori; (fig: proposal) respingere. **(b)** (offer: idea, suggestion) lanciare. **(c)** (calculation, prediction) far sballare.

♦**throw over** vt + adv (person) piantare.

♦**throw together** vt + adv (clothes, meal etc) mettere insieme; (essay) buttar giù; (people) fare incontrare.

♦**throw up 1** vi + adv (fam: vomit) vomitare. **2** vt + adv (ball etc) lanciare in aria; **she threw up her hands in despair** ha alzato le braccia al cielo per la disperazione.

throw·away ['θrəuə‚weɪ] adj (disposable: bottle etc) da buttar via; (casual: remark) buttato(a) lì.

throw·back ['θrəubæk] n: **it's a** ~ **to** (fig) ciò risale a.

throw-in ['θrəuɪn] n (Ftbl) rimessa in gioco.

thrown [θrəun] pp of **throw**.

thru [θruː] (Am) = **through**.

thrush[1] [θrʌʃ] n (bird) tordo.

thrush[2] [θrʌʃ] n (Med: esp in children) mughetto; (: in women) candida.

thrust [θrʌst] (vb: pt, pp **thrust**) **1** n (push) spintone m; (Aer, Space) spinta; (Mil: offensive) attacco, offensiva; **forward** ~ spinta propulsiva. **2** vt (push) spingere con forza; (finger, stick, dagger) cacciare; **he** ~ **a book into my hands** mi ha cacciato un libro tra le mani; **she** ~ **her head out of the window** ha sporto la testa dalla finestra; **to** ~ **o.s. upon sb** (fig) imporre la propria presenza a qn; **they** ~ **the job on me** (fig) mi hanno costretto ad accettare il lavoro; **I** ~ **my way through the crowd** mi sono fatto largo tra la folla; **to** ~ **sb/sth aside** spingere qn/qc da una parte; **to** ~ **an idea aside** scartare un'idea.

thud [θʌd] **1** n tonfo. **2** vi: **to** ~ **to the ground** cadere a terra con un tonfo; **to** ~ **against the wall** colpire il muro con un tonfo.

thug [θʌg] n teppista m/f.

thumb [θʌm] **1** n pollice m; **to be under sb's** ~ (fig) essere succube di qn; **to give sb/sth the** ~**s up** dare la propria approvazione a qn/qc; **to give sth the** ~**s down** disapprovare or bocciare qc. **2** vt: **to** ~ **a lift** or **a ride** fare l'autostop; **to** ~ **one's nose at sb** fare marameo a qn; **to** ~ **one's nose at**

sb/sth *(fig)* beffarsi di qn/qc; **a well-~ed book** un libro vissuto. **3** *vi:* **to ~ through a book/magazine** *etc* sfogliare un libro/una rivista *etc.*

thumb·nail ['θʌmneɪl] **1** *n* unghia del pollice. **2** *cpd:* **~ sketch** *n* descrizione *f* breve.

thumb·tack ['θʌmtæk] *n (Am)* puntina da disegno.

thump [θʌmp] **1** *n (blow)* colpo; *(noise of fall etc)* tonfo; **it came down with a ~** è caduto con un tonfo. **2** *vt (hit hard: person)* picchiare; *(: door)* picchiare su; *(: table)* battere su. **3** *vi (person: on door, table)* picchiare; *(: move heavily)* camminare pesantemente; *(pound: heart)* battere forte.

thump·ing ['θʌmpɪŋ] *adj (fam):* **it's a ~ great book** è un libro enorme; **a ~ headache** un mal di testa martellante.

thun·der ['θʌndə'] **1** *n (Met)* tuono; *(of hooves, traffic etc)* fragore *m*; **with a face like ~** con un volto di fuoco. **2** *vi (Met, voice, fig)* tonare; **the guns ~ed in the distance** i cannoni tonavano in lontananza; **the train ~ed by** il treno è passato rombando; **he ~ed at him to stop** gli urlò di fermarsi.

thunder·bolt ['θʌndəbəʊlt] *n* fulmine *m.*

thun·der·ous ['θʌndərəs] *adj (applause)* fragoroso(a).

thunder·storm ['θʌndəstɔ:m] *n* temporale *m.*

thunder·struck ['θʌndəstrʌk] *adj (fig)* sbigottito(a).

thun·dery ['θʌndərɪ] *adj (weather)* minaccioso(a), da temporale.

Thurs·day ['θɜ:zdɪ] *n* giovedì *m inv; for usage see* Tuesday.

thus [ðʌs] *adv (in this way)* così; *(as a result)* perciò; **~ far** fino ad ora.

thwart [θwɔ:t] *vt* ostacolare.

thy [ðaɪ] *poss adj (old, poet)* il(la) tuo(a).

thyme [taɪm] *n* timo.

thy·roid ['θaɪrɔɪd] *n (also: ~ gland)* tiroide *f.*

ti·ara [tɪ'ɑːrə] *n (women's)* diadema *m; (of pope)* tiara.

Ti·bet [tɪ'bet] *n* Tibet *m.*

Ti·bet·an [tɪ'betən] **1** *adj* tibetano(a). **2** *n* **(a)** *(person)* tibetano/a. **(b)** *(language)* tibetano.

tibia ['tɪbɪə] *n* tibia.

tic [tɪk] *n (Med)* tic *m inv.*

tick¹ [tɪk] **1** *n* **(a)** *(of clock)* tic tac *m inv; (fam: moment)* secondo, attimo; **I shan't be a ~** ci metto un secondo. **(b)** *(mark)* segno; **to put a ~ against sth** fare un segno di fianco a qc. **2** *vt (also: ~ off: name on list etc)* spuntare; **to ~ the right answer** segnare la risposta giusta. **3** *vi (clock)* ticchettare; **I can't understand what makes him ~** *(fig)* non riesco a capire come ragioni.

♦ **tick off** *vt + adv (fam: scold)* sgridare.

♦ **tick over** *vi + adv (engine)* andare al minimo; *(fig: business etc)* andare avanti come al solito.

tick² [tɪk] *n (Zool)* zecca.

tick³ [tɪk] *n (fam):* **to buy sth on ~** comprare qc a credito.

tick·er ['tɪkə'] **1** *n (fam: watch)* orologio; *(: heart)* cuore *m.* **2** *cpd:* **~ tape** *n* nastro di telescrivente; *(for public festivities)* stelle *fpl* filanti.

tick·et ['tɪkɪt] **1** *n (gen)* biglietto; *(for library)* tessera; *(Comm: label)* cartellino; *(: from cash register)* scontrino; *(Am Pol)* lista dei candidati; **to get a (parking) ~** *(Aut)* prendere una multa (per sosta vietata); **return ~,** *(Am)* **round-trip ~** biglietto di andata e ritorno; **admission by ~ only** si ammettono solo le persone munite di biglietto; **that's the ~!** *(fig)* così sì che va bene! **2** *vt (label: goods)* etichettare. **3** *cpd:* **~ agency** *n (Theatre)* agenzia di vendita di biglietti; **~ collector** *n* bigliettaio; **~ holder** *n* persona munita di biglietto; **~ inspector** *n* controllore *m;* **~ office** *n* biglietteria.

tick·ing¹ ['tɪkɪŋ] *n (of clock etc)* ticchettio.

tick·ing² ['tɪkɪŋ] *n (material)* tela da materassi.

ticking-off [,tɪkɪŋ'ɒf] *n (fam):* **to give sb a ~** dare a qn una lavata di testa, sgridare qn.

tick·le ['tɪkl] **1** *vt (person)* fare il solletico a; *(fig: palate etc)* stuzzicare; *(: amuse)* divertire; **it ~d his fancy** stuzzicava la sua fantasia; **to be ~d pink** *(fam)* andare in brodo di giuggiole. **2** *vi:* **it ~s mi** *(or* gli *etc)* fa il solletico. **3** *n:* **to give sb a ~** fare il solletico a qn.

tick·lish ['tɪklɪʃ] *adj,* **tick·ly** ['tɪklɪ] *adj (fam) (easily tickled: person)* che soffre il solletico; *(which tickles: blanket, cough)* che provoca prurito; *(fig: touchy: person)* permaloso(a); *(: delicate: situation, problem)* delicato(a).

tid·al ['taɪdl] *adj (of tide)* di marea; *(affected by the tide)* soggetto(a) alla marea; **~ wave** onda anomala.

tid·dler ['tɪdlə'] *n (small fish)* pesciolino; *(fam: child)* bambinetto/a.

tid·dly ['tɪdlɪ] *adj (-ier, -iest) (fam: drunk)* brillo(a).

tiddly·winks ['tɪdlɪwɪŋks] *nsg* (gioco della) pulce.

tide [taɪd] **1** *n* marea; *(fig: of emotion)* ondata; *(: of events etc)* corso; **the ~ of public opinion** l'orientamento dell'opinione pubblica; **high/low ~** alta/bassa marea; **the ~ has turned** la marea è cambiata; *(fig)* c'è stato un cambiamento (di tendenze); **to go with the ~** *(fig)* seguire la corrente; **to swim against the ~** andare controcorrente. **2** *vt:* **to ~ sb over** *or* **through (until)** dare una mano a qn (fino a); **can you lend me £10 to ~ me over until Friday?** mi puoi prestare 10 sterline per tirare avanti fino a venerdì?

tide·mark ['taɪdmɑːk] *n* linea di marea.

ti·di·ly ['taɪdɪlɪ] *adv* in modo ordinato; **to arrange ~** sistemare; **to dress ~** vestirsi per benino.

ti·di·ness ['taɪdɪnɪs] *n* ordine *m.*

tid·ings ['taɪdɪŋz] *npl* notizie *fpl.*

tidy ['taɪdɪ] **1** *adj (-ier, -iest) (gen)* ordinato(a), in ordine; *(hair)* in ordine, a posto; *(drawing, work etc)* pulito(a); *(person: in appearance)* curato(a); *(: in character)* ordinato(a); *(mind)* organizzato(a); **a ~ sum** *(fam)* una bella sommetta. **2** *vt (also: ~ up: room, toys etc)* mettere in ordine; *(: one's hair)* ravviarsi.

♦ **tidy away** *vt + adv* mettere via.

♦ **tidy out** *vt + adv* mettere in ordine.

♦ **tidy up** *vi + adv* fare ordine. **2** *vt + adv =* **tidy 2.**

tie [taɪ] **1** *n* **(a)** *(necktie etc)* cravatta; *(cord, ribbon)* legaccio; *(fig: bond)* legame *m;* **black/white ~** *(on invitation)* smoking/abito di rigore; **the children are a ~** i bambini sono una schiavitù; **~s of friendship** legami d'amicizia; **family ~s** legami familiari. **(b)** *(Sport etc: draw)* pareggio; *(Pol)* parità *f inv* di voti; **the match ended in a ~** l'incontro è finito con un pareggio; **cup ~** *(Sport: match)* incontro di coppa.

2 *vt (gen, fig)* legare; *(also: ~ up: shoe)* allacciare, allacciarsi; **to ~ a knot (in sth)** fare un nodo (a qc); **to get ~d in knots** *(also fig)* ingarbugliarsi; **to ~ a necktie** fare il nodo a una cravatta; **my job ~s me to London** il mio lavoro mi tiene a Londra; **his hands are ~d** *(fig)* ha le mani legate.

3 *vi* **(a)** *(dress, shoes)* allacciarsi. **(b)** *(Sport etc: draw)* pareggiare.

♦ **tie back** *vt + adv (curtains)* fissare; **to ~ back one's hair** farsi la coda.

♦ **tie down** *vt + adv* assicurare; *(fig):* **to ~ sb down to a promise/a price/a time** obbligare qn a mantenere una promessa/a fissare un prezzo/a venire a una certa ora; **to ~ sb down to sth** *(promise etc)* essere vincolato da qc; **to be ~d down** *(fig)* essere legato mani e piedi.

♦ **tie in 1** *vi + adv*: **to ~ in (with)** *(correspond)* corrispondere (a); *(be connected)* avere legami (con). **2** *vt + adv*: **to ~ in (with)** *(meeting, visit)* far coincidere (con); *(findings)* far combaciare (con).

♦ **tie on** *vt + adv (label etc)* attaccare.

♦ **tie up 1** *vi + adv (Naut)* ormeggiare. **2** *vt + adv (person, parcel etc)* legare; *(boat)* ormeggiare; *(fig: capital)* impegnare; *(: business deal)* concludere; *(: connect)* ricollegare; **to be ~d up (with sb/sth)** *(busy)* essere impegnato (con qn/a fare qc); **the traffic was ~d up by the accident** il traffico è rimasto bloccato per l'incidente.

tie-break(er) ['taɪbreɪk(əʳ)] *n (Tennis)* tie-break *m inv; (in quiz)* spareggio.

tie-in ['taɪɪn] *n (link)* legame *m*.

tie-on [taɪ'ɒn] *adj (label)* volante.

tie·pin ['taɪpɪn] *n* fermacravatta *m inv*.

tier [tɪəʳ] *n (in theatre, stadium etc)* fila; *(layer)* strato; **to arrange in ~s** disporre in file *(or in strati)*.

tie-up ['taɪʌp] *n (connection)* legame *m*.

tiff [tɪf] *n* battibecco; **a lover's ~** un battibecco tra innamorati.

ti·ger ['taɪgəʳ] *n* tigre *f*.

tight [taɪt] **1** *adj* **(a)** *(gen)* stretto(a); *(rope)* teso(a), tirato(a); *(usu pred: firmly fixed, hard to move)* duro(a); *(strict: control, discipline)* severo(a); *(fam: mean)* tirchio(a); **it's a ~ fit** è un po' stretto; **to be in a ~ spot** *(fig)* essere in una situazione difficile; **space/money is a bit ~** siamo un po' stretti/a corto di denaro; **to keep a ~ hold of sth** tenere qc stretto; **to keep a ~ hold on the reins** *(fig)* tenere le redini in pugno. **(b)** *(fam: drunk)* sbronzo(a); **to get ~** sbronzarsi.

2 *adv (hold)* stretto; *(close)* ermeticamente; *(grasp)* saldamente; **to be packed ~** *(suitcase)* essere pieno zeppo; *(people)* essere pigiati; **screw it up ~!** avvitalo stretto!; **pull the door ~!** chiudi bene la porta!; **to hold sb ~** tenere stretto qn; **everybody hold ~!** tenetevi stretti!; **the room was packed ~ with people** la stanza era piena zeppa di persone; **to sleep ~** *(soundly)* dormire sodo.

tight·en ['taɪtn] **1** *vt (also: ~ up: gen)* stringere; *(: rope)* tendere; *(: regulation)* rendere più severo(a); **to ~ one's belt** *(fig)* tirare la cinghia. **2** *vi (also: ~ up: knot)* stringersi; *(rope)* tendersi; *(: grasp)* farsi più stretto.

♦ **tighten up 1** *vi + adv* **(a)** = **tighten 2. (b)**: **to ~ up on sth** rendere qc più severo(a). **2** *vt + adv* = **tighten 1.**

tight-fisted [ˌtaɪt'fɪstɪd] *adj* avaro(a), tirchio(a).

tight-lipped [ˌtaɪt'lɪpt] *adj (annoyed)* a labbra serrate; *(silent)* abbottonato(a).

tight·ly ['taɪtlɪ] *adv* = **tight 2.**

tight·ness ['taɪtnɪs] *n (of lid, screw)* resistenza; *(of discipline)* rigore *m; (of regulations)* rigidità; **you should have seen the ~ of her trousers!** avresti dovuto vedere com'erano stretti i suoi pantaloni!; **I can feel a ~ in my chest** ho un senso di oppressione nel torace.

tight·rope ['taɪtrəup] **1** *n* corda (da acrobata). **2** *cpd*: **~ walker** *n* funambolo/a.

tights [taɪts] *npl* collant *m inv*.

ti·gress ['taɪgrɪs] *n* tigre *f* (femmina).

til·de ['tɪldɪ] *n* tilde *f*.

tile [taɪl] **1** *n (roof ~)* tegola; *(floor ~)* mattonella; *(wall ~, decorative ~)* piastrella; **a night on the ~s** *(fam)* una notte brava. **2** *vt (roof)* rivestire di tegole; *(floor, bathroom etc)* piastrellare.

tiled [taɪld] *adj (floor)* a mattonelle, a piastrelle;

(wall, bathroom) a piastrelle; *(roof)* rivestito(a) di tegole.

till¹ [tɪl] *vt (Agr)* coltivare.

till² [tɪl] = **until.**

till³ [tɪl] *n (for money)* cassa.

till·er ['tɪləʳ] *n (Naut)* barra (del timone).

tilt [tɪlt] **1** *n* **(a)** *(slope)* pendio; **to wear one's hat at a ~** portare il cappello sulle ventitrè. **(b): (at) full ~** a tutta velocità. **2** *vt* inclinare; **~ it this way/ the other way** inclinalo da questa/quella parte; **he ~ed his chair back** ha inclinato la sedia indietro. **3** *vi* inclinarsi; **to ~ to one side** inclinarsi da una parte; **he ~ed back in his chair** si è inclinato indietro con la sedia.

tim·ber ['tɪmbəʳ] *n (material)* legname *m; (trees)* alberi *mpl*; **~!** cade!

tim·bered ['tɪmbəd] *adj (house etc)* rivestito(a) di legno.

tim·bre ['tæmbrə, 'tɪmbəʳ] *n* timbro.

time [taɪm] **1** *n* **(a)** *(gen)* tempo; **~ and space** il tempo e lo spazio; **how ~ flies!** come vola il tempo!; **only ~ will tell** si saprà solo col tempo; **~ is on our side** il tempo è dalla nostra; **all in good ~** senza fretta; **to have (the) ~ (to do sth)** avere il tempo (di fare qc); **to find the ~ for reading** trovare il tempo per leggere; **I've no ~ for them** *(too busy)* non ho tempo da perdere con loro; *(contemptuous)* non li posso soffrire; **he lost no ~ in doing it** l'ha fatto subito senza perdere tempo; **it takes ~ to...** ci vuole tempo per...; **to take one's ~** prenderla con calma; **~ is money** *(Proverb)* il tempo è denaro; **he'll do it in his own ~** *(without being hurried)* lo farà quando ha (un minuto di) tempo; *(out of working hours)* lo farà nel suo tempo libero; **my ~ is my own** dispongo del mio tempo.

(b) *(period of ~)* tempo; **a long ~** molto tempo; **a long ~ ago** molto tempo fa; **a short ~** poco tempo; **in a short ~** she will have left fra poco sarà partita; **in a short ~** they were all gone nel giro di poco tempo se ne erano andati tutti; **a short ~ after** poco tempo dopo; **for a ~** per un po' di tempo; **have you been here all this ~?** sei stato qui tutto questo tempo?; **for the ~ being** per il momento; **in no ~** in un attimo; **in a week's ~** fra una settimana.

(c) *(moment)* momento; *(period)* periodo; **any ~** in qualsiasi momento; **come any ~ you like** vieni quando vuoi; **any ~ now** da un momento all'altro; **at that ~** allora, a quel tempo; **at the present ~** al momento, adesso; **at this ~ of the year** in questo periodo dell'anno; **(by) this ~ next year** in questo periodo l'anno prossimo; **by the ~ he arrived** quando è arrivato; **at the same ~** *(simultaneously)* contemporaneamente; **but at the same ~, I have to admit...** tuttavia devo ammettere...; **at the same ~ as** nello stesso momento in cui; **at ~s** a volte; **at all ~s** in ogni momento, sempre; **from ~ to ~** di tanto in tanto; **now is the ~ to go to Venice** questo è il periodo *or* momento giusto per andare a Venezia; **the ~ has come to leave** è arrivato il momento *or* l'ora di partire; **this is no ~ for jokes** non è il momento di scherzare; **this is neither the ~ nor the place to discuss it** non è né il luogo né il momento adatto per discuterne.

(d) *(by clock)* ora; **what ~ do you make it?** che ora fai?; **have you got the (right) ~?** hai l'ora (esatta)?; **what's the ~?** che ora è?; **Greenwich Mean T~** l'ora di Greenwich; **on ~** *(person)* puntuale; *(train etc)* in orario; **to arrive (just) in ~ for dinner** arrivare (appena) in tempo per cena; **it's ~ for the news** *(on radio)* c'è il giornale radio;

(on television) c'è il telegiornale; **to be 30 minutes behind/ahead of** ~ avere 30 minuti di ritardo/anticipo; **about** ~ **too!** era anche ora!; **it was about** ~ **you had a haircut** era proprio ora che ti tagliassi i capelli.

(e) *(era: often:* ~s) era; *(period)* periodo, epoca; **in modern** ~s nell'era moderna; **in Elizabethan** ~s nel periodo elisabettiano; **in my** ~ ai miei tempi; **during my** ~ **at Lexus** quando ero alla Lexus; **it was before my** ~ non ero ancora nato; ~s **were hard** erano tempi duri; **in** ~s **to come** nel tempo a venire; **to be ahead of one's** ~ essere un precursore; **to be behind the** ~s vivere nel passato.

(f) *(experience):* **to have a good** ~ divertirsi; **to have a bad** *or* **rough** ~ **(of it)** passarsela male.

(g) *(occasion)* volta; **three** ~s tre volte; **this/next** ~ questa/la prossima volta; **the last** ~ **I did it** l'ultima volta che l'ho fatto; ~ **after** ~, ~ **and again** mille volte; **many's the** ~... più di una volta...; **I remember the** ~ when ricordo ancora quando; **for weeks at a** ~ per settimane; **to carry 3 boxes at a** ~ portare 3 scatole per volta.

(h) *(Mus, Mil)* tempo; **to keep** ~ andare a tempo; **to play/march in** ~ suonare/marciare a tempo; **to be out of** ~ essere *or* andare fuori tempo.

(i) *(Math):* **4** ~s **3 is 12** 4 per 3 fa 12; **3** ~s **as fast (as), 3** ~s **faster (than)** 3 volte più veloce (di).

2 *vt* **(a)** *(schedule)* programmare; *(choose* ~ *of: joke, request):* **to** ~ **sth well/badly** scegliere il momento più/meno opportuno per qc, fare qc al momento giusto/sbagliato; **the footballer** ~**d his shot perfectly** il giocatore ha calcolato il tiro alla perfezione; **the bomb was** ~**d to explode 5 minutes later** la bomba era stata regolata in modo da esplodere 5 minuti più tardi.

(b) *(with stopwatch etc)* cronometrare; **to** ~ **an egg** controllare il tempo per la cottura di un uovo; **to** ~ **o.s.** prendere i propri tempi.

3 *cpd:* ~ **bomb** *n* bomba a orologeria; ~ **card** *n*, ~ **sheet** *n* cartellino (da timbrare); ~ **exposure** *n (Phot)* posa continua; ~ **limit** *n* limite *m* di tempo; **to set a** ~ **limit** fissare un limite di tempo; ~ **signal** *n* segnale *m* orario; ~ **switch** *n* timer *m inv*, temporizzatore *m*.

time-and-motion [ˌtaɪmən'məʊʃən] *adj:* ~ **expert** esperto in tempi di produzione.

time-consum·ing ['taɪmkən,sjuːmɪŋ] *adj* che richiede molto tempo.

time-honoured, *(Am)* **time-honored** ['taɪm,ɒnəd] *adj* consacrato(a) dal tempo.

time-lag ['taɪmlæg] *n* intervallo di tempo.

time·less ['taɪmlɪs] *adj (unending)* eterno(a), infinito(a); *(unchanging)* senza tempo.

time·ly ['taɪmlɪ] *adj* tempestivo(a); *(opportune)* opportuno(a).

time·piece ['taɪmpiːs] *n* orologio.

tim·er ['taɪmə^r] *n (egg* ~ *etc)* clessidra; *(Tech)* timer *m inv*, temporizzatore *m*.

time-saving ['taɪm,seɪvɪŋ] *adj* che fa risparmiare tempo.

time·table ['taɪm,teɪbl] *n (for trains etc)* orario; *(programme of events etc)* programma *m*.

tim·id ['tɪmɪd] *adj (shy)* timido(a); *(unadventurous)* timoroso(a).

ti·mid·ity [tɪ'mɪdɪtɪ] *n* timidezza.

tim·id·ly ['tɪmɪdlɪ] *adv* timidamente.

tim·ing ['taɪmɪŋ] *n (of actor)* coordinazione *f*; *(of musician)* tempismo; *(of demonstration)* orario; *(of engine)* messa in fase; *(Industry, Sport)* cronometraggio; **that was good/bad** ~ hai *(or* ha *etc)*

scelto il momento opportuno/sbagliato; **that was perfect** ~! che tempismo!

tim·or·ous ['tɪmərəs] *adj* timoroso(a).

tim·pa·ni ['tɪmpənɪ] *npl (Mus)* timpani *mpl*.

tin [tɪn] **1** *n* **(a)** *(metal)* stagno; (~*plate)* latta. **(b)** *(Brit: container)* barattolo, scatola; *(: for baking)* teglia. **2** *vt* inscatolare. **3** *cpd:* ~ **can** *n* barattolo, scatola; ~ **mine** *n* miniera di stagno; ~ **soldier** *n* soldatino di latta; ~ **whistle** *n (Mus)* zufolo.

tin-foil ['tɪnfɔɪl] *n* carta stagnola.

tinge [tɪndʒ] **1** *n (of colour, fig)* punta; **her hair had a** ~ **of red in it** i suoi capelli avevano dei riflessi rossi. **2** *vt:* **to be** ~**d with** avere una punta di.

tin·gle ['tɪŋgl] **1** *n (of skin)* formicolio; *(thrill)* fremito. **2** *vi (cheeks, skin: from cold)* pungere; *(from bad circulation)* formicolare; **a tingling sensation** un formicolio; **to** ~ **with excitement** fremere dall'eccitazione.

tink·er ['tɪŋkə^r] **1** *n* stagnino ambulante. **2** *vi (also:* ~ **about):** **to** ~ **(with)** *(play)* trastullarsi (con); *(repair)* armeggiare (con).

tin·kle ['tɪŋkl] **1** *n (of bell etc)* tintinnio; **give me a** ~ *(fam)* dammi un colpetto di telefono. **2** *vi* tintinnare.

tin·kling ['tɪŋklɪŋ] **1** *adj (sound)* tintinnante, argentino(a). **2** *n* tintinnio.

tinned [tɪnd] *adj (Brit)* in scatola.

tin·ny ['tɪnɪ] *adj (-ier, -iest) (metallic: sound)* metallico(a); *(pej: car, machine)* che sembra di latta.

tin-open·er ['tɪn,əʊpnə^r] *n (Brit)* apriscatole *m inv*.

tin·plate ['tɪnpleɪt] *n* latta.

tin·sel ['tɪnsəl] *n* fili *mpl* argentati.

tint [tɪnt] **1** *n (gen)* sfumatura; *(for hair)* shampoo *m inv* colorante. **2** *vt (hair)* fare uno shampoo colorante a.

tiny ['taɪnɪ] *adj (-ier, -iest)* minuscolo(a).

tip[1] [tɪp] *n (gen)* punta; *(peak)* cima, vetta; *(of stick etc)* puntale *m*; **it's on the** ~ **of my tongue** *(fig)* ce l'ho sulla punta della lingua; **it was just the** ~ **of the iceberg** *(fig)* era solo la punta dell'iceberg.

tip[2] [tɪp] **1** *n* **(a)** *(gratuity)* mancia. **(b)** *(hint)* suggerimento; *(advice)* consiglio; *(: for horse race)* cavallo; **I'll give you a** ~ ti darò un consiglio. **2** *vt* **(a)** *(porter, waiter)* dare la mancia a; **I** ~**ped him £1** gli ho dato una mancia di 1 sterlina, gli ho dato 1 sterlina di mancia. **(b)** *(predict: winner)* pronosticare; *(: horse)* dare vincente; **he is being** ~**ped for the job** secondo i pronostici dovrebbe avere il posto.

♦ **tip off** *vt* + *adv* fare una soffiata a.

tip[3] [tɪp] **1** *n (rubbish dump)* discarica. **2** *vt (tilt)* inclinare; *(empty: also:* ~ **out)** svuotare; *(overturn: also:* ~ **over)** rovesciare; **to** ~ **sb off his seat** far cadere qn dalla sedia; **to** ~ **away the dishwater** svuotare l'acqua dei piatti; **to** ~ **back a chair** inclinare una sedia all'indietro; **he** ~**ped out the contents of the box** ha rovesciato il contenuto della scatola; **to** ~ **over a glass of wine** rovesciare un bicchiere di vino; **to** ~ **the balance** far pendere la bilancia da una parte. **3** *vi (incline)* pendere, essere inclinato(a); *(also:* ~ **over)** rovesciarsi.

♦ **tip up 1** *vi* + *adv* ribaltarsi. **2** *vt* + *adv* inclinare.

tip-off ['tɪpɒf] *n* soffiata.

tipped [tɪpt] *adj (cigarette)* col filtro.

tip·ping ['tɪpɪŋ] *n:* **'no** ~**'** 'divieto di scarico'.

tip·ple ['tɪpl] *(fam)* **1** *n* drink *m inv* preferito. **2** *vi* alzare il gomito.

tip·pler ['tɪplə^r] *n (fam)* beone *m*.

tip·ster ['tɪpstə^r] *n* chi vende informazioni sui cavalli alle corse, sulle azioni in Borsa.

tip·sy ['tɪpsɪ] *adj (-ier, -iest)* brillo(a).

tip·toe ['tɪptəʊ] **1** *n:* **to walk on** ~ camminare in punta dei piedi. **2** *vi* camminare in punta dei piedi.

tip·top ['tɪp'tɒp] *adj*: **in ~ condition** in ottime condizioni.

ti·rade [taɪ'reɪd] *n* tirata.

tire[1] ['taɪə[r]] **1** *vt (exhaust)* stancare. **2** *vi* stancarsi; **to ~ of sb/sth** stancarsi di qn/qc.
♦ **tire out** *vt + adv* sfinire, spossare.

tire[2] ['taɪə[r]] *(Am)* = **tyre**.

tired ['taɪəd] *adj* **(a)** stanco(a); **to be/feel/look ~** essere/sentirsi/sembrare stanco; **to be ~ of sb/ sth** essere stanco or stufo di qn/qc; **to get** or **grow ~ of doing sth** stancarsi di fare qc. **(b)** *(fig: cliché etc)* trito(a) e ritrito(a); *(: shabby)* consunto(a).

tired·ness ['taɪədnɪs] *n* stanchezza.

tire·less ['taɪəlɪs] *adj* instancabile.

tire·some ['taɪəsəm] *adj (job, person)* noioso(a); *(situation)* seccante; **how ~!** che seccatura!

tir·ing ['taɪərɪŋ] *adj* faticoso(a).

tis·sue ['tɪʃuː] **1** *n* **(a)** *(thin paper)* velina; *(paper handkerchief)* fazzolettino di carta. **(b)** *(Anat)* tessuto. **(c)** *(fig)*: **to weave a ~ of lies** tessere una ragnatela di menzogne. **2** *cpd*: **~ paper** *n* carta velina.

tit[1] [tɪt] *n (bird: also:* **~mouse**) cincia; **great ~** cinciallegra.

tit[2] [tɪt] *n*: **to give ~ for tat** rendere pan per focaccia.

tit[3] [tɪt] *n (fam: breast)* tetta.

ti·ta·nium [tɪ'teɪnɪəm] *n* titanio.

tit·bit ['tɪtbɪt] *n*, *(Am)* **tid·bit** ['tɪdbɪt] *n (of food)* bocconcino, leccornia; *(fig: of news, information etc)* notizia appetitosa.

tit·il·late ['tɪtɪleɪt] *vt (sexually)* titillare.

titi·vate ['tɪtɪveɪt] *vt* agghindare.

ti·tle ['taɪtl] **1** *n* **(a)** *(gen)* titolo; **to hold a ~** detenere un titolo. **(b)** *(Law: right)*: **~** (to) diritto (a). **2** *cpd*: **~ deed** *n (Law)* atto di proprietà; **~ holder** *n (Sport)* detentore/trice del titolo; **~ page** *n* frontespizio; **~ role** *n (Theatre, Cine)* ≈ ruolo di protagonista.

ti·tled ['taɪtld] *adj (person)* titolato(a).

tit·ter ['tɪtə[r]] **1** *n* risatina stupida. **2** *vi* ridacchiare.

tittle-tattle ['tɪtltætl] *(fam)* **1** *n* pettegolezzi *mpl*. **2** *vi* pettegolare.

tiz·zy ['tɪzɪ] *n (fam)*: **to be in/get into a ~ (about sth)** essere in preda al/farsi prendere dal panico (per qc).

T-junction ['tiː'dʒʌŋkʃən] *n* incrocio a T.

to [tuː, *weak form* tə] *prep* **1 (a)** *(direction: gen)* a; *(: to a country)* in; *(: to sb's house, office etc)* da; **to go ~ Paris/school/the station** andare a Parigi/a scuola/alla stazione; **to go ~ the doctor's/to Peter's** andare dal dottore/da Peter; **the road ~ Edinburgh** la strada per Edimburgo; **have you ever been ~ India?** sei mai stato in India?; **~ the left/the right** a sinistra/destra; **a letter ~ his wife** una lettera a sua moglie.

(b) *(next to, with position)* a; **with one's back ~ the wall** con le spalle al muro; **at right angles ~ sth** ad angolo retto con qc; **the door is ~ the left (of)** la porta è a sinistra (di).

(c) *(as far as)* fino a; **from here ~ London** da qui (fino) a Londra; **to count ~ 10** contare fino a dieci; **from 40 ~ 50 people** da 40 a 50 persone; **~ some extent** fino a un certo punto, in parte; **to be wet ~ the skin** essere bagnato fino al midollo.

(d) *(with expressions of time)* a; **it's twenty-five ~ 3** sono or mancano venticinque minuti alle 3, sono le 2 e trentacinque.

(e) *(expressing indirect object)* a; **to give sth ~ sb** dare qc a qn; **it belongs ~ him** gli appartiene, è suo; **the man I sold it ~** or *(frm)* **~ whom I sold it**

l'uomo (a) cui l'ho venduto; **to be kind ~ sb** essere gentile con qn; **a solution ~ the problem** una soluzione al problema; **a monument ~ the fallen** un monumento ai caduti; **to drink ~ sb** bere a qn or alla salute di qn.

(f) *(in relation ~)* (in confronto) a; **A is ~ B as C is ~ D** A sta a B come C sta a D; **superior ~ the others** superiore agli altri; **three goals ~ two** tre goal a due; **that's nothing ~ what is to come** non è nulla in confronto a ciò che ancora deve venire; **10 inhabitants ~ the square kilometre** 10 abitanti per chilometro quadrato; **30 miles ~ the gallon** ≈ 11 chilometri con un litro; **8 apples ~ the kilo** 8 mele in un chilo.

(g) *(about)* di; **what do you say ~ this?** che cosa ne pensi?; **that's all there is ~ it** questo è tutto, è tutto lì.

(h) *(according to)* secondo; **~ my way of thinking** secondo il mio modo di pensare, a mio parere; **~ the best of my recollection** per quanto mi ricordi io; **we danced ~ the music of...** abbiamo ballato con la musica di... .

(i) *(purpose, result)*: **to come ~ sb's aid** venire in aiuto a qn; **to sentence sb ~ death** condannare qn a morte; **~ my great surprise** con mia grande sorpresa.

2 *with vb* **(a)** *(simple infin)*: **~ go** andare; *(following another vb)*: **to want ~ do** voler fare; **to try ~ do** cercare di fare; **to start ~ cry** incominciare or mettersi a piangere.

(b) *(purpose, result)* per; **he did it ~ help you** l'ha fatto per aiutarti; **he came ~ see you** è venuto per vederti.

(c) *(without vb)*: **I don't want ~** non voglio (farlo); **you ought ~** devi (farlo).

(d) *(equivalent to relative clause)* da; **I have things ~ do** ho (delle cose) da fare; **he's not the sort ~ do that** non è il tipo da fare una cosa del genere; **now is the time ~ do it** è ora di farlo; **he has a lot ~ lose** rischia grosso; **he has nothing ~ lose** non ha nulla da perdere.

(e) *(after adj etc)*: **ready ~ go** pronto a partire; **hard ~ believe** difficile da credere; **the first ~ go** il primo ad andarsene; **too old/young ~...** troppo vecchio/giovane per... .

3 *adv* **(a)**: **to push the door ~** *(closed)* accostare la porta.

(b): **to come ~** *(recover consciousness)* riprendere conoscenza.

toad [təʊd] *n* rospo.

toad-in-the-hole ['təʊdɪnðə'həʊl] *n (Culin)* salsicce coperte di pastella e cotte nel forno.

toad·stool ['təʊdstuːl] *n* fungo velenoso.

toady ['təʊdɪ] *(pej)* **1** *n* leccapiedi *m/f inv*. **2** *vi*: **to ~ to sb** leccare i piedi a qn.

toast [təʊst] **1** *n* **(a)** *(bread)* pane *m* tostato; **a piece of ~** una fetta di pane tostato. **(b)** *(drink)* brindisi *m inv*; **to propose/drink a ~ to sb** proporre (di fare)/fare un brindisi a qn; **the ~ of the town/ nation** *(fig)* il vanto della città/nazione. **2** *vt* **(a)** *(bread)* tostare. **(b)** *(drink to)* brindare a.

toast·er ['təʊstə[r]] *n* tostapane *m inv*.

toast-rack ['təʊstræk] *n* portatoast *m inv*.

to·bac·co [tə'bækəʊ] **1** *n* tabacco; **pipe ~** tabacco da pipa. **2** *cpd*: **~ pouch** *n* borsa per il tabacco.

to·bac·co·nist [tə'bækənɪst] *n* tabaccaio.

to·bog·gan [tə'bɒɡən] **1** *n* toboga *m inv*, slittino. **2** *vi* andare in slitta.

to·day [tə'deɪ] **1** *adv* oggi; *(these days)* al giorno d'oggi, oggigiorno; **a fortnight ~** quindici giorni a oggi; **what day is it ~?** che giorno è oggi?; **what date is it ~?** quanti ne abbiamo oggi?; **~ is the 4th of March** (oggi) è il 4 di marzo. **2** *n* oggi *m inv*;

writers of ~ gli scrittori d'oggi; ~'s **paper** il giornale di oggi.

tod·dle ['tɒdl] vi (child): **to** ~ **in/out** etc entrare/uscire etc a passettini; (adult): **he** ~**d off** se n'è andato camminando tranquillamente.

tod·dler ['tɒdlə^r] n (small child) bambino/a che fa i primi passi.

tod·dy ['tɒdɪ] n: **hot** ~ specie di ponce caldo.

to-do [tə'duː] n (fam: fuss): **to cause a** ~ fare delle storie.

toe [təʊ] **1** n (Anat) dito del piede; (of shoe) punta; **big** ~ alluce m; **little** ~ mignolino; **to keep sb on his** ~**s** (fig) tenere qn sull'attenti. **2** vt: **to** ~ **the line** (fig: conform) conformarsi alle regole.

toe·cap ['təʊkæp] n mascherina.

toe·nail ['təʊneɪl] n unghia del piede.

tof·fee ['tɒfɪ] **1** n caramella f mou inv; **he can't do it for** ~ (fam) non lo sa fare per niente. **2** cpd: ~ **apple** n mela caramellata.

to·geth·er [tə'geðə^r] adv **(a)** (gen) insieme; ~ **with** insieme a; **all** ~ tutti insieme; **they were both in it** ~ (pej) vi erano implicati entrambi; **we're in this** ~ siamo nella stessa barca; **to add 3 and 3** ~ fare 3 più 3; **to bring the 2 sides** ~ far mettere d'accordo le 2 parti; **to gather** ~ radunarsi; **to put a meal** ~ mettere insieme un pranzo or una cena. **(b)** (simultaneously) insieme, contemporaneamente; (continuously) di seguito.

to·geth·er·ness [tə'geðənɪs] n solidarietà.

tog·gle ['tɒgl] n (on coat) olivetta di legno.

togs [tɒgz] npl (fam: clothes) vestiti mpl.

toil [tɔɪl] **1** n duro lavoro, fatica. **2** vi lavorare sodo, faticare; **to** ~ **away at sth** sgobbare per fare qc; **to** ~ **up a hill** arrancare su per una collina.

toi·let ['tɔɪlɪt] **1** n **(a)** (lavatory) gabinetto; **to go to the** ~ andare al gabinetto or al bagno; **she's in the** ~ è in gabinetto or in bagno. **(b)** (dressing, washing etc) toilette; **she was at her** ~ si stava facendo la toilette. **2** cpd: ~ **bag** n nécessaire m inv da toilette; ~ **bowl** n vaso or tazza del gabinetto; ~ **paper** n carta igienica; ~ **roll** n rotolo di carta igienica; ~ **water** n acqua di colonia.

toi·let·ries ['tɔɪlɪtrɪz] npl articoli mpl da toilette.

to·ing and fro·ing ['tuːɪŋən'frəʊɪŋ] n andirivieni m inv.

to·ken ['təʊkən] **1** n **(a)** (voucher) buono; (metal disc) gettone m; **book/record** ~ buono per un libro/disco. **(b)** (sign, symbol) segno; **by the same** ~ (fig) per lo stesso motivo. **2** cpd (fee, strike) simbolico(a); (resistance, gesture) formale.

told [təʊld] pt, pp of **tell**.

tol·er·able ['tɒlərəbl] adj (pain, heat etc) sopportabile; (film, food etc) passabile, discreto(a).

tol·er·ably ['tɒlərəblɪ] adv (good, comfortable) abbastanza.

tol·er·ance ['tɒlərəns] n (of pain, hardship) sopportazione f; (of behaviour, Med, Tech) tolleranza.

tol·er·ant ['tɒlərənt] adj tollerante.

tol·er·ate ['tɒləreɪt] vt (gen) tollerare, sopportare.

tol·era·tion [ˌtɒlə'reɪʃən] n tolleranza.

toll¹ [təʊl] **1** n **(a)** (on road) pedaggio. **(b)** (losses, casualties): **the death** ~ **on the roads** il numero di vittime sulle strade; **the severe winter has taken its** ~ **on the crops** l'inverno rigido ha colpito duramente il raccolto. **2** cpd (road, bridge) a pedaggio.

toll² [təʊl] **1** vt, vi (bell) suonare lentamente e solennemente. **2** n (of bell) rintocco.

Tom [tɒm] n: **any** ~, **Dick or Harry** chiunque, il primo venuto.

tom [tɒm] n (also: ~**cat**) gatto.

to·ma·to [tə'mɑːtəʊ] **1** n, pl ~**es** pomodoro. **2** cpd (juice, sauce) di pomodoro.

tomb [tuːm] n tomba.

tom·bo·la [tɒm'bəʊlə] n tombola.

tom·boy ['tɒmbɔɪ] n maschiaccio.

tomb·stone ['tuːmstəʊn] n pietra tombale.

tome [təʊm] n tomo; (hum) librone m.

tom·fool·ery [ˌtɒm'fuːlərɪ] n sciocchezze fpl.

tom·my gun ['tɒmɪ,gʌn] n fucile m mitragliatore.

to·mor·row [tə'mɒrəʊ] adv, n domani (m inv); ~ **morning** domani mattina; ~ **is Sunday** domani è domenica; **the day after** ~ dopodomani; ~ **is another day** (fig) domani è un altro giorno; ~'s **paper** il giornale di domani.

tom-tom ['tɒmtɒm] n tamtam m inv.

ton [tʌn] n (weight: Brit) = 1016 kilogrammi; (metric ~) tonnellata; (Naut) tonnellata di stazza; (: displacement ~) tonnellata inglese; **this suitcase weighs a** ~ (fam) questa valigia pesa una tonnellata; ~**s of sth** (fam) un sacco di qc.

tone [təʊn] **1** n (gen) tono; (of colour) tonalità f inv; (of musical instrument) timbro; **dialling** ~ (Telec) segnale m di libero; **to praise sb in ringing** ~**s** (fig) portare qn alle stelle; **they were speaking in low** ~**s** parlavano a voce bassa; **two different** ~**s of red** due tonalità di rosso; **to raise/lower the** ~ **of sth** migliorare/abbassare il tono di qc. **2** vi (also: ~ **in**: colours) intonarsi.

♦ **tone down** vt + adv (moderate: colour) attenuare; (fig: language, criticism) moderare.

♦ **tone up** vt + adv (muscles) tonificare.

tone-deaf [ˌtəʊn'def] adj che non ha orecchio.

tongs [tɒŋz] npl (for coal) molle fpl; (for sugar, in laboratory) pinza; (curling ~) arricciacapelli m inv.

tongue [tʌŋ] n **(a)** (gen) lingua; (of shoe) linguetta; (of bell) battaglio; **have you lost your** ~? hai perso la lingua?; **hold your** ~! chiudi quella bocca!; **to put out one's** ~ (at sb) mostrare la lingua (a qn); **to say sth** ~ **in cheek** (fig) dire qc ironicamente. **(b)** (language) lingua.

tongue-tied ['tʌŋtaɪd] adj ammutolito(a).

tongue-twister ['tʌŋ,twɪstə^r] n scioglilingua m inv.

ton·ic ['tɒnɪk] n **(a)** (Med) ricostituente m; (skin ~ etc) tonico; **fresh air is the best** ~ **when you have a headache** l'aria fresca è il miglior rimedio per il mal di testa; **this will be a** ~ **to her** questo la tirerà su. **(b)**: ~ (**water**) acqua tonica.

to·night [tə'naɪt] adv (this evening) questa sera, stasera; (this night) questa notte, stanotte; **I'll see you** ~ ci vediamo stasera; ~'s **TV programmes** i programmi della serata.

ton·nage ['tʌnɪdʒ] n tonnellaggio.

tonne [tʌn] n (also: **metric ton**) tonnellata.

ton·sil ['tɒnsl] n tonsilla; **to have one's** ~**s out** farsi operare di tonsille.

ton·sil·li·tis [ˌtɒnsɪ'laɪtɪs] n tonsillite f; **to have** ~ avere la tonsillite.

too [tuː] adv **(a)** (excessively) troppo; **it's** ~ **sweet** è troppo dolce; **it's** ~ **sweet for me to drink** non lo bevo, è troppo dolce per me; **it's** ~ **heavy for me** è troppo pesante per me; **it's** ~ **heavy for me to lift** non riesco a sollevarlo, è troppo pesante per me; **it's** ~ **good to be true** è troppo bello per essere vero; **I'm not** ~ **sure about that** non ne sono troppo sicuro. **(b)** (also) anche; (moreover) per di più; **I went** ~ ci sono andato anch'io; **I speak French and Japanese** ~ parlo il francese e (anche) il giapponese; **not only that, he's blind** ~! non solo, ma è anche cieco!; **he's famous, intelligent and rich** ~ è famoso, intelligente e per di più anche ricco.

took [tʊk] pt of **take**.

tool [tuːl] n **(a)** (gen, Tech) attrezzo, arnese m; (set of) ~**s** (completo di) attrezzi; **the** ~**s of one's**

trade i ferri del mestiere. **(b)** *(fig: person)* strumento; **he was a mere ~ in their hands** non era che uno strumento *or* un fantoccio nelle loro mani.

tool·bag ['tuːlbæg] *n* borsa degli attrezzi.

tool·box ['tuːlbɒks] *n* cassetta degli attrezzi.

tool·kit ['tuːlkɪt] *n* corredo di attrezzi.

tool·shed ['tuːlʃed] *n* capanna per gli attrezzi.

toot [tuːt] **1** *n* colpo di clacson. **2** *vt*: **to ~ one's horn** suonare il clacson.

tooth [tuːθ] *n, pl* **teeth** *(Anat, Tech)* dente *m*; **to clean one's teeth** lavarsi i denti; **to have a ~ out** farsi togliere un dente; **to have a sweet ~** essere ghiotto di dolci; **long in the ~** *(fam: old)* vecchiotto; **to be fed up to the (back) teeth with sb/sth** *(fam)* averne fin sopra i capelli di qn/qc; **to get one's teeth into** *(fig: work)* impegnarsi a fondo in; *(: subject)* immergersi in; **armed to the teeth** armato fino ai denti; **to fight ~ and nail** combattere con le unghie e con i denti; **it sets my teeth on edge** mi fa venire i brividi; **by the skin of one's teeth** per il rotto della cuffia; **in the teeth of great opposition** malgrado la forte opposizione.

tooth·ache ['tuːθeɪk] *n* mal *m* di denti; **to have ~** avere il mal di denti.

tooth·brush ['tuːθbrʌʃ] *n* spazzolino da denti.

tooth·comb ['tuːθkəʊm] *n*: **to go through sth with a fine ~** passare qc al setaccio.

tooth·less ['tuːθlɪs] *adj* sdentato(a).

tooth·paste ['tuːθpeɪst] *n* dentifricio.

tooth·pick ['tuːθpɪk] *n* stuzzicadenti *m inv.*

toothy ['tuːθɪ] *adj* (**-ier, -iest**) *(fam)* che ha una dentatura cavallina; **to give sb a ~ smile** fare a qn un sorriso a trentadue denti.

top[1] [tɒp] **1** *n* **(a)** *(highest point: of hill, tree, stairs etc)* cima; *(: of list, table, queue)* testa; *(: of career)* apice *m*; **at the ~ of the hill** sulla cima della collina; **at the ~ of the stairs/page/street** in cima alle scale/alla pagina/alla strada; **at the ~ of the table** a capotavola; **to be ~ of the pops** essere in testa alla hit-parade; **Liverpool is at the ~ of the league** *(Sport)* il Liverpool è in testa alla classifica; **from ~ to bottom** *(fig)* da cima a fondo; **from ~ to toe** dalla testa ai piedi; **from the ~** dall'alto; **from the ~ of the hill** dalla cima della collina; **on ~** sopra; **to fall on ~ of sb** cadere addosso a qn; **he's going thin on ~** *(fam)* sta incominciando a perdere i capelli; **to reach the ~** *(fig: of career etc)* raggiungere l'apice; **the men at the ~** *(fig)* quelli che sono al potere.

(b) *(surface)* superficie *f*; *(: of box, cupboard)* sopra *m inv*, parte *f* superiore; *(roof: of car)* tetto; *(upper part: of bus)* piano superiore; **the ~ of the table needs wiping** bisogna pulire la superficie *or* il piano della tavola; **oil comes to the ~** l'olio sale alla superficie; **seats on the ~!** ci sono posti di sopra!; **the ~ of the milk** la panna.

(c) *(Dress: blouse etc)* camicia *(or* maglietta *etc)*; *(of pyjamas)* giacca.

(d) *(lid: of bottle)* tappo; *(: of box, jar)* coperchio; *(of pen)* tappo, cappuccio.

(e) *(~ gear)*: **to change into ~** mettere la quarta *(or* quinta).

(f) *(in phrases)*: **on ~ of (all)** that per di più, inoltre; **it's just one thing on ~ of another** è una cosa dietro un'altra; **to feel/be on ~ of the world** *(fam)* essere/sentirsi al settimo cielo; **to be/get on ~ of things** *(fig)* dominare/cominciare a dominare la situazione; **things are getting on ~ of me** *(fam)* mi sta precipitando tutto addosso; **to come out on ~** *(fig)* uscire vincitore; **I can't tell you off the ~ of my head** a mente non te lo posso dire; **at the ~ of one's voice** *(fig)* a squarciagola.

2 *adj* **(a)** *(highest: floor, step)* ultimo(a); *(: shelf, drawer etc)* (ultimo(a)) in alto, più alto(a); *(: price, in rank)* più alto(a); **at ~ speed** a tutta velocità; **~ gear** la marcia più alta; **the ~ men in the party** i dirigenti del partito; **a ~ job** un posto di prestigio; **she's ~ dog at work** *(fig fam)* è un pezzo grosso sul lavoro.

(b) *(best)* migliore; **to get ~ marks** avere i voti migliori; **to come ~ of the class** avere i voti più alti di tutta la classe, riuscire il migliore della classe; **he came ~ in maths** ha avuto i voti migliori in matematica; **the ~ twenty** *(Mus)* i venti migliori dischi (della settimana); **to be on ~ form** *(fam)* sentirsi veramente in forma; **a ~ surgeon** un grande chirurgo.

(c) *(last: layer etc)* ultimo(a); **the ~ coat (of paint)** l'ultima mano (di vernice); **she is in the ~ class at school** sta facendo l'ultimo anno di scuola.

3 *vt* **(a)** sormontare; **a church ~ped by a steeple** una chiesa sormontata da un campanile; **to ~ a cake with cream** coprire una torta di panna.

(b): **to ~ the bill** *(Theatre)* avere il primo posto sul cartellone.

(c) *(exceed)* superare; **and to ~ it all...** *(fig)* e per finire...; **profits ~ped £5000 last year** i profitti hanno superato le 5000 sterline l'anno scorso.

(d) *(vegetables, fruit)* tagliare le punte a; **to ~ and tail fruit** tagliare le punte e i gambi alla frutta.

4 *cpd*: **~ hat** *n* cilindro.

♦ **top up** *vt* + *adv* riempire; **to ~ sb's glass up** riempire il bicchiere a qn, dare ancora da bere a qn; **to ~ up a battery** fare un rabbocco alla batteria.

top[2] [tɒp] *n* **(a)** *(toy)* trottola. **(b)** *(Circus)*: **the big ~** il tendone del circo.

to·paz ['təʊpæz] *n* topazio.

top·coat ['tɒpkəʊt] *n* *(overcoat)* soprabito.

top·flight ['tɒpflaɪt] *adj* di primaria importanza.

top·heavy [ˌtɒp'hevɪ] *adj* *(structure etc)* troppo pesante in alto; **this company is ~** *(fig)* ci sono troppi dirigenti in questa società.

top·ic ['tɒpɪk] *n* *(of conversation)* argomento; *(of essay)* soggetto.

topi·cal ['tɒpɪkəl] *adj* d'attualità; **a highly ~ question** un argomento di grande attualità.

top·less ['tɒplɪs] *adj* *(girl)* a seno scoperto; **~ bathing suit** topless *m inv.*

top·level ['tɒpˌlevl] *adj* ad alto livello.

top·most ['tɒpməʊst] *adj* il(la) più alto(a).

to·pog·ra·phy [tə'pɒgrəfɪ] *n* topografia.

top·per ['tɒpəʳ] *n* *(fam)* cilindro.

top·ping ['tɒpɪŋ] *n* *(Culin)* guarnizione *f.*

top·ple ['tɒpl] *vt* *(fig: overthrow)* far cadere.

♦ **topple over** *vi* + *adv* cadere; **he ~d over a cliff** è caduto da una scogliera.

top·ranking [ˌtɒp'ræŋkɪŋ] *adj* di massimo grado.

top·secret ['tɒp'siːkrɪt] *adj* segretissimo(a).

topsy·turvy ['tɒpsɪ'tɜːvɪ] *adj, adv* sottosopra *(inv).*

top·up ['tɒpʌp] *n* *(Brit fam: refill)*: **would you like a ~?** vuoi che ti riempia la tazza *(or* il bicchiere *etc)*?

torch [tɔːtʃ] *n* *(electric)* torcia elettrica, lampadina tascabile; *(flaming)* torcia, fiaccola; **to carry a ~ for sb** *(fig)* essere innamorato cotto di qn.

tore ['tɔːʳ] *pt of* **tear**[1].

tor·ment ['tɔːment] **1** *n* tormento, tortura; **to be in ~** *(also fig)* soffrire le pene dell'inferno. **2** [tɔː'ment] *vt* *(hurt)* tormentare; *(annoy)* molestare, stuzzicare; **she was ~ed by doubts** era tormentata *or* assillata dai dubbi.

tor·men·tor [tɔːˈmɛntəʳ] *n* tormentatore/trice.

torn [tɔːn] *pp of* **tear**[1].

tor·na·do [tɔːˈneɪdəʊ] *n, pl* **~es** tornado *m inv*.

tor·pe·do [tɔːˈpiːdəʊ] **1** *n, pl* **~es** siluro. **2** *vt* silurare. **3** *cpd*: **~ boat** *n* motosilurante *f*.

tor·pid [ˈtɔːpɪd] *adj* intorpidito(a).

tor·por [ˈtɔːpəʳ] *n* torpore *m*.

tor·rent [ˈtɒrənt] *n (also fig)* torrente *m;* **we got caught in a ~ of rain** una pioggia torrenziale ci ha sorpresi.

tor·ren·tial [tɒˈrɛnʃəl] *adj* torrenziale.

tor·rid [ˈtɒrɪd] *adj* torrido(a); *(fig)* denso(a) di passione.

tor·so [ˈtɔːsəʊ] *n (Anat)* torso; *(Sculpture)* busto.

tor·toise [ˈtɔːtəs] *n* tartaruga.

tortoise·shell [ˈtɔːtəsʃɛl] *n* guscio di tartaruga.

tor·tu·ous [ˈtɔːtjʊəs] *adj* tortuoso(a).

tor·ture [ˈtɔːtʃəʳ] **1** *n* tortura; **it was sheer ~!** *(fig)* è stata una vera tortura. **2** *vt* torturare; *(fig)* tormentare.

tor·tur·er [ˈtɔːtʃərəʳ] *n* torturatore/trice.

Tory [ˈtɔːrɪ] *adj, n* conservatore(trice) *(m/f)*.

toss [tɒs] **1** *n* **(a)** *(movement: of head etc)* movimento brusco; **with a ~ of the head** con una scrollata del capo; **to take a ~** *(from horse)* fare una caduta. **(b)** *(of coin)* lancio; **to win/lose the ~** vincere/ perdere a testa e croce; *(Sport)* vincere/perdere il sorteggio; **it's pointless to argue the ~** *(fam)* è inutile stare a discutere.

2 *vt* **(a)** *(move: head etc)* muovere bruscamente; **the boat was ~ed by the waves** l'imbarcazione era sballottata dalle onde. **(b)** *(throw: ball)* lanciare; *(: head)* buttare all'indietro; *(subj: horse: head)* tirare su; *(: mane)* agitare; *(: rider)* disarcionare; *(subj: bull)* lanciare in aria; **to ~ sth to sb** lanciare qc a qn; **to ~ a pancake** far saltare in aria una crêpe; **to ~ a coin** lanciare in aria una moneta; **I'll ~ you for it** ce lo giochiamo a testa e croce.

3 *vi* **(a)** *(also:* **~ about, ~ around)** agitarsi; *(: boat)* rollare e beccheggiare; **to ~ (in one's sleep), ~ and turn** agitarsi nel sonno, girarsi e rigirarsi. **(b)** *(also:* **~ up)** tirare a sorte, fare a testa e croce; **we ~ed (up) for the last piece of cake** abbiamo fatto a testa e croce per l'ultima fetta di torta.

toss-up [ˈtɒsʌp] *n (fig fam)*: **it's a ~ between going to the cinema and going for a meal** è uguale andare al cinema o a mangiare fuori; **it's a ~ between the two candidates** i due candidati hanno le stesse probabilità.

tot [tɒt] *n* **(a)** *(child)* bimbetto/a. **(b)** *(drink)* bicchierino; **a ~ of rum** un bicchierino di rum.

♦ **tot up** *vt + adv* sommare.

to·tal [ˈtəʊtl] **1** *adj (complete, utter)* totale, completo(a); *(sum)* globale; **the ~ losses amount to...** il totale delle perdite ammonta a...; **a ~ failure** un vero fiasco, un assoluto disastro; **he was in ~ ignorance of the fact that...** non sapeva assolutamente che... . **2** *n* totale *m;* **grand ~** somma globale; **in ~** in tutto. **3** *vt (also:* **~ up:** *add)* sommare; *(: amount to)* ammontare a.

to·tali·tar·ian [ˌtəʊtælɪˈtɛərɪən] *adj* totalitario(a).

to·tal·ity [təʊˈtælɪtɪ] *n* totalità.

to·tal·ly [ˈtəʊtəlɪ] *adv* completamente.

tote[1] [təʊt] *n (Racing)* totalizzatore *m*.

tote[2] [təʊt] **1** *vt (fam)* trascinare; **to ~ a gun** portare il fucile. **2** *cpd*: **~ bag** *n* sporta.

to·tem pole [ˈtəʊtəm pəʊl] *n* totem *m inv*.

tot·ter [ˈtɒtəʳ] *vi (person)* camminare barcollando; *(object, government)* vacillare; **to ~ in/out** *etc* entrare/uscire *etc* barcollando.

touch [tʌtʃ] **1** *n* **(a)** *(sense)* tatto; *(act of ~ing)* contatto; **rough to the ~** ruvido al tatto; **by ~** al tatto; **at the slightest ~** al minimo contatto; **the ~ of her hand** il solo tocco della sua mano; **a soft ~** *(fig fam)* una persona sempre disponibile; **a pianist with a delicate ~** un pianista dal tocco raffinato; **the personal ~** una nota personale; **it has a ~ of genius** è geniale; **to lose one's ~** *(fig)* perdere la mano; *(: with people)* perdere il proprio fascino; **to put the finishing ~es to sth** dare gli ultimi ritocchi a qc.

(b) *(small quantity)* pizzico; **a ~ of irony** una punta d'ironia; **to have a ~ of flu** avere una leggera influenza.

(c) *(contact)* contatto; **to be in ~ with sb** essere in contatto con qn; **I'll be in ~** mi farò sentire; **you can get in ~ with me here** mi puoi rintracciare qui; **to keep in ~ with sb** mantenere i rapporti con qn; **to lose ~ with sb** perdere di vista qn; **to be out of ~ with events** essere tagliato fuori.

(d) *(Ftbl, Rugby)*: **the ball is in ~** la palla è fuori gioco.

2 *vt* **(a)** *(gen)* toccare; *(brush lightly, fig: topic, problem)* sfiorare; **she ~ed his arm** gli ha toccato il braccio; **his hair ~es his shoulders** i capelli gli sfiorano le spalle; **~ wood!** tocchiamo ferro!; **to ~ sb for £5** *(fam)* chiedere 5 sterline in prestito a qn.

(b) *(neg phrases)*: **I never ~ gin** non tocco mai il gin; **you haven't ~ed your cheese** non hai neppure toccato il formaggio; **if you admit nothing, they can't ~ you** *(fig)* se non confessi, non ti possono toccare.

(c) *(move)* commuovere; *(affect)* riguardare; **I am ~ed by your offer** la tua offerta mi commuove; **she was ~ed by his gift** fu commossa dal suo regalo; **it ~es all our lives** riguarda tutti noi, ci tocca tutti.

(d) *(compare)* uguagliare; **nobody can ~ them for quality** per quanto riguarda la qualità non li batte nessuno; **no artist in the country can ~ him** non c'è artista nel paese che lo possa uguagliare.

3 *vi (hands)* toccarsi; *(property, gardens)* confinare; **our hands ~ed** le nostre mani si sono sfiorate; **'do not ~'** 'non toccare'.

♦ **touch down 1** *vt + adv (Rugby)* segnare una meta. **2** *vi + adv (on land)* atterrare; *(on sea)* ammarare; *(on moon)* allunare.

♦ **touch off** *vt + adv (argument etc)* provocare.

♦ **touch on** *vi + prep*: **to ~ on a subject** sfiorare un argomento.

♦ **touch up** *vt + adv* **(a)** *(improve)* ritoccare. **(b)** *(fam: sexually)* mettere le mani addosso a.

touch-and-go [ˌtʌtʃənˈgəʊ] *adj*: **it's ~ whether...** è incerto se...; **it was ~ with the sick man** il malato era tra la vita e la morte.

touch·down [ˈtʌtʃdaʊn] *n (on land)* atterraggio; *(on sea)* ammaraggio; *(on moon)* allunaggio.

touched [tʌtʃt] *adj (fam: crazy)* tocco(a).

touch·ing [ˈtʌtʃɪŋ] *adj* commovente.

touch·line [ˈtʌtʃlaɪn] *n (Ftbl)* linea laterale; *(Rugby)* linea di touche.

touch-type [ˈtʌtʃtaɪp] *vi* dattilografare *(senza guardare i tasti)*.

touchy [ˈtʌtʃɪ] *adj (person)* permaloso(a); *(subject)* delicato(a); **he's ~ about his weight** è molto suscettibile quando si parla del suo peso.

tough [tʌf] **1** *adj* **(-er, -est) (a)** *(substance, fabric)* resistente; *(meat, conditions, regulations)* duro(a); *(journey)* faticoso(a), duro(a); *(task, problem, situation)* difficile; *(fig: resistance, fight)* accanito(a); **as** ~ **as old boots** duro come una suola di scarpa; ~ **opposition** opposizione tenace. **(b)** *(person: hardy, resilient)* robusto(a), resistente; *(: mentally strong)* resistente, tenace; *(: hard: in character)* inflessibile; *(: rough)* violento(a), brutale; **they got** ~ **with the workers** hanno adottato una politica inflessibile con i lavoratori; **he's a** ~ **man to deal with** è un tipo difficile; **a** ~ **guy** un duro; **he's a** ~ **customer** *(fam)* è un prepotente. **(c)** *(unfortunate)*: ~ **luck!** *(fam)* che sfortuna!; **but it was** ~ **on the others** ma è stata una sfortuna per gli altri.

   2 *n* *(fam: person)* delinquente *m/f*.
tough·en ['tʌfn] *vt* *(also:* ~ **up:** *substance)* rinforzare; *(: metal)* indurire; *(: person)* rendere più forte.
tough·ness ['tʌfnɪs] *n* *(see adj)* **(a)** resistenza; durezza; difficoltà; accanimento. **(b)** resistenza; tenacia; inflessibilità; violenza.
tou·pee ['tu:peɪ] *n* toupet *m* *inv.*
tour ['tʊəʳ] **1** *n* *(gen)* giro; *(of building, exhibition, town)* visita; *(by musicians, team, actors)* tournée *f* *inv*; **a round the world** ~ un giro del mondo; **package** ~ viaggio organizzato; **to go on a** ~ **of** *(region, country)* fare il giro di; *(museum, castle)* visitare; **to go on a walking/cycling** ~ **of** Tuscany fare il giro della Toscana a piedi/in bicicletta; **on** ~ *(Theatre)* in tournée; **to go on** ~ andare in tournée; ~ **of inspection** giro d'ispezione. **2** *vt* *(subj: tourists)* fare un giro di, fare un viaggio in; *(: musicians, team etc)* fare una tournée in. **3** *vi*: **to go** ~**ing** andare a fare un viaggio; **a** ~**ing company** *(Theatre)* una compagnia in tournée. **4** *cpd*: ~ **operator** *n* operatore *m* turistico.
tour·ism ['tʊərɪzəm] *n* turismo.
tour·ist ['tʊərɪst] **1** *n* turista *m/f*. **2** *cpd* *(attraction, season)* turistico(a); ~ **agency** *n* agenzia di viaggi e turismo; ~ **class** *n* classe *f* turistica; ~ **office** *n* ufficio del turismo; **the** ~ **trade** il turismo.
tour·na·ment ['tʊənəmənt] *n* torneo; **tennis** ~ torneo di tennis.
tour·ni·quet ['tʊənɪkeɪ] *n* *(Med)* laccio emostatico, pinza emostatica.
tou·sled ['taʊzld] *adj* *(hair)* arruffato(a); *(bedclothes)* sottosopra *inv.*
tout [taʊt] **1** *n* *(for hotels etc)* procacciatore *m* di clienti; *(ticket* ~*)* bagarino; *(Racing)* portaquote *m* *inv*. **2** *vi*: **to** ~ **for business** sollecitare ordinazioni; *(for hotels)* procacciare clienti.
tow [təʊ] **1** *n* rimorchio; **to give sb a** ~ *(Aut)* rimorchiare qn; **on** ~ a rimorchio; **he arrived with a friend in** ~ *(fig fam)* si è portato dietro un amico. **2** *vt* *(boat, car, caravan)* rimorchiare; **to** ~ **a car away** portar via una macchina con il carro attrezzi.
to·ward(s) [təˈwɔːd(z)] *prep* *(gen)* verso; *(of attitude)* nei confronti di, verso; **we walked** ~ **the sea** ci siamo incamminati verso il mare; **the government is moving** ~ **disaster** il governo si avvia al disastro; ~ **noon/the end of the year** verso mezzogiorno/la fine dell'anno; **your attitude** ~ **him** il tuo atteggiamento nei suoi confronti *or* verso di lui; **to feel friendly** ~ **sb** provare un sentimento d'amicizia per qn; **to save** ~ **sth** risparmiare per comprare qc; **half my salary goes** ~ **paying the rent** metà del mio stipendio se ne va per l'affitto *or* in affitto.
tow·el ['taʊəl] **1** *n* *(for hands)* asciugamano; *(tea*~, *dish*~*)* strofinaccio; **to throw in the** ~ *(fig)* gettare la spugna. **2** *cpd*: ~ **rail** *n* portasciugamano. **3** *vt*: **to** ~ **o.s. dry** asciugarsi con l'asciugamano.
tow·el·ling ['taʊəlɪŋ] *n* *(tessuto a)* spugna.
tow·er ['taʊəʳ] **1** *n* *(of castle, church etc)* torre *f*; **the**

T~ **of London** la Torre di Londra; **he was a** ~ **of strength to me** mi è stato di grande appoggio. **2** *vi* *(building, mountain)* innalzarsi; **to** ~ **above** *or* **over sb/sth** sovrastare qn/qc. **3** *cpd*: ~ **block** *n* grattacielo.
tow·er·ing ['taʊərɪŋ] *adj* *(building, figure)* imponente; **in a** ~ **rage** *(fig)* in preda a un violento accesso d'ira.
town [taʊn] **1** *n* città *f* *inv*; **to live in a** ~ vivere in città; **to be out of** ~ essere fuori città; **to go (in) to** ~ andare in città *or* in centro; **in the** ~ in città; **to go out on the** ~ *(fam)* uscire a far baldoria; **to go to** ~ **on sth** *(fig fam)* fare qc in grande. **2** *cpd* *(centre)* della città; *(life)* di città; *(house)* in città; ~ **clerk** *n* segretario comunale; ~ **council** *n* consiglio comunale; ~ **hall** *n* municipio; ~ **planning** *n* pianificazione *f* urbana; *(study)* urbanistica.
towns·people ['taʊnz,pi:pl] *npl* cittadinanza, cittadini *mpl*.
tow·path ['taʊpɑːθ] *n* alzaia.
tow·rope ['taʊrəʊp] *n* cavo per rimorchio.
tox·ic ['tɒksɪk] *adj* tossico(a).
tox·in ['tɒksɪn] *n* tossina.
toy [tɔɪ] **1** *n* giocattolo. **2** *cpd* *(railway, house)* in miniatura; ~ **poodle** *n* barboncino nano; ~ **car** *n* automobilina, modellino; ~ **soldier** *n* soldatino; ~ **train** *n* trenino.
♦ **toy with** *vi* + *prep* **(a)** *(play with: object)* giocherellare con; *(: food)* trastullarsi con; *(: affections)* giocare con. **(b)** *(consider: idea)* accarezzare.
toy·box ['tɔɪbɒks] *n* baule *m* per i giocattoli.
toy·shop ['tɔɪʃɒp] *n* negozio di giocattoli.
trace [treɪs] **1** *n* *(sign)* traccia; **there was no** ~ **of it** non ne restava traccia; **to vanish without** ~ sparire senza lasciar traccia; **I've lost all** ~ **of them** ho perso completamente le loro tracce; **the postmortem revealed** ~**s of poison in the blood** l'autopsia ha rivelato tracce di veleno nel sangue. **2** *vt* **(a)** *(draw)* tracciare; *(: with tracing paper)* ricalcare. **(b)** *(follow)* seguire le tracce di; *(find, locate)* rintracciare; **I cannot** ~ **any reference to the matter** non riesco a rintracciare alcun riferimento alla faccenda. **3** *cpd*: ~ **element** *n* oligoelemento.
♦ **trace back** *vt* + *adv*: **they** ~**ed the weapon back to here** hanno stabilito che l'arma proviene da qui; **to** ~ **back one's family** to rintracciare le origini della propria famiglia fino a.
tra·chea [trəˈkɪə] *n* *(Anat)* trachea.
trac·ing pa·per ['treɪsɪŋ,peɪpəʳ] *n* carta da ricalco.
track [træk] **1** *n* **(a)** *(mark: of person, animal)* orma, impronta; *(: of vehicle)* solco; *(: of ship)* scia; **to be on sb's** ~ essere sulle tracce di qn; **to follow in sb's** ~**s** *(also fig)* seguire le orme di qn; **to keep** ~ **of** *(fig: person)* seguire le tracce di; *(: keep in touch with)* restare in contatto con; *(: event)* essere al corrente di; **to lose** ~ **of** *(fig: person)* perdere le tracce di; *(: lose contact with)* perdere di vista; *(: event)* non essere al corrente di; **to lose** ~ **of an argument** perdere il filo del discorso; **to make** ~**s (for)** *(fig fam)* avviarsi (a *or* verso).

   (b) *(path)* sentiero; *(: of comet, rocket etc)* traiettoria; **to be on the right** ~ *(fig)* essere sulla buona strada; **to be on the wrong** ~ *(fig)* essere fuori strada; **to throw sb off the** ~ *(fig)* mettere qn fuori strada.

   (c) *(Sport)* pista.

   (d) *(Rail)* binario; **on the right/wrong side of the** ~**s** *(Am fam)* nei quartieri alti/nella zona povera della città.

   (e) *(Mus: tape)* pista; **a 4-**~ **tape** un nastro a 4 piste; **the first** ~ **on the record/tape** la prima canzone del disco/nastro.

    2 vt (person, animal) seguire le tracce di.

    3 cpd: ~ **events** npl (Sport) prove fpl su pista; ~ **record** n: **to have a good** ~ **record** (fig) avere un buon curriculum.

♦ **track down** vt + adv (locate: person) seguire le tracce di e catturare; (: letter) rintracciare.

track·er dog ['trækə,dɒg] n cane m poliziotto inv.

track·ing sta·tion ['trækɪŋ ,steɪʃən] n (Space) osservatorio spaziale.

track·suit ['træksuːt] n tuta da ginnastica.

tract[1] [trækt] n **(a)** (area) distesa. **(b)** (Anat): **respiratory** ~ apparato respiratorio.

tract[2] [trækt] n (pamphlet) trattatello.

trac·table ['træktəbl] adj (person) accomodante; (animal) docile.

trac·tion ['trækʃən] **1** n trazione f. **2** cpd: ~ **engine** n trattrice f.

trac·tor ['træktəʳ] n trattore m.

trade [treɪd] **1** n **(a)** (commerce) commercio; (business) affari mpl; **to do** ~ **with sb** fare affari con qn, essere in rapporti commerciali con qn; **foreign** ~ commercio estero; **to do a brisk or roaring** ~ fare affari d'oro; **Board of T**~ (Brit), **Department of T**~ (Am) Ministero del Commercio. **(b)** (industry) industria, settore m; **he's in the cotton/building** ~ è nell'industria cotoniera/edilizia; **the book** ~ l'editoria. **(c)** (profession) mestiere m; **he's a butcher by** ~ di mestiere fa il macellaio; **tailoring is a useful** ~ quello del sarto è un mestiere utile; **to sell to the** ~ vendere all'ingrosso.

    2 vt (fig: exchange sth for sth) barattare; **he** ~**d his tennis racquet for a football** ha barattato la sua racchetta da tennis con un pallone.

    3 vi: **to** ~ **in sth** commerciare in qc; **to** ~ **with sb** fare affari con qn, intrattenere relazioni commerciali con qn.

    4 cpd (association, fair, route etc) commerciale; ~ **agreement** n accordo commerciale; ~ **deficit** n bilancio commerciale in deficit; **T**~ **Descriptions Act** n legge f a tutela del consumatore; ~ **discount** n sconto sul listino; ~ **name** n nome m depositato; (of a company) ragione f sociale; ~ **price/value** n prezzo all'ingrosso; ~ **secret** n segreto di fabbricazione; ~ **wind** n aliseo.

♦ **trade in** vt + adv cedere in permuta.

trade-in ['treɪdɪn] **1** n: **to take as a** ~ accettare in permuta. **2** cpd: ~ **price/value** n prezzo/valore m di permuta.

trade·mark ['treɪdmɑːk] n (Comm) marchio di fabbrica; (fig) marchio.

trad·er ['treɪdəʳ] n commerciante m/f.

trades·man ['treɪdzmən] n, pl **-men** fornitore m; (shopkeeper) negoziante m; ~**'s entrance** ingresso per i fornitori or di servizio.

trade(s) un·ion [,treɪd(z)'juːnjən] **1** n sindacato. **2: trade-union** cpd (official) sindacale.

trade(s) un·ion·ism [,treɪd(z)'juːnjənɪzəm] n sindacalismo.

trade(s) un·ion·ist [,treɪd(z)'juːnjənɪst] n sindacalista m/f.

trad·ing ['treɪdɪŋ] adj (port, centre) commerciale; (nation) che vive di commercio; ~ **estate** (Brit) zona industriale; ~ **stamp** bollo premio.

tra·di·tion [trə'dɪʃən] n tradizione f.

tra·di·tion·al [trə'dɪʃənl] adj tradizionale.

tra·di·tion·al·ly [trə'dɪʃnəlɪ] adv per tradizione.

traf·fic ['træfɪk] (vb: pt, pp ~**ked**) **1** n traffico; **rail** ~ traffico ferroviario; **the** ~ **is heavy during the rush hour** il traffico è molto intenso nelle ore di punta; **closed to heavy** ~ (Aut) divieto di transito

per gli automezzi pesanti; **drug** ~ traffico di droga. **2** vi: **to** ~ **(in)** trafficare (in). **3** cpd (Aut: regulations etc) stradale; ~ **island** n salvagente m, isola f spartitraffico inv; ~ **jam** n ingorgo; **a 5-mile** ~ **jam** una coda di 5 miglia; ~ **lights** npl semaforo; ~ **offence** n infrazione f al codice stradale; ~ **warden** n vigile/essa (urbano(a)).

traf·fick·er ['træfɪkəʳ] n trafficante m/f.

trag·edy ['trædʒɪdɪ] n (gen, Theatre) tragedia; **it is a** ~ **that...** è una vera disgrazia che... .

trag·ic ['trædʒɪk] adj tragico(a).

tragi·cal·ly ['trædʒɪkəlɪ] adv tragicamente.

tragi·com·edy ['trædʒɪ'kɒmɪdɪ] n tragicommedia.

trail [treɪl] **1** n **(a)** (of dust, smoke etc) scia; **the hurricane left a** ~ **of destruction** l'uragano non ha lasciato altro che distruzione dietro di sé. **(b)** (track) orma; **to be on sb's** ~ essere sulle orme di qn. **(c)** (path) sentiero. **2** vt **(a)** (drag) trascinare; **don't** ~ **mud into the house** non portare fango in casa. **(b)** (track: animal) seguire le orme di; (: person) pedinare. **3** vi **(a)** (object) strisciare; (plant) arrampicarsi; **to** ~ **by 2 goals** (Sport) essere in svantaggio di 2 goal. **(b)** (wearily: also: ~ **along**) trascinarsi.

♦ **trail away, trail off** vi + adv (sound) affievolirsi; (interest, voice) spegnersi a poco a poco.

trail·er ['treɪləʳ] n **(a)** (Aut) rimorchio; (for horses) van m inv; (Am: caravan) roulotte f inv. **(b)** (Cine) 'prossimamente' m inv.

train [treɪn] **1** n **(a)** (Rail) treno; **to go by** ~ andare in or col treno; **to travel by** ~ viaggiare in treno; **in** or **on the** ~ in treno, sul treno; **to take the 3.00** ~ prendere il treno delle 3; **to change** ~**s** cambiare treno. **(b)** (line: of animals, vehicles etc) fila; (entourage) seguito; (of admirers) codazzo. **(c)** (series): ~ **of events** serie f di avvenimenti a catena; **my** ~ **of thought** il filo dei miei pensieri; **the earthquake brought great suffering in its** ~ il terremoto ha portato con sé disgrazie e sofferenze. **(d)** (of dress) strascico.

    2 vt **(a)** (instruct) istruire; (Mil) addestrare; (Sport, mind, memory) allenare; (animal) ammaestrare; **to** ~ **sb to do sth** preparare qn a fare qc. **(b)**: **to** ~ **(on)** (direct: gun) puntare (contro); (: camera, telescope) puntare (a or verso).

    3 vi **(a)** (learn a skill) fare pratica, fare tirocinio; **to** ~ **as or to be a lawyer** fare pratica come avvocato; **where did you** ~? dove hai fatto pratica or tirocinio? **(b)** (Sport): **to** ~ **(for)** allenarsi (per).

    4 cpd: ~ **service** n collegamento ferroviario; **electric** ~ **set** n trenino elettrico.

trained [treɪnd] adj (accountant, nurse etc) diplomato(a); (teacher) abilitato(a) all'insegnamento; (Sport: athlete, horse) allenato(a); (animal) ammaestrato(a); **well-**~ (child, dog) ben educato; **I've got him well-**~ (hum) l'ho addomesticato per bene.

trainee [treɪ'niː] **1** n (gen) apprendista m/f; (for profession) tirocinante m/f; **she's a management** ~ sta facendo tirocinio come dirigente. **2** cpd: **he's a** ~ **teacher** sta facendo tirocinio come insegnante; **to be a** ~ **typist** fare pratica come dattilografa.

train·er ['treɪnəʳ] n **(a)** (Sport) allenatore/trice; (of circus animals) domatore/trice. **(b)**: ~**s** pl (shoes) scarpe fpl da ginnastica.

train·ing ['treɪnɪŋ] **1** n (in job) pratica, tirocinio; (Mil) addestramento; (Sport) allenamento; **to be in** ~ essere in allenamento; **to be out of** ~ essere fuori allenamento. **2** cpd (scheme, centre: for job) di formazione professionale; (Sport) di addestramento; ~ **college** n istituto professionale; ~

course n corso di formazione professionale; ~ **shoes** npl scarpe fpl da ginnastica.

train-spotting ['treɪnspɒtɪŋ] n: **to go** ~ andare a osservare i treni.

traipse [treɪps] **1** vi (fam): **to** ~ **in/out** etc entrare/ uscire etc trascinandosi. **2** n: **a long** ~ una camminata sfiancante.

trait [treɪt] n caratteristica.

trai·tor ['treɪtəʳ] n traditore/trice; **to turn** ~ passare al nemico.

tra·jec·tory [trə'dʒɛktərɪ] n traiettoria.

tram [træm] n, **tram·car** ['træmkɑːʳ] n (Brit) tram m inv.

tram·lines ['træmlaɪnz] npl **(a)** rotaie fpl del tram. **(b)** (Tennis) corridoio.

tramp [træmp] **1** n **(a)** (sound of feet) rumore m pesante (di passi). **(b)** (long walk) camminata; **to go for a** ~ **in the hills** andare a fare una camminata sui colli. **(c)** (person) vagabondo/a; **she's a** ~ (fam pej) è una sgualdrina. **2** vt: **to** ~ **the streets looking for sth** battere le strade in cerca di qc. **3** vi camminare a passi pesanti; **the soldiers** ~**ed past** i soldati sono passati marciando pesantemente; **he** ~**ed up to the door** si è avvicinato con passi pesanti alla porta.

tram·ple ['træmpl] vt (crush) calpestare.

♦ **trample on** vi + prep calpestare; **to** ~ **on sb's feelings** (fig) calpestare i sentimenti di qn.

tram·po·line ['træmpəlɪn] n trampolino americano.

trance [trɑːns] n trance f inv; **to go into a** ~ cadere in trance.

tran·quil ['træŋkwɪl] adj tranquillo(a).

tran·quil·lity, (Am) **tran·quil·ity** [træŋ'kwɪlɪtɪ] n tranquillità.

tran·quil·liz·er, (Am) **tran·quil·iz·er** ['træŋkwɪlaɪzəʳ] n (Med) tranquillante m.

trans... [trænz] pref trans... .

trans·act [trænz'ækt] vt (conduct) trattare; (carry through) concludere.

trans·ac·tion [træn'zækʃən] n (business) trattativa; (in bank) operazione f; **cash** ~**s** operazioni in contanti.

trans·at·lan·tic [ˌtrænzət'læntɪk] adj transatlantico(a).

trans·cend [træn'sɛnd] vt trascendere, superare.

trans·cend·ent [træn'sɛndənt] adj trascendente.

tran·scen·den·tal [ˌtrænsɛn'dɛntl] adj trascendentale; ~ **meditation** meditazione f trascendentale.

tran·scribe [træn'skraɪb] vt trascrivere.

tran·scrip·tion [træn'skrɪpʃən] n trascrizione f.

trans·fer ['trænsfəʳ] **1** n **(a)** trasferimento; (Law) cessione f; **by bank** ~ tramite trasferimento bancario. **(b)** (picture) decalcomania. **2** [træns'fɜːʳ] vt: **to** ~ **(from/to)** (move) trasferire (da/a); (Sport) essere ceduto(a) (da/a); **to** ~ **one's affections/ambitions to sb** trasferire i propri sentimenti/le proprie ambizioni su qn; **to** ~ **money from one account to another** trasferire il denaro da un conto su un altro; **to** ~ **sth to sb's name** mettere qc a nome di qn; **to make a** ~**red charge call** fare una chiamata a carico del destinatario. **3** [træns'fɜːʳ] vi (gen) trasferirsi; **she** ~**red from History to Classics** (Univ etc) è passata da Storia a Lettere Antiche.

trans·fer·able [træns'fɜːrəbl] adj trasferibile; **not** ~ non cedibile, personale.

trans·fig·ure [træns'fɪgəʳ] vt trasfigurare.

trans·fix [træns'fɪks] vt trafiggere; (fig): ~**ed with fear** paralizzato dalla paura.

trans·form [træns'fɔːm] vt trasformare.

trans·for·ma·tion [ˌtrænsfə'meɪʃən] n trasformazione f.

trans·form·er [træns'fɔːməʳ] n (Elec) trasformatore m.

trans·fu·sion [træns'fjuːʒən] n trasfusione f; **to give sb a blood** ~ praticare una trasfusione di sangue a qn.

trans·gress [træns'grɛs] vt (go beyond) infrangere; (violate) trasgredire, infrangere.

tran·si·ent ['trænzɪənt] adj transitorio(a).

tran·sis·tor [træn'zɪstəʳ] **1** n (Elec) transistor m inv. **2** cpd: ~ **radio** n (radio f inv a) transistor m inv.

tran·sis·tor·ized [træn'zɪstəraɪzd] adj (circuit) transistorizzato(a).

trans·it ['trænzɪt] **1** n transito; **in** ~ in transito; **their luggage was lost in** ~ il loro bagaglio è stato smarrito durante il trasferimento. **2** cpd: ~ **camp** n campo (di raccolta) profughi; ~ **visa** n visto di transito.

tran·si·tion [træn'zɪʃən] **1** n transizione f. **2** cpd: ~ **period** n periodo di transizione.

tran·si·tive ['trænzɪtɪv] adj transitivo(a).

tran·si·tory ['trænzɪtərɪ] adj transitorio(a).

trans·late [trænz'leɪt] **1** vt: **to** ~ **(from/into)** tradurre (da/in); **it is** ~**d as** si traduce con. **2** vi tradurre; **it won't** ~ è intraducibile.

trans·la·tion [trænz'leɪʃən] n traduzione f.

trans·la·tor [trænz'leɪtəʳ] n traduttore/trice.

trans·lu·cent [trænz'luːsnt] adj traslucido(a).

trans·mis·sion [trænz'mɪʃən] **1** n (Aut, Radio etc) trasmissione f. **2** cpd: ~ **shaft** n (Aut) albero di trasmissione.

trans·mit [trænz'mɪt] vt (illness, programme, message) trasmettere.

trans·mit·ter [trænz'mɪtəʳ] n (Radio, TV, Telec) trasmittente f, emittente f.

trans·mute [trænz'mjuːt] vt: **to** ~ **(into)** tramutare (in).

tran·som ['trænsəm] n traversa.

trans·par·en·cy [træns'pɛərənsɪ] n trasparenza; (Phot) diapositiva.

trans·par·ent [træns'pɛərənt] adj trasparente; **a** ~ **lie** (fig) una menzogna palese.

tran·spire [træns'paɪəʳ] vi **(a)** (Bot, Physiology) traspirare. **(b)** (become known): **it finally** ~**d that...** alla fine si è venuto a sapere che... . **(c)** (happen) succedere.

trans·plant [træns'plɑːnt] **1** vt (also Med) trapiantare. **2** ['trænsplɑːnt] n (Med) trapianto; **to have a heart** ~ subire un trapianto cardiaco.

trans·port ['trænspɔːt] **1** n **(a)** (gen) trasporto; (vehicle) mezzo di trasporto; **public** ~ mezzi pubblici; **Ministry of T**~ Ministero dei Trasporti; **I haven't got any** ~ non ho un mezzo. **(b)** (fig: of delight, rage etc) trasporto; **to go into** ~**s of joy** esultare dalla gioia. **2** [træns'pɔːt] vt **(a)** trasportare; (History: criminals) deportare. **(b)** (fig): ~**ed with delight** deliziato(a); ~**ed with joy** estasiato(a). **3** cpd (system, costs etc) di trasporto; ~ **cafe** n ≃ locanda per camionisti.

trans·por·ta·tion [ˌtrænspɔː'teɪʃən] n **(a)** trasporto; (vehicle) mezzo di trasporto. **(b)** (History: of criminals) deportazione f.

trans·pose [træns'pəʊz] vt **(a)** (words etc) trasporre. **(b)** (Mus) trasportare.

trans·ship [træns'ʃɪp] vt trasbordare.

trans·verse ['trænzvɜːs] adj trasversale.

trans·ves·tite [trænz'vestaɪt] n travestito/a.

trap [træp] **1** n **(a)** trappola; **to set** or **lay a** ~ **(for sb)** tendere una trappola (a qn); **he was caught in his own** ~ si è fregato con le sue stesse mani. **(b)** (fam: mouth) boccaccia; **shut your** ~! chiudi quella boccaccia! **(c)** (carriage) calesse m. **2** vt **(a)** prendere in trappola; **to** ~ **sb into saying sth** far raccontare qc a qn con un trucco. **(b)** (block) bloccare; (: in wreckage) intrappolare; **the miners are ~ped** i minatori sono rimasti intrappolati; **to ~ one's finger in the door** chiudersi il dito nella porta.

trap·door ['træpdɔ:ʳ] n botola.

tra·peze [trə'pi:z] **1** n trapezio. **2** cpd: **~ artist** n trapezista m/f.

trap·per ['træpəʳ] n cacciatore m (che tende trappole).

trap·pings ['træpɪŋz] npl (of public office) bardatura; (fig: of success) segni mpl esteriori.

Trap·pist ['træpɪst] adj, n trappista (m).

trash [træʃ] **1** n (Am: rubbish) rifiuti mpl, spazzatura; (fig: nonsense) sciocchezze fpl, stupidaggini fpl; **the book is ~** il libro è una schifezza; **they're just ~** (fam pej: people) sono dei pezzenti. **2** cpd: **~ can** n bidone m della spazzatura.

trashy ['træʃɪ] adj di scarso valore, di scarto.

trau·ma ['trɔ:mə] n trauma m.

trau·mat·ic [trɔ:'mætɪk] adj (Med) traumatico(a); (Psych, fig) traumatizzante.

trav·el ['trævl] **1** n viaggi mpl; **~ is easier now** viaggiare è più facile al giorno d'oggi; **when are you off on your ~s?** quando parti per uno dei tuoi viaggi?; **if you meet him on your ~s** (fig) se lo incontri in uno dei tuoi giri.

2 vi (a) viaggiare; (make a journey) fare un viaggio; **we shall be ~ling in France** faremo un viaggio in Francia; **to ~ round the world** fare un viaggio intorno al mondo; **to ~ by car** viaggiare in macchina; **they have ~led a lot** hanno viaggiato molto; **they have ~led a long way** sono venuti da lontano; **to ~ light** viaggiare con poco bagaglio; **this wine doesn't ~ well** questo vino non resiste agli spostamenti.

(b) (go at a speed etc) viaggiare, andare; **it ~s at 50 km/h** fa 50 km/h; **light ~s at a speed of...** la velocità della luce è di...; **news ~s fast** le notizie si diffondono molto velocemente.

(c) (Tech: move) spostarsi; **it ~s along this wire** si sposta lungo questo filo.

(d) (Comm) fare il rappresentante (di commercio); **he ~s in furs** fa il rappresentante di pellicce.

3 vt (road, distance) percorrere, fare; **this is a much ~ed road** questa è una strada di grande traffico.

4 cpd: **~ agency** n agenzia (di) viaggi; **~ agent** n agente m di viaggio; **~ brochure** n dépliant m di viaggi; **~ sickness** n (in car/plane/boat) mal m di macchina/d'aria/di mare.

trav·el·ler, (Am) **trav·el·er** ['trævləʳ] n (gen) viaggiatore/trice; (Comm) commesso viaggiatore; **my fellow ~s** i miei compagni di viaggio; **~'s cheque,** (Am) **~'s check** travellers' cheque m inv.

trav·el·ling, (Am) **trav·el·ing** ['trævlɪŋ] adj (salesman) viaggiatore(trice); (circus, exhibition) itinerante; (expenses, allowance) di viaggio; (bag, rug, clock) da viaggio.

trav·elogue ['trævəlɒg] n (book/film) diario/documentario di viaggio; (talk) conferenza sui viaggi.

trav·erse ['trævəs] vt traversare, attraversare.

trav·es·ty ['trævɪstɪ] n: **his trial was a ~ of justice** il suo processo è stato una farsa.

trawl [trɔ:l] **1** n (net) rete f a strascico. **2** vi: **to ~ (for sth)** pescare (qc) con rete a strascico.

trawl·er ['trɔ:ləʳ] n peschereccio (per la pesca a strascico).

tray [treɪ] n vassoio; (filing ~) cestino per la corrispondenza.

treach·er·ous ['tretʃərəs] adj (disloyal: person, act) sleale; (fig: answer) infido(a); **road conditions today are ~** oggi il fondo stradale è pericoloso.

treach·ery ['tretʃərɪ] n slealtà; **an act of ~** un tradimento.

trea·cle ['tri:kl] n melassa.

tread [tred] (vb: pt **trod**, pp **trodden**) **1** n (a) (footsteps) passo; (sound) rumore m di passi; **to walk with (a) heavy ~** avere un'andatura pesante. **(b)** (of stair) pedata; (of tyre) battistrada m inv.

2 vt (ground) calpestare; (path) percorrere; (grapes) pigiare; **to ~ water** tenersi a galla (con la testa dritta) muovendo solo le gambe; **don't ~ mud into the carpet** non infangare il tappeto; **he trod his cigarette end into the mud** ha schiacciato il mozzicone della sigaretta nel fango; **to ~ a dangerous path** (fig) battere un sentiero pericoloso.

3 vi (walk) camminare; **to ~ on sth** calpestare qc; **to ~ on sb's toes** (also fig) pestare i piedi a qn; **we must ~ very carefully** or **warily** dobbiamo muoverci con molta cautela.

trea·dle ['tredl] n pedale m.

tread·mill ['tredmɪl] n (fig): **to go back to the ~** tornare alla solita routine.

trea·son ['tri:zn] n tradimento.

treas·ure ['treʒəʳ] **1** n (no pl: gold, jewels) tesori mpl; (valuable object, fig: person) tesoro; **our charlady is a real ~** la nostra donna a ore è una vera rarità. **2** vt (value: friendship) stimare; (keep: valuables) custodire gelosamente; (: memory) fare tesoro di. **3** cpd: **~ house** n (fig) pozzo; **~ hunt** caccia al tesoro; **~ trove** n reperto archeologico di proprietà dello Stato.

treas·ur·er ['treʒərəʳ] n tesoriere m.

treas·ury ['treʒərɪ] n (a) tesoreria; **the T~** (Brit), **the T~ Department** (Am) il Ministero del Tesoro. **(b)** (fig) pozzo.

treat [tri:t] **1** n (pleasure) piacere m; (present) sorpresa, sorpresina; **as a special birthday ~ they took me to the theatre** mi hanno fatto una piacevole sorpresa per il compleanno portandomi a teatro; **to give sb a ~** fare una sorpresa a qn; **to have a ~ in store** avere una sorpresa in serbo; **he's standing ~** paga or offre lui; **this is my ~** tocca a me offrire.

2 vt (a) (gen, Tech) trattare; **to ~ sb like a child** trattare qn come se fosse un bambino. **(b)** (consider) considerare; **to ~ sth as a joke** considerare qc uno scherzo; **we ~ all applications in the order in which we receive them** prendiamo in considerazione le domande nell'ordine in cui ci arrivano. **(c)** (give, buy for sb): **to ~ sb to sth** offrire qc a qn; **I'm ~ing you** offro io; **he ~ed himself to another drink** si è concesso un altro bicchierino. **(d)** (patient, illness) curare; **he was ~ed with antibiotics/for bronchitis** è stato sottoposto a un trattamento di antibiotici/per la bronchite.

trea·tise ['tri:tɪz] n trattato.

treat·ment ['tri:tmənt] n (a) trattamento; **to give sb preferential ~** fare un trattamento di favore a qn; **he got good/bad ~** è stato trattato bene/male; **our ~ of foreigners** il modo in cui trattiamo gli stranieri. **(b)** (medical) medicazione f; **to give sb medical ~ for sth** curare qc a qn; **to have ~ for sth** farsi curare qc.

trea·ty ['tri:tɪ] n trattato.

tre·ble ['trebl] **1** adv (3 times) tre volte. **2** adj (a) triplo(a). **(b)** (Mus: voice, part) da soprano; (: note, instrument) alto(a); **~ clef** chiave f di sol. **3** n (boy ~) voce f bianca. **4** vt triplicare. **5** vi triplicarsi.

tree [tri:] **1** n (a) (Bot) albero; (fig): **to be at the top of the ~** essere all'apice. **(b)** (for shoes) tendiscarpe m inv. **2** cpd: **~ house** n capanna costruita su un albero; ~ **trunk** n tronco d'albero.

tree-lined ['tri:laɪnd] adj fiancheggiato(a) da alberi.

tree-top ['tri:top] n cima dell'albero.

trek [trɛk] **1** n (hike) spedizione f; (fam) camminata sfiancante. **2** vi (hike) fare una camminata lunga e faticosa; (fam) trascinarsi.

trel·lis ['trɛlɪs] n graticcio.

trem·ble ['trɛmbl] **1** n (of fear) tremito; (of passion, excitement) fremito; **to be all of a** ~ tremare dalla testa ai piedi, tremare come una foglia. **2** vi: **to** ~ **(with)** tremare (per); **to** ~ **at the thought of sth** tremare al pensiero di qc.

tre·men·dous [trə'mɛndəs] adj (huge: difference, pleasure) enorme; (dreadful: storm, blow) tremendo(a); (: speed) spaventoso(a), folle; (terrific: success) strepitoso(a); (fam: excellent) fantastico(a).

tre·men·dous·ly [trə'mɛndəslɪ] adv incredibilmente; **he enjoyed it** ~ gli è piaciuto da morire.

trem·or ['trɛmə'] n (of fear, shock) tremito; (of excitement) fremito; **it sent** ~**s down my spine** mi ha fatto venire i brividi; **earth** ~ scossa di terremoto.

tremu·lous ['trɛmjʊləs] adj (trembling) tremulo(a); (timid) timido(a).

trench [trɛntʃ] **1** n (gen) fosso; (Mil) trincea. **2** cpd: ~ **coat** n trench m inv.

trench·ant ['trɛntʃənt] adj tagliente.

trend [trɛnd] n tendenza; (of prices, events, coastline) andamento; **to set the** ~ dare il via a una tendenza; ~ **towards/away from** tendenza a/ad allontanarsi da; **there is a** ~ **towards doing/away from doing** si tende a fare/a non fare.

trendy ['trɛndɪ] adj (-ier, -iest) (fam) alla moda.

trepi·da·tion [,trɛpɪ'deɪʃən] n trepidazione f.

tres·pass ['trɛspəs] **1** vi: **to** ~ **(on)** (on land) transitare abusivamente (su); (fig: on time, hospitality) abusare (di); **'no** ~**'ing'** 'divieto di transito'. **2** n (on land) transito abusivo.

tres·pass·er ['trɛspəsə'] n trasgressore m; '~**s will be prosecuted'** 'i trasgressori saranno puniti secondo i termini di legge'.

tres·tle ['trɛsl] **1** n cavalletto. **2** cpd: ~ **table** n tavola su cavalletti.

tri... [traɪ] pref tri... .

tri·al ['traɪəl] **1** n (a) (gen) giudizio; (proceedings) processo; ~ **by jury** processo penale con giuria; **to be on** ~ **(for a crime)** essere sotto processo (per un reato); **to bring sb to** ~ **(for a crime)** portare qn in giudizio (per un reato); **to go on** ~, **stand** ~ essere processato; **to be sent for** ~ essere rinviato a giudizio.
(b) (test: gen) prova; (: of drugs) sperimentazione f; (: of machine) collaudo; ~**s** (Athletics, of horses) concorso; (Ftbl) prova di selezione; **a** ~ **of strength** una prova di forza; **by** ~ **and error** per tentativi; **to be on** ~ (drug) essere in via di sperimentazione; (machine) essere al collaudo; **to give sb a** ~ (for job etc) far fare una prova a qn.
(c) (hardship) prova; **it was a great** ~ è stata una dura prova; **that child is a great** ~ **to them** quel bambino è una continua preoccupazione per loro; **the** ~**s and tribulations of life** le tribolazioni della vita.
2 cpd: ~ **basis** n: **on a** ~ **basis** in prova; ~ **flight** n volo di prova; ~ **offer** n offerta di lancio; ~ **period** n periodo di prova; ~ **run** n periodo di prova.

tri·an·gle ['traɪæŋgl] n triangolo.

tri·an·gu·lar [traɪ'æŋgjʊlə'] adj triangolare.

trib·al ['traɪbəl] adj tribale; (warfare) tra tribù.

tribe [traɪb] n tribù f inv.

tribes·man ['traɪbzmən] n, pl -**men** membro di tribù.

tribu·la·tion [,trɪbjʊ'leɪʃən] n (frm) tribolazione f.

tri·bu·nal [traɪ'bju:nl] n tribunale m; ~ **of inquiry** commissione f d'inchiesta.

tribu·tary ['trɪbjʊtərɪ] n (Geog) affluente m.

trib·ute ['trɪbju:t] n tributo; **to pay** ~ **to sb/sth** rendere omaggio a qn/qc; **floral** ~ omaggio floreale.

trice [traɪs] n: **in a** ~ in un batter d'occhio.

trick [trɪk] **1** n (a) (joke, hoax) scherzo; (ruse, catch, special knack) trucco; **to play a** ~ **on sb** giocare un tiro a qn; **dirty** or **mean** ~ scherzo di cattivo gusto; **there must be a** ~ **in it** ci deve essere sotto qualche cosa; **he's up to his old** ~**s again** è tornato ai suoi vecchi trucchetti; **there's a** ~ **to opening this door** c'è un trucco per aprire questa porta; **it's a** ~ **of the light** è un effetto ottico. **(b)** (habit) mania; **he has a** ~ **of turning up when least expected** ha il dono di spuntare quando uno meno se l'aspetta. **(c)** (card ~) presa; (conjuring ~) gioco di prestigio; **that should do the** ~ (fam) vedrai che funziona; **he doesn't miss a** ~ (fig) non gliene scappa mai una.
2 vt (deceive) ingannare; (swindle) imbrogliare; **I've been** ~**ed!** mi hanno imbrogliato!; **to** ~ **sb into doing sth** convincere qn a fare qc con l'inganno; **to** ~ **sb out of sth** fregare qc a qn.
3 cpd: ~ **photography** n fotografia truccata; ~ **question** n domanda f trabocchetto inv.

trick·ery ['trɪkərɪ] n astuzia.

trick·le ['trɪkl] **1** n (of liquid) rivolo; (fig): **we've had a** ~ **of customers** abbiamo avuto pochi clienti; **there was a steady** ~ **of orders** gli ordini erano pochi ma regolari. **2** vi (liquid) gocciolare; **to** ~ **in** (orders, money) arrivare a poco a poco; (people) arrivare alla spicciolata; (ball) rotolare lentamente.

tricky ['trɪkɪ] adj (-ier, -iest) (person: touchy) difficile; (: sly) astuto(a); (situation) difficile.

tri·col·our, (Am) **tri·col·or** ['trɪkələ'] n tricolore m.

tri·cy·cle ['traɪsɪkl] n triciclo.

tried [traɪd] **1** pt, pp of try. **2** adj: ~ **and tested** sperimentato(a).

tri·fle ['traɪfl] n (a) (unimportant thing) cosa di poco valore, sciocchezza; **he worries about** ~**s** si preoccupa per niente; **it's a** ~ **difficult** è piuttosto difficile. **(b)** (Culin) zuppa inglese.

♦ **trifle with** vi + prep prendere alla leggera; **he's not a person to be** ~**d with** non è una persona da prendere alla leggera; **to** ~ **with sb's affections** giocare con i sentimenti di qn.

tri·fling ['traɪflɪŋ] adj insignificante.

trig·ger ['trɪgə'] **1** n (of gun, machine) grilletto; **to pull the** ~ premere il grilletto. **2** vt (also: ~ **off**: fight etc) provocare, scatenare.

trigger-happy ['trɪgə,hæpɪ] adj che ha la pistola facile.

trigo·nom·etry [,trɪgə'nɒmɪtrɪ] n trigonometria.

trill [trɪl] n (of bird, Mus) trillo.

tril·ogy ['trɪlədʒɪ] n trilogia.

trim [trɪm] **1** adj (-mer, -mest) curato(a); **a** ~ **figure** una figura snella. **2** n (a): **in good** ~ (car etc) in buone condizioni; (person) in forma; **to keep in (good)** ~ mantenersi in forma. **(b)** (cut) spuntata; **to have a** ~ farsi spuntare i capelli. **(c)** (decoration) applicazioni fpl; **car with grey interior** ~ macchina con gli interni grigi. **3** vt (a) (cut: hedge, beard, edges) regolare tagliando; (: hair) spuntare. **(b)** (decorate: Christmas tree) decorare; (edge): **to** ~ **sth with sth** mettere un bordo di qc a qc.

trim·ming ['trɪmɪŋ] n (edging) bordura; ~s (extras, embellishments) accessori mpl; (cuttings) ritagli mpl; **turkey with all the ~s** tacchino con contorno e tutto il resto.

Trini·ty ['trɪnɪtɪ] n Trinità; ~ **Sunday** festa della santissima Trinità.

trin·ket ['trɪŋkɪt] n ninnolo.

trio ['triːəu] n trio.

trip [trɪp] **1** n (a) viaggio; (outing) gita; **away on a ~** in viaggio; **to take a ~** fare un viaggio; **she does 3 ~s to Milan a week** va a Milano 3 volte alla settimana; **I've made 2 ~s to the shops already** sono già andata 2 volte a far la spesa. (b) (Drugs slang) trip m inv, viaggio. **2** vi (a) (stumble) inciampare. (b): **to ~ along, go ~ping along** andare saltellando. **3** vt = **trip up 2.**

♦ **trip over 1** vi + adv inciampare. **2** vi + prep inciampare in.

♦ **trip up 1** vi + adv inciampare; (fig: make a mistake) fare un passo falso. **2** vt + adv far inciampare.

tri·par·tite [ˌtraɪˈpɑːtaɪt] adj (agreement) tripartito(a); (talks) a tre.

tripe [traɪp] n (Culin) trippa; (fam) sciocchezze fpl.

tri·ple ['trɪpl] **1** adj triplo(a); **the T~ Alliance** la Triplice Alleanza. **2** adv: ~ **the distance/the speed** tre volte più lontano/più veloce. **3** vt triplicare. **4** vi triplicarsi.

tri·plet ['trɪplɪt] n: **she's just had ~s** ha appena avuto tre gemelli or un parto trigemino.

trip·li·cate ['trɪplɪkɪt] n: **in ~** in triplice copia.

tri·pod ['traɪpɒd] n treppiede m.

trip·tych ['trɪptɪk] n trittico.

trip·wire ['trɪpwaɪəʳ] n filo in tensione che fa scattare una trappola, allarme etc.

trite [traɪt] adj trito(a) e ritrito(a).

tri·umph ['traɪʌmf] **1** n (sense of ~) trionfo; (success) successo; (victory): ~ **(over)** trionfo (su), vittoria (su); **in ~** in trionfo. **2** vi: **to ~ (over)** trionfare (su).

tri·um·phal [traɪˈʌmfəl] adj trionfale.

tri·um·phant [traɪˈʌmfənt] adj (jubilant) trionfante; (: homecoming) trionfale; (victorious) vittorioso(a).

trivia ['trɪvɪə] npl banalità fpl.

triv·ial ['trɪvɪəl] adj (matter) futile; (excuse, comment) banale; (amount) irrisorio(a); (mistake) di poco conto.

trivi·al·ity [ˌtrɪvɪˈælɪtɪ] n frivolezza; (trivial detail) futilità f inv.

trivi·al·ize ['trɪvɪəlaɪz] vt sminuire.

trod [trɒd] pt of **tread.**

trod·den ['trɒdn] pp of **tread.**

trol·ley ['trɒlɪ] **1** n (in station, supermarket, tea ~ etc) carrello; (in hospital) lettiga. **2** cpd: ~ **bus** n filobus m inv.

trom·bone [trɒmˈbəun] n trombone m.

troop [truːp] **1** n (gen, of scouts) gruppo; (Mil) squadrone m; ~**s** (Mil) truppe fpl. **2** vi (walk): **to ~ in/past/off** etc entrare/passare/andarsene etc in gruppo. **3** cpd: ~ **carrier** n (plane) aereo per il trasporto (di) truppe; (Naut: also: ~**ship**) nave f per il trasporto (di) truppe.

troop·er ['truːpəʳ] n (Mil) soldato di cavalleria; (Am: policeman) poliziotto (della polizia di stato); **to swear like a ~** bestemmiare come un turco.

troop·ing ['truːpɪŋ] n: ~ **the colour** cerimonia del saluto alla bandiera.

tro·phy ['trəufɪ] n trofeo.

trop·ic ['trɒpɪk] n tropico; **the ~s** i tropici; **T~ of Cancer/Capricorn** Tropico del Cancro/Capricorno.

tropi·cal ['trɒpɪkəl] adj tropicale.

trot [trɒt] **1** n (a) (pace) trotto; **to break into a ~** (horse, rider) partire al trotto; (person) mettersi a camminare di buon passo; **to go for a ~** (on horse) andare a fare una trottata; **3 weeks on the ~** (fam) 3 settimane di fila; **to be on the ~** (fam) essere sempre in movimento; **the baby keeps her on the ~** il bambino non le concede un attimo di tregua. (b): **the ~s** (fam: diarrhoea) la cacarella. **2** vi (horse, rider) andare al trotto, trottare; (person): **to ~ in/past** etc entrare/passare etc di corsa.

♦ **trot out** vt + adv (excuse, reason) tirar fuori; (names, facts) recitare di fila.

trou·ble ['trʌbl] **1** n (a) (problems) problemi mpl, difficoltà fpl; (: as result of doing wrong) guai mpl, pasticci mpl; (: with sth mechanical) noie fpl; (unrest, fighting) disordini mpl; **to have ~ doing sth** avere delle difficoltà a fare qc; **to be in ~** (having problems) avere qualche problema or difficoltà; (for doing wrong) essere nei guai; **to get into ~** cacciarsi nei guai; **to get sb into ~** mettere or cacciare qn nei guai; **to help sb out of ~** aiutare qn a tirarsi fuori dai guai; **what's the ~?** che cosa c'è (che non va)?; **the ~ is...** c'è che..., il guaio è che...; **don't go looking for ~** non andare in cerca di guai; **engine ~** noie al motore; **heart/back ~** (Med) disturbi mpl al cuore/di schiena.

(b) (effort, bother): **it's no ~** non è un problema; **it's not worth the ~** non vale la pena; **to go to (all) the ~ of doing sth, take the ~ to do sth** darsi la pena di fare qc.

2 vt (a) (worry) preoccupare; **my eyes have been troubling me** ho avuto dei disturbi agli occhi.

(b) (bother, be nuisance to) disturbare; **I'm sorry to ~ you** mi dispiace disturbarla; **I shan't ~ you with all the details** non starò a raccontarle tutti i particolari; **please don't ~ yourself** non si disturbi.

(c) (+ infin: make the effort): **to ~ to do sth** darsi la pena di fare qc.

3 cpd: ~ **spot** n zona calda.

trou·bled ['trʌbld] adj (person, expression) preoccupato(a); (period) travagliato(a).

trouble-free ['trʌbl.friː] adj (life, car, trip) senza problemi; (area, factory) tranquillo(a); (demonstration) pacifico(a).

trouble·maker ['trʌbl.meɪkəʳ] n attaccabrighe m/f inv.

trouble·shooter ['trʌbl.ʃuːtəʳ] n (Tech) esperto/a (chiamato in casi di emergenza); (Pol) mediatore/ trice.

trou·ble·some ['trʌblsəm] adj (person) molesto(a); (headache etc) fastidioso(a); (dispute, problem) difficile.

trough [trɒf] n (a) (feeding ~) mangiatoia. (b) (between waves) cavo; (on graph) punto più basso; (Met): ~ **of low pressure** area di bassa pressione.

troupe [truːp] n (Theatre etc) compagnia, troupe f inv.

trou·ser ['trauzəʳ] cpd (Brit): ~ **press** n stirapantaloni m inv; ~ **suit** n completo m or tailleur m inv pantalone inv.

trou·sers ['trauzəz] npl (Brit) pantaloni mpl, calzoni mpl.

trous·seau ['truːsəu] n corredo (da sposa).

trout [traut] **1** n, pl inv trota. **2** cpd: ~ **fishing** n pesca alla trota.

trow·el ['trauəl] n (for garden) paletta da giardiniere; (builder's) cazzuola.

tru·an·cy ['truənsɪ] n assenze fpl ingiustificate.

tru·ant ['truənt] n (Scol): **to play ~** marinare la scuola.

truce [truːs] n tregua; **to call a** ~ dichiarare la tregua.

truck[1] [trʌk] n: **to have no** ~ **with sb** non volere avere a che fare con qn.

truck[2] [trʌk] n **(a)** (Rail: wagon) carro m merci inv. **(b)** (esp Am: lorry) camion m inv. **(c)** (hand-trolley) carrello.

truck·driver ['trʌk,draɪvəʳ] n, **truck·er** ['trʌkəʳ] n camionista m.

truck·ing ['trʌkɪŋ] n trasporto con camion.

truck·load ['trʌkləud] n carico (di camion).

trucu·lent ['trʌkjʊlənt] adj aggressivo(a), brutale.

trudge [trʌdʒ] vi: **to** ~ **up/down/along** etc trascinarsi pesantemente su/giù/lungo etc.

true [truː] **1** adj (-r, -st) **(a)** (not fiction: story etc) vero(a); (accurate, correct: statement, description) preciso(a); (: portrait, likeness) fedele; **to come** ~ avverarsi; **the same holds** ~ **of** or **for...** lo stesso vale per...; **too** ~! fin troppo vero!; ~, **but... sì, ma...** **(b)** (real, genuine: emotion, interest etc) sincero(a), vero(a); ~ **love** vero amore; **to behave like a** ~ **Englishman** comportarsi da vero inglese; **in the** ~**st sense of the word** nel vero senso della parola. **(c)** (wall, beam) a piombo; (wheel) centrato(a). **(d)** (faithful: friend etc) fedele; **to be** ~ **to sb/sth** essere fedele a qn/qc; **to be** ~ **to one's word** tenere fede alla parola data; ~ **to life** verosimile; **to run** ~ **to type** essere fedele alla propria immagine.

2 n: **to be out of** ~ (wall, beam) non essere a piombo; (wheel) non essere centrato(a).

truf·fle ['trʌfl] n tartufo.

tru·ism ['truːɪzəm] n verità f inv lapalissiana.

tru·ly ['truːlɪ] adv (genuinely: believe, love) veramente, sinceramente; (faithfully: serve, love, reflect) fedelmente; (emphatic: very) veramente, davvero; **well and** ~ per bene; **yours** ~ (in letter-writing) distinti saluti.

trump [trʌmp] **1** n (Cards) atout m inv; **hearts are** ~**s** l'atout è di cuori; **to turn up** ~**s** (fig) fare miracoli. **2** vt (Cards) tagliare, prendere con l'atout. **3** cpd: ~ **card** n atout m inv; (fig) asso nella manica.

trumped-up [,trʌmpt'ʌp] adj (charge) inventato(a), falso(a).

trum·pet ['trʌmpɪt] **1** n tromba. **2** vi (elephant) barrire.

trum·pet·er ['trʌmpɪtəʳ] n suonatore m di tromba; (Mil) trombettiere m.

trun·cate [trʌŋ'keɪt] vt (report, speech) tagliare.

trun·cheon ['trʌntʃən] n manganello.

trun·dle ['trʌndl] **1** vt (push, pull) far rotolare (a fatica). **2** vi (cart etc) avanzare rumorosamente.

trunk [trʌŋk] **1** n (Anat, Bot) tronco; (of elephant) proboscide f; (big suitcase) baule m; (Am: boot of car) bagagliaio. **2** cpd: ~ **call** n (Brit Telec) telefonata interurbana; ~ **road** n strada principale.

trunks [trʌŋks] npl: **swimming** or **bathing** ~**s** calzoncini mpl da bagno.

truss [trʌs] **1** vt (also: ~ **up**) legare stretto. **2** n (Med) cinto erniario.

trust [trʌst] **1** n **(a)**: ~ **(in)** fiducia (in); **to put one's** ~ **in sb** riporre la propria fiducia in qn; **to put one's** ~ **in sth** riporre le proprie speranze in qc; **to be in a position of** ~ ricoprire un incarico di fiducia; **you'll have to take it on** ~ devi credermi sulla parola. **(b)** (charge): **to leave sth in sb's** ~ affidare qc a qn or alle cure di qn. **(c)** (Law, Fin): **in** ~ in amministrazione fiduciaria. **(d)** (Comm: also: ~ **company**) trust m inv.

2 vt **(a)** (have faith, confidence in) avere fiducia in, fidarsi di; (rely on) fare affidamento su; **to** ~ **sb with sth** (entrust) affidare qc a qn; **I wouldn't** ~ **him an inch** non mi fiderei proprio di lui; ~ **you!** (fam) ci avrei scommesso! **(b)** (hope): **to** ~ **(that)** sperare (che).

3 vi (have faith): **to** ~ **in** credere in; (rely): **to** ~ **to luck/fate** etc affidarsi alla fortuna/al destino etc.

4 cpd: ~ **company** n trust m inv; ~ **fund** n fondo fiduciario.

trust·ed ['trʌstɪd] adj (friend etc) fidato(a).

trus·tee [trʌs'tiː] n amministratore m fiduciario; (of school, institution) amministratore.

trust·ful ['trʌstfʊl] adj, **trust·ing** ['trʌstɪŋ] adj fiducioso(a).

trust·worthy ['trʌst,wɜːðɪ] adj (person) fidato(a); (source of news etc) attendibile.

trusty ['trʌstɪ] adj (-ier, -iest) (hum) fidato(a).

truth [truːθ] n verità f inv; **to tell the** ~ dire la verità; **to tell (you) the** ~, ~ **to tell** a dire il vero or la verità; **the** ~ **of the matter is that...** la verità è che...; **the** ~ **hurts** la verità fa male; **there is some** ~ **in what he says** c'è del vero in ciò che dice; **there isn't a word of** ~ **in it** non c'è nulla di vero; ~ **will out** la verità viene sempre a galla.

truth·ful ['truːθfʊl] adj (account) veritiero(a); (person) sincero(a).

truth·ful·ly ['truːθfəlɪ] adv sinceramente.

try [traɪ] **1** n **(a)** (attempt) tentativo; **to give sth a** ~ provare qc; **why don't you give the exam a** ~? perché non provi a fare l'esame?; **to have a** ~ (at doing sth) provare (a fare qc); **it's worth a** ~ vale la pena di tentare. **(b)** (Rugby) meta.

2 vt **(a)** (usu + infin): **to** ~ **to do sth** (attempt) provare a fare qc; (seek) cercare di fare qc; **to** ~ **one's (very) best** or **one's (very) hardest** mettercela tutta. **(b)** (sample: method, car, food etc) provare; **why not** ~ **him for the job?** perché non gli fai fare una prova?; ~ **pressing that switch** prova a schiacciare quell'interruttore. **(c)** (test: strength, vehicle, machine) verificare, collaudare; (tax, strain: patience, person) mettere alla prova; (: eyes) affaticare; **to** ~ **one's hand at sth** (fig) cimentarsi in qc. **(d)** (Law): **to** ~ **sb (for sth)** processare qn (per qc).

3 vi (attempt) provare; ~ **again!** provaci ancora!

♦ **try for** vi + prep mirare a.

♦ **try on** vt + adv (clothes, shoes) provare. **(b)** (fig): **to** ~ **it on (with sb)** cercare di farla (a qn).

♦ **try out** vt + adv (sth new, different) provare; (employee) far fare una prova a; **to** ~ **sth out on sb** far provare qc a qn.

try·ing ['traɪɪŋ] adj (tiring: situation, time etc) difficile, duro(a); (tiresome: person) noioso(a), seccante; **to have a** ~ **time** passare un periodo difficile.

tsar [zɑːʳ] n zar m inv.

tset·se fly ['tsetsɪflaɪ] n mosca f tse-tse inv.

T-shirt ['tiː:ʃɜːt] n maglietta.

T-square ['tiːskweəʳ] n squadra a T.

tub [tʌb] n (for washing clothes) mastello; (for flowers) vasca; (for ice cream) vaschetta; (: individual) coppetta; (bath~) vasca da bagno.

tuba ['tjuːbə] n tuba.

tub·by ['tʌbɪ] adj (-ier, -iest) (fam) grassoccio(a).

tube [tjuːb] **1** n **(a)** (pipe) tubo; (of toothpaste, paint etc) tubetto; (Anat) tuba. **(b)** (Am fam: television) tele f. **(c)** (London underground) metrò m inv. **2** cpd: ~ **station** n stazione f del metrò.

tube·less ['tjuːblɪs] adj (tyre) senza camera d'aria.

tu·ber ['tjuːbəʳ] n (Bot) tubero.

tu·ber·cu·lo·sis [tjuˌbɜːkjuˈləusɪs] n tubercolosi f.

tub·ing ['tjuːbɪŋ] n tubi mpl, tubazione f.

tubu·lar ['tjuːbjuləʳ] adj tubolare.

TUC n (abbr of Trades Union Congress) Confederazione f dei sindacati (britannici).

tuck [tʌk] **1** n (Sewing) pince f inv. **2** vt (put) infilare, cacciare; **she ~ed a blanket round him** lo ha avvolto in una coperta.

♦ **tuck away** vt + adv riporre in un luogo sicuro, nascondere; **she has her money safely ~ed away** ha messo i soldi in un posto sicuro.

♦ **tuck in 1** vi + adv (fam) attaccare (a mangiare). **2** vt + adv (blankets) rimboccare; (shirt) mettere dentro; **to ~ sb in** rimboccare le coperte a qn.

♦ **tuck into** vi + prep (fam: meal) buttarsi su.

♦ **tuck up** vt + adv (skirt, sleeves) tirare su; **to ~ sb up** rimboccare le coperte a qn.

Tues·day ['tjuːzdɪ] n martedì m inv; **the date today is ~ 23rd March** oggi è martedì 23 marzo; **on ~** martedì; **on ~s** di martedì; **every ~** tutti i martedì; **every other ~** ogni due martedì; **last/next ~** martedì scorso/prossimo; **~ next** martedì prossimo; **the following ~** (in past) il martedì successivo; (in future) il martedì dopo; **the ~ before last/after next** martedì di due settimane fa/fra quindici giorni; **a week/fortnight on ~, ~ week/fortnight** martedì fra una settimana/quindici giorni; **~ morning/lunchtime/afternoon/evening** martedì mattina/all'ora di pranzo/pomeriggio/sera; **~ night** martedì sera; (overnight) martedì notte; **the ~ film** (TV) il film del martedì; **~'s newspaper** il giornale di martedì.

tuft [tʌft] n (of hair) ciuffo, ciocca; (of grass etc) ciuffo.

tug [tʌg] **1** n (a) (pull) strattone m; **to give sth a (good) ~** dare uno strattone a qc. (b) (also: **~boat**) rimorchiatore m. **2** vt (pull) tirare con forza. **3** vi: **to ~ (at)** dare uno strattone a (a).

tug-of-war [,tʌgəv'wɔːʳ] n (Sport) tiro alla fune; (fig) braccio di ferro.

tui·tion [tjʊ'ɪʃən] n lezioni fpl.

tu·lip ['tjuːlɪp] n tulipano m.

tulle [tjuːl] n tulle m.

tum·ble ['tʌmbl] **1** n ruzzolone m, capitombolo; **to have a ~, take a ~** fare un ruzzolone or capitombolo. **2** vi (a) (fall) ruzzolare, fare un capitombolo; **to ~ downstairs** ruzzolare giù dalle scale. (b) (rush): **to ~ into/out of bed** buttarsi a/cadere giù dal letto; **the children ~d out of the room/the car** i bambini si sono precipitati fuori dalla stanza/dalla macchina. (c) (suddenly understand): **to ~ to sth** (fam) realizzare qc. **3** cpd: **~ dryer** n asciugatrice f ad aria calda.

tumble-down ['tʌmbldaʊn] adj cadente, in rovina.

tum·bler ['tʌmbləʳ] n (glass) bicchiere m (senza stelo).

tum·my ['tʌmɪ] n (fam) pancia.

tu·mour, (Am) **tu·mor** ['tjuːməʳ] n tumore m.

tu·mult ['tjuːmʌlt] n tumulto.

tu·mul·tu·ous [tjuː'mʌltjʊəs] adj tumultuoso(a).

tuna ['tjuːnə] n (also: **~ fish**) tonno m.

tune [tjuːn] **1** n (a) melodia, aria; **he gave us a ~** ci ha suonato qualcosa; **to change one's ~** (fig) cambiare tono; **to the ~ of** (fig: amount) per la modesta somma di. (b): **in ~** (instrument) accordato(a); (person) intonato(a); **out of ~** (instrument) scordato(a); (person) stonato(a); **to sing in ~** cantare senza stonare; **to sing out of ~** stonare; **in ~ with** (fig) in accordo con. **2** vt (Mus) accordare; (Aut: engine) mettere a punto. **3** vi (Mus: also: **~ up**) accordare.

♦ **tune in** vi + adv (Radio, TV) sintonizzarsi.

tune·ful ['tjuːnfʊl] adj melodioso(a).

tune·less ['tjuːnlɪs] adj poco melodioso(a).

tun·er ['tjuːnəʳ] n (a) (Radio: knob) sintonizzatore

m. (b) (piano ~ etc) accordatore m.

tung·sten ['tʌŋstən] n tungsteno.

tu·nic ['tjuːnɪk] n tunica.

tun·ing fork ['tjuːnɪŋ,fɔːk] n diapason m inv.

Tu·ni·sia [tjuː'nɪzɪə] n Tunisia.

tun·nel ['tʌnl] **1** n (gen) galleria, tunnel m inv; (Min) galleria; **the Mont Blanc ~** il traforo del Monte Bianco. **2** vt: **to ~ one's way out** aprirsi un passaggio scavando; **to ~ a passage** scavare un passaggio. **3** vi scavare una galleria.

tun·ny ['tʌnɪ] n = **tuna**.

tup·pence ['tʌpəns] n (Brit fam) = **twopence**.

tur·ban ['tɜːbən] n turbante m.

tur·bine ['tɜːbaɪn] n turbina.

tur·bo·jet ['tɜːbəʊ'dʒɛt] n turbogetto, turboreattore m.

tur·bo·prop ['tɜːbəʊ'prɒp] n turboelica m inv.

tur·bot ['tɜːbət] n, pl inv rombo gigante.

tur·bu·lence ['tɜːbjʊləns] n turbolenza.

tur·bu·lent ['tɜːbjʊlənt] adj turbolento(a).

tu·reen [tə'riːn] n zuppiera.

turf [tɜːf] **1** n (grass) tappeto erboso; (one piece) zolla erbosa; **the T~** (Racing) l'ippica, le corse ippiche. **2** vt (also: **~ over**) ricoprire di zolle erbose. **3** cpd: **~ accountant** n allibratore m.

♦ **turf out** vt + adv (fam) buttar fuori.

tur·gid ['tɜːdʒɪd] adj (prose etc) ampolloso(a).

Turk [tɜːk] n turco/a.

Tur·key ['tɜːkɪ] n Turchia.

tur·key ['tɜːkɪ] n tacchino.

Turk·ish ['tɜːkɪʃ] **1** adj turco(a); **~ bath** bagno turco; **~ delight** gelatine ricoperte di zucchero a velo. **2** n (language) turco.

tur·mer·ic ['tɜːmərɪk] n curcuma.

tur·moil ['tɜːmɔɪl] n confusione f; **to be in a ~** essere in uno stato di confusione.

turn [tɜːn] **1** n (a) (rotation) giro; **to give sth a ~** girare qc; **done to a ~** (Culin) cotto a puntino.

(b) (change of direction: in road etc) curva; **'no left ~'** 'divieto di svolta a sinistra'; **to do a left ~** (Aut) girare a sinistra; **take the next left ~** prendi la prossima a sinistra; **a road full of twists and ~s** una strada tutta a curve; **to take a ~ in the park** fare un giro nel parco; **at the ~ of the year/century** alla fine dell'anno/del secolo; **at every ~** (fig) a ogni piè sospinto; **things took a new ~** (fig) le cose hanno preso una nuova piega; **to take a ~ for the better** (situation, events) volgere al meglio; (patient, health) migliorare; **to take a ~ for the worse** (situation, events) volgere al peggio; (patient, health) peggiorare; **an odd ~ of mind** una strana disposizione mentale; **~ of phrase** modo di esprimersi.

(c) (Med): **he had a bad ~ last night** la scorsa notte ha avuto una crisi or un peggioramento; **the news gave me quite a ~** (fam) la notizia mi ha scosso profondamente.

(d) (in series etc) turno; **by ~s** a turno; **hot and cold by ~s** ora caldo ora freddo; **and he, in ~, said...** e lui, a sua volta, ha detto...; **they spoke in ~** hanno parlato a turno; **to take ~s at doing sth, take it in ~(s) to do sth** fare qc a turno; **to take/wait/miss one's ~** fare/aspettare/saltare il proprio turno; **it's my ~** è il mio turno, tocca me; **whose ~ is it?** a chi tocca?; **your ~ will come** verrà anche il tuo momento; **to take ~ and ~ about** fare i turni; **to take ~s at the wheel** fare un turno al volante; **to speak out of ~** (fig) parlare a sproposito.

(e) (Theatre) numero; **to do a comedy ~** fare un numero comico.

(f) (action): **to do sb a good ~** rendere un

servizio a qn; **to do sb a bad** ~ fare un brutto tiro a qn; **his good** ~ **for the day** la sua buona azione quotidiana; **one good** ~ **deserves another** una mano lava l'altra.

2 vt **(a)** (wheel, handle etc) girare; (: mechanically etc) far girare; ~ **the key in the lock** gira la chiave nella toppa.

(b) (also: ~ **over**: record, mattress, steak) girare; (: page) girare, voltare; (: soil) rivoltare; **to** ~ **one's ankle** prendere una storta; **it** ~**s my stomach** mi fa rivoltare lo stomaco.

(c) (direct: car, object) voltare; (: attention) rivolgere; (: gun, telescope) puntare; **the fireman** ~**ed the hose on the building** il pompiere ha puntato l'idrante verso l'edificio; **to** ~ **a gun on sb** puntare la pistola contro qn; **to** ~ **one's back on sb** (also fig) voltare le spalle a qn; **to** ~ **one's back on the past** tagliare i ponti col passato; **as soon as his back is** ~**ed** non appena volta le spalle; **power/success** ~**ed his head** il potere/il successo gli ha dato alla testa; **without** ~**ing a hair** senza battere ciglio; **to** ~ **the other cheek** (fig) porgere l'altra guancia; **he** ~**ed his hand to cookery** si è dato alla cucina; **to** ~ **the tables on sb** (fig) capovolgere la situazione a danno di qn; **they** ~**ed him against us** ce l'hanno messo contro.

(d) (go past, round) girare, voltare; **the car** ~**ed the corner** la macchina ha voltato l'angolo; **to have** ~**ed the corner** (fig) aver superato la fase critica; **he's** ~**ed 50** ha passato i 50; **it's** ~**ed four o'clock** sono le quattro passate.

(e) (change): **to** ~ **sb/sth into sth** trasformare qn/qc in qc; **to** ~ **iron into gold** trasformare il ferro in oro; **to** ~ **a book into a film** fare un film da un libro; **it** ~**ed him into a bitter man** lo ha reso un uomo pieno d'amarezza; **the shock** ~**ed her hair white** le sono venuti i capelli bianchi dallo shock; **the heat has** ~**ed the milk** il caldo ha fatto andare a male il latte.

(f) (shape: wood, metal) tornire; **to** ~ **wood on a lathe** lavorare il legno con il tornio; **a well-**~**ed phrase** un'espressione molto elegante; **a well-**~**ed ankle** una caviglia ben tornita.

3 vi **(a)** (rotate) girare; (change direction: person) girarsi, voltarsi; (: vehicle) girare, svoltare; (: ship) virare; (: wind, tide, weather) cambiare; **my head is** ~**ing** (fig) mi gira la testa; **everything** ~**s on his decision** (fig) tutto dipende dalla sua decisione; **to** ~ **and go back** girare or girarsi e tornar indietro; **to** ~ **left** (Aut) girare a sinistra; **the car** ~**ed into a lane** la macchina ha svoltato in una stradina; **to wait for the weather to** ~ aspettare che il tempo cambi; **he** ~**ed to me and smiled** si è girato verso di me e mi ha sorriso; **to** ~ **to sb for help** rivolgersi a qn per aiuto; **she has no-one to** ~ **to** non ha nessuno cui potersi rivolgere; **he** ~**ed to politics** si è messo in politica, si è dato alla politica; **he** ~**ed to drink** si è dato al bere; **I don't know which way to** ~ (fig) non so dove sbattere la testa; **the conversation** ~**ed to religion** la conversazione passò alla religione; **to** ~ **against sb** mettersi contro qn.

(b) (change): **to** ~ **into sth** trasformarsi in qc; **the milk has** ~**ed** il latte è andato a male; **to** ~ **red** arrossire; **to** ~ **nasty** diventare cattivo; **he** ~**ed into a cynic** è diventato un cinico; **they** ~**ed communist** sono diventati comunisti; **a singer** ~**ed songwriter** un cantante divenuto autore.

♦ **turn aside** vi + adv voltarsi dall'altra parte.

♦ **turn away** vi + adv voltarsi dall'altra parte; **he** ~**ed away from the awful sight** ha distolto lo sguardo da quella scena tremenda. **2** vt + adv **(a)**

(move: eyes) distogliere; (: head) girare dall'altra parte; (: gun) spostare. **(b)** (reject: person) mandar via; (: business) rifiutare.

♦ **turn back 1** vi + adv **(a)** (in journey etc) tornare indietro. **(b)** (in book) ritornare. **2** vt + adv **(a)** (fold: bedclothes) ripiegare. **(b)** (send back) far tornare indietro. **(c)** (clock) spostare indietro; **to** ~ **back the clock 20 years** (fig) tornare indietro di 20 anni; **it's no use trying to** ~ **the clock back** è inutile tornare sui propri passi.

♦ **turn down** vt + adv **(a)** (fold down: bedclothes, collar, page) ripiegare. **(b)** (reduce: gas, heat, volume) abbassare. **(c)** (refuse: offer) rifiutare; (candidate) scartare.

♦ **turn in 1** vi + adv **(a)**: **to** ~ **in (to)** girare (in); **she** ~**ed in at the house** ha girato per entrare nella casa. **(b)** (fam: go to bed) andare a letto. **2** vt + adv (hand over) consegnare; **to** ~ **sb in** consegnare qn alla polizia.

♦ **turn off 1** vi + adv **(a)** (person, vehicle) girare. **(b)** (appliance etc) spegnersi. **2** vt + adv **(a)** (appliance, light) spegnere; (tap) chiudere. **(b)** (fam: person: also sexually) far schifo a.

♦ **turn on 1** vi + adv (appliance) accendersi. **2** vt + adv **(a)** (appliance, light, electricity) accendere; (tap) aprire. **(b)** (fam: person, also sexually) sconvolgere.

♦ **turn out 1** vi + adv **(a)** (appear, attend: troops, doctor etc) presentarsi; **to** ~ **out for a meeting** presentarsi ad un'assemblea. **(b)** (prove to be) rivelarsi; **it** ~**ed out to be true** è risultato che era vero; **things will** ~ **out all right** andrà tutto bene; **how did the cake** ~ **out?** com'è venuta la torta?; **it** ~**ed out that...** si è scoperto che.... **2** vt + adv **(a)** (appliance, light) spegnere. **(b)** (produce: goods) produrre; (: novel, good pupils) creare; **to be well** ~**ed out** (fig) essere ben vestito. **(c)** (empty: pockets) vuotare; (tip out: cake) capovolgere. **(d)** (clean out: room) dare una bella pulita a. **(e)** (expel: tenant, employee) mandar via. **(f)** (guard, police) far uscire.

♦ **turn over 1** vi + adv **(a)** (car etc) capovolgersi; (engine) girare; **my stomach** ~**ed over** mi si è rivoltato lo stomaco; **she** ~**ed over onto her back** si è girata sulla schiena. **(b)** (in reading) girare la pagina, voltare la pagina; (in letter): **please** ~ **over** (abbr **PTO**) segue. **2** vt + adv **(a)** (page, mattress, card) girare; (patient) far girare; **to** ~ **sth over in one's mind** riflettere a lungo or rimuginare su qc. **(b)** (hand over: object, person) consegnare.

♦ **turn round 1** vi + adv **(a)** (person) girarsi; (vehicle) girare. **(b)** (rotate) girare; **to** ~ **round and round** girare su se stesso. **2** vt + adv girare.

♦ **turn up 1** vi + adv **(a)** (be found) saltar fuori; (arrive) arrivare; **something will** ~ **up** salterà fuori qualcosa; **we waited but she didn't** ~ **up** abbiamo aspettato ma non si è fatta vedere. **(b)** (point upwards) essere rivolto(a) all'insù; **his nose** ~**s up** ha il naso all'insù. **2** vt + adv **(a)** (collar, sleeve, hem) tirare su; **a** ~**ed-up nose** un naso all'insù; **to** ~ **up one's nose at sth** arricciare il naso davanti a qc. **(b)** (heat, gas, radio etc) alzare. **(c)** (find) scoprire.

turn·about ['tɜːnəbaʊt] n, **turn·around** ['tɜːnəraʊnd] n voltafaccia m inv.

turn·coat ['tɜːnkəʊt] n voltagabbana m/f inv.

turn·ing ['tɜːnɪŋ] **1** n (side road) strada laterale; (fork) biforcazione f; (bend) curva; **the first** ~ **on the right** la prima a destra. **2** cpd: ~ **point** n (fig) svolta decisiva.

tur·nip ['tɜːnɪp] n rapa.

turn·off ['tɜːnɒf] n (in road) strada laterale.

turn·out ['tɜːnaʊt] n (a) (attendance): **there was a poor ~** la partecipazione è stata molto scarsa. **(b)** (clean) ripulita.

turn·over ['tɜːn,əʊvəʳ] n (a) (Comm) giro d'affari; **these goods have a rapid ~** di questi prodotti c'è grande smercio; **there is a rapid ~ in staff** c'è un ricambio molto rapido di personale. **(b)** (Culin): **apple** etc **~** sfogliatella alle mele etc.

turn·pike ['tɜːnpaɪk] n (Am Aut) autostrada (a pagamento).

turn·stile ['tɜːnstaɪl] n cancelletto girevole.

turn·table ['tɜːn,teɪbl] n (of record player) piatto; (for trains, car etc) piattaforma girevole.

turn·up ['tɜːnʌp] n (a) (of trousers) risvolto. **(b):** **that was a ~ for the book** (fam) è stato un colpo di scena.

tur·pen·tine ['tɜːpəntaɪn] **1** n (fam abbr: **turps**) trementina. **2** cpd: **~ substitute** n acquaragia.

tur·quoise ['tɜːkwɔɪz] **1** n (stone, colour) turchese m. **2** adj (ring) di turchesi; (colour) turchese.

tur·ret ['tʌrɪt] n torretta.

tur·tle ['tɜːtl] **1** n tartaruga acquatica, testuggine f; **to turn ~** (boat) scuffiare. **2** cpd: **~ soup** n zuppa di tartaruga.

turtle·dove ['tɜːtldʌv] n tortora.

turtle·neck ['tɜːtlnɛk] n collo alto (pullover).

tusk [tʌsk] n zanna.

tus·sle ['tʌsl] **1** n baruffa; **to have a ~ with** fare baruffa con. **2** vi: **to ~ (with sb for sth)** far baruffa (con qn per qc).

tus·sock ['tʌsək] n ciuffo d'erba.

tut [tʌt] (also: **~-~**) **1** excl non si fa così! **2** vi far schioccare la lingua in segno di disapprovazione.

tu·tor ['tjuːtəʳ] **1** n (private teacher) insegnante m/f privato(a); (Brit Univ) professore responsabile degli studi di uno o più studenti. **2** vt: **to ~ sb in Italian** dare lezioni private d'italiano a qn.

tu·to·rial [tjuː'tɔːrɪəl] n (Univ) esercitazione f, seminario.

tux·edo [tʌk'siːdəʊ] n (Am) smoking m inv.

TV [,tiː'viː] n (abbr of **television**) TV f inv, tivù f inv.

twad·dle ['twɒdl] n scemenze fpl.

twang [twæŋ] **1** n (of wire, bow etc) suono acuto; (of voice): **to speak with a ~** parlare con voce nasale. **2** vt (Mus) pizzicare le corde di.

tweak [twiːk] **1** n: **to give sb's nose/ear a ~** dare un pizzicotto sul naso/una tirata d'orecchie a qn. **2** vt (nose) pizzicare; (ear, hair) tirare.

twee [twiː] adj (fam pej: person) affettato(a); (: decor) lezioso(a).

tweed [twiːd] n (cloth) tweed m; **~s** (suit) abito di tweed.

tweet [twiːt] vi cinguettare.

tweet·er ['twiːtəʳ] n (Stereo) tweeter m inv.

twee·zers ['twiːzəz] npl pinzette fpl.

twelfth [twelfθ] **1** adj dodicesimo(a); **T~ Night** la notte dell'Epifania. **2** n (in series) dodicesimo/a; (fraction) dodicesimo; for usage see **fifth**.

twelve [twelv] adj, n dodici (m) inv; for usage see **five**.

twen·ti·eth ['twentɪɪθ] **1** adj ventesimo(a). **2** n (in series) ventesimo/a; (fraction) ventesimo; for usage see **fifth**.

twen·ty ['twentɪ] adj, n venti (m) inv; for usage see **fifty**.

twerp [twɜːp] n (fam) idiota m/f.

twice [twaɪs] adv due volte; **~ as much, ~ as many** il doppio; **I have ~ as many cigarettes as you** ho il doppio delle sigarette che hai tu; **there's ~ as much wine here as beer** qui c'è vino in quantità due volte superiori alla birra; **~ a week** due volte alla settimana; **she is ~ your age** ha il

doppio dei tuoi anni; **~ as big** due volte più grande.

twid·dle ['twɪdl] vt, vi: **to ~ (with) sth** giocherellare con qc; **to ~ one's thumbs** (fig) girarsi i pollici.

twig[1] [twɪg] n ramoscello.

twig[2] [twɪg] vt, vi (fam) capire.

twi·light ['twaɪlaɪt] n (evening) crepuscolo (also fig); (morning) alba; **at ~** al crepuscolo; all'alba; **in the ~** nella penombra.

twill [twɪl] n (fabric) twill m.

twin [twɪn] **1** adj gemello(a); **~ beds** letti gemelli; **~ town** città gemella. **2** n gemello/a. **3** vt: **to ~ one town with another** fare il gemellaggio di una città con un'altra.

twin-carburettor ['twɪn,kɑːbjʊ'rɛtəʳ] adj a doppio carburatore.

twine [twaɪn] **1** n cordicella. **2** vt intrecciare. **3** vi attorcigliarsi.

twin-engined [,twɪn'ɛndʒɪnd] adj a due motori; **~ aircraft** bimotore m.

twinge [twɪndʒ] n (of pain) fitta; **a ~ of regret/ sadness** una punta di rimpianto/tristezza; **I've been having ~s of conscience** ho i rimorsi di coscienza.

twin·kle ['twɪŋkl] **1** n scintillio; **he had a ~ in his eye** gli scintillavano gli occhi. **2** vi scintillare.

twin·kling ['twɪŋklɪŋ] n: **in the ~ of an eye** in un batter d'occhio.

twin-set ['twɪnset] n completo di golf e cardigan.

twirl [twɜːl] **1** n (of body) piroetta; (in writing) ghirigoro. **2** vt (also: **~ round**: baton, lasso) far roteare; (: knob) far girare; (: moustache) arricciare. **3** vi (also: **~ round**: dancers) volteggiare.

twist [twɪst] **1** n (a) (in wire etc) piega; (of tobacco) treccia; (of paper) cartoccio; (of lemon) fettina. **(b)** (twisting action): **to give sth a ~** far girare qc; **to give one's ankle a ~** (Med) slogarsi la caviglia; **with a quick ~ of the wrist** con un rapido movimento del polso. **(c)** (bend) svolta, piega; (fig: in story etc) sviluppo; **a road full of ~s and turns** una strada a zigzag or tutta a curve; **the plot has an unexpected ~** la trama ha uno sviluppo inatteso; **to go round the ~** (fam) ammattire, impazzire. **(d):** **the ~** (dance) il twist; **to do the ~** ballare il twist.
2 vt (wrench out of shape) far piegare; (turn) girare; (unscrew) svitare; (also: **~ together**) intrecciare; (coil): **to ~ (round)** attorcigliare (intorno a); (fig: sense, words) travisare, distorcere; **his face was ~ed with pain** il suo volto era contratto dal dolore; **to ~ one's ankle/neck/wrist** (Med) slogarsi la caviglia/il collo/il polso; **to ~ sb's arm** (fig) forzare qn.
3 vi (a) (rope etc) attorcigliarsi; (road etc) snodarsi; **the road ~ed and turned** la strada procedeva a zigzag. **(b)** (dance) ballare il twist.

♦ **twist off** vt + adv svitare.

twist·ed ['twɪstɪd] adj (wire, rope) attorcigliato(a); (ankle, wrist) slogato(a); (fig: logic, mind) contorto(a).

twist·er ['twɪstəʳ] n (fam) imbroglione m.

twit [twɪt] n (fam) cretino/a.

twitch [twɪtʃ] **1** n (slight pull) tiratina; (nervous) tic m inv; **to give sth a ~** dare una tiratina a qc. **2** vi (hands, face, muscles) contrarsi; (person) agitarsi; (tail, ears) drizzarsi; (nose) muoversi.

twit·ter ['twɪtəʳ] **1** n (of bird) cinguettio; **to be all of a ~**, **be in a ~** (fam) essere in grande agitazione. **2** vi (bird) cinguettare; (person) cicalare.

two [tuː] **1** adj due inv. **2** n due m inv; **to break sth in ~** spezzare qc in due; **to ~s a due a due; to arrive in ~s and threes** arrivare alla spicciolata; **to put ~ and ~ together** (fig) fare uno più

uno; **that makes ~ of us** e così siamo in due.
two-door [ˌtuːˈdɔːʳ] *adj (car)* a due porte.
two-edged [ˌtuːˈɛdʒd] *adj (also fig)* a doppio taglio.
two-faced [ˌtuːˈfeɪst] *adj (fig)* doppio(a), falso(a).
two-fold [ˈtuːfəʊld] **1** *adv:* **to increase ~** aumentare del doppio. **2** *adj (increase)* doppio(a); *(reply)* in due punti.
two-legged [ˌtuːˈlɛgd] *adj* a due gambe, bipede.
two-party [ˈtuːˌpɑːtɪ] *adj (Pol)* bipartitico(a).
two·pence [ˈtʌpəns] *n (Brit)* due penny; *(: coin)* moneta da due penny.
two-phase [ˈtuːfeɪz] *adj (Elec)* bifase.
two-piece [ˈtuːpiːs] **1** *adj* (a) due pezzi. **2** *n (suit)* due pezzi *m inv.*
two-ply [ˈtuːplaɪ] *adj (wool)* a due capi.
two-seater [ˌtuːˈsiːtəʳ] *n (car)* macchina a due posti; *(plane)* biposto.
two·some [ˈtuːsəm] *n* coppia; **to go out in a ~** uscire in coppia.
two-stroke [ˈtuːstrəʊk] **1** *n (engine)* due tempi *m inv.* **2** *adj* a due tempi.
two-time [ˌtuːˈtaɪm] *vt (fam)* fare le corna a.
two-tone [ˈtuːtəʊn] *adj (colour)* bicolore.
two-way [ˈtuːweɪ] *adj (street)* a doppio senso; *(traffic)* a doppio senso di circolazione; **~ radio** radio *f inv* ricetrasmittente.
two-wheeler [ˌtuːˈwiːləʳ] *n* bicicletta.
ty·coon [taɪˈkuːn] *n* magnate *m.*
tym·pa·num [ˈtɪmpənəm] *n (Anat, Archit)* timpano.
type [taɪp] **1** *n* **(a)** *(gen, Bio etc)* tipo; *(sort)* genere *m,* tipo; *(make: of tea, machine)* marca; **what ~ do you want?** che tipo vuole?; **what ~ of person is he?** che tipo è?; **he's not my ~** non è il mio tipo; **it's my ~ of film** è il mio genere di film; **he's a pleasant ~** è un tipo piacevole. **(b)** *(Typ: one letter)* carattere *m* (tipografico); *(: letters collectively)* caratteri (tipografici), tipi *mpl;* **in bold/italic ~** in grassetto/corsivo. **2** *vt* **(a)** *(also:* **~ out,** **~ up)** battere a macchina. **(b)** *(disease etc)* clas-

sificare. **3** *vi* dattilografare, battere a macchina.
type·cast [ˈtaɪpkɑːst] *pt, pp* **typecast** *vt (Cine, Teatro)* far sempre fare la stessa parte a.
type·face [ˈtaɪpfeɪs] *n* carattere *m* tipografico.
type·script [ˈtaɪpskrɪpt] *n* dattiloscritto.
type·set [ˈtaɪpsɛt] *vt* comporre.
type·set·ter [ˈtaɪpˌsɛtəʳ] *n* compositore *m.*
type·writ·er [ˈtaɪpraɪtəʳ] *n* macchina da scrivere.
type·writ·ten [ˈtaɪprɪtn] *adj* dattiloscritto(a), battuto(a) a macchina.
ty·phoid [ˈtaɪfɔɪd] *n* febbre *f* tifoidea.
ty·phoon [taɪˈfuːn] *n* tifone *m.*
ty·phus [ˈtaɪfəs] *n* tifo.
typi·cal [ˈtɪpɪkəl] *adj* tipico(a); **a ~ case/example** un caso/esempio tipico; **the ~ Spaniard** il tipico spagnolo, lo spagnolo tipo; **(isn't that just) ~!** tipico!; **that's ~ of her!** questo è tipico di lei!
typi·cal·ly [ˈtɪpɪkəlɪ] *adv* tipicamente; **~, he arrived home late** come al solito è arrivato a casa tardi.
typi·fy [ˈtɪpɪfaɪ] *vt (thing)* caratterizzare; *(person)* impersonare.
typ·ing [ˈtaɪpɪŋ] **1** *n (skill)* dattilografia; **have you finished that ~?** hai finito quelle cose che dovevi battere a macchina? **2** *cpd (lesson)* di dattilografia; *(paper)* per macchina da scrivere; *(error)* di battitura; **~ pool** *n* ufficio *m* dattilografia *inv.*
typ·ist [ˈtaɪpɪst] *n* dattilografo/a.
ty·pog·ra·pher [taɪˈpɒgrəfəʳ] *n* tipografo.
ty·po·graph·ic(al) [ˌtaɪpəˈgræfɪk(əl)] *adj* tipografico(a).
ty·pog·ra·phy [taɪˈpɒgrəfɪ] *n* tipografia.
ty·ran·nic(al) [tɪˈrænɪk(əl)] *adj* tirannico(a).
tyr·an·ny [ˈtɪrənɪ] *n* tirannia.
ty·rant [ˈtaɪərənt] *n* tiranno.
tyre [ˈtaɪəʳ] **1** *n (Aut etc)* gomma. **2** *cpd:* **~ gauge** *n* manometro (per pneumatici); **~ pressure** *n* pressione *f* delle gomme.
tzar [zɑːʳ] *n* = **tsar.**

U

U, u [juː] *n (letter)* U, u *f or m inv.*
ubiqui·tous [juːˈbɪkwɪtəs] *adj* onnipresente.
U-boat [ˈjuːbəʊt] *n* sottomarino tedesco, U-boot *m inv.*
ud·der [ˈʌdəʳ] *n* mammella.
UFO [ˈjuːfəʊ] *n abbr (= unidentified flying object)* U.F.O. *m inv.*
Ugan·da [juːˈgændə] *n* Uganda.
ugh [ɜːh] *excl* puah!
ug·li·ness [ˈʌglɪnɪs] *n* bruttezza.
ugly [ˈʌglɪ] *adj* (-ier, -iest) **(a)** *(not pretty)* brutto(a); **as ~ as sin** brutto come la fame; **~ duckling** *(fig)* brutto anatroccolo. **(b)** *(unpleasant, nasty: situation, wound)* brutto(a); *(: rumour)* inquietante; *(: mood, look)* minaccioso(a); *(: crime, sight)* ripugnante; *(: vice)* osceno(a); **an ~ customer** *(fam)* un brutto tipo.
UHF *abbr (= ultra-high frequency)* UHF.
U.K. *abbr of* United Kingdom.
ul·cer [ˈʌlsəʳ] *n (also:* **stomach ~**) ulcera; *(elsewhere)* ulcerazione *f*; **mouth ~** afta.
Ul·ster [ˈʌlstəʳ] *n* Ulster *m.*
ul·te·ri·or [ʌlˈtɪərɪəʳ] *adj*: **~ motive** secondo fine *m.*
ul·ti·mate [ˈʌltɪmɪt] **1** *adj* **(a)** *(final: result)* finale; *(: conclusion)* definitivo(a); *(: destination)* ultimo(a). **(b)** *(greatest: insult)* massimo(a); *(: authority)* supremo(a); **the ~ deterrent** *(Mil)* l'ultimo mezzo di dissuasione. **(c)** *(principle, cause)* fondamentale. **2** *n* non plus ultra *m*; **the ~ in luxury** il non plus ultra del lusso.
ul·ti·mate·ly [ˈʌltɪmɪtlɪ] *adv (in the end; eventually)* in fin dei conti, in definitiva; *(in the last analysis)* in ultima analisi; *(at last)* alla fine.
ul·ti·ma·tum [ˌʌltɪˈmeɪtəm] *n, pl* **~s** *or* **ultimata** [ˌʌltɪˈmeɪtə] *(Mil, fig)* ultimatum *m inv*; **to issue an ~ to** dare l'ultimatum a.
ultra... [ˈʌltrə] *pref* ultra... .
ultra·ma·rine [ˌʌltrəməˈriːn] **1** *adj* oltremarino(a). **2** *n* oltremarino.
ultra·son·ic [ˌʌltrəˈsɒnɪk] *adj* ultrasonico(a).
ultra·sound [ˌʌltrəˈsaʊnd] *n (Med)* ecografia.
ultra·vio·let [ˌʌltrəˈvaɪəlɪt] *adj* ultravioletto(a).
um·ber [ˈʌmbəʳ] **1** *n* terra d'ombra. **2** *adj* color terra d'ombra.
um·bili·cal [ˌʌmbɪˈlaɪkəl] *adj*: **~ cord** cordone *m* ombelicale.
um·brage [ˈʌmbrɪdʒ] *n*: **to take ~ (at sth)** adombrarsi (a *or* per qc), risentirsi (di *or* per qc).
um·brel·la [ʌmˈbrɛlə] *n* ombrello; **under the ~ of** *(fig)* sotto l'egida di.
um·pire [ˈʌmpaɪəʳ] **1** *n* arbitro. **2** *vi* arbitrare.
ump·teen [ˈʌmptiːn] *adj (fam)* non so quanti(e); **~ times** centomila volte *fpl.*
ump·teenth [ˈʌmptiːnθ] *adj (fam)* ennesimo(a).
UN *n abbr of* United Nations.
un·abashed [ˌʌnəˈbæʃt] *adj* imperturbato(a).
un·abat·ed [ˌʌnəˈbeɪtɪd] *adj*: **to be** *or* **continue ~** *(storm, wind)* non accennare a diminuire; *(sb's strength)* non dare segni di cedimento.
un·able [ʌnˈeɪbl] *adj*: **to be ~ to do sth** *(not to know*

how to) non saper fare qc, non essere capace di fare qc; *(not to have it in one's power to)* non poter fare qc, non riuscire a fare qc.
un·abridged [ˌʌnəˈbrɪdʒd] *adj* integrale.
un·ac·cep·table [ˌʌnəkˈsɛptəbl] *adj (proposal, behaviour)* inaccettabile; *(price)* impossibile; **it's ~ that** è inammissibile che + *sub.*
un·ac·com·pa·nied [ˌʌnəˈkʌmpənɪd] *adj (child, person, luggage)* non accompagnato(a); *(singing, song)* senza accompagnamento; *(violin)* solo(a).
un·ac·count·ably [ˌʌnəˈkaʊntəblɪ] *adv* inesplicabilmente.
un·ac·count·ed [ˌʌnəˈkaʊntɪd] *adj*: **two passengers are ~ for** due passeggeri mancano all'appello.
un·ac·cus·tomed [ˌʌnəˈkʌstəmd] *adj* **(a)**: **to be ~ to sth/to doing** non essere abituato(a) a qc/a fare. **(b)**: **with ~ zeal** con insolito zelo.
un·ac·quaint·ed [ˌʌnəˈkweɪntɪd] *adj*: **to be ~ with** *(facts)* ignorare, non essere al corrente di; *(poverty)* non aver mai conosciuto.
un·adul·ter·at·ed [ˌʌnəˈdʌltəreɪtɪd] *adj (gen)* puro(a); *(wine)* non sofisticato(a).
un·af·fect·ed [ˌʌnəˈfɛktɪd] *adj* **(a)** *(person, behaviour)* naturale, spontaneo(a); *(manner, voice)* non affettato(a); *(gratitude)* sincero(a). **(b)** *(emotionally)*: **to be ~ by** non essere toccato(a) da; **she was wholly ~ by the news** la notizia non le ha fatto né caldo né freddo.
un·afraid [ˌʌnəˈfreɪd] *adj*: **to be ~** non aver paura.
un·aid·ed [ʌnˈeɪdɪd] **1** *adv* senza aiuto. **2** *adj*: **by his own ~ efforts** con le sue sole forze, senza l'aiuto di nessuno.
un·al·ter·able [ʌnˈɒltərəbl] *adj* inalterabile.
un·al·tered [ʌnˈɒltəd] *adj* inalterato(a).
un·am·bigu·ous [ˌʌnæmˈbɪgjʊəs] *adj* non ambiguo(a).
un·am·bi·tious [ˌʌnæmˈbɪʃəs] *adj (person)* poco ambizioso(a); *(plan)* senza pretese.
un-Ameri·can [ˈʌnəˈmɛrɪkən] *adj* antiamericano(a).
una·nim·ity [juːnəˈnɪmɪtɪ] *n* unanimità.
unani·mous [juːˈnænɪməs] *adj* unanime.
unani·mous·ly [juːˈnænɪməslɪ] *adv* all'unanimità.
un·an·swer·able [ʌnˈɑːnsərəbl] *adj (question)* senza risposta; *(case, argument)* irrefutabile.
un·an·swered [ʌnˈɑːnsəd] *adj (question, letter)* senza risposta; *(criticism)* non confutato(a).
un·ap·pe·tiz·ing [ʌnˈæpɪtaɪzɪŋ] *adj* poco appetitoso(a).
un·ap·pre·cia·tive [ˌʌnəˈpriːʃɪətɪv] *adj* che non apprezza.
un·ap·proach·able [ˌʌnəˈprəʊtʃəbl] *adj (person)* inavvicinabile, scostante.
un·armed [ʌnˈɑːmd] *adj (person)* disarmato(a); *(combat)* senz'armi.
un·ashamed [ˌʌnəˈʃeɪmd] *adj (brazen)* sfrontato(a), sfacciato(a); **she was quite ~ about it** non se ne vergognava minimamente.
un·asked [ʌnˈɑːskt] *adj (gen)* spontaneamente; *(arrive)* senza essere invitato(a).

un·as·sist·ed [ˌʌnə'sɪstɪd] *adj*, *adv* senza nessun aiuto.

un·as·sum·ing [ˌʌnə'sjuːmɪŋ] *adj* modesto(a), senza pretese.

un·at·tached [ˌʌnə'tætʃt] *adj (part)* staccato(a); *(fig: group, person)* indipendente; *(: soldier)* non assegnato(a); *(not married etc)* libero(a), senza legami.

un·at·tend·ed [ˌʌnə'tɛndɪd] *adj (not looked after: luggage)* incustodito(a); *(: child, patient)* solo(a), senza sorveglianza.

un·at·trac·tive [ˌʌnə'træktɪv] *adj (person)* poco attraente; *(offer)* poco allettante; *(place)* senza attrattiva.

un·author·ized [ʌn'ɔːθəraɪzd] *adj* non autorizzato(a).

un·avail·able [ˌʌnə'veɪləbl] *adj (article, room, book)* non disponibile; *(person)* impegnato(a).

un·avail·ing [ˌʌnə'veɪlɪŋ] *adj (effort)* vano(a), inutile.

un·avoid·able [ˌʌnə'vɔɪdəbl] *adj* inevitabile.

un·avoid·ably [ˌʌnə'vɔɪdəblɪ] *adv (detained)* per cause di forza maggiore.

un·aware [ˌʌnə'wɛəʳ] *adj*: **to be ~ of sth/that...** non rendersi conto di *or* ignorare qc/che... .

un·awares [ˌʌnə'wɛəz] *adv*: **to catch** *or* **take sb ~** prendere qn alla sprovvista.

un·bal·anced [ʌn'bælənst] *adj* non equilibrato(a); *(mentally)* squilibrato(a).

un·bear·able [ʌn'bɛərəbl] *adj* insopportabile.

un·bear·ably [ʌn'bɛərəblɪ] *adv* insopportabilmente.

un·beat·able [ˌʌn'biːtəbl] *adj* imbattibile.

un·beat·en [ʌn'biːtn] *adj (team, army)* imbattuto(a); *(record)* insuperato(a).

un·be·com·ing [ˌʌnbɪ'kʌmɪŋ] *adj (unseemly: language, behaviour)* sconveniente; *(unflattering: garment)* che non dona.

un·be·known(st) [ˌʌnbɪ'nəʊn(st)] *adv*: **~ to all**'insaputa di; **~ to me** a mia insaputa.

un·be·liev·able [ˌʌnbɪ'liːvəbl] *adj* incredibile; **it's ~ that...** è incredibile che... + *sub*.

un·be·liev·ably [ˌʌnbɪ'liːvəblɪ] *adv* incredibilmente.

un·be·liev·ing·ly [ˌʌnbɪ'liːvɪŋlɪ] *adv* con aria incredula; **he looked at me ~** mi ha guardato incredulo.

un·bend [ˌʌn'bɛnd] *pt*, *pp* **unbent 1** *vt (pipe etc)* raddrizzare. **2** *vi (fig: person)* distendersi.

un·bend·ing [ˌʌn'bɛndɪŋ] *adj (fig)* inflessibile, rigido(a).

un·bent [ˌʌn'bɛnt] *pt*, *pp of* **unbend**.

un·bi·as(s)ed [ˌʌn'baɪəst] *adj* obiettivo(a), imparziale.

un·blem·ished [ʌn'blɛmɪʃt] *adj* senza macchia.

un·block [ʌn'blɒk] *vt (pipe, road)* sbloccare.

un·bolt [ˌʌn'bəʊlt] *vt* levare il catenaccio a.

un·born [ˌʌn'bɔːn] *adj* non ancora nato(a).

un·bound·ed [ˌʌn'baʊndɪd] *adj* sconfinato(a), senza limite.

un·break·able [ˌʌn'breɪkəbl] *adj* infrangibile.

un·bri·dled [ʌn'braɪdld] *adj (fig: lust, ambition)* sfrenato(a).

un·bro·ken [ˌʌn'brəʊkən] *adj* **(a)** *(intact)* intatto(a), intero(a); **his spirit remained ~** il suo spirito è rimasto integro. **(b)** *(continuous: sleep, silence)* ininterrotto(a); *(: line of descent)* diretto(a). **(c)** *(record)* insuperato(a). **(d)** *(animal)* non domato(a).

un·buck·le [ˌʌn'bʌkl] *vt* slacciare.

un·bur·den [ʌn'bɜːdn] *vt*: **to ~ o.s. to sb** sfogarsi con qn.

un·business·like [ʌn'bɪznɪslaɪk] *adj (trader)* che

non ha il senso degli affari; *(transaction)* irregolare; *(fig: person)* poco efficiente; **he has an ~ manner** non ha niente dell'uomo d'affare; **it's ~ to do so** ciò dimostra una mancanza di organizzazione.

un·but·ton [ˌʌn'bʌtn] *vt* sbottonare.

uncalled-for [ʌn'kɔːldfɔːʳ] *adj* fuori luogo.

un·can·ni·ly [ʌn'kænɪlɪ] *adv* straordinariamente, incredibilmente.

un·can·ny [ʌn'kænɪ] *adj* **(-ier, -iest)** *(knack, resemblance)* sconcertante; *(sound, atmosphere)* strano(a), inquietante.

uncared-for [ˌʌn'kɛədfɔːʳ] *adj (gen)* trascurato(a); *(nails)* non curato(a).

un·ceas·ing [ʌn'siːsɪŋ] *adj* incessante.

un·ceas·ing·ly [ʌn'siːsɪŋlɪ] *adv* incessantemente, senza sosta.

un·cer·emo·ni·ous ['ʌn,sɛrɪ'məʊnɪəs] *adj (abrupt, rude)* brusco(a); **in ~ haste** in modo sbrigativo.

un·cer·emo·ni·ous·ly ['ʌn,sɛrɪ'məʊnɪəslɪ] *adv* senza tante cerimonie.

un·cer·tain [ʌn'sɜːtn] *adj (unsure, unknown: gen)* incerto(a); *(: aims)* vago(a); *(temper)* instabile; **I'm ~ about what to do** sono incerto sul da farsi; **it is ~ whether** non è sicuro se; **he is ~ whether** non sa bene se; **in no ~ terms** chiaro e tondo, senza mezzi termini.

un·cer·tain·ly [ʌn'sɜːtnlɪ] *adv (say)* senza troppa convinzione, con aria incerta; *(move)* con passo incerto.

un·cer·tain·ty [ʌn'sɜːtntɪ] *n* incertezza; *(doubts)* dubbi *mpl*; **the uncertainties of this life** gli incerti della vita.

un·chal·lenged [ˌʌn'tʃælɪndʒd] *adj (gen, Law)* incontestato(a); **to go ~** non venire contestato, non trovare opposizione; **to let a remark go ~** lasciar passare un'osservazione senza replicare.

un·changed [ˌʌn'tʃeɪndʒd] *adj (plans, situation)* immutato(a), invariato(a); **he's completely ~** non è cambiato minimamente.

un·chang·ing [ʌn'tʃeɪndʒɪŋ] *adj* immutabile.

un·chari·table [ʌn'tʃærɪtəbl] *adj (attitude)* poco generoso(a); *(remark)* cattivo(a).

un·chart·ed [ˌʌn'tʃɑːtɪd] *adj* inesplorato(a).

un·checked [ˌʌn'tʃɛkt] *adj* **(a)** *(unrestrained: anger)* incontrollato(a); **to go ~** *(abuse, violence)* rimanere incontrollato; *(virus, inflation)* dilagare; **to advance ~** avanzare senza incontrare opposizione. **(b)** *(not verified: facts)* non controllato(a), non verificato(a); *(typescript)* non corretto(a).

un·chris·tian [ˌʌn'krɪstjən] *adj* poco cristiano(a).

un·civi·lized [ˌʌn'sɪvɪlaɪzd] *adj (gen)* selvaggio(a); *(fig)* incivile, barbaro(a).

un·claimed [ˌʌn'kleɪmd] *adj (prize, social security benefit)* non ritirato(a); *(property)* non reclamato(a).

un·cle ['ʌŋkl] *n* zio.

un·clean [ˌʌn'kliːn] *adj* sporco(a); *(fig)* immondo(a).

un·clear [ˌʌn'klɪəʳ] *adj* non chiaro(a); **I'm still ~ about what I'm supposed to do** non ho ancora ben capito cosa dovrei fare.

un·cloud·ed [ˌʌn'klaʊdɪd] *adj* senza nuvole; *(fig: mind)* limpido(a); *(: happiness)* senza una nube.

un·coil [ˌʌn'kɔɪl] **1** *vt* srotolare. **2** *vi* srotolarsi, svolgersi.

un·col·lect·ed [ˌʌnkə'lɛktɪd] *adj (luggage, prize)* non ritirato(a); *(rubbish)* non portato(a) via; *(tax)* non riscosso(a).

un·combed [ˌʌn'kəʊmd] *adj* spettinato(a).

un·com·fort·able [ʌn'kʌmfətəbl] *adj* **(a)** *(person, chair)* scomodo(a); *(afternoon)* poco piacevole; **to**

have an ~ time passare un brutto quarto d'ora; **to make life ~ for sb** rendere la vita difficile a qn. **(b)** *(shy, embarrassed)* a disagio, non a proprio agio; **to make sb feel ~** mettere qn a disagio; **I had an ~ feeling that...** ho avuto la sgradevole sensazione che... .

un·com·fort·ably [ʌn'kʌmfətəblɪ] *adv* **(a)** *(dressed)* in modo poco pratico; *(hot)* troppo, eccessivamente. **(b)** *(uneasily: say)* con voce inquieta; *(: think)* con inquietudine; **~ near** a una vicinanza preoccupante.

un·com·mit·ted [ˌʌnkə'mɪtɪd] *adj (attitude, country)* neutrale; **to be ~** *(person)* non essersi impegnato; **to remain ~ to** *(policy, party)* non dare la propria adesione a.

un·com·mon [ʌn'kɒmən] *adj* **(a)** *(unusual)* insolito(a), raro(a); **it's not ~ that** non è raro che + *sub*. **(b)** *(outstanding)* fuori dal comune.

un·com·mu·ni·ca·tive [ˌʌnkə'mjuːnɪkətɪv] *adj* poco comunicativo(a), chiuso(a).

un·com·plain·ing [ˌʌnkəm'pleɪnɪŋ] *adj* che non si lamenta.

un·com·plain·ing·ly [ˌʌnkəm'pleɪnɪŋlɪ] *adv* senza lamentarsi.

un·com·pli·cat·ed [ʌn'kɒmplɪkeɪtɪd] *adj* semplice, poco complicato(a).

un·com·pli·men·ta·ry ['ʌnˌkɒmplɪ'mentərɪ] *adj* poco gentile.

un·com·pro·mis·ing [ʌn'kɒmprəmaɪzɪŋ] *adj (honesty, dedication)* assoluto(a); *(attitude)* intransigente, inflessibile.

un·con·cealed [ˌʌnkən'siːld] *adj* non dissimulato(a).

un·con·cerned [ˌʌnkən'sɜːnd] *adj (unworried)* tranquillo(a); **to be ~ about** non darsi pensiero di, non preoccuparsi di *or* per.

un·con·di·tion·al [ˌʌnkən'dɪʃənl] *adj (surrender, refusal)* incondizionato(a); *(freedom)* senza condizioni, assoluto(a).

un·con·di·tion·al·ly [ˌʌnkən'dɪʃnəlɪ] *adv* incondizionatamente, senza condizioni.

un·con·firmed [ˌʌnkən'fɜːmd] *adj* non confermato(a).

un·con·gen·ial [ˌʌnkən'dʒiːnɪəl] *adj (person)* poco simpatico(a); *(surroundings, work)* poco piacevole.

un·con·nect·ed [ˌʌnkə'nektɪd] *adj* **(a)** *(unrelated)* senza connessione, senza rapporto; **to be ~ with** essere estraneo a. **(b)** *(incoherent)* sconnesso(a).

un·con·scious [ʌn'kɒnʃəs] **1** *adj* **(a)** *(Med)* senza conoscenza, privo(a) di sensi; **to fall ~** svenire, cadere (a terra) privo di sensi; **to knock sb ~** far perdere i sensi a qn con un pugno. **(b)** *(unaware)*: **~ (of)** inconsapevole (di), ignaro(a) (di). **(c)** *(unintentional: action, desire)* inconscio(a). **2** *n (Psych)*: **the ~** l'inconscio.

un·con·scious·ly [ʌn'kɒnʃəslɪ] *adv* inconsciamente, senza rendersi conto.

un·con·sti·tu·tion·al ['ʌnˌkɒnstɪ'tjuːʃənl] *adj* incostituzionale.

un·con·test·ed [ˌʌnkən'testɪd] *adj (champion)* incontestato(a); *(Parliament: seat)* non disputato(a).

un·con·trol·lable [ˌʌnkən'trəʊləbl] *adj (desire, child, epidemic)* incontrollabile; *(laughter)* irrefrenabile; *(temper, reaction)* incontrollato(a).

un·con·trolled [ˌʌnkən'trəʊld] *adj (child, dog, laughter, weeping)* sfrenato(a); *(inflation, price rises)* che sfugge al controllo.

un·con·ven·tion·al [ˌʌnkən'venʃənl] *adj* poco convenzionale.

un·con·vinced [ˌʌnkən'vɪnst] *adj*: **to be** *or* **remain ~** non essere convinto(a).

un·con·vinc·ing [ˌʌnkən'vɪnsɪŋ] *adj* non convincente, poco persuasivo(a).

un·cooked [ˌʌn'kʊkt] *adj* crudo(a).

un·cork [ˌʌn'kɔːk] *vt* stappare.

un·cor·robo·rat·ed [ˌʌnkə'rɒbəreɪtɪd] *adj* non convalidato(a).

un·cou·ple [ˌʌn'kʌpl] *vt* sganciare.

un·couth [ʌn'kuːθ] *adj* maleducato(a), rozzo(a).

un·cov·er [ʌn'kʌvəʳ] *vt* **(a)** *(find out)* scoprire; *(: scandal)* portare alla luce. **(b)** *(remove coverings of)* scoprire; *(: drain)* scoperchiare.

un·criti·cal [ˌʌn'krɪtɪkəl] *adj*: **~ (of)** che manca di senso critico (nei confronti di).

unc·tion ['ʌŋkʃən] *n*: **extreme ~** *(Rel)* estrema unzione *f*.

unc·tu·ous ['ʌŋktjʊəs] *adj* untuoso(a).

un·cul·ti·vat·ed [ˌʌn'kʌltɪveɪtɪd] *adj* incolto(a).

un·cul·tured [ˌʌn'kʌltʃəd] *adj (person)* senza cultura, incolto(a); *(mind)* ignorante.

un·curl [ˌʌn'kɜːl] *vt (gen)* srotolare; *(one's legs)* stendere.

un·dam·aged [ˌʌn'dæmɪdʒd] *adj (goods)* in buono stato; *(fig: reputation)* intatto(a).

un·dat·ed [ˌʌn'deɪtɪd] *adj* senza data.

un·daunt·ed [ˌʌn'dɔːntɪd] *adj*: **~ by** per nulla intimidito(a) da; **to carry on ~** continuare imperterrito.

un·de·cid·ed [ˌʌndɪ'saɪdɪd] *adj (person)* indeciso(a), incerto(a); *(matter)* irrisolto(a); **we are still ~ whether to go** siamo ancora indecisi se andare o meno.

un·de·feat·ed [ˌʌndɪ'fiːtɪd] *adj* imbattuto(a).

un·de·fined [ˌʌndɪ'faɪnd] *adj (idea)* non ben definito; *(number, quantity)* indefinito(a); *(feeling)* vago(a).

un·de·liv·ered [ˌʌndɪ'lɪvəd] *adj* non recapitato(a); **if ~ return to sender** ≃ in caso di mancato recapito rispedire al mittente.

un·de·mon·stra·tive [ˌʌndɪ'mɒnstrətɪv] *adj* riservato(a), poco espansivo(a).

un·de·ni·able [ˌʌndɪ'naɪəbl] *adj* innegabile, fuori discussione.

un·de·ni·ably [ˌʌndɪ'naɪəblɪ] *adv* innegabilmente.

un·der ['ʌndəʳ] **1** *adv* **(a)** *(beneath: position)* sotto; *(: direction)* sotto, di sotto; **to be ~** *(~ anaesthetic)* essere sotto anestesia.

(b) *(less)* al di sotto, meno; **girls of 14 and ~** ragazze dai 14 anni in giù.

2 *prep* **(a)** *(beneath)* sotto; **~ the table** sotto il tavolo; **from ~ the bed** da sotto il letto; **it's ~ there** sta lì sotto; **~ water** sott'acqua.

(b) *(less than)* meno di; *(: in rank, scale)* al di sotto di; **in ~ 2 hours** in meno di 2 ore; **people ~ 50 (years old)** gente al di sotto dei 50.

(c) *(fig: sb's leadership, sign of zodiac, letter in catalogue)* sotto; **~ anaesthetic** sotto anestesia; **~ discussion/repair/construction** in discussione/riparazione/costruzione; **to study ~ sb** studiare con qn *or* sotto la guida di qn; **~ the circumstances** date le circostanze; **~ the Romans** sotto i Romani; **~ a false name** sotto falso nome; **he has 30 workers ~ him** ha 30 operai sotto di sé.

(d) *(according to)* secondo; **~ the new law** secondo quanto previsto dalla nuova legge.

under... ['ʌndəʳ] *pref* **(a)** *(in rank)* sotto..., aiuto...; *(in age)*: **the ~-15s** i ragazzi al di sotto dei 15 anni; **~gardener** aiutogiardiniere *m*. **(b)** *(insufficiently)* sotto...; **~prepared** poco preparato(a); **~cooked** poco cotto(a).

under·age [ˌʌndər'eɪdʒ] *adj* minorenne.

under·arm ['ʌndərɑːm] *adv (throw)* di sotto in su.

under·car·riage [ˈʌndəˌkærɪdʒ] *n (Aer)* carrello (d'atterraggio).

under·charge [ˌʌndəˈtʃɑːdʒ] *vt* far pagare di meno a.

under·clothes [ˈʌndəkləʊðz] *npl* biancheria (intima *or* personale).

under·coat [ˈʌndəkəʊt] *n (of paint)* prima mano *f*.

under·cover [ˈʌndəˌkʌvəʳ] *adj (agent)* segreto(a); *(meeting)* clandestino(a).

under·cur·rent [ˈʌndəˌkʌrənt] *n* corrente *f* sottomarina; *(fig)* vena (nascosta).

under·cut [ˌʌndəˈkʌt] *pt, pp* **undercut** *vt (Comm)* vendere a minor prezzo di.

under·de·vel·oped [ˌʌndədɪˈvɛləpt] *adj (baby, muscles, photo)* non ben sviluppato(a); *(country)* sottosviluppato(a).

under·dog [ˈʌndədɒg] *n*: **the ~** *(in fight)* il(la) più debole; *(in society)* la vittima (del sistema); *(in family, organization)* l'ultima ruota del carro.

under·done [ˌʌndəˈdʌn] *adj* poco cotto(a); *(deliberately: steak)* al sangue.

under·es·ti·mate [ˌʌndərˈɛstɪmeɪt] *vt* sottovalutare.

under·ex·posed [ˌʌndərɪksˈpəʊzd] *adj (Phot)* sottoesposto(a).

under·fed [ˌʌndəˈfɛd] *adj* denutrito(a).

under·floor heat·ing [ˈʌndəflɔːˈhiːtɪŋ] *n* riscaldamento a pavimento.

under·foot [ˌʌndəˈfʊt] *adv* per terra; **to trample ~** *(also fig)* calpestare; **the children are always getting ~** i bambini sono sempre tra i piedi.

under·go [ˌʌndəˈgəʊ] *pt* **underwent**, *pp* **undergone** [ˌʌndəˈgɒn] *vt* sottoporsi a, subire; **to ~ changes** essere sottoposto(a) a modifiche; **the car is ~ing repairs** la macchina è in riparazione.

under·gradu·ate [ˌʌndəˈgrædjʊɪt] **1** *n (also:* **undergrad)** studente(essa) universitario(a). **2** *cpd (opinion, attitudes)* degli studenti; **~ courses** *npl* corsi *mpl* di laurea.

under·ground [ˈʌndəgraʊnd] **1** *adj (passage, cave, railway)* sotterraneo(a); *(fig: political movement, press)* clandestino(a); *(: Art, Cine)* underground *inv*. **2** [ˌʌndəˈgraʊnd] *adv* sottoterra; **to go ~** *(fig)* darsi alla macchia. **3** *n (Brit Rail)* metropolitana; *(Mil, Pol)* movimento clandestino, resistenza; *(Art etc)* controcultura, underground *f*; **to go by ~** *or* **on the ~** andare in *or* con la metropolitana.

under·growth [ˈʌndəgrəʊθ] *n* sottobosco.

under·hand [ˌʌndəˈhænd] *adj (method)* equivoco(a), poco pulito(a); *(trick)* subdolo(a).

under·in·sured [ˌʌndərɪnˈʃʊəd] *adj* non sufficientemente assicurato(a).

under·lie [ˌʌndəˈlaɪ] *pt* **underlay** [ˌʌndəˈleɪ], *pp* **underlain** [ˌʌndəˈleɪn] *vt (fig)* essere alla base di; **an underlying nervousness** un nervosismo di fondo; **the underlying cause** il motivo di fondo.

under·line [ˌʌndəˈlaɪn] *vt (also fig)* sottolineare.

under·ling [ˈʌndəlɪŋ] *n (pej)* galoppino, tirapiedi *m inv*.

under·men·tioned [ˌʌndəˈmɛnʃənd] *adj* (riportato(a)) qui sotto *or* qui di seguito.

under·mine [ˌʌndəˈmaɪn] *vt (fig)* minare; *(: authority)* pregiudicare.

under·neath [ˌʌndəˈniːθ] **1** *prep* sotto, al di sotto di. **2** *adv* sotto, di sotto. **3** *n* parte *f* di sotto.

under·nour·ished [ˌʌndəˈnʌrɪʃt] *adj* denutrito(a).

under·paid [ˌʌndəˈpeɪd] *adj* mal pagato(a).

under·pants [ˈʌndəpænts] *npl* mutande *fpl*, slip *m inv*.

under·pass [ˈʌndəpɑːs] *n (for cars)* sottopassaggio; *(for pedestrians)* sottopassaggio pedonale.

under·pin [ˌʌndəˈpɪn] *vt (Archit)* puntellare; *(fig: argument etc)* corroborare.

under·play [ˌʌndəˈpleɪ] *vt* minimizzare; **to ~ one's hand** *(fig)* non giocare bene le carte.

under·popu·lat·ed [ˌʌndəˈpɒpjʊleɪtɪd] *adj* scarsamente popolato(a), sottopopolato(a).

under·priced [ˌʌndəˈpraɪst] *adj* a un prezzo inferiore al dovuto.

under·privi·leged [ˌʌndəˈprɪvɪlɪdʒd] *adj* svantaggiato(a); **the ~** i diseredati.

under·rate [ˌʌndəˈreɪt] *vt* sottovalutare.

under·seal [ˈʌndəˌsiːl] *vt* rendere stagno il fondo di.

under·sec·re·tary [ˌʌndəˈsɛkrətrɪ] *n* sottosegretario.

under·sell [ˈʌndəˈsɛl] *pt, pp* **undersold** *vt (competitors)* vendere a prezzi più bassi di; *(fig)* non valorizzare a sufficienza.

under·shirt [ˈʌndəʃɜːt] *n (Am)* maglietta, canottiera.

under·side [ˈʌndəsaɪd] *n* parte *f* di sotto.

under·signed [ˈʌndəsaɪnd] *adj, n* sottoscritto(a) *(m/f)*; **I the ~** io sottoscritto.

under·sized [ˌʌndəˈsaɪzd] *adj* piccolo(a) (di statura).

under·skirt [ˈʌndəskɜːt] *n* sottoveste *f*.

under·sold [ˈʌndəˈsəʊld] *pt, pp of* **undersell**.

under·staffed [ˌʌndəˈstɑːft] *adj* a corto di personale.

under·stand [ˌʌndəˈstænd] *pt, pp* **understood** **1** *vt* **(a)** *(gen)* capire; **to make o.s. understood** farsi capire; **I can't ~ a word of it** non ci capisco una parola; **I don't ~ why...** non capisco perché...; **she ~s children** capisce i bambini; **we ~ one another** ci capiamo (tra di noi); **he doesn't ~ how I feel** non mi capisce; **I can ~ his wanting to go** posso ben capire il suo desiderio di andarsene; **is that understood?** chiaro?; **I wish it to be understood that...** sia ben chiaro che...; **~!** *(agreed)* intesi! **(b)** *(believe)* credere; **we understood we were to be paid** a quanto avevamo capito dovevamo essere pagati; **I ~ you have been absent** mi risulta che lei è stato assente; **it's understood that...** resta inteso che...; **he let it be understood that he was leaving** ha dato a intendere che stava per partire; **she is understood to be ill** si dice che stia poco bene.

2 *vi* capire; **I quite ~** capisco benissimo, s'immagini; **she was, I ~, a Catholic** era, se non sbaglio, cattolica.

under·stand·able [ˌʌndəˈstændəbl] *adj* comprensibile.

under·stand·ing [ˌʌndəˈstændɪŋ] **1** *adj (person)* comprensivo(a); *(smile)* indulgente. **2** *n* **(a)** *(intelligence)* comprensione *f*; **his ~ of these problems** il modo in cui vede questi problemi; **it was my ~ that...** era mia convinzione che... + *sub*. **(b)** *(sympathy)* simpatia, comprensione *f*. **(c)** *(agreement)* accordo, intesa; **to come to an ~ with sb** giungere ad un accordo con qn; **on the ~ that he pays** a patto che *or* a condizione che paghi lui.

under·state [ˌʌndəˈsteɪt] *vt* minimizzare, sminuire.

under·state·ment [ˈʌndəˌsteɪtmənt] *n* minimizzare *m*; **that's an ~!** a dir poco!

under·stood [ˌʌndəˈstʊd] *pt, pp of* **understand**.

under·study [ˈʌndəstʌdɪ] **1** *n (Theatre)* doppio. **2** *vt* sostituire.

under·take [ˌʌndəˈteɪk] *pt* **undertook**, *pp* **undertaken** [ˌʌndəˈteɪkən] *vt (task, responsibility etc)* assumersi; **to ~ to do sth** impegnarsi a fare qc.

under·tak·er [ˈʌndəˌteɪkəʳ] *n* impresario di pompe funebri.

under·tak·ing [ˌʌndəˈteɪkɪŋ] *n* **(a)** *(task)* impresa;

it is quite an ~! è una bella impresa! **(b)** *(pledge)* promessa, assicurazione *f;* **to give an** ~ **that...** dare la propria parola che... .

under·tone [ˈʌndətəʊn] *n* **(a)** *(low voice)* tono sommesso; **in an** ~ a mezza voce, a voce bassa. **(b)** *(of criticism etc)* vena, sottofondo.

under·took [ˌʌndəˈtʊk] *pt of* **undertake.**

under·tow [ˈʌndətəʊ] *n* risucchio.

under·value [ˌʌndəˈvæljuː] *vt (Comm etc)* sottovalutare; *(fig)* svalutare, sottovalutare.

under·wa·ter [ˌʌndəˈwɔːtəʳ] **1** *adj (swimming, photography)* subacqueo(a); *(exploration)* sottomarino(a). **2** *adv* sott'acqua.

under·wear [ˈʌndəweəʳ] *n* biancheria (intima).

under·weight [ˌʌndəˈweɪt] *adj (person)* sottopeso *inv; (thing)* al di sotto del giusto peso.

under·went [ˌʌndəˈwɛnt] *pt of* **undergo.**

under·world [ˈʌndəwɜːld] *n (hell)* inferi *mpl; (criminal)* malavita.

under·write [ˈʌndəraɪt] *pt* **underwrote,** *pp* **underwritten** *vt (Fin)* sottoscrivere; *(Insurance)* assicurare.

under·writ·er [ˈʌndəˌraɪtəʳ] *n (Insurance)* assicuratore *m; (Fin)* sottoscrittore *m.*

under·writ·ten [ˈʌndəˌrɪtn] *pp of* **underwrite.**

under·wrote [ˈʌndərəʊt] *pt of* **underwrite.**

un·de·served [ˌʌndɪˈzɜːvd] *adj* immeritato(a).

un·de·serv·ing [ˌʌndɪˈzɜːvɪŋ] *adj:* **to be** ~ **of** non meritare, non essere degno di.

un·de·sir·able [ˌʌndɪˈzaɪərəbl] **1** *adj (effects)* sgradevole; *(behaviour, habits, friendship)* discutibile. **2** *n* persona indesiderabile.

un·de·vel·oped [ˌʌndɪˈvɛləpt] *adj (land, resources)* non sfruttato(a).

un·did [ˌʌnˈdɪd] *pt of* **undo.**

un·dies [ˈʌndɪz] *npl (fam)* biancheria (intima).

un·dig·ni·fied [ʌnˈdɪɡnɪfaɪd] *adj (person)* senza dignità, poco dignitoso(a); *(manner, action)* indecoroso(a), sconveniente.

un·di·lut·ed [ˌʌndaɪˈluːtɪd] *adj (concentrate)* non diluito(a); *(bliss)* perfetto(a), assoluto(a).

un·dip·lo·matic [ˌʌndɪpləˈmætɪk] *adj* poco diplomatico(a).

un·dis·cern·ing [ˌʌndɪˈsɜːnɪŋ] *adj (reader)* poco selettivo(a); *(critic)* di scarso acume.

un·dis·ci·plined [ʌnˈdɪsɪplɪnd] *adj* indisciplinato(a).

un·dis·cov·ered [ˌʌndɪsˈkʌvəd] *adj (areas)* inesplorato(a); *(work of art)* ignoto(a).

un·dis·guised [ˌʌndɪsˈɡaɪzd] *adj (dislike, amusement etc)* palese.

un·dis·mayed [ˌʌndɪsˈmeɪd] *adj:* **to be** ~ **at** non lasciarsi impressionare da.

un·dis·put·ed [ˌʌndɪsˈpjuːtɪd] *adj* incontrastato(a).

un·dis·tin·guished [ˌʌndɪsˈtɪŋɡwɪʃt] *adj* senza infamia e senza lode, mediocre; **an** ~ **poet** un poetucolo; **an** ~ **wine** un vino qualsiasi.

un·dis·turbed [ˌʌndɪsˈtɜːbd] *adj* **(a)** *(sleep)* tranquillo(a); **to work** ~ lavorare in pace; **to leave sth** ~ lasciare qc così com'è. **(b)** *(unworried):* ~ **(by)** indifferente (a); **the Prime Minister is** ~ **by rising inflation** l'inflazione crescente non turba minimamente il primo ministro.

un·di·vid·ed [ˌʌndɪˈvaɪdɪd] *adj:* **I want your** ~ **attention** esigo tutta la tua attenzione.

undo [ʌnˈduː] *pt* **undid,** *pp* **undone** *vt* **(a)** *(unfasten: button, shoelaces)* slacciare; *(: knot)* sciogliere; *(: parcel)* aprire; *(: knitting)* disfare. **(b)** *(reverse: action, wrong)* riparare; *(spoil)* rovinare.

un·do·ing [ʌnˈduːɪŋ] *n* rovina.

un·done [ˌʌnˈdʌn] **1** *pp of* **undo. 2** *adj (unfastened: button)* slacciato(a); **to come** ~ slacciarsi; **to leave** ~ *(shirt)* lasciare aperto *or* sbottonato;

(button) lasciare slacciato; *(job)* non fare, lasciare da fare.

un·doubt·ed [ʌnˈdaʊtɪd] *adj* indubbio(a).

un·doubt·ed·ly [ʌnˈdaʊtɪdlɪ] *adv* indubbiamente, senza dubbio.

un·dreamed [ʌnˈdriːmd] *adj,* **un·dreamt** [ʌnˈdrɛmt] *adj:* ~ **of** mai sognato(a).

un·dress [ˌʌnˈdrɛs] **1** *vt* spogliare. **2** *vi (also:* **get** ~**ed)** spogliarsi, svestirsi.

un·drink·able [ˌʌnˈdrɪŋkəbl] *adj (unpalatable)* imbevibile; *(poisonous)* non potabile.

un·due [ˌʌnˈdjuː] *adj* eccessivo(a), esagerato(a).

un·du·la·ting [ˈʌndjʊleɪtɪŋ] *adj (countryside, surface)* ondulato(a); *(sea)* ondeggiante.

un·du·ly [ˌʌnˈdjuːlɪ] *adv* troppo, eccessivamente.

un·dy·ing [ʌnˈdaɪɪŋ] *adj* imperituro(a).

un·earned [ˌʌnˈɜːnd] *adj (praise, respect)* immeritato(a); ~ **income** rendita.

un·earth [ˌʌnˈɜːθ] *vt* dissotterrare; *(fig: secret)* disseppellire; *(: object)* scovare; *(: evidence)* portare alla luce.

un·earth·ly [ʌnˈɜːθlɪ] *adj (eerie: brightness)* innaturale; *(: noise, sound)* spettrale; ~ **hour** *(fam)* ora impossibile.

un·easi·ly [ʌnˈiːzɪlɪ] *adv (sleep)* male; *(glance, look)* con apprensione; **to be** ~ **balanced** essere in equilibrio precario; **she glanced** ~ **at him** gli lanciò uno sguardo inquieto.

un·easy [ʌnˈiːzɪ] *adj (calm, peace etc)* precario(a); *(night, sleep)* agitato(a); *(silence)* imbarazzato(a); *(person: worried)* inquieto(a), agitato(a); *(: ill at ease)* a disagio; **to feel** ~ **about doing sth** non sentirsela di fare qc; **to become** ~ **about sb/sth** cominciare a preoccuparsi per qn/qc; **to have an** ~ **conscience** non avere la coscienza apposto.

un·eat·en [ˌʌnˈiːtn] *adj* non mangiato(a); *(left over)* avanzato(a); **she left the steak** ~ non ha toccato la bistecca.

un·eco·nom·ic [ˈʌnˌiːkəˈnɒmɪk] *adj (method, process)* antieconomico(a).

un·eco·nomi·cal [ˈʌnˌiːkəˈnɒmɪkəl] *adj (car, machine)* poco economico(a); *(use)* dispendioso(a).

un·edu·cat·ed [ʌnˈɛdjʊkeɪtɪd] *adj (person)* senza istruzione, incolto(a); *(speech)* popolare.

un·emo·tion·al [ˌʌnɪˈməʊʃənl] *adj (person)* freddo(a), impassibile; *(account)* distaccato(a).

un·em·ployed [ˌʌnɪmˈplɔɪd] **1** *adj* disoccupato(a), senza lavoro. **2** *npl:* **the** ~ i disoccupati.

un·em·ploy·ment [ˌʌnɪmˈplɔɪmənt] **1** *n* disoccupazione *f.* **2** *cpd:* ~ **benefit** *n (Brit)* sussidio di disoccupazione.

un·end·ing [ʌnˈɛndɪŋ] *adj* interminabile, senza fine.

un·en·dur·able [ˌʌnɪnˈdjʊərəbl] *adj* insopportabile.

un·en·ter·pris·ing [ʌnˈɛntəpraɪzɪŋ] *adj* poco intraprendente.

un·en·thu·si·as·tic [ˈʌnɪnˌθjuːzɪˈæstɪk] *adj* poco entusiasta.

un·en·vi·able [ʌnˈɛnvɪəbl] *adj* poco invidiabile.

un·equal [ˌʌnˈiːkwəl] *adj (length, objects)* disuguale; *(amounts)* diverso(a); *(division of labour)* ineguale; **to be** ~ **to a task** non essere all'altezza di un compito.

un·equalled, *(Am)* **un·equaled** [ʌnˈiːkwəld] *adj* senza pari, insuperato(a).

un·equivo·cal [ˌʌnɪˈkwɪvəkəl] *adj (answer)* inequivocabile; *(person)* esplicito(a), chiaro(a).

un·equivo·cal·ly [ˌʌnɪˈkwɪvəkəlɪ] *adv* in modo inequivocabile.

un·err·ing [ʌnˈɜːrɪŋ] *adj (aim, taste, instinct)* infallibile.

UNESCO [juːˈnɛskəʊ] *n abbr* (= *United Nations*

Educational, Scientific and Cultural Organization) U.N.E.S.C.O. *f.*

un·eth·i·cal [ˌʌn'eθɪkəl] *adj (methods)* poco ortodosso(a), non moralmente accettabile; *(doctor's behaviour)* contrario(a) all'etica professionale.

un·even [ˌʌn'iːvən] *adj (thickness, work)* ineguale; *(ground)* disuguale, accidentato(a); *(heartbeat)* irregolare.

un·even·ly [ˌʌn'iːvənlɪ] *adv (gen)* in modo irregolare.

un·event·ful [ˌʌnɪ'ventfʊl] *adj* senza sorprese, tranquillo(a).

un·ex·cep·tion·able [ˌʌnɪk'sepʃnəbl] *adj (behaviour)* irreprensibile; *(style)* ineccepibile; *(speech)* inappuntabile.

un·ex·cep·tion·al [ˌʌnɪk'sepʃənl] *adj* che non ha niente d'eccezionale.

un·ex·cit·ing [ˌʌnɪk'saɪtɪŋ] *adj (news)* poco emozionante; *(film, evening)* poco interessante; *(person)* scialbo(a).

un·ex·pec·ted [ˌʌnɪks'pektɪd] *adj* inatteso(a), imprevisto(a).

un·ex·pect·ed·ly [ˌʌnɪks'pektɪdlɪ] *adv* inaspettatamente; *(arrive)* senza preavviso.

un·ex·plained [ˌʌnɪks'pleɪnd] *adj* inspiegato(a).

un·ex·posed [ˌʌnɪks'pəʊzd] *adj (Phot)* vergine.

un·ex·pressed [ˌʌnɪks'prest] *adj* inespresso(a).

un·fail·ing [ʌn'feɪlɪŋ] *adj (remedy)* sicuro(a), infallibile; *(humour)* inesauribile; *(zeal, courage)* immancabile.

un·fail·ing·ly [ʌn'feɪlɪŋlɪ] *adv* immancabilmente, senza fallo.

un·fair [ˌʌn'feəʳ] *adj* **(-er, -est)** *(person, decision, criticism)* ingiusto(a); *(means, tactics)* sleale; *(competition)* scorretto(a); **it's ~ that...** non è giusto che... + *sub;* **to be ~ to sb** essere ingiusto verso qn.

un·fair·ly [ˌʌn'feəlɪ] *adv (treat, criticize)* ingiustamente; *(play)* scorrettamente.

un·faith·ful [ˌʌn'feɪθfʊl] *adj:* **~ (to sb)** infedele (a qn).

un·fa·mil·iar [ˌʌnfə'mɪljəʳ] *adj (subject)* sconosciuto(a); *(experience)* insolito(a); *(surroundings)* estraneo(a); **to be ~ with sth** non essere pratico di qc, non avere familiarità con qc.

un·fash·ion·able [ˌʌn'fæʃnəbl] *adj (clothes)* fuori moda; *(district)* non alla moda; **these trousers are ~** questi pantaloni sono fuori moda *or* non vanno più.

un·fas·ten [ˌʌn'fɑːsn] *vt (buttons, seatbelt)* slacciare; *(scarf, rope)* sciogliere; *(gate)* aprire.

un·fath·om·able [ʌn'fæðəməbl] *adj (anche fig)* insondabile; *(: person)* imperscrutabile.

un·fa·vour·able, *(Am)* **un·fa·vor·able** [ˌʌn'feɪvərəbl] *adj (gen)* sfavorevole; *(report, result)* negativo(a).

un·fa·vour·ably, *(Am)* **un·fa·vor·ably** [ˌʌn'feɪvərəblɪ] *adv (judge, see)* in senso sfavorevole; *(speak)* sfavorevolmente; **to look ~ upon** vedere di malocchio.

un·feel·ing [ʌn'fiːlɪŋ] *adj* insensibile.

un·fin·ished [ˌʌn'fɪnɪʃt] *adj (letter)* non finito(a); *(business)* in sospeso; *(symphony)* incompiuto(a).

un·fit [ˌʌn'fɪt] *adj (unsuitable):* **~ (for)** inadatto(a); *(Sport: injured)* non in grado di giocare *(or* correre *etc)*; *(ill)* non in forma; **~ for habitation** inabitabile; **to be ~ to do sth** non essere in grado di fare qc; **~ for military service** inabile (al servizio militare).

un·flag·ging [ʌn'flægɪŋ] *adj* instancabile.

un·flap·pable [ʌn'flæpəbl] *adj* calmo(a), composto(a).

un·flat·ter·ing [ˌʌn'flætərɪŋ] *adj (dress, hairstyle)*

che non dona; *(portrait, light)* poco lusinghiero(a).

un·flinch·ing [ʌn'flɪntʃɪŋ] *adj* risoluto(a), che non indietreggia.

un·fold [ʌn'fəʊld] **1** *vt (newspaper, map, wings)* spiegare, aprire; *(arms)* distendere; *(fig: plan, idea)* esporre; *(: secret)* svelare. **2** *vi (flower)* schiudersi; *(fig: view)* spiegarsi; *(: story)* svolgersi, snodarsi.

un·fore·see·able ['ʌnfɔː'siːəbl] *adj* imprevedibile.

un·fore·seen [ˌʌnfɔː'siːn] *adj* imprevisto(a).

un·for·get·table [ˌʌnfə'getəbl] *adj* indimenticabile.

un·for·giv·able [ˌʌnfə'gɪvəbl] *adj* imperdonabile.

un·formed [ˌʌn'fɔːmd] *adj (clay)* informe, senza forma; *(foetus, character)* non ancora formato(a); *(ideas)* non definito(a).

un·for·tu·nate [ʌn'fɔːtʃnɪt] **1** *adj (deserving of pity)* povero(a); *(unlucky)* sfortunato(a); *(unsuitable, regrettable: remark, habit)* infelice; **it is most ~ that he left** è un gran peccato che se ne sia andato. **2** *n* sfortunato/a, sventurato/a.

un·for·tu·nate·ly [ʌn'fɔːtʃnɪtlɪ] *adv* purtroppo, sfortunatamente; **an ~ worded speech** un discorso infelice.

un·found·ed [ˌʌn'faʊndɪd] *adj* infondato(a), senza fondamento.

un·friend·ly [ˌʌn'frendlɪ] *adj* **(-ier, -iest)** *(person):* **~ (to)** scostante (con), antipatico(a) (con); *(attitude, reception)* ostile; *(remark)* scortese.

un·ful·filled [ˌʌnfʊl'fɪld] *adj (ambition)* non realizzato(a); *(prophecy)* che non si è avverato(a); *(desire)* insoddisfatto(a); *(promise)* non mantenuto(a); *(terms of contract)* non rispettato(a); *(person)* frustrato(a).

un·furl [ʌn'fɜːl] *vt* spiegare.

un·fur·nished [ˌʌn'fɜːnɪʃt] *adj* non ammobiliato(a).

un·gain·ly [ʌn'geɪnlɪ] *adj* sgraziato(a), goffo(a).

un·get-at-able ['ʌnget'ætəbl] *adj (fam)* inaccessibile.

un·god·ly [ʌn'gɒdlɪ] *adj* empio(a); *(fam):* **at an ~ hour** a un'ora impossibile.

un·gra·cious [ʌn'greɪʃəs] *adj* sgarbato(a), scortese.

un·gram·mati·cal [ˌʌngrə'mætɪkəl] *adj* sgrammaticato(a), scorretto(a).

un·grate·ful [ʌn'greɪtfʊl] *adj* ingrato(a).

un·grudg·ing [ˌʌn'grʌdʒɪŋ] *adj (help)* dato(a) volentieri; *(praise)* sincero(a).

un·guard·ed [ʌn'gɑːdɪd] *adj* **(a)** *(Mil etc)* indifeso(a), sguarnito(a). **(b)** *(fig: careless)* imprudente; **in an ~ moment** in un momento di distrazione.

un·hap·pi·ly [ʌn'hæpɪlɪ] *adv (miserably)* tristemente, con aria infelice; *(unfortunately)* purtroppo, sfortunatamente; **to be ~ married** aver fatto un matrimonio infelice.

un·hap·pi·ness [ʌn'hæpɪnɪs] *n* infelicità.

un·hap·py [ʌn'hæpɪ] *adj* **(-ier, -iest) (a)** *(gen)* infelice; **an ~ state of affairs** una situazione spiacevole. **(b)** *(not pleased)* scontento(a); *(uneasy, worried)* preoccupato(a), inquieto(a); **to be ~ about sth/doing sth** non essere contento di qc/di fare qc. **(c)** *(unfortunate: remark, choice)* infelice; *(: coincidence)* disgraziato(a).

un·harmed [ˌʌn'hɑːmd] *adj* illeso(a), incolume; *(thing)* intatto(a).

un·healthy [ʌn'helθɪ] *adj* **(-ier, -iest)** *(person)* malaticcio(a), poco sano(a); *(climate, place, complexion etc)* malsano(a); *(curiosity etc)* malsano(a), malato(a); *(interest)* morboso(a).

unheard-of [ˌʌn'hɜːdɒv] *adj (unprecedented)*

inaudito(a), senza precedenti; *(outrageous)* dell'altro mondo.

un·heed·ed [ˌʌn'hiːdɪd] *adj*: **the warning went** ~ l'avvertimento fu ignorato.

un·help·ful [ˌʌn'hɛlpfʊl] *adj* poco disponibile.

un·hesi·tat·ing [ʌn'hɛzɪteɪtɪŋ] *adj (loyalty)* che non vacilla; *(reply, offer)* pronto(a), immediato(a); **she was** ~ **in her support** non ha avuto un attimo di esitazione nell'appoggiarmi *(or* nell'appoggiarlo *etc).*

un·hesi·tat·ing·ly [ʌn'hɛzɪteɪtɪŋlɪ] *adv* senza esitazione.

un·hinge [ʌn'hɪndʒ] *vt (door)* scardinare, togliere dai cardini; *(fig: mind)* sconvolgere; *(: person)* far perdere la ragione a.

un·hook [ˌʌn'hʊk] *vt (remove: picture etc)* staccare; *(: trailer)* sganciare; *(undo: gate)* aprire; *(: dress)* slacciare.

unhoped-for [ʌn'həʊptfɔːʳ] *adj* insperato(a).

un·hur·ried [ˌʌn'hʌrɪd] *adj (gen)* tranquillo(a); **after a little** ~ **reflection** dopo averci pensato con calma.

un·hurt [ˌʌn'hɜːt] *adj* sano(a) e salvo(a), illeso(a).

un·hy·gien·ic [ˌʌnhaɪ'dʒiːnɪk] *adj* non igienico(a); *(surroundings)* insalubre.

uni·corn ['juːnɪkɔːn] *n* unicorno.

un·iden·ti·fied [ˌʌnaɪ'dɛntɪfaɪd] *adj* non identificato(a); ~ **flying object** *(abbr* **UFO)** oggetto volante non identificato *(abbr* U.F.O.).

uni·fi·ca·tion [ˌjuːnɪfɪ'keɪʃən] *n* unificazione *f.*

uni·form ['juːnɪfɔːm] **1** *adj (colour, acceleration)* uniforme. **2** *n (Mil, school)* uniforme *f*, divisa; **in full** ~ in alta uniforme; **in/out of** ~ in divisa/borghese.

uni·form·ity [ˌjuːnɪ'fɔːmɪtɪ] *n* uniformità.

uni·form·ly ['juːnɪfɔːmlɪ] *adv* uniformemente.

uni·fy ['juːnɪfaɪ] *vt (country)* unire; *(different parts, systems)* unificare.

uni·lat·er·al [ˌjuːnɪ'lætərəl] *adj* unilaterale.

un·im·agi·nable [ˌʌnɪ'mædʒɪnəbl] *adj* inimmaginabile, inconcepibile.

un·im·agi·na·tive [ˌʌnɪ'mædʒɪnətɪv] *adj* privo(a) di fantasia, a corto di idee.

un·im·paired [ˌʌnɪm'pɛəd] *adj* intatto(a), non danneggiato(a).

un·im·peach·able [ˌʌnɪm'piːtʃəbl] *adj (honesty, character)* irreprensibile; *(conduct)* incensurabile; *(witness)* al di sopra di ogni sospetto.

un·im·por·tant [ˌʌnɪm'pɔːtənt] *adj (gen)* senza importanza, di scarsa importanza; *(detail)* trascurabile.

un·im·pressed [ˌʌnɪm'prɛst] *adj (gen)* niente affatto impressionato(a); *(unconvinced)* niente affatto convinto(a).

un·in·hab·it·ed [ˌʌnɪn'hæbɪtɪd] *adj (house)* disabitato(a); *(island)* deserto(a).

un·in·hib·it·ed [ˌʌnɪn'hɪbɪtɪd] *adj (person, behaviour)* disinibito(a); *(emotion, laughter)* sfrenato(a).

un·ini·ti·at·ed [ˌʌnɪ'nɪʃɪeɪtɪd] *npl*: **the** ~ i profani.

un·in·jured [ˌʌn'ɪndʒəd] *adj (person)* incolume; *(reputation)* intatto(a).

un·in·spired [ˌʌnɪn'spaɪəd] *adj (poem, performance)* privo(a) d'ispirazione, piatto(a); **he was** ~ **by the essay topic** l'argomento del tema non l'ha ispirato.

un·in·tel·li·gent [ˌʌnɪn'tɛlɪdʒənt] *adj* poco intelligente.

un·in·tel·li·gible [ˌʌnɪn'tɛlɪdʒɪbl] *adj* incomprensibile, inintelligibile.

un·in·tend·ed [ˌʌnɪn'tɛndɪd] *adj*, **un·in·ten·tion·al** [ˌʌnɪn'tɛnʃənl] *adj* involontario(a); **it was**

quite ~ non l'ho *(or* l'ha *etc)* fatto apposta.

un·in·ten·tion·al·ly [ˌʌnɪn'tɛnʃnəlɪ] *adv* senza volerlo, involontariamente.

un·in·ter·est·ed [ʌn'ɪntrɪstɪd] *adj (person, attitude)* indifferente; **to be** ~ **in politics** non interessarsi di politica.

un·in·ter·est·ing [ˌʌn'ɪntrɪstɪŋ] *adj (person)* poco interessante; *(book, offer)* privo(a) d'interesse.

un·in·ter·rupt·ed ['ʌn,ɪntə'rʌptɪd] *adj (line, series)* ininterrotto(a); *(work)* senza interruzioni; **to have an** ~ **night's sleep** dormire per una notte di filato.

un·in·vit·ed [ˌʌnɪn'vaɪtɪd] *adj (guest)* non invitato(a); *(criticism)* non richiesto(a); **to arrive** ~ *(at* sb's) piovere in casa (a qn); **to help o.s. to sth** ~ servirsi di qc senza chiedere.

un·in·vit·ing [ˌʌnɪn'vaɪtɪŋ] *adj (place, food)* non invitante, poco invitante; *(offer)* poco allettante.

un·ion ['juːnjən] **1** *n* **(a)** *(gen)* unione *f*; **the U~** *(Am)* gli stati dell'Unione; **U~ of Soviet Socialist Republics** *(abbr* **USSR)** Unione delle Repubbliche Socialiste Sovietiche *(abbr* U.R.S.S.). **(b)** *(trade* ~) sindacato. **(c)** *(club, society)* associazione *f*, circolo. **2** *cpd (leader, movement)* sindacale; ~ **card** *n* tessera sindacale; **U~ Jack** *n* bandiera del *Regno Unito.*

un·ion·ist ['juːnjənɪst] *n* = **trade unionist.**

un·ion·ize ['juːnjənaɪz] *vt* sindacalizzare, organizzare in sindacato.

unique [juː'niːk] *adj* unico(a).

unique·ly [juː'niːklɪ] *adv* eccezionalmente, singolarmente.

unique·ness [juː'niːknɪs] *n* unicità, singolarità.

uni·sex ['juːnɪsɛks] *adj* unisex *inv.*

uni·son ['juːnɪzn] *n*: **in** ~ *(Mus, fig)* all'unisono.

unit ['juːnɪt] **1** *n* **(a)** *(gen, Elec, Math, Mil)* unità *f inv*; **mo≀etary/linguistic** ~ unità monetaria/linguistica; ~ **of length** unità di lunghezza. **(b)** *(division, section)* reparto; *(of furniture)* elemento (componibile); **production** ~ reparto produzione; **sink** ~ blocco lavello; **the basic social** ~ il nucleo sociale di base; **research** ~ *(personnel)* équipe *f inv*; *(building)* sede *f* di ricerca. **2** *cpd*: ~ **trust** *n (Brit Fin)* fondo d'investimento.

unite [juː'naɪt] **1** *vt (join: parts, pieces)* unire; *(unify: parts of country etc)* unificare. **2** *vi (gen)* unirsi; *(companies)* fondersi; **to** ~ **with sb/in doing** *or* **to do sth** unirsi a qn/per fare qc.

unit·ed [juː'naɪtɪd] **1** *adj (family, people)* unito(a); *(effort)* unitario(a); *(efforts)* comune. **2** *cpd*: **U~ Kingdom** *n (abbr* **U.K.)** Regno Unito; **U~ Nations (Organization)** *n (abbr* **UN, UNO)** (Organizzazione *f* delle) Nazioni *fpl* Unite *(abbr* O.N.U.); **U~ States (of America)** *n (abbr* **US, USA)** Stati Uniti (d'America) *(abbr* U.S.A.).

unity ['juːnɪtɪ] *n (gen)* unità; *(of members, individuals)* unione *f*; **in** ~ in armonia, in pieno accordo.

Univ. *abbr of* **university.**

uni·ver·sal [ˌjuːnɪ'vɜːsəl] **1** *adj (phenomenon, disapproval)* generale; *(language, values)* universale; **a** ~ **favourite** un gran favorito. **2** *cpd*: ~ **joint** *n (Tech)* giunto cardanico.

uni·ver·sal·ly [ˌjuːnɪ'vɜːsəlɪ] *adv (known)* universalmente; *(accepted)* all'unanimità.

uni·verse ['juːnɪvɜːs] *n* universo.

uni·ver·sity [ˌjuːnɪ'vɜːsɪtɪ] **1** *n* università *f inv*; **Oxford U~** l'Università di Oxford; **to be at/go to** ~ essere/andare all'università. **2** *cpd (student, professor, education)* universitario(a); ~ **year** anno accademico; ~ **degree** laurea.

un·just [ˌʌn'dʒʌst] *adj* ingiusto(a); **to be** ~ **to sb** essere ingiusto con *or* verso qn.

un·jus·ti·fi·able [ʌn'dʒʌstɪfaɪəbl] *adj* ingiustificabile.

un·jus·ti·fi·ably [ʌn'dʒʌstɪfaɪəblɪ] *adv* senza motivo.

un·jus·ti·fied [ʌn'dʒʌstɪfaɪd] *adj (remark)* ingiustificato(a), immotivato(a); *(suspicion)* infondato(a).

un·just·ly [ʌn'dʒʌstlɪ] *adv* ingiustamente.

un·kempt [ʌn'kɛmpt] *adj (hair)* scarmigliato(a); *(appearance)* trasandato(a).

un·kind [ʌn'kaɪnd] *adj (-er, -est) (person, remark)* poco gentile, scortese; *(: stronger)* villano(a); *(fate, blow)* crudele; **the sun can be ~ to delicate skins** il sole può far male alle pelli delicate.

un·kind·ly [ʌn'kaɪndlɪ] *adv (speak)* in modo sgarbato; *(treat)* male; **don't take it ~ if...** non te la prendere se... .

un·kind·ness [ʌn'kaɪndnɪs] *n* sgarbatezza; *(stronger)* cattiveria.

un·know·ing [ʌn'nəʊɪŋ] *adj* inconsapevole, ignaro(a).

un·know·ing·ly [ʌn'nəʊɪŋlɪ] *adv* senz'accorgersene, senza saperlo.

un·known [ʌn'nəʊn] **1** *adj* sconosciuto(a), ignoto(a); **the murderer is as yet ~** ancora non si sa chi sia l'assassino; **it's ~ for her to get to work on time** quando mai è arrivata al lavoro in orario?; **~ quantity** *(Math, fig)* incognita; **the U~ Soldier** *or* **Warrior** il Milite Ignoto; **his intentions are ~ to me** non conosco le sue intenzioni; **a substance ~ to scientists** una sostanza ignota agli scienziati. **2** *adv*: **~ to me** a mia insaputa. **3** *n* **(a)** *(person)* sconosciuto/a. **(b)** *(Math)* incognita; **the ~** l'ignoto.

un·lady·like [ʌn'leɪdɪlaɪk] *adj* non da signorina perbene; **it's ~ to swear** una signorina perbene non bestemmia.

un·law·ful [ʌn'lɔːfʊl] *adj* illecito(a), illegale.

un·less [ən'lɛs] *conj* a meno che non + *sub*, se non + *indic*, a meno di + *infin*; **we won't get there on time ~ we leave earlier** non arriveremo in tempo a meno di non partire prima *or* a meno che non partiamo prima; **~ otherwise stated** salvo indicazione contraria; **~ I am mistaken** se non mi sbaglio.

un·li·censed [ʌn'laɪsənst] *adj (vehicle)* senza bollo; *(hotel)* senza licenza per la vendita di alcolici.

un·like [ʌn'laɪk] **1** *adj* diverso(a), dissimile. **2** *prep* a differenza di, contrariamente a; **that photo is quite ~ her** quella foto non le somiglia affatto; **it's quite ~ him to do that** non è da lui fare una cosa simile; **I, ~ others...** diversamente dagli *or* a differenza degli altri, io... .

un·like·li·hood [ʌn'laɪklɪhʊd] *n*, **un·like·li·ness** [ʌn'laɪklɪnɪs] *n* improbabilità.

un·like·ly [ʌn'laɪklɪ] *adj (-ier, -iest) (happening)* improbabile; *(explanation)* inverosimile; **in the ~ event that it does happen...** dovesse succedere, cosa assai improbabile...; **it is ~ that he will come, he is ~ to come** è poco probabile che venga.

un·lim·it·ed [ʌn'lɪmɪtɪd] *adj (time, power)* illimitato(a); *(wealth)* smisurato(a).

un·lined [ʌn'laɪnd] *adj (paper)* senza righe; *(garment)* senza fodera, sfoderato(a).

un·lit [ʌn'lɪt] *adj (lamp)* non acceso(a); *(room)* senza luce; *(road)* non illuminato(a).

un·load [ʌn'ləʊd] **1** *vt* **(a)** scaricare. **(b)** *(fam: get rid of)*: **to ~ onto sb** *(problem, children)* scaricare su qn. **2** *vi* scaricare.

un·lock [ʌn'lɒk] *vt* aprire; **she left the door ~ed** non ha chiuso la porta a chiave.

un·loose [ʌn'luːs] *vt*, **un·loos·en** [ʌn'luːsn] *vt (belt)* allentare; *(hair)* sciogliere; *(knot)* slegare, sciogliere.

un·lov·able [ʌn'lʌvəbl] *adj* antipatico(a).

un·luck·i·ly [ʌn'lʌkɪlɪ] *adv* purtroppo, sfortunatamente; **~ for her** per sua sfortuna.

un·lucky [ʌn'lʌkɪ] *adj (-ier, -iest) (person, day)* sfortunato(a); *(decision)* disgraziato(a); *(number, object)* che porta sfortuna, di malaugurio; **she was ~ enough to meet him** ha avuto la sfortuna di incontrarlo; **to be ~** *(person)* essere sfortunato, non avere fortuna; **it's ~ to walk under a ladder** porta sfortuna *or* è di malaugurio passare sotto una scala.

un·man·age·able [ʌn'mænɪdʒəbl] *adj (unwieldy: tool, vehicle)* poco maneggevole; *(: parcel)* ingombrante; *(uncontrollable: teenage son, hair)* intrattabile; *(: situation)* impossibile.

un·manned [ʌn'mænd] *adj (spacecraft)* senza equipaggio.

un·marked [ʌn'mɑːkt] *adj (unstained)* pulito(a), senza macchie; *(without marking: face)* senza una ruga, senza un segno; *(: linen)* senza cifre; *(: banknote)* pulito(a); *(uncorrected: essay)* non corretto(a); **~ police car** civetta della polizia.

un·mar·ried [ʌn'mærɪd] *adj (man)* scapolo, non sposato; *(woman)* nubile, non sposata; **~ mother** ragazza madre.

un·mask [ʌn'mɑːsk] *vt (fig)* smascherare.

un·matched [ʌn'mætʃt] *adj* senza pari, impareggiabile.

un·men·tion·able [ʌn'mɛnʃnəbl] *adj (topic, vice)* innominabile; *(word)* irripetibile.

un·mer·ci·ful [ʌn'mɜːsɪfʊl] *adj* spietato(a).

un·mind·ful [ʌn'maɪndfʊl] *adj*: **to be ~ of** *(frm)* essere incurante di.

un·mis·tak·(e)able [ʌnmɪs'teɪkəbl] *adj (person, sound)* inconfondibile; *(displeasure, meaning)* più che chiaro(a), lampante.

un·mis·tak·(e)ably [ʌnmɪs'teɪkəblɪ] *adv* senza timore di sbagliarsi, inconfondibilmente; **~ clear** inequivocabile.

un·miti·gat·ed [ʌn'mɪtɪgeɪtɪd] *adj (criminal)* incallito(a); *(liar)* matricolato(a); *(disaster)* totale, assoluto(a).

un·mo·ti·vat·ed [ʌn'məʊtɪveɪtɪd] *adj* immotivato(a).

un·moved [ʌn'muːvd] *adj* indifferente.

un·named [ʌn'neɪmd] *adj (nameless)* senza nome; *(anonymous)* anonimo(a).

un·natu·ral [ʌn'nætʃrəl] *adj (gen)* innaturale; *(affected)* affettato(a); *(perverted)* contro natura; **it's ~ for him to behave like that** non è da lui comportarsi così.

un·nec·es·sari·ly [ʌn'nɛsɪsərɪlɪ] *adv (in vain)* inutilmente; *(excessively)* senza che ce ne sia bisogno.

un·nec·es·sary [ʌn'nɛsɪsərɪ] *adj (superfluous)* non necessario(a); *(useless)* inutile; **it was ~ to be rude!** non c'era bisogno di essere sgarbati!; **it's ~ for you to attend** non è necessario che tu venga.

un·nerve [ʌn'nɜːv] *vt (subj: accident)* sgomentare; *(: hostile attitude)* bloccare; *(: long wait, interview)* snervare.

un·no·ticed [ʌn'nəʊtɪst] *adj*: **to go** *or* **pass ~** passare inosservato(a).

UNO *n abbr of* **United Nations Organization.**

un·ob·jec·tion·able [ʌnəb'dʒɛkʃnəbl] *adj (person)* ammodo *inv*; *(conduct)* ineccepibile.

un·ob·serv·ant [ʌnəb'zɜːvənt] *adj*: **to be ~** non avere spirito di osservazione.

un·ob·served [ʌnəb'zɜːvd] *adj (also fig)* inosservato(a); **to go ~** passare inosservato.

un·ob·struct·ed [ˌʌnəb'strʌktɪd] *adj (road)* sgombro(a); *(pipe)* non ostruito(a), non bloccato(a); **an** ~ **view** un'ampia vista.

un·ob·tain·able [ˌʌnəb'teɪnəbl] *adj (food)* introvabile; **this number is** ~ *(Telec)* non si riesce a prendere la linea.

un·ob·tru·sive [ˌʌnəb'truːsɪv] *adj* discreto(a).

un·oc·cu·pied [ˌʌn'ɒkjʊpaɪd] *adj (house)* vuoto(a); *(seat, table, also Mil: zone)* libero(a), non occupato(a); *(person: not busy)* libero(a), senza impegni.

un·of·fi·cial [ˌʌnə'fɪʃəl] *adj (visit)* privato(a), non ufficiale; *(unconfirmed: report, news)* ufficioso(a); **in an** ~ **capacity** in veste ufficiosa; ~ **strike** sciopero a sorpresa.

un·of·fi·cial·ly [ˌʌnə'fɪʃəlɪ] *adv* ufficiosamente.

un·opened [ˌʌn'əʊpənd] *adj (letter)* chiuso(a); *(present)* ancora incartato(a).

un·op·posed [ˌʌnə'pəʊzd] *adj (enter, be elected)* senza incontrare opposizione; **the motion was** ~ **by the committee** il comitato non si è opposto alla mozione.

un·or·gan·ized [ˌʌn'ɔːgənaɪzd] *adj (person)* disorganizzato(a); *(essay, life)* mal organizzato(a).

un·ortho·dox [ˌʌn'ɔːθədɒks] *adj* poco ortodosso(a).

un·pack [ˌʌn'pæk] **1** *vt (suitcases)* disfare; *(belongings)* sballare. **2** *vi* disfare le valige, disfare i bagagli.

un·paid [ˌʌn'peɪd] *adj (bill, debt)* da pagare; *(holiday)* non pagato(a); *(work)* non retribuito(a).

un·pal·at·able [ʌn'pælətəbl] *adj (food)* immangiabile; *(fig: truth)* sgradevole.

un·par·al·leled [ʌn'pærəleld] *adj* senza pari.

un·par·don·able [ʌn'pɑːdnəbl] *adj* imperdonabile.

un·pat·ri·ot·ic ['ʌnˌpætrɪ'ɒtɪk] *adj (person)* poco patriottico(a); *(speech, attitude)* antipatriottico(a).

un·per·turbed [ˌʌnpə'tɜːbd] *adj* imperturbato(a), imperterrito(a); ~ **by sth** per nulla scosso da qc.

un·pick [ˌʌn'pɪk] *vt (seam)* disfare; *(stitches)* togliere.

un·pin [ˌʌn'pɪn] *vt (dress)* togliere gli spilli a; *(hair)* togliere le forcine a; *(notice)* staccare.

un·planned [ˌʌn'plænd] *adj (visit)* imprevisto(a); *(baby)* non previsto(a).

un·pleas·ant [ʌn'plɛznt] *adj (smell, task)* sgradevole, spiacevole; *(person, remark)* antipatico(a); *(day, experience)* brutto(a); **to be** ~ **to sb** essere villano con qn.

un·pleas·ant·ly [ʌn'plɛzntlɪ] *adv* in modo poco piacevole; **the room smelt** ~ **of fish** c'era un odore sgradevole di pesce nella stanza; **it was** ~ **close to the truth** era spiacevolmente vicino al vero; **it's** ~ **warm in here** qui c'è un caldo sgradevole.

un·pleas·ant·ness [ʌn'plɛzntnɪs] *n (quality: of smell, event)* sgradevolezza; *(: of person)* antipatia; *(bad feeling, quarrelling)* tensioni *fpl*.

un·plug [ˌʌn'plʌg] *vt* staccare (dalla presa), togliere la spina a.

un·pol·ished [ˌʌn'pɒlɪʃt] *adj (shoes, furniture)* non lucidato(a); *(diamond)* grezzo(a); *(manners, person)* rozzo(a).

un·pol·lut·ed [ˌʌnpə'luːtɪd] *adj* non inquinato(a).

un·popu·lar [ˌʌn'pɒpjʊləʳ] *adj (gen)* impopolare; **to be** ~ **with sb** *(person, law)* non riscuotere l'approvazione di qn; **to make o.s.** ~ **(with)** rendersi antipatico (a); *(subj: politician etc)* alienarsi le simpatie (di); **I'm** ~ **with the boss at the moment** non sono nelle grazie del capo in questo momento; **he's** ~ **with the rest of the class** è mal visto dal resto della classe.

un·prec·edent·ed [ʌn'prɛsɪdəntɪd] *adj* senza precedenti.

un·pre·dict·able [ˌʌnprɪ'dɪktəbl] *adj* imprevedibile.

un·preju·diced [ʌn'prɛdʒʊdɪst] *adj (not biased)* obiettivo(a), imparziale; *(having no prejudices)* senza pregiudizi.

un·pre·pared [ˌʌnprɪ'pɛəd] *adj (person)* impreparato(a); *(speech)* improvvisato(a); **it caught me** ~ mi ha trovato impreparato; **he was** ~ **for his exam/the interview** è andato all'esame/al colloquio impreparato.

un·pre·pos·sess·ing ['ʌnˌpriːpə'zɛsɪŋ] *adj* insulso(a).

un·pre·ten·tious [ˌʌnprɪ'tɛnʃəs] *adj* senza pretese.

un·prin·ci·pled [ʌn'prɪnsɪpld] *adj* senza scrupoli.

un·pro·duc·tive [ˌʌnprə'dʌktɪv] *adj* improduttivo(a); *(discussion)* sterile.

un·pro·fes·sion·al ['ʌnprə'fɛʃənl] *adj*: ~ **conduct** scorrettezza professionale.

un·prof·it·able [ˌʌn'prɒfɪtəbl] *adj (financially)* non redditizio(a); *(: job, deal)* poco lucrativo(a); *(fig)* infruttuoso(a); **an** ~ **afternoon** un pomeriggio poco produttivo.

un·prom·is·ing [ˌʌn'prɒmɪsɪŋ] *adj* poco promettente.

un·pro·nounce·able [ˌʌnprə'naʊnsəbl] *adj* impronunciabile.

un·pro·tect·ed [ˌʌnprə'tɛktɪd] *adj (town)* indifeso(a); *(house)* esposto(a), non riparato(a).

un·pro·voked [ˌʌnprə'vəʊkt] *adj* non provocato(a).

un·pub·lished [ˌʌn'pʌblɪʃt] *adj* inedito(a).

un·pun·ished [ˌʌn'pʌnɪʃt] *adj*: **to go** ~ restare impunito(a).

un·quali·fied [ˌʌn'kwɒlɪfaɪd] *adj* **(a)** *(worker)* non qualificato(a); *(in professions)* non diplomato(a), non abilitato(a); *(applicant)* senza i requisiti necessari. **(b)** *(absolute: assent, denial)* incondizionato(a); *(: admiration)* senza riserve; *(: success)* sotto tutti gli aspetti; *(idiot)* perfetto(a); *(liar)* matricolato(a).

un·ques·tion·able [ʌn'kwɛstʃənəbl] *adj (fact)* incontestabile, indiscutibile; *(honesty)* indiscusso(a).

un·ques·tion·ably [ʌn'kwɛstʃənəblɪ] *adv* indiscutibilmente.

un·ques·tion·ing [ʌn'kwɛstʃənɪŋ] *adj (obedience, acceptance)* cieco(a).

un·rav·el [ʌn'rævəl] **1** *vt (knitting)* disfare; *(wool)* dipanare; *(threads)* sfilare; *(fig: mystery)* sbrogliare; *(: plot)* venire a capo di. **2** *vi (knitting)* disfarsi; *(threads)* dipanarsi.

un·read·able [ˌʌn'riːdəbl] *adj* illeggibile.

un·real [ˌʌn'rɪəl] *adj* irreale.

un·re·al·is·tic [ˌʌnrɪə'lɪstɪk] *adj (idea)* illusorio(a); *(estimate)* non realistico(a); **you're being** ~ **if you think…** ti fai delle illusioni se credi… .

un·re·al·ity [ˌʌnrɪ'ælɪtɪ] *n* irrealtà.

un·rea·son·able [ʌn'riːznəbl] *adj (behaviour)* irrazionale; *(person, idea)* irragionevole; *(price, time)* irragionevole, assurdo(a); **it is** ~ **to expect that…** è un po' troppo aspettarsi che…+*sub*; **he makes** ~ **demands on me** vuole troppo da me; **he was most** ~ **about it** non ha voluto sentire ragione.

un·rec·og·niz·able [ˌʌn'rɛkəgnaɪzəbl] *adj* irriconoscibile.

un·rec·og·nized [ˌʌn'rɛkəgnaɪzd] *adj (talent, genius)* misconosciuto(a); *(Pol: regime)* non ufficialmente riconosciuto(a); **he walked along the road** ~ **by passers-by** è passato per la strada senza che nessuno lo riconoscesse.

un·re·cord·ed [ˌʌnrɪˈkɔːdɪd] *adj* non documentato(a), non registrato(a).

un·re·fined [ˌʌnrɪˈfaɪnd] *adj* *(sugar, petroleum)* greggio(a); *(person, manners: coarse)* rozzo(a).

un·re·hearsed [ˌʌnrɪˈhɜːst] *adj* *(Theatre etc)* improvvisato(a); *(spontaneous)* imprevisto(a).

un·re·lat·ed [ˌʌnrɪˈleɪtɪd] *adj:* ~ **(to)** *(unconnected)* senza nesso *or* rapporto (con); *(by family)* non imparentato(a) (con), senza legami di parentela (con).

un·re·lent·ing [ˌʌnrɪˈlentɪŋ] *adj* *(rain)* implacabile; *(activity)* senza tregua; *(attack)* che non dà tregua; *(hatred)* irriducibile; *(person, heat)* spietato(a), accanito(a).

un·re·li·able [ˌʌnrɪˈlaɪəbl] *adj* *(person)* su cui non si può contare; *(source)* non attendibile; *(firm)* poco serio(a); *(car, machine)* che non dà affidamento.

un·re·lieved [ˌʌnrɪˈliːvd] *adj* *(pain, gloom)* costante; *(anguish, depression)* totale; *(boredom)* mortale; *(colour)* uniforme.

un·re·mit·ting [ˌʌnrɪˈmɪtɪŋ] *adj* *(activity)* senza sosta; *(kindness)* immancabile; *(hatred)* irriducibile.

un·re·peat·able [ˌʌnrɪˈpiːtəbl] *adj* *(offer, bargain)* unico(a); *(words etc)* irripetibile.

un·re·pent·ant [ˌʌnrɪˈpentənt] *adj* *(smoker, sinner)* impenitente; **to be ~ about sth** non mostrare l'ombra del rimorso per qc.

un·rep·re·sen·ta·tive [ˌʌnreprɪˈzentətɪv] *adj* *(untypical)* atipico(a), poco rappresentativo(a).

un·re·quit·ed [ˌʌnrɪˈkwaɪtɪd] *adj* *(love)* non ricambiato(a).

un·re·served [ˌʌnrɪˈzɜːvd] *adj* **(a)** *(seat)* non prenotato(a), non riservato(a). **(b)** *(person)* aperto(a). **(c)** *(approval, admiration)* senza riserve.

un·re·spon·sive [ˈʌnrɪsˈpɒnsɪv] *adj* che non reagisce; ~ **to** insensibile a.

un·rest [ʌnˈrest] *n* *(Pol)* agitazione *f*.

un·re·strained [ˌʌnrɪˈstreɪnd] *adj* sfrenato(a).

un·re·strict·ed [ˌʌnrɪˈstrɪktɪd] *adj* *(power, time)* illimitato(a); *(access)* libero(a).

un·re·ward·ed [ˌʌnrɪˈwɔːdɪd] *adj* non ricompensato(a); **to go ~** rimanere senza ricompensa.

un·re·ward·ing [ˌʌnrɪˈwɔːdɪŋ] *adj* *(job)* ingrato(a), senza soddisfazione; *(: financially)* poco remunerativo(a).

un·ripe [ʌnˈraɪp] *adj* acerbo(a).

un·ri·valled, *(Am)* **un·ri·valed** [ʌnˈraɪvəld] *adj* senza pari; **to be ~** non avere *or* non temere rivali.

un·roll [ʌnˈrəʊl] **1** *vt* srotolare. **2** *vi* srotolarsi.

un·ruf·fled [ʌnˈrʌfld] *adj* *(person)* calmo(a) e tranquillo(a), imperturbato(a); *(hair)* a posto; *(water)* senza un'increspatura.

un·ru·ly [ʌnˈruːlɪ] *adj* **(-ier, -iest)** *(behaviour)* indisciplinato(a); *(child, mob)* turbolento(a); *(hair)* ribelle.

un·safe [ʌnˈseɪf] *adj* *(machine, car, wiring)* pericoloso(a); *(method)* poco sicuro(a); ~ **to drink** non potabile; ~ **to eat** non commestibile; **to feel ~** non sentirsi sicuro.

un·said [ʌnˈsed] *adj* non detto(a); **consider it ~** come non detto; **it would have been better left ~** sarebbe stato meglio se non fosse stato detto; **much was left ~** molte cose sono rimaste non dette.

un·sale·able, *(Am)* **un·sal·able** [ʌnˈseɪləbl] *adj* invendibile.

un·sat·is·fac·tory [ˈʌnˌsætɪsˈfæktərɪ] *adj* *(result)* poco soddisfacente; *(profits)* al di sotto delle aspettative; *(piece of work, hotel room)* che lascia a desiderare; *(on school report)* insufficiente.

un·sat·is·fied [ʌnˈsætɪsfaɪd] *adj* *(desire, need etc)*

insoddisfatto(a); *(not fulfilled: person)* inappagato(a); *(not convinced):* ~ **(with)** poco convinto(a) (di).

un·sat·is·fy·ing [ˌʌnˈsætɪsfaɪɪŋ] *adj* *(result, work)* insoddisfacente, poco soddisfacente; *(meal)* che non soddisfa.

un·sa·voury, *(Am)* **un·sa·vory** [ʌnˈseɪvərɪ] *adj* *(looks, experience)* sgradevole; *(activity)* equivoco(a); *(character)* poco raccomandabile; *(joke)* di pessimo gusto.

un·scathed [ʌnˈskeɪðd] *adj* senza un graffio; *(fig)* indenne.

un·sci·en·tif·ic [ˈʌnˌsaɪənˈtɪfɪk] *adj* poco scientifico(a).

un·screw [ʌnˈskruː] **1** *vt* svitare. **2** *vi* svitarsi.

un·scru·pu·lous [ʌnˈskruːpjʊləs] *adj* *(person)* senza scrupoli, privo(a) di scrupoli; *(means)* disonesto(a).

un·sea·son·able [ʌnˈsiːznəbl] *adj* *(weather)* non tipico(a) della stagione.

un·seem·ly [ʌnˈsiːmlɪ] *adj* sconveniente, indecoroso(a).

un·seen [ˌʌnˈsiːn] **1** *adj* *(person)* inosservato(a); *(danger)* nascosto(a); *(Scol: translation)* all'impronta, estemporaneo(a). **2** *n* *(Scol)* traduzione *f* nella lingua madre.

un·self·ish [ʌnˈselfɪʃ] *adj* *(person)* altruista; *(act)* disinteressato(a).

un·ser·vice·able [ʌnˈsɜːvɪsəbl] *adj* inservibile.

un·set·tle [ʌnˈsetl] *vt* *(stomach, plans)* scombussolare; *(person)* disorientare.

un·set·tled [ʌnˈsetld] *adj* *(person, future)* incerto(a); *(question)* non risolto(a); *(weather, market)* instabile, variabile; **to feel ~** sentirsi a disagio *or* disorientato.

un·set·tling [ʌnˈsetlɪŋ] *adj* inquietante; **the news had an ~ effect on me** la notizia ha avuto l'effetto di agitarmi *or* mi ha scombussolato.

un·shak(e)·able [ʌnˈʃeɪkəbl] *adj* irremovibile.

un·shak·en [ʌnˈʃeɪkən] *adj* *(person)* nient'affatto scosso(a); *(resolve)* saldo(a) come prima.

un·shav·en [ʌnˈʃeɪvn] *adj* non rasato(a).

un·shrink·able [ʌnˈʃrɪŋkəbl] *adj* irrestringibile.

un·sight·ly [ʌnˈsaɪtlɪ] *adj* non bello(a) a vedersi; *(stronger)* brutto(a).

un·skilled [ʌnˈskɪld] *adj* *(worker, manpower)* non specializzato(a).

un·so·cia·ble [ʌnˈsəʊʃəbl] *adj* *(person)* poco socievole; *(behaviour)* antipatico(a); **he's very ~** è un orso.

un·so·cial [ʌnˈsəʊʃəl] *adj:* ~ **hours** orario sconveniente.

un·sold [ʌnˈsəʊld] *adj* invenduto(a).

un·so·lic·it·ed [ˌʌnsəˈlɪsɪtɪd] *adj* non richiesto(a).

un·solved [ʌnˈsɒlvd] *adj* non risolto(a).

un·so·phis·ti·cat·ed [ˌʌnsəˈfɪstɪkeɪtɪd] *adj* *(person, dress, habits)* semplice; *(machine)* primitivo(a), rudimentale.

un·sound [ʌnˈsaʊnd] *adj* *(health)* debole, cagionevole; *(in construction: floor, foundations)* debole, malsicuro(a); *(argument)* che non regge; *(opinion)* poco fondato(a); *(policy, advice)* poco sensato(a); *(judgment, investment)* poco sicuro(a); *(business)* poco solido(a); **of ~ mind** *(Law)* non in pieno possesso delle sue facoltà mentali.

un·spar·ing [ʌnˈspeərɪŋ] *adj* *(generous):* **to be ~ of** *or* **in** non risparmiare; *(criticism)* spietato(a).

un·speak·able [ʌnˈspiːkəbl] *adj* *(pain, joy)* indicibile, indescrivibile; *(behaviour)* abominevole.

un·speak·ably [ʌnˈspiːkəblɪ] *adv* indicibilmente.

un·spoiled [ʌnˈspɔɪld] *adj,* **un·spoilt** [ʌnˈspɔɪlt] *adj* *(countryside)* non rovinato(a), non deturpato(a); *(child)* non viziato(a); *(person)* genuino(a).

un·spo·ken [ˌʌn'spəʊkən] *adj (words)* non detto(a); *(agreement, approval)* tacito(a).

un·sta·ble [ˌʌn'steɪbl] *adj (gen, Chem, Phys)* instabile; *(mentally)* squilibrato(a).

un·stamped [ˌʌn'stæmpt] *adj* non affrancato(a).

un·steady [ˌʌn'stɛdɪ] *adj (ladder, foothold)* non sicuro(a); *(hand, voice)* tremante; *(economy)* vacillante; **to be ~ on one's feet** non reggersi bene sulle gambe.

un·stint·ing [ˌʌn'stɪntɪŋ] *adj (support)* incondizionato(a); *(generosity)* illimitato(a); *(praise)* senza riserve.

un·stressed [ˌʌn'strɛst] *adj* non accentato(a).

un·stuck [ˌʌn'stʌk] *adj:* **to come ~** *(label etc)* staccarsi, scollarsi; *(fam: plan)* andare a monte; *(: person)* fallire.

un·sub·stan·ti·at·ed [ˌʌnsəb'stænʃɪeɪtɪd] *adj (rumour, accusation)* infondato(a).

un·suc·cess·ful [ˌʌnsək'sɛsfʊl] *adj (gen)* che non ha successo; **to be ~** *(play, book, actor)* non avere successo; *(idea)* non avere fortuna; *(attempt, marriage)* non riuscire; *(negotiation)* fallire; *(application)* avere esito negativo; **to be ~ in an exam** non superare un esame; **to be ~ in doing sth** non riuscire a fare qc.

un·suc·cess·ful·ly [ˌʌnsək'sɛsfəlɪ] *adv* senza successo.

un·suit·able [ˌʌn'suːtəbl] *adj:* **~ (for)** *(clothes, colour)* non adatto(a) (a), inadatto(a) (a); *(moment)* inopportuno(a) (a *or* per); **this film is ~ for children** non è un film adatto ai bambini; **~ for children under 15** sconsigliabile ai minori di 15 anni; **he's ~ for the post** non è la persona adatta per quell'impiego; **the post is ~ for him** quel posto non fa per lui.

un·suit·ed [ˌʌn'suːtɪd] *adj:* **to be ~ for** *or* **to** non essere fatto(a) per.

un·sup·port·ed [ˌʌnsə'pɔːtɪd] *adj (claim)* senza fondamento; *(theory)* non dimostrato(a).

un·sure [ˌʌn'ʃʊə'] *adj:* **~ of, ~ about** incerto(a) su; **to be ~ of o.s.** essere insicuro.

un·sur·passed [ˌʌnsə'pɑːst] *adj* insuperato(a).

un·sus·pect·ed [ˌʌnsəs'pɛktɪd] *adj* insospettato(a).

un·sus·pect·ing [ˌʌnsəs'pɛktɪŋ] *adj (gen)* che non sospetta nulla; *(public)* ignaro(a).

un·sweet·ened [ˌʌn'swiːtnd] *adj* senza zucchero.

un·swerv·ing [ʌn'swɜːvɪŋ] *adj* ferreo(a), incrollabile.

un·sym·pa·thet·ic ['ʌnˌsɪmpə'θɛtɪk] *adj (attitude)* poco incoraggiante; *(person)* antipatico(a); *(response)* gelido(a).

un·sys·tem·at·ic ['ʌnˌsɪstɪ'mætɪk] *adj* poco sistematico(a).

un·tan·gle [ˌʌn'tæŋgl] *vt (knots, wool)* sbrogliare.

un·tapped [ˌʌn'tæpt] *adj* non sfruttato(a).

un·taxed [ˌʌn'tækst] *adj (goods)* esente da imposte; *(income)* non imponibile.

un·teach·able [ˌʌn'tiːtʃəbl] *adj (person)* a cui è impossibile insegnare; *(subject)* impossibile da insegnare.

un·ten·able [ˌʌn'tɛnəbl] *adj (position)* insostenibile.

un·test·ed [ˌʌn'tɛstɪd] *adj (theory)* non sperimentato(a); *(new product, method)* non collaudato(a).

un·think·able [ʌn'θɪŋkəbl] *adj* impensabile.

un·ti·di·ly [ʌn'taɪdɪlɪ] *adv:* **to dress ~** non aver cura nel vestirsi; **to write/work ~** scrivere/lavorare in modo disordinato.

un·ti·di·ness [ʌn'taɪdɪnɪs] *n (of dress)* trascuratezza, sciattezza; *(of person)* aspetto disordinato; *(of room)* disordine *m*.

un·ti·dy [ʌn'taɪdɪ] *adj (-ier, -iest) (person, writing)* disordinato(a); *(room)* in disordine, disordina-

to(a); *(appearance)* sciatto(a).

un·tie [ˌʌn'taɪ] *vt (knot, parcel)* disfare; *(shoelaces)* sciogliere; *(hands, person)* slegare.

un·til [ən'tɪl] **1** *prep* fino a; **~ now** finora; **~ then** fino ad allora; **~ such time as** fino a quando non; **from morning ~ night** dalla mattina alla sera; **~ his arrival** fino al suo arrivo; **I didn't know anything about it ~ 10 minutes ago** non ne sapevo niente fino a 10 minuti fa. **2** *conj* finché (non), fino a quando non; **I won't see her ~ I return** non la vedrò finché non torno *or* fino al mio ritorno; **wait ~ I get back** aspetta finché torno; **he did nothing ~ I told him** non ha mosso un dito finché non gliel'ho detto; **they built the factory we had a view of the river** prima che costruissero la fabbrica potevamo vedere il fiume.

un·time·ly [ʌn'taɪmlɪ] *adj (death, end)* prematuro(a); *(remark)* fuori luogo, inopportuno(a); **to come to an ~ end** *(person)* morire prematuramente; *(project)* naufragare anzitempo.

un·tir·ing [ʌn'taɪərɪŋ] *adj* instancabile, indefesso(a).

un·told [ˌʌn'təʊld] *adj (story, secret)* mai rivelato(a); *(loss, wealth etc)* incalcolabile; *(misery)* indicibile.

un·touch·able [ʌn'tʌtʃəbl] *n* paria *m inv*, intoccabile *m/f*.

un·touched [ˌʌn'tʌtʃt] *adj* **(a)** *(not used etc)* non toccato(a), intatto(a); **she left her breakfast ~** non ha toccato la colazione; **~ by human hand** *(Comm)* manipolato a distanza. **(b)** *(safe: person)* incolume; **the thieves left our cases ~** i ladri non hanno toccato le nostre valigie. **(c)** *(unaffected)*: **~ by** insensibile a.

un·to·ward [ˌʌntə'wɔːd] *adj* increscioso(a).

un·trained [ˌʌn'treɪnd] *adj (person, teacher)* inesperto(a), nuovo(a) del mestiere; **to the ~ eye/ ear** a un occhio inesperto/orecchio non esercitato.

un·trans·lat·able [ˌʌntrænz'leɪtəbl] *adj* intraducibile.

un·tried [ˌʌn'traɪd] *adj (method)* non collaudato(a); *(person)* non messo(a) alla prova; *(Law: criminal)* non processato(a); *(: case)* non portato(a) in tribunale.

un·trou·bled [ʌn'trʌbld] *adj* calmo(a).

un·true [ˌʌn'truː] *adj (statement)* falso(a), non vero(a).

un·trust·wor·thy [ˌʌn'trʌstˌwɜːðɪ] *adj (person)* di cui non ci si può fidare; *(source etc)* poco attendibile, non degno(a) di fede.

un·truth [ˌʌn'truːθ] *n, pl* **~s** [ˌʌn'truːðz] falsità *f inv*.

un·truth·ful [ˌʌn'truːθfʊl] *adj* falso(a), menzognero(a).

un·us·able [ˌʌn'juːzəbl] *adj* inservibile, inutilizzabile.

un·used¹ [ˌʌn'juːzd] *adj (new)* mai usato(a), nuovo(a); *(not made use of)* non usato(a), non utilizzato(a).

un·used² [ˌʌn'juːst] *adj:* **to be ~ to sth/to doing sth** non essere abituato(a) a qc/a fare qc.

un·usual [ʌn'juːʒʊəl] *adj (uncommon)* insolito(a); *(exceptional: event, talent)* non comune, raro(a); **it's ~ for him to be late** è strano che arrivi in ritardo; **that's ~ for her** che strano, non è da lei; **how ~!** che strano!

un·usu·al·ly [ʌn'juːʒʊəlɪ] *adv (unaccustomedly)* insolitamente; *(exceedingly: awkward)* quanto mai; *(tall, gifted)* eccezionalmente; **most ~, she was late** fatto molto strano, era in ritardo.

un·ut·ter·able [ʌn'ʌtərəbl] *adj (joy, boredom)* indicibile.

un·var·ied [ʌnˈvɛərɪd] *adj (routine)* invariato(a); *(diet)* monotono(a).

un·var·nished [ˌʌnˈvɑːnɪʃt] *adj (wood)* non verniciato(a); *(fig: truth)* nudo(a) e crudo(a); *(: account)* senza fronzoli.

un·veil [ʌnˈveɪl] *vt (plan)* svelare; *(monument)* scoprire, inaugurare.

un·voiced [ʌnˈvɔɪst] *adj (consonant)* sordo(a); *(opinion)* inespresso(a).

un·want·ed [ˌʌnˈwɒntɪd] *adj (person, effect)* non desiderato(a); *(clothes)* smesso(a); **to feel ~** sentirsi respinto(a).

un·war·rant·ed [ʌnˈwɒrəntɪd] *adj* ingiustificato(a).

un·wary [ʌnˈwɛərɪ] *adj* incauto(a).

un·wa·ver·ing [ʌnˈweɪvərɪŋ] *adj* fermo(a), incrollabile.

un·wel·come [ʌnˈwɛlkəm] *adj (gen)* non gradito(a); **to feel ~** sentire che la propria presenza non è gradita.

un·well [ˌʌnˈwɛl] *adj* indisposto(a); **to feel ~** non sentirsi bene.

un·whole·some [ˌʌnˈhəʊlsəm] *adj (food)* non genuino(a); *(climate, humour)* malsano(a).

un·wieldy [ʌnˈwiːldɪ] *adj* poco maneggevole.

un·will·ing [ˌʌnˈwɪlɪŋ] *adj* riluttante; **to be ~ to do sth** non essere disposto a fare qc; **he was ~ to admit he was wrong** non voleva ammettere di aver torto.

un·will·ing·ly [ˌʌnˈwɪlɪŋlɪ] *adv* controvoglia, malvolentieri, di malavoglia.

un·wind [ˌʌnˈwaɪnd] *pt, pp* **unwound 1** *vt* srotolare. **2** *vi* srotolarsi; *(fam: relax)* distendersi, rilassarsi.

un·wise [ˌʌnˈwaɪz] *adj (decision, act)* avventato(a); **it was ~ of you to do that** è stato imprudente da parte tua fare questo.

un·wit·ting [ʌnˈwɪtɪŋ] *adj (insult)* non intenzionale, non voluto(a); *(cause)* involontario(a); *(victim)* inconsapevole.

un·wit·ting·ly [ʌnˈwɪtɪŋlɪ] *adv* senza volerlo; **all ~** in tutta innocenza.

un·work·able [ˌʌnˈwɜːkəbl] *adj (plan etc)* inattuabile.

un·world·ly [ˌʌnˈwɜːldlɪ] *adj* staccato(a) dal mondo.

un·wor·thy [ʌnˈwɜːðɪ] *adj* non degno(a), indegno(a); **to be ~ of sth/to do sth** non essere degno di qc/di fare qc.

un·wound [ˌʌnˈwaʊnd] *pt, pp of* **unwind**.

un·wrap [ˌʌnˈræp] *vt (present)* aprire, scartare; *(parcel)* disfare, aprire.

un·writ·ten [ˌʌnˈrɪtn] *adj (agreement)* tacito(a); **it is an ~ law that...** la norma vuole che... .

un·zip [ˌʌnˈzɪp] *vt* aprire (la chiusura lampo di).

up [ʌp] **1** *adv* **(a)** *(upwards, higher)* su, in alto; **~ there** lassù; **~ above** su in alto; **a bit higher ~** un po' più su *or* in alto; **to stop halfway ~** fermarsi a metà (salita); **to throw sth ~ in the air** gettare qc in aria; **~ in the sky/mountains** su nel cielo/in montagna; **my office is 5 floors ~** il mio ufficio è al quinto piano; **'this side ~'** 'alto'; **the sun is ~** è sorto il sole; **the road is ~** ci sono lavori in corso, la strada è interrotta; **to be ~ among** *or* **with the leaders** essere tra i primi; **~ with Leeds United!** viva il Leeds United!; **to walk ~ and down** camminare su e giù; **to bounce ~ and down** saltellare; **he's been ~ and down all evening** non è stato fermo un momento stasera; **she's still a bit ~ and down** *(sick person)* ancora non si è ripresa del tutto.

(b) *(installed, built etc)*: **to be ~** *(building)* essere terminato(a); *(tent)* essere piantato(a); *(cur-*

tains, shutters, wallpaper) essere su; *(picture)* essere appeso(a); *(notice)* essere esposto(a).

(c) *(out of bed)*: **to be ~** essere su; **to be ~ late** star su fino a tardi; **to be ~ and about again** essere di nuovo in piedi.

(d) *(in price, value)*: **to be ~ (by)** essere andato(a) su *(di)*; *(standard, level)*: **to be ~** essere salito(a); **prices are ~ on last year** i prezzi sono più alti dell'anno scorso; **we are 3 goals ~** abbiamo un vantaggio di 3 goal, vinciamo per 3 goal.

(e) *(finished)*: **the lease/his leave is ~** il contratto d'affitto/il suo congedo è scaduto; **when the year was ~** finito l'anno; **time's ~** il tempo è scaduto; **it's all ~ with her** *(fam)* è finita per lei.

(f) *(upwards)*: **from £2 ~** dalle 2 sterline in su.

(g) *(in or towards the north)* su; **to live/go ~ North** vivere/andare su al Nord; **she's ~ from the country** viene dalla campagna; **he's ~ for the day** è qui per la giornata; **he goes ~ to Oxford next year** va a Oxford l'anno prossimo; **~ North/ in Scotland** su al Nord/in Scozia.

(h) *(knowledgeable)*: **he's well ~ in** *or* **on politics** è informatissimo di *or* sulla politica; **I'm not very well ~ on what's going on** non sono bene al corrente di ciò che sta succedendo.

(i) *(fam: wrong)*: **what's ~?** che c'è?; **what's ~ with him?** che ha?, che gli prende?; **there's something ~ with him/with the TV** (lui)/la TV ha qualcosa che non va.

(j): **~ to** *(as far as)* fino a; **~ to now** finora; **~ to here** fin qui, fino a qui; **~ to £10** fino a 10 sterline.

(k): **~ to** *(fam: doing)*: **what are you ~ to?** *(these days)* che fai di bello?; *(at this very moment)* cosa stai combinando?; **he's ~ to something, he's ~ to no good** sta architettando qualcosa.

(l): **~ to** *(equal to)* all'altezza di; **I don't feel ~ to it** non me la sento; **the book isn't ~ to much** *(fam)* il libro non vale un gran che.

(m): **~ to** *(depending on)*: **it's ~ to you to decide** sta a te decidere; **I'd go, but it's ~ to you** io ci andrei, ma dipende da te.

(n): **to be ~ against opposition** trovarsi di fronte a una forte opposizione; **you don't know what you're ~ against** non sai a cosa vai incontro; **he's really ~ against it** sta in un bell'impiccio.

2 *prep*: **to go ~** *(stairs)* salire; *(hill)* salire su per; *(river)* rimontare; **it's ~ that road** è su per quella strada; **to be ~ a tree** essere su un albero; **further ~ the page** più su nella stessa pagina; **halfway ~ the stairs** a metà scala; **he pointed ~ the street** ha indicato in fondo alla strada; **he went off ~ the road** se n'è andato su per la strada; **to travel ~ and down the country** viaggiare su e giù per il paese; **he drives me ~ the wall** *(fig)* mi fa uscire dai gangheri.

3 *n*: **~s and downs** *(in life, career)* alti e bassi *mpl*; **the road is full of ~s and downs** la strada è molto accidentata; **he's on the ~ and ~** le cose gli stanno andando sempre meglio.

4 *adj (train, line)* per la città.

5 *vi (fam)*: **he ~ped and went** ha preso e se n'è andato; **he ~ped and punched him** gli ha mollato un pugno.

up-and-coming [ˈʌpəndˌkʌmɪŋ] *adj* promettente.

up-and-down [ˌʌpənˈdaʊn] *adj (movement)* (in) su e giù; *(business, progress etc)* con molti alti e bassi.

up·bring·ing [ˈʌpˌbrɪŋɪŋ] *n* educazione *f*.

up·country [ˌʌpˈkʌntrɪ] *adv (be)* all'interno; *(go)* verso l'interno.

up·date [ˌʌp'deɪt] *vt* aggiornare.

up·grade [ˌʌp'greɪd] *vt (employee)* promuovere, avanzare di grado.

up·heav·al [ˌʌp'hiːvəl] *n (Geol)* sollevamento; *(Pol)* sconvolgimento; *(fig)* scompiglio.

up·held [ˌʌp'hɛld] *pt, pp* of **uphold**.

up·hill [ˌʌp'hɪl] **1** *adv:* **to go ~** andare in salita. **2** *adj* in salita, in su; *(fig: task)* faticoso(a); **it's ~ all the way** è tutta salita; *(fig)* è una lotta continua.

up·hold [ˌʌp'həʊld] *pt, pp* **upheld** *vt (sustain: honour)* tenere alto(a); *(: law)* far rispettare; *(support: person, decision)* appoggiare; *(Law: verdict)* confermare.

up·hol·stery [ˌʌp'həʊlstərɪ] *n* tappezzeria.

up·keep ['ʌpkiːp] *n* manutenzione *f*.

up·lift [ˌʌp'lɪft] *vt (fig)* sollevare, tirar su; *(spiritually)* elevare, esaltare.

upon [ə'pɒn] *prep* = **on 1**.

up·per ['ʌpəʳ] **1** *adj* **(a)** *(jaw, lip etc)* superiore; *(storey)* superiore, di sopra; **the ~ reaches of the Po** l'alto Po; **to keep a stiff ~ lip** *(fig)* conservare il sangue freddo. **(b)** *(in importance, rank)* superiore, più alto(a), più elevato(a); **the ~ school** gli ultimi anni di scuola superiore; **the ~ income bracket** la fascia di reddito più alto; **the ~ classes** i ceti più elevati; **the ~ middle class** l'alta borghesia; **the ~ crust** *(fam)* l'aristocrazia. **2** *n (of shoe)* tomaia; **to be on one's ~s** *(fig fam)* essere al verde, non avere un soldo bucato.

upper-class [ˌʌpə'klɑːs] *adj (district)* signorile; *(people)* dell'alta borghesia; *(accent)* aristocratico(a); *(attitude)* snob *inv*.

upper·most ['ʌpəməʊst] *adj (thought)* dominante; *(echelon)* più alto(a), più elevato(a); **it was ~ in my mind** è stata la mia prima preoccupazione.

up·pish ['ʌpɪʃ], **up·pi·ty** ['ʌpɪtɪ] *adj (Brit fam)* con la puzza sotto il naso; **to get ~** darsi importanza.

up·right ['ʌpraɪt] **1** *adj* **(a)** *(posture)* ritto(a), eretto(a); *(post)* verticale. **(b)** *(fig)* retto(a), onesto(a). **2** *adv* dritto(a); **to stand ~** *(person)* stare dritto; *(object)* essere in posizione verticale. **3** *n* **(a)** *(post)* supporto verticale; *(of door, window)* montante *m*. **(b)** *(piano)* pianoforte *m* verticale.

up·ris·ing ['ʌpˌraɪzɪŋ] *n* rivolta, insurrezione *f*.

up·roar ['ʌprɔːʳ] *n* trambusto, gran baccano; **the whole place was in ~** c'era un gran baccano.

up·roari·ous [ˌʌp'rɔːrɪəs] *adj (gen)* chiassoso(a); *(laughter)* fragoroso(a); *(welcome)* entusiastico(a); *(very funny: joke, mistake)* da crepar dal ridere.

up·root [ˌʌp'ruːt] *vt* sradicare.

up·set [ˌʌp'sɛt] *(vb: pt, pp* **upset**) **1** *vt* **(a)** *(container, contents)* rovesciare; *(boat)* capovolgere, rovesciare; *(fig: plan, schedule)* scombussolare. **(b)** *(emotionally: disturb)* turbare, *(stronger)* sconvolgere; *(: offend)* offendere; *(: annoy)* contrariare, seccare; **don't ~ yourself** non te la prendere. **(c)** *(make ill: person)* far star male; *(: stomach)* scombussolare.

2 *adj* **(a)** *(emotionally: disturbed)* turbato(a), *(stronger)* sconvolto(a); *(: offended)* offeso(a); *(: annoyed)* contrariato(a), seccato(a); **to get ~** lasciarsi turbare *or* sconvolgere; offendersi; seccarsi; **don't get ~** non te la prendere. **(b): I have an ~ stomach** ho lo stomaco in disordine *or* scombussolato.

3 ['ʌpsɛt] *n* **(a)** *(disturbance: in plans etc)* contrattempo, contrarietà *f inv*; *(emotional)* dispiacere *m*. **(b): to have a stomach ~** avere lo stomaco in disordine *or* scombussolato.

up·set·ting [ʌp'sɛtɪŋ] *adj (saddening)* sconvolgen-

te; *(offending)* offensivo(a); *(annoying)* fastidioso(a).

up·shot ['ʌpʃɒt] *n (result)* risultato; **the ~ of it all was that...** la conclusione è stata che... .

up·side down [ˌʌpsaɪd'daʊn] **1** *adv (person)* a testa in giù; *(object)* alla rovescia, sottosopra; **to turn ~** capovolgere; *(mattress)* rivoltare; *(fig)* mettere sottosopra *or* a soqquadro. **2** *adj (person)* a testa in giù; *(object)* capovolto(a); **the room was ~** *(in disorder)* la stanza era tutta sottosopra.

up·stairs [ˌʌp'stɛəz] **1** *adv* di sopra; **to go ~** andare di sopra; **the people ~** quelli di sopra. **2** *n* piano di sopra. **3** ['ʌpstɛəz] *adj (room)* al piano di sopra.

up·stand·ing [ˌʌp'stændɪŋ] *adj (strong)* aitante; *(honourable)* retto(a).

up·start ['ʌpstɑːt] *n* parvenu *m inv*.

up·stream ['ʌp'striːm] *adv (be)* a monte; *(swim)* controcorrente; **to sail ~** rimontare la corrente.

up·surge ['ʌpsɜːdʒ] *n (of enthusiasm etc)* ondata.

up·take ['ʌptɛɪk] *n (fam):* **slow on the ~** duro(a) di comprendonio; **to be quick on the ~** capire le cose al volo.

up·tight [ʌp'taɪt] *adj (fam)* teso(a).

up-to-date ['ʌptə'deɪt] *adj (figures, edition)* aggiornato(a); *(person)* ben informato(a), aggiornato(a); *(ideas)* attuale, al passo coi tempi; *(clothes)* alla moda; **to bring sb ~ (on sth)** aggiornare qn (su qc).

up-to-the-minute ['ʌptəðə'mɪnɪt] *adj (fashionable: dress, person)* all'ultimissima moda; *(: style)* modernissimo(a); *(latest: information)* dell'ultimo minuto.

up·turn ['ʌptɜːn] *n (fig: improvement)* ripresa; *(in value of currency)* rialzo.

up·turned [ʌp'tɜːnd] *adj (box etc)* capovolto(a), rovesciato(a); *(nose)* all'insù.

up·ward ['ʌpwəd] **1** *adj (movement)* verso l'alto, in su; *(curve)* ascendente; **~ tendency** *(Fin)* tendenza al rialzo. **2** *adv (also:* **~s) (a)** in su, verso l'alto; **to lie face ~** giacere supino. **(b)** *(with numbers):* **from the age of 13 ~s** dai 13 anni in su; **~s of 500** 500 e più.

ura·nium [juə'reɪnɪəm] *n* uranio.

Ura·nus [juə'reɪnəs] *n (Astron)* Urano.

ur·ban ['ɜːbən] *adj* urbano(a).

ur·bane [ɜː'beɪn] *adj* urbano(a), civile.

ur·bani·zation [ˌɜːbənaɪ'zeɪʃən] *n* urbanizzazione *f*.

ur·chin ['ɜːtʃɪn] *n* monello/a.

urge [ɜːdʒ] **1** *n* impulso, stimolo, voglia; **to feel an ~ to do sth** sentire un impulso a fare qc. **2** *vt* **(a)** *(try to persuade)* insistere; **to ~ that** insistere che + *sub;* **to ~ sb to do sth** insistere che qn faccia qc; **he ~d me to visit the Uffizi** mi ha raccomandato vivamente di visitare gli Uffizi; **he needed no urging** non si è fatto pregare. **(b)** *(advocate: measure)* fare pressioni per; *(: caution, acceptance)* raccomandare vivamente; **to ~ sth on** *or* **upon sb** sottolineare a qn l'importanza di qc.

♦ **urge on** *vt + adv (also fig)* incitare, spronare.

ur·gen·cy ['ɜːdʒənsɪ] *n (of case, need)* urgenza; *(of tone of voice, pleas)* insistenza; **it is a matter of ~** è una questione della massima urgenza.

ur·gent ['ɜːdʒənt] *adj* **(a)** *(message, need)* urgente. **(b)** *(earnest, persistent: plea)* pressante; *(: tone)* insistente, incalzante.

ur·gent·ly ['ɜːdʒəntlɪ] *adv (see adj)* d'urgenza, urgentemente; in modo pressante, con insistenza.

uri·nal ['jʊərɪnl] *n (building)* vespasiano; *(vessel)* orinale *m*, pappagallo.

uri·nate ['jʊərɪneɪt] *vi* orinare.

urine ['jʊərɪn] *n* orina.

urn [ɜːn] *n* **(a)** *(vase)* urna. **(b)** *(also:* **tea ~, coffee**

~) contenitore a spina per tè, caffè.

us [ʌs] *pers pron pl* **(a)** *(direct, indirect)* ci; *(stressed, after prep, in comparatives)* noi; **they saw** ~ **ci** hanno visto; **they're older than** ~ sono più vecchi di noi; **we had some suitcases with** ~ avevamo con noi delle valigie; **let's go** andiamo; ~ **Scots** noialtri Scozzesi. **(b)** *(fam: me)*: **give** ~ **a kiss** dammi un bacino.

USA *n abbr of* **United States of America.**

us·able ['juːzəbl] *adj* utilizzabile, usabile.

us·age ['juːzɪdʒ] **1** *n* **(a)** *(custom)* usanza, uso. **(b)** *(Linguistics: use, way of using)* uso; **to be in common** ~ essere nell'uso comune. **(c)** *(treatment, handling)* uso; **it's had some rough** ~ è stato un po' bistrattato.

use [juːs] **1** *n* **(a)** *(gen)* uso, impiego; **a new** ~ **for old tyres** un nuovo modo di utilizzare vecchi copertoni; **directions for** ~ istruzioni per l'uso; **for the** ~ **of the blind** ad uso dei ciechi; **for** ~ **in case of emergency** da usarsi in caso di emergenza; **ready for** ~ pronto per l'uso; **to make** ~ **of sth** far uso di qc, utilizzare qc; **in** ~ in uso; **out of** ~ fuori uso; **is your old radio still in** ~? usi ancora la vecchia radio?; **to be in daily** ~ venire adoperato quotidianamente; **to be no longer in** ~ essere fuori uso; **it's gone** *or* **fallen out of** ~ non lo si usa più; **for one's own** ~ per uso personale; **fit for** ~ che si può ancora usare; **to make good** ~ **of sth, to put sth to good** ~ far buon uso di qc; **to find a** ~ **for sth** trovare il modo di utilizzare qc; **we have no further** ~ **for this** questo non ci serve più.

(b) *(usefulness)*: **to be of** ~ essere utile, servire; **it's (of) no** ~ non serve, è inutile; **it's no** ~! niente da fare!; **it's no** ~ **discussing it further** non serve a niente continuare a discuterne; **what's the** ~ **of all this?** a che serve tutto ciò?; **she's no** ~ **as a teacher** non vale niente come insegnante.

(c) *(ability or right to use)*: **to lose the** ~ **of one's legs** perdere l'uso delle gambe; **can I have the** ~ **of the car?** posso usare la macchina?

2 [juːz] *vt* **(a)** *(gen)* usare; *(opportunity)* sfruttare; **to** ~ **force** usare la forza; **'to be** ~**d only in emergencies'** 'da usare solo in caso d'emergenza'; **to** ~ **sth as a hammer** usare qc come martello; **what's this** ~**d for?** a che serve?; **I could** ~ **a drink** *(fam)* berrei qualcosa; **this room could** ~ **some paint** *(fam)* una passata di vernice non farebbe male a questa stanza; ~ **your head** *or* **brains!** usa la testa *or* il cervello!; ~ **your eyes!** apri gli occhi!

(b) *(make* ~ *of, exploit: influence)* servirsi di, adoperare; *(: opportunity)* approfittare di.

(c) *(*~ *up, consume)* consumare; *(finish)* finire; *(left-overs etc)* usare, utilizzare.

(d) *(old poet: treat)* trattare.

3 *aux vb*: **I** ~**d to go there every day** ci andavo ogni giorno, ero solito andarci ogni giorno; **things are not what they** ~**d to be** non è più come una volta.

♦ **use up** *vt + adv (strength)* usare; *(left-overs)* utilizzare; *(supplies)* dare fondo a; *(petrol, paper, money)* finire.

used[1] [juːzd] *adj (secondhand: clothing)* usato(a); *(: car)* di seconda mano, d'occasione, usato(a).

used[2] [juːzt] *adj*: **to be** ~ **to sth** essere abituato(a) a qc; **to be** ~ **to doing sth** essere abituato a *or* avere l'abitudine di fare qc; **to get** ~ **to** abituarsi a, fare l'abitudine a.

use·ful ['juːsfʊl] *adj* **(a)** *(gen)* utile; **he's a** ~ **man to know** è una conoscenza utile; **that's a** ~ **thing to know** buona a sapersi; **it is very** ~ **to be able to drive** saper guidare è molto utile; **to make o.s.** ~ rendersi utile; **to come in** ~ fare comodo, tornare utile. **(b)** *(fam: capable: player)* bravino(a); **he is** ~ **with a gun** sa maneggiare il fucile.

use·less ['juːslɪs] *adj* **(a)** *(no good: remedy)* inefficace; *(: advice)* inutile; *(unusable: object)* inservibile; **he's** ~ **as a forward** come centravanti non vale niente; **you are** ~! sei un inetto! **(b)** *(pointless)* inutile; **it's** ~ **arguing with him** non serve a niente *or* è inutile discutere con lui.

user ['juːzəʳ] *n (of public service, dictionary etc)* utente *m/f*; *(of petrol, gas etc)* consumatore/trice; **car** ~**s** automobilisti *mpl*; **library** ~**s** lettori *mpl*.

ush·er ['ʌʃəʳ] **1** *n (Law)* usciere *m*; *(in theatre, cinema etc)* maschera; *(at wedding)* valletto che accompagna gli ospiti al loro posti. **2** *vt*: **to** ~ **sb in** far entrare qn; **it** ~**ed in a new era** *(fig)* ha inaugurato una nuova era.

ush·er·ette [ˌʌʃəˈrɛt] *n* maschera.

USSR *n abbr of* **Union of Soviet Socialist Republics.**

usu·al ['juːʒʊəl] **1** *adj (gen)* solito(a); **at the** ~ **time** alla solita ora; **earlier than** ~ prima del solito; **as is** ~ **on these occasions** come vuole la tradizione; **as is** ~ **with this type of housing** come sempre in questo genere di case; **he's not his** ~ **self** di solito non è così; **he'll soon be his** ~ **self again** tornerà presto ad essere quello di sempre; **as** ~ come al solito, come d'abitudine; **'business as** ~**'** l'ufficio *(or* il negozio *etc)* è aperto al pubblico'; **more than** ~ più del solito; **it's not** ~ **for her to be late** non è sua abitudine arrivare in ritardo. **2** *n*: **the** ~, **please!** *(fam: drink)* il solito, per favore!

usu·al·ly ['juːʒʊəlɪ] *adv* di solito; **to be more than** ~ **careful** fare ancora più attenzione del solito.

usu·rer ['juːʒərəʳ] *n* usuraio/a.

usurp [juːˈzɜːp] *vt* usurpare.

uten·sil [juːˈtɛnsl] *n* utensile *m*.

uter·us ['juːtərəs] *n* utero.

utili·tar·ian [ˌjuːtɪlɪˈtɛərɪən] *adj* **(a)** *(furniture)* funzionale. **(b)** *(Philosophy)* utilitarista.

util·ity [juːˈtɪlɪtɪ] **1** *n (usefulness)* utilità; *(public service)* servizio. **2** *cpd*: ~ **room** *n* locale adibito alla stiratura dei panni etc.

uti·li·za·tion [ˌjuːtɪlaɪˈzeɪʃən] *n* utilizzazione *f.*

uti·lize ['juːtɪlaɪz] *vt (spare time)* utilizzare; *(talent, opportunity)* sfruttare.

ut·most ['ʌtməʊst] **1** *adj* **(a)** *(greatest: simplicity, caution)* massimo(a); *(: danger)* estremo(a); **with the** ~ **speed** a tutta velocità; **of the** ~ **importance** della massima importanza; **it is of the** ~ **importance that...** è estremamente importante che... + *sub.* **(b)** *(furthest: limits)* estremo(a). **2** *n*: **to do one's** ~ *(to do sth)* fare tutto il possibile (per fare qc); **to the** ~ **of one's ability** al limite delle proprie capacità.

Uto·pia [juːˈtəʊpɪə] *n* utopia.

Uto·pian [juːˈtəʊpɪən] *adj* utopico(a).

ut·ter[1] ['ʌtəʳ] *adj (disaster, silence)* totale, assoluto(a); *(madness)* puro(a); *(fool)* perfetto(a); **that's** ~ **nonsense** sono tutte sciocchezze.

ut·ter[2] ['ʌtəʳ] *vt (groan, sigh)* emettere; *(cry, insult)* lanciare; *(word)* pronunciare; **she never** ~**ed a word** non ha detto una sola parola.

ut·ter·ly ['ʌtəlɪ] *adv* completamente, del tutto.

utter·most ['ʌtəməʊst] = **utmost.**

U-turn [juːˈtɜːn] *n* inversione *f* a U; *(fig)* voltafaccia *m inv.*

V

V, v [viː] *n (letter)* V, v *f or m inv.*

va·can·cy ['veɪkənsɪ] *n* **(a)** *(emptiness)* vuoto. **(b)** *(in boarding house etc)* stanza libera; **'no vacancies'** 'completo'; **have you any vacancies?** avete una stanza? **(c)** *(job)* posto libero; **have you any vacancies?** avete bisogno di personale?; **'vacancy for a secretary'** 'segretaria cercasi'.

va·cant ['veɪkənt] *adj* **(a)** *(seat, room etc)* libero(a); *(property)* vuoto(a), libero(a); *(post)* scoperto(a), *(frm)* vacante. **(b)** *(look etc)* vuoto(a), vacuo(a).

va·cate [və'keɪt] *vt (house, seat, room)* lasciar libero(a); *(post)* lasciare, dare le dimissioni da.

va·ca·tion [və'keɪʃən] *n (esp Am)* vacanza, ferie *fpl*; *(Univ)* vacanze; **on** ~ in vacanza, in ferie; **to take a** ~ prendere una vacanza, prendere le ferie.

vac·ci·nate ['væksɪneɪt] *vt* vaccinare.

vac·ci·na·tion [ˌvæksɪ'neɪʃən] *n* vaccinazione *f.*

vac·cine ['væksiːn] *n* vaccino.

vac·il·late ['væsɪleɪt] *vi (waver)*: **to** ~ **(between)** oscillare (tra).

vacu·ous ['vækjuəs] *adj (look, expression)* vacuo(a), stupido(a); *(comment)* stupido(a).

vacuum ['vækjum] **1** *n (also fig)* vuoto; **in a** ~ *(fig)* in assoluto isolamento. **2** *cpd:* ~ **cleaner** *n* aspirapolvere *m inv;* ~ **flask** *n* thermos *m inv.*

vacuum-packed ['vækjum,pækt] *adj* confezionato(a) sottovuoto.

vaga·bond ['vægəbɒnd] *n* vagabondo/a.

va·gary ['veɪgərɪ] *n* capriccio.

va·gi·na [və'dʒaɪnə] *n* vagina.

va·gran·cy ['veɪgrənsɪ] *n* vagabondaggio.

va·grant ['veɪgrənt] *n* vagabondo/a.

vague [veɪg] *adj (-r, -st) (gen)* vago(a); *(directions, description)* impreciso(a), confuso(a); *(person: absent minded)* distratto(a); **I have a** ~ **idea that...** penso che...; **I haven't the** ~**st idea** non ho la minima *or* più pallida idea; **the** ~ **outline of a ship** la sagoma indistinta *or* confusa di una nave; **a** ~ **look** uno sguardo assente *or* vuoto.

vague·ly ['veɪglɪ] *adv* vagamente.

vain [veɪn] *adj* **(a)** *(useless, empty)* vano(a); **in** ~ invano; **all our efforts were in** ~ tutti i nostri sforzi sono stati inutili. **(b)** *(-er, -est) (conceited)* vanitoso(a).

vain·ly ['veɪnlɪ] *adv (see adj)* invano; vanitosamente.

val·ance ['væləns] *n* volant *m inv,* balza.

val·en·tine ['væləntaɪn] *n (card)* biglietto di auguri per San Valentino.

val·et ['væleɪ] *n* cameriere *m* personale.

val·iant ['væljənt] *adj (poet)* coraggioso(a); **a** ~ **knight** un prode cavaliere.

val·id ['vælɪd] *adj (ticket, document, excuse)* valido(a); *(claim, objection)* giustificato(a).

vali·date ['vælɪdeɪt] *vt (contract, document)* convalidare; *(argument, claim)* comprovare.

va·lid·ity [və'lɪdɪtɪ] *n (of document)* validità; *(of argument)* fondatezza, validità.

val·ley ['vælɪ] *n* valle *f.*

val·our, *(Am)* **val·or** ['vælə'] *n (frm)* valore *m.*

valu·able ['væljuəbl] **1** *adj (contribution, time)* pre-

zioso(a); *(painting, object)* di valore, costoso(a). **2:** ~**s** *npl* preziosi *mpl.*

valua·tion [ˌvæljuˈeɪʃən] *n* stima, valutazione *f*; **what is your** ~ **of him?** che opinione ti sei fatto di lui?

value ['væljuː] **1** *n* **(a)** valore *m; (usefulness)* utilità; **to lose (in)** ~ *(currency)* svalutarsi; *(property)* perdere (di) valore; **to gain (in)** ~ *(currency)* guadagnare; *(property)* aumentare di valore; **sentimental** ~ valore affettivo; **of no** ~ di nessun valore, senza valore; **to be of great** ~ **to sb** avere molta importanza per qn; **it has been of no** ~ **to him** non gli è servito a nulla; **you get good** ~ **(for money)** in that shop si compra bene in quel negozio; **this dress is good** ~ **(for money)** questo abito ha un buon prezzo. **(b)** *(moral):* ~**s** *pl* valori *mpl.*

2 *vt (financially)* valutare; *(friendship, independence etc)* tenere a; **it is** ~**d at £8** è stato valutato a 8 sterline.

3 *cpd:* ~ **added tax** *n (abbr* **VAT)** imposta sul valore aggiunto *(abbr* I.V.A.); ~ **judgment** *n* giudizio soggettivo *(basato su valori personali o di classe).*

val·ued ['væljuːd] *adj* stimato(a), tenuto(a) in grande considerazione.

valve [vælv] *n (all senses)* valvola.

vam·pire ['væmpaɪə'] **1** *n* vampiro. **2** *cpd:* ~ **bat** *n (Zool)* vampiro.

van¹ [væn] *n (Aut)* furgone *m; (Rail)* vagone *m.*

van² [væn] *n abbr of* **vanguard.**

van·dal ['vændəl] *n* vandalo.

van·dal·ism ['vændəlɪzəm] *n* vandalismo.

van·dal·ize ['vændəlaɪz] *vt* vandalizzare.

vane [veɪn] *n (weather~)* segnavento.

van·guard ['vængɑːd] *n* avanguardia; **to be in the** ~ **of progress** essere all'avanguardia del progresso; **to be in the** ~ **of a movement** essere tra i capostipiti di un movimento.

va·nil·la [və'nɪlə] **1** *n* vaniglia. **2** *adj (ice cream)* alla vaniglia; *(essence)* di vaniglia.

van·ish ['vænɪʃ] *vi* svanire; **to** ~ **into thin air** volatilizzarsi.

van·ish·ing ['vænɪʃɪŋ] *adj:* ~ **point** punto di fuga.

van·ity ['vænɪtɪ] *n* vanità *f inv.*

van·quish ['væŋkwɪʃ] *vt (poet)* sconfiggere.

van·tage ['vɑːntɪdʒ] *n:* ~ **point** punto d'osservazione (favorevole).

vap·id ['væpɪd] *adj* scipito(a).

va·por·ize ['veɪpəraɪz] **1** *vt* vaporizzare. **2** *vi* vaporizzarsi.

va·pour, *(Am)* **va·por** ['veɪpə'] **1** *n* vapore *m.* **2** *cpd:* ~ **trail** *n (Aer)* scia.

vari·abil·ity [ˌvɛərɪə'bɪlɪtɪ] *n* variabilità.

vari·able ['vɛərɪəbl] **1** *adj (output, performance)* non costante; *(weather, wind)* variabile; *(mood)* mutevole. **2** *n* fattore *m* variabile.

vari·ance ['vɛərɪəns] *n:* **to be at** ~ **(with sb over sth)** essere in disaccordo (con qn per qc); **to be at** ~ **(with sth)** *(facts, statements)* discostarsi (da qc).

vari·ant ['vɛərɪənt] *n* variante *f*.

vari·ation [,vɛərɪ'eɪʃən] *n* variazione *f*.

vari·cose ['værɪkəʊs] *adj*: ~ **vein** vena varicosa.

var·ied ['vɛərɪd] *adj (gen)* vario(a); *(life)* movimentato(a); *(diet)* diversificato(a).

varie·gat·ed ['vɛərɪgeɪtɪd] *adj* variegato(a).

va·ri·ety [və'raɪətɪ] **1** *n (type)* varietà *f inv*, tipo; *(range, diversity)* molteplicità, varietà; **in a wide** *or* **large** ~ **of colours** in una vasta gamma di colori; **for a** ~ **of reasons** per una serie di motivi; **for** ~ per variare. **2** *cpd*: ~ **artist** *n* artista *m/f* di varietà; ~ **show** *n* spettacolo di varietà.

vari·ous ['vɛərɪəs] *adj* vario(a), diverso(a); **at** ~ **times** *(different)* in momenti diversi; *(several)* diverse volte; **we all went our** ~ **ways home** ognuno è tornato a casa per la sua strada.

vari·ous·ly ['vɛərɪəslɪ] *adv* in modo vario, variamente.

var·nish ['vɑːnɪʃ] **1** *n (for wood)* vernice *f* trasparente; *(for nails)* smalto. **2** *vt (wood)* dare la vernice a; *(nails)* mettersi lo smalto su.

vary ['vɛərɪ] **1** *vt* variare. **2** *vi (change)*: **to** ~ **(with** *or* **according to)** variare (con *or* a seconda di); *(deviate)*: **to** ~ **(from)** discostarsi (da); **the temperature/her mood varies** la temperatura/il suo umore è variabile; **these items** ~ **in price** il prezzo di questi articoli varia.

vary·ing ['vɛərɪŋ] *adj* variabile, che varia; **with** ~ **degrees of success** con risultati più o meno soddisfacenti.

vase [vɑːz] *n* vaso.

vas·ec·to·my [væ'sɛktəmɪ] *n* vasectomia.

vas·eline ['væsɪliːn] *n* ® vaselina.

vast [vɑːst] *adj* **(-er, -est)** *(territory, expanse)* vasto(a); *(sum, amount)* ingente; *(success, difference, improvement)* enorme; **at** ~ **expense** con enorme dispendio di capitale.

vast·ly ['vɑːstlɪ] *adv (grateful, rich)* enormemente; ~ **superior** di gran lunga superiore a; **he's** ~ **mistaken if...** sbaglia di grosso se...; **the film was** ~ **successful** il film ha avuto un successo strepitoso.

VAT ['viːeɪtiː, væt] *abbr see* **value.**

vat [væt] *n (for wine, dye etc)* tino.

Vati·can ['vætɪkən] *n*: **the** ~ il Vaticano.

vault[1] [vɔːlt] *n (Archit)* volta; *(of bank)* caveau *m inv; (tomb)* sotterraneo; **family** ~ tomba di famiglia.

vault[2] [vɔːlt] *vt, vi*: **to** ~ **(over)** sth saltare qc con un balzo.

vault·ed ['vɔːltɪd] *adj* a volta.

vaunt·ed ['vɔːntɪd] *adj (esp: much* ~) di cui tanto si parla.

V.D. [,viː'diː] *abbr see* **venereal.**

veal [viːl] *n* vitello.

veer [vɪəʳ] *vi (ship)* virare; *(car, wind)* girare; **wind** ~**ing westerly at times** vento con tendenza a provenire da ovest; **the country has** ~**ed to the left** il paese ha fatto una svolta a sinistra; **the conversation** ~**ed round to politics** la conversazione si è spostata sulla politica.

veg·eta·ble ['vɛdʒɪtəbl] **1** *n* **(a)** ortaggio; ~**s** verdura, verdure *fpl*, ortaggi *mpl*; **would you like some** ~**s?** vuoi un po' di verdura? **(b)** *(generic term: plant)* vegetale *m*. **2** *cpd (oil, wax)* vegetale; *(soup)* di verdura; ~ **garden** *n* orto.

veg·etar·ian [,vɛdʒɪ'tɛərɪən] *adj, n* vegetariano(a) *(m/f)*.

veg·etate ['vɛdʒɪteɪt] *vi* vegetare.

veg·eta·tion [,vɛdʒɪ'teɪʃən] *n* vegetazione *f*.

ve·he·mence ['viːɪməns] *n* veemenza.

ve·he·ment ['viːɪmənt] *adj (speech, passions)* veemente, violento(a); *(attack)* feroce; *(dislike,*

hatred) profondo(a); **there was** ~ **opposition** ci fu una resistenza accanita.

ve·hi·cle ['viːɪkl] *n* veicolo; *(fig)* mezzo.

veil [veɪl] **1** *n* velo; **to take the** ~ *(Rel)* prendere il velo; **under a** ~ **of secrecy** *(fig)* protetto da una cortina di segretezza. **2** *vt* velare, coprire con un velo; **the town was** ~**ed in mist** la città era avvolta dalla nebbia.

veiled [veɪld] *adj (also fig)* velato(a).

vein [veɪn] *n (gen)* vena; *(Bot)* venatura; *(in melancholy* ~ d'umore malinconico; **in a different** ~ con uno spirito diverso.

vel·lum ['vɛləm] *n (writing paper)* carta patinata.

ve·loc·ity [vɪ'lɒsɪtɪ] *n* velocità *f inv*.

vel·vet ['vɛlvɪt] **1** *n* velluto. **2** *adj (skirt etc)* di velluto.

vel·vet·een [,vɛlvɪ'tiːn] *n* vellutino.

vel·vety ['vɛlvɪtɪ] *adj* vellutato(a).

ve·nal ['viːnl] *adj* venale.

ven·det·ta [vɛn'dɛtə] *n* vendetta.

vend·ing ma·chine ['vɛndɪŋmə'ʃiːn] *n* distributore *m* automatico.

ven·dor ['vɛndɔːʳ] *n* venditore/trice; **street** ~ venditore ambulante.

ve·neer [və'nɪəʳ] *n* impiallacciatura; *(fig)* parvenza.

ven·er·able ['vɛnərəbl] *adj* venerabile; *(old man, appearance)* venerando(a).

ven·er·ate ['vɛnəreɪt] *vt* venerare.

ven·era·tion [,vɛnə'reɪʃən] *n* venerazione *f*.

ve·nereal [vɪ'nɪərɪəl] *adj*: ~ **disease** *(abbr* **V.D.)** malattia venerea.

venge·ance ['vɛndʒəns] *n* vendetta; **to take** ~ **on** sb vendicarsi su qn; **with a** ~ *(fig)* furiosamente.

ve·nial ['viːnɪəl] *adj* veniale.

Ven·ice ['vɛnɪs] *n* Venezia.

veni·son ['vɛnɪsən] *n* carne *f* di cervo.

ven·om ['vɛnəm] *n (also fig)* veleno.

ven·om·ous ['vɛnəməs] *adj (also fig)* velenoso(a).

vent [vɛnt] **1** *n (Tech, airhole)* presa d'aria; *(of jacket)* spacco; **to give** ~ **to one's anger** sfogare la propria rabbia. **2** *vt*: **to** ~ **one's anger (on sb/sth)** *(fig)* scaricare *or* sfogare la propria rabbia (su qn/qc).

ven·ti·late ['vɛntɪleɪt] *vt* ventilare.

ven·ti·la·tion [,vɛntɪ'leɪʃən] **1** *n* aerazione *f*, ventilazione *f*. **2** *cpd*: ~ **shaft** *n* condotto di aerazione.

ven·ti·la·tor ['vɛntɪleɪtəʳ] *n* ventilatore *m*.

ven·trilo·quist [vɛn'trɪləkwɪst] *n* ventriloquo.

ven·ture ['vɛntʃəʳ] **1** *n* impresa; **a business** ~ un'iniziativa commerciale; **a new** ~ **in publishing** una nuova iniziativa editoriale. **2** *vt (money, reputation, life)* rischiare; *(opinion, guess)* azzardare; **to** ~ **to do sth** azzardarsi a fare qc; **if I may** ~ **an opinion** se posso azzardare *or* arrischiare un parere; **nothing** ~**d, nothing gained** chi non risica non rosica. **3** *vi*: **to** ~ **on sth** avventurarsi in qc; **to** ~ **out (of doors)** arrischiarsi ad uscire (di casa).

venue ['vɛnjuː] *n* luogo d'incontro.

Venus ['viːnəs] *n (Astron)* Venere *m; (Mythology)* Venere *f*.

ve·rac·ity [və'ræsɪtɪ] *n* veridicità.

ve·ran·da(h) [və'rændə] *n* veranda.

verb [vɜːb] *n* verbo.

ver·bal ['vɜːbəl] *adj* verbale.

ver·bal·ly ['vɜːbəlɪ] *adv* a voce.

ver·ba·tim [vɜː'beɪtɪm] *adv, adj* parola per parola.

ver·bi·age ['vɜːbɪɪdʒ] *n* verbosità.

ver·bose [vɜː'bəʊs] *adj* verboso(a).

ver·dict ['vɜːdɪkt] *n (Law)* verdetto; *(opinion)* giudizio, parere *m;* ~ **of guilty/not guilty** verdetto di colpevolezza/non colpevolezza; **his** ~ **on the**

wine was unfavourable ha dato un giudizio sfavorevole sul vino.

verge [vɜːdʒ] **1** n (of road) bordo, margine m; (fig) orlo; **to be on the ~ of** (disaster) essere sull'orlo di; (a discovery) essere alle soglie di; **she was on the ~ of tears** stava quasi per piangere; **to be on the ~ of doing sth** essere sul punto di fare qc. **2** vi: **to ~ on** or **upon** tendere a.

ver·ger ['vɜːdʒə'] n sagrestano.

ver·i·fi·ca·tion [ˌvɛrɪfɪ'keɪʃən] n verifica, accertamento.

veri·fy ['vɛrɪfaɪ] vt (check) verificare, controllare; (prove the truth of) confermare.

veri·table ['vɛrɪtəbl] adj vero(a).

ver·mil·ion [və'mɪljən] adj vermiglio(a).

ver·min ['vɜːmɪn] n insetti mpl (or animali mpl) nocivi; (fig pej) parassiti mpl.

ver·mouth ['vɜːməθ] n vermut m inv.

ver·nacu·lar [və'nækjʊlə'] n vernacolo.

ver·sa·tile ['vɜːsətaɪl] adj (person) versatile; (tool) multiusi inv.

ver·sa·til·ity [ˌvɜːsə'tɪlɪtɪ] n (of person) versatilità.

verse [vɜːs] n (a) (of poem) verso; (: stanza) strofa; (of Bible) versetto. (b) (no pl: poetry) poesia; **in ~** in versi; **blank ~** versi mpl sciolti.

versed [vɜːst] adj: **to be well ~ in sth** essere pratico(a) di qc.

ver·sion ['vɜːʃən] n versione f.

ver·sus ['vɜːsəs] prep (Law, Sport, gen) contro.

ver·te·bra ['vɜːtɪbrə] n, pl **vertebrae** ['vɜːtɪbriː] vertebra.

ver·te·brate ['vɜːtɪbrət] **1** adj vertebrato(a). **2** n vertebrato.

ver·tex ['vɜːtɛks] n, pl **vertices** ['vɜːtɪsiːz] vertice m.

ver·ti·cal ['vɜːtɪkəl] **1** adj (gen) verticale; (cliff) a picco. **2** n verticale f.

ver·ti·go ['vɜːtɪɡəʊ] n vertigine f; **to suffer from ~** soffrire di vertigini.

verve [vɜːv] n (of person) verve f; (of painting, writing) vivacità.

very ['vɛrɪ] **1** adv (a) (extremely) molto; **~ happy** molto felice, felicissimo; **it's ~ cold** fa molto freddo; **~ well** molto bene; **~ little** molto poco; **~ much** molto; **~ much younger** molto più giovane; **are you tired? — (yes,) ~** sei stanco? — (sì,) molto; **he's so ~ poor** è estremamente povero; **~ high frequency** (Radio) altissima frequenza.

    (b) (absolutely): **the ~ first** il primissimo, proprio il primo; **the ~ last** l'ultimissimo, proprio l'ultimo; **the ~ cleverest** di gran lunga il più intelligente; **they are the ~ best of friends** sono grandissimi amici; **to wish sb the ~ best of luck** augurare a qn ogni fortuna; **at the ~ most** al massimo; **at the ~ least** come minimo; **at the ~ latest** al più tardi; **he won't come until 9 o'clock, at the ~ earliest** arriverà alle 9, al più presto; **the ~ same hat** esattamente lo stesso cappello; **it's my ~ own** è proprio mio.

    2 adj (a) (precise) stesso(a); **that ~ day** quello stesso giorno; **his ~ words** le sue stesse parole; **her ~ words were…** le sue parole testuali furono…; **he's the ~ man we want** è proprio l'uomo che cercavamo; **the ~ thing!** proprio quel che ci vuole!

    (b) (mere) solo(a); **the ~ thought (of it) alarms me** il solo pensiero mi spaventa, sono spaventato solo al pensiero; **the ~ idea!** che bell'idea!

    (c) (extreme): **at the ~ bottom/top** proprio in fondo/in cima; **at the ~ end** proprio alla fine; **to the ~ end** fino alla fine; **in the ~ depths of the jungle** nel cuore della giungla.

ves·pers ['vɛspəz] npl vespri mpl.

ves·sel ['vɛsl] n (ship) vascello; (receptacle) recipiente m.

vest[1] [vɛst] **1** n (Brit) canottiera; (Am: waistcoat) panciotto, gilè m inv. **2** cpd: **~ pocket** n (Am) taschino.

vest[2] [vɛst] vt: **to ~ sb with sth** investire qn di qc; **to ~ powers/authority in sb** conferire poteri/autorità a qn.

vest·ed ['vɛstɪd] adj (interest) acquisito(a).

ves·ti·bule ['vɛstɪbjuːl] n atrio, vestibolo.

ves·tige ['vɛstɪdʒ] n vestigio; **not a ~ of truth** nemmeno un briciolo di verità.

vest·ment ['vɛstmənt] n (Rel) paramento.

ves·try ['vɛstrɪ] n sagrestia.

vet [vɛt] **1** n (abbr of **veterinary surgeon**) veterinario. **2** vt (text, application) esaminare; **to ~ sb for a job** raccogliere le informazioni dettagliate su qn prima di offrirgli un posto.

vet·er·an ['vɛtərən] **1** adj: **~ soldier** veterano; **a ~ teacher** un veterano dell'insegnamento; **she's a ~ campaigner for…** lotta da sempre per…; **~ car** vettura d'epoca (anteriore al 1916). **2** n (war ~) veterano.

vet·eri·nary ['vɛtərɪnərɪ] adj veterinario(a); **~ surgeon** veterinario.

veto ['viːtəʊ] **1** n, pl **~es** veto; **to use** or **exercise one's ~** esercitare il proprio diritto di veto; **to put a ~ on** porre il veto a. **2** vt porre il veto a.

vex [vɛks] vt irritare.

vexa·tion [vɛk'seɪʃən] n (state) irritazione f; (problem) contrarietà f inv, cruccio.

vexa·tious [vɛk'seɪʃəs] adj, **vex·ing** ['vɛksɪŋ] adj irritante, fastidioso(a).

vexed [vɛkst] adj (a) irritato(a); **to be/get ~ (with sb about sth)** essere irritato/irritarsi (con qn per qc). (b) (question) controverso(a).

VHF [ˌviːeɪtʃ'ɛf] abbr (= very high frequency) VHF.

via ['vaɪə] prep (place) via; (person) attraverso.

vi·abil·ity [ˌvaɪə'bɪlɪtɪ] n attuabilità.

vi·able ['vaɪəbl] adj (proposal) attuabile; (foetus) in grado di sopravvivere.

via·duct ['vaɪədʌkt] n viadotto.

vibes [vaɪbz] npl (fam abbr of **vibrations**) feeling m.

vi·brant ['vaɪbrənt] adj (sound) vibrante; (colour) vivace, vivo(a); **to be ~ with life** sprizzare vita da tutti i pori.

vi·brate [vaɪ'breɪt] vi (gen, Mus): **to ~ (with)** vibrare (per); (footsteps) risuonare.

vi·bra·tion [vaɪ'breɪʃən] n vibrazione f.

vic·ar ['vɪkə'] n (Church of England) pastore m; (Roman Catholic) vicario.

vic·ar·age ['vɪkərɪdʒ] n canonica (anglicana).

vi·cari·ous [vɪ'kɛərɪəs] adj sofferto(a) al posto di un altro; **to get ~ pleasure out of sth** trarre piacere indirettamente da qc.

vice[1] [vaɪs] **1** n vizio. **2** cpd: **the ~ squad** la (squadra del) buoncostume.

vice[2] [vaɪs] n (Tech) morsa.

vice-chairman [ˌvaɪs'tʃɛəmən] n, pl **-men** vicepresidente m.

vice-chancellor [ˌvaɪs'tʃɑːnsələ'] n (Brit Univ) rettore m (eletto, non onorario).

vice-president [ˌvaɪs'prɛzɪdənt] n vicepresidente m.

vice ver·sa [ˌvaɪsɪ'vɜːsə] adv viceversa.

vi·cin·ity [vɪ'sɪnɪtɪ] n vicinanze fpl.

vi·cious ['vɪʃəs] adj (remark, criticism) maligno(a); (glare) malevolo(a), d'odio; (tongue) velenoso(a); (attack) brutale; (blow, kick) dato(a) con cattiveria; (animal) cattivo(a); **a ~ habit** un vizio; **a ~ circle** un circolo vizioso.

vi·cis·si·tudes [vɪ'sɪsɪtjuːdz] npl vicissitudini fpl.

vic·tim ['vɪktɪm] *n* vittima; **to be the ~ of** essere vittima di; **to fall ~ to** *(fig: desire, sb's charms)* cadere vittima di.

vic·ti·mi·za·tion [,vɪktɪmaɪ'zeɪʃən] *n* punizione *f* ingiusta; **to be the subject of ~ by sb** essere preso di mira da qn.

vic·tim·ize ['vɪktɪmaɪz] *vt* prendere qn di mira.

vic·tor ['vɪktə^r] *n (in sport, battle)* vincitore *m*.

Vic·to·rian [vɪk'tɔːrɪən] *adj, n* vittoriano(a) *(m/f)*.

vic·to·ri·ous [vɪk'tɔːrɪəs] *adj (gen)* vittorioso(a); *(shout)* di vittoria, trionfante.

vic·to·ry ['vɪktərɪ] *n* vittoria; **to win a ~ over sb** riportare una vittoria su qn.

vict·uals ['vɪtlz] *npl* provviste *fpl*.

video ['vɪdɪəʊ] **1** *n (fam: ~ recording machine)* video *m inv*. **2** *cpd:* ~ **cassette** *n* videocassetta; ~ **nasty** *n (fam)* horror-video *m inv*; ~ **recorder** *n* videoregistratore *m*; ~ **recording** *n* registrazione *f* su video.

video·tape ['vɪdɪəʊteɪp] **1** *n* videotape *m inv*. **2** *vt* registrare (su videotape).

vie [vaɪ] *vi:* **to ~ (with sb) for sth** essere in lotta (con qn) per qc; **to ~ with one another for sth** contendersi qc.

Vi·et·nam [,vjet'næm] *n* Vietnam *m*.

Vi·et·nam·ese [,vjetnə'miːz] **1** *adj* vietnamita. **2** *n (person)* vietnamita *m/f*; *(language)* vietnamita *m*.

view [vjuː] **1** *n* **(a)** *(sight)* vista; *(panorama)* veduta; **a splendid ~ of the river** una splendida veduta del fiume; **50 ~s of Venice** 50 vedute di Venezia; **you'll get a better ~ from here** da qui vedrai meglio; **back/front ~ of sth** vista da dietro/davanti; **to be in** *or* **within ~ (of sth)** essere in vista (di qc); **the house is within ~ of the sea** la casa ha la vista sul mare; **to come into** *or* **within ~ (of sth)** arrivare in vista (di qc); **the city suddenly came into ~** la città apparve all'improvviso; **in full ~ of sb** sotto gli occhi di qn; **hidden from ~** nascosto alla vista; **on ~** *(house)* aperto al pubblico; *(exhibit)* in esposizione.

(b) *(opinion)* punto di vista; **in my ~** a mio parere; **to take** *or* **hold the ~ that...** essere dell'opinione che...; **to take a dim** *or* **poor ~ of sth** accogliere male qc; *(survey):* **an overall ~ of the situation** una visione globale della situazione; **in ~ of the fact that...** visto che...; **in ~ of this, ...** visto ciò, ...; *(intention):* **to have in ~** avere in mente; **to keep sth in ~** non perdere qc di vista; **with this in ~** in considerazione di ciò; **with a ~ to doing sth** con l'intenzione di fare qc.

2 *vt (house)* vedere; *(television)* guardare; *(situation)* considerare; **how does the government ~ it?** che cosa ne pensa il governo?

view·er ['vjuːə^r] *n* **(a)** *(TV)* telespettatore/trice. **(b)** *(for slides)* visore *m*.

view·finder ['vjuːfaɪndə^r] *n (Phot)* mirino.

view·point ['vjuːpɔɪnt] *n (on hill etc)* posizione *f*; *(fig)* punto di vista.

vig·il ['vɪdʒɪl] *n* veglia; **to keep ~** vegliare.

vigi·lance ['vɪdʒɪləns] *n* vigilanza.

vigi·lant ['vɪdʒɪlənt] *adj* vigile.

vig·or·ous ['vɪgərəs] *adj (handshake, character)* vigoroso(a); *(speech, protest)* energico(a); *(plant)* forte.

vig·our, *(Am)* **vig·or** ['vɪgə^r] *n (physical)* energia; *(fig)* vigore *m*.

vile [vaɪl] *adj (horrible)* orrendo(a); *(very bad)* pessimo(a); *(: smell)* disgustoso(a); **what a ~ trick!** che scherzo meschino!; **a ~ habit** un vizio detestabile.

vili·fy ['vɪlɪfaɪ] *vt* diffamare.

vil·la ['vɪlə] *n* villa.

vil·lage ['vɪlɪdʒ] **1** *n* paese *m*. **2** *cpd (of a ~, ~s in general)* di paese; *(of one particular ~)* del paese; **a ~ inn** una locanda di paese; **the ~ inn** la locanda del paese; **the ~ idiot** lo scemo del villaggio.

vil·lag·er ['vɪlɪdʒə^r] *n* abitante *m/f* di paese.

vil·lain ['vɪlən] *n* mascalzone *m*; *(hum: rascal)* birbaccione/a; *(in novel, film)* cattivo/a.

vil·lain·ous ['vɪlənəs] *adj* scellerato(a), infame.

vil·lainy ['vɪlənɪ] *n* scelleratezza.

vim [vɪm] *n (fam)* energia.

vin·di·cate ['vɪndɪkeɪt] *vt (prove right)* giustificare; *(prove innocent)* scagionare.

vin·di·ca·tion [,vɪndɪ'keɪʃən] *n (see vb)* giustificazione *f*; scagionare *m*; **in ~ of** per giustificare; **a discolpa di**.

vin·dic·tive [vɪn'dɪktɪv] *adj* vendicativo(a); **to feel ~ towards sb** volersi vendicare di qn.

vine [vaɪn] *n* vite *f*.

vine-growing ['vaɪngrəʊɪŋ] *adj* viticolo(a).

vin·egar ['vɪnɪgə^r] *n* aceto.

vine·yard ['vɪnjəd] *n* vigna, vigneto.

vin·tage ['vɪntɪdʒ] **1** *n (harvest)* vendemmia; *(season)* periodo della vendemmia; *(year)* annata; **what ~ is this wine?** di che anno è questo vino?; **the 1970 ~** il vino del 1970. **2** *cpd:* ~ **wine** *n* vino d'annata; ~ **car** *n* auto *f inv* d'epoca; ~ **year** *n:* **it has been a ~ year for plays** è stata una buona annata per il teatro.

vi·nyl ['vaɪnɪl] **1** *n* vinile *m*. **2** *adj* di vinile, vinilico(a).

vio·la [vɪ'əʊlə] *n (Mus)* viola.

vio·late ['vaɪəleɪt] *vt* violare.

vio·la·tion [,vaɪə'leɪʃən] *n* violazione *f*; **in ~ of sth** violando qc.

vio·lence ['vaɪələns] *n* violenza; **outbreaks of ~** episodi di violenza; **acts of ~** atti di violenza; **robbery with ~** rapina a mano armata; **to do ~ to sth** *(fig)* fare violenza a qc.

vio·lent ['vaɪələnt] *adj (gen)* violento(a); **to die a ~ death** morire di morte violenta; **a ~ temper** un temperamento violento; **to be in a ~ temper** essere furioso; **a ~ dislike of sb/sth** una sentita avversione per qn/qc; **by ~ means** con l'impiego della violenza.

vio·lent·ly ['vaɪələntlɪ] *adv (struggle, react)* in modo violento; *(severely: ill, angry)* terribilmente; **to fall ~ in love with sb** innamorarsi follemente di qn.

vio·let ['vaɪələt] **1** *n (Bot)* viola; *(colour)* violetto. **2** *adj* violetto(a).

vio·lin [,vaɪə'lɪn] **1** *n* violino. **2** *(case, concerto)* per violino.

vio·lin·ist [,vaɪə'lɪnɪst] *n* violinista *m/f*.

VIP [,viːaɪ'piː] *n abbr (= very important person)* Vip *m/f inv*.

vi·per ['vaɪpə^r] *n* vipera.

vir·gin ['vɜːdʒɪn] **1** *n* vergine *f*; **she/he is a ~** lei/lui è vergine; **the Blessed V~** la Beata Vergine. **2** *adj (fig: forest, soil etc)* vergine *inv*; ~ **snow** neve fresca.

vir·gin·ity [vɜː'dʒɪnɪtɪ] *n* verginità.

Vir·go ['vɜːgəʊ] *n (Astron, Astrology)* Vergine *f*; **to be ~** essere della Vergine.

vir·ile ['vɪraɪl] *adj* virile.

vi·ril·ity [vɪ'rɪlɪtɪ] *n* virilità.

vir·tual ['vɜːtjʊəl] *adj* effettivo(a), vero(a); **she's the ~ star of the show** è lei la vera star dello spettacolo; **it was a ~ defeat** di fatto è stata una sconfitta.

vir·tu·al·ly ['vɜːtjʊəlɪ] *adv (in effect)* di fatto; *(to all intents and purposes)* praticamente; **he ~ owns the house** di fatto la casa è sua; **it is ~ impossible**

to do anything è praticamente impossibile fare qualcosa.

vir·tue ['vɜːtjuː] *n* virtù *f inv;* **it has the ~ of simplicity** *or* **of being simple** ha il pregio di essere semplice; **I see no ~ in doing that** non vedo nessun vantaggio nel farlo; **to make a ~ of necessity** fare di necessità virtù; **by ~ of** in virtù di.

vir·tuo·so [,vɜːtjʊˈəʊzəʊ] *n* virtuoso/a.

vir·tu·ous ['vɜːtjʊəs] *adj* virtuoso(a).

viru·lent ['vɪrʊlənt] *adj* virulento(a).

vi·rus ['vaɪərəs] *n* virus *m inv.*

visa ['viːzə] *n* visto.

vis-à-vis ['viːzəviː] *prep* rispetto a, in confronto a.

vis·count ['vaɪkaʊnt] *n* visconte *m.*

vis·cous ['vɪskəs] *adj* viscoso(a).

vise [vaɪs] *n* (*Am*) = **vice**².

vis·ibil·ity [,vɪzɪˈbɪlɪtɪ] *n* visibilità.

vis·ible ['vɪzəbl] *adj* **(a)** visibile; **~ to the naked eye** che si può vedere ad occhio nudo; **to become ~** apparire. **(b)** (*obvious*) evidente.

vis·ibly ['vɪzəblɪ] *adv* visibilmente.

vi·sion ['vɪʒn] *n* **(a)** (*eyesight*) vista, capacità visiva. **(b)** (*imagination, apparition*) visione *f;* **a man of ~** un uomo che vede lontano; **my ~ of the future** la mia visione del futuro; **to see ~s** avere le visioni; **I had ~s of having to walk home** mi sono immaginato di dover andare a casa a piedi.

vi·sion·ary ['vɪʒənərɪ] **1** *n* visionario/a. **2** *adj* chiaroveggente; (*fanciful*) irreale, immaginario(a).

vis·it ['vɪzɪt] **1** *n* visita; (*stay*) soggiorno; **to go on a ~ to** (*person*) andare in visita da; (*place*) andare a visitare; **to pay a ~ to** (*person*) fare una visita a; (*place*) andare a visitare; **on a private/official ~** in visita privata/ufficiale. **2** *vt* **(a)** (*person*) andare a trovare, (*frm*) andare in visita da; (*place: go and see*) visitare; (*: inspect*) ispezionare. **(b)** (*stay with: person*) essere ospite di.

vis·it·ing ['vɪzɪtɪŋ] **1** *adj* (*speaker, professor, team*) ospite. **2** *cpd:* **~ card** *n* biglietto da visita; **~ hours** *npl* orario delle visite.

visi·tor ['vɪzɪtər] *n* (*guest*) ospite *m/f;* (*: in hotel*) cliente *m/f;* (*tourist*) turista *m/f;* (*in hospital*) persona in visita; (*at zoo, exhibition*) visitatore/trice; **~s' book** (*in hotel*) registro dei clienti; (*in museum*) registro dei visitatori; **~s to the town** i visitatori (della città); **you've got a ~** (*in hospital, at home*) c'è una visita per te.

vi·sor ['vaɪzər] *n* (*on helmet etc*) visiera; (*Aut*) aletta parasole.

vis·ta ['vɪstə] *n* (*view*) vista; (*fig*) prospettiva.

vis·ual ['vɪzjʊəl] *adj* visivo(a); **the ~ arts** le arti figurative; **~ aids** (*Scol*) sussidi *mpl* visivi.

visu·al·ize ['vɪzjʊəlaɪz] *vt* (*imagine*) immaginare, immaginarsi; **to ~ sb doing sth** immaginare qn che fa qc.

visu·al·ly ['vɪzjʊəlɪ] *adv:* **~ handicapped** con una menomazione della vista; **~ the film was good** sul piano dell'immagine il film era buono.

vi·tal ['vaɪtl] *adj* **(a)** (*gen*) vitale; (*error*) fatale; **of ~ importance (to sb/sth)** di vitale importanza (per qn/qc); **~ statistics** (*of population*) statistica demografica; (*fam: woman's*) misure *fpl*. **(b)** (*lively*) pieno(a) di vitalità.

vi·tal·ity [vaɪˈtælɪtɪ] *n* vitalità; **his performance lacked ~** la sua esecuzione mancava di brio.

vi·tal·ly ['vaɪtəlɪ] *adv:* **~ important** di vitale importanza; **~ urgent** di estrema urgenza.

vita·min ['vɪtəmɪn] **1** *n* vitamina; **with added ~s** vitaminizzato(a). **2** *cpd:* **~ tablet** *n* confetto di vitamine.

vit·re·ous ['vɪtrɪəs] *adj* (*rock*) vetroso(a); (*china, enamel*) vetrificato(a).

vit·ri·ol·ic [,vɪtrɪˈɒlɪk] *adj* (*fig*) caustico(a).

viva ['vaɪvə] *n* (*also:* **~ voce**) (esame *m*) orale.

vi·va·cious [vɪˈveɪʃəs] *adj* vivace, pieno(a) di brio.

vi·vac·ity [vɪˈvæsɪtɪ] *n* vivacità.

viv·id ['vɪvɪd] *adj* (*colour*) vivo(a), vivido(a); (*dream, impression, recollection, expression on face*) chiaro(a); (*description, memory*) vivido(a); **a ~ imagination** una vivida *or* fervida immaginazione.

viv·id·ly ['vɪvɪdlɪ] *adv* (*describe*) in modo vivido; (*recollect*) chiaramente.

viv·id·ness ['vɪvɪdnɪs] *n* (*of colour, description*) vivacità; (*of impression, recollection*) chiarezza.

vivi·sec·tion [,vɪvɪˈsekʃən] *n* vivisezione *f.*

V-neck ['viːnek] *n* maglione *m* con lo scollo a V.

vo·cabu·lary [vəˈkæbjʊlərɪ] *n* (*gen*) vocabolario, lessico; (*in textbook*) vocabolario; **we have to learn all the new ~** dobbiamo imparare tutti i vocaboli nuovi.

vo·cal ['vəʊkəl] *adj* **(a)** (*gen*) vocale; **~ track** (*on record*) pezzo cantato. **(b)** (*fig fam: vociferous*) rumoroso(a).

vo·cal·ist ['vəʊkəlɪst] *n* cantante *m/f* (*in un gruppo*).

vo·ca·tion [vəʊˈkeɪʃən] *n* vocazione *f;* **to have a ~ for teaching** avere la vocazione dell'insegnamento.

vo·ca·tion·al [vəʊˈkeɪʃənl] *adj* (*training etc*) professionale; **~ guidance** orientamento professionale.

vo·cif·er·ous [vəʊˈsɪfərəs] *adj* rumoroso(a).

vod·ka ['vɒdkə] *n* vodka *f inv.*

vogue [vəʊg] *n* moda; **to be in ~, be the ~** essere di moda.

voice [vɔɪs] **1** *n* (*gen, Gram*) voce *f;* **she is in fine ~ again** ha riacquistato la sua bella voce; **in a loud/soft ~** a voce alta/bassa; **at the top of one's ~** a tutta voce; **with one ~** all'unisono; **to have a ~ in the matter** aver voce in capitolo; **to give ~ to** esprimere. **2** *vt* (*feelings, opinions*) esprimere.

void [vɔɪd] **1** *adj* (*empty*) vuoto(a); (*Law*) nullo(a); **~ of** privo di; **to make** *or* **render a contract ~** invalidare un contratto. **2** *n* vuoto; **to fill the ~** colmare il vuoto.

vola·tile ['vɒlətaɪl] *adj* (*Chem*) volatile; (*fig: situation*) esplosivo(a), teso(a); (*: character*) volubile.

vol·can·ic [vɒlˈkænɪk] *adj* vulcanico(a).

vol·ca·no [vɒlˈkeɪnəʊ] *n, pl* **~es** vulcano.

vole [vəʊl] *n* arvicola.

vo·li·tion [vɒˈlɪʃən] *n:* **of one's own ~** di propria volontà.

vol·ley ['vɒlɪ] *n* (*of shots, stones, insults*) raffica, scarica; (*Tennis*) volée *f inv.*

volley·ball ['vɒlɪbɔːl] *n* pallavolo *f.*

volt [vəʊlt] *n* volt *m inv.*

volt·age ['vəʊltɪdʒ] *n* voltaggio, tensione *f;* **high/low ~** alta/bassa tensione.

volte-face ['vɒltˈfɑːs] *n* voltafaccia *m inv.*

vol·uble ['vɒljubl] *adj* loquace.

vol·ume ['vɒljuːm] *n* **(a)** (*book*) volume *m;* **~ one/two** volume primo/secondo. **(b)** (*size; sound*) volume *m;* (*of tank*) capacità *f inv.* **(c):** **~s** *pl* (*great quantities*) tonnellate *fpl;* **his expression spoke ~s** la sua espressione lasciava capire tutto; **it speaks ~s for his charm** ti fa abbondantemente capire quanto fascino abbia.

vo·lu·mi·nous [vəˈluːmɪnəs] *adj* voluminoso(a); (*writer*) prolifico(a).

vol·un·tari·ly ['vɒləntərɪlɪ] *adv* spontaneamente.

vol·un·tary ['vɒləntərı] *adj (statement, confession)* spontaneo(a); *(attendance)* facoltativo(a); *(unpaid: contribution, work, worker)* volontario(a).

vol·un·teer [,vɒlən'tɪəʳ] **1** *n (Mil, gen)* volontario/a. **2** *vt (one's help, services, suggestion)* offrire spontaneamente; *(information)* spiattellare; **no-one ~ed an answer** nessuno si è offerto di rispondere; **he rarely ~s his opinion** è raro che esprima la propria opinione spontaneamente. **3** *vi (for a task)* offrirsi come volontario(a), offrirsi spontaneamente; *(Mil)* arruolarsi come volontario; **to ~ to do sth** offrirsi spontaneamente di fare qc. **4** *cpd (forces, helpers)* volontario(a); *(corps)* di volontari.

vo·lup·tu·ous [və'lʌptjʊəs] *adj (pleasure, sensation)* voluttuoso(a); *(lips, figure)* sensuale.

vom·it ['vɒmɪt] **1** *n* vomito. **2** *vt, vi* vomitare.

vo·ra·cious [və'reɪʃəs] *adj* vorace; *(reader)* avido(a).

vor·tex ['vɔːtɛks] *n, pl* **vortices** ['vɔːtɪsiːz] vortice *m*; *(fig)* turbine *m*.

vote [vəʊt] **1** *n (ballot, election)* votazione *f*; *(suffrage, single ~)* voto; **~ for/against** voto a favore/contrario; **to pass a ~ of confidence/no confidence** dare il voto di fiducia/sfiducia; **~ of thanks** discorso di ringraziamento; **to put sth to the ~, to take a ~ on sth** mettere qc ai voti; **as the 1931 ~ showed** com'è risultato dalle votazioni del 1931; **the Labour ~ has decreased** il partito laburista ha perso voti.

2 *vt (gen)* votare; *(sum of money etc)* votare a favore di; **the bill was ~ed through parliament** la proposta di legge è stata approvata dal parlamento; **he was ~d secretary** è stato eletto segretario; **to ~ a proposal down** respingere una proposta.

3 *vi*: **to ~ (for sb/sth)** votare (per qn/qc); **to ~ on sth** mettere qc ai voti; **to ~ Labour/Conservative** votare laburista/conservatore; **to ~ to do sth** scegliere di fare qc; **to ~ against/in favour of sth** votare a favore di/contro qc; **I ~ we turn back** *(fam)* io propongo di tornare indietro.

vot·er ['vəʊtəʳ] *n* elettore/trice.

vot·ing ['vəʊtɪŋ] **1** *n* votazione *f*, voto. **2** *cpd*: **~ booth** *n* cabina elettorale; **~ paper** *n* scheda elettorale.

vo·tive ['vəʊtɪv] *adj* votivo(a).

vouch [vaʊtʃ] *vi*: **to ~ for sth** garantire qc; **to ~ for sb** garantire per qn.

vouch·er ['vaʊtʃəʳ] *n* buono; **luncheon ~** buono pasto; **travel ~** voucher *m inv*, tagliando.

vow [vaʊ] **1** *n* voto; **to take** *or* **make a ~ to do sth** fare voto di fare qc; **to take one's ~s** *(Rel)* prendere i voti. **2** *vt (obedience, allegiance)* giurare; **to ~ to do sth/that** giurare di fare qc/che.

vow·el ['vaʊəl] **1** *n* vocale *f*. **2** *cpd*: **~ sound** *n* suono vocalico.

voy·age ['vɔɪɪdʒ] *n* viaggio per mare; **the ~ out/back** il viaggio di andata/di ritorno.

voy·ag·er ['vɔɪədʒəʳ] *n* passeggero/a.

vul·can·ize ['vʌlkənaɪz] *vt* vulcanizzare.

vul·gar ['vʌlgəʳ] *adj (gen, pej)* volgare; **~ Latin** latino volgare; **~ fraction** *(Math)* frazione *f* ordinaria.

vul·gar·ity [vʌl'gærɪtɪ] *n* volgarità; *(expression)* espressione *f* volgare.

vul·ner·able ['vʌlnərəbl] *adj (person)* soggetto(a); *(position)* esposto(a).

vul·ture ['vʌltʃəʳ] *n* avvoltoio.

W

W¹, w [ˈdʌblju] *n (letter)* W, w *f or m inv.*

W² *abbr (* = *west)* O.

wad [wɒd] *n (of cloth)* tampone *m; (of chewing gum, putty)* pallina; *(of cotton wool)* batuffolo; *(of papers, banknotes)* mucchio.

wad·ding [ˈwɒdɪŋ] *n* imbottitura.

wad·dle [ˈwɒdl] *vi* camminare come una papera; **to ~ in/out** *etc* entrare/uscire *etc* camminando come una papera.

wade [weɪd] *vi:* **to ~ through** *(water, mud)* camminare in; *(long grass, corn)* farsi strada attraverso; *(fig: book)* leggere con fatica; **to ~ ashore** raggiungere a piedi la riva; **to ~ into sb** *(fig)* scagliarsi su qn; **he ~d in and helped us** *(fig)* si rimboccò le maniche e ci aiutò.

wad·er [ˈweɪdəʳ] *n (bird)* trampoliere *m; (boot)* stivale *m* da pesca.

wa·fer [ˈweɪfəʳ] *n (Culin)* wafer *m inv; (: with ice cream)* cialda; *(Rel)* ostia.

wafer-thin [ˌweɪfəˈθɪn] *adj* molto sottile.

waf·fle [ˈwɒfl] **1** *n (Culin)* cialda; *(fam: talk)* chiacchiere *fpl,* ciance *fpl.* **2** *vi (fam: also:* **~ on)** ciarlare, chiacchierare. **3** *cpd:* **~ iron** *n* stampo per cialde.

waft [wɑːft] **1** *vt* portare. **2** *vi* diffondersi.

wag¹ [wæg] **1** *n:* **with a ~ of its tail** dimenando la coda. **2** *vt:* **the dog ~ged its tail** il cane scodinzolò; **to ~ one's finger at sb** fare un cenno di rimprovero a qn scuotendo il dito. **3** *vi (tail)* dimenarsi; **that'll set the tongues ~ging** *(fig)* susciterà pettegolezzi; **his tongue never stops ~ging** *(fig)* non sta mai zitto.

wag² [wæg] *n (joker)* buffone/a, burlone/a.

wage [weɪdʒ] **1** *n (often:* **~s)** paga; **a day's ~s** un giorno di paga; **she gets a good ~** è pagata bene; **minimum ~** minimo salariale. **2** *vt (campaign)* intraprendere; **to ~ war** far guerra. **3** *cpd (demand)* salariale; *(negotiations)* sul salario; *(freeze)* dei salari; **~ earner** *n* salariato/a; **the family ~ earner** il sostegno della famiglia; **~ packet** *n* busta *f* paga *inv.*

wa·ger [ˈweɪdʒəʳ] **1** *n:* **~ (on)** scommessa (su). **2** *vt (sum of money):* **to ~ (on)** puntare (su), scommettere (su); **to ~ that...** scommettere che... .

wag·gle [ˈwægl] **1** *n:* **with a ~ of her hips** ancheggiando; **with a ~ of its tail** scodinzolando. **2** *vt (tail)* dimenare; **to ~ one's hips** ancheggiare.

wag·gon, *(Am)* **wag·on** [ˈwægən] *n (horse-drawn)* carro; *(truck)* camion *m inv; (Rail)* vagone *m* merci *inv; (trolley)* carrello; **he's on the ~ again!** *(fam)* ha ripreso a non bere!

waif [weɪf] *n* bambino/a abbandonato(a).

wail [weɪl] **1** *n (of suffering)* gemito; *(of baby)* vagito; *(of siren)* urlo; *(of wind)* ululato; **a ~ of protest** un urlo di protesta. **2** *vi (see n)* gemere; vagire; urlare; ululare.

wail·ing [ˈweɪlɪŋ] *n (of sufferance)* gemito; *(of baby)* vagito; *(of siren)* urlo; *(of wind)* ululato.

waist [weɪst] *n (Anat, of dress)* vita; *(fig: narrow part: of violin)* strozzatura; **stripped to the ~** nudo fino alla cintola, a torso nudo; **to be up to the ~ in mud** essere nel fango fino alla vita.

waist·band [ˈweɪstbænd] *n* cintura.

waist·coat [ˈweɪskəʊt] *n* panciotto, gilè *m inv.*

waist-deep [ˌweɪstˈdiːp] *adv* fino alla cintola, fino alla vita.

waist·ed [ˈweɪstɪd] *adj (dress)* segnato(a) in vita; **high-/low-~** a vita alta/bassa.

waist·line [ˈweɪstlaɪn] *n* vita; **to watch one's ~** essere a dieta.

wait [weɪt] **1** *n:* **~ (for)** attesa (di); **to have a long ~** aspettare a lungo; **a 2-hour ~** un'attesa di 2 ore; **to lie in ~ (for sb)** tendere un agguato (a qn).

  2 *vt (a) (turn, chance)* aspettare, attendere. **(b)** *(Am: delay: dinner* etc*)* ritardare.

  3 *vi (a):* **to ~ (for sb/sth)** aspettare (qn/qc); **to ~ for sb to do sth** aspettare che qn faccia qc; **~ a moment!** (aspetta) un momento!; **~ and see!** aspetta e vedrai!; **we'll have to ~ and see** dobbiamo vedere come vanno le cose; **just you ~!** te la faccio vedere io!; **just you ~ till your father comes home!** vedrai quando torna tuo padre!; **~ till you're older** aspetta di essere cresciuto; **to keep sb ~ing** far aspettare qn; **'repairs while you ~'** 'riparazioni lampo'; **I can't ~ to see his face** non vedo l'ora di vedere che faccia farà; **I can hardly ~!** non vedo l'ora!; **that was worth ~ing for** è valsa la pena di aspettare così tanto. **(b)** *(as servant):* **to ~ on sb** servire qn; **to ~ at table** servire a tavola; **to ~ on sb hand and foot** servire qn in tutto e per tutto.

◆ **wait behind** *vi + adv* trattenersi.

◆ **wait in** *vi + adv* restare ad aspettare.

◆ **wait up** *vi + adv* restare alzato(a) (ad aspettare); **don't ~ up for me** non rimanere alzato per me.

wait·er [ˈweɪtəʳ] *n* cameriere *m.*

wait·ing [ˈweɪtɪŋ] **1** *n* attesa; *(Aut):* **'no ~'** 'divieto di sosta'. **2** *cpd:* **~ game** *n:* **to play a ~ game** temporeggiare; **~ list** *n* lista d'attesa; **~ room** *n* sala d'aspetto *or* d'attesa.

wait·ress [ˈweɪtrɪs] *n* cameriera.

waive [weɪv] *vt (claim)* rinunciare a; *(rule, age limit)* non tener conto di.

waiv·er [ˈweɪvəʳ] *n* rinuncia.

wake¹ [weɪk] *n (of ship)* scia; **to follow in sb's ~** *(fig)* seguire le tracce di qn; **it left a trail of destruction in its ~** ha lasciato una scia di distruzione dietro di sé.

wake² [weɪk] *n (over corpse)* veglia *(funebre).*

wake³ [weɪk] *pt* **woke** *or (old)* **~d,** *pp* **woken** *or (old)* **~d 1** *vi (also:* **~ up)** svegliarsi, destarsi; **~ up!** *(also fig)* svegliati!; **there's enough noise to ~ the dead!** c'è un baccano del diavolo!; **to ~ up to sth** *(fig)* rendersi conto di qc. **2** *vt (also:* **~ up)** svegliare; *(memories, desires)* risvegliare; **to ~ sb (up) to sth** *(fig)* rendere qn consapevole di qc, aprire gli occhi a qn su qc; **to ~ one's ideas up** *(fam)* darsi una mossa.

wake·ful [ˈweɪkfʊl] *adj (person, night)* insonne.

wak·en [ˈweɪkən] = **wake³.**

wak·ing [ˈweɪkɪŋ] *adj:* **in my ~ hours** quando sono sveglio, di giorno.

Wales [weɪlz] *n* Galles *m*.

walk [wɔ:k] **1** *n* **(a)** *(stroll, ramble)* passeggiata; *(path, place to ~)* percorso, sentiero; **to take sb/one's dog for a ~** portare qn/il cane a spasso; **to go for a ~** *(short)* andare a fare quattro passi; *(long)* andare a fare una passeggiata; **it's only a 10-minute ~ from here** ci vogliono solo 10 minuti a piedi da qui; **there's a nice ~ by the river** c'è una bella passeggiata lungo il fiume; **from all ~s of life** *(fig)* di ogni estrazione sociale. **(b)** *(gait)* passo, andatura; **at a ~** *(of person, horse)* al passo; **he has an odd sort of ~** cammina in modo strano.
2 *vt* **(a)** *(distance)* percorrere a piedi; **we ~ed 40 kilometres yesterday** ieri abbiamo percorso 40 chilometri a piedi; **to ~ the streets** vagare per le strade; *(prostitute)* battere il marciapiede; **you can ~ it in a few minutes** puoi arrivarci a piedi in pochi minuti; **he ~ed it** *(fig)* è stato uno scherzo per lui. **(b)** *(cause to ~: invalid)* aiutare a camminare; *(lead: dog)* portare a spasso; *(: horse)* portare; **I'll ~ you home** ti accompagno a casa; **to ~ sb into the ground** *or* **off his feet** far stancare qn (a furia di camminare).
3 *vi* *(gen)* camminare; *(for pleasure, exercise)* passeggiare; *(not drive or ride)* andare a piedi; **to ~ in one's sleep** essere sonnambulo; **can your little boy ~ yet?** sa già camminare il tuo bambino?; **~ a little with me** accompagnami per un pezzo; **to ~ up and down (the room)** camminare su e giù (per la stanza); **we had to ~** abbiamo dovuto andare a piedi; **to ~ home** andare a casa a piedi; **we were out ~ing in the hills** stavamo passeggiando in collina; **to ~ into sth** *(bump into)* andare a sbattere contro qc; *(fig: fall into: trap etc)* cadere in qc.

♦ **walk about, walk around 1** *vi + adv* camminare; **I've been ~ing about all afternoon** sono stato in giro tutto il pomeriggio. **2** *vi + prep*: **to ~ about the room** camminare per la stanza; **to ~ about the town** gironzolare per la città.

♦ **walk away** *vi + adv* allontanarsi (a piedi), andare via; *(fig: unhurt)* uscire illeso(a); **to ~ away with sth** *(fig: win easily)* vincere facilmente qc; *(: steal)* andarsene con qc.

♦ **walk in** *vi + adv* entrare.

♦ **walk off 1** *vi + adv* = **walk away**. **2** *vt + adv* *(lunch)* smaltire; *(headache)* farsi passare (camminando).

♦ **walk on** *vi + adv* *(go on ~ing)* continuare a camminare; *(Theatre)* fare la comparsa.

♦ **walk out** *vi + adv* *(go out)* uscire; *(as protest)* uscire (in segno di protesta); *(strike)* scendere in sciopero; **to ~ out of a meeting** lasciare una riunione (in segno di protesta); **he just ~ed out on his wife** ha piantato in asso la moglie.

♦ **walk over** *vi + prep* *(defeat)* schiacciare; **to ~ all over sb** *(dominate)* mettere i piedi in testa a qn.

♦ **walk up** *vi + adv* *(approach)*: **to ~ up (to)** avvicinarsi (a); **~ up, ~ up!** *(at fair)* avanti!

walk·about ['wɔ:kə,baʊt] *n* *(of celebrity)*: **to go on a ~** mischiarsi con la folla.

walk·er ['wɔ:kə'] *n* *(person)* camminatore/trice; *(for babies)* girello.

walkie-talkie ['wɔ:kı'tɔ:kı] *n* walkie-talkie *m inv*.

walk-in ['wɔ:kın] *adj*: **~ cupboard** stanzino.

walk·ing ['wɔ:kıŋ] **1** *n* camminare *m*; **to do a lot of ~** camminare molto. **2** *adj* *(holiday)* a piedi; *(shoes)* da passeggio; **it's within ~ distance** ci si arriva a piedi; **he's a ~ encyclopaedia** è un'enciclopedia ambulante; **the ~ wounded** i feriti in grado di camminare; **~ stick** bastone *m* da passeggio.

walk-on ['wɔ:kɒn] *adj* *(Theatre: part)* da comparsa.

walk-out ['wɔ:kaʊt] *n* *(from conference)* abbandono; *(strike)* sciopero a sorpresa.

walk-over ['wɔ:k,əʊvə'] *n* *(Sport)* vittoria facile; **the exam was a ~** l'esame è stato un gioco da ragazzi.

walk·way ['wɔ:k,weı] *n* passaggio pedonale.

wall [wɔ:l] **1** *n* *(inside, of mountain)* muro, parete *f*; *(outside)* muro; *(Anat)* parete; *(of tyre)* fianco; *(fig: of smoke etc)* cortina; **the Great W~ of China** la Grande Muraglia Cinese; **the city ~s** le mura della città; **it drives me up the ~** *(fam)* mi fa impazzire *or* infuriare; **to go to the ~** *(fig: firm etc)* fallire. **2** *cpd* *(cupboard, clock)* a muro; **~ light** *n* applique *f inv*; **~ map** *n* carta murale; **~ bars** *npl* *(Sport)* spalliera; **~ hanging** *n* tappezzeria.

♦ **wall in** *vt + adv* *(garden etc)* circondare con un muro.

♦ **wall off** *vt + adv* *(area of land)* recingere (con un muro).

♦ **wall up** *vt + adv* *(entrance etc)* murare.

wal·la·by ['wɒləbı] *n* canguro piccolo.

walled [wɔ:ld] *adj* *(city)* fortificato(a); *(house, garden)* cintato(a).

wal·let ['wɒlıt] *n* portafoglio.

wall·flower ['wɔ:l,flaʊə'] *n* violaciocca (gialla); *(fig)*: **to be a ~** fare tappezzeria.

wal·lop ['wɒləp] *(fam)* **1** *n* *(blow)* cazzotto; *(sound)*: **with a ~** con un tonfo. **2** *vt* *(person)* darle di santa ragione a; **to ~ the table** battere il pugno sul tavolo.

wal·lop·ing ['wɒləpıŋ] *(fam)* **1** *n*: **to give sb a ~** darle di santa ragione a qn. **2** *adj* *(also:* **~ great**) enorme.

wal·low ['wɒləʊ] *vi*: **to ~ (in)** *(in water, mud)* rotolarsi (in); *(in bath)* sguazzare (in); **to ~ in one's grief** crogiolarsi nel proprio dolore; **to ~ in luxury** nuotare nell'oro.

wall·paper ['wɔ:l,peıpə'] *n* carta da parati, tappezzeria.

wall-to-wall [,wɔ:ltə'wɔ:l] *adj*: **~ carpeting** moquette *f*.

wal·nut ['wɔ:lnʌt] **1** *n* *(nut)* noce *f*; *(tree, wood)* noce *m*. **2** *adj* *(wardrobe)* di noce; *(cake)* di noci.

wal·rus ['wɔ:lrəs] *n* tricheco.

waltz [wɔ:lts] **1** *n* valzer *m inv*. **2** *vi* ballare il valzer; **to ~ in/out** *etc* *(gaily)* entrare/uscire *etc* saltellando; *(cheekily)* entrare/uscire *etc* con fare spavaldo.

wan [wɒn] *adj* *(gen)* pallido(a); *(look, person)* triste.

wand [wɒnd] *n* *(magic ~)* bacchetta (magica); *(of usher etc)* mazza.

wan·der ['wɒndə'] **1** *n*: **to go for a ~ around the shops/the town** fare un giro per i negozi/in città. **2** *vi* *(person)* gironzolare; *(river, road)* serpeggiare; *(stray: from path)* allontanarsi; *(fig: thoughts, eyes)* vagare; *(: attention)* diminuire; **to ~ back/out** *etc* tornare indietro/uscire *etc* con calma; **don't go ~ing off** non allontanarti; **to ~ from** *or* **off the point** divagare; **to let one's mind ~** distrarsi. **3** *vt* *(streets, hills)* girovagare per; **to ~ the world** girare il mondo.

wan·der·er ['wɒndərə'] *n* vagabondo/a.

wan·der·ing ['wɒndərıŋ] **1** *adj* *(tribe)* nomade; *(minstrel, actor)* girovago(a); *(path, river)* tortuoso(a); *(glance, mind)* distratto(a). **2**: **~s** *npl* peregrinazioni *fpl*, vagabondaggi *mpl*.

wan·der·lust ['wɒndəlʌst] *n* sete *f* di viaggi.

wane [weın] **1** *vi* *(moon)* calare; *(fig)* declinare. **2** *n*: **to be on the ~** = **to wane**.

wan·gle ['wæŋgl] *(fam)* **1** *n* astuzia. **2** *vt* *(job, ticket)* procurare (con l'astuzia); *(days off)* ottenere (con l'astuzia); **he ~d his way** in riuscì a entrare con l'astuzia.

wan·gler ['wæŋglə'] *n (fam)* furbacchione/a.

wan·gling ['wæŋglɪŋ] *n (fam)* astuzia.

wan·ly *adv* tristemente.

want [wɒnt] **1** *n* **(a)** *(lack):* **~ (of)** mancanza (di); **for ~ of** per mancanza di; **for ~ of anything better to do** non avendo nulla di meglio da fare; **it wasn't for ~ of trying** non si può certo dire che non ci abbia *(or* abbiamo *etc)* provato.

(b) *(poverty)* miseria, povertà; **to be in ~** essere in miseria.

(c) *(need)* bisogno; **to be in ~ of sth** avere bisogno di qc; **my ~s are few** ho poche esigenze; **it fills a long-felt ~** soddisfa un bisogno che si sentiva da tempo.

2 *vt* **(a)** *(gen)* volere; *(wish, desire)* volere, desiderare; **to ~ to do sth** volere *(or* desiderare) fare qc; **to ~ sb to do sth** volere *(or* desiderare) che qn faccia qc; **I ~ you to tell me** voglio che tu mi dica; **I ~ it done now** voglio che sia fatto subito; **what do you ~ with me?** cosa vuoi da me?; **you've got him where you ~ him** *(fig)* ce l'hai in pugno; **you don't ~ much!** *(iro)* ti accontenti di poco!; **she ~s £500 for the car** vuole *or* chiede 500 sterline per la macchina; **I don't ~ you interfering!** non voglio che ti metta in mezzo tu!; **I know when I'm not ~ed** so capire quando non sono desiderato; **you're ~ed on the phone** ti vogliono al telefono; **I don't ~** to non voglio; **'cook ~ed'** 'cercasi cuoco'; **he is ~ed for murder** è ricercato per omicidio; **to ~ sb** *(sexually)* desiderare qn.

(b) *(need, require: subj: person)* avere bisogno di; *(subj: task)* richiedere; *(ought)* dovere; **you ~ to see a doctor** faresti meglio ad *or* dovresti andare dal dottore; **that's the last thing I ~!** *(fam)* è l'ultima cosa che vorrei!; **that's all we ~ed!** *(fam)* è proprio quello che ci voleva!; **you ~ a screwdriver to do that** ti ci vuole un cacciavite per farlo; **it only ~ed the parents to come in...** bastava solo che i genitori entrassero... .

3 *vi (lack):* **to ~ (for)** mancare (di); **she doesn't ~ for friends** gli amici non le mancano; **they ~ for nothing** a loro non manca nulla.

want·ing ['wɒntɪŋ] *adj:* **to be ~ (in)** mancare (di); **humour is completely ~ in his work** la sua opera manca completamente di senso dell'umorismo; **he is ~ in confidence** non è abbastanza sicuro di sé; **he was tried and found ~** fu messo alla prova e trovato inadatto.

wan·ton ['wɒntən] *adj (shameless)* lascivo(a); *(wilful)* gratuito(a), ingiustificato(a).

war [wɔː'] **1** *n* guerra; *(fig):* **~ (on** *or* **against)** lotta (contro); **to be at/go to ~ (with)** essere/entrare in guerra (con); **to make ~ (on)** far guerra (a); **a ~ of words/nerves** una guerra verbale/psicologica; **to have been in the ~s** *(fig hum)* essere malridotto. **2** *vi:* **to ~ (with)** guerreggiare (con), far guerra (a). **3** *cpd (wound, crime, bride)* di guerra; **~ cry** *n* grido di guerra; **~ dance** *n* danza di guerra; **~ game** *n* war game *m inv;* **~ memorial** *n* monumento ai caduti; **~ paint** *n* pittura di guerra.

war·ble ['wɔːbl] **1** *n (of bird)* trillo. **2** *vi (bird)* trillare; *(person)* gorgheggiare.

war·bler ['wɔːblə'] *n* uccello canoro.

ward [wɔːd] *n* **(a)** *(Law)* pupillo/a; **~ of court** minore *m/f* sotto tutela (giudiziaria). **(b)** *(Pol)* distretto (elettorale). **(c)** *(in hospital)* corsia.

♦**ward off** *vt + adv (blow, attack)* parare;

(attacker) respingere; *(danger, depression)* scongiurare.

...ward(s) [wəd(z)] *adj, adv suf:* **town~** verso la città, in direzione della città; **south~** verso il sud.

war·den ['wɔːdn] *n (of institution)* direttore/trice; *(of park, game reserve)* guardiano/a.

war·der ['wɔːdə'] *n* guardia carceraria, secondino.

war·dress ['wɔːdrɪs] *n* guardia carceraria *(donna)*.

ward·robe ['wɔːdrəʊb] *n (cupboard)* guardaroba *m inv,* armadio; *(clothes)* guardaroba; *(Theatre)* costumi *mpl.*

ward·room ['wɔːdrʊm] *n (Naut)* quadrato.

ware·house ['wɛəhaʊs] *n* deposito, magazzino.

wares [wɛəz] *npl* merci *fpl.*

war·fare ['wɔːfɛə'] *n (fighting)* lotta; *(technique)* arte *f* bellica.

war·head ['wɔːhɛd] *n* testata.

war·horse ['wɔːhɔːs] *n (fig):* **old ~** veterano.

wari·ly ['wɛərɪlɪ] *adj* cautamente, con prudenza.

wari·ness ['wɛərɪnɪs] *n* cautela.

war·like ['wɔːlaɪk] *adj* battagliero(a), bellicoso(a).

warm [wɔːm] **1** *adj* **(-er, -est) (a)** *(gen)* caldo(a); **I'm ~, I feel ~** ho caldo; **it's ~ today** oggi fa caldo; **it's ~ work** è un lavoro che ti fa sudare; **come and get ~** vieni a scaldarti; **to keep o.s. ~** non prendere freddo; **it keeps me ~** mi tiene caldo; **to keep sth ~** tenere qc al caldo; **am I getting ~?** *(fig: in game)* fuocherello? **(b)** *(fig: colour)* caldo(a); *(: thanks, congratulations, apologies)* sentito(a); *(: person, greeting)* cordiale; *(: heart)* d'oro; *(: supporter)* convinto(a).

2 *vt (gen)* scaldare; **to ~ o.s. by the fire** scaldarsi vicino al fuoco; **it ~ed my heart** mi ha fatto tanto piacere.

3 *vi (food etc)* scaldarsi; **he ~ed to his subject** si appassionò all'argomento; **I** *or* **my heart ~ed to him** mi è entrato in simpatia.

4 *cpd:* **~ front** *n (Met)* fronte *m* caldo.

♦**warm up 1** *vi + adv (person)* scaldarsi; *(: Sport etc)* scaldarsi (i muscoli); *(fig: party)* ravvivarsi; *(: game)* farsi acceso(a). **2** *vt + adv (food)* scaldare, riscaldare; *(engine)* scaldare; *(fig: party)* ravvivare; *(: audience)* preparare.

warm-blooded ['wɔːm,blʌdɪd] *adj* a sangue caldo.

warm-hearted [,wɔːm'hɑːtɪd] *adj* cordiale, affettuoso(a).

warm·ly ['wɔːmlɪ] *adv (gen)* caldamente; *(fig: welcome, thank, applaud)* caldamente, calorosamente.

war·monger ['wɔː,mʌŋgə'] *n* guerrafondaio.

war·monger·ing ['wɔː,mʌŋgərɪŋ] *n* bellicismo.

warmth [wɔːmθ] *n* calore *m; (fig)* calore, calorosità.

warm-up ['wɔːmʌp] *n (Sport)* riscaldamento.

warn [wɔːn] *vt:* **to ~ (of** *or* **about)** avvertire (di); **to ~ sb not to do sth** *or* **against doing sth** avvertire qn di non fare qc; **you have been ~ed!** sei stato avvertito!; **to ~ sb off** *or* **against sth** mettere qn in guardia contro qc.

warn·ing ['wɔːnɪŋ] **1** *n (gen)* avvertimento, ammonimento; *(by police, judge)* diffida; *(advance notice):* **~ (of)** preavviso (di); **to give sb a ~ that** avvertire qn che; **to give sb due/a few days' ~** avvertire qn a tempo debito/con qualche giorno di anticipo; **without (any) ~** senza preavviso; **let this be a ~ to you!** che ti serva da ammonimento!; **gale ~** *(Met)* avviso di burrasca. **2** *cpd:* **~ light** *n* spia luminosa; **~ shot** *n:* **to fire a ~ shot** sparare in aria per avvertire.

warp [wɔːp] **1** *n (in weaving)* ordito; *(of wood)* curvatura, deformazione *f.* **2** *vt (wood)* deformare, curvare; *(fig: mind, personality, judgment)* influenzare negativamente. **3** *vi (wood)* deformarsi, curvarsi.

war·path ['wɔːpɑːθ] *n*: **to be on the ~** *(fig)* essere sul sentiero di guerra.

warped [wɔːpt] *adj (wood)* curvo(a); *(fig: character, sense of humour etc)* contorto(a).

war·rant ['wɒrənt] **1** *n* **(a)** *(for travel etc)* buono; *(Law)* mandato; **there is a ~ out for his arrest** è stato emesso un mandato di arresto per lui. **(b)** *(justification)* giustificazione *f*. **2** *vt* **(a)** *(justify, merit)* giustificare; **nothing ~s such an assumption** nulla convalida questa ipotesi. **(b)** *(guarantee)* garantire; **I'll ~ you he'll be back soon** scommetto che sarà di ritorno presto. **3** *cpd*: **~ officer** *n (Mil)* ≃ maresciallo.

war·rant·ed ['wɒrəntɪd] *adj (action, remark)* giustificato(a); *(Comm: goods)* garantito(a).

war·ran·ty ['wɒrəntɪ] *n (Comm)* garanzia; **under ~** in garanzia.

war·ren ['wɒrən] *n (rabbit ~)* tana; *(fig)* alveare *m*; **a ~ of little streets** un dedalo di stradine.

war·ring ['wɔːrɪŋ] *adj (interests etc)* opposto(a), in lotta; *(nations)* in guerra.

war·ri·or ['wɒrɪəʳ] *n* guerriero/a.

War·saw ['wɔːsɔː] *n* Varsavia.

war·ship ['wɔːʃɪp] *n* nave *f* da guerra.

wart [wɔːt] *n (Med)* porro.

wart·hog ['wɔːthɒg] *n* facocero.

war·time ['wɔːtaɪm] **1** *n* tempo di guerra; **in ~** in tempo di guerra. **2** *cpd (regulations, rationing etc)* di guerra.

wary ['wɛərɪ] *adj (-ier, -iest) (gen)* prudente; *(manner)* cauto(a); **to be ~ (of)** starci un po' attento (con); **to keep a ~ eye on sth** tenere bene d'occhio qc; **to be ~ about** *or* **of doing sth** andare cauto nel fare qc.

was [wɒz] *1st, 3rd pers sg pt of* **be**.

wash [wɒʃ] **1** *n* **(a)** *(act of ~ing)* lavata; **to give sth a ~** lavare qc; **it needs a ~** ha bisogno di essere lavato; **your jeans are in the ~** i tuoi jeans sono nel bucato; **it ran in the ~** si è stinto nel lavaggio; **it'll all come out in the ~** *(fig: work out)* tutto andrà a posto; *(: become known)* tutto salterà fuori. **(b)** *(of ship)* scia. **(c)** *(Art)* lavatura. **2** *vt* **(a)** *(gen)* lavare; **to ~ o.s.** lavarsi; **to ~ one's hands/hair** lavarsi le mani/i capelli; **to ~ one's hands of sth** *(fig)* lavarsi le mani di qc. **(b)** *(lap: sea, waves)* bagnare, lambire; **an island ~ed by a blue sea** un'isola bagnata da un mare azzurro. **(c)** *(sweep, carry: sea etc)* portare, trascinare; **he was ~ed overboard** fu trascinato in mare (dalle onde). **3** *vi* **(a)** *(have a ~)* lavarsi; *(do the washing)* fare il bucato; **I'll ~ if you wipe** io lavo i piatti se tu li asciughi; **man-made fabrics usually ~ well** di solito è facile lavare i tessuti sintetici; **that excuse won't ~!** *(fam)* quella scusa non regge! **(b)** *(sea etc)*: **to ~ against sth** frangersi contro qc; **to ~ over sth** infrangersi su qc. **4** *cpd*: **~ leather** *n* pelle *f* di daino.

♦ **wash away** *vt + adv (gen)* portare via; *(fig: sins etc)* cancellare.

♦ **wash down** *vt + adv (walls, car)* lavare; *(pill, food)* mandar giù.

♦ **wash off** *vt + adv (stain, dirt)* togliere (lavando).

♦ **wash out** *vt + adv* **(a)** *(stain etc)* togliere (lavando); *(bottle, paintbrush)* sciacquare. **(b)**: **to be ~ed out** *(fam: tired)* essere sfinito(a), essere distrutto(a).

♦ **wash up 1** *vi + adv (Brit: do dishes)* lavare i piatti; *(Am: have a wash)* darsi una lavata. **2** *vt + adv* **(a)** *(Brit: dishes)* lavare, rigovernare. **(b)**

(subj: sea etc) portare, trascinare.

wash·able ['wɒʃəbl] *adj* lavabile.

wash·basin ['wɒʃ,beɪsn] *n*, **wash·bowl** ['wɒʃbəʊl] *n* lavabo.

wash·cloth ['wɒʃklɒθ] *n (Am)* pezzuola (per lavarsi).

wash·day ['wɒʃdeɪ] *n* giorno di bucato.

wash·er ['wɒʃəʳ] *n* **(a)** *(Tech)* rondella. **(b)** *(washing machine)* lavatrice *f*; *(dish~)* lavastoviglie *f inv*.

wash-hand ba·sin ['wɒʃ,hænd,beɪsn] *n* lavabo.

wash·ing ['wɒʃɪŋ] **1** *n* **(a)** *(act)* lavaggio; *(: of clothes)* bucato. **(b)** *(clothes themselves)* bucato; **dirty ~** biancheria da lavare. **2** *cpd*: **~ line** *n* corda del bucato; **~ machine** *n* lavatrice *f*; **~ powder** *n* detersivo (per bucato).

washing-up [,wɒʃɪŋ'ʌp] **1** *n (dishes)* piatti sporchi; **to do the ~** lavare i piatti, rigovernare. **2** *cpd*: **~ bowl** *n* catino; **~ liquid** *n* detersivo liquido (per stoviglie).

wash-out ['wɒʃaʊt] *n (fam: plan, party, person)* disastro.

wash·room ['wɒʃrʊm] *n* gabinetto.

wasn't ['wɒznt] = **was not**.

wasp [wɒsp] *n* vespa.

wasp·ish ['wɒspɪʃ] *adj (character)* litigioso(a); *(comment)* pungente.

wast·age ['weɪstɪdʒ] *n (gen)* spreco; *(of time, Comm: through pilfering)* perdita; *(amount wasted)* scarto.

waste [weɪst] **1** *adj (material)* di scarto; *(food)* avanzato(a); *(energy, heat)* sprecato(a); *(land, ground: in city)* abbandonato(a); *(: in country)* incolto(a); **to lay ~** devastare.

2 *n* **(a)** *(gen)* spreco; *(of time)* perdita; **it's a ~ of money** sono soldi sprecati; **it's a ~ of effort** è fatica sprecata; **to go to ~** andare sprecato. **(b)** *(~ material: industrial, chemical etc)* scorie *fpl*; *(rubbish)* spazzatura, immondizia, rifiuti *mpl*. **(c)** *(land)* immensa distesa desolata; **desert ~** landa desertica.

3 *vt (gen)* sprecare; *(time, opportunity)* perdere, sprecare; **you didn't ~ much time getting here** non ci hai messo tanto ad arrivare qui; **he's ~d in that job** è sprecato in quel lavoro; **sarcasm is ~d on him** lui non capisce il sarcasmo.

4 *vi (food)* andare a male; **~ not, want not** *(Proverb)* chi risparmia guadagna.

5 *cpd*: **~ disposal** *n* raccolta dei rifiuti; **~ disposal unit** *n* tritarifiuti *m inv*; **~ pipe** *n* tubo di scarico; **~ products** *n (Industry)* materiali *mpl* di scarto; *(from body)* materiali *mpl* di rifiuto.

♦ **waste away** *vi + adv* consumarsi, deperire.

waste·bin ['weɪst,bɪn] *n (basket)* cestino (per la carta straccia); *(in kitchen)* pattumiera.

waste·ful ['weɪstfʊl] *adj (person)* sprecone(a); *(process)* dispendioso(a); **to be ~ with** *or* **of sth** sprecare qc.

waste·land ['weɪst,lænd] *n* terra desolata.

waste·paper ['weɪst,peɪpəʳ] **1** *n* carta straccia. **2** *cpd*: **~ basket** *n* cestino (per la carta straccia).

wast·er ['weɪstəʳ] *n (person)* sprecone/a.

watch¹ [wɒtʃ] *n (wrist ~)* orologio; **it's 10 o'clock by my ~** il mio orologio fa le 10.

watch² [wɒtʃ] **1** *n* **(a)** *(vigilance)* sorveglianza; **to be on the ~ for** *(danger)* stare in guardia contro; *(person, vehicle)* guardare se arriva; *(bargain)* essere a caccia di; **to keep ~ over** *(prisoner)* tenere d'occhio; *(patient)* vegliare; **to keep a close ~ on sb/sth** tener bene d'occhio qn/qc; **to keep ~ for sb/sth** dare un'occhiata se arriva qn/qc.

(b) *(period of duty)* guardia; *(Naut)* quarto; *(sentry)* sentinella; **officer of the ~** *(Naut)* ufficiale *m* di quarto.

2 vt **(a)** (guard: gen) tener d'occhio.

(b) (observe: gen) guardare; (subj: police) tenere d'occhio; (monitor: case etc) seguire; **to ~ sb do(ing) sth** osservare qn mentre fa qc; **you can't do that! — just you ~ (me)!** non puoi farlo! — e come no, sta' a vedere!; **to ~ one's chance** aspettare il momento propizio; **to ~ the time** controllare l'ora; **a new actor to be ~ed** un nuovo attore molto promettente or da seguire.

(c) (be careful with) stare attento(a) a; **to ~ one's language** moderare i termini; **~ it!** attento!; **~ how you drive/what you're doing** attento a come guidi/quel che fai; **~ your head** attento alla testa; **we shall have to ~ our spending** dovremo limitare le spese; **to ~ the clock** (fig) avere l'occhio sull'orologio; **to ~ sb's interests** guardare agli interessi di qn.

3 vi (observe) guardare; (pay attention) stare attento(a); (sleeper, sick person) vegliare; **to ~ for sb/sth** aspettare qn/qc; **the doctors are ~ing for any deterioration in his condition** i medici lo tengono in osservazione per scoprire eventuali peggioramenti delle sue condizioni.

♦ **watch out** vi + adv fare attenzione, stare attento(a); **to ~ out for** (keep watch) guardare se arriva (or arrivano); (be on the alert) stare attento a; **~ out!** (also threatening) attento!, attenzione!

♦ **watch over** vi + prep sorvegliare.

watch·dog ['wɒtʃdɒg] n cane m da guardia; (fig) sorvegliante m/f.

watch·er ['wɒtʃəʳ] n (observer) osservatore/trice; (spectator) spettatore/trice.

watch·ful ['wɒtʃful] adj: **to be ~ for** or **against sth** stare attento a or in guardia contro qc; **to keep a ~ eye on sb** tenere bene d'occhio qn.

watch·ful·ness ['wɒtʃfulnɪs] n attenzione f, vigilanza.

watch·maker ['wɒtʃˌmeɪkəʳ] n orologiaio/a.

watch·man ['wɒtʃmən] n, pl **-men** guardiano.

watch·strap ['wɒtʃstræp] n cinturino dell'orologio.

watch·tower ['wɒtʃˌtauəʳ] n torre f di guardia.

watch·word ['wɒtʃwɜːd] n parola d'ordine.

wa·ter ['wɔːtəʳ] **1** n (gen) acqua; **fresh/salt ~** acqua dolce/salata; **I'd like a drink of ~** vorrei un bicchier d'acqua; **the High Street is under ~** la High Street è inondata; **to turn on the ~** aprire l'acqua; **to spend money like ~** spendere e spandere, avere le mani bucate; **a lot of ~ has flowed under the bridge since then** (fig) da allora è passata molta acqua sotto i ponti; **that theory won't hold ~** (fig) quella teoria fa acqua; **to pour cold ~ on sth** (fig) mostrarsi poco entusiasta di qc; **it's like ~ off a duck's back** (fig) è come parlare al muro; **the ~s of the Tiber** le acque del Tevere; **British ~s** acque fpl (territoriali) britanniche; **to take the ~s** passare le acque; **the ~s** (in pregnancy) le acque; **to pass ~** orinare; **~ on the brain** (Med) idrocefalia; **~ on the knee** (Med) sinovite f.

2 vt (garden, plant) innaffiare; (horses, cattle) abbeverare; (wine) annacquare.

3 vi (eyes) piangere; **to make sb's mouth ~ far** venire l'acquolina in bocca a qn.

4 cpd (pressure, supply, tank) dell'acqua; (softener, purifier, power) idrico(a); **~ bed** n materasso ad acqua; **~ biscuit** n cracker m inv (non salato); **~ bottle** n (for drinking) borraccia; (for heat) borsa dell'acqua calda; **~ closet** n (frm) gabinetto; **~ level** n livello dell'acqua; (of flood) livello delle acque; **~ lily** n ninfea; **~ main** n conduttura dell'acqua; **~ polo** n pallanuoto f; **~ vapour** n vapore m acqueo; **~ wings** npl braccioli mpl salvagente.

♦ **water down** vt + adv (milk, wine) diluire; (fig: claim etc) moderare; (: effect) attenuare.

water·colour, (Am) **water·color** ['wɔːtəˌkʌləʳ] n (picture) acquerello; (paints): **~s** colori mpl per acquerello.

water·cooled ['wɔːtəkuːld] adj raffreddato(a) ad acqua.

water·course ['wɔːtəkɔːs] n corso d'acqua.

water·cress ['wɔːtəkres] n crescione m.

water·fall ['wɔːtəfɔːl] n cascata.

water·front ['wɔːtəfrʌnt] n (seafront) lungomare m; (at docks) banchina.

wa·ter·ing can ['wɔːtərɪŋˌkæn] n annaffiatoio.

water·line ['wɔːtəlaɪn] n (Naut) linea di galleggiamento.

water·logged ['wɔːtəlɒgd] n (ground etc) impregnato(a) d'acqua; (fields) allagato(a); (shoes) inzuppato(a).

water·mark ['wɔːtəmaːk] n (in paper) filigrana; (left by tide) segno della marea.

water·melon ['wɔːtəˌmelən] n anguria, cocomero.

water·proof ['wɔːtəpruːf] **1** adj impermeabile. **2** n impermeabile m. **3** vt impermeabilizzare.

water·shed ['wɔːtəʃed] n (Geog, also fig) spartiacque m.

water·side ['wɔːtəsaɪd] **1** n riva. **2** adj sulla riva.

water·skiing ['wɔːtəˌskiːɪŋ] n sci m d'acqua, sci acquatico.

water·tight ['wɔːtətaɪt] adj (compartment etc) stagno(a); (fig: excuse, argument)) inattaccabile; (: alibi) di ferro.

water·way ['wɔːtəweɪ] n corso d'acqua navigabile.

water·wheel ['wɔːtəwiːl] n ruota idraulica.

water·works ['wɔːtəwɜːks] n (sg: place) impianto idrico; (pl: fig fam): **to turn on the ~** scoppiare a piangere; **to have trouble with one's ~** avere dei problemi alla vescica.

wa·tery ['wɔːtərɪ] adj (tea, soup) acquoso(a); (pale: sun, colour) slavato(a); (eyes) umido(a); **to go to a ~ grave** perire tra i flutti.

watt [wɒt] n watt m inv.

watt·age ['wɒtɪdʒ] n wattaggio.

wave [weɪv] **1** n (a) (gen, Phys, Radio) onda; (in hair, on surface) ondulazione f; (fig: of enthusiasm, strikes etc) ondata; **in ~s** a ondate; **short/ medium/long ~** (Radio) onde corte/medie/ lunghe; **the new ~** (Cine, Mus) la new wave. **(b)** (greeting) cenno di saluto; (signal) gesto, cenno; **to give sb a ~** salutare qn con la mano; **with a ~ of his hand** con un cenno della mano.

2 vt **(a)** (brandish: flag, banner, handkerchief) sventolare; (: stick, umbrella) agitare; (beckon, motion) far segno a; **he ~d the ticket under my nose** mi sventolò il biglietto sotto il naso; **to ~ sb goodbye, to ~ goodbye to sb** fare un cenno d'addio a qn; **she ~d a greeting to the crowd** salutò la folla con un cenno della mano; **he ~d us over to his table** ci invitò con un cenno al suo tavolo. **(b)** (hair) ondulare.

3 vi **(a)** (person) gesticolare; **to ~ to** or **at sb** fare un cenno a qn. **(b)** (flag, branches etc) ondeggiare. **(c)** (hair) essere mosso(a) or ondulato(a).

♦ **wave about, wave around** vt + adv (object) agitare; **to ~ one's arms about** (in talking) gesticolare.

♦ **wave aside, wave away** vt + adv (person): **to ~ sb aside** fare cenno a qn di spostarsi; (fig: suggestion, objection) respingere, rifiutare; (: doubts) scacciare.

♦ **wave on** vt + adv (subj: policeman etc) fare segno di avanzare a.

wave·band ['weɪvbænd] n gamma di lunghezze d'onda.

wave·length ['weɪvleŋθ] *n* lunghezza d'onda;
we're not on the same ~ *(fig)* parliamo due linguaggi diversi.

wa·ver ['weɪvəʳ] *vi (flame, needle etc)* oscillare;
(voice) tremare; *(fig: hesitate)*: **to ~ (between)**
oscillare (tra); *(: courage, support)* vacillare; **he's
beginning to ~** comincia a vacillare.

wavy ['weɪvɪ] *adj* **(-ier, -iest)** *(hair, surface)* ondula-
to(a); *(line)* ondeggiante, sinuoso(a).

wax[1] [wæks] **1** *n* cera; *(for skis)* sciolina; *(in ear)*
cerume *m*. **2** *adj* di cera. **3** *vt (furniture, car)* dare
la cera a.

wax[2] [wæks] *vi (moon)* crescere; **to ~ enthusiastic**
entusiasmarsi; **to ~ eloquent about sth** infervorarsi nel parlare di qc.

wax(ed) pa·per ['wæks(t)'peɪpəʳ] *n* carta oleata.

wax·en ['wæksən] *adj (of wax)* di cera; *(fig: pale)*
cereo(a).

wax·work ['wækswɜːk] *n (model)* statua di cera.

wax·works ['wækswɜːks] *nsg or pl* museo delle
cere.

waxy ['wæksɪ] *adj* **(-ier, -iest)** *(fig: complexion)* ce-
reo(a).

way [weɪ] **1** *n* **(a)** *(road, lane etc)* strada; *(in street
names)* via; **private/public ~** strada privata/
pubblica; **the ~ across the fields** il sentiero
attraverso i campi; **the Appian W~** la Via Appia;
across *or* **over the ~** di fronte.

(b) *(route)* strada; **the W~ of the Cross** *(Rel)* la
via crucis; **to ask one's ~ to the station** chiedere
la strada per la stazione; **which is the ~ to the
station?** qual'è la strada per la stazione?; **we
came a back ~** siamo arrivati per strade secondarie; **she went by ~ of Birmingham** è andata
passando per Birmingham; **to go the wrong ~**
andare dalla parte sbagliata; **to lose one's ~**
perdere la strada; **the ~ in** l'entrata; **the ~ out**
l'uscita; **to find one's ~ into a building** riuscire a
entrare in un edificio; **don't bother, I'll find my
own ~ out** non si scomodi, esco da me; **to find a ~
out of a problem** trovare una soluzione a un
problema; **to take the easy ~ out** trovare una
facile soluzione; **on the ~** *(en route)* per strada;
(expected) in arrivo; **on the ~ to work** andando a
lavorare; **you pass it on your ~ home** ci passi
davanti andando a casa; **he's on the ~ to
becoming an alcoholic** è sulla strada dell'alcolismo; **it's time we were on our ~** è ora di andare;
all the ~ (here/home) per tutta la strada (venendo qui/andando a casa); **I'm with you all the ~** *(fig
fam)* sono assolutamente d'accordo con te; **to
make one's (own) ~ home** andare a casa (da
solo); **I know my ~ about town** conosco la città;
to lead the ~ fare strada; *(fig)* essere all'avanguardia; **I don't want to take you out of your ~**
non voglio farti deviare; **the village is rather out
of the ~** il villaggio è abbastanza fuori mano;
that's nothing out of the ~ these days non è nulla
di eccezionale al giorno d'oggi; **to go out of one's
~ to help sb** farsi in quattro per aiutare qn;
**would you see your ~ (clear) to helping me
tomorrow?** pensi di potermi aiutare domani?; **to
go one's own ~** *(fig)* andare per la propria strada,
fare di testa propria; **to make one's ~ in the
world** farsi strada nel mondo; **he worked his ~
up in the company** si è fatto strada nella compagnia; **the company isn't paying its ~** la compagnia è in debito; **he put me in the ~ of some good
contracts** mi ha procurato dei buoni contratti.

(c) *(space sb wants to go through)* strada; **to be
or get in the** *or* **sb's ~** intralciare qn; **am I in your
~?** *(of sb watching sth)* ti tolgo la visuale?; **to
stand in sb's ~** intralciare il passaggio a qn; *(fig)*

fermare qn; **to stand in the ~ of progress** bloc-
care il progresso; **to be** *or* **get out of the** *or* **sb's ~**
lasciare passare qn; **to keep out of sb's ~** evitare
qn; **to move sth out of the ~** togliere di torno qc;
as soon as I've got this essay out of the ~ appena
mi sono liberato di questo tema; **keep those
matches out of his ~** tieni lontano da lui quei
fiammiferi; **to push/elbow one's ~ through the
crowd** farsi strada a spinte/gomitate tra la folla;
he crawled/limped his ~ to the gate andò a
carponi/zoppicando verso il cancello; **to make ~
(for sb/sth)** far strada (a qn/qc); *(fig)* lasciare il
posto *or* far largo (a qn/qc); **to leave the ~ open
for further talks** lasciare aperta la possibilità di
ulteriori colloqui.

(d) *(direction)* direzione *f*; **come this ~** vieni
da questa parte; **this ~ for...** da questa parte
per...; **which ~ did he go?** da che parte è andato?;
which ~ do we go from here? da che parte
dobbiamo andare da qui?; *(fig)* cosa facciamo
adesso?; **are you going my ~?** fai la strada che
faccio io?; **everything is going my ~** *(fig)* mi sta
andando tutto liscio; **this ~ and that** di qua e di
là; **down our ~** dalle nostre parti; **she didn't
know which ~ to look** non sapeva dove guardare; **put it the right ~ up** mettilo in piedi dalla
parte giusta; **to be the wrong ~ round** essere al
contrario; **to look the other ~** *(fig)* guardare
dall'altra parte; **to be in a fair ~ to doing sth**
essere sulla strada giusta per fare qc; **to split sth
three ~s** dividere qc in tre.

(e) *(indicating distance, motion, progress)*: **to
come a long ~** *(also fig)* fare molta strada; **it's a
long ~ away** è molto lontano da qui; **a little ~
along the road** un po' più avanti lungo la strada;
he'll go a long ~ *(fig)* farà molta strada; **we've
come a long ~ since those days** abbiamo fatto
molta strada da quei tempi; **it should go a long ~
towards convincing him** dovrebbe contribuire
molto a convincerlo; **to be under ~** *(work,
project)* essere in corso; **to get under ~** avviarsi;
the job is now well under ~ il lavoro ora è ben
avviato.

(f) *(means)* mezzo; *(manner)* modo; **the
British ~ of life** lo stile di vita britannico; **there
are ~s and means** c'è il modo di farlo; **we'll find
a ~ of doing it** troveremo un modo per farlo; **the
only ~ of doing it** l'unico modo per farlo; **there
are no two ~s about it** la possibilità è una sola; **he
has his own ~ of doing it** ha un modo tutto suo
per farlo; **I'll do it (in) my own ~** lo farò a modo
mio; **they've had it all their own ~ too long** hanno
fatto per troppo tempo a modo loro; **to get one's
own ~** fare come si vuole; **I will help in every ~
possible** aiuterò in tutti i modi possibili; **he
helped in a small ~** ha aiutato un pochino; **in no
~, not in any ~** per nulla; **no ~!** *(fam)* assolutamente no!; **there's no ~ I'll do it** non lo farò per
nessun motivo al mondo; **do it this ~** fallo in
questo modo, fallo così; **in this ~** così, in questo
modo; **it was this ~...** è stato così...; **(in) one ~ or
another** in un modo o nell'altro; **in a ~** in un certo
senso; **in some ~s** in un certo senso; **in many ~s**
per molti versi; **to my ~ of thinking** al mio modo
di vedere; **either ~ I can't help you** non ti posso
aiutare in nessun caso; **to go on in the same old ~**
continuare nel modo di sempre; **the ~ things are**
come stanno le cose; **in the ordinary ~ (of
things)** normalmente.

(g) *(custom)* abitudine *f*; *(manner)* modo di
fare; **the ~s of the Spaniards** i costumi degli
Spagnoli; **foreign ~s** modo di fare da straniero;
he has his little ~s ha le sue piccole abitudini;

it's not my ~ non uso fare così; **he has a ~ with people** lui ci sa fare con la gente; **he has a ~ with him** ci sa fare; **to get into/out of the ~ of doing sth** prendere/perdere l'abitudine di fare qc.

(h) *(state)*: **things are in a bad ~** le cose si mettono male; **he's in a bad ~** è ridotto male; **to be in the family ~** *(fam)* aspettare un bambino.

(i) *(with 'by')*: **by the ~** a proposito; **but that's just by the ~** ma questo è tra parentesi; **by ~ of a warning** come avvertimento; **she's by ~ of being an artist** è una specie di artista.

2 *adv (fam)*: **it happened ~ back** è successo molto tempo fa; **~ back in 1900** nel lontano 1900; **it's ~ out in Nevada** è nel lontano Nevada; **he was ~ out in his estimate** la sua valutazione era decisamente errata.

way·bill ['weɪbɪl] *n (Comm)* bolla di accompagnamento.

way·farer ['weɪˌfeərəʳ] *n (old)* viandante *m/f*.

way·lay ['weɪ'leɪ] *pt, pp* **waylaid** *vt* fermare.

way-out ['weɪ'aʊt] *adj (fam)* eccentrico(a).

way·side ['weɪsaɪd] **1** *n* bordo della strada; **to fall by the ~** *(fig)* perdersi lungo la strada. **2** *cpd (flowers, café)* sul bordo della strada.

way·ward ['weɪwəd] *adj (self-willed)* ribelle.

W.C. *n (abbr of water closet)* W.C. *m inv.*

we [wiː] *pers pron pl* noi; **~ understand** abbiamo capito; *(stressed)* noi sì che abbiamo capito; **here ~ are** eccoci; **~ Italians** noi *or* noialtri Italiani; **as ~ say in Florence...** come si dice a Firenze...; **~ all make mistakes** tutti possiamo sbagliare.

weak [wiːk] *adj* **(-er, -est)** *(gen)* debole; *(tea, coffee)* leggero(a); *(health)* precario(a); **to grow ~(er) = to weaken 2**; **a ~ chin** un mento sfuggente; **to have ~ eyes** *or* **eyesight** avere la vista debole; **her French is ~**, **she is ~ at French** è scarsa in francese; **~ in the head** *(fam)* scemo; **to go ~ at the knees** *(with excitement, hunger etc)* sentirsi mancare le ginocchia.

weak·en ['wiːkən] **1** *vt (gen)* indebolire; *(grip)* allentare; *(influence)* diminuire; *(solution, mixture)* diluire; **this fact ~s your case** questo fatto sminuisce il tuo argomento. **2** *vi (gen)* indebolirsi; *(grip)* allentarsi; *(influence)* diminuire; *(give way)* cedere; **we must not ~ now** non dobbiamo cedere ora.

weak-kneed ['wiːk'niːd] *adj (fig)* debole, codardo(a).

weak·ling ['wiːklɪŋ] *n (physically)* mingherlino/a; *(morally)* smidollato/a.

weak·ly ['wiːklɪ] **1** *adj* deboluccio(a), gracile. **2** *adv* debolmente.

weak·ness ['wiːknɪs] *n* debolezza; **chocolate is one of my ~es** il cioccolato è una delle mie passioni; **to have a ~ for sth** avere un debole per qc.

weak-willed ['wiːk'wɪld] *adj* debole.

weal [wiːl] *n (welt)* livido.

wealth [welθ] *n* ricchezza; *(fig: abundance)*: **~ (of)** ricchezza *or* abbondanza (di).

wealthy ['welθɪ] *adj* **(-ier, -iest)** ricco(a).

wean [wiːn] *vt (baby)* svezzare; **to ~ sb (away) from alcohol** far perdere a qn il vizio del bere.

weap·on ['wepən] *n* arma.

wear [weəʳ] *(vb: pt* **wore**, *pp* **worn**) **1** *n* **(a)** *(use)* uso; **shoes for everyday ~** scarpe da mettere tutti i giorni; **there's still a lot of ~ in these** *(shoes, carpets, tyres)* sono ancora in buono stato; **I've had a lot of ~ out of this jacket** porto questa giacca da anni; **to stand up to a lot of ~** durare a lungo.

(b) *(deterioration through use)* logoramento, logorio; **~ and tear** usura; **the ~ on the engine** l'usura del motore; **she looks the worse for ~**

(old, exhausted) sembra sciupata; *(hung-over)* ha l'aria distrutta.

(c) *(clothing)* abbigliamento; **children's ~** confezioni *fpl* per bambini; **summer ~** abiti *mpl* estivi.

2 *vt* **(a)** *(spectacles, necklace)* portare; *(clothing)* portare, indossare; *(look, smile, beard etc)* avere; **to ~ make-up** truccarsi; **she wore her blue dress** portava il suo vestito blu; **I have nothing to ~ to the dinner** non ho niente da mettermi per la cena; **to ~ one's hair long** avere i capelli lunghi; **he wore a big smile** aveva un grande sorriso.

(b) *(damage through use)* consumare, logorare; **I always manage to ~ my jumpers at the elbow** i miei maglioni sono sempre consumati sui gomiti; **they have worn a path across the lawn** hanno formato un sentiero nel prato a forza di camminarci; **to ~ a hole in sth** bucare qc a furia di usarlo; **the rocks had been worn smooth** le rocce erano levigate.

(c) *(fam: believe, tolerate)* bere; **he won't ~ that** questa non la beve.

3 *vi* **(a)** *(last)* durare; **she has worn well** porta bene i suoi anni; **that theory has worn well** quella teoria è ancora valida.

(b) *(become worn: shoes, inscription etc)* consumarsi; *(: rocks)* levigarsi; **the edges have worn smooth** gli spigoli si sono smussati; **that excuse is ~ing a bit thin** quella scusa non regge più.

♦ **wear away 1** *vt + adv (rock, pattern etc)* consumare. **2** *vi + adv* consumarsi.

♦ **wear down 1** *vt + adv (heel, tyre tread etc)* consumare; *(fig: opposition etc)* fiaccare; **to ~ down sb's patience** far perdere la pazienza a qn. **2** *vi + adv (heels, tyre tread etc)* consumarsi.

♦ **wear off** *vi + adv (plating, paint etc)* consumarsi, logorarsi; *(pain, excitement etc)* calmarsi, diminuire; *(anaesthetic)* non fare più effetto; **after a while the novelty wore off** dopo un po' non era più una novità.

♦ **wear on** *vi + adv* prolungarsi, protrarsi; **as the evening wore on** nel corso della serata.

♦ **wear out 1** *vt + adv* consumare, logorare; *(fig: exhaust)* sfiancare, spossare; *(: patience)* far perdere; **to be worn out** essere consumato; *(fig: person)* essere estenuato *or* distrutto. **2** *vi + adv (shoes, carpet etc)* consumarsi; **his strength wore out** era spossato; **his patience wore out** ha perso la pazienza.

♦ **wear through 1** *vt + adv* consumare. **2** *vi + adv* consumarsi.

wear·able ['weərəbl] *adj* indossabile.

wea·ri·ly ['wɪərɪlɪ] *adv* stancamente.

wea·ri·ness ['wɪərɪnɪs] *n* stanchezza.

wea·ri·some ['wɪərɪsəm] *adj (tiring)* estenuante; *(boring)* noioso(a).

wea·ry ['wɪərɪ] **1** *adj* **(-ier, -iest)** *(tired)* stanco(a), affaticato(a); *(dispirited)* stanco(a), abbattuto(a); *(tiring: wait, day)* estenuante; **to be ~ of sb/sth** essere stanco di qn/qc; **five ~ miles** cinque lunghe miglia. **2** *vt* stancare. **3** *vi*: **to ~ of sb/sth** stancarsi di qn/qc.

wea·sel ['wiːzl] *n* donnola.

weath·er ['weðəʳ] **1** *n* tempo; **in this ~** con questo tempo; **what's the ~ like?** che tempo fa?; **it gets left outside in all ~s** rimane fuori con qualsiasi tempo; **to be under the ~** *(fig: ill)* sentirsi poco bene; **to make heavy ~ of sth** trovare qc difficile. **2** *vt* **(a)** *(wood)* stagionare. **(b)**: **to ~ the storm** *(ship)* resistere alla tempesta; *(fig)* superare le difficoltà. **3** *vi (rocks)* logorarsi; *(wood)* stagionare. **4** *cpd (bureau, ship, chart, station)* meteorologico(a); ~ **eye** n: **to keep a ~ eye on sth** (fig) tener d'occhio qc; ~ **forecast** n previsioni fpl del tempo; ~ **report** n bollettino meteorologico.

weather-beaten ['wɛðə,biːtn] adj (rocks, building) segnato(a) dalle intemperie; (person, skin) segnato(a) dal tempo.

weather·cock ['wɛðəkɒk] n segnavento m inv, banderuola.

weath·ered ['wɛðəd] adj (skin, rocks) segnato(a) dalle intemperie; (wood) stagionato(a).

weather·man ['wɛðəmæn] n, pl -**men** meteorologo.

weather·proof ['wɛðəpruːf] adj (garment) impermeabile.

weather·vane ['wɛðə,veɪn] n = **weathercock**.

weave [wiːv] (vb: pt **wove**, pp **woven**) 1 n trama. 2 vt (threads, basket), (fabric) intrecciare; (fig) tessere; **he wove these details into the story** ha intrecciato nella storia questi dettagli; **he wove a story round these experiences** ha intessuto una storia attorno a queste esperienze. 3 vi tessere; (fig: pt, pp ~**d**: move in and out) zigzagare; **to ~ in and out of the traffic** zigzagare nel traffico.

weav·er ['wiːvəʳ] n tessitore/trice.

weav·ing ['wiːvɪŋ] n tessitura.

web [wɛb] n (of spider) tela, ragnatela; (between toes etc) membrana interdigitale; (fig) insieme m; **it was a ~ of lies** era una ragnatela di bugie.

webbed [wɛbd] adj: ~ **foot** piede m palmato.

web·bing ['wɛbɪŋ] n (on chair) cinghie fpl.

wed [wɛd] 1 vt sposare; **to be** ~**ded to one's job/an idea** essere molto attaccato al proprio lavoro/a un'idea. 2 vi sposarsi.

we'd [wiːd] = **we would; we had**.

wed·ded ['wɛdɪd] adj (wife, husband) legittimo(a); (bliss, life etc) coniugale.

wed·ding ['wɛdɪŋ] 1 n matrimonio, nozze fpl; **silver/golden** etc ~ nozze d'argento/d'oro etc; **to have a church** ~ sposarsi in chiesa. 2 cpd (cake, dress, reception) nuziale; ~ **anniversary** n anniversario di matrimonio; ~ **breakfast** n pranzo nuziale; ~ **day** n giorno delle nozze; ~ **invitation** n partecipazione f di nozze; ~ **night** n prima notte di nozze; ~ **present** n regalo di nozze; ~ **ring** n fede f, vera.

wedge [wɛdʒ] 1 n (of wood etc) zeppa; (for splitting sth) cuneo; (piece: of cheese, cake) spicchio, fetta; **it's the thin end of the** ~ (fig) è l'inizio della fine; **to drive a** ~ **between two people** intaccare il rapporto tra due persone. 2 vt mettere una zeppa sotto (or in); **to** ~ **a door open** tenere aperta una porta con un fermo; **the car was** ~**d between 2 lorries** la macchina era incastrata tra due camion.

wedge-shaped ['wɛdʒʃeɪpt] adj a forma di cuneo.

Wednes·day ['wɛnzdeɪ] n mercoledì m inv; for usage see **Tuesday**.

wee [wiː] adj (-**er**, -**est**) (Scot, fam) piccolo(a); **a ~ bit** un pochettino.

weed [wiːd] 1 n erbaccia. 2 vt (flower bed) diserbare. 3 vi strappare le erbacce.

♦ **weed out** vt + adv eliminare.

weed-killer ['wiːdkɪləʳ] n diserbante m, erbicida m.

weedy ['wiːdɪ] adj (-**ier**, -**iest**) (fam: person) allampanato(a).

week [wiːk] n settimana; **once/twice a** ~ una volta/due volte alla settimana; **this** ~ questa settimana; **next/last** ~ la settimana prossima/scorsa; **in the middle of the** ~ a metà settimana; **a** ~ **today** oggi a otto; **2** ~**s ago** 2 settimane fa; **in 2** ~**s' time** fra 2 settimane, fra 15 giorni; **Tuesday** ~, **a** ~ **on Tuesday** martedì a otto; **to take 3** ~**s' holiday** prendere 3 settimane di ferie; **the** ~ **ending** January 3rd ≃ la prima settimana di gennaio; ~ **in**, ~ **out**, ~ **after** ~ settimana dopo settimana; **every other** ~ una settimana sì, una no; **to knock sb into the middle of next** ~ (fam) darle di santa ragione a qn.

week·day ['wiːkdeɪ] n giorno feriale; (Comm) giornata lavorativa; **on** ~**s** durante la settimana, nei giorni feriali.

week·end [,wiːk'ɛnd] 1 n week-end m inv, fine m settimana inv; **a long** ~ un fine settimana lungo; **at the** ~ durante il fine settimana. 2 cpd (cottage) per il fine settimana; (visit) di fine settimana; ~ **case** n borsa da viaggio.

week·ly ['wiːklɪ] 1 adj settimanale. 2 adv settimanalmente; £15 ~ 15 sterline alla settimana. 3 n (magazine) settimanale m.

weep [wiːp] (vb: pt, pp **wept**) 1 vt (tears) versare, piangere. 2 vi piangere; (Med: wound etc) essudare; **to** ~ **for sb** piangere per qn; **I could have wept!** mi sarei messo a piangere! 3 n: **to have a good** ~ fare un bel pianto.

weep·ing ['wiːpɪŋ] 1 n pianto. 2 cpd: ~ **willow** n salice m piangente.

wee·wee ['wiːwiː] (fam) 1 n pipì f inv. 2 vi fare la pipì.

weft [wɛft] n (Textiles) trama.

weigh [weɪ] 1 vt (a) (also fig) pesare; **it** ~**s a ton** (also fig) pesa una tonnellata; **to** ~ **sth in one's hand** soppesare qc; **to** ~ **sth in one's mind** soppesare mentalmente qc; **to** ~ **the pros and cons** valutare i pro e i contro. (b): **to** ~ **anchor** (Naut) salpare or levare l'ancora. 2 vi (fig: be a worry): **to** ~ **on sb** pesare su qn; (: be important): **to** ~ **with sb** avere importanza or contare per qn; **it** ~**s on her mind** la preoccupa; **that didn't** ~ **with him** quello per lui non aveva importanza.

♦ **weigh down** vt + adv (branches) piegare; (person): **to be** ~**ed down by sth** curvarsi sotto il peso di qc; **to be** ~**ed down with sorrows** essere oppresso dai dispiaceri.

♦ **weigh in** vi + adv (Sport) pesarsi (prima di una gara); **he** ~**ed in at 60 kilos** al controllo del peso era 60 chili.

♦ **weigh out** vt + adv (goods) pesare.

♦ **weigh up** vt + adv (alternatives, situation) pesare, valutare.

weigh·bridge ['weɪbrɪdʒ] n bascula.

weigh·ing ['weɪŋ] adj: ~ **machine** pesa.

weight [weɪt] 1 n (a) (gen, fig) peso; **sold by** ~ venduto a peso; **it** (o he etc) **is worth its** (o his etc) ~ **in gold** vale tanto oro quanto pesa; **to put on/lose** ~ ingrassare/dimagrire; **to carry** ~ (fig) avere peso; **these are arguments of some** ~ questi sono argomenti di un certo peso; **that's a** ~ **off my mind** mi sono tolto un peso; **they won by sheer** ~ **of numbers** hanno vinto solo per superiorità numerica; **to chuck** or **throw one's** ~ **about** (fam) fare il prepotente; **he doesn't pull his** ~ non lavora quanto dovrebbe. (b) (for scales etc) peso; ~**s and measures** pesi e misure.

2 vt (also: ~ **down**) mettere dei pesi su.

weight·less ['weɪtlɪs] adj senza peso.

weight·less·ness ['weɪtlɪsnɪs] n mancanza di peso.

weight·lifter ['weɪt,lɪftəʳ] n pesista m.

weight·lifting ['weɪt,lɪftɪŋ] n sollevamento pesi, pesistica.

weighty ['weɪtɪ] adj (-**ier**, -**iest**) (fig: problems, duties, considerations) importante.

weir [wɪəʳ] n sbarramento.

weird [wɪəd] adj (-**er**, -**est**) strano(a), bizzarro(a).

weir·do ['wɪədəʊ] n (fam) tipo(a) strampalato(a).

welch [wɛlʃ] vi (fam): **to** ~ **on** (promise) venir meno a; (debt) non pagare.

wel·come ['wɛlkəm] **1** *adj* (*gen*) gradito(a); ~! benvenuto!; ~ **to Britain!** benvenuto in Gran Bretagna!; **to be** ~ (*person*) essere il(*or* la) benvenuto(a); **you will always be** ~ **here** qui sarai sempre il benvenuto; **to make sb** ~ accogliere bene qn; **you're** ~ (*after thanks*) prego; **you're** ~ **to try** prova pure; **you're** ~ **to** (**borrow**) it prendilo pure; **it's a** ~ **change** è un piacevole cambiamento.

2 *n* accoglienza; **a cold/warm** ~ un'accoglienza fredda/calda; **to bid sb** ~ dare il benvenuto a qn; **the crowd gave him an enthusiastic** ~ la folla lo accolse con entusiasmo; **what sort of a** ~ **will this product get?** che accoglienza avrà questo prodotto?

3 *vt* accogliere, ricevere; (*also*: **bid** ~) dare il benvenuto a; (*fig: change, suggestion*) accogliere; **I'd** ~ **your help** gradirei il tuo aiuto; **we** ~ **this step** siamo lieti di questo passo.

wel·com·ing ['wɛlkəmɪŋ] *adj* accogliente.

weld [wɛld] **1** *vt* saldare. **2** *n* saldatura.

weld·er ['wɛldəʳ] *n* saldatore *m*.

weld·ing ['wɛldɪŋ] **1** *n* saldatura. **2** *cpd*: ~ **torch** *n* cannello da saldare.

wel·fare ['wɛlfɛəʳ] **1** *n* (**a**) (*gen*) bene *m*; (*comfort*) benessere *m*; **the nation's** ~ il bene della nazione; **spiritual** ~ benessere spirituale; **to look after sb's** ~ preoccuparsi di qn; **child** ~ protezione *f* dell'infanzia. (**b**) (*fam: social aid etc*) assistenza sociale. **2** *cpd* (*aid, organization, work*) di assistenza (sociale); ~ **centre** *n* centro di assistenza sociale; ~ **state** *n* stato assistenziale; ~ **worker** *n* assistente *m/f* sociale.

well¹ [wɛl] **1** *n* (*for water etc*) pozzo; (*of stairs*) tromba; (*of lift*) gabbia. **2** *vi* (*also*: ~ **out**, ~ **up**) sgorgare.

well² [wɛl] (*comp* **better**, *superl* **best**) **1** *adv* (**a**) (*gen*) bene; **very** ~ benissimo; **he did as** ~ **as he could** ha fatto meglio che poteva; **to do** ~ (**in sth**) andare bene (in qc); **to be doing** ~ stare bene; **you did** ~ **to come** hai fatto bene a venire; **he did** ~ **to come tenth** è stato un buon risultato per lui il fatto di essere arrivato decimo; ~ **done!** ben fatto!; **to think** ~ **of sb** avere una buona opinione di qn; **to be** ~ **in with sb** essere in buoni rapporti con qn; **to do** ~ **by sb** trattare bene qn; **it was** ~ **worth it** ne valeva certo la pena; **you're** ~ **out of it** è un bene che tu ne sia uscito; ~ **and truly** completamente; ~ **over a thousand** molto *or* ben più di mille; **all** *or* **only too** ~ anche troppo bene; **and** ~ **I know it!** è proprio vero!; **he's** ~ **away** (*fam: drunk*) è brillo.

(**b**) (*probably, reasonably*): **we might just as** ~ **have...** avremmo fatto bene a...; **she cried, as** ~ **she might** piangeva a buon diritto; **one might** ~ **ask why...** ci si potrebbe ben chiedere perché...; **you may** ~ **ask!** una buona domanda!; **you might as** ~ **tell me** potresti anche dirmelo; **I might** *or* **may as** ~ **come** potrei anche venire; **I couldn't very** ~ **leave** non potevo andarmene così.

(**c**): **as** ~ (*in addition*) anche; **she sings as** ~ **as playing the piano** oltre a suonare il piano, canta; **X as** ~ **as Y** sia X che Y.

2 *adj* (**a**) (*healthy*): **to be** ~ stare bene; **get** ~ **soon!** guarisci presto!; **I don't feel** ~ non mi sento bene.

(**b**) (*acceptable, satisfactory*) buono(a); **all is not** ~ non va tutto bene; **that's all very** ~, **but...** va benissimo, ma..., d'accordo, ma...; ~ **and good** bene; **it would be as** ~ **to ask** sarebbe bene chiedere; **it's just as** ~ **we asked** abbiamo fatto bene a chiedere.

3 *excl* (*gen*) bene; (*resignation, hesitation*) beh;

~, **as I was saying...** dunque, come stavo dicendo...; ~, ~, ~! ma guarda un po'!; **very** ~ **then** va bene; ~ **I never!** ma no!, ma non mi dire!; ~ **there you are then!** ecco, hai visto!

4 *n*: **to wish sb** ~ augurare ogni bene a qn; (*in exam etc*) augurare a qn di riuscire.

well- [wɛl] *pref* bene; ~**dressed** ben vestito(a), vestito(a) bene.

we'll [wiːl] = **we will, we shall**.

well-balanced ['wɛl'bælənst] *adj* equilibrato(a).

well-behaved ['wɛlbɪ'heɪvd] *adj* che si comporta bene.

well-being ['wɛl'biːɪŋ] *n* benessere *m*.

well-bred ['wɛl'brɛd] *adj* educato(a), beneducato(a).

well-built ['wɛl'bɪlt] *adj* (*house*) ben costruito(a); (*person*) ben fatto(a).

well-chosen ['wɛl'tʃəʊzn] *adj* (*remarks, words*) ben scelto(a), appropriato(a).

well-developed ['wɛldɪ'vɛləpt] *adj* sviluppato(a).

well-disposed ['wɛldɪ'spəʊzd] *adj*: ~ **to**(**wards**) bendisposto(a) verso.

well-earned ['wɛl'ɜːnd] *adj* (*rest*) meritato(a).

well-founded ['wɛl'faʊndɪd] *adj* fondato(a).

well-heeled ['wɛl'hiːld] *adj* (*fam: wealthy*) agiato(a).

well-informed ['wɛlɪn'fɔːmd] *adj* (*knowledgeable*) informato(a); (*having knowledge of*) ben informato(a).

well-ing·ton ['wɛlɪŋtən] *n* (*also*: ~ **boot**) stivale *m* di gomma.

well-kept ['wɛl'kɛpt] *adj* (*house, grounds, secret*) ben tenuto(a); (*hair, hands*) ben curato(a).

well-known ['wɛl'nəʊn] *adj* noto(a), famoso(a).

well-meaning ['wɛl'miːnɪŋ] *adj* ben intenzionato(a).

well-nigh ['wɛl'naɪ] *adv*: ~ **impossible** quasi impossibile.

well-off ['wɛl'ɒf] **1** *adj* (*rich*) benestante; **you're** ~ **without him** puoi fare tranquillamente a meno di lui; **you don't know when you're** ~ non sai quanto sei fortunato. **2** *npl*: **the** ~ i benestanti.

well-preserved ['wɛlprɪ'zɜːvd] *adj* (*person*): **to be** ~ portare bene gli anni.

well-read ['wɛl'rɛd] *adj* colto(a).

well-spent ['wɛl'spɛnt] *adj* (*money*) ben speso(a); **that was time** ~ non è stata una perdita di tempo.

well-spoken ['wɛl'spəʊkən] *adj* che parla bene.

well-stocked ['wɛl'stɒkt] *adj* (*shop, larder*) ben fornito(a); (*river*) ricco(a) di pesce.

well-timed ['wɛl'taɪmd] *adj* opportuno(a).

well-to-do ['wɛltə'duː] *adj* ricco(a), benestante.

well-wisher ['wɛl,wɪʃəʳ] *n* ammiratore/trice.

Welsh [wɛlʃ] **1** *adj* gallese. **2** *n* (**a**): **the** ~ (*people*) i Gallesi. (**b**) (*language*) gallese *m*.

welsh [wɛlʃ] *vi* = **welch**.

Welsh·man ['wɛlʃmən] *n*, *pl* **-men** gallese *m*.

Welsh·woman ['wɛlʃ,wʊmən] *n*, *pl* **-women** gallese *f*.

welt [wɛlt] *n* (*bruise*) livido.

wel·ter·weight ['wɛltəweɪt] *n* peso *m* welter *inv*.

wend [wɛnd] *vt*: **to** ~ **one's way home** incamminarsi verso casa.

went [wɛnt] *pt of* **go**.

wept [wɛpt] *pt, pp of* **weep**.

were [wɜːʳ] *2nd pers sg, pl pt of* **be**.

we're [wɪəʳ] = **we are**.

weren't [wɜːnt] = **were not**.

were·wolf ['wɪəwʊlf] *n*, *pl* **-wolves** licantropo, lupo mannaro (*fam*).

west [wɛst] **1** *n* ovest *m*; **the wind is in** *or* **from the** ~ il vento viene da ovest *or* da occidente; (**to the**) ~ **of** a ovest di; **in the** ~ **of** nella parte occidentale di; **the W~** *(Pol)* l'Occidente *m.* **2** *adj (gen)* ovest *inv; (part, coast)* occidentale; *(wind)* di ponente; **the W~ Country** il sud-ovest dell'Inghilterra. **3** *adv* verso ovest; **to sail ~** navigare verso ovest; **a house facing ~** una casa esposta a ovest. **4** *cpd:* **W~ German** *adj, n* tedesco(a) occidentale *(m/f);* **W~ Germany** *n* Germania Occidentale; **W~ Indian 1** *adj* delle Indie Occidentali; **2** *n* abitante *m/f* delle Indie Occidentali; **W~ Indies** *pl* Indie *fpl* Occidentali.

west·bound ['wɛst,baʊnd] *adj (traffic)* diretto(a) a ovest; *(carriageway)* ovest *inv.*

west·er·ly ['wɛstəlɪ] *adj (wind)* di ponente; **in a ~ direction** verso ovest.

west·ern ['wɛstən] **1** *adj (also Pol)* occidentale; **in W~ France/Europe** nella Francia/nell'Europa occidentale. **2** *n (film)* western *m inv; (novel)* romanzo di avventura di cow-boy.

west·erni·za·tion [,wɛstənaɪ'zeɪʃən] *n* occidentalizzazione *f.*

west·ern·ized ['wɛstənaɪzd] *adj* occidentalizzato(a).

west·ward ['wɛstwəd] **1** *adj (direction)* ovest *inv.* **2** *adv (also:* ~s) a ovest, verso ovest.

wet [wɛt] **1** *adj* (**-ter, -test**) (**a**) bagnato(a); *(damp)* umido(a); *(soaked)* fradicio(a); *(paint, varnish, ink)* fresco(a); **in ~ clothes** coi vestiti bagnati; **to get ~** bagnarsi; **to be ~ through** *or* **~ to the skin** essere bagnato fino alle ossa; **what a ~ blanket you are!** *(fam)* che pesante che sei! (**b**) *(rainy)* piovoso(a); **a ~ day** una giornata piovosa. (**c**) *(fam: person)* smidollato(a). **2** *n* (**a**) *(moisture)* umidità; *(rain)* pioggia; **it got left out in the ~** l'hanno lasciato fuori sotto la pioggia. (**b**) *(fam pej: person)* smidollato/a. **3** *vt* bagnare; **to ~ the bed** bagnare il letto; **to ~ one's pants** *or* **o.s.** farsi la pipì addosso.

we've [wiːv] = **we have.**

whack [wæk] **1** *n* (**a**) *(blow)* (forte) colpo. (**b**) *(fam: attempt):* **to have a ~ at sth/at doing sth** provare qc/a fare qc, tentare qc/di fare qc. (**c**) *(fam: share)* parte *f.* **2** *vt (person)* dare un ceffone a; *(table etc)* dare una manata a; *(fam: defeat)* dare una batosta a.

whale [weɪl] *n* balena; **we had a ~ of a time** *(fam)* ci siamo divertiti come pazzi.

whale·bone ['weɪlbəʊn] *n (in corset)* stecca di balena.

whal·er ['weɪlə^r] *n (person)* baleniere *m; (ship)* baleniera *f.*

wharf [wɔːf] *n, pl* ~s *or* **wharves** [wɔːvz] banchina.

what [wɒt] **1** *adj* (**a**) che, quale; **~ time is it?** che ore sono?; **for ~ reason?** per quale motivo?; **to ~ extent?** fino a che punto?; **in ~ way can I help you?** come posso aiutarti?; **~ good would that do?** a che può servire?; **~ a nuisance!** che seccatura!; **~ a fool I was!** che sciocco sono stato!

(**b**): **buy ~ food you like** compra il cibo che vuoi; **~ little I had** il poco che avevo.

2 *pron* (**a**) *(interrog)* che cosa, cosa, che; **~'s happening?** che *or* (che) cosa succede?; **~ were you talking about?** di cosa stavate parlando?; **~ is it** *(or* he *etc)* **called?** come si chiama?; **~'s the weather like?** com'è il tempo?; **~ do you want now?**, **~ is it now?** che cosa vuoi adesso?, che c'è ora?; **~ are you doing that for?** perché lo fai?; **~ is that tool for?** a che *or* a cosa serve quello strumento?; **~ is his address?** sai il suo indirizzo?; **~ will it cost?** quanto sarà? *or* costerà?; **~ is the Italian for 'book'?** come si dice 'book' in italiano?; **it's WHAT?** come?

(**b**) *(rel)* ciò che, quello che; **I wonder ~ he'll do now** mi chiedo cosa farà adesso; **is that ~**

happened? è andata così?; **I don't know ~ to do** non so cosa fare; **tell us ~ you're laughing at** dicci perché stai ridendo; **tell me ~ you're thinking about** dimmi a cosa stai pensando; **he asked me ~ she had said** mi ha chiesto che cosa avesse detto; **~ I want is a cup of tea** ciò che che voglio adesso è una tazza di tè; **it's just ~ I wanted** è proprio ciò che volevo; **say ~ you like** di' quello che vuoi; **he knows ~'s ~** *(fam)* sa il fatto suo; **I'll show her ~'s ~!** le farò vedere io!; **I know ~** *or* **I'll tell you ~, let's go to the cinema** sai cosa facciamo? — andiamo al cinema; **she's not ~ she was** non è più quella che era.

(**c**): **~ about me?** e io?; **~ about a drink?** beviamo qualcosa?; **~ about going to the cinema?** se andassimo al cinema?; **you know John — yes, ~ about him?** conosci John — sì, perché?; **~ about that money you owe me?** e quei soldi che mi dovevi?; **~ about it?** *(what do you think)* cosa ne pensi?; *(so* ~) e allora?; **... and ~ have you, ...** **and ~ not** *(fam)* e chi più ne ha più ne mette; **and ~'s more** e per di più; **~ with one thing and another** tra una cosa e l'altra.

3 *excl (disbelieving)* cosa!, come!; **~, no coffee!** come, non c'è caffè!

what-d'ye-call-him ['wɒtdjə'kɔːl,hɪm], **what·sit** ['wɒtsɪt], **whats-his-name** ['wɒtsɪzneɪm] *etc n (fam)* coso.

what·ev·er [wɒt'ɛvə^r] **1** *pron* (**a**) *(anything that)* (tutto) ciò che, (tutto) quello che; *(no matter what)* qualsiasi cosa + *sub,* qualunque cosa + *sub;* **do ~ you want** fa' quello *or* ciò che vuoi; **~ happens** qualsiasi cosa succeda; **~ it costs** costi quello che costi; **or ~ they're called** o come si chiamano. (**b**) *(emphatic):* **~ do you mean?** cosa vorresti dire?; **~ did you do that for?** perché mai l'hai fatto? **2** *adj, adv (any):* **~ book you choose** qualsiasi *or* qualunque libro tu scelga; *(all):* **give me ~ money you've got** dammi quei soldi che hai; **nothing ~** proprio niente; **it's no use ~** non serve proprio a nulla.

what·so·ev·er ['wɒtsəʊ'ɛvə^r] = **whatever.**

wheat [wiːt] *n* grano, frumento.

wheat·en ['wiːtn] *adj* di frumento, di grano.

wheat·germ ['wiːtdʒɜːm] *n* germe *m* di grano.

wheat·meal ['wiːtmiːl] *n* farina integrale di frumento.

whee·dle ['wiːdl] *vt:* **to ~ sb into doing sth** convincere qn a fare qc (con lusinghe); **to ~ sth out of sb** *(favour etc)* ottenere qc da qn (con lusinghe); *(secret, name)* farsi dire qc da qn (con lusinghe).

wheel [wiːl] **1** *n (gen)* ruota; *(steering* ~) volante *m; (Naut)* timone *m; (potter's* ~) tornio da vasaio; *(spinning* ~) filatoio; **to take the ~** prendere il volante; **the ~ of fortune** la ruota della fortuna. **2** *vt (push: bicycle, pram etc)* spingere; **we ~ed it over to the window** l'abbiamo spinto alla finestra. **3** *vi (birds)* roteare; **to ~ left** *(Mil)* fare una conversione a sinistra; **to ~ round** *(person)* voltarsi.

wheel·bar·row ['wiːl,bærəʊ] *n* carriola.

wheel·base ['wiːlbeɪs] *n* interasse *m.*

wheel·chair ['wiːltʃɛə^r] *n* sedia a rotelle.

wheeler-dealer ['wiːlə,diːlə^r] *n* trafficone *m.*

wheeze [wiːz] *vi* ansimare.

whelk [wɛlk] *n* buccino.

whelp [wɛlp] *n* piccolo *(di animale).*

when [wɛn] **1** *adv* quando; **~ did it happen?** quando è successo?; **I know ~ it happened** so quando è successo; **since ~ do you like Indian food?** da quando (in qua) ti piacciono i cibi indiani?; **say ~!** dimmi quando basta!

2 *conj* (**a**) *(at, during or after the time that)*

quando; ~ **I came in** quando sono entrato; ~ **you've read it** quando l'hai letto; **be careful ~ you cross the road** *or* ~ **crossing the road** stai attento quando attraversi la strada; **even ~** anche quando; ~ **it's finished, it will measure...** quando sarà finito misurerà...; **why walk ~ you can take a bus?** perché camminare se puoi andare in autobus?.

(**b**) *(the time that)*: **that was ~ I needed you** era allora che avevo bisogno di te; **now is ~ I need you** è adesso che ho bisogno di te; **that's ~ the train arrives** il treno arriva a quell'ora; **she told me about ~ she was in Milan** mi parlò di quando era a Milano.

(**c**) *(rel: on or at which)* in cui; **on the day ~** il giorno in cui; **at the very moment ~...** proprio quando...; **in the winter when...** in inverno quando...; **during the time ~ she lived abroad** nel periodo in cui viveva all'estero; **one day ~ it was raining** un giorno che pioveva.

whence [wɛns] *adv (poet: from where)* da dove.

when·ever [wɛn'ɛvəʳ] **1** *conj (rel: at whatever time)* quando, in qualsiasi momento + *sub*; *(: each time)* quando, ogni volta che; **come ~ you like** vieni quando vuoi; **leave ~ it suits you** parti quando ti fa comodo *or* in qualsiasi momento ti faccia comodo; **I go ~ I can** ci vado ogni volta che posso; ~ **you see one of those, stop** fermati quando ne vedi uno. (**b**) *(in questions)*: ~ **did I say that?** quando mai l'ho detto? **2** *adv*: **tomorrow or ~** domani o in qualsiasi momento.

where [wɛəʳ] **1** *adv* (**a**) *(gen)* dove; **there's a cinema ~ the butcher's used to be** dove c'era la macelleria c'è adesso un cinema; ~ **possible** quando è possibile, se possibile; **from ~ I am** da dove sono; so **that's ~ they've got to!** ecco dove erano finiti!; **this is ~ we found it** è qui che l'abbiamo trovato; **that's ~ we got to in the last lesson** è lì dove siamo arrivati nell'ultima lezione; **that's just ~ you're wrong!** è proprio lì che ti sbagli!; **she walked ~ she could have had a lift** ha camminato anche se avrebbe potuto avere un passaggio. (**b**) *(rel: in, on, at which)* dove, in (*or* da, su *etc*) cui; **the town ~ we come from** la città da cui veniamo; **the house ~ I was born** la casa in cui sono nato; **the hill ~ the heather grows** la collina dove *or* su cui cresce l'erica.

where·abouts [ˌwɛərə'bauts] **1** *adv* dove; ~ **did you say you lived?** da che parti hai detto che abiti? **2** *npl*: **to know sb's ~** sapere dove si trova qn.

where·as [wɛər'æz] *conj (on the other hand)* mentre; *(Law)* considerato che.

where·by [wɛə'bai] *adv* per cui.

where·upon [ˌwɛərə'pɒn] *adv* al che.

wher·ever [wɛər'ɛvəʳ] **1** *conj* dovunque + *sub*; ~ **you go I'll go too** dovunque tu vada ci verrò anch'io; ~ **they went they were cheered** venivano acclamati dovunque andassero; **Udine, ~ that is** Udine, dovunque questo posto sia; **sit ~ you like** siediti dove vuoi. **2** *adv* (**a**): **in Naples, Florence, or ~** a Napoli, Firenze o in qualsiasi altro posto. (**b**) *(in questions)* dove; ~ **did he put it?** dove (mai) l'ha messo?

where·with·al [ˈwɛəwɪðɔːl] *n*: **the ~** (**to do sth**) i mezzi (per fare qc).

whet [wɛt] *vt (tool)* affilare; *(appetite, curiosity)* stimolare.

wheth·er [ˈwɛðəʳ] *conj (if)* se; *(no matter ~)* che + *sub*; ~ **you want to or not** che tu la voglia o no; ~ **it's sunny or not** che ci sia il sole o no; **I am not certain ~ he'll come (or not)** non so con certezza se verrà (o no), non sono sicuro che venga; ~ **they come or not** che vengano o meno; **I don't know ~ you know...** non so se lo sai...; **I doubt ~ that's true** dubito che sia vero.

whew [hwuː] *excl* uh!

whey [wei] *n* siero.

which [wɪtʃ] **1** *adj* (**a**) *(interrog)* quale; ~ **pen/book do you want?** quale penna/libro vuoi?; **she didn't say ~ books she wanted** non ha detto quali libri voleva; ~ **books are yours?** quali libri sono i tuoi?; ~ **one/ones do you want?** quale/quali vuoi?; ~ **way did she go?** da che parte è andata? (**b**): **in ~ case** nel qual caso; **he lived in Italy for a year, during ~ time...** ha vissuto in Italia per un anno, periodo in cui...; **by ~ time** e a quel punto.

2 *pron* (**a**) *(interrog, the one or ones that)* quale; ~ **of these are yours?** quali di questi sono tuoi?; ~ **do you want?** quale vuoi?; ~ **of your sisters?** quale delle tue sorelle?; ~ **of you?** chi di voi?; **I can't tell ~** is non riesco a distinguere l'uno dall'altro; **I know ~ I'd rather have** so quale preferirei; **I don't mind ~** non importa quale. (**b**) *(rel: that)* che; *(: indirect)* cui, il(la) quale; **the apple (~)** you ate la mela che hai mangiato; **the apple ~ is on the table** la mela che è sul tavolo; **the meeting (~)** we attended la riunione (a) cui abbiamo partecipato; **the hotel at ~** we stayed l'albergo dove ci siamo fermati; **the chair on ~** la sedia sulla quale *or* su cui; **the book of ~** il libro del quale *or* di cui; **he said he was there,** ~ is true ha detto che c'era, il che è vero; **it rained a lot,** ~ **upset her** ha piovuto tanto e ciò l'ha irritata; **you're late,** ~ **reminds me...** sei in ritardo, il che mi ricorda...; **after ~** dopo di che; **from ~ one can deduce...** dal che si può dedurre... .

which·ever [wɪtʃ'ɛvəʳ] **1** *adj (that one which)* quello(a) che; *(no matter which)* qualsiasi + *sub*, qualunque +*sub*; **take ~ one you prefer** prendi quello che preferisci; **you can choose ~ system you want** puoi scegliere il sistema che vuoi; ~ **system you have there are difficulties** qualsiasi sistema tu abbia ci sono delle difficoltà; ~ **way you look at it** da qualsiasi punto di vista lo consideri. **2** *pron (the one which)* quello(a) che; *(no matter which one)* qualsiasi + *sub*, qualunque + *sub*; ~ **of the methods you choose** qualsiasi metodo tu scelga; **choose ~ you like** scegline uno qualsiasi.

whiff [wɪf] *n (of gas, sth unpleasant)* zaffata; *(of sea air, perfume)* odore *m*; **to catch a ~ of sth** sentire l'odore di qc; **a few ~s of this could knock you out** se annusi un po' di questo svieni.

while [wail] **1** *n* (**a**): **a ~** un po' (di tempo); **for a little ~** per un po'; **for a long ~** per un bel po', a lungo; **after a ~** dopo un po'; **for a ~** per un po', per un certo periodo; **in a ~** tra poco; **once in a ~** ogni tanto, di tanto in tanto; **it will be a good ~ before he gets here** gli ci vorrà un bel po' (di tempo) per arrivare qui; **a little ~ ago** poco fa; **in between ~s** nel frattempo; **all the ~** tutto il tempo. (**b**): **we'll make it worth your ~** faremo in modo che ti valga la pena; **it might be worth your ~ to...** forse ti converrebbe... .

2 *conj* (**a**) *(during the time that)* mentre; *(as long as)* finché, fintantoché, mentre; ~ **this was happening** mentre avveniva questo; **she fell asleep ~ reading** si addormentò mentre stava leggendo; **it won't happen ~ I'm here** non acca-

drà finché sono qui io. **(b)** *(although)* benché +
sub, anche se; ~ **I agree with what you have said**
benché sia d'accordo *or* anche se sono d'accordo
con ciò che hai detto. **(c)** *(whereas)* mentre; **I
enjoy sport,** ~ **he prefers reading** a me piace lo
sport, mentre lui preferisce la lettura.

♦ **while away** *vt + adv (time, hours)* far passare.

whilst [waɪlst] *conj* = **while 2**.

whim [wɪm] *n* capriccio; **a passing** ~ una passione
momentanea; **as the** ~ **takes me** come mi
gira.

whim·per ['wɪmpəʳ] **1** *n (of person)* gemito;
(: whine) piagnucolio; *(of dog)* uggiolio. **2** *vi (see n)*
gemere; piagnucolare; uggiolare.

whim·si·cal ['wɪmzɪkəl] *adj (person)* estroso(a);
(look) curioso(a); *(idea, story)* fantasioso(a); **a** ~
smile un sorrisetto.

whine [waɪn] **1** *n (of dog)* guaito; *(of child)* piagnucolio; *(of engine)* gemito; *(of bullet)* fischio. **2**
vi (dog) guaire; *(child)* piagnucolare; *(engine)*
gemere; *(bullet)* fischiare; *(fig fam: complain)*
piagnucolare, lamentarsi; **don't come whining to
me about it** non venire a piangere da me.

whin·ny ['wɪnɪ] **1** *vi* nitrire. **2** *n* nitrito.

whip [wɪp] **1** *n* **(a)** frusta; *(riding* ~*)* frustino. **(b)**
(Parliament: person) capogruppo; **three-line** ~
ordine *m* tassativo di votare. **(c)** *(Culin)* mousse *f*
inv.

2 *vt* **(a)** frustare; *(Culin: cream etc)* sbattere.
(b) *(fam: move quickly):* **he** ~**ped the book off the
table** tolse rapidamente il libro dal tavolo; **they**
~**ped her into hospital** la portarono d'urgenza
all'ospedale; **he** ~**ped a gun out of his pocket**
estrasse rapidamente una pistola dalla tasca; **the
car** ~**ped round the corner** la macchina
svoltò a gran velocità.

3 *vi:* **she** ~**ped round when she heard me** si
voltò di scatto quando mi sentì.

4 *cpd:* ~ **hand** *n:* **to have the** ~ **hand (over sb)**
avere il predominio (su qn).

♦ **whip up** *vt + adv (cream)* montare, sbattere;
(fam: meal) improvvisare; *(: stir up: support,
feeling)* suscitare, stimolare.

whip·lash ['wɪplæʃ] *n (blow from whip)* frustata;
(Med: also: ~ **injury)** colpo di frusta.

whip·per·snap·per ['wɪpəsnæpəʳ] *n (also:* **young**
~**)** pallone *m* gonfiato.

whip·pet ['wɪpɪt] *n* piccolo levriero inglese.

whip·ping ['wɪpɪŋ] **1** *n:* **to give sb a** ~ fustigare *or*
frustare qn. **2** *cpd:* ~ **boy** *n (fig)* capro espiatorio;
~ **cream** *n* panna da montare.

whip-round ['wɪpraʊnd] *n (fam)* colletta.

whirl [wɜːl] **1** *n (spin)* vortice *m*, turbinio; *(of dust,
water etc)* turbine *m*, vortice; *(of cream)* ricciolo;
my head is in a ~ mi gira la testa; **the social** ~ il
vortice della vita mondana; **let's give it a** ~ *(fam)*
facciamo un tentativo.

2 *vt (also:* ~ **round:** *dance partner)* far roteare,
far volteggiare; **the wind** ~**ed the leaves** il vento
ha sollevato le foglie in un vortice; **he** ~**ed us
round the town** ci ha fatto visitare la città a tutta
velocità *or* in un baleno; **he** ~**ed us off to the
theatre** ci trascinò con sé al teatro.

3 *vi (also:* ~ **round:** *wheel, merry-go-round)* girare; *(: dancers)* volteggiare; *(: leaves, dust)* sollevarsi in un vortice; **the countryside** ~**ed past
us** la campagna sfilava accanto a noi; **the
dancers** ~**ed past us** i danzatori sono passati
accanto a noi volteggiando; **my head was** ~**ing**
mi girava la testa.

whirl·pool ['wɜːlpuːl] *n* mulinello, vortice *m*.

whirl·wind ['wɜːlwɪnd] **1** *n* tromba d'aria. **2** *cpd*
(romance etc) travolgente.

whirr [wɜːʳ] **1** *n (of insect wings, machine)* ronzio. **2**
vi ronzare.

whisk [wɪsk] **1** *n (Culin: hand* ~*)* frusta; *(: electric*
~*)* frullino; **with a** ~ **of its tail** con un colpo di
coda. **2** *vt* **(a)** *(Culin)* frullare; *(: egg whites)* montare a neve. **(b):** ~ **the eggs into the mixture**
mescolare delicatamente le uova all'impasto;
the horse ~**ed the flies away with its tail** il
cavallo scacciava le mosche con la coda; **the
waiter** ~**ed the dishes away** il cameriere tolse in
fretta i piatti; **they** ~**ed him off to a meeting** lo
trascinarono in fretta a una riunione.

whisk·ers ['wɪskəz] *npl (side* ~*)* favoriti *mpl,* basette *fpl; (beard)* barba; *(moustache, of animal)*
baffi *mpl.*

whis·ky, *(Am, Ir)* **whis·key** ['wɪskɪ] *n* whisky *m
inv.*

whis·per ['wɪspəʳ] **1** *n* **(a)** *(gen)* bisbiglio, sussurro;
(of leaves) fruscio, stormire *m;* **to speak in a** ~
bisbigliare. **(b)** *(rumour)* voce *f.* **2** *vt* bisbigliare,
sussurrare; **to** ~ **sth to sb** bisbigliare qc a qn. **3** *vi*
(gen) bisbigliare; *(leaves)* frusciare, stormire; **to**
~ **to sb** bisbigliare a qn.

whis·per·ing ['wɪspərɪŋ] **1** *n* bisbiglio; *(of leaves)*
fruscio; **there's been a lot of** ~ **about her** sono
corse voci sul suo conto. **2** *cpd:* ~ **campaign** *n*
campagna diffamatoria; ~ **gallery** *n* galleria
acustica.

whist [wɪst] *n* whist *m.*

whis·tle ['wɪsl] **1** *n (sound)* fischio; *(instrument)*
fischietto; **the referee blew his** ~ l'arbitro fischiò; **the police searched him, but he was as
clean as a** ~ la polizia lo ha perquisito ma lui era
pulito; **the handle broke off as clean as a** ~ la
maniglia si è staccata di netto; **to blow the** ~ **on**
(inform on) vendere. **2** *vt:* **to** ~ **a tune** fischiettare
un motivetto. **3** *vi (gen)* fischiare; *(in low tone)*
fischiettare; **he** ~**d for a taxi** fischiò per fermare un taxi; **the referee** ~**d for a foul** l'arbitro
fischiò un fallo; **the bullet** ~**d past my ear** la
pallottola mi fischiò vicino all'orecchio; **he's
whistling in the dark** *(fig)* lo fa *(or* dice) per darsi
coraggio.

whistle-stop ['wɪslstɒp] *adj:* ~ **tour** *(Am Pol, fig)*
rapido giro.

Whit [wɪt] **1** *n* Pentecoste *f.* **2** *cpd (holiday, weekend)*
di Pentecoste; ~ **Monday** *n* lunedì *m inv* di Pentecoste.

whit [wɪt] *n:* **not a** ~ neanche un po'; **not a** ~ **of
truth** neanche un briciolo di verità.

white [waɪt] **1** *adj (gen)* bianco(a); **to turn** *or* **go** ~
(person) sbiancare; *(hair)* diventare bianco; **a** ~
man un bianco; **the big** ~ **hope** *(fig)* la grande
promessa; **to be as** ~ **as a sheet** essere bianco
come un lenzuolo.

2 *n* **(a)** *(colour, of eyes)* bianco; *(of egg)* bianco,
albume *m;* **the** ~**s** *(washing)* i capi bianchi; **tennis**
~**s** completo da tennis. **(b)** *(person)* bianco/a.

3 *cpd:* **a** ~ **Christmas** un Natale con la neve; ~
coffee *n* caffellatte *m inv;* ~ **elephant** *n (fam)*
oggetto *(or* progetto) costoso ma inutile; ~ **horse**
n (on wave) cresta di spuma (dell'onda); **the W~
House** *(Am)* la Casa Bianca; ~ **lie** *n* bugia pietosa; ~ **meat** *n* carne *f* bianca; ~ **paper** *n (Pol)* libro
bianco; ~ **pepper** *n* pepe *m* bianco; ~ **sauce** *n*
besciamella; ~ **spirit** *n* acquaragia (sintetica); ~
wedding *n* matrimonio in bianco; ~ **wine** *n*
vino bianco.

white·bait ['waɪtbeɪt] *n* bianchetti *mpl.*

white-collar ['waɪtˌkɒləʳ] *adj:* ~ **worker** colletto
bianco.

white-haired [ˌwaɪt'heəd] *adj* canuto(a), dai capelli bianchi.

white-hot [ˌwaɪt'hɒt] *adj (metal)* incandescente.

white-ness ['waɪtnɪs] *n (gen)* bianco; *(of skin)* candore *m; (pallor)* biancore *m.*

whit-en-ing ['waɪtnɪŋ] *n (substance)* bianchetto.

white-wash ['waɪtwɒʃ] **1** *n* bianco di calce. **2** *vt (wall)* imbiancare (con il bianco di calce); *(fig: person, sb's faults)* coprire; *(: motives)* dissimulare; *(: event, episode)* raccontare in modo da sminuire.

whith-er ['wɪðəʳ] *adv (poet)* dove.

whit-ing ['waɪtɪŋ] *n (fish)* merlango.

whit-ish ['waɪtɪʃ] *adj* biancastro(a), bianchiccio(a).

whit-low ['wɪtləʊ] *n* patereccio.

Whit-sun ['wɪtsən] *n* Pentecoste *f.*

whit-tle ['wɪtl] *vt (wood)* intagliare.

♦ **whittle away** *vt + adv (fig)* ridurre.

♦ **whittle down** *vt + adv (fig)* ridurre, tagliare.

whiz(z) [wɪz] **1** *vi (motorbike, sledge etc)* sfrecciare; *(bullet)* sibilare; **cars were ~ing past** le macchine passavano sfrecciando. **2** *cpd:* ~ **kid** *n (fam)* prodigio.

WHO *n (abbr of World Health Organization)* O.M.S.

who [huː] *pron* **(a)** *(interrog: si può anche usare al posto di 'whom' nella lingua parlata)* chi; ~ **is it?, ~'s there?** chi è?; **I know ~ it was** so chi è stato; ~ **are you looking for?** chi stai cercando?; ~'**s the book by?** chi ha scritto il libro?; ~ **does she think she is?** *(fam)* chi si crede di essere?; **you'll soon find out ~'s ~** presto li conoscerai; ~ **should it be but Neil!** chi poteva essere se non Neil! **(b)** *(rel)* che; **my cousin ~ lives in New York** mio cugino che vive a New York; **those ~ can swim** quelli che sanno nuotare, chi sa nuotare.

who'd [huːd] = **who would; who had.**

who-dun-it [huː'dʌnɪt] *n (fam)* (romanzo) giallo.

who-ever [huː'evəʳ] *pron* **(a)** *(the person that, anyone that)* chiunque *+ sub*, chi; *(no matter who)* chiunque *+ sub*; ~ **said that was an idiot** chiunque l'abbia detto *or* chi l'ha detto è un idiota; ~ **finds it** chiunque lo trovi; **ask ~ you like** chiedi a chiunque; **it won't be easy, ~ does it** non sarà facile, chiunque lo faccia; ~ **she marries** chiunque sposerà, non importa chi sposerà. **(b)** *(in questions)* chi (mai); ~ **told you that?** chi (mai) te l'ha detto?

whole [həʊl] **1** *adj* **(a)** *(entire: + sg n)* intero(a), tutto(a); *(: + pl n)* intero(a); **with my ~ heart** con tutto il mio cuore; **a ~ lot of things** una gran quantità di cose, moltissime cose; **a ~ lot of people** moltissima gente; **a ~ lot better** molto meglio; **the ~ lot** tutto; **3 ~ days** 3 giorni interi; **the ~ day** tutto il giorno, il giorno intero; **I read the ~ book** ho letto tutto il libro *or* il libro per intero; **the ~ world** tutto il mondo, il mondo intero; ~ **villages were destroyed** interi paesi furono distrutti; **is that the ~ truth?** è tutta la *or* l'intera verità?; **but the ~ purpose** *or* **point was to...** ma il vero scopo era di.... **(b)** *(intact, unbroken)* intero(a); *(: series, set)* completo(a); **to swallow sth ~** mandar giù qc intero; *(fig)*: **he swallowed it ~** l'ha bevuta tutta; **to our surprise he came back ~** con nostra sorpresa tornò sano e salvo.

2 *n* **(a)** *(all):* **the ~ of the film** tutto il film, il film intero; **the ~ of the sum** la somma intera, l'intera somma; **the ~ of the time** tutto il tempo; **the ~ of Italy** tutta l'Italia, l'Italia intera; **as a ~** nel suo insieme; **on the ~** nel complesso. **(b)** *(entire unit)* tutto; **they make a ~** formano un tutto; **2 halves make a ~** 2 metà fanno un intero.

3 *cpd:* ~ **milk** *n* latte *m* intero; ~ **note** *n (Am Mus)* semibreve *f.*

whole-hearted [ˌhəʊl'hɑːtɪd] *adj (approval, agreement)* incondizionato(a), totale; *(thanks, congratulations)* sentito(a); **to be ~ in sth** fare qc di tutto cuore.

whole-meal ['həʊlmiːl] *adj (flour, bread)* integrale.

whole-sale ['həʊlseɪl] **1** *adj (prices, trade)* all'ingrosso; *(fig: slaughter, destruction)* in massa; *(acceptance)* in blocco; *(campaign)* su vasta scala; **his work came in for ~ criticism** il suo lavoro è stato criticato in blocco. **2** *adv (see adj)* all'ingrosso; in massa; in blocco; su vasta scala.

whole-sal-er ['həʊlˌseɪləʳ] *n* grossista *m/f.*

whole-some ['həʊlsəm] *adj (gen)* sano(a); *(climate)* salubre.

who'll [huːl] = **who will.**

whol-ly ['həʊlɪ] *adv* completamente.

whom [huːm] *pron* **(a)** *(spesso sostituito da 'who' nella lingua parlata: interrog)* chi; ~ **did you see?** chi hai visto?; **from ~ did you receive it?** da chi l'hai ricevuto? **(b)** *(rel: direct object)* che; *(: indirect)* cui; **the man ~ I saw** l'uomo che ho visto; **those to ~ I spoke** le persone con le quali ho parlato; **the lady with ~ I was talking** la signora con cui stavo parlando; **three policemen, none of ~ wore a helmet** tre poliziotti, nessuno dei quali portava il casco.

whoop [huːp] **1** *n* grido. **2** *vi* gridare; *(Med: when coughing)* tossire in modo convulso.

whoop-ing cough ['huːpɪŋkɒf] *n* pertosse *f.*

whoosh [wʊʃ] *n:* **it came out with a ~** *(sauce etc)* è uscito di getto; *(air)* è uscito con un sibilo.

whop-per ['wɒpəʳ] *n (fam: car/parcel etc)* macchina/pacco *etc* enorme; *(: lie)* grossa bugia.

whop-ping ['wɒpɪŋ] *adj (fam: also: ~ great)* enorme.

whore [hɔːʳ] *n (pej)* puttana.

whorl [wɜːl] *n (of shell)* voluta.

who's [huːz] = **who is; who has.**

whose [huːz] **1** *poss pron* di chi; ~ **is this?** di chi è questo?; **I know ~ it is** so di chi è. **2** *poss adj* **(a)** *(interrog)* di chi; ~ **hat/book is this?** di chi è questo cappello/libro?; ~ **daughter are you?** di chi sei figlia?; ~ **fault was it?** di chi era la colpa? **(b)** *(rel)* il(la) cui; **the woman ~ car was stolen** la donna la cui macchina è stata rubata; **the man ~ wife I was talking to** l'uomo alla cui moglie stavo parlando; **those ~ passports I have** quelli di cui ho il passaporto.

who've [huːv] = **who have.**

why [waɪ] **1** *adv, conj* perché; ~ **is he always late?** perché è sempre in ritardo?; **I wonder ~ he said that** mi chiedo perché l'abbia detto; ~ **don't you come too?** perché non vieni anche tu?; **there's no reason ~...** non c'è motivo per cui... *+ sub*; ~ **not?** perché no?; **so that's ~ he did it!** ecco perché l'ha fatto! **2** *excl (surprise)* guarda guarda!, ma guarda un po'!; *(remonstrating)* ma (via)!; *(explaining)* ebbene!; ~, **it's you!** guarda guarda, or ah, sei tu!; ~, **it's obvious!** ma (via), è ovvio! **3** *n:* **the ~s and (the) wherefores** il perché e il percome.

wick [wɪk] *n* stoppino.

wick-ed ['wɪkɪd] *adj (person, remark, smile)* cattivo(a), malvagio(a); *(: mischievous)* malizioso(a); *(satire)* cruento(a); *(system, policy)* iniquo(a); *(fam: price, weather etc)* terribile; **she has a ~ temper** ha un carattere insopportabile; **that was a ~ thing to do** è stata una cattiveria; **a ~ blow** un brutto *or* duro colpo; **a ~ sense of humour** un perfido senso dell'umorismo.

wick-ed-ness ['wɪkɪdnɪs] *n (see adj)* cattiveria,

malvagità; malizia; crudezza; iniquità.

wick·er ['wɪkə^r] **1** n vimine m. **2** adj di vimini.

wicker·work ['wɪkəwɜːk] n oggetti mpl di vimini.

wick·et ['wɪkɪt] (Cricket) **1** n porta. **2** cpd: ~ **keeper** n ≃ portiere m.

wide [waɪd] **1** adj (gen) largo(a); (survey, study, margin) ampio(a); (ocean, desert) vasto(a); (fig: considerable: variety, choice) grande; **it is 3 metres** ~ è largo 3 metri; **his** ~ **knowledge of the subject** la sua profonda conoscenza dell'argomento; **in the whole** ~ **world** nel mondo intero, in tutto il mondo; **the** ~ **screen** il grande schermo. **2** adv (aim, fall) lontano dal bersaglio; **set** ~ **apart** (houses, eyes) ben distanziati; (legs) divaricati; **to be** ~ **open** (door etc) essere spalancato; **to be** ~ **open to criticism/attack** essere aperto alle critiche/all'attacco; **the ball went** ~ la palla è passata di fianco alla porta.

wide-angle ['waɪdˌæŋgl] adj (lens etc) grandangolare.

wide-awake [ˌwaɪdə'weɪk] adj completamente sveglio(a); (fig) sveglio(a).

wide-eyed [ˌwaɪd'aɪd] adj con gli occhi spalancati.

wide·ly ['waɪdlɪ] adv (spread) largamente; (read etc) molto; (travel) in lungo e in largo; (differing) molto, profondamente; (popularly, by many people) generalmente; **to be** ~ **read** (author) essere molto letto; (reader) essere molto colto; **it is** ~ **believed that** è una credenza diffusa che; **to be** ~ **spaced** (houses, trees) essere molto distanziati.

wid·en ['waɪdn] **1** vt (also fig) ampliare, allargare. **2** vi (also: ~ **out**) ampliarsi.

wide-ranging [ˌwaɪd'reɪndʒɪŋ] adj (survey, report) vasto(a); (interests) svariato(a).

wide·spread ['waɪdspred] adj (disease, belief) diffuso(a); (wings, arms) spalancato(a); **there is** ~ **fear that...** c'è una paura diffusa che... .

wid·ow ['wɪdəʊ] **1** n vedova; **to be left a** ~ restare vedova; **she is a golf** ~ suo marito la lascia per andare a giocare a golf. **2** vt: **to be** ~**ed** restare vedovo(a).

wid·ow·er ['wɪdəʊə^r] n vedovo.

width [wɪdθ] n (see adj) larghezza; ampiezza; vastità; (of fabric) altezza; **it's 7 metres in** ~ è largo 7 metri.

width·ways ['wɪdθwaɪz] adv trasversalmente.

wield [wiːld] vt (sword, axe) maneggiare; (: brandish) brandire; (power, influence) esercitare.

wife [waɪf] n, pl **wives** moglie f; **the** ~ (fam) la padrona; **it's just an old wives' tale** è solo una storiella.

wife·ly ['waɪflɪ] adj coniugale, di moglie.

wig [wɪg] n parrucca.

wig·gle ['wɪgl] **1** n: **with a** ~ **of her hips** ancheggiando. **2** vt (fingers, loose tooth) muovere; **to** ~ **one's hips** ancheggiare. **3** vi (person) dimenarsi, agitarsi; (worm) agitarsi, muoversi; (tooth, screw) traballare.

wig·gly ['wɪglɪ] adj (line) ondulato(a), sinuoso(a).

wig·wam ['wɪgwæm] n wigwam m inv.

wild [waɪld] **1** adj **(a)** (not domesticated: animal, plant) selvatico(a); (countryside) selvaggio(a); **in its** ~ **state** allo stato selvatico; **to grow** ~ (plant) crescere allo stato selvatico; ~ **horses wouldn't make me tell you** (fig) non riuscirai a cavarmelo neanche con la forza; **to sow one's** ~ **oats** (fig) correre la cavallina.

(b) (rough: wind, weather) violento(a); (sea, night) tempestoso(a).

(c) (unrestrained, disorderly: child) sfrenato(a), turbolento(a); (appearance, look) selvaggio(a); (eyes) sbarrato(a); (hair) disordinato(a);

to lead a ~ **life** avere una vita disordinata; **to run** ~ (children) scatenarsi.

(d) (fam: angry) arrabbiato(a), furibondo(a); (: enthusiastic): **to be** ~ **about** andar pazzo(a) per; ~ **with indignation** assolutamente indignato; **to be** ~ **with joy** essere pazzo di gioia; **it makes me** ~ mi fa infuriare; **I'm not** ~ **about the idea** non sono entusiasta dell'idea; **to go** ~ (dog etc) agitarsi come un pazzo; (person): **to go** ~ (**with**) non stare più in sé (da); **the audience went** ~ la folla era in delirio.

(e) (rash, extravagant) folle; (: laughter) sguaiato(a); (erratic: shot, guess) azzardato(a); **it's a** ~ **exaggeration** è una grossa esagerazione; **you've let your imagination run** ~ hai lavorato troppo di fantasia.

2 n: **the** ~ la natura; **to live out in the** ~**s** (hum) vivere a casa del diavolo.

3 cpd: ~ **goose chase** n ricerca inutile; **W~ West** n selvaggio Ovest.

wild·cat ['waɪldkæt] **1** n gatto(a) selvatico(a). **2** cpd: ~ **strike** n ≃ sciopero selvaggio.

wil·der·ness ['wɪldənɪs] n (gen) deserto; (neglected garden) giungla.

wild·fire ['waɪldfaɪə^r] n: **to spread like** ~ propagarsi rapidamente.

wild·life ['waɪldlaɪf] **1** n natura, flora e fauna. **2** cpd (sanctuary, reserve) naturale.

wild·ly ['waɪldlɪ] adv (gen) violentemente; (behave, talk) in modo sfrenato; (rush around) come un pazzo; (exaggerate) largamente; (applaud, cheer) freneticamente; **to guess** ~ tirare a indovinare; ~ **happy/enthusiastic** terribilmente felice/entusiasta; **her heart was beating** ~ il cuore le batteva forte.

wild·ness ['waɪldnɪs] n (gen) violenza; (of countryside, scenery) aspetto selvaggio; (of the weather) avversità; **the** ~ **of his appearance** il suo aspetto selvaggio; **the** ~ **of her imagination** la sua fantasia sfrenata.

wiles [waɪlz] npl astuzie fpl.

wil·ful, (Am) **will·ful** ['wɪlfʊl] adj (self-willed) testardo(a); (deliberate) intenzionale.

wil·ful·ly, (Am) **will·ful·ly** ['wɪlfəlɪ] adv (see adj) testardamente; intenzionalmente.

will¹ [wɪl] (pt **would**) **1** modal aux vb **(a)** (forming future tense): **I** ~ **finish it tomorrow** lo finirò domani; **I** ~ **have finished it by tomorrow** lo finirò entro domani; **you won't lose it,** ~ **you?** non lo perderai, vero?; ~ **you do it?** — **yes, I** ~/**no, I won't** lo farai? — sì (lo farò)/no (non lo farò).

(b) (in conjectures): **he** ~ or **he'll be there by now** dovrebbe essere arrivato a questo punto; **that** ~ **be the postman** sarà il postino.

(c) (in commands, requests, offers): ~ **you be quiet!** vuoi stare tranquillo?; **I won't go — oh yes you** ~, **my lad!** non ci andrò — oh, sì che ci andrai, ragazzo mio!; ~ **you come?** vieni anche tu?; ~ **you be there?** ci sarai anche tu?; ~ **you help me?** mi puoi aiutare?; ~ **you have a cup of tea?** vorresti una tazza di tè?; ~ **you sit down** (politely) prego, si accomodi; (angrily) vuoi metterti seduto!; **won't you come with us?** non vuoi venire con noi?; **I will not** or **won't put up with it!** io non lo accetterò!

(d) (expressing habits, persistence, capability): **he** ~ **often sit there for hours** spesso rimane seduto lì per ore; **the car won't start** la macchina non parte; **the car** ~ **do 100 mph** la macchina fa 100 miglia all'ora; **accidents** ~ **happen** gli incidenti possono capitare; **he** WILL **fidget!** continua a muoversi!

2 vi (wish) volere; (just) as you ~! come vuoi!; say what you ~ di' quello che vuoi.

will² [wɪl] **1** n (a) volontà; to have a ~ of one's own avere una volontà indipendente; to do sth of one's own free ~ fare qc di propria volontà; the ~ to win/live la voglia di vincere/vivere; against sb's ~ contro la volontà or il volere di qn; at ~ a volontà; to work with a ~ lavorare di buona lena; with the best ~ in the world con tutta la più buona volontà del mondo; where there's a ~ there's a way volere è potere. (b) (testament) testamento; the last ~ and testament of le ultime volontà di; to make a ~ fare testamento.

2 vt (a) (urge on by willpower): to ~ sb to do sth pregare (tra sé) perché qn faccia qc; he ~ed himself to stay awake si costrinse a restare sveglio. (b) (leave in one's ~): to ~ sth to sb lasciare qc a qn in eredità.

will·ing ['wɪlɪŋ] **1** adj (a) (obedience, help) spontaneo(a); (helper, worker) volenteroso(a); he's very ~ è pieno di buona volontà; there were plenty of ~ hands erano tutti pronti ad aiutare. (b): to be ~ (to do sth) essere disposto(a) (a fare qc); he wasn't very ~ to help me non aveva una gran voglia di aiutarmi; God ~ se Dio vuole. **2** n: to show ~ dare prova di buona volontà.

will·ing·ly ['wɪlɪŋlɪ] adv volentieri.

will·ing·ness ['wɪlɪŋnɪs] n disponibilità; I don't doubt it ~ non metto in dubbio la sua buona volontà.

will-o'-the-wisp [,wɪləðə'wɪsp] n (also fig) fuoco fatuo.

wil·low ['wɪləʊ] **1** n (also: ~ tree) salice m. **2** cpd: ~ pattern n motivo cinese (in blu su ceramica bianca).

wil·lowy ['wɪləʊɪ] adj slanciato(a).

will·power ['wɪl,paʊəʳ] n forza di volontà.

willy-nilly ['wɪlɪ'nɪlɪ] adv volente o nolente.

wilt [wɪlt] vi (flower) appassire; (fig: person) cominciare a crollare; (: effort, enthusiasm) diminuire.

wily ['waɪlɪ] adj (-ier, -iest) astuto(a).

win [wɪn] (vb: pt, pp won) **1** n (Sport etc) vittoria; their fifth ~ in a row la loro quinta vittoria di seguito. **2** vt (race, cup, prize etc) vincere; (victory) conquistare, aggiudicarsi; (sympathy, support, friendship) conquistare, ottenere; (person) accattivarsi; (contract) aggiudicarsi; I won £10 from him gli ho vinto 10 sterline; to ~ sb's favour/heart conquistare il favore/cuore di qn; she won it at tennis l'ha vinto a tennis; it won him first prize gli ha valso il primo premio; to ~ the day (Mil, fig) avere il sopravvento. **3** vi vincere; O.K., you ~ (fam) bene, ti do ragione.

♦ **win back** vt + adv riconquistare.

♦ **win over, win round** vt + adv convincere; we won him over to our point of view l'abbiamo convinto ad accettare il nostro punto di vista.

♦ **win out, win through** vi + adv uscirne vittorioso(a).

wince [wɪns] **1** n: to give a ~ rabbrividire; (grimace) fare una smorfia. **2** vi rabbrividire; (grimace) fare una smorfia; he ~d at the thought rabbrividì al pensiero.

winch [wɪntʃ] **1** n argano. **2** vt: to ~ up/down sollevare/abbassare con un argano.

wind¹ [wɪnd] **1** n (a) vento; high ~ vento forte; the ~ is in the west il vento viene da ovest; into or against the ~ controvento; to go like the ~ filare come il vento; to run before the ~ (Naut) andare con il vento in poppa; there's something in the ~ (fig) c'è qualcosa nell'aria; to get ~ of sth venire a sapere qc; to get or have the ~ up (fam) agitarsi; to take the ~ out of sb's sails smontare qn; to

sail close to the ~ (fig) spingere le cose troppo in là; (act almost illegally) rasentare l'illegalità; (blue joke) rasentare la volgarità; to throw caution to the ~s disdegnare ogni prudenza. (b) (Med) flatulenza; to break ~ scoreggiare (fam); to bring up ~ (baby) fare il ruttino. (c) (breath) respiro, fiato; to get one's ~ back or one's second ~ riprendere fiato; to be short of ~ essere senza fiato. (d) (Mus): the ~(s) i fiati.

2 vt: to ~ sb (with punch etc) mozzare il fiato a qn; to ~ a baby far fare il ruttino a un bambino.

3 cpd: ~ erosion n erosione f del vento; ~ instrument n (Mus) strumento a fiato; ~ tunnel n galleria aerodinamica or del vento.

wind² [waɪnd] pt, pp wound **1** vt (a) (roll, coil) avvolgere, arrotolare; to ~ sth into a ball aggomitolare qc; to ~ one's way home avviarsi verso casa. (b) (clock, watch, toy) caricare; (key, handle) girare. **2** vi (also: ~ its way: river, path) serpeggiare; (procession) percorrere.

♦ **wind down** vt + adv (car window) abbassare; (fig: production, business) diminuire.

♦ **wind in** vt + adv (fishing line etc) riavvolgere.

♦ **wind on** vt + adv (film) avanzare.

♦ **wind up 1** vt + adv (a) (car window) alzare; (clock, toy) caricare; to ~ sb up (fig fam) innervosire or far venire i nervi a qn. (b) (close: meeting, debate) concludere, chiudere; (: company) chiudere. **2** vi + adv (meeting, debate) concludersi; (fam: end up) finire; we wound up in Rome siamo finiti a Roma.

wind·bag ['wɪndbæg] n (fam: person) chiacchierone/a.

wind·break ['wɪndbreɪk] n frangivento.

wind·cheater ['wɪnd,tʃiːtəʳ] n giacca a vento.

wind·er ['waɪndəʳ] n (on watch) corona di carica.

wind·fall ['wɪndfɔːl] n (apple etc) frutto abbattuto dal vento; (fig) bella sorpresa.

wind·ing ['waɪndɪŋ] adj (road, path) serpeggiante, tortuoso(a).

wind·lass ['wɪndləs] n argano, verricello.

wind·less ['wɪndlɪs] adj senza vento.

wind·mill ['wɪndmɪl] n mulino a vento.

win·dow ['wɪndəʊ] **1** n (gen) finestra; (of car) finestrino; (~ pane) vetro; (stained glass ~) vetrata; (shop ~) vetrina; (of booking office etc) sportello; (in envelope) finestrella; to break a ~ rompere un vetro; to clean the ~s pulire i vetri; to look out of the ~ guardare fuori della finestra.

2 cpd: ~ box n cassetta per i fiori; ~ cleaner n persona che pulisce le finestre; ~ dressing n (Comm) allestimento della vetrina; (fig) fumo negli occhi; ~ ledge n davanzale m; ~ seat n (in house) panchetta fissa vicino alla finestra; (in train) posto vicino al finestrino.

window-shopping ['wɪndəʊ,ʃɒpɪŋ] n: to go ~ andare a vedere le vetrine.

window·sill ['wɪndəʊsɪl] n davanzale m.

wind·pipe ['wɪndpaɪp] n trachea.

wind·screen ['wɪndskriːn], (Am) **wind·shield** ['wɪndʃiːld] **1** n parabrezza m inv. **2** cpd: ~ wiper n tergicristallo.

wind·sock ['wɪndsɒk] n manica a vento.

wind·swept ['wɪndswept] adj (landscape) ventoso(a); (square) spazzato(a) dal vento; (person) scompigliato(a) per il vento.

windy ['wɪndɪ] adj (-ier, -iest) (a) ventoso(a); it's ~ c'è vento. (b) (fam: afraid, nervous): ~ (about) teso(a) (per), nervoso(a) (per).

wine [waɪn] **1** n vino. **2** vt: to ~ and dine sb offrire un ottimo pranzo a qn. **3** cpd (bottle) per il vino; (vinegar, merchant) di vino; ~ cellar n cantina; ~ list n lista dei vini; ~ tasting n degustazione f dei vini; ~ **waiter** n sommelier m inv.

wine·glass ['waɪnglɑːs] n bicchiere m da vino.

wing [wɪŋ] 1 n **(a)** (gen, also Sport, Archit) ala; (Brit Aut) fiancata; **to take sb under one's** ~ prendere qn sotto l'ala; **the left** ~ **of the Conservative Party** la sinistra del Partito Conservatore. **(b)**: ~s (Theatre) quinte fpl. 2 cpd: ~ **mirror** n specchietto retrovisore esterno; ~ **nut** n galletto.

wing·er ['wɪŋəʳ] n (Sport) ala.

wing·span ['wɪŋspæn] n, **wing·spread** ['wɪŋspred] n apertura alare, apertura d'ali.

wink [wɪŋk] 1 n (blink) strizzata d'occhi; (meaningful) occhiolino, strizzatina d'occhi; **to give sb a** ~ ammiccare or fare l'occhiolino a qn; **in a** ~ in un baleno; **I didn't sleep a** ~ non ho chiuso occhio. 2 vi (meaningfully): **to** ~ **(at sb)** fare l'occhiolino (a qn), ammiccare (a qn); (blink) strizzare gli occhi; (light, star etc) baluginare.

win·kle ['wɪŋkl] 1 n litorina. 2 vt: **to** ~ **a secret out of sb** carpire un segreto a qn.

win·ner ['wɪnəʳ] n (gen) vincitore/trice; **to pick a** ~ (horse) scegliere il cavallo vincente; (gen) fare un affare; **it's a** ~! (fam) è eccezionale!

win·ning ['wɪnɪŋ] 1 adj **(a)** (gen) vincente; (hit, shot) decisivo(a); ~ **post** traguardo. **(b)** (charming) affascinante. 2: ~s npl vincite fpl.

win·ter ['wɪntəʳ] 1 n inverno; **in** ~ d'inverno; **the** ~ **of 1981** l'inverno 1981; **it's** ~ è inverno. 2 adj (clothes, weather, day) invernale, d'inverno; ~ **sports** sport mpl invernali.

winter·time ['wɪntətaɪm] n inverno, stagione f invernale.

win·try, win·tery ['wɪntrɪ] adj invernale; (fig: look) freddo(a).

wipe [waɪp] 1 n pulita, passata; **to give sth a** ~ dare una pulita or una passata a qc. 2 vt (gen) pulire; (blackboard) cancellare; **to** ~ **one's eyes** asciugare gli occhi; **to** ~ **one's nose** soffiare il naso; **to** ~ **one's feet** or **shoes** pulirsi i piedi; **to** ~ **one's bottom** pulirsi il sedere; **to** ~ **the dishes** asciugare i piatti; **to** ~ **sth dry** asciugare qc; **to** ~ **the floor with sb** (fig fam) schiacciare qn.

♦ **wipe away** vt + adv (marks) togliere; (tears) asciugare.

♦ **wipe off** vt + adv cancellare; (stains) togliere (strofinando).

♦ **wipe out** vt + adv **(a)** (erase: writing, memory, debt) cancellare. **(b)** (destroy: town, race, enemy) distruggere.

♦ **wipe up** vi + adv (dry dishes) asciugare i piatti. 2 vt + adv asciugare.

wip·er ['waɪpəʳ] n tergicristallo.

wire ['waɪəʳ] 1 n **(a)** (Elec) filo di ferro; (Elec) filo (elettrico); **to get one's ~s crossed** (fam) fraintendersi. **(b)** (telegram) telegramma m. 2 vt **(a)** (Elec: house) fare l'impianto elettrico di; (: circuit) installare; **to** ~ **a room for sound** installare un impianto di sonorizzazione in una stanza. **(b)** (Telec) telegrafare. **(c):** **to** ~ **sth to sth** (tie) attaccare qc a qc con un filo. 3 cpd: ~ **cutters** npl tronchese m or f; ~ **netting** n rete f metallica.

wire·less ['waɪəlɪs] 1 n (also: ~ **set**) radio f inv. 2 cpd (station, programme) radiofonico(a).

wire-tapping ['waɪə,tæpɪŋ] n intercettazione f telefonica.

wir·ing ['waɪərɪŋ] n (Elec) impianto elettrico.

wiry ['waɪərɪ] adj (-ier, -iest) (person) magro(a) e forte; (animal) vigoroso(a); (hair) ispido(a).

wis·dom ['wɪzdəm] 1 n (of person) saggezza; (of remark, action) prudenza. 2 cpd: ~ **tooth** n dente m del giudizio.

wise [waɪz] 1 adj (-r, -st) (gen, person) saggio(a); (: learned) sapiente; (prudent: advice, remark)

prudente; **a** ~ **man** un saggio; **the Three W~ Men** i tre Re Magi; **to be** ~ **after the event** giudicare a posteriori; **it was** ~ **of you not to do that** sei stato saggio a non farlo; **I'm none the** ~r ne so come prima; **to get** ~ **to sb/sth** (fam) imparare a conoscere qn/qc; **to put sb** ~ **to sb/sth** (fam) mettere qn al corrente su qn/qc. 2 cpd: ~ **guy** n (fam) saputello/a, sapientone/a.

wise·crack ['waɪzkræk] n (fam) battuta, spiritosaggine f.

wise·ly ['waɪzlɪ] adv (decide) saggiamente; (nod, smile) con aria saggia.

wish [wɪʃ] 1 n **(a)** desiderio; **I had no** ~ **to upset you** non avevo nessun'intenzione di farti star male; **to go against sb's** ~es andare contro il volere di qn; **I'll grant you 3** ~es ti concedo di esprimere 3 desideri; **you shall have your** ~ realizzerai il tuo desiderio; **to make a** ~ esprimere un desiderio. **(b):** **best** ~es (in greetings) tanti auguri; **with best** ~es con i migliori auguri.

2 vt **(a)** (want) volere, desiderare; **to** ~ **sb to do sth** volere che qn faccia qc; **to** ~ **to do sth** voler fare qc; **I** ~ **he'd shut up** (fam) vorrei che stesse zitto; **I** ~ **I'd gone too** vorrei esserci andato anch'io; **I** ~ **I could!** mi piacerebbe!, magari potessi! **(b)** (foist): **to** ~ **sb on sb** appioppare or affibbiare qn a qn; **to** ~ **sth on sb** rifilare qc a qn. **(c)** (bid, express) augurare; **to** ~ **sb goodbye** dire arrivederci a qn; **to** ~ **sb good luck/a happy Christmas** augurare a qn buona fortuna/buon Natale; **to** ~ **sb well/ill** augurare del bene/male a qn.

3 vi: **to** ~ **for sth** desiderare qc; **she has everything she could** ~ **for** ha tutto ciò che desidera; **what more could you** ~ **for?** cosa vuoi di più?

wish·bone ['wɪʃbəʊn] n (of turkey, chicken etc) forcella.

wish·ful ['wɪʃfʊl] adj: **it's just** ~ **thinking** è solo una pia illusione.

wishy-washy ['wɪʃɪ,wɒʃɪ] adj (fam: colour, person) slavato(a); (: character, argument, ideas) insulso(a).

wisp [wɪsp] n (of straw, smoke) filo; (of hair) ciuffetto.

wist·ful ['wɪstfʊl] adj (look, smile) pieno(a) di rammarico; (: nostalgic) nostalgico(a).

wist·ful·ly ['wɪstfəlɪ] adv (see adj) con occhi pieni di rammarico; nostalgicamente.

wit [wɪt] n **(a)** (understanding) intelligenza; **native** ~ buon senso; **to be at one's** ~'s **end** avere esaurito tutte le risorse, non sapere più che fare; **to have** or **keep one's** ~s **about one** avere presenza di spirito; **use your** ~s! usa il cervello!; **to live by one's** ~s vivere di espedienti; **to collect one's** ~s rimettersi in sesto; **to be frightened** or **scared out of one's** ~s essere spaventato a morte. **(b)** (humour, wittiness) ingegno, arguzia. **(c)** (person) persona arguta, bello spirito.

witch [wɪtʃ] 1 n strega. 2 cpd: ~ **doctor** n stregone m.

witch·craft ['wɪtʃkrɑːft] n stregoneria.

witch-hunt ['wɪtʃ,hʌnt] n (Pol) caccia alle streghe.

with [wɪð, wɪθ] prep **(a)** (gen) con; **I was** ~ **him** ero con lui; **she stayed** ~ **friends** abitava da amici; **he had no money** ~ **him** non aveva denaro con sé; **to rise** ~ **the sun** alzarsi all'alba; **she mixed the sugar** ~ **the eggs** mischiò lo zucchero con le uova; **I'm** ~ **you** (fig) sono con te; **I'm not** ~ **you** (fig) non ti seguo; **she just wasn't** ~ **us** era completamente assente; **to be** ~ **it** (fam: up-to-date) essere alla moda; (: alert) essere sveglia.

(b) (descriptive) con; **a room** ~ **a view** una

stanza con vista sul mare (or sulle montagne etc); **the fellow** ~ **the big beard** il tipo con la grossa barba.

(c) (manner, means, cause) con; **to cut wood** ~ **a knife** tagliare il legno con un coltello; **to walk** ~ **a stick** camminare col bastone; **white** ~ **snow** bianco di neve; **in bed** ~ **measles** a letto con il morbillo; ~ **tears in her eyes** con le lacrime agli occhi; **she's gone down** ~ **flu** ha preso l'influenza; **to shake** ~ **fear** tremare di paura; ~ **that, he** left con ciò se ne andò; ~ **time** col tempo.

(d) (concerning: in the case of): **the trouble** ~ **Harry** il problema con Harry; **you must be patient** ~ **her** devi avere pazienza con lei; **she's good** ~ **children** è brava con i bambini; **how are things** ~ **you?** (fam) come ti va la vita?

(e) (in proportion) a seconda di; **it varies** ~ **the time of year** varia a seconda della stagione.

(f) (in spite of) nonostante; ~ **all his faults I still like him** nonostante i suoi difetti mi piace ancora.

with·draw [wɪθ'drɔː] pt **withdrew,** pp **withdrawn 1** vt: **to** ~ **(from)** (gen) ritirare (da); (money) prelevare (da), ritirare (da); **he withdrew his remarks** ha ritirato quanto aveva detto, ha ritrattato. **2** vi: **to** ~ **from** (gen) ritirarsi da; (move away) allontanarsi da; **to** ~ **in sb's favour** ritirarsi a favore di qn; **to** ~ **to a new position** (Mil) arretrare su una nuova posizione; **to** ~ **into o.s.** chiudersi in se stesso.

with·draw·al [wɪθ'drɔːəl] **1** n (gen) ritiro; (of money) prelievo. **2** cpd: ~ **symptoms** npl crisi f di astinenza.

with·drawn [wɪθ'drɔːn] **1** pp of **withdraw. 2** adj distaccato(a).

with·drew [wɪθ'druː] pt of **withdraw.**

with·er ['wɪðəʳ] **1** vt far appassire. **2** vi (plant) appassire; (limb) atrofizzarsi; (fig: love, passion) spegnersi; (: hope) sfumare; (: beauty) sfiorire.

with·ered ['wɪðəd] adj (plant) appassito(a), vizzo(a); (skin) vizzo(a), inaridito(a); (limb) atrofizzato(a); **a** ~ **old woman** una vecchia rinsecchita.

with·er·ing ['wɪðərɪŋ] adj (tone, look, remark) raggelante.

with·hold [wɪð'həʊld] pt, pp **witheld** vt (money from pay etc) trattenere; (truth, news) nascondere; (refuse: consent) non concedere, negare; **I'm** ~ **ing my rent until the roof is repaired** non pagherò l'affitto finché il tetto non sarà stato riparato.

with·in [wɪð'ɪn] **1** prep **(a)** (inside) dentro; **a voice** ~ **me said...** una voce dentro di me disse...; **to be** ~ **the law** restare nei limiti della legge; **to live** ~ **one's income** vivere nei limiti delle proprie entrate. **(b)** (less than): **we were** ~ **100 metres of the summit** eravamo a meno di 100 metri dalla vetta; ~ **a year of her death** meno di un anno prima della (or dopo la) sua morte; **correct to** ~ **a millimetre** preciso al millimetro; ~ **an hour** entro un'ora; ~ **an hour from now** da qui a un'ora; **he returned** ~ **the week** è tornato la settimana stessa. **2** adv: **'car for sale — apply** ~**'** 'auto in vendita — rivolgersi all'interno'.

with·out [wɪð'aʊt] prep senza; **he did it** ~ **telling me** l'ha fatto senza dirmelo; **he came** ~ **a coat/ any money** è venuto senza cappotto/soldi; ~ **a coat or hat** senza cappotto né cappello; **the bus left** ~ **me** l'autobus è partito senza di me; **he is** ~ **friends** non ha amici; **to be quite** ~ **shame** non avere un minimo di pudore; ~ **anybody knowing** senza che nessuno lo sappia; **to go** or **do** ~ **sth** fare a meno di qc.

with·stand [wɪθ'stænd] pt, pp **withstood** [wɪθ'stʊd] vt resistere a

wit·ness ['wɪtnɪs] **1** n **(a)** (person) testimone m; ~ **for the prosecution/defence** testimone a carico/ discarico; **to call sb as a** ~ chiamare qn a testimoniare. **(b)** (evidence) testimonianza; **to bear** ~ **to sth** (subj: person) testimoniare qc; (: thing, result) provare qc. **2** vt **(a)** (event, crime) essere testimone di; (change, improvement) constatare. **(b)** (attest by signature) autenticare. **3** vi (testify) testimoniare; **to** ~ **to sth/having seen sth** testimoniare qc/di aver visto qc. **4** cpd: ~ **box,** (Am) ~ **stand** n banco dei testimoni.

wit·ti·cism ['wɪtɪsɪzəm] n arguzia.

wit·ty ['wɪtɪ] adj (-ier, -iest) arguto(a), spiritoso(a).

wives [waɪvz] npl of **wife.**

wiz·ard ['wɪzəd] n mago, stregone m; (fig) mago; **he's a financial** ~ è un mago della finanza; **he's a** ~ **at maths** è un genio matematico.

wiz·ened ['wɪznd] adj raggrinzito(a).

wk. abbr (= week) sett.

wob·ble ['wɒbl] **1** n: **to have a** ~ (chair) traballare; **she had a** ~ **in her voice** le tremava la voce. **2** vi (table, wheel, cyclist) traballare; (dancer, acrobat) vacillare; (compass needle) oscillare; (hand, voice) tremare.

wob·bly ['wɒblɪ] adj (-ier, -iest) (hand, voice) tremante; (table, chair) traballante; (object about to fall) che oscilla pericolosamente; (wheel) che ha troppo gioco; **to feel** ~ (person) sentirsi debole.

woe [wəʊ] n (poet, hum) dolore m; ~ **is me!** povero me!; ~ **betide him who...** guai a chi...; **a tale of** ~ una triste storia.

woe·be·gone ['wəʊbɪgɒn] adj triste.

woe·ful ['wəʊfʊl] adj (story, news) triste; (expression) triste, mesto(a); (deplorable) vergognoso(a), deplorevole.

woke [wəʊk] pt of **wake³.**

wok·en ['wəʊkən] pp of **wake³.**

wolf [wʊlf] **1** n, pl **wolves** [wʊlvz] **(a)** lupo; (fig): **a** ~ **in sheep's clothing** un lupo in veste di agnello; **to keep the** ~ **from the door** sbarcare il lunario; **to cry** ~ gridare al lupo. **(b)** (fig fam: womanizer) mandrillo. **2** vt (also: ~ **down**) divorare. **3** cpd: ~ **whistle** n: **he gave a** ~ **whistle** le ha fischiato dietro.

wom·an ['wʊmən] **1** n, pl **women** donna; ~ **is very different from man** la donna è molto diversa dall'uomo; **young** ~ giovane donna; **come along, young** ~! su, signorina!; **I have a** ~ **who comes in to do the cleaning** ho una donna che viene a fare le pulizie; ~ **of the world** donna di mondo; **the little** ~ (hum: wife) la mogliettina; **the** ~ **in his life** la donna della sua vita; **women's page** (Press) rubrica femminile; **women's lib** (fam) movimento femminista; **women's libber** (fam) femminista; **Women's Liberation Movement** Movimento per la Liberazione della Donna. **2** cpd: ~ **doctor** n dottoressa; ~ **driver** n guidatrice; ~ **friend** n amica.

wom·an·ly ['wʊmənlɪ] adj femminile; ~ **behaviour** comportamento da donna.

womb [wuːm] n utero; (fig: of Christianity) culla; (: of nature) grembo.

wom·en ['wɪmɪn] pl of **woman.**

women·folk ['wɪmɪnfəʊk] npl donne fpl.

won [wʌn] pt, pp of **win.**

won·der ['wʌndəʳ] **1** n **(a)** (feeling) meraviglia, stupore m; **in** ~ con stupore; **lost in** ~ stupefatto. **(b)** (object or cause of ~) miracolo, portento; **the** ~**s of science** i miracoli della scienza; **the Seven W**~**s of the World** le Sette Meraviglie del mondo; **it is no** or **little** or **small** ~ **that he left** non c'è da stupirsi se è partito; **the** ~ **of it was that...** la cosa incredibile or sorprendente era che...; **to do**

or **work** ~s fare miracoli; **no** ~! non c'è da stupirsi!; **no** ~ **he got upset** non mi stupisco se si è arrabbiato.

2 *vt* chiedersi, domandarsi; **I** ~ **whether** *or* **if...** mi chiedo se...; **I was** ~**ing if you could give me a lift** mi chiedevo se potessi darmi un passaggio; **I** ~ **where/how/when** mi chiedo dove/come/ quando.

3 *vi* **(a)** *(ask o.s., speculate)*: **to** ~ **about** pensare di; **I was** ~**ing about going out for dinner** pensavo di andare fuori a cena, magari; **does she know about it?** — **I** ~ **lo sa?** — è quello che mi chiedo anch'io. **(b)** *(be surprised)* stupirsi, meravigliarsi; **to** ~ **at sth** stupirsi di qc.

won·der·ful ['wʌndəfʊl] *adj* meraviglioso(a), stupendo(a).

won·der·ing ['wʌndərɪŋ] *adj* stupito(a), stupefatto(a).

wonder·land ['wʌndə‚lænd] *n* paese *m* delle meraviglie.

won·ky ['wɒŋkɪ] *adj* (**-ier, -iest**) *(Brit fam: chair, table)* traballante; *(: person)* debole; **to go** ~ *(TV picture, machine)* avere qualcosa che non va.

won't [wəʊnt] = **will not.**

woo [wuː] *vt* corteggiare; *(fig: fame, audience)* cercare di conquistare.

wood [wʊd] **1** *n* **(a)** *(material)* legno; **touch** ~!, *(Am)* **knock on** ~! tocca legno!; **aged in the** ~ invecchiato in botti di legno. **(b)** *(forest)* bosco; ~**s** boschi *mpl;* **we're not out of the** ~ **yet** *(fig)* non siamo ancora a posto; **he can't see the** ~ **for the trees** *(fig)* si perde in minuzie, gli sfugge l'essenziale. **(c)** *(Golf)* mazza di legno; *(Bowls)* boccia. **2** *cpd* **(a)** *(made of* ~*)* di legno; ~ **pulp** *n* pasta di legno. **(b)** *(living etc in a* ~*)* dei boschi, del bosco; ~ **anemone** *n* anemone *m* dei boschi, silvia; ~ **pigeon** *n* colombaccio, palomba.

wood·bine ['wʊdbaɪn] *n (honeysuckle)* caprifoglio.

wood·carving ['wʊd‚kɑːvɪŋ] *n* scultura in legno.

wood·cock ['wʊdkɒk] *n* beccaccia.

wood·cut ['wʊdkʌt] *n* incisione *f* su legno.

wood·cut·ter ['wʊd‚kʌtə^r] *n* tagliaboschi *m inv.*

wood·ed ['wʊdɪd] *adj* coperto(a) di boschi, boscoso(a).

wood·en ['wʊdn] *adj* **(a)** *(made of wood)* di legno. **(b)** *(fig: movements, manner)* impacciato(a); *(: face, stare)* inespressivo(a); *(: personality)* goffo(a); **to give a** ~ **performance** *(actor)* recitare in maniera impacciata.

wood·land ['wʊdlənd] **1** *n* zona boscosa. **2** *cpd* di bosco, silvestre.

wood·pecker ['wʊd‚pekə^r] *n* picchio.

wood·shed ['wʊdʃed] *n* legnaia.

woods·man ['wʊdzmən] *n, pl* **-men** *(lumberjack)* tagliaboschi *m inv; (forester)* guardaboschi *m inv.*

wood·wind ['wʊdwɪnd] *n, pl (Mus)* legni *mpl.*

wood·work ['wʊdwɜːk] *n* **(a)** *(craft)* falegnameria. **(b)** *(wooden parts)* parti *fpl* in legno.

wood·worm ['wʊdwɜːm] *n* tarlo.

woof [wʊf] **1** *n (of dog)* bau bau *m.* **2** *vi* abbaiare.

woof·er ['wʊfə^r] *n* woofer *m inv.*

wool [wʊl] **1** *n* lana; **all** ~, **pure** ~ pura lana; **knitting** ~ lana per lavorare a maglia; **to pull the** ~ **over sb's eyes** *(fam)* fargliela a qn. **2** *cpd* *(dress)* di lana; *(shop)* di lane, di filati; *(trade, industry)* laniero(a), della lana.

wool·gath·er·ing ['wʊl‚gæðərɪŋ] *n (fig)*: **to be** ~ avere la testa fra le nuvole.

wool·len, *(Am)* **wool·en** ['wʊlən] **1** *adj (cloth, dress)* di lana; *(industry)* laniero(a), della lana. **2**: ~**s** *npl* indumenti *mpl* di lana.

wool·ly, *(Am)* **wooly** ['wʊlɪ] **1** *adj* (**-ier, -iest**) *(jumper etc)* di lana; *(fig: clouds)* come batuffoli;

(: ideas) vago(a); *(: essay, book)* sul vago. **2** *n* indumento di lana.

woozy ['wuːzɪ] *adj* (**-ier, -iest**) *(fam)* intontito(a).

word [wɜːd] **1** *n* **(a)** *(gen)* parola; **what's the** ~ **for 'pen' in Italian?** come si dice 'pen' in italiano?; ~**s** *(of song)* parole *fpl,* testo; **in the** ~**s of Dante** come disse Dante; ~ **for** ~ parola per parola, testualmente; **to put sth into** ~**s** esprimere qc a parole; **silly isn't the** ~ **for it!** sciocco non è la parola esatta!; ~**s fail me** non ho parole; **in a** ~ in una parola; **not in so many** ~**s** non esattamente con queste parole; **those were her very** ~**s** queste sono state le sue parole; **the last** ~ **in** il massimo in; **to have the last** ~ avere l'ultima parola; **to give sb a** ~ **of warning** avvertire qn; **I can't get a** ~ **out of him** non riesco a strappargli una parola di bocca; **by** ~ **of mouth** a (viva) voce; **to take the** ~**s out of sb's mouth** rubare la parola di bocca a qn; **don't put** ~**s into my mouth!** non ho detto questo!; **to have a** ~ **with sb** scambiare due parole con qn; **could I have a** ~ **with you?** posso parlarti un attimo?; **to put in a (good)** ~ **for sb** mettere una buona parola per qn; **without a** ~ senza dire nulla; **don't say** *or* **breathe a** ~ **about it** non farne parola; **to have** ~**s with sb** *(quarrel with)* avere un diverbio con qn.

(b) *(news)* notizia; **is there any** ~ **from Peter yet?** non ci sono ancora notizie da parte di Peter?; ~ **came from headquarters that...** il quartiere generale ci ha fatto sapere che...; **to bring** ~ **of sth to sb** portare la notizia di qc a qn; **to leave** ~ **(with sb, for sb) that...** lasciare scritto (a qn) che...; ~ **of command** ordine *m;* **to give the** ~ **to do sth** dare l'ordine di fare qc; **to preach the W**~ predicare la parola di Dio.

(c) *(promise)* parola; **he is a man of his** ~ è un uomo di parola; **to be as good as one's** ~, **to keep one's** ~ tenere fede alla parola data, mantenere la promessa; **to break one's** ~ mancare di parola; **to give sb one's** ~ **(that...)** dare a qn la propria parola (che...); **I've only got your** ~ **for it** ho solo la tua parola; **to take sb at his** ~ prendere qn in parola; **I take your** ~ **for it** ti prendo in parola.

2 *vt (document, protest)* formulare.

3 *cpd*: ~ **game** *n* gioco di parole; ~ **processing** *n* word processing *m;* ~ **processor** *n (machine)* word processor *m inv.*

word-blind ['wɜːd‚blaɪnd] *adj* dislessico(a).

word·ing ['wɜːdɪŋ] *n (of contract, document)* formulazione *f.*

word-perfect [‚wɜːd'pɜːfɪkt] *adj (speech etc)* imparato(a) a memoria; **to be** ~ *(actor)* sapere a memoria la parte.

wordy ['wɜːdɪ] *adj* (**-ier, -iest**) verboso(a), prolisso(a).

wore [wɔː^r] *pt of* wear.

work [wɜːk] **1** *n* **(a)** *(gen)* lavoro; **it's hard** ~ è un lavoro duro; **to be at** ~ **(on sth)** lavorare (a qc); **it's all in a day's** ~ è una cosa di ordinaria amministrazione; **to get on with one's** ~ continuare il proprio lavoro; **the forces at** ~ gli elementi che influiscono; ~ **on the new school has begun** sono cominciati i lavori per la nuova scuola; **a good piece of** ~ un buon lavoro; **to set sb to** ~ **doing sth** mettere qn a fare qc; **to set to** ~, **to start** ~ mettersi all'opera; **I'm trying to get some** ~ **done** sto cercando di lavorare; **to make short** *or* **quick** ~ **of** *(sth)* sbrigare in fretta; *(fig fam: sb)* sistemare subito.

(b) *(employment, job)* lavoro; **to go to** ~ andare al lavoro; **he's at** ~ **today** oggi è in ufficio *or* al lavoro; **to look for** ~ cercare lavoro; **to be out of** ~ essere disoccupato; **to be in** ~ avere un lavoro; **to put** or **throw sb out of** ~ licenziare qn; **he's off** ~ **this week** non lavora questa settimana; **he hasn't done a full day's** ~ **in his life** non ha mai lavorato un giorno intero nella sua vita.

(c) (product: of writer, musician, scholar etc) opera; **his life's** ~ il lavoro di tutta la sua vita; **he sells a lot of his** ~ vende molti dei suoi lavori; **good** ~**s** opere fpl buone; ~ **of art/reference** opera d'arte/di consultazione; **the** ~**s of Dickens** le opere di Dickens; **he's a nasty piece of** ~ (fig) è un tipaccio.

(d): ~**s** pl (of machine, clock etc) meccanismo; (Admin etc) opere fpl; (Mil) opere, fortificazioni fpl; **road** ~**s** opere stradali; **to give sb the** ~**s** (fam: treat harshly) dare una strigliata a qn.

(e) (factory etc): ~**s** (pl inv) fabbrica, stabilimento; ~**s outing** gita aziendale.

2 vt **(a)** (students, employees) far lavorare; **to** ~ **o.s. to death** ammazzarsi di lavoro.

(b) (operate) azionare; **can you** ~ **the photocopier?** sai usare la fotocopiatrice?; **it is** ~**ed by electricity** va a corrente.

(c) (miracle) fare; (change) operare; **to** ~ **wonders** fare miracoli; **she managed to** ~ **her promotion** è riuscita a garantirsi la promozione; **they** ~**ed it so that she could come** (fam) hanno fatto in modo che potesse venire; **to** ~ **sth into a speech** far scivolare qc in un discorso; **to** ~ **one's passage on a ship** pagarsi il viaggio su una nave lavorando; **to** ~ **one's way through college** lavorare per pagarsi gli studi; **to** ~ **one's way along sth** riuscire ad avanzare lungo qc; **to** ~ **one's hands free** riuscire a liberare le mani; **to** ~ **sth loose** far smollare qc; **to** ~ **one's way through a book** riuscire a leggersi tutto un libro; **to** ~ **one's way up to the top of a company** farsi strada fino al vertice di una compagnia; **to** ~ **o.s. into a rage** infuriarsi.

(d) (shape: metal, dough, clay) lavorare; (exploit: mine) sfruttare; (: land) coltivare; (Sewing: design) ricamare; ~**ed by hand** lavorato a mano.

3 vi **(a)** lavorare; **to** ~ **towards/for sth** lavorare in vista di/per qc; **to** ~ **hard** lavorare sodo; **to** ~ **at** (essay, project) lavorare su qc; **she's** ~**ing at her desk** sta lavorando alla scrivania; **to** ~ **to rule** (Industry) fare uno sciopero bianco; **to** ~ **like a Trojan** lavorare come un pazzo.

(b) (machine, car, plan, brain etc) funzionare; (drug, medicine) fare effetto; **to get sth** ~**ing** far funzionare qc; **it** ~**s off the mains** funziona a corrente; **it** ~**s both ways** (fig) è un'arma a doppio taglio.

(c) (mouth, face, jaws) contrarsi.

(d) (move gradually) muoversi pian piano; **to** ~ **loose** (screw) allentarsi; **he** ~**ed slowly along the cliff** avanzava lentamente lungo la scogliera; **to** ~ **round to a question** formulare una domanda dopo averci girato intorno.

4 cpd: ~ **force** n forza lavoro; ~ **permit** n permesso di lavoro.

♦ **work in 1** vi + adv (arrangement etc) inserirsi. **2** vt + adv (reference etc) inserire, infilare.

♦ **work off** vt + adv (fat) eliminare; (annoyance) sfogare; (debt) pagarsi (lavorando).

♦ **work on** vi + prep **(a)** (task, novel) lavorare a; **he's** ~**ing on the car** sta facendo dei lavori alla macchina; **the police are** ~**ing on the case** la polizia sta facendo indagini sul caso. **(b):** **we've no clues to** ~ **on** non abbiamo indizi su cui basarci; **we're** ~**ing on the principle that...** partiamo dal presupposto che... + sub. **(c)** (persuade, influence): **to** ~ **on sb** lavorarsi qn.

♦ **work out 1** vi + adv **(a)** (problem) risolversi. **(b)**

(amount to): **the cost** ~**ed out at £5** il costo ammontava a 5 sterline. **(c)** (succeed: plan) funzionare; (marriage) andare bene; **I hope it all** ~**s out for you** spero che alla fine ti vada tutto bene; **things aren't** ~**ing out as planned** le cose non stanno andando come previsto. **(d)** (Sport) allenarsi. **2** vt + adv **(a)** (problem, calculation) risolvere; **things will** ~ **themselves out** tutto andrà a posto. **(b)** (devise: plan, details) mettere a punto. **(c)** (understand: behaviour) capire. **(d)** (exhaust: resources) esaurire.

♦ **work up** vt + adv **(a)** (develop: trade) sviluppare; **he** ~**ed his way up from the factory floor** ha cominciato come operaio; **to** ~ **up an appetite** farsi venire appetito; **to** ~ **up enthusiasm for sth** entusiasmarsi per qc. **(b): to** ~ **sb up into a temper/fury** far arrabbiare/infuriare qn; **don't get all** ~**ed up!** non agitarti tanto!

♦ **work up to** vi + prep preparare il terreno a.

work·able ['wɜːkəbl] adj (plan) fattibile, realizzabile; (land) coltivabile; (mine) sfruttabile.

worka·day ['wɜːkədeɪ] adj monotono(a), banale.

work·bench ['wɜːkbentʃ] n banco (da lavoro).

work·er ['wɜːkəʳ] n (gen) lavoratore/trice; (esp Agr, Industry etc) operaio/a; **he's a poor** ~ non lavora bene; **office** ~ impiegato; **management and** ~**s** il padronato e i lavoratori.

work·ing [wɜːkɪŋ] **1** adj (day) feriale; (week) lavorativo(a); (tools, conditions) di lavoro; (clothes) da lavoro; (wife) che lavora; (partner) attivo(a); ~ **capital** (Comm) capitale m d'esercizio; **the** ~ **class** la classe operaia; **an 8-hour** ~ **day** una giornata lavorativa di 8 ore; ~ **knowledge** conoscenza pratica; **a** ~ **man** un operaio; ~ **model** modello operativo; **in** ~ **order** funzionante; ~ **party** commissione f. **2** n **(a)** (work) lavoro. **(b):** ~**s** pl (way sth works) funzionamento; **the** ~**s of his mind** i meccanismi della sua mente. **(c):** ~**s** pl (of quarry) scavi mpl.

working-class [,wɜːkɪŋ'klɑːs] adj: **to be** ~ appartenere alla classe operaia; **to come from a** ~ **background** venire da una famiglia di operai.

work·load ['wɜːkləʊd] n carico di lavoro.

work·man ['wɜːkmən] n, pl **-men** operaio.

work·man·like ['wɜːkmənlaɪk] adj (attitude) professionale; (work) ben fatto(a).

work·man·ship ['wɜːkmənʃɪp] n (of worker) abilità professionale; (of thing) fattura.

work·out ['wɜːkaʊt] n (Sport) allenamento.

work·shop ['wɜːkʃɒp] n officina; (fig): **a music** ~ un incontro di musica.

work·shy ['wɜːkʃaɪ] adj pigro(a), indolente.

work-to-rule [,wɜːktə'ruːl] n sciopero bianco.

world [wɜːld] **1** n **(a)** (gen) mondo; **in the** ~ al mondo; **all over the** ~ in tutto il mondo; **to be on top of the** ~ toccare il cielo con un dito; **it's a small** ~! com'è piccolo il mondo!; **alone in the** ~ solo al mondo; **it's not the end of the** ~! (fam) non è la fine del mondo!; **to live in a** ~ **of one's own** vivere in un mondo tutto proprio; **the business** ~ il mondo degli affari; **the** ~ **we live in** il mondo in cui viviamo; **to come** or **go down/to go up** or **rise in the** ~ scendere/salire nella scala sociale; **to come into the** ~ venire al mondo; **the next** ~ l'aldilà; **to have the best of both** ~**s** avere un doppio vantaggio; **it's out of this** ~! (fam) è la fine del mondo!; **he's not long for this** ~ non gli rimane molto da vivere.

(b) (phrases): **I wouldn't do it for the** ~ or for **anything in the** ~ non lo farei per nessuna cosa al mondo; **what in the** ~ **is he doing?** che cavolo sta facendo?; **to think the** ~ **of sb** tenere molto a qn; **there's a** ~ **of difference between...** c'è un abisso tra...; **to do sb a ~ of good** fare un gran bene a qn; **the ~ and his wife** un miliardo di persone; **they're ~s apart** non hanno niente da spartire; **she looked for all the ~ as if she was dead** sembrava proprio che fosse morta; **the ~'s worst cook** la cuoca peggiore che possa esistere.

2 cpd (record) mondiale; (tour) del mondo; **~ champion** n campione/essa mondiale; **W~ Cup** n (Ftbl) Coppa del Mondo; **W~ War One/Two** n prima/seconda guerra mondiale.

world-famous [,wɜːld'feɪməs] adj di fama mondiale.

world·ly ['wɜːldlɪ] adj (-ier, -iest) (matters, person, pleasures) mondano(a), del mondo; (attitude) materiale.

worldly-wise [,wɜːldlɪ'waɪz] adj esperto(a) della vita.

world-wide ['wɜːldwaɪd] adj mondiale.

worm [wɜːm] **1** n (Zool, also person: pej) verme m; **to have ~s** (Med) avere i vermi; **the ~ will turn** (Proverb) anche la pazienza ha un limite. **2** vt (**a**): **to ~ one's way through a crowd** insinuarsi tra la folla; **to ~ one's way into a group** insinuarsi in un gruppo; **to ~ one's way into sb's confidence** conquistare la confidenza di qn. (**b**): **to ~ a secret out of sb** strappare (a poco a poco) un segreto a qn.

worn [wɔːn] **1** pp of **wear**. **2** adj (carpet, tyre) consumato(a); (person) stanco(a), sfinito(a).

worn-out ['wɔːn,aʊt] adj (thing) consunto(a), logoro(a); (person) estenuato(a).

wor·ried ['wʌrɪd] adj preoccupato(a); **to be ~ about sth** essere preoccupato per qc; **to be ~ sick** (fam) essere preoccupatissimo.

wor·rier ['wʌrɪə'] n ansioso/a.

wor·ry ['wʌrɪ] **1** n preoccupazione f; **what's your ~?** cosa ti preoccupa?, cosa c'è che non va?; **to cause sb a lot of ~** creare un sacco di preoccupazioni a qn; **that's the least of my worries** questa è l'ultima cosa che mi preoccupa. **2** vt (**a**) (cause concern) preoccupare; **to ~ o.s. sick** (about or over sth) preoccuparsi da morire (per qc); **don't ~ yourself** or **your head about it** non fartene un pensiero. (**b**) (bother) disturbare, importunare. (**c**) (subj: dog: bone) azzannare; (: sheep) spaventare. **3** vi: **to ~ about** or **over sth/sb** preoccuparsi di qc/per qn.

wor·ry·ing ['wʌrɪɪŋ] adj (problem) preoccupante; **it's a ~ time for her** è un brutto momento per lei; **she's not the ~ kind** non è il tipo che si preoccupa.

worse [wɜːs] **1** adj (comp of **bad**) peggiore; **~ than** peggio or peggiore di; **it's ~ than ever** è peggio che mai; **it could have been ~!** poteva andare peggio!; **he was the ~ for drink** (fam) aveva un po' bevuto; **he is none the ~ for it** non ha avuto brutte conseguenze; **to get ~, to grow ~** peggiorare; **I don't think any the ~ of you** non per questo ti stimo meno; **it gets ~ and ~** peggiora sempre (di) più; **so much the ~ for you!** tanto peggio per te!; **~ luck!** che sfortuna!, che scalogna!

2 adv (comp of **badly**) peggio; **she behaves ~ than ever** si comporta peggio che mai; **I won't think any the ~ of you** (for having done) non ti stimerò di meno (per aver fatto); **you might do ~ than (to) marry him** sposare lui non è il male peggiore; **he is now ~ off than before** ora è in condizioni peggiori di prima.

3 n peggio; **a change for the ~** un cambiamento in peggio; **~ followed** a questo seguì il peggio; **there is ~ to come** il peggio deve ancora venire.

wors·en ['wɜːsn] **1** vt (health) peggiorare;

(chances) diminuire. **2** vi peggiorare.

wor·ship ['wɜːʃɪp] **1** n (**a**) (adoration) adorazione f, culto; (organized ~) culto; **place of ~** (Rel) luogo di culto. (**b**) (Brit: in titles): **Your W~** (to judge) Vostro Onore; (to mayor) signor sindaco. **2** vt adorare; **she ~s her children** (fig) adora i suoi bambini; **she ~s the ground he treads on** bacia il terreno dove lui cammina. **3** vi (Rel) assistere alle funzioni.

wor·ship·per ['wɜːʃɪpə'] n adoratore/trice; (Christian) fedele m/f.

worst [wɜːst] **1** adj (superl of **bad**) il(la) peggiore; **it was the ~ possible time** era il momento peggiore or meno opportuno; **the ~ film of the three** il film peggiore tra i tre; **the ~ pupil in the school** il peggiore alunno della scuola; **one of his ~ efforts** uno delle sue prove peggiori.

2 adv (superl of **badly**) peggio; **he sings ~ of all** canta peggio di tutti; **to come off ~** (in fight, argument) avere la peggio.

3 n peggio; (of crisis, storm) culmine m; **at (the) ~** alla peggio; **the ~ of it is that...** il peggio è che...; **the ~ is yet to come** il peggio deve ancora venire; **if the ~ comes to the ~** nel peggior dei casi; **to get the ~ of an argument** avere la peggio in una discussione; **he brings out the ~ in me** risveglia in me gli istinti peggiori; **we're over** or **past the ~ of it now** il peggio è passato ora; **do your ~!** sono pronto al peggio!

wor·sted ['wʊstɪd] n (cloth) pettinato.

worth [wɜːθ] **1** adj: **how much is it ~?** quanto vale?; **it's ~ £5** vale 5 sterline; **it's ~ a great deal** vale molto; **it's ~ a great deal to me** (sentimentally) ha un gran valore per me; **he is ~ his weight in gold** vale tanto oro quanto pesa; **I tell you this for what it's ~** ti dico questo per quello che può valere; **what's it ~ to you?** quale valore ha per te?; **to run for all one is ~** correre a gambe levate; **it hardly seemed ~ mentioning** non mi sembrava abbastanza importante da parlarne; **it's well ~ the effort/expense** vale lo sforzo/la spesa; **it's not ~ the paper it's written on** non vale nemmeno la carta su cui è scritto; **it's not ~ it, it's not ~ the trouble** non ne vale la pena; **it's more than my life is ~** è troppo rischioso; **is it ~ doing?** vale la pena di farlo?

2 n valore m; **10 pounds' ~ of books** 10 sterline di libri; **he had no chance to show his true ~** nor ebbe occasione di mostrare quanto valeva.

worth·less ['wɜːθlɪs] adj (effort, action, attempt) inutile; (object) privo(a) di valore; **a ~ individual** un individuo spregevole.

worth·while ['wɜːθ'waɪl] adj (gen) che vale la pena; (book, film) che merita; (life, work) utile; (contribution) valido(a); **a ~ trip** un viaggio che vale la pena di fare.

wor·thy ['wɜːðɪ] **1** adj (-ier, -iest) (gen) degno(a); (cause, aim) lodevole; **~ of** degno di. **2** n (hum) personalità.

would [wʊd] modal aux vb (cond of **will**) (**a**) (cond tense): **if you asked him he ~ do it** se tu glielo chiedessi lo farebbe; **if you had asked him he ~ have done it** se tu gliel'avessi chiesto l'avrebbe fatto; **you'd think she had enough to worry about** si direbbe che aveva abbastanza di cui preoccuparsi.

(**b**) (in indirect speech): **I said I ~ do it** ho detto che l'avrei fatto.

(**c**) (emphatic): **you WOULD be the one to forget!** tu te lo potresti benissimo dimenticare!; **it WOULD have to snow today!** doveva proprio nevicare oggi!; **you WOULD say that, ~n't you!** dovevi dirlo, vero!

(d) *(insistence)*: **she ~n't behave** non ha voluto comportarsi bene; **I told her not to but she ~ do it** le avevo detto di non farlo ma lei l'ha voluto fare.

(e) *(conjecture)*: **what ~ this be?** questo cosa sarebbe?; **it ~ have been about midnight** sarà stato verso mezzanotte; **it ~ seem so** sembrerebbe proprio di sì.

(f) *(wish)*: **what ~ you have me do?** cosa desideri che faccia?; **~ (that) it were not so!** *(old, poet)* magari non fosse così!

(g) *(in offers, invitations, requests)*: **~ you care for some tea?** vorresti *or* gradiresti del tè?; **~ you ask him to come in?** lo faccia entrare per cortesia.

(h) *(habit)*: **he ~ paint it each year** era solito dipingerlo ogni anno.

would-be ['wʊdbiː] *adj*: **a ~ poet/politician** un aspirante poeta/politico.

wouldn't ['wʊdnt] = **would not**.

wound[1] [wuːnd] **1** *n* ferita; **leg/bullet ~** ferita alla gamba/di proiettile. **2** *vt (also fig)* ferire.

wound[2] [waʊnd] *pt, pp of* **wind**[2].

wound-ed ['wuːndɪd] *adj (also fig)* ferito(a); **a ~ man** un ferito. **2** *npl*: **the ~** i feriti.

wove [wəʊv] *pt of* **weave**.

wo-ven ['wəʊvən] *pp of* **weave**.

wow [waʊ] *excl (fam)* accidenti!

wraith [reɪθ] *n* spettro.

wran-gle ['ræŋgl] **1** *n* litigio, alterco. **2** *vi*: **to ~ (about *or* over)** litigare (su).

wrap [ræp] **1** *n (shawl)* scialle *m*; *(housecoat)* vestaglia; *(rug)* coperta; *(cape)* mantellina; **still under ~s** *(fig: plan, scheme)* segreto. **2** *vt (also: ~ up)* avvolgere; *(: with paper)* incartare; **the scheme is ~ped in secrecy** il piano è avvolto nel mistero.

♦ **wrap up 1** *vt + adv* **(a)** *(gen)* avvolgere; *(parcel)* incartare; *(child)* coprire bene; **she ~ped it up a bit, but what she meant was...** ci ha girato un po' intorno, ma intendeva dire che... . **(b)** *(fam: finalize)* concludere. **(c)**: **to be ~ped up in sb/sth** essere completamente preso da sb/qc. **2** *vi + adv* **(a)** *(dress warmly)* coprirsi, vestirsi bene. **(b)** *(fam: be quiet)*: **~ up!** chiudi il becco!

wrap-per ['ræpə'] *n (on chocolate)* carta; *(postal)* fascetta; *(book ~)* foderina, copertina.

wrap-ping ['ræpɪŋ] **1** *n (for chocolate, parcel)* carta. **2** *cpd*: **~ paper** *n (brown)* carta da pacchi; *(gift ~)* carta da regalo.

wrath [rɒθ] *n (poet)* ira, collera.

wreak [riːk] *vt (destruction, havoc)* portare, causare; **to ~ vengeance on** vendicarsi su.

wreath [riːθ] *n, pl* **wreaths** [riːðz] *(of flowers etc)* ghirlanda; *(of smoke, mist etc)* corona.

wreathed [riːðd] *adj*: **a face ~ in smiles** un volto raggiante *or* tutto sorridente; **~ in mist** avvolto dalla nebbia.

wreck [rek] **1** *n (of ship, scheme etc)* naufragio; *(ship itself)* relitto; *(fig: old car etc)* rottame *m*; *(: building)* rudere *m*; **I'm a ~, I feel a ~** sono distrutto. **2** *vt (gen)* distruggere, rovinare; *(ship)* far naufragare; *(train)* far deragliare; *(house)* demolire; *(health)* rovinare; **to be ~ed** *(Naut)* fare naufragio.

wreck-age ['rekɪdʒ] *n (of ship)* relitti *mpl*; *(of car etc)* rottami *mpl*; *(of building)* macerie *fpl*.

wreck-er ['rekə'] *n (Naut: salvager)* ricuperatore *m* (di relitti); *(Am: breaker, salvager)* demolitore *m*; *(Am: breakdown van)* carro *m* attrezzi *inv*.

wren [ren] *n* scricciolo.

wrench [rentʃ] **1** *n* **(a)** *(tug)* strattone *m*; **to give sth a ~** dare uno strattone a qc. **(b)** *(tool)* chiave *f*.

(c) *(fig)* strazio. **2** *vt* **(a)**: **to ~ sth (away) from** *or* **off sb** strappare qc da qn; **he ~ed it out of my hands** me lo ha strappato di mano; **she ~ed herself free** si liberò con uno strattone; **to ~ a door open** aprire una porta bruscamente. **(b)** *(Med)* slogare.

wres-tle ['resl] **1** *n*: **to have a ~ with sb** fare la lotta con qn. **2** *vi* **(a)** lottare, fare la lotta; *(Sport)* praticare la lotta libera. **(b)** *(fig)*: **to ~ with** *(one's conscience, device, machine)* lottare con; *(temptation, sins)* lottare contro.

wres-tler ['reslə'] *n (Sport)* lottatore/trice.

wres-tling ['reslɪŋ] **1** *n (Sport)* lotta libera. **2** *cpd*: **~ match** *n* incontro di lotta libera.

wretch [retʃ] *n* disgraziato/a, sciagurato/a; **little ~!** *(often hum)* birbante!

wretch-ed ['retʃɪd] *adj* **(a)** *(house, conditions)* misero(a), disgraziato(a); *(life)* gramo(a); *(pittance)* misero(a); *(unhappy, depressed)* infelice, triste, depresso(a); **I feel ~** *(fam: ill)* sto male. **(b)** *(very bad: weather, behaviour)* pessimo(a), orribile; *(holiday)* schifoso(a); *(results)* pessimo(a); **I feel ~ about it** *(fam: conscience-stricken)* mi sento un verme; **what ~ luck!** *(fam)* che scalogna!; **where's that ~ dog?** *(fam)* dov'è quel maledetto cane?

wrick [rɪk] *vt*: **to ~ one's ankle** slogarsi la caviglia; **to ~ one's neck** farsi uno strappo al collo.

wrig-gle ['rɪgl] **1** *vt (toes, fingers)* muovere; **to ~ one's way through** *(tunnel)* attraversare strisciando; *(undergrowth)* strisciare in. **2** *vi (also: ~ about *or* around)* agitarsi, dimenarsi; *(: worm, snake, eel)* muoversi sinuosamente; *(fish: on hook)* divincolarsi; **to ~ along/down** avanzare/ scendere strisciando; **to ~ free** liberarsi contorcendosi; **to ~ through a hole** passare contorcendosi un buco; **he managed to ~ out of it** *(fig)* se l'è cavata con un espediente.

wrig-gly ['rɪglɪ] *adj (-ier, -iest)* che si dimena.

wring [rɪŋ] *pt, pp* **wrung** *vt* **(a)** *(also: ~ out: wet cloth, water)* strizzare. **(b)** *(twist)* tirare; **I'll ~ your neck!** *(fam)* ti tirerò il collo!; **she wrung my hand** mi strinse forte la mano; **to ~ one's hands** *(fig: in distress)* torcersi le mani; **to ~ sb's heart** *(fig)* stringere il cuore a qn. **(c)** *(also: ~ out: confession, truth, money)* estorcere.

wring-er ['rɪŋə'] *n* strizzatoio (manuale).

wring-ing ['rɪŋɪŋ] *adj (also: ~ wet)* bagnato(a) fradicio(a).

wrin-kle ['rɪŋkl] **1** *n (on face, skin)* ruga; *(in stockings, paper etc)* grinza. **2** *vt (fabric)* stropicciare; *(nose)* arricciare; *(flat surface, skin)* corrugare. **3** *vi (see vt)* stropicciarsi; arricciarsi; corrugarsi.

wrin-kled ['rɪŋkld] *adj*, **wrin-kly** ['rɪŋklɪ] *adj (fabric, paper)* stropicciato(a); *(nose)* arricciato(a); *(surface)* corrugato(a), increspato(a); *(skin)* rugoso(a).

wrist [rɪst] *n* polso.

wrist-band ['rɪstbænd] *n (of shirt)* polsino; *(of watch)* cinturino.

wrist-watch ['rɪstwɒtʃ] *n* orologio da polso.

writ [rɪt] *n (Law)* mandato; **to issue a ~ against sb, to serve a ~ on sb** notificare un mandato di comparizione a qn.

write [raɪt] *pt* **wrote**, *pp* **written 1** *vt* scrivere; *(form, list)* compilare; *(certificate)* redigere; **she wrote that she'd arrive soon** scrisse che sarebbe arrivata presto; **to ~ sb a letter** scrivere una lettera a qn; **he's just written another novel** ha appena scritto un altro romanzo; **how is his name written?** come si scrive il suo nome?; **she wrote 3 pages** ha scritto 3 pagine; **his guilt was written all over his face** gli si leggeva in faccia che era colpevole. **2** *vi* scrivere; **to ~ to sb** scrivere a qn; **that's nothing to ~ home about** *(fam)* non è niente di speciale; **I'll ~ for the catalogue** scriverò per farmi mandare il catalogo; **to ~ for a paper** scrivere per un giornale.

♦ **write away** *vi + adv*: **to ~ away for** *(information)* richiedere per posta; *(goods)* ordinare per posta.

♦ **write back** *vi + adv* rispondere *(con una lettera)*.

♦ **write down** *vt + adv (make a note of, put in writing)* segnare, annotare.

♦ **write in 1** *vt + adv* inserire. **2** *vi + adv* scrivere; **to ~ in for sth** scrivere per richiedere qc.

♦ **write off 1** *vi + adv* = **write away**. **2** *vt + adv (debt)* estinguere; *(scheme)* porre un termine a; *(smash up: car)* distruggere; **he was written off as useless** *(fig)* fu considerato inutile; **I've written off the whole thing** *(fig)* ci ho messo una croce sopra.

♦ **write out** *vt + adv (gen)* scrivere; *(list, form)* compilare; *(cheque)* fare; *(copy: essay)* ricopiare.

♦ **write up** *vt + adv (notes, diary)* aggiornare; *(write report on: developments etc)* mettere per iscritto; **she wrote the play up in the Glasgow Herald** ha scritto una recensione della commedia sul Glasgow Herald.

write-off ['raɪtɒf] *n (Comm)* perdita; *(fig: car etc)* rottame *m*.

writ·er ['raɪtəʳ] *n (of letter, report etc)* autore/trice; *(as profession)* scrittore/trice; **to be a good/poor ~** essere un bravo/cattivo scrittore; **~'s cramp** crampo dello scrivano.

write-up ['raɪtʌp] *n (review)* recensione *f*.

writhe [raɪð] *vi* contorcersi; **to ~ with embarrassment** voler sprofondare dalla vergogna.

writ·ing ['raɪtɪŋ] **1** *n (art)* scrivere *m*; *(sth written)* scritto; *(handwriting)* scrittura; **to put sth in ~** mettere qc per iscritto; **in my own ~** scritto di mio pugno; **Aubrey's biographical ~s** gli scritti biografici di Aubrey; **~ is my profession** scrivere è la mia professione, faccio lo scrittore di professione; **~ is just a hobby with me** scrivere è solo un hobby per me; **the ~ on the wall** *(fig)* il presagio della rovina. **2** *cpd*: **~ case** *n* necessaire *m inv* per la corrispondenza; **~ desk** *n* scrivania, scrittoio; **~ paper** *n* carta da lettere.

writ·ten ['rɪtn] **1** *pp* of **write**. **2** *adj* scritto(a).

wrong [rɒŋ] **1** *adj* **(a)** *(morally)* sbagliato(a), riprovevole; *(unfair)* ingiusto(a), sbagliato(a); **it's ~ to steal, stealing is ~** è male rubare; **you were ~ to do that** hai sbagliato facendo così; **what's ~ with a drink now and again?** che c'è di male per un bicchierino ogni tanto?

(b) *(incorrect)* sbagliato(a), errato(a); **to be ~** *(answer)* essere sbagliato; *(in doing, saying)* avere torto; **I was ~ in thinking that...** mi sbagliavo nel pensare che....

(c) *(improper, not sought, not wanted)* sbagliato(a); **to say/do the ~ thing** dire/fare qc che non va; **you have the ~ number** *(Telec)* ha sbagliato numero.

(d) *(amiss)*: **is anything** *or* **something ~?** c'è qualcosa che non va?; **what's ~ (with you)?** che cos'hai?, cosa c'è che non va?; **there's nothing ~** va tutto bene; **there is something ~ with my lights** le luci non funzionano bene; **what's ~ with your arm?** cos'hai al braccio?; **what's ~ with the car?** cos'ha la macchina che non va?; **to be ~ in the head** *(fam)* essere un po' tocco.

2 *adv (spell, pronounce)* in modo sbagliato; **you're doing it all ~** stai sbagliando tutto; **you did ~ to do it** hai fatto male agendo così; **to get sth ~** sbagliare qc; **don't get me ~** *(fam)* non fraintendermi; **to go ~** *(on route)* sbagliare strada; *(in calculation)* sbagliarsi, commettere un errore; *(morally)* prendere una cattiva strada; *(plan etc)* andare male, fallire; **something went ~ with the brakes** è successo qualcosa ai freni; **you can't go ~** non puoi sbagliarti; **you won't go far ~ if you follow his advice** non faresti male a seguire il suo consiglio.

3 *n* **(a)** *(evil)* male *m*; **to do ~** far male; **he can do no ~ in her eyes** per lei è perfetto.

(b) *(unjust act)* torto; **to do sb a ~** fare un torto a qn; **to be in the ~** avere torto; **to put sb in the ~** mettere qn dalla parte del torto; **to right a ~** riparare a un torto; **to suffer a ~** subire un torto.

4 *vt* fare (un) torto a.

wrong·doer [ˌrɒŋ'duːəʳ] *n* malfattore/trice.

wrong·ful ['rɒŋfʊl] *adj (unjust: accusation, dismissal)* ingiusto(a); *(unlawful: arrest, imprisonment)* illegale, illecito(a).

wrong-headed [ˌrɒŋ'hɛdɪd] *adj (determined)* ostinato(a); *(mistaken)* sbagliato(a).

wrong·ly ['rɒŋlɪ] *adv (answer, do, count)* erroneamente; *(treat)* ingiustamente; *(accuse, dismiss)* a torto.

wrote [rəʊt] *pt* of **write**.

wrought [rɔːt] **1** *(old, poet)* **(a)** *pt, pp* of **work**. **(b)**: **great changes have been ~** sono avvenuti dei grandi cambiamenti. **2** *adj (silver)* lavorato(a); *(iron)* battuto(a).

wrought-iron [ˌrɔːt'aɪən] *adj* di ferro battuto.

wrought-up [ˌrɔːt'ʌp] *adj*: **to be ~** essere teso(a).

wrung [rʌŋ] *pt, pp* of **wring**.

wry [raɪ] *adj* beffardo(a); **to make a ~ face** fare una smorfia.

wry·ly ['raɪlɪ] *adv* in modo beffardo.

wt. *abbr* of **weight**.

X

X, x [ɛks] *n* (*letter, Maths*) X, x *for m inv*; **if you have ~ dollars a year** se hai x dollari all'anno; **~ marks the spot** il punto è segnato con una croce.

X-certificate [ˌɛksə'tɪfɪkət] *adj* (*film*) vietato ai minori di 18 anni (*secondo un sistema di censura non più in uso*).

Xer·ox ['zɪərɒks] *vt* ® fotocopiare.

Xmas ['ɛksməs, 'krɪsməs] *n abbr of* **Christmas.**

X-ray ['ɛks'reɪ] **1** *n* (*ray*) raggio X; (*photo*) radiografia; **to have an ~** farsi fare una radiografia. **2** *vt* radiografare. **3** *cpd* (*examination*) radiografico(a); **~ picture** *n* lastra.

xy·lo·phone ['zaɪləfəʊn] *n* xilofono.

Y

Y, y [waɪ] *n* (*letter*) Y, y *for m inv*.

yacht [jɒt] **1** *n* yacht *m inv*, panfilo da diporto. **2** *cpd*: **~ club** *n* yacht club *m*, circolo nautico.

yacht·ing ['jɒtɪŋ] *n* yachting *m*, velismo.

yachts·man ['jɒtsmən] *n, pl* **-men** yachtsman *m inv*, velista *m*.

yachts·woman ['jɒtswʊmən] *n, pl* **-women** yachtswoman *f inv*, velista.

yak [jæk] *n* yak *m inv*.

yam [jæm] *n* igname *m*; (*sweet potato*) patata dolce.

Yank [jæŋk], **Yan·kee** ['jæŋkɪ] (*fam*) **1** *n* nordamericano/a, yankee *m/f inv*. **2** *adj* nordamericano(a), yankee *inv*.

yank [jæŋk] **1** *n* strattone *m*. **2** *vt* tirare, dare uno strattone a; **to ~ a nail out** strappare via un chiodo.

yap [jæp] (*of dog*) **1** *n* guaito. **2** *vi* guaire.

yard¹ [jɑːd] *n* (**a**) (*measure*) iarda, yard *f inv* (= 91, 44 cm); **to sell sth by the ~** ≃ vendere qc al metro; **~s of** (*fig*) dei chilometri di. (**b**) (*Naut*) pennone *m*.

yard² [jɑːd] *n* (*court~, farm~*) cortile *m*; (*Am: garden*) giardino; (*worksite*) cantiere *m*; (*for storage*) deposito; **builder's ~** deposito di materiale da costruzione; **back ~** (*Brit*) cortile sul retro; (*Am*) giardino sul retro.

yard·age ['jɑːdɪdʒ] *n* ≃ metraggio.

yard·arm ['jɑːdɑːm] *n* (*Naut*) varea.

yard·stick ['jɑːdstɪk] *n* (*fig*) metro, criterio.

yarn [jɑːn] *n* (**a**) (*wool etc*) filato. (**b**) (*tale*) storia, racconto; **to spin sb a ~** raccontare a qn una grossa balla.

yash·mak ['jæʃmæk] *n* velo (*indossato dalle donne musulmane*).

yawn [jɔːn] **1** *n* sbadiglio. **2** *vi* sbadigliare; (*fig: hole, chasm*) aprirsi; **'yes', she ~ed 'sì'**, disse con uno sbadiglio. **3** *vt*: **to ~ one's head off** continuare a sbadigliare.

yawn·ing ['jɔːnɪŋ] *adj* (*fig: abyss*) spalancato(a).

yd(s). *abbr of* **yard(s).**

ye [jiː] (*old*) **1** *pron* = **you** (*pl*). **2** *art* = **the.**

yea [jeɪ] (*old*) **1** *adv* (*yes*) sì. **2** *n*: **the ~s and the nays** i sì e i no.

yeah [jɛə] *adv* (*fam*) sì.

year [jɪəʳ] *n* (**a**) anno; **this ~** quest'anno; **all (the) ~ round** (per) tutto l'anno; **~ in, ~ out** anno dopo anno; **~ by ~, from ~ to ~** col passar degli anni; **~s and ~s ago** tanti anni fa; **from one ~ to the next** da un anno all'altro; **3 times a ~** 3 volte all'anno; **in the ~ 1869** nell'anno 1869, nel 1869; **in the ~ of grace** nell'anno di grazia; **last ~** l'anno scorso; **next ~** (*looking to future*) l'anno prossimo *or* venturo; **the next ~** (*in past time*) l'anno seguente *or* successivo; **he got 10 ~s** (*in prison*) si è beccato 10 anni; **it takes ~s** ci vogliono anni; **I met him a ~ last January** a gennaio era un anno che l'avevo conosciuto; **a ~ tomorrow** domani tra un anno; **I haven't seen her for ~s** non la vedo da anni, sono anni che non la vedo; **over the ~s** con gli anni; **she's three ~s old** ha tre anni; **she's in her fiftieth ~** compierà cinquant'anni; **it's taken ~s off her** l'ha ringiovanita; **a ~ or per ~** all'anno.

(**b**) (*Scol, Univ*) anno; **he's in the second ~** è al secondo anno.

(**c**) (*of wine*) annata.

(**d**) (*age*): **old/young for one's ~s** vecchio/giovane per i suoi anni *or* per la sua età; **from her earliest ~s** fin dall'infanzia; **he's getting on in ~s** ha i suoi anni ormai.

year·book ['jɪəˌbʊk] *n* annuario.

year·ling ['jɪəlɪŋ] *n* (*racehorse*) yearling *m inv*.

year·ly ['jɪəlɪ] **1** *adj* annuale; **twice-~** semestrale. **2** *adv* annualmente; **three times ~** tre volte all'anno.

yearn [jɜːn] *vi*: **to ~ for sb/sth** desiderare ardentemente qn/qc; **to ~ to do sth** struggersi dal desiderio di *or* anelare a fare qc.

yearn·ing ['jɜːnɪŋ] **1** *adj* (*desire*) intenso(a); (*look, tone etc*) desideroso(a), bramoso(a). **2** *n*: **~ (for)** desiderio struggente (di).

yearn·ing·ly ['jɜːnɪŋlɪ] *adv* con smania, con desiderio.

yeast [jiːst] *n* lievito.

yell [jɛl] **1** *n* urlo; **to give a ~, to let out a ~** lanciare un urlo; **a ~ of laughter** una fragorosa risata. **2** *vi* urlare. **3** *vt (order, name)* urlare.

yel·low ['jɛləʊ] **1** *adj* (**-er, -est**) giallo(a); *(fig: cowardly)* fifone(a); **to go** *or* **turn** ~ *(person)* diventare giallo; *(leaf, paper)* ingiallire. **2** *n (colour)* giallo; *(of an egg)* rosso. **3** *vi* ingiallire.

yel·low·ish ['jɛləʊɪʃ] *adj* giallastro(a), giallognolo(a).

yelp [jɛlp] **1** *n (of dog)* guaito; *(of person)* strillo. **2** *vi (see n)* guaire; strillare.

yen¹ [jɛn] *n (currency)* yen *m inv*.

yen² [jɛn] *n (fam)*: **to have a** ~ **to do sth** avere una gran voglia di fare qc.

yeo·man ['jəʊmən] *n, pl* **-men** *(Brit old)* piccolo proprietario terriero; **Y**~ **of the Guard** Guardiano della Torre di Londra.

yes [jɛs] **1** *adv* sì; *(answering negative question)* (ma) sì; **to say** ~ **(to)** dire di sì (a), acconsentire (a); ~ ~, **but what if it doesn't?** sì, va bene, ma se non lo fa? **2** *n* sì *m inv*. **3** *cpd*: ~ **man** *n* tirapiedi *m inv*.

yes·ter·day ['jɛstədeɪ] *adv* ieri; ~ **morning/ evening** ieri mattina/sera; **the day before** ~ l'altro ieri; **a week** ~ *(past)* una settimana fa, ieri; **late** ~ ieri in serata; **it rained all (day)** ~ ieri ha piovuto tutto il giorno; **the great men of** ~ i grandi uomini del passato *or* di ieri.

yet [jɛt] **1** *adv* **(a)** *(already, up to now, so far)* già; *(now, by now)* ancora; **I wonder if he's come** ~ mi chiedo se non sia già arrivato; **not** ~ non ancora; **he hasn't come** ~ non è ancora arrivato; **I needn't go (just)** ~ non è ancora il momento di andare; **don't go (just)** ~ non andare già via; **this is his best film** ~ finora questo è il suo film migliore; **as** ~ per ora, finora. **(b)** *(still)* ancora; **he may come** ~ può ancora arrivare; **that question is** ~ **to be decided** quella questione è ancora da decidere; **I'll do it** ~! lo farò a tutti i costi! **(c)** *(in addition, even)* ~ **again** di nuovo; ~ **another/more** ancora un altro/più; ~ **once more** ancora una volta. **(d)** *(frm)*: **nor** ~ tanto meno; **I do not like him, nor** ~ **his sister** lui non mi piace, e tanto meno sua sorella.

2 *conj* ma; **and** ~ eppure, tuttavia; **it was funny,** ~ **sad at the same time** era buffo e triste nel contempo; **and** ~ **I enjoyed it** e tuttavia mi è piaciuto.

yeti ['jɛtɪ] *n* yeti *m inv*.

yew [ju:] *n (also:* ~ **tree)** tasso.

Yid·dish ['jɪdɪʃ] *adj, n* yiddish *(m) inv*.

yield [ji:ld] **1** *n (gen, Fin)* resa; *(of crops etc)* raccolto; **a** ~ **of 5%** un profitto *or* un interesse del 5%. **2** *vt* **(a)** *(gen, Fin)* fruttare; *(results etc)* fornire, produrre; *(information, opportunity)* fornire. **(b)** *(surrender: also:* ~ **up)** cedere. **3** *vi (surrender)*: **to** ~ **(to)** cedere (a), arrendersi (a); *(break, collapse)* cedere; *(Am Aut)* dare la precedenza; **to** ~ **to temptation** cedere alla tentazione.

yip·pee [jɪ'pi:] *excl (fam)* hurrà!

yob(bo) ['jɒb(əʊ)] *n* teppista *m/f*.

yo·del ['jəʊdl] **1** *vi* fare lo jodel. **2** *n* jodel *m inv*.

yoga ['jəʊgə] *n* yoga *m*.

yo·ghurt ['jəʊgət] *n* yogurt *m inv*.

yoke [jəʊk] **1** *n* **(a)** *(of oxen, also fig)* giogo. **(b)** *(on dress etc)* sprone *m*. **2** *vt (also:* ~ **together:** *oxen)* aggiogare.

yo·kel ['jəʊkəl] *n* zotico/a, villano/a.

yolk [jəʊk] *n* tuorlo, rosso (d'uovo).

yon·der ['jɒndər] *adv:* **(over)** ~ laggiù, là.

you [ju:] *pers pron* **(a)** *(subj: fam: sg)* tu; *(: polite form)* lei; *(: pl)* voi; *(: very formal)* loro; **if I was** *or* **were** ~ se fossi in te *(or lei etc)*; ~ **are very kind** è molto gentile da parte tua *(or sua etc)*; ~ **Italians** voi *or* voialtri Italiani; ~ **and I will go** tu ed io andiamo; **it's** ~! eccoti!; ~ **angel!** sei un angelo!;

that dress just isn't ~ quel vestito proprio non ti *(or le)* si addice.

(b) *(see* **a)** *(obj: direct)* ti; la; vi; loro *(after vb)*; *(: indirect)* ti; le; vi; loro *(after vb)*; **I'll see** ~ **tomorrow** ti vedrò domani; la vedrò domani; vi vedrò domani; vedrò loro domani; **I gave it to** ~ te l'ho dato; gliel'ho dato; ve l'ho dato; l'ho dato loro.

(c) *(see* **a)** *(stressed, after prep, in comparisons)* te; lei; voi; loro; **I told YOU to do it** ho detto a TE *(or* LEI *etc)* di farlo; **it's for** ~ è per te *(or lei etc)*; **she's younger than** ~ è più giovane di te *(or lei etc)*.

(d) *(impersonal: one)* si; **fresh air does** ~ **good** l'aria fresca fa bene; ~ **never can tell** non si sa mai; ~ **can't do that!** non si fanno queste cose!

you'd [ju:d] = **you would; you had.**

you'll [ju:l] = **you will; you shall.**

young [jʌŋ] **1** *adj* (**-er, -est**) *(gen)* giovane; *(fruit)* verde, acerbo(a); **a** ~ **man** un giovanotto; **a** ~ **lady** una signorina; **they have a** ~ **family** hanno i bambini piccoli; **in my** ~ **days** quand'ero giovane; **she's not so** ~ **as she was** non è più tanto giovane; **the** ~**er son** il figlio minore; **he is 2 years** ~**er than her** ha 2 anni meno di lei; **if I were 15 years** ~**er** se avessi 15 anni di meno; **you're only** ~ **once** si è giovani una volta sola; **she's** ~ **at heart** è giovane dentro; **he looks** ~ **for his age** sembra più giovane di quanto sia in realtà; **the night is** ~ la notte è appena cominciata; **to grow** *or* **get** ~**er** ringiovanire; **the** ~**er generation** la nuova generazione.

2 *npl (of animals)* piccoli *mpl*, prole *f*; **the** ~ *(young people)* i giovani.

young·ster ['jʌŋstər] *n* giovane *m*, giovanotto.

your [jɔːr] *poss adj* **(a)** *(sg: fam)* il(la) tuo(a); *pl* i(le) tuoi(tue); *(: polite)* il(la) suo(a); *pl* i(le) suoi(sue); *(pl)* il(la) vostro(a); *pl* i(le) vostri(e); *(: very formal)* il(la) loro; *pl* i(le) loro; ~ **house** la tua *(or* sua *etc)* casa; ~ **brother** tuo *(or* suo *etc)* fratello. **(b)** *(impersonal: one's)*: **it's bad for** ~ **health** dannaggia la salute; ~ **average Italian** l'italiano medio.

you're [jʊər] = **you are.**

yours [jɔːz] *poss pron (sg: fam)* il(la) tuo(a); *pl* i(le) tuoi(tue); *(: polite)* il(la) suo(a); *pl* i(le) suoi(sue); *(pl)* il(la) vostro(a); *pl* i(le) vostri(e); *(: very formal)* il(la) loro; *pl* i(le) loro; ~ **is red, mine is green** il tuo *(or* suo *etc)* è rosso, il mio è verde; **this is** ~ questo è (il) tuo *(or* suo *etc)*; **a friend of** ~ un tuo *(or* suo *etc)* amico; ~ **faithfully/sincerely** *(in letters)* distinti/cordiali saluti; **what's** ~? *(fam: drink)* tu che prendi?

your·self [jɔ'sɛlf] *pers pron, pl* **yourselves** [jə'sɛlvz] **(a)** *(reflexive: fam)* ti; *(: polite)* si; *(: pl)* vi; *(: very formal)* si; **have you hurt** ~? ti sei *(or* si è) fatto male?; **have you hurt yourselves?** vi siete *(or* si sono) fatti male? **(b)** *(emphatic: fam)* tu stesso(a); *(: polite)* lei stesso(a); *(: pl)* voi stessi(e); *(: very formal)* loro stessi(e); **you** ~ **told me** me l'hai detto proprio tu, tu stesso me l'hai detto. **(c)** *(after prep: fam)* te, te stesso(a); *(: polite)* lei, lei stesso(a); *(: pl)* voi, voi stessi(e); *(: very formal)* loro, loro stessi(e); **(all) by** ~ *(tutto)* da solo. **(d)** *(impersonal: reflexive)* si; *(: emphatic)* se stessi; *(: after prep)* sé, se stessi; *see also* **oneself.**

youth [ju:θ] **1** *n* **(a)** *(gen)* giovinezza, gioventù *f*; **in early** ~ nella prima giovinezza; **in my** ~ da giovane, quando ero giovane. **(b)** *(pl:* ~**s** [ju:ðz]: *boy)* ragazzo, giovane *m*. **(c)** *pl (young people)* giovani *mpl*; **the** ~ **of today** i giovani di oggi. **2** *cpd*: ~ **hostel** *n* ostello per la gioventù; ~ **movement** *n* movimento giovanile.

youth·ful ['ju:θfʊl] *adj (air, figure, manner)* giovanile; *(mistakes)* di gioventù.

youth·ful·ness |'juːθfʊlnɪs| n giovinezza.
you've |juːv| = **you have.**
yowl |jaʊl| **1** n (of dog, person) urlo; (of cat) miagolio. **2** vi (see n) urlare; miagolare.
yo-yo |'jəʊjəʊ| n yo-yo m inv.

Yu·go·slav |ˌjuːgəʊ'slɑːv| adj, n jugoslavo(a) (m/f).
Yu·go·sla·via |ˌjuːgəʊ'slɑːvɪə| n Jugoslavia.
Yule·tide |'juːltaɪd| n (old) periodo natalizio.
yum·my |'jʌmɪ| adj (-ier, -iest) (fam) che fa gola.

Z

Z, z |zɛd. Am ziː| n (letter) Z, z f or m.
Zam·bia |'zæmbɪə| n Zambia m.
zany |'zeɪnɪ| adj (-ier, -iest) pazzoide.
zeal |ziːl| n zelo; ~ **for** ansia di.
zeal·ot |'zɛlət| n zelota m/f.
zeal·ous |'zɛləs| adj zelante.
zeb·ra |'ziːbrə| **1** n zebra. **2** cpd: ~ **crossing** n (Brit) strisce fpl pedonali.
zen·ith |'zɛnɪθ| n (Astron) zenit m inv; (fig) culmine m.
zeph·yr |'zɛfəʳ| n zefiro.
zep·pe·lin |'zɛplɪn| n zeppelin m inv.
zero |'zɪərəʊ| **1** n zero; **5° below** ~ 5° sotto zero. **2** cpd (altitude, gravity) zero inv; (fam: interest, hope) nullo(a); ~ **hour** n ora zero.
zest |zɛst| n **(a)** (enthusiasm): ~ **(for)** gusto (per), entusiasmo (per); (fig: spice) sapore m; ~ **for living** gioia di vivere. **(b)** (Culin: of orange etc) buccia.
zig·zag |'zɪgzæg| **1** n zigzag m inv. **2** vi: **to ~ across/down/up** etc attraversare/scendere/salire etc a zigzag. **3** cpd a zigzag.
zinc |zɪŋk| **1** n zinco. **2** cpd di zinco.
Zi·on·ism |'zaɪənɪzəm| n sionismo.
Zi·on·ist |'zaɪənɪst| **1** adj sionistico(a). **2** n sionista m/f.

zip |zɪp| **1** n **(a)** (also: ~ **fastener**) cerniera (lampo), zip m inv. **(b)** (energy) energia, forza. **2** vt: **to ~ up** chiudere la cerniera di; ~**ped pockets** (with ~s) tasche con cerniera; (~ped up) tasche con la cerniera chiusa; **he ~ped the bag open/closed** ha aperto/chiuso la cerniera della borsa. **3** vi: **to ~ past** sfrecciare davanti; **to ~ along to the shops** fare una corsa per comprare qc. **4** cpd: ~ **code** n (Am Post) codice m di avviamento postale.
zip·per |'zɪpəʳ| n = **zip 1a.**
zith·er |'zɪðəʳ| n cetra.
zo·di·ac |'zəʊdɪæk| n zodiaco.
zom·bie |'zɒmbɪ| n zombie m/f inv.
zone |zəʊn| n zona.
zonked |zɒŋkt| adj (fam: exhausted) distrutto(a).
zoo |zuː| n zoo m inv, giardino zoologico.
zoo·logi·cal |ˌzəʊə'lɒdʒɪkəl| adj zoologico(a).
zo·olo·gist |zəʊ'ɒlədʒɪst| n zoologo/a.
zo·ol·ogy |zəʊ'ɒlədʒɪ| n zoologia.
zoom |zuːm| **1** n **(a)** (sound) rombo. **(b)** (Phot: also: ~ **lens**) zoom m inv. **2** vi **(a)** (go fast): **to ~ off** sfrecciare via; **he ~ed past at 120 mph** ci sfrecciò accanto a 120 miglia all'ora. **(b)** (Phot, Cine): **to ~ in (on sb/sth)** zumare (su qn/qc).
zuc·chi·ni |zuːˈkiːnɪ| n, pl inv (Am) zucchina.
Zulu |'zuːluː| adj, n zulù (m/f) inv.
Zü·rich |'zjʊərɪk| n Zurigo f.

ITALIAN VERBS

1 Gerundio *2* Participio passato *3* Presente *4* Imperfetto *5* Passato remoto *6* Futuro *7* Condizionale *8* Congiuntivo presente *9* Congiuntivo passato *10* Imperativo

accadere *like* **cadere**
accedere *like* **concedere**
accendere *2* acceso *5* accesi, accendesti
accludere *like* **alludere**
accogliere *like* **cogliere**
accondiscendere *like* **scendere**
accorgersi *like* **scorgere**
accorrere *like* **correre**
accrescere *like* **crescere**
addirsi *like* **dire**
addurre *like* **ridurre**
affiggere *2* affisso *5* affissi, affiggesti
affliggere *2* afflitto *5* afflissi, affliggesti
aggiungere *like* **giungere**
alludere *2* alluso *5* allusi, alludesti
ammettere *like* **mettere**
andare *3* vado, vai, va, andiamo, andate, vanno *6* andrò *etc 8* vada *10* va'!, vada!, andate!, vadano!
annettere *2* annesso *5* annessi *or* annettei, annettesti
apparire *2* apparso *3* appaio, appari *o* apparisci, appare *o* apparisce, appaiono *o* appariscono *5* apparvi *o* apparsi, apparisti, apparve *o* appari *o* apparse, apparvero *o* apparirono *o* apparsero *8* appaia *o* apparisca
appartenere *like* **tenere**
appendere *2* appeso *5* appesi, appendesti
apporre *like* **porre**
apprendere *like* **prendere**
aprire *2* aperto *3* apro *5* aprii *o* apersi, apristi *8* apra
ardere *2* arso *5* arsi, ardesti
ascendere *like* **scendere**
aspergere *2* asperso *5* aspersi, aspergesti
assalire *like* **salire**
assistere *2* assistito
assolvere *2* assolto *5* assolsi *or* assolvei *or* assolvetti, assolvesti
assumere *2* assunto *5* assunsi, assumesti
astenersi *like* **tenere**
astrarre *like* **trarre**
attendere *like* **tendere**
attingere *like* **tingere**
AVERE *3* ho, hai, ha, abbiamo, avete, hanno *5* ebbi, avesti, ebbe, avemmo, aveste, ebbero *6* avrò *etc 8* abbia *etc 10* abbi!, abbia!, abbiate!, abbiano!
avvedersi *like* **vedere**
avvenire *like* **venire**
avvincere *like* **vincere**
avvolgere *like* **volgere**
benedire *like* **dire**
bere *1* bevendo *2* bevuto *3* bevo *etc 4* bevevo *etc 5* bevvi *o* bevetti, bevesti *6* berrò *etc 8* beva *etc 9* bevessi *etc*
cadere *5* caddi, cadesti *6* cadrò *etc*
chiedere *2* chiesto *5* chiesi, chiedesti
chiudere *2* chiuso *5* chiusi, chiudesti
cingere *2* cinto *5* cinsi, cingesti
cogliere *2* colto *3* colgo, colgono *5* colsi, cogliesti *8* colga
coincidere *2* coinciso *5* coincisi, coincidesti
coinvolgere *like* **volgere**
commettere *like* **mettere**
commuovere *like* **muovere**

comparire *like* **apparire**
compiacere *like* **piacere**
compiangere *like* **piangere**
comporre *like* **porre**
comprendere *like* **prendere**
comprimere *2* compresso *5* compressi, comprimesti
compromettere *like* **mettere**
concedere *2* concesso *or* conceduto *5* concessi *or* concedei *or* concedetti, concedesti
concludere *like* **alludere**
concorrere *like* **correre**
condurre *like* **ridurre**
confondere *like* **fondere**
congiungere *like* **giungere**
connettere *like* **annettere**
conoscere *2* conosciuto *5* conobbi, conoscesti
consistere *like* **assistere**
contendere *like* **tendere**
contenere *like* **tenere**
contorcere *like* **torcere**
contraddire *like* **dire**
contraffare *like* **fare**
contrarre *like* **trarre**
convenire *like* **venire**
convincere *like* **vincere**
coprire *like* **aprire**
correggere *like* **reggere**
correre *2* corso *5* corsi, corresti
corrispondere *like* **rispondere**
corrompere *like* **rompere**
costringere *like* **stringere**
costruire *5* costrussi, costruisti
crescere *2* cresciuto *5* crebbi, crescesti
cuocere *2* cotto *3* cuocio, cociamo, cuociono *5* cossi, cocesti
dare *3* do, dai, dà, diamo, date, danno *5* diedi *o* detti, desti *6* darò *etc 8* dia *etc 9* dessi *etc 10* da'!, dai!, date!, diano!
decidere *2* deciso *5* decisi, decidesti
decrescere *like* **crescere**
dedurre *like* **ridurre**
deludere *like* **alludere**
deporre *like* **porre**
deprimere *like* **comprimere**
deridere *like* **ridere**
descrivere *like* **scrivere**
desumere *like* **assumere**
detergere *like* **tergere**
devolvere *2* devoluto
difendere *2* difeso *5* difesi, difendesti
diffondere *like* **fondere**
dipendere *like* **appendere**
dipingere *like* **tingere**
dire *1* dicendo *2* detto *3* dico, dici, dice, diciamo, dite, dicono *4* dicevo *etc 5* dissi, dicesti *6* dirò *etc 8* dica, diciamo, diciate, dicano *9* dicessi *etc 10* di'!, dica!, dite!, dicano!
dirigere *2* diretto *5* diressi, dirigesti
discendere *like* **scendere**
dischiudere *like* **chiudere**
disciogliere *like* **sciogliere**
discorrere *like* **correre**
discutere *2* discusso *5* discussi, discutesti
disfare *like* **fare**

disgiungere *like* **giungere**
disilludere *like* **alludere**
disperdere *like* **perdere**
dispiacere *like* **piacere**
disporre *like* **porre**
dissolvere 2 dissolto *or* dissoluto 5 dissolsi *or*
dissolvetti *or* dissolvei, dissolvesti
dissuadere *like* **persuadere**
distendere *like* **tendere**
distinguere 2 distinto 5 distinsi, distinguesti
distogliere *like* **togliere**
distrarre *like* **trarre**
distruggere *like* **struggere**
divenire *like* **venire**
dividere 2 diviso 5 divisi, dividesti
dolere 3 dolgo, duoli, duole, dolgono 5 dolsi,
dolesti 6 dorrò *etc* 8 dolga
DORMIRE 1 *GERUNDIO* dormendo
  2 *PARTICIPIO PASSATO* dormito
  3 *PRESENTE* dormo, dormi, dorme, dormiamo,
dormite, dormono
  4 *IMPERFETTO* dormivo, dormivi, dormiva,
dormivamo, dormivate, dormivano
  5 *PASSATO REMOTO* dormii, dormisti, dormì, dor-
mimmo, dormiste, dormirono
  6 *FUTURO* dormirò, dormirai, dormirà,
dormiremo, dormirete, dormiranno
  7 *CONDIZIONALE* dormirei, dormiresti,
dormirebbe, dormiremmo, dormireste,
dormirebbero
  8 *CONGIUNTIVO PRESENTE* dorma, dorma, dorma,
dormiamo, dormiate, dormano
  9 *CONGIUNTIVO PASSATO* dormissi, dormissi, dor-
misse, dormissimo, dormiste, dormissero
  10 *IMPERATIVO* dormi!, dorma!, dormite!, dormano!
dovere 3 devo *o* debbo, devi, deve, dobbiamo,
dovete, devono *o* debbono 6 dovrò *etc* 8 debba,
dobbiamo, dobbiate, devano *o* debbano
eccellere 2 eccelso 5 eccelsi, eccellesti
eleggere *like* **leggere**
elidere 2 eliso 5 elisi, elidesti
eludere *like* **alludere**
emergere 2 emerso 5 emersi, emergesti
emettere *like* **mettere**
erigere *like* **dirigere**
escludere *like* **alludere**
esigere 2 esatto
esistere 2 esistito
espellere 2 espulso 5 espulsi, espellesti
esplodere 2 esploso 5 esplosi, esplodesti
esporre *like* **porre**
esprimere *like* **comprimere**
ESSERE 2 stato 3 sono, sei, è, siamo, siete, sono 4
ero, eri, era, eravamo, eravate, erano 5 fui, fosti,
fu, fummo, foste, furono 6 sarò *etc* 8 sia *etc* 9
fossi, fossi, fosse, fossimo, foste, fossero 10 sii!,
sia!, siate!, siano!
estendere *like* **tendere**
estinguere *like* **distinguere**
estrarre *like* **trarre**
evadere 2 evaso 5 evasi, evadesti
evolvere 2 evoluto
fare 1 facendo 2 fatto 3 faccio, fai, fa, facciamo,
fate, fanno 4 facevo *etc* 5 feci, facesti 6 farò *etc* 8
faccia *etc* 9 facessi *etc* 10 fa'!, faccia!, fate!,
facciano!
fingere *like* **cingere**
FINIRE 1 *GERUNDIO* finendo
  2 *PARTICIPIO PASSATO* finito
  3 *PRESENTE* finisco, finisci, finisce, finiamo,

finite, finiscono
  4 *IMPERFETTO* finivo, finivi, finiva, finivamo,
finivate, finivano
  5 *PASSATO REMOTO* finii, finisti, finì, finimmo,
finiste, finirono
  6 *FUTURO* finirò, finirai, finirà, finiremo, finirete,
finiranno
  7 *CONDIZIONALE* finirei, finiresti, finirebbe,
finiremmo, finireste, finirebbero
  8 *CONGIUNTIVO PRESENTE* finisca, finisca, finisca,
finiamo, finiate, finiscano
  9 *CONGIUNTIVO PASSATO* finissi, finissi, finisse,
finissimo, finiste, finissero
  10 *IMPERATIVO* finisci!, finisca!, finite!, finiscano!
flettere 2 flesso
fondere 2 fuso 5 fusi, fondesti
frammettere *like* **mettere**
frapporre *like* **porre**
friggere 2 fritto 5 frissi, friggesti
fungere 2 funto 5 funsi, fungesti
giacere 3 giaccio, giaci, giace, giac(c)iamo,
giacete, giacciono 5 giacqui, giacesti 8 giaccia
etc 10 giaci!, giaccia!, giac(c)iamo!, giacete!,
giacciano!
giungere 2 giunto 5 giunsi, giungesti
godere 6 godrò *etc*
illudere *like* **alludere**
immergere *like* **emergere**
immettere *like* **mettere**
imporre *like* **porre**
imprimere *like* **comprimere**
incidere *like* **decidere**
includere *like* **alludere**
incorrere *like* **correre**
incutere *like* **discutere**
indulgere 2 indulto 5 indulsi, indulgesti
indurre *like* **ridurre**
inferire[1] 2 inferto 5 infersi, inferisti
inferire[2] 2 inferito 5 inferii, inferisti
infliggere *like* **affliggere**
infrangere 2 infranto 5 infransi, infrangesti
infondere *like* **fondere**
insistere *like* **assistere**
intendere *like* **tendere**
interdire *like* **dire**
interporre *like* **porre**
interrompere *like* **rompere**
intervenire *like* **venire**
intraprendere *like* **prendere**
introdurre *like* **ridurre**
invadere *like* **evadere**
irrompere *like* **rompere**
iscrivere *like* **scrivere**
istruire *like* **costruire**
ledere 2 leso 5 lesi, ledesti
leggere 2 letto 5 lessi, leggesti
maledire *like* **dire**
mantenere *like* **tenere**
mettere 2 messo 5 misi, mettesti
mordere 2 morso 5 morsi, mordesti
morire 2 morto 3 muoio, muori, muore, moriamo,
morite, muoiono 6 morirò *o* morrò *etc* 8 muoia
mungere 2 munto 5 munsi, mungesti
muovere 2 mosso 5 mossi, movesti
nascere 2 nato 5 nacqui, nascesti
nascondere 2 nascosto 5 nascosi, nascondesti
nuocere 2 nuociuto 3 nuoccio, nuoci, nuoce,
nociamo *o* nuociamo, nuocete, nuocciono 4
nuocevo *etc* 5 nocqui, nuocesti 6 nuocerò *etc* 7
nuoccia

occorrere *like* **correre**
offendere *like* **difendere**
offrire *2* offerto *3* offro *5* offersi *o* offrii, offristi *8* offra
omettere *like* **mettere**
opporre *like* **porre**
opprimere *like* **comprimere**
ottenere *like* **tenere**
parere *2* parso *3* paio, paiamo, paiono *5* parvi *o* parsi, paresti *6* parrò *etc 8* paia, paiamo, paiate, paiano
PARLARE *1 GERUNDIO* parlando
  2 PARTICIPIO PASSATO parlato
  3 PRESENTE parlo, parli, parla, parliamo, parlate, parlano
  4 IMPERFETTO parlavo, parlavi, parlava, parlavamo, parlavate, parlavano
  5 PASSATO REMOTO parlai, parlasti, parlò, parlammo, parlaste, parlarono
  6 FUTURO parlerò, parlerai, parlerà, parleremo, parlerete, parleranno
  7 CONDIZIONALE parlerei, parleresti, parlerebbe, parleremmo, parlereste, parlerebbero
  8 CONGIUNTIVO PRESENTE parli, parli, parli, parliamo, parliate, parlino
  9 CONGIUNTIVO PASSATO parlassi, parlassi, parlasse, parlassimo, parlaste, parlassero
  10 IMPERATIVO parla!, parli!, parlate!, parlino!
percorrere *like* **correre**
percuotere *2* percosso *5* percossi, percotesti
perdere *2* perso *or* perduto *5* persi *or* perdei *or* perdetti, perdesti
permettere *like* **mettere**
persuadere *2* persuaso *5* persuasi, persuadesti
pervenire *like* **venire**
piacere *2* piaciuto *3* piaccio, piacciamo, piacciono *5* piacqui, piacesti *8* piaccia *etc*
piangere *2* pianto *5* piansi, piangesti
piovere *5* piovve
porgere *2* porto *5* porsi, porgesti
porre *1* ponendo *2* posto *3* pongo, poni, pone, poniamo, ponete, pongono *4* ponevo *etc 5* posi, ponesti *6* porrò *etc 8* ponga, poniamo, poniate, pongano *9* ponessi *etc*
posporre *like* **porre**
possedere *like* **sedere**
potere *3* posso, puoi, può, possiamo, potete, possono *6* potrò *etc 8* possa, possiamo, possiate, possano
prediligere *2* prediletto *5* predilessi, prediligesti
predire *like* **dire**
prefiggersi *like* **affiggere**
preludere *like* **alludere**
prendere *2* preso *5* presi, prendesti
preporre *like* **porre**
prescegliere *like* **scegliere**
prescrivere *like* **scrivere**
presiedere *like* **sedere**
presumere *like* **assumere**
pretendere *like* **tendere**
prevalere *like* **valere**
prevedere *like* **vedere**
prevenire *like* **venire**
produrre *like* **ridurre**
proferire *like* **inferire**[2]
profondere *like* **fondere**
promettere *like* **mettere**

promuovere *like* **muovere**
proporre *like* **porre**
prorompere *like* **rompere**
proscrivere *like* **scrivere**
proteggere *2* protetto *5* protessi, proteggesti
provenire *like* **venire**
provvedere *like* **vedere**
pungere *2* punto *5* punsi, pungesti
racchiudere *like* **chiudere**
raccogliere *like* **cogliere**
radere *2* raso *5* rasi, radesti
raggiungere *like* **giungere**
rapprendere *like* **prendere**
ravvedersi *like* **vedere**
ravvolgere *like* **volgere**
recidere *like* **decidere**
redigere *2* redatto
redimere *2* redento *5* redensi, redimesti
reggere *2* retto *5* ressi, reggesti
rendere *2* reso *5* resi, rendesti
reprimere *like* **comprimere**
rescindere *like* **scindere**
respingere *like* **spingere**
restringere *like* **stringere**
ricadere *like* **cadere**
richiedere *like* **chiedere**
riconoscere *like* **conoscere**
ricoprire *like* **coprire**
ricorrere *like* **correre**
ridere *2* riso *5* risi, ridesti
ridire *like* **dire**
ridurre *1* riducendo *2* ridotto *3* riduco *etc 4* riducevo *etc 5* ridussi, riducesti *6* ridurrò *etc 8* riduca *etc 9* riducessi *etc*
riempire *1* riempiendo *3* riempio, riempi, riempie, riempiono
rifare *like* **fare**
riflettere *2* riflettuto *or* riflesso
rifrangere *like* **infrangere**
rifulgere *2* rifulso *5* rifulsi, rifulgesti
rimanere *2* rimasto *3* rimango, rimangono *5* rimasi, rimanesti *6* rimarrò *etc 8* rimanga
rimettere *like* **mettere**
rimordere *like* **mordere**
rimpiangere *like* **piangere**
rinascere *like* **nascere**
rinchiudere *like* **chiudere**
rincrescere *like* **crescere**
rinvenire *like* **venire**
ripercuotere *like* **percuotere**
riporre *like* **porre**
riprendere *like* **prendere**
riprodurre *like* **ridurre**
riscuotere *like* **scuotere**
risolvere *like* **assolvere**
risorgere *like* **sorgere**
rispondere *2* risposto *5* risposi, rispondesti
ritenere *like* **tenere**
ritrarre *like* **trarre**
riuscire *like* **uscire**
rivedere *like* **vedere**
rivivere *like* **vivere**
rivolgere *like* **volgere**
rodere *2* roso *5* rosi, rodesti
rompere *2* rotto *5* ruppi, rompesti
salire *3* salgo, sali, salgono *8* salga
sapere *3* so, sai, sa, sappiamo, sapete, sanno *5* seppi, sapesti *6* saprò *etc 8* sappia *etc 10* sappi!, sappia!, sappiate!, sappiano!
scadere *like* **cadere**

scegliere 2 scelto 3 scelgo, scegli, sceglie, scegliamo, scegliete, scelgono 5 scelsi, scegliesti 8 scelga, scegliamo, scegliate, scelgano 10 scegli!, scelga!, scegliamo!, scegliete!, scelgano!

scendere 2 sceso 5 scesi, scendesti

schiudere like chiudere

scindere 2 scisso 5 scissi, scindesti

sciogliere 2 sciolto 3 sciolgo, sciogli, scioglie, sciogliamo, sciogliete, sciolgono 5 sciolsi, sciogliesti 8 sciolga, sciogliamo, sciogliate, sciolgano 10 sciogli!, sciolga!, sciogliamo!, sciogliete!, sciolgano!

scommettere like mettere

scomparire like apparire

scomporre like porre

sconfiggere 2 sconfitto 5 sconfissi, sconfiggesti

sconvolgere like volgere

scoprire like aprire

scorgere 2 scorto 5 scorsi, scorgesti

scorrere like correre

scrivere 2 scritto 5 scrissi, scrivesti

scuotere 2 scosso 3 scuoto, scuoti, scuote, scotiamo, scotete, scuotono 5 scossi, scotesti 6 scoterò etc 8 scuota, scotiamo, scotiate, scuotano 10 scuoti!, scuota!, scotiamo!, scotete!, scuotano!

sedere 3 siedo, siedi, siede, siedono 8 sieda

seppellire 2 sepolto

smettere like mettere

smuovere like muovere

socchiudere like chiudere

soccorrere like correre

soddisfare like fare

soffriggere like friggere

soffrire 2 sofferto 5 soffersi or soffrii, soffristi

soggiungere like giungere

solere 2 solito 3 soglio, suoli, suole, sogliamo, solete, sogliono 8 soglia, sogliamo, sogliate, sogliano

sommergere like emergere

sopprimere like comprimere

sorgere 2 sorto 3 sorsi, sorgesti

sorprendere like prendere

sorreggere like reggere

sorridere like ridere

sospendere like appendere

sospingere like spingere

sostenere like tenere

sottintendere like tendere

spandere 2 spanto

spargere 2 sparso 5 sparsi, spargesti

sparire 5 sparii or sparvi, sparisti

spegnere 2 spento 3 spengo, spengono 5 spensi, spegnesti 8 spenga

spendere 2 speso 5 spesi, spendesti

spingere 2 spinto 5 spinsi, spingesti

sporgere like porgere

stare 2 stato 3 sto, stai, sta, stiamo, state, stanno 5 stetti, stesti 6 starò etc 8 stia etc 9 stessi etc 10 sta'!, stia!, state!, stiano!

stendere like tendere

storcere like torcere

stringere 2 stretto 5 strinsi, stringesti

struggere 2 strutto 5 strussi, struggesti

succedere like concedere

supporre like porre

svenire like venire

svolgere like volgere

tacere 2 taciuto 3 taccio, tacciono 5 tacqui, tacesti 8 taccia

tendere 2 teso 5 tesi, tendesti etc

tenere 3 tengo, tieni, tiene, tengono 5 tenni, tenesti 6 terrò etc 8 tenga

tergere 2 terso 5 tersi, tergesti

tingere 2 tinto 5 tinsi, tingesti

togliere 2 tolto 3 tolgo, togli, toglie, togliamo, togliete, tolgono 5 tolsi, togliesti 8 tolga, togliamo, togliate, tolgano 10 togli!, tolga!, togliamo!, togliete!, tolgano!

torcere 2 torto 5 torsi, torcesti

tradurre like ridurre

trafiggere like sconfiggere

transigere like esigere

trarre 1 traendo 2 tratto 3 traggo, trai, trae, traiamo, traete, traggono 4 traevo etc 5 trassi, traesti 6 trarrò etc 8 tragga 9 traessi etc

trascorrere like correre

trascrivere like scrivere

trasmettere like mettere

trasparire like apparire

trattenere like tenere

uccidere 2 ucciso 5 uccisi, uccidesti

udire 3 odo, odi, ode, odono 8 oda

ungere 2 unto 5 unsi, ungesti

uscire 3 esco, esci, esce, escono 8 esca

valere 2 valso 3 valgo, valgono 5 valsi, valesti 6 varrò etc 8 valga

vedere 2 visto o veduto 5 vidi, vedesti 6 vedrò etc

VENDERE 1 GERUNDIO vendendo

2 PARTICIPIO PASSATO venduto

3 PRESENTE vendo, vendi, vende, vendiamo, vendete, vendono

4 IMPERFETTO vendevo, vendevi, vendeva, vendevamo, vendevate, vendevano

5 PASSATO REMOTO vendei o vendetti, vendesti, vendé o vendette, vendemmo, vendeste, venderono o vendettero

6 FUTURO venderò, venderai, venderà, venderemo, venderete, venderanno

7 CONDIZIONALE venderei, venderesti, venderebbe, venderemmo, vendereste, venderebbero

8 CONGIUNTIVO PRESENTE venda, venda, venda, vendiamo, vendiate, vendano

9 CONGIUNTIVO PASSATO vendessi, vendessi, vendesse, vendessimo, vendeste, vendessero

10 IMPERATIVO vendi!, venda!, vendete!, vendano!

venire 2 venuto 3 vengo, vieni, viene, vengono 5 venni, venisti 6 verrò etc 8 venga

vincere 2 vinto 5 vinsi, vincesti

vivere 2 vissuto 5 vissi, vivesti

volere 3 voglio, vuoi, vuole, vogliamo, volete, vogliono 5 volli, volesti 6 vorrò etc 8 voglia etc 10 vogli!, voglia!, vogliate!, vogliano!

volgere 2 volto 5 volsi, volgesti

VERBI INGLESI

present	pt	pp	present	pt	pp
arise	arose	arisen	drink	drank	drunk
awake	awoke	awaked	drive	drove	driven
be (am,	was,	been	dwell	dwelt	dwelt
is, are;	were		eat	ate	eaten
being)			fall	fell	fallen
bear	bore	born(e)	feed	fed	fed
beat	beat	beaten	feel	felt	felt
become	became	become	fight	fought	fought
befall	befell	befallen	find	found	found
begin	began	begun	flee	fled	fled
behold	beheld	beheld	fling	flung	flung
bend	bent	bent	fly	flew	flown
beset	beset	beset	forbid	forbad(e)	forbidden
bet	bet,	bet,	forecast	forecast	forecast
	betted	betted	forget	forgot	forgotten
bid	bid,	bid,	forgive	forgave	forgiven
	bade	bidden	forsake	forsook	forsaken
bind	bound	bound	freeze	froze	frozen
bite	bit	bitten	get	got	got, (US)
bleed	bled	bled			gotten
blow	blew	blown	give	gave	given
break	broke	broken	go	went	gone
breed	bred	bred	(goes)		
bring	brought	brought	grind	ground	ground
build	built	built	grow	grew	grown
burn	burnt,	burnt,	hang	hung,	hung,
	burned	burned		hanged	hanged
burst	burst	burst	have	had	had
buy	bought	bought	hear	heard	heard
can	could	(been able)	hide	hid	hidden
cast	cast	cast	hit	hit	hit
catch	caught	caught	hold	held	held
choose	chose	chosen	hurt	hurt	hurt
cling	clung	clung	keep	kept	kept
come	came	come	kneel	knelt,	knelt,
cost	cost,	cost,		kneeled	kneeled
	costed	costed	know	knew	known
creep	crept	crept	lay	laid	laid
cut	cut	cut	lead	led	led
deal	dealt	dealt	lean	leant,	leant,
dig	dug	dug		leaned	leaned
do (3rd	did	done	leap	leapt,	leapt,
person:				leaped	leaped
he/she/			learn	learnt,	learnt,
it does)				learned	learned
draw	drew	drawn	leave	left	left
dream	dreamed,	dreamed,	lend	lent	lent
	dreamt	dreamt	let	let	let

present	pt	pp	present	pt	pp
lie (lying)	lay	lain	sow	sowed	sown, sowed
light	lit, lighted	lit, lighted	speak	spoke	spoken
			speed	sped, speeded	sped, speeded
lose	lost	lost			
make	made	made	spell	spelt, spelled	spelt, spelled
may	might	—			
mean	meant	meant	spend	spent	spent
meet	met	met	spill	spilt, spilled	spilt, spilled
mistake	mistook	mistaken			
mow	mowed	mown, mowed	spin	spun	spun
			spit	spat	spat
must	(had to)	(had to)	spoil	spoiled, spoilt	spoiled, spoilt
pay	paid	paid			
put	put	put	spread	spread	spread
quit	quit, quitted	quit, quitted	spring	sprang	sprung
			stand	stood	stood
read	read	read	steal	stole	stolen
rend	rent	rent	stick	stuck	stuck
rid	rid	rid	sting	stung	stung
ride	rode	ridden	stink	stank	stunk
ring	rang	rung	stride	strode	stridden
rise	rose	risen	strike	struck	struck, stricken
run	ran	run			
saw	sawed	sawed, sawn	strive	strove	striven
			swear	swore	sworn
say	said	said	sweep	swept	swept
see	saw	seen	swell	swelled	swollen, swelled
seek	sought	sought			
sell	sold	sold	swim	swam	swum
send	sent	sent	swing	swung	swung
set	set	set	take	took	taken
shake	shook	shaken	teach	taught	taught
shear	sheared	shorn, sheared	tear	tore	torn
			tell	told	told
shed	shed	shed	think	thought	thought
shine	shone	shone	throw	threw	thrown
shoot	shot	shot	thrust	thrust	thrust
show	showed	shown	tread	trod	trodden
shrink	shrank	shrunk	wake	woke, waked	woken, waked
shut	shut	shut			
sing	sang	sung	wear	wore	worn
sink	sank	sunk	weave	wove, weaved	woven, weaved
sit	sat	sat			
slay	slew	slain	wed	wedded, wed	wedded, wed
sleep	slept	slept			
slide	slid	slid	weep	wept	wept
sling	slung	slung	win	won	won
slit	slit	slit	wind	wound	wound
smell	smelt, smelled	smelt, smelled	wring	wrung	wrung
			write	wrote	written

ALFABETO TELEFONICO

PHONETIC ALPHABET

Italia come	fonetica		phonetics	GB for	USA
Ancona	[a]	A	[eɪ]	Andrew	Abel
Bologna	[bi]	B	[biː]	Benjamin	Baker
Como	[tʃi]	C	[siː]	Charlie	Charlie
Domodossola	[di]	D	[diː]	David	Dog
Empoli	[e]	E	[iː]	Edward	Easy
Firenze	['effe]	F	[ɛf]	Frederick	Fox
Genova	[dʒi]	G	[dʒiː]	George	George
Hotel	['akka]	H	[eɪtʃ]	Harry	How
Imola	[i]	I	[aɪ]	Isaac	Item
I lunga	[i'lunga]	J	[dʒeɪ]	Jack	Jig
Kursaal	['kappa]	K	[keɪ]	King	King
Livorno	['ɛlle]	L	[ɛl]	Lucy	Love
Milano	['ɛmme]	M	[ɛm]	Mary	Mike
Napoli	['ɛnne]	N	[ɛn]	Nellie	Nan
Otranto	[ɔ]	O	[əʊ]	Oliver	Oboe
Padova	[pi]	P	[piː]	Peter	Peter
Quarto	[ku]	Q	[kjuː]	Queenie	Queen
Roma	['ɛrre]	R	[ɑːʳ]	Robert	Roger
Savona	['ɛsse]	S	[ɛs]	Sugar	Sugar
Torino	[ti]	T	[tiː]	Tommy	Tare
Udine	[u]	U	[juː]	Uncle	Uncle
Venezia	[vi, vu]	V	[viː]	Victor	Victor
Washington	[doppio vu]	W	['dʌbljʊ]	William	William
Ics	[iks]	X	[ɛks]	Xmas	X
York, yacht	['ipsilon]	Y	[waɪ]	Yellow	Yoke
Zara	[dzɛta]	Z	[zɛd, *Am* ziː]	Zebra	Zebra